ROSAI AND ACKERMAN'S

Surgical Pathology

NINTH EDITION

Commissioning Editor: Michael Houston
Project Development Manager: Joanne Scott
Project Manager: Naughton Project Management, Aoibhe O'Shea
Design Manager: Sarah Russell
Illustration Manager: Mick Ruddy
Illustrator: Lynda Payne

Cover illustrations: Volume 1: Fig. 5.21
Volume 2: Fig. 5.40

GRACE LIBRARY CARLOW UNIVERSITY
PITTSBURGH PA 15213

ROSAI AND ACKERMAN'S

Surgical Pathology

Juan Rosai MD

Chairman, Department of Pathology
National Cancer Institute
Milan, Italy

Professor, Department of Pathology
Weill Medical College of
Cornell University
New York, New York, USA

Ref.
RD
57
A2
2004
v. 1

NINTH EDITION

 Mosby

An Affiliate of Elsevier

CATALOGUED

MOSBY
An Affiliate of Elsevier

Previous editions copyrighted 1953, 1959, 1964, 1968, 1974, 1981, 1989, 1996
© 2004, Elsevier Inc. All rights reserved.

No part of this publication may be reproduced, stored in a retrieval system, or
transmitted in any form or by any means, electronic, mechanical, photocopying,
recording or otherwise, without either the prior permission of the publishers or a licence
permitting restricted copying in the United Kingdom issued by the Copyright Licensing
Agency, 90 Tottenham Court Road, London W1T 4LP. Permissions may be sought
directly from Elsevier's Health Sciences Rights Department in Philadelphia, USA: phone:
(+1) 215 238 7869, fax: (+1) 215 238 2239, e-mail: healthpermissions@elsevier.com. You may
also complete your request on-line via the Elsevier homepage (http://www.elsevier.com),
by selecting 'Customer Support' and then 'Obtaining Permissions'.

First edition 1953   Fifth edition 1974
Second edition 1959   Sixth edition 1981
Third edition 1964   Seventh edition 1989
Fourth edition 1968   Eighth edition 1996

Part ISBN-13: 9789996000423
Part ISBN-10: 9996000427
Set ISBN-13: 978-0-323-01342-0
Set ISBN-10: 0-323-01342-2

British Library Cataloguing in Publication Data
A catalogue record for this book is available from the British Library

Library of Congress Cataloging in Publication Data
A catalog record for this book is available from the Library of Congress

Notice
Medical knowledge is constantly changing. Standard safety precautions must be
followed, but as new research and clinical experience broaden our knowledge, changes
in treatment and drug therapy may become necessary or appropriate. Readers are
advised to check the most current product information provided by the manufacturer of
each drug to be administered to verify the recommended dose, the method and duration
of administration, and contraindications. It is the responsibility of the practitioner,
relying on experience and knowledge of the patient, to determine dosages and the best
treatment for each individual patient. Neither the Publisher nor the authors assume any
liability for any injury and/or damage to persons or property arising from this
publication.
The Publisher

 your source for books,
journals and multimedia
in the health sciences
www.elsevierhealth.com

Printed in China
Last digit is the print number: 07 06 05 04 03

The
publisher's
policy is to use
**paper manufactured
from sustainable forests**

To my sons,
Alberto, Carlos, and Johnny

And my grandson,
John

Contents

VOLUME 2

Preface
to the ninth edition

The eight years that have elapsed between this and the previous edition have seen momentous changes taking place in the practice of surgical pathology. Immuno-histochemistry has continued its notable expansion and has become an indispensable adjunct for the practice of the specialty. It has truly transformed the practice of surgical pathology in a fashion that no other special technique has done before or after. Newcomers to the specialty take it for granted when ordering their panels, without pausing to think that only thirty years ago none of it was available to the brave pathologists who based all of their diagnoses and their histogenetic considerations on patterns of growth and cell shapes seen in hematoxylin-stained slides, with occasional modest help provided by one or other special stain.

We are now in the midst of another transformation, resulting from the application to surgical pathology specimens of the enormous amount of new knowledge derived from the genetic molecular revolution. The potential, and in some instances, already tangible benefits of this technology are too obvious to be emphasized. It may instead be instructive to reflect on the effect that this barrage of new information is having on the approach to surgical pathology by the new generation of practitioners, and the danger that the tradition of meticulous gross and microscopic examination upon which surgical pathology has been built may be gradually eroding. Some of this may be inevitable and is perhaps not altogether undesirable, yet the amount of information that this time-honored examination can still provide is so rich and dependable that one recoils at the thought of its being ignored or slighted. On that basis, this edition dutifully incorporates the many promising results reached with the new technologies (emphasizing the few in which a clinical validation has occurred), but always matches them against the results and conclusions derived from the morphology-based approach that has served pathologists so well for so long.

Another important change that has taken place during this period concerns the increasing demands for standardization, obedience of regulatory controls, and legal accountability, which have prompted various professional organizations to produce sets of guidelines to help pathologists navigate this increasingly complicated system.

Yet another significant development concerns the pervasive influence acquired by electronic information systems in practically all activities that take place in the surgical pathology laboratory, rendering some degree of computer literacy indispensable to those wishing to practice the specialty.

It has not been easy to accommodate this rapidly changing and continuously expanding universe in the confines of the covers of this book. The amount of information that has to be reviewed, even if often of a merely confirmatory or plainly repetitive nature, is monumental, and the trend for subspecialization of surgical pathology—each with its own rites and language—has accelerated. The sum of these factors has made the production of this book a heavy burden, to the point of making one wonder whether it had grown beyond the capabilities of an individual. Yet, as you can see, don't ask me how, another edition has been completed, once again for the most part written by one author, in the continuing hope that whatever expertise is inevitably missing as a result may be compensated by what somebody referred to as "the ultimate simplicity of one voice speaking." Along those lines, a constant attempt has been made to preserve as much as possible of the pragmatic flavor initially given to this work by its peerless begetter, Dr. Lauren V. Ackerman (1905–1993).

This goal of coherence notwithstanding, it was obvious that there were highly specialized areas that could not have been covered adequately without the contribution of experts. I was fortunate in being able to secure the collaboration of the outstanding individuals listed on the Contributors' page for this purpose, and I am very grateful to them for their generosity in lending their considerable expertise to this effort.

A book that has gone through so many editions is bound to contain strata of text and illustrative material that have been contributed by someone or other at some point and then been covered by other strata, but whose source will still be identifiable to the initiated. Among the many such past contributors, I would like to mention Dr. Morton E. Smith (Chapter 30), Dr. Robert E. Vickers

(Chapter 6), and Dr. John Morrow (sections on Information systems in surgical pathology and Model for an automated anatomic pathology system, Chapter 1).

Thanks are also due to the many colleagues and associates who generously contributed illustrative material from their own files or personal publications. Among them, I would like to single out for the magnitude of their contributions the following: Dr. Robin A. Cooke, from Brisbane, Australia; Dr. Robert Erlandson, from South Berlington, Vermont; Dr. Fabio Facchetti, from Brescia, Italy; Dr. Pedro J. Grases Galofrè, from Barcelona, Spain; and Ms. Loredana Alasio, Chief Cytotechnologist in my Department of Pathology at the Cancer Institute in Milan.

Each of the editions of this book in which I have been involved has been written at a different place: the Fifth at Washington University, the Sixth at the University of Minnesota, the Seventh at Yale University, the Eighth at Memorial Sloan-Kettering Cancer Center, and the present at the National Cancer Institute in Milan. In each place I have learned a great deal from my colleagues and have incorporated many of their comments and suggestions. I am most grateful to the countless staff pathologists, pathology residents, and pathology fellows from each of these places who have unwittingly contributed to the book in this fashion. I suspect that some of them will recognize themselves in some of the statements.

Once again, the contribution made by my wife, Dr. Maria Luisa Carcangiu, has been colossal. It encompassed every aspect of the book production, beginning with psychologic support in the many moments of near collapse to the chore of performing many of my departmental responsibilities in order to allow me to put the final touches to the project, not to speak of the thoughts that were generated during the course of our innumerable exchanges of opinions at work and at home.

The secretarial staff at the Institute has been most supportive. I must confess I was a little apprehensive when all this started in view of the relative inexperience of the person chosen for the transcription task and her less than perfect knowledge of the English language. The way Maria Morelli rose to the task was astounding. After a few stressful initiation chapters, she was typing my handwritten pages (yes, I still did it with pencil and paper) with a speed and accuracy of the kind I have rarely witnessed anywhere, not to speak of the enthusiasm and devotion she threw into the effort. Thanks are also due to Gianni Roncato, the Department's photographer, for his skillful and dedicated contribution to this effort.

So, here it is for you, my fellow surgical pathologist, hoping that it will provide you with some assistance in carrying out our demanding, stressful, wonderful job.

Juan Rosai, MD
Milan, 2004

Preface
to the first edition

This book can be only an introduction to the vast field of surgical pathology: the pathology of the living. It does not pretend to replace in any way the textbooks to general pathology, its purpose being merely to supplement them, assuming that the reader has a background in or access to those texts. The contents are not as complete as they might be because emphasis has been placed on the common rather than the rare lesions and are, to a great extent, based on the author's personal experiences.

This book has been written for the medical student as well as for those physicians who are daily intimately concerned with surgical pathology. This must of necessity include not only the surgeon and the pathologist, but also those physicians in other fields who are affected by its decisions, such as the radiologist and the internist. Gross pathology has been stressed throughout with an attempt to correlate the gross findings with the clinical observations. The many illustrations have been selected as typical of the various surgical conditions, although in a few instances the author has been unable to resist showing some of the more interesting rare lesions he has encountered. Concluding each chapter there is a bibliography listing those references which are not only relatively recent and readily available, but also those which will lead the reader to a more detailed knowledge of the subject.

Dr. Zola K. Cooper, Assistant Professor of Pathology and Surgical Pathology, has written one of the sections on Skin, and Dr. David E. Smith, Assistant Professor of Pathology and Surgical Pathology, has written the chapter on Central Nervous System. Both of these members of the Department are particularly well qualified for their respective roles because of their background and present responsibilities in these fields. Their efforts on my behalf are most gratefully acknowledged.

Many members of the Surgical Staff at Barnes Hospital have given much help both knowingly and unwittingly. I am particularly grateful to Dr. Charles L. Eckert, Associate Professor of Surgery, for letting me bother him rather constantly with my questions and for giving freely of his experience. Dr. Richard Johnson, who succeeded me as Pathologist at the Ellis Fischel State Cancer Hospital, agreeably made available all the material there, and Dr. Franz Leidler, Pathologist at the Veterans Hospital, has been most cooperative.

Thanks must be given to Dr. H.R. McCarroll, Assistant Professor of Orthopedics, for constructively criticizing the chapter on Bone and Joint, and to Dr. C.A. Waldron for helping me with the chapters related to the Oral Cavity. Among other faculty friends and colleagues who were especially helpful, I would like to mention Dr. Carl E. Lischer, Dr. Eugene M. Bricker, Dr. Heinz Haffner, Dr. Thomas H. Burford, Dr. Carl A. Moyer, Dr. Evarts A. Graham, Dr. Robert Elman, Dr. Edward H. Reinhard, Dr. J. Albert Key, Dr. Glover H. Copher, Dr. Margaret G. Smith, and Dr. Robert A. Moore.

Mr. Cramer K. Lewis, of our Department of Illustration, has been very patient with my demands, and his efforts and skill have been invaluable. Miss Marion Murphy, in charge of our Medical Library, and her associates gave untiringly of their time.

Because of recent advances in anesthesia, antibiotics, and pre- and postoperative care, modern surgery permits the radical excision of portions or all of various organs. There is a need today for contemplative surgeons, men with a rich background in the fundamental sciences, whether chemistry, physiology, or pathology. The modern surgeon should not ask himself, "Can I get away with this operation?" but rather, "What does the future hold for this patient?" It is hoped that this book may contribute in some small fashion toward the acquisition of this attitude.

Lauren V. Ackerman, MD
St. Louis, Missouri, USA

List of Contributors

Chapter 13: Liver (Non-neoplastic diseases)
Valeer J. Desmet, MD PhD
Emeritus Professor of Pathology
Universitair Ziekenhuis St Rafael
Leuven, Belgium

Chapter 17: Kidney (Non-neoplastic diseases)
Nelson G. Ordòñez, MD
Professor of Pathology
The University of Texas M.D.Anderson Cancer Center
Houston, Texas, USA

Chapter 23: Bone Marrow
Richard D. Brunning, MD
Professor Emeritus
Department of Laboratory Medicine and Pathology
University of Minnesota Medical School
Minneapolis, Minnesota, USA

Chapter 28: Central Nervous System
Marc K. Rosenblum, MD
Chairman, Department of Pathology
Memorial Hospital
Memorial Sloan-Kettering Cancer Center;
Professor of Pathology
Weill Medical College
Cornell University
New York, New York, USA

Chapter 28: Peripheral Nerves; Skeletal Muscle;
Chapter 29: Pituitary Gland
Juan M. Bilbao, MD
Staff Neuropathologist
Sunnybrook and Women's College Health Sciences Centre
North York, Ontario, Canada;
Office of the Chief Coroner for Ontario, Canada;
Associate Professor of Pathology
University of Toronto Medical School
Toronto, Ontario, Canada

Lee-Cyn Ang, MBBS, FRCPC, FRCPath
Director of Neuropathology
Department of Pathology
London Health Sciences Centre and
University of Western Ontario
London, Ontario, Canada

1 Introduction

Historical perspective

Surgical pathology has come a long way since the time that Velpeau, famous professor of clinical surgery at the University of Paris, stated in his work on diseases of the breast published in 1853*: "The intervention of the microscope is not at all necessary to decide whether such and such a tumor, which has been removed, is or is not of cancerous nature." In the 1870s, Carl Ruge and his associate Johann Veit, of the University of Berlin, introduced the surgical biopsy as an essential diagnostic tool.[2] Despite the controversies that followed, Friedrich von Esmarch, professor of surgery at Kiel and a leading military surgeon, presented forceful arguments at the German Surgical Congress of 1889 on the need to establish a microscopic diagnosis before operating in suspected cases of malignant tumors requiring extensive mutilating procedures. Shortly thereafter, the freezing microtome was introduced, and the frozen section procedure hastened the acceptance of this recommendation.[11] In the United States, the specialty of surgical pathology was conceived and initially developed by surgeons and gynecologists.[2a,10a] It is said that William S. Halsted was the first American surgeon to create a division of surgical

pathology at Hopkins when he made Joseph Colt ("Bloody") Bloodgood the first full-fledged American surgical pathologist.[9] These pioneer efforts, which were initially met with indifference and occasionally scorn by the academic pathology establishment, proved to be hugely successful. In the second phase of its development, the specialty came to be performed by pathology-trained individuals, and this was followed by its logical and perhaps inevitable incorporation into pathology departments.[8] Because of the differences in background, philosophy, and goals between the "surgical" and the "general" pathologists, the merging of the two schools proved to be a slow, complicated, and sometimes frustrating process, and one that is still evolving. The intellectual, logistic, and financial benefits of this arrangement are, however, too obvious for *all* parties involved for any alternative scheme to be a realistic consideration.

Of the many individuals who contributed to consolidate the specialty of surgical pathology in the United States during the first half of the twentieth century, special recognition is due to Arthur Purdy Stout of Columbia-Presbyterian Hospital in New York City and his successor Raffaele Lattes; James Ewing and his successor Fred Stewart of Memorial Hospital, also in New York City; Malcolm Dockerty at the Mayo Clinic; and Lauren V. Ackerman of Barnes Hospital in St. Louis, Missouri[1,3,5,7,8,10] (Fig. 1.1). To these, one feels duty-bound to add the names of Pierre Masson in France and Canada, and Rupert A. Willis in Australia and England.[6]

---

* From Velpeau AALM. Traité des maladies du sein et de la region mammatre. Paris, 1854. Translated into English by Henry M. A treatise on the diseases of the breast and mammary region. London, 1856, pp. 479–480.

Fig. 1.1 Founders of American surgical pathology. **A,** Arthur Purdy Stout, M.D.; **B,** James Ewing, M.D.; **C,** Fred W. Stewart, M.D.; **D,** Malcolm B. Dockerty, M.D.; **E,** Lauren V. Ackerman, M.D. (**A** from Lattes R. Am J Surg Pathol 1986, **10**(Suppl 1): 4–5; **B** from Stewart F. Arch Pathol 1943, **36:** 325–330; **C** from Stout AP. Cancer 1961, **14:** frontispiece; **D** courtesy of Dr. Lewis B. Woolner)

In terms of publications, the most influential textbooks written during this period in the field of oncologic surgical pathology (subspecialties excluded) were James Ewing's *Neoplastic Diseases* (1919), Pierre Masson's *Tumeurs; Diagnostic Histologiques* (1923) Arthur Purdy Stout's *Human Cancer* (1932), Rupert A. Willis's *Pathology of Tumors* (1948), Lauren V. Ackerman's *Surgical Pathology* (1953), and the remarkable *Atlas of Tumor Pathology* collection, begun in 1949. The latter work, colloquially known as the A.F.I.P. Fascicles and currently in its fourth series, has perhaps contributed more than any other to establish the discipline of surgical pathology throughout the world as a result of its comprehensiveness coverage, the expertise of the authors, and the substantially low cost of the individual fascicles. Kudos to the Armed Forces Institute of Pathology—an institution currently in dire financial distress—for their mighty contribution to this effort, not to speak of the consultative and other academic activities they have carried out over the best part of the century with such a distinction and generosity.[4]

Surgical pathology and the pathologist

The basic characteristics of the surgical pathologist were masterfully described by the begetter of this book, Dr. Lauren V. Ackerman. Since these remain virtually unchanged 50 years later, it was deemed appropriate to repeat almost verbatim the comments he made in that regard in the early editions of this book:

A department of pathology in a large medical center should have a division of surgical pathology closely affiliated with the clinical and surgical departments. Surgical pathology implies surgery, but the modern surgical pathologist is closely affiliated with many branches of medicine. This includes all the surgical specialties, internal medicine, dermatology, neurology, diagnostic radiology, radiation therapy, and medical oncology. Although the study of radiology deals with shadows and the study of pathology with substance, the correlation of those shadows with the gross substance strengthens the diagnostic skill of the radiologist, explains errors in radiologic interpretation, and instills humility rather than dogmatism. The radiotherapist and medical oncologist, too, can learn much from the study of surgical pathology, particularly the correlation between sensitivity to therapy and microscopic tumor types and the effects of therapy on normal tissue. Furthermore, explanations for the success or failure of therapy may become apparent by the study of surgical specimens.

The surgical pathologist has the unique opportunity of bridging the gap between the beginning of disease and its end stages, and he should take advantage of this circumstance. He can do this only after a solid foundation of study at the autopsy table, where the ravages of cancer and other diseases are all too clear. With this background, he can then correlate the initial stages of disease seen in specimens from living patients in the surgical pathology laboratory and make fundamental contributions to knowledge. With the integration of clinical findings, pathologic anatomy is still a living science.

By the very nature of the material submitted to him, the surgical pathologist is bound to make some mistakes. He sees the earliest subtle and sometimes bewildering changes in Hodgkin's lymphoma. He may not recognize that the minimal granulomatous response in a lymph node is really a peripheral manifestation of histoplasmosis. The necessity of follow-up on the patient in whom the diagnosis is not certain is mandatory. Time is often a better diagnostician.

The surgical pathologist not only must know his own field thoroughly, but he also must have a rich background in clinical medicine. He needs to understand the clinician's needs and respond to them accordingly. He must be in a position to advise the clinician about the biopsy or the excised material he receives. It is not sufficient for him to say whether a lesion is benign or malignant. He must be able to tell the surgeon the extent of the disease, the grade of malignancy, the adequacy of the excision, and other pertinent information. He should also be able to comment on whether additional therapy may be necessary and give information on the prognosis of the disease. He should communicate with clinicians constantly, informally and through interdepartmental conferences. The ever-increasing complexity of medicine has led to the unavoidable development of subspecialization within surgical pathology. There is no question that in some cases clinicians are best served by patholo-gists who have special expertise in certain areas and fully understand the clinical implications of their pathologic findings. Hematopathology, nephropathology, neuropathology, and dermatopathology are prime examples of such subspecialties.

The exponential growth of knowledge and the incorporation of increasingly sophisticated techniques to the study of pathology makes the need for subspecialization—at least in the academic arena—increasingly apparent. To cite an obvious example, it is hard to believe that the splendid advances made in hematopathology during the past 30 years would have been possible without much concentrated effort on the part of highly specialized individuals.[12]

Surgical pathology and the nonpathologist

By its very nature, surgical pathology depends heavily on the input of clinicians and surgeons who are fully aware of the potentials and limitations of the specialty. They should know that a microscopic diagnosis is a subjective evaluation that acquires full meaning only when the pathologist is fully cognizant of the essential clinical data, surgical findings, and type of surgery. The requisition slip for pathologic study should ideally be completed by a physician familiar with the case; too often the task is delegated to a medical student, a nurse, or the surgery resident who was requested to perform the biopsy. One of the most frustrating and potentially dangerous experiences that a pathologist can suffer is that of the occasional requisition form lacking adequate clinical information.[15] I am not referring to a detailed recounting of the symptoms and radiographic findings of the case. I am talking about not mentioning the fact that a patient with a lung nodule had a sarcoma of the thigh removed 3 years ago, or that a "scar tissue" from the face is from the fourth recurrence of a desmoplastic melanoma. The potential medical, financial and legal possible consequences of this negligence are enormous, and there are not enough immunohistochemical stains or computer programs that will fully protect the pathologist and the patient against them. For some subspecialties, inadequacy of clinical information (including the clinical differential diagnosis in a dermatosis), whether because of ignorance or carelessness, is almost an invitation to an inadequate (or at least incomplete) pathologic interpretation.

One of the best ways for a clinician to acquire a feeling of what the specialty is, and how it can be best used, is to have a full-time rotation in surgical pathology during the residency years. We have found this practice invaluable in establishing a mutually beneficial rapport between surgeons and pathologists. The surgeon will certainly not learn to be a pathologist during this short period, but will leave the rotation with a better feeling for what a surgical pathologist can do and what he cannot, and how best to benefit from the interaction. It is unfortunate that a shortage of trainees and increased clinical demands have made such a rotation so difficult to implement in recent times.

To quote again Dr. Ackerman from an early edition of this book:

> A good surgeon has not only technical dexterity (a fairly common commodity), but also, more importantly, good judgment and a personal concern for his patient's welfare. The surgeon with a prepared mind and a clear concept of the pathology of disease invariably is the one with good judgment. Without this background of knowledge, he will not recognize specific pathologic alterations at surgery nor will he have a clear concept of the limitations of his knowledge, and therefore he will not know when to call the pathologist to help him. Without this basic knowledge, he may improve his technical ability but never his judgment. One might say that with him his ignorance is refined rather than his knowledge broadened.

It is unfortunate that in some specialized areas of pathology (especially, dermatology, gynecology, and gastrointestinal pathology), a conflict still persists in some quarters as to who should be interpreting the microscopic slides and in which department the laboratory should be located. Admittedly, there are exceptional persons who are not trained pathologists but who have made fundamental contributions to pathology in their respective fields of interest; however, there are many reasons why it is inadvisable for clinicians to become their own pathologists. Although it is mandatory for them to have some knowledge of pathology, it is difficult, if not impossible, to be both a competent clinician and a skillful pathologist, just as it is not rational for the surgical pathologist to believe himself capable of performing operations as a sideline. An additional reason is that an objective evaluation of the slide is compromised because of the conscious or unconscious tendency that we all have to agree with ourselves. Furthermore, since the situation so created is one of self-referral, there is an economic incentive to perform more, rather than fewer, microscopic examinations. The situation is comparable to the practice of radiology by nonradiologists, where it has been shown that the nonradiologist physician who owns an x-ray machine uses an average of twice as many x-ray examinations as do colleagues who refer patients to radiologists.[13]

There is a fundamental unity to the morphologic patterns of disease in the human body that can be appreciated only by being familiar with those patterns as they occur in different organ systems. Only by understanding the pathology of disease as a whole can the manifestation of that disease in a given organ be fully comprehended. This is the main reason why a clinician cannot hope to deal adequately with some small branch of surgical pathology. Disease does not cooperate with him by remaining neatly confined to an anatomic system.

It is encouraging to see that the trend in the United States is decidedly toward a restitution to the pathology departments of what logically belongs to them. Interestingly, this development has been largely driven by economic rather than academic factors. Indeed, the ability of bringing back to the Department of Pathology a subspeciality pathology laboratory housed in a clinical department seems inversely proportional to the revenues that this laboratory generates. In any event, medicine has become too complex to be handled with the approach of the Renaissance man. The days in which the gynecologist examined the patient, looked at the x-ray films, performed the surgery, examined the surgical specimen microscopically, and administered radiation therapy are over.

As far as pathology is concerned, the process is likely to be accelerated by the economic factors that are playing an increasingly important role in shaping the practice of medicine. Modern academic surgical pathology can no longer be performed in a laboratory equipped with a tissue processor, a paraffin oven, a set of reagents, and a microscope. It requires facilities for electron microscopy, enzyme histochemistry, immunohistochemistry, and molecular biology techniques. To have these expensive and complicated facilities duplicated within each of the major clinical and surgical departments of a medical center is financially absurd, a fact that has not escaped the attention of hospital administrators and third-party payers. An additional reason why the pathologist interpreting microscopic slides should not belong to a clinical department is that only by remaining independent can he have the unbiased approach necessary for the performance of his functions. He should be in a position to discuss freely with the clinician the indications for the performance of a biopsy, a frozen section, or a surgical procedure. Tissue committees and the important quality-control function that they fulfill depend largely on the pathologist's prerogative, free of any interference, to present facts and question procedures.

At this point, it is only fair to mention that many of the problems alluded to are of our own making. One of the main reasons why clinicians began to act as pathologists and set up pathology minilaboratories in their own departments was because many departments of pathology were unable or unwilling to provide the services that clinicians rightfully demanded. In the past, the diagnosis of tissue removed from a living patient often was delegated to a resident, and reports emanating from the department of pathology not only were delayed, but also often indicated only whether the tissue was benign or malignant. These circumstances sometimes forced clinicians to direct some branch of surgical pathology. Under these conditions, the clinician's diagnoses and recommendations were better than those of the experienced but uninterested pathologist. Fortunately, the situation has changed radically. There is, however, no room for complacency. It is the duty of the current generation of pathologists to improve the quality and quantity of the services provided by continually adapting to the ever-increasing complexity of their task. In this time and age, the overriding challenge comes from molecular biology. It will not make morphology disappear, as some of its more strident apologists have announced in apocalyptic terms, but it will certainly change dramatically the way we practice the specialty.[14,16,17] Actually, it has happened already. It would be a mistake for surgical pathologists not to embrace it, as they have done before with other special techniques. It will no be as natural as it was for electron microscopy or immunohistochemistry, which, after all, had also a morphologic basis. Molecular biology is a seemingly different world, with a different language and pictorial representation. Yet the link is there. Some of the greater advances in medicine and biology have been made by people who combined to their best advantage the tools of two or more disciplines in order to answer a question. Future discoveries will not likely be made by morphologists ignorant of molecular biologic findings or by biologists unaware or scornful of morphologic data but by those willing and capable of integrating them through a team approach.

Surgical pathology report

The delivery of a specimen in the surgical pathology laboratory initiates a complex series of events that culminates in the issuance of the final report.

The surgical pathology report is an important medical document that should describe, as thoroughly and concisely as possible, all the relevant gross and microscopic features of a case, and which should also interpret their significance for the clinician. It should be prompt, accurate, and brief. The pathologist should avoid unnecessary histologic jargon that is of no clinical consequence and concentrate on the aspects that bear a relation to therapy and prognosis. To quote Richard Reed*:

> A competent [pathologist] is not simply a storage site for microscopic verbiage. It is not enough to be able to recite by rote the microscopic findings once the clinical diagnosis is established. The ability to offer clinical differential diagnoses from the interpretation of microscopic findings is the mark of the mature [surgical] pathologist. In addition, he may record data that are prognostically significant or offer suggestions for pertinent clinical tests. The ability to recognize cytologic and histologic features is simply a beginning. The ability to

integrate microscopic findings into a meaningful interpretation is the distinguishing characteristic of a pathologist and is the art of pathology.

The usual surgical pathology report is composed of five major fields, the order of which is to some extent a matter of personal preference. The first, which follows the demographics information, is designated as "History," and contains the essential clinical data known to the pathologist at the time he dictates a description of the gross specimen(s), such as sex and age of the patient, symptoms, surgical findings, and type of surgery. It should also list previous biopsies on the same patient, if any had been taken. We insist on having a "History" section in all of our reports, no matter how brief, because it gives the reader of the report, whether a clinician or another pathologist, an immediate orientation to the nature of the problem that led to that particular operation.

The second field, designated as "Gross," contains the gross description of the specimen(s). This should be precise and thorough, because once the gross specimen is discarded, and unless a picture has been taken, this description remains the only document by which the gross features of the case can be evaluated. It should indicate how the various specimens were identified by the surgeon and whether they were received fresh or fixed, intact or open. The specimens should be described in a logical sequential fashion, with a clear description of gross abnormalities and their location. Lengthy anatomic descriptions of normal structures should be avoided. The size, color, and location of all lesions should be recorded. The metric system is to be used for all measurements. It is advisable to give specific dimensions and descriptions rather than to provide comparisons with common objects such as fruits or vegetables. The weight of the whole specimen, and sometimes the weight of the individual organs or lesions in a specimen, should be recorded whenever indicated. It is important to be accurate, factual, and noncommittal in the gross description, avoiding subjective interpretations as much as possible. Azzopardi[19] rightly commented that the contents of a mammary cyst are better described as amber, brownish, greenish, opaque, or white rather than "blood-stained," "pus," or "milky" because the reason for the color of a secretion is often unknown. This sensible advice should be applied to other lesions as well. We prefer to identify the various sections taken by using letters of the English alphabet sequentially (rather than the first letter of the specimen or some other code), and we list this identification at the end of the gross description rather than after each specimen. The "gross" portion of the report is concluded by noting whether or not all of the tissue was submitted for microscopic examination and by including the name of the pathologist who performed the gross examination.

---

* From Reed RJ. New concepts in surgical pathology of the skin. New York, 1976, John Wiley & Sons, Inc. (Wiley Series in Surgical Pathology, Hartmann W, ed.)

The third field is termed "Microscopic." We regard this as an optional feature of the report, which in many cases is unnecessary. When included, it should be short and to the point. The surgeon usually is not too interested in whether the nucleoli are acidophilic, basophilic, or amphophilic but rather what that means, if anything; if another pathologist is keen on this point, he probably will like to examine the slide himself.

The fourth and most important field of the report is the "Diagnosis." Each specimen received should have a separate diagnosis or diagnoses. Our practice is to divide each diagnosis into two parts, separated by a dash. The first lists the organ, specific site in that organ, and operation; the second gives the morphologic diagnosis (e.g., Bone, femur, biopsy—Osteosarcoma). This is useful for coding purposes, and again, it provides the reader with all the essential information on that particular specimen in a single entry. The SNOMED code should follow.

The fifth field, which is optional, is a "Note" or "Comment." Here, the pathologist may mention the differential diagnosis, give the reasons for this diagnostic interpretation, make some prognostic and therapeutic considerations about the entity, clarify some aspects of the case, and include selected references. When properly used, this becomes one of the most important means of clinicopathologic correlation. Parenthetically, by reading these notes one can tell apart immediately the pure morphologist from the clinically oriented surgical pathologist, who before writing the note in question will ask himself: "If I were the clinician on this case, what would I like to know from this pathologic study?".

If a frozen section has been performed, the information regarding the organ biopsied, the diagnosis given, the names of the pathologist(s) who performed the procedure, and the final diagnosis corresponding to *the frozen sample* should be included in the report, either as a separate field (which we prefer) or incorporated into the History or Gross fields.

The amount of information to be provided in pathology reports—particularly in the case of tumors—has grown exponentially in recent years. Only a few decades ago it was deemed perfectly appropriate to issue a report on a mastectomy specimen as "Invasive carcinoma with three metastatic lymph nodes." Currently, the information expected to be provided in such a specimen is daunting.[20] The desirability of including such information on this and other tumor types in a *consistent* fashion in terms of thoroughness, terminology, and sequence is obvious[18] (Appendix C). Since it is a rare individual who can do it from memory based on experience—exaggerated boasts to the contrary notwithstanding—it follows that the use of standard forms as a guiding hand is to be encouraged.[21] Whether these are to be employed as checklists or as modifiable "canned sentences" in a computer database is of little importance as long as they fulfill their important function. The forms we have developed at Memorial Hospital for the major tumor types are displayed in Appendix D.[24]

In a well-planned survey sponsored by the College of American Pathologists, it was found that the completeness of the pathology report in colectomy specimens from various institutions was more dependent on the use of a standard form than on any other parameter (such as academic status of the institution, number of surgical specimens, and presence of a pathology residency program).[25]

It is medically and legally important that the diagnoses and comments made by the pathologist on a given case be documented as clearly as possible in a written form in the clinical chart via the pathology report. This should be done because sometimes there is a remarkable discrepancy between the diagnostic considerations given verbally by the pathologist to the clinician and the paraphrasing of these considerations by the clinician in the chart. Each remark of importance given verbally should be incorporated into the final pathology report.

When an urgent decision needs to be made on the basis of a pathologic finding, the clinician should not have to wait for that information to reach him by standard printed report. Electronic displays on computer screens, available in stations, clinics, and physicians' offices immediately after the pathologist has "signed" the case electronically, are being routinely used and have proved very effective in shortening the communication gap. However, it is well to remember that no technologic advancement can replace the time-honored practice of two medical specialists discussing, immediately after the facts are known, how best to treat a patient.

Perhaps it should be stated again that a crucial aspect of the work of the surgical pathologist is the timing of his work. Whether this is counted in minutes, as in a frozen section procedure, or in 6 days, as in a routinely processed specimen, it is essential to keep time at a minimum.[22,23] The pathologist who spends minutes enraptured in the examination of a frozen section and shares his excitement with his colleagues should remember that there is somebody else who is spending those same minutes under somewhat different circumstances and in a different frame of mind. The same applies to the surgical pathologist who is earnestly attempting to subclassify an obviously benign sweat gland tumor into one of the innumerable subcategories that have been described. This is a laudable academic exercise and one that may have some clinical implications. However, it would be advisable for him also to think in practical terms; before this process is completed and an authoritative final diagnosis made, he should consider calling the clinician to inform him that the lesion is a benign sweat gland tumor (or a benign adnexal tumor, for that matter), that no further surgery is necessary, that in all likelihood the patient is cured, and that additional studies to classify the lesion precisely are in progress.

Slide review and consultation

A very fortunate aspect of pathology (although some may view it as a curse) is the fact that the material on which the diagnosis is made (i.e., the microscopic slide) is of a permanent nature and can be evaluated by different observers or by the same observer at different times. This feature should be used by the pathologist to the maximum. All slides and paraffin blocks should be stored indefinitely if facilities are available. Whenever a specimen is received in the laboratory, the files should be searched for previous material on the same patient, a search now generally done automatically by computer. If such material is present and is conceivably related to the present illness, the slides and the report should be reviewed. It is mandatory also for the pathologist to review the outside slides of a patient who is referred to his institution with a microscopic diagnosis made elsewhere before therapy is begun.[30] It is the responsibility of the pathology department of the referring institution—as legal custodians of this material—to carefully pack and ship this material with a copy of their pathology report.[33] Whether the slides have been requested by the clinician or the pathology department is immaterial, but eventually they should be examined by the pathologist, and a formal report should be issued, a copy of which should be sent to the referring pathologist. Pathologists should not object to this practice, which is not instituted to question their interpretation but rather to ensure uniformity of diagnosis, grading, and nomenclature in a given institution, to allow comparisons with subsequent material in the same patient, and to enable this material to be presented at interdepartmental conferences.[26] Whenever possible, representative slides should remain in the files of the institution that requested them for a variety of reasons, including the fact that the need for additional review may arise later. This can be easily achieved in most cases by the sender preparing one or more additional slides, a relatively low-cost operation. Obviously, if only one slide shows the diagnostic area or if the specimen is a cytologic preparation, that is a different matter. A satisfactory alternative for such cases is to document photographically the key features of the cases before returning the slides by making use of the now widely available high-resolution photomicroscopy digital cameras.

Consultation with other pathologists in unusual, difficult and controversial cases has become an increasingly popular practice, at least in the United States.[27,29] When done for the right reasons and in the proper fashion, it is a healthy practice that benefits the referring pathologist, the consultant, and the patient. In order to obtain maximum benefit from this procedure, some basic rules need to be observed[28,35,37] (Appendix A). It is important for the referring pathologist to review the clinical history carefully (which should have been done anyway to begin with) and provide all the pertinent information to the consultant, together with a description of the gross findings, all the relevant slides, and his interpretation of the lesion. If the need for immunohistochemistry or other special stains is anticipated, he should include a set of unstained slides or (preferably) a paraffin block. If he is sending the case to more than one consultant, he will be courteous enough to inform each consultant of this fact and, ideally, he will let each expert know what the other expert said. If there is a concrete possibility that the case will end up in court or if it is in the medicolegal arena already, the consultant should be so informed.

It is also expected that the sender of the case will let the consultant know of any subsequent developments on the case, especially those that have a bearing on the diagnosis and evolution; he may do so spontaneously (despite the sense of uneasiness that the "unsolicited follow-up" invariably generates in the mind of the consultant) or when so requested by the consultant. The consultant should be as expeditious and careful with these cases as he is with his own material, if not more so. The medical and legal implications of his diagnoses are of no less importance than those made in his own institution. He also should keep in mind that the case does not become his property just because he was asked to express an opinion on it.

It is a prerogative of the consultant to make general considerations about the expected natural history and possible therapeutic approaches to the case, based on previous experience and review of the literature,[36] and even to express his own preferences. Such considerations, if presented in the right format, are generally welcomed by the submitter and the therapist, especially when dealing with very unusual entities. However, the consultant should keep in mind that the microscopic appearance of the tumor is only one of many criteria upon which the final therapeutic decision should be based.[32] Therefore, it is prudent for the consultant to phrase those considerations in such a way that the physician eventually responsible for deciding upon and implementing the therapy will be helped rather than impeded.

Of course, another aspect of slide review/second opinion is that carried out intradepartmentally on a daily basis. Traditionally, this has been done in an informal way among two or more colleagues, with no permanent record remaining. It is good medical practice to document the action in the written report. The same applies when such a review is carried out on a regular basis at an intradepartmental consensus session. Some authors have suggested that all cases with a diagnosis of malignancy should be confirmed by a second pathologist. Since a high proportion of the errors result from missing the diagnostic area, one could make just the reciprocal recommendation, or go all the way and propose for all cases to be routinely reviewed by a second pathologist.[31,34] The approach is sound but probably not viable on a large scale when considering the substantial additional cost involved.

Limitations of histologic diagnosis

It is as important for the surgical pathologist to know the limitations of his specialty as it is for him to be aware of its strength and potential contributions. This fact has been expressed in a most perceptive and amusing way by Dr. Oscar N. Rambo in an article entitled "The limitations of histologic diagnosis." Excerpts from this essay follow*:

> Pathologists are physicians and human beings. They have as great a capacity for error and susceptibility to subjective distractions as other practitioners of the art of medicine. Because of certain nineteenth century dogmas and because the teaching of pathology used to be relegated primarily to the long-forgotten pre-clinical phase, pathologists traditionally have been regarded to be more scientific than many of their colleagues. A mystic perversion of this assumption prevails among those clinicians who believe that the pathologist, given only a piece of a patient's tissue, has all of the other ingredients necessary to produce a statement of absolute truth at the end of his report. More dangerous to mankind is a pathologist with the same concept…
>
> Incomplete communication between the clinician and pathologist may make diagnosis difficult or impossible. To perform intelligently, a consultant must know all the facts that have any bearing on the case. To render a diagnosis from an inherently puzzling bit of tissue with only vague knowledge of its source and no concept of the clinical problem is as fool-hardy as to undertake an appendectomy on the basis of hearsay evidence that the patient has a pain in his belly.
>
> As an off-duty exercise, pathologists frequently like to play games with slides as "pure unknowns." Sometimes with their brains and microscopes they can give a remarkably accurate reconstruction of the disease process, pronounce the exact diagnosis and flush with pride at the awed applause of those gathered around the optical altar. And sometimes they can be absolutely wrong. Showmanship has no place in life and death diagnosis…
>
> Much of the effort expended in carefully executing a diagnostic biopsy procedure is wasted if the pathologist is regarded as a technician rather than a consultant. In many instances, the physician who will have to interpret the slide can offer valuable advice about the clinical nature of a lesion and where best to sample it if he is [invited] to examine the patient before or during surgery. With historical background, physical findings and precise orientation of anatomic relationships, the [pathologist] can block the tissue

> in the plane that will give the most meaningful sections…
>
> Most physicians are taught that the best biopsy is a cleanly excised, uncrushed wedge that includes a junction between normal and neoplastic tissue. The edge of an ulcerating squamous carcinoma may be indistinguishable from pseudoepitheliomatous hyperplasia; the junction between colonic mucosa and a well differentiated exophytic carcinoma may be sharp, dramatic and unmistakable, but if the biopsy is inadequate in depth or breadth, the pathologist is obliged to append a note stating that he cannot determine from the tissue submitted whether the process is a cancer or a polyp. The normal margin must not be obtained at the expense of representative tumor. Worst of all are expanding soft tissue neoplasms. Junction biopsies may include only a pseudocapsule that can be hard, typically "fish flesh" and grossly more malignant in character than the tumor beneath. Such a barrier found in the retroperitoneum or deep muscle groups of an extremity may achieve a thickness of one centimeter or more…
>
> While it may not always be technically feasible to obtain bigger, better, or multiple biopsies, there are many occasions in which the advantages of a significant increase in the sample of tumor outweigh the risk to the patient. Adequate volume of tissue permits a choice of fixatives, histochemical studies, bioassay or tissue culture. In some instances, one of the specialized examinations may break a morphologic deadlock…
>
> Before a biopsy specimen is delivered to the laboratory, it may be so damaged that the slides prepared from it are worthless. In place of a diagnosis the pathologist must write, "Tissue unsatisfactory for interpretation." A more serious consequence of damage is failure to recognize subtle artefactual changes in cells. False positive, false negative and incorrect histogenetic interpretations have resulted from avoidable mishandling of biopsy fragments…
>
> The complaint of withholding information may also be lodged against the pathologist. The unsophisticated recipient of a pathologist's written consultation will seek out the usually brief, bald diagnostic statement, accept it as the truth and proceed on his definitive therapeutic way. In the majority of instances, the diagnosis is the "truth," assuming certain minimum standards of professional competence and permitting considerable philosophic license with the word. But the appearance of a sample of tumors and diseases difficult to classify may be thoroughly misleading when considered out of context.
>
> There are ways in which the pathologist can and should indicate doubts and alternative possibilities when he suspects that the tissue submitted to him may tell only part of the story of the patient's disease or may be a false representation. Retreat to the smug assertion, "I can see only what is in the tissues you gave me," has been forced on pathologists by colleagues who have sought miracles of extrapolation from inadequate biopsies. Differential diagnoses of tissue have been discouraged by the myth of objectivity, the dogma that pathologists have the final word, and the thundering denunciations of pathologists' speculations by physicians who want a single, solid answer, right or wrong…
>
> With full knowledge of the relativity of the term, we use [the term] "inexperience" with deliberate intent. Neither pride nor pressure should force a pathologist to make a deci-

---

* From Rambo ON. The limitations of histologic diagnosis. Prog Radiat Ther 1962, **2**: 215–224. Reprinted by permission of Grune & Stratton, Inc., and the author.

sion about a disease process that he does not recognize. The nearest approximation or look-alike in his experience may be entirely unrelated. A mismatch may result in mutilation or death of the patient.

Recognition of one's limitations is as great an asset as the sharpest diagnostic eye. There is a chain of command for handling serious and unfamiliar problems. Colleagues immediately available may offer a rapid solution from past experience or from lack of obsessive preconception. The community may be polled. Among the members may be one who has perfect and documented recall of an entity not previously encountered. Such a survey may yield only confusion, but from it one can usually salvage a list of experts with series of entities, ones that may come to the average pathologist only once or twice in his lifetime.

While it is true that world renowned experts are human and fallible and that there is an almost irreducible percentage of undiagnosable tumors, it is every physician's obligation to, submit his insoluble problems to the highest court of appeal. Such a presentation should be made only after thorough deliberation and must be accompanied by all pertinent clinical data. A complete historical review and serial roentgen studies of a bone tumor may be more important diagnostically than a biopsy. It is sportsmanlike and of great educational value to the pathologist [seeking a second opinion] to submit his own report even if it ends with several speculative diagnoses, each preceded by a question mark.

Biopsy

Interpreting biopsies is one of the most important duties of the surgical pathologist. In *incisional* biopsies, only a portion of the lesion is sampled, and therefore the procedure is strictly of a diagnostic nature. In *excisional* biopsies, the entire lesion is removed, usually with a rim of normal tissue, and therefore the procedure serves both a diagnostic and a therapeutic function. The decision whether to perform an incisional or an excisional biopsy depends primarily on the size of the lesion; the smaller it is, the more logical to take it out completely when first encountered. For large lesions, particularly those of deep soft tissues, an incisional biopsy is usually preferable because of the fact that the type and extent of excision vary considerably depending on the tumor type. The danger of incisional biopsies promoting metastatic spread, a hotly debated subject in the past, has proved to be inconsequential.[38]

Biopsies are also classified according to the instrument used to obtain them: cold knife, cautery, needle, or endoscope. Of these, the one usually least suitable for microscopic interpretation is that obtained with a cautery, because this instrument chars and distorts the tissue and prevents proper staining.

Some general rules for the biopsy procedure follow. The fact that they are so obvious makes it particularly bothersome that they are so often violated or ignored.

1 The larger the lesion, the more numerous the biopsies that should be taken from it because of the variability in pattern that may exist and the fact that the diagnostic areas may be present only focally.

2 In ulcerated tumors, biopsy of the central ulcerated area may show only necrosis and inflammation. The most informative biopsy is likely to be one taken from the periphery that includes both normal and diseased tissue; however, the biopsy should not be so peripheral that only normal tissue is obtained.

3 The biopsy should be deep enough that the relationship between tumor and stroma can be properly assessed. Epithelia involved by carcinoma have a tendency to detach from the underlying stroma. This should be avoided whenever possible by careful handling of the tissue.

4 Deeply seated lesions are sometimes accompanied by a prominent peripheral tissue reaction, which may be characterized by chronic inflammation, hyperemia, fibrosis, calcification, and metaplastic bone formation. If the biopsy is too peripheral, this may be the only tissue obtained. Similarly, in a mass of lymph nodes, a deep-seated node may show involvement by a malignant tumor, whereas a superficial node may show only nonspecific hyperplasia.

5 When several fragments of tissue are obtained, they should all be sent to the pathology department and all of them submitted for microscopic examination. Sometimes the smaller or grossly less impressive fragment is the only one that contains the diagnostic elements.

6 Crushing or squeezing of the tissue with forceps at the time of performance of the biopsy by the surgeon, at the time of the gross examination by the pathologists, or at the time of embedding by the histotechnologist should be carefully avoided. The artifacts resulting from it often render a biopsy impossible to interpret.

7 Once the biopsy is obtained, it should be placed immediately into a container with an adequate volume of fixative. The temptation on the part of the surgeon or the pathologist to turn it around, wash it, or scrape the surface should be resisted, since it will not provide any information of diagnostic significance but only create artifacts.

8 Depending on the presumed or known nature of the lesion, consideration should be given *at the time of the biopsy* to the possible need for special studies, such as touch preparations, electron microscopy, cytogenetics, molecular pathology, flow cytometry, or others.

Intraoperative consultation ("frozen section")

The procedure colloquially known as frozen section is one of the most important and difficult procedures that the pathologist performs during his practice.[40] It requires experience, knowledge of clinical medicine and pathology, the capacity to make quick decisions under pressure, good judgment, an attitude that is conservative but not excessively so, and a keen awareness of the limitations of the method. It follows from these requirements that the responsibility for frozen section diagnosis should fall on a well-trained pathologist whose main activity is in the division of surgical pathology and who knows well the surgeon requesting the procedure. To state it bluntly, the pathologist who is primarily engaged in basic research and who rotates through surgical pathology once a week "to keep in touch" is ill-equipped to take the main responsibility for this delicate task.

It is unfortunate that a procedure that is time-consuming, costly, and sometimes stressful is so often misused by some surgeons to satisfy their curiosity, to compensate for deficiencies in recognizing normal anatomic structures, or as a mechanism to communicate the results immediately to the patient's relatives. Frozen sections represent a good source of income to the department (at least under the fee-for-service reimbursement system) and excellent training for the residents who participate in them, but when unnecessary they increase the medical bill needlessly and sometimes hamper a proper pathologic evaluation of the specimen. This has been particularly true in the case of mammographically detected breast lesions[41] (see Chapter 20). There is a very simple question that the surgeon should ask himself in deciding whether a frozen section should be done or not: Will the result of the frozen section examination influence in any way the surgical procedure? If the answer is no, the procedure is not indicated.[57] By using this criterion, we have estimated that almost half of the frozen sections done at a particular institution could have been avoided.[47] It is our impression that this percentage would not have been significantly different if the study had been done in any of the other high-powered places we have worked. The three legitimate purposes of a frozen section are (1) to establish the presence and nature of a lesion; (2) to determine the adequacy of surgical margins; and (3) to establish whether the tissue obtained contains diagnosable material (even if the exact diagnosis cannot be made on the frozen sample) or whether additional sampling is indicated.[43,54,62,65] Sometimes a pathologist cannot reach a decision on the basis of the frozen section. When this is the case, he need not be apologetic. He should state this fact just as affirmatively as when he makes a diagnosis of carcinoma. Sometimes he can add that, according to his evaluation, the tissue removed is representative of the lesion but that the definitive diagnosis will have to wait for the permanent sections. The surgeon will then have to decide, depending on the nature of the case, whether to give the pathologist additional tissue for frozen section or whether to close the incision and wait for the permanent sections.

The indications and limitations of frozen section diagnosis vary from organ to organ and are detailed in the respective chapters.

At the time of a frozen section, the diagnosis given verbally to the surgeon should be transcribed verbatim in an appropriate form and a copy of such form incorporated immediately into the chart. Another copy should remain in the laboratory and be filed with the frozen section slides. If the frozen sections are performed by several individuals on a rotation basis, it is important for a senior pathologist to review the material periodically to ensure that the quality of the sections and the agreement between the frozen section diagnosis and the final diagnosis remain at an acceptable level. These periodic reviews also are useful in pointing out patterns of use and misuse of the procedure by the various departments and their individual members.

The overall accuracy of this procedure has been tested and proved on numerous occasions, in both university hospitals and community hospitals (Table 1.1).[39,42,45,46,47,52,53,57,61] A CAP-sponsored review of over 90,000 frozen sections performed at 461 institutions showed a concordance rate of 98.58%, a remarkable figure.[50] Of the discordant cases, 67.8% were false-negative diagnoses for neoplasm. The main reasons for the discrepancies were:

1 Misinterpretation of the original frozen section (31.8%)
2 Absence of diagnostic tissue in the material frozen but presence in the material not sampled (31.4%)
3 Absence of diagnostic tissue in the frozen section but presence in the corresponding permanent section (30.0%).

A point worth repeating is that the real aim of the frozen section procedure is to influence the course of the operation. Most times, one achieves this purpose by providing a specific diagnosis but this need not be the case. In some instances, telling the surgeon "Widen the surgical margins, " "Do a lobectomy, " or "Stop there" may be far more useful than providing a very sophisticated microscopic diagnosis. Alas, being able to give that right advice requires medical knowledge that sometimes transcends pure morphologic skills.

In terms of turn-around-time, a CAP-sponsored study of almost 33,000 frozen sections done in 700 hospitals from various countries showed that 90% of the procedures were completed within 20 minutes, measured from the time that the pathologist received the specimen to the time that he returned the frozen section diagnosis to the surgeon.[58]

To carry out the task effectively, the pathologist should be thoroughly briefed on the patient's clinical history: ideally the surgeon and the pathologist should have discussed the case beforehand. The pathologist should be prepared to advise the surgeon as to the best area to

Table 1.1 Historical review of frozen-section accuracy

Institution	Year	No. of cases	Overall Accuracy (%)	False positives (%)	False negatives (%)	% Deferred	% Different
Bryan Memorial Hospital (Lincoln, NE)	1938	45	88.9	0	8.9	2.2	
Woman's Hospital (Detroit)	1957	412	94.9	0	1.4	3.5	
Washington Hospital Center (Washington, DC)	1959	1810	97.6	0.16	1.0	1.2	
Barnes Hospital (St. Louis)	1959	1269	98.0	0.30	1.7	0	
Henry Ford Hospital (Detroit)	1962	1093	97.5	0.64	1.9	0	
Miami Valley Hospital (Dayton, OH)	1966	1176	98.1	20	1.7	0.4	
Columbia-Presbyterian (New York City)	1968	3000	97.2	0.27	1.2	1.2	
Bispebjerb Hospital (Memphis)	1970	1964	96.6	0.60	1.8	0.1	0.9
Baptist Memorial Hospital (Memphis)	1972	3249	98.9	0.12	0.95	1.3	
University Hospital of San Diego	1973	2665	96.5	0.15	1.61	1.72	
University of Texas and Ohio State University Hospitals (Galveston and Columbus)	1974	10,000	98.0	0.15	0.88	0.5	0.58*
University of Aberdeen	1976	3556	98.5	0.17	0.61	0	1.76†
Bristol Royal Infirmary	1985	1000	96.5			1.3	2.2‡
Royal Alexandra Hospital for Children (Camperdown, NSW)	1985§	520	90.1	0.40	0.40	5.6	3.5
Meir General Hospital (Kfar Saba)	1986	586	96.1	0.20	2.5	1.2	
Los Angeles County-University of Southern California Medical Center	1987	1414	94.8	0.40	1.1	3.7	
University of Washington (Seattle)	1989	1000	90.4	0.20	2.3	6.1	1.0

Adapted from Oneson RH, Minke JA, Silverberg SG. Intraoperative pathologic consultation. An audit of 1,000 recent consecutive cases. Am J Surg Pathol 1989, **13**: 237–243.

* Grade errors.   † No major discrepancy.   ‡ Insignificant error (0.9) and significant error (1.3).   § Pediatric cases only.

biopsy. He should also be skillful in selecting from the specimen received the portion to be examined microscopically. The cryostat is now routinely used because of the technical excellence of the sections obtained.[62] Freezing the tissue in isopentane (methylbutane) cooled with liquid nitrogen or with an electronic device saves valuable time and results in fewer artifacts than when the tissue is frozen on the cryostat stage. Although all kinds of quick stains have been devised for frozen section use, we prefer hematoxylin–eosin because of the quality of the preparations and the better correlation that this allows with the permanent sections. Technical modification of some special stains such as PAS (30 seconds) and immunostains (7 minutes) have been devised for possible intraoperative use.[48,64] Examination of cytology specimens obtained by touch preparation of the fresh specimen can add a great deal of information to the frozen sections, and sometimes obviates the need for them altogether[39,44,49,55,59] (Fig. 1.2).

A most peculiar variation of the frozen section technique is that incorporated in the concept of Mohs' surgery as applied to skin tumors.[60,63] In this procedure, the tumor is removed with a scalpel angled 45 degrees to the skin, divided into quadrants, color coded, oriented en face, and sectioned in the cryostat horizontally across the bottom. The slides are then examined "by the Mohs'

surgeon serving as his own pathologist," the areas of neoplasm are mapped, and immediate re-excision is carried out if indicated. The difficulties of interpreting sections oriented in this fashion are rarely addressed by the proponents of this technique, and the rationale given for "the Mohs' surgeon serving as his own pathologist" (more often than not lacking any formal pathology

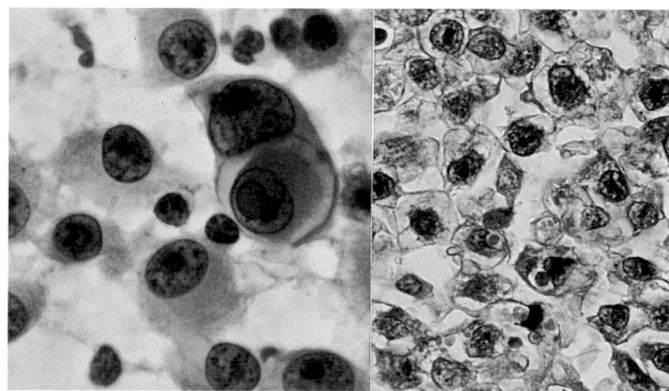

Fig. 1.2 Touch preparation of an axillary mass stained with hematoxylin and eosin at the time of frozen section (left). The diagnosis of metastatic malignant melanoma is more obvious in the cytology specimen than in the corresponding histology section (right). Note the prominent nuclear pseudoinclusion. (Courtesy of Dr. Bodgan Czerniak, Houston, Texas)

training) is less than credible. Suffice it to say that, after having seen this procedure in practice in several institutions, we remain highly skeptical of its scientific validity, despite the claims of its proponents[51,56] (see also Chapter 5).

Diagnostic cytology

Diagnostic cytology, when performed by well-trained, experienced individuals, offers an extremely high degree of reliability.[67] A positive cytologic diagnosis of malignancy made under these circumstances should be given the same weight as one obtained from a surgical biopsy. The cytologist will make a certain number of false-negative diagnoses depending on the source of the material, but false-positive diagnoses should practically never occur, for they will in themselves invalidate the method.

Recently, the procedure came under attack by some clinicians and even the lay press. The claim, sometimes justified, was that in some institutions—particularly some private laboratories—cytologic examinations were being carried out by poorly supervised cytotechnologists under heavy time constraints because of economic incentives, the emphasis being on the number of tests performed rather than on the quality of the procedure.[79] Obviously, it behooves the pathologist to maintain or restore the professional and scientific quality of this procedure if cytology is to remain an integral component of the practice of pathology.

In writing the cytology reports, we have made it our policy, whenever possible, to use the same terminology as that used for the microscopic sections, instead of employing the original grading system of Papanicolaou. A cytologic diagnosis of "squamous cell carcinoma" rendered on a sputum specimen gives the surgeon a better idea about the nature of a pulmonary mass than one of "cytology grade IV." We report cases in which we cannot be certain whether the cells present are malignant or not as "suspicious" and ask for additional material. We have found the guidelines for educational notes, disclaimers and other comments issued by the Papanicolau Society of Cytopathology very useful in transmitting this type of information to the clinician.[84a]

In most organs, a determined effort should be made to substantiate the cytologic diagnosis by a conventional biopsy procedure before decisive treatment is carried out. For instance, if a diagnosis of cancer is obtained from a cervical smear, irradiation or surgical treatment should not be started until a positive formal biopsy is at hand. For other organs, the approach may be quite different. For instance, a positive bronchial cytology in a patient with a pulmonary shadow justifies the administration of definitive therapy (surgery, radiation therapy, or chemotherapy), even if the bronchoscopic biopsy is negative.

Exfoliative cytology is of little practical value for lesions that are readily accessible to incisional biopsy, such as the skin or the oral cavity. Neither does it seem advisable to use this time-consuming method as a screening procedure for asymptomatic patients except under special circumstances. The value of cervicovaginal cytology for the screening of cervical carcinoma has been demonstrated beyond doubt, but this is perhaps the only cytology-based screening technique that has proved its worth in terms of human lives saved when related to the cost of the program.[71,86] The results so far obtained in the screening for other cancers in high-risk populations—such as gastric cytology in patients with pernicious anemia, bronchial cytology in heavy smokers, and nipple aspiration cytology in older women—have not been encouraging.

The technique of fine-needle aspiration (FNA) was developed at Memorial Hospital in New York City in the 1920s.[74,82] Despite the impressive results obtained, the procedure did not catch on in the United States, and it was all but abandoned even at Memorial. It was resurrected years later in Europe, particularly in Scandinavian countries, where its safety and accuracy were fully documented. Eventually, it made it back into the United States, where it has gained great popularity, especially for lesions of the breast, thyroid, salivary glands, and lung.[75,80,81,89] It is generally carried out with a "fine" needle (OD 0.6 to 0.9 mm), sometimes under image guidance.[78] There is no question that the procedure is, in most instances, inexpensive, safe, quick, and—when performed by experienced workers—quite accurate.[73] It has contributed a great deal to transform cytology from a primarily screening tool to a powerful diagnostic technique.[87] However, like any other technique, it has definite limitations that its enthusiastic champions sometimes choose to ignore.[76] It can also induce artifacts of various types in the tissues, which the pathologist should be cognizant of in order to avoid misinterpretation.[68]

It is not often realized that many of the special stains that are routinely used for tissue sections can also be very useful for the evaluation of cytologic material. This includes stains for glycogen, melanin, fat, and mucin. More importantly, cytologic material is also well suited for examination with immunocytochemical, ultrastructural, flow cytometric, cytogenetic, and molecular biologic techniques[69,70,72,84a,87,88] (Figs 1.3 and 1.4). The indications and limitations of this method are discussed further in the individual chapters.

New technologies have been introduced in recent years in an attempt to improve the detection of cytologic abnormalities in PAP and other smears. These include liquid-based, thin-layer cytology (ThinPrep, AutoCyte), computerized rescreening (PAPNET), and algorithm-based computer rescreening (AutoPap). Although the potential of these techniques is considerable,[66,71,85] it is too early to tell whether they will prove superior to the conventional ones in terms of health outcomes or cost

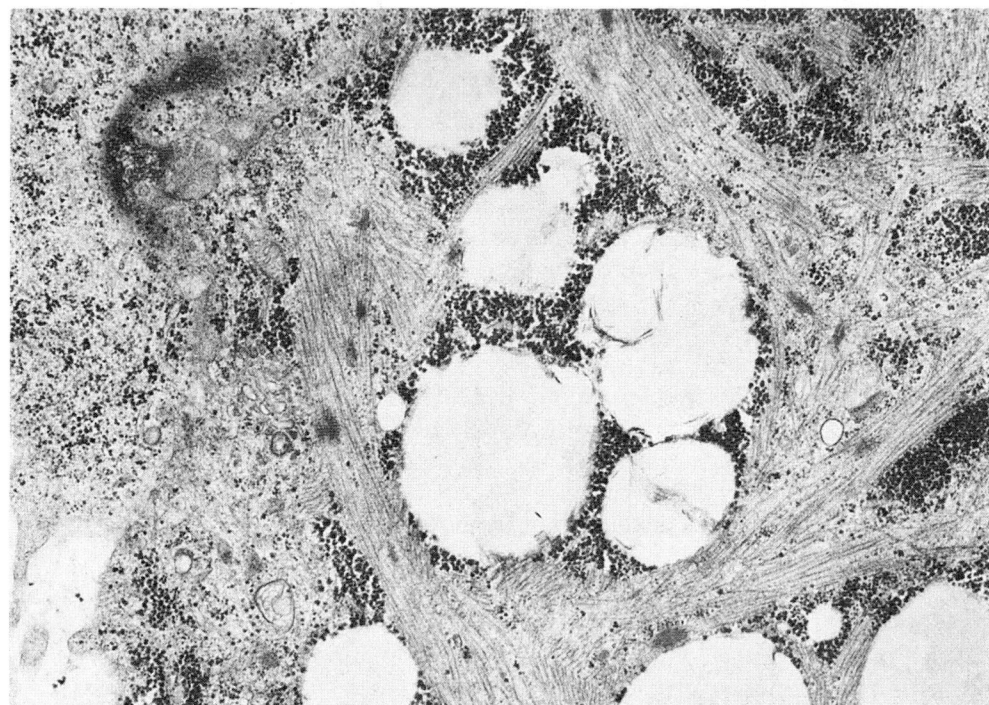

Fig. 1.3 Metastatic alveolar rhabdomyosarcoma to lungs and pleura in a 14-year-old girl. Electron microscopy of pleural fluid shows well-preserved neoplastic cells containing large quantities of glycogen and lipid; thick and thin microfilaments also may be noted. (×16,850)

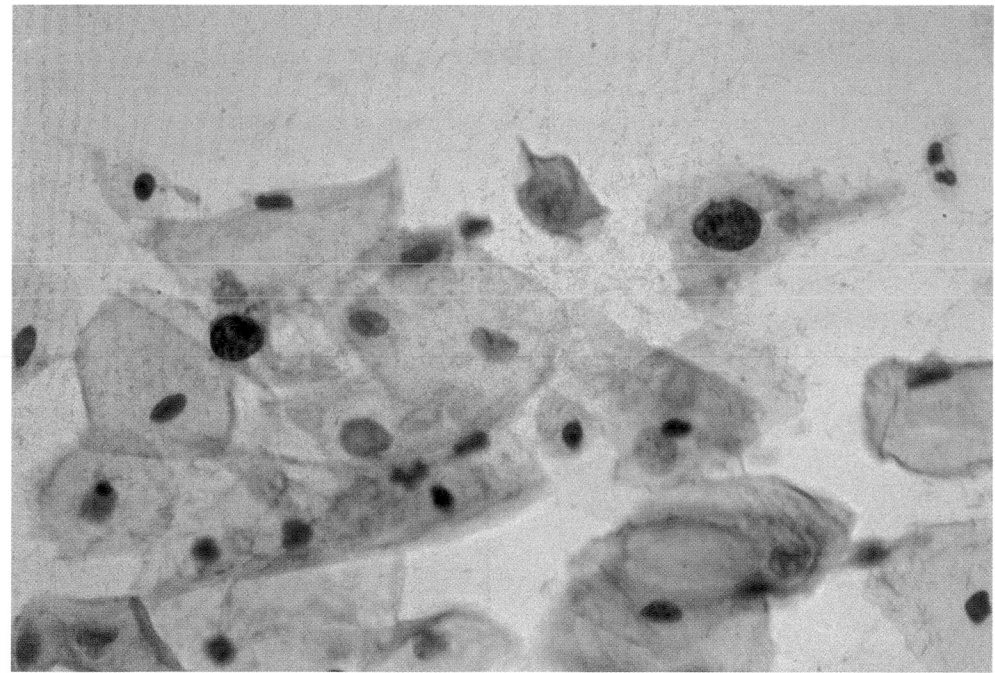

Fig. 1.4 Immunocytochemical demonstration of HPV infection in a cytologic specimen from uterine cervix. (Courtesy of Dr. Patricia Saigo, New York, NY)

effectiveness.[77,83,84] Needless to say, the considerable financial forces that exist behind these initiatives (to which pathologists are not immune) are not particularly conducive to an objective and dispassionate evaluation.

Digital pathology and telepathology

The era of digital pathology has arrived to surgical pathology.[91] It has done so mainly through the many anatomic pathology information systems now on the market[99] and the various devices that exist to capture digital images of gross and microscopic specimens, which can be integrated with the respective pathology reports. This has also allowed for these images to be transmitted electronically to any part of the globe. The latter, in short, is what is meant by *telepathology*. This can be done at various levels, from the e-mail attachment of a few static photographs to sophisticated systems that duplicate almost to perfection the examination of slides under the microscope and are, therefore, accurately referred to as *virtual microscopy*.[97] These instruments allow the remote user to move the microscopic field in any direction, to change magnifications, and even to change the focus, the latter function being particularly useful for cytologic preparations. This can be achieved by moving the components of a microscope located elsewhere by remote control[100] or by scanning the desired images and performing the above operations on those images (whether by accessioning them from a remote server or by unloading them in a local server) rather than the actual slide. For the past few years, we have used an instrument that operates on the latter principle and have found it very suitable for its purpose. The resolution of the images is practically the same as that obtained with the actual slide under the microscope and the program is extremely easy to use. The technique is suitable for routine histologic preparations, immunostains, cytology preparations, and electron micrographs.[98]

Whether this technology will ever replace the time-honored practice of mailing the slides for consultation, it remains to be seen. After all, most pathologists, if given the choice, would rather look at a section on a glass slide than an image, if only because this is what they have been doing since the beginning of recorded pathology history. Besides, few are the consultations that cannot wait 24 or 48 hours for an opinion. As Richard Kempson told me once, "Federal Express is the worse enemy of telepathology." With due apologies to DHL, this is true enough, and it may be difficult to justify the purchase of one of these instruments (the cost of which is not insignificant) for consultation purposed only.[90] However, if one realizes that the instrument can also be used very effectively for teaching purposes, quality control programs, consensus meetings, and as a research tool (for instance, to instantly retrieve any of the cases from a multiblock specimen), a different picture will emerge.[92,94,96] To all these applications, one should add that of "digital" frozen sections, an aspect we have not personally explored.[93,95,101]

Information systems in surgical pathology

Properly implemented, the ability of computers to store, organize, process, and retrieve prodigious amounts of information can measurably enhance the efficiency of the surgical pathology laboratory, improve the quality of the pathologist's service, monitor turnaround times and other quality assurance parameters, aid in research and teaching, and reduce the costs of operation.[107] However, the realization of these benefits is not automatic; it requires that the level of automation in a given installation be carefully matched to the needs of the pathologists, the institution, and the budget. Unfortunately, many surgical pathologists are poorly prepared to make the decisions required to design or choose a suitable automated system. The result, therefore, has too often been the implementation of systems that are little more than word processors with rudimentary patient registration features, or the initiation of extensive but poorly planned "in-house" software development efforts, usually by computer programers with a limited understanding of what features are required. In the former situation, the laboratory is denied most of the benefits of automation; in the latter case, it is likely to experience endless development costs for capabilities that may never materialize and, at the same time, sacrifice most of the benefit of effective automation. Compounding the problem is the relative paucity of information in the literature specifically addressing the problem of automation in surgical pathology, a deficiency that began to be corrected only recently.[103,106] Along these lines, a useful "laundry list" of the "ideal" equipment needs of an Anatomic Pathology laboratory has been published recently in a Spanish pathology journal.[104a]

Automation of surgical pathology laboratories has lagged far behind automation of the clinical laboratory for several reasons: (1) the relatively low volume of specimens; (2) the complexity of the tasks involved; (3) the nonquantitative (textual) nature of the data; and (4) the reluctance of many pathologists to alter their work habits to accommodate automation. Consequently, although automated record-keeping systems that are able to file coded specimen information have been relatively easy to design and introduce, only the most comprehensive systems, beginning with the CAPER system developed at the Massachusetts General Hospital,[102] have been able to offer any degree of practical automation of the routine reporting and administrative tasks of the surgical pathology laboratory. Several technical advances during the past decades have contributed to the increasing sophistication of such systems. The rapid development of microcomputer technology has made the necessary hardware affordable by any surgical pathology laboratory. Improvements in mass information storage technology (e.g. hard disks) now make the storage of enormous amounts of textual information practical for the periods of time routinely required (5 to 10 years). Finally, the development of high-level programing languages especially designed for database and string variable (text) manipulation have allowed the incremental development of sophisticated systems that retain the ability to be easily altered or enhanced to meet new user demands. Thus, pathologists may now reasonably expect that and automated surgical pathology system will "talk" to them in their own language, will not require that they change the way diagnoses are worded and recorded, will not ask them to remember "codes," will accept the information they provide in almost any format, will store this information permanently and reliably, will automatically organize it for recall by any combination of criteria, and will unobtrusively attend to most of the routine administrative chores. More sophisticated systems are also now providing storage of both visual and textual information and "expert" consultative support such as on-line assistance with specimen preparation, grading, staging, diagnosis, and bibliographic retrieval.

Regardless of the level of automation chosen, certain features of the system design become very important if the system is to be both effective and acceptable to the user (see box below). The introduction of an automated system into the diagnostic laboratories inevitably causes concern among the staff, whether they are professional, technical, or administrative. Many of the fears that accompany automation are widely recognized because the introduction of computer technology into any work environment significantly redefines "essential" tasks and shifts the balance of authority toward those with computer literacy. Some of these changes are unavoidable and perhaps not altogether undesirable. However, the best systems minimize the level of computer prowess needed to effectively use the system. This is essential at the profession level.

Few pathologists would welcome a system that asked them to alter the way they phrase their reports, and many would resist systems that force them to use the computer to complete their tasks.[104] Therefore, the first and paramount design requirement of any system must be to allow the pathologist to work independently of the computer, if desired, without sacrificing the advantages of the system. This requirement will become less important as familiarity with computers among anatomic pathologists grows; this is already occurring because of the pervasive presence of this technology in everyday life, and it is also facilitated through the incorporation of informatics training in pathology residency programs.[105] As I am learning the hard way, becoming computer-literate can be a difficult and sometimes painful process for a "senior" pathologist. Yet, I am afraid there is hardly a choice. As Arthur Schlesinger dramatically put in a 1997 issue of Foreign Affairs, "those who skip or flunk the computer will fall into the *blade runner* proletariat, a snarling, embittered, violent underclass."

A second feature desirable for effective automation is the rigorous avoidance of redundant data entry. Each data item relating to a case—be it patient name, number

of blocks processed, special stains prepared, diagnosis, or billing codes—should ideally involve only a single human intervention. All derivative information, including diagnosis codes, should be automatically assigned by the computer whenever possible. This principle should apply even to the inquiry of patient data, to make it possible to retrieve information on a patient by identifying only a portion of the name or to locate a case by providing only a portion of the diagnostic terms used or any one of an unlimited number of synonyms. A corollary to this requirement is that the system must independently track each data item to allow complete flexibility in the compilation of reports, searches, and inquires using arbitrary formats. It follows that systems that capture data from paper records after case processing has begun (rather than in "real time") only give the illusion of automation and can offer little or no significant savings in the workload. Similarly, systems that capture most or all of the patient data as text documents in word processing files are highly limited in their reporting and searching capabilities and are also unlikely to eliminate much redundant data entry.

Real-time integration of information from all aspects of the diagnostic pathology operation is also required. For example, specimens for a patient may be simultaneously received in cytology and surgical microscopy, cell makers, flow cytometry, and so on. Information on previous material may also exist. Good practice demands that the information from all current and previous examinations be considered by the pathologist when rendering an opinion. The system must, therefore, automatically bring to the attention of each user information on all previous specimens, as well as information on all current specimens that are being processed, regardless of their stage of completion. Consequently, an adequate pathology information system must be able to simultaneously correlate the input from multiple users, whether they are all working on different aspects of the same case or different specimens for the same patient, and will automatically inform each user of all pertinent information regardless of where or when the information was entered. The practical consequence of this requirement is that (except for the smallest institutions) all users are likely to share a common device (file server) on which the bulk of the relevant data is kept.

A related design requirement is that the system be able to permanently retain *on-line* all primary information about a case. This includes all demographic and clinical information, the full text of the gross and microscopic description, the full text of the diagnosis and any diagnosis codes, all addenda and special procedures, and all billing and histology laboratory data. Permanent on-line storage of all data is practical and cost effective with current technology and eliminates the need for redundant hard copy storage of patient records if adequate precautions are taken to safeguard the data (see the following

Basic design criteria for an automated system in surgical pathology
1 Pathologist participation not compulsory
2 Elimination of redundant data entry
3 Real-time integration of all data
4 On-line permanent and safe storage of all primary data
5 Rapid response time
6 Flexible and easily modified design

discussion). Conversely, any system that purges patient data (e.g., the gross description or other text fields) becomes an incomplete archive and sacrifices many of the advantages of automation since in such a system neither inquiry nor database searches can be relied on to return all available information on a case. Such crippled systems should be avoided.

If all primary information on every case is to be permanently retained on-line, adequate precautions must be built into the system to prevent permanent loss or corruption of the data. Security checks must prevent unauthorized access to the database, all transactions must be simultaneously recorded on two physically separate storage devices, copies of all data must be made (backed up) daily or as frequently as possible, complete machine-readable copies of the data must be stored off-site, and archival copies of the data on magnetic tape or a similar medium must be saved permanently off-site at regular intervals. Such precautions ensure that data will not be lost even with major system failures (e.g., disk crash) and that only a minimal amount of data will be corrupted or lost even if the whole computer facility were to be destroyed. The permanent storage or archival copies of the data are needed only to ensure against unauthorized database tampering. Although these precautions may seem excessive, they are easily implemented and provide a level of database security that, in most institutions, far exceeds that provided by hard copy (paper, microfiche) records.

An acceptable automated pathology computer system must also provide very rapid response times for all routine tasks. Any system that requires more than 1 second for routine inquiries of any patient-related information or more than a few seconds for simple diagnosis-based searches of all of the patient files is frustrating in daily use. Excellent response times require adequate equipment and well-designed software. Therefore, it is doubtful whether an adequate fully automated surgical pathology system can be developed on hardware that is already dedicated to operating a clinical pathology laboratory, unless the clinical laboratory has significant excess disk and computer capacity. The peaks of computer activity in a clinical laboratory occur around 10:30 AM to 12:00 PM and 2:00 to 3:30 PM, times that correlate closely with peak activity of the surgical pathology laboratory. Therefore, the total capacity of a combined system must far exceed the initial expectation of the capacity thought to be appropriate to ensure adequate system performance at all times. Similarly, the software must be designed to minimize the number of disk operations required to find the data needed on a patient. The best systems make extensive use of indices, which allow the system to immediately identify the information it is seeking without performing time-consuming searches of the database.

A final design criterion must be the ability of the system to be easily modified to accept changing user needs. Obsolescence will come early to any system without this feature, since the need to accommodate new or altered tasks will inevitably arise. This is particularly true when a system designed for one institution is adapted to another.

Model for an automated anatomic pathology system

An overview of one of the major systems currently in use is presented as an example. Many other systems with varying degrees of sophistication have been made available in recent years, the features of which are periodically listed and compared in CAP Today, the official publication of The College of American Pathologists. The latest listing at the time of this writing (the March 2003 issue) included 17 programs to choose from for those not prepared to build their own system (an option which we highly discourage).

The system operates on a computer that is dedicated to anatomic pathology. There are numerous peripheral devices interfaced to the system, including dial-up modems and printers. Terminals linked to the system have been installed in the following places: staff offices; sign-out areas; secretarial areas; administration, cytology, histology, and special laboratories; accession desk; and surgical pathology gross room, autopsy suite, and autopsy room. Similar terminals have also been strategically placed throughout the hospital to facilitate inquiry from authorized users. All functions are available from virtually any terminal; access to specific functions for each user is controlled by password at the time of log-on. Access is also available through the intranet using web technology.

Organization

Overall, the system is organized into the following major sections: (1) surgical pathology; (2) cytology; (3) autopsy; (4) billing; (5) department-wide options (primarily data searches and administrative tasks); (6) system manager; (7) histology and immunohistochemistry laboratory; (8) molecular genetic laboratory; and (9) miscellaneous.

Surgical pathology

The system accomplishes all of the obvious tasks performed in a surgical pathology laboratory. During accessioning of a new specimen, information on the patient, specimen, submitting physician, billing agency, initial billing codes, and so forth is collected. Because all redundant entries are eliminated, it is usually unnecessary to enter the entire physician's name or address, billing agency, billing codes, towns, cities, ZIP codes in the area, any state, any hospital address or patient floor, most dates, or even the patient's name or demographic information (unless the patient is new). Information is also captured at accessioning on the "type of specimen" to allow the computer to obtain preliminary information about the specimen being processed. This date field is designed to allow a secretary to correctly identify broad categories of specimens. For example, if the specimen were a breast resection, the secretary might enter "BRE," to which the computer would respond by asking the user to select from:

1 BREAST: BIOPSY
2 BREAST: RESECTION FOR CANCER
3 BREAST: REDUCTION MAMMOPLASTY (NOT CANCER)

These three categories can be easily distinguished. Yet, this information allows the computer to seek additional information of the user via type-specific questions (e.g., "LUNG CANCER" would elicit questions about the patient's smoking or asbestos history), to anticipate the proper procedure for cutting the specimen, to generate customized data labels for tissue embedding and later the microscope slides, and to provide specific instructions to pathologists and technicians at the time of the gross room examination. All of the information and protocols that are triggered by the selection of a specimen type are derived from user-defined "dictionaries" and may therefore be easily changed at any time. It is also possible to trigger billing code assignments from the specimen type.

All text entries, such as "gross description" or "final diagnosis," are made directly into the appropriate data field using either a simple text editor or a full screen-oriented word processor. The two editors may be used interchangeably at the discretion of the user. All aspects of each case can be edited simultaneously by different users, although the system does not allow editing of the same data item for a particular case by more than one user at a time. All text fields allow free text entry, as well as many choices of user-defined "canned" text. The latter may include the forms and checklists for the standardized reporting of surgical pathology diagnoses for the major tumor types that have been developed by ADASP and/or CAP (see Appendix A). Free text and canned descriptions can be easily intermingled and edited. The diagnosis entered may be either "preliminary" or "final". Preliminary reports are generally used for cases requiring special studies and may read as follows: "poorly differentiated carcinoma, specific type pending immunohistochemistry". Entering of the final diagnosis results in erasure of the preliminary report.

An *inquiry* is fundamentally different from a report. Thus the STANDARD INQUIRY option not only displays the full text of the gross description, diagnosis, information on special procedures, amendments to the diagnosis, and the date each task was completed but also gives detailed information about several other events

such as the names of the staff pathologists, whether gross photographs were taken, frozen or gross tissue saved, special fixatives used, and whether the preparation of microscopic slides has been completed. Separate inquiry options for use outside the department provide a simplified presentation of the diagnostic information, while other options provide detailed information on the status of the microscopic slides and special stains that are being prepared in a given case. This latter option (HISTOLOGY CASSETTE STATUS INQUIRY) allows immediate inquiry into the stage of preparation of all slides and all special stains on the case.

Many standard reports are generated by the system, the two most common being the WORKING DRAFT and the FINISHED FORMAT REPORT. The working draft is printed on completion of the gross dictation. This report contains a synopsis of all previous or current related case material, including cytology, clinical history, demographic and other data, and full text of the gross description (double-spaced for ease of editing). The reviewing pathologist may then record the diagnosis on this sheet for later transcription or enter it directly into the terminal. The finished format report is then signed electronically by the pathologist and made immediately available to the clinicians. This is done by mailing the hard copy of the report, by distributing it by a computer-driven fax device,[116] and by having it displayed on request in the various terminals located in the clinics, the physicians' offices and through the intranet using web technology.

Most other standard reports, such as overdue case lists, conference lists, and consultation logs, are of an administrative nature.

Cytology

In many ways, the operation of the CYTOLOGY section is similar to that of the SURGICAL PATHOLOGY section. The major difference is that it makes extensive use of case/type-specific questionnaires, so that only relevant questions are asked at the time of accessioning. For example, routine PAP smears elicit questions on menstrual history, birth control medication, and previous cancer history; a sputum sample activates a different set of questions.

Reporting of routine gynecologic specimens such as PAP smears is also facilitated by using a "checklist", whereby the cytotechnologist may simply select any number of predefined features that are recognized in the smear. This may be done using the printed checklist for later entry, or the information may be entered directly into the computer as the smear is evaluated. From these checklists the computer will automatically SNOMED-code (see later section) the specimen, decide which specimens need to be reviewed by a pathologist (based on predefined user criteria), capture a percentage of the cases for quality control review, and generate a completed full text report ready for mailing.

At the time of cytology accessioning, slide labels are

automatically generated. These contain the slide designation, cytology number, and patient name. Additional labels with any desired information can also be generated at will.

Autopsy

The AUTOPSY section of the system provides a complete morgue registration system and handles all aspects of autopsy report preparation. As with SURGICAL PATHOLOGY and CYTOLOGY, the AUTOPSY section supports unlimited text and "canned text" entries. The "specimen type" concept is also used in the AUTOPSY section to generate case-specific and informative autopsy worksheets, which enhance the training experience of the pathology residents and provide a measure of increased quality control in the autopsy suite.

Billing

The BILLING feature of the system allows automatic capture of charges for all specimens, including special procedures such as immunohistochemistry. These are compiled into charge batches sorted by user-defined tables into technical and professional components. These charge batches are delivered to the hospital via magnetic tape or to other group practice plans as printed hard copies. The system allows an unlimited number of separate billing groups, each with separate charge codes and fees.

Department-wide options

In the DEPARTMENT-WIDE OPTIONS, one finds the most general search capabilities of the system. Basically, two search options are provided. One type of search that is used frequently by the pathologists involves finding cases with certain diagnoses or combinations of diagnoses. This is most easily done using the SNOMED SEARCH option. Because SNOMED (*Systemized Nomenclature Of Medicine*) is a carefully constructed and rational coding system, indices based on SNOMED-coded cases provide a very accurate and rapid way to search by diagnosis categories.[109,113] Although not generally conceded, under most circumstances SNOMED has proved to be the superior system for the purpose.[111,112] The one drawback to using SNOMED has been the labor involved in properly coding the cases. Increasingly, however, SNOMED coding has been automated. The searches made using SNOMED coding are rapid and precise and are difficult to achieve with less precise coding schemes or by free-text searching. They also have the advantage that they can be conducted without clerical assistance at any time.

The other search option uses a "report generator". This software package allows arbitrary searches over virtually any of the data items captured by the system, as well as over many derived data items, such as words or free-text phrases or intervals between accession and signout. The search may use any unlimited combination of Boolean logic. The output format is also user defined, so that almost any type of report can be compiled with this option. These searches are designed to be run in the background. They are usually performed overnight when system load is reduced so that the many disk accesses required by such searches will not adversely affect overall system performance.

Systems manager

The SYSTEMS MANAGER section allows editing of all dictionaries used in the system and provides a number of other maintenance and administrative features. Almost all transactions in the system leave an audit trail, which may be examined by means of the options in this module. Access to the SYSTEMS MANAGER section is strictly limited to a few staff members of the managerial level.

Histology and Immunohistochemistry laboratory

The HISTOLOGY AND IMMUNOHISTOCHEMISTRY LABORATORY section handles all functions related to the preparation of slides from the specimen. The interaction begins in the gross room, where the pathologist enters directly into a terminal the information on the number of blocks and tissue pieces submitted to the histology laboratory, as well as any special request for stains, recuts, altered processing, and so on. This task is simplified in the case of routine specimens because much of the information needed has already been anticipated by the computer on the basis of the "specimen type" and only needs to be verified by the pathologists. If at any point in the gross handling of a specimen the resident or histotechnologist needs help, the entry of "??" will gain access to the entire gross room manual (Appendix B of this book), which is maintained on-line.

All worksheets in the histology laboratory are generated automatically from the entries in the gross room. These worksheets are sorted in numeric order and contain all information necessary for slide preparation. All requests for special stains, recuts, and so on are entered directly into the system and appear immediately on the SPECIAL STAIN LOG, which is a perpetual log of unfinished stain requests. All slide labels are printed automatically in the histology laboratory: these include patient name, block designation, case and part number, and a computer-assigned block number (which eliminates redundant block labeling). For special stains, the label also contains the type of stain and the date the procedure was done, to facilitate comparison with control slides. In addition, some systems now allow for direct printing of the pathology number directly on the frosted side of the glass slide and on the plastic paraffin block holder ("cassette").

Molecular genetic laboratory

The MOLECULAR LABORATORY provides a separate registration system, which is, however, fully integrated with the surgical pathology and cytology portions of the system for cross reference. It handles all aspects of the preparation of the molecular genetic reports.

Miscellaneous

This section contains items such as grading and staging manual for the major tumor types.

Additional features

An increasing number of systems currently in use allow for high-quality digital images of gross and microscopic material to be automatically linked to individual cases or teaching collections.[114] These images can also be transmitted to other computers anywhere in the world for diagnostic or teaching purposes (telepathology) (see p. 13).

Reporting by digital speech recognition is already being used at several institutions, at the same time that the speech recognition systems themselves are being developed and perfected.[108] The successful implementation of a "continuous speech recognition" system (i.e., one that does not require a pause between words when dictating) would undoubtedly have a great impact on the practice of anatomic pathology.[110,115]

Quality evaluation

The monitoring of the quality of work being carried out in a laboratory of surgical pathology—for the purposes of detecting inadequacies, updating procedures, and improving the final product—is an important responsibility of the laboratory director or his delegate. Traditionally, this has been carried out in an informal and highly personalized fashion. As of late, outside accrediting agencies (notably, in the United States, the Joint Commission on Accreditation of Healthcare Organizations, otherwise known as JCAHO) have mandated a more structured and rigorous system of self-checking, under designations such as quality control, quality assurance, quality improvement, total quality assessment, and the like. Terminological nuances and bureaucratic overtones aside, there is much to be said about a system that will remind people on a regular basis about the performance and documentation of these tasks. Although some general rules apply[117] (Appendix B), the program should be adapted to the idiosyncrasies of the place. A comforting aspect is that most directors will find when setting up the system that in most instances they will be simply identifying and documenting activities that they were already performing. Appendix B is a model for such a program.

Legal aspects of surgical pathology

The surgical pathologist has not remained immune to the wave of legal actions that has hit the medical profession.[120] The most common reasons for surgical pathologists being brought to trial are the claims that (1) a mistaken diagnosis was made on the basis of misinterpretation of the slide; (2) an important lesion or feature present in the specimen was missed, either because of oversight or through failure of sampling; or (3) the pathologic diagnosis failed to give the clinician a clear idea about the nature or extent of the lesion or the adequacy of the sample because of poor wording or omissions in the report. Two essential components of these claims are that the alleged error or omission resulted in physical, emotional, and/or financial damage to the patient and that such an error or omission was below the standards for the practice of pathology in that particular community at that particular time. In legal parlance, the basic elements for the definition of malpractice are[118]:

1 **Duty**: Recognition of an obligation of a physician to treat the patient.
2 **Breach**: Neglect to treat within the standard of care.
3 **Proximal cause**: Breach causes injury in a fairly direct manner.
4 **Damage**: Injury resulted.

On occasion, the pathologist is blamed for not having sought an outside opinion when confronted with an unusually difficult or unusual entity. Although internal and external consultations are desirable under those circumstances and sometimes prove very useful, there is no professional rule that binds the pathologist to such action, and therefore it would seem inappropriate to institute a penalty if such an action is not carried out. A fully-qualified pathologist should be given the prerogative—like any other member of the medical profession—to decide if, when, and with whom to consult, hoping that such a prerogative will be used wisely.[119]

Not infrequently, an accurate diagnosis is impossible because the histologic or cytologic sample provided by the clinician is inadequate. When this is the case, the pathologist has the right and duty to state this fact in the report, however annoying this may prove to the clinician. Such reports might read: "The appearance is consistent with actinic keratosis, but invasive squamous cell carcinoma cannot be ruled out because of the superficial nature of the biopsy" or "Cytologic material insufficient for evaluation." It is also true that sometimes the inadequacy of examination is attributable to the pathologist for not having thoroughly studied the material submitted to the laboratory, as when he selects for microscopic examination an inadequate number of fragments from a specimen of transurethral resection.

A review of 344 pathology claims reported from 1995 to 1997 to a company that insures approximately 10% of US-based pathologists (and is, therefore, likely to be representative of the overall experience) showed that 17% of the total were Pap smear claims (of which 93% involved false negatives). A detailed evaluation of the others revealed some noteworthy facts:

- Four claims resulted from misidentified pathology reports or mislabeled blocks or specimens, resulting in patients being told they had a malignant diagnosis when in fact they did not (and vice-versa).
- Three claims involved a "missed" micrometastasis of breast carcinoma in an axillary lymph node. It was claimed that this error contributed to disease recurrence, which may have been prevented if appropriate chemotherapy had been given.
- Three claims involved a cervical lymph node containing metastatic squamous carcinoma, which was misdiagnosed as a branchial cleft cyst.
- Two claims involved pathologists held liable for diagnostic errors made by the expert consultants to whom they referred the case. This is called vicarious liability, i.e., one can be held responsible for having chosen a negligent consultant.

About half of the claims fell into groups of specimen type or diagnostic category ("systematic errors" or "high-risk" diagnostic areas). They were: breast FNA and biopsy[121,122]; malignant melanoma[123]; malignant lymphoma, prostatic biopsy, and frozen section[124]; urinary bladder and branchial cleft cyst.[125] The remaining cases were random.[126]

The majority of the claims for breast FNA were for false-negative reports resulting from sampling error. Most claims for breast biopsies concerned the over-diagnosis of ductal carcinoma in situ (CIS) or benign proliferative breast disease as invasive carcinoma, the misdiagnosis of lobular CIS involving ducts as ductal CIS, and the failure to recognize small foci of invasive lobular CIS. Amongst the cutaneous melanocytic lesions, the main problem areas were malignant melanomas misdiagnosed as Spitz nevi, and metastatic melanomas to lymph nodes misinterpreted as malignant lymphomas. Overall, 52% of these claims involved a false-positive diagnosis of cancer.

Epstein[118] has written a very useful and thoughtful article in which he provides good advice to pathologists as to how to avoid the judicial process (and how to behave if unsuccessful in that quest). In it, he mentions that almost 60% of all US-based physicians have been sued at least once, a frightful figure. He adds, however, that only 3% of those cases went to the jury and were decided in favor of the plaintiff, and that about 70 to 80% of medical malpractice cases were disposed with no indemnity payment.

Some very practical points on how to behave in court (beginning with the advice "Dress smartly, but not ostentatiously") have also been provided by a firm that offers legal training consultancy in the United Kingdom.[118a]

References

Historical perspective

1 Azar HA. Arthur Purdy Stout (1885–1967). The man and the surgical pathologist. Am J Surg Pathol 1984, **8:** 301–307.

2 Dhom G. History of Pathology, Berlin. Pathologe 2000, **21:** 285–291.

2a Fechner RE. The birth and evolution of American surgical pathology. Chapter 2 of: Guiding the surgeon's hand. The history of American surgical pathology, J. Rosai (ed.). Washington, DC, 1997, The American Registry of Pathology / Armed Forces Institute of Pathology, pp. 7–22.

3 Fitzgerald PJ, Fred W. Stewart, MD, PhD. 1894–1991. Cancer 1991, **67:** 2419–2421.

4 Gorstein F, Mostofi FK. Armed Forces Institute of Pathology in jeopardy - Who should care? (editorial) Hum Pathol 2003, **34:** 203–205.

5 Lattes R. Arthur Purdy Stout and his times. With a history of the laboratory of surgical pathology at the College of Physicians and Surgeons of Columbia University. Am J Surg Pathol 1986, **10**(Suppl 1): 4–13.

6 Moore S, Seemayer TA, Tremblay G. The career and influence of Pierre Masson (1880-1959). Int J Surg Pathol 2001, **9:** 231–236.

7 Rosai J, Lauren V. Ackerman, M.D. Am J Surg Pathol 1994, **18:** 211–213.

8 Rosai J (ed.). Guiding the surgeon's hand. The history of American surgical pathology. Washington, D.C., 1997, Armed Forces Institute of Pathology.

9 Rosen G. Beginnings of surgical biopsy. Am J Surg Pathol 1977, **1:** 361–364.

10 Stewart TW, James Ewing, M.D., 1866–1943. Arch Pathol 1943, **36:** 325–330.

10a Stout AP. Notes on the education of an "oncological" surgical pathologist. Chapter 10 of : Guiding the surgeon's hand. The history of American surgical pathology, J. Rosai (ed.). Washington, DC, 1997, The American Registry of Pathology / Armed Forces Institute of Pathology, pp. 275–286.

11 Wright JR. The development of the frozen section techniques, the evolution of surgical biopsy, and the origins of surgical pathology. Bull Hist Med 1985, **59:** 295–326.

Surgical pathology and the pathologist

12 Dorfman RF. Maude Abbott Lecture. Hematopathology. A crescendo of scholarly activity. Mod Pathol 1994, **7:** 226–241.

Surgical pathology and the nonpathologist

13 Childs AW, Hunter ED. Patterns of primary medical care. Use of diagnostic x-ray by physicians. Berkeley, Calif., 1970. Institute of Business and Economic Research, University of California.

14 Jones D, Fletcher CD. How shall we apply the new biology to diagnostics in surgical pathology? J Pathol 1999, **187:** 147–154.

15 Nakhleh RE, Gephardt G, Zarbo RJ. Necessity of clinical information in surgical pathology. Arch Pathol Lab Med 1999, **123:** 615–619.

16 Pfeifer JD, Hill A, O'Sullivan MJ, Dehner LP. Diagnostic gold standard for soft tissue tumours: morphology or molecular genetics? Histopathology 2001, **37:** 485–500.

17 Rosai J. The continuing role of morphology in the molecular age. Mod Pathol 2001, **14:** 258–260.

Surgical pathology report

18 Association of Directors of Anatomic and Surgical Pathology. Standardization of the surgical pathology report. Am J Surg Pathol 1992, **16:** 84–86.

19 Azzopardi JG. Problems in breast pathology. In Bennington JL (consulting ed.) Major problems in pathology, vol. 11. Philadelphia, 1979, W.B. Saunders Co., pp. 1–2.

20 Cross SS. Bull AD. Is the informational content of histopathological reports increasing? J Clin Pathol 1992, **45**: 179–180.

21 Kempson RL. The time is now. Checklists for surgical pathology reports (editorial). Arch Pathol Lab Med 1992, **116**: 1107–1108.

22 Novis DA, Zarbo RJ. Interinstitutional comparison of frozen section turnaround time. A College of American Pathologists Q-probes study of 32868 frozen section in 700 hospitals. Arch Pathol Lab Med 1997, **121**: 559–567.

23 Novis DA, Zarbo RJ, Saladino AJ. Interstitutional comparison of surgical biopsy diagnosis turnaround time: a College of American Pathologists Q-probes study of 5384 surgical biopsies in 157 small hospitals. Arch Pathol Lab Med 1998, **122**: 951–956.

24 Rosai J. Standardized reporting of surgical pathology diagnoses for the major tumor types. A proposal. The Department of Pathology, Memorial Sloan-Kettering Cancer Center. Am J Clin Pathol 1993, **100**: 240–255.

25 Zarbo RJ. Interinstitutional assessment of colorectal carcinoma surgical pathology report adequacy. A College of American Pathologists Q-Probes study of practice patterns from 532 laboratories and 15,940 reports. Arch Pathol Lab Med 1992, **116**: 1113–1119.

Slide review and consultation

26 Abt AB, Abt LG, Olt GJ. The effect of interinstitution anatomic pathology consultation on patient care. Arch Pathol Lab Med 1995, **119**: 514–517.

27 Arbiser ZK, Folpe AL, Weiss SW. Consultative (expert) second opinions in soft tissue pathology. Analysis of problem-prone diagnostic situations. Am J Clin Pathol 2001, **116**: 473–476.

28 Association of Directors of Anatomic and Surgical Pathology. Consultations in surgical pathology. Am J Surg Pathol 1993, **17**: 743–745.

29 Cooper K, Fitzgibbons PL, Surgical Pathology Committee of the College of American Pathologists and the Association of Directors of Anatomic and Surgical Pathology. Institutional consultations in surgical pathology: how should diagnostic disagreements be handled? Arch Pathol Lab Med 2002, **126**: 650–651.

30 Kronz JD, Westra WH, Epstein JI. Mandatory second opinion surgical pathology at a large referral hospital. Cancer 2000, **86**: 2426–2435.

31 Oxley DK. Crafting a useful surgical pathology report. Am J Clin Pathol 1999, **111**: 424.

32 Pack GT. Functions and dysfunctions of the surgical pathologist. Surgery 1962, **52**: 752–755.

33 Rosen PP. Special report. Perils, problems, and minimum requirements in shipping pathology slides. Am J Clin Pathol 1989, **91**: 348–354.

34 Safrin RE, Bark CJ. Surgical pathology sign-out. Routine review of every case by second pathologist. Am J Surg Pathol 1993, **17**: 1190–1192.

35 Sissons HA. On seeking a second opinion. J Clin Pathol 1978, **31**: 1121–1124.

36 Stout AP. Mesenchymal tumors of the soft tissues. Trans Coll Physicians Phila 1963, **31**: 91–97.

37 Tomaszewski JE, Bear HD, Conally JA, Epstein JI, Feldman M, Foucar K, Layfield L, LiVolsi V, Sirota RL, Stoler MH, Stombler RE. Consensus conference on second opinion in diagnostic anatomic pathology. Who, what, and when. Am J Clin Pathol 2000, **114**: 329–335.

Biopsy

38 Wright JR Jr. The 1917 New York biopsy controversy. A question of surgical incision and the promotion of metastases. Bull Hist Med 1988, **62**: 546–562.

Intraoperative consultation ("frozen section")

39 Abrams J, Silverberg SG. The role of intraoperative cytology in the evaluation of gynecologic disease. Pathol Annu 1989, **24**(Pt 2): 167–187.

40 Acs G, Baloch ZW, LiVolsi VA. Intraoperative consultation: an histological prespective. Semin Diagn Pathol 2002, **19**: 190–191.

41 Recommendations of the Association of Directors of Anatomic and Surgical Pathology. Part I. Immediate management of mammographically detected breast lesions. Hum Pathol 1993, **24**: 689–690.

42 Bianchi S, Palli D, Ciatto S, Galli M, Giorgi D, Vezzosi V, Del Turco MR, Cataliotti L, Cardona G, Zampi G. Accuracy and reliability of frozen section diagnosis in a series of 672 nonpalpable breast lesions. Am J Clin Pathol 1995, **103**: 199–205.

43 Byers RM, Bland KI, Borlase B, Luna M. The prognostic and therapeutic value of frozen section determinations in the surgical treatment of squamous carcinoma of the head and neck. Am J Surg 1978, **136**: 525–528.

44 Czerniak B, Rosai J. Role of cytology in intraoperative diagnosis. A practical guide. Pathol Annu 1995, **30**(Pt 2): 83–102.

45 Dahlin DC. Seventy-five years experience with frozen sections at the Mayo Clinic (editorial). Mayo Clin Proc 1980, **55**: 721–723.

46 Dankwa EK, Davies JD. Frozen section diagnosis. An audit. J Clin Pathol 1985, **38**: 1235–1240.

47 Dehner LP, Rosai J. Frozen section examination in surgical pathology. A retrospective study of one year experience, comprising 778 cases. Minn Med 1977, **60**: 83–94.

48 Dworak O, Wittekind C. A 30-s PAS stain for frozen sections. Am J Surg Pathol 1992, **16**: 87–88.

49 Esteban JM, Zaloudek C, Silverberg SG. Intraoperative diagnosis of breast lesions. Comparison of cytologic with frozen section technics. Am J Clin Pathol 1987, **88**: 681–688.

50 Gephardt GN, Zarbo RJ. Interinstitutional comparison of frozen section consultations: a college of American Pathologists Q-probes study of 90,538 cases in 461 institutions. Arch Pathol Lab Med 1997, **120**: 804–809.

51 Grabski WJ, Salasche SJ, McCollough ML, Berkland ME, Gutierrez JA, Finstuen K. Interpretation of Mohs micrographic frozen sections. A peer review comparison study. J Am Acad Dermatol 1989, **20**: 670–674.

52 Holaday WJ, Assor D. Ten thousand consecutive frozen sections. A retrospective study focusing on accuracy and quality control. Am J Clin Pathol 1974, **61**: 769–777.

53 Howanitz PJ, Hoffman GG, Zarbo RJ. The accuracy of frozen-section diagnoses in 34 hospitals. Arch Pathol Lab Med 1990, **114**: 355–359.

54 Kraemer BB, Silva G. The examination of margins of resection by frozen section. Part I. Surg Pathol 1988, **1**: 437–466.

55 Mair S, Lash RH, Suskin D, Mendelsohn G. Intraoperative surgical specimen evaluation. Frozen section analysis, cytologic examination, or both? A comparative study of 206 cases. Am J Clin Pathol 1991, **96**: 8–14.

56 Miller PK, Roenigk RK, Brodland DG, Randle HW. Cutaneous micrographic surgery. Mohs procedure. Mayo Clin Proc 1992, **67**: 971–980.

57 Nakazawa H, Rosen P, Lane N, Lattes R. Frozen section experience in 3000 cases. Am J Clin Pathol 1968, **49**: 41–51.

58 Novis DA, Zarbo RJ. Interinstitutional comparison of frozen section turnaround time. A College of American Pathologists Q-probes study of 32868 frozen section in 700 hospitals. Arch Pathol Lab Med 1997, **121**: 559–567.

59 Oneson RH, Minke JA, Silverberg SG. Intraoperative pathologic consultation. An audit of 1,000 recent consecutive cases. Am J Surg Pathol 1989, **13**: 237–243.

60 Roenigk RK. Mohs' micrographic surgery. Mayo Clin Proc 1988, **63**: 175–183.

61 Rogers C, Klatt EC, Chandrasoma P. Accuracy of frozen-section

diagnosis in a teaching hospital. Arch Pathol Lab Med 1987, **111:** 514–517.

62 Silva EG, Kraemer BB. Intraoperative pathologic diagnosis. Frozen section and other techniques. Baltimore, 1987, Williams & Wilkins.

63 Swanson NA, Grekin RC, Baker SR. Mohs surgery. Techniques, indications, and applications in head and neck surgery. Head Neck Surg 1983, **6:** 683–692.

64 Tsutsumi Y, Serizawa A, Kawaii K. Enhanced polymer one-step staining (EPOS) for proliferating cell nuclear antigen (PCNA) and Ki-67 antigen. Application to intra-operative frozen diagnosis. Pathol Int 1995, **45:** 108–115.

65 Zarbo RJ, Schmidt WA, Bachner P, Howanitz PJ, Meier FA, Schifman RB, Boone J, Herron RM. Indications and immediate patient outcomes of pathology intraoperative consultations: A College of American Pathologists/Centers for disease control and prevention outcomes Working Group Study. Arch Pathol Lab Med 1996, **120:** 19–25.

Diagnostic cytology

66 Bergeron C, Masseroli M, Ghezi A, Lemarie A, Mango L, Koss LG. Quality control of cervical cytology in high-risk women. PAPNET system compared with manual rescreening. Acta Cytol 2000, **44:** 151–157.

67 Bigner SH, Cohen CG. Cytopathology during the 1980s. Am J Clin Pathol 1991, **96:** S15–S19.

68 Chan JK, Tans SK, Tsang WY, Lee KC, Batsakis JG. Histologic changes induced by fine-needle aspiration. Adv Anat Pathol 1996, **3:** 71–90.

69 Dardick I, Yazdi HM, Brosko C, Rippstein P, Hickey NM. A quantitative comparison of light and electron microscopic diagnoses in specimens obtained by fine-needle aspiration biopsy. Ultrastruct Pathol 1991, **15:** 105–129.

70 Esteban JM, Yokota S, Husain S, Battifora H. Immunocytochemical profile of benign and carcinomatous effusions. A practical approach to difficult diagnosis. Am J Clin Pathol 1990, **94:** 698–705.

71 Felix JC, Amezcua C. In vitro adjuncts to the pap smear. Obstet Gynecol Clin North Am 2002, **29:** 685–699.

72 Flens MJ, van der Valk P, Tadema TM, Huysmans AC, Risse EK, van Tol GA, Meijer CJ. The contribution of immunocytochemistry in diagnostic cytology. Comparison and evaluation with immunohistology. Cancer 1990, **65:** 2704–2711.

73 Frable WJ. Needle aspiration biopsy. Past, present, and future. Hum Pathol 1989, **20:** 504–517.

74 Frable WJ. The history of fine needle aspiration biopsy. The American experience. Cytopathol Annu, Chapter 6, 1994, pp. 91–94.

75 Hajdu SI, Melamed MR. The diagnostic value of aspiration smears. Am J Clin Pathol 1973, **59:** 350–356.

76 Hajdu SI, Melamed MR. Limitations of aspiration cytology in the diagnosis of primary neoplasms. Acta Cytol (Baltimore) 1984, **28:** 337–345.

77 Hartmann KE, Nanda K, Hall S, Myers E. Technologic advances for evaluation of cervical cytology: is newer better? Obstet Gynecol Surv 2001, **56:** 765–774.

78 Jonasson JG, Wang HH, Porter DH, Tyagi G, Ducatman BS. Image-directed percutaneous biopsy. A comparison of cytologic and histologic findings. Cancer 1992, **70:** 2187–2191.

79 Kline TS. The papanicolaou smear: a brief historical perspective and where we are today. Arch Pathol Lab Med 1997, **121:** 205–210.

80 Koss LG. Aspiration biopsy. A tool in surgical pathology. Am J Surg Pathol 1988, **12:** 43–53.

81 Koss LG. Aspiration biopsy. Cytologic interpretation and histologic bases, ed. 2. Igaku-Shoin, 1992, Tokyo.

82 Martin HE, Ellis. Biopsy by needle puncture and aspiration. Ann Surg 1930, **92:** 169–181.

83 Meerding WJ, Doornewaard H, Van Ballegooijen M, Bos A, Van Der Graaf Y, Van Den Tweel JG, Van Der Schouw YT, Habbema JD. Cost analysis of PAPNET-assisted vs. conventional Pap smear evaluation in primary screening of cervical smears. Acta Cytol 2001, **45:** 28–35.

84 Moseley RP, Paget S. Liquid-based cytology: is this the way forward for cervical screening? Cytopathology 2002, **13:** 71–82.

84a Papanicolaou Society of Cytopathology practice guidelines Task Force. Papanicolaou Society of cytopathology guidelines for educational notes, disclaimers, and similar comments on reports of cervical cytology specimens. Diagn Cytopathol 2003, **28:** 282–285.

84b Ross JS. Emergency Cancer Diagnostics: "On Slide" or "Off Slide": That is the question. Am J Clin Pathol 2003, **120:** 822–824.

85 Spitzer M. Cervical screening adjuncts: recent advances. Am J Obstet Gynecol 1998, **179:** 544–556.

86 Spitzer M. In vitro conventional cytology historical strengths and current limitations. Obstet Gynecol Clin North Am 2002, **29:** 673–683.

87 Turbat-Herrera EA, Knowles K. Cytology: screening or diagnostic tool? Hum Pathol 1999, **29:** 1356–1366.

88 Weintraub J, Redard M, Wenger D, Vassilakos P. The application of immunocytochemical techniques to routinely-fixed and stained cytologic specimens. An aid in the differential diagnosis of undifferentiated malignant neoplasms. Pathol Res Pract 1990, **186:** 658–665.

89 Wied GL, Koss LG. Aspiration biopsy cytology. Acta Cytol [Baltimore] 1984, **28:** 195–197.

Digital pathology and telepathology

90 Bamford WM, Rogers N, Kassam M, Rashbass J, Furness PN. The development and evaluation of the UK national telepathology network. Histopathology 2003, **42:** 110–119.

91 Barbareshchi M, Demichelis F, Forti S, Dalla Palma P. Digital pathology: science fiction? Int J Surg Pathol 2001, **8:** 261–263.

92 Cross SS, Dennis T, Start RD. Telepathology: current status and future prospects in diagnostic histopathology. Histopathology 2002, **41:** 91–109.

93 Dawson PJ, Johnson JG, Edgemon LJ, Brand CR, Hall E, Van Buskirk GF. Outpatient frozen sections by telepathology in a veterans administration medical centre. Hum Pathol 2000, **31:** 786–788.

94 Dervan PA, Wootton R. Diagnostic telepathology. Histopathology 1998, **32:** 195–198.

95 Kaplan KJ, Burgess JR, Sandberg GD, Myers CP, Bigott TR, Greenspan RB. Use of robotic telepathology for frozen-section diagnosis: a retrospective trial of a telepathology system for intraoperative consultation. Mod Pathol 2002, **15:** 1197–1204.

96 Kayser K. Interdisciplinary telecommunication and expert teleconsultation in diagnostic pathology: present status and future prospects. J Telemed Telecare 2002, **8:** 325–330.

97 Okada DH, Binder SW, Felten CL, Strauss JS, Marchevsky AM. "Virtual Microscopy" and the internet as telepathology consultation tools: diagnostic accuracy in evaluating melanocytic skin lesions. Am J Dermatopathol 2000, **21:** 525–531.

98 Schroeder JA, Voelkl E, Hofstaedter F. Ultrastructural telepathology-remote EM diagnostic via internet. Ultrastruct Pathol 2001, **25:** 301–307.

99 Sinard JH, Morrow JS. Informatics and anatomic pathology, meeting challenges and charting the future. Hum Pathol 2001, **32:** 143–148.

100 Weinstein RS, Descour MR, Liang C, Bhattacharyya AK, Graham AR, Davis JR, Scott KM, Richter L, Krupinski EA, Szymus J, Klayner K, Dunn BE. Telepathology overview: from concept to implementation. Hum Pathol 2002, **32:** 1283–1299.

101 Winokur TS, McClennan S, Siegal GP, Redden D, Gore P, Lazenby A, Reddy V, Listinsky CM, Conner DA, Goldman J,

Grimes G, Vaughn G, McDonald JM. A prospective trial of telepathology for intraoperative consultation (frozen sections). Hum Pathol 2000, **31:** 781–785.

Information systems in surgical pathology

102 Aller RD, Robboy SJ, Poitras JW, Altshuler BS, Cameron M, Prior MC, Miao S, Barnett GO. Computer assisted pathology encoding and reporting system (CAPER). Am J Clin Pathol 1997, **68:** 715–720.

103 Buffone GJ, Beck JR. Informatics. A subspecialty in pathology. Am J Clin Pathol 1993, **100:** 75–81.

104 Cote RA, Rothwell DJ. The classification-nomenclature issues in medicine. A return to natural language. Med Inf (Lond) 1989, **14:** 25.

104a Rojo MG. Equipamiento informático ideal en un servicio de Anatomia Patológica. Rev Esp Patol 2003, **36:** 235–256.

105 Henricks WH, Healy JC. Informatics training in pathology residency programs. Am J Clin Pathol 2002, **118:** 172–178.

106 McNeely MDD. Advances in medical informatics during the 1980's. Am J Clin Pathol 1991, **96:** S33–S39.

107 Sinard JH, Morrow Jon S. Informatics and anatomic pathology: meeting challenges and charting the future. Hum Pathol 2001, **32:** 143–148.

Model for automated anatomic pathology system

108 Al-Aynati MM, Chorneyko KA. Comparison of voice-automated transcription and human transcription in generating pathology reports. Arch Pathol Lab Med 2003, **127:** 721–725.

109 Berman JJ, Moore GW, Donnelly WH, Massey JK, Craig B. A SNOMED analysis of three years' accessioned cases (40,124) of a surgical pathology department. Implications for pathology-based demographic studies. In Ozbolt JG (ed.): Proceedings of the Eighteenth Annual Symposium on computer applications in medical care. Philadelphia, 1994, Hanley & Belfus, Inc., pp. 188–192.

110 Meijer GA, Baak JPA. Reporting by digital speech recognition (editorial). Hum Pathol 1995, **26:** 813–815.

111 Moore GW, Berman JJ. Performance analysis of manual and automated systemized nomenclature of medicine (SNOMED) coding. Am J Clin Pathol 1994, **101:** 253–256.

112 Moore GW, Berman JJ. Automatic SNOMED coding. JAMA 1994, **1:** S225.

113 Rothwell DJ, Cote RA, Brochu L. The systemized nomenclature of human and veterinary medicine, SNOMED International Microglossary for pathology. Northfield, IL, 1993, College of American Pathologists.

114 Schubert E, Gross W, Siderits RH, Deckenbaugh L, He F, Becich MJ. A pathologist-designed imaging system for anatomic pathology signout, teaching, and research. Semin Diagn Pathol 1994, **11:** 263–273.

115 Teplitz C, Cipriani M, Dicostanzo D, Sarlin J. Automated Speech-recognition Anatomic Pathology (ASAP) reporting. Semin Diagn Pathol 1994, **11:** 245–252.

116 Wick MR, Archer JB, Isaacs HM, Gross W. Distribution of surgical pathology reports by a computer-driven telephone facsimile (FAX) device. Semin Diagn Pathol 1994, **11:** 258–262.

Quality evaluation

117 Association of Directors of Anatomic and Surgical Pathology. Recommendations on quality control and quality assurance in anatomic pathology. Am J Surg Pathol 1991, **15:** 1007–1009.

Legal aspects of surgical pathology

118 Epstein JI. Pathologists and the judicial process: how to avoid it. Am J Surg Pathol 2001, **25:** 527–537.

118a McLaren P. Going to court – some practical advice. RC Path 2003, **122:** 31–33.

119 Tomaszewski JE, LiVolsi VA. Mandatory second opinion of pathologic slides: is it necessary? Cancer 2000, **86:** 2198–2200.

120 Troxel DB. Diagnostic errors in surgical pathology uncovered by a review of malpractice claims. Int J Surg Pathol 2000, **8:** 161–163.

121 Troxel DB. Diagnostic pitfalls in surgical pathology – uncovered by a review of malpractice claims. Part II. Breast fine needle aspirations. Int J Surg Path 2000, **8:** 229–231.

122 Troxel DB. Diagnostic errors in surgical pathology uncovered by a review of malpractice claims. Part III. Breast biopsies. Int J Surg Pathol 2000, **8:** 335–337.

123 Troxel DB. Diagnostic errors in surgical pathology uncovered by a review of malpractice claims. Part IV. Melanoma. Int J Surg Pathol 2001, **9:** 61–63.

124 Troxel DB. Diagnostic pitfalls in surgical pathology – discovered by a review of malpractice claims (Part V – Lymphoma, prostate, and frozen section). Int J Surg Pathol 2001, **9:** 133–136.

125 Troxel DB. Diagnostic errors in surgical pathology – uncovered by a review of malpractice claims. Part VI – urinary bladder and branchial cleft cyst. Int J Surg Pathol 2001, **9:** 227–229.

126 Troxel DB. Diagnostic pitfalls in surgical pathology – discovered by a review of malpractice claims. Part VII – Random errors). Int J Surg Pathol 2001, **9:** 305–308.

2 Gross techniques in surgical pathology

Introduction

The routine work associated with a surgical pathology specimen includes gross and microscopic examination. Of the two, the latter is unquestionably the more popular, perhaps because it is esthetically more pleasing, is not associated with any particular odor, and does not involve any manual work other than moving the slide across the microscope, keeping it in focus, and changing objectives. The smaller the specimen, the less significant the gross examination appears to be. Some view it merely as a purely technical step, analogous to tissue processing. It has been stated that autopsy pathology is gross pathology, whereas surgical pathology is histopathology.

It is unfortunate that this is the prevailing attitude among pathologists. As Chandler Smith stated in his essay, "In praise of the gross examination," it is the gross aspect that shows the size, form, and nature of the process so that it can be understood both in a structural sense and in a clinical context.[1]

For some specimens, such as cardiac valves, a careful gross examination and description provide much more information than the examination of a random microscopic section. In many cases, an inadequate gross dissection and sampling will invalidate the microscopic interpretation. The dissection, gross description, and selection of sections for microscopic study is a crucial part of the pathologic examination, and one that often cannot be remedied if omitted or done poorly at the time of the initial workup. If the microscopic description is inadequate, the slide can be reviewed and the problem corrected; if the dimensions of the specimen are not recorded, the key sections not taken, and the proper special studies not performed at the time of the initial gross examination, the chances of acquiring this information may be lost forever.

Complicated specimens demand experience and knowledge in order to be dissected, described, and sampled adequately. There exists a curious reticence among residents and junior pathologists in consulting with a senior staff member about the proper handling of difficult gross specimens, whereas no inhibition is noticeable when the same individuals are confronted with a difficult microscopic slide. This is unfortunate because sometimes the reason the slide is so difficult to interpret is because of an inadequate sampling of the gross specimen.

Surgical pathology gross room

The size and features of the surgical pathology gross room depend on the number of specimens, number of staff pathologists and residents, and type of institution. The gross room described in the following paragraphs is modeled after a large laboratory in an academic institution, but many of the requirements also apply to laboratories in small hospitals.

First of all, the room should be large enough to permit the simultaneous work of all the pathologists assigned to gross activities; it should be well illuminated and properly ventilated. We have been appalled at the number of pathology departments throughout the country that have woefully inadequate gross room facilities, some consisting merely of a table, a chair, a cutting board, a sink, and a shelf cornered between a cryostat and a secretarial desk.

Each "gross station" should be under a properly ventilated hood and contain the following:

1 A cutting board placed inside a metal box designed in such a fashion that all the fluids will flow directly into the sink
2 Shelves for specimen containers
3 Ready access to a sink with hot and cold water
4 Ready access to formalin
5 Dictation equipment, preferably activated by a pedal
6 Computer terminal
7 Box of instruments, including heavy and small scissors, different-sized smooth and toothed forceps, a malleable probe, a scalpel handle, disposable blades, a long knife, a ruler, and pins for attaching specimens to a cork surface
8 Box with cassettes and labels

In addition, the gross room should contain the following central equipment:

1 A large formalin container—a very convenient arrangement consists of the suspension of a large container from the ceiling, with formalin pumped into it with a mechanical pump and the fixative delivered to the individual dissection areas by a tubing system ending in faucets
2 Containers with other fixatives, with instructions on how to mix them at the time of use
3 Photographic facilities, ideally located within each station for the sake of convenience.
4 A self-contained x-ray unit
5 Large 4°C refrigerator
6 Small 4°C refrigerator (e.g., for electron microscopy fixatives, photographic film)
7 Band saw—preferably one designed for use in butcher shops rather than those used by carpenters—located in a totally enclosed and properly ventilated space
8 Balances—one of large capacity for most specimens and a precision balance for small specimens, such as parathyroid glands
9 Electrically driven, commercial meat cutter—results in excellent cross sections of solid specimens for demonstration and photographic purposes
10 Dissecting microscope
11 X-ray viewbox
12 Large table with sink for the dissection of large specimens (such as amputations)
13 Central table for multiple use (e.g., for placing containers with cassettes to be sent to the histology laboratory, for showing specimens to visitors, for gross conference)
14 Tissue procurement/tissue bank facilities—includes desk space, hood-enclosed cutting board, computer terminal, equipment and supplies for freezing specimens, freezer(s), and refrigerator.

Initial handling of specimens

The best arrangement is to have the surgical pathology laboratory in close proximity to the operating room and to have specimens other than small biopsies submitted to the laboratory in a fresh state immediately after resection. They should be transported in a glass, plastic, or metal container or in a plastic bag without the addition of any fluids. It is better to avoid wrapping the specimen with gauzes, which tend to produce desiccation. If a delay is anticipated in the transport of the specimen to surgical pathology, or in the handling of that specimen in the laboratory, it is advisable to place the container in a refrigerator at 4°C to slow down autolysis. Most small biopsies (needle biopsies, incisional biopsies, endoscopic biopsies) should be placed in the chosen fixative immediately after they are obtained.

Specimens received in the fresh state should be examined as soon as possible, and a determination should be made on the basis of clinical information and gross appearance (and frozen section examination, if necessary) whether special procedures (see following list) other than routine gross and microscopic examination are necessary or desirable. Specific instructions for these procedures are included in Appendix E.

Cultures—bacterial, fungal, viral
Electron microscopy
Histochemical and immunohistochemical stains
Imprints (touch preparations)
Cytogenetic studies
Molecular pathology studies
Photographs, whether conventional or digital
Plastic embedding for light microscopy (1-μm sections)[2,3,6]
X-ray studies
Special fixatives (other than routine formalin)
Tissue culture[4]
Tumor procurement/tumor bank needs

The pathologist should always keep in mind the fact that formalin fixation, paraffin embedding, and microscopic examination of hematoxylin–eosin sections is only one way of performing a pathologic study of a specimen. It is usually the most important, but it is sometimes insufficient and on occasion woefully inadequate. With the present sophistication in the study of lymphoproliferative disease, a "routine" study of these specimens can hardly be regarded as adequate without the performance of imprints, special fixations, cell marker studies, and sometimes, cytogenetics, and gene rearrangement studies. It is the pathologist's responsibility to think beyond the basic task—to be aware of newer techniques and apply them intelligently to cases.

We have found it extremely useful to have a "surgical pathologist assistant" especially trained to perform the technical aspects of these studies in a consistent fashion under the direction and supervision of the surgical pathologist.[5] This assistant should also be proficient in gross photography and radiographic techniques, injection of specimens, cutting and staining for frozen sections, and other technical tasks that are carried out in the gross room. Having this important collaborator not only frees the surgical pathologist for other activities, but it also ensures a consistency and continuity in the performance of these tests that is otherwise very difficult to attain. Ideally, a dedicated area should be made available in or adjacent to the gross room for the assistant to carry out these special tasks, particularly those regarding the processing of tissues for special studies.

It should be emphasized that the role of these individuals should be carefully supervised by a pathologist. As the name indicates, they are *assistants* to the pathologists and not pathologists' surrogates. The CAP Policy on Pathologists' Assistants made this point very clear by stating that:

> "A pathologist may utilize the services of a properly trained pathologist's assistant to gather, screen, and prepare materials that the pathologist must examine in order to make a diagnosis. Thus, a pathologist's assistant may prepare tissue for medical examination by the pathologist if the assistant is acting pursuant to a protocol developed by the pathologist. Indeed, a pathologist's assistant may, pursuant to protocol, developed by the pathologist, perform other tasks that facilitate the practice of medicine by the pathologist in the best interest of patients.
>
> Ultimately, however, making diagnoses and related medical judgments constitutes the practice of medicine. Responsibility for making these diagnoses and judgments must remain with the pathologist. Both quality medical practice and legal requirements preclude delegation of this responsibility to pathologist's assistants."

Fixation

Of the many fixatives that have been proposed, *10% buffered formalin* remains the best compromise under most circumstances. It is inexpensive, the tissue can remain in it for prolonged periods without deterioration, and it is compatible with most special stains including immunohistochemical techniques,[9,10,19] as long as the tissue is placed in fixative shortly (<30 min) after surgical removal, and overfixation (>24 to 48 hours) is avoided.[28] "Pure" formalin is a concentrated (40%) solution of the gas formaldehyde in water. Thus a 10% formalin solution represents a 4% solution of the gas, which is 1.3 molar. If the final dilution is maintained in a range between 8%

and 12%, no noticeable differences will be noted. However, once the concentration of formalin drops below 5%, the quality of the preparation will suffer. This may happen, unknowingly, in places where "pure formalin" is adulterated by diluting it with water. Rodriguez-Martinez et al.[21] have devised a simple-to-follow formula for checking the final dilution of the fixative and correcting it if necessary by measuring the specific gravity of the fluid (Table 2.1). Contrary to popular belief, shrinkage of tissues is minimal in formalin fixation per se.[9,26] Any shrinkage that occurs (and it may be considerable) is due to the contractile qualities of the specimen, as supported by the observation that it tends to occur immediately after excision prior to fixation and that is related to the amount of contractile tissue present.[13] The most obvious example is the external muscle layer of the gastrointestinal tract. It has been calculated that segments of colorectum shrink by 57% of the in vivo length.[12] Much of this can be avoided by pinning down the specimen on a corkboard prior to fixation.

Zenker's (which incorporates mercuric chloride) is an excellent fixative, one of the best that has ever been devised for light microscopic work, but it is expensive, requires careful disposal of the mercury, and necessitates meticulous attention to fixation times and washing procedures to remove the precipitates of mercury. This fixative or sublimate sodium acetate formalin ("B-5") are often used for biopsies of the kidney, bone marrow, lymph node, and testicle.

Bouin's fixative (which contains picric acid) has been especially recommended for testicular biopsies, but Zenker's fluid results in almost identical preparations. Bouin, Zenker and B-5 are excellent fixatives for routine work and for most immunohistochemical stains, but the preservation of nucleic acids is very poor.[25]

Carnoy's fixative is a mixture of ethanol, chloroform, and glacial acetic acid.[20] Thus at the same time that it fixes the tissues, it dissolves most of the fat. This property has been found useful for the identification of lymph nodes in radical resection specimens.

As various special techniques have been incorporated into the diagnostic pathology armamentarium and gained in popularity, attempts have been made to develop fixatives that were equally compatible with routine handling and the performance of the techniques in question. When electron microscopy was in vogue, a "universal fixative" was proposed, made up of a mixture of 4% commercial paraformaldehyde and 1% glutaraldehyde in a neutral buffer.[17] At the crest of the immunohistochemistry wave, fixatives were introduced for the same purpose. With the current excitement with molecular biology techniques, it is not only natural that efforts are being made to develop fixatives that would preserve as much as possible the amount and integrity of the nucleic acids present.[25,27,27a] One such proposal calls for 70% ethanol which—in contrast to formalin—is a noncross-linking

Table 2.1 Formula for the preparation of 10% formalin on the basis of a solution of formaldehyde of unknown concentration

Density of 'pure' formalin	Percentage of formaldehyde	Milliliters of formalin	Milliliters of water
		necessary to prepare 10% formalin	
1.090	40.00	10.00	90.00
1.086	39.00	10.25	89.75
1.083	38.00	10.56	89.44
1.080	37.00	10.84	89.16
1.075	35.15	11.37	88.63
1.070	33.30	12.00	88.00
1.065	31.45	12.70	87.30
1.060	29.60	13.35	86.65
1.055	27.75	14.40	85.60
1.050	25.90	15.44	84.56
1.045	24.05	16.62	83.38
1.040	22.20	18.00	82.00
1.035	20.35	19.61	80.39
1.030	18.50	21.65	78.35
1.025	14.80	27.00	73.00
1.020	12.95	30.92	69.08
1.015	11.10	36.10	63.90
1.012	9.25	43.24	56.74
1.010	7.40	54.00	46.00
1.0085	5.55	72.07	27.93
1.0065	4.00	100.00	0.00

Translated from Rodriguez-Martinez HA, Santos-Estrada L, Rosales MM, Cruz-Ortiz H: Formol o formalina al diez por ciento? Patologia (Mexico) 1971, 9: 233–231.

agent and brings very little chemical change to the DNA except for a reversible collapse.[11,25] Another proposed fixative is methacarn, which is a Carnoy's solution in which methanol is used in place of ethanol.[24] While the search for the all-purpose fixative continues,[11] the most sensible approach is to handle the tissue according to the recommendations for the particular technique being used. Naturally, this implies that enough material is available for the purpose and that one has thought of it while the tissue is still fresh. If these conditions have not been met in a particular case (a not uncommon occurrence), one may console oneself by reflecting on the fact that formalin (a truly remarkable substance) will still allow for most of these techniques to be carried out, however imperfectly. Regarding DNA preservation, the best results are obtained with buffered (rather than acid) formalin at 4°C (rather than at room temperature).[25]

Whenever formalin is used, the volume of fixative should be at least 10 times that of the tissue. The container should have an opening large enough so that the tissue can be removed easily after it has been hardened by the fixation. The fixative should surround the specimen on all sides. Large specimens that float on a fixative should be covered by a thick layer of gauze. In cases of large, flat, heavy specimens that rest on the bottom of the containers, the gauze should be placed between the container bottom and the specimen.

The fixation can be carried out at room temperature or, in the case of large specimens, at 4°C (see following discussion). Tissue should not be frozen once it has been placed in the fixative solution, for a peculiar ice crystal distortion will result.[23] The freezing point of a 10% formalin solution is −3°C.

The speed of penetration of tissue by formalin is about 1 mm/h. However, tissue penetration is not equivalent to fixation. It has been pointed out that formalin penetrates tissues rapidly as methylene glycol but fixes slowly as carbonyl formaldehyde.[25] Therefore, a fixation time of several hours is needed for most specimens.

An easy and inexpensive way of shortening the fixation time for routine specimens is by submerging the specimen in a large beaker containing fixative kept at about 60°C and in continuous motor by the action of a heater–rotor.

Fixation can also be achieved with microwaves, which are defined as electromagnetic waves with a frequency between 300 MHz and 300 GHz. They can be used by themselves or in combination with conventional chemical fixation. Microwaving tissue in formalin gives results somewhat inferior to those obtained by first fixing tissues in formalin for a few hours in at room temperature followed by microwave irradiation for 1 to 2 minutes at 55°C.[25] The decreased fixation time achievable with microwaves is an obvious advantage, but this is upset by the artefacts introduced, which include tissue shrinkage and breakdown of red blood cells. However, these artifacts are very minor if the technique is carried out carefully, so that no appreciable differences with routinely processed material will be evident.[22] As a matter of fact, a procedure has been described combining chemical fixation and microwave that results in a 1-hour processing time, a section quality allegedly equivalent to that of routine processing, and better preservation of RNA.[18]

It should also be taken into account that most laboratories use for this purpose household ovens, which have obvious limitations in terms of reproducibility. Ovens specifically designed for histology use should offer the standardization and calibration that these kitchen instruments sorely lack, and would presumably render the procedure even more satisfactory.

Parenthetically, microwaves are also used in the pathology laboratory for decalcification,[8] processing for electron microscopy,[10a,16] and immunohistochemical staining, including antigen retrieval.[7,14,15]

General principles of gross examination

Proper identification and orientation of the specimen are imperative for the adequate pathologic evaluation of a case. An unlabeled specimen should never be processed; if the biopsy is received in the laboratory without identification, the physician who performed the procedure or, in his absence, one of the assistants should be called to identify and label the specimen. A properly completed surgical pathology requisition form containing the patient's identification, age, and sex; essential clinical data; operation; surgical findings; and tissue submitted should accompany every specimen. If such history is unavailable, the physician or one of his assistants should be contacted and asked to provide it. If this cannot be obtained for one reason or another, the pathologist has the prerogative and obligation, as a medical consultant, to review the chart and even examine the patient personally before rendering an opinion on a slide for which such information is essential.

If there are difficulties with orientation of the specimen, the surgeon should be contacted and cooperation requested in identifying the position, anatomic landmarks, surgical margins, and any other structure of significance.

Careful search and examination of *all* the material submitted are in order. Even the underside of the cover should be searched for tissue fragments. Surgeons should be instructed to submit to the pathology laboratory *all* the material that they have removed, not selected portions from it.[29] The specimen, especially if small, should be handled on a clean cutting board, using spotless, clean instruments. The problem of contamination of a specimen with a fragment from another (the "floater" or "cutting board metastasis") is one of the major catastrophes

that can occur in the pathology laboratory because it can lead to irreparable mistakes (see next section).

Even if the pathologist is not a surgeon or an anatomist, he should have some knowledge of normal anatomy, the extent of most operations, and the number and types of structures to be expected in a given procedure. The first step is a general inspection of the specimen, with identification of all of its normal and abnormal components. He should place the specimen on the cutting board in an anatomic position and record at this point the following information: (1) type of specimen; (2) structures included; (3) dimensions; (4) weight; (5) shape; and (6) color. This is also the time to identify the surgical margins in order to preserve them in subsequent steps and eventually study them microscopically. The pathologist should keep in mind that, in many surgical excisions, the surgeon already knows the microscopic diagnosis of the lesion, and he is now interested in other information, such as extent of the lesion, invasion of neighboring structures, presence of tumor at the surgical margins, vascular invasion, and lymph node metastases. If a surgical margin is involved by tumor, he wants to know where this surgical margin is located. The accumulation of these data requires careful and sometimes tedious, but always rewarding, work.

Before the dissection of the specimen is begun, the advisability of taking gross photographs of the external surface should be considered. While this is a good practice for documentation purposes, it should be remembered that for most specimens the external appearance is merely that of a nondescript mass, whereas a properly made cross section will better demonstrate the important gross features of the lesion.

Three situations may arise during dissection of a surgical specimen:

1 It may be necessary to separate each of its main components in the fresh state, such as in a radical neck dissection.
2 It may be necessary to remove only some components (such as the regional lymph nodes) and leave the rest of the specimen as a single piece.
3 It may be better to fix the entire specimen as a block. This can be achieved in several ways, depending on the size, shape, and presence or absence of a cavity in the specimen. Small specimens without particularly thick areas are simply placed in a fixative at room temperature. Larger specimens that cannot be satisfactorily injected (such as a radical resection of a soft tissue tumor or a nephrectomy specimen) are better fixed overnight in a refrigerator at 4°C to slow down the autolytic process. Hollow specimens are either opened fresh or else fixed simultaneously from the outside and the inside. The latter is achieved either by injecting the cavity with formalin by syringe or catheter or by packing the cavity with gauze or cotton

impregnated with formalin (Figs 2.1 and 2.2). Cystic lesions (such as ovarian cystadenomas) can be injected with formalin after the original fluid has been removed. Multilocular cysts require individual injection of the larger cavities, combined with fixation of the specimen block at 4°C.

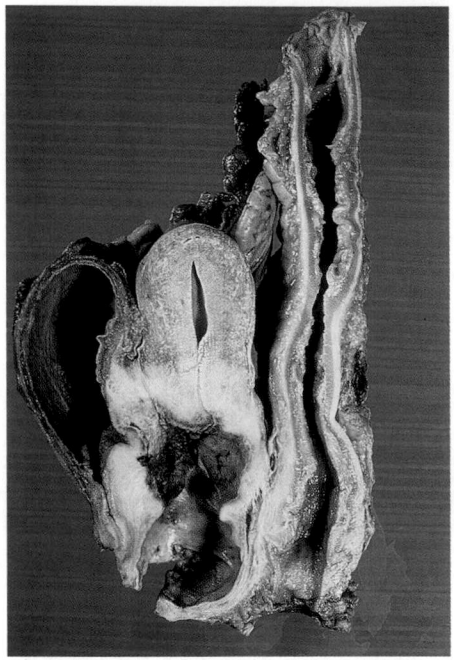

Fig. 2.1 Specimens of pelvic exenteration for carcinoma of the uterine cervix that have been sectioned sagittally after the vesical, vaginal, uterine, and rectal cavities have been adequately fixed. (Courtesy of Dr. H. A. Rodriguez-Martinez, Mexico City, Mexico)

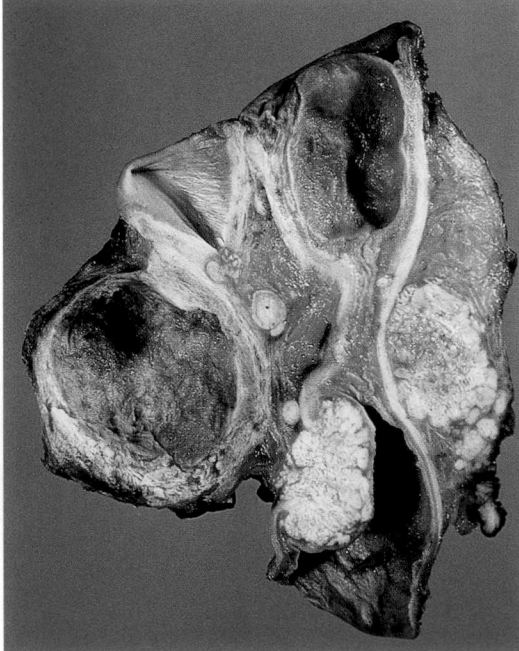

Fig. 2.2 Specimens of pelvic exenteration for carcinoma of the uterine cervix that have been sectioned sagittally after the vesical, vaginal, uterine, and rectal cavities have been adequately fixed. (Courtesy of Dr. H. A. Rodriguez-Martinez, Mexico City, Mexico)

Specimens that contain both soft tissues and bone are handled in a different fashion, depending on the site and type of pathology present. One alternative is to freeze the entire fresh specimen and then prepare parallel slices with the band saw while the specimen is still frozen. Washing these slices with tap water results in excellent specimens for photography and demonstration purposes. Another method, which is employed when the bony structures are not involved by tumor, consists in carefully dissecting out the bone in order to process the remaining soft tissue as a single specimen.

As a general rule, when a specimen is sliced, and assuming that several of the slices show similar features, it is advisable to leave one of the best slices intact for possible photography, gross demonstration, or display as a museum specimen. Under no circumstances should *any portion* of a specimen be discarded before the case is signed out. Actually, it is advisable to save the wet tissue for a minimum of 1 month, but sometimes the shortage of space prevents implementing this practice. A questionnaire revealed a wide variation in the length of time different laboratories throughout the country keep the wet tissues.[30] This ranged anywhere from less than a month (25.6% of the laboratories) to an indefinite period (3.3%). A uniform national guideline seems necessary, but it seems to us that a length of 1 month after the case has been signed out is quite reasonable. We firmly believe that paraffin blocks, microscopic slides, and reports should be kept permanently if space allows, regardless of what the minimum state requirement might be. In the case of paraffin blocks, the fact that this material is suitable for a variety of molecular studies has transformed it into a veritable treasure and vindicated the pathologist who has bravely insisted over the years on preserving this material despite the remonstrations of the administrators on the grounds of space requirements, and having even to endure the misguided humor of some surgical colleagues.[31]

The recording of the features of the gross specimen can be done *pari passu* with the dissection or at the end of the gross procedure, the key measurements having previously been noted. While the former technique allows for some time saving (and is therefore the most popular), the latter often results in a more cohesive description. Regardless of the method used, the description should refer to the features of the specimen rather than the steps the prosector has taken to make them apparent. Statements such as "Upon opening the … it was noted …" should be avoided.

Several speech-recognition programs are currently available, some of them having incorporated a lengthy pathology dictionary. The ones we have tried have not been entirely satisfactory, and we don't use any at present. However, they have certainly come a long way from the first models, which makes us hopeful that the situation will be very different by the time the next edition of this book is written.

Tissue contamination (the "floater")

The albatross always hanging around the pathologist's neck is that of contamination of the tissue with extraneous material, particularly tissue from another patient, i.e., the "floater."[32] This may happen in the operating room or clinic, or during any of the steps of the pathology procedure: at the time the tissue is examined in the gross room and placed in a cassette, when embedding, at the time of cutting the section and spreading it on the slide, and perhaps even during processing, staining, and mounting. Obviously, each of these steps should be carried out in such a way to minimize this occurrence; however, the possibility is still there that it will occur. Furthermore, even if by some miracle one were able to eradicate completely this curse from one's own laboratory, the danger might still come from slides that have been processed elsewhere. What can the pathologist do to identify this occurrence, which otherwise might have untoward consequences? Simply be constantly on the alert, and suspect a "floater" whenever confronted with any of these situations:

1 A fragment of tissue that looks different from all the others by virtue of the thickness of the section and/or staining intensity
2 A fragment of tissue that is on a slightly different plane from the others, especially if superimposed on them
3 A fragment of tissue showing pathologic changes totally different from the others, and of a type that one would not have expected at all under the clinical circumstances of the case.

Whenever the suspicion of a "floater" arises, a series of steps should be taken. The first and most obvious is to look at the other cases that were processed on that day, and most particularly in the same gross station. Stains for blood group or HLA class I antigens have been found useful,[35,37] but the most effective way to prove the extraneous nature of the material is through molecular biology methods such as microsatellite DNA markers following microdissection.[33,34,36,38] Obviously, the latter can also be applied, and in a much easier fashion, to the instances in which there is a suspicion that the *entire* specimen belongs to another patient. Just as obviously, these techniques would not be applicable if the suspected mix-up is from one specimen to another of the *same* patient.

Specimen photography

Documentation of the gross features of a surgical specimen is best achieved by taking one or several gross photographs of the lesion in the form of either color transparencies or digital images, the latter incorporated

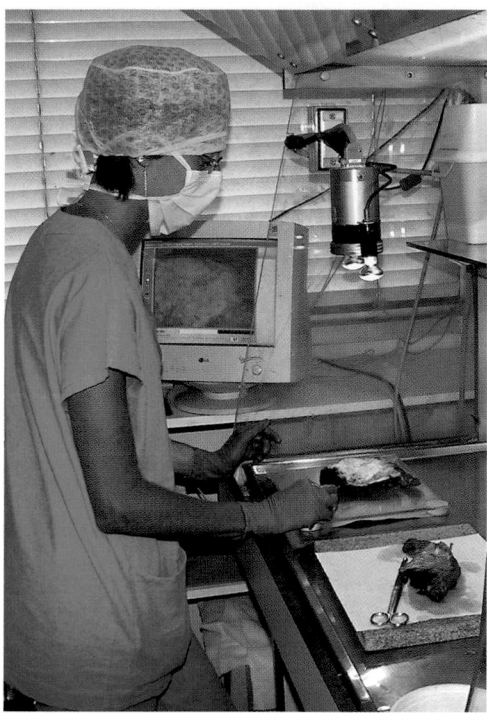

Fig. 2.3 Set-up for digital gross photography, which has been incorporated into each cutting station for the prosecutor's convenience.

into the corresponding case file through the AP information system. Ideally, there should be a digital photography set-up within each gross station for convenience[48] (Fig. 2.3). A similar system has been found very useful for the photographic documentation of autopsies.[40] Not surprisingly, the more practical and the more convenient the system, the larger the number of photographs that will be taken.[40] This is far superior to drawings made by the pathologist or to the use of pre-designed diagrams.

Listed below are some hints that we have found useful in obtaining gross photographs that show the lesion at its best advantage and that are also aesthetically pleasing[39,41,43,44,45,49,50]:

1 A common mistake is to take a photograph of the external surface of the intact tumor (which is often meaningless, other than providing some information on overall size and configuration) but omitting a photograph of the cut surface, which is usually much more informative.
2 Some consideration should be given to what is the best view of the lesion before the picture is taken. If a specimen is cut in two, it is better to photograph one half rather than both halves of a partially cut specimen.
3 Preparation and trimming of the specimen are important. This includes removing fat and other unnecessary tissue around the lesion, opening ducts and vessels, and trimming fat around the latter structures.

4 The background should be spotlessly clean, be kept to a minimum, have no texture, and be illuminated. For color photographs, a gray-toned neutral-intensity color is preferable (we use a light blue). The use of drapes, sponges, and gauzes is to be discouraged.

5 Rulers should be used only when reference to size is important. They should be as unobtrusive as possible, always in the metric system, without advertisements or other distractions, clean, clearly legible, and placed in such a way as to allow a quick determination of the measurements of the lesion. They should be of adequate size and be kept in focus by raising or lowering them according to the height of the specimen.

6 Knife marks in the cut surface should be avoided by using sharp instruments and by cutting the specimens with a continuous, slow motion of the hand.

7 The specimen should be properly oriented, centered, and framed. A common mistake is to use only half or less of the field of a photograph. A close-up often improves the resolution of detail in the specimen without the loss of any important information.

8 Whenever possible, normal structures should be included in the photograph to serve as a frame of reference for the lesion.

9 Objects such as hands, forceps, probes, scissors; and paper clips are distracting and should generally be avoided.

10 Specimen identification by the use of labels on top of the lesion is distracting. It is better to write the pathology number on the frame of the transparency than to include it in the projected photograph.

11 Reflective glare (specular reflections) should be avoided by properly placing the illumination system, by turning off the room lights, by blotting the cut section of the specimen with a gauze, and, if necessary, by using diffusion screens.

12 The proper exposure can be determined with a light meter by trial and error, unless done automatically by the camera. It is always advisable to take several photographs of a lesion, using slightly different exposures.

13 For specimens of substantial height, the lens aperture should be as small as possible (f-stop of 16 or greater) to increase the depth of field.

14 Heightened image clarity and contrast can be obtained by the use of ultraviolet illumination.[42]

Because indefinite storage of gross specimens is unfeasible (having been given up even by the Mayo Clinic), the gross photograph often remains, together with the gross description, the best permanent documentation of the gross features of a lesion. For many years, we have routinely taken Polaroid black-and-white prints of all pertinent specimens and attached them to the surgical pathology report, in some cases together with the specimen x-ray film. Also, we mark the sites of the sections taken for histology on these photographs or in reproductions of the specimen obtained with a Xerox copier or similar duplicating machine.[47] Currently, we have replaced the Polaroid and Xerox images with digital images that we use for the same purpose; these allow us to record the various dimensions of the specimen and to indicate the site of the sections taken for histology.[46]

Specimen radiography

Radiographic examination of surgical specimens sometimes provides important information. Specimens particularly suitable for this type of examination include bone lesions, calcified soft tissue masses, breast biopsies and excisions (especially if they had been studied by mammography), cardiac valves, and lymph node groups in which a lymphangiogram had been performed.[53] Areas of calcification (particularly important in breast biopsies) can be detected even in the paraffin blocks if the cassettes are made of plastic or some other radiolucent material.[56] Radiopaque foreign bodies (such as metal clips) can be spotted easily. Radiologic–pathologic correlations can be made by perfusing radiopaque material within the lumina of ducts or vessels, radiographing the specimen, and comparing the results with both the clinical x-ray film and the gross specimen. Some people have found specimen x-ray films useful for locating lymph nodes in radical resection specimens.[51,54,55] Others have used them to perform a microradiographic analysis of bone.[52] Traditionally, these studies were done by taking the specimen to the radiology department. The availability of a self-contained, fully shielded x-ray machine specially devised for pathology specimens has greatly facilitated the procedure by allowing the pathologist to take his own x-ray studies in the gross room.

Lymph node dissection

Careful dissection of lymph nodes is one of the most important components in the gross evaluation of a radical operation for cancer. The first step consists of dissecting the node-containing fat from the organ in the fresh state, using forceps and sharp scissors. In the gastrointestinal tract and other sites, most of the nodes are found in very close proximity to the muscular wall of the organ, so dissection of fat should be done in such a way as to expose the clean muscular surface. More than once we have seen a resident searching fruitlessly for nodes in an enormous piece of omentum from a gastrectomy specimen without realizing that he had left all of the nodes attached to the lesser and greater curvature of the stomach when he separated the organs. If the number of nodes found in a given specimen is substantially lower than that expected for that operation, it may be advisable to consult with a senior pathologist or the surgeon before proceeding further. Sometimes the explanation is that the nodes exhibit adipose metaplasia (i.e., they are infiltrated by fat except for a thin peripheral semilunar rim) and are therefore difficult to identify grossly.

The individual nodes may be searched for in the fat in the fresh state or after overnight fixation. If the latter course is taken, it is advantageous to fix the specimen in Carnoy's solution, which somewhat clears the specimen by the action of the chloroform at the same time that it fixes it. One should be gentle with the nodes at the time of the dissection; it is too easy to crush them with the forceps and scissors, especially if they are dissected before fixation. Various clearing techniques have been devised for the maximal recovery of lymph nodes.[57] The yield is certainly impressive, but we are not convinced that the extra time, effort, and money that need to be expended are justified from a practical standpoint.

The lymph nodes should be separated and labeled in groups according to the type of specimen (see Appendix E). In some operations, such as radical hysterectomy, this is already done by the surgeon. *All* lymph nodes identified grossly are to be submitted for histologic examination.

Sampling for histologic examination

Tissues submitted for histology must not be more than 3 mm thick and not larger than the dimensions of the cassette used; otherwise they will not be adequately infiltrated by paraffin. Adipose tissue must be cut even thinner. Overfilling of the cassette should be avoided, or the tissue will not be infiltrated. Whenever identified grossly, suture material, metal clips, and other foreign bodies should be removed from the tissues before putting them in cassettes, or the microtome knives will be damaged. Metal clips are especially common in staging laparotomy and lymphadenectomy specimens and can be difficult to detect by plain inspection. If the presence of clips is suspected in a specimen, this can be checked by taking an x-ray. This can even be done with the tissue inside the cassette if the latter is made of a nonradiopaque material. Similarly, discrete areas of calcification or ossification should be dissected out, or else the specimen should be decalcified. Fragments of tissue that are small enough to go through the cassette perforations must be wrapped in thin paper (such as tea bag paper) or else placed between small porous cushions the size of the cassette (available from the cassette manufacturers). If the fragments are very small, it is advisable to stain them with hematoxylin or Mercurochrome before putting them in the cassette to facilitate their identification by the histotechnologist. Slices of sponge placed

inside the cassette may result in peculiar holes in the form of sharply outlined triangles.[61]

Most specimens from solid tissues are cut in the form of pieces measuring 10 to 15 mm on the sides and 2 to 3 mm in thickness; the histotechnologist will orient them in a flat position in the paraffin block, so it will not matter which side is sectioned. However, if one side shows a given feature better than the opposite side, the pathologist can indicate this with India ink on the side *opposite* the one to be cut. Many specimens (in general, those having a luminal side) need to be embedded on edge. If a section of a gallbladder, large bowel, or similar organ is properly taken, the histotechnologist should have no problem orienting the specimen properly. Additional insurance for proper orientation is provided by including in the cassette a paper tag labeled "on edge." In general, better preparations will be obtained in organs covered by folded mucosa (e.g., stomach, bowel) if the sections are taken perpendicular rather than parallel to the mucosal folds. For smaller specimens (e.g., cervical biopsies, peroral small bowel biopsies), orientation is more difficult but just as important. In these cases, the pathologist can help the histotechnologist by showing him the specimen before putting it in the cassette, by embedding it in paraffin himself, or by surrounding it with a material that will keep it in the desired position during the processing steps. We use for this purpose a solution of 3% agar in distilled water, kept in a viscous fluid state at 60°C. The specimen is kept on edge with small forceps on top of a glass slide while 1 or 2 drops of the agar solution are applied to it. Once this solidifies (it should take less than a minute), it is detached from the slide with a sharp blade and transferred to the cassette.[64] Further description of this technique is given in Appendix E.

To ensure adequate sampling, multiple microscopic sections ("various levels" or VL) should be requested for some specimens at the time that the gross description is dictated. This includes biopsies from the respiratory tract, gastrointestinal tract, bladder, lymph nodes, and bone marrow; all needle and punch biopsies; and in general, all specimens measuring 3 mm or less.

A question frequently asked is how much of the tissue received should be submitted for microscopic examination. The cryptic reply of a particularly, experienced and astute surgical pathologist was "just enough." What he meant, of course, was that there are no all-encompassing rules; the nature of the case, appearance of the gross specimen, experience, and common sense should dictate how much is enough. For instance, one cassette is plenty for a case of herniated intervertebral disk submitted in numerous fragments, unless the pathologist has a special interest in the pathology of the nucleus pulposus. Conversely, all tissue usually should be submitted in a diagnostic endometrial curettage. However, if the procedure was done for incomplete abortion and gross examination shows obvious products of conception, one representative section is more than adequate. The main problem is posed by specimens such as prostatic transurethral resections in patients without clinical suspicion of carcinoma. There is no question that the more fragments submitted, the more incidental carcinomas will be found.[62] However, it is impractical and probably not justified to process all the prostatic fragments received regardless of the total amount. The guidelines that we have developed for these specimens are described in Appendix E.

Knowledge of the precise site from which sections were taken for microscopic examination is of great importance, especially when determining whether tumor is present at the surgical margins. This can be achieved by marking these sites and their corresponding numbers or letters in predesigned picture protocols, in a drawing of the specimen made at the time of gross examination, or in a digital photograph using a program specifically devised for that purpose.

Identification of the tissues submitted for histology and other pertinent information should be provided to the histotechnologist in a separate form or entered in the computer terminal at the time of the gross examination.

Failure to perform these relatively simple steps is responsible for a large proportion of the poor and sometimes uninterpretable microscopic slides being produced. Part of the problem arises from the fact that, in most pathology training programs, no exposure is given to basic histology techniques, such as embedding, cutting, and staining. We have found that even a 1- or 2-day learning session in the histology laboratory by the trainee just before his rotation in the gross room is very effective in avoiding many of these problems.

Surgical margins

One of the most important components of a gross examination and sampling is the evaluation of the surgical margins, under the assumption that a positive margin will likely lead to local recurrence if uncorrected.[59] This is usually carried out by "painting" those margins with India ink or a similar pigment before sectioning. This can be done on either the fresh specimen or after fixation by gently wiping the margins with gauze and carefully covering the entire surgical surface with India ink using a cotton swab stick. Special care should be taken to mark the lateral epithelial margins of the specimen when present. If it is of importance to know the exact topography of the margins involved, this can be achieved by the surgeon identifying them individually and the pathologist submitting them for histology with a unique code identifier or by using dyes of different colors. As already stated, the procedure is facilitated a great deal by identifying in an image of the specimen (digital, Xerox, or pencil drawing) the location of the margin in relation to the anatomic landmarks.

Identifying the true surgical margins is done with some specimens better than with others. The smoother the specimen contours and the harder the consistency, the easier the task. Unfortunately, some of the most common specimens on which margins are requested—breast lumpectomies being a prime example—hardly fulfill these desiderata, and the accuracy of the determination is probably much less than that assumed by the pathologist and the surgeon. This possibility is underscored by studies in several anatomic sites showing a lack of statistical correlation between the status of the margins and the incidence of actual recurrence, and the fact that a good number of patients in whom margins are deemed positive but no re-excision is carried out remain free of disease.[58,65] In some of these situations, one wonders whether it might not be preferable for the surgeon to remove the tissue in question, *then* take the margins from the surface that he has just created, and send those for histopathologic evaluation. With such a procedure, there would be no question that those are real surgical margins, nor there will be any issues about their exact location.

Two interesting variations on the theme of surgical margins evaluations have been the proposal to evaluate them on the basis of cytologic ("touch") preparations,[63] and through detection of molecular alterations, such as p53 mutations ("molecular" margins).[60] Although cytologic evaluation can be a great adjunct at the time of intraoperative consultations (sometimes obviating the need for a frozen section altogether), we think it is perilous to rely on it for this specific purpose. As for the "molecular" margins, to depend entirely on them at our present state of knowledge seems foolhardy, to say the least. The reasons, which ought to be self-evident, have been dutifully enumerated by several authors.[58,65]

Guidelines for handling the most common and important surgical specimens

In order to achieve a certain consistency in the way the specimens are handled in the gross room, it is important for a manual of procedures to be available to the person performing the gross examination to assist him in dissecting the specimen, describing it, taking the appropriate sections for microscopic examination, and performing whatever other additional tasks may be required depending on the nature of the case.[66,67,68,69,70] These can be made available in the form of a printed manual, in a microfiche format, or in computer-readable form, with the manual, microfiche reader, or computer terminal placed by the side of the dissecting area (Fig. 2.4).

These devices can be of great utility to pathology residents and other beginners, as long as one recognizes that they have not been designed to replace entirely

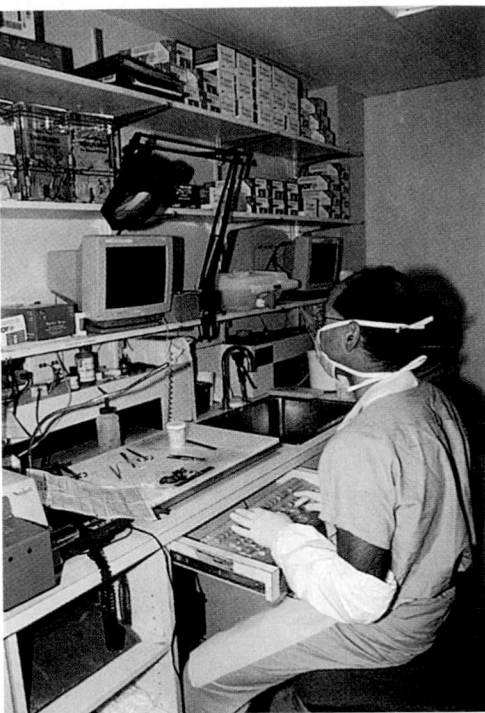

Fig. 2.4 Gross room hood incorporating setting for digital photography, a convenient and time-saving arrangement.

the time-honored system of the seasoned practitioner transmitting to the apprentice, with his own words and hands, the secrets of the trade.

Some of these guidelines for handling of the most common and important surgical specimens (procedure, description, and sections for histology) are given in Appendix C.

References

Introduction

1   Smith JC. In praise of the gross examination. Hum Pathol 1974, **5:** 505–506.

Initial handling of specimens

2   Burns WA, Bretschneider AM, Morrison AB. Embedding in large plastic blocks. Diagnostic light and potential electron microscopy on the same block. Arch Pathol Lab Med 1979, **103:** 177–179.
3   Chang SC. Hematoxylin-eosin staining of plastic-embedded tissue sections. Arch Pathol 1972, **93:** 344–351.
4   Ioachim HL. Tissue culture of human tumors. Its use and prospects. Pathol Annu 1970, **5:** 217–256.
5   Kenney TD, Broda KR. The pathologist's assistant. Hum Pathol 1974, **5:** 503–505.
6   Snodgress AB, Dorsey CH, Bailey GWH, Dickson LG. Convential histopathologic staining methods compatible with Epon-embedded, osmicated tissue. Lab Invest 1972, **26:** 329–337.

Fixation

7   Boon ME, Kok LP. Microwave cookbook of pathology: the art of microscopic visualization. Leinden, 1987, Coulomb Press Leyden.
8   Cunningham CD 3rd, Schulte BA, Bianchi LM, Weber PC, Schmiedt BN. Microwave decalcification of human temporal bones. Laryngoscope 2001, **111:** 278–282.

9   Fox CH, Johnson FB, Whiting J, Roller PP. Formaldehyde fixation. J Histochem Cytochem 1985, **33:** 845–853.
10 Friedman NB. On formalin fixation. Hum Pathol 1992, **23:** 1440–1441.
10a Giberson RT, Austin RL, Charlesworth J, Adamson G, Herrera GA. Microwave and digital imaging technology reduce turnaround times for diagnostic electron microscopy. Ultrastruct Pathol 2003, **27:** 187–196.
11 Gillespie JW, Best CJM, Bichsel VE, Cole KA, Greenhut SF, Hewitt SM, Ahram M, Gathright YB, Merino MJ, Strausberg RL, Epstein JI, Hamilton SR, Gannot G, Baibakova GV, Calvert VS, Flaig MJ, Chuaqui RF, Harring JC, Pfeifer J, Petricoin EF, Linehan WM, Duray PH, Bova GS, Emmert-Buck MR. Evaluation on non-formalin tissue fixation for molecular profiling studies. Am J Pathol 2002, **160:** 449–457.
12 Goldstein NS, Soman A, Sacksner J. Disparate surgical margin lengths of colorectal resection specimens between in vivo and in vitro measurements. Am J Clin Pathol 1999, **111:** 349–351.
13 Johnson RE, Sigman JD, Funck GF, Robinson RA, Hoffman HT. Quantification of surgical margin shrinkage in the oral cavity. Head Neck 1997, **19:** 281–286.
14 Leong AS. Microwaves in diagnostic immunohistochemistry. Eur J Morphol 1996, **34:** 381–383.
15 Leong AS. Microwave fixation and rapid processing in a large throughput histopathology laboratory. Pathology 1991, **23:** 271–273.
16 Leong AS, Sormunen RT. Microwave procedures for electron microscopy and resin-embedded sections. Micron 1998, **29:** 397–409.
17 McDowell EM, Trump BF. Histologic fixatives suitable for diagnostic light and electron microscopy. Arch Pathol Lab Med 1976, **100:** 405–414.
18 Morales AR, Essenfeld H, Essenfeld E, Duboe MC, Vincek V, Nadji M. Continuous-specimen-flow, high-throughout, 1-hour tissue processing: a system for rapid diagnostic tissue preparation. Arch Pathol Lab Med 2002, **126:** 583–590.
19 Puchtler H, Melcan SN. On the chemistry of formaldehyde fixation and its effects on immunohistochemical reactions. Histochemistry 1985, **82:** 201–204.
20 Puchtler H, Waldrop FS, Conner HM, Terry MS. Carnoy fixation. Practical and theoretical considerations. Histochemie 1968, **18:** 361–371.
21 Rodriguez-Martinez HA, Santos-Estrada L, Rosales MM, Cruz-Ortiz H. Formol o formalina al diez por ciento? Patologia (Mexico) 1971, **9:** 223–231.
22 Rohr LR, Layfield LJ, Wallin D, Hardy D. A comparison of routine and rapid microwave tissue processing in a surgical pathology laboratory. Quality of histologic sections and advantages of microwave processing. Am J Clin Pathol 2001, **115:** 703–708.
23 Rosen Y, Ahuja SC. Ice crystal distortion of formalin-fixed tissues following freezing. Am J Surg Pathol 1977, **1:** 179–181.
24 Shibutani M, Uneyama C, Miyazaki K, Toyoda K, Hirose M. Methacarn fixation: a novel tool for analysis of gene expressions in paraffin-embedded tissue specimens. Lab Invest 2000, **80:** 199–208.
25 Srinivasan M, Sedmak D, Jewell S. Effect of fixatives and tissue processing on the content and integrity of nucleic acids. Am J Pathol 2002, **161:** 1961–1971.
26 Stowell RE. Effect of tissue volume of various methods of fixation, dehydration and embedding. Stain Technol 1941, **16:** 67–83.
27 Tbakhi A, Totos G, Hauser-Kronberger C, Pettay J, Baunoch D, Hacker GW, Rubbs RR. Fixation conditions for DNA and RNA in situ hybridisation. A reassessment of molecular morphology dogma. Am J Pathol 1998, **152:** 35–41.
27a Vincek V, Nassiri M, Mehrdad N, Morales AR. A tissue fixative that protects macromolecules (DNA, RNA and Protein) and histomorphology in clinical samples. Lab Invest 2003, **83:** 1427–1435.

28   Werner M, Chott A, Fabiano A, Battifora H. Effect of formalin tissue fixation and processing on immunohistochemistry. Am J Surg Pathol 2000, **24**: 1016–1019.

General principles of gross examination

29   Cotton DWK, Stephenson TJ. Histopathology for minor surgery. Histopathology 1992, **20**: 455–456.

30   Ring AM. How long to keep records and specimens. Med Lab Observer Jan 1977, 97–102.

31   Selzer R. The specimen collectors. In Selzer R (ed.): Confessions of a knife. New York, 1979, Simon and Schuster.

Tissue contamination (the "floater")

32   Gephardt GN, Zarbo RJ. Extraneous tissue in surgical pathology: A College of American Pathologists Q-probes study of 275 laboratories. Arch Pathol Lab Med 2002, **120**: 1009–1014.

33   Hunt JL, Sealsky P, Sasatomi E, Niehouse L, Bakker A, Finkelstein SD. A microdissection and molecular genotyping assay to confirm the identity of tissue floaters in paraffin-embedded tissue blocks. Arch Pathol Lab Med 2003, **127**: 213–217.

34   Kessis TD, Silberman MA, Sherman M, Hedrick L, Cho KR. Rapid identification of patient specimens with microsatellite DNA markers. Mod Pathol 1996, **9**: 183–188.

35   Laggaaij EL, Cramer-Knijnenburg GF, Van Der Pijl JW, Bruijn JA, Fijter JW, Van Krieken JH. Rapid verification of the identity of questionable specimens using immunohistochemistry with monoclonal antibodies directed against HLA-class 1 antigens. Histopathology 1998, **31**: 284–288.

36   O'Briain DS, Sheils O, McElwaine S, McCann SR, Lawler M. Sorting our mix-ups. The provenance of tissue section may be confirmed by PCR using microsatellite markers. Am J Clin Pathol 1997, **106**: 758–764.

37   Ota M, Fukushima H, Akamatsu T, Nakayama J, Katsuyama T, Hasekura H. Availability of immunostaining methods for identification of mixed-up tissue specimens. Am J Clin Pathol 1989, **92**: 665–69.

38   Tsongalis GJ, Berman MM. Application of forensic identity testing in a clinical setting: specimen identification. Diagn Mol Pathol 1997, **6**: 111–114.

Specimen photography

39   Barker NJ. Photography. In Westra WH, Hruban RH, Phelps TH, Isacson C (eds): Surgical pathology dissection. An illustrated guide, ed. 2. New York, 2003, Springer-Verlag, pp. 26–32.

40   Belanger AJ, Lopes AE, Sinard JH. Implementation of a practical digital imaging system for routine gross photography in an autopsy environment. Arch Pathol Lab Med 2000, **124**: 160–165.

41   Burgess CA. Gross specimen photography – a survey of lighting and background techniques. Med Biol Illustr 1975, **25**: 159–166.

42   Cutignola L, Bullough PG. Photographic reproduction of anatomic specimens using ultraviolet illumination. Am J Surg Pathol 1991, **15**: 1096–1099.

43   Edwards WD. Photography of medical specimens. Experiences from teaching cardiovascular pathology. Mayo Clin Proc 1988, **63**: 42–57.

44   Haberlin C. Specimen photography. In Hansell P (ed.): A Guide to Medical Photography. London, 1879, MTP Press, pp. 77–97.

45   Kent TH, Reynolds JAM. Recognition of quality photographs of gross specimens. Audiovisual teaching set. Iowa City, Iowa, 1978, Department of Pathology, University of Iowa.

46   Schubert E, Gross W, Siderits RH, Deckenbaugh L, He F, Becich MJ. A pathologist-designed imaging system for anatomic pathology signout, teaching and research. Sem Diagn Pathol 1994, **11**: 263–273.

47   Start RD, Stephenson TJ, Clelland CA. The photocopier. An overlooked tool in surgical pathology. Pathol Res Pract 1995, **191**: 52–56.

48   Titus K. Every thing in its place. CAP Today, 2000, p. 56.

49   Vetter JP. The color photography of gross specimens. J Coll Am Pathologist 1984, **3**: 155–161.

50   White W. Photomacrography, an introduction. Boston, Mass: 1987, Butterworth, pp. 97–133.

Specimen radiography

51   Andersen J, Jensen J. Lymph node identification. Specimen radiography of tissue predominated by fat. Am J Clin Pathol 1977, **68**: 511–512.

52   Dunn EJ, Beows DW, Rothert SW, Greer RB. Microradiography of bone, a new use for the versatile Faxitron (letter). Arch Pathol 1975, **99**: 62.

53   Fornasier VL. Fine detail radiography in the examination of tissue. Hum Pathol 1975, **6**: 623–631.

54   Jensen J, Anderson J. Lymph node identification in carcinoma of the colon and rectum. Value of tissue specimen radiography. Acta Pathol Microbiol Scand (A) 1978, **86**: 205–209.

55   Wilkinson EJ. Lymph-node identification by specimen radiography and xerography (letter). Am J Clin Pathol 1978, **70**: 308–309.

56   Wilkinson EJ, Gnadt JT, Milbrath J, Clowry LJ. Breast biopsy evaluation by paraffin-block radiography. Arch Pathol Lab Med 1978, **102**: 470–473.

Lymph node dissection

57   Durkin K, Haagensen CD. An improved technique for the study of lymph nodes in surgical specimens. Ann Surg 1980, **191**: 419–429.

Samples for histologic examination

58   Batsakis JG. Surgical excision margins: a pathologist's perspective. Adv Anat Pathol 1999, **6**: 140–148.

59   Brennan MF. The enigma of local recurrence. The Society of Surgical Oncology. Ann Surg Oncol 1997, **4**: 1–12.

60   Brennan JA, Mao L, Hruban RH, Boyle JO, Eby YJ, Kock WM, Goodman SN, Sidransky D. Molecular assessment of histopathological staging in squamous-cell carcinoma of the head and neck. N Engl J Med 1995, **332**: 429–435.

61   Farrell D, Thompson P, Morley A. Tissue artefacts caused by sponges. J Clin Pathol 1992, **45**: 923–924.

62   Lefer LG, Rosier RP. Increased prevalence of prostatic carcinoma due to more thorough microscopical examination (letter). N Engl J Med 1977, **296**: 109.

63   Mair S, Lash RH, Suskin D, Mendelsohn G. Intraoperative surgical specimen evaluation: cytologic examination, or both? A comparative study of 206 cases. Am J Clin Pathol 1991, **96**: 8–14.

64   Ventura L, Bologna M, Ventura T, Colimberti P, Leocata P. Agar specimen orientation technique revisited: a simple and effective method in histopathology. Ann Diagn Pathol 2001, **5**: 107–109.

65   Wick MR, Mills SE. Evaluation of surgical margins in anatomic pathology: technical, conceptual, and clinical considerations. Semin Diagn Pathol 2002, **19**: 207–218.

Guidelines for handling the most common and important surgical specimens

66   Pierson KK. Principles of prosecution. A guide for the anatomic pathologist. New York, 1980, John Wiley & Sons.

67   Rosai J. Manual of surgical pathology gross room procedures. Minneapolis, 1981, University of Minnesota Press.

68   Schmidt WA. Principles and techniques of surgical pathology. Menlo Park Calif., 1983, Addison-Wesley Publishing Co.

69   Westra WH. Surgical pathology dissection: an illustrated upgrade, ed. 2. New York, 2003, Springer.

70   Wilson RR. Methods in morbid anatomy. New York, 1972, Appleton-Century-Crofts.

3 Special techniques in surgical pathology

Introduction

The mainstay of surgical pathology is (and is likely to remain for a long time) the examination of the specimens following fixation in formalin, processing in graded alcohols and xylene or other solvents, embedding in paraffin, cutting of sections with a microtome, and staining with hematoxylin–eosin (H&E). The microtome is usually preset for a 5-μm thickness, and the sections actually obtained come to a pretty close approximation of that figure.[3]

There is hardly a procedure in the whole armamentarium of medicine that gives so much information so quickly and at such a little cost as the H&E technique, despite the obturate criticisms it had to endure over the years.[4]

In the H&E technique, hematoxylin staining of nuclei is followed by counterstaining of cytoplasms and various extracellular materials by eosin. Hematoxylin is extracted from the bark of a tropical wood, *Haematoxylon campechianum* ("Bloody red bark tree" from Campeche, Mexico).[5] In order to function as a nuclear stain, it needs to be oxidized ("ripened") to the purple dye *hematein* and provided with a net positive charge by combining it ("chelating") with a metallic salt ("mordant"). Eosin is an anionic xanthene dye that combines electrostatically with various cytoplasmic components and with tissue such as collagen or muscle, the latter in an amphoteric manner.

This technique has proved one of the most durable in medicine and has remained essentially unchanged— except for automation and time compression of some of the steps,[255a] for over half a century. This may be due in part to a certain resistance to change that has been attributed to the practitioners of pathology, but I believe the main reason is that the technique works extremely well. It is certainly far from ideal: Masson, a master of histologic techniques, regarded formalin as a poor fixative and H&E as a poor stain.[2] Yet it is difficult to argue with success. The technique, imperfect as it is, offers considerable advantages: It is relatively quick, inexpensive, suitable for most situations, and comparatively easy to master. Most important, it allows an accurate microscopic diagnosis of the large majority of specimens sent to the laboratory. However, it simply cannot answer all the questions that a case poses at the plain diagnostic level, and it is clearly insufficient when one engages in an etiologic, histogenetic, or pathogenetic quest. As a consequence, the pathologist has always searched for additional techniques to probe those questions. Colloquially, these techniques have been referred to as "special," simply because they are applied only under special circumstances. Most of them have gone (or are going) through three distinct phases: an initial phase of unrestrained enthusiasm followed by a phase of equally vigorous criticism, the matter eventually settling into a situation in which the techniques are accepted as useful aids only when applied to selected situations and always referring back to conventional morphology as the standard by which they should be interpreted. As Gonzalez-Crussi[1] wisely stated, "however sophisticated and 'modern,' a novel diagnostic technique ought to be suspect if it does violence to a universally agreed upon diagnosis arrived at by more traditional means."

The special techniques that have been found most helpful in diagnostic pathology over the years are discussed in this chapter.

Special stains

Of the hundreds of "special" stains listed in the classical texts dealing with histologic techniques (such as Romeis' monumental *Mikroskopische Technik*, first issued at the beginning of the twentieth century and now in its seventeenth edition),[21] the surgical pathologist will find a relatively small minority to be of real diagnostic utility at present. This is especially true since the advent of immunohistochemistry, which has rendered many of them obsolete. Those most commonly used at present in our laboratory are the following:

1 *PAS (periodic acid–Schiff) stain.* This is an extremely useful and esthetically pleasing technique, to the point that in at least one institution I know it was used as the standard stain in place of H&E. Substances containing vicinal glycol groups or their amino or alkylamino derivatives are oxidized by periodic acid to form dialdehydes, which combine with Schiff's reagent to form an insoluble magenta compound. This stain therefore demonstrates glycogen (in a specific fashion, when used with a diastase-digested control) and neutral mucosubstances, outlines basement membranes, and makes evident most types of fungi and parasites (Fig. 3.1). It is also useful for the demonstration of the intracytoplasmic crystals in alveolar soft part sarcoma.

2 *Stains for microorganisms.* These include techniques for gram-positive and gram-negative bacteria, acid-fast mycobacteria, fungi, and parasites. The Gram stain allows the separation of bacteria into those that retain the crystal violet–iodine complex (gram positive) and those that are decolorized by alcohol or acetone treatment and counterstained by either safranin or fuchsin.[7] Acid fastness depends on the high lipid content (mycolic acids and long-chain fatty acids) in the cell walls of mycobacteria, which confer on the cell the ability to complex basic dyes (such as carbolfuchsin) and to retain them following

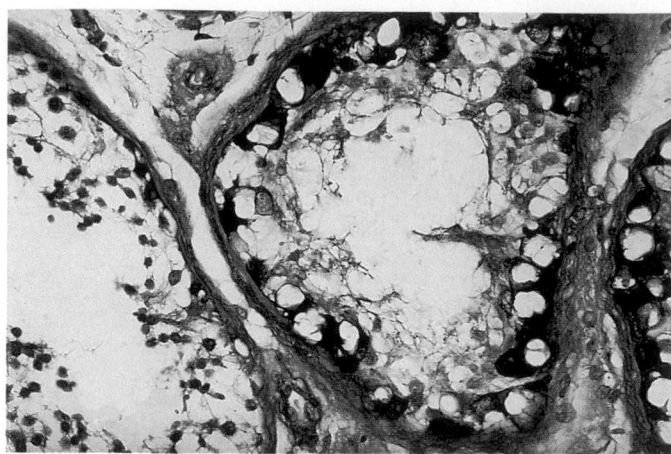

Fig. 3.1 PAS stain in intratubular germ cell neoplasia of the testis. Abundant PAS-positive glycogen is present in the cytoplasm of the tumor cells, in stark contrast with the cells of the normal seminiferous tubule on the left. This material was completely removed by diastase digestion.

strong decoloration with acid–alcohol. The techniques in this group most used are Brown and Brenn (B&B; as a modification of the Gram stain), Ziehl–Neelsen (for acid-fast organisms), Grocott's hexamine–silver (for fungi and *Pneumocystis*), PAS (for fungi, amebae, and *Trichomonas*), and Dieterle or one of its modifications (for *Helicobacter*, *Legionella*, and the organisms of syphilis and Lyme disease).

3 *Argentaffin and argyrophilic stains.* The argentaffin reaction depends on the presence in the tissue of a substance, often of the phenolic group (such as catecholamines or indolamines), that reduces silver (and other metallic) salts[25,26]; we generally use the Fontana–Masson technique in paraffin-embedded material (see later discussion)[22] (Fig. 3.2). In the argyrophilic reaction, an extraneous reducing agent such as hydroquinone or formalin is added; we generally employ the unmodified Grimelius' technique and prefer to use it in Bouin's fixed material whenever available. Others have found the Churukian-Schenk's modification to give better results.[22]

Silver stains are mainly used for the identification of neuroendocrine cells and their tumors,[8] but also for the demonstration of reticulin fibers, melanin, and calcium.

4 *Amyloid stains.* The mysteriously named Congo Red[23] followed by examination with both standard and polarized light (the notorious apple green birefringence) is regarded as the most reliable and practical technique to detect amyloid. It should be realized, however, that the stain does not have chemical specificity, being dependent upon an arrangement of the molecule in an antiparallel beta-pleated sheet. It should also be noted that nonamyloid-related green birefringence can occur as a result of excess dye retained in the tissue and to other technical factors.[9]

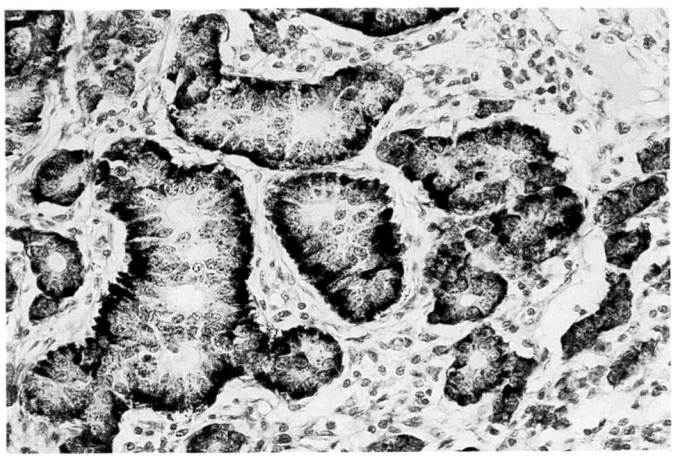

Fig. 3.2 Fontana–Masson argentaffin stain in a carcinoid tumor. The dark brown silver granules have a typical cytoplasmic basal location.

5 *Reticulin stains.* Reticulin stains demonstrate both "reticular fibers" and basement membrane material. Reticular fibers consist of very thin fibers of mainly type III collagen, which are widespread in connective tissue throughout the body. Basement membranes are largely composed of type IV collagen and laminin. In both instances, it appears that the adsorption of silver stains and their PAS positivity are due to a coating of bound proteoglycans. Reticular fibers and reticulin stains should not be equated to reticulum cells, a common misconception. The latter term refers to cells (generally of the accessory immune system, also called dendritic cells) in which the "reticulum" or network is formed not by extracellular material but by thin, complex cytoplasmic prolongations.

Traditionally, the main applications of silver-based reticulin stains (such as Gomori's, Wilder's, and Gordon and Sweet's) in tumor pathology have been in distinguishing: (1) epithelial from nonepithelial neoplasms; (2) various mesenchymal neoplasms from each other; and (3) in situ from invasive carcinoma. In general, foci of carcinoma have reticulin around the tumor nests but not between the individual cells, whereas in most sarcomas and large cell lymphomas the silver-positive material separates single cells. The striking contrast between the two patterns can be readily appreciated by comparing the epithelial and mesenchymal components of a synovial sarcoma. In tumors of endothelial cells, the reticulin that identifies the vessel wall (rather than the one which coats the individual tumor cells) is seen on the outside of the neoplastic population, whereas the reverse is true in tumors of pericytes or vascular smooth muscle cells. In typical cases of leiomyosarcoma the reticulin wraps individual cells completely, whereas in typical cases of malignant peripheral nerve sheath tumor it runs in parallel to the spindle tumor cells without surrounding them at the poles. Reticulin stains have also been used to distinguish ovarian granulosa cell tumors (in which the fibers are scanty and surrounding groups of cells) from fibrothecomas (in which they surround individual tumor cells). Unfortunately, these patterns are well in evidence only in classic cases of these respective entities, i.e., those which are already easily diagnosable with H&E techniques. In the controversial cases, reticulin stains are likely to provide results that are far from conclusive, to the point that we have found them of very limited utility. We agree wholeheartedly with Azzopardi when he stated that "reticulin silver impregnations are virtually valueless in the differentiation of certain sarcomatoid carcinomas from true sarcomas," and that "reticulin impregnations may be deceptive and merely serve to 'confirm' an erroneous diagnosis of sarcoma."[6] The other traditional use for this technique in tumor pathology has been the detection of foci of beginning invasion in carcinoma in situ lesions. This has been largely superseded by various immunohistochemical stains (Fig. 3.3).

6 *Trichrome stains.* In the trichrome methods, such as those devised by Masson (a veritable cornucopia), van Gieson, and Mallory, phosphotungstic or phosphomolybdic acid is used in combination with several anionic dyes. The main value of this group of stains is in the evaluation of the type and amount of extracellular material. The three tissue structures demonstrated by the three component dyes are nuclei, cytoplasm, and extracellular collagen.[17] It is not generally realized that the only component of all trichrome stains having some degree of specificity is that provided by the phosphotungstic or phosphomolybdic acid, which stains the collagen fibers;

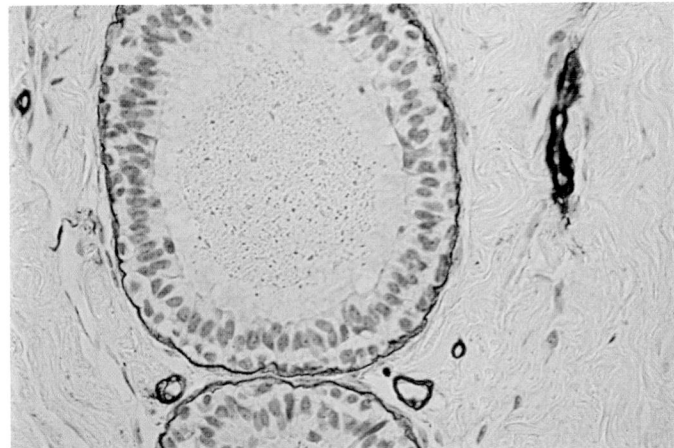

Fig. 3.3 Demonstration of basement membrane material in blood vessels and ducts of breast through the detection of type IV collagen by immunohistochemistry. This technique has largely superseded the demonstration of "reticulin fibers" by silver staining.

everything else is background staining, no better from the point of view of specificity than what is obtained with H&E.[19] The often-used statement that a trichrome stain "proved" the smooth muscle nature of a tumor is therefore inaccurate.

7 *PTAH (phosphotungstic acid–hematoxylin) stain.* This particular variant of trichrome stain has been traditionally used for the demonstration of intracytoplasmic filaments, such as those in muscle and glial cells. It has been largely superseded by the immunohistochemical reactions for the specific microfilaments being searched for. Foraker[12] once made the witty remark that the "special stain" he found most useful as a junior faculty member was a procedure known as the "slow PTAH." This took a week to complete, which was enough time for his boss to come back to look at the H&E sections of the case.

8 *Stains for hemosiderin (Perls), melanin (Fontana–Masson), and calcium (von Kossa).* In the Perls' technique for hemosiderin, hydrochloric acid splits off the protein bound to the iron, allowing the potassium ferrocyanide to combine specifically with the ferric iron to form ferric ferrocyanide (Prussian blue). In the Fontana–Masson method for melanin (already mentioned in connection with the argentaffin reaction), an ammoniacal silver solution is used without a reducing bath. Only substances capable of reducing directly silver salts (i.e., argentaffin) such as melanin are demonstrated. In the von Kossa method for calcium, silver is substituted for calcium in calcium salts; this silver salt is then reduced to black metallic silver by the use of light or a photographic developer.

9 *Stains for neutral lipids.* Most of these stains are based on the principle that the colored compounds used are more soluble in the tissue lipids than in their own solvent. Actually, these compounds do not qualify as dyes in the conventional sense, in that they contain no auxochromic groups but are chromogens. Oil red O is the one most commonly employed.

A limitation of fat stains is the fact that they cannot be performed in paraffin-embedded material because of the fat solubilizing properties of xylene and other clearing materials used for processing. In tumor pathology, the utility of fat stains is minimal and largely limited to the inconsequential distinction between fibroma and thecoma in the ovary, support for the diagnosis of renal cell carcinoma and sebaceous gland tumors of skin, and identification of lipid-rich carcinoma in various organs. Despite ingrained notions to the contrary, fat stains are of little if any use for the diagnosis of liposarcoma; some liposarcomas contain little or no stainable fat, whereas several types of nonadipose tissue neoplasms can contain considerable amounts.

10 *Mucin stains.* Mucin is the traditional term used for a large group of macromolecules containing an acidic group, which is divided into two major categories: the epithelial *O*-glycoproteins (membrane-bound or secreted) composed of a protein core and a sialic acid-containing carbohydrate moiety (whether sulfated or not) and the stromal glycosaminoglycans, which contain hyaluronic acid and which also can be sulfated. Historically, the term "mucin" has been used for the former category, whereas the latter substance has been usually referred to as "myxoid" (hence the term pseudomyxoma for a lesion that may appear myxoid, i.e., stromal, but is really epithelial, i.e., mucinous). The combination of Alcian blue and PAS is probably the best "pan-mucin" stain, since it demonstrates mucosubstances of neutral, slightly acidic, and highly acidic types.[11] Enzymatic pretreatment will show whether the acidic groups are made of sialic acid (digestible with sialidase), hyaluronic acid (digestible with hyaluronidase), or sulfated groups (digestible with neither). Several stains are available for the specific demonstration of highly acidic mucins. These include Alcian blue performed at pH 1.0, colloidal iron, high iron-diamine, and the classic Mayer's mucicarmine. At the risk of sounding old-fashioned, we prefer the latter stain despite its empiric nature.[15] The abnormalities in mucin secretion sometimes present in carcinomas (usually because of incomplete carbohydrate synthesis) can be surmised from the mucin stains but require more sophisticated techniques for their specific identification.[13,27] Hale's colloidal iron stain has become the standard for the identification of renal chromophobe carcinoma (see Chapter 7). Although it should not be necessary, we will mention that Hale's stain is a mucin stain in which iron is used as a reagent, *not* a stain to demonstrate iron.

Mucin stains are also used to classify gastric incomplete metaplasia into subtypes (sialomucin- and sulfomucin-containing) having supposedly different malignant potentials (see Chapter 11).

It should be noted that all of the mucin stains mentioned above demonstrate the carbohydrate component of these glycoproteins. Lately, immunohistochemical identification of the protein core of the same molecules (MUC) is providing a different type of separation of these molecules, which may be of greater diagnostic significance[14,18] (see p. 58).

11 *Giemsa stain.* The most spectacular results with Giemsa and other Romanovsky-type stains are obtained with alcohol-fixed smears.[16] However, reasonably good preparations can also be achieved in paraffin-embedded material, provided one is very scrupulous with the technique and fastidious with the source of the reagents. The technique is most useful for the demonstration of various hematolymphoid elements (including mast cells) and microorganisms.

12 *Elastic fibers.* Weigert-type techniques are reasonably specific for elastin and are regarded by many as the method of choice for the demonstration of these extracellular fibers. However, the Verhoeff–van Gieson (VVG) stain is more popular because it is quick and outlines the elastic fibers with a strong black color. Both techniques are usually set against the esthetically pleasant trichrome background provided by van Gieson's stain.

13 *Myelin stains.* Luxol fast blue is the nonimmunohistochemical method of choice for the demonstration of myelin. It is based on the strong affinity of the copper phthalocyanine dye for the phospholipids and choline bases of myelin.

14 *Formaldehyde-induced fluorescence.* This is a very special type of technique, remarkably sensitive for the demonstration of catecholamines and indolamines but requiring rather costly and cumbersome equipment as originally described. A modified version as applied to touch preparations has made it more accessible to the practicing pathologist,[10,20] but it is hardly used at the present time anyway. It is based on the principle that biogenic amines subjected to formaldehyde vapors produced by heating the polymer paraformaldehyde form highly fluorescent derivatives.

Enzyme histochemistry

After a period of enthusiasm in the 1950s and 1960s for the use of enzyme histochemical techniques in pathology,[39,42] the technique fell in general disuse as far as diagnostic applications were concerned. This was due to the complexity of the techniques, the need for fresh material, and the relative nonspecificity of most of the reactions.[38] At the present time, the enzyme histochemical methods most commonly used for diagnostic purposes are those for skeletal muscle-related enzymes (for the study of myopathies), acetylcholinesterase (for the diagnosis of Hirschsprung's disease), and chloroacetate esterase (for the identification of cells of the myeloid series and mast cells).[40] The latter, known as Leder's technique, benefits from the fact that chloroacetate esterase is one of the few enzymes that resists the effects of formalin fixation and paraffin embedding (Fig. 3.4). Another enzyme that can be demonstrated following routine procedures is acid phosphatase (Fig. 3.5).[30]

Yet another enzyme histochemical technique with diagnostic connotations is the DOPA reaction for cells of the melanocytic series. It depends on the presence of the enzyme tyrosinase and requires the use of fresh tissue (Fig. 3.6). A modified version of the technique allows the demonstration of the precipitation product in paraffin-embedded material.[34]

A plastic embedding technique following paraformaldehyde fixation has been described that combines preservation of various enzymes with excellent morphologic detail.[29,31] Enzyme histochemistry can also be carried out at the ultrastructural level.[37]

Finally, it should be noted the enzymes, being of proteic nature and therefore immunogenic, can also be demonstrated with immunohistochemical techniques in

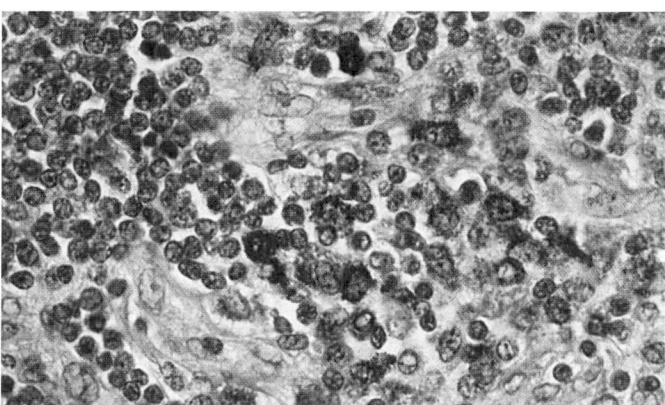

Fig. 3.4 Leder's chloracetate esterase technique. Lymph node involved by systemic mastocytosis. The myeloid precursors stain an intense red color.

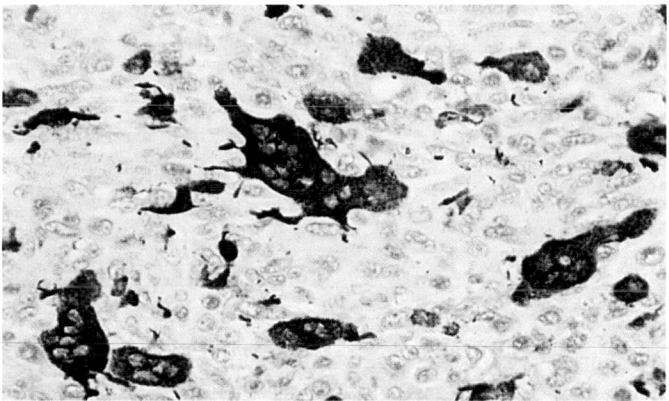

Fig. 3.5 Duray's acid phosphatase technique. Specimen from giant cell tumor of bone fixed in formalin and embedded in paraffin. The osteoclasts show strong acid phosphatase activity.

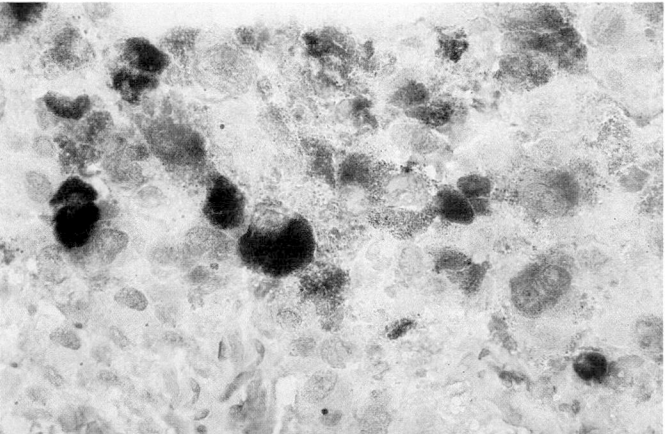

Fig. 3.6 Dopa reaction in a fresh frozen section of malignant melanoma. Deposition of brown pigment in the cytoplasm of the tumor cell is indicative of the presence of tyrosinase.

formalin-fixed, paraffin-embedded material even when no longer enzymatically active.[28,33,35,36,41]

Tissue culture

The pioneer work of Margaret Murray, Arthur Purdy Stout, and Luciano Ozzello at Columbia-Presbyterian Hospital in New York City showed that some histogenetic clues could be obtained from the examination of primary cultures of human tumors such as thymoma, synovial sarcoma, rhabdomyosarcoma, and hemangiopericytoma.[52] The concepts of the existence of fibrous mesothelioma and fibrous histiocytoma (at present greatly challenged) were to a large extent based on tissue culture observations by these investigators.[53,56]

The rationale for the diagnostic application of tissue culture in human tumors is based on the observation that tumor cells can express features of differentiation in vitro that are not exhibited or not appreciable in vivo.[47,49] The classic and often quoted example is neuroblastoma, which is seen to grow neurites within 24 hours of having been placed in a suitable culture medium, as described in a classic paper by the Columbia-Presbyterian group[51] (Fig. 3.7). Another spectacular example is amelanotic melanoma, which sometimes becomes deeply pigmented in vitro[44] (Fig. 3.8). In some instances, this differentiation or maturation has been induced in the culture system by the addition of an exogenous agent, such as cyclic AMP.[48] An interesting development along these lines is the neural differentiation that has been obtained in Ewing's sarcoma—one of the histogenetically most challenging human neoplasms—by the addition of AMP or TPA to the medium.[43] Indeed, the use of short-term tissue culture has been reproposed for the differential diagnosis of small round cell tumors of infancy, including Ewing's sarcoma.

It should be apparent that cells grown in culture can be studied with any of the modern tools such as immunohistochemistry, electron microscopy, ultrastructural immunohistochemistry, cytogenetics, and molecular biologic techniques.[54,55]

Despite these substantial contributions, it should be stated that at a practical, strictly diagnostic level the utility of tissue culture techniques remains very limited, to the point that it is difficult to justify maintaining such operations in a laboratory of surgical pathology. This applies even to the specific situation of small round cell tumors of infancy, in which the technique has been largely superseded by the use of molecular genetic tests. However, those diagnostic pathologists who have access to tissue culture facilities that have been set up elsewhere in their department for primarily investigative purposes will find it interesting and occasionally useful to have some selected tumors evaluated by this technique.[45,46,50]

Some reflections are also worth making vis-à-vis the

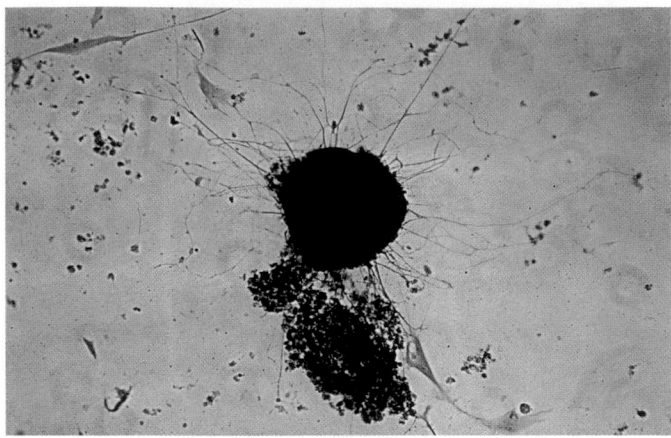

Fig. 3.7 Neuroblastoma showing neurites emanating from a cluster of tumor cells after 24 hours of tissue culture. (Courtesy of Dr. L. Ozzello, New York)

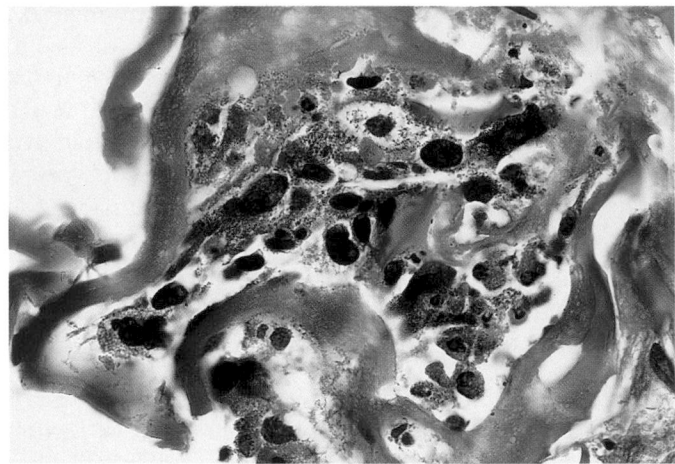

Fig. 3.8 Organ culture of malignant melanoma in Gelfoam, which appears as a homogeneous eosinophilic network. The tumor was amelanotic in vivo, but it is seen producing large amounts of melanin in vitro.

role of special techniques (as exemplified here by tissue culture) in relation to morphology. The concepts of fibrous mesothelioma and malignant fibrous histiocytoma (now largely discredited) were initially proposed mainly on the basis of tissue culture patterns, which were thought to provide better histogenetic evidence than morphology, which in both instances was giving a very different message. A lesson to be learned from these episodes is that great caution should be exercised in the interpretation of novel technology if in direct opposition to the conclusions that have been drawn from the time-honored cytoarchitectural evaluation of tumors.

Quantitative methods (histometry)

Objective measurement of microscopic features has been advocated for decades as a method to make more reproducible and "scientific" the practice of histopathology, but it is only relatively recently that technical advances in computing technology have rendered this procedure suitable for diagnostic and prognostic determinations in surgical pathology.[66,69,72,73] Yet, the adoption of these methods by the surgical pathology community keeps lagging behind. The reason, as a frustrated champion of this technology suggested, may well be "lack of primary innovative leadership among pathologists."[59] There may be other explanations. Traditionally the measurements have been made from photographs, from projected images, or by the use of eyepiece graticules. Currently, semiautomatic or fully automated image analyzers are employed.[67,68,74] Most of the original contributions employing this technique have been in the evaluation of non-neoplastic diseases of skeletal muscle, peripheral nerve, small bowel, and bone.[57,60] At present, the method is also applied with increasing frequency to various aspects of tumor pathology, such as determination of DNA ploidy (in Feulgen-stained preparations)[61,62,65,71]: proliferative index (after staining of the sections with MIB-1 [Ki-67] or analogous markers), nuclear grading,[63] dysplasia grading,[59] and hormone receptor status.[70] In the case of DNA ploidy and proliferative index evaluations, image analysis has been proved to be as accurate as flow cytometry, and clearly superior to it in some specific situations, such as when the amount of tissue is scanty or when the ratio of tumor to non-neoplastic elements is low.[62,65,66]

Needless to say, image analysis can be also applied to cytologic preparations. Actually, a specimen composed of isolated cells in a clear background represents the technically ideal situation on which to employ the method.[75]

X-ray microanalysis

X-ray microanalysis is based on the principle that, when a target atom in a specimen is struck by an electron beam, electron displacement to a higher energy state (orbital shell) and subsequent return will occur. The x-ray photon characteristic for the particular atom is measured, converted to digital form, and expressed in an x-ray spectrogram that allows for identification of elements 11 through 99 (i.e., most of the periodic table).[77] It is preferable to use tissue fixed directly in glutaraldehyde, but material can also be processed following formalin fixation, obtained from the paraffin block, or even retrieved from the original H&E slide by the use of the "pop-off" technique.[76] The examination is performed with either a transmission or scanning electron microscope coupled with an x-ray detector of the energy dispersive type. Currently, the main use of x-ray microanalysis is in the determination of the nature of crystalline (usually foreign) material observed in surgical pathology specimens.[77]

Electron microscopy

The main applications of electron microscopy to diagnostic pathology are in the fields of renal and tumor pathology.[79,80,84–86,87,91–93,95,100,101] The latter aspect is discussed in Chapter 17. In tumor pathology, ultrastructural examinations have proved very useful in determining the histogenesis (or differentiation) of various tumors but, unfortunately, have not shown consistent differences between reactive conditions, benign tumors, and malignant tumors of the same cell type. Lesions of controversial nature in which electron microscopy has provided crucial information and sometimes settled the histogenetic issue include granular cell tumor, schwannoma, Langerhans' cell histiocytosis, spindle cell (sarcomatoid) carcinoma, mesothelioma, spindle cell thymoma, carcinoid tumors and small cell carcinomas of various sites, spermatocytic seminoma of testis, and several others. At the present time, the role of diagnostic electron microscopy has diminished considerably as a result of the advent of immunohistochemistry and other techniques. However, it remains a powerful tool that can be of great utility to the diagnostic pathologist if used selectively and intelligently, with full knowledge of its potential contributions and limitations. The pathologist confronted with a tumor that he finds undiagnosable by light microscopy who sends a sample for electron microscopic study in the hope that some feature of diagnostic significance will be found is likely to be disappointed by the results. The best chance for electron microscopy to be of utility is when the pathologist has already formulated a definite differential diagnosis between two or three entities at the light microscopic level and examines the tissue ultrastructurally searching specifically for the markers to be expected in each of those entities. I believe that this technique is used at its full potential only when the electron microscopic study is carried out by an individual experienced in anatomic pathology who has studied personally the light microscopic preparations of the case, has concluded that electron microscopy is indicated and for what reasons, has examined the thick sections, and has sat down at the electron microscope in order to select the proper photographic fields. Diagnostic electron microscopy observations become fully informative only when closely correlated with the light microscopic features, just as the latter acquire their full significance only when paired with the gross pathology and the clinical features of the case.

The limitations of electron microscopy can be summarized as follows:

1 Sampling, wherein only a small proportion of the neoplasm can be studied
2 Paucity of truly specific ultrastructural features, since the number of organelles or other structures that are exclusive of a cell or tissue type is very small

3 Possible misinterpretation of entrapped non-neoplastic elements as belonging to the tumor. Admittedly, this possibility exists with any technique, but it is particularly noticeable with electron microscopy because of the difficulties in evaluating spatial relationships in a small tissue sample.

The greatest diagnostic potential of electron microscopy has been realized in the following instances:

1 Identification of a tumor as of (neuro)endocrine nature through the detection of dense-core granules of so-called neurosecretory type
2 Assessment of the nature of tumor cells with granular cytoplasm (oncocytes, granular cells, endocrine cells)
3 Identification of epithelial (including glandular and squamous) differentiation in tumors of various types[88a]
4 Identification of a tumor as of melanocytic nature through the detection of melanosomes[88]
5 Identification of a lesion as belonging to the Langerhans' cell histiocytosis group of conditions through the detection of Birbeck's granules
6 Identification of a tumor as composed of steroid-producing cells from adrenal cortex and gonads through the detection of abundant smooth endoplasmic reticulum and mitochondria with tubulovesicular cristae
7 Identification of a tumor as of endothelial cell nature through the detection of Weibel–Palade bodies
8 Identification of skeletal and smooth muscle cells through the detection of the respective systems of cytoplasmic filaments
9 Identification of Schwann cells through the detection of mesoaxons and other features
10 Identification of alveolar soft tissue sarcoma through the detection of the characteristic membrane-bound crystals
11 Identification of smooth muscle, neural, or other types of differentiation in tumors of the GIST family.[82]

The main situations in which electron microscopy is likely to offer information of diagnostic utility are the following:

1 Differential diagnosis among carcinoma, melanoma, and sarcoma[88,90,98]
2 Differential diagnosis between adenocarcinoma and mesothelioma
3 Differential diagnosis of anterior mediastinal tumors among thymoma, thymic carcinoid, malignant lymphoma, and seminoma
4 Differential diagnosis of small round cell tumors of infancy[93,96]
5 Differential diagnosis of spindle cell tumors of soft tissues[99]
6 Differential diagnosis between endocrine and non-endocrine tumors.

Undoubtedly, the best ultrastructural evaluation is made when a small sample of fresh material is fixed, immediately after removal, in a fixative specifically devised for this purpose. Of these, the standard ones are 4% glutaraldehyde and Karnovsky fluid, which is a mixture of glutaraldehyde and formaldehyde (the latter prepared from paraformaldehyde, see below). This is followed by post-fixation in osmium tetroxide, processing, and plastic embedding. The tissue can be stored for long periods (up to 6 months) at 4°C in glutaraldehyde or Karnovsky's fixative without appreciable changes in the preservation.[94] Failure to use these fixatives will result in a number of artifacts that no subsequent procedure can eliminate. Fortunately, the fact remains that some of the structures on which the diagnosis depends (such as desmosomes, dense-core granules, or melanosomes) may still be identifiable despite the artifacts present. Therefore, it is worthwhile in many instances to retrieve material originally processed for routine light microscopic study.[97] Tissue fixed in buffered formaldehyde gives better results than tissue exposed to highly acidic fixatives such as Bouin's, Zenker's, or B-5. As a matter of fact, formaldehyde would be almost as good as a fixative for electron microscopy were not for the fact that commercial formalin preparations contain ethyl alcohol or other extraneous substances introduced to slow down its degradation to formic acid. That is the reason why paraformaldehyde fixation is a good substitute or addition (as in the Karnovsky's fluid) to glutaraldehyde. So-called "paraformaldehyde fixation" is nothing more than fixation using freshly made pure formaldehyde from its polymer.

When retrieving tissue that has been fixed in routine formalin for electron microscopy study, it is advisable to select the sample from the very periphery of the fragments, which is likely to be better fixed than the rest. If wet formalin-fixed material is unavailable, tissue may still be retrieved from the paraffin block, even if the number and magnitude of artifacts will be considerably greater.[102] Finally, tissue can be obtained even from the H&E-stained section itself, a procedure that can be very useful if the structure in question is present only focally.[78]

It should also be remembered that cytologic preparations are also suitable for ultrastructural examination.[89]

Plastic embedding of the type employed for electron microscopic examination (such as glycol methacrylate) is also useful for the examination of biopsy material at the light microscopic level because of the superior cytologic detail it provides.[83]

An issue often raised in these increasingly cost-conscious times is whether it is advisable for a pathology laboratory to have an electron microscopic facility fully devoted to diagnostic work, in view of the high cost of the operation. In our opinion, such a facility is still highly desirable in academic institutions and private laboratories handling a large volume of material. Most other places are probably better served by sending their problem cases to large electron microscopic laboratories that perform referral work or, even better, to an expert consultant who can determine whether electron microscopy or some other special technique is truly needed to solve the diagnostic quandary.[81]

Immunohistochemistry

Briefly stated, immunohistochemistry is the application of immunologic principles and techniques to the study of cells and tissues. The original method, brilliantly conceived by Coons, consisted of labeling with a fluorescent probe an antibody raised in rabbits and searching for it (and therefore for the antigen against which the antibody was directed) in tissue sections examined under a fluorescent microscope following incubation. The technical improvements that supervened in subsequent years have been responsible for these methods becoming a staple of the histopathology laboratory.

Several procedures are available, the two most commonly used at present being the peroxidase– antiperoxidase immune complex method and the biotin–avidin immunoenzymatic technique (Figs 3.9 and 3.10). In the latter procedure, the high affinity of avidin for biotin is used to couple the peroxidase label to the primary antibody.[242,446]

Various methods for increasing the sensitivity of the procedure have been devised. Their aim is to expose antigenic sites (epitopes) that may otherwise be unexposed ("masked"), hence their generic designation as "antigen-unmasking" or "antigen-retrieving" techniques.[337] They

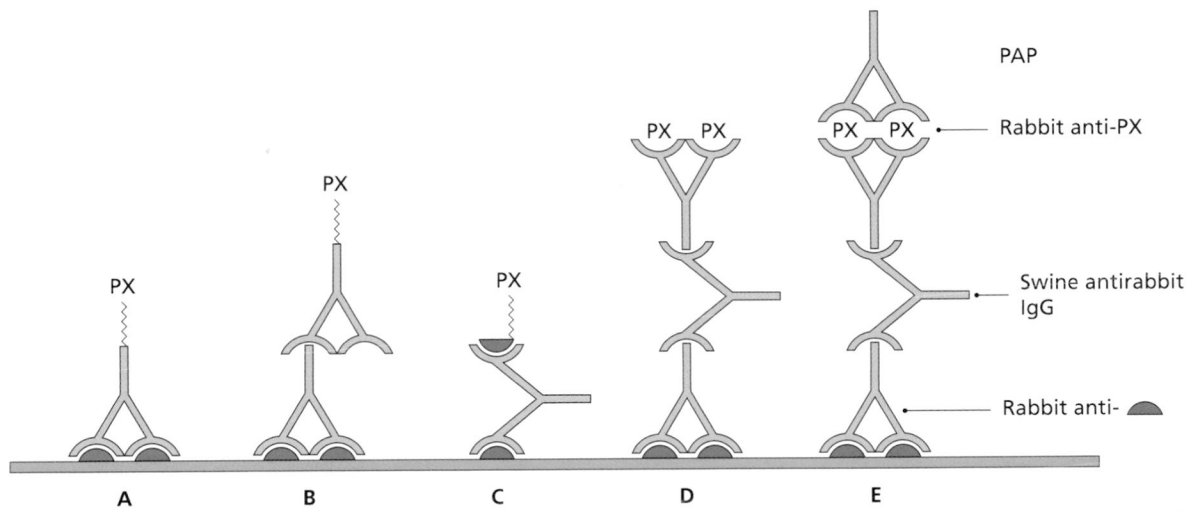

Fig. 3.9 Immunoperoxidase procedures. **A,** Peroxidase (PX) antibody conjugate, direct. **B,** Peroxidase antibody conjugate, indirect. **C,** Labeled antigen method. **D,** Enzyme bridge procedure. **E,** Peroxidase antiperoxidase (PAP) immune complex method. Solid semicircle indicates antigen. (From Falini B, Taylor CR. New developments in immunoperoxidase techniques and their application. Arch Pathol Lab Med 1983, **107:** 105–117)

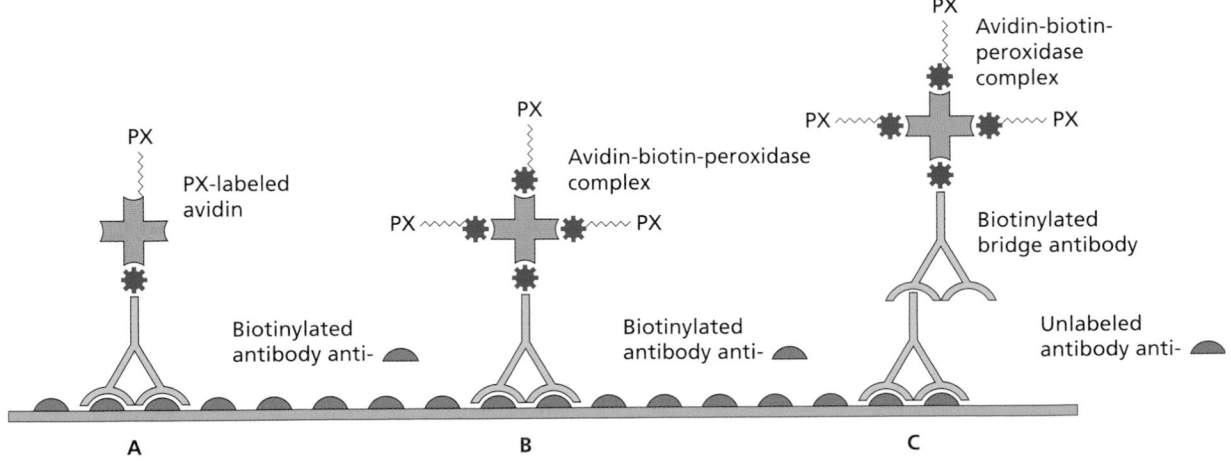

Fig. 3.10 Biotin–avidin immunoenzymatic techniques. Solid semicircle, antigen; PX, peroxidase; *, biotin; shaded open cross, avidin. **A,** Biotinylated primary antibody method. **B,** Biotinylated peroxidase method. **C,** Avidin–biotin–peroxidase complex method. (From Falini B, Taylor CR. New developments in immunoperoxidase techniques and their application. Arch Pathol Lab Med 1983, **107:** 105–117)

include digestion with a variety of proteolytic enzymes, treatment with microwaves, and exposure to the combined action of heat and pressure in a pressure cooker.[217,363]

There is probably no other method that has so revolutionized the field during the past 50 years as the immunohistochemical technique.[146,368,428] The advantages are obvious: remarkable sensitivity and specificity, applicability to routinely processed material (even if stored for long periods), and feasibility of an accurate correlation with the traditional morphologic parameters. It is compatible with most of the fixatives currently in use[252,293] and is feasible even in decalcified material[372] or in previously stained microscopic sections.[392] It is sometimes positive even in totally necrotic material.[257] It can also be adapted to cytologic preparations[149,183,309,375,504] and to electron microscopy.[231,366,426] It can be used in conjunction with conventional techniques (such as silver staining) in the same section.[325] It has replaced and rendered obsolete many of the conventional special stains and—to some extent—many of the diagnostic applications of electron microscopy. However, like any other technique, it presents potential pitfalls that need to be acknowledged by the pathologist interpreting the reaction, in order to prevent the technique being misleading rather than helpful.[308] Many of these pitfalls can be avoided by scrupulous technique, periodic checking of the antibody activity, and proper use of positive and negative controls.

A quick labeling method (<7 min) has been devised for its possible use in intraoperative consultation,[472] such as evaluation of sentinel lymph nodes.[500] A variety of devices for the automation of immunohistology are now available.[493]

An ingenious method for antibody testing—the "sausage tissue block"—that allows the simultaneous evaluation of over 100 different tissue samples on a single slide with one drop of antibody has been devised by Battifora[122] and has now developed into a veritable industry, known as the multiblock or tissue microarray.[139,238,273,358,454] Modern versions of these instruments devised for this purpose allow to place hundreds or even thousand of tissues in a single block.[409,454] It is our impression, however, that some of the manufacturers have gone too far in their quest for squeezing as many specimens as possible in a single block (elegantly expressed as "high throughput tissue microarrays"). The problem is that, if the tissue cylinders are below a certain diameter, they run the risk of not being representative of the lesion and of suffering from the so-called "edge artefact" when immunostained. The diameter we prefer for the tissues we place in multiblocks is that of 3 mm.

False-negative results in immunohistochemistry can occur when:

1 An antibody is inappropriate, denatured, or used at the wrong concentration.

2 There is loss of antigen through autolysis and/or diffusion. This factor plays a much larger role with some antigens (such as factor VIII-related antigen) than with others (such as actin). It should be remembered that most antigens continue to leak out after fixation; therefore, it is always preferable to perform the stains using the original paraffin block rather than tissue left in formalin for long periods.

3 Presence of antigen is at a density below the level of detection with the reagents and techniques used, because of either minimal production or excessive release.

Because of the existence of all these factors, an apparently negative immunohistochemical result should not be used to rule out a diagnosis even in the presence of a positive built-in control, especially if such a diagnosis is strongly suggested by the clinical and morphologic features.

False-positive results, which are even more dangerous, can result from a variety of causes:

1 Cross-reactivity of the antibody with antigens different from the one being sought.

2 Nonspecific binding of the antibody to the tissue.[136]

3 Presence of endogenous peroxidase in—or avidity for the avidin–biotin complex by—some cellular elements.

4 Entrapment of normal tissues by the tumor cells. This problem, which also exists in H&E-stained sections, is amplified through the great sensitivity of the technique. One example of this phenomenon is the entrapment of skeletal muscle by soft tissue tumors, with the resulting misdiagnosis of rhabdomyosarcoma because of positivity for desmin, myoglobin, or some other skeletal muscle marker.[133] Another is the misdiagnosis of malignant lymphoma of thyroid as carcinoma because of the positivity of the entrapped follicular epithelium for thyroglobulin.[427] Still another is the misdiagnosis of Hodgkin's lymphoma or large cell lymphoma of the thymus as malignant thymoma because of the presence of keratin-positive entrapped thymic epithelial cells.[408]

The existence of this phenomenon also makes very difficult the determination of multihormonal secretion in endocrine neoplasms. For instance, the majority of endocrine tumors of the pancreas show positivity for more than one hormone,[367] but the possibility of only one of these hormones representing the neoplastic element and the others expressing the residual non-neoplastic cells should be regarded as an alternative for at least some of the cases. As a matter of fact, the problem of entrapment of normal structures is so subtle and pervasive that it can be eliminated with certainty only if the stain is done in a metastatic site, where entrapped normal tissue from that particular organ would be out of the question.

5 Release of proteins from the cytoplasm of normal cells invaded by the tumor, with subsequent permeation of the interstitium and nonspecific absorption (and possibly phagocytosis) by the tumor cells. Perhaps in some cases this phenomenon—which is the most treacherous of them all—represents an artifact developed after the removal of the tissue, but in most instances it is probably occurring already in vivo. Immunoglobulins are known to exhibit this phenomenon, which explains the positivity of Reed–Sternberg cells for various light and heavy Ig chains.[357] A marker particularly prone to this artifact (probably because of its great diffusing properties) is thyroglobulin. We have seen in the thyroid gland cases of metastatic clear cell carcinoma from the kidney, malignant lymphoma, and metastatic signet ring carcinoma in which the tumor cells around the trapped thyroid follicles showed strong cytoplasmic staining for thyroglobulin, whereas those located at a greater distance or in other organs were totally negative (Fig. 3.11).[141,427] Still another example of this phenomenon is the malignant tumor growing within blood vessels and picking up factor VIII or other endothelial markers from the adjacent non-neoplastic endothelial cells. This may explain some cases of keratin-positive anaplastic carcinomas of the thyroid with a prominent endovascular component showing an apparent positivity for factor VIII.[356] Still another example of this phenomenon is provided by breast carcinoma that invades the pectoralis muscle, the myoglobin liberated from the injured muscle diffusing into the carcinoma cells and rendering them positive for this skeletal muscle-specific antigen.[188]

There are other factors that have contributed to misinterpretations. We are referring to the apparently anomalous positive stains caused by ectopic antigen expression, by hitherto unrecognized cross reactions, or by the fact that some markers originally claimed to be specific for a certain cell tissue or tumor have proved with increased experience to be shared by other tissues or neoplasms. Examples of this phenomenon are plentiful and include neuron-specific enolase,[185] α_1-antitrypsin,[511] S-100 protein (originally claimed to be specific for the central nervous system and now known to be present in a large variety of cells, ranging from dendritic reticulum cells to chondrocytes), vimentin (originally claimed to be specific for mesenchymal cells but later also detected in neuronal cells and many other elements), and epithelial membrane antigen (first thought to be specific for breast, then for breast and skin adnexa, then for epithelial cells in general, and now also demonstrated in several mesenchymal tumors and hematolymphoid neoplasms).[174] Actually, the possibility should always be kept in mind that a marker regarded at the present time as specific for a certain cell type may prove in the future to react with others.

The number of antigens that have been detected with immunohistochemistry in tissue sections is already huge and keeps increasing at a steady rate. Theoretically, any substance that is antigenic and whose antigenicity is at least partially retained in tissue sections can be demonstrated by this technique. With the advent of monoclonal technology, a large number of antibodies have become available for which the antigenic determinant is chemically poorly defined or—in some instances—totally unknown. Although some of these antibodies have proved extremely useful (particularly in the field of hematopathology), one should be particularly careful not to overinterpret the results in terms of presumptive tissue specificity.[208] An area that has acquired a great significance lately is that of transcription factors. These are nuclear proteins necessary for the transcription of certain genes, some of which are tissue-specific. The advantages they offer over the traditional markers located in the cytoplasm, cell membrane or extracellular space is that there is a generally higher degree of specificity and practically no diffusion. Also, since the marker location is nuclear, the stain can be combined with another with a different chromogen aimed at a cytoplasmic or cell membrane marker. Examples of transcription factor that have already proved their diagnostic utility are myogenin, TTF-1, WT-1, and FLI-1. Another area that needs to be explored further is that of the nuclear matrix proteins.[244]

Although strictly speaking not an immunohistochemical technique, the method devised for the in situ labeling of nuclear DNA fragmentation (as seen in apoptosis) is mentioned here. Tissue sections pretreated with protease are wick end labeled with biotinylated poly-dU (introduced by terminal deoxy-transferase) and stained with avidin-conjugated peroxidase.[209]

The most important diagnostic applications of immunohistochemistry are discussed in the respective chapters. Listed subsequently in alphabetical order for

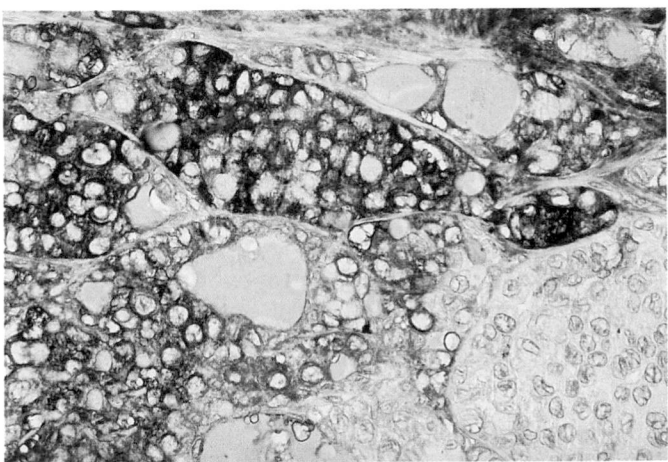

Fig. 3.11 Lobular carcinoma of the breast with signet ring features metastatic to the thyroid, stained for thyroglobulin. There is spurious staining for this marker in the metastatic tumor cells because of diffusion of thyroglobulin from the entrapped thyroid follicles.

easy reference are most of the antigens that have been applied to surgical pathology problems, whether as diagnostic aids or as histogenetic probes. Antigens connected with the hematopoietic system (including all those in the CD series) are discussed in Chapter 21.

Acquaporins. These are membrane proteins of water channels, which show different expressions along the nephron. Acquaporin-1 is expressed in the proximal renal tubule and the descending thin limb of Henle's loop, whereas acquaporin-2 is selectively expressed in collecting ducts.[106,384] Extrarenal acquaporin-1 has been reported in capillary endothelium and red blood cells. Acquaporins can be used to evaluate the possible renal nature of a lesion, together with the various keratins and CD15.[334]

Actin. This is a ubiquitous contractile protein responsible for cell motility. It is an extremely useful marker for the identification of smooth muscle cells and myofibroblasts, and for the evaluation of the participation of myoepithelial cells in lesions of breast, salivary glands, and sweat glands.[371] Various isoforms of this protein exist, including those which are specific for smooth muscle and striated muscle.[455] Antibodies specific for striated muscle (sarcomeric) actin are used as markers for rhabdomyosarcoma.[158,171]

Androgen receptors. See under Hormone receptors.

Albumin. Albumin comprises about one half of the blood serum proteins. It stabilizes extracellular fluid volume and serum pH, and it is a carrier for steroids and other substances. It is manufactured by hepatocytes and, therefore, is potentially a good marker for hepatocellular and hepatoid carcinomas, were it not for the fact that its ubiquitousness renders immunohistochemical demonstration of site of origin (as opposed to diffusion) very difficult. The problem has been obviated by detecting the messenger RNA for albumin with the in-situ hybridization (ISH) technique.[203,278]

ALK. The ALK (anaplastic lymphoma kinase gene) is located on chromosome 2. As a result of the t(2;5) chromosomal translocation it is fused with the NPM (nucleophosphin) gene, leading to the production of a hybrid NPM-ALK protein. This protein is detectable with the ALK-1 (p80) monoclonal antibody, which is therefore useful for the identification of anaplastic large cell lymphoma. Significantly, the expression of the ALK protein also occurs in the inflammatory myofibroblastic tumor and other soft tissue neoplasms.[144a,488a]

Alkaline phosphatase. This group of enzymes consists of membrane-bound glycoproteins that are widely distributed in human tissues. The major isoenzymes are the hepatic, osseous, renal, and placental types. Placental alkaline phosphatase (PLAP) reactivity is seen in all types of gonadal and extragonadal germ cell tumors (including intratubular germ cell neoplasia)[126] but is also present in a variety of non-germ cell neoplasms,[517] including those with muscle differentiation.[212]

Alpha-actinin. This is a constituent protein of sarcomeric muscle, related to Z bands.[182] It has been detected in rhabdomyosarcoma, but its level of sensitivity seems low.[441]

Alpha-amylase. This is a family of digestive enzymes secreted by the pancreatic acinar cells and salivary glands. Therefore, tumors of these organs are often immunoreactive for them. Alas, this is also sometimes true for carcinomas of lung, female genital tract, gastrointestinal tract, liver, and extrahepatic bile ducts.[222,477,494]

Alpha-1-antichymotrypsin. Alpha-1-antichymotrypsin (alpha-1-ACT) is an acute-phase plasma protease inhibitor (molecular weight [MW] 68,000), mainly synthesized in the liver. It shows a high level of homology of DNA sequences with alpha-1-antitrypsin (alpha-1-AT). It has been employed, together with the latter, as a marker for histiocytes and other cells of the accessory immune system. However, it is also found in a large number of other cell types, including epithelial neoplasm.[287] As a result, its diagnostic utility is rather limited.[299] Interestingly, a major portion of prostate specific antigen (PSA) exists in the circulation as a complex with alpha-1-ACT.[533]

Alpha-1-antitrypsin. Alpha-1-AT (alpha-1-proteinase inhibitor) is discussed under the section on alpha-1-ACT.

Alpha-fetoprotein. This glycoprotein is a major plasma component of the fetus, the major sources being the liver and the visceral endoderm of the yolk sac. It is one of the major oncofetal antigens. It is invariably present in yolk sac (endodermal sinus) tumors and also in a high proportion of other germ cell tumors.[282] It is also present in hepatocytic and hepatoid neoplasms, in pancreatic tumors with acinar cell differentiation, and in variety of carcinomas with germ cell-like features.[154,288]

Alpha-lactalbumin. This is a major protein of human milk, synthesized almost exclusively by mammary tissue. It has been detected in normal, fibrocystic, and neoplastic breast tissue. It is present in breast carcinomas of both ductal and lobular type at the primary site and in metastases.[157,301] The only other tumor type in which it has been found is the breast-related hydradenoma papilliferum of vulva.

Alpha-methylacyl-CoA racemase. This is a mitochondrial and peroxisomal enzyme which catalyzes the racemization of alpha-methyl, branched carboxylic coenzyme A thioesters. It has been found to be overexpressed in adenocarcinoma of the prostate and has therefore been proposed as a marker for malignancy in this organ. It is also expressed in other carcinoma types.[253a,532a]

Angiotensin-converting enzyme. This is a membrane-bound enzyme that converts angiotensin I to the biologically active vasopressor angiotensin II and inactivates the depressor substance bradykinin. It is localized in the vascular endothelium of the lung and other tissues and in the epithelial cells of the renal proximal tubule and intestinal mucosa. It has also been detected in renal cell carcinoma.[473] A somatic isoform of the enzyme is present in testicular seminoma and intratubular germ cell neoplasia.[204]

B72.3. B72.3 is a monoclonal antibody that reacts with a high molecular-weight glycoprotein that has been named tumor-associated glycoprotein-72 (TAG-72). It has been proposed that TAG-72 represents the sialated form of Tn[442] (see section on blood group antigens). The antigen has a limited distribution in benign adult tissues but is consistently expressed by a wide variety of adenocarcinomas.[321] One of its most common applications is in the differential diagnosis between mesothelioma (in which it is usually negative) and pulmonary adenocarcinoma.[393] It has also been used for the differential diagnosis between benign and malignant glandular proliferations but with less success.[324]

Basement membrane. This extracellular structure can be manufactured by epithelial, smooth muscle, striated muscle, pericytic, endothelial, schwannian, and melanocytic cells. It has a very complex structure, the two major components being type IV collagen and laminin (see under individual headings).

BCA-225. This glycoprotein (MW 225,000 to 250,000) is a marker isolated from human breast carcinoma tissue. It crossreacts with gp52, the envelope glycoprotein of the mouse mammary tumor virus. It was originally thought to be primarily expressed only in breast carcinomas,[342] but more recent studies have shown that it is also commonly present in carcinomas of the kidney, ovary, and lung and, less frequently, in adenocarcinomas of other organs.[320]

Ber-EP4. This monoclonal antibody is directed against an epitope on the protein molecule of two glycoproteins located on the surface of glandular epithelial cells of endodermal derivation.[429] It is mainly used for the differential diagnosis between adenocarcinoma and mesothelioma.[393]

Blood group antigens. The A, B, and H blood group antigens are glycolipids present in the cell membrane of red blood cells (and in many types of epithelial cells), which can be detected with immunohistochemical methods, with the red blood adherence method, or by the use of lectins (see discussion of lectin receptors).[197,199] Loss of these isoantigens has been observed in carcinomas of various types.[302,509] Furthermore, a correlation has been found between ABH deletion and tumor aggressiveness.[431]

T (Thompsen–Friedenreich) and Tn antigens are precursor antigens of the MN blood group system.[462] They are masked in most, normal adult tissues but are detectable in several types of carcinoma, including breast, large bowel, bladder, and lung.[241] The T antigen is recognized by the lectin peanut agglutinin.[522] It has been shown that the increased expression of the T antigen in

carcinomas results from an alteration of the glycosylation pathway in these tumors.[245]

Bone GLA protein. This is a vitamin K-dependent protein that constitutes approximately 20% of the noncollagenous protein in bone. It has been detected immunohistochemically in osteosarcoma and chondrosarcoma.[251]

CA19-9. This is a carbohydrate antigen recognized by a monoclonal antibody produced by a hybridoma raised against a human colonic carcinoma cell line. It has been characterized as a monosialoganglioside related to the Lewis A blood group antigen. Its most common clinical application has been in the diagnosis and monitoring of pancreatic carcinoma. Immunohistochemically, positive reactions are obtained in most pancreatobiliary adenocarcinomas and transitional cell carcinomas. Adenocarcinomas of other sites can also be positive but with a lower frequency.[206,323]

CA-125. This is a cell surface glycoprotein originally identified in mucinous epithelial ovarian tumors and recognized by the monoclonal antibody OC 125.[270,300] It is also expressed by adenocarcinomas of other sites, including cervix, endometrium, gastrointestinal tract, thyroid, and breast.[267,322,485]

Cadherins. The cadherin family of cell adhesion molecules is a group of transmembrane glycoproteins located in desmosomes.[407] The two types of cadherin better studied are epithelial-type (E-cadherin) and neural type (N-cadherin). They form complexes with catenin,[497] which control several important biological processes, including cell migration, differentiation, proliferation, and apoptosis.[391,458] These complexes are often deficient in carcinomas.[497] The two major kinds are desmoglein and desmocollins I and II.[269] In carcinomas, cadherin expression has been found to be inversely correlated with differentiation.[283,451,459] Cadherins are absent in lobular carcinoma of the breast and present in ductal carcinoma.[103,304] Germ-line and somatic mutations of cadherin play an important role in the pathogenesis of gastric carcinoma of the diffuse type.[326]

Desmosomal glycoprotein (DGI) is a major component of desmosomes that has extensive homology with the cadherins.[516]

Caldesmon. H-caldesmon is a cytoskeleton-associated protein similar to calponin and used for similar purposes (see under calponin).

Calmodulin. See discussion of S-100 protein.

Calponin. This is a cytoskeleton-associated actin-binding protein present in smooth muscle cells, myoepithelial cells, and other contractile cells.[194] It is, therefore, mainly used to document the presence of myoid differentiation.[346]

Calretinin. This is a 29-kD calcium-binding protein expressed by various types of mesothelial, epithelial, and stromal cells.[64,324a] Its main use is in the differential diagnosis between mesothelioma (almost always positive except for the desmoplastic variant) and lung adenocarcinoma (usually but not always negative).[348] It has also been found in carcinoma of other organs,[213] synovial sarcomas,[347] gonadal sex cord-stromal tumors,[140] adamantinomas,[110] and cardiac myxomas.[478]

Cancer-associated carbohydrates. Modified carbohydrate structures present on the surface of carcinoma cells or secreted by them can be detected by monoclonal antibodies. These structures may result from the accumulation of precursor chain because of the decreased activity of synthesizing enzymes, the production of new oligosaccharides resulting from increased or aberrant glycosylation of carbohydrate chains, a change in the density of carbohydrates on the cell surface, or the exposure of chains usually covered by other structures. Alterations in glycolipid synthesis include aberrant fucosylation and/or sialylation of the lacto series, sialylation or fucosylation of the globo series, and syaliation of the ganglio series.[442] Markers related to this type of change include CA 15.3, CA19-9, CA 50, CA-125, CA 242, MCA, SLEX, B72.3, and CEA (see discussions of individual types).

Carbohydrates. See discussion of cancer-associated carbohydrates.

Carbonic anhydrase C. This is a ubiquitous metalloprotein enzyme involved in carbon dioxide hydration and, presumably, in the regulation of ionic and acid–base balance. The C isoenzyme, present in the nervous system, has been suggested as a marker for oligodendrocytes and oligodendrogliomas. However, positivity has also been found in astrocytomas, glioblastomas, schwannomas, meningiomas, and other tumors,[406] including those of adrenal gland.[434]

Carcinoembryonic antigen (CEA). This is a glycoprotein of heterogeneous composition (MW 200,000) normally detected in the glycocalix of fetal epithelial cells, particularly those of mucin-secreting glandular nature.[211,415] It is detectable only in small amounts in normal adult cells and benign tumors but is present in large quantities in carcinomas, particularly in adenocarcinomas of the gastrointestinal tract (including pancreas) and lung and in thyroid medullary carcinoma. Because of the fact that it is primarily expressed by fetal tissues and malignant tumors, it is referred to as an oncofetal antigen. Monoclonal antibodies offer a greater degree of tumor specificity than the conventional antisera.[256] These have been divided into five major groups according to the epitopes they recognize.[187]

Casein. See discussion of epithelial membrane antigen.

Cathepsin D. This is a lysosomal proteinase belonging to the same family as pepsin and chymotrypsin. Early hopes that it could be used as a prognostic marker for breast carcinoma have not materialized.[109] Interestingly, cathepsin D has been found to be a marker of ganglion cell differentiation in the developing and neoplastic human peripheral sympathetic nervous tissues.[328]

Other cathepsin types exist (B, K, L), which have been detected in a large and heterogeneous group of epithelial and mesenchymal neoplasms.[524]

CD10. This antibody, which identifies neprilysin, is reactive for a variety of female genital tract tumors and is particularly useful for the identification of endometrial stromal neoplasms.[151,486] It is also positive in renal cell carcinoma,[152] and solid and pseudopapillary tumor of the pancreas.[386]

CD15 (LeuM1). This is an antibody that recognizes hapten X, a carbohydrate molecule linked to the cell membrane protein of myelomonocytic cells. It has been found to react with adenocarcinomas of various sites and to be of utility in the differential diagnosis between mesothelioma (usually negative) and lung adenocarcinoma (usually positive).[112,412]

CD31. This antibody identifies the hematopoietic progenitor antigen ER-MP12, which is identical to the vascular endothelial adhesion molecule PECAM-1.[313] It has emerged as one of the most useful markers of endothelial cells, although occasionally it may show focal staining of some carcinomas.[179] Among small round cell tumors, it stains regularly malignant lymphomas, and occasionally Ewing's sarcoma/primitive neuroectodermal tumor (PNET).[383]

CD34 (Q BEND 10). This marker stains normal and neoplastic endothelial cells, as well as a variety of soft tissue neoplasms, including dermatofibrosarcoma protuberans, solitary fibrous tumor, gastrointestinal stromal tumors (GISTs), the spindle cell component of a number of adipose tissue neoplasms and benign polyps, and a variety of peripheral nerve sheath tumors.[161,470,512]

CD56 (NCAM). See under intercellular adhesion molecules (ICAMs).

CD57 (Leu7). This is a marker for a subset of normal lymphocytes, which has been found also to react with a variety of neural and neuroendocrine neoplasms and with prostatic adenocarcinomas.[113,343]

CD99 (O13; p30/32; MIC2). This is mainly used for the diagnosis of Ewing's sarcoma/PNET, but it is also present in a large variety of other tumors, including lymphoblastic lymphoma, some rhabdomyosarcomas, retinoblastoma, some desmoplastic small cell tumors, ependymoma, solitary fibrous tumor, synovial sarcoma, neuroendocrine tumors, ovarian granulosa cell tumor, and others.[201,465]

CD117. This antibody identifies c-KIT, a transmembrane tyrosine kinase normally expressed by Cajal's interstitial cells, melanocytes, mast cells, and germ cells. Among neoplasms, it is expressed in mastocytosis, melanoma, germ cell tumors, and the GIST tumor family. In the latter, the expression is ligand-independent and resulting from a mutation of the c-*kit* gene.[240,381,433]

CDX2. This homeobox gene encodes a transcription factor that plays an important role in the proliferation and differentiation of intestinal epithelial cells. The corresponding protein seems to be highly restricted to intestinal epithelium and therefore promises to become a very useful marker for the identification of adenocarcinomas of intestinal origin.[364a,514b]

Chromogranin. The chromogranin family is composed of acidic glycoproteins (MW 20,000 to 100,000) located in the soluble fraction of neurosecretory granules.[194a,316,475] The most abundant is chromogranin A (MW 75,000).[226] Two others have been named chromogranin B (or secretogranin I) and chromogranin C (or secretogranin II).[318] Nearly all types of neuroendocrine tumors are reactive, so that chromogranin stain has become the most widely used "pan-endocrine" marker[294] (Fig. 3.12).

Collagen. Collagen is the major constituent of connective tissue. It is composed of a large family of structurally related proteins with distinct distributions and functions.[498,502] As many as 14 different types have been described, and these have been divided into two major classes:

1 Fibril-forming collagen (types I, II, III, V, and IX). These are characterized by a long central triple helical domain and the formation of highly organized fibrils arranged in a quarter-staggered fashion. Collagen type I predominates in the dermis, tendons, and bone. Type II is associated with cartilage. Type III is widespread in loose connective tissue and constitutes the main component of so-called reticular fibers; it is abundant in fetal skin, scars, and arterial walls. Type V has been found to be increased in the desmoplastic stromal reaction induced by carcinomas.[120]

2 Non-fibril-forming collagen. This comprises the collagen types not listed in the previous group. The better known member is collagen type IV, which is—together with laminin—the major component of the basement membrane[200] (see Fig. 3.3). Stains for type IV collagen are useful for the distinction between in situ and (micro)invasive carcinoma and for the differential diagnosis between tumors that manufacture basement membrane (epithelial, smooth muscle, pericytic,

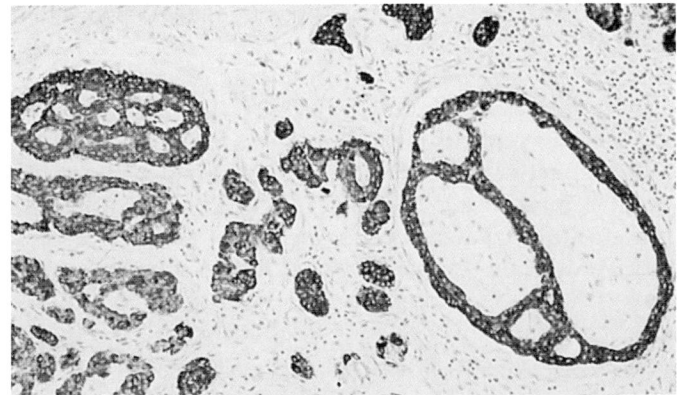

Fig. 3.12 Chromogranin positivity in carcinoid tumor of stomach.

schwannian) and those that do not (fibroblastic, lymphoid).

Type VII collagen is also associated with basement membranes and seems to be restricted to those surrounding or underlying combined epithelia. In malignant tumors, type VII collagen is correlated with squamous differentiation.[515]

Creatine kinase. This widely distributed enzyme of contractile or transport, system is composed of two polypeptide subunits, known as B (brain type) and M (muscle type), that combine to form three dimeric enzymes. The MM isoenzyme is abundant in skeletal muscle and has therefore been used as a diagnostic aid in rhabdomyosarcoma.[492,521] However, it is not entirely specific for this tissue type.[492]

Cytokeratins. See discussion of keratins.

Desmin. This muscle-type intermediate filament (MW 55,000) is found in cells of smooth and striated muscle and in a lesser amount also in myofibroblasts. It is particularly abundant in parenchymal (as opposed to vascular) smooth muscle. Therefore it has been primarily used for the identification of smooth muscle and skeletal muscle tumors.[354,491] Positivity for desmin associated with negativity for actin is a feature of a subset of cells of myofibroblastic appearance,[525] and of those of hormone-dependent stroma (vagina, breast).[239] It is also a feature of desmoplastic small cell tumor (see Chapter 26).

Desmocollin. See discussion of cadherins.

Desmoglein. See discussion of cadherins.

Desmoplakins. Desmoplakins are membrane-bound structures to which intermediate filaments attach to form specialized cell junctions (desmosomes and related structures). They have been found to contain six major high-molecular-weight protein components. Two of them, designated respectively as desmoplakin I (MW 250,000) and desmoplakin II (MW 215,000), have been used as markers for the presence of cell junctions, thus providing indirect evidence about the cell type.[361]

Endorphin. See discussion of opioid peptides.

Endosialin (FB5). This is a cell surface glycoprotein of vascular endothelial cells that has been found to be expressed in malignant vascular tumors. Its specificity still needs to be determined.[422]

Endothelin (ET-1). This is a protein known to exist in many organs and to have several biologic functions, including vasoconstriction. Immunohistochemical studies have localized it to endothelial cells and—to a lesser extent—medial smooth muscle cells.[487] The range of its expression in vascular and other mesenchymal tumor has yet to be explored. Endothelin-1 and its receptor have been found to be expressed in adrenal cortical cells and their tumors.[236]

Enolases. See discussion of neuron-specific enolase.

Enzymes. All enzymes are proteins and therefore demonstrable immunohistochemically even if their specific activity is no longer present. In addition to those listed individually, enzymes that have been demonstrated with this technique include those of the catecholamine-synthesizing pathway,[266] those of the steroid hormone-synthesizing pathway,[435] and leukocyte elastase (a serine protease present in cells of the myeloid series).[166]

EpCam. EpCam protein, also known as ESA or EGP40, is an epithelial transmembrane protein found on the basolateral surface of simple, pseudostratified, and transitional epithelia. It is expressed in many carcinoma types, but most soft tissue and lymphoid tumors are negative.[514a]

Epidermal growth factor receptor (EGFR). This is a tyrosine kinase anchored on the cell membrane, thought to be important for tumor progression. It is present in various types of epithelial tumors, notably breast carcinoma. No convincing relationship with survival or clinicopathologic features has been found.[469] However, it serves as an indicator of probable therapeutic response to EGFR inhibitors.[424]

Epithelial membrane antigen (EMA). This is a glycoprotein present in human milk fat globule membranes[410]; it is probably analogous to the antigen demonstrated with antisera raised against the casein fraction of human milk.[399] It is an excellent marker for most normal and neoplastic epithelia but is not restricted to them (Fig. 3.13).[480] It is also expressed by mesotheliomas, meningiomas, a variety of mesenchymal neoplasms, and even some malignant lymphomas.[416,457,471] It has also been found to be a marker of normal and neoplastic perineurial cells.[114] There is evidence suggesting that monoclonal antibodies raised against various epitopes of human or guinea pig milk fat globule membrane may offer a greater degree of specificity, in the sense of being apparently restricted to epithelial tissues.[220,234,534]

Estrogen receptors. See under Hormone receptors.

Factor VIII-related antigen. Factor VIII-related antigen is one of the three functional components of the antihemophiliac factor (factor VIII).[369] It is synthesized in endothelial cells of blood vessels (where it has been located in the Weibel–Palade bodies) and is also found in megakaryocytes, platelets, and mast cells. It is widely

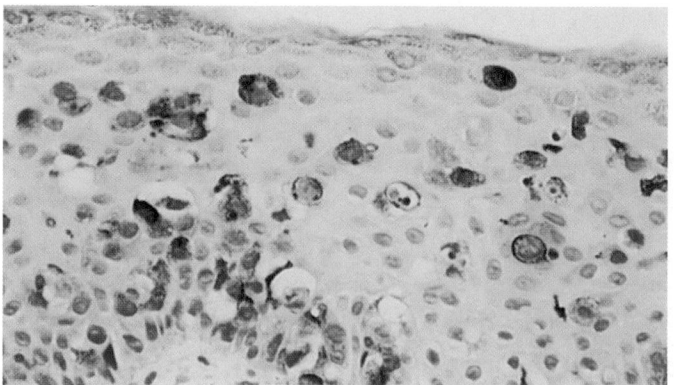

Fig. 3.13 Epithelial membrane antigen (EMA) in Paget's disease of breast.

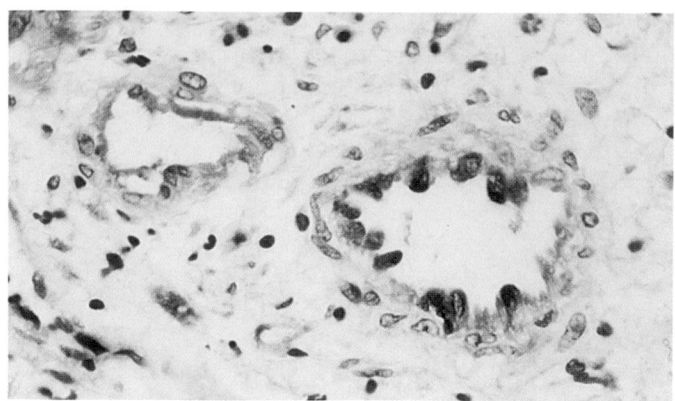

Fig. 3.14 Factor VIII-related antigen in epithelioid vascular tumor of bone.

used as a marker of endothelial cell differentiation (Fig. 3.14).[223,369]

Factor XIIIa. Factor XIII is a protransglutaminase involved in hemostasis. It has a tetrameric structure with two subunits. The activation of this enzyme, which is calcium dependent, follows cleavage of the two subunits and leads to the formation of factor XIIIa. This factor catalyzes the covalent cross-linking and stabilization of fibrin during clot formation. Positive staining for factor XIIIa has been found in megakaryocytes and various types of monocytes/macrophages.[143,177] In the skin, factor XIIIa-positive cells (known as dermal dendrocytes) are scattered throughout the dermis, at the dermoepidermal junction, and in dermal blood vessels. Benign fibrous histiocytomas of skin are strongly positive for this marker.[144]

Fascin. Fascin is an actin-binding protein involved in the formation of dendritic processes. Fascin is normally present in dendritic follicular cells. It has been found to be often expressed in the Reed-Sternberg cells of Hodgkin's lymphoma and also in the tumor cells of anaplastic large cell lymphoma.[189a]

Ferritin. Ferritin, together with transferrin and lactoferrin, is a major iron-binding protein. It has been detected immunohistochemically in hepatocellular carcinoma[160] and breast carcinoma.[147,430]

Fibrin. This is a key component of the coagulation mechanism. It is formed from fibrinogen (MW 340,000), a protein made of three pairs of disulfide-bonded polypeptide chains. Two major forms of fibrin exist, known as I and II. Monoclonal antibodies that distinguish these various components have been described.[128]

Fibronectin. This glycoprotein is found in the extracellular matrix and plasma. It serves as an adhesion protein and mediates cell-matrix interactions. Several molecular variants exist.[274] Abnormal expression of this molecule has been found in some tumors, such as hepatocellular carcinoma,[488] but its diagnostic utility is nil.

Fillagrin. Fillagrin (MW 50,000) is the matrix protein of keratin. It received its name because of its ability to aggregate filaments of keratin into fibers or macrofibrils.[168] It has been used to study disorders of keratinization and various epithelial neoplasms. Its diagnostic utility seems very limited.[501]

FLI-1. The FLI-1 protein is the product of the FLI-1 gene, which is overexpressed in Ewing's sarcoma/PNET as a result of the EWS/FLI-1 gene fusion, and which can be detected immunohistochemically.[201] FLI-1 is also positive in most lymphoblastic lymphomas but, generally, not in other small round cell tumors. It is also normally expressed in endothelial cells and, therefore, it may be used as a marker for endothelial neoplasms.[202]

Fodrin. This molecule is a component of adhesion complexes, together with cadherin and catenin. A disruption of this complex has been found in a variety of epithelial tumors.[461]

Galectin. The galectins constitute a family of lactose-binding proteins sharing affinity for β-galactoside residues and significant sequence similarity in their carbohydrate-binding site.[119] Increased galectin expression has been found in several carcinoma types, including those arising from thyroid, endometrium, head and neck, kidney, bladder, large bowel, and pancreas.[169] Gal-3 has been particularly studied in the thyroid gland, where it stains carcinomas in a stronger and more consistent fashion than adenomas.[317]

Gastricsin. This is an acid protease (MW 35,000) present in the human gastric juice, which is produced in the form of a zymogen (progastricsin), primarily in the stomach but also in the duodenum. A similar enzyme has been found in seminal fluid and in benign and malignant prostatic tissues.[417]

GD3 ganglioside. The disialoganglioside GD3 is a neuroectodermal antigen detected by the monoclonal antibody R24 and expressed by normal melanocytes and malignant melanomas. Its highest expression has been found on the surface of melanoma cells.[496]

Glial fibrillary acidic protein. Glial fibrillary acidic protein (GFAP; MW 48,000 to 52,000) is one of the five major types of cytoplasmic intermediate filaments.[155,170] It is present in normal, reactive, and neoplastic astrocytes; developing, reactive, and neoplastic ependymal cells; and developing and neoplastic oligodendrocytes[406] (Fig. 3.15). Expression of this marker has also been documented in peripheral nerve sheath tumors and in mixed tumors of salivary glands and sweat glands.

GLUT. This is the generic name for a family of key glucose transporters, some of which are overexpressed in a variety of neoplasms.[440] The claim that GLUT5 is highly expressed in breast cancer but absent in normal human breast tissue[529] has not been independently verified. GLUT-1 has been studied in ovarian surface epithelial tumors[261] and juvenile hemangiomas[385]

Gross cystic disease fluid protein-15. Gross cystic disease fluid protein-15 (GCDFP-15; also known as BR-2) is present in the fluid content of fibrocystic disease of the breast and represents a marker of apocrine differentia-

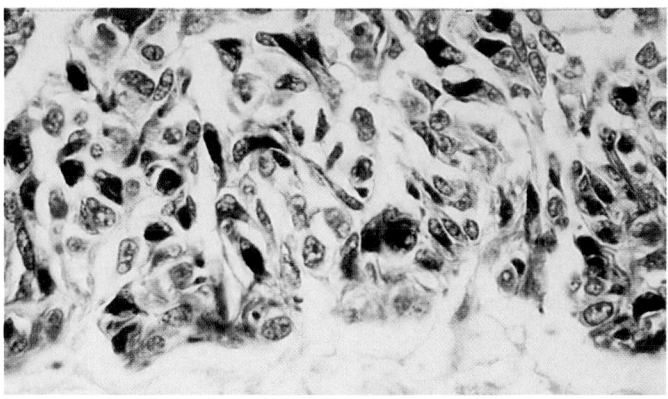

Fig. 3.15 Glial fibrillary acidic protein (GFAP) in malignant astrocytoma.

tion.[335] It is expressed in the normal and neoplastic apocrine glands of the skin, the apocrine metaplasia accompanying fibrocystic disease of the breast, the rare in situ and invasive apocrine carcinomas of the breast, and some breast tumors not showing morphologic evidence of apocrine differentiation.

Hamartin. See under tuberin.

HBME-1. This monoclonal antibody recognizes an unknown antigen located on the microvilli of mesothelial cells.[167,349] It stains most mesotheliomas, but is also positive in a small percentage of adenocarcinomas, a fact that limits its diagnostic utility.[387,393]

Hemoglobin. This is heme-carrying protein specific for cells of the erythroid series, already present at early stages of erythropoiesis. It represents an excellent marker for the identification of normal, megaloblastic, and dysplastic erythroid cells.[411]

Hepatocyte paraffin 1 (Hep-Par1). This antibody recognizes an unidentified mitochondrial antigen present in normal and neoplastic hepatocytes. It has a coarsely granular cytoplasmic quality and is negative in the bile ducts and stromal cells. It is utilized to identify hepatocellular carcinomas, hepatoblastomas, and hepatoid carcinomas,[193,329,514] and seems to have a high degree of specificity.[260,289,295]

HER2/neu (ERBB2). This cell membrane protein is closely related to EGFR. When overexpressed, it acts as an oncogene. This overexpression can be seen in breast carcinoma (22%), lung adenocarcinoma (28%), colorectal carcinoma (17%), lung squamous cell carcinoma (11%), and gastric adenocarcinoma (11%).[271] It is useful for predicting response to Herceptin in carcinoma of breast and other organs,[456] but its value as an independent prognostic factor is minimal.

Histaminase. This oxidative deaminating enzyme, also known as diamine oxidase, is present in normal tissues of various types. It has also been detected in certain tumors with endocrine differentiation, such as pulmonary small cell carcinoma[124] and medullary thyroid carcinoma.[341]

Histocompatibility antigens (HLAs). These are membrane-bound glycoproteins that are important in the regulation of the immune response and in resistance or susceptibility to a large number of diseases.[275] They are responsible for the rejection of transplanted organs. Two major categories exist. The first, known as class I antigens (MW 44,000), is formed by antigens coded by HLA-A, HLA-B, and HLA-C loci and is expressed on virtually all nucleated cells. The second category, known as class II antigens, is coded by the HLA-DR locus. These are also known as HLA-DR or Ia-like antigens and are expressed by most types of histiocytes (including connective tissue macrophages), although they are not specific for them (see discussion of Ia-like antigens).

HMB-45. This is a monoclonal antibody originally obtained from an extract of malignant melanoma, which identifies an oncofetal glycoconjugate associated with immature melanosomes and probably related to the tyrosinase enzymatic system.[116,262] Originally thought to be specific for activated/neoplastic melanocytes, it is now known to be expressed by other neural crest-derived tumors, angiomyolipomas of the kidney and other sites, other components of the tuberous–sclerosis complex ("PEComas"), and occasional carcinomas as well as several other neoplasms.[205]

Hormone receptors. The effect of hormones in target organs is mediated by intracellular (largely intranuclear) peptides known as hormone receptors. Monoclonal antibodies for estrogen, progesterone, and androgen receptors are available.[127,336] Originally the technique worked reliably only in frozen section material,[337,414,418] but now the results in paraffin-embedded material are just as good.[404,449] They compare favorably with those obtained with the conventional biochemical assay.

Hu. The neuron-associated Hu protein family, which includes HuC, HuD, and Hel-N1, can be recognized by the recombinant antibody fragment fab GLN 495. Its localization is both nuclear and cytoplasmic. It labels neurons throughout the central, peripheral, and autonomic nervous system, and is an excellent marker for neural and neuroendocrine differentiation.[224,225] The staining of pulmonary small cell carcinoma is particularly strong.

Human chorionic gonadotropin (hCG). This is normally secreted by the syncytiotrophoblast and is composed of two chains. The alpha chain has an amino acid sequence nearly identical to those of the pituitary glycoprotein hormones follicle-stimulating hormone (FSH), Luteinizing hormone (LH), and thyroid-stimulating hormone (TSH). The beta chain is hormone specific.[230] The antibodies prepared against the latter subunit are employed to detect trophoblastic differentiation in germ cell tumors and ectopic hCG production in other neoplasms[230] (Fig. 3.16).

Human placental lactogen (hPL). This is a placental protein that has been used for the identification of trophoblastic differentiation in germ cell tumors and gesta-

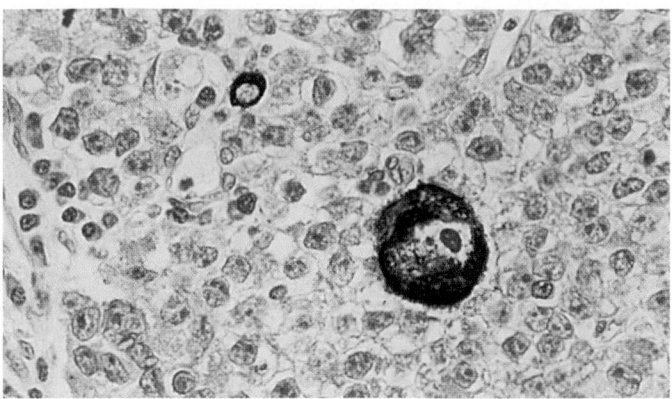

Fig. 3.16 Human chorionic gonadotropin (hCG). Seminoma with trophoblast-like giant cells.

tional neoplasms, particularly those composed of transitional trophoblast (placental site trophoblastic tumor).[423] Several types of carcinomas of somatic organs (such as lung and stomach) can also express this marker.[233]

5-Hydroxytryptamine (5-HT). This indolamine, also known as serotonin, is widely distributed in neuroendocrine cells and is particularly abundant in Kultschisky's type cells of the distal small bowel and appendix.[189,513] Carcinoid tumors (particularly of those sites) and related neuroendocrine neoplasms are usually positive for this marker.

Ia-like antigens. These are membrane-bound glycoproteins composed of polypeptides (MW 34,000 and 28,000) that are coded for by genes located in the major histocompatibility complex. They correspond to HLA-DR antigens (see discussion of HLA) and are detected on histiocytes, B lymphocytes, and activated T lymphocytes. They are believed to regulate cell-to-cell interactions leading to immune effector function. Ia-like antigens have also been detected on cells with no apparent immune function, such as epithelial cells of the kidney, bowel, bronchi, breast, skin, and vascular endothelium.[380] It has been claimed that they are a marker of malignant transformation, particularly for the melanocytic system.[519]

Immunoglobulins. These proteins produced by plasma cells play a key role in the immune response. Five major types exist, designated as IgG, IgM, IgA, IgD, and IgE. They consist of heavy and light polypeptide chains, joined by disulfide bonds. The composition of the heavy chain determines the type of immunoglobulin, and the type of light chain (kappa or lambda) subdivides them into two categories. The usual immunohistochemical method for determining whether a plasma cell population is monotypic or polytypic is to perform a reaction for kappa and lambda light chains.

J chain is a polypeptide around which IgA and IgM molecules polymerize and is produced by immunoglobulin-synthesizing cells. It is present in most B immunoblasts regardless of their class, but it is absent from mature plasma cells. Its presence in a cell indicates that the immunoglobulin molecule is being synthesized at that site.[249]

IgA molecules present in mucosal membranes are attached to a secretory component secreted by the glandular cells (see discussion of secretory component).

Inhibin. This is a peptide hormone produced by ovarian granulosa cells to inhibit FSH. It reacts with sex cord-stromal tumors of ovary and testis,[164,247,338] sex cord-stromal like structures of endometrial stromal tumors,[279] steroid-producing tumors of adrenal cortex and gonads,[255,421] endometrial decidua, and trophoblastic tissue.[272] Curiously, it is also positive in granular cell tumors.[198]

Integrins. Integrins are a family of membrane-spanning cell surface proteins that promote cell-to-cell or cell-to-matrix adhesion and that integrate the pericellular matrix to the cytoskeleton. They are thought to be involved in the differentiation of tissues during development. A subgroup of these molecules—known as VLA integrins—shows a cell lineage-dependent distribution pattern in solid tumors that may prove useful in tumor typing.[350]

Intercellular adhesion molecules (ICAMs). As the name indicates, these are intercellular molecules that bind cells together. ICAM1, which mediates inflammation, is expressed on monocytes, B and T lymphocytes, fibroblasts, and several types of epithelial cells. NCAM (CD56) is normally found on neurons, astrocytes, Schwann cells, myoblasts, and NK lymphocytes. Among tumors, it is mainly expressed in neuroendocrine carcinomas (including pulmonary cell carcinomas) and NK lymphomas, but also some mesotheliomas.[264,290,291,450]

Interleukins (ILs). These constitute a family of glycoproteins produced by macrophages, endothelial cells, T lymphocytes, and other tissues (including epithelia) that serve an important function in the host response to infection. They participate in regulation of the immune response, hematopoiesis, and the acute-phase reaction.[248]

Intermediate filaments. This family of cytoplasmic filaments is so named because their diameter (8 to 10 nm) is intermediate between the diameters of actin (thin) and tubulin (thick). There are at least five biochemically and immunologically distinct types, respectively named cytokeratin, vimentin, desmin, glial fibrillary acidic protein, and neurofilaments[123,173,176,355,377,400,506] (see individual headings). Cytokeratins comprise a complex group of at least 20 polypeptides, whereas each of the other four classes consists of a single polypeptide unit.

Although originally these filaments were thought to be expressed in a stable, cell type-specific, and differentiation-dependent fashion, it has been shown that their coexpression is a common phenomenon in fetal and neoplastic tissues.[159,499]

Involucrin. This is a major structural subunit of a protein envelope synthesized by maturing cells (keratinocytes) of human stratified squamous epithelia, visible in electron micrographs as a 10-nm-thick marginal band.[505] It is absent from basal cells but appears in large amounts as the cells mature. Involucrin has, therefore, been used as a marker of squamous epithelium and as an expression of suprabasal differentiation.[507] In the thyroid gland, it stains papillary carcinoma in a stronger fashion than follicular carcinoma.[310] Its diagnostic utility, however, seems to be very limited.[333]

J chain. See discussion of immunoglobulins.

Keratins. Keratins or cytokeratins are a family of water-insoluble, intracellular fibrous proteins present in almost all epithelia.[345] At least 20 well-defined subclasses of keratins have been identified on the basis of their molecular weight (ranging from 40,000 to 68,000) and isoelectric pH value (ranging from 5 to 8). This combination constitutes the so-called keratin catalog, which shows a tissue-specific distribution throughout the epithelia[162,362,438] and which can be mapped using a battery of monoclonal antibodies[314] (Fig. 3.17). For scanning purposes, several of these antibodies are combined in the form of "cocktails" (such as AE1/AE3).

Keratins represent an excellent marker for epithelial differentiation regardless of whether the tumor is of endodermal, neuroectodermal, mesenchymal, or germ cell derivation (Figs 3.18 and 3.19). However, more sensitive immunohistochemical techniques for the keratin product and PCR determinations of keratin gene expression[490] have shown that some keratins (particularly 8 and 18) are commonly expressed in a wide range of nonepithelial normal tissues and neoplasms.[215] They are particularly common and prominent in synovial sarcoma, epithelioid sarcoma and uterine smooth muscle tumors,[134,344] but examples of keratin positivity have been described in virtually every major tumor type, including most soft tissue sarcomas, many bone sarcomas, small round cell tumors, malignant melanomas, gliomas, plasmacytomas, and even occasional malignant lymphomas.[175,353]

The antibody 34βE12 stains selectively the keratins of basal cells; it has been used in the differential diagnosis between well-differentiated prostatic carcinoma and the benign lesions that simulate it.[520]

The use of individual keratins can provide important information about the site of origin of a given carcinoma, although many exceptions exist.[153] The typically CK7+/CK20+ carcinomas are those from pancreas, bile duct, and urothelium (about 65% each), and one third of gastric carcinomas. The usually CK7+/CK20− tumors include lung, breast, endometrium, ovary, thyroid, and salivary gland, as well as mesothelioma. CK7−/CK20+ tumors are those from large bowel (95%), Merkel cell carcinoma (most), and about one third of the gastric adenocarcinomas. Finally, typically CK7−/CK20− tumors are carcinomas of adrenal cortex, liver, kidney, and adrenal gland.

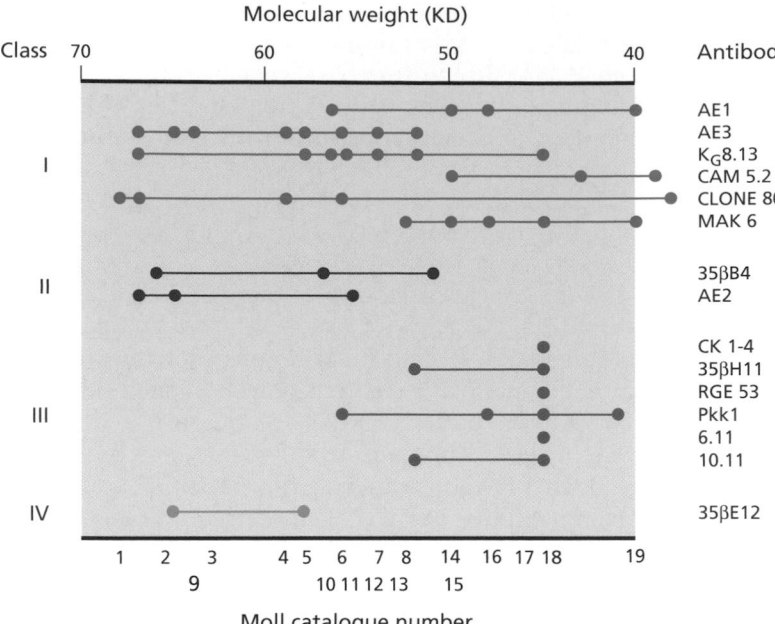

Molecular weight (KD)

Fig. 3.17 Cytokeratin catalog and reactivity of monoclonal antibodies. The acidic cytokeratins (Moll's catalogue No. 10 and 12–19) range in molecular weight from 40,000 to 56,500; the basic cytokeratins (Moll's catalog No. 1–8) range in molecular weight from 53,000 to 67,000. The antibodies have been divided into four classes, based on their pattern of reactivity: I, high- and low-molecular-weight cytokeratins present in squamous, ductal, and simple epithelia, broadly reactive; II, higher-molecular-weight cytokeratins present in squamous epithelium; III, lower-molecular-weight cytokeratins present in simple and ductal epithelium; IV, high-molecular-weight cytokeratins present in both squamous and ductal epithelium. (From DeLellis RA, Kwan P. Technical considerations in the immunohistochemical demonstration of intermediate filaments. Am J Surg Pathol 1988, **1**: 17–23)

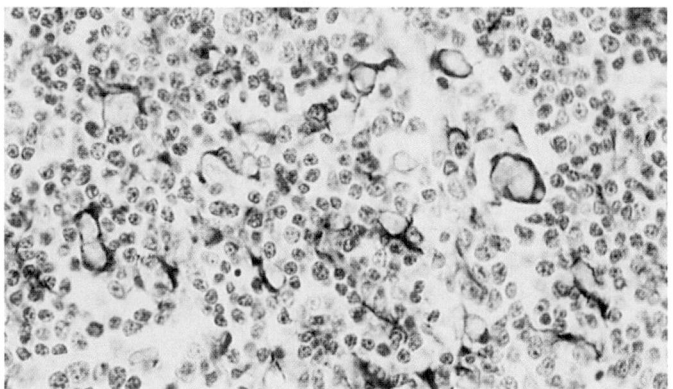

Fig. 3.18 Keratin stain in a type B1 (lymphocyte-rich) thymoma.

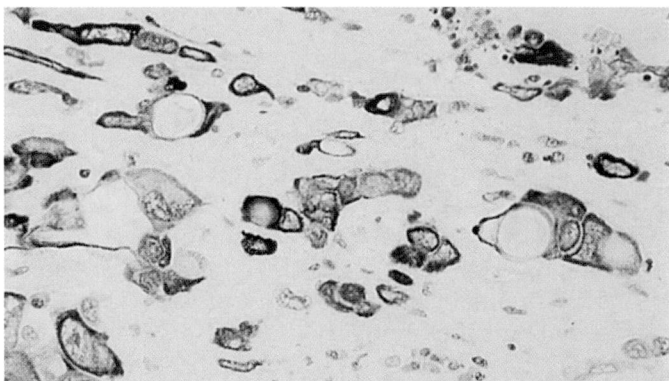

Fig. 3.19 Keratin stain. Anaplastic carcinoma of pancreas.

It should also be mentioned that CK5/6 is an useful marker for the differential diagnosis between malignant mesothelioma (usually positive) and lung adenocarcinoma (usually negative).[394] CK5/6, however, also stains several types of epithelial neoplasms, including squamous cell carcinoma, salivary gland tumors, and thymoma.[150,152a]

Ki-67 (MIB-1). See p. 65.

Ki-S1. See p. 65.

Lactalbumin. See discussion of alpha-lactalbumin.

Lactoferrin. See discussion of ferritin.

Laminin. This structural protein (MW 900,000) is one of the two major components of the basement membrane, together with type IV collagen.[125,274] It is, therefore, present in tumors that produce basement membranes, such as carcinomas, smooth muscle tumors, and tumors of endothelial cells.[351] Laminin is better expressed in blood vessels than lymph vessels, but this feature does not allow a sharp distinction between the two structures.[315]

Lectin receptors. Lectins are plant-derived proteins that bind specifically to simple or complex carbohydrate groups acting as receptors.[445] As such, lectins are useful tools to study the glycoprotein and glycolipid structure of the cell surface.[413] These lectin receptors can be localized by standard immunohistochemical methods. Some lectins (such as concanavalin A) seem to have an affinity for cells of the lymphoid system.[466] The lectin of *Ulex europaeus* combines with the H antigen that corresponds to blood group O.[405] It has been found that it binds to endothelial cells regardless of the individual's blood group and has, therefore, been used as a marker of vessels and vascular neoplasms.[352] Lectins have also been used to map the various segments of the nephron and to correlate the findings with those of renal neoplasms.[495,503]

Leu7. See discussion of lymphoid and other leukocytic antigens.

Leu-M1. See discussion of lymphoid and other leukocytic antigens.

Loricrin. Loricrin is a protein associated with the very late stages of epidermal differentiation in the granular layers of normal human epidermis. Loricrin expression is decreased in diseases associated with parakeratosis (such as psoriasis) and increased in hypergranulotic processes (such as lichen planus).[237]

Lymphoid and other leukocytic antigens. A large number (over 250) of lymphoid-related antigens have been described. Often the same antigen has been given different designations depending on the source of production, resulting in a very confusing state of affairs. Mercifully, a systematized nomenclature has been agreed upon, which has clarified matters considerably. This is referred to as the CD system, which is an abbreviation for *cluster designation*.[490a] Most of these are membrane-associated markers which relate to the various lymphocyte subsets and level of functional maturation. These are further discussed in Chapter 21. Some of these antigens are also expressed in nonlymphoid cells and have been found of utility in the recognition and categorization of a variety of nonlymphoid neoplasms.[150,490a] The most important of these are listed under their respective CD category.

Lysozyme. This bacteriolytic enzyme, also known as muramidase, acts on muramic acid linkages in bacterial cell walls. It is found in human secretions and in neutrophils, cells of the monocyte-histiocyte series (including mast cells) and some epithelial cells.[137,330] It has often been employed as a histiocytic marker, but it lacks specificity.

Mart-1 (Melan-A). This melanocyte-associated marker, which is a target for cytotoxic T cells, is recognized by the antibody A103.[258] In contrast to HMB-45, it is not related to melanosomes. In addition to melanocytes and related melanin-producing cells (peripheral nerve sheath tumors and neoplasms in the angiomyolipoma family),[196] it stains tumors of steroid-producing cells, such as those of adrenal cortex.[138]

Maspin. This is a serine protease inhibitor which inhibits tumor cell motility and invasion in cell culture, and tumor growth and metastases in animal models.[359] It localizes both in the nucleus and cytoplasm, and is utilized as a myoepithelial marker, particularly for breast lesions.[306,419]

Merosin. This is a laminin-like protein that is specifically associated with basement membranes. It has been found in peripheral nerves, striated muscle, and placenta.[186] Study of the expression of merosin in benign peripheral nerve tumors suggests that this protein is induced epigenetically in well-differentiated cells in contact with connective tissue or vascular components.[305]

Mesothelin. This is a surface antigen of unknown function that is strongly expressed in mesothelial cells.[397] It stains almost all mesotheliomas, but is also reactive with a high number of adenocarcinomas of lung and other sites, and therefore its diagnostic utility is limited.[397]

MIB-1 (Ki-67). See p. 65.

Microorganisms. Immunohistochemical methods for a wide variety of viral, bacterial (including mycobacterial), spirochetal, fungal, and parasitic antigens are now available.[118,365,518] Those used with greater frequency for diagnostic purposes are the ones aimed at detecting *Helicobacter pylori*[489] and viruses such as hepatitis B virus, herpes simplex, cytomegalovirus (Fig. 3.20), and human papilloma virus.[104,195] An immunohistochemical method for the detection of *Pneumocystis carinii* in sputum has also been described.[277]

Microphthalmia transcription factor. This is a melanocytic nuclear protein critical for the embryonic development and postnatal viability of melanocytes. It is found in benign nevi and malignant melanomas, including the soft tissue version of this tumor (clear cell sarcoma),[218] but usually not the desmoplastic type.[219] It is also positive in the tumors of the angiomyolipoma family.[530]

Mitochondrial antigens. Two monoclonal antibodies are now available for the detection of mitochondrial antigens, and these can be used for the identification of mitochondria-rich cells/oncocytes. One is monoclonal antibody mES13, originally produced against bacterially expressed BACB *ras* p21.[510] The other, known as 113.1, was obtained using Raji Burkitt's lymphoma cells as immunogen.[402]

MOC-31. This monoclonal antibody recognizes an epithelial-associated transmembrane glycoprotein present in normal and neoplastic epithelial cells. It is positive in practically all lung adenocarcinomas and in over 80% of the nonpulmonary adenocarcinomas, but in only 5% of the mesotheliomas, the latter in a focal fashion.[398] Therefore, it is a very useful tool for the differential diagnosis of these tumors.[387]

Moesin. This is a member of the ERM family (ezrin, radixin, moesin), which is directly associated with the cytoplasmic domain of CD44 and which is thought to be related to the metastatic potential of tumor cells. It has been studied in normal skin and several cutaneous

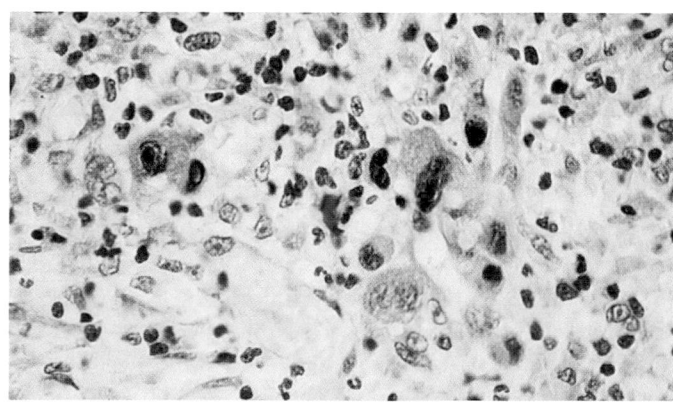

Fig. 3.20 Cytomegalovirus (CMV). Viral colitis in an immunosuppressed patient.

tumors, which show a variation of doubtful significance in its expression.[246]

MUC. This is the abbreviation for the protein core peptide (apomucin) of the glycoproteins of epithelial glandular cells traditionally known as mucins. Eleven mucin genes have been identified, which relate to the various types of glandular epithelium.[105,253,307,332,364] MUC2 is thought to be characteristic of appendiceal mucinous neoplasms and the complication that may result from them, i.e., pseudomyxoma peritonei.[389]

Myelin proteins. Myelin basic protein is a myelin-specific protein present in both central and peripheral myelin sheaths. As such, it can be demonstrated in oligodendrocytes and Schwann cells.[406] However, controversy still exists as to whether it represents a reliable marker for oligodendroglioma and peripheral nerve sheath tumors. The same is true for other myelin-related proteins, such as P2 protein and PO protein.[156]

MyoD1. MyoD1 encodes a nuclear phosphoprotein, the expression of which is restricted to skeletal muscle. Three related myogenic proteins are myogenin, myf5, and MRf4. It is believed that these proteins perform critical functions in the commitment, differentiation, and maintenance of the myogenic lineage.[180] MyoD1 has been demonstrated in a variety of skeletal muscle tumors and other neoplasms with known or presumed skeletal muscle differentiation,[474] but—in contrast to myogenin—it functions reliably only in fresh frozen tissue.

Myogenin. This is another myogenic nuclear protein for which an antibody is available that demonstrates this nuclear marker in formalin-fixed, paraffin-embedded material. It has emerged as one of the top choices for the identification of skeletal muscle differentiation in tumors,[281] although its specificity is not absolute.[295] It is strongly expressed in all types of rhabdomyosarcoma, most particularly in the alveolar subtype.[181]

Myoglobin. This oxygen-binding protein is apparently specific for striated (skeletal and myocardial) muscle and is, therefore, of utility for the identification of rhabdomyosarcomas and other tumors exhibiting skeletal muscle differentiation.[163,370] Unfortunately, the sensitivity is low, and only well-differentiated tumors are likely to exhibit this marker.

Myosin. Two biochemically distinct forms of this contractile protein exist: smooth muscle type (nonsarcomeric) and skeletal muscle type (sarcomeric). Three subtypes of the latter have been described: slow, fast, and fetal. The main use of this marker has been in the identification of skeletal muscle differentiation in tumors.[492] Interestingly, a member of the myosin family known as myosin XVA is consistently present in endocrine tumors of the gastrointestinal tract and pancreas.[292]

Nestin. This is a newly described intermediate filament that is particularly abundant in neuroepithelial stem cells.[484] Nestin has also been detected in primitive neuroectodermal tumors and gliomas,[484] where it said to

be also a marker for the endothelial proliferation that often accompanies these tumors.[467]

Neurofilaments. These represent the intermediate filaments of neurons and their processes. They are protein triplets composed of three major subunits (MW 68,000, 150,000, and 200,000), that are immunochemically distinct.[406] Neurofilaments are expressed in tumors of neuronal origin or tumors displaying neuronal differentiation, such as neuroblastoma, medulloblastoma, and retinoblastoma. Positivity has also been encountered in Merkel's cell tumor of the skin, endocrine tumors of the pancreas, carcinoid tumors, parathyroid tumors, and other neoplasms of endocrine nature[360] (Fig. 3.21).

Neuron-specific enolase. Enolases are widely distributed glycolytic dimeric enzymes that catalyze the interconversion of 2-phosphoglycerate and phosphoenolpyruvate.[406] The gamma-gamma and alpha-gamma isoenzymes of enolase are preferentially found in neurons and neuroendocrine cells and have therefore been designated as neuron-specific enolases (NSEs). Positivity is found in the majority of neuroectodermal and neuroendocrine neoplasms, including carcinoid tumors and malignant melanoma. Unfortunately, NSEs have also been detected in several other types of normal and neoplastic cells, obviously limiting their diagnostic usefulness.[401] The best results are obtained with the use of monoclonal antibodies.[443,444] The beta subunit of enolase has been employed as a marker for striated muscle, but it is not specific for it.[263]

Nup88 (karyoporin). This molecule is associated with the nuclear pore macromolecular structures that regulate the bidirectional nucleocytoplasmic traffic. Overexpression of this marker has been found in several tumor types, its significance being obscure.[216]

Oligosaccharides. See discussion of cancer-associated carbohydrates.

Opioid peptides. Alpha-endorphin, met-enkephalin, and dynorphin B production is a feature of neural and neuroendocrine cells. These substances have also been found in a large number of neural and neuroendocrine

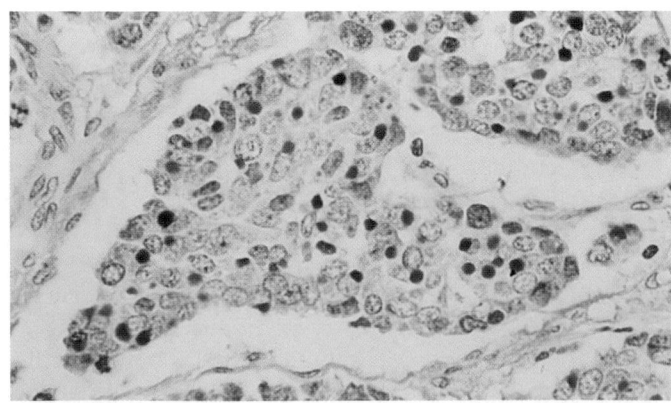

Fig. 3.21 Neurofilaments. Dot-like positivity in Merkel cell tumor of skin.

tumors, including paraganglioma, thyroid medullary carcinoma, and carcinoid tumors. A monoclonal "panopioid" antibody has been developed that recognizes the tetrapeptide Tyr-Gly-Gly-Phe, which is the sequence responsible for the pharmacologic activity of all opioid peptides.[131]

Osteocalcin. This osteoblast-associated procollagen peptide has been employed for the identification of osteosarcoma and other osteoid-forming lesions. It is apparently more specific than osteonectin.[190,191]

Osteonectin. This is a glycoprotein involved in tissue mineralization, cell–extracellular matrix interactions, and angiogenesis. It stains osteosarcomas, but also several other tumor types, including malignant melanomas.[190,191,331]

Osteopontin. Osteopontin is an acidic glycoprotein that has been isolated from rat, bovine, and human bone. It has a cellular attachment activity and is expressed in the early stages of bone formation by osteoblasts and some bone marrow cells. It has also been found in other tissues, such as the brain, kidney, decidua, and placenta. Among tumors, it has been detected in gliomas (particularly anaplastic ones[432]), benign and malignant bone tumors,[468] various types of renal tumors,[284] and borderline ovarian surface tumors[482]

p53. Mutations of the *p53* tumor-suppressor gene represent the most common genetic alteration in human tumors (see p. 70). The product of this gene is a nuclear protein thought to be involved in the control of the cell cycle, apoptosis, and the maintenance of genomic stability. The altered protein product of the mutant gene has a much extended half-life and can be detected with immunohistochemical techniques.[135,312] It should be noted, however, that accumulation of the protein can also occur as a result of epigenetic changes, and therefore it is not an obligatory indicator of a gene mutation.

p63. This is a homolog of p53 which is consistently expressed by basal/stem cells of stratified epithelium, and myoepithelial cells of breast and salivary glands.[117,181a,240,386a,508a] Six different isoforms exist, the functions of which are largely unknown.

Peptide hormones. A huge number of peptide hormones acting as neuroendocrine mediators have been described, and others are likely to be discovered in the future.[460] Those for which antibodies are available and which have been detected immunohistochemically in normal and neoplastic tissue include adrenocorticotrophic hormone (ACTH), antidiuretic hormone (ADH), bombesin, calcitonin (Fig. 3.22), cholecystokinin, enteroglucagon (glycentin), gastrin, growth hormone (GH), glucagon, gastrin-releasing peptide (GRP), insulin (Fig. 3.23), LH, neurotensin, pancreatic polypeptide (PP), prolactin, parathormone (PTH), somatostatin, TSH, P substance, vasopressin, vasoactive intestinal peptide (VIP), Y (NPY) peptide, and YY peptide.

P-glycoprotein. P-glycoprotein is a membrane protein

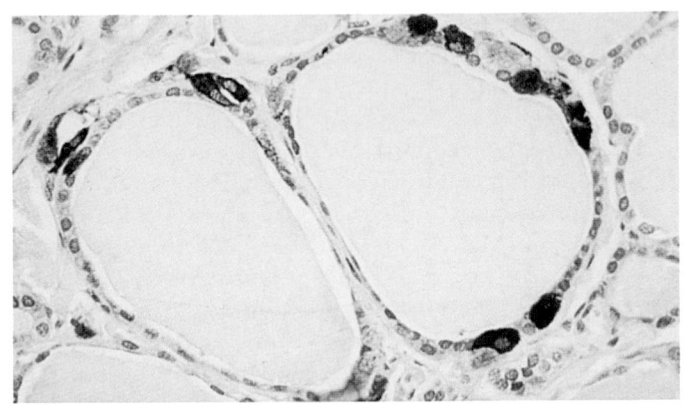

Fig. 3.22 Calcitonin. C-cell hyperplasia of thyroid.

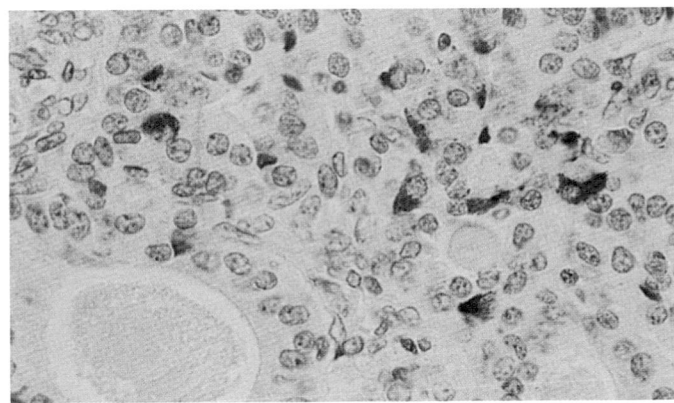

Fig. 3.23 Insulin. Strumal carcinoid of ovary with scattered insulin-reactive cells.

responsible for most cases of multidrug resistance. Three isoforms exist, only two of which (I and II) are associated with this property. The fact that this protein is expressed in one isoform or another in a variety of normal cells (such as endothelial cells, colonic epithelial cells, and adrenal cortical cells) suggest that it has distinct physiologic roles associated with specialized cell functions.[210]

PGP 9.5. Protein gene product 9.5 is a neural protein of unknown function isolated from the brain. It stains neural and neuroendocrine cells and their tumors, but its level of specificity is not high.[229,425,481]

Placental proteins. The placenta is the most active endocrine organ of the human body. Among the many proteins secreted by the trophoblast, the three that have been detected immunohistochemically are human chorionic gonadotropin (hCG), human placental lactogen (hPL), and pregnancy-specific beta-1-glycoprotein (SP1) (see discussion of individual markers).[130]

PLAP. See discussion of alkaline phosphatase.

Prealbumin. Prealbumin (MW 54,900) is a plasma protein that binds thyroxine and retinal for transport in the blood. It is thought to be produced in the liver but is also present in pancreatic islet cells and their tumors.[311]

Pregnancy-specific glycoprotein. Pregnancy-specific beta-1-glycoprotein (SP1) is a placental protein (MW

90,000). Originally thought to be specific for the syncytiotrophoblast, it is now known to be also present in breast carcinomas and a variety of other epithelial malignancies.[280]

Progesterone receptors. See under Hormone receptors.

Proliferating cell nuclear antigen (PCNA). See p. 66.

Prostate-specific antigen (PSA). PSA is a kallikrein-like protease (MW 33,000) that has been extracted from prostatic tissue and that has been found to have a greater degree of specificity for normal, hyperplastic, and neoplastic prostatic tissue than prostatic acid phosphatase. Therefore, immunohistochemical demonstration of PSA has become the method of choice for the identification of prostatic adenocarcinoma.[376,464]

Prostatic acid phosphatase (PAP). This isoenzyme of acid phosphatase is secreted by the normal, hyperplastic, and neoplastic prostatic epithelium (Fig. 3.24). It is a useful marker, but it is not entirely specific for the prostate. Carcinomas of bladder and carcinoid tumors of various sites have also been found to be sometimes reactive.[447]

Racemase. See under alpha-methylacyl-CoA racemase.

Renin. This proteolytic enzyme is produced and stored in the granules of the juxtaglomerular cells surrounding the afferent arterioles of renal glomeruli. Renin acts on the basic substrate angiotensinogen to form angiotensin I, which is subsequently changed by a converting enzyme to angiotensin II. Renin has been demonstrated immunohistochemically in the normal kidney,[192] juxtaglomerular cell tumors, the blood vessels of tumors of lung and other sites,[476] and—allegedly—some soft tissue tumors.[178,373]

Retinal S-antigen. This is a protein (MW 50,000) intimately involved in the phototransduction of vision. Together with opsin, it appears to be a good photoreceptor marker.[406] It has been identified in the retinal photoreceptor cells and pinealocytes and in their neoplastic counterparts (i.e., retinoblastoma and pineocytoma). Focal positivity has also been found in medulloblastomas.[406]

S-100 protein. This is a family of acidic, dimeric calcium-binding proteins (MW 21,000) composed of different combinations of alpha and beta subunits and first isolated in the central nervous system.[340] They are present in the nucleus and cytoplasm of glial and Schwann cells, melanocytes, chondrocytes, adipocytes, myoepithelial cells, and other cells, and in the tumors derived from them[378,406] (Fig. 3.25). A quantitative differentiation distribution has been found between alpha and beta forms.[227] It has both a nuclear and a cytoplasmic localization. As a matter of fact, an apparently positive stain for this marker showing *only* a cytoplasmic pattern should be questioned. The wide expression of this antigen has substantially diminished its diagnostic utility.[232,439] Its main use is in the evaluation of peripheral nerve sheath and melanocytic tumors.[259]

S-100 protein is structurally similar in the calcium-binding domains to calmodulin, and important transducer of calcium-mediated signals.

Secretory component. This glycoprotein is a normal glandular epithelial cell product that combines with dimeric IgA in association with J chain to form intact 11 S secretory IgA molecules.[228] Secretory component is normally present in the epithelial cells lining the various mucosal surfaces and has therefore been employed as a marker for tumors of glandular epithelial origin.[228]

Serotonin. See under 5-hydroxytryptamine.

Steroid hormones and related enzymes. Estradiol, testosterone, and other steroid hormones have been localized immunohistochemically in normal and neoplastic tissues from gonads and adrenal cortex, despite the considerable loss that occurs during embedding because of the use of organic solvents.[283] The capacity for production of several of these closely related steroids by tumor cells has prevented a close correlation between tumor types and hormonal profile and has limited the practical utility of this stain.[283] The various enzymes involved in steroidogenesis can also be evaluated immunohistochemically.[250,434]

Sox9. This is a transcription factor that plays an

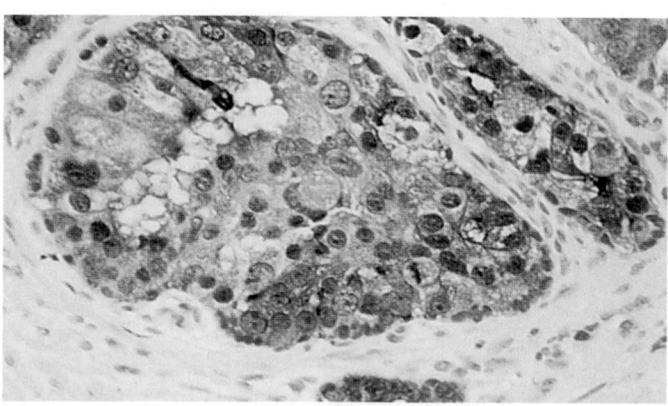

Fig. 3.24 Prostatic acid phosphatase. Prostatic adenocarcinoma of large duct type.

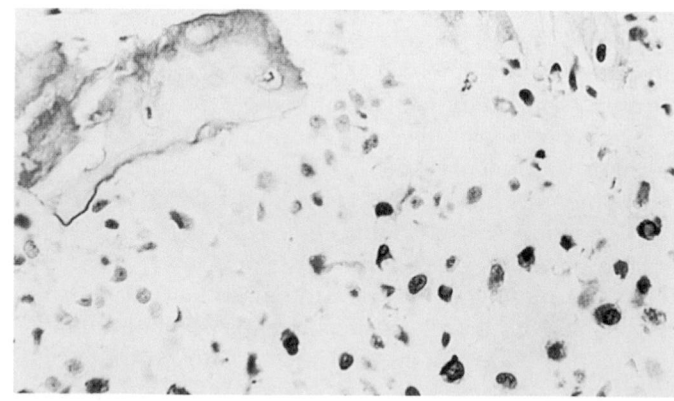

Fig. 3.25 S-100 protein. Chondrosarcoma of bone. There is both cytoplasmic and nuclear staining.

essential role in the early phases of chondrocyte differentiation and thus appears to be a master regulator of chondrogenesis.[303] It has, therefore, been employed to document cartilaginous differentiation in neoplasms.[508]

Surfactant apoprotein (PE-10). This protein is secreted by type II (granular) pneumocytes in the pulmonary alveoli and is, therefore, used as a marker for these cells and their tumors. It is found both in cytoplasmic lamellar formations and in intranuclear inclusions.[453] A related marker found in type II pneumocytes has been named lamino-organel antigen.

Surfactant apoprotein has been found to be expressed in a high proportion of pulmonary adenocarcinomas and is, therefore, of great utility in the differential diagnosis with adenocarcinomas of other organs.[268,528] It has also been found in normal and neoplastic breast epithelium.[132]

Synaptophysin. This is a major glycosylated transmembrane glycoprotein (MW 38,000) that has been isolated from neuronal presynaptic vesicles.[479] It is expressed in normal, reactive, and neoplastic cells of neuroectodermal and neuroendocrine types, including pheochromocytoma, thyroid medullary carcinoma, endocrine pancreatic tumors, and carcinoid tumors.[148,214]

T antigen. See discussion of blood group antigens.

TAU proteins. These are microtubule-associated proteins (MW 50,000 to 70,000) that serve as immunohistochemical markers of Alzheimer's disease and which may occasionally be expressed in glial tumors, and also in myxoid chondrosarcoma and GISTs.[145,243]

Tenascin. This is an extracellular matrix glycoprotein that has been found in the early fetal rat mammary gland. Original claims that it was detectable in the stroma in malignant but not in benign breast tumors[327] have not been confirmed; actually, it has a very wide distribution in normal, reactive, inflammatory, and neoplastic tissues.[276,483]

Thrombomodulin. This is an endothelial cell-associated cofactor located on the cell membrane that forms a 1:1 stoichiometric complex with thrombin.[527] It has been used as a marker for vascular tumors composed of endothelial cells.[111,527] However, thrombomodulin is also expressed by other vascular cells, mesothelial cells, and epidermal keratinocytes, as well as tumors from these tissue types.[286] Among nonvascular tumors, the highest levels of positivity are found in mesotheliomas and in transitional cell (urothelial) carcinomas.[395,396]

Thrombospondin. Thrombospondin is a cytoadhesive protein present in the alpha-granules of platelets. It is presumed to mediate the attachment of malignant cells to the extracellular matrix and may play a role in tumor invasion. In cases of breast carcinoma, thrombospondin is strongly expressed in the desmoplastic stroma and at the basement membrane associated with the malignant cells.[523]

Thymic hormones. It has long been hypothesized that the thymus exerts its endocrine function through the secretion of thymic hormones.[129] Allegedly, alpha-thymosin and some other of these thymic hormones can be detected immunohistochemically in the normal thymus and in thymomas.[437] If these reports were ever to be confirmed, these markers could prove very useful in the evaluation of thymic epithelial neoplasms, since no other antigens specific for these cells are currently available. Unfortunately, our own experience with them has been very disappointing. The fact that there is hardly any literature on the subject in recent years makes us suspect that others have had a similarly negative experience.

Thyroglobulin. This is a large glycoprotein (MW 670,000) formed by two identical subunits. It is produced by the thyroid follicular cells and serves as the substratum for iodination and hormonogenesis. It is a specific marker of thyroid differentiation and is widely used in the evaluation of thyroid neoplasms[463] (Fig. 3.26). In this regard it has been found preferable to the search for the thyroid hormones T_3 and T_4.[108]

Thyroid transcription factor-1 (TTF-1). This is a nuclear transcription factor necessary for the development of thyroid and pulmonary tissue. This DNA-binding protein was first identified in thymocytes (hence its name) and later in pneumocytes.[296] It is expressed in all types of thyroid carcinoma (including medullary carcinoma), except for the anaplastic type. It is also present in most cases of lung carcinoma (including the small cell neuroendocrine type),[379,526] and has become one of the most useful markers in the differential diagnosis between lung carcinoma and carcinomas of other sites on one side and mesotheliomas on the other both in histologic sections and cytologic preparations.[382] As usual, there is a catch: some high-grade neuroendocrine carcinomas of non-pulmonary origin (but not Merkel cell carcinomas) can also stain.[107]

Tissue polypeptide antigen (TPA). This is a nonfilamentous protein located in maturing cells (keratinocytes) of human stratified squamous epithelia. As such, it is absent in basal cells and appears in the suprabasal layers.[319] It has been employed as a marker of squamous epithelium.

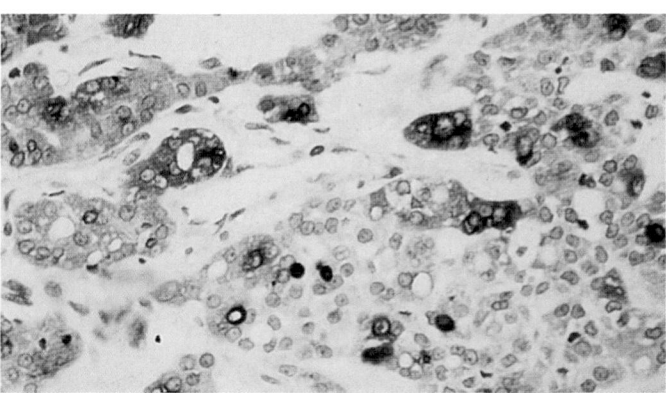

Fig. 3.26 Thyroglobulin. Poorly differentiated (insular) carcinoma of thyroid.

Transferrin. See discussion of ferritin.

Tropomyosin. This protein is a molecular subunit of thin filaments.[297,388] It has been used as a marker for rhabdomyosarcoma, but it does not seem to offer any real advantages over the more usual markers of myogenous differentiation.[441]

Tryptase. This neutral protease is the dominant protein component of human mast cells.[165] It has not been found in human eosinophils, basophils, neutrophils, lymphocytes, or monocytes. Therefore, it has been employed for the selective staining of mast cells.[165]

Tuberin. This is the product of a suppressor gene which is mutated in tuberous sclerosis, the other being hematin. These two molecules are colocalized in most tissues.[254]

Uroplakin. Uroplakins are specific differentiation products of terminally differentiated superficial urothelial cells.[403] A monoclonal antibody against uroplakin III has been found to stain urothelial tumors of bladder, ureter and pelvis, as well as urothelial-type tumors of the ovary (such as Brenner tumor.[390] The marker seems to have a high degree of specificity but only a moderate degree of sensitivity.[265]

VASA. This gene is said to be specific for the germ cell lineage. Its protein product has been detected in seminoma and intratubular germ cell neoplasia (ITGCN), but not in nonseminomatous germ cell tumors or nongerm cell tumors.[531]

Villin. This is an actin bundling and severing protein (MW 95,000) that seems to be restricted in animal tissues to epithelial cells with a brush border. Thus, the enterocytes of the intestine and epithelial cells of proximal but not distal tubules of the kidney are strongly positive, as are the tumor cells of colorectal carcinoma, intestinal-type tumors of other sites, renal cell carcinoma, and various types of neuroendocrine tumors.[221,436,532]

Vimentin. This is one of the five major types of cytoplasmic intermediate filaments (MW 57,000). It is characteristic of cells of mesenchymal nature, such as endothelial cells, fibroblasts, and vascular smooth muscle cells.[298] However, it is not restricted to cells of mesodermal origin but is sometimes also expressed in tumors of epithelial or neural nature, not infrequently in conjunction with keratin and GFAP, respectively.[115] Actually, vimentin is so ubiquitous that some people use it as a control of the immunohistochemical reaction, in the sense of questioning its reliability is there is no staining for vimentin in the tissue. Along these lines, there is no more frustrating conclusion to draw after having done an exhaustive immunohistochemical evaluation of a neoplasm that it is only positive for vimentin.

Viruses. See discussion of microorganisms.

WT-1. This is a transcription factor isolated from kidney and expressed in Wilms' tumor, hence its name. This nuclear marker, which has proved of great diagnostic utility, is also expressed by mesothelioma and müllerian epithelial neoplasms (notably ovarian serous carcinoma).[387,448] Among small round cell tumors, a consistent pattern of cytoplasmic positivity has been seen in rhabdomyosarcoma.[142] In desmoplastic small cell tumor (which because of the EWS-WT1 gene fusion makes only the carboxy terminus portion of the molecule) it is reactive for the antibody WT (C-19), which recognizes the carboxy terminus, but not for the antibody WT(180), which recognizes the amino terminus.[235]

Z-protein. This protein is normally present in the Z band of striated muscle. It has been detected in cases of rhabdomyosarcoma, but it does not seem to offer particular advantages over the other skeletal muscle markers.[297,374]

This is a long list indeed. Few if any laboratories will be expected to offer all these stains, many of which are of only minimal diagnostic value.

The standard surgical pathology laboratory will be well served by acquiring the following selection of antibodies (lymphoid markers not included, see Chapter 21), obviously to be modified according to the type of material handled:

Top choice
Actin (common, smooth muscle, and sarcomeric)
Calcitonin
Calretinin
Chromogranin
CD31
CD34
Desmin
EMA
GFAP
hCG
HER2/neu
HMB-45
Hormone receptors (estrogen, androgen)
Keratin (AE1/AE3 or similar wide-spectrum cocktail, and Cam 5.2)
MIB-1 (Ki-67)
Myogenin
PSA
S-100 protein
Thyroglobulin
TTF-1
Vimentin
WT-1

Desirable
Alpha-fetoprotein
Alpha-lactalbumin
B72.3
CD10
CD117
CEA
Collagen type IV
Factor VIII-related antigen

Hep-Par-1
Inhibin
Keratins (individual, such as CK7, CK20, and 34βE12)
Lysozyme
Mart-1 (Melan-A)
Microorganisms (for selected viruses)
Neurofilaments
Prostatic acid phosphatase
Peptide hormones (selected ones)
PLAP
Synaptophysin
Ulex europaeus I lectin
Optional
All the others

The first-choice antibodies should equip the surgical pathologist with the tools needed to tackle the most common diagnostic problems in tumor pathology, including that which epitomizes them all (i.e., the characterization of the undifferentiated or poorly differentiated malignant tumor, whether primary or metastatic).[121,172,207] Antibody panels are used in some laboratories to standardize the immunohistochemical search depending on the nature of the problem.[121] Thus a pulmonary adenocarcinoma-versus-mesothelioma panel may consist of stains for keratin, CEA, CD15, calretinin, and WT-1. The preparation of these prepackaged formulas is useful in a well-defined situation such as the one just described, but the number of permutations is so large that it would be impractical and perhaps even undesirable to attempt to devise a list of panels that would cover most eventualities.

Flow cytometry

The technique of flow cytometry consists of the measurement of various parameters while a suspension of cells flows through a beam of light past stationary detectors.[544,550,554,558,559,563,570] The instrument focuses hydrodynamically a cell suspension in a sample chamber and passes single cells through a light source, usually a laser. The light scattered at various angles by the cells is registered by detectors and converted to electronic signals, which are then digitized, stored, and analyzed by the computer to produce a histogram (Fig. 3.27). This technique allows the analysis of 5000 to 10,000 cells per second. Cellular features that can be evaluated with flow cytometry include cell size, cytoplasmic granularity, cell viability, cell cycle time (S-phase fraction), DNA content (DNA ploidy), surface marker phenotype, and enzyme content.[540] Technical advances now allow for several of these parameters to be evaluated simultaneously.[569]

Depending on their DNA content, neoplasms are divided into diploid and aneuploid. *Diploid* tumors have

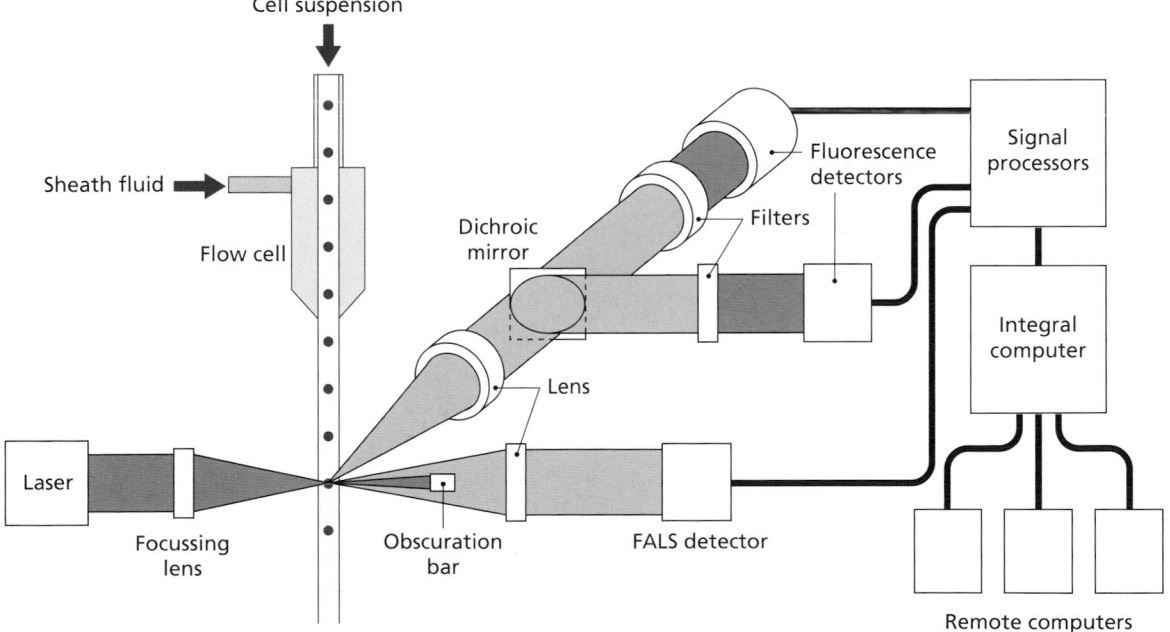

Fig. 3.27 Schematic representation of a flow cytometer suitable for clinical work. Stained cells enter the flow chamber where they pass into the center of a stream of sheath fluid in single file. They are then struck by a focussed laser beam and emit scattered and fluorescent light, which is separated according to wavelength by appropriate mirrors and filters. An obscuration bar protects the forward angle light scatter (FALS) detector from exposure to the direct laser beam. Only two fluorescence detectors are shown, for sake of simplicity, but a typical instrument has three or four such detectors, one of which can be used to measure laser light scattered perpendicular to the laser beam by the cells. Signals from the detectors pass to amplifying processors and then to the integral (on-board) computer, which digitizes the signals, stores them, and displays them. Detailed analysis of the data is often most efficiently done with stand-alone computers. (From Coon JS, Landay AL, Weinstein RS. Biology of disease. Advances in flow cytometry for diagnostic pathology. Lab Invest 1987, **57**: 453–479)

a major population mode at the normal diploid DNA value. *Aneuploid* tumors are those having a cell population with a DNA content other than diploid. The *DNA index* (DI) is the ratio of the DNA content of the aneuploid peak to the DNA content of the diploid peak. *Tetraploid tumors* are a subset of aneuploid tumors in which the DI is 1.9 to 2.1. The *hyperdiploid fraction* is the percentage of cells above the upper bound of the diploid population and constitutes a measure of the S-phase or proliferative fraction of a cell population.

The main limitation of flow cytometry is that cells need to be in a single-cell suspension in order to be analyzed. This requirement is easily achieved in blood and other fluids[541]; indeed, flow cytometric analysis of leukemias and lymphomas has become routine in many institutions.[552] Obtaining satisfactory samples from non-hematopoietic solid tumors is more difficult, but suitable techniques have now been developed for most. As a matter of fact, flow cytometric DNA analysis can even be performed on nuclear suspensions recovered from thick sections of routine formalin-fixed, paraffin-embedded tissue blocks[543,553,562] with similar (although generally inferior) results to those obtained using fresh tissues[545,561] (Fig. 3.28). The potential of this technical development for the performance of large-scale retrospective studies is obvious.

Great attention should be paid to the technical factors in performing the studies.[551] Surveys have shown that interlaboratory consistency is reasonably good in recognizing aneuploid subpopulations, less satisfactory in determining the DNA index, and poor in measuring the S-phase.[567]

At present, the main clinical uses of flow cytometry in solid tumors are to (1) support a diagnosis of malignancy when the morphologic changes are equivocal; (2) subclassify lesions of borderline malignancy; (3) provide prognostic information independent of stage and grade; (4) monitor response to therapy; (5) establish the development of tumor relapse; and (6) establish the origin of synchronous or metachronous tumors.

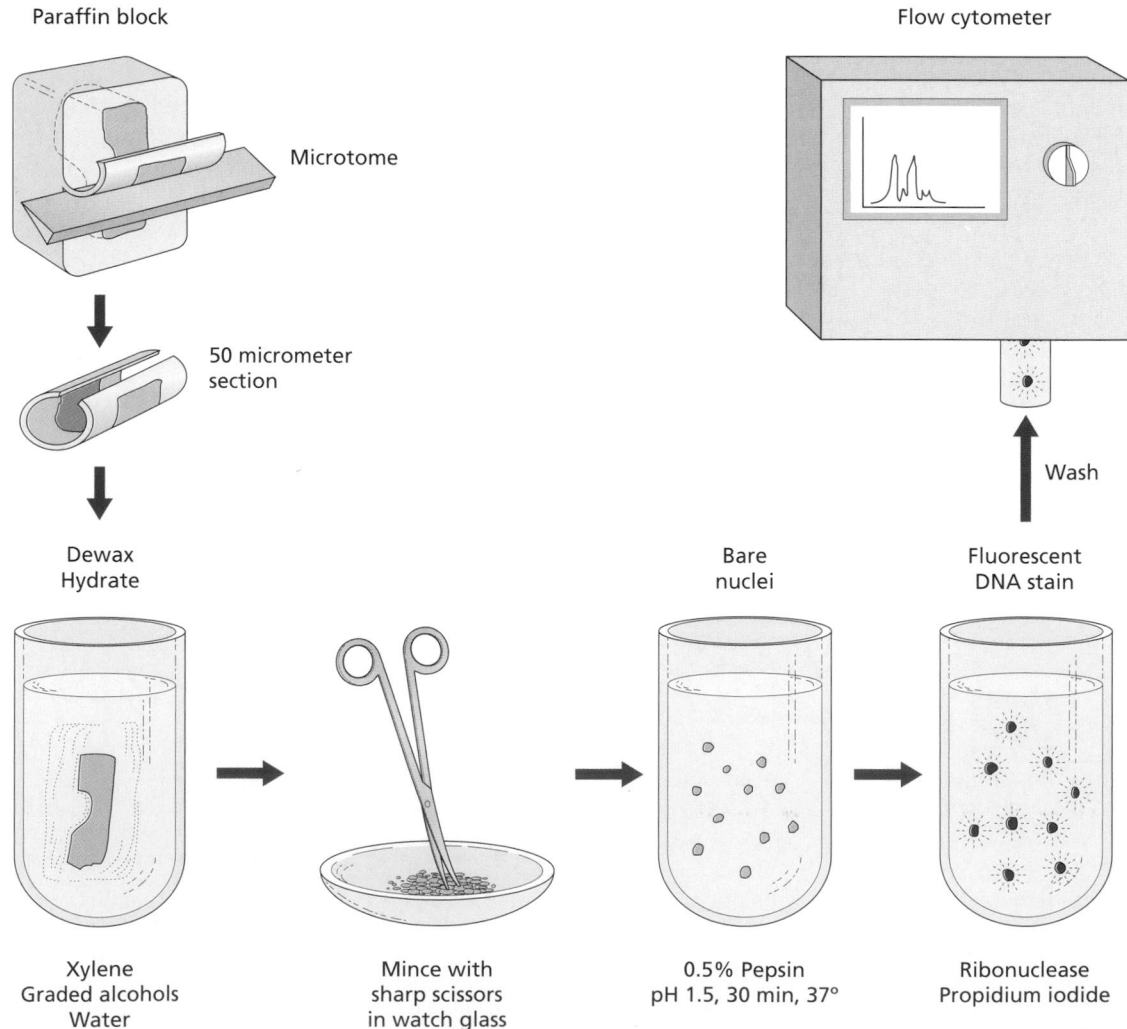

Fig. 3.28 Method of preparing paraffin-embedded tissue for flow cytometry. (From Coon JS, Landay AL, Weinstein RS. Biology of disease. Advances in flow cytometry for diagnostic pathology. Lab Invest 1987, **57**: 453–479)

In all fairness, it should be stated that the role of flow cytometry in the initial diagnosis of tumors is rather limited. Its main role seems to be as a prognostic indicator, as the vast literature on the subject indicates.[557] The tumor categories that have been evaluated more intensively are breast carcinoma,[536,547] non-Hodgkin's lymphoma,[537,538] bladder carcinomas,[535,546,566,568] colorectal carcinoma,[571] prostatic carcinoma,[548,549,555,556,564,565] endocrine neoplasms,[539,572] soft tissue sarcoma,[542] and suspected molar pregnancies.[560] The results are discussed in the respective chapters.

There is no question that DNA ploidy and S-phase fractions correlate with prognosis in many tumor systems. What is not always so clear is whether these correlations remain statistically valid once the tumors have been stratified by conventional clinical and morphologic parameters, including clinical stage, tumor size, microscopic subtype, and nuclear and architectural grading.

Other methods for analysis of cell proliferation

In addition to flow cytometry (S-phase fraction), several other methods are available for the evaluation of the degree of cellular proliferation in tumor tissue.[587,588,596,614]

The older and still widely used method is mitotic count in routinely processed sections, the standard figure employed being the number of mitoses in a certain number (usually 10 to 50) of consecutive "high-power" fields (usually defined as the combination of 10× eyepiece and 40× objective). The method has found its most useful application in the evaluation of mesenchymal neoplasms (particularly uterine smooth muscle tumors), breast carcinoma, neuroblastoma, and GIST, either by itself or as a key component of the grading system. Despite its apparent objectivity, it is subject to considerable variations depending on the thickness of the section, fields chosen, type of microscope used, delay in fixation time, and observer's variability in the identification of mitotic figures.[573,574,582,602,603,610,615] In our opinion, an even greater drawback of this technique as currently used is the blatantly inaccurate and archaic nature of the denominator used (i.e., a microscopic "field"). A considerably more accurate and rational way of making this determination would be by expressing the number of mitotic figures as a function of the percentage of tumor cells, irrespective of the number of non-neoplastic cells and intercellular material present, as investigators counting nuclei labeled with thymidine have always done (see below). We have developed a program adapted to the Bliss Virtual Microscopy system that allows such a count to be made and recorded permanently, and are currently evaluating its applicability and usefulness to routine material.

Another time-honored method for evaluating cell proliferation consists in counting nuclei in S- (DNA synthesis) phase following in vitro thymidine labeling, paraffin embedding, and radioautography.[600] The standard determination of the thymidine labeling index (TL1) is done by counting 2000 tumor nuclei.[599] This method has been used extensively in the study of breast carcinoma[598]; it has been found that patients with carcinomas with high TL1 have an increased incidence of early recurrence and early death.[601] There is a good correlation between the results obtained with thymidine labeling and flow cytometry.

Microspectrophotometric analysis is performed by staining tissue sections obtained from paraffin-embedded material with the Feulgen reaction (which is specific for DNA) and determining the DNA content (expressed in arbitrary units) in a microspectrophotometer using a single wave-length of 560 μm.[612] This tedious technique has been largely replaced by flow cytometry, but it is still being used by some authors.[613]

Cell proliferation can also be investigated with immunohistochemical techniques by staining for nuclear antigens related to cell growth and division and searching for them visually under the microscope or with the help of an image analyzer[590] (see p. 42). Bromodeoxyuridine is a thymidine analog capable of being incorporated into nuclear DNA during S-phase and subsequently detectable by the use of monoclonal antibodies.[595,616,617] Ki-67 is an antigen that corresponds to a nuclear nonhistone protein expressed by cells in the proliferative phases G1, G2, M, and S.[577,586,608] The original antibody against this marker worked only in fresh frozen sections, but monoclonal antibodies have now been developed that detect formalin-resistant epitopes (MIB-1 and MIB-3)[578] (Fig. 3.29). In general, there is a good correlation between Ki-67 staining and mitotic count.[593,606,618]

Ki-S1 is another recently described proliferation marker that is detectable after formalin fixation and

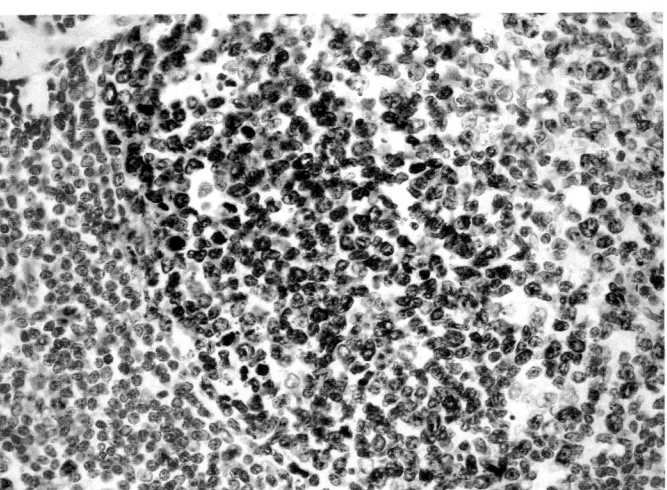

Fig. 3.29 Strong immunostaining for MIB-1 in germinal center of hyperplastic lymph node.

paraffin embedding,[592] and which has been found to be identical with topoisomerase IIα.[576] It functions as a cofactor for polymerase delta during the DNA synthesis phase of the cell cycle.

PCNA is the marker that has most used, together with Ki-67, for the immunohistochemical evaluation of proliferative activity in paraffin embedded material. However, the fact that it has been found to stain resting cells in some tissues and that it seems to be deregulated in some malignant tumors lessens its utility.[579,594,596,597]

Numerous other proteins that act as regulatory elements or checkpoints in different phases of the cell cycle are being characterized and are likely to serve as additional markers of cell proliferation.[575,589,591,609] These include cyclins A, B, C, D, and E, the cyclin-dependent kinases (CDK), the protein kinase catalytic subunits (CdC2), and inhibitory proteins. In turn, some of these inhibitory proteins are regulated by a variety of growth factors. Adding to the complexity is the fact that the tumor-suppressor genes Rb and p53 (see p. 71) are integral components of the cell cycle regulatory system.

Nucleolar organizer region (NOR) evaluation is another indicator of cell proliferation, although of a very different kind. First described as weakly staining chromatinic regions around which nucleoli reorganize during telophase, NORs are now known to contain ribosomal genes (as shown by in situ hybridization) and a number of acidic proteins that have a high affinity for silver (AgNOR proteins).[580] The latter feature has been effectively used for the rapid identification of NORs in light microscopic sections using a simple one-step silver technique.[605,607] NORs appear as black dots of metallic silver, about 0.5 to 1 μm in diameter, localized within secondary constrictions of metaphase chromosomes or within nuclei.

A huge literature appeared in the early 1990s concerning the potential diagnostic and prognostic applications of AgNOR staining.[584] The latter seems more promising than the former, since NOR is intimately related to the proliferative activity of the cell population.[581,583,611] Curiously, and for no apparent reason, the enthusiasm for this technique has waned considerably in recent years, judging from the marked drop of articles on the subject.[604] Specific applications of this technology are discussed in the respective chapters.

Cytogenetics

Karyotypic analysis of human tumors, considered in the past a relatively unrewarding exercise because of the seemingly random and secondary nature of the alterations, has proved to be a powerful tool for the study of these tumors, both in terms of contributing to the definition of the various entities and in providing clues to the molecular mechanisms involved in their pathogenesis.[620] As Sandberg et al[629] have pointed out, the main contributions of cytogenetics in tumor pathology are:

1 Defining subsets within putatively histologically homogeneous tumor types
2 Suggesting connections between histologically diverse tumors
3 Highlighting specific changes in histological subtypes
4 Suggesting the site of the primary when a specific cytogenetic change is found in a metastasis
5 Providing clues to tumor classification, causation, and presence of cancer-related genes.

The detection of nonrandom or specific chromosome abnormalities—such as deletions, amplifications, inversions, and translocations—has been particularly successful in the fields of leukemias and lymphomas,[623] germ cell tumors,[619,626] and mesenchymal neoplasms[621,622,629,632] and less so in carcinomas (Table 3.1). These are further discussed in the respective chapters.

Ideally, conventional cytogenetic analysis requires a minimum sample of 0.5 g of fresh tissue, handled as aseptically as possible, placed in a container with sterile transport medium (phosphate buffered saline; PBS) and sent to the Cytogenetics laboratory. Although immediately processed tissues yield the best results, successful growth of cells can still be obtained from samples processed up to 24 hours after removal, and this allows transport by overnight mail to the reference laboratory. The tissue is then disaggregated, cultured for about a week, harvested, and placed on a slide. The chromosomes are spread out, stained with Giemsa (G-banding), and examined under the microscope.

Because of the labor-intensive, time-consuming nature of this analysis, new techniques have been sought for detecting numerical and structural chromosomal abnormalities in a faster and more efficient fashion. One such technique, interphase cytogenetics, is discussed in a subsequent section. Another recently developed method is **comparative genomic hybridization (CGH)**.[624,627,628] In this procedure, chromosomes are competitively hybridized with two differentially labeled genomic DNAs (one being the test and the other the reference). These, when examined with fluorescence microscopy, show the chromosomal locations of copy number changes in DNA sequences between the two complements (i.e., between tumor and normal DNA). CGH can be applied to fresh-frozen specimens, cell lines, and also DNA extracted from formalin-fixed paraffin-embedded material.[625,633] An ingenious technique has been developed to correlate the microscopic phenotype of solid tumors with their genotype by using universal DNA amplification, CGH, and interphase cytogenetics in formalin-fixed, paraffin-embedded material.[631]

Table 3.1 Specific chromosomal translocations established cytogenetically and the corresponding gene changes in bone and soft-tissue tumors

Tumors	Translocation	Gene fusions
Alveolar rhabdomyosarcoma	t(2;13)(q35;q14)	PAX3-FKHR
	t(1;13)(p36;q14)	PAX7-FKHR
Alveolar soft-part sarcoma	t(X;17)(p11.2;q25)	ASPL-TFE3
Clear-cell sarcoma (malignant melanoma of soft parts)	t(12;22)(q13;q12)	ATF1-EWS
Congenital fibrosarcoma and mesoblastic nephroma	t(12;15)(p13;q25)	ETV6-NTRK3
Dermatofibrosarcoma protuberans (giant-cell fibroblastoma)	t(17;22)(q22;q13)	COL1A1-PDGFB
Desmoplastic round-cell tumor	t(11;22)(p13;q12)	WT1-EWS
Endometrial stromal sarcoma	t(7;17)(p15;q21)	JAZF1-JJAZ1
Ewing sarcoma and peripheral primitive neuroectodermal tumors	t(11;22)(q24;q12)	EWS-FLI1
	t(21;22)(q22;q12)	EWS-ERG
	t(7;22)(p22;q12)	EWS-ETV1
	t(17;22)(q12;q12)	EWS-E1AF
	t(2;22)(q33;q12)	FEV-EWS
Inflammatory myofibroblastic tumor	t(2;19)(p23;p13.1)	ALK-TPM4
	t(1;2)(q22-23;p23)	TPM3-ALK
Myxoid chondrosarcoma, extraskeletal	t(9;22)(q22;q12)	EWS-CHN(TEC)
	t(9;17)(q22;q11)	RBP56-CHN(TEC)
	t(9;15)(q22;q21)	TEC-TCF12
Myxoid liposarcoma	t(12;16)(q13;p11)	TLS(FUS)-CHOP
	t(12;22)(q13;q12)	EWS-CHOP
Synovial sarcoma	t(X;18)(p11;q11)	SYT-SSX1
		SYT-SSX2

From: Cytogenetics and Molecular Genetics of Bone and Soft-Tissue Tumors, Avery A. Sandberg *American Journal of Medical Genetics (Semin. Med. Genet.)* **115**: 189–193 (2002) (with additions)

Molecular pathology

The revolutionary advances made in molecular biology during the past quarter century are having a major impact on the practice of surgical pathology.[634–636,638,639,642–645] Indeed, they have the potential to change this practice in a way that no other techniques ever had before. Advances are occurring at such a rate that it has become very difficult to capture them in a book format, even if highly specialized. Therefore, only a general and, I am afraid, superficial overview of the field will be given, interspersed with some personal reflections.

All of the major molecular methods described in the following paragraphs depend on hybridization techniques based on the application of recombinant DNA technology.[637] The original probes used were nick-translated DNA preparations, but this was soon followed by the use of synthetic oligo(deoxyribo)nucleotides, single-stranded cDNA, and single-stranded antisense RNA. The labeling of the probes is usually done by the incorporation of radionucleotides, but nonradioactive labeling—particularly with biotin and with bromo-deoxyuridine—is also possible (Fig. 3.30).

The immediate significance that molecular techniques have for the surgical pathologist derives from the fact that they can be performed in tissue handled as part of routine work and that many of them are being adapted to their utilization in formalin-fixed, paraffin-embedded material.[640] Along these lines, microdissection instruments have been developed for the DNA analysis of lesions present in tissue sections that measure only a few micrometers, to the point of being limited to a single cell. However, snap frozen material is certainly superior in regard to the yield of extracted DNA and particularly RNA: hence the great importance of the frozen tissue bank in pathology departments.[641]

Filter hybridization

In this form of nucleic acid hybridization, target DNA is extracted from tissues and immobilized on filters made of nitrocellulose or nylon.[652] This can be done directly as "dot blots" or after the performance of restriction enzyme digestion, size fractionation by gel electrophoresis, and subsequent transfer into the filter (Southern blot, named after its inventor, E. M. Southern). This is followed by hybridizing the bound nucleic acid to a labeled probe, masking, and detecting the bound probe (Fig. 3.31). Dot

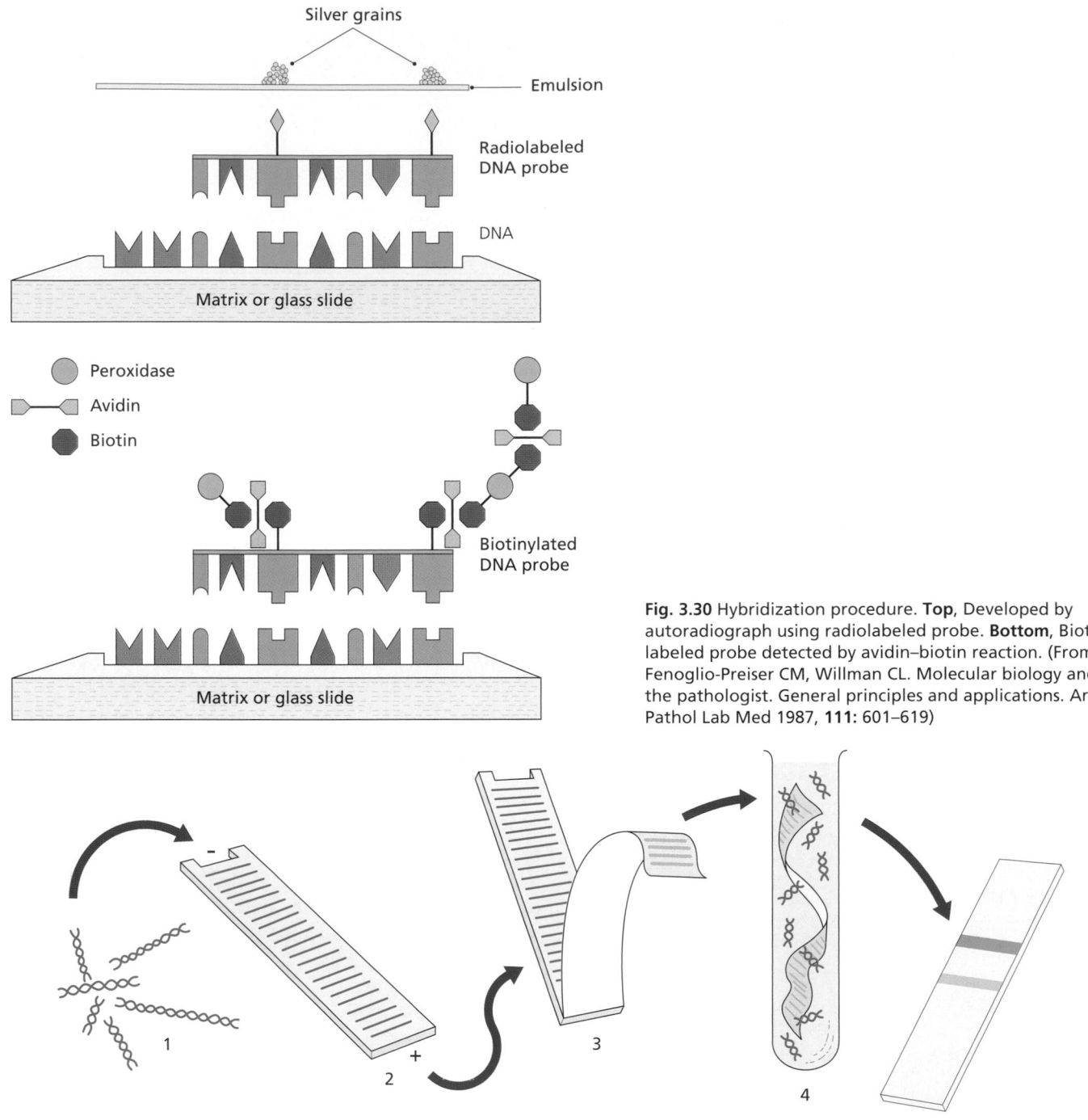

Fig. 3.30 Hybridization procedure. **Top,** Developed by autoradiograph using radiolabeled probe. **Bottom,** Biotin-labeled probe detected by avidin–biotin reaction. (From Fenoglio-Preiser CM, Willman CL. Molecular biology and the pathologist. General principles and applications. Arch Pathol Lab Med 1987, **111:** 601–619)

Fig. 3.31 Steps in Southern blot procedure: (**1**) isolation of DNA; (**2**) polyacrylamide electrophoresis; (**3**) blotting to nitrocellulose; (**4**) hybridization with probe; and (**5**) final product. (From Fenoglio-Preiser CM, Willman CL. Molecular biology and the pathologist. General principles and applications. Arch Pathol Lab Med 1987, **111:** 601–619)

blot hybridization is used when size fractionation of nucleic acid is not required. Procedures analogous to Southern blotting but involving size fractionation of RNA or protein are known as Northern and Western blotting, respectively.[647,649] Although filter hybridization is best done using fresh tissue, good results have been obtained with ethanol-fixed and formalin-fixed, paraffin embedded material.[648,650,653] The attempts being made to develop a fixative suitable for routine work and also capable of preserving as much as possible the integrity of the nucleic acids are discussed in Chapter 2.

The filter hybridization method is ideally suited for the identification and analysis of the following genomic alterations: (1) gene rearrangements/amplifications; (2) gene amplifications; (3) gene deletions; (4) point mutations. It is a powerful technique, but it suffers from a number of technical disadvantages, such as slow turn-around time, the need for radioactive compounds, and the susceptibility of the method to various artifacts. Therefore alternative techniques have been developed, including those discussed in the following sections.[646]

In situ hybridization

In situ hybridization (ISH) consists of the detection of specific DNA or RNA sequences in tissue sections or cell preparations using a labeled complementary nucleic acid sequence or probe.[656,663,668] Under the appropriate conditions, this probe will hybridize (through the establishment of hydrogen bonds) to the target DNA or RNA and be visualized by either radioactive (^{32}P, ^{125}I, ^{35}S, ^{3}H) or nonradioactive (peroxidase, biotin, digoxigenin) labels incorporated into the probe.[654,657,659,660,662,667,673] Both the target and probe nucleic acid need to be single stranded for the hybridization to take place. The main probes currently in use for ISH are cloned RNA and DNA probes and synthetic oligonucleotide probes.

ISH has mainly been used for the detection of viral infections (such as HPV, EBV, and HIV), taking advantage of the ability of the technique to identify directly the viral genome within the infected cell.[655,658,665,666,669] An advantage this offers over immunohistochemistry is that it can detect not only productive but also latent infections, as well as segregate the various virus subtypes, as in HPV. Also, in the area of infectious diseases, it has been found useful for the distinction among *Aspergillus* and other fungal species in tissue sections.[661]

ISH has also been used to detect analysis of gene expression by neoplasms. One such use is the detection of messenger RNA for various peptide hormones[664] and for immunoglobulin light and heavy chains[672]; in many such cases, the technique proved successful when the immunohistochemical detection of the corresponding protein was not. This is explained by the fact that immunohistochemical techniques demonstrate the amount of peptide present in the cell and are, therefore, dependent on the degree of secretion, intracellular degradation, transport, and post-translational processing of the peptides.[670]

The other important use of ISH is for the analysis of proto-oncogene expression during normal fetal development, in normal adult tissues, in inflammatory diseases (as in skin lesions of lupus erythematosus), and in neoplasms.[671]

ISH can be performed in conjunction with immunohistochemistry, combined with PCR (in situ PCR), or carried out at the electron microscopic level by the use of colloidal gold.[656]

Interphase cytogenetics

Briefly stated, interphase cytogenetics refers to the analysis of chromosomes in nondividing cells. As such, it is to be contrasted with the conventional chromosomal analysis performed in metaphase spreads (see p. 66) The latter depends on the presence of a suitable number of dividing cells in the sample, in order to allow the chromosomes to be counted and analyzed after the mitoses have been arrested in metaphase. This method, although proved highly successful under the right circumstances, has many important limitations. The specimen must be fresh, establishment of in vitro culture may be necessary, the dividing cell population may not be representative of the original sample, and the chromosomes may be of poor quality.

Interphase cytogenetics, which is notably free of these shortcomings, has become one of the most rapidly growing fields following the development of extremely sensitive detection methods and an ever-growing number of chromosome specific DNA probes.[674,676,680,684,685] Fluorescent in situ hybridization (FISH) has proved particularly powerful because of its great sensitivity and rapidity.

Three types of DNA probes are used. In the technique known as *chromosome painting*, the probe is a composite one containing both unique sequences from a specific chromosome as well as sequences that are shared with other chromosomes.[675] The latter are blocked in the FISH procedure, the result being an even hybridization along the whole length of the target chromosome. (*Alphoid*) *centromeric probes* are made up of alpha satellite DNA. This represents the major class of centromeric DNA and has chromosome-specific sequences that give very strong signals in the target chromosomes, both in metaphase preparations and in interphase nuclei. *Cosmid probes* are prepared from cosmids, which are vectors specifically designed for cloning large fragments of eukaryotic DNA. They allow the detection of single copy sequences in the human genomes either in metaphase chromosomes or (with more difficulty) in interphase nuclei. The technique has been used for the diagnosis of congenital abnormalities,[682] for the detection of cells of recipient origin in allografts,[677] and for the evaluation of neoplastic diseases. In tumor pathology, the main applications of interphase cytogenetics have been in the field of hematologic malignancies. Technical advances that allow the procedure to be carried out in frozen sections and paraffin sections have led to their increasing use for the study of solid tumors.[675,678,679,681] The technique is most easily applied to the detection of numerical chromosome abnormalities, but it has also been successfully employed for the identification of gene amplification[683] and chromosomal translocations and deletions.[679]

Polymerase chain reaction

Polymerase chain reaction (PCR), a revolutionary technique first introduced in 1985, allows millions of copies of any specific DNA sequence to be generated within a few hours. PCR relies on the ability of DNA polymerases, in the presence of a mixture of deoxynucleotide triphosphates (dATP, dCTP, dGTP, dTTP), to copy a DNA strand using a short complementary DNA fragment as an initiating template.[688,694,705,709]

The steps involved in the procedure are the following[695,698,710]:

1 Synthesis of short DNA fragments (oligonucleotide primers) that are complementary to DNA sequences on opposite strands of the DNA flanking the fragment to be amplified
2 Heat denaturation of the DNA
3 Annealing of the primers to their complementary sequences
4 Extension of the annealed primers with DNA polymerase.

Each cycle of the procedure (from step 2 through step 4) is continuously repeated, each successive cycle doubling the amount of DNA synthesized in the previous one, this chain reaction resulting in the exponential accumulation of the specific DNA target fragment to approximately 2^n, where n is the number of cycles.

The PCR technique can also be used to amplify RNA so that gene expression can be analyzed in small amounts of tissue. For this purpose, extracted RNA is converted to double-stranded cDNA using the retroviral enzyme reverse transcriptase, and this is followed by room temperature PCR (RT-PCR) performed on the cDNA copies.

A major attraction of the PCR technique for the surgical pathologist resides in the fact that it can be utilized to analyze DNA (and, on occasions, also RNA) from samples of formalin-fixed paraffin-embedded material,[686,697,703] and even from microdissected tissue sections.[699]

The applications of PCR technology to medicine in general and pathology in particular are too numerous to be mentioned here.[711] In the specific field of tumor pathology, the main current uses of PCR are the following:

1 Detection of Ig or TCR gene rearrangements, as a means to determine the clonality of B- or T-cell proliferations, respectively[687,692]
2 Detection of the chimeric transcripts resulting from chromosomal translocations in hematologic and solid malignancies [i.e., t(14:18) in follicular lymphomas]. This can be applied for primary diagnosis or for the detection of "residual minimal disease" after treatment[708] (Fig. 3.32)
3 Detection of point mutations in oncogenes and tumor suppressor genes (i.e., activated *ras* oncogenes in pancreatic carcinomas)
4 Detection of gene amplifications, such as N-*myc* in neuroblastoma and c-*erb*B-2 in breast carcinoma
5 Detection of microsatellite instability[707]
6 Detection of microorganisms, including bacteria such as *Mycobacterium tuberculosis*[702,704] and viruses, such as HPV in squamous cell carcinomas, EBV in malignant lymphomas, and HHV-8 in Kaposi's sarcoma[686a]

7 Detection of circulating tumor cells in peripheral blood, through the identification of mRNA for thyroglobulin in thyroid carcinoma, for tyrosinase in melanoma, for PSA in prostatic carcinoma, and others[689,690]

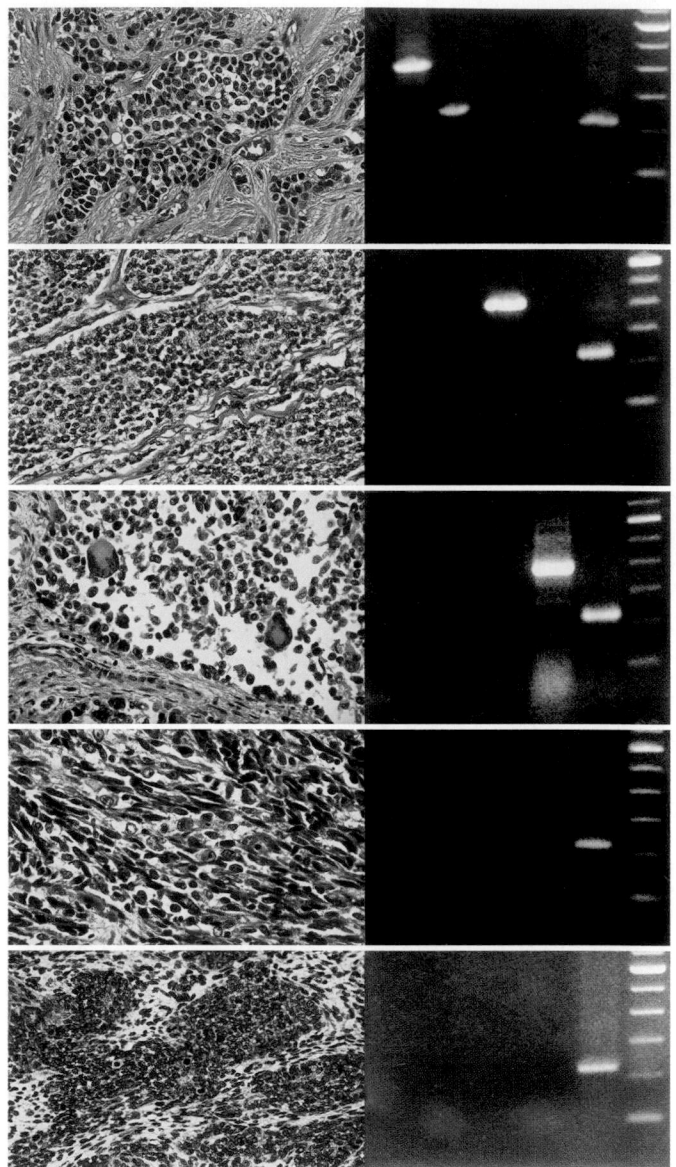

Fig. 3.32 Detection of chimeric transcripts by reverse transcriptase-PCR in five types of pediatric malignant tumors. This composite figure shows a representative photomicrograph and an agarose gel for each tumor type. **First row**: Two cases of desmoplastic small round cell tumor associated with *EWS–WT1* transcripts, one with 268 bp (typical) and one with 451 bp (variant). *EWS–WT1* transcripts are detected in 92% of these tumors. **Second row**: Ewing sarcoma associated with *EWS–FLI-1* transcript. *EWS–FLI-1* and *EWS–ERG* transcripts are found in 81– and 14– of Ewing sarcomas, respectively. **Third row**: Alveolar rhabdomyosarcoma showing amplification of *PAX-3–FKHR* transcript. This alteration is detected in 76– of these tumors, whereas *PAX-7–FKHR* is present in 10– of them. **Fourth row**: Embryonal rhabdomyosarcoma. No chimeric transcript is identified. **Fifth row**: Wilms' tumor of kidney. No chimeric transcript is identified. (Courtesy of Dr. Enrique de Alava, Salamanca, Spain)

8 Distinguishing a *de novo* second malignancy from a tumor recurrence[706]

9 Identification of mismatched specimens and "floaters" (see Chapter 2).

Another exciting development of the PCR technique consists of its in situ application to tissue sections, either by protecting the area of interest from DNA linkage by UV irradiation and following this by conventional PCR analysis, or by combining PCR with in situ hybridization (PISH).[696,700] The latter technique, which has been used to detect latent HIV infection in lymph node sections from asymptomatic virus carriers, is however fraught with technical difficulties, and its practical usefulness to diagnostic pathology still needs to be demonstrated.[693,701]

DNA Microarrays

A radically different approach to the problem is that provided by the DNA microarray ("chip") technology, which allows the simultaneous analysis of tens of thousands of genes in a single step. The main applications have been gene expression analysis and genotyping for point mutations, single nucleotide pleomorphisms, and short tandems repeats.[715] Gene expression analysis is based on nucleic acid hybridization between free targets derived from a biologic sample and an array of DNA fragments (the "probes") which have been anchored to a solid surface. The targets are produced by reverse transcription and simultaneous labeling of RNA molecules; they are part of a complex mixture of distinct cDNA fragments that hybridize with the corresponding probes. The signal generated on each probe reflects the mRNA expression level of the corresponding gene on the sample. After detection, quantification, and integration of signals with specialized software, the intensities are normalized for technical deviations, thus providing a *gene expression profile*. The potential applications, which are enormous, span the whole areas of diagnosis, screening, and prognosis.[712] A particularly promising area is that of determination of the site of origin of the tumor, because of the existence of organ-related gene expression.[693] The field is rapidly evolving, and it remains to be seen which of the methods employed to analyze the gene expressions (nearest neighbor algorithms, linear discriminant analysis, neural networks, support vector machine, or a simple classifier with a pathological tree-based network) will prove to have the greatest discriminatory power.[715a] It is unfortunate that the overenthusiasm and competitiveness in the field sometimes result in the proposal of new tumor classification schemes that seem awfully premature, to say the least.[713,714]

Microdissection

Another technique that has been incorporated recently in surgical pathology laboratories performing molecular work is that of microdissection of tissue sections. As is often the case, the idea is rather old. It had been used extensively by Drs J.R. Oliver and J. Kissane, at Washington University, in St. Louis, in the early 1960s for the microdissection of the nephron. In those halcyon days, the dissection was done with a pair of needles. Now, there are at least three major competing instruments, all employing laser technology and a sophisticated software, that allow the dissection of a pure cell population or even single cells or chromosomes, which—once captured—can be studied with all the available molecular techniques.[716–718]

Oncogenes and tumor-suppressor genes

The genes thought to be directly involved in—and supposedly responsible for—the pathogenesis of tumors have been divided into two major categories: oncogenes and tumor-suppressor genes. The term *oncogene* derives from the transforming capacity that retroviruses were found to have in mammalian tumorigenic systems, with the name proto-oncogene having been adopted for their normal cellular counterpart. These proto-oncogenes (or oncogenes, as they are currently called for short) code for protein products that play key roles in the regulation of cellular proliferation and differentiation. Over 100 of them have been identified in humans, and the list grows monthly.

Tumor-suppressor genes (also known as anti-oncogenes or onco-suppressor genes) are involved in the prevention of uncontrolled cellular proliferation and the promotion of terminal differentiation.[729] Loss of function of these tumor suppressor genes may lead to tumor growth.[722,727,728,731] The most important tumor-suppressor genes are the retinoblastoma (Rb) gene and the p53 gene. The latter is involved in control of the cell cycle, apoptosis, and maintenance of genomic stability. Abnormalities of p53 are the most common genetic abnormality found so far in malignant tumors.[719,721,723,724]

It is becoming increasingly apparent that most malignant tumor display a combination of abnormalities in both oncogenes and tumor suppressor genes, via a multistep process, a theory that fits very well with classic morphologic observations.

Deregulation of oncogene or tumor-suppressor gene activity may occur through a variety of mechanisms:

1 Point mutations (single-base DNA changes) of an oncogene, leading to the production of an abnormal protein (as often happens with *ras* oncogenes). In the case of a tumor-suppressor gene, this mutation needs to be accompanied by loss of the other allele to have a functional effect (see 4 below).

2 Rearrangement or translocation of the oncogene to another genomic site, disrupting the normal regulatory control and resulting in overexpression and/or production of an abnormal protein (as when *c-abl* is translocated from chromosome 9 to chromosome 22).

3 Amplification of the number of copies of the oncogene at the DNA level (as with *neu/c-erb*B-2 in breast carcinoma).[730]

4 Inactivation of a tumor-suppressor gene through loss of one copy of the gene, as detected by loss of heterozygosity (LOH) in the corresponding locus, combined with mutation in the remaining allele, with the resulting reduced expression or inactivation of the corresponding protein product. Mutation of *p53* usually leads to an abnormal protein with a markedly extended half-life, resulting in accumulation of this product, which can be detected immunohistochemically.[733]

From the point of view of their function, oncogenes and tumor-suppressor genes (OTSGs) have been divided into four major categories, allowing for a great deal of overlap:

1 *Mitogenic signal transduction pathways.* This refers to the regulatory pathways that convey the extracellular signal to intracellular components that cause the cell to respond. Typically, the signal begins in a growth factor (usually a protein) binding to a receptor in the form of a transmembrane protein having both extracellular and intracellular domains. This is followed by the signal moving along the various subcellular compartments into the nucleus. The main sites of this extremely intricate process at which OTSGs have been seen to act are at the level of the receptor (as for EGPF, Her2/neu, RET, KIT), the RAS protein (one of the most ubiquitous changes in cancer), the GAP protein (a molecule with homology to the gene responsible for neurofibromatosis), and the transcription factor (such as MYC, WT1, APC, PTEN, and VHL).

2 *Cell cycle regulation.* These include RB1 (responsible for familial retinoblastoma) and p53, which is mutated in a wide variety of cancers. The oncogenes of DNA tumor viruses, including HPV, also fall in this category. It also includes, directly or indirectly, the cyclins (the family of proteins driving the cell through the cell cycle), the cyclin-dependent kinases, and their inhibitors.

3 *DNA replication and repair.* This refers to the group of genes encoding the proteins responsible for maintaining genomic integrity. It includes the mismatch repair genes involved in hereditary non-polyposis colon cancer, the enzyme telomerase (which maintains the length of chromosomes during cell division,[720] and the genes BRC1 and BRC2 (which are mutated in familial breast carcinoma).

4 *Apoptosis.* This refers to gene products involved in programmed cell death, or apoptosis), under the assumption that deficiencies in the mechanism that regulates this process may contribute to the malignant phenotype. The best known example is represented by the bcl-2 family of proteins, which inhibit apoptosis. The opposite function, i.e., that of promoting apoptosis, is provided by the BAX protein family. Both protein groups function by regulating the release of cytochrome *c* from the mitochondria. The p53 protein, already discussed as a transcription factor, is also a cell-cycle checkpoint regulator and a regulator of apoptosis, demonstrating that the function-based classification of OTSGs is, to some extent, artificial. Another example is FHIT, a tumor suppressor gene deleted in about 75% of lung nonsmall cell cancers, which seems to be involved both in apoptosis and cell cycle control.[732]

Concluding remarks

It seems to me that we are still a long way from understanding the key mechanism of cancer development. There are simply too many OTSGs and too may pathways that have been advanced to explain what is, ultimately, a single disease complex. Its clinical and morphologic manifestations are innumerable, but there is clearly a common theme that defines the neoplastic status from a biologic standpoint.[725,726] That common theme calls for a common mechanism that must preside over all the multitudinous and distracting differences. It is very unlikely that this common mechanism could be equally provided by a myriad of pathways driven by hundreds of OTSGs. With all of its evil features, the cancer cell must be acknowledged to be a model of strength, coordination, and purpose. To be able to outgrow its neighbors, to infiltrate the stroma, to find its way into a vessel, to survive in the hostile general circulation, to stop at the right place in order to lodge there and to repeat the cycle, calls for a machinery that can hardly be provided by one, ten, or fifty OTSGs having gone wrong. A machinery that must already have been in the cell in a dormant state and which at some point during embryonic development must have fulfilled an essential role. One need only think of what the trophoblast can do without a single OTSG having gone wrong. Is it possible that the main function of the various OTSGs is to reactivate that mechanism by providing, so to speak, the right passwords to open the program?

References

Introduction

1 Gonzalez-Crussi F. Significance of gene rearrangement (letter to the editor). Am J Surg Pathol 1987, **11**: 491–492.

2 Masson P. Human tumors. Histology, diagnosis and technique, ed. 2. Detroit, 1970, Wayne State University Press.

3 Masuda T, Kawaguchi J, Oikawa H, Yashima A, Suzuiki K, Sato S, Satodate R. How thick are the paraffin-embedded tissue sections routinely prepared in laboratory? A morphometric study using a confocal laser scanning microscope. Pathol Int 1998, **48**: 179–183.

4 Rosai J. The H & E technique: old mistress apologue. Pathologica 1998, **90**: 739–742.

5 Scarani P. Trees with blood-colored wood. Pathologica 2000, **92**: 298–300.

Special stains

6 Azzopardi JG. Problems in breast pathology. Philadelphia, 1979, WB Saunders Co., p. 373.

7 Bottone EJ. The Gram stain. The century-old quintessential rapid diagnostic test. Lab Med 1988, **19**: 288–291.

8 Bussolati G, Volante M, Papotti M. Classic and recent special stains used in differential diagnosis of endocrine tumors. Endocr Pathol 2002, **12**: 379–387.

9 Carson FL, Kingsley WB. Nonamyloid green birefringence following Congo red staining. Arch Pathol Lab Med 1980, **104**: 333–335.

10 DeLellis RA. Formaldehyde-induced fluorescence technique for the demonstration of biogenic amines in diagnostic histopathology. Cancer 1971, **28**: 1704–1710.

11 Filipe MI. Mucins in the human gastrointestinal epithelium. A review. Invest Cell Pathol 1979, **2**: 195–216.

12 Foraker AG. The "H-and-E fuddy dud" and the "histochemical snob." Am J Clin Pathol 1960, **33**: 439–440.

13 Jass JR, Roberton AM. Colorectal mucin histochemistry in health and disease. A critical review. Pathol Int 1994, **44**: 487–504.

14 Jass JR. Mucin core proteins as differentiation markers in the gastrointestinal tract. Histopathology 2001, **37**: 561–564.

15 Laurén PA, Sorvari TE. Mucicarmine staining in the histochemistry of mucosubstances. Scand J Clin Lab Invest 1968, **21**(Suppl 101): 45–46.

16 Marshall PN. Romanowsky-type stains in haematology. Histochem J 1978, **10**: 1–29.

17 Masson P. Some histological methods. Trichrome stainings and their preliminary technique. J Techn Meth 1929, **12**: 75–90.

18 O'Connell JT, Hacker CM, Barsky SH. MUC2 is a molecular marker for pseudomyxoma peritonei. Mod Pathol 2002, **15**: 958–972.

19 Puchtler H, Isler H. The effect of phosphomolybdic acid on the stainability of connective tissues in various dyes. J Histochem 1958, **6**: 265–270.

20 Reynolds CP, German DC, Weinberg AG, Smith RG. Catecholamine fluorescence and tissue culture morphology. Technics in the diagnosis of neuroblastoma. Am J Clin Pathol 1981, **75**: 275–282.

21 Romeis B. Mikroskopische Technik, ed. 17. München, 1989, Urban und Schwarzenberg.

22 Smith DM Jr, Haggitt RC. A comparative study of generic stains for carcinoid secretory granules. Am J Surg Pathol 1983, **7**: 61–68.

23 Steensma DP. Congo red: out of Africa? Arch Pathol Lab Med 2001, **125**: 250–252.

24 Van Noorden CJ, Frederiks WM. Cerium methods for light and electron microscope histochemistry. J Microsc 1993, **171**: 3–16.

25 Vialli M. Argentaffinity and argentophilia. I. A critical review about the technique and the possibilities for histochemical research. Acta Histochem 1977, **60**: 103–120.

26 Vialli M. Argentaffinity and argentophilia. II. The sensitivity of histochemical argentophilic techniques. Acta Histochem 1977, **60**: 211–227.

27 Yamashita Y, Chung YS, Horie R, Kannagi R, Sowa M. Alterations in gastric mucin with malignant transformation. Novel pathway for mucin synthesis. J Natl Cancer Inst 1995, **87**: 441–446.

Enzyme histochemistry

28 Boyle JL, Haupt HM, Stern JB, Multhaupt HA. Tyrosinase expression in malignant melanoma, desmoplastic melanoma, and peripheral nerve tumors. Arch Pathol Lab Med 2002, **126**: 816–822.

29 Cohen MB, Miller TR, Beckstead JH. Enzyme histochemistry and thyroid neoplasia. Am J Clin Pathol 1986, **85**: 668–673.

30 Duray PH, Kaplow L. A simplified Azo dye method for the demonstration of acid phosphatase in paraffin embedded tissue. J Histotechnol 1984, **7**: 69–72.

31 Ferrell LD, Beckstead JH. Plastic embedding. Use of glycol methacrylate-embedded biopsy material at the light microscopic level. Pathol Annu 1990, **25**(Pt 1): 341–360.

32 Leder L-D. The chloroacetate esterase reaction. A useful means of histological diagnosis of hematological disorders from paraffin sections of skin. Am J Dermatopathol 1979, **1**: 39–42.

33 Osamura RY, Yasuda O, Kawai K, Hori S, Suemizu H, Onoda SN, Joh TH. Immunohistochemical localization of catecholamine-synthesizing enzymes in human pheochromocytomas. Endocr Pathol 1990, **1**: 102–108.

34 Rodriguez HA, McGavran MH. A modified dopa reaction for the diagnosis and investigation of pigment cells. Am J Clin Pathol 1969, **52**: 219–227.

35 Sasano H, Kato K, Nagura H, Parkkila S, Parkkila A-K, Rajaniemi H, Sugai N. Carbonic anhydrases in the human adrenal gland and its disorders. Immunohistochemical and biochemical studies of the enzyme. Endocr Pathol 1994, **5**: 100–106.

36 Sasano H, Nagura H, Harada N, Goukon Y, Kimura M. Immunolocalization of aromatase and other steroidogenic enzymes in human breast disorders. Hum Pathol 1994, **25**: 530–535.

37 Schellens JP, Vreeling-Sindelarova H, Fredericks WM. Electron microscopical enzyme histochemistry on unfixed tissues and cells. Bridging the gap between LM and EM enzyme histochemistry. Act Histochem 2003, **105**: 1–19.

38 Sheiban K, Tubbs RR. Enzyme immunohistochemistry. Technical aspects. Semin Diagn Pathol 1984, **1**: 235–250.

39 Sobel HJ. Enzyme cytochemistry for the pathologist. A simple method for the ultrastructural study of tissue alterations with the light microscope. Pathol Annu 1968, **3**: 57–104.

40 Van Noorden CJ, Frederiks WM. Enzyme histochemistry: A laboratory manual of current methods. Oxford, 1992, Oxford University Press.

41 Wick MR, Swanson PE, Manivel JC. Placental-like alkaline phosphatase reactivity in human tumors. An immunohistochemical study of 520 cases. Hum Pathol 1987, **18**: 946–954.

42 Willighagen RGJ. Enzyme histochemistry of human tumors. Beitr Pathol Anat 1970, **141**: 280–282.

Tissue culture

43 Cavazzana AO, Miser JS, Jefferson J, Triche TJ. Experimental evidence for a neural origin of Ewing's sarcoma of bone. Am J Pathol 1987, **127**: 507–518.

44 Costa J, Rosai J, Philpott GW. Pigmentation of "amelanotic" melanoma in culture. Arch Pathol 1973, **95**: 371–373.

45 Doyle A, Griffiths JB. Cell and tissue culture: laboratory procedures in biotechnology. New York, 1998, John Wiley & Sons.

46 Doyle A, Griffiths JB. Cell and tissue culture for medical research. New York, 1998, John Wiley & Sons.

47 Gaillard P. Growth and differentiation of explanted tissues. Int Rev Cytol 1953, **2**: 331–401.

48 Giuffrè L, Schreyer M, Mach J-P, Carrel S. Cyclic AMP induces differentiation in vitro of human melanoma cells. Cancer 1988, **61**: 1132–1141.

49 Ioachim HL. Tissue culture of human tumors. Its use and prospects. Pathol Annu 1970, **5**: 217–256.

50 Mather JP, Barnes DW. Animal cell culture methods. San Diego, 1998, Academic Press.

51 Murray MR, Stout AP. Distinctive characteristics of the sympathicoblastoma cultivated in vitro. A method for prompt diagnosis. Am J Pathol 1947, **23**: 429–441.

52 Murray MR, Stout AP. The classification and diagnosis of human tumors by tissue culture methods. Tex Rep Biol Med 1954, **12**: 898–915.

53 Ozzello L, Stout AP, Murray MR. Cultural characteristics of malignant histiocytomas and fibrous xanthomas. Cancer 1963, **16**: 331–344.

54 Peltonen J, Jaakkola S, Virtanen I, Pelliniemi L. Perineurial cells in culture. An immunocytochemical and electron microscopic study. Lab Invest 1987, **57**: 480–488.

55 Reynolds CP, German DC, Weinberg AG, Smith RG. Catecholamine fluorescence and tissue culture morphology. Technics in the diagnosis of neuroblastoma. Am J Clin Pathol 1981, **75**: 275–282.

56 Stout AP, Murray MR. Localized pleural mesothelioma. Investigation of its characteristics and histogenesis by the method of tissue culture. Arch Pathol 1942, **34**: 951–964.

Quantitative methods (histometry)

57 Baak JPA, Kurver PHJ, Boon ME. Computer-aided application of quantitative microscopy in diagnostic pathology. Pathol Annu 1982, **17**(Pt 2): 287–306.

58 Baak JP. The framework of pathology: good laboratory practice by quantitative and molecular methods. J Pathol 2002, **198**: 277–283.

59 Baak JP, ten Kate FJ, Offerhaus GJ, Van Lanschot JJ, Meijer GA. Routine morphometrical analysis can improve reproducibility of dysplasia grade of Barrett's oesophagus surveillance biopsies. J Clin Pathol 2002, **55**: 910–916.

60 Beck JS, Anderson JM. Quantitative methods as an aid to diagnosis in histopathology. Rec Adv Histopathol 1987, **13**: 255–269.

61 Bosari S, Lee AK, Wiley BD, Heatley GJ, Hamilton WM, Silverman ML. DNA quantitation by image analysis of paraffin-embedded colorectal adenocarcinomas and its prognostic value. Mod Pathol 1992, **5**: 324–328.

62 Coleman K, Baak JPA, van Diest PJ, Curran B, Mullaney J, Fenton M, Leader M. DNA ploidy status in 84 ocular melanomas. A study of DNA quantitation in ocular melanomas by flow cytometry and automatic and interactive static image analysis. Hum Pathol 1995, **26**: 99–105.

63 Dawson AE, Austin RE Jr, Weinberg DS. Nuclear grading of breast carcinoma by image analysis. Classification by multivariate and neural network analysis. Am J Clin Pathol 1991, **95**: S29–S37.

64 Doglioni C, Tos AP, Laurino L, Luzzulino P, Chiarelli C, Celio MR, Viale G. Calretinin: a novel immunocytochemical marker for mesothelioma. Am J Surg Pathol 1996, **20**: 1037–1046.

65 Elsheikh TM, Silverman JF, McCool JW, Riley RS. Comparative DNA analysis of solid tumors by flow cytometric and image analyses of touch imprints and flow cell suspensions. Am J Clin Pathol 1992, **98**: 296–304.

66 Kilpatrick SE, Teot LA, Geisinger KR, Martin PL, Shumate DK, Zbieranski N, Russell GB, Fletcher CDM. Relationship of DNA ploidy to histology and prognosis in rhabdomyosarcoma. Comparison of flow cytometry and image analysis. Cancer 1994, **74**: 3227–3233.

67 Lage JM, Bagg A. Hydatidiform moles: DNA flow cytometry, image analysis and selected topics in molecular biology. Histopathology 1997, **28**: 379–382.

68 Marchevsky AM, Bartels PH, eds. Image analysis. A primer for pathologists. New York, 1994, Raven Press.

69 Proceedings of the fifth international symposium on morphometry in morphological diagnosis. Pathol Res Pract 1989, **185**: 537–824.

70 Remmele W, Schicketanz K. Immunohistochemical determination of estrogen and progesterone receptor content in human breast cancer. Computer-assisted image analysis (QIC score) vs. subjective grading (IRS). Pathol Res Pract 1993, **189**: 862–866.

71 Remmelink M, Salmon I, Petein M, Gras T, Zandona C, Pasteels J-L, Kiss R. Determination of DNA ploidy, nuclear size, and proliferative activity by means of the computer-assisted image analysis of Feulgen-stained nuclei in 68 soft tissue tumors of adults. Hum Pathol 1994, **25**: 694–701.

72 Sorensen FB. Quantitative analysis of nuclear size for objective malignancy grading. A review with emphasis on new, unbiased stereologic methods. Lab Invest 1992, **66**: 4–23.

73 Wells WA, Rainer RO, Memoli VA. Basic principles of image processing. Am J Clin Pathol 1992, **98**: 493–501.

74 Wells WA, Rainer RO, Memoli VA. Equipment, standardization, and applications of image processing. Am J Clin Pathol 1993, **99**: 48–56.

75 Wied GL, Bartels PH, Bibbo M, Dytch HE. Image analysis in quantitative cytopathology and histopathology. Hum Pathol 1989, **20**: 549–571.

X-ray microanalysis

76 Bretschneider A, Burns W, Morrison A. "Pop-off" technique. The ultrastructure of paraffin-embedded sections. Am J Clin Pathol 1981, **76**: 450–453.

77 Terzakis JA. X-ray microanalysis. Problem solving in surgical pathology. Pathol Annu 1985, **20**(Pt 2): 59–81.

Electron microscopy

78 Bretschneider A, Burns W, Morrison A. "Pop-off" technique. The ultrastructure of paraffin-embedded sections. Am J Clin Pathol 1981, **76**: 450–453.

79 Dardick I, Herrera GA. Diagnostic electron microscopy of neoplasms. Hum Pathol 1999, **29**: 1335–1338.

80 Erlandson RA. Application of transmission electron microscopy to human tumor diagnosis. An historical perspective. Cancer Invest 1987, **5**: 487–505.

81 Erlandson RA, Rosai J. A realistic approach to the use of electron microscopy and other ancillary diagnostic techniques in surgical pathology (editorial). Am J Surg Pathol 1995, **19**: 247–250.

82 Eyden B, Chroneyko KA, Shanks JH, Menasce LP, Banerjee SS. Contribution of electron microscopy to understanding cellular differentiation in mesenchymal tumors of the gastrointestinal tract: a study of 82 tumors. Ultrastruct Pathol 2002, **26**: 269–285.

83 Ferrell LD, Beckstead JH. Plastic embedding. Use of glycol methacrylate-embedded biopsy material at the light microscopic level. Pathol Annu 1990, **25**(Pt 1): 341–360.

84 Ghadially FN. Diagnostic electron microscopy of tumours, ed 2. London, 1985, Butterworths.

85 Ghadially FN. Ultrastructural pathology of the cell and matrix. Boston, 1997, Butterworth-Heinemann.

86 Ghadially FN. Diagnostic ultrastructural pathology: a self-evaluation and self-teaching manual. Boston, 1998, Butterworth-Heinemann.

87 Hammar S, Bockus D, Remington F. Metastatic tumors of unknown origin. An ultrastructural analysis of 265 cases. Ultrastruct Pathol 1987, **11**: 209–250.

88 Herrera GA, Turbat-Herrera EA. Current role of electron microscopy on the diagnosis of pigmented tumors. Sem Diagn Pathol 2003, **20**: 60–71.

88a Jackson SB, Strausbach PH, Finley JL, Laich D, Hewan-Lowe KO. Desmosomes and microvilli mean a lot: diagnosis of neoplasms of unknown origin using electron microscopy. Ultrastruct Pathol 2003, **27**: 155–161.

89 Koss LG. Electron microscopy in cytology. Acta Cytol (Baltimore) 1985, **3**: 195–196.

90 Lloreta-Trull JS. The current role of electron microscopy in the diagnosis of epithelial and epithelioid tumors. Semin Diagn Pathol 2003, **20**: 46–59.

91 Mackay B, Silva EG. Diagnostic electron microscopy in oncology. Pathol Annu 1980, **15**(Pt 2): 241–270.

92 Mierau GW, Eyden B. Electron microscopy for tumour diagnosis: is it redundant. Histopathology 1999, **35**: 99–101.

93 Mierau GW, Weeks DA, Hicks MJ. Role of electron microscopy and other special techniques in the diagnosis of childhood round cell tumors. Hum Pathol 1999, **29**: 1347–1355.

94 Mount SL, Schwarz JE, Taatjes DJ. Prolonged storage of fixative for electron microscopy: effects on tissue preservation for diagnostic specimens. Ultrastruct Pathol 1997, **21**: 195–200.

95 Ordóñez NG, Mackay B. Electron microscopy in tumor diagnosis: indications for its use in the immunohistochemical era. Hum Pathol 1999, **29**: 1403–1411.

96 Peydro-Olaya A, Llombart-Bosch A, Carda-Batalla C, Lopez-Guerrero JA. Electron microscopy and other ancillary techniques in the diagnosis of small round cell tumors. Semin Diagn Pathol 2003, **20**: 25–45.

97 Rosai J, Rodriguez HA. Application of electron microscopy to the differential diagnosis of tumors. Am J Clin Pathol 1968, **50**: 535–562.

98 Suo Z, Qvist H, Su W, Holm R, Giercksky KE, Nesland JM. Undifferentiated carcinoma: an immunohistochemical and ultrastructural study. Anticancer Res 1993, **13**: 643–649.

99 Suo Z, Nesland EM. Electron microscopy in diagnosis of spindle cell tumors. Semin Diagn Pathol 2003, **20**: 5–12.

100 Trump BF, Jones RT, eds. Diagnostic electron microscopy, vols 1–4. New York, 1978–1980, 1983, John Wiley & Sons.

101 Tucker JA. The continuing value of electron microscopy in surgical pathology. Ultrastruct Pathol 2001, **24**: 383–389.

102 Wang N-S, Minassian H. The formaldehyde-fixed and paraffin-embedded tissues for diagnostic transmission electron microscopy. A retrospective and prospective study. Hum Pathol 1987, **18**: 715–727.

Immunohistochemistry

103 Acs G, Lawton TJ, Rebbeck TR, LiVolsi VA, Zhang PJ. Differential expression of E-cadherin in lobular and ductal neoplasms of the breast and its biologic and diagnostic implications. Am J Clin Pathol 2001, **115**: 85–98.

104 Adams RL, Springall DR, Levene MM. The immunocytochemical detection of herpes simplex virus in cervical smears. A valuable technique for routine use. J Pathol 1984, **143**: 241–247.

105 Adsay NV, Merati K, Andrea A, Sarkar F, Hruban RH, Wilentz RE, Goggins M, Locobuzio-Donahue C, Longnecker DS, Klimstra DS. The dichotomy in the preinvasive neoplasia to invasive carcinoma sequence in the pancreas: differential expression of MUC1 and MUC2 supports the existence of two separate pathways and carcinogenesis. Mod Pathol 2002, **15**: 1087–1095.

106 Agre P, King LS, Yasui M, Guggino WB, Ottersen OP, Fujiyoshi Y, Engel A, Nielsen S. Aquaporin water channels – from atomic structure to clinical medicine. J Physiol 2002, **542**: 3–16.

107 Agoff SN, Lamps LW, Philip AT, Amin MB, Schmidt RA, True LD, Folpe AL. Thyroid transcription factor-1 is expressed in extrapulmonary small cell carcinomas but not in other extrapulmonary neuroendocrine tumors. Mod Pathol 2000, **13**: 238–242.

108 Albores-Saavedra J, Nedji M, Civantos P, Morales AR. Thyroglobulin in carcinoma of the thyroid. Hum Pathol 1983, **14**: 62–66.

109 Allgayer H, Babic R, Grützner KU, Beyer BCM, Tarabichi A, Schildberg FW, Heiss MM. An immunohistochemical assessment of cathepsin D in gastric carcinoma: its impact on clinical prognosis. Cancer 1997, **80**: 179–187.

110 Altini M, Coleman H, Doglioni C, Favia G, Maiorano E. Calretinin expression in ameloblastomas. Histopathology 2000, **37**: 27–32.

111 Appleton MA, Attanoos RL, Jasani B. Thrombomodulin as a marker of vascular and lymphatic tumours. Histopathology 1997, **29**: 153–157.

112 Arber D, Weiss LM. CD15: A review. Appl Immuno 1993, **1**: 17–30.

113 Arber DA, Weiss LM. CD57: a review. Appl Immuno 1995, **3**: 137–152.

114 Ariza A, Bilbao JM, Rosai J. Immunohistochemical detection of epithelial membrane antigen in normal perineurial cells and perineurioma. Am J Surg Pathol 1988, **12**: 678–685.

115 Azumi N, Battifora H. The distribution of vimentin and keratin in epithelial and nonepithelial neoplasms. A comprehensive immunohistochemical study on formalin- and alcohol-fixed tumors. Am J Clin Pathol 1987, **88**: 286–296.

116 Bacchi CE, Bonetti F, Pea M, Martignoni G, Gown AM. HMB-45: a review. Appl Immuno 1996, **4**: 73–85.

117 Barbareschi M, Pecciarini L, Cangi MG, Macri E, Rizzo A, Viale G, Doglioni C. P63, a p53, is a selective nuclear marker of myoepithelial cells of the human breast. Am J Surg Pathol 2001, **25**: 1054–1060.

118 Barbolini G, Bisetti A, Colizzi V, Damiani G, Migaldi M, Vismara D. Immunohistologic analysis of mycobacterial antigens by monoclonal antibodies in tuberculosis and mycobacteriosis. Hum Pathol 1989, **20**: 1078–1083.

119 Barondes SH, Cooper DN, Gitt MA, Leffler H. Galectins. Structure and function of a large family of animal lectins. J Biol Chem 1994, **269**: 20807–20810.

120 Barsky SH, Rao CN, Grotendorst GR, Liotta LA. Increased content of type V collagen in desmoplasia of human breast carcinoma. Am J Pathol 1982, **108**: 276–283.

121 Battifora H. Recent progress in the immunohistochemistry of solid tumors. Semin Diagn Pathol 1984, **1**: 251–271.

122 Battifora H. The multitumor (sausage) tissue block. Novel method for immunohistochemical antibody testing. Lab Invest 1986, **55**: 244–248.

123 Battifora H. Clinical applications of the immunohistochemistry of filamentous proteins. Am J Surg Pathol 1988, **12**: 24–42.

124 Baylin SB, Abeloff MD, Wieman KC, Tomford JW, Ettinger DS. Elevated histaminase (diamine oxidase) activity in small-cell carcinoma of the lung. N Engl J Med 1975, **293**: 1286–1290.

125 Beck K, Hunter I, Engel J. Structure and function of laminin. Anatomy of a multidomain glycoprotein. FASEB J 1990, **4**: 148–160.

126 Beckstead JH. Alkaline phosphatase histochemistry in human germ cell neoplasms. Am J Surg Pathol 1983, **7**: 341–349.

127 Bergeron C, Ferenczy A, Shyamala G. Distribution of estrogen receptors in various cell types of normal, hyperplastic, and neoplastic human endometrial tissues. Lab Invest 1988, **58**: 338–345.

128 Bini A, Mesa-Tejada R, Fenoglio JJ Jr, Kudryk B, Kaplan KL. Immunohistochemical characterization of fibrin(ogen)-related antigens in human tissues using monoclonal antibodies. Lab Invest 1989, **60**: 814–821.

129 Bodey B. Thymic hormones in cancer diagnostics and treatment. Expert Oncol Biol Ther 2001, **1**: 93–107.

130 Bohn H, Inaba N, Luben G. New placental proteins and their potential diagnostic significance as tumor markers. Oncodev Biol Med 1980, **2**: 141–153.

131 Bostwick DG, Null WE, Holmes D, Weber E, Barchas JD, Bensch KG. Expression of opioid peptides in tumors. N Engl J Med 1987, **317**: 1439–1443.

132 Braidotti P, Cigala C, Craziani D, Del Curto B, Dessy E, Coggi G, Bosari S, Pietra GG. Surfactant protein A expression in human normal and neoplastic breast epithelium. Am J Clin Pathol 2001, **116**: 721–728.

133 Brooks JJ. Immunohistochemistry of soft tissue tumors. Myoglobin as a tumor marker for rhabdomyosarcoma. Cancer 1982, **50**: 1757–1763.

134 Brown DC, Theaker JM, Banks PM, Gatter KC, Mason DY. Cytokeratin expression in smooth muscle and smooth muscle tumours. Histopathology 1987, **11**: 477–486.

135 Bruner JM, Connelly JH, Saya H. p53 protein immunostaining in routinely processed paraffin-embedded sections. Mod Pathol 1993, **6**: 189–194.

136 Buffa R, Crivelli O, Fiocca R, Fontana P, Solcia E. Complement-mediated unspecific binding of immunoglobulins to some endocrine cells. Histochemistry 1979, **63**: 15–21.

137 Burgdorf WHC, Duray P, Rosai J. Immunohistochemical identification of lysozyme in cutaneous lesions of alleged histiocytic nature. Am J Clin Pathol 1981, 75: 162–167.

138 Busam KJ, Iversen K, Coplan KA, Old LJ, Stockert E, Chen YT, McGregor D, Jungbluth A. Immunoreactivity for A103, and antibody to melan-A (Mart-1), in adrenocortical and other steroid tumors. Am J Surg Pathol 1998, 22: 57–63.

139 Callagy G, Cattaneo E, Daigo Y, Happerfield L, Bobrow LG, Pharoah PD, Caldas C. Molecular classification of breast carcinomas using tissue microarrays. Diagn Mol Pathol 2003, 12: 27–34.

140 Cao QJ, Jones JG, Li M. Expression of calretinin in human ovary, testis and ovarian sex cord-stromal tumors. Int J Gynecol Pathol 2001, 20: 346–352.

141 Carcangiu ML, Sibley RK, Rosai J. Clear cell change in primary thyroid tumors. A study of 38 cases. Am J Surg Pathol 1985, 9: 705–722.

142 Carpentieri DF, Nichols K, Chou PM, Matthews M, Pawel B, Huff D. The expression of WT1 in the differentiation of rhabdomyosarcomas from other pediatric small round blue cell tumors. Mod Pathol 2002, 15: 1080–1086.

143 Cerio R, Spaull JR, Oliver GF, Wilson Jones E. A study of factor XIIIa and MAC387 immunolabeling in normal and pathological skin. Am J Dermatopathol 1990, 12: 221–233.

144 Cerio R, Spaull JR, Wilson Jones E. Histiocytoma cutis. A tumour of dermal dendrocytes (dermal dendrocytoma). Br J Dermatol 1990, 120: 197–206.

144a Cessna MH, Zhou H, Sanger WG, Perkins SL, Tripp S, Pickering D, Daines C, Coffin CM. Expression of ALK1 and p80 in inflammatory myobifroblastic tumor and its mesenchymal mimics: a study of 135 cases. Mod Pathol 2002, 15: 931–938.

145 Chambonniere ML, Mosnier-Damet M, Mosnier JF. Expression of microtubule-associated protein tau by gastrointestinal stromal tumors. Hum Pathol 2001, 32: 1166–1173.

146 Chan JK. Advances in immunohistochemistry: impact on surgical pathology practice. Semin Diagn Pathol 2000, 17: 170–177.

147 Charpin C, Lachard A, Pourreau-Schneider N, Jaquemier J, Lavaut MN, Andonian C, Martin PM, Toga M. Localization of lactoferrin and nonspecific cross-reacting antigen in human breast carcinomas. An immunohistochemical study using the avidin-biotin-peroxidase complex method. Cancer 1985, 55: 2612–2617.

148 Chejfec G, Falkmer S, Grimelius L, Jacobsson B, Rodensjö M, Wiedenmann B, Franke WW, Lee I, Gould VE. Synaptophysin. A new marker for pancreatic neuroendocrine tumors. Am J Surg Pathol 1987, 11: 241–247.

149 Chess Q, Hajdu SI. The role of immunoperoxidase staining in diagnostic cytology. Acta Cytol (Baltimore) 1985, 30: 1–7.

150 Chu PG, Arber DA, Weiss LM. Expression of T/NK-cell and plasma cell antigens in nonhematopoietic epithelioid neoplasms: an immunohistochemical study of 447 cases. Am J Clin Pathol 2003, 120: 64–70.

151 Chu PG, Arber DA, Weiss LM, Cheng KL. Utility of CD10 in distinguishing between endometrial stromal sarcoma and uterine smooth muscle tumors: an immunohistochemical comparison of 34 cases. Mod Pathol 2001, 14: 465–471.

152 Chu P, Arber DA. Paraffin section detection of CD10 in 505 nonhematopoietic neoplasms. Frequent expression in renal cell carcinoma and endometrial stromal sarcoma. Am J Clin Pathol 2000, 113: 374–382.

152a Chu PG, Weiss LM. Expression of cytokeratin 5/6 in epithelial neoplasms: an immunohistochemical study of 509 cases. Mod Pathol 2002, 15: 6–10.

153 Chu PG, Weiss LM. Keratin expression in human tissues and neoplasms. Histopathology 2002, 40: 403–439.

154 Cingolani N, Shaco-Levy R, Farruggio A, Klimstra DS, Rosai J. Alpha-fetoprotein production by pancreatic tumors exhibiting acinar cell differentiation: study of five cases, one arising in a mediastinal teratoma. Hum Pathol 2000, 31: 938–944.

155 Clark HB. Immunohistochemistry of nervous system antigens. Diagnostic applications in surgical neuropathology. Semin Diagn Pathol 1984, 1: 309–316.

156 Clark HB, Minesky JJ, Agrawal D, Agrawal HC. Myelin basic protein and P2 protein are not immunohistochemical markers for Schwann cell neoplasms. A comparative study using antisera. Am J Pathol 1985, 121: 96–101.

157 Clayton F, Ordóñez NG, Hanssen GM, Hanssen H. Immunoperoxidase localization of lactalbumin in malignant breast neoplasms. Arch Pathol Lab Med 1982, 106: 268–270.

158 Clement S, Orlandi A, Bocchi L, Pizzolato G, Foschini MP, Eusebi V, Gabbiani G. Actin isoform pattern expression: a tool for the diagnosis and biological characterization of human rhabdomyosarcomas. Virchows Arch 2003, 442: 31–38.

159 Coggi G, Dell'Orto P, Braidotti P, Coggi A, Viale G. Coexpression of intermediate filaments in normal and neoplastic human tissues. A reappraisal. Ultrastruct Pathol 1989, 13: 501–514.

160 Cohen C, Berson SD, Shulman G, Budgeon LR. Immunohistochemical ferritin in hepatocellular carcinoma. Cancer 1984, 53: 1931–1935.

161 Cohen PR, Rapini RP, Farhood AI. Expression of the human hematopoietic progenitor cell antigen CD34 in vascular and spindle cell tumors. J Cutan Pathol 1993, 20: 15–20.

162 Cooper D, Schermer A, Sun T-T. Classification of human epithelia and their neoplasms using monoclonal antibodies to keratins. Strategies, applications, and limitations. Lab Invest 1985, 52: 243–256.

163 Corson JM, Pinkus GS. Intracellular myoglobin. A specific marker for skeletal muscle differentiation in soft tissue sarcomas. An immunoperoxidase study. Am J Pathol 1981, 103: 384–389.

164 Costa MJ, Ames PF, Walls J, Roth LM. Inhibin immunohistochemistry applied to ovarian neoplasms: a novel, effective, diagnostic tool. Hum Pathol 1997, 28: 1247–1254.

165 Craig SS, DeBlois G, Schwartz LB. Mast cells in human keloid, small intestine, and lung by an immunoperoxidase technique using a murine monoclonal antibody against tryptase. Am J Pathol 1986, 124: 427–435.

166 Crocker J, Jenkins R, Burnett D. Immunohistochemical demonstration of leukocyte elastase in human tissues. J Clin Pathol 1984, 37: 1114–1118.

167 Dahlstrom JE, Maxwell LE, Brodie N, Zardawi IM, Jain S. Distinctive microvillous brush border staining with HBME-1 distinguishes pleural mesotheliomas from pulmonary adenocarcinomas. Pathology 2001, 33: 287–291.

168 Dale BA. Filaggrin, the matrix protein of keratin. Am J Dermatopathol 1985, 7: 65–68.

169 Danguy A, Camby I, Kiss R. Galectins and cancer. Biochim Biophys Acta 2002, 1572: 285–293.

170 De Armond SI, Eng LF, Rubinstein U. The application of glial fibrillary acidic (GFA) protein immunohistochemistry in neurooncology. Pathol Res Pract 1980, 168: 374–394.

171 de Jong ASH, van Kessel-van Vark M, Albus-Lutter ChE, Raamsdonk W, Voûte PA. Skeletal muscle actin as tumor marker in the diagnosis of rhabdomyosarcoma in childhood. Am J Surg Pathol 1985, 9: 467–474.

172 DeLellis RA, Dayal Y. The role of immunohistochemistry in the diagnosis of poorly differentiated malignant neoplasms. Semin Oncol 1987, 14: 173–192.

173 DeLellis RA, Kwan P. Technical considerations in the immunohistochemical demonstration of intermediate filaments. Am J Surg Pathol 1988, 12: 17–23.

174 Delsol G, Stein H, Pulford KAF, Gatter KC, Erber WN, Zinne K, Mason DY. Human lymphoid cells express epithelial membrane antigen. Implications for diagnosis of human neoplasms. Lancet 1984, 2: 1124–1129.

175 de Mascarel A, Merlio JP, Coindre JM, Goussot JF, Broustet A. Gastric large cell lymphoma expressing cytokeratin but no leukocyte common antigen. A diagnostic dilemma. Am J Clin Pathol 1989, **91**: 478–481.

176 Denk H, Krepler R, Artlieb U, Gabbiani G, Rungger-Brändle E, Leoncini P, Franke WW. Proteins of intermediate filaments. An immunohistochemical and biochemical approach to the classification of soft tissue tumors. Am J Pathol 1983, **110**: 193–208.

177 Derrick EK, Barker JN, Khan A, Price ML, Macdonald DM. The tissue distribution of factor XIIIa positive cells. Histopathology 1993, **22**: 157–162.

178 DeSchryver-Kecskemeti K, Kraus Fr, Engleman W, Lacy PE. Alveolar soft part sarcoma. A malignant angioreninoma. Histochemical, immunocytochemical, and electron-microscopic study of four cases. Am J Surg Pathol 1982, **6**: 5–18.

179 De Young BR, Frierson HF, Ly MN, Smith D, Swanson PE. CD31 immunoreactivity in carcinomas and mesotheliomas. Am J Clin Pathol 1998, **110**: 374–377.

180 Dias P, Parham D, Shapiro D, Tapscott S, Houghton P. Monoclonal antibodies to the myogenic regulatory protein MyoD1. Epitope mapping and diagnostic utility. Cancer Res 1992, **52**: 6431–6439.

181 Dias P, Chen B, Dilday B, Palmer H, Hosoi H, Singh S, Wu C, Li X, Thompson J, Parham D, Qualman S, Houghton P. Strong immunostaining for myogenin in rhabdomyosarcomas is significantly associated with tumors of the alveolar subclass. Am J Pathol 2000, **156**: 399–408.

181a Di Como CJ, Urist MJ, Babayan I, Drobnjak M, Hedvat CV, Teruya-Feldstein J, Pohar K, Hoos A, Cordon-Cardo C. p63 expression profiles in human normal and tumor tissues. Clin Cancer Res 2002, **8**: 494–501.

182 Dixson JD, Forstner MJ, Garcia DM. The alpha-actinin gene family: a revised classification. J Mol Evol 2003, **56**: 1–10.

183 Domagala W, Lubinski J, Weber K, Osbom M. Intermediate filament typing of tumor cells in fine needle aspirates by means of monoclonal antibodies. Acta Cytol (Baltimore) 1986, **30**: 214–224.

184 Dorudi S, Sheffield JP, Poulsom R, Northover JM, Hart IR. E-cadherin expression in colorectal cancer. An immunocytochemical and in situ hybridization study. Am J Pathol 1993, **142**: 981–986.

185 Dranoff G, Bigner DD. A word of caution in the use of neuron-specific enolase expression in tumor diagnosis. Arch Pathol Lab Med 1984, **108**: 535.

186 Ehrig K, Leivo I, Argraves WS, Ruoslahti E, Engvall E. Merosin, a tissue-specific basement membrane protein, is a laminin-like protein. Proc Natl Acad Sci USA 1990, **87**: 3264–3268.

187 Esteban JM, Paxton R, Mehta P, Battifora H, Shively JE. Sensitivity and specificity of Gold types 1 to 5 anti-carcinoembryonic antigen monoclonal antibodies. Immunohistologic characterization in colorectal cancer and normal tissues. Hum Pathol 1993, **24**: 322–328.

188 Eusebi V, Bondi A, Rosai J. Immunohistochemical localization of myoglobin in nonmuscular cells. Am J Surg Pathol 1984, **8**: 51–55.

189 Facer P, Polak JM, Jaffe BM, Pearse AGE. Immunocytochemical demonstration of 5-hydroxytryptamine in gastrointestinal endocrine cells. Histochem J 1979, **11**: 117–121.

189a Fan G, Kotylo P, Neiman R, Braziel R. Comparison of fascin expression in anaplastic large cell lymphoma and Hodgkin disease. Am J Clin Pathol 2003, **119**: 199–204.

190 Fanburg JC, Rosenberg AE, Weaver DL, Leslie KO, Mann KG, Taatjes DJ, Tracy RP. Osteocalcin and osteonectin immunoreactivity in the diagnosis of osteosarcoma. Am J Clin Pathol 1997, **108**: 464–473.

191 Fanburg-Smith JC, Bratthauer GL, Miettinen M. Osteocalcin and osteonectin immunoreactivity in extraskeletal osteosarcoma: a study of 28 cases. Hum Pathol 1999, **30**: 32–38.

192 Faraggiana T, Gresik E, Tanaka T, Inagami T, Lupo A. Immunohistochemical localization of renin in the human kidney. J Histochem Cytochem 1982, **30**: 459–465.

193 Fasano M, Theise ND, Nalesnik M, Goswami S, Garcia De Davila MT, Finegold MJ, Greco MA. Immunohistochemical evaluation of hepatoblastomas with use of the hepatocyte-specific marker, hepatocyte paraffin 1, and the polyclonal anti-carcinoembryonic antigen. Mod Pathol 1998, **11**: 934–938.

194 Fattoum A, Roustan C, Smyczynski C, Der Terrossian E, Kassab R. Mapping the microtubule binding regions of calponin. Biochemistry 2003, **42**: 1274–1282.

194a Feldman SA, Eiden LE. The chromogranins: Their roles in secretion from neuroendocrine cells and as markers for neuroendocrine neoplasia. Endocrine Pathology 2003, **14**: 3–23.

195 Ferenczy A, Braun L, Shah KV. Human papillomavirus (HPV) in condylomatous lesions of cervix. A comparative ultrastructural and immunohistochemical study. Am J Surg Pathol 1981, **5**: 661–670.

196 Fetsch PA, Fetsch JF, Marcinola FM, Travis W, Batts KP, Abati A. Comparison of melanoma antigen recognized by T Cells (MART-1) to HMB-45: additional evidence to support a common lineage for angiomyolipoma, lymphangiomyomatosis, and clear cell sugar tumor. Mod Pathol 1998, **11**: 699–703.

197 Finan PJ, Wight DG, Lennox ES, Sacks SH, Bleehen NM. Human blood group isoantigen expression in normal and malignant gastric epithelium with anti-A and anti-B monoclonal antibodies. J Natl Canc Inst 1983, **70**: 679–685.

198 Fine SW, Li M. Expression of calretinin and the alpha-subunit on inhibin in granular cell tumors. Am J Clin Pathol 2003, **119**: 259–264.

199 Flanigan RC, King CT, Clark TD, Cash JB, Greenfield B, Sniecinski IJ, Primus FJ. Immunohistochemical demonstration of blood group antigens in neoplastic and normal human urothelium. A comparison with standard red cell adherence. J Urol 1983, **130**: 499–503.

200 Foellmer HG, Madri JA, Furthmayr H. Monoclonal antibodies to type IV collagen. Probes for the study of structure and function of basement membranes. Lab Invest 1983, **48**: 639–649.

201 Folpe AL, Hill CE, Parham DM, O'Shea PA, Weiss SW. Immunohistochemical detection of Fli-1 protein expression: a study of 132 round cell tumors with emphasis on CD99-positive mimics of Ewing's sarcoma/primitive neuroectodermal tumor. Am J Surg Pathol 2000, **24**: 1657–1662.

202 Folpe AL, Chand EM, Goldblum JR, Weiss SW. Expression of Fli-1, a nuclear transcription factor, distinguishes vascular neoplasms from potential mimics. Am J Surg Pathol 2001, **25**: 1061–1066.

203 Foschini MP, Barccarini P, Dal Monte PR, Sinard J, Eusebi V, Rosai J. Albumin gene expression in adenocarcinomas with hepatoid differentiation. Virchows Arch 1999, **433**: 537–541.

204 Franke FE, Pauls K, Kerkman L, Steger K, Klonisch T, Metzger R, Alhenc-Gelas F, Burkhardt E, Bergmann M, Danilov SM. Somatic isoform of angiotensin I-converting enzyme in the pathology of testicular germ cell tumors. Hum Pathol 2001, **31**: 1466–1476.

205 Friedman HD, Tatum AH. HMB-45 positive malignant lymphoma. A case report with literature review of aberrant HMB-45 reactivity. Arch Pathol Lab Med 1991, **115**: 826–830.

206 Gatalica Z, Miettinen M. Distribution of carcinoma antigens CA19-9 and CA15-3: an immunohistochemical study of 400 tumors. Appl Immunohistochem 1994, **2**: 205–211.

207 Gatter KC, Alcock C, Heryet A, Pulford KA, Heyderman E, Taylor-Papadimitriou J, Stein H, Mason DY. The differential diagnosis of routinely processed anaplastic tumours using monoclonal antibodies. Am J Clin Pathol 1984, **82**: 33–43.

208 Gatter KC, Mason DY. The use of monoclonal antibodies for histopathological diagnosis of human malignancy. Semin Oncol 1982, **9**: 517–525.

209 Gavrieli Y, Sherman Y, Ben-Sasson SA. Identification of

programmed cell death in situ via specific labeling of nuclear DNA fragmentation. J Cell Biol 1992, **119**: 493–501.

210 Georges E, Bradley G, Gariepy J, Ling V. Detection of P-glycoprotein isoforms by gene-specific monoclonal antibodies. Proc Natl Acad Sci USA 1990, **87**: 152–156.

211 Gold P, Shuster J, Freedman SO. Carcinoembryonic antigen (CEA) in clinical medicine. Historical perspectives, pitfalls and projections. Cancer 1978, **42**: 1399–1405.

212 Goldsmith JD, Pawel B, Goldblum JR, Pasha TL, Roberts S, Nelson P, Khurana JS, Barr FG, Zhang PJ. Detection and diagnostic utilization of placental alkaline phosphatase in muscular tissue and tumors with myogenic differentiation. Am J Surg Pathol 2002, **26**: 1627–1630.

213 Gotzos V, Wintergerst ES, Musy JP, Spichtin HP, Genton CY. Selective distribution of calretinin in adenocarcinomas of the human colon and adjacent tissues. Am J Surg Pathol 1999, **23**: 701–711.

214 Gould VE. Synaptophysin. A new and promising pen-neuroendocrine marker. Arch Pathol Lab Med 1987, **111**: 791–794.

215 Gould VE. Cytokeratins in epithelial and non-epithelial cells and tumors (editorial). Arq Patol 1994, **26**: 3–9.

216 Gould VE, Orucevic A, Zentgraf H, Gattuso P, Martinez N, Alonso A. Nup88 (karyoporin) in human malignant neoplasms and dysplasias: correlations of immunostaining of tissue sections, cytologic smears, and immunoblot analysis. Hum Pathol 2002, **33**: 536–544.

217 Gown A, de Weber N, Battifora H. Microwave-based antigenic unmasking. A revolutionary new technique for routine immunohistochemistry. Appl Immunohistochem 1993, **1**: 256–266.

218 Granter SR, Weilbaecher KN, Quigley C, Fletcher CD, Fisher DE. Clear cell sarcoma shows immunoreactivity for microphthalmia transcription factor: further evidence for melanocytic differentiation. Mod Pathol 2001, **14**: 6–9.

219 Granter SR, Weilbaecher KN, Quigley C, Fletcher CD, Fisher DE. Microphthalmia transcription factor: not a sensitive or specific marker for the diagnosis of desmoplastic melanoma and spindle cell (non-desmoplastic) melanoma. Am J Dermatopathol 2001, **23**: 185–189.

220 Greenwalt DE, Johnson VG, Kuhajda FP, Eggleston JC, Mather IH. Localization of a membrane glycoprotein in benign fibrocystic disease and infiltrating duct carcinomas of the human breast with the use of monoclonal antibody to guinea pig milk fat globule membrane. Am J Pathol 1985, **118**: 351–359.

221 Gröne H-J, Weber K, Helmchen U, Osborn M. Villin. A marker of brush border differentiation and cellular origin in human renal cell carcinoma. Am J Pathol 1986, **124**: 294–302.

222 Griffin NR, Wells M. Immunolocalization of alpha-amylase in ovarian mucinous tumours. Int J Gynecol Pathol 1990, **9**: 41–46.

223 Guarda LA, Ordonez NG, Smith JL Jr, Hanssen G. Immunoperoxidase localization of factor VIII in angiosarcomas. Arch Pathol Lab Med 1982, **106**: 515–516.

224 Gultekin SH, Rosai J, Demopoulos A, Graus YF, Posner JB, Dalmau J, Rosenblum MK. Hu Immunolabeling as a marker of neural and neuroendocrine differentiation in normal and neoplastic human tissues: assessment using a recombinant anti-hu fab fragment. Int J Surg Pathol 2000, **8**: 109–117.

225 Gultekin SH, Dalmau J, Graus Y, Posner JB, Rosenblum MK. Anti-Hu immunolabeling as an index of neuronal differentiation in human brain tumors: a study of 112 central neuroepithelial neoplasms. Am J Surg Pathol 1998, **22**: 195–200.

226 Hagn C, Schmid KW, Fischer-Colbrie R, Winkler H. Chromogranin A, B, and C in human adrenal medulla and endocrine tissues. Lab Invest 1986, **55**: 405–411.

227 Haimoto H, Hosoda S, Kato K. Differential distribution of immunoreactive S100-α and S100-β proteins in normal nonnervous human tissues. Lab Invest 1987, **57**: 489–498.

228 Harris JP, South MA. Secretory component. A glandular epithelial cell marker. Am J Pathol 1981, **105**: 47–53.

229 Harris MD, Moore IE, Steart PV, Weller RO. Protein gene products (PGP) 9.5 as a reliable marker in primitive neuroectodermal tumours – an immunohistochemical study of 21 childhood cases. Histopathology 1990, **16**: 271–277.

230 Heitz PU, von Herbay G, Klöppel G, Komminoth P, Kasper M, Höfloer H, Müller K-M, Oberholzer M. The expression of subunits of human chorionic gonadotropin (hGC) by nontrophoblastic, nonendocrine, and endocrine tumors. Am J Clin Pathol 1987, **88**: 467–472.

231 Herrera GA. Ultrastructural immunolabeling. A general overview of techniques and applications. Ultrastruct Pathol 1992, **16**: 37–45.

232 Herrera GA, Turbat-Herrera EA, Lott RL. S-100 protein expression by primary and metastatic adenocarcinomas. Am J Clin Pathol 1988, **89**: 168–176.

233 Heyderman E, Chapman DV, Richardson TC, Calvert I, Rosen S. Human chorionic gonadotropin and human placental lactogen in extragonadal tumors. Cancer 1985, **56**: 2674–2682.

234 Hilkens Bujis F, Hilgers J, Hageman Ph, Calafat J, Sonnenberg A, van der Valk M. Monoclonal antibodies against human milk-fat globule membranes detecting differentiation antigens of the mammary gland and its tumors. Int J Cancer 1984, **34**: 197–206.

235 Hill DA, Pfeifer JD, Marley EF, Dehner LP, Humphrey PA, Zhu X, Swanson PE. WT1 staining reliably differentiates desmoplastic small round cell tumor from Ewing sarcoma / primitive neuroectodermal tumor. An immunohistochemical and molecular diagnostic study. Am J Clin Pathol 2000, **114**: 345–353.

236 Hiraki H, Hoshi N, Hasegawa H, Tanigawa T, Emura I, Seito T, Yamaki T, Fukuda T, Watanabe K, Suzuki T. Regular immunohistochemical localization of endothelin-1 and endothelin-B receptor in normal, hyperplastic and neoplastic human adrenocortical cells. Pathol Int 1997, **47**: 117–125.

237 Hohl D. Expression patterns of loricrin in dermatological disorders. Am J Dermatopathol 1993, **15**: 20–27.

238 Hoos A, Cordon-Cardo C. Tissue microarray profiling of cancer specimens and cell lines: opportunities and limitations. Lab Invest 2001, **81**: 1331–1338.

239 Hartmann CA, Sperling M, Stein H. So-called fibroepithelial polyps of the vagina exhibiting an unusual but uniform antigen profile characterized by expression of desmin and steroid hormone receptors but no muscle-specific actin or macrophage markers. Am J Clin Pathol 1990, **93**: 604–608.

240 Hornick JL, Fletcher CD. Immunohistochemical staining for KIT (CD117) in soft tissue sarcomas is very limited in distribution. Am J Clin Pathol 2002, **117**: 188–193.

241 Howard DR, Taylor CR. A method for distinguishing benign from malignant breast lesions utilizing antibody present in normal human sera. Cancer 1979, **43**: 2279–2287.

242 Hsu SM, Raine L, Fanger H. Use of avidin-biotin peroxidase complex (ABC) in immunoperoxidase techniques. A comparison between ABC and unlabeled antibody (PAP) procedures. J Histochem Cytochem 1981, **29**: 557–580.

243 Hu B, McPhaul L, Cornford M, Gaal K, Mirra J, French SW. Expression of Tau protein and tubulin in extraskeletal myxoid chondrosarcoma, chordoma, and other chondroid tumors. Am J Clin Pathol 1999, **112**: 189–193.

244 Hughes JH, Cohen MB. Nuclear Matrix proteins and their potential applications to diagnostic pathology. Am J Clin Pathol 1999, **111**: 267–274.

245 Hull SR, Carraway KL. Mechanism of expression of Thomsen-Friedenreich (T) antigen at the cell surface of a mammary adenocarcinoma. FASEB J 1988, **2**: 2380–2384.

246 Ichikawa T, Masumoto J, Kaneko M, Saida T, Sagara J, Taniguchi S. Expression of moesin and its associated molecule CD44 in epithelial skin tumors. J Cutan Pathol 1998, **25**: 237–243.

247 Iczkowski KA, Bostwick DG, Roche PC, Cheville JC. Inhibin A is a sensitive and specific marker for testicular sex cord-stromal tumors. Mod Pathol 1998, **11**: 774–779.

248 Iglesias M, Plowman GD, Woodworth CD. Interleukin-6 and interleukin-6 soluble receptor regulate proliferation of normal, human papillomavirus-immortalized, and carcinoma-derived cervical cells in vitro. Am J Pathol 1995, **146**: 944–952.

249 Isaacson P. Immunochemical demonstration of J chain. A marker of B-cell malignancy. J Clin Pathol 1979, **32**: 802–807.

250 Ishikura H, Sasano H. Histopathologic and immunohistochemical study of steroidogenic cells in the stroma of ovarian tumors. Int J Gynecol Pathol 1998, **17**: 261–265.

251 Iwasaki R, Yamamuro T, Kotoura Y, Okumura H, Kasai R, Nakashima Y. Immunohistochemical study of bone GLA protein in primary bone tumors. Cancer 1992, **70**: 619–624.

252 Jacobsen M, Jacobsen GK. The influence of various fixatives on the immunohistochemical demonstration of a number of plasma proteins and oncofetal proteins in paraffin embedded material. Acta Pathol Microbiol Immunol Scand (A) 1984, **92**: 461–468.

253 Jass JR. Mucin core proteins as differentiation markers in the gastrointestinal tract. Histopathology 2001, **37**: 561–564.

253a Jiang Z, Fanger GR, Woda BA, Banner BF, Algate P, Dresser K, Xu J, Chu PG. Expression of α-methylacyl-CoA racemase (P504S) in various malignant neoplasms and normal tissues: a study of 761 cases. Hum Pathol **34**: 792–796.

254 Johnson MW, Kerfoot C, Bushnell T, Li M, Vinters HV. Hamartin and tuberin expression in human tissues. Mod Pathol 2001, **14**: 202–210.

255 Jorda M, De MB, Nadji M. Calretinin and inhibin are useful in separating adrenocortical neoplasms from pheochromocytomas. Appl Immuno Mol Morphol 2002, **10**: 67–70.

255a Jorda M, Gomez-Fernandez C, Romaguera R, Poniecka A, Ganjei-Azar P. The impact of a rapid tissue processing method on the turn-around-time of surgical pathology reports: A six-month experience at the University of Miami hospital and clinics. Mod Pathol 2003, **16**: 317a.

256 Jothy S, Brazinsky SA, Chin-A-Loy M, Haggarty A, Krantz MJ, Cheung M, Fuks A. Characterization of monoclonal antibodies to carcinoembryonic antigen with increased tumor specificity. Lab Invest 1986, **54**: 108–117.

257 Judkins AR, Montone KT, LiVolsi VA, van de Rijn M. Sensitivity and specificity of antibodies on necrotic tumor tissue. Am J Clin Pathol 1998, **110**: 641–646.

258 Jungbluth AA, Busam KJ, Gerald WL, Stockert E, Complan KA, Iversen K, MacGregor DP, Old LJ, Chen YT. A103: an anti-melan-A monoclonal antibody for the detection of malignant melanoma in paraffin-embedded tissues. Am J Surg Pathol 1998, **22**: 595–602.

259 Kahn HJ, Marks A, Thom H, Baumal R. Role of antibody of S100 protein in diagnostic pathology. Am J Clin Pathol 1983, **79**: 341–347.

260 Kakar S, Muir T, Murphy LM, Lloyd RV, Burgart LJ. Immunoreactivity of Hep Par 1 in hepatic and extrahepatic tumors and its correlation with albumin in situ hybridisation hepatocellular carcinoma. Am J Clin Pathol 2003, **119**: 361–366.

261 Kalir T, Wang BY, Goldfischer M, Haber RS, Reder I, Demopoulos R, Cohen CJ, Burstein DE. Immunohistochemical staining in GLUT1 in benign, borderline, and malignant ovarian epithelia. Cancer 2002, **94**: 1078–1082.

262 Kapur RP, Bigler SA, Skelly M, Gown AM. Anti-melanoma monoclonal antibody HMB-45 identifies an oncofetal glycoconjugate associated with immature melanosomes. J Histochem Cytochem 1992, **40**: 207–212.

263 Kato K, Ishiguro Y, Ariyoshi Y. Enolase isozymes and disease markers. Distribution of three enolase subunits (α, β and γ) in various human tissues. Dis Markers 1983, **1**: 213–220.

264 Kaufmann O, Georgi T, Dietel M. Utility of 123C3 monoclonal antibody against CD56 (NCAM) for the diagnosis of small cell carcinomas on paraffin sections. Hum Pathol 1998, **28**: 1373–1378.

265 Kaufmann O, Volmerig J, Dietel M. Uroplakin III is a highly specific and moderately sensitive immunohistochemical marker for primary and metastatic urothelial carcinomas. Am J Clin Pathol 2000, **113**: 683–687.

266 Kawai K, Takahashi H, Ikuta F, Tanimura K, Homda Y, Yamazaki H. The occurrence of catecholamine neurons in a parietal lobe ganglioglioma. Cancer 1987, **60**: 1532–1536.

267 Keen CE, Szakacs S, Okon E, Rubin JS, Bryant BM. CA125 and thyroglobulin staining in papillary carcinomas of thyroid and ovarian origin is not completely specific for site of origin. Histopathology 1999, **34**: 113–117.

268 Khoor A, Whitsett JA, Stahlman MT, Halter SA. Expression of surfactant protein B precursor and surfactant protein B mRNA in adenocarcinoma of the lung. Mod Pathol 1997, **10**: 62–67.

269 Koch PJ, Goldschmidt MD, Zimbelmann R, Troyanovsky R, Franke WW. Complexity and expression patterns of the desmosomal cadherins. Proc Natl Acad Sci USA 1992, **89**: 353–357.

270 Koelma IA, Nap M, Rodenburg CJ, Fleuren GJ. The value of tumour marker CA 125 in surgical pathology. Histopathology 1987, **11**: 187–294.

271 Koeppen HK, Wright BD, Burt AD, Quirke P, Mc Nichol AM, Dybdal NO, Sliwkowski MX, Hillan KJ. Overexpression of HER2/neu in solid tumors: an immunohistochemical survey. Histopathology 2001, **38**: 96–104.

272 Kommoss F, Schmidt D, Coerdt W, Olert J, Muntefering H. Immunohistochemical expression analysis of inhibin-alpha and -beta subunits in partial and complete moles, trophlatic tumors, and endometrial deciduas. Int J Gynecol Pathol 2001, **20**: 380–385.

273 Kononen J, Bubendorf L, Kallioniemi A, Barlund M, Schraml P, Leighton S, Torhorst J, Mihatsch MJ, Sauter G, Kallioniemi OP. Tissue microarrays for high-throughput molecular profiling of tumor specimens. Nat Med 1999, **4**: 844–847.

274 Kosmehl H, Berndt A, Katenkamp D. Molecular variants of fibronectin and laminin: structure, physiological occurrence and histopathological aspects. Virchows Arch 1997, **429**: 311–322.

275 Kostyu D, Amos DB. The major histocompatibility complex. Genetic polymorphism and disease susceptibility. In Stanbury JB et al. (eds): Metabolic basis of inherited disease, ed. 5. New York, 1982, McGraw-Hill Book Co., p. 77.

276 Koukoulis GK, Gould VE, Bhattacharyya A, Gould JE, Howeedy AA, Virtanen I. Tenascin in normal, reactive, hyperplastic, and neoplastic tissues. Biologic and pathologic implications. Hum Pathol 1991, **22**: 636–643.

277 Kovacs JA, Ng VL, Masur H, Leoung G, Hadley WK, Evans G, Lane HC, Ognibene FP, Shelhamer J, Parrillo JE, Gill VJ. Diagnosis of *Pneumocystis carinii* pneumonia. Improved detection in sputum with use of monoclonal antibodies. N Engl J Med 1988, **318**: 589–593.

278 Krishna M, Lloyd RV, Batts KP. Detection of albumin messenger RNA in hepatic and extrahepatic neoplasms: a marker of hepatocellular differentiation. Am J Surg Pathol 1997, **21**: 147–152.

279 Krishnamurthy S, Jungbluth AA, Busam KJ, Rosai J. Uterine tumors resembling ovarian sex-cord tumors have an immunophenotype consistent with true sex-cord differentiation. Am J Surg Pathol 1998, **22**: 1078–1082.

280 Kuhajda FP, Bohn H, Mendelsohn G. Pregnancy-specific beta-1 glycoprotein (SP-1) in breast carcinoma. Pathologic and clinical considerations. Cancer 1984, **54**: 1392–1396.

281 Kumar S, Perlman E, Harris CA, Raffeld M, Tsokos M. Myogenin is a specific marker for rhabdomyosarcomas: an immunohistochemical study in paraffin-embedded tissues. Mod Pathol 2001, **13**: 988–993.

282 Kurman RJ, Ganjei P, Nadji M. Contributions of immunocytochemistry to the diagnosis and study of ovarian neoplasms. Int J Gynecol Pathol 1984, **3**: 3–26.

283 Kurman RJ, Goebelsmann U, Taylor CR. Localization of steroid hormones in functional ovarian tumors. In DeLellis RA (ed.): Diagnostic immunohistochemistry. New York, 1981, Masson Publishing USA, Inc., pp. 137–148.

284 Kuroda N, Toi M, Miyazaki E, Naruse K, Hiroi M, Enzan H. Expression of osteopontin in various types of renal tumors. J Urol Pathol 2002, **12**: 79–92.

285 Kurtin PJ, Pinkus GS. Leukocyte common antigen. A diagnostic discriminant between hematopoietic and nonhematopoietic neoplasms in paraffin sections using monoclonal antibodies. Correlation with immunologic studies and ultrastructural localization. Hum Pathol 1985, **16**: 353–365.

286 Lager DJ, Callaghan EJ, Worth SF, Raife TJ, Lentz SR. Cellular localization of thrombomodulin in human epithelium and squamous malignancies. Am J Pathol 1995, **146**: 933–943.

287 Lai ML, Rizzo N, Liguori C, Zucca G, Faa G. Alpha-1-antichymotrypsin immunoreactivity in papillary carcinoma of the thyroid gland. Histopathology 1999, **33**: 332–336.

288 Lam KY, Lo CY, Wat MS, Fan ST. Malignant insulinoma with hepatoid differentiation: a unique case with alpha-fetoprotein production. Endocr Pathol 2001, **12**: 351–354.

289 Lamps LW, Folpe AL. The diagnostic value of hepatocyte paraffin antibody 1 in differentiation hepatocellular neoplasms from nonhepatic tumors: a review. Adv Anat Pathol 2003, **10**: 39–43.

290 Lantuejoul S, Lavarriere MH, Sturm N, Moro D, Frey G, Brambilla C, Brambilla E. NCAM (neural cell adhesion molecules) expression in malignant mesothelioma. Hum Pathol 2000, **31**: 415–421.

291 Lantuejoul S, Moro D, Michalides RJ, Brambilla C, Brambilla E. Neural cell adhesion molecules (NCAM) and NCAM-PSA expression in neuroendocrine lung tumors. Am J Surg Pathol 1998, **22**: 1267–1276.

292 La Rosa S, Capella C, Lloyd RV. Localization of myosin XVA in endocrine tumor of gut and pancreas. Endocr Pathol 2002, **13**: 29–38.

293 Larsson L. Tissue preparation methods for light microscopic immunohistochemistry. Appl Immunohistochem 1993, **1**: 2–16.

294 Larsson L, Alumets J, Eriksson B, Hakanson R, Lundquist G, Oberg K, Sundler F. Antiserum directed against chromogranin A and B (CAB) is a useful marker for peptide hormone-producing endocrine cells and tumors. Endocr Pathol 1992, **3**: 14–22.

295 Lau SK, Prakash S, Geller SA, Alsabeh R. Comparative immunohistochemical profile of hepatocellular carcinoma, cholangiocarcinoma, and metastatic adenocarinoma. Hum Pathol 2002, **33**: 1175–1181.

296 Lau SK, Luthringer DJ, Eisen RN. Thyroid transcription factor-1: a review. Appl Immuno Mol Morphol 2002, **10**: 97–102.

297 Lazarides E, Granger BL, Gard DL, O'Connor CM, Breckler J, Price M, Danto SI. Desmin- and vimentin-containing filaments and their role in the assembly of the Z disc in muscle cells. Cold Spring Harbor Symp Quant Biol 1982, **46**: 351–378.

298 Leader M, Collins M, Patel J, Henry K. Vimentin. An evaluation of its role as a tumour marker. Histopathology 1987, **11**: 63–72.

299 Leader M, Patel J, Collins M, Henry K. Anti-α1-antichymotrypsin staining of 194 sarcomas, 38 carcinomas, and 17 malignant melanomas. Its lack of specificity as a tumour marker. Am J Surg Pathol 1987, **11**: 133–139.

300 Leake J, Woolas RP, Daniel J, Oram DH, Brown CL. Immunocytochemical and serological expression of CA125: a clinicopathological study of 40 malignant ovarian epithelial tumours. Histopathology 1994, **24**: 57–64.

301 Lee AK, DeLellis RA, Rosen PP, Herbert-Stanton T, Tallberg K, Garcia C, Wolfe HJ. Alpha-lactalbumin as an immunohistochemical marker for breast carcinomas. Am J Surg Pathol 1984, **8**: 93–100.

302 Lee AK, DeLellis RA, Rosen PP, Saigo PE, Gangi MD, Bagin R, Groshen S, Wolfe HJ. ABH blood group isoantigen expression in breast carcinomas. An immunohistochemical evaluation using monoclonal antibodies. Am J Clin Pathol 1985, **83**: 308–319.

303 Lefebvre V, De Crombrugghe B. Toward understanding SOX9 function in chondrocyte differentiation. Matrix Biol 1998, **16**: 529–540.

304 Lehr HA, Folpe A, Yaziji H, Kommoss F, Gown AM. Cytokeratin 8 immunostaining pattern and E-cadherin expression distinguish lobular from ductal breast carcinoma. Am J Clin Pathol 2000, **114**: 190–196.

305 Leivo I, Engvall E, Laurila P, Miettinen M. Distribution of merosin, a laminin-related tissue-specific basement membrane protein, in human Schwann cell neoplasms. Lab Invest 1989, **61**: 426–432.

306 Lele SM, Graves K, Galatica Z. Immunohistochemical detection of maspin is a useful adjunct in distinguishing radial sclerosing lesion from tubular carcinoma of the breast. Appl Immuno Mol Morphol 2000, **8**: 32–36.

307 Leroy X, Zini L, Leteurtre E, Serimech F, Porche TN, Aubert JP, Gosselin B, Copin MC. Morphologic subtyping of papillary renal cell carcinoma: correlation with prognosis and differential expression of MUC1 between the two subtypes. Mod Pathol 2002, **15**: 1126–1130.

308 Lewis RE Jr, Johnson WW, Cruse JM. Pitfalls and caveats in the methodology for immunoperoxidase staining in surgical pathologic diagnosis. Surv Synth Pathol Res 1983, **1**: 134–152.

309 Li C-Y, Lazcano-Villareal O, Pierre RV, Yam LT. Immunocytochemical identification of cells in serous effusions. Technical considerations. Am J Clin Pathol 1987, **88**: 696–706.

310 Liberman E, Weidner N. Papillary and follicular neoplasms of the thyroid gland: differential immunohistochemical staining with high-molecular-weight keratin and involucrin. AIMM 2000, **8**: 42–48.

311 Liddle C, Reid WA, Kennedy JS, Miler ID, Home HW. Immunolocalization of prealbumin. Distribution in normal human tissue. J Pathol 1985, **146**: 107–113.

312 Linden MD, Nathanson SD, Zarbo RJ. Evaluation of anti-P53 antibody staining. Quality control and technical considerations. Appl Immunohistochem 1994, **2**: 218–224.

313 Ling V, Luxenberg D, Wang J, Nickbarg E, Leenen PJ, Neben S, Kobayashi M. Structural identification of the hematopoietic progenitor antigen ER-MP12 as the vascular endothelial adhesion molecule PECAM-1(CD31). Eur J Immol 1997, **27**: 509–514.

314 Listrom MB, Dalton LW. Comparison of keratin monoclonal antibodies MAK6, AE1:AE3, and CAM-5.2. Am J Clin Pathol 1987, **88**: 297–301.

315 Listrom MB, Fenoglio-Preiser CM. Does laminin immunoreactivity really distinguish between lymphatics and blood vessels? Surg Pathol 1988, **1**: 71–74.

316 Lloyd RV. Immunohistochemical localization of chromogranin in normal and neoplastic endocrine tissues. Pathol Annu 1987, **22**(Pt 2): 69–90.

317 Lloyd RV. Distinguishing benign from malignant thyroid lesions: galectin 3 as the latest candidate. Endocr Pathol 2001, **12**: 255–257.

318 Lloyd RV, Cano M, Rosa P, Hille A, Huttner WB. Distribution of chromogranin A and secretogranin I (chromogranin B) in neuroendocrine cells and tumors. Am J Pathol 1988, **130**: 296–304.

319 Loning Th, Kuhler Ch, Caselitz J, Stegner H-E. Keratin and tissue polypeptide antigen profiles of the cervical mucosa. Int J Gynecol Pathol 1983, **2**: 105–112.

320 Loy TS, Chapman RK, Diaz-Arias AA, Bulatao IS, Bickel JT. Distribution of BCA-225 in adenocarcinomas. An immunohistochemical study of 446 cases. Am J Clin Pathol 1991, **96**: 326–329.

321 Loy TS, Nashelsky MB. Reactivity of B72.3 with adenocarcinomas. An immunohistochemical study of 476 cases. Cancer 1993, **72**: 2495–2498.

322 Loy TS, Quesenberry JT, Sharp SC. Distribution of CA 125 in adenocarcinomas. An immunohistochemical study of 481 cases. Am J Clin Pathol 1992, **98**: 175–179.

323 Loy TS, Sharp SC, Andershock CJ, Craig SB. Distribution of CA 19–9 in adenocarcinomas and transitional cell carcinomas. An immunohistochemical study of 527 cases. Am J Clin Pathol 1993, **99**: 726–728.

324 Loy TS, Springer D, Chapman RK, Diaz-Arias AA, Bulatao IS, Bickel JT. Lack of specificity of monoclonal antibody B72.3 in distinguishing chronic pancreatitis from pancreatic adenocarcinoma. Am J Clin Pathol 1991, **96**: 684–688.

324a Lugli A, Forster Y, Haas P, Nocito A, Bucher C, Mirlacher M, Storz M, Mihatsch MJ, Sauter G. Calretinin expression in human normal and neoplastic tissues: a tissue microarray analysis on 5223 tissue samples. Hum Pathol **34**: 994–1000.

325 Lundqvist M, Wilander E. A simple procedure for immunocytochemical- and silver-staining of endocrine cells in the same section. Acta Pathol Microbiol Immunol Scand (A) 1983, **91**: 493–494.

326 Macado JC, Soares P, Carneiro F, Rocha A, Beck S, Blin N, Berx G, Sobrinho-Simoes M. E-Cadherin gene mutations provide a genetic basis for the phenotypic divergence of mixed gastric carcinomas. Lab Invest 1999, **79**: 459–465.

327 Mackie EJ, Chiquet-Ehrismann R, Pearson CA, Inaguma Y, Taya K, Kawarada Y, Sakakura T. Tenascin is a stromal marker for epithelial malignancy in the mammary gland. Proc Natl Acad Sci USA 1987, **84**: 4621–4625.

328 Magro A, Ruggieri M, Fraggetta F, Grasso S, Viale G. Cathepsin D is marker of ganglion cell differentiation in the developing and neoplastic human peripheral sympathetic nervous tissues. Virchows Arch 2000, **437**: 406–412.

329 Maitra A, Murakata LA, Albores-Saavedra J. Immunoreactivity for hepatocyte paraffin-1 antibody in hepatoid adenocarcinomas of the gastrointestinal tract. Am J Clin Pathol 2001, **115**: 689–694.

330 Mason DY, Taylor CR. The distribution of muramidase (lysozyme) in human tissues. J Clin Pathol 1975, **28**: 124–132.

331 Massi D, Franchi A, Borgognoni L, Reali UM, Santucci M. Osteonectin expression correlates with clinical outcome in thin cutaneous malignant melanomas. Hum Pathol 1999, **30**: 339–344.

332 Matsukita S, Nomoto M, Kitajima S, Tanaka S, Goto M, Irimura T, Kim YS, Sato E, Yonezawa S. Expression of mucins (MUC1, MUC2, MUC5AC and MUC6) in mucinous carcinoma of the breast: comparison with invasive ductal carcinoma. Histopathology 2002, **42**: 26–36.

333 Mayall FG, Goddard H, Gibbs AR. An assessment of involucrin as a diagnostically useful immunohistochemical marker in lung tumours. Histopathology 1992, **20**: 53–55.

334 Mazal PR, Schaufler R, Altenhuber-Muller R, Haitel A, Watschinger B, Kratzik C, Krupitza G, Regele H, Meisl FT, Zechner O, Kerjaschki D, Susani M. Derivation of nephrogenic adenomas from renal tubular cells in kidney-transplant recipients. N Engl J Med 2002, **347**: 653–659.

335 Mazoujian G, Pinkus GS, Davis S, Haagensen DE Jr. Immunohistochemistry of a gross cystic disease fluid protein (GCDFP-15) of the breast. A marker of apocrine epithelium and breast carcinomas. Am J Pathol 1983, **110**: 105–112.

336 McCarty KS Jr, McCarty KS Sr. Histochemical approaches to steroid receptor analyses. Semin Diagn Pathol 1984, **2**: 297–308.

337 McCarty KS Jr, Miller LS, Cox EB, Konrath J, McCarty KS Sr. Estrogen receptor analyses. Correlation of biochemical and immunohistochemical methods using monoclonal antireceptor antibodies. Arch Pathol Lab Med 1985, **109**: 716–721.

338 McCluggage WG. Value of inhibin staining in gynaecological pathology. Int J Gynecol Pathol 2001, **20**: 79–85.

339 McNicol AM, Richmond JA. Optimizing immunohistochemistry: antigen retrieval and signal amplification. Histopathology 1998, **32**: 97–103.

340 McNutt NS. The S100 family of multipurpose calcium-binding proteins. J Cutan Pathol 1999, **25**: 521–529.

341 Mendelsohn G, Eggleston JC, Weisburger WR, Gann DS, Baylin SB. Calcitonin and histaminase in C-cell hyperplasia and medullary thyroid carcinoma. A light microscopic and immunohistochemical study. Am J Pathol 1978, **92**: 35–52.

342 Mesa-Tejada R, Palakodety RB, Leon JA, Khatcherian AO, Greaton CJ. Immunocytochemical distribution of a breast carcinoma associated glycoprotein identified by monoclonal antibodies. Am J Pathol 1988, **130**: 305–314.

343 Michels S, Swanson PE, Robb JA, Wick MR. Leu-7 in small cell neoplasms. An immunohistochemical study with ultrastructural correlations. Cancer 1987, **60**: 2958–2964.

344 Miettinen M. Immunoreactivity for cytokeratin and epithelial membrane antigen in leiomyosarcoma. Arch Pathol Lab Med 1988, **112**: 637–640.

345 Miettinen M. Keratin immunohistochemistry. Update of applications and pitfalls. Pathol Annu 1993, **28**(Pt 2): 113–143.

346 Miettinen MM, Sarlomo-Rikala M, Kovatich AJ, Lasota J. Calponin and h-caldesmon in soft tissue tumors: consistent h-caldesmon immunoreactivity in gastrointestinal stromal tumors indicates traits of smooth muscle differentiation. Mod Pathol 1999, **12**: 756–762.

347 Miettinen M, Limom J, Niezabitowski A, Lasota J. Calretinin and other mesothelioma markers in synovial sarcoma: analysis of antigenic similarities and differences with malignant mesothelioma. Am J Surg Pathol 2001, **25**: 610–617.

348 Miettinen M, Sarlomo-Rikala M. Expression of calretinin, thrombomodulin, keratin 5, and mesothelin in lung carcinomas of different types: an immunohistochemical analysis of 596 tumors in comparison with epithelioid mesotheliomas of the pleura. Am J Surg Pathol 2003, **27**: 150–158.

349 Miettinen M, Kovatich AJ. HBME-1A monoclonal antibody useful in the differential diagnosis of mesothelioma, adenocarcinoma, and soft-tissue and bone tumors. Appl Immuno 1995, **3**: 115–122.

350 Miettinen M, Castello R, Wayner E, Schwarting R. Distribution of VLA integrins in, solid tumors. Emergence or tumor-type-related expression. Patterns in carcinomas and sarcomas. Am J Pathol 1993, **142**: 1009–1018.

351 Miettinen M, Foidart J-M, Ekblom P. Immunohistochemical demonstration of laminin, the major glycoprotein of basement membranes, as an aid in the diagnosis of soft tissue tumors. Am J Clin Pathol 1983, **79**: 306–311.

352 Miettinen M, Holthofer H, Lehto V-P, Miettinen A, Virtanen I. *Ulex europaeus* I lectin as a marker for tumors derived from endothelial cells. Am J Clin Pathol 1983, **79**: 32–36.

353 Miettinen M, Kovatich A. Keratins in soft-tissue sarcomas—common phenomenon or technical artifact? Am J Clin Pathol 1991, **96**: 673–675.

354 Miettinen M, Lehto V-P, Badlev RA, Virtanen I. Alveolar rhabdomyosarcoma. Demonstration of the muscle type of intermediate filament protein, desmin, as a diagnostic aid. Am J Pathol 1982, **108**: 246–251.

355 Miettinen M, Lehto V-P, Virtanen I. Antibodies to intermediate filament proteins in the diagnosis and classification of human tumors. Ultrastruct Pathol 1984, **7**: 83–107.

356 Mills SE, Stallings RG, Austin MB. Angiomatoid carcinoma of the thyroid gland. Anaplastic carcinoma with follicular and medullary features mimicking angiosarcoma. Am J Clin Pathol 1986, **86**: 674–678.

357 Mir R, Kahn LB. Immunohistochemistry of Hodgkin's disease. A study of 20 cases. Cancer 1983, **52**: 2064–2071.

358 Moch H, Schrami P, Budendorf L, Mirlacher M, Kononen J, Gasser T, Mihatsch MJ, Kallioniemi OP, Sauter G. High-throughput tissue microarray analysis to evaluate genes uncovered by CDNA microarray screening in renal cell carcinoma. Am J Pathol 1999, **154**: 981–986.

359 Mohsin SK, Zhang M, Clark GM, Craig Allred D. Maspin expression in invasive breast cancer: association with other prognostic factors. J Pathol 2003, **199**: 432–435.

360 Molenaar WM, Muntinghe FLH. Expression of neural cell adhesion molecules and neurofilament protein isoforms in Ewing's sarcoma of bone and soft tissue sarcomas other than rhabdomyosarcomas. Hum Pathol 1999, **30**: 1207–1212.

361 Moll R, Cowin P, Kapprell H-P, Franke WW. Desmosomal proteins. New markers for identification and classification of tumors. Lab Invest 1986, **54**: 4–25.

362 Moll R, Franke WW, Schiller DL, Geiger B, Krepler R. The catalog of human cytokeratins. Patterns of expression in normal epithelia, tumors and cultured cells. Cell 1982, **31**: 11–24.

363 Momose J, Mehta P, Battifora J. Antigen retrieval by microwave irradiation in lead thiocyanate. Comparison with protease digestion retrieval. Appl Immunohistochem 1993, **1**: 69–76.

364 Moniaux N, Escande F, Porchet N, Aubert JP, Batra SK. Structural organization and classification of the human mucin genes. Front Biosci 2001, **6**: 1192–1206.

364a Moskaluk CA, Zhang H, Powell SM, Cerilli LA, Hampton GM, Frierson Jr HF. Cdx2 protein expression in normal and malignant human tissues: an immunohistochemical survey using tissue microarrays. Mod Pathol 2003, **16**: 913–919.

365 Moskowitz LB, Ganjei P, Ziegels-Weissman J, Cleary TJ, Penneys NS, Nadji M. Immunohistologic identification of fungi in systemic and cutaneous mycoses. Arch Pathol Lab Med 1986, **110**: 433–436.

366 Mount SL, Taatjes DJ, von Turkovich M, Tindle BH, Trainer TD. Diagnostic immunoelectron microscopy in surgical pathology. Assessment of various tissue fixation and processing protocols. Ultrastruct Pathol 1993, **17**: 547–556.

367 Mukai K, Grotting JC, Greider MH, Rosai J. Retrospective study of 77 pancreatic endocrine tumors using the immunoperoxidase method. Am J Surg Pathol 1982, **6**: 387–399.

368 Mukai K, Rosai J. Applications of immunoperoxidase techniques in surgical pathology. In Wolff M, Fenoglio CM (eds): Progress in surgical pathology, vol. 1. New York, 1980, Masson Publishing USA, Inc., pp. 15–99.

369 Mukai K, Rosai J, Burgdorf WHC. Localization of factor VIII-related antigen in vascular endothelial cells using an immunoperoxidase method. Am J Surg Pathol 1980, **4**: 273–276.

370 Mukai K, Rosai J, Hallaway BE. Localization of myoglobin in normal and neoplastic human skeletal muscle cells using an immunoperoxidase method. Am J Surg Pathol 1979, **3**: 373–376.

371 Mukai K, Schollmeyer JV, Rosai J. Immunohistochemical localization of actin. Applications in surgical pathology. Am J Surg Pathol 1981, **5**: 91–97.

372 Mukai K, Yoshimura S, Anzai M. Effects of decalcification on immunoperoxidase staining. Am J Surg Pathol 1986, **10**: 413–419.

373 Mukai M, Iri H, Nakajima T, Hirose S, Torikata C, Kageyama K, Ueno N, Murakami K. Alveolar soft-part sarcoma. A review on its histogenesis and further studies based on electron microscopy, immunohistochemistry, and biochemistry. Am J Surg Pathol 1983, **7**: 679–689.

374 Mukai M, Iri H, Torikata C, Kageyama K, Morikawa Y, Shimizu K. Immunoperoxidase demonstration of a new muscle protein (Z-protein) in myogenic tumors as a diagnostic aid. Am J Pathol 1984, **114**: 164–170.

375 Nadji M, Ganjei P. Special report. Immunocytochemistry in diagnostic cytology. A 12-year perspective. Am J Clin Pathol 1990, **94**: 470–475.

376 Nadji M, Tabei SZ, Castro A, Chu TM, Murphy GP, Wang MC, Morales AR. Prostatic-specific antigen. An immunohistologic marker for prostatic neoplasms. Cancer 1984, **48**: 1229–1232.

376a Nadji M, Werner B, Ganjei-Azar P, Morales AR. Cost effective diagnostic immunohistochemistry: a three-year experience with 12,605 cases. Mod Pathol 2003, **16**: 317A.

377 Nagle RB. Intermediate filaments. A review of the basic biology. Am J Surg Pathol 1988, **12**: 4–16.

378 Nakajima T, Watanabe S, Sato Y, Kameya T, Shimosato Y. An immunoperoxidase study of S-100 protein distribution in normal and neoplastic tissues. Am J Surg Pathol 1982, **6**: 715–727.

379 Nakamura N, Miyagi E, Murata S, Kawaoi A, Katoh R. Expression of thyroid transcription factor-1 in normal and neoplastic lung tissues. Mod Pathol 2002, **15**: 1058–1067.

380 Natali PG, deMartino C, Quaranta V, Nicotra R, Frezza F, Pellegrino MA, Ferrone S. Expression of a la-like antigens in normal human non-lymphoid tissues. Transplantation 1981, **31**: 75–78.

381 Natkunam Y, Rouse RV. Utility of paraffin section immunohistochemistry for C-KIT (CD117) in the differential diagnosis of systemic mast cell disease involving the bone marrow. Am J Surg Pathol 2000, **24**: 81–91.

382 Ng WK, Chow JC, Ng PK. Thyroid transcription factor-1 is highly sensitive and specific in differentiating metastatic pulmonary from extrapulmonary adenocarcinoma in effusion fluid cytology specimens. A study of 36 cases. Cancer 2002, **96**: 43–48.

383 Nicholson SA, McDermott MB, DeYoung BR, Swanson PE. CD31 immunoreactivity in small cell round tumors. AIMM 2000, **8**: 19–24.

384 Nielsen S, Frokiaer J, Marples D, Kwon TH, Agre P, Knepper MA. Aquaporis in the kidney: from molecules to medicine. Physiol Rev 2002, **82**: 205–244.

385 North PE, Waner M, Mizeraki A, Mihm MC. GLUT1: a newly discovered immunohistochemical marker for juvenile hemangiomas. Hum Pathol 2000, **31**: 11–22.

386 Notohara K, Hamazaki S, Tsukayama C, Nakamoto S, Kawabata K, Mizobuchi K, Sakamoto K, Okada S. Solid-pseudopapillary tumor of the pancreas: immunohistochemical localization of neuroendocrine markers and CD10. Am J Surg Pathol 2000, **24**: 1361–1371.

386a Nylander K, Vojtesek B, Nenutil R, Lindgren B, Roos G, Zhanxiang W, Sjostrom B, Dahlqvist A, Coates PJ. Differential expression of p63 isoforms in normal tissues and neoplastic cells. J Pathol 2002, **198**: 417–27.

387 Oates J, Edwards C. HBME-1, MOC-31, WT1 and calretinin: an assessment of recently described markers for mesothelioma and adenocarcinoma. Histopathology 2000, **36**: 341–347.

388 Obinata T, Maruyama K, Sugita H, Kohama K, Ebashi S. Dynamic aspects of structural proteins in vertebrate skeletal muscle. Muscle Nerve 1981, **4**: 456–488.

389 O'Connell JT, Hacker CM, Barsky SH. MUC2 is a molecular marker for pseudomyxoma peritonei. Mod Pathol 2002, **15**: 958–972.

390 Ogawa K, Johansson SL, Cohen SM. Immunohistochemical analysis of uroplakins, urothelial specific proteins, in ovarian Brenner tumors, normal tissues, and benign and neoplastic lesions of the female genital tract. Am J Surg Pathol 1999, **155**: 1047–1050.

391 Ohene-Abuakwa Y, Pignatelli M. Adhesion molecules as diagnostic tools in tumor pathology. Int J Surg Pathol 2000, **8**: 191–200.

392 Ordóñez NG, Brooks T, Thompson S, Batsakis JG. Use of *Ulex europaeus* agglutinin I in the identification of lymphatic and blood vessel invasion in previously stained microscopic slides. Am J Surg Pathol 1987, **11**: 543–550.

393 Ordóñez NG. Immunohistochemical diagnosis of epithelioid mesotheliomas a critical review of old markers, new markers. Hum Pathol 2002, **33**: 953–967.

394 Ordóñez NG. Value of cytokeratin 5/6 immunostaining in distinguishing epithelial mesothelioma of the pleura from lung adenocarcinomas. Am J Surg Pathol 1998, **22**: 1215–1221.

395 Ordóñez NG. Value of thrombomodulin immunostaining in the diagnosis of mesothelioma. Histopathology 1997, **31:** 25–30.

396 Ordóñez NG. Thrombomodulin expression in transitional cell carcinoma. Am J Clin Pathol 1998, **110:** 385–390.

397 Ordóñez NG. Value of mesothelin immunostaining in the diagnosis of mesothelioma. Mod Pathol 2003, **16:** 192–197.

398 Ordóñez NG. Value of the MOC-31 monoclonal antibody in differentiating epithelial pleural mesothelioma from lung adenocarcinoma. Hum Pathol 1998, **29:** 16–169.

399 Ormerod MG, Bussolati G, Sloane JP, Steele K, Gugliotta P. Similarities of antisera to casein and epithelial membrane antigen. Virchows Arch [A] 1982, **397:** 327–333.

400 Osborne M, Weber K. Tumor diagnosis by intermediate filament typing. Lab Invest 1983, **48:** 372–394.

401 Pahlman S, Esscher T, Nilsson K. Expression of γ-subunit of enolase, neuronspecific enolase, in human non-neuroendocrine tumors and derived cell lines. Lab Invest 1986, **54:** 554–560.

402 Papotti M, Gugliotta P, Forte G, Bussolati G. Immunocytochemical identification of oxyphilic mitochondrion-rich cells. Appl Immunohistochem 1994, **2:** 261–267.

403 Parker DC, Folpe AL, Bell J, Olive E, Young RH, Cohen C, Amin MB. Potential utility of uroplakin III, thrombomodulin, high molecular weight cytokeratin, and cytokeratin 20 in non-invasive, invasive, and metastatic urothelial (transitional cell) carcinoma. Am J Surg Pathol 2002, **27:** 1–10.

404 Pascal RR, Santeusanio G, Sarrell D, Johnson CE. Immunohistologic detection of estrogen receptors in paraffin-embedded breast cancers. Correlation with cytosol measurements. Hum Pathol 1986, **17:** 370–375.

405 Pereira MEA, Kisalus EC, Gruezo G, Kabat EA. Immunohistochemical studies on the combining site of the blood group H-specific lectin I from *Ulex europaeus* seeds. Arch Biochem Biophys 1978, **185:** 108–115.

406 Perentes E, Rubinstein U. Recent applications of immunoperoxidase histochemistry in human neuro-oncology. An update. Arch Pathol Lab Med 1987, **111:** 796–812.

407 Perez-Moreno M, Jamora C, Fuchs E. Sticky business: orchestrating cellular signals at adherens junctions. Cell 2003, **112:** 535–548.

408 Perrone T, Frizzera G, Rosai J. Mediastinal diffuse large-cell lymphoma with sclerosis. A clinicopathologic study of 60 cases. Am J Surg Pathol 1986, **10:** 176–191.

409 Petrosyan K, Press MF. Multispecimen tissue blocks in pathology: an improved technique of preparation. Lab Invest 1997, **77:** 541–542.

410 Pinkus GS, Kurtin PJ. Epithelial membrane antigen. A diagnostic discriminant in surgical pathology. Immunohistochemical profile in epithelial, mesenchymal, and hematopoietic neoplasms using paraffin sections and monoclonal antibodies. Hum Pathol 1985, **16:** 929–940.

411 Pinkus GS, Said JW. Intracellular hemoglobin. A specific marker for erythroid cells in paraffin sections. An immunoperoxidase study of normal, megaloblastic, and dysplastic erythropoiesis, including erythroleukemia and other myeloproliferative disorders. Am J Pathol 1971, **102:** 308–313.

412 Pinkus GS, Said JW. Leu-M1 immunoreactivity in nonhematopoietic neoplasms and myeloproliferative disorders. An immunoperoxidase study of paraffin sections. Am J Clin Pathol 1986, **85:** 278–282.

413 Porta EA, Monserrat AJ. Revisión sobre el valor y aplicación de lectinohistoquímica en patolgía. Patolgia (Mex) 1999, **37:** 41–58.

414 Press MF, Greene GL. An immunocytochemical method for demonstrating estrogen receptor in human uterus using monoclonal antibodies to human estrophilin. Lab Invest 1984, **50:** 480–486.

415 Primus FJ, Clark CA, Goldenberg DM. Immunohistochemical detection of carcinoembryonic antigen. In DeLellis RA (ed.): Diagnostic immunohistochemistry. New York, 1981, Masson Publishing USA, Inc., pp. 263–276.

416 Rabkin MS, Kjeldsberg CR. Epithelial membrane antigen staining patterns of histiocytic lesions. Arch Pathol Lab Med 1987, **111:** 337–338.

417 Reid WA, Liddle CN, Svasti J, Kay J. Gastricsin in the benign and malignant prostate. J Clin Pathol 1985, **38:** 639–643.

418 Reiner A, Spona J, Reiner G, Schemper M, Kolb R, Kwasny W, Függer R, Jakesz R, Holzner JH. Estrogen receptor analysis on biopsies and fine-needle aspirates from human breast carcinoma. Correlation of biochemical and immunohistochemical methods using monoclonal antireceptor antibodies. Am J Pathol 1986, **125:** 443–449.

419 Reis-Filho JS, Milanezi F, Silva P, Schmitt FC. Maspin expression in myoepithelial tumors of the breast. Pathol Res Pract 2001, **197:** 817–821.

420 Reis-Filho JS, Schmitt FC. Taking advantage of basic research: p63 is a reliable myoepithelial and stem cell marker. Adv Anat Pathol 2002, **9:** 280–289.

421 Renshaw AA, Granter SR. A comparison of A103 and inhibin reactivity in adrenal cortical tumors: distinction from hepatocellular carcinoma and renal tumors. Mod Pathol 1999, **11:** 1160–1164.

422 Rettig WJ, Garin-Chesa P, Healey JH, Su SL, Jaffe EA, Old LJ. Identification of endosialin, a cell surface glycoprotein of vascular endothelial cells in human cancer. Proc Natl Acad Sci USA 1992, **89:** 10832–10836.

423 Rhoton-Vlasak A, Wagner JM, Rutgers JL, Baergen RN, Young RH, Roche PC, Plummer TB, Gleich GJ. Placental site trophoblastic tumor: human placental lactogen and pregnancy-associated major basic protein as immunohistologic markers. Hum Pathol 1998, **29:** 280–288.

424 Ritter CA, Arteaga CL. The epidermal growth factor receptor-tyrosine kinase: a promising therapeutic target in solid tumors. Semin Oncol 2003, **30:** 3–11.

425 Rode J, Dhillon AP, Doran JF, Jackson P, Thompson RJ. PGP9.5, a new marker for human neuroendocrine tumours. Histopathology 1985, **9:** 147–158.

426 Rooney N, Day C, Gray T, Underwood JCE. Electron microscopic localization of cell-surface markers in tissue sections using monoclonal and gold-conjugated antibodies. J Pathol 1986, **148:** 29–34.

427 Rosai J, Carcangiu ML. Pitfalls in the diagnosis of thyroid neoplasms. Pathol Res Pract 1987, **182:** 169–179.

428 Rosai J. A consultant's apologia of immunohistochemistry. Appl Immunohistochem 1994, **2:** 229–230.

429 Rossen K, Thomsen HK. Ber-EP4 immunoreactivity depends on the germ layer origin and maturity of the squamous epithelium. Histopathology 2001, **39:** 386–389.

430 Rossiello R, Carriero MV, Giordano GG. Distribution of ferritin, transferrin and lactoferrin in breast carcinoma tissue. J Clin Pathol 1984, **37:** 51–55.

431 Sadoughi N, Misna J, Guinan P, Rubenstone A. Prognostic value of cell surface antigens using immunoperoxidase methods in bladder carcinoma. Urology 1982, **20:** 143–146.

432 Saitoh Y, Kuratsu J-I, Takeshima H, Yamamoto S, Ushio Y. Expression of osteopontin in human glioma. Its correlation with the malignancy. Lab Invest 1995, **72:** 55–63.

433 Sarlomo-Rikala M, Kovatich AJ, Barusevicius A, Miettinen M. CD117: a sensitive marker for gastrointestinal stromal tumors that is more specific than CD34. Mod Pathol 1998, **11:** 728–734.

434 Sasano H, Kato K, Nagura H, Parkkila S, Parkkila AK, Rajaniemi H, Sugai N. Carbonic anhydrases in the human adrenal gland and its disorders: immunohistochemical and biochemical studies of the enzymes. Endocr Pathol 1994, **5:** 100–106.

435 Sasano H, Nagura H, Harada N, Goukon Y, Kimura M. Immunolocalization of aromatase and other steroidogenic

enzymes in human breast disorders. Hum Pathol 1994, **25:** 530–535.

436 Savera AT, Torres FX, Linden MD, Bacchi CE, Gown AM, Zarbo RJ. Primary versus metastatic pulmonary adenocarcinoma: an immunohistochemical study using villin and cytokeratins 7 and 20. Appl Immuno 1996, **4:** 86–94.

437 Savino W, Manganella G, Verley J-M, Wolff A, Berrih S, Levasseur P, Binet J-P, Dardenne M, Bach J-F. Thymoma epithelial cells secrete thymic hormone but do not express class II antigens of the major histocompatibility complex. J Clin Invest 1985, **76:** 1140–1146.

438 Schaafsma HE, Ramaekers FC. Cytokeratin subtyping in normal and neoplastic epithelium. Basic principles and diagnostic applications. Pathol Annu 1994, **29**(Pt 1): 21–62.

439 Schmitt FC, Bacchi CE. S-100 protein. Is it useful as a tumor marker in diagnostic immunocytochemistry? Histopathology 1989, **15:** 281–288.

440 Schonberger J, Ruschoff J, Grimm D, Marienhagen J, Rummele P, Meyringer R, Kossmehl P, Hofstaedter F, Eilles C. Glucose transporter 1 gene expression is related to thyroid neoplasms with an unfavorable prognosis: an immunohistochemical study. Thyroid 2002, **12:** 747–754.

441 Scupham R, Gilbert EF, Wilde J, Wiedrich TA. Immunohistochemical studies of rhabdomyosarcoma. Arch Pathol Lab Med 1986, **110:** 818–821.

442 Sell S. Cancer-associated carbohydrate identified by monoclonal antibodies. Hum Pathol 1990, **21:** 1003–1019.

443 Seshi B, Bell CE Jr. Preparation and characterization of monoclonal antibodies to human neuron-specific enolase. Hybridoma 1985, **4:** 13–25.

444 Seshi B, True L, Carter D, Rosai J. Immunohistochemical characterization of a set of monoclonal antibodies to human neuron-specific enolase. Am J Pathol 1988, **131:** 258–269.

445 Sharon N, Lis H. Lectins as cell recognition molecules. Science 1989, **246:** 227–234.

446 Sheibani K, Tubbs RR. Enzyme immunohistochemistry. Technical aspects. Semin Diagn Pathol 1984, **1:** 235–250.

447 Shevchuk MM, Romas NA, Ng PY, Tannenbaum M, Olsson CA. Acid phosphatase localization in prostatic carcinoma. A comparison of monoclonal antibody to heteroantisera. Cancer 1983, **52:** 1642–1646.

448 Shimizu M, Toki T, Takagi Y, Konishi I, Fujii S. Immunohistochemical detection of the Wilm's tumor gene (WT1) in epithelial ovarian tumors. Int J Gynecol Pathol 2000, **19:** 158–163.

449 Shintaku IP, Said JW. Detection of estrogen receptors with monoclonal antibodies in routinely processed formalin-fixed paraffin sections of breast carcinoma. Use of Dnase pretreatment to enhance sensitivity of the reaction. Am J Clin Pathol 1987, **87:** 161–167.

450 Shipley WR, Hammer RD, Lennington WJ, Macon WR. Paraffin immunohistochemical detection of CD56, a useful marker for neural cell adhesion molecule (NCAM), in normal and neoplastic fixed tissues. Appl Immuno 1997, **5:** 87–93.

451 Shiozaki H, Tahara H, Oka H, Miyata M, Kobayashi K, Tamura S, Iihara K, Doki Y, Hirano S, Takeichi M, et al. Expression of immunoreactive E-cadherin adhesion molecules in human cancers. Am J Pathol 1991, **139:** 17–23.

452 Simpson JF, Page DL. Altered expression of a structural protein (fodrin) within epithelial proliferative disease of the breast. Am J Pathol 1992, **141:** 285–289.

453 Singh G, Katyal SL. Surfactant apoprotein immunohistochemistry. In DeLellis RA (ed.): Advances in immunohistochemistry. New York, Masson Publishing USA, Inc., pp. 263–275.

454 Skacel M, Skilton B, Pettay JD, Tubbs RR. Tissue microarrays: a powerful tool for high-throughput analysis of clinical specimens:
a review of the method with validation data. Appl Immunohistochem Mol Morphol 2002, **10:** 1–6.

455 Skalli O, Gabbiani G, Babai F, Seemayer TA, Pizzolato G, Schürch W. Intermediate filament proteins and actin isoforms as markers for soft tissue tumor differentiation and origin. II. Rhabdomyosarcomas. Am J Pathol 1988, **130:** 515–531.

456 Slamon DJ, Leyland-Jones B, Shak S, Fuchs H, Paton V, Bajamonde A, Fleming T, Eiermann W, Wolter J, Pegram M, Baselga J, Norton J. Use of chemotherapy plus a monoclonal antibody against Her2 for metastatic breast cancer that overexpresses Her2. N Engl J Med 2001, **344:** 783–842.

457 Sloane JP, Ormerod MG. Distribution of epithelial membrane antigen in normal and neoplastic tissues and its value in diagnostic tumor pathology. Cancer 1981, **47:** 1786–1795.

458 Smith ME, Pignatelli M. The molecular histology of neoplasia: the role of the cadherin/catenin complex. Histopathology 1997, **31:** 107–111.

459 Sobrinho-Simoes M, Oliveira C. Different types of epithelial cadherin alternations play different roles in human carcinogenesis. Adv Anat Pathol 2002, **9:** 329–337.

460 Solcia E, Capella C, Buffa R, Usellini L, Fiocca R, Sessa F, Tortora O. The contribution of immunohistochemistry to the diagnosis of neuroendocrine tumors. Semin Diagn Pathol 1984, **1:** 285–296.

461 Sormunen R, Eskelinen S, Leong AS. Fodrin immunolocalization in epithelial tumors. Appl Immunohistochem 1997, **5:** 179–184.

462 Springer GF. T and Tn, general carcinoma autoantigens. Science 1984, **224:** 1198–1206.

463 Stanta G, Carcangiu ML, Rosai J. The biochemical and immunohistochemical profile of thyroid neoplasia. Pathol Annu 1988, **23**(Pt 1): 129–157.

464 Stein BS, Vangore S, Petersen RO, Kendall AR. Immunoperoxidase localization of prostate-specific antigen. Am J Surg Pathol 1982, **6:** 553–557.

465 Stevenson AJ, Chatten J, Bertoni F, Miettinen M. CD99 (p30/32 MIC2) neuroectodermal/Ewing's sarcoma antigen as an immunohistochemical marker: review of more than 600 tumors and the literature experience. Appl Immunohistochem 1994, **2:** 231–240.

466 Strauchen JA. Lectin receptors as markers of lymphoid cells. I. Demonstration in tissue section by peroxidase technique. Am J Pathol 1984, **116:** 297–304.

467 Sugawara K, Kurihara H, Negishi M, Saito N, Nakazato T, Takeuchi T. Nestin as a marker for proliferative endothelium in gliomas. Lab Invest 2002, **82:** 345–351.

468 Sulzbacher I, Birner P, Trieb K, Lang S, Chott A. Expression of osteopontin and vascular endothelial growth factor in benign and malignant bone tumors. Virchows Arch 2002, **441:** 345–349.

469 Suo Z, Risberg B, Karlsson MG, Villman K, Skovlund E, Nesland JM. The expression of EGFR family ligands in breast carcinomas. Int J Surg Pathol 2002, **10:** 91–99.

470 Suster S, Fisher C. Immunoreactivity for the human hematopoietic progenitor cell antigen (CD34) in lipomatous tumors. Am J Surg Pathol 1997, **21:** 195–200.

471 Swanson PE, Manivel CJ, Scheithauer BW, Wick MR. Epithelial membrane antigen reactivity in mesenchymal neoplasms. An immunohistochemical study of 306 soft tissue sarcomas. Surg Pathol 1989, **2:** 313–322.

472 Tabibzadeh SS, Shah KD. Application of a quick immunoenzymatic labeling as an adjunct to frozen-section diagnosis. Am J Clin Pathol 1989, **91:** 63–66.

473 Takada Y, Hiwada K, Yokoyama M, Ochi K, Takeuchi M, Kokubu T. Angiotensin converting enzyme. A possible histologic indicator for human renal cell carcinoma. Cancer 1985, **56:** 130–133.

474 Tallini G, Parham DM, Dias P, Cordon-Cardo C, Houghton PJ, Rosai J. Myogenic regulatory protein expression in adult soft

tissue sarcomas. A sensitive and specific marker of skeletal muscle differentiation. Am J Pathol 1994, **144**: 693–701.

475 Taupenot L, Harper KL, O'Connor DT. The chromogranin-secretogranin family. N Engl J Med 2003, **348**: 1134–1149.

476 Taylor GM, Cook HT, Sheffield EA, Hanson C, Peart WS. Renin in blood vessels in human pulmonary tumors. An immunohistochemical and biochemical study. Am J Pathol 1988, **130**: 543–551.

477 Terada T, Nakanuma Y. An immunohistochemical survey of amylase isoenzymes in cholangiocarcinoma and hepatocellular carcinoma. Arch Pathol Lab Med 1993, **117**: 160–162.

478 Terracciano LM, Mhawech P, Suess K, D'Armiento M, Lehmann FS, Jundt G, Moch H, Sauter G, Mihatsch MJ. Calretinin as a marker for cardiac myxoma, diagnostic and histogenetic considerations. Am J Clin Pathol 2000, **114**: 754–759.

479 Thomas L, Hartung K, Langosch D, Rehm H, Bamberg E, Franke WW, Betz H. Identification of synaptophysin as a hexameric channel protein of the synaptic vesicle membrane. Science 1988, **242**: 1050–1053.

480 Thomas P, Battifora H. Keratins versus epithelial membrane antigen in tumor diagnosis. An immunohistochemical comparison of five monoclonal antibodies. Hum Pathol 1987, **18**: 728–734.

481 Thompson EM, Evans DJ. The significance of PGP 9.5 in tumours: an immunohistochemical study of gastrointestinal stromal tumours. Histopathology 1990, **17**: 175–177.

482 Tiniakos DG, Yu H, Liapis H. Osteopontin expression in ovarian carcinomas and tumors of low malignant potential (LMP). Hum Pathol 1998, **29**: 1230–1254.

483 Titta O, Sipponen P, Gould V, Virtanen I. Tenascin expression in inflammatory, dysplastic and neoplastic lesions of the human stomach. Virchows Arch 1994, **425**: 369–374.

484 Tohyama T, Lee VM, Rorke LB, Marvin M, McKay RD, Trojanowski JQ. Nestin expression in embryonic human neuroepithelium and in human neuroepithelial tumor cells. Lab Invest 1992, **66**: 303–313.

485 Toki T, Shiozawa T, Hosaka N, Ishii K, Nikaido T, Fujii S. Minimal deviation adenocarcinoma of the uterine cervix has abnormal expression of sex steroid receptors, CA125, and gastric mucin. Int J Gynecol Pathol 1997, **16**: 111–116.

486 Toki T, Shimizu M, Takagi Y, Ashida T, Konishi I. CD10 is a marker for normal and neoplastic endometrial stromal cells. Int J Gynecol Pathology 2002, **21**: 41–47.

487 Tokunaga O, Fan J, Watanabe T, Kobayashi M, Kumazaki T, Mitsui Y. Endothelin. Immunohistologic localization in aorta and biosynthesis by cultured human aortic endothelial cells. Lab Invest 1992, **67**: 210–217.

488 Torbenson M, Wang J, Choti M, Ashfaq R, Maitra A, Wilentz RE, Boitnott J. Hepatocellular carcinomas show abnormal expression of fibronectin protein. Mod Pathol 2002, **15**: 826–830.

488a Tort F, Pinyol M, Pulford K, Roncador G, Hernandez L, Nayach I, Kluin-Nelemans C, Kluin P, Touriol C, Delsol G, Mason D, Campo E. Molecular characterization of a new ALK translocation involving moesin (MSN-ALK) in anaplastic large cell lymphoma. Lab Invest 2001, **81**: 419–426.

489 Toulaymat M, Marconi S, Garb J, Otis C, Nash S. Endoscopic biopsy pathology of helicobacter pylori gastritis: comparison of bacterial detection by immunohistochemistry and Genta stain. Arch Pathol Lab Med 1999, **123**: 778–781.

490 Traweek ST, Liu J, Battifora J. Keratin gene expression in non-epithelial tissues. Detection with polymerase chain reaction. Am J Pathol 1993, **142**: 1111–1118.

490a True L, Liu A. A challenge for the diagnostic immunohistopathologist: adding the CD phenotypes to our diagnostic toolbox. Am J Clin Pathol 2003, **120**: 13–15.

491 Truong LD, Rangdaeng S, Cagle P, Ro JY, Hawkins H, Font RL. The diagnostic utility of desmin. A study of 584 cases and review of the literature. Am J Clin Pathol 1990, **93**: 305–314.

492 Tsokos M, Howard R, Costa J. Immunohistochemical study of alveolar and embryonal rhabdomyosarcoma. Lab Invest 1983, **48**: 148–155.

493 Tubbs RR, Bauer TW. Automation of immunohistology. Arch Pathol Lab Med 1989, **113**: 653–657.

494 Ueda G, Yamasaki M, Inoue M, Tanake Y, Inoue Y, Nishino T, Ogawa M. Immunohistochemical demonstration of amylase in endometrial carcinomas. Int J Gynecol Pathol 1986, **5**: 47–51.

495 Ulrich W, Horvat R, Krisch K. Lectin histochemistry of kidney tumors and its pathomorphological relevance. Histopathology 1985, **9**: 1037–1050.

496 Urmacher C, Cordon-Cardo C, Houghton AN. Tissue distribution of GD3 ganglioside detected by mouse monoclonal antibody R24. Am J Dermatopathol 1989, **11**: 577–581.

497 Van Aken E, De Weder O, Coirreia Da Rocha AS, Mareel M. Defective E-Cadherin/catenin complexes in human cancer. Virchows Arch 2001, **439**: 725–751.

498 van der Rest M, Garrone R. Collagen family of proteins. FASEB J 1991, **5**: 2814–2823.

499 Van Muijen BNP, Ruiter DJ, Warnaar SO. Coexpression of intermediate filament polypeptides in human fetal and adult tissues. Lab Invest 1987, **57**: 359–369.

500 Viale G, Bosari S, Mazzarol G, Galimberti V, Luini A, Veronesi P, Paganelli G, Bedoni M, Orvieto E. Intraoperative examination of axillary sentinel lymph nodes in breast carcinoma patients. Cancer 1999, **85**: 2433–2438.

501 Vigneswaran N, Haneke E, Hornstein OP. Are differences in filaggrin expression suitable for discriminating benign, premalignant and malignant skin lesions? An immunohistochemical study. Pathol Res Pract 1989, **184**: 402–409.

502 Vuorio E, de Crombrugghe B. The family of collagen genes. Annu Rev Biochem 1990, **39**: 837–872.

503 Walker RA. The use of lectins in histopathology. Pathol Res Pract 1989, **185**: 826–835.

504 Walts AE, Said JW. Specific tumor markers in diagnostic cytology. Immunoperoxidase studies of carcinoembryonic antigen, lysozyme and other tissue antigens in effusions, washes and aspirates. Acta Cytol (Baltimore) 1983, **27**: 408–416.

505 Walts AE, Said JW, Siegel MB, Banks-Schlegel S. Involucrin, a marker of squamous and urothelial differentiation. An immunohistochemical study on its distribution in normal and neoplastic tissues. J Pathol 1985, **145**: 329–340.

506 Wang E, Fischman D, Liem RKH, Sun T-T, eds. Intermediate filaments. Ann NY Acad Sci 1985, **455**: 1–829.

507 Warhol MJ, Antonioli DA, Pinkus GS, Burke L, Rice RH. Immunoperoxidase staining for involucrin. A potential diagnostic aid in cervicovaginal pathology. Hum Pathol 1982, **13**: 1095–1099.

508 Wehrli BM, Huang W, De Crombrugghe B, Ayala AG, Czerniak B. Sox9, a master regulator of chondrogenesis, distinguishes mesenchymal chondrosarcoma from other small blue round cell tumors. Hum Pathol 2003, **34**: 263–269.

508a Weinstein MH, Signoretti S, Loda M. Diagnostic utility of immunohistochemical staining for p63, a sensitive marker of prostatic basal cells. Mod Pathol 2002, **15**: 1302–08.

509 Weinstein RS, Coon J, Alroy J, Davidsohn I. Tissue-associated blood group antigens in human tumors. In DeLellis RA (ed.): Diagnostic immunohistochemistry. New York, 1981, Masson Publishing USA, Inc., pp. 239–261.

510 Weiss LM, Gaffey MJ, Warhol MJ, Mehta P, Bonsib SM, Bruder E, Santos E, Mederios LJ. Immunocytochemical characterization of a monoclonal antibody directed against mitochondria reactive in paraffin-embedded sections. Mod Pathol 1991, **4**: 596–601.

511 Weiss LM, Trela MJ, Cleary ML, Turner RR, Warnke RA, Sklar J. Frequent immunoglobulin and T-cell receptor gene rearrangements in "histiocytic" neoplasms. Am J Pathol 1985, **121**: 369–373.

512 Weiss SW, Nickoloff BJ. CD34 is expressed by a distinctive cell population in peripheral nerve sheath tumors and related lesions. Am J Surg Pathol 1993, **17:** 1039–1045.

513 Wells CA, Taylor SM, Cuello AC. Argentaffin and argyrophil reactions and serotonin content of endocrine tumours. J Clin Pathol 1985, **38:** 49–53.

514 Wennerberg AE, Nalesnik MA, Coleman WB. Hepatocyte paraffin 1: a monoclonal antibody that reacts with hepatocytes and can be used for differential diagnosis of hepatic tumors. Am J Pathol 1993, **143:** 1050–1054.

514a Werling RW, Yaziji H, Bacchi CE, Gown AM. CDX2, a highly sensitive and specific marker of adenocarcinomas of intestinal origin: an immunohistochemical survey of 476 primary and metastatic carcinoma. Am J Surg PAthol 2003, **27:** 303–310.

514b Went PTH, Lugli A, Meier S, Bundi M, Mirlacher M, Sauter G, Dirnhofer S. Frequent EpCam protein expression in human carcinomas. Hum Pathol (In press).

515 Wetzels RH, Robben HC, Leigh IM, Schaafsma HE, Vooijs GP, Ramaekers FC. Distribution patterns of type VII collagen in normal and malignant human tissues. Am J Pathol 1991, **139:** 451–459.

516 Wheeler GN, Parker AE, Thomas DL, Ataliotis P, Poynter D, Arnemann J, Rutman AJ, Pidsley SC, Watt FM, Rees DA, et al. Desmosomal glycoprotein DGI, a component of intercellular desmosome junctions, is related to the cadherin family of cell adhesion molecules. Proc Natl Acad Sci USA 1991, **88:** 4796–4800.

517 Wick MR, Swanson PE, Manivel JC. Placental-like alkaline phosphatase reactivity in human tumors. An immunohistochemical study of 520 cases. Hum Pathol 1987, **18:** 946–954.

518 Wiley EL, Mulhollan TJ, Beck B, Tyndall JA, Freeman RG. Polyclonal antibodies raised against bacillus Calmette-Guerin, *Mycobacterium duvalii*, and *Mycobacterium paratuberculosis* used to detect mycobacteria in tissue with the use of immunohistochemical techniques. Am J Clin Pathol 1990, **94:** 307–312.

519 Wilson BS, Herzig MA, Lloyd RV. Immunoperoxidase staining for Ia-like antigens in paraffin-embedded tissues from human melanoma and lung carcinoma. Am J Pathol 1984, **115:** 102–116.

520 Wojno KJ, Epstein JI. The utility of basal cell-specific anti-cytokeratin antibody (34βE12) in the diagnosis of prostate cancer. A review of 228 cases. Am J Surg Pathol 1995, **19:** 251–260.

521 Wold LE, Li C-Y, Homburger HA. Localization of the B and M polypeptide subunits of creatine kinase in normal and neoplastic human tissues by an immunoperoxidase technic. Am J Clin Pathol 1981, **75:** 327–332.

522 Wolf MF, Koerner U, Schumacher K. Specificity of reagents directed to the Thomsen-Friedenreich antigen and their capacity to bind to the surface of human carcinoma cell lines. Cancer Res 1986, **46:** 1779–1782.

523 Wong SY, Purdie AT, Han P. Thrombospondin and other possible related matrix proteins in malignant and benign breast disease. An immunohistochemical study. Am J Pathol 1992, **140:** 1473–1482.

524 Wurl P, Taubert H, Meye A, Dansranjavin R, Weber E, Gunther D, Berger D, Schmidt H, Dralle H, Rath FW. Immunohistochemical and clinical evaluation of cathepsin expression in soft tissue sarcoma. Virchows Arch 1997, **430:** 221–225.

525 Yang P, Hirose T, Seki K, Hasegawa T, Hizawa K, Sano T. Myofibroblastic tumor of soft tissue displaying desmin-positive and actin-negative immunophenotypes. Pathol Int 1997, **46:** 696–703.

526 Yatabe Y, Mitsudomi T, Takahashi T. TTF-1 expression in pulmonary adenocarcinomas. Am J Surg Pathol 2002, **26:** 767–773.

527 Yonezawa S, Maruyama I, Sakae K, Igata A, Majerus PW, Sato E. Thrombomodulin as a marker for vascular tumors. Comparative study with factor VIII and *Ulex europaeus* I lectin. Am J Clin Pathol 1987, **88:** 405–411.

528 Zamecnik J, Kodet R. Value of thyroid transcription factor-1 and surfactant apoprotein A in the differential diagnosis of pulmonary carcinomas: a study of 109 cases. Virchows Arch 2002, **440:** 353–361.

529 Zamora-Leon SP, Golde DW, Concha II, Rivas CI, Delgado-Lopez F, Baselga J, Nualart F, Vera JC. Expression of the fructose transporter GLUT5 in human breast cancer. Proc Natl Acad Sci USA 1996, **93:** 1847–1852.

530 Zavala-Pompa A, Folpe AL, Jimenez RE, Lim SD, Cohen C, Eble JN, Amin MB. Immunohistochemical study of microphthalmia transcription factor and tyrosinase in angiomyolipoma of the kidney, renal cell carcinoma, and renal and retroperitoneal sarcomas: comparative evaluation with traditional diagnostic markers. Am J Surg Pathol 2000, **25:** 65–70.

531 Zeeman AM, Stoop H, Boter M, Gillis AJM, Castrillon DH, Oosterhuis JW, Looijenga LH. Vasa is a specific marker for both normal and malignant germ cells. Lab Invest 2002, **82:** 159–166.

532 Zhang PJ, Harris KR, Alobeid B, Brooks JJ. Immunoexpression of villin in neuroendocrine tumors and its diagnostic implications. Arch Pathol Lab Med 1999, **123:** 812–816.

532a Zhou M, Chimmaiyan AM, Kleer CG, Lucas PC, Rubin MA. Alpha-Methylacyl-CoA racemase: a novel tumor marker over-expressed in several human cancer and their precursor lesions. Am J Surg Pathol 2002, **26:** 926–931.

533 Zhu L, Leinonen J, Zhang WM, Finne P, Stenman UH. Dual-label immunoassay for simultaneous measurement of prostate-specific antigen (PSA)-alpha1- antichymotrypsin complex together with free or total PSA. Clin Chem 2003, **49:** 97–103.

534 Zotter S, Lossnitzer A, Kunze K-D, Müller M, Hilkens J, Hilgers J, Hageman P. Epithelial markers for paraffin-embedded human tissues. Immunohistochemistry with monoclonal antibodies against milk fat globule antigens. Virchows Arch [A] 1985, **406:** 237–251.

Flow cytometry

535 Aamodt RL, Coon JS, Deitch A, White RWD, Koss LG, Melamed MR, Weinstein RS, Wheeless LL. Flow cytometric evaluation of bladder cancer. Recommendations of the NCI flow cytometry network for bladder cancer. World J Urol 1992, **10:** 63–67.

536 Bergers E, Baak JP, Van Diest PJ, Willig AJ, Los J, Peterse JL, Ruitenberg HM, Schapers RF, Somsen JG, Van Beek MW, Bellot SM, Fijnheer J, Van Gorp LH. Prognostic value of DNA ploidy using flow cytometry in 1301 breast cancer patients: results of the prospective multicenter morphometric mammary carcinoma projects. Mod Pathol 1997, **10:** 762–768.

537 Braylan RD. Flow-cytometric DNA analysis in the diagnosis and prognosis of lymphoma. Am J Clin Pathol 1993, **99:** 374–380.

538 Braylan RC. Lymphomas. In Bauer KD, Duque RE, Shankey TV (eds): Flow cytometry. Principles and applications. Baltimore, 1993, Williams & Wilkins, pp. 203–234.

539 Brown HM, Komorowski RA, Wilson SD, Demeure MJ, Zhu YR. Predicting metastasis of pheochromocytomas using DNA flow cytometry and immunohistochemical markers of cell proliferation: a positive correlation between MIB-1 staining and malignant tumor behaviour. Cancer 1999, **86:** 1583–1589.

540 Camplejohn RS, Brock A, Barnes DM, et al. Ki-S1, a novel proliferative marker. Flow cytometric assessment of staining in human breast carcinoma cells. Br J Cancer 1993, **67:** 657–662.

541 Chen LM, Lazcano O, Katzmann JA, Kimlinger TK, Li CY. The role of conventional cytology, immunocytochemistry, and flow cytometric DNA ploidy in the evaluation of body cavity fluids. A prospective study of 52 patients. Am J Clin Pathol 1998, **109:** 712–721.

542 Collin F, Chassevent A, Bonichon F, Bertrand G, Terrier P, Coindra JM. Flow cytometric DNA content analysis of 185 soft tissue neoplasms indicates that S-phase fraction is a prognostic factor for sarcomas, French Federation of Cancer Centers (FNCLCC) sarcoma Group. Cancer 1997, **79**: 2371–2379.

543 Coon JS, Landay AL, Weinstein RS. Flow cytometric analysis of paraffin embedded tumors. Implications for diagnostic pathology. Hum Pathol 1986, **17**: 435–437.

544 Darzynkiewicz Z, Crissman HA, Robinson JP. Cytometry. American Soc for cell Biology. San Diego, 2001, Academic Press.

545 Frierson HF Jr. Flow cytometric analysis of ploidy in solid neoplasms. Comparison of fresh tissues with formalin-fixed paraffin-embedded specimens. Hum Pathol 1988, **19**: 290–294.

546 Giella JG, Ring K, Olsson CA, Karp FS, Benson MC. The predictive value of flow cytometry and urinary cytology in the followup of patients with transitional cell carcinoma of the bladder. J Urol 1992, **148**: 293–296.

547 Gnant MFX, Blijham GH, Reiner A, Reinder G, Reynders M, Schutte R, van Asche C, Steger G, Jakesz R. DNA ploidy and other results of DNA flow cytometry as prognostic factors in operable breast cancer. 10 year results of a randomized study. Eur J Cancer 1992, **28**: 711–716.

548 Haugen OA, Mjølnerød O. DNA-ploidy as a prognostic factor in prostatic carcinoma. Int J Cancer 1990, **45**: 224–228.

549 Humphrey PA, Walther PJ, Currin SM, Vollmer RT. Histologic grade, DNA ploidy and intraglandular tumor extent as indicators of tumor progression of clinical stage B prostatic carcinoma. A direct comparison. Am J Surg Pathol 1991, **15**: 1165–1170.

550 Keren DF, McCoy JP, Carey JL. Flow cytometry in clinical diagnosis. Chicago, 2001, ASCP Press.

551 Koss LG, Czerniak B, Herz F, Wersto RP. Flow cytometric measurements of DNA and other cell components in human tumors. A critical appraisal. Hum Pathol 1989, **20**: 528–548.

552 Krause JR, Penchansky L, Contis L, Kaplan SS. Flow cytometry in the diagnosis of acute leukemia. Am J Clin Pathol 1988, **89**: 341–346.

553 Lee JY, Dong SM, Kim SY, Yoo NJ, Lee SH, Park WS. A simple, precise and economical microdissection technique for analysis of genomic DNA from archival tissue sections. Virchows Arch 1998, **433**: 305–310.

554 Melamed MR, Lindmo T, Mendelsohn ML, eds. Flow cytometry and sorting, ed. 2. New York, 1990, Wiley-Liss.

555 Miller J, Horsfall DJ, Marshall VR, Rao DM, Leong SY. The prognostic value of deoxyribonucleic acid flow cytometric analysis in stage D2 prostatic adenocarcinoma. J Urol 1991, **145**: 1192–1196.

556 Nagel R, Al-Abadi H. The prognostic significance of ploidy and DNA-heterogeneity in the primary diagnosis and monitoring of patients with locally advanced prostatic carcinoma. Scand J Urol Nephrol 1991, **138**: 83–92.

557 Nap M, Brockhoff G, Brandt B, Knuechel R, Leers MP, Schmidt H, De Angelis G, Heltze E, Semjonow A. Flow cytometric DNA and phenotype analysis in pathology. A meeting report of a symposium at the annual conference of the German Society of Pathology, Kiel, Germany, 6–9 June 2000. Virchows Arch 2001, **438**: 425–432.

558 Nguyun DT, Diamond LW, Braylan RC. Flow cytometry in hematopathology: a visual approach to data analysis and interpretation. Totowa, NJ, 2003, Humana Press.

559 Ormerod MG. Flow cytometry. A practical approach. Oxford, 1990, IRL Press.

560 Paradinas FJ, Browne P, Fisher RA, Foskett M, Bagshawe KD, Newlands E. A clinical, histopathological and flow cytometric study of 149 complete moles, 146 partial moles and 107 non-molar hydropic abortions. Histopathology 1996, **28**: 101–110.

561 Pelstring RJ, Hurtubise PE, Swerdlow SH. Flow-cytometric DNA analysis of hematopoietic and lymphoid proliferations. A comparison of fresh, formalin-fixed and B5-fixed tissues. Hum Pathol 1990, **21**: 551–558.

562 Schultz DS, Zarbo RJ. Comparison of eight modifications of Hedley's method for flow cytometric DNA ploidy analysis of paraffin-embedded tissue. Am J Clin Pathol 1992, **98**: 291–295.

563 Shapiro HM. Practical flow cytometry. New York, 2002, Wiley-Liss.

564 Song J, Cheng WS, Cupps RE, Earle JD, Farrow GM, Lieber MM. Nuclear deoxyribonucleic acid content measured by static cytometry. Important prognostic association for patients with clinically localized prostate carcinoma treated by external beam radiotherapy. J Urol 1992, **147**: 794–797.

565 Visakorpi T, Kallioniemi OP, Paronen IY, Isola JJ, Heikkinen AI, Koivula TA. Flow cytometric analysis of DNA ploidy and S-phase fraction from prostatic carcinomas. Implications for prognosis and response to endocrine therapy. Br J Cancer 1991, **64**: 578–582.

566 Wheeless LL, Badalament RA, de Vere White RW, Fradet Y, Tribukait B. Consensus review of the clinical utility of DNA cytometry in bladder cancer. Report of the DNA Cytometry Consensus Conference. Cytometry 1993, **14**: 478–481.

567 Wheeless LL, Coon JS, Cox C, Deitch AD, de Vere White RW, Fradet Y, Koss LG, Melamed MR, O'Connell MJ, Reeder JE, et al. Precision of DNA flow cytometry in inter-institutional analyses. Cytometry 1991, **12**: 405–412.

568 Wijkstrom H, Nilsson B, Tribukait B. DNA analysis in predicting survival of irradiated patients with transitional cell carcinoma of bladder. Br J Urol 1992, **69**: 49–55.

569 Willman CL, Stewart CC. General principles of multiparameter flow cytometric analysis. Applications of flow cytometry in the diagnostic pathology laboratory. Semin Diagn Pathol 1989, **6**: 3–12.

570 Wilson JV. Introduction to flow cytometry. Cambridge, 1990, Cambridge University Press.

571 Zarbo RJ, Nakhleh RE, Brown RD, Kubus JJ, Ma CK, Mackowiak P. Prognostic significance of DNA ploidy and proliferation in 309 colorectal carcinomas as determined by two-color multiparametric DNA flow cytometry. Cancer 1997, **79**: 2073–2086.

572 Zbieranowski I, Murray D. The study of endocrine tumors by flow and image cytometry. Endocr Pathol 1992, **3**: 63–82.

Other methods for analysis of cell proliferation

573 Barry M, Sinha SK, Leader MB, Kay EW. Poor agreement in recognition of abnormal mitoses: requirement for standardized and robust definitions. Histopathology 2001, **38**: 68–72.

574 Bergers E, Jannink I, Van Diest PI, Cuesta MA, Meyer S, Van Mourik JC, Baak JP. The influence of fixation delay on mitotic activity and flow cytometric cell cyle variables. Hum Pathol 1997, **289**: 95–100.

575 Bodey B, Williams RT, Carbonaro-Hall DA, Horvath A, Tolu VT, Luck J Jr, Taylor CR, Hall FL. Immunocytochemical detection of cyclin A and cyclin D in formalin-fixed, paraffin-embedded tissues. Novel, pertinent markers of cell proliferation. Mod Pathol 1995, **7**: 846–852.

576 Boege F, Andersen A, Jensen S, Zeidler R, Kreipe H. Proliferation-associated nuclear antigen Ki-S1 is identical with topoisomerase IIα. Delineation of a carboxyl-terminal epitope with peptide antibodies. Am J Pathol 1995, **146**: 1302–1308.

577 Brown DC, Gatter KC. Monoclonal antibody Ki-67. Its use in histopathology. Histopathology 1990, **17**: 489–503.

578 Cattoretti G, Becker MH, Key G, Duchrow M, Schluter C, Galle J, Gerdes J. Monoclonal antibody against recurrent parts of the Ki-67 antigen (MIB 1 and MIB 3) detect proliferating cells in immune-processed formalin-fixed paraffin sections. J Pathol 1992, **168**: 357–363.

579 Coltrera M, Skelly M, Gown A. Anti-PCNA antibody PC10 yields unreliable proliferation indexes in routinely processed, deparaffinized, formalin-fixed tissue. Appl Immunohistochem 1993, **1**: 193–200.

580 Crocker J. Nucleolar organizer regions. Curr Top Pathol 1990, **82**: 91–149.

581 Crocker J, Nar P. Nucleolar organizer regions in lymphomas. J Pathol 1987, **151**: 111–118.

582 Cross SS, Start RD. Estimating mitotic activity in tumours. Histopathology 1997, **29**: 485–488.

583 Derenzini M, Romagnoli T, Mingazzini P, Marinozzi V. Interphasic nucleolar organizer region distribution as a diagnostic parameter to differentiate benign from malignant epithelial tumors of human intestine. Virchows Arch [Cell Pathol] 1988, **54**: 334–340.

584 Derenzini M, Trerè D. Importance of interphase nucleolar organizer regions in tumor pathology. Virchows Arch [Cell Pathol] 1991, **61**: 1–8.

585 Garcia RL, Coltrera MD, Gown AM. Analysis of proliferative grade using anti-PCNA/cyclin monoclonal antibodies in fixed, embedded tissues. Comparison with flow cytometric analysis. Am J Pathol 1989, **134**: 733–739.

586 Gerdes J, Li L, Schlueter C, Duchrow M, Wohlenberg C, Gerlach C, Stahmer I, Kloth S, Brandt E, Flad HD. Immunobiochemical and molecular biologic characterization of the cell proliferation-associated nuclear antigen that is defined by monoclonal antibody Ki-67. Am J Pathol 1991, **138**: 867–873.

587 Hall PA, Coates PJ. Assessment of cell proliferation in pathology. What next? Histopathology 1995, **26**: 105–112.

588 Hall PA, Levison DA, Wright NA. Assessment of cell proliferation in clinical practice. Berlin, 1992, Springer-Verlag.

589 Hunter T, Pines J. Cyclins and cancer II. Cyclin D and inhibitors come of age. Cell 1994, **79**: 573–582.

590 Kelleher L, Magee HM, Dervan PA. Evaluation of cell-proliferation antibodies reactive in paraffin sections. Appl Immunohistochem 1994, **2**: 164–170.

591 King RW, Jackson PK, Kirschner MW. Mitosis in transition. Cell 1994, **79**: 563–571.

592 Kreipe H, Alm P, Olsson H, Hauberg M, Fischer L, Parwaresch R. Prognostic significance of a formalin-resistant nuclear proliferation antigen in mammary carcinomas as determined by the monoclonal antibody Ki-SI. Am J Pathol 1993, **651**: 651–657.

593 Lehr HA, Hansen DA, Kussick S, Li M, Hwang H, Krummenauer F, Trouet S, Gown AM. Assessment of proliferative activity in breast cancer: MIB-1 immunohistochemistry versus mitotic figure count. Hum Pathol 1999, **30**: 1314–1320.

594 Leong A, Milios J, Tang S. Is immunolocalisation of proliferating cell nuclear antigen (PCNA) in paraffin sections a valid index of cell proliferation? Appl Immunohistochem 1993, **1**: 127–135.

595 Lloveras B, Garin-Chesa P, Myc A, Melamed M. In vitro bromodeoxyuridine labeling of malignant neoplasms. A comparative study with flow cytometry cell-cycle analysis. Am J Clin Pathol 1994, **101**: 703–707.

596 Lloyd RV. Proliferation markers in the study of endocrine diseases (editorial). Endocr Pathol 1995, **6**: 83–86.

597 McCormick D, Hall PA. The complexities of proliferating cell nuclear antigen. Histopathology 1992, **21**: 591–594.

598 McDivitt RW, Stone KR, Craig RB, Meyer JS. A comparison of human breast cancer cell kinetics measured by flow cytometry and thymidine labeling. Lab Invest 1985, **52**: 287–291.

599 Meyer JS. Cell proliferation in normal human breast ducts, fibroadenomas, and other ductal hyperplasias measured by nuclear labeling with tritiated thymidine. Effects of menstrual phase, age, and oral contraceptive hormones. Hum Pathol 1977, **8**: 67–81.

600 Meyer JS, Connor RE. In vitro labeling of solid tissues with tritiated thymidine for autoradiographic detection of S-phase nuclei. Stain Technol 1977, **52**: 185–195.

601 Meyer JS, Friedman E, McCrate MM, Bauer WC. Prediction of early course of breast carcinoma by thymidine labeling. Cancer 1983, **51**: 1879–1886.

602 Molenaar WM, Plaat BE, Berends ER, Te Meerman GJ. Observer reliability in assessment of mitotic activity and MIB-1 determined proliferation rate in pediatric sarcomas. Ann Diagn Pathol 2000, **4**: 228–235.

603 O'Leary TJ, Steffes MW. Can you count on the mitotic index? Hum Pathol 1996, **27**: 147–151.

604 Pich A, Margaria E, Chiusa L. Significance of AgNORs in tumour pathology. Pathologica 2002, **94**: 2–9.

605 Ploton D, Menager M, Jeannesson P, Himber G, Pigeon F, Adnet J-J. Improvement in the staining and in the visualization of the argyrophilic proteins of the nucleolar organizer region at the optical level. Histochem J 1986, **18**: 5–14.

606 Rudalph P, Peters J, Lorenz D, Schmidt D, Parwaresch R. Correlation between mitotic and Ki-67 labeling indices in paraffin-embedded carcinoma specimens. Hum Pathol 1998, **29**: 1216–1222.

607 Ruschoff J, Plate K, Bittinger A, Thomas C. Nucleolar organizer regions (NORs). Basic concepts and practical application in tumor pathology. Pathol Res Pract 1989, **185**: 878–885.

608 Sahin AA, Ro JY, el-Naggar AK, Wilson PL, Teague K, Blick M, Ayala AG. Tumor proliferative fraction in solid malignant neoplasms. A comparative study of Ki-67 immunostaining and flow cytometric determinations. Am J Clin Pathol 1991, **96**: 512–519.

609 Sherr CJ. Gl phase progression. Cycling on cue. Cell 1994, **79**: 551–555.

610 Silverberg SG. Reproducibility of the mitosis count in the histologic diagnosis of smooth muscle tumors of the uterus. Hum Pathol 1976, **7**: 451–454.

611 Smith R, Crocker J. Evaluation of nucleolar organizer region-associated proteins in breast malignancy. Histopathology 1988, **12**: 113–125.

612 Swift H, Rasch E. Microspectrophotometry with visible light. In Orster G, Pollister AW (eds): Physical techniques in biological research – cells and tissue, vol. 3. New York, 1966, Academic Press, pp. 354–400.

613 Talerman A, Fu YS, Okagaki T. Spermatocytic seminoma. Ultrastructural and microspectrophotometric observations. Lab Invest 1984, **51**: 343–349.

614 Thiele J, Fischer R. Bone marrow tissue and proliferation markers. Results and general problems (editorial). Virchows Arch [A] 1993, **423**: 409–416.

615 Thunnissen FB, Ambergen AW, Koss M, Travis WD, O'Leary TJ, Ellis IO. Mitotic counting in surgical pathology: sampling bias, heterogeneity and statistical uncertainty. Histopathology 2001, **39**: 1–8.

616 van Dierendonck JH, Wijsman JH, Keijzer R, van de Velde CJ. Cornelisse CJ. Cell-cycle-related staining patterns of anti-proliferating cell nuclear antigen monoclonal antibodies. Comparison with BrdUrd labeling and Ki-67 staining. Am J Pathol 1991, **138**: 1165–1172.

617 Waldman FM, Chew K, Ljung BM, Goodson W, Hom J, Duarte LA, Smith HS, Mayall B. A comparison between bromodeoxyuridine and 3H thymidine labeling in human breast tumors. Mod Pathol 1991, **4**: 718–722.

618 Weidner N, Moore DH, Vartanian R. Correlation of Ki-67 antigen expression with mitotic figure index and tumor grade in breast carcinomas using the novel "paraffin"-reactive M1B1 antibody. Hum Pathol 1994, **25**: 337–342.

Cytogenetics

619 Chaganti RS, Rodriguez E, Bosl GJ. Cytogenetics of male germ-cell tumors. Urol Clin North Am 1993, **20**: 55–66.

620 Dal Cin P, Trent JM. What should oncologists know about cytogenetics in solid tumors? Ann Oncol 1993, **4:** 821–824.

621 Dal Cin P. Cytogenetics of soft tissue tumours. Verh Dtsch Ges Pathol 1999, **82:** 47–58.

622 Fletcher CD, Akerman M, Dal Cin P, De Wever I, Mandahl N, Mertens F, Mitelman F, Rosai J, Rydholm A, Sciot R, Tallini G, Van Der Berghe H, Van De Ven W, Vanni R, Willen H. Correlation between clinicopathologic features and karyotype in lipomatous tumors. A report of 178 cases from the chromosomes and morphology (CHAMP) collaborative study group. Am J Pathol 1996, **148:** 623–630.

623 Gauwerky CE, Croce CM. Chromosomal translocations in leukemia. Semin Cancer Biol 1993, **4:** 333–340.

624 Hermsen MA, Meijer GA, Baak JP, Joenji H, Walboomers JJ. Comparative genomic hybridisation: a new tool in cancer pathology. Hum Pathol 1996, **27:** 342–349.

625 Houldsworth J, Chaganti RS. Comparative genomic hybridization. An overview. Am J Pathol 1994, **145:** 1253–1260.

626 Ilson DH, Motzer RJ, Rodriguez E, Chaganti RS, Bosl GJ. Genetic analysis in the diagnosis of neoplasms of unknown primary tumor site. Semin Oncol 1993, **20:** 229–237.

627 Jeuken JW, Sprenger SH, Wesseling P. Comparative genomic hybridisation: practical guidelines. Diagn Mol Pathol 2002, **4:** 193–203.

628 Lisitsyn NA, Lisitsina NM, Dalbagni G, Barker P, Sanchez CA, Gnarra J, Linehan WM, Reid BJ, Wigler MH. Comparative genomic analysis of tumors. Detection of DNA losses and amplification. Proc Natl Acad Sci USA 1995, **92:** 151–155.

629 Sandberg AA, Bridge JA. The cytogenetics of bone and soft tissue tumors. Austin, 1994, RG Landes Co.

630 Schneider NR. Cytogenetic evaluation of childhood neoplasms. Arch Pathol Lab Med 1993, **117:** 1220–1224.

631 Speicher MR, Jauch A, Walt H, du Manoir S, Ried T, Jochum W, Sulser T, Cremer T. Correlation of microscopic phenotype with genotype in a formalinfixed, paraffin-embedded testicular germ cell tumor with universal DNA amplification, comparative genomic hybridization, and interphase cytogenetics. Am J Pathol 1995, **146:** 1332–1340.

632 Sreekantaiah C, Ladanyi M, Rodriguez E, Chaganti RS. Chromosomal aberrations in soft tissue tumors. Relevance to diagnosis, classification, and molecular mechanisms. Am J Pathol 1994, **144:** 1121–1134.

633 Struski S, Doco-Fenzy M, Cornillet-Lefebvre P. Compilation of published comparative genomic hybridisation studies. Cancer Genet Cytogenet 2002, **135:** 63–90.

Molecular pathology

634 Arends MJ, Bird CC. Recombinant DNA technology and its diagnostic applications. Histopathology 1992, **21:** 303–313.

635 Cline MJ. Molecular diagnosis of human cancer. Lab Invest 1989, **61:** 368–380.

636 Crocker J, ed. Molecular Medical Science Series. Molecular biology in histopathology. Chichester, 1994, John Wiley & Sons.

637 El-Naggar AK. Methods in molecular surgical pathology 2002, **19:** 56–71.

638 Gabrielson E, Berg K, Anbazhagan R. Functional genomics, gene arrays, and the future of pathology. Mod Pathol 2001, **14:** 1294–1299.

639 Grody WW, Gatti RA, Naeim F. Diagnostic molecular pathology. Mod Pathol 1989, **2:** 553–568.

640 Mies C. Molecular pathology of paraffin-embedded tissue. Current clinical applications. Diagn Mol Pathol 1992, **1:** 206–211.

641 Naber SP, Smith LL Jr, Wolfe HJ. Role of the frozen tissue bank in molecular pathology. Diagn Mol Pathol 1992, **1:** 73–79.

642 O'Connor SL, Cho JH, Mc Connell TJ. The application of molecular techniques to solid tumors. Semin Diagn Pathol 2002, **19:** 94–103.

643 Rowley JD, Aster JC, Sklar J. The impact of new DNA diagnostic technology on the management of cancer patients. Survey of diagnostic techniques. Arch Pathol Lab Med 1993, **117:** 1104–1109.

644 Sklar J. DNA hybridization in diagnostic pathology. Hum Pathol 1985, **16:** 654–658.

645 Symposium. Molecular techniques in diagnostic pathology. Hum Pathol 1994, **25:** 555–614.

Filter hybridization

646 Bourguin A, Tung R, Galili N, Sklar J. Rapid, nonradioactive detection of clonal T-cell receptor gene rearrangements in lymphoid neoplasms. Proc Natl Acad Sci USA 1990, **87:** 8536–8540.

647 Castora FJ. Western blotting of proteins. Clin Biotechnol 1989, **1:** 43–49.

648 Dubeau L, Chandler LA, Gralow JR, Nichols PW, Jones PA. Southern blot analysis of DNA extracted from formalin-fixed pathology specimens. Cancer Res 1986, **46:** 2964–2969.

649 Joyce AD, D'Emilia JC, Steele G Jr. Libertino JA, Silverman ML, Summerhayes IC. Detection of altered H-ras proteins in human tumors using western blot analysis. Lab Invest 1989, **61:** 212–218.

650 Mies C, Houldsworth J, Chaganti RS. Extraction of DNA from paraffin blocks for Southern blot analysis. Am J Surg Pathol 1991, **15:** 169–174.

651 Sato Y, Mukai K, Matsuno Y, Furuya S, Kagami Y, Miwa M, Shimosato Y. The AMeX method. A multipurpose tissue-processing and paraffin-embedding method. II. Extraction of spooled DNA and its application to Southern blot hybridization analysis. Am J Pathol 1990, **136:** 267–271.

652 Wright CF, Reid AH. Hybridization and blotting techniques. In O'Leary (ed.): Advanced methods in pathology. Principles, practice, and protocols. Philadelphia, 2003, Saunders, pp. 3–91.

653 Wu AM, Ben-Ezra J, Winberg C, Colombero AM, Rappaport H. Analysis of antigen receptor gene rearrangements in ethanol and formaldehyde-fixed, paraffin-embedded specimens. Lab Invest 1990, **63:** 107–114.

In situ hybridization

654 Bashir R, Hochberg F, Singer RH. Detection of Epstein-Barr virus by in situ hybridization. Progress toward development of a nonisotopic diagnostic test. Am J Pathol 1989, **135:** 1035–1044.

655 Cao M, Beckstead JH. Localization of cytomegalovirus DNA in plastic-embedded sections by in situ hybridization. A methodologic study. Am J Pathol 1989, **134:** 457–463.

656 De Lellis RA. In situ hybridization techniques for the analysis of gene expression. Applications in tumor pathology. Hum Pathol 1994, **25:** 580–585.

657 Grody WW, Cheng L, Lewin KJ. Application of in situ DNA hybridization technology to diagnostic surgical pathology. Pathol Annu 1987, **22**(Pt 2): 151–175.

658 Hamilton-Dutoit SJ, Pallesen G. Detection of Epstein-Barr virus small RNAs in routine paraffin sections using non-isotopic RNA/RNA in situ hybridization. Histopathology 1994, **25:** 101–112.

659 Hankin RC, Lloyd RV. Detection of messenger RNA in routinely processed tissue sections with biotinylated oligonucleotide probes. Am J Clin Pathol 1989, **92:** 166–171.

660 Hara M, Yamada S, Hirata K. Nonradioactive in situ hybridisation: recent techniques and applications. Endocr Pathol 2002, **9:** 21–29.

661 Hayden RT, Isotalo PA, Parrett T, Wolk DM, Qian X, Roberts GD, Lloyd RV. In situ hybridisation for the differentiation of Aspergillus, Fusarium and Pseudallescheria species in tissue sections. Diagn Mol Pathol 2003, **12:** 21–26.

662 Holm R, Karlsen F, Nesland JM. In situ hybridization with nonisotopic probes using different detection systems. Mod Pathol 1992, **5:** 315–319.

663 Kenny-Moynihan MB, Under ER. Immunohistochemical and in-situ hybridisation techniques. In O'Leary TJ (ed.): Advanced methods in pathology. Principles, practice, and protocols. Philadelphia, 2003, Saunders, pp. 3–91.

664 Lloyd R. Introduction to molecular endocrine pathology. Endocr Pathol 1993, **4**: 64–72.

665 Naber SP. Molecular pathology – diagnosis of infectious disease. N Engl J Med 1994, **331**: 1212–1215.

666 Niedobitek G, Finn T, Herbst H, Bornhoft G, Gerdes J, Stein H. Detection of viral DNA by in situ hybridization using bromodeoxyuridine-labeled DNA probes. Am J Pathol 1988, **131**: 1–4.

667 Park JS, Kurman RJ, Kessis TD, Shah KV. Comparison of peroxidase-labeled DNA probes with radioactive RNA probes for detection of human papilloma-viruses by in situ hybridization in paraffin sections. Mod Pathol 1991, **4**: 81–85.

668 Polak JM, McGee JO'D. In situ hybridization: principles and practice. Oxford, 1990, Oxford University Press.

669 Shapshak P, Sun NC, Resnick L, Hsu MY, Tourtellotte WW, Schmid P, Conrad A, Fiala M, Imagawa DT. The detection of HIV by in situ hybridization. Mod Pathol 1990, **3**: 146–153.

670 Strickler JG, Manivel JC, Copenhaver CM, Kubic VL. Comparison of in situ hybridization and immunohistochemistry for detection of cytomegalovirus and herpes simplex virus. Hum Pathol 1990, **21**: 443–448.

671 Walker RA, Senior PV, Jones JL, Critchley DR, Varley JM. An immunohistochemical and *in situ* hybridization study of *c-myc* and *c-erbB2* expression in primary human breast carcinomas. J Pathol 1989, **158**: 97–105.

672 Weiss LM, Movahed LA, Chen YY, Shin SS, Stroup RM, Bui N, Estess P, Bindl JM. Detection of immunoglobulin light-chain mRNA in lymphoid tissues using a practical in situ hybridization method. Am J Pathol 1990, **137**: 979–988.

673 Yap EPH, Martinez-Montero J-C, McGee JO'D. mRNA detection in clinical samples by non-isotopic *in situ* hybridization. In Hemington CS, McGee JO'D (eds): Diagnostic molecular pathology. A practical approach. Oxford, 1992, IRL Press.

Interphase cytogenetics

674 Anastasi J. Interphase cytogenetic analysis in the diagnosis and study of neoplastic disorders. Am J Clin Pathol 1991, **95**: S22–S28.

675 Blough RI, Heerema NA, Ulbright TM, Smolarek TA, Roth LM, Einhorn LH. Interphase chromosome painting of paraffin-embedded tissues in the differential diagnosis of possible germ cell tumors. Mod Pathol 1998, **11**: 634–641.

676 Hopman AHN, van Hooren E, van de Kaa CA, Vooijs PGP, Ramaekers FC. Detection of numerical chromosome aberrations using in situ hybridization in paraffin sections of routinely processed bladder cancers. Mod Pathol 1991, **4**: 503–513.

677 Hruban RH, Long PP, Perlman EJ, Hutchins GM, Baumgartner WA, Baughman KL, Griffin CA. Fluorescence in situ hybridization for the Y-chromosome can be used to detect cells of recipient origin in allografted hearts following cardiac transplantation. Am J Pathol 1993, **142**: 975–980.

678 Kim SY, Lee JS, Ro JY, Gay ML, Hong WK, Hittleman WN. Interphase cytogenetics in paraffin sections of lung tumors by non-isotopic in situ hybridization. Mapping genotype/phenotype heterogeneity. Am J Pathol 1993, **142**: 307–317.

679 Lee W, Han K, Harris CP, Shim S, Kim S, Meisner LF. Use of FISH to detect chromosomal translocations and deletions. Analysis of chromosome rearrangement in synovial sarcoma cells from paraffin-embedded specimens. Am J Pathol 1993, **143**: 15–19.

680 Lichter P, Cremer T. Chromosome analysis by non-isotopic in situ hybridization. In Rooney DE, Czepulowski BH (eds): Human cytogenetics. A practical approach. 1(Constitutional abnormalities), ed. 2. Oxford, 1992, IRL Press.

681 Poddighe PJ, Ramaekers FCS, Hopman AHN. Interphase cytogenetics of tumours. J Pathol 1992, **166**: 215–224.

682 Schad CR, Kraker WJ, Jalal SM, Tallman MS, Londer HN, Cook LP, Jenkins RB. Use of fluorescent in situ hybridization for marker chromosome identification in congenital and neoplastic disorders. Cytogenetics 1991, **96**: 203–210.

683 Shapiro DN, Valentine MB, Røwe ST, Sinclair AE, Sublett JE, Roberts WM, Look AT. Detection of N-myc gene amplification by fluorescence in situ hybridization. Diagnostic utility for neuroblastoma. Am J Pathol 1993, **142**: 1339–1346.

684 Warford A, Lauder I. In situ hybridisation in perspective. J Clin Pathol 1991, **44**: 177–181.

685 Wolman SR. Fluorescence in situ hybridisation. A new tool for the pathologist. Hum Pathol 1994, **25**: 586–590.

Polymerase chain reaction

686 Akoury DA, Seo JJ, James CD, Zaki SR. RT-PCR detection of mRNA recovered from archival glass slide smears. Mod Pathol 1993, **6**: 195–200.

686a Chang F, Syrjanen S, Syrjanen K. Implications of the p53 tumor-suppressor gene in clinical oncology. J Clin Oncol 1995, **13**: 1009–1022.

687 Cossman J, Zehnbauer B, Garrett CT, Smith LJ, Williams M, Jaffe ES, Hanson LO, Love J. Gene rearrangements in the diagnosis of lymphoma/leukemia. Guidelines for use based on a multiinstitutional study. Am J Clin Pathol 1991, **95**: 347–354.

688 Erlich HA, Gelfand D, Sninsky JJ. Recent advances in the polymerase chain reaction. Science 1991, **252**: 1643–1651.

689 Ghossein RA, Bhattacharya S. Molecular detection and characterization of circulating tumor cells and micrometastases in prostatic, urothelial, and renal cellcarcinomas. Semin Surg Oncol 2001, **20**: 304–311.

690 Ghossein RA, Rosai J. Polymerase chain reaction in the detection of micrometastases and circulating tumor cells. Cancer 1996, **78**: 10–16.

691 Giordano TJ, Shedden KA, Scwartz DR, Kuick R, Taylor JM, Lee N, Misek DE, Greenson JK, Kardia SL, Beer DG, Rennert G, Cho KR, Gruber SB, Fearon ER, Hanash S. Organ-specific molecular classification of primary lung, colon and ovarian adenocarcinomas using gene expression profiles. Am J Pathol 2001, **159**: 1231–1238.

692 Griesser H. Applied molecular genetics in the diagnosis of malignant non-Hodgkin's lymphoma. Diagn Mol Pathol 1993, **2**: 177–191.

693 Gu J. Principles and applications of in situ PCR. Cell Vision 1994, **1**: 8–19.

694 Hubbs AE. Amplification methods. In O'Leary TJ (ed.): Advanced methods in pathology. Principles, practice, and protocols. Philadelphia, 2003, Saunders, pp. 3–91.

695 Innis MA, Gelfand DH, Sninsky JJ, White TJ (eds): PCR protocols. A guide to methods and applications. San Diego, 1990, Academic Press.

696 Komminoth P, Long AA. In-situ polymerase chain reaction. An overview of methods, applications and limitations of a new molecular technique. Virchows Arch [Cell Pathol] 1993, **64**: 67–73.

697 Liu H, Huang X, Zhang Y, Ye H, El Hamidi A, Kocjan G, Dogan A, Isaacson PG, Du MQ. Archival fixed histologic and cytologic specimens including stained and unstained materials are amenable to RT-PCR. Diagn Mol Pathol 2002, **11**: 222–227.

698 McPherson MJ, Quirke P, Taylor GR (eds): PCR. A practical approach. Oxford, 1992, IRL Press.

699 Moskaluk CA, Kern SE. Microdissection and polymerase chain reaction amplification of genomic DNA from histological tissue sections. Am J Pathol 1997, **150**: 1547–1552.

700 Nuovo GJ. PCR in situ hybridization. Philadelphia, 1995, Lippincott Raven Publishers.

701 Nuovo GJ, MacConnell P, Forde A, Delvenne P. Detection of human papillo-mavirus DNA in formalin-fixed tissues by in situ hybridization after amplification by polymerase chain reaction. Am J Pathol 1991, **139**: 847–854.

702 Osaki M, Adachi H, Gomyo Y, Yoshida H, Ito H. Detection of mycobacterial DNA in formalin-fixed, paraffin-embedded tissue specimens by duplex polymerase chain reaction: application to histopathologic diagnosis. Mod Pathol 1997, **10**: 78–83.

703 Pan LX, Diss TC, Isaacson PG. The polymerase chain reaction in histopathology. Histopathology 1995, **26**: 201–217.

704 Perosio PM, Frank TS. Detection and species identification of mycobacteria in paraffin sections of lung biopsy specimens by the polymerase chain reaction. Am J Clin Pathol 1993, **100**: 643–647.

705 Remick DG, Kunkel SL, Holbrook EA, Hanson CA. Theory and applications of the polymerase chain reaction. Am J Clin Pathol 1990, **93**: S49–S54.

706 Rolston R, Sasatomi E, Hunt J, Swalsky P, Finkelstein SD. Distinguishing do novo second cancer formation from tumor recurrence: mutational fingerprinting by microdissection genotyping. J Mol Diagn 2001, **3**: 129–132.

707 Ruschoff J, Bocker T, Schlegel J, Stumm G, Hofstaedter F. Microsatellite instability. New aspects in the carcinogenesis of colorectal carcinoma. Virchows Archiv 1995, **426**: 215–222.

708 Sawyers CL, Timson L, Kawasaki ES, Clark SS, Witte ON, Champlin R. Molecular relapse in chronic myelogenous leukemia patients after bone marrow transplantation detected by polymerase chain reaction. Proc Natl Acad Sci USA 1990, **87**: 563–567.

709 Templeton NS. The polymerase chain reaction. History, methods, and applications. Diagn Mol Pathol 1992, **1**: 58–72.

710 Tham KM, Chow VT, Singh P, Tock EP, Ching KC, Lim-Tan SK, Sng IT, Bernard HU. Diagnostic sensitivity of polymerase chain reaction and Southern blot hybridization for the detection of human papillomavirus DNA in biopsy specimens from cervical lesions. Am J Clin Pathol 1991, **95**: 638–646.

711 Wright PA, Wynford-Thomas D. The polymerase chain reaction. Miracle or mirage? A critical review of its uses and limitations in diagnosis and research. J Pathol 1990, **162**: 99–117.

DNA microarrays

712 Bertucci F, Viens P, Tagett R, Nguyen C, Houlgatte R, Birnbaum D. DNA arrays in clinical oncology: promises and challenges. Lab Invest 2003, **83**: 305–316.

713 Callagy G, Cattaneo E, Daigo Y, Happerfield L, Bobrow LG, Pharoah PD, Caldas C. Molecular classification of breast carcinomas using tissue microarrays. Diagn Mol Pathol 2003, **12**: 27–34.

714 Golub TR, Slonim Dk, Tamayo P, Huatd C, Gaasenbeek M, Mesirov JP, Coller H, Loh ML, Dowing JR, Caliguri MA, Bloomfield CD, Lander ES. Molecular classification of cancer: class discovery and class prediction by gene expression monitoring. Science 1999, **286**: 531–537.

715 Heller MJ. DNA microarray technology: devices, systems, and applications. Annu Rev Biomed Eng 2002, **4**: 129–153.

715a Shedden KA, Taylor JMG, Giordano TJ, Kuick R, Misek DE, Rennert G, Schwartz DR, Gruber SB, Logsdon C, Simeone D, Kardia SLR, Greenson JK, Cho KR, Beer DG, Fearon ER, Hanash S. Accurate molecular classification of human cancers based on gene expression using a simple classifier with a pathological tree-based framework. Am J Pathol 2003, **163**: 1985–1995.

Microdissection

716 Eltoum IA, Siegal GP, Frost AR. Microdissection of histologic sections: past, present, and future. Adv Anat Pathol 2002, **9**: 316–322.

717 Willenberg HS, Walters R, Bornstein SR. Use of laser microdissection in complex tissue. Methods Enzymol 2002, **356**: 216–223.

718 Wittliff JL, Erlander MG. Laser capture microdissection and its applications in genomic and proteomics. Methods Enzymol 2002, **356**: 12–25.

Oncogenes and tumor-suppressor genes

719 Chang F, Syrjanen S, Syrjanen K. Implications of the p53 tumor-suppressor gene in clinical oncology. J Clin Oncol 1995, **13**: 1009–1022.

720 Dhaene K, Van Marck E, Parwaresch R. Telomeres, telomerase and cancer: an up-date. Virchows Archiv 2000, **437**: 1–16.

721 Dowell SP, Hall PA. The clinical relevance of the p53 tumour suppressor gene. Cytopathology 1994, **5**: 133–145.

722 Dunlop MG. Allele losses and onco-suppressor genes. J Pathol 1991, **163**: 1–5.

723 Greenblatt MS, Bennett WP, Hollstein M, et al. Mutations in the p53 tumor suppressor gene. Clues to cancer etiology and molecular pathogenesis. Cancer Res 1994, **54**: 4855–4878.

724 Harris CC, Hollstein M. Clinical implications of the p53 tumor-suppressor gene. N Engl J Med 1993, **329**: 1318–1327.

725 Hanahan D, Weinberg R. The hallmarks of cancer. Cell 2000, **100**: 57–70.

726 Huxley J. Biologic aspects of cancer. Brace & Co 1958.

727 Knudson AG. Antioncogenes and human cancer. Proc Natl Acad Sci USA 1993, **90**: 10914–10921.

728 Levine AJ. The tumor suppressor genes. Annu Rev Biochem 1993, **62**: 623–651.

729 Locker J. Tumor suppressor genes and the practice of surgical pathology. Hum Pathol 1995, **26**: 359–361.

730 Maguire HC Jr., Greene MI. The neu (c-erbB-2) oncogene. Semin Oncol 1989, **16**: 148–155.

731 Paul J. Tumour suppressor genes. Oncogenesis update. Histopathology 1989, **15**: 1–9.

732 Sard L, Accornero P, Tornielli S, Delia D, Bunone G, Campiglio M, Colombo MP, Gramegna M, Croce CM, Pierotti MA, Sozzi G. The tumor-suppressor gene FHIT is involved in the regulation of apoptosis and in cell cycle control. Proc Natl Acad Sci USA 1999, **96**: 8489–8492.

733 Taylor D, Koch WM, Zahurak M, Shah K, Sidransky D, Westra WH. Immunohistochemical detection of p53 protein accumulation in head and neck cancer: correlation with p53 gene alterations. Hum Pathol 1999, **30**: 1221–1225.

4 Skin

Dermatoses
Tumors and tumorlike conditions

Dermatoses

Introduction to dermatopathology

The entities described in this section are a select group taken from the large number of diseases that affect the skin. They have been chosen to encompass the types of non-neoplastic material generally seen in surgical pathology laboratories. Many of the infrequently biopsied, histologically nonspecific, and rare dermatoses are excluded. Their characteristics are described in texts devoted wholly to dermatopathology and in the dermatologic literature.[1–11]

The fact that isolated histopathologic analysis has distinct limitations becomes more evident in the evaluation of the reactive processes associated with diseases of the skin than in most other organs. It is imperative that the clinical differential diagnosis be correlated with the gross and microscopic observations in order to render a clinically meaningful diagnosis.

Skin biopsies are often small and have minimal gross changes. Ideally, the lesion should be examined by the pathologist on the patient, but, in lieu of this, an accurate clinical description and differential diagnosis should accompany each biopsy. All biopsies should be taken from grossly characteristic areas. It is a waste of time and money to biopsy ruptured bullae, secondarily infected or heavily scratched areas, or the incipient or involuting lesion. Multiple biopsies may be advisable when the lesions present differing forms and stages. In diseases in which the expected changes are quantitative rather than qualitative (i.e., hyperkeratosis, acanthosis, increase in dermal thickness), the evaluation of these changes is best made by taking a punch biopsy also of clinically normal skin nearby, which represents the best possible control. Formalin, 10% buffered, is an adequate and widely available fixative. Bouin's and Zenker's fixatives may be used but have no unique merits. Incisional and punch biopsies can be kept from curling during fixation by placing them on a piece of file card prior to immersion. When the specimen is 0.3 mm or less in diameter, it is best processed into paraffin in one piece. It may then be sampled at various levels in the block. This prevents loss of tissue during the facing-up of the block and allows more adequate sampling. These technical niceties prevent delays, mishaps, and some mistakes.

Normal anatomy

The skin or integument is a complex organ with many functions and with three main anatomic components: epidermis and skin adnexa, melanocytic system, and dermis and subcutis.[16,22,23,33]

The **epidermis** is a stratified squamous epithelium that differentiates to form the outer protective layer of keratin. It is composed of keratinocytes arranged in four layers: basal, squamous (prickle, malpighian), granular, and cornified (horny). The *basal cells* are the mitotically active cells that give rise to all other keratinocytes; they contain low-molecular-weight keratin and are separated from the dermis by a continuous basal layer, to which they are attached by hemidesmosomes. The *basal membrane* is a complex antigenic structure that plays an important role in many cutaneous diseases.[13] The dermoepidermal junction is thrown into undulating folds of interlocking ridges of epidermis (*rete ridges*) and *dermal papillae*. Thus the undersurface of the epidermis seen in whole mounts presents an anastomosing and reticulated pattern of ridges and valleys. The pattern and size of these ridges vary from area to area. With age, they diminish in size, and the dermoepidermal junction becomes flattened.

The *squamous layer* is composed of several layers of cells, which become larger, more flattened, and more eosinophilic as they approach the surface. This correlates with the intracytoplasmic accumulation of filaments, which are the precursors of keratin, and a diminution of ribosomes. Some cells in the squamous layer exhibit a clear, vacuolated cytoplasm (sometimes resulting in nuclear indentation), which should not be confused with

that of melanocytes or Paget cells. When the cells are separated, as a result of fixation and dehydration or intercellular edema, these areas of attachment are seen via the light microscope as fine spiny ("intercellular") bridges, with a dot-like structure at their center (Bizzozero's nodule), representing the desmosome. The epidermal cells are not a syncytium, and true intercellular bridges do not exist. Destruction of these attachments causes the cells to lose their cohesiveness. This process, termed *acantholysis*, is seen in pemphigus vulgaris and related diseases. The *granular layer* is composed of one to three layers of flattened cells containing keratohyaline granules. These coarse, intensely basophilic granules are rich in histidine and represent the precursors of the protein *filaggrin*, which is responsible for the aggregation of keratin filaments. The cornified layer contains multiple layers of polyhedral cells that have lost their nuclei and that are arranged in a basket-weave pattern (except for the acral regions, in which this layer is thick and compact). The skin from the palms and soles features an additional layer—the stratum lucidum—located between the granular and the cornified layers and appearing as a homogeneous eosinophilic zone.

The major proteins of basal keratinocytes are keratins 5 and 14, which form an extensive network of 10-nm cytoskeletal filaments. As keratinocytes differentiate, they downregulate this pair of keratins and switch on expression of other pairs, the nature of which is dependent on the site. In the epidermis, terminally differentiated keratinocytes express keratins 1 and 10.[17]

The keratinization cycle usually takes 30 to 45 days. Many dermatoses result in alterations in the pattern and speed of this process. Abnormal keratinization may be manifest by *hyperkeratosis*, in which the stratum corneum is thickened, usually in association with a more prominent granular layer, or by *parakeratosis*, in which the cells of the stratum corneum retain their nuclei and the granular layer is diminished or absent.

Certain descriptive terms are applied to alterations in the pattern of the epidermis. It may become *atrophic* or thinned with age or disease. It may be thickened, and as it proliferates the rete ridges extend deeper into the dermis, a process known as *acanthosis*. Outward overgrowth of the epidermis accompanied by elongation of the dermal papillae is *papillomatosis*. A degenerative process in which the basal cells become vacuolated, separated, and disorganized is called *liquefactive or hydropic degeneration*. Various combinations of these changes are seen in the dermatoses, and this descriptive jargon allows succinct communication.

In addition to keratinocytes, the normal epidermis contains melanocytes, Langerhans' cells, and Merkel cells. Melanocytes are described on p. 154. Langerhans' cells are bone marrow-derived dendritic cells whose function is to present antigens to immunologically competent T cells. They are scattered throughout the upper part of the squamous layer and are difficult to identify in routinely stained sections. Ultrastructurally, they have a characteristic organelle—the Birbeck granule—a rod-shaped structure with zipper-like striations and sometimes a bulbous end. Immunohistochemically, they express CD1a, and S-100 protein; they have receptor sites for the Fc portion of the IgG molecule and the third component of complement.[32]

Merkel cells, also extremely difficult to identify in H&E sections and even with special stains, are concentrated in the glabrous skin of the digits, lips, outer root sheath of hair follicles, and tactile hair disks. Ultrastructurally, they contain cytoplasmic dense core (neurosecretory-type) granules, often arranged beneath the cell membrane or located within unmyelinated neurites. Spinous processes projecting from the cytoplasm anchor these cells to adjacent keratinocytes. Immunohistochemically, Merkel cells are reactive for NSE, neurofilaments, keratin (including CK20) and a variety of peptide hormones.[15,21]

The skin adnexa are represented by the hair follicles, sebaceous glands, sweat (eccrine) glands, and apocrine glands. The hair follicle, sebaceous gland, erector pili muscle, and (in certain regions) the apocrine gland constitute a functional complex known as the *pilar unit.*

The hair follicle is responsible for the formation of hair, a cyclic process that proceeds in three phases: anagen or growing phase, catagen or involuting phase, and telogen or resting phase. The mitotically active cells of the hair follicles lining the dermal papilla are the matrix (generative) cells. These cells give rise to the hair shaft and the inner root sheath. The outer layer of the latter structure is surrounded by a layer of large clear (glycogen-rich) cells known as the outer root sheath. At the level of the isthmus, these cells undergo an abrupt type of keratinization, which occurs without the interposition of a granular layer; this is referred to as trichilemmal keratinization, and, by extension, the layer itself is known as the trichilemmal sheath. By contrast, the keratinization in the infundibular portion of the follicle is similar to that of the adjacent epidermis. It is not unusual to find *Demodex folliculorum* mites, clumps of *Staphylococcus epidermidis*, and yeasts of *Pityrosporum* inside the pilar infundibulum.

The sebaceous glands are lobulated structures containing an outer layer of germinative cells that, as they differentiate, move toward the inside and accumulate intracytoplasmic lipid droplets. These result in a typical multivacuolated appearance, with multiple indentations of the centrally located nucleus. The excretory duct of the sebaceous glands opens into the infundibulum of the hair follicle.

Sweat glands are of three types: eccrine (responsible for thermoregulation and, therefore, the only "true" sweat glands), apocrine, and mixed (apoeccrine glands). Eccrine sweat glands are tubular structures with a secretory and an excretory portion. The secretory coil, located in the deep dermis or sometimes in the subcutis, is composed of secretory cells (further divided into clear and dark cells) and myoepithelial cells. The excretory portion is composed of a dermal (straight) and an intraepidermal (spiral) portion, the latter also known as *acrosyringium.*

Apocrine glands are concentrated in the axillae, groin, perineum, but they also occur in small numbers on the face and elsewhere. Like eccrine glands, they have a secretory and an excretory component. It is the former that gives them their highly characteristic appearance. The cells have an abundant acidophilic cytoplasm, which may contain lipid, iron, and lipofuscin.

Immunohistochemically, the various epithelial components of eccrine and apocrine glands stain for CEA, EMA, keratin, S-100 protein, the enzyme carbonic anhydrase, ferritin, secretory immunoglobulin, and pregnancy-specific β-I-glycoprotein (SPI). In addition, apocrine glands express the marker known as GCDFP-15.[26] The myoepithelial cells stain for actin, calponin, caldesmon, and S-100 protein.[14,19,20,24–27,30,31]

The epidermal adnexa are seldom the sites of primary changes. However, diagnostic changes do occur: heterotopias as in nevus sebaceous of Jadassohn, in which apocrine glands are found in the scalp; pigmentation of eccrine gland basement membranes in argyria and hemochromatosis; atrophy, as in scleroderma; duct obstruction with subsequent retention, as in the various forms of miliaria; and deposition of aggregates of granules of mucoprotein in the eccrine gland cells in myxedematous patients.

The **dermis** is a connective tissue structure composed of collagen and elastic fibers bathed in ground substance and containing adnexal structures, vessels, and nerves. It is divided into two layers: adventitial and reticular. The adventitial dermis comprises the superficial layer located immediately beneath the epidermis—the papillary dermis—and that located around adnexal structures—the periadnexal dermis.[32]

The adventitial dermis is largely composed of a delicate network of collagen fibers (mainly type I, with a scattering of type III or "reticulin" fibers), whereas the reticular dermis is made up of thick bundles of type I collagen intermixed with thick elastic fibers.

The thickness of the dermis varies considerably from area to area; it is particularly thick in the back, a feature that is sometimes misinterpreted as being abnormal in biopsies.

The subcutaneous tissue (subcutis) is composed of lobules of mature adipose tissue separated by thin bands of connective tissue-like interlobular septa. The dermal blood vessels are divided into a deep plexus (located in the reticular dermis) and a superficial plexus (located in the papillary dermis), with communicating vessels in between. From the superficial vascular plexus, capillary loops extend into the dermal papillae. The acral skin contains specialized arteriovenous anastomoses—the *Sucquet–Hoyer canals*—surrounded by a row of modified smooth muscle—the *glomus cells*—which have a round shape, clear cytoplasm, and well-defined cytoplasmic borders. The lymphatics of the skin are also divided into a deep and a superficial plexus.

Specialized nerve end organs present in the skin are the *Wagner–Meissner* corpuscles (with a tactile function; mainly located in the papillary dermis of the palms and soles) and *Pacinian corpuscles* (sensitive to pressure; mainly located in the deep dermis and subcutis of weight-bearing areas). With age, and more so in areas exposed to sunlight, the collagen and elastica undergo structural and tinctorial changes called basophilic degeneration of the collagen and senile (actinic) elastosis, respectively.[18,28] These changes should not be attributed to some suspect disease and should be distinguished from pathologic connective tissue changes.

The dermis is the site of inflammatory reactions. In normal skin, a few fibroblasts, macrophages, mast cells, lymphocytes, and dermal dendrocytes are present. The latter represent a population of mononuclear dendritic cells located in the papillary and upper reticular dermis and are thought to function as antigen-presenting cells. They express the coagulation factor XIIIa (also known as fibrin stabilizing factor) and are known to increase in number in a large number of inflammatory and neoplastic disorders.[12,29]

The perivascular and periadnexal spaces and the papillary layer of the dermis are the usual sites in which inflammatory cells aggregate. Certain dermatoses, such as lichen planus and chronic discoid lupus erythematosus, have distinct patterns of inflammatory reaction. Others, such as urticaria pigmentosa, have a specific cellular population. Changes in the nerves, visible in sections stained with hematoxylin–eosin, are infrequent but when present are of note (see section on leprosy, p. 99).

Inflammatory diseases of known etiology

Viral diseases

The viral lesions of skin most commonly seen histologically are warts and condylomas. However, vesiculobullous lesions caused by herpes simplex and herpes zoster and the varicelliform eruption following vaccination of atopic individuals may occasionally be biopsied.[35] These lesions are formed by ballooning and reticular degeneration of the epidermal cells. The fine points of differentiation were described in the classic work by Ebert and Otsuka.[34] The viruses of herpes, vaccinia, and warts can be detected in the vesicular fluid or tissue by electron microscopy, immunohistochemistry, or in situ hybridization.

Warts

Warts are cutaneous (and sometimes mucosal) lesions caused by one of the several human papilloma viruses (HPV), which are members of the papova group.[38,46,52] Several variants of warts occur,[40] depending primarily on the HPV subtype but also on the anatomic features of the region.[41,42,53] *Verruca vulgaris* (generally associated with HPV-2) usually occurs on the hands as an elevated, hard, rough, flesh-colored lesion. The top may be peeled off, leaving a pink granular surface. *Verruca plantaris* occurs on the sole of the foot, is covered by a callus, and is often painful. *Verruca plana* (usually associated with HPV-10) is, as its name indicates, a flatter lesion usually seen in crops or clusters on the face and hands. Flat warts disseminated throughout the body are a feature of the genetically determined *epidermodysplasia verruciformis*.[48,54] *Condyloma acuminatum* or "venereal wart" (usually caused by HPV-6) occurs around the anus and vulva, on the glans penis, and sometimes in other mucosal membranes such as the oral cavity.

The histologic characteristics of these lesions are those of focal epidermal hyperplasia manifested by hyperkeratosis and parakeratosis, varying degrees of acanthosis, and (except for verruca plana) papillomatosis (Fig. 4.1). A trichilemmal type of keratinization may be present.[49] Distinct vacuolization of the cells in the upper portion of the malpighian layer is a feature in early lesions; some of these abnormal cells have large cytoplasmic eosinophilic aggregates. Smaller vacuolated cells with pyknotic nuclei may also be seen in the lower portions of the

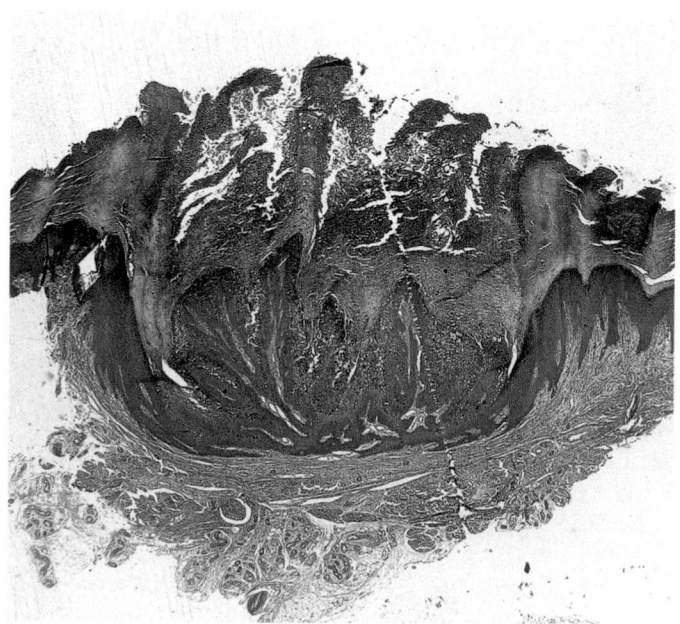

Fig. 4.1 Verruca vulgaris. The lesion is cup-shaped and highly keratotic.

thickened stratum corneum. In condyloma acuminatum, acanthosis may be florid, and tangential cuts can show isolated nests of squamous cells surrounded by inflamed dermis. Care should be taken not to overdiagnose such lesions as squamous cell carcinoma. Older verrucae may not show the microscopic changes that allow their recognition; they may appear simply as papillomas or keratoses. Flat warts undergoing involution exhibit marked mononuclear dermal and intraepidermal inflammation associated with degenerative epidermal changes.[36,37,44] The viral nuclear inclusions are basophilic, Feulgen positive, and DNAse resistant. They can be demonstrated immunohistochemically and with in situ hybridization techniques[46,51] (Fig. 4.2). The eosinophilic cytoplasmic masses are not made of viral material but rather represent accumulations of tonofilaments.

Occasionally, benign or malignant skin tumors and tumorlike conditions of various types (such as seborrheic keratosis, Bowen's disease, and invasive squamous cell carcinoma) are seen superimposed on HPV-induced lesions, suggesting a causal relationship.[43,47,55] Epidermodysplasia verruciformis is the most obvious example.[39,45,50] Changes in keratin expression occur in the keratinocytes as a result of the viral infection, and further changes develop when a neoplastic process supervenes.[51,56]

Molluscum contagiosum

Molluscum contagiosum is a skin disease produced by MCV, a virus specific to humans, present worldwide, and passed by direct skin to skin contact.[63] It is characterized by small, firm, usually multiple nodules that, when fully developed, have central cores from which white keratinous material can be expressed (Fig. 4.3A). The microscopic picture is characteristic. The dermis is indented by a sharply delimited and lobulated mass of proliferating epithelium (Fig. 4.3B). As the cells differentiate within the mass, their cytoplasm gradually is filled

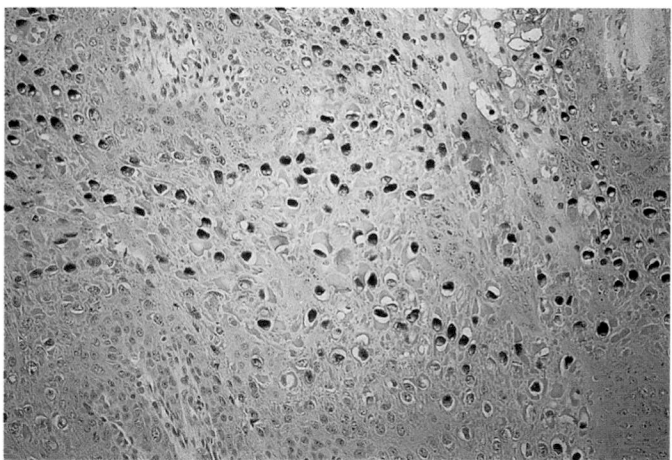

Fig. 4.2 Immumohistochemical demonstration of Papova virus in nuelei of keratinocytes in verruca vulgaris.

by a faintly granular eosinophilic inclusion that displaces the nucleus and enlarges the cells (Fig. 4.3C). These molluscum bodies are formed of viral particles that are similar in size and mode of formation to the poxviruses.[64] Inflammation in the surrounding dermis is intense, sometimes in the form of an abscess,[58] and sometimes in the form of a pleomorphic T-cell infiltrate that can simulate a lymphomatous/leukemic process.[57,59] Metaplastic ossification has been occasionally observed.[61]

Reed and Parkinson[62] believe that molluscum contagiosum arises on the basis of follicular neogenesis, based on their findings of areas of hair bulb differentiation at the periphery, occasionally associated with areas of sebaceous gland differentiation. However, the disease can also appear in places where there are no hair follicles, such as the palms, indicating that the epidermis itself may be affected.[60]

Herpes zoster

Herpes zoster is a painful disease caused by the same virus that causes chickenpox (varicella). It may vary from relatively benign pruritic lesions on the trunk, usually unilateral and in the distribution of a single dermatome, to severe involvement of the first division of the trigeminal nerve with herpetic keratitis and corneal ulceration.[65,68] Postherpetic neuralgia is the unpleasant sequela. Patients with leukemia and malignant lymphoma develop herpes zoster more frequently.[67] The histopathologic features of varicella–herpes zoster lesions differ in several respects from those of herpes simplex lesions.[66]

Bacterial diseases

Folliculitis

The term folliculitis refers to an inflammatory process distributed around hair follicles and involving the follicular opening or adjacent perifollicular skin.[71] They have been divided microscopically into:

1 Infectious
   Superficial (usually suppurative): resulting from fungi, bacteria, syphilis, or viruses
   Deep (usually granulomatous): resulting from fungi or bacteria
2 Noninfectious
   Superficial (usually suppurative): acne vulgaris, rosacea, follicular mucinosis, steroid-induced, etc.
   Deep (usually granulomatous): acne vulgaris (conglobate and keloidal forms), perforating forms, etc.
   Spongiotic: Fox–Fordyce disease, atopic dermatitis, pruritic folliculitis of pregnancy
3 Perifolliculitis
   Predominantly lymphocytic: lichen planopilaris, pityriasis rubra pilaris, etc.
   Predominantly granulomatous: perioral dermatitis, rosacea, etc.

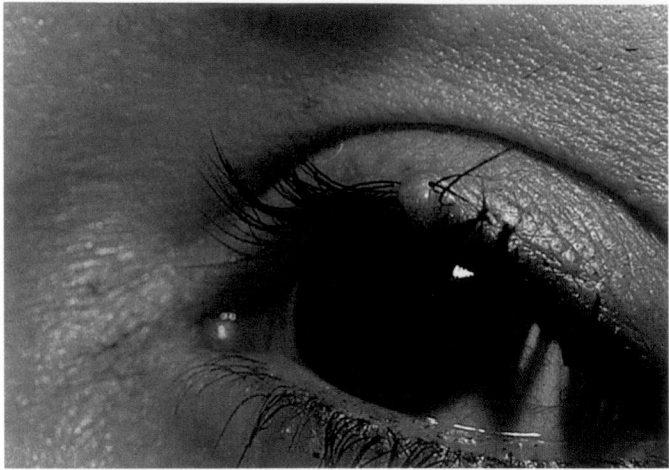

A

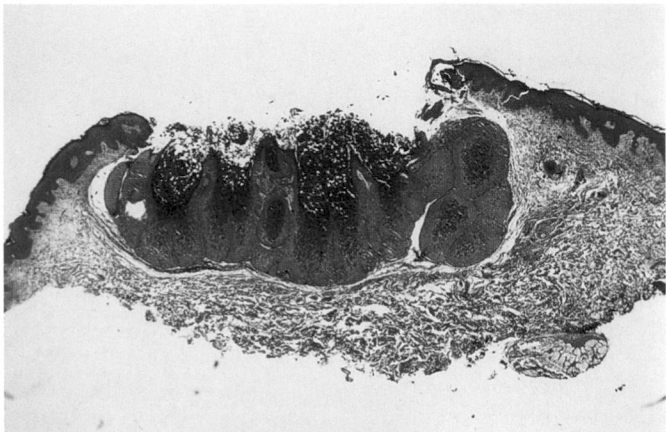

B

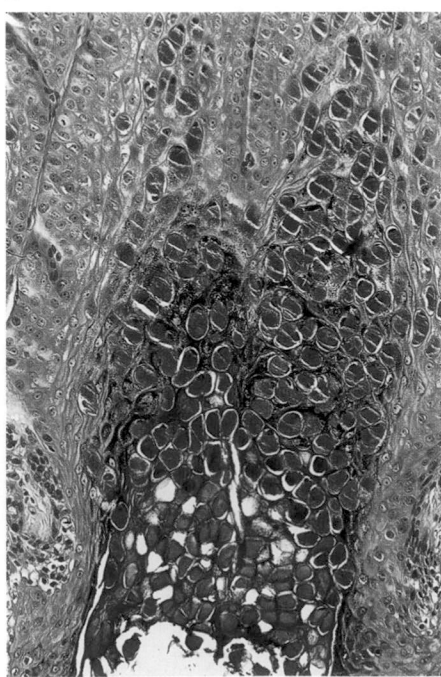

C

Fig. 4.3 Molluscum contagiosum. **A,** Clinical appearance of lesion located in eyelid; **B,** Low-power view of cup-shaped lesion; **C,** High-power view showing numerous molluscum bodies. (**A,** Courtesy of Dr. Carlos Ramos, Belleville, IL)

Demodex mites are more frequent in inflamed follicles than in normal ones, but it is not clear whether they play an etiologic role.[74] *Eosinophilic folliculitis*, as seen in adults and infants, is an HIV-related dermatosis[72,73] (see p. 117). The term *pseudolymphomatous folliculitis* has been proposed for a skin lesion usually located in the face characterized histologically by a dense lymphocytic infiltrate of mixed nature centered around hair follicles, with infiltration of the follicular epithelium.[69] The suggestion has been made that at least of the cases diagnosed as solitary sclerotic fibroma of the skin may be the end stage of a folliculitis.[70]

Hidradenitis suppurativa

Hidradenitis suppurativa is caused by bacterial infection in and about apocrine glands, usually in the axilla but occasionally involving the perineum or vulva[76] (Fig. 4.4). Anaerobic organisms are the most important pathogens. Abscesses, sinuses, and perianal fistulas occur with subsequent scarring.[77] The process tends toward chronicity, and in refractory cases excision of the involved skin may be required.[78,79] The follicles into which the apocrine glands open are plugged by keratin and infection develops following stasis.[80] The end stages are similar to those of severe acne vulgaris and the more chronic disfiguring lesions of *acne aggregata seu conglobata*, in which squamous carcinoma may eventuate.[75]

Tuberculosis and atypical mycobacteriosis

Cutaneous tuberculosis is an uncommon disease in the United States, although its incidence is on the rise.[81] It has various clinical and morphologic forms depending on the mode of entry and whether it is a primary or secondary infection.[81]

Lupus vulgaris is a reactivation type of tuberculosis. It generally involves the face, and the lesions are formed

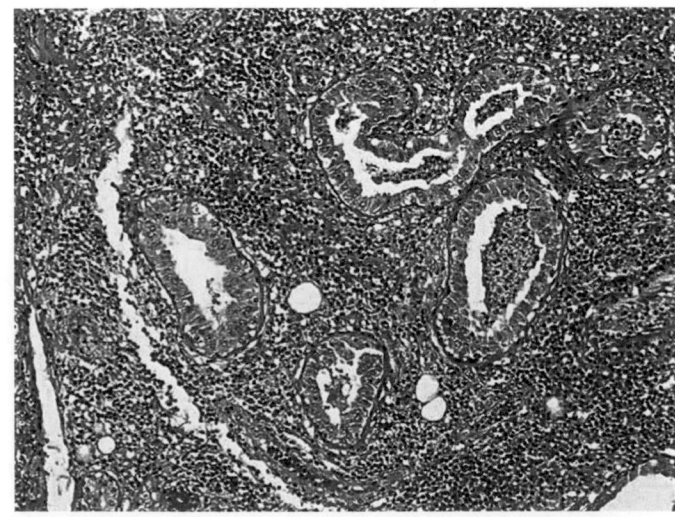

Fig. 4.4 Hidradenitis suppurativa. A heavy neutrophilic infiltrate is present around apocrine glands and in their dilated lumina. (Courtesy Dr. Raffaele Gianotti, Milano, Italy)

of red patches in which small, firm nodules reside[87] (Fig. 4.5). When pressed with a glass slide (diascopy), these nodules have a pale tan color. Microscopically, non-necrotic (sarcoid-like) and—less commonly—necrotic granulomas are found in the dermis (Fig. 4.6). Acid-fast bacilli are difficult to demonstrate but may be found. Cultures are recommended. The organisms can also be demonstrated with PCR methods.[81,94] Ulceration of the skin may occur. In long-standing cases, frank squamous cell carcinoma may arise from these lesions.

Papulonecrotic tuberculid is a skin lesion associated with tuberculosis but typically devoid of organisms; it is seen both in adults and children,[85] and is characterized microscopically by dermal necrosis, a poorly formed granulomatous infiltrate, vasculitis, and edema.[86] Rarely, the vasculitis is in the form of a nodular granulomatous phlebitis.[83]

Erythema induratum of Bazin is a form of tuberculid presenting as recurrent tender subcutaneous nodules that occur mainly on the calves of women with tuberculin hypersensitivity.[90] Mycobacterial DNA has been found in these lesions by PCR.[91]

Atypical mycobacteria can also affect the skin and result in a variety of lesions, including ulceration, abscesses, granulomas, diffuse histiocytic reactions, panniculitis, and rheumatoid-like nodules.[82,88,89,92] *M. kansasii*, *M. marinum*, and *M. ulcerans* are the organisms most commonly implicated.[84,93]

Leprosy

In most regions of the United States, leprosy is a rarity. However, an increased number of cases have been seen during the past decades as the result of the influx of immigrants from Asia and other regions of the world in which the disease is still endemic. Therefore, the pathologist should consider it in the differential diagnosis of dermal granulomas and histiocytic tumors.[96,99] In lepromatous leprosy the *lepra* or *Virchow cells*, filled with acid-fast bacilli, are plentiful (Figs 4.7 and 4.8), but in tuberculoid and indeterminate leprosy, bacilli are very scanty.[95] As for tuberculosis, a PCR-based diagnosis of leprosy is now available.[98] A diagnosis of leprosy should be suspected whenever the granulomas or the lymphocytic infiltration is located in and around the cutaneous nerves or when seen infiltrating and destroying arrectores pilorum muscle[97] (Fig. 4.9). Subcutaneous nodules are seen only in the lepromatous form and are sometimes designated *erythema nodosum leprorum*.

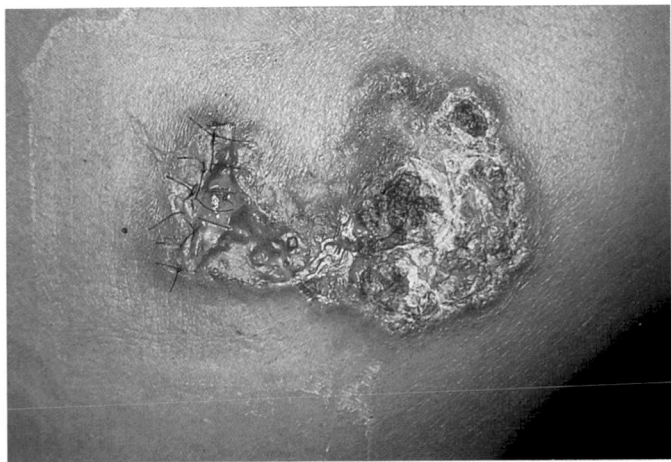

Fig. 4.5 Clinical appearance of lupus vulgaris. The lesion presents in the form of an irregularly shaped red patch with elevated borders.

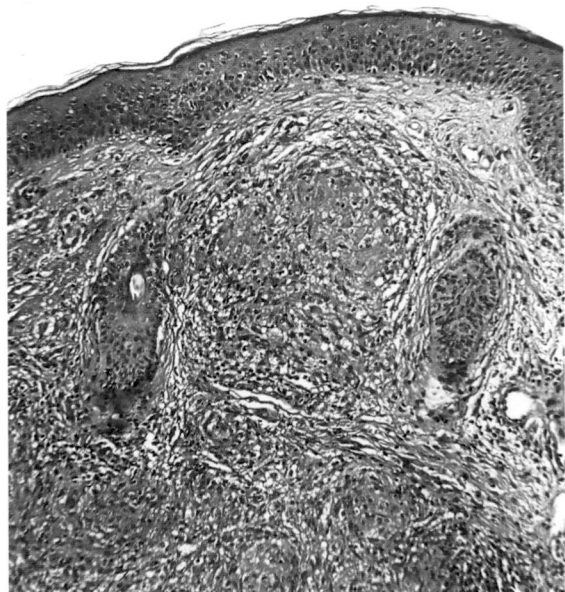

Fig. 4.6 Tuberculosis of skin (lupus vulgaris). Well-formed granulomas with necrotic centers are present in the dermis.

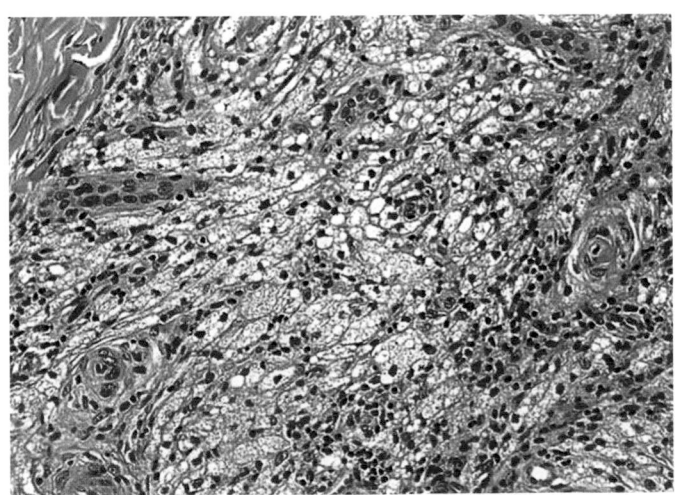

Fig. 4.7 Lepromatous leprosy. Large collections of foamy macrophages (Virchow cells) infiltrate the dermis.

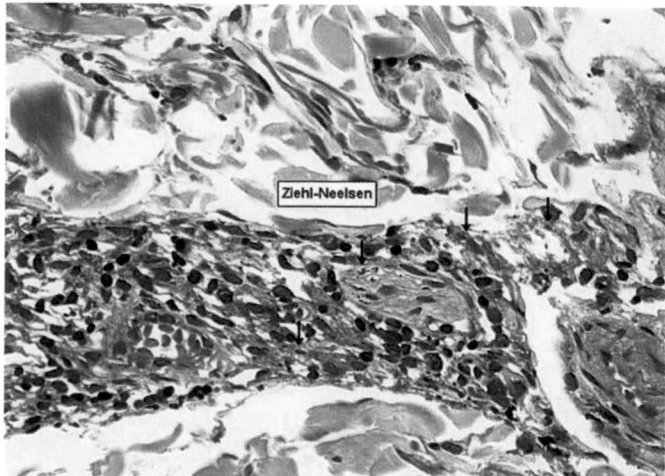

Fig. 4.8 Acid-fast stain shows leprosy organisms (arrows) in a perineurial inflammatory infiltrate. (Courtesy of Dr. Raffaele Gianotti, Milan, Italy)

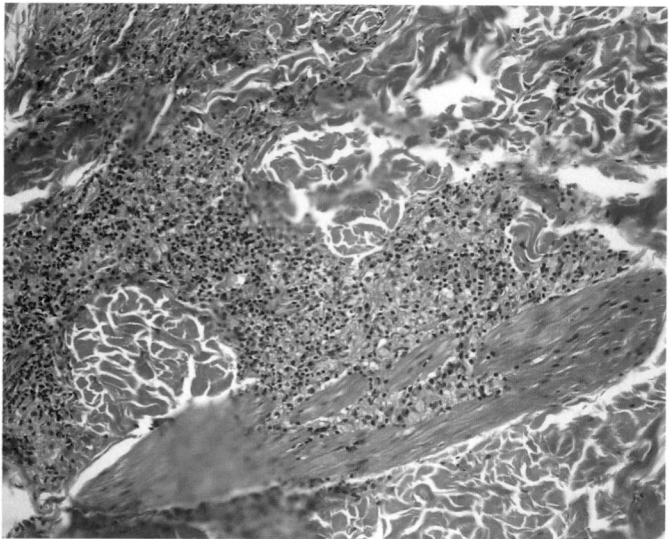

Fig. 4.9 Infiltration of the arrectores piloris muscle by inflammatory cells. This is a diagnostic clue for the diagnosis of leprosy.

Malakoplakia

A few cutaneous examples of this disease have been reported, the histiocytes having the typical Michaelis–Gutmann bodies and sometimes containing identifiable gram-negative organisms.[101,102] Some of the cases have occurred in HIV-infected patients.[100] For a more detailed account of this disorder, the reader is referred to Chapter 17.

Spirochetal diseases

Syphilis

The cutaneous lesions of secondary syphilis are of the maculopapular type and can be confused clinically with drug eruption, lichen planus, psoriasis, and other dermatoses (Fig. 4.10). It can also present in the form of moth-eaten alopecia.[105] The microscopic appearance can be nonspecific, especially in the macular lesions. The

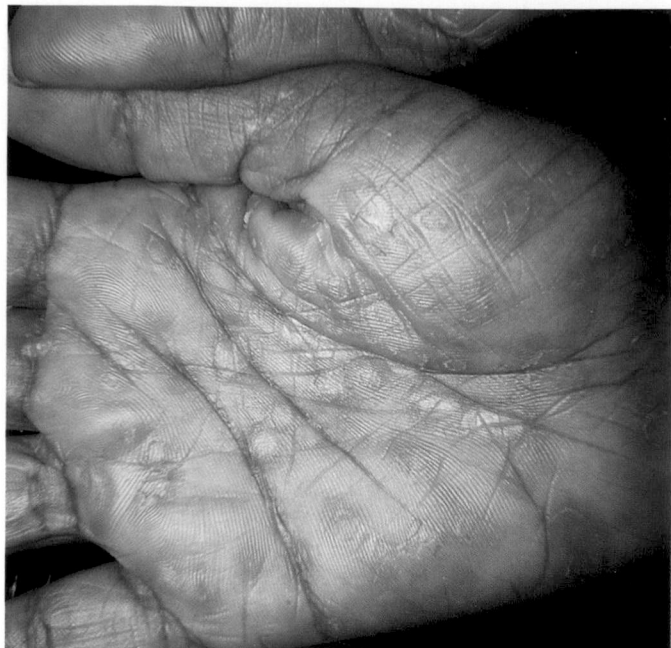

Fig. 4.10 Palmar lesions of secondary syphilis.

late papular lesions are more likely to exhibit the distinctive microscopic appearance of a dense perivascular or diffuse infiltrate predominantly or exclusively composed of plasma cells[103] (Fig. 4.11). Noncaseating granulomas may also be present. The blood vessels characteristically show marked endothelial swelling and often proliferation. The cutaneous lesions of syphilis occurring in HIV-infected individuals do not differ significantly at the microscopic level from those seen in immunocompetent persons.[107]

Engelkens et al.[104] identified spirochetes with the Steiner staining in 71% of their cases of secondary syphilis. A sensitive and specific PCR method to detect *Treponema pallidum* in biopsies and biological fluid has been developed.[106]

Lyme disease

Lyme disease, a multisystem disorder caused by the spirochete *Borrelia burgdorferi*, is most commonly transmitted to humans by a tick bite.[113] It may be manifest in the skin as erythema chronicum migrans (currently regarded as pathognomonic of the disease),[115] acrodermatitis chronica atrophicans, and cutaneous lymphoid hyperplasia ("borrelial lymphocytoma").[108–110,112,117] In the early stages, the predominant microscopic finding is a superficial and deep perivascular infiltrate largely composed of lymphocytes but also containing plasma cells and/or eosinophils (Fig. 4.12). Spirochetes can be demonstrated with the Warthin–Starry silver stain[114]: the organisms have also been detected by PCR in synovial fluid.[118]

It has been suggested that some cases of morphea, lichen sclerosus et atrophicus, anetoderma, and atropho-

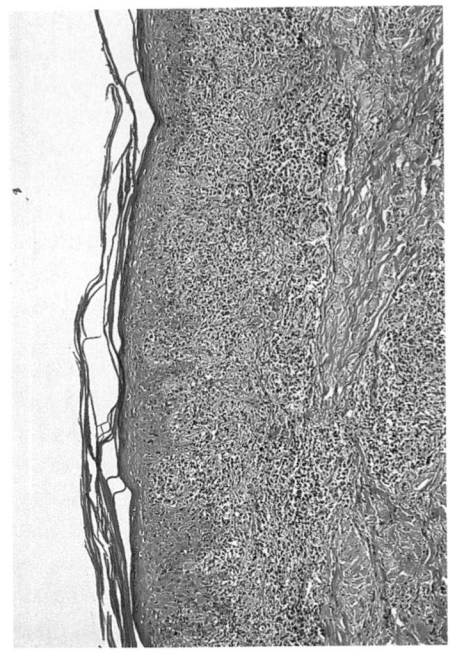
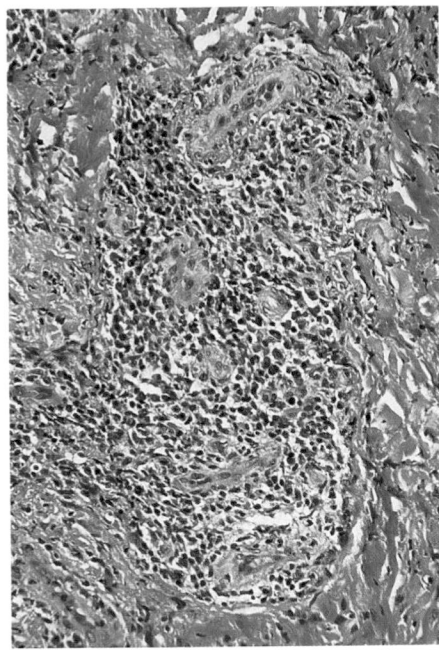

A

B

Fig. 4.11 Secondary syphilis. **A,** Low-power view showing a dense infiltrate predominantly affecting the upper dermis. **B,** High-power view showing markedly hyperplastic blood vessels surrounded by a lymphoplasmacytic infiltrate.

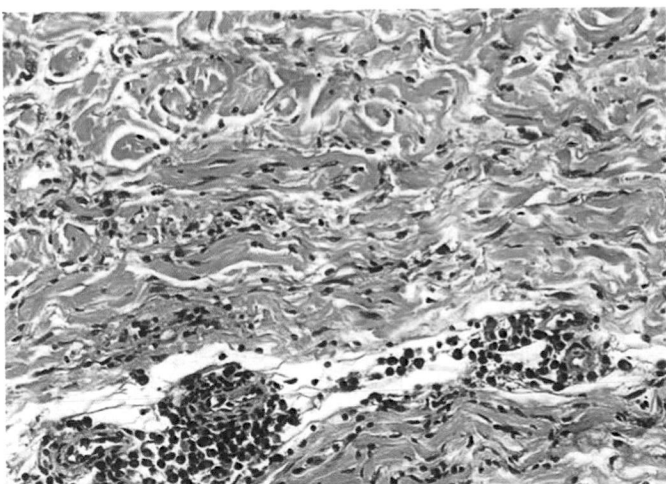

Fig. 4.12 Lyme disease. A perivascular infiltrate of lymphocytes and plasma cells is seen.

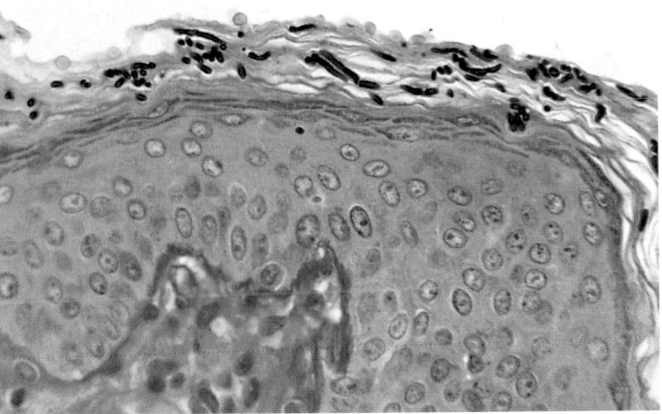

Fig. 4.13 Dermatophytosis due to *Trichophyton*, demonstrated by PAS stain.

derma of Pasini and Pierini may also be caused by borrelial organisms.[111,116] Other organs that may be involved by Lyme disease besides skin include the heart, joints, and nervous system.

Fungal diseases

Tinea (dermatophytoses)

In the dermatophytoses, the fungal spores and hyphae are found in the stratum corneum and in or about hair shafts[119] (Fig. 4.13). Mild epidermal changes such as focal intercellular edema and varying amounts of dermal inflammation may be seen. The fungal elements are readily seen in sections stained by the periodic acid–Schiff or Gomori's methenamine silver methods. Occasionally,

atypical clinical forms of tinea are biopsied, and the fungi are readily missed if not sought. Bacterial folliculitis and perifolliculitis may be superimposed on tinea of the scalp and beard. These lesions are known as *kerion celsi* and *sycosis barbae*, respectively, and may, on occasion, be mistaken for infected tumors. Histologically, cellulitis, abscesses, pseudoepitheliomatous hyperplasia, and a few fungi in the hair follicles and adjacent tissues are seen. A related disorder is *Majocchi's granuloma* (nodular granulomatous perifolliculitis), in which inflammation of dermal and subcutaneous tissue by dermatophytes is present; *Trichophyton rubrum* is the organism most commonly involved.[120]

It should be kept in mind that dermatophytes can be found superimposed on an inflammatory or neoplastic lesion of the skin. We have seen cases of mycosis fungoides that were missed originally because the atypical dermal lymphoid infiltrate was attributed to the fungi seen in the horny layer.

North American blastomycosis

Isolated cutaneous blastomycosis is an uncommon lesion. Usually the skin lesion is secondary to pulmonary involvement, which may be subclinical.[122,123] The causative organism, *Blastomyces dermatitidis*, is a spheric, double-contoured 12 μm ± 4 μm yeast. It reproduces by budding, and this characteristic allows its identification in sections. The skin lesions are slowly enlarging verrucous plaques in which numerous small abscesses are present[121] (Fig. 4.14). Microscopically, they are characterized by marked pseudoepitheliomatous hyperplasia and a mixed granulomatous and acute polymorphonuclear infiltrate.[123] The organism is generally found in giant cells. Smears and cultures are recommended diagnostic adjuncts.

Chromoblastomycosis

Chromoblastomycosis is an indolent cutaneous disease with a verrucous or nodular gross appearance often misdiagnosed clinically as carcinoma and excised.[125,126,128] Hematogenous dissemination occurs very rarely.[124] The spores are brown, hence their name, and the tissue reaction is similar to that seen in blastomycosis. These fungi, closely related species of *Phialophora*, *Fonsecaëa*, and *Cladosporium*, multiply by cross wall formation and splitting. Their color, cross walls, and lack of budding distinguish them from *Blastomyces dermatitidis*. Sometimes, fungi with an identical appearance are found in subcutaneous abscesses.[127]

Other granulomatous diseases

Sarcoidosis

Sarcoidosis affects the skin as well as the lymph nodes and viscera. Microscopically, sarcoidosis is a diagnosis of exclusion, inasmuch as granulomas with an identical microscopic appearance can also appear in the skin in a variety of infectious diseases, including tuberculosis,

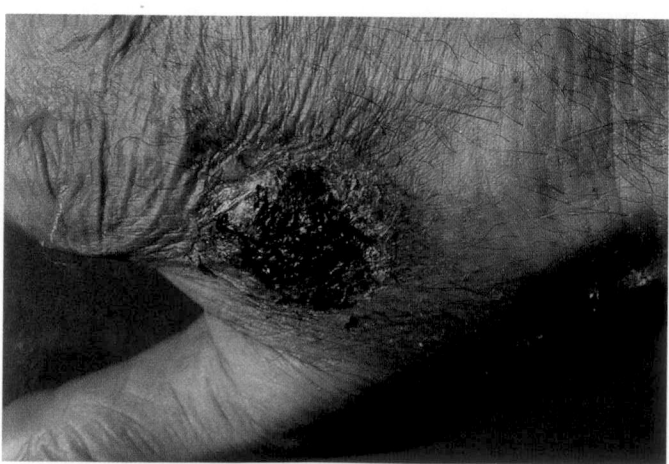

Fig. 4.14 Clinical appearance of North American blastomycosis.

atypical mycobacteriosis, and syphilis; as a reaction to zirconium, beryllium, and tattoos; and as a secondary change in malignant lymphoma.[130] However, the existence of a distinct clinical syndrome, both systemic and dermatologic, designated as sarcoidosis is widely accepted.[129,137] It is discussed here, despite the fact that its etiology is unknown,[131] because of its morphologic similarities with infectious granulomatous diseases and the fact that a mycobacterial etiology seems the most likely, as suggested by the identification of mycobacterial DNA in a high percentage of these lesions.[136]

Usually impaired immune responses—including anergy to delayed hypersensitivity skin tests, reduced phytohemagglutinin-induced blast transformation, and overactivity of B cells, as manifested by elevated serum levels of immunoglobulins and circulating immunocomplexes—suggest that sarcoidosis is an immune-mediated disease.[139] Clinically, the cutaneous manifestations of the disease vary a great deal from case to case. The lesions can be single or multiple and can range from macules to large plaques and nodules.[132,140] Their basic microscopic appearance, however, is similar. The dermis is infiltrated by nests and clusters of noncaseating epithelioid tubercles all but devoid of associated inflammatory cells. In particular, Langhans' giant cells are scarce (Fig. 4.15). The often-mentioned asteroids, seen in giant cells, and the calcified Schaumann bodies are uncommon and nonspecific.

The Kveim (or Kveim–Siltzbach) test was used extensively in the past to confirm a clinical impression of sarcoidosis. Sterilized brei of sarcoid tissue, usually spleen, was injected intradermally, and 6 weeks later the area was biopsied.[138] The presence of a typical sarcoidal reaction was considered a positive test.[134] When the antigen is potent, the test is reliable, and very few false-positive results are found.[135] However, foreign body and nonspecific inflammatory reactions do occur following injections of the Kveim antigen. Furthermore, Hurley and Shelley[133] reported the formation of sarcoid granulomas in 5 of 50 normal individuals following the inoculation of PPD. Because of these findings, the fact that it takes over a month to obtain a result, and also the difficulties in obtaining a suitable antigen, this test is rarely carried out at present, at least in the United States.

Foreign body reaction

Silica, talc, exogenous lipids, zirconium, and beryllium induce granulomatous reactions within the dermis.[141,143,144] Residual particles of talc, silica, and lipids are demonstrable in tissue by routine or polariscopic microscopy. Beryllium, previously a component of the phosphorus in fluorescent lights, induces a distinct necrotizing and granulomatous reaction.[142]

Arthropod bites (often incorrectly called insect bites) may, on occasion, cause inflammatory and granulomatous reactions that can be mistaken for lymphomas[145] (Fig. 4.16).

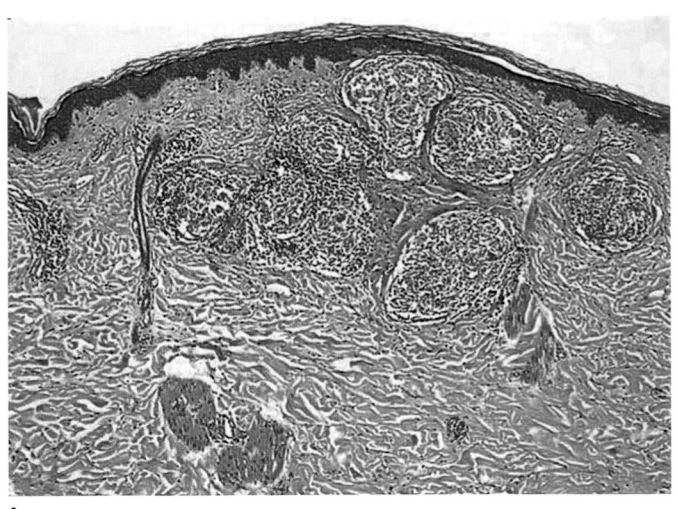
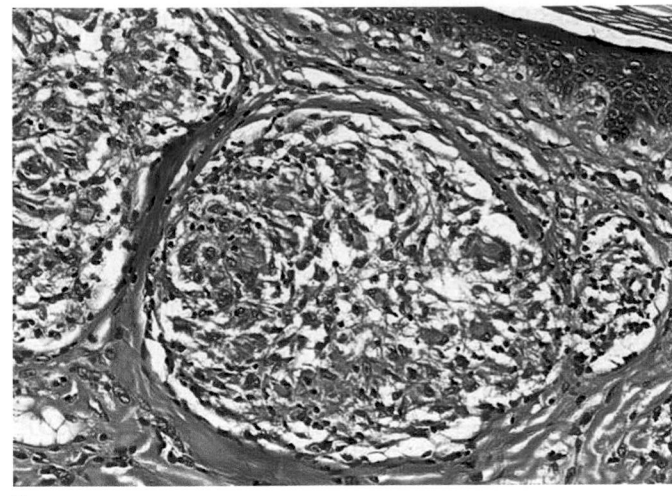

A   **B**

Fig. 4.15 A and **B**, Low and higher power views of cutaneous sarcoidosis.

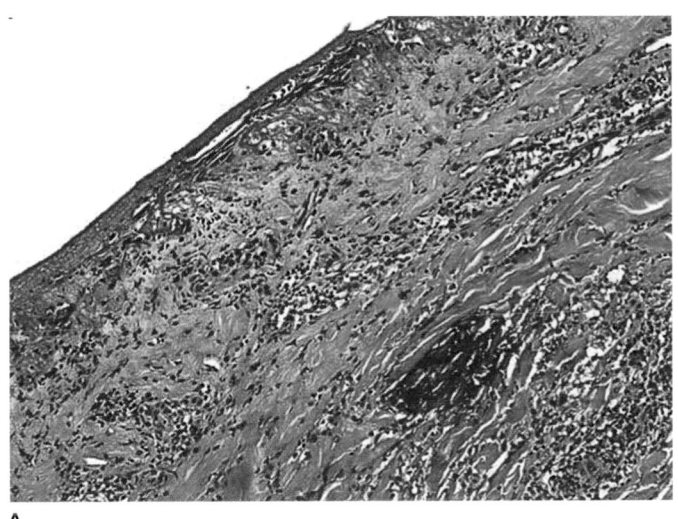

A

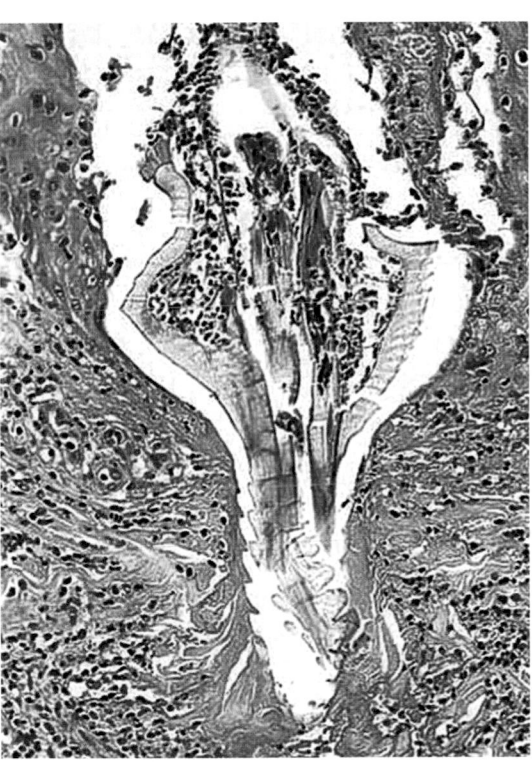

Fig. 4.16 Arthropod bite. **A**, Heavy inflammatory dermal infiltrate around necrotic focus; **B**, Section of the arthropod. (Courtesy of Dr. Raffaele Gianotti, Milan, Italy)

B

Other dermatoses

Psoriasis

Psoriasis is one of the more common dermatoses. Estimates of its incidence vary between 0.5% and 1.5% of the population.[151] It is a chronic, bilaterally symmetric, nonpruritic lesion formed by erythematous plaques covered by fine silvery scales.[152] Typically, it involves the extensor surfaces such as the elbows, the knees, the back, and the scalp. Generalized lesions also occur. Biochemical, histochemical, enzymatic, epidemiologic, and ultrastructural studies have failed so far to determine its cause.[149]

The morphologic characteristics are those of incomplete keratinization manifested as parakeratosis, which is thought to result from a markedly shortened turnover time.[159,161] Keratinocytic differentiation is maintained despite the increased basal cell proliferation.[154,160] This hyperproliferation may be caused by the overexpression of transforming growth factors.[150]

Acanthosis in which there is a regular elongation of the rete ridges, seen as pegs in two dimensions, is prominent. Above the tips of the dermal papillae, the layer of epidermal cells is distinctly attenuated, a feature known as "suprapapillary thinning." Within the dermal papillae, the capillaries are prominent. There is also a polymorphic inflammatory infiltrate composed of lymphocytes, macrophages (some supposedly belonging to a particular subset), and neutrophils.[148] Transmigration of polymorphonuclear leukocytes through the reactive epidermis into the parakeratotic scale results in the formation of Munro microabscesses[153] (Fig. 4.17). When these subcorneal abscesses are particularly prominent, the disease is designated as *pustular psoriasis*, a condition that may be pathogenetically related to *subcorneal pustular dermatosis*.[155,162] Macrophages are present along the dermoepidermal junction and can be a prominent feature of the infiltrate.[148]

Typical psoriasis is seldom biopsied. The atypical cases often are, and they create diagnostic difficulties. These difficulties are caused by the fact that irritated epidermis—from lichen simplex chronicus, florid seborrheic dermatitis, pityriasis rubra pilaris, mycosis fungoides, Reiter's syndrome, or other causes—can develop comparable morphologic changes, which are often referred to as psoriasiform.[146,147,156] Certain fine points of differentiation, such as the extent of suprapapillary thinning, the regularity of the acanthosis, and the lack of hyperkeratosis, may be used but are not absolute. Again, synthesis of all the information is required.

Psoriatic patients treated with photochemotherapy (psoralen) and ultraviolet A radiation (PUVA) are at an increased risk for the development of squamous cell carcinoma and malignant melanoma of skin.[157,158]

Exfoliative dermatitis and erythroderma

Exfoliative dermatitis and erythroderma can be seen secondary to a variety of disorders, including drug reaction, allergic contact dermatitis, psoriasis, pityriasis rubra pilaris, and various malignancies.[167] The dermatopathic lymphadenitis (lipomelanotic reticulosis) associated with these skin diseases should not be confused with malignant lymphoma (see Chapter 21). Usually, the histologic changes in the skin are nonspecific and need to be distinguished from those of Sézary's syndrome and erythrodermic mycosis fungoides.[163–166,168] Sometimes, the microscopic picture is that of a lichenoid dermatitis.[166]

Lichen planus

Lichen planus is a pruritic, violaceous, subacute to chronic, papulosquamous dermatitis of unknown etiology[173,176,187] (Fig. 4.18). It usually involves the flexor surfaces of the arms and the legs, but it may be found in many other sites.[169] Lesions may be confined to the oral mucosa,[170,171] or they may precede or accompany the skin changes. Histologically, the well-developed lesions are rather distinct (Fig. 4.19). The epidermis is hyperkeratotic, the granular layer is prominent, and the hyperplastic epithelium forms irregular acanthotic pegs. The papillary dermis is heavily infiltrated by lymphocytes and histiocytes that form a band-like infiltrate that involves and destroys the dermoepidermal junction. Eosinophilic PAS-positive round or oval formations (colloid, hyaline, or Civatte bodies) are often seen in the basal layer and sometimes also in the upper dermis and

Fig. 4.17 Typical appearance of psoriasis. Note the engorgement of papillae and Munro microabscesses.

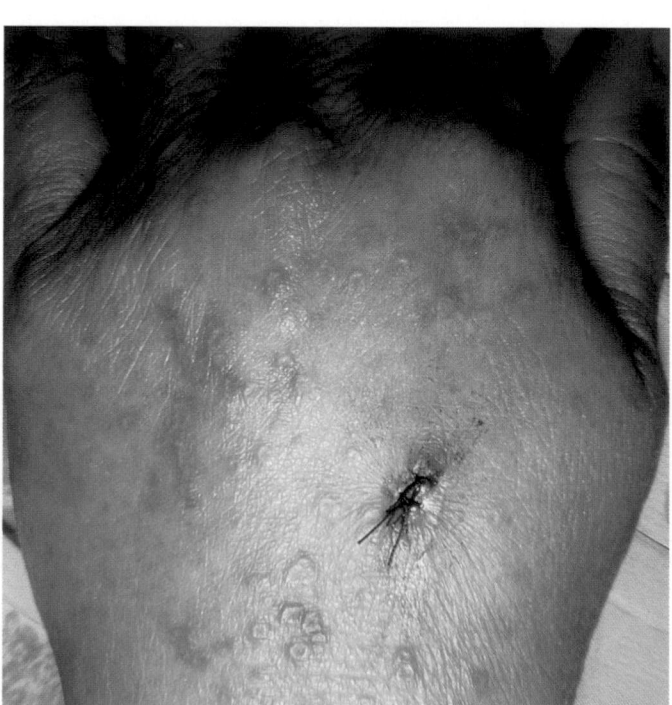

Fig. 4.18 Clinical appearance of lichen planus affecting the dorsum of the hand. One of the lesions has been biopsied.

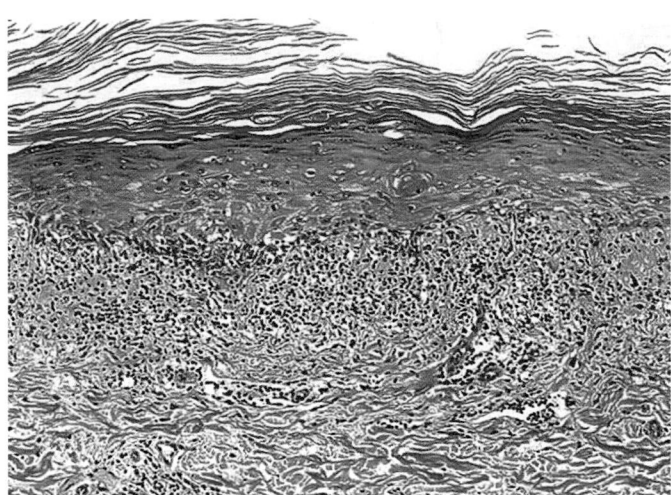

Fig. 4.19 Microscopic appearance of lichen planus. There is orthotopic hyperkeratosis, hypergranulosis, hydropic degeneration of the basal layer, and a band-like inflammatory infiltrate with melanin-containing macrophages.

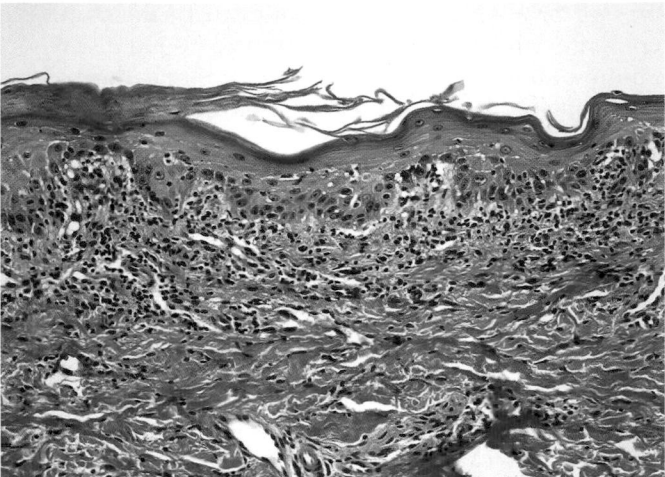

Fig. 4.20 Microscopic changes of acute graft-versus-host reaction.

malpighian layer. They show strong immunoreactivity for immunoglobulins and keratin, the latter supporting the interpretation that they represent degenerated keratinocytes.[178] Immunoglobulin deposition is also present along the dermoepidermal junction. The lymphocytes present in the dermis are almost entirely of T cells, most of them of the helper/ inducer type.[175]

On occasion subepidermal cleavage occurs with the formation of bullae. The border of the inflammatory infiltrate is sharply delimited so that the reticular dermis is uninflamed. Histologically, the absence of atypia and dyskeratotic cells in oral lichen planus assists in distinguishing it from keratosis with atypia (lichenoid dysplasia; see Chapter 5). Clinicopathologic variants of lichen planus include bullous, pemphigoid, hypertrophic, atrophic, and follicular (lichen planopilaris) forms.[180,184,189]

A morphologic pattern akin to that of lichen planus and designated as *lichenoid dermatitis* or lichenoid tissue reaction can be seen in a variety of conditions.[181] This includes drug eruptions, lichenoid actinic keratosis (also known as lichen planus-like keratosis [LPLK], benign lichenoid keratosis, and solitary lichen planus[177,179,183]), lupus erythematosus, acute graft-versus-host reaction, and several other conditions.[182,185,188] A lichenoid reaction is the rule in regressing melanoma (a notorious pitfall),[174] and can also be seen in the epidermis overlying a dermatofibroma.[186] The appearance of the lichenoid inflammatory process resembles a delayed hypersensitive reaction and is thought to represent the morphologic expression of a cell-mediated rejection reaction.[172]

Graft-versus-host disease

Graft-versus-host disease is an important cause of morbidity and mortality following bone marrow transplanta-

tion. The early stages are characterized microscopically by vacuolation of the basal layer, spongiosis, and individual cell necrosis, associated with mononuclear cell infiltration of the upper dermis[194] (Fig. 4.20). Sometimes these epidermal changes occur in the absence of an inflammatory infiltrate.[190] The amount of inflammation seems to be the most important prognostic determinator.[191] This has been quantitated through the Lerner grading system, which has a high degree of interobserver concordance,[193] but which is of limited use in predicting the likelihood of a skin rash progressing to a clinically more significant disease.[192]

In the chronic stage of graft-versus-host disease, the microscopic appearance resembles scleroderma.[195] Granular or linear deposition of IgM in the basement membrane zone is often present, particularly in the chronic form. Evaluation of LN-3 (specific for HLA class II antigens) is said to be useful for the estimation of the severity of the disease.[196]

Vasculitis

There is a large group of cutaneous diseases in which the basic alteration is an inflammatory change in the wall of the dermal and/or subcutaneous vessels (i.e., a vasculitis).[197,212,226] The mechanism is in all likelihood immune mediated for the majority of them, through the action of immune complexes.[227,233] The disease can be restricted to the skin or also involve internal organs; if limited to the skin, it may be generalized or localized to a single focus.[214] The vessels involved may be the capillaries of the papillary dermis, arterioles and venules of the deep dermis and subcutaneous tissue, or deep-seated medium-sized vessels. Red cell extravasation is a constant feature.

The inflammatory infiltrate can be predominantly neutrophilic (usually accompanied by leukocytoclasis), lymphocytic, or granulomatous. Necrotizing changes (usually of fibrinoid type) of the vessel wall may be present or absent. Secondary changes in the overlying epidermis and in the sweat glands are frequent.[198] Direct immunofluorescence often shows granular deposits of immunoglobulins, complement, and fibrin in and about vessel walls.[201,219]

Taking into account all of the foregoing features, morphologic classifications of cutaneous vasculitides have been proposed that correlate well with a variety of clinical conditions.[208,215–217,237]

Lymphocytic non-necrotizing vasculitis involving small superficial vessels is seen in drug eruption, erythema multiforme, Mucha–Habermann disease, some viral infections,[210] collagen-vascular diseases, the group of diseases known as pigmented purpuric dermatosis, and several other conditions[203,222] (Fig. 4.21A). Neutrophilic vasculitis of small vessels accompanied by fibrinoid necrosis and leukocytoclasis (*leukocytoclastic or allergic vasculitis*) usually presents as purpuric palpable lesions, most commonly on the lower part of the legs. Systemic involvement, particularly of the kidneys, is frequently found in the form known as *Henoch–Schönlein purpura*[207,222] (Fig. 4.21B). Other distinct subtypes of leukocytoclastic vasculitis are those associated with chronic idiopathic urticaria, hypocomplementemia, and essential mixed cryoglobulinemia.[230,232,234,235] The presence of systemic disease is more likely when the vasculitis extends deeply into the reticular dermis or subcutaneous fat,[236] but in general the morphologic features of the systemic and the purely cutaneous form are the same.[205,209,220]

Etiologic agents include infections, foreign proteins, chemicals, drugs, and a variety of diseases.[212] Some patients with acute leukemia develop cutaneous vasculitis, the suggestion having been made that the vascular injury is mediated by the leukemic blasts.[223]

Granuloma faciale, erythema elevatum diutinum, and localized chronic fibrosing vasculitis of the skin (described in the following section) represent localized types of non-necrotizing vasculitis involving vessels slightly larger than capillaries. In *malignant atrophic papulosis* (Degos' disease), the main change is an ischemic infarct of the skin resulting from intimal proliferation of a deep-seated arteriole.[200,229,231] In *segmented hyalinizing vasculitis* (atrophie blanche of Milian), the dermal capillaries show focal endothelial proliferation, marked thickening of the wall by PAS-positive eosinophilic hyaline material, and eventually occlusion of the lumen by a fibrin thrombus.[218,228]

Involvement of larger vessels, often accompanied by necrotizing changes, is seen in allergic granulomatosis of Churg and Strauss,[204,211,213] polyarteritis nodosa (systemic or limited to the skin), giant cell arteritis, and Wegener's granulomatosis.[199] Prominent vascular involvement without necrotizing changes is also seen in the cutaneous lesions of lymphomatoid granulomatosis,[221,225] currently regarded as a form of malignant lymphoma (see Chapter 7).

Cutaneous vasculitis should be distinguished from *acute febrile neutrophilic dermatosis* (Sweet's syndrome), a disease characterized by a massive outpouring of neutrophils in the dermis but unaccompanied by bona fide vasculitis.[224] Sweet's syndrome may occur as a cutaneous paraneoplastic manifestation in patients with hematologic malignancies and, with lesser frequency, solid tumors.[202,206]

Granuloma faciale and related lesions

Granuloma faciale typically presents on the face of adults as a thickened, purplish patch, which clinically is often confused with infected nevus, tumor, or sarcoid[241] (Fig.

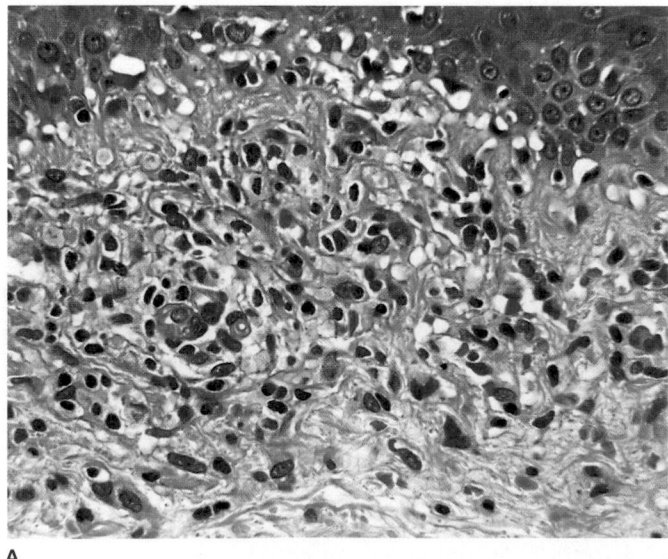

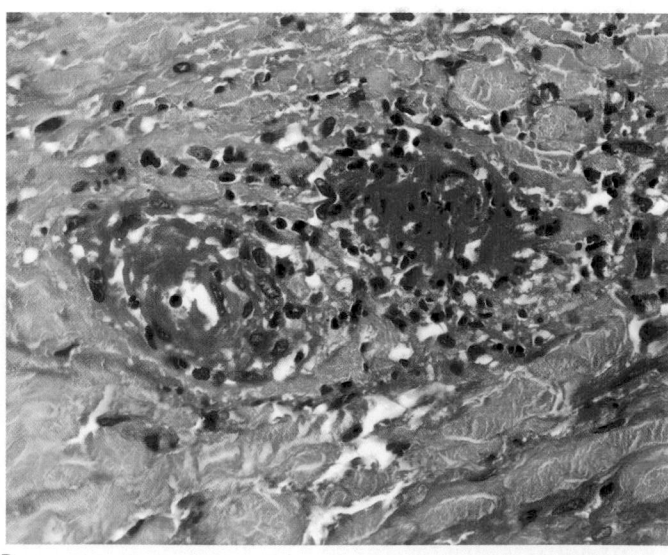

A
B

Fig. 4.21 Cutaneous vasculitis. **A,** Chronic non-necrotizing vasculitis in pigmented purpuric dermatosis; **B,** Acute necrotizing changes in leukocytoclastic vasculitis.

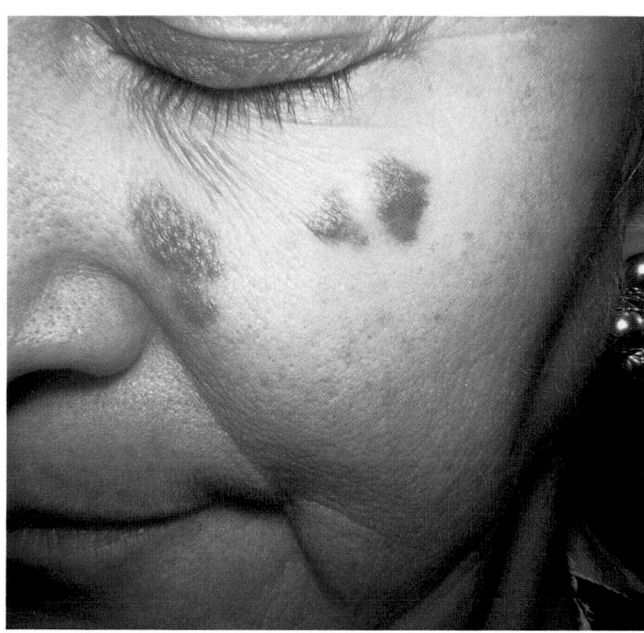

Fig. 4.22 Clinical appearance of granuloma faciale. The lesion appears as thickened purplish patches.

4.22). For this reason, it is often excised or biopsied, and acquaintance with its histologic appearance is helpful. The generally unaltered epidermis is separated from the zone of dermal inflammation by a narrow band of uninvolved dermis. The inflammatory reaction is formed by lymphocytes, histiocytes, and large numbers of eosinophils. The latter may be concentrated about the vessels and a mild to moderate vasculitis observed[240] (Fig. 4.23). Granuloma faciale differs from the tumor stage of mycosis fungoides by the lack of epidermal involvement (Pautrier microabscesses) and of atypical lymphoid cells. Infected arthropod bites may have considerable eosinophilic infiltrate but seldom occur on the face.[238]

Erythema elevatum diutinum shares some morphologic features with granuloma faciale and is thought to be pathogenetically related to it.[244] It generally presents in systemically ill patients as bilaterally symmetrical plaques, papules, or nodules, often over the dorsa of joints. Microscopically, it initially presents as a leukocytoclastic vasculitis and later resolves with storiform or concentric fibrosis.[242] In contrast to granuloma faciale, eosinophils are scanty or absent. Sometimes the disease has a nodular quality that mimics a neoplastic process.[243]

The microscopic appearance of granuloma faciale or erythema elevatum diutinum can be seen in cases not fitting the clinical picture of either disease; such cases have been descriptively designated as *localized chronic fibrosing vasculitis.*[239]

Erythema nodosum and related lesions

The painful, red, subcutaneous lesions that characterize erythema nodosum occur on the anterior surface of the legs. Typically, they involute within a few days or weeks, leaving slightly depressed pigmented areas. They do not ulcerate, as do the lesions of erythema induratum. It seems certain that the pathogenesis is immune mediated, but the precise mechanism is unknown.[259] In an old series of a British population with erythema nodosum, 45% of the patients had antecedent streptococcal infections, 6% had tuberculosis, 36% had sarcoid, and 13% had a variety of lesions.[258] Several other infectious agents can be involved.[251] Some cases are associated with chronic ulcerative colitis and others with Behçet's syndrome.[246–248,250] In the endemic areas of the United States, coccidioidomycosis is a common antecedent.

Histologically, the junction of the dermis and the subcutis is inflamed. An inflammatory infiltrate extends along the fibrous septa between the fat and about the vessels of the dermis. The composition depends largely on the age of the lesion. It may be predominantly neutrophilic, lymphocytic, or histiocytic, with isolated giant cells or noncaseating granulomas[249,261] (Figs 4.24 and 4.25). Varying degrees of vasculitis, chiefly of veins, may be seen.

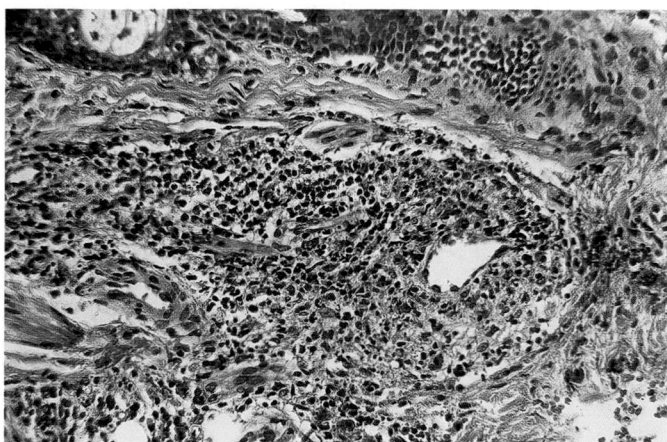

Fig. 4.23 Vascular changes in granuloma faciale.

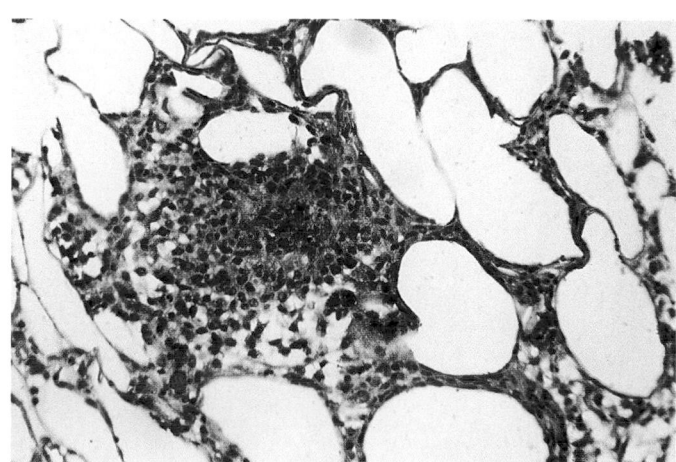

Fig. 4.24 Erythema nodosum. Granuloma-like formation in subcutaneous.

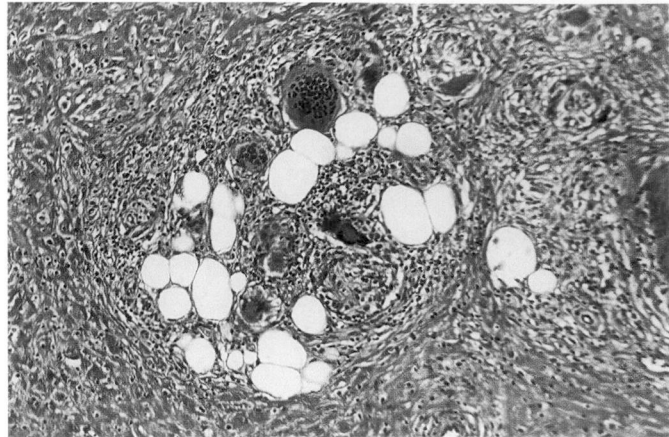

Fig. 4.25 Panniculitis with scattered multinucleated giant cells in erythema nodosum.

A characteristic lesion seen in the early stages of the disease is represented by a cluster of small histiocytes radially arranged around a central cleft (*Miescher's radial granuloma*).[256]

Other nodular lesions of the leg that are probably the result of antigen–antibody precipitates with ensuing vasculitis are *nodular vasculitis* and *subacute nodular migratory panniculitis*.[252] A common feature of these panniculitides, some of which are associated with collagen-vascular diseases, is their predominantly *septal* distribution.[245,254,257,260] In contrast, the panniculitis of Weber–Christian disease has a predominantly *lobular* distribution.[253,255]

Granuloma annulare and related lesions

Granuloma annulare occurs most frequently on the dorsum of the hands and arms as circinate or grouped clusters of pink nodules with slight central depressions (Fig. 4.26). Occasionally, the disease is generalized.[264]

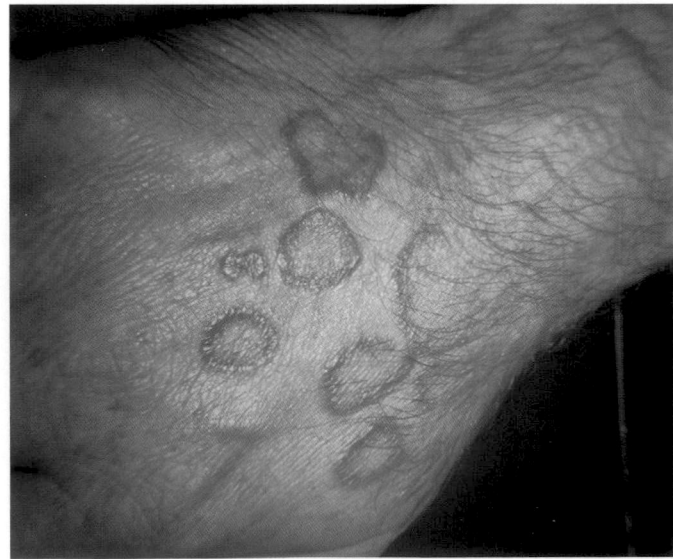

Fig. 4.26 Clinical appearance of multiple lesions of granuloma annulare of dorsum of hand.

Associated systemic diseases are present only exceptionally.[270,277] Early claims that it may represent in some cases a reaction to Bartonella infection have not been substantiated.[276] Histologically, the key component of the lesion is the so-called necrobiotic collagen or palisading granuloma.[267] This is characterized by a well-demarcated zone of disintegrating extracellular material with the appearance of collagen mixed with cell debris that is found in the mid-dermis surrounded by a cuff of radially oriented fibroblasts mixed with lymphocytes and histiocytes (Fig. 4.27). Occasional foreign body giant cells and foci of vasculitis may be found, and mucin is present in the areas of altered collagen. In many lesions, the abnormal collagen is not so distinctly demarcated, and multiple sections are necessary to arrive at a specific diagnosis. Tangential sections not showing the "necrobiotic" areas may be misinterpreted as vasculitis or as one of the histiocytoses.[265] Immunohistochemically, the "histiocytes" of granuloma annulare stain for vimentin and lysozyme but not for other histocytic markers such as Ham 54 or KP-1.[272] Ultrastructural studies have shown an important component of degenerated elastic (rather than collagen) fibers.[266]

The subcutaneous nodules of rheumatoid arthritis and rheumatic fever share with granuloma annulare the presence of the necrobiotic collagen granuloma, but the combination of clinical and microscopic features usually allows an easy distinction.[278]

Isolated, large, rather deep, necrobiotic collagen granulomas are sometimes seen on the extremities or occiput in children.[271] They have been referred to as *deep, subcutaneous, or giant granuloma annulare* and as *pseudorheumatoid nodules*.[272,273] These children do not develop rheumatic or rheumatoid disease, and prolonged prophylaxis is not indicated. Occasionally, siblings may be affected.[263] A presumably analogous disease has been seen limited to the penis.[268]

Granuloma annulare needs also to be distinguished from a peculiar erythematous or brownish annular

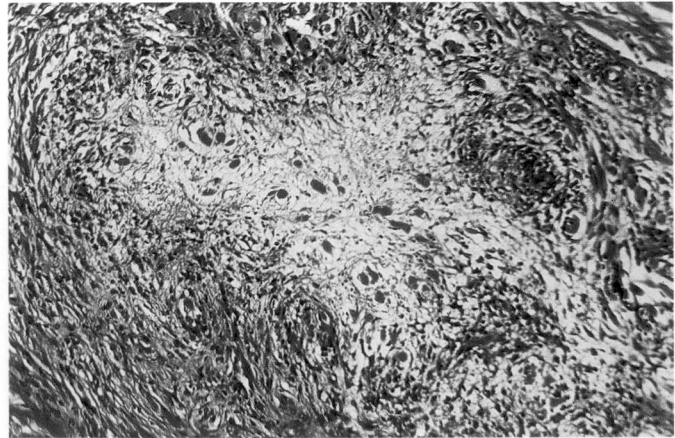

Fig. 4.27 Typical lesion of granuloma annulare, with palisading of histiocytes around "necrobiotic collagen" center.

infiltrate sometimes encountered in the faces of elderly people and variously designated as *O'Brien's actinic granuloma*, Miescher's granuloma, and annular elastolytic giant cell granuloma.[269,275] The presence of elastic fibers in the giant cells, as seen by light and electron microscopy, is one of its most important distinguishing features.[262,279]

Necrobiosis lipoidica

Necrobiosis lipoidica typically presents as atrophic, yellow, depressed plaques involving the legs of diabetic patients[281,286] (Fig. 4.28); however, it can also occur in other sites and in the absence of clinical diabetes.[280,282–284] Microscopically, ill-defined areas of disintegrating dermal collagen are seen surrounded by a lymphohistiocytic infiltrate often arranged in a palisading fashion. Thickening of the blood vessel wall is usually prominent. In contrast with granuloma annulare, stains for mucin and immunoreactivity for lysozyme tend to be negative.[285] The differential diagnosis also includes *necrobiotic xanthogranuloma*, a disease occurring in the head, neck, and trunk of patients with paraproteinemia (see p. 187).

Weber–Christian disease and other lobular panniculitides

The microscopic changes seen in Weber–Christian disease are acute to subacute inflammation of the subcutaneous adipose tissue with necrosis of fat cells, followed by resolution by macrophagic ingestion and subsequent fibrosis. The distribution of the inflammation is lobular rather than septal.[291] The lesions are tender and usually accompanied by malaise and remittent fever. In contrast, *lipogranulomatosis subcutanea of Rothmann and Makai* has no associated systemic symptoms and does not appear in crops.[287] Changes similar to those of Weber–Christian disease can be seen as a complication of α_1-antitrypsin deficiency,[292] chronic pancreatitis, and pancreatic endocrine tumors.[288] A clue to the diagnosis of the latter two conditions is the presence of large foci of fat necrosis containing the "ghosts" of the fat cells and the thick "shadows" of their walls.

Cytophagic histiocytic panniculitis presents clinically with spiking fever, erythematous subcutaneous skin nodules, anemia, and leukopenia. Microscopically, the skin lesions show a florid lobular panniculitis featuring large histiocytes with their cytoplasm filled with fragmented leukocytes ("bean bag cells").[290] This condition is currently regarded as a form of cutaneous malignant T-cell lymphoma[289] (see p. 198).

Mastocytosis

Mastocytosis of the skin can manifest in the form of *urticaria pigmentosa, (solitary) mastocytoma, diffuse and erythrodermic cutaneous mastocytosis,* and *telangiectasia macularis eruptiva perstans.*[296,300,307,309] Urticaria pigmentosa, which is by far the most common, usually has its onset during childhood in the from of multiple brown macules.[295] On occasion, it makes its first appearance in adults.[295] The brown macules may be diffusely distributed or, less frequently, may be single.[300,310] When the lesions are stroked, the skin urticates because of the release of histamine.

A systemic form of the disease exists, characterized by involvement of the spleen, liver, bone marrow, and lymph nodes, with or without cutaneous lesions.[294,302] This form runs a malignant clinical course, and on occasion it is accompanied by circulating mast cells ("*mast cell leukemia*"). In general, it is not possible on morphologic grounds to distinguish urticaria pigmentosa with systemic involvement from that having skin disease only,[308] but some prediction along these lines is possible by the use of a pH-dependent toluidine blue stain.[301] The diagnosis of urticaria pigmentosa in a skin biopsy can be easily missed unless the cytologic features of mast cells in sections stained with hematoxylin–eosin are remembered[305] (Figs 4.29). Some of the cells have large, pale nuclei, distinct cytoplasmic boundaries, and a faintly granular cytoplasm. Others are elongated and closely simulate fibroblasts or perithelial cells. In sections stained with toluidine blue or Giemsa, the metachromatic granules are obvious. The Leder (chloroacetate esterase) stain will also demonstrate the mast cells in routinely processed sections. Immunohistochemically, mast cells can be demonstrated with tryptase, calretinin, and CD117 (c-kit)[293,299,303,304] (Fig. 4.30). Mutations of c-kit have been documented in patients with mastocytosis.[297] Eosinophils usually are mixed with the mast cells in the dermis.

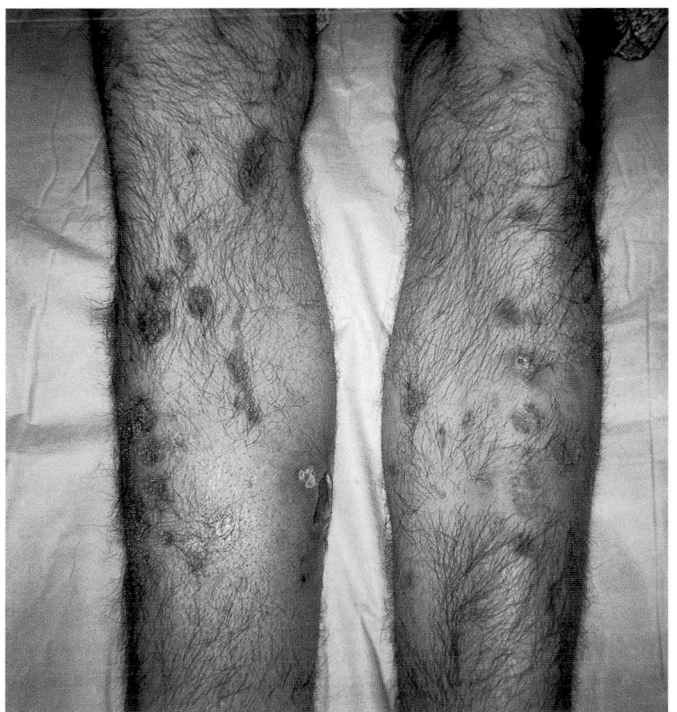

Fig. 4.28 Clinical appearance of lesions of necrobiosis lipoidica.

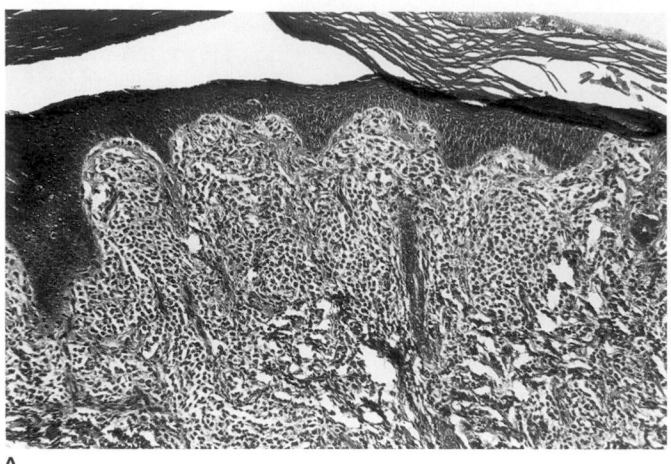

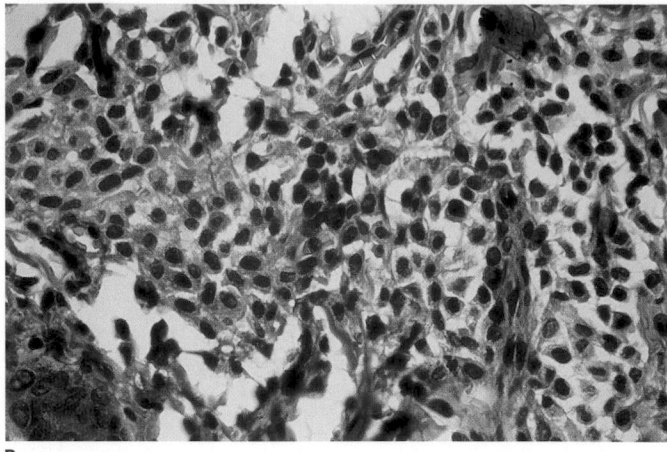

A   **B**

Fig. 4.29 Urticaria pigmentosa. **A**, Diffuse dermal infiltrate of mast cells admixed with eosinophils; **B**, High-power view of the infiltrate.

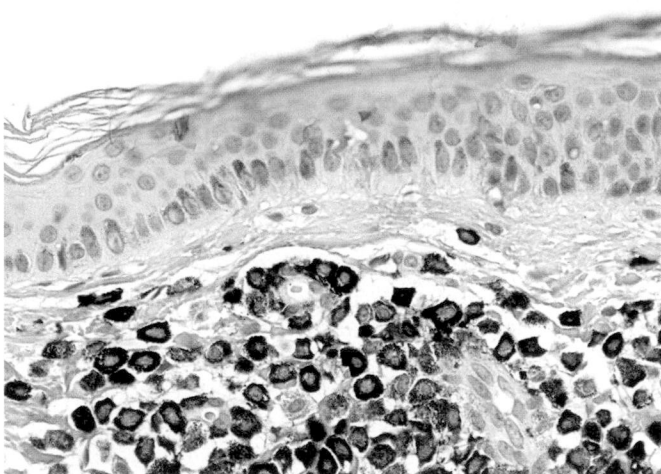

Fig. 4.30 Urticaria pigmentosa. Immunohistochemical demonstration of mast cells with tryptase. (Courtesy of Dr. Raffaele Gianotti, Milan, Italy)

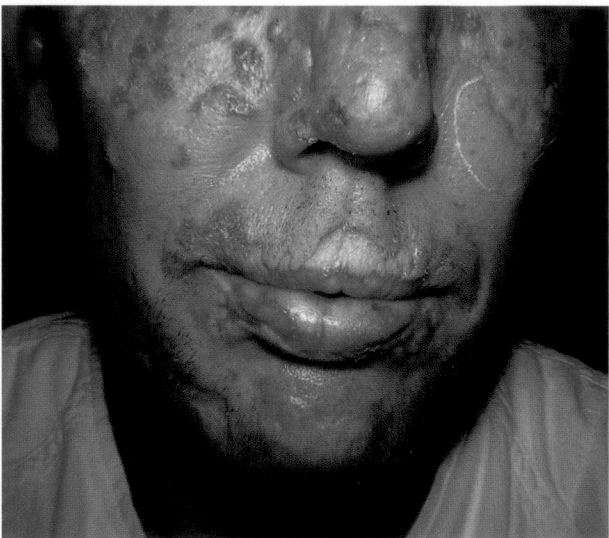

Fig. 4.31 Extensive facial lesions of chronic discoid lupus erythematosus.

Mast cell tumors of the skin are common in the dog[306] and also occur in the cat and ox.[298]

Lupus erythematosus

Chronic discoid lupus erythematosus and *systemic* lupus erythematosus represent distinct and almost uniformly separable entities, even if occasional examples of the former progressing into the latter are on record.[313,319] Some authors accept the existence of an intermediate form and designate it subacute cutaneous lupus erythematosus.[311,316,322]

Chronic discoid lupus erythematosus is a relatively common condition with a distinct preference for women, presenting as delimited erythematous to hyperkeratotic to atrophic patches on the face, neck, scalp, and, less frequently, the arms and trunk[313,324] (Fig. 4.31). Sunlight may cause exacerbations. Histologically, the lesions are characterized by predominantly follicular hyperkeratosis, epidermal atrophy with liquefactive degeneration of the

basal layer, and a distinct, patchy, periadnexal lymphocytic infiltrate[317] (Fig. 4.32). The changes seen in biopsies reflect the stage and type of lesion sampled. None of the changes is pathognomonic. Occasionally, lesions of lupus erythematosus appear as verrucous, hyperkeratotic lesions on the upper extremities resembling keratoacanthomas or hypertrophic lichen planus.[325] Polymorphous light eruption (including chronic actinic dermatitis) and lymphocytic infiltration of the skin may be difficult to distinguish from chronic discoid lupus erythematosus.[320,323,328] As a matter of fact, so-called Jessner's lymphocytic infiltration of the skin may simply be a form of chronic discoid lupus erythematosus without epidermal changes.[327]

Systemic lupus erythematosus is an immune-mediated disease in which antibodies to homologous and heterologous DNA have been demonstrated. It manifests a protean symptomatology usually characterized by fatigue, fever, arthritis, various cutaneous lesions of

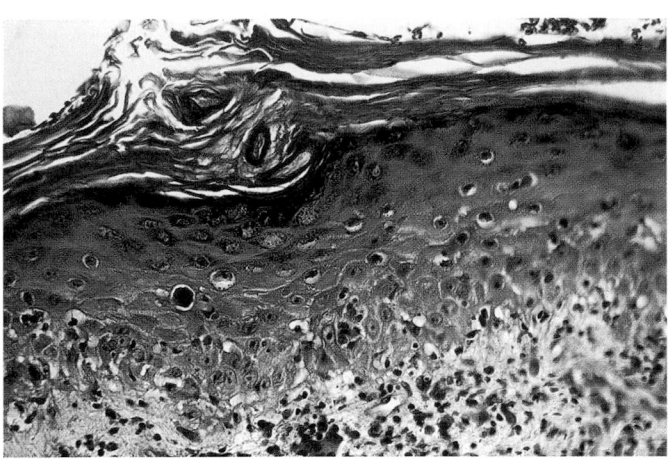

Fig. 4.32 Lesion of chronic discoid lupus erythematosus showing hyperkeratosis and hydropic degeneration of basal layer.

which the erythematous bimalar "butterfly" blush is most common, signs of renal involvement, lymphadenopathy, and panserositis.[326] The typical, but not always present, dermal histologic picture—masterfully described in the original article by Klemperer et al.[321]—is fibrinoid necrosis at the dermoepidermal junction accompanied by atrophy and liquefactive degeneration of the epidermis.[315]

Direct immunofluorescence will show the presence of immunoglobulins (usually IgG and IgM) and so-called membrane attack complex (C5b, C6, C7, C8, and C9) in about 90% of specimens obtained from clinically involved skin of patients with either systemic or chronic discoid lupus erythematosus.[312,329] The deposition consists of coalescing clumps along the dermoepidermal junction, resulting in the formation of an irregular band, a finding that is of great diagnostic importance but not entirely specific for this entity.[330] Clinically uninvolved areas will show deposition of immunoglobulins in about half of the patients with systemic lupus erythematosus but no deposition of the membrane attack complex.[312,318] With few exceptions, direct immunofluorescence is negative in the lesions of polymorphous light eruption and lymphocytic infiltration.

Dermatomyositis

Dermatomyositis is an inflammatory disorder affecting skeletal muscle and skin, characterized clinically by proximal, symmetric muscle weakness and cutaneous lesions. Microscopically, the skin changes may be those of a nonspecific chronic dermatitis or may acquire features very similar to those of systemic lupus erythematosus.[333,334] By immunofluorescence, features favoring dermatomyositis over lupus erythematosus are a negative "lupus band test" and deposition of C5b–q (the membrane attack complex of complement)[335] biopsies of the afflicted muscles show distinct myositis with necrosis of myofibers, fragmentation, phagocytosis, and some sarcolemmal nuclear proliferation. In the later stages,

fibrosis, fat infiltration, and fascicular atrophy appear.[332,336] Much has been written about the incidence or coincidence of adenocarcinoma with dermatomyositis.[337] A review of the literature carried out by Williams many years ago[338] found that 15% of the patients had neoplasms of the stomach, breast, ovary, lung, or colon. Remissions of the dermatomyositis have occurred following resection of the neoplasm. Therefore, careful investigation of adults with dermatomyositis for undetected carcinoma is certainly worthwhile. However, in the majority none will be found.[337]

In longstanding dermatomyositis, and in lupus erythematosus, acrodermatitis atrophicans, and mycosis fungoides, a secondary change called *poikiloderma atrophicans vasculare* may appear. The histologic changes are generally those of the associated disease.

In polymyositis, the muscle abnormalities are similar to those of dermatomyositis, but skin changes are absent.[331]

Scleroderma and eosinophilic fasciitis

Scleroderma is manifest in two distinct forms: *localized scleroderma* or *morphea*[340,357,358] and *systemic scleroderma*, in which the skin, particularly of the face, the upper trunk, hands, and arms (acrosclerosis), the esophagus, the heart, and the lungs are diseased. Most patients are adults but the disease can also present in childhood.[347,355]

Sometimes, visceral disease typical of systemic scleroderma occurs in the absence of cutaneous involvement. A few cases of morphea have been associated with generalized or systemic disease.

The dominant microscopic change in scleroderma is an increase in the amount of collagen, which is morphologically, ultrastructurally, and biochemically unremarkable.[343,344] The relative proportions and distribution of type I and type III collagens are also closely similar to those found in the normal dermis.[348] Thus the histologic diagnosis depends on the evaluation of increments in the amount and distribution of collagen. The "smudging," "homogenization," and variable tinctorial changes seen in sections stained with hematoxylin–eosin do not necessarily indicate structural changes in the collagen. In fact, some care should be exercised not to confuse the changes of senile (actinic) elastosis and basophilic degeneration of collagen and the normally thicker dermis of the fingers and dorsum with scleroderma.[353]

In scleroderma, the dermis, particularly the papillary portion, becomes a dense feltwork of closely woven collagen bundles. The sclerosis may extend in depth to encircle the secretory coils of the eccrine sweat glands. Concomitantly, the epidermis becomes atrophic. Varying amounts of mild and nonspecific inflammatory reaction may be seen in the dermis, more so at the advancing edge of a patch of morphea. The inflammatory infiltrate and vascular damage are particularly pronounced in the early stages of the disease, suggesting that the fibrosis may represent a secondary phenomenon.[342,345] Direct immunofluorescence studies are almost uniformly negative. Dystrophic calcification may occur in scleroderma, and in some patients the dominant patterns is that of acrosclerosis preceded by, or associated with, Raynaud's phenomenon.

Scleroderma needs to be distinguished from *eosinophilic fasciitis (Shulman's disease)*, a condition characterized clinically by swelling, tenderness, and stiffness of an extremity, often involving the lower forearm and sometimes associated with carpal tunnel syndrome.[341,346,350] The most important difference on histologic grounds is that in the latter condition there is marked inflammation and thickening of the deep fascia (with or without eosinophils), whereas in scleroderma this structure tends to show minimal or no abnormalities.[349] Whether there is a relationship between these two entities remains controversial.[351,356]

Scleroderma is also distinguishable from lichen sclerosus et atrophicus (with which it may coexist[354]) and acrodermatitis chronic atrophicans on morphologic and immunohistochemical grounds.[339,352]

Drug eruptions

Allergic reactions to drugs may result in a large variety of dermatoses, some of which are indistinguishable from those occurring in the absence of drug administration. These include urticaria, erythema multiforme, erythema nodosum, folliculitis, pustules, purpura, hyperpigmentation, and several others.[361] Vasculitis of either the leukocytoclastic or lymphocytic type can also occur. Numerous eosinophils and marked thickening of the vessel walls are common features of drug-induced lymphocytic vasculitis. In fixed drug eruption, the features are similar to those of erythema multiforme (Fig. 4.33). Some drugs (particularly procainamide) may induce a disease identical clinically and histologically to systemic lupus erythematosus.

Chemotherapeutic agents may result in acute necrotiz-

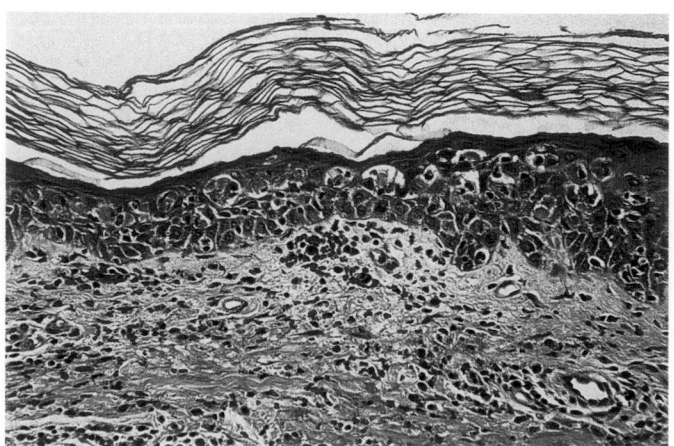

Fig. 4.33 Fixed drug eruption. The infiltrate is rich in eosinophils and is accompanied by necrotic keratinocytes.

ing changes in sweat glands (*neutrophilic eccrine hidradenitis*) and *syringosquamous metaplasia*.[359,360,362] Parenthetically, the latter change can also occur as a consequence of other stimuli (such as necrosis and ulceration of overlying skin) and result in a picture simulating microscopically squamous cell carcinoma; the process seems pathogenetically analogous to that of necrotizing sialometaplasia of minor salivary glands[364] (see Chapter 5). In drug-induced coma, the first cutaneous structure to undergo necrosis is the secretory portion of the eccrine sweat coil, followed by the sweat duct, hair follicle, sebaceous glands, and—lastly—the epidermis.[363]

Pyoderma gangrenosum

Pyoderma gangrenosum is associated with a systemic disorder (such as inflammatory bowel disease) in about half of the cases.[365] It begins with an acute-phase necrotic pustule or furuncle and can evolve to a large and deep necrotic ulcer with a violaceous border and a surrounding halo of erythema.[366] Most lesions are found on the extremities. The majority are deeply seated, but they can also be superficial.[367] Microscopically, the changes are those of hemorrhagic necrosis with abscess formation in the early stage and represented by a heavy infiltrate of lymphocytes and plasma cells in the late stage. Marked epidermal hyperplasia can be seen at the edges. The pathogenesis is probably immune mediated.

Vesiculobullous diseases

The key morphologic features in the microscopic evaluation of vesiculobullous lesions are the level of the plane of separation and the type of cellular change seen, particularly the presence or absence of acantholysis—as masterfully described in the classic monograph by Lever[389] (Table 4.1), now supplemented by their immunofluorescent pattern (Table 4.2). Vesicles and bullae (large vesicles) are divided according to their location into subepidermal and intraepidermal, which in turn may be suprabasal or subcorneal. In making this distinction, one should be aware of the fact that a bulla that was originally subepidermal can become intraepidermal because of regrowth of epithelium across its base, a process that can be very rapid. Actually, large intraepidermal bullae unassociated with acantholytic changes should be suspected of being healed subepidermal bullae. Biopsying early lesions (less than 24 hours old) minimizes this problem.

Subepidermal bullous dermatoses include dermatitis herpetiformis, bullous pemphigoid, erythema multiforme, porphyria cutanea tarda, epidermolysis bullosa, and cicatricial pemphigoid[378] (Figs 4.34 and 4.35). They can also be seen as a secondary event in any dermatosis associated with liquefactive degeneration of the basal layer, such as lupus erythematosus, scleroderma, and

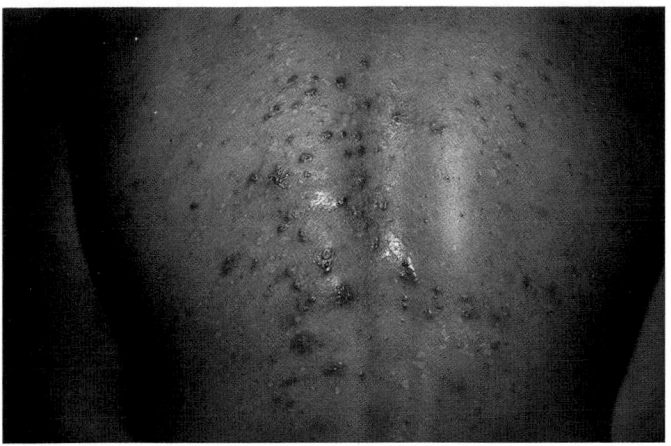

Fig. 4.34 Clinical lesions of dermatitis herpetiformis. Note the small size of the vesicles and their symmetric distribution.

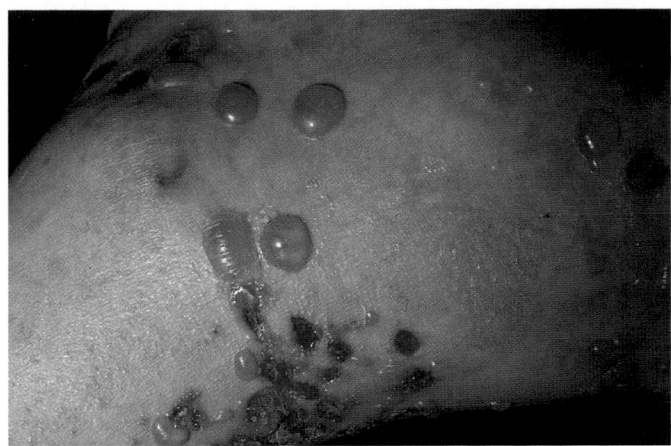

Fig. 4.35 Clinical appearance of bullous pemphigoid. Large bullae are present, some of which have ruptured.

lichen planus.[404] Occasionally, two of these diseases are seen to coexist.[409] The differential diagnosis should be made on the basis of the combined clinical, microscopic, and immunohistochemical findings.[388,396] Some of these disorders are easily recognizable on clinical grounds. This is particularly true of dermatitis herpetiformis (an IgA-mediated skin disease) because of its symmetric distribution, intense pruritus, frequent association with gluten-sensitive enteropathy, and response to sulfapyridine and diaxone.[379,391]

Microscopically, a distinction between these various subepidermal processes is not always possible[388]; how-

ever, careful evaluation of a set of criteria as seen in routinely stained sections results in a high level of concordance with the clinical diagnosis[403,406] (Tables 4.1 and 4.2). The most consistent histologic features of *bullous pemphigoid* are festooning of the dermal papillae, absence of adjacent microabscesses, and a unilocular blister with a mild dermal infiltrate. The most useful criterion for the diagnosis of *dermatitis herpetiformis* is the presence of papillary microabscesses forming a multilocular subepidermal bulla (Fig. 4.36). Eosinophils tend to be particularly numerous in this condition. The most characteristic features of bullous *erythema multiforme*

Table 4.1 Grouping of cutaneous bullous diseases according to the location and mechanism of formation of the bullae

Intraepidermal	Subepidermal
Subcorneal/glandular	**Basal keratinocyte necrosis, cytologic, or damage**
Miliaria crystallina	Epidermolysis bullosa simplex
Staphylococcal scalded skin syndrome	Thermal injury (some)
Pemphigus foliaceus and variants	Erythema multiforme
Bullous impetigo	Herpes gestationis
IgA pemphigus	**Epidermal basement membrane zone destruction or disruption**
Subcorneal pustular dermatosis	Lamina lucida
Erythema toxicum neonatorum	Bullous pemphigoid
Transient neonatal pustular melanosis	Cicatricial pemphigoid
Acropustulosis of infancy	Herpes gestationis
Spinous	Dermatitis herpetiformis
Spongiotic dermatitis	Linear IgA dermatosis
Friction blister (may extend into dermis)	Epidermolysis bullosa acquisita
Miliara rubra	Porphyria cutanea tarda
Incontinentia pigmenti	Epidermolysis bullosa letalis (junctional)
IgA pemphigus	Suction blister
Epidermolytic hyperkeratosis	Thermal injury (some)
Hailey-Hailey disease	Sublamina densa
Suprabasal	Cicatricial pemphigoid
Pemphigus vulgaris and variants	Linear IgA dermatosis
Paraneoplastic pemphigus	Epydermolysis bullosa dystrophica
Darier disease	Epidermolysis bullosa acquisita
	Bullous systemic lupus erythematosus
	Dermal
	Penicillamine-induced blisters (iatrogenic)

Table 4.2 Usual immunofluorescence patterns in the various types of vesicobullous dermatoses. It should be noted that immunoglobulins other than those listed above may also be present, although less commonly and less intensely

Dermatosis	Principle immunoreactant	Location	Pattern
Pemphigus			
All types except below	IgG	ISR	Lacelike
IgA type	IgA	ISR	Lacelike
Paraneoplastic type	IgG	ISR	Lacelike
	C3, IgG	EBMZ	Linear
	C3, IgG	EBMZ	Granular
Bullous pemphigoid	C3, IgG	EBMZ	Linear
Cicatricial pemphigoid	C3, IgG	EBMZ	Linear
Herpes gestationis	C3	EBMZ	Linear
Epidermolysis bullosa acquisita	C3, IgG	EBMZ	Linear
Bullous systemic lupus eryth.	C3, IgG	EBMZ	Linear
	C3, IgG	EBMZ	Granular
Dermatitis herpetiformis	IgA	EBMZ	Granular
Linear IgA dermatosis	IgA	EBMZ	Linear
Erythema multiforme	C3, IgM	EBMZ	Granular
	C3, IgM	Vessels	Granular

ISR: Intercellular squamous region; EBMZ, Epidermal basement membrane zone.

(which progresses clinically from papular erythema to a characteristic target lesion) are subepidermal edema, the presence of basement membrane in the roof of the bulla, abundant nuclear dust in the dermis, and occasional vasculitis, epidermal spongiosis, and epidermal necrosis.[383] Eosinophils can also be present.[401] It should be realized that a wide spectrum of histologic changes exists in erythema multiforme, ranging from a predominantly dermal disturbance to a necrotizing epidermal reaction similar to the adult type of toxic epidermal necrolysis.[371,399] Thus the bullae of erythema multiforme can be subepidermal, with the basal lamina at the top of the blister (as a result of dermal edema), or dermoepidermal, with the basal lamina at the floor of the bulla (as a result of epidermal damage).[397]

Somewhat similar considerations apply to the group of more than 12 genetically determined disorders collectively known as *epidermolysis bullosa*,[375–377,398] in which the site of cleavage can be in the dermis (dermolytic form), at the dermoepidermal junction (junctional form), or in the epidermis (epidermolytic form) (Fig. 4.37).

Squamous cell carcinoma of the skin remains a major cause of morbidity and mortality in patients with epidermolysis bullosa, especially the Hallopeau–Siemens recessive dystrophic form.[394]

Immunofluorescent studies in bullous diseases have been shown to be of considerable diagnostic value, especially in distinguishing bullous pemphigoid from epidermolysis bullosa and dermatitis herpetiformis.[384,393,413] In bullous pemphigoid there is in vivo subepidermal linear

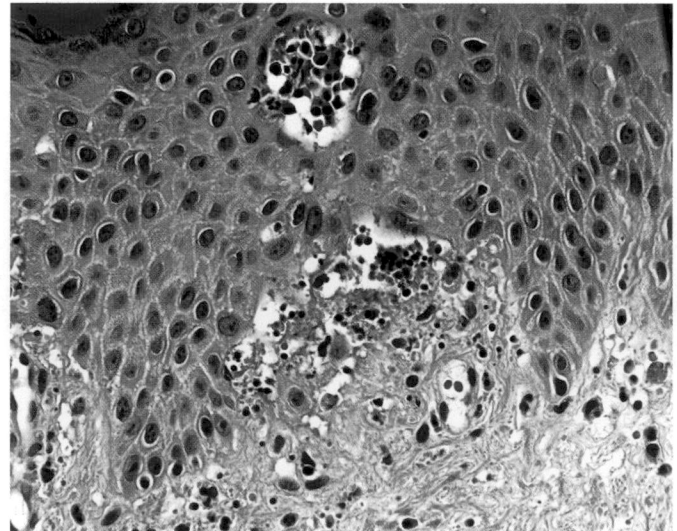

Fig. 4.36 Typical appearance of early lesion of dermatitis herpetiforms.

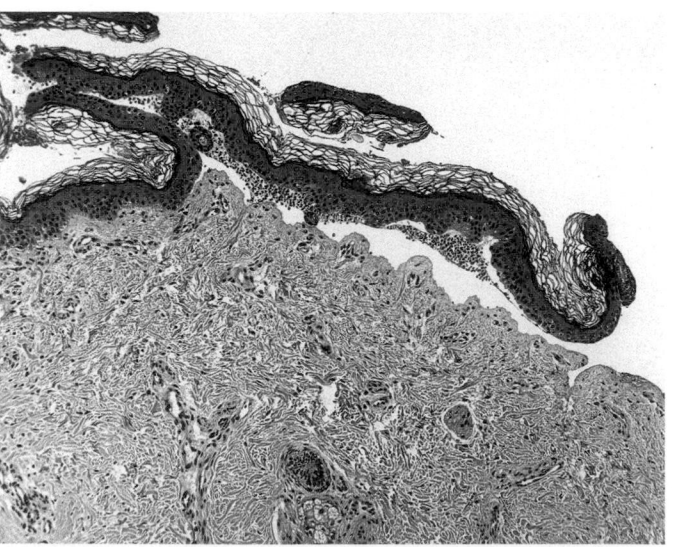

Fig. 4.37 Clean subepidermal bulla of epidermolysis bullosa.

binding of IgG and complement with an occasional mixture of IgA and IgM; there are also circulating antibodies that bind to the basement zone of normal skin or mucous membrane in 70% of patients.[390] In dermatitis herpetiformis, there are no circulating antibodies, and the in vivo immunofluorescent pattern is that of subepidermal granular binding of IgA, mainly at the tips of dermal papillae. The presence of these antibodies is better demonstrated by immunofluorescence on snap-frozen tissue, but positive results can also be obtained in most cases by immunoperoxidase on paraffin-embedded material.[396,410,412]

Intraepidermal bullous dermatoses include *pemphigus vulgaris* and a variant thereof, *pemphigus vegetans*. In these diseases, the cleavage plane is just above the basal layer and is caused by acantholysis (Fig. 4.38). In contrast, the separation in *pemphigus foliaceus*[402] and *pemphigus erythematosus*[369,385] is in or just below the granular layer (Fig. 4.39). Indirect immunofluorescent stains performed with sera of patients with pemphigus demonstrate the presence of antiepithelial autoantibodies in most cases, although the test may be negative in the early stages[374,411] (Fig. 4.40). In addition, immunoglobulins can be detected in over 90% of cases in the epidermal intercellular spaces by a direct immunofluorescence technique.[410] These autoantibodies—some of which are directed against adhering-junction molecules—are thought to play an important role in the pathogenesis of pemphigus vulgaris.[373,380,386,392,407] Despite earlier reports, indirect immunofluorescence is unreliable for evaluating the status of the disease or for gauging therapy in patients with pemphigus. Some cases of pemphigus are seen in association with internal organ malignancies ("paraneoplastic pemphigus").[370,395]

A statistically increased incidence of internal malignancies has been observed in patients with pemphigus, in addition to the well-known association between pemphigus and thymoma.[415]

Acantholysis can be seen in several other dermatologic conditions, such as *familial benign pemphigus* or *Hailey–Hailey disease* (often located in inguinal folds and clinically resembling candidiasis and condylomas),[387] viral vesicles, the pemphigus-like lesions induced by D-penicillamine,[405] actinic keratosis, and the type of squamous cell carcinoma arising from it (adenoid or pseudoglandular), Darier's disease, warty dyskeratoma, and *transient acantholytic dermatosis (Grover's disease)*. The latter is characterized by transient edematous and excoriated papules and vesicles located predominantly on the trunk, thought to be the result of the combined action of heat and sweating.[382,400] According to Chalet et al.,[372] the most important clue to the diagnosis is the association of acantholysis and spongiosis. In addition, focal acantholytic dyskeratotic changes (sometimes limited to a single rete ridge) totally devoid of clinical significance can be found in association with a variety of localized lesions, such as dermatofibroma, basal cell carcinoma, melanocytic nevus, and malignant melanoma.[368,414]

In *subcorneal pustular dermatosis*,[408] the vesicles are just beneath the keratin layer, as they are in *impetigo contagiosa*.[381] Another subcorneal vesicular lesion that has been mistaken clinically for junctional nevus is the *blood*

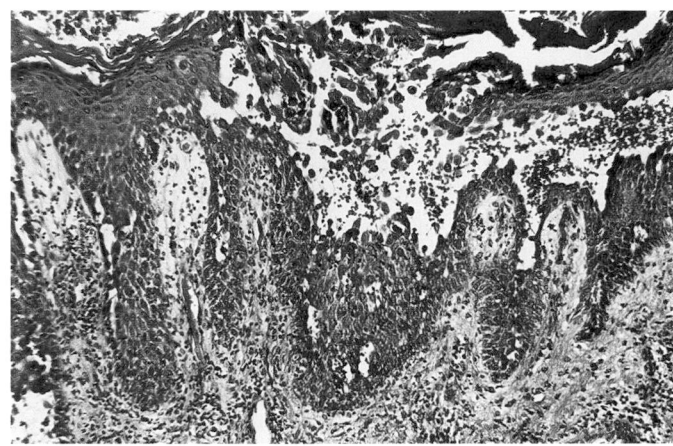

Fig. 4.38 Pemphigus vulgaris. The bulla is in a suprabasal location.

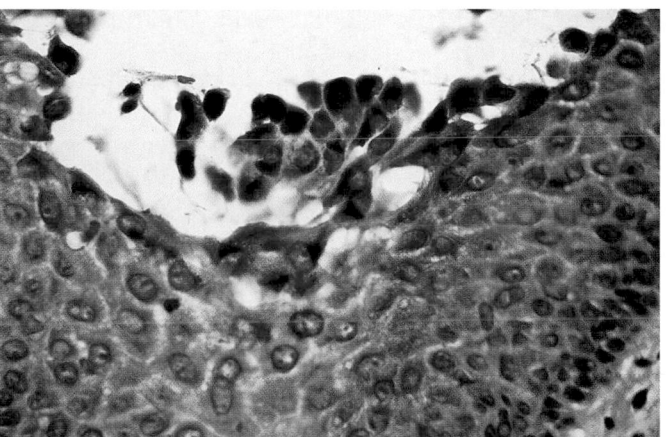

Fig. 4.39 Pemphigus erythematosus. The acantholytic cells are in a superficial location.

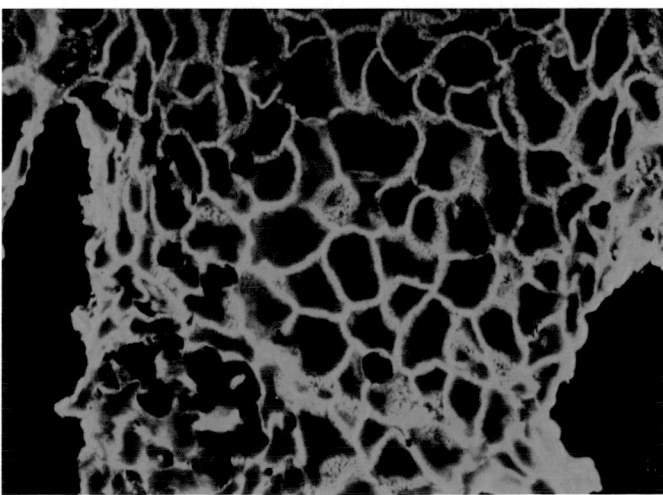

Fig. 4.40 Immunofluorescent demonstration of anti-pemphigus vulgaris antibody.

blister, in which the erythrocytes are trapped beneath the thick stratum corneum of the toes or fingers.

Degenerative and miscellaneous diseases

Lichen sclerosus et atrophicus

Lichen sclerosus et atrophicus occurs most often on the upper trunk and neck, flexor surface of the wrist, and the anogenital areas. When this disease is located in the vulva it is also designated as *kraurosis* and when in the glans penis as *balanitis xerotica obliterans*. The disease occurs most commonly in women, often at or around menopause, but it can also be seen in children and young adults.[417] The etiology is unknown, but there is a strong association with autoimmune disorders and a link with HLA DQ7.[419] Epidermal atrophy, hyperkeratosis, and hydropic degeneration of the basal layer are associated with complete obliteration of the structure of the upper dermis. The latter is replaced by an edematous (rather than sclerotic), hypocellular, faintly staining band beneath which a moderate chronic inflammatory infiltrate appears (Fig. 4.41). In older lesions, some hyalinization and angiectasia occur in this band. In early lesions, the inflammatory infiltrate may be abutting against the epidermal basal layer, without much of a band in between. Such lesions may closely simulate lichen planus.[416]

Lichen sclerosus et atrophicus should be clearly distinguished from localized scleroderma (morphea), although the two diseases may coexist[418] (see p. 111). It should also be separated from the hyperplastic mucosal lesions accompanied by various degrees of atypia (keratoses).

Elastosis perforans

In elastosis perforans, clumps and strands of abnormally coarse elastic fibers penetrate the epidermis and produce a focal epidermal hyperplasia.[420,422,426] The typical site of involvement is the back of the neck in adolescent boys. The altered elastica in the papillary dermis is easily missed and recognition usually requires elastic tissue stains.

Elastosis perforans needs to be distinguished from other perforating dermatoses, such as *reactive perforating collagenosis, perforating folliculitis,* and *Kyrle's disease*.[423–428] The nosologic identity of the latter two disorders and their relationship to each other remains controversial. A high proportion of them are seen in patients with chronic renal failure or diabetes mellitus.[421,428]

Pseudoxanthoma elasticum

The dermal changes in pseudoxanthoma elasticum are manifestations of a heritable disease also having ocular and vascular lesions resulting from degeneration of elastic fibers and due to mutations of the *ABCC/MRP6* gene (which codes for an ATP-binding protein).[429,430] Angioid streaks in the retina and degenerative changes in arteries leading to occlusion or rupture are described. Yellow streaks and plaques of the skin, particularly in areas of creases such as the neck, axillae, and groin, account for the name *pseudoxanthoma*. Histologically, the mid and lower dermis contains clumps and strands of altered, basophilic connective tissue that stain intensely with aldehyde fuchsin and Verhoeff's elastic tissue stain (Fig. 4.42). The basophilic staining quality of the elastic material is due to dystrophic calcification of the fibers.

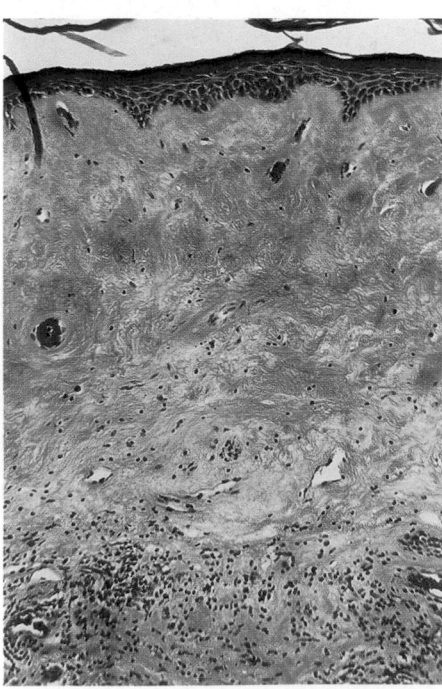

Fig. 4.41 Lichen sclerosus et atrophicus.

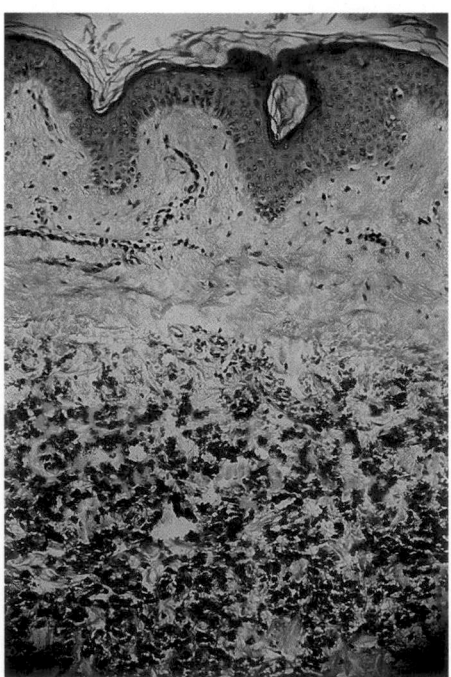

Fig. 4.42 Pseudoxanthoma elasticum.

Cutaneous mucinoses

Pretibial myxedema is characterized by sometimes large nodular lesions that occur on the legs of patients who are or have been thyrotoxic.[441] When particularly extreme, the disease has been referred to as *elephantiasic*.[442] The accumulation of mucopolysaccharides in the dermis is similar to that in the orbital tissues, which is caused by excess TSH secretion by the pituitary gland. Histologically, the dermal collagen is separated by aggregates of faintly basophilic material that stains with Mayer's mucicarmine, Hale's colloidal iron and PAS (diastase resistant).

Other conditions associated with the deposition of large amounts of acid mucopolysaccharides in the dermis are the *generalized myxedema* of hypothyroidism, *papular mucinosis* (lichen myxedematosus), *myxoid cyst*, cutaneous *focal mucinosis*, and *follicular mucinosis*.[434–440,443–445] The latter condition is a reaction pattern of follicular epithelium that is particularly prominent in alopecia mucinosa but that can also be seen in a variety of other diseases, including mycosis fungoides.[435,440] Morphologically, the idiopathic and mycosis fungoides-related forms of the disease are similar; follow-up studies on patients with the idiopathic form have shown little or no progression toward mycosis fungoides, despite the presence in some cases of a clonal T-cell population.[431,433] Cutaneous myxoid nodules are an important component of Carney's syndrome, that also includes cardiac myxomas, spotty hyperpigmentation, and endocrine hyperactivity.[432]

Acanthosis nigricans

Acanthosis nigricans manifests clinically as brown, velvety plaques most often found in the axillae, back of the neck, and other flexural areas. Two major forms exist, one associated with internal malignant neoplasms (particularly of the gastrointestinal tract) and the other with a heterogeneous group of disorders having as common denominator the presence of tissue resistance to insulin.[446,448,449] The latter form includes diabetes, obesity, and Cushing's syndrome. Microscopically, the changes are similar in both types and are characterized by papillomatosis and hyperkeratosis (rather than by acanthosis and hyperpigmentation, as suggested by the name). In the cases associated with malignancy, the disease may be the result of production of epidermal growth factors by the tumor cells.[447,450]

Darier's disease

Darier's disease is an uncommon genodermatosis usually presenting with a symmetrical distribution of keratotic reddish-brown papules over the "seborrheic" areas of the body (Fig. 4.43). Unilateral and localized variants have been described.[452] Microscopically, the skin lesions are characterized by suprabasal clefts in which acantholytic cells called *grains* are found[451] (Fig. 4.44). The dermal papillae covered by a layer of basal cells form

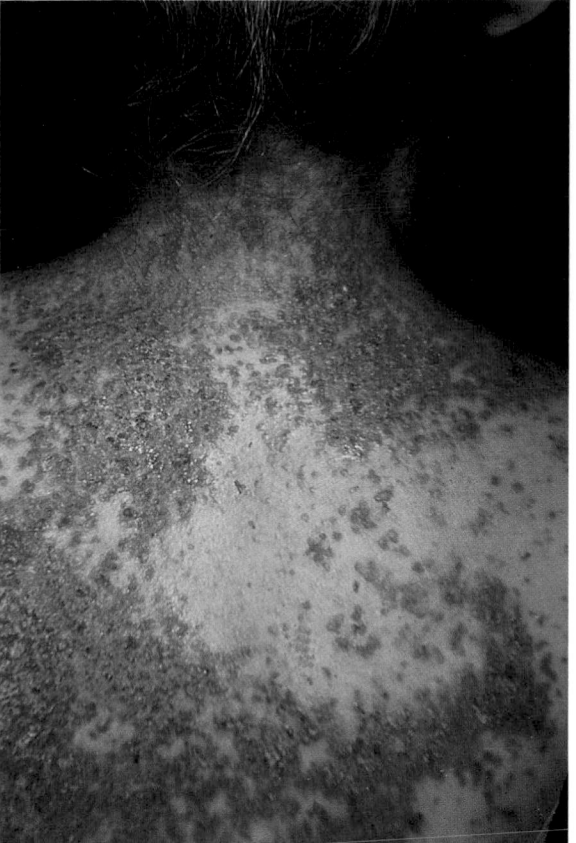

Fig. 4.43 Clinical appearance of Darier's disease. The lesion typically affects the back and presents in the form of reticulated keratotic lesions.

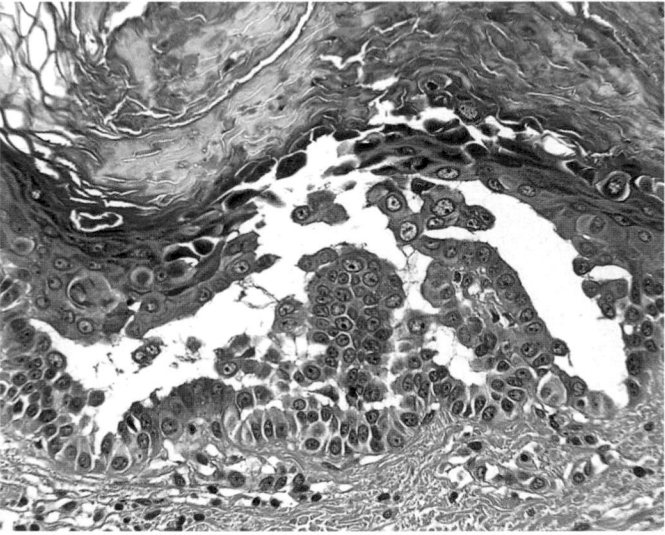

Fig. 4.44 Darier disease.

small villi at the base of the lesion. In addition, within the epidermis large individually dyskeratotic cells called *corps ronds* are found. When the lesions are closely spaced, the skin assumes a verrucous appearance. The back is the most common site of involvement. The oral mucosa and hairless skin may be involved, showing that the disease is not limited to the hair follicle as suggested by the synonym *keratosis follicularis*. Warty dyskeratoma, an isolated follicular lesion, is histologically similar but unrelated to Darier's disease (see p. 152).

Dermatoses in HIV-infected patients

HIV-infected patients may develop a large variety of skin diseases, ranging from inconspicuous macular rashes to Kaposi's sarcoma, the latter being the condition that contributed in the mid 1980s to the recognition of this immune deficiency syndrome.[456,457]

Non-neoplastic skin manifestations of HIV infection include the following:

1 *Maculopapular eruptions*. In acute HIV disease, about a quarter of patients develop a maculopapular erythematous eruption in the trunk that may extend to involve the extremities. Microscopically, there is a nonspecific perivascular collection of lymphocytes and histiocytes in the upper dermis, sometimes associated with small papulovesicular foci with necrotic keratinocytes and a few neutrophils.[453,454]

2 *Papular pruritic eruptions*. These lesions, which may develop after the acute HIV phase, have a tendency for waxing and waning and can occur anywhere in the body. Microscopically, there is a superficial and mid-dermal perivascular lymphocytic dermatitis, often featuring eosinophils, acanthosis, and parakeratosis.[458]

3 *Vasculitis*. A few cases of leukocytoclastic vasculitis have been reported. Some have been said to be the direct result of HIV infection[455] and others of cytomegalovirus (CMV) infection.[466]

4 *Folliculitis and syringitis*. The clinical observation has been made that full-blown AIDS is often preceded by some manifestation of folliculitis.[464] Microscopically, the usual appearance is that of a mixed perifollicular chronic inflammatory infiltrate, sometimes associated with follicle rupture. In some cases the inflammation has a prominent eosinophilic component (*HIV-associated eosinophilic folliculitis*)[461,467,469]

(Fig. 4.45). Herpetic syringitis (i.e., inflammation of the acrosyringium of the sweat glands) has been described, sometimes accompanied by squamous syringometaplasia.[465]

5 *Seborrheic dermatitis*. This common complication of HIV infection differs from that seen in immunocompetent individuals in that it tends to involve the trunk and extremities and is clinically more severe.[463] Microscopically, the changes depend on the stage of the lesion and are qualitatively similar to those seen in the usual form of the disease.[472]

6 *Psoriasis*.

7 *Drug reaction*.

8 *Parasitic* (scabies), *fungal* (cryptococcosis, histoplasmosis, dermatophytosis), and *bacterial* (mycobacteriosis, syphilis, bacillary angiomatosis) *infections*.

9 *Viral infections* (other than these already mentioned). Herpes simplex occurs in about 20% of HIV-infected patients, usually in the form of a painful ulcer in the perianal or perioral regions[470] (Figs 4.46 and 4.47).

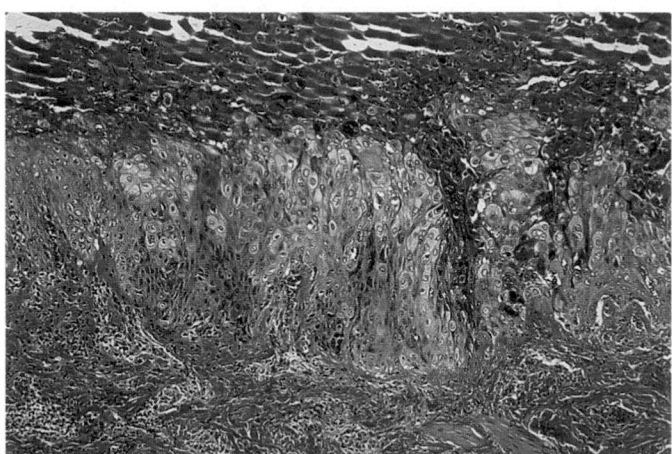

Fig. 4.46 Herpes simplex in a 10-year-old child affected by AIDS.

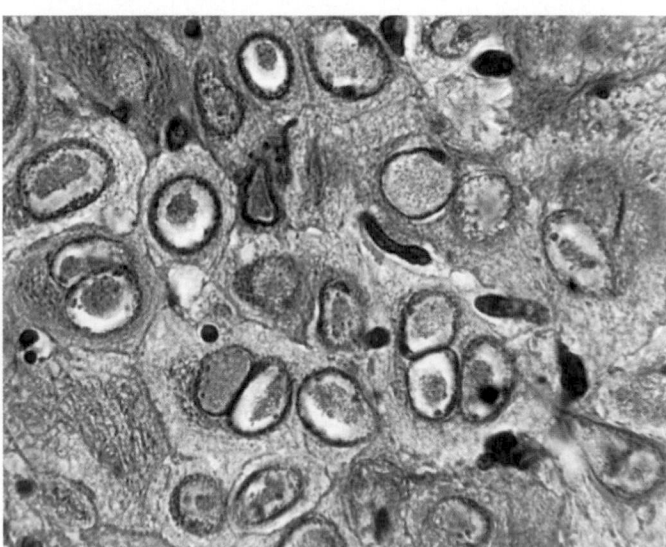

Fig. 4.47 Large intranuclear inclusions in cutaneous herpes simplex infection.

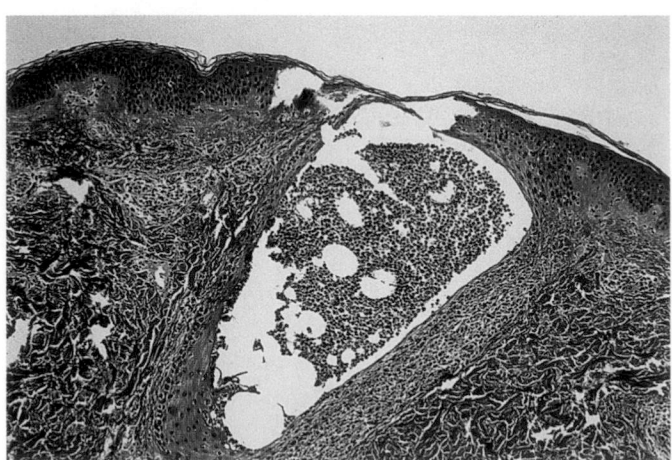

Fig. 4.45 Eosinophilic folliculitis in an HIV-infected patient.

Varicella–herpes zoster infection can be severe and widespread, sometimes with involvement of numerous dermatomes.[459,460,462] CMV may be detected in ulcerative lesions at mucocutaneous junctions. Other viral infections include molluscum contagiosum, oral hairy leukoplakia, and HPV-induced lesions (such as anal warts and bowenoid papulosis).[468]

10 *Papular neutrophilic xanthoma.* This HIV-associated lesion is characterized by collections of foamy macrophages, extracellular nuclear dust, and hyaline necrosis of collagen fibers.[471]

References

Introduction to dermatopathology

1 Ackerman AB. Histologic diagnosis of inflammatory skin disease. An algorithmic method based on pattern analysis, ed. 2, Baltimore, 1997, Williams & Williams.

2 Ackerman AB. Differential diagnosis in dermatopathology II, ed. 2. New York, 2001, Ardor Scribendi.

3 Demis D (ed). Clinical dermatology. Hagerstown, MD, Harper & Row, 1972 to present.

4 Farmer ER, Hood AF (eds). Pathology of the skin, ed. 2. New York, 2000, McGraw-Hill.

5 Fitzpatrick TB, Freedberg I (eds). Fitzpatrick's dermatology in general medicine, ed. 6. New York, 2003, McGraw-Hill.

6 Johnson BL Jr, Honig PJ, Jaworsky C. Pediatric dermatopathology. Clinical and pathologic correlations. Boston, 1994, Butterworth-Heinemann.

7 Lever WF, Elder DE. Lever's histopathology of the shin, ed. 8. Philadelphia, 1997, Lippincott-Raven.

8 McKee P. Essential skin pathology. London, 1999, Mosby.

9 Mehregan AH. Pinkus' guide to dermatohistopathology. ed. 6. Norwalk, 1995, Appleton & Lange.

10 Rook A, Wilkinson DS, Ebling FJG, Champion RH. Rook/Wilkinson/Ebling textbook of dermatology. ed. 6. Oxford, 1998, Blackwell Science.

11 Weedon D, Strutton G. Skin pathology, ed. 2. London, 2002, Churchill Livingstone.

Normal anatomy

12 Derrick E, Barker J, Khan A, Price M, McDonald D. The tissue distribution of factor XIIIa positive cells. Histopathology 1993, **22:** 157–162.

13 Fine J-D. Structure and antigenicity of the skin basement membrane zone. J Cutan Pathol 1991, **18:** 401–409.

14 Foschini MP, Scarpellini F, Gown AM, Eusebi V. Differential expression of myoepithelial markers in salivary, sweat and mammary glands. Int J Surg Pathol 2000, **8:** 29–37.

15 Gould VE, Moll R, Moll I, Lee I, Franke WW. Neuroendocrine (Merkel) cells of the skin. Hyperplasias, dysplasias and neoplasias. Lab Invest 1985, **52:** 334–353.

16 Horstman E. Die Haut. In Möllendorff WV (ed.): Handbuch der microskopichen Anatomie des Menschen, vol. 3, part 3. Berlin, 1957, Springer-Verlag, pp. 1–488.

17 Leask A, Byrne C, Fuchs E. Transcription factor AP2 and its role in epidermal-specific gene expression. Proc Natl Acad Sci USA 1991, **88:** 7948–7952.

18 Lund HZ, Sommerville RL. Basophilic degeneration of the cutis. Am J Clin Pathol 1957, **27:** 183–190.

19 Maiorana A, Nigrisoli E, Papotti M. Immunohistochemical markers of sweat gland tumors. J Cutan Pathol 1986, **13:** 187–196.

20 Metze D, Jurecka W, Gebhart W, Schuller-Petrovic S. Secretory immunoglobulin A in sweat gland tumors. J Cutan Pathol 1989, **16:** 126–132.

21 Moll R, Moll I, Franke WW. Identification of Merkel cells in human skin by specific cytokeratin antibodies. Changes of cell density and distribution in fetal and adult plantar epidermis. Differentiation 1984, **28:** 136–154.

22 Montagna W, Parakkal PF. The structure and function of the skin, ed 3. New York, 1974, Academic Press, Inc.

23 Montagna W, Kligman AM, Carlisle KS. Atlas of normal human skin. New York, 1992, Springer-Verlag.

24 Noda Y, Horike H, Watanabe Y, Mori M. Immunohistochemical identification of epithelial membrane antigen in sweat gland tumours by the use of a monoclonal antibody. Pathol Res Pract 1987, **182:** 797–804.

25 Noda Y, Oosumi H, Morishima T, Tsujimura T, Mori M. Immunohistochemical study of carbonic anhydrase in mixed tumours and adenomas of sweat and sebaceous glands. J Cutan Pathol 1987, **14:** 285–290.

26 Pagani A, Eusebi V, Bussolati G. Detection of PIP-GCDFP-15 gene expression in apocrine epithelium of the breast and salivary glands. Appl Immunohistochem 1994, **2:** 29–35.

27 Penneys NS, Zlatkiss I. Immunohistohemical demonstration of ferritin in sweat gland and sweat gland neoplasms. J Cutan Pathol 1990, **17:** 32–36.

28 Sams WM Jr, Smith JG Jr. The histochemistry of chronically sun-damaged skin. J Invest Dermatol 1961, **37:** 447–453.

29 Sueki H, Whitaker D, Buchsbaum M, Murphy GF. Novel interactions between dermal dendrocytes and mast cells in human skin. Implications for hemostasis and matrix repair. Lab Invest 1993, **69:** 133–135.

30 Tamaki K, Furue M, Matsukawa A, Ohara K, Mizoguchi M, Hino H. Presence and distribution of carcinoembryonic antigen and lectin-binding sites in benign apocrine sweat gland tumours. Br J Dermatol 1985, **113:** 565–571.

31 Tsubura A, Senzaki H, Sasaki M, Hilgers J, Morii S. Immunohistochemical demonstration of breast-derived and/or carcinoma-associated glycoproteins in normal skin appendages and their tumors. J Cutan Pathol 1992, **19:** 73–79.

32 Urmacher C. Histology of normal skin. Am J Surg Pathol 1990, **14:** 671–686.

33 Urmacher CD. Normal skin. In Sternberg S (ed.): History of Pathologists, ed. 2. Philadelphia, 1997, Lippincott-Raven.

Inflammatory diseases of known etiology
Viral diseases

34 Ebert MH, Otsuka M. Virus diseases of skin, with special reference to elementary and inclusion bodies. Arch Dermatol 1943, **48:** 635–649.

35 McSorely J, Shapiro L, Braunstein MA, Hsu KC. Herpes simplex and varicella-zoster. Comparative histopathology of 77 cases. Int J Dermatol 1979, **13:** 69–75.

Warts

36 Aiba S, Rokugo M, Tagami H. Immunohistologic analysis of the phenomenon of spontaneous regression of numerous flat warts. Cancer 1986, **58:** 1246–1251.

37 Berman A, Winkelmann RK. Flat warts undergoing involution. Histopathological findings. Arch Dermatol 1977, **113:** 1219–1221.

38 Brentjens MH, Yeung-Yue KA, Lee PC, Tyring SK. Human papilloma virus: a review. Dermatol Clin 2002, **20:** 315–351.

39 Dhillon I, Zouzias D, Geronemus R. Invasive squamous cell carcinoma in a patient with epidermodysplasia verruciformis. J Dermatol Surg Oncol 1991, **17:** 300–302.

40 Dvoretzky I, Lowy DR. Infections by human papillomavirus (warts). Am J Dermatopathol 1982, **4:** 85–89.

41 Egawa K, Inaba Y, Yoshimura K, Ono T. Varied clinical

morphology of HPV-1 induced warts, depending on anatomical factors. Br J Dermatol 1993, **128:** 271–276.

42 Gross G, Pfister H, Hagedorm M. Correlation between human papillomavirus type and histology of warts. J Invest Dermatol 1982, **78:** 160–164.

43 Inaba Y, Egawa K, Yoshimura K, Ono T. Demonstration of human papillomavirus type 1 DNA in a wart with bowenoid histologic changes. Am J Dermatopathol 1993, **15:** 172–175.

44 Iwatsuki K, Tagami H, Takigawa M, Yamada M. Plane warts under spontaneous regression. Immunopathologic study on cellular constituents leading to the inflammatory reaction. Arch Dermatol 1986, **122:** 655–659.

45 Jacyk WK, Dreyer L, de Villiers EM. Seborrheic keratoses of black patients with epidermodysplasia verruciformis contain human papillomavirus DNA. Am J Dermatopathol 1993, **15:** 1–6.

46 Jenson AB, Sommer S, Payling-Wright C, Pass F, Link CC Jr, Lancaster WD. Human papillomavirus. Frequency and distribution in plantar and common warts. Lab Invest 1982, **47:** 491–497.

47 Kao GF, Kao WH. Malignant transformation of keratinocytes by human papilomaviruses. J Cutan Pathol 1994, **21:** 193–199.

48 Kawashima M. Epidermodysplasia verruciformis. J Dermatol 1992, **19:** 707–709.

49 Kimura S, Komatsu T, Ohyama K. Common and plantar warts with trichilemmal keratinization-like keratinizing process. A possible existence of pseudotrichilemmal keratinization. J Cutan Pathol 1982, **9:** 391–395.

50 Majewski S, Jablonska S. Do epidermodysplasia verruciformis human papillomaviruses contribute to malignant and benign epidermal proliferations. Arch Dermatol 2002, **138:** 649–654.

51 Mullink H, Jiwa NM, Walboomers JM, Horstman A, Vos W, Meijer CJ. Demonstration of changes in cytokeratin expression in condylomata accuminata in relation to the presence of human papilloma virus as shown by a combination of immunohistochemistry and in situ hybridization. Am J Dermatopathol 1991, **13:** 530–537.

52 Nebesio CL, Mirowski GW, Chuang TY. Human papillomavirus: clinical significance and malignant potential. Int J Dermatol 2001, **40:** 373–379.

53 Nuovo G, Lastarria DA, Smith S, Lerner J, Comite SL, Eliezri YD. Human papillomavirus segregation patterns in genital and nongenital warts in prepubertal children and adults. Am J Clin Pathol 1991, **95:** 467–474.

54 Obalek S, Favre M, Szymanczyk J, Misiewicz J, Jablonska S, Orth G. Human papillomavirus (HPV) types specific of epidermodysplasia verruciformis detected in warts induced by HPV3 or HPV3-related types in immunosuppressed patients. J Invest Dermatol 1992, **98:** 936–941.

55 Phillips ME, Ackerman AB. "Benign" and "malignant" neoplasms associated with verrucae vulgares. Am J Dermatopathol 1982, **4:** 61–84.

56 Proby C, Churchill L, Purkis P, Glover M, Sexton C, Leigh I. Keratin 17 expression as a marker for epithelial transformation in viral warts. Am J Pathol 1993, **143:** 1667–1678.

Molluscum contagiosum

57 Ackerman AB, Tanski EV. Pseudoleukemia cutis. Report of a case in association with molluscum contagiosum. Cancer 1977, **40:** 813–817.

58 Cribier B, Scrivener Y, Grosshans E. Molluscum contagiosum: histologic patterns and associated lesions. A study of 578 cases. Am J Dermatopathol 2001, **23:** 99–103.

59 Guitart J, Hurt MA. Pleomorphic T-cell infiltrate associated with molluscum contagiosum. Am J Dermatopathol 1999, **21:** 178–180.

60 Legrain A, Pierard GE. Molluscum contagiosum may affect primarily the epidermis without involving hair follicles. Am J Dermatopathol 1985, **7:** 131–132.

61 Naert F, Lachapelle JM. Multiple lesions of molluscum contagiosum with metaplastic ossification. Am J Dermatopathol 1989, **11:** 238–241.

62 Reed RJ, Parkinson RP. The histogenesis of molluscum contagiosum. Am J Surg Pathol 1977, **1:** 161–166.

63 Smith KJ, Skelton H. Molluscum contagiosum: recent advances in pathogenic mechanisms, and new therapies. Am J Clin Dermatol 2002, **3:** 535–545.

64 Sutton JS, Burnett JW. Ultrastructural changes in dermal and epidermal cells of skin infected with molluscum contagiosum virus. J Ultrastruct Res 1969, **26:** 177–196.

Herpes zoster

65 Gnann JW Jr, Whitley RJ. Clinical practice. Herpes zoster. N Engl J Med 2002, **347:** 340–346.

66 McSorely J, Shapiro L, Braunstein MA, Hsu KC. Herpes simplex and varicella-zoster. Comparative histopathology of 77 cases. Int J Dermatol 1979, **13:** 69–75.

67 Merselis JG, Kaye D, Hook EW. Disseminated herpes zoster. Report of 17 cases. Arch Intern Med 1964, **113:** 679–686.

68 Molin I. Aspects of the natural history of herpes zoster. Acta Derm Venereol (Stockh) 1969, **48:** 569–583.

Bacterial diseases
Folliculitis

69 Arai E, Okubo H, Tsuchida T, Kitamura K, Katyayama I. Pseudolymphomatous folliculitis: a clinicopathologic study of 15 cases of cutaneous pseudolymphoma with follicular invasion. Am J Surg Pathol 1999, **23:** 1313–1319.

70 Chang SN, Chun SI, Moon TK, Park WH. Solitary sclerotic fibroma of the skin: degenerated sclerotic change of inflammatory conditions, especially folliculitis. Am J Dermatopathol 2000, **22:** 22–25.

71 Herman LE, Harawi SJ, Ghossein RA, Kurban AK. Folliculitis. A clinicopathologic review. Pathol Annu 1991, **26**(Pt 2): 201–246.

72 McCalmont TH, Althemus D, Mauer T, Berger TG. Eosinophilic folliculitis: the histologic spectrum. Am J Dermatopathol 1996, **17:** 439–446.

73 Ramdial PK, Morar N, Dlova NC, Aboobaker J. HIV-associated eosinophilic folliculitis in an infant. Am J Dermatopathol 1999, **21:** 241–246.

74 Vollmer RT. Demodex-associated folliculitis. Am J Dermatopathol 1997, **18:** 589–591.

Hidradenitis suppurativa

75 Dillon JS, Spjut HJ. Acne aggregata seu conglobata. Ann Surg 1964, **195:** 451–455.

76 Heller DS, Haefner HK, Hameed M, Lieberman RW. Vulvar hidradenitis suppurativa. Immunohistochemical evaluation of apocrine and eccrine involvement. J Reprod Med 2002, **47:** 695–700.

77 Jemec GB. Hidradenitis suppurativa. J Cutan Med Surg 2003, **7:** 47–56.

78 Masson JK. Surgical treatment for hidradenitis suppurativa. Surg Clin North Am 1969, **49:** 1043–1052.

79 Mitchell KM, Beck DE. Hidradenitis suppurativa. Surg Clin North Am 2002, **82:** 1187–1197.

80 Shelley WB, Cahn MM. The pathogenesis of hidradenitis suppurativa in man. Arch Dermatol 1955, **72:** 562–569.

Tuberculosis and atypical mycobacteriosis

81 Barbagallo J, Tager P, Ingleton R, Hirsch RJ, Weinberg JM. Cutaneous tuberculosis: diagnosis and treatment. Am J Clin Dermatol 2002, **3:** 319–328.

82 Beyt BE Jr, Ortbals DW, Santa Cruz DJ, Kobayaski GS, Eisen AZ, Medoff G. Cutaneous mycobacteriosis. Analysis of 34 cases with

a new classification of the disease. Medicine (Baltimore) 1980, **60:** 95–109.

83 Hara K, Tsuzuki T, Takagi N, Shimokata K. Nodular granulomatous phlebitis of the skin: a fourth type of tuberculid. Histopathology 1997, **30:** 129–134.

84 Hayman J, McQueen A. The pathology of *Mycobacterium ulcerans* infection. Pathology 1985, **17:** 594–600.

85 Jordaan HF, Schneider JW, Schaaf HS, Victor TS, Geiger DH, Van Heiden PD, Rossouw DJ. Papulonecrotic tuberculid in children: a report of eight patients. Am J Dermatopathol 1996, **18:** 172–185.

86 Jordaan HF, Van Niekerk DJ, Louw M. Papulonecrotic tuberculid. A clinical, histopathological, and immunohistochemical study of 15 patients. Am J Dermatopathol 1994, **16:** 474–485.

87 Marcoval J, Servitje O, Moreno A, Jucgla A, Peyri J. Lupus vulgaris. Clinical, histopathologic, and bacteriologic study of 10 cases. J Am Acad Dermatol 1992, **26**(3 Pt 2): 404–407.

88 Santa Cruz DJ, Strayer DS. The histologic spectrum of the cutaneous mycobacterioses. Hum Pathol 1982, **13:** 485–495.

89 Saxe N. Mycobacterial skin infections. J Cutan Pathol 1985, **12:** 300–312.

90 Schneider JW, Jordaan HF. The histopathologic spectrum of erythema induratum of Bazin. Am J Dermatopathol 1997, **19:** 323–333.

91 Schneider JW, Jordaan HF, Geiger DH, Victor T, Van Helden PD, Rossouw DJ. Erythema induratum of Bazin: a clinicopathological study of 20 cases and detection of mycobacterium tuberculosis DNA in skin lesions by polymerase chain reaction. Am J Dermatopathol 1996, **17:** 350–356.

92 Street ML, Umbert-Millet IJ, Roberts GD, Su WP. Nontuberculous mycobacterial infections of the skin. Report of fourteen cases and review of the literature. J Am Acad Dermatol 1991, **24:** 208–215.

93 Travis WD, Travis LB, Roberts GD, Su DW, Weiland LW. The histopathologic spectrum in *Mycobacterium marinum* infection. Arch Pathol Lab Med 1985, **109:** 1109–1113.

94 Victor T, Jordaan H, van Niekerk D, Louw M, Jordaan A, van Helden P. Papulonecrotic tuberculid. Identification of *Mycobacterium tuberculosis* DNA by polymerase chain reaction. Am J Dermatopathol 1992, **14:** 491–495.

Leprosy

95 Bhatia AS, Katoch K, Narayanan RB, Ramu G, Mukherjee A, Lavania RK. Clinical and histopathological correlation in the classification of leprosy. Int J Lepr Other Mycobact Dis 1993, **61:** 433–438.

96 Mansfield RE. Histoid leprosy. Arch Pathol 1969, **87:** 580–585.

97 Porichha D, Misra AK, Dhariwal AC, Samal RC, Reddy BN. Ambiguities in leprosy histopathology. Int J Lepr Other Mycobact Dis 1993, **61:** 428–432.

98 Torres P, Camarena JJ, Gomez JR, Nogueira JM, Gimeno V, Navarro JC, Olmos A. Comparison of PCR mediated amplification of DNA and the classical methods for detection of mycobacterium leprae in different types of clinical samples in leprosy patients and contacts. Lepr Rev 2003, **74:** 18–30.

99 Triscott JA, Nappi O, Gerrara G, Wick MR. "Pseudoneoplastic" leprosy. Leprosy revisited. Am J Dermatopathol 1995, **17:** 297–302.

Malakoplakia

100 Barnard M, Chalvardjian A. Cutaneous malakoplakia in a patient with acquired immunodeficiency syndrome (AIDS). Am J Dermatopathol 1998, **20:** 185–188.

101 Mehregan DR, Mehregan AH, Mehregan DA. Cutaneous malakoplakia: a report of two cases with the use of anti-BCG for the detection for micro-organisms. J Am Acad Dermatol 2000, **43:** 351–354.

102 Nieland ML, Silverman AR, Borochovitz D, Saferstein HL. Cutaneous malakoplakia. Am J Dermatopathol 1981, **3:** 287–291.

Spirochetal diseases
Syphilis

103 Alessi E, Innocenti M, Ragusa G. Secondary syphilis. Clinical morphology and histopathology. Am J Dermatopathol 1983, **5:** 11–17.

104 Engelkens HJ, ten Kate FJ, Vuzevski VD, van der Sluis JJ, Stolz E. Primary and secondary syphilis. A histopathological study. Int J STD AIDS 1991, **2:** 280–284.

105 Jordan HF, Louw M. The moth-eaten alopecia of secondary syphilis. A histopathological study of 12 patients. Am J Dermatopathol 1995, **17:** 158–162.

106 Liu H, Rodes B, Chen CY, Steiner B. New tests for syphilis: rational design of a PCR method for detection of Treponema pallidum in clinical specimens using unique regions of the DNA polymerase 1 gene. J Clin Microbiol 2001, **39:** 1941–1946.

107 McBroom RL, Styles AR, Chiu MJ, Clegg C, Cockerell CJ, Radolf JD. Secondary syphilis in persons infected with and not infected with HIV-1: a comparative immunohistologic study. Am J Dermatopathol 1999, **21:** 432–441.

Lyme disease

108 Abele DC, Anders KH. The many faces and phases of borreliosis. I. Lyme disease. J Am Acad Dermatol 1990, **23:** 167–186.

109 Abele DC, Anders KH. The many faces and phases of borreliosis. II. J Am Acad Dermatol 1990, **23:** 401–410.

110 Aberer E, Klade H. Cutaneous manifestation of Lyme borreliosis. Infection 1991, **19:** 284–286.

111 Aberer E, Stanek G. Histological evidence for spirochetal origin of morphea and lichen sclerosus et atrophicans. Am J Dermatopathol 1987, **9:** 374–379.

112 Asbrink E. Cutaneous manifestations of Lyme borreliosis. Clinical definitions and differential diagnoses. Scand J Infect Dis Suppl 1991, **77:** 44–50.

113 Baumgarten JM, Montiel NJ, Sinha AA. Lyme disease – part 1: epidemiology and etiology. Cutis 2002, **69:** 349–352.

114 Berger BW, Clemmensen OJ, Ackerman AB. Lyme disease is a spirochetosis. A review of the disease and evidence for its cause. Am J Dermatopathol 1983, **5:** 111–124.

115 Edlow JA. Erythema migrans. Med Clin North Am 2002, **86:** 239–260.

116 Malane MS, Grant-Kels JM, Feder HM Jr, Luger SW. Diagnosis of Lyme disease based on dermatologic manifestations. Ann Intern Med 1991, **114:** 490–498.

117 Montiel NJ, Baumgarten JM, Sinha AA. Lyme disease – part II: clinical features and treatment. Cutis 2002, **69:** 443–448.

118 Nocton JJ, Dressler F, Rutledge BJ, Rys PN, Persing DH, Steere AC. Detection of *Borrelia burgdorferi* DNA by polymerase chain reaction in synovial fluid from patients with Lyme arthritis. N Engl J Med 1994, **330:** 229–234.

Fungal diseases
Tinea (dermatophytoses)

119 Graham JH, Johnson WC, Burgoon CF, Helwig EB. Tinea capitis. Arch Dermatol 1964, **89:** 528–543.

120 Smith KJ, Neafie RC, Skleton HG III, Barrett TL, Graham JH, Lupton GP. Majocchi's granuloma. J Cutan Pathol 1991, **18:** 28–35.

North American blastomycosis

121 Body BA. Cutaneous manifestations of systemic mycoses. Dermatol Clin 1996, **14:** 125–135.

122 Harrell ER, Curtis AC. North American blastomycosis. Am J Med 1959, **27:** 750–766.

123 Lemos LB, Baliga M, Guo M. Blastomycosis: the great pretender can also be an opportunist. Initial clinical diagnosis and underlying diseases in 123 patients. Ann Diagn Pathol 2002, **6:** 194–203.

Chromoblastomycosis

124 Azulay RD, Serruya J. Hematogenous dissemination in chromoblastomycosis. Arch Dermatol 1966, **95:** 57–60.
125 Bonifaz A, Carrasco-Gerard E, Saul A. Chromoblastomycosis: clinical and mycologic experience of 5 cases. Mycoses 2001, **44:** 1–7.
126 French AJ, Russell SR. Chromoblastomycosis. Arch Dermatol 1953, **67:** 129–134.
127 Kempson RL, Sternberg WH. Chronic subcutaneous abscesses caused by pigmented fungi, a lesion distinguishable from cutaneous chromoblastomycosis. Am J Clin Pathol 1963, **39:** 598–606.
128 Minotto R, Bernardi CD, Mallmann LF, Edelweiss MI, Scroferneker ML. Chromoblastomycosis: a review of 100 cases in the state of Rio Grande du Sul, Brazil. J Am Acad Dermatol 2001, **44:** 585–592.

Other granulomatous diseases

Sarcoidosis

129 Cronin E. Skin changes in sarcoidosis. Postgrad Med J 1970, **46:** 507–509.
130 Dickinson JA. Sarcoidal reactions in tattoos. Arch Dermatol 1969, **100:** 315–319.
131 Du Bois RM, Goh N, McGrath D, Cullinan P. Is there a role for microorganisms in the pathogenesis of sarcoidosis? J Intern Med 2003, **253:** 4–17.
132 Giuffrida TJ, Kerdel FA. Sarcoidosis. Dermatol Clin 2002, **20:** 435–447.
133 Hurley HJ, Shelley WB. Sarcoid granulomas with intradermal tuberculin in normal human skin. Arch Dermatol 1960, **82:** 65–72.
134 Israel HL, Goldstein RA. Relations of Kveim-antigen reaction to lymphadenopathy. N Engl J Med 1971, **284:** 345–349.
135 James DG, Williams WJ. Kveim-Silzbach test revisited. Sarcoidosis 1991, **8:** 6–9.
136 Li N, Bajoghli A, Kubba , Bhawan J. Identification of mycobacterial DNA in cutaneous lesions of sarcoidosis. J Cutan Pathol 1999, **26:** 271–278.
137 Maycock RL, Bertrand P, Morrison CE, Scott JH. Manifestations of sarcoidosis. Am J Med 1963, **35:** 67–89.
138 Siltzbach LE. The Kveim test in sarcoidosis. JAMA 1961, **178:** 476–482.
139 Thomas PD, Hunninghake GW. Current concepts of the pathogenesis of sarcoidosis. Am Rev Respir Dis 1987, **135:** 747–760.
140 Young RJ III, Gilson RT, Yanase D, Elston DM. Cutaneous sarcoidosis. Int J Dermatol 2001, **40:** 249–253.

Foreign body reaction

141 Epstein E. Silica granuloma of the skin. Arch Dermatol 1955, **71:** 24–35.
142 Helwig EB. Chemical (beryllium) granulomas of the skin. Milit Surg 1951, **109:** 540–558.
143 Newcomer VD, Graham JH, Schaffert RR, Kaplan L. Sclerosing lipogranuloma resulting from exogenous lipids. Arch Dermatol 1956, **73:** 361–371.
144 Shelley WB, Hurley HJ. The pathogenesis of silica granulomas in man. A non-allergic colloidal phenomenon. J Invest Dermatol 1960, **34:** 107–123.
145 Zhu YI, Stiller MJ. Arthropods and skin diseases. Int J Dermatol 2002, **41:** 533–549.

Other dermatoses

Psoriasis

146 Albert J, Crone RI. Keratosis blenorrhagica (Reiter's disease?) and its treatment. Arch Dermatol 1959, **79:** 581–586.

147 Barr RJ, Young EM Jr. Psoriasiform and related papulosquamous disorders. J Cutan Pathol 1985, **12:** 412–425.
148 Boehncke WH, Wortmann S, Kaufmann R, Mielke V, Sterry W. A subset of macrophages located along the basement membrane ("lining cells") is a characteristic histopathologic feature of psoriasis. Am J Dermatopathol 1995, **17:** 139–144.
149 Champion RH. Psoriasis. Br Med J (Clin Res) 1986, **292:** 1693–1969.
150 Elder JT, Fisher GJ, Lindquist PB, Bennett BL, Pittelkow MR, Coffey RJ Jr, Ellingsworth L, Derynck R, Voorhees JJ. Overexpression of transforming growth factor a in psoriatic epidermis. Science 1989, **243:** 811–814.
151 Farber EM, McClintock RP. A current review of psoriasis. Calif Med 1968, **108:** 440–457.
152 Fox BJ, Odom RB. Papulosquamous diseases. A review. J Am Acad Dermatol 1985, **12:** 597–624.
153 Helwig EB. Pathology of psoriasis. Ann NY Acad Sci 1958, **73:** 924–935.
154 Leigh IM, Pulford KA, Ramaekers FCS, Lane EB. Psoriasis. Maintenance of an intact monolayer basal cell differentiation compartment in spite of hyperproliferation. Br J Dermatol 1985, **113:** 53–64.
155 Sanchez NP, Perry HO, Muller SA, Winkelmann RK. Subcorneal pustular dermatosis and pustular psoriasis. A clinicopathologic correlation. Arch Dermatol 1983, **119:** 715–721.
156 Soeprono FF. Histologic criteria for the diagnosis of pityriasis rubra pilaris. Am J Dermatopathol 1986, **8:** 277–283.
157 Stern RS, Lunder EJ. Risk of squamous cell carcinoma and methoxsalen (psoralen) and UV-A radiation (PUVA). A meta-analysis. Arch Dermatol 1998, **134:** 1582–1585.
158 Stern RS, Nichols KT, Vakeva LH. Malignant melanoma in patients treated for psoriasis and methoxsalen (psoralen) and ultraviolet A radiation (PUVA). The PUVA follow-up study. N Engl J Med 1997, **336:** 1041–1045.
159 Thewes M, Stadler R, Korge B, Mischke D. Normal psoriatic epidermis expression of hyperproliferation-associated keratins. Arch Dermatol Res 1991, **283:** 465–471.
160 Van Erp PEJ, Rijzewijk JJ, Boezeman JBM, Leenders J, De Mare S, Schalkwijk J, van de Kerkhof PCM, Ramaekers FCS, Bauer FW. Flow cytometric analysis of epidermal subpopulations from normal and psoriatic skin using monoclonal antibodies against intermediate filaments. Am J Pathol 1989, **135:** 865–869.
161 Weinstein GD, van Scott EJ. Autoradiographic analysis of turnover times of normal and psoriatic epidermis. J Invest Dermatol 1965, **45:** 257–262.
162 Zelickson BD, Muller SA. Generalized pustular psoriasis. A review of 63 cases. Arch Dermatol 1991, **127:** 1339–1345.

Exfoliative dermatitis and erythroderma

163 Abrahams I, McCarthy JT, Sanders SL. One hundred and one cases of exfoliative dermatitis. Arch Dermatol 1963, **87:** 96–101.
164 Kohler S, Kim YH, Smoller BR. Histologic criteria for the diagnosis of erythrodermic mycosis fungoides and Sezary syndrome: a critical reappraisal. J Cutan Pathol 1997, **24:** 292–297.
165 Nicolis GD, Helwig EB. Exfoliative dermatitis. Arch Dermatol 1973, **108:** 788–797.
166 Patterson JW, Berry AD III, Darwin BS, Gottlieb A, Wilkerson MG. Lichenoid histopathologic changes in patients with clinical diagnoses of exfoliative dermatitis. Am J Dermatopathol 1991, **13:** 358–364.
167 Rothe MJ, Bialy TL, Grant-Kels JM. Erythroderma. Dermatol Clin 2000, **18:** 405–415.
168 Sentis HJ, Willemze R, Scheffer E. Histopathologic studies in Sezary syndrome and erythrodermic mycosis fungoides. A comparison with benign forms of erythroderma. Am Acad Dermatol 1986, **15:** 1217–1226.

Lichen planus

169 Altman J, Perry HO. The variations and course of lichen planus. Arch Dermatol 1961, **84:** 179–191.

170 Andreasen JO. Oral lichen planus. A histologic evaluation of 97 cases. Oral Surg 1968, **25:** 158–166.

171 Bagan-Sebastian JV, Milian MMA, Penarrocha DM, Jiminez Y. A clinical study of 205 patients with oral lichen planus. J Oral Maxillofac Surg 1992, **50:** 116–118.

172 Berman A, Herszenson S, Winkelmann RK. The involuting lichenoid plaque. Arch Dermatol 1982, **118:** 93–96.

173 Boyd AS, Neldner KH. Lichen planus. J Am Acad Dermatol 1991, **25:** 593–619.

174 Dalton SR, Baptista MA, Libow LF, Elston DM. Lichenoid tissue reaction in malignant melanoma. A potential diagnostic pitfall. Am J Clin Pathol 2002, **117:** 766–770.

175 DePanfilis G, Manara G, Sansoni P, Allegra F. T-cell infiltrate in lichen planus. Demonstration of activated lymphocytes using monoclonal antibodies. J Cutan Pathol 1983, **10:** 52–58.

176 Fox, BJ, Odom RB. Papulosquamous disease. A review. J Am Acad Dermatol 1985, **12:** 597–624.

177 Frigy AF, Cooper PH. Benign lichenoid keratosis. Am J Clin Pathol 1985, **83:** 439–443.

178 Gomes MA, Staquet MJ, Thivolet J. Staining of colloid bodies by keratin antisera in lichen planus. Am J Dermatopathol 1981, **3:** 341–347.

179 Lumpkin LR, Helwig EB. Solitary lichen planus. Arch Dermatol 1966, **93:** 54–55.

180 Mehregan DA, Van Hale HM, Muller SA. Lichen planopilaris. Clinical and pathologic study of forty-five patients. J Am Acad Dermatol 1992, **27:** 935–942.

181 Patterson JW. The spectrum of lichenoid dermatitis. J Cutan Pathol 1991, **18:** 67–74.

182 Pinkus H. Lichenoid tissue reactions. Arch Dermatol 1973, **107:** 840–846.

183 Prieto VG, Casal M, McNutt NS. Lichen planus-like keratosis. A clinical and histological reexamination. Am J Surg Pathol 1993, **17:** 259–263.

184 Ragaz A, Ackerman AB. Evolution, maturation, and regression of lesions of lichen planus. New observations and correlations of clinical and histologic findings. Am J Dermatopathol 1981, **3:** 5–25.

185 Sale GE, Lerner KG, Barker EA, Shulman HM, Thomas ED. The skin biopsy in the diagnosis of acute graft-versus-host disease in man. Am J Pathol 1977, **89:** 621–635.

186 Sanchez Yus E, Soria L, De Eusebio E, Requena L. Lichenoid, erosive and ulcerated dermatofibromas. Three additional clinico-pathologic variants. J Cutan Pathol 2000, **27:** 112–117.

187 Scully C, El-Kom M. Lichen planus. Review and update on pathogenesis. J Oral Pathol 1985, **14:** 431–458.

188 Weedon D. The lichenoid tissue reaction. J Cutan Pathol 1985, **12:** 279–281.

189 Willsteed E, Bhogal BS, Das AK, Wojnarowska F, Black MM, McKee PH. Lichen planus pemphigoides. A clinicopathologic study of nine cases. Histopathology 1991, **19:** 147–154.

Graft-versus-host disease

190 Elliott CJ, Sloane JP, Sanderson KV, Vincent M, Shepherd V, Powles R. The histological diagnosis of cutaneous graft versus host disease. Relationship of skin changes to marrow purging and other clinical variables. Histopathology 1987, **11:** 145–155.

191 Hymes SR, Farmer ER, Lewis PG, Tutschka PJ, Santos GW. Cutaneous graft-versus-host reaction. Prognostic features seen by light microscopy. J Am Acad Dermatol 1985, **12:** 468–474.

192 Kohler S, Hendrickson MR, Chao NJ, Smoller BR. Value of skin biopsies in assessing prognosis and progression of acute graft-versus-host disease. Am J Surg Pathol 1997, **21:** 988–996.

193 Massi D, Franchi A, Pimpinelli N, Laszlo D, Bosi A, Santucci M.

A reappraisal of the histopathologic criteria for the diagnosis of cutaneous allogeneic acute graft-vs-host disease. Am J Clin Pathol 1999, **112:** 791–800.

194 Snover DC. Biopsy interpretation in bone marrow transplantation. Pathol Annu 1989, **24**(Pt 2): 63–101.

195 Spielvogel RL, Goltz RW, Kersey JH. Scleroderma-like changes in chronic graft vs host disease. Arch Dermatol 1977, **113:** 1424–1428.

196 Synovec MS, Braddock SW, Linder J. LN-3. A diagnostic adjunct in cutaneous graft-versus-host disease. Mod Pathol 1990, **3:** 643–647.

Vasculitis

197 Ackerman AB, Jones RE Jr. Making chronic nonspecific dermatitis specific. How to make precise diagnoses of superficial perivascular dermatitides devoid of epidermal involvement. Am J Dermatopathol 1985, **7:** 307–323.

198 Akosa AB, Lampert IA. The sweat gland in cutaneous vasculitis. Histopathology 1991, **18:** 553–558.

199 Barksdale SK, Hallahan CW, Kerr GS, Fauci AS, Stern JB, Travis WD. Cutaneous pathology in Wegener's granulomatosis. A clinicopathologic study of 75 biopsies in 46 patients. Am J Surg Pathol 1995, **19:** 161–172.

200 Black MM, Wilson Jones E. Malignant atrophic papulosis (Degos syndrome). Br J Dermatol 1971, **85:** 290–292.

201 Boom BW, Mommaas AM, Vermeer BJ. Presence and interpretation of vascular immune deposits in human skin. The value of direct immunofluorescence. J Dermatol Sci 1992, **3:** 26–34.

202 Callen JP. Neutrophilic dermatoses. Dermatol Clin 2002, **20:** 409–419.

203 Carlson AJ, Mihm MC, LeBoit PE. Cutaneous lymphocytic vaculitis: a definition, a review, and a proposed classification. Semin Diagn Pathol 1996, **13:** 72–90.

204 Chumbley LC, Harrison EG Jr, DeRemee RA. Allergic granulomatosis and angiitis (Churg-Strauss syndrome). Report and analysis of 30 cases. Mayo Clin Proc 1977, **52:** 477–484.

205 Churg J, Churg A. Idiopathic and secondary vasculitis. A review. Mod Pathol 1989, **2:** 144–160.

206 Cohen PR, Holder WR, Tucker SB, Kono S, Kurzrock R. Sweet syndrome in patients with solid tumors. Cancer 1993, **72:** 2723–2731.

207 Conn DL. Update on systemic necrotizing vasculitis. Mayo Clin Proc 1989, **64:** 535–543.

208 Copeman PWM, Ryan TJ. The problems of classification of cutaneous angiitis with reference to histopathology and pathogenesis. Br J Dermatol 1970, **82:** 2–14.

209 Cribier B, Couilliet D, Meyer P, Grosshans E. The severity of histopathological changes of leukocytoclastic vasculitis is not predictive of extracutaneous involvement. Am J Dermatopathol 2000, **21:** 532–536.

210 Curtis JL, Egbert BM. Cutaneous cytomegalovirus vasculitis. An unusual clinical presentation of a common opportunistic pathogen. Hum Pathol 1982, **13:** 1138–1141.

211 Diri E, Buscemi DM, Nugent KM. Churg-Strauss syndrome: diagnostic difficulties and pathogenesis. Am J Med Sci 2003, **325:** 101–105.

212 Ekenstam E, Callen JP. Cutaneous leukocytoclastic vasculitis. Clinical and laboratory features of 82 patients seen in private practice. Arch Dermatol 1984, **120:** 484–489.

213 Finan MC, Winkelmann RK. The cutaneous extravascular necrotizing granuloma (Churg-Strauss granuloma) and systemic disease. A review of 27 cases. Medicine (Baltimore) 1983, **62:** 142–157.

214 Fiorentino DF. Cutaneous vasculitis. J Am Acad Dermatol 2003, **48:** 311–340.

215 Gibson LE. Cutaneous vasculitis. Approach to diagnosis and systemic associations. Mayo Clin Proc 1990, **65:** 221–229.

216 Gibson LE. Cutaneous vasculitis update. Dermatol Clin 2001, **19:** 603–615.

217 Gilliam JN, Smiley JD. Cutaneous necrotizing vasculitis and related disorders. Ann Surg 1976, **37**: 328–339.

218 Gray HR, Graham JH, Johnson W, Burgoon CF Jr. Atrophie blanche. Periodic painful ulcers of the lower extremities. Arch Dermatol 1966, **93**: 187–193.

219 Harrist TJ, Mihm MC Jr. The diagnostic use of direct and indirect immunofluorescence techniques in dermatologic disease. Hum Pathol 1979, **10**: 625–653.

220 Hodge SJ, Callen JP, Ekenstam E. Cutaneous leukocytoclastic vasculitis. Correlation of histopathological changes with clinical severity and course. J Cutan Pathol 1987, **14**: 279–284.

221 James WD, Odom RB, Katzenstein A-LA. Cutaneous manifestations of lymphomatoid granulomatosis. Report of 44 cases and a review of the literature. Arch Dermatol 1981, **117**: 196–202.

222 Jennette JC, Falk RJ. Small-vessel vasculitis. N Engl J Med 1997, **337**: 1512–1523.

223 Jones D, Dorfman DM, Barnhill RL, Granter SR. Leukemic vasculitis. A feature of leukemia cutis in some patients. Am J Clin Pathol 1997, **107**: 637–642.

224 Jordaan HF. Acute febrile neutrophilic dermatosis. A histopathological study of 37 patients and a review of the literature. Am J Dermatopathol 1989, **11**: 99–111.

225 Kessler S, Lund HZ, Leonard DD. Cutaneous lesions of lymphomatoid granulomatosis. Comparison with lymphomatoid papulosis. Am J Dermatopathol 1981, **3**: 115–127.

226 Lie JT. Systemic and isolated vasculitis. A rational approach to classification and pathologic diagnosis. Pathol Annu 1989, **24**(Pt 1): 25–114.

227 Mackel SE, Jordon RE. Leukocytoclastic vasculitis. A cutaneous expression of immune complex disease. Arch Dermatol 1982, **118**: 296–301.

228 Maessen-Visch MB, Koedam MI, Hamulyak K, Neumann HA. Atrophie blanche. Int J Dermatol 1999, **38**: 161–172.

229 Magrinat G, Kerwin KS, Gabriel DA. The clinical manifestations of Degos' syndrome. Arch Pathol Lab Med 1989, **113**: 354–362.

230 Mehregan DR, Hall MJ, Gibson LE. Urticarial vasculitis. A histopathologic and clinical review of 72 cases. J Am Acad Dermatol 1992, **26**: 441–448.

231 Molenaar WM, Rosman JB, Donker AJM, Houthoff HJ. The pathology and pathogenesis of malignant atrophic papulosis (Degos' disease). A case study with reference to other vascular disorders. Pathol Res Pract 1987, **182**: 98–106.

232 Peteiro C, Toribio J. Incidence of leukocytoclastic vasculitis in chronic idiopathic urticaria. Study of 100 cases. Am J Dermatopathol 1989, **11**: 528–533.

233 Ryan TJ. Cutaneous vasculitis. J Cutan Pathol 1985, **12**: 381–387.

234 Sams WM Jr, Claman HN, Kohler PF, McIntosh RM, Small P, Mass MF. Human necrotizing vasculitis. Immunoglobulins and complement in vessel walls of cutaneous lesions and normal skin. J Invest Dermatol 1975, **64**: 441–445.

235 Sams WM Jr, Thorne EG, Small P, Mass MF, McIntosh RM, Stanford RE. Leukocytoclastic vasculitis. Arch Dermatol 1976, **112**: 219–226.

236 Sanchez NP, Van Hale HM, Su WPD. Clinical and histopathologic spectrum of necrotizing vasculitis. Report of findings in 101 cases. Arch Dermatol 1985, **121**: 220–224.

237 Winkelmann RK, Ditto WB. Cutaneous and visceral syndromes of necrotizing or "allergic" angiitis. A study of 38 cases. Medicine (Baltimore) 1964, **43**: 59–89.

Granuloma faciale and related lesions

238 Allen AC. Persistent "insect bites" (dermal eosinophilic granulomas) simulating lymphoblastomas, histiocytoses, and squamous cell carcinomas. Am J Pathol 1948, **24**: 367–387.

239 Carlson JA, LeBoit PE. Localized chronic fibrosing vasculitis of the skin: an inflammatory reaction that occurs in settings other than erythema elevatum diutinum and granuloma faciale. Am J Surg Pathol 1997, **21**: 698–705.

240 Johnson WC, Higdon RS, Helwig EB. Granuloma faciale. Arch Dermatol 1959, **79**: 42–52.

241 Pedace FJ, Perry HO. Granuloma faciale. Arch Dermatol 1966, **94**: 387–395.

242 Sangueza OP, Pilcher B, Martin Sangueza J. Erythema elevatum diutinum: a clinicopathological study of eight cases. Am J Dermatopathol 1997, **19**: 214–222.

243 Shanks JH, Banerjee SS, Bishop PW, Pearson JM, Eyden BP. Nodular erythema elevatum diutinum mimicking cutaneous neoplasms. Histopathology 1997, **31**: 91–96.

244 Yiannias JA, El-Azhary RA, Gibson LE. Erythema elevatum diutinum. A clinical and histopathologic study of 13 patients. J Am Acad Dermatol 1992, **26**: 38–44.

Erythema nodosum and related lesions

245 Black MM. Panniculitis. J Cutan Pathol 1985, **12**: 366–380.

246 Boh EE, Al-Smadi RM. Cutaneous manifestations of gastrointestinal diseases. Dermatol Clin 2002, **20**: 533–546.

247 Chun SI, Su WPD, Lee S, Rogers RS III. Erythema nodosum-like lesions in Behçet's syndrome. A histopathologic study of 30 cases. J Cutan Pathol 1989, **16**: 259–265.

248 Crawford GH, Kim S, James WD. Skin signs of systemic disease: an update. Adv Dermatol 2002, **18**: 1–27.

249 Förström L, Winkelmann RK. Acute panniculitis. A clinical and pathologic study of 34 cases. Arch Dermatol 1977, **113**: 909–917.

250 Mir-Madjlessi SH, Taylor JS, Farmer RG. Clinical course and evolution of erythema nodosum and pyoderma gangrenosum in chronic ulcerative colitis. A study of 42 patients. Am J Gastroenterol 1985, **80**: 615–620.

251 Patterson JW, Brown PC, Broecker AH. Infection-induced panniculitis. J Cutan Pathol 1989, **16**: 183–193.

252 Perry HO, Winkelmann RK. Subacute nodular migratory panniculitis. Arch Dermatol 1964, **89**: 170–179.

253 Reed RJ, Clark WH, Mihm MC. Disorders of the panniculus adiposus. Hum Pathol 1973, **4**: 219–229.

254 Requena L, Sanchez Yus E. Panniculitis. Part I. Mostly septal panniculitis. J Am Acad Dermatol 2001, **45**: 163–183.

255 Requena L, Sanchez Yus E. Panniculitis. Part II. Mostly lobular panniculitis. J Am Acad Dermatol 2001, **45**: 325–361.

256 Sánchez Yus E, Sanz Vico MD, de Diego V. Miescher's radial granuloma. A characteristic marker of erythema nodosum. Am J Dermatopathol 1989, **11**: 434–442.

257 Ter Poorten MC, Thiers BH. Panniculitis. Dermatol Clin 2002, **20**: 421–433.

258 Vesey CMR, Wilkinson DS. Erythema nodosum. A study of 70 cases. Br J Dermatol 1959, **71**: 139–155.

259 White WL, Wieselthier JS, Hitchcock MG. Panniculitis: recent developments and observations. Semin Cutan Med Surg 1997, **15**: 278–299.

260 Winkelmann RK. Panniculitis in connective tissue disease. Arch Dermatol 1983, **119**: 336–344.

261 Winkelmann RK, Förström L. New observations on the histopathology of erythema nodosum. J Invest Dermatol 1975, **65**: 441–446.

Granuloma annulare and related lesions

262 Al-Hoqail IA, Al-Ghamdi AM, Martinka M, Crawford RI. Actinic granuloma is a unique and distinct entity: a comparative study with granuloma annulare. Am J Dermatopathol 2002, **24**: 209–212.

263 Arner S, Aspegren N. Familial granuloma annulare. Acta Derm Venereol (Stockh) 1968, **48**: 253–254.

264 Friedman-Birnbaum R, Weltfriend S, Munichor M, Lichtig C. A

comparative histopathologic study of generalized and localized granuloma annulare. Am J Dermatopathol 1989, **11**: 144–148.

265 Guitart J, Zemtsov A, Bergfeld WF, Tomecki KJ. Diffuse dermal histiocytosis. A variant of generalized granuloma annulare. Am J Dermatopathol 1991, **13**: 174–178.

266 Hanna WM, Moreno-Merlo F, Andrighetti L. Granuloma annulare: an elastic tissue disease? Case report and literature review. Ultrastruct Pathol 1999, **23**: 33–38.

267 Johnson WC. Necrobiotic granulomas. J Cutan Pathol 1984, **12**: 289–299.

268 Kossard S, Collins AG, Wegman A, Hughes MR. Necrobiotic granulomas localised to the penis. A possible variant of subcutaneous granuloma annulare. J Cutan Pathol 1990, **17**: 101–104.

269 Lindlbauer SR, Gschnait F. Annular elastolytic giant cell granuloma. J Cutan Pathol 1990, **10**: 321–326.

270 Magro CM, Crowson AN, Regaver S. Granuloma annulare and necrobiosis lipoidica tissue reactions as a manifestation of systemic disease. Hum Pathol 1996, **27**: 50–56.

271 Mesara BW, Brody GL, Oberman HA. "Pseudorheumatoid" subcutaneous nodules. Am J Clin Pathol 1966, **45**: 684–691.

272 Mullans E, Helm KF. Granuloma annulare. An immunohistochemical study. J Cutan Pathol 1994, **21**: 135–139.

273 Patterson JW. Rheumatoid nodule and subcutaneous granuloma annulare. A comparative histologic study. Am J Dermatopathol 1988, **10**: 1–8.

274 Rubin M, Lynch FW. Subcutaneous granuloma annulare. Comment on familial granuloma annulare. Arch Dermatol 1966, **93**: 416–429.

275 Schwarz TH, Lindlbauer R, Gschnait F. Annular elastolytic giant cell granuloma. J Cutan Pathol 1983, **10**: 321–326.

276 Smoller BR, Madhusudhan KT, Scott MA, Horn TD. Granuloma annulare: another manifestation of Bartonella infection? Am J Dermatopathol 2002, **23**: 510–513.

277 Wells RS, Smith MA. The natural history of granuloma annulare. Br J Dermatol 1963, **75**: 199–205.

278 Wood MG, Beerman H. Necrobiosis lipoidica, granuloma annulare and rheumatoid nodule. J Invest Dermatol 1960, **34**: 139–147.

279 Yanagihara M, Kato F, Mori S. Extra- and intra-cellular digestion of elastic fibers by macrophages in annular elastolytic giant cell granuloma. An ultrastructural study. J Cutan Pathol 1987, **14**: 303–308.

Necrobiosis lipoidica

280 Bauer M, Levan NE. Diabetic dermangiopathy. A spectrum including pigmented pretibial patches and necrobiosis lipoidica diabeticorum. Br J Dermatol 1970, **83**: 528–535.

281 Ferringer T, Miller F III. Cutaneous manifestations of diabetes mellitus. Dermatol Clin 2002, **20**: 483–492.

282 Fisher ER, Danowski TS. Histologic, histochemical, and electron microscopic features of the shin spots of diabetes mellitus. Am J Clin Pathol 1968, **50**: 547–554.

283 Magro CM, Crowson AN, Regauer S. Granuloma annulare and necrobiosis lipoidica tissue reactions as a manifestation of systemic disease. Hum Pathol 1996, **27**: 50–56.

284 Muller SA, Winkelmann RK. Necrobiosis lipoidica diabeticorum. Histopathologic study of 98 cases. Arch Dermatol 1966, **94**: 1–10.

285 Padilla RS, Mukai K, Dahl MV, Burgdorf WH, Rosai J. Differential staining pattern of lysozyme in palisading granulomas. An immunoperoxidase study. J Am Acad Dermatol 1983, **8**: 634–638.

286 Sibbald RG, Landolt SJ, Toth D. Skin and diabetes. Endocrinol Metab Clin North Am 1996, **25**: 463–472.

Weber–Christian disease and other lobular panniculitides

287 Laymon CW, Peterson WC Jr. Lipogranulomatosis subcutanea (Rothmann-Makai). An appraisal. Arch Dermatol 1964, **90**: 288–292.

288 Lewis CT, Tschen JA, Klima M. Subcutaneous fat necrosis associated with pancreatic islet cell carcinoma. Am J Dermatopathol 1991, **13**: 52–56.

289 Marzano AV, Berti E, Paulli M, Caputo R. Cytophagic histiocytic panniculitis and subcutaneous panniculitis-like T-cell lymphoma: report of 7 cases. Arch Dermatol 2000, **136**: 889–896.

290 Petterson T, Kariniemi AL, Tervonen S, Franssila K. Cytophagic histiocytic panniculitis. A report of four cases. Br J Dermatol 1992, **127**: 635–640.

291 Requena L, Sanchez Yus E. Panniculitis. Part II. Mostly lobular panniculitis. J Am Acad Dermatol 2001, **45**: 325–361.

292 Su WPD, Smith KC, Pittelkow MR, Winkelmann RK. α 1-antitrypsin deficiency panniculitis. A histopathologic study of four cases. Am J Dermatopathol 1987, **9**: 483–490.

Mastocytosis

293 Arber DA, Tamayo R, Weiss LM. Paraffin section detection of the c-kit gene product (CD117) in human tissues: value in the diagnosis of mast cell disorders. Hum Pathol 1998, **29**: 498–504.

294 Brunning RD, McKenna RW, Rosai J, Parkin JL, Risdall R. Systemic mastocytosis. Extracutaneous manifestations. Am J Surg Pathol 1983, **7**: 425–438.

295 Caplan RM. The natural course of urticaria pigmentosa. Analysis and follow-up of 112 cases. Arch Dermatol 1963, **87**: 144–157.

296 Escribano L, Akin C, Castells M, Orfao A, Metcalf DD. Mastocytosis: current concepts in diagnosis and treatment. Ann Hematol 2002, **81**: 677–690.

297 Feger F, Ribadeau Dumas A, Leriche L, Valent P, Arock M. Kit and c-kit mutations in mastocytosis: a short overview with special reference to novel molecular and diagnostic concepts. Int Arch Allergy Immunol 2002, **127**: 110–114.

298 Head KW. Cutaneous mast cell tumors in the dog, cat, and ox. Br J Dermatol 1958, **70**: 390–408.

299 Horny HP, Sillaber C, Menke D, Kaiserling E, Wehrmann M, Stehberger B, Chott A, Lechner K, Lennert K, Valent P. Diagnostic value of immunostaining for tryptase in patients with mastocytosis. Am J Surg Pathol 1998, **22**: 1132–1140.

300 Johnson WC, Helwig EB. Solitary mastocytosis (urticaria pigmentosa). Arch Dermatol 1961, **84**: 806–815.

301 Klatt EC, Lukes RJ, Meyer PR. Benign and malignant mast cell proliferations. Diagnosis and separation using a pH-dependent toluidine blue stain in tissue section. Cancer 1983, **51**: 1119–1124.

302 Lennert K, Parkaresch MR. Mast cells and mast cell neoplasia. A review. Histopathology 1979, **3**: 349–365.

303 Li CY. Diagnosis of mastocytosis: value of cytochemistry and immunohistochemistry. Leuk Res 2001, **25**: 537–541.

304 Mangini J, Silverman JF, Dabbs DJ, Tung MY, Silverman AR. Diagnostic value of calretinin in mast cell lesions of the skin. Int J Surg Pathol 2000, **8**: 119–122.

305 Mihm MC, Clark WH, Reed RJ, Caruso MG. Mast cell infiltrates of the skin and the mastocytosis syndrome. Hum Pathol 1973, **4**: 231–239.

306 Nielsen SW, Cole CR. Canine mastocytoma. A report of one hundred cases. Am J Vet Res 1958, **19**: 417–432.

307 Soter NA. The skin in mastocytosis. J Invest Dermatol 1991, **96**: 32S–38S.

308 Travis WD, Li C-Y, Su WPD. Adult-onset urticaria pigmentosa and systemic mast cell disease. Am J Clin Pathol 1985, **84**: 710–714.

309 Valent P, Horny HP, Escribano L, Longley BJ, Li CY, Schwartz LB, Marone G, Nunez R, Akin C, Sotlar K, Sperr WR, Wolff K, Brunnin RD, Parwaresch RM, Austen KF, Lennert K, Metcalfe DD, Vardima JW, Bennett JM. Diagnostic criteria and classification of mastocytosis: a consensus proposal. Leuk Res 2001, **25**: 603–625.

310 Wolff K, Komar M, Petzelbauer P. Clinical and histopathological aspects of cutaneous mastocytosis. Leuk Res 2001, **25**: 519–528.

Lupus erythematosus

311 Bangert JL, Freeman RG, Sontheimer RD, Gilliam JN. Subacute cutaneous lupus erythematosus and discoid lupus erythematosus. Comparative histopathologic findings. Arch Dermatol 1984, **120**: 332–337.

312 Biesecker G, Lavin L, Ziskind M, Koffler D. Cutaneous localization of the membrane attack complex in discoid and systemic lupus erythematosus. N Engl J Med 1982, **306**: 264–270.

313 Callen JP. Systemic lupus erythematosus in patients with chronic cutaneous (discoid) lupus erythematosus. Clinical and laboratory findings in seventeen patients. J Am Acad Dermatol 1985, **12**: 278–288.

314 Clark SK. Cutaneous lupus erythematosus. Recognition of its many forms. Postgrad Med 1986, **79**: 195–203.

315 Clark WH, Reed RJ, Mihm MC. Lupus erythematosus. Histopathology of cutaneous lesions. Hum Pathol 1973, **4**: 157–163.

316 Crowson AN, Magro CM. Subacute cutaneous lupus erythematosus arising in the setting of calcium channel blocker therapy. Hum Pathol 1997, **28**: 67–73.

317 Crowson AN, Magro C. The cutaneous pathology of lupus erythematous: a review. J Cutan Pathol 2001, **28**: 1–23.

318 Harrist TJ, Mihm MC Jr. The diagnostic use of direct and indirect immunofluorescence techniques in dermatologic disease. Hum Pathol 1979, **10**: 625–653.

319 Harvey AM, Schulman LE, Tumulty PA, Conley CL, Schoenrich EH. Systemic lupus erythematosus. Review of the literature and clinical analysis of 138 cases. Medicine (Baltimore) 1954, **33**: 291–437.

320 Heller P, Wieczorek R, Waldo E, Meola T, Buchness MR, Soter NA, Lim HW. Chronic actinic dermatitis. An immunohistochemical study of its T-cell antigenic profile, with comparison to cutaneous T-cell lymphoma. Am J Dermatopathol 1994, **16**: 510–516.

321 Klemperer P, Pollack AD, Baehr G. Pathology of disseminated lupus erythematosus. Arch Pathol 1941, **32**: 569–631.

322 Murphy JK, Stephens C, Hartley T, Das AK, Hughes GR, McKee PH. Subacute cutaneous lupus erythematosus – the annular variant. A histological and ultrastructural study of five cases. Histopathology 1991, **19**: 329–336.

323 Norris PG, Hawk JL. Polymorphic light eruption. Photodermatol Photoimmunol Photomed 1990, **7**: 186–191.

324 Tuffanelli DL. Lupus erythematosus. Arch Dermatol 1972, **106**: 553–566.

325 Uitto J, Santa-Cruz DJ, Zeisen A, Leone P. Verrucous lesions in patients with discoid lupus erythematosus. Br J Dermatol 1978, **98**: 507–520.

326 Wechsler HL. Lupus erythematosus. A clinician's coign of vantage. Arch Dermatol 1983, **119**: 877–882.

327 Weyers W, Bonczkowitz M, Weyers I. LE or not LE - that is the question: an unsuccessful attempt to separate lymphocytic infiltration from the spectrum of discoid lupus erythematosus. Am J Dermatopathol 1998, **20**: 225–232.

328 Willemze R, Verneer BJ, Meijer CJ. Immunohistochemical studies in lymphocytic infiltration of skin (Jessner) and discoid lupus erythematosus. A comparative study. J Am Acad Dermatol 1984, **11**: 832–840.

329 Williams REA, Mackie RM, O'Keefe R, Thomson W. The contribution of direct immunofluoresence to the diagnosis of lupus erythematosus. J Cutan Pathol 1989, **16**: 122–125.

330 Wojnarowska F, Bhogal B, Black MM. The significance of an IgM band at the dermoepidermal junction. J Cutan Pathol 1986, **13**: 359–362.

Dermatomyositis

331 Dalakas MC. Polymyositis, dermatomyositis, and inclusion-body myositis. N Engl J Med 1991, **325**: 1487–1498.

332 Dalakas MC. Muscle biopsy findings in inflammatory myopathies. Rheum Dis Clin North Am 2002, **28**: 779–798.

333 Golitz LE. Collagen diseases. J Cutan Pathol 1985, **12**: 358–365.

334 Janis JF, Winkelmann RK. Histopathology of the skin in dermatomyositis. Arch Dermatol 1968, **97**: 640–649.

335 Magro CM, Crowson AN. The immunofluorescent profile of dermatomyositis: a comparative study with lupus erythematous. J Cutan Pathol 1998, **24**: 543–552.

336 Mastaglia FL, Garlepp MJ, Phillips BA, Zilko PJ. Inflammatory myopathies: clinical, diagnostic and therapeutic aspects. Muscle Nerve 2003, **27**: 407–425.

337 Sigurgeirsson B, Lindelof B, Edhag O, Allander E. Risk of cancer in patients with dermatomyositis or polymyositis. A population-based study. N Engl J Med 1992, **326**: 363–367.

338 Williams RC Jr. Dermatomyositis and malignancy. A review of the literature. Ann Intern Med 1959, **50**: 1174–1181.

Scleroderma and eosinophilic fasciitis

339 Aberer E, Klade H, Hobisch G. A clinical, histological, and immunohistochemical comparison of acrodermatitis chronica atrophicans and morphea. Am J Dermatopathol 1991, **13**: 334–341.

340 Asboe-Hansen G. Scleroderma. J Am Acad Dermatol 1987, **17**: 102–108.

341 Barnes L, Rodnan GP, Medsger TA Jr, Short D. Eosinophilic fasciitis. A pathologic study of twenty cases. Am J Pathol 1979, **96**: 493–518.

342 Doyle JA, Connolly SM, Winkelmann RK. Cutaneous and subcutaneous inflammatory sclerosis syndromes. Arch Dermatol 1982, **118**: 886–890.

343 Fisher ER, Rodnan GP. Pathological observations concerning the cutaneous lesion of progressive systemic sclerosis. An electron microscopic histochemical and immunohistochemical study. Arthritis Rheum 1960, **3**: 536–545.

344 Fleischmajer R. The collagen in scleroderma. Arch Dermatol 1964, **89**: 437–441.

345 Fleischmajer R, Perlish JS, Duncan M. Scleroderma. A model for fibrosis. Arch Dermatol 1983, **119**: 957–962.

346 Jones HR Jr, Beetham WP Jr, Silverman ML, Margles SW. Eosinophilic fasciitis and the carpal tunnel syndrome. J Neurol Neurosurg Psychiatry 1986, **49**: 324–327.

347 Krafchik BR. Localized cutaneous scleroderma. Semin Dermatol 1992, **11**: 65–72.

348 Lovell CR, Nicholls AC, Duance VC, Bailey AJ. Characterization of dermal collagen in systemic sclerosis. Br J Dermatol 1979, **100**: 359–369.

349 Michet CJ Jr, Doyle JA, Ginsburg WW. Eosinophilic fasciitis. Report of 15 cases. Mayo Clin Proc 1981, **56**: 27–34.

350 Moutsopoulos HM, Webber BL, Pavlidis NA, Fostiropoulos G, Goules D, Shulman LE. Diffuse fasciitis with eosinophilia. A clinicopathologic study. Am J Med 1980, **68**: 701–709.

351 Person JR, Su WPD. Subcutaneous morphea. A clinical study of sixteen cases. Br J Dermatol 1979, **100**: 371–380.

352 Rahbari H. Histochemical differentiation of localized morphea-scleroderma and lichen sclerosus et atrophicus. J Cutan Pathol 1990, **16**: 342–347.

353 Reed RJ, Clark WH, Mihm MC. The cutaneous collagenoses. Hum Pathol 1973, **4**: 165–186.

354 Shono S, Imura M, Ota M, Osaku A, Shinomiya S, Toda K. Lichen sclerosus et atrophicus, morphea, and coexistence of both diseases. Histological studies using lectins. Arch Dermatol 1991, **127**: 1352–1356.

355 Singsen BH. Scleroderma in childhood. Pediatr Clin North Am 1986, **33**: 1119–1139.

356 Su WPD, Person JR. Morphea profunda. A new concept and a histopathologic study of 23 cases. Am J Dermatopathol 1981, **3**: 251–260.

357 Winkelmann RK. Classification and pathogenesis of scleroderma. Mayo Clin Proc 1971, **46:** 83–91.

358 Young EM Jr, Barr RJ. Sclerosing dermatoses. J Cutan Pathol 1985, **12:** 426–441.

Drug eruptions

359 Bernstein EF, Spielvogel RL, Topolsky DL. Recurrent neutrophilic eccrine hidradenitis. Br J Dermatol 1992, **127:** 529–533.

360 Bhawan JAG, Malhotra R. Syringosquamous metaplasia. A distinctive eruption in patients receiving chemotherapy. Am J Dermatopathol 1990, **12:** 1–6.

361 Burrows NP, Russell Jones RR. Pustular drug eruptions. A histopathological spectrum. Histopathology 1993, **22:** 569–573.

362 Fitzpatrick J. The cutaneous histopathology of chemotherapeutic reactions. J Cutan Pathol 1993, **20:** 1–14.

363 Sanchez Yus E, Requena L, Simon P. Histopathology of cutaneous changes in drug-induced coma. Am J Dermatopathol 1993, **15:** 208–216.

364 Serrano T, Saez A, Moreno A. Eccrine squamous syringometaplasia. A prospective clinicopathologic study. J Cutan Pathol 1993, **20:** 61–65.

Pyoderma gangrenosum

365 Boh EE, Al-Smadi RM. Cutaneous manifestations of gastrointestinal diseases. Dermatol Clin 2002, **20:** 533–546.

366 Powell FC, Schroeter AL, Su WPD, Perry HO. Pyoderma gangrenosum. A review of 86 patients. Q J Med 1985, **55:** 173–186.

367 Wilson-Jones E, Winkelmann RK. Superficial granulomatous pyoderma. A localized vegetative form of pyoderma gangrenosum. J Am Acad Dermatol 1988, **18:** 511–521.

Vesiculobullous diseases

368 Ackerman AB. Focal acantholytic dyskeratosis. Arch Dermatol 1972, **106:** 702–706.

369 Amerian ML, Ahmed AR. Pemphigus erythematosus. Senear-Usher syndrome. Int J Dermatol 1985, **24:** 16–25.

370 Anhalt GJ, Kim SC, Stanley JR, Korman NJ, Jabs DA, Kory M, Izumi H, Ratrie H, Mutasim D, Ariss-Abdo L, Labib RS. Paraneoplastic pemphigus. N Engl J Med 1990, **323:** 1729–1735.

371 Bedi TR, Pinkus H. Histopathological spectrum of erythema multiforme. Br J Dermatol 1976, **95:** 243–250.

372 Chalet M, Grover R, Ackerman AB. Transient acantholytic dermatosis. A re-evaluation. Arch Dermatol 1977, **113:** 431–435.

373 Chidgey M. Desmosomes and disease: an update. Histol Histopathol 2002, **17:** 1179–1192.

374 Devries DT, Warren SJ. Recent advances in intraepidermal blistering diseases. Adv Dermatol 2002, **18:** 203–245.

375 Dunnill MG, Leigh IM. The molecular basis of inherited skin disorders. Progress Pathol 2001, **5:** 103–119.

376 Eady RA. Epidermolysis bullosa: scientific advances and therapeutic challenges. J Dermatol 2001, **28:** 638–640.

377 Epstein EH. Molecular genetics of epidermolysis bullosa. Science 1992, **256:** 799–804.

378 Farmer ER. Subepidermal bullous diseases. J Cutan Pathol 1985, **12:** 316–321.

379 Fry L. Dermatitis herpetiformis: problems, progress and prospects. Eur J Dermatol 2002, **12:** 523–531.

380 Hertl M, Veldman C. Pemphigus-paradigm of autoantibody-mediated autoimmunity. Skin Pharmacol Appl Skin Physiol 2001, **14:** 408–418.

381 Hirschmann JV. Impetigo: etiology and therapy. Curr Clin Top Infect Dis 2002, **22:** 42–51.

382 Hu C-H, Michel B, Farber EM. Transient acantholytic dermatosis (Grover's disease). A skin disorder related to heat and sweating. Arch Dermatol 1985, **121:** 1439–1441.

383 Imamura S, Horio T, Yanase K, Taniguchi S, Miyachi Y, Tachibana T, Yoshioka A, Fujita M. Erythema multiforma. Pathomechanism of papular erythema and target lesion. J Dermatol 1992, **19:** 524–533.

384 Jablonska S (with Working and Organizing Committee). Cooperative study. Uses for immunofluorescence tests of skin and sera. Utilization of immunofluorescence in the diagnosis of bullous diseases, lupus erythematosus and certain other dermatoses. Arch Dermatol 1975, **111:** 371–381.

385 Jordon RE. Commentary. Pemphigus erythematosus. A unique member of the pemphigus group. Arch Dermatol 1982, **118:** 742.

386 Korman NJ, Eyre RW, Klaus-Kovtun V, Stanley JR. Demonstration of an adhering-junction molecule (plakoglobin) in the autoantigens of pemphigus foliaceus and pemphigus vulgaris. N Engl J Med 1989, **321:** 631–635.

387 Langenberg A, Berger TG, Cardelli M, Rodman OG, Estes S, Barron DR. Genital benign chronic pemphigus (Hailey-Hailey disease) presenting as condylomas. J Am Acad Dermatol 1992, **26:** 951–955.

388 Lazaro-Medina A, Robbins TO, Bystryn J-C, Ackerman AB. Limitations in the diagnosis of vesiculobullous diseases. Am J Dermatopathol 1983, **5:** 7–10.

389 Lever WF. Pemphigus and pemphigoid. Springfield, IL, 1965, Charles C Thomas.

390 Liu Z, Diaz LA. Bullous pemphigoid: end of the century overview. J Dermatol 2001, **28:** 647–650.

391 Lyell A. Dermatitis herpetiformis enteropathy. Br J Dermatol 1968, **81:** 228–229.

392 Maize JC, Provost TT. Value of immunofluorescent techniques in studies of bullous disease. Am J Dermatopathol 1983, **5:** 67–72.

393 Mallipeddi R. Epidermolysis bullosa and cancer. Clin Exp Dermatol 2002, **27:** 616–623.

394 McMillan JR, Shimizu H. Desmosomes: structure and function in normal and diseased epidermis. J Dermatol 2001, **28:** 291–298.

395 Mehregan D, Oursler J, Leiferman K, Muller S, Anhalt G, Peters M. Paraneoplastic pemphigus. A subset of patients with pemphigus and neoplasia. J Cutan Pathol 1993, **20:** 203–210.

396 Mutasim DF, Diaz LA. The relevance of immunohistochemical techniques in the differentiation of subepidermal bullous diseases. Am J Dermatopathol 1991, **13:** 77–83.

397 Orfanos CE, Schaumburg-Lever G, Lever WF. Dermal and epidermal types of erythema multiforme. A histopathologic study of 24 cases. Arch Dermatol 1974, **109:** 682–688.

398 Pai S, Marinkovich MP. Epidermolysis bullosa: new and emerging trends. Am J Clin Dermatol 2002, **3:** 371–380.

399 Paquet P, Pierard GE. Erythema multiforme and toxic epidermal necrolysis: a comparative study. Am J Dermatopathol 1997, **19:** 127–132.

400 Parsons JM. Transient acantholytic dermatosis (Grover's disease): a global perspective. J Am Acad Dermatol 1996, **35:** 653–666.

401 Patterson JW, Parsons JM, Blaylock K, Mills AS. Eosinophils in skin lesions of erythema multiforme. Arch Pathol Lab Med 1989, **113:** 36–39.

402 Perry HO, Brunsting LA. Pemphigus foliaceus. Further observations. Arch Dermatol 1965, **91:** 10–23.

403 Piérard J, Whimster I. The histological diagnosis of dermatitis herpetiformis, bullous pemphigoid and erythema multiforme. Br J Dermatol 1961, **73:** 253–266.

404 Rencic A, Goyal S, Mofid M, Wigley F, Nousari HC. Bullous lesions in scleroderma. Int J Dermatol 2002, **41:** 335–339.

405 Santa Cruz DJ, Prioleau PG, Marcus MD, Uitto J. Pemphigus-like lesions induced by D-penicillamine. Analysis of clinical, histopathological, and immunofluorescence features in 34 cases. Am J Dermatopathol 1981, **3:** 85–92.

406 Saxe N, Kahn LB. Subepidermal bullous disease. A correlated clinico-pathologic study of 51 cases. J Cutan Pathol 1976, **3:** 83–94.

407 Scully C, Challacombe SJ. Pemphigus vulgaris: update on

etiopathogenesis, oral manifestations and management. Crit Rev Oral Biol Med 2002, **13:** 397–408.

408 Sneddon IB, Wilkinson DS. Subcorneal pustular dermatosis. Br J Dermatol 1956, **68:** 385–394.

409 Stoll DM, King LE Jr. Association of bullous pemphigoid with systemic lupus erythematosus. Arch Dermatol 1984, **120:** 362–366.

410 Thivolet J, Faure M. Immunohistochemistry in cutaneous pathology. J Cutan Pathol 1983, **10:** 1–32.

411 Tuffanelli DL. Clinical importance of autoantibodies in pemphigus. Arch Dermatol 1982, **118:** 844–845.

412 Turbitt ML, Mackie RM, Young H, Campbell I. The use of paraffin-processed tissue and the immunoperoxidase technique in the diagnosis of bullous diseases, lupus erythematosus and vasculitis. Br J Dermatol 1982, **106:** 411–418.

413 Valeski JE, Kumar V, Beutner EH, Cartone C, Kasprzyk K. Differentiation of bullous pemphigoid from epidermolysis bullosa acquisita on frozen skin biopsies. Int J Dermatol 1992, **31:** 37–41.

414 Waldo ED, Ackerman AB. Epidermolytic hyperkeratosis and focal acantholytic dyskeratosis. A unified concept. Pathol Annu 1978, **13:** 149–175.

415 Younus J, Ahmed AR. The relationship of pemphigus to neoplasia. J Am Acad Dermatol 1990, **23:** 498–502.

Degenerative and miscellaneous diseases
Lichen sclerosus et atrophicus

416 Fung MA, LeBoit PE. Light microscopic criteria for the diagnosis of early vulvar lichen sclerosis: a comparison with lichen planus. Am J Surg Pathol 1998, **22:** 473–478.

417 Helm KF, Gibson LE, Muller SA. Lichen sclerosus et atrophicus in children and young adults. Pediatr Dermatol 1992, **9:** 311.

418 Patterson JAK, Ackerman AB. Lichen sclerosus et atrophicus is not related to morphea. A clinical and histologic study of 24 patients in whom both conditions were reputed to be present simultaneously. Am J Dermatopathol 1984, **6:** 323–335.

419 Tasker GL, Wojnarowska F. Lichen sclerosus. Clin Exp Dermatol 2003, **28:** 128–133.

Elastosis perforans

420 Golitz L. Follicular and perforating disorders. J Cutan Pathol 1985, **12:** 282–288.

421 Hood AF, Hardegen GL, Zarate AR, Nigra TP, Gelfand MC. Kyrle's disease in patients with chronic renal failure. Arch Dermatol 1982, **118:** 85–88.

422 Mehregan AH. Elastosis perforans serpiginosa. Arch Dermatol 1968, **97:** 381–393.

423 Millard PR, Young E, Harrison DE, Wojnarowska F. Reactive perforating collagenosis. Light, ultrastructural and immunohistological studies. Histopathology 1986, **10:** 1047–1056.

424 Patterson JW. The perforating disorders. J Am Acad Dermatol 1984, **10:** 561–581.

425 Poliak SC, Lebwohl MG, Parris A, Prioleau PG. Reactive perforating collagenosis associated with diabetes mellitus. N Engl J Med 1982, **306:** 81–84.

426 Reed RJ, Clark WH, Mihm MC. The cutaneous elastoses. Hum Pathol 1973, **4:** 187–199.

427 Sehgal VN, Jain S, Thappa DM, Bhattacharya SN, Logani K. Perforating dermatoses: a review and report of four cases. J Dermatol 1993, **20:** 329–340.

428 White CR Jr, Heskel NS, Pokorny DJ. Perforating folliculitis of hemodialysis. Am J Dermatopathol 1982, **4:** 109–116.

Pseudoxanthoma elasticum

429 Hu X, Plomp A, Wijnholds J, Ten Brink J, Van Soest S, Van Den Born LI, Leys A, Peek R, De Jong PT, Bergen AA. ABCC6/MRP6 mutations: further insight into the molecular pathology of pseudoxanthoma elasticum. Eur J Hum Genet 2003, **11:** 215–224.

430 Ohtani T, Furukawa F. Pseudoxanthoma elasticum. J Dermatol 2002, **29:** 615–620.

Cutaneous mucinoses

431 Brown HA, Gibson LE, Pujol RM, Lust JA, Pittelkow MR. Primary follicular mucinosis: long-term follow-up of patients younger than 40 years with and without clonal T-cell receptor gene rearrangement. J Am Aced Dermatol 2002, **47:** 856–862.

432 Carney JA, Headington JT, Su WPD. Cutaneous myxomas. A major component of the complex of myxomas, spotty pigmentation, and endocrine overactivity. Arch Dermatol 1986, **122:** 790–798.

433 Cerroni L, Fink-Puches R, Back B, Kerl H. Follicular mucinosis: a critical reappraisal of clinicopathologic features and association with mycosis fungoides and Sezary syndrome. Arch Dermatol 2002, **138:** 182–189.

434 Farmer ER, Hambrick GW Jr, Shulman LE. Papular mucinosis. A clinicopathologic study of four patients. Arch Dermatol 1982, **118:** 9–13.

435 Hempstead RW, Ackerman AB. Follicular mucinosis. A reaction pattern in follicular epithelium. Am J Dermatopathol 1985, **7:** 245–257.

436 Hierholzer K, Finke R. Myxedema. Kidney Int Suppl 1997, **59:** S82–S89.

437 Jackson EM, English JC III. Diffuse cutaneous mucinoses. Clin Dermatol 2002, **20:** 493–501.

438 Johnson WC, Graham JH, Helwig EB. Cutaneous myxoid cyst. A clinicopathological and histochemical study. JAMA 1965, **191:** 109–114.

439 Johnson WC, Helwig EB. Cutaneous focal mucinosis. A clinicopathological and histochemical study. Arch Dermatol 1966, **93:** 13–20.

440 Mehregan DA, Gibson LE, Muller SA. Follicular mucinosis. Histopathologic review of 33 cases. Mayo Clin Proc 1991, **66:** 387–390.

441 Niepomniszcze H, Amad RH. Skin disorders and thyroid diseases. J Endocrinol Invest 2001, **24:** 628–638.

442 Rapoport B, Alsabeh R, Aftergood D, McLachlan SM. Elephantiasic pretibial myxedema: insight into and a hypothesis regarding the pathogenesis of the extrathyroidal manifestations of Graves' disease. Thyroid 2000, **10:** 685–692.

443 Reed RJ, Clark WH, Mihm MC. The cutaneous mucinoses. Hum Pathol 1973, **4:** 201–205.

444 Rongioletti F, Rebora A. Updated classification of popular mucinosis, lichen myxedematosus, and scleromyxedema. J Am Acad Dermatol 2001, **44:** 273–281.

445 Steigleder GK, Küchmeister B. Cutaneous mucinous deposits. J Cutan Pathol 1985, **12:** 334–347.

Acanthosis nigricans

446 Brown J, Winkelmann RK. Acanthosis nigricans. A study of 90 cases. Medicine (Baltimore) 1968, **47:** 33–51.

447 Ellis DL, Kafka SP, Chow JC, Nanney LB, Inman WH, McCadden ME, King LE Jr. Melanoma, growth factors, acanthosis nigricans, the sign of Leser-Trélat, and multiple acrochordons. A possible role for alpha-transforming growth factor in cutaneous paraneoplastic syndromes. N Engl J Med 1987, **317:** 1582–1587.

448 Stuart CA, Driscoll MS, Lundquist KF, Gilkison CR, Shaheb S, Smit MM. Acanthosis nigricans. J Basic Clin Physiol Pharmacol 1998, **9:** 407–418.

449 Taylor SL, Arioglu E. Syndromes associated with insulin resistance and acanthosis nigricans. J Basic Clin Physiol Pharmacol 1998, **9:** 419–439.

450 Torley D, Bellus GA, Munro CS. Genes, growth factors and acanthosis nigricans. Br J Dermatol 2002, **147:** 1096–1101.

Darier's disease

451 Gottlieb SK, Lutzner MA. Darier's disease. Arch Dermatol 1973, **107**: 225–230.

452 O'Malley MP, Haake A, Goldsmith L, Berg D. Localized Darier disease. Implications for genetic studies. Arch Dermatol 1997, **133**: 1134–1138.

Dermatoses in HIV-infected patients

453 Balslev E, Thomsen HK, Weismann K. Histopathology of acute human immunodeficiency virus exanthema. J Clin Pathol 1990, **43**: 201–202.

454 Brehmer-Andersson E, Torssander J. The exanthema of acute (primary) HIV infection. Identification of a characteristic histopathological picture? Acta Derm Venereol (Stockh) 1990, **70**: 85–87.

455 Farthing CF, Staughton RC, Rowland Payne CM. Skin disease in homosexual patients with acquired immune deficiency syndrome (AIDS) and lesser forms of human T cell leukaemia virus (HTL V III) disease. Clin Exp Dermatol 1985, **10**: 3–12.

456 Francis N. Non-neoplastic, cutaneous and mucocutaneous manifestations of HIV infection. Histopathology 1993, **23**: 297–305.

457 Harawi SJ, Ghossein RA, Kurban RS, Kurban AK. Cutaneous diseases associated with HIV infection. Pathol Annu 1991, **26** (Pt 1): 265–309.

458 Hevia O, Jimenez-Acosta F, Ceballos PI, Gould EW, Penneys NS. Pruritic papular eruption of the acquired immunodeficiency syndrome. A clinicopathologic study. J Am Acad Dermatol 1991, **24**: 231–235.

459 Hoppenjans WB, Bibler MR, Orme RL, Solinger AM. Prolonged cutaneous herpes zoster in acquired immunodeficiency syndrome. Arch Dermatol 1990, **126**: 1048–1050.

460 Jacobson MA, Berger TG, Fikrig S, Becherer P, Moohr JW, Stanat SC, Biron KK. Acyclovir-resistant varicella zoster virus infection after chronic oral acyclovir therapy in patients with the acquired immunodeficiency syndrome (AIDS). Ann Intern Med 1990, **112**: 187–191.

461 Mathes BM, Douglass MC. Seborrheic dermatitis in patients with acquired immunodeficiency syndrome. J Am Acad Dermatol 1985, **13**: 947–951.

462 McCalmont TH, Altemus D, Mauer T, Berger TG. Eosinophilic folliculitis: the histologic spectrum. Am J Dermatopathol 1996, **17**: 439–446.

463 McNutt NS, Kindel S, Lugo J. Cutaneous manifestations of measles in AIDS. J Cutan Pathol 1992, **19**: 315–324.

464 Muhlemann MF, Anderson MG, Paradinas FJ, Key PR, Dawson SG, Evans BA, Murray-Lyon IM, Cream JJ. Early warning skin signs in AIDS and persistent generalized lymphadenopathy. Br J Dermatol 1986, **114**: 419–424.

465 Muñoz E, Valks R, Fernández-Herrera J, Fraga J. Herpetic syringitis associated with eccrine squamous syringometaplasia in HIV-positive patients. J Cutan Pathol 1997, **24**: 425–428.

466 Penneys NS, Hicks B. Unusual cutaneous lesions associated with acquired immunodeficiency syndrome. J Am Acad Dermatol 1985, **13**: 845–852.

467 Ramdial PK, Morar N, Dlova NC, Aboobaker J. HIV-associated eosinophilic folliculitis in an infant. Am J Dermatopathol 1999, **21**: 241–246.

468 Rolighed J, Sorensen IM, Jacobsen NO, Lindeberg H. The presence of HPV types 6/11, 13, 16 and 33 in bowenoid papulosis in an HIV-positive male, demonstrated by DNA in situ hybridization. APMIS 1991, **99**: 583–585.

469 Rosenthal D, Le Boit PE, Klumpp L, Berger TG. Human immunodeficiency virus-associated with advanced human immunodeficiency virus infection. Arch Dermatol 1991, **127**: 206–209.

470 Siegal FP, Lopez C, Hammer GS, Brown AE, Kornfeld SJ, Gold J, Hassett J, Hirschman SZ, Cunningham-Rundles C, Adelsberg BR, et al. Severe acquired immunodeficiency in male homosexuals, manifested by chronic perianal ulcerative herpes simplex lesions. N Engl J Med 1981, **305**: 1439–1444.

471 Smith KJ, Yeager J, Skelton HG. Histologically distinctive popular neutrophilic xanthomas in HIV-1+ patients. Am J Surg Pathol 1997, **21**: 545–549.

472 Soeprono FF, Schinella RA, Cockerell CJ, Comite SL. Seborrheic-like dermatitis of acquired immunodeficiency syndrome. A clinicopathologic study. J Am Acad Dermatol 1986, **14**: 242–248.

Tumors and tumorlike conditions

The skin is, contrary to the ubiquitous simplistic concept, a remarkably heterogeneous organ. The nodular lesions (hamartomatous, reactive, and neoplastic) that occur in the skin are more numerous than those produced by any other organ. For example, the eccrine sweat gland alone gives rise to 10 or more histologically distinct adenomas. This diversity, combined with a body of descriptive data (clinical, histologic, histochemical, immunohistochemical, and ultrastructural) amassed over the past century and dispersed in varying literatures, produces confusion, chiefly in the area of nomenclature. Within the limits inherent in this book, it is impossible to pursue finite segmentation, interesting and accurate as it may be. The more common lesions will be discussed in some detail and pertinent references provided for the rare lesions.

Most of the mesenchymal tumors that may involve the dermis are discussed in the chapter on soft tissues. Only those showing exclusive or preferential involvement of the skin are included in this chapter.

Epidermis

Seborrheic keratosis

Seborrheic keratoses are common, benign, pigmented, predominantly basal keratinocytic proliferations occurring chiefly on the trunk of adults. They may be single or multiple. The sudden appearance of, or increase in the number and size of, seborrheic keratoses in association with internal malignant disease is known as the *Leser–Trélat sign*.[3]

Grossly, the lesions of seborrheic keratosis protrude above the surface of the skin, are soft, and vary in color from tan to black. The single, heavily pigmented seborrheic keratosis may be confused clinically with malignant melanoma.

Microscopically, the number of epidermal basal cells is greatly increased, presumably as a result of a maturation defect. The *acanthotic* pattern is the most frequent, in which a thick layer of basal cells is seen interspersed with pseudohorny cysts (Fig. 4.48). Some of these cells contain melanin, as the result of transfer from neighboring melanocytes (see p. 154). Other microscopic patterns of seborrheic keratosis are the *hyperkeratotic*, the *adenoid*, *acantholytic*,[2] and *desmoplastic*. The latter may simulate invasive squamous cell carcinoma.[4a]

Immunohistochemically, the keratinocytes of seborrheic keratosis invariably express low-molecular-weight keratin but often exhibit a deficiency of the high-molecular-weight keratins.[6,10]

In *irritated seborrheic keratosis*, squamous metaplasia is pronounced; this should not be misdiagnosed as basosquamous carcinoma. This phenomenon does not seem to be related to human papilloma virus (HPV).[12] Instead, HPV can be identified in the seborrheic kerato-

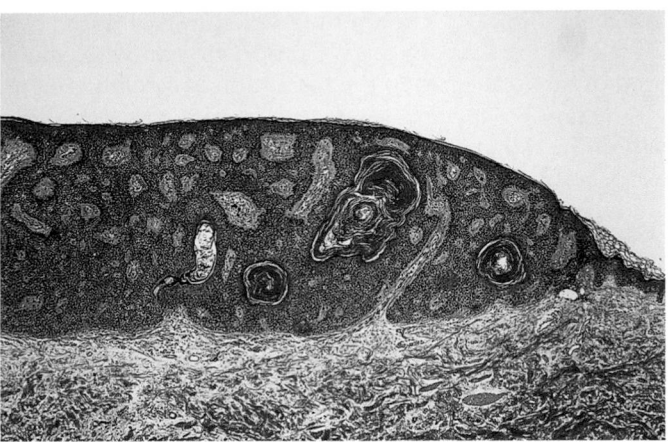

Fig. 4.48 Seborrheic keratosis with mild pigmentation in a senior pathologist. Pseudohorny cysts are evident.

sis-like lesions of patients with epidermodysplasia verruciformis,[4,8] and in those exhibiting bowenoid changes.[7,11] The latter should probably be interpreted as condylomas rather than as true seborrheic keratoses.[5]

Malignant skin neoplasms of various types (particularly basal cell carcinoma) may be seen contiguous or adjacent to lesions of seborrheic keratosis.[1]

Multiple, small seborrheic keratoses are readily treated by superficial curettage or freezing.[9]

Acrochordon

Acrochordon is the preferred name for a common and inconsequential skin lesion also known as fibroepithelial papilloma, fibroepithelial polyp, fibroma molle, and skin tag. As these various names indicate, it is a polypoid lesion composed of varying amounts of stroma covered by a papillomatous epidermis. It is probably not a specific entity but a pattern of growth that may result from seborrheic keratosis, warts, and perhaps other benign processes.

A distinctive variant of this exophytic fibroepithelial process is represented by the *acquired (digital) fibrokeratoma*, characterized by collagenous protrusions covered by hyperkeratotic epidermis, usually occurring around interphalangeal joints but sometimes in other sites.[13]

Actinic keratosis

In that portion of the epidermis exposed to sunlight, chiefly that of the near ultraviolet spectrum, a sequence of atrophic, hyperplastic, and eventually dysplastic changes known as actinic or solar keratosis may develop.[15] The term "senile" keratosis, often used as a synonym, is inappropriate. An increased incidence of these changes has been found in renal transplant recipients, particularly in the lip region.[17] Histologically, actinic keratoses involve the interfollicular epidermis, sparing the follicular apparatus and the intraepidermal portion of the sweat duct, as demonstrated in the classic article by Pinkus.[19] The stratum corneum is replaced by a parakeratotic scale. Excessive production and accumulation of this scale lead to the formation of *cutaneous horns*. The granular layer is generally absent except at and about the follicular orifices. The malpighian layer shows disorderly maturation as well as individually dysplastic and dyskeratotic cells (Fig. 4.49). Morphologic variations on the theme of actinic keratosis include basaloid proliferations resembling early basal cell carcinomas, suprabasal acantholysis producing vesicles similar to those of pemphigus vulgaris, a marked degree of keratinocytic atypia throughout the malpighian layer (bowenoid actinic keratosis), and the presence of large atypical clear cells (pagetoid actinic keratosis).[18] Not infrequently, the basal melanocytes participate in the proliferation and atypia, resulting in a combination of actinic keratosis and actinic melanosis. Such cases appear clinically as heavily pigmented lesions.[16]

The papillary dermis is often chronically inflamed, and basophilic degenerative changes are prominent in the collagen. In florid forms of actinic keratosis, the atypical epithelial proliferation produces irregularly elongated acanthotic ridges, and this process extends down the external root sheaths of the hair follicles. In such cases, the differential diagnosis with superficially invasive squamous carcinoma inevitably arises (see p. 134).

Accumulation of p53 protein, presumably as a result of mutation, has been found in almost three fourths of actinic keratosis lesions and found to correlate with the degree of atypia.[20]

Actinic keratoses may be treated by a variety of methods—freezing, superficial curettage, application of antineoplastic chemotherapeutic agents, and surgical excision.[21] Excision is, in fact, unnecessarily radical therapy except for the more florid and infiltrative types and those not responding to topical 5-fluorouracil.[14]

Cutaneous horn

Cutaneous horn (cornu cutaneum) is the traditional picturesque term for a protruding skin lesion largely composed of keratin and resembling a horn in shape.[22] The lesion can reach a gigantic size and truly resemble an animal horn.[25] The clinical appearance of cutaneous horn can result from a variety of diseases: therefore, cutaneous horn should not be used as a pathologic term. Most cases are caused by actinic keratosis, but others may be the result of verruca, seborrheic keratosis, inverted follicular keratosis, or squamous cell carcinoma.[28] The keratin formed is usually of epidermal type, but occasionally it has trichilemma-like features, i.e., it contains deep red granules. When this is the case, the lesion has been referred to as *trichilemmal keratosis*, *verrucous trichilemmal tumor*, and *trichilemmal horn*.[23,24,26,27]

Bowen's disease

Bowen's disease consists clinically of indolent, scaly, erythematous plaques occurring predominantly on skin unexposed to sunlight (Fig. 4.50). Histologically, the lesions show a variety of atypical epithelial changes, such as cytoplasmic vacuolization, nuclear hyperchromasia, multinucleated keratinocytes, individual cell dyskeratosis, and increased number of mitoses, including atypical forms (Fig. 4.51). The maturation pattern is markedly altered, but some surface flattening and keratinization are almost always present. Extension of the process into the eccrine sweat glands may occur.[29] In its fully developed stage, Bowen's disease can be regarded as a carcinoma in situ of the skin or as a form of squamous intraepidermal neoplasia, a concept supported by

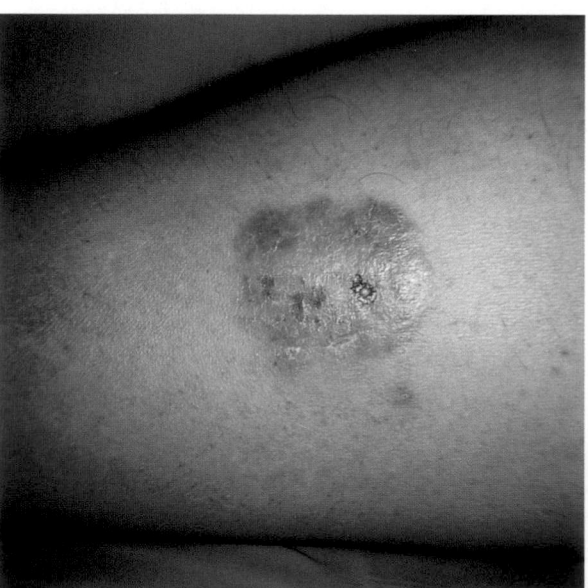

Fig. 4.50 Clinical appearance of Bowen's disease. A slightly elevated red patch of irregular contours is seen. This clinical appearance conforms to the syndrome originally described by Bowen.

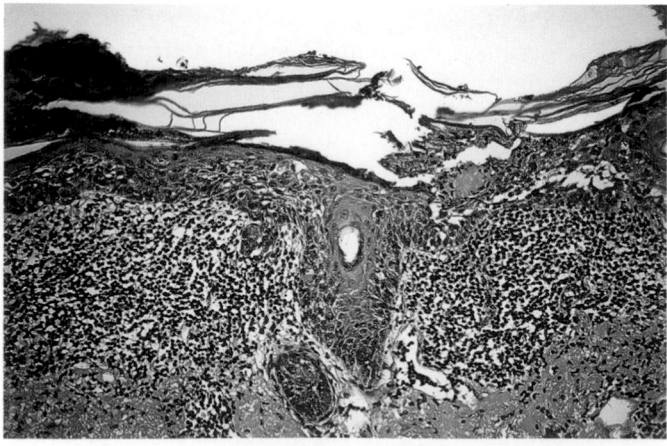

Fig. 4.49 Actinic keratosis. Note the hyperparakeratosis, moderate malpighian atypia, and dermal inflammatory infiltrate.

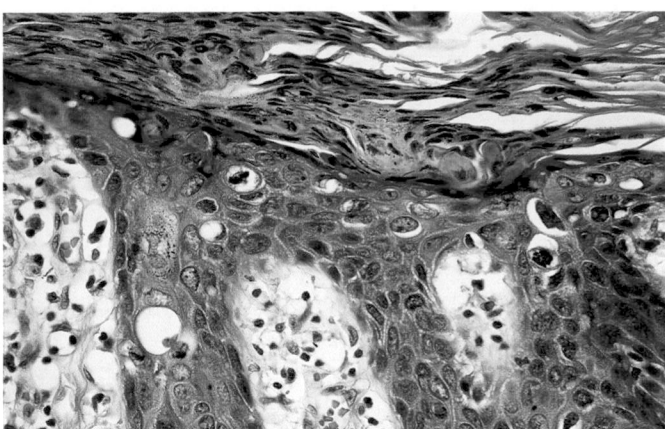

Fig. 4.51 Microscopic appearance of Bowen's disease. The atypia involves the full thickness of the epithelium.

the presence of the expression of mutant p53 protein,[34,36] and of distinct aneuploidy in flow cytometric studies.[35] It should be emphasized that the diagnosis of Bowen's disease is a clinicopathologic one.[33] Lesions showing similar microscopic changes but located in sun-exposed areas and having the clinical appearance of actinic keratosis should not be diagnosed as Bowen's disease but rather as bowenoid actinic keratosis. Occasionally, lesions of Bowen's disease contain large atypical clear cells simulating Paget's disease (pagetoid Bowen's disease)[37]; even more rarely, the two processes coexist.

Some studies[30,32] have shown an apparent increase in the incidence of visceral cancer in patients with Bowen's disease, but others have failed to document such an association. Since arsenic is capable of inducing hyperplastic and dysplastic epidermal changes that may lead to the development of invasive squamous cell carcinoma, this element has been looked for in lesions of Bowen's disease, but the search has proved inconclusive.[31]

Squamous cell carcinoma

General features

The large majority of squamous cell (epidermoid) carcinomas of the skin are actinic induced,[38,55,60] one of the postulated pathogenetic mechanisms being the induction of p53 mutations by ultraviolet light[41] (Fig. 4.52). The incidence of this tumor is directly related to the amount of exposure to the sun and the lack of pigmentation of the skin. Blond, blue-eyed, fair-skinned people living in Texas have a higher incidence of skin cancer than do their counterparts in Minnesota. Squamous cell carcinoma in black people is a very rare disease. In urban populations, frankly invasive squamous cell carcinoma is uncommon, whereas in rural populations it is common.[68] Nearly all of these actinic-induced tumors are preceded and accompanied by lesions of actinic keratosis.[64]

Squamous cell carcinomas of the skin can also be seen as a complication of the following:

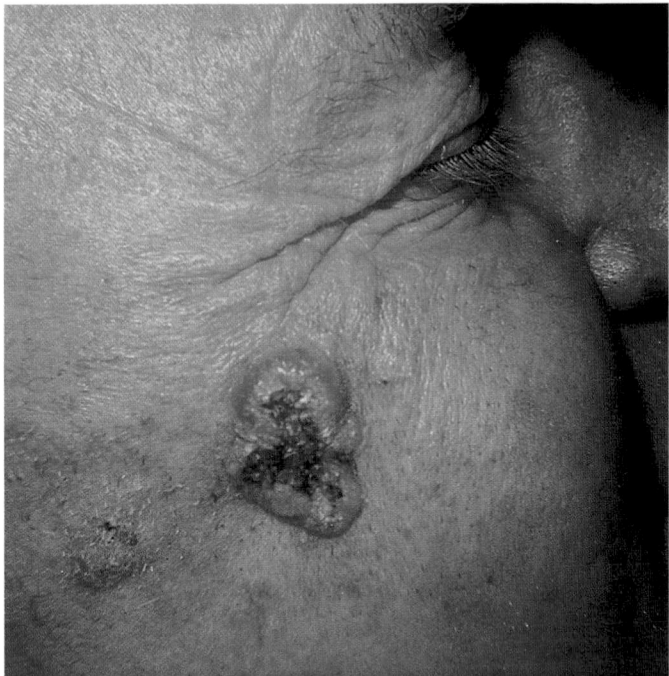

A

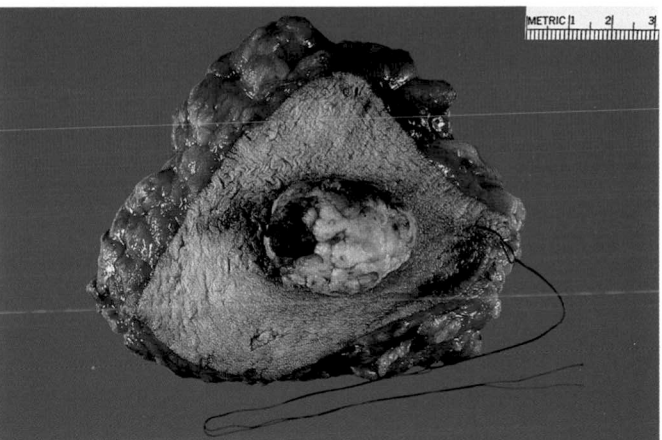

B

Fig. 4.52 Squamous cell carcinoma. **A,** Tumor of the face with rolled edges and depressed center; **B,** Tumor of the leg with exophytic appearance.

1 Xeroderma pigmentosum, a genetically determined condition characterized by a diminished capacity for DNA repair following ultraviolet light irradiation.[43,67] These patients may also develop basal cell carcinomas and malignant melanomas.

2 Epidermodysplasia verruciformis, a generalized virally induced dermatosis.[53]

3 Cutaneous scars of various types: from burns (Marjolin's ulcer), x-rays, epidermolysis bullosa, chronic osteomyelitic sinuses, necrobiosis lipoidica, acne aggregata seu conglobata, or hidradenitis suppurativa.[39,40,48,49,51,54,56,62]

4 Chemical exposure: arsenic, coal tars, soot, and a variety of oils and distillation products.[42]

5 Organ transplantation.[61] In these patients the carcinomas are often associated with severe actinic keratosis or, less commonly, widespread warts.[58] HPV has been detected in these lesions.[45,65] The clinical course can be very aggressive.[57]

6 PUVA-treated psoriatic patients, in whom the risk is dose dependent.[47,66]

7 HIV infection. There may be an increased risk for both squamous cell and basal cell carcinoma in this population.[69]

8 Ichthyosis,[52] epidermal nevus,[50] porokeratosis,[59] and congenital lymphedema.[44,46] Only a few cases have been reported in each of these disorders.

Smoller et al.[63] have shown that an "activated" keratinocyte phenotype—characterized by a particular staining pattern for ψ-3, involucrin, filaggrin, and keratins—is the common denominator for the conditions that predispose to squamous cell carcinoma.

Microscopic features

Over 80% of squamous cell carcinomas are well differentiated and, as such, produce large amounts of keratin (Fig. 4.53). Some of this is seen in the form of horn pearls, particularly in the better differentiated tumors; characteristically, keratohyaline granules within these pearls are sparse or absent. Intercellular bridges can be found with ease in most cases. The pattern of growth may be polypoid or even papillary,[72] or may have a deep penetrating quality. Sometimes the tumors are cup-shaped in the manner of keratoacanthomas.

Invasion of the dermis is *sine qua non* for the diagnosis, but this may be a very subjective evaluation in the early stages. A lesion interpreted by some as florid actinic keratosis may be interpreted by others as a superficially invasive squamous cell carcinoma.[71] This is a reflection of the fact that actinic keratosis and squamous cell carcinoma are part of a continuous spectrum of squamous neoplasia. Fortunately, the issue is of no great practical importance, since the treatment and prognosis for borderline lesions are essentially the same.

Squamous cell carcinoma may contain a population of non-neoplastic dendritic melanocytes, with transfer of some of the melanin granules into the cytoplasm of the tumor cells (*pigmented squamous cell carcinoma*); this phenomenon is analogous to that seen more commonly in basal cell carcinoma.

Occasionally, the cytoplasm of the tumor cells has a clear cell appearance throughout, raising the differential diagnosis with a variety of adnexal tumors.[73] Even more rarely, the tumors may have a component of signet ring cells.[70]

Immunohistochemical and molecular genetic features

Squamous cell carcinomas of the skin exhibit immunoreactivity for high-molecular-weight keratins, involucrin (a precursor of the cross-linked envelope protein of the stratum corneum), epithelial membrane antigen (EMA), and often also CEA.[79,81,82] They also express *Ulex europaeus* agglutinin I lectin-binding sites, in contrast to most basal cell carcinomas.[78] Poorly differentiated tumors can also be immunoreactive for vimentin.[80] In contrast to basal cell carcinomas, squamous cell carcinomas are negative for BerEP4.[74,83] Basement membrane components such as laminin and type IV collagen can be found surrounding some of the tumor nests.[75]

Accumulation of p53 protein, presumably as a result of mutation, has been detected in close to half of cases.[77] Various chromosomal alterations have been detected, but none of them seems to be distinctive.[76]

Other microscopic types

Spindle squamous cell carcinoma (metaplastic carcinoma) usually occurs in sun-exposed areas and is relatively common in the lip (see Fig. 4.54). The differential

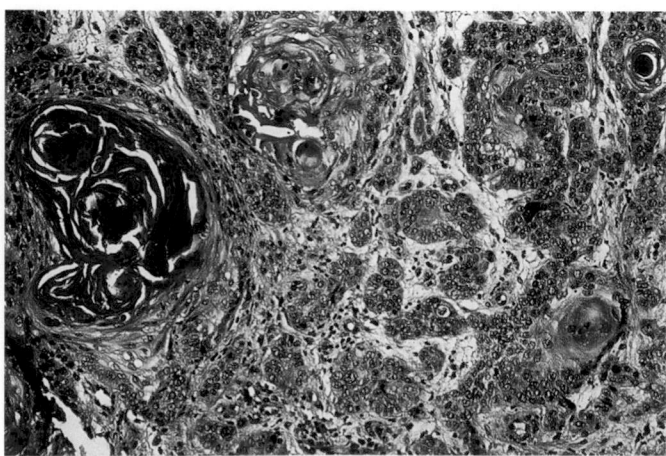

Fig. 4.53 Deeply invasive well-differentiated squamous cell carcinoma.

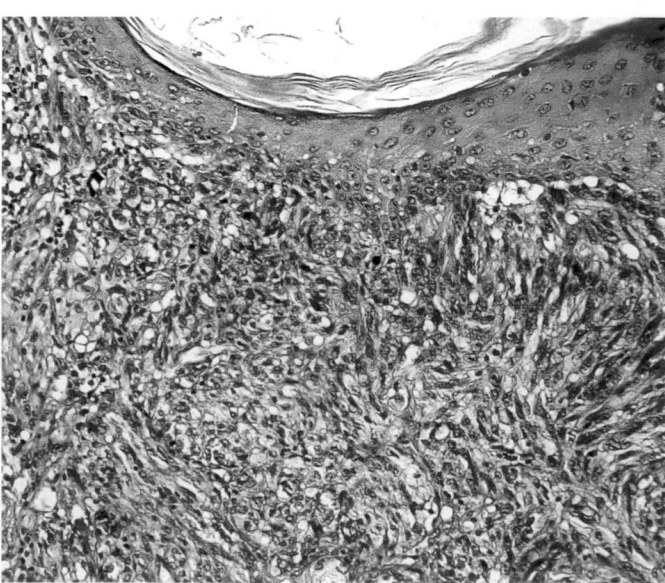

Fig. 4.54 Squamous cell carcinoma with spindle metaplastic features.

diagnosis includes malignant melanoma and atypical fibroxanthoma. Continuity of tumor cells with the basal layer of the epidermis, foci of clear-cut squamous change, and keratin immunoreactivity are the most important distinguishing features.[88,93] Vimentin is consistently coexpressed by these tumors.[98] *Carcinosarcoma* is the term used when there is a sharp segregation between the epithelial and the sarcoma-like components.[91] When the distinction between spindle cell carcinoma and a mesenchymal tumor is not possible (a not uncommon occurrence), it is preferable to use the noncommittal term *sarcoma-like tumor of the skin*[89] (see p. 185).

Adenoid (pseudoglandular; acantholytic) squamous cell carcinoma results from acantholysis, i.e., lack of cell cohesiveness caused by a desmosomal defect (Fig. 4.55). Sometimes the pattern simulates instead an angiosarcoma (*pseudoangiomatous carcinoma*).[84,96] Nearly all cases occur in sun-exposed areas, and many are associated with actinic keratosis with acantholysis. Immunohistochemically, there is a preferential reduction of the cell adhesion molecule syndecan-1.[86] The differential diagnosis includes primary or metastatic adenocarcinoma, true *adenosquamous carcinoma* of the skin, a rare aggressive neoplasm that exhibits squamous differentiation and mucin production,[85,99] and *mucoepidermoid carcinoma*, an even rarer tumor of probable sweat gland nature.[94]

Verrucous carcinoma is an extremely well-differentiated type of squamous cell carcinoma, also known in the skin as *carcinoma* or *epithelioma cuniculatum*.[87,97] It appears as an ulcerated, fungating, and polypoid mass with openings of sinus tracts onto the skin surface. Most cases are located in the sole of the foot (Fig. 4.56). Local invasion is the rule, and extension to bone is frequent, but nodal metastases are exceptional.[92,95] It is regarded as the cutaneous counterpart of the more common verrucous carcinoma of the oral cavity and other mucosal membranes, and, like them, it may be positive for HPV.[90]

Treatment

Complete excision remains the treatment of choice for most squamous cell carcinomas.[101,102] Careful pathologic examination, including marking of the surgical margins with India ink or silver nitrate, allows identification of those cases in which the tumor has been transected. Depending on the size and location of the tumor and the general condition of the patient, alternative therapies include curettage and electrodesiccation, cryotherapy, and radiation therapy.[100]

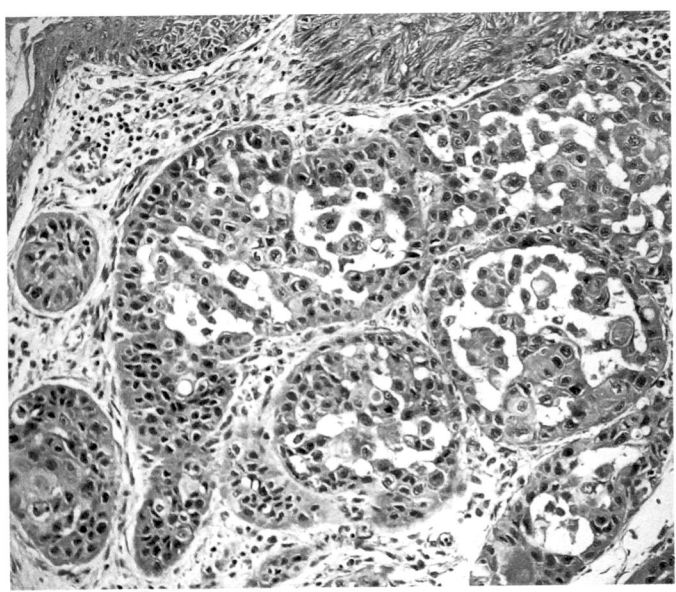

Fig. 4.55 Acantholytic squamous cell carcinoma, resulting in a pseudoglandular appearance.

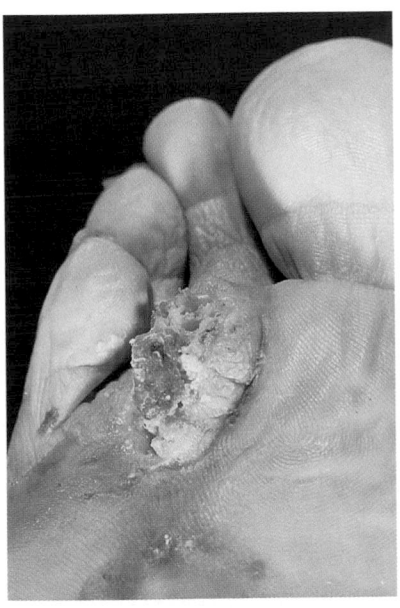

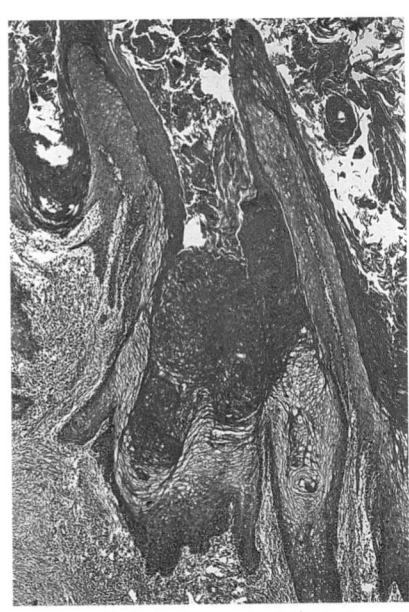

A **B**

Fig. 4.56 Verrucous carcinoma of skin. **A**, Typical appearance of lesion located in sole of foot. **B**, Papillomatous growth associated with hyperkeratosis and pushing type of invasion into the underlying dermis. (Courtesy of Dr. Daniel Santa Cruz, St. Louis)

Prognosis

The overall prognosis of squamous cell carcinoma is excellent, particularly for the actinic-induced tumors. Superficially invasive cancers (less than 1.5 cm) metastasize only occasionally.[106] Even in lesions larger than 2 cm with unequivocal invasion into the reticular dermis, the incidence of regional lymph node metastases is less than 5%. The best prognostic determinators are staging (see Appendix C), level of dermal invasion, and vertical tumor thickness.[104,105] In one series, all tumors that recurred were 4 mm or more thick and involved the deep half of the dermis or deeper; all tumors that proved fatal were at least 1 cm in maximum thickness, and most extended into the subcutaneous fat or beyond.[104] The presence or absence of actinic keratosis at the edge of a squamous cell carcinoma is not as useful a predictor of behavior as tumor thickness or level of invasion.[103]

Pseudoepitheliomatous hyperplasia

At sites of trauma, chronic irritation, and ulcers, the reparative hyperplasia of the epidermis may produce seemingly invasive tongues of epithelial cells. This abnormality, known as pseudoepitheliomatous (pseudocarcinomatous) hyperplasia, can also be caused by mycotic infections (particularly North American blastomycosis), bromoderma, pyoderma vegetans, tuberculosis, syphilis, granular cell tumor, and melanocytic lesions (particularly Spitz nevi but also malignant melanoma[108,109]). The epithelial proliferation is generally associated with a dermal fibrocytic and vascular proliferation and a prominent acute or subacute inflammatory infiltrate. Characteristically, the proliferating strands of epithelium are thin, markedly elongated, anastomosing, and heavily infiltrated by inflammatory cells[107] (Fig. 4.57). Clear separation of pseudoepitheliomatous hyperplasia from squamous cell carcinoma is not always easy. The width of the strands (thin in hyperplasia and broad in carcinomas) and the degree of keratinocytic atypia (greater in the carcinoma) are the main distinguishing features. It should be kept in mind that the presence of an intraepidermal inflammatory infiltrate, no matter how heavy, does not rule out the diagnosis of squamous cell carcinoma. We have seen several cases with clear-cut architectural and cytologic features of carcinoma that were repeatedly underdiagnosed as pseudoepitheliomatous hyperplasia because of their association with a prominent lymphocytic, neutrophilic, eosinophilic, or granulomatous infiltrate.

Basal cell carcinoma

General features

Basal cell carcinoma derives its name from the cytologic similarity of the tumor cells to the normal basal cells of the epidermis and the traditional belief that it arises from them. In our opinion, *all* basal cell carcinomas attempt to differentiate toward adnexal structures (particularly pilosebaceous units), but most of them remain at a stage so primitive as to render this recognition not immediately apparent.[132] The belief that basal cell carcinomas represent primitive "adnexal" carcinomas has been voiced over the years by several authors,[112,123] and is supported by the marked immunohistochemical similarities that exist between basal cell carcinoma and tumors of indubitable hair follicle derivation.[117–119,129,134] Some authorities who initially doubted the concept have now gone as far as flatly stating that basal cell carcinoma is a trichoblastic carcinoma.[127]

Basal cell carcinoma is the most frequent form of skin cancer; it occurs predominantly on sun-exposed skin in direct proportion to the number of pilosebaceous units present therein, a feature supporting the previous histogenetic interpretation.[115,125] Fair-skinned, blue-eyed persons engaged in outdoor occupations suffer a higher incidence of these tumors.[113] Synchronous and metachronous tumors are frequent.[131] Exceptionally, children and young adults are affected.[126,130]

Basal cell carcinomas may also develop in sunlight-protected skin,[124] in nevus sebaceus of Jadassohn (see p. 147), in the lower leg in association with chronic venous stasis and other preexistent conditions,[110,128,133] over arteriovenous malformations,[111] and following arsenic ingestion, x-ray exposure, skin injury, chickenpox scars, tattoos, hair transplantation scars, and immune suppression.[121]

The clinical appearance of basal cell carcinoma is as variable as its histologic patterns. Nodular, ulcerative, superficial, erythematous, and sclerosing (morphea-like) forms occur (Fig. 4.58).

Basal cell nevus syndrome (Gorlin's syndrome) is characterized by multiple basal cell carcinomas, palmar pits, calcification of dura, keratinous cysts of the jaws, skeletal anomalies, and occasional abnormalities of the central nervous system, mesentery, and endocrine organs[114,116] (Fig. 4.59). Microscopically, the basal cell

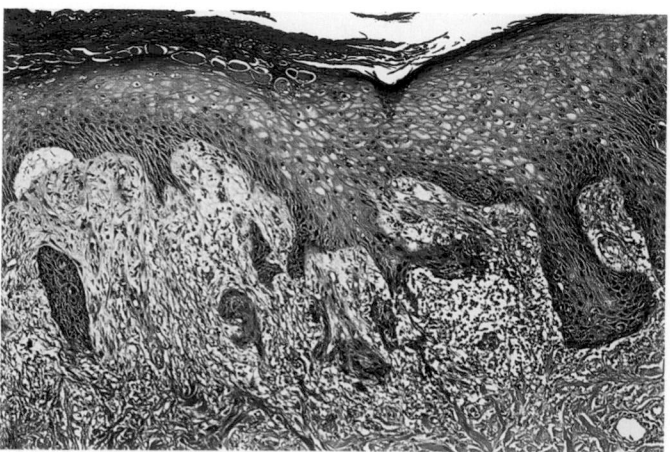

Fig. 4.57 Pseudoepitheliomatous hyperplasia following removal of a benign nevus.

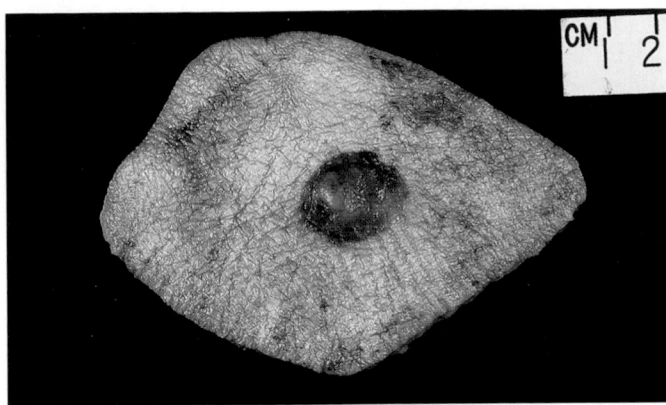

Fig. 4.58 Gross appearance of basal cell carcinoma of forehead. The lesion is nodular and pigmented.

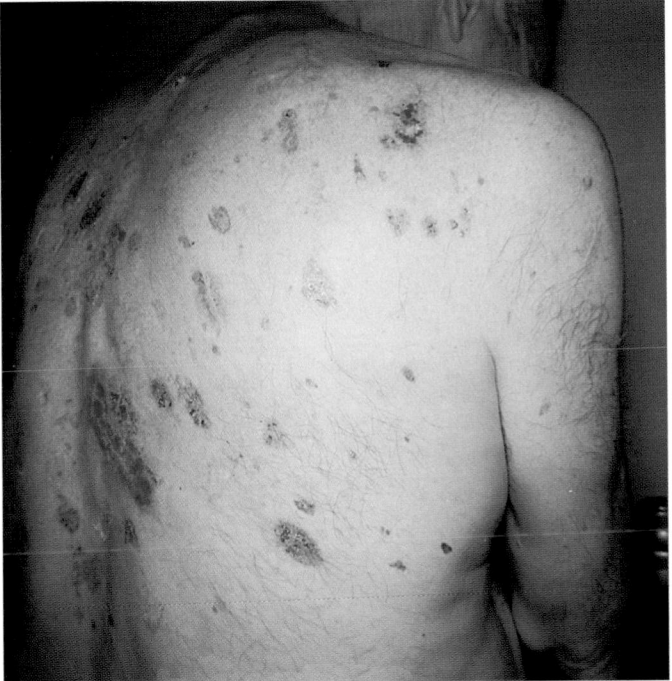

Fig. 4.59 Multiple basal cell carcinomas in the skin of the back of an elderly patient.

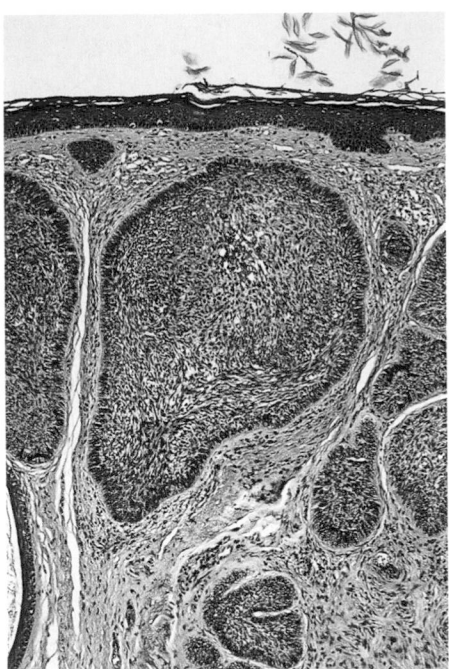

Fig. 4.60 Typical nodular appearance with peripheral palisading of cutaneous basal cell carcinoma.

carcinomas exhibit a broader spectrum of subtypes than the sporadic tumors.[120] The syndrome should be suspected when basal cell carcinomas are seen in young people who have multiple tumors, many of which are of the superficial multicentric type and in which osteoid is an occasional finding.[122]

Microscopic features

Basal cell carcinomas arise from basally located cells of the epidermis and pilosebaceous units and differentiate incompletely in the direction of adnexal (primarily follicular) structures.[143] Epidermal attachment is present in nearly all cases. The tumors may have solid, cystic, adenoid, keratotic, pigmented, infiltrating, and sclerosing (morphea-like) patterns[146,147] (Fig. 4.60). The keratotic pattern probably represents an expression of differentiation

toward the infundibular portion of hair follicles, has no clinical significance, and should be distinguished from so-called "basosquamous carcinoma" (see p. 138).

The nests of basal cell carcinoma show prominent palisading and are surrounded by a typical loose stroma, which contains myofibroblasts and often exhibits mucinous change.[150] Cleft-like retraction spaces, some of artifactual nature and others resulting from the accumulation of stromal mucin, are often seen between the epithelial nests and the stroma.[145] Melanin can accumulate in dermal macrophages between the tumor nests and result in a "pigmented" appearance clinically (Fig. 4.61). Langerhans' cells can also be present.[141] Intercellular amyloid material is not infrequent, sometimes accompanied by the deposition of immunoglobulins.[144,153] Oval to spindle tumor cells with hyaline eosinophilic cytoplasm have been found in a few cases[152] and interpreted by some authors as evidence of myoepithelial differentiation[155] (see also under Other microscopic types). Mitotic activity (sometimes accompanied by atypical forms), marked atypia with the appearance of bizarre ("monster") tumor cells, and giant cell formation may occur, but there is no convincing evidence that any of these features carries prognostic significance.[138,140,151] In other instances the atypia is present in the reactive stromal cells, and equally inconsequential.[149] The stroma may undergo osseous metaplasia, sometimes to a considerable degree[154]; in other instances, it may contain peculiar collagen crystal-like structures.[156]

Rarely, matrical (shadow cell formation), eccrine differentiation, or markedly thickened basement membrane is seen in otherwise typical basal cell carcinoma, further

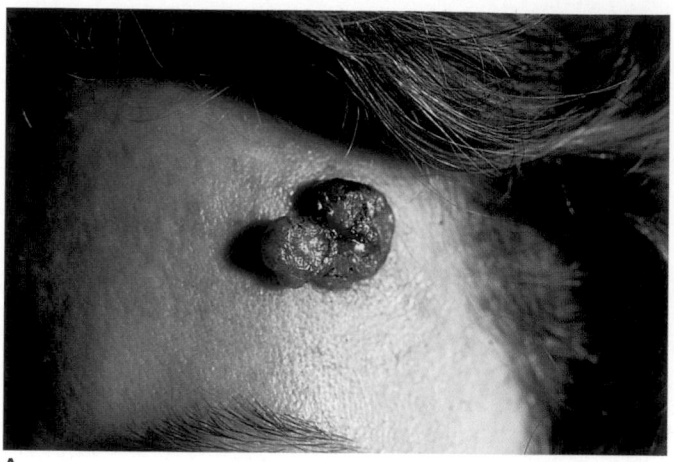
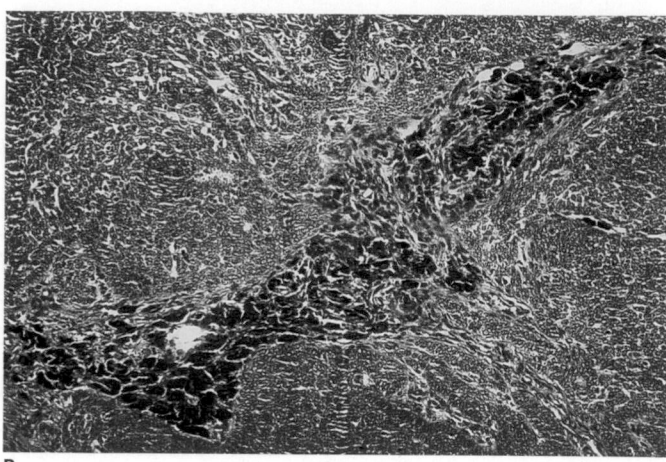

Fig. 4.61 A and **B**, Clinical and microscopic appearance of pigmented basal cell carcinoma. Melanin is largely present in macrophages located in the stroma between tumor lobules.

supporting the close relationship of these tumors with adnexal structures.[135,139,142] Perineurial or endoneurial invasion by tumor cells is rarely present.[148] Sometimes, a basal cell carcinoma is seen adjacent to a benign melanocytic nevus, the juxtaposition being a coincidental event.[136]

The differential diagnosis of basal cell carcinoma includes the areas of highly organoid basaloid proliferation sometimes seen on top of dermatofibromas[137] and the more atypical foci of basaloid proliferation that may be found in association with actinic keratosis and Bowen's disease (see respective discussions).

Histochemical and immunohistochemical features

Immunohistochemically, the cells of basal cell carcinoma are positive for keratin (particularly low-molecular-weight type[166,170,172]) but usually negative for EMA, CEA, and involucrin.[162,165] The basement membrane that surrounds the tumor nests reacts with antibodies against laminin, types IV and V collagen, and bullous pemphigoid antigen.[164,171] The pattern of staining for these markers tends to be attenuated and discontinuous, as an expression of the disruption of this structure.[163,167] This feature is more prominent in the aggressive tumors.[158]

A suggestion was made some years ago to the effect that basal cell carcinomas may show neuroendocrine differentiation[159]; although the relatively common finding of argyrophilia may seem to support this contention, immunoreactivity for neuroendocrine markers such as chromogranin or neuron-specific enolase is an exceptionally rare event.[160]

It has been shown that most basal cell carcinomas stain for BerEP4 whereas most squamous cell carcinomas do not[157,168,169]; the reverse is true regarding the expression of *Ulex europaeus* agglutinin I lectin-binding sites.[161]

Molecular genetic features

More than 80% of basal cell carcinomas overexpress p53 protein,[176] and this figure is even higher in the more

aggressive types (see below). They also commonly express bcl-2, a feature of alleged value in the differential diagnosis with actinic keratosis.[174]

Clonal chromosome aberrations are frequent, most often represented by the numerical changes +18, +9, +20, +7, and +5.[173] Loss of heterozygosity at 9q22.3 and trisomy 6 have also been detected, the latter supposedly correlating with the metastatic potential of the tumor.[175,177]

Other microscopic types

Superficial basal cell carcinoma arises in skin with sparse, fine hairs and epidermis that is thin, such as that of the trunk. It grows chiefly in a lateral direction, beneath a relatively flat epidermis, and exhibits a high recurrence rate.[185,188,189]

Basosquamous (metatypical) carcinoma has the general configuration of a basal cell carcinoma, but it also contains atypical squamous cells. This variant is more aggressive than the conventional basal cell carcinoma. A high proportion of the metastasizing basal cell tumors belong to this type, which should be distinguished from the keratotic form of basal cell carcinoma.[181,187]

Granular basal cell carcinoma contains tumor cells with cytoplasmic granules analogous in every way to those seen in granular cell tumor of the dermis and other locations.[180,182,184] No clinical significance is ascribed to this variety.

Clear cell basal cell carcinoma contains tumor cells with prominent cytoplasmic vacuoles[178,179,190]; in other cases the tumor cells may even have a signet ring configuration,[193] perhaps indicative of myoepithelial cell differentiation.[186]

Fibroepithelial tumor (Pinkus' tumor; fibroepithelioma) is a polypoid variant of basal cell carcinoma, often occurring on the back, in which the stroma is very abundant[183] (Fig. 4.62). It has been suggested that the fibroadenoma-like pattern of this tumor is the result of eccrine duct spread.[191]

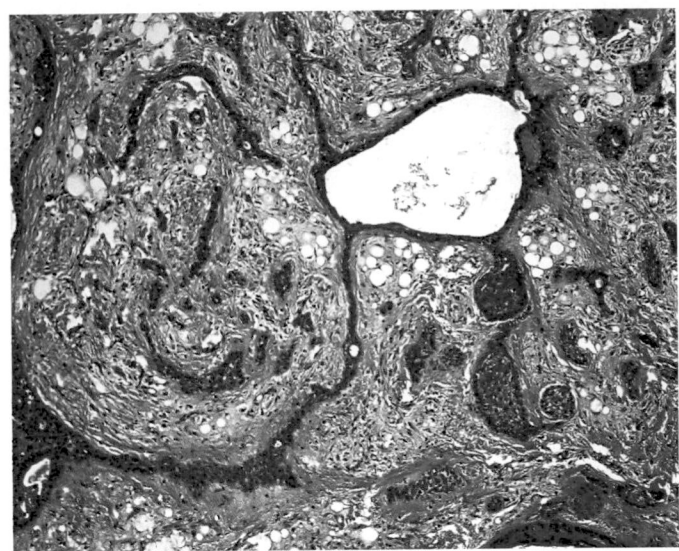

Fig. 4.62 Highly organoid appearance of Pinkus' fibroepithelioma.

Infundibulocytic basal cell carcinoma is a variant of basal cell carcinoma in which evidence of hair follicle differentiation is much more evident and advanced than in the ordinary type; it could be viewed as being situated between the latter and trichoepithelioma in terms of the differentiation spectrum.[192]

Spread and metastases

Basal cell carcinoma usually grows in a slow and indolent fashion. However, if untreated, the tumor may invade the subcutaneous fat, skeletal muscle, and bone ("ulcus rodens"). Tumors of the face may invade skull, nares, orbit, or temporal bone via the auditory canal. They can thus reach the central nervous system and produce lethal meningitis. Microscopically, the locally more aggressive tumors tend to show loss of peripheral palisading and a dense, fibrous stroma rather than a loose stroma.[203] At a statistical level, they also show decreased expression of syndecan-1[196] and bcl-2,[206] greater expression of p53,[195] higher AgNOR count,[199] and higher incidence of aneuploidy[202] than the others. In terms of location, local recurrence is more common in tumors of the nasolabial fold, inner canthus, and postauricular region.[204] This is probably the combined result of the highly irregular infiltrative pattern that these tumors often exhibit, and the fact that in these locations the distance to the surgical margins tends to be rather close.[198,201] In general, the microscopic appearance of the recurrence is not substantially different from that of the original tumor.[200] Distant metastases are extraordinarily rare, but over 100 cases have been reported.[194,207,208] These include cases associated with the basal cell nevus syndrome.[197] Approximately 60% to 75% of these metastases involved the regional lymph nodes, and the others affected organs such as lung, bone, and liver. Metastases in basal cell carcinoma are more likely in the basosquamous types, in those with perineurial spread, and in tumors located on sunlight-protected skin.[205]

Treatment

Excision, curettage and desiccation, and irradiation used appropriately cure most basal cell carcinomas.[209,216] Even when these tumors extend to the margin of surgical excision (an occurrence of approximately 5% in large series), only one third will show evidence of recrudescence over the ensuing 2 to 5 years.[211] Thus immediate reexcision is not always indicated under these circumstances. Actually, it has been suggested that evaluation of the pattern of tumor growth (widely dispersed versus tightly clustered nests) is a better predictor of local recurrence than presence or absence of tumor at the surgical margins.[215]

Recurrent basal cell carcinomas can be treated with radiation therapy or surgical reexcision.[217] In some institutions, these recurrent tumors (and increasingly, many others, whether recurrent or not) are being treated by a procedure known as Mohs' micrographic surgery.[212–214] The catch phrases that allegedly render this a special procedure are the following:

1 "Chemical cauterization" with zinc chloride paste. This practice, initially recommended by Mohs himself as a key feature of the procedure, has largely since been abandoned in favor of the conventional scalpel.

2 "Microscopically controlled." This is an elegant way of expressing the fact that the adequacy of the surgical margins is checked by frozen section, a practice that has been in existence in surgical pathology laboratories for almost a century.

3 "En face" orientation of the specimen to be frozen. Once again, this is hardly a novelty in histology or pathology, the technique having been described over a century ago. Depending on the circumstances, it may provide more information than the conventional vertical section, or it may not; it is certainly more difficult to interpret (as all tangential sections are), and it may be very misleading.

4 "The Mohs surgeon acts as his own pathologist." In other words, the entire procedure of cutting, staining, and interpreting the frozen sections from the various margins is done by the surgeon himself, with the aid of a technician. This is not the place to discuss the medicolegal, quality assurance, and financial conflicts of interest that this policy raises; suffice it to say that they are of great proportions.

Somebody has commented that the statements made by many Mohs surgeons regarding the merits, superiority, and uniqueness of their technique have alienated "the great majority of dermatologists, plastic surgeons, [and] head and neck surgeons."[210] I would like to add "pathologists" (at least one of them) to that list.

Skin adnexa

The large majority of skin adnexal tumors differentiate only along one adnexal line, and this results in the formation of reasonably distinct types whose structure, cytochemistry, and immunohistochemistry can be correlated with those of the corresponding adnexa or even a subdivision thereof.[218,222–224,228,230] However, since all cutaneous adnexa share the same origin, it is not surprising that the tumors arising from them have many features in common, not only among themselves, but also with those of surface epidermal type. As a matter of fact, it is not unusual to find evidence of differentiation along two or more adnexal lines in different tumors occurring in the same individual or sometimes even within the same neoplasm, whether benign or malignant.[219,226,229,232] The tumors described as *cutaneous adnexal carcinomas with divergent differentiation* are an expression of the latter phenomenon.[225]

Lymphoepithelioma-like carcinoma of the skin may also represent a primitive adnexal neoplasm. As the name indicates, this lesion shows a morphologic resemblance to the tumor of the upper respiratory tract that bears that name, but it also exhibits features suggestive of beginning sweat gland and/or follicular differentiation[220,231] (Fig. 4.63). However, cases have been described with divergent differentiation toward apocrine structures.[221] It does not seem to be related to Epstein–Barr virus (EBV).[227]

Eccrine sweat glands

Eccrine poroma

Eccrine poromas occur chiefly on the palms and soles but have been reported in many other sites. They often show a moat and hillock pattern and, histologically, are characterized by a sharp junction between the proliferating, nonpigmented, small keratinocytes and the adjacent epidermis (Fig. 4.64). Within these cords and nests, ducts and sharply outlined squamous islands may be formed.[236] The tumor may be purely intraepidermal, purely intradermal (also referred to as dermal duct tumor), or (more commonly) involve both areas.[235] Purely intraepidermal poromas have been described in the past as hydroacanthoma simplex.[238,241] Heavily pigmented variants of this tumor have been reported. Ultrastructural, enzymatic, histochemical, and immunohistochemical studies show that the predominant cell of eccrine poroma has features similar to those of the eccrine gland acrosyringium.[234,242] EMA immunoreactivity is consistently present.[240] The dermis beneath often shows a distinct proliferation of reactive vessels and some inflammation. The main differential diagnosis of eccrine poroma is with basal cell carcinoma and seborrheic keratoses.

Eccrine poroma should also be distinguished from *acrosyringeal adenomatosis* (eccrine syringofibroadenoma), a peculiar condition in which papular lesions spread gradually and symmetrically to cover large areas of the body. Microscopically, they are formed by a diffuse proliferation of acrosyringium-related cells in the epidermis and dermis.[233,237]

The behavior of eccrine poroma is benign, but a malignant counterpart of the tumor, known as eccrine porocarcinoma, exists[239] (see p. 144).

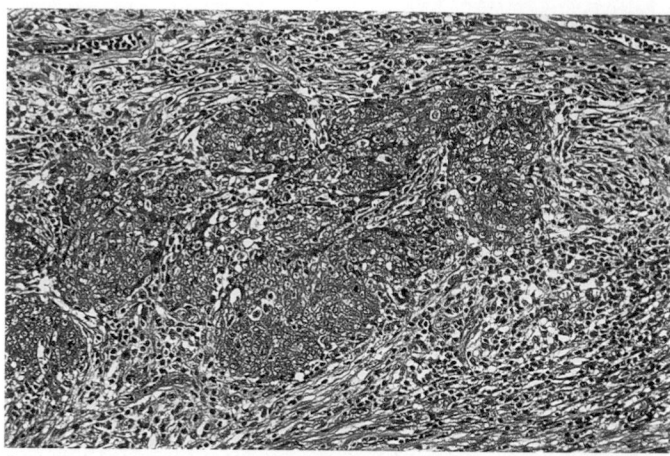

A

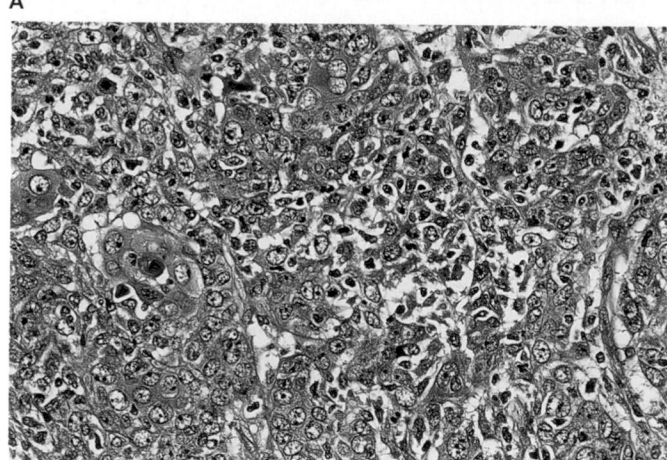

B

Fig. 4.63 A and **B,** Low and high-power views of lymphoepithelioma-like carcinoma.

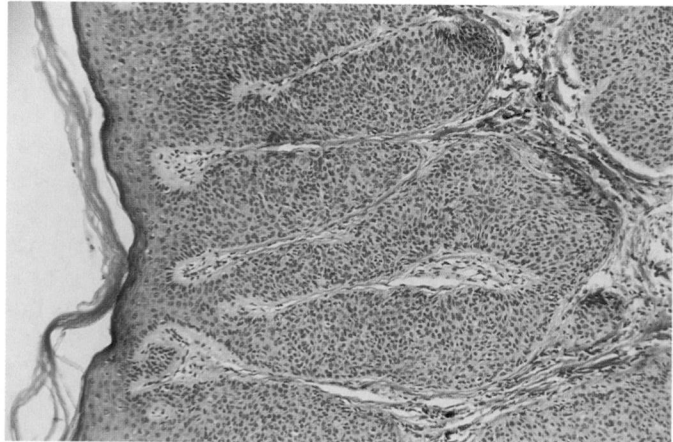

Fig. 4.64 Eccrine poroma. The tumor characteristically grows in the form of cords and nest of small tumor cells attached to the epidermis.

Eccrine acrospiroma

Eccrine acrospiroma, also known as solid–cystic or nodular hidradenoma, arises from the distal excretory duct.[246] It forms nodules with occasional cystic foci high in the dermis (Fig. 4.65). Some of the proliferating cells are cytologically similar to those of the poroma. Others have an abundant clear cytoplasm (hence the other synonym, clear cell hidradenoma), and still others exhibit prominent squamous metaplasia.[245] Immunohistochemically, there is reactivity for keratin, EMA, CEA, S-100 protein, and vimentin.[243] Johnson and Helwig[244] regard eccrine poroma as a subtype of eccrine acrospiroma. The differential diagnosis of eccrine acrospiroma includes glomus tumor because of the presence in both entities of round clear cells and marked vascularity; the distinction between the two entities is easily made by immunohistochemical evaluation.[243]

Syringoma

Syringomas are generally multiple, yellowish, papulonodular lesions that occur chiefly on the neck and face (particularly lower eyelids) of women. Other forms are vulvar syringoma, acral syringoma (limited to the dorsal proximal and middle phalanges of the hand), and eruptive syringoma (see below). Microscopically, these tumors are formed by clusters of small ducts lined by epithelium two cells thick, occasionally with comma-shaped extensions (Fig. 4.66). A clear cell variety has been described, resulting from intracellular accumulation of glycogen.[248] The ultrastructural[250] and histochemical[252] findings indicate that these lesions are of eccrine rather than apocrine nature. Specifically, the pattern of cytokeratin expression suggests that syringoma differentiates toward the portion of the sweat duct located in the uppermost portion of the dermis and lower portion of the epidermis (sweat duct ridge).[247]

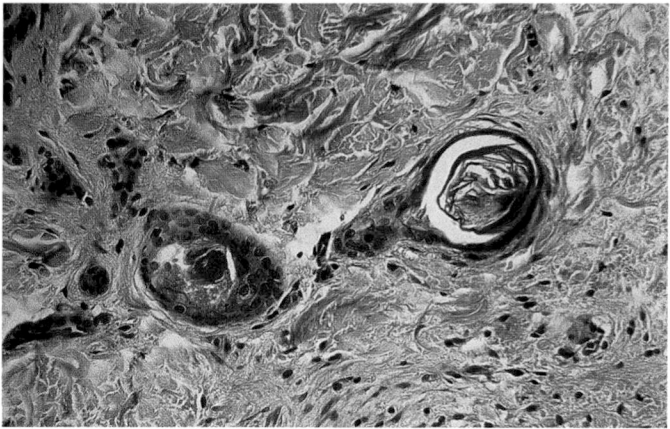

Fig. 4.66 Syringoma. Small glandular structures with little "tails" are typical of this entity.

Eruptive syringoma appears as multiple yellow–brown papules on the neck, anterior trunk, axillae, shoulder, anterior surfaces of the arms, abdomen, and pubic areas of young people[251]; the process may be reactive rather than neoplastic.[249]

Chondroid syringoma (mixed tumor) and myoepithelioma

Chondroid syringomas are benign, nodular, nonulcerated tumors that occur predominantly on the face, head, and neck but also on the extremities and trunk.[262] Histologically, immunohistochemically, and ultrastructurally, their appearance is comparable to that of mixed tumors of salivary gland origin.[258,260,267] This includes the presence of cells with an abundant hyaline cytoplasm.[254,256,263] Sometimes, eosinophilic globules with radiating fibrillary structures are seen within and around the lumina, their appearance being analogous to those seen in collagenous spherulosis of the breast.[253,255] Immunohistochemically, the inner layer cells express cytokeratin, CEA, and EMA; the outer cell layers are positive for vimentin, S-100 protein, NSE, and—sometimes—glial fibrillary acidic protein.[255,257,259] Immunoreactivity for smooth muscle actin has also been found, in keeping with the presence of a myoepithelial cell component.[264,266] Although most of these tumors are thought to be of eccrine type, a variety exhibiting clear-cut evidence of apocrine differentiation has been well documented; this is often admixed with follicular and sebaceous components.[265] Despite the occasionally atypical appearance of the cartilaginous component, the large majority of these tumors are benign.

Tumors having a similar myoepithelial cell component but lacking the epithelial element are known as **myoepitheliomas**;[258a] some of these behave in a malignant fashion, apparently with a higher frequency than the homologous salivary gland neoplasms.[264]

Tumors with an appearance similar to cutaneous chondroid syringomas and myoepitheliomas can also be seen in the deep soft tissue[261] (see Chapter 25).

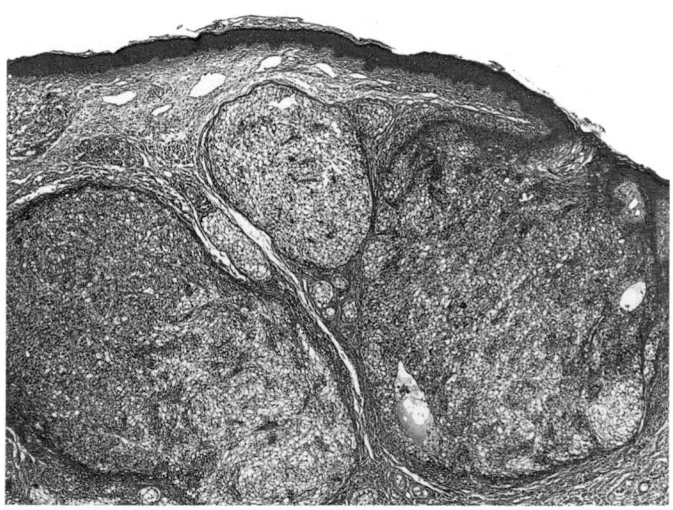

Fig. 4.65 Eccrine acrospiroma. The lesion is lobulated and shows a prominent clear cell component.

Eccrine cylindroma

Classically, cylindroma of the skin has been described as a large, multicentric tumor of the scalp (*turban tumor*) (Fig. 4.67). In fact, the majority of these slow-growing adenomas are solitary and small, and approximately 10% occur on sites other than the head and neck.[269] Exceptionally, they are seen in association with microscopically identical tumors in the major salivary glands.[276] Microscopically, the heavy accumulation of basement membrane material around and within the tumor lobules is the most important distinguishing feature (Fig. 4.68). The ultrastructural and immunohistochemical features indicate differentiation toward the intradermal coiled duct region of eccrine sweat glands,[268,272,275] provide evidence for the participation of myoepithelial cells,[270,277,278] and are very similar to those of eccrine spiradenoma.[273] Sometimes, features of cylindroma and eccrine spiradenoma coexist in the same lesion (spiradenocylindromas).[271,274] Several examples of eccrine cylindroma undergoing malignant transformation are on record (see p. 144).

Multiple cylindromas are caused by a mutation in the CYLD gene, found in chromosome 16; both copies of this tumor-suppressor gene must be inactivated for the syndrome to occur.[267a]

Eccrine spiradenoma

Eccrine spiradenomas are sharply delimited, lobular adenomas that can occur almost anywhere in the body and can be extremely painful. They originate from the lower portion of the eccrine duct and are microscopically very cellular[282,286] (Fig. 4.69). The scanty cytoplasm and marked cellularity may lead the unwary to an erroneous diagnosis of malignancy.[284] We have seen them confused with synovial sarcoma and with metastatic carcinoma. They can also be confused clinically and microscopically with vascular tumors because of their high degree of vascularity[280] (Fig. 4.70). Ultrastructural and immunohistochemical studies have shown that these tumors contain an admixture of epithelial (secretory) and myoepithelial cells.[279,281,283]

In some spiradenomas, a heavy infiltration by lymphocytes (mainly of T-cell type) is present between the tumor cells; the resulting appearance is reminiscent of a thymoma, to the point that Masson referred to it as "reticulo-epithelial (?thymoid) evolution."[287] The analogy is accentuated by the presence of perivascular spaces containing lymphocytes.[290]

The tumor entity known as *cutaneous lymphadenoma*

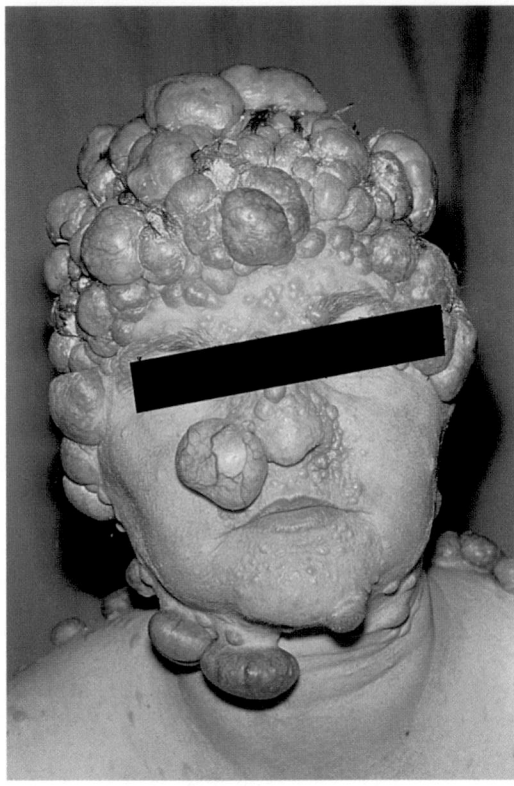

Fig. 4.67 Clinical appearance of multiple dermal eccrine cylindroma extensively involving the scalp and other sites of the head and neck. This is sometimes referred to as turban tumor.

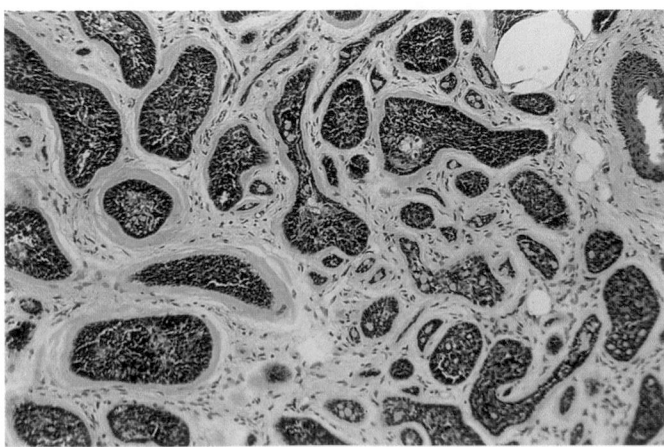

Fig. 4.68 Eccrine dermal cylindroma. Compact nests of tumor cells surrounded by thick basement membrane.

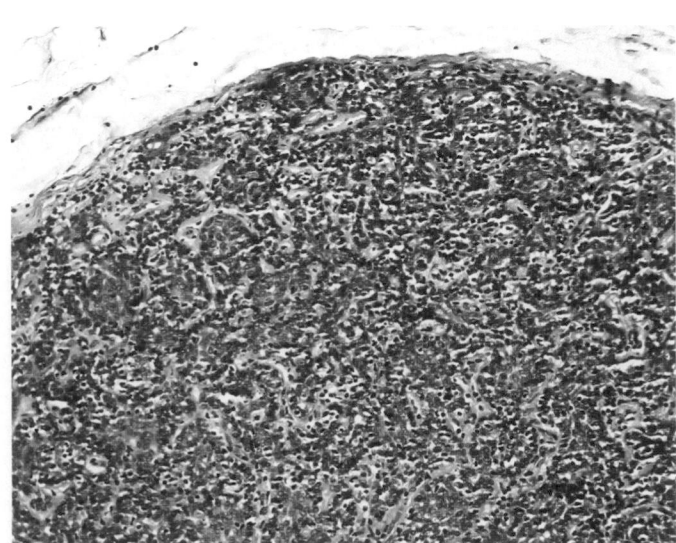

Fig. 4.69 Eccrine spiradenoma. The lesion is highly cellular and infiltrated by lymphocytes.

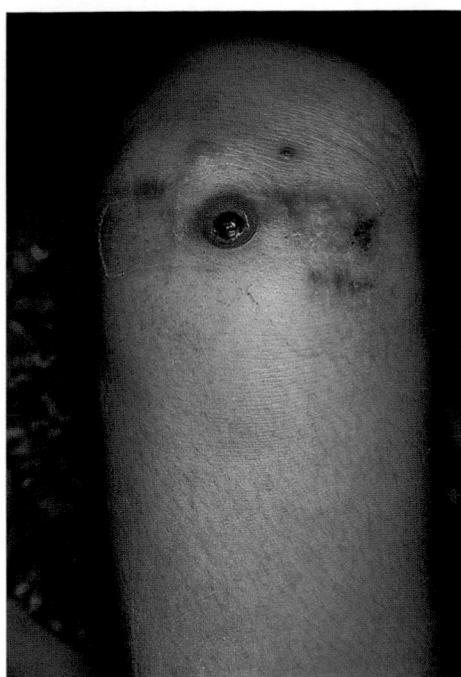

Fig. 4.70 Clinical appearance of eccrine spiradenoma of the knee associated with a prominent vascular component that resulted in a hemangioma-like appearance clinically.

seems to represent a closely related phenomenon. It presents as multiple rounded lobules of basaloid cells with some peripheral palisading, foci of keratinization, and sometimes duct formation, which are admixed with an intense infiltrate of small lymphocytes.[288,289] The immunohistochemical profile of this tumor has suggested to some authors a histogenetic link with trichoblastoma.[285]

On rare occasions, eccrine spiradenoma has been seen to undergo transformation to a high-grade malignancy (see p. 144).

Papillary syringadenoma

Papillary syringadenomas are verrucous, moist tumors that occur chiefly on the scalp, neck, and face but may be found elsewhere on the skin. They are seen from childhood to senescence, and often there is a history of slow growth or of a recent change in a "birthmark." Microscopically, a glandular papillary proliferation connected to the skin surface is seen. Dense plasma cell infiltration is common. These plasma cells are predominantly of the IgG and IgA classes.[293,294] Juxtaposed nevus sebaceus was found in one third and basal cell carcinoma in one tenth of the patients reported in the classic article by Helwig and Hackney.[292]

A malignant counterpart of this neoplasm (syringocystadenocarcinoma papilliferum) has been described,[291] as well as a variant containing a prominent fibrous component, known as *eccrine syringofibroadenoma* and sometimes developing in peristomal skin.[291a]

Papillary eccrine adenoma

Papillary eccrine adenoma is a distinctive sweat gland tumor, most often located on the distal extremities of black people.[299] Microscopically, tubular structures resembling eccrine ducts are seen; many are dilated and exhibit intraluminal papillomatosis. Local recurrence may supervene, but none of the reported lesions has metastasized. Immunohistochemically and ultrastructurally, the pattern suggests differentiation toward the secretory epithelium of sweat glands.[295–297] The main differential diagnosis is with low-grade eccrine carcinoma.[298]

Aggressive digital papillary adenoma

Another sweat gland neoplasm with a marked predilection for the digits is aggressive digital papillary adenoma.[301] Microscopically, tubuloalveolar and ductal structures alternate with areas of papillary projections protruding into cystic lumina (Fig. 4.71). The appearance is somewhat reminiscent of carcinoma of the breast. Local recurrence is common.[301] A malignant counterpart of this tumor—recognized by its poor glandular differentiation and by necrosis, cellular atypia, and invasiveness—metastasizes in a high proportion of cases, particularly to the lung.[300,301]

Clear cell acanthoma and other "acanthomas"

Degos' clear cell acanthoma[304] is a morphologically distinct intraepithelial tumor composed of clear, glycogen-filled keratinocytes associated with dermal inflammation. A minor melanocytic population may also be present.[306,308] Clear cell acanthoma is seen almost

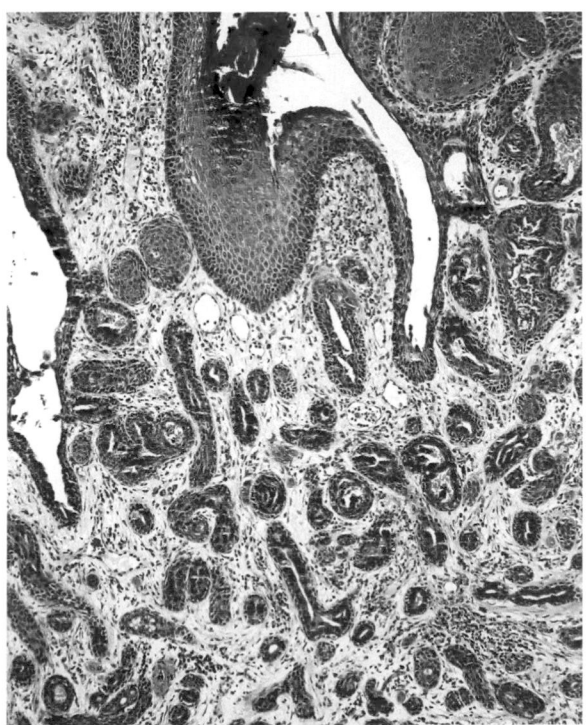

Fig. 4.71 Aggressive digital eccrine adenoma.

invariably in the leg of females, is occasionally multiple, and is thought to arise from intraepidermal eccrine ducts. Similar cytologic changes ("pale cell acanthosis") can be seen focally in seborrheic keratosis and several other skin disorders as an expression of a reaction pattern of epidermal epithelium.[307] As a matter of fact, clear cell acanthoma itself may be an exaggerated form of this process rather than a true neoplasm.

One could mention here that *acanthoma* is a generic term that has been used for "benign tumors of epidermal keratinocytes."[303] It comprises a large number of probably unrelated lesions, most of which are actually non-neoplastic, such as seborrheic keratosis, verrucous acanthoma, epidermolytic hyperkeratosis, warty dyskeratoma, acantholytic acanthoma,[305,307a,309] and large cell acanthoma.[302,310,311] Consequently, the term acanthoma has very little meaning when used without a qualifier, and only a little more when used with one.

Intraepidermal epithelioma

The lesion traditionally known as *intraepithelial epithelioma of Borst–Jadassohn* is probably composed of a heterogeneous group of disorders, the two most common being irritated seborrheic keratosis and eccrine poroma (and related intraepidermal sweat gland tumors).[312,313]

Sweat gland carcinoma

Adenocarcinomas arising from eccrine glands constitute only a minute fraction of sweat gland neoplasms.[319,344,355,360] (Figs 4.72 and 4.73). Most occur in adults, but they have also been reported in children.[318] They can be very difficult to recognize at the microscopic level. Those with well-developed ductal differentiation simulate metastatic carcinoma, particularly from the breast,[361,363] a similarity highlighted by the fact that they can also exhibit immunoreactivity for GCDF-15 and estrogen receptor protein.[359] The sweat gland carcinomas with large clear

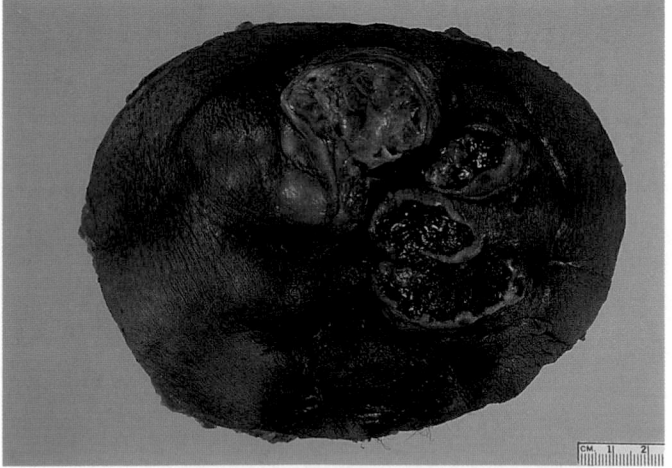

Fig. 4.72 Gross appearance of resected specimen of sweat gland carcinoma of the axilla. The tumor grows in a multinodular fashion, and it shows several areas of ulceration.

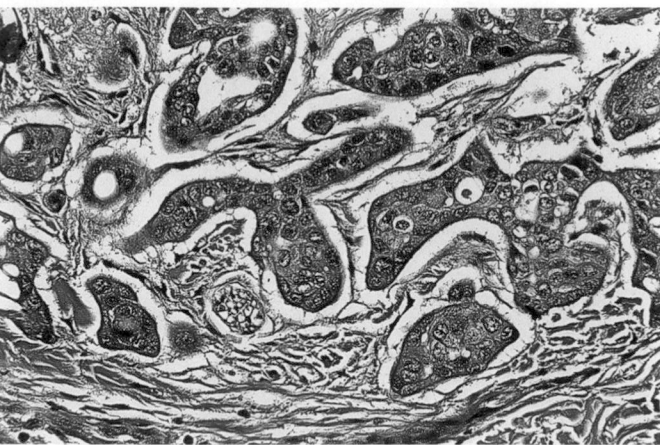

Fig. 4.73 Typical branching configuration of sweat gland carcinoma.

cells resemble metastatic renal cell carcinoma,[323] and those with prominent basaloid formations may be confused with basal cell carcinoma.[342]

Some sweat gland carcinomas retain morphologic features that allow them to be recognized as the malignant counterparts of the various types of sweat gland adenomas,[316,324] as already alluded to in some of the previous sections.

Malignant eccrine poroma (porocarcinoma) is the most frequent member of this group.[342,353,357] Most cases occur in the lower extremities, like their benign counterparts. Some of the lesions are pedunculated. Microscopically, the architecture is similar to that of eccrine poroma, but there is obvious atypia and high mitotic activity. Epidermotropism is a common feature of this tumor, the resulting picture being that of extramammary Paget's disease.[336,345] Foci of squamous differentiation and clear cell features may be present.[350,366] Pigmentation may occur and lead to a mistaken diagnosis of malignant melanoma.[330] Metastases occur most frequently in the regional lymph node, this often following repeated local recurrences.[334]

Other distinct varieties of sweat gland carcinoma include *malignant chondroid syringoma,*[332] (malignant mixed tumor) and the closely related *malignant myoepithelioma* (Fig. 4.74), *malignant dermal cylindroma,*[338,354] *malignant syringoma* (*syringoid eccrine carcinoma*[314,339,347]), *malignant acrospiroma,*[331,342] *aggressive digital papillary adenocarcinoma,*[325] (Fig. 4.75) and *apocrine carcinoma.*[346,349]

In addition to these presumably de novo lesions, eccrine acrospiroma, spiradenoma, syringoma, and cylindroma can undergo malignant transformation, the phenomenon manifesting clinically as enlargement of a cutaneous nodule of long standing.[315,321,328,337,365] This transformation is usually in the form of a high-grade carcinoma, including the variant known as sarcomatoid carcinoma or carcinosarcoma.[340]

Several other distinctive types of sweat gland carcinoma occur. One is **mucinous (adenocystic) carcinoma,**

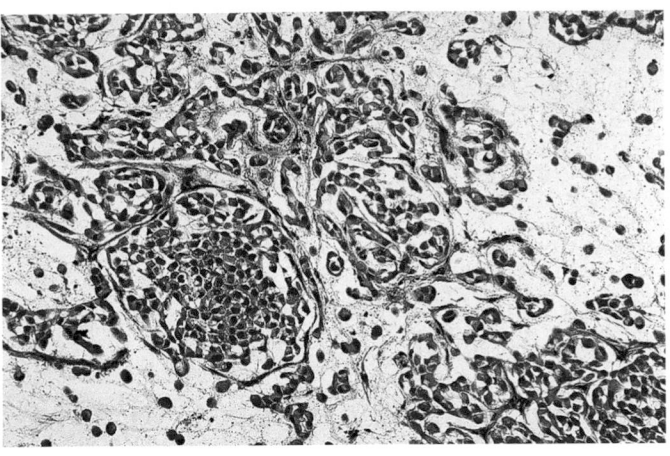
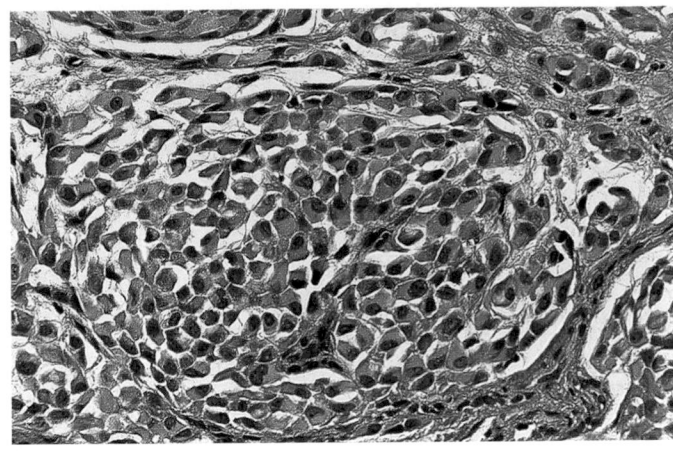

A   B

Fig. 4.74 A and **B**, Sweat gland carcinoma of myoepithelial type located in the toe.

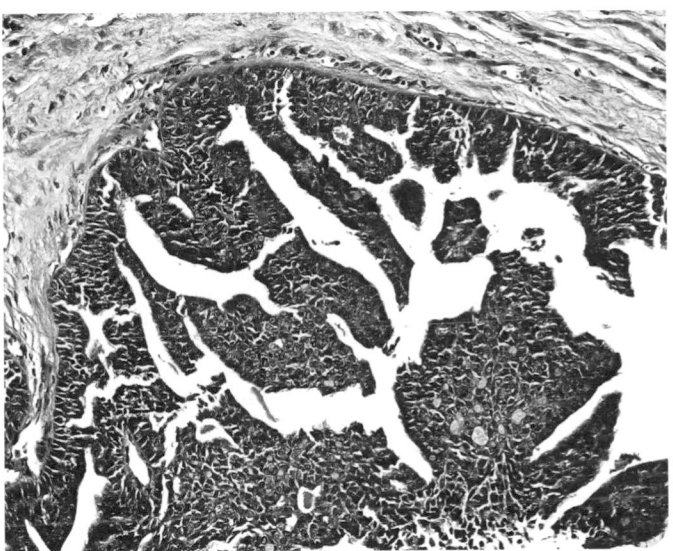

Fig. 4.75 Aggressive digital papillary adenocarcinoma metastatic to lymph node.

often appearing in the scalp of elderly patients.[343,356] Its microscopic appearance resembles mucinous carcinoma of the breast by virtue of the presence of clusters of tumor cells floating in lakes of mucin. The similarity is reinforced by the fact that, on occasion, the mucinous pattern is associated with an infiltrating ductal pattern.[367] The immunohistochemical profile of mucinous carcinoma suggests differentiation toward the eccrine secretory coil,[326] but some cases have been thought to exhibit apocrine-type features.[362]

This tumor should be distinguished from the even rarer primary **adenoid cystic carcinoma** of the skin, a tumor morphologically and immunohistochemically equivalent to the salivary gland neoplasm that bears that name.[320,327,335,364] More important, it should be distinguished from *mucinous syringometaplasia*, a non-neoplastic reactive change that can be accompanied by prominent epithelial hyperplasia.[341]

Another variant of sweat gland carcinoma, originally designated as microcystic adnexal carcinoma and later renamed **sclerosing sweat duct carcinoma**, appears as a slow-growing, indurated nodule or plaque, usually on the face.[322,329,348] The upper lip is a particularly common location. Microscopically and immunohistochemically, the tumor shares several features with benign syringoma.[333] Cords and nests of uniform keratinocytes, keratin-containing cysts, and foci of ductal differentiation are present (Figs 4.76 and 4.77). Exceptionally, there is sebaceous differentiation.[352] The stroma has a dense, collagenous quality. The tumor has invasive properties, sometimes extending into the subcutaneous fat and/or perineurial spaces.[322] Recurrence is common, but metastases are extremely rare.[317]

Nearly all types of sweat gland carcinoma exhibit immunoreactivity for cytokeratin, CEA, and EMA, like their benign counterparts.[351,358]

Extramammary Paget's disease

Extramammary Paget's disease results from the presence in the epidermis of carcinoma cells with signs of glandular differentiation. Concomitant involvement of eccrine glands and/or hair follicles is nearly always present, whereas dermal invasion is seen in a minority of cases, the frequency varying according to the location (extremely rare in the vulva and more common in the perianal region).[376] Cases limited to the epidermis are explained by postulating an origin from the intraepidermal portion of the sweat glands or from primitive basal cells with the capacity to differentiate toward glandular elements.[371,374] The latter hypothesis would explain the occasional occurrence of lesions combining the features of Paget's disease and Bowen's disease.[386]

The labia majora, scrotum, and perineum are the most frequent sites, with adjacent areas following. The lesions are grossly circinate, annular, erythematous, and eczematoid plaques. Histologically, large, pale, vacuolated cells are seen concentrated just above the basal layer. They may be single or arranged in rows, small nests, or glandular

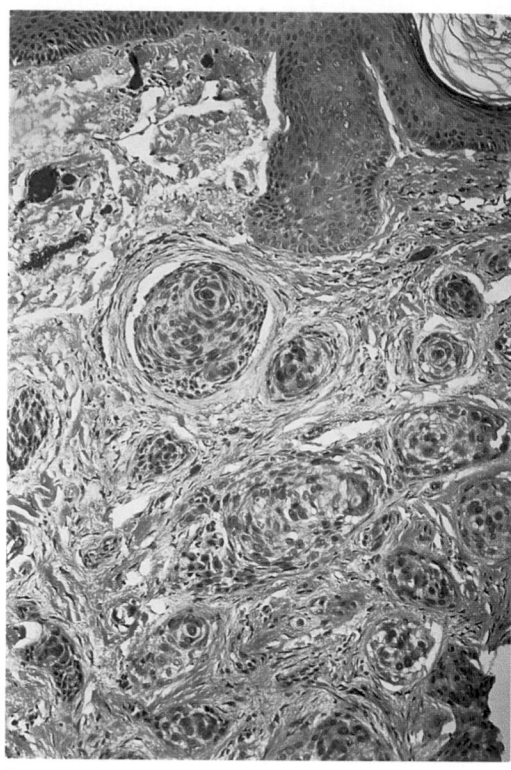

A

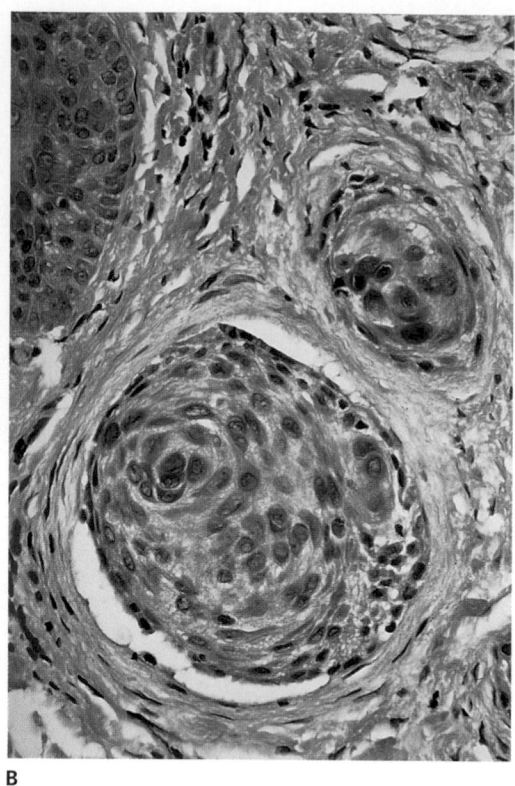

B

Fig. 4.76 Sclerosing sweat gland carcinoma composed of nests of keratinocytes in a whorling pattern. This tumor was located in skin of upper lip in a 28-year-old woman.

formations. A cleft-like separation is often seen between the Paget's cells and the adjacent non-neoplastic keratinocytes. Electron microscopic examination shows that Paget's cells are not altered keratinocytes or melanocytes but rather cells with glandular differentiation.[379] In contrast to Paget's disease of the breast, the extramammary form is consistently positive for mucin stains; these tinctorial differences seem to result from minor changes in the chemical structure of the sialomucins present in the respective tumors.[368,375] Immunohistochemically, the tumor cells show reactivity for EMA, CEA, and the type of low-molecular-weight cytokeratin present in simple epithelia[372,373,377,383,389] (Fig. 4.78).

The theme common to all forms of Paget's disease is the origin of the tumor from epithelial cells with the capacity to differentiate toward the glandular structures of the region. These are the mammary glands in the breast, the apocrine glands in the vulva, and the perianal and/or rectal glands in the perianal region. This probably explains the fact that there is heterogeneity in the immunohistochemical profile of Paget's disease depending on the site of occurrence but in concordance with that of the corresponding normal glands and adenocarcinomas of the region. Thus, vulvar Paget's disease is positive for GCDFP-15 and hormone receptors (curiously, androgen rather than estrogen or progesterone),[369,370] and

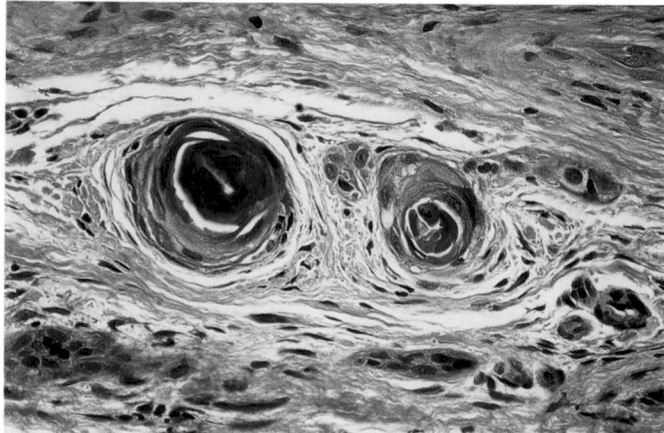

Fig. 4.77 Sclerosing sweat gland carcinoma (microcystic adnexal carcinoma).

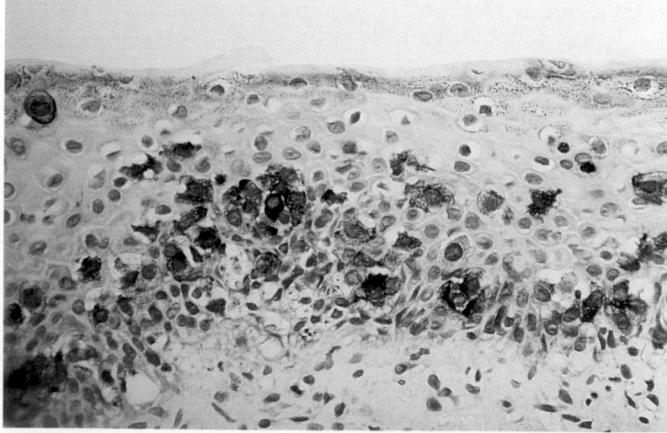

Fig. 4.78 Paget's disease of the skin immunostained for epithelial membrane antigen.

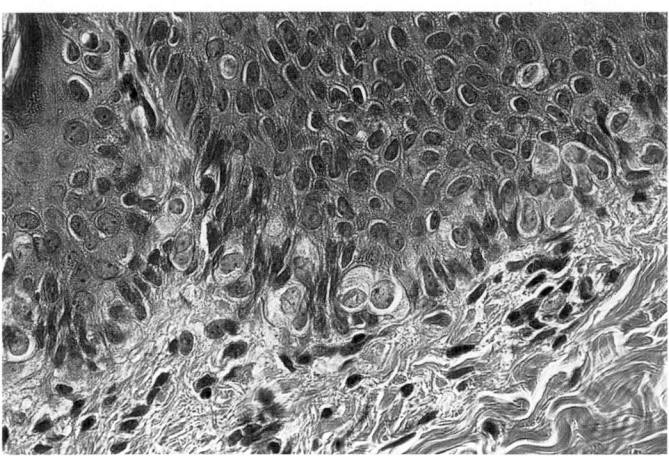

Fig. 4.79 Clear cell papulosis of skin. Large clear cells arranged singly or in small clusters are seen in the basal portions of the epidermis. (Slide contributed by Dr. T.T. Kuo, Taipei, Taiwan)

shows a pattern of lectin-binding sites similar to that of apocrine glands.[381,385,390,391] Conversely, perianal Paget's disease often shows positivity for keratin 20, a feature of colorectal glands.[384,387]

Complete surgical excision is the treatment of choice, but this may be difficult to achieve because of the ill-defined gross edges of the lesion.

The differential diagnosis of extramammary Paget's disease includes pagetoid Bowen's disease, pagetoid actinic keratosis, benign and malignant melanocytic lesions, metastatic epidermotropic carcinomas from breast and other sites,[388] and so-called "clear cell papulosis."[378,380] Most of the reported cases of the latter condition have been in children below the age of 4 years and have been characterized by multiple small whitish maculopapular lesions that, microscopically, are seen to contain pale cells with a similar immunohistochemical profile to that of Paget's cells[382] (Fig. 4.79). These cells are probably related to the so-called "Toker's cells" as seen in the nipple (see Chapter 20).

Apocrine glands

It is possible that some of the sweat gland tumors already described, particularly papillary syringadenoma, cylindroma, and chondroid syringoma, exhibit apocrine differentiation[393]; as a matter of fact, the existence of eccrine and apocrine forms of the latter has been proposed. Furthermore, stains for the apocrine marker GCDFP-15 are often positive in sweat gland neoplasms.[393] However, tumors composed exclusively of apocrine glands are extremely rare.

Apocrine cystadenoma is discussed on p. 152.

Tubular apocrine adenoma is characterized by dermal and subcutaneous tubular structures of apocrine type arranged in a lobular fashion.[394] The lesion is very similar if not identical to papillary syringadenoma.[392]

Papillary hydradenoma and **ceruminous adenoma**

have been traditionally regarded as tumors of apocrine glands. They are discussed in Chapters 19 and 31, respectively.

Apocrine carcinoma is described on p. 144.

Sebaceous glands

Senile sebaceous hyperplasia

The most common nodular lesion of the sebaceous glands is due to hyperplasia. It occurs chiefly on the nose and cheeks of elderly persons, hence the name senile sebaceous nevus or, preferably, senile sebaceous hyperplasia.[395]

Nevus sebaceus of Jadassohn and epidermal nevus

Nevus sebaceus of Jadassohn is a distinct clinicopathologic type of epithelial nevus.[398] It is composed of a hamartomatous conglomerate of large sebaceous glands associated with heterotopic apocrine glands, defective hair follicles, acanthosis, and papillomatosis (Fig. 4.80). The lesions occur on the scalp and face, are present from infancy, and gradually enlarge.[396,399] Basal cell carcinomas, a variety of adnexal tumors (particularly trichoblastomas) and, very rarely, squamous cell carcinomas can arise within this lesion.[397,402]

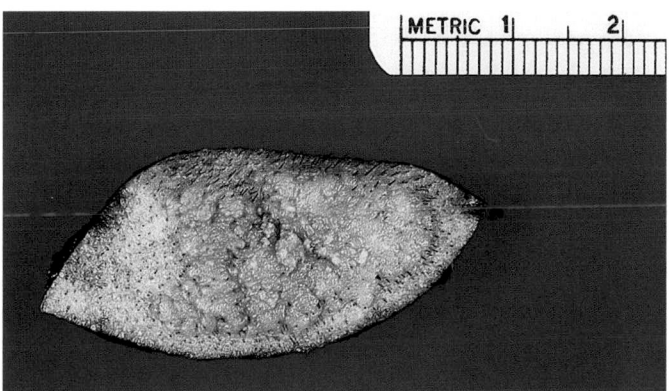

A

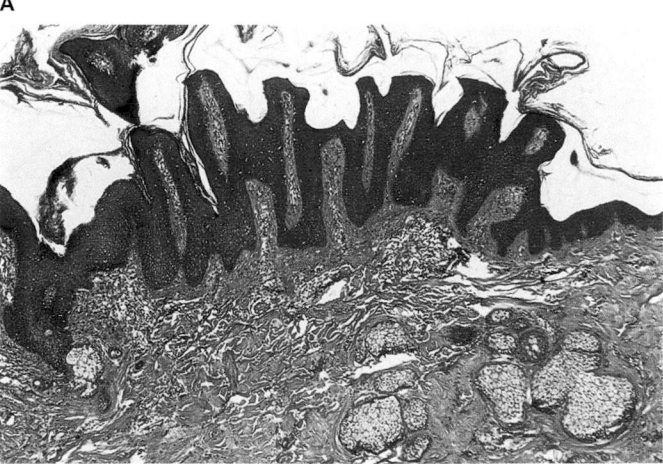

B

Fig. 4.80 Nevus sebaceous of Jaddassohn. **A,** Gross appearance; **B,** Microscopic appearance, showing epidermal papillomatous hyperplasia and increased number of sebaceous glands.

Epithelial nevi without an adnexal component are generically referred to as **epidermal nevi**. They are characterized microscopically by hyperkeratosis, papillomatosis, and acanthosis and are sharply demarcated from the adjacent skin. Several clinicopathologic varieties exist, one of them having a characteristic linear distribution (linear epidermal nevus).[398,400,401]

Sebaceous adenoma

Sebaceous adenoma presents as a nodular lobulated growth with generative cells at the periphery and cells showing varying degrees of sebaceous differentiation toward the center[404] (Fig. 4.81). Although well differentiated, it lacks the distinctly organoid quality of senile sebaceous hyperplasia. It should be realized that the so-called "sebaceous adenoma" occurring on the face of patients with the tuberous sclerosis syndrome is not a sebaceous neoplasm but a fibrovascular proliferation process ("angiofibroma") accompanied by a mild degree of sebaceous hyperplasia. Morphologic variations on the theme of benign sebaceous gland tumors include *sebaceoma*[403,406] and *mantleoma*.[405]

Sebaceous carcinoma

Bona fide sebaceous carcinoma is extremely rare.[420] Those occurring in the eyelids, in caruncles, and in the orbit are much more aggressive than those located elsewhere in the skin,[408,423] but an unfavorable clinical course can occasionally also be seen with the latter.[418] Some of the cases have followed irradiation therapy to the area.[415] Microscopically, sebaceous carcinomas exhibit, together with evidence of sebaceous differentiation, prominent atypia, increased mitotic activity, and invasive features

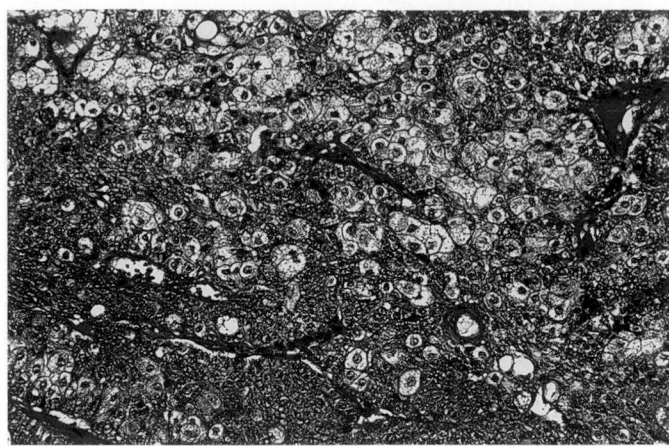

Fig. 4.82 Sebaceous carcinoma. The tumor is well-differentiated but had invasive borders.

(Fig. 4.82). Immunoreactivity for keratin and cytokeratin, EMA, and Leu-M1 is present; CEA and S-100 protein are absent.[407,422] Sebaceous carcinoma shows a greater expression of the Thomsen–Friedenreich (T) antigen than sebaceous adenoma, and it may show reactivity for androgen receptors, a feature that it shares with sebaceous adenomas.[409]

Sebaceous carcinoma should be distinguished from basal cell carcinomas with sebaceous differentiation,[412] and from squamous cell carcinomas accompanied by hydropic changes in the tumor cells.[416] Necrosis and lack of lymphoid cell reaction have been found to be associated with a more aggressive course.[414]

Sebaceous adenoma and carcinoma may be seen as a component of *Muir–Torre syndrome*.[413,417,419] In this condition, multiple cutaneous tumors exhibiting varying degrees of sebaceous and hair follicle differentiation occur in association with multiple internal malignancies.[410,411] The tumors, whether benign or malignant, have a characteristically cystic pattern of growth which should be a clue to the association.[421]

Hair follicles

A myriad of neoplasms, hamartomas, and cysts can develop from the hair follicle. In an exhaustive review of the subject, Headington[425] listed 26 entries, and several additional ones have been described since.[424,426–430] One wonders how useful or sensible it will be to further continue this subdivision, which is largely irrelevant on clinical grounds, as opposed to using a more encompassing term such as *benign trichogenic tumor*.[431] In any event, only the more common and better established varieties of hair follicle tumors will be described here.

Inverted follicular keratosis

The lesions of inverted follicular keratosis occur mostly on the face of elderly patients, the eyelid being a preferred location. Clinically, they present as a papule or nodule, practically always single, usually projecting

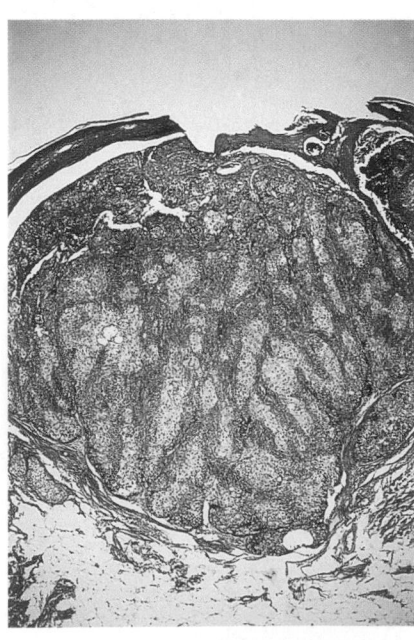

Fig. 4.81 Sebaceous adenoma. The tumor has a distinctly lobular architecture. The light and dark areas correspond to well-differentiated sebaceous cells and generative cells, respectively.

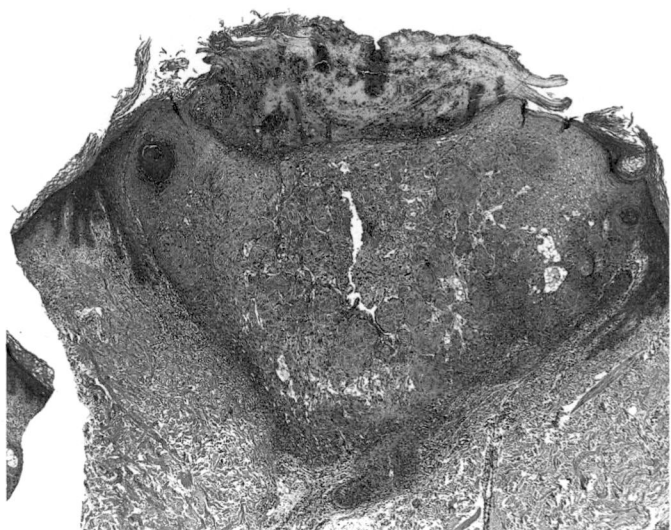

Fig. 4.83 Inverted follicular keratosis. There are numerous "keratotic eddies."

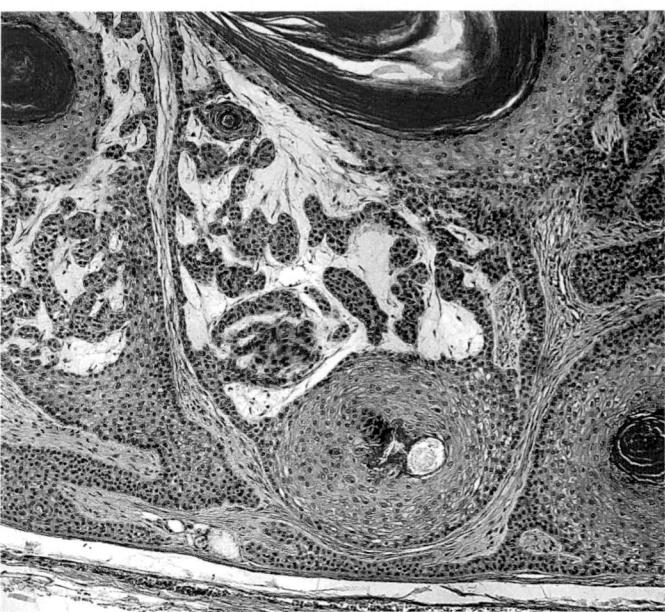

Fig. 4.84 Organoid pattern in trichoepithelioma.

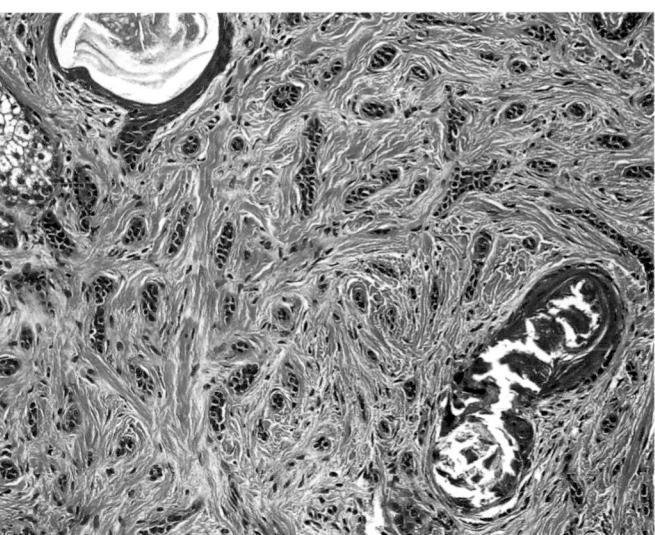

Fig. 4.85 Desmoplastic trichoepithelioma. This benign tumor is not to be confused with basal cell carcinoma.

from the surface. Microscopically, the most distinctive feature is the presence of squamous eddies[434] (Fig. 4.83). They usually have a papillomatous, as well as an acanthotic inverted component. In contrast to keratoacanthoma, the borders are sharply outlined, and inflammation is usually lacking.[432]

The histogenesis and pathogenesis are controversial. Some view it as a unique keratotic lesion of the infundibular portion of the hair follicle (hence the name),[433] whereas others regard it as an irritated form of seborrheic keratosis or verruca vulgaris.[435]

Trichoepithelioma

Trichoepitheliomas are hair follicle tumors of long standing,[439] a good number of which occur in children.[441] They are often multiple, do not ulcerate, and may attain a huge size.[440] Some are seen in a familial setting.[438] Histologically, a stromal element surrounds abortive pilar differentiation (Fig. 4.84). The main differential diagnosis is with basal cell carcinoma, which is histogenetically a closely related tumor; the most helpful features are the frondlike arrangement of the basaloid cells, the presence of epithelial tracts comprising two or more layers of basaloid cells, and the formation of papillary mesenchymal bodies, which represent attempts to form the papillary mesenchyme responsible for hair follicle induction.[436] A variant of this tumor, appropriately known as *desmoplastic trichoepithelioma*, is accompanied by extensive fibrous proliferation that surrounds and distorts the epithelial islands[437] (Fig. 4.85). In contrast with the conventional form, this variant is usually single. Its main differential diagnosis is with the morphea-like form of basal cell carcinoma.[442] Immunostaining for stromalysin-3 (a matrix metalloproteinase) is said to be of help in this regard, in the sense of being always negative in desmoplastic trichoepithelioma and positive in most cases of basal cell carcinoma.[443]

Trichilemmoma

Trichilemmoma (tricholemmoma) is a benign solid tumor that presents as a lobular formation or plate-like growth of glycogen-rich clear cells, often surrounded by palisading and sometimes exhibiting central keratinization (Fig. 4.86). Multiple trichilemmomas are associated with acral keratoses, sclerotic fibromas of skin, papillomas of the oral mucosa, and, occasionally, tumors of the breast, thyroid, and gastrointestinal tract—a condition known as *Cowden's disease* or multiple hamartoma syndrome.[445,446,450]

A *desmoplastic* variety of trichilemmoma that simulates an invasive carcinoma has been described.[447]

Trichilemmal (tricholemmal) carcinoma is a tumor that combines features of trichilemma-type keratinization with atypical features such as brisk mitotic activity,

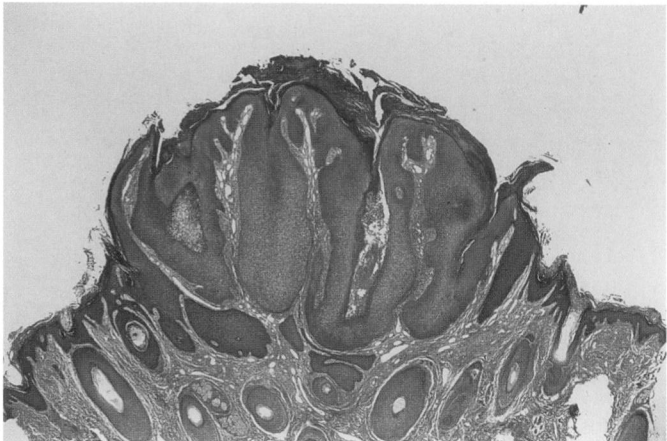

Fig. 4.86 Trichilemmoma. The tumor presents as a lobular growth of glycogen-rich clear cells. (Courtesy of Dr. D. Santa Cruz, St. Louis)

invasion of reticular dermis, and ulceration.[449,451] Clear tumor cells are a conspicuous feature of this neoplasm, and it may well be that some reported cases of "clear cell carcinoma" of the skin belong to this category.[448] The clinical course of trichilemmal carcinoma is very indolent, and the incidence of metastatic behavior is extremely low.[444,452]

Trichofolliculoma

Trichofolliculomas are solitary, nodular, highly organoid hamartomatous lesions that recapitulate the anagen, catagen, and telogen phases of the normal hair follicle. They should be distinguished from trichoepitheliomas and basal cell carcinomas.[455] Their characteristic dilated central follicle is surrounded by proliferating epithelium showing various stages of pilar formation (Fig. 4.87). Merkel cells are often present,[456] as they also are in other hair follicle tumors such as trichoblastoma.[453]

The occurrence of multiple fibrofolliculomas in association with trichodiscomas (another type of benign hair follicle tumor) and acrochordons (fibroepithelial polyps) constitutes a genetically determined syndrome.[454]

Keratoacanthoma

Keratoacanthoma typically presents as a dome-shaped lesion with a central crater filled with keratin (Fig. 4.88). It occurs in males three or four times more frequently than in females. When compared with conventional squamous cell carcinoma of the skin, keratoacanthoma is seen to occur in a somewhat younger population and to have a similar but not identical distribution.[483] The most important microscopic feature is the architecture of the lesion as seen on cross section: overhanging edges, a keratin-filled crater, and hemispheric shape (Fig. 4.89). Cytologic criteria are of little use in the differential diagnosis with conventional squamous cell carcinoma.[465] Most of the epithelium is well differentiated, with abundant ground glass cytoplasm, but nuclear abnormalities and mitotic activity can be prominent. The growing edge is usually of the pushing type, a feature accentuated by the heavy rim of inflammatory cells, in which eosinophils may be prominent. However, in some instances there is extension into the underlying skeletal muscle, perineurial invasion, or even blood vessel invasion.[462,468,471] It should be noted that eosinophilic infiltration can also occur in squamous cell carcinoma and may actually be more frequent in it.[475] Florid proliferation of sweat ducts entrapped by the keratoacanthomas is a common feature of probable reactive nature.

Many special techniques have been used in the differential diagnosis between keratoacanthoma and conventional squamous cell carcinoma. These include

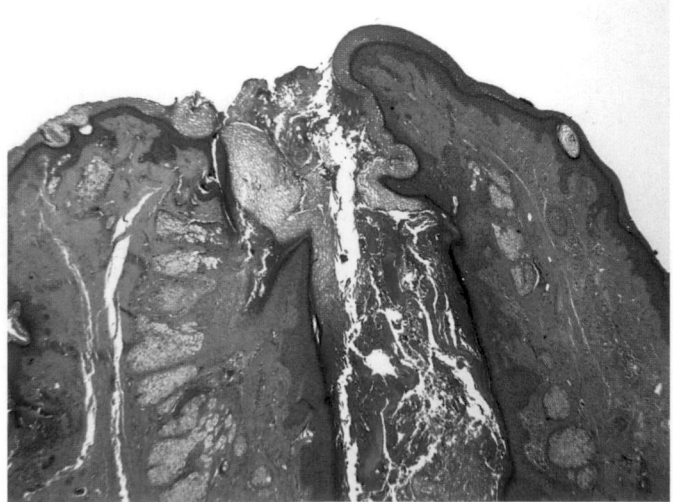

Fig. 4.87 Highly organoid pattern of trichofolliculoma.

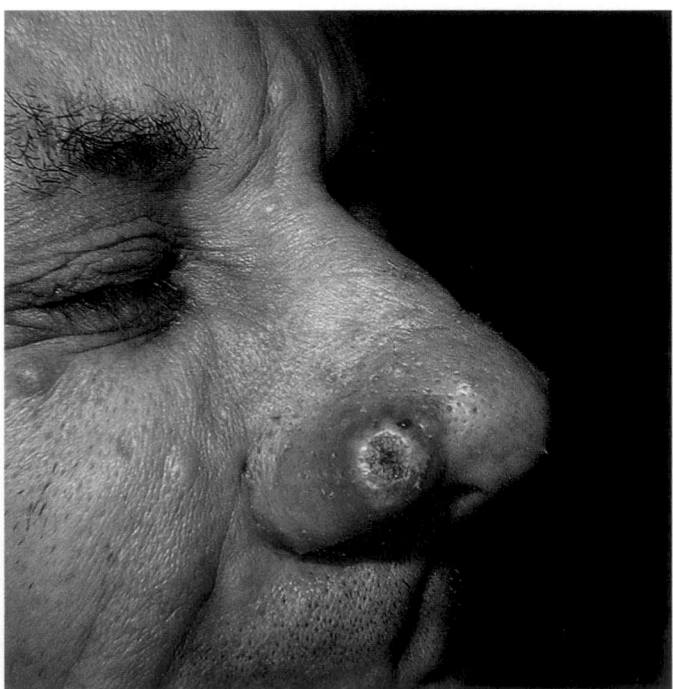

Fig. 4.88 Clinical appearance of keratoacanthoma.

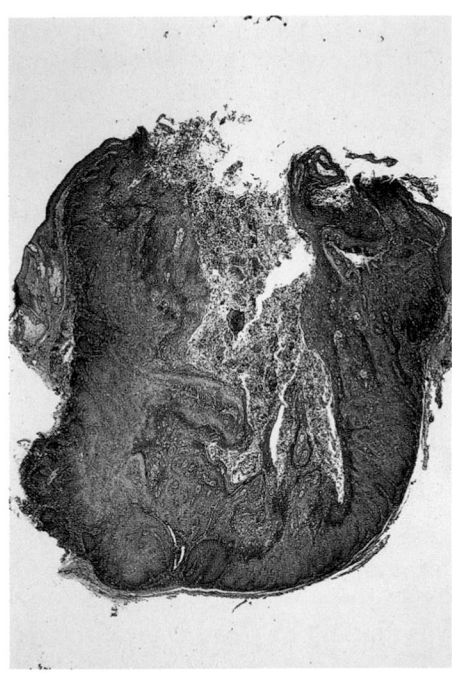

Fig. 4.89 Low-power appearance of keratoacanthoma.

immunohistochemical staining for filaggrin (a histidine-rich protein normally present in the granular and horny layers of the epidermis),[470] transforming growth factor alpha expression,[466] VCAM and ICAM,[476] MIB-1 expression,[459] PCNA distribution,[478] DNA content,[479,481] and p53 expression,[461,474,479] but it is doubtful whether any of these achieves a sharp separation between the two entities (perhaps simply because such a sharp separation does not exist).

Keratoacanthoma is thought to represent a proliferation of the infundibular portion of hair follicles rather than of the epidermis. In its most typical form, it arises from previously normal skin, grows rapidly for 4 to 6 weeks, and then undergoes spontaneous regression over the following 4 to 6 weeks to leave a slightly depressed, annular scar.[460] However, many variations exist. Some lesions grow slowly, some lesions do not regress spontaneously, some develop at the site of previous trauma,[477] and some lesions (referred to as *actinic keratoacanthomas*) are seen in sun-exposed skin in association with typical changes of actinic keratosis.[472,482] Perhaps keratoacanthoma is a pattern of proliferation of the infundibular epithelium rather than a specific entity. Some have been reported in association with inflammatory dermatoses, congenital skin lesions, genetic diseases, and scars. Some patients have numerous eruptive lesions (Gryzbowski type), and others have multiple ulcerating tumors with atypical distribution (Ferguson–Smith type).[469] Some keratoacanthomas may actually represent a subtype of well-differentiated squamous cell carcinomas, as supported by the chromosomal aberrations they exhibit.[463] This would explain the fact that, occasionally, lesions with the characteristic clinical and microscopic features

of keratoacanthoma have been found to grow to huge sizes and/or to metastasize to regional lymph nodes, particularly when the patient's immunity is impaired.[467,480] However, to state that keratoacanthoma is simply a squamous cell carcinoma is to ignore the fact that, in its most typical expression, it shows many clinical and pathologic differences with conventional squamous cell carcinoma. At the very least, it should be regarded as a distinct (?deficient) subtype of squamous cell carcinoma, for the same reasons that bronchioloalveolar carcinoma is regarded as a distinct subtype of pulmonary adenocarcinoma.[458,473,484,485]

Yet another variant of this process is so-called **subungual keratoacanthoma,** thought to arise from the nail matrix, which presents as a rapidly growing mass in the tip of a finger or toe, often associated with a lytic cup-shaped defect of the distal phalanx.[457,464]

Keratinous cyst

Keratinous cysts have been known for many years as sebaceous cysts, a misnomer born of a mistaken gross interpretation of the cyst content and perpetuated by uncritical repetition.[487,491]

Two types of keratinous cyst occur, with occasional hybrid forms. The more common (90%), known as the **epidermal** or **epidermoid type,** is lined by cornified epithelium, has a distinct granular layer, and contains lamellated keratin without calcification (Fig. 4.90). Although some of these cysts (particularly those located in the fingers)[489] result from traumatic inclusion of epidermis—hence the term epidermal inclusion cyst—the majority probably arise from the infundibular portion of hair follicles. A few of these cysts exhibit seborrheic keratosis-like changes in their wall.[492]

The other keratinous cyst is the **pilar** or **trichilemmal** type[488,490,491] (Fig. 4.91). It occurs preferentially on the scalp and is microscopically characterized by a trichilemmal type of keratinization, i.e., sudden keratinization without the formation of a granular layer and an uneven

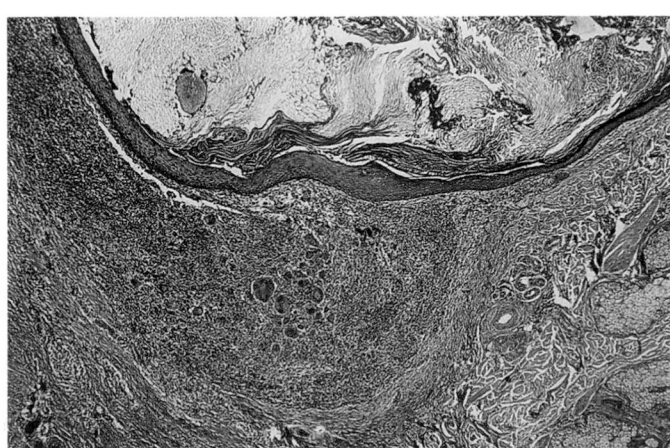

Fig. 4.90 Keratinous cyst of epidermal type with secondary inflammation.

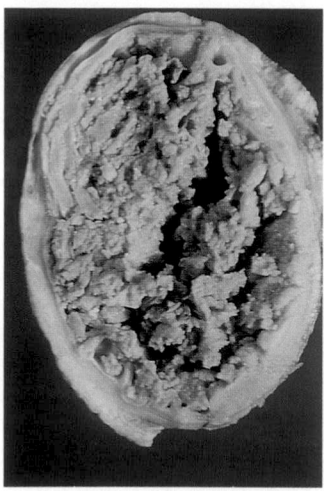

Fig. 4.91 Gross appearance of keratinous cyst of trichilemmal type. Grumous material composed of pilar-type keratin occupies the lumen.

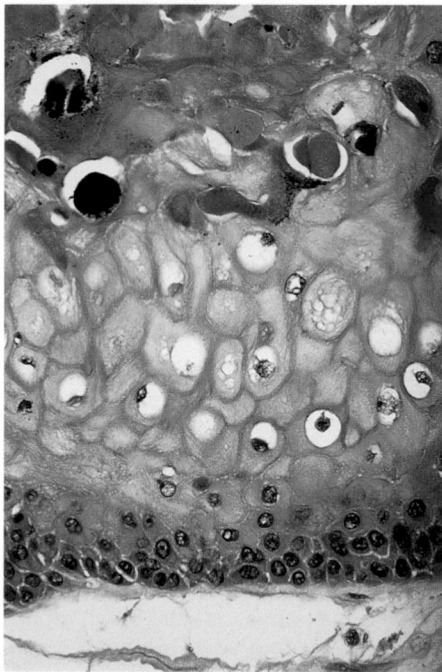

Fig. 4.92 Keratinous cyst of pilar type showing trichilemmal pattern of keratinization.

interphase between the keratinized and nonkeratinized cells (Fig. 4.92). The keratin inside the cyst is not lamellated, some of the nuclei are retained, and focal calcification is frequent. Ultrastructural and immunohistochemical studies also support a trichilemmal derivation for this lesion.[486]

HPV (usually 57 or 60) has been found in cases of keratinous cysts of palmoplantar and other locations, suggesting that it may play an etiologic role.[487a]

Other cutaneous cysts

Several other varieties of cutaneous cysts occur, sometimes in combination.[493,495,504] Although some of them are not of hair follicle derivation, they are listed here for comparison purposes.

1 **Dermoid cyst.** These are microscopically similar in most respects to keratinous cysts of the epidermal type except for the fact that they contain hair adnexa in their wall opening into the cavity.[510] Most of them are found in the face of children along lines of embryonic closure.

2 **Steatocystoma.** This is lined by a thin layer of stratified squamous epithelium resembling the ductal portion of a sebaceous gland; lobules of sebaceous glands and small hair follicles are present. It may occur as a solitary lesion,[496] as multiple lesions on the face,[507] or in the more common disseminated form known as *steatocystoma multiplex*.[497,503]

3 **Hydrocystoma** (solitary or multiple, usually on the face) and **apocrine cystadenoma**. Both of these are lined by a layer of sweat duct-like epithelium, which in some of the lesions has apocrine features.[498,505]

4 **Cutaneous ciliated cyst (cystadenoma).** This is usually seen in the extremities of young females shortly after puberty and is thought by some to be of müllerian derivation.[494,500,501] However, some cases have been described in males.[509]

5 **Vellus hair cyst.** This presents as small, multiple, eruptive cysts over the chest wall and extremities of young individuals. It is lined by a layer of flattened, follicular sheath epithelium and contains numerous vellus hairs and soft keratinous material.[499]

6 **Pigmented follicular cyst.** This is a hyperpigmented lesion with epidermal-type keratinization, which contains laminated keratin, many pigmented hair shafts, and some growing hair follicles.[506]

7 **So-called "bronchogenic cyst."** This is usually discovered at birth or soon thereafter in the suprasternal notch.[502] The lining is made up of pseudostratified columnar ciliated epithelium. Despite its name, the lesion is probably of branchial cleft derivation rather than of bronchial origin.[508]

8 **Cutaneous metaplastic synovial cyst.** This is discussed on p. 203.

Warty dyskeratoma

Warty dyskeratoma (isolated follicular keratosis) is a small papulonodular lesion usually occurring in sun-exposed skin and characterized microscopically by a peculiar follicular acantholysis and dyskeratosis. Despite the microscopic similarities with Darier's disease, it does not represent an isolated manifestation of the latter (which is not a follicle-based process). Instead, it is probably a primary proliferative process of hair follicles, which has been viewed either as the follicular counterpart of actinic keratosis (isolated follicular keratosis) or as a sui generis follicular neoplasm (follicular dyskeratoma).[511]

Pilar tumor (proliferating trichilemmal cyst)

Pilar tumor represents the neoplastic counterpart of the pilar (trichilemmal) cyst, and it therefore exhibits the same predilection for the scalp and base of neck of women.[513,516,519] All types of transitional forms can be found between the ordinary pilar cyst and the full-blown pilar tumor. In some instances the pilar tumor presents as a mural nodule in a lesion having otherwise the appearance of a pilar cyst, and in others the two lesions coexist in the same individual.[515] The overlying epidermis is usually involved, but in some cases the lesion opens into the surface. Pilar tumor can reach huge proportions[521] (Fig. 4.93). In the past, some of these lesions have been misinterpreted as squamous cell carcinomas arising from sebaceous cysts.

Microscopically, pilar tumors have a predominantly solid appearance and pushing borders. Occasionally, they open into the skin surface. Interlacing bands of squamous epithelium exhibiting trichilemma-type keratinization are characteristic (Fig. 4.94). Nuclear atypia may be prominent, and some irregularities at the interphase between epithelium and stroma can be observed. Sometimes focal invasion of the stroma is identified.[518] This lesion is neoplastic rather than hyperplastic, a hypothesis supported by the finding of nondiploid DNA content in some of the cases.[524] The behavior is generally benign; several instances of local recurrence have been reported, but metastases are exceptionally rare.[513,517,522] The few well-documented instances of metastases have occurred in tumors with clear-cut malignant microscopic features.[512,523] The malignant component may have the appearance of a focal trichilemmal carcinoma or, exceptionally, a spindle cell (sarcomatoid) carcinoma.[514,520,525]

Pilomatrixoma

Pilomatrixoma (pilomatricoma), formerly known as calcified epithelioma of Malherbe, is a nodular, subepidermal benign tumor arising from the hair matrix (Fig. 4.95). It occurs predominantly in children and young adults, and most of the cases are located on the head, neck, and upper extremities.[527] Microscopically, it is composed of solid nests of small basaloid cells that may lead to a mistaken diagnosis of basal cell carcinoma,[534] particularly on cytologic examination.[540,542] The key feature is the fact that these basaloid cells undergo abrupt keratinization, leading to the formation of "ghost" and "shadow" cells (Fig. 4.96). Foreign body reaction, calcification, and ossification are common secondary events. This may be accompanied by extramedullary hematopoiesis.[532] Transepidermal elimination or perforation can occur.[537] The histochemical, immunohistochemical, and ultrastructural features are in keeping with an origin from the hair matrix.[531,533,536,541] It should be remarked that focal features of hair matrix differentiation can sometimes be seen in lesions other than pilomatrixoma.[535]

Cases of pilomatrixoma with atypical histologic features and a tendency for local invasiveness and local recurrence have been designated as aggressive pilomatrixomas.[537,543] *Malignant pilomatrixoma* (pilomatrix

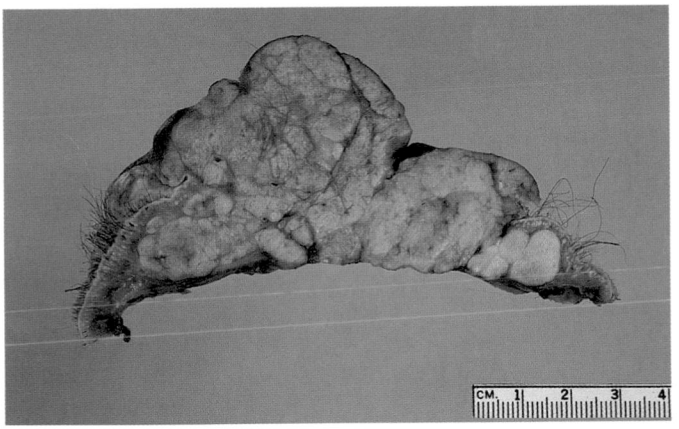

Fig. 4.93 Cut surface of a pilar tumor. It has a multinodular appearance, with both an exophytic and an endophytic component.

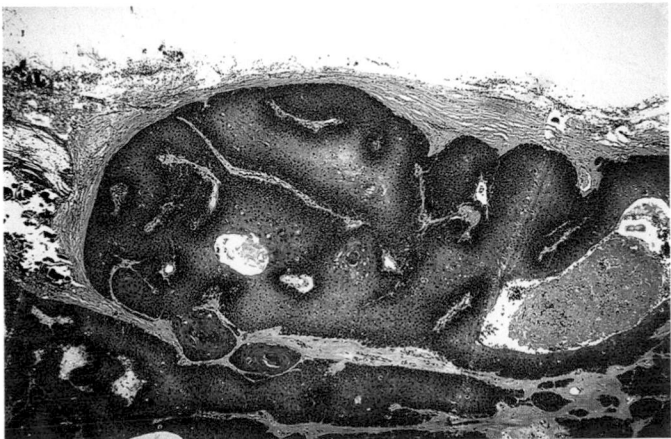

Fig. 4.94 Low-power appearance of pilar tumor. The lobulated contour is characteristic.

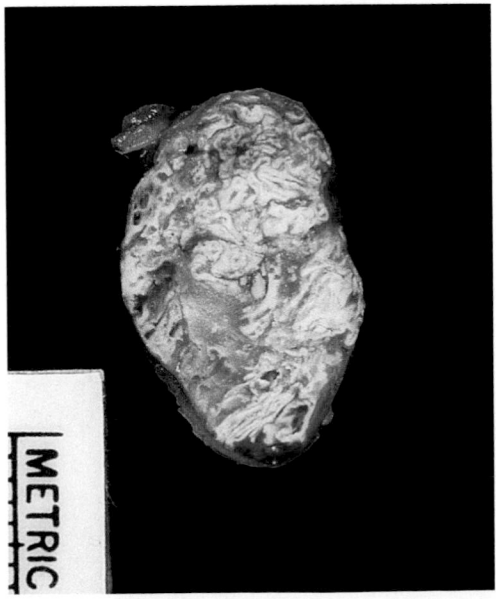

Fig. 4.95 Appearance of pilomatrixoma.

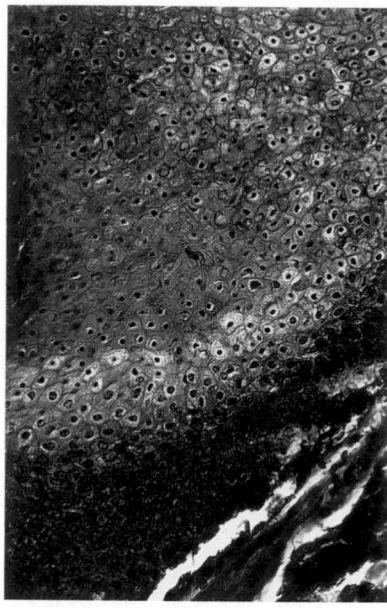

Fig. 4.96 Microscopic appearance of pilomatrixoma. The basal cells keratinize, as does cortex of hair without granular layer, and produce "ghost" cells.

carcinoma) exhibits cytologic atypia, an infiltrating border, transitions to squamous cells, clear cells, necrosis, and mitoses.[530] Sarcomatoid features may be present.[529] Local recurrence is common, and metastases to distant sites can occur.[526,528,538,539,544]

Melanocytes

Melanocytes are neural crest-derived cells located in the basal layer of skin, hair follicles, most squamous-covered mucosal membranes, leptomeninges, and several other sites. Their function is to produce an insoluble pigment known as *melanin*, using tyrosine as a substrate, and to transfer this product through the process of cytocrinia to the adjacent epithelial cells. The neuroectodermal origin of melanocytes, proposed many years ago by Masson and others,[554] has been proved by a variety of techniques, among which the chick–quail chimera model of LeDouarin is the most elegant and convincing.[551]

The ratio of melanocytes to basal keratinocytes varies from 1:4 to 1:10 depending on the site of the body. Racial differences in skin pigmentation are due to differences in the amount of melanin contained in the keratinocytes rather than the number of melanocytes. The functional unit composed of a melanocyte and the adjacent keratinocytes receiving melanin from it is referred to as the *epidermal melanin unit*.

Normal melanocytes with scant pigment appear as pale cells in routinely stained sections (hence the former name "Masson's clear cells"), but other intraepidermal clear cells are of keratinocytic nature.[547] Melanocytes possess slender cytoplasmic processes (dendrites) that emanate from the cell body and extend between keratinocytes; these become particularly apparent when containing increased melanin pigment through either increased production or a block in the transfer mechanism.

Melanocytes are generally positive for melanin stains (such as the Fontana–Masson silver stain), tyrosinase, DOPA reaction, S-100 protein, NSE, Mart-1 (A103), microphthalmia transcription factor, and vimentin; the intensity of these reactions shows marked variability, possibly depending on the functional status of the cell.[546,549,550,553] Stains for neurofilaments and glial fibrillary acidic protein are negative.[555] Stains for HMB-45 are generally negative in normal resting melanocytes but positive in activated melanocytes, particularly those of malignant melanoma (see p. 170).[545,558] Keratin is another marker that is consistently absent in normal melanocytes but sometimes expressed in their neoplastic counterparts (see p. 170). The fact that normal melanocytes show strong immunoreactivity for the *bcl*-2 proto-oncogene product has been recorded.[559] This is also expressed in benign nevi but less commonly in malignant melanomas.[556,557]

Ultrastructurally, the hallmark of the melanocyte is the melanin-synthesizing organelle known as the *melanosome*. The development of this Golgi-derived structure, which has a specific appearance in its fully developed form because of the striated appearance of its electron-dense content, is preceded by the ultrastructurally nonspecific premelanosome and followed by the mature melanin granule.

The term *melanocyte* should be reserved for the mature melanin-forming cell. Its immature counterpart is the *melanoblast*. Dermal macrophages with phagocytosed melanin are melanophages. The *melanophore* is a melanin-containing "contractile cell" found in amphibians.[548] *Nevus cell* or *nevocyte* are terms that have been traditionally used for the cells of benign ordinary nevi; some authors regard them as nothing but melanocytes and have suggested abandoning the term altogether.[552]

Nevi

The word nevus (L. *naevus*, birthmark) can be properly applied to any circumscribed growth of the skin of congenital origin. However, it is usually used as a synonym for mole (L. *moles*, a shapeless mass) to designate a localized benign abnormality of the melanocytic system. The adjectives *melanocytic* (which we prefer), *nevocellular*, and *pigmented* refer specifically to this type of nevus.

Melanocytic nevi are usually acquired, in the sense that they become clinically apparent after the first year of life. Most of them will appear between the second and sixth years, and nearly all will have become manifest by the age of 20 years. They follow a rather predictable evolution, which only rarely is upset by some dramatic event, such as spontaneous resolution, activation, or malignant transformation.[561] Their proliferative activity roughly correlates with the age of the patient.[565a] Every Caucasian person has a variable number of nevi, the average being between 20 and 30.[566] Their distribution frequency is different from that of malignant melanoma. They are much more common in the skin of the head, neck, and trunk, whereas a high percentage of malignant melanomas occur in the lower extremities. Nevi of every conceivable size, shape, and degree of pigmentation occur, and they may be more or less hairy. Nevi have been variously classified, but it is best to divide them according to the location of the melanocytes inasmuch as their position bears a definite relationship to the likelihood of malignant transformation.

Melanocytic nevi straddle the fence between malformation and neoplasia. Cellular blue nevi and Spitz nevi have morphologic and behavioral features consistent with a true neoplastic process, whereas the usual compound nevus has such a distinctive organoid configuration (with adnexal participation) as to strongly suggest a developmental abnormality, perhaps related to atavistic structures such as the tactile corpuscles of reptiles.[565] However, the finding that these lesions are clonal and that they exhibit loss of heterozygosity speaks in favor of a neoplastic nature.[562,567] Masson suggested that the ordinary compound mole has a dual origin from intraepidermal melanoblasts (some of which become intradermal) and dermal Schwann cells.[568,569] Many ultrastructural, histochemical, immunohistochemical, and experimental studies support his proposal that the cells from the upper portion of compound nevi have melanocytic properties, whereas those in the deep portion have features strongly suggesting differentiation toward specialized peripheral nerve structures (not necessarily schwannian related).[560,564,570]

The overwhelming majority of nevi are located in the skin, but they can also be found in any mucosal membrane covered by squamous epithelium (see respective sections). Clusters of benign nevus cells can also be seen in the capsule of a lymph node, the axillary region being the most common location.[563,571] These nests, which do not penetrate into the node itself, should not be confused with metastatic malignant melanoma, a mistake particularly likely to occur when they are found in specimens from axillary lymphadenectomy performed because of cutaneous melanoma (see Chapter 21).

Junctional, intradermal, and compound nevi
Ordinary nevi are classified according to the location of the nevus cells in relation to the major epidermal and dermal landmarks. **Junctional nevus** is defined as a nevus in which the melanocytic proliferation is restricted to the basal portion of the epidermis ("junctional" area). Nevi of the palms and soles are nearly always of the junctional type,[578] with most of the intraepidermal melanocytes concentrated in the skin furrows.[587] Grossly, junctional nevus is flat or slightly elevated, nonhairy, and fawn colored. Microscopically, it is characterized by the presence of melanocytic nests ("theques") on the epider-

mal side of the dermoepidermal junction (Fig. 4.97). Malignant melanomas may arise from this lesion.

Lentigo simplex is generally regarded as the first phase in the evolution of common nevi ("*nevi incipientes*") and therefore a precursor of junctional nevus. It consists of a proliferation of melanocytes in the epidermal basal layer, and it differs from junctional nevus in that the melanocytes are individually arranged rather than in theques. Multiple lentigines occur in Peutz–Jeghers syndrome, centrofacial lentiginosis, Moynahan's syndrome, LEOPARD syndrome, Carney's syndrome, and xeroderma pigmentosum.[584]

Intradermal nevus is the term given to a nevus in which all the melanocytes are in the dermis. This is the common adult type of nevus. It may be papillomatous, pedunculated, or flat, and it is often hairy. Microscopically, small nests or bundles of melanocytes are seen in the upper dermis, with a tendency to concentrate around pilosebaceous units. The degree of pigmentation and cellularity varies widely. The lower half of the lesion tends to be less cellular and less pigmented, and is composed of spindle cells with fibrillary cytoplasm arranged in bundles.[582] Sometimes, structures resembling tactile (Wagner–Meissner) corpuscles are present. Although these areas are immunohistochemically different from neurofibromas,[579] we favor the interpretation that they represent the expression of the neural component of the nevus; it is hard for us to dismiss these highly organoid structures as simply the result of atrophy, as others have done.[585] Occasionally, a storiform pattern of growth is present in this deep portion, establishing a link—at least on morphologic grounds—with the dermal tumor known as storiform neurofibroma.[572] Multinucleated melanocytes can be seen scattered throughout the nevus, particularly in the upper half; many of these cells have a characteristic "mulberry" shape. Ultrastructurally and immunohistochemically, the intradermal nevus cells are surrounded by basement membrane components.[586,591]

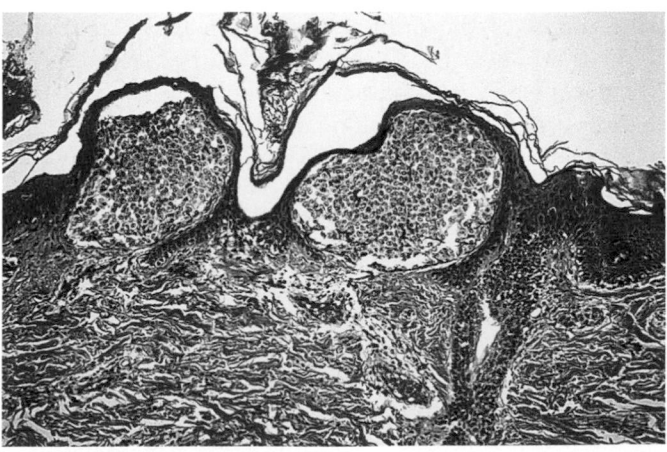

Fig. 4.97 Typical junctional nevus. Two large theques of melanocytes expand the basal layer of the epidermis.

Malignant melanomas practically never arise from intradermal nevi, although a few convincing examples are on record.[589]

Compound nevus combines the features of the junctional and intradermal types, i.e., it has both an epidermal and a dermal component. The percentage of nevi with junctional changes decreases as the age of the patient increases.[588] As for the other types of nevi, the amount of melanin deposition is highly variable and sometimes very abundant (*hypermelanotic nevus*)[575]; as a general rule, it is concentrated in the superficial half of the lesion, particularly the intraepidermal portion. As with other nevi, lymphocytes and other mononuclear cells may be seen at the base of the lesion[573]; they tend to be in clusters rather than exhibiting the bandlike quality more commonly seen in melanoma.

The microscopic appearance of nevi shows some interesting variations depending on the site in which they occur. Nevi of the palms and soles tend to remain junctional throughout life. Nevi of the scalp often exhibit a prominent neural component. Nevi located on the vulvar skin (vulvar or genital nevi) tend to have larger, more irregularly shaped, and more irregular theques than those located elsewhere, and they have a tendency to be accompanied by lentiginous melanocytic hyperplasia; because of these features, they can be misdiagnosed as malignant melanomas.[574]

Many morphologic variations have been observed in otherwise typical compound or intradermal nevi. These include the presence of marked sclerosis (*desmoplastic* or *sclerotic nevus*),[580] nodular myxoid changes,[583] amyloid deposition, elastosis, and metaplastic bone in the stroma; folliculitis and abscess formation; association with keratinous cysts[576] and psammoma bodies; cytoplasmic vacuolization (sometimes resulting in lipoblast-like cells); oncocytic changes[581]; and eczematous or focal acantholytic keratotic changes in the overlying epidermis.[577,590]

Blue, cellular, and epithelioid blue nevi

Blue nevus of the ordinary type is usually small and located in the head, neck, or upper extremity.[599] Microscopically, it is characterized by an ill-defined deep dermal proliferation of elongated and/or dendritic dermal melanocytes, sometimes extending into the subcutis. Melanin pigment is usually abundant (Fig. 4.98). There is a band of uninvolved dermis between the epidermis and the lesion, and junctional activity is consistently absent. Blue nevi are sometimes misdiagnosed as benign fibrous histiocytomas because the melanin present in them is misinterpreted as hemosiderin. They are positive for melanin stains, S-100 protein, and all other melanocytic stains, including HMB-45.[618]

Blue nevi have also been reported in the sclera, hard palate,[602] breast, vagina, cervix,[598] prostate,[604] spermatic cord, and lymph nodes.[597] The microscopic appearance of

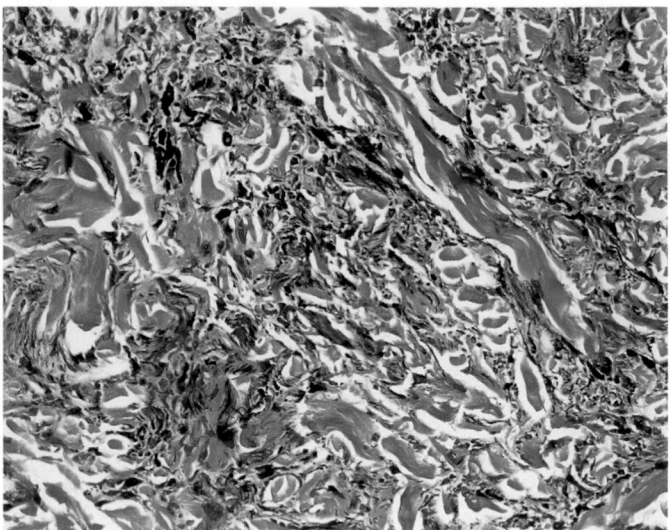

Fig. 4.98 Blue nevus of the ordinary type. The cells are spindle-shaped and heavily pigmented.

the cells of blue nevi and their distribution are so reminiscent of those seen in the pigmented cells of reptiles as to suggest the possibility that they represent atavistic structures rather than true neoplasms, a hypothesis that has also been advanced for ordinary nevi (see p. 154).

The differential diagnosis of blue nevus includes dermatofibrosarcoma (if the melanin pigment is mistaken for hemosiderin) and—more importantly—metastatic melanoma from the skin or eye, which can simulate it closely.[593,622]

Cellular blue nevus is a distinctive variety of blue nevus, often clinically suspected of being malignant because of its large size and intense pigmentation.[607,616] The most common locations are the buttock and sacrococcygeal areas; less common sites include the scalp, face, and dorsa of hands and feet.[616] Microscopically, these lesions are extremely cellular, hence their name. Extension into the subcutis is the rule, and pigment can be easily found. They differ microscopically from malignant melanomas by the absence of junctional activity, epidermal invasion, peripheral inflammation, and necrosis; the presence of pushing margins, biphasic pattern, fasciculation, and neuroid structures; the inconspicuousness of the nucleoli; and the relative lack of atypia and mitotic figures[616] (Fig. 4.99).

Morphologic variations that cellular blue nevi can exhibit on occasion include the presence of a prominent cellular stroma between the tumor nests (*desmoplastic cellular blue nevus*),[608] focal balloon cell change,[613] and paucity of pigmentation (*amelanotic cellular blue nevus*).[624]

Immunohistochemically, cellular blue nevi are positive for S-100 protein, Melan-A, and HMB-45. Some congenital cellular blue nevi have also been found to be reactive for CD34.[617]

The behavior of cellular blue nevus is nearly always benign, but a few cases with local recurrence or

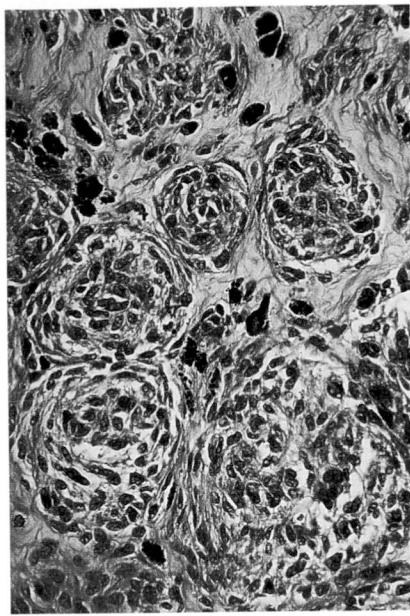 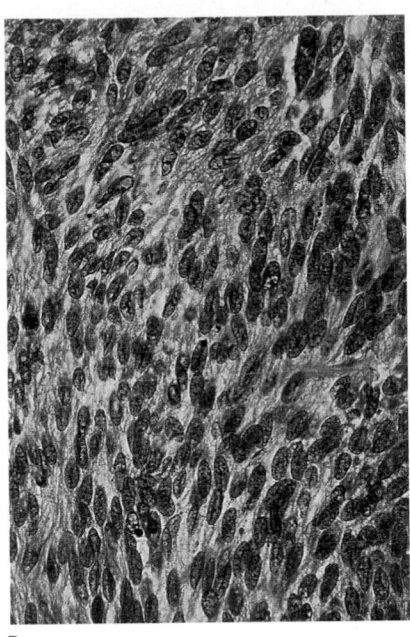

Fig. 4.99 Large cellular blue nevus. **A**, A distinct nesting pattern is present, with most of the melanin being located in macrophages situated in the intervening stroma. **B**, Numerous oval to spindle tumor cells with indistinct nucleoli. There is no mitotic activity.

involvement of regional lymph nodes have been documented.[616] However, even these patients are cured by excision of the primary lesion and involved nodes, in the sense that the disease does not progress further.

These cases should be distinguished from malignant melanoma arising from cellular blue nevus (I have seen two such cases in the breast) and from a type of malignant tumor that has most of the morphologic features of cellular blue nevus but that exhibits a malignant behavior.[595,600,611,619] The latter, which has also been referred to as *blue melanoma*, is more common in the scalp and foot (especially heel). Microscopic features that should raise this possibility in a lesion with the architectural features of a cellular blue nevus are marked nuclear atypia, numerous mitoses, atypical mitoses, necrosis (sometimes with palisading at the edges), and the occurrence of epithelioid tumor cells.[600,605] It has been claimed that malignant blue nevi have higher AgNOR counts and higher proliferative activity (as measured by PCNA) than cellular blue nevi.[614]

Cellular blue nevi with architectural and/or cytologic atypia but not sufficient to be placed in one of the two former malignant categories have been noncommittally designated as *atypical*.[620] In a series of 9 cases, there were no recurrences or metastases, indicating that a conservative diagnostic and therapeutic approach is justified for these morphologically borderline lesions.

Both ordinary and cellular blue nevi are usually immunoreactive for S-100 protein, HMB-45, and the other melanocytic markers,[618,623] but exceptions occur.[596]

Variations on the theme of either ordinary or cellular blue nevus include cases forming large plaques up to 17 cm in diameter,[621] cases with a target-like appearance,[592] and cases in which there is a second component of ordinary type (junctional, compound, or intradermal).

The latter represents the most common type of *combined nevi*.[606,615]

Epithelioid blue nevus is a multicentric familial form of blue nevus that is part of the Carney complex together with cardiac myxoma, psammomatous melanotic schwannoma, and other abnormalities. Microscopically, these nevi are heavily pigmented, poorly circumscribed dermal lesions composed of two types of melanocytes: one intensely pigmented and globular, and the other lightly pigmented, polygonal, and spindle.[594] Epithelioid blue nevi can also be seen outside the Carney complex,[610,612] and their status as a distinct subtype of blue nevus has been questioned.[601]

* * *

Other benign skin lesions containing deeply seated dendritic melanocytes include *Mongolian spot* (an ill-defined area of bluish discoloration, up to several centimeters in size, usually in the lumbosacral region), *Ota's nevus* (located in the ophthalmomaxillary area), *Ito's nevus* (located in the shoulder region), and *Sun's nevus* (a bilateral speckled pigmentation of the zygomatic region in Chinese people).[603,609]

Spitz nevus and related nevi

Spitz nevus (spindle and/or epithelioid cell nevus) characteristically occurs before puberty, but it may also appear in adult life.[632,639] The most typical presentation is in the form of a raised, pink or red nodule in the skin of the face. It may be multiple, either in a clustered (agminate) or disseminated fashion[634]; this should not be mistaken for the satellite lesions of malignant melanoma.

Microscopically, most Spitz nevi are of the compound type, with a prominent intraepidermal component. About 5% to 10% are junctional, and 20% or more are intradermal.[641,642] They are composed of spindle cells, epithelioid cells, or an admixture of both.

The spindle cell variant is characterized by cigar-shaped cells with large nuclei and prominent nucleoli (Fig. 4.100). The cells of the epithelioid type have similar nuclei and a large, polygonal cytoplasm with distinct borders (Fig. 4.101). A variant of the latter is a multi-nucleated giant melanocyte containing up to 10 or 20 nuclei. Mitoses are found in approximately half of the cases,[651,654] but atypical mitoses are exceptional. Pigmentation is usually scanty, but a deeply pigmented variant (often of recent onset and located on the proximal extremities of young adults) exists; this is referred to as *pigmented spindle cell nevus* (Reed's nevus) and is regarded by some as a separate entity from Spitz nevus[626,644,648] (Fig. 4.102).

Sometimes, Spitz nevi of predominantly dermal location are accompanied by an extensive stromal desmoplasia, which encircles the individual cells and simulates an invasive pattern (*desmoplastic Spitz nevus*).[627] This feature is more commonly seen in adults, and this adds to the diagnostic difficulty.[642] Other features occasionally present in Spitz nevi are predominantly intraepidermal growth (*pagetoid Spitz nevus*),[630] invasion of lymph vessels,[637] florid pseudoepitheliomatous hyperplasia,[645] "tubular" pattern of growth,[629] plexiform pattern of growth (*plexiform Spitz nevus*),[630a,649] halo reaction,[636] and prominent vasculature (*angiomatoid Spitz nevus*)[631] (Fig. 4.103). Features that favor a diagnosis of Spitz nevus over one of malignant melanoma are symmetric shape; sharp lateral demarcation; maturation in depth; arrangement of the spindle cells perpendicularly to the skin surface; presence of tadpole and multinucleated giant cells; lack of upward epidermal spread (but see above); presence of telangiectasia, edema, and fibrosis; presence of eosinophilic hyaline bodies along the dermoepidermal junction thought to be made of basement membrane material (Kamino's bodies); and lack of ulceration.[628,643,646,652,653] In addition, the cytoplasm of

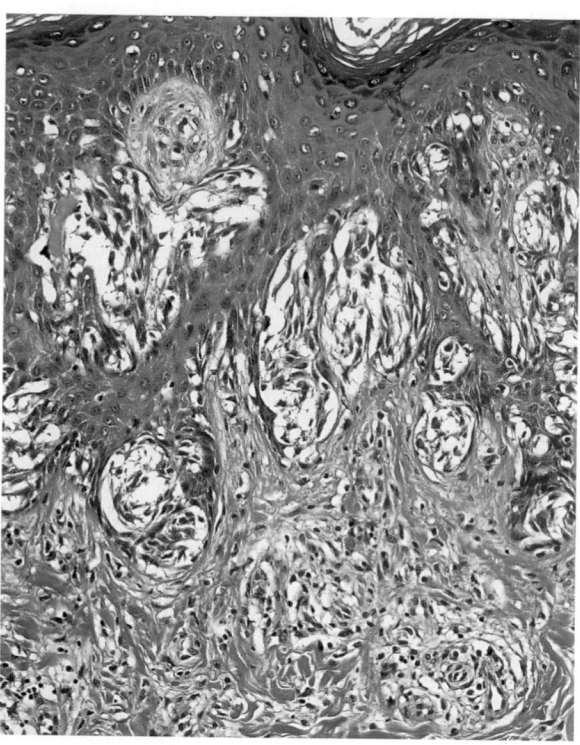

Fig. 4.100 Spitz nevus of spindle cell type. This example is predominantly junctional in location.

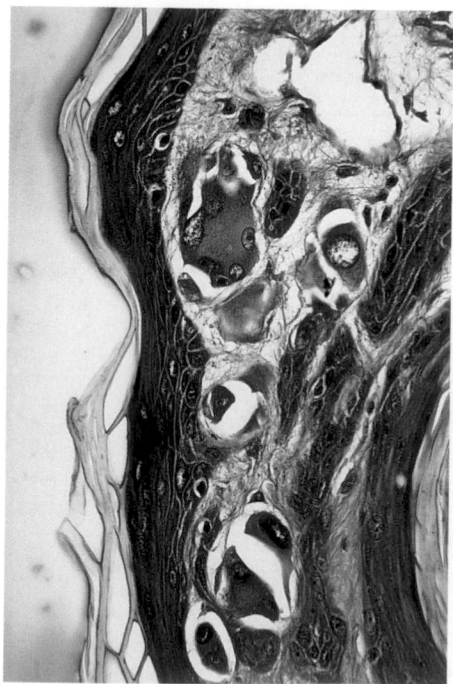

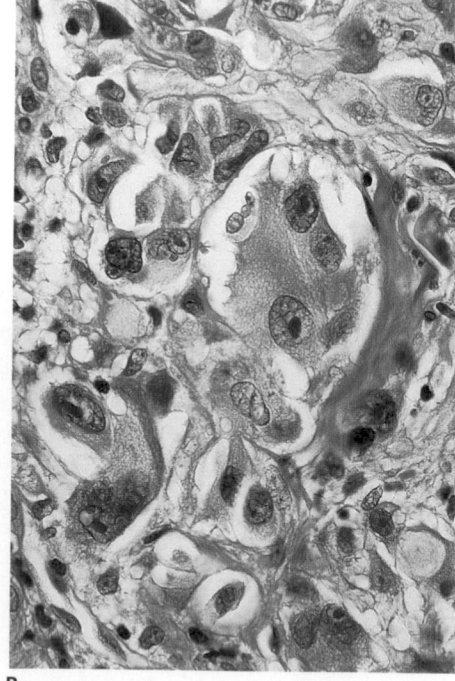

Fig. 4.101 A and **B,** Spitz nevus of epithelioid type. The tumor cells feature large size, polygonal shape, occasional multinucleation, and a strongly eosinophilic cytoplasm.

A

B

benign epithelioid nevi has a homogeneous acidophilic ground glass appearance, whereas that of melanoma cells tends to be more irregular in configuration and staining reaction. Unfortunately, immunohistochemical stains have proved of very little value in this important differential diagnosis, except for a recent claim (in urgent need of confirmation) concerning S100A6 protein expression.[638,643a]

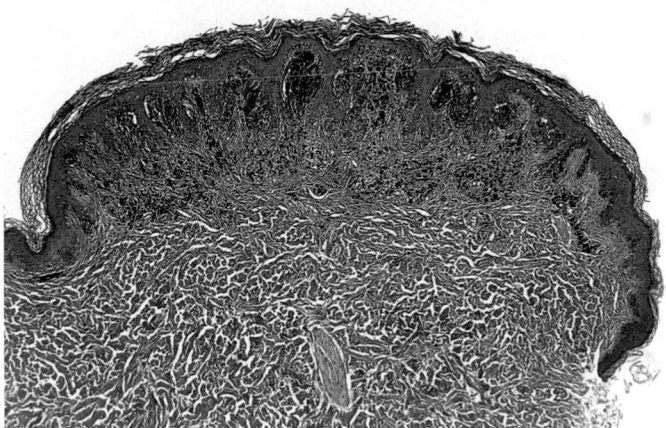

Fig. 4.102 Reed nevus. The tumor is heavily pigmented, in contrast to the usual type of Spitz nevus.

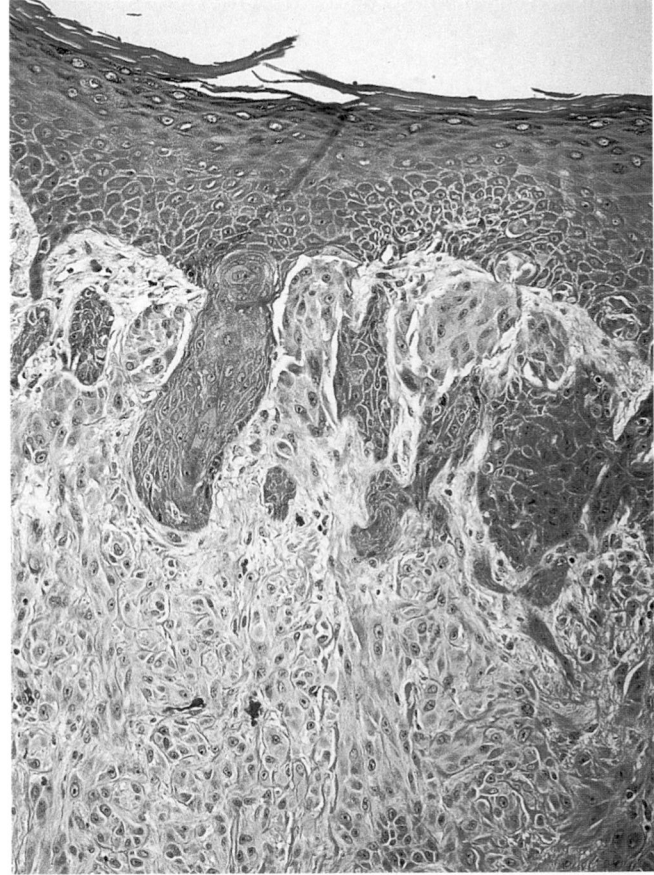

Fig. 4.103 Spitz nevus of the spindle cell type associated with pseudoepitheliomatous hyperplasia.

The behavior of Spitz nevi is almost uniformly benign, but local recurrences may result from incomplete excision; these may show greater architectural irregularities than the original lesion.[635] In addition, several cases of Spitz nevi associated with regional lymph node involvement have been reported.[647,653] These "malignant Spitz nevi" tend to be large and deep, with pushing penetration of the dermis and subcutis. None of the patients reported by Smith et al.[647] went on to develop distant disease. However, we have seen a clinically and histologically typical case of Spitz nevus in the cheek of a young girl previously affected by acute leukemia that recurred locally, then metastasized to a regional node, and eventually led to widespread metastases and death.[633]

The argument as to whether malignant Spitz tumor exists or not is largely semantic. There is no question—as the cases described above illustrate—that, on occasion, cutaneous melanocytic tumors fulfilling the morphologic features of Spitz tumor behave in a malignant fashion. Whether one calls them malignant Spitz tumors or Spitz-type malignant melanomas is immaterial, but to call them malignant melanomas without a qualifier does not fully convey the clinicopathologic identity of this rare but important entity. In this scheme, and following a reasoning similar to that adopted for cellular blue nevus (see previous section), Spitz nevi that show worrisome microscopic features not sufficient to place them in a straightforward malignant category could be designated as *atypical*, while fully acknowledging the subjective nature of this evaluation.[625] In two series of cases of diagnostically controversial lesions with spitzoid features in which sentinel lymph node biopsy was carried out, metastatic deposits were found in 44% and 50% of them, respectively; these distressingly high figures indicate the need for sentinel node biopsy under these circumstances.[640,650]

Congenital nevus

Congenital nevus differs from the more common acquired variety because of its generally larger size (Fig. 4.104); tendency to involve the reticular dermis and subcutaneous tissue; single cell permeation of dermal collagen bundles; and involvement of skin adnexa, arrector pili muscles, nerves, and vessels.[669,673,675] However, there are too many exceptions to allow for an absolute distinction based on microscopic criteria alone.[669] Neuroid differentiation, such as the formation of Wagner–Meissner-like corpuscles, is common. The term *neuronevus* has been applied to congenital (and some acquired) nevi in which this feature is particularly prominent. When looking at these formations, one marvels at the fact that some authors deny the participation of specialized peripheral nerve structures in the formation of these lesions. The arrangement of round nevus cells in and around vessel walls may simulate the appearance of a glomus tumor[662] (Fig. 4.105). When removed a few months after birth, these congenital nevi can show pagetoid intraepidermal proliferation of melanocytes, simulating the appearance of superficially spreading melanoma.[663,664] Some congenital nevi also resemble melanoma at the clinical level, especially when located in acral sites[657] or when growing in a very rapid fashion.[656]

Giant congenital nevus is a variant of congenital nevus characterized by its extensive size, its surface area being by definition 144 cm² or larger. It has a tendency to distribute along a dermatome and often has a "bathing trunk" or "garment" configuration. It is also referred to as giant pigmented nevus and giant hairy nevus. It may involve a whole extremity, the entire scalp, and most of the trunk and even extend into the placenta.[658] It is often associated with smaller ("satellite") nevi and with nevi in mucosal membranes.[671] When in the scalp, it may result in convoluted folds of greatly thickened skin; this is known as cerebriform congenital nevus and is the usual histologic substratum of so-called "cutis verticis gyrata."[660] Its microscopic appearance is qualitatively similar to that of the more common (non-giant) congenital nevus; occasionally, it has a component of pigmented large epithelioid cells similar to those seen in epithelioid blue nevus.[666]

Giant congenital nevus is sometimes associated with meningeal or cerebral melanosis (so-called "neurocutaneous melanosis"),[661,674] or it may occur as a component of melanophakomatosis, together with numerous satellite nevi. It may give rise to malignant melanoma of the skin or central nervous system and to related malignant neuroectodermal tumors with a variety of patterns, including malignant peripheral nerve sheath tumor, so-called "cutaneous malignant melanotic neurocristic tumor," rhabdomyosarcoma, liposarcoma, and round cell or spindle cell undifferentiated forms.[659,667,668,672] Exceptionally, this malignancy occurs *outside* the region of the congenital nevus.[670] Whether the smaller congenital nevi are also subject to an increased risk of malignant transformation has not yet been established with certainty.[655,665]

Other nevi

Halo nevus (leukoderma acquisitum centrifugum) is the clinical term used to describe a melanocytic nevus surrounded by a zone of depigmented skin[680] (Fig. 4.106). It is most commonly found on the trunk of young patients, and it can be multiple.[683] Microscopically, it is characterized by a heavy infiltration of the nevus by lymphocytes and histiocytes and is thought to represent the expression of a host immune response (Figs 4.107 and 4.108).

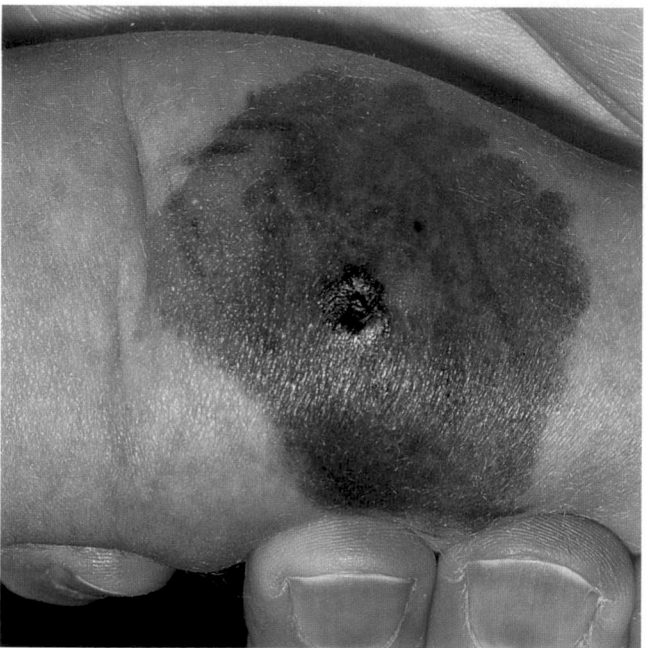

Fig. 4.104 Congenital nevus with central hyperpigmented area. This corresponded microscopically to a pagetoid intraepidermal proliferation of melanocytes.

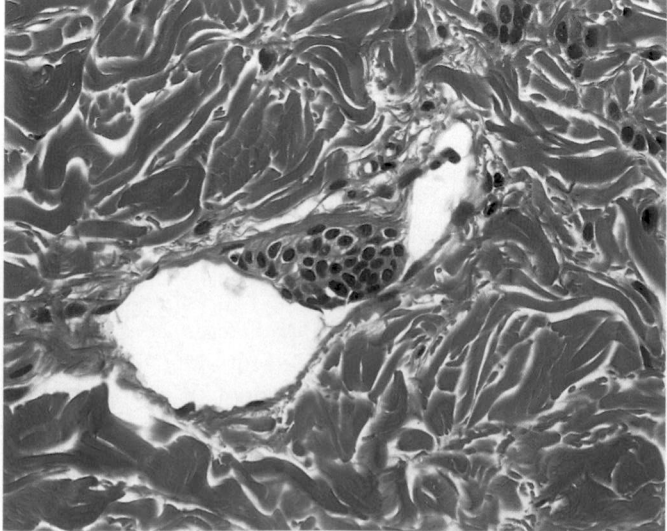

Fig. 4.105 Vascular involvement in congenital nevus. This is not a sign of malignancy.

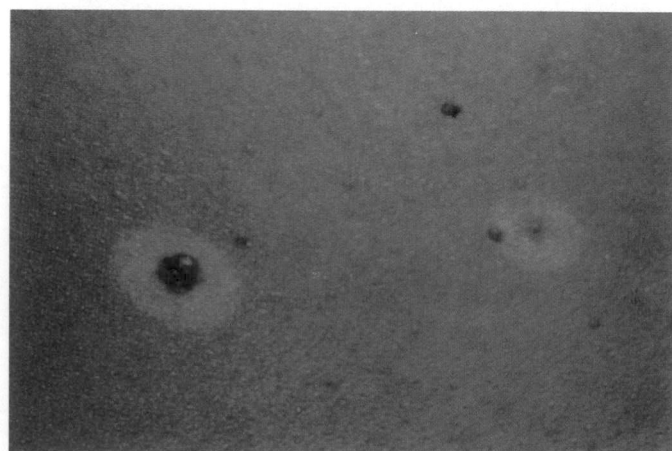

Fig. 4.106 Typical clinical appearance of halo nevus. Heavily pigmented center is surrounded by sharply defined oval area of depigmentation. Pigmented nevus may be situated in center, as here, or be eccentric. (Courtesy of Dr. A.W. Kopf, New York)

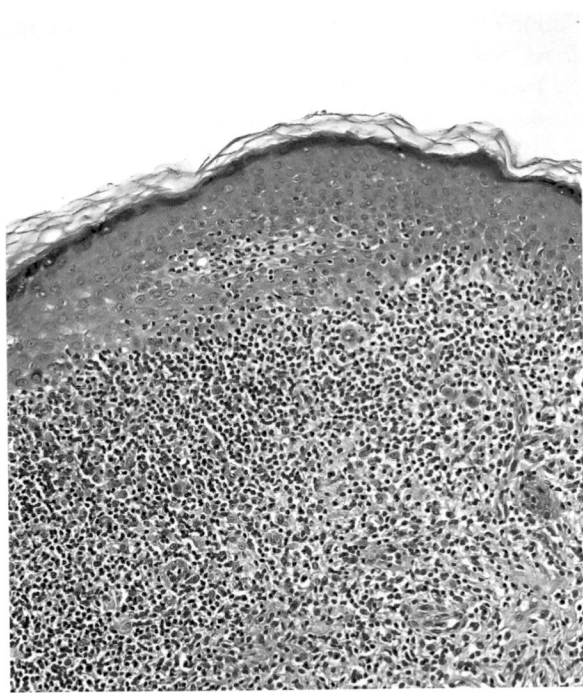

Fig. 4.107 Halo nevus. The low-power view is that of an inflammatory dermal nodule.

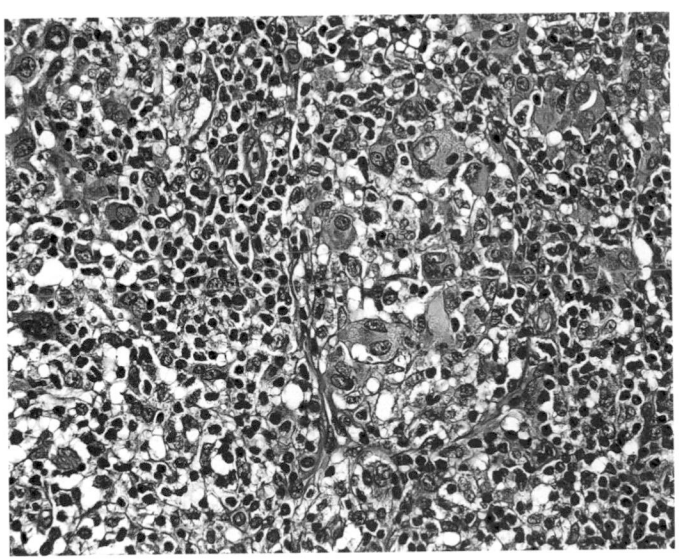

Fig. 4.108 Halo nevus. High-power view showing residual melanocytes amidst a heavy inflammatory infiltrate.

The lesion can be confused with melanoma, lymphoma, and dermatitis. Ultrastructurally, melanocytes in various stages of degeneration can be identified amid the lymphohistiocytic elements.[679] It should be mentioned that malignant melanoma may also be surrounded by a halo of depigmented skin.[680] However, in this instance the halo tends to be irregular, and the pigmented spot is usually off center.

Balloon cell nevus is another unusual variety of nevus, identified by the presence of large pale melanocytes with foamy cytoplasm, perhaps the result of a biochemical

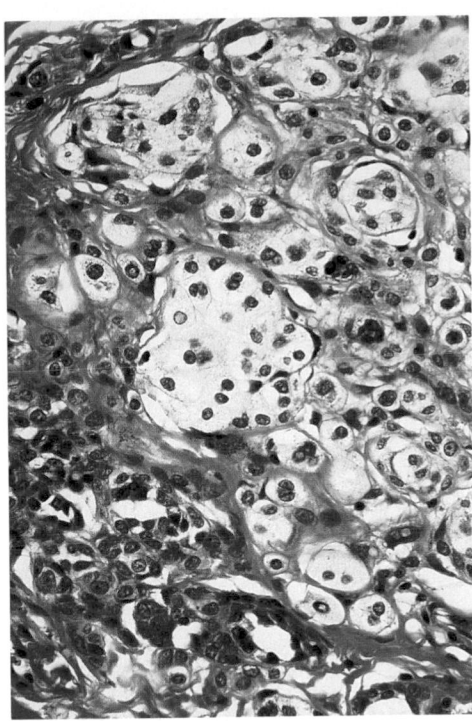

Fig. 4.109 Balloon cell nevus. The tumor cells are arranged in nests and have a voluminous pale cytoplasm.

alteration in melanin synthesis[681] (Fig. 4.109). Balloon cells also can occur in blue nevi and malignant melanomas.[677]

Cockarde nevus is characterized clinically by a concentric pattern of pigmentation; a central pink to darkly pigmented papule is surrounded by a stippled pigmented circle, with a clear zone in between.[678] Microscopically, the central lesion is a junctional or compound nevus without inflammatory changes, the peripheral portion (ring) shows multiple junctional melanocytic nests, and the intermediate zone is basically unremarkable.

Deep penetrating nevus is the name given to a variant of compound nevus in which the dermal component extends deeply into the reticular dermis and sometimes even into the subcutaneous fat.[682] The junctional component is usually inconspicuous, whereas the dermal component is cellular, nested or fascicular, abundantly pigmented, and cytologically mildly atypical. Mitoses are nil, and there is little or no inflammatory infiltrate. Sometimes deep penetrating nevus is seen admixed with other types of nevi, as a form of combined nevus.[676]

Treatment

Since every Caucasian adult has, on average, 20 to 30 nevi, it is obvious that specific indications are needed for their removal, other than those dictated by cosmetic considerations. The presence of a junctional component per se is not an indication; most plantar and palmar nevi are junctional, but they are too common and the possibility of malignant transformation too remote to warrant routine removal.[688,691] Definite indications for excision include the appearance of a pigmented lesion in an adult, chronic mechanical irritation of a nevus, or the appearance of any of the following changes in a preexisting nevus: deepening of pigmentation or spread of the pigment beyond the gross confines of the lesion, appearance of flat areas of depigmentation within the nevus, appearance of a red inflamed zone around the nevus, rapid growth, ulceration, itching, oozing of serum, or bleeding with trivial trauma.[685]

Removal of a nevus should be carried out with a cold knife rather than a cautery to prevent the distortion of tissue and peculiar staining reactions associated with the latter.

Incomplete removal may result in local recurrence.[686,689,690] The recurrent lesion often shows junctional activity, even if this feature was not present in the original excision.[684] This, together with the nuclear enlargement and nucleolar prominence that often accompany these recurrences, has sometimes resulted in a mistaken diagnosis of malignant melanoma, hence the term *pseudomelanoma* that has been proposed for this phenomenon[687] (Fig. 4.110).

Early surgical removal of the giant form of congenital nevus is also recommended because of their greater tendency to undergo malignant transformation; unduly large lesions have to be excised in the course of several sessions.

Active and dysplastic nevi

Active nevus ("hot nevus") is a term that has been applied to benign melanocytic nevi that show prominence of the junctional component and hyperplasia of individual basal melanocytes, often associated with increased overall cellularity and dermal inflammatory infiltrate. Activation of nevi, thus defined, has been reported as a result of sunlight exposure[702] or ultraviolet irradiation,[716] in pregnancy,[699] following the use of contraceptive pills,

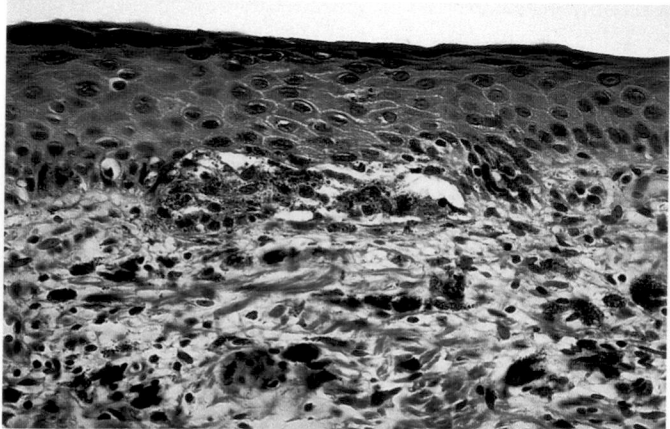

Fig. 4.110 Recurrent nevus following shave excision. There is an irregular proliferation of melanocytes along the dermo-epidermal junction, associated with some dermal fibrosis and clusters of melanin-laden macrophages. This lesion should not be overdiagnosed as malignant melanoma.

in association with malignant melanoma elsewhere in the skin,[718] in recurrent nevi,[704] and sometimes for no obvious reason. It has been suggested that HIV infection is yet another cause of melanocytic activation.[714] Exceptionally, a myriad of "eruptive" nevi with the microscopic signs of activation unassociated with any recognizable cause will appear in an adult.[697]

Dysplastic nevus remains a highly controversial concept.[696] This lesion seems to blend or at least exhibit some morphologic similarities with the phenomenon of activation of nevi as already described. In its better defined form, it occurs as a genetically determined syndrome in families prone to develop malignant melanoma (dysplastic nevus syndrome).[700,705] The nevi are clinically atypical, with a relatively large size (>5 mm), irregular outline, and variegated appearance; they appear in adolescence and continue to develop in adult life[706,717] (Fig. 4.111). Microscopically, most dysplastic nevi are compound nevi exhibiting marked lentiginous proliferation of melanocytes at the dermoepidermal junction, with or without theques. The latter are irregularly sized and shaped. These theques bridge adjacent rete ridges, which are themselves of irregular shape and orientation. If a dermal component is present, the junctional component is seen to extend beyond its lateral margins. The dermis shows eosinophilic and lamellar fibroplasia, focal perivascular lymphocytic infiltrate, and vascular dilatation.[695,698,707] These features, collectively referred to as *architectural atypia*, are usually matched by a mild to moderate degree of *cytologic atypia*, manifested by nuclear hyperchromasia, prominent nucleoli, and dusty melanin pigment. The melanocytes can be spindle shaped or epithelioid; the former tend to be arranged parallel to the skin surface[693,705] (Fig. 4.112).

Proposals have been made to grade dysplastic nevi depending on the severity of atypia, but the criteria are far from standardized.[701,711,715] It has been further suggested that the degree of atypia in these nevi correlates with the risk for developing melanoma.[692a] It should be remarked that only a minority of the clinically atypical nevi fulfill the microscopic criteria for dysplastic nevus.[694,709]

Ultrastructurally, a variety of melanosomal alterations have been described in these lesions.[710] DNA ploidy studies have shown that nearly all dysplastic nevi are diploid,[713] despite previous claims to the contrary.

Although the importance of having identified a familial syndrome with a predisposition toward melanoma cannot be overemphasized, the application of this concept to the solitary pigmented lesions remains questionable in terms of morphologic criteria, molecular markers, and biologic significance.[692,703,712,719] On the basis of present evidence, we think that solitary melanocytic nevi with "dysplastic" features should be regarded as clinically benign and handled as such for all practical purposes.

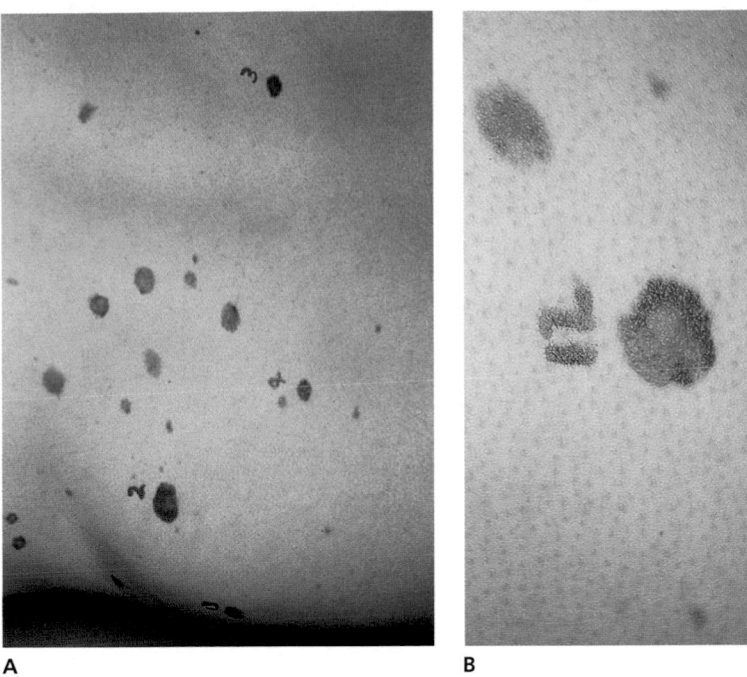

A

B

Fig. 4.111 A and **B**, Clinical appearance of dysplastic nevi in patient with the dysplastic nevus syndrome. These nevi are large, have an irregular outline, and feature a variegated appearance. (Courtesy of Dr. D. Santa Cruz, St. Louis)

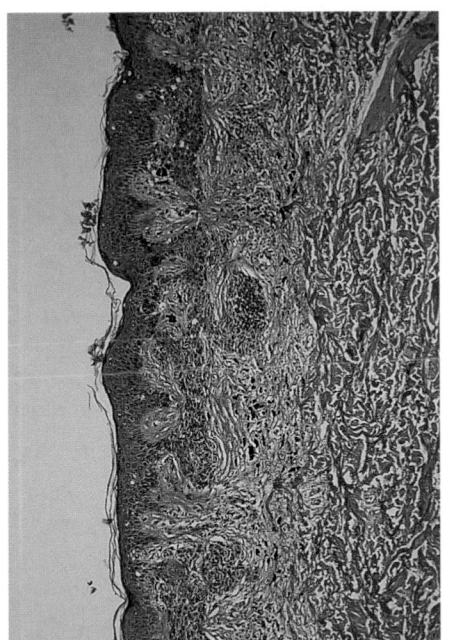

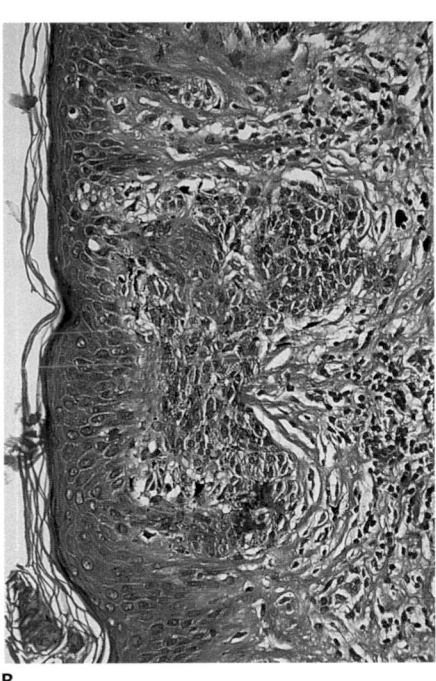

A

B

Fig. 4.112 A and **B**, So-called dysplastic nevus. There is dermal fibrosis, inflammation, and a proliferation of melanocytes at the dermo-epidermal junction, with bridging of rete ridges.

A more general approach to the problem can be taken by acknowledging the fact that one encounters, not infrequently, a melanocytic nevus (usually of the compound type) with atypical changes of the intraepidermal component. If the atypia is of a degree such as to indicate the emergence of a bona fide malignant neoplasm, we designate such lesion an *in situ malignant melanoma arising in a compound nevus*. For the considerably more common cases in which the atypia is below the threshold of melanoma (fully acknowledging the subjective nature of this determination), we use the term *compound nevus with* *atypia of the junctional component*, with the addition "(*so-called dysplastic nevus*)" if the above listed features for this "entity" are present. For the borderline cases, we err on the conservative side (i.e., we use the latter terminology), comforted by the knowledge that a complete surgical excision will be curative in practically every instance.

Other authors have taken a similar approach for intradermal nevi having atypical melanocytes in the basal layer in insufficient numbers to be considered compound nevi, the proposed term being *intradermal nevus with benign atypical junctional melanocytic hyperplasia*.[708]

Malignant melanoma

General features

The large majority of melanomas are associated with sunlight exposure and thought to be due to ultraviolet radiation.[731] Therefore, most are found in the head and neck area and on the lower extremities, the latter location being particularly common in females.[733,749] Rare but well-known locations of cutaneous melanomas are the subungual region ("melanotic whitlow")[726,742,739a,746] and the palms and soles. White people, particularly those of fair complexion, red hair, and a tendency to burn or develop freckles after exposure to sunlight,[724] are particularly susceptible to the development of melanomas. The few melanomas developing in black people tend to occur in the palms, soles, nail beds, or mucous membranes.

The overwhelming majority of melanomas arise after puberty. However, there is no question that they can also occur in children.[721,728,729,739,739a,747] These melanomas have the same microscopic pattern as those in adults and, therefore, can be distinguished in most cases on morphologic grounds from Spitz nevi.[723,735,738]

The presence of a large number of melanocytic nevi represents a risk factor for melanoma, even if these nevi are not of the dysplastic type.[732,736,745] The genetically determined disease xeroderma pigmentosum predisposes to the development of melanoma, and cases have been reported of melanoma in association with type I Recklinghausen's disease.[744]

Malignant melanomas can present as multiple primary tumors.[725,737] In a series of 712 patients with melanomas, 38 (5.3%) had more than one primary melanoma: 24 had 2 primary lesions, 11 had 3, 2 had 4, and one had 8.[740] The prognosis was more dependent on the type and stage of the largest lesion than on the number of primary lesions. Multiple primary melanomas should be distinguished from the phenomenon of nevus activation in patients with melanomas.[748]

The existence of hereditary forms of malignant melanoma has been known for a long time.[720] Members of melanoma-prone families often exhibit numerous atypical melanocytic lesions ("dysplastic nevi") that serve as a cutaneous marker of those at higher risk[727,743] (see p. 162). Melanoma can be associated with generalized melanosis[730,741] and with lesions resembling vitiligo.[722]

The fact that malignant melanomas can develop from nevi can be no longer denied, but the exact percentage is not clear. It is obvious that only an infinitesimal portion of acquired nevi become malignant. The percentage is higher for congenital nevi and—allegedly—for dysplastic nevi, but the exact figures are again unknown. Remnants of dysplastic nevi are said to be present in anywhere from less than 5% to almost half of all melanomas, this wide range undoubtedly reflecting the difficulties in distinguishing lateral melanoma spread from a preexisting lesion.[734]

Clinical appearance and clinicopathologic types

For the purposes of clinical and microscopic description, it is useful to divide melanomas into four categories by following the criteria championed by Clark et al.[754,765] in the United States and McGovern[759,761] in Australia, even acknowledging the fact that the clinicopathologic or prognostic differences among them are not as sharp as originally claimed.[750,768] These categories are melanoma arising in Hutchinson's freckle (lentigo maligna–melanoma), superficially spreading melanoma, nodular melanoma, and acral lentiginous melanoma. A high degree of accuracy in the differential diagnosis among these types is possible on the basis of location and gross appearance.[764]

Hutchinson's freckle (lentigo maligna) typically occurs in the sun-exposed areas of elderly white persons, most commonly on the cheek.[760,771] It is a flat, slowly growing lesion, its color varying from tan to black.[753] Microscopically, it is characterized by a proliferation of atypical melanocytes in the basal layer, distributed individually as well as in nests (Fig. 4.113). Retraction of the cytoplasm and pleomorphism are prominent. Hutchinson's freckle is an actinically induced atypia of melanocytes; as such, it could be regarded as the melanocytic analog of actinic keratosis. As a matter of fact, both components may coexist in the same lesion. A more descriptive term for Hutchinson's freckle, which also may be applied to histologically similar lesions that do not quite fit this clinical picture, is *actinic melanosis*.

The proliferation of atypical basal melanocytes in the deep portion of the rete ridges can simulate invasion, especially in a tangential section. It is advisable to be very conservative in the evaluation of this lesion, just as one should be in actinic keratosis. If no clear-cut dermal infiltration can be demonstrated despite the examination of multiple sections, it is better not to classify the lesion as a melanoma.

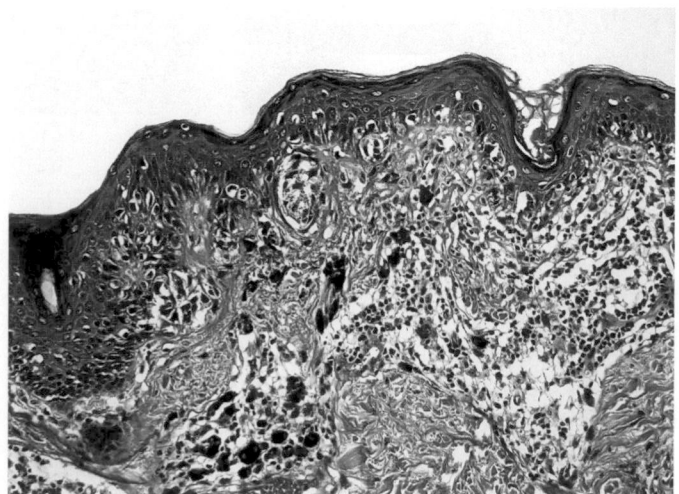

Fig. 4.113 So-called lentigo maligna. The atypical melanocytes are present along the basal layer individually and in theques.

The malignant melanoma that develops on the basis of Hutchinson's freckle is often of the spindle cell type and is endowed with a low degree of aggressiveness. Of 85 cases studied by Wayte and Helwig,[771] 45 were thought to contain an invasive melanoma in the center of the lesion, but the criteria might have been somewhat liberal. In any event, of the 85 cases, only 3 patients died of the tumor; a fourth developed lymph node metastases but remained well after resection of the involved nodes. Another type of melanoma that can develop on the basis of Hutchinson's freckle, also of spindle cell type but endowed with a much more aggressive behavior, is *desmoplastic melanoma*[755] (see below). This tumor tends to recur locally as well as to metastasize distantly.[757] It can also be seen in connection with other pigmented lesions.[752,770]

Superficial spreading melanoma is the most common form of melanoma. It has also been called premalignant melanosis or pagetoid melanoma, and it can occur anywhere on the body surface. It has a variegated appearance, the colors including hues of tan, brown, black, blue, pink, and white. The telltale color of early superficially spreading melanoma is most frequently a shade of blue admixed with tan, brown, or dark brown.[764] The surface is slightly elevated, and the margins are barely palpable (Fig. 4.114). The white areas correspond to areas of spontaneous regression. They are related to tumor size but not to the level of invasion or prognosis.[762] Pink and blue areas also correspond to areas of tumor regression, associated with dermal fibrosis and accumulation of melanin-laden macrophages. The borders of the lesion are irregular and usually include a prominent indentation or notch. Deep invasion generally is accompanied by the appearance of an elevated nodule on the surface. Microscopically, the noninvasive areas are composed of uniform atypical melanocytes with nest formation and pagetoid appearance (Fig. 4.115).

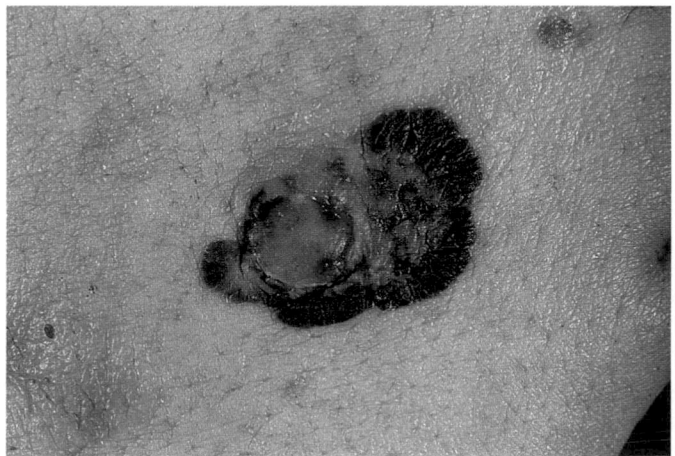

Fig. 4.114 Clinical appearance of melanoma of superficially spreading type. The nodular light area corresponds to a focus of amelanotic malignant melanoma featuring deep dermal invasion.

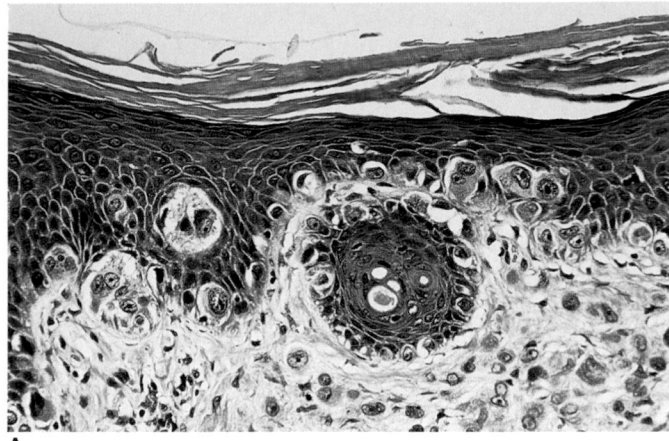

A

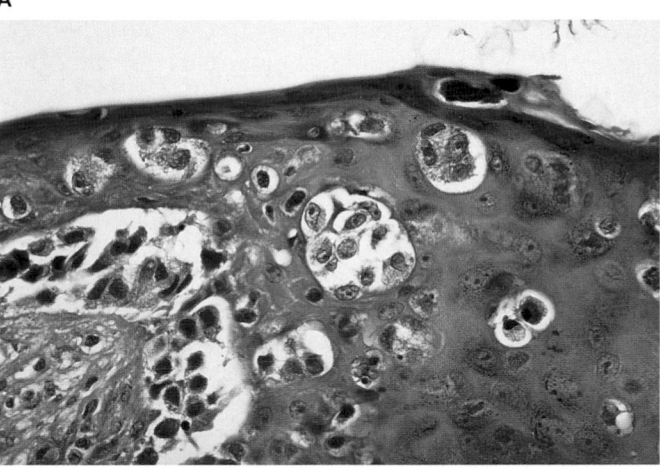

B

Fig. 4.115 A, Pagetoid appearance of melanocytes in superficially spreading malignant melanoma. **B,** Malignant melanoma showing transepidermal migration. There is also individual necrosis of neoplastic melanocytes. Some of the melanin has reached the horny layer (so-called pigmented parakeratosis).

Nodular melanoma can present as a smooth nodule covered by normal epidermis, as an elevated blue–black plaque, or as a polypoid, frequently ulcerated mass.[763] A lateral flat component is not seen clinically or microscopically. This type of melanoma affects all body surfaces, is usually of short duration, and occurs in a younger age group than either of the foregoing two categories.

(Acral) lentiginous melanoma has an intraepidermal component of lentiginous type, which is similar in many respects to that seen in Hutchinson's freckle.[751,756,769] In contrast to the latter, however, the intraepidermal melanocytes tend to be bizarre, the involved epidermis is markedly hyperplastic rather than atrophic, and the papillary dermis in this region is widened and inflamed. Tumors with these features have been seen on the palms, soles, subungual areas, mucocutaneous junction of the oral and nasal cavities, and anus.[767] This type of melanoma is more common in black and Oriental people.[766]

* * *

The clinical differential diagnosis of malignant melanoma includes a wide variety of lesions, particularly those containing melanin or hemosiderin pigment: benign nevi of various types, benign fibrous histiocytoma, inflamed or thrombosed hemangioma, pigmented seborrheic keratosis, and pigmented basal cell carcinoma.[758] Conversely, malignant melanomas that are amelanotic or covered by a thick layer of keratin can simulate a pyogenic granuloma or a callus, respectively.

Microscopic features

The typical example of malignant melanoma is easily identified microscopically because of its junctional activity; prominent melanin pigmentation; invasion of the surrounding tissue; marked cytologic atypia; nuclear grooves, folds, and pseudoinclusions; large eosinophilic nucleoli; and abundant mitotic figures, some of them atypical.[774] Alas, this is not always the case. As a matter of fact, malignant melanoma is notorious for the great microscopic variability that it may exhibit.[773,793] The cells can be epithelioid, spindle shaped, or extremely bizarre. Their size can range from small (lymphocyte-like)[784] to that of giant multinucleated forms (Figs 4.116 and 4.117). The cytoplasm can be eosinophilic, basophilic, foamy, of

signet ring type,[772,806] rhabdoid,[776,778,806a] oncocytic or completely clear (*balloon cell melanoma*).[790] Melanin can be abundant, scanty, or absent (*amelanotic melanoma*). Sometimes the amount of melanin production is so massive as to obscure the cellular details; such cases have been inelegantly called *animal-type* melanoma on the grounds that they resemble melanocytic neoplasms in horses and other mammals.[779]

The pattern of growth of melanoma may be pseudoglandular, pseudopapillary, peritheliomatous, hemangiopericytoma-like resembling Spitz nevus (*spitzoid melanoma*), trabecular, or verrucous (*nevoid or pseudonevoid melanoma*)[792,793,797,809,810] (Figs 4.118 and 4.119). The tumor can be accompanied by marked fibroblastic response, myxoid changes[785,807] (Fig. 4.120), metaplastic or neoplastic bone and cartilage,[794,796] osteoclast-like giant cells,[780,781] or pseudoepitheliomatous hyperplasia of the overlying epidermis.[788] Occasionally, formations suggesting differentiation toward Schwann cells, tactile corpuscles, ganglion cells, and other neuroid structures are observed.[782,783,801] Sometimes the lymph node and other metastases of a melanoma acquire an appearance that is practically indistinguishable from that of a malignant peripheral nerve sheath tumor.[791]

An additional variation is the already mentioned *desmoplastic melanoma*, which represents a subtype of spindle cell melanoma.[803] This is an important type of melanoma because of its degree of aggressivity and the fact that it can be easily misdiagnosed, sometimes with serious consequences. Microscopically, it is formed of spindle cells surrounded by a heavy desmoplastic stroma. The tumor cells can be very scanty and not overly atypical. The difficulty is compounded by the fact that these cells are positive for S-100 protein but usually not for HMB-45, Melan-A, or any of the other more specific melanoma markers, while sometimes acquiring mesenchymal markers such as actin.[804] The differential diagnosis of desmoplastic melanoma includes hypertrophic scar (which may contain S-100 protein-positive

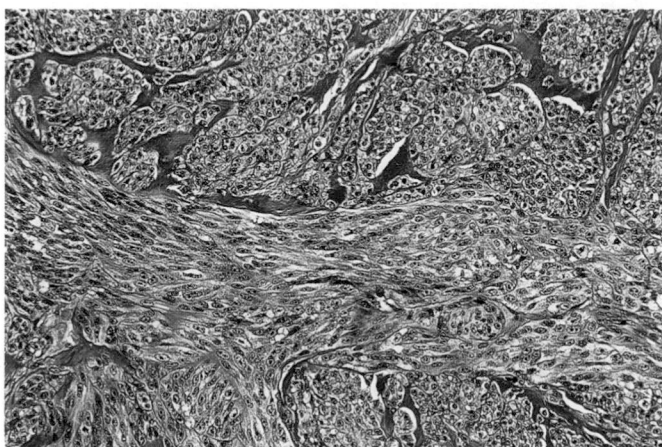

Fig. 4.116 Malignant melanoma in the region of the Achilles tendon showing prominent spindling. This is a common finding in tumors at this site.

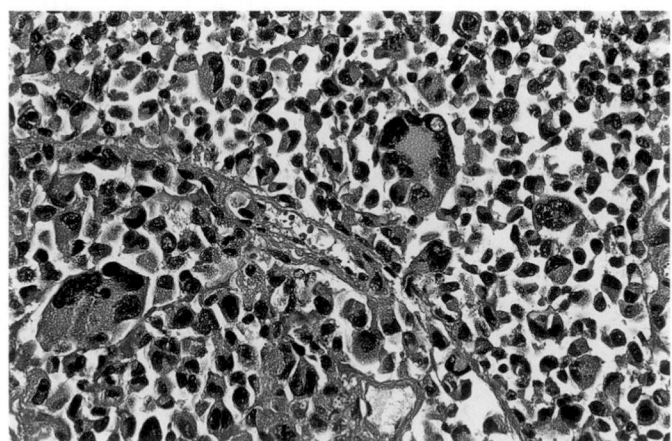

Fig. 4.117 Melanoma containing highly anaplastic tumor cells.

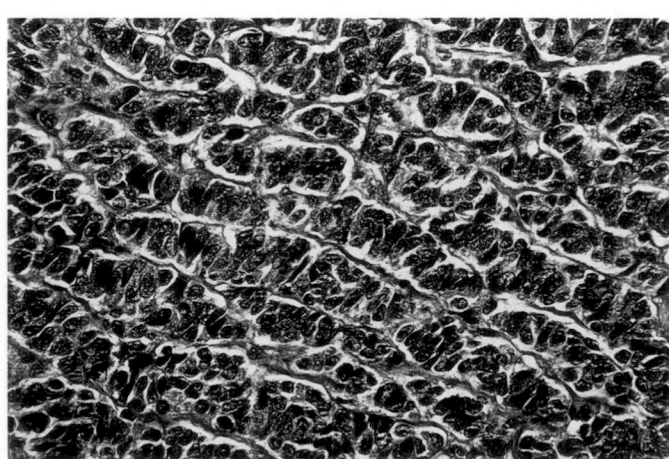

Fig. 4.118 Prominent trabecular pattern of growth in melanoma.

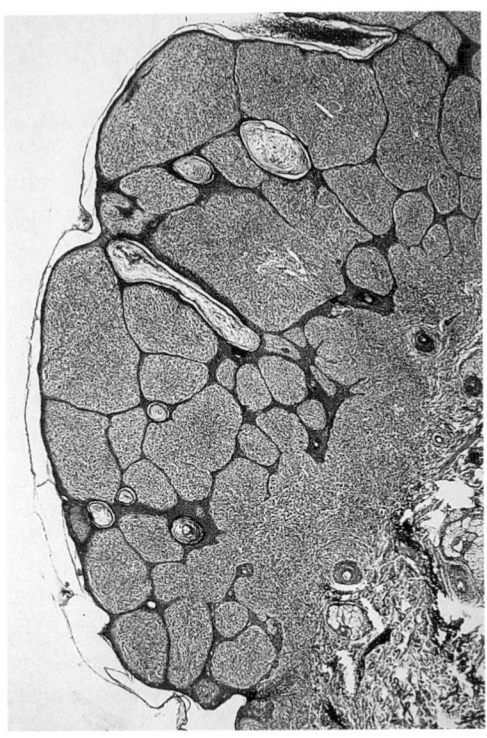

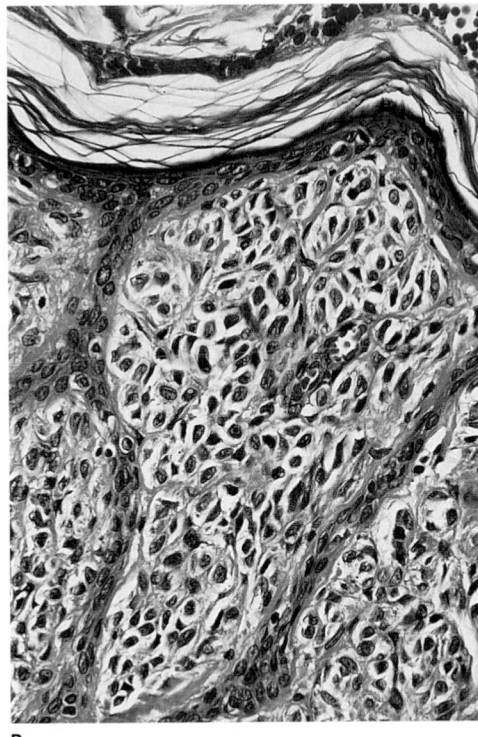

Fig. 4.119 Malignant melanoma with nevoid pattern of growth. A, Low-power view showing a polypoid configuration suggestive of a benign intradermal nevus. B, High-power view showing only minimal atypicality of the tumor cells. This tumor recurred locally and eventually metastastized to regional lymph nodes. (Slide contributed by Dr. Paul Duray, Bethesda, MD.)

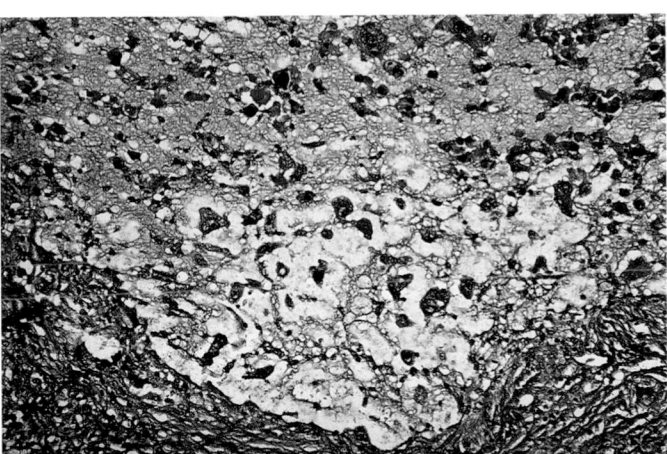

Fig. 4.120 Myxoid changes in malignant melanoma. This secondary alteration is more common at metastatic sites, but can also be seen in the primary lesion.

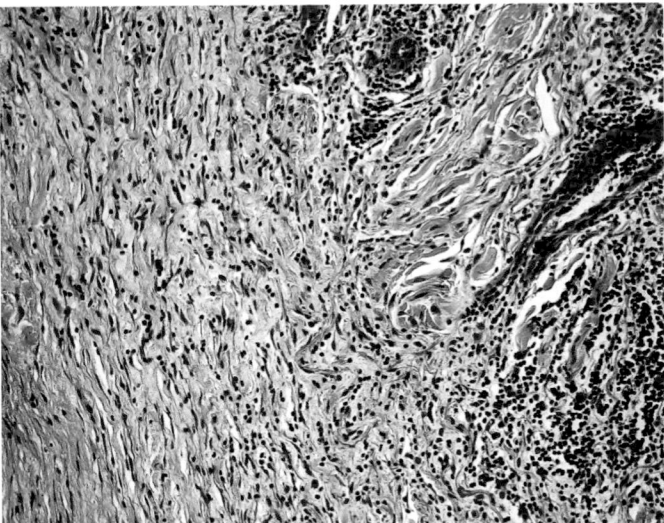

Fig. 4.121 Desmoplastic malignant melanoma. The spindle cells have a deceptively bland appearance. The collections of lymphocytes are a characteristic feature.

cells),[805] atypical fibroxanthoma, spindle squamous cell carcinoma, and peripheral nerve sheath tumors. Clues to the diagnosis at the hematoxylin–eosin level are focal fascicular pattern of growth, deep invasion, infiltration of nerves, round collections of lymphocytes at the tumor periphery (sometimes so prominent as to resemble cutaneous lymphoid hyperplasia/pseudolymphoma), and presence of a lesion with the features of Hutchinson's freckle in the overlying epidermis[789] (Fig. 4.121). Alas, many of these features will often be absent in the individual case. *Neurotropic melanoma* is a variant of desmoplastic/spindle cell melanoma growing in a peripheral nerve sheath pattern, either because the tumors invade preexisting nerves or because they differentiate along peripheral nerve structures.[777,800,808] Along these lines, it is interesting that spindle cell melanomas have often been found to express the p75 neurotrophin receptor, a feature further supporting their differentiation along neural lines.[787]

Yet another proposed type of melanoma is the *borderline* or *minimal deviation melanoma*, a controversial concept that includes the previously cited verrucous and spitzoid melanoma, as well as a halo nevus-like type.[775,798,802] As a result of all these variations, malignant melanoma can simulate carcinoma, various types of sarcoma, malignant lymphoma, and several other neoplasms.

Nearly all malignant melanomas exhibit an intraepidermal component ("junctional activity") during their initial phase. Therefore, a melanoma lying entirely within the dermis should be suspected of being metastatic. However, many well-documented cases of primary intradermal melanoma exist, the possible explanations for their occurrence being total regression of the intraepidermal component or origin from an intradermal nevus.

At a practical level, there are two major diagnostic challenges in this field. The first is how to identify as melanoma an obviously malignant tumor when melanin formation is not apparent in routine sections. Features suggestive of melanoma in hematoxylin–eosin sections are cells with abundant acidophilic, finely granular cytoplasm; pseudonuclear inclusions; a combination of epithelial and spindle cell patterns of growth; a fascicular arrangement of tumor cells; and pseudoalveolar arrangement. Special stains, immunohistochemical stains, and ultrastructural examination are of great utility in establishing the diagnosis in controversial cases (see next section). The other important diagnostic problem is the determination of whether a skin lesion of obvious melanocytic nature is benign or malignant. Benign lesions most commonly overdiagnosed as melanomas are Spitz nevi (especially the desmoplastic type of pure epithelioid nevus), halo nevi, activated and dysplastic nevi, vulvar (genital-type) nevi, and nevi that have recurred following incomplete excision. Conversely, the type of melanoma that is more likely to be underdiagnosed as benign is a level I or II superficially spreading type. We have found the criteria listed here to be the most useful for the identification of early malignant melanoma.[799] Unfortunately, none of them is pathognomonic. The diagnosis of melanoma can be made only on the basis of a combination of features.

1 Poor circumscription (lack of cohesiveness) of the intraepidermal melanocytic component. The nests are not as sharply defined as those of benign lesions, and the individual cells within the nests are separated from each other.
2 Lateral extension of individual melanocytes. Benign lesions usually exhibit a sharp cutoff, whereas in most malignant lesions there is a trailing off of atypical melanocytes spreading from the center of the lesion.
3 Extension of melanocytes, individually and in nests, throughout the malpighian layer and within adnexal epithelium. This phenomenon of transepidermal migration results in a pagetoid appearance of the lesion, hence the term "pagetoid melanoma" that is sometimes used. The melanin pigment can reach the horny layer, a process known as pigmented parakeratosis; this is rare in benign nevi, but appears with some frequency in some variants of benign lentigo and in "activated" benign lesions.
4 Size variation, shape variation, and confluence of melanocytic nests.
5 Asymmetry. This pertains to many of the items described in this list, such as lateral extension, the extent of the dermal component, architectural features of the nests, cell type, the distribution and appearance of the melanin, and the degree of inflammation and fibrosis.
6 Lack of maturation of dermal melanocytes.
7 Melanocytic atypia, evidenced by the prominence of nuclei and nucleoli and an increase of the nucleocytoplasmic ratio.
8 The presence of mitoses in melanocytes. Most benign nevi have a very small number of mitotic figures, although some spindle and epithelioid cell nevi may contain many. The presence of atypical mitoses is a strong indication that the lesion is malignant. The same is true for the presence of mitoses in the *dermal* component of melanocytic lesions other than Spitz nevi. Some benign and malignant melanocytic lesions are associated with marked hyperplasia of the epidermis: in these cases, one should be careful to distinguish mitoses in keratinocytes from mitoses in melanocytes.
9 Melanocytes with an abundant clear cytoplasm having a finely dispersed ("dusty") chromatin. This has been interpreted as a sign of degeneration and is a particularly useful sign.
10 Necrosis of individual melanocytes. This phenomenon should be distinguished from the eosinophilic hyaline bodies seen most often in Spitz nevi.
11 Dermal infiltrate of chronic inflammatory cells, mainly lymphocytes. This is particularly prominent in the early lesions and tends to have a bandlike distribution instead of the patchy appearance usually seen in irritated nevi.

So far, no reliable ultrastructural, immunohistochemical, or molecular genetic differences between benign and malignant melanocytic lesions have been described. At the ultrastructural level, there is a greater tendency for abnormal melanosome formation in malignant melanomas than in the benign lesion, but there is a great degree of overlap.[795] It has been further claimed that the melanosomes in Hutchinson's freckle melanoma tend to be ellipsoidal (resembling those of normal melanocytes), whereas those of superficial spreading and nodular melanoma are most often spheroidal and abnormal in appearance,[786] but there is too much overlap for these differences to be useful at a practical level.

Histochemical and immunohistochemical features
At the outset, it should be restated that all of the markers listed in this section are useful (to a greater or lesser

degree) to distinguish normal or neoplastic melanocytes from other cell types, but none of them is of great utility in the separation between benign and malignant melanocytic neoplasms.

Melanin stains are silver based and rely on the reducing properties of melanin granules. These *argentaffin* stains (of which the Fontana–Masson is the most widely used) are particularly useful in two situations: detecting finely dispersed granules that are not immediately apparent in hematoxylin–eosin sections, or demonstrating (when used in conjunction with iron stain) that the brown pigment seen in the routine sections is melanin rather than hemosiderin.

Immunohistochemically, the typical melanoma is reactive for vimentin, S-100 protein, HMB-45, Melan-A, tyrosinase, and microphthalmia transcription factor.[826,836] Of these, vimentin is the more consistent (seen in practically 100% of the cases) but the least useful diagnostically. Positivity for S-100 protein, although also nonspecific, is of greater practical importance because it is negative in most of the tumors that enter in the differential diagnosis[829,833] (Fig. 4.122). This reactivity is both nuclear and cytoplasmic, and it is present in over 90% of the cases.[812]

HMB-45 is a much more specific marker than S-100 protein[813] (Fig. 4.123). It is particularly useful when the differential diagnosis includes a nonmelanocytic tumor that can also be S-100 protein positive, such as breast carcinoma.[815] It may be detected in S-100 protein-negative melanomas, but on the whole it is less sensitive than the latter. It recognizes a premelanosomal glycoprotein (g100) related to the tyrosinase system, which explains why it may be negative in undifferentiated amelanotic neoplasms.[823,831,835] Antibodies NK/1 beteb and HMB-50 recognize different epitopes on the same antigen.[811] As already indicated, HMB-45 is generally negative in desmoplastic malignant melanoma.

Melan-A (Mart-1) is a melanocyte differentiation antigen originally identified as a target for cytotoxic T cells,

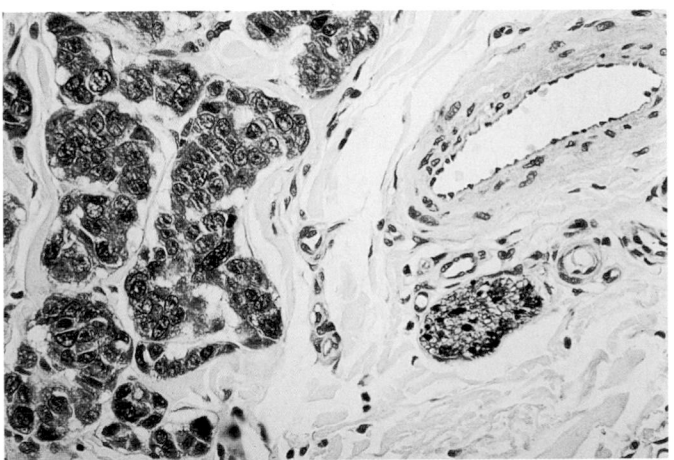

Fig. 4.122 Malignant melanoma of skin immunostained for S-100 protein. Strong nuclear and cytoplasmic reactivity is present.

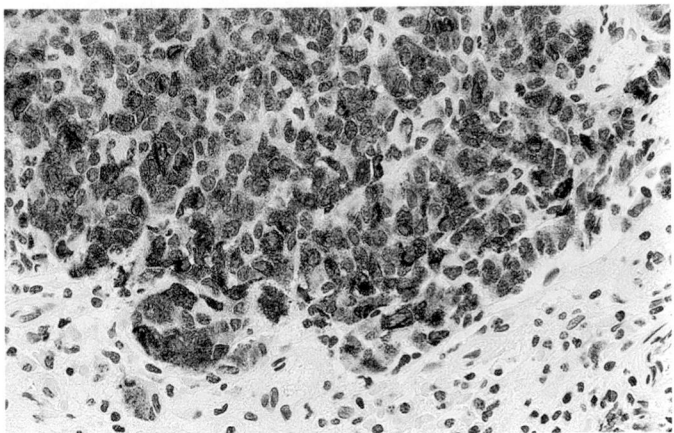

Fig. 4.123 HMB-45 immunoreactivity in melanoma.

which is detected with the monoclonal antibody A103. It is positive in approximately 80% of melanomas and has become a widely used marker for this tumor; it also stains steroid-producing cells from adrenal cortex, ovary, and testis, and the tumors originating from them.[822]

Tyrosinase is a key enzyme for the production of melanin from tyrosine; it can be detected with conventional enzyme histochemical methods (which require fresh tissue) but now also with immunohistochemistry or RT-PCR in paraffin-embedded material.[814,820,821] At the immunohistochemical level, the positivity is in the range of over 90%.[814,821] Other tumors reacting to this marker are peripheral nerve sheath and neuroendocrine neoplasms.

Microphthalmia transcription factor (MiTF) is a nuclear protein needed for the development and postnatal viability of melanocytes, through its function as a master regulator of extracellular signals. It stains nearly all melanomas of conventional type,[824] but—like most other markers—it fails to stain most spindle cell/desmoplastic melanomas,[819] despite early statements to the contrary; furthermore, it can also be positive in a variety of nonmelanocytic spindle cell tumors, including dermatofibroma and smooth muscle tumors.[819]

NK1/C3 has also been advocated for the identification of melanoma, but it suffers from its considerable cross-reactivity with many other neoplasms.[830,834]

Neuron-specific enolase also stains melanoma cells, in keeping with the neuroectodermal nature of these cells, but the stain is of little practical utility.

It is important to recognize that, contrary to previous claims, a significant number of melanomas exhibit immunoreactivity for low-molecular-weight keratins (such as those demonstrated with the Cam 5.2 antibody)[827,837]; some cases are also positive for CEA,[832] EMA,[827] α_1-antichymotrypsin,[825] and CD68 (KP-1).[817]

The DOPA (di-hydroxyphenylalanine) reaction demonstrates the presence of the enzyme dopa-oxidase (which transforms dopa into a melanin-like pigment), but the fact that it requires fresh tissue represents an important limitation of the method. Theoretically, this could be circumvented by developing an immunohisto-chemical reaction for this enzyme, similar to that being used for tyrosinase.

Melanin precursors in the cytoplasm of the tumor cells can be detected by formaldehyde-induced fluorescence, both in touch preparations and in freeze-dried sections.[828]

Some malignant melanomas that are amelanotic in vivo can produce large amounts of melanin when placed in a tissue culture system.[816]

AgNOR counts are significantly higher in malignant melanomas than in any of the benign melanocytic lesions, but whether this observation will turn into a useful diagnostic test at the practical level remains doubtful.[818]

Electron microscopic features

Electron microscopy has contributed greatly to the confirmation of a diagnosis of malignant melanoma through the identification of melanosomes and the less specific premelanosomes[839,841,842] (Figs 4.124 and 4.125), and it still does—although to a lesser extent—following the advent of immunohistochemistry. The utility of this technique was brought dramatically to light in a case we examined in an axillary lymph node, which was very suggestive of

melanoma in the H&E section but which was negative for S-100 protein and HMB-45 while being positive for low-molecular-weight keratin. Ultrastructurally, the tumor cells had well-developed melanosomes and lacked epithelial features. A regressed primary tumor in the adjacent skin was later detected.

Occasionally, melanoma cells can have well-developed microvilli similar to those more commonly seen in adenocarcinoma cells.[840] Various chromosomal aberrations and gene mutations have been described in melanomas, one of the most frequent affecting 9p21, which contains the p16 locus, a critical site for the normal progression of the cell cycle.[844]

No alterations of p53 expression have been found in most melanomas.[838,843]

Molecular genetic features

Genetic abnormalities detected in melanoma include CDKN2A and PTEN inactivation, RAS mutation (especially N-RAS), and the recently described BRAF mutation.[844b,844c,844d] The genetic make-up of melanomas seems to differ markedly depending on anatomical location and sun-exposure pattern.[844a]

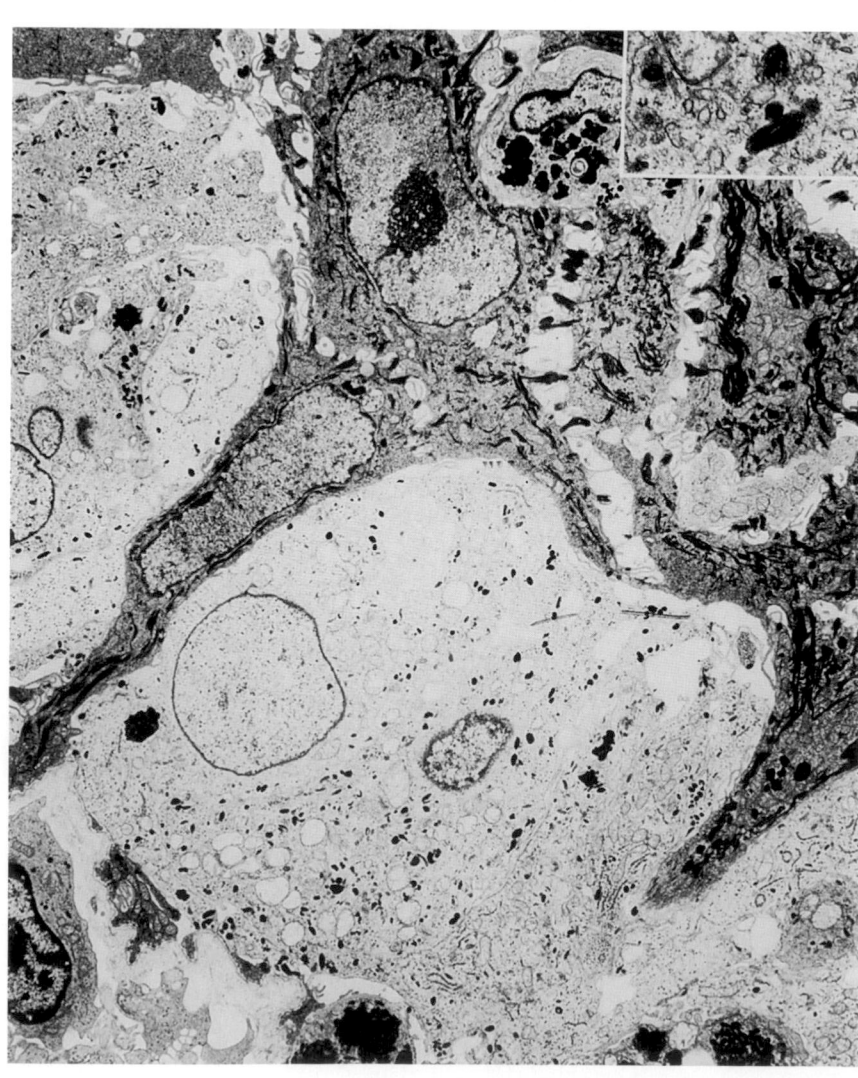

Fig. 4.124 Electron microscopy of superficially spreading melanoma of right ear demonstrating junctional melanocytes among keratinocytes. Inset, Stage 3 melanosomes present in neoplastic cells. (x3850; inset x25,270)

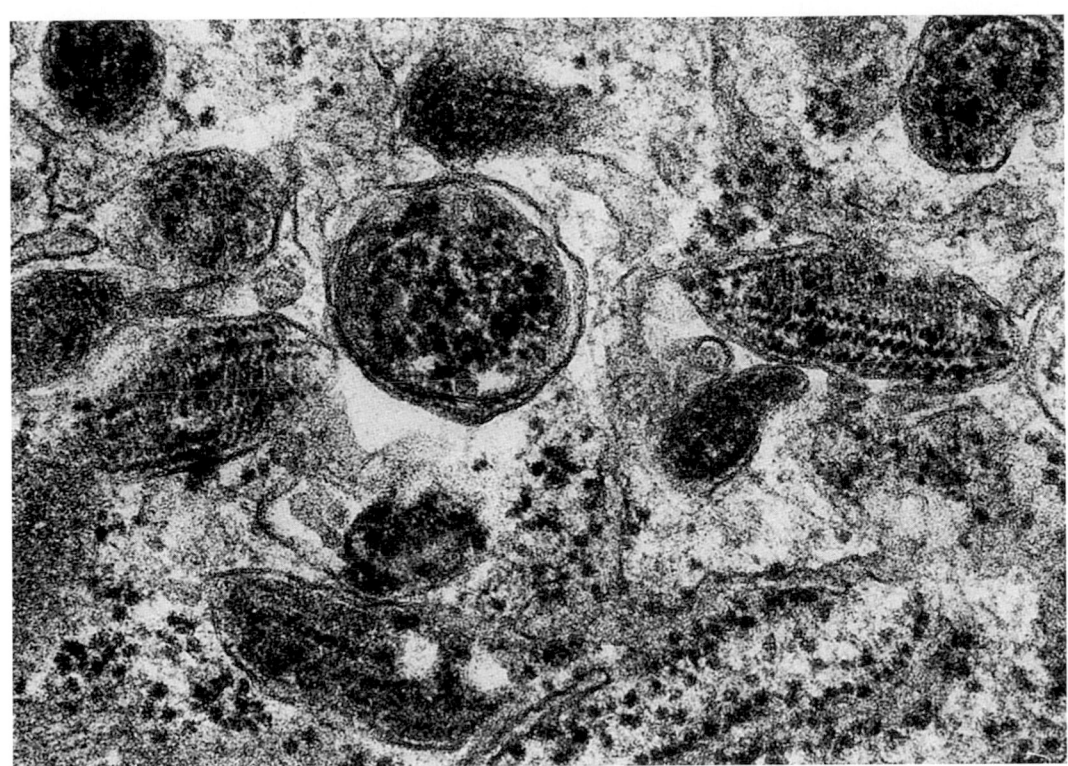

Fig. 4.125 Stage 2 and stage 3 melanosomes with characteristic lattice arrangement in malignant melanoma of skin metastatic to lung (x81,000)

Biopsy and frozen section

There is no evidence that *incisional* biopsy of a malignant melanoma increases the probability of spread. Comparison of patients on whom incisional biopsy was done and those who had excision without biopsy has shown no differences in survival rate.[846,847] However, whenever feasible, an elliptical *excisional* biopsy with narrow margins (down to the subcutaneous fat) constitutes the best procedure for the initial evaluation of pigmented skin lesions.[851] If the lesion proves malignant, a reexcision should be carried out. Punch biopsies or incisional biopsies are indicated in the case of extensive lesions (such as giant congenital nevi or lentigo maligna) or for lesions located in certain areas (such as the subungual region).

In experienced hands, the diagnosis of malignant melanoma by frozen section is reliable.[845,848,850] However, one can hardly justify its routine use on practical grounds, other than for the evaluation of surgical margins.[849,852]

Regression

Partial regression is a common feature in melanoma, particularly in the Hutchinson's freckle type. Total regression is much less common, but numerous cases in which the primary tumor regressed completely after giving rise to nodal and distant metastases have been documented.[854,859] This phenomenon may also explain some apparent discrepancies between expected and observed prognosis based on tumor thickness[855,857] and also the fact that in 5% to 15% of patients with metastatic melanoma the primary tumor is never found.[853,856]

Clinically, the spontaneous regression of melanoma is often heralded by the sudden onset of an irregular halo around the tumor. Microscopically, the early stage of regression is characterized by a dense infiltrate of lymphocytes similar to that seen in spontaneously disappearing nevi. This change may be partial or complete. In the late stage, vascular scar tissue with a variable number of melanin-laden macrophages is present (Fig. 4.126). Several distinctive clinical patterns result from this process. It has been pointed out that only melanomas with an intraepidermal component have been found to undergo spontaneous regression.[858]

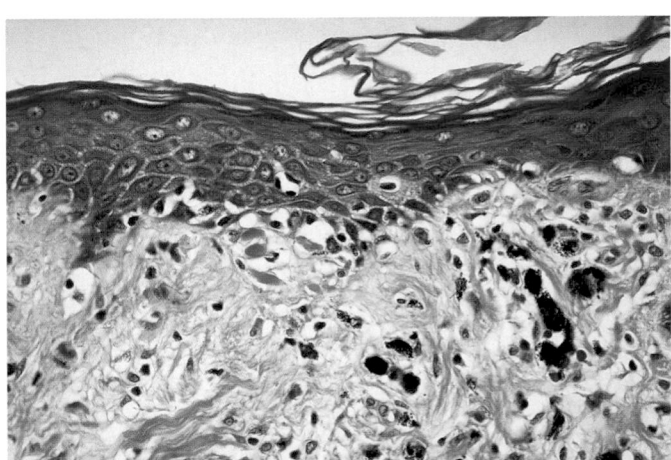

Fig. 4.126 Area of regression in malignant melanoma. There is extensive dermal fibrosis, epidermal atrophy, numerous dermal melanophages, and dyskeratotic cells in the dermo-epidermal junction. Viable tumor was present in other areas.

Atypical in situ melanocytic lesions

One of the most controversial aspects in the pathology of the melanocytic system is the evaluation and nomenclature of atypical melanocytic lesions that are limited to the epidermis. Such changes may be seen at the periphery of an obvious malignant melanoma,[862,865] in the epidermal component of a compound nevus, or as an isolated finding. Terms such as atypical (intraepidermal, premalignant) melanocytic hyperplasia, lentiginous dysplastic nevus, melanocytic dysplasia, melanocytic intraepidermal neoplasia (MIN), premalignant melanosis, and melanoma in situ have been used for this process, depending on location, some variations in morphologic appearance, and—most of all—observer's bias.[860–865] In a broad sense, Hutchinson's freckle and dysplastic nevi also fall into this category. In general, we have avoided the term malignant melanoma in situ for lesions of this sort in order to prevent unnecessary surgical procedures and undue concern on the part of the patient. We believe that descriptive names such as *atypical melanocytic hyperplasia* or equivalent terms such as intraepithelial atypical melanocytic proliferation and intraepithelial melanocytic neoplasia identify the nature of the process while avoiding the many undesirable consequences of the words "malignant" and "melanoma."[866]

Spread and metastases

Malignant melanoma spreads by growing along the dermoepidermal junction and upper dermis and later by invading the deep dermis and eventually the subcutis and deeper structures, the latter feature being evaluated in a semiquantitative manner by determining the Clark level and Breslow thickness (further discussed on p. 184). A laudable but misguided attempt of adapting basic biologic concepts to surgical pathology specimens has been that of designating a particular morphologic pattern of malignant melanoma as *vertical growth phase* (as opposed to *radial growth phase*).[869] The term refers to the presence in the dermis of one or more aggregates of tumor cells which are often amelanotic and which may resemble each other closely but which differ from the tumor cells above and around them. The term is misleading because the identification depends largely on cytologic criteria rather than location or presumed direction of growth. *Tumorigenic melanoma* is just as unsatisfactory, and *intralesional tumor progression* only slightly better for a phenomenon that in any other tumor type would be simply regarded as the morphologic expression of a lesser differentiated and biologically more aggressive tumor component.

Some melanomas show a remarkable tendency for vascular invasion ("angiotropic malignant melanoma").[874]

Metastases in regional lymph nodes are common even if the nodes appear clinically negative (see next section).

Distant metastases occur most often in the liver, lungs, gastrointestinal tract, bone, and central nervous system

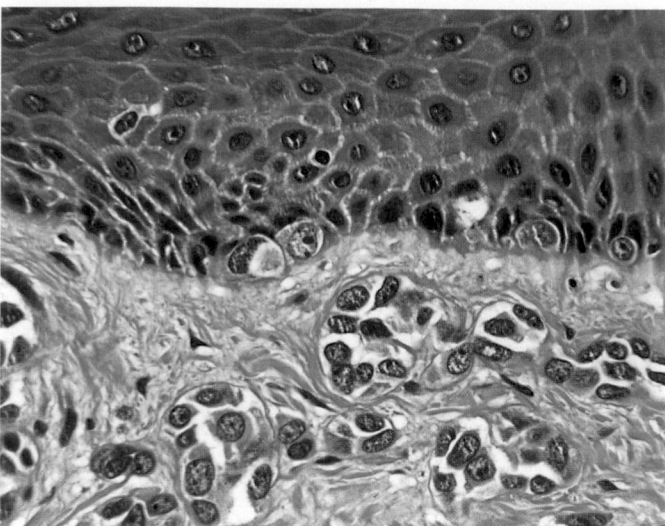

Fig. 4.127 Metastatic malignant melanoma with secondary epidermal involvement.

but can occur anywhere.[868] At autopsy, metastases to the heart are found in one half of the patients.[871] A certain pattern in the distribution of these metastases, related to the embryologic origin of the organs involved, has been noted.[870] Cutaneous metastases are also common. Many of them are located close to the tumor ("satellite nodules"), suggesting a lymphatic rather than a blood vessel mechanism. Cutaneous and subcutaneous metastases located between the site of the primary tumor and the regional lymph node are sometimes referred to as "in-transit metastases." Both satellite nodules and in-transit metastases are usually indicators of disseminated systemic disease.[873] Cutaneous metastases from melanoma can be difficult to distinguish from a primary lesion because the metastases may develop a secondary intraepidermal component ("epidermotropic" metastases) (Fig. 4.127). A useful differential feature is the fact that in metastatic carcinoma with secondary intraepithelial spread, the dermal component is much wider than the epidermal one, whereas the opposite is generally true for the primary lesion.[872] However, some epidermotropic metastatic malignant melanomas are primarily intraepidermal, simulating malignant melanoma in situ.[867]

The behavior of malignant melanoma is very unpredictable. Deaths from metastatic melanoma have been documented 15 years or more after the initial therapy.[875] Conversely, some patients with widespread satellite nodules in one extremity may survive for many years without evidence of tumor spread beyond that extremity. Immunologic factors probably play an important although still ill-understood role in the evolution of this neoplasm.

Sentinel lymph node

During the course of the past decade, the performance of sentinel lymph node biopsy in melanoma has become routine.[879,886] This procedure is based on the mechanistic concept that the pattern of metastatic spread of melanoma to the nodes is orderly, and that if the sentinel node (defined as the first node on the direct lymphatic drainage path from the primary tumor) is negative, the likelihood is very high that this will also be true for the other nodes of that region. Therefore, if the sentinel node is positive, a lymphadenectomy is carried out. Although there are strong voices of dissent,[885a] most workers in the field maintain that sentinel node biopsy is an accurate staging procedure and a powerful prognostic indicator.[880]

Sentinel node biopsy is recommended for all melanomas measuring 1 mm or more in thickness. The node is identified with a dye or an isotope,[878] and submitted to the pathology department, where preferably it will be submitted in toto for paraffin embedding (after bivalving, if necessary) rather than subjecting it to frozen section.

Controversy still exists as to the best method for the pathologic evaluation of the sentinel node that will ensure a high detection rate while preventing the other activities of the histology laboratory coming to a full halt. In general, the recommendation is for the examination of a certain number of hematoxylin–eosin step sections plus one or more immunostains.[883,884,888] Following an exhaustive pathologic study of 105 sentinel lymph node procedures carried out at Memorial Sloan-Kettering Cancer Center, we concluded that the performance of 3 levels at 250-μm intervals, each level being composed of a set of 3 sections stained with H&E, S-100 protein, and HMB-45, will detect the overwhelming majority of the nodal metastases present, and that is therefore the procedure we recommend to the laboratories that have or can obtain the manpower needed to do it.[889] We would regard as the absolute minimum the performance of 3 "step" H&E sections (with about 10 discarded sections in between) plus one immunostain, among which we and most others prefer HMB-45[876] (Fig. 4.128).

It remains to be seen whether molecular techniques for the detection of isolated tumor cells (such as the RT-PCR procedure for tyrosinase) will be a useful adjunct to the combined morphologic and immunohistochemical method just described.[877,882]

The differential diagnosis of metastatic melanoma to lymph node includes benign nevus cells (nodal nevi) and histiocytes. Benign nevus cell inclusions are usually limited to the nodal capsule (although they can also be intraparenchymal),[876a] have a typical semilunar shape, lack nuclear atypia, and stain for S-100 protein and Melan-A but weakly or not at all for HMB-45 or MIB-1 (Ki-67).[885] Histiocytes and other cells of the accessory immune system can be a problem because of their immunoreactivity for S-100 protein and occasional positivity for HMB-45, as well as the fact that melanomas can be positive for some of the histiocyte-associated markers.[887] However, they should lack nuclear atypia and be positive for PG-M1 (which melanoma cells are not).[881]

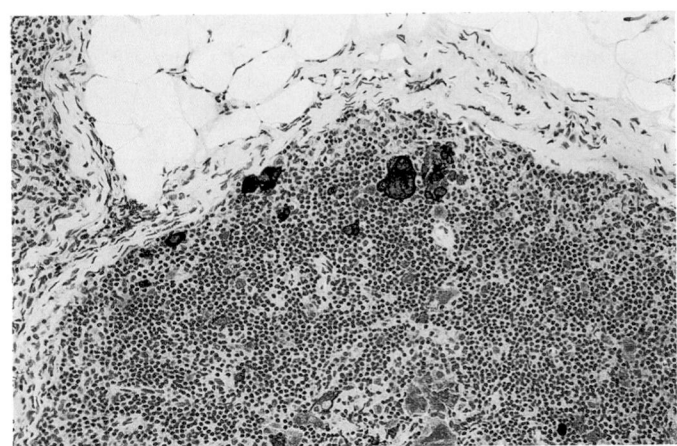

Fig. 4.128 Isolated melanoma cells in sentinel lymph node, demonstrated with HMB-45 immunostain.

Treatment

The treatment of choice of most malignant melanomas is wide excision of the primary lesion. A margin of 2 to 3 cm or perhaps even 1 cm is probably sufficient for the average sized tumor, even if some surgeons in the past have recommended a margin of 5 cm.[891,899,899a,900] Balch et al.[892] recommended a margin of 2 cm for thin melanomas (less than 0.76 mm in thickness) and a margin of 3 to 5 cm for thicker lesions, but even this proposal has been questioned in view of the fact that survival in melanoma is unrelated to the width of the margins, irrespective of the width of the tumor.[890,895,898,906] Indeed, the same group of authors has shown that even in intermediate-thickness melanoma (1 to 4 mm), a surgical margin of 2 cm is sufficient.[893]

If the regional lymph nodes are clinically considered to be involved, a radical lymph node dissection should be performed. Removal of clinically negative lymph nodes has always been a very controversial subject. Some authors have been in favor of the procedure based on the finding of microscopic foci of malignant melanoma in almost a fourth of clinically negative nodes.[894,902] However, most series have failed to show an improvement of survival in the patients so treated.[897,903–905] A prospective randomized study of stage I melanoma of the limbs showed no differences in survival between the patients who had regional node dissection at the time of the original excision and those who had it only when clinically detectable metastases appeared.[908,909] As already indicated in the preceding section, the field has been revolutionized in the last decade with the introduction of the sentinel lymph node biopsy as a guide for planning therapy and gauging prognosis.

An alternative to surgery for Hutchinson's freckle is represented by radiation therapy[901]; Dancuart et al.[896] have reported very good results with this technique. Unfortunately, radiation therapy, chemotherapy, and immunotherapy have so far proved largely ineffective in invasive or metastatic melanoma, despite the occasional spectacular result.[907] Dacarbazine remains the drug of choice in disseminated melanoma; interleukin, biochemotherapy, and interferon have given good results, but only in a small percentage of patients.[901]

Prognosis

The death rate for malignant melanoma is still unacceptably high if one considers the fact that this lesion is diagnosable at a stage when it can be cured in nearly every instance. In a series of nearly 3000 patients with melanoma in Norway, the overall 5-year relative survival rate was about 60%.[948]

There are many clinical and pathologic factors that have been studied in regard to their influence on prognosis.[934,969] Before offering the reader this imposing list, we should mention as an introduction that an analysis of 17,600 patients with melanoma showed that: (1) in the Tumor (T) staging category, the most powerful predictors of survival were tumor thickness and ulceration, whereas the level of invasion had a significant impact only within the subgroup of thin (<1 mm) melanomas; (2) in the Node (N) category, the independent prognostic factors were the number of metastatic nodes, and whether the nodal metastases were clinically occult or clinically apparent; (3) in the metastases (M) category, nonvisceral metastases were associated with a better survival than visceral metastases.[914]

Now as to the individual factors:

1 *Tumor stage.* This is by far the most important prognostic parameter. In one large series using a previous stage system, the 10-year survival rate was almost 70% for localized disease and less than 20% for metastatic disease.[948]

    The simpler staging system for melanoma divides it into three stages: I, localized disease; II, regional cutaneous (satellite or in transit) metastasis or regional lymph node metastasis; and III, distant metastasis. More elaborate systems have been proposed, mainly for the purpose of further subdividing localized disease. Of these, the one most widely used is that proposed by the American Joint Committee on Cancer staging system[911,912] (see Appendix C).

2 *Level of invasion and tumor thickness.* These are two important prognostic determinators. In Clark's system, melanomas are divided into five levels of invasion according to the following scheme:

    I   Intraepidermal (in situ)
    II   In the papillary dermis
    III Filling the papillary dermis and stopping at the interphase between the papillary and reticular dermis
    IV   In the reticular dermis
    V   In the subcutaneous fat.

    A direct relationship exists between the level of invasion and the incidence of lymph node metastases

and, therefore, the prognosis.[920] In one series, regional node metastases were present in 32% of the patients with level III invasion, 67% with level IV, and 66% with level V[940]; patients with level I and level II did not undergo node dissection, but none of them had clinical evidence of metastases. In the series of Wanebo et al.,[966,967] the 5-year disease-free survival after surgery was 100% in patients with level II invasion, 88% in those with level III, 66% in those with level IV, and 15% in those with level V.

The tumor thickness is evaluated by the microstage or Breslow's system. The tumor is measured with an ocular micrometer at right angles to the surface of the adjacent normal skin, *from* the top of the granular layer of the overlying epidermis or *from* the ulcer base over the deepest point of invasion *to* the deepest invasive tumor cells. Traditionally, the system has assigned the melanomas into low-, intermediate-, and high-risk categories depending on whether their depth is less than 0.76 mm, between 0.76 and 1.5 mm, or greater than 1.5 mm, respectively.[917] The 5-year disease-free survival is 98% for the first group, 44% to 63% for the third, and somewhere in between for the second.[913,916,919,967] In one series, the 3-year actuarial incidence of subsequent regional metastases in patients initially treated by wide local excision of the melanoma was 0% for lesions less than 0.76 mm, 25% for 0.76 to 1.50 mm lesions, 51% for 1.50 to 3.99 mm lesions, and 62% for lesions over 4 mm in thickness.[913] There is also a close correlation between melanoma thickness and occult metastases in sentinel lymph nodes.[943]

Note should be taken of the fact that, in recent publications (including the new staging system of melanoma), the groups are divided according to 1 mm increments rather than in the fashion originally devised by Breslow and his followers.[912,914]

Superficially, it would seem that the methods of level of invasion and tumor thickness are comparable, yet they examine different parameters. In Clark's level system, what is being evaluated is the ability of the tumor cells to invade the dermis. For instance, a large and rather thick melanoma may stop at the bottom of the papillary dermis with very sharp margins (level III), whereas a smaller and thinner melanoma can be seen freely invading the reticular dermis. The microstage system defines the *amount* of invasive tumor present in the section, and is therefore a surrogate for tumor volume. There is actually little correlation between the two methods, and a lively controversy took place over which is the better of the two.[917,918] Thickness seems to have emerged as the most important determinant, despite the nihilistic attitude of some observers.[935,942,959] Yet, it is prudent for the pathologist to record both the thickness and the level of invasion in each case. Both methods present problems of interpretation. A common problem with the level system is the assignment of a higher level than the real one because of the failure to recognize that a seemingly deep collection of malignant melanocytes actually may be attached to a pilosebaceous unit or that a melanoma can massively expand the papillary dermis but still be limited to this layer. Another difficulty is the fact that in some parts of the body the boundary between papillary and reticular dermis is a very indistinct one. A potential problem to keep in mind with the microstage method is that, with tangential cutting of a lesion, an artificial increase of the tumor thickness will result. Another factor to keep in mind is that the measured thickness is a function of the number of sections examined.[958]

An extension of the concept that tumor amount is an important prognostic parameter is the proposal that tumor *volume* is even more accurate than thickness.[931,961]

As important as the concept of tumor thickness is, it should be kept in mind that "thin" melanomas (less than 1.0 mm or even 0.76 mm) can still result in metastases and death.[950,970]

3 *Shape of the lesion.* This feature, as determined clinically, is closely related to the tumor thickness as evaluated by the Breslow system. Thus prognosis is related to the maximum tumor elevation and is worse for polypoid than for dome-shaped lesions.[933,945] This is not because of the polypoid shape itself but rather the greater tumor thickness usually associated with these lesions.[953]

4 *Sex.* In one large series,[948] the 5-year survival rate was 50.5% for males and 70.5% for females. This improved survival for females results from a variety of factors, such as location and depth of invasion.[951] However, it seems to remain somewhat better even after these factors have been corrected.

5 *Age.* It has been claimed that younger age is associated with a more favorable prognosis in males but not in females.[964] One study has shown the adverse prognostic significance of old age, but this is at least partially due to the large percentage of thick melanomas in this age group.[926]

6 *Effect of pregnancy.* This remains a controversial subject. Isolated case reports have strongly suggested an adverse effect, but several large studies showed no statistical differences in prognosis.[928a,952,968] Perhaps part of the difficulty resides in the fact that this alleged influence may be dependent on the stage of the melanoma. Shiu et al.[957] found no statistical difference in stage I disease but a significantly lower survival rate in pregnant patients (29%) with stage II lesions as compared with nonparous (51%) or nulliparous (55%) patients. Parenthetically, malignant melanoma cells do not contain hormone receptors at

the immunohistochemical level, and this also applies to pregnant patients.[929]

7 *Anatomic location.* Rogers et al.[955] have defined the following as high-risk sites: scalp, mandibular area, midline of trunk, upper medial thighs, hands, feet, popliteal fossae, and genitalia. Some but not all of these differences are attributable to their association with thickness. Subungual melanomas have a notoriously bad prognosis, which is probably largely due to their late detection.

8 *Size.* The diameter of the melanoma has no independent prognostic significance once this parameter has been corrected for tumor thickness.

9 *Clinicopathologic type.* Early articles describing the three major types of malignant melanoma claimed a better prognosis for melanoma arising in Hutchinson's freckle, a worse prognosis for nodular melanoma, and an intermediate prognosis for superficially spreading melanoma.[922,923] More recent studies have shown that, once depth of invasion is entered into the equation, most of these differences are erased. The behavior of acral lentiginous melanoma is particularly aggressive, but again this may be the consequence of its propensity for deep invasion and ulceration: In the series of Coleman et al.,[927] the average 3-year survival rate was 11%.

10 *Cytologic features.* Whether the melanoma cells are spindle, epithelioid, or any other shape seems to bear no direct relationship to the prognosis.[925,946]

11 *Degree of pigmentation.* This feature does not seem to influence prognosis.[925]

12 *Mitotic activity.* Although controversy exists, most authors have shown a relationship between mitotic activity and prognosis independently from other parameters.[965] As a matter of fact, a study of 3661 patients from a single center showed that tumor mitotic rate is a more powerful prognostic indicator than ulceration.[910]

13 *Cell proliferative activity.* Melanomas have been stained for cell proliferation markers such as MIB-1 (Ki-67) and PCNA. A relationship has been demonstrated between this parameter and the thickness of the tumor, but there is controversy as to whether it offers independent prognostic information.[930,939,954,962,963,971]

14 *Dermal inflammatory infiltrate.* It has been found that a dense lymphocytic infiltrate around the melanoma is associated with a better prognosis, particularly if the lymphocytes are closely intermingled with the neoplastic melanocytes ("tumor-infiltrating lymphocytes").[960] The intensity of this reaction has been graded using the odd terminology *brisk*, *non-brisk*, and *absent*, and found to have a strong predictive value in melanomas with a vertical growth phase.[924] Conversely, the presence of numerous plasma cells in the infiltrate is said to correlate with an increased probability of lymph node metastases.[949] However,

the significance of these findings diminishes greatly after correcting for tumor thickness.

15 *Ulceration.* The presence of ulceration has emerged as one of the most important prognostic determinators of the primary tumors, as reflected in the change that has been made in the staging system. The prognostic value remains after the tumor is matched with nonulcerated lesions by thickness, type, and stage.[915,947,956] Furthermore, the diameter of the ulceration is related to prognosis, and therefore this parameter should be included in the pathology report.

16 *Regression.* It has been claimed that the presence of focal areas of regression in a malignant melanoma may modify the significance of the level or thickness of the residual tumor (Fig. 4.126). This may explain why relatively superficial melanomas exhibiting focal regression are associated with an incidence of lymph node metastases higher than that expected on the basis of these determinations.[936] However, more recent studies have failed to confirm this claim.[928,941,944] Parenthetically, the prognosis of patients with metastatic malignant melanoma and unknown (presumably regressed) primary is the same as for patients with an overt primary malignancy.[921]

17 *Staining pattern.* No consistent relationships have been detected between any histochemical or immunohistochemical staining patterns in melanoma and prognosis.[937]

18 *Microscopic satellites.* The presence of microscopic satellites, defined as tumor nests over 50 μm in diameter separate from the main tumor mass, shows a high association with regional lymph node metastases and, therefore, with prognosis.[938]

19 *Preexisting benign nevus.* In one large series, the prognosis of melanoma was significantly better when the tumor had histologic evidence of a coexisting acquired melanocytic nevus.[932]

Other pigmented skin lesions

There are several types of benign and (less commonly) malignant skin lesions that are neither melanocytic nevi nor malignant melanoma.

Hyperpigmentation, whether regional or generalized, is the result of stimulation of melanocytes by a variety of stimuli, such as sunlight, heat, drugs, hormones (as in pregnancy), dietary deficiency (as in kwashiorkor), metabolic disorders (such as Gaucher's disease), scars, and a variety of dermatoses (generically referred to as postinflammatory hyperpigmentation).[973] The only microscopic change (rarely seen because of the infrequency of biopsies in this group of conditions) is increased pigmentation of basal keratinocytes, accompanied by increased transfer of melanin into the adjacent keratinocytes.

Ephelis (freckle) arises in sun-exposed skin of susceptible individuals and shows microscopically mild hyperpigmentation of basal keratinocytes, associated with a normal epidermal architecture.

Solar lentigo shows elongation of rete ridges and increased pigmentation of the basal and suprabasal layers; this lesion is related to keratosis rather than to simple lentigo, and it may have a reticulated appearance[972] (Fig. 4.129).

Café-au-lait spot, as seen in von Recklinghausen's disease but also in other genetically determined disease and in 10% of the general population, is characterized microscopically by basal hyperpigmentation of the epidermis and, at the ultrastructural level, by the presence of macromelanosomes.

Becker's nevus, typically seen in the shoulder, chest, or lower back, shows increased epidermal pigmentation associated with mild acanthosis and sometimes hypertrichosis.

Pigmentation can also occur in several types of non-melanocytic skin neoplasms because of increased activity of melanocytes or increased retention of pigment in the epithelial cells. The most striking example is *melanoacanthoma*, in which dendritic melanocytes and keratinocytes participate in the formation of this benign lesion, which some authors regard as an entity and others (including ourselves) as a variant of seborrheic keratosis.[974]

Other lesions that may be heavily pigmented are ordinary seborrheic keratosis, acrochordon, dermatosis papulosa nigra, actinic keratosis, Bowen's disease and bowenoid papulosis, basal cell carcinoma, and some adnexal tumors (particularly trichoepithelioma, pilomatrixoma, and eccrine poroma). In pigmented basal cell carcinoma, both participation of dendritic melanocytes and retention of pigment in the neoplastic epithelial cells occur.

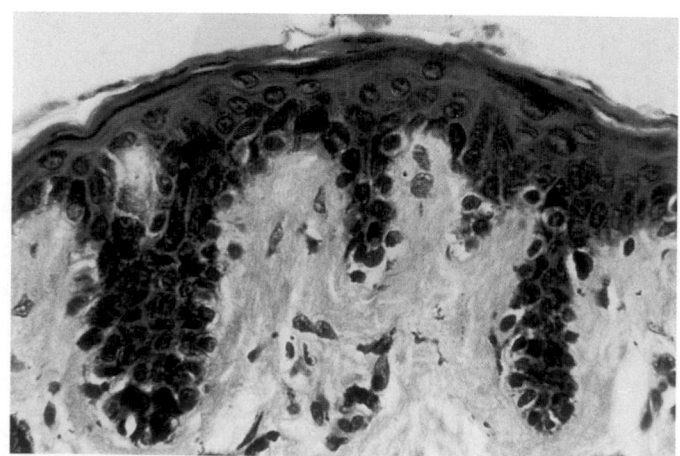

Fig. 4.129 Microscopic appearance of lentigo. There is elongation of rete ridges associated with hyperpigmentation of the basal layer.

Neuroendocrine cells

Merkel cell carcinoma

Merkel cell carcinoma is the currently preferred term for a distinctive cutaneous malignancy originally described as trabecular carcinoma[1025,1026] and also known as Merkel cell tumor, small cell carcinoma, endocrine carcinoma, and neuroendocrine carcinoma of the skin.[1020] It occurs mainly in adults and elderly individuals, but a few cases have been described in children.[1009] The face and extremities are the most common locations.[1005,1007,1016] (Figs 4.130 and 4.131). Clinically, it appears as a nodular, sometimes ulcerated lesion with a reddish or violaceous

hue. Microscopically, the tumor is centered in the dermis or sometimes in the subcutaneous tissue, with the overlying epidermis being usually uninvolved.[975] The monotonous nature of the dermal round cell infiltrate and the diffuse pattern of infiltration of the subcutaneous fat are responsible for its occasional misdiagnosis as malignant lymphoma[1018,1031] (Fig. 4.132). The pattern of growth can also be trabecular, but it is rare for this to be the predominant feature (hence the inappropriateness of the term trabecular carcinoma).[1028] The diagnosis of Merkel cell carcinoma can be made on the basis of the cytologic features as seen in a good hematoxylin and eosin-stained slide (Fig. 4.133). The cytoplasm is scanty but visible as a thin acidophilic rim; the nuclei are round and vesicular, with a typically fine granular ("dusty") chromatin and multiple nucleoli. Mitotic figures and fragmented nuclei (probably as the result of apoptosis) are plentiful. The stroma may contain proliferated vessels with plump endothelial cells, a feature that these tumors share with many other malignant neoplasms having a primitive neural phenotype.[988]

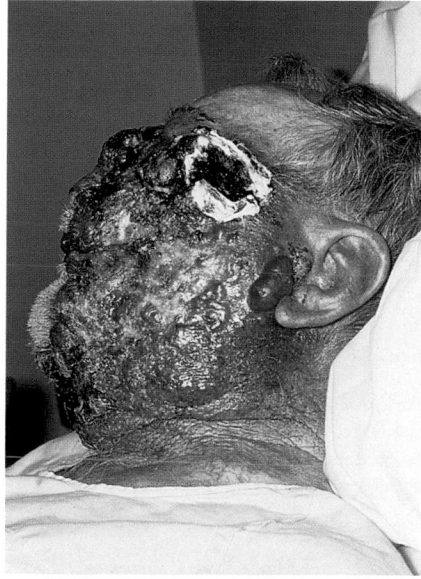

Fig. 4.130 Merkel cell carcinoma. This unfortunate patient had involvement of almost the entire face by a partially ulcerated neoplasm that failed to respond with chemotherapy after an initial diagnosis of malignant lymphoma.

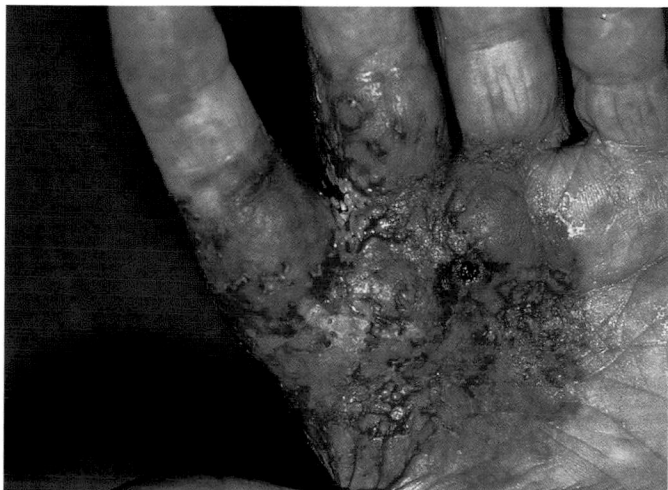

Fig. 4.131 Merkel cell carcinoma involving the hand. This particular lesion was associated with Bowen's disease of the overlying epidermis.

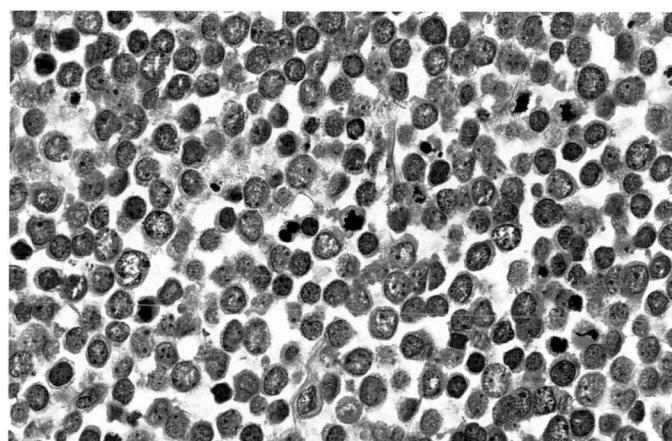

Fig. 4.132 Medium- and high-power views of Merkel cell carcinoma. Note the finely granular, dusty quality of the chromatin and the small nucleoli.

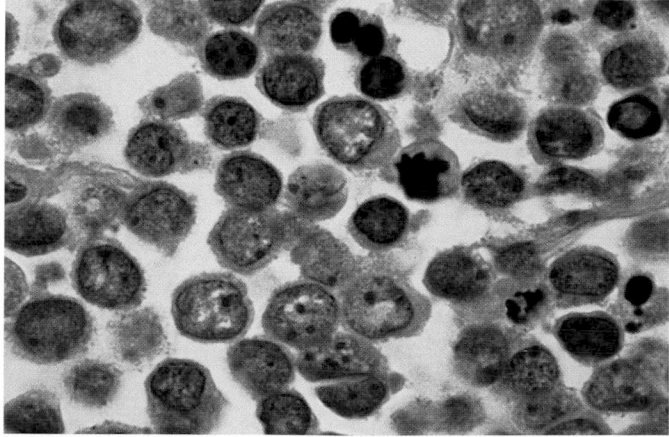

Fig. 4.133 Medium- and high-power views of Merkel cell carcinoma. Note the finely granular, dusty quality of the chromatin and the small nucleoli.

Merkel cell carcinoma can be seen in association with in situ or invasive squamous cell carcinoma, with duct-like structures of eccrine type, and with basal cell carcinoma-like areas, suggesting that it originates from a multipotential stem cell of ectodermal derivation.[980,991,992,996] Rarely, it exhibits focal or extensive intraepidermal pagetoid spread[995] (Fig. 4.134). Even more rarely, the entire tumor can be intraepidermal.[978]

Exceptionally, Merkel cell carcinoma can show foci resembling leiomyosarcoma or atypical fibroxanthoma, either in the primary tumor or in the recurrences as a result of dedifferentiation/divergent differentiation.[976,983]

When examined ultrastructurally, the tumor cells are seen to contain dense-core neurosecretory granules (sometimes arranged immediately beneath the cell membrane) and tightly packed perinuclear intermediate filaments[986,1018,1019] (Fig. 4.135). Filament-rich cytoplasmic spikes similar to those seen in normal Merkel cells have

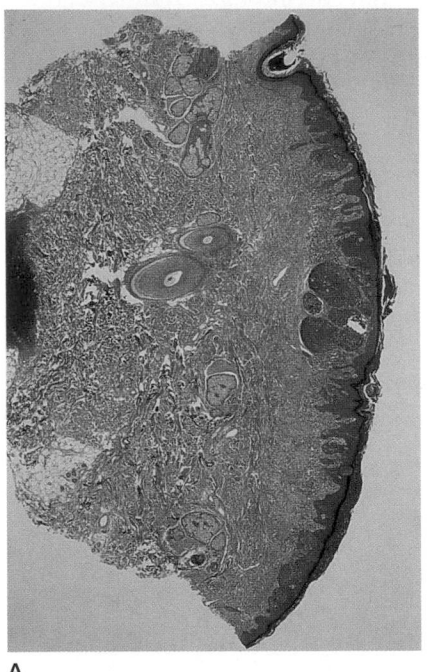

A

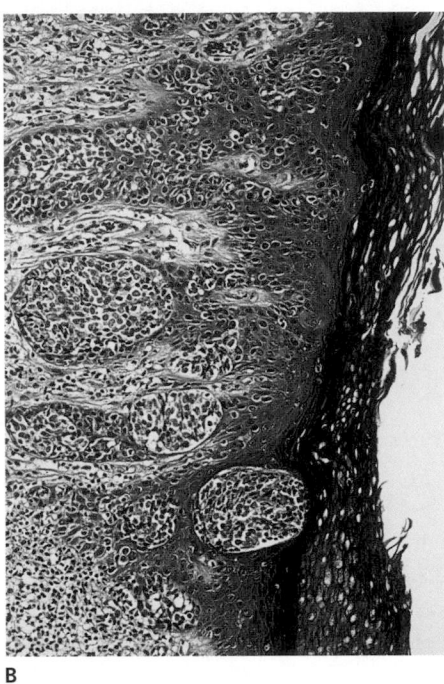

B

Fig. 4.134 A and **B**, Merkel cell carcinoma showing marked degree of epidermotropism. (Slide contributed by Dr. Philip LeBoit, San Francisco)

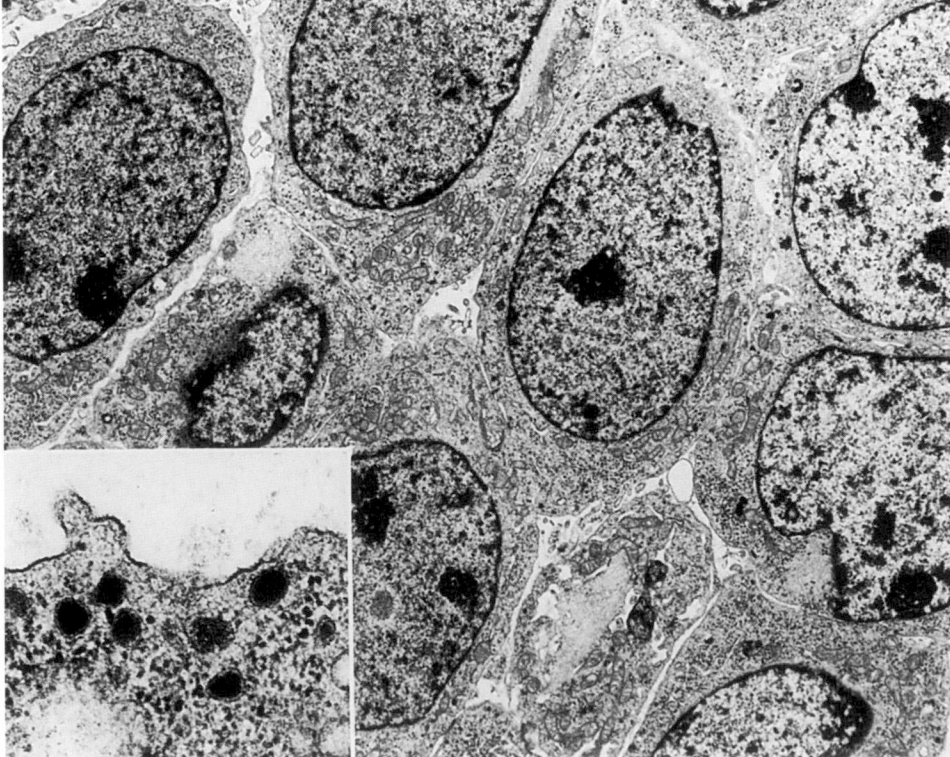

Fig. 4.135 Same tumor shown in Figs 4.132 and 4.133. Ultrastructurally, neurosecretory-type granules are seen in periphery of cytoplasm beneath cell membrane. (x4400; inset x41,100)

been detected in a few cases.[1017,1029] Occasionally, innumerable filiform cell prolongations are present, resulting in an "anemone cell" appearance.[1033]

The tumor cells are argyrophilic with the Grimelius reaction, especially if the tissue has been fixed in Bouin's solution.

Immunohistochemically, positivity for low-molecular-weight keratin, neurofilaments, and neuron-specific enolase is usually obtained[997,1001,1032] (Fig. 4.136). The positivity for keratin is predominantly of type 20[981,1004,1011] and has a distinct perinuclear dot-like quality, a feature found only exceptionally in small cell carcinomas of internal organs (we have seen it in isolated cases of neuroendocrine tumors of the salivary gland, pancreas, and thyroid). The consistent positivity for CK20 and neurofilaments and the negativity for TTF-1 are important in the differential diagnosis with small cell neuroendocrine carcinoma of lung.[979,981,982,994,1010,1012] Exceptions, however, occur, such as cases that are positive for CK7 while negative for CK20.[998]

In addition to the markers just listed, some cases of Merkel cell carcinoma have shown focal reactivity for chromogranin (less than half of the cases), synaptophysin, vasoactive intestinal peptide, pancreatic polypeptide, calcitonin, substance P, somatostatin, ACTH, other peptide hormones, and for CD117.[977,993,1000,1015,1021,1022]

At the cytogenetic level, one group found abnormalities of chromosomes 1, 11, and 12 in over one third of the cases.[1002] A distal deletion involving 1p35–36 seems particularly relevant, inasmuch as it has been detected in other malignant tumors showing neural differentiation.[1027] Another recently described chromosomal aberration is trisomy 6.[987]

Merkel cell carcinoma is an aggressive neoplasm. Regional nodal metastases are common, and distant metastases also occur, particularly to the lungs, liver, and bones,[989,1030] but also to unusual sites such as the testis.[1008] Occasionally, a typical Merkel cell carcinoma is found in a lymph node (most often inguinal) in the absence of a primary skin tumor.[984] The most likely explanation for this occurrence is spontaneous regression of the primary tumor (a phenomenon analogous to that which has been well documented in melanoma),[999,1024] but the alternative of at least some of these tumors possibly arising from nodal neuroendocrine cells has been raised.[984]

The recommended initial treatment for Merkel cell carcinoma is wide resection of the primary site and regional lymph node dissection.[990,1006] Radiation therapy can be effective as an adjunct,[1003] and chemotherapy has been employed for metastatic tumors.[985,1013,1023] Locoregional recurrence carries an ominous prognostic significance.[1014]

Other neuroendocrine tumors

Sometimes, tumors with an appearance identical to pulmonary **small cell neuroendocrine carcinoma** are found in the skin. They probably represent morphologic variants of Merkel cell carcinoma, but the possibility of a metastasis from an internal organ should always be ruled out.[1036] Most cases reported as *peripheral neuroblastomas* of skin also fit into the category of Merkel cell carcinoma; others are clearly different and of unquestionable neural derivation.[1040] Still others belong to the Ewing's sarcoma/PNET category.[1037] **Carcinoid tumors** of both insular and trabecular types, allegedly primary in the skin, have also been reported.[1034,1035,1038,1039] These should be distinguished from skin metastases from carcinoid tumor of internal organs, particularly lung.

Dermis

Fibroblastic tumors and tumorlike conditions

Keloid is an abnormal pattern of dermal reaction to injury (which may be clinically inapparent), seen most commonly in black persons[1061] (Fig. 4.137). The earlobe is one of the most common locations. It can be separated on morphologic grounds from a *hyperplastic scar* (which may precede it) because of the formation of wide acidophilic bands of collagen, with fibroblasts and myofibroblasts running in parallel between them[1041,1047] (Fig. 4.138). The immunohistochemical profile is also different.[1066] This distinction is useful in estimating the probability of recrudescence, which is much higher for keloids than for hypertrophic scars. Another differential diagnosis is with so-called "keloidal dermatofibroma," in which an otherwise typical dermatofibroma exhibits an area similar to keloid in its superficial portion.[1056]

In keloids that have been injected with steroids, pools of mucinous material can be found.[1065] The myofibroblasts present in these lesions are immunoreactive for vimentin, actin, nonmuscle myosin, and fibronectin.[1046] Scattered mast cells are also present. A keloid-type

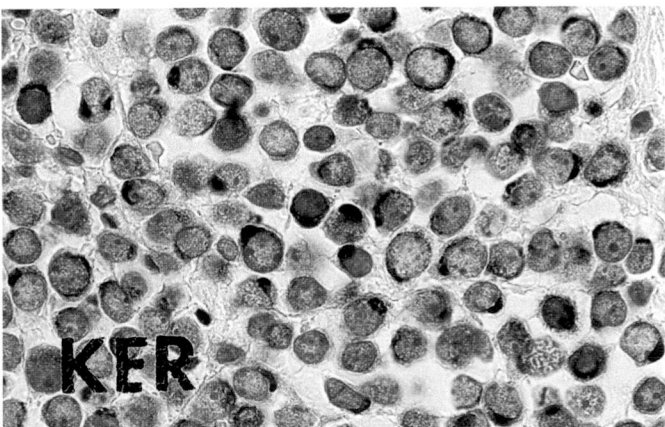

Fig. 4.136 Dot-like immunoreactivity for keratin in Merkel cell carcinoma.

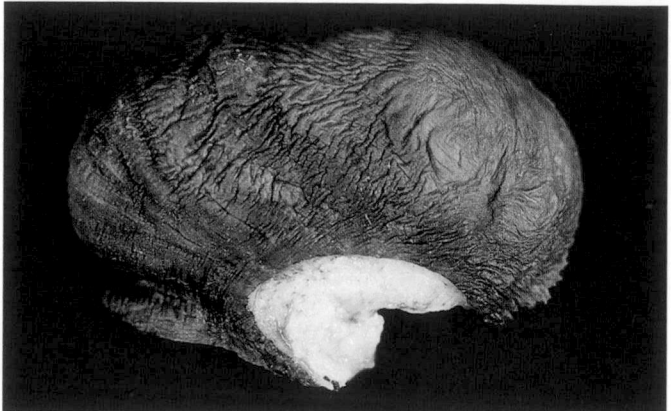

Fig. 4.137 Gross appearance of keloid of ear. The lesion has a polypoid shape.

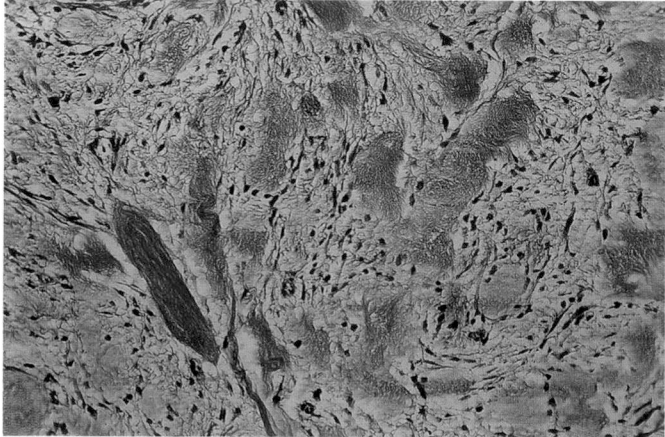

Fig. 4.138 Microscopic appearance of keloid, with characteristic wide bands of hyalinized collagen.

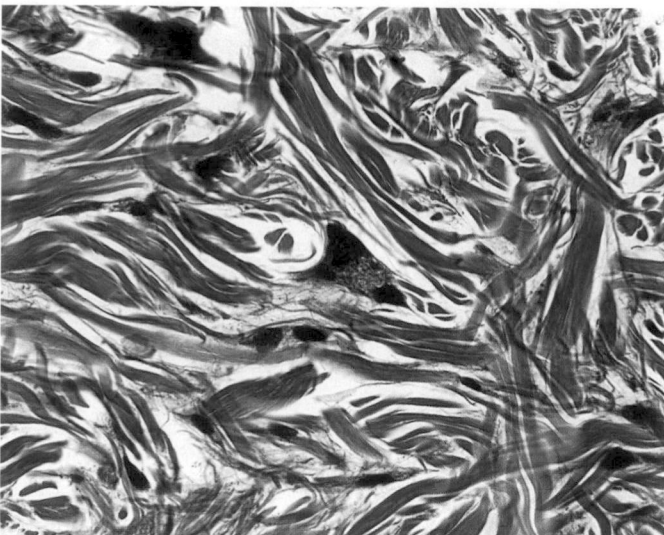

Fig. 4.139 Pleomorphic fibroma. A large triangular cell with hyperchromatic nuclei is encased within dense fibrous tissue.

change is sometimes seen as a complication of acne ("acne keloidalis").[1053]

Soft fibroma (acrochordon, cutaneous tag) is a misnomer for a non-neoplastic polypoid lesion composed of a loose connective tissue stalk covered by a normal to slightly hyperplastic (sometimes hyperkeratotic) epidermis.

Pleomorphic fibroma has a denser collagenous background, and it contains scattered bizarre cells with hyperchromatic nuclei and stellate cytoplasm, unaccompanied by mitotic activity[1044] (Fig. 4.139); the lesion is the cutaneous equivalent of the more common polypoid lesion seen in squamous-covered mucosal membranes, such as nasal cavity, oral cavity, and urogenital tract[1054] (see respective chapters). It is probably closely related to *giant cell collagenoma*,[1063] but distinct (also on immunohistochemical grounds) from dermatofibroma with monster cells.[1064]

Recurrent infantile digital fibroma is discussed in Chapter 25.

Fibrous papule of the face appears clinically as a solitary, dome-shaped, firm lesion, and the nose is by far the most common site (hence the alternative term "fibrous

papule of the nose").[1049] Microscopically, there are increased vessels with a dilated lumen separated by a fibroblastic stroma containing stellate and sometimes multinucleated cells similar to those of pleomorphic fibroma.[1057] The numerous hair follicles are surrounded by a concentric array of collagen fibers. This lesion, which anatomically is best described as an angiofibroma, should be distinguished from a fibrosing (involuting) melanocytic nevus, a not always easy but practically inconsequential task.[1042]

Sclerosing (sclerotic) fibroma is characterized by the heavy deposition of collagen in a markedly hypocellular lesion having well-circumscribed outlines. The collagen is predominantly of type I,[1067] and there is expression of CD34.[1051] This is probably a heterogeneous condition, with some of the cases representing the end stage of a folliculitis.[1043] Multiple fibromas of the face, scalp, and subungual region are seen in tuberous sclerosis, together with angiofibroma of the face and "shagreen patches" in the lumbosacral region. Multiple sclerotic fibromas are also a marker for Cowden's disease.[1062] A solitary form of sclerosing fibroma has been referred to as *circumscribed storiform collagenoma*.[1058]

Collagenous fibroma (desmoplastic fibroblastoma) is a different lesion from sclerosing (sclerotic) fibroma despite the misleadingly similar terminology. It is typically subcutaneous, sometimes associated with fascial involvement, and is characterized microscopically by bland stellate and spindle-shaped fibroblasts embedded in a collagenous or myxocollagenous matrix.[1048,1052,1059]

Dermatomyofibroma (cutaneous myofibroma) is a benign cutaneous, plaque-like proliferation of fibroblasts and myofibroblasts (the latter confirmed ultrastructurally[1060]) centered in the deep dermis and subcutis. It is most commonly found in and around the shoulder of young women.[1050,1055,1068] When hemorrhagic, it may simulate plaque-stage Kaposi sarcoma.[1057a]

Solitary fibrous tumor has been reported in the skin, its microscopic appearance being similar to that of its more common deep-seated counterpart.[1045]

Fibrohistiocytic tumors and tumorlike conditions

Benign fibrous histiocytoma

Benign fibrous histiocytoma (also known as subepidermal nodular fibrosis, dermatofibroma, histiocytoma, and sclerosing hemangioma) refers to a spectrum of firm, nodular, nonencapsulated, often pigmented lesions that occur chiefly on the extremities.[1071,1075] Clinically, they may be single or multiple and have a flat polypoid or depressed shape. Most of them are less than 1 cm in diameter, but some can reach huge proportions. When heavily pigmented, they may be confused clinically with nevi, malignant melanoma, Kaposi's sarcoma, and other vascular tumors. On transection, they are usually solid and rather well circumscribed but not encapsulated, the color ranging from white to yellow to dark brown, depending on the relative amounts of fibrous tissue, fat, and hemosiderin. Microscopically, there is a cellular fibroblastic proliferation with varying amounts of collagen deposition, admixed with a variable number of macrophages, most of which contain fat (thereby acquiring a foamy appearance) or hemosiderin. Some of these histiocytes are multinucleated and may acquire the features of Touton's giant cells. Much more rarely, they have osteoclast-like features, with or without accompanying bone formation.[1091,1093] The lesion is characteristically centered in the upper dermis, but it can involve the deep dermis and occasionally extend into the subcutis.[1090,1111] The fibrohistiocytic proliferation is set in a fine vascular network, which can be very prominent (Fig. 4.140). The presence of this vascular component is responsible for this lesion having been regarded in the past as a sclerosing hemangioma and for the fact that it is still occasionally misdiagnosed as Kaposi's sarcoma, especially when occurring in HIV-infected individuals. Focal storiform features may be seen, but they are rarely as well developed as in dermatofibrosarcoma protuberans. Smooth muscle proliferation may be present within the adjacent dermis.[1095] The lesions blend imperceptibly into the adjacent dermis. The overlying epidermis can be normal, atrophic, or acanthotic. Sometimes there is a proliferation of hair germ-like structures in the basal layer of this epithelium, and rarely a full-blown basal cell carcinoma develops[1079,1080,1083] (Fig. 4.141); the epidermal growth factor receptor is said to play a role in this interesting phenomenon.[1098]

Exceptionally, the overlying epidermis shows squamous cell carcinoma in situ.[1086]

Morphologic variations of dermatofibroma include prominent palisading similar to that seen in peripheral

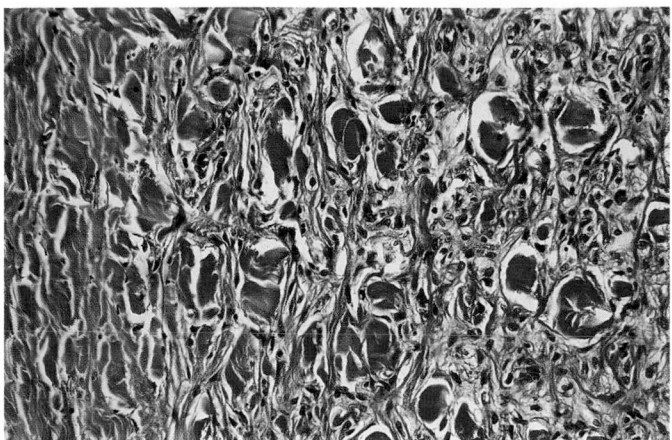

A

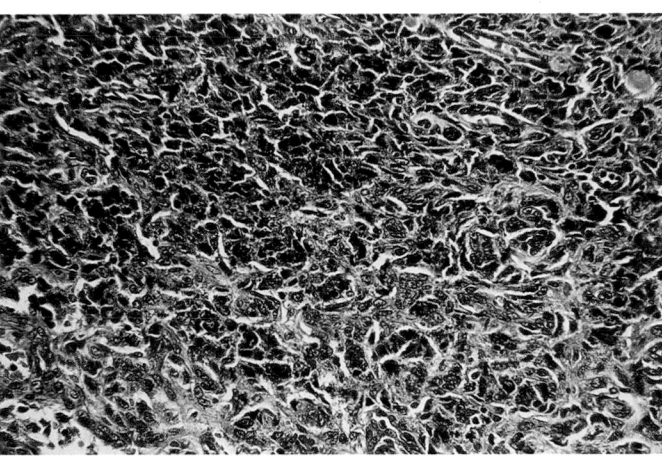

B

Fig. 4.140. Benign fibrous histiocytoma of skin. The tumor depicted in **A** is predominantly fibrous, whereas that shown in **B** is mainly composed of hemosiderin-laden macrophages.

nerve tumors,[1103] keloid-like changes,[1092] myxoid changes,[1110] granular cells,[1105,1113] markedly lipidized cells,[1087] clear cells,[1099,1108] diffuse eosinophilic infiltrate,[1070] and lichenoid, erosive, and ulcerated features.[1101] Sometimes two or more of these variations coexist.[1112] Marked focal cellular atypia (manifested by the presence of "monster cells"),[1096,1106] extreme cellularity (sometimes associated with necrosis),[1077] and the presence of large cystic changes filled with blood may also occur. The latter lesion, referred to as *hemorrhagic, aneurysmal*, or *angiomatoid*, should be distinguished from the angiomatoid malignant fibrous histiocytoma seen in deeper sites in younger patients (see Chapter 25)[1076,1102] (Fig. 4.142). *Epithelioid cell histiocytoma* is probably yet another variation on the theme; this is characterized by the presence of large "angulated" epithelioid cells as the main constituent[1082,1104,1109] (Fig. 4.143). This tumor is notorious for its ability to simulate vascular and melanocytic neoplasms.[1081]

Immunohistochemically, the proliferating spindle cells of benign fibrous histiocytoma are positive for vimentin but usually negative for lysozyme and other histiocytic

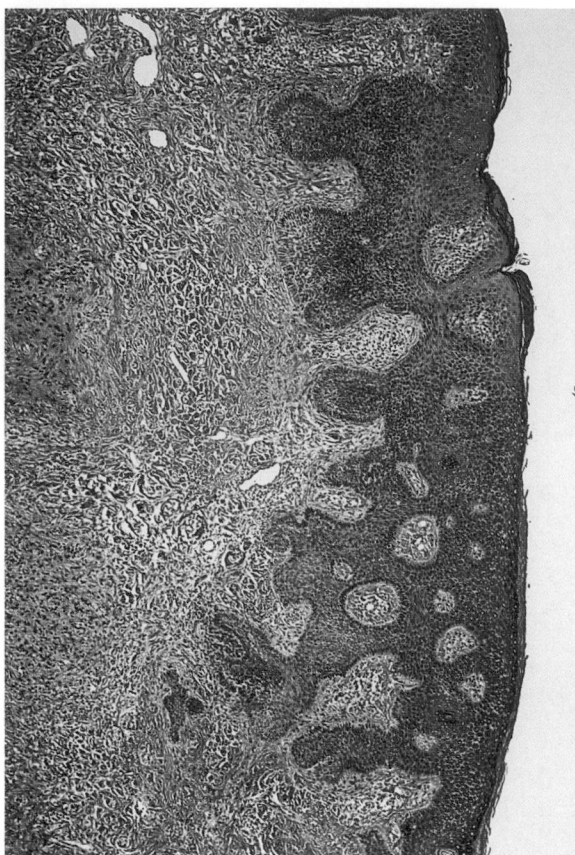

Fig. 4.141 Benign fibrous histiocytoma. This lesion is associated with basaloid proliferation of the overlying skin. This change does not represent a basal cell carcinoma.

markers; these results raise questions about their alleged histiocytic nature.[1073,1084] They have also been found to be reactive for FXIIIa, a proenzyme known to be present in so-called "dermal dendrocytes"[1069,1100]; in contrast with dermatofibrosarcoma protuberans, they are negative for CD34,[1069,1094] and positive for tenascin.[1089] Another group of markers that dermatofibromas often exhibit are those associated with smooth muscle/myofibroblastic differentiation, such as actin, desmin, and myosin; this is not generally known and has led to misdiagnoses such as leiomyoma or—worse—leiomyosarcoma.[1072,1114]

There is a long standing controversy as to whether dermatofibroma is a neoplastic or reactive condition, but the occurrence of aggressive and even metastasizing forms of the disease (see below) and the evidence of clonality at the molecular level[1074,1078,1107] favor the former possibility.

The behavior of dermatofibroma is generally very indolent, to the extent that local recurrence is very rare even if the margins are inadequate. However, cases with locally aggressive behavior and even with distant metastases are on record. This is seen more commonly with lesions located in the face and those exhibiting deep extension into the subcutaneous tissue and/or cellular fascicles of mitotically active spindle cells, but it remains an exceptionally rare occurrence.[1085,1088,1097]

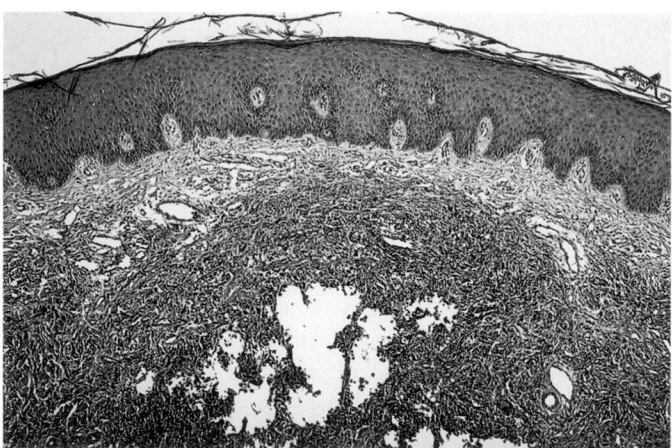

A

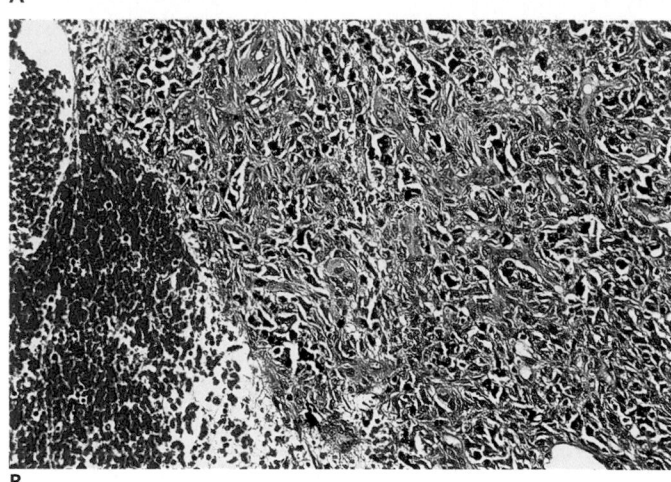

B

Fig. 4.142 Aneurysmal benign fibrous histiocytoma. **A,** Low-power appearance. The empty space in the center of the lesion was occupied by blood; **B,** Higher-power view, showing recent and old hemorrhage.

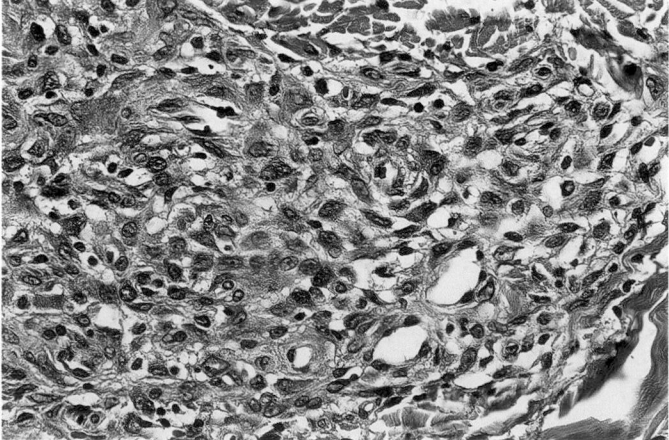

Fig. 4.143 Epithelioid histiocytoma.

Atypical fibroxanthoma

Atypical fibroxanthomas are nodular, sometimes ulcerated tumors that typically occur on the sun-exposed skin of elderly persons and are often regarded clinically as carcinomas[1122,1124,1125] (Fig. 4.144). Similar lesions have

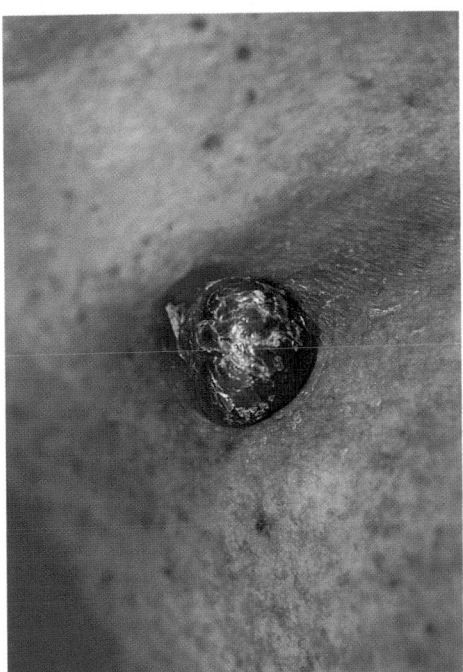

Fig. 4.144 Clinical appearance of atypical fibroxanthoma. The lesion is characteristically elevated, reddish, and ulcerated.

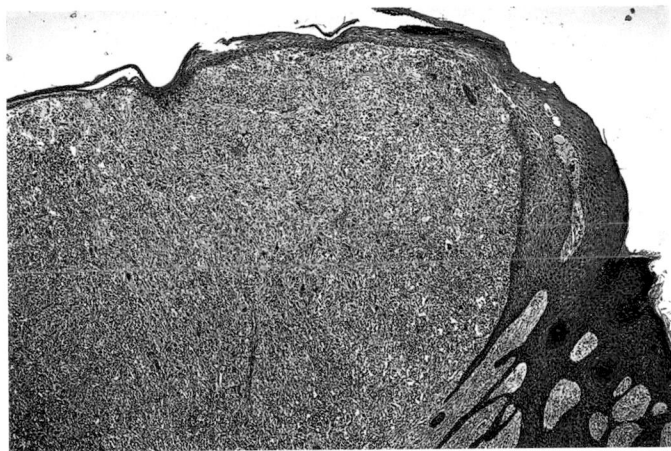

Fig. 4.145 Low-power view of atypical fibroxanthoma. The lesion is typically polypoid and ulcerated.

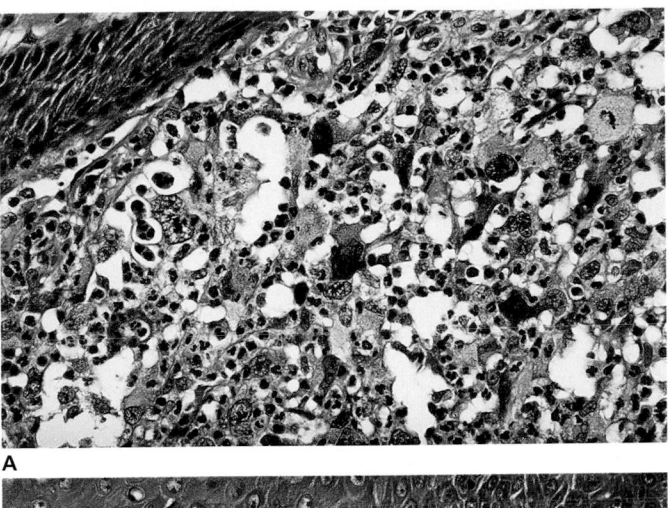

A

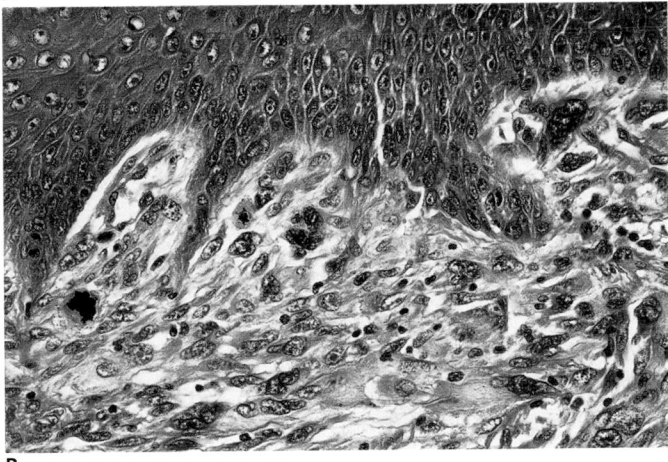

B

Fig. 4.146 A and **B**, High-power views of atypical fibroxanthoma, showing highly anaplastic cells in the dermis surrounded by an inflammatory infiltrate.

been reported with different names at sites of irradiation damage.[1115,1133] Others have been seen in sun-protected areas of younger individuals. Histologically, the tumor is often polypoid and ulcerated, especially when occurring at the classical sites (Fig. 4.145). Bizarre tumor cells are seen scattered within a spindle cell stroma with varying amounts of inflammation (Fig. 4.146). Mitoses are plentiful, some of them being atypical. A helpful point to remember is that the scattered tumor cells are very abnormal, but that the background in which they are situated has an inflammatory or reactive appearance. However, in some instances there is little pleomorphism and a predominance of spindle cells.[1117] The overlying epidermis may be normal, atrophic, hyperplastic, or ulcerated, but by definition it should not show continuity

with the tumor. Morphologic variations include tumors with pigmentation,[1120,1138] with osteoclast-like giant cells,[1126] with clear cells,[1118,1134] (which should be distinguished from other clear cell mesenchymal neoplasms)[1127a] and with granular cells.[1132]

Immunohistochemically, the various components of the lesion may show reactivity for vimentin, actin, calponin, h-caldesmon, CD68 (detected with monoclonal antibody KP-1), α_1-antitrypsin, a_1-antichymotrypsin, cathepsin-B, FXIIIa (focal), S-100 protein (focal) and CD99, and negativity for keratin, EMA, and desmin.[1129–1131,1135,1136] Surprisingly, the large majority of these tumors have been found to be diploid on flow cytometry.[1139] Furthermore, and despite the bizarre microscopic features that suggest a high-grade lesion, atypical fibroxanthomas are relatively indolent lesions that are usually cured by local excision.[1119] However, some cases have resulted in local recurrence, and a few have metastasized.[1123] Factors that portend aggressive behavior and possible metastases in atypical fibroxanthoma are vascular invasion, extension into deep tissues, tumor necrosis, local recurrence, and history of immunosuppression.[1123] The accumulated evidence suggests that atypical fibroxanthoma is a malignant tumor that is statistically associated with an excellent prognosis because of its generally small size and superficial location. The view has been advanced that this tumor is a distinct subtype of malignant fibrous histiocytoma, based on morphologic, ultrastructural, and immunohistochemical criteria.[1128] However, we do not believe that the matter of histogenesis has been entirely settled. Some unquestionable squamous cell carcinomas and malignant melanomas (of the so-called "desmoplastic" variety) exhibit in their deep portions a pattern of growth that is indistinguishable from that of atypical fibroxanthoma.[1127] This being the case, one cannot help wondering whether some or perhaps most of the tumors presently included among the atypical fibroxanthomas may not actually be carcinomas or melanomas in disguise. Evans and Smith[1121] favored this point of view and therefore used for them the noncommittal term *sarcoma-like tumors* of the skin. They made the interesting observation that the prognosis was not significantly different whether there was a definite component of squamous cell carcinoma in them or not, an experience which has been duplicated by others.[1137]

In summary, it seems likely that atypical fibroxanthoma (like malignant fibrous histiocytoma) is the expression of a pattern of growth that can be exhibited by true mesenchymal neoplasms but also by squamous cell carcinoma, malignant melanoma, skin adnexal tumors, and even Merkel cell carcinoma.[1116]

Dermatofibrosarcoma protuberans

Dermatofibrosarcomas protuberans (DFSP) are slow-growing, nodular, polypoid neoplasms that are found almost exclusively in the dermis, from which they often invade the subcutaneous tissue (Fig. 4.147). Most of the cases occur in adults, but they have also been seen in infancy and childhood.[1161] As a group, these tumors are much larger than benign fibrous histiocytomas; however, the diagnosis of DFSP should not be made or ruled out on the basis of size alone. Microscopically, the appearance of radial whorls of spindle cells producing the storiform or cartwheel pattern is characteristic although not pathognomonic (Fig. 4.148). Other features of diagnostic importance are the high cellularity, monomorphic appearance, moderate-to-high mitotic activity, lack or inconspicuousness of foamy or hemosiderin-laden macrophages and/or multinucleated giant cells, and entrapment of isolated fat cells when the subcutis is infiltrated (Fig. 4.149). Myxoid features can be present focally and sometimes be the dominant feature of the tumor.[1154,1171] Bundles of plumper spindle cells of myxoid appearance can be seen.[1146] Regressive areas with atrophy may also occur, and these are likely to be underdiagnosed.[1148,1177] Granular cell change may be present in areas.[1143]

Immunohistochemically, these tumors are positive for vimentin, actin (focally and inconstantly), and CD34

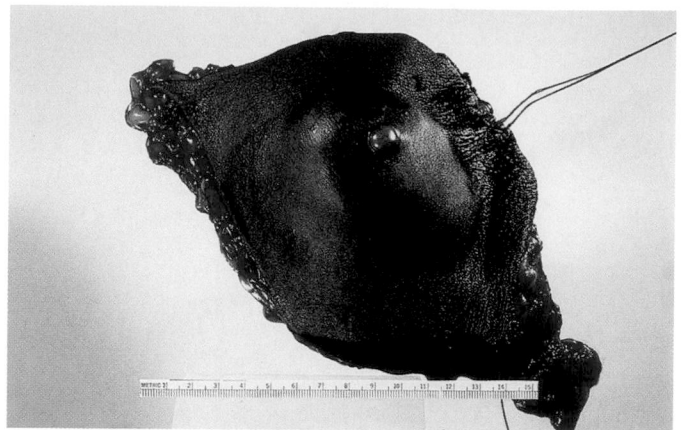

Fig. 4.147 Gross appearance of dermatofibrosarcoma protuberans, showing typical bulging above the skin.

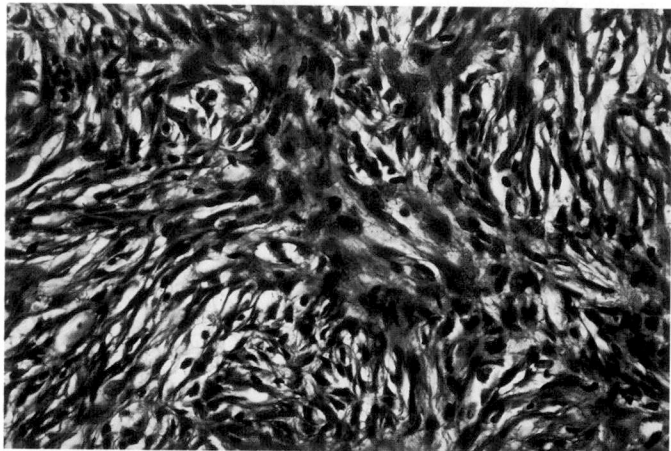

Fig. 4.148 Storiform or cartwheel pattern of dermatofibrosarcoma protuberans.

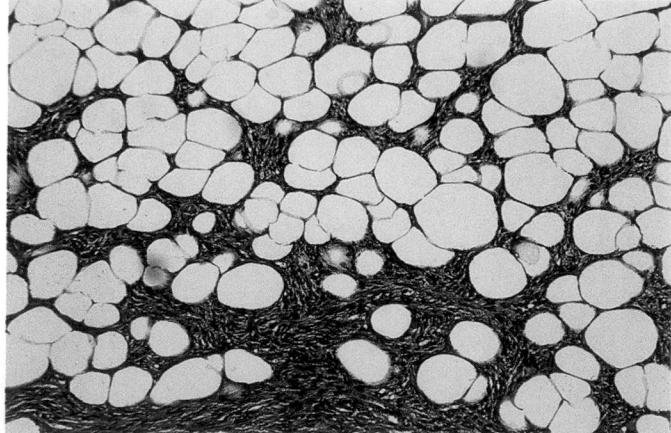

Fig. 4.149 Typical pattern of invasion of subcutaneous fat by dermatofibrosarcoma protuberans.

(strongly and consistently).[1151,1155] Conversely, they are negative for S-100 protein, HMB-45, keratin, and factor XIIIa (although some dendritic cells that are reactive for the latter marker are usually found).[1140,1158–1160] The diagnosis of DFSP can be made or at least suspected on the basis of fine needle aspiration material.[1167]

Cytogenetically, DFSP shows supernumerary rings derived from chromosome 22 or a linear translocation in the same chromosome, both of them leading to the gene fusion *COL1A1* with *PDGF*.[1169,1172] This molecular alteration is also found in the morphologic variants of this tumor, including the high-grade areas when present.[1162]

Dermatofibrosarcoma protuberans has been placed for many years under the malignant fibrous histiocytoma umbrella. The histogenesis of this tumor is, however, far from clear. The occasional occurrence of histologically identical tumors containing melanin (see following discussion), some of their ultrastructural features,[1157] and the consistent reactivity they exhibit for CD34 and nerve growth factor receptor raise the alternative possibility that DFSP may be a peculiar type of nerve sheath tumor (but composed of cells other than Schwann cells or perineural cells).[1153,1175]

The natural history of DFSP is characterized by an extremely high tendency for local recurrence following limited resection.[1145,1173] Very rare instances of metastases to regional nodes and/or internal organs have also been documented.[1141]

A close relationship exists between DFSP and giant cell fibroblastoma (see Chapter 25), which is mainly manifested by the occurrence of hybrid or combined tumors, either simultaneously or sequentially,[1142,1144,1164,1170] and by their common molecular alterations.[1168,1174]

DFSP can undergo "progression" to a fibrosarcoma, the latter areas acquiring the typical herringbone appearance of that tumor type and no longer exhibiting a storiform pattern of growth: it is not clear whether this morphologic change is reflected in a more aggressive clinical form,[1147,1149,1156,1163,1176] although the logical expectation is that it should; occasionally, the tumor progression is toward a more pleomorphic neoplasm with the appearance of a malignant fibrous histiocytoma[1165] or a malignant giant cell tumor of soft parts.[1152]

Pigmented DFSP (Bednar's tumor, pigmented storiform neurofibroma) is a neoplasm having the overall appearance of an ordinary DFSP but containing, in addition, a variable (but usually small and patchy) population of dendritic cells containing large amounts of melanin pigment.[1150] Although this finding obviously raises the possibility of schwannian/melanocytic derivation, the tumor is negative for S-100 protein and other melanocyte-related markers and should not be equated with malignant melanoma of conventional, desmoplastic, or soft tissue (clear cell sarcoma) types. The similarity with DFSP extends even to the occasional development in Bednar's tumor of fibrosarcomatous areas and of distant metastatic spread.[1166]

Malignant fibrous histiocytoma

A tumor morphologically analogous to the pleomorphic-storiform type of malignant fibrous histiocytoma of soft tissues occurs in the skin, but its separation from atypical fibroxanthoma and dermatofibrosarcoma protuberans with dedifferentiation or "progression" is not always clear-cut. Perhaps the term should be restricted to pleomorphic malignant fibrohistiocytic tumors of skin that infiltrate deeply into the subcutis, fascia, or muscle and have considerable necrosis.[1179,1182] Some of the reported cases have occurred in chronic ulcers or scars,[1181] and others have shown the features of the myxoid variant (myxofibrosarcoma).[1179a] Tumors having architectural and cytologic features intermediate between those of benign fibrous histiocytoma (dermatofibroma) and malignant fibrous histiocytoma are best designated as *borderline or atypical fibrous histiocytomas*, regarded as potential recurring lesions, and treated with wide local excision. A group of such lesions occurring in children and adolescents has been described as *atypical fibrous histiocytomas*, a term that is microscopically accurate but which may lead to confusion with atypical fibroxanthoma, an altogether different lesion.[1180]

As in the case of atypical fibroxanthoma, before making the diagnosis of malignant fibrous histiocytoma of the skin one should take into consideration (in addition to the above mentioned entities) the possibilities of anaplastic carcinoma and malignant melanoma.[1178]

Xanthoma

Xanthomas are non-neoplastic nodules resulting from the accumulation of fat-laden histiocytes in the dermis and subcutis or deeply in the tendons, synovium, and bone (Figs 4.150 and 4.151). They are usually periarticular and few in number, but disseminated forms occur.[1183] They are often associated with hyperlipidemia, either primary (familial) or secondary to diabetes mellitus, hypothyroidism, multiple myeloma, malignant lymphoma, leukemia, and obstructive liver disease. Flat xanthomas of the eyelid, referred to as *xanthelasma*, show a similar

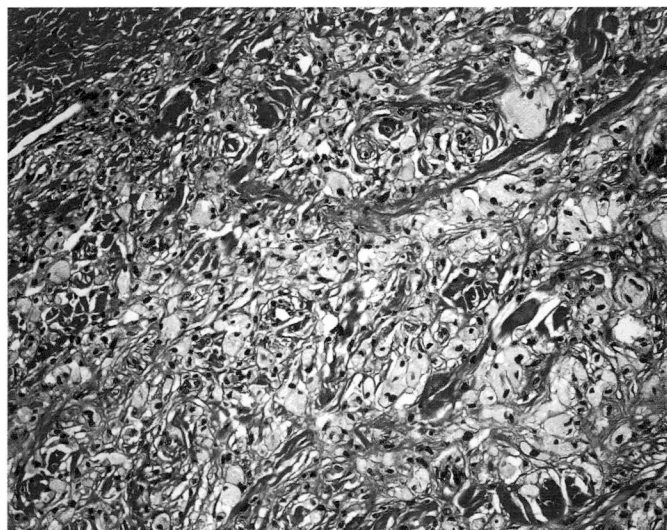

Fig. 4.150 Cutaneous xanthoma showing ill-defined collection of foamy macrophages in the dermis.

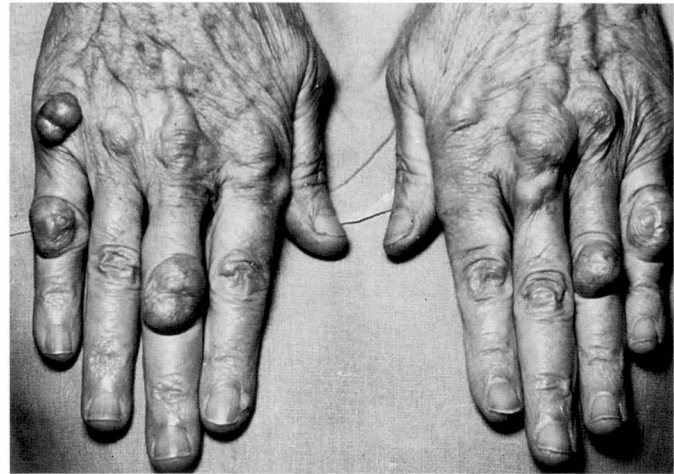

Fig. 4.151 Xanthoma tuberosum multiplex in patient with hypercholesterolemia.

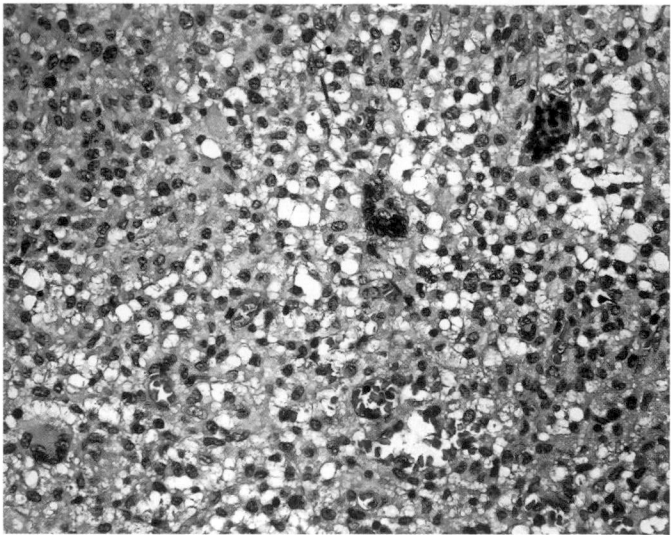

Fig. 4.152 Juvenile xanthogranuloma. Scattered multinucleated histiocytes are seen among numerous mononuclear elements.

microscopic appearance. Only a minority of these patients have hyperlipidemia. Papular xanthoma is usually found in the trunk or extremities of males.[1184] In *eruptive xanthoma*, there is an abrupt onset of crops of yellowish papules with erythematous halos on the extensor surfaces. It can be confused with granuloma annulare at the microscopic level.[1186] In *verruciform xanthoma*, there is a papillomatous, verruca-like change of the overlying epidermis.[1188,1191]

Xanthogranulomas with scanty foamy macrophages and giant cells may closely mimic malignant melanoma, also because of their immunoreactivity for S-100 protein.[1185]

Necrobiotic xanthogranuloma is a destructive dermal and subcutaneous xanthogranulomatous process that most frequently involves the face (particularly the periorbital region) and trunk. It is commonly accompanied by a monoclonal gammopathy and sometimes by cryoglobulins.[1189] Mucosal, muscle, and systemic lesions may be present.[1187,1190]

Juvenile xanthogranuloma

Juvenile xanthogranuloma (nevoxanthoendothelioma) occurs most often in the skin, but it can also be found in the subcutaneous tissue, skeletal muscle,[1191b] ocular globe, peripheral nerves,[1192] testis,[1198] and other sites.[1193,1199] It usually presents in infants, hence the prefix "nevo," in the form of a congenital mark.[1191a] However, it also occurs in adults, having in them a slightly different microscopic appearance.[1201] The upper part of the body is most commonly involved. The skin lesions are multiple in approximately 20% of cases[1200]; adult cases are more often solitary. Glaucoma and amblyopia, caused by involvement of the iris and ciliary body, can sometimes be seen as the initial manifestation of the disease. It has been reported in association with type I neurofibromatosis, epilepsy, Niemann–Pick disease, urticaria pigmentosa, and cytomegalovirus (CMV) infection.[1201]

Microscopically, the lesion is characterized by a histiocytic proliferation that in later stages is accompanied by foamy and Touton giant cell forms (Fig. 4.152). Lymphocytes, eosinophils, proliferating vessels, and fibroblasts may also be present. Ultrastructurally, the histiocytes do not contain Birbeck's granules; some have instead a variable number of cytoplasmic lipid vacuoles.[1197] Immunohistochemically, most cases show positivity for α_1-antichymotrypsin, lysozyme, and other histiocytic markers,[1195] whereas S-100 protein is essentially negative; the lesion is thought to be a proliferation of (non-Langerhans') cells belonging to the so-called "accessory immune system," whether conventional macrophages or plasmacytoid monocytes.[1194,1196]

A variant of xanthogranuloma is predominantly composed of spindle cells; solitary and generalized forms have been described.[1202]

Other histiocytic proliferations

Many other types of histiocytic infiltrates of the skin occur, a high percentage of them in children.[1203,1207,1211,1212] *Giant cell reticulohistiocytoma* can present in a solitary or multicentric form, the latter sometimes associated with articular involvement ("lipoid dermatoarthritis").[1205,1209,1216] Microscopically, there is an infiltration of mononuclear and multinucleated histiocytes with a characteristic ground glass cytoplasm, admixed with other inflammatory cells.[1215] Immunohistochemically, the main proliferating cells have markers of histiocytes, with an important secondary component of dermal dendrocytes.[1210,1213] Some authors believe that reticulohistiocytoma and multicentric reticulohistiocytosis represent different entities.[1218]

In *Langerhans' cell histiocytosis* (histiocytosis X), scattered ordinary histiocytes are seen admixed with eosinophils and S-100 protein and CD1-positive Langerhans' cells, the latter defining the nature of the disorder (see Chapter 21). Invasion of the epidermis by the infiltrate is an important diagnostic sign.

Rosai–Dorfman disease (sinus histiocytosis with massive lymphadenopathy) may involve the skin[1217] (Figs 4.153 and 4.154); in most instances the diagnosis is obvious because of the presence of prominent cervical lymphadenopathy, but in a large number of cases the cutaneous lesions represent the predominant or exclusive manifestation of the disease.[1206,1208,1214]

Leprosy can be easily confused with fibrous histiocytoma when the infiltrate is composed of a mixture of histiocytes and fibroblasts (so-called "histioid form").[1204]

Smooth muscle tumors

Leiomyomas of skin can be divided into three distinct types: the genital lesions located in the nipple or scrotum; the multiple superficial nodules of nevoid or hamartomatous type derived from arrectores pilorum muscle (pilar leiomyoma)[1229]; and the solitary angioleiomyoma (vascular leiomyoma), which is usually subcutaneous rather than dermal[1222] (see Chapter 25). Cutaneous leiomyomas can be very painful. Microscopically, they show intersecting fascicles of smooth muscle, without atypia, mitotic activity, or necrosis. Occasionally, scattered bizarre hyperchromatic nuclei are present in either angioleiomyosarcomas[1224] or pilar leiomyomas.[1226] As in analogous situations in other parts of the body, these tumors—which behave in a benign fashion—are variously called pleomorphic, symplasmic, or atypical.

Familial cutaneous leiomyomatosis is a genetically determined condition sometimes associated with a distinct morphologic type of renal cell carcinoma.[1225]

Leiomyosarcomas are larger, more cellular, and mitotically active and may contain areas of necrosis.[1219,1221,1223] Some of them exhibit a prominent vascular pattern, suggesting that they may represent the malignant counterpart of vascular leiomyoma.[1231] Others have clear cell ("leiomyoblastomatous") features[1227,1230] and still others have a desmoplastic quality.[1220] Cutaneous leiomyosarcomas often recur. However, they metastasize only exceptionally if at all, in stark contrast with their subcutaneous counterpart[1221] (see Chapter 25). Some of the recently reported cases have occurred in HIV-infected patients.[1228]

Skeletal muscle tumors

Striated muscle hamartoma (rhabdomyosarcomatous mesenchymal hamartoma) is a benign process of infants usually located centrally on the chin or near the ala of the nose, sometimes in association with other congenital abnormalities. Microscopically, the lesion is formed by a central core containing bundles and individual fibers of skeletal muscle and other mesenchymal elements.[1232,1236] Occasionally, lesions with a similar appearance (and also of presumed choristomatous or hamartomatous nature) present as multiple nodules in the skin.[1234,1235]

Adult rhabdomyoma has been reported in the lip and eyelid.[1237]

Cutaneous sarcomas exhibiting **rhabdomyoblastic** differentiation are exceptional, but a few convincing cases are on record.[1238] Rhabdomyosarcoma can represent the malignant component of congenital melanocytic nevus.[1233]

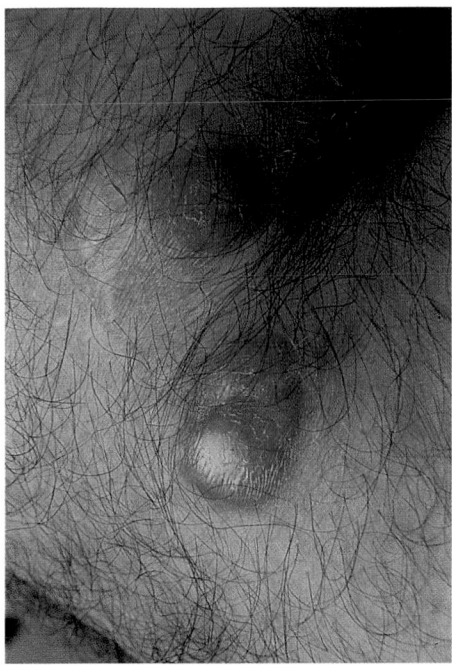

Fig. 4.153 Clinical appearance of Rosai-Dorfman disease of the skin. In this case the lesion presented in the form of multiple elevated erythematous nodules.

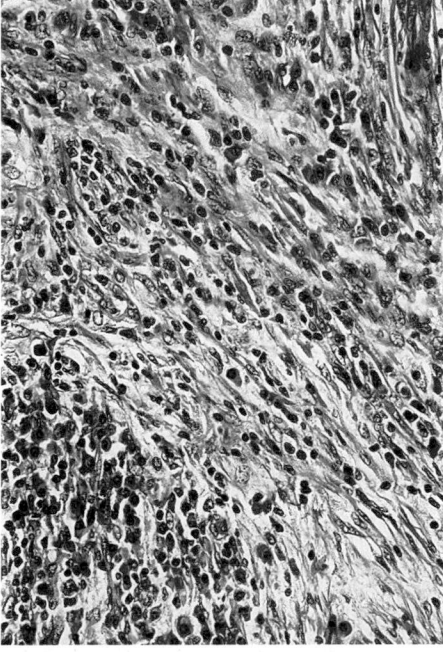

Fig. 4.154 Microscopic appearance of cutaneous Rosai-Dorfman disease. A polymorphic infiltrate composed of lymphocytes, plasma cells, and histiocytes is present. As is often the case in extranodal lesions, there is a moderate degree of fibrosis.

Peripheral nerve tumors

Of the various types of peripheral nerve tumors, those with a predilection for cutaneous (dermal)—as opposed to subcutaneous or deeper—involvement are neurofibroma, granular cell tumor (not all of which are neural), neurothekeoma, and palisaded encapsulated neuroma.[1255] The first two tumors are discussed in Chapter 25, but it should be mentioned here that dermal neurofibromas can result in proliferation of entrapped sweat glands or folliculosebaceous structures which can be confusing.[1245]

Neurothekeoma (nerve sheath myxoma, cutaneous lobular neuromyxoma) is a benign neoplasm of presumed peripheral nerve derivation characterized microscopically by a myxoid background enclosing nests of epithelioid cells sometimes exhibiting a mild to moderate degree of atypia.[1248,1249] The staining pattern with S-100 is variable. A cellular variant of this tumor has been described: it is invariably negative for S-100 protein and other neural markers (except for PGP9.5[1261]) and can be confused with malignant melanoma and other melanocytic tumors,[1241,1250,1258] particularly when exhibiting atypical features[1242] (Fig. 4.155). The exact nature of this variant and its relationship with the usual (myxoid) form of neurothekeoma and other skin neoplasms are debatable.[1240,1243,1252,1262] However, the fact that intermediate forms exist suggests that they are part of the same spectrum. We have seen several cases in which typical neurothekeoma areas blended with a pattern very similar to that of plexiform fibrohistiocytic tumor, suggesting a relationship between the two entities.[1251]

Palisaded encapsulated neuroma (solitary circumscribed neuroma) presents as a small solitary papule, usually located in the face.[1253] Microscopically, it is a spindle cell lesion exhibiting varying degrees of nuclear palisading (Fig. 4.156).[1254] Occasionally, the cells are epithelioid rather than spindle.[1260] Misinterpretation of this benign process (which is probably hyperplastic rather than neoplastic) as a neurofibroma or leiomyoma is common. Immunohistochemically, the spindle cells are strongly reactive for S-100 protein, in keeping with their presumed schwannian nature.[1239,1247] Axons can be demonstrated with special stains.

Epithelial sheath neuroma is a most peculiar skin lesion characterized by a proliferation of nerve fibers coated by squamous epithelium[1256]; it is not clear whether this process is neoplastic or reactive.

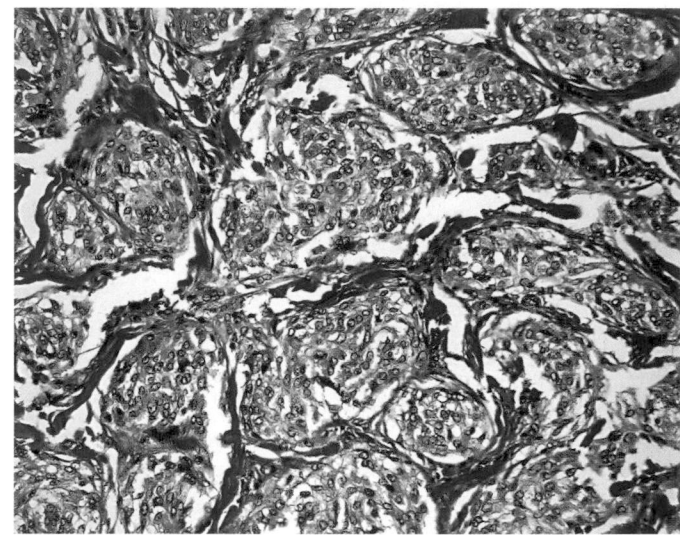

Fig. 4.155 Cellular neurothekeoma. The tumor cells are arranged in compact nests.

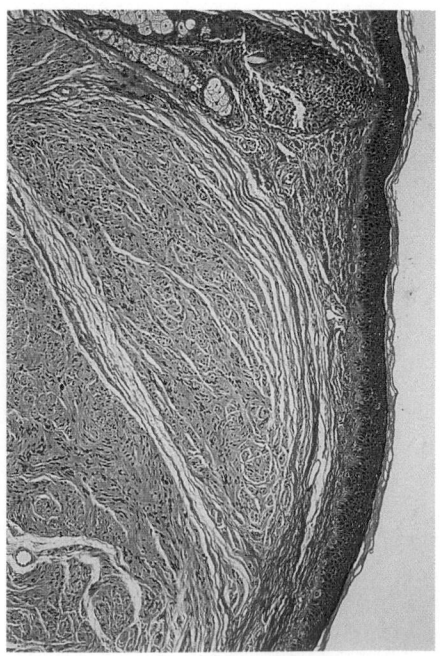
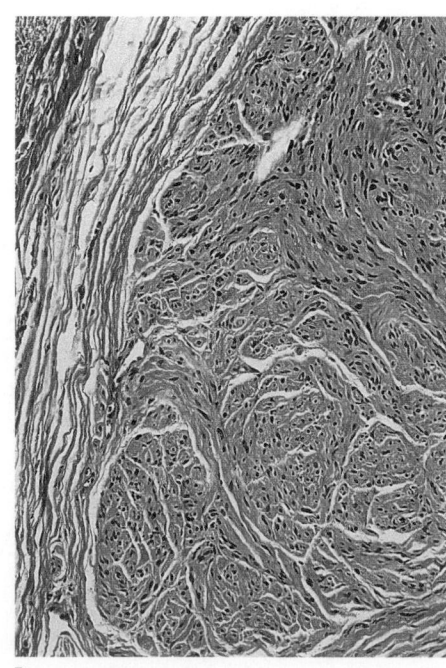

A

B

Fig. 4.156 A and **B,** Palisaded encapsulated neuroma. The fascicular pattern is well developed. This lesion should not be confused with leiomyoma of skin.

Perineurioma can occur in the skin in the form of either an epithelioid neoplasm (often misdiagnosed as epithelioid histiocytoma) or as a sclerosing lesion (which simulates a fibroma). EMA immunoreactivity is an important clue to the diagnosis in either case.[1246,1257]

Although the large majority of **malignant peripheral nerve sheath tumors (MPNST)** are located in the deep soft tissues, cutaneous examples have been described in patients with or without type I Recklinghausen's disease.[1244,1259]

Vascular tumors and tumorlike conditions

A large variety of tumors and ectasias arising from blood and lymph vessels of the skin exists,[1263,1264] and several new types have been described in recent years.[1265] Most of these lesions are discussed in Chapter 25. Only those features pertaining to their cutaneous location will be mentioned in this section.

Hemangioma

The more distinctive types of benign blood vessel tumors of skin are capillary hemangioma, benign (infantile) hemangioendothelioma (Fig. 4.157), cavernous hemangioma, angiokeratomas of various types,[1271] verrucous hemangioma,[1272] acral arteriovenous tumor,[1268] microvenular hemangioma,[1266,1270] arteriovenous hemangioma,[1275] glomeruloid hemangioma (Fig. 4.158; a distinctive vascular proliferation seen in Castleman's disease associated with the POEMS syndrome),[1267,1274] hobnail hemangioma (including targetoid hemosiderotic heman-

gioma)[1269,1276] (Fig. 4.159), and glomus tumor (see Chapter 25). The hemangiomas associated with Maffucci's syndrome, blue rubber bleb nevus, and Kasabach–Merritt syndrome are of the cavernous type.

Spider angioma, venous lake, capillary aneurysm, angioma serpiginosum, and the lesion of hereditary hemorrhagic telangiectasia are not true neoplasms but rather telangiectatic processes of either hamartomatous or acquired nature.[1273] This may also be true for some of the lesions listed in the preceding paragraph.

Lymphangioma

Cutaneous lymphangiomas usually present in infancy, the majority being present by the age of 5 years.[1281] Sites of predilection are the neck, axilla, breasts, chest, buttocks, and thighs. The lesions are divided into superficial (lymphangioma circumscriptum), deep (lymphangioma cavernosum), and cystic (cystic hygroma) varieties. Recurrence develops in about 25% of cases.[1278] This is apparently caused by the presence of large muscle-coated lymphatic cisterns lying deep in the subcutis and feeding the superficial vesicles.[1284] Lymphangioma circumscriptum sometimes follows surgical and/or radiation therapy for breast carcinoma.[1282]

Benign lymphangioendothelioma is the name that has been proposed for the benign lymph vessel tumor originally described as acquired progressive lymphangioma.[1280,1283] It presents as a bruise-like lesion and simulates angiosarcoma because of the presence of anastomosing vascular channels. However, atypia of

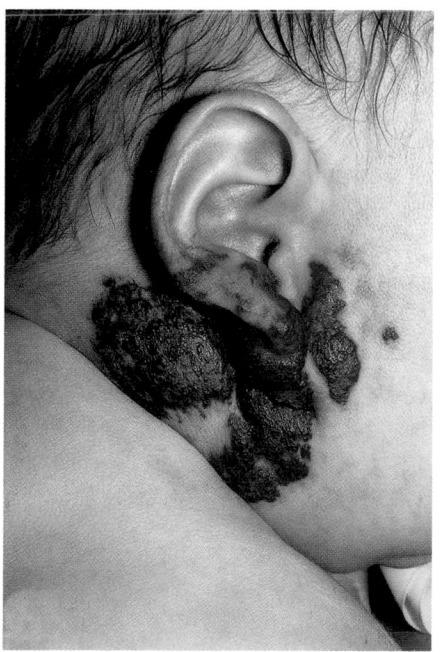
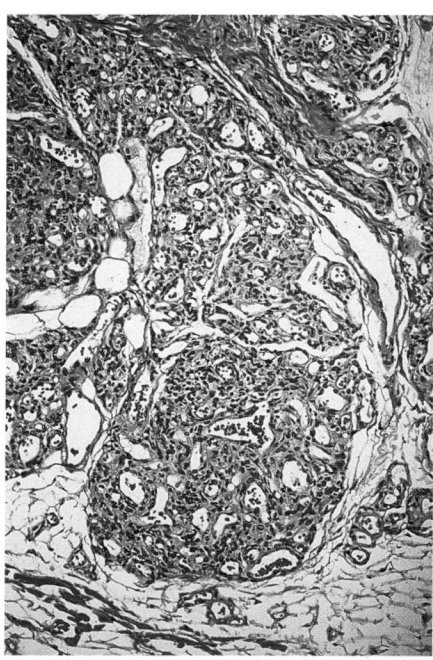
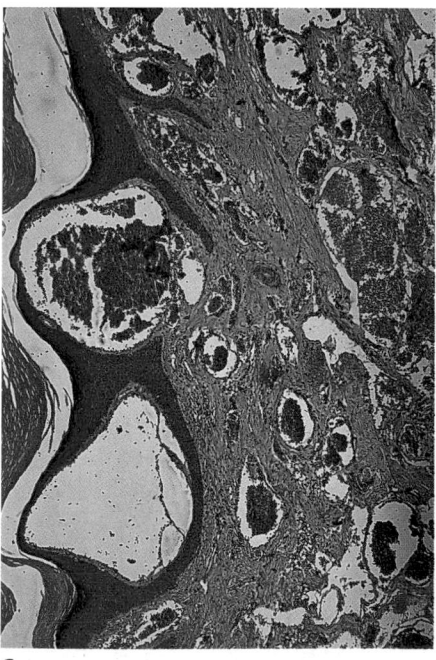

A   **B**   **C**

Fig. 4.157 A,Clinical appearance of infantile hemangioma (benign hemangioendothelioma) (A, courtesy of Dr. RA Cooke, Brisbane, Australia; From Cooke RA, Stewart B: Colour atlas of Anatomical Pathology, Edinburgh, Churchill Livingstone, 2004). **B,** Benign hemangioendothelioma. Notice marked hypercellularity and lobular configuration. **C,** Cavernous hemangioma of skin. Vessels are markedly dilated and result in elevation of the overlying atrophic epidermis.

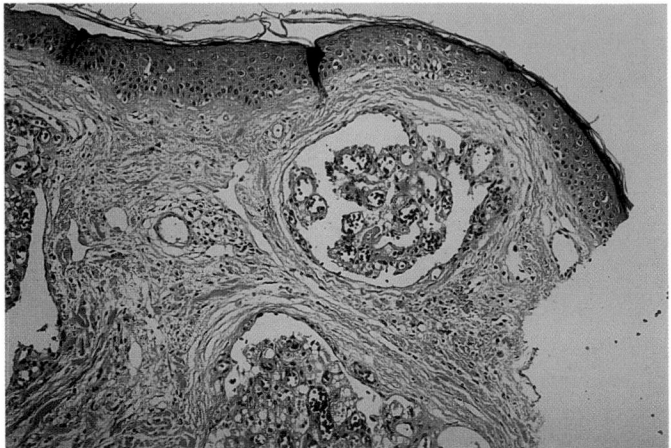

Fig. 4.158 Glomeruloid hemangioma in a patient with POEMS syndrome. Microscopic appearance of the individual lesions is reminiscent of renal glomeruli.

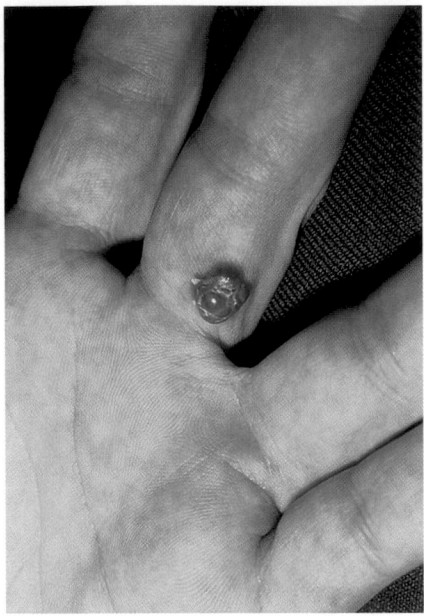

Fig. 4.160 Clinical appearance of typical pyogenic granuloma.

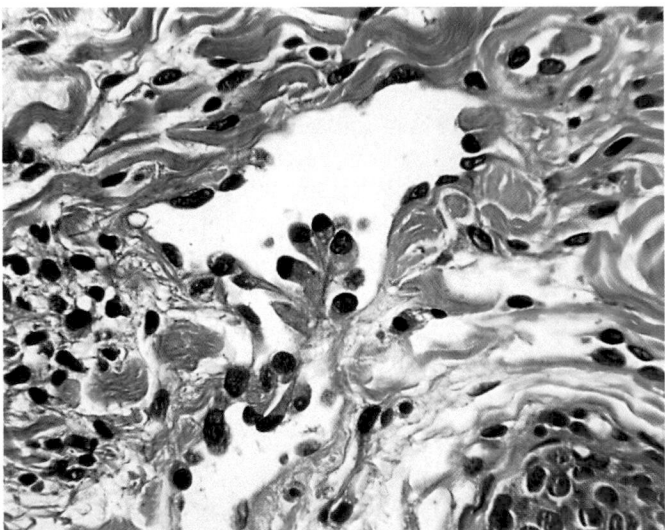

Fig. 4.159 Hobnail hemangioma. The endothelial cells protrude into the vessel lumina.

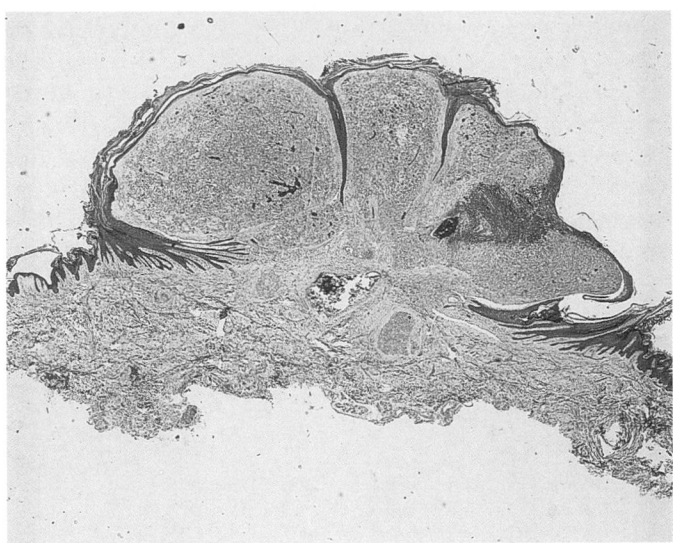

Fig. 4.161 Low-power microscopic view of typical pyogenic granuloma.

endothelial cells is totally absent.[1283] Before this diagnosis is made, care should be exercised in ruling out the lymphangioma-like form of Kaposi's sarcoma.[1277,1279]

Pyogenic granuloma and related lesions

Pyogenic granuloma (granuloma pyogenicum) presents clinically as a rapidly growing polypoid red mass, surrounded by a collarette of thickened epidermis. The fingers and lips are the most common locations (Fig. 4.160). Sometimes it appears in connection with a keratinous cyst.[1287] Microscopically, there are vascular proliferation, edema, and inflammation. The epidermis is thinned and sometimes ulcerated at the top, and there are acanthosis and hyperkeratosis at the sides (Fig. 4.161). The most distinctive feature is the so-called *vascular (capillary) lobule*, a central branching vessel usually devoid of red blood cells, surrounded by a hypercellular proliferation of neoformed endothelial and perithelial

cells[1291,1293] (Fig. 4.162). High cellularity and abundant mitotic activity may be present (particularly in lesions of the lips), but these are not indicative of an aggressive behavior.[1288,1295] On the contrary, the lesion is self-limited, and spontaneous regression is the rule. Excision is usually curative, although some examples located on the trunk may recur as multiple satellites.[1297] Lobular capillary hemangioma can also occur in a disseminated form,[1292] develop within port-wine stains,[1296] be located in the deep dermis or subcutaneous tissue,[1286] or present as a polypoid mass within a vein (intravenous pyogenic granuloma).[1285] Deeply seated lesions usually lack the edema and inflammation seen in the more superficial examples. Despite some clinical features that suggest a

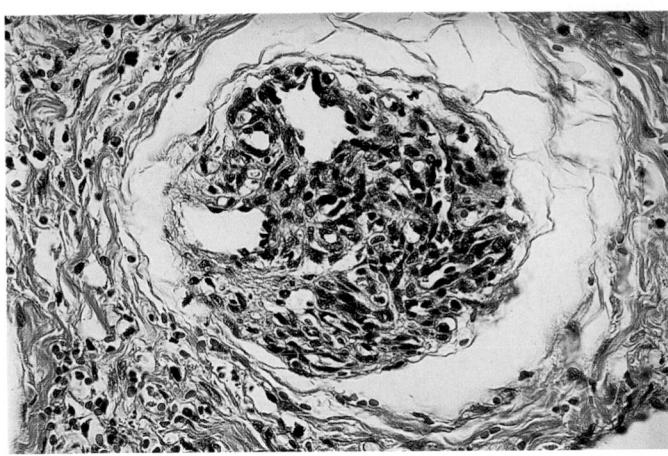

Fig. 4.162 So-called capillary or vascular lobule. This formation is almost always an indicator of a benign process.

hormonal dependency of the lesion, immunohistochemical studies for steroid hormone receptors have given negative results.[1293]

Pyogenic granuloma is by far the most common member of a family of benign vascular proliferation of the skin featuring the just described vascular lobule.[1289] Another member is *acquired (tufted) angioma* (Nakagawa's angioblastoma), which typically presents as multiple red plaques on the shoulders and upper back of children and adolescents and is characterized microscopically by multiple vascular lobules, which tend to be more cellular than those of pyogenic granuloma and to have a semilunar vessel at the periphery rather than a more open one at the center.[1294,1298]

Vascular lobules can also be seen in benign (infantile) hemangioendothelioma and in a variety of reactive conditions, such as venous stasis and acrodermatitis, so-called "reactive (benign) angioendotheliomatosis,"[1290] verruga peruana, and bacillary angiomatosis[1289] (see below). At a practical level, it is important to remember that the presence of a well-developed lobular pattern in a vascular proliferative lesion strongly favors a benign diagnosis, no matter how cellular and mitotically active that lesion may be.

Masson's hemangioma

Masson's hemangioma (vegetant intravascular hemangioendothelioma; Masson's pseudoangiosarcoma; intravascular papillary endothelial hyperplasia) is in all likelihood the result of exuberant organization and recanalization of a thrombus.[1300] It may develop in a previously normal vessel as a result of trauma, or it may superimpose itself on a pyogenic granuloma or cavernous hemangioma.[1301–1303] It is characterized microscopically by a papillary proliferation of endothelial cells (which are plump but lack atypia) located entirely within the lumen of a dilated vessel. The core of the papillae has a deeply acidophilic quality, resulting at least in part from fibrin deposition. The immunohistochemical profile of

the predominant element is that of activated endothelial cells.[1299]

Epithelioid hemangioma

Epithelioid hemangioma (histiocytoid hemangioma, angiolymphoid hyperplasia with eosinophilia) presents clinically as inflammatory-looking nodules, the head and neck (particularly the periauricular region) being the preferred locations.[1306,1314,1317] Despite earlier claims to the contrary, this disease is clearly distinct from *Kimura's disease* as seen in the Orient.[1307,1310,1321] Microscopically, a central area of proliferated blood vessels is infiltrated and surrounded by a heavy inflammatory infiltrate rich in eosinophils and containing lymphoid follicles with germinal centers. In a variation of the theme, the proliferation may acquire a lobular solid pattern that may result in overdiagnosis.[1304a] The defining feature of this entity is the peculiar epithelioid or histiocytoid appearance of the endothelial cells (Figs 4.163 and 4.164). Sometimes the inflammatory infiltrate is nil or absent.[1305] These lesions, as they occur in the skin, are of an indolent nature, and there is controversy as to whether they are reactive or neoplastic.[1309] They represent the "benign"

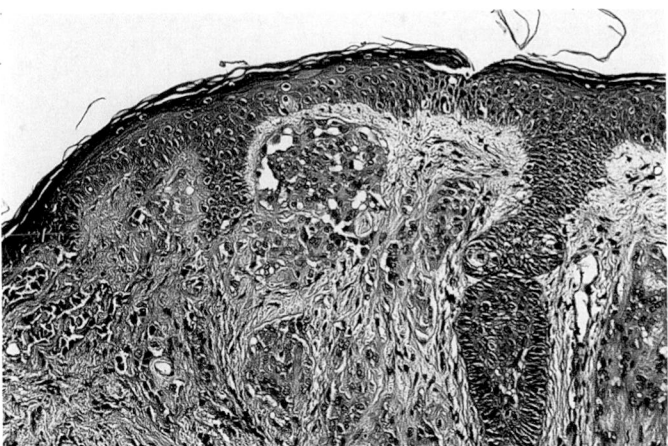

Fig. 4.163 Benign cutaneous vascular tumor largely composed of epithelioid vascular cells, with focal glomeruloid features.

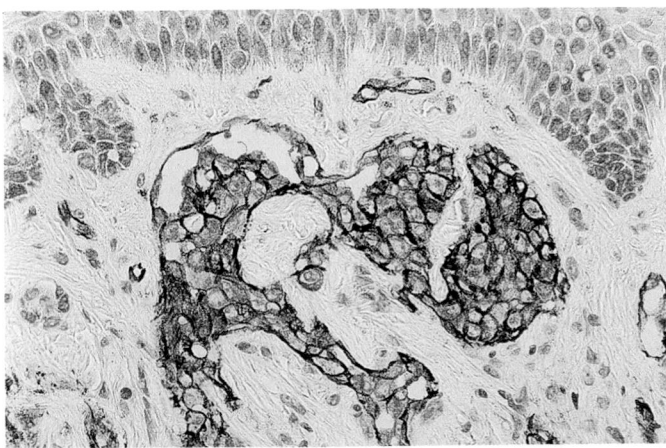

Fig. 4.164 Same case as above immunostained for CD31.

end of the spectrum of a family of vascular proliferations having as a common denominator the presence of epithelioid (histiocytoid) endothelial cells, which also includes epithelioid hemangioendothelioma (a low-grade malignant tumor) and epithelioid angiosarcoma (a high-grade malignant tumor).[1304,1308,1319,1320] A distinction among these entities is possible in the majority of the cases on the basis of location (most epithelioid hemangiomas are cutaneous, whereas most epithelioid hemangioendotheliomas and angiosarcomas are not), cellularity, atypia, and some architectural features.[1309] However, many types of exceptions to these rules and numerous overlaps occur. Tumors with the appearance of epithelioid hemangioendothelioma[1312,1316,1318] and epithelioid angiosarcoma[1311] can occur in the skin, whereas tumors with the appearance of epithelioid hemangioma can be seen in deep sites such as bone.[1313] Furthermore, one occasionally encounters a lesion with the features of epithelioid hemangioma in the skin overlying a soft tissue or bone tumor with the features of epithelioid hemangioendothelioma.[1315] An interesting subtype of epithelioid hemangioendothelioma has been described on the tip of digits ("acral" variety).[1322]

Kaposi's sarcoma

In its classic form, Kaposi's sarcoma is infrequent in the United States but relatively common in some regions of the Mediterranean basin and even more so in equatorial Africa, where it comprises 10% of all malignant tumors.[1324,1349] The incidence of Kaposi's sarcoma in the United States has increased several hundred-fold during the last two decades through its occurrence in the AIDS population and, to a lesser degree, in persons with other forms of immunosuppression, such as organ transplant recipients.[1325,1326,1373] An association with the systemic form of Castleman's disease and with angioimmunoblastic lymphadenopathy (two disorders of the immune system) has also been reported.[1337,1378] In patients with AIDS, Kaposi's sarcoma is predominantly a feature of the homosexual population, although it has also been seen in heterosexual drug users.[1341]

In classic Kaposi's sarcoma, the disease manifests itself by multiple blue dermal plaques or nodules starting on the feet and legs (Fig. 4.165). These nodules progress up the extremity and occasionally assume a pedunculated appearance reminiscent of pyogenic granuloma (Fig. 4.166). By angiographic techniques, clinically inapparent subcutaneous nodules can be identified. Temporary control is effected by irradiation, chemotherapy, or, if the lesion is sharply delimited, excision. The course of Kaposi's sarcoma is variable although usually prolonged. Some elderly persons die of intercurrent disease. An increased incidence of malignant tumors, particularly of lymphoid type, has been documented.[1368] In patients in whom the disease runs its full course, widespread visceral involvement may be found.[1348] Lymph nodes and

the gastrointestinal tract are the organs most commonly involved. Visceral involvement can precede the development of skin lesions or occur in their absence.[1375] Indicators of poor outcome in classic Kaposi's sarcoma are immunosuppression and age over 50 years.[1330]

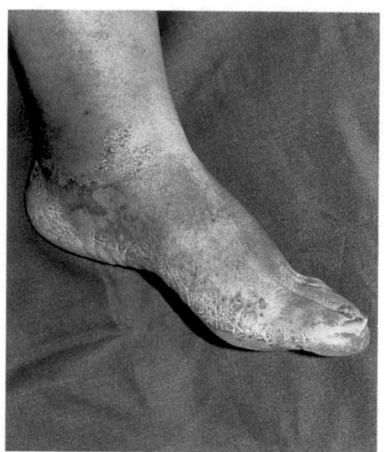

A

B

Fig. 4.165 Clinical appearance of Kaposi's sarcoma. **A,** Diffuse violaceous lesions in skin of foot and ankle. This is the most common location of the classical form. **B,** Early lesion of Kaposi's sarcoma in an HIV-infected patient.

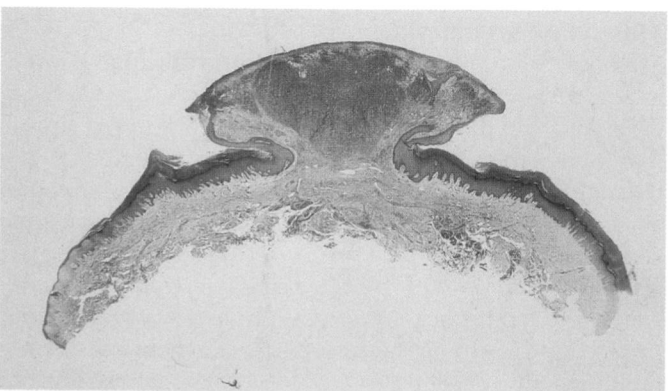

Fig. 4.166 Low-power view of a lesion of Kaposi's sarcoma having a prominent polypoid shape that stimulates pyogenic granuloma.

Other clinical forms of Kaposi's sarcoma have been described in the African cases.[1377] In the AIDS population, the lesions of Kaposi's sarcoma have a more erratic distribution, a wider variety of clinical appearance, and a more rapidly aggressive clinical course,[1353,1382] with frequent involvement of the lymph nodes, lung, and/or gastrointestinal tract.[1354]

Microscopically, the most typical feature of Kaposi's sarcoma is the presence of spindle cells forming slits containing red blood cells (Fig. 4.167). Mitotic activity is only moderate, and pleomorphism is usually absent. Admixed in this lesion are lymphocytes, hemosiderin-laden macrophages, and other inflammatory cells. Variously sized hyaline bodies, which are PAS positive, are often seen in the cytoplasm of the proliferating cells and sometimes extracellularly (Fig. 4.168). These probably represent the result of ingestion and degradation of erythrocytes and—although diagnostically useful—are not specific for Kaposi's sarcoma.[1339,1351]

In early lesions, the spindle proliferation may be limited to the papillary dermis and to the vascular plexus surrounding the secretory coil of sweat glands[1366] (Fig. 4.169). The changes can be very subtle and limited to a few irregularly dilated vascular spaces and aggregates of plumper (epithelioid) cells[1361]; at this stage, the microscopic appearance may be nondiagnostic, and the pathologist should not be afraid of stating this, no matter how suggestive the clinical picture may be.

Histochemical, immunohistochemical, and ultrastructural studies have shown that Kaposi's sarcoma is derived from vasoformative mesenchyme with multipotential capabilities[1362] (Figs 4.170 and 4.171). At this point, it seems reasonable to conclude that the spindle cells of Kaposi's sarcoma differentiate toward endothelial

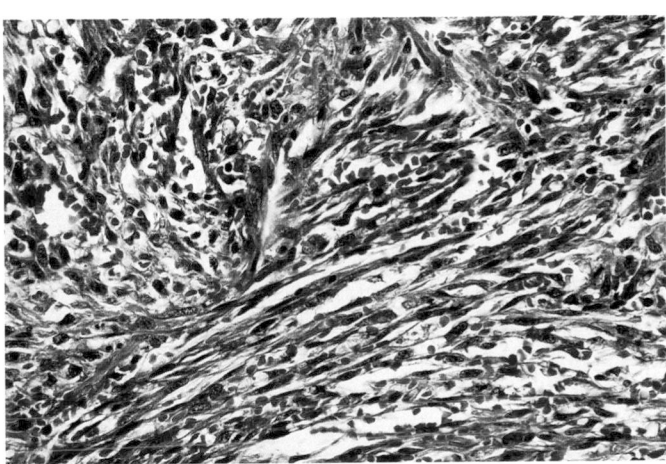

Fig. 4.167 Microscopic appearance of Kaposi's sarcoma. Elongated spindle cells showing minimal atypia are separated by slits containing red blood cells.

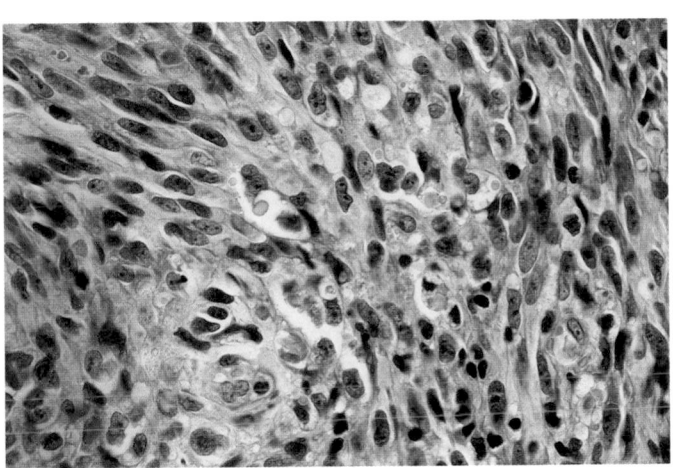

Fig. 4.168 Lesion of Kaposi's sarcoma showing numerous eosinophilic hyaline bodies. This feature, although not pathognomonic, is a helpful diagnostic clue.

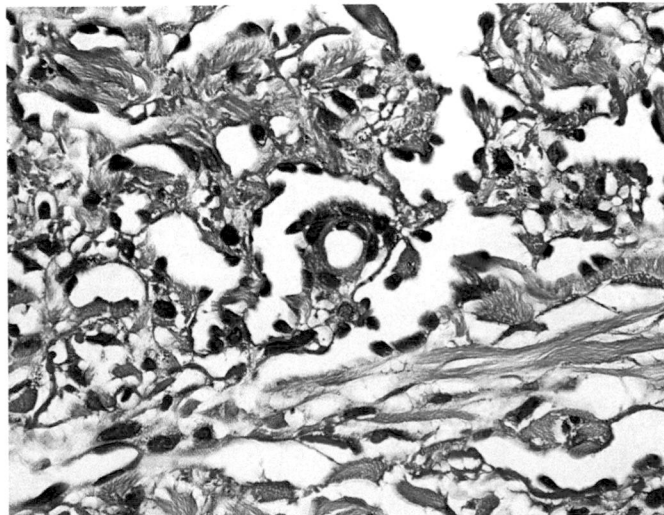

Fig. 4.169 Early changes of Kaposi's sarcoma, manifested by vascular proliferation in the dermis. These changes often center around skin adnexae.

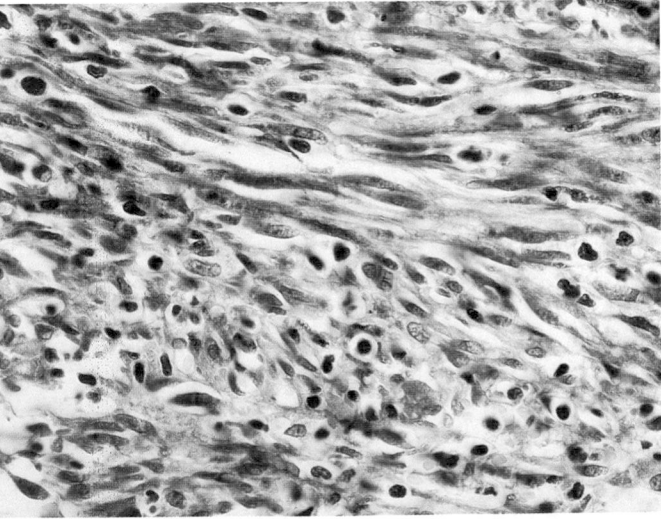

Fig. 4.170 Immunoreactivity for Factor VIII-related antigen in Kaposi's sarcoma.

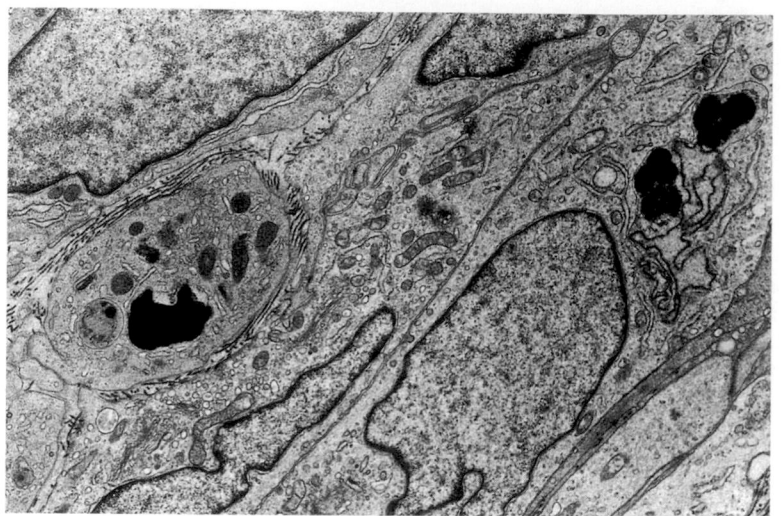

Fig. 4.171 Electron microscopic appearance of Kaposi's sarcoma involving submental lymph node in a 32-year-old man affected by AIDS. Poorly differentiated dermal spindle-shaped tumor cells containing electron-dense remains of phagocytized red cells. (x7200) (Courtesy of Dr. Robert E. Erlandson, Memorial Sloan-Kettering Cancer Center)

cells,[1340,1379] probably of lymph vessel rather than blood vessel nature.[1336,1380] Indeed, FVIII-related antigen, CD31, CD34, angiotensin-converting enzyme, thrombomodulin, leukocyte adhesion molecule-1, and other endothelial markers have been detected in at least some of the cases,[1335,1344,1346,1359,1371,1381] even acknowledging the fact that the many immunohistochemical and ultrastructural studies that have been performed on this disorder have given confusing and often contradictory results.[1328,1331,1334,1356,1367] An important component of FXIIIa-positive dermal dendrocytes is present,[1360] although it does not appear to represent the primary proliferating element.[1343]

It should be realized that not all of the vascular lesions of the skin present in AIDS patients have the morphologic features of Kaposi's sarcoma. Some exhibit anastomosing vascular channels resembling those of angiosarcoma, others are composed of plump (histiocytoid or epithelioid) endothelial cells,[1328] others are solid and undifferentiated,[1370] and still others have a lymphangioma-like appearance.[1333] It seems likely that all these morphologic forms of AIDS-related vascular proliferation are pathogenetically and histogenetically related.

Controversy also reigns concerning the pathogenesis of Kaposi's sarcoma, particularly whether it should be regarded as a multicentric hyperplastic or as a neoplastic process.[1327] The fact that nearly all these lesions have been found to be diploid on flow cytometric studies[1338] would seem to favor the former mechanism, which could be mediated by the action of oncogenes and growth factors that stimulate local angiogenesis.[1347,1372] The clonal nature of the lesions and their sometimes markedly aggressive behavior favor instead a neoplastic nature.[1364,1365] Remarkably, it has been shown that post-transplant Kaposi's sarcoma originates from the seeding of donor-derived progenitors.[1327a]

The most important recent development in this field has been the discovery that a new human herpes virus (HHV-8) is present in almost 100% of Kaposi's sarcoma lesions, whether HIV-related, classic, endemic, or iatro-genic.[1323] HHV-8, also known as Kaposi sarcoma-associated herpes virus (KSHV), is a gamma-herpesvirus closely related to Epstein–Barr virus (EBV).[1358] It is believed to be necessary but not sufficient to cause the disease, with other factors (such as immunosuppression) probably playing a major contributory role. Parenthetically, HHV-8 is also involved in the pathogenesis of multicentric Castleman's disease and primary effusion lymphoma.[1342,1363,1369] DNA sequences of the virus and the protein encoded by this virus (ORF-73) have been detected in the spindle cells by in situ hybridization, PCR, and immunohistochemistry (the latter by using monoclonal antibody ORF-73).[1345,1350,1352,1355,1363a]

In terms of differential diagnosis, benign lesions that can be microscopically confused with Kaposi's sarcoma include arteriovenous malformations, acroangiodermatitis, pyogenic granuloma and other vascular proliferations exhibiting a lobular pattern of growth (such as tufted angioma), spindle cell tumor of lymph nodes with amianthoid fibers (nearly always located in the inguinal region), bacillary angiomatosis, pigmented purpuric dermatosis, and the predominantly vascular or hemorrhagic forms of benign fibrous histiocytoma[1329,1332,1357,1374,1376] (see p. 181).

Bacillary angiomatosis and verruga peruana

Bacillary angiomatosis is due to infection by a rickettsia-like organism of the *Rochalimaea* species now known as *Bartonella henselae*.[1387,1394] The cutaneous lesions, which present clinically as reddish papules and nodules, are characterized microscopically by lobules of capillaries with plump (epithelioid or histiocytoid) endothelial cells[1389] (Fig. 4.172A). Thus, this entity shows some of the architectural features of pyogenic granuloma and some of the cytologic features of epithelioid hemangioma. Clues to the diagnosis are represented by clusters of neutrophils (many of them fragmented) and the presence of a granular purplish-staining extracellular material (Fig. 4.172B). The latter results from the accumulation of a

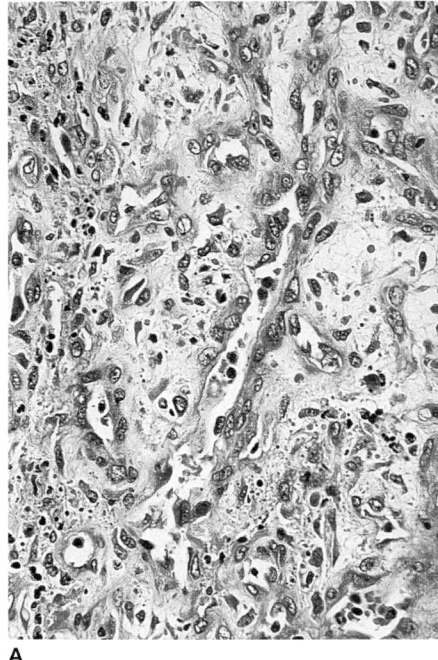
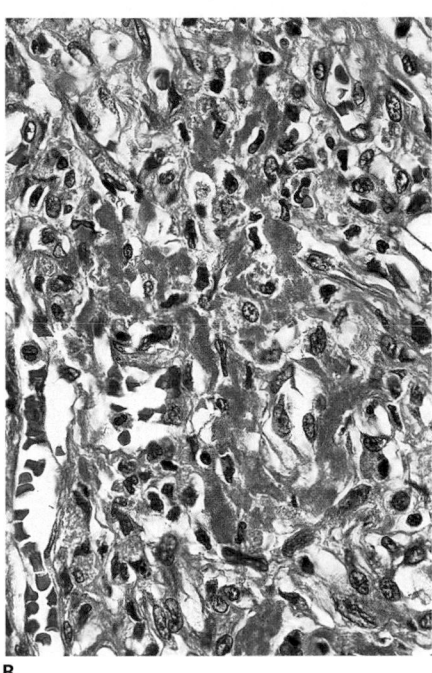

A **B**

Fig. 4.172 Bacillary angiomatosis. **A**, Note epithelioid appearance of the endothelial cells in the proliferating vessels and neutrophilic infiltrate with marked karyorrhexis. **B**, An amphophilic granular material is seen in the stroma, due to the accumulation of myriads of microorganisms.

myriad of organisms, as demonstrated with silver stains or electron microscopy.[1388,1390,1391]

Bacillary angiomatosis can also involve soft tissues (sometimes in the absence of skin disease),[1392] lymph nodes,[1385] and internal organs.[1386,1393] It can also be seen in association with Kaposi's sarcoma.[1393]

The differential diagnosis of bacillary angiomatosis includes *verruga peruana*, another vascular proliferative process induced by an infectious organism, in this instance *Bartonella bacilliformis*.[1383,1384] Identification of Rocha-Lima's inclusions is the most important clue for the diagnosis of this disease, which is endemic to Peru.

Other non-neoplastic lesions of skin that can be seen in HIV-infected patients are discussed on p. 117.

Angiosarcoma

Angiosarcoma (malignant hemangioendothelioma) of the skin is almost exclusively restricted to the head and neck of elderly persons[1400,1409,1410,1419] if the varieties associated with long standing lymphedema or radiation therapy are excluded[1394a,1396–1398,1413,1416] (Fig. 4.173). It characteristically presents as a violaceous flat lesion of ill-defined margins, on which elevated nodules may develop.[1403,1405] Occasionally, the tumor acquires a verrucous appearance because of hyperplasia of the overlying epidermis.[1401] Microscopically, three distinct patterns are seen, singly or in combination: undifferentiated foci, which can simulate carcinoma or malignant melanoma; freely anastomosing channels lined by atypical endothelial cells, surrounding skin adnexa, and dissecting dermal collagen fibers; and areas resembling Kaposi's sarcoma[1419,1421] (Fig. 4.174). The tumor cells have ultrastructural and immunohistochemical features of endothelial cells, although these can be lost in the poorly differentiated tumors.[1404,1407,1415] There have been contradictory reports regarding the presence of HHV-8 in cutaneous angiosarcoma.[1406,1408]

Occasionally, the tumor cells have an epithelioid morphology (**epithelioid angiosarcoma**).[1411,1417] This tumor should be distinguished from epithelioid hemangioendothelioma and—more importantly—from epithelioid hemangioma.[1412,1418] In other instances, focal granular cell changes are encountered. In contrast to Kaposi's sarcoma, flow cytometric studies of angiosarcoma have usually shown a nondiploid pattern.[1402] Angiosarcoma is a slow-growing but highly aggressive neoplasm that stubbornly recurs following surgery or radiation therapy to involve extensive areas of the scalp and face and eventually metastasizes to the regional lymph nodes, the lung, and other organs.[1419,1421] Any vascular lesion of the skin diagnosed as angiosarcoma in a young patient or not located in the head and neck should be suspected of

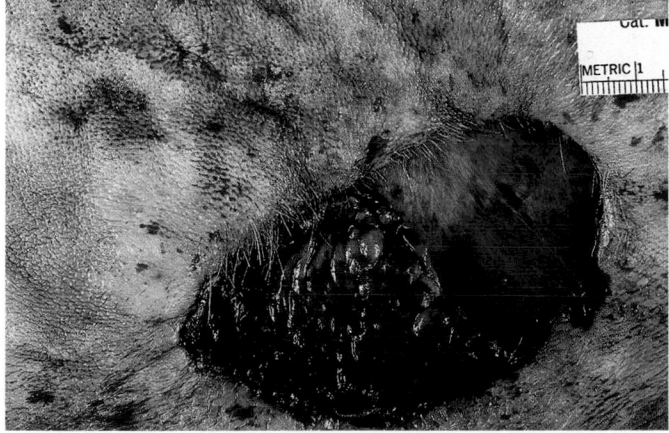

Fig. 4.173 Gross appearance of angiosarcoma of scalp.

being something else and, more often than not, a benign process.[1399] Two malignant tumors notorious for their ability to simulate angiosarcoma are squamous cell carcinoma[1414] and epithelioid sarcoma.[1420] A benign and probably not even neoplastic lesion that we have seen confused with angiosarcoma is hamartoma of the scalp with ectopic meningothelial elements (see p. 202).

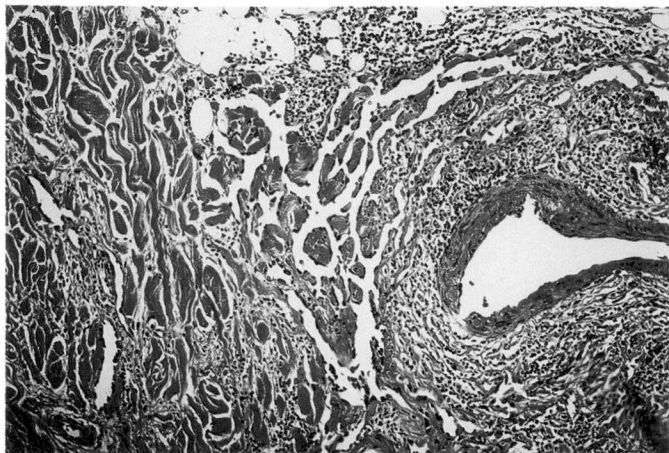

A

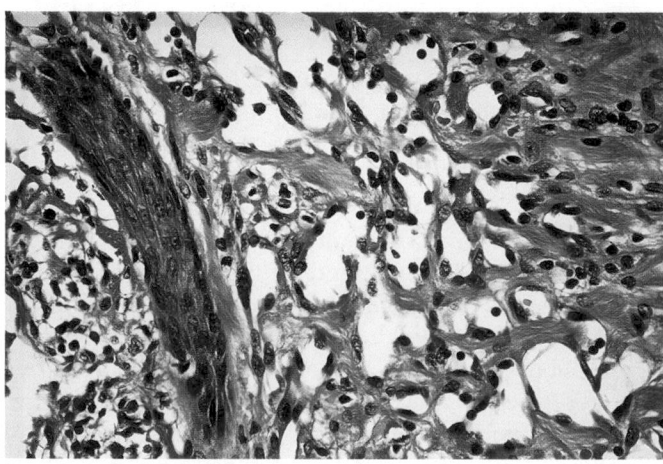

B

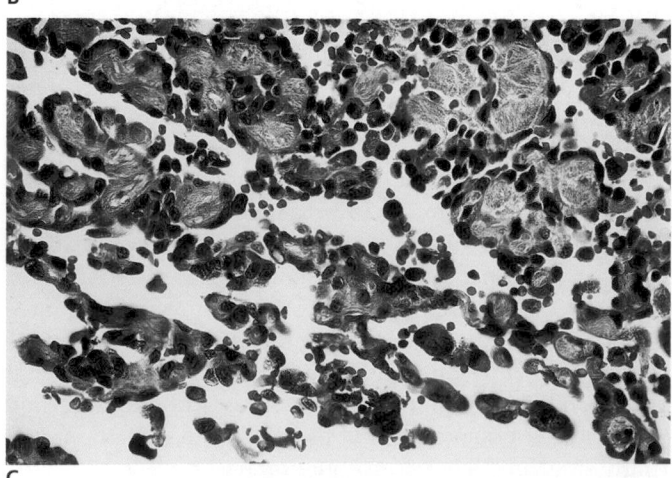

C

Fig. 4.174 Angiosarcoma of skin. **A,** Dissection of dermal collagen fibers by neoplastic vessels; **B,** Freely anastomosing vessels lined by atypical cells; **C,** Papillary projections.

Retiform hemangioendothelioma is a distinctive low-grade variant of angiosarcoma usually occurring in the distal extremities of young individuals, sometimes associated with hyperkeratotic changes in the overlying epidermis.[1395] Microscopically, there is a complex ("retiform") network of vessels in the dermis and subcutaneous tissue, lined by endothelial cells having round (lymphocyte-like) nuclei and scanty cytoplasm. These cells protrude into the lumen of the neoplastic vessels in a hobnail fashion. Similar areas are sometimes seen in angiosarcomas, but here they are accompanied by a greater degree of atypia and pleomorphism.

Lymphoid tumors and tumorlike conditions
Cutaneous lymphoid hyperplasia
Cutaneous lymphoid hyperplasia (also known as lymphoplasia, lymphadenoma, lymphocytoma benigna cutis, lymphadenosis benigna cutis, and Spiegler–Fendt sarcoid) occurs predominantly on the face of women as livid nodules or plaques, usually solitary.[1425] It probably represents a response to trauma, insect bites, and other undetermined stimuli.[1424] Microscopically, an infiltrate predominantly composed of lymphocytes and histiocytes is present in the dermis[1429] (Fig. 4.175). The morphologic and immunoarchitectural features of the lesion are very similar to those of reactive lymph nodes.[1439]

Features that have traditionally been used to favor a diagnosis of lymphoid hyperplasia over one of malignant lymphoma are the following: multiplicity of cell types, including plasma cells and eosinophils; formation of lymphoid follicles, with or without germinal centers; phagocytosis of nuclear debris; vascular proliferation; predominantly perivascular or periadnexal distribution of the infiltrate; and prominent epidermal hyperplasia.[1430] With the realization that marginal zone lymphoma can occur in the skin,[1428a] a modification of these criteria

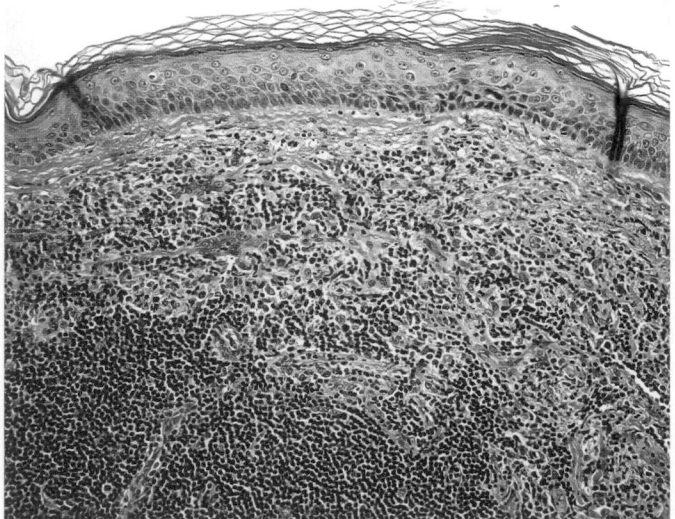

Fig. 4.175 Cutaneous lymphoid hyperplasia. Note the numerous hyperplastic vessels with plump endothelial cells.

has become necessary. To wit, reactive follicles are regularly seen in this condition, the diagnosis of which should be favored in the presence of marginal zone cells, sheets of plasma cells, and/or Dutcher bodies.[1423]

Immunohistochemically, cutaneous lymphoid hyperplasia shows a mixed lymphocytic infiltrate with abundant representation of B and T lymphocytes. Some of the larger lymphoid cells may show reactivity for the Ki-1 antibody.[1427] Molecular genetic analysis may be useful for the differential diagnosis with malignant lymphoma.[1437] In that regard, reported cases of cutaneous lymphoid hyperplasia containing a monotypic plasma cell population[1433] should probably be reinterpreted as marginal zone lymphomas.

Most lesions of cutaneous lymphoid hyperplasia are characterized by a benign clinical course, with resolution following antibiotic or x-ray therapy or occurring spontaneously. Some cases, however, have been documented to progress to malignant lymphoma.[1429a,1440]

Jessner's lymphocytic infiltration of the skin is regarded by many as a clinicopathologic variant of cutaneous lymphoid hyperplasia related to chronic discoid lupus erythematosus (see p. 110), but controversy about its nature persists.[1431,1438] Plasmacytoid monocytes are often present in the infiltrate and are regarded as a clue to the diagnosis.[1436] Other clinically benign lymphocytic infiltrates that can microscopically simulate malignant lymphoma are related to molluscum contagiosum,[1422] syphilis,[1426] nodular scabies,[1435] and actinic reticuloid.[1428] Those that simulate microscopically the appearance of mycosis fungoides have been generically referred to as cutaneous pseudo-T-cell lymphomas.[1432,1434]

Mycosis fungoides and related peripheral T-cell lymphomas

Mycosis fungoides is a distinct clinicopathologic type of peripheral T-cell lymphoma[1468,1485,1492,1504] (Fig. 4.176). A viral etiology has been suspected because of certain similarities to HTLV-1-associated adult T-cell leukemia–lymphoma,[1483] but has never been substantiated.[1501,1508] The large majority of cases occur in adult and elderly individuals, but adolescents and young adults can also be affected.[1449,1461] It has various manners of presentation and progression, most identified by eponymic designations.[1443] Traditionally, mycosis fungoides is divided into three stages: premycotic, mycotic, and tumorous. In the premycotic stage, the skin is erythematous, scaly, and pruritic. Clinical variations characterized by solitary, follicular, granulomatous, pustular, bullous, hyperkeratotic, verrucous, and hypopigmented forms exist.[1441,1445,1450,1456,1467,1474–1476] Large plaque parapsoriasis is a clinically defined entity that is known to "convert" to mycosis fungoides in a high percentage of cases; whether or not this entity is malignant from the beginning has been argued for a long time, but the accumulated evidence strongly suggests that this is indeed the

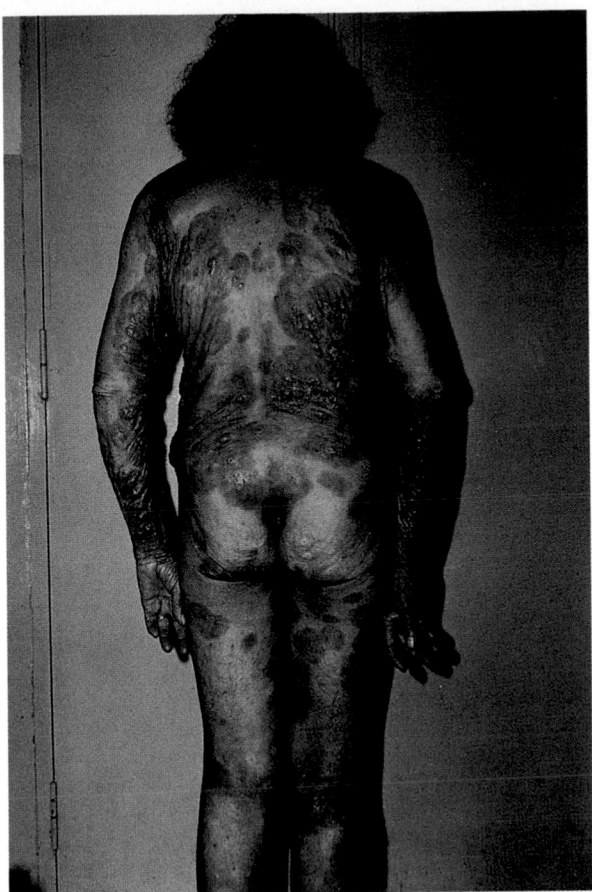

Fig. 4.176 Clinical appearance of mycosis fungoides showing infiltrative plaques over virtually entire body.

case (some authors claim that this is also true for small plaque parapsoriasis/digitate dermatosis).[1479]

In the premycotic stage, the microscopic appearance may be nondiagnostic and represented by a chronic nonspecific dermatitis associated with psoriasiform changes in the epidermis.[1460a] In the mycotic stage, infiltrative plaques appear, and biopsies show a polymorphous inflammatory infiltrate in the dermis that contains small numbers of frankly atypical lymphoid cells.[1491] These cells may invade the epidermis to form Pautrier's microabscesses or, more often, to line up individually along the epidermal basal layer[1489] (Figs 4.177 and 4.178). The latter finding, if unaccompanied by spongiosis, is strongly suggestive of mycosis fungoides. The lymphoid infiltrate may be predominantly located around hair follicles and can be accompanied by follicular mucinosis.[1479,1497] In rare instances there is infiltration of the eccrine sweat glands.[1464] In the tumorous stage, dense infiltrates of atypical lymphoid cells expand the dermis. The characteristic cell of mycosis fungoides is a small or medium-sized lymphocyte with a cerebroid nucleus. This term refers to the highly irregular contour of the thick nuclear membrane, which results in an appearance somewhat reminiscent of brain convolutions[1442] (Fig. 4.179). Thin, well-prepared sections are necessary to identify this feature.[1446] These cerebroid cells are of T-cell type; their phenotype is usually that of helper T cells (CD4+), but sometimes it is suppressor/cytotoxic or aberrant.[1487,1505] Interestingly, several differences in antigen expression have been found between intra-epidermal and intradermal lymphocytes.[1453,1482,1486] In advanced stages of the disease, these cells may express CD15.[1503]

Although the presence of cerebroid cells is necessary to make a diagnosis of mycosis fungoides, they are not pathognomonic of the disease. Scattered cells with these nuclear features can be seen in other lymphomas and in some types of spongiotic acute and chronic dermatitis.[1457,1459,1490,1506] Conversely, it should be noted that a reactive B-cell component (with plasma cells and follicle formation) can accompany the T-cell neoplastic infiltrate of mycosis fungoides.[1491]

On the basis of immunocytochemical studies of the T-cell population performed in fresh frozen tissue, it has been suggested that loss of the differentiation antigens CD2, CD3, CD5, and CD7 occurs in neoplastic T lymphocytes but not in reactive conditions.[1452,1484,1496] Greater diagnostic assistance is provided by molecular studies (such as the analysis of T-cell receptor genes) for the identification of T-cell clones in skin biopsy specimens from patients with early disease.[1499,1502,1507]

The course of mycosis fungoides is usually protracted over a period of years. Clinical signs associated with poor prognosis are the presence of generalized plaques or tumors, diffuse erythema, and lymphadenopathy.[1460,1462] A correlation exists between the histologic findings and the clinical course,[1498] which applies primarily to the number and cytologic features of the neoplastic T cells but also to the density of epidermal Langerhans' cells,[1481] but the prognostic significance of the microscopic features as seen in a single biopsy is negligible.[1493] Parenthetically, Langerhans' cells have been implicated in the pathogenesis of the disease, together with dermal dendrocytes.[1453,1458]

In approximately one half to two thirds of patients with mycosis fungoides of the skin, involvement of lymph nodes and internal viscera occurs. In most instances, the internal disease is microscopically still recognizable as mycosis fungoides by the polymorphism of the infiltrate and, most important, the cerebroid quality of the nuclei of the tumor cells.[1478,1488] In other cases, the internal malignancy has morphologic features indistinguishable from those of a diffuse large cell lymphoma.[1451] The internal infiltrates of mycosis fungoides can be found in the lymph nodes, lung, spleen, liver, kidney, bone marrow, central nervous system, and practically every other organ.[1444,1465,1488] The disease can even present as a primary extracutaneous lesion, either in the lymph nodes or in internal organs.[1447,1500]

Sepsis is a frequent terminal complication. The forms of therapy for disease limited to the skin include total skin electron beam irradiation, topical chemotherapy, and PUVA.[1463,1473]

Sézary's syndrome is a variant of mycosis fungoides characterized clinically by infiltrative erythroderma with

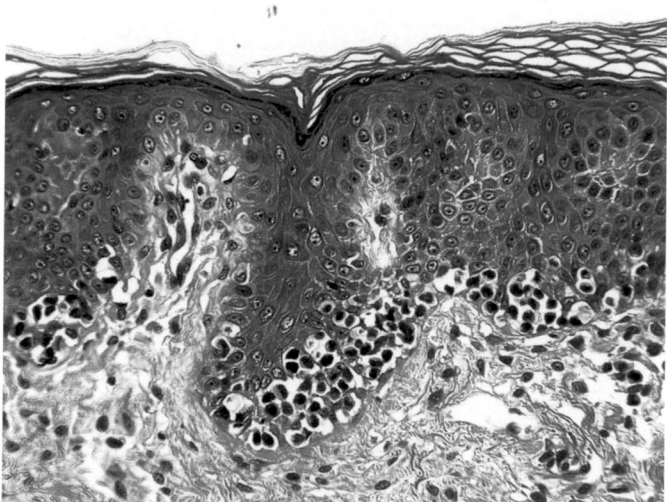

Fig. 4.177 Epidermotropism of neoplastic lymphoid cells in mycosis fungoides.

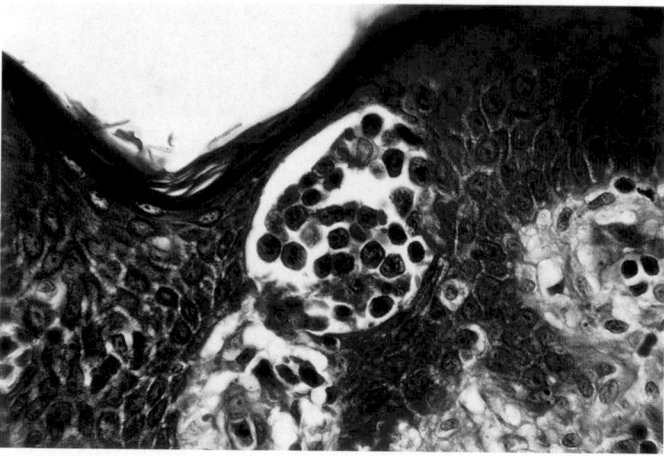

Fig. 4.178 So-called Pautrier microabscess in mycosis fungoides.

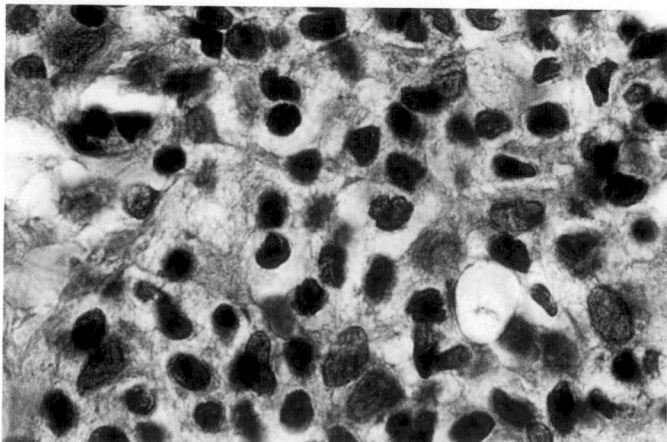

Fig. 4.179 High-power view of mycosis fungoides cell, showing marked nuclear irregularities.

pruritus, lymphadenopathy, and the presence of large or small cerebroid cells (Sézary cells) in the peripheral blood.[1448,1470,1494] PAS-positive cytoplasmic granules are present in their cytoplasm. The distinction between mycosis fungoides and Sézary's syndrome is to some extent artificial because circulating cerebroid cells of the same phenotype are found in approximately 20% of patients with mycosis fungoides. However, minor morphologic differences exist, such as a smaller number of cerebroid cells in the epidermis and fewer lymphocytes aligned within the basal layer, which may render the diagnosis more difficult.[1472]

Woringer–Kolopp disease (pagetoid reticulosis) is another T-cell cutaneous proliferative disorder, which is characterized morphologically by a monomorphic *intraepidermal* infiltrate of cells with cerebroid nuclei, indistinguishable from those of the usual mycosis fungoides and Sézary's syndrome.[1454,1455,1477] The lesion presents clinically as a solitary erythematosquamous patch, and the evolution is extremely slow.

Other forms of T-cell lymphoma that can involve the skin are adult T-cell leukemia–lymphoma,[1466,1483] lymphoepithelioid lymphoma (Lennert's lymphoma),[1469] and multilobulated T-cell lymphoma.[1495]

Subcutaneous T-cell lymphoma presents as deep-seated nodules, most frequently on the extremities.[1480]

Lymph nodes in mycosis fungoides

Lymphadenopathy is common in patients with mycosis fungoides. The pathologic changes may be those of dermatopathic lymphadenitis, involvement by mycosis fungoides, or both.[1509,1512] The distinction between these processes can be extremely difficult to make. Preservation or distortion of the nodal architecture and the number of atypical lymphoid cells in T-cell-dependent paracortical areas are the two most important prognostic features.[1510,1511] Immunophenotyping and determination of clonal rearrangement of T-cell receptor genes offer a more sensitive and reliable means to make the distinction[1513,1514] (see Chapter 21).

Lymphomatoid papulosis and anaplastic large cell lymphoma

Lymphomatoid papulosis is the original term given to a self-healing, recurrent papular eruption with a generally indolent clinical course and characterized microscopically by a polymorphic dermal infiltrate usually located superficially (Figs 4.180 and 4.181). This infiltrate often exhibits a distinct perivascular distribution (an important diagnostic sign)[1516] but it may also surround pilosebaceous units.[1517,1528] It contains scattered, markedly atypical lymphoid cells, some resembling Reed–Sternberg cells,[1532,1535] except for the fact that their cytoplasm tends to be more eosinophilic and the nuclei tend to arrange themselves in a wreath-like fashion (Fig. 4.182). Their phenotype is that of cytotoxic T cells, and they characteristically express CD30.[1520,1527,1530] An impor-

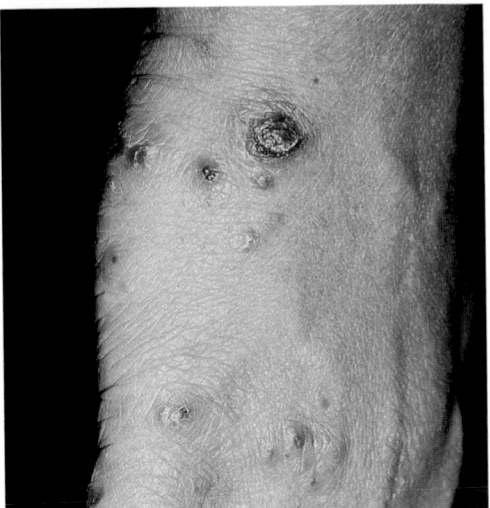
Fig. 4.180 Lymphomatoid papulosis. Clinical appearance. Multiple lesions are present, the larger ones showing ulceration.

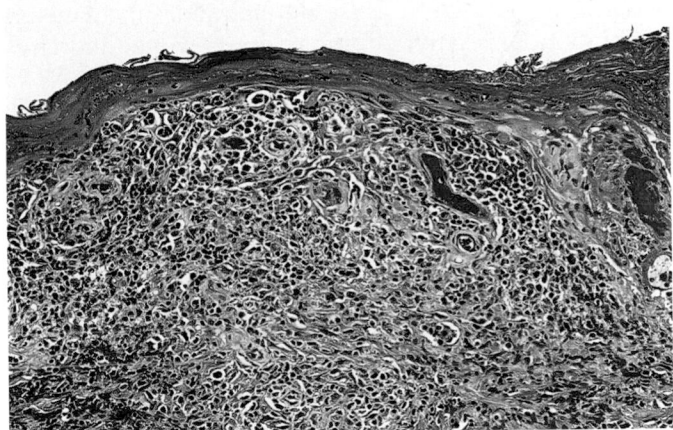
Fig. 4.181 Low-power view of lymphomatoid papulosis showing heavy dermal infiltrate with epidermal thinning.

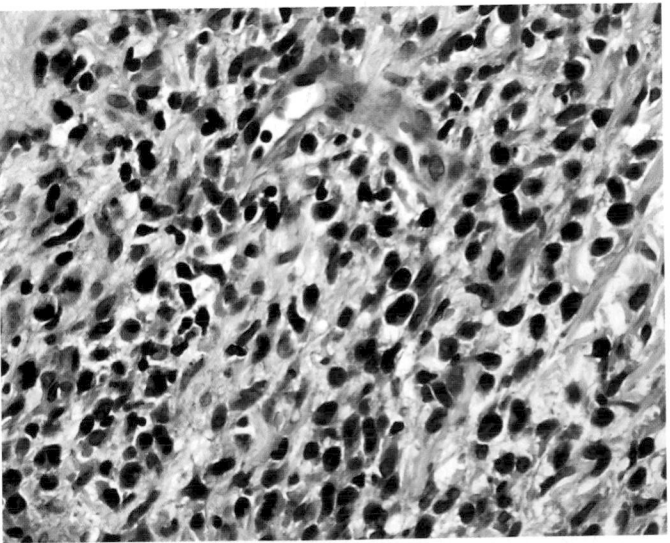
Fig. 4.182 Lymphomatoid papulosis. High-power view, showing pleomorphism and large atypical lymphoid cells.

tant differential diagnosis is with arthropod bite, in which CD30-positive cells are usually absent.[1529]

The nature of lymphomatoid papulosis remains controversial. It was originally regarded either as a specific dermatosis or as a variant of pityriasis lichenoides acuta (Mucha–Habermann disease). The fact that there is a clonal population of T cells,[1522,1534] that some of the cases show the *NPM–ALK* transcript (see below), and that in 10% to 20% of cases there is an association with, or evolution into, malignant lymphoma[1533] favors instead the interpretation that lymphomatoid papulosis is a lymphoproliferative disease closely related to anaplastic large cell lymphoma (discussed immediately below), of which it may represent the self-healing "benign" form (just as keratoacanthoma could be viewed as the self-healing "benign" form of squamous cell carcinoma of the skin).[1518]

Anaplastic large cell lymphoma of skin presents clinically as solitary or multiple, often ulcerated skin lesions, and it affects predominantly elderly males. Microscopically, there is a diffuse dermal and subcutaneous infiltration by a polymorphic infiltrate containing large anaplastic tumor cells with an appearance similar to those described in lymphomatoid papulosis.[1523] Indeed, the similarities with the latter condition are many, except for the greater amount of the infiltrate and the greater number of atypical cells. Pseudoepitheliomatous hyperplasia is a common accompanying feature. Morphologic variants include monomorphic, small cell predominant, myxoid, lymphohistiocytic, sarcomatoid, and Hodgkin's lymphoma-like.[1524]

The large lymphoid cells show strong positivity for CD30 in the form of diffuse membrane staining, as well as a paranuclear dot-like reaction in the Golgi area. Lineage markers are usually of T-cell type, but they can also be null (but not B-cell type).[1524,1530] At the genetic level, this tumor is characterized by the chromosomal translocation t(2;5), which generates the chimeric *NPM–ALK* transcript. This can be detected by immunohistochemistry, RT-PCR and in situ hybridization in the lesional tissue.[1515,1521]

Three clinicopathologic forms of anaplastic large cell lymphoma are recognized: primary cutaneous, primary systemic ALK+, and primary systemic ALK–.[1525,1530] The primary cutaneous form is associated with a good prognosis, as secondary systemic dissemination is only rarely observed.

It should be mentioned that the disease originally described as *regressing atypical histiocytosis* is identical to the regressing phase of cutaneous anaplastic large cell lymphoma.[1519,1526,1531]

It also needs to be pointed out that the presence of CD30-positive atypical lymphoid cells in a skin lesion is not diagnostic of lymphomatoid papulosis/anaplastic large cell lymphoma, in as much as they can also be seen in a variety of non-neoplastic cutaneous infiltrates.[1515a]

Other malignant lymphomas

Malignant lymphoma (other than mycosis fungoides and related T-cell lymphomas) presenting as skin nodules in adults may represent an expression of generalized disease or may be the only manifestation of the tumor[1543,1557] (Fig. 4.183). Some have been reported in the setting of HIV infection or organ transplantation.[1540,1558] For those tumors with initial skin involvement, the head and neck are the most common sites.[1541] Another relatively frequent site is the upper back, for which the eponymic designation of *Crosti's disease* is sometimes used.[1539]

The classification of cutaneous lymphomas should follow the general rules of lymphoma classification (along REAL/WHO lines) rather than being organ-based, but at the same time it should be recognized that the clinical features play an important prognostic role and should be used for guiding therapy.[1549,1563]

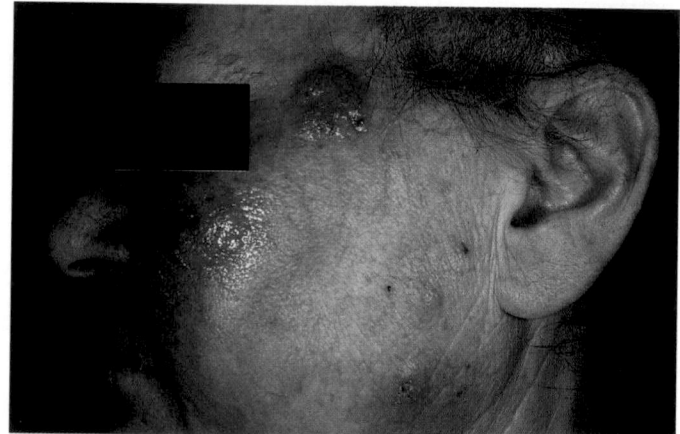

Fig. 4.183 Malignant lymphoma of skin. The lesion appears in the form of markedly erythematous nodules on the face.

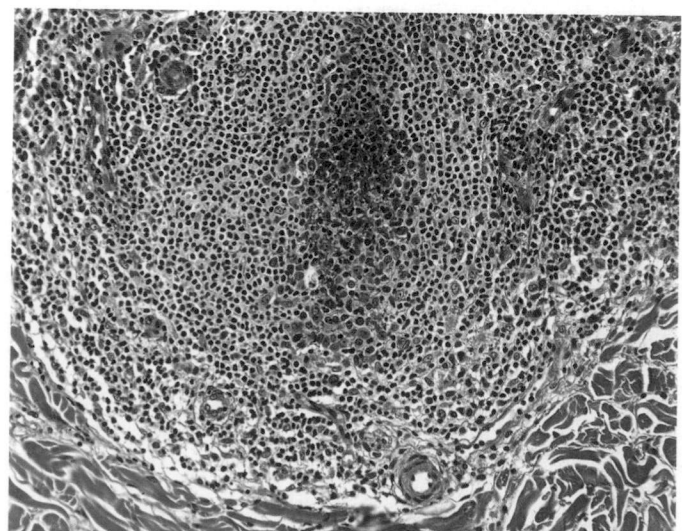

Fig. 4.184 Marginal zone B-cell lymphoma of skin. A small residual germinal center is present.

Most of the primary cutaneous lymphomas other than mycosis fungoides are of B-cell nature.[1536,1542,1547,1553,1562] They include diffuse large cell lymphoma, follicle center cell lymphoma, marginal zone lymphoma, and mantle zone lymphoma[1538,1546,1548,1556,1556a,1560] (Fig. 4.184).

Important features for microscopic recognition include the surrounding and destruction of cutaneous structures by the infiltrate; blood vessel involvement, with fragmentation or destruction of the vessel wall; and linear arrays (Indian file arrangement) of abnormal cells along the collagen fibers. The lymphomas most difficult to identify microscopically are those composed of small lymphocytes; in many cases, only a noncommittal diagnosis of "cutaneous lymphocytic infiltrate" or "small lymphocytic proliferation" can be made, with an indication for the clinician to investigate further the possibility of lymphoma.[1545] Cell marker analysis has provided evidence that the majority of these proliferations are clonal and therefore presumably neoplastic, but it has not greatly improved our ability to predict the clinical outcome. It is well to remember that the majority of these diffuse, small lymphocytic lesions, whether polyclonal or monoclonal, are characterized by a very indolent clinical course and long survival with only minimal therapeutic intervention.[1554]

Occasionally, the cutaneous lymphomatous infiltrate is accompanied by a florid sarcoid-like granulomatous reaction.[1551,1565,1566] Some cases of T-cell lymphoma have been accompanied by panniculitis.[1537]

Lymphoblastic lymphoma is very unusual, but it represents the predominant type of cutaneous lymphoma in children.[1550,1564,1579]

Blastic natural killer cell leukemia/lymphoma is a CD56+ TdT+ systemic malignancy with frequent cutaneous involvement and a highly aggressive clinical course.[1544,1552,1578]

Hodgkin's lymphoma of the skin presents in most instances as papules and nodules forming distally to involved lymph nodes; they are an indication of stage IV disease and probably result from retrograde lymphatic spread.[1575] A few well-documented cases of primary Hodgkin's lymphoma of the skin have been reported[1571,1575] (some of them in HIV-infected patients[1569]), but many of the cases published in the past under this rubric were examples of lymphomatoid papulosis.

Plasmacytoma may exceptionally present in the form of localized cutaneous disease.[1561,1574,1577]

True histiocytic lymphoma of the skin probably exists,[1572] but most cases previously reported as malignant histiocytosis would probably be reclassified as anaplastic malignant lymphoma at present.

Intravascular (angiotropic) lymphoma is the currently preferred term for the disease originally described as malignant (systemic, neoplastic) angioendotheliomatosis and characterized by accumulations of large, round, malignant cells in the lumen (and sometimes

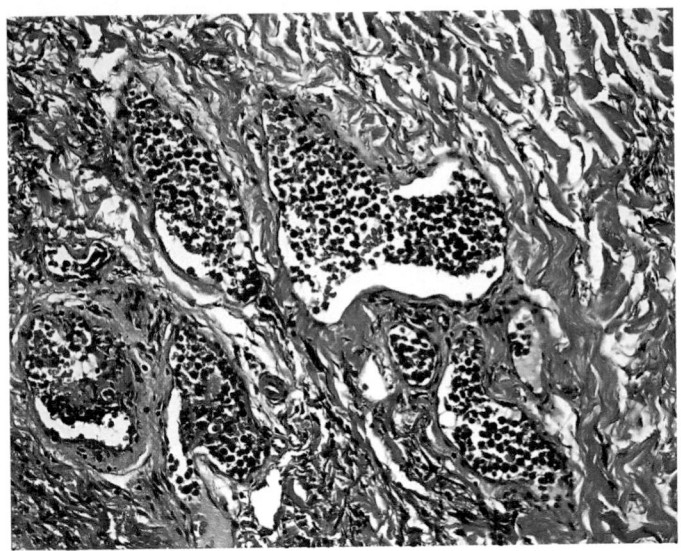

Fig. 4.185 Angiotropic malignant lymphoma. The dermal vessels are packed with malignant lymphoid cells.

wall) of vessels[1567] (Fig. 4.185). The cutaneous and neurologic manifestations dominate the clinical presentation, but the disease may present initially in the uterine cervix, prostate, nasal cavity, bone, skeletal muscle, or other sites.[1573,1576] It was originally regarded as a systemic malignancy of vascular endothelium, but immunocytochemical studies have shown that it represents an angiotropic form of malignant lymphoma, usually of B-cell but sometimes of T-cell type.[1559,1568,1570] The term "angiotropic lymphoma" should not be equated with that of "angiocentric lymphoma," a T-cell malignancy with a different organ distribution and microscopic appearance (see Chapter 7). It should also be mentioned that a true reactive form of cutaneous angioendotheliomatosis exists.[1555]

Leukemia

Involvement of the skin in the form of multiple papules or nodules ("leukemia cutis") occurs in approximately 10% of patients with monocytic leukemia, 8% with chronic lymphocytic leukemia, and 5% with chronic granulocytic leukemia.[1580,1584,1589] Most patients have an abnormal blood count at the time of diagnosis, but in some instances the skin lesions represent the first clinical manifestation of the disease and are accompanied by a normal peripheral blood ("aleukemic" forms).[1589] Granulocytic leukemia of skin is usually a manifestation of recurrence in treated patients or a late development in association with widespread dissemination.[1586] Rarely, the disease manifests initially as multiple tumors in the skin: these cases tend to be misdiagnosed as large cell lymphoma.[1587] In chronic lymphocytic leukemia, the dermal infiltrate can be perivascular and periadnexal, nodular/diffuse, or bandlike.[1581] Immunohistochemical evaluation plays an important role in the identification of this process, particularly if fresh frozen tissue is available.[1588,1589] This includes the use of CD99 for acute lymphoblastic and acute myelogenous leukemia.[1583]

It is well to remember that a large proportion of the skin lesions occurring in leukemic patients are histologically nonspecific inflammatory reactions and are not caused by infiltration by neoplastic cells.[1582] This includes leukemic vasculitis, although in this condition is not clear whether the cells infiltrating the vessel walls are reactive or neoplastic.[1585]

Other primary tumors and tumorlike conditions

Endometriosis can present in women of reproductive age in the umbilicus or groin without antecedent surgery. When present in other cutaneous sites, there is nearly always an associated surgical scar.[1607] Microscopically, the combination of endometrial glands and stroma is characteristic; the lesion should not be confused with a sweat gland tumor or, worse, with a metastatic adenocarcinoma. Marked hemorrhage or decidual changes in the stroma may render the recognition difficult and lead to an overdiagnosis of malignancy.[1603,1604]

Benign cystic teratoma exceptionally presents as a skin nodule; the presence of tissue components from all three germinal layers distinguishes it from the more common dermoid cyst (see p. 152).[1593,1610]

Meningioma can occur as a skin nodule, either in the scalp or along the vertebral axis, with or without an associated skin defect (see Chapter 28). *Hamartoma of the scalp with ectopic meningothelial elements* (rudimentary meningocele) is pathogenetically related to meningioma of the skin; it appears as a scalp nodule, usually during infancy, and is characterized by a dermal and sub-cutaneous proliferation of polygonal to spindle meningothelial cells, sometimes arranged in whorls and sometimes dissecting collagen fibers in a fashion reminiscent of angiosarcoma (Fig. 4.186). Psammoma bodies and islands of cartilage may be present. A long cleft is sometimes seen in the center of the lesion, in keeping with its presumed malformative pathogenesis. The ectopic meningothelial cells are immunoreactive for vimentin and EMA and negative for CD31 and FVIII-related antigen.[1602,1608]

Meningioma-like tumor of the skin (not to be confused with cutaneous meningioma or with hamartoma of the scalp with ectopic meningothelial elements) is yet another recently described benign lesion of obscure histogenesis, characterized by a whorled configuration of spindle-shaped cells, some arranged around blood vessels.[1590]

Nasal glioma is a form of glial heterotopia that is seen in neonates at the root of the nose, sometimes immediately beneath the skin (see Chapter 7).

Ganglioneuroma can exceptionally present as a primary cutaneous neoplasm.[1610a]

Extraosseous chondromas are usually located in the soft tissues, but a few dermal examples are on record.[1600]

Osteomas of skin are probably not true neoplasms, but rather examples of metaplastic ossification of other lesions, such as pilomatrixomas or melanocytic nevi.[1594]

Metaplastic synovial cyst (synovial metaplasia of the skin) is a peculiar postsurgical intradermal cystic formation associated with transepidermal fistulas and lined microscopically by tissue resembling hyperplastic synovium.[1591,1592,1595,1597] The rare cutaneous *ganglion cyst* probably has a similar pathogenesis.[1606]

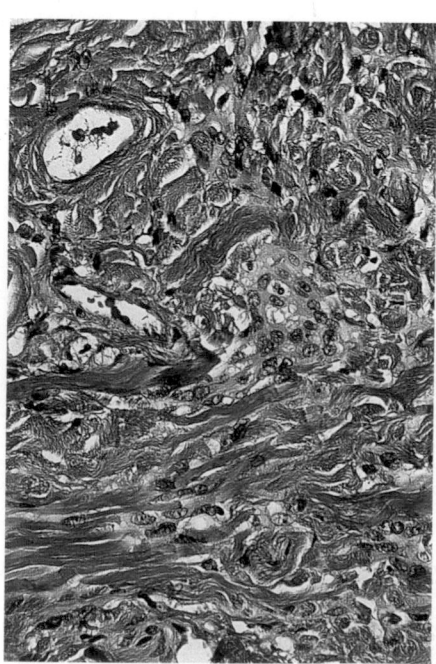 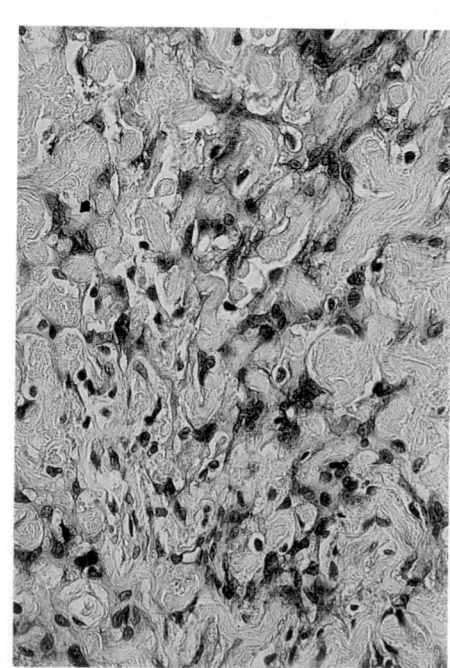

A   B

Fig. 4.186 Hamartoma of the scalp with ectopic meningothelial elements. **A,** Meningothelial cells are present in the deep dermis, some of them arranged in clusters and others individually among collagen fibers. **B,** Positive immunostain for epithelial membrane antigen (EMA).

Inflammatory pseudotumor presents as a small, deeply seated dermal nodule; microscopically, it has a fibrosed (sometimes hyalinized) and vascularized center containing a polymorphic infiltrate rich in plasma cells surrounded by a rim of lymphoid follicles, the overall appearance resembling a lymph node on low-power examination.[1601] The process is probably truly inflammatory and not related to so-called "inflammatory myofibroblastic tumor."

Chordomoid nodule is a peculiar skin nodule that has been found in infants and that has a morphologic resemblance to chordoma; its histogenesis is unknown.[1609]

Soft tissue-type tumors of various types can sometimes present as cutaneous (dermal) neoplasms. In addition to those that have already been mentioned, the list includes lipomas and atypical lipomatous tumors,[1596] giant cell tumor,[1599] Ewing's sarcoma/PNET,[1598] and synovial sarcoma.[1605]

Metastatic carcinoma

In males, the most common sources of metastatic tumor to the skin are lung (25%), large bowel, skin (melanoma), kidney, and upper aerodigestive tract. In females, the breast is by far the most common source (69%), followed by the lung, skin (melanoma), kidney, and ovary.[1612,1613,1617] Most cases are multiple and appear as firm, nonulcerated nodules.[1615] When solitary, they may be misdiagnosed as primary skin tumors (Fig. 4.187). This is particularly true for renal cell carcinoma, which is often misinterpreted as a sweat gland tumor[1614,1616]; the presence of dilated sinusoidal vessels, extravasated red blood cells in the glandular lumina, and nuclear atypia should suggest the

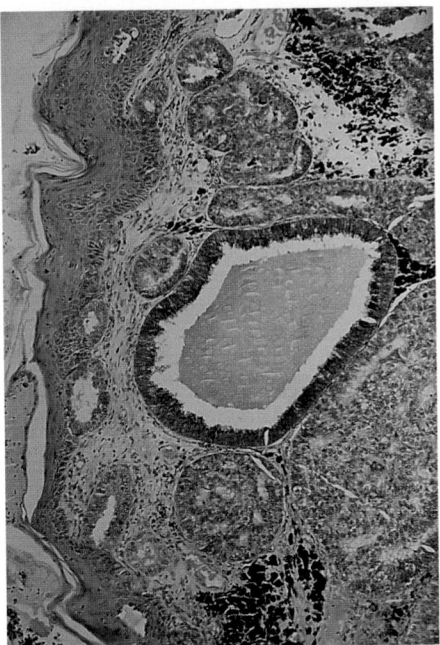

Fig. 4.188 Metastatic adenocarcinoma of breast to skin. Tumor has epidermotropic qualities, thus simulating primary carcinoma of sweat gland derivation.

correct diagnosis. Occasionally, metastatic signet ring carcinomas from the stomach or other sites elicit a brisk fibroblastic reaction with storiform features, thus closely resembling the appearance of a dermatofibrosarcoma protuberans.

Occasionally, the metastatic dermal nodules invade the overlying epidermis, simulating the appearance of a primary tumor ("epidermotropic carcinomas")[1611,1618,1620] (Fig. 4.188). Another source of error is the solitary cutaneous metastasis from a small cell carcinoma of the lung, endocrine tumor of the pancreas, or carcinoid tumor of the small bowel that is misdiagnosed as Merkel cell carcinoma or some other primary neuroendocrine carcinoma of skin.[1619]

The most common sites for skin metastases are the chest and abdomen, followed by the head and neck; location in the extremities is rare. Those metastases situated in the scalp can be associated with alopecia ("alopecia neoplastica"). The interesting observation has been made that the skin metastases tend to be close to the site of the primary tumor: chest in lung carcinoma, abdominal wall in gastrointestinal tumors, and lower back in renal cell carcinoma.[1613]

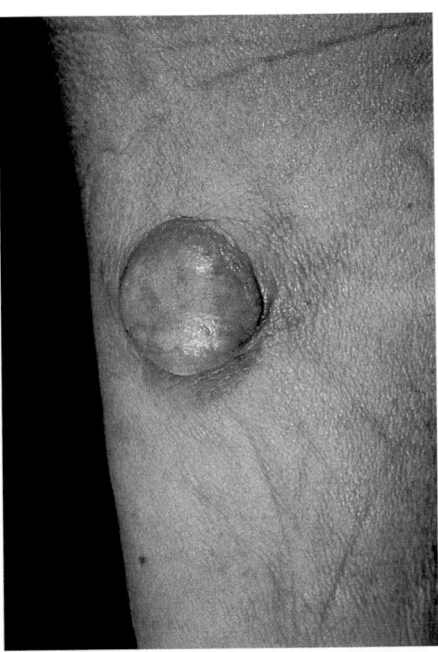

Fig. 4.187 Squamous cell carcinoma of uterine cervix metastatic to skin of arm.

References

Epidermis
Seborrheic keratosis

1 Cascajo CD, Reichel M, Sanchez JL. Malignant neoplasms associated with seborrheic keratoses: an analysis of 54 cases. Am J Dermatopathol 1996, **18**: 278–282.

2 Chen M, Shinmori H, Takemiya M, Miki Y. Acantholytic variant of seborrheic keratosis. J Cutan Pathol 1990, **17**: 27–31.

3 Holdiness MR. The sign of Leser-Trélat. Int J Dermatol 1986, **25**: 564–572.

4 Jacyk W, Dreyer L, De Villiers E. Seborrheic keratoses of black patients with epidermodysplasia verruciformis contain human papillomavirus DNA. Am J Dermatopathol 1993, **15**: 1–6.

4a King R, Page RN, Googe PB. Desmoplastic seborrheic keratosis. Am J Dermatopathol 2003, **25**: 210–214.

5 Li J, Ackerman AB. "Seborrheic keratoses" that contain human papillomavirus are condylomata acuminata. Am J Dermatopathol 1994, **16**: 398.

6 Nindl M, Nakagawa H, Furue M, Ishibashi Y. Simple epithelial cytokeratin-expression in seborrheic keratosis. J Cutan Pathol 1992, **19**: 415–422.

7 Rahbari H. Bowenoid transformation of seborrheic verrucae (keratoses). Br J Dermatol 1979, **101**: 459–463.

8 Roncalli De Oliveira W, Neto CF, Rady PL, Tyring SK. Seborrheic keratosis-like lesions in patients with epidermodysplasia verruciformis. J Dermatol 2003, **30**: 48–53.

9 Scully JP. Treatment of seborrheic keratosis. JAMA 1970, **213**: 1498.

10 Shimizu N, Ito M, Tazawa T, Sato Y. Immunohistochemical study on keratin expression in certain cutaneous epithelial neoplasms. Basal cell carcinoma, pilomatricoma, and seborrheic keratosis. Am J Dermatopathol 1989, **11**: 534–540.

11 Zhao Y, Lin Y, Luo R, Huang X, Liu M, Xia M, Jin H. Human papillomavirus (HPV) infection in seborrheic keratosis. Am J Dermatopathol 1989, **11**: 209–212.

12 Zhu WY, Leonardi C, Kinsey W, Penneys NS. Irritated seborrheic keratoses and benign verrucous acanthomas do not contain papillomavirus DNA. J Cutan Pathol 1991, **18**: 449–452.

Acrochordon

13 Cooper PH, Mackel SE. Acquired fibrokeratoma of the heel. Arch Dermatol 1985, **121**: 386–388.

Actinic keratosis

14 Dinehart SM. The treatment of actinic keratoses. J Am Acad Dermatol 2000, **42**: 25–28.

15 Fu W, Cockerell CJ. The actinic (solar) keratosis: a 21st-century perspective. Arch Dermatol 2003, **139**: 66–70.

16 James MP, Wells GC, Whimster IW. Spreading pigmented actinic keratoses. Br J Dermatol 1978, **98**: 373–379.

17 King GN, Healy CM, Glover MT, Kwan JT, Williams DM, Leigh IM, Worthington HV, Thornhill MH. Increased prevalence of dysplastic and malignant lip lesions in renal-transplant recipients. N Engl J Med 1995, **332**: 1052–1057.

18 Mai KR, Alhalouly T, Landry D, Stinson WA, Perkins DG, Yadzi HM. Pagetoid variant of actinic keratosis with or without squamous cell carcinoma of sun-exposed skin: a lesion simulating extramammary Paget's disease. Histopathology 2002, **41**: 331–336.

19 Pinkus H. Keratosis senilis. A biologic concept of its pathogenesis and diagnosis based on the study of normal epidermis and 1730 seborrheic and senile keratoses. Am J Clin Pathol 1958, **29**: 193–207.

20 Sim CS, Slater S, McKee PH. Mutant p53 expression in solar keratosis. An immunohistochemical study. J Cutan Pathol 1992, **19**: 302–308.

21 Spira M, Freeman R, Arfai P, Gerow FJ, Hardy SB. Clinical comparison of chemical peeling, dermabrasion and 5-FU for senile keratoses. Plast Reconstr Surg 1970, **46**: 61–66.

Cutaneous horn

22 Bondeson J. Everard Home, John Hunter, and cutaneous horns: a historical review. Am J Dermatopathol 2001, **23**: 362–369.

23 DiMaio DJ, Cohen PR. Trichilemmal horn: case presentation and literature review. J Am Acad Dermatol 1998, **39**: 368–371.

24 Kimura S. Trichilemmal keratosis (horn). A light and electron microscopic study. J Cutan Pathol 1983, **10**: 59–68.

25 Michal M, Bisceglia M, Di Mattia A, Requena L, Fanburg-Smith JC, Mukensnabl P, Hes O, Cada F. Gigantic cutaneous horns of the scalp: lesions with a gross similarity to the horns of animals: a report of four cases. Am J Surg Pathol 2002, **26**: 789–794.

26 Nakamura K. Two cases of trichilemmal-like horn. Arch Dermatol 1984, **120**: 386–387.

27 Poblet E, Jimenez-Reyes J, Gonzalez-Herrada C, Granados R. Trichilemmal keratosis: a clinicopathologic and immunohistochemical study of two cases. Am J Dermatopathol 1997, **18**: 543–547.

28 Yu RC, Pryce DW, Macfarlane AW, Stewart TW. A histopathological study of 643 cutaneous horns. Br J Dermatol 1991, **124**: 449–452.

Bowen's disease

29 Argenyi ZB, Hughs AM, Balogh K, Vo T-L. Cancerization of eccrine sweat ducts in Bowen's disease as studied by light microscopy, DNA spectrophotometry and immunohistochemistry. Am J Dermatopathol 1990, **12**: 433–440.

30 Callen JP, Headington J. Bowen's and non-Bowen's squamous intradermal neoplasia of the skin. Relationship to internal malignancy. Arch Dermatol 1980, **116**: 422–426.

31 Centeno JA, Mullick FG, Martinez L, Page NP, Gibb H, Longfellow D, Thompson C, Ladich ER. Pathology related to chronic arsenic exposure. Environ Health Perspect 2002, **110**: 883–886.

32 Graham JH, Helwig EB. Bowen's disease and its relationship to systemic cancer. Arch Dermatol 1959, **80**: 133–159.

33 Kossard S, Rosen R. Cutaneous Bowen's disease. An analysis of 1001 cases according to age, sex, and site. J Am Acad Dermatol 1992, **27**: 406–410.

34 Kuo TT, Hu S, Lo SK, Chan HL. p53 expression and proliferative activity in Bowen's disease with or without chronic arsenic exposure. Hum Pathol 1997, **28**: 786–790.

35 Newton JA, Camplejohn RS, McGibbon DH. Aneuploidy in Bowen's disease. Br J Dermatol 1986, **114**: 691–694.

36 Sim CS, Slater SD, McKee PH. Mutant p53 protein is expressed in Bowen's disease. Am J Dermatopathol 1992, **14**: 195–199.

37 Williamson JD, Colome MI, Sahin A, Ayala AG, Medeiros LJ. Pagetoid Bowen disease: a report of 2 cases that express cytokeratin 7. Arch Pathol Lab Med 2000, **124**: 427–430.

Squamous cell carcinoma
General features

38 Alam M, Ratner D. Cutaneous squamous-cell carcinoma. N Engl J Med 2001, **344**: 975–983.

39 Alexander SJ. Squamous cell carcinoma in chronic hydradenitis suppurativa. A case report. Cancer 1979, **43**: 745–748.

40 Barr LH, Menard JW. Marjolin's ulcer. The LSU experience. Cancer 1983, **52**: 173–175.

41 Brash DE, Rudolph JA, Simon JA, Lin A, McKenna GJ, Baden HP, Halperin AJ, Ponten J. A role for sunlight in skin cancer. UV-induced p53 mutations in squamous cell carcinoma. Proc Natl Acad Sci USA 1991, **88**: 10124–10128.

42 Centeno JA, Mullick FG, Martinez L, Page NP, Gibb H, Longfellow D, Thompson C, Ladich ER. Pathology related to chronic arsenic exposure. Environ Health Perspect 2002, **110**: 883–886.

43 Cleaver JE, Crowley E. UV damage, DNA repair and skin carcinogenesis. Front Biosci 2002, **1**: 1024–1042.

44 Epstein JI, Mendelsohn G. Squamous carcinoma of the foot arising in association with long-standing verrucous hyperplasia in a patient with congenital lymphedema. Cancer 1984, **54:** 943–947.

45 Euvrard S, Kanitakis J, Claudy A. Skin cancers after organ transplantation. N Engl J Med 2003, **348:** 1681–1691.

46 Furukawa H, Yamamoto Y, Minakawa H, Sugihara T. Squamous cell carcinoma in chronic lymphedema: case report and review of the literature. Dermatol Surg 2002, **28:** 951–953.

47 Gasparro FP. The role of PUVA in the treatment of psoriasis. Photobiology issues related to skin cancer incidence. Am J Clin Dermatol 2000, **1:** 337–348.

48 Johnson LL, Kempson RL. Epidermoid carcinoma in chronic osteomyelitis. Diagnostic problems and management. J Bone Joint Surg (A) 1965, **47:** 133–145.

49 Kim J, Su W, Kurtin P, Ziesmer S. Marjolin's ulcer. Immunohistochemical study of 17 cases and comparison with common squamous cell carcinoma and basal cell carcinoma. J Cutan Pathol 1992, **19:** 278–285.

50 Levin A, Amazon K, Rywlin AM. A squamous cell carcinoma that developed in an epidermal nevus. Report of a case and a review of the literature. Am J Dermatopathol 1984, **6:** 51–55.

51 McGrath J, Schofield O, Mayou B, McKee P, Eady R. Epidermolysis bullosa complicated by squamous cell carcinoma. Report of 10 cases. J Cutan Pathol 1992, **19:** 116–123.

52 Madariaga J, Fromowitz F, Phillips M, Hoover HC Jr. Squamous cell carcinoma in congenital ichthyosis with deafness and keratitis. A case report and review of the literature. Cancer 1986, **57:** 2026–2029.

53 Majewski S, Jablonska S. Do epidermodysplasia verruciformis human papillomavirus contribute to malignant and benign epidermal proliferation? Arch Dermatol 2002, **138:** 649–654.

54 Mallipeddi R. Epidermolysis bullosa and cancer. Clin Exp Dermatol 2002, **27:** 616–623.

55 Marks R. An overview of skin cancers. Incidence and causation. Cancer 1995, **75:** 607–612.

56 Martin H, Strong E, Spiro RH. Radiation-induced skin cancer of the head and neck. Cancer 1970, **25:** 61–71.

57 Martinez JC, Otley CC, Stasko T, Euvrard S, Brown C, Schanbachen CF, Weaver AL, Transplant-Skin Cancer Collaborative. Defining the clinical course of metastatic skin cancer in organ transplant recipients: a multicenter collaborative study. Arch Dermol 2003, **139:** 301–306.

58 Mullen DL, Silverberg SG, Penn I, Hammond WS. Squamous cell carcinoma of the skin and lip in renal homograft recipients. Cancer 1976, **37:** 729–734.

59 Otsuka F, Umebayashi Y, Watanabe S, Kawashima M, Hamanaka S. Porokeratosis large skin lesions are susceptible to skin cancer development. Histological and cytological explanation for the susceptibility. J Cancer Res Clin Oncol 1993, **119:** 395–400.

60 Preston D, Stern R. Nonmelanoma cancers of the skin. N Engl J Med 1992, **327:** 1649–1662.

61 Rubel JR, Milford EL, Abdi R. Cutaneous neoplasms in renal transplant recipients. Eur J Dermatol 2002, **12:** 532–535.

62 Schwartz RA, Birnkrant AP, Rubenstein DJ, Kim U, Burgess GH, Stoll HL Jr, Chai SW, Southwick GJ, Milgrom H. Squamous cell carcinoma in dominant type epidermolysis bullosa dystrophica. Cancer 1981, **47:** 615–620.

63 Smoller BR, Krueger J, McNutt NS, Hsu A. "Activated" keratinocyte phenotype is unifying feature in conditions which predispose to squamous cell carcinoma of the skin. Mod Pathol 1990, **3:** 171–175.

64 Sober AJ, Burstein JM. Precursors to skin cancer. Cancer 1995, **75:** 645–650.

65 Soler C, Chardonnet Y, Allibert P, Euvrard S, Schmitt D, Mandrand B. Detection of mucosal human papillomavirus types 6/11 in cutaneous lesions from transplant recipients. J Invest Dermatol 1993, **101:** 286–291.

66 Stern RS, Laird N, Melski J, Parrish JA, Fitzpatrick TB, Bleich HL. Cutaneous squamous-cell carcinoma in patients treated with PUVA. N Engl J Med 1984, **310:** 1156–1161.

67 Tsao H. Genetics of nonmelanoma skin cancer. Arch Dermatol 2001, **137:** 1486–1492.

68 Urbach F. Geographic pathology of skin cancer. In Urbach F (ed.): International conference on the biologic effects of ultraviolet radiation (with emphasis on the skin). New York, 1969, Pergamon Press, pp. 635–650.

69 Wang C-Y, Brodland DG, Su WPD. Skin cancers associated with acquired immunodeficiency syndrome. Mayo Clin Proc 1995, **70:** 766–772.

Microscopic features

70 Cramer SF, Heggeness LM. Signet-ring squamous cell carcinoma. Am J Clin Pathol 1989, **91:** 488–491.

71 Jones RE Jr (ed.). What is the boundary that separates a thick solar keratosis and a thin squamous-cell carcinoma? Am J Dermatopathol 1984, **6:** 301–306.

72 Landman G, Taylor RM, Friedman KJ. Cutaneous papillary squamous cell carcinoma. A report of two cases. J Cutan Pathol 1990, **17:** 105–110.

73 Requena L, Sanchez M, Requena I, Alegre V, Sanchez Yus E. Clear cell squamous cell carcinoma. A histologic, immunohistologic, and ultrastructural study. J Dermatol Surg Oncol 1991, **17:** 656–660.

Immunohistochemical and molecular genetic features

74 Beer TW, Shepherd P, Theaker JM. Ber EP4 and epithelial membrane antigen aid distinction of basal cell, squamous cell and basosquamous carcinoma of the skin. Histopathology 2000, **37:** 218–223.

75 Gusterson BA, Clinton S, Gough G. Studies of early invasive and intraepithelial squamous cell carcinomas using an antibody to type IV collagen. Histopathology 1986, **10:** 161–169.

76 Heim S, Mertens F, Jin YS, Mandahl N, Johansson B, Biorklund A, Wennerberg J, Jonsson N, Mitelman F. Diverse chromosome abnormalities in squamous cell carcinomas of the skin. Cancer Genet Cytogenet 1989, **39:** 69–76.

77 Helander SD, Peters MS, Pittelkow MR. Expression of p53 protein in benign and malignant epidermal pathologic conditions. J Am Acad Dermatol 1993, **29:** 741–748.

78 Heng MC, Fallon-Friedlander S, Bennett R. Expression of *Ulex europaeus* agglutinin I lectin-binding sites in squamous cell carcinomas and their absence in basal cell carcinomas. Indicator of tumor type and differentiation. Am J Dermatopathol 1992, **14:** 216–219.

79 Heyderman E, Graham RM, Chapman DV, Richardson TC, McKee PH. Epithelial markers in primary skin cancer. An immunoperoxidase study of the distribution of epithelial membrane antigen (EMA) and carcinoembryonic antigen (CEA) in 65 primary skin carcinomas. Histopathology 1984, **8:** 423–434.

80 Iyer PV, Leong A S-Y. Poorly differentiated squamous cell carcinomas of the skin can express vimentin. J Cutan Pathol 1992, **19:** 34–39.

81 Perkins W, Campbell I, Leigh I, Mackie R. Keratin expression in normal skin and epidermal neoplasms demonstrated by a panel of monoclonal antibodies. J Cutan Pathol 1992, **19:** 476–482.

82 Said JW, Sassoon AF, Shintaku IP, Banks-Schlegel S. Involucrin in squamous and basal cell carcinomas of the skin. An immunohistochemical study. J Invest Dermatol 1984, **82:** 449–452.

83 Swanson PE, Fitzpatrick MM, Ritter JH, Glusac EJ, Wick MR.

Immunohistologic differential diagnosis of basal cell carcinoma, squamous cell carcinoma, and trichoepithelioma in small cutaneous biopsy specimens. J Cutan Pathol 1998, **25**: 153–159.

Other microscopic types

84   Banerjee S, Eyden B, Wells S, McWilliam L, Harris M. Pseudoangiosarcomatous carcinoma. A clinicopathologic study of seven cases. Histopathology 1992, **21**: 13–24.

85   Banks ER, Cooper PH. Adenosquamous carcinoma of the skin. A report of 10 cases. J Cutan Pathol 1991, **18**: 227–234.

86   Bayer-Garner IB, Smoller BR. The expression of syndecan-1 is preferentially reduced compared with that of E-cadherin in acantholytic squamous cell carcinoma. J Cutan Pathol 2001, **28**: 83–89.

87   Brownstein MH, Shapiro L. Verrucous carcinoma of skin. Epithelioma cuniculatum plantare. Cancer 1976, **38**: 1710–1716.

88   Eusebi V, Ceccarelli C, Piscioli F, Cristofolini M, Azzopardi JG. Spindle cell tumours of the skin of debatable origin. An immunocytochemical study. J Pathol 1984, **144**: 189–199.

89   Evans HL, Smith JL. Spindle cell squamous carcinomas and sarcoma-like tumors of the skin. A comparative study of 38 cases. Cancer 1980, **45**: 2687–2697.

90   Garven TC, Thelmo WL, Victor J, Pertschuk L. Verrucous carcinoma of the leg positive for human papillomavirus DNA 11 and 18. A case report. Hum Pathol 1991, **22**: 1170–1172.

91   Izaki S, Hirai A, Yoshizawa Y, Kitamura K, Inoue T, Hatoko M, Itoyama S, Inazu M. Carcinosarcoma of the skin. Immunohistochemical and electron microscopic observations. J Cutan Pathol 1993, **20**: 272–278.

92   Kao GF, Graham JH, Helwig EB. Carcinoma cuniculatum (verrucous carcinoma of the skin). A clinicopathologic study of 46 cases with ultrastructural observations. Cancer 1982, **49**: 2395–2403.

93   Kuwano H, Hashimoto H, Enjoji M. Atypical fibroxanthoma distinguishable from spindle cell carcinoma in sarcoma-like skin lesions. A clinicopathologic and immunohistochemical study of 21 cases. Cancer 1985, **55**: 172–180.

94   Landman G, Farmer ER. Primary cutaneous mucoepidermoid carcinoma. Report of a case. J Cutan Pathol 1991, **18**: 56–59.

95   McKee PH, Wilkinson JD, Black MM, Whimster IW. Carcinoma (epithelioma) cuniculatum. A clinico-pathological study of nineteen cases and review of the literature. Histopathology 1981, **5**: 425–436.

96   Nappi O, Wick MR, Pettinato G, Ghiselli RW, Swanson PE. Pseudovascular adenoid squamous cell carcinoma of the skin. A neoplasm that may be mistaken for angiosarcoma. Am J Surg Pathol 1992, **16**: 429–438.

97   Reingold IM, Smith BR, Graham JH. Epithelioma cuniculatum pedis, a variant of squamous cell carcinoma. Am J Clin Pathol 1978, **69**: 561–565.

98   Smith KJ, Skelton HG III, Morgan AM, Barrett TL, Lupton GP. Spindle cell neoplasms coexpressing cytokeratin and vimentin (metaplastic squamous cell carcinoma). J Cutan Pathol 1992, **19**: 286–293.

99   Weidner N, Foucar E. Adenosquamous carcinoma of the skin. An aggressive mucin- and gland-forming squamous carcinoma. Arch Dermatol 1985, **121**: 775–779.

Treatment

100   Alam M, Ratner D. Cutaneous squamous-cell carcinoma. N Engl J Med 2001, **344**: 975–983.

101   Fleming ID, Amonette R, Monaghan T, Fleming MD. Principles of management of basal and squamous cell carcinoma of the skin. Cancer 1995, **75**: 699–704.

102   Sober AJ. Diagnosis and management of skin cancer. Cancer 1983, **51**: 2448–2452.

Prognosis

103   Dinehart SM, Nelson-Adesokan P, Cockerell C, Russell S, Brown R. Metastatic cutaneous squamous cell carcinoma derived from actinic keratosis. Cancer 1997, **79**: 920–923.

104   Friedman HI, Cooper PH, Wanebo HJ. Prognostic and therapeutic use of microstaging of cutaneous squamous cell carcinoma of the trunk and extremities. Cancer 1985, **56**: 1099–1105.

105   Immerman SC, Scanlon EF, Christ M, Knox KL. Recurrent squamous cell carcinoma of the skin. Cancer 1983, **51**: 1537–1540.

106   Lund HZ. How often does squamous cell carcinoma metastasize? Arch Dermatol 1965, **92**: 635–637.

Pseudoepitheliomatous hyperplasia

107   Civatte J. Pseudo-carcinomatous hyperplasia. J Cutan Pathol 1985, **12**: 214–223.

108   Kamino H, Tam ST, Alvarez L. Malignant melanoma with pseudocarcinomatous hyperplasia – an entity that can simulate squamous cell carcinoma. A light-microscopic and immunohistochemical study of four cases. Am J Dermatopathol 1990, **12**: 446–451.

109   Scott G, Chen KTK, Rosai J. Pseudoepitheliomatous hyperplasia in Spitz's nevi. A possible source of confusion with squamous cell carcinoma. Arch Pathol Lab Med 1989, **113**: 61–63.

Basal cell carcinoma

General features

110   Black MM, Walkden VM. Basal cell carcinomatous changes on the lower leg. A possible association with chronic venous stasis. Histopathology 1983, **7**: 219–227.

111   Feinmesser M, Taube E, Bandani E, Kristt D. Basal cell carcinoma arising over arteriovenous malformations: some speculation on the theme. Am J Dermatopathol 1998, **19**: 575–579.

112   Foot NC. Adnexal carcinoma of the skin. Am J Pathol 1947, **23**: 1–27.

113   Gellin GE, Kopf AW, Garfinkel L. Basal cell epithelioma. A controlled study of associated factors. Arch Dermatol 1965, **91**: 38–45.

114   Gorlin RJ, Vickers RA, Kelln E, Williamson JJ. The multiple basal-cell nevi syndrome. An analysis of a syndrome consisting of multiple nevoid basal cell carcinoma, jaw cysts, skeletal anomalies, medulloblastoma, and hyporesponsiveness to parathormone. Cancer 1965, **18**: 89–104.

115   Graham PG, McGavran MH. Basal-cell carcinomas and sebaceous glands. Cancer 1964, **17**: 803–806.

116   Howell JB, Anderson DE. The nevoid basal cell carcinoma syndrome. Arch Dermatol 1982, **118**: 824–826.

117   Jih DM, Lyle S, Elenitsas R, Elder DE, Cotsarelis G. Cytokeratin 15 expression in trichoepitheliomas and a subset of basal cell carcinomas suggests they originate from hair follicle stem cells. J Cutan Pathol 1999, **26**: 113–118.

118   Kore-eda S, Horiguchi Y, Ueda M, Toda K, Imamura S. Basal cell carcinoma cells resemble follicular matrix cells rather than follicular bulge cells: immunohistochemical and ultrastructural comparative studies. Am J Dermatopathol 1998, **20**: 362–369.

119   Kurzen H, Esposito L, Langbein L, Hartschuh W. Cytokeratins as markers of follicular differentiation: an immunohistochemical study of trichoblastoma and basal cell carcinoma. Am J Dermatopathol 2002, **23**: 501–509.

120   Lindeberg H, Jepsen FL. The nevoid basal cell carcinoma syndrome. Histopathology of the basal cell tumors. J Cutan Pathol 1983, **10**: 68–73.

121   Mason JK, Helwig EB, Graham JH. Pathology of the nevoid basal cell carcinoma syndrome. Arch Pathol 1965, **79**: 401–408.

122 Masson P. Human tumors. Histology, diagnosis and technique, ed 2. Detroit, 1970, Wayne State University Press, pp. 416–430.

123 McGibbon DH. Malignant epidermal tumours. J Cutan Pathol 1985, **12:** 224–238.

124 Mehregan AH. Aggressive basal cell epithelioma on sunlight-protected skin. Report of eight cases, one with pulmonary and bone metastases. Am J Dermatopathol 1983, **5:** 221–229.

125 Miller SJ. Biology of basal cell carcinoma. Parts I and II. J Am Acad Dermatol 1991, **24:** 1–13, 161–175.

126 Milstone EB, Helwig EB. Basal cell carcinoma in children. Arch Dermatol 1973, **108:** 523–527.

127 Misago N, Ackerman AB. Trichoblastic (basal-cell) carcinoma with tricholemmal (at the bulb) differentiation. Dermatopathology 1999, **5:** 200–204.

128 Nogita T, Kamikawa T, Kawashima M. Significance of pre-existent conditions in basal cell carcinoma on the lower extremities. Int J Dermatol 1993, **32:** 350–353.

129 Poniecka AW, Alexis JB. An immunohistochemical study of basal cell carcinoma and trichoepithelioma. Am J Dermatopathol 1999, **21:** 332–336.

130 Rahbari H, Mehregan AH. Basal cell epitheliomas (carcinoma) in children and teenagers. Cancer 1982, **49:** 350–353.

131 Robinson JK. Risk of developing another basal cell carcinoma. A 5-year prospective study. Cancer 1987, **60:** 118–120.

132 Rosai J. Basal cell carcinoma with follicular differentiation (Letters to the Editor I and II). Am J Dermatopathol 1989, **10:** 457–458, 1988, **11:** 479–480.

133 Ryan JF. Basal cell carcinoma and chronic venous stasis. Histopathology 1989, **14:** 657–659.

134 Schirren CG, Rutten A, Kauderwitz P, Diaz C, McClain S, Burgdorf WH. Trichoblastoma and basal cell carcinoma are neoplasms with follicular differentiation sharing the same profile of cytokeratin intermediate filaments. Am J Dermatopathol 1997, **19:** 341–350.

Microscopic features

135 Ambrojo P, Aguilar A, Simon P, Requena L, Sanchez Yus E. Basal cell carcinoma with matrical differentiation. Am J Dermatopathol 1992, **14:** 293–297.

136 Boyd AS, Rapini RP. Cutaneous collision tumors. An analysis of 69 cases and review of the literature. Am J Dermatopathol 1994, **16:** 253–257.

137 Cheng L, Amini SB, Tarif Zaim MT. Follicular basal cell hyperplasia overlying dermatofibroma. Am J Surg Pathol 1997, **21:** 711–718.

138 Cutlan RT, Maluf HM. Immunohistochemical characterization of pleomorphic giant cells in basal cell carcinoma. J Cutan Pathol 1999, **26:** 353–356.

139 El-Shabrawi L, Le Boit PE. Basal cell carcinoma with thickened basement membrane: a variant that resembles some benign adnexal neoplasms. Am J Dermatopathol 1998, **19:** 568–574.

140 Elston D, Bergfeld W, Petroff N. Basal cell carcinoma with monster cells. J Cutan Pathol 1993, **20:** 70–73.

141 Florell SR, Zone JJ, Gerwels JW. Basal cell carcinomas are populated by melanocytes and Langerhans cells. Am J Dermatopathol 2001, **23:** 24–28.

142 Heenan PJ, Bogle MS. Eccrine differentiation in basal cell carcinoma. I Invest Dermatol 1993, **100:** 295S–299S.

143 Kint A. Histogenetic study of the basal cell epithelioma. Curr Probl Dermatol 1970, **3:** 82–123.

144 Looi LM. Localized amyloidosis in basal cell carcinoma. A pathologic study. Cancer 1983, **52:** 1833–1836.

145 McArdle JP, Roff BT, Muller HK. Characterization of retraction spaces in basal cell carcinoma using an antibody to type IV collagen. Histopathology 1984, **8:** 447–455.

146 McGibbon DH. Malignant epidermal tumours. J Cutan Pathol 1985, **12:** 224–238.

147 Maloney ME, Jones DB, Sexton FM. Pigmented basal cell carcinoma. Investigation of 70 cases. J Am Acad Dermatol 1992, **27:** 74–78.

148 Mark GJ. Basal cell carcinoma with intraneural invasion. Cancer 1977, **40:** 2181–2187.

149 Meehan SA, Egbert BM, Rouse RV. Basal cell carcinoma with tumor epithelial and stromal giant cells: a variant of pleomorphic basal cell carcinoma. Am J Dermatopathol 1999, **21:** 473–478.

150 Nagao S, Nemoto H, Suzuki M, Satoh N, Iijima S. Myofibroblasts in basal cell epithelioma. With special reference to the phagocytic function of myofibroblasts. J Cutan Pathol 1986, **13:** 261–267.

151 Pritchard B, Youngberg G. Atypical mitotic figures in basal cell carcinoma. A review of 208 cases. Am J Dermatopathol 1993, **15:** 549–552.

152 Sahin AA, Ro JY, Grignon DJ, Ordonez NG. Basal cell carcinoma with hyaline inclusions. Arch Pathol Lab Med 1989, **113:** 1015–1018.

153 Satti MB, Azzopardi JG. Amyloid deposits in basal cell carcinoma of the skin. J Am Acad Dermatol 1990, **22:** 1082–1087.

154 Shoji T, Burlage AM, Bhawan J. Basal cell carcinoma with massive ossification. Am J Dermatopathol 1999, **21:** 34–36.

155 Suster S, Ramon y Cajal S. Myoepithelial differentiation in basal cell carcinoma. Am J Dermatopathol 1991, **13:** 350–357.

156 Zamecnki M, Skalova A, Michal M. Basal cell carcinoma with collagenous crystalloids. Arch Pathol Lab Med 1996, **120:** 581–582.

Histochemical and immunohistochemical features

157 Beer TW, Shepherd P, Theaker JM. Ber EP4 and epithelial membrane antigen aid distinction of basal cell, squamous cell and basosquamous carcinomas of the skin. Histopathology 2000, **37:** 218–223.

158 De Rosa G, Barra E, Guarino M, Staibano S, Donofrio V, Boscaino A. Fibronectin, laminin, type IV collagen distribution, and myofibroblastic stromal reaction in aggressive and nonaggressive basal cell carcinoma. Am J Dermatopathol 1994, **16:** 258–267.

159 Eusebi V, Mambelli V, Tison V, DeLellis R, Betts CM. Endocrine differentiation in basal cell carcinoma. Tumori 1979, **65:** 191–199.

160 George E, Swanson PE, Wick MR. Neuroendocrine differentiation in basal cell carcinoma. An immunohistochemical study. Am J Dermatopathol 1989, **11:** 131–135.

161 Heng MC, Fallon-Friedlander S, Bennett R. Expression of *Ulex europaeus* agglutinin I lectin-binding sites in squamous cell carcinomas and their absence in basal cell carcinomas. Indicator of tumor type and differentiation. Am J Dermatopathol 1992, **14:** 216–219.

162 Heyderman E, Graham RM, Chapman DV, Richardson TC, McKee PH. Epithelial markers in primary skin cancer. An immunoperoxidase study of the distribution of epithelial membrane antigen (EMA) and carcinoembryonic antigen (CEA) in 65 primary skin carcinomas. Histopathology 1984, **8:** 423–434.

163 Kirihara Y, Haratake J, Horie A. Clinicopathological and immunohistochemical study of basal cell carcinoma with reference to the features of basement membrane. J Dermatol 1992, **19:** 161–169.

164 Rasmussen HB, Teisner B, Andersen JA, Brandup F, Purkis T, Leigh I. Immunohistochemical studies on the localization of fetal antigen 2 (FA2), laminin, and collagen type 4 in basal cell carcinoma. J Cutan Pathol 1991, **18:** 215–219.

165 Said JW, Sassoon AF, Shintaku IP, Banks-Schlegel S. Involucrin in squamous and basal cell carcinomas of the skin. An

immunohistochemical study. J Invest Dermatol 1984, **82:** 449–452.

166 Shimizu N, Ito M, Tazawa T, Sato Y. Immunohistochemical study on keratin expression in certain cutaneous epithelial neoplasms. Basal cell carcinoma, pilomatricoma, and seborrheic keratosis. Am J Dermatopathol 1989, **11:** 534–540.

167 Stanley JR, Beckwith JB, Fuller RP, Katz SI. A specific antigenic defect of the basement membrane is found in basal cell carcinoma but not in other epidermal tumors. Cancer 1982, **50:** 1486–1490.

168 Swanson PE, Fitzpatrick MM, Ritter JH, Glusac EJ, Wick MR. Immunohistologic differential diagnosis of basal cell carcinoma, squamous cell carcinoma, and trichoepithelioma in small cutaneous biopsy specimens. J Cutan Pathol 1998, **25:** 153–159.

169 Tellechea O, Reis JP, Domingues JC, Baptista AP. Monoclonal antibody Ber EP4 distinguishes basal-cell carcinoma from squamous-cell carcinoma of the skin. Am J Dermatopathol 1993, **15:** 452–455.

170 Thomas P, Said JW, Nash G, Banks-Schlegel S. Profiles of keratin proteins in basal and squamous cell carcinomas of the skin. An immunohistochemical study. Lab Invest 1984, **50:** 36–41.

171 Van Cauwenberge D, Pierard GE, Foidart JM, Lapiere ChM. Immunohistochemical localization of laminin, type IV and type V collagen in basal cell carcinoma. Br J Dermatol 1983, **108:** 163–170.

172 Viac J, Reano A, Thivolet J. Cytokeratins in human basal and squamous cell carcinomas. Biochemical, immunohistological findings and comparisons with normal epithelia. J Cutan Pathol 1982, **9:** 377–390.

Molecular genetic features

173 Jin Y, Mertens F, Persson B, Warloe T, Gullestad HP, Salemark L, Jin C, Jonsson N, Risberg B, Mandahl N, Mitelman F, Heim S. Nonrandom numerical chromosome abnormalities in basal cell carcinomas. Cancer Genet Cytogenet 1998, **103:** 35–42.

174 Mills AE. Solar keratosis can be distinguished from superficial basal cell carcinoma by expression of bcl-2. Am J Dermatopathol 1997, **19:** 443–445.

175 Nangia R, Sait SN, Block AM, Zhang PJ. Trisomy 6 in basal cell carcinomas correlates with metastatic potential: a dual color fluorescence in situ hybridization study on paraffin sections. Cancer 2001, **91:** 1927–1932.

176 Shea CR, McNutt NS, Volkenandt M, Lugo J, Prioleau PG, Albino AP. Overexpression of p53 protein in basal cell carcinomas of human skin. Am J Pathol 1992, **141:** 25–29.

177 Shen T, Park WS, Boni R, Saini N, Pham T, Lash AE, Vortmeyer AO, Zhuang Z. Detection of loss of heterozygosity on chromosome 9q22.3 in microdissected sporadic basal cell carcinoma. Hum Pathol 1999, **30:** 284–287.

Other microscopic types

178 Barnadas MA, Freeman RG. Clear cell basal cell epithelioma. Light and electron microscopic study of an unusual variant. J Cutan Pathol 1988, **15:** 1–7.

179 Barr RJ, Alpern KS, Santa Cruz DJ, Fretzin DF. Clear cell basal cell carcinoma. An unusual degenerative variant. J Cutan Pathol 1993, **20:** 308–316.

180 Barr RJ, Graham JH. Granular cell basal cell carcinoma. A distinct histopathologic entity. Arch Dermatol 1979, **115:** 1067.

181 Farmer ER, Helwig EB. Metastatic basal cell carcinoma. A clinicopathologic study of seventeen cases. Cancer 1980, **46:** 748–757.

182 Garcia P, Lopez Carreira M, Martinez-Gonzalez MA, Ballestin C, Gil R, De Prada I. Granular cell basal cell carcinoma. Light

microscopy, immunohistochemical and ultrastructural study. Virchows Arch [A] 1993, **422:** 173–177.

183 Gellin GE, Bender B. Giant premalignant fibroepithelioma. Arch Dermatol 1966, **94:** 70–73.

184 Hayden AA, Shamma NH. Ber-EP4 and MNF-116 in a previously undescribed morphologic pattern of granular basal cell carcinoma. Am J Dermatopathol 2002, **23:** 530–532.

185 Imayama S, Yashima Y, Higuchi R, Urabe H. A new concept of basal cell epitheliomas based on the three-dimensional growth pattern of the superficial multicentric type. Am J Pathol 1987, **128:** 497–504.

186 Kim YC, Vandersteen DP, Chung YJ, Myong NH. Signet ring cell basal cell carcinoma: a basal cell carcinoma with myoepithelial differentiation. Am J Dermatopathol 2002, **23:** 525–529.

187 Lopes De Faria J, Navarrete MA. The histopathology of the skin basal cell carcinoma with areas of intermediate differentiation. A metatypical carcinoma? Pathol Res Pract 1991, **187:** 978–985.

188 McGibbon DH. Malignant epidermal tumours. J Cutan Pathol 1985, **12:** 224–238.

189 Rippey JJ. Why classify basal carcinomas? Histopathology 1998, **32:** 393–398.

190 Starink TM, Blomjous CEM. Clear cell basal cell carcinoma. Histopathology 1990, **17:** 401–406.

191 Stern JB, Haupt HM, Smith RRL. Fibroepithelioma of Pinkus. Eccrine duct spread of basal cell carcinoma. Am J Dermatopathol 1994, **16:** 585–587.

192 Walsh N, Ackerman AB. Infundibulocystic basal cell carcinoma. A newly described variant. Mod Pathol 1990, **3:** 599–608.

193 White GM, Barr RJ, Liao SY. Signet ring cell basal cell carcinoma. Am J Dermatopathol 1991, **13:** 288–292.

Spread and metastases

194 Andrews RJ, Sercarz JA, Fu YS, Calcaterra TC. Metastatic basal cell carcinoma from head and neck primary lesions. Int J Surg Pathol 1998, **6:** 17–22.

195 Auepemkiate S, Boonyaphiphat P, Thongsuksai P. p53 expression related to the aggressive infiltrative histopathological feature of basal cell carcinoma. Histopathology 2002, **40:** 568–573.

196 Bayer-Garner IB, Dilday B, Sanderson RD, Smoller BR. Syndecan-1 expression is decreased with increasing aggressiveness of basal cell carcinoma. Am J Dermatopathol 2000, **22:** 119–122.

197 Berardi RS, Korba J, Melton J, Chen H. Pulmonary metastasis in nevoid basal cell carcinoma syndrome. Int Surg 1991, **76:** 64–66.

198 Breuninger H, Dietz K. Prediction of subclinical tumor infiltration in basal cell carcinoma. J Dermatol Surg Oncol 1991, **17:** 574–578.

199 De Rosa G, Staibano S, Barra E, Zeppa P, Salvatore G, Vetrani A, Palombini L. Nucleolar organizer regions in aggressive and nonaggressive basal cell carcinoma of the skin. Cancer 1992, **69:** 123–126.

200 Dixon AY, Lee SH, McGregor DH. Histologic evolution of basal cell carcinoma recurrence. Am J Dermatopathol 1991, **13:** 241–247.

201 Dixon AY, Lee SH, McGregor DH. Histologic features predictive of basal cell carcinoma recurrence. Results of a multivariate analysis. J Cutan Pathol 1993, **20:** 137–142.

202 Herzberg AJ, Garcia JA, Kerns BJ, Jordan PA, Pence JC, Rotter SM, Dzubow LM. DNA ploidy of basal cell carcinoma determined by image cytometry of fresh smears. J Cutan Pathol 1993, **20:** 216–222.

203 Jacobs GH, Rippey JJ, Altini M. Prediction of aggressive behavior in basal cell carcinoma. Cancer 1982, **49:** 533–537.

204 McGibbon DH. Malignant epidermal tumours. J Cutan Pathol 1985, **12:** 224–238.

205 Mehregan AH. Aggressive basal cell epithelioma on sunlight-protected skin. Report of eight cases, one with pulmonary and bone metastases. Am J Dermatopathol 1983, **5**: 221–229.

206 Ramdial PK, Madaree A, Reddy R, Chetty R. bcl-2 protein expression in aggressive and non-aggressive basal cell carcinomas. J Cutan Pathol 2000, **27**: 283–291.

207 Snow SN, Sahl W, Lo JS, Mohs FE, Warner T, Dekkinga JA, Feyzi J. Metastatic basal cell carcinoma. Report of five cases. Cancer 1994, **73**: 328–335.

208 Wermuth BM, Fajardo LF. Metastatic basal cell carcinoma. A review. Arch Pathol 1970, **90**: 458–462.

Treatment

209 Fleming ID, Amonette R, Monaghan T, Fleming MD. Principles of management of basal and squamous cell carcinoma of the skin. Cancer 1995, **75**: 699–704.

210 Friedman NR. Recurrent basal cell carcinoma and Mohs surgery (correspondence). J Am Acad Dermatol 1988, **19**: 908.

211 Gooding CA, White G, Yatsuhashi M. Significance of marginal extension in excised basal cell carcinoma. N Engl J Med 1965, **273**: 923–924.

212 Headington JT. A dermatopathologist looks at Mohs micrographic surgery (editorial). Arch Dermatol 1990, **126**: 950–951.

213 Mikhail GR (ed.). Mohs micrographic surgery. Philadelphia, 1991, WB Saunders Co.

214 Miller PK, Roenigk RK, Brodland DG, Randle HW. Cutaneous micrographic surgery. Mohs procedure. Mayo Clin Proc 1992, **67**: 971–980.

215 Seidman JD, Berman JJ, Moore GW. Basal cell carcinoma. Importance of histologic discontinuities in the evaluation of resection margins. Mod Pathol 1991, **4**: 325–330.

216 Wilder RB, Kittelson JM, Shimm DS. Basal cell carcinoma treated with radiation therapy. Cancer 1991, **68**: 2134–2137.

217 Wilder RB, Shimm DS, Kittelson JM, Rogoff EE, Cassady JR. Recurrent basal cell carcinoma treated with radiation therapy. Arch Dermatol 1991, **127**: 1668–1672.

Skin adnexa

218 Abenoza P, Ackerman AB. Neoplasms with eccrine differentiation. Philadelphia, 1990, Lea & Febiger.

219 Buchi ER, Peng Y, Eng AM, Tso MO. Eccrine acrospiroma of the eyelid with oncocytic, apocrine and sebaceous differentiation. Further evidence for pluripotentiality of the adnexal epithelia. Eur J Ophthalmol 1991, **1**: 187–193.

220 Carr KA, Bulengo-Ransby SM, Weiss LM, Nickoloff BJ. Lymphoepithelioma-like carcinoma of the skin. A case report with immunophenotypic analysis and in situ hybridization for Epstein-Barr viral genome. Am J Surg Pathol 1992, **16**: 909–913.

221 Harvell JD, Kerschmann RL, LeBoit PE. Eccrine or apocrine poroma? Six poromas with divergent adnexal differentiation. Am J Dermatopathol 1996, **18**: 1–9.

222 Massa MC, Medenica M. Cutaneous adnexal tumors and cysts. A review. Part I. Tumors with hair follicular and sebaceous glandular differentiation and cysts related to different parts of the hair follicle. Pathol Annu 1985, **20**(Pt 2): 189–233.

223 Massa MC, Medenica M. Cutaneous adnexal tumors and cysts. A review. Part II. Tumors with apocrine and eccrine glandular differentiation and miscellaneous cutaneous cysts. Pathol Annu 1987, **22**(Pt 1): 225–276.

224 Murphy GF, Elder DE. Non-melanocytic tumors of the skin. Third Series, fasc. 1, Washington, DC, 1991, Armed Forces Institute of Pathology.

225 Nakhleh RE, Swanson PE, Wick MR. Cutaneous adnexal carcinomas with divergent differentiation. Am J Dermatopathol 1990, **12**: 325–334.

226 Sanchez Yus E, Requena L, Simon P, Sanchez M. Complex adnexal tumor of the primary epithelial germ with distinct patterns of superficial epithelioma with sebaceous differentiation, immature trichoepithelioma, and apocrine adenocarcinoma. Am J Dermatopathol 1992, **14**: 245–252.

227 Shek TWH, Leung EY, Luk IS, Loong F, Chan AC, Yik YH, Lam LK. Lymphoepithelioma-like carcinoma of the skin. Am J Dermatopathol 1997, **18**: 637–644.

228 Smith KJ, Skelton HG, Holland TT. Recent advances and controversies concerning adnexal neoplasms. Dermatol Clin 1992, **10**: 117–160.

229 Weyers W, Nilles M, Eckert F, Schill WB. Spiradenomas in Brooke-Spiegler syndrome. Am J Dermatopathol 1993, **15**: 156–161.

230 Wick MR, Swanson PE. Cutaneous adnexal tumors. A guide to pathologic diagnosis. Chicago, 1991, ASCP Press.

231 Wick MR, Swanson PE, LeBoit PE, Strickler JG, Cooper PH. Lymphoepithelioma-like carcinoma of the skin with adnexal differentiation. J Cutan Pathol 1991, **18**: 93–102.

232 Wong TY, Suster S, Cheek RF, Mihm MC. Benign cutaneous adnexal tumors with combined folliculosebaceous, apocrine, and eccrine differentiation: Clinicopathologic and immunohistochemical study of eight cases. Am J Dermatopathol 1996, **18**: 124–136.

Eccrine sweat glands
Eccrine poroma

233 Hara K, Mizuno E, Nitta Y, Ikeya T. Acrosyringeal adenomatosis (eccrine syringofibroadenoma of Mascaro). A case report and review of the literature. Am J Dermatopathol 1992, **14**: 328–339.

234 Hashimoto K, Lever WF. Eccrine poroma. Histochemical and electron microscopic studies. J Invest Dermatol 1964, **43**: 237–247.

235 Kakinuma H, Miyamoto R, Iwasawa U, Baba S, Suzuki H. Three subtypes of poroid neoplasia in a single lesion. Eccrine poroma, hidroacanthoma simplex, and dermal duct tumor. Histologic, histochemical, and ultrastructural findings. Am J Dermatopathol 1994, **16**: 66–72.

236 Kohda M, Manabe T, Ueki H. Squamous islands in eccrine neoplasma. Am J Dermatopathol 1990, **12**: 344–349.

237 Lui H, Stewart WD, English JC, Wood WS. Eccrine syringofibroadenomatosis. A clinical and histologic study and review of the literature. J Am Acad Dermatol 1992, **26**: 805–813.

238 Rahbari H. Hidroacanthoma simplex. A review of 15 cases. Br J Dermatol 1983, **109**: 219–225.

239 Robson A, Greene J, Ansari N, Kim B, Seed PT, McKee PH, Calonje E. Eccrine porocarcinoma (malignant eccrine poroma): a clinicopathologic study of 69 cases. Am J Surg Pathol 2001, **25**: 710–720.

240 Takanashi M, Urabe A, Nakayama J, Hori Y. Distribution of epithelial membrane antigen in eccrine poroma. Dermatologica 1991, **183**: 187–190.

241 Warner TFCS, Goell WS, Cripps DJJ. Hidroacanthoma simplex. An ultrastructural study. J Cutan Pathol 1982, **9**: 189–195.

242 Watanabe S, Mogi S, Ichikawa E, Takahashi H, Minami H, Harada S. Immunohistochemical analysis of keratin distribution in eccrine poroma. Am J Pathol 1993, **142**: 231–239.

Eccrine acrospiroma

243 Haupt HM, Stern JB, Berlin SJ. Immunohistochemistry in the differential diagnosis of nodular hidradenoma and glomus tumor. Am J Dermatopathol 1992, **14**: 310–314.

244 Johnson BL Jr, Helwig EB. Eccrine acrospiroma. Cancer 1969, **23**: 641–657.

245   Stanley RJ, Sanchez NP, Massa MC, Cooper AJ, Crotty CP, Winkelmann RK. Epidermoid hidradenoma. A clinicopathologic study. J Cutan Pathol 1982, **9**: 293–302.

246   Winkelmann RK, Wolff K. Solid-cystic hidradenoma of the skin. Clinical and histopathologic study. Arch Dermatol 1968, **97**: 651–661.

Syringoma

247   Eckert F, Nilles M, Schmid U, Altmannsberger M. Distribution of cytokeratin polypeptides in syringomas. An immunohistochemical study on paraffin-embedded material. Am J Dematopathol 1992, **14**: 115–121.

248   Feibelman GE, Maize JC. Clear-cell syringoma. A study of conventional and electron microscopy. Am J Dermatopathol 1984, **6**: 139–150.

249   Guitart J, Rosenbaum MM, Requena L. "Eruptive syringoma": a misnomer for a reactive eccrine gland ductal proliferation? J Cutan Pathol 2003, **30**: 202–205.

250   Hashimoto K, Gross BG, Lever WF. Syringoma. Histochemical and electron microscopic studies. J Invest Dermatol 1966, **46**: 150–166.

251   Soler-Carrillo J, Estrach T, Mascaro JM. Eruptive syringoma: 27 new cases and review of the literature. J Eur Acad Dermatol Venereol 2001, **15**: 242–246.

252   Winkelmann RK, Gottlieb BF. Syringoma. An enzymatic study. Cancer 1963, **16**: 665–669.

Chondroid syringoma (mixed tumor)

253   Argenyi ZB, Balogh K. Collagenous spherulosis in chondroid syringomas. Am J Dermatopathol 1992, **14**: 62–64.

254   Argenyi ZB, Goeken JA, Balogh K. Hyaline cells in chondroid syringomas. A light-microscopic, immunohistochemical, and ultrastructural study. Am J Dermatopathol 1989, **11**: 403–412.

255   Banerjee SS, Harris M, Eyden BP, Howell S, Wells S, Mainwaring AR. Chondroid syringoma with hyaline cell change. Histopathology 1993, **22**: 235–245.

256   Ferreiro JA, Nascimento AG. Hyaline-cell rich chondroid syringoma. A tumor mimicking malignancy. Am J Surg Pathol 1995, **19**: 912–917.

257   Hassab-el-Naby HM, Tam S, White WL, Ackerman AB. Mixed tumors of the skin. A histological and immunohistochemical study. Am J Dermatopathol 1989, **11**: 413–428.

258   Hirsch P, Helwig EB. Chondroid syringoma. Arch Dermatol 1961, **84**: 835–847.

258a Hornick JL, Fletcher CDM. Cutaneous myoepithelioma: a clinicopathologic and immunohistochemical study of 14 cases. Hum Pathol (In press, 2004).

259   Iglesias FD, Forcelledo FF, Sanchez TS, Garcia LF, Zapatero AH. Chondroid syringoma. A histological and immunohistochemical study of 15 cases. Histopathology 1990, **17**: 311–318.

260   Jaworski RC. The ultrastructure of chondroid syringoma (mixed tumor of skin). Ultrastruct Pathol 1984, **6**: 153–159.

261   Kilpatrick SE, Hitchcock MG, Kraus MD, Calonje E, Fletcher CD. Mixed tumors and myoepitheliomas of soft tissue: a clinicopathologic study of 19 cases with a unifying concept. Am J Surg Pathol 1997, **21**: 13–22.

262   Kunikane H, Ishikura H, Yamaguchi J, Yoshiki T, Itoh T, Aizawa M. Chondroid syringoma (mixed tumor of the skin). A clinicopathological study of 13 cases. Acta Pathol Jpn 1987, **37**: 615–625.

263   Mambo NC. Hyaline cells in a benign chondroid syringoma. Report of a case and findings by conventional and electron microscopy. Am J Dermatopathol 1984, **6**: 265–272.

264   Nakayama H, Miyazaki E, Hiroi M, Kiyoku H, Naruse K, Enzan H. So-called neoplastic myoepithelial cells in chondroid

syringomas/mixed tumors of the skin: their subtypes and immunohistochemical analysis. Pathol Int 1998, **48**: 245–253.

265   Requena L, Sanchez Yus E, Santa Cruz DJ. Apocrine type of cutaneous mixed tumor with follicular and sebaceous differentiation. Am J Dermatopathol 1992, **14**: 186–194.

266   Wiley EL, Milchgrub S, Freeman RG, Kim ES. Sweat gland adenomas. Immunohistochemical study with emphasis on myoepithelial differentiation. J Cutan Pathol 1993, **20**: 337–343.

267   Yoneda K, Kitajima Y, Furuta H, Tsuneda Y, Mori S. The distribution of keratin type intermediate-sized filaments in so-called mixed tumour of the skin. Br J Dermatol 1983, **109**: 393–400.

Eccrine cylindroma

267a Bignell GR, Warren W, Seal S, Takahashi M, Rapley E, Barfoot R, Green H, Brown C, Biggs PJ, Lakhani SR, Jones C, Hansen J, Blaif E, Hofmann B, Siebert R, Turner G, Evans DG, Schrander-Stumpel C, Beemer FA, Van Den Ouweland A, Halley D, Delpech B, Cleveland MG, Leigh I, Leisti J, Rasmussen S. Indentification of the familial cylindromatosis tumour-supressor gene. Nat Genet 2000, **25**: 160–165.

268   Cotton DWK, Braye SG. Dermal cylindromas originate from the eccrine sweat gland. Br J Dermatol 1984, **111**: 53–61.

269   Crain RC, Helwig EB. Dermal cylindroma (dermal eccrine cylindroma). Am J Clin Pathol 1961, **35**: 504–515.

270   Eckert F, Betke M, Schmoeckel C, Neuweiler J, Schmid U. Myoepithelial differentiation in benign sweat gland tumors. Demonstrated by a monoclonal antibody to alpha-smooth muscle actin. J Cutan Pathol 1992, **19**: 294–301.

271   Goette DK, McConnell MA, Fowler VR. Cylindroma and eccrine spiradenoma coexistent in the same lesion. Arch Dermatol 1982, **118**: 273–274.

272   Kallioinen M. Immunoelectron microscope demonstration of the basement membrane components laminin and type IV collagen in the dermal cylindroma. J Pathol 1985, **147**: 97–102.

273   Meybehm M, Fischer HP. Spiradenoma and dermal cylindroma: comparative immunohistochemical analysis and histogenetic considerations. Am J Dermatopathol 1997, **19**: 154–161.

274   Michal M, Lamovec J, Mukensnabl P, Pizinger K. Spiradenocylindromas of the skin: tumors with morphological features of spiradenoma and cylindroma in the same lesion: report of 12 cases. Pathol Int 1999, **49**: 419–425.

275   Penneys N, Kaiser M. Cylindroma expresses immunohistochemical markers linking it to eccrine coil. J Cutan Pathol 1993, **20**: 40–43.

276   Reingold IM, Keasbey LE, Graham JH. Multicentric dermal-type cylindromas of the parotid glands in a patient with florid turban tumor. Cancer 1977, **40**: 1702–1710.

277   Tellechea O, Reis JP, Ilheu O, Poiares Baptista A. Dermal cylindroma. An immunohistochemical study of thirteen cases. Am J Dermatopathol 1995, **17**: 260–265.

278   Wollina U, Rulke D, Schaarschmidt H. Dermal cylindroma. Expression of intermediate filaments, epithelial and neuroectodermal antigens. Histol Histopathol 1992, **7**: 575–582.

Eccrine spiradenoma

279   al-Nafussi A, Blessing K, Rahilly M. Non-epithelial cellular components in eccrine spiradenoma. A histological and immunohistochemical study of 20 cases. Histopathology 1991, **18**: 155–160.

280   Cotton DWK, Slater DN, Rooney N, Goepel JR, Mills PM. Giant vascular eccrine spiradenomas. A report of two cases with histology, immunohistology and electron microscopy. Histopathology 1986, **10**: 1093–1099.

281   Eckert F, Betke M, Schmoeckel C, Neuweiler J, Schmid U. Myoepithelial differentiation in benign sweat gland tumors.

Demonstrated by a monoclonal antibody to alpha-smooth muscle actin. J Cutan Pathol 1992, **19:** 294–301.

282 Hashimoto K, Gross BG, Nelson RG, Lever WF. Eccrine spiradenoma. Histochemical and electron microscopic studies. J Invest Dermatol 1966, **46:** 347–365.

283 Jitsukawa K, Sucki H, Sato S, Anzai T. Eccrine spiradenoma. An electron microscopic study. Am J Dermatopathol 1987, **9:** 99–108.

284 Kersting DW, Helwig EB. Eccrine spiradenoma. Arch Dermatol 1956, **73:** 199–227.

285 McNiff JM, Eisen RN, Glusac EJ. Immunohistochemical comparison of cutaneous lymphadenoma, trichoblastoma, and basal cell carcinoma: support for classification of lymphadenoma as a variant of trichoblastoma. J Cutan Pathol 1999, **26:** 119–124.

286 Mambo NC. Eccrine spiradenoma. Clinical and pathologic study of 49 tumors. J Cutan Pathol 1983, **10:** 312–320.

287 Masson P. Human tumors. Histology, diagnosis and technique, ed. 2. Detroit, 1970, Wayne State University Press, pp. 440–441.

288 Requena L, Sanchez Yus E. Cutaneous lymphadenoma with ductal differentiation. J Cutan Pathol 1992, **19:** 429–433.

289 Santa Cruz DJ, Barr RJ, Headington JT. Cutaneous lymphadenoma. Am J Surg Pathol 1991, **15:** 101–110.

290 van den Oord JJ, De Wolf-Peeters C. Perivascular spaces in eccrine spiradenoma. A clue to its histological diagnosis. Am J Dermatopathol 1995, **17:** 266–270.

Papillary syringadenoma

291 Bondi R, Urso C. Syringocystadenocarcinoma papilliferum. Histopathology 1997, **28:** 475–477.

291a Clarke LE, Ioffreda M, Abt AB. Eccrine syringofibroadenoma arising in peristomal skin. Int J Surg Pathol 2003, **11:** 61–63.

292 Helwig EB, Hackney VC. Syringadenoma papilliferum. Arch Dermatol 1955, **71:** 361–372.

293 Mambo NC. Immunohistochemical study of the immunoglobulin classes of the plasma cells in papillary syringadenoma. Virchows Arch [A] 1982, **397:** 1–6.

294 Vanatta PR, Bangert JL, Freeman RG. Syringocystadenoma papilliferum. A plasmacytotropic tumor. Am J Surg Pathol 1985, **9:** 678–683.

Papillary eccrine adenoma

295 Guccion JG, Patterson RH, Nayar R, Saini NB. Papillary eccrine adenoma: an ultrastructural and immunohistochemical study. Ultrastruct Pathol 1998, **22:** 263–269.

296 Ichikawa E, Okabe S, Umebayashi Y, Iijima S, Otsuka F, Watanabe S. Papillary eccrine adenoma: immunohistochemical studies of keratin expression. J Cutan Pathol 1997, **24:** 564–570.

297 Mizuoka H, Senzaki H, Shikata N, Uemura Y, Tsubura A. Papillary eccrine adenoma: immunohistochemical study and literature review. J Cutan Pathol 1998, **25:** 59–64.

298 Nova MP, Kress Y, Jennings TA, Halperin AJ, Axiotis CA. Papillary eccrine adenoma and low-grade eccrine carcinoma. A comparative histologic, ultrastructural, and immunohistochemical study. Surg Pathol 1990, **3:** 179–188.

299 Rulon DB, Helwig EB. Papillary eccrine adenoma. Arch Dermatol 1977, **113:** 596–598.

Aggressive digital papillary adenoma

300 Duke WH, Sherrod TT, Lupton GP. Aggressive digital papillary adenocarcinoma (aggressive digital papillary adenoma and adenocarcinoma revisited). Am J Surg Pathol 2000, **24:** 775–784.

301 Kao GF, Helwig EB, Grahan JH. Aggressive digital papillary adenoma and adenocarcinoma. A clinicopathological study of 57 patients, with histochemical, immunopathological, and ultrastructural observations. J Cutan Pathol 1987, **14:** 129–146.

Clear cell acanthoma and other "acanthomas"

302 Argenyi ZB, Huston BM, Argenyi EE, Maillet MW, Hurt MA. Large-cell acanthoma of the skin. A study by image analysis cytometry and immunohistochemistry. Am J Dermatopathol 1994, **16:** 140–144.

303 Brownstein MH. The benign acanthomas. J Cutan Pathol 1985, **12:** 172–188.

304 Brownstein MH, Fernando S, Shapiro L. Clear cell acanthoma. Clinicopathologic analysis of 37 new cases. Am J Clin Pathol 1973, **59:** 306–311.

305 Cohen PR, Ulmer R, Theriault A, Leight IM, Duvic M. Epidermolytic acanthomas: clinical characteristics and immunohistochemical features. Am J Dermatopathol 1997, **19:** 232–241.

306 Fanti PA, Passarini B, Varotti C. Melanocytes in clear cell acanthoma. Am J Dermatopathol 1990, **12:** 373–376.

307 Fukushiro S, Takei Y, Ackerman AB. Pale-cell acanthosis. A distinctive histologic pattern of epidermal epithelium. Am J Dermatopathol 1985, **7:** 515–527.

307a Giannotti MA, Alves AC, Silva MJ, Giannotti Filho O. Epidermolytic acanthoma. A study of 45 cases. Mod Pathol 2003, **16:** 91a.

308 Langer K, Wuketich S, Konrad K. Pigmented clear cell acanthoma. Am J Dermatopathol 1994, **16:** 134–139.

309 Megahed M, Scharffetter-Kochaneck K. Acantholytic acanthoma. Am J Dermatopathol 1993, **15:** 283–285.

310 Mehregan DR, Hamzavi F, Brown K. Large cell acanthoma. Int J Dermatol 2003, **42:** 36–39.

311 Roewert HJ, Ackerman AB. Large-cell acanthoma is a solar lentigo. Am J Dermatopathol 1992, **14:** 122–132.

Intraepidermal epithelioma

312 Mehregan AH, Pinkus H. Intraepidermal epithelioma. A critical study. Cancer 1964, **17:** 609–636.

313 Steffen C, Ackerman AB. Intraepidermal epithelioma of Borst-Jadassohn. Am J Dermatopathol 1985, **7:** 5–24.

Sweat gland carcinoma

314 Alessi E, Caputo R. Syringomatous carcinoma of the scalp presenting as a slowly enlarging patch of alopecia. Am J Dermatopathol 1993, **15:** 503–505.

315 Argenyi ZB, Nguyen AV, Balogh K, Sears JK, Whitaker DC. Malignant eccrine spiradenoma. A clinicopathologic study. Am J Dermatopathol 1992, **14:** 381–390.

316 Berg JW, McDivitt RW. Pathology of sweat gland carcinoma. Pathol Annu 1968, **3:** 123–144.

317 Chiller K, Passaro D, Scheuller M, Singer M, McCalmont T, Grekin RC. Microcystic adnexal carcinoma: forty-eight cases, their treatment, and their outcome. Arch Dermatol 2000, **136:** 1355–1359.

318 Chow CW, Campbell PE, Burry AF. Sweat gland carcinomas in children. Cancer 1984, **53:** 1222–1227.

319 Cooper PH. Carcinomas of sweat glands. Pathol Annu 1987 **22(Pt 1):** 83–124.

320 Cooper PH, Adelson GL, Holthaus WH. Primary cutaneous adenoid cystic carcinoma. Arch Dermatol 1984, **120:** 774–777.

321 Cooper PH, Frierson HF, Morrison AG. Malignant transformation of eccrine spiradenoma. Arch Dermatol 1985, **121:** 1445–1448.

322 Cooper PH, Mills SE, Leonard DD, Santa Cruz DJ, Headington JT, Barr RJ, Katz DA. Sclerosing sweat duct (syringomatous) carcinoma. Am J Surg Pathol 1985, **9:** 422–433.

323 Cooper PH, Robinson CR, Greer KE. Low-grade clear cell eccrine carcinoma. Arch Dermatol 1984, **120:** 1076–1078.

324 Dissanayake RVP, Salm R. Sweat-gland carcinomas. Prognosis related to histological type. Histopathology 1980, **4:** 445–466.

325 Duke WH, Sherrod TT, Lupton GP. Aggressive digital papillary adenocarcinoma (aggressive digital papillary adenoma and adenocarcinoma revisited). Am J Surg Pathol 2000, **24**: 775–784.

326 Eckert F, Schmid U, Hardmeier T, Altmannsberger M. Cytokeratin expression in mucinous sweat gland carcinomas. An immunohistochemical analysis of four cases. Histopathology 1992, **21**: 161–165.

327 Fukai K, Ishii M, Kobayashi H, Chanoki M, Furukawa M, Nakagawa K, Hamada T, Abe Y, Ooshima A. Primary cutaneous adenoid cystic carcinoma. Ultrastructural study and immunolocalization of types I, III, IV and V collagens and laminin. J Cutan Pathol 1990, **17**: 374–380.

328 Gerretsen AL, van der Putte SC, Deenstra W, van Vloten WA. Cutaneous cylindroma with malignant transformation. Cancer 1993, **72**: 1618–1623.

329 Goldstein DJ, Barr RJ, Santa Cruz DJ. Microcystic adnexal carcinoma. A distinct clinicopathologic entity. Cancer 1982, **50**: 566–572.

330 Hara K, Kamiya S. Pigmented eccrine porocarcinoma. A mimic of malignant melanoma. Histopathology 1995, **27**: 86–88.

331 Headington JT, Niederhuber JE, Beals TF. Malignant clear cell acrospiroma. Cancer 1978, **41**: 641–647.

332 Ishimura E, Iwamoto H, Kobashi Y, Yamabe H, Ichijima K. Malignant chondroid syringoma. Report of a case with widespread metastasis and review of pertinent literature. Cancer 1983, **52**: 1966–1973.

333 Kato H, Mizuno N, Nakagawa K, Furukawa M, Hamada T. Microcytic adnexal carcinoma. A light microscopic, immunohistochemical and ultrastructural study. J Cutan Pathol 1990, **17**: 87–95.

334 Kolde G, Macher E, Grundmann E. Metastasizing eccrine porocarcinoma. Report of two cases with fatal outcome. Pathol Res Pract 1991, **187**: 477–481.

335 Kuramoto Y, Gagami H. Primary adenoid cystic carcinoma masquerading as syringoma of the scalp. Am J Dermatopathol 1990, **12**: 169–174.

336 Landa NG, Winkelmann RK. Epidermotropic eccrine porocarcinoma. J Am Acad Dermatol 1991, **24**: 27–31.

337 Lin PY, Fatteh SM, Lloyd KM. Malignant transformation in a solitary dermal cylindroma. Arch Pathol Lab Med 1987, **111**: 765–767.

338 Lo JS, Peschen M, Snow SN, Oriba HA, Mohs FE. Malignant cylindroma of the scalp. J Dermatol Surg Oncol 1991, **17**: 897–901.

339 McKee PH, Fletcher CDM, Rasbridge SA. The enigmatic eccrine epithelioma (eccrome syringomatous carcinoma). Am J Dermatopathol 1990, **12**: 552–561.

340 McKee PH, Fletcher CDM, Stavrinos P, Pambakian H. Carcinosarcoma arising in eccrine spiradenoma. A clinicopathologic and immunohistochemical study of two cases. Am J Dermatopathol 1990, **12**: 335–343.

341 Madison JF, Cooper PH, Burgdorf WHC. Mucinous syringometaplasia with prominent epithelial hyperplasia and deep dermal involvement. J Cutan Pathol 1990, **17**: 220–224.

342 Mehregan AH, Hashimoto K, Rahbari H. Eccrine adenocarcinoma. A clinicopathologic study of 35 cases. Arch Dermatol 1983, **119**: 104–114.

343 Mendoza S, Helwig EB. Mucinous (adenocystic) carcinoma of the skin. Arch Dermatol 1971, **103**: 68–78.

344 Miller WL. Sweat gland carcinoma. Am J Clin Pathol 1967, **47**: 767–780.

345 Misago N, Toda S, Hikichi Y, Iyadomi M, Kohda H. A unique case of extramammary Paget's disease. Derivation from eccrine porocarcinoma? Am J Dermatopathol 1992, **14**: 553–559.

346 Nishikawa Y, Tokusashi Y, Saito Y, Ogawa K, Miyokawa N, Katagiri M. A case of apocrine adenocarcinoma associated with hamartomatous apocrine gland hyperplasia of both axillae. Am J Surg Pathol 1994, **18**: 832–836.

347 Ohnishi T, Kaneko S, Egi M, Takizawa H, Watanabe S. Syringoid eccrine carcinoma: report of a case with immunohistochemical analysis of cytokeratin expression. Am J Dermatopathol 2002, **24**: 409–413.

348 Ohtsuka H, Nagamatsu S. Microcystic adnexal carcinoma: review of 51 Japanese patients. Dermatology 2002, **204**: 190–193.

349 Paties C, Taccagni GL, Papotti M, Valente G, Zangrandi A, Aloi F. Apocrine carcinoma of the skin. A clinicopathologic, immunocytochemical, and ultrastructural study. Cancer 1993, **71**: 375–381.

350 Pena J, Suster S. Squamous differentiation in malignant eccrine poroma. Am J Dermatopathol 1993, **15**: 492–496.

351 Penneys NS, Nadji M, Ziegels-Weissman J, Ketabchi M, Morales AR. Carcinoembryonic antigen in sweat-gland carcinomas. Cancer 1982, **50**: 1608–1611.

352 Pujol RM, LeBoit PE, Su WP. Microcystic adnexal carcinoma with extensive sebaceous differentiation. Am J Dermatopathol 1997, **19**: 358–362.

353 Robson A, Greene J, Ansari N, Kim B, Seed PT, McKee PH, Calonje E. Eccrine porocarcinoma (malignant eccrine poroma): a clinicopathologic study of 69 cases. Am J Surg Pathol 2001, **25**: 710–720.

354 Rockerbie N, Solomon AR, Woo TY, Beals TF, Ellis CN. Malignant dermal cylindroma in a patient with multiple dermal cylindromas, trichoepitheliomas, and bilateral dermal analogue tumors of the parotid gland. Am J Dermatopathol 1989, **11**: 353–359.

355 Santa Cruz DJ. Sweat gland carcinomas. A comprehensive review. Semin Diagn Pathol 1987, **4**: 38–74.

356 Santa Cruz DJ, Meyers JH, Gnepp DR, Perez BM. Primary mucinous carcinoma of the skin. Br J Dermatol 1978, **98**: 645–653.

357 Shaw M, McKee PH, Lowe D, Black MM. Malignant eccrine poroma. A study of twenty-seven cases. Br J Dermatol 1982, **107**: 675–680.

358 Swanson PE, Cherwitz DL, Neumann MP, Wick MR. Eccrine sweat gland carcinoma. An histologic and immunohistochemical study of 32 cases. J Cutan Pathol 1987, **14**: 65–86.

359 Swanson PE, Mazoujian G, Mills SE, Campbell RJ, Wick MR. Immunoreactivity for estrogen receptor protein in sweat gland tumors. Am J Surg Pathol 1991, **15**: 835–841.

360 Urso C, Bondi R, Paglierani M, Salvadori A, Anichini C, Giannini A. Carcinomas of sweat glands: report of 60 cases. Arch Pathol Lab Med 2001, **125**: 498–505.

361 Urso C, Paglierani M, Bondi R. Histologic spectrum of carcinomas with eccrine ductal differentiation (sweat-gland ductal carcinomas). Am J Dermatopathol 1993, **15**: 435–440.

362 Wako M, Nishimaki K, Kawamura N, Harima N, Kubota T, Yoneda K, Manabe M, Ansai S. Mucinous carcinoma of the skin with apocrine-type differentiation: immunohistochemical studies. Am J Dermatopathol 2003, **25**: 66–70.

363 Wick MR, Goellner JR, Wolfe JT III, Su WPD. Adnexal carcinomas of the skin. I. Eccrine carcinomas. Cancer 1985, **56**: 1147–1162.

364 Wick MR, Swanson PE. Primary adenoid cystic carcinoma of the skin. A clinical, histological, and immunocytochemical comparison with adenoid cystic carcinoma of salivary glands and adenoid basal cell carcinoma. Am J Dermatopathol 1986, **8**: 2–13.

365 Wick MR, Swanson PE, Kaye VN, Pittelkow MR. Sweat gland carcinoma ex eccrine spiradenoma. Am J Dermatopathol 1987, **9**: 90–98.

366 Wong TY, Suster S, Nogita T, Duncan LM, Dickersin RG, Mihm MC Jr. Clear cell eccrine carcinomas of the skin.

A clinicopathologic study of nine patients. Cancer 1994, **73**: 1631–1643.

367 Yamamoto O, Nakayama K, Asahi M. Sweat gland carcinoma with mucinous and infiltrating duct-like patterns. J Cutan Pathol 1992, **19**: 334–339.

Extramammary Paget's disease

368 Battles OE, Page DL, Johnson JE. Cytokeratins, CEA, and mucin histochemistry in the diagnosis and characterization of extramammary Paget's disease. Am J Clin Pathol 1997, **108**: 6–12.

369 Diaz de Leon E, Carcangiu ML, Prieto VG, McCue PA, Burchette JL, To G, Norris BA, Kovatich AJ, Sanchez RL, Krigman HR, Gatalica Z. Extramammary Paget's disease is characterized by the consistent lack of estrogen and progesterone receptors but frequently expresses androgen receptor. Am J Clin Pathol 2000, **113**: 572–575.

370 Fujimoto A, Takata M, Hatta N, Takehara K. Expression of structurally unaltered androgen receptor in extramammary Paget's disease. Lab Invest 2000, **80**: 1465–1471.

371 Guarner J, Cohen C, Derose PB. Histogenesis of extramammary and mammary Paget cells. An immunohistochemical study. Am J Dermatopathol 1989, **11**: 313–318.

372 Guldhammer B, Nørgaard T. The differential diagnosis of intraepidermal malignant lesions using immunohistochemistry. Am J Dermatopathol 1986, **8**: 295–301.

373 Helm KF, Goellner JR, Peters MS. Immunohistochemical stains in extramammary Paget's disease. Am J Dermatopathol 1992, **14**: 402–407.

374 Helwig EB, Graham JH. Anogenital (extramammary) Paget's disease. A clinicopathological study. Cancer 1963, **16**: 387–403.

375 Inokuchi K, Sasai Y. Histochemical analysis of sialomucin Paget cells of mammary and extramammary Paget's disease. Acta Histochem 1992, **92**: 216–223.

376 Jones RE Jr, Austin C, Ackerman AB. Extramammary Paget's disease. A critical reexamination. Am J Dermatopathol 1979, **1**: 101–132.

377 Kariniemi A-L, Ramaekers F, Lehto V-P, Virtanen I. Paget cells express cytokeratins typical of glandular epithelia. Br J Dermatol 1985, **112**: 179–183.

378 Kohler S, Rouse RV, Smoller BR. The differential diagnosis of pagetoid cells in the epidermis. Mod Pathol 1998, **11**: 79–92.

379 Koss LG, Brockunier A Jr. Ultrastructural aspects of Paget's disease of the vulva. Arch Pathol 1969, **87**: 592–600.

380 Kuo T-T, Chan H-L, Hsueh S. Clear cell papulosis of the skin. A new entity with histogenetic implications for cutaneous Paget's disease. Am J Surg Pathol 1987, **11**: 827–834.

381 Merot Y, Mazoujian G, Pinkus G, Momtaz T-K, Murphy GF. Extramammary Paget's disease of the perianal and perineal regions. Evidence of apocrine derivation. Arch Dermatol 1985, **121**: 750–752.

382 Mohanty SK, Arora R, Kakkar N, Kumar B. Clear cell papulosis of the skin. Ann Diagn Pathol 2002, **6**: 385–388.

383 Nagle RB, Lucas DO, McDaniel KM, Clark VA, Schmalzel GM. Paget's cells. New evidence linking mammary and extramammary Paget cells to a common cell phenotype. Am J Clin Pathol 1985, **83**: 431–438.

384 Nowak MA, Guerriere-Kovach P, Pathan A, Campbell TE, Deppisch LM. Perianal Paget's disease: distinguishing primary and secondary lesions using immunohistochemical studies including gross cystic disease fluid protein-15 and cytokeratin 20 expression. Arch Pathol Lab Med 1999, **122**: 1077–1081.

385 Ordóñez NG, Awalt H, Mackay B. Mammary and extramammary Paget's disease. An immunocytochemical and ultrastructural study. Cancer 1987, **59**: 1173–1183.

386 Peralta OC, Barr RJ, Romansky SG. Mixed carcinoma *in situ*.

An immunohistochemical study. J Cutan Pathol 1983, **10**: 350–358.

387 Ramalingam P, Hart WR, Goldblum JR. Cytokeratin subset immunostaining in rectal adenocarcinoma and normal anal glands. Arch Pathol Lab Med 2001, **125**: 1074–1077.

388 Requena L, Sanchez Yus E, Nunez C, White CR, Sangueza OP. Epidermotropically metastatic breast carcinomas: rare histopathologic variants mimicking melanoma and Paget's disease. Am J Dermatopathol 1997, **18**: 385–395.

389 Shah KD, Tabizadeh SS, Gerber MA. Immunohistochemical distinction of Paget's disease from Bowen's disease and superficial spreading melanoma with the use of monoclonal cytokeratin antibodies. Am J Clin Pathol 1987, **88**: 689–695.

390 Tamaki K, Hino H, Ohara K, Furue M. Lectin-binding sites in Paget's disease. Br J Dermatol 1985, **113**: 17–24.

391 Vanstapel M-J, Gatter KC, DeWolf-Peeters C, Millard PR, Desmet VJ, Mason DY. Immunohistochemical study of mammary and extra-mammary Paget's disease. Histopathology 1984, **8**: 1013–1023.

Apocrine glands

392 Ishiko A, Shimizu H, Inamoto N, Nakmura K. Is tubular apocrine adenoma a distinct clinical entity? Am J Dermatopathol 1993, **15**: 482–487.

393 Mazoujian G, Margolis R. Immunohistochemistry of gross cystic disease fluid protein (GCDFP-15) in 65 benign sweat gland tumors of the skin. Am J Dermatopathol 1988, **10**: 28–35.

394 Umbert P, Winkelmann RK. Tubular apocrine adenoma. J Cutan Pathol 1976, **3**: 75–87.

Sebaceous glands
Senile sebaceous hyperplasia

395 Mehregan AH. Sebaceous tumors of the skin. J Cutan Pathol 1985, **12**: 196–199.

Nevus sebaceus of Jadassohn and epidermal nevus

396 Alessi E, Sala F. Nevus sebaceus. A clinicopathologic study of its evolution. Am J Dermatopathol 1986, **8**: 27–31.

397 Jaqueti G, Requena L, Yus E. Trichoblastoma is the most common neoplasm developed in nevus sebaceus of Jadassohn: a clinicopathologic study of a series of 155 cases. Am J Dermatopathol 2000, **22**: 108–118.

398 Mehregan AH, Pinkus H. Life history of organoid nevi. Special reference to nevus sebaceus of Jadassohn. Arch Dermatol 1965, **91**: 274–289.

399 Morioka S. The natural history of *nevus sebaceus*. J Cutan Pathol 1985, **12**: 200–213.

400 Prayson RA, Kotagal P, Wyllie E, Bingaman W. Linear epidermal nevus and nevus sebaceus syndromes: a clinicopathologic study of 3 patients. Arch Pathol Lab Med 1999, **123**: 301–305.

401 Su WPD. Histopathologic varieties of epidermal nevus. A study of 160 cases. Am J Dermatopathol 1982, **4**: 161–170.

402 Wilson Jones E, Heyl T. Naevus sebaceus. A report of 140 cases with special regard to the development of secondary malignant tumours. Br J Dermatol 1970, **82**: 99–117.

Sebaceous adenoma

403 Misago N, Mihara I, Ansai S, Narisawa Y. Sebaceoma and related neoplasms with sebaceous differentiation: a clinicopathologic study of 30 cases. Am J Dermatopathol 2002, **24**: 294–304.

404 Rulon DB, Helwig EB. Cutaneous sebaceous neoplasms. Cancer 1974, **33**: 82–102.

405 Steffen C. Mantleoma. A benign neoplasm with mantle differentiation. Am J Dermatopathol 1993, **15**: 306–310.

406 Troy JL, Ackerman AB. Sebaceoma. A distinctive benign neoplasm of adnexal epithelium differentiating toward sebaceous cells. Am J Dermatopathol 1984, **6**: 7–13.

Sebaceous carcinoma

407 Ansai S, Hashimoto H, Aoki T, Hozumi Y, Aso K. A histochemical and immunohistochemical study of extra-ocular sebaceous carcinoma. Histopathology 1993, **22**: 127–133.

408 Bailet JW, Zimmerman MC, Arnstein DP, Wollman JS, Mickel RA. Sebaceous carcinoma of the head and neck. Case report and literature review. Arch Otolaryngol head Neck Surg 1992, **118**: 1245–1249.

409 Bayer-Garner IB, Givens V, Smoller B. Immunohistochemical staining for androgen receptors: a sensitive marker of sebaceous differentiation. Am J Dermatopathol 1999, **21**: 426–431.

410 Burgdorf WHC, Pitha J, Fahmy A. Muir-Torre syndrome. Histologic spectrum of sebaceous proliferation. Am J Dermatopathol 1986, **8**: 202–208.

411 Finan MC, Connolly SM. Sebaceous gland tumors and systemic disease. A clinicopathologic analysis. Medicine (Baltimore) 1984, **63**: 232–242.

412 Friedman KJ, Boudreau S, Farmer ER. Superficial epithelioma with sebaceous differentiation. J Cutan Pathol 1987, **14**: 193–197.

413 Graham R, McKee P, McGibbon D, Heyderman E. Torre-Muir syndrome. An association with isolated sebaceous carcinoma. Cancer 1985, **55**: 2868–2873.

414 Hasebe T, Mukai K, Yamaguchi N, Ishihara K, Kaneko A, Takasaki Y, Shimosato Y. Prognostic value of immunohistochemical staining for proliferating cell nuclear antigen, p53, and c-*erb*B-2 in sebaceous gland carcinoma and sweat gland carcinoma: comparison with histopathological parameter. Mod Pathol 1994, **7**: 37–43.

415 Hood IC, Qizilbash AH, Salama SS, Young JEM, Archibald SD. Sebaceous carcinoma of the face following irradiation. Am J Dermatopathol 1986, **8**: 505–508.

416 Kuo T. Clear cell carcinoma of the skin. Am J Surg Pathol 1980, **4**: 573–583.

417 Misago N, Narisawa Y. Sebaceous neoplasms in Muir-Torre syndrome. Am J Dermatopathol 2000, **22**: 155–161.

418 Moreno C, Jacyk WK, Judd MJ, Requena L. Highly aggressive extraocular sebaceous carcinoma. Am J Dermatopathol 2002, **23**: 450–455.

419 Paraf F, Sasseville D, Watters AK, Narod S, Ginsburg O, Shibata H, Jothy S. Clinicopathological relevance of the association between gastrointestinal and sebaceous neoplasms. The Muir-Torre syndrome. Hum Pathol 1995, **26**: 422–427.

420 Rulon DB, Helwig EB. Cutaneous sebaceous neoplasms. Cancer 1974, **33**: 82–102.

421 Rutten A, Burgdorf W, Hugel H, Kutzner H, Hosseiny-Malayeri HR, Friedl W, Propping P, Kruse R. Cystic sebaceous tumors as marker lesions for the Muir-Torre syndrome: a histopathologic and molecular genetic study. Am J Dermatopathol 1999, **21**: 405–413.

422 Swanson PE, Campbell RJ, Wick MR. Sebaceous carcinoma. An immunohistochemical study of 36 ocular and 5 extraocular neoplasms (abstract). J Cutan Pathol 1987, **14**: 374.

423 Wick MR, Goellner JR, Wolfe JT III, Su WPD. Adnexal carcinomas of the skin. II. Extraocular sebaceous carcinomas. Cancer 1985, **56**: 1163–1172.

Hair follicles

424 Barr RJ, Goodman MM. Neurofollicular hamartoma. A light microscopic and immunohistochemical study. J Cutan Pathol 1990, **16**: 336–341.

425 Headington JT. Tumors of the hair follicle. A review. Am J Pathol 1976, **85**: 480–505.

426 Massa MC, Medenica M. Cutaneous adnexal tumors and cysts. A review. Part I. Tumors with hair follicular and sebaceous glandular differentiation and cysts related to different parts of the hair follicle. Pathol Annu 1985, **20**(Pt 2): 189–233.

427 Mehregan AH. Hair follicle tumors of the skin. J Cutan Pathol 1985, **12**: 189–195.

428 Mehregan AH, Brownstein MH. Pilar sheath acanthoma. Arch Dermatol 1978, **114**: 1495–1497.

429 Rosen LB. A review and proposed new classification of benign acquired neoplasms with hair follicle differentiation. Am J Dermatopathol 1990, **12**: 496–516.

430 Sau P, Lupton GP, Graham JH. Trichogerminoma. Report of 14 cases. J Cutan Pathol 1992, **19**: 357–365.

431 Wong TY, Reed JA, Suster S, Flynn SD, Mihm MC Jr. Benign trichogenic tumours. A report of two cases supporting a simplified nomenclature. Histopathology 1993, **22**: 575–580.

Inverted follicular keratosis

432 Azzopardi JG, Laurini R. Inverted follicular keratosis. J Clin Pathol 1975, **28**: 465–471.

433 Mehregan AH. Inverted follicular keratosis. Arch Dermatol 1964, **89**: 229–235.

434 Sim-Davis D, Marks R, Wilson Jones E. The inverted follicular keratosis. A surprising variant of seborrheic wart. Acta Derm Venereol (Stockh) 1976, **56**: 337–344.

435 Spielvogel RL, Austin C, Ackerman AB. Inverted follicular keratosis is not a specific keratosis but a verruca vulgaris (or seborrheic keratosis) with squamous eddies. Am J Dermatopathol 1983, **5**: 427–442.

Trichoepithelioma

436 Bettencourt MS, Prieto VG, Shea CR. Trichoepithelioma: a 19-year clinicopathologic re-evaluation. J Cutan Pathol 1999, **26**: 398–404.

437 Brownstein MH, Shapiro L. Desmoplastic trichoepithelioma. Cancer 1977, **40**: 2979–2986.

438 Clarke J, Ioffreda M, Helm KF. Multiple familial trichoepitheliomas: a folliculosebaceous-apocrine genodermatosis. Am J Dermatopathol 2002, **24**: 402–405.

439 Gray HR, Helwig EB. Epithelioma adenoides cysticum and solitary trichoepithelioma. Arch Dermatol 1963, **87**: 102–114.

440 Lorenzo MJ, Yebra-Pimentel MT, Peteiro C, Toribio J. Cystic giant solitary trichoepithelioma. Am J Dermatopathol 1992, **14**: 155–160.

441 Marrogi AJ, Wick MR, Dehner LP. Benign cutaneous adnexal tumors in childhood and young adults, excluding pilomatrixoma. Review of 28 cases and literature. J Cutan Pathol 1991, **18**: 20–27.

442 Takei Y, Fukushiro S, Ackerman AB. Criteria for histologic differentiation of desmoplastic trichoepithelioma (sclerosing epithelial hamartoma) from morphea-like basal-cell carcinoma. Am J Dermatopathol 1985, **7**: 207–221.

443 Thewes M, Worret WI, Engst R, Ring J. Stromelysin-3: a potent marker for histopathologic differentiation between desmoplastic trichoepithelioma and morphealike basal cell carcinoma. Am J Dermatopathol 1998, **20**: 140–142.

Trichilemmoma

444 Boscaino A, Terracciano LM, Donofrio V, Ferrarra G, De Rosa G. Tricholemmal carcinoma. A study of seven cases. J Cutan Pathol 1992, **19**: 94–99.

445 Brownstein MH, Wolf M, Bikowski JB. Cowden's disease. A cutaneous marker of breast cancer. Cancer 1978, **41**: 2393–2398.

446 Carlson GJ, Nivatvongs S, Snover DC. Colorectal polyps in Cowden's disease (multiple hamartoma syndrome). Am J Surg Pathol 1984, **8**: 763–770.

447 Hunt SJ, Kilzer B, Santa Cruz DJ. Desmoplastic trichilemmoma. Histologic variant resembling invasive carcinoma. J Cutan Pathol 1990, **17**: 45–52.

448 Lee JY, Tang CK, Leung YS. Clear cell carcinoma of the skin. A tricholemmal carcinoma? J Cutan Pathol 1989, **16**: 31–39.

449 Reis JP, Tellechea O, Cunha MF, Baptista AP. Trichilemmal carcinoma. Review of 8 cases. J Cutan Pathol 1993, **20**: 44–49.

450 Requena L, Gutierrez J, Sanchez Yus E. Multiple sclerotic fibromas of the skin. A cutaneous marker of Cowden's disease. J Cutan Pathol 1992, **19**: 346–351.

451 Swanson PE, Marrogi AJ, Williams DJ, Cherwitz DL, Wick MR. Tricholemmal carcinoma. Clinicopathologic study of 10 cases. J Cutan Pathol 1992, **19**: 100–109.

452 Wong TY, Suster S. Tricholemmal carcinoma. A clinicopathologic study of 13 cases. Am J Dermatopathol 1994, **16**: 463–473.

Trichofolliculoma

453 Collina G, Eusebi V, Capella C, Rosai J. Merkel cell differentiation in trichoblastoma. Virchows Arch 1998, **433**: 291–296.

454 Fujita WG, Barr RJ, Headley JL. Multiple fibrofolliculomas with trichodiscomas and acrochordons. Arch Dermatol 1981, **117**: 32–35.

455 Gray HR, Helwig EB. Trichofolliculoma. Arch Dermatol 1962, **86**: 619–625.

456 Hartschuh W, Schulz T. Immunohistochemical investigation of the different developmental stages of trichofolliculoma with special reference to the Merkel cell. Am J Dermatopathol 1999, **21**: 8–15.

Keratoacanthoma

457 Allen CA, Stephens M, Steel WM. Subungual keratoacanthoma. Histopathology 1994, **25**: 181–183.

458 Beham A, Regauer S, Soyer HP, Beham-Schmid C. Keratoacanthoma: a clinically distinct variant of well differentiated squamous cell carcinoma. Adv Anat Pathol 1999, **5**: 269–280.

459 Biesterfeld S, Josef J. Differential diagnosis of keratoacanthoma and squamous cell carcinoma of the epidermis by MIB-1 immunohistometry. Anticancer Res 2002, **22**: 3019–3023.

460 Blessing K, al Nafussi A, Gordon PM. The regressing keratoacanthoma. Histopathology 1994, **24**: 381–384.

461 Cain CT, Niemann TH, Argenyi ZB. Keratoacanthoma versus squamous cell carcinoma. An immunohistochemical reappraisal of p53 protein and proliferating cell nuclear antigen expression in keratoacanthoma-like tumors. Am J Dermatopathol 1995, **17**: 324–331.

462 Calonje E, Wilson Jones E. Intravascular spread of keratoacanthoma. An alarming but benign phenomenon. Am J Dermatopathol 1992, **14**: 414–417.

463 Clausen OP, Beigi M, Bolund L, Kolvraa S, Gjersvik PJ, Mork G, de Angelis PM. Keratoacanthomas frequently show chromosomal aberration as assessed by comparative genomic hybridization. J Invest Dermatol 2002, **119**: 1367–1372.

464 Cramer SF. Subungual keratoacanthoma. A benign bone-eroding neoplasm of the distal phalanx. Am J Clin Pathol 1981, **75**: 425–429.

465 Fisher ER, McCoy MM, Wechsler HL. Analysis of histopathologic and electron microscopic determinants of keratoacanthoma and squamous cell carcinoma. Cancer 1972, **29**: 1387–1397.

466 Ho T, Horn T, Finzi E. Transforming growth factor alpha expression helps to distinguish keratoacanthomas from squamous cell carcinomas. Arch Dermatol 1991, **127**: 1167–1171.

467 Hodak E, Jones RE, Ackerman AB. Solitary keratoacanthoma is a squamous-cell carcinoma. Three examples with metastases. Am J Dermatopathol 1993, **15**: 332–342.

468 Janecka IP, Wolff M, Crikelair F, Cosman B. Aggressive histological features of keratoacanthoma. J Cutan Pathol 1978, **4**: 342–348.

469 Kingman J, Callen JP. Keratoacanthoma. A clinical study. Arch Dermatol 1984, **120**: 736–740.

470 Klein-Szanto AJP, Barr RJ, Reiners JJ Jr, Mamrack MD. Filaggrin distribution in keratoacanthomas and squamous cell carcinoma. Arch Pathol Lab Med 1984, **108**: 888–890.

471 Lapius NA, Helwig EB. Perineurial invasion by keratoacanthoma. Arch Dermatol 1980, **116**: 791–793.

472 Lawrence N, Reed RJ. Actinic keratoacanthoma. Speculations on the nature of the lesion and the role of cellular immunity in its evaluation. Am J Dermatopathol 1990, **12**: 517–533.

473 LeBoit PE. Can we understand keratoacanthoma? Am J Dermatopathol 2002, **24**: 166–168.

474 Lee YS, Teh M. p53 expression in pseudoepitheliomatous hyperplasia, keratoacanthoma, and squamous cell carcinoma of skin. Cancer 1994, **73**: 2317–2323.

475 Lowe D, Fletcher CDM, Shaw MP, McKee PH. Eosinophil infiltration in keratoacanthoma and squamous cell carcinoma of the skin. Histopathology 1984, **8**: 619–625.

476 Melendez ND, Smoller BR, Morgan M. VCAM (CD-106) and ICAM (CD-54) adhesion molecules distinguish keratoacanthomas from cutaneous squamous cell carcinomas. Mod Pathol 2003, **16**: 8–13.

477 Pattee SF, Silvis NG. Keratoacanthoma developing in sites of previous trauma: a report of two cases and review of the literature. J Am Acad Dermatol 2003, **48**: S35–S38.

478 Phillips P, Helm KF. Proliferating cell nuclear antigen distribution in keratoacanthoma and squamous cell carcinoma. J Cutan Pathol 1993, **20**: 424–428.

479 Pilch H, Weiss J, Heubner C, Heine M. Differential diagnosis of keratoacanthomas and squamous cell carcinomas. J Cutan Pathol 1994, **21**: 507–513.

480 Piscioli F, Boi S, Zumiani G, Cristofolini M. A gigantic, metastasizing keratoacanthoma. Report of a case and discussion on classification. Am J Dermatopathol 1984, **6**: 123–129.

481 Randall MB, Geisnger KR, Kute TE, Buss DH, Prichard RW. DNA content and proliferative index in cutaneous squamous cell carcinoma and keratoacanthoma. Am J Clin Pathol 1990, **93**: 259–262.

482 Reed RJ. Actinic keratoacanthoma. Arch Dermatol 1972, **106**: 858–864.

483 Rook A, Champion RH. Keratoacanthoma. Natl Cancer Inst Monogr 1963, **10**: 257–274.

484 Sanchez Yus E, Simon P, Requena L, Ambrojo P, de Eusebio E. Solitary keratoacanthoma: a self-healing proliferation that frequently becomes malignant. Am J Dermatopathol 2000, **22**: 305–310.

485 Sleater JP, Beers BB, Stephens CA, Hendricks JB. Keratoacanthoma. A deficient squamous cell carcinoma? Study of *bcl*-2 expression. J Cutan Pathol 1994, **21**: 514–519.

Keratinous cyst

486 Cotton DWK, Kirkham N, Young BJJ. Immunoperoxidase anti-keratin staining of epidermal and pilar cysts. Br J Dermatol 1984, **111**: 63–68.

487 Kligman AM. The myth of the sebaceous cyst. Arch Dermatol 1964, **89**: 253–256.

487a Lee S, Lee W, Chung S, Kim D, Sohn M, Kim M, Kim J, Bae H, Kam S. Detection of human papillomavirus 60 in epidermal cysts of nonpalmoplantar location. Am J Dermatopathol 2003, **25**: 243–247.

488 Leppard BJ, Sanderson KV. The natural history of trichilemmal cysts. Br J Dermatol 1976, **94**: 379–390.

489 Lucas GL. Epidermoid inclusion cysts of the hand. J South Orthop Assoc 1999, **8**: 188–192.

490 McGavran MH, Binnington B. Keratinous cysts of the skin. Arch Dermatol 1966, **94**: 499–508.

491 Pinkus H. "Sebaceous cysts" are trichilemmal cysts. Arch Dermatol 1969, **99**: 544–553.

492 Rahbari H. Epidermoid cysts with seborrheic verruca-like cyst walls. Arch Dermatol 1982, **118**: 326–328.

Other cutaneous cysts

493 Ahn SK, Chung J, Lee WS, Lee SH, Choi EH. Hybrid cysts showing alternate combination of eruptive vellus hair cyst, steatocystoma multiplex, and epidermoid cyst, and an association among the three conditions. Am J Dermatopathol 1997, **18**: 645–649.

494 al-Nafussi AI, Carder P. Cutaneous ciliated cyst. A case report and immunohistochemical comparison with fallopian tube. Histopathology 1990, **16**: 595–598.

495 Andersen WK, Rao BK, Bhawan J. The hybrid epidermoid and apocrine cyst: a combination of apocrine hidrocystoma and epidermal inclusion cyst. Am J Dermatopathol 1997, **18**: 364–366.

496 Brownstein MH. Steatocystoma simplex. A solitary steatocystoma. Arch Dermatol 1982, **118**: 409–411.

497 Cho S, Chang SE, Choi JH, Sung KJ, Moon KC, Koh JK. Clinical and histologic features of 64 cases of steatocystoma multiplex. J Dermatol 2002, **29**: 152–156.

498 De Viragh PA, Szeimies RM, Eckert F. Apocrine cystadenoma, apocrine hidrocystoma, and eccrine hidrocystoma: three distinct tumors defined by expression of keratins and human milk fat globulin 1. J Cutan Pathol 1997, **24**: 249–255.

499 Esterly NB, Fretzin DF, Pinkus H. Eruptive vellus hair cysts. Arch Dermatol 1979, **113**: 500–503.

500 Farmer ER, Helwig EB. Cutaneous ciliated cysts. Arch Dermatol 1978, **114**: 70–73.

501 Fontaine DG, Lau H, Murray SK, Fraser RB, Wright JR Jr. Cutaneous ciliated cyst of the abdominal wall: a case report with a review of the literature and discussion of pathogenesis. Am J Dermatopathol 2002, **24**: 63–66.

502 Fraga S, Helwig EB, Rosen SM. Bronchogenic cysts in the skin and subcutaneous tissue. Am J Clin Pathol 1971, **56**: 230–238.

503 Kligman AM, Kirschbaum JD. Steatocystoma multiplex. A dermoid tumor. J Invest Dermatol 1964, **42**: 383–387.

504 Kurban RS, Bhawan J. Cutaneous cysts lined by nonsquamous epithelium. Am J Dermatopathol 1991, **13**: 509–517.

505 Mehregan AH. Apocrine cystadenoma. A clinicopathologic study with special reference to the pigmented variety. Arch Dermatol 1964, **90**: 274–279.

506 Mehregan AH, Medenica M. Pigmented follicular cysts. J Cutan Pathol 1982, **9**: 423–427.

507 Requena L, Martin L, Renedo G, Arias D, Espinel ML, de Castro A. A facial variant of steatocystoma multiplex. Cutis 1993, **51**: 449–452.

508 Shareef DS, Salm R. Ectopic vestigial lesions of the neck and shoulders. J Clin Pathol 1981, **34**: 1155–1162.

509 Trotter SE, Rassi DM, Saad M, Sharif H, Ali M. Cutaneous ciliated cyst occurring in a male. Histopathology 1994, **25**: 492–493.

510 Yamaki T, Higuchi R, Sasaki K, Nozaki M. Multiple dermoid cysts on the forehead. Case report. Scand J Plast Reconstr Surg Hand Surg 1996, **30**: 321–324.

Warty dyskeratoma

511 Kaddu S, Dong H, Mayer G, Kerl H, Cerroni L. Warty dyskeratoma—"follicular dyskeratoma": analysis of clinicopathologic features of a distinctive follicular adnexal neoplasm. J Am Acad Dermatol 2002, **47**: 423–428.

Pilar tumor (proliferating trichilemmal cyst)

512 Amaral ALMP, Nascimento AG, Goellner JR. Proliferating pilar (trichilemmal) cyst. Report of two cases, one with carcinomatous transformation and one with distant metastases. Arch Pathol Lab Med 1984, **108**: 808–810.

513 Brownstein MH, Arluk DJ. Proliferating trichilemmal cyst. A simulant of squamous cell carcinoma. Cancer 1981, **48**: 1207–1214.

514 Haas N, Audring H, Sterry W. Carcinoma arising in proliferating trichilemmal cyst expresses fetal and trichilemmal hair phenotype. Am J Dermatopathol 2002, **24**: 340–344.

515 Hendricks DL, Liang MD, Borochovitz D, Miller T. A case of multiple pilar tumors and pilar cysts involving the scalp and back. Plast Reconstr Surg 1991, **87**: 763–767.

516 Hohnes EJ. Tumors of the lower hair sheath. Cancer 1968, **21**: 234–248.

517 Jones EW. Proliferating epidermoid cysts. Arch Dermatol 1966, **94**: 11–19.

518 Lopez-Rios F, Rodriquez-Peralto JL, Aguilar A, Hernandez L, Gallego M. Proliferating trichilemmal cyst with focal invasion: report of a case and a review of the literature. Am J Dermatopathol 2000, **22**: 183–187.

519 Mann B, Salm R, Azzopardi JG. Pilar tumour. A distinctive type of trichilemmoma. Diagn Histopathol 1982, **5**: 157–167.

520 Mori O, Hachisuka H, Sasai Y. Proliferating trichilemmal cyst with spindle cell carcinoma. Am J Dermatopathol 1990, **12**: 479–484.

521 Poiares Baptista A, Garcia E Silva L, Born MC. Proliferating trichilemmal cyst. J Cutan Pathol 1983, **10**: 178–187.

522 Reed RJ, Lamar LM. Invasive hair matrix tumors of the scalp. Invasive pilomatrixoma. Arch Dermatol 1966, **94**: 310–316.

523 Rutty GN, Richman PI, Laing JH. Malignant change in trichilemmal cysts. A study of cell proliferation and DNA content. Histopathology 1992, **21**: 465–468.

524 Sleater J, Beers B, Stefan M, Kilpatrick T, Hendricks J. Proliferating trichilemmal cyst. Report of four cases, two with nondiploid DNA content and increased proliferation index. Am J Dermatopathol 1993, **15**: 423–428.

525 Takata M, Rehman I, Rees JL. A trichilemmal carcinoma arising from a proliferating trichilemmal cyst: the loss of the wild-type p53 is a critical event in malignant transformation. Hum Pathol 1998, **29**: 193–195.

Pilomatrixoma

526 De Galvez-Aranda MV, Herrera-Ceballos E, Sanchez-Sanchez P, Bosch-Garcia RJ, Matilla-Vicente A. Pilomatrix carcinoma with lymph node pulmonary metastasis: report of a case arising on the knee. Am J Dermatopathol 2002, **24**: 139–143.

527 Forbis RJ, Helwig EB. Pilomatrixoma. Arch Dermatol 1961, **83**: 606–618.

528 Gould E, Kurzon R, Kowalczyk AP, Saldana M. Pilomatrix carcinoma with pulmonary metastasis. Report of a case. Cancer 1984, **54**: 370–372.

529 Hanly MG, Allsbrook WC, Pantazis CG, Lane R, Porubsky ES, Mann ES. Pilo-matrical carcinosarcoma of the cheek with subsequent pulmonary metastases. A case report. Am J Dermatopathol 1994, **16**: 196–200.

530 Hardisson D, Linares MD, Cuevas-Santos J, Contreras F. Pilomatrix carcinoma: a clinicopathologic study of six cases and review of the literature. Am J Dermatopathol 2002, **23**: 394–401.

531 Hashimoto K, Nelson RG, Lever WF. Calcifying epithelioma of Malherbe. Histochemical and electron microscopic studies. J Invest Dermatol 1966, **46**: 391–408.

532 Kaddu S, Beham-Schmid C, Soyer HP, Hodl S, Beham A, Kerl H. Extra-medullary hematopoiesis in pilomatricomas. Am J Dermatopathol 1995, **17**: 126–130.

533 Kaddu S, Soyer HP, Hodl S, Kerl H. Morphological stages of pilomatricoma. Am J Dermatopathol 1997, **18:** 333–338.

534 Kaddu S, Soyer KS, Wolf IH, Kerl H. Proliferating pilomatricoma. A histopathologic simulator of matrical carcinoma. J Cutan Pathol 1997, **24:** 228–234.

535 LeBoit PE, Parslow TG, Choy S-H. Hair matrix differentiation. Occurrence in lesions other than pilomatricoma. Am J Dermatopathol 1987, **9:** 399–405.

536 McGavran MH. Ultrastructure of pilomatrixoma (calcifying epithelioma). Cancer 1965, **18:** 1445–1456.

537 Marrogi AJ, Wick MR, Dehner LP. Pilomatrical neoplasms in children and young adults. Am J Dermatopathol 1992, **14:** 87–94.

538 O'Donovan DG, Freemont A, Adams JE, Markham DE. Malignant pilomatrixoma with bone metastasis. Histopathology 1993, **23:** 385–386.

539 Sau P, Lupton GP, Graham JH. Pilomatrix carcinoma. Cancer 1993, **71:** 2491–2498.

540 Solanki P, Ramzy I, Durr N, Henkes D. Pilomatrixoma. Cytologic features with differential diagnostic considerations. Arch Pathol Lab Med 1987, **111:** 294–297.

541 Tateyama H, Eimoto T, Tada T, Niwa T. Malignant pilomatricoma. An immuno-histochemical study with antihair keratin antibody. Cancer 1992, **69:** 1271–32.

542 Wang J, Cobb CJ, Martin SE, Venegas R, Wu N, Greaves TS. Pilomatrixoma: clinicopathologic study of 51 cases with emphasis on cytologic features. Diagn Cytopathol 2002, **27:** 167–172.

543 Wickremaratchi T, Collins CM. Pilomatrixoma or calcifying epithelioma of Malherbe invading bone. Histopathology 1992, **21:** 79–81.

544 Wood MG, Parhizgar B, Beerman H. Malignant pilomatricoma. Arch Dermatol 1984, **120:** 770–773.

Melanocytes

545 Bacchi CE, Bonetti F, Pea M, Martignoni G, Gown AM. HMB-45: a review. Appl Immunohistochem 1996, **4:** 73–85.

546 Boyle JL, Haupt HM, Stern JB, Multhaupt HAB. Tyrosinase expression in malignant melanoma, desmoplastic melanoma, and peripheral nerve tumors: an immunohistochemical study. Arch Pathol Lab Med 2002, **126:** 816–822.

547 Clark WH Jr, Watson MC, Watson BEM. Two kinds of "clear" cells in the human epidermis. With a report of a modified DOPA reaction for electron microscopy. Am J Pathol 1961, **39:** 333–344.

548 Fitzpatrick TB, Lerner AB. Terminology of pigment cells. Science 1953, **117:** 640.

549 Jungbluth AA, Busam KJ, Gerald WL, Stockert E, Coplan KA, Iversen K, MacGregor DP, Old LJ, Chen YT. A103: an anti-Melan-A monoclonal antibody for the detection of malignant melanoma in paraffin-embedded tissues. Am J Surg Pathol 1998, **22:** 595–602.

550 King R, Weilbaecher KN, McGill G, Cooley E, Mihm M, Fisher DE. Microphthalmia transcription factor. A sensitive and specific melanoctye marker for melanoma diagnosis. Am J Pathol 1999, **155:** 731–738.

551 Le Douarin N. Cell migration in early vertebrate development studied in inter-specific chimaeras. In Embryogenesis in mammals. Ciba Foundation Symposium. Amsterdam, 1976, Elsevier Excerpta Medica – North Holland, pp. 71–101.

552 Magana-Garcia M, Ackerman AB. What are nevus cells? Am J Dermatopathol 1990, **12:** 93–102.

553 Mangini J, Li N, Bhawan J. Immunohistochemical markers of melanocytic lesions: a review of their diagnostic usefulness. Am J Dermatopathol 2002, **24:** 270–281.

554 Masson P. Pigment cells in man. In Miner RW (ed.): The biology of melanomas (special publication). New York, 1948, The New York Academy of Sciences, vol. 4, pp. 15–51.

555 Miettinen M, Lehto V-P, Virtanen I. Presence of fibroblast type intermediate filaments (vimentin) and absence of neurofilaments in pigmented nevi and malignant melanomas. J Cutan Pathol 1983, **10:** 188–192.

556 Plettenberg A, Ballaun C, Pammer J, Mildner M, Strunk D, Weninger W. Human melanocytes and melanoma cells constitutively express the *Bcl*-2 proto-oncogene in situ and in cell culture. Am J Pathol 1995, **146:** 651–659.

557 Ramsay JA, From L, Kahn HJ. *bcl*-2 protein expression in melanocytic neoplasms of the skin. Mod Pathol 1995, **8:** 150–154.

558 Smoller BR, McNutt NS, Hsu A. HMB-45 recognizes stimulated melanocytes. J Cutan Pathol 1989, **16:** 49–53.

559 van den Oord JJ, Vandeghinste N, De Ley M, De Wolf-Peeters C. *Bcl*-2 expression in human melanocytes and melanocytic tumors. Am J Pathol 1994, **145:** 294–300.

Nevi

560 Argenyi ZB, Rodgers J, Wick M. Expression of nerve growth factor and epidermal growth factor receptors in neural nevi with nevic corpuscles. Am J Dermatopathol 1997, **18:** 460–464.

561 Cochran A, Bailly C, Paul E, Dolbeau D. Nevi, other than dysplastic and spitz nevi. Semin Diagn Pathol 1993, **10:** 18–35.

562 Hui P, Perkins AS, Glusac E. Assessment of clonality in melanocytic nevi. J Cutan Pathol 2001, **28:** 140–144.

563 Johnson WT, Helwig EB. Benign nevus cells in the capsule of lymph nodes. Cancer 1969, **23:** 747–753.

564 Kroumpouzos G, Cohen LM. Intradermal melanocytic nevus with prominent schwannian differentiation. Am J Dermatopathol 2002, **24:** 39–42.

565 Laidlaw GF, Murray MF. Melanoma studies. Theory of pigmented moles. Their relation to evolution of hair follicles. Am J Pathol 1933, **9:** 827–838, Addendum: Theory of pigmented moles. Am J Pathol 1934, **10:** 319–320.

565a Lu D, Hoch B, Dehner LP, Lind AC. Proliferative activity in melanocytic nevi from patients grouped by age. Mod Pathol 2003, **16:** 94a.

566 Mackie RM, English J, Aitchison TC, Fitzsimons CP, Wilson P. The number and distribution of benign pigmented moles (melanocytic naevi) in a healthy British population. Br J Dermatol 1985, **113:** 167–174.

567 Maitra A, Gazdar AF, Moore TO, Moore AY. Loss of heterozygosity analysis of cutaneous melanoma and benign melanocytic nevi: laser capture microdissection demonstrates clonal genetic changes in acquired nevocellular nevi. Hum Pathol 2002, **33:** 191–197.

568 Masson P. Les naevi pigmentaires, tumeurs nerveuses. Ann Anat Pathol (Paris) 1926, **3:** 417–453, 657–696.

569 Masson P. My conception of cellular nevi. Cancer 1951, **4:** 9–38.

570 Misago N. The relationship between melanocytes and peripheral nerve sheath cells (part 1): melanocytic nevus (excluding so-called "blue nevus") with peripheral nerve sheath differentiation. Am J Dermatopathol 2000, **22:** 217–229.

571 Ridolfi RL, Rosen PP, Thaler H. Nevus cell aggregates associated with lymph nodes. Estimated frequency and clinical significance. Cancer 1977, **39:** 164–171.

Junctional, intradermal, and compound nevi

572 Bednár B. Storiform neurofibroma in the core of naevocellular naevi. J Pathol 1970, **101:** 199–201.

573 Benz G, Holzel D, Schmoeckel C. Inflammatory cellular infiltrates in melanocytic nevi. Am J Dermatopathol 1991, **13:** 538–542.

574 Clark WH, Hood AF, Tucker MA, Jampel RM. Atypical

melanocytic nevi of the genital type with a discussion of reciprocal parenchymal-stromal interactions in the biology of neoplasia. Hum Pathol 1998, **29:** S1–S24.

575 Cohen LM, Bennion SC, Johnson TW, Golitz LE. Hypermelanotic nevus: clinical, histopathologic, and ultrastructural features in 316 cases. Am J Dermatopathol 1997, **19:** 23–30.

576 Cohen PR, Rapini RP. Nevus with cyst. A report of 93 cases. Am J Dermatopathol 1993, **15:** 229–234.

577 Conlin PA, Rapini RP. Epidermolytic hyperkeratosis associated with melanocytic nevi: a report of 53 cases. Am J Dermatopathol 2002, **24:** 23–25.

578 Fallowfield ME, Collina G, Cook MG. Melanocytic lesions of the palm and sole. Histopathology 1994, **24:** 463–467.

579 Gray MH, Smiller BR, McNutt NS, Hsu A. Neurofibromas and neurotized melanocytic nevi are immunohistochemically distinct neoplasms. Am J Dermatopathol 1990, **12:** 234–241.

580 Harris GR, Shea CR, Horenstein MG, Reed JA, Burchette JL, Prieto VG. Desmoplastic (sclerotic) nevus: an underrecognized entity that resembles dermatofibroma and desmoplastic melanoma. Am J Surg Pathol 1999, **23:** 786–794.

581 Jih DM, Morgan MB, Bass J, Tuthill R, Somach S. Oncocytic metaplasia occurring in a spectrum of melanocytic nevi. Am J Dermatopathol 2002, **24:** 468–472.

582 Masson P. My conception of cellular nevi. Cancer 1951, **4:** 9–38.

583 Mehregan DR, Mehregan DA, Mehregan AH. Nodular myxoid change in melanocytic nevi: a report of two cases. Am J Dermatopathol 1997, **18:** 400–402.

584 Mooi WJ, Krausz T. Biopsy pathology of melanocytic disorders. Biopsy Pathology Series 17. London, 1992, Chapman & Hall.

585 Paesschen MAV, Goovaerts G, Buyssens N. A study of the so-called neurotization of nevi. Am J Dermatopathol 1990, **12:** 242–248.

586 Schaumburg-Lever G, Lever I, Fehrenbacher B, Moller H, Bischof B, Kaiserling E, Garbe C, Rassner G. Melanocytes in nevi and melanomas synthesize basement membrane and basement membrane-like material: an immunohistochemical and electron microscopic study including immunoelectron microscopy. J Cutan Pathol 2000, **27:** 67–75.

587 Signoretti S, Annessi G, Puddu P, Faraggiana T. Melanocytic nevi of palms and soles: a histological study according to the plane of sections. Am J Surg Pathol 1999, **23:** 283–287.

588 Stegmaier OC, Montgomery H. Histopathologic studies of pigmented nevi in children. J Invest Dermatol 1953, **20:** 51–64.

589 Tajima Y, Nakajima T, Sugano I, Nagao K, Kondo Y. Malignant melanoma within an intradermal nevus. Am J Dermatopathol 1994, **16:** 301–306.

590 Weedon D. Unusual features of nevocellular nevi. J Cutan Pathol 1982, **9:** 284–392.

591 Yaar M, Woodley DT, Gilchrest BA. Human nevocellular nevus cells are surrounded by basement membrane components. Immunohistologic studies of human nevus cells and melanocytes in vivo and in vitro. Lab Invest 1988, **58:** 157–162.

Blue, cellular, and epithelioid blue nevi

592 Bondi EE, Elder D, Guerry DP IV, Clark WH. Target blue nevus. Arch Dermatol 1983, **119:** 919–920.

593 Busam KJ. Metastatic melanoma to the skin simulating blue nevus. Am J Surg Pathol 1999, **23:** 276–282.

594 Carney JA, Ferreiro JA. The epithelioid blue nevus: a multicentric familial tumor with important associations, including cardiac myxoma and psammomatous melanotic schwannoma. Am J Surg Pathol 1997, **20:** 259–272.

595 Connelly J, Smith JL. Malignant blue nevus. Cancer 1991, **67:** 2653–2657.

596 Dei Tos AP, Khurana JS, Kurtin PJ, Nacimento AG. Absence of S-100 protein immunoreactivity in cellular blue nevus: a potential diagnostic pitfall. Appl Immunohistochem 1999, **7:** 255–259.

597 Epstein JL, Erlandson RA, Rosen PP. Nodal blue nevi. A study of three cases. Am J Surg Pathol 1984, **8:** 907–915.

598 Goldman RL, Friedman NB. Blue nevus of the uterine cervix. Cancer 1967, **20:** 210–214.

599 Gonzalez-Campora R, Galera-Davidson H, Vazquez-Ramirez FJ, Diaz-Cano S. Blue nevus. Classical types and new related entities. A differential diagnostic review. Pathol Res Pract 1994, **190:** 627–635.

600 Granter SR, McKee PH, Calonje E, Mihm MC, Busam K. Melanoma associated with blue nevus and melanoma mimicking cellular blue nevus: a clinicopathologic study of 10 cases on the spectrum of so called "malignant blue nevus". Am J Surg Pathol 2001, **25:** 316–323.

601 Groben PA, Harvell JD, White WL. Epithelioid blue nevus: neoplasm sui generis or variation on a theme? Am J Dermatopathol 2001, **22:** 473–488.

602 Harper JC, Waldron CA. Blue nevus of palate. Oral Surg 1965, **20:** 145–149.

603 Hirayama T, Suzuki T. A new classification of Ota's nevus based on histopathological features. Dermatologica 1991, **183:** 169–172.

604 Jao W, Fretzin DF, Christ ML, Prinz LM. Blue nevus of the prostate gland. Arch Pathol 1971, **91:** 187–192.

605 Kao GF, Graham JH, Helwig EB. Cutaneous malignant blue melanoma (abstract). Lab Invest 1981, **44:** 33.

606 Leopold JG, Richards DB. The interrelationship of blue and common naevi. J Pathol Bacteriol 1968, **95:** 37–46.

607 Masson P. Neuro-nevi "bleu." Arch De Vecchi Anat Patol 1950, **14:** 1–28.

608 Michal M, Kerekes Z, Kinkor Z, Ondrias F, Pizinger K. Desmoplastic cellular blue nevi. Am J Dermatopathol 1995, **17:** 230–235.

609 Mooi WJ, Krausz T. Biopsy pathology of melanocytic disorders. Biopsy Pathology Series 17. London, 1992, Chapman & Hall.

610 Moreno C, Requena L, Kutzner H, de la Cruz A, Jaqueti G, Yus ES. Epithelioid blue nevus: a rare variant of blue nevus not always associated with the Carney complex. J Cutan Pathol 2000, **27:** 218–223.

611 Nakano S, Groth W, Gartmann H, Steigleder GK. Malignant blue nevus with metastases to lung. Am J Dermatopathol 1988, **10:** 436–441.

612 O'Grady TC, Barr RJ, Billman G, Cunningham BB. Epithelioid blue nevus occurring in children with no evidence of Carney complex. Am J Dermatopathol 1999, **21:** 483–486.

613 Perez MT, Suster S. Balloon cell change in cellular blue nevus. Am J Dermatopathol 1999, **21:** 181–184.

614 Pich A, Chiusa L, Margaria E, Aloi F. Proliferative activity in the malignant cellular blue nevus. Hum Pathol 1993, **24:** 1323–1329.

615 Pulitzer DR, Martin PC, Cohen AP, Reed RJ. Histologic classification of the combined nevus. Analysis of the variable expression of melanocytic nevi. Am J Surg Pathol 1991, **15:** 1111–1122.

616 Rodriguez H, Ackerman LV. Cellular blue nevus. Cancer 1968, **21:** 393–405.

617 Smith KJ, Germain M, Williams J, Skelton H. CD34-positive cellular blue nevi. J Cutan Pathol 2001, **28:** 145–150.

618 Sun J, Morton TH, Gown AM. Antibody HMB-45 identifies the cells of blue nevi. An immunohistochemical study on paraffin sections. Am J Surg Pathol 1990, **14:** 748–751.

619 Temple-Camp CRE, Saxe N, King H. Benign and malignant cellular blue nevus. A clinicopathologic study of 30 cases. Am J Dermatopathol 1988, **10:** 289–296.

620 Tran TA, Carlson JA, Basaca PC, Mihm MC. Cellular blue nevus

with atypia (atypical cellular blue nevus): a clinicopathologic study of nine cases. J Cutan Pathol 1998, **25**: 252–258.

621 Tsoitis G, Kanitakis C, Kapetis E. Naevus bleu multinodulaire en plaque, superficiel et neuroide. Ann Dermatol Venereol 1983, **110**: 231–235.

622 Wieselthier JS, White WL. Cutaneous metastasis of ocular malignant melanoma: an unusual presentation simulating blue nevi. Am J Dermatopathol 1996, **18**: 289–295.

623 Wood WS, Tron VA. Analysis of HMB-45 immunoreactivity in common and cellular blue nevi. J Cutan Pathol 1991, **18**: 261–263.

624 Zembowicz A, Granter SR, McKee PH, Mihm MC. Amelanotic cellular blue nevus: a hypopigmented variant of the cellular blue nevus: clinicopathologic analysis of 20 cases. Am J Surg Pathol 2002, **26**: 1493–1500.

Spitz nevus and related nevi

625 Barnhill RL, Argenyi ZB, From L, Glass LF, Maize JC, Mihm MC Jr, Rabkin MS, Ronan SG, White WL, Piepkorn M. Atypical Spitz nevi/tumors: lack of consensus for diagnosis, discrimination from melanoma, and prediction of outcome. Hum Pathol 1999, **30**: 513–520.

626 Barnhill RL, Barnhill MA, Berwick M, Mihm MC. The histologic spectrum of pigmented spindle cell nevus. A review of 120 cases with emphasis on atypical variants. Hum Pathol 1991, **22**: 52–58.

627 Barr RJ, Morales RV, Graham JH. Desmoplastic nevus. A distinct histologic variant of mixed spindle cell and epithelioid cell nevus. Cancer 1980, **46**: 557–564.

628 Binder S, Asnong C, Paul E, Cochran A. The histology and differential diagnosis of Spitz nevus. Semin Diagn Pathol 1993, **10**: 36–46.

629 Burg G, Kempf W, Hochil M, Huwyler T, Panizzon RG. "Tubular" epithelioid cell nevus: a new variant of Spitz's nevus. J Cutan Pathol 1999, **25**: 475–478.

630 Busam KJ, Barnhill RL. Pagetoid spitz nevus. Intraepidermal Spitz tumor with prominent pagetoid spread. Am J Surg Pathol 1995, **19**: 1061–1067.

630a Clarke B, Essa A, Chetty R. Plexiform spitz nevus. Int J Surg Pathol 2002, **10**: 69–73.

631 Diaz-Cascajo C, Borghi S, Weyers W. Angiomatoid Spitz nevus: a distinct variant of desmoplastic Spitz nevus with prominent vasculature. Am J Dermatopathol 2000, **22**: 135–139.

632 Echevarria R, Ackerman LV. Spindle and epithelioid cell nevi in the adult. A clinicopathologic report of 26 cases. Cancer 1967, **20**: 175–189.

633 Goldes J, Holmes S, Satz M, Cich J, Dehner L. Melanoma masquerading as Spitz nevus following acute lymphoblastic leukaemia. Pediatr Dermatol 1984, **1**: 295–298.

634 Hamm H, Happle R, Bröcker E. Multiple agminate Spitz naevi. Review of the literature and report of a case with distinctive immunohistological features. Br J Dermatol 1987, **117**: 511–522.

635 Harvell JD, Bastian BC, LeBoit PE. Persistent (recurrent) Spitz nevi: a histopathologic, immunohistochemical and molecular pathologic study of 22 cases. Am J Surg Pathol 2002, **26**: 654–661.

636 Harvell JD, Meehan SA, LeBoit PE. Spitz's nevi with halo reaction: a histopathologic study of 17 cases. J Cutan Pathol 1998, **24**: 611–619.

637 Howat AJ, Variend S. Lymphatic invasion in Spitz nevi. Am J Surg Pathol 1985, **9**: 125–128.

638 Kanter-Lewenshohn L, Hedblad MA, Wejde J, Larsson O. Immunohistochemical markers for distinguishing Spitz nevi from malignant melanomas. Mod Pathol 1997, **10**: 917–920.

639 Kernen JA, Ackerman LV. Spindle cell nevi and epithelioid cell nevi (so-called juvenile melanomas) in children and

adults. A clinicopathologic study of 27 cases. Cancer 1960, **13**: 612–625.

640 Lohmann CM, Coit DG, Brady MS, Berwick M, Busam KJ. Sentinel lymph node biopsy in patients with diagnostically controversial spitzoid melanocytic tumors. Am J Surg Pathol 2001, **26**: 47–55.

641 Mooi WJ. Spitz nevus and its histologic simulators. Adv Anat Pathol 2002, **9**: 209–221.

642 Paniago-Pereira C, Maize JC, Ackerman AB. Nevus of large spindle and/or epithelioid cells (Spitz's nevus). Arch Dermatol 1978, **114**: 1811–1823.

643 Peters MS, Goellner JR. Spitz naevi and malignant melanomas of childhood and adolescence. Histopathology 1986, **10**: 1289–1302.

643a Ribé A, McNutt S. S100A6 protein expression is different in spitz nevi and melanomas. Mod Pathol 2003, **16**: 505–511.

644 Sagebiel RW, Chinn EK, Egbert BM. Pigmented spindle cell nevus. Clinical and histologic review of 90 cases. Am J Surg Pathol 1984, **8**: 645–653.

645 Scott G, Chen KTK, Rosai J. Pseudoepitheliomatus hyperplasia in Spitz's nevi. A possible source of confusion with squamous cell carcinoma. Arch Pathol Lab Med 1989, **113**: 61–63.

646 Skelton HG, Miller ML, Lupton GP, Smith KJ. Eosinophilic globules in spindle cell and epithelioid cell nevi: composition and possible origin. Am J Dermatopathol 1999, **20**: 547–550.

647 Smith KJ, Skleton HG, Lupton GP, Graham JH. Spindle cell and epithelioid cell nevi with atypia and metastasis (malignant Spitz nevus). Am J Surg Pathol 1989, **13**: 931–939.

648 Smith NP. The pigmented spindle cell tumor of Reed. An underdiagnosed lesion. Semin Diagn Pathol 1987, **4**: 75–87.

649 Spatz A, Peterse S, Fletcher CD, Barnhill RL. Plexiform Spitz nevus: an intradermal Spitz nevus with plexiform growth pattern. Am J Dermatopathol 2000, **21**: 542–546.

650 Su LD, Fullen DR, Sondak VK, Johnson TM, Lowe L. Sentinel lymph node biopsy for patients with problematic spitzoid melanocytic lesions. Cancer 2003, **97**: 499–507.

651 Tu P, Miyauchi S, Miki Y. Proliferative activities in Spitz nevus compared with melanocytic nevus and malignant melanoma using expression of PCNA/cyclin and mitotic rate. Am J Dermatopathol 1993, **15**: 311–314.

652 Walsh N, Crotty K, Palmer A, McCarthy S. Spitz nevus versus spitzoid malignant melanoma: an evaluation of the current distinguishing histopathologic criteria. Hum Pathol 1998, **29**: 1105–1112.

653 Weedon D. Borderline melanocytic tumors. J Cutan Pathol 1985, **12**: 266–270.

654 Weedon D, Little JH. Spindle and epithelioid cell nevi in children and adults. A review of 211 cases of the Spitz nevus. Cancer 1977, **40**: 217–225.

Congenital nevus

655 Alper JC. Congenital nevi. The controversy rages on. Arch Dermatol 1985, **121**: 734–735.

656 Angelucci D, Natali PG, Amerio PL, Ramenghi M, Musiani P. Rapid perinatal growth mimicking malignant transformation in a giant congenital melanocytic nevus. Hum Pathol 1991, **22**: 297–300.

657 Botet MV, Caro FR, Sánchez JL. Congenital acral melanocytic nevi clinically simulating acral lentiginous melanoma. J Am Acad Dermatol 1981, **5**: 406–410.

658 Demian SDE, Donnelly WH, Frias JL, Monif GRG. Placental lesions in congenital giant pigmented nevi. Am J Clin Pathol 1974, **61**: 438–442.

659 Hendrickson MR, Ross JC. Neoplasms arising in congenital giant nevi. Morphologic study of seven cases and a review of the literature. Am J Surg Pathol 1981, **5**: 109–135.

660 Jeanfils S, Tennstedt D, Lachapelle JM. Cerebriform intradermal

nevus. A clinical pattern resembling cutis verticis gyrata. Dermatology 1993, **186**: 294–297.

661 Kadonaga JN, Frieden IJ. Neurocutaneous melanosis. Definition and review of the literature. J Am Acad Dermatol 1991, **24**: 747–755.

662 Kaye VM, Dehner LP. Cutaneous glomus tumor. A comparative immunohistochemical study with pseudoangiomatous intradermal melanocytic nevi. Am J Dermatopathol 1991, **13**: 2–6.

663 Kerl H, Smolle J, Hödl S, Soyer HP. Kongenitales Pseudomelanom. Zeitschr Hautkrankh 1989, **64**: 564–568.

664 Mancianti ML, Clark WH, Hayes FA, Herlyn M. Malignant melanoma simulants arising in congenital melanocytic nevi do not show experimental evidence for a malignant phenotype. Am J Pathol 1990, **136**: 817–829.

665 Mark GJ, Mihm MC Jr, Liteplo MG, Reed RJ, Clark WH Jr. Congenital melanocytic nevi of the small and garment type. Clinical, histologic and ultrastructural study. Hum Pathol 1973, **4**: 395–418.

666 Martinez-Barba E, Polo-Garcia LA, Ferri-Naguez B, Ruiz-Macia JA, Kurtzner H, Requena L. Congenital giant melanocytic nevus with pigmented epithelioid cells: a variant of epithelioid blue nevus. Am J Dermatopathol 2002, **24**: 30–35.

667 Pearson JP, Weiss SW, Headington JT. Cutaneous malignant melanotic neurocristic tumors arising in neurocristic hamartomas: a melanocytic tumor morphologically and biologically distinct from common melanoma. Am J Surg Pathol 1996, **20**: 665–677.

668 Reed WB, Becker SW, Becker SW Jr, Nickel WR. Giant pigmented nevi, melanoma, and leptomeningeal melanocytosis. A clinical and histopathological study. Arch Dermatol 1965, **91**: 100–119.

669 Rhodes AR, Silverman RA, Harrist TJ, Melski JW. A histologic comparison of congenital and acquired nevomelanocytic nevi. Arch Dermatol 1985, **121**: 1266–1273.

670 Roth MJ, Medeiros LJ, Kapur S, Wexler LH, Mims S, Horowtiz ME, Tsokos M. Malignant schwannoma with melanocytic and neutroepithelial differentiation in an infant with congenital giant melanocytic nevus. A complex neurocristopathy. Hum Pathol 1993, **24**: 1371–1375.

671 Ruiz-Maldonado R, Tamayo L, Laterza AM, Duran C. Giant pigmented nevi. Clinical, histopathologic, and therapeutic considerations. J Pediatr 1992, **120**: 906–911.

672 Schmitt FC, Bittencourt A, Mendonca N, Dorea M. Rhabdomyosarcoma in a congenital pigmented nevus. Pediatr Pathol 1992, **12**: 93–98.

673 Silvers DN, Helwig EB. Melanocytic nevi in neonates. J Am Acad Dermatol 1981, **4**: 166–175.

674 Slaughter JC, Hordman JM, Kempe LG, Earle KM. Neurocutaneous melanosis and leptomeningeal melanomatosis in children. Arch Pathol 1969, **88**: 298–304.

675 Walsh MY, MacKie RM. Histological features of value in differentiating small congenital melanocytic naevi from acquired naevi. Histopathology 1988, **12**: 145–154.

Other nevi

676 Cooper PH. Deep penetrating (plexiform spindle cell) nevus. A frequent participant in combined nevus. J Cutan Pathol 1992, **19**: 172–180.

677 Gardner WA Jr, Vazquez MD. Balloon cell melanoma. Arch Pathol 1970, **89**: 470–472.

678 Guzzo C, Johnson B, Honig P. Cockarde nevus. A case report and review of the literature. Pediatr Dermatol 1988, **4**: 250–253.

679 Hashimoto K. Ultrastructural studies of halo nevus. Cancer 1974, **34**: 1653–1666.

680 Mooney MA, Barr RJ, Buxton MG. Halo nevus or halo phenomenon? A study of 142 cases. J Cutan Pathol 1995, **22**: 342–348.

681 Schrader WA, Helwig EB. Balloon cell nevi. Cancer 1967, **20**: 1502–1514.

682 Seab JA, Graham JH, Helwig EB. Deep penetrating nevus. Am J Surg Pathol 1989, **13**: 39–44.

683 Wayte DM, Helwig EB. Halo nevi. Cancer 1968, **22**: 69–90.

Treatment

684 Cox AJ, Walton RG. The induction of junctional changes in pigmented nevi. Arch Pathol 1965, **79**: 428–434.

685 Davis NC, Herron J, McLeon GR. The macroscopic appearance of malignant melanoma of the skin. Med J Aust 1966, **2**: 883–886.

686 Estrada JA, Pierard-Franchimont C, Pierard GE. Histogenesis of recurrent nevus. Am J Dermatopathol 1990, **12**: 370–372.

687 Kornberg R, Ackerman AB. Pseudomelanoma. Recurrent melanocytic nevus following partial surgical removal. Arch Dermatol 1975, **111**: 1588–1590.

688 Mundth ED, Gurainick EA, Raker JW. Malignant melanoma. A clinical study of 427 cases. Ann Surg 1965, **162**: 15–28.

689 Park HK, Leonard DD, Arrington JH III, Lund HZ. Recurrent melanocytic nevi. Clinical and histologic review of 175 cases. J Am Acad Dermatol 1987, **17**: 285–292.

690 Sexton M, Sexton CW. Recurrent pigmented melanocytic nevus. A benign lesion, not to be mistaken for malignant melanoma. Arch Pathol Lab Med 1991, **115**: 122–126.

691 Wilson FC Jr, Andersonk PC. A dissenting view on the prophylactic removal of plantar and palmar nevi. Cancer 1961, **14**: 102–104.

Active and dysplastic nevi

692 Ackerman AB, Mihara I. Dysplasia, dysplastic melanocytes, dysplastic nevi, the dysplastic nevus syndrome, and the relation between dysplastic nevi and malignant melanomas. Hum Pathol 1985, **16**: 87–91.

692a Arumi-Uria M, McNutt S, Finnerty B. Grading of atypia in nevi: correlation with melanoma risk. Mod Pathol 2003, **16**: 764–771.

693 Barnhill RL, Roush GC, Duray PH. Correlation of histologic architectural and cytoplasmic features with nuclear atypia in atypical (dysplastic) nevomelanocytic nevi. Hum Pathol 1990, **21**: 51–58.

694 Black WC, Hunt WC. Histologic correlations with the clinical diagnosis of dysplastic nevus. Am J Surg Pathol 1990, **14**: 44–52.

695 Brodell RT, Santa Cruz DJ. Borderline and atypical melanocytic lesions. Semin Diagn Pathol 1985, **2**: 63–86.

696 Cockerell CJ. A rational approach to the understanding and management of the dysplastic nevus syndrome concept. Pathol Annu 1993, **28** (Pt 1): 121–144.

697 Eady RAJ, Gilkes JJH, Jones EW. Eruptive naevi. Report of two cases, with enzyme histochemical, light and electron microscopical findings. Br J Dermatol 1977, **97**: 267–278.

698 Elder D, Clark W, Elenitsas R, Guerry D, Halpern A. The early and intermediate precursor lesions of tumor progression in the melanocytic system. Common acquired nevi and atypical (dysplastic) nevi. Semin Diagn Pathol 1993, **10**: 18–35.

699 Foucar E, Bentley TJ, Laube DW, Rosai J. A histopathologic evaluation of nevocellular nevi in pregnancy. Arch Dermatol 1985, **121**: 350–354.

700 Greene MH, Clark WH Jr, Tucker MA, Elder DE, Kraemer KH, Guerry DP IV, Witmer WK, Thompson J, Matozzo I, Fraser MC. Acquired precursors of cutaneous malignant melanoma. The familial dysplastic nevus syndrome. N Engl J Med 1985, **312**: 91–97.

701 Hastrup N, Clemmensen OJ, Spaun E, Sondergaard K. Dysplastic naevus. Histological criteria and their inter-observer reproducibility. Histopathology 1994, **24**: 503–509.

702 Holman CDJ, Heenan PJ, Caruso V, Glancy RJ, Armstrong BK. Seasonal variation in the junctional component of pigmented naevi. Int J Cancer 1983, **31**: 213–215.

703 Hussein MR, Wood GS. Molecular aspect of melanocytic dysplastic nevi. J Mol Diagn 2002, **4**: 71–80.

704 Kornberg R, Ackerman AB. Pseudomelanoma. Recurrent melanocytic nevus following partial surgical removal. Arch Dermatol 1975, **111**: 1588–1590.

705 Lynch HT, Fusaro RM, Pester J, Lynch JF. Familial atypical multiple mole melanoma (FAMMM) syndrome. Genetic heterogeneity and malignant melanoma. Br J Cancer 1980, **42**: 58–70.

706 McBride A, Rivers JK, Kopf AW, Cockerell CJ, Bart RS, Grin CM, Silverman MK, Vossaert KA. Clinical features of dysplastic nevi. Dermatol Clin 1991, **9**: 717–722.

707 Mihm MC, Rilke F, Cascinelli N, Fitzpatrick TB, Sober AJ. Histopathologic diagnosis of dysplastic nevi. Concordance among pathologists convened by the World Health Organization melanoma programme. Hum Pathol 1991, **22**: 313–319.

708 Okamura JM, Barr RJ, Cantos KA. Benign atypical junctional melanocytic hyperplasia associated with intradermal nevi: a common finding that may be confused with melanoma in situ. Mod Pathol 2000, **13**: 857–860.

709 Peter RU, Worret WI, Nickolay-Kiesthardt J. Prevalance of dysplastic nevi in healthy young men. Int J Dermatol 1992, **31**: 327–330.

710 Rhodes AR, Seki Y, Fitzpatrick TB, Stern RS. Melanosomal alterations in dysplastic melanocytic nevi. A quantitative, ultrastructural investigation. Cancer 1988, **61**: 358–369.

711 Rivers JK, Cockerell CJ, McBride A, Kopf AW. Quantification of histologic features of dysplastic nevi. Am J Dermatopathol 1990, **12**: 42–50.

712 Roth ME, Grant-Kels JM, Ackerman AB, Elder DE, Friedman RF, Heilman ER, Maize JC, Sagebiel RW. The histopathology of dyplastic nevi. Continued controversy. Am J Dermatopathol 1991, **13**: 38–51.

713 Sangueza OP, Hyder DM, Bakke AC, White CR Jr. DNA determination in dysplastic nevi. A comparative study between flow cytometry and image analysis. Am J Dermatopathol 1993, **15**: 99–105.

714 Smith KJ, Skelton HG, Heimer W, Baxter D, Angritt P, Frisman D, Wagner KF. Melanocytic activation in HIV-1 disease. HMB-45 staining in common acquired nevi. Military Medical Consortium for the Advancement of Retroviral Research. J Am Acad Dermatol 1993, **29**: 539–544.

715 Smoller BR, Egbert BM. Dysplastic nevi can be diagnosed and graded reproducibly. A longitudinal study. J Am Acad Dermatol 1992, **27**: 399–402.

716 Tronnier M, Wolff HH. UV-irradiated melanocytic nevi simulating melanoma in situ. Am J Dermatopathol 1995, **17**: 1–6.

717 Tucker MA, Fraser MC, Goldstein AM, Struewing JP, King MA, Crawford JT, Chiazze EA, Zametkin DP, Fontaine LS, Clark WH. A natural history of melanomas and dysplastic nevi: an atlas of lesion in melanoma-prone families. Cancer 2002, **94**: 3192–3209.

718 Tucker SB, Horstmann JP, Hertel B, Aranha G, Rosai J. Activation of nevi in patients with malignant melanoma. Cancer 1980, **46**: 822–827.

719 Urso C. Atypical histologic features in melanocytic nevi. Am J Dermatopathol 2001, **22**: 391–396.

Malignant melanoma

General features

720 Anderson DE, Smith JL JR, McBride CM. Hereditary aspects of malignant melanoma. JAMA 1967, **200**: 741–746.

721 Bader JL, Li FP, Olmstead PM, Strickman NA, Green DM. Childhood malignant melanoma. Incidence and etiology. Am J Pediatr Hematol Oncol 1985, **7**: 341–345.

722 Balasanov K, Andreev VC, Tchernozemski I. Malignant melanoma and vitiligo. Dermatologica 1969, **139**: 211–219.

723 Barnhill RL. Childhood melanoma. Semin Diagn Pathol 1998, **15**: 189–194.

724 Beral V, Evans S, Shaw H, Milton G. Cutaneous factors related to the risk of malignant melanoma. Br J Dermatol 1983, **109**: 165–172.

725 Blackwood MA, Holmes R, Synnestvedt M, Young M, George C, Yang H, Elder DE, Schuchter LM, Guerry D, Ganguly A. Multiple primary melanoma revisited. Cancer 2002, **94**: 2248–2255.

726 Blessing K, Kernohan NM, Park KGM. Subungual malignant melanoma. Clinicopathological features of 100 cases. Histopathology 1991, **19**: 425–430.

727 Carey WP Jr, Thompson CJ, Synnestvedt M, Guerry D, Halpern A, Schultz D, Elder DE. Dysplastic nevi as a melanoma risk factor in patients with familial melanoma. Cancer 1994, **74**: 3118–3125.

728 Ceballos PI, Ruiz-Maldonado R, Mihm MC Jr. Melanoma in children. N Engl J Med 1995, **332**: 656–662.

729 Crotty KA, McCarthy SW, Palmer AA, Ng AB, Thompson JF, Gianoutsos MP, Shaw HM. Malignant melanoma in childhood. A clinicopathologic study of 13 cases and comparison with Spitz nevi. World J Surg 1992, **16**: 179–185.

730 Eide J. Pathogenesis of generalized melanosis with melanuria and melanoptysis secondary to malignant melanoma. Histopathology 1981, **5**: 285–294.

731 Gilchrest BA, Eller MS, Geller AC, Yaar M. The pathogenesis of melanoma induced by ultraviolet radiation. N Engl J Med 1999, **340**: 1341–1348.

732 Grob JJ, Gouvernet J, Aymar D, Mostaque A, Romano MH, Collet AM, Noe MC, DiConstanzo MP, Bonerandi JJ. Count of benign melanocytic nevi as a major indicator of risk for nonfamilial nodular and superficial spreading melanoma. Cancer 1990, **66**: 387–395.

733 Gussack GS, Reintgen D, Cox E, Fisher SR, Cole TB, Seigler HF. Cutaneous melanoma of the head and neck. A review of 399 cases. Arch Otolaryngol 1983, **109**: 803–808.

734 Hastrup N, Osterlind A, Drzewiecki KT, Hou-Jensen K. The presence of dysplastic nevus remnants in malignant melanomas. A population-based study of 551 malignant melanomas. Am J Dermatopathol 1991, **13**: 378–385.

735 Helwig EB. Malignant melanoma in children. In Neoplasms of the skin and malignant melanoma. Proceedings of the 20th Annual Clinical Conferences on Cancer, Houston, Texas, 1975. Chicago, 1976, Year Book Medical Publishers, pp. 11–26.

736 Holly EA, Kelly JW, Shpall SN, Chiu S-H. Number of melanocytic nevi as a major risk factor for malignant melanoma. J Am Acad Dermatol 1987, **17**: 459–468.

737 Kang S, Barnhill R, Mihm M, Sober A. Multiple primary cutaneous melanomas. Cancer 1992, **70**: 1911–1916.

738 Lerman RI, Murray D, O'Hara JM, Booher RH, Foote FW Jr. Malignant melanoma of childhood. A clinicopathologic study and a report of 12 cases. Cancer 1970, **25**: 436–449.

739 McCarthy SW, Crotty KA, Palmer AA, Ng AB, McCarthy WH, Shaw HM. Cutaneous malignant melanoma in teenagers. Histopathology 1994, **24**: 453–461.

739a Mones JM, Ackerman AB. Melanomas in prepubescent children. Am J Dermatopathol 2003, **25**: 223–238.

740 Moseley HS, Giuliano AE, Storm FK III, Clark WH, Robinson DS, Morton DL. Multiple primary melanoma. Cancer 1979, **43**: 939–944.

741 Murray C, D'Intino Y, MacCormick R, Nassar B, Walsh N. Melanosis in association with metastatic malignant melanoma:

report of a case and a unifying concept of pathogenesis. Am J Dermatopathol 1999, **21:** 28–30.

742 Patterson H, Helwig EB. Subungual malignant melanoma. A clinical-pathologic study. Cancer 1980, **46:** 2074–2087.

743 Reimer RR, Clark WH Jr, Greene MH, Ainsworth AM, Fraumeni JF Jr. Precursor lesions in familial melanoma. A new genetic preneoplastic syndrome. JAMA 1978, **239:** 744–746.

744 Stokkel M, Kroon B, van der Sande J, Neering H. Malignant cutaneous melanoma associated with neurofibromatosis in two sisters from a family with atypical multiple mole melanoma syndrome. Case reports and review of the literature. Cancer 1993, **72:** 2370–2375.

745 Swerdlow AJ, English J, MacKie RM, O'Doherty CJ, Hunter JA, Clark J, Hole DJ. Benign melanocytic naevi as a risk factor for malignant melanoma. Br Med J 1986, **292:** 1555–1559.

746 Takematsu H, Obata M, Tomita Y, Kato T, Takahashi M, Abe R. Subungual melanoma. A clinicopathologic study of 16 Japanese cases. Cancer 1985, **55:** 2725–2731.

747 Tate PS, Ronan SG, Feucht KA, Eng MA, Das Gupta TK. Melanoma in childhood and adolescence. Clinical and pathological features of 48 cases. J Pediatr Surg 1993, **28:** 217–222.

748 Tucker SB, Horstmann JP, Hertel B, Aranha G, Rosai J. Activation of nevi in patients with malignant melanoma. Cancer 1980, **46:** 822–827.

749 Urist MM, Balch CM, Soong S-J, Milton GW, Shaw HM, McGovern VJ, Murad TM, McCarthy WH, Maddox WA. Head and neck melanoma in 534 clinical stage I patients. A prognostic factors analysis and results of surgical treatment. Ann Surg 1984, **200:** 769–775.

Clinical appearance and clinicopathologic types

750 Ackerman AB, David KM. A unifying concept of malignant melanoma. Biologic aspects. Hum Pathol 1986, **17:** 438–440.

751 Arrington JH III, Reed RJ, Ichinose H, Krementz ET. Plantar lentiginous melanoma. A distinctive variant of human cutaneous malignant melanoma. Am J Surg Pathol 1977, **1:** 131–143.

752 Bruijn JA, Mihm MC, Barnhill RL. Desmoplastic melanoma. Histopathology 1992, **20:** 197–206.

753 Clark WH Jr, Mihm MC Jr. Lentigo maligna and lentigo-maligna melanoma. Am J Pathol 1969, **55:** 39–67.

754 Clark WH Jr, Elder DE, Van Horn M. The biologic forms of malignant melanoma. Hum Pathol 1986, **17:** 443–450.

755 Conley J, Lattes R, Orr W. Desmoplastic malignant melanoma (a rare variant of spindle cell melanoma). Cancer 1971, **28:** 914–936.

756 Krementz ET, Reed RJ, Coleman WP III, Sutherland CM, Carter RD, Campbell M. Acral lentiginous melanoma. A clinicopathologic entity. Ann Surg 1982, **195:** 632–645.

757 Labrecque PG, Hu C-H, Winkelmann RK. On the nature of desmoplastic melanoma. Cancer 1976, **38:** 1205–1213.

758 Levene A. An experience of malignant melanoma. Pathology 1985, **17:** 266–270.

759 McGovern VJ. Malignant melanoma. Clinical and histological diagnosis. New York, 1976, John Wiley & Sons.

760 McGovern VJ. The nature of melanoma. A critical review. J Cutan Pathol 1982, **9:** 61–81.

761 McGovern VJ, Cochran AJ, Van Der Esch EP, Little JH, MacLennan R. The classification of malignant melanoma, its histological reporting and registration. A revision of the 1972 Sydney classification. Pathology 1986, **18:** 12–21.

762 McLean DI, Lew RA, Sober AJ, Mihm MC, Fitzpatrick TB. On the prognostic importance of white depressed areas in the primary lesion of superficial spreading melanoma. Cancer 1979, **43:** 157–161.

763 Manci EA, Balch CM, Murad TM, Soong S-J. Polypoid

melanoma, a virulent variant of the nodular growth pattern. Am J Clin Pathol 1981, **75:** 810–815.

764 Mihm MC Jr, Fitzpatrick TB. Early detection of malignant melanoma. Cancer 1976, **37:** 597–603.

765 Mihm MC Jr, Clark WH Jr, From L. The clinical diagnosis, classification and histogenetic concepts of the early stages of cutaneous malignant melanomas. N Engl J Med 1971, **284:** 1078–1082.

766 Mishima Y, Nakanishi T. Acral lentiginous melanoma and its precursor. Heterogeneity of palmo-plantar melanomas. Pathology 1985, **17:** 258–265.

767 Paladugu RR, Winberg CD, Yonemoto RH. Acral lentiginous melanoma. A clinicopathologic study of 36 patients. Cancer 1983, **52:** 161–168.

768 Søndergaard K. Histological type and biological behavior of primary cutaneous malignant melanoma. Part 1. An analysis of 1916 cases. Virchows Arch [A] 1983, **401:** 315–331.

769 Søndergaard K. Histological type and biological behavior of primary cutaneous malignant melanoma. Part 2. An analysis of 86 cases located on so-called acral regions as plantar, palmar, and sub-parungual areas. Virchows Arch [A] 1983, **401:** 333–343.

770 Valensi QJ. Desmoplastic malignant melanoma. A report on two additional cases. Cancer 1977, **39:** 286–292.

771 Wayte DM, Helwig EB. Melanotic freckle of Hutchinson. Cancer 1968, **21:** 893–911.

Microscopic features

772 Al-Talib RK, Theaker JM. Signet-ring cell melanoma. Light microscopic, immunohistochemical and ultrastructural features. Histopathology 1991, **18:** 572–575.

773 Banerjee SS, Harris M. Morphological and immunophenotypic variations in malignant melanoma. Histopathology 2000, **36:** 387–402.

774 Barnhill R, Mihm M. The histopathology of cutaneous malignant melanoma. Semin Diagn Pathol 1993, **10:** 47–75.

775 Blessing K, Evans A, Al-Nafussi A. Verrucous naevoid and keratotic malignant melanoma. A clinico-pathological study of 20 cases. Histopathology 1993, **23:** 453–458.

776 Borek BT, McKee PH, Freeman JA, Maguire B, Brander WL, Calonje E. Primary malignant melanoma with rhabdoid features: a histologic and immunocytochemical study of three cases. Am J Dermatopathol 1998, **20:** 123–127.

777 Carlson JA, Dickersin GR, Sober AJ, Barnhill RL. Desmoplastic neurotropic melanoma. A clinicopathologic analysis of 28 cases. Cancer 1995, **75:** 478–494.

778 Chang ES, Wick MR, Swanson PE, Dehner LP. Metastatic malignant melanoma with "rhabdoid" features. Am J Clin Pathol 1994, **102:** 426–431.

779 Crowson AN, Magro CM, Mihm MC. Malignant melanoma with prominent pigment synthesis: "Animal type" melanoma – a clinical and histological study of six cases with a consideration of other melanocytic neoplasms with prominent pigment synthesis. Hum Pathol 1999, **30:** 543–550.

780 DaRoca PJ, Reed R, Martin PC. Metastatic amelanotic melanoma simulating giant-cell tumor of bone. Hum Pathol 1990, **21:** 978–979.

781 Denton KJ, Stretch J, Athanasou N. Osteoclast-like giant cells in malignant melanoma. Histopathology 1992, **20:** 179–180.

782 DiMaio SM, Mackay B, Smith JL Jr, Dickersin GR. Neurosarcomatous transformation in malignant melanoma. An ultrastructural study. Cancer 1982, **50:** 2345–2354.

783 Grayson W, Mare LR. Ganglioneuroblastic differentiation in a primary cutaneous malignant melanoma. Am J Dermatopathol 2003, **25:** 40–44.

784 Hanson IM, Banerjee SS, Menasce LP, Prescott RJ. A study of eleven cutaneous malignant melanomas in adults with small-

785 Hitchcock MG, McCalmont TH, White WL. Cutaneous melanoma with myxoid features: twelve cases with differential diagnosis. Am J Surg Pathol 1999, 23: 1506–1513.

786 Hunter JAA, Zaynoun S, Paterson WD, Bleehen SS, Mackie R, Cochran AJ. Cellular fine structure in the invasive nodules of different histogenetic types of malignant melanoma. Br J Dermatol 1978, 98: 255–272.

787 Iwamoto S, Burrows RC, Agoff SN, Piepkorn M, Bothwell M, Schmidt R. The p75 neurotrophin receptor, relative to other schwann cell and melanoma markers, is abundantly expressed in spindled melanomas. Am J Dermatopathol 2001, 23: 288–294.

788 Kamino H, Tam ST, Alvarez L. Malignant melanoma with pseudocarcinomatous hyperplasia – an entity that can simulate squamous cell carcinoma. A light microscopic and immunohistochemical study of four cases. Am J Dermatopathol 1990, 12: 446–451.

789 Kaneishi NK, Cockerell CJ. Histologic differentiation of desmoplastic melanoma from cicatrices. Am J Dermatopathol 1998, 20: 128–134.

790 Kao GF, Helwig EB, Graham JH. Balloon cell malignant melanoma of the skin. A clinicopathologic study of 34 cases with histochemical, immunohistochemical, and ultrastructural observations. Cancer 1992, 69: 2942–2952.

791 King R, Busam K, Rosai J. Metastatic malignant melanoma resembling malignant peripheral nerve sheath tumor: report of 16 cases. Am J Surg Pathol 1999, 23: 1499–1505.

792 Kuehnl-Petzoldt Ch, Berger H, Wiebelt H. Verrucous-keratotic variations of malignant melanoma. A clinicopathological study. Am J Dermatopathol 1982, 4: 403–410.

793 Levene A. On the histological diagnosis and prognosis of malignant melanoma. J Clin Pathol 1980, 33: 101–124.

794 Lucas D, Tazelaar H, Unni K, Wold L, Oakada K, Dimarzio D, Rolfe B. Osteogenic melanoma. A rare variant of malignant melanoma. Am J Surg Pathol 1993, 17: 400–409.

795 Mintzis MM, Silvers DN. Ultrastructural study of superficial spreading melanoma and benign simulants. Cancer 1978, 42: 502–511.

796 Nakagawa H, Imakado S, Nogita T, Ishibashi Y. Osteosarcomatous changes in malignant melanoma. Immunohistochemical and ultrastructural studies of a case. Am J Dermatopathol 1990, 12: 162–168.

797 Nakhleh RE, Wick MR, Rocamora AN, Swanson PE, Dehner LP. Morphologic diversity in malignant melanomas. Am J Clin Pathol 1990, 93: 731–740.

798 Phillips ME, Margolis RJ, Merot Y, Sober AJ, Reed RJ, Muhlbauer JE, Mihm MC Jr. The spectrum of minimal deviation melanoma. A clinicopathologic study of 21 cases. Hum Pathol 1986, 17: 796–806.

799 Price NM, Rywlin AM, Ackerman AB. Histologic criteria for the diagnosis of superficial spreading malignant melanoma. Formulated on the basis of proven metastatic lesions. Cancer 1976, 38: 2434–2441.

800 Quinn MJ, Crotty KA, Thompson JF, Coates AS, O'Brien CJ, McCarthy WH. Desmoplastic and desmoplastic neurotropic melanoma: experience with 280 patients. Cancer 1998, 83: 1128–1135.

801 Reed RJ, Leonard DD. Neurotropic melanoma. A variant of desmoplastic melanoma. Am J Surg Pathol 1979, 3: 301–311.

802 Reed RJ, Webb SV, Clark WH. Minimal deviation melanoma (halo nevus variant). Am J Surg Pathol 1990, 14: 53–68.

803 Reiman HM, Goellner JR, Woods JE, Mixter RC. Desmoplastic melanoma of the head and neck. Cancer 1987, 60: 2269–2274.

804 Riccioni L, Di Tommaso L, Collina G. Actin-rich desmoplastic malignant melanoma: report of three cases. Am J Dermatopathol 2000, 21: 537–541.

805 Robson A, Allen P, Hollowood K. S100 expression in cutaneous scars: a potential diagnostic pitfall in the diagnosis of desmoplastic melanoma. Histopathology 2001, 38: 135–140.

806 Sheibani K, Battifora H. Signet-ring cell melanoma. A rare morphologic variant of malignant melanoma. Am J Surg Pathol 1988, 12: 28–34.

806a Somach S, Morgan MB. Oncocytic melanoma: an ultrastructural and prognostic study. Mod Pathol 2003, 16: 100a.

807 Urso C, Giannotti B, Bondi R. Myxoid melanoma of the skin. Arch Pathol Lab Med 1990, 114: 527–528.

808 Warner TFCS, Lloyd RV, Hafez GR, Angevine JM. Immunocytochemistry of neurotropic melanoma. Cancer 1984, 53: 254–257.

809 Wong T-Y, Suster S, Duncan LM, Mihm MC Jr. Nevoid melanoma. A clinico-pathological study of seven cases of malignant melanoma mimicking spindle and epithelioid cell nevus and verrucous dermal nevus. Hum Pathol 1995, 26: 171–179.

810 Zembowicz A, McCusker M, Chiarelli C, Dei Tos AP, Granter SR, Calonje E, McKee PH. Morphological analysis of nevoid melanoma: a study of 20 cases with a review of the literature. Am J Dermatopathol 2001, 23: 167–175.

Histochemical and immunohistochemical features

811 Adema G, de Boer A, Hullenaar R, Denijn M, Ruiter D, Vogel A, Figdor C. Melanocyte lineage-specific antigens recognized by monoclonal antibodies NKI-beteb, HMB-50, and HMB-45 are encoded by a single cDNA. Am J Pathol 1993, 143: 1579–1585.

812 Argenyi ZB, Cain C, Bromley C, Nguyen AV, Abraham AA, Kerschmann R, Le Boit PE. S-100 protein–negative malignant melanoma. Fact or fiction? A light-microscopic and immunohistochemical study. Am J Dermatopathol 1994, 16: 233–240.

813 Bacchi CE, Bonetti F, Pea M, Martignoni G, Gown AM. HMB-45: a review. Appl Immunohistochem 1996, 4: 73–85.

814 Boyle JL, Haupt HM, Stern JB, Multhaupt HAB. Tyrosinase expression in malignant melanoma, desmoplastic melanoma, and peripheral nerve tumors: an immunohistochemical study. Arch Pathol Lab Med 2002, 126: 816–822.

815 Colombari R, Bonetti F, Zamboni G, Scarpa A, Marino F, Tomezzoli A, Capelli P, Menestrina F, Chilosi M, Fiore-Donati L. Distribution of melanoma specific antibody (HMB-45) in benign and malignant melanocytic tumors. An immunohistochemical study on paraffin sections. Virchows Arch [A] 1988, 413: 17–24.

816 Costa J, Rosai J, Philpott GW. Pigmentation of "amelanotic" melanoma in culture. A finding of diagnostic relevance. Arch Pathol 1973, 95: 371–373.

817 Facchetti F, Bertalot G, Grigolato PG. KP1 (CD68) staining of malignant melanomas. Histopathology 1991, 19: 141–145.

818 Friedman RJ, Grin CM, Heilman E, Weiser J, Gottlieb GJ, Wlado E, Rigel DS, Kopf AW. Distinguishing benign and malignant melanocytic lesions with the AgNOR method. Dermatol Clin 1991, 9: 689–693.

819 Granter SR, Weilbaecher KN, Quigley C, Fletcher CD, Fisher DE. Microphthalmia transcription factor: not a sensitive or specific marker for the diagnosis of desmoplastic melanoma and spindle cell (non-desmoplastic) melanoma. Am J Dermatopathol 2001, 23: 185–189.

820 Guo J, Cheng L, Wen DR, Huang RR, Cochran AJ. Detection of tyrosinase mRNA in formalin-fixed, paraffin-embedded archival sections of melanoma, using the reverse transcriptase in situ polymerase chain reaction. Diagn Mol Pathol 1998, 7: 10–15.

821 Hofbauer GF, Kamarashev J, Geertsen R, Boni R, Dummer R. Tyrosinase immunoreactivity in formalin-fixed, paraffin-embedded primary and metastatic melanoma: frequency and distribution. J Cutan Pathol 1998, 25: 204–209.

822 Jungbluth AA, Busam KJ, Gerald WL, Stockert E, Coplan KA, Iversen K, MacGregor DP, Old LJ, Chen YT. A103: an anti-Melan-A monoclonal antibody for the detection of malignant melanoma in paraffin-embedded tissues. Am J Surg Pathol 1998, **22**: 595–602.

823 Kapur RP, Bigler SA, Skelly M, Gown AM. Anti-melanoma monoclonal antibody HMB45 identifies an oncofetal glycoconjugate associated with immature melanosomes. J Histochem Cytochem 1992, **40**: 207–212.

824 King R, Weilbaecher KN, McGill G, Cooley E, Mihm M, Fisher DE. Microphthalmia transcription factor: a sensitive and specific melanocyte marker for melanoma diagnosis. Am J Pathol 1999, **155**: 731–738.

825 Leader M, Patel J, Collins M, Henry K. Anti-α-1-antichymotrypsin staining of 194 sarcomas, 38 carcinomas, and 17 malignant melanomas. Its lack of specificity as a tumour marker. Am J Surg Pathol 1987, **11**: 133–139.

826 Mangini J, Li N, Bhawan J. Immunohistochemical markers of melanocytic lesions: a review of their diagnostic usefulness. Am J Dermatopathol 2002, **24**: 270–281.

827 Miettinen M, Franssila K. Immunohistologic spectrum of malignant melanoma. The common presence of keratins. Lab Invest 1989, **61**: 623–628.

828 Morishima T, Nagashima N, Hanawa S, Fukada E, Kanematsu S, Shibata A. Quick diagnosis of malignant melanoma with the touch-fluorescence method during operation. Cancer 1986, **57**: 2037–2041.

829 Nakajima T, Watanabe S, Sato Y, Kameya T, Shimosato Y, Ishihara K. Immunohistochemical demonstration of S 100 protein in malignant melanoma and pigmented nevus, and its diagnostic application. Cancer 1982, **50**: 912–918.

830 Nakanishi T, Hashimoto K. The differential reactivity of benign and malignant nevomelanocytic lesions with mouse monoclonal antibody TNKH1. Cancer 1987, **59**: 1340–1344.

831 Schaumburg-Lever G, Metzler G, Kaiserling E. Ultrastructural localization of HMB-45 binding sites. J Cutan Pathol 1991, **18**: 432–435.

832 Selby W, Nance K, Park H. CEA immunoreactivity in metastatic malignant melanoma. Mod Pathol 1992, **5**: 415–419.

833 Springall DR, Gu J, Cocchia D, Michetti F, Levene A, Levene MM, Marangos PJ, Bloom SR, Polak JM. The value of S-100 immunostaining as a diagnostic tool in human malignant melanomas. A comparative study using S-100 and neuron-specific enolase antibodies. Virchows Arch [A] 1983, **400**: 331–343.

834 Vennegoor C, Hageman Ph, Van Nouhuijs H, Ruiter DJ, Calafat J, Ringens PJ, Rumke Ph. A monoclonal antibody specific for cells of the melanocyte lineage. Am J Pathol 1988, **130**: 179–192.

835 Wagner SN, Wagner C, Höfler H, Atkinson MJ, Goos M. Expression cloning of the cDNA encoding a melanoma-associated Ag recognized by mAb HMB-45. Identification as melanocyte-specific Pmel 17cDNA. Lab Invest 1995, **73**: 229–235.

836 Yaziji H, Gown AM. Immunohistochemical markers of melanocytic tumors. Int J Surg Pathol 2003, **11**: 11–15.

837 Zarbo RJ, Gown AM, Nagle RB, Visscher DW, Crissman JD. Anomalous cytokeratin expression in malignant melanoma. One- and two-dimensional Western blot analysis and immunohistochemical survey of 100 melanomas. Mod Pathol 1990, **3**: 494–501.

Electron microscopic features

838 Barnhill RL, Castresana JS, Rubio MP, Martin MT, Idoate M, Vazquez JJ, Thor AD. p53 expression in cutaneous malignant melanoma. An immunohistochemical study of 87 cases of primary, recurrent, and metastatic melanoma. Mod Pathol 1994, **7**: 533–535.

839 Bhuta S. Electron microscopy in the evaluation of melanocytic tumors. Semin Diagn Pathol 1993, **10**: 92–101.

840 Carstens P, Hollander J. Metastatic spindle cell malignant melanoma with prominent microvilli. Ultrastruct Pathol 1992, **16**: 587–592.

841 Erlandson RA. Ultrastructural diagnosis of amelanotic malignant melanoma. Aberrant melanosomes, myelin figures or lysosomes? Ultrastruct Pathol 1987, **11**: 191–208.

842 Mazur MT, Katzenstein AL. Metastatic melanoma. The spectrum of ultrastructural morphology. Ultrastruct Pathol 1980, **1**: 337–356.

843 Saenz-Santamaria MC, McNutt NS, Bogdany JK, Shea CR. p53 expression is rare in cutaneous melanomas. Am J Dermatopathol 1995, **17**: 344–349.

844 Slominski A, Wortsman J, Carlson AJ, Matsuoka LY, Balch CM, Mihm MC. Malignant melanoma: an update. Arch Pathol Lab Med 2001, **125**: 1295–1306.

Molecular genetic features

844a Bastian BC, Olshen AB, LeBoit PE, Pinkel D. Classifying melanocytic tumors based on DNA copy number changes. Am J Pathol 2003, **163**: 1765–1770.

844b Omholt K, Karsberg S, Platz A, et al: Screening of N-ras codon 61 mutations in paired primary and metastatic cutaneous melanomas: Mutations occur early and persist throughout tumor progression. Clin Cancer Res 2002, **8**: 3468–3474.

844c Pollock PM, Trent JM. The genetics of cutaneous melanoma. Clin Lab Med 2000, **20**: 667–690.

844d Uribe P, Wistuba II, González S. BRAF mutation. A frequent event in benign, atypical and malignant melanocytic lesions of the skin. Am J Dermatopathol 2003, **25**: 365–370.

Biopsy and frozen section

845 Braun-Falco O, Korting HC, Konz B. Histological and cytological criteria in the diagnosis of malignant melanomas by cryostat sections. Virchows Arch [A] 1981, **393**: 115–121.

846 Epstein E, Bragg K, Linden G. Biopsy and prognosis of malignant melanoma. JAMA 1969, **208**: 1369–1371.

847 Lees VC, Briggs JC. Effect of initial biopsy procedure on prognosis in Stage 1 invasive cutaneous malignant melanoma. Review of 1086 patients. Br J Surg 1991, **78**: 1108–1110.

848 Little JH, Davis NC. Frozen section diagnosis of suspected malignant melanoma of the skin. Cancer 1974, **34**: 1163–1172.

849 McGovern VJ, McPeak C, Reed RJ, Sugarbaker EV. Malignant melanoma. A clinical and pathologic symposium. Pathol Annu 1982, **17**(Pt 2): 361–393.

850 Shafir R, Hiss J, Tsur H, Bubis JJ. Pitfalls in frozen section diagnosis of malignant melanoma. Cancer 1983, **51**: 1168–1170.

851 Swanson NA, Lee KK, Gorman A, Lee HN. Biopsy techniques. Diagnosis of melanoma. Dermatol Clin 2002, **20**: 677–680.

852 Zitelli JA, Moy RL, Abell E. The reliability of frozen sections in the evaluation of surgical margins for melanoma. J Am Acad Dermatol 1991, **24**: 102–106.

Regression

853 Anbari KK, Schuchter LM, Bucky LP, Mick R, Synnestvedt M, Guerry D, Hamilton R, Halpern AC. Melanoma of unknown primary site: presentation, treatment, and prognosis – a single institution study for the University of Pennsylvania Pigmented Lesion Study Group. Cancer 1997, **79**: 1816–1821.

854 Avril MF, Charpentier P, Margulis A, Guillaume JC. Regression of primary melanoma with metastases. Cancer 1992, **69**: 1377–1381.

855 Blessing K, McLaren KM, McLean A, Davidson P. Thin malignant melanomas (<1.5mm) with metastasis. A histological study and survival analysis. Histopathology 1990, **17**: 397–400.

856 Chang P, Knapper WH. Metastatic melanoma of unknown primary. Cancer 1982, **49**: 1106–1111.

857 Gromet MA, Epstein WL, Blois MS. The regressing thin malignant melanoma. A distinctive lesion with metastatic potential. Cancer 1978, **42**: 2282–2292.

858 McGovern VJ. Spontaneous regression of melanoma. Pathology 1975, **7**: 91–99.

859 Smith JL Jr, Stehlin JS Jr. Spontaneous regression of primary malignant melanomas with regional metastases. Cancer 1965, **18**: 1399–1415.

Atypical in situ melanocytic lesions

860 Ackerman AB. Malignant melanoma in situ. The flat, curable stage of malignant melanoma. Pathology 1985, **17**: 298–300.

861 Clark WH, Evans HL, Everett MA, Farmer EV, Freeman RG, Graham JH, Mihm MC Jr, Rosai J, Sagebiel RW, Wick MR. Early melanoma. Histologic terms. J Cutan Pathol 1991, **18**: 477–479.

862 Cook MG, Robertson I. Melanocytic dysplasia and melanoma. Histopathology 1985, **9**: 647–658.

863 Dubow BE, Ackerman AB. Ideas in pathology – malignant melanoma in situ. The evolution of a concept. Mod Pathol 1990, **3**: 734–745.

864 Kossard S, Commens C, Symons M, Doyle J. Lentiginous dysplastic naevi in the elderly. A potential precursor for malignant melanoma. Australas J Dermatol 1991, **32**: 27–37.

865 McGovern VJ, Shaw HM, Milton GW. Histogenesis of malignant melanoma with an adjacent component of the superficial spreading type. Pathology 1985, **17**: 251–254.

866 Rywlin AM. Intraepithelial melanocytic neoplasia (IMN) versus intraepithelial atypical melanocytic proliferation (IAMP). Am J Dermatopathol 1988, **10**: 92–93.

Spread and metastases

867 Abernethy JL, Soyer HP, Kerl H, Jorizzo JL, White WL. Epidermotropic metastatic malignant melanoma simulating melanoma in situ. A report of 10 examples from two patients. Am J Surg Pathol 1994, **18**: 1140–1149.

868 Adair C, Ro JY, Sahin AA, El-Naggar AK, Ordonez NG, Ayala AG. Malignant melanoma metastatic to gastrointestinal tract. A clinicopathologic study. Int J Surg Pathol 1994, **2**: 3–10.

869 Clark WH, Elder DE, Van Horn M. The biologic forms of malignant melanoma. Hum Pathol 1986, **17**: 443–450.

870 de la Monte SM, Moore GW, Hutchins GM. Patterned distribution of metastases from malignant melanoma in humans. Cancer Res 1983, **43**: 3427–3433.

871 Gibbs P, Cebon JS, Calafiore P, Robinson WA. Cardiac metastases from malignant melanoma. Cancer 1999, **85**: 78–84.

872 Kornberg R, Harris M, Ackerman AB. Epidermotropically metastatic malignant melanoma. Differentiating malignant melanoma metastatic to the epidermis from malignant melanoma primary in the epidermis. Arch Dermatol 1978, **114**: 67–69.

873 Roses DF, Harris MN, Rigel D, Carrey Z, Friedman R, Kopf AW. Local and intransit metastases following definitive excision for primary cutaneous malignant melanoma. Ann Surg 1983, **198**: 65–69.

874 Shea CR, Kline MA, Lugo J, McNutt NS. Angiotropic metastatic malignant melanoma. Am J Dermatopathol 1995, **17**: 58–62.

875 Steiner A, Wolf C, Pehamberger H, Wolff K. Late metastases of cutaneous malignant melanoma. Br J Dermatol 1986, **114**: 737–740.

Sentinel lymph node

876 Baisden BL, Askin FB, Lange JR, Westra WH. HMB-45 immunohistochemical staining of sentinel lymph nodes: a specific method for enhancing detection of micrometastases in patients with melanoma. Am J Surg Pathol 2000, **24**: 1140–1146.

876a Biddle DA, Evans HL, Kemp BL, El-Naggar AK, Harvell JD, White WL, Iskandar SS, Prieto VG. Intraparenchymal nevus cell aggregates in lymph nodes. Am J Surg Pathol 2003, **27**: 673–681.

877 Bostick PJ, Morton DL, Turner RR, Huynh KT, Wang HJ, Elashoff R, Essner R, Hoon DS. Prognostic significance of occult metastases detected by sentinel lymphadenectomy and reverse transcriptase-polymerase chain reaction in early-stage melanoma patients. J Clin Oncol 2000, **17**: 3238–3244.

878 Czerniecki BJ, Bedrosian I, Faries M, Alavi A. Revolutionary impact of lymphoscintigraphy and intraoperative sentinel node mapping in the clinical practice of oncology. Semin Nucl Med 2001, **31**: 158–164.

879 Gennari R, Bartolomei M, Testori A, Zurrida S, Stoldt HS, Audisio Geraghty JG, Paganelli G, Veronesi U. Sentinel node localization in primary melanoma: preoperative dynamic lymphoscintigraphy, intraoperative gamma probe, and vital dye guidance. Surgery 2000, **127**: 19–25.

880 Gershenwald JE, Thompson W, Mansfield PF, Lee JE, Colome MI, Tseng C, Lee JJ, Balch CM, Reintgen DS, Ross MI. Multi-institutional melanoma lymphatic mapping experience: the prognostic value of sentinel lymph node status in 612 stage I or II melanoma patients. J Clin Oncol 1999, **17**: 976–983.

881 Groisman GM, Amar M, Schafer I. The histiocytic marker PG-M1 is helpful in differentiating histiocytes and histiocytic tumors from melanomas. Appl Immunohistochem Mol Morphol 2002, **10**: 205–209.

882 Gutzmer R, Kaspari M, Brodensen JP, Mommert S, Volker B, Kapp A, Werfel T, Kiehl P. Specificity of tyrosinase and HMB45 PCR in the detection of melanoma metastases in sentinel lymph node biopsies. Histopathology 2002, **41**: 510–518.

883 Hauschild A, Christophers E. Sentinel node biopsy in melanoma. Virchows Arch 2001, **438**: 99–106.

884 Lawrence WD, Association of Directors of Anatomic and Surgical Pathology. ADASP recommendations for processing and reporting of lymph node specimens submitted for evaluation of metastatic disease. Virchows Arch 2001, **439**: 601–603.

885 Lohmann CM, Iversen K, Jungbluth AA, Bervick M, Busam KJ. Expression of melanocyte differentiation antigens and Ki-67 in nodal nevi and comparison of Ki-67 expression with metastatic melanoma. Am J Surg Pathol 2002, **26**: 1351–1357.

885a Medalie NS, Ackerman AB. Sentinel lymph node biopsy has no benefit with primary cutaneous melanoma metastatic to a lymph node: an assertion based on comprehensive, critical analysis Part 1. Am J Dermatopathol 2003, **25**: 399–417.

886 Morton DL. Lymphatic mapping and sentinel lymphadenectomy for melanoma: past, present, and future. Ann Surg Oncol 2001, **8**: 22S–28S.

887 Pernick NL, DaSilva M, Gangi MD, Crissman J, Adsay V. "Histiocytic markers" in melanoma. Mod Pathol 1999, **12**: 1072–1077.

888 Prieto VG, Clark SH. Processing of sentinel lymph nodes for detection of metastatic melanoma. Ann Diagn Pathol 2002, **6**: 257–264.

889 Spanknebel KA, Coit DG, Beiligk SC, Gonen M, Rosai J, Klimstra DS. Characterization of micrometastatic disease in melanoma sentinel lymph nodes by enhanced pathology: recommendations for standardizing pathological analysis. Am J Surg Pathol (submitted for publication).

Treatment

890 Ackerman AB, Scheiner AM. How wide and deep is wide and deep enough? A critique of surgical practice in excisions of primary cutaneous malignant melanoma. Hum Pathol 1983, **14**: 743–744.

891 Aitken DR, Clausen K, Klein JP, James AG. The extent of primary melanoma excision. A re-evaluation – how wide is wide? Ann Surg 1983, **198**: 634–641.

892 Balch CM, Murad TM, Soong S-J, Ingalls AL, Richards PC, Maddox WA. Tumor thickness as a guide to surgical management of clinical stage I melanoma patients. Cancer 1979, **43**: 883–888.

893 Balch CM, Urist MM, Karakousis CP, Smith TJ, Temple WJ, Drzewiecki K, Jewell WR, Bartolucci AA, Mihm MC Jr, Barnhill R. Efficacy of 2-cm surgical margins for intermediate-thickness melanomas (1 to 4 mm). Results of a multi-institutional randomized surgical trial. Ann Surg 1993, **218**: 262–267.

894 Cochran AJ, Wen DR, Morton DL. Occult tumor cells in the lymph nodes of patients with pathological stage I malignant melanoma. An immunohistological study. Am J Surg Pathol 1989, **13**: 430–432.

895 Cosimi AB, Sober AJ, Mihm MC, Fitzpatrick TB. Conservative surgical management of superficially invasive cutaneous melanoma. Cancer 1984, **53**: 1256–1259.

896 Dancuart F, Harwood AR, Fitzpatrick PJ. The radiotherapy of lentigo maligna and lentigo maligna melanoma of the head and neck. Cancer 1980, **45**: 2279–2283.

897 Elder DE, Guerry DP IV, Van Horn M, Hurwitz S, Zehngebot L, Goldman LI, LaRossa D, Hamilton R, Bondi EE, Clark WH Jr. The role of lymph node dissection for clinical stage I malignant melanoma of intermediate thickness (1.51–3.99 mm). Cancer 1985, **56**: 413–418.

898 Heenan PJ, English DR, Holman CDJ, Armstrong BK. The effects of surgical treatment on survival and local recurrence of cutaneous malignant melanoma. Cancer 1992, **69**: 421–426.

899 Kelly JW, Sagebiel RW, Calderon W, Murillo L, Dakin RL, Blois MS. The frequency of local recurrence and microsatellites as a guide to reexcision margins for cutaneous malignant melanoma. Ann Surg 1984, **200**: 759–763.

899a Khayat D, Rixe O, Martin G, Soubrane C, Banzet M, Bazex J-A, Lauret P, Vérola O, Auclerc G, Harper P, Banzet P. Surgical margins in cutaneous melanoma (2cm versus 5cm for lesions measuring less than 2.1-mm thick). Cancer 2003, **97**: 1941–1946.

900 Landthaler M, Braun-Falco O, Leitl A, Konz B, Hölzel D. Excisional biopsy as the first therapeutic procedure versus primary wide excision of malignant melanoma. Cancer 1989, **64**: 1612–1616.

901 Lang PG. Current concepts in the management of patients with melanoma. Am J Clin Dermatol 2002, **3**: 401–426.

902 McNeer G. Malignant melanoma. Surg Gynecol Obstet 1965, **120**: 343–344.

903 Sandeman TF. The radical treatment of enlarged lymph nodes in malignant melanoma. Am J Roentgenol Radium Ther Nucl Med 1966, **97**: 969–979.

904 Sim FH, Taylor WF, Ivins JC, Pritchard DJ, Soule EH. A prospective randomized study of the efficacy of routine elective lymphadenectomy in management of malignant melanoma. Preliminary results. Cancer 1978, **41**: 948–956.

905 Sim FH, Taylor WF, Pritchard DJ, Soule EH. Lymphadenectomy in the management of stage I malignant melanoma. A prospective randomized study. Mayo Clin Proc 1986, **61**: 697–705.

906 Urist MM, Balch CM, Soong S-J, Shaw HM, Milton GW, Maddox WA. The influence of surgical margins and prognostic factors predicting the risk of local recurrence in 3445 patients with primary cutaneous melanoma. Cancer 1985, **55**: 1398–1402.

907 Veronesi U, Adamus J, Aubert C, Bajetta E, Beretta G, Bonadonna G, Bufalino R, Cascinelli N, Cocconi G, Durand J, DeMarsillac J, Ikonopisov RL, Kiss B, Lejeune F, MacKie R, Madej G, Mulder H, Mechl Z, Milton GW, Morabito A, Peter H, Priario J, Paul E, Rumke P, Sertoli R, Tomin R. A randomized trial of adjuvant chemotherapy and immunotherapy in cutaneous melanoma. N Engl J Med 1982, **307**: 913–916.

908 Veronesi U, Adamus J, Bandiera DC, Brennhovd IO, Caceres E, Cascinelli N, Claudio F, Ikonopisov RL, Javorski VV, Kirov S,

Kulakowski A, Lacour J, Lejeune F, Mechl Z, Morabito A, Rodé I, Sergeev S, van Slooten E, Szczygiel K, Trapeznikov NN, Wagner RI. Stage I melanoma of the limbs. Immediate versus delayed node dissection. Tumori 1980, **66**: 373–396.

909 Veronesi U, Adamus J, Bandiera DC, Brennhovd IO, Caceres E, Cascinelli N, Claudio F, Ikonopisov RL, Javorski VV, Kirov S, Kulakowski A, Lacour J, Lejeune F, Mechl Z, Morabito A, Rodé I, Sergeev S, van Slooten E, Szczygiel K, Trapeznikov NN, Wagner RI. Delayed regional lymph node dissection in stage I melanoma of the skin of the lower extremities. Cancer 1982, **49**: 2420–2430.

Prognosis

910 Azzola MF, Shaw HM, Thompson JF, Soong SJ, Scolyer RA, Watson GF, Colman MH, Zhang Y. Tumor mitotic rate is a more powerful prognostic indicator than ulceration in patients with primary cutaneous melanoma: an analysis of 3661 patients from a single center. Cancer 2003, **97**: 1488–1498.

911 Balch CM, Buzaid AC, Atkins MB, Cascinelli N, Coit DG, Fleming ID, Houghton A, Kirkwood JM, Mihm MF, Morton DL, Reintgen D, Ross MI, Sober A, Soong SJ, Thompson JA, Thompson JF, Gershenwald JE, McMasters KM. A new American Joint Committee on Cancer staging system for cutaneous melanoma. Cancer 2000, **88**: 1484–1491.

912 Balch CM, Buzaid AC, Soong SJ, Atkins MB, Cascinelli N, Coit DG, Fleming ID, Gershenwald JE, Houghton A, Kirkwood JM, McMasters KM, Mihm MF, Morton DL, Reintgen DS, Ross MI, Sober A, Thompson JA, Thompson JF. Final version of the American Joint Committee on Cancer staging system for cutaneous melanoma. J Clin Oncol 2001, **19**: 3635–3648.

913 Balch CM, Murad TM, Soong S-J, Ingalls AL, Halpern NB, Maddox WA. A multifactorial analysis of melanoma. Prognostic histopathological features comparing Clark's and Breslow's staging methods. Ann Surg 1978, **188**: 732–742.

914 Balch CM, Soong SJ, Gershenwald JE, Thompson JF, Reintgen DS, Cascinelli N, Urist M, McMasters KM, Ross MI, Kirkwood JM, Atkins MB, Thompson JA, Coit DG, Byrd D, Desmond R, Zhang Y, Liu PY, Lyman GH, Morabito A. Prognostic factors analysis of 17,600 melanoma patients: validation of the American Joint Committee on Cancer melanoma staging system. J Clin Oncol 2001, **19**: 3622–3634.

915 Balch CM, Wilkerson JA, Murad TM, Soong S-J, Ingalls AL, Maddox WA. The prognostic significance of ulceration of cutaneous melanoma. Cancer 1980, **45**: 3012–3017.

916 Breslow A. Thickness, cross-sectional areas and depth of invasion in the prognosis of malignant melanoma. Ann Surg 1970, **172**: 902–908.

917 Breslow A. Tumor thickness, level of invasion and node dissection in stage I cutaneous melanoma. Ann Surg 1975, **182**: 572–575.

918 Breslow A. Problems in the measurement of tumor thickness and level of invasion in cutaneous melanoma. Hum Pathol 1977, **8**: 1–2.

919 Breslow A, Cascinelli N, van der Esch EP, Morabito A. Stage I melanoma of the limbs. Assessment of prognosis by levels of invasion and maximum thickness. Tumori 1978, **64**: 273–284.

920 Buttner P, Garbe C, Bertz J, Burg G, d'Hoedt B, Drepper H, Guggenmoos-Holzmann I, Lechner W, Lippold A, Orfanos CE, Peters A, Rassner G, Stadler R, Stroebel W. Primary cutaneous melanoma. Optimized cutoff points of tumor thickness and importance of Clark's level for prognostic classification. Cancer 1995, **75**: 2499–2506.

921 Chang P, Knapper WH. Metastatic melanoma of unknown primary. Cancer 1982, **49**: 1106–1111.

922 Clark WH Jr, From L, Bernardino EA, Mihm MC. The histogenesis and biologic behavior of primary human malignant melanomas of the skin. Cancer Res 1969, **29**: 705–726.

923 Clark WH Jr, Goldman LI, Mastrangelo MJ. Human malignant melanoma. Clinical Oncology Monographs. New York, 1979, Grune & Stratton.

924 Clemente CG, Mihm MC Jr, Bufalino R, Zurrida S, Collini P, Cascinelli N. Prognostic value of tumor infiltrating lymphocytes in the vertical growth phase of primary cutaneous melanoma. Cancer 1996, 77: 1303–1310.

925 Cochran AJ. Histology and prognosis in malignant melanoma. J Pathol 1969, 97: 459–468.

926 Cohen HJ, Cox E, Manton K, Woodbury M. Malignant melanoma in the elderly. J Clin Oncol 1987, 5: 100–106.

927 Coleman WP, Loria PR, Reed RJ, Krementz ET. Acral lentiginous melanoma. Arch Dermatol 1980, 116: 773–776.

928 Cooper PH, Wanebo HJ, Hagar RW. Regression in thin malignant melanoma. Microscopic diagnosis and prognostic importance. Arch Dermatol 1985, 121: 1127–1131.

928a Daryanani D, Plukker JT, DeHullu JA, Kuiper H, Nap RE, Hoekstra HJ. Pregnancy and early-stage melanoma. Cancer 2003, 97: 2248–2253.

929 Duncan LM, Travers RL, Koerner FC, Mihm MC Jr, Sober AJ. Estrogen and progesterone receptor analysis in pregnancy-associated melanoma. Absence of immunohistochemically detectable hormone receptors. Hum Pathol 1994, 25: 36–41.

930 Frahm SO, Schubert C, Parwarech R, Rudolph P. High proliferative activity may predict early metastasis of thin melanomas. Hum Pathol 2002, 32: 1376–1381.

931 Friedman RJ, Rigel DS, Kopf AW, Grin CM, Heilman E, Bart RS, Kamino H, Harris MN, Roses DF, Postel AH, et al. Volume of malignant melanoma is superior to thickness as a prognostic indicator. Preliminary observation. Dermatol Clin 1991, 9: 643–648.

932 Friedman RJ, Rigel DS, Kopf AW, Lieblich L, Lew R, Harris MN, Roses DF, Gumport SL, Ragaz A, Waldo E, Levine J, Levenstein M, Koenig R, Bart RS, Trau H. Favorable prognosis for malignant melanomas associated with acquired melanocytic nevi. Arch Dermatol 1983, 119: 455–462.

933 Funk W, Schmoeckel CH, Hölzel D, Braun-Falco O. Prognostic classification of malignant melanoma by clinical criteria. Br J Dermatol 1984, 111: 129–138.

934 Garbe C, Buttner P, Bertz J, Burg G, d'Hoedt B, Drepper H, Guggenmoos-Holzmann I, Lechner W, Lippold A, Orfanos CE, Peters A, Rassner G, Stadler R, Stroebel W. Primary cutaneous melanoma. Identification of prognostic groups and estimation of individual prognosis for 5093 patients. Cancer 1995, 75: 2484–2491.

935 Green M, Ackerman B. Thickness is not an accurate gauge of prognosis of primary cutaneous melanoma. Am J Dermatopathol 1993, 15: 461–473.

936 Gromet MA, Epstein WL, Blois MS. The regressing thin malignant melanoma. A distinctive lesion with metastatic potential. Cancer 1978, 42: 2282–2292.

937 Hagen EC, Vennegoor C, Schlingemann RO, Van Der Velde EA, Ruiter DJ. Correlation of histopathological characteristics with staining patterns in human – melanoma assessed by (monoclonal) antibodies reactive on paraffin sections. Histopathology 1986, 10: 689–700.

938 Harrist TJ, Rigel DS, Day CL Jr, Sober AJ, Lew RA, Rhodes AR, Harris MN, Kopf AW, Friedman RJ, Golomb FM, Cosimi AB, Gorstein F, Malt RA, Wood WC, Postel A, Hennessey P, Gumport SL, Roses DF, Mintzis MM, Raker JW, Fitzpatrick TB, Mihm MC Jr. "Microscopic satellites" are more highly associated with regional lymph node metastases than is primary melanoma thickness. Cancer 1984, 53: 2183–2187.

939 Hazan C, Melzer K, Panageas KS, Li E, Kamino H, Kopf A, Cordon-Cardo C, Osman I, Polsky D. Evaluation of the proliferation marker MIB-1 in the prognosis of cutaneous malignant melanoma. Cancer 2002, 95: 634–640.

940 Holmes EC, Clark W, Morton DL, Eilber FR, Bochow AJ. Regional lymph node metastases and the level of invasion of primary melanoma. Cancer 1976, 37: 199–201.

941 Kelly JW, Sagebiel RW, Blois MS. Regression in malignant melanoma. A histologic feature without independent prognostic significance. Cancer 1985, 56: 2287–2291.

942 Lee Y-TN. Diagnosis, treatment and prognosis of early melanoma. The importance of depth of microinvasion. Ann Surg 1980, 191: 87–97.

943 Lens MB, Dawes M, Newton-Bishop JA, Goodacre T. Tumour thickness as a predictor of occult lymph node metastases in patients with stage I and II melanoma undergoing sentinel lymph node biopsy. Br J Surg 2002, 89: 1223–1227.

944 McGovern VJ, Shaw HM, Milton GW. Prognosis in patients with thin malignant melanoma. Influence of regression. Histopathology 1983, 7: 673–680.

945 McGovern VJ, Shaw HM, Milton GW. Prognostic significance of a polypoid configuration in malignant melanoma. Histopathology 1983, 7: 663–672.

946 McGovern VJ, Shaw HM, Milton GW, Farago GA. Prognostic significance of the histological features of malignant melanoma. Histopathology 1979, 3: 385–393.

947 McGovern VJ, Shaw HM, Milton GW, McCarthy WH. Ulceration and prognosis in cutaneous malignant melanoma. Histopathology 1982, 6: 399–407.

948 Magnus K. Prognosis in malignant melanoma of the skin. Significance of stage of disease, anatomical site, sex, age and period of diagnosis. Cancer 1977, 40: 389–397.

949 Mascaro JM, Molgo M, Castel T, Castro J. Plasma cells within the infiltrate of primary cutaneous malignant melanoma of the skin. A confirmation of its histoprognostic value. Am J Dermatopathol 1987, 9: 497–499.

950 Naruns PL, Nizze JA, Cochran AJ, Lee MB, Morton DL. Recurrence potential of thin primary melanomas. Cancer 1986, 57: 545–548.

951 O'Doherty CJ, Prescott RJ, White H, McIntyre M, Hunter JAA. Sex differences in presentation of cutaneous malignant melanoma and in survival from stage I disease. Cancer 1986, 58: 788–792.

952 Pack GT, Scharnagel IM. The prognosis for malignant melanoma in the pregnant woman. Cancer 1951, 4: 324–334.

953 Reed KM, Bronstein BR, Mihm MC Jr, Sober AJ. Prognosis for polypoidal melanoma is determined by primary tumor thickness. Cancer 1986, 57: 1201–1203.

954 Rieger E, Hofmann-Wellenhof R, Soyer HP, Kofler R, Cerroni L, Smolle J, Kerl H. Comparison of proliferative activity as assessed by proliferating cell nuclear antigen (PCNA) and Ki-67 monoclonal antibodies in melanocytic skin lesions. A quantitative immunohistochemical study. J Cutan Pathol 1993, 20: 229–236.

955 Rogers GS, Kopf AW, Rigel DS, Friedman RJ, Levine JL, Levenstein M, Bart RS, Mintzis MM. Effect of anatomical location on prognosis in patients with clinical stage I melanoma. Arch Dermatol 1983, 119: 644–649.

956 Shaw HM, Balch CM, Soong S-J, Milton GW, McCarthy WH. Prognostic histopathological factors in malignant melanoma. Pathology 1985, 17: 271–274.

957 Shiu MH, Schottenfeld D, Maclean B, Fortner JG. Adverse effects of pregnancy on melanoma. A reappraisal. Cancer 1976, 37: 181–187.

958 Solomon AR, Ellis CN, Headington JT. An evaluation of vertical growth in thin superficial spreading melanomas by sequential serial microscopic sections. Cancer 1983, 52: 2338–2341.

959 Sondergaard K. Depth of invasion and tumor thickness in primary cutaneous malignant melanoma. A study of 2012 cases. Acta Pathol Microbiol Immunol Scand (A) 1985, 93: 49–55.

960 Sondergaard K, Schou G. Therapeutic and clinicopathological factors in the survival of 1469 patients with primary cutaneous malignant melanoma in clinical stage I. Virchows Arch A [A] 1985, **408:** 249–258.

961 Sorensen FB, Kristensen IG, Grymer F, Jakobsen A. DNA level, tumor thickness, and stereological estimates of nuclear volume in stage I cutaneous malignant melanomas. A comparative study with analysis of prognostic impact. Am J Dermatopathol 1991, **14:** 11–19.

962 Soyer HP. Ki 67 immunostaining in melanocytic skin tumors. Correlation with histologic parameters. J Cutan Pathol 1991, **18:** 264–272.

963 Takahashi H, Strutton GM, Parsons PG. Determination of proliferating fractions in malignant melanomas BVY anti-PCNA/cyclin monoclonal antibody. Histopathology 1991, **18:** 221–228.

964 Thörn M, Ponten F, Bergstrom R, Sparen P, Adami HO. Clinical and histopathologic predictors of survival in patients with malignant melanoma. A population-based study in Sweden. J Natl Cancer Inst 1994, **86:** 761–769.

965 Van Der Esch EP, Cascinelli N, Preda F, Morabita A, Bufalino R. Stage I melanoma of the skin. Evaluation of prognosis according to histologic characteristics. Cancer 1981, **48:** 1668–1673.

966 Wanebo HJ, Fortner JG, Woodruff J, MacLean B, Binkowski E. Selection of the optimum surgical treatment of stage I melanoma by depth of microinvasion. Use of the combined microstage technique (Clark-Breslow). Ann Surg 1975, **182:** 302–315.

967 Wanebo HJ, Woodruff J, Fortner JG. Malignant melanoma of the extremities. A clinicopathologic study using levels of invasion (microstage). Cancer 1975, **35:** 666–676.

968 White LP, Linden G, Breslow L, Harzfeld L. Studies on melanoma. The effect of pregnancy on survival in human melanoma. JAMA 1961, **177:** 235–238.

969 Wick MR. Prognostic factors for cutaneous melanoma. Am J Clin Pathol 1998, **110:** 713–718.

970 Woods JE, Soule EH, Creagan ET. Metastasis and death in patients with thin melanomas (less than 0.76 mm). Ann Surg 1983, **198:** 63–64.

971 Woolsey JT, Dietrich DR. Prognostic significance of PCNA grade in malignant melanoma. J Cutan Pathol 1993, **20:** 498–503.

Other pigmented skin lesions

972 Bolognia JL. Reticulated black solar lentigo ("ink spot" lentigo). Arch Dermatol 1992, **128:** 934–940.

973 Duve S, Schmoeckel C, Burgdorf WH. Melanocytic hyperplasia in scars: a histopathological investigation of 722 cases. Am J Dermatopathol 1996, **18:** 236–240.

974 Mishima Y, Pinkus H. Benign mixed tumor of melanocytes and malpighian cells. Melanoacanthoma. Its relationship to Bloch's benign nonnevoid melanoepithelioma. Arch Dermatol 1960, **81:** 539–550.

Neuroendocrine cells
Merkel cell carcinoma

975 Bayrou O, Avril MF, Charpentier P, Caillou B, Guillaume JC, Prade M. Primary neuroendocrine carcinoma of the skin. Clinicopathologic study of 18 cases. J Am Acad Dermatol 1991, **24:** 198–207.

976 Boutilier R, Desormeau L, Cragg F, Roberts P, Walsh N. Merkel cell carcinoma: squamous and atypical fibroxanthoma-like differentiation in successive local tumor recurrences. Am J Dermatopathol 2001, **23:** 46–49.

977 Brinkschmidt C, Stolze P, Fahrenkamp AG, Hundeiker M, Fischer-Colbrie R, Zelger B, Bocker W, Schmid KW. Immunohistochemical demonstration of chromogranin A, chromogranin B, and secretoneurin in Merkel cell carcinoma of the skin. An immunohistochemical study on 18 cases suggesting two types of Merkel cell carcinoma. Appl Immunohistochem 1995, **3:** 37–44.

978 Brown HA, Sawyer DM, Woo T. Intraepidermal Merkel cell carcinoma with no dermal involvement. Am J Dermatopathol 2000, **22:** 65–69.

979 Byrd-Gloster AL, Khoor A, Glass LF, Messina JL, Whitsett JA, Livingstone SK, Cagle PT. Differential expression of thyroid transcription factor 1 in small cell lung carcinoma and Merkel cell tumor. Hum Pathol 2000, **31:** 58–62.

980 Cerroni L, Kerl H. Primary cutaneous neuroendocrine (Merkel cell) carcinoma in association with squamous- and basal-cell carcinoma. Am J Dermatopathol 1998, **19:** 610–613.

981 Chan JK, Suster S, Wenig BM, Tsang WY, Chan JB, Lau AL. Cytokeratin 20 immunoreactivity distinguishes Merkel cell (primary cutaneous neuroendocrine) carcinomas and salivary gland small cell carcinomas from small cell carcinomas of various sites. Am J Surg Pathol 1997, **21:** 226–234.

982 Cheuk W, Kwan MY, Suster S, Chan JK. Immunostaining for thyroid transcription factor 1 and cytokeratin 20 aids the distinction of small cell carcinoma from Merkel cell carcinoma, but not pulmonary from extrapulmonary small cell carcinomas. Arch Pathol Lab Med 2001, **125:** 228–231.

983 Cooper L, De Bono R, Alsanjari N, Al-Nafussi A. Merkel cell tumours with leiomyosarcomatous differentiation. Histopathology 2000, **36:** 540–543.

984 Eusebi V, Capella C, Cossu A, Rosai J. Neuroendocrine carcinoma within lymph nodes in the absence of a primary tumor, with special reference to Market cell carcinoma. Am J Surg Pathol 1992, **16:** 658–666.

985 Fenig E, Brenner B, Katz A, Rakovsky E, Hana MB, Sulkes A. The role of radiation therapy and chemotherapy in the treatment of Merkel cell carcinoma. Cancer 1997, **80:** 881–885.

986 Frigerio B, Capella C, Eusebi V, Tenti P, Azzopardi JG. Merkel cell carcinoma of the skin. The structure and origin of normal Merkel cells. Histopathology 1983, **7:** 229–249.

987 Gancberg D, Feoli F, Hamels J, de Saint-Aubain N, Andre J, Rouas G, Verhest A, Larsimont D. Trisomy 6 in Merkel cell carcinoma: a recurrent chromosomal aberration. Histopathology 2000, **37:** 445–451.

988 Gaudin PB, Rosai J. Florid vascular proliferation associated with neural and neuroendocrine neoplasms: a diagnostic clue and potential pitfall. Am J Surg Pathol 1995, **19:** 642–652.

989 Goepfert H, Remmler D, Silva E, Wheeler B. Merkel cell carcinoma (endocrine carcinoma of the skin) of the head and neck. Arch Otolaryngol 1984, **110:** 707–712.

990 Gollard R, Weber R, Kosty MP, Greenway HT, Massullo V, Humberson C. Merkel cell carcinoma: review of 22 cases with surgical, pathologic, and therapeutic considerations. Cancer 2000, **88:** 1842–1851.

991 Gomez LG, DiMaio S, Silva EG, Mackay B. Association between neuroendocrine (Merkel cell) carcinoma and squamous carcinoma of the skin. Am J Surg Pathol 1983, **7:** 171–177.

992 Gould E, Albores-Saavedra J, Dubner N, Smith W, Payne CM. Eccrine and squamous differentiation in Merkel cell carcinoma. An immunohistochemical study. Am J Surg Pathol 1988, **12:** 768–772.

993 Haneke E, Schulze HJ, Mahrle G. Immunohistochemical and immunoelectron microscopic demonstration of chromogranin A in formalin-fixed tissue of Merkel cell carcinoma. J Am Acad Dermatol 1993, **28:** 222–226.

994 Hanly AJ, Elgart GW, Jorda M, Smith J, Nadji M. Analysis of thyroid transcription factor-1 and cytokeratin 20 separates Merkel cell carcinoma from small cell carcinoma of the lung. J Cutan Pathol 2000, **27:** 118–120.

995 Hashimoto K, Lee MW, D'Annunzio DR, Balle MR, Narisawa

Y. Pagetoid Merkel cell carcinoma: epidermal origin of the tumor. J Cutan Pathol 1999, **25**: 572–579.

996 Heenan PJ, Cole JM, Spagnolo DV. Primary cutaneous neuroendocrine carcinoma (Merkel cell tumor). An adnexal epithelial neoplasm. Am J Dermatopathol 1990, **12**: 7–16.

997 Hofler H, Kerl H, Lackinger E, Helleis G, Denk H. The intermediate filament cytoskeleton of cutaneous neuroendocrine carcinoma (Merkel cell tumour). Immunohistochemical and biochemical analyses. Virchows Arch [A] 1985, **406**: 339–350.

998 Jensen K, Kohler S, Rouse RV. Cytokeratin staining in Merkel cell carcinoma: an immunohistochemical study of cytokeratins 5/6, 7, 17, and 20. Appl Immunohistochem Mol Morphol 2000, **8**: 310–315.

999 Kayashima K, Ono T, Johno M, Kojo Y, Yamashita N, Matsunaga W. Spontaneous regression in Merkel cell (neuroendocrine) carcinoma of the skin. Arch Dermatol 1991, **127**: 550–553.

1000 Layfield L, Ulich T, Liao S, Barr R, Cheng L, Lewin KL. Neuroendocrine carcinoma of the skin. An immunohistochemical study of tumor markers and neuroendocrine products. J Cutan Pathol 1986, **13**: 268–273.

1001 Leff EL, Brooks JSJ, Trojanowski JQ. Expression of neurofilament and neuronspecific enolase in small cell tumors of skin using immunohistochemistry. Cancer 1985, **56**: 625–631.

1002 Leonard JH, Leonard P, Kearsley JH. Chromosomes 1, 11, and 13 are frequently involved in karyotypic abnormalities in metastatic Merkel cell carcinoma. Cancer Genet Cytogenet 1993, **67**: 65–70.

1003 Marks ME, Kim RY, Salter MM. Radiotherapy as an adjunct in the management of Merkel cell carcinoma. Cancer 1990, **65**: 60–64.

1004 Miettinen M. Keratin 20. Immunohistochemical marker for gastrointestinal, urothelial, and Merkel cell carcinomas. Mod Pathol 1995, **8**: 384–388.

1005 Pilotti S, Rilke F, Lombardi L. Neuroendocrine (Merkel cell) carcinoma of the skin. Am J Surg Pathol 1982, **6**: 243–254.

1006 Raaf JH, Urmacher C, Knapper WK, Shiu MH, Cheng EWK. Trabecular (Merkel cell) carcinoma of the skin. Treatment of primary, recurrent, and metastatic disease. Cancer 1986, **57**: 178–182.

1007 Ratner D, Nelson BR, Brown MD, Johnson TM. Merkel cell carcinoma. J Am Acad Dermatol 1993, **29**: 143–156.

1008 Ro JY, Ayala AG, Tetu B, Ordonez NG, el-Naggar A, Grignon DJ, Mackay B. Merkel cell carcinoma metastatic to the testis. Am J Clin Pathol 1990, **94**: 384–389.

1009 Schmid CH, Beham A, Feightinger J, Aubock L, Dietze O. Recurrent and subsequently metastasizing Merkel cell carcinoma in a 7-year-old girl. Histopathology 1992, **20**: 437–438.

1010 Schmidt U, Muller U, Metz KA, Leder KD. Cytokeratin and neurofilament protein staining in Merkel cell carcinoma of the lung. Am J Dermatopathol 1998, **20**: 346–351.

1011 Scott MP, Helm KF. Cytokeratin 20: a marker for diagnosing Merkel cell carcinoma. Am J Dermatopathol 1999, **21**: 16–20.

1012 Shah IA, Netto D, Schlageter MO, Muth C, Fox I, Manne RK. Neurofilament immunoreactivity in Merkel-cell tumors. A differentiating feature from small-cell carcinoma. Mod Pathol 1993, **6**: 3–9.

1013 Sharma D, Flora G, Grunberg SM. Chemotherapy of metastic Merkel cell carcinoma. Case report and review of the literature. Am J Clin Oncol 1991, **14**: 166–169.

1014 Shaw JH, Rumball E. Merkel cell tumour. Clinical behaviour and treatment. Br J Surg 1991, **78**: 138–142.

1015 Sibley RK, Dahl D. Primary neuroendocrine (Merkel cell) carcinoma of the skin. II. An immunocytochemical study of 21 cases. Am J Surg Pathol 1985, **9**: 109–116.

1016 Sibley RK, Dehner LP, Rosai J. Primary neuroendocrine (Merkel cell?) carcinoma of the skin. I. A clinicopathologic and ultrastructural study of 43 cases. Am J Surg Pathol 1985, **9**: 95–108.

1017 Sibley RK, Rosai J, Foucar E, Dehner LP, Bosl G. Neuroendocrine (Merkel cell) carcinoma of the skin. A histologic and ultrastructural study of two cases. Am J Surg Pathol 1980, **4**: 211–221.

1018 Sidhu GS, Feiner H, Flotte TJ, Mullins JD, Schaefler K, Schultenhover SJ. Merkel cell neoplasms. Histology, electron microscopy, biology, and histogenesis. Am J Dermatopathol 1980, **2**: 101–119.

1019 Silva E, Mackay B. Neuroendocrine (Merkel cell) carcinomas of the skin. An ultrastructural study of nine cases. Ultrastruct Pathol 1981, **2**: 1–9.

1020 Silva EG, Mackay B, Goepfert H, Burgess MA, Fields RS. Endocrine carcinoma of the skin (Merkel cell carcinoma). Pathol Annu 1984, **19**(Pt 2): 1–30.

1021 Silva EG, Ordóñez NG, Lechago J. Immunohistochemical studies in endocrine carcinoma of the skin. Am J Clin Pathol 1984, **81**: 558–562.

1022 Su LD, Fullen DR, Lowe L, Uherova P, Schnitzer B, Valder R. CD117 (KIT receptor) expression in Merkel cell carcinoma. Am J Dermatopathol 2002, **24**: 289–293.

1023 Tai PT, Yu E, Winquist E, Hammond A, Stitt L, Tonita J, Gilchrist J. Chemotherapy in neuroendocrine/Merkel cell carcinoma of the skin: case series and review of 204 cases. J Clin Oncol 2000, **18**: 2493–2499.

1024 Takenaka H, Kishimoto S, Shibagaki R, Nagura M, Yasumo H. Merkel cell carcinoma with partial spontaneous regression: an immunohistochemical, ultrastructural, and TUNEL labeling study. Am J Dermatopathol 1998, **19**: 614–618.

1025 Tang C-K, Toker C. Trabecular carcinoma of the skin. An ultrastructural study. Cancer 1978, **42**: 2311–2321.

1026 Toker C. Trabecular carcinoma of the skin. Arch Dermatol 1972, **105**: 107–110.

1027 Vortmeyer AO, Merino MJ, Boni R, Liotta LA, Cavazzana A, Zhuang Z. Genetic changes associated with primary Merkel cell carcinoma. Am J Clin Pathol 1998, **109**: 565–570.

1028 Walsh NM. Primary neuroendocrine (Merkel cell) carcinoma of the skin. Morphologic diversity and implications thereof. Hum Pathol 2001, **32**: 680–689.

1029 Warner TFCS, Uno H, Hafez GR, Burgess J, Bolles C, Lloyd RV, Oka M. Merkel cells and Merkel cell tumors. Ultrastructure, immunocytochemistry and review of the literature. Cancer 1983, **52**: 238–245.

1030 Wick MR, Goellner JR, Scheithauer BW, Thomas JR III, Sanchez NP, Schroeter AL. Primary neuroendocrine carcinomas of the skin (Merkel cell tumors). A clinical, histologic, and ultrastructural study of thirteen cases. Am J Clin Pathol 1983, **79**: 6–13.

1031 Wick MR, Kaye VN, Sibley RK, Tyler R, Frizzera G. Primary neuroendocrine carcinoma and small-cell malignant lymphoma of the skin. A discriminant immunohistochemical comparison. J Cutan Pathol 1986, **13**: 347–358.

1032 Wick MR, Scheithauer BW, Kovacs K. Neuron-specific enolase in neuroendocrine tumors of the thymus, bronchus, and skin. Am J Clin Pathol 1983, **79**: 703–707.

1033 Wills EJ. Anemone cell tumor with neuroendocrine differentiation (presumed Merkel cell carcinoma). Ultrastruct Pathol 1990, **14**: 161–172.

Other neuroendocrine tumors

1034 Collina G, Quarto F, Eusebi V. Trabecular carcinoid of the skin with cellular stroma. Am J Dermatopathol 1988, **10**: 430–435.

1035 Courville P, Joly P, Thomine E, Ziade J, Soubrane JC, Kuhn JM, Lauret P. Primary cutaneous carcinoid tumour. Histopathology 2000, **36**: 566–567.

1036 Gould VE, Moll R, Moll I, Lee I, Franke WW. Neuroendocrine (Merkel) cells of the skin. Hyperplasias, dysplasias, and neoplasms. Lab Invest 1985, **52:** 334–353.

1037 Hasegawa SL, Davison JM, Rutten A, Fletcher JA, Fletcher CD. Primary cutaneous Ewing's sarcoma: immunophenotypic and molecular cytogenetic evaluation of five cases. Am J Surg Pathol 1998, **22:** 310–318.

1038 Smith PA, Chappell RH. Another possible primary carcinoid tumour of skin? Virchows Arch [A] 1985, **408:** 99–103.

1039 van Dijk C, ten Seldam REJ. A possible primary cutaneous carcinoid. Cancer 1975, **36:** 1016–1020.

1040 Van Nguyen A, Argenyi ZB. Cutaneous neuroblastoma. Peripheral neuroblastoma. Am J Dermatopathol 1993, **15:** 7–14.

Dermis

Fibroblastic tumors and tumorlike conditions

1041 Blackburn WR, Cosman B. Histologic basis of keloid and hypertrophic scar differentiation. Clinicopathologic correlation. Arch Pathol 1966, **82:** 65–71.

1042 Cerio R, Rao BK, Spaull J, Wilson Jones E. An immunohistochemical study of fibrous papule of the nose. 25 cases. J Cutan Pathol 1989, **16:** 194–198.

1043 Chang SN, Chun SI, Moon TK, Park WH. Solitary sclerotic fibroma of the skin: degenerated sclerotic change of inflammatory conditions, especially folliculitis. Am J Dermatopathol 2000, **22:** 22–25.

1044 Chen TM, Purohit SK, Wang AR. Pleomorphic sclerotic fibroma: a case report and literature review. Am J Dermatopathol 2002, **24:** 54–58.

1045 Cowper SE, Kilpatrick T, Proper S, Morgan MB. Solitary fibrous tumor of the skin. Am J Dermatopathol 1999, **21:** 213–219.

1046 Eddy RJ, Petro JA, Tomasek JJ. Evidence for the nonmuscle nature of the "myofibroblast" of granulation tissue and hypertrophic scar. An immunofluorescence study. Am J Pathol 1988, **130:** 252–260.

1047 Ehrlich HP, Desmouliere A, Diegelmann RF, Cohen IK, Compton CC, Garner WL, Kapanci Y, Gabbiani G. Morphological and immunochemical differences between keloid and hypertrophic scar. Am J Pathol 1994, **145:** 105–113.

1048 Fukunaga M, Ushigome S. Collagenous fibroma (desmoplastic fibroblastoma): a distinctive fibroblastic soft tissue tumor. Adv Anat Pathol 1999, **6:** 275–280.

1049 Graham JH, Sanders JB, Johnson WC, Helwig EB. Fibrous papule of the nose. A clinicopathological study. J Invest Dermatol 1965, **45:** 194–203.

1050 Guitart J, Ritter JH, Wick MR. Solitary cutaneous myofibromas in adults: report of six cases and discussion of differential diagnosis. J Cutan Pathol 1997, **23:** 437–444.

1051 Hanft VN, Shes CR, McNutt NS, Pullitzer D, Horenstein MG, Prieto VG. Expression of CD34 in sclerotic (plywood) fibromas. Am J Dermatopathol 2000, **22:** 17–21.

1052 Hasegawa T, Shimoda T, Hirohashi S, Hizawa K, Sano T. Collagenous fibroma (desmoplastic fibroblastoma): report of four cases and review of the literature. Arch Pathol Lab Med 1998, **122:** 455–460.

1053 Herzberg AJ, Dinehart SM, Kerns BJ, Pollack SV. Acne keloidalis. Transverse microscopy, immunohistochemistry, and electron microscopy. Am J Dermatopathol 1990, **12:** 109–121.

1054 Kamino H, Lee Y-Y, Berke A. Pleomorphic fibroma of the skin. A benign neoplasm with cytologic atypia. A clinicopathologic study of eight cases. Am J Surg Pathol 1989, **13:** 107–113.

1055 Kamino H, Reddy VB, Gero M, Greco MA. Dermatomyofibroma. A benign cutaneous, plaque-like proliferation of fibroblasts and myofibroblasts in young adults. J Cutan Pathol 1992, **19:** 85–93.

1056 Kuo TT, Hu S, Chan HL. Keloidal dermatofibroma: report of 10 cases of a new variant. Am J Surg Pathol 1998, **22:** 564–568.

1057 Meigel WN, Ackerman AB. Fibrous papule of the face. Am J Dermatopathol 1979, **1:** 329–340.

1057a Mentzel T, Kutzner H. Haemorrhagic dermatomyofibroma (plaque-like dermal fibromatosis) : clinicopathological and immunohistochemcial analysis of three cases resembling plaque-stage Kaposi's sarcoma. Histopathology 2003, **42:** 594–598.

1058 Metcalf JS, Maize JC, Leboit PE. Circumscribed storiform collagenoma (sclerosing fibroma). Am J Dermatopathol 1991, **13:** 122–129.

1059 Miettinen M, Fetsch JF. Collagenous fibroma (desmoplastic fibroblastoma): a clinicopathologic analysis of 63 cases of a distinctive soft tissue lesion with stellate-shaped fibroblasts. Hum Pathol 1998, **29:** 676–682.

1060 Ng WK, Cheung MF, Ma L. Dermatomyofibroma: further support of its myofibroblastic nature by electronmicroscopy. Histopathology 1996, **29:** 181–183.

1061 Rahban SR, Garner WL. Fibroproliferative scars. Clin Plast Surg 2003, **30:** 77–89.

1062 Requena L, Gutierrez J, Yus ES. Multiple sclerotic fibromas of the skin. A cutaneous marker of Cowden's disease. J Cutan Pathol 1992, **19:** 346–351.

1063 Rudolph P, Schubert C, Harms D, Parwaresch R. Giant cell collagenoma: a benign dermal tumor with distinctive multinucleate cells. Am J Surg Pathol 1998, **22:** 557–563.

1064 Rudolph P, Schubert C, Zelger BG, Zelger B, Parwaresch R. Differential expression of CD34 and Ki-M1p in pleomorphic fibroma and dermatofibroma with monster cells. Am J Dermatopathol 1999, **21:** 414–419.

1065 Santa Cruz DJ, Ulbright TM. Mucin-like changes in keloids. Am J Clin Pathol 1981, **75:** 18–22.

1066 Santucci M, Borgognoni L, Reali UM, Gabbiani G. Keloids and hypertrophic scars of Caucasians show distinctive morphologic and immunophenotypic profiles. Virchows Arch 2001, **438:** 457–463.

1067 Shitabata PK, Crouch ED, Fitzgibbon JF, Swanson PE, Adesokan PN, Wick MR. Cutaneous sclerotic fibroma. Immunohistochemical evidence of a fibroblastic neoplasm with ongoing type I collagen synthesis. Am J Dermatopathol 1995, **17:** 339–343.

1068 Smith KJ, Skleton HG, Barrett TL, Lupton GP, Graham JH. Cutaneous myofibroma. Mod Pathol 1989, **2:** 603–609.

Fibrohistiocytic tumors and tumorlike conditions

Benign fibrous histiocytoma

1069 Abenoza P, Lillemoe T. CD34 and Factor XIIIa in the differential diagnosis of dermatofibroma and dermatofibrosarcoma protuberans. Am J Dermatopathol 1993, **15:** 429–434.

1070 Aiba S, Terui T, Tagami H. Dermatofibroma with diffuse eosinophilic infiltrate. Am J Dermatopathol 2000, **22:** 281–284.

1071 Black WC III, McGavran MH, Graham P. Nodular subepidermal fibrosis. Arch Surg 1969, **98:** 296–300.

1072 Bruecks AK, Trotter MJ. Expression of desmin and smooth muscle myosin heavy chain in dermatofibromas. Arch Pathol Lab Med 2002, **126:** 1179–1183.

1073 Burgdorf WHC, Duray P, Rosai J. Immunohistochemical identification of lysozyme in cutaneous lesions of alleged histiocytic nature. Am J Clin Pathol 1981, **75:** 162–167.

1074 Calonje E. Is cutaneous benign fibrous histiocytoma (dermatofibroma) a reactive inflammatory process or a neoplasm? (Commentary.) Histopathology 2000, **37:** 278–280.

1075 Calonje E, Fletcher CDM. Cutaneous fibrohistiocytic tumors. An update. Adv Anat Pathol 1994, **1:** 2–15.

1076 Calonje E, Fletcher CDM. Aneurysmal benign fibrous histiocytoma. Clinico pathological analysis of 40 cases of a tumour frequently misdiagnosed as a vascular neoplasm. Histopathology 1995, **26**: 323–332.

1077 Calonje E, Mentzel T, Fletcher CD. Cellular benign fibrous histiocytoma. Clinicopathologic analysis of 74 cases of a distinctive variant of cutaneous fibrous histiocytoma with frequent recurrence. Am J Surg Pathol 1994, **18**: 668–676.

1078 Chen TC, Kuo T, Chan HL. Dermatofibroma is a clonal proliferative disease. J Cutan Pathol 2000, **27**: 36–39.

1079 Cheng L, Amini SB, Tarif Zaim M. Follicular basal cell hyperplasia overlying dermatofibroma. Am J Surg Pathol 1997, **21**: 711–718.

1080 Dalziel K, Marks R. Hair follicle-like change over histiocytomas. Am J Dermatopathol 1986, **8**: 462–466.

1081 Glusac EJ, McNiff JM. Epithelioid cell histiocytoma: a simulant of vascular and melanocytic neoplasms. Am J Dermatopathol 1999, **21**: 1–7.

1082 Glusac EJ, Barr RJ, Everett MA, Pitha J, Santa Cruz DJ. Epithelioid cell histiocytoma. A report of 10 cases including a new cellular variant. Am J Surg Pathol 1994, **18**: 583–590.

1083 Goette DK, Helwig EB. Basal cell carcinomas and basal cell carcinoma-like changes overlying dermatofibromas. Arch Dermatol 1975, **111**: 589–592.

1084 Gonzalez BS. Benign fibrous histiocytoma of the skin. An immunohistochemical analysis of 30 cases. Pathol Res Pract 1985, **180**: 486–489.

1085 Guillou L, Gebhard S, Salmeron M, Coindre JM. Metastasizing fibrous histiocytoma of the skin: a clinicopathologic and immunohistochemical analysis of three cases. Mod Pathol 2000, **13**: 654–660.

1086 Herman KL, Kantor GR, Katz SM. Squamous cell carcinoma in-situ overlying dermatofibroma. J Cutan Pathol 1990, **17**: 385–387.

1087 Iwata J, Fletcher CD. Lipidized fibrous histiocytoma: clinicopathologic analysis of 22 cases. Am J Dermatopathol 2000, **22**: 126–134.

1088 Kaddu S, McMenamin ME, Fletcher CD. Atypical fibrous histiocytoma of the skin: clinicopathologic analysis of 59 cases with evidence of infrequent metastasis. Am J Surg Pathol 2002, **26**: 35–46.

1089 Kahn HJ, Fekete E, From L. Tenascin differentiates dermatofibroma from dermatofibrosarcoma protuberans: comparison with CD34 and factor XIIIa. Hum Pathol 2001, **32**: 50–56.

1090 Kamino H, Jacobson M. Dermatofibroma extending into the subcutaneous tissue. Differential diagnosis from dermatofibrosarcoma protuberans. Am J Surg Pathol 1990, **14**: 1156–1164.

1091 Kuo TT, Chan HL. Ossifying dermatofibroma with osteoclast-like giant cells. Am J Dermatopathol 1994, **16**: 193–195.

1092 Kuo TT, Hu S, Chan HL. Keloidal dermatofibroma: report of 10 cases of a new variant. Am J Surg Pathol 1998, **22**: 564–568.

1093 Kutchemeshgi M, Barr R, Henderson C. Dermatofibroma with osteoclast-like giant cells. Am J Dermatopathol 1992, **14**: 397–401.

1094 Kutzner H. Expression of the human progenitor cell antigen CD34 (HCPA-1) distinguishes dermatofibrosarcoma protuberans from fibrous histiocytoma in formalin-fixed, paraffin-embedded tissue. J Am Acad Dermatol 1993, **28**: 613–617.

1095 Le Boit PE, Barr RJ. Smooth-muscle proliferation in dermatofibromas. Am J Dermatopathol 1994, **16**: 155–160.

1096 Leyva WH, Santa Cruz DJ. Atypical cutaneous fibrous histiocytoma. Am J Dermatopathol 1986, **8**: 467–471.

1097 Mentzel T, Kutzner H, Rutten A, Hugel H. Benign fibrous histiocytoma (dermatofibroma) of the face: clinicopathologic and immunohistochemical study of 34 cases associated with an aggressive clinical course. Am J Dermatopathol 2002, **23**: 419–426.

1098 Morgan MB, Howard HG, Everett MA. Epithelial induction in dermatofibroma: a role for the epidermal growth factor (EGF) receptor. Am J Dermatopathol 1997, **19**: 35–40.

1099 Paties C, Vassallo G, Taccogni GL. Clear cell dermatofibroma. Am J Surg Pathol 1997, **21**: 250–252.

1100 Prieto VG, Reed JA, Shea CR. Immunohistochemistry of dermatofibromas and benign fibrous histiocytomas. J Cutan Pathol 1995, **22**: 336–341.

1101 Sanchez Yus E, Soria L, de Eusebio E, Requena L. Lichenoid, erosive and ulcerated dermatofibromas. Three additional clinico-pathologic variants. J Cutan Pathol 2000, **27**: 112–117.

1102 Santa Cruz DJ, Kyriakos M. Aneurysmal ("angiomatoid") fibrous histiocytoma of the skin. Cancer 1981, **47**: 2053–2061.

1103 Schwob VS, Santa Cruz DJ. Palisading cutaneous fibrous histiocytoma. J Cutan Pathol 1986, **13**: 403–407.

1104 Singh Gomez C, Calonje E, Fletcher CD. Epithelioid benign fibrous histiocytoma of skin. Clinico-pathological analysis of 20 cases of a poorly known variant. Histopathology 1994, **24**: 123–129.

1105 Soyer HP, Metze D, Kerl H. Granular cell dermatofibroma. Am J Dermatopathol 1997, **19**: 168–173.

1106 Tamada S, Ackerman AB. Dermatofibroma with monster cells. Am J Dermatopathol 1987, **9**: 380–387.

1107 Vanni R, Fletcher CD, Sciot R, Dal Cin P, DeWever I, Mandahl N, Mertens F, Mitelman F, Rosai J, Rydholm A, Tallini G, van den Berghe H, Willen H. Cytogenetic evidence of clonality in cutaneous benign fibrous histiocytomas: a report of the CHAMP study group. Histopathology 2000, **37**: 212–217.

1108 Wambacher-Gasser B, Zelger B, Zelger BG, Steiner H. Clear cell dermatofibroma. Histopathology 1997, **30**: 64–69.

1109 Wilson Jones E, Cerio R, Smith N. Epithelioid cell histiocytoma. A new entity. Br J Dermatol 1989, **120**: 185–195.

1110 Zelger BG, Calonje E, Zelger B. Myxoid dermatofibroma. Histopathology 1999, **34**: 357–364.

1111 Zelger B, Sidoroff A, Stanzl U, Fritsch PO, Ofner D, Jasani B, Schmid KW. Deep penetrating dermatofibroma versus dermatofibrosarcoma protuberans. A clinicopathologic comparison. Am J Surg Pathol 1994, **18**: 677–686.

1112 Zelger BG, Sidoroff A, Zelger B. Combined dermatofibroma: co-existence of two or more variant patterns in a single lesion. Histopathology 2000, **36**: 529–539.

1113 Zelger BG, Steiner H, Kutzner H, Rütten A, Zelger B. Granular cell dermatofibroma. Histopathology 1998, **31**: 258–262.

1114 Zelger BW, Zelger BG, Rappersberger K. Prominent myofibroblastic differentiation: a pitfall in the diagnosis of dermatofibroma. Am J Dermatopathol 1997, **19**: 138–146.

Atypical fibroxanthoma

1115 Bourne RG. Paradoxical fibrosarcoma of skin (pseudosarcoma). A review of 13 cases. Med J Aust 1963, **1**: 504–510.

1116 Boutilier R, Desormeau L, Cragg F, Roberts P, Walsh N. Merkel cell carcinoma: squamous and atypical fibroxanthoma-like differentiation in successive local tumor recurrences. Am J Dermatopathol 2001, **23**: 46–49.

1117 Calonje E, Wadden C, Wilson-Jones E, Fletcher C. Spindle-cell non-pleomorphic atypical fibroxanthoma. Analysis of a series and delineation of a distinctive variant. Histopathology 1993, **22**: 247–254.

1118 Crowson AN, Carlson-Sweet K, Macinnis C, Taylor JR, Battaglia T, LaMar WL, Minor D, Sutter S, Hill T. Clear cell atypical fibroxanthoma: a clinicopathologic study. J Cutan Pathol 2002, **29**: 374–381.

1119 Dahl I. Atypical fibroxanthoma of the skin. A clinicopathological study of 57 cases. Acta Pathol Microbiol Scand (A) 1976, **84**: 183–197.

1120 Diaz-Cascajo C, Weyers W, Borghi S. Pigmented atypical fibroxanthoma: a tumor that may be easily mistaken for malignant melanoma. Am J Dermatopathol 2003, **25**: 1–5.

1121 Evans HL, Smith JL. Spindle cell squamous carcinomas and sarcoma-like tumors of the skin. A comparative study of 38 cases. Cancer 1980, **45**: 2687–2697.

1122 Fretzin DF, Helwig EB. Atypical fibroxanthoma of the skin. A clinicopathologic study of 140 cases. Cancer 1973, **31**: 1541–1552.

1123 Helwig EB, May D. Atypical fibroxanthoma of the skin with metastasis. Cancer 1986, **57**: 368–376.

1124 Hudson AW, Winkelmann RK. Atypical fibroxanthoma of the skin. A reappraisal of 19 cases in which the original diagnosis was spindle-cell squamous carcinoma. Cancer 1972, **29**: 413–422.

1125 Kempson RL, McGavran MH. Atypical fibroxanthomas of the skin. Cancer 1964, **17**: 1463–1471.

1126 Khan Z, Cockerell CJ. Atypical fibroxanthoma with osteoclast-like multinucleated giant cells. Am J Dermatopathol 1997, **19**: 174–179.

1127 Kuwano H, Hashimoto H, Enjoji M. Atypical fibroxanthomas distinguishable from spindle cell carcinoma in sarcoma-like skin lesions. A clinicopathologic and immunohistochemical study of 21 cases. Cancer 1985, **55**: 172–180.

1127a Lazar AJF, Fletcher DCM. Distinctive dermal clear cell mesenchymal neoplasm: analysis of 6 cases. Mod Pathol 2003, **16**: 93a.

1128 Leong AS-Y, Milios J. Atypical fibroxanthoma of the skin. A clinicopathological and immunohistochemical study and a discussion of its histogenesis. Histopathology 1987, **11**: 463–475.

1129 Longacre T, Smoller B, Rouse R. Atypical fibroxanthoma. Multiple immunohistologic profiles. Am J Surg Pathol 1993, **17**: 1199–1209.

1130 Ma CK, Zarbo RJ, Gown AM. Immunohistochemical characterization of atypical fibroxanthoma and dermatofibrosarcoma protuberans. Am J Clin Pathol 1992, **97**: 478–483.

1131 Monteagudo C, Calduch L, Navarro S, Joan-Figueroa A, Llombart-Bosch A. CD99 immunoreactivity in atypical fibroxanthoma: a common feature of diagnostic value. Am J Clin Pathol 2002, **117**: 126–131.

1132 Orosz Z, Kelemen J, Szentirmay Z. Granular cell variant of atypical fibroxanthoma. Pathol Oncol Res 1996, **2**: 244–247.

1133 Rachmaninoff N, McDonald JR, Cook JC. Sarcoma-like tumors of the skin following irradiation. Am J Clin Pathol 1961, **36**: 427–437.

1134 Requena L, Sangueza OP, Yus ES, Furio V. Clear-cell atypical fibroxanthoma: an uncommon histopathologic variant of atypical fibroxanthoma. J Cutan Pathol 1997, **24**: 176–182.

1135 Sakamoto A, Oda Y, Yamamoto H, Oshiro Y, Miyajima K, Itakura E, Tamiya S, Honda Y, Ishihara A, Iwamoto Y, Tsubeyoshi M. Calponin and h-caldesmon expression in atypical fibroxanthoma and superficial leiomyosarcoma. Virchows Arch 2002, **440**: 404–409.

1136 Silvis NG, Swanson PE, Manivel JC, Kaye VN, Wick MR. Spindle-cell and plemorphic neoplasms of the skin. A clinicopathologic and immunohistochemical study of 30 cases, with emphasis on "atypical fibroxanthomas." Am J Dermatopathol 1988, **10**: 9–19.

1137 Smith KJ, Skleton HG III, Morgan AM, Barrett TL, Lupton GP. Spindle cell neoplasms coexpressing cytokeratin and vimentin (metaplastic squamous cell carcinoma). J Cutan Pathol 1992, **19**: 286–293.

1138 Tomaszewski MM, Lupton GP. Atypical fibroxanthoma: an unusual variant with osteoclast-like giant cells. Am J Surg Pathol 1997, **21**: 213–218.

1139 Worrell TJ, Ansari Q, Ansari J, Cockerell C. Atypical fibroxanthoma. DNA ploidy analysis of 14 cases with possible histogenetic implications. J Cutan Pathol 1993, **20**: 211–215.

Dermatofibrosarcoma protuberans

1140 Abenoza P, Lillemoe T. CD34 and Factor XIIIa in the differential diagnosis of dermatofibroma and dermatofibrosarcoma protuberans. Am J Dermatopathol 1993, **15**: 429–434.

1141 Adams JT, Saltzstein SL. Metastasizing dermatofibrosarcoma protuberans. Report of two cases. Am Surg 1963, **29**: 879–886.

1142 Alguacil-Garcia A. Giant cell fibroblastoma recurring as dermatofibrosarcoma protuberans. Am J Surg Pathol 1991, **15**: 798–801.

1143 Banerjee SS, Harris M, Eyden BP, Hamid BNA. Granular cell variant of dermatofibrosarcoma protuberans. Histopathology 1990, **17**: 375–378.

1144 Beham A, Fletcher CDM. Dermatofibrosarcoma protuberans with areas resembling giant cell fibroblastoma. Report of two cases. Histopathology 1990, **17**: 167–169.

1145 Bowne WB, Antonescu CR, Leung DH, Katz SC, Hawkins WG, Woodruff JM, Brennan MF, Lewis JJ. Dermatofibrosarcoma protuberans: a clinicopathologic analysis of patients treated and followed at a single institution. Cancer 2000, **88**: 2711–2720.

1146 Calonje E, Fletcher CD. Myoid differentiation in dermatofibrosarcoma protuberans and its fibrosarcomatous variant: clinicopathologic analysis of 5 cases. J Cutan Pathol 1996, **23**: 30–36.

1147 Connelly J, Evans HL. Dermatofibrosarcoma protuberans. A clinicopathologic review with emphasis on fibrosarcomatous areas. Am J Surg Pathol 1992, **16**: 921–925.

1148 Davis DA, Sanchez RL. Atrophic and plaquelike dermatofibrosarcoma protuberans. Am J Dermatopathol 1998, **20**: 498–501.

1149 Ding J, Hashimoto H, Enjoji M. Dermatofibrosarcoma protuberans with fibrosarcomatous areas. A clinicopathologic study of nine cases and a comparison with allied tumors. Cancer 1989, **64**: 721–729.

1150 Ding J, Hashimoto H, Sugimoto T, Tsuneyoshi M, Enjoji M. Bednar tumor (pigmented dermatofibrosarcoma protuberans). An analysis of six cases. Acta Pathol Jpn 1990, **40**: 744–754.

1151 Dominguez-Malagon HR, Ordóñez NG, Mackay B. Dermatofibrosarcoma protuberans. Ultrastructural and immunocytochemical observations. Ultrastruct Pathol 1995, **19**: 281–290.

1152 Eisen RN, Tallini G. Metastatic dermatofibrosarcoma protuberans with fibrosarcomatous change in the absence of local recurrence. A case report of simultaneous occurrence with a malignant giant cell tumor of soft parts. Cancer 1993, **72**: 462–468.

1153 Fanburg-Smith JC, Miettinen M. Low-affinity nerve growth factor receptor (p75) in dermatofibrosarcoma protuberans and other nonneural tumors: a study of 1,150 tumors and fetal and adult normal tissues. Hum Pathol 2001, **32**: 976–983.

1154 Frierson HF, Cooper PH. Myxoid variant of dermatofibrosarcoma protuberans. Am J Surg Pathol 1983, **7**: 445–450.

1155 Goldblum JR, Tuthill RJ. CD34 and factor-XIIIa immunoreactivity in dermatofibrosarcoma protuberans and dermatofibroma. Am J Dermatopathol 1997, **19**: 147–153.

1156 Goldblum JR, Reith JD, Weiss SW. Sarcomas arising in dermatofibrosarcoma protuberans: a reappraisal of biologic behavior in eighteen cases treated by wide local excision with extended clinical follow-up. Am J Surg Pathol 2000, **24**: 1125–1130.

1157 Hashimoto K, Brownstein MH, Jakobiec FA. Dermatofibrosarcoma protuberans. A tumor with perineural and endoneural cell features. Arch Dermatol 1974, **110**: 874–885.

1158 Kutzner H. Expression of the human progenitor cell antigen CD34 (HPCA-1) distinguishes dermatofibrosarcoma protuberans from fibrous histocytoma in formalin-fixed, paraffin-embedded tissue. J Am Acad Dermatol 1993, **28:** 613–617.

1159 Leong ASY, Lim MHT. Immunohistochemical characteristics of dermatofibrosarcoma protuberans. Appl Immunohistochem 1994, **2:** 42–47.

1160 Ma CK, Zarbo RJ, Gown AM. Immunohistochemical characterization of atypical fibroxanthoma and dermatofibrosarcoma protuberans. Am J Clin Pathol 1992, **97:** 478–483.

1161 McKee PH, Fletcher CDM. Dermatofibrosarcoma protuberans presenting in infancy and childhood. J Cutan Pathol 1991, **18:** 241–246.

1162 Maire G, Pedeutour F, Coindre JM. COL1A1-PDGFB gene fusion demonstrates a common histogenetic origin for dermatofibrosarcoma protuberans and its granular cell variant. Am J Surg Pathol 2002, **26:** 932–937.

1163 Mentzel T, Beham A, Katenkamp D, Dei Tos AP, Fletcher CD. Fibrosarcomatous ("high-grade") dermatofibrosarcoma protuberans: clinicopathologic and immunohistochemical study of a series of 41 cases with emphasis on prognostic significance. Am J Surg Pathol 1998, **22:** 576–587.

1164 Michal M, Zamecnik M. Giant cell fibroblastoma with a dermatofibrosarcoma protuberans component. Am J Dermatopathol 1992, **14:** 549–552.

1165 O'Dowd J, Laidler P. Progression of dermatofibrosarcoma protuberans to malignant fibrous histiocytoma. Report of a case with implications for tumor histogenesis. Hum Pathol 1988, **19:** 368–370.

1166 Onoda N, Tsutsumi Y, Kakudo K, Ozawa A, Niizuma K, Ohkido M, Osamura RY. Pigmented dermatofibrosarcoma protuberans (Bednar tumor). An autopsy case with systemic metastases. Acta Pathol Jpn 1990, **40:** 935–940.

1167 Powers CN, Hurt MA, Frable WJ. Fine-needle aspiration biopsy. Dermatofibrosarcoma protuberans. Diagn Cytopathol 1993, **9:** 145–150.

1168 Rubin BP, Fletcher JA, Fletcher CDM. The histologic, genetic, and biological relationships between dermatofibrosarcoma protuberans and giant cell fibroblastoma: an unexpected story. Adv Anat Pathol 1997, **4:** 336–341.

1169 Sandberg AA, Bridge JA. Updates on the cytogenetics and molecular genetics of bone and soft tissue tumors. Dermatofibrosarcoma protuberans and giant cell fibroblastoma. Cancer Genet Cytogenet 2003, **140:** 1–12.

1170 Shmookler B, Enzinger FM, Weiss SW. Giant cell fibroblastoma. A juvenile form of dermatofibrosarcoma protuberans. Cancer 1989, **64:** 2154–2161.

1171 Sigel JE, Bergfeld WF, Goldblum JR. A morphologic study of dermatofibrosarcoma protuberans: expansion of a histologic profile. J Cutan Pathol 2000, **27:** 159–163.

1172 Sirvent N, Maire G, Pedeutour F. Genetics of dermatofibrosarcoma protuberans family of tumors: from ring chromosomes to tyrosine kinase inhibitor treatment. Genes Chromosomes Cancer 2003, **37:** 1–19.

1173 Taylor HB, Helwig EB. Dermatofibrosarcoma protuberans. Cancer 1962, **15:** 717–725.

1174 Terrier-Lacombe MJ, Guillou L, Maire G, Terrier P, Vince DR, de Saint Aubain Somerhausen N, Collin F, Pedeutour F, Coindre JM. Dermatofibrosarcoma protuberans, giant cell fibroblastoma, and hybrid lesions in children: clinicopathologic comparative analysis of 28 cases with molecular data – a study from the French Federation of Cancer Centers Sarcoma Group. Am J Surg Pathol 2002, **27:** 27–39.

1175 Weiss S, Nickoloff B. CD-34 is expressed by a distinctive cell population in peripheral nerve, nerve sheath tumors, and related lesions. Am J Surg Pathol 1993, **17:** 1039–1045.

1176 Wrotnowski U, Cooper PH, Shmookler BM. Fibrosarcomatous change in dermatofibrosarcoma protuberans. Am J Surg Pathol 1988, **12:** 287–293.

1177 Zelger BW, Ofner D, Zelger BG. Atrophic variants of dermatofibroma and dermatofibrosarcoma protuberans. Histopathology 1995, **26:** 519–528.

Malignant fibrous histiocytoma

1178 Helm KF. Malignant melanoma masquerading as malignant fibrous histiocytoma. Am J Dermatopathol 1997, **19:** 473–476.

1179 Kuwano H, Hashimoto H, Enjoji M. Atypical fibroxanthomas distinguishable from spindle cell carcinoma in sarcoma-like skin lesions. A clinicopathologic and immunohistochemical study of 21 cases. Cancer 1985, **55:** 172–180.

1179a Mansoor A, White CR. Myxofibrosarcoma presenting in the skin: clinicopathological features and differential diagnosis with cutaneous myxoid neoplasms. Am J Dermatopathol 2003, **25:** 281–286.

1180 Marrogi AJ, Dehner LP, Coffin CM, Wick MR. Atypical fibrous histiocytoma of the skin and subcutis in childhood and adolescence. J Cutan Pathol 1992, **19:** 268–277.

1181 Routh A, Hickman BT, Johnson WW. Malignant fibrous histiocytoma arising from chronic ulcer. Arch Dermatol 1985, **121:** 529–531.

1182 Wick MR, Fitzgibbon J, Swanson PE. Cutaneous sarcomas and sarcomatoid neoplasms of the skin. Semin Diagn Pathol 1993, **10:** 148–158.

Xanthoma

1183 Altman J, Winkelman RI. Xanthoma disseminatum. Arch Dermatol 1962, **86:** 582–596.

1184 Breier F, Zelger B, Reiter H, Gschnait F, Zelger BW. Papular xanthoma: a clinicopathological study of 10 cases. J Cutan Pathol 2002, **29:** 200–206.

1185 Busam KJ, Rosai J, Iversen C, Jungbluth AA. Xanthogranulomas with inconspicuous foam cells and giant cells mimicking malignant melanoma: a clinical, histologic, and immunohistochemical study of three cases. Am J Surg Pathol 2000, **24:** 864–869.

1186 Cooper PH. Eruptive xanthoma. A microscopic simulant of granuloma annulare. J Cutan Pathol 1986, **13:** 207–215.

1187 Cornblath WT, Dotan SA, Trobe JD, Headington JT. Varied clinical spectrum of necrobiotic xanthogranuloma. Ophthalmology 1992, **99:** 103–107.

1188 Duray PH, Johnston YE. Verruciform xanthoma of the nose in an elderly male. Am J Dermatopathol 1986, **8:** 237–240.

1189 Jeziorska M, Hassan A, Mackness MI, Woolley DE, Tullo AB, Lucas GS, Durrington PN. Clinical, biochemical, and immunohistochemical features of necrobiotic xanthogranulomatosis. J Clin Pathol 2003, **56:** 64–68.

1190 Mehregan DA, Winkelmann RK. Necrobiotic xanthogranuloma. Arch Dermatol 1992, **128:** 94–100.

1191 Mohsin SK, Lee MW, Amin MB, Stoler MH, Eyzaguirre E, Ma CK, Zarbo RJ. Cutaneous verruciform xanthoma: a report of five cases investigating the etiology and nature of xanthomatous cells. Am J Surg Pathol 1998, **22:** 479–487.

Juvenile xanthogranuloma

1191a Dehner LP. Juvenile xanthogranulomas in the first two decades of life. Am J Surg Pathol 2003, **27:** 579–593.

1191b Fanburg-Smith JC, Rubin BP, Miettinen M. Deep juvenile xanthogranuloma. A study of 30 intramuscular and 19 subcutaneous cases. Mod Pathol 2004, **16:** 11a.

1192 George DH, Scheitauer BW, Hilton DL, Fakhouri AJ, Kraus EW. Juvenile xanthogranuloma of peripheral nerve: a report of two cases. Am J Surg Pathol 2001, **25:** 521–526.

1193 Janney CG, Hurt MA, Santa Cruz DJ. Deep juvenile

xanthogranuloma. Subcutaneous and intramuscular forms. Am J Surg Pathol 1991, **15**: 1017–1018.

1194 Kraus MD, Haley JC, Ruiz R, Essry L, Moran CA, Fletcher CD. "Juvenile" xanthogranuloma: an immunophenotypic study with a reappraisal of histogenesis. Am J Dermatopathol 2001, **23**: 104–111.

1195 Marrogi AJ, Dehner LP, Coffin CM, Wick MR. Benign cutaneous histiocytic tumors in childhood and adolescence, excluding Langerhans' cell proliferations. A clinicopathologic and immunohistochemical analysis. Am J Dermatopathol 1992, **14**: 8–18.

1196 Nascimento AG. A clinicopathologic and immunohistochemical comparative study of cutaneous and intramuscular forms of juvenile xanthogranuloma. Am J Surg Pathol 1997, **21**: 645–652.

1197 Sangüeza OP, Salmon JK, White CR Jr, Beckstead JH. Juvenile vanthogranuloma. A clinical, histopathologic and immunohistochemical study. J Cutan Pathol 1995, **22**: 327–335.

1198 Senger C, Gonzalez-Crussi F. Testicular juvenile xanthogranuloma: a case report. J Urol Pathol 1999, **10**: 159–168.

1199 Sonoda T, Hashimoto H, Enjoji M. Juvenile xanthogranuloma. Clinicopathologic analysis and immunohistochemical study of 57 patients. Cancer 1985, **56**: 2280–2286.

1200 Tahan SR, Pastel-Levy C, Bhan AK, Mihm MC Jr. Juvenile vanthogranuloma Clinical and pathologic characterization. Arch Pathol Lab Med 1989, **113**: 1057–1061.

1201 Zelger B, Cerio R, Orchard G, Wilson-Jones E. Juvenile and adult xanthogranuloma. Am J Surg Pathol 1994, **18**: 126–135.

1202 Zelger BWH, Staudacher C, Orchard G, Wilson-Jones E, Burgdorf WHC. Solitary and generalized variants of spindle cell xanthogranuloma (progressive nodular histiocytosis). Histopathology 1995, **27**: 11–20.

Other histiocytic proliferations

1203 Alexis JB, Poppiti RJ, Turbat-Herrera E, Smith MD. Congenital self-healing reticulohistiocytosis. Report of a case with 7-year follow-up and a review of the literature. Am J Dermatopathol 1991, **13**: 189–194.

1204 Azulay RD. Histopathology of skin lesions in leprosy. Int J Lepr 1971, **39**: 244.

1205 Barrow MV, Holubar K. Multicentric reticulohistiocytosis. A review of 33 patients. Medicine 1969, **48**: 287–305.

1206 Brenn T, Calonje E, Granter SR, Leonard N, Grayson W, Fletcher CD, McKee PH. Cutaneous Rosai-Dorfman disease is a distinct clinical entity. Am J Dermatopathol 2002, **24**: 385–391.

1207 Caputo R, Alessi E, Berti E. Cutaneous histiocytoses in children. Histopathologic, ultrastructural, and immunohistochemical findings. Prog Surg Pathol 1989, **10**: 111–126.

1208 Chu P, Leboit PE. The histologic features of cutaneous sinus histiocytosis. A study of cases both with and without systemic involvement. J Cutan Pathol 1992, **19**: 201–206.

1209 Luz FB, Gaspar TAP, Kalil-Gaspar N, Ramos-e-Silva M. Multicentric reticulohistiocytosis. J Eur Acad Dermatol Venereol 2001, **15**: 524–531.

1210 Mangi MH, Mufti GJ. Multicentric reticulohistiocytosis. Detailed immunophenotyping confirms macrophage origin. Am J Surg Pathol 1990, **14**: 687–693.

1211 Marrogi AJ, Dehner LP, Coffin CM, Wick MR. Benign cutaneous histiocytic tumors in childhood and adolescence, excluding Langerhans' cell proliferations. A clinicopathologic and immunohistochemical analysis. Am J Dermatopathol 1992, **14**: 8–18.

1212 Mihm MC Jr, Clark WH, Reed RJ. The histiocytic infiltrates of the skin. Hum Pathol 1974, **5**: 45–54.

1213 Perrin C, Lacour J, Michiels J, Flory P, Ziegler G, Ortonne J. Multicentric reticulohistiocytosis. Immunohistological and

ultrastructural study – a pathology of dendritic cell lineage. Am J Dermatopathol 1992, **14**: 418–425.

1214 Perrin C, Michiels JF, Lacour JP, Chagnon A, Fuzibet JG. Sinus histiocytosis (Rosai-Dorfman disease) clinically limited to the skin. An immunohistochemical and ultrastructural study. J Cutan Pathol 1993, **20**: 368–374.

1215 Purvis WE III, Helwig EB. Reticulohistiocytic granuloma ("reticulohistiocytoma") of the skin. Am J Clin Pathol 1954, **24**: 1005–1015.

1216 Tani M, Hori K, Nakanishi T, Iwasaki T, Ogawa Y, Jimbo T. Multicentric reticulohistiocytosis. Electron microscopic and ultracytochemical studies. Arch Dermatol 1981, **117**: 495–499.

1217 Thawerani H, Sanchez RL, Rosai J, Dorfman RF. The cutaneous manifestations of sinus histiocytosis with massive lymphadenopathy. Arch Dermatol 1978, **114**: 191–197.

1218 Zelger B, Cerio R, Soyer HP, Misch K, Orchard G, Wilson-Jones E. Reticulohistiocytoma and multicentric reticulohistiocytosis. Histopathologic and immunophenotypic distinct entities. Am J Dermatopathol 1994, **16**: 577–584.

Smooth muscle tumors

1219 Dahl I, Angervall L. Cutaneous and subcutaneous leiomyosarcoma. A clinicopathologic study of 47 patients. Pathol Europ 1974, **9**: 307–315.

1220 Diaz-Cascajo C, Borghi S, Weyers W. Desmoplastic leiomyosarcoma of the skin. Am J Dermatopathol 2000, **22**: 251–256.

1221 Fields JP, Helwig EB. Leiomyosarcoma of the skin and subcutaneous tissue. Cancer 1981, **47**: 156–169.

1222 Hachisuga T, Hashimoto H, Enjoji M. Angioleiomyoma. A clinicopathologic reappraisal of 562 cases. Cancer 1984, **54**: 126–130.

1223 Kaddu S, Beham A, Cerroni L, Humer-Fuchs U, Salmhofer W, Kerl H, Soyer HP. Cutaneous leiomyosarcoma. Am J Surg Pathol 1997, **21**: 979–987.

1224 Kawagishi N, Kashiwagi T, Ibe M, Manabe A, Ishida-Yamamoto A, Hashimoto Y, Iizuka H. Pleomorphic angioleiomyoma. Am J Dermatopathol 2000, **22**: 268–271.

1225 Kiuru M, Launonen V, Hietala M, Aittomaki K, Vierimaa O, Salovaara R, Arola J, Pukkala E, Sistonen P, Herva R, Aaltonen LA. Familial cutaneous leiomyomatosis is a two-hit condition associated with renal cell cancer of characteristic histopathology. Am J Pathol 2001, **159**: 825–829.

1226 Mahalingam M, Goldberg LJ. Atypical pilar leiomyoma: cutaneous counterpart of uterine symplastic leiomyoma? Am J Dermatopathol 2001, **23**: 299–303.

1227 Massi D, Biancalani M, Franchi A, Santucci M. Clear-cell smooth muscle tumor of the skin. Mod Pathol 1998, **11**: 1021–1025.

1228 Orlow SJ, Kamino H, Lawrence RL. Multiple subcutaneous leiomyosarcomas in an adolescent with AIDS. Am J Pediatr Hematol Oncol 1992, **14**: 265–268.

1229 Raj S, Calonje E, Kraus M, Kavanagh G, Newman PL, Fletcher CD. Cutaneous pilar leiomyoma: clinicopathologic analysis of 53 lesions in 45 patients. Am J Dermatopathol 1997, **19**: 2–9.

1230 Suster S. Epithelioid leiomyosarcoma of the skin and subcutaneous tissue. Clinicopathologic, immunohistochemical, and ultrastructural study of five cases. Am J Surg Pathol 1994, **18**: 232–240.

1231 Varela-Duran J, Oliva H, Rosai J. Vascular leiomyosarcoma. The malignant counterpart of vascular leiomyoma. Cancer 1979, **44**: 1684–1691.

Skeletal muscle tumors

1232 Farris PE, Manning S, Vuitch F. Rhabdomyomatous mesenchymal hamartoma. Am J Dermatopathol 1994, **16**: 73–75.

1233 Hoang MP, Sinkre P, Albores-Saavedra J. Rhabdomyosarcoma arising in a congenital melanocytic nevus. Am J Dermatopathol 2002, **24:** 26–29.

1234 O'Connell JX, Rosenberg AE. Multiple cutaneous neuromuscular choristomas. Report of a case and a review of the literature. Am J Surg Pathol 1990, **14:** 93–96.

1235 Sahn EE, Garen PD, Pai GS, Levkoff AH, Hagerty RC, Maize JC. Multiple rhabdomyomatous mesenchymal hamartomas of the skin. Am J Dermatopathol 1990, **12:** 485–491.

1236 Sanchez RL, Raimer SS. Clinical and histologic features of striated muscle hamartoma. Possible relationship to Delleman's syndrome. J Cutan Pathol 1994, **21:** 40–46.

1237 Verdolini R, Goteri G, Brancosini D, Collina G, Simonetti O, Offidani A, Giangiacomi M. Adult rhabdomyoma: report of two cases of rhabdomyoma of the lip and of eyelid. Am J Dermatopathol 2000, **22:** 264–267.

1238 Wong T-Y, Suster S. Primary cutaneous sarcomas showing rhabdomyoblastic differentiation. Histopathology 1995, **26:** 25–32.

Peripheral nerve tumors

1239 Argenyi ZB. Immunohistochemical characterization of palisaded, encapsulated neuroma. J Cutan Pathol 1990, **17:** 329–335.

1240 Argenyi Z, Leboit P, Santa Cruz D, Swanson P, Kutzner H. Never sheath myxoma (neurothekeoma) of the skin. Light microscopic and immunohistochemical reappraisal of the cellular variant. J Cutan Pathol 1993, **20:** 294–303.

1241 Barnhill RL, Mihm MC Jr. Cellular neurothekeoma. A distinctive variant of neurothekeoma mimicking nevomelanocytic tumors. Am J Surg Pathol 1990, **14:** 113–120.

1242 Busam KJ, Mentzel T, Colpaert C, Barnhill RL, Fletcher CD. Atypical or worrisome features in cellular neurothekeoma: a study of 10 cases. Am J Surg Pathol 1998, **22:** 1067–1072.

1243 Calonje E, Wilson-Jones E, Smith N, Fletcher CDM. Cellular "neurothekeoma." An epithelioid variant of pilar leiomyoma? Morphological and immunohistochemical analysis of a series. Histopathology 1992, **20:** 397–404.

1244 Dabski C, Reiman H, Muller S. Neurofibrosarcoma of skin and subcutaneous tissues. Mayo Clin Proc 1990, **65:** 164–282.

1245 del Rio E, Sanchez Yus E, Simon P, Vazquez Veiga HA. Stimulation of folliculo-sebaceous proliferations by neurofibromas: a report of two cases. J Cutan Pathol 1998, **25:** 228–232.

1246 Fetsch JF, Miettinen M. Sclerosing perineurioma: a clinicopathologic study of 19 cases of a distinctive soft tissue lesion with a predilection for the fingers and palms of young adults. Am J Surg Pathol 1997, **21:** 1433–1442.

1247 Fletcher CDM. Solitary circumscribed neuroma of the skin (so-called palisaded, encapsulated neuroma). A clinicopathologic and immunohistochemical study. Am J Surg Pathol 1989, **13:** 574–580.

1248 Gallager RL, Helwig EB. Neurothekeoma. A benign cutaneous tumor of neural origin. Am J Clin Pathol 1980, **74:** 759–764.

1249 Holden CA, Wilson Jones E, MacDonald DM. Cutaneous lobular neuromyxoma. Br J Dermatol 1982, **106:** 211–215.

1250 Husain S, Silvers DN, Halperin AJ, McNutt NS. Histologic spectrum of neurothekeoma and the value of immunoperoxidase staining for S-100 protein in distinguishing it from melanoma. Am J Dermatopathol 1994, **16:** 496–503.

1251 Jaffer S, Eusebi V, Rosai J. Neurothekeomas and plexiform fibrohistiocytic tumors: a relationship? Lab Invest 2000, **80:** 11A.

1252 Laskin WB, Fetsch JF, Miettinen M. The "neurothekeoma": immunohistochemical analysis distinguishes the true nerve sheath myxoma from its mimics. Hum Pathol 2000, **31:** 1230–1241.

1253 Megahed M. Palisaded encapsulated neuroma (solitary circumscribed neuroma). A clinicopathologic and immunohistochemical study. Am J Dermatopathol 1994, **16:** 120–125.

1254 Reed RJ, Fine RM, Meltzer HD. Palisaded, encapsulated neuromas of the skin. Arch Dermatol 1972, **106:** 865–870.

1255 Requena L, Sangu-za OP. Benign neoplasms with neural differentiation. A review. Am J Dermatopathol 1995, **17:** 75–96.

1256 Requena L, Grosshans E, Kutzner H, Ryckaert C, Cribier B, Resnik KS, LeBoit PE. Epithelial sheath neuroma: a new entity. Am J Surg Pathol 2000, **24:** 190–196.

1257 Robson AM, Calonje E. Cutaneous perineurioma: a poorly recognized tumour often misdiagnosed as epithelioid histiocytoma. Histopathology 2000, **37:** 332–339.

1258 Rosati LA, Fratamico CM, Eusebi V. Cellular neurothekeoma. Appl Pathol 1986, **4:** 186–191.

1259 Sanguza OP, Requena L. Neoplasms with neural differentiation: a review. Part II: malignant neoplasms. Am J Dermatopathol 1998, **20:** 89–102.

1260 Tsang WYW, Chan JKC. Epithelioid variant of solitary circumscribed neuroma of the skin. Histopathology 1992, **20:** 439–441.

1261 Wang AR, May D, Bourne P, Scott G. PGP9.5: a marker for cellular neurothekeoma. Am J Surg Pathol 1999, **23:** 1401–1407.

1262 Zelger BG, Steiner H, Kutzner H, Maier H, Zelger B. Cellular 'neurothekeoma': an epithelioid variant of dermatofibroma? Histopathology 1998, **32:** 414–422.

Vascular tumors and tumorlike conditions

1263 Johnson WC. Pathology of cutaneous vascular tumors. Int J Dermatol 1976, **15:** 239–270.

1264 Ryan TJ, Cherry GW. Vascular birthmarks. Pathogenesis and management. New York, 1987, Oxford Press.

1265 Tsang WY, Chan JK, Fletcher CD. Recently characterized vascular tumours of skin and soft tissues. Histopathology 1991, **19:** 489–501.

Hemangioma

1266 Aloi F, Tomasini C, Pippione M. Microvenular hemangioma. Am J Dermatopathol 1993, **15:** 534–538.

1267 Chan JKC, Fletcher CDM, Hicklin GA, Rosai J. Glomeruloid hemangioma. A distinctive cutaneous lesion of multicentric Castleman's disease associated with POEMS syndrome. Am J Surg Pathol 1990, **14:** 1036–1046.

1268 Connelly MG, Winkelmann RK. Acral arteriovenous tumor. A clinicopathologic review. Am J Surg Pathol 1985, **9:** 15–21.

1269 Guillou L, Calonje E, Speight P, Rosai J, Fletcher CD. Hobnail hemangioma: a pseudomalignant vascular lesion with a reappraisal of targetoid hemosiderotic hemangioma. Am J Surg Pathol 1999, **23:** 97–105.

1270 Hunt SJ, Santa Cruz DJ, Barr RJ. Microvenular hemangioma. J Cutan Pathol 1991, **18:** 235–240.

1271 Imperial R, Helwig E. Angiokeratoma. A clinicopathologic study. Arch Dermatol 1967, **95:** 166–175.

1272 Imperial R, Helwig E. Verrucous hemangioma. A clinico-pathologic study of 21 cases. Arch Dermatol 1967, **96:** 247–253.

1273 Johnson WC. Pathology of cutaneous vascular tumors. Int J Dermatol 1976, **15:** 239–270.

1274 Kishimoto S, Takenaka H, Shibagaki R, Noda Y, Yamamoto M, Yasuno H. Glomeruloid hemangioma in POEMS syndrome shows two different immunophenotypic endothelial cells. J Cutan Pathol 2000, **27:** 87–92.

1275 Koutlas IG, Jessurun J. Arteriovenous hemangioma. A clinicopathological and immunohistochemical study. J Cutan Pathol 1994, **21:** 343–349.

1276 Mentzel T, Partanen TA, Kutzner H. Hobnail hemangioma

("targetoid hemosiderotic hemangioma"): clinicopathologic and immunohistochemical analysis of 62 cases. J Cutan Pathol 1999, **26**: 279–286.

Lymphangioma

1277 Cossu S, Satta R, Cottoni F, Massarelli G. Lymphangioma-like variant of Kaposi's sarcoma: clinicopathologic study of seven cases with review of the literature. Am J Dermatopathol 1997, **19**: 16–22.

1278 Flanagan BP, Helwig EB. Cutaneous lymphangioma. Arch Dermatol 1977, **113**: 24–30.

1279 Gange RW, Jones EW. Lymphangioma-like Kaposi's sarcoma. A report of three cases. Br J Dermatol 1979, **100**: 327–334.

1280 Guillou L, Fletcher CD. Benign lymphangioendothelioma (acquired progressive lymphangioma): a lesion not to be confused with well-differentiated angiosarcoma and patch stage Kaposi's sarcoma: clinicopathologic analysis of a series. Am J Surg Pathol 2000, **24**: 1047–1057.

1281 Peachey R, Whimster I. Lymphangioma of skin. A review of 65 cases. Br J Dermatol 1970, **83**: 519–527.

1282 Prioleau PG, Santa Cruz DJ. Lymphangioma circumscriptum following radical mastectomy and radiation therapy. Cancer 1978, **42**: 1989–1991.

1283 Watanabe M, Kishiyama K, Ohkawara A. Acquired progressive lymphangioma. J Am Acad Dermatol 1983, **8**: 663–667.

1284 Whimster IW. The pathology of lymphangioma circumscriptum. Br J Dermatol 1976, **94**: 473–486.

Pyogenic granuloma and related lesions

1285 Cooper PH, McAllister HA, Helwig EB. Intravenous pyogenic granuloma. Am J Surg Pathol 1979, **3**: 221–228.

1286 Cooper PH, Mills SE. Subcutaneous granuloma pyogenicum. Lobular capillary hemangioma. Arch Dermatol 1982, **118**: 30–33.

1287 Hunt SJ. Two pyogenic granulomas arising in an epidermoid cyst. Am J Dermatopathol 1989, **11**: 360–363.

1288 Kapadia SB, Heffner DK. Pitfalls in the histopathologic diagnosis of pyogenic granuloma. Eur Arch Otorhinolaryngol 1992, **249**: 195–200.

1289 Leboit PE. Lobular capillary proliferation. The underlying process in diverse benign cutaneous vascular neoplasms and reactive conditions. Semin Dermatol 1990, **8**: 298–310.

1290 McMenanim ME, Fletcher CD. Reactive angioendotheliomatosis: a study of 15 cases demonstrating a wide clinicopathologic spectrum. Am J Surg Pathol 2002, **26**: 685–697.

1291 Mills SE, Cooper PH, Fechner RE. Lobular capillary hemangioma. The underlying lesion of pyogenic granuloma. A study of 73 cases from the oral and nasal mucous membranes. Am J Surg Pathol 1980, **4**: 471–479.

1292 Nappi O, Wick MR. Disseminated lobular capillary hemangioma (pyogenic granuloma). A clinicopathologic study of two cases. Am J Dermatopathol 1986, **8**: 379–385.

1293 Nichols G, Gaffey M, Mills S, Weiss L. Lobular capillary hemangioma. An immunohistochemical study including steroid hormone receptor status. Am J Clin Pathol 1992, **97**: 770–775.

1294 Padilla RS, Orkin M, Rosai J. Acquired "tufted" angioma (progressive capillary hemangioma). A distinctive clinicopathologic entity related to lobular capillary hemangioma. Am J Dermatopathol 1987, **9**: 292–300.

1295 Renshaw A, Rosai J. Benign atypical vascular lesions of the lip. A study of 12 cases. Am J Surg Pathol 1993, **17**: 557–565.

1296 Swerlick RA, Cooper PH. Pyogenic granuloma (lobular capillary hemangioma) within port-wine stains. J Am Acad Dermatol 1983, **8**: 627–630.

1297 Warner J, Wilson Jones E. Pyogenic granuloma recurring with multiple satellites. A report of 11 cases. Br J Dermatol 1968, **80**: 218–227.

1298 Wilson-Jones E, Orkin M. Tufted angioma (angioblastoma). A benign progressive angioma, not to be confused with Kaposi's sarcoma or low-grade angiosarcoma. J Am Acad Dermatol 1989, **20**: 214–225.

Masson's hemangioma

1299 Albrecht S, Kahn HJ. Immunohistochemistry of intravascular papillary endothelial hyperplasia. J Cutan Pathol 1990, **17**: 16–21.

1300 Barr RJ, Graham JH, Sherwin LA. Intravascular papillary endothelial hyperplasia. A benign lesion mimicking angiosarcoma. Arch Dermatol 1978, **114**: 723–726.

1301 Clearkin KP, Enzinger FM. Intravascular papillary endothelial hyperplasia. Arch Pathol Lab Med 1976, **100**: 441–444.

1302 Hashimoto H, Daimaru Y, Enjoji M. Intravascular papillary endothelial hyperplasia. A clinicopathologic study of 91 cases. Am J Dermatopathol 1983, **5**: 539–546.

1303 Kuo T, Sayers CP, Rosai J. Masson's "vegetant intravascular hemangioendothelioma." A lesion often mistaken for angiosarcoma. Study of seventeen cases located in the skin and soft tissues. Cancer 1976, **38**: 1227–1236.

Epithelioid hemangioma

1304 Allen PW, Ramakrishna B, MacCormac LB. The histiocytoid hemangiomas and other controversies. Pathol Annu 1992, **27**(Pt 2): 51–88.

1304a Brenn T, Fletcher CDM. Cutaneous epithelioid angiomatous nodule. A distinct vascular lesion in the morphologic spectrum of epithelioid hemangioma. Mod Pathol 2003, **16**: 88a.

1305 Burrall BA, Barr RJ, King F. Cutaneous histiocytoid hemangioma. Arch Dermatol 1982, **118**: 166–170.

1306 Castro C, Winkelmann RK. Angiolymphoid hyperplasia with eosinophilia in the skin. Cancer 1974, **34**: 1696–1705.

1307 Chan JKC, Hui PK, Ng CS, Yuen NWF, Kung ITM, Gwi E. Epithelioid haemangioma (angiolymphoid hyperplasia with eosinophilia) and Kimura's disease in Chinese. Histopathology 1989, **15**: 557–574.

1308 Cooper PH. Is histiocytoid hemangioma a specific pathologic entity? Am J Surg Pathol 1988, **12**: 815–817.

1309 Fetsch JF, Weiss SW. Observations concerning the pathogenesis of epithelioid hemangioma (angiolymphoid hyperplasia). Mod Pathol 1991, **4**: 449–455.

1310 Helander SD, Peters MS, Kuo T-T, Su WPD. Kimura's disease and angiolymphoid hyperplasia with eosinophilia. New observations from immunohisto-chemical studies of lymphocyte markers, endothelial antigens, and granulocyte proteins. J Cutan Pathol 1995, **22**: 319–326.

1311 Marrogi AJ, Hunt SJ, Santa Cruz DJ. Cutaneous epithelioid angiosarcoma. Am J Dermatopathol 1990, **12**: 350–356.

1312 Mentzel T, Beham A, Calonje E, Katenkamp D, Fletcher CD. Epithelioid hemangioendothelioma of skin and soft tissues: clinicopathologic and immunohistochemical study of 30 cases. Am J Surg Pathol 1997, **21**: 363–374.

1313 O'Connell J, Kattapuram S, Mankin H, Bhan A, Rosenberg A. Epithelioid hemangioma of bone. A tumor often mistaken for low-grade angiosarcoma or malignant hemangioendothelioma. Am J Surg Pathol 1993, **17**: 610–617.

1314 Olsen TG, Helwig EB. Angiolymphoid hyperplasia with eosinophilia. A clinicopathologic study of 116 patients. J Am Acad Dermatol 1985, **12**: 781–796.

1315 Ose D, Vollmer R, Shelburne J, McComb R, Harrelson J. Histiocytoid hemangioma of the skin and scapula. A case report with electron microscopy and immunohistochemistry. Cancer 1983, **51**: 1656–1662.

1316 Quante M, Patel NK, Hill S, Merchant W, Courtauld E,

Newman P, McKee PH. Epithelioid hemangioendothelioma presenting in the skin: a clinicopathologic study of eight cases. Am J Dermatopathol 1999, **20**: 541–546.

1317 Reed RJ, Terazakis N. Subcutaneous angioblastic lymphoid hyperplasia with eosinophilia (Kimura's disease). Cancer 1972, **29**: 489–497.

1318 Resnik K, Kantor G, Spielvogel R, Ryan E. Cutaneous epithelioid hemangioendothelioma without systemic involvement. Am J Dermatopathol 1993, **15**: 272–276.

1319 Rosai J, Gold J, Landy R. The histiocytoid hemangiomas. A unifying concept embracing several previously described entities of skin, soft tissues, large vessels, bone and heart. Hum Pathol 1979, **10**: 707–730.

1320 Tsang WY, Chan JK. The family of epithelioid vascular tumors. Histol Histopathol 1993, **8**: 187–212.

1321 Urabe A, Tsuneyoshi M, Enjoji M. Epithelioid hemangioma versus Kimura's disease. A comparative clinicopathologic study. Am J Surg Pathol 1987, **11**: 758–766.

1322 Verret J-L, Avenel M, Francois H, Baudouin M, Alain P. Hemangiomes histiocytoides des pulpes digitales. Ann Dermatol Venereol 1983, **110**: 251–257.

Kaposi's sarcoma

1323 Ablashi DV, Chatlynne LG, Whitman JE Jr, Cesarman E. Spectrum of Kaposi's sarcoma-associated herpesvirus, or human herpesvirus 8, diseases. Clin Microbiol Rev 2002, **15**: 439–464.

1324 Ackerman LV, Murray JF (eds). Symposium on Kaposi's sarcoma. Acta Un Int Cancer 1962, **18**: 312–511.

1325 Akhtar M, Bunuan H, Ali MA, Godwin JT. Kaposi's sarcoma in renal transplant recipients. Ultrastructural and immunoperoxidase study of four cases. Cancer 1984, **53**: 258–266.

1326 Antman K, Chang Y. Kaposi's sarcoma. N Engl J Med 2000, **342**: 1027–1038.

1327 Auerbach HE, Brooks JJ. Kaposi's sarcoma. Neoplasia or hyperplasia? Surg Pathol 1989, **2**: 19–28.

1327a Barozzi P, Luppi M, Facchetti F, Mecucci C, Alu M, Sarid R, Rasini V, Ravazzini L, Rossi E, Festa S, Crescenzi B, Wolf DG, Schultz TF, Torelli G. Post-transplant Kaposi sarcoma originates from the seeding donor-derived progenitors. Nat Med 2003, **9**: 554–561.

1328 Beckstead JH, Wood GS, Fletcher V. Evidence for the origin of Kaposi's sarcoma from lymphatic endothelium. Am J Pathol 1985, **119**: 294–300.

1329 Blumenfeld W, Egbert BM, Sagebiel RW. Differential diagnosis of Kaposi's sarcoma. Arch Pathol Lab Med 1985, **109**: 123–127.

1330 Brenner B, Weissmann-Brenner A, Rakowsky E, Weltfriend S, Fenig E, Friedman-Birnbaum R, Sulkes A, Linn S. Classical Kaposi sarcoma: prognostic factor analysis of 248 patients. Cancer 2002, **95**: 1982–1987.

1331 Burgdorf WHC, Mukai K, Rosai J. Immunohistochemical identification of factor VIII-related antigen in endothelial cells of cutaneous lesions of alleged vascular nature. Am J Clin Pathol 1981, **75**: 167–171.

1332 Chor PJ, Santa Cruz DJ. Kaposi's sarcoma. A clinicopathologic review and differential diagnosis. J Cutan Pathol 1992, **19**: 6–20.

1333 Cossu S, Satta P, Cottoni F, Massarelli G. Lymphangioma-like variant of Kaposi's sarcoma: clinicopathologic study of seven cases with review of the literature. Am J Dermatopathol 1997, **19**: 16–22.

1334 Dictor M, Andersson C. Lymphaticovenous differentiation in Kaposi's sarcoma. Cellular phenotypes by stage. Am J Pathol 1988, **130**: 411–417.

1335 Flotte TJ, Hatcher VA, Friedman-Kien AE. Factor VIII-related antigen in Kaposi's sarcoma in young homosexual men. Arch Dermatol 1984, **120**: 180–182.

1336 Folpe AL, Veikkola T, Valtola R, Weiss SW. Vascular endothelial growth factor receptor-3 (VEGFR-3): a marker of vascular tumors with presumed lymphatic differentiation, including Kaposi's sarcoma, kaposiform and Dabska-type hemangioendotheliomas, and a subset of angiosarcomas. Mod Pathol 2000, **13**: 180–185.

1337 Frizzera G, Banks PM, Massarelli G, Rosai J. A systemic lymphoproliferative disorder with morphologic features of Castleman's disease. Pathological findings in 15 patients. Am J Surg Pathol 1983, **7**: 211–231.

1338 Fukunaga M, Silverberg SG. Kaposi's sarcoma in patients with acquired immune deficiency syndrome. A flow cytometric DNA analysis of 26 lesions in 21 patients. Cancer 1990, **66**: 758–764.

1339 Fukunaga M, Silverberg SG. Hyaline globules in Kaposi's sarcoma. A light microscopic and immunohistochemical study. Mod Pathol 1991, **4**: 187–190.

1340 Gallo RC. The enigmas of Kaposi's sarcoma. Science 1998, **282**: 1837–1839.

1341 Garrett TJ, Lange M, Ashford A, Thomas L. Kaposi's sarcoma in heterosexual intravenous drug users. Cancer 1985, **55**: 1146–1148.

1342 Geraminejad P, Memar O, Aronson I, Rady PL, Hengge U, Tyring S. Kaposi's sarcoma and other manifestations of human herpesvirus 8. J Am Acad Dermatol 2002, **47**: 641–655.

1343 Gray MH, Trimble CL, Zim J, McNutt NS, Smoller BR, Varghese M. Relationship of Factor XIIIa positive dermal dendrocytes to Kaposi's sarcoma. Arch Pathol Lab Med 1991, **115**: 791–796.

1344 Guarda LG, Silva EG, Ordóñez NG, Smith JL Jr. Factor VIII in Kaposi's sarcoma. Am J Clin Pathol 1981, **76**: 197–200.

1345 Herman PS, Shogreen ME, White WL. The evaluation of human herpesvirus 8 (Kaposi's sarcoma-associated herpesvirus) in cutaneous lesions of Kaposi's sarcoma: a study of formalin-fixed paraffin-embedded tissue. Am J Dermatopathol 1998, **20**: 7–11.

1346 Hoerl HD, Goldblum JR. Immunoreactivity pattern of CD31 and CD68 in 28 cases of Kaposi's sarcoma: evidence supporting endothelial differentiation in the spindle cell component. Appl Immunohistochem 1997, **5**: 173–178.

1347 Huang YQ, Li JJ, Moscatelli D, Basilico C, Nicolaides A, Zhang WG, Poiesz BJ, Friedman-Kien AE. Expression of int-2 oncogene in Kaposi's sarcoma lesions. J Clin Invest 1993, **91**: 1191–1197.

1348 Ioachim HL, Adsay VB, Giancotti FR, Dorsett B, Melamed J. Kaposi's sarcoma of internal organs. A multiparameter study of 86 cases. Cancer 1995, **75**: 1376–1385.

1349 Iscovich J, Boffetta P, Franceshi S, Azizi E, Sarid R. Classic Kaposi sarcoma: epidemiology and risk factors. Cancer 2000, **88**: 500–517.

1350 Jin YT, Tsai ST, Yan JJ, Hsiao JH, Lee YY, Su IJ. Detection of Kaposi's sarcoma-associated herpesvirus-like DNA sequence in vascular lesions. A reliable diagnostic marker for Kaposi's sarcoma. Am J Clin Pathol 1996, **105**: 360–363.

1351 Kao GF, Johnson FB, Sulica VI. The nature of hyaline (eosinophilic) globules and vascular slits of Kaposi's sarcoma. Am J Dermatopathol 1990, **12**: 256–267.

1352 Katano H, Sato Y, Kurata T, Mori S, Sata T. High expression of HHV-8-encoded ORF73 protein in spindle-shaped cells of Kaposi's sarcoma. Am J Pathol 1999, **155**: 47–52.

1353 Krigel RL, Friedman-Kien AE. Epidemic Kaposi's sarcoma. Semin Oncol 1990, **17**: 350–360.

1354 Lee WA, Hutchins GM. Cluster analysis of the metastatic patterns of human immunodeficiency virus-associated Kaposi's sarcoma. Hum Pathol 1992, **23**: 306–311.

1355 Li JJ, Huang YQ, Cockerell CJ, Friedman-Kien AE. Localization of human herpes-like virus type 8 in vascular endothelial cells and perivascular spindle-shaped cells of Kaposi's sarcoma lesions by in situ hybridization. Am J Pathol 1996, **148**: 1741–1748.

1356 McNutt NS, Fletcher V, Conant MA. Early lesions of Kaposi's sarcoma in homosexual men. An ultrastructural comparison with other vascular proliferations in skin. Am J Pathol 1983, **111**: 62–77.

1357 Marshall ME, Hatfield ST, Hatfield DR. Arteriovenous malformation simulating Kaposi's sarcoma (pseudo-Kaposi's sarcoma). Arch Dermatol 1985, **121**: 99–101.

1358 Martinelli PT, Tyring SK. Human herpesvirus 8. Dermatol Clin 2002, **20**: 307–314.

1359 Nickoloff BJ. The human progenitor cell antigen (CD34) is localized on endothelial cells, dermal dendritic cells, and perifollicular cells in formalinfixed normal skin, and on proliferating endothelial cells and stromal spindle-shaped cells in Kaposi's sarcoma. Arch Dermatol 1991, **127**: 523–529.

1360 Nickoloff BJ, Griffiths CEM. Factor XIIIa-expressing dermal dendrocytes in AIDS-associated cutaneous Kaposi's sarcoma. Science 1989, **243**: 1736–1737.

1361 Niedt WG, Myskowski PL, Urmacher A, Niedzwiecki D, Chapman D, Safai B. Histology of early lesions of AIDS-associated Kaposi's sarcoma. Mod Pathol 1990, **3**: 64–70.

1362 O'Connell KM. Kaposi's sarcoma. Histopathological study of 159 cases from Malawi. J Clin Pathol 1977, **30**: 687–695.

1363 Parravicini C, Chandran B, Corbellino M, Berti E, Paulli M, Moore PS, Chang Y. Differential viral protein expression in Kaposi's sarcoma-associated herpesvirus-infected diseases. Kaposi's sarcoma, primary effusion lymphoma, and multicentric Castleman's disease. Am J Pathol 2000, **156**: 743–749.

1363a Patel RM, Goldblum JR, His Ed. Utility of the immunohistochemical detection of HHV-8 in the diagnosis of Kaposi's sarcoma. Mod Pathol 2003, **16**: 19a.

1364 Rabkin CS, Janz S, Lash A, Coleman AE, Musaba E, Liotta L, Biggar RJ, Zhuang Z. Monoclonal origin of multicentric Kaposi's sarcoma lesions. N Engl J Med 1997, **336**: 988–993.

1365 Reitz MS, Nerurkar LS, Gallo RC. Perspective on Kaposi's sarcoma: facts, concepts, and conjectures. J Natl Cancer Inst 1999, **91**: 1453–1458.

1366 Ruszczak Zb, Mayer-Da Silva A, Orfanos CE. Kaposi's sarcoma in AIDS. Multicentric angioneoplasia in early skin lesions. Am J Dermatopathol 1987, **9**: 388–398.

1367 Rutgers JL, Wieczorek R, Bonetti F, Kaplan KL, Posnett DN, Friedman-Kien AE, Knowles DM II. The expression of endothelial cell surface antigens by AIDS-associated Kaposi's sarcoma. Evidence for a vascular endothelial cell origin. Am J Pathol 1986, **122**: 493–499.

1368 Safai B, Mike V, Giraldo G, Beth E, Good RA. Association of Kaposi's sarcoma with second primary malignancies. Possible etio-pathogenic implications. Cancer 1980, **45**: 1472–1479.

1369 Sarid R, Klepfish A, Schattner A. Virology, pathogenetic mechanisms, and associated diseases of Kaposi sarcoma-associated herpesvirus ("human herpesvirus 8"). Mayo Clin Proc 2002, **77**: 941–949.

1370 Schwartz RA, Kardashian JF, McNutt NS. Crain WR, Welch KL, Choy SH. Cutaneous angiosarcoma resembling anaplastic Kaposi's sarcoma in a homosexual man. Cancer 1983, **51**: 721–726.

1371 Scully PA, Steinman HK, Kennedy C, Trueblood K, Frisman DM, Voland JR. AIDS-related Kaposi's sarcoma displays differential expression of endothelial surface antigens. Am J Pathol 1988, **130**: 244–251.

1372 Sinkovics JG. Kaposi's sarcoma. Its "oncogenes" and growth factors. Crit Rev Oncol Hematol 1991, **11**: 87–107.

1373 Stribling J, Weitzner S, Smith GV. Kaposi's sarcoma in renal allograft recipients. Cancer 1978, **42**: 442–446.

1374 Strutton G, Weedon D. Acro-angiodermatitis. A simulant of Kaposi's sarcoma. Am J Dermatopathol 1987, **9**: 85–89.

1375 Sunter JP. Visceral Kaposi's sarcoma. Occurrence in a patient suffering from celiac disease. Arch Pathol Lab Med 1978, **102**: 543–545.

1376 Suster S, Rosai J. Intranodal hemorrhagic spindle-cell tumor with "amianthoid" fibers. Report of six cases of a distinctive mesenchymal neoplasm of the inguinal region that simulates Kaposi's sarcoma. Am J Surg Pathol 1989, **13**: 347–357.

1377 Taylor JF, Templeton AC, Vogel CL, Ziegler JL, Kyalwazi SK. Kaposi's sarcoma in Uganda. A clinicopathological study. Int J Cancer 1971, **8**: 122–135.

1378 Varsano S, Manor Y, Steiner Z, Griffel B, Klajman A. Kaposi's sarcoma and angioimmunoblastic lymphadenopathy. Cancer 1984, **54**: 1582–1585.

1379 Way DL, Witte MH, Fiata M, Ramirez G, Nagle RB, Bermas MJ, Dictor M, Borgs P, Witte CL. Endothelial transdifferentiated phenotype and cell-cycle kinetics of AIDS-associated Kaposi sarcoma cells. Lymphology 1993, **26**: 79–89.

1380 Weninger W, Partanen TA, Breiteneder-Geleff S, Mayer C, Kowalski H, Mildner M, Pammer J, Sturzl M, Kerjaschki D, Alitalo K, Tschachler E. Expression of vascular endothelial growth factor receptor-3 and podoplanin suggests a lymphatic endothelial cell origin of Kaposi's sarcoma tumor cells. Lab Invest 1999, **79**: 243–251.

1381 Zhang Y-M, Bachmann S, Hemmer C, van Lunzen J, von Stemm A, Kern P, Dietrich M, Ziegler R, Waldherr R, Nawroth PP. Vascular origin of Kaposi's sarcoma. Expression of leukocyte adhesion molecule-1, thrombomodulin, and tissue factor. Am J Pathol 1994, **144**: 51–59.

1382 Ziegler JL, Templeton AC, Vogel CL. Kaposi's sarcoma. A comparison of classical, endemic, and epidemic forms. Semin Oncol 1984, **11**: 47–52.

Bacillary angiomatosis and verruga peruana

1383 Arias-Stella J, Lieberman PH, Erlandson RA, Arias-Stella J Jr. Histology, immunohistochemistry, and ultrastructure of the verruga in Carrion's disease. Am J Surg Pathol 1986, **10**: 595–610.

1384 Arias-Stella J, Lieberman PH, Garcia-Caceres U, Erlandson RA, Kruger H, Arias-Stella J Jr. Verruga peruana mimicking malignant neoplasms. Am J Dermatopathol 1987, **9**: 279–291.

1385 Chan JKC, Lewin KJ, Lombard CM, Teitelbaum S, Dorfman RF. Histopathology of bacillary angiomatosis of lymph node. Am J Surg Pathol 1991, **15**: 430–437.

1386 Finet JF, Abdalsamad I, Bakdach H, Maitre B, Laporte JL, Le Charpentier YL. Intrathoracic localization of bacillary angiomatosis. Histopathology 1996, **28**: 183–185.

1387 Koehler J, Quinn F, Berger T, Leboit P, Tappero J. Isolation of *Rochalimaea* species from cutaneous and osseous lesions of bacillary angiomatosis. N Engl J Med 1992, **327**: 1625–1631.

1388 Kostianovsky M, Lamy Y, Greco MA. Immunohistochemical and electron microscopic profiles of cutaneous Kaposi's sarcoma and bacillary angiomatosis. Semin Diagn Pathol 1992, **9**: 629–640.

1389 LeBoit PE, Berger TG, Egbert BM, Beckstead JH, Yen TS, Stoler MH. Bacillary angiomatosis. The histopathology and differential diagnosis of a pseudoneoplastic infection in patients with human immunodeficiency virus disease. Am J Surg Pathol 1989, **13**: 909–920.

1390 Reed J, Brigati D, Flynn S, McNutt NS, Min K-W, Welch D, Slater L. Immunocytochemical identification or *Rochalimaea henselae* in bacillary (epithelioid) angiomatosis, parenchymal bacillary peliosis, and persistent fever with bacteremia. Am J Surg Pathol 1992, **16**: 650–657.

1391 Relman DA, Loutit JS, Schmidt TM, Falkow S, Tompkins LS. The agent of bacillary angiomatosis. An approach to the identification of uncultured pathogens. N Engl J Med 1990, **323:** 1573–1580.

1392 Schinella RA, Greco MA. Bacillary angiomatosis presenting as a soft-tissue tumor without skin involvement. Hum Pathol 1990, **21:** 567–568.

1393 Steeper TA, Rosenstein H, Weiser J, Inampudi S, Snover DC. Bacillary epithelioid angiomatosis involving the liver, spleen, and skin in an AIDS patient with concurrent Kaposi's sarcoma. Am J Clin Pathol 1992, **97:** 713–718.

1394 Tsang WYW, Chan JKC. Bacillary angiomatosis. A "new" disease with a broadening clinicopathologic spectrum. Histol Histopath 1992, **7:** 143–152.

Angiosarcoma

1394a Billings SD, McKenney JK, Folpe AL, Weiss SW. Post-radiation cutaneous angiosarcoma of the breast, an analysis of 26 cases. Mod Pathol 2003, **16:** 88a.

1395 Calonje E, Fletcher CDM, Wilson-Jones E, Rosai J. Retiform hemangioendothelioma. A distinctive form of low-grade angiosarcoma delineated in a series of 15 cases. Am J Surg Pathol 1994, **18:** 115–125.

1396 Cancellieri A, Eusebi V, Mambelli V, Ricotti G, Gardini G, Pasquinelli G. Well-differentiated angiosarcoma of the skin following radiotherapy. Report of two cases. Pathol Res Pract 1991, **187:** 301–306.

1397 Capo V, Ozzello L, Fenoglio CM, Lombardi L, Rilke F. Angiosarcomas arising in edematous extremities, immunostaining for factor VIII-related antigen and ultrastructural features. Hum Pathol 1985, **16:** 144–145.

1398 Chen TKK, Gilbert EF. Angiosarcoma complicating generalized lymphangiectasia. Arch Pathol Lab Med 1979, **103:** 86–88.

1399 Connors RC, Ackerman AB. Histologic pseudomalignancies of the skin. Arch Dermatol 1976, **112:** 1767–1780.

1400 Cooper PH. Angiosarcomas of the skin. Semin Diagn Pathol 1987, **4:** 2–17.

1401 Diaz-Cascajo C, Weyers W, Borghi S, Reichel M. Verrucous angiosarcoma of the skin: a distinct variant of cutaneous angiosarcoma. Histopathology 1998, **32:** 556–561.

1402 Dictor M, Ferno M, Baldetorp B. Flow cytometric DNA content in Kaposi's sarcoma by histologic stage. Comparison with angiosarcoma. Anal Quant Cytol Histol 1991, **13:** 201–208.

1403 Haustein UF. Angiosarcoma of the face and scalp. Int J Dermatol 1991, **30:** 851–856.

1404 Holden CA, Spaull J, Das AK, McKee PH, Wilson Jones E. The histogenesis of angiosarcoma of the face and scalp. An immunohistochemical and ultrastructural study. Histopathology 1987, **11:** 37–51.

1405 Holden CA, Spittle MF, Wilson Jones E. Angiosarcoma of the face and scalp, prognosis and treatment. Cancer 1987, **59:** 1046–1057.

1406 Lasota J, Miettinen M. Absence of Kaposi's sarcoma-associated virus (human herpesvirus-8) sequences in angiosarcoma. Virchows Arch 1999, **434:** 51–56.

1407 Leader M, Collins M, Patel J, Henry K. Staining for factor VIII related antigen and *Ulex europaeus* agglutinin I (UEA-I) in 230 tumours. An assessment of their specificity for angiosarcoma and Kaposi's sarcoma. Histopathology 1986, **10:** 1153–1162.

1408 McDonagh DP, Liu J, Gaffry MJ, Layfield LJ, Azumi N, Traweek ST. Detection of Kaposi's sarcoma-associated herpesvirus-like DNA sequences in angiosarcoma. Am J Pathol 1996, **149:** 1363–1368.

1409 Maddox JC, Evans HL. Angiosarcoma of skin and soft tissue. A study of forty-four cases. Cancer 1981, **48:** 1907–1921.

1410 Mark RJ, Tran LM, Sercarz J, Fu YS, Calcaterra TC, Juillard GF. Angiosarcoma of the head and neck. The UCLA experience 1955 through 1990. Arch Otolaryngol Head Neck Surg 1993, **119:** 973–978.

1411 Marrogi AJ, Hunt SJ, Santa Cruz DJ. Cutaneous epithelioid angiosarcoma. Am J Dermatopathol 1990, **12:** 350–356.

1412 Mentzel T, Beham A, Calonje E, Katenkamp D, Fletcher CD. Epithelioid hemangioendothelioma of skin and soft tissues: clinicopathologic and immunohistochemical study of 30 cases. Am J Surg Pathol 1997, **21:** 363–374.

1413 Moskaluk CA, Merino MJ, Danforth DN, Medeiros LJ. Low-grade angiosarcoma of the skin of the breast. A complication of lumpectomy and radiation therapy for breast carcinoma. Hum Pathol 1992, **23:** 710–714.

1414 Nappi O, Wick MR, Pettinato G, Ghiselli RW, Swanson PE. Pseudovascular adenoid squamous cell carcinoma of the skin. A neoplasm that may be mistaken for angiosarcoma. Am J Surg Pathol 1992, **16:** 429–438.

1415 Orchard GE, Zelger B, Jones EW, Jones RR. An immunocytochemical assessment of 19 cases of cutaneous angiosarcoma. Histopathology 1997, **28:** 235–240.

1416 Otis CN, Peschel R, McKhann C, Merino M, Duray PH. The rapid onset of cutaneous angiosarcoma after radiotherapy for breast carcinoma. Cancer 1986, **57:** 2130–2134.

1417 Prescott RJ, Banerjee SS, Eyden BP, Haboubi NY. Cutaneous epithelioid angiosarcoma. A clinicopathological study of four cases. Histopathology 1994, **25:** 421–430.

1418 Quante M, Patel NK, Hill S, Merchant W, Courtauld E, Newman P, McKee PH. Epithelioid hemangioendothelioma presenting in the skin: a clinicopathologic study of eight cases. Am J Dermatopathol 1999, **20:** 541–546.

1419 Rosai J, Summer HW, Kostianovsky M, Perez-Mesa C. Angiosarcoma of the skin. A clinicopathologic and fine structural study. Hum Pathol 1976, **7:** 83–109.

1420 von Hochstetter AR, Meyer VE, Grant JW, Honegger HP, Schreiber A. Epithelioid sarcoma mimicking angiosarcoma. The value of immunohistochemistry in the differential diagnosis. Virchows Arch [A] 1991, **418:** 271–278.

1421 Wilson Jones E. Malignant vascular tumours. Clin Exp Dermatol 1976, **1:** 287–312.

Lymphoid tumors and tumorlike conditions
Cutaneous lymphoid hyperplasia

1422 Ackerman AB, Tanski EV. Pseudoleukemia cutis. Report of a case in association with molluscum contagiosum. Cancer 1977, **40:** 813–817.

1423 Baldassano MF, Bailey EM, Ferry JA, Harris NL, Duncan LM. Cutaneous lymphoid hyperplasia and cutaneous marginal zone lymphoma: comparison of morphologic and immunophenotypic features. Am J Surg Pathol 1999, **23:** 88–96.

1424 Caro Wa, Helwig EB. Cutaneous lymphoid hyperplasia. Cancer 1969, **24:** 487–502.

1425 Cerio R, MacDonald DM. Benign cutaneous lymphoid infiltrates. J Cutan Pathol 1985, **12:** 442–452.

1426 Cochran REI, Thomson J, Fleming KA, Strong AMM. Histology simulating reticulosis in secondary syphilis. Br J Dermatol 1976, **95:** 251–254.

1427 Eckert F, Schmid U, Kaudewitz P, Burg G, Braun-Falco O. Follicular lymphoid hyperplasia of the skin with high content of Ki-positive lymphocytes. Am J Dermatopathol 1989, **11:** 345–352.

1428 Ive FA, Magnus IA, Warin RP, Jones EW. "Actinic reticuloid." A chronic dermatosis association with severe photosensitivity and the histological resemblance to lymphoma. Br J Dermatol 1969, **81:** 469–485.

1428a Li C, Inagaki H, Kuo T-t, Hu S, Okabe M, Eimoto T. Primary cutaneous marginal zone b-cell lymphoma. Am J Surg Pathol 2004, **27:** 1061–1069.

1429 Mach KW, Wilgram GF. Characteristic histopathology of cutaneous lymphoplasia (lymphocytoma). Arch Dermatol 1966, **94:** 26–34.

1429a Nihal M, Mikkola D, Horvath N, Gilliam AC, Stevens SR, Spiro T, Cooper KD, Wood GS. Cutaneous lymphoid hyperplasia: a lymphoproliferative continuum with lymphomatous potential. Hum Pathol 2003, **34**: 617–622.

1430 Rijlaarsdam JU, Meijer CJLM, Willemze R. Differentiation between lymphadenosis benigna cutis and primary cutaneous follicular center cell lymphomas. A comparative clinicopathologic study of 57 patients. Cancer 1990, **65**: 2301–2306.

1431 Rijlaarsdam JU, Nieboer C, De Vries E, Willemze R. Characterization of the dermal infiltrates in Jessner's lymphocytic infiltrate of the skin, polymorphous light eruption and cutaneous lupus erythematosus. Differential diagnostic and pathogenetic aspects. J Cutan Pathol 1990, **17**: 2–8.

1432 Rijlaarsdam JU, Scheffer E, Meijer CJLM, Willemze R. Cutaneous pseudo-T-cell lymphomas. A clinicopathologic study of 20 patients. Cancer 1992, **69**: 717–724.

1433 Schmid U, Eckert F, Griesser H, Steinke C, Cogliatti SB, Kaudewitz P, Lennert K. Cutaneous follicular lymphoid hyperplasia with monotypic plasma cells. A clinicopathologic study of 18 patients. Am J Surg Pathol 1995, **19**: 12–20.

1434 Smolle J, Torne R, Soyer HP, Kerly H. Immunohistochemical classification of cutaneous pseudolymphomas. Delineation of distinct patterns. J Cutan Pathol 1990, **17**: 149–159.

1435 Thomson J, Cochrane T, Cochran R, McQueen A. Histology simulating reticulosis in persistent nodular scabies. Br J Dermatol 1974, **90**: 421–429.

1436 Toonstra J, van der Putte SCJ. Plasmacytoid monocytes in Jessner's lymphocytic infiltration of the skin. A valuable clue for the diagnosis. Am J Dermatopathol 1991, **13**: 321–328.

1437 Wechsler J, Bagot M, Henni T, LeCouedic J-P, Gaulard P, Zafrani ES. Gene analysis in 18 cases of cutaneous lymphoid infiltrates of uncertain significance. Arch Pathol Lab Med 1995, **119**: 157–162.

1438 Willemze R, Dijkstra A, Meijer CJLM. Lymphocytic infiltration of the skin (Jessner). A T-cell lymphoproliferative disease. Br J Dermatol 1984, **110**: 523–529.

1439 Wirt DP, Grogan TM, Jolley CS, Rangel CS, Payne CM, Hansen PC, Lynch PJ, Schuchardt M. The immunoarchitecture of cutaneous pseudolymphoma. Hum Pathol 1985, **6**: 492–510.

1440 Wood GS, Ngan B-Y, Tung R, Hoffman TE, Abel EA, Hoppe RT, Warnke RA, Cleary ML, Sklar J. Clonal rearrangements of immunoglobulin genes and progression to B cell lymphoma in cutaneous lymphoid hyperplasia. Am J Pathol 1989, **135**: 13–19.

Mycosis fungoides and related peripheral T-cell lymphomas

1441 Argenyi ZB, Goeken JA, Piette WW, Madison KC. Granulomatous mycosis fungoides. Clinicopathologic study of two cases. Am J Dermatopathol 1992, **14**: 200–210.

1442 Barcos M. Mycosis fungoides. Diagnosis and pathogenesis. Am J Clin Pathol 1993, **99**: 452–458.

1443 Blasik LG, Newkirk RE, Dimond RL, Clendenning WE. Mycosis fungoides d'emblée. A rare presentation of cutaneous T-cell lymphoma. Cancer 1982, **49**: 742–747.

1444 Bodensteiner DC, Skikne B. Central nervous system involvement in mycosis fungoides, Diagnosis, treatment and literature review. Cancer 1982, **50**: 1181–1184.

1445 Breathnach SM, McKee PH, Smith NP. Hypopigmented mycosis fungoides. Report of five cases with ultrastructural observations. Br J Dermatol 1982, **106**: 643–649.

1446 Brehmer-Andersson E. Mycosis fungoides and its relation to Sézary's syndrome, lymphomatoid papulosis, and primary cutaneous Hodgkin's disease. A clinical, histopathologic and cytologic study of fourteen cases and a critical review of the literature. Acta Derm Venereol (Stockh) 1976, **56**(Suppl 75): 1–142.

1447 Brousset P, Pages M, Chittal SM, Gorguet B. Tumour phase of mycosis fungoides in the tongue. Histopathology 1992, **20**: 87–89.

1448 Buechner SA, Winkelmann RK. Sézary syndrome. A clinicopathologic study of 39 cases. Arch Dermatol 1983, **119**: 979–986.

1449 Burns MK, Ellis CN, Cooper KD. Mycosis fungoides-type cutaneous T-cell lymphoma arising before 30 years of age. Immunophenotypic, immunogenotypic and clinicopathologic analysis of nine cases. J Am Acad Dermatol 1992, **27**: 974–978.

1450 Cerroni L, Fink-Puches R, El-Shabrawi-Caelen L, Soyer HP, LeBoit PE, Kerl H. Solitary skin lesions with histopathologic features of early mycosis fungoides. Am J Dermatopathol 2000, **21**: 518–524.

1451 Cerroni L, Rieger E, Hodl S, Kerl H. Clinicopathologic and immunologic features associated with transformation of mycosis fungoides to large-cell lymphoma. Am J Surg Pathol 1992, **16**: 543–552.

1452 Chu A, Patterson J, Berger C, Vonderheid E, Edelson R. In situ study of T-cell subpopulations in cutaneous T-cell lymphoma. Diagnostic criteria. Cancer 1984, **54**: 2414–2422.

1453 Cooper KD. Skin-infiltrating lymphocytes in normal and disordered skin. Activation signals and functional roles in psoriasis and mycosis fungoides-type cutaneous T-cell lymphoma. J Dermatol 1992, **19**: 731–737.

1454 Degreef H, Holvoet C, Van Vloten WA, Desmet V, De Wolf-Peeters C. Woringer-Kolopp disease. An epidermotropic variant of mycosis fungoides. Cancer 1976, **38**: 2154–2165.

1455 Deneau DG, Wood GS, Beckstead J, Hoppe RT, Price N. Woringer-Kolopp disease (pagetoid reticulosis). Four cases with histopathologic, ultrastructural, and immunohistologic observations. Arch Dermatol 1984, **120**: 1045–1051.

1456 El Shabrawi-Caelen L, Cerroni L, Medeiros LJ, McCalmont TH. Hypopigmented mycosis fungoides: frequent expression of a CD8+ T-cell phenotype. Am J Surg Pathol 2002, **26**: 450–457.

1457 Fisher ER, Horvat BC, Wechsler HL. Ultrastructural features of mycosis fungoides. Am J Clin Pathol 1972, **58**: 99–110.

1458 Fivenson DP, Douglass MC, Nickoloff BJ. Cutaneous expression of Thy-1 in mycosis fungoides. Am J Pathol 1992, **141**: 1373–1380.

1459 Flaxman BA, Zelasny G, Van Scott EJ. Nonspecificity of characteristic cells in mycosis fungoides. Arch Dermatol 1971, **104**: 141–147.

1460 Fuks ZY, Bagshaw MA, Farber EM. Prognostic signs and management of the mycosis fungoides. Cancer 1973, **32**: 1385–1395.

1460a Glusac EJ. Criterion by criterion, mycosis fungoides. Am J of Dermatopathol 2003, **25**: 264–269.

1461 Gordon BG, Weisenburger DD, Warkentin PI, Anderson J, Sanger WG, Bast M, Gnarra D, Vose JM, Bierman PJ, Armitage J. Peripheral T-cell lymphoma in childhood and adolescence. A clinicopathologic study of 22 patients. Cancer 1993, **71**: 257–263.

1462 Green SB, Byar DP, Lamberg SI. Prognostic variables in mycosis fungoides. Cancer 1981, **47**: 2671–2677.

1463 Hamminga L, Hermans J, Noordijk EM, Meijer CJLM, Scheffer E, Van Vloten WA. Cutaneous T-cell lymphoma. Clinicopathological relationships, therapy and survival in ninety-two patients. Br J Dermatol 1982, **107**: 145–156.

1464 Hitchcock MG, Burchette JL Jr, Olsen EA, Ratech H, Kamino H. Eccrine gland infiltration by mycosis fungoides. Am J Dermatopathol 1997, **18**: 447–453.

1465 Huberman MS, Bunn PA Jr, Matthews MJ, Ihde DC, Gazdar AF, Cohen MH, Minna JD. Hepatic involvement in the cutaneous T-cell lymphomas. Results of percutaneous biopsy and peritoneoscopy. Cancer 1980, **45**: 1683–1688.

1466 Jimbow K, Maeda K, Ito Y, Ishida O, Takami T. Heterogeneity of cutaneous T-cell lymphoma. Phenotypic and ultrastructural characterization of four unusual cases. Cancer 1985, **56:** 2458–2469.

1467 Kartsonis J, Brettschneider F, Weissman A, Rosen L. Mycosis fungoides bullosa. Am J Dermatopathol 1990, **12:** 76–80.

1468 Kerl H, Cerroni L, Burg G. The morphologic spectrum of T-cell lymphomas of the skin. A proposal for a new classification. Semin Diagn Pathol 1991, **8:** 55–61.

1469 Kiesewetter F, Haneke E, Lennert K, Hornstein OP, Fartasch M. Cutaneous lymphoepithelioid lymphoma (Lennert's lymphoma). Combined immunohistological, ultrastructural, and DNA flow-cytometry analysis. Am J Dermatopathol 1989, 11: 549–554.

1470 Kim YH, Hoppe RT. Mycosis fungoides and the Sezary syndrome. Semin Oncol 1999, **26:** 276–289.

1471 King-Ismael D, Ackerman AB. Guttate parapsoriasis/digitate dermatosis (small plaque parapsoriasis) is mycosis fungoides. Am J Dermatopathol 1992, **14:** 518–530.

1472 Kohler S, Kim YH, Smoller BR. Histologic criteria for the diagnosis of erythrodermic mycosis fungoides and Sezary syndrome: a clinical reappraisal. J Cutan Pathol 1997, **24:** 292–297.

1473 Kuzel TM, Roenigk HH Jr, Rosen ST. Mycosis fungoides and the Sézary syndrome. A review of pathogenesis, diagnosis, and therapy. J Clin Oncol 1991, **9:** 1298–1313.

1474 Lacour JP, Castanet J, Perrin C, Ortonne JP. Follicular mycosis fungoides. A clinical and histologic variant of cutaneous T-cell lymphoma. Report of two cases. J Am Acad Dermatol 1993, **29:** 330–334.

1475 LeBoit PE. Variants of mycosis fungoides and related cutaneous T-cell lymphomas. Semin Diagn Pathol 1991, **8:** 73–81.

1476 LeBoit PE, Zackheim HS, White CR Jr. Granulomatous variants of cutaneous T-cell lymphoma. The histopathology of granulomatous mycosis fungoides and granulomatous slack skin. Am J Surg Pathol 1988, **12:** 83–95.

1477 Lever WF. Localized mycosis fungoides with prominent epidermotropism. Woringer-Kolopp disease. Arch Dermatol 1977, **113:** 1254–1256.

1478 Long JC, Mihm MC. Mycosis fungoides with extra-cutaneous dissemination. A distinct clinicopathologic entity. Cancer 1974, **34:** 1745–1755.

1479 Mehregan DA, Gibson LE, Muller SA. Follicular mucinosis. Histopathologic review of 33 cases. Mayo Clin Proc 1991, **66:** 387–390.

1480 Mehregan DA, Su WP, Kurtin PJ. Subcutaneous T-cell lymphoma. A clinical, histopathologic, and immunohistochemical study of six cases. J Cutan Pathol 1994, **21:** 110–117.

1481 Meissner K, Loning T, Rehpenning W. Epidermal Langerhans cells and prognosis of patients with mycosis fungoides and Sezary syndrome. In Vivo 1993, **7:** 277–280.

1482 Michie SA, Abel EA, Hoppe RT, Warnke RA, Wood GS. Discordant expression of antigens between intraepidermal and intradermal T-cells in mycosis fungoides. Am J Pathol 1990, **137:** 1447–1451.

1483 Nagatani T, Matsuzaki T, Iemoto G, Kim ST, Baba N, Miyamoto H, Nakajima H. Comparative study of cutaneous T-cell lymphoma and adult T-cell leukemia/lymphoma. Clinical, histopathologic, and immunohistochemical analyses. Cancer 1990, **66:** 2380–2386.

1484 Nasu K, Said J, Vonderheid E, Olerud J, Sako D, Kadin M. Immunopathology of cutaneous T-cell lymphomas, Am J Pathol 1985, **119:** 436–447.

1485 National Cancer Institute, Division of Cancer Treatment. Proceedings of the workshop on cutaneous T-cell lymphomas (mycosis fungoides and Sézary syndrome). Cancer Treat Rep 1979, **63:** 561–736.

1486 Nickoloff J, Griffiths CEM. Intradermal but not dermal T

lymphocytes are positive for a cell-cycle-associated antigen (K167-) in mycosis fungoides. Am J Pathol 1990, **136:** 261–266.

1487 Ralfkiaer E, Wantzin GL, Mason DY, Hou-Jensen K, Stein H, Thomsen K. Phenotypic characterization of lymphocyte subsets in mycosis fungoides. Comparison with large plaque parapsoriasis and benign chronic dermatoses. Am J Clin Pathol 1985, **84:** 610–619.

1488 Rappaport H, Thomas LB. Mycosis fungoides. The pathology of extracutaneous involvement. Cancer 1974, **34:** 1198–1229.

1489 Sanchez JL, Ackerman A. The patch of mycosis fungoides. Am J Dermatopathol 1979, **1:** 5–26.

1490 Santucci M, Biggeri A, Feller AC, Massi D, Burg G. Efficacy of histologic criteria for diagnosing early mycosis fungoides: an EORTC Cutaneous Lymphoma Study Group investigation. Am J Surg Pathol 2000, **24:** 40–50.

1491 Shapiro PE, Pinto FJ. The histologic spectrum of mycosis fungoides/Sezary syndrome (cutaneous T-cell lymphoma). A review of 222 biopsies, including newly described patterns and the earliest pathologic changes. Am J Surg Pathol 1994, **18:** 645–667.

1492 Shum DT, Roberts JT, Smout MS, Wells GA, Simon GT. The value of nuclear contour index in the diagnosis of mycosis fungoides. An assessment of current ultrastructural morphometric diagnostic criteria. Cancer 1986, **57:** 298–304.

1493 Smoller BR, Detwiler SP, Kohler S, Hoppe RT, Kim YH. Role of histology in providing prognostic information in mycosis fungoides. J Cutan Pathol 1998, **25:** 311–315.

1494 Trotter MJ, Whittaker SJ, Orchard GE, Smith NP. Cutaneous histopathology of Sezary syndrome: a study of 41 cases with a proven circulating T-cell clone. J Cutan Pathol 1997, **24:** 286–291.

1495 Van der Putte SCJ, Toonstra J, De Weger RA, Van Unnik JAM. Cutaneous T-cell lymphoma, multilobated type. Histopathology 1982, **6:** 35–54.

1496 Van der Putte SCJ, Toonstra J, Van Wichen DF, van Unnik JA, van Vloten WA. Aberrant immunophenotypes in mycosis fungoides. Arch Dermatol 1988, **124:** 373–380.

1497 van Doorn R, Scheffer E, Willemze R. Follicular mycosis fungoides, a distinct disease entity with or without associated follicular mucinosis: a clinicopathologic and follow-up study of 51 patients. Arch Dermatol 2002, **138:** 191–198.

1498 Vonderheid EC, Tam DW, Johnson WC, Van Scott EJ, Wallner PE. Prognostic significance of cytomorphology in the cutaneous T-cell lymphomas. Cancer 1981, **47:** 119–125.

1499 Weinberg JM, Rook AH, Lessin SR. Molecular diagnosis of lymphocytic infiltrates of the skin. Arch Dermatol 1993, **129:** 1491–1500.

1500 Weisenburger DD, Nathwani BN, Forman SJ, Rappaport H. Noncutaneous peripheral T-cell lymphoma histologically resembling mycosis fungoides. Cancer 1982, **49:** 1839–1847.

1501 Whittaker SJ, Ng YL, Rustin M, Levene G, McGibbon DH, Smith NP. HTLV-I-associated cutaneous disease. A clinicopathological and molecular study of patients from the U.K. Br J Dermatol 1993, **128:** 483–492.

1502 Whittaker SJ, Smith NP, Jones RR, Luzzatto L. Analysis of beta, gamma, and delta T-cell receptor genes in mycosis fungoides and Sezary syndrome. Cancer 1991, **68:** 1572–1582.

1503 Wieczorek R, Suhrland M, Ramsay D, Reed ML, Knowles DM II. Leu-M1 antigen expression in advanced (tumor) stage mycosis fungoides. Am J Clin Pathol 1986, **86:** 25–32.

1504 Willemze R, Beljaards RC, Meijer CJ. Classification of primary cutaneous T-cell lymphomas. Histopathology 1994, **24:** 405–415.

1505 Wood GS, Edinger A, Hoppe RT, Warnke RA. Mycosis fungoides skin lesions contain CD8+ tumor-infiltrating lymphocytes expressing an activated. MHC-restricted cytotoxic T-lymphocyte phenotype. J Cutan Pathol 1994, **21:** 151–156.

1506 Yeh YA, Hudson AR, Prieto VG, Shea CR, Smoller BR.

Reassessment of lymphocytic atypia in the diagnosis of mycosis fungoides. Mod Pathol 2001, **14**: 285–288.

1507 Zelickson BD, Peters MS, Muller SA, Thibodeau SN, Lust JA. Quam LM, Pittelkow MR. T-cell receptor gene rearrangement analysis. Cutaneous T cell lymphoma, peripheral T cell lymphoma, and premalignant and benign cutaneous lymphoproliferative disorders. J Am Acad Dermatol 1991, **25**: 787–796.

1508 Zucker-Franklin D, Hooper WC, Evatt BL. Human lymphotropic retroviruses associated with mycosis fungoides. Evidence that human T-cell lymphotropic virus type II (HTLV-II) as well as HTLV-I may play a role in the disease. Blood 1992, **80**: 1537–1545.

Lymph nodes in mycosis fungoides

1509 Colby TV, Burke JS, Hoppe RT. Lymph node biopsy in mycosis fungoides. Cancer 1981, **47**: 351–359.

1510 Sausville EA, Worsham GF, Matthews MJ, Makuch RW, Fischmann AB, Schechter GP, Gazdar AF, Bunn PA Jr. Histologic assessment of lymph nodes in mycosis fungoides/Sézary syndrome (cutaneous T-cell lymphoma). Clinical correlations and prognostic import of a new classification system. Hum Pathol 1985, **16**: 1098–1109.

1511 Schechter GP, Bunn PA, Fischmann AB, Young SW, Fukes Z. Blood and lymph node T-lymphocytes in cutaneous T-cell lymphoma. Evaluation by light microscopy. Cancer Treat Rep 1979, **63**: 581–586.

1512 Scheffer E, Meijer CJ, van Vloten WA. Dermatopathic lymphadenopathy and lymph node involvement in mycosis fungoides. Cancer 1980, **45**: 137–148.

1513 Weiss LM, Hu E, Wood GS, Moulds C, Cleary ML, Warnke R, Sklar J. Clonal rearrangements of T-cell receptor genes in mycosis fungoides and dermatopathic lymphadenopathy. N Engl J Med 1985, **313**: 539–544.

1514 Weiss LM, Wood GS, Warnke RA. Immunophenotypic differences between dermatopathic lymphadenopathy and lymph node involvement in mycosis fungoides. Am J Pathol 1985, **120**: 179–185.

Lymphomatoid papulosis and anaplastic large cell lymphoma

1515 Beylot-Barry M, Lamant L, Vergier B, de Muret A, Fraitag S, Delord B, Dubus P, Vaillant L, Delaunay M, MacGrogan G, Beylot C, de Mascarel A, Delsol G, Merlio JP. Detection of t(2;5)(p23;q35) translocation by reverse transcriptase polymerase chain reaction and in situ hybridization in CD30-positive primary cutaneous lymphoma and lymphomatoid papulosis. Am J Pathol 1996, **149**: 483–492.

1515a Cepeda LT, Pieretti M, Chapman SF, Horenstein MG. CD30-positive atypical lymphoid cells in common non-neoplastic cutaneous infiltrates rich in neutrophils and eosinophils. Am J Surg Pathol 2003, **27**: 912–918.

1516 Chan JK. The perivascular cuff of large lymphoid cells: a clue to diagnosis of anaplastic large cell lymphoma. Int Surg Pathol 2001, **8**: 153–156.

1517 Cockerell CJ, Stetler LD. Accuracy in diagnosis of lymphomatoid papulosis. Am J Dermatopathol 1991, **13**: 20–25.

1518 Drews R, Samel A, Kadin ME. Lymphomatoid papulosis and anaplastic large cell lymphomas of the skin. Semin Cutan Med Surg 2000, **19**: 109–117.

1519 Flynn KJ, Dehner LP, Gajl-Peczalska KJ, Dahl MV, Ramsay N, Wang N. Regressing atypical histiocytosis. A cutaneous proliferation of atypical neoplastic histiocytes with unexpectedly indolent biologic behavior. Cancer 1982, **49**: 959–970.

1520 Kadin ME. Lymphomatoid papulosis. Am J Dermatopathol 1995, **17**: 197–208.

1521 Kadin ME, Morris SW. The t(2;5) in human lymphomas. Leuk Lymphoma 1998, **29**: 249–256.

1522 Kadin ME, Vonderheid EC, Sako D, Clayton LK, Olbricht S. Clonal composition of T cells in lymphomatoid papulosis. Am J Pathol 1987, **126**: 13–17.

1523 Kaudewitz P, Stein H, Dallenbach F, Eckert F, Bieber K, Burg G, Braun-Falco O. Primary and secondary cutaneous Ki-1+ (CD30+) anaplastic large cell lymphomas. Morphologic, immunohistologic, and clinical characteristics. Am J Pathol 1989, **135**: 359–367.

1524 Kinney MC, Kadin ME. The pathologic and clinical spectrum of anaplastic large cell lymphoma and correlation with ALK gene dysregulation. Am J Clin Pathol 1999, **111**: S56–S67.

1525 Macgrogan G, Vergier B, Dubus P, Beylot-Barry M, Belleannee G, Delaunay MM, Eghbali H, Beylot C, Rivel J, Trojani M, Vital C, De Mascarel A, Bloch B, Merlio JP. CD30-positive cutaneous large cell lymphomas. A comparative study of clinicopathologic and molecular features of 16 cases. Am J Clin Pathol 1996, **105**: 440–450.

1526 Motley RJ, Jasani B, Ford AM, Poynton CH, Calonje-Daly JE, Holt PJ. Regressing atypical histiocytosis, a regressing cutaneous phase of Ki-1-positive anaplastic large cell lymphoma. Immunocytochemical, nucleic acid, and cytogenetic studies of a new case in view of current opinion. Cancer 1992, **70**: 476–483.

1527 Ralfkiaer E, Stein H, Wantzin GL, Thomsen K, Ralfkiaer N, Mason DY. Lymphomatoid papulosis. Characterization of skin infiltrates by monoclonal anti-bodies. Am J Clin Pathol 1985, **84**: 587–593.

1528 Requena L, Sanchez M, Coca S, Sanches Yus E. Follicular lymphomatoid papulosis. Am J Dermatopathol 1990, **12**: 67–75.

1529 Smoller B, Longacre T, Warnke R. Ki-1 (CD30) expression in differentiation of lymphomatoid papulosis from arthropod bite reactions. Mod Pathol 1992, **5**: 492–496.

1530 Stein H, Foss HD, Durkop H, Marafioti T, Delsol G, Pulford K, Pileri S, Falini B. CD30(+) anaplastic large cell lymphoma: a review of its histopathologic, genetic, and clinical features. Blood 2000, **96**: 3681–3695.

1531 Turner ML, Gilmour HM, McLaren KM, Langlands K, Craig JI, Parker AC. Regressing atypical histiocytosis. Report of two cases with progression to high grade T-cell non-Hodgkin's lymphoma. Hematol Pathol 1993, **7**: 33–47.

1532 Valentino LA, Helwig EB. Lymphomatoid papulosis. Arch Pathol 1973, **96**: 409–416.

1533 Wantzin GL, Thomsen K, Brandrup F, Larsen JK. Lymphomatoid papulosis. Development into cutaneous T-cell lymphoma. Arch Dermatol 1985, **121**: 792–794.

1534 Weiss LM, Wood GS, Trela M, Warnke RA, Sklar J. Clonal T-cell populations in lymphomatoid papulosis. Evidence of a lymphoproliferative origin for a clinically benign disease. N Engl J Med 1986, **315**: 475–479.

1535 Willemze R, Meyer CJLM, Van Vloten WA, Scheffer E. The clinical and histological spectrum of lymphomatoid papulosis. Br J Dermatol 1982, **107**: 131–144.

Other malignant lymphomas

1536 Aguilera NS, Tomaszewski MM, Moad JC, Bauer FA, Taubenberger JK, Abbondanzo SL. Cutaneous follicle center lymphoma: a clinicopathologic study of 19 cases. Mod Pathol 2001, **14**: 828–835.

1537 Aronson IK, West DP, Variakojis D, Ronan SG, Iossifides I, Zeitz HJ. Panniculitis associated with cutaneous T-cell lymphoma and cytophagocytic histiocytosis. Br J Dermatol 1985, **112**: 87–96.

1538 Baldassano MF, Bailey EM, Ferry JA, Harris NL, Duncan LM. Cutaneous lymphoid hyperplasia and cutaneous marginal zone lymphoma: comparison of morphologic and immunophenotypic features. Am J Surg Pathol 1999, **23:** 88–96.

1539 Berti E, Alessi E, Caputo R. Reticulohistiocytoma of the dorsum (Crosti's disease) and other B-cell lymphomas. Semin Diagn Pathol 1991, **8:** 82–90.

1540 Beylot-Barry M, Vergier B, Masquelier B, Bagot M, Joly P, Souteyrand P, Vaillant L, Avril MF, Franck N, Fraitag S, Delaunay M, Laroche L, Estave E, Courville P, Dechelotte P, Beylot C, De Mascarel A, Wechsler J, Merlio JP. The spectrum of cutaneous lymphomas in HIV infection: a study of 21 cases. Am J Surg Pathol 1999, **23:** 1208–1216.

1541 Burke JS, Hoppe RT, Cibull ML, Dorfman RF. Cutaneous malignant lymphoma. A pathologic study of 50 cases with clinical analysis of 37. Cancer 1981, **47:** 300–310.

1542 Cerroni L, Kerl H. The clinicopathological spectrum of cutaneous B-cell lymphomas. Prog Pathol 2001, **5:** 1–16.

1543 Charlotte F, Wechsler J, Joly P, Bagot M, Lessana-Leibowitch M, Gaulard P, Zafrani ES. Nonepidermotropic cutaneous lymphomas. A histopathological and immunohistological study of 52 cases. Arch Pathol Lab Med 1994, **118:** 56–63.

1544 DiGiuseppe JA, Louie DC, Williams JE, Miller DT, Griffin CA, Mann RB, Borowitz MJ. Blastic natural killer cell leukemia/lymphoma: a clinicopathologic study. Am J Surg Pathol 1997, **21:** 1223–1230.

1545 Evans HL, Winkelmann RK, Banks PM. Differential diagnosis of malignant and benign cutaneous lymphoid infiltrates. A study of 57 cases in which malignant lymphoma had been diagnosed or suspected in the skin. Cancer 1979, **44:** 699–717.

1546 Fernandez-Vasquez A, Rodriguez-Peralto JL, Martinez MA, Platon EM, Algara P, Camacho FI, Lopez-Rio F, Zarco C, Sanchez-Yus E, Fresno MF, Barthe L, Aliaga A, Fraga M, Forteza J, Oliva H, Piris MA. Primary cutaneous large B-cell lymphoma: the relation between morphology, clinical presentation, immunohistochemical markers, and survival. Am J Surg Pathol 2001, **25:** 307–315.

1547 Franco R, Fernandez-Vazquez A, Rodriguez-Peralto JL, Bellas C, Lopez-Rios F, Saez A, Villuendas R, Navarrete M, Fernandez I, Zarco C, Piris MA. Cutaneous follicular B-cell lymphoma: description of a series of 18 cases. Am J Surg Pathol 2001, **25:** 875–883.

1548 Garcia CF, Weiss LM, Warnke RA, Wood GS. Cutaneous follicular lymphoma. Am J Surg Pathol 1986, **10:** 454–463.

1549 Gilliam AC, Wood GS. Primary cutaneous lymphomas other than mycosis fungoides. Semin Oncol 1999, **26:** 290–306.

1550 Grümayer ER, Ladenstein RL, Slavc I, Urban C, Radaszkiewicz T, Bettelheim P, Gadner H. B-cell differentiation pattern of cutaneous lymphomas in infancy and childhood. Cancer 1988, **61:** 303–308.

1551 Kahn LB, Gordon W, Camp R. Florid sarcoid reaction associated with lymphoma of the skin. Cancer 1974, **33:** 1117–1122.

1552 Khoury JD, Medeiros LJ, Manning JR, Sulak LE, Bueso-Ramos C, Jones D. CD56+ TdT+ blastic natural killer cell tumor of the skin: a primitive systemic malignancy related to myelomonocytic leukemia. Cancer 2002, **94:** 2401–2408.

1553 Kim BK, Surti U, Pandya AG, Swerdlow SH. Primary and secondary cutaneous diffuse large B-cell lymphomas: a multiparameter analysis of 25 cases including fluorescence in situ hybridization for t(14;18) translocation. Am J Surg Pathol 2003, **27:** 356–364.

1554 Knowles DM II, Jakobiec FA. Cell marker analysis of extranodal lymphoid infiltrates. To what extent does the determination of mono- or polyclonality resolve the diagnostic dilemma of malignant lymphoma vs pseudolymphoma in an extranodal site? Semin Diagn Pathol 1985, **2:** 163–168.

1555 Krell JM, Sanchez RL, Solomon AR. Diffuse dermal

angiomatosis. A variant of reactive cutaneous angioendotheliomatosis. J Cutan Pathol 1994, **21:** 363–370.

1556 Kurtin PJ, Di Caudo DJ, Habermann TM, Chen MG, Su WP. Primary cutaneous large cell lymphomas. Morphologic, immunophenotypic, and clinical features of 20 cases. Am J Surg Pathol 1994, **18:** 1183–1191.

1556a Li C, Inagaki H, Kuo T-t, Hu S, Okabe M, Eimoto T. Primary cutaneous marginal zone b-cell lymphoma. Am J Surg Pathol 2004, **27:** 1061–1069.

1557 Long JC, Mihm MC, Qazi R. Malignant lymphoma of the skin. A clinico-pathologic study of lymphoma other than mycosis fungoides diagnosed by skin biopsy. Cancer 1976, **38:** 1282–1296.

1558 McGregor JM, Yu CC, Lu QL, Cotter FE, Levison DA, MacDonald DM. Post-transplant cutaneous lymphoma. J Am Acad Dermatol 1993, **29:** 549–554.

1559 Molina A, Lombard C, Donlon T, Bangs CD, Dorfman RF. Immunohisto-chemical and cytogenetic studies indicate that malignant angioendotheliomatosis is a primary intravascular (angiotropic) lymphoma. Cancer 1990, **66:** 474–479.

1560 Pandolfino TL, Siegel RS, Kuzel TM, Rosen ST, Guitart J. Primary cutaneous B-cell lymphoma: review and current concepts. J Clin Oncol 2000, **18:** 2152–2168.

1561 Prost C, Reyes F, Wechsler J, Gaston A, Richard I, Poirier J. High-grade malignant cutaneous plasmacytoma metastatic to the central nervous system. A case report with electron microscopy, immunohistological, and neuropathological studies. Am J Dermatopathol 1987, **9:** 30–36.

1562 Salama S. Primary cutaneous B-cell lymphoma and lymphoproliferative disorders of skin: current status of pathology and classification. Am J Clin Pathol 2000, **114:** S104–S128.

1563 Sander CA, Flaig MJ, Kaudewitz P, Jaffe ES. The Revised European-American classification of Lymphoid neoplasms (REAL): a preferred approach for the classification of cutaneous lymphomas. Am J Dermatopathol 1999, **21:** 274–278.

1564 Sander CA, Medeiros LJ, Abruzzo LV, Horak ID, Jaffe ES. Lymphoblastic lymphoma presenting in cutaneous sites. A clinicopathologic analysis of six cases. J Am Acad Dermatol 1991, **25:** 1023–1031.

1565 Saxe N, Kahn LB, King H. Lymphoma of the skin. A comparative clinicopathologic study of 50 cases including mycosis fungoides and primary and secondary cutaneous lymphoma. J Cutan Pathol 1977, **4:** 111–122.

1566 Scarabello A, Leinweber B, Ardigo M, Rutten A, Feller AC, Kerl H, Cerroni L. Cutaneous lymphomas with prominent granulomatous reaction: a potential pitfall in the histopathologic diagnosis of cutaneous T- and B-cell lymphomas. Am J Surg Pathol 2002, **26:** 1259–1268.

1567 Scott PWB, Silvers DN, Helwig EB. Proliferating angioendotheliomatosis. Arch Pathol 1975, **99:** 323–326.

1568 Sepp N, Schuler G, Romani N, Geissler D, Gattringer C, Burg G, Bartram CR, Fritsch P. Intravascular lymphomatosis (angioendotheliomatosis). Evidence for a T-cell origin in two cases. Hum Pathol 1990, **21:** 1051–1058.

1569 Shaw MT, Jacobs SR. Cutaneous Hodgkin's disease in a patient with human immunodeficiency virus infection. Cancer 1989, **64:** 2585–2587.

1570 Sheibani K, Battifora H, Winberg CD, Burke JS, Ben-Ezra J, Ellinger GM, Quigley NJ, Fernandez BB, Morrow D, Rappaport H. Further evidence that "malignant angioendotheliomatosis" is an angiotropic large-cell lymphoma. N Engl J Med 1986, **314:** 943–948.

1571 Sioutos N, Kerl H, Murphy SB, Kadin ME. Primary cutaneous Hodgkin's disease. Unique clinical, morphologic, and immunophenotypic findings. Am J Dermatopathol 1994, **16:** 2–8.

1572 Soria C, Orradre J, Garcia-Almagro D, Martinez B, Algara P, Piris M. True histiocytic lymphoma (monocytic sarcoma). Am J Dermatopathol 1992, **14:** 511–517.

1573 Stroup RM, Sheibani K, Moncada A, Purdy LJ, Battifora H. Angiotropic (intravascular) large cell lymphoma. A clinicopathologic study of seven cases with unique clinical presentations. Cancer 1990, **66:** 1781–1788.

1574 Walker E, Robertson AG, Boorman JG, McNicol AM. Primary cutaneous plasmacytoma. The use of in situ hybridization to detect monoclonal immunoglobulin light-chain mRNA. Histopathology 1992, **20:** 135–138.

1575 White RW, Patterson JW. Cutaneous involvement in Hodgkin's disease. Cancer 1985, **55:** 1136–1145.

1576 Wick MR, Mills SE. Intravascular lymphomatosis. Clinicopathologic features and differential diagnosis. Semin Diagn Pathol 1991, **8:** 91–101.

1577 Wong KF, Chan JK, Li LP, Yau TK, Lee AW. Primary cutaneous plasmacytoma. Report of two cases and review of the literature. Am J Dermatopathol 1994, **16:** 392–397.

1578 Wong KF, Chan JK, Ng CS, Lee KC, Tsang WY, Cheung MM. CD56 (NKH1)-positive hematolymphoid malignancies. An aggressive neoplasm featuring frequent cutaneous/mucosal involvement, cytoplasmic azurophilic granules, and angiocentricity. Hum Pathol 1992, **23:** 798–804.

1579 Zaatari GS, Chan WC, Kim TH, Williams DL, Kletzel M. Malignant lymphoma of the skin in children. Cancer 1987, **59:** 1040–1045.

Leukemia

1580 Baer MR, Barcos M, Farrell H, Raza A, Preisler HD. Acute myelogenous leukemia with leukemia cutis. Eighteen cases seen between 1969 and 1986. Cancer 1989, **63:** 2192–2200.

1581 Cerroni L, Zenahlik P, Hofler G, Kaddu S, Smolle J, Kerl H. Specific cutaneous infiltrates of B-cell chronic lymphocytic leukemia: a clinicopathologic and prognostic study of 42 patients. Am J Surg Pathol 1996, **20:** 1000–1010.

1582 Desch JK, Smoller BR. The spectrum of cutaneous disease in leukemias. J Cutan Pathol 1993, **20:** 407–410.

1583 Dorfman DM, Kraus M, Perez-Atayde AR, Barnhill RL, Pinkus GS, Granter SR. CD99 (p30/32^MIC2^) immunoreactivity in the diagnosis of leukemia cutis. Mod Pathol 1997, **10:** 283–288.

1584 Greenwood R, Barker DJ, Tring FC, Parapia L, Reid M, Scott CS, Lauder I. Clinical and immunohistological characterization of cutaneous lesions in chronic lymphocytic leukemia. Br J Dermatol 1985, **113:** 447–453.

1585 Jones D, Dorfman DM, Barnhill RL, Granter SR. Leukemic vasculitis: a feature of leukemia cutis in some patients. Am J Clin Pathol 1997, **107:** 637–642.

1586 Kaiserling E, Horny HP, Geerts ML, Schmid U. Skin involvement in myelogenous leukemia. Morphologic and immunophenotypic heterogeneity of skin infiltrates. Mod Pathol 1994, **7:** 771–779.

1587 Long JC, Mihm MC. Multiple granulocytic tumors of the skin. Report of six cases of myelogenous leukemia with initial manifestations in the skin. Cancer 1977, **39:** 2004–2016.

1588 Ratnam KV, Su WP, Zeismer SC, Li CY. Value of immunohistochemistry in the diagnosis of leukemia cutis. Study of 54 cases using paraffin-section markers. J Cutan Pathol 1992, **19:** 193–200.

1589 Sepp N, Radaszkiewicz T, Meijer CJ, Smolle J, Seewann H, Fritsch P, Kerl H. Specific skin manifestations in acute leukemia with monocytic differentiation. A morphologic and immunohistochemical study of 11 cases. Cancer 1993, **71:** 124–132.

Other primary tumors and tumorlike conditions

1590 Barr RJ, Yi ES, Jensen JL, Wuerker RB, Liao SY. Meningioma-like tumor of the skin. An ultrastructural and immunohistochemical study. Am J Surg Pathol 1993, **17:** 779–787.

1591 Beham A, Fletcher CDM, Feichtinger J, Zelger B, Schmid C, Humer U. Synovial metaplasia of the skin. Virchows Arch [A] 1993, **423:** 315–318.

1592 Bhawan J, Dayal Y, Gonzalez-Serva A, Eisen R. Cutaneous metaplastic synovial cyst. J Cutan Pathol 1990, **17:** 22–26.

1593 Camacho F. Benign cutaneous cystic teratoma. J Cutan Pathol 1982, **9:** 345–351.

1594 Conlin PA, Jimenez-Quintero LP, Rapini RP. Osteomas of the skin revisited: a clinicopathologic review of 74 cases. Am J Dermatopathol 2002, **24:** 479–483.

1595 Fowler MR, Nathan CA, Abreo F. Synovial metaplasia, a specialized form of repair. Arch Pathol Lab Med 2002, **126:** 727–730.

1596 French CA, Mentzel T, Kutzner H, Fletcher CD. Intradermal spindle cell/pleomorphic lipoma: a distinct subset. Am J Dermatopathol 2002, **22:** 496–502.

1597 Gonzalez JG, Ghiselli RW, Santa Cruz DJ. Synovial metaplasia of the skin. Am J Surg Pathol 1987, **11:** 343–350.

1598 Hasegawa SL, Davison JM, Rutten A, Fletcher JA, Fletcher CD. Primary cutaneous Ewing's sarcoma: immunophenotypic and molecular cytogenetic evaluation of five cases. Am J Surg Pathol 1998, **22:** 310–318.

1599 Hoang MP, Rogers BB, Albores-Saavedra J. Giant cell tumor of the skin: a morphologic and immunohistochemical study of five cases. Ann Diagn Pathol 2002, **6:** 288–293.

1600 Hsueh S, Santa Cruz DJ. Cartilaginous lesions of the skin and superficial soft tissue. J Cutan Pathol 1982, **9:** 405–416.

1601 Hurt MA, Santa Cruz DJ. Cutaneous inflammatory pseudotumor. Lesions resembling "inflammatory pseudotumors" or "plasma cell granulomas" of extracutaneous sites. Am J Surg Pathol 1990, **14:** 764–773.

1602 Marrogi AJ, Swanson PE, Kyriakos M, Wick MR. Rudimentary meningocele of the skin. Clinicopathologic features and differential diagnosis. J Cutan Pathol 1991, **18:** 178–188.

1603 Nogales F, Martin F, Linares J, Naranjo R, Concha A. Myxoid change in decidualized scar endometriosis mimicking malignancy. J Cutan Pathol 1993, **20:** 87–91.

1604 Pellegrini AE. Cutaneous decidualized endometriosis. A pseudomalignancy. Am J Dermatopathol 1982, **4:** 171–174.

1605 Pollock AM, Sweeney EC. Primary cutaneous synovial sarcoma: a case report. Am J Dermatopathol 1998, **20:** 509–512.

1606 Radice F, Gianotti R. Cutaneous ganglion cell tumor of the skin. Case report and review of the literature. Am J Dermatopathol 1993, **15:** 488–491.

1607 Steck WD, Helwig EB. Cutaneous endometriosis. JAMA 1965, **191:** 167–170.

1608 Suster S, Rosai J. Hamartoma of the scalp with ectopic meningothelial elements. A distinctive benign soft tissue lesion that may simulate angiosarcoma. Am J Surg Pathol 1990, **14:** 1–11.

1609 Tang TT, Dunn DK, Hodach AE, Harrist TJ, Mihm MC Jr. Subcutaneous and skeletal chordomoid nodules in an infant. Am J Dermatopathol 1981, **3:** 303–310.

1610 Tsai TF, Chuan MT, Hsiao CH. A cystic teratoma of the skin. Histopathology 1997, **29:** 384–386.

1610a Wallace CA, Hallman JR, Sangueza OP. Primary cutaneous ganglioneuroma. A report of two cases and literature review. Am J Dermatopathol 2003, **25:** 239–242.

Metastatic carcinoma

1611 Aguilar A, Schoendorff C, Lopez Redondo MJ, Ambrojo P, Requena L, Sanchez Yus E. Epidermotropic metastases from internal carcinomas. Am J Dermatopathol 1991, **13:** 452–458.

1612 Brownstein MH, Helwig EB. Metastatic tumors of the skin. Cancer 1972, **29:** 1298–1307.

1613 Brownstein MH, Helwig EB. Patterns of cutaneous metastases. Arch Dermatol 1972, **105:** 862–868.

1614 Conner DH, Taylor HB, Helwig EB. Cutaneous metastasis of renal cell carcinoma. Arch Pathol 1963, **76:** 339–346.

1615 McKee PH. Cutaneous metastases. J Cutan Pathol 1985, **12:** 239–250.

1616 Menter A, Boyd AS, McCaffree DM. Recurrent renal cell carcinoma presenting as skin nodules: two case reports and review of the literature. Cutis 1989, **44:** 305–308.

1617 Reingold IM. Cutaneous metastases from internal carcinoma. Cancer 1966, **19:** 162–168.

1618 Requena L, Sanchez Yus E, Nunez C, White CR, Sangueza OP. Epidermotropically metastatic breast carcinomas: rare histopathologic variants mimicking melanoma and Paget's disease. Am J Dermatopathol 1997, **18:** 385–395.

1619 Rodriguez G, Villamizar R. Carcinoid tumor with skin metastasis. Am J Dermatopathol 1992, **14:** 263–269.

1620 Youngberg GA, Berro J, Young M, Leicht SS. Metastatic epidermotropic squamous carcinoma histologically simulating primary carcinoma. Am J Dermatopathol 1989, **11:** 457–465.

5 Oral cavity and oropharynx

Normal anatomy

The oropharyngeal region represents the upper portion of the digestive tract; in addition, the oropharynx constitutes a portion of the upper respiratory tract. The oropharynx and hypopharynx share many of the diseases of the two adjacent digestive tract organs—oral cavity and esophagus—whereas the nasopharynx shares them with the two other components of the upper respiratory tract, i.e., the nasal cavity and paranasal sinuses.

For the purposes of the topographic characterization of lesions that occur in this area (particularly squamous cell carcinoma), the oropharyngeal region is divided into the following regions: (1) *Lip*, including only the vermilion surface and comprising an upper and lower lip joined at the commissures of the mouth; (2) *floor of the mouth*, a U-shaped area bounded by the lower gingiva and the oral tongue; (3) *oral tongue*, defined as the portion of the tongue anterior to the circumvallate papillae; (4) *buccal mucosa*, which covers the inner surface of the cheeks and lips; (5) *gingiva* (alveolar ridge), the mucosa covering the mandible or maxilla from the gingivobuccal gutter to the origin of the mobile mucosa; (6) *retromolar trigone*, a small triangular surface behind the third molar covering the ascending ramus of the mandible; (7) *hard palate*, a semilunar area located between the upper alveolar ridge and the mucous membrane covering the palatine process of the maxillary bones; (8) *base of the tongue*, bound anteriorly by the circumvallate papillae, laterally by the glossotonsillar sulci, and posteriorly by the epiglottis; (9) *tonsillar area*, which includes the anterior and posterior tonsillar pillars and the tonsillar fossa; (10) *soft palate*; and (11) *pharyngeal walls*.[1,1a]

The surface epithelium of this region is of stratified squamous type throughout, with greater depth than the epithelium of the skin and lacking hair follicles and sweat glands. It keratinizes in the areas most exposed to mastication (gingivae, hard palate, and dorsum of tongue) but not in others. The lamina propria is composed of loose connective tissue and contains mucous and serous glands of minor salivary gland type. Minor but distinctive variations exist among the various areas of this region.

There is a long-standing argument as to whether all routine tonsil and adenoid specimens from otherwise healthy pediatric patients with recurrent infections or obstructive sleep apnea should be examined microscopically or not. We, like others, favor the policy of examining all the cases grossly and submitting for microscopic examination only those cases in which there is a suspicion of significant pathology on the basis of either the clinical or gross findings (such as specimen assymetry).[6a]

Regarding the normal anatomy of the tonsillar region, it has been noted that skeletal muscle is present in close contact with the lymphoid tissue of the region; therefore, its detection in routine tonsillectomy specimens is not an indication of inappropriate surgical technique.[2]

The oral cavity is the site of numerous diseases, both congenital and acquired, affecting a large variety of tissues and systems. Only those that occur commonly enough to be of interest to the surgical pathologist are discussed here. For a more thorough discussion of these diseases and the rarer diseases, the reader is referred to specialized textbooks on the subject.[3–6]

Congenital abnormalities

Dermoid cysts are seen in the midline of the floor of the mouth. Although present at birth, they may become evident only later on when secondarily inflamed.[12] They are lined by squamous epithelium and contain skin adnexa.[16] **Heterotopic gastric or intestinal epithelium** has been reported in the tongue and floor of the mouth, sometimes resulting in cystic formations.[13] Minute **cysts of odontogenic origin** are commonly seen in the alveolar and palatal mucosa of newborns and older infants; they need not be biopsied (see Chapter 6). Nodules of **heterotopic nerve tissue** in the palate or parapharyngeal space, mainly composed of glial elements and ependyma-lined clefts, have been reported[7,9]; in rare cases, a neoplasm may arise from them.[8] **White sponge nevus,** an autosomal dominantly inherited disease, is characterized by large white plaques in the oral mucosa (Figs 5.1 and 5.2). Microscopically there is striking intracellular edema throughout the malpighian layer.[17] **Fordyce's disease** refers to the presence of normal sebaceous glands inside the oral cavity, a very common occurrence. Sometimes

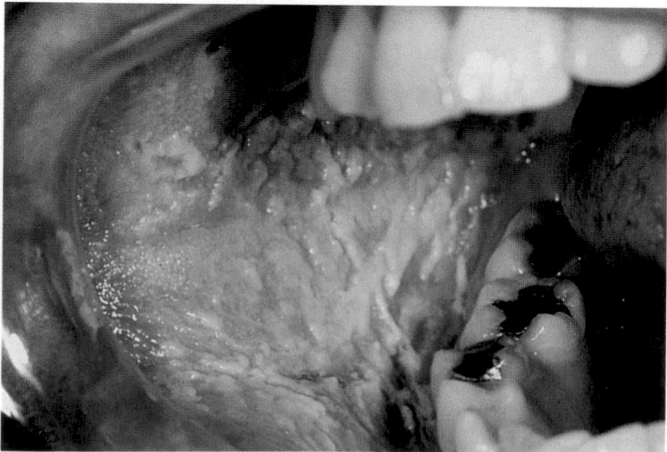

Fig. 5.1 Clinical appearance of white sponge nevus. (Courtesy Dr James Sciubba, Long Island Jewish Medical Center, Long Island, New York)

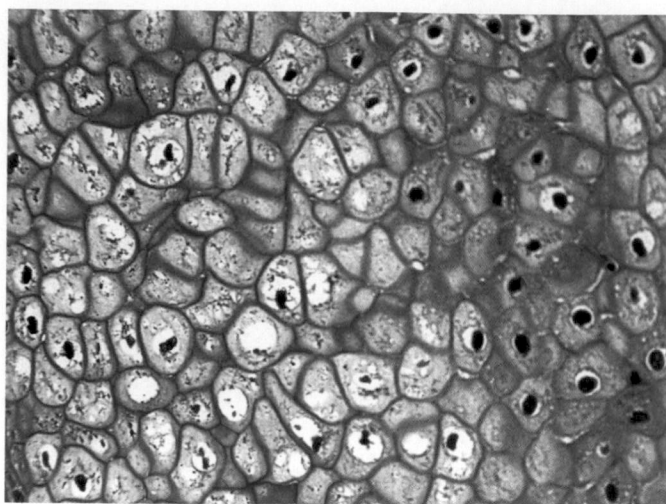

Fig. 5.2 White sponge nevus. There is a marked pallor of the cytoplasm due to intracellular edema.

these glands undergo hyperplastic changes and appear as discrete nodules.[10] The entity **lingual thyroid** is discussed in Chapter 9.

Although it does not represent a congenital anomaly, the occurrence of **epithelial nests** in intraoral sensory nerve endings should be mentioned here.[11,15] Their importance relates to the fact that pathologists unaware of their existence might easily confuse them with perineural invasion by epidermoid carcinoma. These formations are normally occurring neuroepithelial structures of alleged receptor function, known by anatomists as the *organ of Chievitz,* Chievitz's paraparotid organ, and juxtaoral organ[9a,18,19] (Fig. 5.3). They lie deep to the internal pterygoid muscle near the pterygomandibular raphe and are associated with small branches from the buccal nerve. These structures can undergo nodular hyperplasia.[14]

Inflammatory diseases

Chronic inflammatory lesions of nonspecific type are produced in the oral cavity by ill-fitting dentures; ragged, sharp teeth; and poor dental hygiene. Removal of the offending agent allows the pathologic process to subside. Microscopically, a combination of hyperplastic epithelium, fibrous tissue, and inflammatory cells in varying proportions is seen. Bhaskar et al.[24] described 341 such cases, all associated with the use of dentures, under the term *inflammatory papillary hyperplasia;* 82.7% of the lesions were located in the palate. Localized overgrowth of the epithelium with or without ulceration is frequent, and it is not rare to see large pseudotumors made up of fibrous tissue and chronic inflammatory cells, among which plasma cells may be prominent.[21] The inflammation distorts the epithelial pegs and may produce areas in which squamous cells are isolated from the overlying epithelium.[20] Lesions in which the fibrous pro-

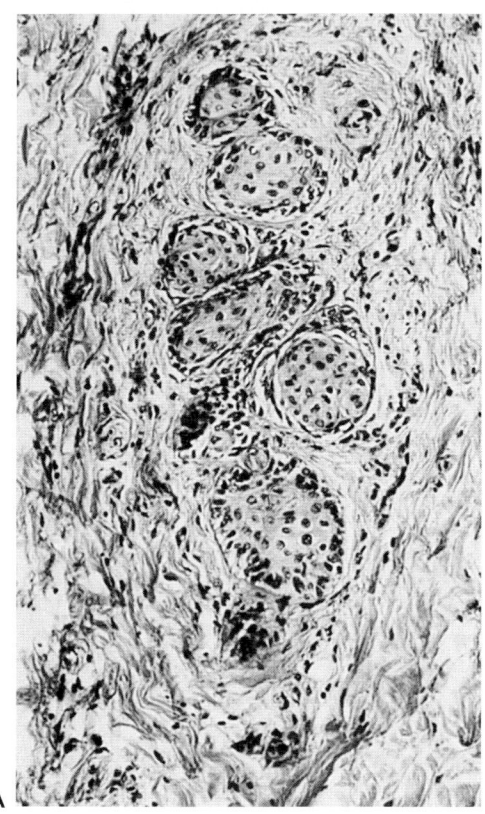 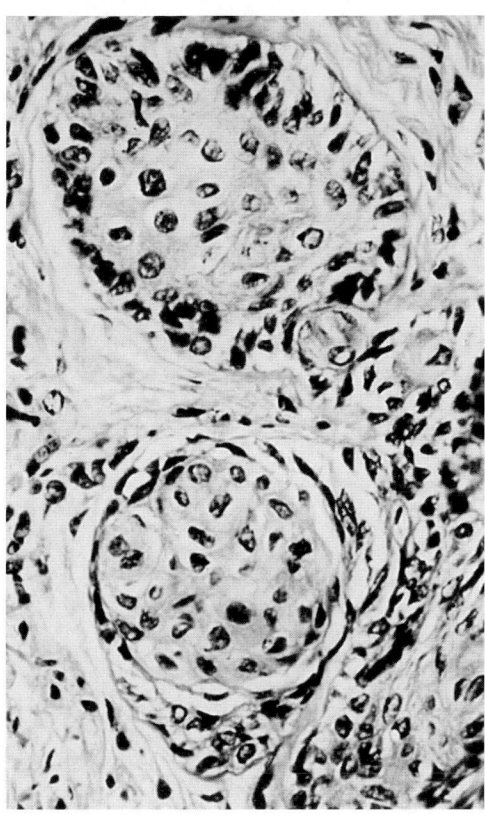

A   B

Fig. 5.3 Low-power (**A**) and high-power (**B**) views of juxtaoral organ of Chievitz. (From Tschen JA, Fechner RE. The juxtaoral organ of Chievitz. Am J Surg Pathol 1979, **3**: 147–150.)

liferation predominates are sometimes inaccurately described as *irritation fibromas*. Scattered stellate and multinucleated giant cells can be seen throughout the fibrous tissue, in which case the term *giant cell fibroma* has been used.[34,41]

Geographic tongue (benign migratory glossitis, glossitis migrans) is a relatively common condition (affecting 1% to 2% of the population) of unknown cause, which is usually asymptomatic. Most patients are adults, but it has also been seen in children. It often occurs in association with fissured tongue. Clinically, it appears as an erythematous flat zone on the dorsum of the tongue resulting from loss of the filiform papillae (Fig. 5.4). The microscopic appearance is that of a psoriasiform process; there is acanthosis with migration of neutrophils throughout the epithelium to form microabscesses near the surface, accompanied by a mild inflammatory infiltrate in the lamina propria.[46]

Tuberculosis is a rare lesion within the oral cavity. It is usually seen on the tongue as a painful ulcer, but it also may occur on the buccal mucosa. It nearly always is associated with advanced pulmonary disease. Microscopically, there are typical tubercles.[30]

Syphilis may produce a gumma in the tongue or palate appearing as a painless indurated mass. Microscopically, there is a granuloma with giant cells, numerous plasma cells, and prominent vascular changes. A relationship was said to exist between syphilis and tongue cancer, although the percentage of patients with such association keeps dropping. Thus, a

study of 243 patients with cancer of the tongue revealed that only 15 (6.1%) had a history of syphilis.[37]

Histoplasmosis can occur anywhere in the oral cavity and can closely simulate squamous cell carcinoma on clinical examination. Indurated ulcers, nodular lesions, or verrucous masses can be present. The usual microscopic appearance is that of a granuloma, although sometimes only a nonspecific inflammatory reaction is

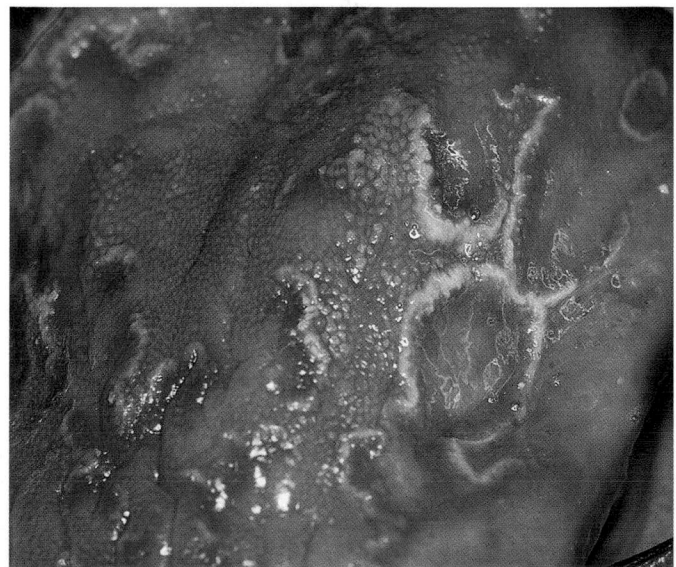

Fig. 5.4 Clinical appearance of geographic tongue. (Courtesy of Dr. James Sciubba, Long Island Medical Center Long Island, New York)

seen. Special stains (Gomori's methenamine-silver or PAS-Gridley) are necessary for the identification of the fungi.[23]

Crohn's disease can involve the oral cavity and pharynx, sometimes as the initial manifestation.[31,40] Oral lesions develop in about 6% of patients with Crohn's disease at some stage of this disorder. The most common locations are lips, gingiva, vestibular sulci, and buccal mucosa.[40] The lesions can manifest as edema, ulcers, or polypoid papulous hyperplastic mucosa. Microscopically, there are edema, dilatation of lymph vessels, chronic inflammation, scattered giant cells, and rarely, noncaseating granulomas.[22,42]

Sarcoidosis may affect the oral mucosa, gingiva, tongue, hard palate, and major salivary glands. Random biopsy of the lower lip has been successfully used to support a diagnosis of sarcoidosis; in a series of 75 consecutive patients, noncaseating granulomas were found by this procedure in 58%.[38]

Melkersson–Rosenthal syndrome is composed of the triad of orofacial swelling, peripheral facial nerve paralysis, and plicated tongue. *Cheilitis granulomatosa* is probably an abortive variant of this syndrome, the etiology and pathogenesis of which remain obscure.[47] Microscopically, there is a granulomatous inflammation primarily involving the stroma of the lip (Fig. 5.5). The differential diagnosis includes sarcoidosis and Crohn's disease.

Granulomatous tonsillitis is occasionally found in specimens of tonsillectomy performed because of chronic recurrent tonsillar enlargement; in most cases, no specific organism is recovered, and the course is benign.[45]

Waldeyer's ring lymphoid hyperplasia is an often symptomatic complication of HIV infection. Characteristically, the process is accompanied by a scattering of multinucleated giant cells adjacent to the tonsillary crypt of surface epithelium.[36] These cells, which harbor significant amounts of HPV, exhibit histiocytic markers and probably belong to the accessory immune system.[25]

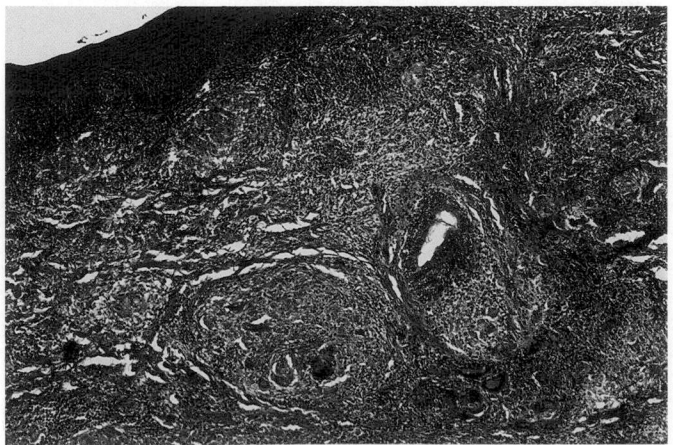

Fig. 5.5 Lip biopsy in a patient with Melkersson–Rosenthal syndrome. Numerous non-necrotizing granulomas are seen beneath a normal epithelium.

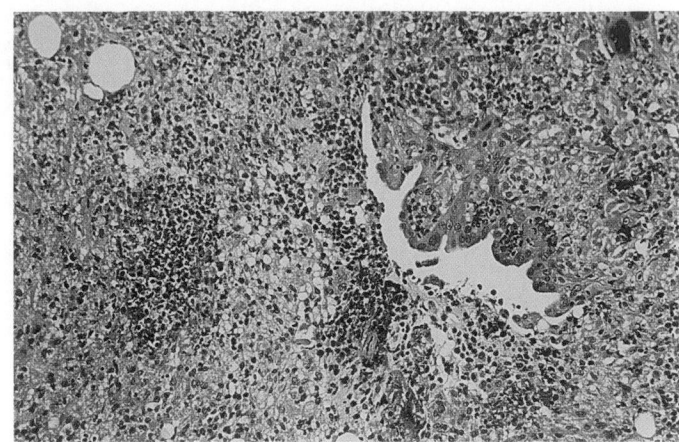

Fig. 5.6 Tongue ulceration with eosinophilia. A mixed inflammatory infiltrate rich in eosinophils is present, together with dilated vessels.

Wegener's granulomatosis may manifest in the oral cavity as a red to purple hyperplastic gingiva; in about 5% of the cases it is the first manifestation of the disease.[39] On microscopic examination, there are epithelioid histiocytes, giant cells, eosinophils, pseudoepitheliomatous hyperplasia, and, in rare cases, vasculitis.[32] Both this condition and the so-called **lethal midline granuloma**, which may present initially as a nonhealing ulcer of the hard palate, are described in more detail in Chapter 7.

Behçet's disease affects primarily skin, oral mucosa, and eyes and is characterized microscopically by a leukocytoclastic vasculitis.[33] **Cytomegalovirus infection** can manifest in the oral cavity as an ulcerated lesion.[28,35]

Tongue ulceration with eosinophilia (eosinophilic ulcer; ulcerative eosinophilic granuloma; Riga–Fede disease) may mimic carcinoma clinically. Microscopically, it shows a polymorphic inflammatory infiltrate rich in eosinophils, extending into the submucosa, muscle, and minor salivary glands[26,44] (Fig. 5.6). The initiating event is presumably traumatic (crush injury to the tongue muscle), hence its alternative designation as *traumatic (ulcerative) granuloma*.[27,48]

Atypical histiocytic granuloma is the name given to a reactive nodule in the oral cavity characterized by a heavy histiocytic infiltration; the cellularity and mitotic activity may lead to confusion with a malignant process.[29]

Post-traumatic spindle cell nodule, analogous to that originally described in the urogenital system, can occur in the oral cavity and lead to the same interpretative error, i.e., its overdiagnosis as leiomyosarcoma.[43]

Other non-neoplastic lesions

Leukoedema presents as a diffuse opalescent lesion of the cheek mucosa that can extend to the lips; microscopically, the main alteration is vacuolization or intracellular edema of the malpighian cells, a change of a probably degenerative nature.[71]

Fibrous hyperplasia of the gingiva has been traditionally described as a complication of diphenylhydantoin (Dilantin) therapy, but most cases seen today are genetically inherited, idiopathic, or associated with other drugs, such as cyclosporin A.[68,72] The gingival thickening can be so extreme as to necessitate surgical removal.

Oral submucosal fibrosis, as seen mainly in Indians and Pakistanis, is a reactive process characterized microscopically by subepithelial fibrosis and chronic inflammation, accompanied by hyalinization and loss of vascularity. The overlying epithelium may be either atrophic or hyperplastic and is often hyperkeratotic.[65] The pathogenesis is unknown. The disease is thought to predispose the patient to the development of squamous cell carcinoma.[64]

Mucous cyst (mucocele), when applied to a lesion of the oral cavity, refers to two different processes. The first and more common is referred to as *extravasation mucocele* and represents a focus of stromal reaction to spillage of mucus from a traumatically injured minor salivary gland.[66] It is often seen in young individuals, the lower lip being the classic location, and the microscopic pattern is that of granulation tissue surrounding one or more spaces containing mucin[60] (Fig. 5.7). Sometimes the cysts are very superficial and simulate vesicobullous diseases clinically.[56] An anatomic variant of this process is known as *ranula* when it occurs as a blue-domed cyst in a sublingual location, and as *plunging ranula* when it extends into the neck above the hyoid bone.[59,62]

The second type, named *retention mucocele*, occurs most often in older patients and in other locations in the oral cavity, such as the floor of the mouth and the inside of the cheek. Microscopically, a mucus-filled cyst completely lined by cylindric, cuboidal, or flattened cells is seen.[55]

Oral focal mucinosis is the oral counterpart of the more common cutaneous focal mucinosis[69]; this condition is located in oral cavity sites other than the lip and lacks the granulation tissue wall and inflammatory cells consistently seen in extravasation mucocele.

Necrotizing sialometaplasia is a reactive condition involving minor or—less commonly—major salivary glands; its importance lies in the fact that it can be confused histologically with squamous cell or mucoepidermoid carcinoma.[49,51,52] The disease usually presents as an ulcerating lesion of the hard palate characterized by vascular proliferation, prominent inflammatory infiltrate, and partial necrosis of salivary glands, associated with regeneration and squamous metaplasia of the adjacent duct and acini. Cases also have been described in the nasal cavity, gingiva, lip, hypopharynx, maxillary sinus, and major salivary glands. The morphologic changes are somewhat similar to those seen in this region after radiation therapy. The pathogenesis is probably ischemic, and some cases have been seen as a complication of vasculitis and other primary vascular disorders. The lobular configuration that these lesions exhibit on low-power examination is an important sign in the differential diagnosis with squamous cell carcinoma[53] (Fig. 5.8).

Amyloidosis of the tongue is a common microscopic finding in older individuals, usually as an isolated event but sometimes as the manifestation of a systemic disease.[61] Only in a small proportion of cases are the deposits extensive enough to result in clinically evident disease in the form of diffuse macroglossia or a localized tumor.[70,73]

Malakoplakia has been reported as a unilateral tonsillar lesion.[57]

Dermatologic disorders of various types can involve the oral cavity, including *lichen planus,*[50,58] *lupus erythematosus,*[58,67] *pemphigus vulgaris,*[54] and *pityriasis lichenoides acuta (Mucha–Habermann disease).*[63]

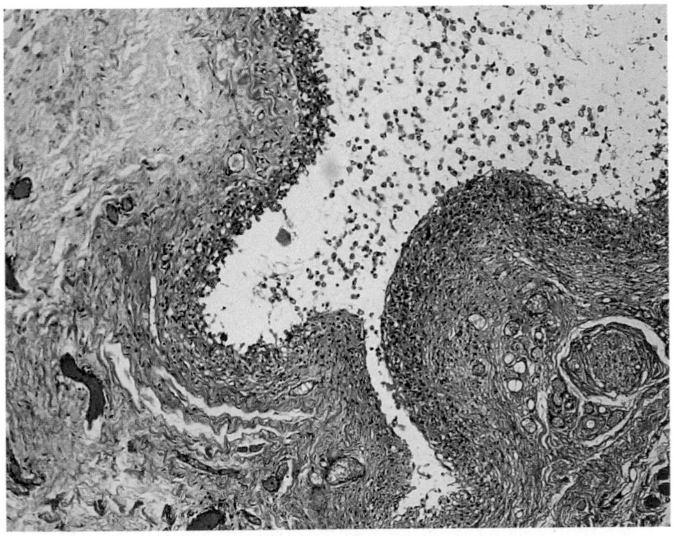

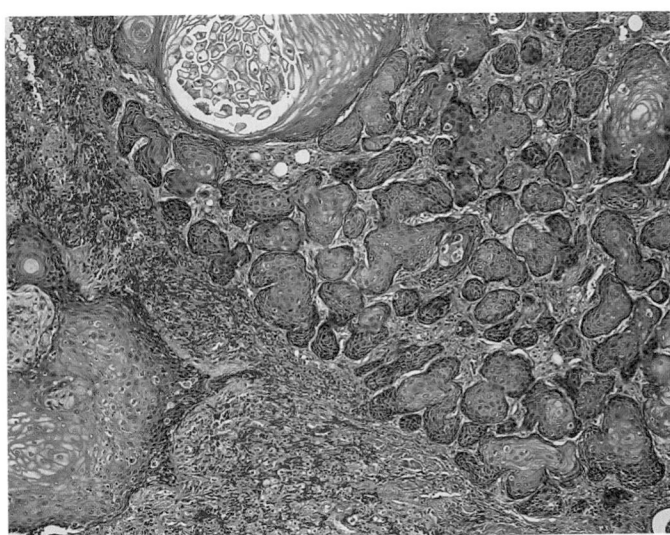

Fig. 5.7 Extravasation mucocele. The lining of the cyst is made up of histiocytes rather than epithelial cells.

Fig. 5.8 Necrotizing sialometaplasia. The retained lobular configuration is an important diagnostic clue.

Tumors and tumorlike conditions of surface epithelium

Intraepithelial proliferative lesions

It has been rightly pointed out that the lesions grouped under this generic term "continue to be among the most widely discussed, reclassified, and semantically tortured conditions in the medical literature".[99] Part of the problem resides in the fact that different clinical and pathologic terms have been introduced independently over the years and that the correlations between them—although certainly present, as will be shown below—are less than perfect. Among the clinical terms, **leukoplakia** remains the most widely used.[82,99,103] It has been defined as "a white patch or plaque, not less than 5 mm in diameter, that cannot be removed by rubbing and cannot be classified as any other diagnosable disease", and it implies nothing about the histologic appearance. It is equivalent to the term *keratosis* as used more often at other sites (such as larynx) and is sometimes subclassified (always on clinical grounds) as homogeneous, nonhomogeneous (speckled; nodular; erythroleukoplakia), erythroplakia (which is red rather than white), and proliferative verrucous leukoplakia.[76,90,99] The most common location of leukoplakia, as defined above, is the buccal gingival gutter.[91] The speckled type of leukoplakia is superinfected by *Candida albicans* in over 60% of the cases.[92]

At the histopathologic level, terms such as keratosis, squamous hyperplasia and verrucous hyperplasia have been used interchangeably, the choice depending on minor architectural differences but mainly on personal preference. When dysplasia is present, this is added to the diagnosis and the changes are graded as mild, moderate and severe, the latter merging with squamous cell carcinoma in situ and therefore grouped with it, as it is at other sites[79,83,85,96] (Figs 5.9 to 5.12). The microscopic criteria for the diagnosis of severe dysplasia/CIS are the same as for other mucosal membranes: epithelial disarray with full thickness atypia, no flattening or horizontal elongation of the surface layer, and a basement membrane that appears intact in routinely stained sections (although it may show thinning and discontinuities in immunostains for basement membrane components such as type IV collagen and laminin[94]).

The atypical proliferative changes characteristically involve the surface epithelium, but they can also extend to the ducts of minor salivary glands.[77] When the dysplastic changes are accompanied by hyperkeratosis, prominent granular layer, irregular basal layer, sawtoothed rete pegs, and bandlike lymphocytic infiltrate, the condition is referred to as *lichenoid dysplasia*[75,81,86] (Fig. 5.13). Because of the often subtle degree of the dysplastic changes, this condition is often underdiagnosed as lichen planus, a mistake that may have serious consequences.[86]

The alternative terminology that has been proposed for this group of lesions is that of *oral intraepithelial*

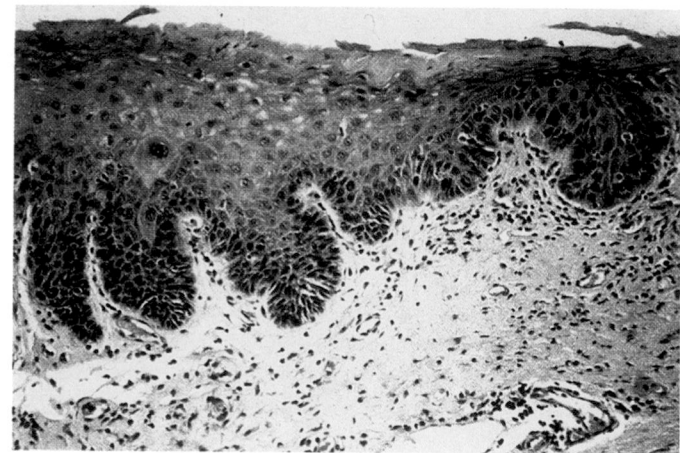

Fig. 5.10 Mild dysplasia. (From Pindborg JJ, Reichart PA, van der Waal I. Histological typing of cancer and precancer of the oral mucosa, World Health Organization International Classification of Tumours, ed 2, Berlin, Springer, 1997.)

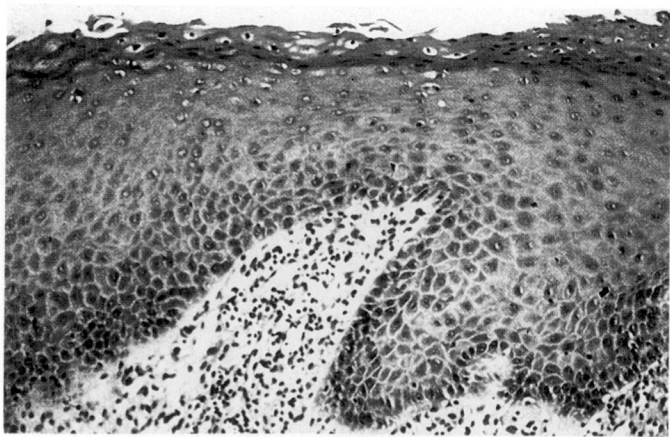

Fig. 5.9 Keratosis without dysplasia. (From Pindborg JJ, Reichart PA, Smith CJ, van der Waal I. Histological typing of cancer and precancer of the oral mucosa, World Health Organization International Classification of Tumours, ed 2, Berlin, Springer, 1997.)

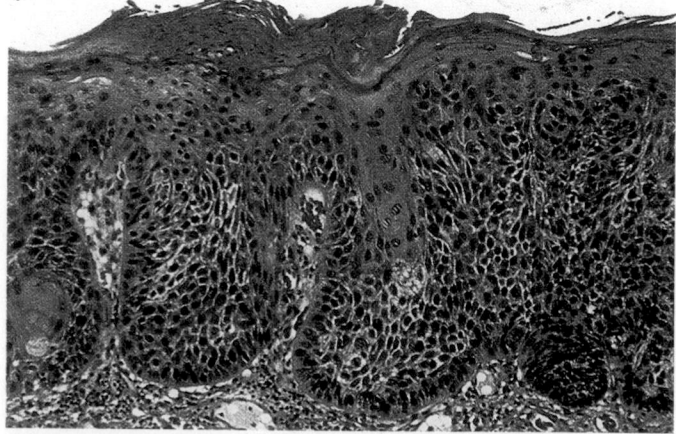

Fig. 5.11 Moderate dysplasia. (From Pindborg JJ, Reichart PA, Smith CJ, van der Waal I. Histological typing of cancer and precancer of the oral mucosa, World Health Organization International Classification of Tumours, ed 2, Berlin, Springer, 1997.)

neoplasia (OIN), grade I (equivalent to mild dysplasia), grade II (equivalent to moderate dysplasia), and grade III (equivalent to severe dysplasia/CIS). Unless the latter terminology were to be adopted (and there is no sign that it will happen soon), our preference is to use *keratosis* as the generic term, to qualify it if indicated and—most importantly—to indicate the presence and degree of dysplasia, according to the scheme in Table 5.1. It should be acknowledged that, no matter what terminology is used, the determination is subjective and marred by a marked degree of interobserver variability.

At the immunohistochemical level, the main distinction between keratosis without and with dysplasia is a quantitative one: whereas in the former the expressions

Table 5.1 Classification of keratosis

Generic term	Qualifiers	Dysplasia
Keratosis	(NOS)	Absent
	Lichenoid	Mild
	Verrucous	Moderate
	Proliferative verrucous	Severe/CIS

Examples:
- Keratosis, with no dysplasia
- Keratosis, lichenoid, with mild dysplasia
- Keratosis, with severe dysplasia/CIS

of keratin 19, epidermal growth factor and proliferation-related antigens (such as Ki-67) are all limited to the basal layer, in the latter they are also expressed in suprabasal cells. Of these markers, Ki-67 (MIB-1) seems the most consistent and therefore the most useful for the identification and grading of the dysplasia.[78,80] DNA ploidy studies have shown that about one third of "leukoplakic" lesions are hyperploid or aneuploid, but that the relationship of this parameter with the grade of dysplasia is poor.[93,100] NOR distribution counts in dysplasia have an intermediate grade between those seen in normal mucosa and in invasive carcinoma, but there is a great deal of overlap.[102] Overexpression of p53 has been found in only a small minority of dysplasias, in keeping with the known late occurrence of this event in the Knori genesis chain.[78,88,89]

In terms of clinicopathologic correlations, severe dysplastic changes are much more likely to be present in lesions with the clinical appearance of erythroplakia than those of homogeneous leukoplakia, with erythroleukoplakia occupying an intermediate position.[74] Thus, of 158 "early" asymptomatic squamous cell carcinomas studied by Mashberg et al.[87], 143 (90.5%) had red velvety ("erythroplastic") components, whereas only 10 (9.8%) had white components; only four lesions were solely white, and there was no color distinction between in situ and invasive carcinoma.[74] Presence of induration almost guaranteed the presence of stromal invasion.

There is also a correlation between the location of the leukoplakia and the chance of it exhibiting dysplastic changes microscopically, in the sense of this probability being much higher for the lesions located in the floor of the mouth.[101]

The most important issue concerning this group of lesions is the likelihood of them evolving into invasive carcinomas of either squamous or verrucous type. There is no question that this prediction is more accurate when made on the basis of the severity of the dysplasia as judged microscopically than when attempted on the basis of clinical features. If all cases fitting the clinical definition of dysplasia are included, the incidence of subsequent malignancy is very low. Pindborg et al.[90] followed 248 patients with oral leukoplakia (mostly of the speckled type) for 1 to 10 years, and found that only

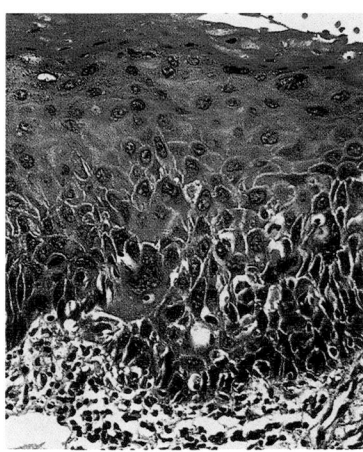

Fig. 5.12 Severe dysplasia. (From Pindborg JJ, Reichart PA, Smith CJ, van der Waal I. Histological typing of cancer and precancer of the oral mucosa, World Health Organization International Classification of Tumours, ed 2, Berlin, Springer, 1997.)

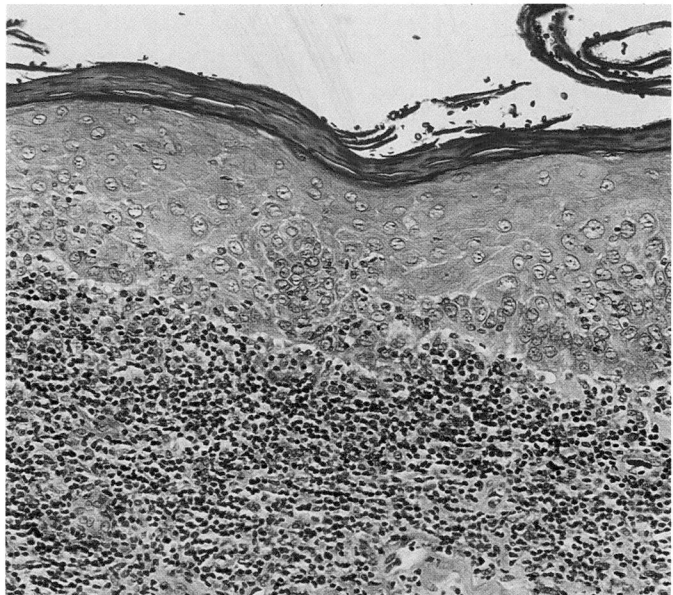

Fig. 5.13 Lichenoid dysplasia. There is a bandlike lymphocytic infiltrate beneath the squamous epithelium, with some infiltration of lymphocytes in the lower third. This lesion is commonly underdiagnosed.

4.4% developed squamous cell carcinoma. In Einhorn and Wersäll's series[80] of 782 patients with a mean follow-up of 11.7 years, the incidence of invasive carcinoma was 2.4% after 10 years and 4% after 20 years. Most other series quote figures ranging from <1% to 6%,[97,98] the outstanding exception being a series of 257 patients from San Francisco followed for an average period of 7.2 years in which the incidence of carcinoma was 17.5%.[98]

From a microscopic standpoint, the implicit assumption is that the greater the atypia, the higher the premalignant potential. It is, however, important to remember that some squamous cell carcinomas of the mouth present without any evidence of adjacent or preceding dysplasia,[79] and that a lesion with the features of severe dysplasia/CIS may simply be the peripheral expression of an invasive carcinoma that has not been properly sampled.

There is hope that some special procedure will eventually allow a more accurate and reproducible prediction of the premalignant potential of these lesions.[95] One such technique is the determination of the nuclear DNA content (ploidy). Sudbo et al.[100] analyzed 150 patients with microscopically confirmed dysplasias and a mean follow-up of 103 months. The incidence of carcinoma was 3% for those with diploid lesions, 60% for those with tetraploid lesions, and 84% for those with tetraploid lesions. These remarkable results are in obvious need of independent confirmation.

Actinic cheilitis is the equivalent in the lip vermilion of actinic keratosis of the skin on morphologic, pathogenetic, and behavioral grounds; it should therefore not be equated with the leukoplakic–dysplastic conditions within the oral cavity previously discussed. An increased prevalence of dysplastic and malignant lip lesions has been documented in renal transplant recipients and other immunosuppressed individuals.[84]

Oral lesions and human papilloma virus (HPV)

The oral cavity can be the site of a variety of HPV-related lesions, some of which are microscopically and behaviorally analogous to those located in the genital tract.[113] These include *focal epithelial hyperplasia (Heck's disease)*,[116] *verruca vulgaris*,[111] *condyloma acuminatum*,[120] and *squamous papilloma*[104,115] (Fig. 5.14).

Heck's disease presents clinically as a well-circumscribed, sessile, pale elevation of the buccal mucosa. Microscopically, the most prominent feature is the presence of balloon cells in the malpighian layers. This disorder is very common among Native Americans and Eskimos.[116]

The verrucae, condylomas, and papillomas often exhibit koilocytosis as a sign of cytopathic effect. Atypical nuclear changes may be present, especially in HIV-positive patients.[117]

An etiologic role for HPV has also been suggested for verrucous carcinoma[109] and squamous cell carcinoma, including some of its variants.[108,115b,118,124] The benign oral

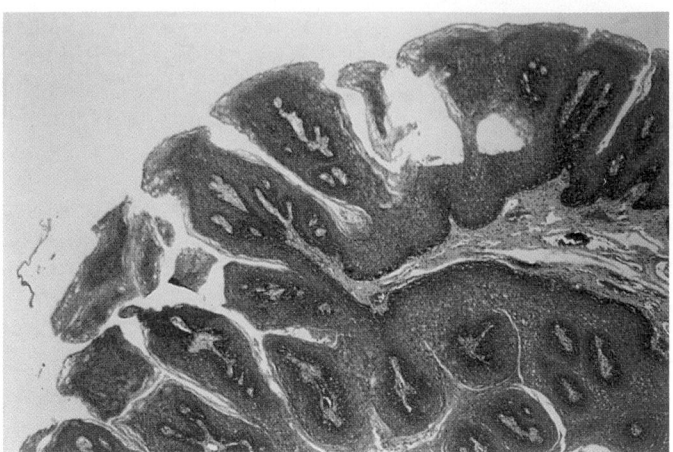

Fig. 5.14 Squamous papilloma of the oral cavity.

lesions are statistically associated with HPV types 2, 4, 6, 11, 13, and 32, and the malignant ones with HPV types 16, 18, and 33.[107,113] Among the carcinomas, those with the highest incidence of HPV detection are the poorly differentiated nonkeratinizing tumors of the tonsil seen in young individuals.[109a,123] Parenthetically, many of the latter tumors express p16 protein.[115a] HPV-positive oropharyngeal cancers are also more likely to exhibit a basaloid morphology.[114]

Not all squamous papillomas of the oral cavity are virally induced. Some may be the result of mechanical irritation, and others (although possibly viral related) are genetically determined, such as those occurring as a component of Cowden's syndrome.[121,122]

Hairy leukoplakia was originally thought to be associated with HPV but is now believed to be due to EBV.[105,106] This lesion develops in patients with HIV infection and is characteristically located along the lateral edges of the tongue.[110] Microscopically, it shows parakeratosis, acanthosis, and intranuclear inclusions in keratinocytes, associated with ballooned or ground-glass cytoplasm (Fig. 5.15).[112,119] There is a high incidence of superinfection by *Candida* organisms.

Squamous cell carcinoma

General features

Practically speaking, cancer of the oral cavity mucosa is synonymous with squamous cell (epidermoid) carcinoma. Known predisposing factors vary according to the location of the tumor. For carcinoma of the lip, they include sunlight, fair complexion, and—to a lesser extent—smoking and mechanical irritation.[126,128,130] Transplant recipients are also at an increased risk, presumably as a result of immunosuppression.[129,134] This risk is greater among younger patients.[129]

Oropharyngeal carcinomas have been related mainly to tobacco and alcohol, but also to syphilis, oral sepsis, iron deficiency, oral candidiasis, and Fanconi's anemia.[125–127,134a,136,137] Most cases occur in men over the age of

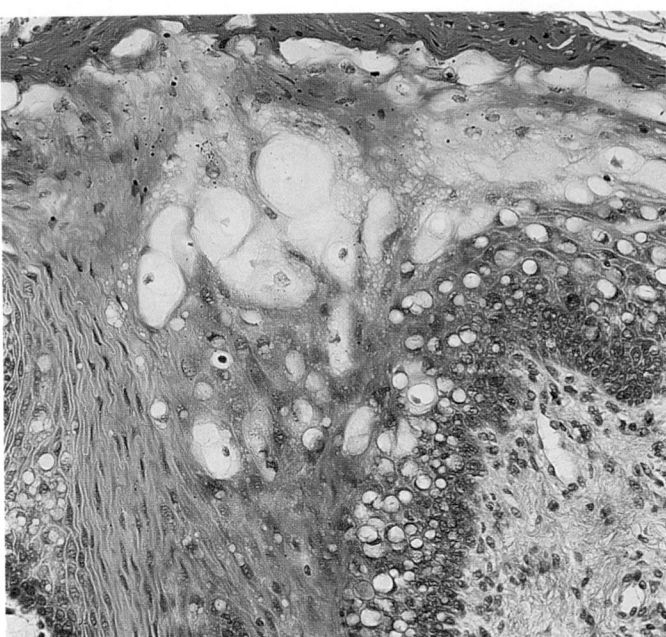

Fig. 5.15 Hairy leukoplakia. There is prominent ballooning of the squamous cells in the upper half of the epithelium, associated with mild inflammation in the underlying stroma.

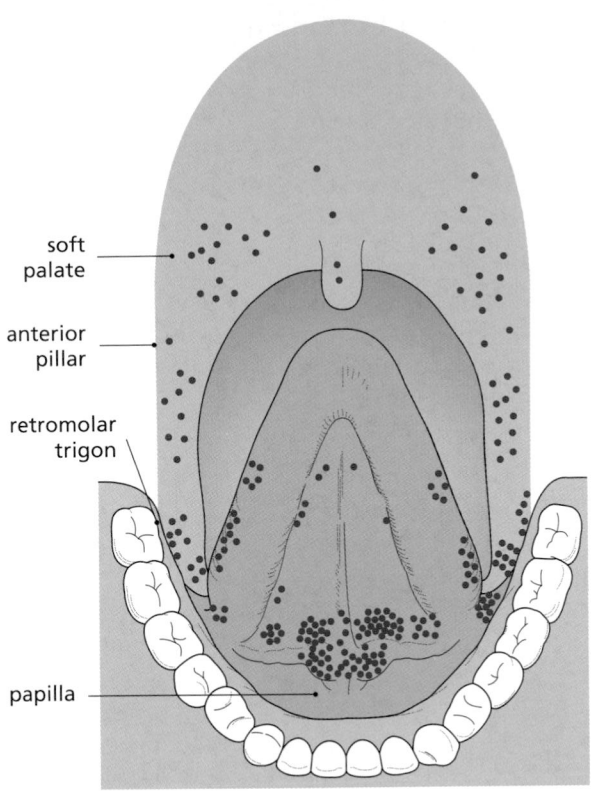

Fig. 5.16 Scattergram indicating site of origin of over 200 asymptomatic early squamous cell carcinomas. Note concentration of lesions around papilla at exit of Wharton's duct, ventrolateral aspect of tongue, lingual aspect of retromolar trigone (R), anterior pillar (P), and soft palate (SP). (Adapted from Mashberg A, Meyers H. Anatomic site and size of 222 early asymptomatic oral squamous cell carcinomas. A continuing prospective study of oral cancer. II. Cancer 1976, **37**: 2149–2157.)

50, although the relative incidence among women and younger patients seems to be increasing.[131–133,135] Some cases have been documented in children, particularly in the tongue.[138] Their alleged association with HPV is discussed in p. 254.[115b,132a]

Location
In a large series from the M.D. Anderson Hospital in Houston, Texas,[144] the location of the tumors within the oral cavity was listed as follows: lip, 45%; tongue, 16%; floor of mouth, 12%; buccal mucosa, 10%; lower gingiva, 12%; and upper gingiva and hard palate, 5%. Of the lip tumors, over 90% involve the lower lip. In a careful study of early asymptomatic squamous cell carcinomas of the oral cavity proper, Mashberg and Meyers[145] found that the overwhelming majority of them occurred in three locations: floor of the mouth (especially at the papilla at the exit of Wharton's duct), soft palate–anterior pillar–retromolar complex, and ventrolateral aspect of the mobile portion of the tongue (Fig. 5.16). These "high-risk areas" have in common a lining of thin nonkeratinized squamous epithelium, with short or absent rete ridges and a narrow lamina propria.

Multiplicity of tumors is common[141]; in such cases, the tongue is one of the most commonly affected sites.[143] Patients with carcinoma of the oral cavity have a hundred-fold probability of developing a second primary tumor in the region.[139,142,147] The chances of this occurrence are particularly high when the carcinoma is associated with dysplastic changes elsewhere in the oral cavity, which are the morphologic indicators of the important biologic phenomenon known as *field cancerization*.[147,149]

The analysis of the karyotype and pattern of p53 mutation in these multiple tumors has shown that in some cases they are clonally related (taken to indicate that they represent metastases from a single lesion), whereas others—probably the majority—are truly multiple primary tumors.[140,146,147a,148,150]

Microscopic features
Intraoral squamous cell carcinomas range widely in their degree of differentiation. Those located at the base of the tongue or in the tonsil tend to be particularly undifferentiated and solid, thereby creating diagnostic confusions with large cell malignant lymphoma. The epithelium adjacent to the invasive tumor often shows carcinoma in situ or dysplastic changes.[153] Some variations in the microscopic appearance of this tumor exist. A few squamous cell carcinomas are massively infiltrated with mature eosinophils, a feature that may create diagnostic difficulties and that is said to be associated with an improved prognosis.[151] Others may be colonized by melanocytes.[152]

Histochemical and immunohistochemical features
Immunohistochemically, these tumors are invariably positive for keratin. In the study by Suo et al.,[155] all cases

expressed CK8 and 19, most expressed 5/6 and 13 (the latter only in the metastases), and none expressed CK20. These tumors also exhibit reactivity for involucrin[155] and desmosome-related proteins.[154]

For the special features of the tonsillar tumors associated with cystic metastases in cervical lymph nodes, see under *Spread and metastases.*

Molecular genetic features

The most common oncogene alterations identified in oral squamous cell carcinoma involve p16 (approximately 80% of the cases), p53 (50%), cyclin D1 (30%), p63 (30%), PTEN (10%), Rb (<10%), and EGFR (<10%).[131,158–161]

Evaluation of these changes has led to the proposal of a model of molecular progression, which is esthetically appealing but which should be viewed only as a working hypothesis.[156,157]

Biopsy, cytology, and frozen section

Dentists have the best opportunity to discover early lesions of the oral cavity. It is their responsibility to examine the oral cavity carefully and to refer patients with suspicious lesions for proper evaluation and possible biopsy.[162] The diagnosis is usually obvious in a well-taken sample. A biopsy specimen that is often much more difficult to interpret is the one taken from an abnormal-appearing mucosa some time after irradiation therapy for an invasive squamous cell carcinoma has been completed. Under these circumstances, it is better to refrain from making a diagnosis of carcinoma unless there is definite stromal invasion, because from a cytologic standpoint it is often impossible to distinguish residual carcinoma in situ from radiation atypia. Generally speaking, it is better to wait a minimum of 6 to 8 weeks after completion of the therapy before taking a new biopsy.

Cytologic examination of clinically evident oral tumors is of little practical value,[165] but scrapings with cytologic analysis of inconspicuous red or white lesions by the dentist may allow the detection of a carcinoma in situ and save a patient's life. It is a shame that it is not done more often.[163b] FNA is a very convenient and efficient way to confirm the presence of cervical lymph node metastases.[163a]

The main role of frozen section in oropharyngeal squamous cell carcinoma is in the evaluation of surgical margins. A good correlation has been found between presence or closeness of the tumor at the margin and the probability of local recurrence and mortality.[164]

The evaluation of the surgical margins through the molecular search for p53 mutations (positive "molecular" margins) has been proposed,[163] but the wisdom and feasibility of this extravagant approach needs to be properly assessed.

Spread and metastases

The pattern of direct spread of oropharyngeal carcinoma is dictated by the anatomic features of the primary site.[166]

Carcinoma of the lip invades adjacent skin, the orbicular muscle, and—when advanced—the buccal mucosa, the adjacent mandible, and the mental nerve. Tumors of the floor of the mouth penetrate early beneath the mucosa into the sublingual gland, into the midline muscles, and extend toward the gingiva and mandible.[172] Tumors of the oral tongue, which usually arise on the lateral surfaces and undersurfaces, tend to remain localized for long periods but eventually invade the floor of the mouth and root of the tongue, resulting in fixation of the organ. Tumors of the buccal mucosa invade the underlying muscles and may eventually penetrate into the skin. Tumors of gingiva extend quickly into the periosteum, the adjacent buccal mucosa, and the floor of mouth. Tumors of the hard palate may spread into the underlying bone, but extension into the maxillary antrum is very rare. Tumors of retromolar trigone spread to adjacent buccal mucosa, anterior tonsillar pillar, maxilla, pterygomandibular space, medial pterygoid muscle, and buccinator muscle.

Invasion of the mandible usually involves the body of the bone, from which it may spread to the ramus; direct invasion of the latter structure may also occur, particularly after radiation therapy.[170] Metastases occur primarily by the lymphatic route, the distribution of lymph node involvement depending on the location of the primary tumor.[175] The more anterior the tumor, the lower the position of the cervical nodal metastasis. Carcinomas of the base of the tongue and oropharynx tend to metastasize to the deep retropharyngeal lymph nodes.

Metastases to the posterior triangle region (level V) are rare; they occur in 6% of the oropharyngeal tumors and 1% of the oral tumors.[168] Features of the primary tumor associated with the likelihood of nodal metastases in the neck are location (higher for the posterior portion of the tongue and oropharynx, intermediate for the anterior portion of the tongue, and low for the lip, floor of mouth, cheek mucosa, hard palate, and gingiva), poor microscopic differentiation, and depth of invasion.[169,176,178,179] Occasionally, the cervical node metastases from these squamous cell carcinomas undergo cystic degeneration. This, plus the well-differentiated nature of the lesion, may easily lead to a mistaken diagnosis of branchial cyst with malignant transformation ("branchial carcinoma").[167] The occult primary lesion is often located in the lingual or faucial tonsil, and it may take 10 years or more for it to be detected.[171,177] Interestingly, a high proportion of tonsillar tumors associated with cystic lymph node metastases are immunoreactive for keratin 7, a putative marker of ductal differentiation, suggesting an origin from (or a line of differentiation toward) large excretory ducts of submucosal glands.[173] Another peculiar morphologic pattern that squamous cell carcinoma can exhibit when metastasizing to cervical nodes is that of an extensive foreign body giant cell reaction around clumps of keratin, without viable tumor cells; this is particularly common if the tumor has been previously irradiated.[174]

Treatment

The two pillars of therapy for oropharyngeal carcinoma are surgery and radiation therapy, used either singly or in combination.[182a] For most early stage lesions, the results of irradiation and surgery are very similar, so that the final decision as to which to use often depends on factors such as functional and cosmetic results, the patient's general status, and the physician's bias.[181,183,185,186] Advanced cases are treated by a combination of radiation therapy and chemotherapy.[131,182,186] It has been claimed that absence of p53 expression associated with a high cell proliferation rate (as measured by Ki-67) predicts an excellent outcome after radiation therapy, whereas tumors that express p53 and have a low growth fraction (Ki-67 <20%) usually do not respond to this therapeutic modality.[184]

The treatment of metastatic squamous cell carcinoma to the cervical lymph nodes without detectable primary is largely dependent on the specific location of the lymphadenopathy.[180]

Prognosis

Listed below are the most important prognostic determinators in carcinomas of the oral cavity.

1   **Location**. The overall 5-year survival rates are about 90% for carcinomas of the lower lip; 60% for tumors of the anterior tongue; 40% for tumors of the posterior tongue, floor of mouth, tonsil, gingiva, and hard palate; and 20–30% for tumors of the soft palate.[191,193,194,197,198,200] However, these figures are heavily influenced by and largely dependent upon the tumor stage.

2   **Stage**. As usual, this parameter is of the utmost significance (Appendix C). Thus, the recurrence-free 5-year survival rates for "mucosal cancer" of this region in a series of over 3000 cases were: stage I, 91.0%; stage II, 77.2%; stage III, 61.2%; stage IVA, 32.4%; stage IVB, 25.3%; stage IVC, 3.6%.[199]

3   **Grade**. This parameter has proved to be of independent prognostic value.[187,190] It has been noted that grading of the deep invasive margins of the tumor provides better prognostic information than grading of the entire tumor.[189,203]

4   **Depth of invasion**. This is an important factor, at least in some locations.[192,193,204] This feature is incorporated into the staging systems.

5   **Tumor size**. This feature does not correlate closely with clinical outcome, except for the very small tumors.[201]

6   **Desmoplastic reaction**. Presence of a florid desmoplastic reaction to a squamous cell carcinoma of the lip has been found to be a marker of aggressive behavior, including a much higher likelihood of metastases.[188]

7   **Tissue eosinophilia**. Intense infiltration of the carcinoma by eosinophils is said to be a favorable prognostic factor.[192a]

8   **Lymph node involvement**. Naturally, presence of lymph node metastases is an important prognostic criterion and, as such, it is a key feature of the staging system.[195] Extracapsular spread (i.e., spread of the metastases beyond the lymph node capsule) is an indicator of a further decrease in survival rates.[202]

9   **DNA ploidy**. Half of the oral carcinomas are polyploid or aneuploid, either in part or throughout. The nondiploid tumors tend to be clinically more advanced than the diploid ones.[205] DNA ploidy correlates with the microscopic grade of the tumor and with prognosis, but its value as an *independent* prognostic determinator is still a matter of contention.[187,196,205]

10 **H antigen**. It has been claimed that loss of expression of blood group antigen is associated with a greater tendency for invasiveness and distant spread.[191]

11 **p21gene**. Overexpression of this gene (the product of which is the downstream regulatory protein of p53) was found to be an independent indicator of unfavorable prognosis in lingual squamous cell carcinoma.[206]

12 **3q26.3 locus**. Amplification of this genetic locus has been found to be associated with tumor progression and poor prognosis.[203a]

Verrucous carcinoma

Verrucous carcinoma (Ackerman's tumor) is a variant of well-differentiated squamous cell carcinoma endowed with enough clinical, pathologic, and behavioral peculiarities to justify its being regarded as a specific tumor entity.[207,212,215,217] The oral cavity is its classic location, but this lesion also has been reported in the larynx, nasal cavity, esophagus, penis, anorectal region, vulva, vagina, uterine cervix, and skin (particularly in the sole of the foot). Within the oral cavity, the most common sites are the buccal mucosa and lower gingiva.[213,214] Most patients are elderly males, and there is a close connection with the use of tobacco, especially chewing or snuff dipping.[219] Grossly, it presents as a large, fungating, soft papillary growth that tends to become infected and slowly invades contiguous structures (Fig. 5.17). It may grow through the soft tissues of the cheek, penetrate into the mandible or maxilla, and invade perineurial spaces.[210] Regional lymph node metastases are exceedingly rare, and distant metastases have not been reported.

The microscopic diagnosis of verrucous carcinoma may be difficult because of its well-differentiated character. A superficial biopsy will show only hyperkeratosis, acanthosis, and benign-appearing papillomatosis. Sections of an adequate biopsy show swollen and voluminous rete pegs that extend into the deeper tissues, where their pattern becomes quite complex[208] (Fig. 5.18). The most important differential feature with squamous cell carcinoma is the good cytologic differentiation

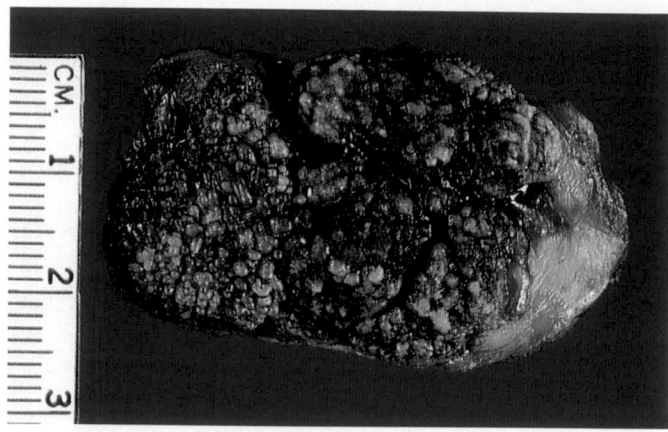

Fig. 5.17 Gross appearance of verrucous carcinoma with extensive involvement of the tongue.

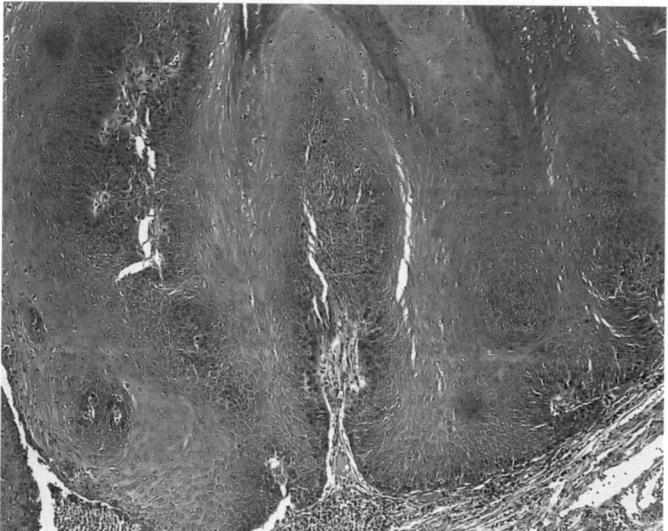

Fig. 5.18 Verrucous carcinoma of tongue. Extremely well differentiated squamous rete pegs push into the underlying stroma.

throughout the tumor. Dr Lauren Ackerman, who first described the entity, used to express this fact by stating: "If a lesion looks cytologically like carcinoma, it is not verrucous carcinoma." Image analysis studies have confirmed the size differences among the cells of these two tumors.[209] Interestingly, in about one fifth of the cases, cytologically identifiable foci of squamous cell carcinoma occur within a lesion that looks otherwise like a verrucous carcinoma, hence the importance of thorough sampling.[216] These *hybrid (verrucous–squamous) tumors* are said to be associated with a higher recurrence rate than pure verrucous carcinoma.[216]

Resection is the treatment of choice. If surgery is inadequate, the tumor will recur.[207] Radiation therapy is not recommended, since it may alter the nature of the tumor to a highly malignant, rapidly metastasizing, poorly differentiated squamous cell carcinoma.[213] This has occurred in as many as 30% of the cases in some series, the average postirradiation interval being 6 months.

It is likely that most of the cases reported in the past as *oral florid papillomatosis*[220] represent early and noninvasive stages of verrucous carcinoma. Along the same lines, the similar if not identical conditions known as *verrucous hyperplasia*,[218] *proliferative verrucous leukoplakia*,[211] *verrucous keratosis*, and *leukoplakia verrucosa* can be regarded as precursor lesions of verrucous carcinoma, from which they are distinguished by the fact that the verrucous process is *superficial* to the adjacent squamous epithelium.

Other microscopic types

Carcinomas of surface epithelial origin other than squamous cell carcinoma of either the conventional or verrucous carcinoma types include the following:

1 **Adenoid (pseudoglandular) squamous cell carcinoma.** This tumor exhibits a pseudoglandular or alveolar appearance because of acantholysis. Most examples are located in the lip and, like their more common cutaneous counterparts, are associated with and probably induced by actinic radiation; however, a few are seen in the gingiva or tongue, where an actinic pathogenesis cannot be invoked.[240]

2 **Adenosquamous carcinoma.** In contrast to the type listed previously, the rare adenosquamous carcinoma shows areas of squamous differentiation mixed with others having true glandular differentiation.[228,235] Some of these cases may be of minor salivary gland derivation.

3 **Basaloid squamous cell carcinoma.** This is an aggressive variant of squamous cell carcinoma that has a predilection for the upper aerodigestive tract (oral cavity, oropharynx, esophagus, and larynx) but also occurs in other sites such as lung.[221,225,234] We view so-called "cloacogenic carcinoma of the anal canal" as also belonging to this category. It seems likely that the "basaloid" pattern represents an attempt at glandular differentiation of one type or another, wherever it occurs. As such, this tumor is histogenetically related to adenosquamous carcinoma although microscopically distinct from it. In basaloid carcinoma, areas with obvious squamous differentiation are admixed with solid tumor islands that exhibit peripheral palisading and a thick basement membrane[242] (Fig. 5.19). Cystic spaces containing mucoid or hyaline material are present, resulting in a resemblance to adenoid cystic carcinoma. The prominence of basal lamina material is one of the most striking attributes of this tumor at both the ultrastructural and immunohistochemical level.[225] Immunoreactivity for high molecular weight keratin (detected with the 34βE12 antibody) is a consistent feature of this tumor.[236] Occasional examples have a spindle cell component.[237] The differential diagnosis includes minor salivary gland tumors (particularly adenoid cystic carcinoma)[241] and peripheral ameloblastoma (see p. 261).

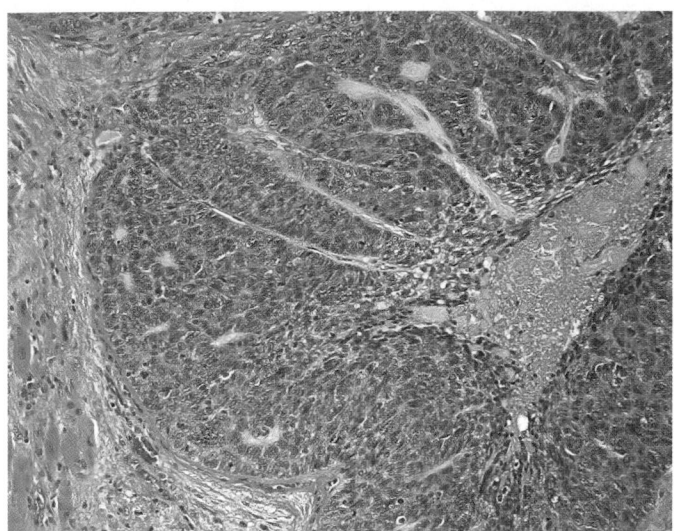

Fig. 5.19 Basaloid squamous cell carcinoma. Note the lobular configuration and the deposition of basement membrane material.

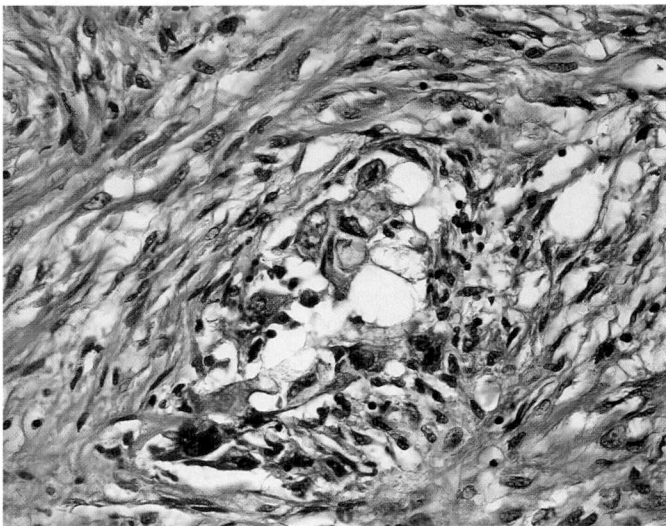

Fig. 5.20 Spindle cell (sarcomatoid) carcinoma. The central island is clearly identifiable as epithelial, whereas the peripheral component has a sarcoma-like appearance.

Adenoid cystic carcinoma shows a lower nuclear grade and exhibits focal glandular differentiation, whereas basaloid squamous cell carcinoma shows squamous differentiation, a feature also appreciated ultrastructurally.[230] Both adenoid cystic carcinoma and basaloid squamous cell carcinoma are immunoreactive for 34βE12.[236]

4 **Spindle cell (sarcomatoid) carcinoma**. This may appear as an ulcerated and infiltrative mass or as a polypoid growth in the lip, tongue, or other portions of the oral cavity. Sometimes the sarcoma-like formation blends with areas of obvious squamous cell carcinoma, is associated with squamous cell carcinomas elsewhere in the oral cavity, or represents the recurrence of what originally was an obvious squamous cell carcinoma[222,223,229,232] (Fig. 5.20). These findings, plus a wealth of electron microscopic, immunohistochemical and molecular data, indicate that the sarcoma-like component represents a metaplastic change of the originally epithelial neoplasm.[224a,226,243,244] The sarcoma-like component may look like so-called malignant fibrous histiocytoma of soft tissue or it may show evidence of specific mesenchymal differentiation, particularly along muscle lines.[238] Hyaline globules ("thanatosomes") may be found in the cytoplasm of the larger tumor cells.[239] The nodal and distal metastases of this tumor may be purely carcinomatous, have a mixed appearance as in the primary neoplasm, or, in rare cases, be entirely composed of sarcoma-like elements. The prognosis is closely related to the depth of invasion and is not significantly different from ordinary squamous cell carcinoma of equivalent stage and thickness.[233,243]

5 **Small cell carcinoma**. The appearance is similar to that of the homonymous lung carcinoma.[224] It may be pure or associated with a squamous component, and its behavior is very aggressive.[231]

6 **Lymphoepithelioma-like carcinoma**. A tumor microscopically similar to the lymphoepithelioma of the nasopharynx and tonsil is occasionally found in the oral cavity.[227]

Tumors and other lesions of minor salivary glands

Minor salivary glands, present in practically all structures within the oral cavity, participate in many of the diseases affecting their major counterparts, a feature that can be exploited for diagnostic purposes. Thus biopsy of the lower lip has shown involvement of the minor salivary glands in cases of *cystic fibrosis*[276] and *Sjögren's syndrome*[253] and has also been used to diagnose end-stage *chronic graft-versus-host disease*.

Salivary gland choristoma presents as a gingival nodule microscopically composed of disorganized seromucinous salivary gland tissue mixed with sebaceous glands.[250]

Adenomatoid hyperplasia is a term used for a localized hyperplastic process of minor salivary glands appearing clinically as a nodule, usually in the hard palate but occasionally in the retromolar area.[248]

Intraoral minor salivary glands can give rise to a variety of benign and malignant tumors. The hard palate is the most common location, but the tumors also occur in the soft palate, cheek, tonsil, floor of the mouth, tongue, lip (usually the upper), gingiva, and jaw. It is important to remember that tumors arising in the deep lobe of the parotid gland may present as primary intraoral masses. With a few exceptions, minor salivary gland tumors are morphologically analogous to those located in the major glands[265,273] (see Chapter 12); however, they differ from the latter in their relative incidence and, to some extent, in their natural history.[252]

Benign mixed tumors pleomorphic adenomas), which constitute over 75% of all parotid neoplasms, make up only about half of the salivary gland tumors of the palate.[255,257,260] They may be overdiagnosed as malignant because of increased cellularity, nuclear atypia in the often predominant myoepithelial component (see under Myoepithelioma), or pseudoepitheliomatous hyperplasia of the overlying mucosa.[275]

Adenoid cystic carcinoma, mucoepidermoid carcinoma, and **polymorphous low-grade adenocarcinoma** (see later section) comprise the large majority of intraoral malignant salivary gland tumors, in contrast to the more even distribution of tumor types seen in the parotid gland. A few cases of **acinic cell carcinoma** have also been described.[247] The prognosis of adenoid cystic carcinoma is said to be better when the tumor is located in the palate than when present in the parotid or submaxillary gland,[257] but this may be at least partially due to the inclusion among the palatal tumors of some cases of polymorphous low-grade carcinomas. The prognostic difference among the various morphologic subtypes of this tumor, which has been noted for the major salivary gland, seems to apply also to this location.[254] Of the salivary gland tumors located in the lip, about 80% are benign. Among the malignant types, adenoid cystic carcinoma and mucoepidermoid carcinoma are the most frequent.[271]

Some types of salivary gland tumors occur predominantly or, in some instances, almost exclusively in the minor salivary glands of the oral cavity. They include the following:

1 **Basal cell adenoma.** This tumor, characterized by a canalicular pattern of growth, has a predilection for the upper lip and palate (often at the junction between the hard and soft regions), where it is sometimes confused with adenoid cystic carcinoma.[249,260,274] As discussed in Chapter 12, some authors like to distinguish this tumor from other basal cell adenomas and designate it as *canalicular adenoma* (Fig. 5.21).

2 **Myoepithelioma.** This lesion, composed of hyaline or plasmacytoid cells, usually involves the hard palate (Fig. 5.22). The differential diagnosis includes plasmacytoma, oncocytoma, and even skeletal muscle neoplasms. Despite its high cellularity and the occasional presence of atypical hyperchromatic nuclei and intravascular tumor cells, the behavior is generally benign[256,267] (see Chapter 12).

3 **Sialadenoma papilliferum.** This lesion is a papillary lesion of the oral cavity, usually located in the hard palate and characterized microscopically by a biphasic composition. An exophytic mass of well-differentiated squamous epithelium is seen covering a glandular component consisting of cleftlike cystic spaces lined by cuboidal or columnar epithelium; some of these glands may contain oncocytic cells, and others may exhibit squamous metaplasia.[261,262] The appearance is

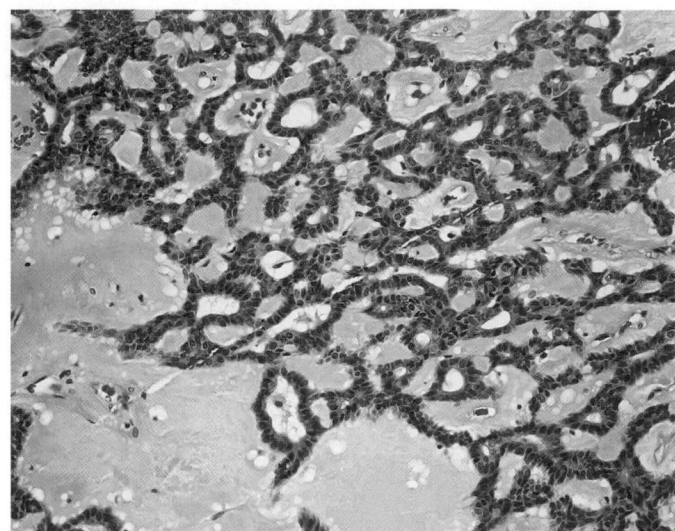

Fig. 5.21 Canalicular adenoma. This type of benign salivary gland tumor is particularly common in the lip.

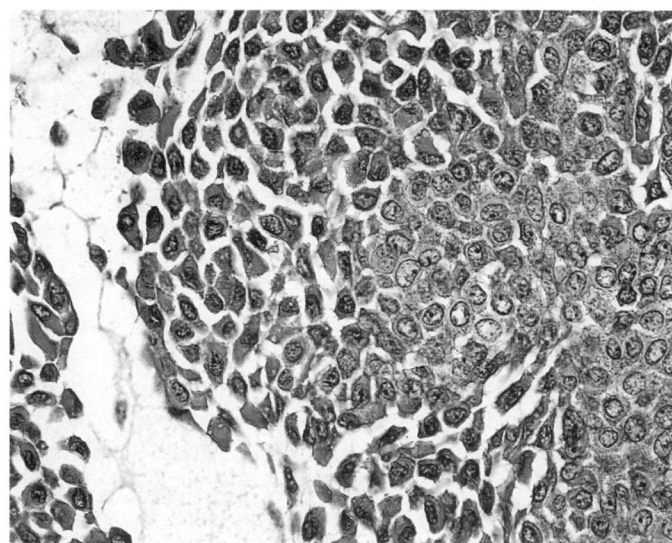

Fig. 5.22 Myoepithelioma exclusively composed of so-called "hyaline" or "plasmacytoid" cells.

reminiscent of both Warthin's tumor of the parotid gland and papillary syringocystadenoma of skin, both at the light and electron microscopic level.[261]

4 **Inverted ductal papilloma.** This tumor has a pattern of growth similar to that of inverted papilloma of the nasal cavity. It appears clinically as a small submucosal mass in the oral cavity of adults. Microscopically, there are complex invaginations formed by well-differentiated, predominantly squamous epithelium-associated microcysts, occasional mucous cells, and a lining of columnar cells. The behavior is benign.[277]

5 **Syringoma.** This neoplasm has an appearance similar to that of the homonymous skin tumor of sweat gland origin.[266]

6 **Polymorphous low-grade adenocarcinoma.**[251,259] This is the currently preferred term for a low-grade

malignant tumor that has also been called *low-grade papillary adenocarcinoma*,[246,270] *terminal duct carcinoma*,[263] and *lobular carcinoma*.[245] Adult females are most commonly affected.[251] The palate is the most common location; polymorphous low-grade adenocarcinoma is the second most common type of salivary gland carcinoma in this location following adenoid cystic carcinoma.[258] Microscopically, there is uniformity of cell type but a marked variation in architectural patterns, which is responsible for the various names that this tumor has received.[272] Tubular, cribriform, papillary, solid, and fascicular formations may appear, with frequent combinations and transitions (Figs 5.23 and 5.24). The periphery of the tumor has invasive features, sometimes in an Indian-file pattern, which has led to a strained analogy with invasive lobular carcinoma of the breast. Perineurial invasion is also common. Mitotic activity is inconspicuous. S-100 protein immunoreactivity is present, suggesting an important myoepithelial participation.[268,278] The differential diagnosis includes benign mixed tumor, basal cell adenoma (both of which lack infiltrative features), and particularly adenoid cystic carcinoma.[263] However, the last lacks the plump and columnar cells of polymorphous low-grade adenocarcinoma, as well as its papillary and fascicular growth patterns. The behavior of this tumor is that of a low-grade malignancy. In one series of 69 cases, recurrences developed in 12% and regional lymph node metastases in 10%, but there were no distant metastases, and there was only one tumor-related death.[268] In another series comprising 164 cases, 97.6% of the patients were either alive or had died of other disease.[251] Tumors with a conspicuous papillary component are associated with a higher incidence of lymph node metastases.[259] Rarely, polymorphous low-grade

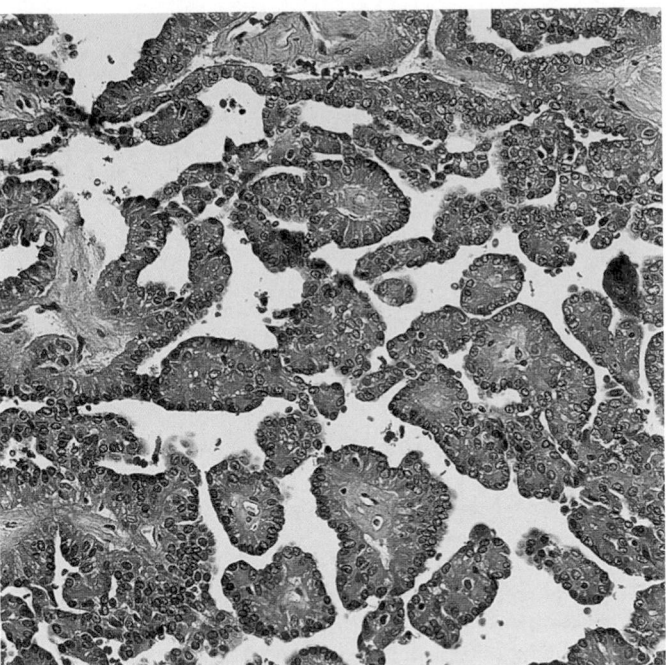

Fig. 5.24 Polymorphous low-grade adenocarcinoma. In this particular example the papillary formations are very prominent.

adenocarcinoma may undergo transformation to a high-grade tumor.[271a,274a]

The recently described *cribriform adenocarcinoma of the tongue* is mentioned here despite its obscure histogenesis because it may well be of minor salivary gland derivation, and also because its differential diagnosis includes several types of salivary gland tumors. Morphologically, it resembles the solid and follicular variants of papillary thyroid carcinoma (to the point of raising the possibility of an origin from the thyroglossal duct anlage), but thyroglobulin stains are negative.[269]

The treatment of minor salivary gland tumors is primarily surgical. It has been emphasized that the first excision should be the most definitive and comprehensive and that treatment of recurrent disease is rarely curative.[264] Postoperative irradiation is generally recommended for all high-grade malignancies, including adenoid cystic carcinoma.[264]

Tumors of odontogenic epithelium

Peripheral ameloblastoma is a tumor of the oral cavity, not involving bone but exhibiting microscopic features of ameloblastic differentiation (Fig. 5.25). As a matter of fact, its appearance is indistinguishable from that of ameloblastoma of the jaw[279] (see Chapter 6). Most of the reported cases have occurred in the gingiva, and several have been published in the past as basal cell carcinomas.

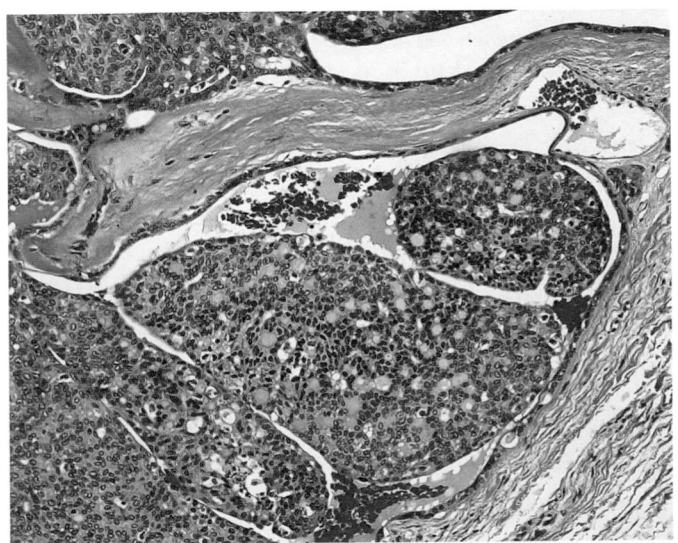

Fig. 5.23 Polymorphous low-grade adenocarcinoma. In this area the tumor has an orderly microglandular configuration.

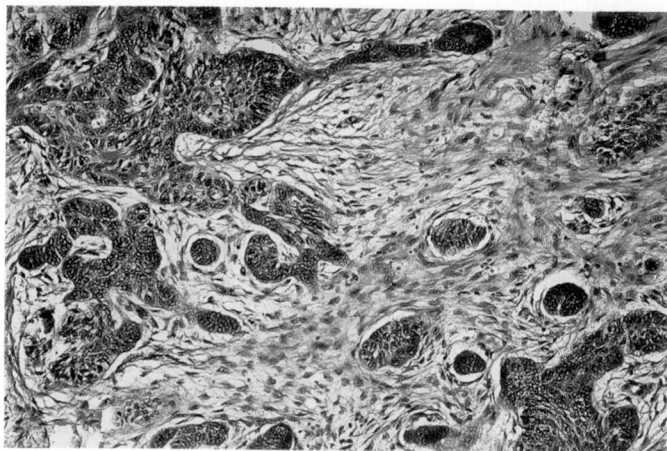

Fig. 5.25 Peripheral ameloblastoma. This tumor connected with the lining epithelium of the gingival mucosa and did not involve the jawbones.

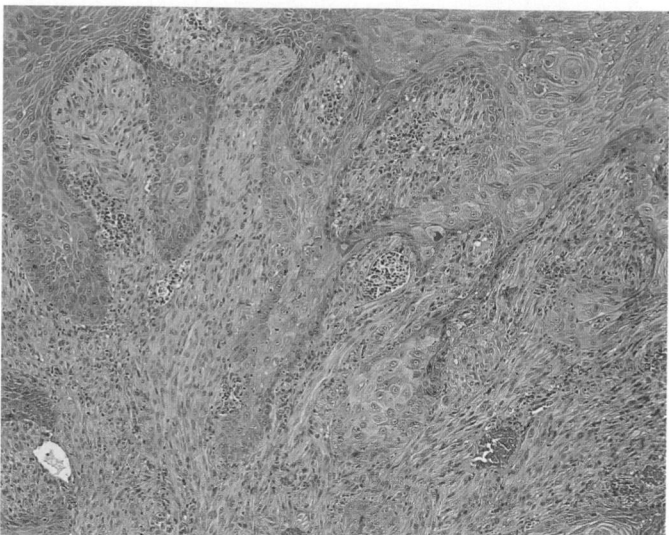

Fig. 5.26 Spitz's nevus of tongue accompanied by intense pseudoepitheliomatous hyperplasia of the overlying squamous epithelium.

They may arise from remnants of the dental lamina within the gingiva ("rests of Serres") or from surface epithelium that has retained the capacity to differentiate along odontogenic structures. They are relatively innocuous and are generally cured by local excision.[279]

Tumors of melanocytes

Ephelis and **lentigo** (melanotic macules) can present as solitary lesions of the oral cavity, usually the lower lip.[290,297] They are more common in females and are characterized microscopically by hyperpigmentation of the basal layer, associated in the latter with elongation of the rete ridges. The term *melanoacanthoma* has been used when the melanocytic proliferation extends above the basal layer and is found mixed intimately with the keratinocytes.[287a,289,297] Multiple pigmented macules of the lip are one of the components of the Peutz–Jeghers syndrome (see Chapter 11, small bowel). The presence of pigmented patches within the oral cavity (usually located in the hard palate or gingiva) is known as **melanosis**.

Melanocytic nevi may involve the lips and, in rare cases, the inside of the oral cavity.[284–286] In one series, there were 3 junctional, 30 compound, 32 intramucosal (equivalent of the cutaneous intradermal), and 6 blue nevi.[299] The nevus of Ota may also involve the oral cavity in the region of the palate.[293]

We have seen three cases of Spitz nevus of the tongue associated with pseudoepitheliomatous hyperplasia which simulated both malignant melanoma and squamous cell carcinoma[287] (Fig. 5.26).

Malignant melanoma of the oral cavity is particularly common in people of Japanese and black African origin.[298] The palate and gingiva are the most common locations.[282,294] Both pigmented and amelanotic varieties

occur.[281] Some of the tumors have desmoplastic features, especially when occurring in the lower lip. These are often underdiagnosed because of their scarce cellularity and sometimes less than prominent atypia. The diagnosis should be suspected in the presence of a spindle cell proliferation in the lamina propria with a fascicular pattern of growth, particularly if accompanied by prominent clusters of lymphocytes.[291] The diagnosis is supported by the S-100 protein positivity, which however is usually accompanied by negativity for HMB-45.[295] Conventional melanoma, by contrast, is usually positive for both markers.[295] Oral "melanosis" adjacent to the area of invasive tumor is found in about 30% of the cases[298]; in most instances, there is some degree of atypia in this intraepithelial component. Arrington et al.[280] regard this as a distinct subtype of melanoma and designate it as *(acral) lentiginous melanoma*.[292] Lymph node and distant metastases are common, and the prognosis is extremely poor.[283,288,296] The histologic parameters used for predicting prognosis of cutaneous melanomas do not apply as well.[295a]

Tumors and tumorlike conditions of lymphoid tissue

Benign nodules made of well-differentiated lymphocytes, with or without an admixture of histiocytes, are not uncommon in the oral cavity. They may represent enlarged buccal lymph nodes or hypertrophic buccal tonsils or may be associated with cystic glandular structures ("*lymphoepithelial cysts*").[302] The most prominent of these benign lymphoid proliferations are designated *lymphoid polyps or pseudolymphomas*.[314] We have also seen several cases of nodular collections of mature lymphocytes in the hard palate accompanied by florid epimyoepithelial islands of minor salivary gland derivation. Although these patients did not have clinical abnormalities in the major salivary glands, we think that these cases could be regarded as oral cavity counterparts of Mikulicz's disease (see Chapter 12).

Malignant lymphoma most commonly occurs in the Waldeyer's ring, particularly in the palatine and lingual tonsil, but it can also develop in the gingival area, buccal mucosa, or palate. Most patients are in their sixth or seventh decades. The disease seems to be more common in Europe than in other parts of the world. The typical clinical presentation is that of a soft, bulky mass covered by normal or ulcerated mucosa. Microscopically, most cases are of B-cell nature and follicular center cell origin, of large size and with a generally diffuse pattern of growth.[301,305,311,316a,317,320] It is common for these tumors to exhibit a peculiar artifact characterized by a marked elongation (streaking) of nuclei that can render the diagnosis very difficult.[319] In about 40% of the cases, there is evidence of disease outside the oral cavity, particularly in the cervical lymph nodes and gastrointestinal tract.[315] A high proportion of the latter represent cases of mantle cell lymphoma or lymphoma of so-called "MALT type".[305,313] T-cell lymphomas can also occur in this location[316] (including mycosis fungoides),[303] as well as anaplastic large cell lymphomas.[317] An increasing number of AIDS-related malignant lymphomas of the oral cavity of both B- and T-cell type have been reported, the former predominating.[318] In contrast to non-Hodgkin lymphomas of the nasal/nasopharyngeal region, those of tonsil and tongue are nearly always negative for EBV.[307]

As for malignant lymphomas elsewhere, clinical staging and microscopic typing are the two most important prognostic factors.[301]

Plasmacytomas can occur in the soft tissues of the oral cavity, although not so commonly as in the upper air passages.[301a] It is important to distinguish them from the more common *plasma cell granulomas* of reactive nature,[300] including so-called *"mucous membrane plasmacytosis"*.[309] These disorders are composed of mature plasma cells, have a mixture of other inflammatory cells, and are associated with fibrosis. Immunohistochemical staining for immunoglobulin types may help in this differential diagnosis.

Hodgkin's disease and **true histiocytic malignancies** presenting initially in the oral cavity are extremely rare and some even questionable, but several reported cases are on record.[315a,317]

Langerhans' cell granulomatosis (histiocytosis X) can involve the oral cavity, either as an isolated focus or as an expression of multisystem disease.[312] The lesions are most often found in the gingiva but also can affect the hard palate.[310]

Leukemia of acute myelocytic or myelomonocytic type is associated with gingival involvement in about 4% of the cases, with or without concomitant skin involvement.[308] In rare cases, oral cavity disease is the first manifestation of granulocytic sarcoma.[304]

Follicular dendritic cell tumors (dendritic reticulum cell tumors) have been observed in the palate and tonsil.[306] These are fully discussed in Chapter 21.

Other tumors and tumorlike conditions

Peripheral giant cell granuloma (giant cell epulis) is seen in all age groups and is more common in females.[342] Maxilla and mandible are affected with equal frequency. A soft-to-firm mass forms in the gingiva, pushes the teeth aside, and may erode the underlying bone. Microscopically, the lesion shows numerous osteoclast-like giant cells, an active vascular stroma, and, at times, small amounts of neoformed bone (Fig. 5.27). This common lesion is benign and probably of reactive nature.

Granular cell tumor can involve any portion of the oral cavity, the tongue being the most common site (Fig. 5.28). The overlying epithelium often shows florid pseudoepitheliomatous hyperplasia.[336,360,385] An exceptionally rare malignant counterpart of this lesion has also been described.[388] A lesion that is indistinguishable from granular cell tumor by light microscopy is seen occasionally in the gingiva of newborn infants and is called *congenital epulis* (Fig. 5.29). This lesion occurs almost exclusively in females and it behaves in a benign fashion even if incompletely excised.[354] Ultrastructural studies have suggested a mesenchymal (fibroblastic, pericytic, or smooth muscle) rather than an odontogenic origin.[347,353,390] Staining for S-100 protein is negative, in contrast to the adult form of this lesion.[355,387]

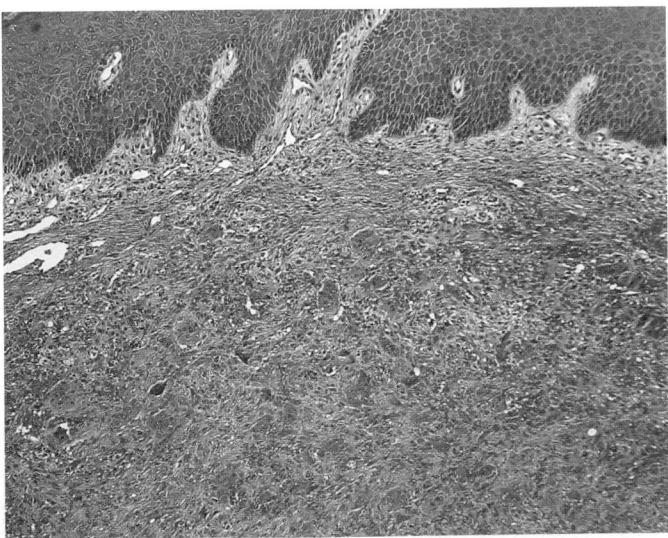

Fig. 5.27 Peripheral giant cell granuloma beneath a slightly hyperplastic squamous epithelium.

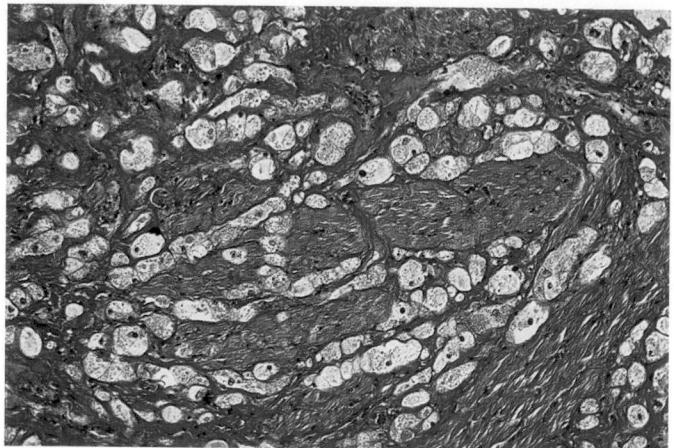

Fig. 5.28 Granular cell tumor. The lesion shows a pseudoinfiltrative pattern that may lead to overdiagnosis.

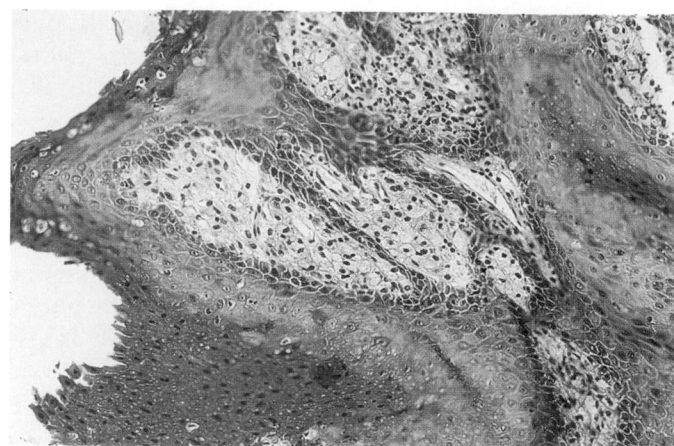

Fig. 5.30 Verruciform xanthoma. Clusters of foamy macrophages are seen expanding the stroma beneath a hyperkeratotic epithelium.

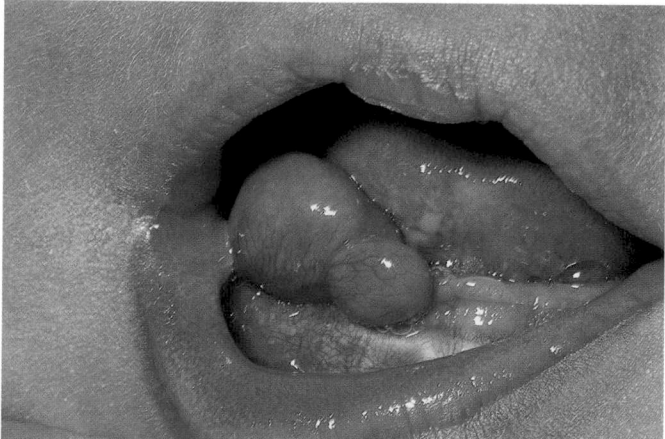

Fig. 5.29 Clinical appearance of congenital epulis. (Courtesy of Dr. RA Cooke, Brisbane, Australia; From Cooke RA, Stewart B: Colour atlas of Anatomical Pathology, Edinburgh, Churchill Livingstone, 2004.)

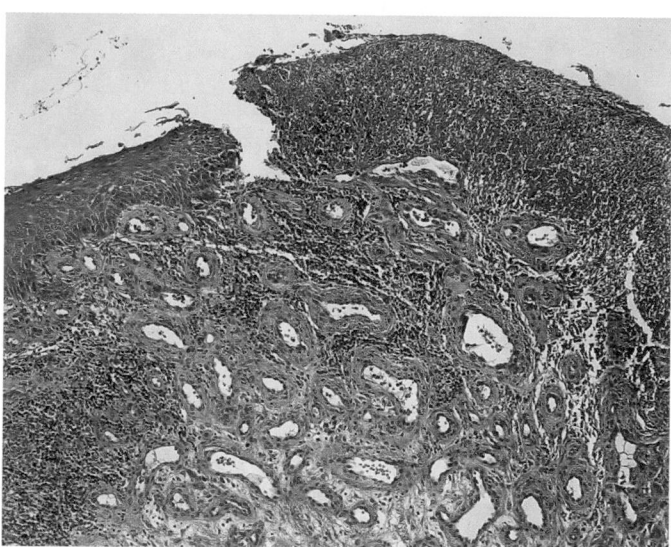

Fig. 5.31 Pyogenic granuloma. Numerous neoformed vessels are separated from each other by an inflamed and edematous stroma. The overlying mucosa is partially ulcerated.

Verruciform xanthoma presents in middle-aged persons as a raised, granular, or verrucous lesion of the oral cavity, usually in the gingiva or alveolar ridge.[361,367] Collections of foamy macrophages in the lamina propria are covered by a verrucous and acanthotic epithelium[366] (Fig. 5.30). The lesion is probably a reactive process rather than a true neoplasm.[365]

Skin adnexal type tumorlike conditions are sometimes seen in the oral cavity. These include *keratoacanthoma* (common in the lip but occasionally situated intraorally),[337] *inverted follicular keratosis* (most often in the lower lip),[321] and *warty dyskeratoma*.[330,345]

Hairy polyp is a rare congenital malformation arising from the oropharynx or nasopharynx. Microscopically, the lesion is polypoid and composed of epidermis, hair follicles, sebaceous glands, and eccrine sweat glands. Adipose tissue, smooth muscle, striated muscle, and cartilage may be present in the core.[383]

Vascular proliferations of the oral cavity are benign in the vast majority of cases. The two most common types are probably not even neoplastic, although their ability to simulate a malignant process should not be underestimated.[375] The first is *pyogenic granuloma (lobular capillary hemangioma)*, which appears as an elevated, dark red lesion that may or may not be ulcerated[386a] (Fig. 5.40). Large masses of proliferating endothelial cells are separated by an edematous stroma containing inflammatory cells (Fig. 5.31). Characteristically, the covering epithelium almost meets at the base of the lesion. The lesion may regress completely or heal as a residual fibrous mass or fibroepithelial papilloma.[350] An identical lesion occurring during pregnancy has been referred to as granuloma gravidarum or pregnancy tumor.[358] The second is *intravascular papillary endothelial hyperplasia (Masson's hemangioma)*, which can occur de novo or superimposed on a pre-existing hemangioma (Figs 5.32 and 5.33).[328] Both this lesion and pyogenic granuloma occur most commonly in the lip, their features sometimes overlapping.[375]

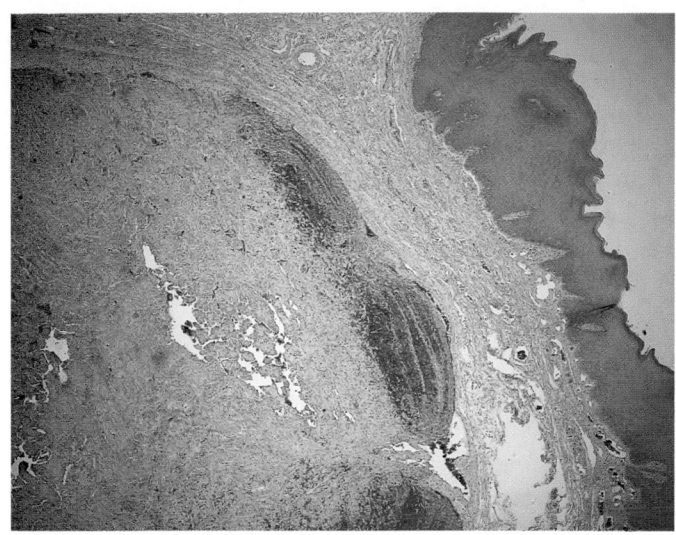

Fig. 5.32 Intravascular papillary endothelial hyperplasia. Remnants of the original thrombus can be seen in the more superficial portion of the nodule.

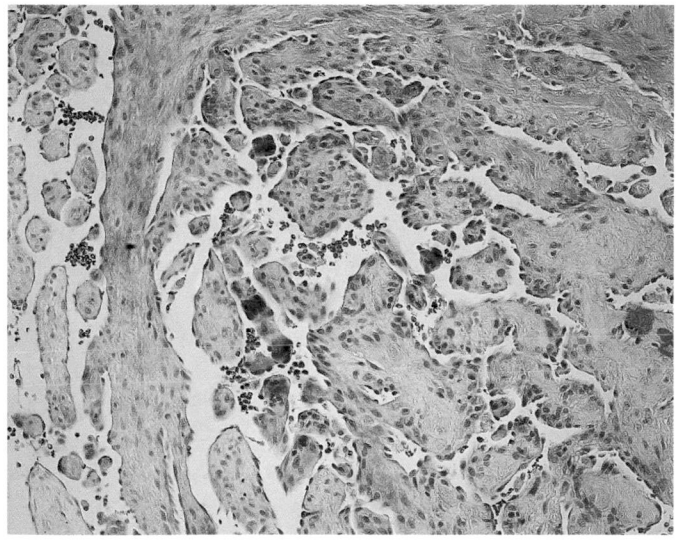

Fig. 5.33 Intravascular papillary endothelial hyperplasia. Papillary projections lined by endothelial cells are seen within the vascular lumen.

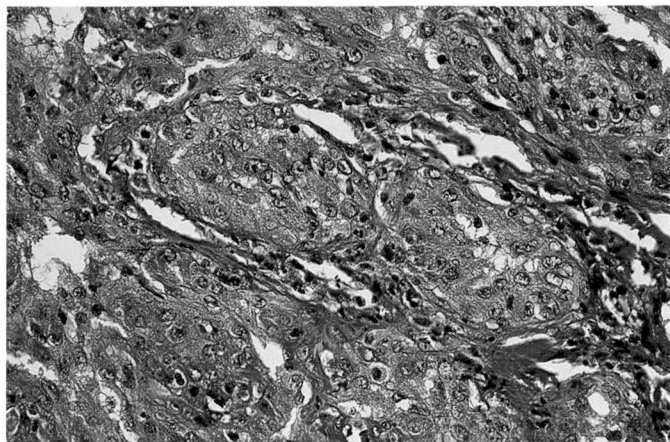

Fig. 5.34 Epithelioid hemangioma of soft tissues of oral cavity. This lesion tends to be overdiagnosed as a malignant vascular neoplasm and sometimes is confused with carcinoma.

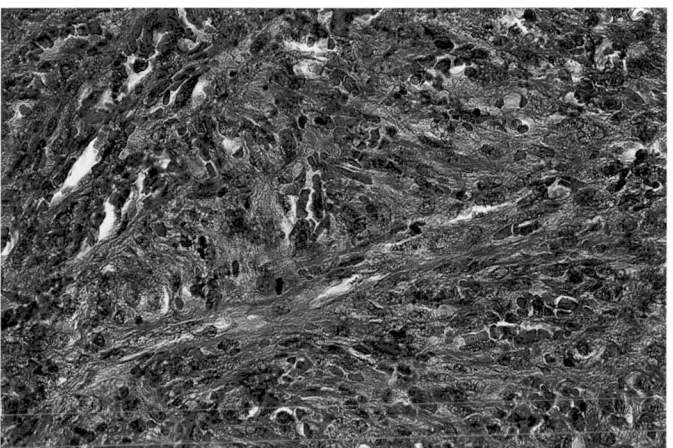

Fig. 5.35 Kaposi's sarcoma of oral cavity. Atypical spindle cells form slits containing red blood cells.

Benign vascular tumors are largely represented by *hemangiomas* and *lymphangiomas*.[326] Most of these are located in the tongue, where they can result in soft cystic masses large enough to interfere with speech and mastication. Microscopically, most of these lesions have markedly dilated ("cavernous") vascular or lymphatic channels. The treatment is surgical. *Tonsillar lymphangiomatous polyps* present as unilateral tonsillar masses composed of dilated lymph channels covered by hyperplastic squamous epithelium, resulting in a typical polypoid configuration.[348] Other benign or borderline vascular tumors that may present intraorally are *glomus tumor*,[381] *hemangiopericytoma*,[370] *epithelioid hemangioma* (angiolymphoid hyperplasia with eosinophilia),[371,372] and *epithelioid* hemangioendothelioma (Fig. 5.34).[339]

Kaposi's sarcoma of the oral cavity has been seen with increasing frequency in relation to AIDS infection. Sometimes the oral lesion is the first manifestation of the disease. The palate is the most common site. Clinically, the lesions may appear as small, well-delineated macular lesions or as larger, infiltrative nodules.[374] Microscopically and immunohistochemically, the features are generally similar to those of its cutaneous counterpart (Fig. 5.35).[373] In addition to pyogenic granuloma, the differential diagnosis includes *bacillary angiomatosis* (another AIDS-related vascular proliferative process).[374] *Angiosarcoma* of the oral cavity is very rare.[327,337b,369] We have seen a case appearing many years after irradiation of a lymphangioma, and a similar case has been reported.[363] Before making a diagnosis of angiosarcoma in the oral cavity (particularly if the lesion is in the lip or tongue), the much more likely possibility of a benign vascular process of one of the types previously described should be considered.[375]

Smooth muscle tumors can also occur in this location.[357,364] Most *leiomyomas* are located in the tongue, and many are of vascular type. *Leiomyosarcomas* are more common in the cheek region (Fig. 5.36). Involvement of the jawbones can occur.[335]

Solitary fibrous tumor presents as a well-circumscribed submucosal mass; the behavior of the reported cases has been benign.[322,389a]

Rhabdomyomas have a special predilection for the oral cavity and neck. Most are seen in adults. The floor of the mouth is the most common location,[332,340] but they also occur in the tongue.[382] Both adult and fetal forms have been described, as well as intermediate ("juvenile") forms.[333] The adult types are usually well circumscribed and may be multiple.[324,341] They may recur locally and display cytogenetic abnormalities, features more in keeping with a neoplastic than a hamartomatous process.[343]

Rhabdomyosarcomas of embryonal type have been described in the tongue and other oral sites in children (Figs 5.37 and 5.38).

Peripheral nerve tumors and tumorlike conditions of the oral cavity and pharynx include *schwannoma* (often located in the tongue),[356,389] *neurofibroma*,[368] *traumatic neuromas* (some containing mature ganglion cells),[334] and the *multiple mucosal neuromas* seen as a component of multiple endocrine adenomatosis type III. The individual lesions resemble plexiform neurofibromas and may be found in the lips, tongue, conjunctiva, nasal cavity, and larynx.[344] They are made up of all the elements of the normal nerve, including a thickened EMA-positive perineurial layer.[329] *Malignant peripheral nerve sheath tumors* of the oral cavity, some of which are pigmented, have also been described.[346]

Other **benign soft tissue tumors** that have been reported in this location are *lipoma* (including some variants such as myxoid lipoma, spindle cell lipoma, and lipoma with osseous and chondroid metaplasia)[323,331,380] *chondroma*,[362] and *angiolipoma*.[338] The mesenchymal tumors exhibiting myxochondroid features have been grouped under the term *ectomesenchymal chondromyxoid tumor;* most have occurred in the anterior tongue (Fig. 5.39).[386] Microscopically, they are characterized by a lobular proliferation of oval and spindle cells in a

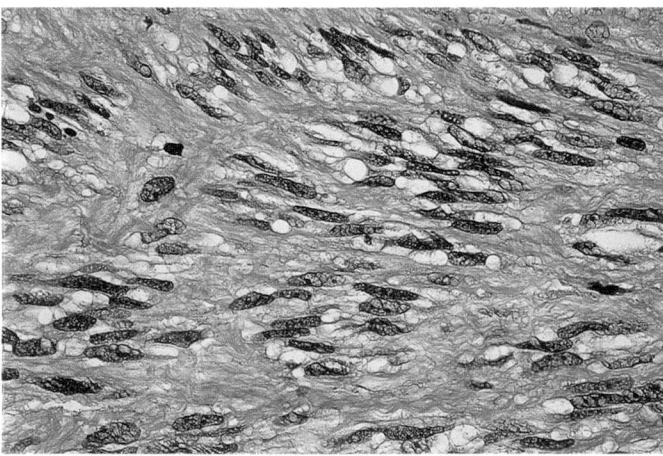

Fig. 5.36 Leiomyosarcoma of oral cavity. Note the prominent cytoplasmic vacuoles indenting to the nuclear poles.

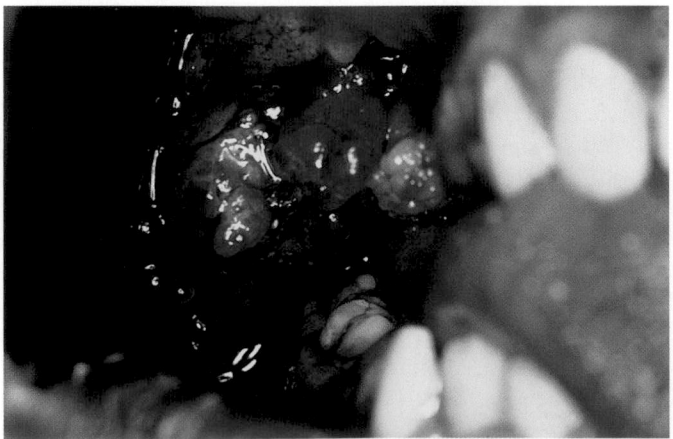

Fig. 5.37 Clinical appearance of embryonal rhabdomyosarcoma of oral cavity in an infant.

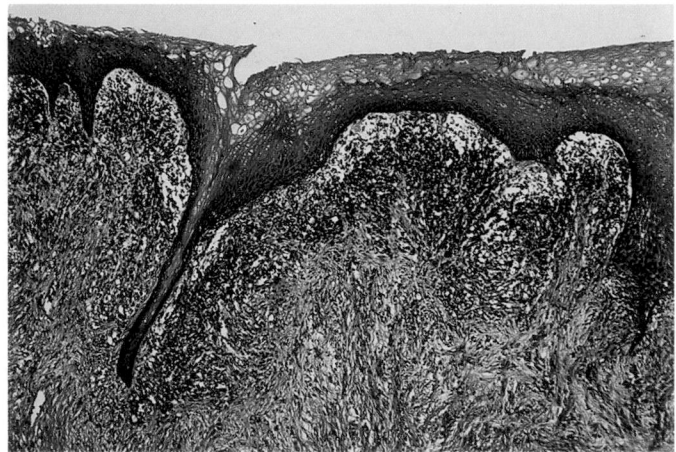

Fig. 5.38 Low-power appearance of embryonal rhabdomyosarcoma of oral cavity. A prominent cambium layer is present.

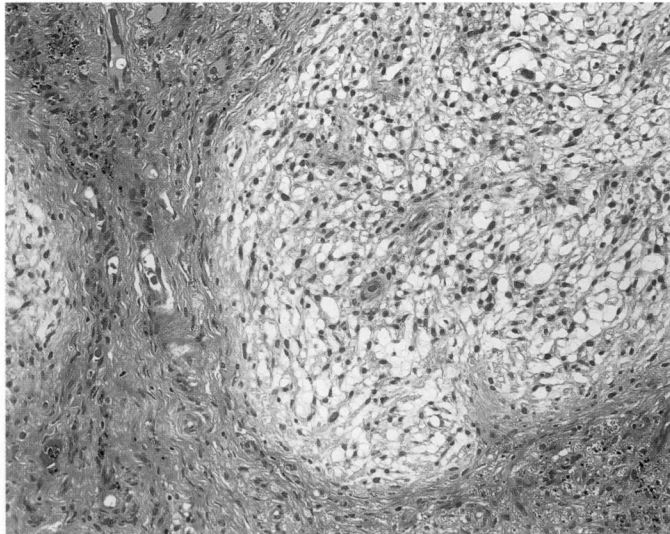

Fig. 5.39 Ectomesenchymal chondromyxoid tumor of tongue. (Slide courtesy of Dr. D Heffner, Washington, D.C.)

chondromyxoid background. Immunohistochemically, the tumor cells are reactive for GFAP and keratin, and less frequently for smooth muscle actin and S-100 protein (but not for EMA and desmin).

Synovial sarcomas can occur as primary tumors in the pharynx, tonsil, cheek, tongue, or palate of young adults[359,384]; the main differential diagnosis is with salivary gland tumors, particularly benign mixed tumor (Fig. 5.40).

Other reported sarcomas of the oral cavity include **alveolar soft part sarcoma**,[337c,352] **extraskeletal osteosarcoma**,[376] **fibrosarcoma**, and **liposarcoma** (Fig. 5.41).[337a,363a,378,379]

Metastatic tumors may present as primary intraoral masses. The gingiva is the classic location, with or without oral involvement. The lung is the most common site of the primary lesion.[349,351] Metastatic renal cell carcinoma can masquerade clinically and microscopically as a pyogenic granuloma. Other sites for the primary tumor include breast, skin (melanoma), prostate, endometrium, large bowel, and mesothelioma.[325,377,389c,391] Chordoma of cervical vertebrae can protrude into the oral cavity.[389b]

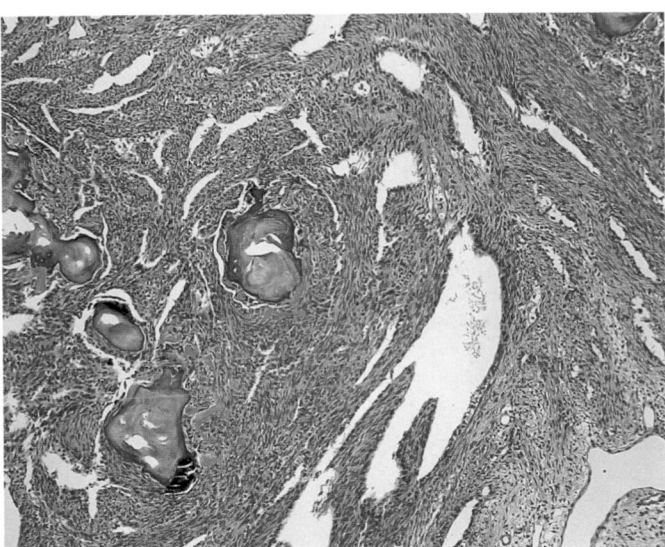

Fig. 5.40 Synovial sarcoma of pharynx. Note the hemangiopericytoma-like areas and the foci of ossification.

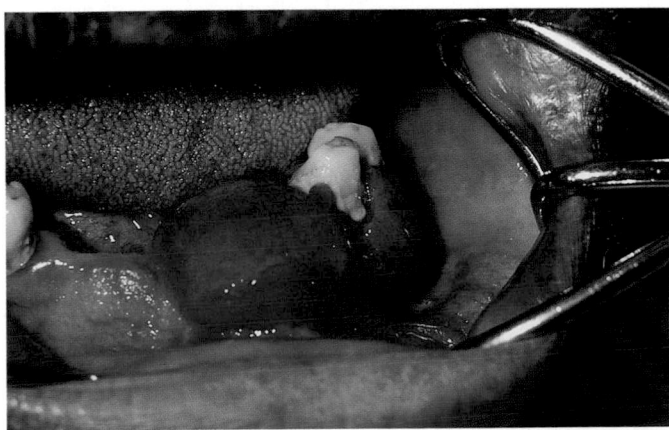

Fig. 5.41 Clinical appearance of primary fibrosarcoma of the oral cavity, presenting as a sessile polypoid mass in the gingiva.

References

Normal anatomy

1 Balogh K. Mouth, Nose and Paranasal Sinuses. In S Sternberg (ed.): Histology for pathologists, ed 2. Philadelphia, 1997, Lippincott-Raven, pp 367–390.

1a Barnes L, Johnson JT. Pathologic and clinical considerations in the evaluation of major head and neck specimens resected for cancer. I. Pathol Annu 1986, **21:** 173–250.

2 Gnepp DR, Souther J. Skeletal muscle in routine tonsillectomy specimens: a common finding. Hum Pathol 2000, **31:** 813–816.

3 Gorlin RJ, Goldman HM. Thoma's oral pathology, ed. 6. St. Louis, 1970, The C. V. Mosby Co.

4 Odell EW, Morgan PR. Biopsy pathology of the oral tissues, ed. 1. London, 1998, Chapman & Hall Medical.

5 Regezi JA, Sciubba J. Oral pathology: clinical pathologic correlations, ed. 3. Philadelphia, 1999, Saunders.

6 Soames JV, Southam JC. Oral pathology, ed. 3. Oxford, 1998, Oxford University Press.

6a Williams MD, Brown HM. The adequacy of gross pathological examination of routine tonsils and adenoids in patients 21 years old and younger. Hum Pathol **34:** 1053–1057.

Congenital abnormalities

7 al-Nafussi A, Hancock K, Sommerlad B, Carder PJ. Heterotopic brain presenting as a cystic mass of the palate. Histopathology 1990, **17:** 81–84.

8 Bossen EH, Hudson WR. Oligodendroglioma arising in heterotopic brain tissue of the soft palate and nasopharynx. Am J Surg Pathol 1987, **11:** 571–574.

9 Broniatowski M, Witt WJ, Shah AC, Galloway PG, Abramowsky CR. Glial tissue in the parapharyngeal space. Arch Otolaryngol 1981, **107:** 638–641.

9a Pantanowitz L. Images in Pathology. Int J Surg Pathol 37.

10 Daley T. Pathology of intraoral sebaceous glands. J Oral Pathol Med 1993, **22:** 241–245.

11 Dunlap CL, Barker BF. Diagnostic problems in oral pathology. Semin Diagn Pathol 1985, **2:** 16–30.

12 Gibson WS Jr, Fenton NA. Congenital sublingual dermoid cyst. Arch Otolaryngol 1982, **108:** 745–748.

13 Gorlin RJ, Jirasek JE. Oral cysts containing gastric or intestinal mucosa. An unusual embryological accident or heterotopia. Arch Otolaryngol 1970, **91:** 594–597.

14 Leibl W, Pflüger H, Kerjaschki D. A case of nodular hyperplasia of the juxtaoral organ in man. Virchows [Arch Pathol Anat] 1976, **371:** 389–391.

15 Lutman GB. Epithelial nests in intraoral sensory nerve endings simulating perineural invasion in patients with oral carcinoma. Am J Clin Pathol 1974, **61:** 275–284.

16 Meyer I. Dermoid cysts (dermoids) of the floor of the mouth. Oral Surg Oral Med Oral Pathol 1955, **8:** 1149–1164.

17 Simpson HE. White sponge nevus. J Oral Surg 1966, **24:** 463–466.

18 Tschen JA, Fechner RE. The juxtaoral organ of Chievitz. Am J Surg Pathol 1979, **3:** 147–150.

19 Zenker W, Salzer G. Die histologie des chievitzen organs. Acta Anat [Basel] 1961, **44:** 286–321.

Inflammatory diseases

20 Ackerman LV, McGavran MH. Proliferating benign and malignant epithelial lesions of the oral cavity. J Oral Surg 1958, **16:** 400–413.

21 Barker DS, Lucas RB. Localized fibrous overgrowths of the oral mucosa. Br J Oral Surg 1967, **5**: 86–92.

22 Basu MK, Asquith P, Thompson RA, Cooke WT. Oral manifestations of Crohn's disease. Gut 1975, **16**: 249–254.

23 Bennett DE. Histoplasmosis of the oral cavity and larynx. A clinicopathologic study. Arch Intern Med 1967, **120**: 417–427.

24 Bhaskar SN, Beasley JD, Cutright DE. Inflammatory papillary hyperplasia of the oral mucosa. Report of 341 cases. J Am Dent Assoc 1970, **81**: 949–952.

25 Dargent JL, Lespagnard L, Kornreich A, Hermans P et al. HIV-associated multinucleated giant cells in lymphoid tissue of the Waldeyer's ring: a detailed study. Mod Pathol 2000, **13**: 1293–1299.

26 el-Mofty SK, Swanson PE, Wick MR, Miller AS. Eosinophilic ulcer of the oral mucosa. Report of 38 new cases with immunohistochemical observations. Oral Surg Oral Med Oral Pathol 1993, **75**: 716–722.

27 Elzay RP. Traumatic ulcerative granuloma with stromal eosinophilia (Riga–Fede's disease and traumatic eosinophilic granuloma). Oral Surg Oral Med Oral Pathol 1983, **55**: 497–506.

28 Epstein JB, Sherlock CH, Wolber RA. Oral manifestations of cytomegalovirus infection. Oral Surg Oral Med Oral Pathol 1993, **75**: 443–451.

29 Eversole LR, Leider AS, Jacobsen PL, Kidd PM. Atypical histiocytic granuloma. Light microscopic, ultrastructural, and histochemical findings in an unusual pseudomalignant reactive lesion of the oral cavity. Cancer 1985, **55**: 1722–1729.

30 Eveson JW. Granulomatous disorders of the oral mucosa. Semin Diagn Pathol 1996, **13**: 118–127.

31 Halme L, Meurman JH, Laine P, von Smitten K, Syrjanen S, Lindqvist C, Strand-Pettinen I. Oral findings in patients with active or inactive Crohn's disease. Oral Surg Oral Med Oral Pathol 1993, **76**: 175–181.

32 Handlers JP, Waterman J, Abrams AM, Melrose RJ. Oral features of Wegener's granulomatosis. Arch Otolaryngol 1985, **111**: 267–270.

33 Helm TN, Camisa C, Allen C, Lowder C. Clinical features of Behçet's disease. Report of four cases. Oral Surg Oral Med Oral Pathol 1991, **72**: 30–34.

34 Houston GD. The giant cell fibroma. A review of 464 cases. Oral Surg Oral Med Oral Pathol 1982, **53**: 582–586.

35 Jones AC, Freedman PD, Phelan JA, Baughan RA, Kerpel SM. Cytomegalovirus infections of the oral cavity. A report of six cases and review of the literature. Oral Surg Oral Med Oral Pathol 1993, **75**: 76–85.

36 Kapadia SB, Wiley CA, Soontornniyomkij V, Wang G, Swerdlow SH. HIV-associated Waldeyer's ring lymphoid hyperplasias: characterization of multinucleated giant cells and the role of Epstein–Barr virus. Hum Pathol 1999, **30**: 1383–1388.

37 Meyer I, Abbey LM. Relationship of syphilis to primary carcinoma of tongue. Oral Surg Oral Med Oral Pathol 1970, **30**: 678–681.

38 Nessan VJ, Jacoway JR. Biopsy of minor salivary glands in the diagnosis of sarcoidosis. N Engl J Med 1979, **301**: 922–924.

39 Patten SF, Tomecki KJ. Wegener's granulomatosis: cutaneous and oral mucosal disease. J Am Acad Dermatol 1993, **28**: 710–718.

40 Plauth M, Jenss H, Meyle J. Oral manifestations of Crohn's disease. An analysis of 79 cases. J Clin Gastroenterol 1991, **13**: 29–37.

41 Regezi JA, Courtney RM, Kerr DA. Fibrous lesions of skin and mucous membranes which contain stellate and multinucleated cells. Oral Surg Oral Med Oral Pathol 1975, **39**: 605–614.

42 Schnitt SJ, Antonioli DA, Jaffe B, Peppercorn MA. Granulomatous inflammation of minor salivary gland ducts. A new oral manifestation of Crohn's disease. Hum Pathol 1987, **18**: 405–407.

43 Sellers RA, Bicket WJ, Parker MG. Posttraumatic spindle cell nodule of the buccal mucosa. Oral Surg Oral Med Oral Pathol 1992, **74**: 212–215.

44 Tang TT, Glicklich M, Hodach AE, Oechler HW, McCreadie SR. Ulcerative eosinophilic granuloma of the tongue. A light- and electron-microscopic study. Am J Clin Pathol 1981, **75**: 420–425.

45 Taxy JB. Granulomatous tonsillitis. An unusual host response with benign clinical evolution. Int J Surg Pathol 1995, **3**: 23–28.

46 Weathers DR, Baker G, Archard HO, Burkes EJ Jr. Psoriasiform lesions of the oral mucosa (with emphasis on "ectopic geographic tongue"). Oral Surg Oral Med Oral Pathol 1974, **37**: 872–887.

47 Worsaae N, Christensen KC, Schiødt M, Reibel J. Melkersson-Rosenthal syndrome and cheilitis granulomatosa. A clinicopathologic study of thirty-three patients with special reference to their oral lesions. Oral Surg Oral Med Oral Pathol 1982, **54**: 404–413.

48 Wright JM, Rankin KV, Wilson JW. Traumatic granuloma of the tongue. Head Neck Surg 1983, **5**: 363–366.

Other non-neoplastic lesions

49 Abrams AM, Melrose RJ, Howell FV. Necrotizing sialometaplasia. A disease simulating malignancy. Cancer 1973, **32**: 130–135.

50 Bouquot JE, Gorlin RJ. Leukoplakia, lichen planus, and other oral keratoses in 23,616 white Americans over the age of 35 years. Oral Surg Oral Med Oral Pathol 1986, **61**: 373–381.

51 Dunlap CL, Barker BF. Necrotizing sialometaplasia. Report of five additional cases. Oral Surg Oral Med Oral Pathol 1974, **37**: 722–727.

52 Dunlap CL, Barker BF. Diagnostic problems in oral pathology. Semin Diagn Pathol 1985, **2**: 16–30.

53 Fechner RE. Necrotizing sialometaplasia. A source of confusion with carcinoma of the palate. Am J Clin Pathol 1977, **67**: 315–317.

54 Handlers JP, Melrose RJ, Abrams AM, Taylor CR. Immunoperoxidase technique in diagnosis of oral pemphigus vulgaris. An alternative method to immunofluorescence. Oral Surg Oral Med Oral Pathol 1982, **54**: 207–212.

55 Harrison JD. Salivary mucoceles. Oral Surg Oral Med Oral Pathol 1975, **39**: 268–278.

56 Jensen JL. Superficial mucoceles of the oral mucosa. Am J Dermatopathol 1990, **12**: 88–92.

57 Kalfayan B, Seager GM. Malakoplakia of palatine tonsil. Am J Clin Pathol 1982, **78**: 390–394.

58 Konttinen YT, Malmström M, Reitamo S, Tolvanen E, Seppä A, Sirelius K. Oral lesions in lichen planus and systemic lupus erythematosus. A histochemical and immunohistochemical study. Acta Pathol Microbiol Immunol Scand [A] 1982, **90**: 295–299.

59 Langlois N, Kohle P. Plunging ranula: a case report and literature review. Hum Pathol 1992, **23**: 1306–1308.

60 Lattanand A, Johnson WC, Graham JH. Mucous cyst (mucocele). A clinicopathologic and histochemical study. Arch Dermatol 1970, **101**: 673–678.

61 Madani M, Harwick RD, Chen SY, Miller AS. Amyloidosis of the oral cavity: report of five cases. Compendium 1991, **12**: 336, 338–342.

62 McClatchey KD, Appelblatt NH, Zarbo RJ, Merrel DM. Plunging ranula. Oral Surg Oral Med Oral Pathol 1984, **57**: 408–412.

63 McDaniel RK, White JW Jr, Edwards PA. Mucha-Habermann's disease with oral lesions. Oral Surg Oral Med Oral Pathol 1982, **53**: 596–601.

64 Pillai R, Balaram P, Reddiar KS. Pathogenesis of oral submucous fibrosis: relationship to risk factors associated with oral cancer. Cancer 1992, **69**: 2011–2020.

65 Pindborg JJ, Poulsen HE, Zachariah J. Oral epithelial changes in thirty Indians with oral cancer and submucous fibrosis. Cancer 1967, **20**: 1141–1146.

66 Praetorius F, Hammarstrom L. A new concept of the pathogenesis of oral mucous cysts based on a study of 200 cases. J Dent Assoc S Afr 1992, **47**: 226–231.

67 Schiødt M. Oral discoid lupus erythematosus. III. A histopathologic study of sixty-six patients. Oral Surg Oral Med Oral Pathol, 1984, **57**: 281–293.

68 Takagi M, Yamamoto H, Mega H, Hsieh KJ, Shioda S, Enomoto S. Heterogeneity in the gingival fibromatoses. Cancer 1991, **68**: 2202–2212.

69 Tomich CE. Oral focal mucinosis. A clinicopathologic and histochemical study of eight cases. Oral Surg Oral Med Oral Pathol 1974, **38**: 714–724.

70 van der Wal N, Henzen-Logmans S, van der Kwast WAM, van der Waal I. Amyloidosis of the tongue. A clinical and postmortem study. J Oral Pathol 1984, **13**: 632–639.

71 van Wyk CW, Ambrosio SC. Leukoedema. Ultrastructural and histochemical observations. J Oral Pathol 1983, **12**: 319–329.

72 Wysocki GP, Gretzinger HA, Laupacis A, Ulan RA, Stiller CR. Fibrous hyperplasia of the gingiva. A side effect of cyclosporin A therapy. Oral Surg Oral Med Oral Pathol 1983, **55**: 274–278.

73 Yamaguchi A, Nasu M, Esaki Y, Shimada H, Yoshiki S. Amyloid deposits in the aged tongue. A postmortem study of 107 individuals over 60 years of age. J Oral Pathol 1982, **11**: 237–244.

Tumors and tumorlike conditions of surface epithelium
Intraepithelial proliferative lesions

74 Amagasa T, Yokoo E, Sato K, Tanaka N, Shioda S, Takagi M. A study of the clinical characteristics and treatment of oral carcinoma in situ. Oral Surg Oral Med Oral Pathol 1985, **60**: 50–55.

75 Bánóczy J. Oral leukoplakia and other white lesions of the oral mucosa related to dermatological disorders. J Cutan Pathol 1983, **10**: 238–256.

76 Batsakis JG, Suarez P, el-Naggar AK. Proliferative verrucous leukoplakia and its related lesions. Oral Oncol 1999, **35**: 354–359.

77 Browne RM, Potts AJC. Dysplasia in salivary gland ducts in sublingual leukoplakia and erythroplakia. Oral Surg Oral Med Oral Pathol 1986, **62**: 44–48.

78 Coltrera MD, Zarbo MJ, Sakr WA, Gown AM. Markers for dysplasia of the upper aerodigestive tract. Suprabasal expression of PCNA, p53, and CK19 in alcohol-fixed, embedded tissue. Am J Pathol 1992, **141**: 817–825.

79 Crissman JD, Gnepp DR, Goodman ML, Hellquist H, Johns ME. Preinvasive lesions of the upper aerodigestive tract. Histologic definitions and clinical implications. A symposium. Pathol Annu 1987, **22**: 311–352.

80 Einhorn J, Wersäll J. Incidence of oral carcinoma in patients with leukoplakia of the oral mucosa. Cancer 1967, **20**: 2189–2193.

81 Eisenberg E, Krutchkoff DJ. Lichenoid lesions of oral mucosa. Diagnostic criteria and their importance in the alleged relationship to oral cancer. Oral Surg Oral Med Oral Pathol 1992, **73**: 699–704.

82 Fischman SL, Ulmansky M, Sela J, Bab I, Gazit D. Correlative clinicopathological evaluation of oral premalignancy. J Oral Pathol 1982, **11**: 283–289.

83 Katz HC, Shear M, Altini M. A critical evaluation of epithelial dysplasia in oral mucosal lesions using the Smith-Pindborg method of standardization. J Oral Pathol 1985, **14**: 476–482.

84 King GN, Healy CM, Glover MT, Kwan JTC, Williams DM, Leign IM, Worthington HV, Thornhill MH. Increased prevalence of dysplastic and malignant lip lesions in renal-transplant recipients. N Engl J Med 1995, **332**: 1052–1057.

85 King OH. Intraoral leukoplakia? Cancer **17**: 131–136, 1964.

86 Krutchkoff DJ, Eisenberg E. Lichenoid dysplasia. A distinct histopathologic entity. Oral Surg Oral Med Oral Pathol 1985, **30**: 308–315.

87 Mashberg A, Morrissey JB, Garfinkel L. A study of the appearance of early asymptomatic oral squamous cell carcinoma. Cancer 1973, **32**: 1436–1445.

88 Nishioka H, Hiasa Y, Hiyashi I, Kitahori Y, Konishi N, Sugimura M. Immunohistochemical detection of p53 oncoprotein in human oral squamous cell carcinomas and leukoplakias: comparison with proliferating cell nuclear antigen staining and correlation with clinicopathological findings. Oncology 1993, **50**: 426–429.

89 Ogden GR, Kiddie RA, Lunny DP, Lane DP. Assessment of p53 protein expression in normal, benign, and malignant oral mucosa. J Pathol 1992, **166**: 389–394.

90 Pindborg JJ, Jølst O, Renstrup G, Roed-Petersen B. Studies in oral leukoplakia. A preliminary report on the period prevalence of malignant transformation in leukoplakia based on a follow-up study of 248 patients. J Am Dent Assoc 1968, **76**: 767–771.

91 Renstrup G. Leukoplakia of the oral cavity. A clinical and histopathologic study. Acta Odontol Scand 1958, **16**: 99–111.

92 Renstrup G. Occurrence of *Candida* in oral leukoplakias. Acta Pathol Microbiol Scand [B] 1970, **78**: 421–424.

93 Saito T, Notani K, Miura H, Fukuda H, Mizuno S, Shindoh M, Amemiya A. DNA analysis of oral leukoplakia by flow cytometry. Int J Oral Maxillofac Surg 1991, **20**: 259–263.

94 Sakr WA, Zarbo RJ, Jacobs JR, Crissman JD. Distribution of basement membrane in squamous cell carcinoma of the head and neck. Hum Pathol 1987, **18**: 1043–1050.

95 Scully C, Burkhardt A. Tissue markers of potentially malignant human oral epithelial lesions. J Oral Pathol Med 1993, **22**: 246–256.

96 Shafer WG. Oral carcinoma in situ. Oral Surg Oral Med Oral Pathol 1975, **39**: 227–238.

97 Silverman S Jr, Bhargava K, Mani NJ, Smith LW, Malaowalla AM. Malignant transformation and natural history of oral leukoplakia in 57,518 industrial workers in Gujarat, India. Cancer 1976, **38**: 1790–1795.

98 Silverman S Jr, Gorsky M, Lozada F. Oral leukoplakia and malignant transformation. A follow-up study of 257 patients. Cancer 1984, **53**: 563–568.

99 Suarez P, Batsakis JG, el-Naggar AK. Leukoplakia: still a gallimaufry or is progress being made?—A review. Adv Anat Pathol 1998, **5**: 137–155.

100 Sudbo J, Kildal W, Risberg B, Koppang HS, Danielsen HE, Reith A. DNA content as a prognostic marker in patients with oral leukoplakia. N Engl J Med 2001, **344**: 1270–1278.

101 Waldron CA, Shafer WG. Leukoplakia revisited. A clinicopathologic study of 3256 oral leukoplakias. Cancer 1975, **36**: 1386–1392.

102 Warnokulasuriya KA, Johnson NW. Nucleolar organizer region (NOR) distribution as a diagnostic marker in oral keratosis, dysplasia and squamous cell carcinoma. J Oral Pathol Med 1993, **22**: 77–81.

103 WHO Collaborating Centre for Oral Precancerous Lesions. Definition of leukoplakia and related lesions. An aid to studies on oral precancer. Oral Surg Oral Med Oral Pathol 1978, **46**: 518–539.

Oral lesions and human papilloma virus (HPV)

104 Abby LJ, Page DG, Sawyer DR. The clinical and histopathologic features of a series of 464 oral squamous cell papillomas. Oral Surg Oral Med Oral Pathol 1980, **49**: 419–428.

105 Adler-Storthz K, Ficarra G, Woods KV, Gaglioti D, DiPietro M, Shillitoe EJ. Prevalence of Epstein-Barr virus and human papillomavirus in oral mucosa of HIV-infected patients. J Oral Pathol Med 1992, **21**: 164–170.

106 Becker J, Leser U, Marschall M, Langford A, Jilg W, Gelderblom H, Reichart P, Wolf H. Expression of proteins encoded by Epstein-Barr virus trans-activator genes depends on the differentiation of epithelial cells in oral hairy leukoplakia. Proc Natl Acad Sci USA 1991, **88**: 8332–8336.

107 Bouda M, Gorgoulis G, Kastrinakis NG, Giannoudis A, Tsoli E, Danassi-Afentaki D, Foukas P, Kyroudi A, Laskaris G, Herrington CS, Kittas C. 'High risk' HPV types are frequently detected in potentially malignant and malignant oral lesions, but not in normal oral mucosa. Mod Pathol 2000, **13:** 644–653.

108 de Villiers E-M, Weidauer H, Otto H, zur Hausen H. Papillomavirus DNA in human tongue carcinomas. Int J Cancer 1985, **36:** 575–578.

109 Eisenberg E, Rosenberg B, Krutchkoff DJ. Verrucous carcinoma. A possible viral pathogenesis. Oral Surg Oral Med Oral Pathol 1985, **59:** 52–57.

109a El-Mofty SK, Lu DW. Prevalence of human papillomavirus type 16DNA in squamous cell carcinoma of the palatine tonsil, and not the oral cavity, in young patients. Am J Surg Pathol 2003 **27:** 1463–1470.

110 Eversole LR, Jacobsen P, Stone CE, Freckleton V. Oral condyloma planus (hairy leukoplakia) among homosexual men. A clinicopathologic study of thirty-six cases. Oral Surg Oral Med Oral Pathol 1986, **61:** 249–255.

111 Eversole LR, Laipis PJ, Greer TL. Human papillomavirus type 2 DNA in oral and labial verruca vulgaris. J Cutan Pathol 1987, **14:** 319–325.

112 Fernández JF, Benito MAC, Lizaldez EB, Monatañés MA. Oral hairy leukoplakia. A histopathologic study of 32 cases. Am J Dermatopathol 1990, **12:** 571–578.

113 Garlick JA, Taichman LB. Human papillomavirus infection of the oral mucosa. Am J Dermatopathol 1991, **13:** 386–395.

114 Gillison ML, Koch WM, Capone RB, Spafford M, Westra WH, Wu L, Zahurak ML, Daniel RW, Viglione M, Symer DE, Shah KV, Sidransky D. Evidence for a causal association between human papillomavirus and a subset of head and neck cancers. J Natl Cancer Inst 2000, **92(9):** 709–720.

115 Jenson AB, Lancaster WD, Hartmann D-P, Shaffer EL Jr. Frequency and distribution of papillomavirus structural antigens in verrucae, multiple papillomas, and condylomata of the oral cavity. Am J Pathol 1982, **107:** 212–218.

115a Klussmann JP, Gü ltekin E, Weissenborn SJ, Wieland U, Dries V, Dienes HP, Eckel HE, Pfister HJ and Fuchs PG. Expression of p16 Protein identifies a distinct entity of Tonsillar Carcinomas associated with Human Papillomavirus. Am J Pathol 2003, **162:** 747–753.

115b Mork J, Lie AK, Glattre E, Hallmans G, Jellum E, Koskela P, Møller B, Pukkala E, Schiller JT, Youngman L, Lehtinen M, and Dillner J. Human Papillomavirus infection as a risk factor for squamous-cell carcinoma of the head and neck. N Engl J Med 2001, **15:** 1125–1131.

116 Pilgard G. Focal epithelial hyperplasia. Report of nine cases from Sweden and review of the literature. Oral Surg Oral Med Oral Pathol 1983, **57:** 540–543.

117 Regezi JA, Greenspan D, Greenspan JS, Wong E, McPhail LA. HPV-associated epithelial atypia in oral warts in HIV+ patients. J Cutan Pathol 1994, **21:** 217–223.

118 Shroyer KR, Greer RO Jr. Detection of human papillomavirus DNA by in situ DNA hybridization and polymerase chain reaction in premalignant and malignant oral lesions. Oral Surg Oral Med Oral Pathol 1991, **71:** 708–713.

119 Southam JC, Felix DH, Wray D, Cubie HA. Hairy leukoplakia—a histological study. Histopathology 1991, **19:** 63–67.

120 Swan RH, McDaniel RK, Dreiman BB, Rome WC. Condyloma acuminatum involving the oral mucosa. Oral Surg Oral Med Oral Pathol 1981, **51:** 503–508.

121 Swart JGN, Lekkas C, Allard RHB. Oral manifestations in Cowden's syndrome. Report of four cases. Oral Surg Oral Med Oral Pathol 1985, **59:** 264–268.

122 Welch TB, Barker BF, Williams C. Peroxidase-antiperoxidase evaluation of human oral squamous cell papillomas. Oral Surg Oral Med Oral Pathol 1986, **61:** 603–606.

123 Wilczynski SP, Lin BTY, Xie Y, Paz B. Detection of human papillomavirus DNA and oncoprotein overexpression are associated with distinct morphological patterns of tonsillar squamous cell carcinoma. Am J Pathol 1998, **152:** 145–156.

124 Woods KV, Shillitoe EJ, Spitz MR, Schantz SP, Adler Storthz K. Analysis of human papillomavirus DNA in oral squamous cell carcinomas. J Oral Pathol Med 1993, **22:** 101–108.

Squamous cell carcinoma
General features

125 Binnie WH, Rankin KV. Epidemiological and diagnostic aspects of oral squamous cell carcinoma. J Oral Pathol 1984, **13:** 333–341.

126 Binnie WH, Rankin KV, Mackenzie IC. Etiology of oral squamous cell carcinoma. J Oral Pathol 1983, **12:** 11–29.

127 Chen J, Katz RV, Krutchkoff DJ. Intraoral squamous cell carcinoma: epidemiologic patterns in Connecticut from 1935 to 1985. Cancer 1990, **66:** 1288–1296.

128 Chen J, Katz R, Krutchkoff D, Eisenberg E. Lip cancer. Incidence trends in Connecticut, 1935–1985. Cancer 1992, **70:** 2025–2030.

129 Curtis RE, Rowlings PA, Deeg HJ, Shriner DA, Socie G, Travis LB, Horowitz MM, Witherspoon RP, Hoover RN, Sobacinski KA, Fraumeni JF Jr., Boice JD. Solid cancers after bone marrow transplantation. N Engl J Med 1997, **336:** 897–904.

130 Douglass CW, Gammon MD. Reassessing the epidemiology of lip cancer. Oral Surg Oral Med Oral Pathol 1984, **57:** 631–642.

131 Forastiere A, Koch W, Trotti A, Sidransky D. Head and neck cancer. N Engl J Med 2001, **345:** 1890–1900.

132 Ildstad ST, Tollerud DJ, Bigelow ME, Remensnyder JP. Squamous cell carcinoma of the head and neck at the Massachusetts General Hospital. A comparison of biologic characteristics in men and women. Surgery 1986, **99:** 7–14.

132a Mork J, Lie AK, Glattre E, Hallmans G, Jellum E, Koskela P, Møller B, Pukkala E, Schiller JT, Youngman L, Lehtinen M, and Dillner J. Human Papillomavirus infection as a risk factor for squamous-cell carcinoma of the head and neck. N Engl J Med 2001, **15:** 1125–1131.

133 Muir C, Weiland I. Upper aerodigestive tract cancers. Cancer 1995, **75:** 147–153.

134 Mullen DL, Silverberg SG, Penn I, Hammond WS. Squamous cell carcinoma of the skin and lip in renal homograft recipients. Cancer 1976, **37:** 729–734.

134a Neville BW and Day TA. Oral cancer and precancerous lesions. CA Cancer J Clin 2002, **52:** 195–215.

135 Newman AN, Rice DH, Ossoff RH, Sisson GA. Carcinoma of the tongue in persons younger than 30 years of age. Arch Otolaryngol 1983, **109:** 302–304.

136 Reed K, Ravikumar TS, Gifford RRM, Grage TB. The association of Fanconi's anemia and squamous cell carcinoma. Cancer 1983, **52:** 926–928.

137 Rich AM, Radden BG. Squamous cell carcinoma of the oral mucosa. A review of 244 cases in Australia. J Oral Pathol 1984, **13:** 459–471.

138 Usenius T, Kärjä J, Collan Y. Squamous cell carcinoma of the tongue in children. Cancer 1987, **60:** 236–239.

Location

139 Boysen M, Loven JO. Second malignant neoplasms in patients with head and neck squamous cell carcinomas. Acta Oncol 1993, **32:** 283–288.

140 Braakhuis BJ, Tabor MP, Rene Leemans C, Van Der Waal I, Snow GB, Brakenhoff RH. Second primary tumors and field cancerization in oral and oropharyngeal cancer: Molecular techniques provide new insights and definitions. Head Neck 2002, **24:** 198–206.

141 Gluckman JL, Crissman JD, Donegan JO. Multicentric squamous-cell carcinoma of the upper aerodigestive tract. Head Neck Surg 1980, **3:** 90–96.

142 Ildstad ST, Bigelow ME, Remensnyder JP. Intra-oral cancer at the Massachusetts General Hospital. Squamous cell carcinoma of the floor of the mouth. Ann Surg 1983, **197**: 34–41.

143 Jovanovic A, Schulten EA, Kostense PJ, Snow GB, van der Waal I. Squamous cell carcinoma of the lip and oral cavity in the Netherlands. An epidemiological study of 740 patients. J Craniomaxillofac Surg 1993, **21**: 149–152.

144 MacComb WS, Fletcher GH, Healey JE. Intra-oral cavity. In MacComb WS, Fletcher GH (eds): Cancer of the head and neck. Baltimore, 1967, The Williams & Wilkins Co., pp. 89–151.

145 Mashberg A, Meyers H. Anatomical site and size of 222 early asymptomatic oral squamous cell carcinomas. A continuing prospective study of oral cancer. II. Cancer 1976, **37**: 2149–2157.

146 Nakanishi Y, Noguchi M, Matsuno Y, Saikawa M, Mukai K, Shimosato Y, Hirohashi S. p53 expression in multicentric squamous cell carcinoma and surrounding squamous epithelium of the upper aerodigestive tract. Immunohistochemical analysis of 95 lesions. Cancer 1995, **75**: 1657–1662.

147 Shibuya H, Amagasa T, Seto K-I, Ishibashi K, Horiuchi J-I, Suzuki S. Leukoplakia-associated multiple carcinomas in patients with tongue carcinoma. Cancer 1986, **57**: 843–846.

147a Tabor MP, Brakenhoff RH, Ruijter-Schippers HJ, van der Wal JE, Snow GB, Leemans CR and Braakhuis BJM. Multiple Head and Neck Tumors frequently originate from a single Preneoplastic lesion. American Journal of Pathology 2002, **161**: 1051–1161.

148 Van Oijen MG, Leppers vd Straat FG, Tilanus MG, Slootweg PJ. The origins of multiple squamous cell is carcinoma in the aerodigestive tract. Cancer 2000, **88**: 884–893.

149 Van Rees BP, Cleton-Jansen AM, Cense HA, Polak MM, Clement MJ, Drillenburg P, Van Lanschot JJB, Offerhaus GJ. Molecular evidence of field cancerization in a patient with 7 tumors of the aerodigestive tract. Hum Pathol 2000, **31**: 269–271.

150 Worsham MJ, Wolman SR, Carey TE, Zarbo RJ, Benninger MS, Van Dyke DL. Common clonal origin of synchronous primary head and neck squamous cell carcinomas. Analysis by tumor karyotypes and fluorescence in situ hybridization. Hum Pathol 1995, **26**: 251–261.

Microscopic features

151 Lowe D, Fletcher CDM. Eosinophilia in squamous cell carcinoma of the oral cavity, external genitalia, and anus—clinical correlations. Histopathology 1984, **8**: 627–632.

152 Modica LA, Youngberg GA, Avila FO. Melanocyte colonization of an oral carcinoma. Histopathology 1990, **17**: 477–478.

153 Wright A, Shear M. Epithelial dysplasia immediately adjacent to oral squamous cell carcinoma. J Oral Pathol 1985, **14**: 559–564.

Histochemical and immunohistochemical features

154 Harada T, Shinohara M, Nakamura S, Shimada M, Oka M. Immunohistochemical detection of desmosomes in oral squamous cell carcinomas: correlation with differentiation, mode of invasion, and metastatic potential. Int J Oral Maxillofac Surg 1992, **21**: 346–349.

155 Suo Z, Holm R, Nesland JM. Squamous cell carcinomas. An immunohistochemical study of cytokeratins and involucrin in primary and metastatic tumours. Histopathology 1993, **23**: 45–54.

Molecular genetic features

156 Califano J, Van Der Reit P, Westra W, Nawroz H, Clayman G, Piantadosi S, Corio R, Lee D, Greenberg B, Koch W, Sidransky D. Genetic progression model for head and neck cancer: implications for field cancerization. Cancer Res 1996, **56**: 2488–2492.

157 Califano J, Westra WH, Meininger G, Corio R, Koch WM, Sidransky D. Genetic progression and clonal relationship of recurrent premalignant head and neck lesions. Clin Cancer Res 2000, **6**: 347–352.

158 El-Nagger AK, Lai S, Clayman GL, Zhou JH, Tucker SA, Myers J, Luna MA, Benedict WF. Expression of p.16 Rb. And cyclin D1 gene products in oral and laryngeal squamous carcinoma: biological and clinical implications. Hum Pathol 1999, **30**: 1013–1018.

159 Nakanishi Y, Noguchi M, Matsuno Y, Mukai K, Shimosato Y, Hirohashi S. p53 expression in squamous cell carcinoma and dysplasia of the vocal cords and oral cavity. Appl Immunohistochem 1993, **1**: 101–107.

160 Satoh M, Hatakeyama S, Sashima M, Suzuki A. Immunohistochemical detection of *ras* 21 in oral squamous cell carcinomas. Oral Surg Oral Med Oral Pathol 1992, **64**: 469–472.

161 Warnakulasuriya KA, Johnson NW. Expression of p53 mutant nuclear phosphoprotein in oral carcinoma and potentially malignant oral lesions. J Oral Pathol Med 1992, **21**: 404–408.

Biopsy, cytology, and frozen section

162 Bhaskar SN. Oral pathology in the dental office. Survey of 20,575 biopsy specimens. J Am Dent Assoc 1968, **76**: 761–766.

163 Brennan JA, Mao L, Hruban RH, Boyle JO, Eby YJ, Koch WM, Goodman SN, Sidransky D. Molecular assessment of histopathological staging in squamous-cell carcinoma of the head and neck. N Engl J Med 1995, **332**: 429–435.

163a Cerilli LA and Wick MR, Fine needle aspiration biopsies of the head and neck: the surgical pathologist's perspective. International Journal of Surgical Pathology 2000, **8**: 17–18.

163b Koss L.G. Diagnostic cytology and its histopathologic bases, ed 4. Philadelphia, 1992, J.B. Lippincott, pp. 874–879.

164 Looser KG, Shah JP, Strong EW. The significance of "positive" margins in surgically resected epidermoid carcinomas. Head Neck Surg 1978, **1**: 107–111.

165 Shklar G, Cataldo E, Meyer I. Reliability of cytologic smear in diagnosis of oral cancer. A controlled study. Arch Otolaryngol 1970, **91**: 158–160.

Spread and metastases

166 Barnes L, Johnson JT. Pathologic and clinical considerations in the evaluation of major head and neck specimens resected for cancer. Part I. Pathol Annu 1986, **21**: 173–250.

167 Compagno J, Hyams VJ, Safavian M. Does branchiogenic carcinoma really exist? Arch Pathol Lab Med 1976, **100**: 311–314.

168 Davidson BJ, Kulkarny V, Delacure MD, Shah JP. Posterior triangle metastases of squamous cell carcinoma of the upper aerodigestive tract. Am J Surg 1993, **166**: 295–298.

169 Frierson HF Jr, Cooper PH. Prognostic factors in squamous cell carcinoma of the lower lip. Hum Pathol 1986, **17**: 346–354.

170 McGregor AD, MacDonald DG. Patterns of spread of squamous cell carcinoma to the ramus of the mandible. Head Neck 1993, **15**: 440–444.

171 Micheau C, Cachin Y, Caillou B. Cystic metastases in the neck revealing occult carcinoma of the tonsil. A report of six cases. Cancer 1974, **33**: 228–233.

172 O'Brien CJ, Carter RL, Soo K-C, Barr LC, Hamlyn PJ, Shaw HJ. Invasion of the mandible by squamous carcinomas of the oral cavity and oropharynx. Head Neck Surg 1986, **8**: 247–256.

173 Regauer S, Beham A, Mannweiler S. CK7 expression in carcinomas of the Waldeyer's ring area. Hum Pathol 2000, **31**: 1096–1101.

174 Safaii H, Azar HA. Keratin granulomas in irradiated squamous cell carcinoma of various sites. Cancer Res 1966, **26**: 500–508.

175 Shah JP, Candela FC, Poddar AK. The patterns of cervical lymph node metastases from squamous carcinoma of the oral cavity. Cancer 1990, **66**: 109–113.

176 Shear M, Hawkins DM, Farr HW. The prediction of lymph node

metastases from oral squamous carcinoma. Cancer 1976, **37**: 1901–1907.

177 Thompson LDR, Heffner DK. The clinical importance of cystic squamous cell carcinomas in the neck: a study of 136 cases. Cancer 1998, **82**: 944–956.

178 Umeda M, Yokoo S, Take Y, Omori A, Nakanishi K, Shimada K. Lymph node metastasis in squamous cell carcinoma of the oral cavity. Correlation between histologic features and the prevalence of metastasis. Head Neck 1992, **14**: 263–272.

179 Yamamoto E, Miyakawa A, Kohama G-I. Mode of invasion and lymph node metastasis in squamous cell carcinoma of the oral cavity. Head Neck Surg 1984, **6**: 938–947.

Treatment

180 De Braud F, al-Sarraf M. Diagnosis and management of squamous cell carcinoma of unknown primary tumor site of the neck. Semin Oncol 1993, **20**: 273–278.

181 Korb LJ, Spaulding CA, Constable WC. The role of definitive radiation therapy in squamous cell carcinoma of the oral tongue. Cancer 1991, **67**: 2733–2738.

182 Merlano M, Vitale V, Rosso R, Benasso M, Corvo R, Cavallari M, Sanguinetti G, Bacigalupo A, Badellino F, Margarino G, Brema F, Pastorino G, Marziano C, Grimaldi A, Scasso F, Sperati G, Pallestrini E, Garaventa G. Treatment of advanced squamous-cell carcinoma of the head and neck with alternating chemotherapy and radiotherapy. N Engl J Med 1992, **327**: 1115–1121.

182a Parsons JT, Mendenhall WM, Stringer SP, Amdur RJ, Hinerman RW, Villaret DB, Moore-Higgs GJ, Greene BD, Speer TW, Cassisi NJ, Million RR. Squamous cell carcinoma of the Oropharynx. Cancer 2002, **94**: 2967–2980.

183 Perez CA, Purdy JA, Breaux SR, Ogura JH, Von Essen S. Carcinoma of the tonsillar fossa. A nonrandomized comparison of preoperative radiation and surgery or irradiation alone. Long-term results. Cancer 1982, **50**: 2314–2322.

184 Raybaud-Diogene H, Fortin A, Morency R, Roy J, Monteil RA, Tetu B. Markers of radioresistance in squamous cell carcinomas of the head and neck: a clinicopathologic and immunohistochemical study. J Clin Oncol 1997, **15**: 1030–1038.

185 Rodgers LW Jr, Stringer SP, Mendenhall WM, Parsons JT, Cassisi NJ, Million RR. Management of squamous cell carcinoma of the floor of mouth. Head Neck 1993, **15**: 16–19.

186 Vokes E, Weichselbaum R, Lippman S, Hong W. Head and neck cancer. N Engl J Med 1993, **328**: 184–194.

Prognosis

187 Anneroth G, Hansen LS, Silverman S Jr. Malignancy grading in oral squamous cell carcinoma I. Squamous cell carcinoma of the tongue and floor of mouth. Histologic grading in the clinical evaluation. J Oral Pathol 1986, **15**: 162–168.

188 Breuninger H, Schaumburg-Lever G, Holzschuh J, Horny HP. Desmoplastic squamous cell carcinoma of skin and vermilion surface: a highly malignant subtype of skin cancer. Cancer 1997, **79**: 915–919.

189 Bryne M, Koppang HS, Lilleng R, Kjaerheim A. Malignancy grading of the deep invasive margins of oral squamous cell carcinomas has high prognostic value. J Pathol 1992, **166**: 375–381.

190 Bryne M, Nielsen K, Koppang HS, Dabelsteen E. Reproducibility of two malignancy grading systems with reportedly prognostic value for oral cancer patients. J Oral Pathol Med 1991, **20**: 369–372.

191 Bryne M, Thrane PS, Dabelsteen E. Loss of expression of blood group antigen H is associated with cellular invasion and spread of oral squamous cell carcinomas. Cancer 1991, **67**: 613–618.

192 Crissman JD, Gluckman J, Whiteley J, Quenelle D. Squamous-cell carcinoma of the floor of the mouth. Head Neck Surg 1980, **3**: 2–7.

192a Dorta RG, Landman G, Kowalski LP, Lauris JRP, Latorre MRDO,

Oliveira DT. Tumor-associated tissue eosinophilia as a prognostic factor in oral squamous cell carcinomas. Histopathology 2002, **41**: 152–157.

193 Frierson HF Jr, Cooper PH. Prognostic factors in squamous cell carcinoma of the lower lip. Hum Pathol 1986, **17**: 346–354.

194 Givens CD Jr, Johns ME, Cantrell RW. Carcinoma of the tonsil. Analysis of 162 cases. Arch Otolaryngol 1981, **107**: 730–734.

195 Grandi C, Alloisio M, Moglia D, Podrecca S, Sala L, Salvatori P, Molinari R. Prognostic significance of lymphatic spread in head and neck carcinomas. Therapeutic implications. Head Neck Surg 1985, **8**: 67–73.

196 Hemmer J, Kreidler J. Flow cytometric DNA ploidy analysis of squamous cell carcinoma of the oral cavity: comparison with clinical staging and histologic grading. Cancer 1990, **66**: 317–320.

197 Ildstad ST, Bigelow ME, Remensnyder JP. Intra-oral cancer at the Massachusetts General Hospital. Squamous cell carcinoma of the floor of the mouth. Ann Surg 1983, **197**: 34–41.

198 Ildstad ST, Bigelow ME, Remensnyder JP. Squamous cell carcinoma of the alveolar ridge and palate. A 15-year survey. Ann Surg 1984, **199**: 445–453.

199 Iro H, Waldfahrer F. Evaluation of the newly updated TNM classification of head and neck carcinoma with data from 3247 patients. Cancer 1998, **83**: 2201–2207.

200 Marks JE, Smith PG, Sessions DG. Pharyngeal wall cancer. A reappraisal after comparison of treatment methods. Arch Otolaryngol 1985, **111**: 79–85.

201 Moore C, Flynn MB, Greenberg RA. Evaluation of size in prognosis of oral cancer. Cancer 1986, **58**: 158–162.

202 Myers JN, Greenberg JS, Mo V, Roberts D. Extracapsular spread. A significant predictor of treatment failure in patients with squamous cell carcinoma of the tongue. Cancer 2001, **92**: 3030–3036.

203 Odell EW, Jani P, Sherriff M, Ahluwalia SM, Hibbert J, Levison DA, Morgan PR. The prognostic value of individual histologic grading parameters in small lingual squamous cell carcinomas. The importance of the pattern of invasion. Cancer 1994, **74**: 789–794.

203a Singh B, Stoffel A, Gogineni S, Poluri A, Pfister DG, Shaha AR, Pathak A, Bosl A, Cordon-Cardo C, Shah JP, Rao PH. Short Communication: amplification of the 3q26.3 Locus is associated with progression to invasive cancer and is a negative prognostic factor in head and neck squamous cell carcinomas. American Journal of Pathology 2002, **161**: 365–371.

204 Stein AL, Tahan SR. Histologic correlates of metastasis in primary invasive squamous cell carcinoma of the lip. J Cutan Pathol 1994, **21**: 16–21.

205 Tytor M, Wingren S, Olofsson J. Heterogeneity of squamous cell carcinomas of the oral cavity studied by flow cytometry. Pathol Res Pract 1991, **187**: 30–35.

206 Yuen PW, Chow V, Choy J, Lam KL, Ho WK, Wei WI. The clinicopathologic significance of p53 and p21: expression in the surgical management of lingual squamous cell carcinoma. Am J Clin Pathol 2001, **116**: 240–245.

Verrucous carcinoma

207 Ackerman LV. Verrucous carcinoma of the oral cavity. Surgery 1948, **23**: 670–678.

208 Batsakis JG, Hybels R, Crissman JD, Rice DH. The pathology of head and neck tumors. Verrucous carcinoma. Part 15. Head Neck Surg 1982, **5**: 29–38.

209 Cooper JR, Hellquist HB, Michaels L. Image analysis in the discrimination of verrucous carcinoma and squamous papilloma. J Pathol 1992, **166**: 383–387.

210 Demian SDE, Bushkin FL, Echevarria RA. Perineural invasion and anaplastic transformation of verrucous carcinoma. Cancer 1973, **32**: 395–401.

211 Hansen LS, Olson JA, Silverman S Jr. Proliferative verrucous

leukoplakia. A long-term study of thirty patients. Oral Surg Oral Med Oral Pathol 1985, **60**: 285–298.

212 Koch BB, Trask DK, Hoffman HT, Karnell LH, Robinson RA, Zhen W, Menck HR. National survey of head and neck verrucous carcinoma: patterns of presentation care, and outcome. Cancer 2001, **92**: 110–120.

213 Kraus FT, Perez-Mesa C. Verrucous carcinoma. Clinical and pathologic study of 105 cases involving oral cavity, larynx and genitalia. Cancer 1966, **19**: 26–38.

214 McCoy JM, Waldron CA. Verrucous carcinoma of the oral cavity. A review of forty-nine cases. Oral Surg Oral Med Oral Pathol 1981, **52**: 623–629.

215 McDonald JS, Crissman JD, Gluckman JL. Verrucous carcinoma of the oral cavity. Head Neck Surg 1982, **5**: 22–28.

216 Medina JE, Dichtel W, Luna MA. Verrucous-squamous carcinoma of the oral cavity. A clinicopathologic study of 104 cases. Arch Otolaryngol 1984, **110**: 437–440.

217 Prioleau PG, Santa Cruz DJ, Meyer JS, Bauer WC. Verrucous carcinoma. A light and electron microscopic, autoradiographic, and immunofluorescence study. Cancer 1980, **45**: 2849–2857.

218 Shear M, Pindborg JJ. Verrucous hyperplasia of the oral mucosa. Cancer 1980, **46**: 1855–1862.

219 Sundström B, Mörnstad H, Axéll T. Oral carcinomas associated with snuff dipping. Some clinical and histological characteristics of 23 tumours in Swedish males. J Oral Pathol 1982, **11**: 245–251.

220 Wechsler HL, Risher ER. Oral florid papillomatosis. Clinical, pathological and electron microscopic observations. Arch Dermatol 1962, **86**: 140–152.

Other microscopic types

221 Banks E, Frierson H, Mills S, George E, Zarbo R, Swanson P. Basaloid squamous cell carcinoma of the head and neck: a clinicopathologic and immunohistochemical study of 40 cases. Am J Surg Pathol 1992, **16**: 939–946.

222 Batsakis JG, Suarez P. Sarcomatoid carcinomas of the upper aerodigestive tracts. Adv Anat Pathol 2000, **7**: 282–293.

223 Batsakis JG, Rice HD, Howard DR. The pathology of head and neck tumors. Spindle cell lesions (sarcomatoid carcinomas, nodular fasciitis, and fibrosarcoma) of the aerodigestive tracts. Part 14. Head Neck Surg 1982, **4**: 499–513.

224 Baugh RF, Wolf GT, McClatchey KD. Small cell carcinoma of the head and neck. Head Neck Surg 1986, **8**: 343–354.

244a Choi HR, Sturgis EM, Rosenthal DI, Luna MA, Batsakis JG, El-Naggar AK. Sarcomatoid carcinoma of the head and neck. Molecular evidence for evolution and progression from conventional squamous cell carcinomas. Am J Surg Pathol 2003, **27**: 1216–1220.

225 Coppola D, Catalano E, Tang CK, Elfenbein IB, Harwick R, Mohr R. Basaloid squamous cell carcinoma of floor of mouth. Cancer 1993, **72**: 2299–2305.

226 Ellis GL, Langloss JM, Heffner DK, Hyams VJ. Spindle-cell carcinoma of the aerodigestive tract. An immunohistochemical analysis of 21 cases. Am J Surg Pathol 1987, **11**: 335–342.

227 Evans AT, Guthrie W. Lymphoepithelioma-like carcinoma of the uvula and soft palate: a rare lesion in an unusual site. Histopathology 1991, **19**: 184–186.

228 Gerughty RM, Hennigar GR, Brown FM. Adenosquamous carcinoma of the nasal, oral and laryngeal cavities. A clinicopathologic survey of ten cases. Cancer 1968, **22**: 1140–1155.

229 Green GW Jr, Bernier J. Spindle cell squamous carcinoma of the lip. Report of four cases. Oral Surg Oral Med Oral Pathol 1959, **12**: 1008–1016.

230 Hewan-Lowe K, Dardick I. Ultrastructural distinction of basaloid-squamous carcinoma and adenoid cystic carcinoma. Ultrastruct Pathol 1995, **19**: 371–381.

231 Hull MT, Eble JN, Warfel KA. Extrapulmonary oat-cell carcinoma

of the tongue. An electron-microscopic study. J Oral Pathol 1984, **13**: 489–496.

232 Leifer C, Miller AS, Putong PB, Min BH. Spindle-cell carcinoma of the oral mucosa. A light and electron microscopic study of apparent sarcomatous metastasis to cervical lymph nodes. Cancer 1974, **34**: 597–605.

233 Leventon GS, Evans HL. Sarcomatoid squamous cell carcinoma of the mucous membranes of the head and neck. A clinicopathologic study of 20 cases. Cancer 1981, **48**: 994–1003.

234 Luna MA, Naggar AE, Parichatikanond P, Weber RS, Batsakis JG. Basaloid squamous carcinoma of the upper aerodigestive tract: clinicopathologic and DNA flow cytometric analysis. Cancer 1990, **66**: 537–542.

235 Martinez-Madrigal F, Baden E, Casiraghi O, Micheau C. Oral and pharyngeal adenosquamous carcinoma. A report of four cases with immunohistochemical studies. Eur Arch Otorhinolaryngol 1991, **248**: 255–258.

236 Morice WG, Ferreiro JA. Distinction of basaloid squamous cell carcinoma from adenoid cystic and small cell undifferentiated carcinoma by immunohistochemistry. Hum Pathol 1998, **29**: 609–612.

237 Muller S, Barnes L. Basaloid squamous cell carcinoma of the head and neck with a spindle cell component. An unusual histologic variant. Arch Pathol Lab Med 1995, **119**: 181–182.

238 Nakhleh R, Zarbo R, Ewing S, Carey J, Gown A. Myogenic differentiation in spindle cell (sarcomatoid) carcinomas of the upper aerodigestive tract. Appl Immunohistochem 1993, **1**: 58–68.

239 Papadimitriou JC, Drachenberg CB, Brenner DS, Newkirk C, Trump BF, Silverberg SG. 'Thanatosomes': a unifying morphogenetic concept for tumor hyaline globules related to apoptosis. Hum Pathol 2000, **31**: 1455–1465.

240 Takagi M, Sakota Y, Takayama S, Ishikawa G. Adenoid squamous cell carcinoma of the oral mucosa. Report of two autopsy cases. Cancer 1977, **40**: 2250–2255.

241 Tsang WYW, Chan JKC, Lee KC, Ldung AKF, Fu YT. Basaloid-squamous carcinoma of the upper aerodigestive tract and so-called adenoid cystic carcinoma of the oesophagus; the same tumour type? Histopathology 1991, **19**: 35–46.

242 Wain SL, Kier R, Vollmer RT, Bossen EH. Basaloid-squamous carcinoma of the tongue, hypopharynx, and larynx. Report of 10 cases. Hum Pathol 1986, **17**: 1158–1166.

243 Weidner N. Sarcomatoid carcinoma of the upper aerodigestive tract. Semin Diagn Pathol 1987, **4**: 157–168.

244 Zarbo RJ, Crissman JD, Venkat H, Weiss MA. Spindle-cell carcinoma of the upper aerodigestive tract mucosa. An immunohistologic and ultrastructural study of 18 biphasic tumors and comparison with seven monophasic spindle-cell tumors. Am J Surg Pathol 1986, **10**: 741–753.

Tumors and other lesions of minor salivary glands

245 Aberle AM, Abrams AM, Bowe R, Melrose RJ, Handlers JP. Lobular (polymorphous low-grade) carcinoma of minor salivary glands. A clinicopathologic study of twenty cases. Oral Surg Oral Med Oral Pathol 1985, **60**: 387–395.

246 Allen MS Jr, Fitz-Hugh GS, Marsh WL Jr. Low-grade papillary adenocarcinoma of the palate. Cancer 1974, **33**: 153–158.

247 Anavi Y, Calderon S, Gal G, Sandbank J. Intraoral acinic cell carcinoma. Ann Dent 1993, **52**: 26–29.

248 Arafat A, Brannon RB, Ellis GL. Adenomatoid hyperplasia of mucous salivary glands. Oral Surg Oral Med Oral Pathol 1981, **52**: 51–55.

249 Batsakis JG. Oral monomorphic adenomas. Ann Otol Rhinol Laryngol 1991, **100**: 348–350.

250 Brannon RB, Houston GD, Wampler HW. Gingival salivary gland choristoma. Oral Surg Oral Med Oral Pathol 1986, **61**: 185–188.

251 Castle JT, Thompson LD, Frommelt RA, Wenig BM, Kessler HP.

Polymorphous low-grade adenocarcinoma: a clinicopathologic study of 164 cases. Cancer 1999, **86:** 207–219.

252   Chaudhry AP, Vickers RA, Gorlin RJ. Intraoral minor salivary gland tumors. An analysis of 1414 cases. Oral Surg Oral Med Oral Pathol 1961, **14:** 1194–1226.

253   Chisholm DM, Mason DK. Labial salivary gland biopsy in Sjögren's disease. J Clin Pathol 1968, **21:** 656–660.

254   Chomette G, Auriol M, Tranbaloc P, Vaillant JM. Adenoid cystic carcinoma of minor salivary glands. Analysis of 86 cases. Clinicopathological, histoenzymological and ultrastructural studies. Virchows Arch [Pathol Anat] 1982, **395:** 289–301.

255   Coates HLC, Devine KD, DeSanto LW, Weiland LH. Glandular tumors of the palate. Surg Gynecol Obstet 1975, **140:** 589–593.

256   Coleman H, Altini M. Intravascular tumour in intra-oral pleomorphic adenomas: a diagnostic and therapeutic dilemma. Histopathology 1999, **35:** 439–444.

257   Eneroth C-M. Incidence and prognosis of salivary-gland tumors at different sites. A study of parotid, submandibular and palatal tumors in 2632 patients. Acta Otolaryngol [Stockh] 1970, **263:** 174–178.

258   Evans HL, Batsakis JG. Polymorphous low-grade adenocarcinoma of minor salivary glands. A study of 14 cases of a distinctive neoplasm. Cancer 1984, **53:** 935–942.

259   Evans HL, Luna MA. Polymorphous low-grade adenocarcinoma: a study of 40 cases with long-term follow-up and an evaluation of the important of papillary areas. Am J Surg Pathol 2000, **24:** 1319–1328.

260   Eveson JW, Cawson RA. Tumours of the minor (oropharyngeal) salivary gland. A demographic study of 336 cases. J Oral Pathol 1985, **14:** 500–509.

261   Fantasia JE, Nocco CE, Lally ET. Ultrastructure of sialadenoma papilliferum. Arch Pathol Lab Med 1986, **110:** 523–527.

262   Freedman PD, Lumerman H. Sialadenoma papilliferum. Report of 2 cases. Oral Surg Oral Med Oral Pathol 1978, **45:** 88–94.

263   Frierson HF Jr, Mills SE, Garland TA. Terminal duct carcinoma of minor salivary glands. A nonpapillary subtype of polymorphous low-grade adenocarcinoma. Am J Clin Pathol 1985, **84:** 8–14.

264   Gates GA. Malignant neoplasms of the minor salivary glands. N Engl J Med 1982, **306:** 718–722.

265   Isacsson G, Shear M. Intraoral salivary gland tumors. A retrospective study of 201 cases. J Oral Pathol 1983, **12:** 57–62.

266   Johnston CA, Toker C. Syringomatous tumors of minor salivary gland origin. Hum Pathol 1982, **13:** 182–184.

267   Lomax-Smith JD, Azzopardi JG. The hyaline cell. A distinctive feature of "mixed" salivary tumors. Histopathology 1978, **2:** 77–92.

268   Luna MA, Batsakis JG, Ordóñes NG, Mackay B, Tortoledo ME. Salivary gland adenocarcinomas. A clinicopathologic analysis of three distinctive types. Semin Diagn Pathol 1987, **4:** 117–135.

269   Michal M, Skalova A, Simpson RH, Raslan WF, Curik R, Leivo I, Mukensmabl P. Cribriform adenocarcinoma of the tongue: a hitherto unrecognized type of adenocarcinoma characteristically occurring in the tongue. Histopathology 1999, **35:** 495–501.

270   Mills SE, Garland TA, Allen MS Jr. Low-grade papillary adenocarcinoma of palatal salivary gland origin. Am J Surg Pathol 1984, **8:** 367–374.

271   Owens OT, Calcaterra TC. Salivary gland tumors of the lip. Arch Otolaryngol 1982, **108:** 45–47.

271a Pelkey TJ and Mills SE. Histologic transformation of polymorphous low-grade adenocarcinoma of salivary gland. Am J Clin Pathol 1999, **111:** 785–91.

272   Perez-Ordonez B, Linkov I, Huvos AG. Polymorphous low-grade adenocarcinoma of minor salivary glands: a study of 17 cases with emphasis on cell differentiation. Histopathology 1998, **32:** 521–529.

273   Regezi JA, Lloyd RV, Zarbo RJ, McClatchey KD. Minor salivary gland tumors. A histologic and immunohistochemical study. Cancer 1985, **55:** 108–115.

274   Suarez P, Hammond HL, Luna MA, Stimson PG. Palatal canalicular adenoma: report of 12 cases and review of the literature. Ann Diagn Pathol 1998, **2:** 224–228.

274a Simpson RHW, Reis-Filho JS, Pererira EM, Ribeiro AC, Abdulkadir A. Polymorphous low-grade adenocarcinoma of the salivary glands with transformation to high-grade carcinoma. Histopathology 2002, **41:** 250–59.

275   Takeda Y, Sasou S, Obata K. Pleomorphic adenoma of the minor salivary gland with pseudoepitheliomatous hyperplasia of the overlying oral mucosa: report of two cases. Pathol Int 1998, **48:** 389–395.

276   Warwick WJ, Bernard B, Meskin LH. The involvement of the labial mucous salivary gland in patients with cystic fibrosis. Pediatrics 1964, **34:** 621–638.

277   White DK, Miller AS, McDaniel RK, Rothman BN. Inverted ductal papilloma. A distinctive lesion of minor salivary gland. Cancer 1982, **49:** 519–524.

278   Zarbo RJ, Regezi JA, Batsakis JG. S-100 protein in salivary gland tumors. An immunohistochemical study of 129 cases. Head Neck Surg 1986, **8:** 268–275.

Tumors of odontogenic epithelium

279   Gardner DG. Peripheral ameloblastoma. A study of 21 cases, including 5 reported as basal cell carcinoma of the gingiva. Cancer 1977, **39:** 1625–1633.

Tumors of melanocytes

280   Arrington JH III, Reed RJ, Ichinose H, Krementz ET. Plantar lentiginous melanoma. A distinctive variant of human cutaneous malignant melanoma. Am J Surg Pathol 1977, **1:** 131–143.

281   Batsakis JG, Suarez P. Mucosal melanomas: a review. Adv Anat Pathol 2000, **7:** 167–280.

282   Batsakis JG, Regezi JA, Solomon AR, Rice DH. The pathology of head and neck tumors. Mucosal melanomas. Part 13. Head Neck Surg 1982, **4:** 404–418.

283   Berthelsen A, Andersen AP, Jensen TS, Hansen HS. Melanomas of the mucosa in the oral cavity and the upper respiratory passages. Cancer 1984, **54:** 907–912.

284   Buchner A, Hansen LS. Pigmented nevi of the oral mucosa. A clinicopathologic study of 32 new cases and review of 75 cases from the literature. Part I. Oral Surg Oral Med Oral Pathol 1979, **48:** 131–142.

285   Buchner A, Hansen LS. Pigmented nevi of the oral mucosa. A clinicopathologic study of 32 new cases and review of 75 cases from the literature. Part II. Oral Surg Oral Med Oral Pathol 1980, **49:** 55–62.

286   Devildos LR, Langlois CC. Intramucosal cellular nevi. Oral Surg Oral Med Oral Pathol 1981, **52:** 162–166.

287   Dorji T, Cavazza A, Nappi O, Rosai J. Spitz nevus of the tongue with pseudoepitheliomatous hyperplasia: report of three cases of a pseudomalignant condition. Am J Surg Pathol 2002, **26:** 774–777.

287a Fornatora M, Reich R, Haber S, Solomon F, Freedman P. Oral Melanoacanthoma: A report of 10 cases, review of literature, and immunohistochemical analysis for HMB-45 reactivity. American Journal of Dermatopathology 2003, **25:** 12–15.

288   Eisen D, Voorhees JJ. Oral melanoma and other pigmented lesions of the oral cavity. J Am Acad Dermatol 1991, **24:** 527–537.

289   Goode RK, Crawford BE, Callihan MD, Neville BW. Oral melanoacanthoma. Review of the literature and report of ten cases. Oral Surg Oral Med Oral Pathol 1983, **56:** 622–628.

290   Kaugars GE, Heise AP, Riley WT, Abbet LM, Svirksy JA. Oral melanotic macules. A review of 353 cases. Oral Surg Oral Med Oral Pathol 1993, **76:** 59–61.

291   Kilpatrick SE, White WL, Browne JD. Desmoplastic malignant melanoma of the oral mucosa: an underrecognized diagnostic pitfall. Cancer 1996, **78:** 383–389.

292 McDonald JS, Miller RL, Wagner W, Giammara B. Acral lentiginous melanoma of the oral cavity. Head Neck Surg 1983, **5**: 257–262.

293 Page DG, Svirsky JA, Kaugars GE. Nevus of Ota with associated palatal involvement. Oral Surg Oral Med Oral Pathol 1985, **59**: 282–284.

294 Panje WR, Moran WJ. Melanoma of the upper aerodigestive tract. A review of 21 cases. Head Neck Surg 1986, **8**: 309–312.

295 Prasad ML, Jungbluth AA, Iversen K, Huvos AG, Busam KJ. Expression of melanocytic differentiation markers in malignant melanomas of the oral and sinonasal mucosa. Am J Surg Pathol 2001, **25**: 782–787.

295a Prasad M, Patel S, Hoshaw-Woodard S, Escrig M, Shah J, Huvos A, Busam K. Prognostic factors for malignant melanoma of the squamous mucosa of the head and neck. American Journal of Surgical Pathology 2002, **26**: 883–92.

296 Rapini RP, Golitz LE, Greer RO Jr, Krekorian EA, Poulson T. Primary malignant melanoma of the oral cavity. A review of 177 cases. Cancer 1985, **55**: 1543–1551.

297 Sexton FM, Maize JC. Melanotic macules and melanoacanthomas of the lip. A comparative study with census of the basal melanocyte population. Am J Dermatopathol 1987, **9**: 438–444.

298 Takagi M, Ishikawa G, Mori W. Primary malignant melanoma of the oral cavity in Japan. With special reference to mucosal melanosis. Cancer 1974, **34**: 358–370.

299 Tradahl JN, Sprague WG. Benign and malignant melanocytic lesions of the oral mucosa. An analysis of 135 cases. Cancer 1970, **25**: 812–823.

Tumors and tumorlike conditions of lymphoid tissue

300 Ballesteros E, Osborne BM, Matsushima AY. Plasma cell granuloma of the oral cavity: A report of two cases and review of the literature. Mod Pathol 1998, **11**: 60–64.

301 Barton JH, Osborne BM, Butler JJ, Meoz RT, Kong J, Fuller LM, Sullivan JA. Non-Hodgkin's lymphoma of the tonsil. A clinicopathologic study of 65 cases. Cancer 1984, **53**: 86–95.

301a Batsakis J, Medeiros J, Luna M, El-Naggar A. Plasma cell dyscrasias and the head and neck. Annals of Diagnostic Pathology 2002, **6**: 129–140.

302 Bernier JL, Bhaskar SN. Lymphoepithelial lesions of salivary glands. Histogenesis and classification based on 186 cases. Cancer 1958, **11**: 1156–1179.

303 Brousset P, Pages M, Chittal SM, Gorguet B. Tumour phase of mycosis fungiodes in the tongue. Histopathology 1992, **20**: 87–90.

304 Castella A, Davey FR, Elbadawi A, Gordon GB. Granulocytic sarcoma of the hard palate. Report of the first case. Hum Pathol 1984, **15**: 1190–1192.

305 Chan JKC, Ng CS, Lo STH. Immunohistological characterization of malignant lymphomas of the Waldeyer's ring other than the nasopharynx. Histopathology 1987, **11**: 885–899.

306 Chan JK, Tsang WY, Ng CS, Tang SK, Yu HC, Lee AW. Follicular dendritic cell tumors of the oral cavity. Am J Surg Pathol 1994, **18**: 148–157.

307 Chan JK, Yip TT, Tsang WY, Ng CS, Lau WH, Poon YF, Wong CC, Ma VW. Detection of Epstein-Barr viral RNA in malignant lymphomas of the upper aerodigestive tract. Am J Surg Pathol 1994, **18**: 938–946.

308 Dreizen S, McCredie KB, Keating MJ, Luna MA. Malignant gingival and skin "infiltrates" in adult leukemia. Oral Surg Oral Med Oral Pathol 1983, **55**: 572–579.

309 Ferreiro JA, Egorshin EV, Olsen KD, Banks PM, Weiland LH. Mucous membrane plasmacytosis of the upper aerodigestive tract. A clinicopathologic study. Am J Surg Pathol 1994, **18**: 1048–1053.

310 Gorsky M, Silverman S Jr, Lozada F, Kushner J. Histiocytosis X. Occurrence and oral involvement in six adolescent and adult patients. Oral Surg Oral Med Oral Pathol 1983, **55**: 24–29.

311 Handlers JP, Howell RE, Abrams AM, Melrose RJ. Extranodal oral lymphoma. Part I. A morphologic and immunoperoxidase study of 34 cases. Oral Surg Oral Med Oral Pathol 1986, **61**: 362–367.

312 Harman KS. Histiocytosis X. A review of 114 cases with oral involvement. Oral Surg Oral Med Oral Pathol 1980, **49**: 38–54.

313 Paulsen J, Lennert K. Low-grade B-cell lymphoma of mucosa-associated lymphoid tissue type in Waldeyer's ring (see comments). Histopathology 1994, **24**: 1–11.

314 Saltzstein SL. Extranodal malignant lymphomas and pseudolymphomas. Pathol Annu 1969, **4**: 159–164.

315 Saul SH, Kapadia SB. Primary lymphoma of Waldeyer's ring. Clinicopathologic study of 68 cases. Cancer 1985, **56**: 157–166.

315a Sidhu J, Rigotti R, Schotanus P. Primary adenoidal Hodgkin's disease: report of a case with an unusual morphology and review of the literature. International Journal of Surgical Pathology 2000, **8**: 241–246.

316 Sirois DA, Miller AS, Harwick RD, Vonderheid EC. Oral manifestations of cutaneous T-cell lymphoma. A report of eight cases. Oral Surg Oral Med Oral Pathol 1993, **75**: 700–705.

316a Solomides C, Miller A, Christman R, Talwar J, Simpkins H. Lymphomas of the oral cavity: histology, immunologic type, and incidence of Epstein-Barr virus infection. Hum Pathol 2002, **33**: 153–157.

317 Takahashi H, Fujita S, Okabe H, Tsuda N, Tezuka F. Immunophenotypic analysis of extranodal non-Hodgkin's lymphomas in the oral cavity. Pathol Res Pract 1993, **189**: 300–311.

318 Thomas JA, Cotter F, Hanby AM, Long LQ, Morgan PR, Bramble B, Bailey BM. Epstein-Barr virus-related oral T-cell lymphoma associated with human immunodeficiency virus immunosuppression. Blood 1993, **81**: 3350–3356.

319 Tomich CE, Shafer WG. Lymphoproliferative disease of the hard palate. A clinicopathologic entity. A study of twenty-one cases. Oral Surg Oral Med Oral Pathol 1975, **39**: 754–768.

320 Yamanaka N, Harabuchi Y, Sambe S, Shido F, Matsuda F, Kataura A, Ishii Y, Kikuchi K. Non-Hodgkin's lymphoma of Waldeyer's ring and nasal cavity. Clinical and immunologic aspects. Cancer 1985, **56**: 768–776.

Other tumors and tumorlike conditions

321 Adrian JC. Inverted follicular keratosis of the lip. Oral Surg Oral Med Oral Pathol 1984, **57**: 625–630.

322 Alawi F, Stratton D, Freedam PD. Solitary fibrous tumor of the oral soft tissues: a clinicopathologic and immunohistochemical study of 16 cases. Am J Surg Pathol 2001, **25**: 900–910.

323 Allard RHB, Blok P, van der Kwast WAM, van der Waal I. Oral lipomas with osseous and chondrous metaplasia. Report of two cases. J Oral Pathol 1982, **11**: 18–25.

324 Assor D, Thomas JR. Multifocal rhabdomyoma. Report of a case. Arch Otolaryngol 1969, **90**: 489–491.

325 Baden E, Duvillard P, Micheau C. Metastatic papillary endometrial carcinoma of the tongue: case report and review of the literature. Arch Pathol Lab Med 1992, **116**: 965–968.

326 Batsakis JG, Rice DH. The pathology of head and neck tumors. Vasoformative tumors. Part 9A. Head Neck Surg 1981, **3**: 231–239.

327 Batsakis JG, Rice DH. The pathology of head and neck tumors. Vasoformative tumors. Part 9B. Head Neck Surg 1981, **3**: 326–339.

328 Bodner L, Dayan D. Intravascular papillary endothelial hyperplasia of the mandibular mucosa. Int J Oral Maxillofac Surg 1991, **20**: 263–274.

329 Cangiarella J, Jagirdar J, Adelman H, Budzilovich G, Greco MA. Mucosal neuromas and plexiform neurofibromas: an immunocytochemical study. Pediatr Pathol 1993, **13**: 281–288.

330 Chau MNY, Radden BG. Oral warty dyskeratoma. J Oral Pathol 1984, **13**: 546–556.

331 Chen S-Y, Fantasia JE, Miller AS. Myxoid lipoma of oral soft tissue. A clinical and ultrastructural study. Oral Surg Oral Med Oral Pathol 1984, **57:** 300–307.

332 Corio RL, Lewis DM. Intraoral rhabdomyomas. Oral Surg Oral Med Oral Pathol 1979, **48:** 525–531.

333 Crotty PL, Nakhleh RE, Dehner LP. Juvenile rhabdomyoma. An intermediate form of skeletal muscle tumor in children. Arch Pathol Lab Med 1993, **117:** 43–47.

334 Daneshvar A. Pharyngeal traumatic neuromas and traumatic neuromas with mature ganglion cells (pseudoganglioneuromas). Am J Surg Pathol 1990, **14:** 565–571.

335 Dry SM, Jorgensen JL, Fletcher CDM. Leiomyosarcomas of the oral cavity: an unusual topographic subset easily mistaken for nonmesenchymal tumours. Histopathology 2000, **36:** 210–220.

336 Dunlap CL, Barker BF. Diagnostic problems in oral pathology. Semin Diagn Pathol 1985, **2:** 16–30.

337 Eversole LR, Leider AS, Alexander G. Intraoral and labial keratoacanthoma. Oral Surg Oral Med Oral Pathol 1982, **54:** 663–667.

337a Fanburg-Smith J, Furlong M, Childers E. Liposarcoma of the oral and salivary gland region: a clinicopathologic study of 18 cases with emphasis on specific sites, morphologic subtypes, and clinical outcome. Mod Pathol 2002, **15:** 1020.

337b Fanburg-Smith J, Furlong M, Childers E. Oral and salivary gland angiosarcoma: a clinicopathologic study of 29 cases. Mod Pathol 2003, **16:** 263.

337c Fanburg-Smith J, Miettinen M, Folpe A, Weiss S, Childers E. Alveolar soft part sarcoma of the tongue: 14 cases. Mod Pathol 2003, **16:** 11A.

338 Flaggert JJ III, Heldt LV, Keaton WM. Angiolipoma of the palate. Report of a case. Oral Surg Oral Med Oral Pathol 1986, **60:** 333–336.

339 Flaitz CM, McDaniel RK, Mackay B, Kennady MC, Luna MA, Hicks MJ. Primary intraoral epithelioid hemangioendothelioma presenting in childhood. Review of the literature and case report. Ultrastruct Pathol 1995, **19:** 275–280.

340 Gardner DG, Corio RL. Fetal rhabdomyoma of the tongue, with a discussion of the two histologic variants of this tumor. Oral Surg Oral Med Oral Pathol 1983, **56:** 293–300.

341 Gardner DG, Corio RL. Multifocal adult rhabdomyoma. Oral Surg Oral Med Oral Pathol 1983, **56:** 76–78.

342 Giansanti JS, Waldron CA. Peripheral giant cell granuloma. Review of 720 cases. J Oral Surg 1969, **27:** 787–791.

343 Gibas Z, Miettinen M. Recurrent parapharyngeal rhabdomyoma: evidence of neoplastic nature of the tumor from cytogenetic study. Am J Surg Pathol 1992, **16:** 721–728.

344 Gorlin RJ, Sedano HO, Vickers RA, Cervenka J. Multiple mucosal neuromas, pheochromocytoma and medullary carcinoma of the thyroid. A syndrome. Cancer 1968, **22:** 293–299.

345 Harrist TJ, Murphy GF, Mihm MC Jr. Oral warty dyskeratoma. Arch Dermatol 1980, **116:** 929–931.

346 Janzer RC, Makek M. Intraoral malignant melanotic schwannoma. Ultrastructural evidence for melanogenesis by Schwann's cells. Arch Pathol Lab Med 1983, **107:** 298–301.

347 Kameyama Y, Mizohata M, Takehana S, Murata H, Manabe H, Mukai Y. Ultrastructure of the congenital epulis. Virchows Arch [Pathol Anat] 1983, **401:** 251–260.

348 Kardon DE, Wenig BM, Heffner DK, Thompson LDR. Tonsillar lymphangiomatous polyps: a clinicopathologic series of 26 cases. Modern Pathol 2000, **13:** 1128–1133.

349 Kaugars GE, Svirsky JA. Lung malignancies metastatic to the oral cavity. Oral Surg Oral Med Oral Pathol 1981, **51:** 179–186.

350 Kerr DA. Granuloma pyogenicum. Oral Surg Oral Med Oral Pathol 1951, **4:** 158–176.

351 Kim RY, Perry SR, Levy DS. Metastatic carcinoma to the tongue. Cancer 1979, **43:** 386–389.

352 Komori A, Takeda Y, Kakiichi T. Alveolar soft-part sarcoma of the tongue. Report of a case with electron microscopic study. Oral Surg Oral Med Oral Pathol 1984, **57:** 532–539.

353 Lack EE, Perez-Atayde AR, McGill TJ, Vawter GF. Gingival granular cell tumor of the newborn (congenital "epulis"). Ultrastructural observations relating to histogenesis. Hum Pathol 1982, **13:** 686–689.

354 Lack EE, Worsham GF, Callihan MD, Crawford BE, Vawter GF. Gingival granular cell tumors of the newborn (congenital "epulis"). A clinical and pathologic study of 21 patients. Am J Surg Pathol 1981, **5:** 37–46.

355 Lifshitz MS, Flotte TJ, Greco MA. Congenital granular cell epulis. Immunohistochemical and ultrastructural observations. Cancer 1984, **53:** 1845–1848.

356 López JI, Ballestin C. Intraoral schwannoma. A clinicopathologic and immunohistochemical study of nine cases. Arch Anat Cytol Pathol 1993, **41:** 18–23.

357 MacDonald DG. Smooth muscle tumours of the mouth. Br J Oral Surg 1969, **6:** 207–214.

358 MacVicar J, Dunn MF. Pregnancy tumour of the gums. J Obstet Gynaecol Br Commonw 1969, **76:** 260–263.

359 Massarelli G, Tanda F, Salis B. Synovial sarcoma of the soft palate. Report of a case. Hum Pathol 1978, **9:** 341–345.

360 Matthews JB, Mason GI. Oral granular cell myoblastoma. An immunohistochemical study. J Oral Pathol 1982, **11:** 343–352.

361 Mostafa KA, Takata T, Ogawa I, Ijuhin N, Nikai H. Verruciform xanthoma of the oral mucosa. A clinicopathologic study with immunohistochemical findings relating to pathogenesis. Virchows Arch A Pathol Anat Histopathol 1993, **423:** 243–248.

362 Munro JM, Singh MP. Chondroma of the tongue: report of a case and a consideration of the histogenesis of such lesions. Arch Pathol Lab Med 1990, **114:** 541–542.

363 Nagata M, Semba I, Ooya K, Urago A, Yonezawa S, Sakae K. Malignant endothelial neoplasm arising in the area of lymphangioma. Immunohistochemical and ultrastructural observation. J Oral Pathol 1984, **13:** 560–572.

363a Nascimento A, Má irín E, Menamin M, Fletcher C. Liposarcomas/atypical lipomatous tumors of the oral cavity: a clinicopathologic study of 23 cases. Annals of Diagnostic Pathology 2002, **6:** 83–93.

364 Natiella JR, Neiders ME, Greene GW. Oral leiomyoma. Report of six cases and a review of the literature. J Oral Pathol 1982, **11:** 353–365.

365 Neville BW. The verruciform xanthoma. A review and report of eight new cases. Am J Dermatopathol 1986, **8:** 247–253.

366 Neville BW, Weathers DR. Verruciform xanthoma. Oral Surg Oral Med Oral Pathol 1980, **49:** 429–434.

367 Nowparast B, Howell FV, Rick GM. Verruciform xanthoma. A clinicopathologic review and report of fifty-four cases. Oral Surg Oral Med Oral Pathol 1981, **51:** 619–625.

368 Oberman HA, Sullenger G. Neurogenous tumors of the head and neck. Cancer 1967, **20:** 1992–2001.

369 Oliver AJ, Gibbons SD, Radden BG, Busmanis I, Cook RM. Primary angiosarcoma of the oral cavity. Br J Oral Maxillofac Surg 1991, **29:** 38–41.

370 Perez-Atayde AR, Kozakewich HW, McGill T, Fletcher JA. Hemangiopericytoma of the tongue in a 12-year-old child: ultrastructural and cytogenetic observations. Hum Pathol 1994, **25:** 425–429.

371 Peters E, Altini M, Kola AH. Oral angiolymphoid hyperplasia with eosinophilia. Oral Surg Oral Med Oral Pathol 1986, **61:** 73–79.

372 Razquin S, Mayayo E, Citores MA, Alvira R. Angiolymphoid hyperplasia with eosinophilia of the tongue: report of a case and review of the literature. Hum Pathol 1991, **22:** 837–839.

373 Regezi JA, MacPhail LA, Daniels TE, DeSouza YG, Greenspan JS, Greenspan D. Human immunodeficiency virus-associated oral Kaposi's sarcoma. A heterogeneous cell population dominated by spindle-shaped endothelial cells. Am J Pathol 1993, **143:** 240–249.

374 Regezi JA, MacPhail LA, Daniels TE, Greenspan JS, Greenspan D,

Dodd CL, Lozada-Nur F, Heinic GS, Chinn H, Silverman S. Oral Kaposi's sarcoma. A 10-year retrospective histopathologic study. J Oral Pathol Med 1993, **22:** 292–297.

375 Renshaw A, Rosai J. Benign atypical vascular lesions of the lip. A study of 12 cases. Am J Surg Pathol 1993, **17:** 557–565.

376 Reyes JM, Vangore SK, Putong PB, Harwick R, Miller AS, Chen S-Y. Osteogenic sarcoma of the tongue. Oral Surg Oral Med Oral Pathol 1981, **51:** 421–425.

377 Rusthoven JJ, Fine S, Thomas G. Adenocarcinoma of the rectum metastatic to the oral cavity. Two cases and a review of the literature. Cancer 1984, **54:** 1110–1112.

378 Saddik M, Oldring DJ, Mourad WA. Liposarcoma of the base of tongue and tonsillar fossa: a possibly underdiagnosed neoplasm. Arch Pathol Lab Med 1996, **120:** 292–295.

379 Sadeghi EM, Sauk JJ Jr. Liposarcoma of the oral cavity. Clinical, tissue culture, and ultrastructure study of a case. J Oral Pathol 1982, **11:** 263–275.

380 Said-Al-Naief N, Zahurullah FR, Sciubba JJ. Oral spindle cell lipoma. Ann Diagn Pathol 2001, **5:** 207–215.

381 Saku T, Okabe H, Matsutani K, Sasaki M. Glomus tumor of the cheek. An immunohistochemical demonstration of actin and myosin. Oral Surg Oral Med Oral Pathol 1985, **60:** 65–71.

382 Sangueza O, Sangueza P, Jordan J, White CR. Rhabdomyoma of the tongue. Am J Dermatopathol 1990, **12:** 492–495.

383 Sexton M. Hairy polyp of the oropharynx. A case report with speculation on nosology. Am J Dermatopathol 1990, **12:** 294–298.

384 Shmookler BM, Enzinger FM, Brannon RB. Orofacial synovial sarcoma. A clinicopathologic study of 11 new cases and review of the literature. Cancer 1982, **50:** 269–276.

385 Slootweg P, de Wilde P, Vooijs P, Ramaekers F. Oral granular cell lesions. An immunohistochemical study with emphasis on intermediate-sized filaments proteins. Virchows Arch [Pathol Anat] 1983, **402:** 35–45.

386 Smith BC, Ellis GL, Meis-Kindblom JM, Williams SB. Ectomesenchymal chondromyxoid tumor of the anterior tongue. Nineteen cases of a new clinicopathologic entity. Am J Surg Pathol 1995, **19:** 519–530.

386a Toida M, Hasegawa T, Watanabe F, Kato K, Makita H, Fujitsuka H, Kato Y, Miyamoto K, Shibata T, Shimokawa K. Lobular capillary hemangioma of the oral mucosa: clinicopathological study of 43 cases with special reference to immunohistochemical characterization of the vascular elements. Pathology International 2003, **53:** 1–7.

387 Tucker MC, Rusnock EJ, Asumi N, Hoy GR, Lack EE. Gingival granular cell tumors of the newborn. An ultrastructural and immunohistochemical study. Arch Pathol Lab Med 1990, **114:** 895–898.

388 Wetzel W, Leipzig B, Grunow W, Kenna M, Kalderon A, Morgan B. Malignant granular cell tumor of the tongue. Arch Otolaryngol 1982, **108:** 603–605.

389 Williams HK, Cannell H, Silvester K, Williams DM. Neurilemmoma of the head and neck. Br J Oral Maxillofac Surg 1993, **31:** 32–35.

389a Wu SL, Vang R, Clubb F, Connelly J. Solitary fibrous tumor of the tongue: report of a case with immunohistochemical and ultrastructural studies. Annals of Diagnostic Pathology 2002, **6:** 168–171.

389b Yamashita A, Hatakeyama K, Marutsuka K, Fujita S, Ono S, Torihara K, Tamura S, Komune S, Asada Y. Chordoma of cervical vertebra protruding into the oral cavity. Pathology International 2002, **56:** 59–62.

389c Zanconati F, DelConte A, Bonifacio-Gori D, Falconieri G. Metastatic pleural mesothelioma presenting with solitary involvement of the tongue. International Journal of Surgical Pathology 2003, **11:** 51–55.

390 Zarbo RJ, Lloyd RV, Beals TF, McClatchey KD. Congenital gingival granular cell tumor with smooth muscle cytodifferentiation. Oral Surg Oral Med Oral Pathol 1983, **56:** 512–520.

391 Zohar Y, Ben-Tovim R, Gal R, Laurian N. Metastatic carcinoma of oral soft tissue. Head Neck Surg 1985, **7:** 484–486.

6 Mandible and maxilla

Normal anatomy

In most respects, the microscopic features of the mandible and maxilla differ in no significant way from those of any other bones. Their peculiarity is derived from their close proximity to the mucosal surface of the oral cavity and the fact that they enclose the odontogenic apparatus, a highly specialized structure that gives rise to a large variety of malformative, inflammatory, and neoplastic conditions.

The odontogenic structures are unique in the sense that they contain primitive embryonic structures from early fetal development to about 25 years of age. They have a combined ectodermal and mesodermal derivation; the mesodermal component has the added peculiarity that it originates from the neural crest.

The odontogenic development as seen in a tooth germ is a striking example of reciprocal inductive phenomena between two different types of tissue. The first is composed of an invagination of the ectodermally derived primitive oral cavity (dental lamina), which subsequently acquires a bell shape and develops along its inner (concave) aspects a layer of cuboidal to columnar cells, the *ameloblasts*, which are responsible for the secretion of enamel matrix. At this stage, it is also referred to as the enamel organ.

The second component, which is mesodermally derived and enclosed within the above described bell, is formed by the *dental papilla*, having initially the appearance of a loose stellate reticulum and later undergoing a maturation of its outer aspect (i.e., that contiguous to the ameloblastic layer) that results in the emergence of *odontoblasts* (i.e., the cells responsible for the formation of the dentinal matrix).

An increase in the cellularity of the dental papilla adjacent to the maturing ameloblastic (enamel-forming) epithelium leads to the formation of the *dental sac* or *follicle*, which is in turn responsible for the formation of a dense fibrous sheath enveloping the tooth known as *periodontium*. In addition, the inner cells of this sac become *cementoblasts* and deposit cement over the newly formed dentin, whereas the more peripheral cells of this structure are thought to become osteoblasts and contribute to the production of alveolar bone.

The major extracellular components of the tooth are dentin, enamel, and cementum. *Dentin* is easily recognized because of its radially striated appearance caused by the presence of innumerable minute canals (the dentinal tubules) containing cytoplasmic processes from the odontoblasts. If these canals are absent, it may be difficult to distinguish between atypical poorly mineralized dentin (dentinoid) and osteoid. *Enamel* consists of thin rods or prisms that on cross section are separated by concentric lines (lines of Retzius). *Cementum* is very similar to bone in physicochemical characteristics and is indeed regarded as a special type of bundle bone. It may be cellular or acellular, and it is identified microscopically mainly because of its intense basophilia. When less than entirely typical, its distinction from bone may become impossible. It must be recognized that cementum-like material may be encountered in parts of the skeletal system, other than the maxilla or mandible, in which participation of odontogenic tissue is out of the question.

The presence of rounded, strongly basophilic *cementicles* within the periodontal ligament is a normal feature, and it should not be misinterpreted as evidence of Paget's disease, as it often is by the neophyte.

The *dental pulp* has a myxoid hypocellular appearance that is essentially identical to that of myxoma and that sometimes can be confused with it by the same neophyte. It differs from the latter grossly because of its most compact appearance (as an oral pathologist wit put it: "If you drop it on the cutting board, it bounces; a myxoma doesn't") and microscopically because a layer of odontoblasts may be recognizable at the periphery.

Nests of odontogenic epithelium (with or without their associated mesenchymal counterpart) are normally found in the jaw and have the potential to develop into cysts or tumors. Those nests located in the alveolar mucosa and resulting from the breakup of the dental lamina are referred to as *nests of Serres*, whereas those embedded within the periodontium are known as *rests of Malassez*.

Another source of cysts in this region is related to the breakdown of ectodermal lining cells during the union or fusion of the various embryonic processes of the region, through the formation of entrapped epithelium-lined nests.

The surgical pathology of the maxilla and mandible encompasses the spectrum of pathology, because both systemic and unique diseases occur in these locations. Conditions previously considered "dental" or removed from the consideration of the general surgical pathologist are being encountered with increasing frequency. This discussion concentrates on commonly found and surgically related conditions of the jaws. A more detailed discussion of these conditions, as well as of others that are less common, may be found in specialized texts.[1–6]

Inflammatory diseases

The majority of inflammatory conditions of the jaws have a dental origin. Untreated dental caries eventually leads to inflammation of the pulpal or soft tissue portions of teeth that are unable to respond and heal adequately.[14,19,20] This results in inflammation of the cancellous bone and connective tissue surrounding the dental root apices that follows a predictable, albeit variable, clinical and pathologic course.

Dental granuloma (localized osteitis) is ordinarily detected in a dental roentgenogram. Grossly, the lesion rarely measures over 1.5 cm in diameter. Microscopically, it consists of a rounded collection of chronic inflammatory cells rich in histiocytes and surrounded by dense fibrous tissue. Degeneration can occur in the center, leading to cavity formation and the development of a *radicular* or *periapical cyst*[16,17] (see p. 285).

Hyaline ring-like structures may be seen in areas of chronic periostitis. These rings enclose vessels, giant cells, other inflammatory cells, and bundles of collagen fibrils. This inconsequential microscopic oddity, variously referred to as *pulse granuloma, lentil granuloma, oral vegetable granuloma,* and *giant cell hyaline angiopathy,* has given rise to numerous theories about its nature, as can be deduced from the names it has received.[7,8,15,18] The two leading hypotheses are a reaction to legume parenchymatous cells at various stages of digestion ("pulse" being the edible seed of legumes) and a degenerative change in vessel walls resulting from localized vasculitis. The latter explanation seems more reasonable.

Osteomyelitis of the jaws usually represents an additional consequence and extension of dental or periodontal infection.[13] Acute, subacute, and chronic forms exist.[21] Some of the latter are of the sclerosing (Garré) type.[9,11] Hematogenous osteomyelitis has been encountered rarely.[22] Symptoms such as pain, fever, and soft tissue swelling or redness in later stages are usually present. Smooth, regular, and atrophic loss of the covering mucosa is a late finding, and the exposed bone appears dull and devitalized. Roentgenographic features of osteomyelitis are subtle, irregular, ill-defined, and predominantly radiolucent lesions. A sequestrum is more often identified at the time of surgical exploration than during examination of x-ray films. Acute suppurative inflammation and resorptive scalloping of margins of nonvital bone within a large portion of maxilla or mandible are the main microscopic findings.

Staphylococcus aureus is the organism most commonly cultured. Anaerobic bacteria have also been demonstrated to be important.[12] Tuberculosis, mucormycosis, aspergillosis, and candidiasis have also been causally identified in osteomyelitis of the jaws.[10]

Simple bone cyst

Simple bone cyst usually occurs in young patients as a sharply outlined unilocular radiolucent mass (Fig. 6.1). It is usually located in the body or symphyseal area of the mandible and can assume sizable proportions.[23,27] In older patients it may also involve the maxilla.[28] It is also known as traumatic, solitary, or hemorrhagic cyst, but there is a history of trauma in only one half of the cases, and the content of the cyst is rarely hemorrhagic.[24] Actually, little is observed within the cavity at surgery in the typical case; this feature is analogous to that seen in solitary (unicameral) bone cyst, of which simple bone cyst may be the gnathic counterpart. Morphologically, the cavity is entirely intraosseous and not lined by epithelium. Surgical samples from the periphery show instead a delicate fibrovascular lining of unremarkable appearance. A few osteoclast-like giant cells and hemosiderin-laden macrophages may be present. Surgical exploration with thorough curettage is the treatment of choice.[25] Recurrence has been observed but is distinctly uncommon; it is said to be more frequent in the cysts having a thickened wall with dysplastic bone formation.[26]

The differential diagnosis of simple bone cyst includes aneurysmal bone cyst (particularly when the latter is associated with a benign fibro-osseous lesion) and so-called *latent bone cavity*, a symptomless open cavity situated below and behind the inferior dental canal near the angle of the mandible and often containing salivary gland tissue.[24]

Central giant cell granuloma and other giant cell-containing lesions

Lesions of the jaws that feature large numbers of osteoclast-like, multinucleated giant cells include the following entities: central giant cell granuloma, cherubism, giant cell tumor (osteoclastoma), fibro-osseous lesions, bone lesion of hyperparathyroidism, hereditary hyperparathyroidism and jaw tumors syndrome, and aneurysmal bone cyst. **Central giant cell granuloma** is by far the most common. Its pathogenesis is unknown. It has been suggested that it is the result of the organization of slow, minute, recurrent hemorrhages, hence the alternative name *reparative giant cell granuloma* given to it by Jaffe in his classic paper on the subject.[34] A history of trauma is often ascertained.

A lesion with the same microscopic appearance can occur at extreognathic sites, where it has received a variety of names (see Chapter 24).[40a] This condition affects children and young adults, predominantly females, and occurs almost twice as frequently in the mandible as in the maxilla, particularly in the anterior region.[34,40] It produces a cystic lesion of the bone, which microscopically shows large numbers of multinucleated giant cells, rather cellular vascular stroma, and often new bone formation (Figs 6.2 and 6.3). The osteoclast-like giant cells have a patchy distribution usually associated with areas of hemorrhage. Ultrastructurally, the proliferating cells include fibroblasts, myofibroblasts, and histiocytes.[32]

These lesions are treated by surgical removal and thorough curettage. Recurrence is treated similarly but only after the diagnosis has been confirmed.[30,40]

Cherubism (hereditary and intraosseous fibrous swellings of the jaws) is indistinguishable microscopically from the lesions of central giant cell granuloma.[41]

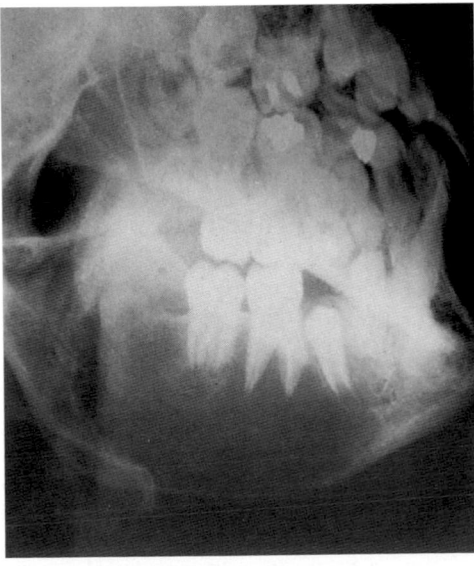

Fig. 6.1 Simple bone cyst of mandible in an 11-year-old girl. Note thin shell of remaining mandible.

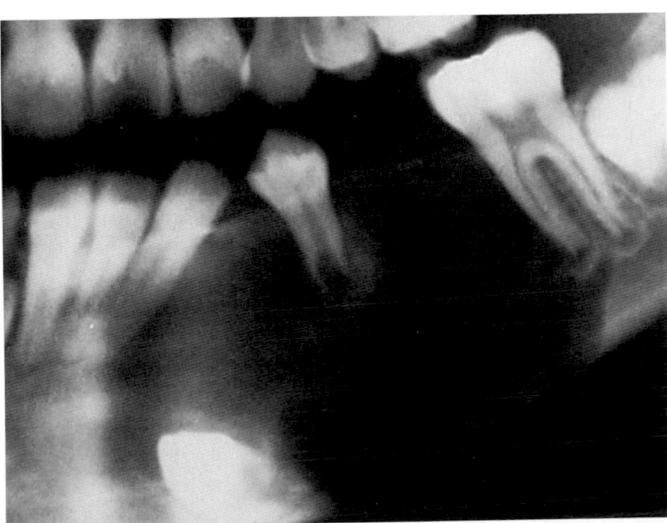

Fig. 6.2 Radiographic appearance of recurrent giant cell granuloma in a 10-year-old girl. The inferior border of mandible has been eroded.

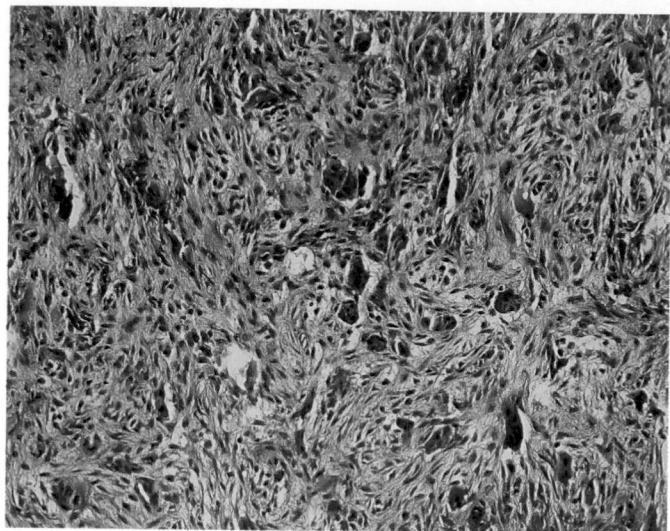

Fig. 6.3 Reparative giant cell granuloma. Osteoclast-like giant cells are scattered within a fibroblastic matrix.

However, the bilateral presentation of mandibular and maxillary involvement in a young individual with an autosomal dominant mode of inheritance, the sometimes more delicate fibrovascular stroma without bone formation, and the differing behavior and response to treatment clearly justify a nosologic separation between the two. The gene responsible for cherubism has been mapped to chromosome 4p16.3,[35] and identified as encoding c-Abl-binding protein SH3BP2.[38]

Hyperparathyroidism,[36] giant cell tumor,[29,33,37] and other conditions containing areas resembling giant cell granuloma (especially at the periphery) may constitute a basis for histologic misinterpretation as well. Fortunately, these are encountered much less commonly and are usually associated with additional clinical or laboratory information that aids delineation.[31]

Benign fibro-osseous lesions

Several types of tumors and tumorlike conditions composed of benign fibro-osseous tissue exist. Their histologic features are very similar, while their clinical behavior can be very different.[42–46] Their accurate diagnosis depends on an integration of the microscopic picture with the medical, family and dental history, the radiographic and operative appearance, skeletal survey and laboratory tests; furthermore, it may need to be revised on the basis of the course of the disease and response to treatment. The pathologist who relies on histology alone for the interpretation of these lesions is less likely to contribute to the successful management of these patients.

Fibrous dysplasia and related lesions

Fibrous dysplasia can be polyostotic or monostotic, the microscopic appearance of the two forms being essentially

the same.[57,58] The polyostotic form may be accompanied by pigmented skin lesions, endocrine dysfunction presenting with precocious puberty in females, and other anomalies (Albright's syndrome). Both monostotic fibrous dysplasia and Albright's syndrome are associated with a somatic mutation of the *GNAS1* gene.[48,55] Fibrous dysplasia confined to jawbones is sometimes referred to as the *craniofacial form* of the disease. Congenital or hereditary fibrous dysplasia in siblings has been reported[49,56] and should not be confused with cherubism.

Clinically, painless and sometimes dramatic swellings of the maxilla or mandible are observed that are characteristically unilateral. Young individuals of both sexes may be affected, the mean age at time of diagnosis in most series being from 25 to 35 years. The lesions tend to become static as skeletal maturity is reached.[54] The roentgenographic appearance varies from cystic or radiolucent to sclerotic or radiopaque, and the margins tend to be ill-defined.

The histologic appearance of fibrous dysplasia in its usual, most recognizable form is characterized by the presence of C-shaped or Chinese figure-like trabeculae of woven or immature bone within a proliferating fibroblastic stroma (Figs 6.4). Osteoblastic rimming of these trabeculae is usually absent, but its presence focally (particularly at the periphery of the lesion) does not rule out a diagnosis of fibrous dysplasia.

The two main morphologic variations on this theme are represented by lesions in which there is deposition of either lamellar bone with prominent osteoblastic rimming, or rounded psammoma-like masses resembling cement. The former have been designated as **ossifying fibroma** (fibrous osteoma), the latter as **cementifying fibroma**, and those lesions exhibiting both patterns as **cemento-ossifying fibroma**[50–53] (Figs 6.5 and 6.6). A further variation in the theme is represented by the *juvenile*

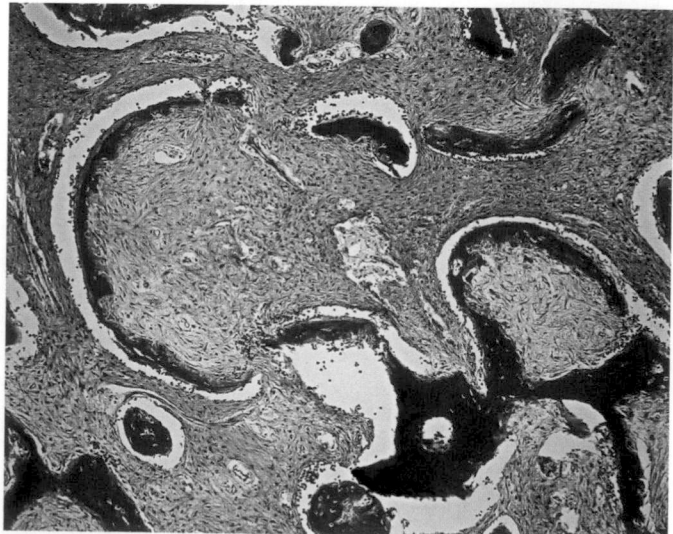

Fig. 6.4 Fibrous dysplasia. Curved bone trabeculae are surrounded by a dense fibrous stroma. Osteoclasts are lacking.

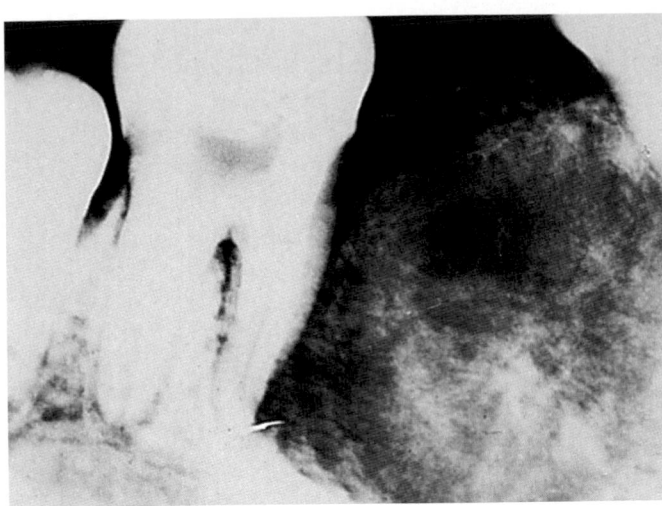

Fig. 6.5 Ossifying fibroma in a 17-year-old girl. Note the sharp border of the lesion. (Courtesy of Dr CA Waldron, Atlanta.)

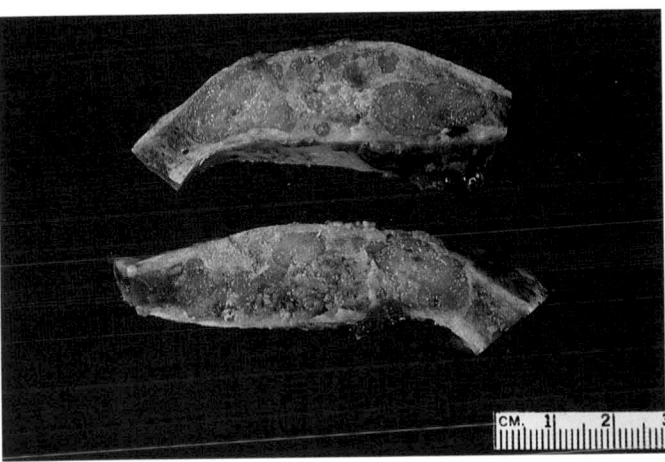

Fig. 6.6 Gross appearance of cementifying fibroma. The lesion is hard, whitish, and ill defined.

(aggressive) ossifying fibroma, an actively growing lesion in young patients and characterized microscopically by an unduly cellular fibrous stroma.[60] It seems likely that all of these lesions have a periodontal ligament origin. These lesions show a marked predilection for females and for the molar-premolar region of the mandible. Some authors have stressed the importance of separating fibrous dysplasia from the "fibroma" group of lesions because the latter are well-demarcated lesions that are amenable to surgical enucleation or to curettage.[51] Although these practical considerations justify a segregation for therapeutic and prognostic purposes, the pathogenetic relationship between these entities remains controversial.[47,59]

Cementoma and related lesions

There are additional fibrous and ossifying, calcifying, or cementifying conditions of the jaws that may be linked to fibro-osseous lesions because of their histologic resemblance, although some of them may be of odontogenic nature.

Cementoma (periapical and focal cemental or cemento-osseous dysplasia) is a relatively common disorder, being detectable radiographically in 0.3% of the adult population. It is usually multiple and asymptomatic, is limited to small regions surrounding apices of teeth, and ordinarily does not require treatment. It is thought to be of periodontal ligament origin and non-neoplastic in nature.[72] An autosomal dominant form of this disorder has been described (Fig. 6.7).[68]

Mandibular incisor regions of female adults usually are involved. Occasionally, a single tooth is affected, and this may become a surgical specimen. Microscopically, the most typical feature is the presence of curvilinear trabeculae ("ginger root" pattern) or irregularly shaped cementum-like masses. The main differential diagnosis is with cemento-ossifying fibroma, which shows thin isolated trabeculae with prominent osteoblastic rimming.[66,71]

Benign osteoblastoma can occur in the jaw, sometimes in intimate relationship to a dental root surface. When the latter is the case, the alternative designations of *(benign) cementoblastoma* and *true cementoma* are sometimes used (Figs 6.8 and 6.9).[62,67,69]

The clinical course is usually innocuous: the lesion often stabilizes as a heavily calcified nodule. However, the fact that some lesions are locally aggressive indicates that surgical excision is the treatment of choice.

Microscopically, this lesion features irregular osteoid and bone formation (or cementum, the differences between these tissues being very subtle) within proliferative fibrovascular connective tissues.[64,70] Plump osteoblasts are seen rimming the newly formed trabeculae (Fig. 6.10). Osteoblastomas exhibiting a prominent epithelioid configuration of the osteoblasts are referred to as *aggressive* and are regarded by some as low-grade (non-metastasizing) osteosarcomas (see Chapter 24).

Other lesions of the jaw featuring bone or cementum formation within proliferative fibrous connective tissue are solitary **large** or **"gigantiform" cementomas,**[61] **multiple**

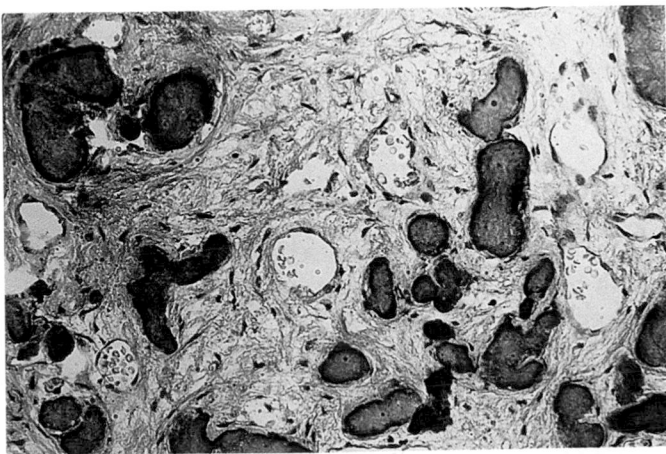

Fig. 6.7 Periapical cemental dysplasia. (From Pindborg JJ, Kramer IRH, Torloni H. Histological typing of odontogenic tumours, jaw cysts, and allied lesions. Geneva, 1971, World Health Organization.)

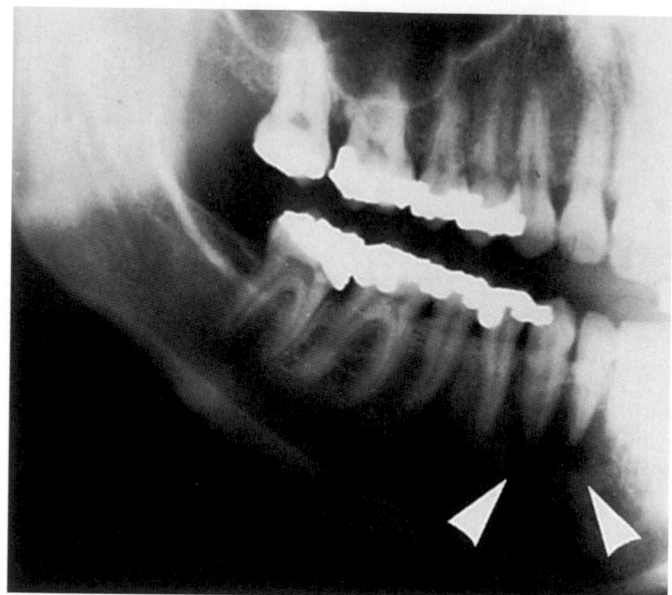

Fig. 6.8 Radiograph illustrating mandibular benign osteoblastoma or cementoblastoma without calcification that was associated with periapical regions of permanent premolars (arrows).

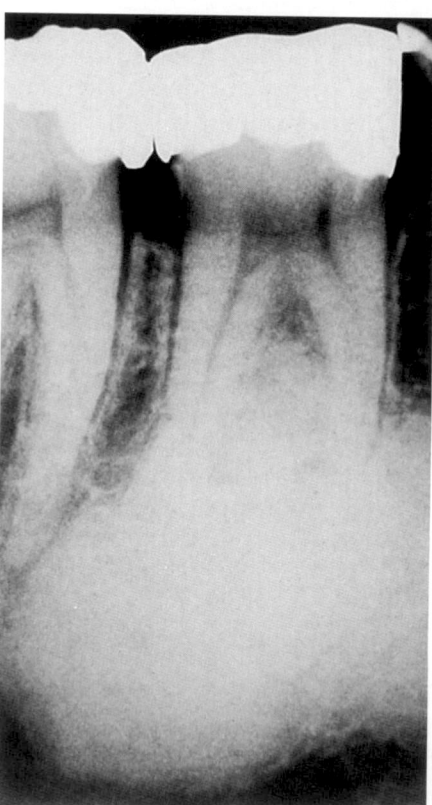

Fig. 6.9 Typical radiographic appearance of cementoblastoma. A dense, homogeneous mass is seen in continuity with the tooth root. (Courtesy of Dr. C.A. Waldron, Atlanta.)

cementomas in black female patients, and **osteomas** (especially those observed in patients with the osteomatosis–intestinal polyposis syndrome).[73] Inflammatory lesions of the jaws during their sclerotic or healing phases, and Paget's disease also enter in the differential diagnosis.[63,65]

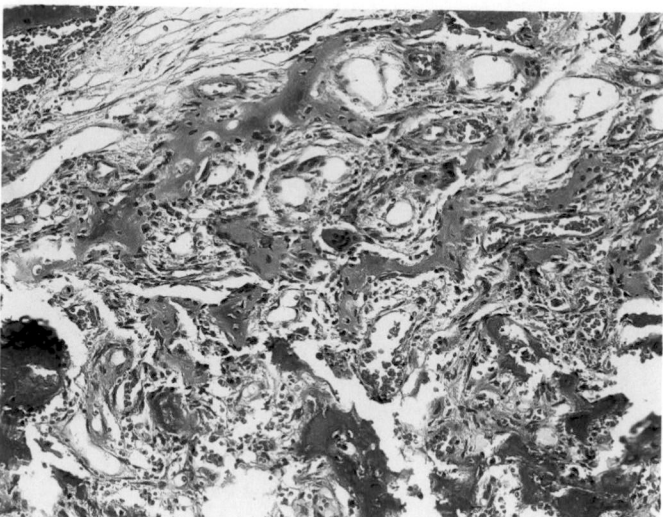

Fig. 6.10 Osteoblastoma. Numerous neoformed osteoid trabeculae are lined by osteoblasts and separated by a highly vascularized matrix.

Epithelial cysts

Epithelium-lined cysts of the maxilla or mandible are among the more commonly encountered oral diseases from both the clinician's and the pathologist's perspective.[118] Most cannot be identified specifically on the basis of their histologic appearance alone, with the exception of keratocysts and calcifying and keratinizing cysts. Therefore integration of radiographic, surgical, and microscopic findings is necessary to reach a specific diagnosis.[93,94,112,120]

Two major categories of cyst exist: odontogenic and fissural (nonodontogenic). *Odontogenic* cysts arise from the odontogenic epithelium and are located within the jaw (or, rarely, in the adjacent soft tissues). *Fissural (nonodontogenic) cysts* are thought to arise from epithelial inclusions within soft or bony portions of the region which lack the embryologic and tooth-forming heritage of odontogenic epithelium. They occur along embryologic fissure lines. Several subtypes of these two major categories exist.

Odontogenic cysts
   Dentigerous cyst
   Eruption cyst
   Gingival cyst
   Lateral periodontal cysts
   Keratinizing and calcifying odontogenic cyst
   Radicular or periapical cyst (including residual cyst)
   Keratocysts
      Solitary or primordial
      Multiple (nevoid basal cell carcinoma syndrome)
   Glandular odontogenic cyst
Fissural and other nonodontogenic cysts
   Nasoalveolar (Klestadt or nasolabial) cyst

Nasopalatine (median anterior palatal) cyst
Fissural cysts of tongue and floor of the mouth
Dermoid and epidermoid cysts
Palatal cyst

Dentigerous cysts surround or are associated with unerupted teeth and usually are found in young adults. They are present in almost 1% of individuals having complete dental roentgenograms.[83,95,104] They arise from alterations of reduced enamel epithelium after development of enamel and are associated with the tooth crown, at least initially. Swelling and, rarely, pain are symptoms, but they occur late or with infection and inflammation.

Microscopically, the uncomplicated dentigerous cyst has a thin fibrous wall lined by keratinized stratified squamous epithelium.[83] Secondary changes in the form of chronic inflammation, ulceration, reactive hyperplasia, metaplasia, calcification, and clusters of histiocytes containing hemosiderin and lipofuscin are common.[95,126] Dysplasia and carcinoma can also develop in them.[80,85,90]

Surgical excision is the treatment of choice for dentigerous cysts. Recurrence is very unusual. When it occurs, incomplete removal, keratocysts, other cystlike conditions of the jaws, and failure to recognize ameloblastoma in early or cystic examples should be considered.[125]

Eruption cyst is a subtype of dentigerous cyst that may be unilateral or bilateral, single or multiple. It presents as a gingival swelling above erupting primary or, rarely, permanent teeth. Surgical exposure of the affected tooth reveals a subacutely inflamed and hemorrhagic cyst wall lined by usually thin and nonkeratinizing stratified squamous epithelium.

Gingival cysts of newborn infants (Bohn's nodules) present as minute cystic or nodular formations; they are seen in most neonates and gradually disappear, usually in a matter of weeks.[95,104] Microscopically, they are lined by stratified squamous epithelium, sometimes parakeratotic.[84,92] Occasionally, gingival cysts are seen in adults.[113]

Lateral periodontal cysts probably represent cystic remnants of the dental lamina. They are remarkable by virtue of their anatomic location, usually apposing gingival or root surfaces of teeth in adults.[103] Mandibular premolar regions are the most frequent sites of occurrence. Microscopically, they are lined by an extremely thin epithelium (one or two layers thick).[123]

Keratinizing and calcifying odontogenic cyst is characterized by prominent basal palisading and large masses of keratinized "ghost" cells[76,77,91] (Fig. 6.11). Some of the cells may exhibit clear cell changes, and others may contain melanin pigment.[121] Some examples show a remarkable similarity with ameloblastoma and craniopharyngioma, from which they are distinguished by the presence of the characteristic ghost cells and dentinoid.[78,96,101,109a] It has been proposed that lesions in which this proliferation is particularly florid represent the neoplastic counterpart of the calcifying odontogenic cyst,

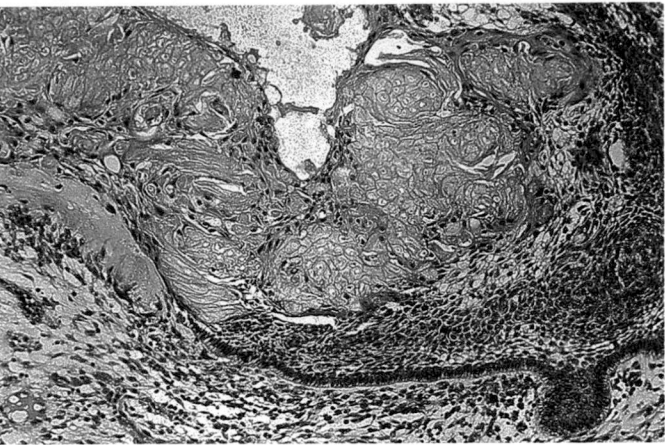

Fig. 6.11 Calcifying odontogenic cyst. The appearance is highly proliferative, suggesting that this lesion may actually be neoplastic. (From Pindborg JJ, Kramer IRH, Torloni H. Histological typing of odontogenic tumours, jaw cysts, and allied lesions. Geneva, 1971, World Health Organization.)

and the term *odontogenic ghost cell tumor* has been proposed for them.[89,129] Indeed, it may well be that all of the lesions in this category are tumors exhibiting varying (and sometimes very extensive) degrees of cystic change, a possibility supported by the common presence of molecular alterations in the form of β-catenin mutations.[119a]

Radicular or periapical cysts are another sequela of dental inflammatory disease and represent the most frequently encountered cyst of the jaws.[111] They occur in all age groups but are more commonly diagnosed during the third and fourth decades. Those observed within the maxilla or the mandible after tooth extraction are called *residual cysts*. Roentgenographically, they present as a well-circumscribed radiolucency at the apex of the affected tooth (Figs 6.12 to 6.14). Microscopically, they are lined by stratified squamous epithelium, the thickness of which varies according to the degree of inflammation present. Ulceration is common, and epithelium may be difficult to identify. Metaplasia, calcification, and hyaline bodies occasionally may be identified in the epithelium. The inflammatory infiltrate in the wall may be acute, chronic, or mixed. Aggregates of cholesterol crystals, foamy macrophages, multinucleated giant cells, and plasma cells are common. The cyst usually is easily curetted from the surrounding bone, and recurrence is rare. At surgery, the cyst may be found attached to the apex of the extracted tooth. Ramachandran et al.[114] have divided them into two categories—apical true cyst and apical pocket cysts—depending on their relation to the tooth canal.

Keratocysts constitute approximately 10% of cysts of the jaw and ordinarily can be diagnosed on the basis of their histologic features.[79,99] They have been divided into *solitary or primordial* (90%) and *multiple* (10%). The latter are a component of the nevoid basal cell carcinoma syndrome (Gorlin's syndrome), together with cutaneous

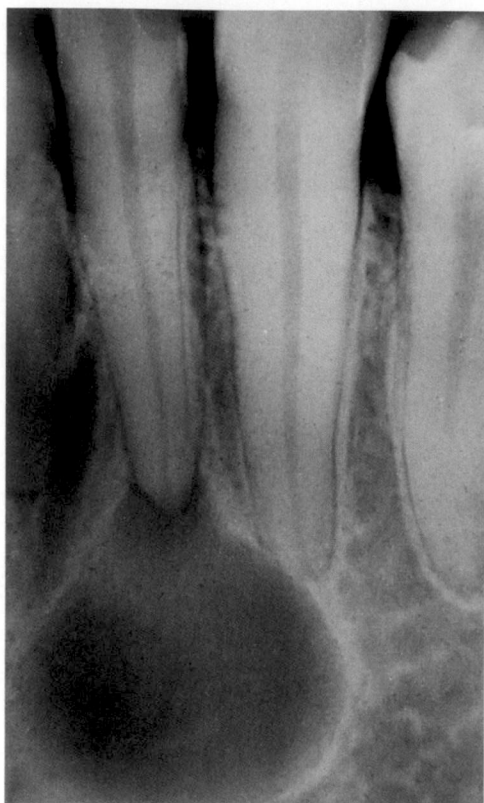

Fig. 6.12 Radicular periodontal cyst demonstrating continuity with pulp canal of nonvital tooth.

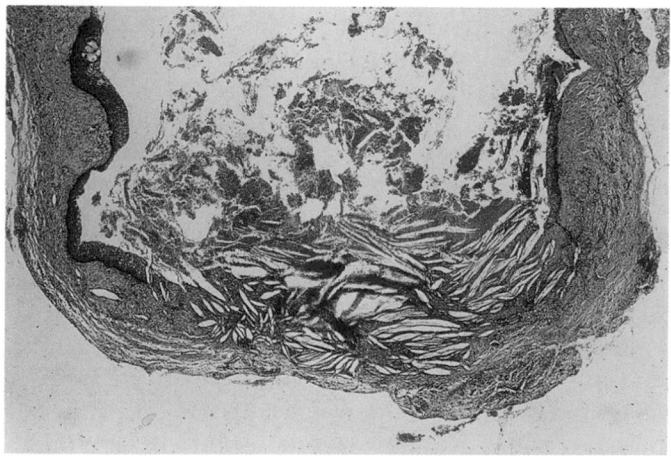

Fig. 6.13 Radicular cyst. The cavity is filled with squamous material and the lining is partially ulcerated. (From Pindborg JJ, Kramer IRH, Torloni H. Histological typing of odontogenic tumours, jaw cysts, and allied lesions. Geneva, 1971, World Health Organization.)

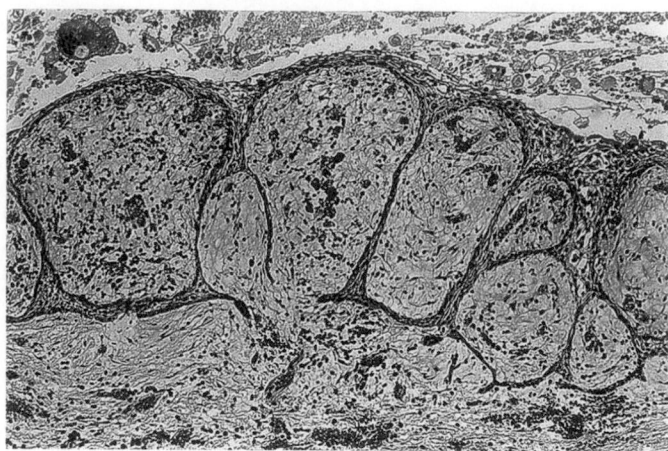

Fig. 6.14 Radicular cyst with secondary epithelial hyperplasia. (From Pindborg JJ, Kramer IRH, Torloni H. Histological typing of odontogenic tumours, jaw cysts, and allied lesions. Geneva, 1971, World Health Organization.)

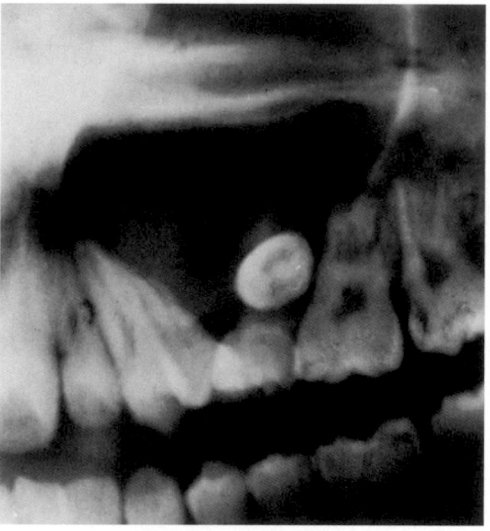

Fig. 6.15 Radiograph demonstrating portion of maxillary odontogenic keratocyst in a 15-year-old with a 2-week history of facial swelling.

nevoid basal cell carcinomas and numerous skeletal abnormalities.[98,115] Rarely, ketatocysts of similar appearance are present in various skin locations.[98a] This syndrome is transmitted by an autosomal dominant gene having high penetrance and variable expressivity.[88,97] Mutation of the human homologue of Drosophila patched (PTC) gene is thought to be the molecular defect in this syndrome.[130]

Keratocysts occur most frequently in the third molar region of the mandible (Figs 6.15 and 6.16). The mean age of the patients is 40 years. The cysts are more frequently multilocular and more commonly associated with swelling and pain than are dentigerous cysts.

Grossly, the cyst cavity contains a cheesy material consisting of keratinous debris that, when flushed away, reveals a white, subtly wrinkled surface. Microscopically, the epithelial lining is characterized by regimentation of the basal layer and a wavy, corrugated, or mildly verrucous surface of parakeratotic squamous epithelium.[107,108,128] Some authors have proposed to separate these from the cystic lesions exhibiting an orthokeratinized lining, on the basis of a lesser degree of aggressiveness associated with the latter.[109,127]

Keratocysts have a high rate of recurrence, which has reached up to 60% in some series. This has been variously attributed to technical difficulties with curettement due

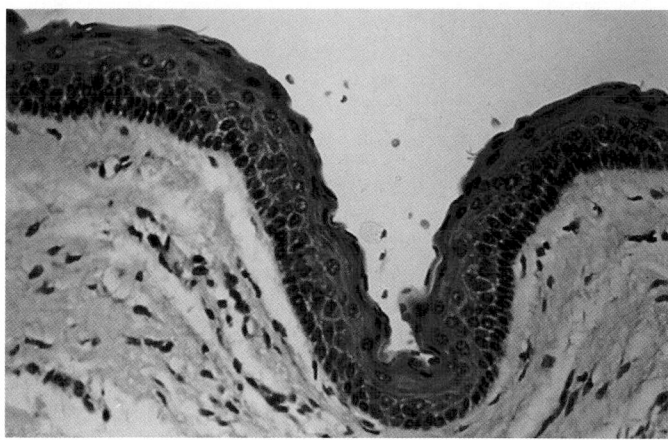

Fig. 6.16 Odontogenic keratocyst. Note the corrugated surface. (From Pindborg JJ, Kramer IRH, Torloni H. Histological typing of odontogenic tumours, jaw cysts, and allied lesions. Geneva, 1971, World Health Organization.)

to the multilocularity of the cysts and the friability of the material, presence of epithelial remnants in the wall, and budding of the epithelial lining within the cyst wall.[124]

Glandular odontogenic cyst (sialo-odontogenic cyst) contains mucous cells and ductlike structures and can therefore be confused with mucoepidermoid carcinoma.[106,117]

Nasoalveolar (Klestadt or nasolabial) cyst predominantly occurs in females, and is commonly bilateral. Originally thought to arise from epithelial rests at the embryologic junction of the globular, lateral nasal, and maxillary processes, development from the caudal end of the nasolacrimal rod or duct is currently favored.[102,119] The nasoalveolar cyst occurs near the base of the nostril, outside the alveolar process of the maxilla. It eventually obliterates the nasolabial fold and gently presses its way toward the nasal mucosa. Microscopically, the lining may be of stratified squamous or respiratory type.

Nasopalatine (median anterior palatal) cyst may be intraosseous or be located within the soft tissues of the palatine papilla. It represents cyst formation of embryologic remnants of the incisive canal joining the oral and nasal cavities,[74] and is the most common type of fissural or nonodontogenic cyst. Microscopically, it is lined by respiratory or stratified squamous epithelium or a combination of both.[81,87,116]

Fissural cysts of the tongue and floor of the mouth are infrequent.[75] "Globulomaxillary cysts" are probably not fissural cysts, and justification for their inclusion in this category has been challenged.[86,110] Similarly, the fissural nature of "median mandibular cyst" is doubtful.[82,122]

Dermoid cysts have a squamous lining and cutaneous adnexa, whereas **epidermoid cysts** lack the latter component.[100,105]

Palatal cysts in newborn infants (Epstein's pearls) are located at the junction of the hard and soft palate and are microscopically similar to gingival cysts.[92]

Odontogenic tumors

Odontogenic tumors are neoplasms of the jaws which differentiate toward tooth structures. Despite their rarity there is a great variety of types, with numerous transitional forms.[131,141] This has resulted in many classification attempts, beginning with the histologic scheme proposed by Broca in 1867. Thoma and Goldman[140] in 1946 classified them histogenetically into epithelial, mesodermal and mixed, whereas Pindborg and Clausen[137] in 1958 stressed the phenomenon of induction (as a mechanism of differentiation) over histogenesis. Subsequent authors[133,134,139] have slightly rearranged these types and added a few, most of which are included in the current classification scheme from the World Health Organization.[135]

The following grouping presents odontogenic tumors in a simplified fashion for the general surgical pathologist. It emphasizes their clinical behavior, which is benign for most types.[136]

It should be noted that peripheral (extraosseous) equivalents of most central odontogenic tumors have been described, located in the mandibular or maxillary gingiva, either from the surface mucosa or dental lamina nests in the submucosa,[132] or in the sinonasal tract.[138]

Benign tumors
    Adenomatoid odontogenic tumor (adenoameloblastoma)
    Calcifying epithelial odontogenic tumor (Pindborg's tumor)
    Squamous odontogenic tumor
    Ameloblastic fibroma
    Odontoma
        Complex
        Compound
        Ameloblastic (odonto-ameloblastoma)
    Cementoma
    (Odontogenic) myxoma, fibroma, and myxofibroma
Borderline tumors
    Ameloblastoma (adamantinoma)
Malignant tumors
    Ameloblastic carcinoma
    Ameloblastic fibrosarcoma
    Clear cell odontogenic carcinoma

Benign tumors

Adenomatoid odontogenic tumor (adenoameloblastoma)

Adenomatoid odontogenic tumor is a benign lesion that probably arises from the odontogenic epithelium of the dental lamina complex or its remnants.[142,143,145,149] It is more common in females, occurs most frequently in the second decade of life, and the most common location is the anterior maxilla.[143] Frequently, it is associated with an unerupted canine tooth ("follicular" type) (Fig. 6.17) and

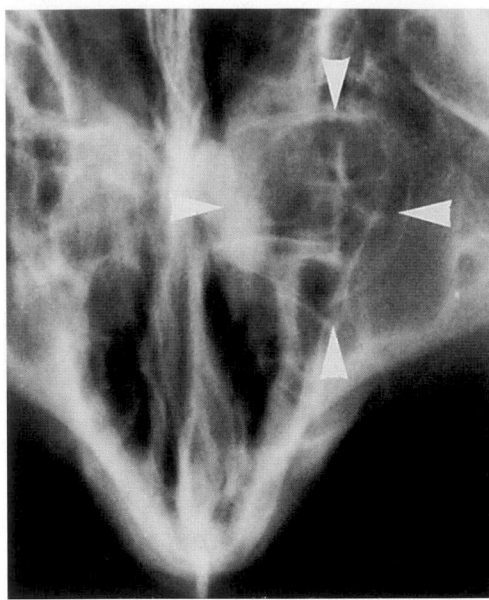

Fig. 6.17 Adenomatoid odontogenic tumor of maxilla in an edentulous patient. Radiographically, a dentigerous cyst is suggested (arrows).

may appear cystic roentgenographically. A peripheral variety of this tumor exists.[149] Although the tumor expands, it is not invasive and does not recur after conservative surgical therapy.[148]

Grossly, it is rounded and predominantly cystic, to the point of simulating an odontogenic cyst; however, focal solid areas are usually also present. The low-power microscopic appearance is reminiscent of an odontogenic cyst. However, examination of the thicker areas of the epithelial lining reveals numerous ductal structures lined by cuboidal or tall columnar cells (Fig. 6.18). Homogeneous zones of hyaline material and calcified deposits may be scattered throughout the epithelial lining.[142,144,147]

Melanin deposition may be present.[150] Ultrastructurally, there is clearcut evidence of glandular differentiation.[146]

Calcifying epithelial odontogenic tumor

Calcifying epithelial odontogenic tumor (Pindborg's tumor) occurs more commonly in the fourth and fifth decades.[151] There is no sex predilection. Most of the reported cases have arisen in the mandibular premolar-molar area in association with an embedded tooth,[160] and a few have been found peripherally located in the gingiva.[162]

Microscopically, the tumor is composed of closely packed polyhedral epithelial cells accompanied by scanty stroma (Fig. 6.19). The epithelial cells frequently demonstrate nuclear pleomorphism. Intracellular degeneration results in numerous spherical spaces filled with eosinophilic homogeneous material that in time becomes calcified. This has been shown to be amyloid or a similar substance.[153,157,158,161] Ultrastructurally, two cell populations exist.[156] High activity of alkaline phosphatase and adenosine triphosphatase has been found in the cytoplasmic membrane, an enzyme histochemical profile similar to that of the stratum intermedium cells of the normal dental germ.[154] Hybrids of this neoplasm and adenomatoid odontogenic tumor have been described.[155]

Calcifying epithelial odontogenic tumor may be invasive and recur locally, but on the whole it is a less aggressive lesion than ameloblastoma.[159,163] A single instance of metastasis to a regional lymph node has been reported.[152]

Squamous odontogenic tumor

Squamous odontogenic tumor is a benign neoplasm that occurs in a wide age range and has a predilection for the anterior maxilla and posterior mandible. Tumors in the former location tend to be more aggressive.[164,165,167] Radiographically, the lesion appears as a well-circumscribed semicircular radiolucency surrounded by

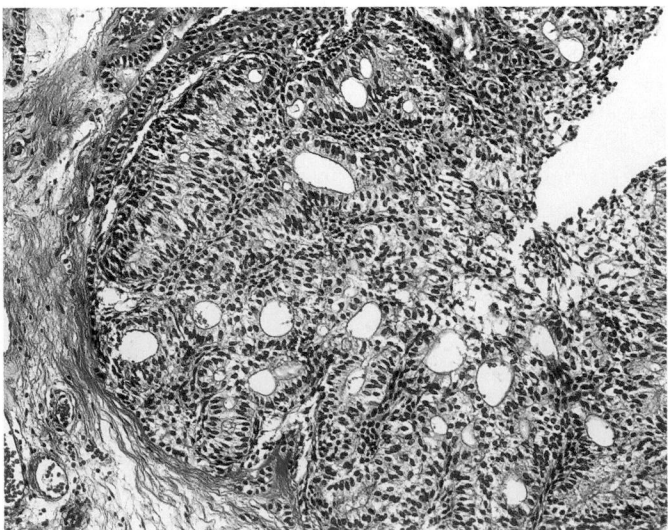

Fig. 6.18 Adenomatoid odontogenic tumor. Regularly shaped glandular structures are set back-to-back.

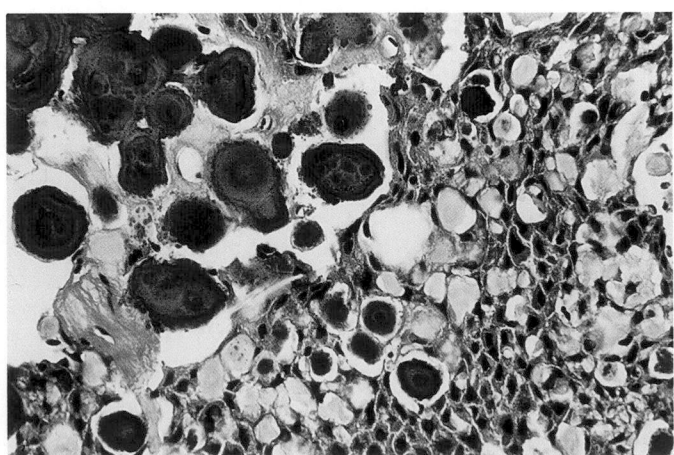

Fig. 6.19 Calcifying epithelial odontogenic tumor. (From Pindborg JJ, Kramer IRH, Torloni H. Histological typing of odontogenic tumours, jaw cysts, and allied lesions. Geneva, 1971, World Health Organization.)

a sclerotic border. Microscopically, it is composed of nests and islands of well-differentiated squamous epithelium lacking atypia or mitotic activity, located within a collagenous stroma of low to moderate cellularity[165,166] (Fig. 6.20). An extraosseous variety of this tumor has been described.[164]

Ameloblastic fibroma

Ameloblastic fibroma often resembles a cyst roentgenographically (Fig. 6.21). In contrast to ameloblastoma, the tumor with which it is most commonly mistaken, ameloblastic fibroma usually occurs in a young age group, rarely being seen in individuals older than 21 years of age. It is usually solid, although a cystic variety has been described.[170]

Microscopically, it is composed of strands and buds of epithelial cells embedded in a cellular connective tissue stroma (Fig. 6.22). The presence of this mesenchymal component is the main distinguishing feature with ameloblastoma. Hard tooth structures such as enamel or dentin are absent.[172] For the most part, the cells composing the epithelial strands are cuboidal and two cell layers thick. Only occasionally a stellate reticulum is present. A *granular cell variety* of ameloblastic fibroma has been described.[169]

The clinical behavior of ameloblastic fibroma is benign.[168] Therefore, and in contrast to ameloblastoma, simple curettage is usually adequate.[171]

Odontoma

Odontomas are defined as odontogenic tumors featuring production of calcified parts of teeth. They usually occur in the alveolar ridge of the mandible or maxilla, but a few examples have been reported in the middle ear.[177] Three subtypes of odontoma are recognized.

Complex odontoma is a poorly differentiated lesion, with a variety of calcified patterns but not enough coordinated production of enamel, dentin, or cementum to reach a point where an actual tooth can be identified (Fig. 6.23). It is more frequent in molar areas of the mandible in female patients (Fig. 6.24). Although the tumors occasionally achieve considerable proportions, they are entirely benign and usually represent incidental findings in routine roentgenographic examinations.

Compound odontoma exhibits a higher degree of differentiation than does complex odontoma, so that the individual lesion characteristically consists of masses of small misshapen teeth known as denticles (Fig. 6.25). Most lesions have only a few of these structures, but cases containing as many as 2000 are on record. Complex odontomas behave in an entirely benign fashion. They are more commonly encountered in anterior regions of the jaws, and in the maxilla more often than in the mandible.

Ameloblastic odontoma (odonto-ameloblastoma) is a solid or cystic lesion characterized by the presence of a

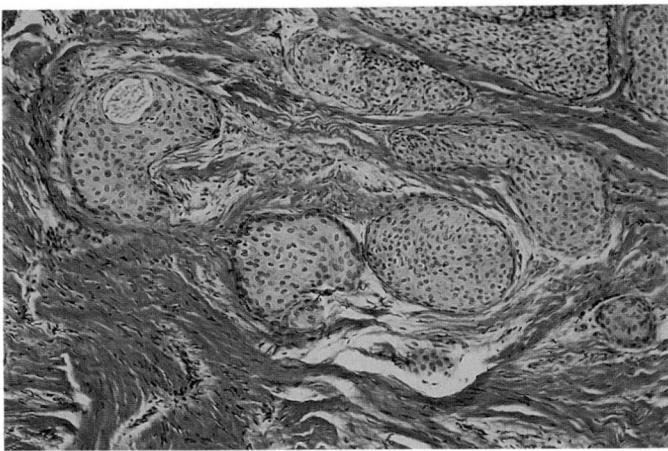

Fig. 6.20 Squamous odontogenic tumor. Well-defined nests of monotonous clear cells are separated by an abundant collagen stroma.

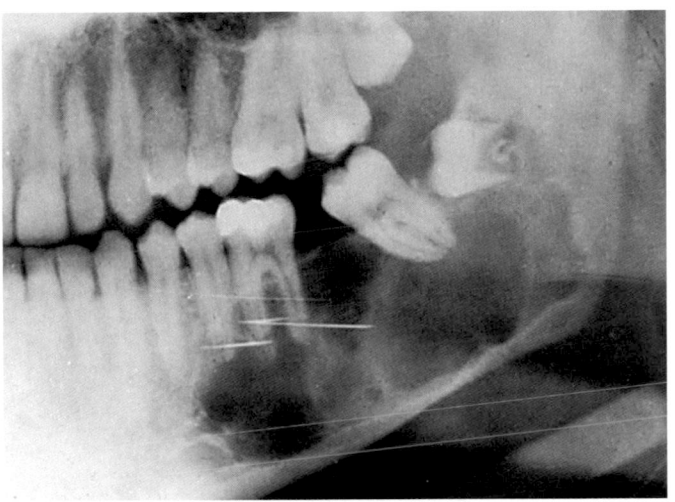

Fig. 6.21 Radiographical appearance of ameloblastic fibroma of mandible in a 17-year-old youth. The defect is multilocular but suggests irregularity.

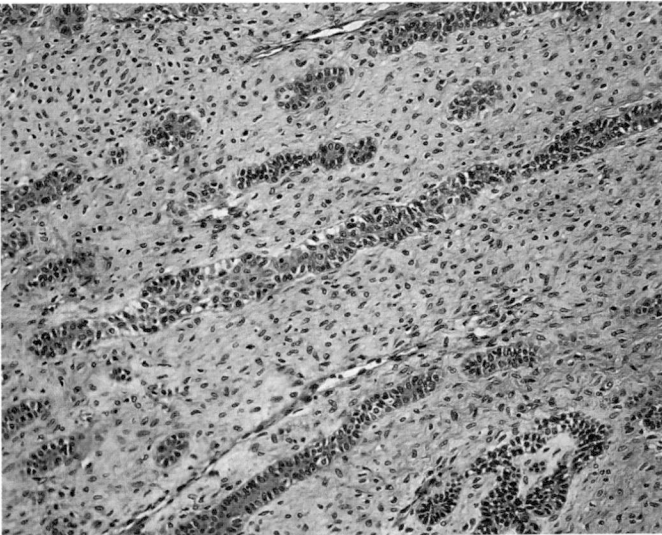

Fig. 6.22 Ameloblastic fibroma. The neoplastic fibrous stroma encloses thin strips of ameloblastic epithelium.

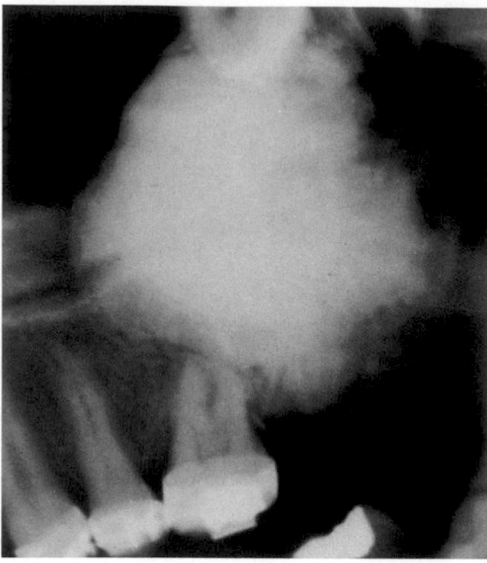

Fig. 6.23 Radiograph illustrating benign complex odontoma involving posterior maxilla of a 16-year-old girl. Note molar superiorly and absence of one molar.

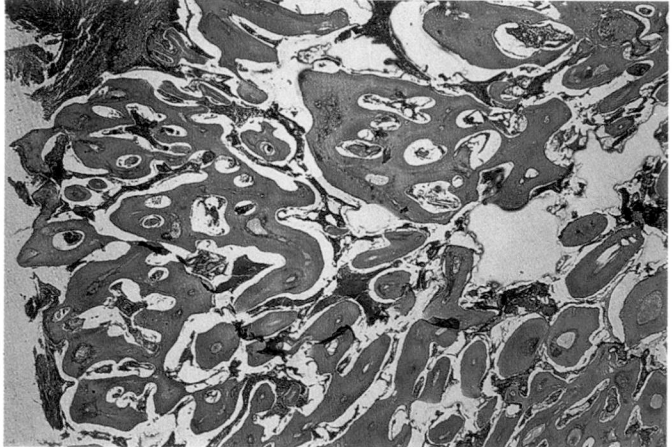

Fig. 6.24 Complex odontoma. (From Pindborg JJ, Kramer IRH, Torloni H. Histological typing of odontogenic tumours, jaw cysts, and allied lesions. Geneva, 1971, World Health Organization.)

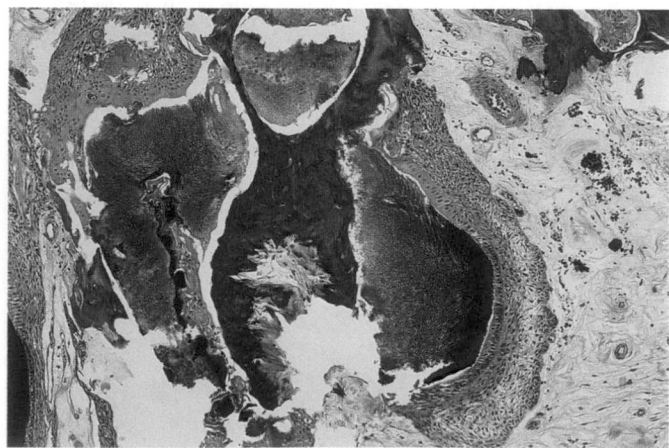

Fig. 6.25 Compound odontoma having the appearance of a misshapen tooth.

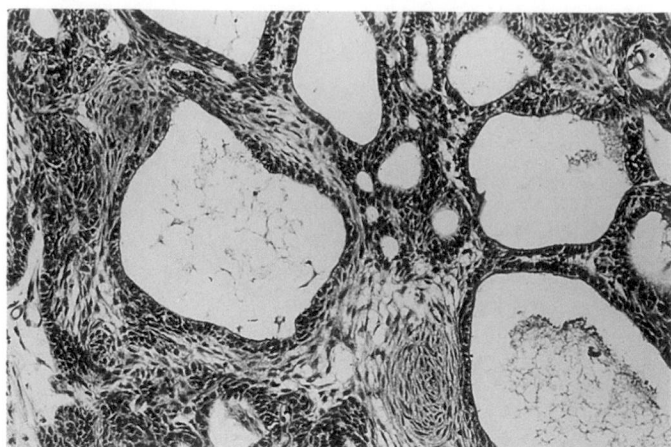

Fig. 6.26 Odontoameloblastoma. (From Pindborg JJ, Kramer IRH, Torloni H. Histological typing of odontogenic tumours, jaw cysts, and allied lesions. Geneva, 1971, World Health Organization.)

prominent epithelial component resembling ameloblastoma in addition to dental hard and soft tissues, such as enamel and dentin (Fig. 6.26).[173,175,176,178] It is currently regarded as a form of immature complex odontoma and different from both ameloblastoma and ameloblastic fibroma despite some morphologic resemblances.[174,179] It is generally benign but on occasion it behaves aggressively and recurs locally after conservative surgical removal.[175,176,178]

Immunohistochemical expression of the enamel sheath protein *sheathlin* has been detected in odontomas and other odontogenic tumors with inductive dental hard tissue formation.[180]

Cementoma

This lesion is discussed on page 283.

(Odontogenic) myxoma, myxofibroma, and fibroma

Myxoma of the jaws is generally regarded as of tooth germ origin and specifically derived from the dental papilla, hence the qualifier *odontogenic* usually applied to it.[182,183,189] It is often related to malformed or missing teeth.[181] Approximately 60% occur during the second or third decades, and there is an equal incidence of mandible and maxilla involvement. Radiographically, these tumors often present as cystic lesions, but they can attain a large size and result in marked facial deformity. Recurrence after conservative removal is not unusual (Fig. 6.27).

Microscopically, myxoma consists of loose stellate cells with long, branching cytoplasmic processes (Fig. 6.28). Occasionally, strands of odontogenic epithelium thought to represent rests of Malassez are noted. The myxoma cells are immunohistochemically reactive for vimentin and negative for S-100 protein.[191]

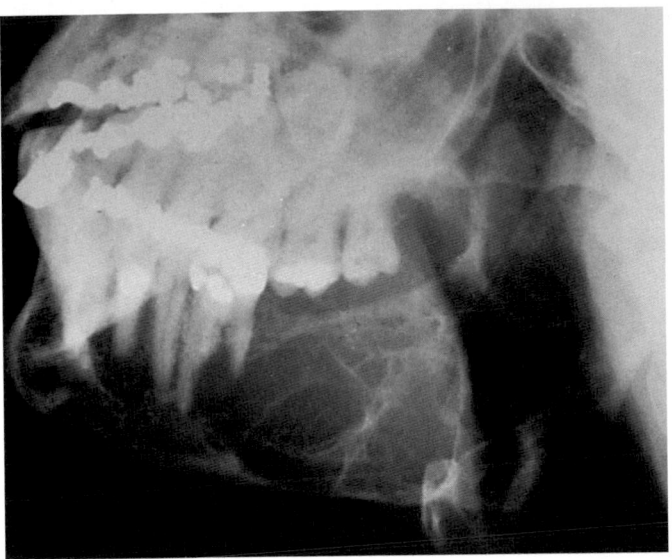

Fig. 6.27 Radiograph illustrating a large recurrent odontogenic myxoma of mandible in male adult.

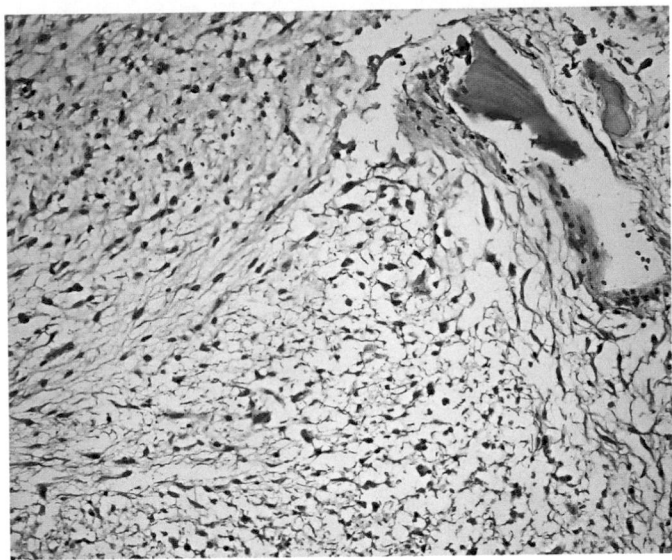

Fig. 6.28 Odontogenic myxoma. The lesion is highly myxoid, hypocellular, and devoid of atypia.

Odontogenic fibroma differs microscopically from the myxoma by the presence of fibrous tissue and greater numbers of odontogenic epithelial rests.[185,186,190,193] This lesion occurs most frequently in the maxilla anterior to the molars and displays a marked female predilection.[188] Tumors in which the myxomatous and the fibrous components are equally represented are designated as *myxofibromas*.[194] Cases combining features of odontogenic fibroma and central giant cell granulomas exist.[192]

Peripheral counterparts of these lesions occurring in the gingiva have been described.[184,187]

Borderline tumors

Ameloblastoma

General and clinical features

Ameloblastoma (adamantinoma) is the most common of the epithelial odontogenic tumors,[199] but it is still comparatively rare, comprising about 1% of tumors and cysts arising in the jaws. It may arise from the epithelial lining of a dentigerous cyst, from the remnants of the dental lamina and enamel organ, or from the basal layer of the oral mucosa, sometimes in a multicentric fashion[196,197,202,204,205] (see Chapter 5).

Ameloblastoma appears most commonly in the third to fifth decades, but it has also been described in children.[195,203] No sex or racial preference is noted. Over 80% occur in the mandible, with 70% of these arising in the molar-ramus area. The usual radiographic appearance is that of a lytic expansile lesion. Clinical duration may range from a few weeks to 50 years[198,200] (Fig. 6.29). The diagnosis can be made by fine needle aspiration.[201]

Peripheral ameloblastomas located in the oral cavity are discussed in Chapter 5, and peripheral ameloblastomas of the sinonasal tract are discussed in Chapter 7.

Morphologic features

Traditionally, ameloblastoma has been divided into solid and (multi)cystic types, but this distinction is arbitrary in as much as nearly all ameloblastomas demonstrate some degree of cystic change (Fig. 6.30). Microscopically, many subtypes or patterns have been described: follicular, plexiform (Fig. 6.31 and 6.32), acanthomatous (Fig. 6.33), papilliferous-keratotic, granular cell, desmoplastic, vascular, and with dentinoid induction (dentinoameloblastoma).[206,207,207a,209,210,212,214] Two or more types may coexist within the same tumor, and there is little evidence to suggest that one subtype is more aggressive than another.

The two predominant patterns are follicular and plexiform. In the follicular type, there is an attempt to mimic the dental organ epithelium. The outermost cells resemble those of the inner dental epithelium of the developing tooth follicle (i.e., the ameloblastic layer). The cells are tall columnar, with polarization of the nuclei away from the basement membrane.[211] The central portion of the epithelial island is composed of a loose network of cells resembling stellate reticulum. Squamous metaplasia within the stellate reticulum gives rise to the acanthomatous type. The epithelial islands demonstrate little inductive influence on the fibrous connective tissue stroma. Enamel and dentin are not formed by ameloblastoma. The plexiform pattern demonstrates irregular masses and interdigitating cords of epithelial cells with a minimum of stroma.[208,211] Occasionally, multinucleated giant cells of osteoclastic type are present in the stroma.[213]

Histochemical and immunohistochemical features

Immunohistochemically, the tumor cells exhibit strong reactivity for keratin and are surrounded by a continuous layer of laminin in a pattern similar to that seen in the developing tooth.[217] The major keratins expressed are

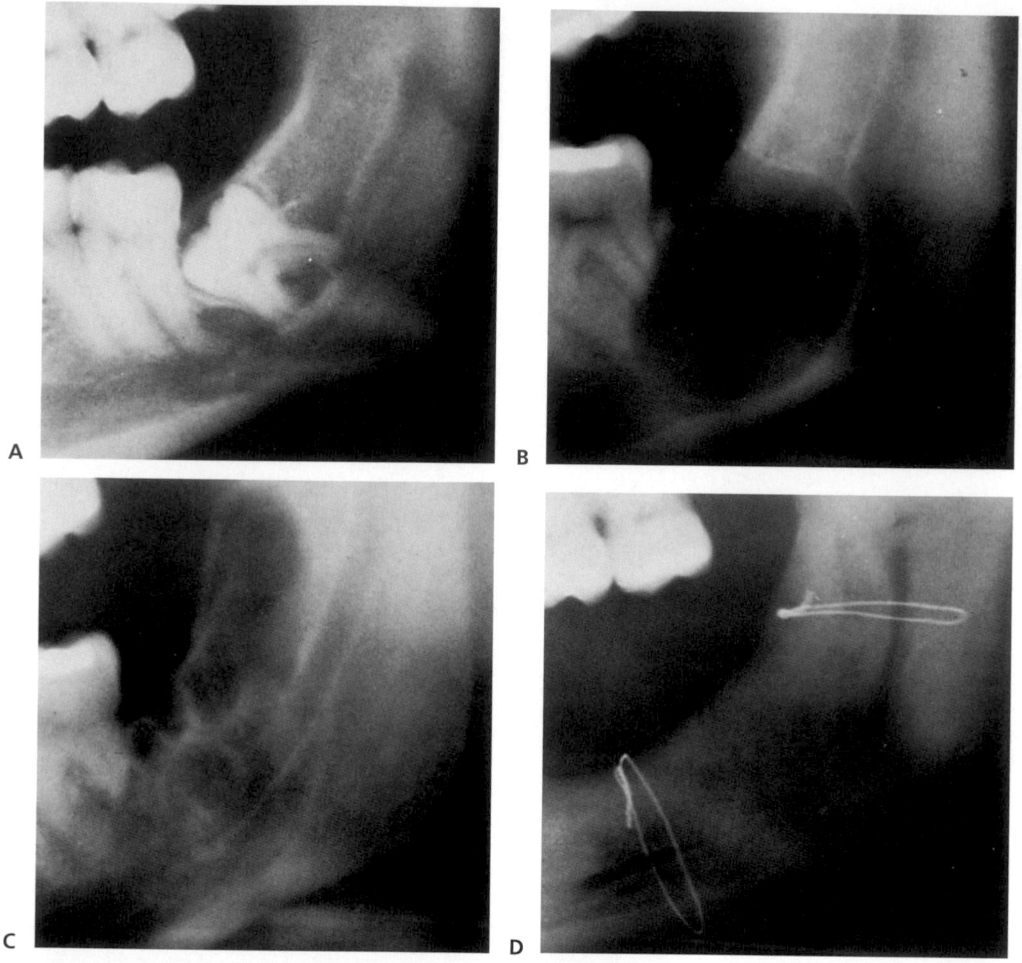

A

B

C

D

Fig. 6.29 Four radiographs illustrating history of ameloblastoma associated with impacted third molar tooth in a 19-year-old female patient. **A** (April, 1971), Subtle, atypical radiolucency can be discerned below tooth. Tooth was surgically removed. No surgical specimen was obtained. **B** (September, 1974), Routine dental roentgenogram revealed residual or recurrent cystic lesion. Surgical curettage was performed and "early" ameloblastoma demonstrated. No further treatment was given. **C** (February, 1978), Multilocular radiolucency of more typical character. Tumor was resected. **D** (December, 1978), There is no evidence of residual tumor. (Courtesy of Dr. William Randall and Dr. Clark Borstad, Minneapolis.)

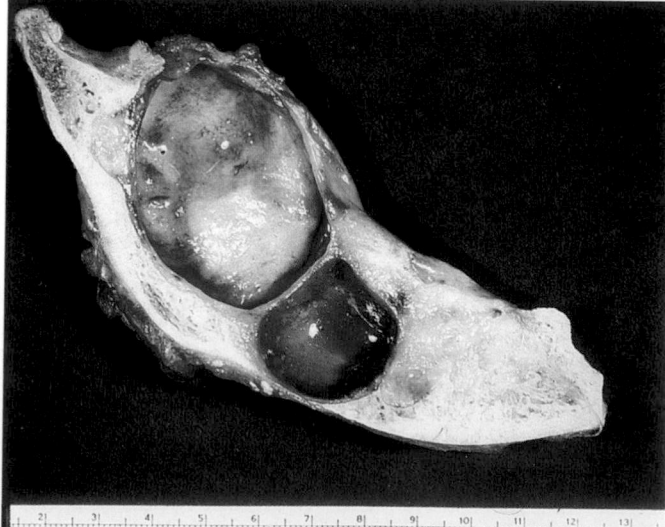

Fig. 6.30 Gross appearance of ameloblastoma of mandible.

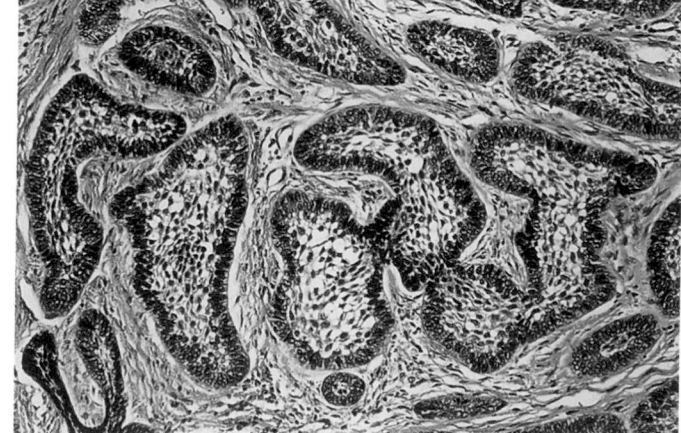

Fig. 6.31 Ameloblastoma exhibiting the classic basaloid ("follicular") appearance. (From Pindborg JJ, Kramer IRH, Torloni H. Histological typing of odontogenic tumours, jaw cysts, and allied lesions. Geneva, 1971, World Health Organization.)

CKs 5 and 14, whereas coexpression of CKs 8, 18, and 19 is a feature of the cells in the stellate reticulum-like areas.[218] Curiously, carletinin has been found to be positive in the overwhelming majority of solid and multicystic ameloblastomas (as well as in the unicystic tumors, see below).[215] The staining, which is almost always restricted to the stellate reticulum-like epithelium, may be of diagnostic aid for the identification of these tumors.

Granular cell ameloblastoma is positive for keratin and negative for S-100 protein, in keeping with its ameloblastic nature and in contrast to the ordinary granular cell tumor; however, and like the latter, it is also

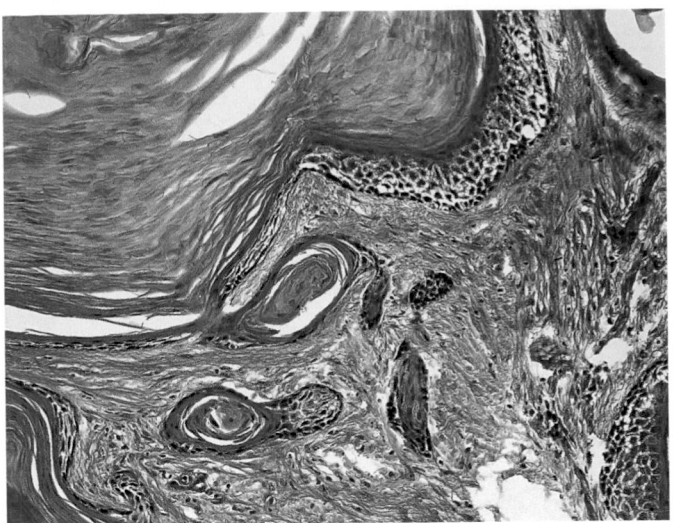

Fig. 6.32 Keratotic ameloblastoma. Ameloblastic epithelium surrounds large keratin-filled cavities.

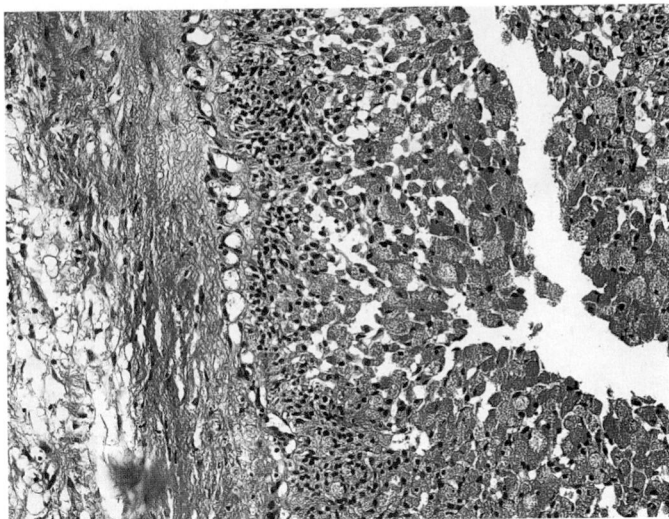

Fig. 6.33 Granular cell ameloblastoma. Most of the tumor cells have an abundant, deeply granular cytoplasm.

positive for CD68, indicating that the granular cell change is here too due to lysosomal overload.[216]

Electron microscopic features

Ultrastructurally, the tumor cells show clearcut evidence of epithelial differentiation in the form of bundles of tonofilaments and complex desmosomes, with some differences existing between the follicular and the plexiform types.[219–221] The granular variety shows the same type of lysosomal formations seen in granular cell tumor in other locations.[222,223]

Spread and metastasis

Ameloblastoma has invasive properties and a tendency to recur. It is because of these properties that we have placed it in a borderline (low-grade malignant) rather than a benign category, in contrast to the approach taken in this regard by most oral pathologists and rendered official by the WHO classification.

Furthermore, distant metastases have been documented in rare instances, especially to the lungs but also to the central nervous system.[224–226,228,229,231] The term *malignant ameloblastoma* is accepted by the WHO for those metastasizing tumors that retain the typical morphology of ameloblastoma[230] (as opposed to ameloblastic carcinoma, see next section). In the majority of these cases, the distant metastases have been preceded by several local recurrences.[227]

Differential diagnosis

A particularly vexing problem in this area is the differential diagnosis between focal reactive hyperplasia in a dentigerous cyst and so-called *unicystic ameloblastoma*, the latter representing either malignant ameloblastic transformation to a dentigerous cyst or a predominantly cystic form of ameloblastoma.

The minimal criterion for the diagnosis of ameloblastoma under these circumstances is the finding of a

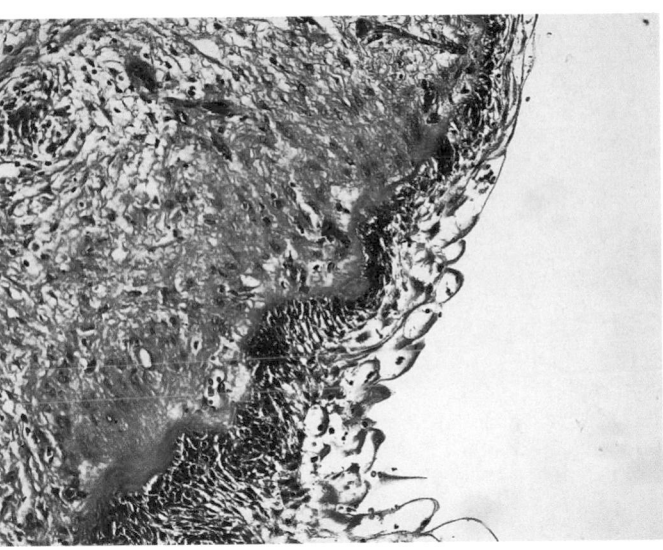

Fig. 6.34 Unicystic ameloblastoma fulfilling the minimum criteria for this entity, which should be distinguished from reactive epithelial changes in a radicular cyst (see Fig. 6.14).

palisaded basal layer with stellate reticulum-like epithelium above[234,236,238,239] (Fig. 6.34). Immunoreactivity for calretinin supports the diagnosis.[232] Enucleation of the lesion is usually curative, but local recurrence may develop, particularly if there are ameloblastic islands embedded in the cyst wall.[233,235,237]

Malignant tumors

Ameloblastic carcinoma

Ameloblastic carcinoma is defined as a tumor having the overall microscopic architectural features of ameloblastoma but also manifesting malignant cytologic features, such as marked nuclear atypia and numerous mitotic figures[241,242] (Fig. 6.35). It is possible that at least some of the reported *intraosseous carcinomas* of the jaw

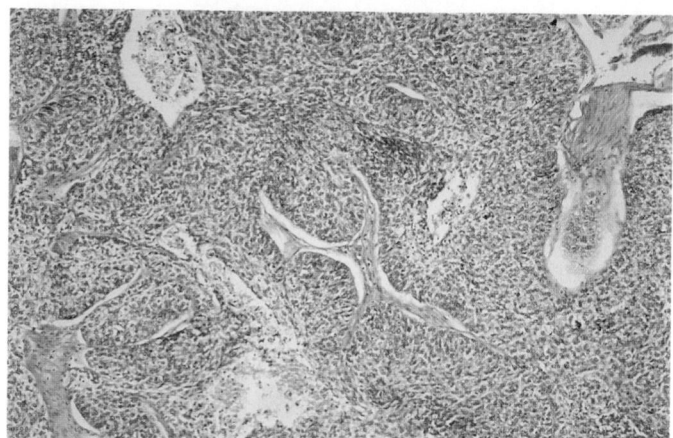

Fig. 6.35 Ameloblastic carcinoma. The geographic configuration of the tumor nests and the overall basophilic staining quality give this lesion a distinctly basaloid quality.

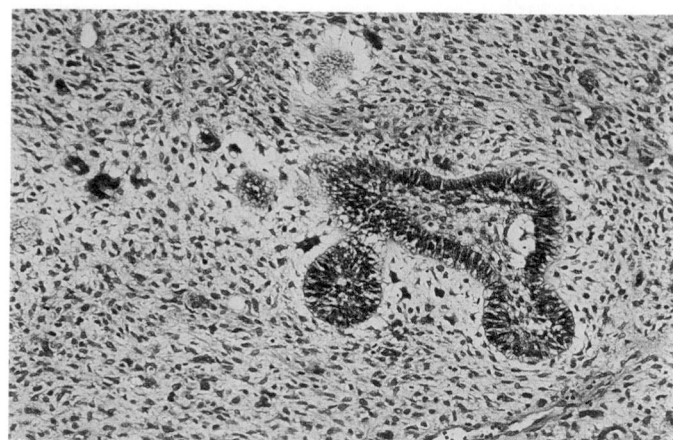

Fig. 6.37 Ameloblastic fibrosarcoma. Islands of well-differentiated ameloblastic epithelium are separated by a neoplastic stroma showing marked pleomorphism and mitotic activity.

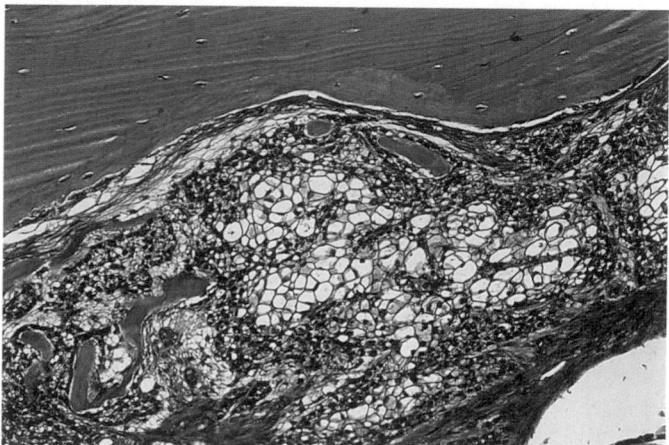

Fig. 6.36 Malignant intraosseous clear cell tumor of probable odontogenic origin. It may be difficult to distinguish this neoplasm from a minor salivary gland tumor or a metastatic carcinoma.

and ameloblastic fibrosarcoma (*ameloblastic carcinosarcoma*) have been described.[248,250]

Clear cell odontogenic carcinoma

Clear cell odontogenic carcinoma is a rare epithelial lesion of the jaw of putative odontogenic origin that may simulate a clear cell carcinoma of salivary gland type of metastatic origin. The clear cells are arranged in nests surrounded by a mature collagenous stroma, are devoid of mucin, and contain glycogen.[251] Although originally regarded as benign, it is now thought of as malignant, with occasional examples having metastasized to regional lymph nodes.[252–254]

Other tumors and tumorlike conditions

Paget's disease of the mandible and maxilla can occur as a dominant clinical expression of a generalized process or as the only localization in the monostotic form of the disease. The process may be complicated by the appearance of osteosarcoma or giant cell tumor. Actually, the possibility of Paget's disease should always be investigated when either of these two neoplasms is found in the jaw. Normal cementicles within the periodontal ligament should not be confused with Paget's disease (see p. 280).

Langerhans' cell histiocytosis (eosinophilic granuloma; histiocytosis X) of bone has a marked predilection for the jaw—more often the mandible—where it can cause a localized ragged zone of destruction (see Chapter 21).[273,301]

Aneurysmal bone cyst can produce massive expansion of the mandible (Fig. 6.38). Because of its high content of giant cells, the lesion can be confused microscopically with central giant cell granuloma (see p. 281).[262,299]

represent ameloblastic carcinomas with a marked degree of squamous change[240,244] (Fig. 6.36); others appear to arise in keratocysts and other types of odontogenic cysts.[243]

Ameloblastic fibrosarcoma

Ameloblastic fibrosarcoma (odontogenic sarcoma; odontogenic fibrosarcoma) shows histopathologic features similar to those of ameloblastic fibroma but differs from it by virtue of cytologic atypia, increased cellularity, diminution or absence of the epithelial component, and aggressive behavior (Fig. 6.37).[245,249] Sometimes these features appear in recurrences of tumors originally diagnosed as ameloblastic fibromas. Ultrastructurally, most of the tumor cells have features of fibroblasts.[246]

Pain is a common symptom, in contrast with most other odontogenic tumors. Death follows extensive local recurrence and extension.[247] Distant metastases from this tumor are exceptionally rare.

Cases combining features of ameloblastic carcinoma

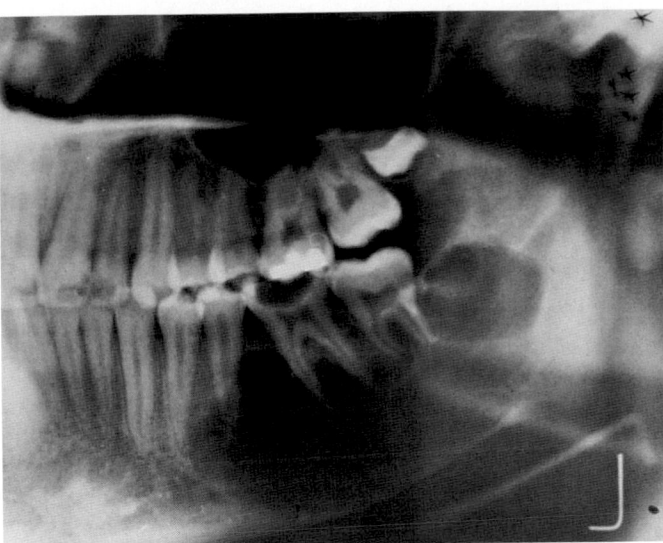

Fig. 6.38 Radiograph illustrating cystlike appearance of aneurysmal bone cyst of mandible in a 19-year-old man.

Benign tumors of the jaw include, among others, hemangioma of either cavernous or Masson's type,[290,318] benign peripheral nerve tumors,[275,307] nonossifying fibroma[277] (not to be confused with the ossifying fibroma discussed on p. 282), desmoplastic fibroma[260,284,312] (which has a definite predilection for the mandible), chondromyxoid fibroma,[294] chondroblastoma,[315] the already mentioned osteoblastoma, osteochondroma (often located in the coronoid process of the mandible),[289] and so-called "osteoma". The last lesion occurs almost exclusively in the jaw and is present in more than 80% of patients with Gardner's syndrome.[283]

Salivary gland tumors may present as primary intraosseous masses, usually in the mandible. Mucoepidermoid carcinoma is the most common type[264]; other types include adenoid cystic carcinoma, acinic cell carcinoma, and hyalinizing clear cell carcinoma.[258,278,295,298]

Meningioma has been seen in the mandible, presumably arising from ectopic nests of arachnoidal cells or related perineurial cells.[292] Parenthetically, we have seen two microscopically similar cases located in the ramus of the pubic bone.

Pigmented neuroectodermal tumor of infancy (melanotic progonoma; retinal anlage tumor) is a rare neoplasm of neuroectodermal derivation previously thought to arise from odontogenic epithelium[288,309] (Figs 6.39 and 6.40). The maxilla is the most common location; however, it also occurs in the mandible, skull, long bones, epididymis, mediastinum, and soft tissues of extremities[285] (see Chapter 25). Immunohistochemical and ultrastructural studies and the occasional demonstration of both neuronal differentiation and vanillylmandelic acid production have confirmed the neural nature of this neoplasm.[263] The behavior is generally benign, but some cases with aggressive local behavior and a few that have resulted in distant metastases have been documented.[272,285,308]

Myofibromatosis is another proliferative process that may involve the mandible of infants or children (see Chapter 25).[321]

True giant cell tumors of the jawbone are exceptional[306]; most of them are seen in patients with Paget's disease.[261] It should be remembered that the overwhelming majority of osteoclast-containing lesions of bone represent examples of entities other than giant cell tumor.

Osteosarcoma is the most common primary malignant tumor of the jaw. The mandible is affected slightly more often than the maxilla[280,297] (Fig. 6.41). The majority

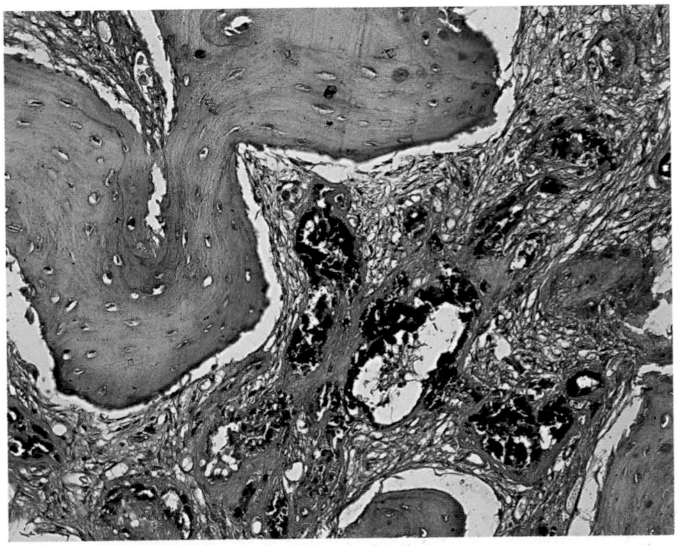

Fig. 6.39 Pigmented neuroectodermal tumor of infancy. The neoplastic islands located between the bone trabeculae contain abundant melanin pigment.

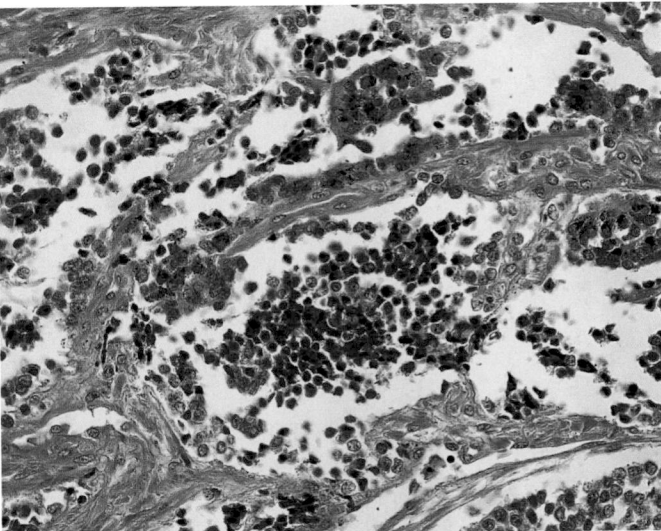

Fig. 6.40 Pigmented neuroectodermal tumor of infancy. This example shows the classic pattern of neuroblast-like cells surrounded by larger melanin-containing cells.

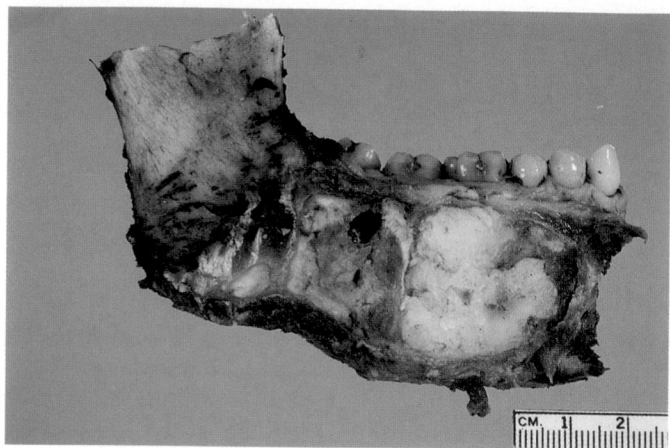

Fig. 6.41 Gross appearance of osteosarcoma of mandible.

of the maxillary tumors occur in the alveolar ridge.[259] Most cases arise de novo, but others represent complications of radiation therapy, Paget's disease, or fibrous dysplasia.[311] The majority are of the usual intramedullary type, but parosteal examples have been reported.[313] Microscopically, most have a conventional appearance, with many exhibiting a prominent chondroblastic component (Fig. 6.42). Others have a telangiectatic quality that may lead to confusion with aneurysmal bone cyst.[265] The prognosis for osteosarcoma of the jaw is, as a group, more favorable than for osteosarcoma of long bones. It is best for the tumors located in the mandibular symphysis and worst for those involving the maxillary antrum.[280] Multimodality therapy similar to that used for osteosarcomas of the extremities is used for them.

Chondrosarcoma of the jaw shows a marked predilection for the maxilla.[282,314] It can be central or peripheral, and microscopically it may exhibit conventional, mesenchymal, or dedifferentiated features.[267,317]

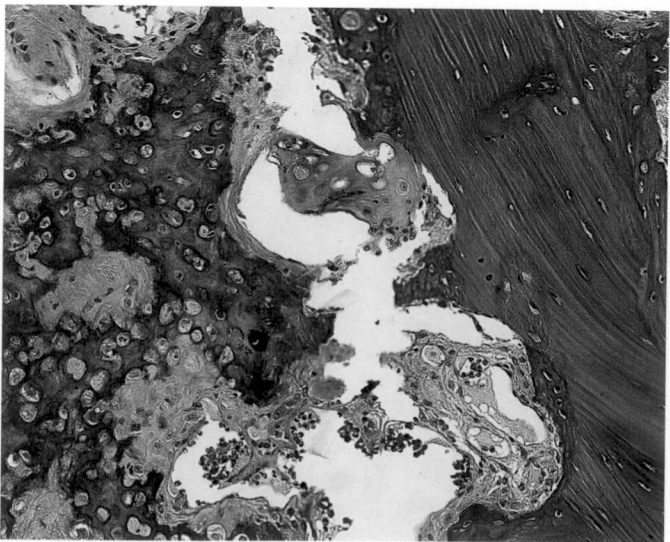

Fig. 6.42 Osteosarcoma of jaw. The neoplastic bone (left) is clearly distinguishable from the residual normal bone (right).

Fibrosarcoma has a predilection for the mandible. It is slow-growing and locally aggressive.[320]

Ewing's sarcoma can present as a primary tumor of the jaw; most of the reported cases have been located in the maxilla.[257,266]

Kaposi's sarcoma of the oral cavity may erode the underlying jawbone; in exceptional cases it presents as a primary intraosseous lesion.[293]

Other sarcomas of jaw are *leiomyosarcoma*,[291,305] *rhabdomyosarcoma*,[294] *malignant peripheral nerve sheath tumor*[286] (including its melanotic variant[281]), *angiosarcoma* (including the epithelioid variety[279]), and *so-called malignant fibrous histiocytoma*.[255,319] The last is a very aggressive neoplasm.

Malignant lymphoma that involves the jaws is nearly always of the non-Hodgkin type.[310] In adults, most cases are of a large cell type, whereas in children there is a predominance of undifferentiated types.[274] The high frequency of jaw involvement in Burkitt's lymphoma is well known.[274]

Hodgkin's disease with primary presentation in the jaw is a curiosity; less than a handful of cases have been reported, and the authenticity of some is in question.[269]

Acute leukemia may involve the jaw and oral cavity in children, sometimes as the initial sign of the disease.[304,316]

Plasma cell neoplasms can present in the jaw, either as part of a generalized process (multiple myeloma) or as the only manifestation of the disease (plasmacytoma).[270,287]

Direct invasion of the mandible by squamous cell carcinoma of the oral cavity is not uncommon. Extension along the mandibular canal can be seen at a great distance from the primary tumor.[296,302]

Metastatic tumors to the jaw in adults most often originate from breast, lung, large bowel, prostate, kidney, thyroid, or testis.[256,303] In children, metastases to the jaw originate most frequently from adrenal neuroblastoma, embryonal rhabdomyosarcoma, and Wilms' tumor.[268,271]

The tooth-bearing area of the body and molar regions of the mandible are the most frequent sites for these metastases, possibly because of greater blood supply in these regions. In about one half of the cases, oral metastasis is the first sign of systemic disease. Swelling, pain, and anesthesia are the most common symptoms.[268,276,300]

Diseases of the temporomandibular joint

Hypoplasia of the mandibular condyle may be unilateral or bilateral, and it is characterized by facial asymmetry and abnormality of function. It often represents diminished or retarded development and may be associated with anomalies of the ear or temporal bone and with macrostomia. It may also be the result of acquired conditions, especially mandibular fracture or other traumas during the growth period.

Hyperplasia of the mandibular condyle usually manifests as an isolated finding in the form of unilateral facial enlargement in adults, but it may be also seen in association with hemihypertrophy.[323] Grossly, the condyle appears larger than normal. Microscopic examination reveals a thick and irregular layer of hyaline or fibrohyaline cartilage covering the articular surface of the condyle. This disease is probably related to, if not identical with, *synovial chondromatosis* or *osteochondromatosis*.[322,325] When the cellularity of the cartilaginous nodules is marked, the possibility of overdiagnosing the case as chondrosarcoma exists.

Tophaceous pseudogout (tumoral calcium pyrophosphate dihydrate crystal deposition disease) results from the deposition of calcium pyrophosphate dihydrate crystals.[328] Microscopically, the presence of chondromyxoid tissue with atypical chondrocytes can result in a mistaken diagnosis of chondrosarcoma. The identification by polarized light of birefringent crystals associated with a granulomatous reaction is the clue to the diagnosis (Fig. 6.43).[324]

Traumatic, inflammatory, and degenerative conditions may all result in the so-called *temporomandibular joint pain–dysfunction syndrome*. The features of this syndrome include limitation of jaw movement with discomfort or pain, tenderness of masticatory muscles, and, sometimes, clicking of the joint during mastication. The gross and microscopic anatomy of joint components (capsule, articulating portions of the mandibular condyle, and the meniscus) displays markedly altered relationships in such instances. Less altered, individual components of the temporomandibular joint, such as a meniscus or condylar head, may be surgically removed

and submitted for pathologic examination. Although it is sometimes possible to demonstrate specific inflammatory or degenerative conditions of this joint such as rheumatoid arthritis, osteoarthritis (osteoarthrosis), or osteochondromatosis, in most cases the pathologic features are nonspecific.[326]

Tendosynovial giant cell tumor can occur in the region of the temporomandibular joint. Lack of familiarity with this fact coupled with the high cellularity of the lesion may result in overinterpretation as a malignant process.[327]

Other conditions that have been reported in the temporomandibular joint include osteoma and osteoblastoma, ganglion and synovial cyst, aneurysmal bone cyst, epidermal inclusion cyst, hemangioma, nonossifying fibroma, Langerhans' cell histiocytosis, and plasma cell myeloma.[327]

References

Normal anatomy

1 Cawson RA. Oral diseases: clinical and pathologic correlations, ed. 3. Edinburgh, 2001, Mosby.
2 Cawson RA. Lucas's Pathology of tumors of the oral tissues, ed. 5. London, 1998, Churchill Livingstone.
3 Gorlin RJ, Goldman HM (eds). Thoma's Oral pathology, ed. 6. St. Louis, 1970, Mosby.
4 Kramer IRH, Pindborg JJ, Shear M. Histological typing of odontogenic tumours, ed. 2. In World Health Organization: International Histological Classification of Tumours. Berlin, 1992, Springer-Verlag.
5 Regezi JA, Sciubba JJ. Oral pathology: clinical pathologic correlations, ed. 3. Philadelphia, 1999, Saunders.
6 Sciubba JJ, Fantasia JE, Khan LB. Tumors and cysts of the jaws. Atlas of tumor pathology, series 3, fascicle 29. Washington D.C., 2001, Armed Forces Institute of Pathology.

Inflammatory diseases

7 Barker BF, Dunlap CL. Hyaline rings of the oral cavity. The so-called "pulse" granuloma redefined. Semin Diagn Pathol 1987, **4:** 237–242.
8 El-Labban NG, Kramer IRH. The nature of the hyaline rings in chronic periostitis and other conditions. An ultrastructural study. Oral Surg Oral Med Oral Pathol 1981, **51:** 509–515.
9 Ellis DJ, Winslow JR, Indovina AA. Garre's osteomyelitis of the mandible. Report of a case. Oral Surg Oral Med Oral Pathol 1977, **44:** 183–189.
10 Gorlin RJ, Goldman HM (eds). Thoma's Oral pathology, ed. 6. St. Louis, 1970, Mosby.
11 Jacobsson S, Heyden G. Chronic sclerosing osteomyelitis of the mandible. Histologic and histochemical findings. Oral Surg Oral Med Oral Pathol 1977, **43:** 357–364.
12 Kannangara DW, Thadepalli H, McQuirter JL. Bacteriology and treatment of dental infections. Oral Surg Oral Med Oral Pathol 1980, **50:** 103–109.
13 Lieblich SE, Piecuch JF. Infections of the jaws, including infected fractures, osteomyelitis and osteoradionecrosis. Atlas Oral Maxillofac Surg Clin North Am 2000, **8:** 121–132.
14 Massler M, Pawlak J. The affected and infected pulp. Oral Surg Oral Med Oral Pathol 1977, **43:** 929–947.
15 McMillan MD, Kardos TB, Edwards JL, Thorburn DN, Adams DB, Palmer DK. Giant cell hyalin angiopathy or pulse granuloma. Oral Surg Oral Med Oral Pathol 1981, **52:** 178–186.

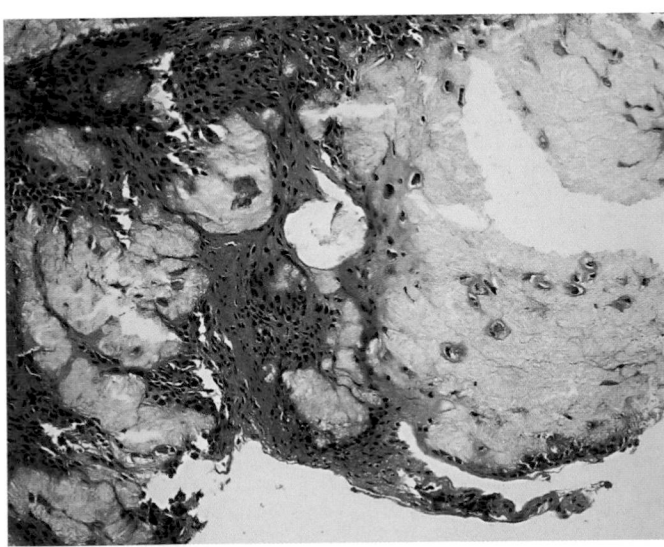

Fig. 6.43 Tophaceous pseudogout. The lobules have the appearance of slightly atypical cartilage.

16 Mortensen M, Winthee JE, Birn H. Periapical granulomas and cysts. An investigation of 1,600 cases. Scand J Dent Res 1970, **78:** 241–250.

17 Moursh F. A roentgenographic study of dentigerous cysts. Oral Surg Oral Med Oral Pathol 1964, **18:** 466–473.

18 Sapp JP, Jensvold J. The distribution and morphologic variation of hyaline deposits in odontogenic lesions. Oral Surg Oral Med Oral Pathol 1983, **55:** 151–161.

19 Seltzer S, Rainey E, Gluskin AH. Correlation of scanning electron microscope and light microscope findings in uninflamed and pathologically involved human pulps. Oral Surg Oral Med Oral Pathol 1977, **43:** 910–928.

20 Shaw JH. Causes and control of dental caries. N Engl J Med 1987, **317:** 996–1002.

21 Titterington WP. Osteomyelitis and osteoradionecrosis of the jaws. J Oral Med 1971, **26:** 7–16.

22 Waldvogel FA, Medoff G, Swartz MN. Osteomyelitis. Clinical features, therapeutic considerations and unusual aspects. Springfield, Ill., 1971, Charles C. Thomas.

Simple bone cyst

23 Gait C. Solitary bone cyst of the mandible. Report of a case. Br J Surg 1976, **13:** 250–253.

24 Howe GL. "Haemorrhagic cysts" of the mandible. Br J Oral Surg 1965, **3:** 55–76, 77–91.

25 Huebner GR, Turlington EG. So-called traumatic (hemorrhagic) bone cysts of the jaws. Oral Surg Oral Med Oral Pathol 1971, **31:** 354–365.

26 Matsumura S, Murakami S, Kakimoto N, Furukawa S, Kishino M, Ishida T, Fuchihata H. Histopathologic and radiographic findings of the simple bone cyst. Oral Surg Oral Med Oral Pathol Oral Radiol Endod 1998, **85:** 619–625.

27 Regezi JA, Courtney RM, Batsakis JG. The pathology of head and neck tumors. Part 12. Cysts of the jaws. Head Neck Surg 1981, **4:** 48–57.

28 Saito Y, Hoshina Y, Nagamine T, Nakajima T, Suzuki M, Hayashi T. Simple bone cyst. A clinical and histopathologic study of fifteen cases. Oral Surg Oral Med Oral Pathol 1992, **74:** 487–491.

Central giant cell granuloma and other giant cell-containing lesions

29 Dahlin DC, Cupps RE, Johnson EW Jr. Giant-cell tumor. A study of 195 cases. Cancer 1970, **25:** 1061–1070.

30 Dehner LP. Tumors of the mandible and maxilla in children. I. Clinicopathologic study of 46 histologically benign lesions. Cancer 1973, **31:** 364–384.

31 Dorfman HD, Czerniak B. Bone tumors. St. Louis, 1998, Mosby.

32 El-Labban NG, Lee KW. Myofibroblasts in central giant cell granuloma of the jaws. An ultrastructural study. Histopathology 1983, **7:** 907–918.

33 Goldenberg RR, Campbell CJ, Bonfiglio M. Giant cell tumor of bone. An analysis of two hundred and eighteen cases. J Bone Joint Surg [Br] 1970, **52:** 619–664.

34 Jaffe HL. Giant cell reparative granuloma, traumatic bone cyst, and fibrous (fibro-osseous) dysplasia of the jawbones. Oral Surg Oral Med Oral Pathol 1953, **6:** 159–175.

35 Mangion J, Rahman N, Edkins S, Barfoot R, Nguyen T, Sigurdsson A, Townend JV, Fitzpatrick DR, Flanagan AM, Stratton MR. The gene for cherubism maps to chromosome 4p16.3. Am J Hum Genet 1999, **65:** 151–157.

36 Masson EA, MacFarlane IA, Bodmer CW, Vaughan ED. Parathyroid carcinoma presenting with a brown tumour of the mandible in a young man. Br J Oral Maxillofac Surg 1993, **31:** 117–119.

37 McGrath PJ. Giant-cell tumour of bone. An analysis of fifty-two cases. J Bone Joint Surg 1972, [Br] **54:** 216–229.

38 Ueki Y, Tiziani V, Santanna C, Fukai N, Maulik C, Garfinkle J,

Ninoyima C, doAmaral C, Peters H, Habal M, Rhee-Morris L, Doss JB, Kreiborg S, Olsen BR, Reichenberger E. Mutations in the gene encoding c-Abl-binding protein SH3BP2 cause cherubism. Nat Genet 2001, **28:** 125–126.

39 Waldron CA. Intraosseous fibrous swelling of jaws. In Bergsma D (ed.): Birth defects. Atlas and compendium. Baltimore, 1973, Williams & Wilkins.

40 Waldron CA, Shafer WG. The central giant cell reparative granuloma of the jaws. An analysis of 38 cases. Am J Clin Pathol 1966, **45:** 437–447.

40a Yamaguchi T, Dorfman H. Giant cell reparative granuloma: A comparative clinicopathologic study of lesions in gnathic and extragnathic sites. Int J Surg Pathol 2001, **9:** 189–200.

41 Yamaguchi T, Dorfman HD, Eisig S. Cherubism: clinicopathologic features. Skeletal Radiol 1999, **28:** 350–353.

Benign fibro-osseous lesions

42 Dehner LP. Tumors of the mandible and maxilla in children. I. Clinicopathologic study of 46 histologically benign lesions. Cancer 1973, **31:** 364–384.

43 Eversole LR, Sabes WR, Rovin S. Fibrous dysplasia, a nosologic problem in the diagnosis of fibro-osseous lesions of the jaws. J Oral Pathol 1972, **1:** 189–220.

44 Talib AN, Gaston GW. Biopsy technique for fibro-osseous and osteolytic lesions of the jaws. Oral Surg Oral Med Oral Pathol 1977, **44:** 177–182.

45 Waldron CA. Intraosseous fibrous swelling of jaws. In Bergsma D (ed.): Birth defects. Atlas and compendium. Baltimore, 1973, Williams & Wilkins.

46 Waldron CA, Giansanti JS. Benign fibro-osseous lesions of the jaws. Oral Surg Oral Med Oral Pathol 1973, **35:** 190–201, 340–350.

Fibrous dysplasia and related lesions

47 Brannon RB, Fowler CB. Benign fibro-osseous lesions: a review of current concepts. Adv Anat Pathol 2001, **8:** 126–143.

48 Cohen MM Jr, Howell RE. Etiology of fibrous dysplasia and McCune-Albright syndrome. Int J Oral Maxillofac Surg 1999, **28:** 366–371.

49 El Deeb M, Waite DE, Gorlin RJ. Congenital monostotic fibrous dysplasia. A new possibly autosomal recessive disorder. J Oral Surg 1979, **37:** 520–525.

50 El-Mofty SK. Cemento-ossifying fibroma and benign cementoblastoma. Semin Diagn Pathol 1999, **16:** 301–307.

51 Eversole LR, Leider AS, Nelson K. Ossifying fibroma. A clinicopathologic study of sixty-four cases. Oral Surg Oral Med Oral Pathol 1985, **60:** 505–511.

52 Eversole LR, Sabes WR, Rovin S. Fibrous dysplasia, a nosologic problem in the diagnosis of fibro-osseous lesions of the jaws. J Oral Pathol 1972, **1:** 189–220.

53 Hamner JE III, Scofield HH, Cornyn J. Benign fibroosseous jaw lesions of periodontal membrane origin. An analysis of 249 cases. Cancer 1968, **22:** 861–878.

54 Harris WH, Dudley HR, Barry RJ. The natural history of fibrous dysplasia. J Bone Joint Surg [Am] 1962, **44:** 207–233.

55 Lania A, Mantovani G, Spada A. G protein mutations in endocrine diseases. Eur J Endocrinol 2001, **145:** 543–559.

56 Pierce AM, Wilson DF, Goss AN. Inherited craniofacial fibrous dysplasia. Oral Surg Oral Med Oral Pathol 1985, **60:** 403–409.

57 Reed RJ. Fibrous dysplasia of bone. Arch Pathol 1963, **75:** 480–495.

58 Schmaman A, Smith I, Ackerman LV. Benign fibro-osseous lesions of the mandible and maxilla. A review of 35 cases. Cancer 1970, **26:** 303–312.

59 Voytek TM, Ro JY, Edeiken J, Ayala AG. Fibrous dysplasia and cementoossifying fibroma. A histologic spectrum. Am J Surg Pathol 1995, **19:** 775–781.

60 Williams HK, Mangham C, Speight PM. Juvenile ossifying fibroma. An analysis of eight cases and a comparison with other fibro-osseous lesions. J Oral Pathol Med 2000, **29**: 13–18.

Cementoma and related lesions

61 Abdelsayed RA, Eversole LR, Singh BS, Scarbrough FE. Gigantiform cementoma: Clinicopathologic presentation of 3 cases. Oral Surg Oral Med Oral Pathol Oral Radiol Endod 2001, **91**: 438–444.

62 Corio RL, Crawford BE, Schaberg SJ. Benign cementoblastoma. Oral Surg Oral Med Oral Pathol 1976, **41**: 524–530.

63 Ellis DJ, Winslow JR, Indovina AA. Garre's osteomyelitis of the mandible. Report of a case. Oral Surg Oral Med Oral Pathol 1977, **44**: 183–189.

64 El-Mofty SK. Cemento-ossifying fibroma and benign cementoblastoma. Semin Diagn Pathol 1999, **16**: 301–307.

65 Jacobsson S, Heyden G. Chronic sclerosing osteomyelitis of the mandible. Histologic and histochemical findings. Oral Surg Oral Med Oral Pathol 1977, **43**: 357–364.

66 Kramer IRH, Pindborg JJ, Shear M. Histological typing of odontogenic tumours, ed. 2. In World Health Organization: International Histological Classification of Tumours. Berlin, 1992, Springer-Verlag.

67 Larsson A, Forsberg O, Sjögren S. Benign cementoblastoma. Cementum analogue of benign osteoblastoma? J Oral Surg 1978, **36**: 299–303.

68 Sedano HO, Kuba R, Gorlin RJ. Autosomal dominant cemental dysplasia. Oral Surg Oral Med Oral Pathol 1982, **54**: 642–646.

69 Slootweg PJ. Cementoblastoma and osteoblastoma: a comparison of histologic features. J Oral Pathol Med 1992, **21**: 385–389.

70 Steiner GC. Ultrastructure of osteoblastoma. Cancer 1977, **39**: 2127–2136.

71 Su L, Weathers DR, Waldron CA. Distinguishing features of focal cemento-osseous dysplasias and cemento-ossifying fibromas: I. A pathologic spectrum of 316 cases. Oral Surg Oral Med Oral Pathol Oral Radiol Endod 1997, **84**: 301–309.

72 Summerlin DJ, Tomich CE. Focal cemento-osseous dysplasia: a clinicopathologic study of 221 cases. Oral Surg Oral Med Oral Pathol 1994, **78**: 611–620.

73 Swanson KS, Guttu RL, Miller ME. Gigantic osteoma of the mandible: report of a case. J Oral Maxillofac Surg 1992, **50**: 635–638.

Epithelial cysts

74 Abrams AM, Howell FV, Bullock WK. Nasopalatine cysts. Oral Surg Oral Med Oral Pathol 1963, **16**: 306–332.

75 Akinosi JO. Multiple sublingual dermoid cysts. Br J Oral Surg 1974, **12**: 235–239.

76 Altini M, Farman AG. The calcifying odontogenic cyst. Oral Surg Oral Med Oral Pathol 1975, **40**: 751–759.

77 Anneroth G, Nordenram A. Calcifying odontogenic cyst. Oral Surg Oral Med Oral Pathol 1975, **39**: 794–801.

78 Bernstein ML, Buchino JJ. The histologic similarity between craniopharyngioma and odontogenic lesions. A reappraisal. Oral Surg Oral Med Oral Pathol 1983, **56**: 502–511.

79 Brannon RB. The odontogenic keratocyst. Oral Surg Oral Med Oral Pathol 1976, **42**: 54–72.

80 Browne RM, Gough NG. Malignant change in the epithelial lining of odontogenic cysts. Cancer 1972, **29**: 1199–1207.

81 Buchner A, Mlinek A. Palatal opening of the nasopalatine duct. A developmental anomaly. Oral Surg Oral Med Oral Pathol 1972, **34**: 440–444.

82 Buchner A, Ramon Y. Median mandibular cyst. A rare lesion of debatable origin. Oral Surg Oral Med Oral Pathol 1974, **37**: 431–437.

83 Cabrini RL, Barras RE, Albano H. Cysts of the jaw. A statistical analysis. J Oral Surg 1970, **28**: 485–489.

84 Cataldo E, Berkman MD. Cysts of the oral mucosa in newborns. Am J Dis Child 1968, **116**: 44–48.

85 Chretien PB, Carpenter DF, White NS, Harrah JD, Lightbody PM. Squamous carcinoma arising in a dentigerous cyst. Presentation of a fatal case and review of four previously reported cases. Oral Surg Oral Med Oral Pathol 1970, **30**: 809–816.

86 Christ TF. The globulomaxillary cyst. An embryologic misconception. Oral Surg Oral Med Oral Pathol 1970, **30**: 515–526.

87 Courage GR, North AF, Hansen LS. Median palatine cysts. Review of the literature and report of a case. Oral Surg Oral Med Oral Pathol 1974, **37**: 745–753.

88 Donatsky O, Hjörting-Hansen E, Philipsen HP, Fejerskov O. Clinical, radiologic, and histopathologic aspects of 13 cases of nevoid basal cell carcinoma syndrome. Int J Oral Surg 1976, **5**: 19–28.

89 Ellis GL. Odontogenic ghost cell tumor. Semin Diagn Pathol 1999, **16**: 288–292.

90 Eversole LR, Sabes WR, Rovin S. Aggressive growth and neoplastic potential of odontogenic cysts. With special reference to central epidermoid and mucoepidermoid carcinomas. Cancer 1975, **35**: 270–282.

91 Freedman PD, Lumerman H, Gee JK. Calcifying odontogenic cysts. A review and analysis of seventy cases. Oral Surg Oral Med Oral Pathol 1975, **40**: 93–106.

92 Fromm A. Epstein's pearls, Bohn's nodules and inclusion-cysts of the oral cavity. J Dent Child 1967, **34**: 275–287.

93 Gardner DG, Sapp JP, Wysocki GP. Odontogenic and "fissural" cysts of the jaws. Pathol Annu 1978, **13**(Pt 1): 177–200.

94 Gorlin RJ. Potentialities of oral epithelium manifest by mandibular dentigerous cysts. Oral Surg Oral Med Oral Pathol 1957, **10**: 271–284.

95 Gorlin RJ. Cysts of the jaws, oral floor, and neck. In Gorlin RJ, Goldman HM (eds): Thoma's oral pathology, ed. 6. St. Louis, 1970, Mosby.

96 Gorlin RJ, Pindborg JJ, Clausen FP, Vickers RA. The calcifying odontogenic cyst. A possible analogue of the cutaneous calcifying epithelioma of Malherbe. An analysis of fifteen cases. Oral Surg Oral Med Oral Pathol 1962, **15**: 1235–1243.

97 Gorlin RJ, Pindborg JJ, Cohen MM Jr. Syndromes of the head and neck, ed. 2. New York, 1976, McGraw-Hill.

98 Gorlin RJ, Vickers RA, Kelly E, Williamson JJ. The multiple basal cell nevi syndrome. Cancer 1965, **18**: 89–104.

98a Hamel AF, den Dunnen AFA, Suurmeiger AJH. The cutaneous keratocyst: a rare hallmark of the nevoid Basal cell carcinoma syndrome. Int J Surg Pathol 2003, **11**: 36.

99 Hodgkinson DJ, Woods JE, Dahlin DC, Tolman DE. Keratocysts of the jaw. Cancer 1978, **41**: 803–813.

100 Howell WE, Stein H, Tomaro AJ. Sublingual dermoid cyst in an infant. Report of a case. J Oral Surg 1972, **30**: 437–441.

101 Kalnins V. Calcification and amelogenesis in craniopharyngiomas. Oral Surg Oral Med Oral Pathol 1971, **31**: 366–379.

102 Karmody CS, Gallagher JC. Nasoalveolar cysts. Ann Otol Rhinol Laryngol 1972, **81**: 278–283.

103 Kerezoudis NP, Donta-Bakoyianni C, Siskos G. The lateral periodontal cyst: aetiology, clinical significance and diagnosis. Endod Dent Traumatol 2000, **16**: 144–150.

104 Killey HC, Kay IW. An analysis of 471 benign cystic lesions of the jaws. Int Surg 1966, **46**: 540–545.

105 Kinnman J, Suh KW. Dermoid cysts of the floor of the mouth. J Oral Surg 1968, **26**: 190–193.

106 Koppang HS, Johannessen S, Haugen LK, Haanaes HR, Solheim T, Donath K. Glandular odontogenic cyst (sialo-odontogenic cyst): report of two cases and literature review of 45 previously reported cases. J Oral Pathol Med 1998, **27**: 455–462.

107 Kramer IRH, Pindborg JJ, Shear M. Histological typing of odontogenic tumours, ed. 2. In World Health Organization:

International Histological Classification of Tumours. Berlin, 1992, Springer-Verlag.

108 Kramer IRH, Toller PA. The use of exfoliative cytology and protein estimations in preoperative diagnosis of odontogenic keratocysts. Int J Oral Surg 1973, **2**: 143–151.

109 Li T-J, Kitano M, Chen X-M, Itoh T, Kawashima K, Sugihara K, Nozoe E, Mimura T. Orthokeratinized odontogenic cyst: a clinicopathologic and immunocytochemical study of 15 cases. Histopathology 1998, **32**: 242–251.

109a Li T-J, Yu S-F. Clinicopathologic spectrum of the so-called calcifying odontogenic cysts: A study of 21 intraosseous cases with reconsideration of the terminology and classification. Am J Surg Pathol 2003, **27**: 372–384.

110 Little JW, Jakobsen J. Origin of the globulomaxillary cyst. J Oral Surg 1973, **31**: 188–195.

111 Mortensen M, Winther JE, Birn H. Periapical granulomas and cysts. An investigation of 1,600 cases. Scand J Dent Res 1970, **78**: 241–250.

112 Moursh F. A roentgenographic study of dentigerous cysts. Oral Surg Oral Med Oral Pathol 1964, **18**: 466–473.

113 Nxumalo TN, Shear M. Gingival cyst in adults. J Oral Pathol Med 1992, **21**: 309–313.

114 Ramachandran Nair PN, Pajarola G, Schroeder HE. Types and incidence of human periapical lesions obtained with extracted teeth. Oral Surg Oral Med Oral Pathol Oral Radiol Endod 1996, **81**: 92–102.

115 Rayner CRW, Towers JF, Wilson JSP. What is Gorlin's syndrome? The diagnosis and management of the basal cell naevus syndrome, based on a study of thirty-seven patients. Br J Plast Surg 1977, **30**: 62–67.

116 Redman RS. Nasopalatine duct cyst with pigmented lining suggestive of olfactory epithelium. Oral Surg Oral Med Oral Pathol 1974, **37**: 421–428.

117 Regezi JA. Odontogenic cysts, odontogenic tumors, fibroosseous, and giant cell lesions of the jaws. Mod Pathol 2002, **15**: 331–341.

118 Regezi JA, Courtney RM, Batsakis JG. The pathology of head and neck tumors. Part 12. Cysts of the jaws. Head Neck Surg 1981, **4**: 48–57.

119 Roed-Petersen B. Nasolabial cysts. A presentation of five patients with a review of the literature. Br J Oral Surg 1969, **7**: 84–94.

119a Sekine S, Sato S, Takata T, Fukuda Y, Isheda T, Kishino M, Shibata T, Kanai Y, Hirohashi S. β-catenin mutations are frequent in calcifying odontogenic cysts, but rare in ameloblastomas. Am J Pathol 2003, **163**: 1707–1712.

120 Shear M. Cysts of the oral region. Bristol, 1976, John Wright & Sons, Ltd.

121 Soames JV. A pigmented calcifying odontogenic cyst. Oral Surg Oral Med Oral Pathol 1982, **53**: 395–400.

122 Soskolne WA, Shteyer A. Median mandibular cyst. Oral Surg Oral Med Oral Pathol 1977, **44**: 84–88.

123 Standish SM, Shafter WG. The lateral periodontal cyst. J Periodontol 1958, **29**: 27–33.

124 Stoelinga PJW, Cohen MM Jr, Morgan AF. The origin of keratocysts in the basal cell nevus syndrome. J Oral Surg 1975, **33**: 659–663.

125 Vickers RA, Gorlin RJ. Ameloblastoma. Delineation of early histopathologic features of neoplasia. Cancer 1970, **26**: 699–710.

126 Wright JM. Squamous odontogenic tumor-like proliferation in odontogenic cysts. Oral Surg Oral Med Oral Pathol 1979, **47**: 354–358.

127 Wright JM. The odontogenic keratocyst. Orthokeratinized variant. Oral Surg Oral Med Oral Pathol 1981, **51**: 609–618.

128 Wysocki GP, Sapp JP. Scanning and transmission electron microscopy of odontogenic keratocysts. Oral Surg Oral Med Oral Pathol 1975, **40**: 494–501.

129 Yoshida M, Kumamoto H, Ooya K, Mayanagi H. Histopathological and immunohistochemical analysis of calcifying odontogenic cysts. J Oral Pathol Med 2001, **30**: 582–588.

130 Zedan W, Robinson PA, High AS. A novel polymorphism in the PTC gene allows easy identification of allelic loss in basal cell nevus syndrome lesions. Diagn Mol Pathol 2001, **10**: 41–45.

Odontogenic tumors

131 Anneroth G, Hansen LS. Variations in keratinizing odontogenic cysts and tumors. Oral Surg Oral Med Oral Pathol 1982, **54**: 530–546.

132 Batsakis JG, Hicks MJ, Flaitz CM. Peripheral epithelial odontogenic tumors. Ann Otol Rhinol Laryngol 1993, **102**: 322–324.

133 Eversole LR, Tomich CE, Cherrick HM. Histogenesis of odontogenic tumors. Oral Surg Oral Med Oral Pathol 1971, **32**: 569–581.

134 Gorlin RJ, Chaudhry AP, Pindborg JJ. Odontogenic tumors. Classification, histopathology, and clinical behavior in man and domesticated animals. Cancer 1961, **14**: 73–101.

135 Kramer IRH, Pindborg JJ, Shear M. Histological typing of odontogenic tumours, ed. 2. In World Health Organization: International Histological Classification of Tumours. Berlin, 1992, Springer-Verlag.

136 Melrose RJ. Benign epithelial odontogenic tumors. Semin Diagn Pathol 1999, **16**: 271–287.

137 Pindborg JJ, Clausen F. Classification of odontogenic tumors. Suggestion. Acta Odontol Scand 1958, **16**: 293–301.

138 Schafer DR, Thompson LDR, Smith BC, Wenig BM. Primary ameloblastoma of the sinonasal tract: a clinicopathologic study of 24 cases. Cancer 1998, **82**: 667–674.

139 Spouge JD. Odontogenic tumors. Oral Surg Oral Med Oral Pathol 1967, **24**: 392–403.

140 Thoma KH, Goldman HM. Odontogenic tumors. Classification based on observations of epithelial, mesenchymal and mixed varieties. Am J Pathol 1946, **22**: 433–471.

141 Tomich CE. Benign mixed odontogenic tumors. Semin Diagn Pathol 1999, **16**: 308–316.

Benign tumors

Adenomatoid odontogenic tumor (adenoameloblastoma)

142 Abrams AM, Melrose RJ, Howell FV. Adenoameloblastoma. Cancer 1968, **22**: 175–185.

143 Courtney RM, Kerr DA. The odontogenic adenomatoid tumor. Oral Surg Oral Med Oral Pathol 1975, **39**: 424–435.

144 el-Labban NG. The nature of the eosinophilic and laminated masses in the adenomatoid odontogenic tumor: A histochemical and ultrastructural study. J Oral Pathol Med 1992, **21**: 75–81.

145 Giansanti JS, Someren A, Waldron CA. Odontogenic adenomatoid tumor (adenoameloblastoma). Survey of 111 cases. Oral Surg Oral Med Oral Pathol 1970, **30**: 69–88.

146 Hatakeyama S, Suzuki A. Ultrastructural study of adenomatoid odontogenic tumor. J Oral Pathol 1978, **7**: 395–410.

147 Kramer IRH, Pindborg JJ, Shear M. Histological typing of odontogenic tumours, ed. 2. In World Health Organization: International Histological Classification of Tumours. Berlin, 1992, Springer-Verlag.

148 Philipsen HP, Reichart PA, Zhang KH, Nikai H, Yu QX. Adenomatoid odontogenic tumor: Biologic profile based on 499 cases. J Oral Pathol Med 1991, **20**: 149–158.

149 Philipsen HP, Samman N, Ormiston IW, Wu PC, Reichart PA. Variants of the adenomatoid odontogenic tumor with a note on tumor origin. J Oral Pathol Med 1992, **21**: 348–352.

150 Warter A, George-Diolombi G, Chazal M, Ango A. Melanin in a dentigerous cyst and associated adenomatoid odontogenic tumor. Cancer 1990, **66**: 786–788.

Calcifying epithelial odontogenic tumor

151 Ai-Ru L, Zhen L, Jian S. Calcifying epithelial odontogenic tumors. A clinicopathologic study of nine cases. J Oral Pathol 1982, **11**: 399–406.

152 Basu MK, Matthews JB, Sear AJ, Browne RM. Calcifying epithelial odontogenic tumour. A case showing features of malignancy. J Oral Pathol 1984, **13**: 310–319.

153 Chaudhry AP, Hanks CT, Leifer C, Gargiulo EA. Calcifying epithelial odontogenic tumor. A histochemical and ultrastructural study. Cancer 1972, **30**: 1036–1045.

154 Chomette G, Auriol M, Guilbert F. Histoenzymological and ultrastructural study of a bifocal calcifying epithelial odontogenic tumor. Characteristics of epithelial cells and histogenesis of amyloid-like material. Virchows Arch [A] 1984, **403**: 67–76.

155 Damm DD, White DK, Drummond JF, Poindexter JB, Henry BB. Combined epithelial odontogenic tumor. Adenomatoid odontogenic tumor and calcifying epithelial odontogenic tumor. Oral Surg Oral Med Oral Pathol 1982, **55**: 487–496.

156 El-Labban NG, Lee KW, Kramer IRH. The duality of the cell population in calcifying epithelial odontogenic tumor (CEOT). Histopathology 1984, **8**: 679–691.

157 El-Labban NG, Lee KW, Kramer IRH, Harris M. The nature of the amyloid-like material in a calcifying epithelial odontogenic tumor. An ultrastructural study. J Oral Pathol 1983, **12**: 366–374.

158 Franklin CD, Martin MV, Clark A, Smith CJ, Hindle MO. An investigation into the origin and nature of "amyloid" in a calcifying epithelial odontogenic tumour. J Oral Pathol 1981, **10**: 417–429.

159 Kramer IRH, Pindborg JJ, Shear M. Histological typing of odontogenic tumours, ed. 2. In World Health Organization: International Histological Classification of Tumours. Berlin, 1992, Springer-Verlag.

160 Pindborg JJ. The calcifying epithelial odontogenic tumor. Review of the literature and report of an extra-osseous case. Acta Odontol Scand 1966, **24**: 419–430.

161 Ranlov P, Pindborg JJ. The amyloid nature of the homogeneous substance in the calcifying epithelial odontogenic tumour. Acta Pathol Microbiol Scand 1966, **68**: 169–174.

162 Takeda Y, Suzuki A, Sekiyama S. Peripheral calcifying epithelial odontogenic tumor. Oral Surg Oral Med Oral Pathol 1983, **56**: 71–75.

163 Vap DR, Dahlin DC, Turlington EG. Pindborg tumor. The so-called calcifying epithelial odontogenic tumor. Cancer 1970, **25**: 629–636.

Squamous odontogenic tumor

164 Baden E, Doyle J, Mesa M, Fabie M, Lederman D, Eichen M. Squamous odontogenic tumor. Report of three cases including the first extraosseous case. Oral Surg Oral Med Oral Pathol 1993, **75**: 733–738.

165 Goldblatt LI, Brannon RB, Ellis GL. Squamous odontogenic tumor. Report of five cases and review of the literature. Oral Surg Oral Med Oral Pathol 1982, **54**: 187–196.

166 Leventon GS, Happonen R-P, Newland JR. Squamous odontogenic tumor. Report of two cases and review of the literature. Am J Surg Pathol 1981, **5**: 671–677.

167 Pullon PA, Shafer WG, Elzay RP, Kerr DA, Corio RL. Squamous odontogenic tumor. Report of six cases of a previously undescribed lesion. Oral Surg Oral Med Oral Pathol 1975, **40**: 616–630.

Ameloblastic fibroma

168 Chuong R, Kaban LB. Diagnosis and treatment of jaw tumors in children. J Oral Maxillofac Surg 1985, **43**: 323–332.

169 Couch RD, Morris EE, Vellios F. Granular cell ameloblastic fibroma. Report of 2 cases in adults, with observations of its similarity to congenital epulis. Am J Clin Pathol 1962, **37**: 398–404.

170 Meyers AD, Poulson T, Pettigrew J, Clark M. Cystic ameloblastic fibroma. Ear Nose Throat J 1991, **70**: 729–732.

171 Trodahl JN. Ameloblastic fibroma. A survey of cases from the Armed Forces Institute of Pathology. Oral Surg Oral Med Oral Pathol 1972, **33**: 547–558.

172 van Wyk CW, van der Vyver PC. Ameloblastic fibroma with dentinoid formation/immature dentinoma. A microscopic and ultrastructural study of the epithelial-connective tissue interface. J Oral Pathol 1983, **12**: 37–46.

Odontoma

173 Dunlap CL, Fritlen TJ. Cystic odontoma with concomitant adenoameloblastoma. Oral Surg Oral Med Oral Pathol 1972, **34**: 450–457.

174 Gardner DG. The mixed odontogenic tumors. Oral Surg Oral Med Oral Pathol 1984, **58**: 166–168.

175 Jacobsohn PH, Quinn JH. Ameloblastic odontomas. Report of three cases. Oral Surg Oral Med Oral Pathol 1968, **26**: 829–836.

176 Kramer IRH, Pindborg JJ, Shear M. Histological typing of odontogenic tumours, ed. 2. In World Health Organization: International Histological Classification of Tumours. Berlin, 1992, Springer-Verlag.

177 McClatchey KD, Hakimi M, Batsakis JG. Retrotympanic odontoma. Am J Surg Pathol 1981, **5**: 401–404.

178 Olech E, Alvares O. Ameloblastic odontoma. Oral Surg Oral Med Oral Pathol 1967, **23**: 487–492.

179 Slootweg PJ. An analysis of the interrelationship of the mixed odontogenic tumors—ameloblastic fibroma, ameloblastic fibro-odontoma, and the odontomas. Oral Surg Oral Med Oral Pathol 1981, **51**: 266–276.

180 Takata T, Zhao M, Uchida T, Kudo Y, Sato S, Nikai H. Immunohistochemical demonstration of an enamel sheath protein, sheathlin, in odontogenic tumors. Virchows Archiv 2000, **436**: 324–329.

(Odontogenic) myxoma, myxofibroma, and fibroma

181 Allphin AL, Manigilia AJ, Gregor RT, Sawyer R. Myxomas of the mandible and maxilla. Ear Nose Throat J 1993, **72**: 280–284.

182 Barker BF. Odontogenic myxoma. Semin Diagn Pathol 1999, **16**: 297–301.

183 Barros RE, Dominguez FV, Cabrini RL. Myxoma of the jaws. Oral Surg Oral Med Oral Pathol 1969, **27**: 225–236.

184 de Villiers Slabbert H, Altini M. Peripheral odontogenic fibroma: a clinicopathologic study. Oral Surg Oral Med Oral Pathol 1991, **72**: 86–90.

185 Dunlap CL. Odontogenic fibroma. Semin Diagn Pathol 1999, **16**: 293–296.

186 Dunlap CL, Barker BF. Central odontogenic fibroma of the WHO type. Oral Surg Oral Med Oral Pathol 1984, **57**: 390–394.

187 Gardner DG. The peripheral odontogenic fibroma. An attempt at clarification. Oral Surg Oral Med Oral Pathol 1982, **54**: 40–48.

188 Handlers JP, Abrams AM, Melrose RJ, Danforth R. Central odontogenic fibroma: clinicopathologic features of 19 cases and review of the literature. J Oral Maxillofac Surg 1991, **49**: 46–54.

189 Hasleton PS, Simpson W, Craig RD. Myxoma of the mandible. A fibroblastic tumor. Oral Surg Oral Med Oral Pathol 1978, **46**: 396–406.

190 Heimdal A, Isacsson G, Nilsson L. Recurrent odontogenic fibroma. Oral Surg Oral Med Oral Pathol 1980, **50**: 140–145.

191 Moshiri S, Oda D, Worthington P, Myall R. Odontogenic myxoma: Histochemical and ultrastructural study. J Oral Pathol Med 1992, **21**: 401–403.

192 Odell EW, Lombardi T, Barrett AW, Morgan PR, Speight PM. Hybrid central giant cell granuloma and central odontogenic fibroma-like lesions of the jaws. Histopathology 1997, **39**: 165–171.

193 Wesley RK, Wysocki GP, Mintz SM. The central odontogenic fibroma. Oral Surg Oral Med Oral Pathol 1975, **40**: 235–245.

194 Zimmerman DC, Dahlin DC. Myxomatous tumors of jaws. Oral Surg Oral Med Oral Pathol 1958, **11**: 1069–1080.

Borderline tumors
Ameloblastoma
General and clinical features

195 Daramola JO, Ajaglae HA, Oluwasanmi JO. Ameloblastoma of the jaws in Nigerian children. A review of sixteen cases. Oral Surg Oral Med Oral Pathol 1975, **40**: 458–463.

196 Gardner DG. Peripheral ameloblastoma. A study of 21 cases, including 5 reported as basal cell carcinoma of the gingiva. Cancer 1977, **39**: 1625–1633.

197 Gorlin RJ. Odontogenic tumors. In Gorlin RJ, Goldman HM (eds): Thoma's oral pathology, ed. 6. St. Louis, 1970, Mosby.

198 Hoffman PJ, Baden E, Rankow RM, Potter GD. Fate of uncontrolled ameloblastoma. Oral Surg Oral Med Oral Pathol 1968, **26**: 419–426.

199 Larsson Å, Almrén H. Ameloblastoma of the jaws. Acta Pathol Microbiol Scand [A] 1978, **86**: 337–349.

200 Mehlisch DR, Dahlin DC, Masson JK. Ameloblastoma. A clinicopathologic report. J Oral Surg 1972, **30**: 9–22.

201 Radhika S, Nijhawan R, Das A, Dey P. Ameloblastoma of the mandible: Diagnosis by fine-needle aspiration cytology. Diagn Cytopathol 1993, **9**: 310–313.

202 Richardson JF, Greer RO. Ameloblastoma of mucosal origin. Arch Otolaryngol 1974, **100**: 174–175.

203 Sehdev MK, Huvos AG, Strong EW, Gerold FP, Willis GW. Ameloblastoma of maxilla and mandible. Cancer 1974, **33**: 324–333.

204 Vickers RA, Gorlin RJ. Ameloblastoma. Delineation of early histopathologic features of neoplasia. Cancer 1970, **26**: 699–710.

205 Wesley RK, Borninski ER, Mintz S. Peripheral ameloblastoma. Report of a case and review of the literature. J Oral Surg 1977, **35**: 670–672.

Morphologic features

206 Altini M, Slabbert HD, Johnston T. Papilliferous keratoblastoma. J Oral Pathol Med 1991, **20**: 46–48.

207 Burkes EJ Jr, Wallace DA. Granular cell ameloblastoma. J Oral Surg 1976, **34**: 742–744.

207a Collini P, Zuchini N, Vessecchia G, Guzzo M. Papilliferous keratoameloblastoma of mandible: a papillary ameloblastic carcinoma. Report of a case with a 6-year follow-up and review of the literature. Int J Surg Pathol 2002, **10**: 149–155.

208 Gorlin RJ. Odontogenic tumors. In Gorlin RJ, Goldman HM (eds): Thoma's oral pathology, ed. 6. St. Louis, 1970, Mosby.

209 Hartman KS. Granular-cell ameloblastoma. Oral Surg Oral Med Oral Pathol 1974, **38**: 241–243.

210 Higuchi Y, Nakamura N, Ohishi M, Tashiro H. Unusual ameloblastoma with extensive stromal desmoplasia. J Craniomaxillofac Surg **19**: 323–327, 1991.

211 Kramer IRH, Pindborg JJ, Shear M. Histological typing of odontogenic tumours, ed. 2. In World Health Organization: International Histological Classification of Tumours. Berlin, 1992, Springer-Verlag.

212 Nasu M, Takagi M, Yamamoto H. Ultrastructural and histochemical studies of granular-cell ameloblastoma. J Oral Pathol 1984, **13**: 448–456.

213 Richard BM, Thyveetil M, Sharif H, Athanasou NA. Ameloblastoma with stromal multinucleated giant cells. Histopathology 1994, **25**: 497–500.

214 Slabbert H, Altini M, Crooks J, Uys P. Ameloblastoma with dentinoid induction: Dentinoameloblastoma. J Oral Pathol Med 1992, **21**: 46–48.

Histochemical and immunohistochemical features

215 Altini M, Coleman H, Doglioni C, Favia G, Maiorano E. Calretinin expression in ameloblastomas. Histopathology 2000, **37**: 27–32.

216 Dina R, Marchetti C, Vallania G, Corinaldesi G, Eusebi V. Granular cell ameloblastoma – an immunocytochemical study. Pathol Res Pract 1996, **192**: 541–546.

217 Thesleff I, Ekblom P. Distribution of keratin and laminin in ameloblastoma. Comparison with developing tooth and epidermoid carcinoma. J Oral Pathol 1984, **13**: 85–96.

218 Vigneswaran N, Whitaker SB, Bodnick SD, Waldron CA. Expression patterns of epithelial differentiation antigens and lectin-binding sites in ameloblastomas: A comparison with basal cell carcinomas. Hum Pathol 1993, **24**: 49–67.

Electron microscopic features

219 Larsson Å, Almrén H. Ameloblastoma of the jaws. Acta Pathol Microbiol Scand [A] 1978, **86**: 337–349.

220 Mehlisch DR, Dahlin DC, Masson JK. Ameloblastoma. A clinicopathologic report. J Oral Surg 1972, **30**: 9–22.

221 Nasu M, Ishikawa G. Ameloblastoma. Light and electron microscopic study. Virchows Arch [A] 1983, **399**: 163–175.

222 Navarrete AR, Smith M. Ultrastructure of granular cell ameloblastoma. Cancer 1971, **27**: 948–955.

223 Tandler B, Rossi EP. Granular cell ameloblastoma. Electron microscopic observations. J Oral Pathol 1977, **6**: 401–412.

Spread and metastasis

224 Gorlin RJ. Odontogenic tumors. In Gorlin RJ, Goldman HM (eds): Thoma's oral pathology, ed. 6. St. Louis, 1970, Mosby.

225 Hoke HF Jr, Harrelson AB. Granular cell ameloblastomas with metastases to cervical vertebrae. Cancer 1967, **20**: 991–999.

226 Ikemura K, Tashiro H, Fujino H, Ohbu D, Nakajima K. Ameloblastoma of the mandible with metastasis to the lungs and lymph nodes. Cancer 1972, **29**: 930–940.

227 Kunze E, Donath K, Luhr HG, Engelhardt W, De Vivie R. Biology of metastasizing ameloblastoma. Pathol Res Pract 1985, **180**: 526–535.

228 Madiedo G, Choi H, Kleinman JG. Ameloblastoma of the maxilla with distant metastases and hypercalcemia. Am J Clin Pathol 1981, **75**: 585–591.

229 Phillips SD, Corio RL, Brem H, Mattox D. Ameloblastoma of the mandible with intracranial metastasis. A case study. Arch Otolaryngol Head Neck Surg 1992, **118**: 861–863.

230 Slootweg PJ, Müller H. Malignant ameloblastoma or ameloblastic carcinoma. Oral Surg Oral Med Oral Pathol 1984, **57**: 168–176.

231 White RM, Patterson JW. Distant skin metastases in a long-term survivor of malignant ameloblastoma. J Cutan Pathol 1986, **13**: 383–389.

Differential diagnosis

232 Coleman H, Altini M, Ali H, Doglioni C, Favia G, Maiorano E. Use of calretinin in the differential diagnosis of unicystic ameloblastomas. Histopathology 2001, **38**: 312–317.

233 Gardner DG. Plexiform unicystic ameloblastoma. A diagnostic problem in dentigerous cysts. Cancer 1981, **47**: 1358–1363.

234 Gardner DG, Corio RL. The relationship of plexiform unicystic ameloblastoma to conventional ameloblastoma. Oral Surg Oral Med Oral Pathol 1983, **56**: 54–60.

235 Gardner DG, Corio RL. Plexiform unicystic ameloblastoma. A variant of ameloblastoma with a low-recurrence rate after enucleation. Cancer 1984, **53**: 1730–1735.

236 Leider AS, Eversole LR, Barkin ME. Cystic ameloblastoma. A clinicopathologic analysis. Oral Surg Oral Med Oral Pathol 1985, **60**: 624–630.

237 Li T-J, Wu Y-T, Yu S-F, Yu G-Y. Unicystic ameloblastoma: a clinicopathologic study of 33 chinese patients. Am J Surg Pathol 2000, **24**: 1385–1392.

238 McMillan MD, Smillie AC. Ameloblastomas associated with dentigerous cysts. Oral Surg Oral Med Oral Pathol 1981, **51**: 689–696.

239 Vickers RA, Gorlin RJ. Ameloblastoma. Delineation of early histopathologic features of neoplasia. Cancer 1970, **26**: 699–710.

Malignant tumors
Ameloblastic carcinoma

240 Bruce RA, Jackson IT. Ameloblastic carcinoma. Report of an aggressive case and review of the literature. J Craniomaxillofac Surg 1991, **19**: 267–271.

241 Eversole LR. Malignant epithelial odontogenic tumors. Semin Diagn Pathol 1999, **16**: 317–324.

242 McClatchey KD. Tumors of the dental lamina. A selective review. Semin Diagn Pathol 1987, **4**: 200–204.

243 Müller S, Waldron CA. Primary intraosseous squamous carcinoma. Report of two cases. Int J Oral Maxillofac Surg 1991, **20**: 362–365.

244 Nagai N, Takeshita N, Nagatsuka H, Inoue M, Nishijima K, Nojima T, Yamasaki M, Hoh C. Ameloblastic carcinoma: Case report and review. J Oral Pathol Med 1991, **20**: 460–463.

Ameloblastic fibrosarcoma

245 Chomette G, Auriol M, Guilbert F, Delcourt A. Ameloblastic fibrosarcoma of the jaws—report of three cases. Clinico-pathologic, histoenzymological and ultrastructural study. Pathol Res Pract 1983, **178**: 40–47.

246 Nasu M, Matsubara O, Yamamoto H. Ameloblastic fibrosarcoma. An ultrastructural study of the mesenchymal component. J Oral Pathol 1984, **13**: 178–187.

247 Pindborg JJ. Pathology of the dental hard tissues. Philadelphia, 1970, W.B. Saunders.

248 Slater LJ. Odontogenic sarcoma and carcinosarcoma. Semin Diagn Pathol 1999, **16**: 325–332.

249 Sözeri B, Ataman M, Ruacan S, Gediköglu G. Ameloblastic fibrosarcoma. Int J Pediatr Otorhinolaryngol 1993, **25**: 255–259.

250 Tanaka T, Ohkubo T, Fujitsuke H, Tatematsu N, Oka N, Kojima T, Morishita Y, Yoshimi N, Mori H. Malignant mixed tumor (malignant ameloblastoma and fibrosarcoma) of the maxilla. Arch Pathol Lab Med 1991, **115**: 84–87.

Clear cell odontogenic carcinoma

251 Eversole LR, Belton CM, Hansen LS. Clear cell odontogenic tumor. Histochemical and ultrastructural features. J Oral Pathol 1985, **14**: 603–614.

252 Li T-J, Yu S-F, Gao Y, Wang E-B. Clear cell odontogenic carcinoma: a clinicopathologic and immunocytochemical study of 5 cases. Arch Pathol Lab Med 2001, **125**: 1566–1571.

253 Maiorano E, Altini M, Viale G, Piattelli A, Favia G. Clear cell odontogenic carcinoma: report of two cases and review of the literature. Am J Clin Pathol 2001, **116**: 107–114.

254 Milles M, Doyle JL, Mesa M, Raz S. Clear cell odontogenic carcinoma with lymph node metastasis. Oral Surg Oral Med Oral Pathol 1993, **76**: 82–89.

Other tumors and tumorlike conditions

255 Abdul-Karim FW, Ayala AG, Chawla SP, Jing B-S, Goepfert H. Malignant fibrous histiocytoma of jaws. A clinicopathologic study of 11 cases. Cancer 1985, **56**: 1590–1596.

256 Al-Ani S. Metastatic tumors to the mouth. J Oral Surg 1973, **31**: 120–122.

257 Arafat A, Ellis GL, Adrian JC. Ewing's sarcoma of the jaws. Oral Surg Oral Med Oral Pathol 1983, **55**: 589–596.

258 Berho M, Huvos AG. Central hyalinizing clear cell carcinoma of the mandible and the maxilla: a clinicopathologic study of two cases with an analysis of the literature. Hum Pathol 1999, **30**: 101–104.

259 Bertoni F, Dallera P, Bacchini P, Marchetti C, Campobassi A. The Istituto Rizzoli-Beretta experience with osteosarcoma of the jaw. Cancer 1991, **68**: 1555–1563.

260 Bertoni F, Present D, Marchetti C, Bacchini P, Stea G. Desmoplastic fibroma of the jaw. The experience of the Istituto Beretta. Oral Surg Oral Med Oral Pathol 1986, **61**: 179–184.

261 Bhambhani M, Lamberty BG, Clements MR, Skingle MR, Crisp AJ. Giant cell tumours in mandible and spine: A rare complication of Paget's disease of bone. Ann Rheum Dis 1992, **51**: 1335–1337.

262 Bhaskar SN, Bernier JL, Godby F. Aneurysmal bone cyst and other giant cell lesions of the jaws. Report of 104 cases. J Oral Surg 1959, **17**: 30–41.

263 Borello ED, Gorlin RJ. Melanotic neuroectodermal tumor of infancy. A neoplasm of neural crest origin. Cancer 1966, **19**: 196–206.

264 Brookstone MS, Huvos AG. Central salivary tumors of the maxilla and mandible: A clinicopathologic study of 11 cases with an analysis of the literature. J Oral Maxillofac Surg 1992, **50**: 229–236.

265 Chan CW, Kung TM, Ma L. Telangiectatic osteosarcoma of the mandible. Cancer 1986, **58**: 2110–2115.

266 Chan RC, Sutow WW, Lindberg RD, Samuels ML, Murray JA. Management and results of localized Ewing's sarcoma. Cancer 1979, **43**: 1001–1006.

267 Christensen RE Jr. Mesenchymal chondrosarcoma of the jaws. Oral Surg Oral Med Oral Pathol 1982, **54**: 197–206.

268 Clausen F, Poulsen H. Metastatic carcinoma to the jaws. Acta Pathol Microbiol Scand 1963, **57**: 361–374.

269 Cohen MA, Bender S, Struthers PJ. Hodgkin's disease of the jaws. Review of the literature and report of a case. Oral Surg Oral Med Oral Pathol 1984, **57**: 413–417.

270 Corwin J, Lindberg RD. Solitary plasmacytoma of bone vs. extramedullary plasmacytoma and their relationship to multiple myeloma. Cancer 1979, **43**: 1007–1013.

271 Dehner LP. Tumors of the mandible and maxilla in children. II. A study of 14 primary and secondary malignant tumors. Cancer 1973, **32**: 112–120.

272 Dehner LP, Sibley RK, Sauk JJ Jr, Vickers RA, Nesbit ME, Leonard AS, Waite DE, Neeley JE, Ophoven J. Malignant melanotic neuroectodermal tumor of infancy. Cancer 1979, **43**: 1389–1410.

273 Domboski ML. Eosinophilic granuloma of bone manifesting mandibular involvement. Oral Surg Oral Med Oral Pathol 1980, **50**: 116–123.

274 Eisenbud L, Sciubba J, Mir R, Sachs SA. Oral presentations in non-Hodgkin's lymphoma. A review of thirty-one cases. Part II. Fourteen cases arising in bone. Oral Surg Oral Med Oral Pathol 1984, **57**: 272–280.

275 Ellis GL, Abrams AM, Melrose RJ. Intraosseous benign neural sheath neoplasms of the jaws. Report of seven new cases and review of the literature. Oral Surg Oral Med Oral Pathol 1977, **44**: 731–743.

276 Ellis GL, Jensen JL, Reingold IM, Barr RJ. Malignant neoplasms metastatic to gingivae. Oral Surg Oral Med Oral Pathol 1977, **44**: 238–245.

277 Elzay RP, Mills S, Kay S. Fibrous defect (nonossifying fibroma) of the mandible. Oral Surg Oral Med Oral Pathol 1984, **58**: 402–407.

278 Flood TR, Mahajara BB, MacDonald DG, Giri DD. Central acinic carcinoma of the mandible: Report of a case. Br J Oral Maxillofac Surg 1991, **29**: 26–28.

279 Freedman PD, Kerpel SM. Epithelioid angiosarcoma of the maxilla. A case report and review of the literature. Oral Surg Oral Med Oral Pathol 1992, **74**: 319–325.

280 Garrington GE, Scofield HH, Cornyn J, Hooker SP. Osteosarcoma of the jaws. Analysis of 56 cases. Cancer 1967, **20**: 377–391.

281 Grätz KW, Makek M, Sailer HF. Malignant melanotic schwannoma of the oral cavity. Int J Oral Maxillofac Surg 1991, **20**: 236–238.

282 Hackney FL, Aragon SB, Aufdemorte TB, Holt GR, Van Sickels JE. Chondrosarcoma of the jaws: Clinical findings, histopathology, and treatment. Oral Surg Oral Med Oral Pathol 1991, **71**: 139–143.

283 Ida M, Nakamura T, Utsunomiya J. Osteomatous changes and tooth abnormalities found in the jaws of patients with adenomatosis coli. Oral Surg Oral Med Oral Pathol 1981, **52**: 2–11.

284 Inwards CY, Unni KK, Beabout JW, Sim FH. Desmoplastic fibroma of bone. Cancer 1991, **68**: 1978–1983.

285 Johnson RE, Scheithauer BW, Dahlin DC. Melanotic

neuroectodermal tumor of infancy. A review of seven cases. Cancer 1983, **52**: 661–666.

286 Kameyama Y, Maeda H, Nakane S, Maeda S, Takai Y, Fukaya M. Malignant schwannoma of the maxilla in a patient without neurofibromatosis. Histopathology 1987, **11**: 1205–1210.

287 Kanazawa H, Shoji A, Yokoe H, Midorikawa S, Takamiya Y, Sato K. Solitary plasmacytoma of the mandible. Case report and review of the literature. J Craniomaxillofac Surg 1993, **21**: 202–206.

288 Kapadia SB, Frisman DM, Hitchcock CL, Ellis GL, Popek EJ. Melanotic neuroectodermal tumor of infancy. Clinicopathological, immunohistochemical, and flow cytometry study. Am J Surg Pathol 1993, **17**: 566–573.

289 Kerscher A, Piette E, Tideman H, Wu PC. Osteochondroma of the coronoid process of the mandible. Report of a case and review of the literature. Oral Surg Oral Med Oral Pathol 1993, **75**: 559–564.

290 Komori A, Koike M, Kinjo T, Azuma T, Yoshinari M, Inaba H, Hizawa K. Central intravascular papillary endothelial hyperplasia of the mandible. Virchows Arch [A] 1984, **403**: 453–459.

291 Kratochvil FJ III, MacGregor SD, Budnick SD, Hewan-Lowe K, Allsup HW. Leiomyosarcoma of the maxilla. Report of a case and review of the literature. Oral Surg Oral Med Oral Pathol 1982, **54**: 647–655.

292 Landini G, Kitano M. Meningioma of the mandible. Cancer 1992, **69**: 2917–2920.

293 Langford A, Pohle HD, Reichart P. Primary intraosseous AIDS-associated Kaposi's sarcoma. Report of two cases with initial jaw involvement. Int J Oral Maxillofac Surg 1991, **20**: 366–368.

294 Lingen MW, Solt DB, Polverini PJ. Unusual presentation of a chondromyxoid fibroma of the mandible. Report of a case and review of the literature. Oral Surg Oral Med Oral Pathol 1993, **75**: 615–621.

294a Loducca SV, Mantesso A, de Oliveira EMF, de Araújo VC. Intraosseous rhabdomyosarcoma of the mandible: a case report. Int J Surg Pathol 2003, **11**: 57–60.

295 Lopez JI, Elizalde JM, Landa S. Central mucoepidermoid carcinoma. Report of a case and review of the literature. Pathol Res Pract 1993, **189**: 365–367.

296 Lukinmaa PL, Hietanen J, Söderholm AL, Lindqvist C. The histologic pattern of bone invasion by squamous cell carcinoma of the mandibular region. Br J Oral Maxillofac Surg 1992, **30**: 2–7.

297 Mark RJ, Sercarz JA, Tran L, Dodd LG, Selch M, Calcaterra TC. Osteogenic sarcoma of the head and neck. The UCLA experience. Arch Otolaryngol Head Neck Surg 1991, **117**: 761–766.

298 Martinez-Madrigal F, Pineda-Daboin K, Casiraghi A, Luna MA. Salivary gland tumors of the mandible. Ann Diagn Pathol 2000, **4**: 347–353.

299 Matt BJ. Aneurysmal bone cyst of the maxilla: Case report and review of the literature. Int J Pediatr Otorhinolaryngol 1993, **25**: 217–226.

300 McDaniel RK, Luna MA, Stimson PG. Metastatic tumors in the jaws. Oral Surg Oral Med Oral Pathol 1971, **31**: 380–386.

301 McGavran MH, Spady HA. Eosinophilic granuloma of bone. A study of twenty-eight cases. J Bone Joint Surg 1960, [Am] **42**: 979–992.

302 McGregor AD, MacDonald DG. Patterns of spread of squamous cell carcinoma to the ramus of the mandible. Head Neck 1993, **15**: 440–444.

303 Meyer I, Shklar G. Malignant tumors metastatic to mouth and jaws. Oral Surg Oral Med Oral Pathol 1965, **20**: 350–362.

304 Michaud M, Baehner RL, Bixler D, Kafrawy AH. Oral manifestations of acute leukemia in children. J Am Dent Assoc 1977, **95**: 1145–1150.

305 Miettinen M, Lehto V-P, Ekblom P, Tasanen A, Virtanen I. Leiomyosarcoma of the mandible. Diagnosis as aided by immunohistochemical demonstration of desmin and laminin. J Oral Pathol 1984, **13**: 373–381.

306 Mintz GA, Abrams AM, Carlsen GD, Melrose RJ, Fister HW. Primary malignant giant cell tumor of the mandible. Report of a

case and review of the literature. Oral Surg Oral Med Oral Pathol 1981, **51**: 164–171.

307 Mori H, Kakuta S, Yamaguchi A, Nagumo M. Solitary intraosseous neurofibroma of the maxilla: Report of a case. J Oral Maxillofac Surg 1993, **51**: 688–690.

308 Navas Palacios JJ. Malignant melanotic neuroectodermal tumor. Light and electron microscopic study. Cancer 1980, **46**: 529–536.

309 Pettinato G, Manivel JC, d'Amore ES, Jaszez W, Gorlin RJ. Melanotic neuroectodermal tumor of infancy. A reexamination of a histogenetic problem based on immunohistochemical, flow cytometric, and ultrastructural study of 10 cases. Am J Surg Pathol 1991, **15**: 233–245.

310 Pileri SA, Montanari M, Falini B, Poggi S, Sabattini E, Baglioni P, Bacchini P, Bertoni F. Malignant lymphoma involving the mandible: Clinical, morphologic, and immunohistochemical study of 17 cases. Am J Surg Pathol 1990, **14**: 652–659.

311 Present D, Bertoni F, Enneking WF. Osteosarcoma of the mandible arising in fibrous dysplasia. A case report. Clin Orthop 1986, **204**: 238–244.

312 Rabhan WN, Rosai J. Desmoplastic fibroma. Report of ten cases and review of the literature. J Bone Joint Surg [Am] 1968, **50**: 487–502.

313 Roca AN, Smith JL Jr, Jing B-S. Osteosarcoma and parosteal osteogenic sarcoma of the maxilla and mandible. Study of 20 cases. Am J Clin Pathol 1970, **54**: 625–636.

314 Ruark DS, Schlehaider UK, Shah JP. Chondrosarcomas of the head and neck. World J Surg 1992, **16**: 1010–1015.

315 Spahr J, Elzay RP, Kay S, Frable WJ. Chondroblastoma of the temporomandibular joint arising from articular cartilage. A previously unreported presentation of an uncommon neoplasm. Oral Surg Oral Med Oral Pathol 1982, **54**: 430–435.

316 Stafford R, Sonis S, Lockhart P, Sonis A. Oral pathoses as diagnostic indicators in leukemia. Oral Surg Oral Med Oral Pathol 1980, **50**: 134–139.

317 Takahashi K, Sato K, Kanazawa H, Wang XL, Kimura T. Mesenchymal chondrosarcoma of the jaw—report of a case and review of 41 cases in the literature. Head Neck 1993, **15**: 459–464.

318 Taylor BG, Etheredge SN. Hemangiomas of mandible and maxilla presenting as surgical emergencies. Am J Surg 1964, **108**: 574–577.

319 Thompson SH, Shear M. Fibrous histiocytomas of the oral and maxillofacial regions. J Oral Pathol 1984, **13**: 282–294.

320 Unni KK, Dahlin DC. Dahlin's Bone tumors: general aspects and data on 11,087 cases, ed. 5. Philadelphia, 1996, Lippincott-Raven.

321 Vigneswaran N, Boyd DL, Waldron CA. Solitary infantile myofibromatosis of the mandible. Report of three cases. Oral Surg Oral Med Oral Pathol 1992, **73**: 84–88.

Diseases of the temporomandibular joint

322 Blankestijn J, Panders AK, Vermey A, Scherpbier AJJA. Synovial chondromatosis of the temporo-mandibular joint. Report of three cases and a review of the literature. Cancer 1985, **55**: 479–485.

323 Gorlin RJ, Pindborg JJ, Cohen MM Jr. Syndromes of the head and neck, ed. 2. New York, 1976, McGraw-Hill.

324 Ishida T, Dorfman HD, Bullough PG. Tophaceous pseudogout (tumoral calcium pyrophosphate dehydrate crystal deposition disease). Hum Pathol 1995, **26**: 587–593.

325 Sanders B, McKelvy B. Osteochondromatous exostosis of the condyle. J Am Dent Assoc 1977, **95**: 1151–1153.

326 Shapiro BL. Disorders of the temporomandibular joint. In Gorlin RJ, Goldman HM (eds): Thoma's oral pathology, ed. 6. St. Louis, 1970, Mosby.

327 Warner BF, Luna MA, Robert Newland T. Temporomandibular joint neoplasms and pseudotumors. Adv Anat Pathol 2000, **7**: 365–381.

328 Yamakawa K, Iwasaki H, Ohjimi Y, Kikuchi M, Iwashita A, Isayama T, Naito M. Tumoral calcium pyrophosphate dihydrate crystal deposition disease. A clinicopathologic analysis of five cases. Pathol Res Pract 2001, **197**: 499–506.

7 Respiratory tract

Nasal cavity, paranasal sinuses, and nasopharynx
Larynx and trachea
Lung and pleura

Nasal cavity, paranasal sinuses, and nasopharynx

Normal anatomy

The nasal cavity, paranasal sinuses, and nasopharynx form a functional unity that is reflected in the communality of the pathologic processes that involve the region. This is particularly the case for the first two components, which are often grouped under the term *sinonasal*.

The two main types of epithelia lining these structures are stratified squamous and respiratory-type pseudostratified columnar. The interphase between them is sharp in some areas, whereas in others there is an intervening zone of transitional (intermediate) epithelium. The latter resembles the transitional epithelium of bladder and other urothelia at the light microscopic but not at the ultrastructural level.[1]

Each of these epithelial types has its own distinctive cytokeratin profile as determined immunohistochemically.[1a]

Numerous submucosal seromucinous (salivary gland-type) glands are present throughout, being particularly numerous in the region of the eustachian tube opening in the nasopharynx. Focal oncocytic metaplasia of these glands is common with advancing age.

Collections of small lymphocytes are present submucosally throughout the nasopharynx, less so in the sinonasal region. In addition to the pharyngeal tonsil, they are abundant in the rim of the eustachian tube opening (Gerlach's tonsil).

Inflammatory ("allergic") polyp

Nasal polyps are not true neoplasms. Their formation is associated with inflammation, allergy, or mucoviscidosis.[2] Clinically, they appear as soft polypoid masses that extend laterally from the mucosa into the anterior part of the middle meatus.[9] Bilaterality is the rule. With time, they can fill the entire nasal cavity and even extend upward into the cranial cavity.[16] A morphologically similar type of polyp can be seen arising from one of the paranasal sinuses; this is referred to as *choanal polyp* and is subdivided according to its specific location into antrochoanal (the most common), sphenochoanal, and ethmoidochoanal.[3] Microscopically, the polyps are composed of a loose mucoid stroma and mucous glands and are covered by respiratory epithelium, which often exhibits foci of squamous metaplasia. They are infiltrated by lymphocytes, plasma cells, mast cells, neutrophils, and eosinophils.[7] Among the lymphocytes, there is a predominance of CD8+ (suppressor/cytotoxic) over CD4+ (helper/inducer) cells.[14] The eosinophils are immunoreactive for E62 (an activation marker), suggesting that they play a role in the pathogenesis of these polyps.[15] These eosinophils are not restricted to the polyps having a presumed allergic pathogenesis, although they are more numerous in them[5] (Fig. 7.1). Prominent thickening of the basal membrane is a common finding.

Occasionally, the stromal cells are large and pleomorphic, with bizarre hyperchromatic nuclei, and can simulate rhabdomyosarcoma or other malignancies[4,8,13] (Fig. 7.2). These cells are of a reactive nature and are similar to those sometimes seen in polyps of the oral cavity, vagina, and other mucosa-covered sites. Choanal polyps may show a prominent component of dilated vessels

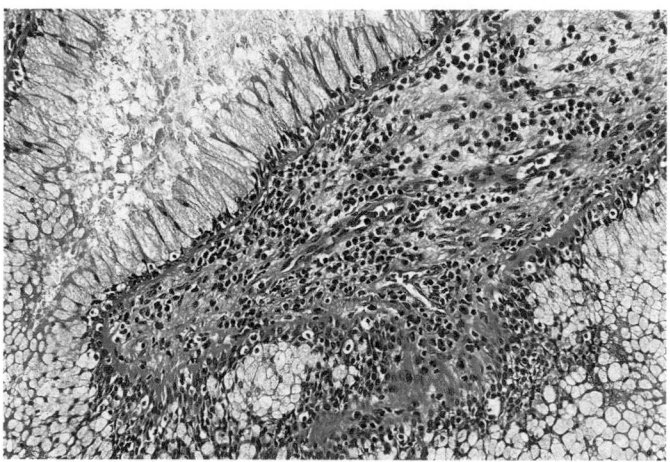

Fig. 7.1 Allergic nasal polyp showing a large number of eosinophils and hyperplasia of mucous glands.

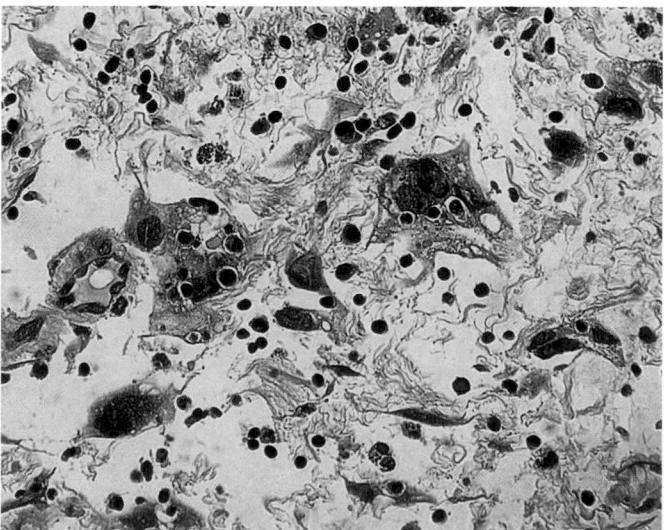

Fig. 7.2 Bizarre stromal cells in a nasal polyp, set against an edematous and inflammatory background.

("angiomatous or angiectatic polyps"), sometimes associated with thrombosis and infarct.[3,17]

From 6% to 10% of patients with mucoviscidosis (cystic fibrosis) develop polyps in the nasal cavity and paranasal sinuses. Therefore children presenting with nasal polyps should be investigated for this genetically determined condition. Microscopically, the polyps differ from the ordinary variety by the presence of large cystic glands with inspissated secretion in their lumina, lack of extensive infiltration by eosinophils, degranulation of mast cells, preponderance of neutral mucin, and lack of submucosal hyalinization.[6,11,12] Nasal polyps can also develop as a complication of mucopolysaccharoidosis (Hurler-Scheie syndrome).[10]

Local recurrence is common following the surgical removal of sinonasal polyps, probably because of persistence of the inciting pathogenetic factors.

Other inflammatory lesions

Chronic sinusitis has been traditionally divided into purulent and nonpurulent types. The maxillary sinus is by far the most commonly involved site. The disease is caused by various microbial organisms. The main microscopic features are inflammatory infiltrate, edema, glandular hyperplasia, basement membrane thickening, and squamous metaplasia.[44] Eosinophils may also be present and are occasionally numerous.[29] The underlying bone may show thickening and remodeling, with prominent osteoblastic rimming and fibrosis of the bone marrow spaces.

Mucocele of the maxillary sinus represents a complication of chronic sinusitis in which the accumulation of inflammatory exudate and the mucin secreted by the hyperplastic glands lifts the epithelial lining of the sinus and the periosteum away from the underlying bone. It is also sometimes referred to as *pseudocyst*.[28] The process gradually expands the cavity and causes destruction of contiguous bones to the point that it can be mistaken for a malignant neoplasm.[30]

Mycotic infections of the upper respiratory tract are usually located in the paranasal sinuses.[25] *Mucormycosis* is one of the most frequent. It usually occurs in association with poorly controlled diabetes mellitus, especially when complicated with ketoacidosis. It is also seen in the immunocompromised population. The infection may spread rapidly to involve orbit and brain ("invasive fungal sinusitis"). Characteristically, the organisms invade blood vessels and cause thrombosis, hemorrhage, and infarction.[34]

Allergic fungal sinusitis is a term used for an infection of the sinus caused by *Aspergillus*, *Curvularia*, or other fungal organisms that results in the formation of so-called allergic mucin, made up of pools of mucin-containing eosinophils, numerous Charcot–Leyden crystals, and fungal hyphae.[21,32,45,46]

Rhinosporidiosis is an inflammatory disease endemic in India, but it has also been reported in other parts of the world.[48] It is characterized by hyperplastic polypoid lesions of the nasal cavity and—rarely—other mucous membranes. The diagnosis is readily made by the identification of numerous globular cysts measuring up to 200 nm in diameter (Fig. 7.3). Each of these cysts represents a thick-walled sporangium containing numerous spores. The precise nature of this organism remains enigmatic.[18]

Tuberculosis can involve the nasal cavity, nasopharynx, or paranasal sinuses. Many of the cases are associated with cervical lymphadenopathy; most seem to represent an isolated upper respiratory tract infection rather than secondary spread from pulmonary infection.[49]

Sarcoidosis may first present with nasal manifestations and may result in perforation of the septum.[23,40]

Scleroma (rhinoscleroma) is an inflammatory disease of the nose, pharynx, and larynx caused by an organism of the *Klebsiella* group. Microscopically, the predominant cells are foamy macrophages and plasma cells (Fig. 7.4).

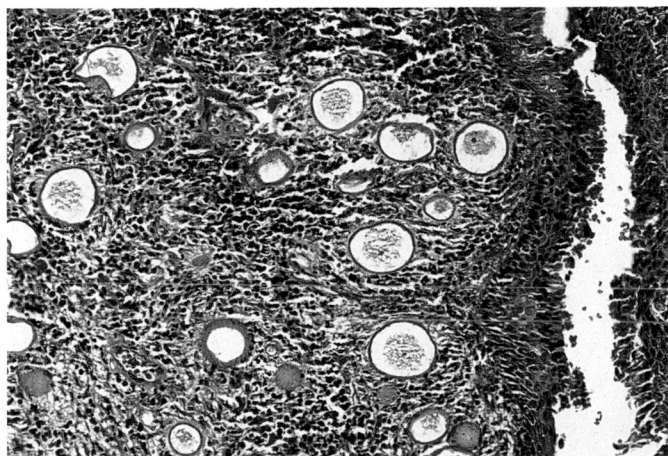

Fig. 7.3 Rhinosporidiosis. Large globular cysts are present surrounded by a heavy inflammatory reaction.

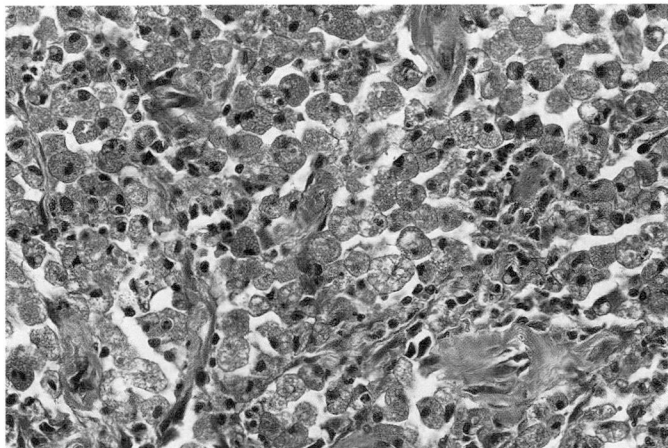

Fig. 7.4 Rhinoscleroma. The infiltrate is mainly of histiocytic character, some of the cells having foamy features. The main differential diagnosis is with nasal involvement by Rosai-Dorfman disease.

Vasculitis, ulceration, and pseudoepitheliomatous hyperplasia may be present.[20] The organisms can be identified using periodic acid-Schiff (PAS) or Hotchkiss–McManus stains or by an immunocytochemical technique.[38]

Rosai–Dorfman disease (sinus histiocytosis with massive lymphadenopathy) can affect various head and neck sites, including the nasal cavity (in the form of polyps), paranasal sinuses, and nasopharynx. Concomitant cervical nodal involvement may or may not be present.[27,50]

Wegener's granulomatosis in its classic form is a rapidly progressive condition in which nasal involvement is accompanied by pulmonary and renal disease. Microscopically, a leukocytoclastic vasculitis with geographic necrosis surrounded by palisaded histiocytes, lymphocyte-poor granulomatous reaction, and epithelial ulceration is seen.[22,36,37]

In one series,[26] vasculitis, necrosis, and granulomatous inflammation *together* were seen in only 16% of the biopsy specimens; both vasculitis and granulomatous inflammation were seen in 21%, and vasculitis and necrosis in 23%. In another series,[24] the nasal biopsy was diagnostic of Wegener's granulomatosis in 53% of the patients; samples larger than 5 mm in greatest diameter were more likely to contain diagnostic features than were smaller samples. Elastic tissue stains are helpful in identifying remnants of badly damaged vessels. Wegener's granulomatosis should be distinguished from tuberculosis and other specific infections; from malignant lymphoma, whether conventional or angiocentric (see p. 319); so-called eosinophilic angiocentric fibrosis (see below); cocaine-induced lesions[48a]; and from other immune-mediated diseases, such as lupus erythematosus.[42]

It should be remembered that Wegener's granulomatosis is not a lymphocyte-rich process, whether in the upper respiratory tract or in the lung; therefore a biopsy from the sinonasal region containing a dense lymphocytic infiltrate renders such a diagnosis unlikely, and the alternative possibility of a malignant lymphoma is a real one.[39]

Eosinophilic angiocentric fibrosis is an inflammatory disease of unknown cause characterized by a perivascular "onion-skin" fibrosis and a mixed inflammatory infiltrate rich in eosinophils. There are no granulomas, necrosis or vasculitis. It has been viewed as the mucosal counterpart of granuloma faciale and can involve any portion of the upper respiratory tract.[19,41,45]

Granulomas of foreign body-type can develop in nasal mucous membranes after local steroid injections.[52] They contain an amorphous foreign material in their center. **Cholesterol granulomas** of the paranasal sinuses of unknown etiology have been reported by Coup et al.[23]

Myospherulosis is another iatrogenically induced granulomatous condition of the nose and paranasal sinuses.[33] It is a form of lipogranuloma that develops

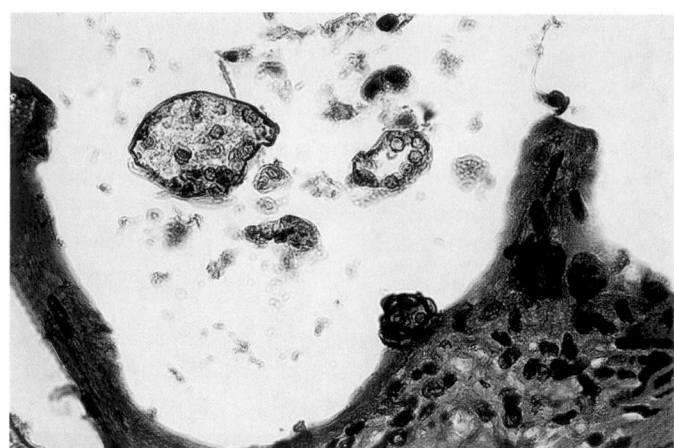

Fig. 7.5 Myospherulosis of paranasal sinus following an operation in the region for fibromatosis. A "bag" containing round structures is seen floating in a tissue cavity surrounded by fibrous tissue.

after hemostatic packing with petrolatum-based ointments and gauze, and it is microscopically analogous to a disease previously described in the subcutaneous tissues of East Africans.[35] Microscopically, its distinctive feature is the presence of large tissue spaces containing saclike structures with brown "spherules" resembling fungi (Fig. 7.5). It turns out that these mysterious formations are simply erythrocytes that have been altered and clumped by the action of the petrolatum.[31,43,48]

Tumors

Sinonasal papilloma

Sinonasal papillomas are benign neoplasms of the respiratory mucosa most commonly presenting in adult men with nasal stuffiness, nasal obstruction, or epistaxis. They can also occur in children.[56] In rare cases, they may extend into the cranial cavity.[74] Many adjectives have been attached to them, such as inverted, cylindrical cell, transitional, squamous, and schneiderian[55,75,79,80] (Fig. 7.6). Excluded from this group are the verrucous hyperkeratotic squamous papillomas arising from the stratified squamous epithelium lining the nasal vestibule, which are analogous to tumors occurring elsewhere in the skin. In contrast to inflammatory polyps, sinonasal papillomas are unilateral in the large majority of cases.[61] Microscopically, the papillomas are composed of proliferating columnar and/or squamous epithelial cells, with an admixture of mucin-containing cells and numerous microcysts[68,71] (Fig. 7.7). Some tumors are partially or entirely composed of swollen, granular, eosinophilic cells with features of oncocytes[53] (Fig. 7.8). Occasional mitoses are present in the basal layer. Atypia is mild to moderate, and there is an orderly maturation pattern. The tumor cells are able to synthesize secretory component and to take up IgA and IgM.[63] The dual composition

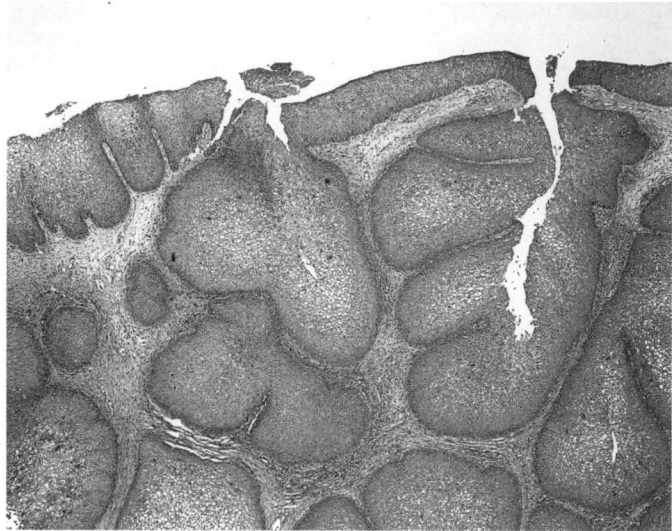

Fig. 7.6 Sinonasal papilloma with inverted pattern of growth.

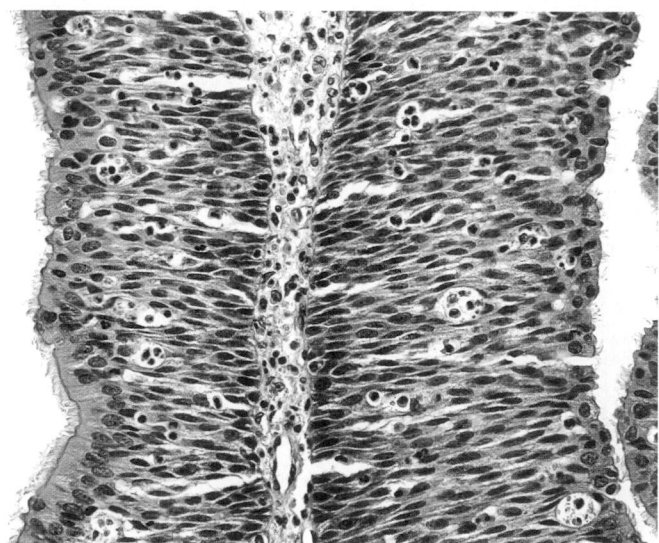

Fig. 7.7 Stratified lining by cylindrical cells in sinonasal papilloma.

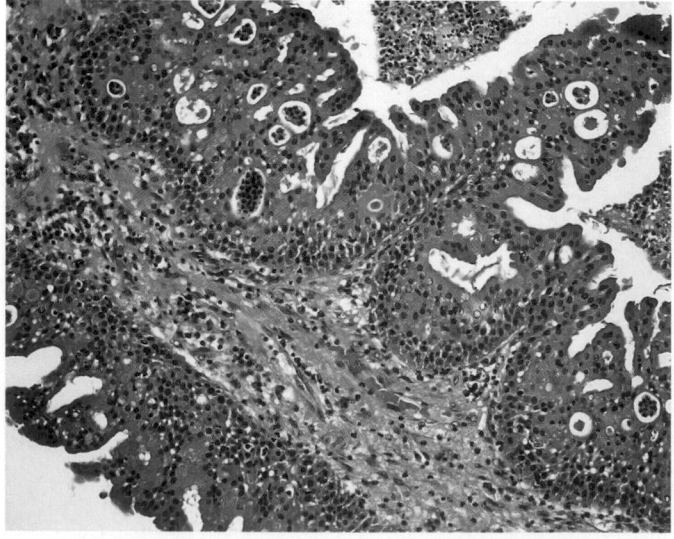

Fig. 7.8 Sinonasal papilloma lined by oncocytic epithelium.

of columnar and squamous cells is also apparent at the immunohistochemical level, in the sense that there is expression of keratin corresponding to both cell types.[77]

The papillomas arising in the nasal septum are usually exophytic and mushroom-shaped ("fungiform" or "everted"), with a thin central core of connective tissue[72] (Fig. 7.9). Those located in the lateral wall (middle meatus or middle or inferior turbinate) are of the inverted type, with inward growth of the epithelium into the stroma. The latter feature can be misinterpreted as invasion and the lesion incorrectly diagnosed as carcinoma.

Sinonasal papillomas have a tendency to recur, this feature being particularly common with the inverted type.[68] They also have a complex and often misunderstood relationship with malignancy, which may manifest in three ways:

1 Development of obvious carcinoma months or years after the excision of a papilloma, with or without recurrences of the papilloma in the interim.[64,70] This event occurs in about 3% of all papillomas and is associated with a 25% survival rate.
2 Presence of focal invasive carcinoma in an otherwise typical papilloma at the time of the first excision.[54,73] This complication, seen in about 3% of the cases, is associated with an excellent prognosis.[57]
3 Occurrence of a tumor having a pattern of growth very similar to that of papilloma but with subtle cytologic features indicative of malignancy (see p. 310).[68] The survival rate for this group is as poor as for carcinoma after papilloma (that is, in the neighborhood of 25%).

The potential for malignant transformation exists in all papilloma subtypes, including those composed of oncocytic epithelium.[67]

Many studies have been done in recent years with in situ hybridization or polymerase chain reaction (PCR) techniques demonstrating the presence of human papilloma virus (HPV) in sinonasal papillomas, even if the detection rate varied considerably.[59,60,62,66,76,78] HPV 6/11 has been the type most often detected.[58] In several of the series the incidence of positivity was notably higher for the fungiform than for the inverted papillomas, which often show histologic evidence of viral infection in the form of koilocytosis.[60,62] Despite early claims to the contrary,[65] it would seem that Epstein–Barr virus (EBV) is not present in sinonasal papillomas.[60]

The treatment of sinonasal papillomas is surgical removal. Computed tomography (CT) scanning is being increasingly used in management planning. The standard therapy is lateral rhinotomy and en bloc excision of the lateral nasal wall, followed by removal of all the mucosa in the ipsilateral paranasal sinuses.[69]

Sinonasal carcinoma

General features

Sinonasal carcinoma is an unusual tumor responsible for less than 1% of cancer deaths in the United States.[90] A marked left-sided preponderance has been noted for ethmoid tumors, suggestive of an exogenous pathogenesis.[89] An occupational group known to be at an increased risk is nickel refiners.[90] Studies from Europe, Australia, and North America have shown that another profession at risk is that of woodworkers, with most of the tumors in this group being adenocarcinomas.[83,85,86,87] In contrast to sinonasal papilloma, only a small minority of the carcinomas of this region that have been investigated for evidence of HPV infection have yielded positive results.[82,84] They also lack evidence of EBV infection, whether their histology is that of squamous cell carcinoma or undifferentiated carcinoma.[81,88]

Location and spread

Intranasal carcinomas occur more commonly in the vestibule and lateral wall and only rarely in the septum.[93–95] In one series of paranasal sinus tumors, 76% occurred in the ethmoid sinus, 16% in the sphenoid sinus, and 2% in the frontal sinus.[92] Sinonasal carcinomas often are diagnosed late in their course, when extensive bone destruction is already present. Intranasal tumors may extend into the medial wall of the antrum, ethmoid sinuses, orbit, anterior skull bone, and upper lip. Tumors of the infrastructure of the maxillary sinus spread inferiorly into the alveolar process or gingivobuccal sulcus, anteriorly into the soft tissues of the cheek beneath the zygoma, or medially into the nasal cavity and hard palate. Those of the suprastructure may extend superiorly and medially into the orbit, ethmoid sinus, and cribriform plate; posterolaterally into the pterygoid space, sphenoid sinus, or base of the skull; anterolaterally into the zygoma; or posterolaterally into the infratemporal fossa.[91]

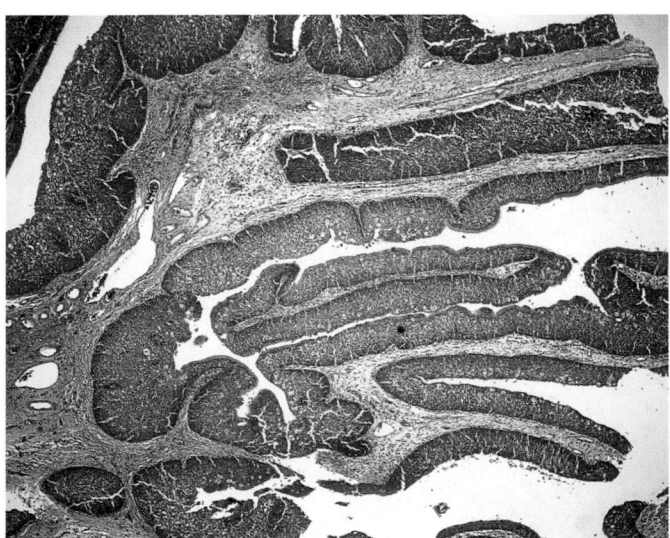

Fig. 7.9 Sinonasal papilloma with everted pattern of growth.

Microscopic features

Squamous cell carcinoma is the most common microscopic type of sinonasal carcinoma, as already showed in the monumental study by Ringertz in 1938.[115] Most of the cases are high-grade lesions, with varying degrees of keratinization[98] (Fig. 7.10).

Cylindrical (transitional) cell carcinoma is closely related to squamous cell carcinoma. Foci of intracellular mucin production may be present. In most instances the microscopic diagnosis is obvious because of the atypicality and stromal infiltration. In others the identification is more difficult because the growth pattern is similar to that of a papilloma in the sense that stromal invasion is not immediately apparent. The differential diagnosis must be made on the basis of cellular abnormalities, such as gross disturbance of polarity and atypical nuclear changes[109,112] (Fig. 7.11). However, mitoses and some degree of nuclear hyperchromasia also can be present in benign lesions. In rare cases these cylindrical cell carcinomas have been found to have focal *yolk saclike* features.[108]

The differential diagnosis of squamous cell or cylindric cell carcinoma also includes the sometimes bizarre atypical epithelial changes that can develop following chemotherapy.[120]

Verrucous carcinoma, basaloid squamous cell carcinoma, and sarcomatoid carcinoma (spindle cell carcinoma, carcinosarcoma) are three types of malignant tumors that have been rarely observed in the sinonasal region. They are similar in all regards to their more common counterparts in the upper digestive tract and larynx.[114,118,119,121]

Adenocarcinoma without a specific salivary gland pattern usually arises on the middle turbinate or in the ethmoid sinus and from there extends laterally into the orbit and upward into the anterior cranial fossa. The majority seem to arise from the mucosal lining rather than from the subjacent glands.[103,111a] Microscopically, they show a wide range of differentiation and patterns, most of them having a well-differentiated tubulopapillary architecture[101,104] (Figs 7.12 and 7.13). Some of these tumors (referred to as colonic-type) have an appearance strongly reminiscent of colorectal carcinoma, including the presence of goblet cells[96,107,116] (Fig. 7.14). Others, referred to as enteric-type, resemble small intestinal

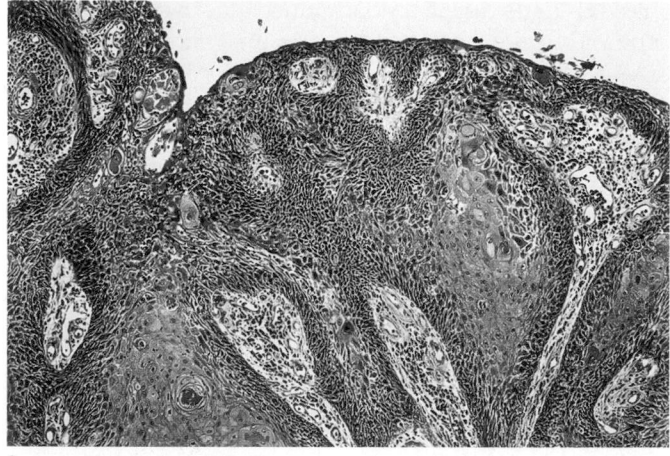

A

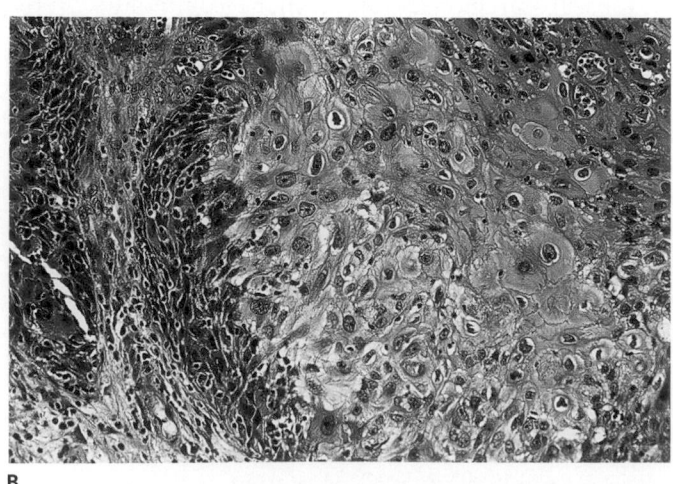

B

Fig. 7.10 Low- and high-power views of sinonasal squamous cell carcinoma.

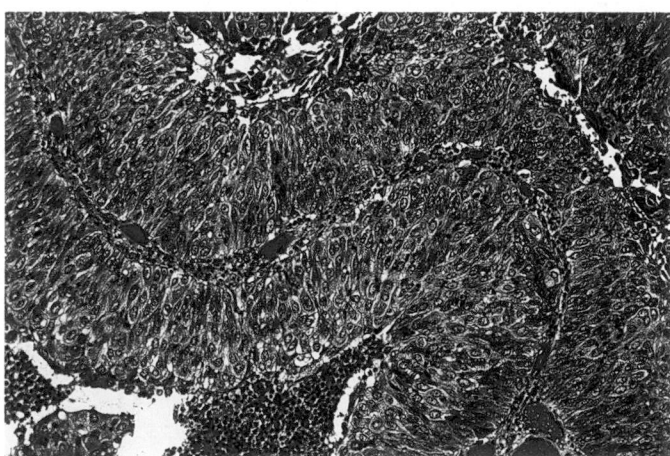

Fig. 7.11 Sinonasal carcinoma of "transitional" type. There is moderate but clearly evident nuclear atypia.

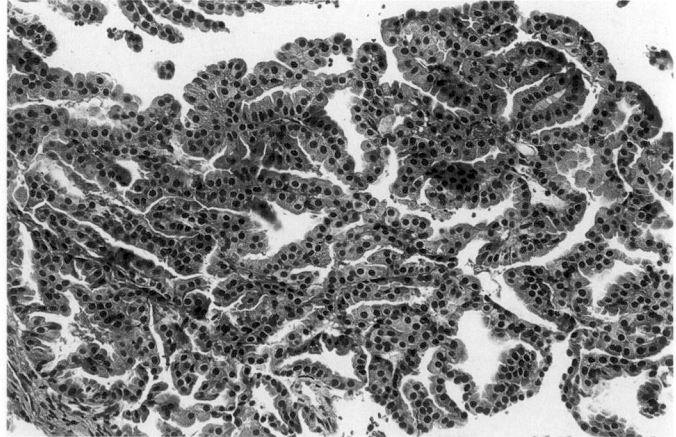

Fig. 7.12 Sinonasal adenocarcinoma with complex arborizing papillary pattern and extremely well differentiated cytologic appearance.

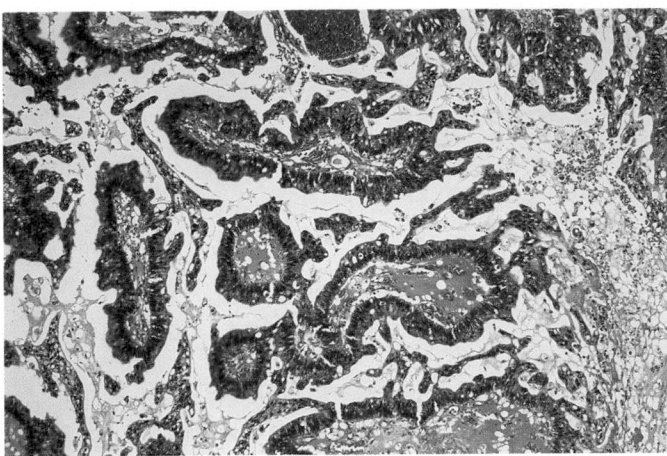

Fig. 7.13 Adenocarcinoma of the nasal cavity. The tumor is well differentiated and has a distinctly papillary configuration.

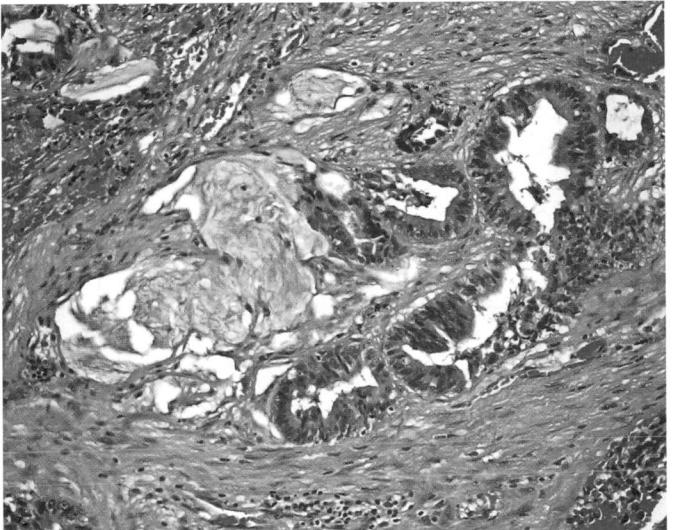

Fig. 7.14 Sinonasal adenocarcinoma of colonic type. Some of the mucin produced by the tumor has spilled into the stroma, resulting in a mucocele-like effect.

mucosa, with the formation of resorptive, goblet, Paneth, and argentaffin cells.[97,111,117] In rare cases the neuroendocrine component is present in the form of atypical carcinoid, resulting in the formation of a composite neoplasm.[99] The morphologic similarities with intestinal-type adenocarcinomas are not matched at the molecular level in terms of K-*ras* and p53 abnormalities.[122] Adenocarcinomas are locally aggressive tumors, with a propensity for local recurrence despite their well-differentiated nature.[111] Lymph node metastases are rare.

Small cell neuroendocrine carcinoma has a morphologic, immunohistochemical, and ultrastructural appearance similar to that of its pulmonary homolog.[113] The main differential diagnosis is with undifferentiated (anaplastic) carcinoma (see below) and with olfactory neuroblastoma (see p. 316).

Undifferentiated (anaplastic) carcinoma of the nasal cavity or paranasal sinuses is characterized microscopi-

cally by nests, trabeculae, and sheets of medium-sized cells having a high mitotic rate, extensive necrosis, and prominent vascular invasion.[106] These neoplasms, which (in contrast to the type just discussed) do not show evidence of neuroendocrine differentiation, are extremely aggressive.[100,102,105,110]

Differences in the keratin profile of these sinonasal carcinomas related to their microscopic subtype have been detected.[100a]

Treatment and prognosis

The recommended treatment for sinonasal carcinoma is a combination of surgery and radiation therapy.[128] The 5-year survival rates with this modality have been in the neighborhood of 60%.[123,124,133] Relapse occurs almost always within 2 years after the initial treatment.[130] As usual, the most important prognostic factor is tumor stage[124,131] (Appendix C). In a multivariate analysis of a large retrospective cohort, extension to the pterygomaxillary fossa and invasion of the dura remained independent prognostic factors.[124]

Histology-wise, it would seem that adenocarcinoma carries a slightly better prognosis than squamous cell carcinoma.[124] Among the adenocarcinomas, there is a relationship between degree of differentiation and prognosis.[125] Tubulopapillary tumors showing minimal atypia run an indolent clinical course.[126] The prognosis of undifferentiated (anaplastic) carcinoma is extremely poor.[127,129,132]

It has been claimed that the apoptotic index is an independent prognostic factor in sinonasal squamous cell carcinoma.[122a]

Nasopharyngeal carcinoma

General features

Carcinoma of the nasopharynx is a leading cause of death for large populations in southeast Asia and, to a lesser degree, in northern Africa.[134,140,159] The age-incidence curve is bimodal, with a peak occurring between 15 and 25 years and another between 60 and 69 years.[139,145,154] Cases showing familial aggregation have been reported both in the United States and in the Orient.[138] The accumulated evidence strongly suggests that this tumor results from the combined action of genetic predisposition, environmental factors, and the Epstein–Barr virus (EBV).[136,142,146–148] Specifically, it has been proposed that tumor initiation requires EBV expression but that the induction of preneoplastic events and maintenance of tumor-cell phenotype require critical cellular genes.[156]

Within the tumor, the EBV DNA is homogeneous and clonal with regard to repeat sequences.[151] Expression of specific viral messenger RNAs or gene products is consistently detected within all of the tumor cells.[135,153]

The virus can be demonstrated in the tumor tissue with in situ hybridization and immunohistochemical techniques, the former being the most reliable[155,157,158,160] (Fig.

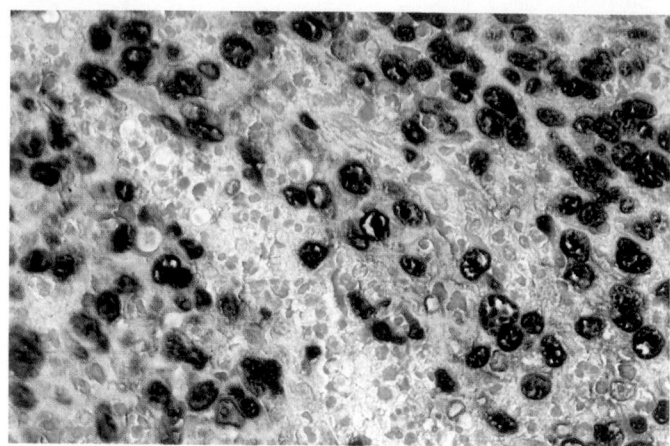

Fig. 7.15 Immunohistochemical demonstration of EBER in nasopharyngeal undifferentiated carcinoma.

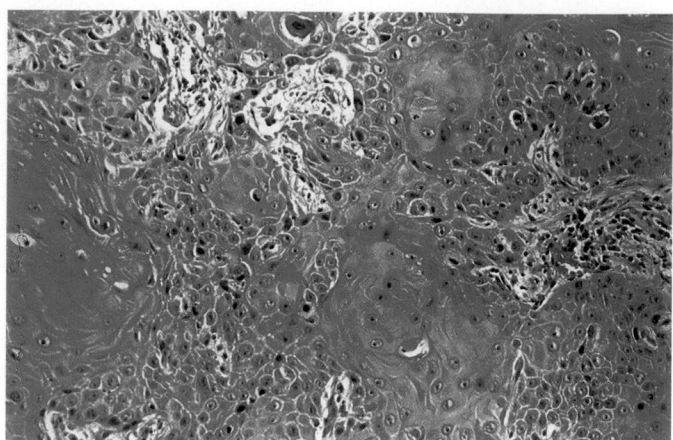

Fig. 7.16 Nasopharyngeal carcinoma of keratinizing squamous cell type. (From Shanmugaratuam K, Sobin LH. Histological typing of upper respiratory tract tumours. Geneva, 1978, World Health Organization)

7.15). It has also been detected with the PCR technique in material obtained by fine needle aspiration of metastatic cervical nodes.[141,150] The virus has been found in all microscopic types of nasopharyngeal carcinoma—including cases exhibiting glandular differentiation[144]—although with different frequencies (see below). The consistent detection of IgG antibodies (which are directed against the early EBV antigen) and of IgA antibodies (which are directed against the capsid viral antigen) has been used in the United States to support a presumptive diagnosis of nasopharyngeal carcinoma.[143,149,152] However, the presence of 30% false-positive results for the former test and 9% to 18% for the latter indicates that the diagnosis of nasopharyngeal carcinoma cannot be based solely on serologic tests. These tests have also been used in areas with a high incidence of nasopharyngeal carcinoma as a risk predictor. In one such study, carried out in Taiwan, in which almost 10,000 men were enrolled, blood samples were examined for IgA antibodies against EBV-specific capsid antigen and neutralizing antibodies against EBV-specific DNase. It was found that the risk for cancer development was 4.0 for subjects with one marker and 32.8 for subjects with both markers, as compared with subjects with neither marker.[137]

Gross features

Grossly, the tumor may be very difficult to detect. Random ("blind") biopsies from the nasopharyngeal area should be taken whenever the diagnosis is suspected, particularly from the fossa of Rosenmüller.[161]

Microscopic features

Microscopically, the crucial distinction to be made in nasopharyngeal carcinoma is between tumors that show clearcut evidence of keratinization and those that do not.[168] The former, designated **(keratinizing) squamous cell carcinomas**, do not show as high an association with EBV as the others and occur in an older age group[170,171] (Fig. 7.16). The tumors in the second category, which represent the large majority, have been designated

nonkeratinizing carcinomas and subdivided into *differentiated* and *undifferentiated*[162,167] (Figs 7.17 and 7.18). The former have a stratified or pavimented arrangement and well-defined cell margins, whereas the latter exhibit a syncytial appearance and indistinct cell margins. Some of the tumor cells may be spindle-shaped. A high proportion of these tumors (particularly in the undifferentiated subgroup) is accompanied by a prominent inflammatory infiltrate rich in lymphocytes, a fact responsible for the designation *lymphoepithelioma* that these neoplasms have traditionally received. The term is a misnomer inasmuch as the lymphocytic population is not neoplastic. As a matter of fact, it may be accompanied by other inflammatory cells, such as plasma cells, eosinophils,[166] and—on rare occasions—epithelioid and multinucleated giant cells; however, the term "lymphoepithelioma", inaccurate as it may be, should perhaps be retained in view of the characteristic appearance of this

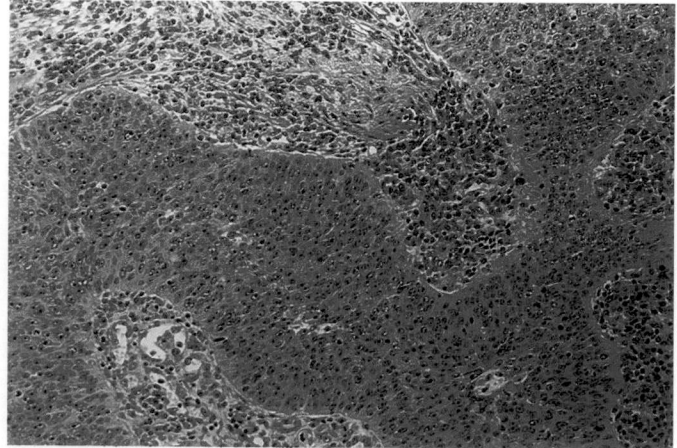

Fig. 7.17 Nasopharyngeal carcinoma of differentiated nonkeratinizing type. (From Shanmugaratuam K, Sobin LH. Histological typing of upper respiratory tract tumours. Geneva, 1978, World Health Organization)

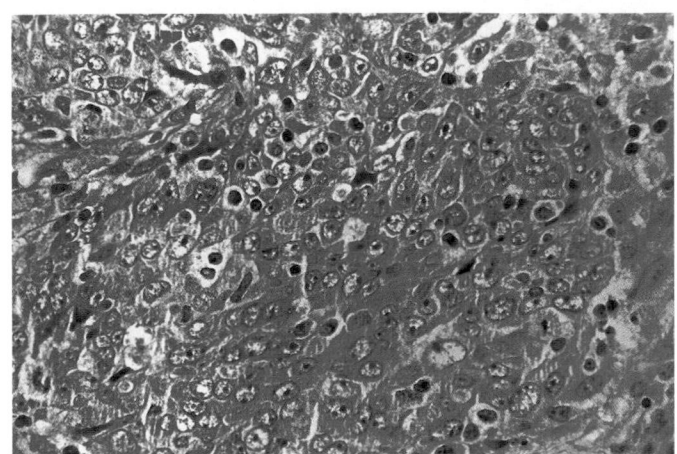

Fig. 7.18 Nasopharyngeal carcinoma of undifferentiated type. (From Shanmugaratuam K, Sobin LH. Histological typing of upper respiratory tract tumours. Geneva, 1978, World Health Organization)

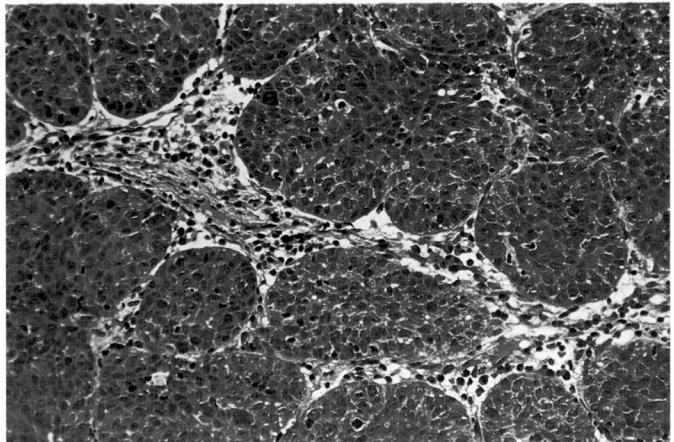

Fig. 7.19 Undifferentiated nasopharyngeal carcinoma composed of tumor cells arranged in compact nests (so-called "Regaud type"). (From Shanmugaratuam K, Sobin LH. Histological typing of upper respiratory tract tumours. Geneva, 1978, World Health Organization)

neoplasm, which is not properly addressed by any of the alternative names proposed.

Two patterns of growth may be seen, sometimes in combination. The first, inaccurately referred to as *Regaud's-type*, consists of well-defined aggregates of epithelial cells surrounded by fibrous tissue and lymphoid cells (Fig. 7.19). In the second, designated just as incorrectly as the *Schmincke-type*, the neoplastic epithelial cells grow diffusely and are closely intermingled with inflammatory cells. The latter type is apt to be confused with large cell malignant lymphoma (Fig. 7.20). Careful examination of the tumor cell nuclei should establish the diagnosis in most instances. The nuclei of nasopharyngeal carcinoma tend to be vesicular, with a smooth outline and a single, large, sharply etched eosinophilic nucleolus[165] (Fig. 7.20). The nuclei of malignant lymphoma are usually more irregularly shaped, the chromatin is coarser, and the nucleoli are smaller and either basophilic or amphophilic. Occasionally, the tumor cells have an oval or spindle shape (Fig. 7.21).

An in situ carcinoma component can be identified in only a minority of cases.[163] Even rarer but well documented is the nasopharyngeal carcinoma that is entirely in situ.[164] Amyloid deposition has been detected in a few cases in the tumor stroma.[169]

Rare microscopic forms of nasopharyngeal carcinoma include **basaloid squamous cell carcinoma**[173] and **papillary adenocarcinoma**.[172] The latter tumor is gland forming, papillary, mucin producing, immunoreactive for keratin and CEA, and associated with an excellent prognosis.[172]

Immunohistochemical features

Immunohistochemically, nasopharyngeal carcinoma (including the lymphoepithelioma-type) shows reactivity for keratin (always), epithelial membrane antigen (usually), and CEA (occasionally).[174,175,177,178] Thus keratin

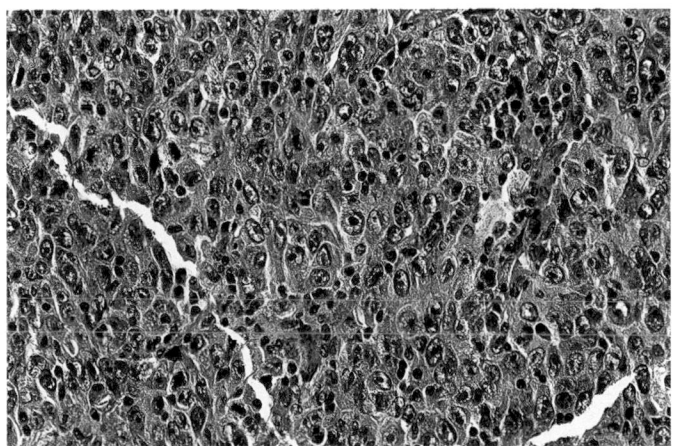

Fig. 7.20 Undifferentiated nasopharyngeal adenocarcinoma composed of cells growing in a diffuse "syncytial" pattern (so-called "Schmincke type").

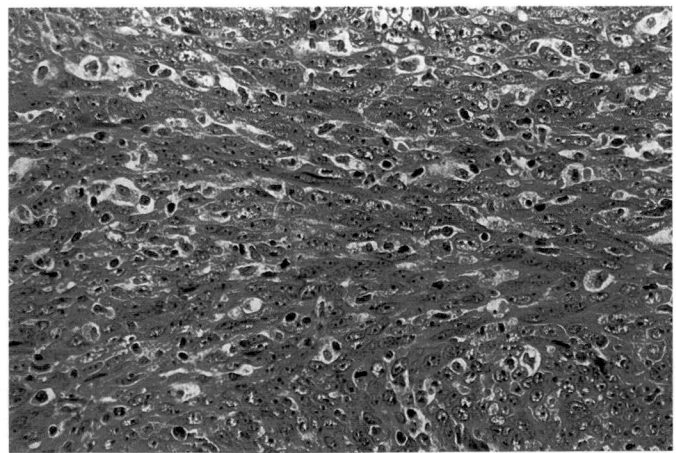

Fig. 7.21 Undifferentiated nasopharyngeal carcinoma composed of oval and spindle tumor cells.

is the most reliable marker for the identification of this neoplasm. A population of S-100 protein-positive dendritic cells may also be present.[176]

Electron microscopic features

Ultrastructurally, tonofilaments and complex desmosomes are present in the tumor cells.[184] The electron microscopic features suggest an origin from the cells of the basal layers of pseudostratified and stratified epithelia.[182]

Molecular genetic features

Nasopharyngeal carcinomas often show overexpression of the p53 product, a finding that seems to correlate with the presence of EBV infection.[181,183] They have also been shown frequently to lack the p16/MTS1 tumor suppressor protein, consistently to express the Rb gene product, and to show overrepresentation of c-myc and Int-2 often.[179,180]

Staging and grading

Several staging systems for nasopharyngeal carcinoma have been proposed. In a comparative study, it was concluded that the system devised by Ho was the best predictor of prognosis.[185]

Spread and metastases

Nasopharyngeal carcinoma arising from the fossa of Rosenmuller frequently extends to the paranasopharyngeal space, from which it can grow along the preneurial space of the trigeminal nerve.[189]

Nasopharyngeal carcinoma has a great propensity to metastasize to regional nodes; in fact, the appearance of unilateral cervical lymphadenopathy is the most common form of presentation. Microscopically, these nodal metastases may closely simulate a large cell lymphoma.[186] The focal (predominantly sinusal) nature of the involvement and the large vesicular nuclei with a single prominent nucleolus seen in metastatic carcinoma are useful features in the differential diagnosis. In some cases the metastatic tumor is accompanied by a marked infiltration by eosinophils, which may result in a mistaken diagnosis of Hodgkin's lymphoma.[187,191] In other cases the lymph node metastases are accompanied by a granulomatous reaction with varying degrees of necrosis[188] (Fig. 7.22). In yet others, it undergoes marked cystic changes, simulating a benign branchial cleft cyst (Fig. 7.23).

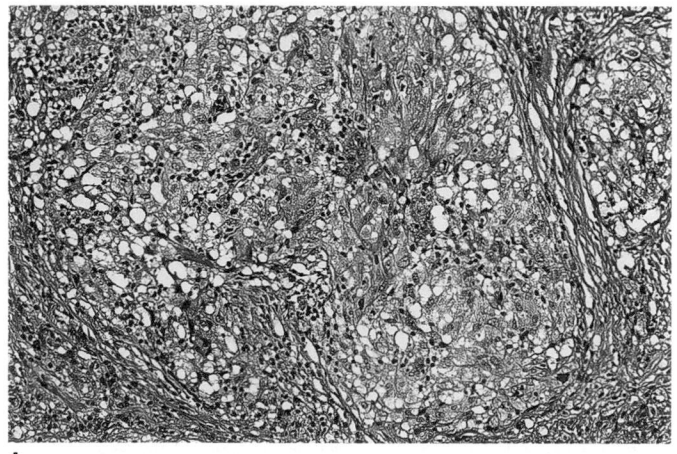
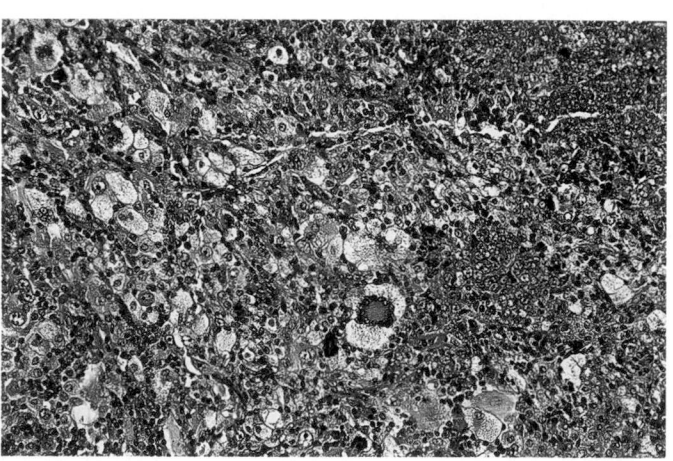

A   B

Fig. 7.22 A and **B**, Patterns of nasopharyngeal undifferentiated carcinoma metastatic to cervical lymph node: **A**, associated with granuloma formation; **B**, associated with xanthogranulomatous reaction.

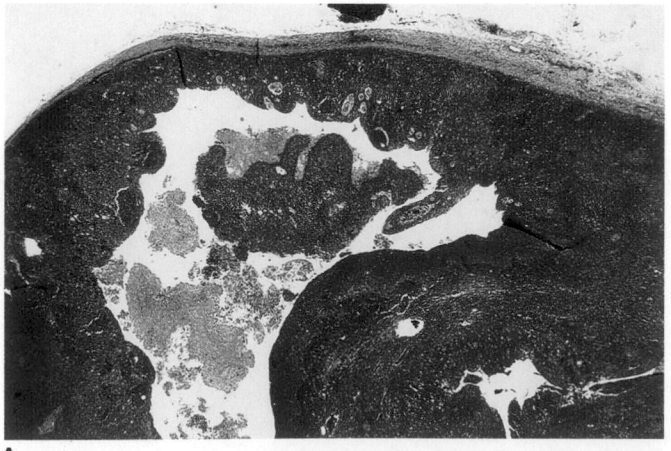
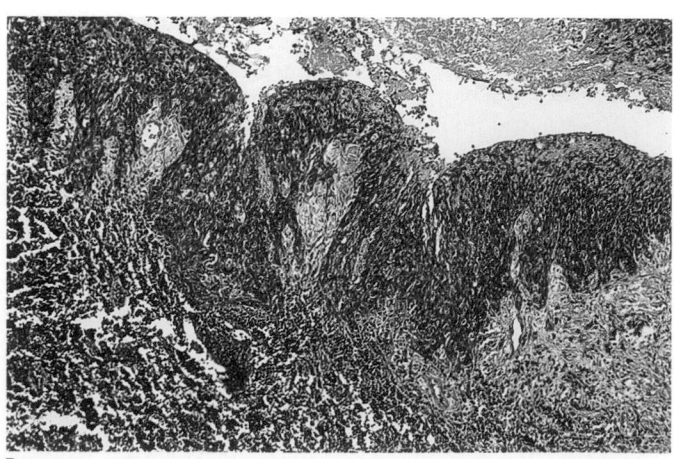

A   B

Fig. 7.23 A and **B**, Cystic metastasis of nasopharyngeal lymphoepithelioma to cervical lymph node simulating the pattern of growth of branchial cleft cyst.

Metastases can also develop in distant sites, such as the skeletal system.[190,192]

Treatment and prognosis

The treatment of choice for nasopharyngeal carcinoma is radiation therapy, which some authors suggest combining with chemotherapy.[200,204] In a series of over 5000 cases from Hong Kong, complete remission after radiation therapy was obtained in 83%; the overall actuarial 10-year survival rate was 43%, and the corresponding failure-free survival was 34%.[198] Survival is significantly affected by patient age (better in young individuals), clinical staging,[196,202] and the location of the regional metastases (better for homolateral rather than contralateral metastases and for metastases that are limited to the upper neck as opposed to the lower cervical regions).[193] Cranial nerve, orbit, and intracranial involvement confer a particularly unfavorable prognosis.[196] At a microscopic level, survival has been found to be worse for the keratinizing squamous cell carcinoma than for the others.[197,203] For the latter category, it has been claimed that the prognosis is worse for tumors exhibiting one or more of these features:

1 marked anaplasia and/or pleomorphism[195];
2 high cell proliferation rate (measured with mitotic count or with proliferation-related immunomarkers)[194];
3 lack of lymphocytic infiltrate[203];
4 high density of S-100 protein-positive dendritic cells[195,199];
5 high microvessel count[201];
6 presence of c-*erb* B-2 expression.[201]

Salivary gland tumors

Tumors of minor salivary gland origin occur in the nasal cavity as well as in the sinuses but much less commonly in the nasopharynx. Their relative frequency conforms to the density and distribution of the seromucous (salivary gland-type) glands of the region—hence their predilection for the nasal (septum and turbinates) or ostial regions.[212] Of the paranasal tumors, the majority are found in the antrum. Of 37 cases reviewed by Rafla,[214] 21 were in the antrum, nine in the ethmoid, five in the nasal fossa, and two in the sphenoid. Most tumors of the paranasal sinuses are malignant; **adenoid cystic carcinoma** is the most common variety.[209] In the nasal cavity there is a relatively high proportion of benign neoplasms in the form of **benign mixed tumor**. The large majority arise from the mucosa of the bony or cartilaginous septum.[206] Their microscopic appearance is similar to that of their homologs in the major salivary glands, but exceptionally they have been found to contain adult skeletal muscle.[211] Recurrence is rare. Rare cases of metastasizing benign mixed tumors of the nasal septum are on record.[208,215]

Several other types of salivary gland tumors have been reported in the sinonasal region, including **mucoepidermoid carcinoma**, **acinic cell carcinoma**, and

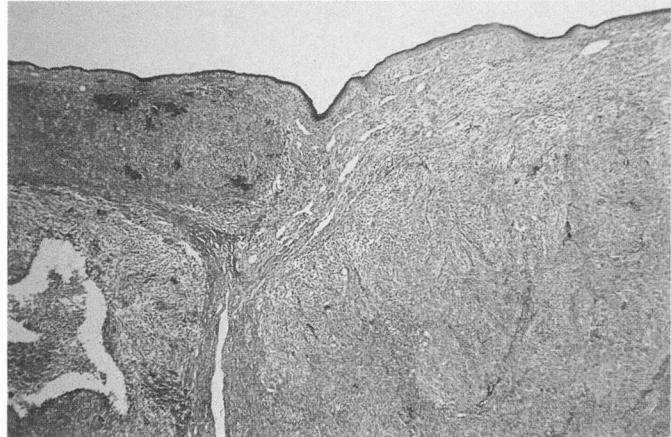

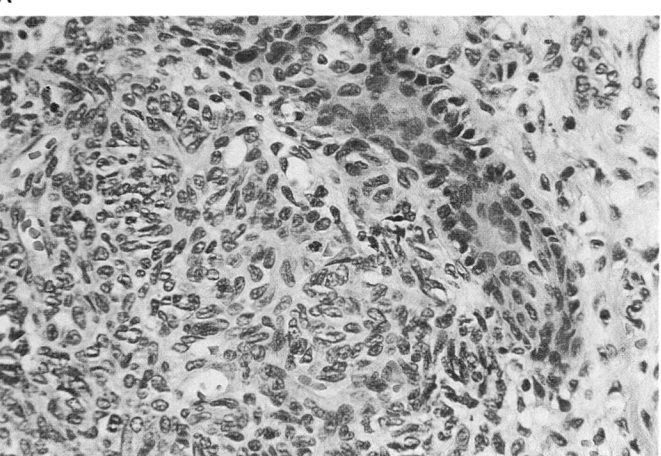

Fig. 7.24 A and **B**, Salivary gland anlage tumor. **A**, The solid, multinodular growth with a focal cyst is the characteristic appearance of this polypoid growth. **B**, A solid focus is composed of stromal cells with interspersed small duct-like structures. Solid or duct like structures adjacent to the nodules are typically present in the loose fibrous stroma between the solid nodules.

myoepithelioma.[205,211–213] Most are low-grade lesions, but local recurrence is a common event.[212] In contrast to the oral cavity, polymorphous low-grade carcinomas are very uncommon in the sinonasal region.

Salivary gland anlage tumor is the term proposed for a distinctive polypoid lesion of the nasopharynx that presents at birth or soon thereafter with respiratory distress. Microscopically, it is characterized by a biphasic pattern of squamous nests and duct like structures at the periphery of the lesion that blend into solid nodules centrally (Fig. 7.24). It is a benign, perhaps hamartomatous process, but it can be life-threatening because of its location.[207]

Neurogenous and related tumors and tumorlike conditions

Encephaloceles and **glial heterotopias** (commonly called *nasal gliomas*) are related malformational tumorlike conditions usually affecting newborns and older infants.[226] They may present as subcutaneous masses at the base of the nose or as intranasal polyps. Microscopically, they are composed of mature glial tissue, with occasional multinucleated glial cells that may simulate neurons (Fig. 7.25). Immunohistochemically, there is reactivity for both S-100 protein and GFAP.[239] In some cases a true neuronal component is also present.[250] Associated bony defects are the rule with the encephaloceles, but they are unusual with the glial heterotopias, a feature to be evaluated at the time of removal.

Meningiomas located intracranially may invade the sphenoid or frontal sinuses secondarily. They can also present as primary intranasal or paranasal masses.[233,258,267] The key diagnostic features are a whorled growth pattern, psammoma bodies, and a combined EMA and vimentin immunoreactivity.[270]

Astrocytomas and other glial tumors can also extend into the root of the nasal cavity from their initial intracranial location.[220,260]

Olfactory neuroblastoma (esthesioneuroblastoma) is a specific type of malignant neuroectodermal tumor thought to arise from neuroepithelial elements in the olfactory membrane or neuroectodermal elements of the olfactory placode.[225,252] In the normal human fetus this olfactory neuroepithelium extends from the roof of the nasal cavity to the midportion of the nasal septum and onto the superior turbinate in a continuous fashion. In adults many of these areas are replaced by respiratory epithelium.[251] Olfactory neuroblastoma shows a wide range of age distribution (3 to 79 years), the median age being about 50 years.[249] Grossly, the tumor appears as a reddish gray, highly vascular polypoid mass of generally soft consistency located in the roof of the nasal fossa. Rare cases have been described as arising in the nasopharynx, maxillary sinus, and ethmoid sinus.[245,252] Microscopically, several patterns have been described, which often merge with each other[228,255] (Fig. 7.26). The most easily recognizable

and common appearance is that of a cellular tumor composed of uniform small cells with round nuclei, scanty cytoplasm, indistinct nuclear membrane, and a prominent fibrillary or reticular background, similar to that seen in other neurogenic tumors (such as ganglioneuroblastoma) (Fig. 7.26C). Rosettes of the Homer Wright-type may be present, but differentiation into mature ganglion cells

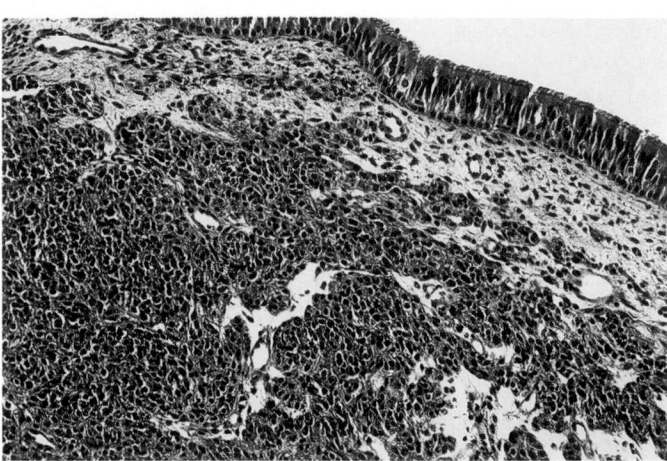

A

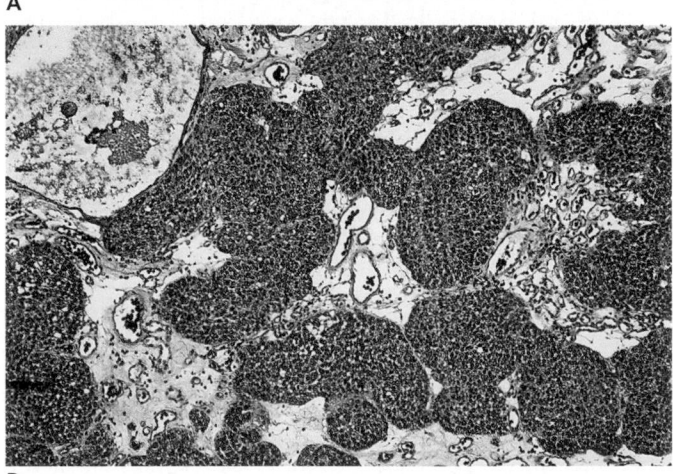

B

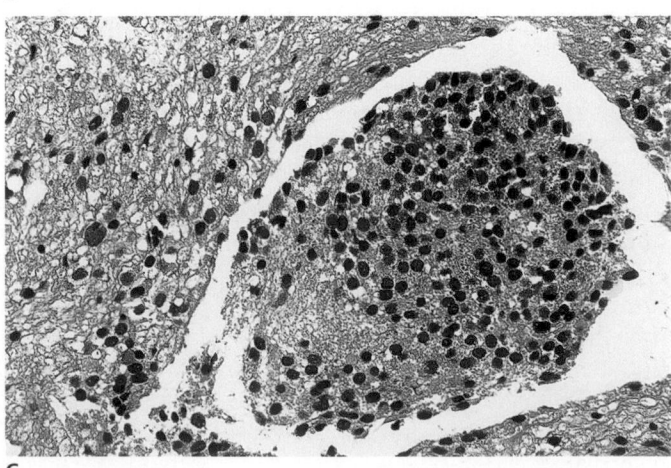

C

Fig. 7.26 A to **C,** Olfactory neuroblastoma. The pattern of growth is nesting in **A** and diffuse in **B.** The tumor depicted in **C** shows typical neurofibrillary background.

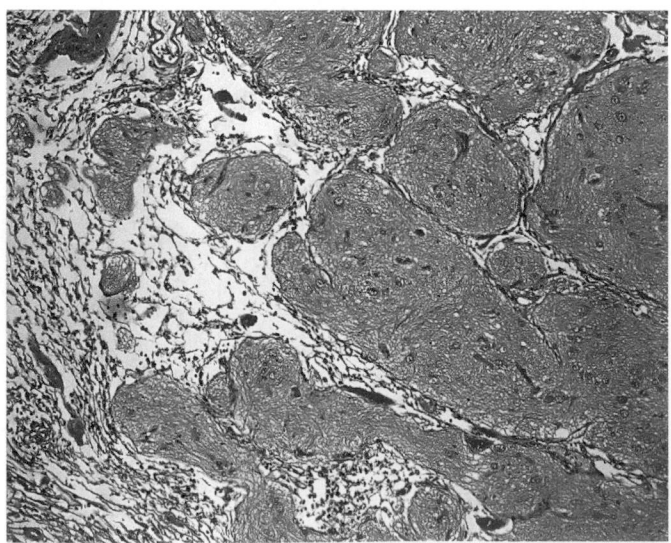

Fig. 7.25 Glial heterotopia in nasal cavity.

takes place only in rare cases.[221] Fibrovascular stroma may be abundant and separate the tumor cells in clusters. The vascular proliferation can be so florid as to obscure the true nature of the tumor[227] (Fig. 7.27). Melanin may in some cases be found in the cytoplasm of the tumor cells.[224] The differential diagnosis of tumors with this appearance is with malignant lymphoma, plasmacytoma, embryonal/alveolar rhabdomyosarcoma, and the Ewing sarcoma/PNET tumor family (see below).

In other examples the tumor cells are larger, have more abundant cytoplasm, and grow in solid nests, thus exhibiting an epithelial appearance. This type is often confused with undifferentiated carcinoma.[237] The suggestion has been made that these two patterns may correspond to two different tumor types, the former being similar (although not identical) to *neuroblastomas* and the latter representing *small cell neuroendocrine carcinomas* (Fig. 7.28)[263] (see p. 311). The fact that in some of these tumors there is a component of adenocarcinoma or

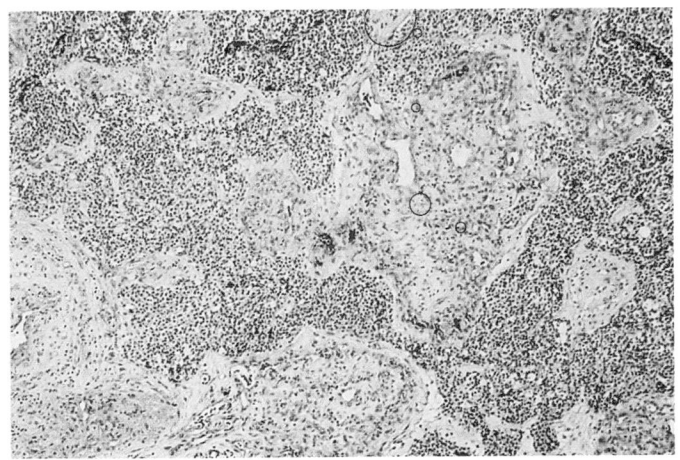

Fig. 7.27 Olfactory neuroblastoma associated with a striking lobular proliferation of blood vessels. This proliferation is a feature often seen in neuroepithelial and neuroendocrine neoplasms.

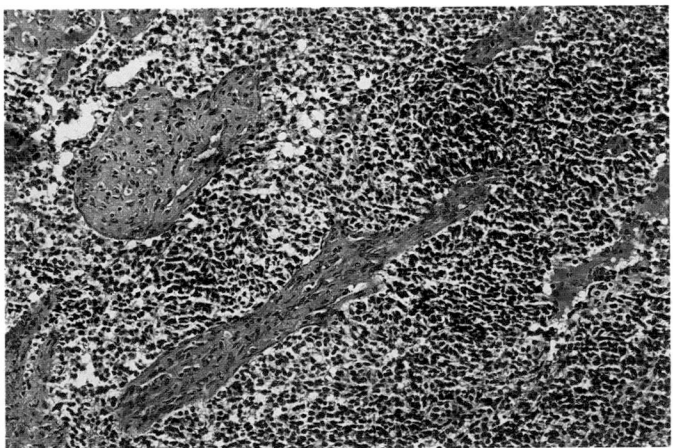

Fig. 7.28 Small cell carcinoma of the nasal cavity. The lesion is extremely cellular and monotonous, with no obvious evidence of neural differentiation.

squamous cell carcinoma would seem to support this contention.[244,248] Other authors have described a similar morphologic dichotomy but favored the existence of a spectrum of differentiation rather than the existence of two separate neoplasms, in view of the many shared ultrastructural and immunohistochemical features.[269] We have also observed "biphasic" cases which combined typical features of the two subtypes, suggesting a close histogenetic relationship. These considerations notwithstanding, we believe that in most cases the distinction between olfactory neuroblastoma and small cell neuroendocrine carcinoma is possible and that it should be attempted.[257]

Another contentious issue has been the relationship between olfactory neuroblastoma and tumors in the Ewing sarcoma/PNET family. Despite early claims to the contrary,[266] it would seem that olfactory neuroblastoma lacks the EWS/FLI1 gene fusion that characterizes the latter, and therefore it should be considered distinct from it.[218,240]

Catecholamines can be demonstrated in olfactory neuroblastoma by fluorescent techniques after formaldehyde vapor or glyoxylic acid treatment[232]; the enzyme dopamine β-hydroxylase and the hormone ACTH have been detected by biochemical and immunocytochemical methods.[247] Parenthetically, a case has been described of Cushing's syndrome secondary to olfactory neuroblastoma.[216] Other substances detected immunohistochemically in the tumor include neuron-specific enolase, chromogranin, neurofilaments, Hu, and keratin[219,223,269,271] (Fig. 7.29). In addition, S-100 protein has been found in isolated cells, often located at the edge of the tumor nests, and GFAP has been detected in scattered astrocyte-like cells.[223,269]

Electron microscopy shows the consistent presence of neurofilaments, neurotubules, and dense-core neurosecretory cytoplasmic granules and may be of considerable help in difficult cases.[241,243,268]

The behavior of olfactory neuroblastoma is mainly characterized by local invasiveness into the paranasal sinuses, nasopharynx, palate, orbit, base of skull, and brain.[229,246] Distant metastases occur in about one fifth of cases; the most common sites are the cervical lymph nodes and lungs.[234] The 5-year survival rate is between 50% and 66%.[222,254] Late recurrence is common.[217,252] This tumor has been shown to be radiosensitive, and a combination of surgery and radiation therapy offers the best chances of cure.[222,236,253] No convincing relationship has been shown between microscopic pattern or ultrastructural features and behavior.[249,254]

Carcinoid tumor has been found in rare cases to present as an intranasal tumor. One such case, in a child, had oncocytic features and was also associated with a bronchial carcinoid.[265]

Pituitary adenoma can present as a primary lesion of the nasopharynx or nasal cavity, presumably arising

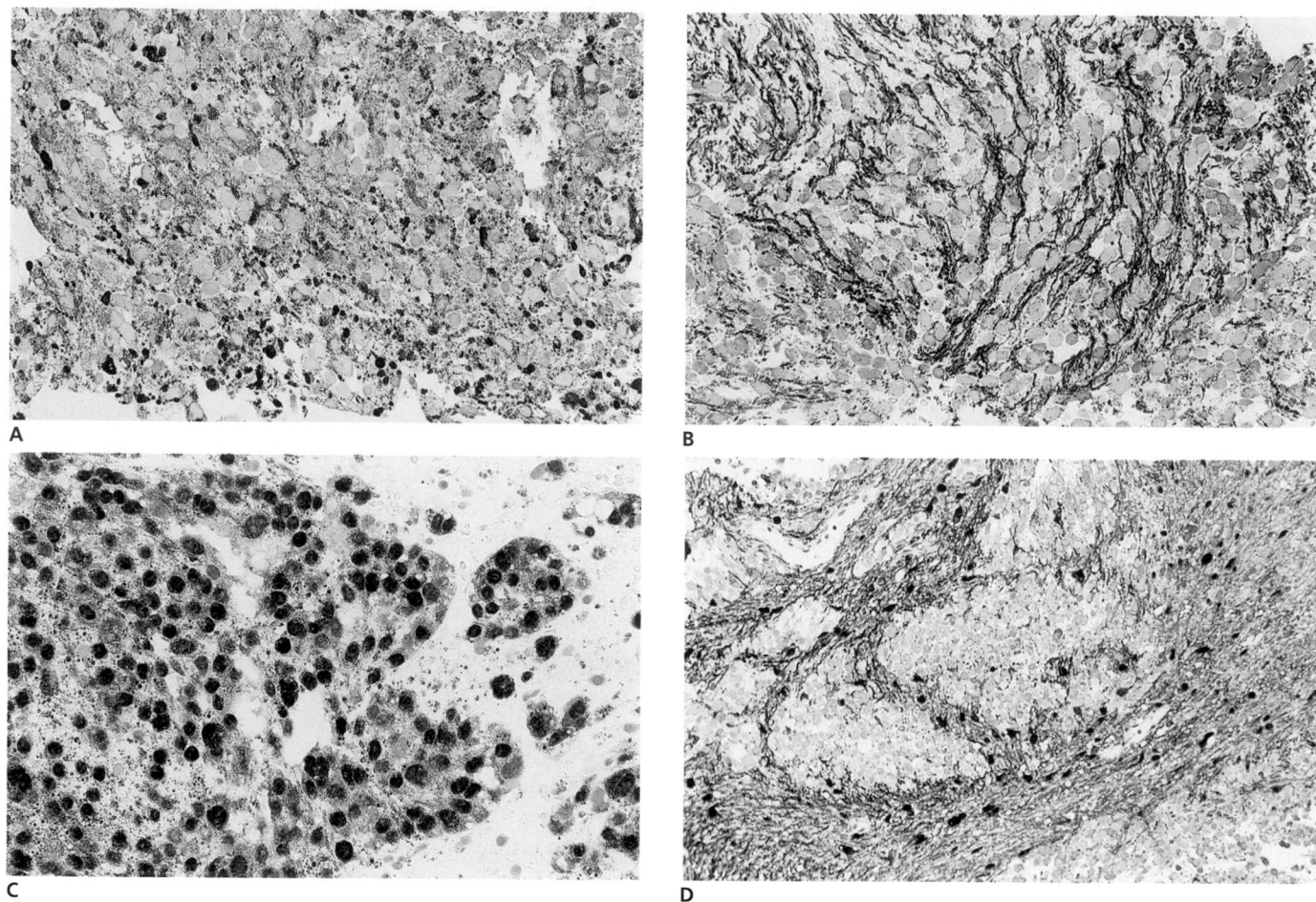

Fig. 7.29 A to **D**, Olfactory neuroblastoma: **A**, chromogranin; **B**, neurofilaments; **C**, Hu; **D**, S-100 protein.

from ectopic anterior pituitary-like cells. These tumors, which are typically of the chromophobe-type, should be distinguished from pituitary adenomas that have extended downward from the sella through the sphenoid bone.[235,238] One should suspect the diagnosis when confronted with a ribbony or rosettoid pattern of growth and a prominent delicate vascularized stroma.[242]

Paragangliomas have been reported both intranasally and in the nasopharynx.[256,261] One of the reported cases had an appearance similar to that of *gangliocytic paraganglioma* of the periampullary region, which we view as unrelated to true paraganglioma (see Chapter 11).[264]

Peripheral nerve tumors of the sinonasal region are extremely rare.[259,262] They presumably arise from the ophthalmic and maxillary branches of the trigeminal nerve and from branches of the autonomic nervous system. The most common type is the schwannoma, which may cause diagnostic problems because of hypercellularity and the fact that—in contrast to its more common counterpart in the soft tissue—it is often unencapsulated.[230] Neurofibromas (including the plexiform variety) and malignant peripheral nerve sheath tumors have also been observed.[231] Some of the latter have exhibited focal skeletal muscle differentiation ("Triton tumor").[231] Some peripheral nerve tumors occur in association with Recklinghausen's disease.

Tumors of melanocytes

Primary sinonasal malignant melanomas usually present as solid polypoid growths.[272,277,278] Their most common location is the nasal cavity, followed by antrum, ethmoid, and frontal sinuses.[277] They arise from melanocytes usually located in the epithelium and stroma of the respiratory mucosa.[279] One case has been reported arising from the mucosa of an inverted papilloma.[276] Most sinonasal melanomas are easily recognizable microscopically, but some can be missed because of their lack of pigmentation, pleomorphic features, or prominent spindle cell appearance[274,276,277] (Fig. 7.30). Occasional examples have shown prominent myxoid features,[273] and others have been accompanied by metaplastic bone formation.[275] The epithelial basal layer should be searched for the presence of theque-like growth or "junctional" activity.[274] Immunohistochemically, these tumors are reactive for vimentin, S-100 protein, and HMB-45, i.e. they have a profile similar to that of their cutaneous counterparts.[274] The prognosis is extremely poor, with most patients dying of metastatic tumor in less than 5 years.[274,277,278a]

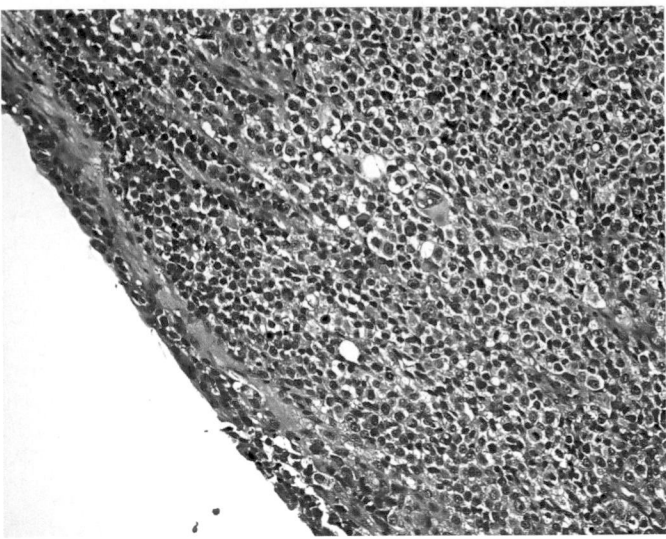

Fig. 7.30 Malignant melanoma of nasal cavity. The diffuse pattern of growth and lack of pigmentation often result in misdiagnoses.

Lymphoid tumors and tumorlike conditions

Malignant lymphoma can present initially as a mass in the sinonasal region or nasopharynx.[318,324] Nearly all cases are of non-Hodgkin-type[28,294,316] and the large majority fall into one of three categories: (1) natural killer (NK)/T-cell type; (2) B-cell type; (3) peripheral T-cell-type.[288] There is a marked geographic difference in their relative frequency: B-cell lymphomas predominate in series from the USA and Western Europe, whereas NK/T-cell lymphomas are prevalent in series from the Far East and Latin America.[283,288,289,296,322]

NK/T-cell lymphoma is a recently delineated distinct clinicopathologic entity, which is highly associated with EBV.[287,314] Morphologically, it is characterized by a broad cytologic spectrum, ranging from small or medium-sized to large transformed cells. Necrosis is nearly always present. Angioinvasion by tumor cells is a very frequent and diagnostically important feature, and this is sometimes accompanied by epitheliotropism reminiscent of that seen in mycosis fungoides. An admixture of reactive histiocytes, some exhibiting erythrophagocytosis, is a frequent feature, probably representing an expression of the virus-associated hemophagocytic syndrome.[310,312] Because of the remarkable pattern of blood vessel involvement, this type of lymphoma is sometimes referred to as *angiocentric lymphoma*. However, angiocentric growth is not always present in nasal NK/T-cell lymphoma, and it can also be seen in other types of lymphoma.[309] The immunophenotype of NK/T-cell lymphoma is characteristic: positive for CD2 and CD56, and usually negative for surface CD3.[299] Cytoplasmic CD3 can be detected in paraffin sections. There is no clonal rearrangement of the T-cell receptor gene. Tumors with a similar phenotype occurring at other extranodal sites (such as skin, subcutaneous tissue, and gastro-

intestinal tract) are referred to as nasal-type NK/T-cell lymphoma.[285] Blastoid and leukemic forms of this lymphoma occur.[286,303] CD56 positivity is a key diagnostic feature, but it should be kept in mind that this can also be seen in a variety of non-lymphoid neoplasms, including Ewing sarcoma/PNET.[302,305] It has been hypothesized that the necrotizing features of this tumor type are mediated by perforin and the Fas–Fas ligand (CD95/CD95L) mechanism.[310,312,313] There is also frequent overexpression of p53.[321a]

It has become apparent that a high percentage of cases of *lethal midline granuloma* (a clinical syndrome characterized by slowly progressive ulceration and destruction of the nose and paranasal cavities, with frequent erosion of the soft tissues, bone, and cartilage of the region) (Fig. 7.31) are due to NK/T-cell lymphoma.[298] In the past, these cases have received terms such as polymorphic

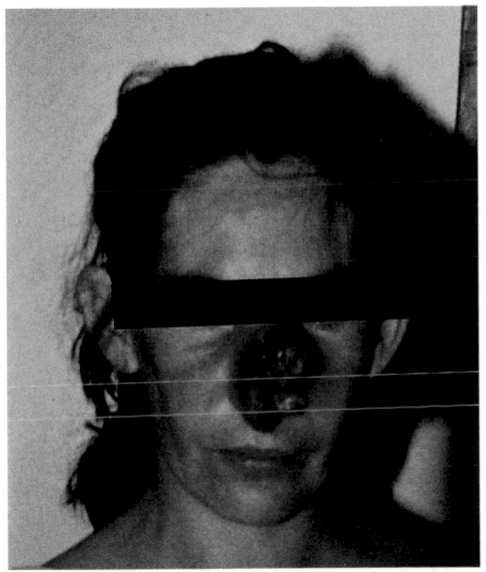

A

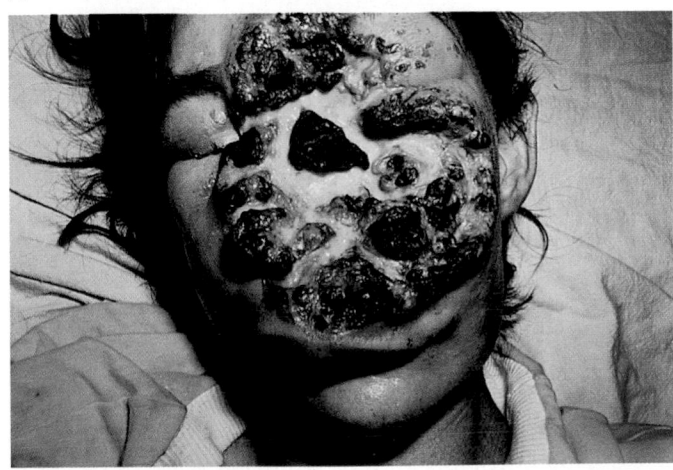

B

Fig. 7.31 A, A young female with clinical diagnosis of lethal midline granuloma. **B,** Same patient a few years later. There was no evidence of systemic disease at the time. This unfortunate individual died a few weeks after this second photograph was taken.

reticulosis,[282,284,291,292,298,316,320,322] malignant histiocytosis,[282] and midline malignant reticulosis.[292] Other cases having the clinical features of lethal midline granuloma represent particularly aggressive example of Wegener's granulomatosis. Still others have been found to be the result of cocaine abuse and are characterized microscopically by nonspecific inflammation and necrosis without vasculitis.[290,319]

Although nasal NK/T-cell lymphomas have been linked by some authors to pulmonary lymphomatoid granulomatosis (because of their angiocentric qualities and other shared morphologic features) under the term *angiocentric immunoproliferative lesion*,[291] this is no longer thought to be appropriate in view of the current belief that lymphomatoid granulomatosis is an EBV-linked B-cell lymphoma with a florid T-cell reaction (see Chapter 7).

B-cell lymphoma of the sinonasal region usually presents as a large cell lymphoma with a diffuse pattern of growth and a relatively monomorphic appearance. It is much more common in the paranasal sinuses than in the nasal cavity (an important point in the differential diagnosis with NK/T-cell lymphoma) and it constitutes the most common type of sinonasal lymphoma in the USA and Western Europe.[326] B-cell lymphomas with a diffuse undifferentiated (Burkitt-like) appearance are the predominant form of sinonasal lymphoma in the pediatric US population.[325]

Peripheral T-cell lymphoma does not express CD56 and usually lacks the necrotizing and angiocentric features of NK/T-cell lymphoma.[300] In contrast to the latter, it shows rearrangement of the T-cell receptor gene.[300]

The behavior of sinonasal lymphoma is difficult to assess because of the fact that one of its major types (NK/T-cell) has been only recently defined, that some of the reported series do not include a thorough immunophenotypic evaluation, and that many cases of NK/T-cell lymphoma go unrecognized for years. In the Far East (where NK/T-cell lymphoma predominates), about 70% to 80% of patients with sinonasal lymphoma present with stage IE or IIE disease, have a complete response rate of 75%, and a 2-year overall survival of 50%.[288] In one series from the USA (where B-cell lymphoma is prevalent), the overall survival rate was 52%.[306]

Plasmacytoma arising in the nasal cavity or nasopharynx may present primarily in the nose as a soft bleeding mass.[281,295,301,304] Microscopic examination shows a monomorphic infiltration by immature plasma cells.[284a] The majority of patients with apparently solitary plasma cell tumors of the upper air passages in whom there is adequate follow-up develop disseminated myeloma.[297] In some patients, this process takes 10 or more years to become manifest. Local control of the disease can usually be achieved with radiation therapy.[302]

Angiotropic (intravascular) lymphoma is not be confused with angiocentric lymphoma (see Chapter 21). In this condition, the neoplastic lymphocytes are predominantly within the lumen of the vessels rather than infiltrating the vessel wall. This unusual type of lymphoma can present initially as an intranasal lesion.[321]

Hodgkin's lymphoma presenting as a primary disease in this region is exceptional, but isolated cases of this occurrence have been reported.[308]

Granulocytic sarcoma has been seen limited to the sinonasal region and simulating malignant lymphoma in routinely stained sections.[293]

Pseudolymphoma (lymphoid hyperplasia) may present as a polypoid intranasal mass.[317]

Lymphoid lesions involving the nasopharyngeal tonsil are discussed together with those of the palatine tonsil in Chapter 5.

Nasopharyngeal angiofibroma

Nasopharyngeal angiofibroma occurs almost exclusively in males between 10 and 25 years of age[337]; however, well-documented cases in older patients and in females are on record. Several cases have been reported in patients with familiar colonic polyposis, but alterations of the APC gene have not been found in the tumors.[334] The great predilection for young males strongly suggests that this lesion is androgen-dependent, a theory confirmed by the fact that stromal and endothelial nuclear immunostaining for androgen receptors is found in 75% of cases; by contrast, very few are positive for progesterone receptors and none for estrogen receptors.[339] It has also been found that nasopharyngeal angiofibroma contains protein basic fibroblast growth factor (bFGF)[345] and that there is a strong nuclear expression of β-catenin.[349a]

This neoplasm arises from a distinctive erectile-like fibrovascular stroma located in the posterolateral wall of the roof of the nose, where the sphenoidal process of the palatine bone meets the horizontal ala of the vomer and the root of the pterygoid process of the sphenoid bone. Grossly, it presents as a polypoid mass that bleeds severely on manipulation and biopsy (Fig. 7.32). It can grow to occlude the involved nares completely. It may protrude below the free edge of the soft palate, extend into the antrum, and grow to the external orifice of the nares, posteriorly into the nasopharynx, or even into the orbit and cranial cavity.[336,337] Selective carotid arteriograms were often used to determine the gross confines of the tumor, but this method has been largely replaced by noninvasive techniques such as CT scan and MRI.

Microscopically, nasopharyngeal angiofibroma is composed of an intricate mixture of blood vessels and fibrous stroma (Fig. 7.33). The latter varies from loose and edematous, with stellate fibroblasts and numerous mast cells, to a dense, acellular, and highly collagenized tissue. The latter is particularly striking and diagnostic. The vessels range from capillary size to venous size; the larger vessels are located at the base of the lesion, whereas the smaller capillary-like vessels with plump endothelial cells are particularly common at the "growing edge" of

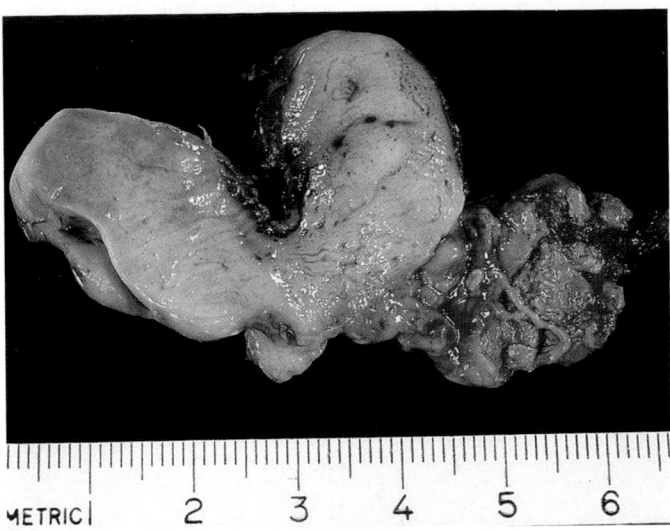

Fig. 7.32 Nasopharyngeal angiofibroma. The cut surface shows the characteristic spongy appearance and well-circumscribed outline.

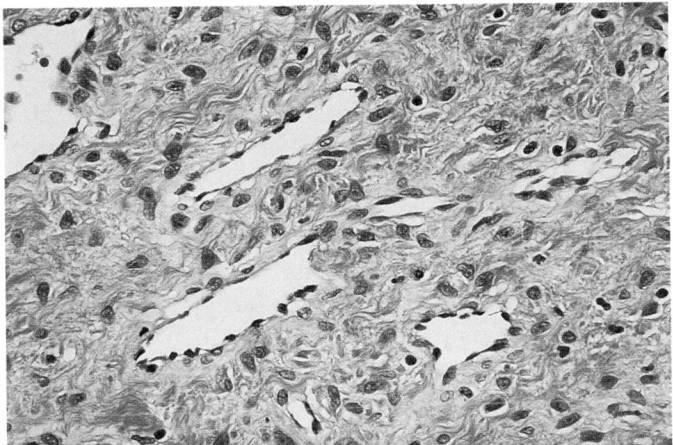

Fig. 7.33 Nasopharyngeal angiofibroma. The dense fibrous quality of the stroma and the numerous thin-walled vessels are characteristic of this entity.

the tumor.[327,347] The large vessels may have an irregular or incomplete smooth muscle coat, but they lack elastic fibers. It is important to distinguish angiofibromas from capillary hemangiomas because of the different natural history of these lesions. In general, hemangiomas are accompanied by a lesser amount of fibrous tissue, often showing some degree of lobulation, and their vessels do not have the "erectile tissue" appearance so characteristic of nasopharyngeal angiofibroma. Location of the tumor is very important in this regard; a diagnosis of angiofibroma should be questioned for any tumor not located in the area described in the preceding paragraph, and particularly for these limited to the nasal cavity. Ultrastructurally, distinctive electron-dense granules composed of tightly bound RNA–protein complexes have been found in the nuclei of the proliferating cells.[348]

There is no doubt that some large angiofibromas regress after puberty, especially after incomplete surgical removal or radiation therapy. Spontaneous total regres-

sion, however, is very rare;[331] in a patient with symptoms, treatment is indicated. There is controversy as to whether surgery or radiation is the treatment of choice, but most writers favor the use of surgery for early lesions.[329,330,340,343,349] Preoperative embolization is used in some cases.[335,344] Radiation therapy or even chemotherapy may be necessary for the more advanced and aggressive tumors.[332,333] Most of the post-therapy recurrences have developed within the first year.[341,342] Meticulous removal of the angiofibroma is essential to prevent recurrence, particularly the portion of the tumor which infiltrates the pterygoid canal and basisphenoid.[338] A few cases of sarcomatous transformation after radiation therapy have been described.[328,346]

Other tumors and tumorlike conditions

Dermoid cysts are dorsal developmental anomalies located in the midline. They may be associated with bony defects and sinus tracts.[376] They can extend intracranially and result in CNS infection.[354]

True teratomas have been reported in the sinuses and nasopharynx of infants and children. The large majority are benign.[376,400]

Nasal chondromesenchymal hamartoma is a benign and probably non-neoplastic process which presents as an intranasal and paranasal polypoid mass in infants and occasionally in older children.[379,382] It is composed microscopically of mature cartilage, myxoid stroma, and aneurysmal bone cystlike formations, and it has been regarded as the upper respiratory tract homolog of chest wall mesenchymal hamartoma (see Chapter 24).

Vascular tumors are relatively common and include a large variety of types. *Lobular capillary hemangioma* is a common tumor of the nasal cavity, where it can reach a large size (Fig. 7.34). This tumor is often misinterpreted

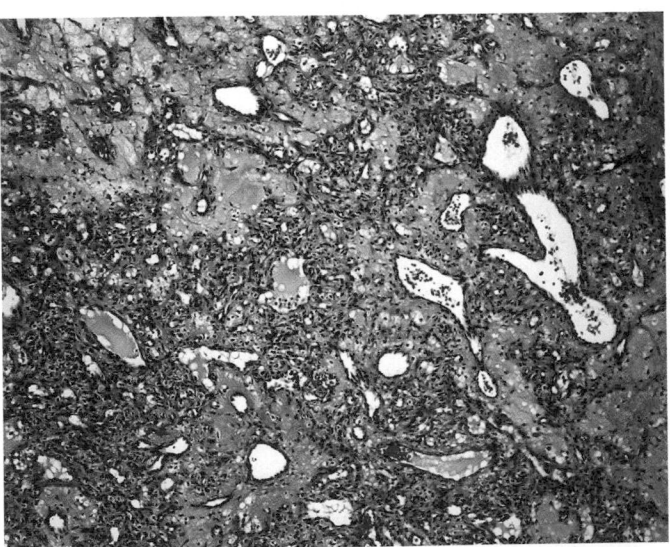

Fig. 7.34 Lobular capillary hemangioma of nasal cavity. Numerous capillary lobules are seen. This lesion should not be confused with nasopharyngeal angiofibroma.

as a nasopharyngeal angiofibroma, or—worse—as an angiosarcoma, the latter because of the marked cellularity and high mitotic activity that it may exhibit. Detection of a *lobular* pattern of growth within the lesion (as opposed to freely anastomosing vascular channels) is a key diagnostic feature. Support for the diagnosis is obtained by the immunohistochemical demonstration of the presence of CD31-positive endothelial cells and actin-positive prethelial/smooth muscle cells, *the latter predominating*.[387] *Hemangiopericytoma-like tumor* is a vascular mesenchymal neoplasm that may arise either in a paranasal sinus or in the nasal cavity.[359,361] The clinical diagnosis is often that of allergic polyp. Microscopically, the lesions appear vascular and highly cellular, but they have little atypia, necrosis, or mitotic activity (Fig. 7.35). Immunohistochemically, there is strong reactivity for vimentin and focal reactivity for actin.[361] Ultrastructurally, the most consistent features are basal lamina material enwrapping the individual cells, tapered cytoplasmic extensions, and orderly bundles of filaments.[361] We view this tumor as being closer to Stout's original concept of hemangiopericytoma than most others that have received this term, in the sense that it is composed of vascular myoid cells closely related to glomus cells.[400a,400b] Local recurrences may develop, but metastases do not occur.[359,361]

Other vascular tumors of the region include *hemangioma*, *lymphangioma*, conventional *glomus tumor*, *Masson's hemangioma* (Fig. 7.36) (papillary endothelial hyperplasia), *angioleiomyoma* (vascular leiomyoma), *Kaposi's sarcoma*, and the exceptionally rare *angiosarcoma*.[353,358,362,373–375,391,399] Before making the latter diagnosis in the nasal cavity, other possibilities should be considered, such as a particularly florid form of lobular capillary hemangioma, the reactive vascular changes in cocaine abusers,[350] and the prominent angiectatic changes sometimes seen in nasal polyps.[404]

Solitary fibrous tumor is a nasopharyngeal neoplasm morphologically and immunohistochemically analogous

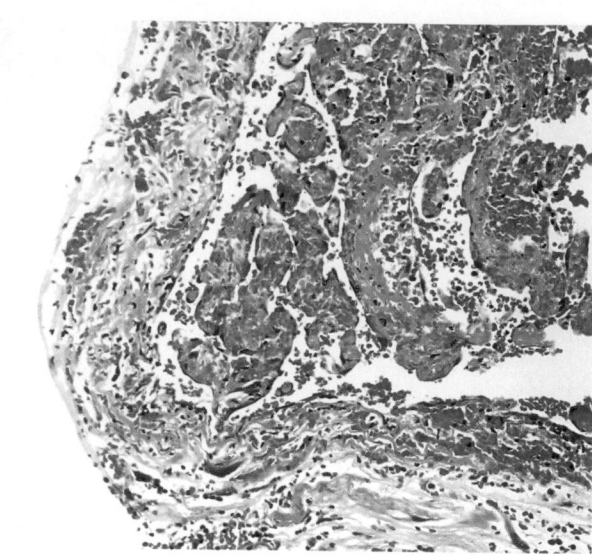

Fig. 7.36 So-called "Masson hemangioma" (papillary endothelial hyperplasia). The intraluminal papillary fronds have a fibrin core and are covered by endothelial cells.

to solitary fibrous tumor of the pleura (so-called solitary fibrous mesothelioma)[403,405] and very closely related histogenetically to hemangiopericytoma (although probably not to hemangiopericytoma-like tumor)[402] (Fig. 7.37). Intranasal extension is common.

Ameloblastoma having a microscopic appearance indistinguishable from that of its more common counterpart in the jaw can present as a primary tumor in the sinonasal tract. The fact that there is often continuity of the tumor with the surface epithelium suggests that most of these tumors are primary in this region rather than extensions of jaw neoplasms.[395] As such, they are analogous to the peripheral ameloblastomas of the oral cavity (see Chapter 6). The differential diagnosis includes

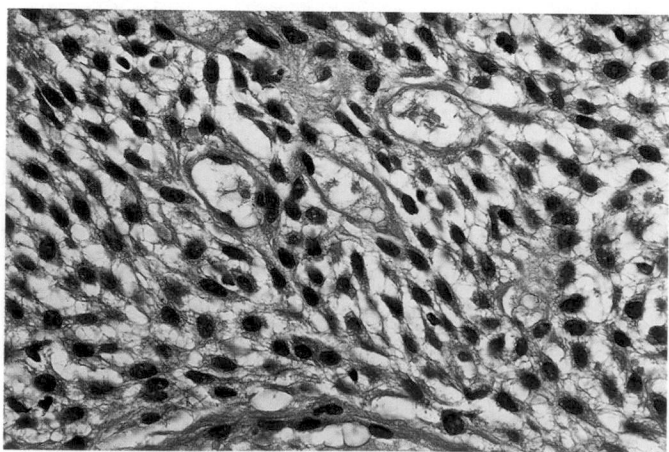

Fig. 7.35 Hemangiopericytoma-like tumor of nasal cavity. Predominantly oval tumor cells arrange themselves around blood vessels.

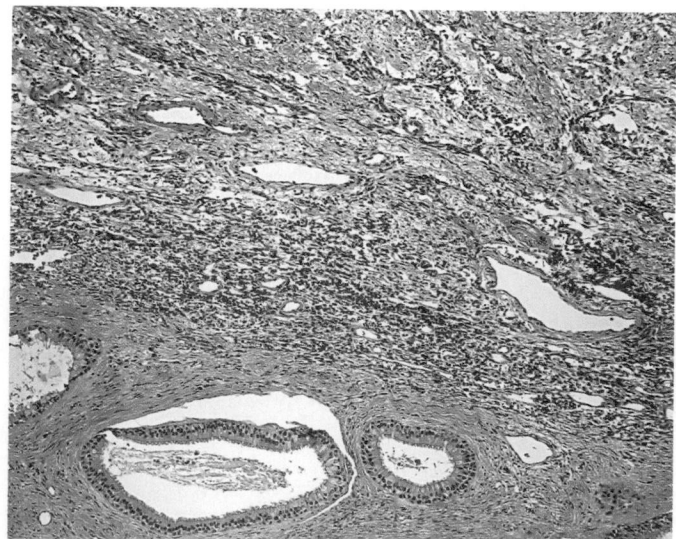

Fig. 7.37 Solitary fibrous tumor of paranasal sinus. The tumor is highly vascularized and shows an alternation of hyper- and hypocellular foci.

sinonasal extension of craniopharyngioma, the nature of which should be apparent on MRI or CT scan examinations.[355,395]

Chordoma of the sphenoid region is another example of a primary cranial/intracranial tumor that can secondarily invade the nasopharynx.[351,393]

Rhabdomyosarcoma of the embryonal-type is one of the three most common types of nasopharyngeal malignancy in children, the other two being lymphoepithelioma and malignant lymphoma[360,380] (Fig. 7.38). Both embryonal and alveolar rhabdomyosarcoma can also develop in this region in adults.[383,385] The alveolar-type may develop clear cell changes because of glycogen accumulation and simulate other neoplasms.[357]

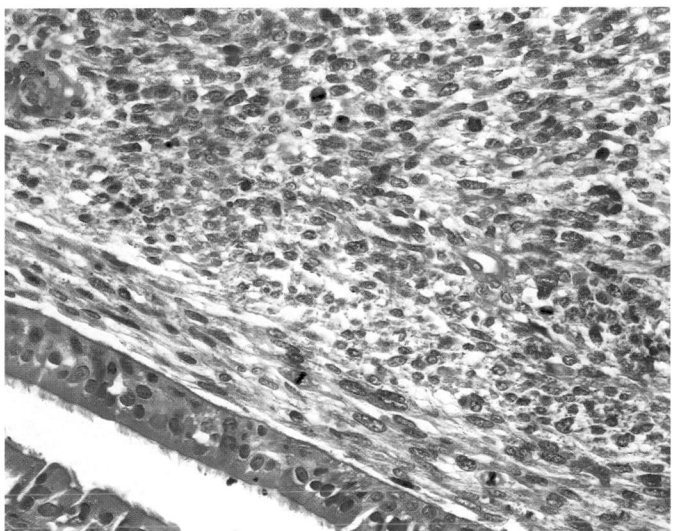

Fig. 7.38 Embryonal rhabdomyosarcoma of nasopharynx. The lesion is extremely cellular and mitotically active.

Teratoid carcinosarcoma (teratocarcinosarcoma) is a unique sinonasal tract neoplasm that combines features of carcinosarcoma and teratoma, the latter including primitive neuroepithelial elements with well-formed rosettes.[388] The histogenesis remains uncertain, but it has been proposed on the basis of ultrastructural and immunohistochemical observations that it represents a neuroectodermal tumor with divergent differentiation.[397] It seems likely that at least some of the reported cases of combined olfactory neuroblastoma and craniopharyngioma are morphologic variants in the theme of teratoid carcinosarcoma[386] (Fig. 7.39). The patients are adults, and the prognosis is poor, with 60% of the patients not surviving beyond 3 years.[378,396]

Soft tissue tumors of this region include, in addition to the entities already described, the following types: osseous and fibro-osseous lesions,[363] cartilaginous tumors,[364,394] smooth muscle tumors,[365,379a,381] benign skeletal muscle tumors,[366,370] fibrous tissue tumors (fibromatosis, "fibromas", and fibrosarcomas)[367,371,377] myxomas,[368] adipose tissue tumors,[369,371a] monotypic angiomyolipoma,[350a] fibrous histiocytomas,[389,392] synovial sarcomas,[398] extraskeletal Ewing's sarcoma/PNET[390] (Fig. 7.40), and desmoplastic small cell tumor.[361a]

Follicular dendritic cell tumor (follicular dendritic cell sarcoma) is a malignant neoplasm arising from the follicular subset of the dendritic/reticulum cells family. Its features are similar to those of its more common counterpart in the lymph nodes (see Chapter 21). In the nasopharynx, its misdiagnosis as lymphoepithelioma is likely. The nucleoli are not as large or eosinophilic as in the latter, and there is immunoreactivity for CD21 and/or CD35 instead of keratin.[352] Some cases have arisen against a background of Castleman's disease of the hyaline–vascular-type.[356]

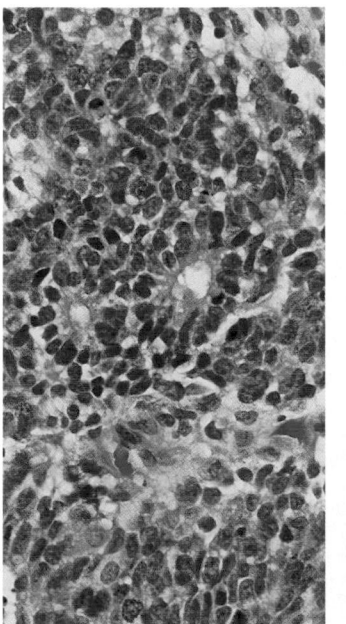
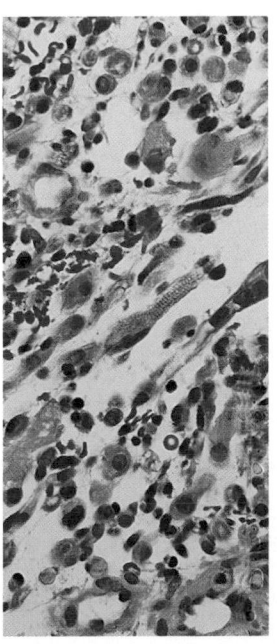
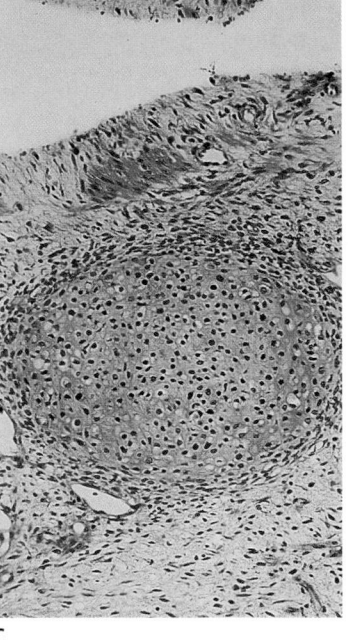

A   B   C

Fig. 7.39 Teratocarcinosarcoma of sinonasal region. This composite photomicrograph shows three different components: adenocarcinomatous with neural-type rosette formations (left), myosarcomatous areas (center), and cartilaginous foci (right). (Courtesy of Dr. Dennis K. Heffner, Washington, D.C.)

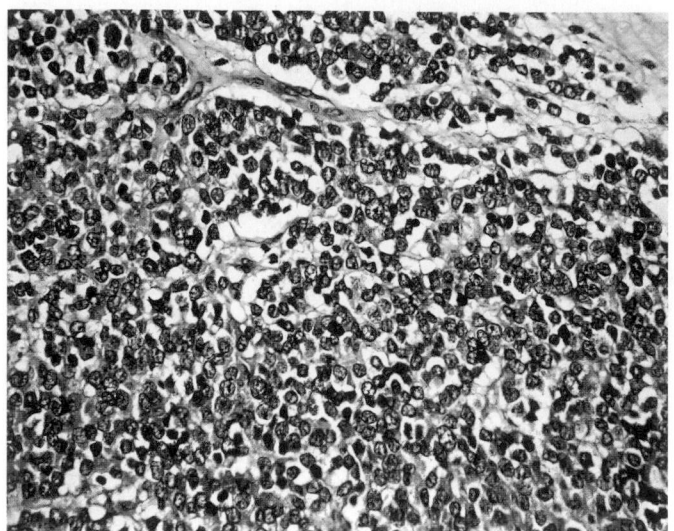

Fig. 7.40 Ewing's sarcoma/PNET of sinonasal region. This tumor type is distinct from olfactory neuroblastoma.

Metastatic tumors to this region are exceptional, but well-documented cases are on record. As usual, renal cell carcinoma, malignant melanoma, and breast carcinoma head the list.[401]

Tumorlike conditions of the region include, in addition to those already mentioned, *giant cell reparative granuloma*,[372] and primary localized *amyloidosis*.[384]

References

Normal anatomy

1 Balogh K. Mouth, nose, and paranasal sinuses. Histology of Pathologists 1997, **2**: 367–390.
1a Stosiek P, Kasper M, Moll R. Changes in cytokeratin expression accompany squamous metaplasia of the human respiratory epithelium. Virchows Arch [A] 1992, **421**: 133–141.

Inflammatory ("allergic") polyp

2 Batsakis JG. The pathology of head and neck tumors. Nasal cavity and paranasal sinuses. Part 5. Head Neck Surg 1980, **2**: 410–419.
3 Batsakis JG, Sneige N. Choanal and angiomatous polyps of the sinonasal tract. Ann Otol Rhinol Laryngol 1992, **101**: 623–625.
4 Compagno J, Hyams VJ, Lepore ML. Nasal polyposis with stromal atypia. Review and follow-up study of 14 cases. Arch Pathol Lab Med 1976, **100**: 224–226.
5 Davidsson A, Hellquist HB. The so-called "allergic" nasal polyp. ORL J Otorhinolaryngol Relat Spec 1993, **55**: 30–35.
6 Henderson WR Jr, Chi EY. Degranulation of cystic fibrosis nasal polyp mast cells. J Pathol 1992, **166**: 395–404.
7 Kawabori S, Denburg JA, Schwartz LB, Irani AA, Wong D, Jordana G, Evans S, Dolovich J. Histochemical and immunohistochemical characteristics of mast cells in nasal polyps. Am J Respir Cell Mol Biol 1992, **6**: 37–43.
8 Kindblom L-G, Angervall L. Nasal polyps with atypical stroma cells. A pseudosarcomatous lesion. A light and electron-microscopic and immunohistochemical investigation with implications on the type and nature of the mesenchymal cells. Acta Pathol Microbiol Immunol Scand (A) 1984, **92**: 65–72.
9 Larsen PL, Tos M. Origin of nasal polyps. Laryngoscope 1991, **101**: 305–312.
10 MacArthur CJ, Gliklick R, McGill TJ, Perez-Atayde A. Sinus complications in mucopolysaccharidosis IH/S (Hurler-Scheie syndrome). Int J Pediatr Otorhinolaryngol 1993, **26**: 79–87.
11 Oppenheimer EA, Rosenstein BJ. Differential pathology of nasal polyps in cystic fibrosis and atopy. Lab Invest 1979, **40**: 445–449.
12 Schwachman H, Kulczycki LL, Mueller HL, Flake CG. Nasal polyposis in cystic fibrosis. Pediatrics 1962, **30**: 389–401.
13 Smith CJ, Echevarria R, McLelland CA. Pseudosarcomatous changes in antrochoanal polyps. Arch Otolaryngol 1974, **99**: 228–230.
14 Stoop AE, van der Heijden HA, Biewanga J, van der Baan S. Lymphocytes and nonlymphoid cells in human nasal polyps. J Allergy Clin Immunol 1991, **87**: 470–475.
15 Stoop AE, van der Heijden HA, Biewenga J, van der Baan S. Eosinophils in nasal polyps and nasal mucosa. An immunohistochemical study. J Allergy Clin Immunol 1993, **91**: 616–622.
16 Yazbak PA, Phillips JM, Ball PA, Rhodes CH. Benign nasal polyposis presenting as an intracranial mass. Case report. Surg Neurol 1991, **36**: 380–383.
17 Yfantis HG, Drachenberg CB, Gray W, Papadimitriou JC. Angiectatic nasal polyps that clinically simulate a malignant process: report of two cases and review of the literature. Arch Pathol Lab Med 2000, **124**: 406–410.

Other inflammatory lesions

18 Ahluwalia KB. New interpretations in rhinosporidiosis, enigmatic disease of the last nine decades. J Submicrosc Cytol Pathol 1992, **24**: 109–114.
19 Altemani AM, Pilch BZ, Sakano E, Altemani JM. Eosinophilic angiocentric fibrosis of the nasal cavity. Mod Pathol 1997, **10**: 391–393.
20 Batsakis JG, el-Naggar AK. Rhinoscleroma and rhinosporidiosis. Ann Otol Rhinol Laryngol 1992, **101**: 879–882.
21 Chang T, Teng MM, Wang SF, Li WY, Cheng CC, Lirng JF. Aspergillosis of the paranasal sinuses. Neuroradiology 1992, **34**: 520–523.
22 Colby TV, Tazelaar HD, Specks U, Deremee RA. Nasal biopsy in Wegener's granulomatosis (editorial). Hum Pathol 1991, **22**: 101–104.
23 Coup AJ, Hopper IP. Granulomatous lesions in nasal biopsies. Histopathology 1980, **4**: 293–308.
24 Del Buono EA, Flint A. Diagnostic usefulness of nasal biopsy in Wegener's granulomatosis. Hum Pathol 1991, **22**: 107–110.
25 DeShazo RD, Chapin K, Swain RE. Fungal sinusitis. N Engl J Med 1997, **337**: 254–259.
26 Devaney KO, Travis WD, Hoffman G, Leavitt R, Lebovics R, Fauci AS. Interpretation of head and neck biopsies in Wegener's granulomatosis. A pathologic study of 126 biopsies in 70 patients. Am J Surg Pathol 1990, **14**: 555–564.
27 Foucar E, Rosai J, Dorfman RF. Sinus histiocytosis with massive lymphadenopathy. Ear, nose and throat manifestations. Arch Otolaryngol 1978, **104**: 687–693.
28 Gardner DG. Pseudocysts and retention cysts of the maxillary sinus. Oral Surg Oral Med Oral Pathol 1984, **58**: 561–567.
29 Hamilos DL, Leung DY, Wood R, Meyers A, Stephens JK, Barkans J, Meng Q, Cunningham L, Bean DK, Kay AB, et al. Chronic hyperplastic sinusitis. Association of tissue eosinophilia with mRNA expression of granulocyte-macrophage colony-stimulating factor and interleukin-3. J Allergy Clin Immunol 1993, **92**: 39–48.
30 Heffner DK. Problems in pediatric otorhinolaryngic pathology. I. Sinonasal and nasopharyngeal tumors and masses with myxoid features. Int J Pediatr Otorhinolaryngol 1983, **5**: 77–91.
31 Kakizaki H, Shimada K. Experimental study of the cause of myospherulosis. Am J Clin Pathol 1993, **99**: 249–256.
32 Katzenstein A-LA, Sale SR, Greenberger PA. Pathologic findings

in allergic aspergillus sinusitis. A newly recognized form of sinusitis. Am J Surg Pathol 1983, **7**: 439–443.

33 Kyriakos M. Myospherulosis of the paranasal sinuses, nose and middle ear. A possible iatrogenic disease. Am J Clin Pathol 1977, **67**: 118–130.

34 Lehrer RI, Howard DH, Sypherd PS, Edwards JE, Segal GP, Winston DJ. Mucormycosis. Ann Intern Med 1980, **93**: 93–108.

35 McClatchie S, Warambo MW, Bremner AD. Myospherulosis. A previously unreported disease? Am J Clin Pathol 1969, **51**: 699–704.

36 McDonald TJ, DeRemee RA, Kern EB, Harrison EG Jr. Nasal manifestations of Wegener's granulomatosis. Laryngoscope 1974, **84**: 2101–2112.

37 Matsubara O, Yoshimura N, Doi Y, Tamura A, Mark EJ. Nasal biopsy in the early diagnosis of Wegener's (pathergic) granulomatosis. Significance of palisading granuloma and leukocytoclastic vasculitis. Virchows Archiv 1996, **428**: 13–20.

38 Meyer PR, Shum TK, Becker TS, Taylor CR. Scleroma (rhinoscleroma). A histologic immunohistochemical study with bacteriologic correlates. Arch Pathol Lab Med 1983, **107**: 377–383.

39 Noorduyn LA, Torenbeek R, van der Valk P, Drosten PB, Snow GB, Balm AJ, Ossenkoppele GJ, Meyer CJ. Sinonasal non-Hodgkin's lymphomas and Wegener's granulomatosis. A clinicopathologic study. Virchows Arch [A] 1991, **418**: 235–240.

40 Patey O, Bonnieux P, Roucayrol AM, Lafaix C. Sarcoidosis of the nose. Report of a case with nasal perforation. Sarcoidosis 1990, **7**: 123–124.

41 Roberts PF, McCann BG. Eosinophilic angiocentric fibrosis of the upper respiratory tract. A mucosal variant of granuloma faciale? A report of three cases. Histopathology 1985, **9**: 1217–1225.

42 Robson AK, Burge SM, Millard PR. Nasal mucosal involvement in lupus erythematosus. Clin Otolaryngol 1992, **17**: 341–343.

43 Rosai J. The nature of myospherulosis of the upper respiratory tract. Am J Clin Pathol 1978, **69**: 475–481.

44 Stierna P, Carlsöö B. Histopathological observations in chronic maxillary sinusitis. Acta Otolaryngol 1990, **110**: 450–458.

45 Thompson LD, Heffner DK. Sinonasal tract eosinophilic angiocentric fibrosis. A report of three cases. Am J Clin Pathol 2001, **115**: 243–248.

46 Torres C, Ro JY, el-Naggar AK, Sim SJ, Weber RS, Ayala AG. Allergic fungal sinusitis: a clinicopathologic study of 16 cases. Hum Pathol 1996, **27**: 793–799.

47 Travis WD, Kwon-Chung KJ, Kleiner DE, Geber A, Lawson W, Pass HI, Henderson D: Unusual aspects of allergic bronchopulmonary fungal disease. Report of two cases due to *Curvularia* organisms associated with allergic fungal sinusitis. Hum Pathol 1991, **22**: 1240–1248.

48 Travis WD, Li C-Y, Weiland LH. Immunostaining for hemoglobin in two cases of myospherulosis. Arch Pathol Lab Med 1986, **110**: 763–765.

48a Trimarchi M, Gregorini G, Facchetti F, Morassi ML, Manfredini C, Maroldi R, Nicolai P, Russell KA, McDonald TJ, Specks U. Cocain-induced midline destructive lesions: clinical, radiographic, histopathologic, and serologic features and the differentiation from Wegener granulomatosis. Medicine (Baltimore) 2001, **80**: 391–404.

49 van der Coer JM, Marres HA, Wielinga EW, Wong-Alcala LS. Rhinosporidiosis in Europe. J Laryngol Otol 1992, **106**: 440–443.

50 Waldron J, Van Hasselt CA, Skinner DW, Arnold M. Tuberculosis of the nasopharynx. Clinicopathological features. Clin Otolaryngol 1992, **17**: 57–59.

51 Wenig BM, Abbondanzo SL, Childers EL, Kapadia SB, Heffner DR. Extranodal sinus histiocytosis with massive lymphadenopathy (Rosai–Dorfman disease) of the head and neck. Hum Pathol 1993, **24**: 483–492.

52 Wolff M. Granulomas in nasal mucoid membranes following local steroid injections. Am J Clin Pathol 1974, **62**: 775–782.

Tumors

Sinonasal papilloma

53 Barnes L, Bedetti C. Oncocytic schneiderian papilloma. A reappraisal of cylindrical cell papilloma of the sinonasal tract. Hum Pathol 1984, **15**: 344–351.

54 Benninger MS, Roberts JK, Sebek BA, Levine HL, Tucker HM, Lavertu P. Inverted papillomas and associated squamous cell carcinomas. Otolaryngol Head Neck Surg 1990, **103**: 457–461.

55 Christensen WN, Smith RRL. Schneiderian papillomas. A clinicopathologic study of 67 cases. Hum Pathol 1986, **17**: 393–400.

56 D'Angelo AJ Jr, Marlowe A, Marlowe FI, McFarland M. Inverted papilloma of the nose and paranasal sinuses in children. Ear Nose Throat J 1992, **71**: 264–266.

57 Fechner RE, Alford DO. Inverted papilloma and squamous carcinoma. An unusual case. Arch Otolaryngol 1968, **88**: 507–512.

58 Fu YS, Hoover L, Franklin M, Cheng L, Stoler MH. Human papillomavirus identified by nucleic acid hybridization in concomitant nasal and genital papillomas. Laryngoscope 1992, **102**: 1014–1019.

59 Furuta Y, Shinohara T, Sano K, Nagashima K, Inoue K, Tanaka K, Inuyama Y. Molecular pathologic study of human papillomavirus infection in inverted papilloma and squamous cell carcinoma of the nasal cavities and paranasal sinuses. Laryngoscope 1991, **101**: 79–85.

60 Gaffey MJ, Frierson HF, Weiss LM, Barber CM, Baber GB, Stoler MH. Human papillomavirus and Epstein–Barr virus in sinonasal schneiderian papillomas. An in situ hybridization and polymerase chain reaction study. Am J Clin Pathol 1996, **106**: 475–482.

61 Hyams VJ. Papillomas of the nasal cavity and paranasal sinuses. A clinicopathologic study of 315 cases. Ann Otol Rhinol Laryngol 1971, **80**: 192–206.

62 Judd R, Zaki SR, Coffield LM, Evatt BL. Sinonasal papillomas and human papillomavirus. Human papillomavirus 11 detected in fungiform schneiderian papillomas by in situ hybridization and the polymerase chain reaction. Hum Pathol 1991, **22**: 550–556.

63 Krisch I, Neuhold N, Krisch K. Demonstration of secretory component, IgA, and IgM by the peroxidase-antiperoxidase technique in inverted papillomas of the nasal cavities. Hum Pathol 1984, **15**: 915–920.

64 Lasser A, Rothfeld RP, Shapiro RS. Epithelial papilloma and squamous cell carcinoma of the nasal cavity and paranasal sinuses. A clinicopathological study. Cancer 1976, **38**: 2503–2510.

65 Macdonald MR, Le KT, Freeman J, Hui MF, Cheung RK, Dosch HM. A majority of inverted sinonasal papillomas carries Epstein–Barr virus genomes. Cancer 1995, **75**: 2307–2312.

66 McLachlin CM, Kandel RA, Colgan TJ, Swanson DB, Witterick IJ, Ngan BY. Prevalence of human papillomavirus in sinonasal papillomas. A study using polymerase chain reaction and in situ hybridization. Mod Pathol 1992, **5**: 406–409.

67 Maitra A, Baskin LB, Lee EL. Malignancies arising in oncocytic schneiderian papillomas: a report of two cases and review of a literature. Arch Pathol Lab Med 2001, **125**: 1365–1367.

68 Michaels L. Benign mucosal tumors of the nose and paranasal sinuses. Semin Diagn Pathol 1996, **13**: 113–117.

69 Myers EN, Fernau JL, Johnson JT, Tabet JC, Barnes EL. Management of inverted papilloma. Laryngoscope 1990, **100**: 481–490.

70 Nielsen PL, Buchwald C, Nielsen LH, Tos M. Inverted papilloma of the nasal cavity. Pathological aspects in a follow-up study. Laryngoscope 1991, **101**: 1094–1101.

71 Oberman HA. Papillomas of the nose and paranasal sinuses. Am J Clin Pathol 1964, **42**: 245–258.

72 Outzen KE, Grontved A, Jorgensen K, Clausen PP. Inverted

papilloma of the nose and paranasal sinuses. A study of 67 patients. Clin Otolaryngol 1991, **16**: 309–312.

73 Pelausa EO, Fortier MA. Schneiderian papilloma of the nose and paranasal sinuses. The University of Ottawa experience. J Otolaryngol 1992, **21**: 9–15.

74 Peterson IM, Heim C. Inverted squamous papilloma with neuro-ophthalmic features. J Clin Neuroophthalmol 1991, **11**: 35–38.

75 Ridolfi RL, Liberman PH, Erlandson RA, Moore OS. Schneiderian papillomas. A clinicopathologic study of 30 cases. Am J Surg Pathol 1977, **1**: 43–53.

76 Sarkar FH, Visscher DW, Kintanar EB, Zarbo RJ, Crissman JD. Sinonasal schneiderian papillomas. Human papillomavirus typing by polymerase chain reaction. Mod Pathol 1992, **5**: 329–332.

77 Schwerer MJ, Kraft K, Baczako K, Maier H. Coexpression of cytokeratins typical for columnar and squamous differentiation in sinonasal inverted papillomas. Am J Clin Pathol 2001, **115**: 747–754.

78 Shen J, Tate JE, Crum CP, Goodman ML. Prevalance of human papillomaviruses (HPV) in benign and malignant tumors of the upper respiratory tract. Mod Pathol 1996, **9**: 15–20.

79 Snyder RN, Perzin KH. Papillomatosis of nasal cavity and paranasal sinuses (inverted papilloma, squamous papilloma). A clinicopathologic study. Cancer 1972, **30**: 668–690.

80 Vrabec DP. The inverted schneiderian papilloma. A clinical and pathological study. Laryngoscope 1975, **85**: 186–220.

Sinonasal carcinoma
General features

81 Cerilli LA, Holst VA, Brandwein MS, Stoler MH, Mills SE. Sinonasal undifferentiated carcinoma: immunohistochemical profile and lack of EBV association. Am J Surg 2001, **25**: 156–163.

82 Furuta Y, Takasu T, Asai T, Shinohara T, Sawa H, Nagashima K, Inuyama Y. Detection of human papillomavirus DNA in carcinomas of the nasal cavities and paranasal sinuses by polymerase chain reaction. Cancer 1992, **69**: 353–357.

83 Ironside P, Matthews J. Adenocarcinoma of the nose and paranasal sinuses in woodworkers in the state of Victoria, Australia. Cancer 1975, **36**: 1115–1121.

84 Judd R, Zaki SR, Coffield LM, Evatt BL. Human papillomavirus type 6 detected by the polymerase chain reaction in invasive sinonasal papillary squamous cell carcinoma. Arch Pathol Lab Med 1991, **115**: 1150–1153.

85 Kleinsasser O, Schroeder HG. What's new in tumors of the nasal cavity? Adenocarcinomas arising after exposure to wood dust. Pathol Res Pract 1989, **184**: 554–558.

86 Moran CA, Wenig BM, Mullick FG. Primary adenocarcinoma of the nasal cavity and paranasal sinuses. Ear Nose Throat J 1991, **70**: 821–828.

87 Nuñez F, Suarez C, Alvarez I, Losa JL, Barthe P, Fresno M. Sinonasal adenocarcinoma. Epidemiological and clinico-pathological study of 34 cases. J Otolaryngol 1993, **22**: 86–90.

88 Paulino AF, Singh B, Carew J, Shah JP, Huvos AG. Epstein–Barr virus in squamous carcinoma of the anterior nasal cavity. Ann Diagn Pathol 2000, **4**: 7–10.

89 Robin PE, Shortridge RTJ. Lateralisation of tumours of the nasal cavity and paranasal sinuses and its relationship to aetiology. Lancet 1979, **1**: 695–696.

90 Rousch GC. Epidemiology of cancer of the nose and paranasal sinuses. Current concepts. Head Neck Surg 1979, **2**: 3–11.

Location and spread

91 Barnes L, Johnson JT. Pathologic and clinical considerations in the evaluation of major head and neck specimens resected for cancer. Part 1. Pathol Annu 1986, **21**: 173–250.

92 Cheng VST, Wang CC. Carcinomas of the paranasal sinuses. A study of sixty-six cases. Cancer 1977, **40**: 3038–3041.

93 Fradis M, Podoshin L, Gertner R, Sabo E. Squamous cell carcinoma of the nasal septum mucosa. Ear Nose Throat J 1993, **72**: 217–221.

94 Patel P, Tiwari R, Karim AB, Nauta JJ, Snow GB. Squamous cell carcinoma of the nasal vestibule. J Laryngol Otol 1992, **106**: 332–336.

95 Taxy JB. Squamous carcinoma of the nasal vestibule: an analysis of five cases and literature review. Am J Clin Pathol 1997, **107**: 698–703.

Microscopic features

96 Barnes L. Intestinal-type adenocarcinoma of the nasal cavity and paranasal sinuses. Am J Surg Pathol 1986, **10**: 192–202.

97 Batsakis JG, Mackay B, Ordoñez NG. Enteric-type adenocarcinoma of the nasal cavity. An electron microscopic and immunocytochemical study. Cancer 1984, **54**: 855–860.

98 Batsakis JG, Rice DH, Solomon AR. The pathology of head and neck tumors. Squamous and mucous-gland carcinomas of the nasal cavity, paranasal sinuses, and larynx. Part 6. Head Neck Surg 1980, **2**: 497–508.

99 Bonato M, Frigerio B, Capella C, Chiaravalli AM, Cerati M. Composite enteric-type adenocarcinoma-carcinoid of the nasal mucosa. Endocrinol Pathol 1993, **4**: 40–47.

100 Cerilli LA, Holst VA, Brandwein MS, Stoler MH, Mills SE. Sinonasal undifferentiated carcinoma: immunohistochemical profile and lack of EBV association. Am J Surg 2001, **25**: 156–163.

100a Franchi A, Moroni M, Massi D, Paglierani M, Santucci M. Sinonasal undifferentiated carcinoma, nasopharyngeal-type undifferentiated carcinoma, and keratinizing and nonkeratinizing squamous cell carcinoma express different cytokeratin patterns. Am J Surg Pathol 2002, **26**: 1597–1604.

101 Franquemont DW, Fechner RE, Mills SE. Histologic classification of sinonasal intestinal-type adenocarcinoma. Am J Surg Pathol 1991, **16**: 368–375.

102 Frierson HF Jr, Mills SE, Fechner RE, Taxy JB, Levine PA. Sinonasal undifferentiated carcinoma. An aggressive neoplasm derived from schneiderian epithelium and distinct from olfactory neuroblastoma. Am J Surg Pathol 1986, **10**: 771–779.

103 Gnepp DR, Heffner DK. Mucosal origin of sinonasal tract adenomatous neoplasms. Mod Pathol 1989, **2**: 365–371.

104 Heffner DK, Hyams VJ, Hauck KW, Lingeman C. Low-grade adenocarcinoma of the nasal cavity and paranasal sinuses. Cancer 1982, **50**: 312–322.

105 Helliwell TR, Yeoh LH, Stell PM. Anaplastic carcinoma of the nose and paranasal sinuses. Light microscopy, immunohistochemistry and clinical correlation. Cancer 1986, **58**: 2038–2045.

106 Houston GD, Gillies E. Sinonasal undifferentiated carcinoma: a distinctive clinicopathologic entity. Adv Anat Pathol 1999, **6**: 317–323.

107 McKinney CD, Mills SE, Franquemont DW. Sinonasal intestinal-type adenocarcinoma. Immunohistochemical profile and comparison with colonic adenocarcinoma. Mod Pathol 1995, **8**: 421–426.

108 Manivel C, Wick MR, Dehner LP. Transitional (cylindric) cell carcinoma with endodermal sinus tumor-like features of the nasopharynx and paranasal sinuses. Clinicopathologic and immunohistochemical study of two cases. Arch Pathol Lab Med 1986, **110**: 198–202.

109 Michaels L. Benign mucosal tumors of the nose and paranasal sinuses. Semin Diagn Pathol 1996, **13**: 113–117.

110 Mills SE, Fechner RE. "Undifferentiated" neoplasms of the sinonasal region. Differential diagnosis based on clinical, light microscopic, immunohistochemical, and ultrastructural features. Semin Diagn Pathol 1989, **6**: 316–328.

111 Mills SE, Fechner RE, Cantrell RW. Aggressive sinonasal lesion resembling normal intestinal mucosa. Am J Surg Pathol 1982, **6**: 803–809.

111a Neto AG, Pineda-Daboin K, Luna MA. Sinonasal tract

seromucous adenocarcinomas: a report of 12 cases. Ann Diagn Pathol 2003, **7**: 154–159.

112 Osborn DA. Nature and behavior of transitional tumors in the upper respiratory tract. Cancer 1970, **25**: 50–60.

113 Perez-Ordonez B, Caruana SM, Huvos AG, Shah JP. Small cell neuroendocrine carcinoma of the nasal cavity and paranasal sinuses. Hum Pathol 1998, **29**: 826–832.

114 Piscioli F, Aldovini D, Bondi A, Eusebi V. Squamous cell carcinoma with sarcoma-like stroma of the nose and paranasal sinuses. Report of two cases. Histopathology 1984, **8**: 633–639.

115 Ringertz N. Pathology of malignant tumors arising in the nasal and paranasal cavities and maxilla. Acta Otolaryngol (Stockholm) 1938, **27**(Suppl): 1–405.

116 Sanchez-Casis G, Devine KD, Weiland LH. Nasal adenocarcinomas that closely simulate colonic carcinomas. Cancer 1971, **28**: 714–720.

117 Schmid KO, Aubock L, Albegger K. Endocrine-amphircrine enteric carcinoma of the nasal mucosa. Virchows Arch [A] 1979, **383**: 329–343.

118 Shindo ML, Stanley RB Jr, Kiyabu MT. Carcinosarcoma of the nasal cavity and paranasal sinuses. Head Neck 1990, **12**: 516–519.

119 Wan SK, Chan JK, Tse KC. Basaloid-squamous carcinoma of the nasal cavity. J Laryngol Otol 1992, **106**: 370–371.

120 Westra WH, Holmes GH, Eisele DW. Bizarre epithelial atypia of the sinonasal tract after chemotherapy. Am J Surg Pathol 2001, **25**: 652–656.

121 Wieneke JA, Thompson LD, Wenig BM. Basaloid squamous cell carcinoma of the sinonasal tract. Cancer 1999, **85**: 841–854.

122 Wu TT, Barnes L, Bakker A, Swalsky PA, Finkelstein SD. K-ras-2 and p53 genotying of intestinal-type adenocarcinoma of the nasal cavity and paranasal sinuses. Mod Pathol 1996, **9**: 199–204.

Treatment and prognosis

122a Bandoh N, Hayashi T, Kishibe K, Takahara M, Imada M, Nonaka S, Harabuchi Y. Prognostic value of p53 mutations, bax, and spontaneous apoptosis in maxillary sinus squamous cell carcinoma. Cancer 2002, **94**: 1968–1980.

123 Cheng VST, Wang CC. Carcinomas of the paranasal sinuses. A study of sixty-six cases. Cancer 1977, **40**: 3038–3041.

124 Dulguerov P, Jacobsen MS, Allal AS, Lehmann W, Calcaterra T. Nasal and paranasal sinus carcinoma: are we making progress? A series of 220 patients and a systematic review. Cancer 2001, **92**: 3012–3029.

125 Franchi A, Gallo O, Santucci M. Clinical relevance of the histological classification of sinonasal intestinal-type adenocarcinomas. Hum Pathol 1999, **30**: 1140–1145.

126 Franquemont DW, Fechner RE, Mills SE. Histologic classification of sinonasal intestinal-type adenocarcinoma. Am J Surg Pathol 1991, **16**: 368–375.

127 Frierson HF Jr, Mills SE, Fechner RE, Taxy JB, Levine PA. Sinonasal undifferentiated carcinoma. An aggressive neoplasm derived from schneiderian epithelium and distinct from olfactory neuroblastoma. Am J Surg Pathol 1986, **10**: 771–779.

128 Giri SPG, Reddy EK, Gemer LS, Krishnan L, Smalley SR, Evans RG. Management of advanced squamous cell carcinomas of the maxillary sinus. Cancer 1992, **69**: 657–661.

129 Helliwell TR, Yeoh LH, Stell PM. Anaplastic carcinoma of the nose and paranasal sinuses. Light microscopy, immunohistochemistry and clinical correlation. Cancer 1986, **58**: 2038–2045.

130 Kondo M, Inuyama Y, Ando Y, Tsutsui T, Yamashita S, Hashimoto T, Kunieda E, Uematsu M, Hashimoto S. Patterns of relapse of squamous cell carcinoma of the maxillary sinus. Cancer 1984, **53**: 2206–2210.

131 Kondo M, Ogawa K, Inuyama Y, Yamashita S, Tominaga S, Shigematsu N, Nishiguchi I, Hashimoto S. Prognostic factors influencing relapse of squamous cell carcinoma of the maxillary sinus. Cancer 1985, **55**: 190–196.

132 Mills SE, Fechner RE. "Undifferentiated" neoplasms of the sinonasal region. Differential diagnosis based on clinical, light microscopic, immunohistochemical, and ultrastructural features. Semin Diagn Pathol 1989, **6**: 316–328.

133 St-Pierre S, Baker SR. Squamous cell carcinoma of the maxillary sinus: analysis of 66 cases. Head Neck Surg 1983, **5**: 508–513.

Nasopharyngeal carcinoma
General features

134 Ablashi DV, Levine PH, Prasad U, Pearson GR. Fourth International Symposium on nasopharyngeal carcinoma. Application of field and laboratory studies to the control of NPC. Cancer Res 1983, **43**: 2375–2378.

135 Ambinder RF, Mann RB. Detection and characterization of Epstein–Barr virus in clinical specimens. Am J Pathol 1994, **145**: 239–252.

136 Chan SH, Day NE, Kunaratnam N, Chia KB, Simons MJ. HLA and nasopharyngeal carcinoma in Chinese. A further study. Int J Cancer 1983, **32**: 171–176.

137 Chien YC, Chen JY, Lie MY, Yang HI, Hsu MM, Chen CJ, Yang CS. Serologic markers of Epstein–Barr virus infection and nasopharyngeal carcinoma in Taiwasnese men. N Engl J Med 2001, **345**(26): 1877–1882.

138 Coffin CM, Rich SS, Dehner LP. Familial aggregation of nasopharyngeal carcinoma and other malignancies. A clinicopathologic description. Cancer 1991, **68**: 1323–1328.

139 Easton JM, Levine PH, Hyams VJ. Nasopharyngeal carcinoma in the United States. A pathologic study of 177 US and 30 foreign cases. Arch Otolaryngol 1980, **106**: 88–91.

140 Fandi A, Altun M, Azi N, Armand JP, Cvitkovic E. Nasopharyngeal cancer. Epidemiology, staging and treatment. Semin Oncol 1994, **21**: 392–397.

141 Feinmesser R, Miyazaki I, Cheung R, Freeman JL, Noyek AM, Dosch HM. Diagnosis of nasopharyngeal carcinoma by DNA amplification of tissue obtained by fine-needle aspiration. N Engl J Med 1992, **326**: 58–59.

142 Gaffey MJ, Weiss LM. Association of Epstein–Barr virus with human neoplasia. Pathol Annu 1992, **27**(Pt 1): 55–74.

143 Henle G, Henle W. Epstein–Barr virus-specific IgA serum antibodies as an outstanding feature of nasopharyngeal carcinoma. Int J Cancer 1976, **17**: 1–7.

144 Jain D, Parkash V, Li M, Gill J, Crouch J, Howe J, Tallini G. Epstein–Barr virus RNA detection and glandular differentiation in nasopharyngeal carcinoma: report of two cases. Arch Pathol Lab Med 2000, **124**: 1369–1372.

145 Jenkin RDT, Anderson JR, Jereb B, Thompson JC, Pyesmany A, Wara WM, Hammond D. Nasopharyngeal carcinoma. A retrospective review of patients less than thirty years of age. A report from Children's Cancer Study Group. Cancer 1981, **47**: 360–366.

146 Liebowitz D. Nasopharyngeal carcinoma. The Epstein–Barr virus association. Semin Oncol 1994, **21**: 382–397.

147 Lopategui JR, Gaffey MJ, Frierson HF Jr, Chan JKC, Mills SE, Chang KL, Chen Y-Y, Weiss LM. Detection of Epstein–Barr viral RNA in sinonasal undifferentiated carcinoma from Western and Asian patients. Am J Surg Pathol 1994, **18**: 391–398.

148 Lu SJ, Day NE, Degos L, Lepage V, Wang PC, Chan SH, Simons M, McKnight B, Easton D, Zeng Y, et al. Linkage of a nasopharyngeal carcinoma susceptibility locus to the HLA region. Nature 1990, **346**: 470–471.

149 Naegele RF, Champion J, Murphy S, Henle G, Henle W. Nasopharyngeal carcinoma in American children. Epstein–Barr virus-specific antibody titers and prognosis. Int J Cancer 1982, **29**: 209–212.

150 Ohshima K, Kikuchi M, Masuda Y, Sumiyoshi Y, Eguchi F, Mohtai H, Takeshita M, Kimura N. Epstein–Barr viral genomes in carcinoma metastatic to lymph nodes. Association with nasopharyngeal carcinoma. Acta Pathol Jpn 1991, **41**: 437–443.

151 Pathmanathan R, Prasad U, Sadler R, Flynn K, Raab Traub N. Clonal proliferations of cells infected with Epstein–Barr virus in preinvasive lesiions related to nasopharyngeal carcinoma. N Engl J Med 1995, **333**: 693–698.

152 Pearson GR, Weiland LH, Neal HB III, Taylor W, Earle J, Mulroney SE, Goepfert H, Lanier A, Talvot ML, Pilch B, Goodman M, Huang A, Levine PH, Hyans V, Moran E, Henle G, Henle W. Application of Epstein–Barr virus (EBV) serology to the diagnosis of North American nasopharyngeal carcinoma. Cancer 1983, **51**: 260–268.

153 Raab-Traub N. Epstein–Barr virus and nasopharyngeal carcinoma. Semin Cancer Biol 1992, **3**: 297–307.

154 Sham JS, Poon YF, Wei WI, Choy D. Nasopharyngeal carcinoma in young patients. Cancer 1990, **65**: 2606–2610.

155 Stewart JP, Arrand JR. Expression of the Epstein–Barr virus latent membrane protein in nasopharyngeal carcinoma biopsy specimens. Hum Pathol 1993, **24**: 239–242.

156 Sun Y, Hegamyer G, Cheng Y-J, Hildesheim A, Chen J-Y, Chen I-H, Cao Y, Yao K-T, Colburn NH. An infrequent point mutation of the p53 gene in human nasopllaryngeal carcinoma. Proc Natl Acad Sci USA 1992, **89**: 6516–6520.

157 Tsai ST, Jin YT, Mann RB, Ambinder RF. Epstein–Barr virus detection in nasopharyngeal tissues of patients with suspected nasopharyngeal carcinoma. Cancer 1998, **82**: 1449–1453.

158 Weiss LM, Movahed LA, Butler AE, Swanson SA, Frierson HF, Cooper PH, Colby TV, Mills SE. Analysis of lymphoepithelioma and lymphoepithelioma-like carcinomas for Epstein–Barr viral genomes by in situ hybridization. Am J Surg Pathol 1989, **13**: 625–631.

159 Wenig BM. Nasopharyngeal carcinoma. Ann Diagn Pathol 1999, **3**: 374–385.

160 Wu TC, Mann RB, Epstein JI, MacMahon E, Lee WA, Charache P, Hayward SD, Kurnlan RJ, Hayward GS, Ambinder RF. Abundant expression of EBER 1 small nuclear RNA in nasopharyngeal carcinoma. A morphologically distinctive target for detection of Epstein–Barr virus in formalin-fixed paraffin-embedded carcinoma specimens. Am J Pathol 1991, **138**: 1461–1469.

Gross features

161 Wei WI, Sham JS, Zong YS, Choy D, Ng MH. The efficacy of fiberoptic endoscopic examination and biopsy in the detection of early nasopharyngeal carcinoma. Cancer 1991, **67**: 3127–3130.

Microscopic features

162 Batsakis JG, Solomon AR, Rice DH. The pathology of head and neck tumors. Carcinoma of the nasopharynx. Part 11. Head Neck Surg 1981, **3**: 511–524.

163 Chan CW, Nicholls JM, Sham JS, Dickens P, Choy D. Nasopharyngeal carcinoma in situ in nasopharyngeal carcinoma. J Clin Pathol 1992, **45**: 898–901.

164 Chaung F, Pang SW, Hioe F, Cheung KN, Lee A, Yau TK. Nasopharyngeal carcinoma in situ: two cases of an emerging diagnostic entity. Cancer 1998, **83**: 1069–1073.

165 Heffner DK. Problems in pediatric otorhinolaryngic pathology. IV. Epithelial and lymphoid tumors of the sinonasal tract and nasopharynx. Int J Pediatr Otorhinolaryngol 1983, **6**: 219–237.

166 Leighton SE, Teo JG, Leung SF, Cheung AY, Lee JC, van Hasselt CA. Prevalence and prognostic significance of tumor-associated tissue eosinophilia in nasopharyngeal carcinoma. Cancer 1996, **77**: 436–440.

167 Micheau C. What's new in histological classification and recognition of nasopharyngeal carcinoma (NPC). Pathol Res Pract 1986, **181**: 249–253.

168 Nicholls JM. Nasopharyngeal carcinoma: classification and histologic appearances. Adv Anat Pathol 1997, **4**: 71–84.

169 Prathap K, Looi LM, Prasad U. Localized amyloidosis in nasopharyngeal carcinoma. Histopathology 1984, **8**: 27–34.

170 Tamada A, Makimoto K, Yamabe H, Imai J, Hinuma Y, Oyagi A, Araki T. Titers of Epstein–Barr virus-related antibodies in nasopharyngeal carcinoma in Japan. Cancer 1984, **53**: 430–440.

171 Tsai ST, Jin YT, Su IJ. Expression of EBER1 in primary and metastatic nasopharyngeal carcinoma tissues using in situ hybridization. A correlation with WHO histologic subtypes. Cancer 1996, **77**: 231–236.

172 Wenig BM, Hyams VJ, Heffner DK. Nasopharyngeal papillary adenocarcinoma. A clinicopathologic study of a low-grade carcinoma. Am J Surg Pathol 1988, **12**: 946–953.

173 Zaatari GS, Santoianni RA. Adenoid squamous cell carcinoma of the nasopharynx and neck region. Arch Pathol Lab Med 1986, **110**: 542–546.

Immunohistochemical features

174 Bosq J, Gatter KC, Micheau C, Mason DY. Role of immunohistochemistry in diagnosis of nasopharyngeal tumours. J Clin Pathol 1985, **38**: 845–848.

175 Gusterson BA, Mitchell DP, Warburton MJ, Carter RL. Epithelial markers in the diagnosis of nasopharyngeal carcinoma. An immunocytochemical study. J Clin Pathol 1983, **36**: 628–631.

176 Lauriola L, Michetti F, Sentinelli S, Cocchia D. Detection of S-100 labelled cells in nasopharyngeal carcinoma. J Clin Pathol 1984, **37**: 1235–1238.

177 Miettinen M, Lehto V-P, Virtanen I. Nasopharyngeal lymphoepithelioma. Histological diagnosis as aided by immunohistochemical demonstration of keratin. Virchows Arch [Cell Pathol] 1982, **40**: 163–169.

178 Oppedal BR, Bohler PJ, Marton PF, Brandtzaeg P. Carcinoma of the nasopharynx. Histopathological examination with supplementary immunohistochemistry. Histopathology 1987, **11**: 1161–1169.

Electron microscopic features

179 Fan C-S, Wong N, Leung SF, To KF, Lo KW, Mok TS, Johnson PJ, Huang DP. Frequent c-myc and Int-2 overrepresentation in nasopharyngeal carcinoma. Hum Pathol 2000, **31**: 169–178.

180 Gulley ML, Nicholls JM, Schnieder BG, Amin MB, Ro JY, Geradts J. Nasopharyngeal carcinomas frequently lack the p16/MTS1 tumor suppressor protein but consistently express the retinoblastoma gene product. Am J Pathol 1998, **152**: 865–869.

181 Leung SY, Chau JY, Yuen ST, Chu KM, Branicki FJ, Chung LP. P53 overexpression is different in Epstein–Barr virus-associated with Epstein–Barr virus-negative carcinoma. Histopathology 1998, **33**: 311–317.

182 Lin H-S, Lin C-S, Yeh S, Tu S-M. Fine structure of nasopharyngeal carcinoma with special reference to the anaplastic-type. Cancer 1969, **23**: 390–405.

183 Murono S, Yoshizaki T, Park CS, Furukawa M. Association of Epstein–Barr virus infection with p53 protein accumulation but not bcl-2 protein in nasopharyngeal carcinoma. Histopathology 1999, **34**: 432–438.

184 Taxy JB, Hidvegi DF, Battifora H. Nasopharyngeal carcinoma. Antikeratin immunohistochemistry and electron microscopy. Am J Clin Pathol 1985, **83**: 320–325.

Staging and grading

185 Teo PM, Leung SF, Yu P, Tsao SY, Foo W, Shiu W. A comparison of Ho's, International Union Against Cancer, and American Joint Committee stage classifications for nasopharyngeal carcinoma. Cancer 1991, **67**: 434–439.

Spread and metastases

186 Carbone A, Micheau C. Pitfalls in microscopic diagnosis of undifferentiated carcinoma of nasopharyngeal-type (lymphoepithelioma). Cancer 1982, **50:** 1344–1351.

187 Giffler RF, Gillespie JJ, Ayala AG, Newland JR. Lymphoepithelioma in cervical lymph nodes of children and young adults. Am J Surg Pathol 1977, **1:** 293–302.

188 Rennke H, Lennert K. Käsig-tuberkuloide Reaktion bei Lymphknotenmetastasen lymphoepithelialer Carcinome (Schmincke-Tumoren). Virchows Arch [A] 1973, **358:** 241–247.

189 Su CY, Lui CC. Perineural invasion of the trigeminal nerve in patients with nasopharyngeal carcinoma. Imaging and clinical correlations. Cancer 1996, **78:** 2063–2069.

190 Tesh NB. Epidermoid carcinoma of the nasopharynx among Chinese. A study of 31 necropsies. J Pathol Bacteriol 1957, **73:** 451–465.

191 Zarate-Osorno A, Jaffe ES, Medeiros LJ. Metastatic nasopharyngeal carcinoma initially presenting as cervical lymphadenopathy. A report of two cases taht resembled Hodgkin's disease. Arch Pathol Lab Med 1992, **116:** 862–865.

192 Zen HG, Jame JM, Chang AY, Li WY, Law CK, Chen KY, Lin CZ. Nasopharyngeal carcinoma with bone marrow metastasis. Am J Clin Oncol 1991, **14:** 66–70.

Treatment and prognosis

193 Baker SR, Wolfe RA. Prognostic factors of the nasopharyngeal malignancy. Cancer 1982, **49:** 163–169.

194 Faccioli S, Cavicchi O, Caliceti U, Ceroni AR, Chieco P. Cell proliferation as an independent predictor of survival for patients with advanced nasopharyngeal carcincoma. Mod Pathol 1997, **10:** 884–894.

195 Giannini A, Bianchi S, Messerini L, Gallo O, Gallina E, Asprella Libonati G, Omi P, Zampi G. Prognostic significance of accessory cells and lymphocytes in nasopharyngeal carcinoma. Pathol Res Pract 1991, **187:** 496–502.

196 Heng DM, Wee J, Fong KW, Lian LG, Sethi VK, Chua ET, Yang TL, Tan HS, Lee KS, Lee KM, Tan T, Chua EJ. Prognostic factors in 677 patients in Singapore with nondisseminated nasopharynegeal carcinoma. Cancer 1999, **86:** 1912–1920.

197 Hsu H-C, Chen C-L, Hsu M-M, Lynn T-C, Tu S-M, Huang S-C. Pathology of nasophayngeal carcinoma. Proposal of a new histologic classification correlated with prognosis. Cancer 1987, **59:** 945–951.

198 Lee AW, Poon YF, Foo W, Law SC, Cheung FK, Chan DK, Tung SY, Thaw M, Ho JH. Retrospective analysis of 5037 patients with nasopharyngeal carcinoma treated during 1976–1985. Overall survival and patterns of failure. Int J Radiat Oncol Biol Phys 1992, **23:** 261–270.

199 Nomori H, Watanabe S, Nakajima T, Shimosata Y, Kameya T. Histiocytes in nasopharyngeal carcinoma in relation to prognosis. Cancer 1986, **57:** 100–105.

200 Rahima M, Rakowsky E, Barzilay J, Sidi J. Carcinoma of the nasopharynx. An analysis of 91 cases and a comparison of differing treatment approaches. Cancer 1986, **58:** 843–849.

201 Roychowdhury DF, Tseng A Jr, Fu KK, Weinberg V, Weidner N. New prognostic factors in nasopharyngeal carcinoma; tumor angiogenesis and c-erbB2 expression. Cancer 1996, **77:** 1419–1426.

202 Sham JS, Choy D. Prognostic factors of nasopharyngeal carcinoma. A review of 759 patients. Br J Radiol 1990, **63:** 51–58.

203 Shanmugaratnam K, Chan SH, de-The G, Goh JEH, Khor TH, Simons MJ, Tye CY. Histopathology of nasopharyngeal carcinoma. Correlations with epidemiology, survival rates, and other biological characteristics. Cancer 1979, **44:** 1029–1044.

204 Tsujii H, Kamada T, Tsuji H, Takamura A, Matsuoka Y, Usubuchi H, Irie G. Improved results in the treatment of nasopharyngeal carcinoma using combined radiotherapy and chemotherapy. Cancer 1989, **63:** 1668–1672.

Salivary gland tumors

205 Begin LR, Rochon L, Frenkiel S. Spindle cell myoepithelioma of the nasal cavity. Am J Surg Pathol 1991, **15:** 184–190.

206 Compagno J, Wong RT. Intranasal mixed tumors (pleomorphic adenomas). A clinicopathologic study of 40 cases. Am J Clin Pathol 1977, **68:** 213–218.

207 Dehner LP, Valbuena L, Perez-Atayde A, Reddick RL, Askin FB, Rosai J. Salivary gland anlage tumor ("congenital pleomorphic adenoma"). A clinicopathologic, immunohistochemical and ultrastructural study of nine cases. Am J Surg Pathol 1994, **18:** 25–36.

208 Freeman SB, Kennedy KS, Parker GS, Tatum SA. Metastasizing pleomorphic adenoma of the nasal septum. Arch Otolaryngol Head Neck Surg 1990, **116:** 1331–1333.

209 Goepfert H, Luna MA, Lindberg RD, White AK. Malignant salivary gland tumors of the paranasal sinuses and nasal cavity. Arch Otolaryngol 1983, **109:** 662–668.

210 Graddt van Roggen JF, Baatenburg-de Jong RJ, Verschuur HP, Baluizen JC, Slootweg PJ, Van Krieken JH. Myoepithelial carcinoma (malignant myoepithelioma): first report of an occurrence in the maxillary sinus. Histopathology 1998, **32:** 239–241.

211 Lam PW, Chan JK, Sin VC. Nasal pleomorphic adenoma with skeletal muscle differentiation: potential misdiagnosis as rhabdomyosarcoma. Hum Pathol 1997, **28:** 1299–1301.

212 Manning JT, Batsakis JG. Salivary-type neoplasms of the sinonasal tract. Ann Otol Rhinol Laryngol 1991, **100:** 691–694.

213 Perzin KH, Cantor JO, Johannessen JV. Acinic cell carcinoma arising in nasal cavity. Report of a case with ultrastructural observations. Cancer 1981, **47:** 1818–1822.

214 Rafla S. Mucous gland tumors of paranasal sinuses. Cancer 1969, **24:** 683–691.

215 Wenig BM, Hitchcock CL, Ellis CL, Gnepp DR. Metastasizing mixed tumor of salivary glands. A clinicopathologic and flow cytometric analysis. Am J Surg Pathol 1992, **16:** 845–858.

Neurogenous and related tumors and tumorlike conditions

216 Amesen MA, Scheithauer BW, Freeman S. Cushing's syndrome secondary to olfactory neuroblastoma. Ultrastruct Pathol 1994, **18:** 61–68.

217 Appelblatt NH, McClatchey KD. Olfactory neuroblastoma. A retrospective clinicopathologic study. Head Neck Surg 1982, **5:** 108–113.

218 Argani P, Perez-Ordonez B, Xiao H, Caruana SM, Huvos AG, Ladanyi M. Olfactory neuroblastoma is not related to the Ewing family of tumours: absence of EWS/FLI1 gene fusion and MIC2 expression. Am J Surg Pathol 1998, **22:** 391–398.

219 Axe S, Kuhajda FP. Esthesioneuroblastoma. Intermediate filaments, neuroendocrine, and tissue-specific antigens. Am J Clin Pathol 1987, **88:** 139–145.

220 Chan JK, Lau WH. Nasal astrocytoma or nasal glia heterotopia? Arch Pathol Lab Med 1989, **113:** 943–945.

221 Chan JK, Lau WH, Yuen RWS. Ganglioneuroblastic transformation of olfactory neuroblastoma. Histopathology 1989, **14:** 425–428.

222 Chao KS, Kaplan C, Simpson JR, Haughey B, Spector GJ, Sessions DG, Arquette M. Esthesioneuroblastoma: the impact of treatment modality. Head Neck 2001, **23:** 749–757.

223 Choi H-SH, Anderson PJ. Immunohistochemical diagnosis of olfactory neuroblastoma. J Neuropathol Exp Neurol 1985, **44:** 18–31.

224 Curtis JL, Rubinstein LJ. Pigmented olfactory neuroblastoma. A new example of melanotic neuroepithelial neoplasm. Cancer 1982, **49:** 2136–2143.

225 Devaney K, Wenig BM, Abbondanzo SL. Olfactory neuroblastoma and other round cell lesions of the sinonasal region. Mod Pathol 1996, **9:** 658–663.

226 Fletcher CDM, Carpenter G, McKee PH. Nasal glioma. A rarity. Am J Dermatopathol 1986, **8**: 341–346.

227 Gaudin PB, Rosai J. Florid vascular proliferation associated with neural and neuroendocrine neoplasms. A diagnostic clue and potential pitfall. Am J Surg Pathol 1995, **19**: 642–652.

228 Gerard-Marchant R, Micheau C. Microscopical diagnosis of olfactory esthesioneuromas. General review and report of five cases. J Natl Cancer Inst 1965, **35**: 75–82.

229 Harrison D. Surgical pathology of olfactory neuroblastoma. Head Neck Surg 1984, **7**: 60–64.

230 Hasegawa SL, Mentzel T, Fletcher CD. Schwannomas of the sinonasal tract and nasopharynx. Mod Pathol 1997, **10**: 777–784.

231 Heffner DK, Gnepp DR. Sinonasal fibrosarcomas, malignant schwannomas, and "Triton" tumors. A clinicopathologic study of 67 cases. Cancer 1992, **70**: 1089–1101.

232 Hirano T, Aida T, Moriyama M, Asano G, Suzuki I, Yuge K. Primary neuroblastoma of the nasal cavity and review of literature. Acta Pathol Jpn 1985, **35**: 183–191.

233 Ho KL. Primary meningioma of the nasal cavity and paranasal sinuses. Cancer 1980, **46**: 1442–1447.

234 Hutter RVP, Lewis JS, Foote FW Jr, Tollefsen HR. Esthesioneuroblastoma. Am J Surg 1963, **106**: 748–753.

235 Iwai Y, Hakuba A, Khosla VK, Nishikawa M, Katsuyama J, Inoue Y, Nishimura S. Giant basal prolactinoma extending into the nasal cavity. Surg Neurol 1992, **37**: 280–283.

236 Kadish S, Goodman M, Wang CC. Olfactory neuroblastoma. A clinical analysis of 17 cases. Cancer 1976, **37**: 1571–1576.

237 Kahn LB. Esthesioneuroblastoma. A light and electron microscopic study. Hum Pathol 1974, **5**: 364–371.

238 Kay S, Lees JK, Stout AP. Pituitary chromophobe tumors of the nasal cavity. Cancer 1950, **3**: 695–704.

239 Kindblom LG, Angervall L, Haglid K. An immunohistochemical analysis of S-100 protein and glial fibrillary acidic protein in nasal glioma. Acta Pathol Microbiol Immunol Scand (A) 1984, **92**: 387–389.

240 Kumar S, Periman E, Pack S, Davis M, Zhang H, Meltzer P, Tsokos M. Absence of EWS/FLI1 fusion in olfactory neuroblastomas indicates thses tumors do not belong to the Ewing's sarcoma family. Hum Pathol 1999, **30**: 1356–1360.

241 Lloreta-Trull J, Mackay B, Troncoso P, Ribalta-Farres T, Smith T, Khorana S. Neuroendocrine tumors of the nasal cavity. An ultrastructural and morphometric study of 24 cases. Ultrastruct Pathol 1992, **16**: 165–175.

242 Luk IS, Chan JK, Chow SM, Leung S. Pituitary adenoma presenting as sinonasal tumor: pitfalls in diagnosis. Hum Pathol 1996, **27**: 605–609.

243 McCluggage WG, Napier SS, Primrose WJ, Adair RA, Toner PG. Sinonasal neuroendocrine carcinoma exhibiting amphicrine differentiation. Histopathology 1995, **27**: 79–82.

244 Mackay B, Luna MA, Butler JJ. Adult neuroblastoma. Electron microscopic observations in nine cases. Cancer 1976, **37**: 1334–1351.

245 Mashberg A, Thoma KH, Wasilewski EJ. Olfactory neuroblastoma (esthesioneuroepithelioma) of the maxillary sinus. Oral Surg Oral Med Oral Pathol 1960, **13**: 908–912.

246 Meneses MS, Thurel C, Mikol J, Ramina R, Maniglia JJ, Arruda WO, Cophignon J. Esthesioneuroblastoma with intracranial extension. Neurosurgery 1990, **27**: 813–819.

247 Micheau C. A new histochemical and biochemical approach to olfactory esthesioneuroma. A nasal tumor of neural crest origin. Cancer 1977, **40**: 314–318.

248 Miller DC, Goodman ML, Pilch BZ, Shi SR, Dickersin GR, Halpern H, Norris CM Jr. Mixed olfactory neuroblastoma and carcinoma. A report of two cases. Cancer 1984, **54**: 2019–2028.

249 Mills SE, Frierson HF Jr. Olfactory neuroblastoma. A clinicopathologic study of 21 cases. Am J Surg Pathol 1985, **9**: 317–327.

250 Mirra SS, Pearl GS, Hoffman JC, Campbell WG Jr. Nasal "glioma" with prominent neuronal component. Report of a case. Arch Pathol Lab Med 1981, **105**: 540–541.

251 Nakashima T, Kimmelman CP, Snow JB Jr. Structure of human fetal and adult olfactory neuroepithelium. Arch Otolaryngol 1984, **110**: 641–646.

252 Oberman HA, Rice DH. Olfactory neuroblastomas. A clinicopathologic study. Cancer 1976, **38**: 2494–2502.

253 O'Connor TA, McLean P, Juillard GJF, Parker RG. Olfactory neuroblastoma. Cancer 1989, **63**: 2426–2428.

254 Olsen KD, DeSanto LW. Olfactory neuroblastoma. Biologic and clinical behavior. Arch Otolaryngol 1983, **109**: 797–802.

255 Ordoñéz NG, Mackay B. Neuroendocrine tumors of the nasal cavity. Pathol Annu 1993, **(28–2)**: 77–111.

256 Parisier SC, Sinclair GM. Glomus tumor of the nasal cavity. Laryngoscope 1968, **78**: 2013–2024.

257 Perez-Ordonez B, Caruana SM, Huvos AG, Shah JP. Small cell neuroendocrine carcinoma of the nasal cavity and paranasal sinuses. Hum Pathol 1998, **29**: 826–832.

258 Perzin KH, Pushparaj N. Nonepithelial tumors of the nasal cavity, paranasal sinuses, and nasopharynx. A clinicopathologic study. XIII. Meningiomas. Cancer 1984, **54**: 1860–1869.

259 Perzin KH, Panyu H, Wechter S. Nonepithelial tumors of the nasal cavity, paranasal sinuses, and nasopharynx. A clinicopathologic study. XII. Schwann cell tumors (neurilemoma, neurofibroma, malignant schwannoma). Cancer 1982, **50**: 2193–2202.

260 Pompili A, Calvosa F, Caroli F, Mastrostefano R, Occhipinti E, Raus L, Sciarretta F. The transdural extension of gliomas. J Neurooncol 1993, **15**: 67–74.

261 Schuller DE, Lucas JG. Nasopharyngeal paraganglioma. Report of a case and review of literature. Arch Otolaryngol 1982, **108**: 667–670.

262 Shugar JMA, Som PM, Biller HF, Som ML, Krespi YP. Peripheral nerve sheath tumors of the paranasal sinuses. Head Neck Surg 1981, **4**: 72–76.

263 Silva EG, Butler JJ, Mackay B, Goepfert H. Neuroblastoma and neuroendocrine carcinomas of the nasal cavity. A proposed new classification. Cancer 1982, **50**: 2388–2405.

264 Sinkre P, Lindberg G, Albores-Saavedra J. Nasopharyngeal gangliocytic paraganglioma. Arch Pathol Lab Med 2001, **125**: 1098–1100.

265 Siwersson U, Kindblom L-G. Oncocytic carcinoid of the nasal cavity and carcinoid of the lung in a child. Pathol Res Pract 1984, **178**: 562–569.

266 Sorensen PH, Wu JK, Berean KW, Lim JF, Donn W, Frierson HF, Reynolds CP, Lopez-Terrada D, Triche TJ. Olfactory neuroblastoma is a peripheral primitive neuroectodermal tumor related to Ewing sarcoma. Proc Natl Acad Sci USA 1996, **93**: 1038–1043.

267 Taxy JB. Meningioma of the paranasal sinuses. A report of two cases. Am J Surg Pathol 1990, **14**: 82–86.

268 Taxy JB, Hidvegi DF. Olfactory neuroblastoma. An ultrastructural study. Cancer 1977, **39**: 131–138.

269 Taxy JB, Bharani NK, Mills SE, Frierson HF Jr, Gould VE. The spectrum of olfactory neural tumors. A light-microscopic immunohistochemical and ultrastructural analysis. Am J Surg Pathol 1986, **10**: 687–695.

270 Thompson LD, Heffner DK. Sinonasal tract eosinophilic angiocentric fibrosis. A report of three cases. Am J Clin Pathol 2001, **115**: 243–248.

271 Trojanowski JQ, Lee V, Pillsbury N, Lee S. Neuronal origin of human esthesioneuroblastoma demonstrated with anti-neurofilament monoclonal antibodies. N Engl J Med 1982, **307**: 159–161.

Tumors of melanocytes

272 Berthelsen A, Andersen AP, Jensen S, Hansen HS. Melanomas of the mucosa in the oral cavity and the upper respiratory passages. Cancer 1984, **54**: 907–912.

273 Chetty R, Slavin JL, Pitson GA, Dowling JP. Melanoma botryoides. A distinctive myxoid pattern of sinonasal malignant melanoma. Histopatholgy 1994, **24**: 377–380.

274 Franquemont DW, Mills SE. Sinonasal malignant melanoma. A clinicopathologic and immunohistochemical study of 14 cases. Am J Clin Pathol 1991, **96**: 689–697.

275 Friedmann I. Osteoid and bone formation in a nasal mucosal melanoma and its metastasis. Histopathology 1998, **33**: 88.

276 Gouldesbrough DR, Martin-Hirsch DP, Lannigan F. Intranasal malignant melanoma arising in an inverted papilloma. Histopathology 1992, **20**: 523–526.

277 Holdcraft J, Gallagher JC. Malignant melanomas of the nasal and paranasal sinus mucosa. Ann Otol Rhinol Laryngol 1969, **78**: 5–20.

278 Lund VJ. Malignant melanoma of the nasal cavity and paranasal sinuses. Ear Nose Throat J 1993, **72**: 285–290.

278a Thompson LDR, Wieneke JA, Miettinen M. Sinonasal tract and nasopharyngeal melanomas. Am J Surg Pathol 2003, **27**: 594–611.

279 Uehara T, Matsubara O, Kasuga T. Melanocytes in the nasal cavity and paranasal sinus. Incidence and distribution in Japan. Acta Pathol Jpn 1987, **37**: 1105–1114.

Lymphoid tumors and tumorlike conditions

280 Abbondanzo SL, Wenig BM. Non-Hodgkin's lymphoma of the sinonasal tract. A clinicopathologic and immunophenotypic study of 120 cases. Cancer 1995, **75**: 1281–1291.

281 Alexiou C, Kau RJ, Dietzfelbinger H, Kremer M, Spiess JC, Schratzenstaller B, Arnold W. Extramedullary plasmacytoma: tumor occurrence and therapeutic concepts. Cancer 1999, **85**: 2305–2314.

282 Aozasa K. Biopsy findings in malignant histiocytosis presenting as lethal midline granuloma. J Clin Pathol 1982, **35**: 599–605.

283 Arber DA, Weiss LM, Albujar PF, Chen YY, Jaffe ES. Nasal lymphomas in Peru. High incidence of T-cell immunophenotype and Epstein–Barr virus infection. Am J Surg Pathol 1993, **17**: 392–399.

284 Batsakis JG, Luna MA. Midfacial necrotizing lesions. Semin Diagn Pathol 1987, **4**: 90–116.

284a Batsakis JG, Medeiros JL, Luna MA, El-Naggar AK. Plasma cell dyscrasias and the head and neck. Ann Diagn Pathol 2002, **6**: 129–140.

285 Chan JK. Peripheral T-cell and NK-cell neoplasms: an integrated approach to diagnosis. Mod Pathol 1999, **12**: 177–199.

286 Chan JK, Sin VC, Wong KF, Ng CS, Tsang WY, Chan CH, Cheung MM, Lau WH. Non-nasal lymphoma expressing the natural killer cell marker CD56: a clinicopathologic study of 49 cases of an uncommon aggressive neoplasm. Blood 1997, **89**: 4501–4513.

287 Chan JK, Yip TTC, Tsang WYM, Ng CS, Lau WH, Poon YF, Wong CCS, Ma VWS. Detection of Epstein-Barr viral RNA in malignant lymphomas of the upper aerodigestive tract. Am J Surg Pathol 1994, **18**: 938–946.

288 Cheung MM, Chan JK, Lau WH, Foo W, Chan PT, Ng CS, Ngan RK. Primary non-Hodgkin's lymphoma of the nose and nasopharynx: clinical features, tumor immunophenotype, and treatment outcome in 113 patients. J Clin Oncol 1998, **16**: 70–77.

289 Cuadra-Garcia I, Proulx GM, Wu CL, Wang CC, Pilch BZ, Harris NL, Ferry JA. Sinonasal lymphoma: a clinicopatholic analysis of 58 cases from the Massachusetts general hospital. Am J Surg Pathol 1999, **23**: 1356–1369.

290 Daggett RB, Haghighi P, Terkeltaub RA. Nasal cocaine abuse causing an aggressive midline intransal and pharyngeal destructive process mimicking midline reticulosis and limited Wegener's granulomatosis. J Rheumatol 1990, **117**: 838–840.

291 DeRemee RA, Weiland LH, McDonald TJ. Polymorphic reticulosis, lymphomatoid granulomatosis. Two diseases or one? Mayo Clin Proc 1978, **53**: 634–640.

292 Fechner RE, Lamppin DW. Midline malignant reticuloses. A clinicopathologic entity. Arch Otolaryngol 1972, **95**: 467–476.

293 Fellbaum C, Hansmann ML. Immunohistochemical differential diagnosis of granulocytic sarcomas and malignant lymphomas on formalin-fixed material. Virchows Arch [A] 1990, **416**: 351–355.

294 Ferry JA, Sklar J, Zukerberg LR, Harris NL. Nasal lymphoma. A clinicopathologic study with immunophenotypic and genotypic analysis. Am J Surg Pathol 1991, **15**: 268–279.

295 Fu Y-S, Perzin KH. Nonepithelial tumors of the nasal cavity, paranasal sinuses and nasopharynx. A clinicopathologic study. IX. Plasmacytomas. Cancer 1978, **42**: 2399–2406.

296 Fu Y-S, Perzin KH. Nonepithelial tumors of the nasal cavity, paranasal sinuses and nasopharynx. A clinicopathologic study. X. Malignant lymphomas. Cancer 1979, **43**: 611–621.

297 Gaal K, Sun NC, Hernandez AM, Arber DA. Sinonasal NK/T-cell lymphomas in the United States. Am J Surg Pathol 2000, **24**: 1511–1517.

298 Ho FC, Choy D, Loke SL, Kung IT, Fu KH, Liang R, Todd D, Khoo RK. Polymorphic reticulosis and conventional lymphomas of the nose and upper aerodigestive tract. A clinicopathologic study of 70 cases, and immunophenotypic studies of 16 cases. Hum Pathol 1990, **21**: 1041–1050.

299 Ishii Y, Yamanaka N, Ogawa K, Yoshida Y, Takami T, Matsuura A, Isago H, Kataura A, Kikuchi K. Nasal T-cell lymphoma as a type of so-called "lethal midline granuloma." Cancer 1982, **50**: 2336–2344.

300 Jaffe ES, Chan JK, Su IJ, Frizzera G, Mori S, Feller AC, Ho FC. Report of the workshop on nasal and related extranodal angiocentric T/natural killer cell lymphomas. Definitions, differential diagnosis, and epidemiology. Am J Surg Pathol 1996, **20**: 103–111.

301 Jaffe ES, Krenacs L, Kumar S, Kingma DW, Raffeld M. Extranodal peripheral T-cell and NK-cell neoplasms. Am J Clin Pathol 1999, **111**(suppl.): S46–S55.

302 Kapadia SB, Desai U, Cheng VS. Extramedullary plasmacytoma of the head and neck. A clinicopathologic study of 20 cases. Medicine (Baltimore) 1982, **61**: 317–328.

303 Kinney MC. The role of morphologic features, phenotype, genotype, and anatomic site in defining extranodal T-cell or NK-cell neoplasms. Am J Clin Pathol 1999, **111**(suppl.): S104–S118.

304 Kobashi Y, Nakamura S, Sasajima Y, Koshikawa T, Yatabe Y, Kitoh K, Mori S, Ueda R, Yamabe H, Suchi T. Inconsistent association of Epstein–Barr virus with CD56 (NCAM)-positive angiocentric lymphoma occurring in sites other than the upper and lower respiratory tract. Histopathology 1996, **28**: 111–120.

305 Kotner LM, Wang CC. Plasmacytoma of the upper air and food passages. Cancer 1972, **30**: 414–418.

306 Liu Q, Ohshima K, Sumie A, Suzushima H, Iwasaki H, Kikuchi M. Nasal DC56-positive small round cell tumors. Differential diagnosis of haematological, neurogenic, and myogenic neoplasms. Virchows Arch 2001, **438**: 271–279.

307 Logsdon MD, Ha CS, Kavadi VS, Cabanillas F, Hess MA, Cox JD. Lymphoma of the nasal cavity and paranasal sinuses: improved outcome and altered prognostic factors with combined modality therapy. Cancer 1997, **80**: 477–488.

308 MacNaughton DM, Tewfik TL, Bernstein ML. Hodgkin's disease in the nasopharynx. J Otolaryngol 1990, **19**: 282–284.

309 Medeiros LJ, Peiper ST, Elwood L, Yano T, Raffeld M, Jaffe ES. Angiocentric immunoproliferative lesions. A molecular analysis of eight cases. Hum Pathol 1991, **22**: 1150–1157.

310 Michaels L, Gregory MM. Pathology of "nonhealing (midline) granuloma." J Clin Pathol 1977, **30**: 317–327.

311 Mori N, Yatabe Y, Oka K, Kinoshita T, Kobayashi T, Ono T, Asai J. Expression of perforin in nasal lymphoma. Additional evidence of its natural killer cell derivation. Am J Pathol 1996, **149**: 699–705.

312 Ng CS, Chan JK, Cheng PNM, Szeto S-C. Nasal T-cell lymphoma

associated with hemophagocytic syndrome. Cancer 1986, **58:** 67–71.

313 Ng CS, Lo ST, Chan JK. Peripheral T- and putative natural killer cell lymphomas commonly coexpress CD95 and DC95 ligand. Hum Pathol 1999, **30:** 48–54.

314 Ohshima K, Suzumiya J, Shimazaki K, Kato A, Tanaka T, Kanda M, Kikuchi M. Nasal T/NK-cell lymphomas commonly express perforin and Fas ligand; important mediators of tissue damage. Histopathology 1997, **31:** 444–450.

315 Ott G, Kalla J, Ott MM, Müller-Hermelink HK. The Epstein–Barr virus in malignant non-Hodgkin's lymphoma of the upper aerodigestive tract. Diagn Mol Pathol 1997, **6:** 134–139.

316 Ratech H, Burke JS, Blayney DW, Sheibani K, Rappaport H. A clinicopathologic study of malignant lymphomas of the nose, paranasal sinuses, and hard palate, including cases of lethal midline granuloma. Cancer 1989, **64:** 2525–2531.

317 Rimarenko S, Schwartz IS. Polypoid nasal pseudolymphoma. Am J Clin Pathol 1985, **83:** 507–509.

318 Robbins KT, Fuller LM, Vlasak M, Osborne B, Jing BS, Velasquez WS, Sullivan JA. Primary lymphomas of the nasal cavity and paranasal sinuses. Cancer 1985, **56:** 814–819.

319 Sercarz JA, Strasnick B, Newman A, Dodd LG. Midline nasal destruction in cocaine abusers. Otolaryngol Head Neck Surg 1991, **105:** 694–701.

320 Strickler JG, Meneses MF, Habermann TM, Ilstrup DM, Earle JD, McDonald TJ, Chang KL, Weiss LM. Polymorphic reticulosis. A reappraisal. Hum Pathol 1994, **25:** 659–665.

321 Stroup RM, Sheibani K, Moncada A, Purdy LJ, Battifora H. Angiotropic (intravascular) large cell lymphoma. A clinicopathologic study of seven cases with unique clinical presentations. Cancer 1990, **66:** 1781–1788.

321a Takahara M, Kishibe K, Bandoh N, Nonaka S, Harabuchi Y. P53, N- and K-Ras, and ß-catenin gene mutations and prognostic factors in nasal NK/T-cell lymphoma from Hokkaido, Japan. Hum Pathol 2004 (in press).

322 Tsokos M, Fauci AS, Costa J. Idiopathic midline destructive disease (IMDD). A subgroup of patients with the "mid-line granuloma" syndrome. Am J Clin Pathol 1982, **77:** 162–168.

323 Van de Rijn M, Bhargava V, Molina-Kirsch H, Carlos-Bregni R, Warnke RA, Cleary ML, Karnel OW. Extranadal head and neck lymphomas in Guatemala: high frequency of Epstein–Barr virus-associated sinonasal lymphomas. Hum Pathol 1997, **28:** 834–839.

324 Wilder WH, Harner SG, Banks PM. Lymphoma of the nose and paranasal sinuses. Arch Otolaryngol 1983, **109:** 310–312.

325 Wollner N, Mandell L, Filippa D, Exelby P, McGowan N, Lieberman P. Primary nasal-paranasal oropharyngeal lymphoma in the pediatric age group. Cancer 1990, **65:** 1438–1444.

326 Ye YL, Zhou MH, Lu XY, Dai YR, Wu WX. Nasopharyngeal and nasal malignant lymphoma. A clinicopathological study of 54 cases. Histopathology 1992, **20:** 511–516.

Nasopharyngeal angiofibroma

327 Beham A, Beham-Schmid C, Regauer S, Aubock L, Stammberger H. Nasopharyngeal angiofibroma: true neoplasm or vascular malformation? Adv Anat Pathol 2000, **7:** 36–46.

328 Chen KTK, Bauer FW. Sarcomatous transformation of nasopharyngeal angiofibroma. Cancer 1982, **49:** 369–371.

329 Cummings BJ. Relative risk factors in the treatment of juvenile nasopharyngeal angiofibroma. Head Neck Surg 1980, **3:** 21–26.

330 Deschler DG, Kaplan MJ, Boles R. Treatment of large juvenile nasopharyngeal angiofibroma. Otolaryngol Head Neck Surg 1992, **106:** 278–284.

331 Dohar JE, Duvall AJ III. Spontaneous regression of juvenile nasopharyngeal angiofibroma. Ann Otol Rhinol Laryngol 1992, **101:** 469–471.

332 Fields JN, Halverson KJ, Devineni VR, Simpson JR, Perez CA. Juvenile nasopharyngeal angiofibroma. Efficacy of radiation therapy. Radiology 1990, **176:** 263–265.

333 Goepfert H, Cangir A, Lee Y-Y. Chemotherapy for aggressive juvenile nasopharyngeal angiofibroma. Arch Otolaryngol 1985, **111:** 285–289.

334 Guertl B, Beham A, Zechner R, Stammberger H, Hoefler G. Nasopharyngeal angiofibroma: an APC-gene-associated tumor? Hum Pathol 2000, **31:** 1411–1413.

335 Gullane PJ, Davidson J, O'Dwyer T, Forte V. Juvenile angiofibroma. A review of the literature and a case series report. Laryngoscope 1992, **102:** 928–933.

336 Harma RA. Nasopharyngeal angiofibroma. Acta Otolaryngol (Stockholm) 1958, **146**(Suppl): 1–74.

337 Hicks JL, Nelson JF. Juvenile nasopharyngeal angiofibroma. Oral Surg Oral Med Oral Pathol 1973, **35:** 807–817.

338 Howard DJ, Lloyd G, Lund V. Recurrence and its avoidance in juvenile angiofibroma. Laryngoscope 2001, **111**(9): 1509–1511.

339 Hwang HC, Mills SE, Patterson K, Gown AM. Expression of androgen receptors in nasopharyngeal angiofibroma: an immunohistochemical study of 24 cases. Mod Pathol 1998, **11:** 1122–1126.

340 Kasper ME, Parsons JT, Mancuso AA, Mendenhall WM, Stringer SP, Cassisi NJ, Million RR. Radiation therapy for juvenile angiofibroma. Evaluation by CT and MRI, analysis of tumor regression, and selection of patients. Int J Radiat Oncol Biol Phys 1993, **25:** 689–694.

341 McCombe A, Lund VJ, Howard DJ. Recurrence in juvenile angiofibroma. Rhinology 1990, **28:** 97–102.

342 McGavran MH, Sessions DG, Dorfman RD, Davis DO, Ogura JH. Nasopharyngeal angiofibroma. Arch Otolaryngol 1969, **90:** 94–104.

343 Neel HB III, Whicker JH, Devine KD, Weiland LH. Juvenile angiofibroma. Review of 120 cases. Am J Surg 1973, **126:** 547–556.

344 Paris J, Guelfucci B, Moulin G, Zanaret M, Triglia JM. Diagnosis and treatment of juvenile nasopharyngeal angiofibroma. Eur Arch Otorhinolaryngol 2001, **258**(3): 120–124.

345 Schiff M, Gonzalez AM, Ong M, Baird A. Juvenile nasopharyngeal angiofibroma contains an angiogenic growth factor. Basic FGF. Laryngoscope 1992, **102:** 940–945.

346 Spagnolo DV, Papadimitriou JM, Archer M. Postirradiation malignant fibrous histiocytoma arising in juvenile nasopharyngeal angiofibroma and producing alpha-1 antitrypsin. Histopathology 1984, **8:** 339–352.

347 Sternberg SS. Pathology of juvenile nasopharyngeal angiofibroma. A lesion of adolescent males. Cancer 1954, **7:** 15–28.

348 Topilko A, Zakrewski A, Pichard E, Viron A. Ultrastructural cytochemistry of intranuclear dense granules in nasopharyngeal angiofibroma. Ultrastruct Pathol 1984, **6:** 221–228.

349 Waldman SR, Levine HL, Astor F, Wood BG, Weinstein M, Tucker HM. Surgical experience with nasopharyngeal angiofibroma. Arch Otolaryngol 1981, **107:** 677–682.

349a Zhang PJ, Weber R, Liang H-H, Pasha TL, LiVolsi VA. Growth factors and receptors in juvenile nasopharyngeal angiofibroma and nasal polyps. An immunohistochemcial study. Arch Pathol Lab Med 2003, **127:** 1480–1484.

Other tumors and tumorlike conditions

350 Alameda F, Fontain J, Corominas JM, Lioreta J, Serrano S. Reactive vascular lesion of nasal septum simulating agiosarcoma in a cocaine abuser. Hum Pathol 2000, **31:** 239–240.

350a Banerjee SS, Trenholm PW, Sheikh MY, Wakamatsu K, Ancans J, Rosai A. Monotypic angiomyolipoma of the nasal cavity: a heretofore undescribed occurrence. Int J Surg Pathol 2001, **9:** 309–315.

351 Batsakis JG, Solomon AR, Rice DH. The pathology of head and

neck tumors. Neoplasms of cartilage, bone, and the notochord. Part 7. Head Neck Surg 1980, **3**: 43–57.

352 Beham-Schmid C, Heham A, Jakse R, Aubock L, Hofler G. Extranodal follicular dendritic cell tumour of the nasopharynx. Virchows Arch 1998, **432**: 293–298.

353 Beneck D, Abati AD, Greco MA. Lymphangioma presenting as a nasal polyp in an infant. Arch Pathol Lab Med 1985, **109**: 773–775.

354 Brydon HL. Intracranial dermoid cysts with nasal dermal sinuses. Acta Neurochir (Wein) 1992, **118**: 185–188.

355 Byrne MN, Sessions DG. Nasopharyngeal craniopharyngioma. Case report and literature review. Ann Otol Rhinol Laryngol 1990, **99**: 633–639.

356 Chan AC, Chan KW, Chan JK, Au WY, Ho WK, Ng WM. Development of follicular dendritic cell sarcoma in hyaline-vascular Castleman's disease of nasopharynx: tracing it evolution by sequential biopsies. Histopathology 2001, **38**: 510–518.

357 Chan JK, Ng H-K, Wan KY, Tsao SY, Leung TWT, Tse KC. Clear cell rhabdomyosarcoma of the nasal cavity and paranasal sinuses. Histopathology 1989, **14**: 391–399.

358 Chu PG, Chang KL, Wu AY, Weiss LM. Nasal glomus tumors: report of two cases with emphasis on immunohistochemical features and differential diagnosis. Hum Pathol 1999, **30**: 1259–1261.

359 Compagno J, Hyams VJ. Hemangiopericytoma-like intranasal tumors. A clinicopathologic study of 23 cases. Am J Clin Pathol 1976, **66**: 672–683.

360 Deutsch M, Mercado R Jr, Parsons JA. Cancer of the nasopharynx in children. Cancer 1978, **41**: 1128–1133.

361 Eichhorn JH, Dickersin GR, Bhan AK, Goodman ML. Sinonasal hemangiopericytoma. A reassessment with electron microscopy, immunohistochemistry, and long-term follow-up. Am J Surg Pathol 1990, **14**: 856–866.

361a Finke NM, Lae ME, Lloyd RV, Gehani SK, Nascimento AG. Sinonasal desmoplastic small round cell tumor. Am J Surg Pathol 2002, **26**: 799–803.

362 Fu Y-S, Perzin KH. Nonepithelial tumors of the nasal cavity, paranasal sinuses and nasopharynx. A clinicopathologic study. I. General features and vascular tumors. Cancer 1974A, **33**: 1275–1288.

363 Fu Y-S, Perzin KH. Nonepithelial tumors of the nasal cavity, paranasal sinuses and nasopharynx. A clinicopathologic study. II. Osseous and fibroosseous lesions, including osteoma, fibrous dysplasia, ossifying fibroma, osteoblastoma, giant cell tumor, and osteosarcoma. Cancer 1974B, **33**: 1289–1305.

364 Fu Y-S, Perzin KH. Nonepithelial tumors of the nasal cavity, paranasal sinuses and nasopharynx. A clinicopathologic study. III. Cartilaginous tumors (chondroma, chondrosarcoma). Cancer 1974C, **34**: 453–463.

365 Fu Y-S, Perzin KH. Nonepithelial tumors of the nasal cavity, paranasal sinuses and nasopharynx. A clinicopathologic study. IV. Smooth muscle tumors (leiomyoma, leiomyosarcoma). Cancer 1975, **35**: 1300–1308.

366 Fu Y-S, Perzin KH. Nonepithelial tumors of the nasal cavity, paranasal sinuses and nasopharynx. A clinicopathologic study. V. Skeletal muscle tumors (rhabdomyoma and rhabdomyosarcoma). Cancer 1976A, **37**: 364–376.

367 Fu Y-S, Perzin KH. Nonepithelial tumors of the nasal cavity, paranasal sinuses and nasopharynx. A clinicopathologic study. VI. Fibrous tissue tumors (fibroma, fibromatosis, fibrosarcoma). Cancer 1976B, **37**: 2912–2928.

368 Fu Y-S, Perzin KH. Nonepithelial tumors of the nasal cavity, paranasal sinuses and nasopharynx. A clinicopathologic study. VII. Myxomas. Cancer 1977A, **39**: 195–203.

369 Fu Y-S, Perzin KH. Nonepithelial tumors of the nasal cavity, paranasal sinuses and nasopharynx. A clinicopathologic study. VIII. Adipose tissue tumors (lipoma and liposarcoma). Cancer 1977B, **40**: 1314–1317.

370 Gale N, Rott T, Kambic V. Nasopharyngeal rhabdomyoma. Report of case (light and electron microscopic studies) and review of the literature. Pathol Res Pract 1984, **178**: 454–460.

371 Gnepp DR, Henley J, Weiss S, Heffner D. Desmond fibromatosis of the sinonasal tract and nasopharynx: a clinicopathologic study of 25 cases. Cancer 1996, **78**: 2572–2579.

371a Gonzàlez-Lois C, Ibarrola C, Ballestín C, Martínez-Tello FJ. Dedifferentiated liposarcoma of the pyriform sinus. Report of a case and review of the literature. Int J Surg Pathol 2002, **10**: 75–79.

372 Govett GS, Amedee RG. Giant cell reparative granuloma presenting as a midline nasal mass. Ear Nose Throat J 1991, **70**: 137–139.

373 Hachisuga T, Hashimoto H, Enjoji M. Angioleiomyoma. A clinicopathologic reappraisal of 562 cases. Cancer 1984, **54**: 126–130.

374 Hayes MM, Van der Westhuizen N, Holden GP. Aggressive glomus tumor of the nasal region. Report of a case with multiple local recurrences. Arch Pathol Lab Med 1993, **117**: 649–652.

375 Heffner DK. Problems in pediatric otorhinolaryngic pathology. II. Vascular tumors and lesions of the sinonasal tract and nasopharynx. Int J Pediatr Otorhinolaryngol 1983A, **5**: 125–138.

376 Heffner DK. Problems in pediatric otorhinolaryngic pathology. III. Teratoid and neural tumors of the nose, sinonasal tract, and nasopharynx. Int J Pediatr Otorhinolaryngol 1983B, **6**: 1–21.

377 Heffner DK, Gnepp DR. Sinonasal fibrosarcomas, malignant schwannomas, and "Triton" tumors. A clinicopathologic study of 67 cases. Cancer 1992, **70**: 1089–1101.

378 Heffner DK, Hyams VJ. Teratocarcinosarcoma (malignant teratoma?) of the nasal cavity and paranasal sinuses. A clinicopathologic study of 20 cases. Cancer 1984, **53**: 2140–2154.

379 Hsueh C, Hsueh S, Gonzalez-Crussi F, Lee TJ, Su J. Nasal chondromesenchymal harmartoma in children: report of two cases with review of the literature. Arch Pathol Lab Med 2001, **125**: 400–403.

379a Huang H-Y, Antonescu CR. Sinonasal smooth muscle cell tumors. Arch Pathol Lab Med 2003, **127**: 297–304.

380 Kapadia SB, Propek EJ, Barnes I. Pediatric otorhinolaryngic pathology. Diagnosis of selected lesions. Pathol Annu 1994, **29**(Pt 1): 159–210.

381 Kuruvilla A, Wenig BM, Humphrey DM, Heffner DK. Leiomyosarcoma of the sinonasal tract. A clinicopathologic study of nine cases. Arch Otolaryngol Head Neck Surg 1990, **116**: 1278–1286.

382 McDermott MB, Ponder TB, Dehner LP. Nasal chondromesenchymal hamartoma: an upper respiratory tract analogue of the chest wall mesenchymal hamartoma. Am J Surg Pathol 1998, **22**: 425–433.

383 Manon JK, Soule EH. Embryonal rhabdomyosarcoma of the head and neck. Report on eighty-eight cases. Am J Surg 1965, **110**: 585–591.

384 Mufarrij AA, Busaba NY, Zaytoun GM, Gallo GR, Feiner HD. Primary localized amyloidosis of the nose and paranasal sinuses. A case report with immunohistochemical observations and a review of the literature. Am J Surg Pathol 1990, **14**: 379–383.

385 Nakhleh RE, Swanson PE, Dehner LP. Juvenile (embryonal and alveolar) rhabdomyosarcoma of the head and neck in adults. A clinical, pathologic, and immunohistochemical study of 12 cases. Cancer 1991, **67**: 1019–1024.

386 Naresh KN, Pai SA. Foci resembling olfactory neuroblastoma and craniopharyngioma are seen in sinonasal teratocarcinosarcomas. Histpathology 1997, **30(4)**: 378–382.

387 Nichols GE, Gaffey MJ, Mills SE, Weiss LM. Lobular capillary hemangioma. An immunohistochemical study including steroid hormone receptor status. Am J Clin Pathol 1992, **97**: 770–775.

388 Pai SA, Naresh KN, Masih K, Ramarao C, Borges AM. Teratocarcinosarcoma of the paranasal sinuses:

a clinicopathologic and immunohistochemical study. Hum Pathol 1998, **29:** 718–722.

389 Perzin KH, Fu Y-S. Non-epithelial tumors of the nasal cavity, paranasal sinuses and nasopharynx. A clinicopathologic study. XI. Fibrous histiocytomas. Cancer 1980, **45:** 2616–2626.

390 Pontius KI, Sebek BA. Extraskeletal Ewing's sarcoma arising in the nasal fossa. Light- and electron-microscopic observations. Am J Clin Pathol 1981, **75:** 410–415.

391 Potter AJ Jr, Khatib G, Peppard SB. Intranasal glomus tumors. Arch Otolaryngol 1984, **110:** 755–756.

392 Rice DH, Batsakis JG, Headington JT, Boles R. Fibrous histiocytomas of the nose and paranasal sinuses. Arch Otolaryngol 1974, **100:** 398–401.

393 Richter HJ, Batsakis JG, Boles R. Chordomas. Nasopharyngeal presentation and atypical long survival. Ann Otol Rhinol Laryngol 1975, **84:** 327–332.

394 Ruark DS, Schlehaider UK, Shah JP. Chondrosarcomas of the head and neck. World J Surg 1992, **16:** 1010–1015.

395 Schafer DR, Thompson LD, Smith BC, Wenig BM. Primary ameloblastoma of the sinonasal tract; a clinicopathologic study of 24 cases. Cancer 1998, **82:** 667–674.

396 Shanmugaratnam K, Kunaratnam N, Chia KB, Chiang GSC, Finniah R. Teratoid carcinosarcoma of the paranasal sinuses. Pathology 1983, **15:** 413–419.

397 Shimazaki H, Aida S, Tamai S, Miyazawa T, Nakanoubou M. Sinonasal teratocarcinosarcoma: ultrastructural and immunohistochemical evidence of neuroectodermal origin. Ultrastruct Pathol 2000, **24:** 115–122.

398 Shmookler BM, Enzinger FM, Brannon RB. Orofacial synovial sarcoma. Cancer 1982, **50:** 269–276.

399 Stern Y, Braslavsky D, Segal K, Shpitzer T, Abraham A. Intravascular papillary endothelial hyperplasia in the maxillary sinus. A benign lesion that may be mistaken for angiosarcoma. Arch Otolaryngol Head Neck Surg 1991, **117:** 1182–1184.

400 Tharrington CL, Bossen EH. Nasopharyngeal teratomas. Arch Pathol Lab Med 1992, **116:** 165–167.

400a Thompson LDR, Miettinen M, Wenig BM. Sinonasal-type hemangiopericytoma. Am J Surg Pathol 2003, **27:** 737–749.

400b Tse LLY, Chan JKC. Sinonasal haemangiopericytoma-like tumour: a sinonasal glomus tumour or a haemangiopericytoma? Histopathology 2002, **40:** 510–517.

401 Wanamaker JR, Kraus DH, Eliacher I, Lavertu P. Manifestations of metastatic breast carcinoma to the head and neck. Head Neck 1993, **15:** 257–262.

402 Watanabe K, Saito A, Suzuki M, Yamanobe S, Suzuki T. True hemangiopericytoma of the nasal cavity. Arch Pathol Lab Med 2001, **125:** 686–690.

403 Witkin GB, Rosai J. Solitary fibrous tumor of the upper respiratory tract. A report of six cases. Am J Surg Pathol 1991, **15:** 842–848.

404 Yfantis HG, Drachenberg CB, Gray W, Papadimitriou JC. Angiectatic nasal polyps that clinically simulate a malignant process: report of two cases and review of the literature. Arch Pathol Lab Med 2000, **124:** 406–410.

405 Zukerberg LR, Rosenberg AE, Randolph G, Pilch BZ, Goodman ML. Solitary fibrous tumor of the nasal cavity and paranasal sinuses. Am J Surg Pathol 1991, **15:** 126–130.

Larynx and trachea

Larynx

Normal anatomy

The larynx is a complex organ composed of various stromal and epithelial tissues.[3a] The supraglottic portion is derived from the third and fourth branchial pouches, whereas the glottis and subglottis originate from the sixth branchial pouch. The major cartilages of the larynx (cricoid, thyroid, and arytenoid) are of hyaline-type, whereas the epiglottis is of elastic-type, with numerous fenestrations. Calcification of the thyroid and cricoid cartilages increases with age; the thyroid cartilage also undergoes ossification.

The larynx is usually divided into three major compartments[7-9]:

1 **Supraglottic**, which extends from the tip of the epiglottis to the true cord and includes the aryepiglottic folds, false vocal cords, and ventricles (saccules)
2 **Glottic**, which consists of the true vocal cords and the anterior commissure that bridges them anteriorly
3 **Subglottic**, which is the area between the lower border of the true vocal cords (where the squamous epithelium ends) and the first tracheal cartilage.

The epithelium of the normal larynx varies from stratified squamous to respiratory-type ciliated, depending on the location, according to the following scheme:

Epiglottis

Lingual (anterior) surface	Stratified squamous
Laryngeal (posterior) surface	Stratified squamous merging into respiratory-type

Larynx

Supraglottic portion	Respiratory-type
Glottis	Stratified squamous
Intraglottic portion	Respiratory-type

The junction between the two epithelial types may be abrupt or separated by a transitional zone. Patches of squamous epithelium are frequently seen within the respiratory-type epithelial regions; these are particularly prominent in smokers. Dendritic melanocytes may be seen in the basal layer, particularly in blacks.

Seromucinous glands are present in most of the larynx; these often show oncocytic metaplasia in older individuals.[3,4,6]

Reinke's space is the term used for the lamina propria of the true vocal cord, bound by the base of the squamous epithelium on one side and the vocal ligament on the other. It contains a few capillaries but lacks lymphatic vessels.

Biopsy specimens from the larynx may show normal or metaplastic cartilaginous formations that can be confused with cartilaginous neoplasms. One is the vocal process of the arytenoid cartilage, which may be seen as a sharply circumscribed nodule of uniformly mature elastic-type cartilage in biopsies from the posterior portion of the true cord. Another is *chondroid metaplasia* of the true cord, a common asymptomatic finding in the mid or posterior portion of this structure; it is characterized by blurred margins and a peripheral zone of myxoid connective tissue.[1]

Two pairs of paraganglia are normally found in the larynx, sometimes in ectopic or aberrant positions.[2]

It is not unusual to find microscopic islands of *thyroid tissue* within the fibrous capsule of the larynx and trachea, just external to the cricothyroid membrane.[5]

Cysts and laryngocele

The two most common types of **cysts** of the larynx have been divided by DeSanto et al.[10] according to their mechanism of formation into *saccular* (24%) and *ductal* (75%).

The former arise from cystic distention of the laryngeal saccule. They are large and deep and are often found inside the ventricle. Saccular cysts differ from laryngoceles only in that they contain mucus, whereas the latter contain air. Ductal cysts, which are the result of dilatation of mucous glands, are small and superficial and are usually located in the true cord or epiglottis. Both types can be lined by either squamous or respiratory epithelium or a combination of both. Saccular cysts may be a cause of neonatal airway obstruction.[16]

A third type of laryngeal cyst, which perhaps represents a subtype of the ductal cyst, is referred to as *oncocytic cyst* because of the fact that it is lined partially or completely by oncocytes.[15] Papillary infoldings are usually present, but the condition is regarded as a metaplastic and hyperplastic change rather than a true neoplasia.[11,13] In rare cases the entire larynx is involved in a diffuse fashion by this process.[17] Oncocytic cysts have a tendency to recur.[11]

A fourth type of laryngeal cyst is the *tonsillar cyst*.[14] It has squamous-lined crypt-like structures and abundant follicular lymphoid tissue in the wall.

The term **laryngocele** refers to an air-containing dilatation of the tip of the laryngeal ventricle that communicates with the lumen of the ventricle by a narrow stalk.[12] The *internal* variety causes hoarseness, dyspnea, or reflex cough, whereas the *external* type appears as a soft mass in the lateral aspect of the neck. Combined forms occur. Laryngoceles may became infected and accumulate purulent material (*laryngopyoceles*).

Inflammation

Chronic (nonspecific) laryngitis can be the result of infection, overuse of the voice, exposure to chemical or physical agents, or irritation by tobacco and alcohol. Microscopically, a lymphocytic infiltrate is seen beneath the mucosa with an inconstant admixture of plasma cells and histiocytes, accompanied by some hyperplasia of the overlying epithelium.

Acute epiglottitis (acute supraglottitis) is a relatively rare but potentially lethal disease because of respiratory tract obstruction caused by massive edema.[22] It is usually a disease of children but also occurs in adults.[30] As a matter of fact, it has been suggested that George Washington died of it.[38] It is a bacterial infection, and *Haemophilus influenzae* type B is the most common organism involved. Grossly, the epiglottis appears red and edematous; microscopically, there is an intense acute inflammatory infiltrate associated with edema that extends to the adjacent soft tissues.

Tuberculosis of the larynx begins with edema of the posterior interarytenoid space, from which it spreads to the epiglottis, aryepiglottic fold, and vocal cords.[18,36] It can simulate carcinoma on laryngoscopic examination.[43]

Roentgenographic examination of the chest may show active advanced tuberculosis, although not as frequently as in the past.[31] Laryngeal biopsy shows typical granulomas, with or without caseation necrosis. Demonstration of acid-fast bacilli is necessary to document the diagnosis.

Histoplasmosis and **blastomycosis** are the two most common types of mycotic laryngitis in the United States.[35] In histoplasmosis, the early lesions are frequently located in the vocal cords and epiglottis.[21] A granulomatous lesion involving *only* the anterior portions of the larynx (especially the epiglottis) or having associated oral lesions is more likely to be histoplasmosis than tuberculosis. **Aspergillosis** and **cryptococcosis** may also involve this organ.[24,32] **Actinomycosis** of the larynx is extremely rare; only a handful of cases have been reported.[34] Several of these mycotic infections (particularly histoplasmosis and blastomycosis, but also aspergillosis) can induce a marked pseudoepitheliomatous hyperplasia of the overlying epithelium that can be confused microscopically with carcinoma.

Leprosy of the larynx is not rare in areas of the world where the disease is endemic.[39]

Crohn's disease can be accompanied by ulcerative and granulomatous lesions in the larynx, particularly the epiglottis.[20,26,40]

Sarcoidosis has been reported to present as epiglottic enlargement.[33]

Laryngeal granulomas resulting from endotracheal trauma caused by intubation can occur bilaterally on the vocal process of the arytenoid cartilage and may be mistaken for a neoplasm.[19] Injection of *Teflon* into paralyzed vocal cords, used as a means of augmentation in cases of recurrent nerve paralysis, may lead to the formation of an exuberant **foreign body granuloma** ("teflonoma")[42] (Fig. 7.41). A case of laryngeal **malakoplakia** and another of **Kimura's disease** have been described.[25,27] **Radiation changes** may present in the form of granulation tissue-

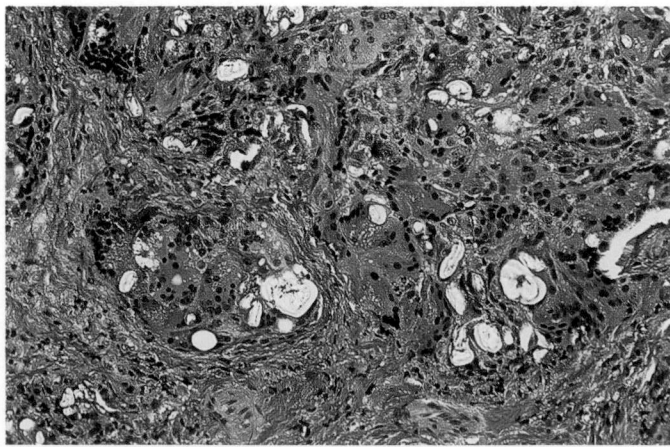

Fig. 7.41 So-called "teflonoma" of larynx. A granulomatous reaction is seen around a foreign body.

type reactions with bizarre mesenchymal cells that can simulate malignancy.[41] **Arthritis** of the cricoarytenoid joint is commonly associated with generalized rheumatoid arthritis.[23,28] **Pemphigus vulgaris** may rarely involve the surpraglottic larynx.[37] **Gout** may result in the deposit of tophi in the true vocal cords.[29] **Rosai–Dorfman disease (sinus histiocytosis with massive lymphadenopathy)** can affect the subglottic region and trachea.

Laryngeal nodule and contact ulcer

Laryngeal nodule represents a peculiar noninflammatory reaction to injury causing hoarseness, which is seen more commonly in people who misuse their voices. It occurs chiefly on the anterior third of the vocal cords and has also been called singers' nodule, amyloid tumor, polyp, and varix.

The microscopic appearance varies depending on the stage of evolution, as carefully recorded in the classic article by Ash and Schwartz on the subject[44] (Fig. 7.42). In

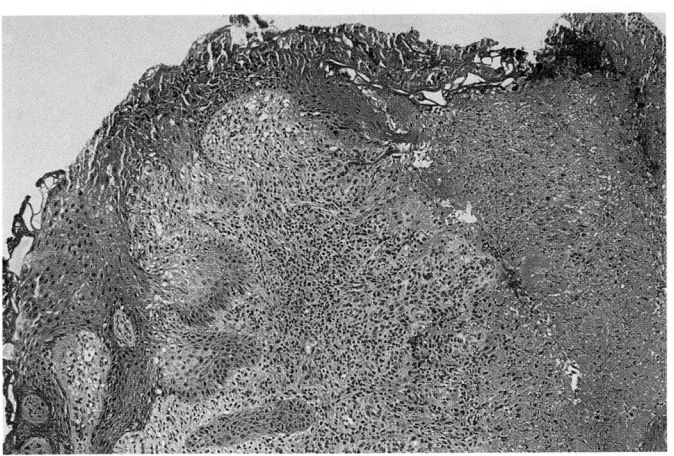

Fig. 7.43 Contact ulcer of larynx. A polypoid mass is seen resulting from a heavily inflamed stroma covered by a partially ulcerated epithelium.

the early stages, there are edema and proliferation of young fibroblasts. Later, dilated blood vessels and hyalinization of the stroma appear. Cases with a prominent vascular component may be mistaken for hemangioma. The hyaline stage was previously designated as "amyloid tumor". This is a misnomer because the material is hyalinized collagen rather than amyloid.

Contact ulcer (granulomatous ulcer, posterior commissure ulcer) is a lesion sometimes erroneously equated with laryngeal nodule but having a different presentation, microscopic appearance, and behavior. It is almost always found at the level of the posterior commissure, in the area of the vocal process of the arytenoid cartilage, at a site where the amount of subepithelial stroma is scantier. Microscopically, it has the appearance of exuberant granulation tissue; it is often confused with a pyogenic granuloma but lacks the characteristic lobular pattern of the latter.[45] The epithelium may be ulcerated or exhibit hyperplastic changes, sometimes of a pseudoepitheliomatous degree[46] (Fig. 7.43). The lesion stubbornly recurs after local excision, but eventually it subsides. Conservative management is strongly recommended, in as much as the trauma associated with the surgical excision can induce further recurrences.

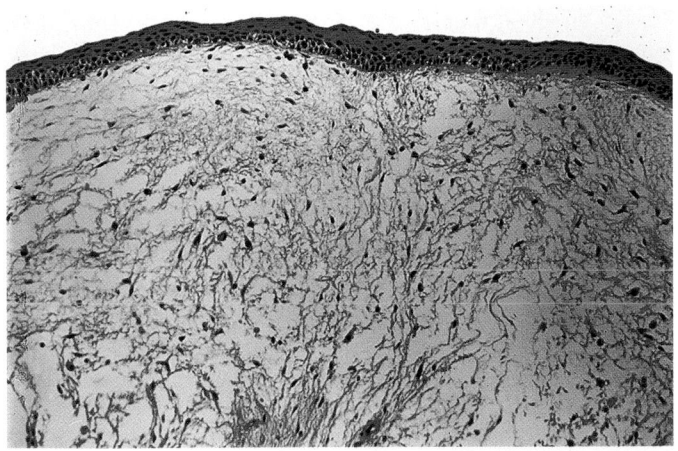

A

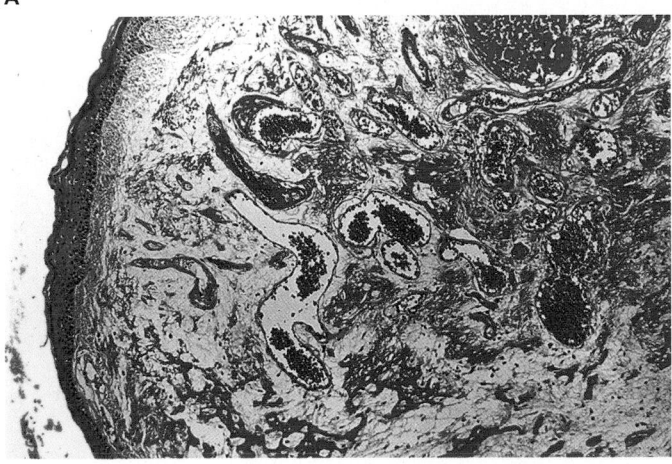

B

Fig. 7.42 A and **B**, Vocal nodule. The lesion shown in **A** has a fibromyxoid quality, whereas that depicted in **B** has angiomatoid features. (From Shanmugaratuam K, Sobin LH. Histological typing of upper respiratory tract tumours. Geneva, 1978, World Health Organization)

Other non-neoplastic lesions

Amyloidosis may involve the tracheobronchial tree as a localized phenomenon.[51,53] It is usually asymptomatic but may result in hoarseness and bleeding.[48] Monoclonal light chain deposition can be detected in most cases.[52] The disease can recur locally and become systemic or multicentric, but none of the patients studied by Thompson et al.[55] developed myeloma or lymphoma.

Eosinophilic angiocentric fibrosis is the term proposed for a peculiar inflammatory lesion of the upper respiratory tract thought to represent a mucosal variant of granuloma faciale and which occurs more commonly in the nasal cavity (see p. 307)[47,54]; some of the reported cases have involved the subglottic region of the trachea and the larynx.[49,54] One of the reported cases involved the sub-glottis.[54] The differential diagnosis includes Wegener's granulomatosis and specific infections.

Focal mucinosis has been rarely reported in the larynx and other portions of the upper aerodigestive tract.[50]

Necrotizing sialometaplasia similar to that more commonly seen in the oral cavity can occur in the larynx.[56]

Tumors and tumorlike conditions

Papilloma and papillomatosis

Juvenile laryngeal papillomas present in children or adolescents with multiple papillary tumors on the true cords, from which they may spread to the false cords, epiglottis, subglottic area, and in rare cases, even the trachea and bronchi. When extensive, papillomatosis may cause extreme respiratory difficulty and even death (Fig. 7.44).

The viral etiology of juvenile laryngeal papillomatosis has been proved by ultrastructural examination,[67] immunohistochemical demonstration of HPV antigens,[61] and in situ hybridization.[76,80] Viral DNA has also been found in uninvolved sites in patients with active disease and also in patients in remission.[80] The types of HPV that have been specifically associated with laryngeal papillomas are HPV11 and HPV6.[59] The high level of epidermal growth factor receptor that has been detected in the cells of this lesion may be responsible, at least in part, for their increased proliferative activity.[68,81]

The microscopic appearance is that of a papillary or acanthotic growth of well-differentiated squamous cells that retain an orderly maturation pattern[71] (Fig. 7.45). Mitotic activity is common, and some degree of koilocytosis and nuclear atypia are the rule.[73] When the process involves the respiratory mucosa, the maturation pattern, which is constant in the squamous epithelium, is not so apparent. This may lead to an overdiagnosis of carcinoma in situ. Mild chronic inflammation and hyperemia are usually present beneath the epithelium.[71]

These tumors tend to recur over a long period. It has been pointed out that the recurrences occur more often at junctions of stratified squamous and respiratory-type epithelium.[69] In rare cases they may extend into the tracheostomy stoma and soft tissues of the larynx or wrap around the carotid artery, while maintaining their well-differentiated nature (Fig. 7.46). Such a process has been designated *invasive papillomatosis*.[65] Treatment has included hormones, vaccines, cautery, cryosurgery, CO(2) laser, interferon, and photo dynamic therapy, with mixed but generally limited results.[57,62,63,78] In cases with very extensive involvement, laryngectomy may become necessary.[77]

Rarely, an obviously malignant squamous cell carcinoma develops in association with laryngeal papillo-

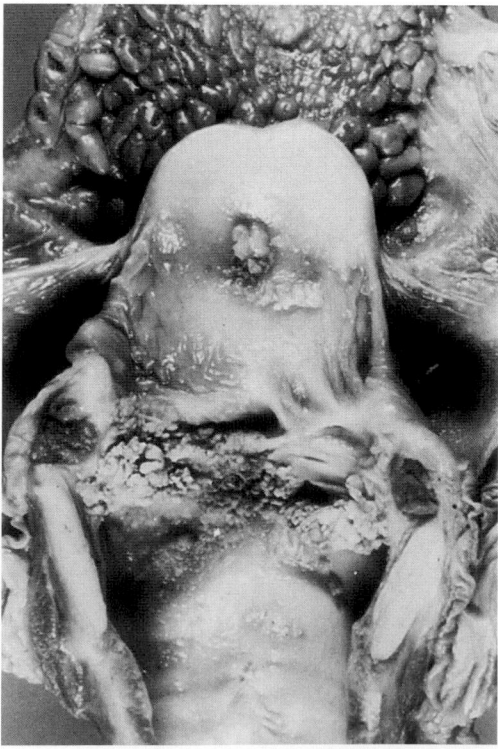

Fig. 7.44 Extensive papillomatosis in an 18-year-old boy. The patient had had almost 50 resections of this process, beginning at 7 years of age, and finally died of suffocation.

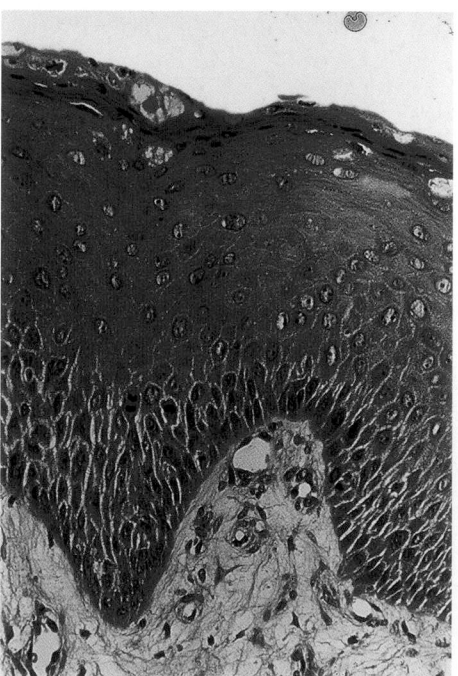

Fig. 7.45 Squamous papilloma of larynx. The lesion shows an orderly pattern of maturation. (From Shanmugaratuam K, Sobin LH. Histological typing of upper respiratory tract tumours. Geneva, 1978, World Health Organization)

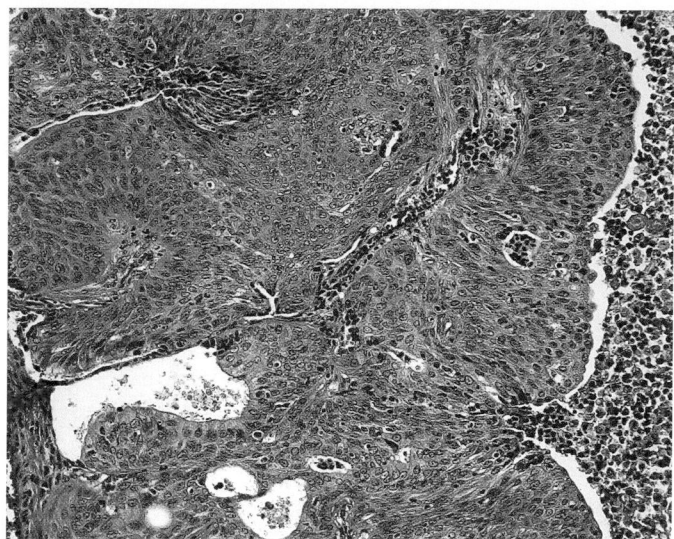

Fig. 7.46 Laryngeal papillomatosis spreading beyond the confines of the organ (so-called "invasive papillomatosis").

matosis. In practically all the reported cases of this complication, irradiation therapy had been administered previously for the papillomas; however, a few cases have been documented in which malignancy developed in the absence of radiation therapy.[75] The carcinoma is usually located in the larynx, but in cases with extensive papillomatosis of the tracheobronchial tree, it may also be found in the trachea or bronchi.[59,66,74,79] Interestingly, in all of the reported cases of juvenile-onset respiratory papillomatosis complicated by the development of pulmonary squamous cell carcinoma, HPV11 was identified in association with the malignant tumor.[60]

Adult laryngeal papillomas have a male predominance, are most commonly solitary, show a greater degree of inflammatory reaction, do not tend to spread, and recur less frequently than the juvenile form. As for the juvenile form, the viral types usually involved are HPV6 and 11.[72]

Verruca vulgaris is another HPV-related lesion that may occur in the larynx and be confused with squamous cell or verrucous carcinoma.[58,64]

Inflammatory pseudotumor has been described involving the subglottic region.[70]

Intraepithelial proliferative lesions

Keratosis of the larynx involves most commonly the true cords and interarytenoid area. It is also designated as simple hyperplasia, epithelial hyperplasia, squamous hyperplasia, and leukoplakia, even if the latter term is not used as often by the clinicians as in the oral cavity. It often occurs in smokers, singers, and others who use their voices excessively.[93] Patients may complain of hoarseness, and laryngoscopic examination may show white thickening of the involved areas. Presence of reddening should alert the clinician to the possible existence

of a more significative lesion (dypslasia/CIS, see below). Cases of keratosis which exhibit an undulating warty configuration are referred to as *verrucous keratosis*. When the process of keratinization is extensive and advanced, the picturesque term *pachyderma laryngis* has been used. Microscopically, keratotic lesions are characterized by hyperkeratotic epithelium (often with a granular layer) and acanthosis, without atypia.

Dysplasia/carcinoma in situ refers to a microscopic change present in some cases of keratosis (and sometimes independently from it) that is characterized by varying degrees of cellular atypia, loss of normal maturation, and loss of stratification.[83,103] The dysplasia is graded as mild, moderate, or severe on the basis of the degree of nuclear abnormalities (including changes in polarity)[105] and the level of the epithelium showing loss of stratification, the severe degree merging with (and to some authors being practically equivalent to) carcinoma in situ. The WHO Collaborating Center for the Histological Classification of Upper Respiratory Tract Tumors described and illustrated the criteria for this grading system as follows[103] (Figs 7.47 to 7.50):

1. **Mild dysplasia.** The nuclear abnormalities are slight and are most marked in the basal third of the epithelial thickness. They are minimal in the upper layers where the cells show maturation and stratification. A few mitoses may be present in the parabasal layers; there are no abnormal mitoses. Keratosis and chronic inflammation are usually present.

2. **Moderate dysplasia.** The nuclear abnormalities are more marked than in mild dysplasia, and nucleoli tend to be prominent. These changes are most marked in the lower two thirds of the epithelial thickness. Moderate nuclear abnormalities may persist up to the surface, but cell maturation and stratification are

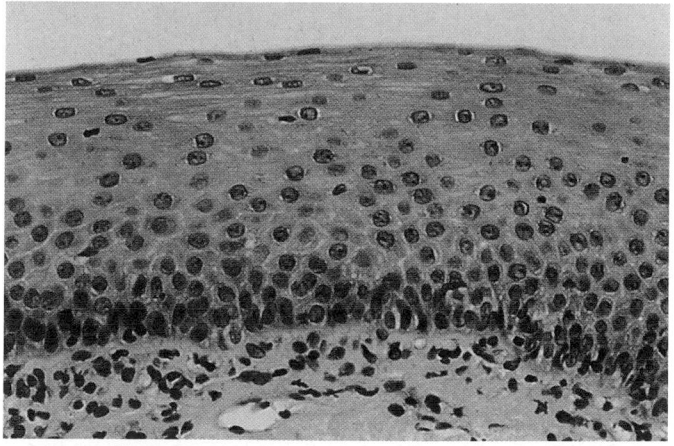

Fig. 7.47 Mild dysplasia of larynx. There is mild nuclear atypia with retained maturation and stratification of upper layers. (From Shanmugaratnam K, Sobin H. Histological typing of tumours of the upper respiratory tract and ear, ed. 2. New York, 1991, Springer-Verlag)

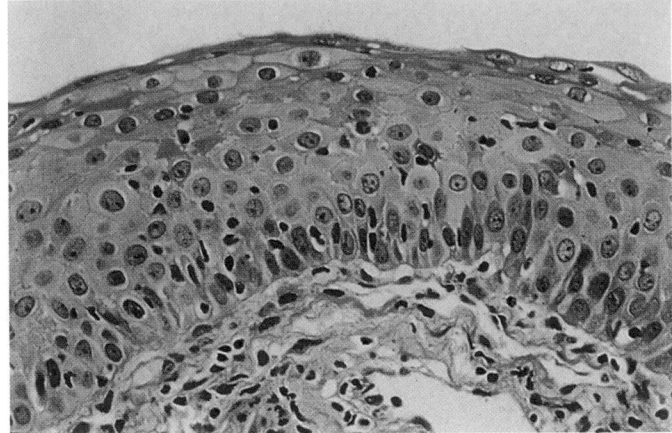

Fig. 7.48 Moderate dysplasia of larynx. There is moderate nuclear atypia with prominent nuclei, but the stratification of the upper layers is retained. (From Shanmugaratnam K, Sobin H. Histological typing of tumours of the upper respiratory tract and ear, ed. 2. New York, 1991, Springer-Verlag)

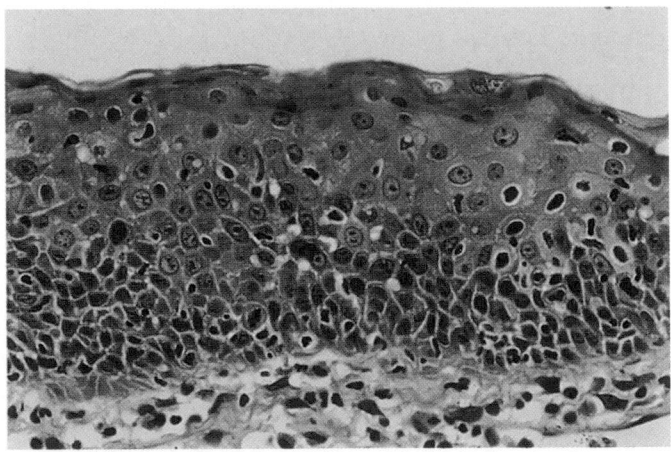

Fig. 7.49 Severe dysplasia of larynx. There is severe nuclear atypia and increased mitotic activity, associated with some maturation and stratification of the most superficial layers. (From Shanmugaratnam K, Sobin H. Histological typing of tumours of the upper respiratory tract and ear, ed. 2. New York, 1991, Springer-Verlag)

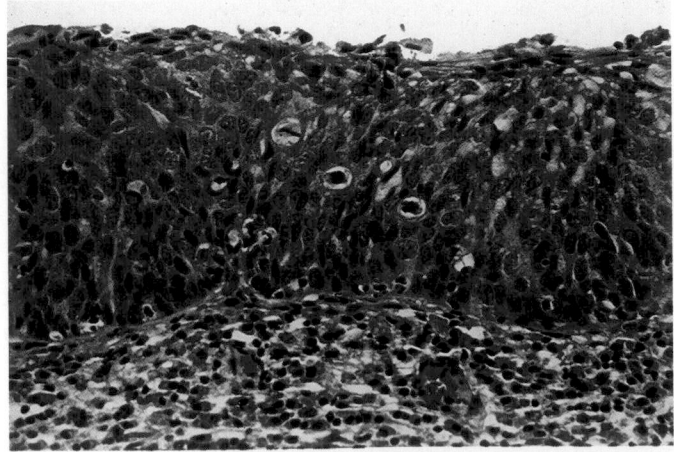

Fig. 7.50 Squamous cell carcinoma in situ of larynx.

evident in the upper layers. Mitoses are present in the parabasal and intermediate layers; there are no abnormal mitoses. The lesion may be associated with keratosis.

3 **Severe dysplasia.** The epithelium shows marked nuclear abnormalities and loss of maturation involving more than two thirds of the epithelial thickness with some of the stratification of the most superficial layers. Nuclear pleomorphism is common, and some of the cells may have bizarre nuclei. In some areas the nucleoli are very prominent, but in others all the nuclei are hyperchromatic. Mitoses are present high up in the epithelium, and atypical mitoses may be found. The cells are generally not as crowded as in classic carcinoma in situ and are usually more differentiated with intercellular bridges between the atypical cells. The presence of some maturation and stratification of the cells in the most superficial layers distinguishes the lesion from carcinoma in situ. The lesion is frequently associated with keratosis.

4 **Carcinoma in situ.** A lesion in which the full thickness of the squamous epithelium shows the cellular features of carcinoma without stromal invasion.

It should be noted that the WHO scheme reproduced here makes a distinction between severe dysplasia and CIS (discussed below), whereas in most other sites these two conditions are currently grouped because of the considerable difficulty in distinguishing them consistently and because of their seemingly similar natural history.

Most cases of carcinoma in situ of the larynx are composed of keratinized cells (spinous or well-differentiated type), whereas a minority are formed of basal-like cells similar to those seen in carcinoma in situ of the uterine cervix (basal-type). There is no evidence that these two subcategories differ from the point of view of their clinical significance.

Papillary carcinoma in situ is a variant of CIS characterized by papillary fronds with a fibrovascular stroma covered by squamous epithelium with cytologic features similar to those seen in the conventional variety.[103] Going back to the latter, it needs to be pointed out again that its boundaries with severe dysplasia are very blurred, to the point that the two diagnoses should be regarded as essentially equivalent for clinical purposes. It should also be kept in mind that a lesion of dysplasia/CIS may simply represents the peripheral portion of an invasive carcinoma. Indeed, about 75% of invasive squamous cell carcinomas of the larynx have an associated in situ component.[82]

The alternative terminologies of *squamous intraepithelial neoplasia (SIN)* or *laryngeal intraepithelial neoplasia (LIN)* have not gained wide acceptance.[72] Yet another proposed alternative grading system, colloquially known as the Ljubljana classification,[88,96] divides the cases as follows:

1 *Simple hyperplasia;*
2 *Abnormal hyperplasia;*
3 *Atypical hyperplasia ("risky" epithelium)[94];*
4 *Carcinoma in situ.*

The first two categories are viewed as benign, the third as potentially malignant, and the fourth as actually malignant. The authors stress the lack of significance of the presence of a surface keratin layer in the differential diagnosis between carcinoma in situ and lesser lesions, an important difference with the WHO scheme. The Ljubljana types are not easily translatable into those in the WHO system, and no compelling evidence has been brought forward that this system will improve the admittedly unsatisfactory rate of interobserver agreement with the WHO system[101] or that it can provide more accurate prognostic information.

A correlation exists between the grade of dysplasia/CIS and the incidence of aneuplody,[84–86] immunohistochemical reactivity for epidermal growth factor receptor,[102] cell proliferation (as measured by Ki-67 immunostaining,[89,106] and expression of the p53 product.[90]

Obviously, the most important question in this group of patients is the estimation of the risk for the development of invasive squamous cell carcinoma. On the whole, the risk is rather small, but this is probably because there is a great predominance of patients with low-grade lesions. In a classic study by McGavran et al.,[100] of 84 patients with laryngeal keratosis with varying degrees of dysplasia followed between 5 and 15 years, only three developed carcinoma and only one of these patients died as a result. In the series of Hellquist,[96] 7% of the patients with mild dysplasia progressed to more severe dysplasia or carcinoma, 24% of those with moderate dysplasia progressed to carcinoma in situ or invasive carcinoma, and 25% of those with severe dysplasias progressed to invasive carcinoma. Similar results were obtained by Gillis et al.[92] and Kambic et al.[98] In the series of Stenersen et al.,[84] 46% of untreated carcinoma in situ developed invasive carcinoma within 4 years. The progression of the disease can be very slow; it is not unusual for patients to have documented CIS for 5 years or more without an invasive component developing in this period.[94] None of the special techniques that have been applied to these lesions up to now have proved superior to simple morphologic assessment, as subjective and unsatisfactory this assessment may be.

The treatment of these conditions need to be individualized in the basis of the patient's age, reliability, extent of the lesion, and—last but not least—the presence and degree of microscopic changes of dysplasia/CIS. Cases of keratosis without dysplasia or mild dysplasia can be simply watched. Cases with more significant changes can be treated with vocal cord stripping, endoscopic laser resection, extensive surgery, or radiation therapy.[87,89,91,99,104]

Invasive carcinoma

General features

Carcinoma of the larynx accounts for 2.2% of all cancers in men and 0.4% in women. Most patients are in their fifth decade of life or beyond, but cases occurring in much younger patients are on record.[113,114] About 96% of the patients are males. Smoking is the main risk factor, this risk being enhanced by heavy alcohol consumption.[109,115,116] HPV does not seem to play an important role in the early development of laryngeal squamous cell carcinoma; at most, it may play a contributory role in the late stages of the tumor.[110] Interestingly, a difference in the incidence of the location of the tumor within the larynx has been found depending on the site of residence of the patient.[107] Hoarseness is a common early symptom for glottic tumors but not for those located elsewhere.

Patients with laryngeal carcinoma are at an increased risk for the development of a second tumor in the upper aerodigestive tract or lung.[108,117]

The "T" classification for cancer of the larynx is shown in Appendix C. It is based on a combination of clinical, endoscopic, and radiologic parameters.[111] A lucid discussion of its deficiencies with suggestions for improvement is provided by Kleinsasser.[112]

Types, spread, and therapy

Spread of laryngeal carcinoma can be accurately predicted from the site of origin and knowledge of the anatomic barriers produced by the different laryngeal compartments.[119] Accordingly, these tumors have been traditionally divided, depending on their location, into four major types[120] (Figs 7.51 to 7.54). This classification has been largely based on laryngoscopic evaluation, but the use of CT scan and MRI has resulted in greater accuracy.[118] MRI is more sensitive but less specific than CT in

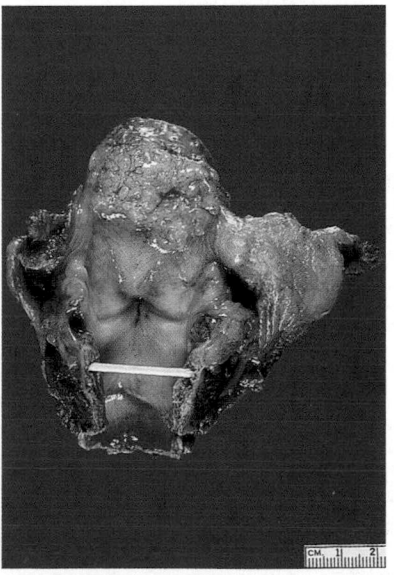

Fig. 7.51 Supraglottic carcinoma of the larynx replacing most of the epiglottis.

detecting cartilage invasion by tumor; it tends to overestimate it, whereas CT tends to underestimate it.[144] The four types are as follows:

1 **Glottic** (60% to 65% of all cases). These tumors arise from the true vocal cords, the anterior third of the glottis being the most common location. They tend to remain localized for long periods because of the surrounding cartilaginous wall and the paucity of lymphatic vessels. In time they may spread across the anterior commissure to the opposite cord, posteriorly to involve the arytenoids, superiorly to involve the supraglottic portion, inferiorly to extend into the subglottic area, and anteriorly to penetrate the thyroid cartilage with subsequent growth into the soft tissues of the anterior neck. In one series, ipsilateral lymph node metastases were not found in any of 41 T1 lesions and in only 7.3% of T2 tumors[136]; therefore prophylactic lymph node dissection is not indicated.

Early cases can be treated by irradiation therapy with excellent results.[122,130] If irradiation fails, surgery still saves most of the patients.[126,129] Small, superficially

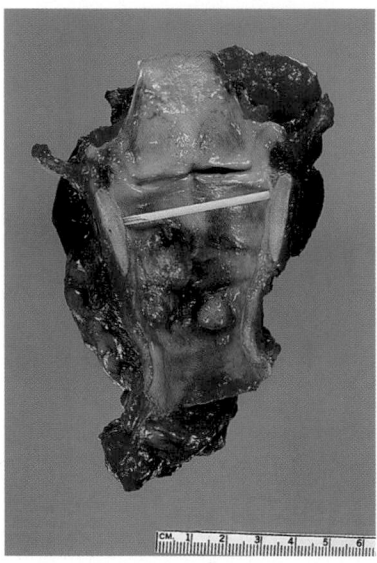

Fig. 7.52 Infraglottic carcinoma appearing as multiple polypoid masses.

Fig. 7.53 Gross appearance of transglottic carcinoma.

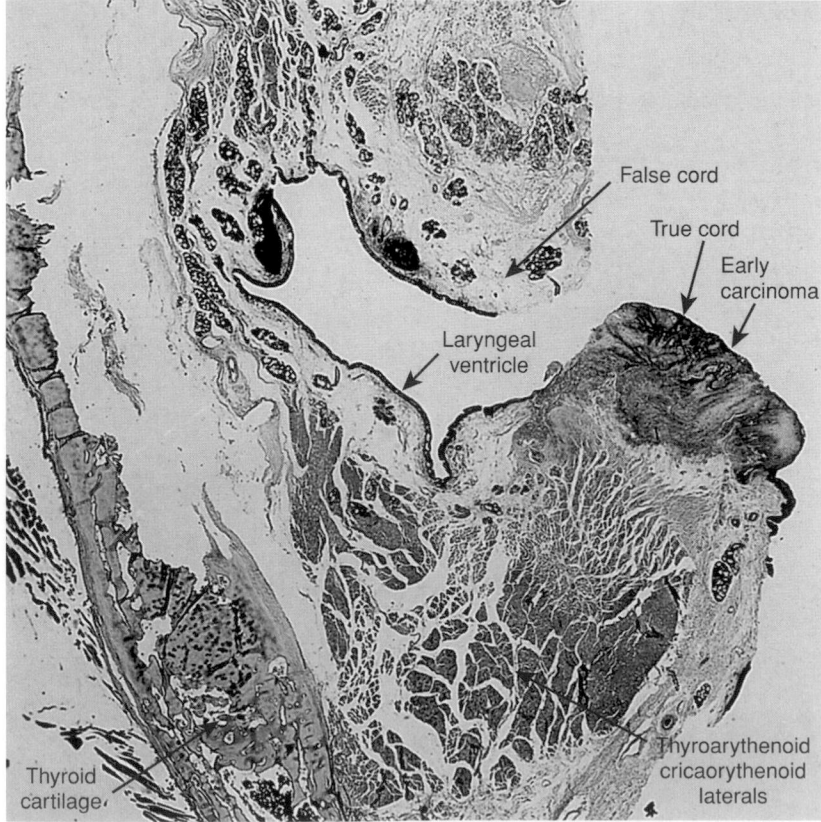

Fig. 7.54 Superficial carcinoma of true vocal cord, as seen in a sagittal section. This lesion is equally curable by resection or radiation therapy.

invasive squamous cell carcinomas of the true cord can also be cured by endoscopic removal (cordectomy) alone with results essentially identical to those obtained in carcinoma in situ.[138,142,143] T2 glottic cancers are best treated by hemilaryngectomy.[121,137]

2 **Supraglottic** (30% to 35% of all cases). These tumors involve the false cord, the ventricle (including those arising in a laryngocele[127]), and/or the laryngeal or lingual surface of the epiglottis.[128] One third of the supraglottic cancers arise from the latter structure. These tumors have a marked tendency to spread toward the pre-epiglottic space, but the oropharynx is protected by the thick hyoepiglottic ligament.[134,140] They may erupt at the laryngeal surface of the epiglottis, leading to confusion with primary tumors of this area. Only 1% of supraglottic carcinomas invade the glottis. Invasion of cartilage is also rare and is largely restricted to cases in which the cartilage had undergone osseous metaplasia.[124]

The incidence of lymph node metastases averages 40%. About 20% to 35% of patients with clinically negative nodes harbor occult metastases on microscopic examination.[119] Supraglottic tumors can be treated by irradiation or laryngectomy.[122,132]

3 **Transglottic** (less than 5% of all cases). This term is applied to cancers that cross the laryngeal ventricle.[135] They have the highest incidence of lymph node involvement (52%). Of sixteen transglottic cancers examined by McGavran et al.,[133] five (31%) had clinically undetected node metastases. This figure indicates that elective lymph node dissection should be performed for tumors in this location, in addition to a total laryngectomy.[139]

4 **Infraglottic** (subglottic) (less than 5% of all cases). Under this category are included cancers involving the true cord with a subglottic extension of more than 1 cm (Fig. 7.55) as well as tumors entirely confined to the subglottic area. The latter are very unusual.[141] Lateral spread to the cricoid cartilage is the rule. Also common is destruction by tumor of the weak interthyrocricoid membrane, with invasion of the prelaryngeal wall and thyroid gland.[131,134] Because of the frequent extension to the trachea, this structure should be resected as distally as possible. Metastases to cervical nodes occur in 15% to 20% of the cases, and metastases to paratracheal nodes occur in about 50%.[119,133] Therefore radical node dissection with clearance of paratracheal nodes is indicated.

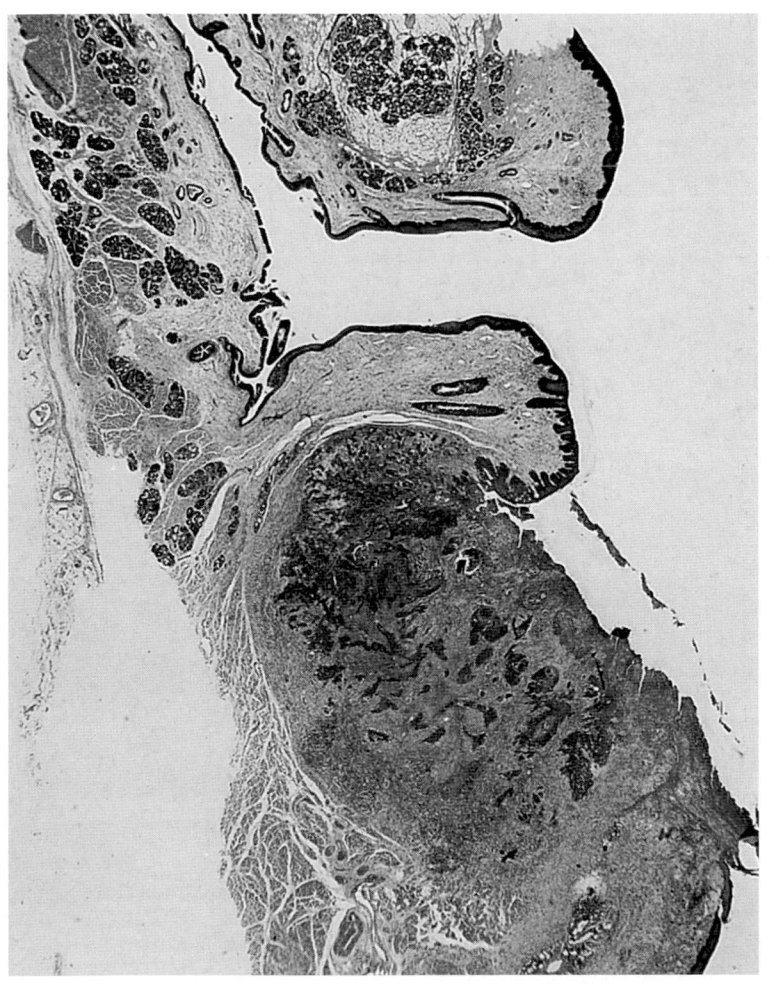

Fig. 7.55 True infraglottic squamous cell carcinoma in a 42-year-old man. Hemilaryngectomy was performed. All margins were free. This was the third infraglottic carcinoma out of 600 consecutive laryngectomies.

Tumors situated on the pyriform sinus or postcricoid areas are considered of pharyngeal origin.

The most common sites of metastases from laryngeal carcinoma, regardless of site of the primary tumor, are the regional lymph nodes, followed by the lungs. Thyroid gland and jugular vein involvement are usually the result of direct extension; the latter is seen only in the presence of extensive nodal involvement and indicates a high probability of systemic dissemination.[123] Cervical node metastases can be accurately diagnosed with the technique of fine needle aspiration.[125]

Pathologic features

Grossly, laryngeal carcinomas are generally described as a protruding pink to gray mass that is often ulcerated. Vocal cord lesions tend to have a keratotic appearance.

Microscopically, over 90% of laryngeal carcinomas are of the squamous cell-type. They are graded into well, moderately, and poorly differentiated on the basis of the degree of differentiation, cellular pleomorphism, and mitotic activity.[146] Most glottic carcinomas are well to moderately differentiated, whereas a high percentage of those located in other regions of the larynx (particularly in the subglottis) are moderately to poorly differentiated. In general, the smaller the tumor, the better differentiated its appearance. Those neoplasms in which the stromal invasion is limited to the most superficial layers just below the basement membrane are designated as superficially invasive, microinvasive, or "early." The last term should be avoided, not only because it may be inaccurate, but also because it is used by clinicians with a somewhat different meaning, specifically, to indicate whether the mobility of the cord is normal or impaired.

Occasionally, the tumor extends over a large surface of the larynx while retaining its superficial character.[145]

Papillary squamous cell carcinoma is a variant of squamous cell carcinoma with an exophytic pattern of growth and the features of CIS associated with foci of invasion. These foci can be inconspicuous and require thorough sampling for their identification. This tumor is distinguished from verrucous carcinoma on the basis of the cytologic atypia it exhibits. It shows a greater degree of association with HPV than ordinary squamous cell carcinoma, and it has a relatively good outlook (in contrast to its counterpart in the sinonasal region).[148]

The diagnosis of postirradiation persistence of squamous cell carcinoma is often difficult to make. If dysplastic or atypical cells are present but limited to the mucosa it is better to err on the conservative side because of the great difficulty in distinguishing tumor recurrence from postirradiation atypia.[147]

Histochemical and immunohistochemical features

Immunoreactivity for keratin is universally present, but the keratin types being expressed vary considerably from tumor to tumor.[151]

Epidermal growth factor receptor has been consistently found with immunohistochemical techniques in laryngeal squamous cell carcinoma, its expression apparently being related to the microscopic grade of the tumor.[149,152] There is also a correlation between the tumor grade and the amount of basement membrane components retained around the tumor cells, and this seems to be particularly true for collagen IV.[150]

Molecular genetic features

Overexpression of the p53 product has been detected in approximately 50% to 60% of the cases.[155a] It may be associated with mutations of the p53, but in most cases it is accompanied by a wild type p53.[154,156] Absence of p16 is common (about 90% of the cases) and may constitute an early tumorigenic event.[152] Instead, loss of Rb protein expression, seen in about 20% of the cases, seems to play only a minor role in this tumor.[155]

Other microscopic types

Verrucous carcinoma is a rare variant of squamous cell carcinoma with a distinctly polypoid appearance and an extremely well-differentiated microscopic appearance[167] (Figs 7.56 and 7.57). Like its counterpart in the oral cavity and other locations, it may show extensive local invasion but practically never metastasizes.[173] HPV sequences have been demonstrated both in the tumor and in adjacent normal tissues in some studies but not in

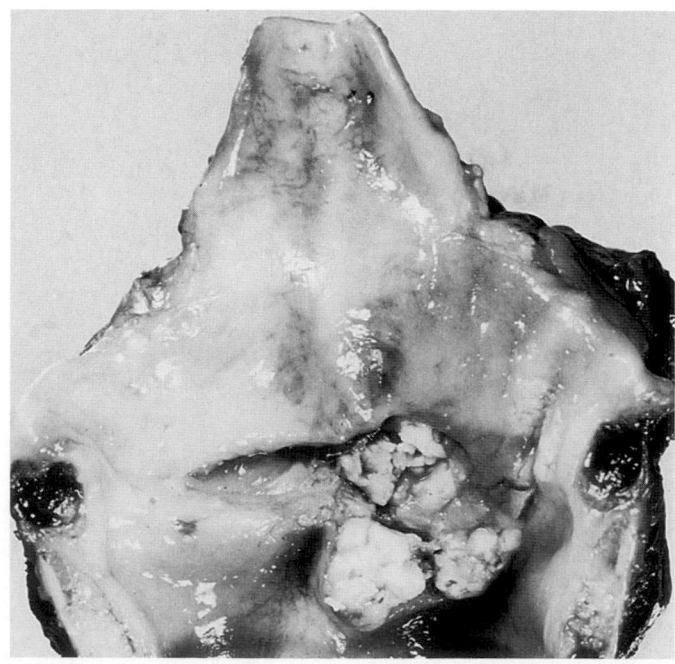

Fig. 7.56 Verrucous carcinoma of larynx with obliteration of right vocal cord and extension into subglottis. (From Kraus FT, Perez-Mesa C. Verrucous carcinoma. Clinical and pathologic study of 105 cases involving oral cavity, larynx, and genitalia. Cancer 1966, **19:** 26–28)

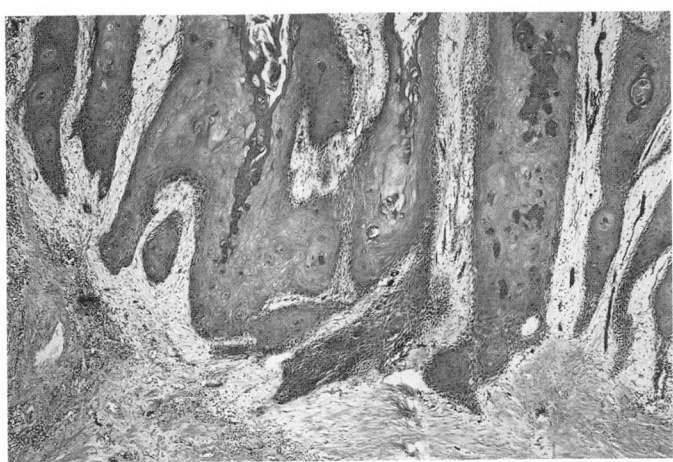

Fig. 7.57 Verrucous carcinoma. Well-differentiated tongues of squamous epithelium impinge on the underlying stroma.

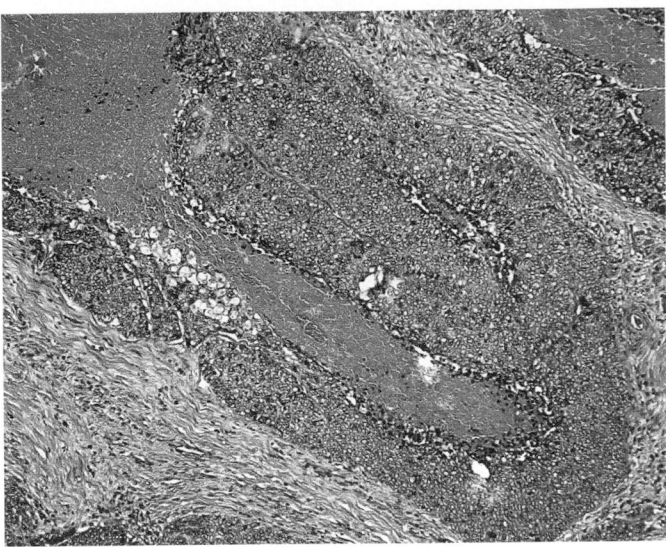

Fig. 7.58 Basaloid carcinoma of larynx. The basophilic staining quality and the high-grade nature of the tumor are evident.

others.[157,172,178] Verrucous carcinoma should be distinguished from the verrucous form of keratosis (verrucous hyperplasia). The differential diagnosis is based on the presence or absence of invasion and can therefore be impossible to make on a small biopsy.[163] Sometimes verrucous carcinoma coexists with conventional squamous cell carcinoma (*hybrid carcinoma*).[183] The primary treatment of verrucous carcinoma is surgical. Radiation therapy may be followed by anaplastic transformation of the tumor.[171] Hybrid carcinomas should be treated as conventional squamous cell carcinomas.

Small cell (neuroendocrine) carcinoma is an unusual type of laryngeal carcinoma (less than 0.5% of all cases) that most often presents in the sixth and seventh decades in men who are heavy smokers.[168] Its microscopic appearance is identical to that of its pulmonary counterpart.[182] Like the latter, it usually contains a few dense-core secretory granules on ultrastructural examination and exhibits a variable (sometimes very scanty) degree of immunoreactivity for neural/neuroendocrine markers.[161] As in other sites, it may be pure or associated with other patterns.[181,184] Cervical, nodal, and distal metastases are very common, and the prognosis is poor.[181] It should be distinguished from atypical carcinoid/large cell neuroendocrine carcinoma (see p. 347).

Basaloid squamous carcinoma is a highly malignant laryngeal tumor characterized by areas of typical in situ and/or invasive squamous cell carcinoma associated with nests of small crowded cells (Fig. 7.58). These cells have hyperchromatic nuclei, scant cytoplasm, small cystic spaces, necrosis, prominent hyalinization, and peripheral palisading.[190,192] The overall appearance suggests an attempt of differentiation toward adnexal (glandular) structures. This tumor, which also occurs in the tongue, pharynx, and esophagus, should not be confused with true adenoid cystic carcinoma, which has a different clinical course.[188] Most of the patients with basa-

loid squamous cell carcinoma are heavy smokers who present with advanced disease and sometimes with other primary tumors in the area.[186] The behavior is extremely aggressive.[159,179]

Lymphoepithelioma-like carcinoma (lymphoepithelial carcinoma) of the larynx is often accompanied by (and sometimes presents initially with) cervical lymph node metastases. Alterations of p53 are common, but no relationship with EBV has been found. The clinical course is aggressive.[180,187]

Adenocarcinoma of nonsalivary gland-type is a very rare neoplasm; most of the reported cases have been in the supraglottic or infraglottic regions rather than in the glottis itself.[162,166] Many of these cases seem to arise from the surface epithelium rather than preexisting glands.[160] A few are of the mucinous-type.[189]

Sarcomatoid carcinoma (spindle-cell carcinoma; carcinoma with sarcoma-like stroma; carcinosarcoma) is a peculiar neoplasm with a high predilection for the upper aerodigestive tract.[158,169] Tumors of this type located in the larynx, as elsewhere, often have a polypoid configuration[185] (Fig. 7.59) and may simulate a laryngeal polyp. Most are located in the supraglottic region. Microscopically, they have an element of squamous cell carcinoma (often inconspicuous and frequently in situ) and a pleomorphic sarcoma-like component, which makes up the bulk of the lesion. The sarcomatoid component may be so bland as to simulate granulation tissue or have a bizarre appearance reminiscent of malignant fibrous histiocytoma, malignant giant cell tumor of soft parts, or osteosarcoma[176] (Fig. 7.60).

Lymph node metastases may be composed of the carcinomatous component alone, both patterns as in the primary tumor, or—in rare cases—the sarcoma-like elements exclusively. Variations on the theme are

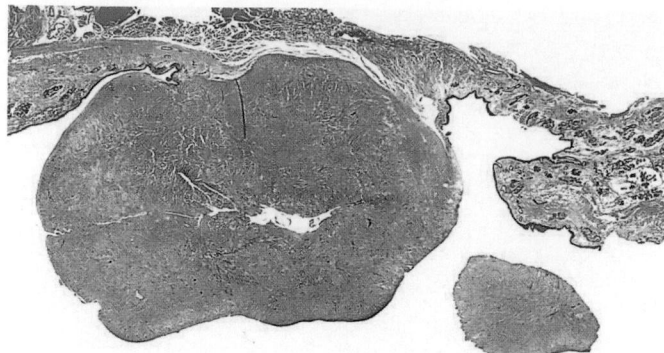

Fig. 7.59 Whole mount of laryngeal sarcomatoid squamous cell carcinoma, showing typical polypoid shape.

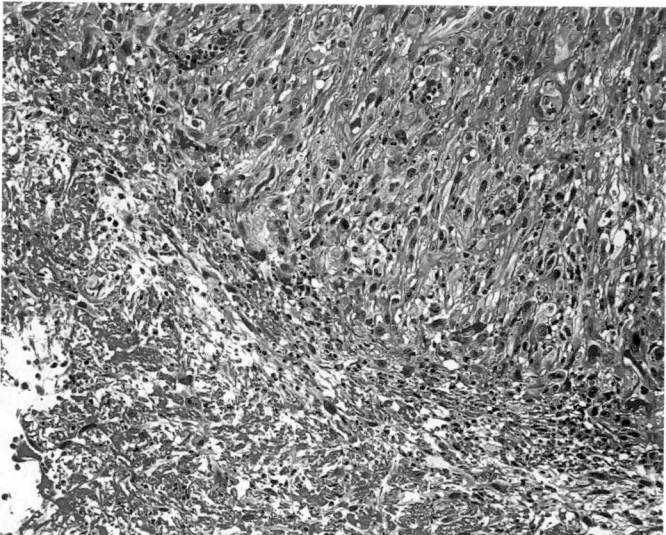

Fig. 7.60 Sarcomatoid carcinoma of larynx with superficial ulceration.

represented by carcinomas showing rhabdomyosarcomatous features only in the metastasis,[170] and carcinomas showing a combination of sarcomatoid and neuroendocrine features.[164] Whether the sarcoma-like stroma is of mesenchymal derivation or a carcinoma in disguise has been a matter of controversy since the entity was first defined in the classic paper by Lane.[175] Current evidence strongly favors the latter interpretation. Immunohistochemical markers of epithelial differentiation such as keratin are detected in at least some of the spindle cells in most cases, even in those with a relatively monomorphic appearance.[165,177,193] Reactivity for α-1-antitrypsin and α-1-chymotrypsin can also be detected, but this is a relatively nonspecific finding that should not be construed as evidence of histiocytic differentiation.[165] The fact that the two tumor components harbor the same p53 mutation is further proof of their common pathway of tumorigenesis.[157a]

Surgical excision is the treatment of choice.[185] The prognosis is better for the polypoid tumors than for

deeply invasive neoplasms with similar microscopic features.[174,191] Stage by stage, it does not seem to be significantly different from that of conventional squamous cell carcinoma.[177]

Prognosis

The factors found to be of prognostic significance in laryngeal squamous cell carcinoma are the following:

1 *Clinical stage* and *site*. These two factors are interrelated (see Appendix C) and are therefore usually evaluated together.[194,200,203] The approximate 5-year survival rates for the different types are the following, allowing for the usual differences from series to series:
Glottic: 80%
I: 90%; II: 85%; III: 60%; IV: <5%
Supraglottic: 65%
I: 85%; II: 75%; III: 45%; IV: <5%
Transglottic: 50%
Subglottic: 40%
   Among supraglottic carcinomas, those located in the aryepiglottic folds have the worst prognosis.[204]
2 *Microscopic grade.* While this parameter is related to the clinical stage of the tumor, it has been shown that it is an independent prognostic determinator.[207]
3 *Field size.* Among T1 glottic carcinomas treated with radiation therapy, a large tumor field size is associated with an increased risk of local recurrence.[205]
4 *Lymph nodes.* In patients with metastatic lymph nodes, the prognosis is affected by the number of involved nodes, their size, and the presence or absence of extranodal extension.[195]
5 *DNA ploidy.* Aneuploid tumors are associated with an increased risk of recurrence.[206]
6 *Host reaction.* It has been claimed that a high density of S-100 protein-positive Langerhans cells in the tumor stroma is a favorable prognostic sign.[197,200]
7 *Keratin expression.* No prognostic significance seems to be attached to the type of keratin expression by the tumor, as evaluated immunohistochemically.[199]
8 *p53 overexpression.* It has been proposed that this parameter is an independent prognostic factor,[202] but the claim has not been substantiated by others.[196,198]

Salivary gland-type tumors

The most common form of salivary gland-type tumor of the larynx is **adenoid cystic carcinoma**.[213] Almost all of these tumors are located in areas other than the true vocal cords, in keeping with the distribution of normal salivary glands in the region. They grow slowly but eventually prove fatal in most instances.[212] This tumor should be distinguished from the more rapidly growing basaloid squamous cell carcinoma (see p. 345).

Other neoplasms in this category include mucoepidermoid carcinoma,[215,216] acinic cell carcinoma,[208,214] benign mixed tumor (pleomorphic adenoma),[210] and myoepithelioma.[209,211]

Carcinoid tumor and paraganglioma

In addition to the already mentioned small cell neuroendocrine carcinoma (see p. 345), the larynx can be the site of two other tumors with neuroendocrine differentiation, i.e., carcinoid tumor and related tumors, and paraganglioma.[218,221,229]

Carcinoid tumor of the *typical* variety looks in all respects like its more common bronchial counterpart at the morphologic, immunohistochemical, and ultrastructural levels.[236] Some are predominantly composed of oncocytic cells (*oncocytic carcinoid tumors*),[235] others have an appearance indistinguishable from that of medullary thyroid carcinoma,[220,223] and still others are composed of clear cells (Fig. 7.61). Most of these tumors are located in the supraglottic region, particularly in the arytenoid and aryepiglottic fold.[219] The prognosis is generally good.

The larynx is much more commonly the site of *atypical carcinoid tumor* (moderately differentiated neuroendocrine carcinoma) and *large cell neuroendocrine carcinoma*.[226–228,230,236] Both of these tumor types are characterized by pleomorphism, mitotic activity, and necrosis (Fig. 7.62). The distinction between them, not always attempted in the articles that have been written on the subject, is made using the same guidelines as those used for the homonymous pulmonary tumors (see p. 407). Argyrophilia, immunoreactivity for chromogranin, and presence of densecore neurosecretory granules on ultrastructural examination are the rule.[225,238] Most patients are elderly males with a history of heavy smoking. Nearly all tumors are located in the supraglottic region, particularly on the arytenoid cartilage.[223,238] They run an aggressive clinical course, with frequent metastases to lymph nodes and distant sites. Mortality is approximately 50%.[238] As in other sites, there may be tumors combining endocrine and exocrine features (so-called amphicrine carcinomas).[224]

Paraganglioma of the larynx is usually located in the supraglottic region, from where it often extends to the

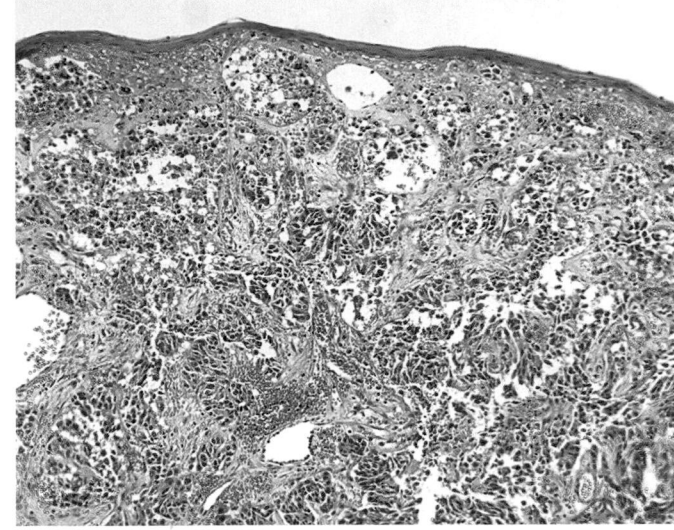

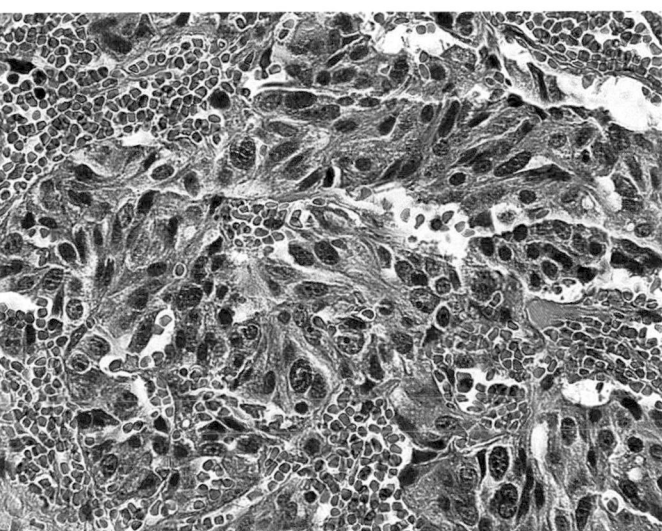

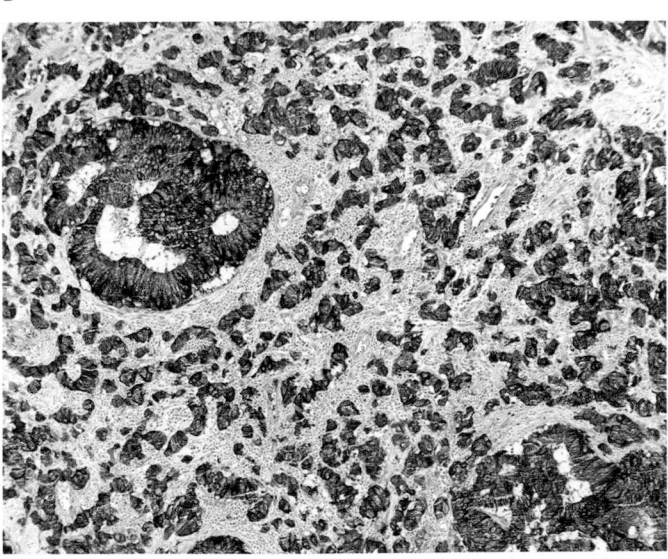

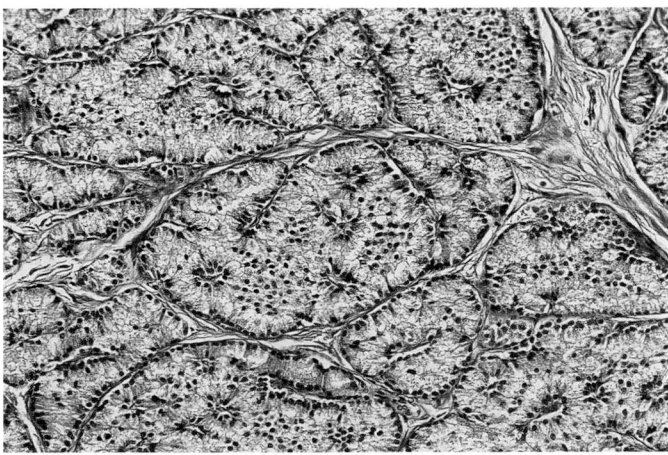

Fig. 7.61 Carcinoid tumor of the larynx showing marked cytoplasmic clear change.

Fig. 7.62 A to **C**, High-grade neuroendocrine carcinoma of larynx: **A**, low-power view; **B**, high-power view; **C**, chromogranin stain.

ipsilateral aryepiglottic fold.[222] However, it can also present as a subglottic tumor.[232] Metastases have been documented in about a fifth of the reported cases.[231] Most are nonfunctioning.[217] Calcitonin and vasoactive intestinal peptide (VIP) have been detected in some of the cases in addition to the usual panendocrine markers.[234] Sustentacular cells, which are immunoreactive for S-100 protein and GFAP, are present at the periphery of the nests and constitute an important diagnostic sign.[231,237]

Other tumors and tumorlike conditions

Hemangioma of the larynx characteristically presents in infants as a sessile, poorly circumscribed mass in the subglottic area, immediately beneath the true vocal cord. Symptoms of upper respiratory tract obstruction may be severe. One half of the patients have associated hemangiomas in the skin, an important diagnostic sign. Biopsy can precipitate massive bleeding. Treatment modalities include endoscopic excision with CO(2) laser, systemic steroids, interferon, and intralesional corticosteroid injection with short-term intubation.[257] Hemangiomas of the larynx are exceptionally also seen in adults.[261]

Angiosarcoma can present as a polypoid mass in the epiglottis (Fig. 7.63) or elsewhere in the larynx.[272] Some of the reported cases have been associated with previous radiation to the area.[262]

Granular cell tumor may involve the true cord or other sites in the larynx.[246,247] Some of the reported cases have been in children.[248] Most are located posteriorly. They are small and yellow and are covered by epithelium. The clinical diagnosis is usually that of laryngeal papilloma or nodule. Their microscopic appearance is typical (see Chapter 25), but they can be mistaken microscopically for invasive squamous cell carcinoma because of the pseudoepitheliomatous hyperplasia that often accompanies this lesion.[243]

Myofibromatosis of the larynx in the neonate may result in severe laryngeal obstruction.[270]

Inflammatory myofibroblastic tumor (inflammatory pseudotumor) can involve the larynx and be confused with a clinically more aggressive process.[259]

Rhabdomyoma has a predilection for the head and neck area, including the larynx. Cross striations are often found in the tumor cells, in addition to peculiar crystal-like intracytoplasmic particles.[241] The adult type is more common than the fetal variety.[280]

Rhabdomyosarcoma also occurs; it is restricted to infancy and childhood and is almost always of the embryonal variety, including the botryoid subtype.[240,250]

Leiomyomas and **leiomyosarcomas** are extremely unusual; some of the former have been of epithelioid or atypical (bizarre) types.[254,264]

Cartilaginous tumors are the most common mesenchymal neoplasms of the larynx.[267,274a] They often arise from the cricoid cartilage and appear posteriorly in the subglottic region (Figs 7.64 and 7.65). Goethals et al.[252] classified four of their 22 cases as *chondromas* and all of the others as *chondrosarcomas* by applying the microscopic criteria used for the homonymous skeletal tumors; none of the tumors metastasized, and only six recurred locally. Although subsequently there have been reported cases with pulmonary metastases, these

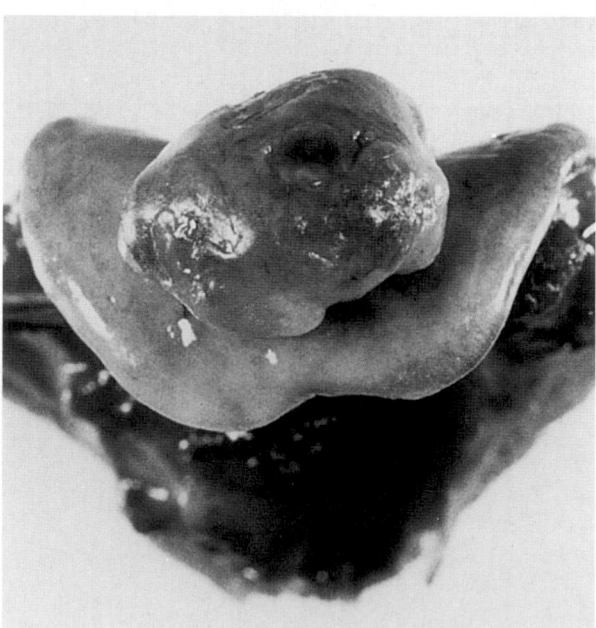

Fig. 7.63 Well-differentiated angiosarcoma of epiglottis. The tumor has a distinctly polypoid appearance and is partially ulcerated. (Courtesy of Dr. J. Costa, Lausanne, Switzerland)

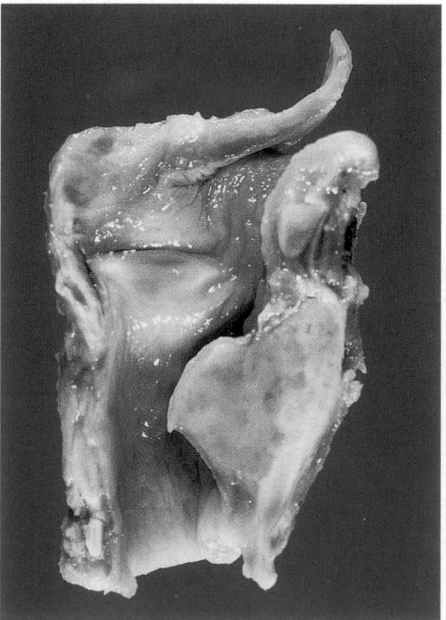

Fig. 7.64 Gross appearance of well-differentiated chondrosarcoma of larynx.

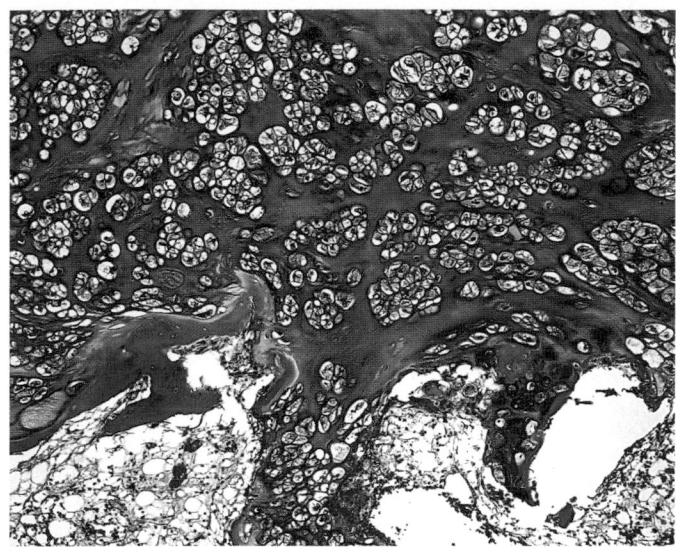

Fig. 7.65 Low-power microscopic view of chondrosarcoma of larynx. Most of these tumors are very well differentiated.

findings indicate that surgery should be as conservative as possible for cartilaginous neoplasms occurring in this location. Rarely, the tumor may be of the clear cell variety or exhibit dedifferentiated foci.[244,260]

Osteosarcomas also occur; they should be distinguished from chondrosarcomas with osseous metaplasia and sarcomatoid carcinomas (carcinosarcomas).[263]

Lipoma of the spindle cell variety was reported in the larynx by Nonaka et al.,[268] and **hibernoma** has been seen in the pre-epiglottic area.[273]

Liposarcoma of the well-differentiated type (atypical lipomatous tumor) can present as a pedunculated laryngeal mass, almost always located in the supraglottic portion of the hypopharynx.[279] As in other sites it can undergo dedifferentiation.[253a]

Malignant fibrous histiocytomas of the larynx also have been described,[251] but one wonders how many of them actually represent sarcomatoid carcinomas in which the epithelial component (which may be very inconspicuous) has either been overlooked or else has been destroyed by tumor ulceration.

Isolated cases of **giant cell tumor**,[265,279a] **aneurysmal bone cyst**,[249] **polypoid xanthoma**,[265] **solitary fibrous tumor**,[271] and **synovial sarcoma**[252] have been reported.

Malignant melanoma can be primary in the larynx,[239,278] but the possibility of metastasis should always be ruled out before entertaining such a diagnosis.[269]

Lymphoid tumors and tumorlike conditions can also involve the larynx, although the event is rare.[256] Reported cases include non-Hodgkin's lymphoma (including the "lethal midline granuloma"-type of probable NK/T-cell nature), and plasmacytoma.[245,255,274] Although the latter lesion may be initially localized, dissemination is likely to occur.[277] Plasmacytoma should be distinguished from chronic inflammation and so-called *mucous membrane*

plasmacytosis, a reactive condition of unknown cause. *Acute leukemia* can present initially with laryngeal obstruction.[258,275] We have also seen a case of a *pseudolymphoma* presenting as a polypoid intralaryngeal mass.

Metastatic tumors to the larynx can arise from various sites; skin (melanoma), kidney, breast, and lung are the most common.[242,276]

Trachea

Non-neoplastic lesions

Tracheopathia osteoplastica presents as multiple submucosal nodules composed of mature bone and cartilage.[281] Its etiology is unknown.

Amyloidosis of the tracheobronchial tree is characterized by the formation of solitary or multiple nodules, usually asymptomatic.

Necrotizing sialometaplasia similar to that more commonly seen in the palate has been described in the trachea after prolonged translaryngeal intubation.[283]

Rheumatoid nodules are occasionally seen in the trachea of patients with rheumatoid arthritis.[282]

Tumors

Papilloma and **papillomatosis** of the trachea are morphologically similar to the homonymous lesions seen in the larynx[304] (Fig. 7.66). Cases seen in conjunction with laryngeal lesions usually begin in infancy and have a very low incidence of malignant transformation. Those limited to the trachea and bronchi usually begin in adulthood and have a greater tendency for malignant change. As in the larynx, some of these well-differentiated papillomatous tumors exhibit invasive tendencies.[290]

Squamous cell carcinoma is the most common primary malignant tumor of the trachea[284,295,311] (Fig. 7.67).

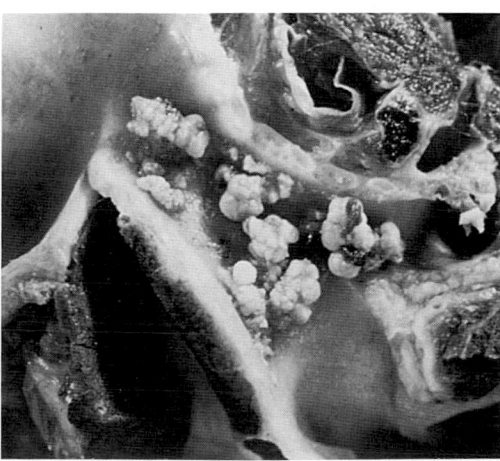

Fig. 7.66 Extensive papillomatosis of trachea and bronchi.

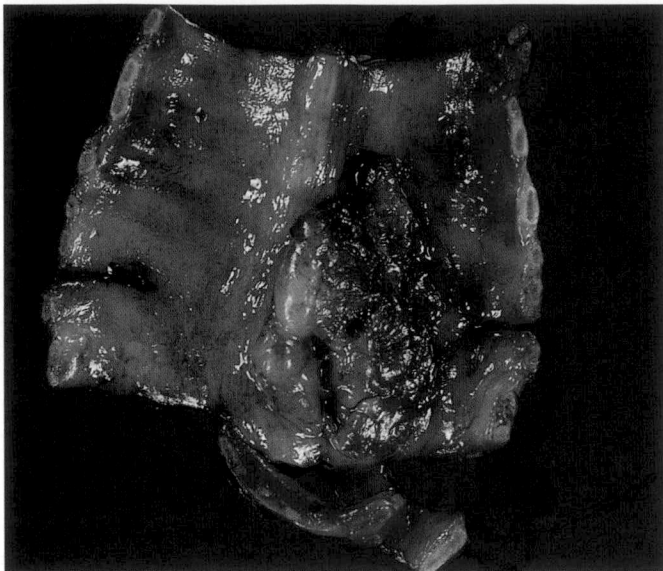

Fig. 7.67 Squamous cell carcinoma of trachea growing as a polypoid mass. The tumor was treated by segmental resection.

The majority arise in the lower third. The clinical course is rapid, and the prognosis is poor. The primary treatment is surgical, usually consisting of circumferential resection of the involved segment with end-to-end anastomosis.[305] Radiation therapy is used for advanced cases.[288]

Adenoid cystic carcinoma is the second most common type. Its appearance is similar to that of the homonymous tumor in the major salivary glands (Fig. 7.68). Most cases are located in the upper third of the trachea.[292] The clinical course is very slow, but the long-term prognosis is poor.

Small cell neuroendocrine carcinoma has an appearance and a behavior similar to that of the bronchial

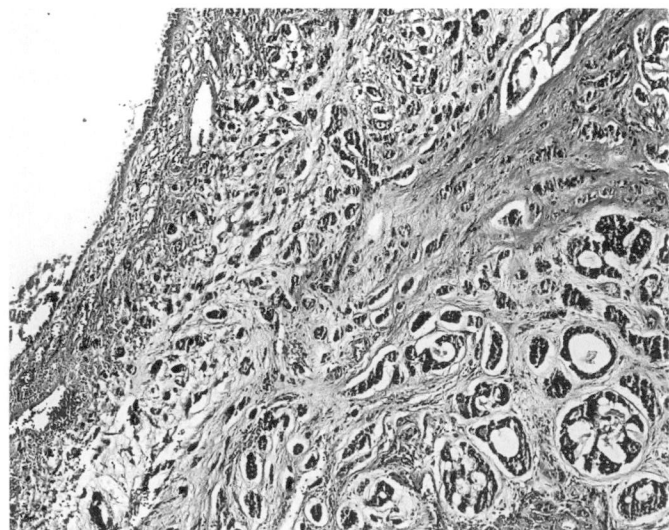

Fig. 7.68 Adenoid cystic carcinoma of trachea growing beneath normal epithelium and showing typical cribriform pattern of growth.

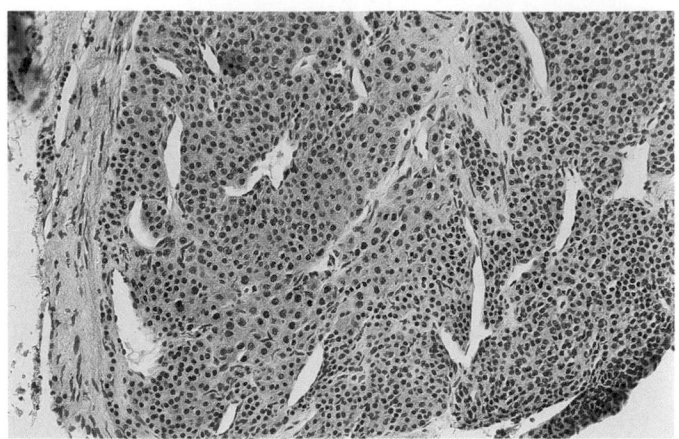

Fig. 7.69 Glomus tumor of trachea. The microscopic appearance is identical to that of the homonymous tumor of the skin.

tumor of the same type, an extension from which should always be considered in the differential diagnosis.[290]

Adenocarcinoma (mucin-producing) and **lymphoepithelioma-like carcinoma** have been observed in the lower third of the organ.[292,306]

Carcinoid tumor may arise in the trachea and be cured by segmental resection with primary reconstruction.[286]

Benign mixed tumors (pleomorphic adenomas) and other salivary gland-type tumors occur, but not nearly as often as adenoid cystic carcinoma.[293,294,300,301]

Other primary tumors of the trachea, all exceptionally rare, include glomus tumor (Fig. 7.69)[291,297] (including its oncocytic variety),[310] hemangiopricytoma,[285] juvenile hemangioma,[303] granular cell tumor,[287] "fibromyxoma,"[308] schwannoma,[302,307] paraganglioma,[298] benign clear cell tumor ("sugar tumor"),[298] fibrosarcoma,[305] benign and malignant fibrous histiocytoma,[309] plasmacytoma, and malignant lymphoma.[289,296] Hodgkin's lymphoma can present initially as a tracheal mass as a result of invasion from adjacent nodes.

Secondary tumors are much more common than primary neoplasms. Most of them arise in the bronchi, esophagus, or larynx and involve the trachea by direct extension.

References

LARYNX

Normal anatomy

1 Hill MJ, Taylor CL, Scott GBD. Chondromatous metaplasia in the human larynx. Histopathology 1980, **4:** 205–214.
2 Lawson W, Zak FG. The glomus bodies ("paraganglia") of the human larynx. Laryngoscope 1974, **84:** 98–111.
3 Lundgren J, Olofsson J, Hellquist H. Oncocytic lesions of the larynx. Acta Otolaryngol (Stockholm) 1982, **94:** 335–344.
3a Mills SE, Fechner RE. Larynx and Pharynx. In: Sternberg S, Ed: Histology for pathologists, 2nd edn, Philadelphia, Lippincott-Raven Publishers, 1997, pp 391–404.
4 Nassar VH, Bridger GP. Topography of the laryngeal mucous glands. Arch Otolaryngol 1971, **94:** 490–498.

5 Richardson GM, Assor D. Thyroid tissue within the larynx. Case report. Laryngoscope 1971, **81:** 120–125.

6 Ritter JH, Nappi O. Ozyphilic proliferations of the respiratory tract and paranasal sinuses. Semin Diagn Pathol 1999, **16:** 105–116.

7 Stell PM, Gregory I, Watt J. Morphology of the human larynx. II. The subglottis. Clin Otolaryngol 1980, **5:** 389–395.

8 Stell PM, Gregory I, Watt J. Morphometry of the epithelial lining of the human larynx. II. The glottis. Clin Otolaryngol 1981, **6:** 259–264.

9 Stell PM, Gudron R, Watt J. Morphology of the human larynx. III. The supraglottis. Clin Otolaryngol 1981, **6:** 389–393.

Cysts and laryngocele

10 DeSanto LW, Devine KD, Weiland LH. Cysts of the larynx. Classification. Laryngoscope 1970, **80:** 145–176.

11 Gallagher JC, Puzon BQ. Oncocytic lesions of the larynx. Ann Otol Rhinol Laryngol 1969, **78:** 307–318.

12 Giovaniello J, Grieco RV, Bartone NF. Laryngocele. Am J Roentgenol Radium Ther Nucl Med 1970, **108:** 825–829.

13 Martin-Hirsch DP, Lannigan FJ, Irani B, Batman P. Oncocytic papillary cystadenomatosis of the larynx. J Laryngol Otol 1992, **106:** 656–658.

14 Newman BH, Taxy JB, Laker HI. Laryngeal cysts in adults. A clinicopathologic study of 20 cases. Am J Clin Pathol 1984, **81:** 715–720.

15 Oliveira CA, Roth JA, Adams GL. Oncocytic lesions of the larynx. Laryngoscope 1977, **87:** 1718–1725.

16 Weber PC, Kenna MA, Casselbrant ML. Laryngeal cysts: a cause of neonatal airway obstruction. Otolaryngol Head Neck Surg 1993, **109:** 129–134.

17 Yamase HT, Putman HC. Oncocytic papillary cystadenomatosis of the larynx. A clinicopathologic entity. Cancer 1979, **44:** 2306–2311.

Inflammation

18 Bailey CM, Windle-Taylor PC. Tuberculous laryngitis. A series of 37 patients. Laryngoscope 1981, **91:** 93–100.

19 Barton RT. Observation on the pathogenesis of laryngeal granuloma due to endotracheal anesthesia. N Engl J Med 1953, **248:** 1097–1099.

20 Basu MK, Asquith P, Thompson RA, Coake WT. Oral manifestations of Crohn's disease. Gut 1975, **16:** 249–254.

21 Bennett DE. Histoplasmosis of the oral cavity and larynx. A clinicopathologic study. Arch Intern Med 1967, **120:** 417–427.

22 Berenberg W, Kevy S. Acute epiglottitis in childhood. A serious emergency, readily recognized at the bedside. N Engl J Med 1958, **258:** 870–874.

23 Bienestock H, Ehrlich GE, Freyberg RH. Rheumatoid arthritis of the cricoarytenoid joint. A clinicopathologic study. Arthritis Rheum 1963, **6:** 48–63.

24 Browning DG, Schwartz DA, Juraoo RL. Cryptococcosis of the larynx in a patient with AIDS. An unusual cause of fungal laryngitis. South Med J 1992, **85:** 762–764.

25 Cho MS, Kim ES, Kim HJ, Yang WI. Kimura's disease of the epiglottis. Histopathology 1997, **30:** 592–594.

26 Croft CB, Wilkinson AR. Ulceration of the mouth, pharynx, and larynx in Crohn's disease of the intestine. Br J Surg 1972, **59:** 249–252.

27 Gabrielides CG, Karkavelas G, Triarides C, Kouloulas A. Malakoplakia of the larynx. Pathol Res Pract 1981, **172:** 53–57.

28 Geterud A, Bake B, Berthlesen B, Bjelle A, Ejnell H. Laryngeal involvement in rheumatoid arthritis. Acta Otolaryngol 1991, **111:** 990–998.

29 Guttenplan MD, Hendrix RA, Townsend MJ, Balsara G. Laryngeal manifestations of gout. Ann Otol Rhinol Laryngol 1991, **100:** 899–902.

30 Hawkins DB, Miller AH, Sachs GB, Benz RT. Acute epiglottitis in adults. Laryngoscope 1973, **83:** 1211–1220.

31 Hunter AM, Millar JW, Wightman AJA, Horne NW. The changing pattern of laryngeal tuberculosis. J Laryngol Otol 1981, **95:** 393–398.

32 Kheir SM, Flint A, Moss JA. Primary aspergillosis of the larynx simulating carcinoma. Hum Pathol 1983, **14:** 184–186.

33 McHugh K, deSilva M, Kilham HA. Epiglottic enlargement secondary to laryngeal sarcoidosis. Pediatr Radiol 1993, **23:** 71.

34 Nelson EG, Tybor AG. Actinomycosis of the larynx. Ear Nose Throat J 1992, **71:** 356–358.

35 Reder PA, Neel HB III. Blastomycosis in otolaryngology. Review of a large series. Laryngoscope 1993, **103:** 53–58.

36 Richter B, Fradis M, Kohler G, Ridder GJ. Epiglottic tuberculosis: differential diagnosis and treatment. Case report and review of the literature. Ann Otol Rhinol Laryngol 2001, **110:** 197–201.

37 Saunders MS, Gentile RD, Lobritz RW. Primary laryngeal and nasal septal lesions in pemphigus vulgaris. J Am Osteopath Assoc 1992, **92:** 933–937.

38 Scheidemandel HH. Did George Washington die of quinsy? Arch Otolaryngol 1976, **102:** 519–521.

39 Soni NK. Leprosy of the larynx. J Laryngol Otol 1992, **106:** 518–520.

40 Ulnick KM, Perkins J. Extraintestinal Crohn's disease: case report and review of the literature. Ear Nose Throat J 2001, **80:** 97–100.

41 Weidner N, Askin FB, Berthrong M, Hopkins MB, Kute TE, McGuirt FW. Bizarre (pseudomalignant) granulation-tissue reactions following ionizing-radiation exposure. A microscopic, immunohistochemical, and flow-cytometric study. Cancer 1987, **59:** 1509–1514.

42 Wenig BM, Heffner DK, Oertel YC, Johnson FB. Teflonomas of the larynx and neck. Hum Pathol 1990, **21:** 617–623.

43 Yarnal JR, Golish JA, van der Kuyp F. Laryngeal tuberculosis presenting as carcinoma. Arch Otolaryngol 1981, **107:** 503–505.

Laryngeal nodule and contact ulcer

44 Ash JE, Schwartz L. The laryngeal (vocal cord) nodule. Trans Am Acad Ophthalmol Otolaryngol 1944, **48:** 323–332.

45 Fechner RE, Cooper PH, Mills SE. Pyogenic granuloma of the larynx and trachea. A causal and pathologic misnomer for granulation tissue. Arch Otolaryngol 1981, **107:** 30–32.

46 Wenig BM, Heffner DK. Contact ulcers of the larynx. A reacquaintance with the pathology of an often underdiagnosed entity. Arch Pathol Lab Med 1990, **114:** 825–828.

Other non-neoplastic lesions

47 Burns BV, Roberts PF, De Carpentier J, Zarod AP. Eosinophilic angiocentric fibrosis affecting the nasal cavity. A mucosal variant of the skin lesion granuloma faciale. J Laryngol Otol 2001, **115:** 223–226.

48 Chow LT, Chow WH, Shum BS. Fatal massive upper digestive tract haemorrhage: an unusal complication of localized amyloidosis of the larynx. J Laryngol Otol 1993, **107:** 51–53.

49 Fageeh NA, Mai KT, Odell PF. Eosinophilic angiocentric fibrosis of the subglottic region of the larynx and upper trachea. J Otolaryngol 1996, **25:** 276–278.

50 Gnepp DR, Vogler C, Sotelo-Avila C, Kielmovitch IH. Focal mucinosis of the upper aerodigestive tract in children. Hum Pathol 1990, **21:** 856–858.

51 Hui AN, Koss MN, Hochholzer L, Wehunt WD. Amyloidosis presenting in the lower respiratory tract. Clinicopathologic, radiologic, immunohistochemical, and histochemical studies on 48 cases. Arch Pathol Lab Med 1986, **110:** 212–218.

52 Lewis JE, Olsen KD, Kurtin PJ, Kyle RA. Laryngeal amyloidosis. A clinicopathologic and immunohistochemical review. Otolaryngol Head Neck Surg 1992, **106:** 372–377.

53 Raymond AK, Sniege N, Batsakis JG. Amyloidosis in the upper

aerodigestive tracts. Ann Otol Rhinol Laryngol 1992, **101:** 794–796.

54 Roberts PF, McCann BG. Eosinophilic angiocentric fibrosis of the upper respiratory tract. A mucosal variant of granuloma faciale? A report of three cases. Histopathology 1985, **9:** 1217–1225.

55 Thompson LDR, Derringer GA, Wenig BM. Amyloidosis of the larynx: a clinicopathologic study of 11 cases. Mod Pathol 2000, **13:** 528–535.

56 Wenig BM. Necrotizing sialometaplasia of the larynx. A report of two cases and a review of the literature. Am J Clin Pathol 1995, **103:** 609–613.

Tumors and tumorlike conditions
Papilloma and papillomatosis

57 Abramson AL, Shikowitz MJ, Mullooly VM, Steinberg BM, Amella CA, Rothstein HR. Clinical effects of photodynamic therapy on recurrent laryngeal papillomas. Arch Otolaryngol Head Neck Surg 1992, **118:** 25–29.

58 Barnes L, Yunis EJ, Krebs FJ III, Sonmez-Aplan E. Verruca vulgaris of the larynx. Demonstration of human papillomavirus types 6/11 by in situ hybridization. Arch Pathol Lab Med 1991, **115:** 895–899.

59 Byrne JC, Tsao M-S, Fraser RS, Howley PM. Human papilloma virus-11 DNA in a patient with chronic laryngotracheobronchial papillomatosis and metastatic squamous-cell carcinoma of the lung. N Engl J Med 1987, **317:** 873–878.

60 Cook JR, Hill DA, Humphrey PA, Pfeifer JD, El-Mofty SK. Squamous cell carcinoma arising in recurrent respiratory papillomatosis with pulmonary involvement: emerging common pattern of clinical features and human papillomavirus serotype association. Mod Pathol 2000, **13:** 914–918.

61 Costa J, Howley PM, Bowling MC, Howard R, Bauer WC. Presence of human papilloma viral antigens in juvenile multiple laryngeal papilloma. Am J Clin Pathol 1981, **75:** 194–197.

62 Dedo HH, Yu KC. Co(2) laser treatment in 244 patients with respiratory papillomas. Laryngoscope 2001, **111:** 1639–1644.

63 Derkay CS, Darrow DH. Recurrent respiratory papillomatosis of the larynx: current diagnosis and treatment. Otalaryngol Clin North Am 2000, **33:** 1127–1142.

64 Fechner RE, Mills SE. Verruca vulgaris of the larynx. A distinctive lesion of probable viral origin confused with verrucous carcinoma. Am J Surg Pathol 1982, **6:** 357–362.

65 Fechner RE, Goepfert H, Alford BR. Invasive laryngeal papillomatosis. Arch Otolaryngol 1974, **99:** 147–151.

66 Guillou L, Sahli R, Chaubert P, Monnier O, Cuttat JF, Costa J. Squamous cell carcinoma of the lung in a nonsmoking, nonirradiated patient with juvenile laryngotracheal papillomatosis. Evidence of human papillomavirus-11 DNA in both carcinoma and papillomas. Am J Surg Pathol 1991, **15:** 891–898.

67 Incze JS, Lui PS, Strong MS, Vaughan CW, Clements MP. The morphology of human papillomas of the upper respiratory tract. Cancer 1977, **39:** 1634–1646.

68 Johnston D, Hall H, DiLorenzo TP, Steinberg BM. Elevation of the epidermal growth factor receptor and dependent signalling in human papillomarvirus-infected laryngeal papillomas. Cancer Res 1999, **59:** 968–974.

69 Kashima H, Mounts P, Leventhal B, Hruban RH. Sites of predilection in recurrent respiratory papillomatosis. Ann Otol Rhinol Laryngol 1993, **102:** 580–583.

70 Manni JJ, Mulder JJ, Schaafsma HE, van Haelst UJ. Inflammatory pseudotumor of the subglottis. Eur Arch Otorhinolaryngol 1992, **249:** 16–19.

71 Nikolaidis ET, Trost DC, Buchholz CL, Wilkinson EJ. The relationship of histologic and clinical factors in laryngeal papillomatosis. Arch Pathol Lab Med 1985, **109:** 24–29.

72 Pou AM, Rimell FL, Jordan JA, Shoemaker DL, Johnson JT, Barua P, Post JC, Ehrlich GD. Adult respiratory papillomatosis: human papillomavirus type and viral coinfections as predictors of prognosis. Ann Otol Rhinol Larynol 1995, **104:** 758–762.

73 Quick CA, Foucar E, Dehner LP. Frequency and significance of epithelial atypia in laryngeal papillomatosis. Laryngoscope 1979, **89:** 550–560.

74 Rabbett WF. Juvenile laryngeal papillomatosis. Relation of irradiation to malignant degeneration in this disease. Ann Otol Rhinol Laryngol 1965, **74:** 1149–1163.

75 Rehberg E, Kleinsasser O. Malignant transformation in non-irradiated juvenile laryngeal papillomatosis. Eur Arch Otorhinolaryngol 1999, **256:** 450–454.

76 Rimell F, Maisel R, Dayton V. In situ hybridization and laryngeal papillomas. Ann Otol Rhinol Laryngol 1992, **101:** 119–126.

77 Robbins KT, Howard D. Multiple laryngeal papillomatosis requiring laryngectomy. Arch Otolaryngol 1983, **109:** 765–769.

78 Robbins KT, Woodson GE. Current concepts in the management of laryngeal papillomatosis. Head Neck Surg 1984, **6:** 861–866.

79 Runckler D, Kessler S. Bronchogenic squamous carcinoma in nonirradiated juvenile laryngotracheal papillomatosis. Am J Surg Pathol 1980, **4:** 293–296.

80 Steinberg BM, Topp WC, Schneider PS, Abramson AL. Laryngeal papillomavirus infection during clinical remission. N Engl J Med 1983, **308:** 1261–1264.

81 Vambutas A, Di Lorenzo TP, Steinberg BM. Laryngeal papilloma cells have high levels of epidermal growth factor receptor and respond to epidermal growth factor by a decrease in epithelial differentiation. Cancer Res 1993, **53:** 910–914.

Intraepithelial proliferative lesions

82 Bauer WC, McGavran MH. Carcinoma-in-situ and evaluation of epithelial changes in laryngo-pharyngeal biopsies. JAMA 1972, **221:** 72–75.

83 Crissman JD. Laryngeal keratosis preceding laryngeal carcinoma. A report of four cases. Arch Otolaryngol 1982, **108:** 445–448.

84 Crissman JD, Fu YS. Intraepithelial neoplasia of the larynx. A clinicopathologic study of six cases with DNA analysis. Arch Otolaryngol Head Neck Surg 1986, **112:** 522–528.

85 Crissman JD, Zarbo RJ. Quantitation of DNA ploidy in squamous intraepithelial neoplasia of the laryngeal glottis. Arch Otolarygnol Head Neck Surg 1991, **117:** 182–188.

86 Crissman JD, Gnepp DR, Goodman ML, Hellquist H, Johns ME. Preinvasive lesions of the upper aerodigestive tract. Histologic definitions and clinical implications. Part 1. Pathol Annu 1987, **22:** 311–352.

87 Elman AJ, Goodman M, Wang CC, Pilch B, Busse J. In situ carcinoma of the vocal cords. Cancer 1979, **43:** 2422–2428.

88 Gale N, Kambic V, Michaels L, Cardesa A, Hellquist H, Zidar N, Poljak M. The Ljubljana classification: a practical strategy for the diagnosis of laryngeal precancerous lesions. Adv Anat Pathol 2000, **7:** 240–251.

89 Gallo A, De Vincentiis M, Manciocco V, Simonelli M, Fiorella ML, Shah JP. CO2 laser Cordectomy for early-stage glottic carcinoma: a long-term follow-up of 156 cases. Laryngoscope 2002, **112:** 370–374.

90 Gallo O, Franchi A, Chiarelli I, Porfirio B, Grande A, Simonetti L, Bocciolini C, Fini-storchi O. Potential biomarkers in predicting progression of epithelial hyperplastic lesions of the larynx. Acta Otolaryngol Suppl 1997, **527:** 30–38.

91 Garcia-Serra A, Hinerman RW, Amdur Rj, Morris CG, Mendenhall WM. Radiotherapy for carcinoma in situ of the true vocal cords. Head Neck 2002, **24:** 390–394.

92 Gillis TM, Incze J, Strong MS, Vaughan CW, Simpson GT. Natural history and management of keratosis, atypia, carcinoma in situ and microinvasive cancer of the larynx. Am J Surg 1983, **146:** 512–516.

93 Goodman ML. Keratosis (leukoolakia) of the larynx. Otolaryngol Clin North Am 1984, **17:** 179–183.

94 Helliwell TR. Commentary: "Risky" epithelium in the larynx—a practical diagnosis? Histopathology 1999, **34**: 262–265.

95 Hellquist H, Lundgren J, Olofsson J. Hyperplasia, dysplasia and carcinoma in situ of the vocal cords. A follow-up study. Clin Otolaryngol 1982, **7**: 11–27.

96 Hellquist H, Cardesa A, Gale N, Kambic V, Michaels L. Criteria for grading in the Ljubljana classification of epithelial hyperplastic laryngeal lesions. A study by members of the Working Group on Epithelial Hyperplastic Laryngeal Lesions of the European Society of Pathology. Histopathology 1999, **34**: 226–233.

97 Hintz BL, Kagan AR, Nussbaum H, Rao AR, Chan PY, Miles J. A "watchful waiting" policy for in situ carcinoma of the vocal cords. Arch Otolaryngol 1981, **107**: 746–751.

98 Kambiè V, Gale N, Ferluga D. Laryngeal hyperplastic lesions, follow-up study and application of lectins and anticytokeratins for their evaluation. Pathol Res Pract 1992, **188**: 1067–1077.

99 Le QT, Takamiya R, Shu HK, Smitt M, Singer M, Terris DJ, Fee WE, Goffinet DR, Fu KK. Treatment results of carcinoma in situ of the glottis: an analysis of 82 cases. Arch Otolaryngol Head Neck Surg 2000, **126**: 1305–1312.

100 McGavran MH, Bauer WC, Ogura JH. Isolated laryngeal keratosis. Its relation to carcinoma of the larynx based on a clinicopathologic study of 87 consecutive cases with long-term follow-up. Laryngoscope 1960, **70**: 932–951.

101 McLaren KM, Burnett RA, Goodlad JR, Howatson SR, Lang S, Lee FD, Lessells AM, Ogston S, Robertson AJ, Simpson JG, Smith GD, Tavadia HB, Walker F. Consistency of histopathological reporting of laryngeal dysplasia. The Scottish Pathology Consistency Group. Histopathology 2000, **37**: 460–467.

102 Miyaguchi M, Olofsson J, Hellquist HB. Immunohistochemical study of epidermal growth factor receptor in severe dysplasia and carcinoma in situ of vocal cords. Acta Otolaryngol (Stockholm) 1991, **111**: 149–152.

103 Shanmugaratnam K and others. Histological typing of tumours of the upper respiratory tract and ear. Berlin, 1991, Springer-Verlag.

104 Spayne JA, Warde P, O'Sullivan B, Payne D, Liu FF, Waldron J, Gullane PJ, Cummings BJ. Carcinoma-in-situ of the glottic larynx: results of treatment with radiation therapy. Int J Radiat Oncol Biol Phys 2001, **49**: 1235–1238.

105 Stenersen TC, Boysen M, Juhng SW, Reith A. Quantitative histopathological evaluation of vocal cord dysplasia with particular emphasis on nuclear orientation. Pathol Res Pract 1992, **188**: 524–530.

106 Zidar N, Gale N, Cor A, Kambic V. Expression of Ki-67 antigen and proliferating cell nuclear antigen in benign and malignant epithelial lesions of the larynx. J Laryngol Otol 1996, **110**: 440–445.

Invasive carcinoma
General features

107 Barnes L, Johnson JT. Pathologic and clinical considerations in the evaluation of major head and neck specimens resected for cancer. Part 1. Pathol Annu 1986, **21**: 173–250.

108 Boysen M, Loven JO. Second malignant neoplasms in patients with head and neck squamous cell carcinomas. Acta Oncol 1993, **32**: 283–288.

109 DeStefani E, Correa P, Oreggia F, Leiva J, Rivero S, Femandez G, Deneo-Pellegrini H, Zavala D, Fontham E. Risk factors for laryngeal cancer. Cancer 1987, **60**: 3087–3091.

110 Gorgoulis VG, Zacharatos P, Kotsinas A, Kyroudi A, Rassidakis AN, Ikonomopoulos JA, Barbatis C, Herrington CS, Kittas C. Human papilloma virus (HPV) is possibly involved in laryngeal but not in lung carcinogenesis. Hum Pathol 1999, **30**: 274–283.

111 Karim AB, Kralendonk JH, Njo KH, Gort G. A critical look at the TNM classification for laryngeal carcinoma. Cancer 1990, **65**: 1918–1922.

112 Kleinsasser O. Revision of classification of laryngeal cancer, is it long overdue? (Proposals for an improved TN-classification). J Laryngol Otol 1992, **106**: 197–204.

113 Lee S-S, Ro JY, Luna MA, Batsakis JG. Squamous cell carcinoma of the larynx in young adults. Semin Diagn Pathol 1987, **4**: 150–152.

114 Mendez P Jr, Maves MD, Panje WR. Squamous cell carcinoma of the head and neck in patients under 40 years of age. Arch Otolaryngol 1985, **111**: 762–764.

115 Muscat JE, Wynder EL. Tobacco, alcohol, asbestos, and occupational risk factors for laryngeal cancer. Cancer 1992, **69**: 2244–2251.

116 Rafferty MA, Fenton JE, Jones AS. The history, aetiology and epidemiology of laryngeal carcinoma. Clin Otolaryngol 2001, **26**: 442–446.

117 Roberts TJ, Epstein B, Lee DJ. Second neoplasms in patients with carcinomas of the vocal cord. Incidence and implications for survival. Int J Radiat Oncol Biol Phys 1991, **21**: 583–589.

Types, spread, and therapy

118 Archer CR, Yeager VL, Herbold DR. Improved diagnostic accuracy in laryngeal cancer using a new classification based on computed tomography. Cancer 1984, **53**: 44–57.

119 Barnes L, Johnson JT. Pathologic and clinical considerations in the evaluation of major head and neck specimens resected for cancer. Part I. Pathol Annu 1986, **21**: 173–250.

120 Bauer WC, Edwards DL, McGavran MH. A critical analysis of laryngectomy in the treatment of epidermoid carcinoma of the larynx. Cancer 1962, **15**: 263–270.

121 Biller HF, Ogura JH, Pratt LL. Hemilaryngectomy for T2 glottic cancers. Arch Otolaryngol 1971, **93**: 238–243.

122 DeSanto LW. The options in early laryngeal carcinoma. N Engl J Med 1982, **306**: 910–912.

123 Djalilian M, Weiland LH, Devine KD, Beahrs OH. Significance of jugular vein invasion by metastatic carcinoma in radical neck dissection. Am J Surg 1973, **126**: 566–569.

124 Dyess CL, Carter D, Kirchner JA, Baron RE. A morphometric comparison of the changes in the laryngeal skeleton associated with invasion by tumor and by external-beam radiation. Cancer 1987, **59**: 1117–1122.

125 Feldman PS, Kaplan MJ, Johns ME, Cantrell RW. Fine-needle aspiration in squamous cell carcinoma of the head and neck. Arch Otolaryngol 1983, **109**: 735–742.

126 Fisher AJ, Caldarelli DD, Chacko DC, Holinger LD. Glottic cancer. Surgical salvage for radiation failure. Arch Otolaryngol Head Neck Surg 1986, **112**: 519–521.

127 Gerard-Marchant R, Micheau C, Cachin Y. Epithélioma laryngé et laryngocèle—une forme anatomo-clinique particulière. Compte-rendu de 7 observations. Ann Otolaryngol 1969, **86**: 437–442.

128 Johns ME, Farrior E, Boyd JC, Cantrell RW. Staging of supraglottic cancer. Arch Otolaryngol 1982, **108**: 700–702.

129 Jose B, Calhoun DL, Mohammed A. Recurrences after irradiation in early vocal cord cancer with literature review. J Surg Oncol 1984, **27**: 224–227.

130 Kaplan MJ, Johns ME, Clark DA, Cantrell RW. Glottic carcinoma. The roles of surgery and irradiation. Cancer 1984, **53**: 2641–2648.

131 Lam KH. Extralaryngeal spread of cancer of the larynx. A study with whole-organ sections. Head Neck Surg 1983, **5**: 410–424.

132 Maceri DP, Lampe HB, Makielski KH, Passamani PP, Krause CJ. Conservation laryngeal surgery. A critical analysis. Arch Otolaryngol 1985, **111**: 361–365.

133 McGavran MH, Bauer WC, Ogura JH. The incidence of cervical lymph node metastases from epidermoid carcinoma of the larynx and their relationship to certain characteristics of the primary tumor. A study based on the clinical and pathological findings for 96 patients treated by primary en bloc laryngectomy and radical neck dissection. Cancer 1961, **14**: 55–65.

134 Michaeu C, Luboinski B, Sancho H, Cachin Y. Modes of invasion of cancer of the larynx. A statistical, histological, and radioclinical analysis of 120 cases. Cancer 1976, **38**: 346–360.

135 Mittal B, Marks JE, Ogura JH. Transglottic carcinoma. Cancer 1984, **53**: 151–161.

136 Ogura JH, Biller HF. Neck dissection for carcinoma of the larynx and hypopharynx. Proceedings of the Sixth National Cancer Conference. Philadelphia, 1970, JB Lippincott Co.

137 Ogura JH, Sessions DG, Spector GJ. Analysis of surgical therapy for epidermoid carcinoma of the laryngeal glottis. Laryngoscope 1975, **85**: 1522–1530.

138 Olsen KD, Thomas JV, DeSanto LW, Suman VJ. Indications and results of cordectomy for early glottic carcinoma. Otolaryngol Head Neck Surg 1993, **108**: 277–282.

139 Robbins KT, Michaels L. Feasibility of subtotal laryngectomy based on whole-organ examination. Arch Otolaryngol 1985, **111**: 356–360.

140 Russ JE, Sullivan C, Gallager HS, Jesse RH. Conservation surgery of the larynx. A reappraisal based on whole organ study. Am J Surg 1979, **138**: 588–596.

141 Sessions DG, Ogura JH, Fried MP. Carcinoma of the subglottic area. Laryngoscope 1975, **85**: 1417–1423.

142 Steiner W. Results of curative laser microsurgery of laryngeal carcinomas. Am J Otolaryngol 1993, **14**: 116–121.

143 Stutsman AC, McGavran MH. Ultraconservative management of superficially invasive epidermoid carcinoma of the true vocal cord. Ann Otol Rhinol Laryngol 1971, **80**: 507–512.

144 Zbaren P, Becker M, Lang H. Pretherapeutic staging of laryngeal carcinoma: clinical findings, computed tomography, and magnetic resonance imaging compared with histopathology. Cancer 1996, **77**: 1263–1273.

Pathologic features

145 Carbone A, Volpe R, Barzan L. Superficial extending carcinoma (SEC) of the larynx and hypopharynx. Pathol Res Pract 1992, **188**: 729–735.

146 Chung CK, Stryker JA, Abt AB, Cunningham DE, Strauss M, Connor GH. Histologic grading in the clinical evaluation of laryngeal carcinoma. Arch Otolaryngol 1980, **106**: 623–624.

147 Crissman JD, Gnepp DR, Goodman ML, Hellquist H, Johns ME. Preinvasive lesions of the upper aerodigestive tract. Histologic definitions and clinical implications (a symposium). Part I. Pathol Annu 1987, **22**: 311–352.

148 Suarez PA, Adler-Storthz K, Luna MA, El-Naggar AK, Abdul-Karim FW, Batsakis JG. Papillary squamous cell carcinomas of the upper aerodigestive tract: a clinicopathologic and molecular study. Head Neck 2000, **22**: 360–368.

Histochemical and immunohistochemical features

149 Christensen ME, Therkildsen MH, Hansen BL, Hansen GN, Bretlau P. Immunohistochemical detection of epidermal growth factor receptor in laryngeal squamous cell carcinomas. Acta Otolaryngol (Stockholm) 1992, **112**: 734–738.

150 Hagedorn H, Schreiner M, Wiest I, Tubel J, Schleicher ED, Nerlich AG. Defective basement membrane in laryngeal carcinomas with heterogeneous loss of distinct components. Hum Pathol 1998, **29**: 447–454.

151 Mallofre C, Cardesa A, Campo E, Condom E, Palacin A, Garin-Chesa P, Traserra J. Expression of cytokeratins in squamous cell carcinomas of the larynx. Immunohistochemical analysis and correlation with prognostic factors. Pathol Res Pract 1993, **189**: 275–282.

152 Scambia G, Panici PB, Battaglia F, Ferrandina G, Almadon G, Paludetti G, Maurizi M, Mancuso S. Receptors for epidermal growth factor and steroid hormones in primary laryngeal tumors. Cancer 1991, **67**: 1347–1351.

Molecular genetic features

153 El-Naggar AK, Lai S, Clayman GL, Zhou JH, Tucker SA, Myers J, Luna MA, Benedict WF. Expression of p16, Rb, and cyclin D1 gene products in oral and laryngeal squamous carcinoma: biological and clinical implications. Hum Pathol 1999, **30**: 1013–1018.

154 Maestro R, Dolcetti R, Gasparotto D, Doglioni C, Pelucchi S, Barzan L, Grandi E, Boiocchi M. High frequency of p53 gene alterations associated with protein overexpression in human squamous cell carcinoma of the larynx. Oncogene 1992, **7**: 1159–1166.

155 Mizokami H, Sawatsubashi M, Tokunaga O, Shin T. Loss of retinoblastoma protein expression in laryngeal squamous cell carcinoma. Mod Pathol 1999, **12**: 47–53.

155a Nadal A, Cardesa A. Molecular biology of laryngeal squamous cell carcinoma. Virchows Arch 2003, **442**: 1–7.

156 Pruneri G, Pignataro L, Fracchiolla NS, Ferrero S, Capaccio P, Carboni N, Ottaviani A, Maiolo AT, Neri A, Buffa R. P53 protein expression in laryngeal squamous cell carcinomas bearing wild type and mutated p53 gene. Histopathology 1996, **28**: 513–520.

Other microscopic types

157 Abramson AL, Brandsma J, Steinberg B, Winkler B. Verrucous carcinoma of the larynx. Possible human papillomavirus etiology. Arch Otolaryngol 1985, **111**: 709–715.

157a Ansari-Lari MA, Hoque MO, Califano J, Westra WH. Immunohistochemical p53 expression patterns in sarcomatoid carcinomas of the upper respiratory tract. Am J Surg Pathol 2002, **26**: 1024–1031.

158 Appelman HD, Oberman HA. Squamous cell carcinoma of the larynx with sarcoma-like stroma. A clinicopathologic assessment of spindle cell carcinoma and "pseudosarcoma." Am J Clin Pathol 1965, **44**: 135–145.

159 Banks ER, Frierson HF Jr, Mills SE, George E, Zarbo R, Swanson PE. Basaloid squamous cell carcinoma of the head and neck. A clinicopathologic and immunohistochemical study of 40 cases. Am J Surg Pathol 1992, **16**: 939–946.

160 Batsakis JG, Luna MA, el-Naggar AK. Nonsquamous carcinomas of the larynx. Ann Otol Rhinol Laryngol 1992, **101**: 1024–1026.

161 Benisch BM, Tawfik B, Breitenbach EE. Primary oat cell carcinoma of the larynx. An ultrastructural study. Cancer 1975, **36**: 145–148.

162 Cady B, Rippey JH, Frazell EL. Non-epidermoid cancer of the larynx. Ann Surg 1968, **167**: 116–120.

163 Crissman JD, Gnepp DR, Goodman ML, Hellquist H, Johns ME. Preinvasive lesions of the upper aerodigestive tract. Histologic definitions and clinical implications (a symposium). Pathol Annu 1987, **22**(Pt 1): 311–352.

164 Doglioni C, Ferlito A, Chiamenti C, Viale G, Rosai J. Laryngeal carcinoma showing multidirectional epithelial neuroendocrine and sarcomatous differentiation. ORL J Otorhinolaryngol Relat Spec 1990, **52**: 316–326.

165 Ellis GL, Langloss JM, Heffner DK, Hyams VJ. Spindle-cell carcinoma of the aerodigestive tract. An immunohistochemical analysis of 21 cases. Am J Surg Pathol 1987, **11**: 335–342.

166 Ferlito A. Histological classification of larynx and hypopharynx cancers and their clinical implications. Acta Otolaryngol 1976, **342**(Suppl): 1–88.

167 Ferlito A, Recher G. Ackerman's tumor (verrucous carcinoma) of the larynx. A clinicopathologic study of 77 cases. Cancer 1980, **46**: 1617–1630.

168 Gnepp DR. Small cell neuroendocrine carcinoma of the larynx. A critical review of the literature. ORL J Otorhinolaryngol Relat Spec 1991, **53**: 210–219.

169 Goellner JR, Devine KD, Weiland LH. Pseudosarcoma of the larynx. Am J Clin Pathol 1973, **59**: 312–326.

170 Goldman RL, Weidner NL. Pure squamous cell carcinoma of the larynx with cervical nodal metastasis showing rhabdomyosarcomatous differentiation. Am J Surg Pathol 1993, **17:** 415–421.

171 Hagen P, Lyons GD, Haindel C. Verrucous carcinoma of the larynx. Role of human papillomavirus, radiation, and surgery. Laryngoscope 1993, **103:** 253–257.

172 Johnson TL, Plieth DA, Crissman JD, Sarkar FH. HPV detection by polymerase chain reaction (PCR) in verrucous lesions of the upper aerodigestive tract. Mod Pathol 1991, **4:** 461–465.

173 Kraus FT, Perez-Mesa C. Verrucous carcinoma. Clinical and pathologic study of 105 cases involving oral cavity, larynx, and genitalia. Cancer 1966, **19:** 26–28.

174 Lambert PR, Ward PH, Berei G. Pseudosarcoma of the larynx. A comprehensive analysis. Arch Otolaryngol 1980, **106:** 700–708.

175 Lane N. Pseudosarcoma (polypoid sarcoma like masses) associated with squamous cell carcinoma of the mouth, fauces and larynx. Report of ten cases. Cancer 1957, **10:** 19–41.

176 Lasser KH, Naeim F, Higgins J, Cove H, Waisman J. "Pseudosarcoma" of the larynx. Am J Surg Pathol 1979, **3:** 397–404.

177 Lewis JE, Olsen KD, Sebo TJ. Spindle cell carcinoma of the larynx: review of 26 cases including DNA content and immuhistochemistry. Hum Pathol 1997, **28:** 664–673.

178 Lopez-Amado M, Garcia-Caballero T, Lozano-Ramirez A, Labella-Caballero T. Human papillomavirus and p53 oncoprotein in verrucous carcinoma of the larynx. J Laryngol Otol 1996, **110:** 742–747.

179 Luna MA, el-Naggar A. Parichatikanond P, Weber RS, Batsakis JG. Basaloid squamous carcinoma of the upper aerodigestive tract. Clinicopathologic and DNA flow cytometric analysis. Cancer 1990, **66:** 537–542.

180 MacMillan C, Kapadia SB, Finkelstein SD, Nalesnik MA, Barnes L. Lymphoepithelial carcinoma of the larynx and hypopharynx: study of eight cases with relationship to Epstein–Barr virus and p53 gene alterations, and review of the literature. Hum Pathol 1996, **27:** 1172–1179.

181 Mills SE, Cooper PH, Garland TA, Johns ME. Small cell undifferentiated carcinoma of the larynx. Report of two patients and review of 13 additional cases. Cancer 1983, **51:** 116–120.

182 Olofsson J, van Nostrand AWP. Anaplastic small cell carcinoma of larynx. Ann Otol Rhinol Laryngol 1972, **81:** 284–287.

183 Orvidas LJ, Olsen KD, Lewis JE, Suman VJ. Verrucous carcinoma of the larynx: a review of 53 patients. Head Neck 1998, **20:** 197–203.

184 Paladugu RR, Nathwani BN, Goodstein J, Dardi LE, Memoli VE, Gould VE. Carcinoma of the larynx with mucosubstance production and neuroendocrine differentiation. An ultrastructural and immunohistochemical study. Cancer 1982, **49:** 343–349.

185 Randall G, Alonso WA, Ogura JH. Spindle cell carcinoma (pseudosarcoma) of the larynx. Arch Otolaryngol 1975, **101:** 63–66.

186 Seidman JD, Berman JJ, Yest BA, Iseri OA. Basaloid squamous carcinoma of the hypopharynx and laryax associated with second primary tumors. Cancer 1991, **68:** 1545–1549.

187 Tardio JC, Cristobal E, Burgos F, Menarguez J. Absence of EBV genome in lymphoepithelioma-like carcinomas of the larynx. Histopathology 1997, **30:** 126–128.

188 Tsang WY, Chan JK, Lee KC, Leung AK, Fu YT. Basaloid-squamous carcinoma of the upper aerodigestive tract and so-called adenoid cystic carcinoma of the oesophagus. The same tumour type? Histopathology 1991, **19:** 35–46.

189 Tsang YW, Ngan KC, Chan JK. Primary mucoid adenocarcinoma of the larynx. J Laryngol Otol 1991, **105:** 315–317.

190 Wain SL, Kier R, Vollmer RT, Bossen EH. Basaloid-squamous carcinoma of the tongue, hypopharynx, and larynx. Report of 10 cases. Hum Pathol 1986, **17:** 1158–1166.

191 Weidner N. Sarcomatoid carcinoma of the upper aerodigestive tract. Semin Diagn Pathol 1987, **4:** 157–168.

192 Wenig BM. Variants of squamous cell carcinoma of the upper aerodigestive tract. Anat Pathol 1998, **3:** 17–52.

193 Zarbo RJ, Crissman JD, Venkat H, Weiss MA. Spindle-cell carcinoma of the upper aerodigestive tract mucosa. An immunohistologic and ultrastructural study of 18 biphasic tumors and comparison with seven monophasic spindle-cell tumors. Am J Surg Pathol 1986, **10:** 741–753.

Prognosis

194 Barnes L, Johnson JT. Pathologic and clinical considerations in the evaluation of major head and neck specimens resected for cancer. Part 1. Pathol Annu 1986, **21:** 173–250.

195 Barona de Guzmàn R, Martorell MA, Basterra J, Armengot M, Alvarez-Valdès R, Garin L. Prognostic value of histopathological parameters in 51 supraglottic squamous cell carcinomas. Laryngoscope 1993, **103:** 538–540.

196 Friedman M, Lim JW, Manders E, Schaffner AD, Kirschenbaum GL, Tanyeri HM, Caldarelli DD, Coon JS. Prognostic significance of Bcl-2 and p53 expression in advanced laryngeal squamous cell carcinoma. Head Neck 2001, **23:** 280–285.

197 Gallo O, Libonati GA, Gallina E, Fini-Storchi O, Giannini A, Urso C, Bondi R. Langerhans cells related to prognosis in patients with laryngeal carcinoma. Arch Otolaryngol Head Neck Surg 1991, **117:** 1007–1010.

198 Kokoska MS, Piccirillo JF, El-Mofty SK, Emami B, Haughey BH, Scholnick SB. Prognostic significance of clinical factors and p53 expression in patients with glottic carcinoma treated with radiation therapy. Cancer 1996, **78:** 1693–1700.

199 Mallofrè C, Cardesa A, Campo E, Condom E, Palacin A, Garin-Chesa P, Traserra J. Expression of cytokeratins in squamous cell carcinomas of the larynx. Immunohistochemical analysis and correlation with prognostic factors. Pathol Res Pract 1993, **189:** 275–282.

200 Manni JJ, Terhaard CH, de Boer MF, Croll GA, Hilgers FJ, Annyas AA, van der Meij AG, Hordijk GJ. Prognostic factors for survival in patients with T3 laryngeal carcinoma. Am J Surg 1992, **164:** 682–687.

201 Nakashima T, Yano G, Hayashi I, Katsuta Y. Epithelial membrane antigen and S-100 protein-labeled cells in primary and metastatic laryngeal carcinomas. Head Neck 1992, **14:** 445–451.

202 Narayana A, Vaughan ATM, Gunaratne S, Kathuria S, Walter SA, Reddy SP. Is p53 an independent prognostic factor in patients with laryngeal carcinoma? Cancer 1998, **82:** 286–291.

203 Pera E, Moreno A, Galindo L. Prognostic factors in laryngeal carcinoma. A multifactorial study of 416 cases. Cancer 1986, **58:** 928–934.

204 Silvestri F, Bussani R, Stanta G, Cosatti C, Ferlito A. Supraglottic versus glottic laryngeal cancer. Epidemiological and pathological aspects. ORL J Otorhinolaryngol Relat Spec 1992, **54:** 43–48.

205 Small W Jr, Mittal BB, Brand WN, Shetty RM, Rademaker AW, Beck GG, Hoover SV. Results of radiation therapy in early glottic carcinoma. Multivariate analysis of prognostic and radiation therapy variables. Radiology 1992, **183:** 789–794.

206 Westerbeek HA, Mooi WJ, Hilgers FJ, Baris G, Begg AC, Balm AJ. Ploidy status and the response of T1 glottic carcinoma to radiotherapy. Clin Otolaryngol 1993, **18:** 98–101.

207 Wiernik G, Millard PR, Haybittle JL. The predictive value of histological classification into degrees of differentiation of squamous cell carcinoma of the larynx and hypophayrnx compared with the survival of patients. Histopathology 1991, **19:** 411–417.

Salivary gland-type tumors

208 Crissman JD, Rosenblatt A. Acinous cell carcinoma of the larynx. Arch Pathol Lab Med 1978, **102:** 233–236.

209 Ibrahim R, Bird DJ, Sieler MW. Malignant myoepithelioma of the larynx with massive metastatic spread to the liver. An ultrastructural and immunocytochemical study. Ultrastruct Pathol 1991, **15:** 69–76.

210 MacMillan RH III, Fechner RE. Pleomorphic adenoma of the larynx. Arch Pathol Lab Med 1986, **110:** 245–247.

211 Martinez-Madrigal F, Payan HS, Meneses A, Malogon HD, Rojas ME. Plasmacytoid myoepithelioma of the laryngeal region. A case report. Hum Pathol 1995, **26:** 802–803.

212 Olofsson J, van Nostrand AWP. Adenoid cystic carcinoma of the larynx. A report of four cases and a review of the literature. Cancer 1977, **40:** 1307–1313.

213 Spiro RH, Hajdu SI, Lewis JS, Strong EW. Mucus gland tumors of the larynx and laryngopharynx. Ann Otol 1976, **85:** 498–503.

214 Squires JE, Mills SE, Cooper PH, Innes DJ Jr, McLean WC. Acinic cell carcinoma. Its occurrence in the laryngotracheal junction after thyroid radiation. Arch Pathol Lab Med 1981, **105:** 200–208.

215 Tomita T, Lotuaco L, Taibett L, Watanabe I. Mucoepidermoid carcinoma of the subglettis. An ultrastructural study. Arch Pathol Lab Med 1977, **101:** 145–148.

216 Whicker JH, Weiland LH, Neel HB III, Devine KD. Adenocarcinoma of the larynx. Ann Otol Rhinol Laryngol 1974, **83:** 487–490.

Carcinoid tumor and paraganglioma

217 Barnes L. Paraganglioma of the larynx. A critical review of the literature. ORL J Otorhinolaryngol Relat Spec 1991, **53:** 220–234.

218 Batsakis JG, el-Naggar AK, Luna MA. Neuroendocrine tumors of larynx. Ann Otol Rhinol Laryngol 1992, **101:** 710–714.

219 el-Naggar AK, Batsakis JG. Carcinoid tumor of the layrnx. A critical review of the literature. ORL J Otorhinolaryngol Relat Spec 1991, **53:** 188–193.

220 el-Naggar AK, Batsakis JG, Vassilopoulou-Sellin R, Ordonez NG, Luna MA. Medullary (thyroid) carcinoma-like carcinoids of the larynx. J Laryngol Otol 1991, **105:** 683–686.

221 Ferlito A, Rosai J. Terminology and classification of neuroendocrine neoplasms of the larynx. ORL J Otorhinolaryngol Relat Spec 1991, **53:** 185–187.

222 Gallivan MVE, Chun B, Rowden G, Lack EE. Laryngeal paraganglioma. Case report with ultrastructural analysis and literature review. Am J Surg Pathol 1979, **3:** 85–92.

223 Laccourreye O, Brasnu D, Carnot F, Fichaux P, Laccourreye H. Carcinoid (neuroendocrine) tumor of the arytenoid. Arch Otolaryngol Head Neck Surg 1991, **117:** 1395–1399.

224 McCluggage WG, Bharucha H, Cameron CHS, Toner PG. Amphicrine carcinoma of the larynx. Histopathology 1994, **24:** 393–394.

225 McCluggage WG, Cameron CHS, Arthur K, Toner PG. Atypical carcinoid tumor of the larynx: an immunohistochemical, ultrastructural, and flow cytometric analysis. Ultrastruct Pathol 1997, **21:** 431–438.

226 Mills SE. Neuroectodermal neoplasms of the head and neck with emphasis on neuroendocrine carcinomas. Mod Pathol 2002, **15:** 264–278.

227 Mills SE, Johns ME. Atypical carcinoid tumor of the larynx. A light microscopic and ultrastructural study. Arch Otolaryngol 1984, **110:** 58–62.

228 Milroy CM, Rode J, Moss E. Laryngeal paragangliomas and neuroendocrine carcinomas. Histopathology 1991, **18:** 201–209.

229 Moisa II. Neuroendocrine tumors of the larynx. Head Neck 1991, **13:** 498–508.

230 Nonomura A, Shintani T, Kono N, Kamimura R, Ohta G. Primary carcinoid tumor of the larynx and review of the literature. Acta Pathol Jpn 1983, **33:** 1041–1049.

231 Ohsawa M, Kurita Y, Horie A, Kurita K. Malignant chemodectoma (paraganglioma) of the larynx. A case report with electron microscopy and biochemical assay. Acta Pathol Jpn 1983, **33:** 1279–1288.

232 Peterson KL, Fu YS, Calcaterra T. Subglottic paraganglioma. Head Neck 1997, **19:** 54–56.

233 Smets G, Warson F, Dehou MF, Storme G, Sacrè R, Van Belle S, Somers G, Gepts W, Klöppel G. Metastasizing neuroendocrine carcinoma of the larynx with calcitonin and somatostatin secretion and CEA production, resembling medullary thyroid carcinoma. Virchows Arch [A] 1990, **416:** 539–543.

234 Sneige N, Mackay B, Ordonez NG, Batsakis JG. Laryngeal paraganglioma. Report of two tumors with immunohistochemical and ultrastructural analysis. Arch Otolaryngol 1983, **109:** 113–117.

235 Stanley RJ, DeSanto LW, Weiland LH. Oncocytic and oncocytoid carcinoid tumors (well-differentiated neuroendocrine carcinomas) of the larynx. Arch Otolaryngol Head Neck Surg 1986, **112:** 529–535.

236 Tamai S, Iri H, Maruyama T, Kasahara M, Akatsuka S, Sakurai S, Murakami Y. Laryngeal carcinoid tumor. Light and electron microscopic studies. Cancer 1981, **48:** 2256–2259.

237 Wasserman PG, Savargaonkar P. Paragangliomas: classification, pathology, and differential diagnosis. Otolaryngol Clin North Am 2001, **34:** 845–862.

238 Woodruff JM, Senie RT. Atypical carcinoid tumor of the larynx. A critical review of the literature. ORL J Otorhinolaryngol Relat Spec 1991, **53:** 194–209.

Other tumors and tumorlike conditions

239 Amin HH, Petruzzelli GJ, Husain AN, Nickoloff BJ. Primary malignant melanoma of the larynx. Arch Pathol Lab Med 2001, **125:** 271–273.

240 Batsakis JG, Fox JE. Rhabdomyosarcoma of the larynx. Arch Otolaryngol 1970A, **91:** 136–140.

241 Batsakis JG, Fox JE. Supporting tissue neoplasms of the larynx. Surg Gynecol Obstet 1970B, **131:** 989–997.

242 Batsakis JG, Luna MA, Byers RM. Metastases to the larynx. Head Neck Surg 1984, **7:** 458–460.

243 Booth JB, Osborn DA. Granular cell myoblastoma of the larynx. Acta Otolaryngol (Stockholm) 1970, **70:** 279–293.

244 Brandwein M, Moore S, Som P, Biller H. Laryngeal chondrosarcomas. A clinicopathologic study of 11 cases, including two "dedifferentiated" chondrosarcomas. Laryngoscope 1992, **102:** 858–867.

245 Chen KTK. Localized laryngeal lymphoma. J Surg Oncol 1984, **26:** 208–209.

246 Coates HL, Devine KD, McDonald TJ, Weiland LH. Granular cell tumors of the larynx. Ann Otol 1976, **85:** 504–507.

247 Compagno J, Hyams VJ, Ste-Marie P. Benign granular cell tumors of the larynx. A review of 36 cases with clinicopathologic data. Ann Otol 1975, **84:** 308–314.

248 Conley SF, Milbrath MM, Beste DJ. Pediatric laryngeal granular cell tumor. J Otolaryngol 1992, **21:** 450–453.

249 Della Libera D, Falconaeiri G, Zanella M. Embryonal "botryoid" rhabdomyosarcoma of the larynx: a clinicopathologic and immunohistochemical study of two cases. Ann Diagn Pathol 1999, **3:** 341–349.

250 Della Libera D, Redlich G, Bittesini L, Falconieri G. Aneurysmal bone cyst of the larynx presenting with hypoglottic obstruction; a case report and review of the literature. Arch Pathol Lab Med 2001, **125:** 673–676.

251 Ferlito A. Histiocytic tumors of the larynx. A clinicopathological study with review of the literature. Cancer 1978, **42:** 611–622.

252 Ferlito A, Caruso G. Endolaryngeal synovial sarcoma. An update on diagnosis and treatment. ORL J Otorhinolaryngol Relat Spec 1991, **53:** 116–119.

253 Goethals PL, Dahlin DC, Devine KD. Cartilaginous tumors of the larynx. Surg Gynecol Obstet 1963, **117:** 77–82.

253a González-Lois C, Ibarrola C, Ballestín C, Martínez-Tello FJ. Dedifferentiated liposarcoma of the pyriform sinus. Int J Surg Pathol 2002, **10**: 75–79.

254 Hellquist HB, Hellquist HH, Vejlens L, Lindholm CE. Epithelioid leiomyoma of the larynx. Histopathology 1994, **24**: 155–160.

255 Ho FC, Choy D, Loke SL, Kung IT, Fu KH, Liang R, Todd D, Khoo RK. Polymorphic reticulosis and conventional lymphomas of the nose and upper aerodigestive tract. A clinicopathologic study of 70 cases, and immunophenotypic studies of 16 cases. Hum Pathol 1990, **21**: 1041–1050.

256 Horny H-P, Kaiserling E. Involvement of the larynx by hemopoietic neoplasms. An investigation of autopsy cases and review of the literature. Pathol Res Pract 1995, **191**: 130–138.

257 Hughes CA, Rezaee A, Ludemann JP, Holinger LD. Management of congenital subglottic hemangioma. J Otolaryngol 1999, **28**: 223–228.

258 Jones RV. Laryngeal involvement in acute leukemia. J Laryngol 1968, **82**: 123–128.

259 Kendall CH, Johnston MN. Pseudo-malignant laryngeal nodule (inflammatory myofibroblastic tumour). Histopathology 1998, **32**: 286–287.

260 Kleist B, Poetsch M, Lang C, Bankau A, Lorenz G, Suess-Fridrich K, Jundt G, Wolf E. Clear cell chondrosaracoma of the larynx: a case report of a rare histologic variant in an uncommon localization. Am J Surg Pathol 2002, **26**: 386–392.

261 Lomeo P, McDonald J, Finneman J. Adult laryngeal hemangioma: report of four cases. Ear Nose Throat J 2000, **79**: 594, 597–598.

262 Loos BM, Wieneke JA, Thompson LD. Laryngeal angiosarcoma: a clinicipathologic study of five cases with a review of the literature. Laryngoscope 2001, **111**: 1197–1202.

263 Madrigal FM, Godoy LM, Daboin KP, Casiragi O, Garcia AM, Luna MA. Laryngeal osteosarcoma: a clinicopathologic analysis of four cases and comparison with a carcinosarcoma. Ann Diagn Pathol 2002, **6**: 1–9.

264 Matsumoto T, Nishiya M, Ichikawa G, Gujii H. Leiomyoma with atypical cells (atypical leiomyoma) in the larynx. Histopathology 1999, **34**: 532–536.

265 Matsumoto T, Nobukawa B, Kobayashi K, Watanabe M, Hosokawa A, Tomaru K, Ichikawa G. Solitary polypoid xanthoma in the larynx. Histopathology 1999, **34**: 475–477.

266 Murrell GL, Lantz HJ. Giant cell tumor of the larynx. Ear Nose Throat J 1993, **72**: 360–361.

267 Nicolai P, Ferlito A, Sasaki CT, Kirchner JA. Laryngeal chondrosarcoma. Incidence, pathology, biological behavior, and treatment. Ann Otol Rhinol Laryngol 1990, **99**: 515–523.

268 Nonaka S, Enomoto K, Kawabori S, Unno T, Muraoka S. Spindle cell lipoma within the larynx. A case report with correlated light and electron microscopy. ORL J Otorhinolaryngol Relat Spec 1993, **55**: 147–149.

269 Pau H, De S, Spencer MG, Steele PR. Metastatic malignant melanoma of the larynx. J Laryngol Otol 2001, **115**: 925–927.

270 Rosenberg HS, Vogler C, Close LG, Warshaw HE. Laryngeal fibromatosis in the neonate. Arch Otolaryngol 1981, **107**: 513–517.

271 Safneck JR, Alguacil-Garcia A, Dort JC, Phillips SM. Solitary fibrous tumour. Report of two new locations in the upper respiratory tract. J Laryngol Otol 1993, **107**: 252–256.

272 Sciot R, Delaere P, Van Damme B, Desmet V. Angiosarcoma of the larynx. Histopathology 1995, **26**: 177–180.

273 Sellari Franceschini S, Segnini G, Berrettini S, Bruschini P, Cagno MC, Testi C. Hibernoma of the larynx. Review of the literature and a new case. Acta Otorhinolaryngol Belg 1993, **47**: 51–53.

274 Swerdlow JB, Merl SA, Davey FR, Gacek RR, Gottlieb AJ. Non-Hodgkin's lymphoma limited to the larynx. Cancer 1984, **53**: 2546–2549.

274a Thompson LDR, Gannon FH. Chondrosarcoma of the larynx. Am J Surg Pathol 2002, **26**: 836–851.

275 Ti M, Villafuerte R, Chase PH, Dosik H. Acute leukemia presenting as laryngeal obstruction. Cancer 1974, **34**: 427–430.

276 Wanamaker JR, Kraus DH, Eliacher I, Lavertu P. Manifestations of metastatic breast carcinoma to the head and neck. Head Neck 1993, **15**: 257–262.

277 Weissman JL, Myers JN, Kapadia SB. Extramedullary plasmacytoma of the larynx. Am J Otolaryngol 1993, **14**: 128–131.

278 Wenig BM. Laryngeal mucosal malignant melanoma. A clinicopathologic, immunohistochemical, and ultrastructural study of four patients and a review of the literature. Cancer 1995, **75**: 1568–1577.

279 Wenig BM, Weiss SW, Gnepp DR. Laryngeal and hypopharyngeal liposarcoma. A clinicopathologic study of 10 cases with a comparison to soft-tissue counterparts. Am J Surg Pathol 1990, **14**: 134–141.

279a Wieneke JA, Gannon FH, Heffner DK, Thompson LDR. Giant cell tumor of the larynx: A clinicopathologic series of eight cases and a review of the literature. Mod Pathol 2001, **14**: 1209–1215.

280 Wood GS, Brammer R, Durham JC, Dichtel W. Adult rhabdomyoma of the larynx. Ear Nose Throat J 1993, **72**: 296–298.

TRACHEA

Non-neoplastic lesions

281 Ashley DJ. Bony metaplasia in trachea and bronchi. J Pathol 1970, **102**: 186–188.

282 Ip MS, Wong MP, Wong KL. Rheumatoid nodules in the trachea. Chest 1993, **103**: 301–303.

283 Romagosa V, Bella MR, Truchero C, Moya J. Necrotizing sialometaplasia (ade nometaplasia) of the trachea. Histopathology 1992, **21**: 280–282.

Tumors

284 Allen M. Malignant tracheal tumors. Mayo Clin Proc 1993, **68**: 680–684.

285 Ballard RW, Yarington CT Jr. Hemangiopericytoma of the tracheal wall. Arch Otolaryngol 1981, **107**: 558–560.

286 Briselli M, Mark GJ, Grillo HC. Tracheal carcinoids. Cancer 1978, **42**: 2870–2879.

287 Burton DM, Heffner DK, Patow CA. Granular cell tumors of the trachea. Laryngoscope 1992, **102**: 807–813.

288 Fechner RE, Fitz-Hugh GS. Invasive tracheal papillomatosis. Am J Surg Pathol 1980, **4**: 79–86.

289 Fidias P, Wright C, Harris NL, Urba W, Grossbard ML. Primary tracheal non-Hodgkin's lymphoma: a case report and review of the literature. Cancer 1996, **77**: 2332–2338.

290 Fields JN, Rigaud G, Emami BN. Primary tumors of the trachea. Results of radiation therapy. Cancer 1989, **63**: 2429–2433.

291 Garcìa-Prats MD, Sotelo-Rodrìguez MT, Ballestìn C, Martìnez-Gonzàlez MA, Roca R, Alfaro J, De Miguel E. Glomus tumor of the trachea. Report of a case with microscopic, ultrastructural and immunohistochemical examination and review of the literature. Histopathology 1991, **19**: 459–464.

292 Hajdu SI, Huvos AG, Goodner JT, Foote FW Jr, Beattie EJ Jr. Carcinoma of the trachea. Clinicopathologic study of 41 cases. Cancer 1970, **25**: 1448–1456.

293 Heard BE, Dewar A, Firmin RK, Lennox SC. One very rare and one new tracheal tumour found by electron microscopy. Glomus tumour and acinic cell tumour resembling carcinoid tumours by light microscopy. Thorax 1982, **37**: 97–103.

294 Horinouchi H, Ishihara T, Kawamura M, Kato R, Kikuchi K, Kobayashi K, Maenaka Y, Torikata C. Epithelial myoepithelial tumour of the tracheal gland. J Clin Pathol 1993, **46**: 185–187.

295 Houston HE, Payne WS, Harrison EG Jr, Olsen AM. Primary cancers of the trachea. Arch Surg 1969, **99**: 132–140.

296 Kaplan MA, Pettit CL, Zukerberg LR, Harris NL. Primary lymphoma of the trachea with morphologic and immunophenotypic characteristics of low-grade B-cell lymphoma of mucosa-associated lymphoid tissue. Am J Surg Pathol 1992, **16:** 71–75.

297 Kim YI, Kim JH, Suh J-S, Ham EK, Suh KP. Glomus tumor of the trachea. Report of a case with ultrastructural observation. Cancer 1989, **64:** 881–886.

298 Küng M, Landa JF, Lubin J. Benign clear cell tumor ("sugar tumor") of the trachea. Cancer 1984, **54:** 517–519.

299 Liew S-H, Leong AS-Y, Tang HMK. Tracheal paraganglioma. A case report with review of the literature. Cancer 1981, **47:** 1387–1393.

300 Lopez-Terrada D, Bloom MGK, Cagle PT, Ostrowski ML. Oncocytic mucoepidermoid carcinoma of the trachea. Arch Pathol Lab Med 1999, **123:** 635–637.

301 Ma CK, Fine G, Lewis J, Lee MW. Benign mixed tumor of the trachea. Cancer 1979, **44:** 2260–2266.

302 Ma CK, Raju U, Fine G, Lewis JW Jr. Primary tracheal neurilemoma. Report of a case with ultrastructural examination. Arch Pathol Lab Med 1981, **105:** 187–189.

303 Messineo A, Wesson DE, Filler RM, Smith CR. Juvenile hemangiomas involving the thoracic trachea in children. Report of two cases. J Pediatr Surg 1992, **27:** 1291–1293.

304 Naka Y, Nakao K, Hamaji Y, Nakahara M, Tsujimoto M, Nakahara K. Solitary squamous cell papilloma of the trachea. Ann Thorac Surg 1993, **55:** 189–193.

305 Olmedo G, Rosenberg M, Fonseca R. Primary tumors of the trachea. Clinicopathologic features and surgical results. Chest 1982, **81:** 701–706.

306 Onizuka M, Doi M, Mitsui K, Ogata T, Hori M. Undifferentiated carcinoma with prominent lymphocytic infiltration (so-called lymphoepithelioma) in the trachea. Chest 1990, **98:** 236–237.

307 Pang LC. Primary neurilemoma of the trachea. South Med J 1989, **82:** 785–787.

308 Pollak ER, Naunheim KS, Little AG. Fibromyxoma of the trachea. A review of benign tracheal tumors. Arch Pathol Lab Med 1985, **109:** 926–929.

309 Sandstrom RE, Proppe KH, Trelstad RL. Fibrous histiocytoma of the trachea. Am J Clin Pathol 1978, **70:** 429–433.

310 Shin DH, Park SS, Lee JH, Park MH, Lee JD. Oncocytic glomus tumor of the trachea. Chest 1990, **98:** 1021–1023.

311 Weber AL, Grillo HC. Tracheal tumors. Radiol Clin North Am 1978, **16:** 227–246.

Lung and pleura

Pleura

Normal anatomy

Both pleural layers have a lining of mesothelial cells endowed with a continuous basement membrane and resting on a layer of well-vascularized connective tissue.[2,5,6] All of these elements are mesodermally derived.

The normal mesothelial cell is flat or low cuboidal. Ultrastructurally, it features apical tight junctions, desmosomes, surface microvilli, and bundles of cytoplasmic tonofilaments. Immunohistochemically, it shows reactivity for both low- and high-molecular-weight keratins.[1,7,8] Secretory component and parathyroid hormone-like peptide have also been localized to normal and reactive mesothelial cells.[3,4]

The normal subserosal cells have the ultrastructural features of fibroblasts and express the intermediate filament vimentin but not keratin; however, when these "multipotential subserosal cells" proliferate in reactive conditions, they co-express keratin and vimentin and develop surface differentiation.[1]

Pleuritis and other non-neoplastic lesions

Inflammatory diseases of the lung may spread to the pleura.[9] The pulmonary lesion may completely resolve but leave a pleural *symphysis* (fusion between the two layers) secondary to prominent pleural fibrosis, which can be several centimeters thick. The underlying lung parenchyma may be perfectly normal, but its expansion is prevented by the surrounding rigid and contracted thickened pleura. If this thickened pleura is peeled off, pulmonary function improves markedly. It is likely that the process designated *shrinking pleuritis with atelectasis, folded lung syndrome,* or *rounded atelectasis* represents a variation on this theme (see p. 387).[11,15]

Marked inflammatory pleural thickening may also occur as the result of organization of a hematoma formed after a penetrating wound of the thorax. The best time to perform a decortication of this lesion is 3 to 5 weeks after the injury, as classical studies carried out in World War II soldiers have shown.[21] Microscopically, the material obtained represents an organized hematoma composed of fibrous tissue. Elastic fibers are absent, an indication that the underlying pleura is not part of the process.

Tuberculosis can involve the pleura in various ways: as a complication of a subpleural primary infection, by direct extension from reinfection disease, and as a result of hematogenous spread.[11,12,16]

Rheumatoid disease occasionally involves the lung and pleura (see p. 387) (Fig. 7.70). In the latter site, it induces a diffuse inflammatory reaction with effusion.[20] The microscopic appearance of the pleural biopsy is often nonspecific. In some instances, however, the presence of palisaded spindle histiocytes underlying a layer of fibrin and arranged perpendicularly to the pleural surface should make the pathologist suspect a rheumatoid pathogenesis.[10,18] Cytologically, the pleural fluid shows epithelioid cells, giant cells, and cholesterol crystals, accompanied by a remarkably small number of mesothelial cells.[15]

Endometriosis of the pleura and diaphragm has been reported. Most of the cases have occurred in the right side and have been associated with widespread intra-abdominal endometriosis.[22]

Amyloidosis can involve the pleura; the diagnosis is possible with needle biopsy.[17]

Reactive eosinophilic pleuritis is discussed on p. 384.

Nodular histiocytic/mesothelial hyperplasia is a reactive process composed of histiocytes/monocytes and

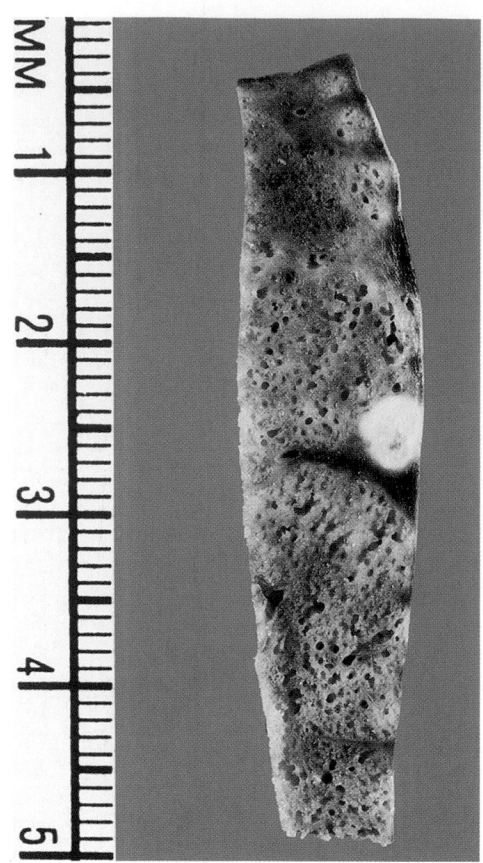

Fig. 7.70 Subpleural rheumatoid nodule in a patient with rheumatoid arthritis. The lung showed interstitial fibrosis. (Courtesy of Dr. RA Cooke, Brisbane, Australia; from Cooke RA, Stewart B: Colour Atlas of Anatomical Pathology. Edinburgh, Churchill Livingstone, 2004).

mesothelial cells. It is more common in hernia sacs and heart (where it is known acronymically as MICE, see Chapter 27), but can also occur in the lung and pleura.[13]

Asbestosis and the pleura

Asbestos is a family of fibrous hydrated silicates that are divided into two groups: the serpentines and the amphiboles.[26] Those of commercial importance are chrysolite in the first group, and amosite and crocidolite in the second.[28,29] These minerals were a component of a large variety of manufactured products, particularly in the construction industry.[36] Proof of the widespread use of this material in the recent past is the finding of asbestos bodies in lung smears (particularly in the lower lobes) in approximately 40% of persons autopsied in the United States.[23,24] Inhalation of these fibers can result in various pathologic processes, which depend on the type of mineral, the dimensions and concentration of the fibers, and the duration of the exposure. The main pleural manifestations of asbestos exposure are pleural plaques and mesothelioma.

Pleural plaques are made up of hyalinized fibrous

tissue. They are usually but not always associated with asbestos (mainly amosite and crocidolite) exposure.[30,32,38,45] The occurrence of these plaques correlates well with the duration and intensity of exposure. They are instead not topographically related to so-called *pleural black spots* (i.e., foci of accumulation of inhaled particles), suggesting that there is no pathogenetic connection between the two processes.[35]

Pleural plaques are characteristically located on the parietal side, mainly in the intercostal spaces on the anterior and posterolateral aspects of the chest wall and on the dome of the diaphragm, at sites where the visceral and parietal pleuras approximate during respiratory excursions.[43] Over time, they become calcified and therefore detectable on chest x-ray film.

The relationship between asbestos and **mesothelioma**, first identified by Wagner et al.[44] in South Africa, has now been documented all over the world.[27,31,41,42] The average prevalence of mesothelioma in people with prolonged heavy exposure to asbestos is 2% to 3% but has reached up to 10% in some series. The latency period is usually 20 years or longer. It should be pointed out that one third of mesothelioma cases are not associated with a history of asbestos exposure,[36] a fact that needs to be taken into account in medicolegal actions.[29a] Amosite and crocidolite are the fiber types found in most cases of mesothelioma.[25,34,39] There can be superimposed deposition of oxalate salts.[34a]

Asbestos bodies are more commonly found in the lung than within the mesothelioma. They can also be found in pulmonary hilar nodes.[40] Microscopic examination is a very insensitive and nonspecific method for the detection and identification of asbestos bodies. Extraction methods to increase their yield and biophysical techniques (such as electron microprobe analysis) are necessary to properly study their true incidence and composition.[23,33]

Tumors

Benign mesothelioma

Benign (papillary) mesothelioma is relatively common in the peritoneal cavity (see Chapter 26) but extremely rare in the pleura. Grossly, it presents as a soft friable mass, mottled pink, gray, and yellow. Microscopically, papillary processes lined by one or several layers of cuboidal mesothelial cells are seen. The distinction with malignant epithelial mesothelioma is made on the basis of the lack of significant atypia and the well-circumscribed, solitary nature of the lesion. The diagnosis of benign papillary mesothelioma should be entertained only if the mesothelial proliferation is well-differentiated throughout and grossly localized, a combination that is very rarely encountered in the pleural cavity. Well-differentiated papillary mesotheliomas that are multicentric or extensive

should be regarded with great caution, inasmuch as some of them will follow an aggressive clinical course.[47]

Two types of benign mesothelial proliferation that are common in the peritoneal cavity but very unusual in the pleura and genital region, respectively, are so-called **benign multicystic mesothelioma** and **adenomatoid tumor**; however, a few convincing cases in this location are on record. They raise the same issue as they do in the peritoneum, that is, whether the mesothelial proliferation is of a neoplastic or reactive nature.[46,48]

Malignant mesothelioma

Generalities

Malignant mesothelioma is usually seen in older adults, although well-documented cases in young individuals are on record.[50] In some instances a familial clustering has been demonstrated.[49] Typically, the tumor presents with chest pain and pleural effusion. In most instances the initial involvement is in the lower half of a hemithorax, but spread to the rest of the pleural cavity is the rule.

Morphologic features

Grossly, the classical presentation is that of multiple gray or white ill-defined nodules in a diffusely thickened pleura (Figs 7.71 and 7.72). It is much rarer for it to present as a localized pleural mass.[52] Pleural effusion is almost always present. Microscopically, the neoplastic formations may form papillae lae or pseudoacini or grow as solid nests[51] (Fig. 7.73). The cytoplasm is abundant and acidophilic. Early cases must be distinguished from reactive mesothelial hyperplasia, as seen in association with inflammatory or neoplastic diseases of the underlying lung, or sometimes with no apparent cause.[53,56,58] Features in favor of malignancy include infiltration of deep tissues, obvious cytologic atypia, prominent cell groupings, and necrosis.[54] The diagnosis of malignant mesothelioma in the absence of detectable invasion ("mesothelioma in situ")[57] should be made only in the presence of clearcut cytologic aberrations and with great caution. Generally speaking, a conservative approach is

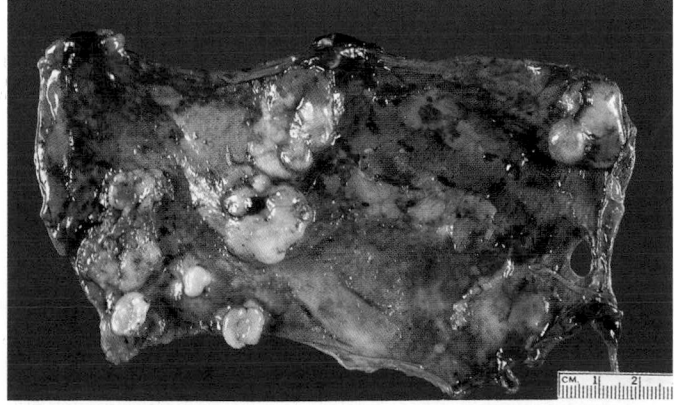

Fig. 7.71 Malignant mesothelioma growing as multiple nodules on the parietal pleura.

indicated; if the lesion is a mesothelioma, usually this becomes apparent in a few months.[54] Obviously malignant mesotheliomas need to be distinguished from metastatic carcinoma, particularly pulmonary adenocarcinoma. This may be a very difficult or even impossible task at the hematoxylin–eosin level in a biopsy specimen and sometimes even in a surgical specimen because of the capacity of some pulmonary adenocarcinomas to grow in a mesothelioma-like fashion.[55] In general, the cells of mesothelioma are more uniform and regular than those of adenocarcinoma, with a more constant nucleocytoplasmic ratio. Their shape is usually cuboidal; a substantial number of columnar-shaped cells favors a diagnosis of adenocarcinoma. Cellular crowding and nuclear molding also favor adenocarcinoma.

Histochemical, immunohistochemical, and electron microscopic features

Mesotheliomas usually produce large amounts of hyaluronic acid, which can be demonstrated with the Alcian blue or colloidal iron stains,[71,74] and also immunohistochemically.[60] This material is nearly always mucicarmine-negative, and the Alcian blue positivity can be removed almost entirely by pretreatment with hyaluronidase. The presence of obvious droplets of mucicarmine-positive or PAS-positive material *in the cytoplasm of the tumor cells* makes the diagnosis of mesothelioma very unlikely, although it does not rule it out completely, inasmuch as the existence of rare mucin-positive mesotheliomas has been documented.[67,75,76]

Glycogen is usually absent, although exceptions occur in the form of *glycogen-rich mesotheliomas*.[80]

Electron microscopy played at one point a pivotal role in the differential diagnosis between mesothelioma and metastatic carcinoma, to the point of being considered the gold standard.[83,84] This was primarily based on the appearance of the microvilli in the apical surface of the tumor cells, which in mesothelioma are longer and more slender than those in adenocarcinoma (Fig. 7.74).[61,64,89,92] The validity of this observation stands, but its practical utility has decreased markedly as a result of the development of an immunohistochemical panel that achieves the distinction in the large majority of the cases.

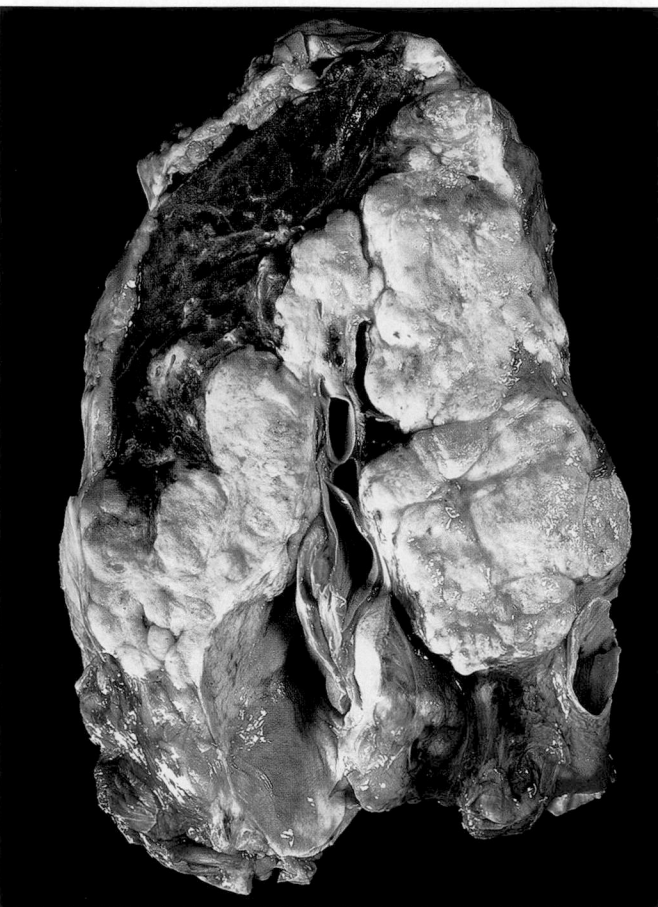

Fig. 7.72 Classical pattern of spread of advanced pleural mesothelioma. (Courtesy of Dr. RA Cooke, Brisbane, Australia; from Cooke RA, Stewart B: Colour Atlas of Anatomical Pathology. Edinburgh, Churchill Livingstone, 2004).

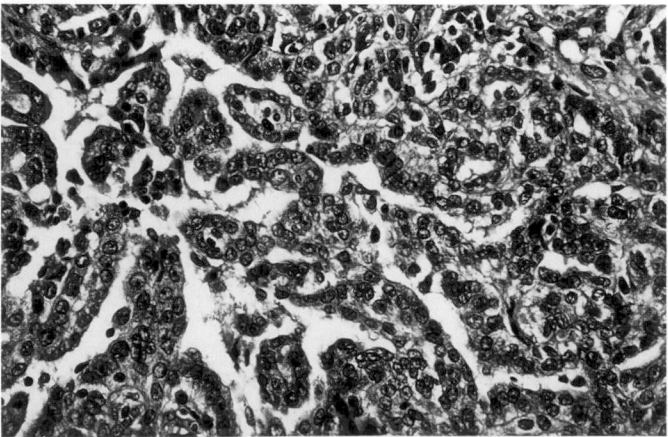

Fig. 7.73 Malignant pleural mesothelioma with a predominantly papillary pattern of growth.

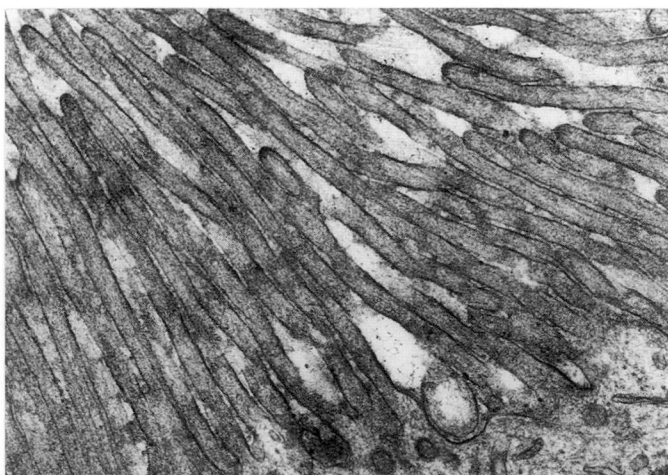

Fig. 7.74 Electron micrograph of a malignant mesothelioma of the pleura. Detail of profuse, long, thin, nonintestinal-type microvilli devoid of a glycocalyx and actin rootlets. (×37,800; courtesy of Dr. Robert E. Erlandson, Memorial Sloan-Kettering Cancer Center)

Because the usual issue in immunohistochemistry is whether a malignant tumor involving the pleura is a mesothelioma or a metastatic pulmonary adenocarcinoma, the markers that have been used for the purpose of differential diagnosis can be segregated into the following groups:

1 *Markers that are usually present in both tumors*: pankeratin, EMA, basement membrane components (also demonstrable ultrastructurally[65]), and S-100 protein (the latter in an erratic fashion)[69,70,85];

2 *Markers that are usually expressed in pulmonary adenocarcinoma but not in mesothelioma*: CEA, CD15, B72.3, Ber-Ep4, Bg8, MOC-31, TTF-1, and secretory component[66,73,81,86–88,90,93];

3 *Markers that are usually expressed in mesothelioma but not in pulmonary adenocarcinoma*: calretinin, WT-1, keratin 5/6, thrombomodulin, vimentin[59,63,78,81] (Fig. 7.75).

As far as calretinin is concerned, it has been emphasized that the best results are obtained using the human recombinant antibodies.[81]

As useful as these markers are in this difficult diagnosis, it should be realized that few if any of them are 100% specific.[77] It should also be remembered as a practical rule that a negative immunoreaction never rules out a diagnosis. Finally, it should be kept in mind that the above listing applies primarily to pulmonary adenocarcinoma but not necessarily to other types of lung cancer, and even less so to metastatic carcinoma from other organs.[77] Thus, a pulmonary squamous cell carcinoma will not necessarily be reactive for B72.3, and a metastatic renal cell carcinoma will not be positive for CEA or TTF-1, but rather for CD10.[82] Conversely, keratin 5/6 will not stain pulmonary adenocarcinoma but is likely to be positive in pulmonary squamous cell carcinoma or in metastatic transitional cell carcinoma.

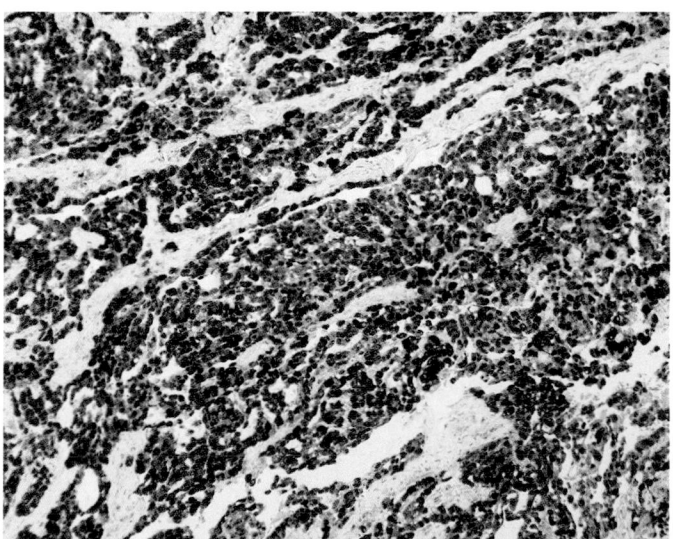

Fig. 7.75 Strong nuclear and cytoplasmic immunoreactivity for calretinin in mesothelioma.

In terms of practical considerations and taking into account the plethora of available markers, a selection needs to be made. Ordonez[79a,81] has concluded that calretinin, cytokeratin 5/6 and WT1 are at present the best "positive" markers of mesothelioma, and that CEA, B72.3 and MOC-31 are the best "negative" markers. He also indicated that a panel of four markers—calretinin, cytokeratin 5/6 (or WT1), CEA, and MOC-31 (or B72.3)—enables a correct diagnosis in nearly every instance.

Additional markers that have been proposed in this situation but whose utility is limited include N-cadherin, E-cadherin, CD445, mesothelin, HBME-1, and HMFG-2.[79b,79c,81]

Other markers that have been detected occasionally in mesothelioma are desmin[68] and human chorionic gonadotropin, the latter less frequently than in pulmonary non-small cell carcinoma.[79] C-kit (CD117) is usually not expressed despite earlier claims to the contrary.[67a]

Differences between lectin-binding patterns have been described between mesothelioma and adenocarcinoma, but they do not seem to have a sharp discriminatory ability.[72]

Unfortunately, no immunomarkers have been described that tell apart a reactive from a neoplastic mesothelioma proliferation. EMA and p53 stains are more commonly positive in mesotheliomas than in reactive conditions, whereas the reverse is true for desmin.[51a] However, there are enough exceptions to limit greatly their diagnostic utility.[62,91]

Molecular genetic features

Evaluation of DNA ploidy is of some assistance, being that aneuplody is present in about 75% of the adenocarcinomas but only in less than 15% of the mesotheliomas.[94,95]

Overexpression of p53 is found in about half of malignant mesotheliomas, regardless of whether they are related to asbestos exposure or not.[96]

Mesothelioma variants

Spindle cell or sarcomatoid mesothelioma is a form of malignant mesothelioma predominantly or entirely composed of spindle tumor cells. These tumors tend to be more nodular and less plaque-like than those composed of cuboidal mesothelial cells and are often accompanied by hemorrhage, necrosis, and cystic change[109] (Fig. 7.76). Pleural effusion is present in most but not all of the cases. Microscopically, the tumor is highly cellular, formed by interwoven bundles of spindle cells. Nuclear atypia is present, and mitotic figures are common. In rare cases, foci of osseous and cartilaginous metaplasia are encountered.[98,112] Cases in which spindle tumor cells coexist with plumper epithelial-like cells may show a resemblance to synovial sarcoma.[104] Spindle cell mesotheliomas show consistent immunohistochemical positivity for keratin.[104a,108] They are also immunoreactive for vimentin and sometimes for smooth muscle actin.[103]

Desmoplastic mesothelioma is a subtype of spindle

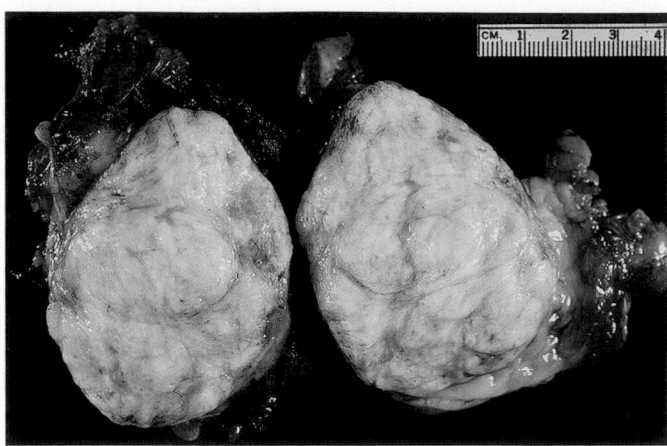

Fig. 7.76 Gross appearance of sarcomatoid mesothelioma. The tumor is better circumscribed than the usual type of mesothelioma.

cell malignant mesothelioma accompanied by abundant deposition of fibrous tissue.[97] The main differential diagnosis is with the more cellular types of solitary fibrous tumors of pleura, some of which may be malignant themselves. Immunohistochemical positivity for keratin, calretinin, and WT-1 is the best evidence in favor of the former. Ultrastructurally, evidence of rudimentary epithelial differentiation may be demonstrated in them.[102]

Desmoplastic mesotheliomas also need to be distinguished from areas of dense inflammatory fibrosis. A claim was made some time ago to the effect that immunohistochemical positivity for keratin in the spindle cells established a diagnosis of mesothelioma, but this turned out not to be the case; the reactive mesothelial cells entrapped in the fibrous plaques can be just as positive.[99] Thus the differential diagnosis is largely based on the appearance of the proliferating cells in routinely stained sections.[106] Features favoring malignancy are nuclear atypia, necrosis, presence of well-developed fascicular, storiform, or other complex tissue patterns, and infiltration of adjacent tissues.[105,106] As in the case of the proliferation of the more typical cuboidal mesothelial cells, a conservative approach is strongly recommended in dubious cases.

Lymphohistiocytoid mesothelioma is another subtype of sarcomatoid mesothelioma characterized microscopically by a diffuse proliferation of atypical histiocyte-like malignant mesothelial cells admixed with numerous lymphocytes and a lesser number of plasma cells. The phenotype of the histiocyte-like elements is that of mesothelial cells.[101] The behavior of this tumor is very aggressive.[99a]

Deciduoid mesothelioma is characterized by the presence of large tumor cells with an abundant ground glass cytoplasm that simulates the appearance of decidual cells. Originally described in the abdominal cavity of young women, it has now also been seen in the pleural cavity, in an older age group, and in patients of both sexes.[110,111]

Malignant mesothelioma with squamous differentiation (pleural squamous cell carcinoma) has been described in patients with a history of chronic empyema or therapeutic pneumothorax,[100] but some of these cases might have been lung carcinomas with extensive pleural extension. Similar histogenetic questions apply to the recently described primary **mucoepidermoid carcinoma** of the pleura.[108a]

A small cell variant of malignant mesothelioma has been described; interestingly, most of the reported cases have been immunoreactive not only for keratin, but also for neuron-specific enolase and occasionally Leu 7.[107]

Spread and metastases

The typical pattern of spread of malignant mesothelioma is by contiguity and perhaps implantation. Through either mechanism it may spread to the entire pleural space, both pleurae, interlobular septa, pericardiun, chest wall, diaphragm, and even the peritoneum.[113] Extension into the subpleural portions of the lung is also common, and intraparenchymal spread can occur,[116] but the presence of nodular masses within the lung parenchyma favors a primary lung cancer with prominent pleural spread. Distant metastases in mesothelioma generally occur only in the late stages of the disease, if at all.[115] Therefore, presence of prominent hilar and supraclavicular lymphadenopathy at the time of initial presentation favors carcinoma over mesothelioma. However, we and others have seen pleural mesotheliomas that have presented initially with lymph node involvement in the cervical or axillary region.[114,117] We have also seen cases of mesothelioma presenting with distant metastases in most unusual places, such as the tongue.[118]

Treatment and prognosis

There is no satisfactory treatment of malignant mesothelioma at present. Surgical excision is often attempted, sometimes of heroic proportions (pneumonectomy, parietal and mediastinal pleurectomy, diaphragmectomy), but on the whole the results have been disappointing. On the other hand, bulk resection of the tumor combined with radiation therapy and/or systemic chemotherapy has sometimes resulted in long-term remissions.[120,122,128]

Prognostic factors that need to be mentioned in relation to malignant mesothelioma are the following:

1 *Stage.* There is a definite relationship between tumor stage (see Appendix B), and prognosis, even if the latter is generally poor in all stages.[123,125–127]
2 *Gender.* The prognosis seems to be poorer in males than in females.
3 *Tumor subtype.* Spindle cell and desmoplastic mesothelioma are associated with a shorter survival than the conventional type, whereas the reverse is true for the deciduoid and especially for the well-differentiated variants.[90,121,124]

Solitary fibrous tumor

Solitary fibrous tumor of pleura (formerly called solitary fibrous mesothelioma) is usually asymptomatic, although on occasion patients present with pain, cough, dyspnea, hypoglycemia-related symptoms, and/or prominent pulmonary osteoarthropathy that rapidly regress when the tumor is removed.[129,138] This tumor is not associated with asbestosis. On rare occasions, it is found in association with a microscopically similar tumor in the peritoneum or retroperitoneum.[135] Grossly, the lesion is well circumscribed, firm, lobulated, gray-white to yellow-white, with frequent whorling and fasciculation. The mean diameter is 6 cm. The appearance is reminiscent of uterine leiomyoma (Fig. 7.77). Cystic degeneration is very unusual, but solitary fibrous tumor can present as a mural nodule within a large pleural-lined cyst. It may be found attached to the visceral pleura (80%) or parietal pleura, within an interlobar fissure, or sometimes within the lung parenchyma without a pleural connection.[148] Lesions with an identical microscopic appearance occur in the peritoneum, retroperitoneum (including kidney), mediastinum, nasopharynx, orbit, breast, and many other sites (see respective chapters).

Microscopically, both benign and malignant forms occur, the former greatly predominating.[134] The distinction between them can be difficult.[139] In the typical benign case, there is a tangled network of fibroblast-like cells, squeezed in between abundant collagen fibers, many of which have a keloid-like quality (Fig. 7.78). The degree of cellularity varies a great deal from area to area. Hemangiopericytoma-like areas are frequent, and some tumors have prominent myxoid features[132] (Fig. 7.79).

The differential diagnosis of the more sclerotic types of solitary fibrous tumor include fibrous plaque, fibromatosis (desmoid tumor), and calcifying fibrous pseudotumor.[140,147] Myxoid tumors need to be distinguished from low grade myxofibrosarcoma and low-grade fibromyxoid tumors. The most cellular types may be misdiagnosed as fibrosarcoma or malignant peripheral nerve sheath tumor. If proper attention is

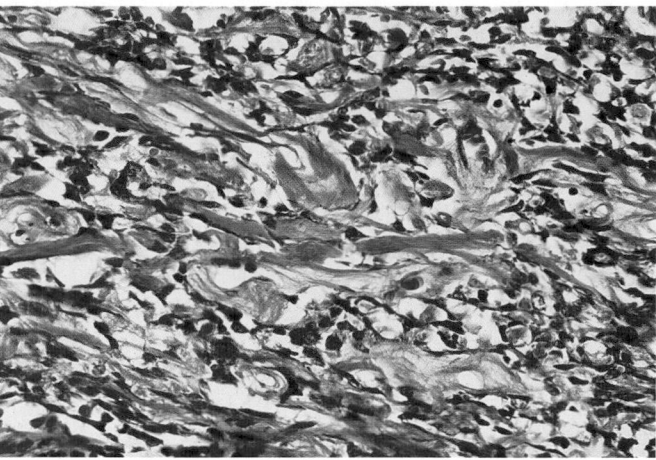

Fig. 7.78 Solitary fibrous tumor of pleura. The proliferation of mesenchymal spindle cells separated by thick bands of keloid-type collagen is characteristic of this entity.

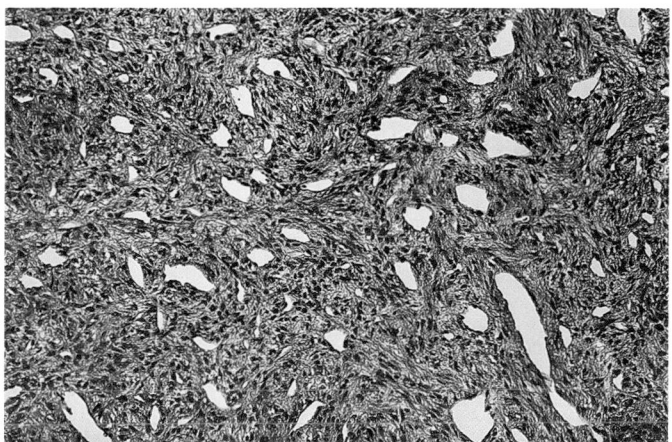

Fig. 7.79 Prominent hemangiopericytoma-like pattern in solitary fibrous tumor.

paid to the lack of nuclear aberrations and the rarity or absence of mitoses, confusion is unlikely to occur. In some instances, clusters of cuboidal cells forming papillae, tubules, or solid nests are found at the periphery of predominantly fibrous tumors; these represent entrapped mesothelium or bronchioloalveolar epithelium and should not be misconstrued as evidence of a biphasic composition of the tumor. The malignant types are characterized by increased cellularity, atypia, mitotic activity, and necrosis.

This neoplasm has been regarded for many years as a form of mesothelioma, largely on the basis of the pattern of growth that the tumor cells exhibit in tissue culture[144]; however, on ultrastructural examination these cells show fibroblast-like rather than mesothelial-like features, and by immunohistochemistry they are reactive for vimentin and sometimes desmin rather than keratin.[130,131,137,141–143] The most likely interpretation of this tumor, therefore, is that it arises from noncommitted mesenchymal cells present in the areolar tissue subjacent to the mesothelial lining.[136] This has led to the proposal of alternative terms

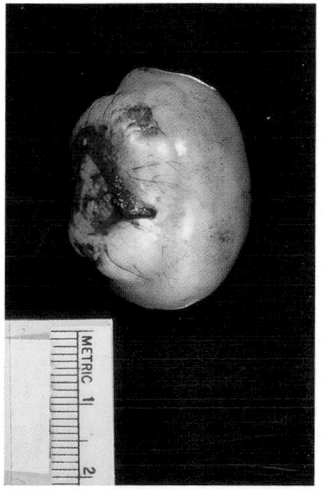
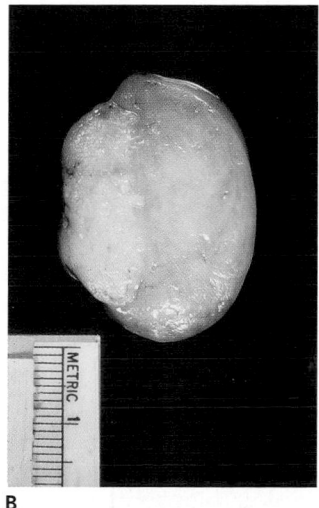

A   **B**

Fig. 7.77 A and **B**, Outer aspect and cut surface of solitary fibrous tumor of pleura. This example was heavily hyalinized.

Fig. 7.80 Malignant solitary fibrous tumor of pleura resulting in numerous serosal implants.

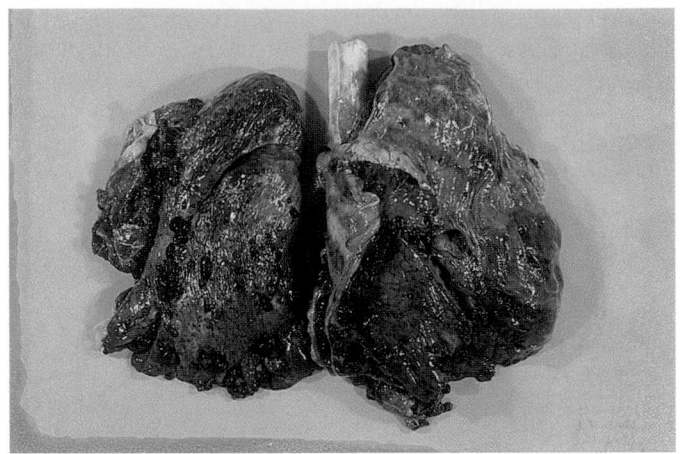

Fig 7.81 Epithelioid angiosarcoma of pleura. The tumor coats the pleural surface in a fashion similar to that of diffuse malignant mesothelioma. (Courtesy of Dr. Juan Segura, San Jose, Costa Rica)

such as submesothelioma or submesothelial fibroma which, however, have not caught on.

The tumor cells of this lesion stain strongly and consistently for CD34 and bcl-2, a finding that may be of use in the differential diagnosis with some of the entities already described.[133,141,145,146]

Almost 90% of these neoplasms are cured by surgical excision. In a thorough review of the literature, Briselli et al.[129] found that 12% had caused death because of extensive intrathoracic growth (Fig. 7.80). Indicators of good prognosis were presence of a pedicle, good circumscription, and absence of nuclear pleomorphism or mitotic activity.

Other primary tumors

Soft tissue-type tumors of various types can occur in the pleura. These need to be distinguished from the more common sarcomatoid mesothelioma (see p. 363) and the malignant form of solitary fibrous tumor (see previous section).

Epithelioid hemangioendothelioma and *angiosarcoma* may coat diffusely the pleura in a fashion simulating mesothelioma[153,154,168] (Fig. 7.81). Some of the angiosarcomas have occurred against a background of chronic pyothorax.[149]

Synovial sarcoma has now been recognized as sometimes arising in the pleura.[152] In the past, most of these cases were diagnosed as malignant mesotheliomas or malignant solitary fibrous tumors. Both biphasic and monophasic forms occur.[154] A molecular search for the SYT-SSX gene fusion that characterizes this tumor may be necessary to confirm the diagnosis.[151] Other soft tissue tumors and tumorlike conditions that have been reported in the pleura are *fibromatosis* (desmoid tumor), *calcifying fibrous pseudotumor*, *liposarcoma*, *chondrosarcoma*, and *malignant fibrous histiocytoma*.[155,162,163,166,167]

Malignant lymphoma centered in the pleural cavity can develop on the basis of longstanding pyothorax.[157]

This tumor, which has been referred to as *pyothorax-associated* or *effusion-associated lymphoma*, is composed of a population of large lymphoid cells with frequent plasmacytoid differentiation. They are thought to be B-cell tumors with occasional aberrant expression of T-cell markers,[165] and show a strong association with EBV.[156,158,160,165]

Other tumors that can present as primary masses in the pleura are *thymoma*[150,161] and *desmoplastic small cell tumor*[164]; in both instances, diagnostic confusion with mesothelioma is possible.

Metastatic tumors

About 75% of metastatic tumors in the pleura are of a carcinomatous nature, metastatic carcinoma being the most common malignant tumor in the pleura. It is second only to congestive heart failure as the cause of pleural effusions in patients over 50 years of age. Dyspnea, cough, and chest pain are the most common presenting symptoms. Most malignant pleural effusions are greater than 500 ml. The fluid is most often serous to serosanguineous, but it may be frankly hemorrhagic.

The most common sites for the primary lesion are lung (33%), breast (20.9%), and stomach (7.3%).[169] Approximately 90% of the lung, breast, and ovarian malignant effusions are ipsilateral to the primary lesion. A malignant pleural effusion may be the first evidence of the existence of cancer.

The fact that lung adenocarcinoma can reach the pleura and spread in a fashion that closely simulates a malignant mesothelioma[170] is discussed on p. 392, and the criteria used for making the differential diagnosis between the two entities are presented on p. 362.

Biopsy and cytology

Needle biopsy of the parietal pleura is very useful for the differential diagnosis between inflammatory and neoplastic processes.[192] Aaron et al.[171] combined pleural biopsy with biopsy of the lung parenchyma and hilar lymph nodes in the study of 89 patients with diffuse pulmonary disease and/or hilar adenopathy and persistent pleural effusion, and reached a definite diagnosis in 62 cases. If tuberculosis is suspected, part of the pleural biopsy should be cultured. Levine et al.[185] found that culture of a single specimen from pleural biopsy was positive with greater frequency than multiple cultures of pleural fluid.

If pleural effusion is present, cytologic examination of the fluid has been found to be more effective in detecting malignancy than pleural biopsy.[189] Therefore when the possibility of malignancy is considered in the presence of pleural effusion, a cytologic examination of the pleural fluid should always be performed, regardless of the gross appearance of the fluid.

Traditionally, longstanding pleural effusions have been regarded as probably malignant if bloody and probably tuberculous if serous. Actually, there is very little relation between the appearance of the fluid and the nature of the disease.[173] The differential cell count of the effusion is of no great help either, as 93% of the effusions caused by tuberculosis and 67% of those caused by cancer are predominantly lymphocytic[187]; however, the presence of numerous mesothelial cells virtually excludes tuberculosis.

There is probably no area in diagnostic cytology that is more difficult to interpret than that of effusions in serous cavities.[181,183,188] This is mainly because proliferating reactive mesothelial cells can acquire features dangerously similar to those of cells of mesothelioma and even metastatic carcinoma. The cells of mesotheliomas can occur singly or in clusters with scalloped borders. The cytoplasm is dense and often has small, regular, centrally located vacuoles.[172] Nuclei are atypical, the nucleocytoplasmic ratio is greatly altered, and multinucleated forms may be present. Cytologic preparations can be stained for PAS, mucicarmine, various enzymes, keratin, CEA, CD15, calretinin, WT-1, TTF-1, and also examined ultrastructurally.[175,177–180,184,186,190] In the huge series by Johnston,[182] a cytopathologic diagnosis conclusive for cancer was obtained in the first specimen of fluid in 90.5% of the cases; there were no false-positive diagnoses.

The presence of a high content of hyaluronic acid in a pleural effusion favors the diagnosis of mesothelioma.[174,191] Chromosomal analysis has also been used in conjunction with cytologic analysis to improve the diagnostic yield.[176]

Lung

Normal anatomy

The two main components of the lung parenchyma are the bronchi and bronchioles (airways) and the alveoli.

The alveoli are lined by type I pneumocytes and type II (granular) pneumocytes; the latter produce surfactant and are the main proliferating component after alveolar injury.[199] The alveolar walls contain capillaries whose basement membrane fuses with that of the alveolar epithelium to constitute a single alveolar capillary membrane.[205,209]

The main cell types of the bronchial-bronchiolar epithelium are basal cells, neuroendocrine (Kulchitsky-type) cells, ciliated cells, serous cells, Clara cells, and goblet cells. Goblet and ciliated cells decrease in number as one approaches the terminal bronchioles, whereas the number of Clara cells increases proportionally. The Clara cells have a secretory function and represent the main progenitor cells after bronchiolar injury. They are recognized—whether in normal, reactive, or neoplastic conditions—by the presence of apical secretory granules that are PAS-positive and diastase-resistant and have a dense appearance ultrastructurally. Kulchitsky-type cells are part of the diffuse neuroendocrine system.[207,208] They are numerous in the bronchial and bronchiolar epithelium of the fetus and neonate, but very scanty and difficult to demonstrate in the adult.

Small clusters of neuroendocrine cells located within the epithelium of bronchi and bronchioles (and sometimes also at the level of alveoli) are referred to as neuroepithelial bodies; their function is unknown.

Submucosal glands are associated with the larger bronchi; they are composed of both serous and mucous cells and are invested by a myoepithelial cell layer. In older individuals, these glands may exhibit oncocytic changes. Lymph vessels are present along bronchovascular structures and pulmonary veins, in septa, and beneath the pleural surface, but not in the alveolar walls.[206] The vasculature of the lung derives from the pulmonary vessels and bronchial vessels, the latter belonging to the systemic circulation. Pulmonary arteries have both an internal and external elastic membrane, whereas pulmonary veins have a single (outer) elastic layer.

Structures sometimes seen in alveolar luminae, which are of no diagnostic significance by themselves, are fresh red blood cells (usually the result of surgical trauma), scattered alveolar macrophages, corpora amylacea (common in elderly people), and blue bodies (composed primarily of calcium carbonate).[195,197,200,203] The interstitium of the lung in adult city dwellers invariably contains variable amounts of anthracotic pigment (carbon); scattered birefringent silica crystals may also be found, a feature which, by itself, is not diagnostic of silicosis (see p. 382).

It is not rare to find scattered megakaryocytes in the alveolar walls; the large, hyperchromatic, and distorted nuclei of these cells should not be misinterpreted as evidence of malignancy or viral infection.[197]

Metaplastic bone is an age-related change sometimes

seen in the bronchial cartilage; it may be accompanied by calcification and by bone marrow elements.[194] More rarely, mature bone is seen in the wall of normal alveoli as the burned-out expression of an air space exudate.

Lymph vessels follow the bronchovascular structures and are found mainly beneath the pleura and in septa. They drain to intrapulmonary peribronchial and hilar lymph nodes. The drainage is mainly cephalad, primarily through mediastinal lymph node groups, but also to abdominal lymph nodes.

Intrapulmonary lymph nodes may be found in the peribronchial region, but sometimes also in the peripheral lung, whether in septae or subpleurally.[204]

Ectopic tissues sometimes found in otherwise normal lung include skeletal muscle[198] (sometimes present extensively in the newborn lung, a condition known as rhabdomyomatosis),[196] neuroglial elements,[202] pancreas,[201] and adrenal cortex.[193] Whether ectopic normal thyroid tissue can occur in the lung or whether all such cases represent metastases from well-differentiated carcinomas remains a controversial issue.[195]

Non-neoplastic lesions

Biopsy

It is imperative for the pathologist to know the clinical history and radiographic findings of the case before attempting to interpret a lung biopsy, especially in non-neoplastic lesions. Basic facts such as localized versus diffuse pattern of the process, presence and degree of functional impairment, and occupational or travel history are extremely important in this regard.

The type of lung biopsy obtained is also of importance. Transbronchial biopsies are useful for infections, sarcoidosis, and neoplasms but not for the usual interstitial pneumonia.[213] For the latter, open lung biopsy represents the ideal material.[210] The lingula or right middle lobe tips should be avoided because of their tendency to show more fibrosis than elsewhere.[212] Areas of extreme scarring and honeycombing are likely to show only end-stage disease and therefore are not very informative. Ideally, samples from two or three different areas should be obtained.[211]

Cystic diseases

Congenital cystic disease is a generic term for any cystic process of the lung thought to be already present at birth.[220] The condition is often overdiagnosed. It can be simulated by various acquired processes, such as a healed abscess. The absence of coal pigment in the cystic area has been used as a sign that the lesion is congenital but is not pathognomonic. Morphologic types of congenital cystic disease include pulmonary sequestration (see p. 369), congenital lobar emphysema, bronchogenic cyst,

the nebulous "congenital bronchiectasis," and cystic adenomatoid transformation.[227,228,230]

Congenital lobar emphysema (congenital lobar hyperinflation) occurs in young children. It affects only one of the upper lobes or the right middle lobe of the lung. Theories for its occurrence include mucosal folds, mucous plugs, and deficiencies in the bronchial cartilages. The pathologic change consists of massive overdistention of the alveolar spaces, not accompanied by tissue destruction. It is therefore not truly a cystic or an emphysematous process. Severe compression of the other pulmonary lobes may result from this lesion.

Cystic adenomatoid transformation is characterized by the presence of variously sized intercommunicating cysts lined by an "adenomatoid" cuboidal-to-ciliated pseudostratified columnar epithelium[214,223,229] (Figs 7.82 and 7.83). It may be seen in association with bronchial

Fig. 7.82 Gross appearance of cystic adenomatoid transformation of lung.

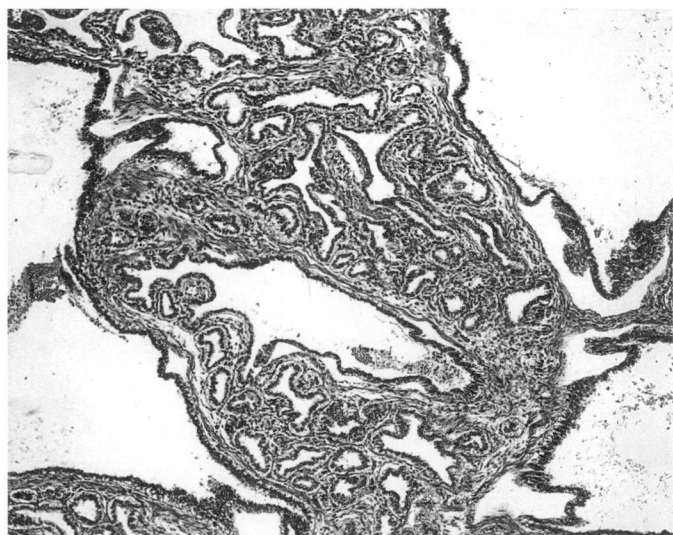

Fig. 7.83 Microscopic appearance of cystic adenomatoid transformation. The air spaces are unevenly dilated and lined by cuboidal epithelium with a gland-like appearance.

atresia. It usually presents with respiratory distress in neonates, but it has also been found in older children and in adults.[215] Three morphologic varieties have been described depending on the size and number of the cysts.[229] Solitary lesions usually involve a lower lobe. Some of the patients have associated pulmonary or extra-pulmonary anomalies. Lobectomy is the treatment of choice.[224]

Acquired cystic diseases of the lung result, for the most part, from emphysema or honeycombing. The latter represents the end stage of interstitial pneumonia or other inflammatory diseases and is discussed on p. 378. Lung cysts can also develop in the Ehlers–Danlos syndrome.[218] On occasion, unilateral multicystic lung disease presents as gelatinous vesicular or grape-like structures that resemble normal or molar placental tissue ("placentoid bullous lesion").[222]

Emphysema is defined as an increase beyond the normal in the size of airspaces distal to the terminal bronchiole associated with destruction of their walls.[226] Emphysema is the most important morphologic substrate of chronic obstructive pulmonary disease, which in turn is a leading case of disability and death.[216,217] Emphysematous *bullae* are large (1 cm or greater) cystic spaces covered by a thin, stretched pleura. Giant bullae can result in an appearance vaguely reminiscent of chorionic villi, a change that has been designated as *placental transmogrification*.[219] Symptoms may result from hemorrhage, infection, compression of adjacent lung, or pneumothorax. Large bullae can be treated by simple excision of the walls with closure of bronchiolar fistulas and obliteration of the pleural space.[225] *Blebs* are formed by the rupture of an alveolus directly beneath the pleura and the escape of air into the areolar layer of the pleura, which results in interstitial emphysema. They are less than 1 cm in diameter. A bleb may rupture into the free pleural space, causing pneumothorax, and sometimes the microscopic change termed *reactive eosinophilic pleuritis* (see p. 384).

Mesenchymal cystic hamartoma is a multifocal and bilateral lung lesion characterized by the formation of small (up to 1 cm) cysts lined by normal or metaplastic respiratory epithelium resting on a cellular "cambium layer" of mesenchymal cells.[221]

Bronchopulmonary sequestration

Bronchopulmonary sequestration is characterized by partial or complete separation of a portion of a lobe of the lung, with no connection to the bronchial tree.

In the **extralobar** variety, the tissue is enveloped by its own pleural covering and exists as a nodule apart from the lung, at any level from the thoracic inlet to the diaphragm, or even within the abdominal cavity[233] (Fig. 7.84). About 90% of cases occur in the left side. Other congenital malformations especially diaphragmatic hernias, occur in approximately 20% of patients.[235] On occasion,

Fig. 7.84 Extralobar type of pulmonary sequestration. The lung has a spongy appearance and is covered by normal pleura.

the sequestered lung communicates with the foregut.[231] An association with polyhydramnios and edema has been observed.[237] The arterial supply is usually by one or several small arteries from the aorta or one of its branches. The venous drainage is into the azygos system.

The **intralobar** variety, which is much more likely to be symptomatic, is characteristically located within the lower lobe, especially in the posterior basal segment[239] (Fig. 7.85). About 60% of the cases occur on the left side. The segment is supplied by a *large* artery arising from the aorta or one of its branches; this artery arises above the diaphragm in 75% of the patients and below the

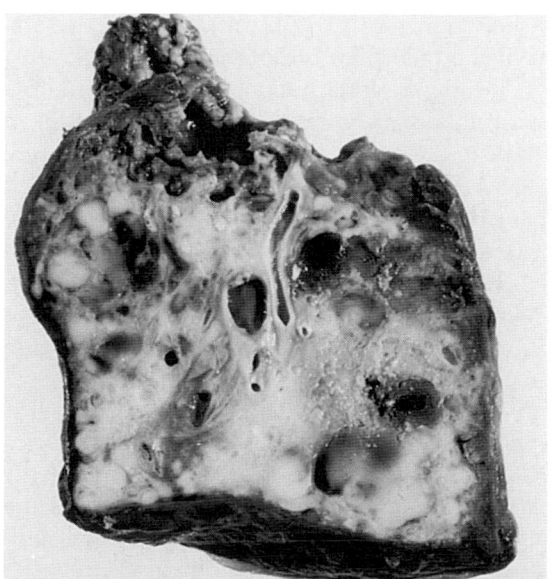

Fig. 7.85 Intralobar type of pulmonary sequestration. As is often the case with this variety, there are extensive secondary inflammatory changes. (Courtesy of Dr. J. Costa, Lausanne, Switzerland)

diaphragm in the remainder. Failure of the surgeon to appreciate this fact may result in the patient's death from hemorrhage. Despite its origin, the artery is always of the elastic pulmonary type. Shunts between the anomalous arteries and intrapulmonary vessels have been demonstrated.[232]

Intralobular sequestrations have been divided into types I, II, and III, depending on whether the overlap between the pulmonary and the anomalous systemic arteries is extensive, slight, or absent, respectively.[236] Venous blood flows into the pulmonary venous system. Grossly, the sequestered portion may present as a single cyst, as a multicystic area, or as a solid mass. Microscopically, there is usually chronic inflammation and fibrosis. Obliterative changes of blood vessels are prominent.

The pathogenesis of this condition is controversial. Persistence of the systemic arterial supply and defects in the pulmonary arterial development have been postulated.[234,238] Other authors favor an acquired origin related to repeated episodes of chronic pneumonia, citing in favor of this interpretation the almost complete absence of this disease in neonates or infants, the infrequency of associated anomalies, and the almost universal presence of chronic inflammation and fibrosis.[236]

Bronchiectasis

Bronchiectasis refers to the permanent dilatation of bronchial lumina, usually associated with destruction of some elements of the bronchial wall and inflammatory changes in the surrounding lung parenchyma. It represents the end stage of a variety of unrelated disorders and can be divided into two categories: obstructive and nonobstructive (postinflammatory).[240]

The obstructive variety results from partial or total obliteration of the bronchial lumen by a neoplasm, foreign body, localized inflammatory process in the bronchial wall, inspissated mucus secretion (as seen in cystic fibrosis), or extended compression (as produced, for instance, by a greatly enlarged lymph node).[241,248] It can occur in any area of the lung and follows the branching pattern of the obstructed bronchus. If the source of obstruction is relieved at an early stage, the bronchiectatic changes will regress; otherwise, the secondary inflammatory and fibrotic changes will render the condition irreversible.

Nonobstructive (postinflammatory) bronchiectasis is thought to result from repeated episodes of pneumonia. It is a disease usually contracted in youth; 69% of the cases studied in a classic series[249] first manifested during the first two decades of life. A history of antecedent pulmonary infection can often be elicited: in a group of children with bronchiectasis reported in another classic study by Field in 1949,[242] there was a history of pneumonia in 35% and of pertussis in 30%. Two other disorders associated with chronic sinonasal infection and frequent

formation of bronchiectasis are *Kartagener's* or *immotile cilia syndrome*, associated with complete situs inversus and infertility, and *Young's syndrome*, associated with infertility caused by azoospermia but lacking ultrastructural ciliary abnormalities.[243,250]

The pathogenesis for the formation of nonobstructive bronchiectasis seems to be mediated by pneumonitis and atelectasis. These lead to an increase of the negative intrapleural pressure, which is then transmitted through the solid nonexpansible pulmonary tissue to the elastic and expansible bronchial walls, which dilate as a result.[242,247]

Nonobstructive bronchiectasis involves the left lung more often than the right, possibly because of a difficulty in draining caused by the physiologic constriction imposed on the left bronchus by the pulmonary artery. The lower lobes are the more frequent sites of the disease. However, bronchiectasis of the left lower lobe is almost always accompanied by involvement of the lingular division of the left upper lobe, and bronchiectasis of the right lower lobe by involvement of the right middle lobe and pectoral branch of the right upper lobe. Bronchiectasis is an important component of so-called middle lobe syndrome.[245]

It is important to realize that the process is usually focal and that the extent of the disease depends entirely on the primary insult. Once bronchiectasis has become established in an area of the lung, it tends to remain confined to that area *unless* there is additional pulmonary infection and atelectasis. For instance, of 114 patients reported by Perry and King,[249] only 6 developed a spread of the disease, and all of them had intercurrent pneumonia.

Bronchiectasis is broadly classified into *saccular*, *cystic*, and *cylindric* types, according to the shape of the bronchial dilatation (Fig. 7.86). The region of involvement is usually in the secondary bronchi; it can be segmental or diffuse. The bronchial walls are irregularly

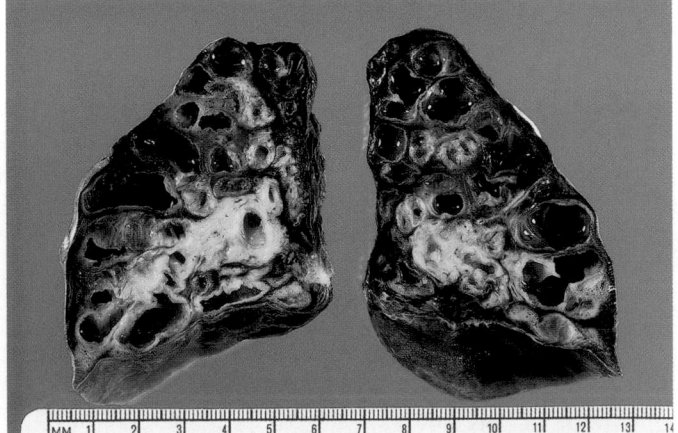

Fig. 7.86 Extensive lung involvement by bronchiectasis accompanied by secondary inflammation and fibrosis. (Courtesy of Dr. RA Cooke, Brisbane, Australia; from Cooke RA, Stewart B: Colour Atlas of Anatomical Pathology. Edinburgh, Churchill Livingstone, 2004).

thickened. The bronchial cartilage may undergo ossification and ulcerate into the lumen. The intervening lung parenchyma shows variable degrees of inflammation and fibrosis; peribronchial abscesses may be seen. The pleura is frequently thickened.

Microscopically, chronic inflammation of the bronchial wall is a constant finding. Lymphocytes predominate, and germinal centers can be encountered, particularly in younger patients. Areas of ulceration are common, but the residual epithelium is usually ciliated and otherwise normal; squamous metaplasia can occur, but it is unusual. In a more advanced stage, granulation tissue develops in the lamina propria, the cartilage is fragmented or destroyed, and the muscle is erased or undergoes focal hyperplastic changes. The mucous glands persist longer than other structures. The bronchial arteries often become greatly enlarged, tortuous, and thick walled.[246] Anastomoses between them and branches of the pulmonary artery develop along the bronchi of the fourth order. The changes in the adjacent lung parenchyma vary from none to advanced organizing pneumonia. Multiple small solid foci of proliferating spindle cells may be seen microscopically in association with saccular bronchiectasis. These formations, traditionally known as *tumorlets*, represent nodular hyperplasia of Kulchitsky-type neuroendocrine cells and are histogenetically related to carcinoid tumors (see p. 407).

Various immunologic abnormalities have been reported in patients with bronchiectasis, and several types of immunemediated diseases have been shown to be associated with this disease.[244]

Complications of bronchiectasis such as bronchopleural fistula with empyema, brain abscess, and amyloidosis are no longer frequent. At present, conservative medical treatment for the cases with an inflammatory pathogenesis is sufficient to control the disease in most instances. Surgical resection is indicated in patients with predominantly unilateral disease, in those with hemorrhage and/or repeated pulmonary infections, and in those with the obstructive variety of the disease.

Abscess

In the pre-antibiotic era, solitary lung abscesses often followed tonsillectomies and other ear, nose, and throat operations. Presently, most lung abscesses follow the aspiration of foreign material or represent secondary infections of lung carcinomas (Fig. 7.87). Embolism from distant sources does not cause unilocular abscesses but can cause multiple bilateral abscesses.

The most common locations of lung abscesses are the right lower lobe, the right upper lobe (particularly the subapical segment), and the left lower lobe, in that order of frequency[251,252] (Fig. 7.88). The apical segment of the lower lobes is particularly vulnerable in patients who must assume a supine position. Anaerobic organisms are

Fig. 7.87 Bronchopneumonia with abscess formation in a 2-year-old boy secondary to aspiration of a foreign body (timothy grass inflorescence). The first recorded case of this condition seems to be that recorded in a book entitled *Some account of Lord Boringdon's accident on July 21st, 1817, and its consequences* as follows: "In 1662, Armand de Boutree, son of the Compte de Nogent, was seized with a violent fever, accompanied by a great difficulty in breathing, a dry cough, afterwards spotting of blood, sleeplessness, and great pain in the right side. A tumor at length appeared on that side, and a surgeon extracted from it an ear of barley almost entire which was quite green and had undergone no change." (From Kissane JIM. Pathology of infancy and childhood, ed. 2. St. Louis, 1975, Mosby)

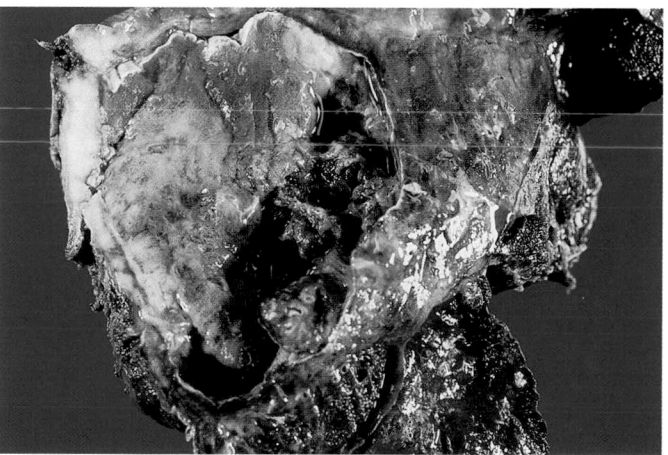

Fig. 7.88 Large lung abscess.

the agents that are most commonly responsible. Chronic abscesses have thick fibrotic walls and are surrounded by areas of organizing pneumonia.

Complications of untreated lung abscesses include overgrowth of fungi (particularly *Mucor* and *Aspergillus*) in the cavity, spread of the process to other portions of the lung, massive hemorrhage, bronchopleural fistula with empyema, and brain abscess.

For small unilocular abscesses, partial resection of the lobe may be curative.[253] However, in most cases lobectomy is preferable because it is associated with a much lesser probability of postoperative complications such as bronchopleural fistula and empyema.

Granulomatous inflammation

A large number of the granulomatous processes involve the lung; some of them radiographically and grossly simulate neoplastic processes. Often, microscopic examination is insufficient to establish a specific diagnosis; therefore it is important to submit a sample for bacteriologic and mycologic examination and to perform stains for *Mycobacteria* and fungi in the sections in every case.[254–256]

Tuberculosis

The material received in the pathology laboratory in cases of pulmonary tuberculosis may be a biopsy obtained with the fiberoptic bronchoscope,[262] material procured via fine needle aspiration,[259] an open-lung biopsy,[265] or a surgical specimen. Despite the use of modern drugs, there are still some patients with pulmonary tuberculosis who, because of inadequate response to drug therapy, become candidates for surgery. Most of the surgical procedures done at the present time for tuberculosis are resectional—wedge excision, subsegmental resection, lobectomy, and pneumonectomy. Strieder et al.[268] summarized the indications for pulmonary resection as follows:

1 Open cavity (with or without positive sputum) after a suitable period (4 to 6 months) on a satisfactory drug regimen
2 Residual caseous or fibrocaseous disease, with or without positive sputum
3 Irreversible destructive lesion, such as bronchostenosis or bronchiectasis
4 Recurrent or persistent hemorrhage, usually arising in a cavity or bronchiectasis
5 Thoracoplasty failure
6 Unexpandable lobe or lung, with associated chronic encapsulated tuberculous empyema
7 Suspected neoplasm

In most reported series of surgically treated tuberculous patients, 80% to 85% have inactive disease 2 to 5 years after surgery. Most complications of surgery, such as bronchopleural fistula, occur in patients with positive sputum preoperatively.[264]

Grossly, most of the tissue resected consists of inflamed, fibrotic, and otherwise nonfunctioning lung parenchyma. Bronchial involvement may lead to stricture formation, with distal bronchiectasis, atelectasis, and superimposed infection[266] (Fig. 7.89). The bronchiectatic changes are more often accompanied by extensive active tuberculosis in the lower than in the upper lobe because of differences in drainage. Peribronchial tuberculous lymph nodes may infect the bronchial mucous glands by direct extension or penetrate the bronchial wall and erode into the lumen, especially when these nodes are calcified.

Tuberculous cavities removed in patients after prolonged antimicrobial therapy may show healing by the

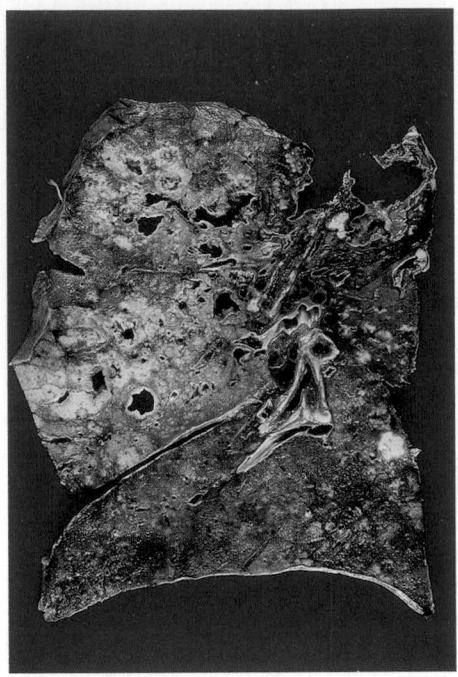

Fig. 7.89 Massive destruction of lung parenchyma by tuberculosis.

process of approximation of the walls, granulation tissue, fibrosis, and the formation of a stellate scar.[270] In other patients the lesion stabilizes as a chronic open cavity. Potential danger exists when this healing occurs with inspissation of caseous material because of the long-term persistence of viable organisms in this material.[257] The most complete form of healing, relatively rare, results in a thin fibrous wall with a smooth surface that has no lining except for a short squamous segment at the point where the bronchus enters the cavity.[258,271] Examination of these healed cavities for acid-fast organisms is invariably negative.[269] Metaplastic bone formation may develop, sometimes extensively.[261]

Tuberculomas are usually seen in adults and are an expression of tuberculous reinfection rather than a primary Ghon focus. In the series by Steele,[267] tuberculomas made up 25% of the solitary lung granulomas and 14% of all solitary pulmonary nodules. In only 14% of the cases of tuberculoma, there was a previous history of tuberculosis. Grossly, tuberculomas present as round discrete firm nodules; they are usually solitary and located immediately beneath a white or slightly yellowish pleura.[265a] On section the lesions may show concentric laminations, central calcification, or cavitation.[260] Microscopically, there are often persistent areas of caseation, in which acid-fast bacilli may be found. A thick fibrous wall surrounds the caseous center, with a variable number of Langhans' giant cells, epithelioid histiocytes, and lymphocytes in between. There is also prominent subpleural fibrous thickening. Communication of the tuberculoma with a bronchus and small active tubercles may be found in the immediate vicinity of the main lesion.

Tuberculomas are treated surgically because of the difficulty of ruling out malignancy and the fact that they represent the nidus for potential spread of infection.

It should be remarked that there is not a single microscopic feature that is pathognomonic of tuberculosis in any of its forms. The identification of the organism therefore is essential for diagnosis. This is usually done by staining the sections with the Ziehl-Neelsen technique, but fluorescent and immunoperoxidase techniques are also available.[263]

Atypical mycobacteriosis

An increasing number of granulomatous infections of the lung is caused by "atypical" or "unclassified" acid-fast mycobacteria.[276] Many of these cases are seen in immune-compromised hosts[272] and/or in patients with preexisting lung disease, including chronic obstructive lung disease, previous tuberculosis, pneumoconiosis, bronchiectasis, and lung carcinoma.[273] These infections cannot be distinguished from tuberculosis on the basis of their microscopic appearance, and therefore culture of the organism is required; however, the diagnosis can be suspected from the appearance of the organisms in acid-fast preparations, since they tend to be longer (about 20 µm), thicker, more coarsely beaded, and much more bent than tubercle bacilli.[275] The surgical approach follows the same general rules as for tuberculosis.[274]

Sarcoidosis

Sarcoidosis can present in the thoracic cavity in various ways: moderate to marked perihilar node involvement without pulmonary disease, diffuse pulmonary disease without roentgenographic evidence of node involvement, a combination of lymph node enlargement and diffuse pulmonary disease, pulmonary interstitial fibrosis, and localized bronchostenosis with distal bronchiectasis and atelectasis. The great majority of the cases fall into the first and third categories. Microscopically, the hallmark of the disease is a noncaseating granuloma mainly composed of epithelioid cells but also containing Langhans' giant cells and lymphocytes. The latter are predominantly of helper T-cell type, many of which show features of activation.[279]

There are many variations in this morphologic theme. Hyalinization of the granuloma and diffuse interstitial fibrosis may render the diagnosis difficult. Small foci of necrosis having a bright eosinophilic ("fibrinoid") appearance may be found in the center of some granulomas. Intracellular and extracellular inclusions of several kinds may be seen, but none is specific (see Chapter 21). Most of the granulomas in sarcoidosis are located in the interstitium and seem to be distributed along lymphatic pathways. They are often seen surrounding bronchioles (but not large bronchi); because of this, transbronchial lung biopsy is positive in more than 80% of the cases.[280] Pleural involvement is less common, in the neighborhood of 10%.[285] The granulomas also can be present around blood vessels and even within the walls of branches of the pulmonary artery and may result in pulmonary hypertension.[283,284]

Necrotizing sarcoid granulomatosis is the name given by Liebow[282] to a pulmonary disease characterized by extensive vascular granulomas that infiltrate, destroy, and occlude pulmonary arteries and veins and are accompanied by widespread necrosis of lung tissue (Fig. 7.90). It is not clear whether this condition is a variant of sarcoidosis or a type of sarcoid-like granulomatous vasculitis, but the former interpretation is favored.[277,278] Most of the patients are female adults and often are asymptomatic. The lesions may be bilateral or unilateral, diffuse or localized. Response to steroid and immunosuppressive drugs is good, and excision of the localized lesion is usually curative.[281]

Wegener's granulomatosis

Wegener's granulomatosis is the best known member of the group of diseases designated by Liebow as *pulmonary angiitis and granulomatosis*. It is becoming apparent that the latter term comprises a number of totally unrelated entities, and it is doubtful whether it should be retained.[288,289,294]

Classic Wegener's granulomatosis is characterized by the triad of necrotizing angiitis, aseptic necrosis (involving both the upper respiratory tract and the lungs), and focal glomerulitis (Fig. 7.91).[301] Other vessels may be involved, such as the temporal artery and cutaneous small vessels.[286] This may result in the formation of tumefactions at extrapulmonary sites.[291,296] If left untreated, the disease runs an accelerated clinical course; however, it has proved quite responsive to cytotoxic drugs (particularly cyclophosphamide). The main morphologic changes in the lungs are liquefactive and/or coagulative necrosis, a large number of eosinophils, scanty benign-appearing lymphocytes and plasma cells, multinucleated giant cells that generally do not form well-defined

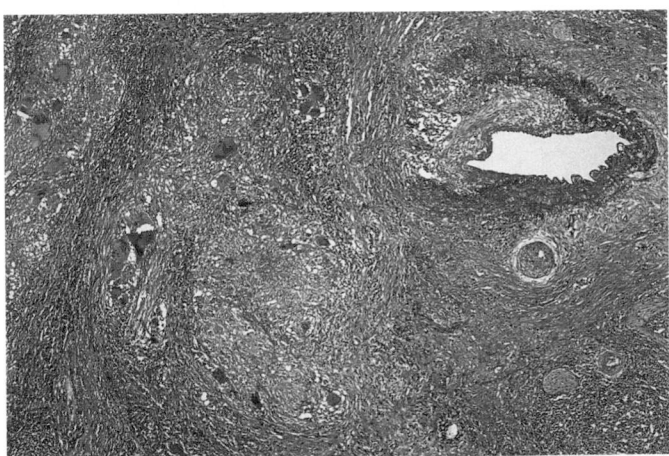

Fig. 7.90 Necrotizing sarcoidal granulomatosis. There is extensive involvement of large vessels by the inflammatory infiltrate, which has a necrotizing quality.

granulomas as in tuberculosis or sarcoidosis,[292] and a destructive, leukocytolytic angiitis involving arteries and veins[290,299,302] (Figs 7.92 and 7.93). Rarely, the changes are centered in the bronchial wall.[303] A *fulminant type* with a predominance of exudative changes and a *fibrous scar type*

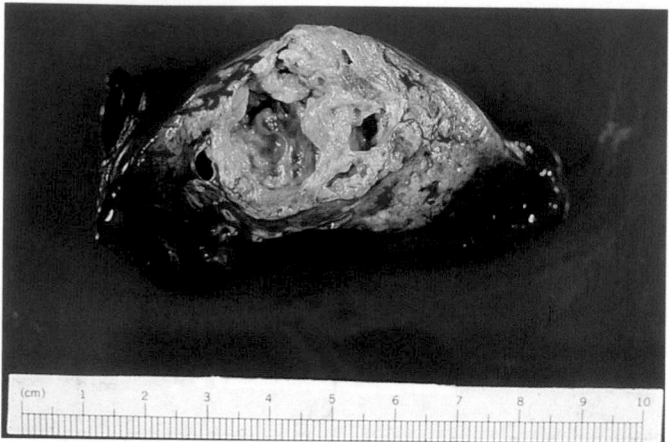

Fig. 7.91 Wegener's granulomatosis. The lesion is well circumscribed, with a granulomatous and partially necrotic appearance.

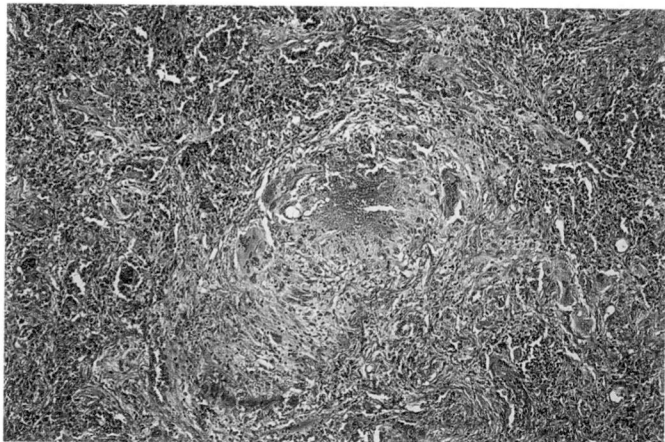

Fig. 7.92 Wegener's granulomatosis. Ill-defined granulomas containing multinucleated giant cells are present.

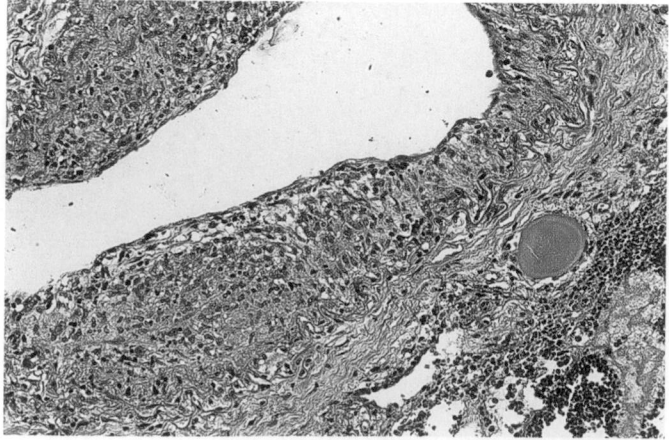

Fig. 7.93 Wegener's granulomatosis showing involvement of the vessel wall.

with abundant deposition of collagen also exist.[302] In rare cases the disease is accompanied by diffuse pulmonary hemorrhage.[298] The diagnosis of Wegener's granulomatosis can be made or suggested in transbronchial biopsy specimens.[295]

Limited Wegener's granulomatosis is confined to the lungs and has a more protracted clinical course.[287] Specifically, there is no glomerulitis. Steroids and cytotoxic drugs are highly effective. Grossly, there are multiple, bilateral nodules, some round and others infarctlike, frequently located in the lower lobes. Microscopically, the disease is indistinguishable from the classic variety. As in the latter, lymphocytes and plasma cells are scanty.[297] Angiitis is a requisite for the diagnosis. However, it should be recognized that vessels located within ordinary infectious (tuberculous or mycotic) granulomas can exhibit secondary inflammatory changes. Therefore the presence of angiitis *away* from the areas of necrosis and massive inflammation should be searched for to document the diagnosis. The diagnosis of Wegener's granulomatosis should be made with great caution in granulomas that appear solitary by radiographic examination.[293,300]

Bronchocentric granulomatosis and allergic granulomatosis

Bronchocentric granulomatosis is a pulmonary granulomatous disease in which all or nearly all the granulomas are centered in bronchi and bronchioles, leading to their destruction.[314] Most of the patients are adults, and some are remarkably asymptomatic despite the extensive nature of the process. The lesions are usually solitary and appear on chest roentgenograms as areas of consolidation or atelectasis rather than discrete nodules. The involved bronchi contain an extremely viscous material, which is composed microscopically of a mixture of mucus, neutrophils, and eosinophils, sometimes agglutinated into a dense mass that is surrounded by foreign body giant cells[315] (Fig. 7.94). This condition is always limited to the lungs, in contrast to the pulmonary granulomatous angiitides, which frequently are accompanied by extrapulmonary manifestations.[316] It should be remembered that bronchocentric granulomas can also be seen in Wegener's granulomatosis (see p. 373). The prognosis is generally favorable.

Cases of bronchocentric granulomatosis occurring in asthmatics tend to contain numerous eosinophils and are usually the result of *allergic bronchopulmonary aspergillosis*[304]; most of those cases seen in nonasthmatics show a predominance of neutrophils, and the sensitizing agent usually remains unidentified.[311] Allergic bronchopulmonary fungal disease can also be due to other fungi, such as *Curvularia* organisms.[317]

Mucus or **mucoid impaction** is a process in which proximal bronchi become filled with thick inspissated mucus. This change, when extensive, may cast a

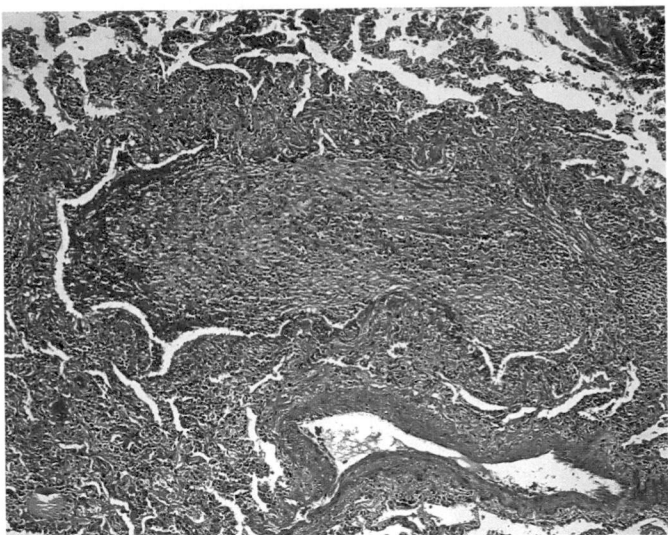

Fig. 7.94 Bronchocentric granulomatosis. A large mucous plug containing eosinophils and other inflammatory cells distends a bronchial space.

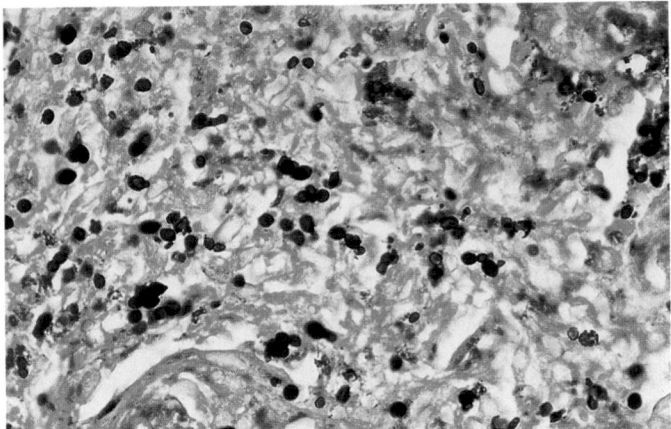

Fig. 7.95 Pulmonary histoplasmosis. The organisms are demonstrated with the Grocott stain.

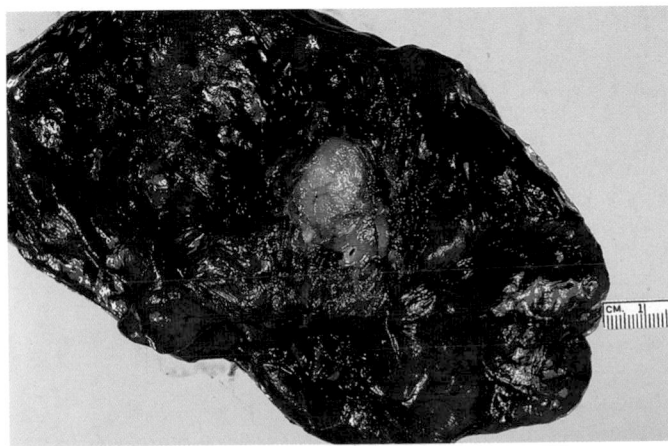

Fig. 7.96 Gross appearance of cryptococcosis of lung.

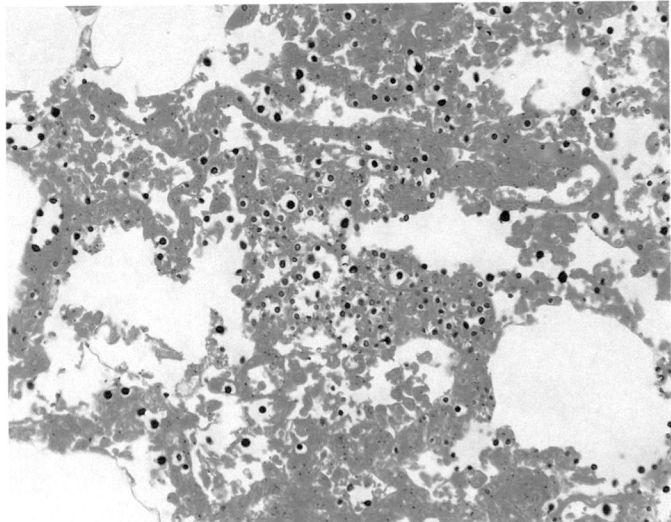

Fig. 7.97 Microscopic appearance of cryptococcosis in a Grocott stain. Note the clear halo around the organisms.

staghorn shadow on the x-ray films.[307] The disease can also involve smaller bronchi and bronchioles. It overlaps microscopically with allergic bronchopulmonary aspergillosis and bronchocentric granulomatosis, but it lacks granulomatous inflammation.[309,318]

Allergic granulomatosis (Churg–Strauss syndrome) presents a clinical picture of systemic vasculitis resembling polyarteritis nodosa but is typically associated with a history of asthma, peripheral eosinophilia (up to 80%), and a high incidence of pulmonary involvement.[305,312]

Microscopically, both the pulmonary and the extrapulmonary lesions are characterized by a prominent eosinophilic infiltrate, foci of necrosis (some associated with eosinophils and some unrelated to them), a granulomatous reaction around some of these necrotic foci, and eosinophilic vasculitis.[308,310] The disease is very rare, and some authors even doubt that it represents a distinct entity.[313] Others have taken the opposite view and have made the point that cases are missed because of the lack of vasculitis, whether because of steroid therapy or the fact that the biopsy was taken at too early of a stage.[306]

Other granulomatous inflammations

Other granulomatous diseases of the lung that may be encountered in biopsies or surgical specimens are those caused by *histoplasmosis*,[327] *blastomycosis*,[329,330] *sporotrichosis*,[324] *cryptococcosis*,[328] *coccidioidomycosis*,[336] *mucormycosis*,[320] *actinomycosis*,[332] and *aspergillosis*[333] (Figs 7.95 to 7.99). Aspergillosis may present as a secondary colonization of a lung abscess or some other cavitary process ("aspergilloma"), in the form of allergic bronchopulmonary aspergillosis (see p. 374), or as invasive or necrotizing pulmonary aspergillosis; the latter usually occurs in the immunocompromised host.[319,321,323,331,333] The chronic form of necrotizing pulmonary aspergillosis can present in several morphologic guises depending upon the relative degree of involvement of the bronchi and lung parenchyma.[335]

Dirofilariasis of the lung usually presents as an incidental solitary nodule on x-ray examination, but it can

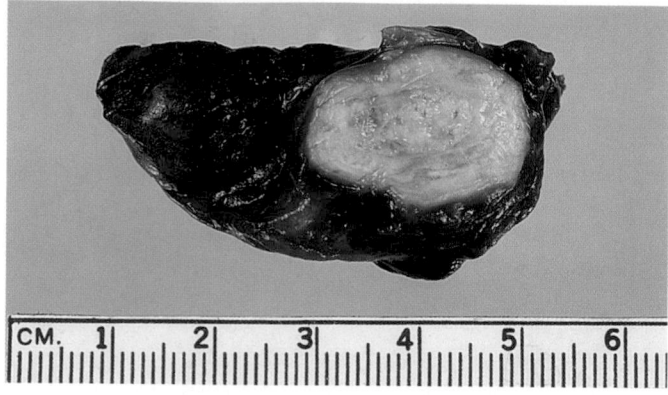

Fig. 7.98 Coccidioidomycotic granuloma. The necrotic center is surrounded by fibrous tissue showing concentric lamination.

Fig. 7.99 Large necrotizing nodule due to pulmonary aspergillosis. (Courtesy of Dr. RA Cooke, Brisbane, Australia; from Cooke RA, Stewart B: Colour Atlas of Anatomical Pathology. Edinburgh, Churchill Livingstone, 2004).

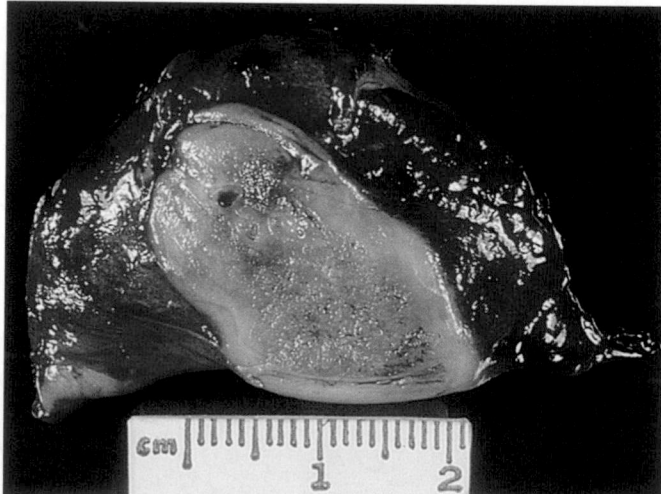

Fig. 7.100 Sharply outlined lung infarct resulting from Dirofilaria infestation.

also be multiple and/or symptomatic (Fig. 7.100). Microscopically, there is a histiocyte-rimmed necrotic nodule containing fragments of *Dirofilaria inmitis*.[325]

Granulomas may also be seen in eosinophilic pneumonia (see p. 380), in bronchial chondromalacia, as a result of exposure to talc in drug abusers through inhala-tion,[326] from industrial exposure to metal dust,[322] and as an expression of hypersensitivity in the group of disorders known as extrinsic allergic alveolitis (see p. 383).[322a] Cholesterol granulomas, sometimes seen as an incidental finding in a lung specimen, may be the result of a prior alveolar hemorrhage. Lipogranulomas may also be encountered incidentally, particularly in diabetic patients.[334]

Acute pulmonary injury and interstitial pneumonias

Acute pulmonary injury is the generic term used for the acute (days or weeks) effects of a variety of noxious agents on the terminal air spaces. It can be divided into several reasonably well-defined clinicopathologic entities, with the caveat that some degree of overlap exists and that some cases defy classification.[337,378] These entities are diffuse alveolar damage, acute interstitial pneumonia, and bronchiolitis obliterans–organizing pneumonia.

Diffuse alveolar damage (DAD) is usually diffuse and bilateral, and it may be caused by infectious agents (particularly viruses), inhalants (such as oxygen), drugs (especially chemotherapeutic agents and amiodarone, the latter used for the treatment of refractory anemia), ingestants (such as kerosene or paraquat), shock, sepsis, radiation, and many other agents.[373,376,382,387] It represents the usual underlying pathologic change of the clinically defined *adult respiratory distress syndrome*.[395] The morphologic changes are of a nonspecific nature, and therefore the etiologic agent cannot be determined from the microscopic picture alone. The earliest stages consist of edema, intra-alveolar hemorrhage, and fibrin deposition. This is followed by hyaline membrane formation (most prominent 3 to 7 days after the injury), a sparse interstitial inflammatory infiltrate, fibrin thrombi (inconstant), and hyperplasia of the alveolar lining cells. These cells, which are mainly of type II (granular) pneumocytic type, may exhibit atypia, mitotic activity, intracytoplasmic lipid accumulation, and cytoplasmic hyaline (Mallory) bodies.[386] The epithelial atypia is said to be more common and pronounced in the cases caused by chemotherapy.[389] The combination of squamous metaplasia and cytologic atypia can be pronounced enough to mimic a squamous cell carcinoma.[380] Foamy macrophages may also be present; they are said to be more common in the cases resulting from amiodarone.[376] In a later (organizing) stage, there is interstitial and intraluminal fibroblastic proliferation, associated with persistence of the hyperplastic lining cells. The epitheliums of the adjacent bronchioles may show mitotic, regenerative, and metaplastic (squamous) changes, but this is not a prominent feature.

Acute interstitial pneumonia (AIP) is a rapidly progressive form of interstitial pneumonia and is synonymous with the *Hamman-Rich syndrome*[365,381] (Fig. 7.101). By

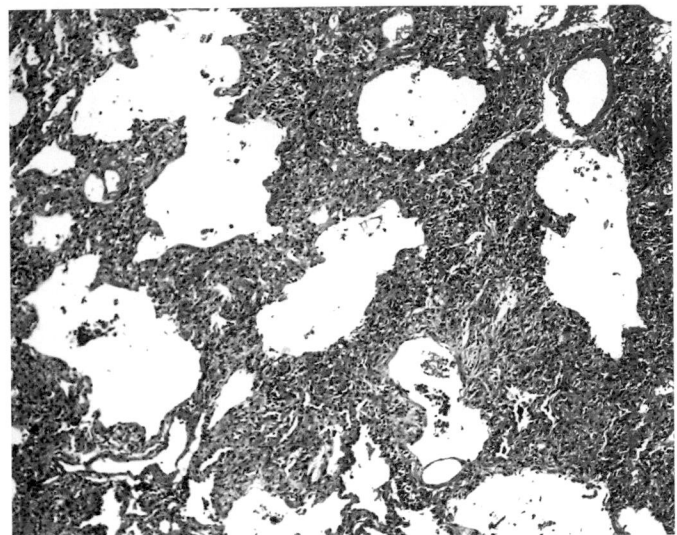

Fig. 7.101 Acute changes of interstitial pneumonia. The clinical features were those of the Hamman–Rich syndrome.

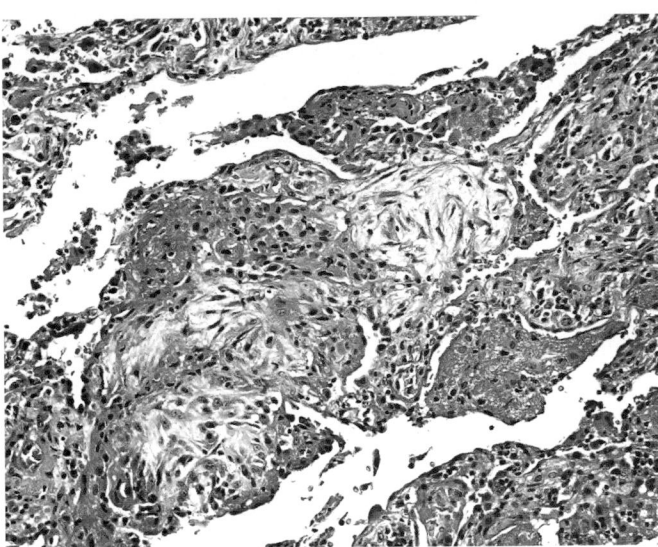

Fig. 7.102 So-called "BOOP." A plug of spindle mesenchymal cells obstructs a terminal bronchiole. There is fibrin deposition and chronic inflammation in the surrounding parenchyma.

definition, there is no identifiable initiating event. The typical patient is a young adult who presents with dyspnea following a influenza-like illness. The prognosis is very poor, with most patients dying within 2 months of onset. Microscopically, the appearance is equivalent to that of the organizing phase of DAD, the most striking feature being the brisk interstitial fibroblastic proliferation.

Bronchiolitis obliterans–organizing pneumonia (BOOP) may also be associated with several conditions, including infections, inhalants (including silo-filler lung), drugs, and collagen-vascular diseases.[347] The onset is usually acute and characterized by cough, dyspnea, fever, and malaise.[353,366] The prognosis is generally excellent.[394] Morphologically, the hallmark of the disease is represented by fibroblastic plugs ("Masson's bodies") filling air spaces (Fig. 7.102). These plugs have a typical elongated to serpiginous shape and are formed by spindle to stellate fibroblasts embedded in a pale-staining matrix. Other changes include clusters of foamy macrophages, a few scattered neutrophils, and thickening of the alveolar septa. It is characteristic for the process to have a patchy appearance on low-power examination, a feature of importance in the differential diagnosis with usual interstitial pneumonia (see below). The rare cases of BOOP with unfavorable outcome (steroid-unresponsive) have shown scarring and remodeling of the lung parenchyma on microscopic examination.[400]

Cases of bronchiolitis obliterans unassociated with abnormalities in the more distal air spaces are extremely rare; Katzenstein and Askin[366] prefer to designate them as *obliterative bronchiolitis*.

The chronic forms of interstitial pneumonia include the following conditions: usual interstitial pneumonia, desquamative interstitial pneumonia, lymphoid interstitial pneumonia, giant cell interstitial pneumonia, and a few others, including the wastebasket term *nonspecific interstitial pneumonia*.[346,362,363]

Usual interstitial pneumonia (UIP) has an insidious onset and a chronic evolution, many of the patients dying of respiratory failure after an average of 4 to 5 years. Some instances of UIP show a pattern of familial incidence suggestive of genetic predisposition,[341] and others are associated with neurofibromatosis[396] or pulmonary venoocclusive disease (see p. 385). Still others are associated with immune-mediated diseases, such as systemic lupus erythematosus, rheumatoid arthritis, scleroderma, Sjögren's syndrome, chronic active hepatitis, Raynaud's phenomenon, ulcerative colitis, and thyroid disease (Fig. 7.103). In a study of 130 cases of "idiopathic interstitial fibrosis," rheumatoid arthritis was found in 18%, transient polyarthritis in 12%, and Sjögren's syndrome in 3%.[393] Approximately 30% of

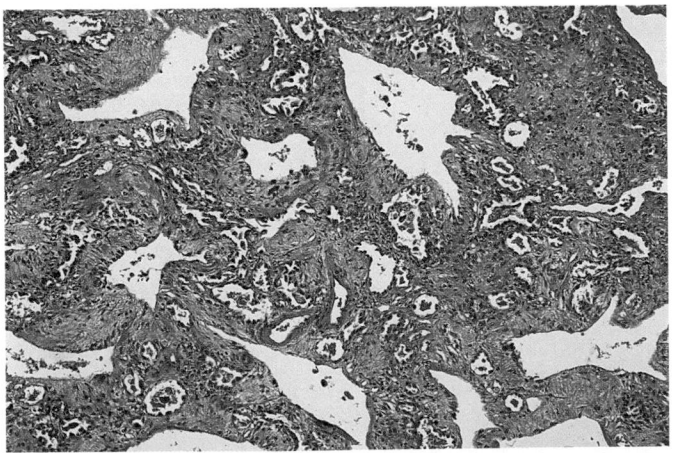

Fig. 7.103 Late stage of interstitial pneumonitis in a patient with lupus erythematosus.

patients with UIP have circulating antinuclear antibodies. Immunofluorescent studies in the lung tissue have demonstrated deposition of immunoglobulins and C3,[393] and the presence of circulating immune complexes has been documented in most cases.[350] All these facts suggest that most cases of UIP represent a form of immune-complex lung disease.[385] The recent finding of aberrant Wnt/β-catenin pathway activation in this condition is of interest because of the possible pathogenetic role that it may play in the abnormal remodeling of lung tissue.[343a]

Microscopically, UIP is a primarily interstitial inflammatory and fibrosing process. According to Katzenstein et al., the single most important feature that distinguishes UIP from the other interstitial pneumonias (including so-called nonspecific interstitial pneumoma) is the marked regional variations in the nature and degree of the infiltrate, with a distinct patchwork appearance and evidence of architectural derangement.[360] These criteria apply both to biopsy and explant specimens, there being a close correlation among the two.[367] Ultrastructural studies suggest that the fibrosis results largely from migration of activated mesenchymal cells through defects in the epithelial lining and its basement membrane, from the interstitial into the intraluminal compartment.[339,344] Other mechanisms that may contribute to the changes are permanent exudates.[360] A pathogenetic role for transforming growth factor-beta 1 and for monocyte chemoattractant protein-1 has been postulated.[348,359]

On occasions, the typical microscopic picture of UIP is complicated by the presence of eosinophilic pneumonia-like areas.[397]

In the late stages of UIP, there are irregular fibrosis, smooth-muscle proliferation, and microcystic formation.[351] *Honeycombing* is a gross descriptive term applied to a localized or diffuse area of coarsening of the lung parenchyma with increased porosity, distinguishable from emphysema by virtue of the fibrosis present and representing the result of interstitial pneumonia or other inflammatory parenchymal disorders, such as Langerhans' cell histiocytosis (Fig. 7.104). It should be regarded neither as an entity nor as an indication of a specific lung disease. The term *bronchiolar emphysema* has been used inappropriately for this condition in the past. There is no evidence that honeycombing is ever congenital. The superior portions of the upper and lower lobes are the most common sites of involvement. Atypical foci of acinar and squamous proliferation are often seen in late stages of honeycombing. This is regarded as a precancerous change, in view of its frequent association with malignant tumors, particularly adenocarcinomas.[375] Several cases of carcinoma arising in lungs with diffuse interstitial fibrosis have been reported.[355,368]

Desquamative interstitial pneumonia (DIP) is characterized by a filling of the alveolar spaces by large mononuclear cells, associated with relatively minor interstitial changes[356,370,372] (Fig. 7.105). In cases examined

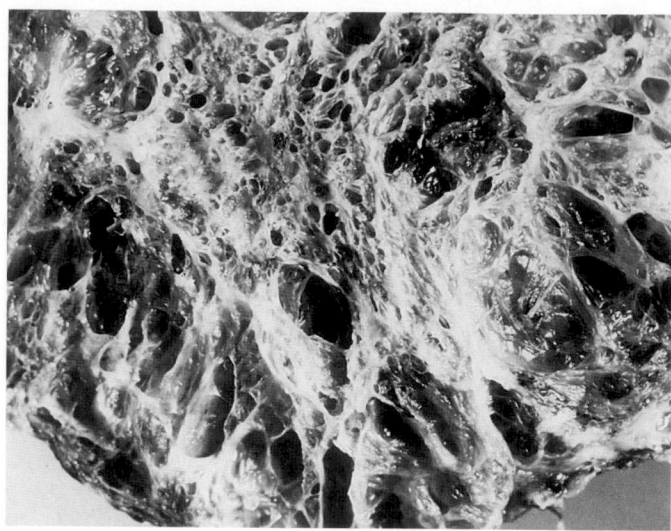

Fig. 7.104 Extensive honeycombing of the right upper lobe in a 63-year-old woman who had associated adenocarcinoma. Regional lymph nodes were negative.

electron microscopically, the desquamated cells have features of macrophages rather than of granular pneumocytes, although hyperplasia of the latter is present in the alveolar wall. Necrosis, hyaline membranes, and fibrin are absent. Radiographically, a ground-glass type of opacification is seen bilaterally in the periphery of the lung bases. Most cases are seen in adults, but pediatric cases also have been reported.[388] Good response to steroids was noted by Liebow et al.[372] in their original series of eighteen patients.

Scadding and Hinson[383,384] have proposed the pathogenetically more satisfactory term *diffuse* or *cryptogenic fibrosing alveolitis* to embrace UIP and DIP. They call them the *mural type* and the *desquamative type* of diffuse fibrosing alveolitis, respectively, and regard them as the opposite ends of a continuous spectrum rather than as

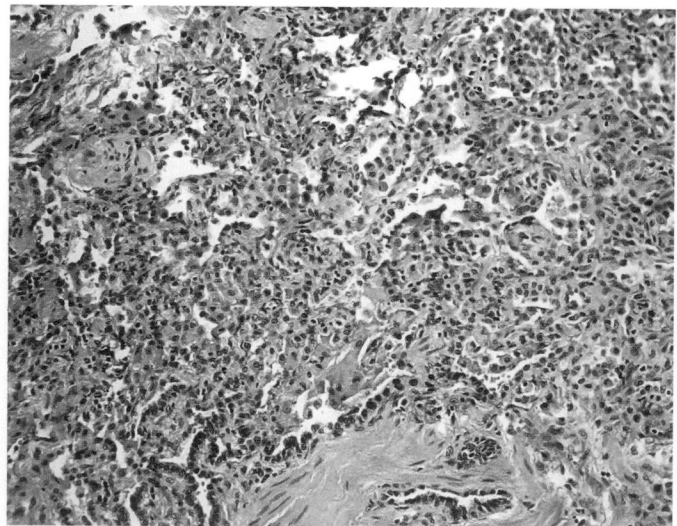

Fig. 7.105 Desquamative interstitial pneumonia. Most of the cells filling the alveolar spaces are histiocytes.

two separate entities.[342,352] Specifically, the proposal is that DIP represents the cellular phase of fibrosing alveolitis.[349,391] Regardless of which viewpoint is correct, it seems clear that it is worthwhile to separate the two conditions in view of their different course and response to therapy. In the series of Carrington et al.,[343] the mortality in DIP was 27.5% and mean survival 12.2 years, in contrast with 66% and 5.6 years in UIP.

Without treatment, 21.9% of the patients with DIP but none with UIP improved. With corticosteroid therapy, 61.5% with DIP and only 11.5% with UIP improved, whereas 27% and 69.2% worsened, respectively. Other series have shown a closer correlation with patient's age, duration of symptoms, functional and radiographic findings, and initial response to steroid therapy than with differences in microscopic appearance.[392]

Respiratory bronchiolitis-associated interstitial lung disease (RBILD). Respiratory bronchiolitis is a common incidental finding in heavy smokers,[354] but in some instances the disease becomes symptomatic.[379] Histologically, the disease is characterized by an accumulation of alveolar macrophages within respiratory bronchioles spilling into neighbouring alveoli. The changes differ from those of DIP in that the histiocytic accumulation is centroacinar instead of diffuse. A variation on the theme having some morphologic resemblances to hypersensitivity pneumonitides has been named *idiopathic bronchiolocentric interstitial pneumonia*.[398]

It could be mentioned here that other forms of lung disease characterized by bronchiolitis are asthma-associated changes, the bronchiolar changes associated with chronic bronchitis and emphysema, cellular bronchiolitis (including the follicular subtype mentioned below), the already mentioned BOOP, and a few other poorly understood disorders.[345]

Lymphoid (lymphocytic) interstitial pneumonia (LIP) is characterized by a lymphocytic infiltrate, often admixed with histiocytes and plasma cells, occupying the lung interstitium.[357,369,371] Serum immunoglobin abnormalities may also be present. A third of the cases have been associated with Sjögren's syndrome.[340] The roentgenographic appearance is that of consolidation and perivascular infiltrative densities.[358] The response to steroids is poor. An etiologic role for the EBV has been suggested for the non-HIV-related cases.[374]

The differential diagnosis includes **follicular bronchitis and bronchiolitis**, a nonspecific inflammatory reaction in which reactive germinal centers are seen adjacent to airways in the absence of chronic obstructive pulmonary disease.[399] It also includes small lymphocytic lymphoma (see p. 416), a difficult problem further complicated by the occasional instance of lymphoma developing in cases of longstanding LIP.[338]

Giant cell interstitial pneumonia (GIP) is the rarest form of interstitial pneumonia. As the name indicates, it contains multinucleated giant cells mixed with the other inflammatory components. Recently, GIP has been removed from the group of idiopathic interstitial pneumonias as it is now regarded as a pneumocomosis associated with hard metal exposure.[378]

Chronic pneumonitis of infancy is a rare form of interstitial lung disease occurring in early childhood and characterized microscopically by marked alveolar thickening, alveolar pneumocyte hyperplasia, and alveolar exudate.[364]

Nonspecific interstitial pneumonia/fibrosis is a term used for cases that cannot be classified into any of the major categories of interstitial pneumonia.[377] They seem to have varying etiologies and a relatively good prognosis.[361] As in the case of the usual/desquamative interstitial pneumomas, there is a prognostic significance among these idiopathic nonspecific interstitial pneumomas depending whether the predominant morphologic pattern is fibrosing or cellular, the prognosis being less favorable with the former.[390]

Organizing pneumonia

Pneumonia is not usually considered a surgical problem. However, if the disease—instead of resolving—organizes, shadows occurring in the lung may be mistaken for tumor (Fig. 7.106). Some of these radiographic shadows have a round or oval shape, hence the alternative term *round* or *spherical pneumonia* that has been applied to them in the radiologic literature.[402,403] The patients present with cough, hemoptysis, and weight loss, further suggesting the existence of a malignant process.[401] *Haemophilus influenzae* and *Streptococcus pneumoniae* have

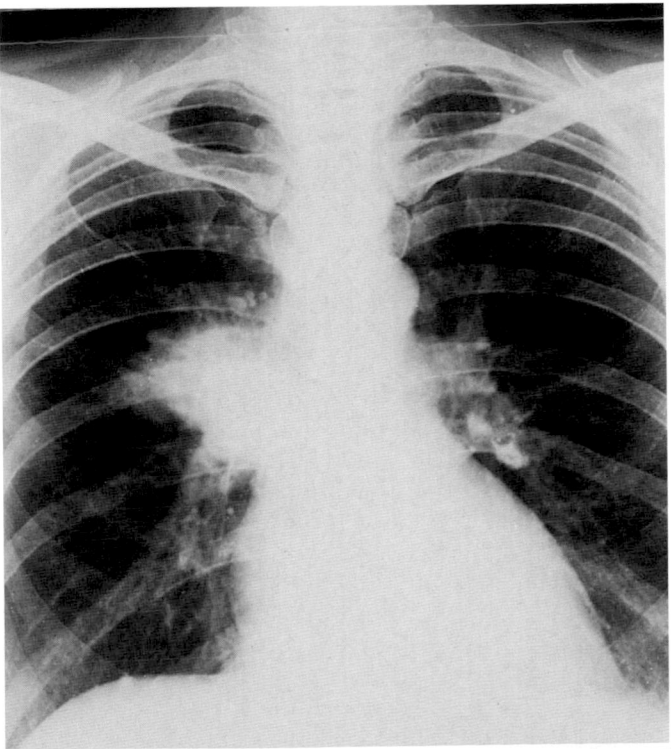

Fig. 7.106 Hilar mass that was considered radiographically to be carcinoma but proved pathologically to be organized pneumonia.

been identified as the etiologic agents in some of the cases.[402] Grossly, the involved area is sharply outlined and very firm, but the pattern of the lung persists. The cut surface is solid and gray-red to light yellow in color. The process extends to the pleura, which is invariably thickened. Microscopically, there is an exudate composed of fibrin and acute inflammatory cells in various degrees of organization, sometimes accompanied by necrotizing changes in the bronchi. In later stages, alveolar collections of foamy macrophages appear as a result of bronchiolar obstruction.

The variant of this process known as bronchiolitis obliterans organizing pneumonia has been discussed in the preceding section. The morphologic features of organizing pneumonia overlap with those of inflammatory pseudotumor, in which a more severe disruption of the underlying lung architecture is evident (see p. 413).

Lipoid pneumonia

Lipoid pneumonia is often a complication of debilitating disease found as an incidental post mortem finding. However, the local expression of this process may be confused with a malignant neoplasm and consequently may become a surgical problem.

Lipoid pneumonia can be divided into two types: exogenous and endogenous. In the *exogenous* type, now seen only rarely, lipoid material from nasal sprays or other sources reaches the lung through the tracheobronchial tree. The *endogenous* type is associated with bronchial obstruction by carcinoma or some other process; the fat accumulated is of endogenous origin. Grossly, the lesion is well circumscribed and firm.[404] In the exogenous type, the lymphatic vessels over the surface of the lung are often prominent, suggesting lymphatic permeation by carcinoma, and fat droplets may be seen flowing from the fresh cut surface.[405] Microscopically, both forms exhibit sudanophilic lipoid

material, inflammatory cells, proliferating alveolar cells, and young fibroblasts occupying large spaces. There may also be reactive endarteritis. The marked hyperplasia of alveolar cells and histiocytes may cause confusion in cytology or frozen section interpretation.

Eosinophilic pneumonia

Eosinophilic pneumonia is a generic term that embraces all pulmonary infiltrations associated with peripheral eosinophilia, as well as infiltrations of the lung by eosinophils with or without peripheral eosinophilia[407] (Fig. 7.108). Langerhans' cell granulomatosis is excluded. The acute form of eosinophilic pneumonia, characterized by fleeting pulmonary infiltrates accompanied by eosinophilia and lasting no more than a month, is commonly referred to as *Löffler's syndrome*. Most cases of eosinophilic pneumonia are of a chronic nature, although the onset can be quite sudden. This is a disease of women, usually between the ages of 20 and 50 years.

Clinically, it is characterized by fever, weight loss, dyspnea, frequent peripheral eosinophilia, and pulmonary infiltrates. The radiographic appearance is very characteristic because of the distinctly peripheral distribution of the infiltrate. The most notable microscopic change is alveolar and interstitial infiltration by eosinophils, but there are also plasma cells and histiocytes. Charcot–Leyden crystals may be found. Additional features seen occasionally include mild angiitis, granulomatosis with giant cell formation, some fibrosis with organization, mucous plugging, and bronchiolitis with necrosis.

Eosinophilic pneumonia has been described in association with rheumatoid arthritis, polyarteritis nodosa, malignant lymphoma, breast carcinoma, nephrotic syndrome, scleroderma, ulcerative colitis, and hypersensitivity to nitrofurantoin (a drug used in the treatment of urinary tract infection).[406,408] Helminths, drugs, *Filaria*,

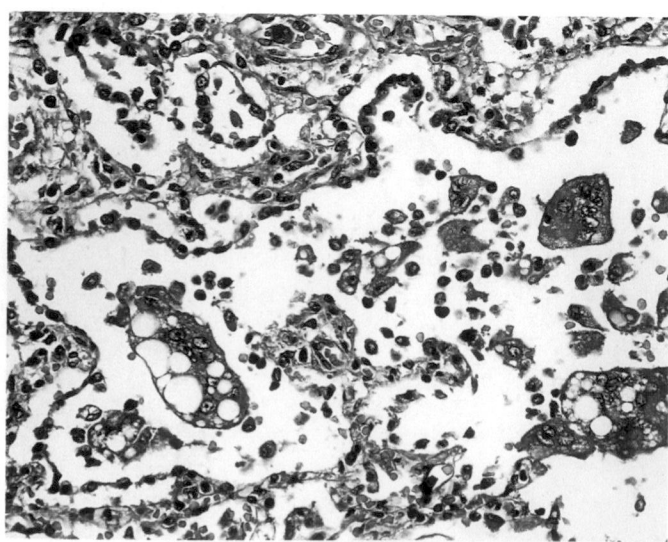

Fig. 7.107 Exogenous lipoid pneumonia due to Vaseline inhalation.

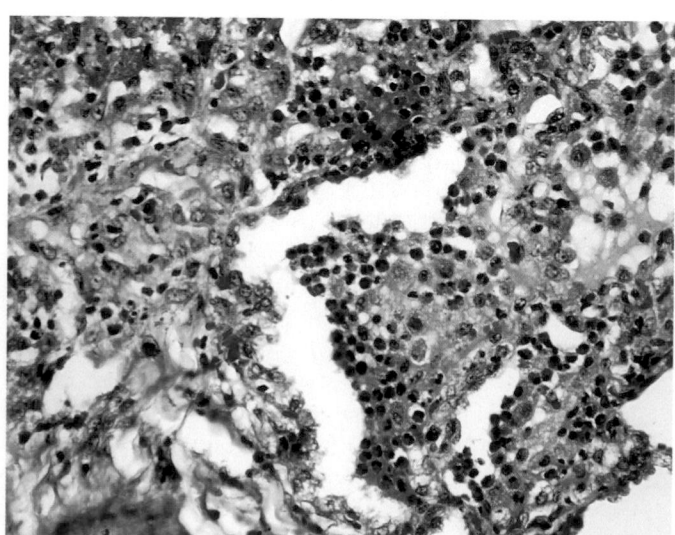

Fig. 7.108 Eosinophilic pneumonia. Numerous mature eosinophils are admixed with histiocytes and granular pneumocytes.

Dirofilaria, and especially *Aspergillus* have been identified as the etiologic agents in some of the cases.[409] When chronic eosinophilic pneumonia develops in a patient who has longstanding asthma, it is usually on the basis of allergic aspergillosis.[410] If the changes of eosinophilic pneumonia are accompanied by necrotizing vasculitis, there is a good probability of extrapulmonary involvement. In *dirofilariasis*, the presentation may also be in the form of single or multiple subpleural infarcts with a central thrombosed artery containing the parasite[411] (see Fig. 7.100).

Pneumocystis carinii pneumonia

Pneumocystis carinii pneumonia is a nonbacterial opportunistic infection.[425] Most cases are seen in individuals who are chronically debilitated and immunosuppressed, such as those receiving therapy for neoplastic disease or affected with AIDS.[415,422,427,429] In severely immunocompromised patients, the infection may spread to extrapulmonary sites and become disseminated.[416]

Microscopically, the typical case is characterized by a foamy or honeycombed intra-alveolar exudate accompanied by a lymphoplasmacytic interstitial infiltrate (Fig. 7.109). However, these features may be inconspicuous or absent in some cases, which may exhibit instead epithelioid granulomas, focal multinucleated giant cells, marked interstitial fibrosis, vasculitis, and severe infiltration by alveolar macrophages.[426,430]

Calcification may also develop.[417] The diagnosis depends on the microscopic identification of the organism, since at present no reliable microbiologic or serologic tests are available.[418] This detection can be carried out in sputum or pulmonary secretions, or in tissue specimens from transbronchial, percutaneous, or open biopsies.[413,423] The specimen should be cultured (to rule out the possibility of other infectious processes), imprints should be taken, and the rest of the tissue should be either fixed in formalin and processed routinely or subjected to frozen section examination.[421] If *Pneumocystis carinii* is present, the imprints are almost invariably positive. The most reliable stain for detecting the organism is Gomori's methenamine silver (GMS). Its disadvantage has been the fact that in its original description the procedure takes 3 hours to perform; however, technical modifications have now cut the time to less than 20 minutes.[419] Immunoperoxidase techniques using monoclonal antibodies and PCR methods are also available.[412,414,420] The cyst forms of the organism appear with the silver stain as round structures, up to 5 μm in diameter, containing single or paired discrete "intracystic bodies" measuring 1 to 2 μm.[424,428] Some of the cysts are crumpled and others are collapsed, with a crescentic shape.

Other pneumonias

Cytomegalovirus pneumonia is usually seen in immunocompromised patients, such as those with AIDS or lymphoid malignancies, transplant recipients, and those receiving cytotoxic drugs. Radiographically, it may present in the form of small (2 to 4 cm) peripherally located nodules, as an acute miliary pattern, or as a diffuse interstitial process. Coalescence and consolidation may occur. Microscopically, a predominantly mononuclear inflammatory infiltrate is seen in conjunction with edema and hyperplasia of the alveolar epithelium. In the diffuse pattern, these changes are associated with spherical areas of hemorrhagic necrosis. Viral inclusion bodies can be detected in most but not all of the cases. These are found both in the nucleus and in the cytoplasm. The latter are stained with both PAS and GMS, a fact that may lead to a mistaken diagnosis of *Pneumocystis carinii* pneumonia.[436]

Herpes simplex pneumonia may result in an interstitial process with mononuclear inflammation and alveolar cell hyperplasia, or in a necrotizing bronchopneumonia.[437] Intranuclear viral inclusions can be found at the edge of the necrotic areas, but they are less numerous than in cytomegalovirus pneumonia (Fig. 7.110).

Adenovirus pneumonia has a rather characteristic microscopic appearance, by virtue of the combination of

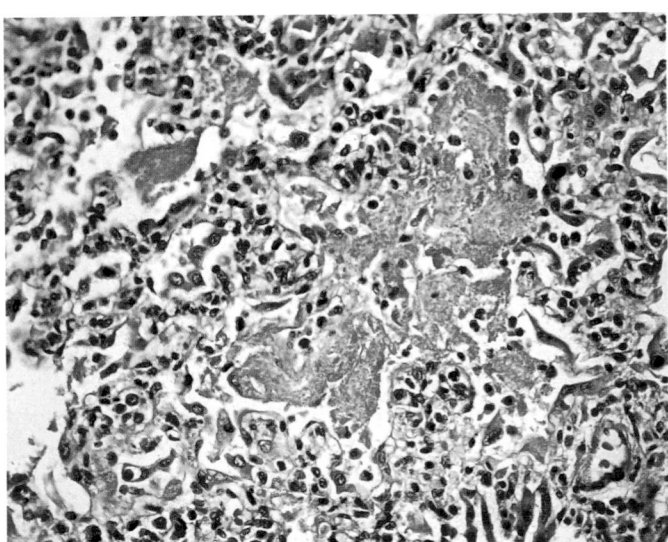

Fig. 7.109 Frothy alveolar exudate in *P. carinii* pneumonia.

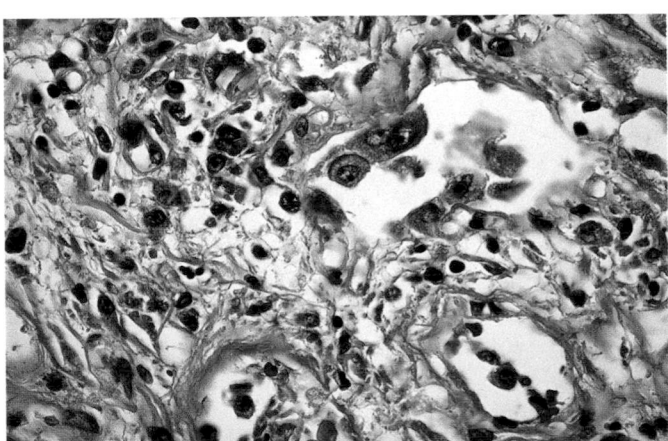

Fig. 7.110 Intranuclear inclusions in herpes simplex pneumonitis.

smudged nuclei, bricklike intranuclear inclusions in epithelial cells, and bronchiolitis obliterans.[431,432,442]

Legionnaires' disease became an instant media sensation in 1976, when it occurred in a small epidemic form among persons attending a convention in a hotel in downtown Philadelphia.[434] It turns out that it is anything but a new disease; apparently, sporadic cases have been seen by the thousands over previous decades.[433] Occasionally, an open or transbronchial lung biopsy is performed in these patients. Microscopically, the process is characterized by intra-alveolar accumulation of neutrophils, macrophages, and fibrin.[444] In this respect, it does not differ much from lobar pneumococcal pneumonia. However, many cases also show a leukocytoclastic neutrophilic inflammatory infiltrate, small vessel vasculitis, and necrosis.[445] The Dieterle silver impregnation stain has proved to be the most reliable for identifying the short gram-negative bacillus that is the etiologic agent. Involvement of the hilar lymph nodes occurs in nearly half of the autopsied cases, and in about one quarter of the cases there is hematogenous spread to other organs.[443]

Nocardiosis is another opportunistic lung infection, and its frequency appears to be increasing.[439] Approximately one half of the reported cases have occurred in patients who have a history of organ transplantation, immunosuppression, steroid usage, or chemotherapy.[435,440] The diagnosis may require an open lung biopsy. Microscopically, the picture is that of a focal bronchopneumonia, with the formation of microabscesses and ill-defined granulomas. Gram stain shows slender, slightly beaded, branching filamentous bacilli.

Mycoplasma pneumoniae pneumonia, formerly known as *atypical pneumonia*, is dominated by bronchiolitis and shifting pulmonary infiltrates. Parenchymal disease takes the form of both interstitial and intra-alveolar involvement; it presents as a pneumonia or bronchopneumonia and may be accompanied by regional lymph node involvement.[438] Microscopically, there is a nonspecific neutrophilic infiltrate in the bronchiolar lumina, bronchiolar metaplasia, lymphoplasmacytic infiltrate in the bronchial wall, and hyperplasia of granular pneumocytes.[441]

Influenza pneumonia can result in a wide range of morphologic changes, from necrotizing pneumonia to mild acute lung injury accompanied by bronchiolitis obliterans and organizing features.[446]

Hantavirus pulmonary syndrome is a severe pulmonary disease caused by a previously unrecognized Hantavirus. A recent outbreak has occurred in the Southwestern United States. The usual morphologic findings are interstitial pneumonitis with a variable mononuclear cell infiltrate, edema, and focal hyaline membranes.[447]

Severe acute respiratory syndrome (SARS) is an infectious condition caused by a coronavirus. It emerged from Guangdong Province in China in November 2002 and resulted in widely publicized outbreaks in Hong Kong, Vietnam and Singapore. Microscopically, the predominant pattern is that of diffuse alveolar damage, the changes depending on the duration of the illness.[434a,434b]

Lung in AIDS

Pulmonary disease occurs frequently during the course of AIDS and often necessitates bronchoalveolar lavage, transbronchial biopsy, or open lung biopsy for appropriate management.[448,450] The open lung biopsy gives the highest diagnostic yield, but the combination of lavage and transbronchial biopsy comes very close to those figures.[453,456] The abnormalities seen in this background include cytomegalovirus pneumonia, *Pneumocystis* pneumonia, atypical mycobacteriosis and tuberculosis, candidiasis, aspergillosis, toxoplasmosis, cryptococcosis, histoplasmosis, blastomycosis, microsporidiosis, and Kaposi's sarcoma, often in combination.[449,454,455,458] Sometimes the morphologic changes are nonspecific, the features being those of the usual, desquamative, or lymphocytic interstitial pneumonia.[451,452,457,459]

Lung in bone marrow transplantation

Most nonleukemic deaths after bone marrow transplantation are caused by graft-versus-host disease and interstitial pneumonia.[462] The incidence of the latter ranges from 20% to 50%, with a fatality rate of 50% to 70%. The most common type is infectious, with cytomegalovirus as the most frequently encountered pathogen.[460] The other form, labeled idiopathic, probably results from pulmonary toxicity of chemotherapy and irradiation, although the possibility has been suggested that some cases represent the pulmonary manifestation of graft-versus-host disease.[461]

Pneumoconiosis

Pneumoconiosis is defined as the non-neoplastic reaction of the lungs to inhaled mineral or organic dust, exclusive of asthma, bronchitis, and emphysema.

Anthracosis refers to the presence of carbon particles in the lung and it is not a pathologic condition per se. The particles are concentrated around bronchovascular bundles, in interlobular septa, and beneath the pleura, therefore along the lymphatic vessel network. Carbon is relatively inert, and even if present in large amounts, it usually elicits little or no fibrosis. When it does elicit fibrosis, the result is *coal worker's pneumoconiosis*, which may present either as "coal nodules" (of little functional significance) or as progressive massive fibrosis (which results in pulmonary function abnormalities).[463]

Silicosis results from the deposition in the lung of particles of silica (quartz, silicon dioxide). The lesions are characterized by micronodular scars along the lymphatic network, particularly around bronchovascular bundles. Early lesions appear as cellular nodules composed of fibroblasts and histiocytes containing abundant silica particles; older nodules are less cellular and hyalinized. They may fuse to produce large masses, undergo necrosis, and cavitate. The edges of the nodule have a characteristic stellate shape. The arteries often show intimal and medial thickening.

The silica particles are best demonstrated under polarized light. They appear as birefringent spicules with pointed ends, 5 μm or less in length. They may be found intracellularly or extracellularly. It should be emphasized that the mere presence of silica particles in a lung specimen does not establish the diagnosis of silicosis. Such a diagnosis should be reserved for cases showing silica in association with the characteristic fibrous scars.[468]

Silicosis is often complicated by tuberculosis. The occurrence of silicosis in the presence of rheumatoid arthritis (which subsumes the morphologic changes in the silicotic nodules that result from it) are referred to as *Caplan's syndrome*.[464]

Mixed dust fibrosis is the term used for the pneumoconiosis resulting from mixed dust exposure, including silica and quartz. It affects foundry workers, arc welders, hematite miners, and boiler scalers.

Asbestosis manifests in the early stages as interstitial pneumonia with predominantly "mural" or desquamative features.[465] Hyperplastic alveolar cells may contain intracytoplasmic Mallory's hyaline tissue, a finding that is not specific for this disorder.[467] In later stages the interstitial fibrosis becomes more diffuse and results in honeycomb lung (Fig. 7.111). The involvement is more prominent in the basal segments. The morphologic features are not specific, and the diagnosis of asbestosis therefore requires the identification of asbestos bodies in the lesions, by conventional microscopy, electron microscopy, or incineration.[466] The typical asbestos body is a long, thin, symmetric, beaded structure with bulbous ends (Fig. 7.112). It is usually straight, but it may be bent or branched. Its core is translucent, and its coat is brown because of its iron content.

The chemical and environmental features of asbestos fibers and the pleural manifestations of the disease are discussed on p. 360.

Other pneumoconioses include siderosis (seen in iron

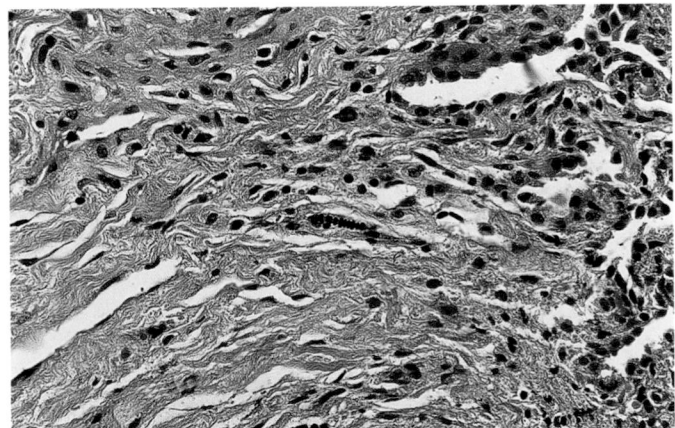

Fig. 7.111 Pulmonary asbestosis showing fibrosis of pleura and subjacent lung. A typical asbestos body is present in the center.

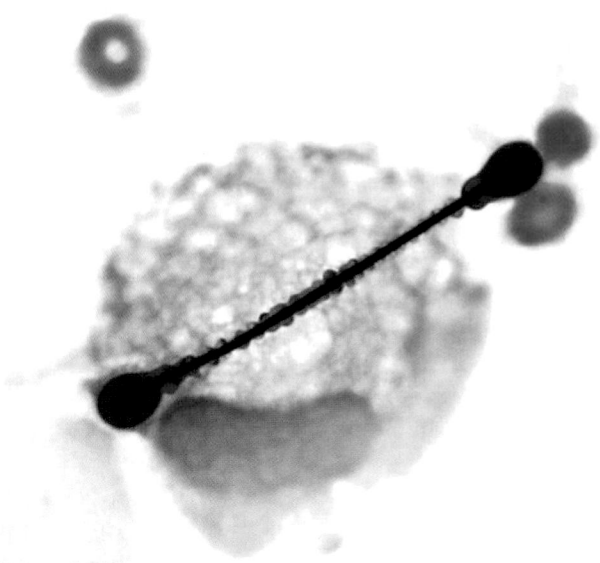

Fig. 7.112 Spectacular asbestos body. (Courtesy of Dr. F. Facchetti, Brescia, Italy)

workers, hematite miners, and welders), berylliosis, and disorders resulting from talc and other silicates, aluminum, hard metals, and silicon carbide.

Extrinsic allergic alveolitis

Extrinsic allergic alveolitis (hypersensitivity alveolitis) is the generic term given to an inflammatory process centered in the alveoli and representing a tissue reaction to an inhaled allergen.[470–472] Patients suffering from this condition have both cellular and humoral immune processes directed against the organic particulate. In a typical case, fever and dyspnea develop a few hours after inhalation of the material. With repeated exposures, a chronic lung disease develops.

Microscopically, there is interstitial and intra-alveolar alveolitis with a predominance of lymphocytes, granulomas, intra-alveolar "buds" made up of fibroblasts and other mesenchymal cells, and fibrosis.[471]

Some of the diseases included in this category are farmer's lung, maple-bark stripper's lung, pigeon-breeder's lung, budgerigar-fancier's lung, and mushroom-picker's lung. Thermophilic actinomycetes from air conditioners or humidifiers can produce acute pulmonary infiltrates or a chronic granulomatous process.[469]

Silo-filler's disease should be clearly separated from the aforementioned group, since it is a form of chemical pneumonitis secondary to nitrogen dioxide inhalation and is not characterized by the presence of granulomas.

Langerhans' cell histiocytosis and other histiocytic disorders

Langerhans' cell histiocytosis (histiocytosis X, eosinophilic granuloma) of the lung is most commonly seen in the third and fourth decades of life.[475,487,488] It is associated with smoking and it can present either as a circumscribed or as a diffuse process.[478] It predominates in the upper lobes and can produce nodular as well as cavitary lesions.[485] Honeycombing of the lung is a characteristic feature in the late stage of the disease. In approximately 20% of the patients, there is associated extrapulmonary involvement, usually in bones or the pituitary region. Spontaneous pneumothorax is a common complication. Microscopically, there is a compact interstitial infiltrate, often subpleural, composed of Langerhans' cells, numerous eosinophils, and reactive mesothelial cells (Fig. 7.113). Langerhans' cells are the essential element for the diagnosis; they have an abundant acidophilic cytoplasm and a vesicular nucleus, with typical grooves and indentations (however, similar grooves also can be seen in reactive mesothelial cells) (Fig. 7.114). Hemosiderin deposition and foci of necrosis are common.[480] Vasculitis may be present. In the healing stage, the disease may no longer be diagnosed microscopically. In these instances, immunohistochemical staining for S-100 protein, HLA-DR, and CD1a can be very helpful.[477,484,489] These stains can also be applied to cells from bronchoalveolar lavage fluid.[474]

Clonality studies with the HUMARA test has shown that the individual lesions can be either nonclonal (most often) or clonal, leaving open the question whether this condition should be regarded as reactive or neoplastic.[491]

The typical microscopic appearance of Langerhans' cell histiocytosis can be obscured by a superimposed infection by *Pneumocystic carinii* pneumonia.[479] Cases have also been reported of coexistent pulmonary Langerhans' cell histiocytosis and carcinoma, but it is not clear whether the two processes are pathogenetically related or not.[481,486]

In most patients with Langerhans' cell histiocytosis of the lung, the disease resolves or stabilizes, with few or no residual foci. A few patients develop progressive pulmonary disease that is ultimately fatal.[478]

Reactive eosinophilic pleuritis is a nonspecific reaction to pleural injury that may closely simulate Langerhans' cell histiocytosis because of the mixture of eosinophils and mesothelial cells (which can look very similar to the Langerhans' cells); in contrast to true eosinophilic granuloma, this lesion does not show interstitial lung disease on radiographic examination or Birbeck's granules on electron microscopic examination.[473] However, in some instances it may be accompanied by eosinophilic infiltration of the pulmonary vessels.[482]

Erdheim–Chester disease is another idiopathic histiocytic disorder which can affect the lung, in conjunction with bones (the latter often in the form of symmetric osteosclerosis) and the central nervous system.[473a] The pulmonary involvement is typically septal (lymphatic) in distribution and characterized by an infiltrate of foamy histiocytes, lymphocytes, and Touton giant cells (Fig. 7.115). The histiocytes are consistently positive for CD68,

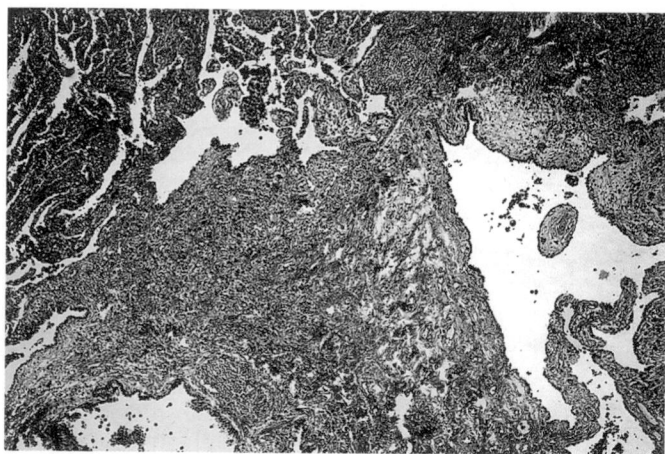

Fig. 7.113 Langerhans' cell histiocytosis. Marked interstitial widening due to mixed cellular infiltrate and associated fibrosis.

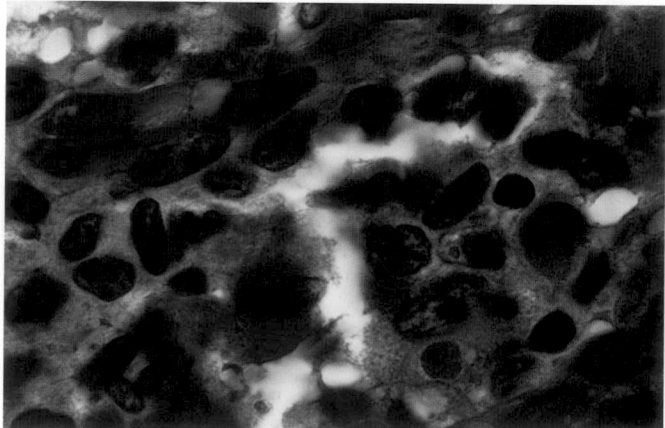

Fig. 7.114 Prominent longitudinal grooves in the nuclei of Langerhans' cells in a case of pulmonary Langerhans' cell histiocytosis.

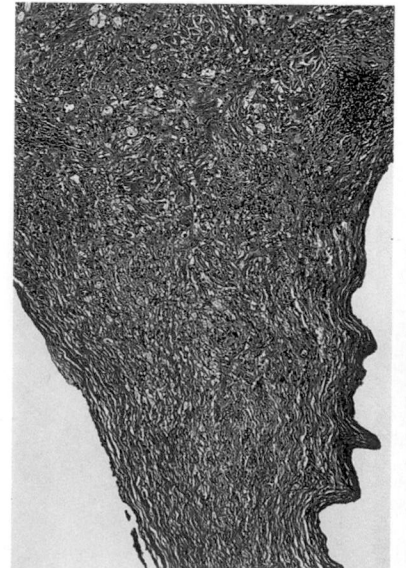
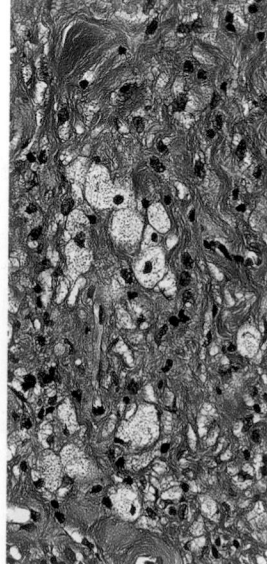

Fig. 7.115 A and **B**, Pulmonary manifestations of Erdheim–Chester disease. The septal pattern of involvement is characteristic. On high power, foamy macrophages encased in dense fibrous tissue are seen.

sometimes reactive for S-100 protein, and negative for CD1a. Birbeck's granules are absent.[476,483]

Rosai–Dorfman disease (sinus histiocytosis with massive lymphadenopathy) is seen in the lung parenchyma only exceptionally, in contrast to its relatively frequent involvement of the upper respiratory tract.[490]

Vascular diseases

Open lung biopsies are sometimes performed in patients with congenital heart disease and pulmonary hypertension to decide whether the state of the pulmonary vessels would allow corrective surgery.[492,499] The status of the arteries, veins, lymphatics, and lung parenchyma should be carefully evaluated in hematoxylin-eosin and elastic tissue stains.[493] Wagenvoort[501] considers pulmonary vascular disease reversible when the arterial lesions are restricted to medial hypertrophy, intimal thickening on the basis of longitudinal smooth muscle, post-thrombotic intimal fibrosis, or cellular intimal proliferation. Concentric-laminar intimal fibrosis of moderate or severe degree probably does not regress. Fibrinoid necrosis and/or plexiform (plexogenic) lesions are regarded as contraindications to surgery unless the nature of the defect is such that one lung is spared.[495] An increase in the number of neuroendocrine cells has been detected in hypertensive pulmonary vascular diseases.[498]

Pulmonary veno-occlusive disease predominantly affects children and adolescents, especially females.[494,500] Pulmonary hypertension develops because of the widespread occlusion of many large and medium-sized branches of the pulmonary veins, accompanied by recanalization and pseudoangiomatous changes.[502] Arterial thickening, as well as prominent hemosiderosis, also is present.[497] The etiology of the disease is unknown; an influenza-like illness has been found to precede many cases of this condition, and an immune-complex pathogenesis has been suggested.[496]

Other non-neoplastic diseases

Arteriovenous fistulas (aneurysms) are roentgenographically discernible, frequently multiple lesions that occur most often in the right lower and middle lobes (Figs 7.116 and 7.117). They are probably congenital and are made up of large vascular channels with arteriovenous communications.[526] Microscopically, the vessels are abnormal, often showing deficiencies and excesses of muscle, which make it impossible to distinguish artery from vein. Because of the shunt, there are bruit, cyanosis, polycythemia, and low oxygen content of arterial blood. Excision is curative.

Broncholithiasis can be seen as a complication of food aspiration, bronchiectasis, or granulomatous diseases (particularly tuberculosis and histoplasmosis).[504,524] The term *broncholith* has been used for any calcification that impinges on and distorts a bronchus. Others prefer to

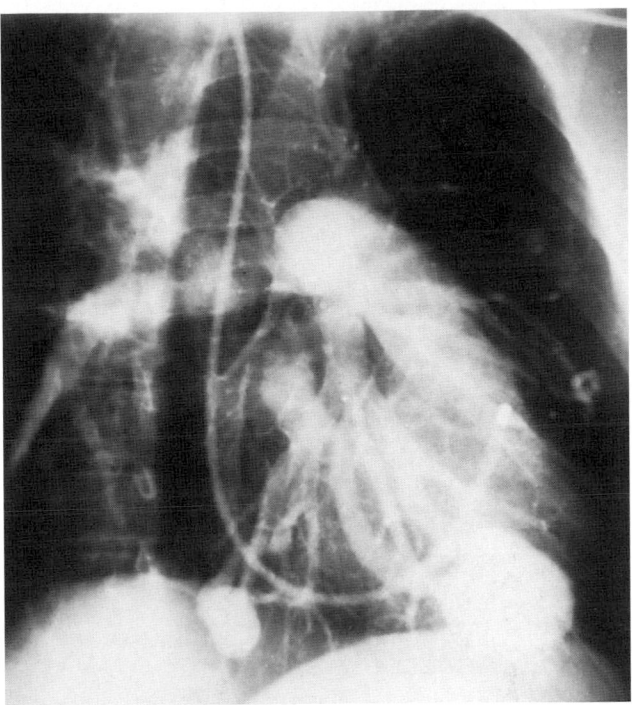

Fig. 7.116 Angiogram of a 28-year-old man with multiple arteriovenous fistulas. The patient had Rendu–Osler–Weber syndrome. After left lower lobectomy, oxygen saturation rose from 86% to 95%.

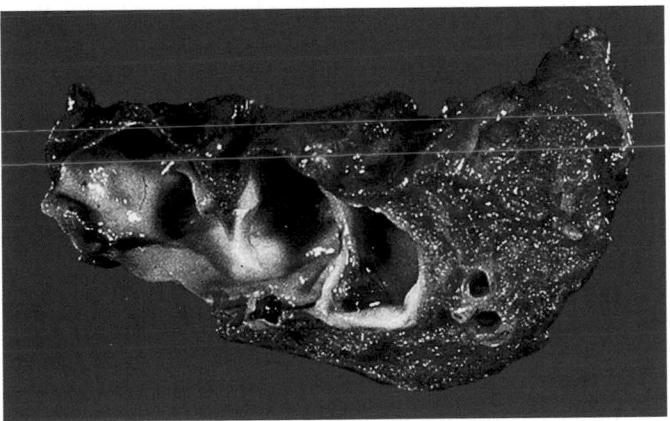

Fig. 7.117 Gross appearance of pulmonary arteriovenous fistula.

restrict the term to a calcified tissue fragment found floating within the bronchial lumen.

Infarcts are usually identified as such on radiographic examination because of their pleural-based triangular shape. However, occasionally they simulate a malignant tumor and are resected surgically (Fig. 7.118).

Alveolar proteinosis is perihilar in distribution, roentgenographically resembling the picture of pulmonary edema. It is being increasingly recognized as an important cause of diffuse pulmonary disease in immunocompromised patients.[508] Consequently, it is now generally regarded as a type of response to alveolar injury rather than as a specific entity. Its occasional coexistence with other conditions, such as nocardiosis,

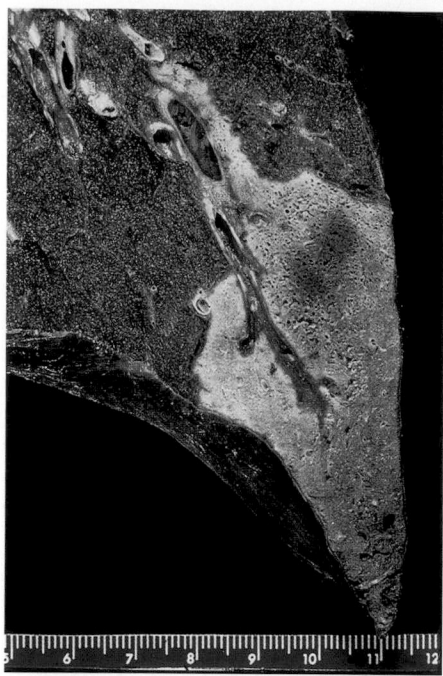

Fig. 7.118 Typical wedge-shaped appearance of pleural-based pulmonary infarct. A large occluding thrombus is evident in the vessel leading to the area of the infarct.

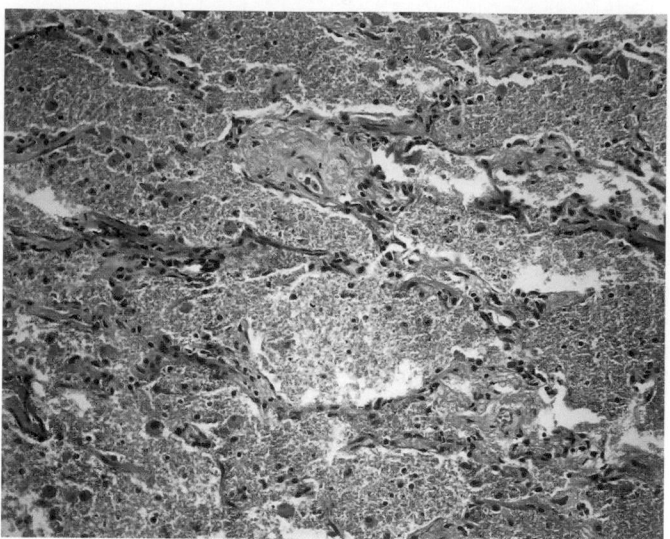

Fig. 7.119 Filling of alveolar spaces by amorphous grumous material in alveolar proteinosis.

histoplasmosis, cryptococcosis, aspergillosis, tuberculosis, cytomegalovirus infection, and a wide range of hematologic malignancies, supports this contention.[506,531,536]

Microscopically, the hallmark of the process is the accumulation of an amorphous eosinophilic (but sometimes basophilic) PAS-positive material of predominantly phospholipid nature in the alveolar lumina, associated with some proliferation and desquamation of granular pneumocytes, small lymphoid accumulations in the interstitium, and some degree of fibrosis[532] (Fig. 7.119). The disease results from an accumulation of surfactant apoprotein through either increased secretion by granular pneumocytes or abnormal uptake and handling of this material by alveolar macrophages.[509,533] It is usually treated by whole-lung lavage.[514]

Idiopathic hemosiderosis classically presents in young adults with hemoptysis and refractory anemia.[535] Roentgenograms of the lung often show a granular perihilar infiltrate. Microscopically, large accumulations of hemosiderin-laden macrophages in the alveolar lumina are accompanied by proliferation of alveolar lining cells. Necrosis, vasculitis, granulomas, and lymphoid follicles do not occur, and there are no deposits of IgG on the alveolar basement membranes.[513] The latter finding is important in the differential diagnosis with Goodpasture's syndrome, which it may simulate in routine sections.[503,512]

In **Goodpasture's syndrome** there are an associated glomerulonephritis, circulating antiglomerular basement membrane antibodies, and linear deposits of IgG along glomerular and alveolar basement membranes.[522a] The differential diagnosis of hemorrhagic lung disorders also includes those diseases known to cause secondary pulmonary alveolar bleeding and hemosiderosis, such as mitral stenosis, periarteritis nodosa, lupus erythematosus, and other forms of systemic vasculitis.[515,524,527,540]

Hematoma of the lung can present as a distinct round mass that radiographically resembles a neoplasm; it usually develops as a result of blunt trauma to the thorax.[517]

Amyloidosis of the lung can be divided into four categories on the basis of distribution: vascular (never a serious clinical problem), nodular bronchial, nodular parenchymal, and diffuse alveolar septal.[507,510,525,538,539] Radiographically, lesions in the second and third categories can be solitary or multiple and can simulate tuberculosis or a metastatic neoplasm. Lesions of the fourth type lead to a severe impairment of lung function, a diffuse infiltrate on roentgenographic examination, and a poor prognosis.[523,525] The amyloid material is mostly made up of AL protein.

Hyalinizing granuloma is usually multiple and bilateral.[516] Microscopically, the central portion is made up of hyalinized, keloid-like collagen. This is surrounded by a foreign body response, the overall appearance simulating nodular amyloidosis. However, special stains for amyloid are negative. Necrotic areas and non-necrotizing epithelioid granulomas are distinctly unusual in this condition, which is of importance in the differential diagnosis. No infectious agents have been identified (except for a case associated with *Aspergillus* infection),[529] and the pathogenesis remains unknown. Four of the cases reported by Engleman et al.[516] were complicated by sclerosing mediastinitis and one by retroperitoneal fibrosis. In another series, more than half of the patients had autoimmune phenomena or previous exposures to mycobacterial or fungal antigens.[542] This suggests that hyalinizing granuloma represents a peculiar immune reaction.

Endometriosis of the lung may present with recurrent catamenial hemoptysis, or as asymptomatic nodules discovered on routine chest x-ray film.[521] Most of the reported cases have been located on the right side (see p. 360). The disease often extends to the pleural surface. A related condition is *ectopic deciduosis*.[518]

Pulmonary alveolar microlithiasis is a rare disease characterized by the presence of microliths or calcospherites within the alveoli of an otherwise normal lung. The process is diffuse and bilateral, and the clinical course is extremely long. The chest x-ray appearance is virtually diagnostic.[530]

Rheumatoid lung disease can present in a wide variety of patterns: diffuse interstitial fibrosis, bronchiolitis obliterans, coarse scarring, marked arterial sclerosis, necrotizing vasculitis, interstitial lymphocytic infiltration with germinal center formation, nodular fibrosis associated with pneumoconiosis (Caplan's syndrome), juxtabronchiolar microgranulomas, rheumatoid nodules, and pleuritis.[519,528,541] The latter is discussed on p. 360.

Apical caps are biconvex zones of fibrosis with focal chronic inflammatory changes found in the lung apices; they are nonspecific, unrelated to tuberculosis, and perhaps having a vascular ischemic pathogenesis.[543]

Rounded atelectasis (also known as folded lung syndrome and shrinking pleuritis) represents a localized area of subpleural lung collapse associated with pleural fibrosis.[511] A history of exposure to asbestos is common.[522] Radiographically, the lesion may simulate a malignant tumor.[537] Most cases are in the posterior aspect of a lower lobe. Grossly, the lung beneath an irregularly thickened pleura shows an ill-defined area of atelectasis that may

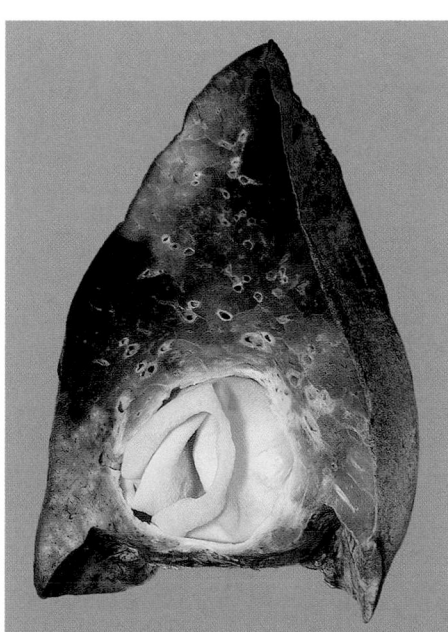

Fig. 7.120 Gross appearance of hydatidosis of lung. (Courtesy of Dr. RA Cooke, Brisbane, Australia; from Cooke RA, Stewart B: Colour Atlas of Anatomical Pathology. Edinburgh, Churchill Livingstone, 2004).

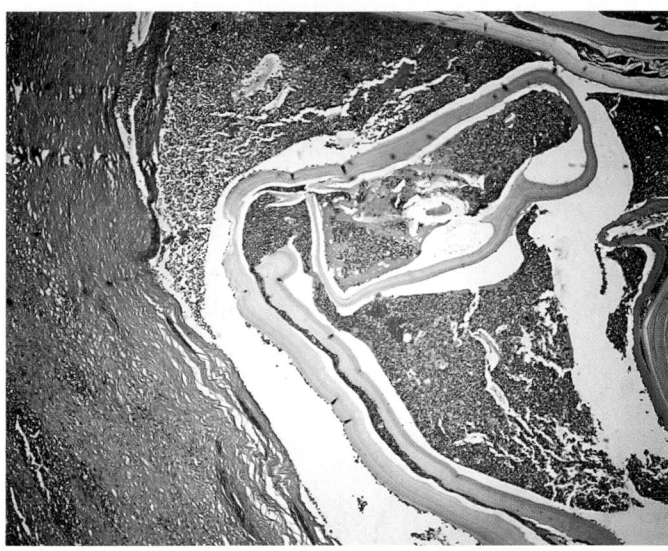

Fig. 7.121 Microscopic appearance of pulmonary hydatidosis.

contain deeply invaginated pleural folds. It is typical for the lesion to "vanish" while being dissected. Microscopically, there are pleural fibrosis and invagination (the latter well demonstrated with elastic tissue stains), associated with atelectasis of the subjacent lung.

Malakoplakia of the lung is very rare; most of the reported cases have been in immunocompromised patients.[505,534,540] The microscopic appearance is similar to that seen in the bladder and other sites (see Chapter 17).

Hydatidosis (echinococcosis) results from infestation by Echinococcus granulosus (which is usually cystic) and only rarely by infestation by Echinococcus multilocularis (which causes alveolar echinococcosis) (Figs 7.120 and 7.121).[519a]

Carcinoma

General and clinical features

Carcinoma of the lung has become increasingly frequent during the past 60 years. This increase is seen in male and especially in female patients and applies to all the major microscopic types.[583] Much has been written about the cause of this phenomemon.[553] Many factors thought in the past to be of pathogenetic importance—such as tuberculosis, tarring of roads, the 1918 influenza epidemic, anthracosis, and anthracosilicosis—are now considered to be totally unrelated to cancer or to account for only a minimal fraction of cases. Exposure to asbestos; polycyclic aromatic hydrocarbons; arsenic, nickel, and chromium compounds; BCME; CMME; vinyl chloride; radiation (as seen in uranium workers and in people with high radon concentration in their houses); and other occupational agents undoubtedly account for some of the cases.[546,552,565,578,584,585,589,590] This is particularly true for asbestosis, which is thought to be responsible for about 5% of all lung carcinoma deaths.[548,573] However, the significance of all these factors pales by comparison with the role played by cigarette smoking, both in males and in females.[567] This is true for all major histologic types of lung carcinoma.[574] The fact that smokers living in urban areas and/or exposed to asbestos are at a higher risk for lung carcinoma than others suggests the potentiating effect of air pollution and asbestos on the carcinogenic effect of tobacco, a possibility that is supported by some experimental models.[560] Significantly, in animals there is a nearly total absence of spontaneous lung tumors that are histologically similar to the smoking-related human lung cancers.[562]

The relationship of cigarette smoking with malignant, dysplastic, and metaplastic alterations of the tracheobronchial tree has also been thoroughly documented by the meticulous histologic observations of Auerbach et al.[547] and confirmed by others[582]; at autopsy, the former authors found an almost linear correlation between the severity of the changes and the degree of cigarette consumption.

Another factor thought to be related to the development of carcinoma is pulmonary fibrosis, through a preceding stage of atypical proliferation of the terminal bronchiolar epithelium. Malignant tumors arising at the site of scars resulting from bullets or other foreign bodies have been well documented. Carcinomas arising adjacent to old granulomas are also on record.[593] However, these constitute an infinitesimal fraction of lung cancers. In most of the peripheral lung tumors diagnosed as "scar carcinomas," the scar is probably the result rather than the cause of the cancer (see also p. 392). A somewhat related problem is posed by the diffuse fibrosis seen in interstitial lung disease with honeycombing; of 153 resected lung tumors evaluated in a classic study by Meyer and Liebow,[569] 22% were associated with—and presumably preceded by—honeycombing and atypical epithelial proliferation. Most of these tumors were in the upper lobe, and one third of them were adenocarcinomas.

Along the same lines, the concept of atypical adenomatous hyperplasia of type 2 alveolar cells or bronchioloalveolar cell adenomas as a precursor of adenocarcinoma has been proposed in several recent articles.[550,564,570,575-577]

A few cases of lung carcinoma have been found to originate from a malignant transformation of papillomatosis of the respiratory tract (see p. 421).[551,556] On the whole, however, HPV does not seem to play an important role in the genesis of lung carcinoma.[586]

Lung carcinoma is more common in males than females, but the difference is decreasing because of a proportionally higher increase in women.[588] The current male:female ratio is 1.5:1. More than 90% of the patients are over 40 years old at the time of the diagnosis,[563] but cases have also been reported in young adults and adolescents.[572]

Lung carcinoma is multiple in about 2% to 5% of the cases[549] (either synchronous or metachronous) and is associated with independent cancer of the head and neck region in about 20% of the cases.[557,568] Genetic molecular studies have shown that at least half of the multicentric lung tumors (whether synchronous or metachronous) show evidence of a different clonal origin and that they are therefore independent from each other.[559]

Most lung cancers are of considerable size when first detected, and about 60% are incurable as a result of extensive local spread and/or distant metastases.[544] Symptoms and signs develop relatively late in the course of the disease, are usually related to partial or complete bronchial obstruction, and may lead to confusion with a primary inflammatory process.[579]

The most common symptoms, in decreasing order of frequency, are cough, weight loss, pain, increased sputum production, hemoptysis, malaise, fever, and those resulting from paraneoplastic manifestations. Peripherally located lesions are clinically silent until they reach a sufficient size to ulcerate into a bronchus or to involve the pleural space. Carcinomas located in the superior pulmonary sulcus result in a clinical picture peculiar to their location, known as *Pancoast's syndrome*.[545,581] This is characterized by pain in the distribution of the ulnar nerve and is often accompanied by Horner's syndrome secondary to involvement of the sympathetic chain.

Sometimes lung carcinoma presents as a solitary circumscribed mass ("coin lesion") on the chest x-ray film of an asymptomatic individual. About 35% to 50% of pulmonary coin lesions in adults represent lung carcinoma.[587] The percentage is higher for patients older than 60 years and for noncalcified lesions. The incidence of malignancy in coin lesions exhibiting obvious calcification is less than 1%. Lung neoplasms are sometimes associated with extrapulmonary manifestations not related to the presence of metastatic disease.[552a,580] Although exceptions occur, there is a fairly good correlation between some morphologic parameters and the systemic effect produced.[591] These are summarized in Table 7.1. These manifestations are caused by the tumor's secretion of biologically active compounds. In the case of the Lambert-Eaton syndrome associated with small cell carcinoma, voltage-gated calcium antibodies have a pathophysiologic role.[566] Additional substances that have been detected in some cases of lung carcinoma include amylase, calcitonin, CEA, α–fetoprotein (AFP), β-pregnancy-specific glycoprotein, and epidermal growth factor receptors. A preponderance of small cell carcinomas exists in this group; however, the correlation between the presence of a tumor marker and the microscopic type is generally poor.[554,555,558,561,563,571,592]

Table 7.1 Systemic effects of lung carcinoma and their statistical relationship with tumor type

Systemic effect and hormone responsible	Tumor type
Cushing syndrome (ACTH)	Small cell carcinoma
	Bronchial carcinoid
Carcinoid syndrome	Bronchial carcinoid
	Small cell carcinoma
Hyponatremia (ADH)	Small cell carcinoma
Hyperparathyroidism (parathormone)	Squamous cell carcinoma
Gynecomastia (HCG)	All tumor types
Clubbing of fingers and hypertrophic pulmonary osteoarthropathy	Unrelated to tumor type; mainly dependent on proximity to pleural surface
Mental syndromes (i.e., toxic confusional psychosis)	Small cell carcinoma
Cortical cerebellar degeneration	All tumor types
Encephalomyelitis	Small cell carcinoma
Sensory neuropathy	Small cell carcinoma
Myopathic-myasthenic syndrome (Lambert-Eaton syndrome)	Small cell carcinoma

Pathologic and generic immunohistochemical features

Several microscopic classifications of lung carcinoma exist. The one most widely used derives from the scheme originally proposed by Kreyberg[606] and adopted with the unavoidable changes made necessary by new advances in the field—by the WHO Committee[615] and the authors of the *3rd Series Atlas of Tumor Pathology*.[596] It includes the following major categories:

1 Squamous cell carcinoma

   a Well differentiated
   b Moderately differentiated
   c Poorly differentiated

2 Adenocarcinoma

   a Not otherwise specified (NOS)
   b Bronchioloalveolar

3 Adenosquamous carcinoma
4 Small cell carcinoma

   a Classic
   b Mixed small cell/large cell
   c Combined

5 Undifferentiated large cell carcinoma
6 Giant cell carcinoma

Several independent studies have shown the applicability and reproducibility of this classification and the fact that there is a very close correlation in tumor type among the biopsy specimen, the surgical specimen, and the lymph node metastases.[604] The greater degree of interobserver variability is found in identifying undifferentiated large cell carcinomas vis-à-vis poorly differentiated adenocarcinomas and poorly differentiated squamous cell carcinoma.[598,603,605] Fortunately, these morphologic distinctions have few practical implications. Greater discrimination is obtained when ultrastructural examination is carried out in every tumor, but one fails to appreciate the practical value of such a costly effort.[594,595] In this regard, it is important to emphasize that the WHO classification of lung tumors is based on light microscopic criteria.

Part of the difficulty in sharply separating lung carcinomas into the previously described categories stems from the fact that many of them show a combination of patterns.[597,608,614] In a study of 100 consecutive cases of lung carcinoma in which either the entire tumor or ten blocks were examined, only 34% were composed of a single histologic type.[611] Early hopes that immunocytochemical determinations would provide a sharper separation into distinct types have not materialized; on the contrary, there is evidence for considerable overlap of antigenic profile between different histologic types.[599,600] At a practical level, one should also realize that the method used to classify the tumors will greatly influence the results. Thus adenosquamous carcinoma will constitute a much higher proportion of cases in series studied by electron microscopy than in those based exclusively on routine light microscopy.[603,612]

The histochemical, immunohistochemical, ultrastructural and molecular-genetic features of lung carcinoma are discussed with the respective cases. Suffice to say here that the most important generic immunomarkers of lung carcinomas are:

- *Keratins.* They are present in all types of lung carcinomas, but the expression of the individual keratins is dependent upon the tumor subtype;
- *Surfactant apoprotein A.* This is primarily a product of type 2 (granular) pneumocytes. It is expressed in about half of the adenocarcinomas and in about one quarter of the other non-small cell lung carcinomas.

Surfactant apoprotein A is detected with the antibody PE-10, which unfortunately it is not widely available[617];

- *TTF-1.* Thyroid transcription factor-1, which is consistently expressed in the normal pulmonary airways, has emerged as one of the most useful markers of epithelial lung tumors.[607] It is expressed in about three quarters of the adenocarcinomas and in a smaller percentage of the other lung carcinoma types.[616] Therefore, its detection in metastases in brain or other sites is an almost certain indicator that the primary tumor is in the lung.[613] There is only one major proviso: as its name indicates, the other tissue in which TTF-1 is consistently expressed is the thyroid epithelium.[609,610,616,617] Parenthetically, the detection of this marker is also possible in cytologic preparations.[601]

Squamous cell carcinoma

The majority of squamous cell carcinomas occur in males. Most cases are centered in segmental bronchi (Fig. 7.122) and therefore present as hilar or perihilar masses in chest x-ray film. However, they can also be found peripherally and even subpleurally.[623a,631] As a group, they are larger than the other types at the time of the diagnosis.[618] Signs of bronchial obstruction, such as obstructive pneumonitis or atelectasis, are found in approximately half of the patients. Exfoliated malignant cells are more commonly identified in sputum cytology specimens than for other types of lung carcinoma. The tumors have a special tendency to undergo central necrosis with cavitation (Fig. 7.123). On the other hand, calcification is extremely unusual. Rarely, squamous cell carcinoma presents as an intrabronchial polypoid mass with only minor extrabronchial spread.[623] Microscopically, the diagnosis of malignancy is based on cell atypia and invasiveness, and the diagnosis of squamous cell type on the detection of keratin and/or intercellular bridges (Fig. 7.124). Keratin formation may be seen in isolated cells or, more commonly, in the form of "keratin

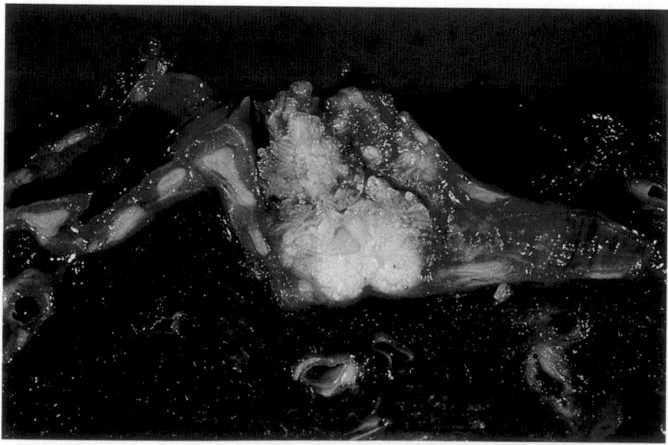

Fig. 7.122 Intraluminal bronchial growth of squamous cell carcinoma.

Fig. 7.123 Large squamous cell carcinoma extending into the pleura and associated with central cavitation.

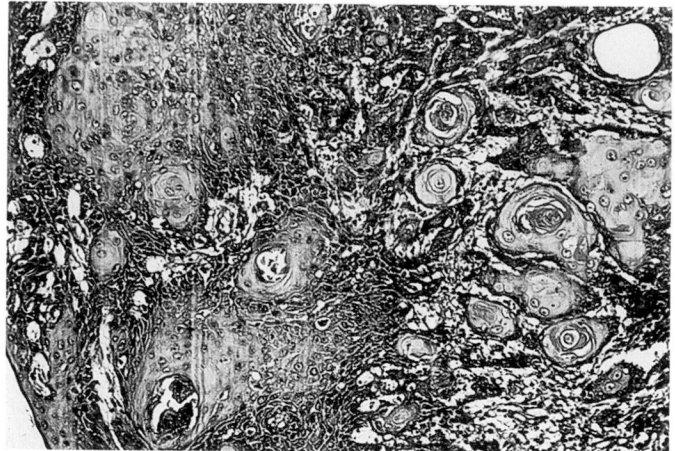

Fig. 7.124 Microscopic appearance of well-differentiated squamous cell carcinoma.

pearls." Isolated necrotic cells should not be confused with keratinized cells. Whorl formation and definite stratification of tumor cells have been used by some as presumptive evidence of squamous differentiation in the absence of the features listed, but according to the WHO classification, these tumors should be placed in an undifferentiated large cell category.

The finding of an occasional intracytoplasmic mucin droplet in an otherwise typical squamous cell carcinoma should not lead to a reclassification of the tumor. Only when substantial components of adenocarcinoma and/or small cell carcinoma are present is the designation of *mixed carcinoma* (followed by a listing of the specific components) justified.

Other morphologic features that can be encountered in squamous cell carcinoma include oncocytoid appearance of the tumor cells (due to increased mitochondrial density); giant cell foreign body reaction to keratin; palisaded granulomas; extensive infiltration by neutrophils and other inflammatory cells (simulating inflammatory malignant fibrous histiocytoma); and lepidic type of growth into air spaces at the tumor periphery.[625] In addition, morphologic features may be present that are distinctive enough to place the tumor into a special subset, as follows:

1 *Small cell variant.* The tumor cells are small, with only focal keratinization. The distinction from small cell carcinoma (and combined small cell/squamous cell carcinoma) can be difficult. In the small cell variant of squamous cell carcinoma, the nuclei are more vesicular and have better defined nucleoli, the tumor nests are more sharply outlined, the stroma is more mature, and there is less necrosis.

2 *Clear cell variant.* Clear cells are numerous (usually because of glycogen accumulation), but the tumor still shows clearcut evidence of keratinization. It should be remembered that clear cell changes occur more frequently in other types of lung carcinoma, particularly adenocarcinoma.

3 *Well-differentiated papillary.* This presents as a delicate intrabronchial papillary lesion with little or no stromal invasion and practically no necrosis.

4 *Basaloid.* This is an important subgroup, characterized by a very aggressive clinical course.[623b,626] The morphologic features are analogous to those of the homonymous tumor in the upper aerodigestive tract (see Chapters 5 and 11).

5 *Spindle cell (sarcomatoid)/carcinosarcoma* (see p. 397).

Squamous cell carcinomas are graded into well, moderately, and poorly differentiated on the basis of the amount of keratinization present; this determination should be based on the features of the predominant component. Electron microscopic examination shows abundant tonofilaments, complex desmosomes, and basal lamina formation (Fig. 7.125).[621,624] Immunohistochemically, there is reactivity for low- and high-molecular-weight keratin, and for involucrin.[627–629]

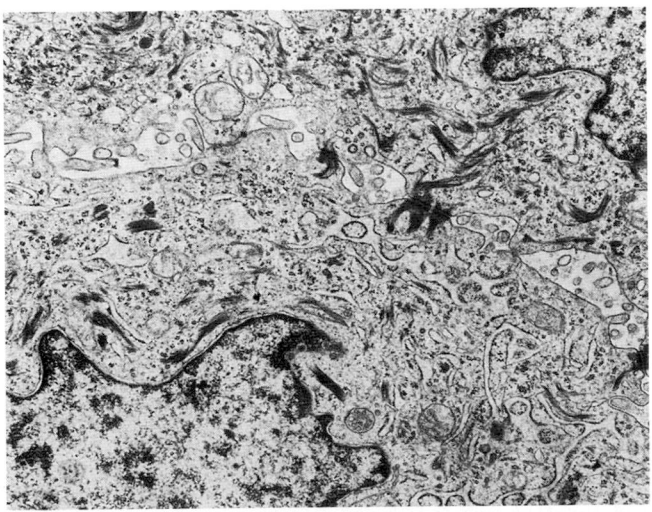

Fig. 7.125 Squamous cell carcinoma of lung. Neoplastic cells with numerous tonofilaments, some of them attached to desmosomes. This is characteristic of squamous differentiation. (×16,850)

The latter is a precursor of the cross-linked envelope protein or marginal band present in the stratum corneum. Immunoreactivity has also been found in at least some of the cases for vimentin, EMA, human milk fat globule (HMF6-2), S-100 protein, Leu-M1, and CEA.

p53 mutations are common and seem to appear at an early stage.[622,635] The product p63 (a p53-homologous nuclear protein) is consistently expressed in pulmonary squamous cell carcinoma but not in small cell carcinoma, and therefore it constitutes a potentially useful tool to distinguish these two tumors.[633]

The bronchial mucosa adjacent to the tumor usually shows squamous metaplasia and sometimes carcinoma in situ, occasionally extending several centimeters from the main mass.[620]

Presence of HPV has been documented in close to 20% of squamous cell carcinomas, the percentage being substantially higher in those showing condylomatous features in the adjacent epithelium (see also p. 421).[619]

At the genetic molecular level, the most common abnormality so far detected in squamous cell carcinoma is loss of FHIT protein,[630,632] followed in frequency by alterations of p53 and p16, but only rarely of the Rb gene.[634]

Adenocarcinoma

Adenocarcinomas comprise approximately half of all lung carcinomas in females and a lower percentage of those in males.[643,689] In absolute numbers, however, they are more common in males than in females. There is epidemiologic evidence suggesting that adenocarcinoma is becoming progressively more prevalent as compared with other microscopic types of lung cancer,[688] to the extent that in some recent series it has become the most common form.[646,686] Grossly, adenocarcinomas usually present as poorly circumscribed gray–yellow lesions (Fig. 7.126). They may be single or multiple.[665] If they secrete abundant mucin, they have a mucoid, glairy appearance. Cavitation is extremely unusual. About 65% of the cases are located peripherally, and 77% involve the

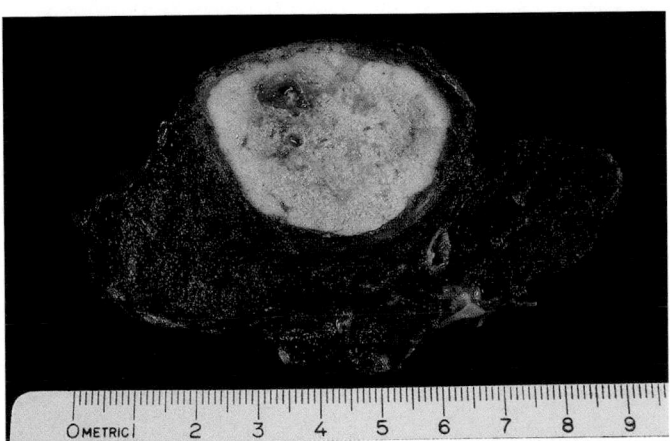

Fig. 7.126 Typical peripheral location of pulmonary adenocarcinoma.

visceral pleura at the time of excision, often resulting in pleural fibrosis or "puckering" (Fig. 7.127). Occasionally, a small peripheral adenocarcinoma spreads massively into the pleural space and coats both pleural layers so as to closely simulate the appearance of diffuse mesothelioma (*pseudomesotheliomatous carcinoma*)[647,650,660,661] (Fig. 7.128). Even rarer is the presentation of adenocarcinoma as a large endobronchial polypoid mass.[659]

A high percentage of adenocarcinomas arise in association with a peripheral scar or honeycombing and may show foci of atypical bronchiolar and alveolar proliferation in the neighboring air spaces.[640,667,671,675,681,692] In a series of eighty-two "scar cancers" reviewed by Auerbach et al.,[639] 72% were adenocarcinomas and 18% were squamous cell carcinomas, the rest being large cell undifferentiated carcinomas. There were no small cell carcinomas. Some controversy has arisen as to whether the scar precedes the appearance of the carcinoma or whether the fibrosis represents a desmoplastic host reaction to the tumor. Immunophenotyping of the collagen present in the scar suggests that the latter mechanism is the most prevalent.[642,644,662,666]

Microscopically, adenocarcinomas exhibit a wide range of differentiation, one extreme blending with bronchioloalveolar carcinoma and the other with undifferentiated large cell carcinoma.[664,683a] The two morphologic signs of glandular differentiation, often found together, are formation of tubules or papillae and secretion of mucin (Fig. 7.129). Depending on the relative prominence of these features, adenocarcinomas have been subdivided into *acinar*, *papillary*, and *solid (adeno)carcinomas with mucin production*, but considerable overlap exists among these groups. *Papillary carcinoma* is a particularly interesting form of pulmonary carcinoma because of its controversial relationship with bronchioloalveolar carcinoma, and its sometimes close morphologic similarity with metastatic papillary thyroid carcinoma, the latter complicated by the fact that the two tumors share immunoreactivity for TTF-1. It has been stated that lung adenocarcinomas with a predominantly

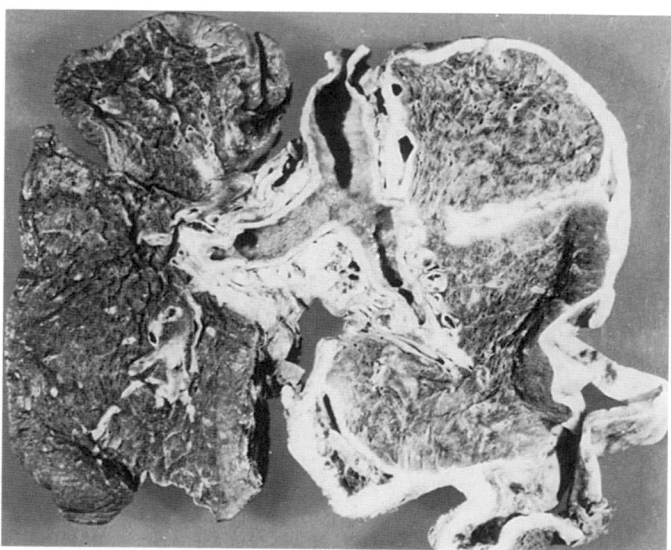

Fig. 7.128 Peripheral adenocarcinoma of lung spreading diffusely to pleural surfaces and closely simulating the gross appearance of malignant mesothelioma. Note metastases in perihilar and intertracheobronchial nodes.

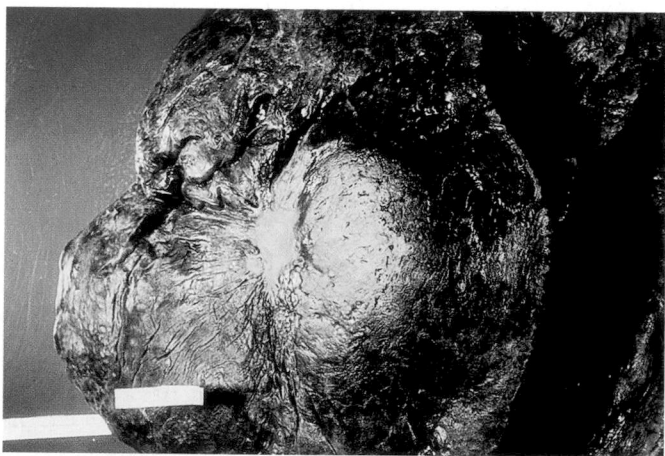

A

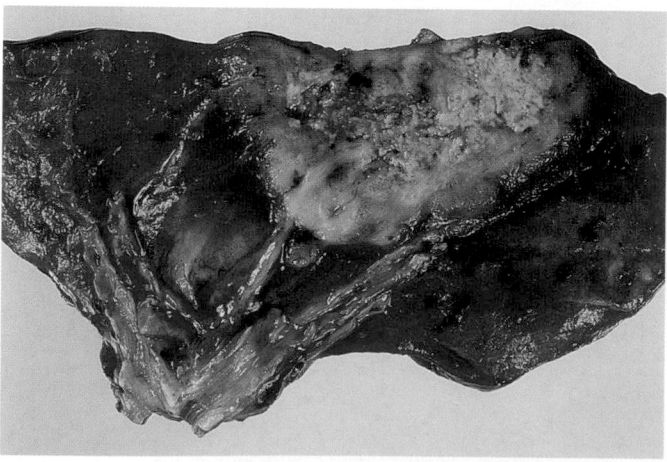

B

Fig. 7.127 A and **B**, Outer aspect and cut section of two pulmonary adenocarcinomas showing pleural retraction.

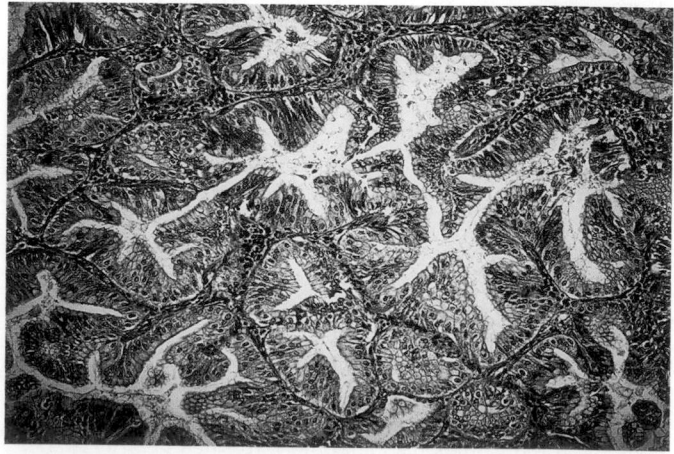

Fig. 7.129 Well-differentiated adenocarcinoma.

micropapillary of growth are associated with a poor prognosis.[637,668] Rare variants of adenocarcinoma include *signet ring adenocarcinoma*[658,695] (Fig. 7.130), *mucinous carcinoma*,[670] *adenocarcinoma with enteric (goblet cell)*[650,684] and *hepatoid differentiation*,[638,654] and *adenocarcinoma with choriocarcinomatous foci*.[636]

It should be remembered that lining of tumor cells along alveolar walls, a pattern of growth that many primary or metastatic tumor types may exhibit, can simulate gland formation. A much rarer phenomenon is pagetoid spread along the mucosa of large bronchi.[652] On occasion, the adenocarcinoma cells exhibit prominent eosinophilic intracytoplasmic globules.[677]

Blood vessel invasion was identified by Bennett et al.[643] in 86% of the 100 adenocarcinomas they examined. In the same series, metastases to peribronchial or hilar lymph nodes were found in half of patients. The resectability rate was 71%, about twice the overall rates for the lung carcinoma.

By electron microscopy, neoplastic counterparts of all the major cells lining the bronchial tree may be found in adenocarcinoma; this includes goblet cells, mucous cells, nonciliated bronchiolar cells, and Clara cells.[648,653,657,683]

Immunohistochemically, there is reactivity for low molecular weight keratins, EMA, CEA, and secretory components.[641,656,674,676] Expression of keratin 7 has been taken as evidence of glandular differentiation in lung carcinoma.[687] Sometimes there is coexpression of keratin and vimentin.[685] S-100 protein-positive Langerhans' cells are frequent in the stroma.[649] In about half of cases there is positivity for surfactant apoprotein (PE-10), a feature of use in the differential diagnosis with other types of primary lung carcinoma and—most important—with metastatic adenocarcinoma.[669,672] Cathepsin B and basement membrane components are also encountered.[682] Lung adenocarcinomas also show consistent expression of Lewis X and Y blood group antigens, a feature that may be of some differential diagnostic value.[655,678]

Overexpression of the p53 tumor suppressor gene product in pulmonary adenocarcinoma has been found to be specifically associated with cigarette smoking[690] and to represent a very early event in the genesis of this tumor.[663] The detection of K-*ras* oncogene activation in lung adenocarcinomas from former smokers suggests that K-*ras* mutations constitute an early and irreversible event in the development of this tumor type.[691] K-*ras* mutation also occurs in atypical bronchioloalveolar hyperplasia[673] and is said to be an indicator of poor prognosis in adenocarcinoma.[679]

Undifferentiated large cell carcinoma

Undifferentiated large cell carcinomas are pleomorphic malignant epithelial tumors without definite evidence of either squamous or glandular differentiation.[710,716] The tumor cells are large, at least in comparison with those of small cell carcinoma (Fig. 7.131). These tumors probably do not represent a specific entity but are rather poorly differentiated variants of squamous cell carcinoma, adenocarcinoma, and perhaps even small cell carcinoma.[720] Electron microscopic studies have supported this interpretation by demonstrating in many cases the presence of intracellular and extracellular lumina (as evidence of glandular differentiation) or well-formed desmosomes with numerous tonofilaments (as evidence of squamous cell carcinoma).[693,703,709] The location of these tumors (as seen radiographically) and the combination of ultrastructural and immunohistochemical features suggests a closer relation to adenocarcinoma than to the other tumor types.[697,706] Some large cell carcinomas are associated with marked peripheral eosinophilia or leukocytosis[694,711]; this seems to be caused by the production of granulocyte colony-stimulating factor by the tumor.[715]

In addition to the usual type of undifferentiated large cell carcinoma composed of solid sheets of relatively uniform large tumor cells, several less common patterns have been observed, some of them qualifying as variants of this tumor type, as follows:

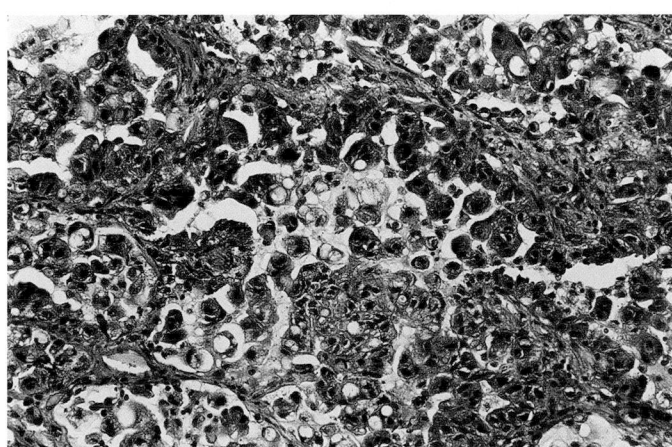

Fig. 7.130 Primary pulmonary adenocarcinoma with signet ring cells, a most unusual finding in this location.

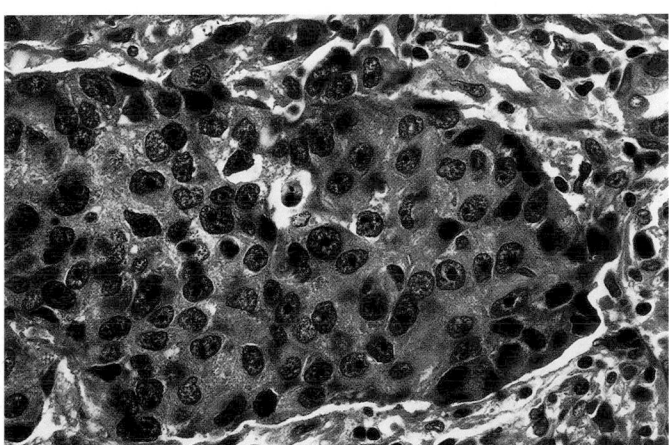

Fig. 7.131 Large cell undifferentiated carcinoma.

1 *Giant cell carcinoma*. This is characterized by the presence of bizarre multinucleated giant cells that alternate with mononuclear forms in a solid fashion simulating sarcoma (Fig. 7.132).[701,705,718] A heavy neutrophilic infiltration can be seen between and inside the tumor cells and may be accompanied by peripheral leukocytosis. Most tumors are peripheral in location and are quite extensive at the time of diagnosis. In some cases, foci of glandular differentiation and/or mucin production have been identified, suggesting that some of these tumors represent "dedifferentiated" forms of adenocarcinoma,[708] and that pulmonary giant cell carcinoma is a morphologic phenotype rather than a pathological entity.[695] As in other organs (such as thyroid and breast), lung carcinomas with tumor giant cells should be distinguished from those containing osteoclast-like giant cells (with the understanding that the two cell types can coexist in the same neoplasm).[712]

2 *Lymphoepithelioma-like carcinoma*. This variant is morphologically analogous to the homonymous tumor in the upper respiratory tract and, as such, characterized by a seemingly syncytial pattern of growth, large vesicular nuclei, prominent eosinophilic nucleoli, and a heavy lymphocytic infiltration.[696] In some cases the latter feature is so prominent that it results in a mistaken diagnosis of either inflammatory pseudotumor or malignant lymphoma.[713] The presence of the EBV genome has been documented in several cases of pulmonary lymphoepithelioma-like carcinoma,[699,704,714] but this seems to be more often the case in Oriental than in Western countries.[698,700] The prognosis of lymphoepithelioma-like carcinoma is better than that of any of the conventional non-small cell carcinomas of equivalent stage.[702,707]

3 *Large cell neuroendocrine carcinoma* and *non-small cell carcinoma with neuroendocrine features*.[717,719] These are discussed on p. 407.

Clear cell carcinoma

Clear cell carcinoma is defined as a type of lung carcinoma predominantly or exclusively composed of clear cells. This lesion probably does not represent a specific microscopic type of lung cancer.[721,722] Focal or extensive areas of clear cell changes can be seen in both squamous cell carcinoma and adenocarcinoma. These clear cells usually contain abundant glycogen and may also contain mucin. The possibility of metastatic renal cell carcinoma should always be considered in the presence of a lung tumor with a prominent clear cell component.

Bronchioloalveolar carcinoma and related tumors

Bronchioloalveolar carcinoma (BAC) can present grossly in various forms that bear an important relationship to its microscopic type and prognosis: a single peripheral nodule, multiple nodules, and a diffuse pneumonic-like infiltrate[724,730,737,744] (Fig. 7.133). The latter two forms may involve several lobes or even be bilateral. In these instances, the surgeon is often unaware that the lesion is a neoplasm. Microscopically, BACs have been divided into *mucinous* and *nonmucinous* types. The **mucinous type** has a glistening appearance on gross examination; there is usually preservation of the underlying lung architecture, with occasional distortion of air spaces by pools of mucus. Microscopically, the tumor is formed by well-differentiated mucin-containing columnar cells that line respiratory spaces without invading the stroma (Fig. 7.134). The tumor nodules have a topographic association with bronchioles rather than bronchi. Continuity between tumor cells lining alveoli and the epithelium of

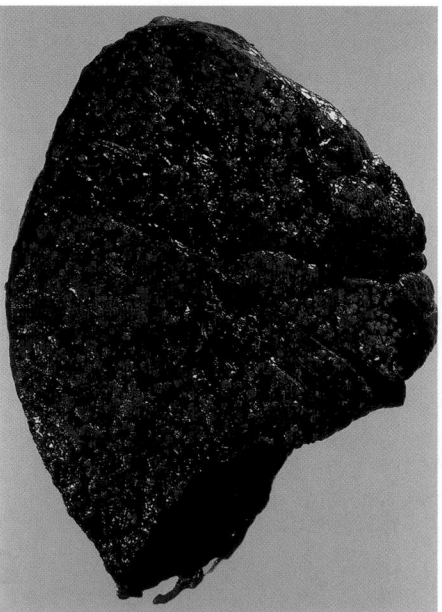

Fig. 7.133 Diffuse lung involvement by bronchioloalveolar carcinoma. (Courtesy of Dr. RA Cooke, Brisbane, Australia; from Cooke RA, Stewart B: Colour Atlas of Anatomical Pathology. Edinburgh, Churchill Livingstone, 2004).

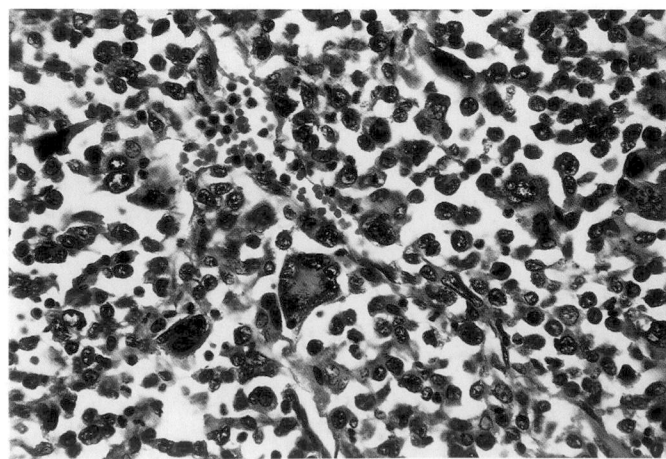

Fig. 7.132 So-called giant cell carcinoma.

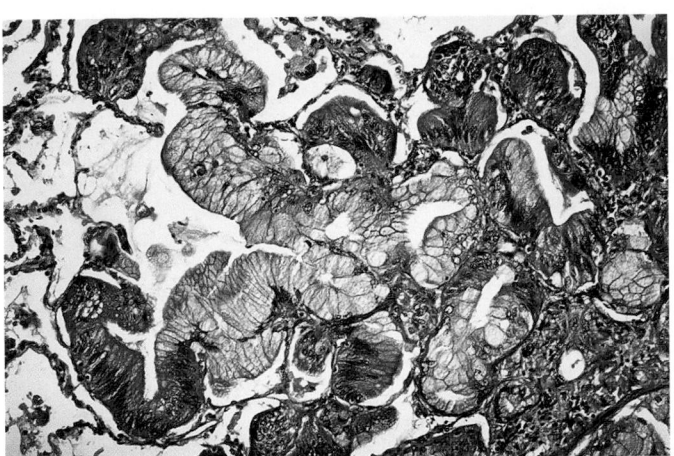

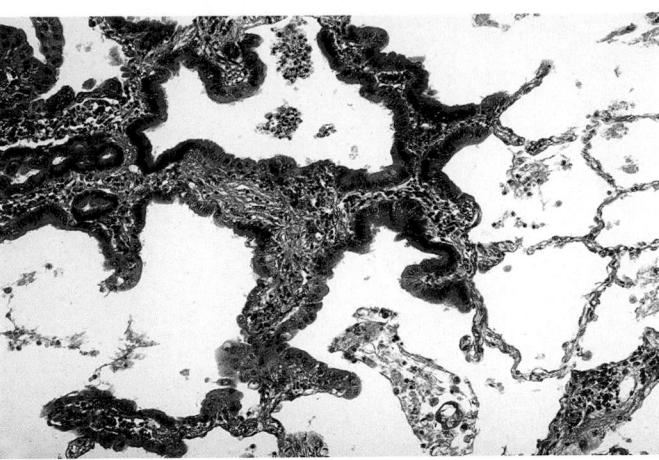

Fig. 7.134 Bronchioloalveolar carcinoma of the bronchiolar (mucinous) type. Extremely well differentiated mucin-producing columnar cells line the alveolar spaces.

Fig. 7.135 In this example of bronchioloalveolar carcinoma, the tumor cells are cuboidal and lack mucin secretion.

respiratory bronchioles or alveolar ducts can be demonstrated. A sharp separation is often found between the neoplastic and the normal cells, a useful diagnostic feature.

The reported cases of benign, borderline, and well-differentiated malignant *mucinous lung tumors* are probably histogenetically related to the mucinous type of BAC.[732,736,742,749] The differential diagnosis includes primary adenocarcinoma of the conventional type and metastatic adenocarcinoma[754] (see p. 422). Multicentric bronchioloalveolar carcinoma can coexist with ordinary adenocarcinoma in the same lung,[747] and an overlapping of bronchioloalveolar and conventional adenocarcinoma features can be seen within the same lesion.[726] The main differences encountered between the two tumors are a higher incidence of multiplicity and a slightly better survival rate in the patients with BAC.[726] Most authors, however, believe that the features of BAC are distinctive enough to warrant its separation from the other subtypes of adenocarcinoma. Interestingly, the incidence of BAC seems to be on the rise.[723]

The **nonmucinous type** of BAC (which comprises 60% to 75% of the cases) presents grossly as gray-white foci of parenchymal consolidation, sometimes associated with a central scar. Microscopically, the tumor cells are cuboidal rather than columnar and often have a bright eosinophilic neoplasm (Fig. 7.135). The degree of nuclear atypia and nucleolar prominence is greater than in the mucinous variety. Apical spouts may be present as indicators of Clara cell differentiation. Hobnail cells may be present. Cilia are exceptionally rare; their presence should suggest the alternative possibility of a reactive condition. Eosinophilic intranuclear inclusions, which are PAS-positive and which are made ultrastructurally of bundles of microfilaments, are commonly seen[738,757a,760] (Fig. 7.136). They represent an useful diagnostic sign, but it should be noted that intranuclear inclusion of similar or different appearances can also be seen in adenocarcinomas of the conventional types.[740]

In contrast to the mucinous type, various degrees of interstitial fibrosis and chronic inflammatory cells (some of which are S-100 protein-positive) are usually present.[751] When the fibrosis is extensive, the tumor is referred to as the *sclerosing variant*. Psammoma bodies are found in 13% of the cases.[726]

Ultrastructurally and immunohistochemically, mucinous BAC show differentiation toward bronchiolar goblet cells,[725,743] whereas the nonmucinous types comprise cells with features of Clara cells and/or type 2 pneumocytes, the former predominating.[731,741,748,753,757]

At the electron microscopic level, type 2 pneumocytes are identified mainly because of the presence of cytoplasmic lamellar inclusion bodies. These correspond to surfactant apoprotein, which is detected immunohistochemically with the antibody PE-10[727,750,759,761] (Fig. 7.137). α-1-Antitrypsin is a useful immunomarker of Clara cell differentiation.[764] A note of caution is needed concerning the keratin profile of these tumors. Whereas conventional adenocarcinomas are usually CK7+/CK20– and therefore readily distinguishable from the CK7–/CK20+ metastatic colorectal adenocarcinomas, the mucinous type of bronchioloalveolar carcinoma is usually immunoreactive for CK20.[755] Both the mucinous and the nonmucinous types of BAC are usually TTF-1-positive.

In terms of mucin production, BAC is characterized by the aberrant expression of MUC3 and MUC6, in contrast to the ordinary type of adenocarcinoma.[729] Exceptionally, foci of endocrine differentiation are detected in BAC.[756]

The nonmucinous type of BAC is more likely to be solitary and has a better prognosis than the mucinous type.[745] Sputum or bronchial washing cytology is almost invariably negative in cases that present as single peripheral nodules but is often positive (up to 88% of the cases)

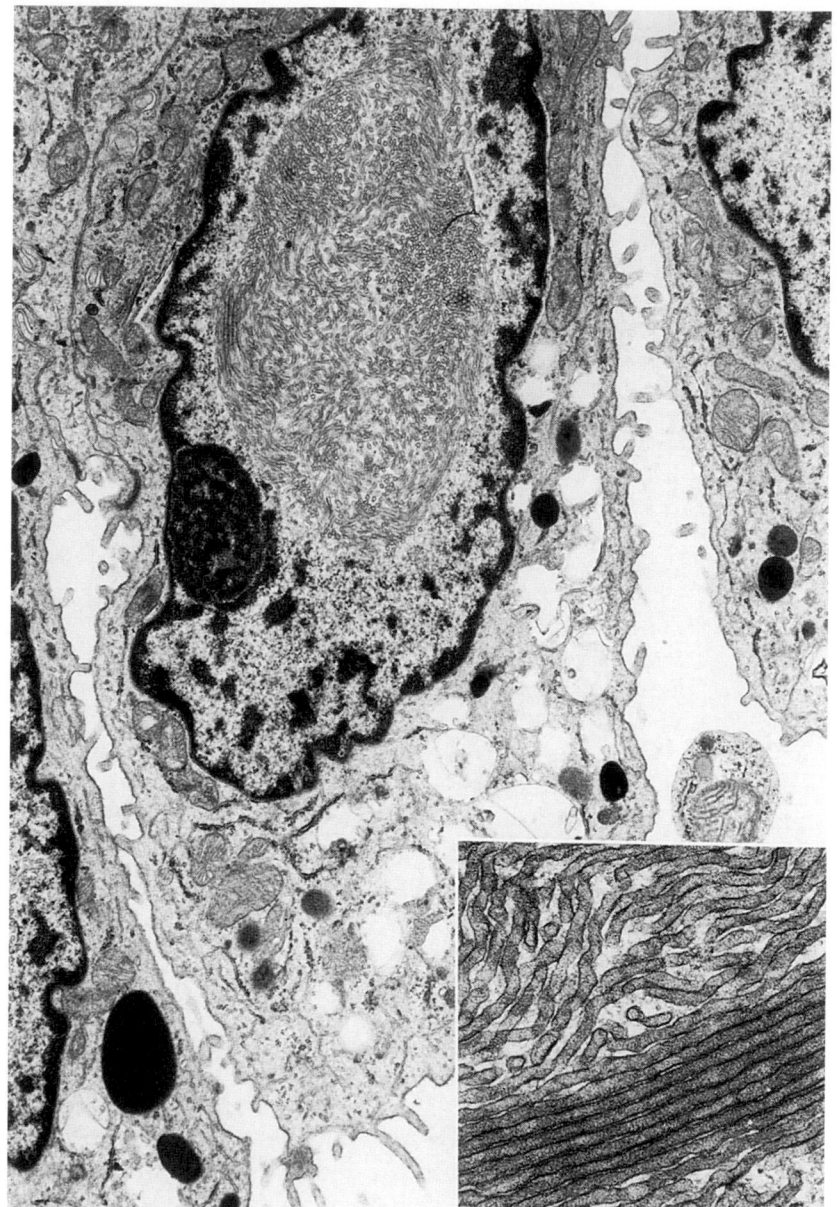

Fig. 7.136 Electron micrograph of bronchioloalveolar carcinoma showing an intranuclear inclusion formed by serpiginous and parallel tubular arrays, better appreciated in the high-power inset. Short microvilli protrude from the surface. Scattered dense bodies may be seen in the cytoplasm. The significance of the intranuclear inclusion is uncertain. (×11,200; inset ×41,000)

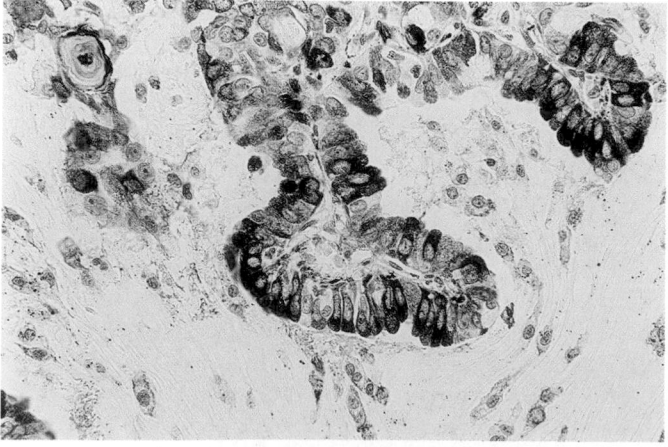

Fig. 7.137 Presence of surfactant apoprotein in bronchioloalveolar carcinoma, as demonstrated immunohistochemically with the PE-10 antibody.

for the multinodular and pneumonic-like forms.[762,763] Percutaneous fine needle aspiration has been used successfully for the detection of this tumor.[758]

The existence of benign counterparts of nonmucinous BAC has been postulated, and the terms *papillary adenoma* and *alveolar adenoma* have been proposed for them.[728,733–735,739,746,752] Another benign tumor which some authors have proposed is composed of type 2 pneumocytes is so-called sclerosing hemangioma (see p. 412).

Adenosquamous carcinoma

The term adenosquamous carcinoma is used for lung tumors in which unquestionable evidence of squamous and glandular differentiation is found in the same neoplasm in a roughly equivalent amount[765] (Fig. 7.138). Squamous cell carcinomas having occasional mucin-producing cells or adenocarcinomas with minute foci of

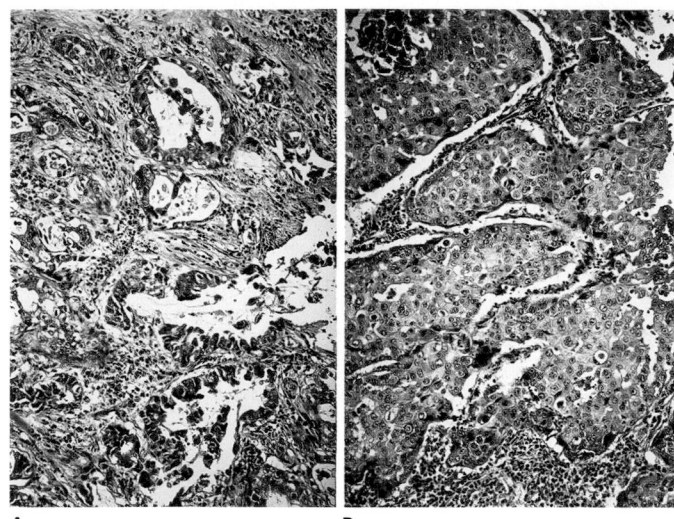

Fig. 7.138 A and **B**, Adenosquamous carcinoma of lung showing an admixture of squamous (**A**) and glandular (**B**) components in the same tumor.

squamous differentiation are named according to their predominant component. Thus defined, adenosquamous carcinomas account for less than 10% of lung cancers. Most of the cases are located peripherally and often are associated with a scar, suggesting a closer relationship with adenocarcinoma than with squamous cell carcinoma.[766,767]

Sarcomatoid carcinoma and carcinosarcoma

As in other organs (particularly in the upper aerodigestive tract), there exists in the lung a family of carcinomas having sarcoma-like features.[779,783a,784] The names these tumors have received have been dependent upon minor variations in their microscopic appearance and the histogenetic biases of the observer. When containing a large number of tumor giant cells, they have been designated as *giant cell carcinomas* (see previous sections). When predominantly composed of spindle cells but still identifiable as epithelial on morphologic, ultrastructural or immunohistochemical grounds they have been called *spindle cell* or *sarcomatoid carcinomas*.[771,773,777,778] Some authors have used the term *pleomorphic (anaplastic) carcinoma* to embrace both the giant cell and spindle cell form, in a fashion analogous to that used for the thyroid gland.[783] When the carcinomatous and sarcoma-like components are segregated, the term *carcinosarcoma* has been employed. Studies of large series of cases with morphologic, immunohistochemical, and molecular techniques have rendered apparent the fact that these represent various manifestations of the same biologic phenomenon, by which the neoplastic cells lose in part or completely their epithelial markers and acquire mesenchymal ones.[769,772]

Grossly, these tumors can appear either as intraparenchymal or intrabronchial polypoid masses.[775] Micro-

scopically, the identifiable epithelial elements, when present, are usually of squamous type but may also have a glandular appearance. The sarcoma-like component may be nondescript (i.e., with a fibrosarcoma- or MFH-like appearance), or resemble chondrosarcoma, osteosarcoma, rhabdomyosarcoma, or angiosarcoma.[768,774,780–782] Osteoclast-like giant cells can be present.[776] As indicated, the interphase between the carcinomatous and sarcoma-like components can be indistinct or sharp. Bronchoscopic biopsy may show one or both elements.

The prognosis of this tumor is poor, and roughly comparable to that of lung carcinoma of the conventional type.[770]

Pulmonary blastoma and pulmonary endodermal tumor

Pulmonary blastoma typically presents in adults, in contrast to most blastomas of other organs (and to pleuropulmonary blastoma, see below). It is also known as embryoma and is usually peripherally located, solitary, well circumscribed, and large (Fig. 7.139).[790,792,795,804] Microscopically, it is characterized by the presence of well-differentiated tubular glands in a cellular stroma typically composed of undifferentiated small oval or spindle cell[793] (Fig. 7.140). The overall appearance resembles fetal lung between 10 and 16 weeks' gestation and is also reminiscent of Wilms' tumor.[788,792] The glandular cells often show subnuclear and supranuclear cytoplasmic vacuoles. Solid balls of cells with abundant acidophilic cytoplasm ("morules") are common; curiously, the nuclei in these formations often have a ground-glass (optically clear) appearance, said to be due to the accumulation of biotin (see below). Glycogen is abundant in the epithelial cells. The stromal component may show differentiation toward skeletal muscle, cartilage, or bone.[791] Intestinal differentiation has been found in some cases,[796] yolk sac differentiation in others,[803] and a component of malignant melanoma in yet others.[786] Metastases supervene in close to half of the cases.

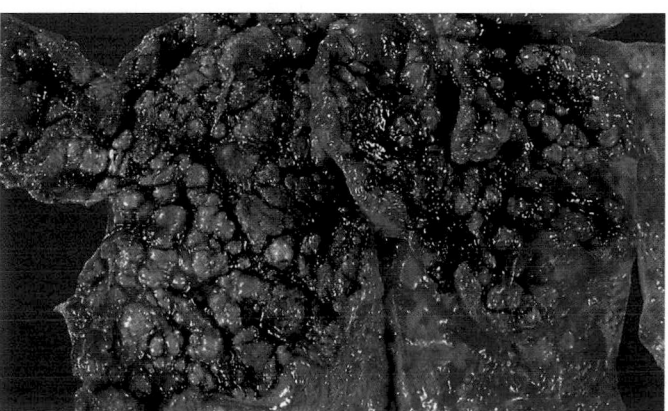

Fig. 7.139 Pulmonary blastoma. Polypoid tumor nodules are seen on the cut surface, in association with extensive hemorrhage.

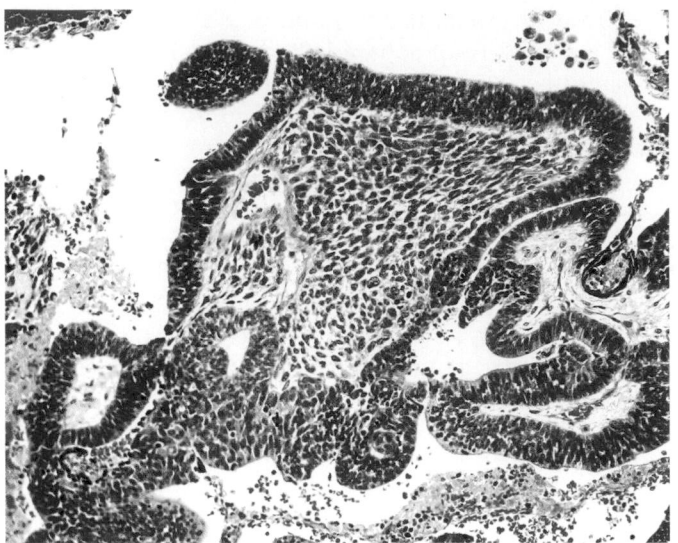

Fig. 7.140 Pulmonary blastoma showing typical biphasic pattern of growth and "fetal" appearance of the epithelial component.

Low-grade and high-grade forms of this tumor have been described, the former being more common in the elderly and the latter in the middle aged.[800]

The occasional presence of combined or transitional forms between pulmonary blastoma and sarcomatoid carcinoma/carcinosarcoma (particularly the latter form) and their similar immunohistochemical and ultrastructural features suggest that they are histogenetically closely related and that in a given case the distinction may not be possible or even warranted.[785,787,802] The prognosis of these two tumor types is also similar, despite early claims to the contrary.[789]

Pulmonary blastoma should not be confused with pleuropulmonary blastoma, a pediatric malignancy with a totally different presentation and morphologic appearance (see p. 420).

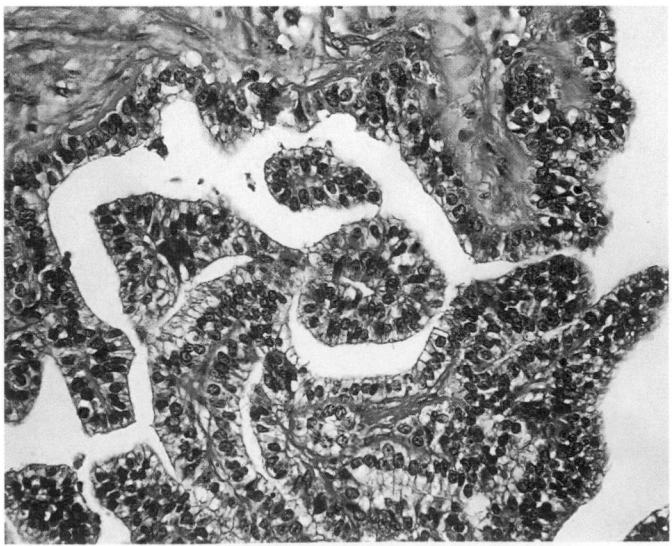

Fig. 7.141 Pulmonary endodermal tumor. In contrast to pulmonary blastoma, a mesenchymal component is absent.

Pulmonary endodermal tumor (*adenocarcinoma of fetal type*) is a lung tumor with glandular component similar to that of blastoma but lacking the sarcomatous elements of the latter[794,798,799] (Fig. 7.141). The glands may have a striking endometrioid appearance.[797] Optically clear nuclei are often present; these have been found to be rich in biotin.[801]

Small cell carcinoma

Small cell carcinoma comprises 10% to 20% of all lung cancers. Most of the patients are males, their median age is 60 years, and 85% or more are smokers.[816] The importance of its distinction from other types of lung carcinoma rests in its clinical behavior, systemic nature, and responsiveness to chemotherapy. Its uniqueness along these lines can be easily gathered from the fact that it has become the custom to divide lung carcinomas simply into small cell and non-small cell categories for clinical purposes.

Small cell carcinoma is typically a lesion of the central portions of the lung, but occasionally it is found in a peripheral location.[807,821] Bronchoscopic biopsy is often positive, even if no gross abnormalities are seen. Grossly, the tumor is white-tan, soft, friable, and extensively necrotic. When centered in a large bronchus (the usual situation), it may involve it in a circumferential fashion and/or spread widely beneath the normal mucosa (Fig. 7.142). The bronchus may be totally occluded in the late stages, but pure or predominant endobronchial involvement is highly unusual. Microscopically, small cell carcinoma should be viewed as a distinctive tumor type rather than as an undifferentiated form of lung cancer. The pattern of growth is generally solid, but there may be streams and ribbons, rosettes and pseudorosettes, or tubules and ductules, as pointed out in the classic article by Azzopardi.[806]

The subclassification of small cell carcinoma has been primarily based on cytologic criteria.[828] The terminology has changed over the years, as follows[814,847,852]:

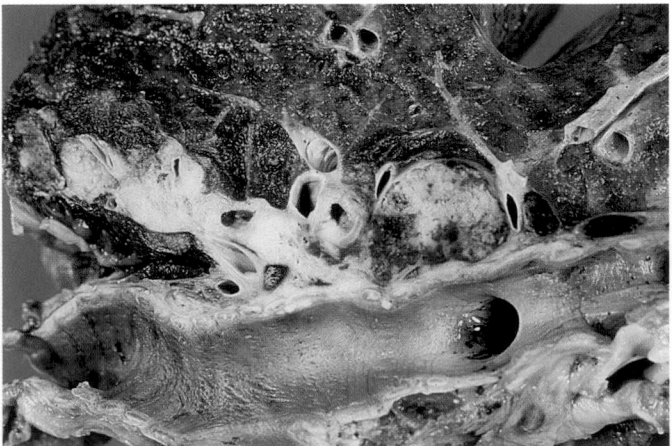

Fig. 7.142 Small cell carcinoma of the lung. The tumor is growing diffusely along the wall of segmental bronchi, and it has metastasized to an adjacent lymph node.

Kreyberg (1962)
Oat cell
Polygonal
WHO (1967)
Lymphocyte-like
Polygonal
Fusiform
WHO (1981)
Oat cell
Intermediate
Combined
International Association for the Study of Lung Cancer (IASLC) (1988)
Small cell (classic)
Mixed small cell/large cell
Combined

None of these schemes are entirely satisfactory, and further attempts at improvement are likely to be proposed. In the currently preferred scheme, which is the one proposed by the IASLC in 1988, three categories are recognized: small cell (classic), mixed small cell/large cell, and combined.[814]

The *classic* form of small cell carcinoma is characterized by small round or oval cells resembling lymphocytes[846,848] (Fig. 7.143). The nuclei are finely granular and very hyperchromatic, nucleoli are inconspicuous, mitoses are frequent, and the cytoplasm is so scanty as to be almost unrecognizable in routine preparations. In some instances the cells have an elongated (fusiform) shape. Nuclear "molding," a change first described in cytologic smears, can also be appreciated in microscopic preparations. A very common artifact, particularly prominent in small biopsy specimens, is elongation of the nuclei, with deformation, clumping, and diffusion of the chromatin. If present throughout the specimen, it may make diagnosis impossible. Interestingly, the classic appearance of small cell carcinoma is seen almost exclusively in small bronchial biopsies. In specimens obtained

from lymph node or distant metastases or from the rare resection specimens of the primary tumor, the tumor cells are usually larger and with more abundant cytoplasm.[834] This suggests that some degree of artifactual shrinkage is at least partially responsible for the "small cell" phenotype.

Chromatin diffusion secondary to necrosis may spread to the wall of the blood vessels, which appear strongly hematoxyphilic.[806] These foci, sometimes referred to as Azzopardi's effect, are positive for the Feulgen reaction (Fig. 7.144).

Mixed small cell/large cell carcinoma is defined as a tumor exhibiting an admixture of small and large tumor cells. This remains a poorly defined category for which interobserver agreement is poor.[820] Actually, the designation is not entirely accurate. Most of these tumors are not composed of an admixture of two cell populations, one small and the other large, as the term seems to imply. Rather, they display tumor cells with nuclear features similar to those of classic small cell carcinoma but having a larger size (Fig. 7.145). Early claims that mixed small

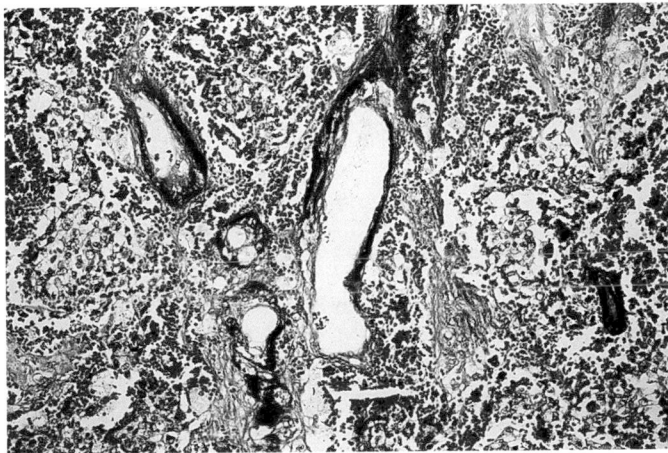

Fig. 7.144 Small cell carcinoma with extensive necrosis associated with hematoxyphilic staining of the vessel walls (so-called "Azzopardi's effect").

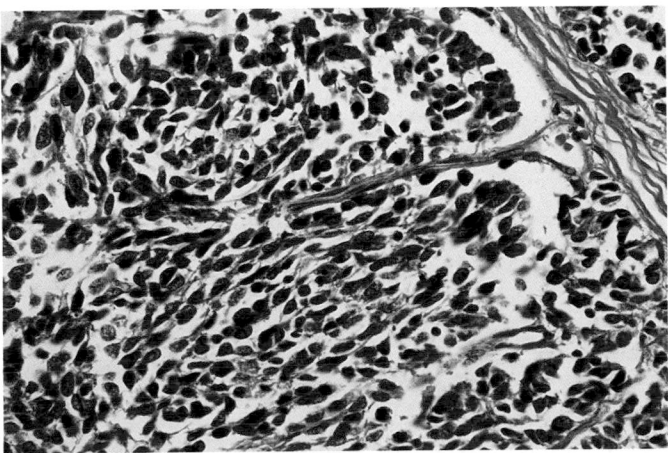

Fig, 7.143 Small cell carcinoma showing cells with darkly staining oval to spindle nuclei and extremely scanty cytoplasm.

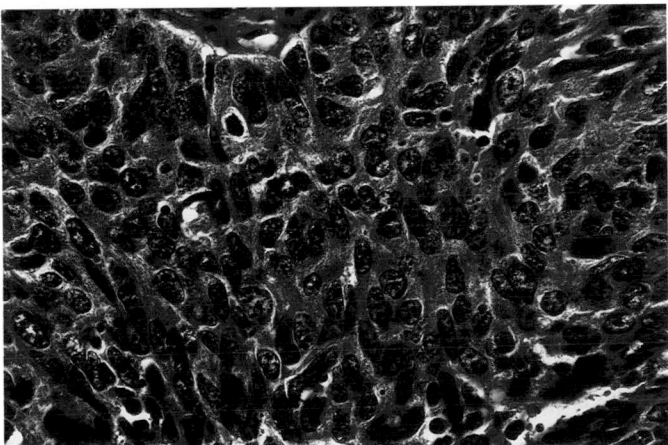

Fig. 7.145 Small cell carcinoma composed of cells having larger ("intermediate-sized") nuclei than those seen in the classic type.

cell/large carcinoma was associated with a worse survival have not been substantiated in more recent series.[805,819,836]

Combined small cell carcinoma is defined as a tumor with the overall features of small cell carcinoma but having in addition a minor (5% or less) component of either squamous cell carcinoma or adenocarcinoma (including the bronchioloalveolar type)[822] (Fig. 7.146). It makes only 1% to 3% of all cases.

In rare cases, small cell carcinomas that are otherwise typical may contain scattered giant tumor cells; this change is seen more commonly after chemotherapy, but it can also be encountered in the initial specimen.[809]

The key factor in determining whether a lung tumor belongs to the small cell category or not, in either a pure or a combined form, is not the detection of neuroendocrine differentiation (as discussed in the following paragraph) or the nuclear size, but rather the chromatin and nucleolar patterns as determined by light microscopic examination of routinely stained material.[823] The chromatin should be finely dispersed, without prominent clumps; more important, nucleoli should be inconspicuous, if detectable at all.

Cytoplasmic argyrophilia may be found in some cases.[842] Ultrastructurally, a few dense-core neurosecretory-type granules are found in at least some of the tumor cells in about 80% of the cases[810,817] (Fig. 7.147). Immunohistochemically, there is variable positivity for neural markers, such as neurofilaments,[826,844] Leu7,[831] chromogranin, synaptophysin, histidine decarboxylase,[830] and neuron-specific enolase[811,838]; the last marker has also been found to be elevated in the serum of many of these patients, rendering it useful in monitoring the disease.[818,825] The tumor cells also exhibit positivity for keratin,[844] often simultaneously with the neural markers. Some of the molecular alterations (such as tumor suppressor gene losses) are common to small cell carcinoma of lung and extrapulmonary sites, but others are associated with the pulmonary location and therefore

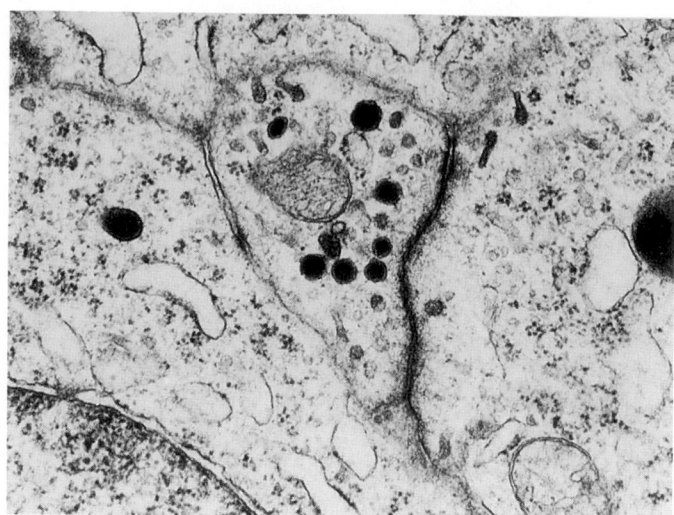

Fig. 7.147 Small cell carcinoma of lung. A few uniform, round, dense-core, membrane-bound granules are present. These granules are difficult to find and are usually present at the periphery of cells. (×41,200)

potentially useful for the assessment of the tumor primary site.[815] In contrast to Ewing sarcoma/PNET, small cell carcinoma is usually unreactive for CD99.[817] Small cell carcinoma cells often express bcl-2 protein.[808] Among the keratins, those usually expressed are of low-molecular weight. In contrast to non-small cell carcinomas, there is usually negativity for 34βE12,[840,845] TTF-1 is positive in about 85% of the cases,[841] whereas surfactant apoprotein (PE-10) is consistently negative.[854]

This combination of morphologic, ultrastructural, and immunohistochemical features, plus the well-known association of small cell carcinoma with a wide variety of endocrine-related syndromes (including inappropriate secretion of antidiuretic hormone, Cushing's syndrome, the Eaton–Lambert or myasthenic-like syndrome, and the carcinoid syndrome)[832,835,837,850] suggests that the cells of this neoplasm are differentiating in the direction of neuroendocrine (Kulchitsky-type) cells. A further argument favoring this interpretation is the existence of cases with a microscopic appearance intermediate between small cell carcinoma and bronchial carcinoid (see p. 411).[829] However, these considerations do not necessarily indicate that small cell carcinoma arises from bronchial Kulchitsky cells, as some have claimed.[843] It is more likely that it originates in primitive cells of the basal bronchial epithelium, which in the process of neoplastic change undergoes partial differentiation toward neuroendocrine cells.[812,839,853] Such an occurrence would explain why small cell carcinoma is so closely related epidemiologically to the other types of lung carcinoma, why some tumors with the small cell carcinoma pattern lack neurosecretory granules by electron microscopy and contain instead desmosomes and tonofilaments,[813,824] and why—as previously indicated—one may see in the same tumor a mixture of small cell carcinoma and squamous

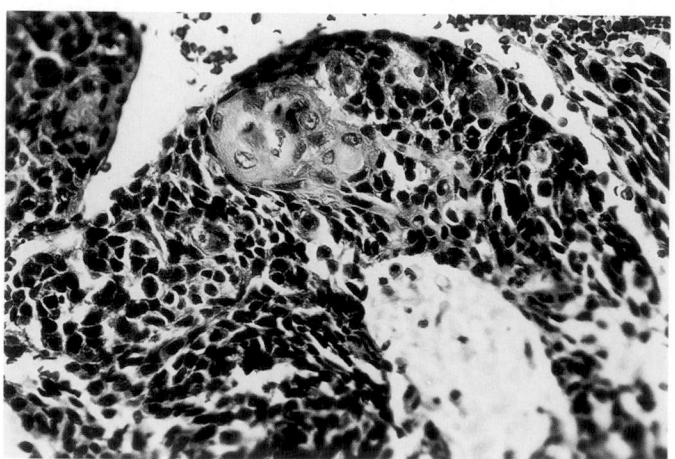

Fig. 7.146 Combined small cell–squamous cell carcinoma.

cell carcinoma, adenocarcinoma, or undifferentiated large cell carcinoma.

Lung carcinomas showing evidence of neuroendocrine differentiation but not fitting the morphologic criteria for small cell carcinoma are discussed on p. 411.

At the genetic molecular level, small cell carcinoma is characterized by a frequent deletion in chromosome 3 (p14–p23)[833,849] mutation of p53 in over 90%, inactivation of Rb gene in over 90%, inactivation of FHIT in 50% to 70%, and lack of abnormalities of p16 (the latter in stark contrast to the non-small cell carcinoma.[851]

Carcinoma in situ

It has been shown that squamous cell carcinomas of the lung have a long preclinical stage in which the lesion progresses from dysplasia to carcinoma in situ, microinvasive carcinoma, and frank invasive carcinoma.[856,857,859,862] Detailed morphologic studies of these very early cases have demonstrated that most cases arise unifocally in a segmental bronchus[855,862] (Fig. 7.148). Grossly, the bronchial mucosa may show slight irregularities in the form of granularity, papillation, and loss of rugae or it may appear unremarkable. Microscopically, the diagnostic criteria are similar to those applied for this diagnosis elsewhere, including a full-thickness change with an intact basement membrane. There is often extension into the ducts of the submucosal glands, a change that may be difficult to distinguish from broad-based early submucosal invasion. The presence of stromal desmoplasia favors the latter. The terms "early invasive" and "intramucosal" carcinoma have been used somewhat interchangeably (and somewhat inaccurately) to designate tumors exhibiting superficial invasion of the stroma that does not extend to the level of the bronchial cartilage; most of these are well-differentiated to moderately differentiated tumors[866,867] (Fig. 7.149). They have been divided into "creeping" (with extensive surface involvement but little invasion) and "penetrating" (having the reverse qualities).[864]

Aberrant expression of p53 and EGF receptor is frequently found in early bronchial neoplasia.[865]

The obvious but still unrealized expectation is that identification of tumors at this early stage should lead to an increase in the cure rate. Woolner et al.[866] collected twenty-eight such cases seen at the Mayo Clinic in a 23-year period. The prognosis in their series was good; only three patients died of the cancer, and in two of the three there was evidence of multicentricity. However, more recent studies from this group and from other authors have not substantiated these early optimistic figures, quoting a high death rate as a result of recurrence or development of a second tumor.[861,867]

Unfortunately, mass roentgenographic screening programs have not been successful in detecting early carcinoma.[858] Cytologic screening programs have also been generally disappointing. Melamed et al.[862] screened 4000 asymptomatic cigarette-smokers over the age of 45 in New York City and found lung cancer in nine men with normal chest roentgenograms. Seven had in situ or incipient invasive squamous cell carcinomas.

In another project, conducted by the Mayo Clinic, a high-risk population was screened by means of periodic sputum cytology examinations and chest x-ray studies; 54% of incidence cancers in the group that were being rescreened every 4 months were detected at an early, potentially curable stage. Sputum cytology proved highly effective for the early detection of squamous cell

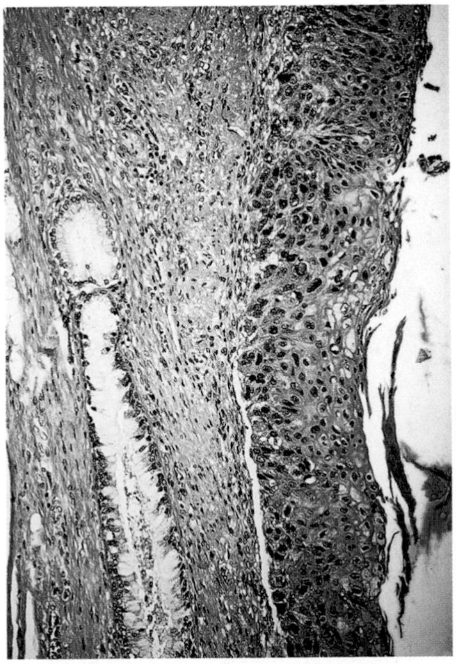

Fig. 7.148 Carcinoma in situ of bronchial mucosa.

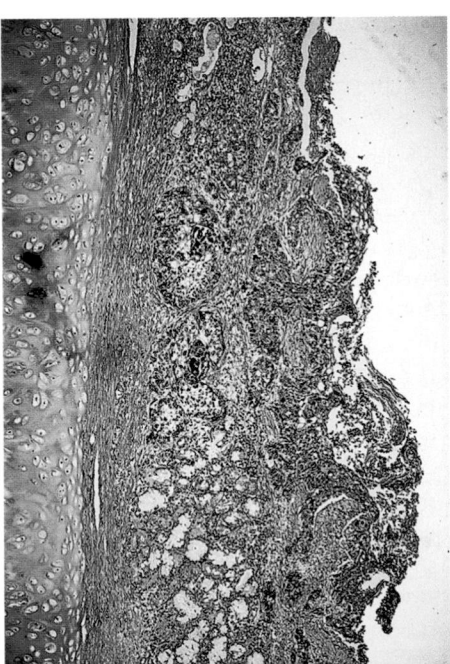

Fig. 7.149 Microinvasive squamous cell carcinoma of bronchial mucosa.

carcinoma but not for adenocarcinomas or undifferentiated large cell carcinomas; there were very few small cell carcinomas.[868]

The latest effort in this Herculean task has been the introduction of helical computer tomography. Assessment of the efficacy and advisability of this test will have to wait until the next edition of this book.[860]

Cases of carcinoma in situ involving a short bronchial segment can be treated with segmentectomy or sleeve resection.[863]

Biopsy

The advent of fiberoptic bronchoscopy has dramatically expanded the potential of the bronchoscopic biopsy.[877] The instrument is easily inserted, is well accepted by patients, enables exploration of both segmental and subsegmental bronchi and the adjacent parenchyma, and can be performed at the bedside in acutely ill patients.[871,874] Biopsy with the rigid bronchoscope provided positive specimens in only one third of operable cases in patients with lung carcinomas, but the fiberoptic bronchoscope has increased these figures substantially, particularly for peripherally located lesions.[873,875] However, it has made things more difficult for the pathologist because of the smaller size of the sample obtained.[869]

Careful correlation among the bronchoscopic appearance, site of the biopsy, and microscopic evaluation is important. A fragment with the microscopic features of carcinoma in situ may be representative of the entire lesion if taken from the center of an area of slight thickening or irregularity of the mucosa but may represent just the peripheral component of an invasive lesion if taken at the edge of a polypoid or ulcerating mass. The presence of squamous metaplasia in a bronchial biopsy should be regarded as a nonspecific change that may be present by itself or accompanied by inflammation, dysplasia, in situ or invasive carcinoma, or even carcinoid tumor. Sometimes the main bronchial specimen is unremarkable, but clumps of cells with diagnostic features of carcinoma may be present separately from it.

One of the most serious problems in small bronchial biopsies is the identification of small, crushed, blue nuclei as belonging to a small cell carcinoma, as opposed to a lymphoma or even a reactive lymphocytic population. Careful handling of the material reduces this problem but does not eliminate it entirely. In some cases, this artifactual distortion is of such magnitude that a differential diagnosis simply becomes impossible, even in the presence of a large number of these cells, much to the bewilderment and irritation of the bronchoscopist.

Biopsy of various lymph node groups has been advocated in the preoperative evaluation of patients with suspected lung carcinomas to avoid thoracotomy in inoperable patients.[872] The nodes most commonly sampled are cervical (especially scalene) and mediastinal.

The latter can be obtained through limited incisions in the second intercostal space or—with increasing frequency—by mediastinoscopy.[870,876]

If bronchoscopic biopsy (with or without lymph node biopsy) fails to establish the diagnosis of carcinoma but the clinical suspicion is high, an exploratory thoracotomy should be performed without delay. At present, this procedure carries practically no operative mortality. Early exploratory thoracotomy will increase the number of tumors suitable for resection.

Thoracotomy with lung biopsy is also indicated in patients with bilateral disseminated disease in which bronchoscopic biopsies and other procedures have failed to establish a diagnosis. This method allows a proper pathologic evaluation and also the performance of microbiologic studies and chemical analyses. The site of the incision is planned according to the distribution of the lesions.

Cytology

Pulmonary cytology has reached a high level of accuracy since Wandall's classic monograph on the subject.[879,882,895] By examination of the sputum and/or bronchial brushings, it is now possible to make a diagnosis in 80% to 90% of patients with lung carcinoma.[881] Most authors agree that bronchial washing does not add significant information to that obtained from the brushings and that the preparations are of inferior quality.[878,884,885,890,891] A single sputum specimen will be positive in 40% to 60% of the patients with lung carcinoma, but this rate rises to 80% or more when five sputum specimens are examined.[880]

In most instances the tumor cells are easily recognized (Figs 7.150 to 7.153). False-positive diagnoses have been made in patients with infarct, bronchiectasis, mycotic infections, viral pneumonia, irradiation changes, and lipoid pneumonia. Usually, the cells that are misinterpreted as malignant are either macrophages or altered alveolar lining cells.

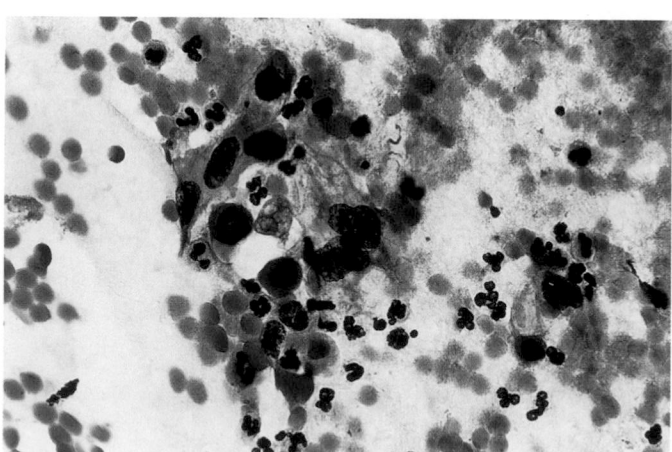

Fig. 7.150 Cytologic appearance of squamous cell carcinoma.

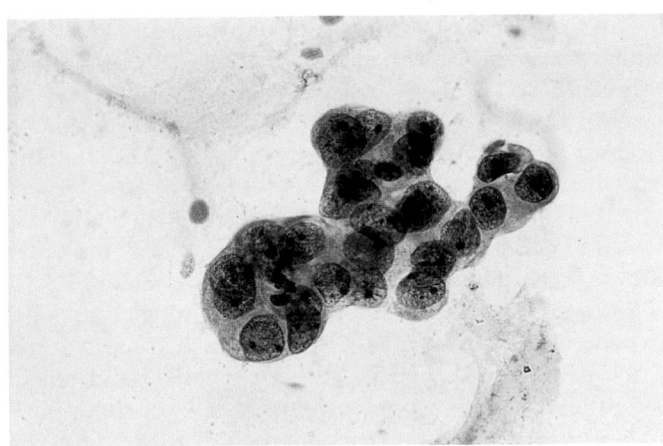

Fig. 7.151 Cytologic appearance of adenocarcinoma.

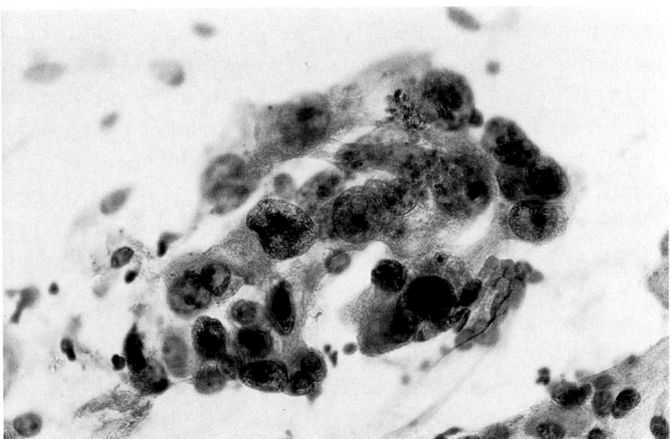

Fig. 7.152 Cytologic appearance of large cell undifferentiated carcinoma.

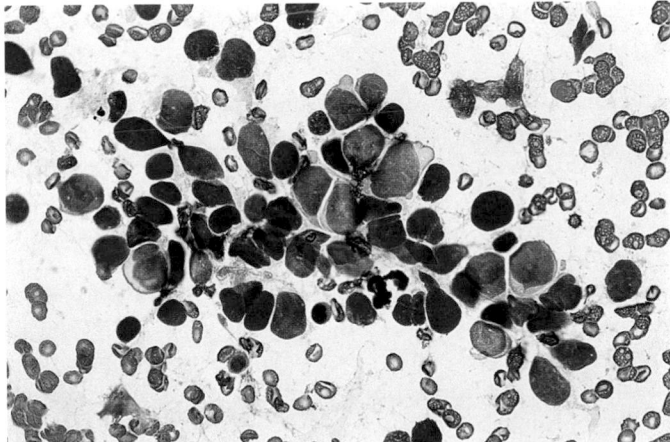

Fig. 7.153 Cytologic appearance of small cell carcinoma.

The diagnosis of exfoliative material from sputum specimens should be made on a conservative basis. Our reports read as follows:

1 "Unsatisfactory (saliva only)" when no macrophages are present in the smear
2 "Negative" when no abnormal cells are observed in a technically satisfactory smear

3 "Benign atypia" when epithelial bronchial cells with hyperplastic and metaplastic changes secondary to inflammation are identified
4 "Suspicious but not diagnostic" (this report is an indication for repeat examination)
5 "Positive for malignant cells"

It should be remembered that malignant cells present in sputum may also originate in any portion of the upper aerodigestive tract.[886] If a patient with a negative chest x-ray film is found to have a positive sputum cytology, a thorough inspection of the bronchial tree with the fiberoptic scope should be carried out, and this should be combined with an equally thorough examination of the upper aerodigestive tract.[897]

An increasingly popular cytologic specimen is that provided by fine needle aspiration. The technique is associated with minimal morbidity, and the diagnostic yield is very high, especially for peripherally located lesions.[889,893,896]

Yet another source of cytologic material is pleural fluid. The incidence of false-negatives is higher in this specimen type than in others, particularly for small cell carcinoma.[888,892]

In addition to making a diagnosis of carcinoma, the pathologist examining cytologic specimens from any of these sites should attempt to establish the specific cell type involved. The overall agreement rate between cytology and histology ranges from 70% to 90%.[887,894] It is particularly high for well-differentiated squamous cell carcinoma, well-differentiated adenocarcinoma, and small cell carcinoma.[881,883] Most difficulties are encountered in the differential diagnosis between poorly differentiated squamous cell carcinoma and large cell undifferentiated carcinoma.

Frozen section

Frozen section is an important procedure in debatable lesions of the lung and has its greatest value in peripherally located lesions. In patients with resectable lung carcinoma, bronchoscopic and/or cytologic examination will be positive in about 80% of the cases. This means that a number of patients with cancer will undergo surgery without a definite preoperative diagnosis. For peripheral lesions, it is better to excise them entirely with a margin of normal lung. This excision may be in the form of lobectomy. Frozen section is then done. Frequently, the lesion proves to be a benign process such as a hamartoma, organizing pneumonia, or granulomatous inflammation, in which case no additional surgery is necessary. If it is carcinoma, the surgeon will decide whether to enlarge the excision.

It is much more important that the pathologist make a definite diagnosis in lesions of the lung than in lesions of the breast, for a second thoracotomy carries with it considerable morbidity and additional risk. One must not be misled into making a diagnosis of carcinoma in highly cellular inflammatory lesions such as organizing pneumonia, lipoid pneumonia, or inflammatory pseudotumor. Conversely, some of the poorly differentiated neoplasms of the lung may have a considerable inflammatory infiltrate and be incorrectly diagnosed as non-neoplastic.

Spread and metastases

Lung cancer spreads by direct extension proximally and distally along the bronchus of origin and may reach the trachea at the level of the carina. It also grows into the lung parenchyma, from where it may reach the mediastinum or pleura. The latter event may result in seeding in both pleural layers and extension into the chest wall and diaphragm. Pleural effusion is very common under these circumstances. Occasionally, the entire pleural space is seeded in a fashion mimicking mesothelioma (see p. 392). Invasion of blood vessels is very common (over 80% of the cases); sometimes, this may lead to extensive tumor emboli and cor pulmonale, a phenomenon seen more commonly with adenocarcinoma.[900] It has been postulated that tumor cells also spread by "aerogenous dissemination," with seeding through the air passages and development of secondary deposits at some distance from the main mass.

Lymph node metastases occur first in the hilar region, then in the mediastinal and lower cervical (supraclavicular) groups, and less commonly in axillary and subdiaphragmatic sites.

Distant metastases are more common in liver, other areas of lung, adrenal, bone and bone marrow, kidney, and central nervous system.[903,904] Less common sites include the gastrointestinal tract, pancreas, thyroid, spleen, pituitary gland, skin, and skeletal muscle.[902,905] Brain metastases seem to be more common in adenocarcinoma and may be the first manifestation of the disease.[898,906] The occurrence of metastases to other portions of the lung raises the differential diagnosis with a second primary lung cancer, an event detected by LeGal and Bauer[901] in 6.4% of sixty-three patients who had survived at least 30 months after excision of a lung cancer. The presence of distant metastases at the time of initial diagnosis is particularly high in small cell carcinoma. In one series, 84% of patients had "extensive" or extrathoracic disease at the time of diagnosis, 14% had metastases to the central nervous system, and 47% had bone marrow metastases.[899]

Treatment

The standard therapy for operable non-small cell carcinoma of the lung is complete surgical excision through thoracotomy.[908,911,913] The excision can be in the form of pneumonectomy, lobectomy, or (very rarely) segmental resection, depending on the location and type of the tumor.

The first successful lung resection for squamous cell carcinoma was performed by Dr. Evarts A. Graham at Barnes Hospital in St Louis, Missouri, in 1933. The patient, a physician, died 30 years later of an unrelated disease (Fig. 7.154). Ironically, he survived Dr. Graham, who died as a result of lung carcinoma.

In patients with stage I disease, surgical therapy is regarded as sufficient, whereas a combined modality therapy is usually applied to higher tumor stages.[918]

Radiation therapy can effectively control the local growth of lung cancer and sometimes results in long-term survival,[924,925] but like surgery, it fails to cure most patients, mainly because as many as 50% of them have distant metastases when diagnosed or shortly following the initial diagnosis.[920,922] It also fails to decrease the incidence of recurrence in the cases showing microscopic evidence of involvement of the bronchial margin.[916] It can reduce local recurrences after resection of squamous cell carcinoma, but it does not increase survival rates.[917] The role of radiation therapy seems to be greater, whether given alone or as a preoperative measure, for tumors of the superior pulmonary sulcus[907,910,915,919] and as an adjunctive measure in the treatment of small cell carcinoma.[909,921] Preoperative chemotherapy has resulted in a modest increase in median survival in patients with non-small cell lung carcinoma.[923]

Multidrug chemotherapy is currently the treatment of choice for small cell carcinoma,[912,914] although some workers believe that a selected group is still best treated with surgery alone.[926] There is no question that the initial tumor response to chemotherapy and its short-term results are distinctly better than for the other types of lung carcinoma; yet long-term cures are rarely achieved.

Prognosis

The long-term prognosis of lung carcinoma remains disappointingly poor, no substantial improvement having been made in recent years in long-term survival rates. In a series of 1008 cases of lung carcinoma treated at a single institution from 1948 to 1955, the 5-year survival rate was 21.3% for the resected cases and 8% for the entire group.[931] Similar figures have been obtained from various other groups during the last 30 years.[941,966] Recent statistics from the National Cancer Institute show a 13% 5-year survival for whites and 11% for blacks for all stages of lung carcinoma.[928]

The prognosis of lung carcinomas has been related to a large number of factors:

1 *Age*. Patients who are younger than 40 years of age have a very poor prognosis, probably because most have advanced disease at presentation.[969]
2 *Sex*. Women have been found to have a worse survival rate than men; this has been partially attributed to the fact that they have a higher incidence of advanced lesions and of tumors with an adenocarcinomatous pattern.[951,952]

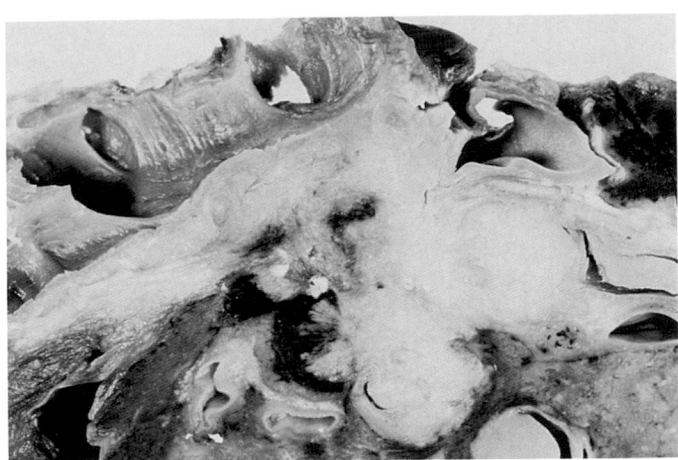

A

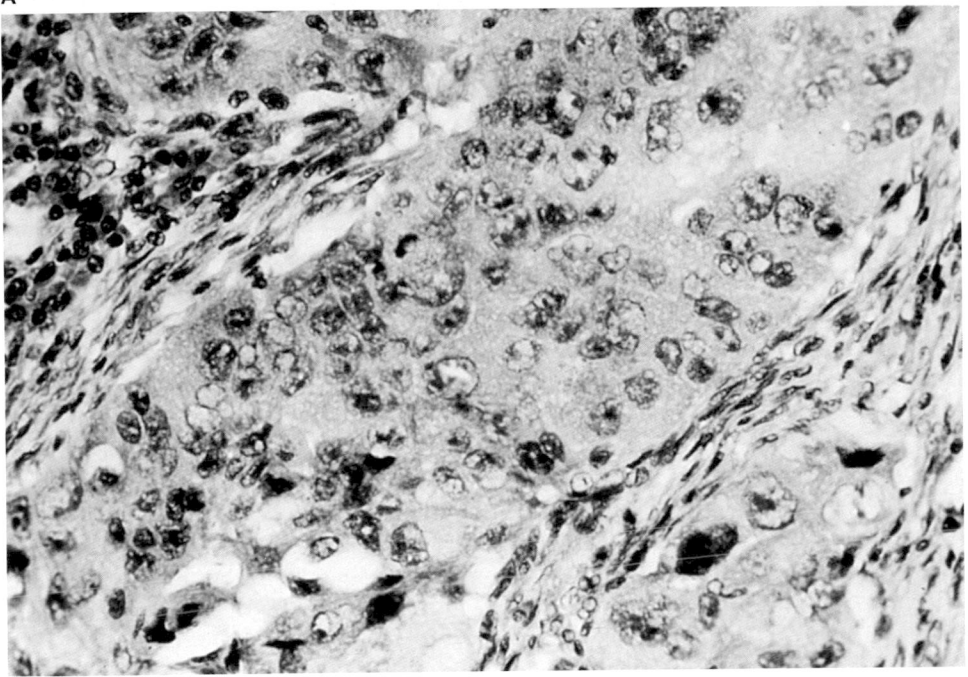

B

Fig. 7.154 A, Squamous cell carcinoma of lung resected by Dr. Evarts A. Graham in 1933. Note extension into surrounding lung and involvement of two regional lymph nodes. The patient died in 1962 without evidence of cancer. **B,** Poorly differentiated squamous cell carcinoma shown in **A.**

3 *Location.* It has been claimed that tumors of the superior pulmonary sulcus have a better prognosis than the others, the reported 5-year survival rates oscillating between 20% and 34%.[927,937,954,968] However, these findings have not been confirmed in more recent series.[946] For squamous cell carcinomas, those located at the periphery are said to do better than those located centrally.[980]

4 *Stage.* A direct relationship is evident between clinical stage and survival rates, particularly for non-small cell carcinoma (see Appendix B).[939] Actually, TNM stage is regarded by most as the single most important prognostic parameter in lung carcinoma, as it is in many other tumors throughout the body.[930,942]

5 *Tumor size.* Large tumors have a worse prognosis than smaller neoplasms of the same histologic type.[967] For the peripheral neoplasms, this relationship no longer holds once the tumor reaches a diameter of 6 cm.[981]

6 *Cell type and degree of differentiation.* Squamous cell carcinoma is the most curable form of lung cancer.[933,972,978] In series of long-term survivors of lung carcinomas, about half of the cases are squamous cell carcinomas.[950] The 5-year survival rate in patients undergoing resection for cure is about 40% for well-differentiated tumors, 20% for moderately differentiated tumors, and 7% for the poorly differentiated tumors. For adenocarcinomas, the corresponding figure is about 25%, apparently not influenced by the degree of differentiation. As a group, the prognosis of bronchioloalveolar carcinoma is only slightly better than that of ordinary adenocarcinoma. However, the localized form of the former (usually having a nonmucinous histology) is curable in a high proportion of cases.[934,960,962] Undifferentiated large cell carcinomas give a figure close to 15%. In one series, undifferentiated large cell histology and presence of tumor giant cells in any histologic type were significantly

associated with a worse outcome.[958] Giant cell carcinoma is practically never curable.[949] Small cell carcinoma has been traditionally associated with a dismal prognosis, the 5-year survival rate being less than 2% in most early series.[948] A substantial short-term improvement has come as a result of chemotherapy, but the long-term outlook remains bleak. Much has been written about the relationship between the small cell carcinoma subtypes and prognosis.[936,947,965] Although some controversy persists, the consensus is that no appreciable prognostic differences exist among the various subtypes.[947,965,974]

7 *Blood vessel invasion.* This feature has ominous prognostic connotations. When associated with lymph node metastases, the adverse effect on survival is additive.[977]

8 *Chest wall invasion.* Surprisingly, tumors associated with obvious invasion of the chest wall have been found to have a prognosis not significantly different from those lacking this feature when all other staging parameters are the same; the operative mortality, however, is substantially higher.[970]

9 *Pleural effusion.* This feature carries a poor prognostic connotation regardless of histologic subtype or cytologic findings in the fluid. The presence of tumor cells in intraoperative pleural lavage is also said to be an indicator of poor prognosis.[929]

10 *Presence of a scar.* It has been claimed that peripheral adenocarcinomas or undifferentiated large cell carcinomas associated with a well-defined fibrotic area (scar) have a worse prognosis than tumors lacking this feature.[959,975]

11 *Lymph node involvement.* This parameter, which is a component of the staging system, is one of the most important prognostic determinators. This applies not only to the presence of nodal metastasis but also to the anatomic level of these deposits.[958,964] It should be pointed out, however, that a 5-year disease-free survival is possible in patients with involvement of mediastinal nodes.[961]

12 *Inflammatory reaction.* The presence of a prominent lymphoplasmacytic reaction around the tumor is a favorable prognostic sign.[958] Also, it has been claimed that tumors associated with regional lymph nodes showing lymphocyte or germinal center predominance have a better prognosis than those in which the nodes have lymphocyte depletion or appear unstimulated.[953]

13 *Carbohydrate antigens.* Loss of expression of blood group A and H/LEy/LEb antigens have been shown to correlate with poor survival.[957,963]

14 *TTF-1.* It has been claimed that a strong expression of this nuclear transcription factor predicts a better survival for patients with non-small cell carcinoma.[944,977a]

15 *DNA ploidy.* There is a suggestion that determination of tumor DNA ploidy by flow cytometry may con-tribute to the prognostic assessment of lung carcinoma, provided that material is obtained by multiple site sampling.[932,973,979]

16 *Oncogene expression.* Expression of *ras* oncogene is enhanced in non-small cell carcinoma, and amplification of at least three *mic* genes has been shown in small cell carcinoma lines.[935,955,956,971] Whether analysis of these proto-oncogenes will provide insight into the pathogenesis of lung cancer and aid in predicting its behavior remains to be determined. Preliminary claims have been made that increased expression of *ras* p21 expression in non-small cell carcinoma, and of N-*myc* in small cell carcinoma, predict poor prognosis.[938,940,945,976] It has also been shown that overexpression of p53 and HER2/*neu* are predictors of poor survival.[943]

Other primary tumors

Hamartoma

Hamartoma (chondroid hamartoma, chondroid adenoma, chondroma, mesenchymoma) generally occurs in adults and is more common in males. It is usually solitary but can be multiple.[988] Its most common location is the lung parenchyma just beneath the pleura, and it presents in most instances as an asymptomatic clearcut shadow on a chest x-ray film. It is usually small, although occasionally it may occupy the entire lobe. Radiographically, a characteristic popcorn pattern of calcification is seen in one third of the cases. Grossly, it is sharply delineated and lobulated (Fig. 7.155). The cut surface is characterized by glistening nodules of cartilage separated by ill-defined clefts. A less common presentation is as a polypoid mass inside a large bronchus[984,990]; this type may result in symptoms caused by bronchial obstruction.

This lesion has been designated as a hamartoma because it conforms to the original definition of this term by Albrecht[982]:

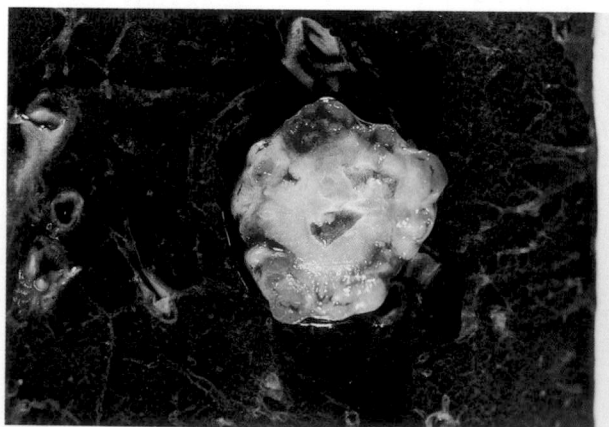

Fig. 7.155 Lobulated shape and shiny cut surface of pulmonary hamartoma. (Courtesy of Dr. RA Cooke, Brisbane, Australia; from Cooke RA, Stewart B: Colour Atlas of Anatomical Pathology. Edinburgh, Churchill Livingstone, 2004).

Hamartomata are tumor-like malformations in which occurs only abnormal mixing of the normal components of the organ. The abnormalities may take the form of a change in quantity, arrangement, or degree, or may comprise all three.

Microscopically, the peripheral hamartoma is made up of normal cartilage arranged in islands, fat, smooth muscle, and clefts lined by ciliated or nonciliated respiratory epithelium (Fig. 7.156). The cartilage often shows calcification and, rarely, ossification. Anthracotic pigment is absent. The endobronchial lesions have fewer epithelial clefts, a decreased amount of cartilage, and an increased amount of the adipose tissue.[990] Sometimes pulmonary hamartoma is seen associated with the peculiar change known as *placental transmogrification*, characterized by the formation of placental villus-like formation in the lung parenchyma[991] (see also p. 369).

There is clinical, morphologic, and ultrastructural evidence to suggest that this lesion is acquired and that it represents a primary overgrowth of mesenchymal tissues of the bronchial wall, with secondary entrapment of bronchial epithelium in the more peripheral lesions.[983,989] Immunohistochemically, some of the spindle cells of this lesion have features of myoepithelial cells, such as positivity for actin and S-100 protein; indeed, we have seen a myoepithelioma arising from a pulmonary hamartoma.

Cytogenetically, there is a consistent chromosome 6p21 breakpoint within the HMG-I (Y) gene or its immediate surroundings, supporting the neoplastic nature of this process.[987]

Carney[985,986] has identified a nonfamilial syndrome ("Carney's triad") characterized by pulmonary chondromas, gastric epithelioid leiomyosarcomas (which would be currently categorized as GISTs), and functioning extra-adrenal paragangliomas.

The treatment of hamartoma is usually in the form of conservative surgery: wedge resection or enucleation of peripheral lesions and sleeve resection of endobronchial lesions.

Carcinoid tumor and other endocrine neoplasms

Carcinoid tumor comprises less than 5% of primary pulmonary neoplasms.[993] For the purposes of discussion, it is advisable to divide pulmonary carcinoid tumor into three major categories—central, peripheral, and atypical—acknowledging the fact that all of them differentiate in the direction of Kulchitsky-type neuroendocrine cells as normally seen in the bronchial mucosa,[992,994–996] that there are intermediate forms, and that neuroendocrine differentiation may also be seen in other types of lung carcinoma (notably small cell carcinoma but also large cell undifferentiated carcinoma and adenocarcinoma). These are discussed in the section on atypical carcinoid tumors.

Central carcinoid tumor

Central carcinoid tumor is the most common type. It usually presents as a slow-growing, solitary polypoid mass within a major bronchus (Figs 7.157 and 7.158); because of its location and high vascularity, hemoptysis and pulmonary infection caused by blockage of distal bronchi are common.[1002] Most cases occur in adults, but they can also develop in children. As a matter of fact,

Fig. 7.157 Central carcinoid tumor showing well-circumscribed quality and connection with a large bronchus.

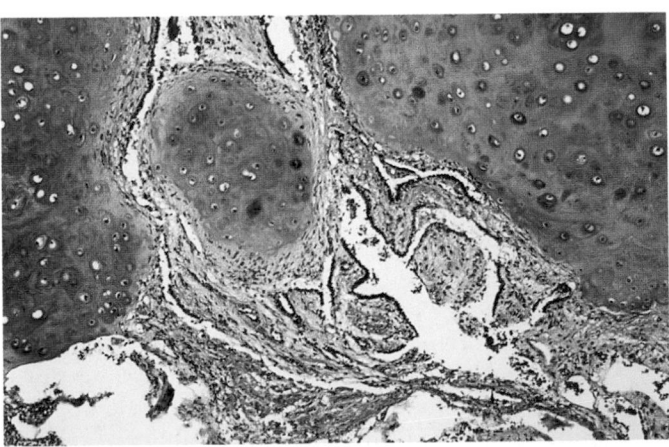

Fig. 7.156 Close intermingling of hyaline cartilage and bronchial epithelium in pulmonary hamartoma.

Fig. 7.158 Whole mount of central carcinoid tumor showing polypoid endobronchial growth.

they constitute the most common primary lung neoplasm in the latter age group.[1016] The sex incidence is almost equal. Most cases are endocrinologically silent at the clinical level. However, cases with typical carcinoid syndrome and elevated 5-HIAA in the urine have been documented. In some instances the tumor has been found to secrete 5-hydroxytryptophan instead of serotonin.[1034] Cases have been reported to be associated with Cushing's syndrome caused by ACTH production,[1007] with endocrine tumors of other sites,[1010] and with MEN I.[1011]

Grossly, central carcinoid tumors are predominantly intrabronchial but also infiltrate the bronchial wall, may extend to the surrounding parenchyma, and may even reach the pleura or the myocardium (Fig. 7.159). Some examples show a predominant extrabronchial component. They are covered by bronchial mucosa, which is only rarely ulcerated. The cut surface is grayish yellow, sometimes divided by fibrous septa, and very well vascularized. Islands of bronchial cartilage totally surrounded by tumor may be evident.

Microscopically, the tumor is made up of small uniform cells having central nuclei with scanty or no mitotic activity and a moderate amount of finely granular cytoplasm. It may grow in the form of compact nests, ribbons, and festoons; in a diffuse solid fashion; and—rarely—in a pseudopapillary or true papillary configuration[1015] (Fig. 7.160). Small glands with a rosette-like appearance are only rarely present. Vascularity is pronounced. The stroma can be heavily hyalinized and may exhibit focal calcification or ossification. Some of the bone present may represent osseous metaplasia by entrapped bronchial cartilage (Fig. 7.161). Tumor cells may be seen within lymph vessels in or around the tumor. Occasionally, prominent nuclear (endocrine-type) pleomorphism is seen in a carcinoid tumor in the absence of necrosis or mitoses; this feature by itself is not sufficient to place the tumor in the atypical carcinoid category. Exceptionally, the cytoplasm of the tumor cells is optically clear.[1013]

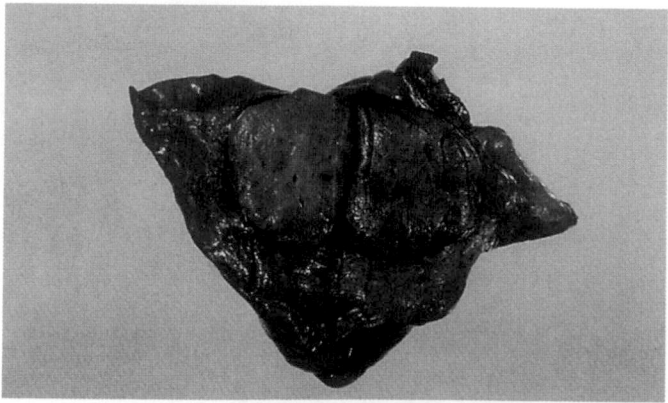

Fig. 7.159 Gross appearance of carcinoid tumor. The tumor is solid, fleshy, and well-circumscribed.

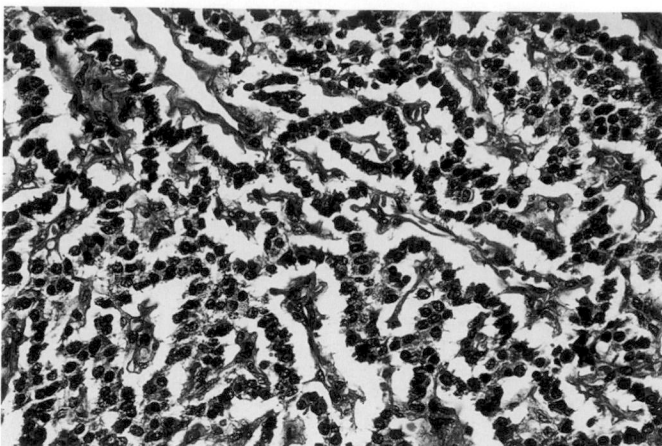

Fig. 7.160 Central carcinoid tumor showing prominent trabecular pattern of growth.

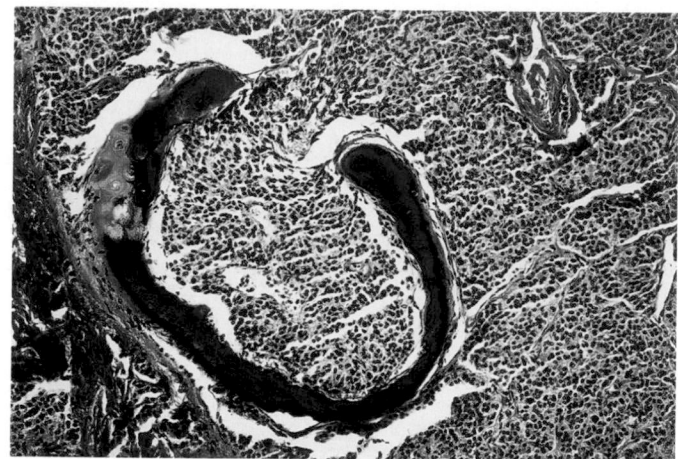

Fig. 7.161 Osseous metaplasia of bronchial cartilage induced by central carcinoid tumor. This is a relatively common finding.

Mucin stains are usually negative, but focal positivity may be found in the glandular lumina.[1033]

Argentaffin cells are rare in formalin-fixed, paraffin embedded sections of bronchial carcinoid, whereas argyrophilic cells (as detected by the Grimelius or Sevier-Munger techniques) can be consistently demonstrated.

The morphologic and immunohistochemical features of bronchial carcinoid tumor resemble those of carcinoid tumor of thymus and larynx (and to some extent those of medullary carcinoma of the thyroid) rather than those of gastrointestinal carcinoid tumors. By electron microscopy, the cells contain numerous dense-core secretory granules that vary considerably in shape and size and are sometimes aligned along the cell membrane (Fig. 7.162). Some variability in the appearance of these granules exists from case to case, which has led to the suggestion that at least two different endocrine types are involved.[1004] Occasionally, abundant cytoplasmic fibrillary inclusions are found.[998]

Immunohistochemically, there is variable but usually positive reactivity for keratin, serotonin, neuron-specific enolase, chromogranin A and B, secretoneurin,

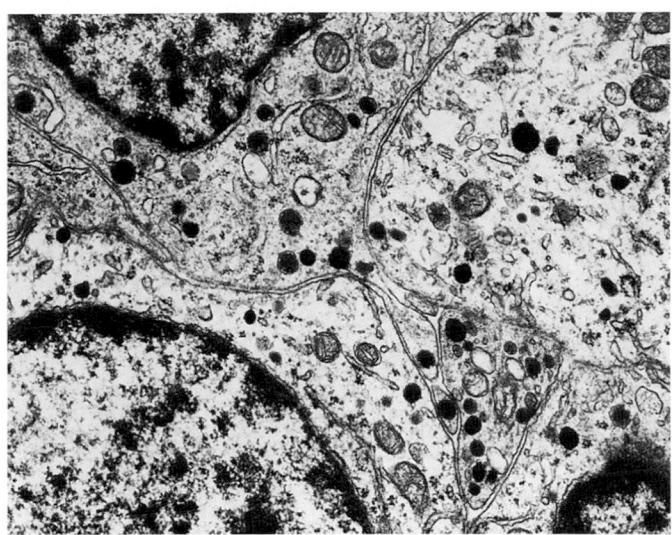

Fig. 7.162 Ultrastructural appearance of carcinoid tumor of lung in a woman with multiple endocrine neoplasia. Moderate numbers of fairly uniform electron-dense neurosecretory granules are present. (×25,270)

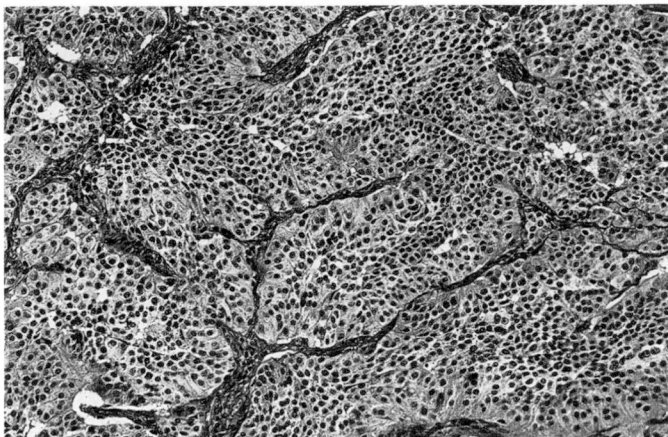

Fig. 7.163 Central carcinoid tumor with paraganglioma-like pattern of growth.

synaptophysin, opioid peptides, Leu7, and neurofilaments.[1001,1023,1024,1037,1042,1043,1049] In addition, many peptide hormones have been detected in individual tumors, sometimes in combination. They include the following: somatostatin, bombesin, gastrin-releasing peptide, growth-hormone-releasing peptide, gastrin, substance P, pancreatic polypeptide, VIP, ACTH, and calcitonin.[1000,1006,1018,1031,1035,1045,1046,1048]

In addition to the many neuroendocrine-type markers above described, pulmonary carcinoid tumors consistently display immunoreactivity for the nuclear transcription factor TTF-1, thus rendering this marker an important tool for the differential diagnosis between primary and metastatic carcinoid tumors in the lung.[1029,1038] Their usual keratin profiles CK7+/CK20–.[1003]

The interesting observation has been made that neuroendocrine lung tumors produce exclusively the alpha subunit of hCG (hCα).[1008]

An additional marker of carcinoid tumor and other neuroendocrine tumors of the lung (including small cell carcinoma) is microtubule-associated protein-2. This is a member of the cytoskeleton family proteins that seems to be specifically expressed in neuronally-differentiate cells.[1025]

Carcinoid tumors with a prominent nesting pattern of growth may acquire a "paraganglioid" appearance, which is accentuated by the presence of S-100 protein-positive sustentacular cells at the periphery of the nests[1012,1016,1030] (Fig. 7.163). In exceptional cases, carcinoid tumor is found to contain melanin granules in the tumor cells ("melanotic carcinoid tumor").[1005,1014]

Flow cytometry studies have shown that aneuploidy is more common in the atypical carcinoid than in central carcinoid, but that it is still seen in one third of the latter

and that it is not necessarily associated with a poor prognosis.[1009,1020,1022,1050]

Cytogenetically, typical (as well as atypical) carcinoid tumors are characterized by 11q deletions.[1044]

Metastases to regional lymph nodes occur in about 5% of the cases; rare instances of distant metastases have also been documented. Those located in bone are characteristically of the osteoblastic type.[1041]

From a diagnostic viewpoint, central carcinoid tumors are easily identifiable with the bronchoscope in the majority of cases.[1047] Bronchoscopic biopsy is usually positive, although severe hemorrhage may result because of the marked vascularity of the tumors. The microscopic diagnosis is generally easy, although small samples with crushing artifact can be confused with small cell carcinoma as we have seen on several occasions.[1019,1027] The diagnosis can also be made on cytologic examination, but the well-differentiated nature of the tumor cells and the fact that the tumor is usually covered by normal or metaplastic mucosa conspire to render most specimens nondiagnostic.[1015] Instead, fine-needle aspiration is often diagnostic.[1040]

The treatment is surgical. Removal through the bronchoscope is not adequate because of the infiltrative nature of the tumor.[846] Depending on the location of the tumor along the bronchial tree and the status of the distal lung, operation may be a segmental bronchial resection, a lobectomy (the usual procedure), or a pneumonectomy.[997,1038,1047,1047] The overall prognosis is excellent.[1028] It has been suggested that carcinoid tumors exhibiting immunoreactivity for CEA are associated with a more aggressive behavior manifested by a greater propensity for nodal metastases.[999]

Oncocytic carcinoid is a variant of carcinoid tumor (usually of the central type) in which the tumor cells have an abundant, granular acidophilic cytoplasm[1021] (Fig. 7.164). At the ultrastructural level, the cytoplasm contains numerous mitochondria and also dense-core secretory granules.[1032,1036] The differential diagnosis is with oncocy-

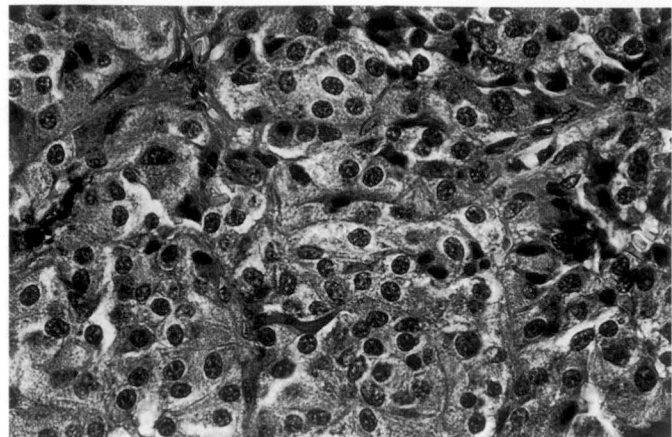

Fig. 7.164 Oncocytic variant of carcinoid tumor.

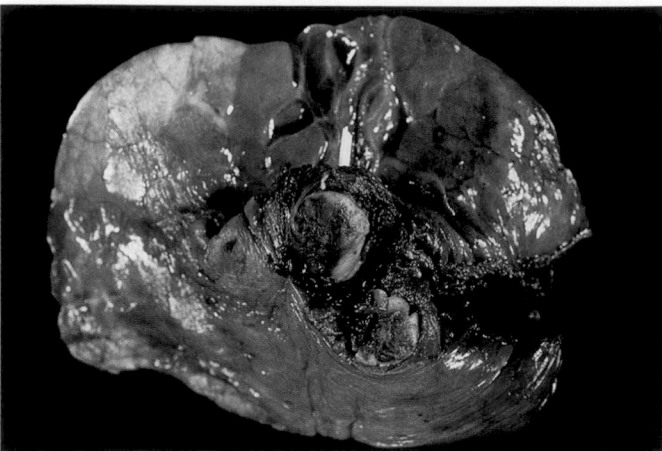

Fig. 7.165 Typical subpleural location of peripheral carcinoid tumor.

toma (see p. 419), and the behavior appears similar to that of central carcinoid tumor of the usual type.

Peripheral carcinoid tumor

As the name indicates, peripheral carcinoid tumor arises in the peripheral lung, often immediately beneath the pleura (Fig. 7.165). Because of its location, it is usually asymptomatic and discovered incidentally. It tends to be multiple and presents grossly as a nonencapsulated gray to tan nodule not bearing an anatomic relationship with a bronchus. Microscopically, it is composed of spindle cells that may closely simulate the appearance of smooth muscle cells; it is not unusual for this lesion to be misdiagnosed as leiomyoma as a result[1054] (Fig. 7.166). The arrangement of the cells is disorderly and there is a certain degree of pleomorphism.[1060] The stroma can be prominent, sometimes of such a degree and amount as to produce restrictive and obstructive lung disease when multiple tumors are present.[1060] As in the case of central carcinoid tumor, the peripheral type may acquire paraganglioma-like features because of the presence of S-100 protein-positive sustentacular cells.[1062]

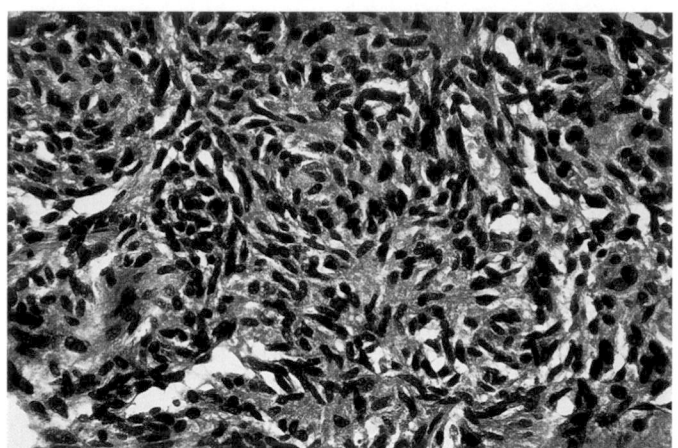

Fig. 7.166 Spindle cell appearance of peripheral carcinoid tumor, which may simulate a mesenchymal neoplasm.

Amyloid and melanin may be found, and calcitonin reactivity may be demonstrated immunohistochemically[1059]; these features establish a close histogenetic link between peripheral lung carcinoid, thymic carcinoid, and thyroid medullary carcinoma. Most other immunohistochemical reactions are similar to those of central carcinoid tumor.[1067] A case has been reported in association with Merkel cell tumor of the skin.[1063]

The prognosis of peripheral carcinoid tumor is excellent; regional node metastases are very rare, and most cases are cured by limited surgery.[1065] Lobectomy is preferable to wedge resection because of the possibility of multicentricity; enucleation should not be attempted.

Tumorlet (carcinoid tumorlet) is the term given to a nodular proliferation of small spindle cells seen in relation to bronchioles, often in association with bronchiectasis and other conditions associated with scarring, including that associated with intralobular

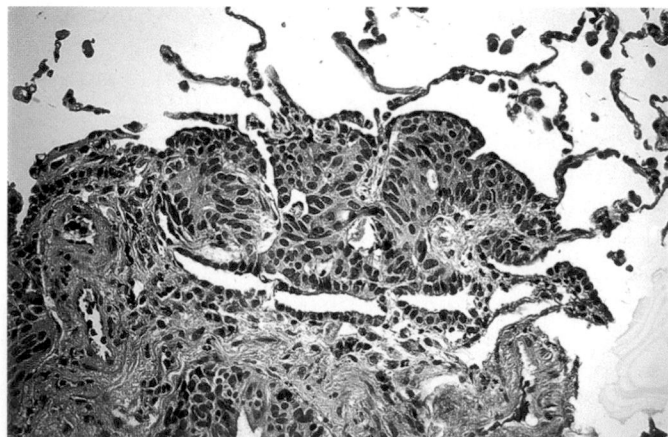

Fig. 7.167 So-called pulmonary tumorlet. The proliferating cells have a close anatomic relationship with terminal bronchioles.

sequestration[1064] (Fig. 7.167). In rare cases, a *diffuse* proliferation of neuroendocrine cells is seen in the context of interstitial lung disease.[1052,1053]

The cells of pulmonary tumorlet have been found to have the same ultrastructural and immunohistochemical features as those of peripheral carcinoid tumor.[1055,1058,1068]

Therefore they have been regarded as either nodular proliferations of endocrine cells or minute carcinoid tumors; indeed, sometimes one sees them in association with a typical peripheral carcinoid.[1061,1066] It has been suggested that a size of 0.5 cm should be used as a criterion for the distinction between tumorlet and carcinoid tumor. The fact that at the cytogenetic level the tumorlets generally lack the 11q13 allelic imbalance that is characteristic of carcinoid tumors suggest a different molecular pathogenesis for the two lesions and provides a further tool for their differential diagnosis.[1057]

The behavior of tumorlet is generally benign, although isolated instances of metastatic behavior have been reported.[1056]

Atypical carcinoid tumor (with a discussion on related neuroendocrine tumors)

Some lung tumors exhibit the overall architectural, ultrastructural, and immunohistochemical features of carcinoid tumor but also exhibit atypical features in the form of increased mitotic activity, nuclear hyperchromasia, and foci of necrosis[1070,1090,1096] (Fig. 7.168). These have been referred to as atypical (intermediate, grade IV) carcinoid tumors. Like their more typical counterparts, they may express various neuroendocrine and neural markers,[1076] and be occasionally accompanied by amyloid deposition in the stroma.[1069] It has been suggested that these neoplasms represent a link between typical carcinoid tumor and small cell carcinoma.[1091] Whether such a histogenetic link exists or not—and there is strong evidence against it[1078,1080]—there is no question that, for prognostic and therapeutic purposes, typical carcinoid tumors of either the central or peripheral types should be sharply separated from the atypical variety.[1097] In one series the incidence of lymph node metastases for atypical carcinoid was almost 70%, as opposed to an incidence of about 5% for the typical carcinoid.[1070] Therefore the treatment should be more aggressive and not different from that for ordinary lung carcinoma of non-small cell type.[1098] In one recent large series, the 5- and 10-year survival of atypical carcinoid was 56% and 35%, respectively.[1095] Features of adverse prognostic significance are female gender, high tumor stage, large tumor size (over 3.5 cm), high mitotic rate, pleomorphism, and aerogenous spread, whereas rosette formation is said to be a favorable sign.[1072]

It would be inappropriate to leave the subject of atypical carcinoid tumors without commenting on the fact that serious problems still exist in the proper categorization of this family of tumors. These problems stem from the fact that there are lung neoplasms exhibiting evidence of neuroendocrine differentiation in which there is difficulty deciding to which of these three categories they belong and still others that do not seem to fit the criteria for any of them.[1073,1082,1083,1093] Travis et al.[1074] have made a brave attempt in putting some order into this chaotic situation by separating these tumors into the following categories:

1 *Typical carcinoid tumors*, whether central or peripheral. These have a characteristically low nuclear grade, practically no mitotic activity or necrosis, very well-developed neuroendocrine architecture, and equally well-developed neuroendocrine phenotype at the ultrastructural and immunohistochemical level.
2 *Atypical carcinoid tumors*. These have a higher nuclear grade, more mitoses (2 to 10 per 10 HPF) and more necrosis but retain a highly developed neuroendocrine architecture and ultrastructural/immunohistochemical phenotype.
3 *Large cell neuroendocrine carcinomas*. These tumors are composed of larger cells than the atypical carcinoid. Their nuclear grade is just as high, and so is the number of mitoses (over 10 per 10 HPF) and amount of necrosis. However, their neuroendocrine architecture is not nearly as well developed. It is manifested—at most—by nesting with peripheral palisading and some rosette-like structures. Despite this, there is clearcut evidence of a neuroendocrine phenotype at the ultrastructural and/or immunohistochemical level.[1085,1089]
4 *Non-small cell carcinomas with neuroendocrine features*. These tumors look like ordinary non-small cell carcinomas of one type or another at the hematoxylin-and-eosin (H&E) level (i.e., they do not have a detectable neuroendocrine architecture at all), but ultrastructural, immunohistochemical or other special studies demonstrate neuroendocrine markers in them.[1079]
5 *Small cell carcinomas*. These have the typical cytoarchitectural features of this tumor, as described on p. 398. The neuroendocrine architecture is very poorly developed, if present at all. Ultrastructural and immunohistochemical studies will show some evidence of a neuroendocrine phenotype in most (although apparently not in all) of the cases but in a much lesser degree than for all the other types listed.

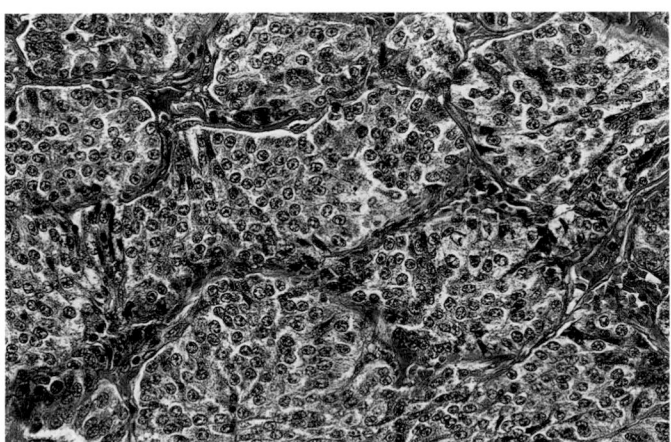

Fig. 7.168 Atypical carcinoid tumor. This case was included in the original report of this entity by Arrigoni et al.[1070]

Great difficulties may be encountered in placing a given tumor into one category or another, whether using this or analogous schemes.[1075] A simple-minded approach that can be used as a first approximation to the differential diagnosis is the following:

- If the tumor strikes the observer immediately as a carcinoid, but on closer inspection one realizes that it has atypical features, it probably belongs to category 2.
- If the tumor strikes the observer on first look as a non-small cell carcinoma, but on closer inspection one realizes that there is some degree of neuroendocrine architecture and neuroendocrine-type nuclear features (and this suspicion is confirmed by special techniques), it probably belongs to category 3.
- If the tumor looks like a non-small cell carcinoma of one conventional type or another (with the possibility of neuroendocrine differentiation not having arisen even after closer inspection), but ultrastructural and/or immunohistochemical studies done for whatever reason bring the surprising news that the tumor cells have a neuroendocrine phenotype, the tumor probably belongs to category 4.
- If the tumor has all the cytoarchitectural features that one associates with small cell carcinoma, but closer inspection reveals that the nuclei of the tumor cells are larger than they ought to be, the tumor probably still belongs to one of the subsets of the small cell carcinoma family, that is, category 5.

It should be obvious to the reader that this remains an imperfect, arbitrary, and conceptually unsatisfactory scheme and that additional work is needed in this area. Hopefully, determination of objective parameters such as nucleocytoplasmic ratio (as evaluated by image analysis), different sets of cell markers, DNA ploidy, and expression of various oncogenes will provide a more sensible and reproducible way to predict prognosis and response to therapy in this family of tumors.[1071,1073,1074,1077,1081,1084,1086–1088,1092]

Paraganglioma and other endocrine neoplasms

Paragangliomas have been exceptionally described in the lung, presenting as solitary (usually peripheral) masses. Their histologic appearance is identical to that of paragangliomas in other sites.[1099,1102,1105] Excision is usually curative, but malignant cases have also been reported.[1101] The differential diagnosis with carcinoid tumor may be extremely difficult, even after applying electron microscopic and immunohistochemical techniques, and this had led some authors to doubt the very existence of pulmonary paragangliomas. The presence of ribbons, festoons, rosettes, and positivity for mucin, CEA and especially keratin, favor carcinoid, whereas a prominent "Zellballen" pattern throughout the tumor and the presence of a population of S-100 protein-positive sustentacular cells at the periphery of the nests favor paraganglioma.

Occasionally, a patient with a paraganglioma of the carotid body presents with a miliary pulmonary infiltrate made up of innumerable minute nodules of similar appearance intimately connected with blood vessels.[1106] These have been interpreted as pulmonary metastases from such a tumor, but the possibility of multicentric growth for at least some of these cases also must be considered.

Other endocrine tumors that have been described in the lung include *ganglioneuroblastoma*[1104] (one combined with carcinoid tumor),[1100] and *gangliocytic paraganglioma*.[1103,1104a] It is difficult to escape from the suspicion that these are histogenetically closely related tumors that have been interpreted and named just a little differently.

Minute meningothelioid nodules and meningioma

Minute meningothelioid nodule (MMN) is the term currently preferred for a curious, clinically inconsequential pulmonary lesion originally described as multiple pulmonary paragangliomas (chemodectomas). It is occasionally seen as an incidental finding in surgically excised lung, the lesions presenting as 1 to 3 mm tan–yellow nodules intimately connected with blood vessels. Ultrastructural studies have shown a total lack of neurosecretory granules or other features suggestive of neuroendocrine derivation. The cells have instead an appearance similar to that of arachnoidal cells and the cells of meningioma.[1112] Immunohistochemically, they are negative for keratin and positive for vimentin, EMA, CEA, and progesterone receptors, a pattern again similar to that of meningothelial cells.[1110,1114,1116] Their genotypical features are more in keeping with a reactive rather than a neoplastic process.[1110a]

Meningioma of lung presenting as a primary pulmonary nodule has also been described,[1107–1109,1113] including a malignant variety.[1115] These should be distinguished from metastatic meningiomas to the lung, a rare but well-documented occurrence.[1111]

So-called sclerosing hemangioma

Sclerosing hemangioma is a distinctive lesion that occurs mostly in adult females, being generally detected as an asymptomatic small, solitary nodule on the chest x-ray film. On serial films, the lesion is found to be stable or, at the most, very slow-growing. Grossly, it is well circumscribed but not encapsulated, solid, and tan or yellow, sometimes with hemorrhagic areas (Fig. 7.169). Occasionally it may be cystic.[1125a] Microscopically, there is a compact growth of polygonal cells with relatively abundant eosinophilic cytoplasm, arranged in a solid as well as a papillary or sclerotic pattern; this growth may be continuous with that of identifiable bronchiolar epithelium[1117,1126] (Figs 7.170 and 7.171). Foci of fresh and old hemorrhage are frequent, and aggregates of xanthoma cells may be present. Exceptionally, there is an accompanying florid granulomatous reaction.[1127] The histogenesis of this lesion has been highly controversial since its description as an entity, which has been variously proposed to be of endothelial, histiocytic, mesothelial and

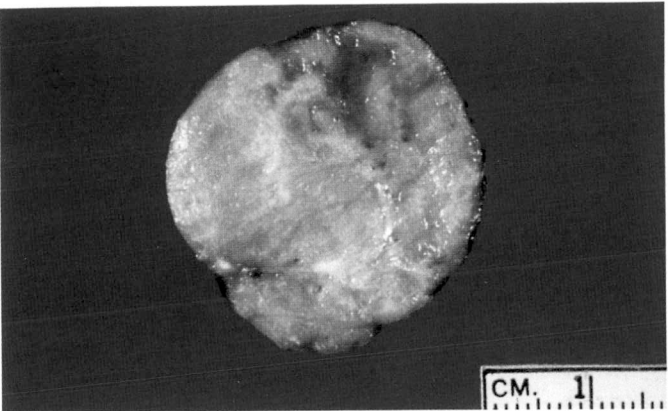

Fig. 7.169 So-called sclerosing hemangioma. Yellow solid areas alternate with foci of fresh hemorrhage and fibrosis.

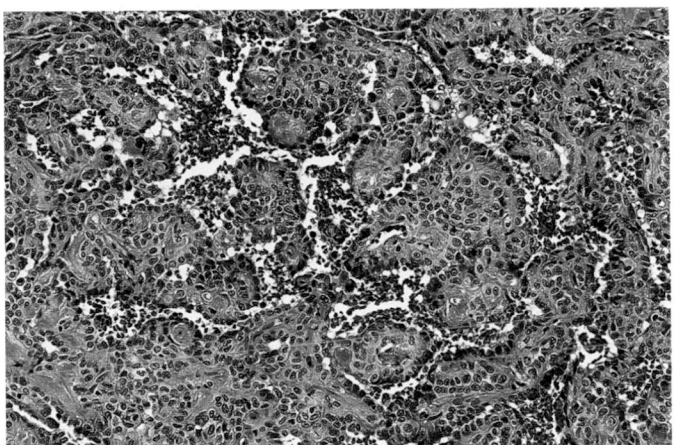

Fig. 7.170 So-called sclerosing hemangioma. A papillary pattern of growth is appreciated on low-power examination.

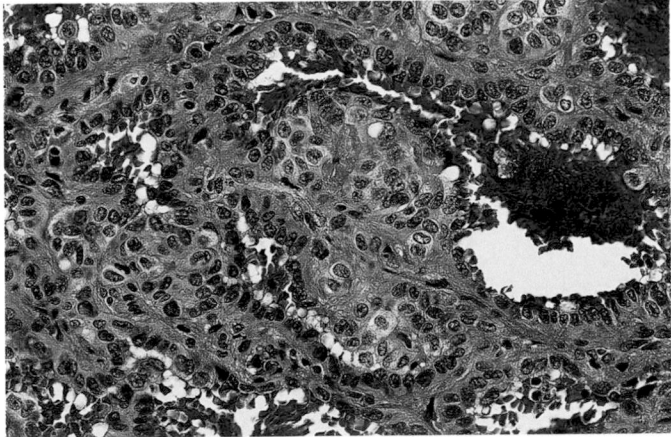

Fig. 7.171 So-called sclerosing hemangioma. The neoplastic "stromal cells" are surrounded by non-neoplastic bronchioloalveolar epithelium.

epithelial nature. Immunohistochemically, there are two distinct components. One is of clearly epithelial nature and reactive for EMA, keratin, CD15, Ber-EP4, apocrine epithelial antigen, and surfactant apoprotein.[1122,1123,1128–1130] Some of these reactivities correspond to those of type II (granular) pneumocytes, as supported by the ultrastructural finding of a microvillous-like folding of the cell membrane and lamellar inclusion. The second—and numerically more prominent—component (referred to as *round* or *stromal cells*) is negative for most of these markers except EMA. However, it is immunoreactive for TTF-1, a feature which it shares with the first component and that suggests an origin from primitive respiratory epithelium.[1118,1120,1124] The proposal has been made by some authors to give this tumor the name of papillary or sclerosing pneumocytoma,[1119,1121,1122] but since it is not yet clear whether the granular pneumocytic component is neoplastic or not, this change in terminology may be a little premature.

From a clinical standpoint, sclerosing hemangioma is a generally benign lesion cured by conservative surgery, although a few malignant examples that have metastasized to the regional nodes are on record.[1120,1126a]

Inflammatory pseudotumor and related lesions

There is a group of pulmonary lesions presenting as more or less circumscribed nodules, having as a common feature the presence of large numbers of inflammatory cells (Figs 7.172 and 7.173). Wide variations on this basic theme occur from case to case or even within the same case and are responsible for the many names and histogenetic interpretations that this group of lesions has received. These variations include vascular proliferation, fibrosis, hyalinization, myxoid change, fat accumulation with the formation of xanthoma cells, hemosiderin deposition, proliferation of alveolar cells, and the presence of inflammatory cells such as lymphocytes and plasma cells.[1133,1138]

It seems likely that many of the lesions diagnosed as inflammatory pseudotumor, inflammatory myofibroblastic tumor, plasma cell granuloma, fibroxanthoma,

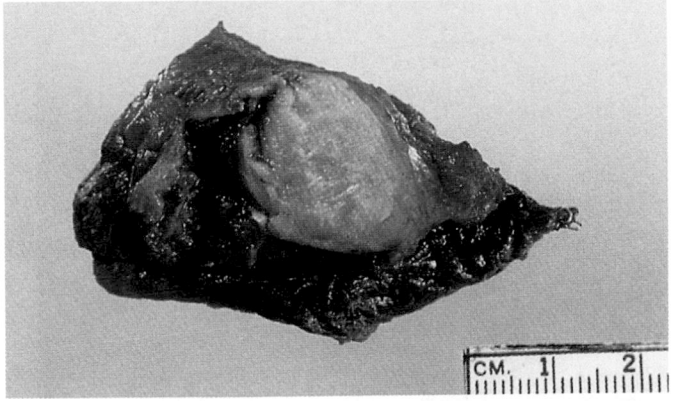

Fig. 7.172 Inflammatory pseudotumor. The lesion is relatively well circumscribed, whitish, and firm.

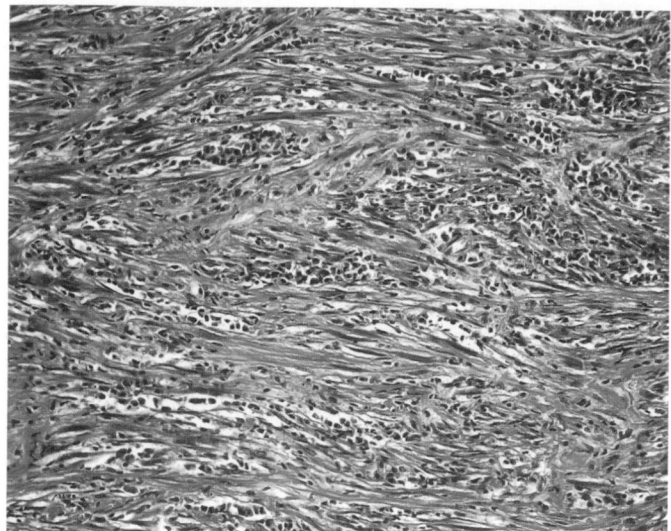

Fig. 7.173 Inflammatory myofibroblastic tumor (inflammatory pseudotumor). Elongated myoid cells are heavily infiltrated by inflammatory cells.

and histiocytoma are closely related processes. Some cases diagnosed as sclerosing hemangioma and hyalinizing granuloma probably fall into this category as well. As is the case with these lesions elsewhere, their inflammatory versus neoplastic nature is in doubt.[1136] Many cases seem to have a clearly reactive evolution and appearance, whereas others are microscopically atypical and clinically aggressive.[1134]

In recent years, a subset has emerged having a reasonably distinct morphologic appearance, for which the term *inflammatory myofibroblastic tumor* has been proposed. In this condition, the predominant element is a spindle cell with immunohistochemical and ultrastructural features (actin reactivity, cytoplasmic filaments) consistent with that of myofibroblastic, or possibly the

cells of the accessory immune system known as fibroblastic (myoid) reticulum (dendritic) cells. These are accompanied by a heavy mononuclear (predominantly lymphocytic) infiltrate which is intimately admixed with the spindle cells, in a fashion reminiscent of that seen in other reticulum (dendritic) cell tumors. The consistent finding of chromosomal rearrangements involving 2p23 and ALK-1 expression supports the neoplastic nature of this subset.[1132]

Most cases diagnosed as inflammatory pseudotumors of the lung occur in adults, but a good number of those rich in plasma cells are seen in children. Actually, they constitute the most common isolated primary lesion of the lung in patients under 16 years of age. The majority present as asymptomatic solitary, small peripheral nodules, yellow and firm, covered by an intact pleura (Fig. 7.174). In rare instances there is extension to the pleura or mediastinum. Other cases present as polypoid endobronchial masses and may lead to distal inflammatory changes.[1131,1137]

Surgical excision is usually curative, but some aggressive examples have been described, especially when the appearance corresponds to that of an inflammatory myofibroblastic tumor or is reminiscent of malignant fibrous histiocytoma of soft tissues. On occasion, the known long duration of the lesion and the presence at the microscopic level of a biphasic pattern with benign and malignant-appearing components suggest the malignant transformation of a preexisting indolent process.[1140]

As above stated, the treatment of choice is surgical excision. However, radiation therapy is an accepted therapeutic option for selected cases.[1135]

Spindle cell inflammatory pseudotumors have been seen as a result of *Mycobacterium tuberculosis* infection in immunosuppressed patients.[1139]

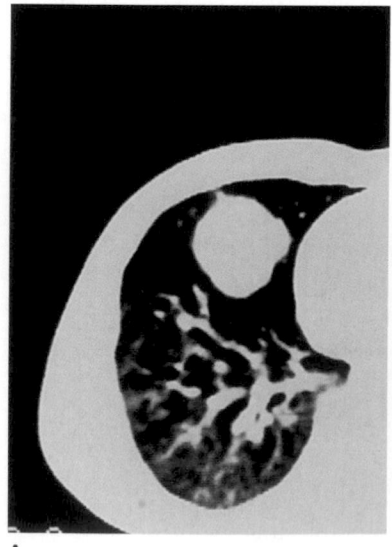

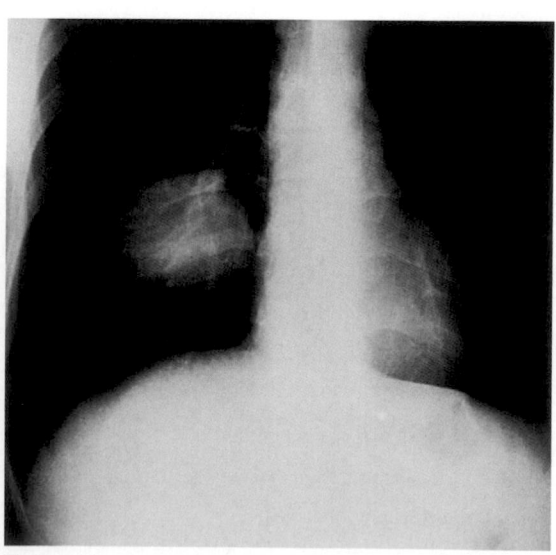

A   B

Fig. 7.174 CT scan and plain radiographic appearance of inflammatory pseudotumor of lung. The lesion has a sharply outlined nodular quality that closely simulates a neoplastic process. (Courtesy of Dr. J. Costa, Lausanne, Switzerland)

Vascular tumors

Vascular tumors of the lung are extremely rare.[1180] Bonafide **hemangioma** is seen more commonly in children[1157]; it can be either endobronchial or parenchymal and should not be equated with so-called sclerosing hemangioma, a nonvascular lesion (see p. 412).

Hemangiomatosis, which is typically multifocal, can present with symptoms and signs of pulmonary hypertension (pulmonary capillary hemangiomatosis) or with the picture of interstitial lung disease.[1153,1154,1175,1177]

Hemangiopericytoma has been described as a primary lung tumor,[1165] but most such cases would be placed in other categories at present, particularly pleuropulmonary solitary fibrous tumor. A particularly notorious trap is the misdiagnosis of a solitary lung metastasis of endometrial stromal sarcoma as a hemangiopericytoma.[1141,1144]

Glomus tumor can exceptionally involve the lung, its appearance being similar to that of its more common cutaneous and soft tissue counterparts; one malignant example of this entity (*glomangiosarcoma*) is also on record.[1142,1156,1161]

Kaposi's sarcoma primary in the lung is usually a manifestation of AIDS[1167,1171] but can also occur in immunocompetent individuals.[1143,1171] The distribution of the disease typically follows lymphatic channels.[1171]

Angiosarcoma can present as a single mass or as diffuse pulmonary infiltrates as an expression of a primary lung malignancy, but the more likely possibility of a metastasis from a distant site should always be ruled out[1170,1179] (see also p. 423).

Lymphangioma and **diffuse lymphangiomatosis** are extremely rare; both of these conditions are more common in children.[1148,1159,1166,1174]

Lymphangiomyomatosis may diffusely involve both lungs.[1150] It occurs *exclusively* in women, generally during their reproductive years. Some patients are affected by tuberous sclerosis and renal angiomyolipomas.[1162,1172] It often leads to respiratory insufficiency, spontaneous pneumothorax, and chylous pleural effusion. Grossly, early cases may simply suggest emphysematous changes, whereas more advanced cases show widespread cystic spaces separated by thick, whitish gray septa. The microscopic features are the same as those of the similarly named lesion of soft tissues[1164] (Fig. 7.175) (see Chapter 25). The proliferating cells share HMB-45 immunoreactivity and other features with the other members of the family of tumors of epithelioid vascular cells, i.e., angiomyolipoma, clear cell (sugar) tumor of lung, and so-called Pecoma[1149] (Fig. 7.176). Indeed, tumors with the appearance of **angiomyolipoma** have been described in the lung.[1160] Progesterone receptors have been identified in the tumor cells,[1146,1158,1169] and objective response to progestational agents or oophorectomy has been documented.[1145,1163] The prognosis of lymphangiomyomatosis is variable[1173]; some patients die

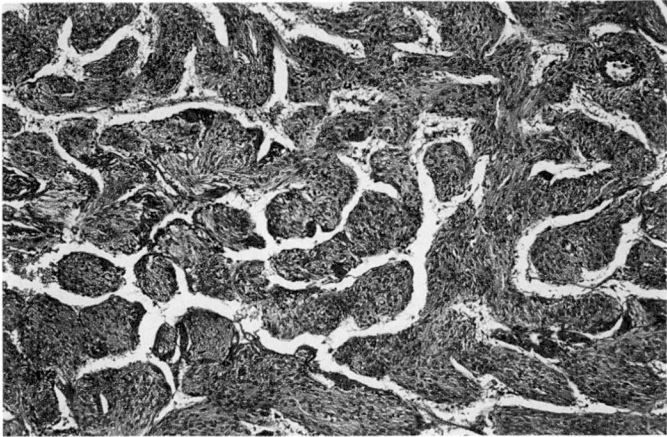

Fig. 7.175 Anastomosing vascular channels surrounded by bland spindle cells in pulmonary lymphangiomyomatosis.

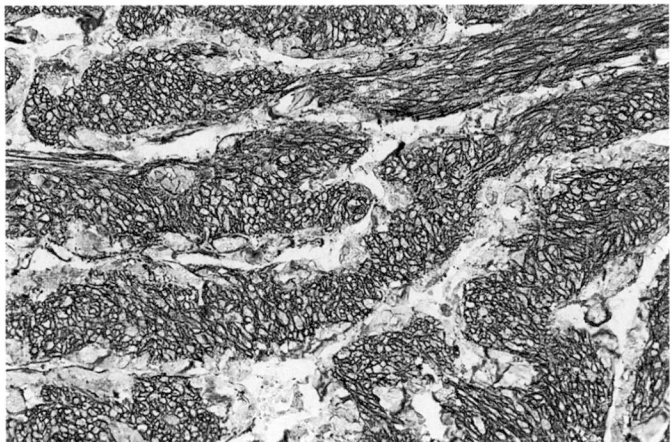

Fig. 7.176 Strong immunostaining for smooth muscle actin in lymphangiomyomatosis. The lesion was also reactive for HMB-45.

as a result of pulmonary insufficiency related to the emphysema-like changes present in the disease, presumably due to the degradation of elastic fibers.[1155]

Epithelioid hemangioendothelioma is the currently used term for the neoplastic process originally described in the lung as intravascular bronchioloalveolar tumor (IV-BAT) and typically appearing as multiple nodules. Many of the patients are young adults, and over 80% are females.[1151] Microscopically, a thin rim of plump acidophilic endothelial cells that may resemble epithelium, histiocytes, cartilage, or decidua is seen surrounding an eosinophilic mass of hyalinized stroma, which is sometimes calcified (Figs 7.177 and 7.178). These polypoid formations fill alveoli and occasionally bronchioles. The lumen of both arteries and veins may also be occupied by tumor, even at a distance from the main mass. Although originally interpreted as a variant of bronchioloalveolar carcinoma, ultrastructural and immunohistochemical studies have shown that the tumor is composed of endothelial cells and that it represents the pulmonary version of epithelioid hemangioendothelioma[1147,1152,1178] (Fig. 7.179).

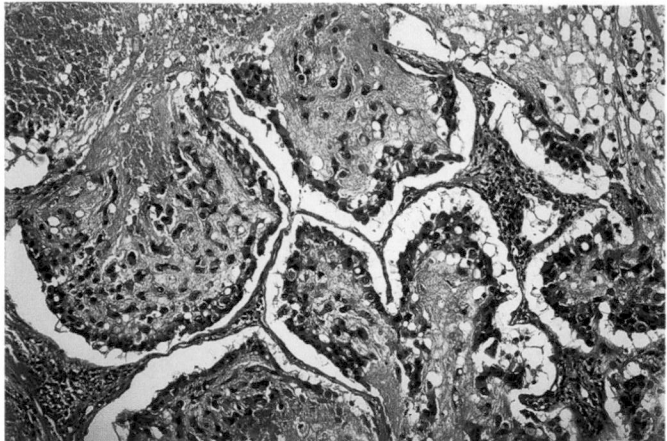

Fig. 7.177 Epithelioid hemangioendothelioma. Nodular intra-alveolar aggregates of tumor cells are seen enclosing an amorphous eosinophilic material.

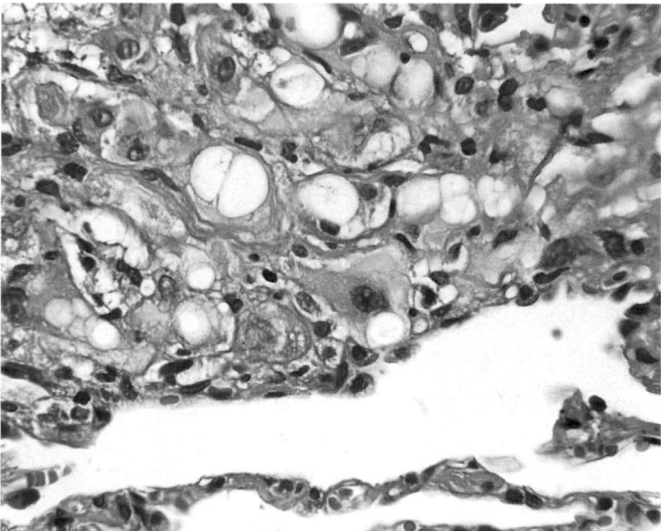

Fig. 7.178 Prominent intracytoplasmic lumen formation in epithelioid hemangioendothelioma.

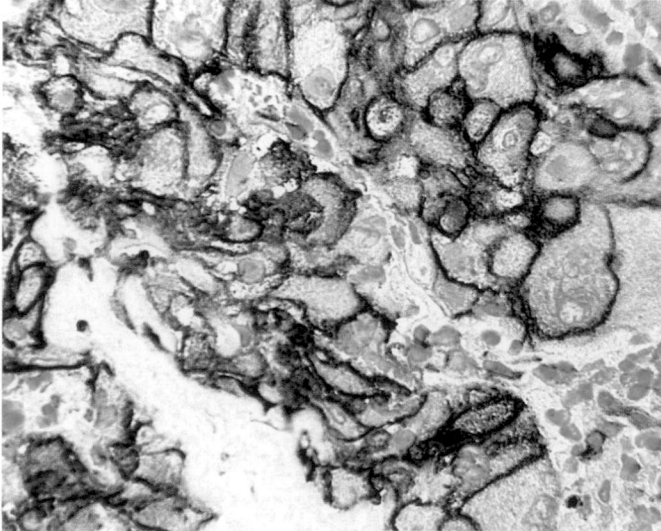

Fig. 7.179 Strong immunoreactivity for CD31 in epithelioid hemangioendothelioma.

The tumor grows in a very slow but progressive fashion, with a tendency to remain restricted to the thoracic cavity. Some patients die as a result of pulmonary insufficiency.[1151] Most of these tumors are primary in the lung, but others with an identical appearance have been interpreted as representing lung metastases from epithelioid hemangioendotheliomas located elsewhere, particularly liver.[1176] The alternative possibility of these being multicentric tumors has also been considered.[1168]

Lymphoid tumors and tumorlike conditions

The lung can be involved by various lymphoproliferative processes, either secondarily or as the only manifestation of the disease.[1195,1204] For purposes of discussion, these can be divided into six broad categories: large cell lymphoma of conventional type, small lymphocytic proliferations, plasmacytoma, Hodgkin's lymphoma, leukemias, and lymphomatoid granulomatosis.[1188,1233]

Large cell lymphoma of conventional type presents as a large mass, occupying most of a lobe and is often accompanied by foci of necrosis.[1189] Occasionally, the pattern of growth is predominantly intrabronchial.[1227] Microscopically, a monomorphic infiltrate of large lymphoid cells is present. Most cases are of B-cell type categories.[1203,1210] Anaplastic large cell (Ki-1) lymphomas also occur.[1186,1228]

Small lymphocytic proliferations resulting in pulmonary nodules are often difficult to interpret. Most of the patients are elderly and asymptomatic, the lesion presenting as a solitary nodule or infiltrate on a chest x-ray film. Grossly, they appear as a relatively well-defined but encapsulated mass, which on cut surface has a homogeneous gray appearance (Fig. 7.180). Some of these lesions are of reactive nature and have been traditionally referred to as pseudolymphomas,[1206,1218] a term which is

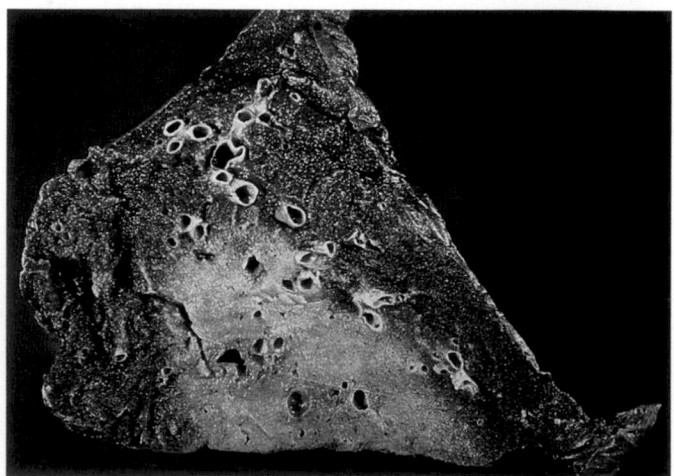

Fig. 7.180 Gross appearance of a lung lesion composed microscopically of a diffuse growth of small lymphocytes. Formerly interpreted as a pseudolymphoma, it is now thought to represent a low-grade B-cell lymphoma of marginal zone type.

probably wise to avoid altogether. Microscopic features said to favor this diagnosis are absence of hilar lymph node involvement, numerous germinal centers, and the presence of other inflammatory cells. In rare cases this reactive lymphoid hyperplasia acquires the features of Castleman's disease,[1216] whereas in others the lymphoid infiltrate acquires a distinctly nodular configuration (*nodular lymphoid hyperplasia*).[1181] Other lesions are neoplastic in nature and represent small lymphocytic ("well-differentiated") lymphomas, with or without plasmacytoid differentiation.[1203,1209] Features in favor of malignancy are the monomorphic nature of the infiltrate; the presence of plasmacytoid features (as opposed to mature plasma cells); the presence of amyloid in the stroma; the invasion of bronchial cartilage, wall of large vessels, or visceral pleura; and a lymphangitic pattern of infiltration[1202,1203,1234] (Fig. 7.181).

In recent years, there has been a reassessment of the well-differentiated lymphocytic lesions of the lung on the basis of immunohistochemical evaluations, the consensus being that most of these lesions are monoclonal and therefore malignant, even when exhibiting morphologic features suggestive of benignancy.[1182,1198,1202,1237] An additional suggestion that has been made is that many of these processes arise from bronchus-associated lymphoid tissue (BALT) and that they therefore represent a subset of mucosa-associated lymphoid tissue (MALT) lymphomas.[1182,1208] This would explain their tendency to infiltrate the overlying epithelium ("lymphoepithelial lesions") and for the circulating cells to "home" to other MALT sites.[1208] The main problem is that it is very difficult to predict on the basis of the morphologic and immunohistochemical features the evolution of these lesions.[1192,1202] By and large, they run a very indolent clinical course and have an excellent outcome,[1234] which is upset in a small minority of cases by the emergence of a high-grade lymphoma.[1202,1207]

Plasmacytoma should be used as a diagnostic term only for neoplastic lesions composed almost entirely of mature and immature plasma cells.[1183,1199,1205] Tumors with a prominent lymphoid component should be classified with the malignant lymphomas. Plasmacytomas of lung may be intraparenchymal or endobronchial, may be associated with nodal or bone involvement, and usually exhibit production of an M protein,[1232,1239] which may appear in the tissue in the form of nodular deposits.[1217]

Hodgkin's lymphoma involving the lung parenchyma is usually associated with nodal involvement, direct extension from mediastinal nodes being frequent in the nodular sclerosis form (Figs 7.182 and 7.183). However, rare cases of primary pulmonary Hodgkin's lymphoma have been well documented.[1223] They occur most frequently in women and older individuals and usually appear as nodular lesions on chest x-ray film.[1231,1241] Endobronchial involvement can also occur, either in the form of a plaque-like infiltrate or as a polypoid mass.[1197]

Leukemic involvement of the lung is found at autopsy in 30% to 40% of the chronic lymphocytic forms, in about 15% to 20% of the chronic myelogenous types, and in over 60% of the adult acute forms, but most of them do not result in clinical manifestations.[1220,1236]

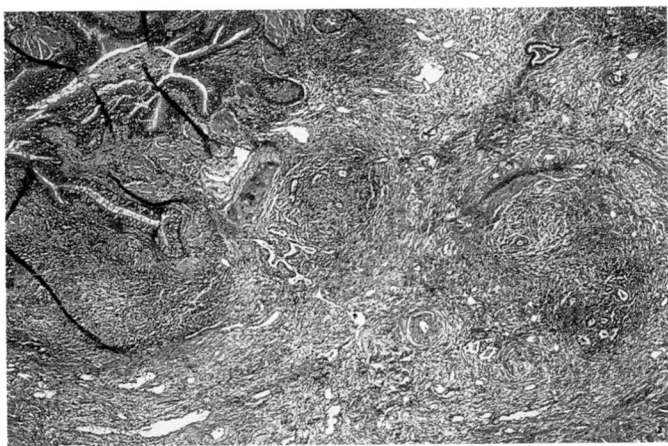

Fig. 7.182 Nodular sclerosis Hodgkin's lymphoma involving lung.

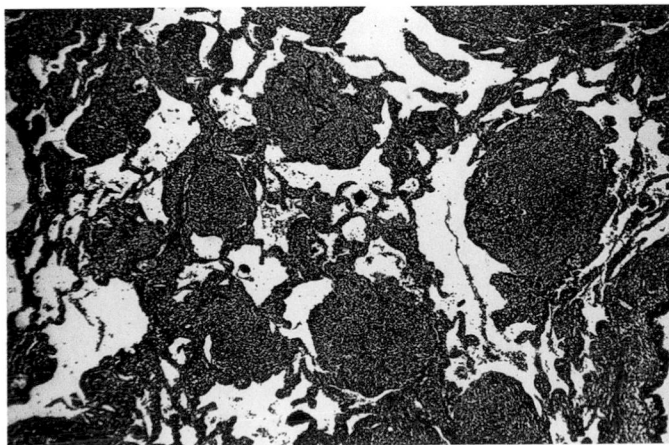

Fig. 7.181 Marginal zone B-cell lymphoma of lung showing a distinct multinodular pattern of growth.

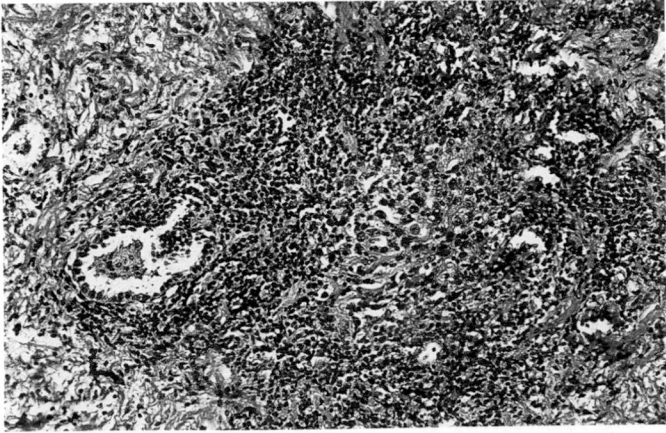

Fig. 7.183 Same case as Fig. 7.183 seen at high power. The mixed nature of the infiltrate and the presence of atypical cells can be appreciated.

Occasionally, however, significant pulmonary impairment results from the infiltrate of chronic lymphocytic leukemia acquiring a selective bronchiolocentric distribution.[1191,1220] In rare cases, acute granulocytic leukemia presents with widespread pulmonary nodules (granulocytic sarcoma).[1184]

Lymphomatoid granulomatosis, originally included by Liebow in his pulmonary angiitis and granulomatosis group,[1210,1211] is now placed among the lymphoproliferative disorders. It usually presents in middle age with well-defined bilateral rounded mass densities, which radiographically may resemble metastases.[1221] Cases of lymphomatoid granulomatosis and similar atypical lymphoproliferative processes have been reported in immunosuppressed transplant recipients,[1196,1224] in association with Sjögren's syndrome, and in HIV-infected patients.[1215] The key microscopic picture is the presence of a polymorphic infiltrate rich in plasma cells, immunoblasts, and atypical large lymphoid cells, with a tendency to involve the walls of pulmonary vessels and to collect in the subendothelial spaces (Fig. 7.184). The multinucleated giant cells and necrotizing changes of Wegener's granulomatosis are not present.

Extrapulmonary involvement occurs in over 80% of the cases.[1229] The most common sites are the skin (particularly in the lower extremities), central nervous system, and kidneys. Other sites include liver, spleen, adrenal glands, heart, and gastrointestinal tract.[1225] The histologic appearance is similar in all of these sites. In rare cases the microscopic changes of lymphomatoid granulomatosis are seen in an extrapulmonary site in the absence of pulmonary involvement.[1185,1230]

It has become increasingly evident that both the morphologic features of lymphomatoid granulomatosis and its clinical course are more in keeping with a malignant

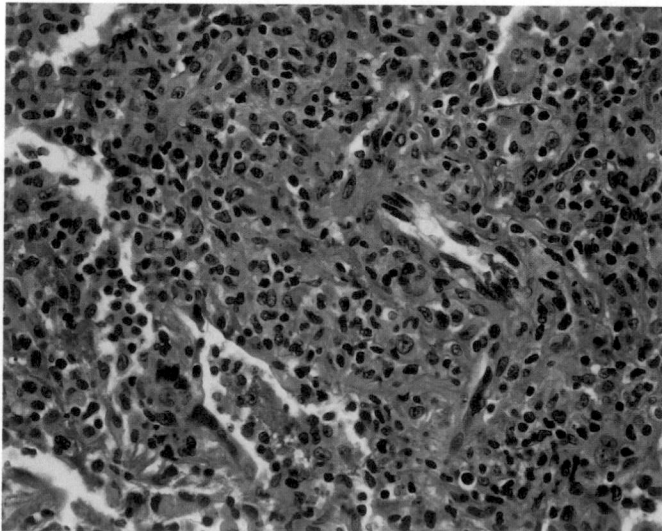

Fig. 7.184 So-called "lymphomatoid granulomatosis." An atypical lymphoid infiltrate containing scattered large lymphoid cells is seen surrounding vascular structures.

than a reactive process[1229] and that it is common for large cell lymphomas of the lung to exhibit vascular infiltration.[1187] Accordingly, lymphomatoid granulomatosis is currently viewed as a primary lymphoproliferative disease that either is or has a great tendency to become malignant lymphoma[1214] An association with EBV has been documented in 50% to 70% of the cases.[1190,1201,1213] On the basis of a combined immunohistochemical and in situ hybridization study, it has been proposed that most cases of lymphomatoid granulomatosis represent a proliferation of EBV-infected B cells associated with a prominent T-cell reaction and vasculitis.[1194,1219]

Response to steroids is poor, but multidrug chemotherapy induces complete remission in about half of cases.[1193,1222] The larger the number of atypical lymphoid cells, the worse the prognosis is said to be.[1200] In a series of 152 cases reported by Katzenstein et al., in the late 1970s,[1200] 63.5% of the patients died as a result of the disease, the median survival being 14 months. Most of the deaths were caused by extensive destruction of the pulmonary parenchyma, sepsis being a common complication. At autopsy, an infiltrate similar to that seen in the lungs was often found in the kidneys, liver, brain, and spleen. Eighteen patients (12%) developed a monomorphic large cell lymphoid infiltrate with the features of malignant lymphoma of the large cell type. Many of these lymphomas had morphologic "immunoblastic" features. Some cases are generalized, whereas others are found restricted to the central nervous system.[1226]

A problem of nosology and terminology arises with the occasional pulmonary processes that show a prominent angiocentric benign-appearing lymphocytic infiltrate. These lesions are not Wegener's granulomatosis of either the classic or limited type, but it is not clear whether they represent a variant of lymphoid interstitial pneumonia with angiitis, a variant of peripheral T-cell lymphoma,[1235] or a distinct entity. Saldana et al.[1229] and others[1238] favor the third interpretation and propose the term *benign lymphocytic angiitis and granulomatosis* for them.

Intravascular lymphomatosis (angiotropic lymphoma) rarely presents with a picture of interstitial lung disease, with dyspnea, fever, and diffuse radiographic infiltrates.[1240]

Salivary gland-type tumors

Several types of epithelial tumors with patterns analogous to those of salivary gland neoplasms occur in the lung, probably arising from submucous bronchial glands. Most of them are located within the main bronchi.[1254]

Adenoid cystic carcinoma is the most common type (Fig. 7.185). It is usually centered in the major bronchi and often involves the trachea,[1257] although peripheral examples are also on record.[1250] Metastases to regional lymph nodes and lung parenchyma are frequent. The primary treatment is surgical excision. Irradiation

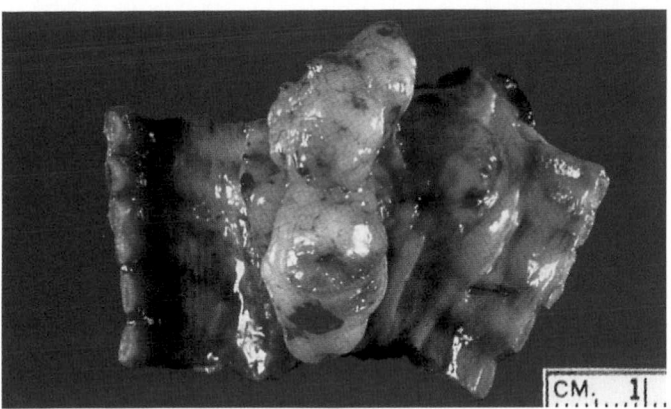

Fig. 7.185 Adenoid cystic carcinoma presenting as a large polypoid intrabronchial mass.

therapy may induce marked regression, but it is not curative. The total duration of the disease is long, but the ultimate prognosis is very poor.[1254] This tumor should be distinguished from basaloid carcinoma with adenoid cystic carcinoma-like pattern (see p. 391).

Mucoepidermoid carcinomas of the lung can be divided into low-grade and high-grade varieties, like their salivary gland counterparts (Fig. 7.186). As in their most common location, they are composed of a combination of mucus-secreting cells, squamous cells, and cells of intermediate type. Several of these cases have occurred in children.[1253] The tumor has a low malignant potential, characterized mainly by local invasion[1266]; however, a few cases have behaved in an unexpectedly aggressive fashion.[1242] Many reported cases of high-grade mucoepidermoid carcinoma are better classified as adenosquamous carcinomas arising from the surface bronchial epithelium. Not surprisingly, they carry a very poor prognosis.[1263]

Cases of lung carcinoma with adenosquamous features, a suggestion of myoepithelial cell differentiation (such as positivity for S-100 protein), and amyloid-like stroma made up of basement membrane material have been recently reported.[1265]

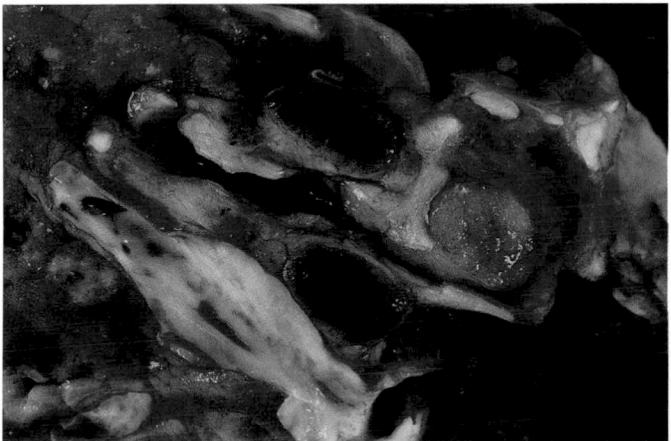

Fig. 7.186 Endobronchial growth of mucoepidermoid carcinoma.

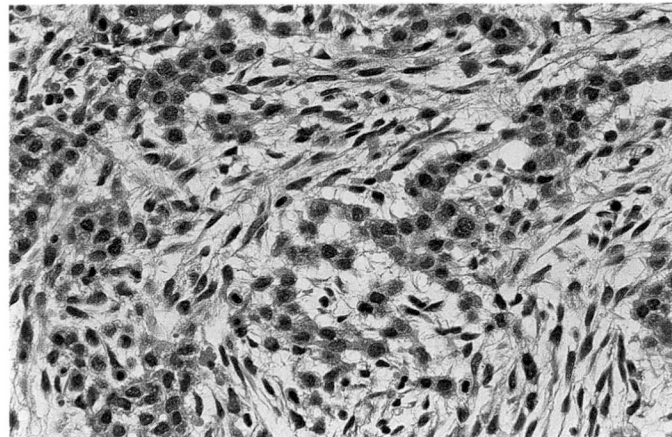

Fig. 7.187 Myoepithelioma of lung. This particular tumor had arisen from a typical hamartoma.

Other tumors in this category include **mucous gland adenoma**,[1244,1248,1252,1262] **mucous gland adenocarcinoma**,[1249] **benign mixed tumor** (pleomorphic adenoma),[1255,1259,1260] its *malignant counterpart*,[1247,1255] **epithelial–myoepithelial carcinoma** (adenomyoepithelioma),[1246,1264] **acinic cell carcinoma** (Fechner tumor),[1251,1256] and pure **oncocytoma**.[1245,1261] The last, which can be malignant, should be distinguished from oncocytic carcinoid tumor, a task that may require ultrastructural or immunohistochemical evaluation.[1258]

We have seen a case of acinic cell carcinoma combined with a typical carcinoid tumor.[1259a]

As already commented upon (p. 407), we have also seen a case of pulmonary myoepithelioma arising from a hamartoma (Fig. 7.187).

Although strictly speaking not of salivary gland, it could be mentioned here the fact that a case of a *sebaceous carcinoma* arising from a bronchus has been reported.[1243]

Clear cell tumor

Clear cell tumor ("sugar tumor") presents grossly as a round or ovoid mass of small size, usually located in the peripheral lung.[1271] It usually occurs in adults, but it has also been reported in children.[1070] Grossly, it is generally small, sharply outlined, and red–tan. Microscopically, it is made up of large cells with clear to eosinophilic granular cytoplasm crowded with glycogen granules (Fig. 7.188). Some cells have a "spidery" appearance. Fat is absent. Mitoses are not seen. There is scanty intervening stroma, but thin-walled vessels may be prominent, as well as extracellular amorphous eosinophilic material (sometimes calcified).

Immunohistochemically, there is diffuse positivity for HMB-45, HMB-50, and cathepsin B; focal reactivity for S-100 protein; and inconstant positivity for neuron-specific enolase (NSE) and synaptophysin.[1270,1273] By electron microscopy, most of the glycogen is usually membrane bound in lysosome-like organelles, in a pattern reminiscent of glycogenosis II.[1268,1274] Intracytoplasmic filaments may be present. Dense-core granules compatible with

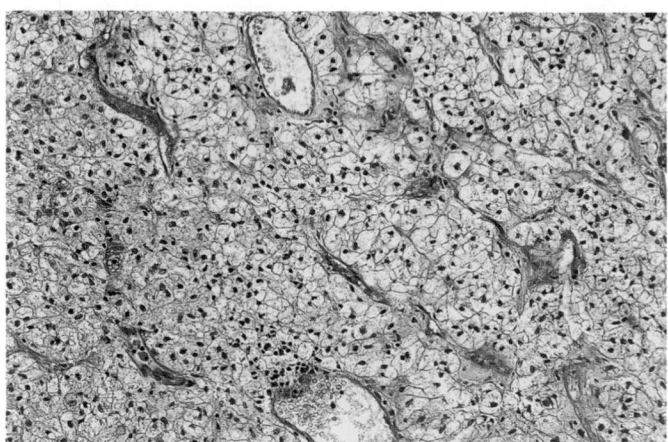

Fig. 7.188 Clear cell tumor of lung. Medium-sized clear cells grow in a solid pattern, separated by a prominent vasculature.

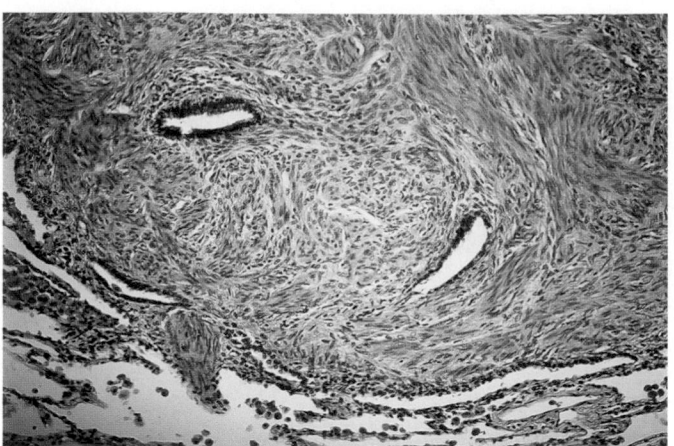

Fig. 7.189 So-called fibroleiomyomatous hamartoma. Fascicles of well-differentiated smooth muscle are seen entrapping bronchiolar structures.

premelanosomes have been found in a few of the cells; in rare cases, well-developed melanosomes occur.[1272] Basal lamina often surrounds the tumor cells.

The histogenesis of this tumor has been a source of great controversy. Pericytes, smooth muscle cells, neuroendocrine cells, Clara cells, and epithelial cells have all been proposed at one time or another.[1267] The HMB-45 immunoreactivity, occasional detection of melanosomes, and other similarities with renal angiomyolipoma suggest that it belongs to the family of tumors of perivascular epithelioid smooth muscle cells (so-called Pecomas), which also includes lymphangiomyomatosis. Indeed, cases have been described of tumors with this appearance outside the lung and kidney (such as in the soft tissues) which have been called primary extrapulmonary sugar tumors (PESTs), but which could just as easily have been designated as extrarenal epithelioid monotypic angiomyolipomas.[1276,1277]

The differential diagnosis of clear cell tumor of lung includes primary carcinoma with clear cell pattern and metastatic carcinoma, particularly from the kidney.[1275] Local excision is curative.

Muscle tumors

Leiomyoma presenting as a primary solitary pulmonary mass exists,[1289,1291] but some peripherally located lesions that have been so diagnosed are actually spindle cell carcinoid tumors. They can be either endobronchial or intraparenchymal and have been described in HIV-infected children in association with EBV.[1281] Multiple leiomyomas of lung, esophagus, and uterus have been described in MEN 1 patients.[1287]

Occasionally, a middle-aged asymptomatic or minimally symptomatic female is seen with multiple small pulmonary nodules composed of well-differentiated smooth muscle, sometimes enclosing epithelial-lined clefts[1282] (Fig. 7.189). Concomitant or preexistent uterine smooth muscle tumors are invariably present. A contro-

versy exists as to whether the pulmonary nodules represent metastases from an extremely well-differentiated uterine leiomyosarcoma (**benign metastasizing leiomyoma**)[1293] or multicentric benign leiomyomatous growths (**leiomyomatous** or **fibroleiomyomatous hamartoma**).[1280] Some support for the latter interpretation is provided by the fact that regression of these lesions during pregnancy or after oophorectomy has been observed.[1279,1283]

Leiomyosarcoma primary in the lung does occur both in adults and children,[1284,1288,1292] but in the presence of a malignant smooth muscle tumor in the lung—even if solitary—the chances are overwhelming that the lesion is metastatic. Most are intraparenchymal masses, some associated with an endobronchial component. Leiomyosarcomas arising from the pulmonary veins can invade secondarily the lung parenchyma.[1290]

Some reported cases of congenital leiomyosarcomas have been reinterpreted as *myofibroblastic tumors* and have been found to be characterized by an indolent clinical course.[1286]

Rhabdomyosarcoma can present in its *pleomorphic* form in the lungs of adults,[1278] or as an expression of the *embryonal* variety in the lungs of children; in the latter, it tends to occur against a background of cystic changes,[1285] and it blends with the pleuropulmonary blastomas having a prominent rhabdomyoblastic component (see below).

Pleuropulmonary blastoma

Pleuropulmonary blastoma (PPB) is a dysontogenetic (embryonal, blastomatous) malignant pediatric neoplasm that is pulmonary- and/or pleural-based.[1295,1297,1299] It is unrelated to pulmonary blastoma, which is a tumor of adults (see p. 397). PPB is characterized histologically by an admixture of primitive blastomatous and sarcomatous elements. The latter may exhibit evidence of skeletal muscle and cartilaginous differentiation.[1296,1300] Some of the tumors are predominantly cystic.[1299,1301] An epithelial component is either lacking or present only in the form of benign-looking, presumably entrapped epithelium.[1294,1298] The behavior of this tumor is aggressive, particularly for the more solid form.[1299]

Miscellaneous primary tumors

Squamous papillomas of the large bronchi can occur alone or, more commonly, in association with morphologically similar tracheal and laryngeal lesions.[1323,1328] Like the latter, they are believed to be caused by HPV.[1335] About one third of the solitary cases presenting during adult life show squamous dysplasia, carcinoma in situ, or foci of invasive squamous cell carcinoma.[1312,1340,1341]

Granular cell tumor can present as a polypoid intrabronchial mass and produce signs of bronchial obstruction.[1307,1311] Multicentric lesions have been described.[1347]

Benign lung tumors other than those already mentioned include intrapulmonary *thymoma*,[1329,1334] *schwannoma*,[1303,1309] *neurofibroma*[1325] (Fig. 7.190), *ganglioneuroblastoma*,[1306] *blue nevus*,[1310] and bronchial *lipoma* *(endobronchial, peripheral, and atypical)*.[1315,1323,1330] Bronchial lipoma is probably of malformative nature and related to hamartoma[1344] (see p. 406).

Solitary fibrous tumor can be entirely intrapulmonary and should therefore be considered in the differential diagnosis of spindle cell tumors of this organ (see p. 364).

Primary sarcomas of lung other than those already mentioned are rare.[1302,1318] *Fibrosarcoma*,[1332,1333] *malignant fibrous histiocytoma*,[1313,1320,1326] *hyalinizing spindle cell tumor with giant rosettes*,[1322] *chondrosarcoma*[1314] (including the mesenchymal variety[1319]), *osteosarcoma*,[1305,1321] *malignant peripheral nerve sheath tumor* (including *malignant triton tumor*[1331,1337]), *monophasic synovial sarcomas*[1348] (Fig. 7.191), *Ewing sarcoma/PNET*,[1345] *desmoplastic cell tumor*,[1343] *follicular dendritic cell tumor*,[1338] and *alveolar soft part sarcoma* have been described in the lung. Some of the spindle cell sarcomas involve diffusely the pulmonary vasculature (Figs 7.192 and 7.193). In the presence of any

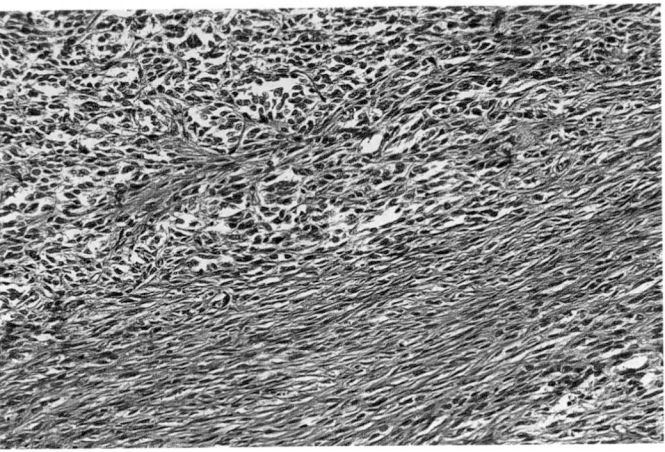

Fig. 7.191 Primary monophasic synovial sarcoma of lung. Some areas have a fibroblastic appearance, whereas in others the cells are slightly plumper, although still lacking an identifiable epithelial organization. There was focal immunoreactivity for keratin.

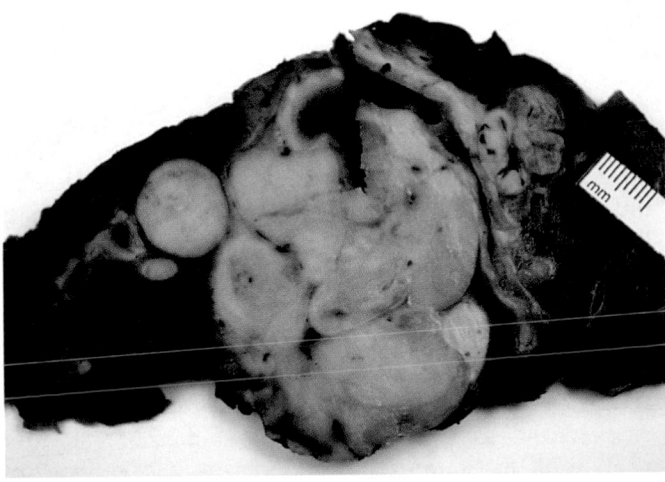

Fig. 7.192 Spindle cell sarcoma of lung with a multinodular pattern of growth centered around large pulmonary vessels.

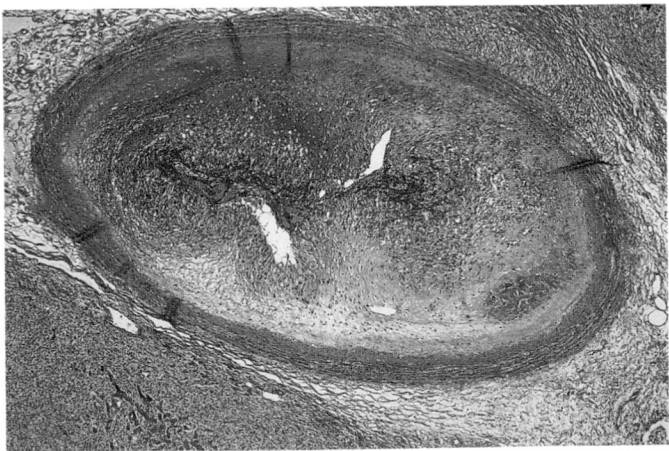

Fig. 7.193 Sarcoma of the lung with prominent involvement of a large intrapulmonary vessel. There was no evidence of tumor outside the lung. Liebow referred to lesions with this pattern as "pulmonary sarcomatosis."

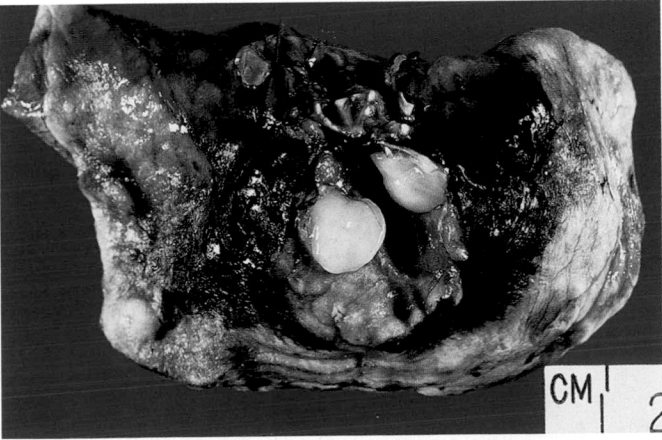

Fig. 7.190 Neurofibroma of lung, an exceptional occurrence.

of these tumors, all efforts should be made to rule out the possibility of a primary tumor elsewhere and/or of a primary lung carcinoma with a sarcoma-like appearance. This applies particularly to the cases reported as *rhabdoid tumor* or *rhabdoid sarcoma* of lung, most of which seem to be dedifferentiated forms of lung carcinoma.[1304,1327,1339,1343a]

Malignant melanoma primary in the lung is yet another tumor type that should be diagnosed with great caution. Although reasonably convincing examples exist (supported by the presence of a "junctional" bronchial component),[1317,1346] the large majority represent metastatic deposits from known or occult primaries.

Germ cell tumors of choriocarcinomatous and other (nonseminomatous) types allegedly primary in the lung have been described.[1316,1336,1342] They need to be distinguished from pulmonary metastases of gonadal germ cell tumors and from primary lung carcinomas with germ cell-like features, both of which are much more common. As already indicated in another section of this Chapter, neuroendocrine lung carcinomas have the capacity to secrete the alpha subunit of hCG.[1308]

Metastatic tumors

The lung is a very common site of metastatic disease, sometimes as the only expression of distant tumor spread. Most metastases are multiple, bilateral, sharply outlined, and rapidly growing; this is particularly true for metastases from carcinomas of breast, gastrointestinal tract, and kidney, sarcomas, and melanomas.[1366] They range from miliary nodules to "cannonball" lesions and are more common in the lower lobes. Other metastases (particularly from carcinomas of stomach, breast, pancreas, and prostate) tend to present as widespread neoplastic involvement of the pulmonary perivascular and peribronchial lymphatics (so-called *lymphangitic carcinomatosis*), which may result in severe dyspnea and pulmonary hypertension, sometimes in the absence of chest x-ray abnormalities.[1379]

In other instances the metastases present as isolated nodules and may simulate the appearance of primary tumors (Figs 7.194 to 7.198). Central cavitation can occur in them; this is particularly common in squamous cell carcinomas of the upper aerodigestive tract, adenocarcinomas of large bowel, and leiomyosarcomas.[1381]

Another type of lung metastasis that can be confused with a primary tumor results from the penetration of intraparenchymal or nodal deposits into the wall of a major bronchus and their presentation as polypoid intrabronchial masses.[1355,1356] This occurs more often with metastatic tumors from breast, kidney, and large bowel.

Yet another pattern of lung metastases is in the form of tumor embolization, in which intraluminal tumor clusters are seen at any level of the pulmonary arterial vasculature; this is more common with carcinomas of

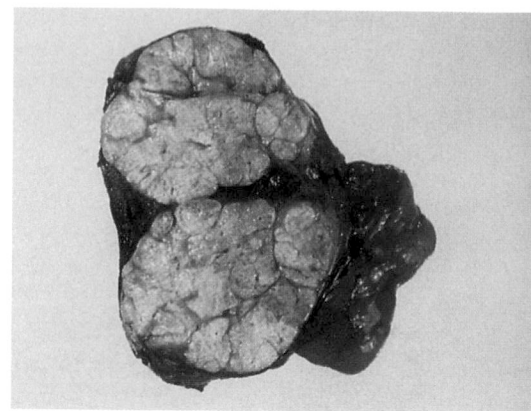

Fig. 7.194 Metastatic renal cell carcinoma to lung. The lesion is well circumscribed, multinodular, and golden yellow.

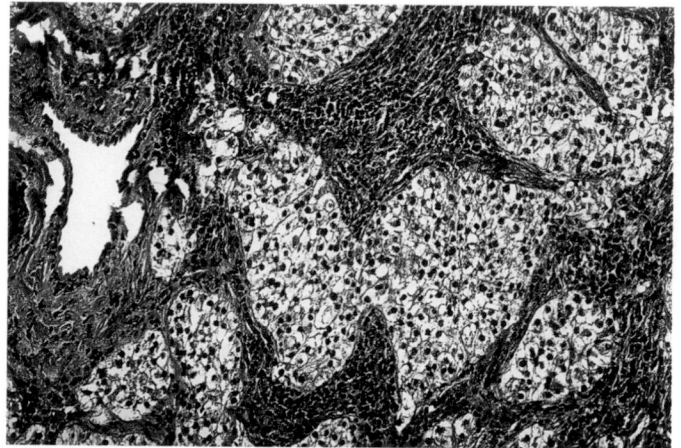

Fig. 7.195 Renal cell carcinoma of clear cell type metastatic to lung.

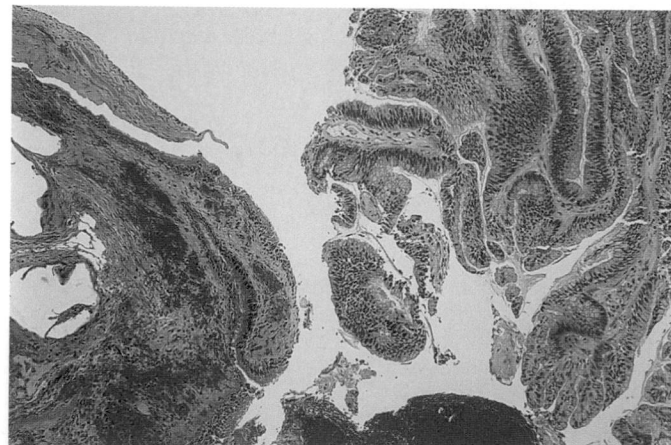

Fig. 7.196 Well-differentiated colonic adenocarcinoma metastatic to lung, diagnosed in a bronchial biopsy.

breast, stomach, and liver, and with choriocarcinoma.[1380] Metastases to the pleura are discussed on p. 366.

The differential diagnosis between primary and metastatic lung carcinoma can be difficult and sometimes impossible. Multiplicity of lesions and extensive lymphatic permeation favor a metastasis. The presence

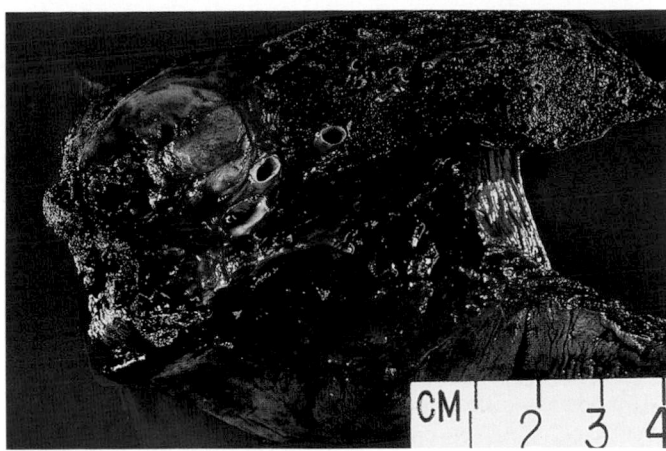

Fig. 7.197 Malignant melanoma metastatic to lung.

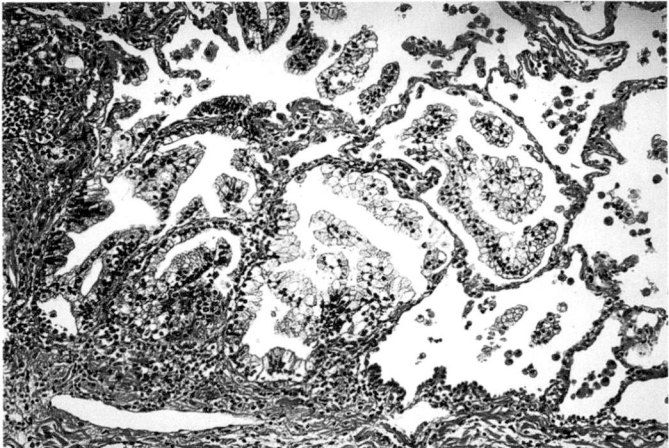

Fig. 7.198 Well-differentiated prostatic adenocarcinoma metastatic to lung, simulating the appearance of bronchioloalveolar carcinoma.

of atypical or in situ changes in the bronchial mucosa adjacent to a squamous cell carcinoma and of honeycombing and atypical hyperplasia of bronchiolar epithelium in the parenchyma surrounding an adenocarcinoma favor a primary tumor. However, it should be remembered that many metastatic cancers to the lung (particularly from large bowel and pancreas) line the alveolar walls in a "lepidic" fashion, simulating bronchioloalveolar carcinomas.[1377] Metastatic adenocarcinomas tend to be more pleomorphic and necrotic than their primary counterparts.

Immunohistochemical staining may provide great assistance in some situations. The presence of GCDFP-15, estrogen receptor protein and/or S-100 protein, favors a breast metastasis over a primary tumor of the lung.[1376] Obviously, positivity for prostatic specific antigen (PSA) and/or prostatic acid phosphatase (PAP) points toward a prostatic origin.[1358] Conversely, immunoreactivity for surfactant apoprotein or protein A is said to be present in about 50% of primary lung adenocarcinomas, but not in metastatic tumors[1369]; however, care should be exercised in distinguishing proliferating

reactive granular pneumocytes from tumor cells. Different patterns of CEA and keratin reactivity help in the distinction between metastatic colorectal carcinoma and primary lung adenocarcinoma.[1364,1368] Specifically, lung adenocarcinoma is likely to be CK7+/CK20−, whereas the reverse is generally true for metastatic colorectal carcinoma. In addition, the latter is usually immunoreactive for CDX-2 (the product of a homeobox gene necessary for intestinal organogenesis).[1352,1383a]

The greatest advance in this field is represented by the detection of TTF-1, a nuclear transcription factor detectable immunohistochemically which, for all practical purposes, is present only in pulmonary and thyroid epithelium. Therefore, its presence in a malignant tumor located in the lung is a reasonably safe indicator that the tumor in question is primary at this site if one can exclude the alternative possibilities of metastatic thyroid carcinoma and extrapment of normal lung structures. The technique can also be applied for the same purpose to cytologic specimens.[1379]

It has been claimed that the presence of microvilli having core rootlets and glycocalyceal bodies on ultrastructural examination of the cells of an adenocarcinoma favors a metastasis from the gastrointestinal tract, but the number of exceptions is such as to severely limit the value of this determination.[1360,1362,1382] Some authors have suggested that different patterns of oncogene expression (such as p53) may provide assistance in this differential diagnosis.[1372]

Among the sarcomas, there are some that are notorious for their ability to simulate primary lung processes. Some metastatic spindle cell sarcomas grow extensively along bronchi and vessels, a pattern that Liebow referred to as *pulmonary sarcomatosis*. Some metastatic angiosarcomas masquerade as either primary vascular tumors or as diffuse pulmonary hemorrhage.[1349,1354] Among uterine tumors, well-differentiated leiomyosarcomas are well known for their ability to simulate leiomyomatous hamartomas, and endometrial stromal sarcomas have often been confused with primary hemangiopericytomas, spindle carcinoid tumors, and other lung primary neoplasms. The fact that the interval between the removal of the original tumors and the appearance of the (often single) lung metastasis can be measured in years or decades contributes to the potential diagnostic pitfall.[1350]

When the pulmonary metastatic foci are few and sharply circumscribed, they are amenable to surgical excision.[1365,1374] Generally, the neoplasms most favorable for resection are well-differentiated sarcomas, and the least favorable are melanomas.[1357,1361,1363,1370] These resectable tumors do not usually cause any pulmonary symptoms and are discovered on radiographs of the chest taken at properly spaced intervals. An important prognostic sign is the interval between the primary operation and the appearance of a metastasis. This was found to be directly proportional to survival time thereafter in the series of Edlich et al.[1359] when the group was considered as a whole. Poor prognostic signs are multiplicity of metastases and presence of hilar lymph node involvement.[1367,1373,1378] In recent years, a particularly aggressive approach has been taken toward lung metastases in children, especially those from osteosarcoma or Wilms' tumor; the excision may be followed by radiation therapy or chemotherapy, depending on the nature of the tumor.[1351] Five-year survival rates of 25% to 40% have been obtained, a remarkable achievement.[1353,1375,1383]

References

PLEURA
Normal anatomy

1   Bolen JW, Hammar SP, McNutt MA. Reactive and neoplastic serosal tissue. A light-microscopic, ultrastructural, and immunocytochemical study. Am J Surg Pathol 1986, **10:** 34–47.

2   Carter D, True L, Otis CN. Serous membranes. In Sternberg S (ed.): Histology for pathologists, ed. 2. Philadelphia, 1997, Lippincott-Raven, pp. 223–242.

3   Ernst CS, Brooks JJ. Immunoperoxidase localization of secretory component in reactive mesothelium and mesotheliomas. J Histochem Cytochem 1981, **29:** 1102–1104.

4   McAuley P, Asa SL, Chiu B, Henderson J, Goltzman D, Drucker DJ. Parathyroid hormone-like peptide in normal and neoplastic mesothelial cells. Cancer 1990, **66:** 1975–1979.

5   Sahn SA. State of the art. The pleura. Am Rev Respir Dis 1988, **138:** 184–234.

6   Wang NS. Anatomy and physiology of the pleural space. Clin Chest Med 1985, **6:** 3–16.

7   Whitaker D, Papadimitriou JM, Walters MNI. The mesothelium. Techniques for investigating the origin, nature, and behaviour of mesothelial cells. J Pathol 1980A, **132:** 263–271.

8   Whitaker D, Papadimitriou JM, Walters MNI. The mesothelium. A histochemical study of resting mesothelial cells. J Pathol 1980B, **132:** 273–284.

Pleuritis and other non-neoplastic lesions

9   Artigas J, Grosse G, Niedobitek F. Reactive lesions of the pleura. Pathol Res Pract 1990, **186:** 228–237.

10 Aru A, Engel U, Francis D. Characteristic and specific histological findings in rheumatoid pleurisy. Acta Pathol Microbiol Immunol Scand (A) 1986, **94:** 57–62.

11 Auerbach O. Pleural, peritoneal and pericardial tuberculosis. A review of 209 cases uncomplicated by treatment of secondary infection. Am Rev Tuberc 1950, **61:** 845–861.

12 Berger HW, Mejia E. Tuberculous pleurisy. Chest 1973, **63:** 88–92.

13 Chan JK, Loo KT, Yau BK, Lam SY. Nodular histiocytic/mesothelial hyperplasia: a lesion potentially mistaken for a neoplasm in transbronchial biopsy. Am J Surg Pathol 1997, **21:** 658–663.

14 Dernevik L, Gatzinsky P, Hultman E, Selin K, William-Olsson G, Zettergren L. Shrinking pleuritis with atelectasis. Thorax 1982, **37:** 252–258.

15 Engel U, Aru A, Francis D. Rheumatoid pleurisy. Specificity of cytological findings. Acta Pathol Microbiol Immunol Scand (A) 1986, **94:** 53–56.

16 George RB, Penn RL, Kinasewitz GT. Mycobacterial, fungal, actinomycotic, and nocardial infections of the pleura. Clin Chest Med 1985, **6:** 63–75.

17 Knapp MJ, Roggli VL, Kim J, Moore JO, Shelburne JD. Pleural amyloidosis. Arch Pathol Lab Med 1988, **112:** 57–60.

18 Martel W, Abell RM, Mikkelsen WM, Whitehouse WM. Pulmonary and pleural lesions in rheumatoid disease. Radiology 1968, **90:** 641–653.

19 Menzies R, Fraser R. Round atelectasis. Pathologic and pathogenetic features. Am J Surg Pathol 1987, **11:** 674–681.

20 Petty TL, Wilkins M. The five manifestations of rheumatoid lung. Dis Chest 1966, **49:** 75–82.

21 Samson PC, Burford TH. Total pulmonary decortication. J Thorac Surg 1947, **16:** 127–145.

22 Yeh TJ. Endometriosis within the thorax. Metaplasia, implantation, or metastasis? J Thorac Cardiovasc Surg 1967, **53:** 201–205.

Asbestosis and the pleura

23 Bhagavan BS, Koss LG. Secular trends in prevalence and concentration of pul monary asbestos bodies – 1940 to 1972. Arch Pathol Lab Med 1976, **100:** 539–541.

24 Cauna D, Totten RS, Gross P. Asbestos bodies in human lungs at autopsy. JAMA 1965, **192:** 371–373.

25 Churg A. Malignant mesothelioma in British Columbia in 1982. Cancer 1985, **55:** 672–674.

26 Churg AM, Warnock ML. Asbestos and other ferruginous bodies. Their formation and clinical significance. Am J Pathol 1981, **102:** 447–456.

27 Craighead JE. Current pathogenetic concepts of diffuse malignant mesothelioma. Hum Pathol 1987, **18:** 544–557.

28 Craighead JE, Mossman BT. The pathogenesis of asbestos-associated diseases. N Engl J Med 1982, **306:** 1446–1455.

29 Gaensler EA, Addington WW. Asbestos or ferruginous bodies. N Engl J Med 1969, **280:** 288–292.

29a Ghio AJ, Roggli VL, Richards JH, Crissman KM, Stonehuerner JD, Piantadosi CA. Oxalate deposition on asbestos bodies. Hum Pathol 2003, **34:** 737–742.

30 Hourihane DO'B, Lessof L, Richardson PC. Hyaline and calcified pleural plaques as an index of exposure to asbestos. A study of radiological and pathological features of 100 cases with a consideration of epidemiology. Br Med J 1966, **1:** 1069–1074.

31 Kannerstein M, Churg J, McCaughey WTE. Asbestos and mesothelioma. A review. Pathol Annu 1978, **13:** 81–129.

32 Kannerstein M, Churg J, McCaughey WTE, Selikoff IJ. Pathogenic effects of asbestos. Arch Pathol Lab Med 1977, **101:** 623–628.

33 Langer AM, Rubin IB, Selikoff LJ. Chemical characterization of asbestos body cores by electron microprobe analysis. J Histochem Cytochem 1972, **20:** 723–734.

34 Leigh J, Rogers AJ, Ferguson DA, Mulder HB, Ackad M, Thompson R. Lung asbestos fiber content and mesothelioma cell type, site and survival. Cancer 1991, **68:** 130–134.

34a Marchevsky AM, Wick MR. Current controversies regarding the role of asbestos exposure in the causation of malignant mesothelioma: the need for the evidence-based approach to develop medicolegal guidelines. Ann Diagn Pathol 2003, **7:** 321–332.

35 Mitchev K, Dumortier P, De Vuyst P. "Black spots" and hyaline pleural plaques on the parietal pleura of 150 urban necropsy cases. Am J Surg Pathol 2002, **26:** 1198–1206.

36 Mossman BT, Bignon J, Corn M, Seaton A, Gee JBL. Asbestos. Scientific developments and implications for public policy. Science 1990, **247:** 204–301.

37 Peterson JT Jr, Greenberg SD, Buffler PA. Non-asbestos-related malignant mesothelioma. A review. Cancer 1984, **54:** 951–960.

38 Ren H, Lee DR, Hruban RH, Kuhlman JE, Fishman EK, Wheeler PS, Hutchins GM. Pleural plaques do not predict asbestosis. High-resolution computed tomography and pathology study. Mod Pathol 1991, **4:** 201–209.

39 Rogers AJ, Leigh J, Berry G, Ferguson DA, Mulder HB, Ackad M. Relationship between lung asbestos fiber type and concentration and relative risk of mesothelioma. A case-control study. Cancer 1991, **67**: 1912–1920.

40 Roggli VL, Benning TL. Asbestos bodies in pulmonary hilar lymph nodes. Mod Pathol 1990, **3**: 513–517.

41 Roggli VL, Kolbeck J, Sanfilippo F, Shelburne JD. Pathology of human mesothelioma. Etiologic and diagnostic considerations. Pathol Annu 1987, **22**: 91–131.

42 Roggli VL, Sharma A, Butnor KJ, Sporn T, Vollmer RT. Malignant mesothelioma and occupational exposure to asbestos: a clinicopathologic correlation of 1445 cases. Ultrastruct Pathol 2002, **26**: 55–65.

43 Rous V, Studeny J. Aetiology of pleural plaques. Thorax 1970, **25**: 270–284.

44 Wagner JC, Sleggs CA, Marchand P. Diffuse pleural mesothelioma and asbestos exposure in the North Western Cape Province. Br J Intern Med 1960, **17**: 260–271.

45 Warnock ML, Prescott BT, Kuwahara TJ. Numbers and types of asbestos fibers in subjects with pleural plaques. Am J Pathol 1982, **109**: 37–46.

Tumors
Benign mesothelioma

46 Ball NJ, Ubanski SJ, Green FHY, Kieser T. Pleural multicystic mesothelial proliferation. The so-called multicystic mesothelioma. Am J Surg Pathol 1990, **14**: 375–378.

47 Butnor KJ, Sporn TA, Hammar SP, Roggli VL. Well-differentiated papillary mesothelioma. Am J Surg Pathol 2001, **25**: 1304–1309.

48 Kaplan MA, Tazelaar HD, Hayashi T, Schroer KR, Travis WD. Adenomatoid tumors of the pleura. Am J Surg Pathol 1996, **20**: 1219–1223.

Malignant mesothelioma
Generalities

49 Dawson A, Gibbs A, Browne K, Pooley F, Griffiths M. Familial mesothelioma. Details of 17 cases with histopathologic findings and mineral analysis. Cancer 1992, **70**: 1183–1187.

50 Kane MJ, Chahinian P, Holland JF. Malignant mesothelioma in young adults. Cancer 1990, **65**: 1449–1455.

Morphologic features

51 Attanoos RL, Gibbs AR. Pathology of malignant mesothelioma. Histopathology 1997, **30**: 403–418.

51a Attanoos RL, Griffin A, Gibbs AR. The use of immunohistochemistry in distinguishing reactive from neoplastic mesothelium. A novel use of desmin and comparative evaluation with epithelial membrane antigen, p53, platelet-derived growth factor-receptor, P-glycoprotein and Bcl-2. Histopathology 2003, **43**: 231–238.

52 Crotty TB, Myers JL, Katzenstein AL, Tazelaar HD, Swensen SJ, Churg A. Localized malignant mesothelioma. A clinicopathologic and flow cytometric study. Am J Surg Pathol 1994, **18**: 357–363.

53 Hansen RM, Caya JG, Clowry LJ Jr, Anderson T. Benign mesothelial proliferation with effusion. Clinicopathologic entity that may mimic malignancy. Am J Med 1984, **77**: 887–892.

54 McCaughey WTE, Al-Jabi M. Differentiation of serosal hyperplasia and neoplasia in biopsies. Part 1. Pathol Annu 1986, **21**: 271–293.

55 Shah IA, Salvatore JR, Kummet T, Gani OS, Wheeler LA. Pseudomesotheliomatous carcinomas involving pleura and peritoneum: a clinicopathologic and immunohistochemical study of three cases. Ann Diagn Pathol 1999, **3**: 148–159.

56 Suzuki Y. Diagnostic criteria for human diffuse malignant mesothelioma. Acta Pathol Jpn 1992, **42**: 767–786.

57 Whitaker D, Henderson D, Shilkin K. The concept of mesothelioma in situ: Implications for diagnosis and histogenesis. Semin Diagn Pathol 1992, **9**: 151–161.

58 Yokoi T, Mark EJ. Atypical mesothelial hyperplasia associated with bronchogenic carcinoma. Hum Pathol 1991, **22**: 695–699.

Histochemical, immunohistochemical, and electron microscopic features

59 Amin KM, Litzky LA, Smythe WR, Mooney AM, Morris JM, Mews DJY, Pass HI, Kari C, Rodeck U, Rauscher FJ III, Kaiser LR, Albelda SM. Wilms' tumor 1 susceptibility (WT1) gene products are selectively expressed in malignant mesothelioma. Am J Pathol 1995, **146**: 344–356.

60 Azumi N, Underhill CB, Kagan E, Sheibani K. A novel biotinylated probe specific for hyaluronate. Its diagnostic value in diffuse malignant mesothelioma. Am J Surg Pathol 1992, **16**: 116–121.

61 Burns TR, Greenberg SD, Mace ML, Johnson EH. Ultrastructural diagnosis of epithelial malignant mesothelioma. Cancer 1985, **56**: 2036–2040.

62 Cagle PT, Brown RW, Lebovitz RM. p53 immunostaining in the differentiation of reactive processes from malignancy in pleural biopsy specimens. Hum Pathol 1994, **25**: 443–448.

63 Collins C, Ordonez N, Schaffer R, Cook C, Xie S, Granger J, Hsu P, Fink L, Hsu S. Thrombomodulin expression in malignant pleural mesothelioma and pulmonary adenocarcinoma. Am J Pathol 1992, **141**: 827–833.

64 Dardick I, Jabi M, McCaughey WTE, Deodhare S, van Nostrand AWP, Srigley JR. Diffuse epithelial mesothelioma. A review of the ultrastructural spectrum. Ultrastruct Pathol 1987, **11**: 503–533.

65 Di Muzio M, Spoletini L, Strizzi L, Vianale G, Fontana V, Orenga MA, Tassi G, Casalini G, Mutti L, Procopio A. Prognostic significance of presence and reduplication of basal lamina in malignant pleural mesothelioma. Hum Pathol 2000, **31**: 1341–1345.

66 Gaffey M, Mills SE, Swanson P, Zarbo R, Shah A, Wick MR. Immunoreactivity for BER-EP4 in adenocarcinomas, adenomatoid tumors, and malignant mesotheliomas. Am J Surg Pathol 1992, **16**: 593–599.

67 Hammar SP, Bockus DE, Remington FL, Rohrbach KA. Mucin-positive epithelial mesotheliomas: a histochemical, immunohistochemical, and ultrastructural comparison with mucin-producing pulmonary adenocarcinomas. Ultrastruct Pathol 1996, **20**: 293–325.

67a Horvai AE, Li L, Xu Z, Kramer MJ, Jablons DM, Treseler PA. c-Kit is not expressed in malignant mesothelioma. Mod Pathol 2003, **16**: 818–822.

68 Hurlimann J. Desmin and neural marker expression in mesothelial cells and mesotheliomas. Hum Pathol 1994, **25**: 753–757.

69 Jasani B, Edwards RE, Thomas ND, Gibbs AR. The use of vimentin antibodies in the diagnosis of malignant mesothelioma. Virchows Arch [A] 1985, **406**: 441–448.

70 Kallianpur AR, Carstens PHB, Liotta LA, Frey KP, Siegal GP. Immunoreactivity in malignant mesotheliomas with antibodies to basement membrane components and their receptors. Mod Pathol 1990, **3**: 11–18.

71 Kannerstein M, Churg J, Magner D. Histochemistry in the diagnosis of malignant mesothelioma. Ann Clin Lab Sci 1973, **3**: 207–211.

72 Kawai T, Suzuki M, Torikata C, Suzuki Y. Expression of blood group-related antigens and helix pomatia agglutinin in malignant pleural mesothelioma and pulmonary adenocarcinoma. Hum Pathol 1991, **22**: 118–124.

73 Kondi-Paphitis A, Addis BJ. Secretory component in pulmonary adenocarcinoma and mesothelioma. Histopathology 1986, **10**: 1279–1287.

74 Kwee WS, Veldhuizen RW, Golding RP, Mullink H, Stam J, Donner R, Boon ME. Histologic distinction between malignant mesothelioma, benign pleural lesion and carcinoma metastasis. Evaluation of the application of morphometry combined with histochemistry and immunostaining. Virchows Arch [A] 1982, **397**: 287–299.

75 MacDougall D, Wang S, Zidar B. Mucin-positive epithelial mesothelioma. Arch Pathol Lab Med 1992, **116**: 874–879.

76 Mayall F, Goddard H, Gibbs A. The frequency of p53 immunostaining in asbestos-associated and non-asbestos-associated mesotheliomas. Histopathology 1993, **22**: 383–386.

77 Miettinen M, Sarlomo-Rikala M. Expression of calretinin, thrombomudulin, keratin 5, and mesothelin in lung carcinomas of different types. Am J Surg Pathol 2003, **27**: 150–158.

78 Oates J, Edwards C. HBME-1, MOC-31, WT1 and calretinin: an assessment of recently described markers for mesothelioma and adenocarcinoma. Histopathology 2000, **36**: 341–347.

79 Okamoto H, Matsuno Y, Noguchi M, Morinaga S, Fujioka Y, Tsuchiya R, Tamura T, Shimosato Y. Malignant pleural mesothelioma producing human chorionic gonadotropin. Report of two cases. Am J Surg Pathol 1992, **16**: 969–974.

79a Ordóñez NG. The immunohistochemical diagnosis of mesothelioma. Am J Surg Pathol 2003, **27**: 1031–1051.

79b Ordóñez NG. Value of E-cadherin and N-cadherin immunostaining in the diagnosis of mesothelioma. Hum Pathol 2003, **34**: 749–755.

79c Ordóñez NG. Application of mesothelin immunostaining in tumor diagnosis. Am J Surg Pathol 2003, **27**: 1418–1428.

80 Ordonez NG. Immunohistochemical diagnosis of epithelioid mesotheliomas: a clinical review of old markers, new markers. Hum Pathol 2002, **33**: 953–967.

81 Ordonez NG, Mackay B. Glycogen-rich mesothelioma. Ultrastruct Pathol 2000, **23**: 401–406.

82 Osborn M, Pelling N, Walker MM, Fisher C, Nicholson AG. The value of "mesothelium-associated" antibodies in distinguishing between metastatic renal cell carcinomas and mesotheliomas. Histopathology 2002, **41**: 301–307.

83 Otis CN, Carter D, Cole S, Battifora H. Immunohistochemical evaluation of pleural mesothelioma and pulmonary adenocarcinoma. A bi-institutional study of 47 cases. Am J Surg Pathol 1987, **11**: 445–456.

84 Oury TD, Hammar SP, Roggli VL. Ultrastructural features of diffuse malignant mesotheliomas. Hum Pathol 1999, **29**: 1382–1392.

85 Rasmusser OO, Larsen KE. S-100 protein in malignant mesotheliomas. Acta Pathol Microbiol Immunol Scand (A) 1985, **93**: 199–201.

86 Riera JR, Astengo-Osuna C, Longmate JA, Battifora H. The immunohistochemical diagnostic panel for epithelial mesothelioma : a reevaluation after heat-induced epitope retrieval. Am J Surg Pathol 1998, **21**: 1309–1419.

87 Ruitenbeek T, Gouw AS, Poppema S. Immunocytology of body cavity fluids. MOC-31, a monoclonal antibody discriminating between mesothelial and epithelial cells. Arch Pathol Lab Med 1994, **118**: 265–269.

88 Sheibani K, Shin SS, Kezirian J, Weiss LM. BER-EP4 antibody as a discriminant in the differential diagnosis of malignant mesothelioma versus adenocarcinoma. Am J Surg Pathol 1991, **15**: 79–84.

89 Suzuki Y, Churg J, Kannerstein M. Ultrastructure of human malignant diffuse mesothelioma. Am J Pathol 1976, **85**: 241–252.

90 Szpak CA, Johnston WW, Roggli V, Kolbeck J, Lottich C, Vollmer R, Thor A, Schlom J. The diagnostic distinction between malignant mesothelioma of the pleura and adenocarcinoma of the lung as defined by monoclonal antibody (B72.3). Am J Pathol 1986, **122**: 252–260.

91 Walts AE, Said JW, Koeffler HP. Is immunoreactivity for p53 useful in distiguishing benign from malignant effusions? Localization of p53 gene product in benign mesothelial and adenocarcinoma cells. Mod Pathol 1994, **7**: 462–468.

92 Warhol MJ, Corson JM. An ultrastructural comparison of mesotheliomas with adenocarcinomas of the lung and breast. Hum Pathol 1985, **16**: 50–55.

93 Wick MR, Loy T, Mills SE, Legier JF, Manivel JC. Malignant epithelioid pleural mesothelioma versus peripheral pulmonary adenocarcinoma. A histochemical, ultrastructural, and immunohistological study of 103 cases. Hum Pathol 1990, **21**: 759–766.

Molecular genetic features

94 el-Naggar AK, Ordonez NG, Garnsey L, Batsakis JG. Epithelioid pleural mesotheliomas and pulmonary adenocarcinomas. A comparative DNA flow cytometric study. Hum Pathol 1991, **22**: 972–978.

95 Esteban J, Sheibani K. DNA ploidy analysis of pleural mesotheliomas. Its usefulness for their distinction from lung adenocarcinomas. Mod Pathol 1992, **5**: 625–630.

96 Mayall F, Goddard H, Gibbs A. The frequency of p53 immunostaining in asbestos-associated and non-asbestos-associated mesotheliomas. Histopathology 1993, **22**: 383–386.

Mesothelioma variants

97 Cantin R, Al-Jabi M, McCaughey WTE. Desmoplastic diffuse mesothelioma. Am J Surg Pathol 1982, **6**: 215–222.

98 Donna A, Betta PG, Bianchi V, Ribotta M, Bellingeri D, Robutti F, Marchesini A. A new insight into the histogenesis of "mesodermomas" – malignant mesotheliomas. Histopathology 1991, **19**: 239–244.

99 Epstein JI, Budin RE. Keratin and epithelial membrane antigen immunoreactivity in nonneoplastic fibrous pleural lesions. Implications for the diagnosis of desmoplastic mesothelioma. Hum Pathol 1986, **17**: 514–519.

99a Galateau-Salle F, Vigaud JM, Burke I, Launoy G, Abdalsamad I, Brambilla E, Capron F, DeLajartre AY, de Mascarel A, Garbe L, Groussard O, Guillou L, Piquenot JM, Thivolet F, Pairon JC, Brochard P, deQuillacq A, Goldberg M, CHU Caen, Caen, Normandy, France. Lymphohistiocytoid mesothelioma, a series of 21 cases. Mod Pathol 2003, **16**: 307A.

100 Hillerdal G, Berg J. Malignant mesothelioma secondary to chronic inflammation and old scars. Two new cases and review of the literature. Cancer 1985, **55**: 1968–1972.

101 Khalidi HS, Medeiros LJ, Battibora H. Lymphohistiocytoid mesothelioma: an often misdiagnosed variant of sarcomatoid malignant mesothelioma. Am J Clin Pathol 2000, **113**: 649–654.

102 Klima M, Bossart MI. Sarcomatous type of malignant mesothelioma. Ultrastruct Pathol 1983, **4**: 349–358.

103 Kung ITM, Thallas V, Spencer EJ, Wilson SM. Expression of muscle actins in diffuse mesotheliomas. Hum Pathol 1995, **26**: 565–570.

104 Lewis RJ, Sisler GE, Mackenzie JW. Diffuse, mixed malignant pleural mesothelioma. Ann Thorac Surg 1981, **31**: 53–60.

104a Lucas DR, Pass HI, Madan SK, Adsay NV, Wali A, Tabaczka P, Lonardo F. Sarcomatoid mesothelioma and its histological mimics: a comparative immunohistochemical study. Histopathology 2003, **42**: 270–279.

105 McCaughey WTE, Al-Jabi M. Differentiation of serosal hyperplasia and neoplasia in biopsies. Part 1. Pathol Annu 1986, **21**: 271–293.

106 Mangano WE, Cagle PT, Churg A, Vollmer RT, Roggli VL. The diagnosis of desmoplastic malignant mesothelioma and its distinction from fibrous pleurisy. A histologic and immunohistochemical analysis of 31 cases including p53 immunostaining. Am J Clin Pathol 1998, **110**: 191–199.

107 Mayall FG, Gibbs AR. The histology and

immunohistochemistry of small cell mesothelioma. Histopathology 1992, **20**: 47–52.

108 Montag AG, Pinkus GS, Corson JM. Keratin protein immunoreactivity of sarcomatoid and mixed types of diffuse malignant mesothelioma. An immunoperoxidase study of 30 cases. Hum Pathol 1988, **19**: 336–342.

108a Moran CA, Suster S. Primary mucoepidermoid carcinoma of the pleura. A clinicopathologic study of two cases. Am J Clin Pathol 2003, **120**: 381–385.

109 Ratzer ER, Pool JL, Melamed MR. Pleural mesotheliomas. Clinical experiences with thirty-seven patients. Am J Roentgenol Radium Ther Nucl Med 1967, **99**: 863–880.

110 Shanks JH, Harris M, Banerjee SS, Eyden BP, Joglekar VM, Nicol A, Hasleton PS, Nicholson AG. Mesotheliomas with deciduoid morphology: a morphologic spectrum and a variant not confined to young females. Am J Surg Pathol 2000, **24**: 285–294.

111 Shia J, Erlandson RA, Klimstra DS. Deciduoid mesothelioma: a report of five cases and literature review. Ultrastruct Pathol 2003, **26**: 355–363.

112 Yousem SA, Hochholzer L. Malignant mesotheliomas with osseous and cartilaginous differentiation. Arch Pathol Lab Med 1987, **111**: 62–66.

Spread and metastases

113 Brenner J, Sordillo PP, Magill GB, Golbey RB. Malignant mesothelioma of the pleura. Review of 123 patients. Cancer 1982, **49**: 2431–2435.

114 Lloreta J, Serrano S. Pleural mesothelioma presenting as an axillary lymph node metastasis with anemone cell appearance. Ultrastruct Pathol 1994, **18**: 293–298.

115 Nauta RJ, Osteen RT, Antman KH, Koster JK. Clinical staging and the tendency of malignant pleural mesotheliomas to remain localized. Ann Thorac Surg 1982, **34**: 66–70.

116 Nind NR, Attanoos RL, Gibbs AR. Unusual intraparenchymal growth patterns of malignant pleural mesotheliom. Histopathology 2003, **42**: 150–155.

117 Sussman J, Rosai J. Lymph node metastasis as the initial manifestation of malignant mesothelioma. Report of six cases. Am J Surg Pathol 1990, **14**: 819–828.

118 Zanconati F, DelConte A, Bonifacio-Gori D, Falconieri G. Metastatic pleural mesothelioma presenting with solitary involvement of the tongue. Int J Surg Pathol 2003, **11**: 51–55.

Treatment and prognosis

119 Adams VI, Unni KK, Muhm JR, Ilstrup DM, Bernatz PE. Diffuse malignant mesothelioma of pleura. Diagnosis and survival in 92 cases. Cancer 1986, **58**: 1540–1551.

120 Aisner J, Wiernik PH. Chemotherapy in the treatment of malignant mesothelioma. Semin Oncol 1981, **8**: 335–343.

121 Curran D, Sahmoud T, Therasse P, Van Meerbeeck J, Postmus PE, Giaccone G. Prognostic factors in patients with pleural mesothelioma: the European Organization for Research and Treatment of Cancer Experience. J Clin Oncol 1998, **16**: 145–152.

122 Klima M, Spjut HJ, Seybold WD. Diffuse malignant mesothelioma. Am J Clin Pathol 1976, **65**: 583–600.

123 Law MR, Gregor A, Hodson ME, Bloom HJG, Turner-Warwick M. Malignant mesothelioma of the pleura. A study of 52 treated and 64 untreated patients. Thorax 1984, **39**: 255–259.

124 Law MR, Hodson ME, Heard B. Malignant mesothelioma of the pleura. Relation between histological type and clinical behaviour. Thorax 1982, **37**: 810–815.

125 Legha SS, Muggia FM. Pleural mesothelioma. Clinical features and therapeutic implications. Ann Intern Med 1977, **87**: 613–621.

126 Ratzer ER, Pool JL, Melamed MR. Pleural mesotheliomas. Clinical experiences with 37 patients. Am J Roentgenol Radium Ther Nucl Med 1967, **99**: 863–880.

127 Vogelzang NJ, Schultz SM, Iannucci AM, Kennedy BJ. Malignant mesothelioma. The University of Minnesota experience. Cancer 1984, **53**: 377–383.

128 Wanebo HJ, Martini N, Melamed MR, Hilaris B, Beattie EJ Jr. Pleural mesothelioma. Cancer 1976, **38**: 2481–2488.

Solitary fibrous tumor

129 Briselli M, Mark EJ, Dickersin GR. Solitary fibrous tumors of the pleura. Eight new cases and review of 360 cases in the literature. Cancer 1981, **47**: 2678–2689.

130 Dalton WT, Zolliker AS, McCaughey WTE, Jacques J, Kannerstein M. Localized primary tumors of the pleura. An analysis of 40 cases. Cancer 1979, **44**: 1465–1475.

131 Dervan PA, Tobin B, O'Connor M. Solitary (localized) fibrous mesothelioma. Evidence against mesothelial cell origin. Histopathology 1986, **10**: 867–875.

132 De Saint Aubain Somerhausen N, Rubin BP, Fletcher CD. Myxoid solitary fibrous tumor: a study of seven cases with emphasis on differential diagnosis. Mod Pathol 1999, **12**: 463–471.

133 Flint A, Weiss SW. CD-34 and keratin expression distinguishes solitary fibrous tumor (fibrous mesothelioma) of pleura from desmoplastic mesothelioma. Hum Pathol 1995, **26**: 428–431.

134 Gold JS, Antonescu CR, Hajdu C, Ferrone CR, Hussain M, Lewis JJ, Brennan MF, Coit DG. Clinicopathologic correlates of solitary fibrous tumors. Cancer 2002, **94**: 1057–1068.

135 Ibrahim N, Briggs J, Corrin B. Double primary localized fibrous tumours of the pleura and retroperitoneum. Histopathology 1993, **22**: 282–283.

136 Janssen JP, Wagenaar SJSC, van den Bosch JMM, Vanderschueren RGJRA, Planteydt HT. Benign localized mesothelioma of the pleura. Histopathology 1985, **9**: 309–313.

137 Kawai T, Zakumaru K, Mikata A, Kageyama K, Torikata C. Solitary (localized) pleural mesothelioma. A light- and electron-microscopic study. Am J Surg Pathol 1978, **2**: 365–375.

138 McPeak CJ, Papaiannou AN. Nonpancreatic tumors associated with hypoglycemia. Arch Surg 1966, **93**: 1019–1024.

139 Moran C, Suster S, Koss M. The spectrum of histologic growth patterns in benign and malignant fibrous tumors of the pleura. Semin Diagn Pathol 1992, **9**: 169–180.

140 Pinkard NB, Wilson RW, Lawless N, Dodd LG, McAdams HP, Koss MN, Travis WD. Calcifying fibrous pseudotumor of pleura. A report of three cases of a newly described entity involving the pleura. Am J Clin Pathol 1996, **105**: 189–194.

141 Renshaw AA, Pinkus GS, Corson JM. CD34 and AE1/AE3. Diagnostic discriminants in the distinction of solitary fibrous tumor of the pleura from sarcomatoid mesothelioma. Appl Immunohistochem 1994, **3**: 94–102.

142 Said JW, Nash G, Banks-Schlegel S, Sassoon AF, Shintaku IP. Localized fibrous mesothelioma. An immunohistochemical and electron microscopic study. Hum Pathol 1984, **15**: 440–443.

143 Steinetz C, Clarke R, Jacobs GH, Abdul-Karin FW, Petrelli M, Tomashefski JF. Localized fibrous tumors of the pleura. Correlation of histopathological, immunohistochemical and ultrastructural features. Pathol Res Pract 1990, **186**: 344–357.

144 Stout AP, Murray MR. Localized pleural mesothelioma. Investigation of its characteristics and histogenesis by the method of tissue culture. Arch Pathol 1951, **34**: 50–64.

145 van de Rijn M, Lombard CM, Rouse RV. Expression of CD34 by solitary fibrous tumors of the pleura, mediastinum, and lung. Am J Surg Pathol 1994, **18**: 814–820.

146 Westra WH, Gerald WL, Rosai J. Solitary fibrous tumor. Consistent CD34 reactivity and occurrence in the orbit. Am J Surg Pathol 1994, **18**: 992–998.

147 Wilson RW, Gallateau-Salle F, Moran CA. Desmoid tumors of the pleura: a clinicopathologic mimic of localized fibrous tumor. Mod Pathol 1999, **12**: 9–14.

148 Yousem SA, Flynn SD. Intrapulmonary localized fibrous tumor. Intraparenchymal so-called localized fibrous mesothelioma. Am J Clin Pathol 1988, **89**: 365–369.

Other primary tumors

149 Aozasa K, Naka N, Tomita Y, Ohsawa M, Kanno H, Uchida A, Ono K. Angiosarcoma developing from chronic pyothorax. Hum Pathol 1994, **7**: 906–911.

150 Attanos RL, Galateau-Salle F, Gibbs AR, Muller S, Ghandour F, Dojcinov SD. Primary thymic epithelial tumours of the pleura mimicking malignant mesothelioma. Histopathology 2002, **41**: 42–49.

151 Aubry MC, Bridge JA, Wickert R, Tazelaar HD. Primary monophasic synovial sarcoma of the pleura: five cases confirmed by the presence of SYT–SSX fusion transcript. Am J Surg Pathol 2001, **25**: 776–781.

152 Essary LR, Vargas SO, Fletcher CD. Primary pleuropulmonary synovial sarcoma: reappraisal of a recently described anatomic subset. Cancer 2002, **94**: 459–469.

153 Falconieri G, Bussani R, Mirra M, Zanella M. Pseudomesotheliomatous angiosarcoma: a pleuropulmonary lesion simulating malignant pleural mesothelioma. Histopathology 1997, **30**: 419–424.

154 Gaertner E, Zeren EH, Fleming MV, Colby TV, Travis WD. Biphasic synovial sarcomas arising in the pleural cavity: a clinicopathologic study of five cases. Am J Surg Pathol 1996, **20**: 36–45.

155 Goetz SP, Robinson RA, Landas SK. Extraskeletal myxoid chondrosarcoma of the pleura. Report of a case clinically simulating mesothelioma. Am J Clin Pathol 1992, **97**: 498–502.

156 Ibuka T, Fukayama M, Hayashi Y, Funata N, Koike M, Ikeda T, Mizutani S: Pyothorax-associated pleural lmphoma. A case evolving from T-cell-rich lymphoid infiltration to overt B-cell lymphoma in association with Epstein-Barr virus. Cancer 1994, **73**: 738–744.

157 Ichi K, Ichimiya A, Akashi A, Mizuta T, Lee Y-E, Tada H, Mori T, Sawamura K, Lee Y-S, Furuse K, Yamamoto S, Aozasa K. Non-Hodgkin's lymphoma of the pleural cavity developing from long-standing pyothorax. Cancer 1987, **60**: 1771–1775.

158 Kukayama M, Ibuka T, Hayashi Y, Ooba T, Koike M, Mizutani S. Epstein–Barr virus in pyothorax-associated pleural lymphoma. Am J Pathol 1993, **143**: 1044–1049.

159 Lin BT, Colby T, Gown AM, Hammar SP, Mertens RB, Churg A, Battifora H. Malignant vascular tumors of the serous membranes mimicking mesothelioma: a report of 14 cases. Am J Surg Pathol 1996, **20**: 1431–1439.

160 Martin A, Capron F, Ligoury-Brunaud M-D, De Frejacques C, Pluot M, Diebold J. Epstein–Barr virus-associated primary malignant lymphomas of the pleural cavity occurring in longstanding pleural chronic inflammation. Hum Pathol 1994, **25**: 1314–1318.

161 Moran CA, Travis WD, Rosado de Christenson M, Koss MN, Rosai J. Thymomas presenting as pleural tumors. Report of eight cases. Am J Surg Pathol 1992, **16**: 138–144.

162 Myoui A, Aozasa K, Iuchi K, Mori T, Yamamoto S, Kuratsu S, Ohsawa M, Ono K, Matsumoto K. Soft tissue sarcoma of the pleural cavity. Cancer 1991, **68**: 1550–1554.

163 Okby NT, Travis WD. Liposarcoma of the pleural cavity: clinical and pathologic features of four cases with a review of the literature. Arch Pathol Lab Med 2000, **124**: 699–703.

164 Parkash V, Gerald WL, Parma A, Miettinen M, Rosai J. Desmoplastic small round cell tumor of the pleura. Am J Surg Pathol 1995, **19**: 659–665.

165 Petitjean B, Jardin F, Joly B, Martin-Garcia N, Tilly H, Picquenot JM, Briare J, Danel C, Mehaut S, Abd-Al-Samad I, Copie-Bergman C, Delfau-Larue MH, Gaulard P. Pyothorax-associated lymphoma: a peculiar clinicopathologic entity derived from B cells at the late stage of differentiation and with

occasional aberrant dual B- and T-cell phenotype. Am J Surg Pathol 2002, **26**: 724–732.

166 Pinckard JK, Rosenbluth DB, Patel K, Dehner LP, Pfeifer JD. Pulmonary hyalinizing granuloma associated with Aspergillus infection. Int J Surg Pathol 2003, **11**: 39–42.

167 Wilson RW, Gallateau-Salle F, Moran CA. Desmoid tumors of the pleura: a clinicopathologic mimic of localized fibrous tumor. Mod Pathol 1999, **12**: 9–14.

168 Zhang PJ, LiVolsi VA, Brooks JJ. Malignant epithelioid vascular tumors of the pleura: report of a series and literature review. Hum Pathol 2000, **31**: 29–34.

Metastatic tumors

169 Chernow B, Sahn SA. Carcinomatous involvement of the pleura. An analysis of 96 patients. Am J Med 1977, **63**: 695–702.

170 Koss MN, Fleming M, Przgodzki RM, Sherrod A, Travis W, Hochholzer L. Adenocarcinoma simulating mesothelioma: a clinicopathologic and immunohistochemical study of 29 cases. Ann Diagn Pathol 1998, **2**: 93–102.

Biopsy and cytology

171 Aaron BL, Bellinger SB, Shepard BM, Doohen DJ. Open lung biopsy. A strong stand. Chest 1971, **59**: 18–22.

172 Boon ME, Veldhuizen RW, Ruinaard C, Snieders MW, Kwee WS. Qualitative distinctive differences between the vacuoles of mesothelioma cells and of cells from metastatic carcinoma exfoliated in pleural fluid. Acta Cytol (Baltimore) 1984, **28**: 443–449.

173 Broghamer WL Jr, Richardson ME, Faurest SE. Malignancy-associated serosanguinous pleural effusions. Acta Cytol (Baltimore) 1984, **28**: 46–50.

174 Chiu B, Churg A, Tengblad A, Pearce R, McCaughey WTE. Analysis of hyaluronic acid in the diagnosis of malignant mesothelioma. Cancer 1984, **54**: 2195–2199.

175 Cibas ES, Corson JM, Pinkus GS. The distinction of adenocarcinoma from malignant mesothelioma in cell blocks of effusions. The role of routine mucin histochemistry and immunohistochemical assessment of carcinoembryonic antigen, keratin proteins, epithelial membrane antigen, and milk fat globule-derived antigen. Hum Pathol 1987, **18**: 67–74.

176 Dewald G, Dines DE, Weiland LH, Gordon H. Usefulness of chromosome examination in the diagnosis of malignant pleural effusions. N Engl J Med 1976, **295**: 1494–1500.

177 Ehya H. The cytologic diagnosis of mesothelioma. Semin Diagn Pathol 1986, **3**: 196–203.

178 Esteban JM, Yokota S, Husain S, Battifora H. Immunocytochemical profile of benign and carcinomatous effusions. Am J Clin Pathol 1990, **94**: 698–705.

179 Frisman D, McCarthy W, Schleiff P, Buckner S, Nocito J, O'Leary T. Immunocytochemistry in the differential diagnosis of effusions. Use of logistic regression to select a panel of antibodies to distinguish adenocarcinomas from mesothelial proliferations. Mod Pathol 1993, **6**: 179–184.

180 Herbert A, Gallagher PJ. Interpretation of pleural biopsy specimens and aspirates with the immunoperoxidase technique. Thorax 1982, **37**: 822–827.

181 Jarvi OH, Kunnas RJ, Laitio MT, Tyrkko JES. The accuracy and significance of cytologic cancer diagnosis of pleural effusions. Acta Cytol (Baltimore) 1972, **16**: 152–158.

182 Johnston WW. The malignant pleural effusion. A review of cytopathologic diagnoses of 584 specimens from 472 consecutive patients. Cancer 1985, **56**: 905–909.

183 Kuhlmann L, Berghauser KH, Schaffer R. Distinction of mesothelioma from carcinoma in pleural effusions. Pathol Res Pract 1991, **187**: 467–471.

184 Leong A, Stevens M, Mukherjee T. Malignant mesothelioma.

Cytologic diagnosis with histologic, immunohistochemical, and ultrastructural correlation. Semin Diagn Pathol 1992, **9:** 141–150.

185 Levine H, Metzger W, Lacera D, Kay L. Diagnosis of tuberculous pleurisy by culture of pleural biopsy specimen. Arch Intern Med 1970, **126:** 269–271.

186 Li C-Y, Lazcano-Villareal O, Pierre RV, Yam LT. Immunocytochemical identification of cells in serous effusions. Technical considerations. Am J Clin Pathol 1987, **88:** 696–706.

187 Light RW, Erozan YS, Ball WC. Cells in pleural fluid. Their value in differential diagnosis. Arch Intern Med 1973, **132:** 854–860.

188 Lopez Cardozo P. A critical evaluation of 3000 cytologic analyses of pleural fluid, ascitic fluid and pericardial fluid. Acta Cytol (Baltimore) 1966, **10:** 455–460.

189 Nance KV, Shermer RW, Askin FB. Diagnostic efficacy of pleural biopsy as compared with that of pleural fluid examination. Mod Pathol 1991, **4:** 320–324.

190 Nance KV, Silverman JF. Immunocytochemical panel for the identification of malignant cells in serous effusions. Am J Clin Pathol 1991, **95:** 867–873.

191 Roboz J, Greaves J, Silides D, Chahinian AP, Holland JF. Hyaluronic acid content of effusions as a diagnostic aid for malignant mesothelioma. Cancer Res 1985, **45:** 1850–1854.

192 Von Hoff DD, LiVolsi V. Diagnostic reliability of needle biopsy of the parietal pleura. A review of 272 biopsies. Am J Clin Pathol 1975, **64:** 200–203.

LUNG
Normal anatomy

193 Armin A, Castell M. Congenital adrenal tissue in the lung with adrenal cytomegaly. Am J Clin Pathol 1984, **82:** 225–228.

194 Ashley DJB. Bony metaplasia in trachea and bronchi. J Pathol 1970, **102:** 186–188.

195 Bando T, Keiichiro G, Ishikawa K, Kuniyoshi M, Kuda T. Ectopic intrapulmonary thyroid. Chest 1993, **103:** 1278–1279.

196 Chen MF, Onerheim R, Wang NS, Hüttner I. Rhabdomyomatosis of newborn lung. A case report with immunohistochemical and electron microscopic characterization of striated muscle cells in the lung. Pediatr Pathol 1991, **11:** 123–129.

197 Colby TV, Yousem SA. Lungs. In Sternberg S (ed.): Histology for pathologists, ed. 2. Philadelphia, 1997, Lippincott-Raven, pp. 433–460.

198 Fraggetta F, Davenport M, Magro G, Cacciaguerra S, Nash R. Striated muscle cells in non-neoplastic lung tissue: a clinicopathologic study. Hum Pathol 2001, **31:** 1477–1481.

199 Gail DB, Lenfant CJM. Cells of the lung. Biology and clinical implications. Am Rev Respir Dis 1983, **127:** 366–387.

200 Hollander DH, Hutchins GM. Central spherules in pulmonary corpora amylacea. Arch Pathol Lab Med 1978, **102:** 629–630.

201 Kellett HA, Lipphard D, Willis RA. Two unusual examples of heteroplasia in the lung. J Pathol Bacteriol 1962, **84:** 421–425.

202 Kershisnik M, Kaplan C, Craven C, Carey J, Townsend J, Knisely A. Intrapulmonary neuroglial heterotopia. Arch Pathol Lab Med 1992, **116:** 1043–1046.

203 Koss MN, Johnson FB, Hochholzer L. Pulmonary blue bodies. Hum Pathol 1981, **12:** 258–266.

204 Kradin RL, Spirn PW, Mark EJ. Intrapulmonary lymph nodes. Chest 1985, **87:** 662–667.

205 Kuhn C. Normal anatomy and histology. In Thurlbeck WM (ed.). Pathology of the lung. New York, 1988, Thieme.

206 Okada Y. Lymphatic system of the human lung. Kyoto, Japan, 1989, Kinpodo.

207 Tamai S. Update. Lung endocrine cells and their pathology. Endocrinol Pathol Update 1990, **1:** 171–188.

208 Tsusumi Y. Immunohistochemical analysis of neuroendocrine substances in nonneoplastic lung and in neuroendrocrine lung tumors. Endocrinol Pathol Update 1990, **1:** 189–214.

209 Weibel E. Design and structure of the human lung. In Fishman AP (ed.): Pulmonary diseases and disorders, ed. 3. New York, 1988, McGraw-Hill Book Co.

Non-neoplastic lesions
Biopsy

210 Burt ME, Flye W, Webber BL, Wesley RA. Prospective evaluation of aspiration needle, cutting needle, transbronchial, and open lung biopsy in patients with pulmonary infiltrates. Ann Thorac Surg 1981, **32:** 146–153.

211 Churg A. Pathologist and pulmonologist. Ever the two shall meet? Hum Pathol 1986, **17:** 763–764.

212 Newman SI, Michel RP, Wang NS. Lingular lung biopsy. Is it representative? Am Rev Respir Dis 1985, **132:** 1084–1086.

213 Wall CP, Gaensler EA, Carrington CB, Wall CP, Gaensler EA, Carrington CB, Hayes JA. Comparison of transbronchial and open biopsies in diffuse infiltrative lung disease. Am Rev Respir Dis 1981, **123:** 280–285.

Cystic diseases

214 Alt B, Shikes RH, Stanford RE, Silverberg SG. Ultrastructure of congenital cystic adenomatoid malformation of the lung. Ultrastruct Pathol 1982, **3:** 217–228.

215 Avitabile AM, Greco MA, Hulnick DH, Feiner HD. Congenital cystic adenomatoid malformation of the lung in adults. Am J Surg Pathol 1984, **8:** 193–202.

216 Barnes PJ. Chronic obstructive pulmonary disease. N Engl J Med 2000, **343:** 269–280.

217 Barnes PJ. New concepts in chronic obstructive pulmonary disease. Annu Rev Med 2003, **54:** 113–129.

218 Corrin B, Simpson CGB, Fisher C. Fibrous pseudotumours and cyst formation in the lungs in Ehlers-Danlos syndrome. Histopathology 1990, **17:** 478–479.

219 Fidler ME, Koomen M, Sebek B, Greco MA, Rizk CC, Askin FB. Placental transmogrification of the lung, a histologic variant of giant bullous emphysema. Clinicopathological study of three further cases. Am J Surg Pathol 1995, **19:** 563–570.

220 Luck SR, Reynolds M, Raffensberger JG. Congenital bronchopulmonary malformations. Curr Probl Surg 1986, **23:** 245–314.

221 Mark EJ. Mesenchymal cystic hamartoma of the lung. N Engl J Med 1986, **315:** 1255–1259.

222 Mark EJ, Muller K-M, McChesney T, Dong-Hwan S, Honig C, Mark MA. Placentoid bulbous lesion of the lung. Hum Pathol 1995, **26:** 74–79.

223 Moerman P, Fryns J, Vandenberghe K, Devlieger H, Lauweryns J. Pathogenesis of congenital cystic adenomatoid malformation of the lung. Histopathology 1992, **21:** 315–322.

224 Nishibayashi SW, Andrassy RJ, Woolley MM. Congenital cystic adenomatoid malformation. A 30-year experience. J Pediatr Surg 1981, **16:** 704–706.

225 Potgieter PD, Benatar SR, Hewitson RP, Ferguson AD. Surgical treatment of bullous lung disease. Thorax 1981, **36:** 885–890.

226 Pride NB. Definitions of emphysema, chronic bronchitis, asthma, and airflow obstruction. 25 years on from the Ciba symposium. Thorax 1984, **39:** 81–85.

227 Soosay G, Badouin S, Hanson P, Gontana G, Jagjivan A, Goldstraw P, Collins J, Sheppard M. Symptomatic cysts in otherwise normal lungs of children and adults. Histopathology 1992, **20:** 517–522.

228 Stocker JT. Congenital and developmental diseases. In Dail DH, Hammer SP (eds): Pulmonary pathology. New York, 1988, Springer-Verlag.

229 Stocker JT, Madewell JE, Drake RM. Congenital cystic adenomatoid malformation of the lung. Classification and morphologic spectrum. Hum Pathol 1977, **8:** 155–171.

230 Wesley JR, Heidelberger KP, DiPietro MA, Cho KJ, Coran AG. Diagnosis and management of congenital cystic disease of the lung in children. J Pediatr Surg 1986, **3:** 202–207.

Bronchopulmonary sequestration

231 Hruben RH, Sjorel SB, Dumler JS, Baker RR, Hutchins GM. Congenital bronchopulmonary sequestrations communicating with the foregut. Am J Clin Pathol 1989, **91:** 403–409.

232 Johnston DG. Inflammatory and vascular lesions of bronchopulmonary sequestration. Am J Clin Pathol 1956, **26:** 636–644.

233 Lager DJ, Kuper KA, Haake GK. Subdiaphragmatic extralobular pulmonary sequestration. Arch Pathol Lab Med 1991, **115:** 536–538.

234 Pryce DM, Sellors TH, Blair LG. Intralobar sequestration of lung associated with an abnormal pulmonary artery. Br J Surg 1947, **35:** 18–29.

235 Savic B, Birtel FJ, Tholen W, Funke HD, Knoche R. Lung sequestration. Report of seven cases and review of 540 published cases. Thorax 1979, **34:** 96–101.

236 Stocker JT. Sequestrations of the lung. Semin Diagn Pathol 1986, **3:** 106–121.

237 Stocker JT, Kagan-Hallet K. Extralobar pulmonary sequestration. Analysis of 15 cases. Am J Clin Pathol 1979, **72:** 917–926.

238 Tandon M, Warnock M. Plexogenic angiopathy in pulmonary intralobular sequestrations. Pathogenetic mechanisms. Hum Pathol 1993, **24:** 263–273.

239 Telander RL, Lennox C, Sieber W. Sequestration of the lung in children. Mayo Clin Proc 1976, **51:** 578–584.

Bronchiectasis

240 Barker AF. Bronchiectasis. N Engl J Med 2002, **346:** 1383–1393.

241 Bolman RM III, Wolfe WG. Bronchiectasis and bronchopulmonary sequestration. Surg Clin North Am 1980, **60:** 867–881.

242 Field CE. Bronchiectasis in childhood. Pediatrics 1949, **4:** 21–45, 231–248, 355–372.

243 Handelsman DJ, Conway AJ, Boylan LM, Turtle JR. Young's syndrome. Obstructive azoospermia and chronic sinopulmonary infections. N Engl J Med 1984, **310:** 3–9.

244 Hilton AM, Hasleton PS, Bradlow A, Leahy BC, Cooper KM, Moore M. Cutaneous vasculitis and immune complexes in severe bronchiectasis. Thorax 1984, **39:** 185–191.

245 Kwon KY, Myers JL, Swensen SJ, Colby TV. Middle lobe syndrome. A clinicopathological study of 21 patients. Hum Pathol 1995, **26:** 302–307.

246 Liebow AA, Hales MR, Lindskog GE. Enlargement of the bronchial arteries and their anastomoses with the pulmonary arteries in bronchiectasis. Am J Pathol 1949, **25:** 211–232.

247 Mallory TB. The pathogenesis of bronchiectasis, bronchial infection and atelectasis. N Engl J Med 1947, **237:** 795–798.

248 Oppenheimer EH, Esterly JR. Pathology of cystic fibrosis. Review of the literature and comparison with 146 autopsied cases. Perspect Pediatr Pathol 1975, **2:** 241–278.

249 Perry KMA, King DS. Bronchiectasis. Study of prognosis based on follow-up of 400 patients. Am Rev Tuberc 1940, **41:** 531–548.

250 Smallman LA, Gregory J. Ultrastructural abnormalities of cilia in the human respiratory tract. Hum Pathol 1986, **17:** 848–855.

Abscess

251 Bosher LH Jr. A review of surgically treated lung abscess. J Thorac Surg 1951, **21:** 370–376.

252 Hagan JL, Hardy JD. Lung abscess revisited. A survey of 184 cases. Ann Surg 1983, **197:** 755–762.

253 Myers RT, Bradshaw HH. Conservative resection of chronic lung abscess. Ann Surg 1950, **131:** 985–993.

Granulomatous inflammation

254 Renshaw AA. The relative sensitivity of special stains and culture in open lung biopsies. Am J Clin Pathol 1994, **102:** 736–740.

255 Ulbright TM, Katzenstein AL. Solitary necrotizing granulomas of the lung. Differentiating features and etiology. Am J Surg Pathol 1980, **4:** 13–28.

256 Zimmerman LE. Demonstration of *Histoplasma* and *Coccidioides* in so-called tuberculomas of lung. Arch Intern Med 1954, **94:** 690–699.

Tuberculosis

257 Auerbach O, Hobby GL, Small MJ, Lenert TF, Comer JV. The clinicopathologic significance of the demonstration of viable tubercle bacilli in resected lesions. J Thorac Surg 1955, **29:** 109–132.

258 Auerbach O, Small MJ. The syndrome of persistent cavitation and noninfectious sputum during chemotherapy and its relation to the open healing of cavities. Am Rev Tuberc 1957, **75:** 242–258.

259 Bailey TM, Akhtar M, Ali MA. Fine needle aspiration biopsy in the diagnosis of tuberculosis. Acta Cytol (Baltimore) 1985, **29:** 732–736.

260 Black H, Ackerman LV. The clinical and pathologic aspects of tuberculoma of the lung. An analysis of 18 cases. Surg Clin North Am 1950, **30:** 1279–1297.

261 Chow L, Shum B, Chow W, Tso C. Diffuse pulmonary ossification – a rare complication of tuberculosis. Histopathology 1992, **20:** 435–436.

262 Danek SJ, Bower JS. Diagnosis of pulmonary tuberculosis by flexible fiberoptic bronchoscopy. Am Rev Respir Dis 1979, **119:** 677–679.

263 Humphrey DM, Weiner MH. Mycobacterial antigen detection by immunohistochemistry in pulmonary tuberculosis. Hum Pathol 1987, **18:** 701–708.

264 Malave G, Foster ED, Wilson JA, Munro DD. Bronchopleural fistula. Presentday study of an old problem. A review of 52 cases. Ann Thorac Surg 1971, **11:** 1–10.

265 Marchevsky A, Damsker B, Gribetz A, Tepper S, Geller SA. The spectrum of pathology of nontuberculous mycobacterial infections in open-lung biopsy specimens. Am J Clin Pathol 1982, **78:** 695–700.

265a Ost D, Fein AM, Feinsilver SH. The solitary pulmonary nodule. N Engl J Med 2003, **348:** 2535–2542.

266 Parker EF, Brailsford LE, Gregg DB. Tuberculous bronchiectasis. Am Rev Respir Dis 1968, **98:** 240–249.

267 Steele JD. The solitary pulmonary nodule. Springfield, Ill., 1964, Charles C Thomas, Publisher.

268 Strieder JW, Laforet EG, Lynch JP. The surgery of pulmonary tuberculosis. N Engl J Med 1967, **276:** 960–965.

269 Sutinen S. Evaluation of activity in tuberculous cavities of the lung. A histopathologic and bacteriologic study of resected specimens with clinical and roentgenographic correlations. Scand J Respir Dis 1968, **67**(Suppl): 5–78.

270 Sweany HC, Seiler HH. The pathology and bacteriology of resected lesions in pulmonary tuberculosis. Dis Chest 1956, **29:** 119–152.

271 Thompson JR. "Open healing" of tuberculous cavities. Am Rev Tuberc 1955, **72:** 601–612.

Atypical mycobacteriosis

272 Chester AC, Winn WC Jr. Unusual and newly recognized patterns of nontuberculous mycobacterial infection with emphasis on the immunocompromised host. Part 1. Pathol Annu 1986, **21:** 251–270.

273 Davidson PT, Khanijo V, Goble M, Moulding TS. Treatment of disease due to *Mycobacterium intracellulare*. Rev Infect Dis 1981, **3:** 1052–1059.

274 Hattler BG Jr, Young WG Jr, Sealy WC, Gentry WH, Cox CB. Surgical management of pulmonary tuberculosis due to atypical mycobacteria. J Thorac Cardiovasc Surg 1970, **59**: 366–371.

275 Snijder J. Histopathology of pulmonary lesions caused by atypical mycobacteria. J Pathol Bacteriol 1965, **90**: 65–73.

276 Wolinsky E. Nontuberculous mycobacteria and associated diseases. Am Rev Respir Dis 1979, **119**: 107–159.

Sarcoidosis

277 Churg A. Pulmonary angiitis and granulomatosis revisited. Hum Pathol 1983, **14**: 868–883.

278 Churg A, Carrington CB, Gupta R. Necrotizing sarcoid granulomatosis. Chest 1979, **76**: 406–413.

279 Hancock WW, Kobzik L, Colby AJ, O'Hara CJ, Cooper AG, Godleski JJ. Detection of lymphokines and lymphokine receptors in pulmonary sarcoidosis. Am J Pathol 1986, **123**: 1–8.

280 Koerner SK, Sakowitz AJ, Appelman RI, Becker NH, Schoenbaum SW. Transbronchial lung biopsy for the diagnosis of sarcoidosis. N Engl J Med 1975, **293**: 268–270.

281 Koss MN, Hochholzer L, Feigin DS, Garancis JC, Ward PA. Necrotizing sarcoid-like granulomatosis. Clinical, pathologic, and immunopathologic findings. Hum Pathol 1980, **11**: 510–519.

282 Liebow AA. Pulmonary angiitis and granulomatosis. Am Rev Respir Dis 1973, **108**: 1–18.

283 Rosen Y, Moon S, Huang C-T, Gourin A, Lyons HA. Granulomatous pulmonary angiitis in sarcoidosis. Arch Pathol Lab Med 1977, **101**: 170–174.

284 Takemura T, Matsui Y, Saiki S, Mikami R. Pulmonary vascular involvement in sarcoidosis. A report of 40 autopsy cases. Hum Pathol 1992, **23**: 1216–1223.

285 Wilen SB, Rabinowitz JG, Ulreich S, Lyons HA. Pleural involvement in sarcoidosis. Am J Med 1974, **57**: 200–209.

Wegener's granulomatosis

286 Barksdale SK, Hallahan CW, Kerr GS, Fauci AS, Stern JB, Travis WD. Cutaneous pathology in Wegener's granulomatosis. A clinicopathologic study of 75 biopsies in 46 patients. Am J Surg Pathol 1995, **19**: 161–172.

287 Carrington CB, Liebow AA. Limited forms of angiitis and granulomatosis of Wegener's type. Am J Med 1966, **41**: 497–527.

288 Churg A. Pulmonary angiitis and granulomatosis revisited. Hum Pathol 1983, **14**: 868–883.

289 Dunnill MS. Pulmonary granulomatosis and angiitis. Histopathology 1991, **19**: 297–302.

290 Fienberg R. The protracted superficial phenomenon in pathergic (Wegener's) granulomatosis. Hum Pathol 1981, **12**: 458–467.

291 Goulart RA, Mark EJ, Rosen S. Tumefactions as an extravascular manifestation of Wegener's granulomatosis. Am J Surg Pathol 1995, **19**: 161–172.

292 Heffner DK. Wegener's granulomatosis is not a granulomatous disease. Ann Diagn Pathol 2002, **6**: 329–333.

293 Katzenstein AL, Locke WK. Solitary lung lesions in Wegener's granulomatosis. Pathologic findings and clinical significance in 25 cases. Am J Surg Pathol 1995, **19**: 545–552.

294 Leavitt RY, Fauci AS. Pulmonary vasculitis. Am Rev Respir Dis 1986, **134**: 149–166.

295 Lombard CM, Duncan SR, Rizk NW, Colby TV. The diagnosis of Wegener's granulomatosis from transbronchial biopsy specimens. Hum Pathol 1990, **21**: 838–842.

296 Nishino H, Deremee R, Rubino F, Parisi J. Wegener's granulomatosis associated with vasculitis of the temporal artery. Report of five cases. Mayo Clin Proc 1993, **68**: 115–121.

297 Saldana MJ, Patchefsky AS, Israel HI, Atkinson GW. Pulmonary angiitis and granulomatosis. The relationship between histological features, organ involvement, and response to treatment. Hum Pathol 1977, **8**: 391–409.

298 Travis WD, Carpenter HA, Lie JT. Diffuse pulmonary hemorrhage. An uncommon manifestation of Wegener's granulomatosis. Am J Surg Pathol 1987, **11**: 702–708.

299 Travis WD, Hoffman GS, Leavitt RY, Pass HI, Fauci AS. Surgical pathology of the lung in Wegener's granulomatosis. Review of 87 open lung biopsies from 67 patients. Am J Surg Pathol 1991, **15**: 315–333.

300 Ulbright TM, Katzenstein AL. Solitary necrotizing granulomas of the lung. Differentiating features and etiology. Am J Surg Pathol 1980, **4**: 13–28.

301 Yi ES, Colby TV. Wegener's granulomatosis. Semin Diagn Pathol 2001, **18**: 34–46.

302 Yoshikawa Y, Watanabe T. Pulmonary lesions in Wegener's granulomatosis. A clinicopathologic study of 22 autopsy cases. Hum Pathol 1986, **17**: 401–410.

303 Yousem SA. Bronchocentric injury in Wegener's granulomatosis. A report of five cases. Hum Pathol 1991, **22**: 535–540.

Bronchocentric granulomatosis and allergic granulomatosis

304 Bosken CH, Myers JL, Greenberger PA, Katzenstein A-LA. Pathologic features of allergic bronchopulmonary aspergillosis. Am J Surg Pathol 1988, **12**: 216–222.

305 Churg A. Pulmonary angiitis and granulomatosis revisited. Hum Pathol 1983, **14**: 868–883.

306 Churg A. Recent advances in the diagnosis of Churg–Strauss syndrome. Mod Pathol 2001, **14**: 1284–1293.

307 Jelihovsky T. The structure of bronchial plugs in mucoid impaction, bronchocentric granulomatosis and asthma. Histopathology 1983, **7**: 153–167.

308 Katzenstein AL. Diagnostic features and differential diagnosis of Churg–Strauss syndrome in the lung. Am J Clin Pathol 2000, **114**: 767–772.

309 Katzenstein AL, Liebow AA, Friedman PJ. Bronchocentric granulomatosis, mucoid impaction, and hypersensitivity reaction to fungi. Am Rev Respir Dis 1975, **111**: 497–537.

310 Koss MN, Antonovych T, Hochholzer L. Allergic granulomatosis (Churg-Strauss syndrome). Pulmonary and renal morphologic findings. Am J Surg Pathol 1981, **5**: 21–28.

311 Koss MN, Robinson RG, Hochholzer L. Bronchocentric granulomatosis. Hum Pathol 1987, **12**: 632–638.

312 Lanham JG, Elkon KB, Pusey CD, Hughes GR. Systemic vasculitis with asthma and eosinophilia. A clinical approach to the Churg-Strauss syndrome. Medicine (Baltimore) 1984, **63**: 65–81.

313 Leavitt RY, Fauci AS. Pulmonary vasculitis. Am Rev Respir Dis 1986, **134**: 149–166.

314 Liebow AA. Pulmonary angiitis and granulomatosis (The J. Burns Amberson Lecture). Am Rev Respir Dis 1973, **108**: 1–18.

315 Nagata N, Sueishi K, Tanaka K, Iwata Y. Pulmonary aspergillosis with bronchocentric granulomas. Am J Surg Pathol 1990, **14**: 485–488.

316 Saldana MJ. Bronchocentric granulomatosis. Clinicopathologic observations in 17 patients (abstract). Lab Invest 1979, **40**: 281–282.

317 Travis WD, Kwon-Chung KJ, Kleiner DE, Geber A, Lawson W, Pass HI, Henderson D. Unusual aspects of allergic bronchopulmonary fungal disease. Report of two cases due to curvularia organisms associated with allergic fungal sinusitis. Hum Pathol 1991, **22**: 1240–1248.

318 Urschel HC Jr, Paulsen DL, Shaw RR. Mucoid impaction of the bronchi. Ann Thorac Surg 1966, **2**: 1–16.

Other granulomatous inflammations

319 Ahmad M, Dar MA, Weinstein AJ, Mehta AC, Golish JA. Thoracic aspergillosis. II. Primary pulmonary aspergillosis, allergic bronchopulmonary aspergillosis. and related conditions. Cleve Clin Q 1984, **51**: 631–653.

320 Bigby TD, Serota ML, Tierney LM Jr, Matthay MA. Clinical spectrum of pulmonary mucormycosis. Chest 1986, **89**: 435–439.

321 Binder RE, Faling LJ, Pugatch RD, Mahasaen C, Snider GL. Chronic necrotizing pulmonary aspergillosis. A discrete clinical entity. Medicine (Baltimore) 1982, **61**: 109–124.

322 Chen WJ, Monnat RJ Jr, Chen M, Mottet NK. Aluminum induced pulmonary granulomatosis. Hum Pathol 1978, **9**: 705–711.

322a Cheung OY, Muhm JR, Helmers RA, Aubry M-C, Tazelaar HD, Khoor A, Leslie KO, Cholby TV. Surgical pathology of granulomatous interstitial pneumonia. Ann Diagn Pathol 2003, **7**: 127–138.

323 Dar MA, Ahmad M, Weinstein AJ, Mehta AC, Golish JA. Thoracic aspergillosis. I. Overview and aspergilloma. Cleve Clin Q 1984, **51**: 615–630.

324 England DM, Hochholzer L. Primary pulmonary sporotrichosis. Report of eight cases with clinicopathologic review. Am J Surg Pathol 1985, **9**: 193–204.

325 Flieder DB, Moran CA. Pulmonary dirofilariasis: a clinicopathologic study of 41 lesions in 39 patients. Hum Pathol 1999, **30**: 251–256.

326 Gibbs A, Pooley F, Griffiths D, Mitha R, Craighead J, Ruttner J. Talc pneumoconiosis. A pathologic and mineralogic study. Hum Pathol 1992, **23**: 1344–1354.

327 Goodwin RA Jr, Des Prez RM. Histoplasmosis. Am Rev Respir Dis 1978, **117**: 929–956.

328 Hammerman KJ, Powell KE, Christianson CS, Huggin PM, Larsh HW, Vivas JR, Tosh FE. Pulmonary cryptococcosis. Clinical forms and treatment. Am Rev Respir Dis 1973, **108**: 1116–1123.

329 Lemos LB, Baliga M, Guo M. Blastomycosis: the great pretender can also be an opportunist. Initial clinical diagnosis and underlying diseases in 123 patients. Ann Diagn Pathol 2002, **6**: 194–203.

330 Lemos L, Guo M, Baliga M. Blastomycosis: organ involvement and etiologic diagnosis: a review of 123 patients in Mississippi. Ann Diagn Pathol 2001, **4**: 391–406.

331 Mehta AC, Dar MA, Ahmad M, Weinstein AJ, Golish JA. Thoracic aspergillosis. III. Invasive pulmonary and disseminated aspergillosis. Cleve Clin Q 1984, **51**: 655–665.

332 Oddò D, González S. Actinomycosis and nocardiosis. A morphologic study of 17 cases. Pathol Res Pract 1986, **181**: 320–326.

333 Rafferty P, Biggs BA, Crompton GK, Grant IWB. What happens to patients with pulmonary aspergilloma? Analysis of 23 cases. Thorax 1983, **38**: 579–583.

334 Reinila A. Perivascular xanthogranulomatosis in the lungs of diabetic patients. Arch Pathol Lab Med 1976, **100**: 542–543.

335 Yousem SA. The histological spectrum of chronic necrotizing forms of pulmonary aspergillosis. Hum Pathol 1997, **28**: 650–656.

336 Zimmerman LE. Demonstration of *Histoplasma* and *Coccidioides* in so-called tuberculomas of lung. Arch Intern Med 1954, **94**: 690–699.

Acute pulmonary injury and interstitial pneumonias

337 American Thoracic Society, European Respiratory Society. American Thoracic Society/European Respiratory Society International Multidisciplinary Consensus Classification of the Idiopathic Interstitial Pneumonias. Am J Respir Crit Care Med 2002, **165**: 277–304.

338 Banerjee D, Ahmad D. Malignant lymphoma complicating lymphocytic interstitial pneumonia. A monoclonal B-cell neoplasm arising in a polyclonal lymphoproliferative disorder. Hum Pathol 1982, **13**: 780–782.

339 Basset F, Ferrans VJ, Soler P, Takemura T, Fukuda Y, Crystal RG. Intraluminal fibrosis in interstitial lung disorders. Am J Pathol 1986, **122**: 443–461.

340 Bloch KJ, Buchanan WW, Wohl MJ, Bunim JJ. Sjögren's syndrome. A clinical, pathological, and serological study of sixty-two cases. Medicine (Baltimore) 1965, **44**: 187–231.

341 Bonanni PP, Frymoyer JW, Jacox RF. A family study of idiopathic pulmonary fibrosis. Am J Med 1965, **39**: 411–421.

342 Britton J, Hubbard R. Review: recent advances in the etiology of cryptogenic fibrosing alveolitis. Histopathology 2000, **37**: 387–392.

343 Carrington CB, Gaensler EA, Coutu RE, Fitzgerald MX, Gupta RG. Natural history and treated course of usual and desquamative interstitial pneumonia. N Engl J Med 1978, **298**: 801–809.

343a Chilosi M, Poletti V, Zamò A, Lestani M, Montagna L, Piccoli P, Pedron S, Bertaso M, Scarpa A, Murer B, Cancellieri A, Maestro R, Semenzato G, Doglioni C. Aberrant Wnt/Beta-catenin pathway activation in idiopathic pulmonary fibrosis. Am J Pathol 2003, **162**: 1495–1502.

344 Coalson JJ. The ultrastructure of human fibrosing alveolitis. Virchows Arch [A] 1982, **395**: 181–199.

345 Colby TV. Bronchiolitis, pathologic considerations. Am J Clin Pathol 1998, **109**: 101–109.

346 Colby TV, Yousem SA. Lungs. In Sternberg S (ed.): Histology for pathologists, ed. 2. Philadelphia, 1997, Lippincott-Raven, pp. 433–460.

347 Cordier J-F, Loire R, Brune J. Idiopathic bronchiolitis obliterans organizing pneumonia. Definition of characteristic clinical profiles in a series of 16 patients. Chest 1989, **96**: 999–1004.

348 Corrin B, Butcher D, McAnulty BJ, Dubois RM, Black CM, Laurent GJ, Farrison NK. Immunohistochemical localization of transforming growth factor-beta 1 in the lungs of patients with systemic sclerosis, cryptogenic fibrosing alveolitis and other lung disorders. Histopathology 1994, **24**: 145–150.

349 Crystal RG. Alveolitis. The key to the interstitial lung disorders. Thorax 1982, **37**: 1–10.

350 Dreisin RB, Schwartz MI, Theofilopoulos AN, Stanford RE. Circulating immune complexes in the idiopathic interstitial pneumonias. N Engl J Med 1978, **298**: 353–357.

351 Dunnill MS. Pulmonary fibrosis. Histopathology 1990, **16**: 321–329.

352 Editorial. Interstitial pneumonia (fibrosing alveolitis). Lancet 1978, **2**: 191–192.

353 Epler GR, Colby TV, McLoud TC, Carrington CB, Gaensler EA. Bronchiolitis obliterans organizing pneumonia. N Engl J Med 1985, **312**: 152–158.

354 Fraig M, Shreesha U, Savici D, Katzenstein AL. Respiratory bronchiolitis: a clinicopathologic study in current smokers, ex-smokers, and never-smokers. Am J Surg Pathol 2002, **26**: 647–653.

355 Fraire AE, Greenberg SD. Carcinoma and diffuse interstitial fibrosis of lung. Cancer 1973, **31**: 1078–1086.

356 Gaensler EA, Goff AM, Prowse CM. Desquamative interstitial pneumonia. N Engl J Med 1966, **274**: 113–128.

357 Greenberg SD, Haley MD, Jenkins DE, Fischer SP. Lymphoplasmacytic pneumonia with accompanying dysproteinemia. Arch Pathol 1973, **96**: 73–80.

358 Heitzman ER, Markarian B, DeLise CT. Lymphoproliferative disorders of the thorax. Semin Roentgenol 1975, **10**: 73–81.

359 Iyonaga K, Takeya M, Saita N, Sakamoto O, Yoshimura T, Ando M, Takahashi K. Monocyte chemoattractant protein-1 in idiopathic pulmonary fibrosis and other interstitial lung diseases. Hum Pathol 1994, **25**: 455–463.

360 Katzenstein AL. Pathogenesis of "fibrosis" in interstitial pneumonia. An electron microscopic study. Hum Pathol 1985, **16**: 1015–1024.

361 Katzenstein AL, Fiorelli RF. Nonspecific interstitial pneumonia/fibrosis. Histologic features and clinical significance. Am J Surg Pathol 1994, **18**: 136–147.

362 Katzenstein AL, Myers JL. Idiopathic pulmonary fibrosis: clinical relevance of pathologic classification. Am J Respir Crit Care Med 1998, **157**: 1201–1315.

363 Katzenstein AL, Myers JL. Non-specific interstitial pneumonia and other idiopathic interstitial pneumonias: classification and diagnostic criteria. Am J Surg Pathol 2000, **24**: 1–3.

364 Katzenstein AL, Gordon LP, Oliphant M, Swender PT. Chronic pneumonitis of infancy. A unique form of interstitial lung disease occurring in early childhood. Am J Surg Pathol 1995, **19**: 439–447.

365 Katzenstein AL, Myers JL, Mazur MT. Acute interstitial pneumonia. A clinicopathologic, ultrastructural, and cell kinetic study. Am J Surg Pathol 1986, **10**: 256–267.

366 Katzenstein AL, Myers JL, Prophet WD, Corley LS III, Shin MS. Bronchiolitis obliterans and usual interstitial pneumonia. A comparative clinicopathologic study. Am J Surg Pathol 1986, **10**: 373–381.

367 Katzenstein AL, Zisman DA, Litzky LA, Nguyen BT, Kotloff RM. Usual interstial pneumonia: histologic study of biopsy and explant specimens. Am J Surg Pathol 2002, **26**: 1567–1577.

368 Kitamura H, Kitamura H, Tsugu S. Combined epidermoid and adenocarcinoma in diffuse interstitial pulmonary fibrosis. Hum Pathol 1982, **13**: 580–583.

369 Koss M, Hochholzer L, Langloss J, Wehunt W, Lazarus A. Lymphoid interstitial pneumonia. Clinicopathological and immunopathological findings in 18 cases. Pathology 1987, **19**: 178–185.

370 Liebow AA. New concepts and entities in pulmonary disease. In Liebow AA, Smith DE (eds.): The lung (monograph of the International Academy of Pathology). Baltimore, 1968, Williams & Wilkins Co.

371 Liebow AA, Carrington CB. Diffuse pulmonary lymphoreticular infiltrations associated with dysproteinemia. Med Clin North Am 1973, **57**: 809–843.

372 Liebow AA, Steer A, Billingsley JG. Desquamative interstitial pneumonia. Am J Med 1965, **39**: 369–404.

373 Luna MA, Bedrossian CWM, Lichtiger B, Salem PA. Interstitial pneumonitis associated with bleomycin therapy. Am J Clin Pathol 1972, **58**: 501–510.

374 Malamou-Mitsi V, Tsai M, Gal A, Koss M, O'Leary T. Lymphoid interstitial pneumonia not associated with HIV infection. Role of Epstein-Barr virus. Mod Pathol 1992, **5**: 487–491.

375 Meyer EC, Liebow AA. Relationship of interstitial pneumonia honeycombing and atypical epithelial proliferation to cancer of the lung. Cancer 1965, **18**: 322–351.

375 Myers JL, Kennedy JI, Plumb VJ. Amiodarone lung. Pathologic findings in clinically toxic patients. Hum Pathol 1987, **18**: 349–354.

377 Nagai S, Kitaichi M, Itoh H, Nishimura K, Izumi T, Colby TV. Idiopathic nonspecific interstitial pneumonia/fibrosis: comparison with idiopathic pulmonary fibrosis and BOOP. Eur Respir J 1998, **12**: 1010–1019.

378 Nicholson AG. Classification of idiopathic interstitial pneumonias: making sense of the alphabet soup. Histopathology 2002, **41**: 381–391.

379 Nicholson AG, Wotherspoon AC, Diss TC, Singh N, Butcher DN, Pan LX, Isaacson PG, Corrin B. Lymphomatoid granulomatosis: evidence that some cases represent Epstein–Barr virus-associated B-cell lymphoma. Histopathology 1996, **29**: 317–324.

380 Ogino S, Franks TJ, Yong M, Koss MN. Extensive squamous metaplasia with cytologic atypia in diffuse alveolar damage mimicking squamous cell carcinoma: a report of two cases. Hum Pathol 2002, **33**: 1052–1054.

381 Olson J, Colby TV, Elliott CG. Hamman-Rich syndrome revisited. Mayo Clin Proc 1990, **65**: 1538–1548.

382 Rosenow EC III. The spectrum of drug-induced pulmonary disease. Ann Intern Med 1972, **77**: 977–991.

383 Scadding JG. Diffuse pulmonary alveolar fibrosis. Thorax 1974, **29**: 271–281.

384 Scadding JG, Hinson KFW. Diffuse fibrosing alveolitis (diffuse interstitial fibrosis of the lungs). Correlation of histology at biopsy with prognosis. Thorax 1967, **22**: 291–304.

385 Schatz M, Patterson R, Fink J. Immunologic lung disease. N Engl J Med 1979, **300**: 1310–1320.

386 Shimizu S, Kobayashi H, Watanabe H, Ohnishi Y. Mallory body-like structures in the lung. Acta Pathol Jpn 1986, **36**: 105–112.

387 Sostman HD, Mattay RA, Putman CE. Cytotoxic drug-induced lung disease. Am J Med 1977, **62**: 608–615.

388 Stillwell PC, Norris DG, O'Connell EJ, Rosenow EC, Weiland LH, Harrison EG Jr. Desquamative interstitial pneumonia in children. Chest 1980, **77**: 165–171.

389 Topilow AA, Rothenberg SP, Cottrell TS. Interstitial pneumonia after prolonged treatment with cyclophosphamide. Am Rev Respir Dis 1973, **108**: 114–117.

390 Travis WD, Matsui K, Moss J, Ferrans VJ. Idiopathic nonspecific interstitial pneumonia: prognostic significance of cellular and fibrosing patterns: survival comparison with usual interstitial pneumonia and desquamative interstitial pneumonia. Am J Surg Pathol 2000, **24**: 19–33.

391 Tubbs RR, Benjamin SP, Reich NE, McCormack LJ, Van Ordstrand HS. Desquamative interstitial pneumonitis. Cellular phase of fibrosing alveolitis. Chest 1977, **72**: 159–165.

392 Tukiainen P, Taskinen E, Holsti P, Korhola O, Valle M. Prognosis of cryptogenic fibrosing alveolitis. Thorax 1983, **38**: 349–355.

393 Turner-Warwick M. Immunological aspects of systemic diseases of the lungs. Proc R Soc Med 1974, **67**: 541–547.

394 Uner AH, Rozum-Slota B, Katzenstein AL. Bronchiolitis obliterans-organizing pneumonia (BOOP)-like variant of Wegener's granulomatosis: a clinicopathologic study of 16 cases. Am J Surg Pathol 1996, **20**: 794–801.

395 Ware LB, Matthay MA. The acute respiratory distress syndrome. N Engl J Med 2000, **342**: 1334–1349.

396 Webb WR, Goodman PC. Fibrosing alveolitis in patients with neurofibromatosis. Radiology 1977, **122**: 289–293.

397 Yousem SA. Eosinophilic pneumonia-like areas in idiopathic usual interstitial pneumonia. Mod Pathol 2000, **13**: 1280–1284.

398 Yousem SA, Dacic S. Idiopathic bronchiolocentric interstitial pneumonia. Mod Pathol 2002, **15**: 1148–1153.

399 Yousem SA, Colby TV, Carrington CB. Follicular bronchitis/bronchiolitis. Hum Pathol 1985, **16**: 700–706.

400 Yousem SA, Lohr RH, Colby TV. Idiopathic bronchiolitis obliterans organizing pneumonia/cryptogenic organizing pneumonia with unfavourable outcome: pathologic predictors. Mod Pathol 1997, **10**: 864–871.

Organizing pneumonia

401 Ackerman LV, Elliott GV, Alanis M. Localized organizing pneumonia. Its resemblance to carcinoma. Review of its clinical, roentgenographic and pathologic features. Am J Roentgenol 1954, **71**: 988–996.

402 Hershey CO, Panaro V. Round pneumonia in adults. Arch Intern Med 1988, **148**: 1155–1157.

403 Rose RW, Ward BH. Spherical pneumonias in children

simulating pulmonary and mediastinal masses. Radiology 1973, **106:** 179–182.

Lipoid pneumonia

404 Berg R Jr, Burford TH. Pulmonary paraffinoma (lipoid pneumonia). J Thorac Surg 1950, **20:** 418–428.

405 Wagner JC, Adler DI, Fuller DN. Foreign body granulomata of the lungs due to liquid paraffin. Thorax 1955, **10:** 157–170.

Eosinophilic pneumonia

406 Grantham JG, Meadows JA III, Gleich GJ. Chronic eosinophilic pneumonia. Evidence for eosinophil degranulation and release of major basic protein. Am J Med 1986, **80:** 89–94.

407 Liebow AA, Carrington CB. The eosinophilic pneumonias. Medicine (Baltimore) 1969, **48:** 251–285.

408 Magee F, Wright JL, Chan N, Currie W, Karr G, Hogg J, Thurlbeck WM. Two unusual pathological reactions to nitrofurantoin. Case reports. Histopathology 1986, **10:** 701–706.

409 Neafie RC, Piggott J. Human pulmonary dirofilariasis. Arch Pathol 1971, **92:** 342–349.

410 Warnock ML, Fennessy J, Rippon J. Chronic eosinophilic pneumonia. A manifestation of allergic aspergillosis. Am J Clin Pathol 1974, **62:** 73–81.

411 White V, Luna M, Green L, Ayala A. Pulmonary dirofilariasis (abstract). Lab Invest 1988, **58:** 96A.

Pneumocystis carinii pneumonia

412 Amin M, Mezger E, Zarbo RJ. Detection of *Pneumocystis carinii*. Comparative study of monoclonal antibody and silver staining. Am J Clin Pathol 1992, **98:** 13–18.

413 Blumenfeld W, McCook O, Grississ JM. Detection of antibodies to *Pneumocystis carinii* in bronchoalveolar lavage fluid by immunoreactivity to *Pneumocystis carinii* within alveoli, granulomas, and disseminated sites. Mod Pathol 1992, **5:** 107–113.

414 Blumenfeld W, McCook O, Holodniy M, Katzenstein DA. Correlation of morphologic diagnosis of *Pneumocystis carinii* with the presence of *Pneumocystis* DNA amplified by the polymerase chain reaction. Mod Pathol 1992, **5:** 103–106.

415 Burke B, Good RA. *Pneumocystis carinii* infection. Medicine 1973, **52:** 23–51.

416 Cote RJ, Rosenblum M, Telzak EE, May M, Unger PD, Cartun RW. Disseminated *Pneumocystis carinii* infection causing extrapulmonary organ failure. Clinical, pathologic, and immunohistochemical analysis. Mod Pathol 1990, **3:** 25–30.

417 Lee MM, Schinella RA. Pulmonary calcification caused by *Pneumocystis carinii* pneumonia. A clinicopathologic study of 13 cases in acquired immune deficiency syndrome patients. Am J Surg Pathol 1991, **15:** 376–380.

418 Macfarlane JT. *Pneumocystis carinii* pneumonia. Thorax 1985, **40:** 561–570.

419 Mahan CT, Sale GE. Rapid methenamine silver stain for *Pneumocystis* and fungi. Arch Pathol Lab Med 1978, **102:** 351–352.

420 Radio SJ, Hansen S, Goldsmith J, Linder J. Immunohistochemistry of *Pneumocystis carinii* infection. Mod Pathol 1990, **3:** 462–469.

421 Rosen PP. Frozen section management of a lung biopsy for suspected *Pneumocystis* pneumonia. Am J Surg Pathol 1977, **1:** 79–82.

422 Rosen PP, Armstrong DA, Ramos C. *Pneumocystis carinii* pneumonia. A clinicopathologic study of 20 patients with neoplastic diseases. Am J Med 1972, **53:** 428–436.

423 Rosen PP, Martini N, Armstrong DA. *Pneumocystis carinii* pneumonia. Diagnosis by lung biopsy. Am J Med 1975, **56:** 794–802.

424 Schwartz DA, Munger RG, Katz SM. Plastic embedding evaluation of *Pneumocystis carinii* pneumonia in AIDS. Simultaneous demonstration of cyst and sporozoite forms. Am J Surg Pathol 1987, **11:** 304–309.

425 Sidhu GS, Cassai ND, Pei Z. Pneumocystis carinii: an update. Ultrastructural Pathology 2003, **27:** 115–122.

426 Travis WD, Pittaluga S, Lipschick GY, Ognibene FP, Suffredini AF, Masur H, Feuerstein I, Kovascs J, Pass HI, Condron PS, Shelhamer JH. Atypical pathologic manifestations of *Pneumocystis Carinii* pneumonia in the acquired immune deficiency syndrome. Review of 123 lung biopsies from 76 patients with emphasis on cysts, vascular invasion, vasculitis, and granulomas. Am J Surg Pathol 1990, **14:** 615–625.

427 Walzer PD, Perl P, Krogstad DJ, Rawson PG, Schultz MG. *Pneumocystis carinii* pneumonia in the United States. Ann Intern Med 1974, **80:** 83–93.

428 Watts JC, Chandler FW. *Pneumocystis carinii* pneumonitis. The nature and diagnostic significance of the methenamine silver-positive "intracystic bodies." Am J Surg Pathol 1985, **9:** 744–751.

429 Watts JC, Chandler FW. Evolving concepts of infection by *Pneumocystis carinii*. Part 1. Pathol Annu 1991, **26:** 93–138.

430 Weber WR, Askin FB, Dehner LP. Lung biopsy in *Pneumocystis carinii* pneumonia. A histopathologic study of typical and atypical features. Am J Clin Pathol 1977, **67:** 11–19.

Other pneumonias

431 Aherne W, Bird T, Court SDM, Gardner PS, McQuillin J. Pathologic changes in virus infections of the lower respiratory tract in children. J Clin Pathol 1970, **23:** 7–18.

432 Becroft DMO. Histopathology of fatal adenovirus infection of the respiratory tract in young children. J Clin Pathol 1967, **20:** 561–569.

433 Blackmon JA, Chandler FW, Cherry WB, England AC III, Feeley JC, Hicklin MD, McKinney RM, Wilkinson HW. Legionellosis. Am J Pathol 1981, **103:** 429–465.

434 Blackmon JA, Hicklin MD, Chandler FW. Legionnaires' disease. Pathological and historical aspects of a "new" disease. Arch Pathol Lab Med 1978, **102:** 337–343.

434a Yan KW, Chan JKC. Pulmonary pathology of severe acute respiratory syndrome (SARS). Int J Surg Pathol 2003, **11:** 118.

434b Franks TJ, Chong PY, Chui P, Galvin JR, Lourens RM, Reid AH, Selbs E, McEvoy PL, Hayden DL, Fukuoka J, Taubenberger JK, Travis WD. Lung pathology of severe acute respiratory syndrome (SARS); a study of 8 autopsy cases from Singapore. Hum Pathol 2003, **34:** 743–748.

435 Frazier AR, Rosenow EC III, Roberts GD. Nocardiosis. A review of 25 cases occurring during 24 months. Mayo Clin Proc 1975, **50:** 657–663.

436 Gorelkin L, Chandler FW, Ewing EP Jr. Staining qualities of cytomegalovirus inclusions in the lungs of patients with the acquired immunodeficiency syndrome. A potential source of diagnostic misinterpretation. Hum Pathol 1986, **17:** 926–929.

437 Graham BS, Snell JD Jr. Herpes simplex virus infection of the adult lower respiratory tract. Medicine 1983, **62:** 384–393.

438 Murray HW, Masur H, Senterfit LB, Roberts RB. The protean manifestations of *Mycoplasma pneumoniae* infection in adults. Am J Med 1975, **58:** 229–242.

439 Oddò D, Gonzalez S. Actinomycosis and nocardiosis. A morphologic study of 17 cases. Pathol Res Pract 1986, **181:** 320–326.

440 Palmer DL, Harvey RL, Wheeler JK. Diagnostic and therapeutic considerations in *Nocardia asteroides* infection. Medicine (Baltimore) 1974, **53:** 391–401.

441 Rollins S, Colby T, Clayton F. Open lung biopsy in *Mycoplasma pneumoniae* pneumonia. Arch Pathol Lab Med 1986, **110:** 34–41.

442 Schaefer HE. Inflammatory disease of the human lung of definite or presumed viral origin. Cytologic and histologic topics. Curr Topics Pathol 1983, **73:** 153–206.

443 Weisenburger DD, Helms CM, Renner ED. Sporadic Legionnaires' disease. A pathologic study of 23 fatal cases. Arch Pathol Lab Med 1981, **105**: 130–137.

444 Winn WC Jr, Glavin FL, Perl DP, Keller JL, Andres TL, Brown TM, Coffin CM, Sensecqua JE, Roman LN, Craighead JE. The pathology of Legionnaires' disease. Fourteen fatal cases from the 1977 outbreak in Vermont. Arch Pathol Lab Med 1978, **102**: 344–350.

445 Winn WC Jr, Myerowitz RL. The pathology of the *Legionella* pneumonias. A review of 74 cases and the literature. Hum Pathol 1981, **12**: 401–442.

446 Yeldandi AV, Colby TV. Pathologic features of lung biopsy specimens from influenza pneumonia cases. Hum Pathol 1994, **25**: 47–53.

447 Zaki SR, Greer PW, Coffield LM, Goldsmith CS, Nolte KB, Foucar K, Fedderson RM, Zumwalt RE, Miller GL, Khan AS, Rollin PE, Ksiazek TG, Nichol ST, Mahy BWJ, Peters CJ. Hantavirus pulmonary syndrome. Pathogenesis of an emerging infectious disease. Am J Pathol 1995, **146**: 552–579.

Lung in AIDS

448 Blumenfeld W, Wagar E, Hadley WK. Use of the transbronchial biopsy for diagnosis of opportunistic pulmonary infections in acquired immunodeficiency syndrome (AIDS). Am J Clin Pathol 1984, **81**: 1–5.

449 Denning DW, Follansbee SE, Scolaro M, Norris S, Edelstein H, Stevens DA. Pulmonary aspergillosis in the acquired immunodeficiency syndrome. N Engl J Med 1991, **324**: 654–662.

450 Gal AA, Klatt EC, Koss MN, Strigle SM, Boylen CT. The effectiveness of bronchoscopy in the diagnosis of *Pneumocystis carinii* and cytomegalovirus pulmonary infections in acquired immunodeficiency syndrome. Arch Pathol Lab Med 1987, **111**: 238–241.

451 Joshi VV, Oleske JM, Minnefor AB, Saad S, Klein KM, Singh R, Zabala M, Dadzie C, Simpser M, Rapkin RH. Pathologic pulmonary findings in children with the acquired immunodeficiency syndrome. A study of ten cases. Hum Pathol 1985, **16**: 241–246.

452 Marchevsky A, Rosen MJ, Chrystal G, Kleinerman J. Pulmonary complications of the acquired immunodeficiency syndrome. A clinicopathologic study of 70 cases. Hum Pathol 1985, **16**: 659–670.

453 McKenna RJ Jr, Campbell A, McMurtrey MJ, Mountain CF. Diagnosis for interstitial lung disease in patients with acquired immunodeficiency syndrome (AIDS). A prospective comparison of bronchial washing, alveolar lavage, transbronchial lung biopsy, and open-lung biopsy. Ann Thorac Surg 1986, **41**: 318–321.

454 Nash G, Fligiel S. Pathologic features of the lung in the acquired immune deficiency syndrome (AIDS). An autopsy study of seventeen homosexual males. Am J Clin Pathol 1984, **81**: 6–12.

455 Nash G, Kerschmann RL, Herndier B, Dubey JP. The pathological manifestations of pulmonary toxoplasmosis in the acquired immunodeficiency syndrome. Hum Pathol 1994, **25**: 652–658.

456 Orenstein M, Webber CA, Cash M, Heurich AE. Value of broncholaveolar lavage in the diagnosis of pulmonary infection in acquired immune deficiency syndrome. Thorax 1986, **41**: 345–349.

457 Ramaswamy G, Jagadha V, Tchertkoff V. Diffuse alveolar damage and interstitial fibrosis in acquired immunodeficiency syndrome patients without concurrent pulmonary infection. Arch Pathol Lab Med 1985, **109**: 408–412.

458 Schwartz D, Visvesvara G, Leotch G, Tashjikian L, Pollack M, Holden J, Bryan R. Pathology of symptomatic microsporidial (*Encephalitozoon hellem*) bronchiolitis in the acquired immunodeficiency syndrome. A new respiratory pathogen diagnosed from lung biopsy, bronchoalveolar lavage, sputum, and tissue. Hum Pathol 1993, **24**: 937–943.

459 Travis W, Fox C, Devaney K, Weiss L, O'Leary T, Ognibene F, Suffredini A, Rosen M, Cohen M, Shelhamer J. Lymphoid pneumonitis in 50 adult patients infected with the human immunodeficiency virus. Lymphocytic interstitial pneumonitis versus nonspecific interstitial pneumonitis. Hum Pathol 1992, **23**: 529–541.

Lung in bone marrow transplantation

460 Sloane JP, Depledge MH, Powles RL, Morgenstern GR, Trickey BS, Dady PJ. Histopathology of the lung after bone marrow transplantation. J Clin Pathol 1983, **36**: 546–554.

461 Urbanski SJ, Kossakowska AE, Curtis J, Chan CK, Hutcheon MA, Hyland RH, Messner H, Minden M, Sculier JP. Idiopathic small airways pathology in patients with graft-versus-host disease following allogeneic bone marrow transplantation. Am J Surg Pathol 1987, **11**: 965–971.

462 Yousem SA. The histological spectrum of pulmonary graft-versus-host disease in bone marrow transplant recipients. Hum Pathol 1995, **26**: 668–675.

Pneumoconiosis

463 Davis JM, Chapman J, Collings P, Douglas AN, Fernie J, Lamb D, Ruckley VA. Variations in the histological patterns of the lesions of coal workers' pneumoconiosis in Britain and their relationship to lung dust content. Am Rev Respir Dis 1983, **128**: 118–124.

464 Gouch J, Rivers D, Seal RME. Pathological studies of modified pneumoconiosis in coal miners with rheumatoic arthritis (Caplan's syndrome). Thorax 1955, **10**: 9–18.

465 Hammars SP. Controversies and uncertainties concerning the pathologic features and pathologic diagnosis of asbestosis. Semin Diagn Pathol 1992, **9**: 102–109.

466 Hyers T, Ohar J, Crim C. Clinical controversies in asbestos-induced lung diseases. Semin Diagn Pathol 1992, **9**: 97–101.

467 Kuhn C III, Kuo TT. Cytoplasmic hyalin in asbestosis. Arch Pathol 1973, **95**: 190–194.

468 Naeye RL. The anthracotic pneumoconioses. Curr Top Pathol 1971, **55**: 37–68.

Extrinsic allergic alveolitis

469 Fink JN, Banaszak EF, Baroriak JJ, Hensley GT, Kurup VP, Scanlon GT, Schleuter DP, Sosman AJ, Thiede WH, Unger GF. Interstitial lung disease due to contamination of forced air systems. Ann Intern Med 1976, **85**: 406–413.

470 Hammar S. Hypersensitivity pneumonitis. Part 1. Pathol Annu 1988, **23**: 195–215.

471 Kawanami O, Basset F, Barrios R, Lacronique JG, Ferrans VJ, Crystal RG. Hypersensitivity pneumonitis in man. Light- and electron-microscopic studies of 18 lung biopsies. Am J Pathol 1983, **110**: 275–289.

472 Nicholson DP. Extrinsic allergic pneumonias. Am J Med 1972, **53**: 131–136.

Langerhans' cell histiocytosis and other histiocytic disorders

473 Askin FB, McCann BG, Kuhn C. Reactive eosinophilic pleuritis. A lesion to be distinguished from pulmonary eosinophilic granuloma. Arch Pathol Lab Med 1977, **101**: 187–191.

473a Bisceglia M, Cammisa M, Suster S, Colby TV. Erdheim-Chester disease: clinical and pathologic spectrum of four cases from the Arkadi M. Rywlin slide seminars. Adv Anat Pathol 2003, **10**: 160–171.

474 Chollet S, Soler P, Dournovo P, Richard MS, Ferrans VJ, Basset F. Diagnosis of pulmonary histiocytosis X by immunodetection of Langerhans' cells in bronchoalveolar lavage fluid. Am J Pathol 1984, **115**: 225–232.

475 Colby TV, Lombard C. Histiocytosis X in the lung. Hum Pathol 1983, **14**: 847–856.

476 Egan AJM, Boardman LA, Tazelaar HD, Swensen SJ, Jett JR, Yousem SA, Myers JL. Erdheim–Chester disease: clinical, radiologic, and histopathologic findings in five patients with interstitial lung disease. Am J Surg Pathol 1999, **23**: 17–26.

477 Flint A, Lloyd RV, Colby TV, Wilson BW. Pulmonary histiocytosis X. Immunoperoxidase staining for HLA-DR antigen and S 100 protein. Arch Pathol Lab Med 1986, **110**: 930–933.

478 Friedman PJ, Liebow AA, Sokoloff J. Eosinophilic granuloma of lung. Clinical aspects of primary pulmonary histiocytosis in the adult. Medicine 1981, **60**: 385–396.

479 Gold J, L'Heureux P, Dehner LP. Ultrastructure in the differential diagnosis of pulmonary histiocytosis and pneumocystosis. Arch Pathol Lab Med 1977, **101**: 243–247.

480 Lewis JG. Eosinophilic granuloma and its variants with special reference to lung involvement. Q J Med 1964, **33**: 337–359.

481 Lombard CM, Medeiros LJ, Colby TV. Pulmonary histiocytosis X and carcinoma. Arch Pathol Lab Med 1987, **111**: 339–341.

482 Luna E, Tomashefski JF Jr, Brown D, Clarke RE, Kleinerman J. Reactive eosinophilic pulmonary vascular infiltration in patients with spontaneous pneumothorax. Am J Surg Pathol 1994, **18**: 195–199.

483 Rush WL, Andriko JA, Galateau-Salle F, Brambilla E, Brambilla C, Ziany-bey I, Rosado-de-Christenson ML, Travis WD. Pulmonary pathology of Erdheim–Chester disease. Mod Pathol 2000, **13**: 747–754.

484 Soler P, Chollet S, Jacque C, Fukuda Y, Ferrans VJ, Basset F. Immunocytochemical characterization of pulmonary histiocytosis X cells in lung biopsies. Am J Pathol 1985, **118**: 439–451.

485 Soler P, Kambouchner KR, Valeyre D, Hance AJ. Pulmonary Langerhans' cell granulomatosis (histiocytosis X). Annu Rev Med 1992, **43**: 105–115.

486 Tomashefski JF, Khiyami A, Kleinerman J. Neoplasms associated with pulmonary eosinophilic granuloma. Arch Pathol Lab Med 1991, **115**: 499–506.

487 Travis WD, Borok Z, Roum JH, et al. Pulmonary Langerhans' cell granulomatosis (histiocytosis X). A clinicopathologic study of 48 cases. Am J Surg Pathol 1993, **17**: 971–986.

488 Vassallo R, Ryu JH, Colby TV, Hartman T, Limper AH. Pulmonary Langerhans'-cell histiocytosis. N Engl J Med 2000, **342**: 1969–1978.

489 Webber D, Tron V, Askin F, Churg A. S-100 staining in the diagnosis of eosinophilic granuloma of lung. Am J Clin Pathol 1985, **84**: 447–453.

490 Wright DH, Richards DB. Sinus histiocytosis with massive lymphadenopathy (Rosai–Dorfman disease): report of a case with widespread nodal and extra nodal dissemination. Histopathology 1981, **5**: 697–709.

491 Yousem SA, Colby TV, Chen YY, Chen WG, Weiss LW. Pulmonary Langerhans' cell histiocytosis: molecular analysis of clonality. Am J Surg Pathol 2001, **25**: 630–636.

Vascular diseases

492 Bjornsson J, Edwards WD. Primary pulmonary hypertension. A histopathologic study of 80 cases. Mayo Clin Proc 1985, **60**: 16–25.

493 Burke AP, Farb A, Virmani R. Short course. The pathology of primary pulmonary hypertension. Mod Pathol 1991, **4**: 269–282.

494 Carrington CB, Liebow AA. Pulmonary veno-occlusive disease. Hum Pathol 1970, **1**: 322–324.

495 Caslin AW, Heath D, Madden B, Yacoub M, Gosney R, Smith P. The histopathology of plexogenic pulmonary arteriopathy. Histopathology 1990, **16**: 9–20.

496 Corrin B, Spencer H, Turner-Warwich M, Beales SJ, Hamblin JJ. Pulmonary veno-occlusion. An immune complex disease? Virchows Arch [A] 1974, **364**: 81–91.

497 Hasleton PS, Ironside JW, Whittaker JS, Kelly W, Ward C, Thompson GS. Pulmonary veno-occlusive disease. A report of four cases. Histopathology 1986, **10**: 933–944.

498 Health D, Yacoub M, Madden GB, Caslin AW, Smith P. Pulmonary endocrine cells in hypertensive pulmonary vascular diseases. Histopathology 1990, **16**: 21–28.

499 Hughes JD, Rubin LJ. Primary pulmonary hypertension. An analysis of 28 cases and a review of the literature. Medicine 1986, **65**: 56–72.

500 Thadani U, Burrow C, Whitaker W, Health D. Pulmonary veno-occlusive disease. Q J Med 1975, **44**: 133–159.

501 Wagenvoort CA. Open lung biopsies in congenital heart disease for evaluation of pulmonary vascular disease. Predictive value with regard to corrective operability. Histopathology 1985, **9**: 417–436.

502 Wagenvoort CA, Wagenvoort N. The pathology of pulmonary veno-occlusive disease. Virchows Arch [A] 1974, **364**: 69–79.

Other non-neoplastic diseases

503 Abboud RT, Chase WH, Ballon HS. Goodpasture's syndrome. Diagnosis by transbronchial lung biopsy. Ann Intern Med 1978, **89**: 635–638.

504 Arrigoni MG, Bernatz PE, Donoghue FE. Broncholithiasis. J Thorac Cardiovasc Surg 1971, **62**: 231–237.

505 Byard R, Bourne A, Thorner P. Malacoplakia of the lung. A review. Surg Pathol 1991, **4**: 301–308.

506 Carnovale R, Zornoza J, Goldman AM, Luna M. Pulmonary alveolar proteinosis. Its association with hematologic malignancy and lymphoma. Radiology 1977, **122**: 303–306.

507 Chen KTK. Amyloidosis presenting in the respiratory tract. Part 1. Pathol Annu 1989, **24**: 253–273.

508 Colon AR, Lawrence RD, Mills SD, O'Connell EJ. Childhood pulmonary alveolar proteinosis (PAP). Report of a case and review of the literature. Am J Dis Child 1971, **121**: 481–485.

509 Crouch E, Persson A, Chang D. Accumulation of surfactant protein D in human pulmonary alveolar proteinosis. Am J Pathol 1993, **142**: 241–248.

510 Da Costa P, Corrin B. Amyloidosis localized to the lower respiratory tract. Probable immunoamyloid nature of the tracheobronchial and nodular pulmonary forms. Histopathology 1985, **9**: 703–710.

511 Dernevik L, Gatzinsky O. Pathogenesis of shrinking pleuritis with atelectasis – "rounded atelectasis." Eur J Respir Dis 1987, **71**: 244–249.

512 Donald KJ, Edwards RL, McEvoy JDS. Alveolar capillary basement membrane lesions in Goodpasture's syndrome and idiopathic pulmonary hemosiderosis. Am J Med 1975, **59**: 642–649.

513 Donlan CJ Jr, Srodes CH, Duffy FD. Idiopathic pulmonary hemosiderosis. Electron microscopic, immunofluorescent, and iron kinetic studies. Chest 1975, **68**: 577–580.

514 Du Bois RM, McAllister WAC, Branthwaite MA. Alveolar proteinosis. Diagnosis and treatment over a 10-year period. Thorax 1983, **38**: 360–363.

515 Eagen JW, Memoli VA, Roberts JL. Pulmonary hemorrhage in systemic lupus erythematosus. Medicine (Baltimore) 1978, **57**: 545–560.

516 Engleman P, Liebow AA, Gmelich J, Friedman PJ. Pulmonary hyalinizing granuloma. Am Rev Respir Dis 1977, **115**: 997–1008.

517 Errion AR, Hauk VN, Kettering DL. Pulmonary hematoma due to blunt non-penetrating thoracic trauma. Am Rev Respir Dis 1963, **88**: 384–392.

518 Flieder DB, Moran CA, Travis WD, Koss MN, Mark EJ. Pleuropulmonary endometriosis and pulmonary ectopic

deciduosis: a clinicopathologic and immunohistochemical study of 10 cases with emphasis on diagnostic pitfalls. Hum Pathol 1998, **29**: 1495–1503.

519 Geddes DM, Corrin B, Brewerton DA, Davies RJ, Turner-Warwick M. Progressive airway obliteration in adults and its association with rheumatoid disease. Q J Med 1977, **46**: 427–444.

519a Gottstein B, Reichen J. Hydatid lung disease (echinococcosis/hydatidosis). Clin Chest Med 2002, **23**: 397–408.

520 Groves LK, Effler DB. Broncholithiasis. A review of twenty-seven cases. Am Rev Tuberc 1956, **73**: 19–30.

521 Hibbard LT, Schumann WR, Goldstein GE. Thoracic endometriosis. A review and report of two cases. Am J Obstet Gynecol 1981, **140**: 227–232.

522 Hillerdal G. Rounded atelectasis. Clinical experience with 74 patients. Chest 1989, **95**: 836–841.

522a Hudson BG, Tryggvason K. Alport's syndrome, Goodpasture's syndrome, and type IV collagen. N Engl J Med 2003, **348**: 2543–2556.

523 Hui AN, Koss MN, Hochholzer L, Wehunt WD. Amyloidosis presenting in the lower respiratory tract. Clinicopathologic, radiologic, immunohistochemical, and histochemical studies on 48 cases. Arch Pathol Lab Med 1986, **110**: 212–218.

524 Leatherman JW, Davies SF, Hoidal JR. Alveolar hemorrhage syndromes. Diffuse microvascular lung hemorrhage in immune and idiopathic disorders. Medicine 1984, **63**: 343–360.

525 Lee S-C, Johnson HA. Multiple nodular pulmonary amyloidosis. A case report and comparison with diffuse alveolar-septal pulmonary amyloidosis. Thorax 1975, **30**: 178–185.

526 Lingskog GE, Liebow AA, Kausel H, Janzen A. Pulmonary arteriovenous aneurysm. Ann Surg 1950, **132**: 591–606.

527 Mark EJ, Ramirez JF. Pulmonary capillaritis and hemorrhage in patients with systemic vasculitis. Arch Pathol Lab Med 1985, **109**: 413–418.

528 Petty IL, Wilkins M. The five manifestations of rheumatoid lung. Dis Chest 1966, **49**: 75–82.

529 Pinckard JK, Rosenbluth DB, Patel K, Dehner LP, Pfeifer JD. Pulmonary hyalinizing granuloma associated with Aspergillus infection. Int J Surg Pathol 2003, **11**: 39–42.

530 Prakash UBS, Barham SS, Rosenow EC III, Brown ML, Payne WS. Pulmonary alveolar microlithiasis. A review including ultrastructural and pulmonary function studies. Mayo Clin Proc 1983, **58**: 290–300.

531 Ranchod M, Bissell M. Pulmonary alveolar proteinosis and cytomegalovirus infection. Arch Pathol Lab Med 1979, **103**: 139–142.

532 Rosen SH, Castleman B, Liebow AA. Pulmonary alveolar proteinosis. N Engl J Med 1958, **258**: 1123–1142.

533 Schober R, Bensch KG, Kosek JC, Northway WH. On the origin of the membranous intraalveolar material in pulmonary alveolar proteinosis. Exp Mol Pathol 1974, **21**: 246–258.

534 Schwartz DA, Ogden PO, Blumberg HM, Honig E. Pulmonary malacoplakia in a patient with the acquired immunodeficiency syndrome. Differential diagnostic considerations. Arch Pathol Lab Med 1990, **114**: 1267–1272.

535 Soergel KH, Sommers SC. Idiopathic pulmonary hemosiderosis and related syndromes. Am J Med 1962, **32**: 499–511.

536 Steer A. Focal pulmonary alveolar proteinosis in pulmonary tuberculosis. Arch Pathol 1969, **87**: 347–352.

537 Szydlowski GW, Cohn HE, Steiner RM, Edie RN. Rounded atelectasis. A pulmonary pseudotumor. Ann Thorac Surg 1992, **53**: 817–821.

538 Thompson PJ, Citron KM. Amyloid and the lower respiratory tract. Thorax 1983, **38**: 84–87.

539 Toyoda M, Ebihara Y, Kato H, Kita S. Tracheobronchial amyloidosis. Histologic, immunohistochemical, ultrastructural, and immunoelectron microscopic observations. Hum Pathol 1993, **24**: 970–976.

540 Travis WD, Colby TV, Lobard C, Carpenter HA. A clinicopathologic study of 34 cases of diffuse pulmonary hemorrhage with lung biopsy confirmation. Am J Surg Pathol 1990, **14**: 1112–1125.

541 Walker WC, Wright V. Pulmonary lesions and rheumatoid arthritis. Medicine (Baltimore) 1968, **47**: 501–520.

542 Yousem SA, Hochholzer L. Pulmonary hyalinizing granuloma. Am J Clin Pathol 1987, **87**: 1–6.

543 Yousem SA, Colby TV, Chen YY, Chen WG, Weiss LW. Pulmonary Langerhans' cell histiocytosis: molecular analysis of clonality. Am J Surg Pathol 2001, **25**: 630–636.

Carcinoma

General and clinical features

544 Aisner J, Belani C. Lung cancer. Recent changes and expectations of improvements. Semin Oncol 1993, **20**: 383–393.

545 Arcasoy SM, Jett JR. Superior pulmonary sulcus tumors and Pancoast's syndrome. N Engl J Med 1997, **337**: 1370–1376.

546 Auerbach O, Garfinkel L, Parks VR, Conston AS, Galdi VA, Joubert L. Histologic type of lung cancer and asbestos exposure. Cancer 1984, **54**: 3017–3021.

547 Auerbach O, Gere JB, Forman JB, Petrick TG, Smolin HJ, Muehsam GE, Kassouny DY, Stout AP. Changes in the bronchial epithelium in relation to smoking and cancer of the lung. N Engl J Med 1957, **256**: 97–104.

548 Cagle PT. Criteria for attributing lung cancer to asbestos exposure. Am J Clin Pathol 2002, **117**: 9–15.

549 Carey FA, Donnelly SC, Walker WS, Cameron EWJ, Lamb D. Synchronous primary lung cancers. Prevalence in surgical material and clinical implications. Thorax 1993, **48**: 344–346.

550 Carey FA, Wallace WAH, Fergusson RJ, Kerr KM, Lamb D. Alveolar atypical adenomatous hyperplasia in association with primary pulmonary adenocarcinoma. A clinicopathologic study of ten cases. Thorax 1992, **47**: 1041–1043.

551 Cook JR, Hill DA, Humphrey PA, Pfeifer JD, El-Mofty SK. Squamous cell carcinoma arising in recurrent respiratory papillomatosis with pulmonary involvement: emerging common pattern of clinical features and human papillomavirus serotype association. Mod Pathol 2000, **13**: 914–918.

552 Craighead JE. Do silica and asbestos cause lung cancer? Arch Pathol Lab Med 1992, **116**: 16–21.

552a Darnell RB, Posner JB. Paraneoplastic syndromes involving the nervous system. N Engl J Med 2003, **349**: 1543–1554.

553 Davila D, Williams D. The etiology of lung cancer. Mayo Clin Proc 1993, **68**: 170–182.

554 Fukayama M, Hayashi Y, Koike M, Hajikano H, Endo S, Okumura H. Human chorionic gonadotropin in lung and lung tumors. Immunohistochemical study on unbalanced distribution of subunits. Lab Invest 1986, **55**: 433–443.

555 Harach HR, Skinner M, Gibbs AR. Biological markers in human lung carcinoma. An immunopathological study of six antigens. Thorax 1983, **38**: 937–941.

556 Helmuth RA, Strate RW. Squamous carcinoma of the lung in a nonirradiated, nonsmoking patient with juvenile laryngotracheal papillomatosis. Am J Surg Pathol 1987, **11**: 643–650.

557 Heyne KH, Lippman SM, Lee JJ, Lee JS, Hong WK. The incidence of second primary tumors in long-term survivors of small-cell lung cancer. J Clin Oncol 1992, **10**: 1519–1524.

558 Hirata Y, Matsukura S, Imura H, Yakura T, Ihjima S, Nagase C, Itoh M. Two cases of multiple hormone-producing small cell carcinoma of the lung. Coexistence of tumor ADH, ACTH, and β-MSH. Cancer 1976, **38**: 2575–2582.

559 Hiroshima K, Toyozaki T, Kohno H, Ohwada H, Fujisawa T. Synchronous and metachronous lung carcinomas: molecular evidence for multicentricity. Pathol Int 1998, **48**: 869–876.

560 Humphrey EW, Ewing SL, Wrigley JV, Northrup WF III,

Kersten TE, Mayer JE, Varco RL. The production of malignant tumors of the lung and pleura in dogs from intratracheal asbestos instillation and cigarette smoking. Cancer 1981, **47**: 1994–1999.

561 Hwang DL, Tay Y-C, Lin SS, Lev-Ran A. Expression of epidermal growth factor receptors in human lung tumors. Cancer 1986, **58**: 2260–2263.

562 Ilgren EB, Griner L, Benirschke K, Pang LSC. A comparative study of pulmonary tumors from the San Diego Zoological Gardens and the tumor reference collection, Imperial Cancer Research Fund, London. Part 2. Pathol Annu 1982, **17**: 331–351.

563 Jubelirer SJ, Wilson RA. Lung cancer in patients younger than 40 years of age. Cancer 1991, **67**: 1436–1438.

564 Koga T, Hashimoto S, Sugio K, Yonemitsu Y, Nakashima Y, Yoshino I, Matsuo Y, Mojtahedzadeh S, Sugimachi K, Sueishi K. Lung adenocarcoma with bronchioloaveolar carcinoma component is frequently associated with foci of high-grade atypicial adenomatous hyperplasia. Am J Clin Pathol 2002, **117**: 464–470.

565 Krauss S, Macy S, Ichiki AT. A study of immunoreactive calcitonir (CT), adrenocorticotropic hormone (ACTH) and carcinoembryonic antigen (CEA) in lung cancer and other malignancies. Cancer 1981, **47**: 2485–2492.

566 Lennon VA, Kryzer TJ, Griesmann GE, O'Suilleabhain PE, Windebank AJ, Woppmann A, Miljanich GP, Lambert EH. Calcium-channel antibodies in the Lambert-Eaton syndrome and other paraneoplastic syndromes. N Engl J Med 1995, **332**: 1467–1474.

567 Loeb LA, Ernster VL, Warner KE, Abbotts J, Laszio J. Smoking and lung cancer. An overview. Cancer Res 1984, **44**: 5940–5958.

568 Marks PH, Schechter FG. Multiple primary carcinomas of the head, neck, and lung. Ann Thorac Surg 1982, **33**: 324–332.

569 Meyer EC, Liebow AA. Relationship of interstitial pneumonia honeycombing and atypical epithelial proliferation to cancer of the lung. Cancer 1965, **18**: 322–351.

570 Miller RR. Bronchioalveolar cell adenomas. Am J Surg Pathol 1990, **14**: 904–912.

571 Miyake M, Ito M, Mitsuoka A, Taki T, Wada H, Hitomi S, Kino T, Matsui Y. Alpha-fetoprotein and human chorionic gonadotropin-producing lung cancer. Cancer 1987, **59**: 227–232.

572 Mizushima Y, Yokoyama A, Ito M, Manabe H, Hirai T, Minami H, Anzai Y, Sato H, Kusajima R, Yamashita R, Kobayashi K, Sugiyama S, Kobayashi M. Lung carcinoma in patients age younger than 30 years. Cancer 1999, **85**: 1730–1733.

573 Mollo F, Magnani C, Bo P, Burlo P, Cravello M. The attribution of lung cancers to asbestos exposure. A pathologic study of 924 cases. Am J Clin Pathol 2002, **117**: 90–95.

574 Morabia A, Wynder EL. Cigarette smoking and lung cancer cell types. Cancer 1991, **68**: 2074–2078.

575 Mori M, Rao SK, Popper HH, Cagle PT, Fraire AE. Atypical adenomatous hyperplasia of the lung: a probable forerunner in the development of adenocarcinoma of the lung. Mod Pathol 2001, **14**: 72–84.

576 Nakanishi K. Alveolar epithelial hyperplasia and adenocarcinoma of the lung. Arch Pathol Lab Med 1990, **114**: 363–368.

577 Nakayama H, Noguchi M, Tsuchiya R, Kodama T, Shimosato Y. Clonal growth of atypical adenomatous hyperplasia of the lung. In situ fluorometric analysis of nuclear DNA content. Mod Pathol 1990, **3**: 314–320.

578 Pastorino U, Berrino F, Gervasio A, Pesenti V, Riboli E, Crosignani P. Proportion of lung cancers due to occupational exposure. Int J Cancer 1984, **33**: 231–237.

579 Patel A, Peters S. Clinical manifestations of lung cancer. Mayo Clin Proc 1993, **68**: 273–277.

580 Patel AM, Davila DG, Peter SG. Paraneoplastic syndromes associated with lung cancer. Mayo Clin Proc 1993, **68**: 278–287.

581 Paulson DL. Carcinomas in the superior pulmonary sulcus. J Thorac Cardiovasc Surg 1975, **70**: 1095–1104.

582 Peters EJ, Morice R, Benner SE, Lippman S, Lukeman J, Lee JS, Ro JY, Hong WK. Squamous metaplasia of the bronchial mucosa and its relationship to smoking. Chest 1993, **103**: 1429–1432.

583 Richardson J, Johnson B. The biology of lung cancer. Semin Oncol 1993, **20**: 105–127.

584 Sankila RJ, Karjalainen ES, Oksanen HM, Hakulinen TR, Teppo LHI. Relationship between occupation and lung cancer as analyzed by age and histologic type. Cancer 1990, **65**: 1651–1656.

585 Sikl H. The present status of knowledge about the Jachymov disease (cancer of the lungs in the miners of the radium mines). Acta Un Int Cancer 1950, **6**: 1366–1375.

586 Szabo I, Sepp R, Nakamoto K, Maeda M, Sakamoto H, Uda H. Human papil lomavirus not found in squamous and large cell lung carcinomas by polymerase chain reaction. Cancer 1994, **73**: 2740–2744.

587 Toomes H, Delphendahl A, Manke H-G, Vogt-Moykopf I. The coin lesion of the lung. A review of 955 resected coin lesions. Cancer 1983, **51**: 534–537.

588 Travis WD, Travis LB, Devesa SS. Lung cancer. Cancer 1995, **75**: 191–202.

589 Warnock ML, Kuwahara TJ, Wolery G. The relation of asbestos burden to asbestosis and lung cancer. Part 2. Pathol Annu 1983, **18**: 109–145.

590 Whitesell P, Drage C. Occupational lung cancer. Mayo Clin Proc 1993, **68**: 183–188.

591 Yesner R. Spectrum of lung cancer and ectopic hormones. Part 1. Pathol Annu 1978, **13**: 207–240.

592 Yokoyama M, Natsuizaka T, Ishii Y, Ohshima S, Kasagi A, Tateno S. Amylase-producing lung cancer. Ultrastructural and biochemical studies. Cancer 1977, **40**: 766–772.

593 Yoneda K. Scar carcinomas of the lung in a histoplasmosis endemic area. Cancer 1990, **65**: 164–168.

Pathologic and generic immunohistochemical features

594 Auerbach O, Frasca JM, Parks VR, Carter HW. A comparison of World Health Organization (WHO) classification of lung tumors by light and electron microscopy. Cancer 1982, **50**: 2079–2088.

595 Bombi JA, Martinez A, Ramarez J, Grau JJ, Nadal A, Fernandez PL, Palacan A, Cardesa A. Ultrastructural and molecular hetergeneity in non-small cell lung carcinomas : study of 110 cases and review of the literature. Ultrastruct Pathol 2002, **26**: 211–218.

596 Colby TV, Koss MN, Travis WD. Tumors of the lower respiratory tract. Atlas of tumor pathology, third series, fascide 13, Washington, DC, 1995, Armed Forces Institute of Pathology.

597 Dunnill MS, Gatter KC. Cellular heterogeneity in lung cancer. Histopathology 1986, **10**: 461–475.

598 Feinstein AR, Gelfman NA, Yesner R, Auerbach O, Hackel DB, Pratt PC. Observer variability in the histopathologic diagnosis of lung cancer. Am Rev Respir Dis 1970, **101**: 671–684.

599 Gatter KC, Dunnill MS, Heryet A, Mason DY. Human lung tumours. Does intermediate filament co-expression correlate with other morphological or immunocytochemical features? Histopathology 1987, **11**: 705–714.

600 Gatter KC, Dunnill MS, Pulford KAF, Heryet A, Mason DY. Human lung tumours. A correlation of antigenic profile with histological type. Histopathology 1985, **9**: 805–823.

601 Gomez-Fernandez C, Jorda M, Delgado PI, Ganjei-Azar P. Thyroid transcription factor 1. A marker for lung adenocarcinoma in body cavity fluids. Cancer 2002, **96**: 289–293.

602 Hammar SP, Bolen JW, Bockus D, Remington F, Friedman S. Ultrastructural and immunohistochemical features of common lung tumors. An overview. Ultrastruct Pathol 1985, **9**: 283–318.

603 Haratake J, Horie A, Tokudome S, Era S, Fujii H, Kawachi J, Miyamoto Y, Suko S, Tokunaga M, Tsuji K, Ikeda M, Kuratsune M. Inter- and intra-pathologist variability in histologic diagnoses of lung cancer. Acta Pathol Jpn 1987, **37**: 1053–1060.

604 Hinson KFW, Miller AB, Tall R. An assessment of the World Health Organization classification of the histologic typing of lung tumors applied to biopsy and resected material. Cancer 1975, **35**: 399–405.

605 Keehn R, Auerbach O, Nambu S, Carter D, Shimosato Y, Greensberg SD, Tateishi R, Saccomanno G, Tokuoka S, Land C. Reproducibility of major diagnoses in a binational study of lung cancer in uranium miners and atomic bomb survivors. Am J Clin Pathol 1994, **101**: 478–482.

606 Kreyberg L. Main histological types of primary epithelial lung tumours. Br J Cancer 1961, **15**: 206–210.

607 Lau SK, Luthringer DJ, Eisen RN. Thyroid transcription factor-1: a review. Appl Immunohistochem Mol Morphol 2002, **10**: 97–102.

608 Mooi WJ, Dingemans KP, Wagenaar SS, Hart AAM, Wagenvoort CA. Ultrastructural heterogeneity of lung carcinomas. Representativity of samples for electron microscopy in tumor classification. Hum Pathol 1990, **21**: 1227–1234.

609 Ordonez NG. Value of thyroid transcription factor-1 immunostaining in distinguishing small cell lung carcinomas from other small cell carcinomas. Am J Surg Pathol 2000, **24**: 1217–1223.

610 Pelosi G, Fraggetta F, Pasini F, Maisonneuve P, Sonzogni A, Iannuc A, Terzi A, Bresaola E, Valduga F, Lupo C, Viale G. Immunoreactivity for thyroid transcription factor-1 in stage non-small cell carcinomas of the lung. Am J Surg Pathol 2001, **25** : 363–372.

611 Roggli VL, Vollmer RT, Greenberg SD, McGavran MH, Spjut HJ, Yesner R. Lung cancer heterogeneity. A blinded and randomized study of 100 consecutive cases. Hum Pathol 1985, **16**: 569–579.

612 Saba SR, Espinoza CG, Richman AV, Azar HA. Carcinomas of the lung. An ultrastructural and immunocytochemical study. Am J Clin Pathol 1983, **80**: 6–13.

613 Srodon M, Westra WH. Immunohistochemical staining for thyroid transcription factor-1: a helpful aid in discerning primary site of tumor origin in patients with brain metastases. Hum Pathol 2002, **33**: 642–645.

614 Taccagni GL, Rovere E, Terreni MR, Gambini S, Cantaboni A. Divergent differentiative histogenetic lines in lung tumors. Identification of histotypes with pure or mixed ultrastructural phenotype and their prognostic significance. Ultrastruct Pathol 1995, **19**: 61–74.

615 Travis WD, Colby TV, Corrin B, Shimosato Y, Brambilla E. Histological typing of lung and pleural tumours, ed. 3. Berlin, 1999, Springer.

616 Yatabe Y, Mitsudomi T, Takahashi T. TTF-1 expression in pulmonary adenocarcinomas. Am J Surg Pathol 2002, **26**: 767–773.

617 Zamecnik J, Kodet R. Value of thyroid transcription factor-1 and surfactant apoprotein A in the differential diagnosis of pulmonary carcinomas: a study of 109 cases. Virchows Arch 2002, **440**: 353–361.

Squamous cell carcinoma

618 Bateson EM. The solitary circumscribed bronchogenic carcinoma. A radiological study of 100 cases. Br J Radiol 1964, **37**: 598–607.

619 Bejui-Thivolet F, Liagre N, Chignol MC, Chardonnet Y, Patricot LM. Detection of human papillomavirus DNA in squamous bronchial metaplasia and squamous cell carcinomas of the lung by in situ hybridization using biotinylated probes in paraffin-embedded specimens. Hum Pathol 1990, **21**: 111–116.

620 Black H, Ackerman LV. The importance of epidermoid carcinoma in situ in the histogenesis of carcinoma of the lung. Ann Surg 1952, **136**: 44–55.

621 Dingemans KP, Mooi WJ. Ultrastructure of squamous cell carcinoma of the lung. Part 1. Pathol Annu 1984, **19**: 249–273.

622 Dosaka-Akita H, Shindoh M, Fujino M, Kinoshita I, Akie K, Katoh M, Kawakami Y. Abnormal p53 expression in human lung cancer is associated with histologic subtypes and patient smoking history. Am J Clin Pathol 1994, **102**: 660–664.

623 Dulmet-Brender E, Jaubert F, Huchon G. Exophytic endobronchial epidermoid carcinoma. Cancer 1986, **57**: 1358–1364.

623a Funai K, Yokose T, Ishii G, Araki K, Yoshida J, Nishimura M, Nagai K, Nishiwaki Y, Ochiai A. Clinicopathologic characteristics of peripheral squamous cell carcinoma of the lung. Am J Surg Pathol 2003, **27**: 978–984.

623b Green LK. Basaloid squamous cell carcinoma of the lung: a review of 292 cases (Abstract). Mod Pathol 2003, **16**: 307a.

624 Havenith MG, Dingemans KP, Cleutjens JPM, Wagenaar SS, Bosman FT. Basement membranes in bronchogenic squamous cell carcinoma. An immunohistochemical and ultrastructural study. Ultrastruct Pathol 1990, **14**: 51–64.

625 Kolin A, Hiruki T. Palisading granulomas associated with lung cancer. Arch Pathol Lab Med 1990, **114**: 697–699.

626 Moro D, Brichon PY, Brambilla E, Veale D, Labat F, Brambilla C. Basaloid bronchial carcinoma. A histologic group with a poor prognosis. Cancer 1994, **73**: 2734–2739.

627 Nelson WG, Sun T-T. The 50- and 58-kdalton keratin classes as molecular markers for stratified squamous epithelia. Cell culture studies. J Cell Biol 1983, **97**: 244–251.

628 Said J. Immunohistochemistry of lung tumors. Lung Biol Health Dis 1990, **44**: 635–651.

629 Said JW, Nash G, Sassoon AF, Shintaku IP, Banks-Schlegel S. Involucrin in lung tumors. A specific marker for squamous differentiation. Lab Invest 1983, **49**: 563–568.

630 Sozzi G, Pastorini U, Moiraghi L, Tagliabue E, Pezzella F, Ghirelli C, Tornielli S, Sard L, Huebner K, Pierotti MA, Croce CM, Pilotti S. Loss of FHIT function in lung cancer and preinvasive bronchial lesions. Cancer Res 1998, **58**: 5032–5037.

631 Tomashefsky JF, Connors AF, Rosenthal ES, Hsiue IL. Peripheral vs. central squamous cell carcinoma of the lung. A comparison of clinical features, histopathology, and survival. Arch Pathol Lab Med 1990, **114**: 468–474.

632 Tomizawa Y, Nakajima T, Kohno T, Saito R, Yamaguchi N, Yokota J. Clinicopathologic significance of Fhit protein expression in stage 1 non-small cell lung carcinoma. Cancer Res 1998, **58**: 5478–5483.

633 Wang BY, Gil J, Kaufman D, Gan L, Kohtz S, Burstein DE. P63 in pulmonary squamous neoplasms, and other pulmonary tumors. Hum Pathol 2002, **33**: 921–926.

634 Wistuba II, Gazdar AF, Minna JD. Molecular genetics of small cell lung carcinoma. Semin Oncol 2001, **28**: 3–13.

635 Zheng J, Shu Q, Li Z-H, Tsao J-I, Weiss LM, Shibata D. Patterns of p53 mutations in squamous cell carcinoma of the lung. Acquisition at a relatively early age. Am J Pathol 1994, **145**: 1444–1449.

Adenocarcinoma

636 Adachi H, Aki T, Yoshida H, Yumoto T, Wakahara H. Combined choriocarcinoma and adenocarcinoma of the lung. Acta Pathol Jpn 1989, **39**: 147–152.

637 Amin MB, Tamboli P, Merchant SH, Ordonez NG, Ro J, Ayala AG, Ro JY. Micropapillary component in lung adenocarcinoma: a distinctive histologic feature with possible prognostic significance. Am J Surg Pathol 2002, **26**: 358–364.

638 Arnould L, Drouot F, Fargeot P, Bernard A, Foucher P, Collin F, Petrella T. Hepatoid adenocarcinoma of the lung: report of a

case of an unusual alphafetoprotein-producing lung tumor. Am J Surg Pathol 1997, **21**: 1113–1118.

639 Auerbach O, Garfinkel L, Parks VR. Scar cancer of the lung. Increase over a 21 year period. Cancer 1979, **43**: 636–642.

640 Bakris GL, Mulopulos GP, Korchik R, Ezdinli EZ, Ro J, Yoon B-H. Pulmonary scar carcinoma. A clinicopathologic analysis. Cancer 1983, **52**: 493–497.

641 Banks-Schlegel SP, McDowell EM, Wilson TS, Trump BF, Harris CC. Keratin proteins in human lung carcinomas. Combined use of morphology, keratin immunocytochemistry, and keratin immunoprecipitation. Am J Pathol 1984, **114**: 273–286.

642 Barsky SH, Huang SJ, Bhuta S. The extracellular matrix of pulmonary scar carcinomas is suggestive of a desmoplastic origin. Am J Pathol 1986, **124**: 412–419.

643 Bennett DE, Sasser WF, Ferguson T. Adenocarcinoma of the lung in men. A clinicopathologic study of 100 cases. Cancer 1969, **23**: 431–439.

644 Cagle PT, Cohle SD, Greenberg SD. Natural history of pulmonary scar cancers. Clinical and pathologic implications. Cancer 1985, **56**: 2031–2035.

645 Castro CY, Moran CA, Flieder DG, Suster S. Primary signet ring cell adenocarcinomas of the lung: a clinicopathological study of 15 cases. Histopathology 2001, **39**: 397–401.

646 Cox JD, Yesner RA. Adenocarcinoma of the lung. Recent results from the Veterans Administration Lung Group. Am Rev Respir Dis 1979, **120**: 1025–1029.

647 Dessy E, Pietra GG. Pseudomesotheliomatous carcinoma of the lung. An immunohistochemical and ultrastructural study of three cases. Cancer 1991, **68**: 1747–1753.

648 Eimoto T, Teshima K, Shirakusa T, Kikuchi M. Ultrastructure of well-differentiated adenocarcinomas of the lung with special reference to bronchioloalveolar carcinoma. Ultrastruct Pathol 1985, **8**: 177–190.

649 Furukawa T, Watanabe S, Kodama T, Sato Y, Shimosato Y, Suemasu K. T-zone histiocytes in adenocarcinoma of the lung in relation to postoperative prognosis. Cancer 1985, **56**: 2651–2656.

650 Gemma A, Noguchi M, Hirohashi S, Tsugane S, Tsuchiya R, Niitani H, Shimosato Y. Clinicopathologic and immunohistochemical characteristics of goblet cell type adenocarcinoma of the lung. Acta Pathol Jpn 1991, **41**: 737–743.

651 Harwood TR, Gracey DR, Yokoo H. Pseudomesotheliomatous carcinoma of the lung. A variant of peripheral lung cancer. Am J Clin Pathol 1976, **65**: 159–167.

652 Higashiyama M, Doi O, Kodama K, Tateishi R, Kurokawa E. Extramammary Paget's disease of the bronchial epithelium. Arch Pathol Lab Med 1991, **115**: 185–188.

653 Horie A, Kotoo Y, Ohta M, Kurita Y. Relation of fine structure to prognosis for papillary adenocarcinoma of the lung. Hum Pathol 1984, **15**: 870–879.

654 Ishikura H, Kanda M, Ito M, Nosaka K, Mizuno K. Hepatoid adenocarcinoma. A distinctive histological subtype of alpha-fetoprotein-producing lung carcinoma. Virchows Arch [A] 1990, **417**: 73–80.

655 Jordon D, Jagirdar J, Kaneko M. Blood group antigens, Lewisx and Lewisy in the diagnostic discrimination of malignant mesothelioma versus adenocarcinoma. Am J Pathol 1989, **135**: 931–937.

656 Kawai T, Torikata C, Suzuki M. Immunohistochemical study of pulmonary adenocarcinoma. Am J Clin Pathol 1988, **89**: 455–462.

657 Kimula Y. A histochemical and ultrastructural study of adenocarcinoma of the lung. Am J Surg Pathol 1978, **2**: 253–264.

658 Kish JK, Ro JY, Ayala AG, McMurtrey MJ. Primary mucinous adenocarcinoma of the lung with signet-ring cells. A histochemical comparison with signet-ring cell carcinomas of other sites. Hum Pathol 1989, **20**: 1097–1102.

659 Kodama T, Shimosato Y, Koide T, Watanabe S, Yoneyama T.

660 Koss MN, Fleming M, Przgodzki RM, Sherrod A, Travis W, Hochholzer L. Adenocarcinoma simulating mesothelioma: a clinicopathologic and immunohistochemical study of 29 cases. Ann Diagn Pathol 1998, **2**: 93–102.

661 Koss M, Travis W, Moran C, Hochholzer L. Pseudomesotheliomatous adenocarcinoma. A reappraisal. Semin Diagn Pathol 1992, **9**: 117–123.

662 Kung ITM, Lui IOL, Loke SL, Khin MA, Mok CK, Lam WK, So SY. Pulmonary scar cancer. A pathologic reappraisal. Am J Surg Pathol 1985, **9**: 391–400.

663 Li ZH, Zheng J, Weiss LM, Shibata D. c-k-ras and p53 mutations occur very early in adenocarcinoma of the lung. Am J Pathol 1994, **144**: 303–309.

664 Linnoila RI. Pathology of non-small cell lung cancer. New Diagnostic approaches. Hematol Oncol Clin North Am 1990, **4**: 1027–1051.

665 Madri JA, Carter D. Scar cancers of the lung. Origin and significance. Hum Pathol 1984, **15**: 625–631.

666 McElvaney G, Miller RR, Muller NL, Nelems B, Evans KG, Ostrow DN. Multicentricity of adenocarcinoma of the lung. Chest 1989, **95**: 151–154.

667 Meyer EC, Liebow AA. Relationship of interstitial pneumonia honeycombing and atypical epithelial proliferation to cancer of the lung. Cancer 1965, **18**: 322–351.

668 Miyoshi T, Satoh Y, Okumura S, Nakagawa K, Shirakusa T, Tsuchiya E, Ishikawa Y. Early-stage lung adenocarcinomas with a micropapillary pattern, a distinct pathologic marker for a significantly poor prognosis. Am J Surg Pathol 2002, **27**: 101–109.

669 Mizutani Y, Nakajima T, Morinaga S, Gotoh M, Shimosato Y, Akino T, Suzuki A. Immunohistochemical localization of pulmonary surfactant apoproteins in various lung tumors. Special reference to nonmucus producing lung adenocarcinomas. Cancer 1988, **61**: 532–537.

670 Moran C, Hochholzer L, Fishback N, Travis W, Koss M. Mucinous (so-called colloid) carcinomas of lung. Mod Pathol 1992, **5**: 634–638.

671 Nakanishi K. Alveolar epithelial hyperplasia and adenocarcinoma of the lung. Arch Pathol Lab Med 1990, **114**: 363–368.

672 Nicholson AG, McCormick CJ, Shimosato Y, Butcher DN, Sheppard MN. The value of PE-10, a monoclonal antibody against pulmonary surfactant, in distinguishing primary and metastatic lung tumours. Histopathology 1995, **27**: 57–60.

673 Ohshima S, Shimizu Y, Takahama M. Detection of c-Ki-*ras* gene mutation in paraffin sections of adenocarcinoma and atypical bronchioloalveolar cell hyperplasia of human lung. Virchows Archiv 1994, **424**: 129–134.

674 Ramaekers F, Puts J, Moesker O, Kant A, Jap P, Vooijs P. Demonstration of keratin in human adenocarcinomas. Am J Pathol 1983, **111**: 213–223.

675 Rao SK, Fraire AE. Alveolar cell hyperplasia in association with adenocarcinoma of lung. Mod Pathol 1995, **8**: 165–169.

676 Said JW, Nash G, Tepper G, Banks-Schlegel S. Keratin proteins and carcinoembryonic antigen in lung carcinoma. An immunoperoxidase study of fifty-four cases, with ultrastructural correlations. Hum Pathol 1983, **14**: 70–76.

677 Scroggs MW, Roggli VL, Fraire AE, Sanfilippo F. Eosinophilic intracytoplasmic globules in pulmonary adenocarcinomas. A histochemical, immunohistochemical, and ultrastructural study of six cases. Hum Pathol 1989, **20**: 845–849.

678 Shimizu T, Yonezawa S, Tanaka S, Sato E. Expression of Lewis X-related antigens in adenocarcinomas of lung. Histopathology 1993, **22**: 549–556.

679 Silini EM, Bosi F, Pellegata NS, Volpato G, Romano A, Nazari S, Tinelli C, Ranzani GN, Solcia E, Fiocca R. K-ras gene mutations: an unfavorable prognostic marker in stage I lung adenocarcinoma. Virchows Arch 1994, **424**: 367–373.

680 Silver SA, Askin FB. True papillary carcinoma of the lung: a distinct clinicopathologic entity. Am J Surg Pathol 1997, **21**: 43–51.

681 Solomon MD, Greenberg SD, Spjut HJ. Morphology of bronchial epithelium adjacent to adenocarcinoma of the lung. Mod Pathol 1990, **3**: 684–687.

682 Sukoh N, Abe S, Nakajima I, Ogura S, Isobe H, Inoue K, Kawakami Y. Immunohistochemical distributions of cathepsin B and basement membrane antigens in human lung adenocarcinoma: association with invasion and metastasis. Virchows Archiv 1994, **424**: 33–38.

683 Taccagni G, Dell'Antonio G, Terreni MR, Cantaboni A. Heterogeneous sub cellular morphology of lung adenocarcinoma cells. Identification of different cytotypes on cytological material. Ultrastruct Pathol 1990, **14**: 65–80.

683a Terasaki H, Niki T, Matsuno Y, Yamada T, Maeshima A, Asamura H, Hayabuchi N, Hirohashi S. Lung adenocarcinoma with mixed bronchioloalveolar and invasive components. Am J Surg Pathol 2003, **27**: 937–951.

684 Tsao M-S, Fraser RS. Primary pulmonary adenocarcinoma with enteric differentiation. Cancer 1991, **68**: 1754–1757.

685 Upton MP, Hirohashi S, Tome Y, Miyazawa N, Suemasu K, Shimosato Y. Expression of vimentin in surgically resected adenocarcinomas and large cell carcinomas of lung. Am J Surg Pathol 1986, **10**: 560–567.

686 Valaitis J, Warren S, Gamble D. Increasing incidence of adenocarcinoma of the lung. Cancer 1981, **47**: 1042–1046.

687 Van de Molengraft F, van Niekerk C, Jap P, Poels L. OV-TL 12/30 (keratin 7 antibody) is a marker of glandular differentiation in lung cancer. Histopathology 1993, **22**: 35–38.

688 Vincent RG, Pickren JW, Lane WW, Bross I, Takita H, Houten L, Gutierrez AC, Rzepka T. The changing histopathology of lung cancer. A review of 1682 cases. Cancer 1977, **39**: 1647–1655.

689 Vincent TN, Satterfield JV, Ackerman LV. Carcinoma of the lung in women. Cancer 1965, **18**: 559–570.

690 Westra W, Offerhaus J, Goodman S, Slebos R, Polak M, Baas I, Rodenuis S, Hruban R. Overexpression of the p53 tumor suppressor gene product in primary lung adenocarcinomas is associated with cigarette smoking. Am J Surg Pathol 1993, **17**: 213–220.

691 Westra W, Slebos R, Offerhaus J, Goodman S, Evers S, Kensler T, Askin F, Rodehuis S, Hruban R. K-ras oncogene activation in lung adenocarcinomas from former smokers. Evidence that K-ras mutations are an early and irreversible event in the development of adenocarcinoma of the lung. Cancer 1993, **72**: 432–438.

692 Yamashiro K, Yasuda S, Nagase A, Hirata T, Nojima T, Nagashima K. Prognostic significance of an interface pattern of central fibrosis and tumor cells in peripheral adenocarcinoma of the lung. Hum Pathol 1995, **26**: 67–73.

Undifferentiated large cell carcinoma

693 Albain KS, True LD, Golomb HM, Hoffman PC, Little AG. Large cell carcinoma of the lung. Ultrastructural differentiation and clinicopathologic correlations. Cancer 1985, **56**: 1618–1623.

694 Ascensao JL, Oken MM, Ewing SL, Goldberg RJ, Kaplan ME. Leukocytosis and large cell lung cancer. A frequent association. Cancer 1987, **60**: 903–905.

695 Attanoos RL, Papagiannis A, Suttinont P, Goddard H, Papotti M, Gibbs AR. Pulmonary giant cell carcinoma: pathological entity of morphological phenotype? Histopathology 1998, **32**: 225–231.

696 Butler AE, Colby TV, Weiss L, Lombard C. Lymphoepithelioma-like carcinoma of the lung. Am J Surg Pathol 1989, **13**: 632–639.

697 Byrd RB, Miller WE, Carr DT, Payne WS, Woolner LB. The roentgenographic appearance of large cell carcinoma of the bronchus. Mayo Clin Proc 1968, **43**: 333–336.

698 Castro CY, Ostrowski ML, Barrios R, Green LK, Popper HH, Powell S, Cagle PT, Ro JY. Relationship between Epstein–Barr virus and lymphoepithelioma-like carcinoma of the lung: a clinicopathologic study of six cases and review of the literature. Hum Pathol 2001, **32**: 863–872.

699 Chan JKC, Hui PK, Yip TTC, Tsang WYW, Law CK, Poon YF, Ma VWS. Detection of Epstein-Barr virus only in lymphoepithelial carcinomas among primary carcinomas of the lung. Histopathology 1995, **26**: 576–578.

700 Chang YL, Wu CT, Shih JY, Lee YC. New aspects in clinicopathologic and oncogene studies of 23 pulmonary lymphoepithelioma-like carcinomas. Am J Surg Pathol 2002, **26**: 715–723.

701 Chejfee G, Candel A, Jansson DS, Warren WH, Koukoulis GK, Gould JE, Manderino GL, Gooch GT, Gould VE. Immunohistochemical features of giant cell carcinoma of the lung. Patterns of expression of cytokeratins, vimentin, and the mucinous glycoprotein recognized by monoclonal antibody A-80. Ultrastruct Pathol 1991, **15**: 131–138.

702 Chen FF, Yan JJ, Lai WW, Jin YT, Su IJ. Epstein–Barr virus-associated non-small cell lung carcinoma: undifferentiated "lymphoepithelioma-like" carcinoma as a distinct entity with better prognosis. Cancer 1998, **82**: 2334–2342.

703 Churg A. The fine structure of large cell undifferentiated carcinoma of the lung. Evidence for its relation to squamous cell carcinomas and adenocarcinomas. Hum Pathol 1978, **9**: 143–156.

704 Gal AA, Unger ER, Koss MN, Yen TSB. Distinctive case – detection of Epstein-Barr virus in lymphoepithelioma-like carcinoma of the lung. Mod Pathol 1991, **4**: 264–268.

705 Ginsberg SS, Buzaid AC, Stern H, Carter D. Giant cell carcinoma of the lung. Cancer 1992, **70**: 606–610.

706 Hammar S. Adenocarcinoma and large cell undifferentiated carcinoma of the lung. Ultrastruct Pathol 1987, **11**: 263–291.

707 Han AJ, Xiong M, Gu XY, Lin SX, Xiong M. Lymphoepithelioma-like carcinoma of the lung with a better prognosis. A clinicopathologic study of 32 cases. Am J Clin Pathol 2001, **115**: 841–850.

708 Herman DL, Bullock WK, Waken JK. Giant cell adenocarcinoma of the lung. Cancer 1966, **19**: 1337–1346.

709 Horie A, Ohta M. Ultrastructural features of large cell carcinoma of the lung with reference to the prognosis of patients. Hum Pathol 1981, **12**: 423–432.

710 Ishida T, Kaneko S, Tateishi M, Oka T, Mitsudomi T, Sugimachi K, Hara N, Ohta M. Large cell carcinoma of the lung. Am J Clin Pathol 1990, **93**: 176–182.

711 Kodama T, Takada K, Kameya T, Shimosato Y, Tsuchiya R, Okabe T. Large cell carcinoma of the lung associated with marked eosinophilia. A case report. Cancer 1984, **54**: 2313–2317.

712 Leung CS, Morava-Protzner I. Large cell carcinoma of lung with osteoclast-like giant cells. Histopathology 1998, **32**: 4842–4844.

713 Matsui K, Kitagawa M, Wakaki K, Masuda S. Lung carcinoma mimicking malignant lymphoma. Report of three cases. Acta Pathol Jpn 1993, **43**: 608–614.

714 Pittaluga S, Wong MP, Chung LP, Loke S-L. Clonal Epstein-Barr virus in lymphoepithelioma-like carcinoma of the lung. Am J Surg Pathol 1993, **17**: 678–682.

715 Sawyers CL, Golde DW, Quan S, Nimer SD. Production of granulocyte-macrophage colony-stimulating factor in two patients with lung cancer, leukocytosis, and eosinophilia. Cancer 1992, **69**: 1342–1346.

716 Shimosato Y, Sobin L, Spencer H, et al. (eds). Histological typing of lung tumours. Geneva, 1981, World Health Organization.

717 Visscher DW, Zarbo RJ, Trojanowski JW, Sakr W, Crissman JD. Neuroendocrine differentiation in poorly differentiated lung

carcinomas. A light microscopic and immunohistologic study. Mod Pathol 1990, **3**: 508–512.

718 Wang N-S, Seemayer TA, Ahmed MN, Knaack J. Giant cell carcinoma of the lung. A light and electron microscopic study. Hum Pathol 1976, **7**: 3–16.

719 Wick M, Berg L, Hertz M. Large cell carcinoma of the lung with neuroendocrine differentiation. A comparison with large cell "undifferentiated" pulmonary tumors. Am J Clin Pathol 1992, **97**: 796–805.

720 Yesner R. Large cell carcinoma of the lung. Semin Diagn Pathol 1985, **2**: 255–269.

Clear cell carcinoma

721 Edwards C, Charlie A. Clear cell carcinoma of the lung. J Clin Pathol 1985, **38**: 880–885.

722 Katzenstein AL, Prioleau PG, Askin FB. The histologic spectrum and significance of clear-cell change in lung carcinoma. Cancer 1980, **45**: 943–947.

Bronchioloalveolar carcinoma and related tumors

723 Barsky SH, Cameron R, Osann KE, Tomita D, Holmes EC. Rising incidence of bronchioloalveolar lung carcinoma and its unique clinicopathologic features. Cancer 1994, **73**: 1163–1170.

724 Barsky SH, Grossman DA, Ho J, Holmes EC. The multifocality of bronchioalveolar lung carcinoma. Evidence and implications of a multiclonal origin. Mod Pathol 1994, **7**: 633–640.

725 Bedrossian CWM, Weilbaecher DG, Bentinck DC, Greenberg SD. Ultrastructure of human bronchioloalveolar cell carcinoma. Cancer 1975, **36**: 1399–1413.

726 Bennett DE, Sasser WF. Bronchiolar carcinoma. A valid clinicopathologic entity? A study of 30 cases. Cancer 1969, **24**: 876–887.

727 Bonikos DS, Hendrickson M, Bensch KG. Pulmonary alveolar cell carcinoma. Fine structural and in vitro study of a case and critical review of this entity. Am J Surg Pathol 1977, **1**: 93–108.

728 Burke LM, Rush WI, Khoor A, Mackay B, Oliveira P, Whitsett JA, Singh G, Turnicky R, Fleming MV, Koss MN, Travis WD. Alveolar adenoma: a histochemical, immunohistochemical, and ultrastructural analysis of 17 cases. Hum Pathol 1999, **30**: 158–167.

729 Copin MC, Buisine MP, Leteurtre E, Marquette CH, Porte H, Auber JP, Gosselin B, Porchet N. Mucinous bronchioloalveolar carcinomas display a specific pattern of mucin gene expression among primary lung adenocarcinomas. Hum Pathol 2001, **32**: 274–281.

730 Daly RC, Trastek VF, Pairolero PC, Murtaugh PA, Huang M-S, Allen MS, Colby TV. Bronchioloalveolar carcinoma. Factors affecting survival. Ann Thorac Surg 1991, **51**: 368–377.

731 Dermer GB. Origin of bronchioloalveolar carcinoma and peripheral bronchial adenocarcinoma. Cancer 1982, **49**: 881–887.

732 Dixon AY, Moran JF, Wesselius LJ, McGregor DH. Pulmonary mucinous cystic tumor. Case report with review of the literature. Am J Surg Pathol 1993, **17**: 722–728.

733 Fantone JC, Geisinger KR, Appelman HD. Papillary adenoma of the lung with lamellar and electron dense granules. An ultrastructural study. Cancer 1982, **50**: 2839–2844.

734 Fine G, Chung C-H. Adenoma of type 2 pneumocytes with oncocytic features. Arch Pathol Lab Med 1991, **115**: 797–801.

735 Fukuda T, Ohnishi Y, Kanai I, Emura I, Watanabde T, Kitazawa M, et al. Papillary adenoma of the lung. Histological and ultrastructural findings in two cases. Acta Pathol Jpn 1992, **42**: 56–61.

736 Graeme-Cook F, Mark EJ. Pulmonary mucinous cystic tumors of borderline malignancy. Hum Pathol 1991, **22**: 185–190.

737 Greco RJ, Steiner RM, Goldman S, Cotler H, Patchefsky A, Cohn HE. Bronchoalveolar cell carcinoma of the lung. Ann Thorac Surg 1986, **41**: 652–656.

738 Greenberg SD, Smith MN, Spjut HJ. Bronchiolo-alveolar carcinoma. Cell of origin. Am J Clin Pathol 1975, **63**: 153–167.

739 Hegg CA, Flint A, Singh S. Papillary adenoma of the lung. Am J Clin Pathol 1992, **97**: 393–397.

740 Hiroshima K, Toyozaki T, Iyoda A, Ohwada H, Kado S, Shirasawa H, Fujisawa T. Ulstructural study of intranuclear inclusion bodies of pulmonary adenocarcinoma. Ultrastruct Pathol 2000, **23**: 383–390.

741 Jacques J, Currie W. Bronchiolo-alveolar carcinoma. Clara cell tumor? Cancer 1977, **40**: 2171–2180.

742 Kragel PJ, Devaney KO, Meth BM, Linnoila I, Frierson HF, Travis WD. Mucinous cystadenoma of the lung. Arch Pathol Lab Med 1990, **114**: 1053–1056.

743 Kuhn C III. Fine structure of bronchioloalveolar cell carcinoma. Cancer 1972, **30**: 1107–1118.

744 Kurokawa T, Matsuno Y, Noguchi M, Mizuno S, Shimosato Y. Surgically curable "early" adenocarcinoma in the periphery of the lung. Am J Surg Pathol 1994, **18**: 431–438.

745 Manning JT Jr, Spjut HJ, Tschen JA. Bronchioloalveolar carcinoma. The significance of two histopathologic types. Cancer 1984, **54**: 525–534.

746 Miller RR. Bronchioloalveolar cell adenomas. Am J Surg Pathol 1990, **14**: 904–912.

747 Miller RR, Nelems B, Evans KG, Muller NL, Ostrow DN. Glandular neoplasia of the lung. A proposed analogy to colonic tumors. Cancer 1988, **61**: 1009–1014.

748 Montes M, Binette JP, Chaudhry AP, Adler RH, Guarino R. Clara cell adenocarcinoma. Light and electron microscope studies. Am J Surg Pathol 1977, **1**: 245–253.

749 Moran CA, Hochholzer L, Fishback N, Travis WD, Koss MN. Mucinous (so-called colloid) carcinomas of lung. Mod Pathol 1992, **5**: 634–638.

750 Morningstar WA, Hassan MO. Bronchiolo-alveolar carcinoma with nodal metastases. Am J Surg Pathol 1979, **3**: 273–278.

751 Nakajima T, Kodama T, Tsumuraya M, Shimosato Y, Kameya T. S-100 protein-positive Langerhans cells in various human lung cancers, especially in peripheral adenocarcinomas. Virchows Arch [A] 1985, **407**: 177–189.

752 Noguchi M, Kodama T, Shimosato Y, Koide T, Naruke T, Singh G, Katyal SL. Papillary adenoma of type 2 pneumocytes. Am J Surg Pathol 1986, **10**: 134–139.

753 Ogata T, Endo K. Clara cell granules of peripheral lung cancers. Cancer 1984, **54**: 1635–1644.

754 Rosenblatt MB, Lisa JR, Collier F. Primary and metastatic bronchioloalveolar carcinoma. Dis Chest 1967, **52**: 147–152.

755 Shah RN, Badve S, Papreddy K, Schindler S, Laskin WB, Yeldandi AV. Expresson of cytokeratin 20 in mucinous bronchioloaveolar carcinoma. Hum Pathol 2002, **33**: 915–920.

756 Sheppard MN, Thurlow NP, Dewar A. Amphicrine differentiation in bronchioloalveolar cell carcinoma. Ultrastruct Pathol 1994, **18**: 437–441.

757 Sidhu GS, Forrester EM. Glycogen-rich Clara cell-type bronchioloalveolar carcinoma. Light and electron microscopic study. Cancer 1977, **40**: 2209–2215.

757a Sidhu GS, Wieczorek R, Cassai ND, Zhu C-C. The concept of bronchioloalveolar cell adenocarcinoma: redefinition, a critique of the 1999 WHO classification, and an ultrastructural analysis of 155 cases. Int J Surg Pathol 2003, **11**: 89–99.

758 Silverman JF, Finley JL, Park HK, Strausbauch P, Unverferth M, Carney M. Fine needle aspiration cytology of bronchioloalveolar-cell carcinoma of the lung. Acta Cytol 1985, **29**: 887–896.

759 Singh G, Katyal SL, Torikata C. Carcinoma of type II pneumocytes. Immunodiagnosis of a subtype of "bronchioloalveolar carcinomas." Am J Pathol 1981, **102**: 195–208.

760 Singh G, Katyal SL, Torikata C. Carcinoma of type II

pneumocytes. PAS staining as a screening test for nuclear inclusions of surfactant specific apoprotein. Cancer 1982, **50:** 946–948.

761 Singh G, Scheithauer BW, Katyal SL. The pathobiologic features of carcinomas of type II pneumocytes. An immunocytologic study. Cancer 1986, **57:** 994–999.

762 Spriggs AI, Cole M, Dunnill MS. Alveolar-cell carcinoma. A problem in sputum cytodiagnosis. J Clin Pathol 1982, **35:** 1370–1379.

763 Tao LC, Delarue NC, Sanders D, Weisbrod G. Bronchiolo-alveolar carcinoma. A correlative clinical and cytologic study. Cancer 1978, **42:** 2759–2767.

764 Tomashefski JF Jr, Buzatu T, Petrelli M, Kleinerman J. α1-Antitrypsin is a marker for Clara cell carcinomas of the lung (abstract). Lab Invest 1988, **58:** 94A.

Adenosquamous carcinoma

765 Fitzgibbons PL, Kern WH. Adenosquamous carcinoma of the lung. A clinical and pathologic study of seven cases. Hum Pathol 1985, **16:** 463–466.

766 Ishida T, Kaneko S, Yokoyama H, Inoue T, Sugio K, Sugimachi K. Adenosquamous carcinoma of the lung. Clinicopathologic and immunohistological features. Am J Clin Pathol 1992, **97:** 678–685.

767 Takamori S, Noguchi M, Morinaga S, Goya T, Tsugane S, Kakegawa T, Shimosato Y. Clinicopathologic characteristics of adenosquamous carcinoma of the lung. Cancer 1991, **67:** 649–654.

Sarcomatoid carcinoma and carcinosarcoma

768 Banerjee SS, Evden BP, Wells S, McWilliam IJ, Harris M. Pseudoangiosarcomatous carcinoma. A clinicopathologic study of seven cases. Histopathology 1992, **21:** 13–23.

769 Dacic S, Finkelstein SD, Sasatomi E, Swalsky PA, Yousem SA. Molecular pathogenesis of pulmonary carcinosarcoma as determined by microdissection-bases allelotyping. Am J Surg Pathol 2002, **26:** 510–516.

770 Davis MP, Eagan RT, Weiland LH, Pairolero PC. Carcinosarcoma of the lung. Mayo Clinic experience and response to chemotherapy. Mayo Clin Proc 1984, **59:** 598–603.

771 Fishback NF, Travis WD, Moran CA, Guinee DG Jr, McCarthy WF, Koss MN. Pleomorphic (spindle/giant cell) carcinoma of the lung. A clinicopathologic correlation of 78 cases. Cancer 1994, **73:** 2925–2936.

772 Fletcher JA, Pinkus GS, Weidner N, Morton CC. Lineage-restricted clonality in biphasic solid tumors. Am J Pathol 1991, **138:** 1199–1207.

773 Hammar SP, Hallman KO. Unusual primary lung neoplasms. Spindle cell and undifferentiated lung carcinomas expressing only vimentin. Ultrastruct Pathol 1990, **14:** 407–422.

774 Humphrey PA, Scroggs MW, Roggli VL, Shelburne JD. Pulmonary carcinomas with a sarcomatoid element. An immunocytochemical and ultrastructural analysis. Hum Pathol 1988, **19:** 155–165.

775 Koss MN, Hochholzer L, Frommelt RA. Carcinosarcomas of the lung: a clinicopathologic study of 66 patients. Am J Surg Pathol 1999, **23:** 1514–1526.

776 Love GL, Daroca PJ Jr. Bronchogenic sarcomatoid squamous cell carcinoma with osteoclast-like giant cells. Hum Pathol 1983, **14:** 1004–1006.

777 Matsui K, Kitagawa M. Spindle cell carcinoma of the lung: a clinicopathologic study of three cases. Cancer 1991, **67:** 2361–2367.

778 Matsui K, Kitagawa M, Miwa A. Lung carcinoma with spindle cell components. Sixteen cases examined by immunohistochemistry. Hum Pathol 1992, **23:** 1289–1297.

779 Nakajima M, Kasai T, Hashimoto H, Iwata Y, Manabe H.

Sarcomatoid carcinoma of the lung: a clinicopathologic study of 37 cases. Cancer 1999, **86:** 608–616.

780 Nappi O, Wick MR. Sarcomatoid neoplasms of the respiratory tract. Semin Diagn Pathol 1993, **10:** 137–147.

781 Nappi O, Swanson PE, Wick MR. Pseudovascular adenoid squamous cell carcinoma of the lung. Clinicopathologic study of the cases and comparison with true pleuropulmonary angiosarcoma. Hum Pathol 1994, **25:** 373–378.

782 Rainosek DE, Ro JY, Ordonez NG, Kulaga AD, Ayala AG. Sarcomatoid carcinoma of the lung. A case with atypical carcinoid and rhabdomyosarcomatous components. Am J Clin Pathol 1994, **102:** 360–364.

783 Ro JY, Chen JL, Lee JS, Sahin AA, Ordonez NG, Ayata AG. Sarcomatoid carcinoma of the lung. Immunohistochemical and ultrastructural studies of 14 cases. Cancer 1992, **69:** 376–386.

783a Rossi G, Cavazza A, Sturm N, Migaldi M, Facciolongo N, Longo L, Maiorana A, Brambilla E. Pulmonary carcinomas with pleomorphic, sarcomatoid, or sarcomatous elements. Am J Surg Pathol 2003, **27:** 311–324.

784 Wick MR, Ritter JH, Humphrey PA. Sarcomatoid carcinomas of the lung: a clinicopathologic review. Am J Clin Pathol 1997, **108:** 40–53.

Pulmonary blastoma and pulmonary endodermal tumor

785 Clerick SJ, Fann CC, Ryoo JW. Mixed pulmonary blastoma and carcinosarcoma. Histopathology 1994, **25:** 171–174.

786 Cohen RE, Weaver MG, Montenegro HD, Abdul-Karim FW. Pulmonary blastoma with malignant melanoma component. Arch Pathol Lab Med 1990, **114:** 1076–1078.

787 Cupples J, Wright J. An immunohistochemical comparison of primary lung carcinosarcoma and sarcoma. Pathol Res Pract 1990, **186:** 326–329.

788 Dail DH, Liebow AA, Gmelich JT, Friedman PJ, Miyai K, Myer W, Patterson SD, Hammar SP. Intravascular, bronchiolar, and alveolar tumor of the lung (IVBAT). An analysis of twenty cases of a peculiar sclerosing endothelial tumor. Cancer 1983, **51:** 452–464.

789 Davis MP, Eagan RT, Weiland LH, Pairolero PC. Carcinosarcoma of the lung. Mayo Clinic experience and response to chemotherapy. Mayo Clin Proc 1984, **59:** 598–603.

790 Francis D, Jacobsen M. Pulmonary blastoma. Curr Top Pathol 1983, **73:** 265–294.

791 Heckman CJ, Truong LD, Cagle PT, Font RL. Pulmonary blastoma with rhabdomyosarcomatous differentiation. An electron microscopic and immunohistochemical study. Am J Surg Pathol 1988, **12:** 35–40.

792 Inoue H, Kasai K, Shinada J, Toshimura H, Kameya T. Pulmonary blastoma – comparison between its epithelial component and fetal bronchial epithelium. Acta Pathol Jpn 1992, **42:** 884–892.

793 Jacobsen M, Francis D. Pulmonary blastoma. A clinico-pathological study of 11 cases. Acta Pathol Microbiol Scand (A) 1980, **88:** 151–160.

794 Kodama T, Shimosato Y, Watanabe S, Koide T, Naruke T, Shimase J. Six cases of well-differentiated adenocarcinoma simulating fetal lung tubules in pseudoglandular stage. Comparison with pulmonary blastoma. Am J Surg Pathol 1984, **8:** 735–744.

795 Koss MN, Hochholzer L, O'Leary T. Pulmonary blastomas. Cancer 1991, **67:** 2368–2381.

796 Marcus PB, Dieb TM, Martin JH. Pulmonary blastoma. An ultrastructural study emphasizing intestinal differentiation in lung tumors. Cancer 1982, **49:** 1829–1833.

797 Mardini G, Pai U, Chavez AM, Tomashefski JF Jr. Endobronchial adenocarcinoma with endometrioid features and prominent neuroendocrine differentiation. A variant of fetal adenocarcinoma. Cancer 1994, **73:** 1383–1389.

798 Müller-Hermelink HK, Kaiserling E. Pulmonary adenocarcinoma of fetal type. Alternating differentiation argues in favour of a common endodermal stem cell. Virchows Arch [A] 1986, **409**: 195–210.

799 Nakatani Y, Dickersin G, Mark E. Pulmonary endodermal tumor resembling fetal lung. A clinicopathologic study of five cases with immunohistochemical and ultrastructural characterization. Hum Pathol 1990, **21**: 1097–1107.

800 Nakatani Y, Kitamura H, Inayama Y, Kamijo S, Nagashima Y, Shimoyama K, Nakamura N, Sano J, Ogawa N, Shibagaki T, Resl M, Mark EJ. Pulmonary adenocarcinomas of the fetal lung type: a clinicopathologic study indicating differences in histology, epidemiology, and natural history of low-grade and high-grade forms. Am J Surg Pathol 1998, **22**: 399–411.

801 Nakatani Y, Kitamura H, Inayama Y, Ogawa N. Pulmonary endodermal tumor resembling fetal lung. The optically clear nucleus is rich in biotin. Am J Surg Pathol 1994, **18**: 637–642.

802 Roth JA, Elguezabal A. Pulmonary blastoma evolving into carcinosarcoma. A case study. Am J Surg Pathol 1978, **2**: 407–413.

803 Siegel R, Bueso-Ramos C, Cohen C, Koss M. Pulmonary blastoma with germ cell (yolk sac) differentiation. Report of two cases. Mod Pathol 1991, **4**: 566–570.

804 Yousem S, Wick M, Randhawa P, Manivel J. Pulmonary blastoma. An immunohistochemical analysis with comparison with fetal lung in its pseudoglandular stage. Am J Clin Pathol 1990, **93**: 167–175.

Small cell carcinoma

805 Albain K, Crowley J, Hutchins L, Gandara D, O'Bryan R, Von Hoff D, Griffin B, Livingston R. Predictors of survival following relapse or progression of small cell lung cancer. Southwest oncology group study 8605 report and analysis of recurrent disease data base. Cancer 1993, **72**: 1184–1191.

806 Azzopardi JG. Oat cell carcinoma of the bronchus. J Pathol Bacteriol 1959, **78**: 513–519.

807 Baines CJ, To T. Small cell lung cancer presenting as a solitary pulmonary nodule. Cancer 1990, **66**: 577–582.

808 Ben-Ezra JM, Kornstein MJ, Grimes MM, Krystal G. Small cell carcinomas of the lung express the Bcl-2 protein. Am J Pathol 1994, **145**: 1036–1040.

809 Begin P, Sahai S, Wang N-S. Giant cell formation in small cell carcinoma of the lung. Cancer 1983, **52**: 1875–1879.

810 Bensch KG, Corrin B, Pariente R, Spencer H. Oat-cell carcinoma of the lung. Its origin and relationship to bronchial carcinoid. Cancer 1968, **22**: 1163–1172.

811 Bergh J, Esscher T, Steinholtz L, Nilsson K, Phlman S. Immunocytochemical demonstration of neuron-specific enolase (NSE) in human lung cancers. Am J Clin Pathol 1985, **84**: 1–7.

812 Carter D. Small-cell carcinoma of the lung. Am J Surg Pathol 1983, **7**: 787–795.

813 Churg A, Johnston WH, Stulbarg M. Small cell and squamous-small cell anaplastic carcinomas of the lung. Am J Surg Pathol 1980, **4**: 255–263.

814 Colby TV, Koss MN, Travis WD. Tumors of the lower respiratory tract. Atlas of tumor pathology, third series, fascicle 13. Washington, DC, 1995, Armed Forces Institute of Pathology.

815 Dacic S, Finkelstein SD, Baksh FK, Swalsky PA, Barnes LE, Yousem SA. Small-cell neuroendocrine carcinoma displays unique profiles of tumor-suppressor gene loss in relationship to the primary site of formation. Hum Pathol 2002, **33**: 927–932.

816 Diggs CH, Engeler JE, Prendergast EJ, Kramer K. Small cell carcinoma of the lung. Cancer 1992, **69**: 2075–2083.

817 Elema JD, Keuning HM. The ultrastructure of small cell lung carcinoma in bronchial biopsy specimens. Hum Pathol 1985, **16**: 1133–1140.

818 Esscher T, Steinholtz L, Bergh J, Nou E, Nilsson K, Phlman S. Neurone specific enolase. A useful diagnostic serum marker for small cell carcinoma of the lung. Thorax 1985, **40**: 85–90.

819 Fraire AE, Johnson E, Yesner R, Zhang X, Spjut H, Greenberg SD. Prognostic significance of histopathologic subtype and stage in small cell lung cancer. Hum Pathol 1992, **23**: 520–528.

820 Fushimi H, Kikui M, Morino H, Hosono Y, Fukuoka M, Kusunoki Y, Aozasa K, Matsumoto K. Detection of large cell component in small cell lung carcinoma by combined cytologic and histologic examinations and its clinical implication. Cancer 1992, **70**: 599–605.

821 Gephardt GN, Grady KJ, Ahmad M, Tubbs RR, Mehta AC, Shepard KV. Peripheral small cell undifferentiated carcinoma of the lung. Clinicopathologic features of 17 cases. Cancer 1988, **61**: 1002–1008.

822 Griffiths AP, Mearns A, Horsfield GI. Combined small cell and bronchioloalveolar cell carcinoma. Histopathology 1990, **17**: 380.

823 Guinee DG Jr, Fishback NF, Koss MN, Abbondanzo SL, Travis WD. The spectrum of immunohistochemical staining of small-cell lung carcinoma in specimens from transbronchial and open-lung biopsies. Am J Clin Pathol 1994, **102**: 406–414.

824 Hage E, Hansen M, Hirsch FR. Electron microscopic sub-classification of small cell carcinoma of the lung. Acta Pathol Jpn 1983, **33**: 671–681.

825 Johnson DH, Marangos PJ, Forbes JT, Hainsworth JD, Van Welch R, Hande KR, Greco FA. Potential utility of serum neuron-specific enolase levels in small cell carcinoma of the lung. Cancer Res 1984, **44**: 5409–5414.

826 Lehto VP, Stenman S, Miettinen M, Dahl D, Virtanen I. Expression of a neural type of intermediate filament as a distinguishing feature between oat cell carcinoma and other lung cancers. Am J Pathol 1983, **110**: 113–118.

827 Lumadue JA, Askin FB, Perlman EJ. MIC2 analysis of small cell carcinoma. Am J Clin Pathol 1994, **102**: 692–694.

828 McCue PA, Finkel GC. Small-cell lung carcinoma. An evolving histopathological spectrum. Semin Oncol 1993, **20**: 153–162.

829 Mark EJ, Ramirez JF. Peripheral small-cell carcinoma of the lung resembling carcinoid tumor. A clinical and pathologic study of 14 cases. Arch Pathol Lab Med 1985, **109**: 263–269.

830 Matsuki Y, Tanimoto A, Hamada T, Sasaguri Y. Histidine decarboxylase expression as a new sensitive and specific marker for small cell lung carcinoma. Mod Pathol 2003, **16**: 72–78.

831 Michels S, Swanson PE, Robb JA, Wick MR. Leu-7 in small cell neoplasms. An immunohistochemical study with ultrastructural correlations. Cancer 1987, **60**: 2958–2964.

832 Morris CS, Esiri MM, Marx A, Newsom-Davis J. Immunocytochemical characteristics of small cell lung carcinoma associated with the Lambert-Eaton myasthenic syndrome. Am J Pathol 1992, **140**: 839–845.

833 Naylor SL, Johnson BE, Minna JD, Sakaguchi AY. Loss of heterozygosity of chromosome 3p markers in small-cell lung cancer. Nature 1987, **329**: 451–454.

834 Nicholson SA, Beasley MB, Brambilla E, Hasleton PS, Colby TV, Sheppard MN, Falk R, Travis WD. Small cell lung carcinoma (SCLC): a clinicopathologic study of 100 cases with surgical specimens. Am J Surg Pathol 2002, **26**: 1184–1197.

835 Patel A, Davila D, Peters S. Paraneoplastic syndromes associated with lung cancer. Mayo Clin Proc 1993, **68**: 278–287.

836 Radice PA, Matthews MJ, Ihde DC, Gazdar AF, Carney DN, Bunn PA, Cohen MH, Fossieck BE, Makuch RW, Minna JD. The clinical behavior of "mixed" small cell/large cell bronchogenic carcinoma compared to "pure" small cell subtypes. Cancer 1982, **50**: 2894–2902.

837 Salyer D, Eggleston JC. Oat cell carcinoma of the bronchus and the carcinoid syndrome. Arch Pathol 1975, **99**: 513–515.

838 Sheppard MN, Corrin B, Bennett MH, Marangos PJ, Bloom SR,

Polak JM. Immunocytochemical localization of neuron specific enolase in small cell carcinomas and carcinoid tumours of the lung. Histopathology 1984, **8**: 171–181.

839 Sidhu GS. The endodermal origin of digestive and respiratory tract APUD cells. Histopathologic evidence and a review of the literature. Am J Pathol 1979, **96**: 5–20.

840 Sturm N, Rossi G, Lantuejoul S, Lavveriere MH, Papotti M, Brichon PY, Brambilla C, Brambilla E. 34βE12 expression along the whole spectrum of neuroendocrine proliferations of the lung, from neuroendocrine cell hyperplasia to small cell carcinoma. Histopathology 2003, **42**: 156–166.

841 Sturm N, Rossi G, Lantuejoul S, Papotti M, Frachon S, Claraz C, Brichon PY, Brambilla C, Brambilla E. Expression of thyroid transcription factor-1 in the spectrum of neuroendocrine cell lung proliferations with special interest in carcinoids. Hum Pathol 2002, **33**: 175–191.

842 Tateishi R, Horai T, Hattori S. Demonstration of argyrophil granules in small cell carcinoma of the lung. Virchows Arch [A] 1978, **377**: 203–210.

843 Tischler AS. Small cell carcinoma of the lung. Cellular origin and relationship to other neoplasms. Semin Oncol 1978, **5**: 244–252.

844 van Muijen GNP, Ruiter DJ, van Leeuwen C, Prins FA, Rietsema K, Warnaar SO. Cytokeratin and neurofilament in lung carcinomas. Am J Pathol 1984, **116**: 363–369.

845 Viberti L, Bongiovanni M, Croce S, Bussolati G. 34betaE12 cytokeratin immunodetection in the differential diagnosis of small cell tumors of lung. Int J Surg Pathol 2000, **8**: 317–322.

846 Vollmer RT. The effect of cell size on the pathologic diagnosis of small and large cell carcinomas of the lung. Cancer 1982, **50**: 1280–1383.

847 Vollmer RT, Birch R, Ogden L, Crissman JD. Subclassification of small cell cancer of the lung. The Southeastern Cancer Study Group experience. Hum Pathol 1985, **16**: 247–252.

848 Warren WM, Memoli VA, Jordan AG, Gould VE. Reevaluation of pulmonary neoplasms resected as small cell carcinomas. Significance of distinguishing between well-differentiation and small cell neuroendocrine carcinomas. Cancer 1990, **65**: 1003–1010.

849 Whang-Peng J. 3p Deletion and small cell lung carcinoma (editorial). Mayo Clin Proc 1989, **64**: 256–260.

850 Williams ED, Azzopardi JG. Tumors of lung and carcinoid syndrome. Thorax 1960, **15**: 30–36.

851 Wistuba II, Gazdar AF, Minna JD. Molecular genetics of small cell lung carcinoma. Semin Oncol 2001, **28**: 3–13.

852 World Health Organization. The World Health Organization histological typing of lung tumours. Am J Clin Pathol 1982, **77**: 123–136.

853 Yesner R. Small cell tumors of the lung. Am J Surg Pathol 1983, **7**: 775–785.

854 Zamecnik J, Kodet R. Value of thyroid transcription factor-1 and surfactant apoprotein A in the differential diagnosis of pulmonary carcinomas: a study of 109 cases. Virchows Arch 2002, **440**: 353–361.

Carcinoma in situ

855 Carter D. Pathology of early squamous cell carcinoma of the lung. Part 1. Pathol Annu 1978, **13**: 131–147.

856 Carter D. Squamous cell carcinoma of the lung. An update. Semin Diagn Pathol 1985, **2**: 226–234.

857 Carter D, Marsh BR, Baker R, Erozan YS, Frost JK. Relationships of morphology to clinical presentation in ten cases of early squamous cell carcinoma of the lung. Cancer 1976, **37**: 1389–1396.

858 Cohen MH. Lung cancer. A status report (editorial). J Natl Cancer Inst 1975, **55**: 505–511.

859 Hirano T, Franzen B, Kato H, Ebihara Y, Auer G. Genesis of squamous cell lung carcinoma. Sequential changes of proliferation, DNA ploidy, and p53 expression. Am J Pathol 1994, **144**: 296–302.

860 Mahadevia PJ, Fleisher LA, Frick KD, Eng J, Goodman SN, Powe NR. Lung cancer screening with helical computed tomography in older adult smokers: a decision and cost-effectiveness analysis. JAMA 2003, **289**: 313–322.

861 Mason MK, Jordan JW. Outcome of carcinoma in situ and early invasive carcinoma of the bronchus. Thorax 1982, **37**: 453–456.

862 Melamed MR, Zaman MB, Flehinger BJ, Martini N. Radiologically occult in situ and incipient invasive epidermoid lung cancer. Detection by sputum cytology in a survey of asymptomatic cigarette smokers. Am J Surg Pathol 1977, **1**: 5–16.

863 Nagamoto N, Saito Y, Sato M, Sagawa M, Kamma K, Takahashi S, Usuda K, Endo C, Fujimura S, Nakada T, Ohkuda K. Clinicopathologic analysis of 19 cases of isolated carcinoma in situ of the bronchus. Am J Surg Pathol 1993, **17**: 1234–1243.

864 Nagamoto N, Saito Y, Suda H, et al. Relationship between length of longitudinal extension and maximal depth of transmural invasion and roentgenographically occult squamous cell carcinoma of the bronchus (non-polypoid type). Am J Surg Pathol 1989, **13**: 11–20.

865 Rusch V, Klimstra D, Linkov I, Dmitrovsky E. Aberrant expression of p53 or the epidermal growth factor receptor is frequent in early bronchial neoplasia and coexpression precedes squamous cell carcinoma development. Cancer Res 1995, **55**: 1365–1372.

866 Woolner LB, David E, Fontana RS, Andersen HA, Bernatz PE. In situ and early invasive bronchogenic carcinoma. Report of 28 cases with postoperative survival data. J Thorac Cardiovasc Surg 1970, **60**: 275–290.

867 Woolner LB, Fontana RS, Cortese DA, Sanderson DR, Bernatz PE, Payne WS, Pairolero PC, Piehler JM, Taylor WF. Roentgenographically occult lung cancer. Pathologic findings and frequency of multicentricity during a 10-year period. Mayo Clin Proc 1984, **59**: 453–466.

868 Woolner LB, Fontana RS, Sanderson DR, Miller WE, Muhm JR, Taylor WF, Uhlenhopp MA. Mayo lung project. Evaluation of lung cancer screening through December 1979. Mayo Clin Proc 1981, **56**: 544–555.

Biopsy

869 Chuang MT, Marchevsky A, Teirstein AS, Kirschner P, Kleinerman J. Diagnosis of lung cancer by fibreoptic bronchoscopy. Problems in the histological classification of non-small cell carcinomas. Thorax 1984, **39**: 175–178.

870 Coughlin M, Deslauriers J, Beaulieu M, Fournier B, Piraux M, Rouleau J, Tardif A. Role of mediastinoscopy in pretreatment staging of patients with primary lung cancer. Ann Thorac Surg 1985, **40**: 556–560.

871 Nguyen G-K, York EL, Jones RL, King EG. Transmucosal needle aspiration biopsy via the fiberoptic bronchoscope. Value and limitations in the cytodiagnosis of tumors and tumor-like lesions of the lung. Part 1. Pathol Annu 1992, **27**: 105–132.

872 Pearson FG, Nelems JM, Henderson RD, Delarue NC. The role of mediastinoscopy in the selection of treatment for bronchial carcinoma with involvement of superior mediastinal lymph nodes. J Thorac Cardiovasc Surg 1972, **64**: 382–390.

873 Popp W, Rauscher H, Ritschka L, Redtenbacher S, Zwich H, Dutz W. Diagnostic sensitivity of different techniques in the diagnosis of lung tumors with the flexible fiberoptic bronchoscope. Comparison of brush biopsy, imprint cytology of forceps biopsy, and histology of forceps biopsy. Cancer 1991, **67**: 72–75.

874 Sackner MA. Bronchofiberscopy. Am Rev Respir Dis 1975, **111**: 62–88.

875 Szabo E, Birer M, Mulshine J. Early detection of lung cancer. Semin Oncol 1993, **20**: 374–382.

876   Unruh H, Chu-Jeng R. Mediastinal assessment for staging and treatment of carcinoma of the lung. Ann Thorac Surg 1986, **41**: 224–229.

877   Zavala DC. Diagnostic fiberoptic bronchoscopy. Techniques and results of biopsy in 600 patients. Chest 1975, **68**: 12–19.

Cytology

878   Chopra SK, Genovesi MG, Simmons DH, Gothe B. Fiberoptic bronchoscopy in the diagnosis of lung cancer. Comparison of pre- and post-bronchoscopy sputa washings, brushings and biopsies. Acta Cytol (Baltimore) 1977, **21**: 524–527.

879   Erozan YS. Cytopathologic diagnosis of pulmonary neoplasms in sputum and bronchoscopic specimens. Semin Diagn Pathol 1986, **3**: 188–195.

880   Fontana RS, Carr DT, Woolner LB, Miller FK. An evaluation of methods of inducing sputum production in patients with suspected cancer of the lung. Proc Staff Meet Mayo Clin 1962, **37**: 113–121.

881   Johnston WW, Bossen EH. Ten years of respiratory cytopathology at Duke University Medical Center. II. The cytopathologic diagnosis of lung cancer during the years 1970 to 1974, with a comparison between cytopathology and histopathology in the typing of lung cancer. Acta Cytol (Baltimore) 1981, **25**: 499–505.

882   Johnston WW, Frable WJ. The cytopathology of the respiratory tract. A review. Am J Pathol 1976, **84**: 372–414.

883   Kanhouwa SB, Matthews MJ. Reliability of cytologic typing of lung cancer. Acta Cytol (Baltimore) 1976, **20**: 229–232.

884   Kvale PA, Frederick RB, Kini S. Diagnostic accuracy in lung cancer. Comparison of techniques used in association with flexible fiberoptic bronchoscopy. Chest 1976, **69**: 752–757.

885   Ng ABP, Horak GC. Factors significant in the diagnostic accuracy of lung cytology in bronchial washing and sputum samples. I. Bronchial washings. Acta Cytol (Baltimore) 1983, **27**: 391–396.

886   Pearson FG, Thompson DW, Delarue NC. Experience with the cytologic detection, localization, and treatment of radiographically undemonstrable bronchial carcinoma. J Thorac Cardiovasc Surg 1967, **54**: 371–382.

887   Pilotti S, Rilke F, Gribaudi G, Spinelli P. Cytologic diagnosis of pulmonary carcinoma on bronchoscopic brushing material. Acta Cytol (Baltimore) 1982, **26**: 655–660.

888   Salhadin A, Nasiell M, Nasiell K, Silfverswärd C, Hjerpe A, Wadas AM, Enstad I. The unique cytologic picture of oat cell carcinoma in effusions. Acta Cytol (Baltimore) 1976, **20**: 298–302.

889   Sinner WN. Pulmonary neoplasms diagnosed with transthoracic needle biopsy. Cancer 1979, **43**: 1533–1540.

890   Skitarelie K, Von Haam E. Bronchial brushings and washings. A diagnostically rewarding procedure? Acta Cytol (Baltimore) 1974, **18**: 321–324.

891   Solomon DA, Solliday NH, Gracey DR. Cytology in fiberoptic bronchoscopy. Comparison of bronchial brushing, washing and post bronchoscopy sputum. Chest 1974, **65**: 616–619.

892   Spriggs AI, Boddington MM. Oat-cell bronchial carcinoma. Identification of cells in pleural fluid. Acta Cytol (Baltimore) 1976, **20**: 525–529.

893   Todd TRJ, Weisbrod G, Tao LC, Sanders DE, Delarue NC, Chamberlain DW, Ilves R, Pearson FG, Cass W, Cooper JD. Aspiration needle biopsy of thoracic lesions. Ann Thorac Surg 1981, **32**: 154–161.

894   Truong LD, Underwood RD, Greenberg SD, McLarty JW. Diagnosis and typing of lung carcinomas by cytopathologic methods. A review of 108 cases. Acta Cytol 1985, **23**: 379–384.

895   Wandall HH. A study on neoplastic cells in sputum as a contribution to the diagnosis of primary lung cancer. Acta Chir Scand 1944, **91**(Suppl 93): 1–143.

896   Zaman MB, Hajdu SI, Melamed MR, Watson RC. Transthoracic aspiration cytology of pulmonary lesions. Semin Diagn Pathol 1986, **3**: 176–187.

897   Zavala DC. Diagnostic fiberoptic bronchoscopy. Techniques and results of biopsy in 600 patients. Chest 1975, **68**: 12–19.

Spread and metastases

898   Cox JD, Yesner RA. Adenocarcinoma of the lung. Recent results from the Veterans Administration Lung Group. Am Rev Respir Dis 1979, **120**: 1025–1029.

899   Eagan RT, Maurer LH, Forcier RJ, Tulloh M. Small cell carcinoma of the lung. Staging, paraneoplastic syndromes, treatment, and survival. Cancer 1974, **33**: 527–532.

900   Gonzalez-Vitale JC, Garcia-Bunuel R. Pulmonary tumor emboli and cor pulmonale in primary carcinoma of the lung. Cancer 1976, **38**: 2105–2110.

901   LeGal Y, Bauer WG. Second primary bronchogenic carcinoma. J Thorac Cardiovasc Surg 1961, **41**: 114–124.

902   McNeill PM, Wagman LD, Neifeld JP. Small bowel metastases from primary carcinoma of the lung. Cancer 1987, **59**: 1486–1489.

903   Onuigbo WIB. Patterns in metastasis in lung cancer. A review. Cancer Res 1961, **21**: 1077–1085.

904   Rosen ST, Aisner J, Makuch RW, Matthews MJ, Ihde DC, Whitacre M, Glatstein EJ, Wiernik PH, Lichter AS, Bunn PA Jr. Carcinomatous leptomeningitis in small cell lung cancer. A clinicopathologic review of the National Cancer Institute experience. Medicine 1982, **61**: 45–53.

905   Sridhar KS, Rao RK, Kunhardt B. Skeletal muscle metastases from lung cancer. Cancer 1987, **59**: 1530–1534.

906   Trillet V, Catajar JF, Croisile B, Turjman F, Aimard G, Bourrat C, Bret P, Carrie C, Chassard JL, Chauvin F, Confavreux C, Cordier JF, Deruty R, Duquesnel J, Fischer G, Gamondes JP, Gerard JP. Cerebral metastases as first symptom of bronchogenic carcinoma. A prospective study of 37 cases. Cancer 1991, **67**: 2935–2940.

Treatment

907   Ahmad K, Fayos JV, Kirsh MM. Apical lung carcinoma. Cancer 1984, **54**: 913–917.

908   Bains MS. Surgical treatment of lung cancer. Chest 1991, **100**: 826–837.

909   Choi NC, Carey RW, Kaufman SD, Grillo HC, Younger J, Wilkins EW Jr. Small cell carcinoma of the lung. A progress report of 15 years' experience. Cancer 1987, **59**: 6–14.

910   Devine JW, Mendenhall WM, Million RR, Carmichael MJ. Carcinoma of the superior pulmonary sulcus treated with surgery and/or radiation therapy. Cancer 1986, **57**: 941–943.

911   Flehringer B, Kimmel M, Melamed M. The effect of surgical treatment on survival from early lung cancer. Implications for screening. Chest 1992, **101**: 1013–1018.

912   Ihde D. Chemotherapy of lung cancer. N Engl J Med 1992, **327**: 1434–1441.

913   Jett JR. Current treatment of unresectable lung cancer. Mayo Clin Proc 1993, **68**: 603–611.

914   Johnson BE. Management of small cell lung cancer. Clin Chest Med 2002, **23**: 225–239.

915   Komaki R, Roh J, Cox JD, Lopes da Conceicao A. Superior sulcus tumors. Results of irradiation of 36 patients. Cancer 1981, **48**: 1563–1568.

916   Law MR, Henk JM, Lennox SC, Hodson ME. Value of radiotherapy for tumour on the bronchial stump after resection for bronchial carcinoma. Thorax 1982, **37**: 496–499.

917   Lung Cancer Study Group. Effects of postoperative mediastinal radiation on completely resected stage II and stage III epidermoid cancer of the lung. N Engl J Med 1986, **315**: 1377–1381.

918 Machtay M, Glatstein E. Combined modality therapy for non-small cell lung carcinoma. Cancer J 2002, **8**: S55–S67.

919 Paulson DL. Carcinomas in the superior pulmonary sulcus. J Thorac Cardiovasc Surg 1975, **70**: 1095–1104.

920 Perez CA. Radiation therapy in the management of carcinoma of the lung. Cancer 1977, **39**: 901–916.

921 Perry MC, Eaton WL, Propert KJ, Ware JH, Zimmer B, Chahinian AP, Skarin A, Carey RW, Kreisman H, Faulkner C, Comis R, Green MR. Chemotherapy with or without radiation therapy in limited small-cell carcinoma of the lung. N Engl J Med 1987, **316**: 912–918.

922 Petrovich Z, Stanley K, Cox JD, Paig C. Radiotherapy in the management of locally advanced lung cancer of all cell types. Final report of randomized trial. Cancer 1981, **48**: 1335–1340.

923 Rosell R, Gomez-Codina J, Camps C, Maestre J, Padille J, Canto A, Mate JL, Li S, Roig J, Olazabal A, et al. A randomized trial comparing preoperative chemotherapy plus surgery with surgery alone in patients with non-small-cell lung cancer. N Engl J Med 1994, **330**: 153–158.

924 Shaw EG, Bonner JA, Foote RL, Martenson JA, Frytak S, Dechamps C, McDougall JC. Role of radiation therapy in the management of lung cancer. Mayo Clin Proc 1993, **68**: 593–602.

925 Sherman DM, Weichselbaum R, Hellman S. The characteristics of long-term survivors of lung cancer treated with radiation. Cancer 1981, **47**: 2575–2580.

926 Sprensen HR, Lund C, Alstrup P. Survival in small cell lung carcinoma after surgery. Thorax 1986, **41**: 479–482.

Prognosis

927 Ahmad K, Fayos JV, Kirsh MM. Apical lung carcinoma. Cancer 1984, **54**: 913–917.

928 Boring CC, Squires TS, Tong T. Cancer statistics, 1992. CA Cancer J Clin 1992, **42**: 19–38.

929 Buhr J, Berghauser KH, Morr H, Dobroschke J, Ebner HJ. Tumor cells in intraoperative pleural lavage. An indicator for the poor prognosis of bronchogenic carcinoma. Cancer 1990, **65**: 1801–1804.

930 Bulzebruck H, Bopp R, Drings P, Bauer E, Krysa S, Probst G, van Kaick G, Muller K, Vogt-Moykopf I. New aspects in the staging of lung cancer. Prospective validation of the International Union Against Cancer TNM Classification. Cancer 1992, **70**: 1102–1110.

931 Burford TH, Ferguson TB, Spjut HJ. Results in the treatment of bronchogenic carcinoma. J Thorac Surg 1958, **36**: 316–328.

932 Carey FA, Lamb D, Bird CC. Intratumoral heterogeneity of DNA content in lung cancer. Cancer 1990, **65**: 2266–2269.

933 Carter D. Squamous cell carcinoma of the lung. An update. Semin Diagn Pathol 1985, **2**: 226–234.

934 Clayton F. Bronchioloalveolar carcinomas. Cell types, patterns of growth, and prognostic correlates. Cancer 1986, **57**: 1555–1564.

935 Cline MJ, Battifora H. Abnormalities of protooncogenes in non-small cell lung cancer. Correlations with tumor type and clinical characteristics. Cancer 1987, **60**: 2669–2674.

936 Davis S, Stanley KE, Yesner R, Kuang DT, Morris JF. Small-cell carcinoma of the lung. Survival according to histologic subtype. A Veterans Administration Lung Group study. Cancer 1981, **47**: 1863–1866.

937 Devine JW, Mendenhall WM, Million RR, Carmichael MJ. Carcinoma of the superior pulmonary sulcus treated with surgery and/or radiation therapy. Cancer 1986, **57**: 941–943.

938 Funa K, Steinholtz L, Nou E, Bergh J. Increased expression of N-myc in human small cell lung cancer biopsies predicts lack of response to chemotherapy and poor prognosis. Am J Clin Pathol 1987, **88**: 216–220.

939 Gail MH, Eagan RT, Feld R, Ginsberg R, Goodell B, Hill L, Holmes EC, Lukeman JM, Mountain CF, Oldham RK, Pearson FG, Wright PW, Lake WH Jr, The Lung Cancer Study Group: Prognostic factors in patients with resected stage I non-small cell lung cancer. A report from the Lung Cancer Study Group. Cancer 1984, **54**: 1802–1813.

940 Gazdar AF. Molecular markers for the diagnosis and prognosis of lung cancer. Cancer 1992, **69**: 1592–1599.

941 Gibbon JH Jr, Albritten FF Jr. Templeton JY III, Nealon TF Jr. Cancer of the lung. An analysis of 532 consecutive cases. Ann Surg 1953, **138**: 489–501.

942 Greenberg SD, Fraire AE, Kinner BM, Johnson EH. Tumor cell type versus staging in the prognosis of carcinoma of the lung. Part 2. Pathol Annu 1987, **22**: 387–405.

943 Han H, Landreneau RJ. Santucci TS, Tung MY, Macherey RS, Shackney SE, Sturgis CD, Raab SS, Silverman JF. Prognostic value of immunohistochemical expressions of p53, HER-2/neu, and bcl-2 in stage 1 non-small-cell lung cancer. Hum Pathol 2002, **33**: 105–110.

944 Haque AK, Syed S, Lele SM, Freeman DH, Adegboyega PA. Immunohistochemical study of thyroid transcription factor-1 and HER2/neu in non-small cell lung cancer: strong thyroid transcription factor-1 expression predicts better survival. Appl Immunohistochem Mol Morphol 2002, **10**: 103–109.

945 Harada M, Dosaka-Akita H, Myamoto H, Kusumaki N, Kawakami Y. Prognostic significance of the expression of ras oncogene product in non-small cell lung cancer. Cancer 1992, **69**: 72–77.

946 Herbert SH, Curran WJ Jr, Stafford PM, Rosenthal SA, McKenna WG, Hughes EN. Comparison of outcome between clinically staged, unresected superior sulcus tumors and other stage II non-small cell lung carcinomas treated with radiation therapy alone. Cancer 1992, **69**: 363–369.

947 Hirsch FR, Osterlind K, Hansen HH. The prognostic significance of histopathologic subtyping in small cell carcinoma of the lung according to the classification of the World Health Organization. A study of 375 consecutive patients. Cancer 1983, **52**: 2144–2150.

948 Kato Y, Ferguson TB, Bennett DE, Burford TH. Oat cell carcinoma of the lung. A review of 138 cases. Cancer 1969, **23**: 517–524.

949 Kemeny M, Block LR, Braun DW Jr, Martini N. Results of surgical treatment of carcinoma of the lung by stage and cell type. Surg Gynecol Obstet 1978, **147**: 865–871.

950 Kern WH, Tucker BL. The pathology of lung cancer in ten-year survivors (abstract). Am J Clin Pathol 1986, **86**: 397.

951 Kirsh MM, Rotman H, Argenta L, Bove E, Cimmino V, Tashian J, Ferguson P, Sloan H. Carcinoma of the lung. Results of treatment over ten years. Ann Thorac Surg 1976, **21**: 371–377.

952 Kirsh MM, Tashian J, Sloan H. Carcinoma of the lung in women. Ann Thorac Surg 1982, **34**: 34–39.

953 Kitaichi M, Asamoto H, Izumi T, Furuta M. Histological classification of regional lymph nodes in relation to postoperative survival in primary lung cancer. Hum Pathol 1981, **12**: 1000–1005.

954 Komaki R, Roh J, Cox JD, Lopes da Conceicao A. Superior sulcus tumors. Results of irradiation of 36 patients. Cancer 1981, **48**: 1563–1568.

955 Kratzke RA, Shimizu E, Kaye FJ. Oncogenes in human lung cancer. Cancer Treat Res 1992, **63**: 61–85.

956 Lee I, Gould VE, Radosevich JA, Thor A, Ma Y, Schlom J, Rosen ST. Immuno-histochemical evaluation of ras oncogene expression in pulmonary and pleural neoplasms. Virchows Arch [Cell Pathol] 1987, **53**: 146–152.

957 Lee JS, Ro JY, Sahini AA, Hong WK, Brown BW, Mountain CF, Hittelman WN. Expression of blood-group antigen A – a favorable prognostic factor in non-small cell lung cancer. N Engl J Med 1991, **324**: 1084–1090.

958   Lipford EH III, Eggleston JC, Lillemoe KD, Sears DL, Moore GW, Baker RR. Prognostic factors in surgically resected limited-stage, non-small cell carcinoma of the lung. Am J Surg Pathol 1984, **8**: 357–365.

959   Maeshima AM, Niki T, Maeshima A, Yamada T, Kondo H, Matsuno Y. Modified scar grade: a prognostic indicator in small peripheral lung adenocarcinoma. Cancer 2002, **95**: 2546–2554.

960   Manning JT Jr, Spjut HJ, Tschen JA. Bronchioloalveolar carcinoma. The significance of two histopathologic types. Cancer 1984, **54**: 525–534.

961   Martini N, Flehinger BJ, Zaman MB, Beattie EJ Jr. Results of resection in non-oat cell carcinoma of the lung with mediastinal lymph node metastases. Ann Surg 1983, **198**: 386–397.

962   Miller WT, Husted J, Freiman D, Atkinson B, Pietra GG. Bronchioloalveolar carcinoma. Two clinical entities with one pathologic diagnosis. AJR 1978, **130**: 905–912.

963   Miyake M, Taki T, Hitomi S, Hakomori S. Correlation of expression of H/LEy/LEb antigens with survival in patients with carcinoma of the lung. N Engl J Med 1992, **327**: 14–18.

964   Naruke T, Suemasu K, Ishikawa S. Lymph node mapping and curability at various levels of metastasis in resected lung cancer. J Thorac Cardiovasc Surg 1978, **76**: 832–839.

965   Nixon DW, Murphy GF, Sewell CW, Kutner M, Lynn MJ. Relationship between survival and histologic type in small cell anaplastic carcinoma of the lung. Cancer 1979, **44**: 1045–1049.

966   Nõu E. The natural five-year course in bronchial carcinoma. Epidemiologic results. Cancer 1984, **53**: 2211–2216.

967   Patel AM, Dunn WF, Trastek VF. Staging systems of lung cancer. Mayo Clin Proc 1993, **68**: 475–482.

968   Paulson DL. Carcinomas in the superior pulmonary sulcus. J Thorac Cardiovasc Surg 1975, **70**: 1095–1104.

969   Pemberton JH, Nagorney DM, Gilmore JC, Taylor WF, Bernatz PE. Bronchogenic carcinoma in patients younger than 40 years. Ann Thorac Surg 1983, **36**: 509–515.

970   Piehler JM, Pairolero PC, Weiland LH, Offord KP, Payne WS, Bernatz PE. Bronchogenic carcinoma with chest wall invasion. Factors affecting survival following en bloc resection. Ann Thorac Surg 1982, **34**: 684–691.

971   Rodenhuis S, van de Wetering ML, Mooi WJ, Evers SG, van Zandwijk N, Bos JL. Mutational activation of the K-*ras* oncogene. A possible pathogenetic factor in adenocarcinoma of the lung. N Engl J Med 1987, **319**: 929–935.

972   Rosenthal SA, Curran WJ. The significance of histology in non-small cell lung cancer. Cancer Treat Rev 1990, **17**: 409–425.

973   Sahin Aysegul A, Ro Jae Y, El-Naggar Adel K, Lee Jin S, Ayala Alberto G, Teague Kim, Hong Waun K. Flow cytometric analysis of the DNA content of non-small cell lung cancer. Ploidy as a significant prognostic indicator in squamous cell carcinoma of the lung. Cancer 1990, **65**: 530–537.

974   Sehested M, Hirsch FR, Osterlind K, Olsen JE. Morphologic variations of small cell lung cancer. A histopathologic study of pretreatment and posttreatment specimens in 104 patients. Cancer 1986, **57**: 804–807.

975   Shimosato Y, Hashimoto T, Kodama T, Kameya T, Suzuki A, Nishiwaki Y, Yoneyama T. Prognostic implications of fibrotic focus (scar) in small peripheral lung cancers. Am J Surg Pathol 1980, **4**: 365–373.

976   Slebos RJC, Kibbelaar RE, Dalesio O, Kooistra A, Stam J, Meijer CJLM, Wagenaar SS, Vanderschueren RGJRA, van Zanwijk N, Mooi WJ, Bos JL, Rodenhuis S. K-ras oncogene activation as a prognostic marker in adenocarcinoma of the lung. N Engl J Med 1990, **323**: 561–565.

977   Spjut HJ, Roper CL, Butcher HR Jr. Pulmonary cancer and its prognosis. A study of the relationship of certain factors to survival of patients treated by pulmonary resection. Cancer 1961, **14**: 1251–1258.

977a   Tan D, Li Q, Deeb G, Ramnath N, Slocum HK, Brooks J, Cheney R, Wiseman S, Anderson T, Loewen G. Thyroid transcription factor-1 expression prevalence and its clinical implications in non-small cell lung cancer: a high-throughput tissue microarray and immunohistochemistry study. Hum Pathol 2003, **34**: 597–604.

978   Temeck BK, Flehinger BJ, Martini N. A retrospective analysis of 10-year survivors from carcinoma of the lung. Cancer 1984, **53**: 1405–1408.

979   Tirindelli-Danesi D, Teodori L, Mauro F, Modini C, Botti C, Cicconetti F, Stipa S. Prognostic significance of flow cytometry in lung cancer. A 5-year study. Cancer 1987, **60**: 844–851.

980   Tomashefski FJ Jr, Conners AF Jr, Rosenthal ES, Hsiue IL. Peripheral vs central squamous cell carcinomas of the lung. A comparison of clinical features, histopathology, and survival. Arch Pathol Lab Med 1990, **114**: 468–474.

981   Treasure T, Belcher JR. Prognosis of peripheral lung tumours related to size of the primary. Thorax 1981, **36**: 5–8.

Other primary tumors

Hamartoma

982   Albrecht E. Ueber Hamartome. Verh Dtsch Pathol Ges 1904, **7**: 153–157.

983   Bateson EM. So-called hamartoma of the lung. A true neoplasm of fibrous connective tissue of the bronchi. Cancer 1973, **31**: 1458–1467.

984   Butler C, Kleinerman J. Pulmonary hamartoma. Arch Pathol 1969, **88**: 584–592.

985   Carney JA. The triad of gastric epithelioid leiomyosarcoma, functioning extradrenal paraganglioma, and pulmonary chondroma. Cancer 1979, **43**: 374–382.

986   Carney JA. Gastric stromal sarcoma, pulmonary chondroma, and extra-adrenal paraganglioma (Carney Triad): natural history, adrenocortical component, and possible familiar occurrence. Mayo Clin Proc 1999, **74**: 543–552.

987   Kazmierczak B, Wanschura S, Rommel B, Bartnitzke S, Bullerdiek J. Ten pulmonary chondroid hamartomas with chromosome 6q21 breakpoints within the HMG-1(Y) gene or its immediate surroundings. J Natl Cancer Inst 1996, **88**: 1234–1236.

988   King TE Jr, Christopher KL, Schwarz MI. Multiple pulmonary chondromatous hamartomas. Hum Pathol 1982, **13**: 496–497.

989   Perez-Atayde AR, Seiler MW. Pulmonary hamartoma. An ultrastructural study. Cancer 1984, **53**: 485–492.

990   Tomashefski JF Jr. Benign endobronchial mesenchymal tumors. Their relationship to parenchymal pulmonary hamartomas. Am J Surg Pathol 1982, **6**: 531–540.

991   Xu R, Murray M, Jagirdar J, Delgado Y, Melamed J. Placental transmogrification of the lung is a histologic pattern frequently associated with pulmonary fibrochondromatous hamartoma. Arch Pathol Lab Med 2002, **126**: 562–566.

Carcinoid tumor and related endocrine neoplasms

992   Bonikos DS, Bensch KG. Endocrine cells of bronchial and bronchiolar epithelium. Am J Med 1977, **63**: 765–771.

993   Davila D, Dunn W, Tazelaar H, Pairolero P. Bronchial carcinoid tumors. Mayo Clin Proc 1993, **68**: 795–803.

994   Gould VE, Linnoila RI. Pulmonary neuroepithelial bodies, neuroendocrine cells, and pulmonary tumors. Hum Pathol 1982, **13**: 1064–1066.

995   Hammar SP, Bockus D, Remington F, Cooper L. The unusual spectrum of neuroendocrine lung neoplasms. Ultrastruct Pathol 1989, **13**: 515–560.

996   Tateishi R. Distribution of argyrophil cells in adult human lungs. Arch Pathol 1973, **96**: 198–202.

Central carcinoid tumor

997   Attar S, Miller JE, Hankins J, Thompson BW, Suter CM, Kleger

PJ, McLaughlin JS. Bronchial adenoma. A review of 51 patients. Ann Thorac Surg 1985, **40:** 126–132.

998 Berger G, Berger F, Bejui F, Bouvier R, Rochet M, Feroldi J. Bronchial carcinoid with fibrillary inclusions related to cytokeratins. An immunohistochemical and ultrastructural study with subsequent investigation of 12 foregut APUDomas. Histopathology 1984, **8:** 245–257.

999 Bishopric GA Jr, Ordóñez NG. Carcinoembryonic antigen in primary carcinoid tumors of the lung. Cancer 1986, **58:** 1316–1320.

1000 Bostwick DG, Bensch KG. Gastrin releasing peptide in human neuroendocrine tumours. J Pathol 1985, **147:** 237–244.

1001 Bostwick DG, Null WE, Holmes D, Weber E, Barchas JD, Bensch KG. Expression of opioid peptides in tumors. N Engl Med 1987, **317:** 1439–1443.

1002 Brandt B III, Heintz SE, Rose EF, Ehrenhaft JL. Bronchial carcinoid tumors. Ann Thorac Surg 1984, **38:** 63–65.

1003 Cai YC, Banner B, Glickman J, Odze RD. Cytokeratin 7 and 20 and thyroid transcription factor 1 can help distinguish pulmonary from gastrointestinal carcinoid and pancreatic endocrine tumors. Hum Pathol 2001, **32:** 1087–1093.

1004 Capella C, Gabrielli M, Polak JM, Buffa R, Solcia E, Bordi C. Ultrastructural and histological study of 11 bronchial carcinoids. Evidence for different types. Virchows Arch [A] 1979, **381:** 313–329.

1005 Carlson AJ, Dickersin GR. Melanotic paraganglioid carcinoid tumor. A case report and review of the literature. Ultrastruct Pathol 1993, **17:** 353–376.

1006 Christen B, Trojanowski JQ, Pietra GG. Immunohistochemical demonstration of phosphorylated and nonphosphorylated forms of human neurofilament subunits in human pulmonary carcinoids. Hum Pathol 1987, **18:** 997–1001.

1007 DeStephano DB, Lloyd RV, Schteingart DE. Cushing's syndrome produced by a bronchial carcinoid tumor. Hum Pathol 1984, **15:** 890–892.

1008 Dirnhofer S, Freund M, Rogatsch H, Krabichler S, Berger P. Selective expression of trophoblastic hormones by lung carcinoma: neuroendocrine tumors exclusively produce human chorionic gonadotropin α–subunit (hCGa). Hum Pathol 2000, **31:** 966–972.

1009 el-Naggar AK, Ballance W, Karim FWA, Ordonez NG, McLemore D, Giacco GG, Batsakis JG. Typical and atypical bronchopulmonary carcinoids. A clinicopathologic and flow cytometry study. Anat Pathol 1991, **95:** 828–834.

1010 Eusebi V, Pileri S, Usellini L, Grassigli A, Capella C. Primary endocrine carcinoma of the parotid salivary gland associated with a lung carcinoid. A possible new association. J Clin Pathol 1982, **35:** 611–616.

1011 Farhangi M, Taylor J, Havey A, O'Dorisio TM. Neuroendocrine (carcinoid) tumor of the lung and type I multiple endocrine neoplasia. South J Med 1987, **80:** 1459–1462.

1012 Frigo BM, Carboni LN, Leonardi AGP, Siegal WE. Bronchial carcinoids with S-100-positive sustentacular cells. Pathol Res Pract 1990, **186:** 212–222.

1013 Gaffey MJ, Mills SE, Frierson HF Jr, Askin FB, Maygarden SJ. Pulmonary clear cell carcinoid tumor: another entity in the differential diagnosis of pulmonary clear cell neoplasia. Am J Surg Pathol 1998, **22:** 1020–1025.

1014 Gal AA, Koss MN, Hochholzer L, DeRose PB, Cohen C. Pigmented pulmonary carcinoid tumor. An immunohistochemical and ultrastructural study. Arch Pathol Lab Med 1993, **117:** 832–836.

1015 Gephardt GN, Belovich DM. Cytology of pulmonary carcinoid tumors. Acta Cytol (Baltimore) 1982, **26:** 434–438.

1016 Gosney JR, Denley H, Resl M. Sustentacular cells in pulmonary neuroendocrine tumours. Histopathology 1999, **34:** 211–215.

1017 Hartman GE, Shochat SJ. Primary pulmonary neoplasms of childhood. A review. Ann Thorac Surg 1983, **36:** 108–119.

1018 Huber RM, Schopohl J, Losa M, Wolfram G, Thetter O, Permanetter W, Werder KV. Growth-hormone releasing hormone in a bronchial carcinoid. Cancer 1991, **67:** 2538–2542.

1019 Hurt R, Bates M. Carcinoid tumours of the bronchus. A 33 year experience. Thorax 1984, **39:** 617–623.

1020 Jackson-York GL, Davus BH, Warren WH, Gould VE, Memoli VA. Flow cytometric DNA content analysis in neuroendocrine carcinoma of the lung. Correlation with survival and histologic subtype. Cancer 1991, **68:** 374–379.

1021 Kuwahara T, Maruyama K, Mochizuki S, Seki Y, Sawada K. Oncocytic carcinoid of the lung. An ultrastructural observation. Acta Pathol Jpn 1984, **34:** 355–359.

1022 Larsimont D, Kiss R, de Launoit Y, Melamed MR. Characterization of the morphonuclear features and DNA ploidy of typical and atypical carcinoids and small cell carcinomas of the lung. Am J Clin Pathol 1990, **94:** 378–383.

1023 Lehto V-P, Miettinen M, Dahl D, Virtanen I. Bronchial carcinoid cells contain neural-type intermediate filaments. Cancer 1984, **54:** 624–628.

1024 Lehto V-P, Miettinen M, Virtanen I. A dual expression of cytokeratin and neurofilaments in bronchial carcinoid cells. Int J Cancer 1985, **35:** 421–425.

1025 Liu Y, Sturgis CD, Grzybicki DM, Jasnosz KM, Olson PR, Tong M, Dabbs DD, Raab SS, Silverman JF. Microtubule-associated protein-2: a new sensitive and specific marker for pulmonary carcinoid tumor and small cell carcinoma. Mod Pathol 2001, **14:** 880–885.

1026 Mark EJ, Quay SC, Dickersin GR. Papillary carcinoid tumor of the lung. Cancer 1981, **48:** 316–324.

1027 Markel SF, Abell MR, Haight C, Franch AJ. Neoplasms, of bronchus commonly designated as adenomas. Cancer 1964, **17:** 590–608.

1028 Martini N, Zaman MB, Bains MS, Burt ME, McCormack PM, Rusch VW, Ginsberg RJ. Treatment and prognosis in bronchial carcinoids involving regional lymph nodes. J Thorac Cardiovasc Surg 1994, **107:** 1–7.

1029 Oliveira AM, Tazelaar HD, Myers JL, Erickson LA, Lloyd RV. Thryoid transcription factor-1 distinguishes metastatic pulmonary from well-differentiated neuroendocrine tumors of the other sites. Am J Surg Pathol 2001, **25:** 815–819.

1030 Resl M, Kral B, Simek J, Bukac J. S-100 protein positive (sustentacular) cells in pulmonary carcinoid tumorlets: a quantitive study of 24 cases. Pathol Res Pract 1997, **192:** 414–417.

1031 Said JW, Vimadalal S, Nash G, Shintaku IP, Heusser RC, Sasson AF, Lloyd RV. Immunoreactive neuron-specific enolase, bombesin, and chromogranin as markers for neuroendocrine lung tumors. Hum Pathol 1985, **16:** 236–240.

1032 Sajjad SM, Mackay B, Lukeman JM. Oncocytic carcinoid tumor of the lung. Ultrastruct Pathol 1980, **1:** 171–176.

1033 Salyer DC, Salyer WR, Eggleston JC. Bronchial carcinoid tumors. Cancer 1975, **36:** 1522–1537.

1034 Sandler M, Scheuer PJ, Watt PJ. 5-Hydroxytryptophan-secreting bronchilal carcinoid tumour. Lancet 1961, **2:** 1067–1069.

1035 Sano T, Saito H, Yamasaki R, Hamaguchi K, Ooiwa K, Shimoda T, Hosoi E, Saito S, Hizawa K. Immunoreactive somatostatin and calcitonin in pulmonary neuroendocrine tumor. Cancer 1986, **57:** 64–68.

1036 Sklar JL, Churg A, Bensch KG. Oncocytic carcinoid tumor of the lung. Am J Surg Pathol 1980, **4:** 287–292.

1037 Springall DR, Lackie P, Levene MM, Marangos PJ, Polak JM. Immunostaining of neuron-specific enolase is a valuable aid to the cytological diagnosis of neuroendocrine tumours of the lung. J Pathol 1984, **143:** 259–265.

1038 Statamis G, Freitag L, Greschuchna D. Limited and radical resection for tracheal and bronchopulmonary carcinoid tumor. Report on 227 cases. Eur J Cardiothorac Surg 1990, **4:** 527–532.

1039 Sturm N, Rossi G, Lantuejoul S, Papotti M, Frachon S, Claraz C, Brichon PY, Brambilla C, Brambilla E. Expression of thyroid transcription factor-1 in the spectrum of neuroendocrine cell lung proliferations with special interest in carcinoids. Hum Pathol 2002, **33**: 175–191.

1040 Szyfelbein WM, Ross JS. Carcinoids, atypical carcinoids, and small-cell carcinomas of the lung. Differential diagnosis of fine-needle aspiration biopsy specimens. Diagn Cytopathol 1988, **4**: 1–8.

1041 Thomas BM. Three unusual carcinoid tumours, with particular reference to osteoblastic bone metastases. Clin Radiol 1968, **19**: 221–225.

1042 Totsch M, Muller LC, Hittmair A, Ofner D, Gibbs AR, Schmid KW. Immunohistochemical demonstration of chromogranins A and B in neuroendocrine tumors of the lung. Hum Pathol 1992, **23**: 312–316.

1043 Totsch M, Padberg B-C, Schroder S, Ofner D, Bokher W, Fischer-Colbrie R, Schmid KW. Secretoneurin in bronchopulmonary carcinoids. Immunohistochemical comparison with chromogranins A and B and secretogranin II. Histopathology 1995, **26**: 357–362.

1044 Walch AK, Zitzelsberger HF, Aubelle MM, Mattis AE, Bauchinger M, Candidus S, Prauer HW, Werner M, Hofler H. Typical and atypical carcinoid tumors of the lung are characterized by 11q deletions as detected by comparative genomic hybridization. Am J Pathol 1998, **153**: 1089–1098.

1045 Warren WH, Memoli VA, Gould VE. Immunohistochemical and ultrastructural analysis of bronchopulmonary neuroendocrine neoplasms. I. Carcinoids. Ultrastruct Pathol 1984, **6**: 15–27.

1046 Wick MR. Immunohistology of neuroendocrine and neuroectodermal tumors. Semin Diagn Pathol 2000, **17**: 194–203.

1047 Wilkins EW Jr, Darling RC, Soutter L, Sniffon RC. A continuing survey of ademonas of the trachea and bronchus in a general hospital. J Thorac Cardiovasc Surg 1963, **46**: 279–291.

1048 Wilkins EW Jr, Grillo HC, Moncure AC, Scannell JG. Changing times in surgical management of bronchopulmonary carcinoid tumor. Ann Thorac Surg 1984, **38**: 339–344.

1049 Wilson TS, McDowell EM, Marangos PJ, Trump BI. Histochemical studies of dense-core granulated tumors of the lung. Neuron-specific enolase as a marker for granulated cells. Arch Pathol Lab Med 1985, **109**: 613–620.

1050 Yang K, Ulich T, Taylor I, Cheng L, Lewin KJ. Pulmonary carcinoids. Immunohistochemical demonstration of brain-gut peptides. Cancer 1983, **52**: 819–823.

1051 Yousem S, Taylor SR. Typical and atypical carcinoid tumors of lung. A clinicopathologic and DNA analysis of 20 tumors. Mod Pathol 1990, **3**: 502–507.

Peripheral carcinoid tumor

1052 Aguayo SM, Miller YE, Waldron JA Jr, Bogin RM, Sunday ME, Staton GW Jr, Beam WR, King TE Jr. Brief report. Idiopathic diffuse hyperplasia of pulmonary neuroendocrine cells and airways disease. N Engl J Med 1992, **327**: 1285–1288.

1053 Armas O, White DA, Erlandson R, Rosai J. Diffuse idiopathic pulmonary neuroendocrine cell proliferation presenting as interstitial lung disease. Am J Surg Pathol 1995, **19**: 963–970.

1054 Bonikos DS, Bensch KG, Jamplis RW. Peripheral pulmonary carcinoid tumors. Cancer 1976, **37**: 1977–1998.

1055 Churg A, Warnock ML. Pulmonary tumorlet. A form of peripheral carcinoid. Cancer 1976, **37**: 1469–1477.

1056 D'Agati VD, Perzin KH. Carcinoid tumorlets of the lung with metastasis to a peribronchial lymph node. Report of a case and review of the literature. Cancer 1985, **55**: 2472–2476.

1057 Finkelstein SD, Hasegawa T, Colby T, Yousem SA. 11q13 allelic imbalance discriminates pulmonary carcinoids from tumorlets.

A microdissection-based genotyping approach useful in clinical practice. Am J Pathol 1999, **155**: 633–640.

1058 Gosney J, Green AR, Taylor W. Appropriate and inappropriate neuroendocrine products in pulmonary tumourlets. Thorax 1990, **45**: 679–683.

1059 Grazer R, Cohen SM, Jacobs JB, Lucas P. Melanin-containing peripheral carcinoid of the lung. Am J Surg Pathol 1982, **6**: 73–78.

1060 Miller MA, Mark GJ, Kanarek D. Multiple peripheral pulmonary carcinoids and tumorlets of carcinoid type, with restrictive and obstructive lung disease. Am J Med 1978, **65**: 373–378.

1061 Miller RR, Muller NL. Neuroendocrine cell hyperplasia and obliterative bronchiolitis in patients with peripheral carcinoid tumors. Am J Surg Pathol 1995, **19**: 653–658.

1062 Min KW. Spindle cell carcinoids of the lung with paraglioid features: a reappraisal of their histogenetic origin from paraganglia using immunohistochemical and electromicroscopic techniques. Ultrastruct Pathol 2001, **25**: 207–217.

1063 Nelson EL, Houghton DC. Concurrent spindle cell peripheral pulmonary carcinoid tumor and Merkel cell tumor of the skin. Arch Pathol Lab Med 1990, **114**: 420–422.

1064 Pelosi G, Sancanaro C, Sbabo L, Bresaola E, Martignoni G, Bontempi L. Development of innumerable neuroendocrine tumorlets in pulmonary lobe scarred by intralobular sequestrations: Immunohistochemical and ultrastructural study of an unusual case. Arch Pathol Lab Med 1992, **116**: 1167–1174.

1065 Ranchod M, Levine GD. Spindle-cell carcinoid tumors of the lung. A clinicopathologic study of 35 cases. Am J Surg Pathol 1980, **4**: 315–331.

1066 Salyer DC, Salyer WR, Eggleston JC. Bronchial carcinoid tumors. Cancer 1975, **36**: 1522–1537.

1067 Tamai S, Kameya T, Yamaguchi K, Yanai N, Abe K, Yanaihara N, Yamazaki H, Kageyama K. Peripheral lung carcinoid tumor producing predominantly gastrin-releasing peptide (GRP). Cancer 1983, **52**: 273–281.

1068 Torikata C. Tumorlets of the lung. An ultrastructural study. Ultrastruct Pathol 1991, **15**: 189–195.

Atypical carcinoid tumor (with a discussion on related neuroendocrine tumors)

1069 Abe Y, Utsunomiya H, Tsusumi Y. Atypical carcinoid tumor of the lung with amyloid stroma. Acta Pathol Jpn 1992, **42**: 286–292.

1070 Arrigoni MG, Woolner LB, Bernatz PE. Atypical carcinoid tumors of the lung. J Thorac Cardiovasc Surg 1972, **64**: 413–421.

1071 Battlehner C, Saldiva P, Carvalho C, Takagaki Y, Montes G, Younes R, Capelozzi V. Nuclear/cytoplasmic ratio correlates strongly with survival in nondisseminated neuroendocrine carcinoma of the lung. Histopathology 1993, **22**: 31–34.

1072 Beasley MB, Thunnissen FB, Brambilla E, Hasleton P, Steele R, Hammar SP, Colby TV, Sheppard M, Shimosato Y, Koss MN, Falk R, Travis WD. Pulmonary atypical carcinoid: predicators of survival in 106 cases. Hum Pathol 2000, **31**: 1255–1265.

1073 Berendsen HH, de Leij L, Poppema S, Postmus PE, Boes A, Sluiter HJ, The H. Clinical characterization of non-small cell lung cancer tumors showing neuroendocrine differentiation features. J Clin Oncol 1989, **7**: 1614–1620.

1074 Broers JLV, Mijnheere EP, Rot MK, Schaart G, Sijlmans A, Boerman OC, Ramaekers FCS. Novel antigens characteristic of neuroendocrine malignancies. Cancer 1991, **67**: 619–633.

1075 Capella C, Heitz PU, Hofler H, Solcia E, Kloppel G. Revised classification of neuroendocrine tumours of the lung, pancreas and gut. Virchows Arch 1995, **425**: 547–560.

1076 Doglioni C, Barbareschi M, Balercia G, Bontempino L, Iuzzolino P. Atypical lung carcinoid with GFAP immunoreactive cells. Pathol Res Pract 1993, **189**: 83–89.

1077 el-Naggar AK, Ballance W, Karim FW, Ordóñez NG, McLemore D, Giacco GG, Batsakis JG. Typical and atypical bronchopulmonary carcinoids. A clinicopathologic and flow cytometric study. Am J Clin Pathol 1991, **95**: 828–834.

1078 Fisher ER, Palekar A, Paulson JD. Comparative histopathologic, histochemical, electron microscopic and tissue culture studies of bronchial carcinoids and oatcell carcinomas of lung. Am J Clin Pathol 1978, **69**: 165–172.

1079 Fresvig A, Qvigstad G, Halvorsen TB, Falkmer S, Waldum HL. Neuroendocrine differentiation in bronchial carcinomas of classic squamous cell-type: an immunohistochemical study of 29 cases applying the tyramide signal amplification technique. Appl Immunohistochem Mol Morphol 2001, **9**: 9–13.

1080 Godwin JD II, Brown CC. Comparative epidemiology of carcinoid and oat-cell tumors of the lung. Cancer 1977, **40**: 1671–1673.

1081 Graziano SL, Mazid R, Newman N, Tatum A, Oler A, Mortimer JA, Gullo JJ, DiFino SM, Scalzo AJ. The use of neuroendocrine immunoperoxidase markers to predict chemotherapy response in patients with non-small-cell lung cancer. J Clin Oncol 1989, **7**: 1398–1406.

1082 Hammar SP, Bockus D, Remington F, Cooper L. The unusual spectrum of neuroendocrine lung neoplasms. Ultrastruct Pathol 1989, **13**: 515–560.

1083 Huang Q, Muzitansky A, Mark EJ. Pulmonary neuroendocrine carcinomas: a review of 234 cases and a statistical analysis of 50 cases treated at one institution using a simple clinicopathologic classification. Arch Pathol Lab Med 2002, **126**: 545–553.

1084 Jackson-York GL, Davis BH, Warren WH, Gould VE, Memoli VA. Flow cytometric DNA content analysis in neuroendocrine carcinoma of the lung. Correlation with survival and histologic subtype. Cancer 1991, **68**: 374–379.

1085 Jiang SX, Kameya T, Shoji M, Dobashi Y, Shinada J, Yoshima H. Large cell neuroendocrine carcinoma of the lung: a histologic and immunohistochemical study of 22 cases. Am J Surg Pathol 1998, **22**: 526–537.

1086 Kibbelaar RE, Moolenaar KW, Michalides RJ, Van Bodegom PC, Vanderschueren RG, Wagenaar SS, Dingemans KP, Bitter-Suermann D, Salesio O, Van Zandwijk N. Neural cell adhesion molecule expression, neuroendocrine differentiation and prognosis in lung carcinoma. Eur J Cancer 1991, **27**: 431–435.

1087 Komminoth P, Roth J, Lackie PM, Bitter-Suermann D, Heitz PU. Polysialic acid of the neural cell adhesion molecule distinguishes small cell lung carcinoma from carcinoids. Am J Pathol 1991, **139**: 297–304.

1088 Larsimont D, Kiss R, de Launoit Y, Melamed MR. Characterization of the morphonuclear features and DNA ploidy of typical and atypical carcinoids and small cell carcinomas of the lung. Am J Clin Pathol 1990, **94**: 378–383.

1089 Loy TS, Darkow GV, Quesenberry JT. Immunostaining in the diagnosis of pulmonary neuroendocrine carcinomas. An immunohistochemical study with ultrastructural correlations. Am J Surg Pathol 1995, **19**: 173–182.

1090 Mills SE, Cooper PH, Walker AN, Kron IL. Atypical carcinoid tumor of the lung. A clinicopathologic study of 17 cases. Am J Surg Pathol 1982, **6**: 643–654.

1091 Paladugu RR, Benfield JR, Pak HY, Ross RK, Teplitz RL. Bronchopulmonary Kulchitsky cell carcinomas. A new classification scheme for typical and atypical carcinoids. Cancer 1985, **55**: 1303–1311.

1092 Roncalli M, Doglioni C, Springall D, Papotti M, Pagani A, Polak J, Ibrahim N, Coggi G, Viale G. Abnormal p53 expression in lung neuroendocrine tumors. Diagnostic and prognostic implications. Diagn Mol Pathol 1992, **1**: 129–135.

1093 Tosch M, Kunk B, Dockhorn-Dworniczak B, Ofner D, Fischer-Colbrie R, Mikuz G, Bocker W, Schmid KW. Immunohistochemical demonstration of chromogranin A, chromogranin B, and secretoneurin in primary non-small-cell carcinomas of the lung. Endocr Pathol 1994, **5**: 212–217.

1094 Travis WD, Linnoila RI, Tsokos MG, Hitchcock CL, Cutler GB Jr, Neiman L, Chrousos G, Pass H, Doppman J. Neuroendocrine tumors of the lung with proposed criteria for large-cell neuroendocrine carcinoma. An ultrastructural, immunohistochemical, and flow cytometric study of 35 cases. Am J Surg Pathol 1991, **15**: 529–553.

1095 Travis WD, Rush W, Flieder DB, Falk R, Fleming MV, Gal AA, Koss MN. Survival analysis of 200 pulmonary neuroendocrine tumors with clarification of criteria for atypical carcinoid and it separation from typical carcinoid. Am J Surg Pathol 1998, **22**: 934–944.

1096 Valli M, Fabris GA, Dewar A, Hornall D, Sheppard MN. Atypical carcinoid tumour of the lung. A study of 33 cases with prognostic features. Histopathology 1994, **24**: 363–369.

1097 Warren WH, Memoli VA, Gould VE. Immunohistochemical and ultrastructural analysis of bronchopulmonary neuroendocrine neoplasms. II. Well-differentiated neuroendocrine carcinomas. Ultrastruct Pathol 1984, **7**: 185–199.

1098 Wilkins EW Jr, Grillo HC, Moncure AC, Scannell JG. Changing times in surgical management of bronchopulmonary carcinoid tumor. Ann Thorac Surg 1984, **38**: 339–344.

Paraganglioma and other endocrine neoplasms

1099 Düsseldorf M, Straaten HG. Primary pulmonary paraganglioma. Zentralbl Chir 1990, **115**: 1575–1578.

1100 Freeman JK, Otis CN. Combined carcinoid tumor and ganglioneuroblastoma of the lung: a case report. Int J Surg Pathol 2001, **9**: 169–173.

1101 Hangartner JR, Loosemore TM, Burke M, Pepper JR. Malignant primary pulmonary paraganglioma. Thorax 1989, **44**: 154–156.

1102 Heppleston AG. A carotid-body-like tumour in the lung. J Pathol Bacteriol 1958, **75**: 461–464.

1103 Hironaka M, Fukayana M, Takayashiki N, Saito K, Sohara Y, Funata N. Pulmonary gangliocytic paraganglioma: case report and comparative immunohistochemical study of related neuroendocrine neoplasms. Am J Surg Pathol 2001, **25**: 688–693.

1104 Hochholzer L, Moran CA, Koss MN. Primary pulmonary ganglioneuroblastoma: a clinicopathologic and immunohistochemical study of two cases. Ann Diagn Pathol 1999, **2**: 154–158.

1104a Kee A-R, Forrest CH, Brennan BA, Papadimitriou JM, Glancy RJ. Gangliocytic paraganglioma of the bronchus. A case report with follow-up and ultrastructural assessment. Am J Surg Pathol 2003, **27**: 1380–1385.

1105 Singh G, Lee RE, Brooks DH. Primary pulmonary paraganglioma. Report of a case and review of the literature. Cancer 1977, **40**: 2286–2289.

1106 Tu H, Bottomley RH. Malignant chemodectoma presenting as a miliary pulmonary infiltrate. Cancer 1974, **33**: 244–249.

Minute meningothelioid nodules and meningioma

1107 Chumas JC, Lorelle CA. Pulmonary meningioma. A light- and electron-microscopic study. Am J Surg Pathol 1982, **6**: 795–801.

1108 Drlicek M, Grisold W, Lorber J, Hackl H, Wuketich S, Jellinger K. Pulmonary meningioma. Immunohistochemical and ultrastructural features. Am J Surg Pathol 1991, **15**: 455–459.

1109 Flynn SD, Yousem SA. Pulmonary meningiomas. A report of two cases. Hum Pathol 1991, **22**: 469–474.

1110 Gaffey MJ, Mills SE, Askin FB. Minute pulmonary meningothelial-like nodules. A clinicopathologic study of so-called minute pulmonary chemodectoma. Am J Surg Pathol 1988, **12**: 167–175.

1110a Ionescu DN, Omalu BI, Finkelstein SD, Swalsky PA, Trusky C, Lomago D, Yousem SA, University of Pittsburgh, Pittsburgh,

PA. Pulmonary meningothelial-like nodules – a genotypic comparison with meningiomas. Mod Pathol 2003, **16**: 308a.

1111 Kodama K, Doi O, Higashiyama M, Horai T, Tateishi R, Nakagawa H. Primary and metastatic pulmonary meningioma. Cancer 1991, **67**: 1412–1417.

1112 Kuhn C III, Askin FB. The fine structure of so-called minute pulmonary chemodectomas. Hum Pathol 1975, **6**: 681–691.

1113 Moran CA, Hochholzer L, Rush W, Koss MN. Primary intrapulmonary meningiomas: a clinicopathologic and immunohistochemical study of ten cases. Cancer 1996, **78**: 2328–2333.

1114 Pelosi G, Maffini F, Decarli N, Viale G. Progesterone receptor immunoreactivity in minute menigothelioid nodules of the lung. Virchows Arch 2002, **440**: 543–546.

1115 Prayson RA, Farver CF. Primary pulmonary malignant meningioma. Am J Surg Pathol 1999, **23**: 722–726.

1116 Torikata C, Mukai M. So-called minute chemodectoma of the lung. An electron microscope and immunohistochemical study. Virchows Arch [A] 1990, **417**: 113–118.

So-called sclerosing hemangioma

1117 Aihara T, Nakajima T. Sclerosing hemangioma of the lung: Pathological study and enzyme immunoassay for estrogen and progesterone receptors. Acta Pathol Jpn 1993, **43**: 507–515.

1118 Chan AC, Chan JK. Pulmonary sclerosing hemangioma consistently expresses thyroid transcription factor-1 (TTF-1): a new clue to its histogenesis. Am J Surg Pathol 2000, **24**: 1531–1536.

1119 Chan K-W, Gibbs AR, Lo WS, Newman GR. Benign sclerosing pneumocytoma of lung (sclerosing haemangioma). Thorax 1982, **37**: 404–412.

1120 Devouassoux-Shisheboran M, Hayashi T, Linnoila I, Koss MN, Travis WD. A clinicopathologic study of 100 cases of pulmonary sclerosing hemangioma with immunohistochemical studies: TTF-1 is expressed in both round and surface cells, suggesting an origin from primitive respiratory epithelium. Am J Surg Pathol 2000, **24**: 906–916.

1121 Eggleston JC. The intravascular bronchioloalveolar tumor and the sclerosing hemangioma of the lung. Misnomers of pulmonary neoplasia. Semin Diagn Pathol 1985, **2**: 270–280.

1122 Haimoto H, Tsutsumi Y, Nagura H, Nakashima N, Watanabe K. Immunohistochemical study of so-called sclerosing haemangioma of the lung. Virchows Arch [A] 1985, **407**: 419–430.

1123 Heikkila P, Salminen US. Papillary pneumocytoma of the lung. An immunohistochemical and electron microscopic study. Pathol Res Pract 1994, **190**: 194–200.

1124 Illei PB, Rosai J, Klimstra DS. Expression of thyroid transcription factor-1 and other markers in sclerosing hemangioma of the lung. Arch Pathol Lab Med 2001, **125**: 1335–1339.

1125 Katzenstein AL, Gmelich JT, Carrington CB. Sclerosing hemangioma of the lung. A clinicopathologic study of 51 cases. Am J Surg Pathol 1980, **4**: 343–356.

1125a Khoury JD, Shephard MN, Moran CA. Cystic sclerosing haemangioma of the lung. Histopathology 2003, **43**: 239–243.

1126 Liebow AA, Hubbel DS. Sclerosing hemangioma (histiocytoma, xanthoma) of lung. Cancer 1956, **9**: 53–75.

1126a Miyagawa-Hayashino A, Tazelaar HD, Langel DJ, Colby TV. Pulmonary sclerosing hemangioma with lymph node metastases. Arch Pathol Lab Med 2003, **127**: 321–325.

1127 Moran CA, Zeren H, Koss MN. Sclerosing hemangioma of the lung. Granulomatous variant. Arch Pathol Lab Med 1994, **118**: 1028–1030.

1128 Nagata N, Daitaku M, Ishida T, Sueishi K, Tanaka K. Sclerosing hemangioma of the lung. Immunohistochemical characterization of its origin as related to surfactant apoprotein. Cancer 1985, **55**: 116–123.

1129 Rodriguez-Soto J, Colby TV, Rouse RV. A critical examination of the immunophenotype of pulmonary sclerosing hemangioma. Am J Surg Pathol 2000, **24**: 442–450.

1130 Satoh Y, Tsuchiya E, Weng SY, Kitagawa T, Matsubara T, Nakagawa K, Kinoshita I, Sugano H. Pulmonary sclerosing hemangioma of the lung. A type II pneumocytoma by immunohistochemical and immunoelectron microscopic studies. Cancer 1989, **64**: 1310–1317.

Inflammatory pseudotumor and related lesions

1131 Buell R, Wang N-S, Seemayer TA, Ahmed MN. Endobronchial plasma cell granuloma (xanthomatous pseudotumor). A light and electron microscopic study. Hum Pathol 1976, **7**: 411–426.

1132 Cessna MH, Zhou H, Sanger WG, Perkins SL, Tripp S, Pickering D, Daines C, Coffin CM. Expression of ALK1 and p80 in inflammatory myofibroblastic tumor and its mesenchymal mimics: a study of 135 cases. Mod Pathol 2002, **15**: 931–938.

1133 Chen HP, Lee SS, Berardi RS. Inflammatory pseudotumor of the lung. Ultrastructural and light microscopic study of a myxomatous variant. Cancer 1984, **54**: 861–865.

1134 Gal AA, Koss MN, McCarthy WF, Hochholzer L. Prognostic factors in pulmonary fibrohistiocytic lesions. Cancer 1994, **73**: 1817–1824.

1135 Imperato JP, Folkman J, Sagerman RH, Cassady JR. Treatment of plasma cell granuloma of the lung with radiation therapy. A report of two cases and a review of the literature. Cancer 1986, **57**: 2127–2129.

1136 Katzensteir A-LA, Mauer JJ. Benign histiocytic tumor of lung. A light- and electron-microscopic study. Am J Surg Pathol 1979, **3**: 61–68.

1137 Lund C, Storensen IM, Axelsen F, Larsen K. Pulmonary histiocytomas. Eur J Respir Dis 1983, **64**: 141–149.

1138 Pettinato G, Manivel J, De Rosa N, Dehner L. Inflammatory myofibroblastic tumor (plasma cell granuloma). Clinicopathologic study of 20 cases with immunohistochemical and ultrastructural observations. Am J Clin Pathol 1990, **94**: 538–546.

1139 Sekosan M, Cleto M, Senseng C, Farolan M, Sekosan J. Spindle cell pseudotumors in the lungs due to *Mycobacterium* tuberculosis in a transplant patient. Am J Surg Pathol 1994, **18**: 1065–1068.

1140 Spencer H. The pulmonary plasma cell/histiocytoma complex. Histopathology 1984, **8**: 903–916.

Vascular tumors

1141 Abrams J, Talcott J, Corson JM. Pulmonary metastases in patients with low-grade endometrial stromal sarcoma. Clinicopathologic findings with immunohistochemical characterization. Am J Surg Pathol 1989, **13**: 133–140.

1142 Alt B, Huffer WE, Belchis DA. A vascular lesion with smooth muscle differentiation presenting as a coin lesion in the lung. Glomus tumor versus hemangiopericytoma. Am J Clin Pathol 1983, **80**: 765–771.

1143 Antman KH, Nadler L, Mark EJ, Montella DL, Kirkpatrick P, Halpern J. Primary Kaposi's sarcoma of the lung in an immunocompetent 32-year-old heterosexual white man. Cancer 1984, **54**: 1696–1698.

1144 Aubry MC, Myers JL, Colby TV, Leslie KO, Tazelaar HD. Endometrial stromal sarcoma metastatic to thelung: a detailed analysis of 16 patients. Am J Surg Pathol 2002, **26**: 440–449.

1145 Banner AS, Carrington CB, Emory WB, Kittle F, Leonard G, Ringus J, Taylor P, Addington WW. Efficacy of oophorectomy in lymphangioleiomyomatosis and benign metastasizing leiomyoma. N Engl J Med 1981, **305**: 204–209.

1146 Berger U, Khaghani A, Pomerance A, Yacoub MH, Coombes RC. Pulmonary lymphangioleiomyomatosis and steroid receptors. An immunocytochemical study. Am J Clin Pathol 1990, **93**: 609–614.

1147 Bhagavan BS, Dorfman HD, Murthy MSN, Eggleston JC. Intravascular bronchiolo-alveolar tumor (IVBAT). A low-grade sclerosing epithelioid angiosarcoma of lung. Am J Surg Pathol 1982, **6**: 41–52.

1148 Carlson KC, Parnassus WN, Klatt EC. Thoracic lymphangiomatosis. Arch Pathol Lab Med 1987, **111**: 475–477.

1149 Chan JKC, Tsang WYW, Pau MY, Tang MC, Pang SW, Fletcher CDM. Lymphangiomyomatosis and angiomyolipoma. Closely related entities characterized by hamartomatous proliferation of HMB-45-positive smooth muscle. Histopathology 1993, **22**: 445–455.

1150 Corring B, Liebow AA, Friedman PJ. Pulmonary lymphangiomyomatosis. Am J Pathol 1975, **79**: 348–382.

1151 Dail DH, Liebow AA, Gmelich JT, Friedman PJ, Miyai K, Myer W, Patterson SD, Hammar SP. Intravascular, bronchiolar, and alveolar tumor of the lung (IVBAT). An analysis of twenty cases of a peculiar sclerosing endothelial tumor. Cancer 1983, **51**: 452–464.

1152 Eggleston JC. The intravascular bronchioloalveolar tumor and the sclerosing hemangioma of the lung. Misnomers of pulmonary neoplasia. Semin Diagn Pathol 1985, **2**: 270–280.

1153 Erbersdobler A, Niendorf A. Multifocal distribution of pulmonary capillary haemangliomatosis. Histopathology 2002, **40**: 88–91.

1154 Faber CN, Yousem SA, Dauber JH, Griffith BP, Hardesty RL, Paradis IL. Pulmonary capillary hemangiomatosis. A report of three cases and a review of the literature. Am Rev Respir Dis 1989, **140**: 808–813.

1155 Fukuda Y, Kawamoto M, Yamamoto A, Ishizaki M, Basset F, Masugi Y. Role of elastic fiber degradation in emphysema-like lesions of pulmonary lymphangiomyomatosis. Hum Pathol 1990, **21**: 1252–1261.

1156 Gaertner EM, Steinberg DM, Huber M, Hayashi T, Tsuda N, Askin FB, Bell SW, Nguyen B, Colby TV, Nishimura SL, Miettinen M, Travis WD. Pulmonary and mediastinal glomus tumors: report of five cases including a pulmonary glomangiosarcoma: a clinicopathologic study with literature review. Am J Surg Pathol 2000, **24**: 1105–1114.

1157 Galliani CA, Beatty JF, Grosfeld JL. Cavernous hemangioma of the lung in an infant. Pediatr Pathol 1992, **12**: 105–111.

1158 Graham ML II, Spelsberg TC, Dines DE, Payne WS, Bjornsson J, Lie JT. Pulmonary lymphangiomyomatosis. With particular reference to steroid-receptor assay studies and pathologic correlation. Mayo Clin Proc 1984, **59**: 3–11.

1159 Holden WE, Morris JF, Antonovic R, Gill TH, Kessler S. Adult intrapulmonary and mediastinal lymphangioma causing haemoptysis. Thorax 1987, **42**: 635–636.

1160 Ito M, Sugamura Y, Ikari H, Sekine I. Angiomyolipoma of the lung. Arch Pathol Lab Med 1998, **122**: 1023–1025.

1161 Koss MN, Hochholzer L, Moran CA. Primary pulmonary glomus tumor: a clinicopathologic and immunohistochemical study of two cases. Mod Pathol 1998, **11**: 253–258.

1162 Lack EE, Dolan MF, Finisio J, Grover G, Singh M, Triche TJ. Pulmonary and extrapulmonary lymphangioleiomyomatosis. Report of a case with bilateral renal angiomyolipomas, multifocal lymphangioleiomyomatosis, and a glial polyp of the endocervix. Am J Surg Pathol 1986, **10**: 650–657.

1163 McCarty KS Jr, Mossler JA, McLelland R, Sieker HO. Pulmonary lymphangiomyomatosis responsive to progesterone. N Engl J Med 1980, **303**: 1461–1465.

1164 Matsui K, Tatsuguchi A, Valencia J, Yu Z, Bechtle J, Beasley MB, Avila N, Travis WD, Moss J, Ferrans VJ. Extrapulmonary lymphangioleiomyatosis (LAM): clinicopathologic features in 22 cases. Hum Pathol 2000, **31**: 1242–1248.

1165 Meade JB, Whitwell F, Bickford BJ, Waddington KB. Primary haemangiopericytoma of lung. Thorax 1974, **29**: 1–15.

1166 Milovic I, Oluic D. Lymphangioma of the lung associated with respiratory distress in a neonate. Pediatr Radiol 1992, **22**: 156.

1167 Nash G, Fligiel S. Kaposi's sarcoma presenting as pulmonary disease in the acquired immunodeficiency syndrome. Diagnosis by lung biopsy. Hum Pathol 1984, **15**: 999–1001.

1168 Nerlich A, Berndt R, Schleicher E. Differential basement membrane composition in multiple epithelioid haemangioendotheliomas of liver and lung. Histopathology 1991, **18**: 303–308.

1169 Ohori NP, Yousem SA, Sonmez-Alpan E, Colby TV. Estrogen and progesterone receptors in lymphangioleiomyomatosis, epithelioid hemangioendothelioma, and, sclerosing hemangioma of the lung. Am J Clin Pathol 1991, **96**: 529–535.

1170 Patel AM, Ryu JH. Angiosarcoma in the lung. Chest 1993, **103**: 1531–1535.

1171 Purdy LJ, Colby TV, Yousem SA, Battifora H. Pulmonary Kaposi's sarcoma. Premortem histologic diagnosis. Am J Surg Pathol 1986, **10**: 301–311.

1172 Sobonya RE, Quan SF, Fleishman JS. Pulmonary lymphangioleiomyomatosis. Quantitative analysis of lesions producing airflow limitation. Hum Pathol 1985, **16**: 1122–1128.

1173 Taylor JR, Ryu J, Colby TV, Raffin TA. Lymphangioleiomyomatosis. Clinical course in 32 patients. N Engl J Med 1990, **323**: 1254–1260.

1174 Tazelaar HD, Kerr D, Yousem SA, Saldana MJ, Langston C, Colby TV. Diffuse pulmonary lymphangiomatosis. Hum Pathol 1993, **24**: 1313–1322.

1175 Tron V, Magee F, Wright JL, Colby T, Churg A. Pulmonary capillary hemangiomatosis. Hum Pathol 1986, **17**: 1144–1150.

1176 Verbeken E, Beyls J, Moerman P, Knockaert D, Goddeeris P, Lauweryns JM. Lung metastasis of malignant epithelioid hemangioendothelioma mimicking a primary intravascular bronchioalveolar tumor. A histologic, ultrastructural, and immunohistochemical study. Cancer 1985, **55**: 1741–1746.

1177 Wagenaar SS, Mulder JJS, Wagenvoort CA, Van Den Bosch JMM. Pulmonary capillary haemangiomatosis diagnosed during life. Histopathology 1989, **14**: 212–214.

1178 Weldon-Linne CM, Victor TA, Christ ML, Fry WA. Angiogenic nature of the "intravascular bronchioloalveolar tumor" of the lung. An electron microscopic study. Arch Pathol Lab Med 1981, **105**: 174–179.

1179 Yousem SA. Angiosarcoma presenting in the lung. Arch Pathol Lab Med 1986, **110**: 112–115.

1180 Yousem SA. Pulmonary vascular neoplasia. Prog Surg Pathol 1989, **10**: 27–62.

Lymphoid tumors and tumorlike conditions

1181 Abbondanzo SL, Rush W, Bijwaard KE, Koss MN. Nodular lymphoid hyperplasia of the lung: a clinicopathologic study of 14 cases. **24**: 587–597.

1182 Addis BJ, Hyjek E, Isaacson PG. Primary pulmonary lymphoma. A reappraisal of its histogenesis and its relationship to pseudolymphoma and lymphoid interstitial pneumonia. Histopathology 1988, **13**: 1–17.

1182 Amin R. Extramedullary plasmacytoma of the lung. Cancer 1985, **56**: 152–156.

1184 Callahan M, Wall S, Askin F, Delaney D, Koller C, Orringer EP. Granulocytic sarcoma presenting as pulmonary nodules and lymphadenopathy. Cancer 1987, **60**: 1902–1904.

1185 Chen KTK. Abdominal form of lymphomatoid granulomatosis. Hum Pathol 1977, **8**: 99–108.

1186 Close PM, Macrae MB, Hammond JM, Aronson I, Johnson CA, Potgieter PD, Jacobs P. Anaplastic large-cell Ki-1 lymphoma. Pulmonary presentation mimicking miliary tuberculosis. Am J Clin Pathol 1993, **99**: 631–636.

1187 Colby TV, Carrington CB. Pulmonary lymphomas simulating lymphomatoid granulomatosis. Am J Surg Pathol 1982, **6**: 19–32.

1188 Colby TV, Yousem SA. Pulmonary lymphoid neoplasms. Semin Diagn Pathol 1985, **2**: 183–196.

1189 Cordier J-F, Chailleux E, Lauque D, Reynaud-Gaubert M, Dietemann-Molard A, Dalphin JC, Blanc-Jouvan F, Loire R. Primary pulmonary lymphomas. A clinical study of 70 cases in nonimmunocompromised patients. Chest 1993, **103**: 201–208.

1190 Donner LR, Dobin S, Harrington D, Bassion S, Rappaport ES, Peterson RF. Angiocentric immunoproliferative lesion (lymphomatoid granulomatosis). A cytogenetic, immunophenotypic, and genotypic study. Cancer 1990, **65**: 249–254.

1191 Doran HM, Sheppard MN, Collins PW, Jones L, Newland AC, Van Der Walt JD. Pathology of the lung in leukemia and lymphoma. A study of 87 biopsies. Histopathology 1991, **18**: 211–220.

1192 Evans HL. Extranodal small lymphocytic proliferation. A clinicopathologic and immunocytochemical study. Cancer 1982, **49**: 84–96.

1193 Fauci AS, Haynes BF, Costa J, Katz P, Wolff SM. Lymphomatoid granulomatosis. Prospective clinical and therapeutic experience over 10 years. N Engl J Med 1982, **306**: 68–74.

1194 Guinee D Jr, Jaffe E, Kingma D, Fishback N, Wallberg K, Krishnan J, Frizzera G, Travis W, Koss M. Pulmonary lymphomatoid granulomatosis. Evidence for a proliferation of Epstein-Barr virus infected B-lymphocytes with a prominent T-cell component and vasculitis. Am J Surg Pathol 1994, **18**: 753–764.

1195 Habermann TM, Ryu JH, Inwards DJ, Kurtin PJ. Primary pulmonary lymphoma. Semin Oncol 1999, **26**: 307–315.

1196 Hammar S, Mennemeyer R. Lymphomatoid granulomatosis in a renal transplant recipient. Hum Pathol 1976, **7**: 111–116.

1197 Harper PG, Fisher C, McLennan K, Souhami RL. Presentation of Hodgkin's disease as an endobronchial lesion. Cancer 1984, **53**: 147–150.

1198 Herbert A, Wright DH, Isaacson PG, Smith JL. Primary malignant lymphoma of the lung. Histopathologic and immunologic evaluation of nine cases. Hum Pathol 1984, **15**: 415–422.

1199 Joseph G, Pandit M, Korfhage L. Primary pulmonary plasmacytoma. Cancer 1992, **71**: 721–724.

1200 Katzenstein AL, Carrington CB, Liebow AA. Lymphomatoid granulomatosis. A clinicopathologic study of 152 cases. Cancer 1979, **43**: 360–373.

1201 Katzenstein AL, Peiper SC. Detection of Epstein-Barr virus genomes in lymphomatoid granulomatosis. Analysis of 29 cases by the polymerase chain reaction technique. Mod Pathol 1990, **3**: 435–441.

1202 Kennedy JL, Nathwani BN, Burke JS, Hill LR, Rappaport H. Pulmonary lymphomas and other pulmonary lymphoid lesions. A clinicopathologic and immunologic study of 64 patients. Cancer 1985, **56**: 539–552.

1203 Koss MN, Hochholzer L, Nichols PW, Wehunt WD, Lazarus AA. Primary non-Hodgkin's lymphoma and pseudolymphoma of lung. A study of 161 patients. Hum Pathol 1983, **14**: 1024–1038.

1204 Koss MN. Pulmonary lymphoid disorders. Semin Diagn Pathol 1995, **12**: 158–171.

1205 Koss MN, Hochholzer L, Moran CA, Frizzera G. Pulmonary plasmacytomas: a clinicopathologic and immunohistochemical study of five cases. Ann Diagn Pathol 1999, **2**: 1–11.

1206 Kradin RL, Mark EJ. Benign lymphoid disorders of the lung, with a theory regarding their development. Hum Pathol 1983, **14**: 857–867.

1207 Kradin RL, Young RH, Kradin LA, Mark EJ. Immunoblastic lymphoma arising in chronic lymphoid hyperplasia of the pulmonary interstitium. Cancer 1982, **50**: 1339–1343.

1208 Kurtin PJ, Myers JL, Adlakha H, Strickler JG, Lohse C, Pankratz VS, Inwards DJ. Pathologic and clinical features of primary pulmonary extranodal marginal zone B-cell lymphoma of MALT type. Am J Surg Pathol 2001, **25**: 997–1008.

1209 L'Hoste RJ Jr, Filippa DA, Lieberman PH, Bretsky S. Primary pulmonary lymphomas. A clinicopathologic analysis of 36 cases. Cancer 1984, **54**: 1397–1406.

1210 Li G, Hansmann ML, Zwingers T, Lennert K. Primary lymphomas of the lung. Morphological, immunohistochemical and clinical features. Histopathology 1990, **16**: 519–532.

1211 Liebow AA. Pulmonary angiitis and granulomatosis (The J Burns Amberson Lecture). Am Rev Respir Dis 1973, **108**: 1–18.

1212 Liebow AA, Carrington CRB, Friedman PJ. Lymphomatoid granulomatosis. Hum Pathol 1972, **3**: 457–558.

1213 Medeiros LJ, Jaffe ES, Chen Y-Y, Weiss LM. Localization of Epstein-Barr viral genomes in angiocentric immunoproliferative lesions. Am J Surg Pathol 1992, **16**: 439–447.

1214 Medeiros LJ, Peiper SC, Elwood L, Yano T, Raffeld M, Jaffe ES. Angiocentric immunoproliferative lesions. A molecular analysis of eight cases. Hum Pathol 1991, **22**: 1150–1157.

1215 Mittal K, Neri A, Feiner H, Schinella R, Alfonso F. Lymphomatoid granulomatosis in the acquired immunodeficiency syndrome. Evidence of Epstein–Barr virus infection and B-cell clonal selection without MYC rearrangement. Cancer 1990, **65**: 1345–1349.

1216 Mohamedani AA, Bennett MK. Angiofollicular lymphoid hyperplasia in a pulmonary fissure. Thorax 1985, **40**: 686–687.

1217 Morinaga S, Watanabe H, Gemma A, Mukai K, Nakajima T, Shimosato Y, Goya T, Shinoda T. Plasmacytoma of the lung associated with nodular deposits of immunoglobulin. Am J Surg Pathol 1987, **11**: 989–995.

1218 Nicholson AG, Wotherspoon AC, Diss TC, Hansell DM, DuBois R, Sheppard MN, Isaacson PG, Corrin B. Reactive pulmonary lymphoid disorders. Histopathology 1995, **26**: 405–412.

1219 Nicholson AG, Wotherspoon AC, Diss TC, Singh N, Butcher DN, Pan LX, Isaacson PG, Corrin B. Lymphomatoid granulomatosis: evidence that some cases represent Epstein–Barr virus-associated B-cell lymphoma. Histopathology 1996, **29**: 317–324.

1220 Palosaari DE, Colby TV. Bronchiolocentric chronic lymphocytic leukemia. Cancer 1986, **58**: 1695–1698.

1221 Patton WF, Lynch JP III. Lymphomatoid granulomatosis. Clinicopathologic study of four cases and literature review. Medicine 1982, **61**: 1–11.

1222 Pisani RJ, Deremee RA. Clinical implications of the histopathologic diagnosis of pulmonary lymphomatoid granulomatosis. Mayo Clin Proc 1990, **65**: 151–163.

1223 Radin AI. Primary pulmonary Hodgkin's disease. Cancer 1990, **65**: 550–563.

1224 Randhawa PS, Yousem SA, Paradis IL, Dauber JA, Griffith BP, Locker J. The clinical spectrum, pathology, and clonal analysis of EBV associated lymphoproliferative disorders in heart-lung transplant recipients. Am J Clin Pathol 1989, **92**: 177–185.

1225 Rattinger MD, Dunn TL, Christian CD Jr, Donnell RM, Collins RD, O'Leary JP, Flexner JM. Gastrointestinal involvement in lymphomatoid granulomatosis. Report of a case and review of the literature. Cancer 1983, **51**: 694–700.

1226 Reddick RL, Fauci AS, Valsamis MP, Mann RB. Immunoblastic sarcoma of the central nervous system in a patient with lymphomatoid granulomatosis. Cancer 1978, **42**: 652–659.

1227 Rose RM, Grigas D, Strattemeir E, Harris NL, Linggood RM. Endobronchial involvement with non-Hodgkin's lymphoma. A clinical-radiologic analysis. Cancer 1986, **57**: 1750–1755.

1228 Rush WL, Andriko JA, Taubenberger JK, Nelson AM, Abbondanzo SL, Travis WD, Koss MN. Primary anaplastic large cell lymphoma of the lung: a clinicopathologic study of five patients. Mod Pathol 2000, **13**: 1285–1292.

1229 Saldana MJ, Patchefsky AS, Israel HI, Atkinson GW. Pulmonary angiitis and granulomatosis. The relationship between histological features, organ involvement, and response to treatment. Hum Pathol 1977, 8: 391–409.

1230 Singh G, Hellstrom HR. Lymphomatoid granulomatosis. Report of a case without pulmonary lesions and with ischemic colitis, probably a sequel to granulomatosis. Hum Pathol 1978, 9: 364–366.

1231 Strum SB, Weiss A, McDermed JE, Rosen VJ. Intrathoracic Hodgkin's disease. A case presentation with multiple pulmonary nodules in the absence of mediastinal or hilar node disease. Cancer 1985, 56: 1953–1956.

1232 Tenholder MF, Scialla SJ, Weisbaum G. Endobronchial metastatic plasmacytoma. Cancer 1982, 49: 1465–1468.

1233 Thompson G, Utz J, Tosenow E, Myers J, Swensen S. Pulmonary lymphoproliferative disorders. Mayo Clin Proc 1993, 68: 804–817.

1234 Turner RR, Colby TV, Doggett RS. Well-differentiated lymphocytic lymphoma. A study of 47 patients with primary manifestation in the lung. Cancer 1984, 54: 2088–2096.

1235 Vergier B, Capron F, Trojani M, Labouyrie E, Ferrer J, Eghbali H, Merlio J. Benign lymphocytic angiitis and granulomatosis. A T-cell lymphoma? Hum Pathol 1992, 23: 1191–1193.

1236 Wardman AG, Cooke NJ. Pulmonary infiltrates in adult acute leukaemia. Empirical treatment or lung biopsy? Thorax 1984, 39: 647–650.

1237 Weiss LM, Yousem SA, Warnke RA. Non-Hodgkin's lymphomas of the lung. A study of 19 cases emphasizing the utility of frozen section immunologic studies in differential diagnosis. Am J Surg Pathol 1985, 9: 480–490.

1238 Weiss MA, Rolfes DB, Alvira MA, Cohen LJ. Benign lymphocytic angiitis and granulomatosis. A case report with evidence of an autoimmune etiology. Am J Clin Pathol 1984, 81: 110–116.

1239 Wile A, Olinger G, Peter JB, Dornfeld L. Solitary intraparenchymal pulmonary plasmacytoma associated with production of an M-protein. Report of a case. Cancer 1976, 37: 2338–2342.

1240 Yousem SA, Colby TV. Intravascular lymphomatosis presenting in the lung. Cancer 1990, 65: 349–353.

1241 Yousem SA, Weiss LM, Colby TV. Primary pulmonary Hodgkin's disease. A clinicopathologic study of 15 cases. Cancer 1986, 57: 1217–1224.

Salivary gland-type tumors

1242 Barsky SH, Martin SE, Matthews M, Gazdar A, Costa JC. "Low grade" mucoepidermoid carcinoma of the bronchus with "high grade" biological behavior. Cancer 1983, 51: 1505–1509.

1243 Borczuk AC, Sha KK, Hisler SE, Mann JM, Hajdu SI. Sebaceous carcinoma of the lung: histologic and immunohistochemical characterization of an unusual pulmonary neoplasm: report of a case and review of the literature. Am J Surg Pathol 2002, 26: 795–798.

1244 England DM, Hochholzer L. Truly benign "bronchial adenoma." Report of 10 cases of mucous gland adenoma with immunohistochemical and ultrastructural findings. Am J Surg Pathol 1995, 19: 887–889.

1245 Fechner RE, Bentinck BR. Ultrastructure of bronchial oncocytoma. Cancer 1973, 31: 1451–1457.

1246 Fulford LG, Kamata Y, Okudera K, Dawson A, Corrin B, Sheppard MN, Ibrahim NB, Nicholson AG. Epithelial–myoepithelial carcinomas of the bronchus. Am J Surg Pathol 2001, 25: 1508–1514.

1247 Hayes MM, van der Westhuizen NG, Forgie R. Malignant mixed tumor of the bronchus. A biphasic neoplasm of epithelial and myoepithelial cells. Mod Pathol 1993, 6: 85–88.

1248 Heard BE, Corrin B, Dewar A. Pathology of seven mucous cell adenomas of the bronchial glands with particular reference to ultrastructure. Histopathology 1985, 9: 687–701.

1249 Hirata H, Noguchi M, Shimosato Y, Uei Y, Goya T. Clinicopathologic and immunohistochemical characteristics of the bronchial gland cell type adenocarcinoma of the lung. Am J Clin Pathol 1990, 93: 20–25.

1250 Inoue H, Iwashita A, Kanegae H, Higuchi K, Fujinaga Y, Matsumoto I. Peripheral pulmonary adenoid cystic carcinoma with susbtantial extension to the proximal bronchus. Thorax 1991, 46: 147–148.

1251 Katz DR, Bubis JJ. Acinic cell tumor of the bronchus. Cancer 1976, 38: 830–832.

1252 Kroe DJ, Pitcock JA. Benign mucous gland adenoma of the bronchus. Arch Pathol 1967, 84: 539–542.

1253 Lack EE, Harris GBC, Eraklis AJ, Vawter GF. Primary bronchial tumors in childhood. A clinicopathologic study of six cases. Cancer 1983, 51: 492–497.

1254 Markel SF, Abell MR, Haight C, French AJ. Neoplasms of bronchus commonly designated as adenomas. Cancer 1964, 17: 590–608.

1255 Moran CA, Suster S, Askin FB, Koss MN. Benign and malignant salivary gland-type mixed tumors of the lung. Clinicopathologic and immunohistochemical study of 7 cases, Cancer 1994, 73: 2481–2490.

1256 Moran CA, Suster S, Koss MN. Acinic cell carcinoma of the lung ("Fechner tumor"). A clinicopathologic, immunohistochemical and ultrastructural study of five cases. Am J Surg Pathol 1992, 16: 1039–1050.

1257 Moran CA, Suster S, Koss MN. Primary adenoid cystic carcinoma of the lung. A clinicopathologic and immunohistochemical study of 16 cases. Cancer 1994, 73: 1390–1397.

1258 Nielsen AL. Malignant bronchial oncocytoma. Case report and review of the literature. Hum Pathol 1985, 16: 852–854.

1259 Payne WS, Schier J, Woolner LB. Mixed tumors of the bronchus (salivary gland type). J Thorac Cardiovasc Surg 1965, 49: 663–668.

1259a Rodriguez J, Diment J, Lombardi L, Dominoni F, Tench W, Rosai J. Combined typical carcinoid and acinic cell tumor of the lung: a heretofore unreported occurrence. Hum Pathol 2003, 34: 1061–1065.

1260 Sakamoto H, Uda H, Tanaka T, Oda T, Morino H, Kikui M. Pleomorphic adenoma in the periphery of the lung. Report of a case and review of the literature. Arch Pathol Lab Med 1991, 115: 393–396.

1261 Santos-Briz A, Terrón J, Sastre R, Romero L, Valle A. Oncocytoma of the lung. Cancer 1977, 40: 1330–1336.

1262 Spencer H. Bronchial gland tumours. Virchows Arch [A] 1979, 383: 101–115.

1263 Turnbull AD, Huvos AG, Goodner JT, Foote FW Jr. Mucoepidermoid tumors of bronchial glands. Cancer 1971, 28: 539–544.

1264 Wilson RW, Moran CA. Epithelial–myoepithelial carcinoma of the lung: immunohistochemical and ultrastructural observations and review of the literature. Hum Pathol 1997A, 28: 631–635.

1265 Yousem SA. Pulmonary adenosquamous carcinomas with amyloid-like stroma. Mod Pathol 1989, 2: 420–426.

1266 Yousem SA, Hochholzer L. Mucoepidermoid tumors of the lung. Cancer 1987, 60: 1346–1352.

Clear cell tumor

1267 Andrion A, Mazzucco G, Gugliotta P, Monga G. Benign clear cell ("sugar") tumor of the lung. A light microscopic, histochemical, and ultrastructural study with a review of the literature. Cancer 1985, 56: 2657–2663.

1268 Becker NH, Soifer L. Benign clear cell tumor ("sugar tumor") of the lung. Cancer 1971, 27: 712–719.

1269 Fukuda T, Machinami R, Joshita T, Nagashima K. Benign clear cell tumor of the lung in an 8-year-old girl. Arch Pathol Lab Med 1986, **110**: 664–666.

1270 Gaffey MJ, Mills SE, Askin FB, Ross GW, Sale GE, Kulander BG, Wisscher DW, Yousem SA, Colby TV. Clear cell tumor of the lung. A clinicopathologic, immunohistochemical, and ultrastructural study of eight cases. Am J Surg Pathol 1990, **14**: 248–259.

1271 Gaffey MJ, Mills SE, Frierson HF Jr, Askin FB, Maygarden SJ. Pulmonary clear cell carcinoid tumor: another entity in the differential diagnosis of pulmonary clear cell neoplasia. Am J Surg Pathol 1998, **22**: 1020–1025.

1272 Gaffey MJ, Mills SE, Zarbo RJ, Weiss LM, Gown AM. Clear cell tumor of the lung. Immunohistochemical and ultrastructural evidence of melanogenesis. Am J Surg Pathol 1991, **15**: 644–653.

1273 Gal AA, Koss MN, Hochholzer L, Chefjec G. An immunohistochemical study of benign clear cell ("sugar") tumor of the lung. Arch Pathol Lab Med 1991, **115**: 1034–1038.

1274 Hoch WS, Patchefsk AS, Takeda M, Gordon G. Benign clear cell tumor of the lung. An ultrastructural study. Cancer 1974, **33**: 1328–1336.

1275 Liebow AA, Castleman B. Benign clear cell ("sugar") tumors of the lung. Yale J Biol Med 1971, **43**: 213–222.

1276 Tazelaar HD, Batts K, Srigley JR. Primary extrapulmonary sugar tumor (PEST): a report of four cases. Mod Pathol 2001, **14**: 615–622.

1277 Wick MR. Immunohistology of neuroendocrine and neuroectodermal tumors. Semin Diagn Pathol 2000, **17**: 194–203.

Muscle tumors

1278 Avagnina A, Elsner E, DeMarco L, Bracco AN, Nazar J, Pavlovsky H. Pulmonary rhabdomyosarcoma with isolated small bowel metastasis. A report of a case with immunohistochemical and ultrastructural studies. Cancer 1984, **53**: 1948–1951.

1279 Banner AS, Carringtor CB, Emory WB, Kittle F, Leonard G, Ringus J, Taylor P, Addington WW. Efficacy of oophorectomy in lymphangioleiomyomatosis and benign metastasizing leiomyoma. N Engl J Med 1981, **305**: 204–209.

1280 Burkhardt A, Otto HF, Kaukel E. Multiple pulmonary (hamartomatous?) leiomyomas. Light and electron microscopic study. Virchows Arch [A] 1981, **394**: 133–141.

1281 Chadwick EG, Conner EJ, Hanson CG, Joshi VV, Abu-Farsakh H, Yogev R, McSherry G, McClain K, Murphy SB. Tumors of smooth-muscle origin in HIV-infected children. JAMA 1990, **263**: 3182–3184.

1282 Gal AA, Brooks JSJ, Pietra GG. Leiomyomatous neoplasms of the lung. A clinical, histologic, and immunohistochemical study. Mod Pathol 1989, **2**: 209–215.

1283 Horstmann JP, Pietra GG, Harman JA, Cole NG Jr, Grinspan S. Spontaneous regression of pulmonary leiomyomas during pregnancy. Cancer 1977, **39**: 314–321.

1284 Jimenez JF, Uthman EO, Townsend JW, Gloster ES, Seibert JJ. Primary bronchopulmonary leiomyosarcoma in childhood. Arch Pathol Lab Med 1986, **110**: 348–351.

1285 Krous HF, Sexauer CL. Embryonal rhabdomyosarcoma arising within a congenital bronchogenic cyst in a child. J Pediatr Surg 1981, **16**: 506–508.

1286 McGinnis M, Jacobs G, El-Naggar A, Redline RW. Congenital peribronchial myofibroblastic tumor (so-called "congenital leiomyosarcoma"). A distinct neonatal lung lesion associated with nonimmune hydrops fetalis. Mod Pathol 1993, **6**: 487–492.

1287 McKeeby JL, Li X, Zhuang Z, Vortmeyer AO, Huang S, Pirner M, Skarulis MC, James-Newton L, Marx SJ, Lubensky IA. Multiple leiomyomas of the esophagus, lung, and uterus in multiple endocrine neoplasia type 1. Am J Pathol 2001, **159**: 1121–1127.

1288 Moran CA, Suster S, Abbondanzo SL, Koss MN. Primary leiomyosarcomas of the lung: a clinicopathologic and immunohistochemical study of 18 cases. Mod Pathol 1997, **10**: 121–128.

1289 Naresh KN, Pai SA, Vyas JJ, Soman CS. Leiomyoma of the bronchus. A case report. Histopathology 1993, **22**: 288–289.

1290 Oliai BR, Tazelaar HD, Lloyd RV, Doria MI, Trastek VF. Leiomyosarcoma of the pulmonary veins. Am J Surg Pathol 1999, **23**: 1082–1088.

1291 White SH, Ibrahim NBN, Forrester-Wood CP, Jeyasingham K. Leiomyomas of the lower respiratory tract. Thorax 1985, **40**: 306–311.

1292 Wick MR, Scheithauer BW, Piehler JM, Pairolero PC. Primary pulmonary leiomyosarcomas. A light and electron microscopic study. Arch Pathol Lab Med 1982, **106**: 510–514.

1293 Wolff M, Silva F, Kaye F. Pulmonary metastases (with admixed epithelial elements) from smooth muscle neoplasms. Report of nine cases, including three males. Am J Surg Pathol 1979, **3**: 325–342.

Pleuropulmonary blastoma

1294 Ashworth TG. Pulmonary blastoma. A true congenital neoplasm. Histopathology 1983, **7**: 585–594.

1295 Dehner LP. Pleuropulmonary blastoma is *the* pulmonary blastoma of childhood. Sem Diagn Pathol 1994, **11**: 144–151.

1296 Hatchitanda Y, Aoyama C, Sato J, Shimada H. Pleuropulmonary blastoma in childhood. A tumor of divergent differentiation. Am J Surg Pathol 1993, **17**: 382–391.

1297 Indolfi P, Casale F, Carli M, Bisogno G, Ninfo V, Cecchetto G, Bagnulo S, Santoro N, Giuliano M, Di Tullio MT. Pleuropulmonary blastoma: management and prognosis of 11 cases. Cancer 2000, **89**: 1396–1401.

1298 Minken SL, Craver WL, Adams JT. Pulmonary blastoma. Arch Pathol 1968, **86**: 442–446.

1299 Priest JR, McDermott MB, Bhatia S, Watterson J, Manivel JC, Dehner LP. Pleuropulmonary blastoma: a clinicopathologic study of 50 cases. Cancer 1997, **80**: 147–161.

1300 Sciot R, Dal Cin P, Brock P, Moerman P, Van Damme B, De Wever I, Casteels-Van Daele M, Van den Berghe H, Desmet V. Pleuropulmonary blastoma (pulmonary blastoma of childhood). Genetic link with other embryonal malignacies? Histopathology 1994, **24**: 559–563.

1301 Weinblatt ME, Siegel SE, Isaacs H. Pulmonary blastoma associated with cystic lung disease. Cancer 1982, **49**: 669–671.

Miscellaneous primary tumors

1302 Attanoos RL, Appleton MA, Gibbs AR. Primary sarcomas of the lung: a clinicopathological and immunohistochemical study of 14 cases. Histopathology 1996, **29**: 29–36.

1303 Bosch X, Ramirez J, Font J, Bombi JA, Ferrer J, Vendrell J, Ingelmo M. Primary intrapulmonary benign schwannoma. A case with ultrastructural and immunohistochemical confirmation. Eur Respir J 1990, **3**: 234–237.

1304 Cavazza A, Colby TV, Tsokos M, Rush W, Travis WD. Lung tumors with a rhabdoid phenotype. Am J Clin Pathol 1996, **105**: 182–188.

1305 Colby TV, Bilbao JE, Battifora H, Unni KK. Primary osteosarcoma of the lung. A reappraisal following immunohistologic study. Arch Pathol Lab Med 1989, **113**: 1147–1150.

1306 Cooney TP. Primary pulmonary ganglioneuroblastoma in an adult. Maturation, involution and the immune response. Histopathology 1981, **5**: 451–463.

1307 Deavers M, Guinee D, Koss MN, Travis WD. Granular cell tumors of the lung. Clinicopathologic study of 20 cases. Am J Surg Pathol 1995, **19**: 627–635.

1308 Dirnhofer S, Freund M, Rogatsch H, Krabichler S, Berger P.

Selective expression of trophoblastic hormones by lung carcinoma: neuroendocrine tumors exclusively produce human chorionic gonadotropin alfa subunit (hCGa). Hum Pathol 2000, **31:** 966–972.

1309 Feldhaus RJ, Anene C, Bogard P. A rare endobronchial neurilemmoma (schwannoma). Chest 1989, **95:** 461–462.

1310 Ferrara G, Boscaino A, De Rosa G. Bronchial blue naevus. A previously unreported entity. Histopathology 1995, **26:** 581–584.

1311 Gallivan GJ, Dolan CT, Stam RE, Eggerston BS Jr, Tovey JD. Granular cell myoblastoma of the bronchus. J Thorac Cardiovasc Surg 1966, **52:** 875–881.

1312 Guilloe L, Sahli R, Chaubert P, Monnier P, Cuttat J-F, Costa J. Squamous cell carcinoma of the lung in a nonsmoking, nonirradiated patient with juvenile laryngotracheal papillomatosis. Am J Surg Pathol 1991, **15:** 891–898.

1313 Halyard MY, Camoriano JK, Culligan JA, Weiland LH, Allen MS, Pluth JR, Pairolero PC. Malignant fibrous histiocytoma of the lung: report of four cases and review of the literature. Cancer 1997, **78:** 2492–2497.

1314 Hayashi T, Tsudo N, Iseki M, Kishikawa M, Shinozaki T, Hasumoto M. Primary chondrosarcoma of the lung. A clinicopathologic study. Cancer 1993, **72:** 69–74.

1315 Hirata T, Reshad K, Itoi K, Muro K, Akiyama J. Lipomas of the peripheral lung – a case report and review of the literature. Thorac Cardiovasc Surg 1989, **37:** 385–387.

1316 Hunter S, Hewan-Lowe K, Coasta MJ. Primary pulmonary fetoprotein-producing malignant germ cell tumor. Hum Pathol 1990, **21:** 1074–1075.

1317 Jennings TA, Axiotix CA, Kress Y, Carter D. Primary malignant melanoma of the lower respiratory tract. Report of a case and literature review. Am J Clin Pathol 1990, **94:** 649–655.

1318 Keel SB, Bacha E, Mark EJ, Neilsen GP, Rosenberg AE. Primary pulmonary sarcoma: a clinicopathologic study of 26 cases. Mod Pathol 2000, **12:** 1124–1131.

1319 Kurotaki H, Tateoka H, Takeuchi M, Yasgihashi S, Kama ta Y, Nagain K. Primary mesenchymal chondrosarcoma of the lung. A case report with immunohistochemical and ultrastructural studies. Acta Pathol Jpn 1992, **42:** 364–371.

1320 Lee JT, Shelburne JD, Linder J. Primary malignant fibrous histiocytoma of the lung. A clinicopathologic and ultrastructural study of five cases. Cancer 1984, **53:** 1124–1130.

1321 Loose JH, El-Naggar AK, Ro JY, Huang W-L, McMurtrey MJ, Ayala AG. Primary osteosarcoma of the lung. Report of two cases and review of the literature. J Thorac Cardiovasc Surg 1990, **100:** 867–873.

1322 Magro G, Fraggetta F, Manusia M, Mingrino A. Hyalinizing spindle cell tumor with giant rosettes: a previously undescribed lesion of the lung. Am J Surg Pathol 1998, **22:** 1431–1433.

1323 Matsuba K, Saito T, Ando K, Shirakusa T. Atypical lipoma of the lung. Thorax 1991, **46:** 685.

1324 Maxwell RJ, Gibbons JR, O'Hara MD. Solitary squamous papilloma of the bronchus. Thorax 1985, **40:** 68–71.

1325 McCluggage, Bharucha H. Primary pulmonary tumours of nerve sheath origin. Histopathology 1995, **26:** 357–362.

1326 McDonnell T, Kyriakos M, Roper C, Mazoujian G. Malignant fibrous histiocytoma of the lung. Cancer 1988, **61:** 137–145.

1327 Miyagi J, Tsuhako K, Kinjo T, Iwamasa T, Hashimoto H, Ishikawa S. Rhabdoid tumor of the lung is a dedifferential phenotype of pulmonary adenocarcinoma. Histopathology 2000, **37:** 37–44.

1328 Moore RL, Lattes R. Papillomatosis of larynx and bronchi. Cancer 1959, **12:** 117–126.

1329 Moran CA, Suster S, Fishback NF, Koss MN. Primary intrapulmonary thymoma. A clinicopathologic and immunohistochemical study of eight cases. Am J Surg Pathol 1995, **19:** 304–312.

1330 Moran CA, Suster S, Koss MN. Endobronchial lipomas.

1331 Moran CA, Suster S, Koss MN. Primary malignant "triton" tumour of the lung. Histopathology 1997, **30:** 140–144.

1332 Nascimento AG, Unni KK, Bernatz PE. Sarcomas of the lung. Mayo Clin Proc 1982, **57:** 355–359.

1333 Pettinato G, Manivel JC, Saldana MJ, Peyser J, Dehner LP. Primary bronchopulmonary fibrosarcoma of childhood and adolescence. Reassessment of a low-grade malignancy. Clinicopathologic study of five cases and review of the literature. Hum Pathol 1989, **20:** 463–471.

1334 Pomplun S, Wotherspoon AC, Shah G, Goldstraw P, Ladas G, Nicholson AG. Immunohistochemical makers in the differentiation of thymic and pulmonary neoplasms. Histopathology 2002, **40:** 152–158.

1335 Popper HH, el-Shabrawi Y, Wockel W, Hofler G, Kenner L, Juttner-Smolle FM, Pongratz MG. Prognostic importance of human papilloma virus typing in squamous cell papilloma of the bronchus: comparison of in situ hybridization and the polymerase chain reaction. Hum Pathol 1994, **25:** 1191–1197.

1336 Pushchak MJ, Farhi DC. Primary choriocarcinoma of the lung. Arch Pathol Lab Med 1987, **111:** 477–479.

1337 Roviaro G, Montorsi M, Varoli F, Binda R, Cecchetto A. Primary pulmonary tumours of neurogenic origin. Thorax 1983, **38:** 942–945.

1338 Shah RN, Ozden O, Yeldandi A, Peterson L, Rao S, Laskin WB. Follicular dendritic cell tumor presenting in the lung: a case report. Hum Pathol 2001, **32:** 745–749.

1339 Shimazaki H, Aida S, Sato M, Deguchi H, Ozeki Y, Tamai S. Lung carcinoma with rhabdoid cells: a clinicopathological study and survival analysis of 14 cases. Histopathology 2001, **38:** 425–434.

1340 Smith PS, McClure J. A papillary endobronchial tumor with a transitional cell pattern. Arch Pathol Lab Med 1982, **106:** 503–506.

1341 Spencer H, Dail DH, Arneaud J. Non-invasive bronchial epithelial papillary tumors. Cancer 1980, **45:** 1486–1497.

1342 Sullivan LG. Primary choriocarcinoma of the lung in a man. Arch Pathol Lab Med 1989, **113:** 82–83.

1343 Syed S, Haque AK, Hawkins HK, Sorensen PH, Cowan DF. Desmoplastic small round cell tumor of the lung. Arch Pathol Lab Med 2002, **126:** 1226–1228.

1343a Tamboli P, Toprani TH, Amin MB, Ro JS, Ordóñez NG, Ayala AG, Ro JY. Carcinoma of lung with rhabdoid features. Hum Pathol 2004, (in press).

1344 Tomashefski JR Jr. Benign endobronchial mesenchymal tumors. Their relationship to parenchymal pulmonary hamartomas. Am J Surg Pathol 1982, **6:** 531–540.

1345 Tsuji S, Hisaoka M, Morimitsu Y, Hshimoto H, Jimi A, Watanabe J, Eguchi H, Kaneko Y. Peripheral primitive neuroectodermal tumour of the lung: report of two cases. Histopathology 1999, **33:** 369–374.

1346 Wilson RW, Moran CA. Primary melanoma of the lung: a clinicopathologic and immunohistochemical study of eight cases. Am J Surg Pathol 1997B, **21:** 1196–1202.

1347 Young CD, Gay RM. Multiple endobronchial granular cell myoblastomas discovered at bronchoscopy. Hum Pathol 1984, **15:** 193–194.

1348 Zeren H, Moran CA, Suster S, Fishback NF, Koss MN. Primary pulmonary sarcomas with features of monophasic synovial sarcoma. A clinicopathological, immunohistochemical, and ultrastructural study of 25 cases. Hum Pathol 1995, **26:** 474–480.

Metastatic tumors

1349 Adem C, Aubry MC, Tazelaar HD, Myers JL. Metastatic angiosarcoma masquerading as diffuse pulmonary haemorrhage: clinicopathologic analysis of seven new patients. Arch Pathol Lab Med 2001, **125:** 1562–1565.

1350 Aubry MC, Myers JL, Colby TV, Leslie KO, Tazelaar HD. Endometrial stromal sarcoma metastatic to the lung: a detailed analysis of 16 patients. Am J Surg Pathol 2002, **26**: 440–449.

1351 Baldeyrou P, Lemoine G, Zucker JM, Schweisguth O. Pulmonary metastases in children. The place of surgery. A study of 134 patients. J Pediatr Surg 1984, **19**: 121–125.

1352 Barbareschi M, Murer B, Colby TV, Chilosi M, Macri E, Loda M, Doglioni C. CDX-2 homeobox gene expression is a reliable marker of colorectal adenocarcinoma metastases to the lungs. Am J Surg Pathol 2003, **27**: 141–149.

1353 Beattie EJ Jr. Surgical treatment of pulmonary metastases. Cancer 1984, **54**: 2729–2731.

1354 Bocklage T, Leslie K, Yousem S, Colby T. Extracutaneous angiosarcomas metastatic to the lungs: clinical and pathologic features of 21 cases. Mod Pathol 2001, **14**: 1216–1225.

1355 Bourke SJ, Henderson AF, Stevenson RD, Banham SW. Endobronchial metastases simulating primary carcinoma of the lung. Respir Med 1989, **83**: 151–152.

1356 Carlin BW, Harrell J II, Olson LK, Moser KM. Endobronchial metastases due to colorectal carcinoma. Chest 1989, **69**: 1110–1114.

1357 Casson AG, Putnam JB, Natarajan G, Johnston DA, Mountain C, McMurtrey M, Roth JA. Five-year survival after pulmonary metastasectomy for adult soft tissue sarcoma. Cancer 1992, **69**: 663–668.

1358 Copeland JN, Amin MB, Humphrey PA, Tamboli P, Ro JY, Gal AA. The morphologic spectrum of metastatic prostatic adenocarcinoma to the lung: special emphasis on histologic features overlapping with other pulmonary neoplasms. Am J Clin Pathol 2002, **117**: 552–557.

1359 Edlich RF, Shea MA, Foker JE, Grondin C, Castaneda AR, Varco RL. A review of 26 years' experience with pulmonary resection for metastatic cancer. Dis Chest 1966, **49**: 587–594.

1360 Engstrand DA, England DM, Oberley TD. Limitations of the usefulness of microvillous ultrastructure in distinguishing between carcinoma primary in and metastatic to the lung. Ultrastruct Pathol 1987, **11**: 53–58.

1361 Feldman PS, Kyriakos M. Pulmonary resection for metastatic sarcoma. J Thorac Cardiovasc Surg 1972, **64**: 784–799.

1362 Flint A, Lloyd RV. Pulmonary metastases of colonic adenocarcinoma. Distinction from pulmonary adenocarcinoma. Arch Pathol Lab Med 1992, **116**: 39–42.

1363 Flye MW, Woltering G, Rosenberg SA. Aggressive pulmonary resection for metastatic osteogenic and soft tissue sarcomas. Ann Thorac Surg 1984, **37**: 123–127.

1364 Ghoneium AHA, Brisson ML, Fuks A, Mobasher AMT, Kreisman H. Monoclonal anti-CEA antibodies in the discrimination between primary pulmonary adenocarcinoma and colon carcinoma metastatic to the lung. Mod Pathol 1990, **3**: 613–618.

1365 Girard P, Baldeyrou P, Le Chevalier T, Le Cesne A, Brigandi A, Grunenwald D. Surgery for pulmonary metastases. Who are the 10-year survivors? Cancer 1994, **74**: 2791–2797.

1366 Harpole DH, Johnson CM, Wolfe WG, George SL, Seigler HF. Analysis of 945 cases of pulmonary metastatic melanoma. J Thorac Cardiovasc Surg 1992, **103**: 743–750.

1367 Katzenstein AL, Purvis R Jr, Gmelich J, Askin F. Pulmonary resection for metastatic renal adenocarcinoma. Pathologic findings and therapeutic value. Cancer 1978, **41**: 712–723.

1368 Loy TS, Calaluce RD. Utility of cytokeratin immunostaining in separating pulmonary adenocarcinomas from colonic adenocarcinomas. Am J Clin Pathol 1994, **102**: 764–767.

1369 Mizutani Y, Nakajima T, Morinaga S, Gotoh M, Shimosato Y, Akino T, et al. Immunohistochemical localization of pulmonary surfactant apoproteins in various lung tumors. Special reference to nonmucus producing lung adenocarcinomas. Cancer 1988, **61**: 532–537.

1370 Mountain CF, McMurtrey MJ, Hermes KE. Surgery for pulmonary metastasis. A 20-year experience. Ann Thorac Surg 1984, **38**: 323–330.

1371 Ng WK, Chow JC, Ng PK. Thyroid transcription factor-1 is highly sensitive and specific in differentiating metastatic pulmonary from extrapulmonary adenocarcinoma in effusion fluid cytology specimens. Cancer 2002, **96**: 43–48.

1372 Noguchi M, Maezawa N, Nakanishi Y, Matsuno Y, Shimosato Y, Hirohashi S. Application of the p53 gene mutation pattern for differential diagnosis of primary versus metastatic lung carcinomas. Diagn Mol Pathol 1993, **2**: 29–35.

1373 Piltz S, Meimarakis G, Wichmann MW, Hatz R, Schildberg FW, Fuerst H. Long-term results after pulmonary resection of renal cell carcinoma metastases. Ann Thorac Surg 2002, **73**: 1082–1087.

1374 Pogrebniak HW, Haas G, Lineham WM, Rosenberg SA, Pass HI. Renal cell carcinoma. Resection of solitary and multiple metastases. Ann Thorac Surg 1988, **54**: 33–38.

1375 Putnam JB Jr, Roth JA, Wesley MN, Johnston MR, Rosenberg SA. Survival following aggressive resection of pulmonary metastases from osteogenic sarcoma. Analysis of prognostic factors. Ann Thorac Surg 1983, **36**: 516–523.

1376 Raab SS, Berg LC, Swanson PE, Wick MR. Adenocarcinoma in the lung in patients with breast cancer. A prospective analysis of the discriminatory value of immunohistology. Am J Clin Pathol 1993, **100**: 27–35.

1377 Rosenblatt MB, Lisa JR, Collier F. Primary and metastatic bronchioloalveolar carcinoma. Dis Chest 1967, **52**: 147–152.

1378 Roth JA, Putnam JB Jr, Wesley MN, Rosenberg SA. Differing determinants of prognosis following resection of pulmonary metastases from osteogenic and soft tissue sarcoma patients. Cancer 1985, **55**: 1361–1366.

1379 Shields DJ, Edwards WD. Pulmonary hypertension attributable to neoplastic emboli. An autopsy study of 20 cases and a review of the literature. Cardiovasc Pathol 1992, **1**: 279–287.

1380 Soares F, Pinto A, Landell G, De Oliveira J. Pulmonary tumor embolism to arterial vessels and carcinomatous lymphangitis. A comparative clinicopathological study. Arch Pathol Lab Med 1993, **117**: 824–826.

1381 Traweek T, Rotter AJ, Swartz W, Azumi N. Cystic pulmonary metastatic sarcoma. Cancer 1990, **65**: 1805–1811.

1382 Tsao M-S, Fraser RS. Primary pulmonary adenocarcinoma with enteric differentiation. Cancer 1991, **68**: 1754–1757.

1383 Van Geel AN, Pastorino U, Jauch KW, Judson IR, Van Coevorden F, Buesa JM, Nielsen OS, Boudinet A, Tursz T, Schmitz PI. Surgical treatment of lung metastases: the European Organization for Research and Treatment of Cancer-Soft Tissue and Bone Sarcoma Group study of 255 patients. Cancer 1996, **77**: 675–682.

1383a Werling RW, Yazjii H, Bacchi C, Gown AM. CDX2, a highly sensitive and specific marker of adenocarcinomas of intestinal origin. Am J Surg Pathol 2003, **27**: 303–310.

8 Mediastinum

Generalities

The mediastinum is the portion of the thoracic cavity located between the pleural cavities, extending anteroposteriorly from the sternum to the spine and sagittally from the thoracic inlet to the diaphragm. The numerous organs and structures it contains make it a veritable Pandora's box, within which congenital cysts, benign tumors, and primary and malignant neoplasms may develop.

An arbitrary division of the mediastinum into *superior*, *anterior*, *middle*, and *posterior* compartments has proved useful, since most cysts and neoplasms have a predilection for one compartment over the others. The most common mediastinal lesions are noted in Figure 8.1 according to their frequency and most common site of occurrence in adults.[2,3,7,9,13] As expected, the relative frequencies of these lesions are considerably different in the pediatric population.[1,11]

About half of the patients with mediastinal cysts and tumors are asymptomatic, the lesions being discovered incidentally on chest x-ray films. When symptoms develop, they usually result from compression and/or invasion of adjacent structures, and include chest pain, cough, and dyspnea. Development of the superior vena caval syndrome is usually indicative of malignancy, the two most common causes in adults being metastatic lung carcinoma and malignant lymphoma,[8,10] and in children malignant lymphoma and acute leukemia.[4] However, it can also occur with benign conditions such as fibrosing mediastinitis.[5] Pulmonary stenosis can also occur with mediastinal tumors as a result of compression of the pulmonary artery or the right ventricular outflow tract.[6]

The location of lesions in the mediastinum, together with their configuration, provides important diagnostic

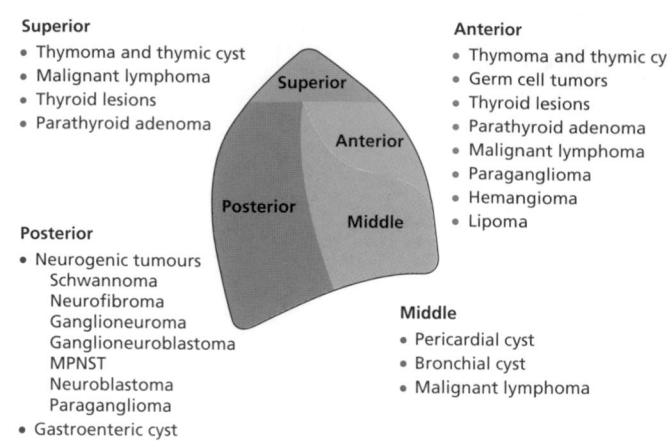

Superior
- Thymoma and thymic cyst
- Malignant lymphoma
- Thyroid lesions
- Parathyroid adenoma

Posterior
- Neurogenic tumours
  Schwannoma
  Neurofibroma
  Ganglioneuroma
  Ganglioneuroblastoma
  MPNST
  Neuroblastoma
  Paraganglioma
- Gastroenteric cyst

Anterior
- Thymoma and thymic cyst
- Germ cell tumors
- Thyroid lesions
- Parathyroid adenoma
- Malignant lymphoma
- Paraganglioma
- Hemangioma
- Lipoma

Middle
- Pericardial cyst
- Bronchial cyst
- Malignant lymphoma

Fig. 8.1 Location of most common lesions of mediastinum.

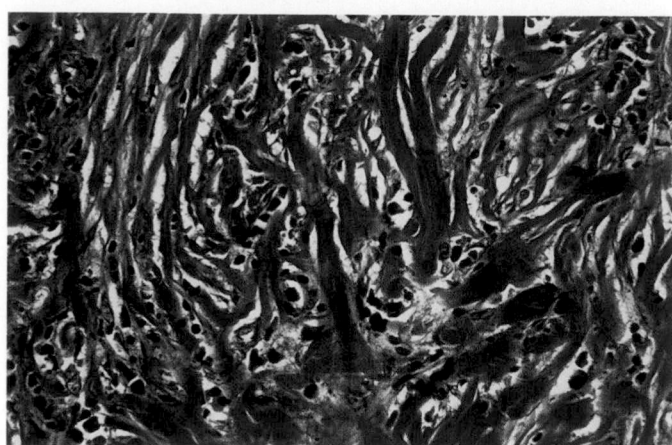

Fig. 8.2 Sclerosing mediastinitis. This is a particularly sclerotic example of this entity, with only a scanty inflammatory infiltrate.

information, but many lesions (both benign and malignant) result in similar radiographic and computed tomographic (CT) scan appearances. Exploration is therefore mandatory in most instances. Preoperative irradiation should be avoided when possible because the changes resulting from it may render the pathologic interpretation difficult or even impossible. Core needle and fine needle aspiration of mediastinal masses has been used successfully, particularly in lesions of the anterosuperior compartment.[12]

Inflammatory diseases

Acute mediastinitis is usually the result of traumatic perforation of the esophagus,[27] or descent of infection from within the neck through the "danger space" anterior to the prevertebral fascia[14,27]; in both cases, it involves predominantly the posterior portion of the mediastinum. The initial lesion may be a neck abscess resulting from dental infection, Ludwig's angina, necrotizing fasciitis,[22] or a pyriform sinus fistula. Abscess formation usually takes place and generally requires surgical drainage.

Other types of mediastinitis are those resulting from spread of infection from the chest wall,[18] and those developing after heart surgery; many of the latter are caused by cytomegalovirus infection.[17]

Chronic mediastinitis can produce compression of the vena cava and simulate a malignant process. The typical location is the anterior mediastinum, in front of the tracheal bifurcation. Microscopically, one may find granulomas, fibrosis, or a combination of both (Fig. 8.2).[30] In some of these cases, a mycotic (particularly histoplasmosis) or tuberculous etiology has been documented.[16,21,29,31] Goodwin et al.[21] studied 38 cases of mediastinal granuloma or fibrosis and found, either by histology or cultures, that they were caused by *Histoplasma* in 26 cases and *Mycobacteria* in 12 cases.

Those caused by *Histoplasma* often were characterized by the formation of a thick fibrous capsule; in those caused by *Mycobacteria* the capsule was quite thin. Cases of *Nocardia* mediastinitis resulting in superior vena caval syndrome have also been reported.[28]

In many instances of chronic mediastinitis, a specific etiology cannot be demonstrated.[19,23] Some of these cases represent examples of **fibrosing mediastinitis** (idiopathic mediastinal fibrosis; idiopathic inflammatory fibrosclerosis of the mediastinum), a member of the group of idiopathic fibrosing (sclerosing) inflammatory conditions, which also includes retroperitoneal fibrosis, sclerosing cholangitis, Riedel's struma, and inflammatory pseudotumor of the orbit. Indeed, fibrosing mediastinitis can be seen in association with one or more of these conditions, particularly retroperitoneal fibrosis.[24,26] This disease should be suspected if any of the following features are present: a particularly cellular fibrous reaction, a polymorphic inflammatory infiltrate rich in plasma cells and eosinophils, and the occurrence of phlebitis.[20] At the same time, one should always keep in mind that some neoplastic disorders may contain extensive areas in which only fibrosis and chronic inflammation are seen[15]; this is particularly true for Hodgkin's lymphoma. The treatment of fibrosing mediastinitis includes steroid therapy and surgical excision.[25]

Cysts (other than thymic)

Pericardial (coelomic) cysts

The pericardial sac is formed by the fusion of multiple disconnected lacunae. Failure of one of the lacunar cavities to merge with the others results in the development of a pericardial (coelomic) cyst. Such cysts are usually located at the right cardiophrenic angle.[32,33] They are soft

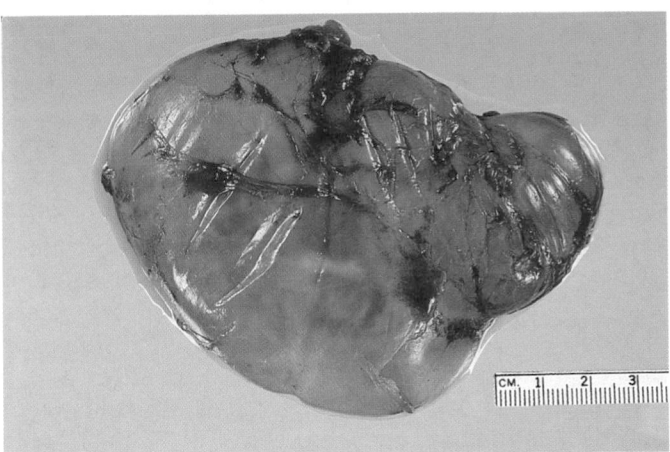

Fig. 8.3 Gross appearance of pericardial cyst. Note the thin translucent quality of the wall, which is partially covered by adipose tissue.

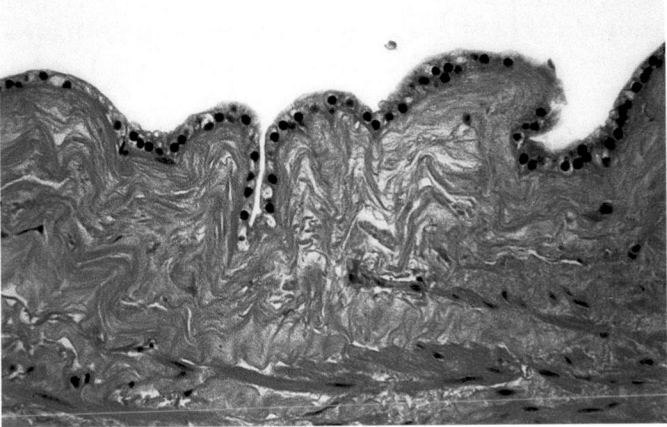

Fig. 8.4 Microscopic appearance of pericardial cyst. The lining is composed of a single layer of mesothelial cells.

and unilocular, usually loosely adherent to the pericardium and attached to the diaphragm; sometimes they communicate with the pericardial cavity (Fig. 8.3). Less commonly, they are seen in a suprapericardial position. At times, multiple cysts may be present. They contain clear fluid unless infected. The blood supply comes from the pericardium. The inner surface of the cyst wall is covered by a flat or cuboidal single layer of mesothelium, which is strongly immunoreactive for keratin (Fig. 8.4).

Foregut cysts

During embryonic development, fusion of the lateral walls that form the tracheoesophageal septum begins caudally. If a small bud or diverticulum of the foregut is pinched off during this process, it will be carried into the mediastinum by the downward growth of the lungs. This structure contains the endoderm and mesoderm that were destined to become part of the trachea, bronchi, esophagus, stomach, or intestine.[34,43]

Bronchial cysts occur along the tracheobronchial tree, their most common location being posterior to the carina.[42,44,45] Rarely, they are located just above the

diaphragm. They can be missed on plain films but are easily detectable on barium-swallow studies or CT scans.[38] These cysts contain clear or gelatinous fluid; are usually unilocular, thin-walled, and spherical; and have an average diameter of 3 to 4 cm[42] (Fig. 8.5). Microscopically, they usually are lined by ciliated columnar epithelium, but focal or extensive squamous metaplasia and/or extreme attenuation of this lining can occur (Fig. 8.6). The wall may contain hyaline cartilage, smooth muscle, bronchial glands, and nerve trunks.

Esophageal cysts probably arise from a persistence, in the wall of the foregut, of vacuoles that form during the solid tube stage of development. Most of them are found embedded in the wall of the lower half of the esophagus. The lining may be squamous, ciliated, columnar, or a mixture of these. Distinction from bronchial cyst may be difficult or even impossible, especially because the latter can be found entirely within the wall of the esophagus. The best evidence that a cyst in this location is of esophageal type is the presence of a definite double layer of smooth muscle in the wall.

Gastric and **enteric cysts** usually are located in the posterior mediastinum in a paravertebral location,

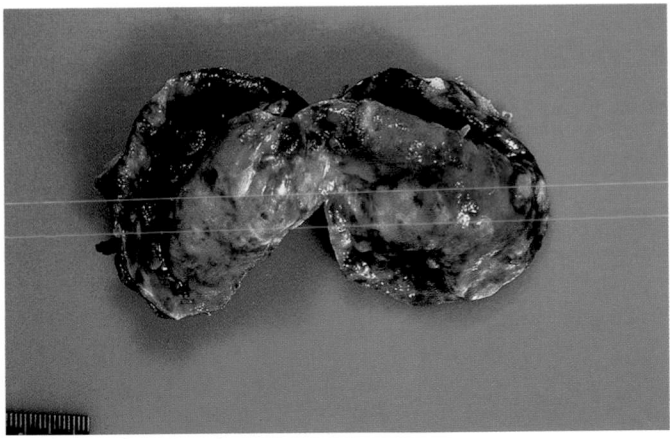

Fig. 8.5 Gross appearance of bronchial mediastinal cyst. The inner lining has a granular quality.

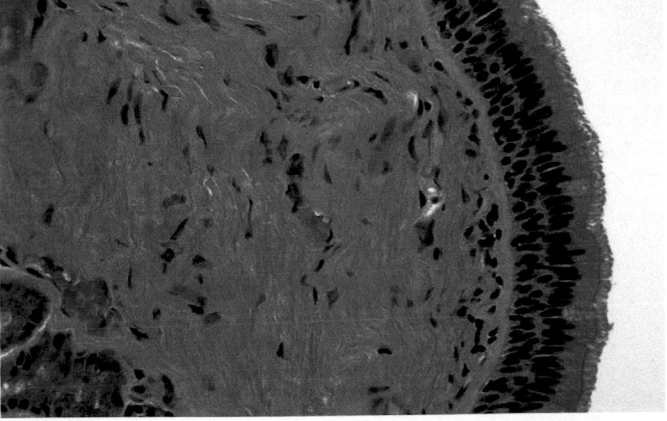

Fig. 8.6 Microscopic appearance of bronchial mediastinal cyst. The lining is composed of pseudostratified ciliated respiratory epithelium.

attached to the wall of the esophagus or even embedded within the muscle layer of this organ. Nearly all cases are associated with vertebral malformations. The gastric variety is made up of the same coats as the stomach, whereas the enteric type simulates the wall of normal intestine. Combined forms occur and are designated as **gastroenteric cysts**. Nerve fibers and ganglia are often present in them.[34]

Pancreatic cysts and pseudocysts may have a primarily mediastinal presentation.[37,39,41] Knowing the tendency of mediastinal germ cell tumors to contain pancreatic tissue, it is logical to assume that some of these pseudocysts may have a teratomatous origin.

• • •

This group of congenital cysts only exceptionally communicates with the tracheobronchial tree or the esophagus. Malignant change takes place within them only exceptionally, usually in the form of adenocarcinoma.[36,40] Symptoms from these cysts depend on their size and location; they are related to pressure phenomena and consist of cough, dysphagia, recurrent pulmonary infection, dyspnea, pain, and rarely hemoptysis. Most bronchial, esophageal, and enteric cysts are asymptomatic and are found incidentally in a routine chest x-ray. In contrast, gastric and gastroenteric cysts are often symptomatic and even life-threatening because of the occurrence of gastric secretion and the resulting hemorrhage, peptic ulcer, or perforation.[35]

Other cysts

Thymic cysts are discussed on p. 464, and **parathyroid cysts** are discussed in the next section.

Cases of mediastinal cysts arising from the **thoracic duct** (the largest lymph vessel in humans) have been reported.[46,47] Some of these perhaps represent examples of cystic lymphangiomas.

Thyroid and parathyroid lesions

Thyroid tumors and tumorlike conditions of several types can present as superior mediastinal masses. The most common pathologic change in mediastinal thyroid glands is nodular hyperplasia, which can reach huge proportions and cause compression symptoms.[50,54] Thyroid nodular hyperplasia in the mediastinum may occur in the form of seemingly independent nodules, a fact that may lead the unwary to regard the lesion as malignant. Actually, malignant change in mediastinal thyroid (except for the clinically inconsequential papillary microcarcinomas) is too unusual to justify excision because of fear of this complication; the main rationale for surgery is the relief of compression symptoms.[48] Nearly all of these lesions can be removed through a collar suprasternal incision.

From a pathogenetic standpoint, the nodular hyperplasia in most instances probably does not arise from ectopic thyroid tissue but rather from cervical thyroid that has been pulled down either into the anterior prevascular compartment or the retrotracheal compartment (so-called "posterior descending goiter") by the nodular enlargement. Support for this interpretation comes from the fact that these masses retain their cervical blood supply through a narrow pedicle. Radioactive iodine scanning yields a positive result in over half of the cases.

Parathyroid tumors and tumorlike conditions can also occur in the mediastinum, a not surprising event in view of the embryologic origin of the parathyroid glands and their intimate relationship with the thymus. About 7% of parathyroid adenomas are found in the superior mediastinum, and most of them can be excised through a collar suprasternal incision.[52] Because of their location, these adenomas can grow to a much larger size than their equivalents in the neck.[49] Mediastinal parathyroid carcinomas have also been reported, some of them being nonfunctioning.[51]

Parathyroid cysts of the mediastinum are usually located in the anterosuperior compartment, and are often functioning.[53]

Thymus

Normal anatomy

The thymus is a lobulated organ covered by a capsule and divided into cortical and medullary portions, the cortex being further subdivided into a subcapsular (outer) and a deep region. The two major cell types are endodermally (with a possible minor ectodermal contribution) derived epithelial cells and bone marrow-derived lymphocytes. The epithelial cells have been divided into several subtypes on the basis of their location, appearance, and phenotypical properties: cortical (dendritic), subcapsular, medullary, and Hassall's corpuscle related.[65,75,76,78] These epithelial cells are keratin positive and express HLA-DR antigens, the keratin profile showing differences related to the anatomic compartment[66] and the functional status (growth phase or involution) of the gland.[67] One or more subsets of these cells are responsible for the differentiation of T lymphocytes.[61,70] It has been assumed for a long time that this process is modulated in the thymic microenvironment through the secretion of thymic hormones[60,70]; however, the specificity, mechanism of action, and exact role of these substances remain elusive despite decades of work on the subject by several groups.[55,74]

Thymic lymphocytes (traditionally known as thymocytes) have a T-cell phenotype; a whole range of differentiation exists among them, the better defined stages being those of subcapsular thymocyte, cortical thymocyte, medullary thymocyte, and mature (peripheral type) T lymphocyte.[63,64,76]

Other cells normally present in the thymus include B cells (present both in the thymic medulla and in the perivascular compartment),[58] interdigitating reticulum cells, Langerhans' cells,[56] mast cells, eosinophils (particularly in neonates),[60] and the usual stromal cells. Aggregates of benign nevus cells have also been described within the substance of the thymus.[68]

A notable subtype of stromal-type cell found in the thymic medulla and possibly playing a role in the pathogenesis of myasthenia gravis is a skeletal muscle cell known as a *myoid cell*, of which a human cell line was recently established.[77] The embryologic origin and functional significance of these enigmatic cells remain controversial.[69]

The thymus undergoes normal involution after puberty, although it never disappears completely.[57,62,71,72] Islands of thymic tissue are consistently found on microscopic examination of the prepericardial fat and sometimes also in the retrocarinal fat.[59] The islands predominantly composed of lymphocytes may be confused with lymph nodes; those mainly made up of epithelial cells show trabecular or rosette-like formations and may be misinterpreted as carcinomatous or neuroendocrine[73] (Fig. 8.7). Occasionally, the epithelial component acquires a nodular character. This has been sometimes interpreted as a microthymoma but is probably a nodular hyperplasia (or a thymic tumorlet, so to speak) (Fig. 8.8).

Primary immunodeficiencies

Thymic dysplasia is the generic term that has been proposed for a congenital thymic alteration thought to be the expression of a failure and/or arrest in the development of the organ.[79,82,83] The most salient features are very small size (less than 5 g), primitive-appearing epithelium without segregation into cortical and medullary regions, presence of tubules and rosettes, absence of Hassall's corpuscles, and almost total absence of lymphocytes. Nezelof[83] has described four morphologic variations on the theme, which are more a reflection of the degree of severity of the process than an indicator of the specific

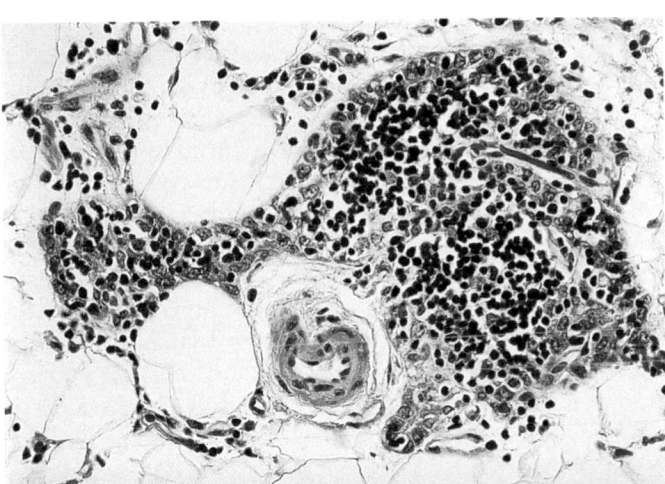

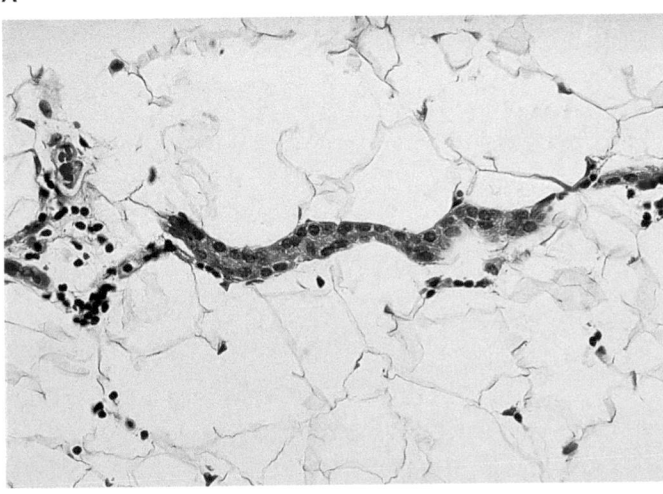

Fig. 8.7 Residual thymic tissue. **A,** This island is predominantly composed of small lymphocytes, but a row of epithelial cells is visible at the periphery. **B,** This thin elongated strand is predominantly composed of oval to spindle epithelial cells.

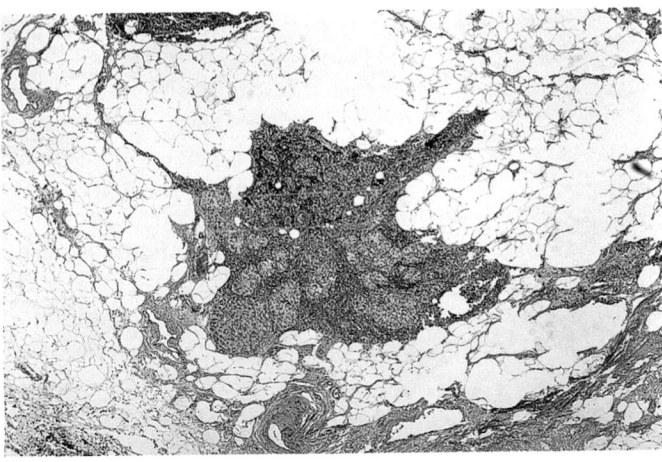

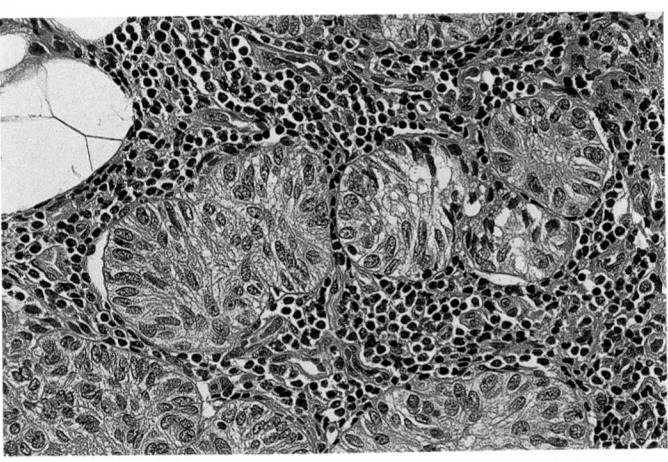

Fig. 8.8 A and **B,** Low-power and higher appearance of nodular hyperplasia of thymic epithelium ("thymic tumorlet").

type of immunodeficiency. Diseases accompanied by thymic dysplasia include the usual X-linked or autosomal recessive form of *severe combined immunodeficiency, ataxia–telangiectasia* and *related chromosomal instability syndromes, Nezelof syndrome*, and the *incomplete form of DiGeorge syndrome*; in the last condition, the thymus is not only dysplastic but often located ectopically.[81,83] In the complete form of DiGeorge syndrome the thymus is by definition absent (i.e., there is *thymic aplasia*).

In most other types of immunodeficiency there is no primary thymic abnormality. These include *congenital agammaglobulinemia* and *adenosine deaminase (ADA) deficiency* (also known as the ADA-negative form of severe combined immunodeficiency).[81]

The main differential diagnosis of thymic dysplasia is with the *acute thymic involution* resulting from "stress" and superimposed infections, which of course are often present in immunosuppressed populations, particularly at autopsy.[84] Acute thymic involution is characterized by marked lymphocytic depletion accompanied by preservation of the lobular architecture and of Hassall's corpuscles.[84] The identification of well-formed Hassall's corpuscles in a thymic biopsy is the best evidence against the diagnosis of primary thymic dysplasia. In some instances, these structures become prominent by virtue of their cystic dilatation, the cysts containing an admixture of keratin, calcium, and mucinous material.

In acute thymic involution, the size of the vessels is large for the size of the lobules, this being another important feature in the differential diagnosis with thymic dysplasia. A scattering of inflammatory cells is present in the interlobular and perilobular tissue, sometimes with a marked predominance of plasma cells. This acute involution process can proceed at a rapid rate, leading to almost complete lymphocytic depletion of the cortex within 1 week.[81]

Distinguishing thymic hyperplasia from acute thymic involution may be difficult in a small biopsy specimen or even at autopsy, a difficulty made greater by the fact that the two conditions often coexist.[80]

Cysts

Thymic cysts can be divided into two distinct types. **Unilocular thymic cysts** are of developmental origin, thought to originate from remnants of the third branchial pouch-derived thymopharyngeal duct. They are generally small, and located in the neck more often than in the mediastinum.[85] The cervical cysts can be found anywhere along a line extending from the angle of the mandible to the manubrium sternum.[92] The wall is thin and translucent, and inflammation is usually lacking. The epithelial lining is flattened, cuboidal, columnar, or (rarely) squamous. Thymic tissue is present in the wall, some of it connecting with the lining epithelium.

Multilocular thymic cyst is in all likelihood an acquired process of a reactive nature.[95] It is by definition

multilocular and always accompanied by inflammation and fibrosis (Fig. 8.9). It can be an incidental microscopic finding or result in a large tumorlike mass adherent to other mediastinal structures, simulating a malignant process at thoracotomy. The lining of the individual cysts may be flat, cuboidal, ciliated columnar, or (often) squamous, either single or stratified (Fig. 8.10). In some areas it may be absent, whereas in others it may have a highly reactive appearance, occasionally acquiring the features of pseudoepitheliomatous hyperplasia.[89,94] Cholesterol granulomas are common. We believe that multilocular thymic cyst is the result of an acquired cystic dilatation of medullary duct epithelium-derived structures, induced by an inflammatory reaction of the thymic parenchyma.[93,95] This inflammation is usually idiopathic, although in some cases a specific etiology (such as HIV infection) can be documented.[90] The so-called *Dubois' abscesses* described in the thymuses of neonates with congenital syphilis probably also belong to this category.[95]

Most importantly, a morphologically similar change can be seen in about half of the thymuses harboring nodular sclerosis Hodgkin's lymphoma or seminoma (germinoma). It can also be seen, although with much lesser frequency, in association with other tumors such as thymoma, large cell lymphoma, and yolk sac tumor. Therefore, in the presence of these cystic changes, it is important to determine whether the changes are purely inflammatory or whether an underlying neoplastic process is present. In regard to the pathogenesis of the lesion, it is of interest that the two malignant tumors most commonly associated with it are those in which a non-neoplastic lymphocytic component is particularly prominent.

We have made the proposal that the process of lymphocyte-induced cystic ductular dilatation resulting in multilocular thymic cyst is also responsible for the

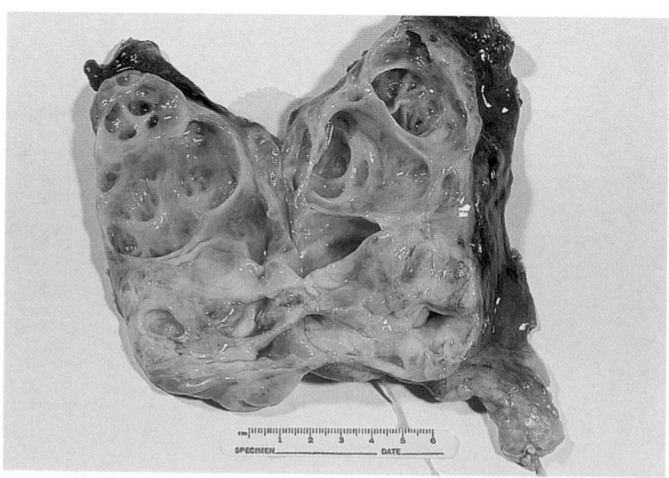

Fig. 8.9 Multilocular thymic cyst. The fibrous septa separating the individual cysts are rather thick. The content of the cysts varied from cloudy to blood tinged.

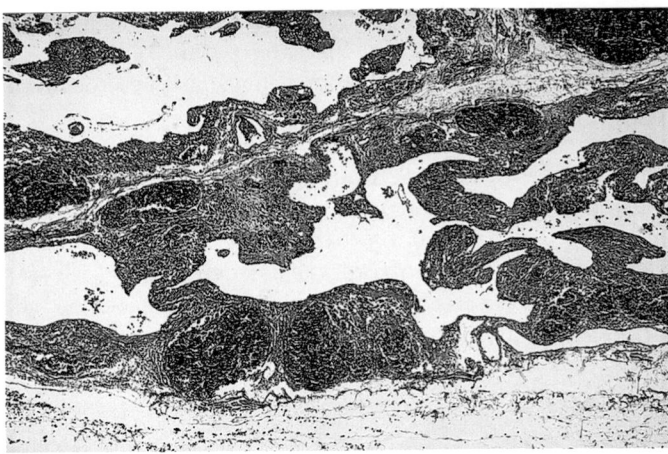

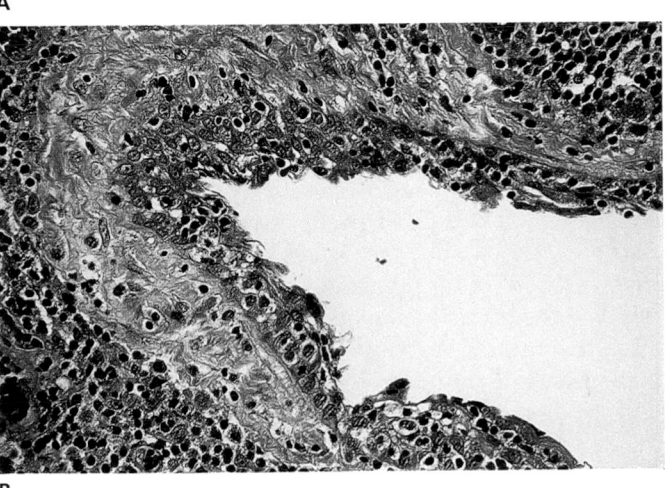

Fig. 8.10 A and **B,** Microscopic appearance of multilocular thymic cyst. This case was associated with thymic Hodgkin's lymphoma, not shown in the photographs. The high-power view shows the stratified squamous lining of the cyst, which is infiltrated by lymphocytes.

development of the following head and neck lesions: branchial cleft cyst, multiple branchial cleft-like cysts in Hashimoto's thyroiditis,[88] benign lymphoepithelial cysts, lymphoepithelial cysts in the parotid glands with HIV infection, and possibly even Warthin's tumor of parotid.[95]

Multilocular thymic cysts must be distinguished from thymomas undergoing cystic degeneration,[86,96] and from cystic lymphangioma.[91] Exceptionally, true squamous cell carcinomas arise from these cysts.[87]

Other non-neoplastic diseases

Ectopic thymus with an entirely normal microscopic appearance can present as a mass in the neck or pleural surface.[112] The maldescended thymic tissue in the neck can be unilateral or bilateral. It is often located adjacent to the thyroid gland and usually associated with a parathyroid gland.[99] Ectopic thymic tissue in the skin of the neck can be a clue to the diagnosis of the branchio-oculo-facial syndrome.[102a]

Ectopic tissues sometimes found in a normally located thymus include *parathyroid gland* (not surprising in view of their common embryogenesis) and *sebaceous glands.*[122]

Acute thymic involution is a constant feature of chronic, debilitating diseases.[113] As already stated, these changes are of a secondary nature and should not be misinterpreted as evidence of a primary immune defect. In patients with HIV infection, thymic involution is particularly pronounced and is accompanied by effacement of the corticomedullary junction, marked lymphocytic depletion, variable degrees of plasma cell infiltration and fibrosis, and inconspicuousness of Hassall's corpuscles.[107,118] Apparently, these late changes are preceded by thymic follicular hyperplasia (see later section).

True thymic hyperplasia is defined as thymic enlargement beyond the upper limits of normal for the age (as determined by weight using the Hammar's table or by volumetric determination) but accompanied by a microscopically normal gland. It has been most often described in infants or children,[98,109] but it has also been found in adults, sometimes after successful chemotherapy for malignant disease.[102,116] In some cases it may simply represent a failure of involution, but in others it is clearly an acquired phenomenon secondary to some therapeutic manipulation.[111]

Thymic follicular hyperplasia (often called simply "thymic hyperplasia," a misleading term) is defined as the presence of lymphoid follicles in the thymus independent of the size of the gland. Actually, the weight of most of the thymuses with lymphoid hyperplasia is within normal limits.[121] These follicles are of secondary type, with germinal center formation (Fig. 8.11), and they are largely composed of B lymphocytes, most of which contain immunoglobulins of the IgM and IgD classes.[110] According to some authors, this is accompanied by a disorderly arrangement and hypertrophy of medullary epithelial cells.[100,114]

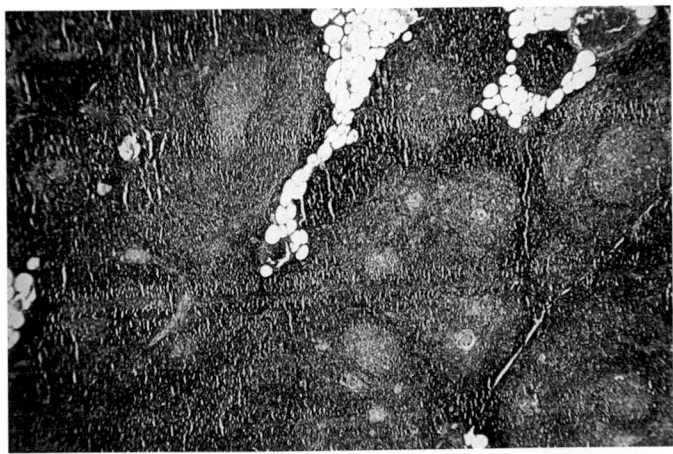

Fig. 8.11 Prominent follicular hyperplasia of thymus in a patient with myasthenia gravis. Florid germinal centers are present throughout the organ.

Follicular hyperplasia is seen in about 65% of the patients with myasthenia gravis (see next section). It is also commonly present in patients with hyperthyroidism, Addison's disease, lupus erythematosus, and other immune-mediated diseases.[115] It has also been described in the early stage of HIV infection, sometimes associated with multilocular cystic formation.[117]

A few germinal centers also may be found in the apparently normal thymus, especially during infancy and childhood; therefore only their presence in a substantial number in adult patients can be viewed as a distinctly abnormal finding.

Langerhans' cell histiocytosis (histiocytosis X) can present as a thymic mass in children, either alone or with involvement of other sites. The microscopic appearance is characteristic, and the overall prognosis is excellent.[119] Exceptionally, it is seen in association with myasthenia gravis.[101,103] It may also coexist with multilocular thymic cyst.[120] Granulomas containing numerous eosinophils and simulating Langerhans' cell histiocytosis can develop in the thymic capsule as a result of diagnostic pneumomediastinum, a procedure that has been largely abandoned[104,105]; they are probably equivalent to the reactive eosinophilic pleuritis seen in patients with pneumothorax.[97]

Other inflammatory diseases that can occasionally involve the thymus are **allergic angiitis and granulomatosis** (Churg–Strauss disease)[106] and **Castleman's disease** (giant lymph node hyperplasia)[108] (see p. 493).

Thymoma

General features

Thymoma is a term that should be restricted to neoplasms of thymic epithelial cells, independently of the presence or number of lymphocytes.[135,139] Seminoma, carcinoid tumor, Hodgkin's lymphoma, and non-Hodgkin's malignant lymphoma can all involve the thymus; thus they can be viewed as thymic tumors but should not be regarded as variants of thymoma.

Nearly all thymomas present in adult life. Thymomas in children are exceptional; most of the cases so diagnosed in the past actually represent lymphoblastic lymphomas of the thymus. However, some well-documented cases exist, most of them occurring near the age of puberty, with an appearance and behavior equivalent to that of their adult counterpart, including an occasional association with myasthenia gravis.[124,128,131,132,140] Some younger children are found to have highly malignant thymic neoplasms with unusual morphologic features, the nature of which has not yet been thoroughly elucidated.[127,141] Familial incidence of thymoma has been recorded only exceptionally.[143]

The usual location of thymoma is the anterosuperior mediastinum; however, this tumor can also occur in other mediastinal compartments (although a posterior location is very rare), in the neck,[136,144] within the thyroid (see later section), within the pericardial cavity,[137] in the pulmonary hilum, within the lung parenchyma,[130,134,141a] or in the pleura itself, sometimes coating it in a mesothelioma-like fashion.[123,129,138]

Radiographically, thymoma usually results in a lobulated shadow that may be calcified (Fig. 8.12). CT scan and magnetic resonance imaging (MRI) are the methods of choice for preoperative diagnosis and evaluation of extent.[133] Fine needle aspiration has been used with success, the diagnosis of thymoma being based on the finding of a dual population of epithelial cells and lymphocytes with the appropriate cytologic features.[125,126,142]

Myasthenia gravis

In patients with myasthenia gravis, the thymus shows follicular hyperplasia (see p. 465) as the only abnormality in about 65% of cases, a thymoma (with or without follicular hyperplasia in the non-neoplastic portion of the gland) in 10%, and no gross or overt microscopic abnormalities in 25% (see later text).[178] Viewed from another angle, this relationship is shown by the fact that about 30% to 45% of patients with thymoma develop myasthenia.[158,176] The tumor may be diagnosed during the investigation of a myasthenic patient, or—less commonly—the myasthenia may develop months or years after the tumor has been excised.[146,166] A patient with myasthenia is more likely to have a thymoma if male and/or developing symptoms after the age of 50.[163] The incidence of malignancy in these tumors seems to be similar to that seen among those with no myasthenic symptoms.[147,164,171] Thymomas associated with myasthenia almost always have epithelial cells of stellate or cuboidal rather than spindle shape, but only a percentage of the tumors with these morphologic features will be associated with myasthenia.

The relative proportion of epithelial cells and lymphocytes does not seem to correlate with the presence of myasthenia. No consistent ultrastructural or immunohistochemical differences have been found between myasthenic and nonmyasthenic thymomas.[179] Actually, the most accurate way to predict the likelihood of myasthenia in a patient with thymoma is to find lymphoid follicles in the adjacent non-neoplastic thymic tissue or, exceptionally, even in the thymoma itself.[145]

In the past, the presence of myasthenia in a patient with thymoma had a profound influence on survival. Thus, in a large series reported by Wilkins et al.,[178] the 10-year cumulative survival rate for patients with thymoma with and without myasthenia was 32% and 67%, respectively. Most of the deaths in the former group resulted from myasthenic crisis. As a consequence of marked improvements in the medical treatment of myasthenia, the picture has changed dramatically.[149] As a matter of fact, the presence or absence of myasthenia in recent series of patients with thymomas shows that this association is no longer of prognostic significance.

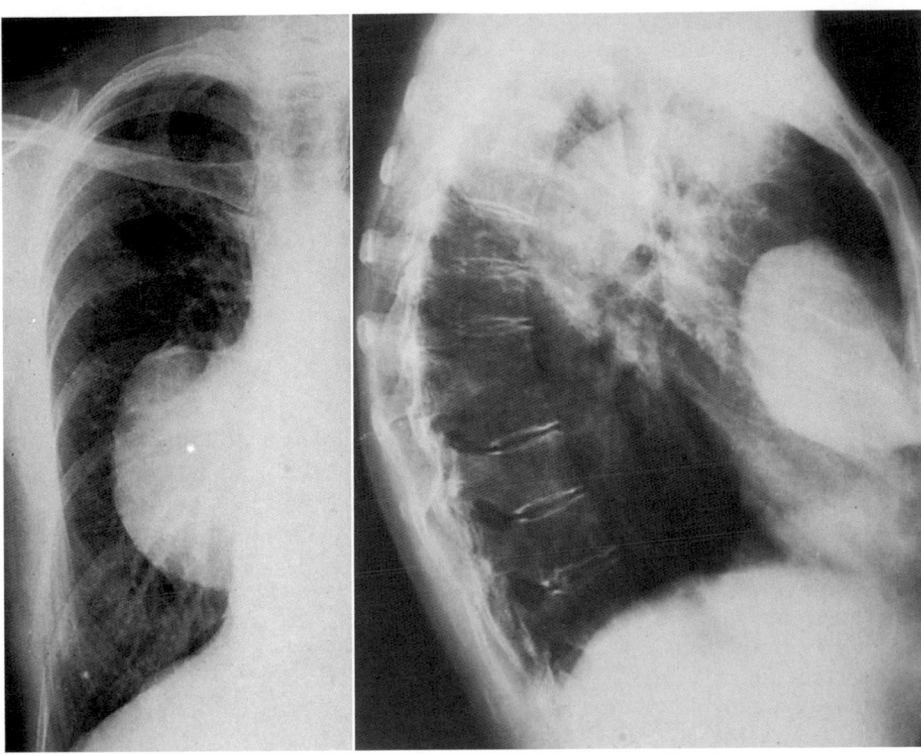

Fig. 8.12 Lobulated large benign thymoma located in anterior portion of mediastinum.

Myasthenia gravis has been found to be related in nearly all cases to a defect in the nicotinic acetylcholine receptor (AChR) located in the subsynaptic membrane of the neuromuscular junction (motor end plate), as a result of circulating autoantibodies that bind to this molecule.[160,173,174]

AChR or a related protein has been detected in the normal thymus.[156,169] Although it has been suggested that this compound might be expressed by thymic epithelial cells, it seems clear that it is mainly, if not entirely, localized to a subset of intrathymic cells that exhibit phenotypical features of skeletal muscle cells (such as cross striations and immunoreactivity for myoglobin and desmin) and that are generally designated as myoid cells.[148,157] It has also been found that non-neoplastic thymuses in myasthenic patients (whether exhibiting obvious follicular hyperplasia or appearing microscopically normal on superficial inspection) often contain cell clusters composed of myoid cells, infiltrating reticulum cells, and CD3+, CD4+ T lymphocytes, that some of these T lymphocytes are AChR-specific, that activated AChR-reactive B cells may also be demonstrated, and that there is increased in situ production of interleukins.[150,151,161] The theory has thus evolved that the autosensitization process leading to myasthenia is initiated in the thymus through an aberrant confrontation of myoid cells with AChR-specific autoimmune T lymphocytes, followed by emigration of these activated thymic T cells to the peripheral immune system and induction of complementary B lymphocytes to produce myasthenogenic autoantibodies.[161,175]

The role that thymoma, when present, plays in this pathogenetic scheme remains unclear. Some have suggested that the two events are not directly related and that the mechanism for the myasthenia is that previously described, independently of the presence or absence of a tumor in the gland. Others have postulated that the thymoma is directly responsible for the myasthenia, through the presence of one or more proteins in the tumor that share an antigenic determinant with the nicotinic AChR or other structures of the neuromuscular junction and that trigger an autoimmune response.[153,159,160]

It should also be noted that myasthenic patients who have thymomas may also feature autoantibodies to striated muscle antigens such as titin,[154,180] even if it is not clear whether these antibodies are important in the development of myasthenia.

About 12% of patients with myasthenia have other autoimmune diseases, such as Graves' disease and rheumatoid arthritis.[165] A most peculiar association that has been recently described is that between myasthenia and generalized hair follicle hamartoma of the skin.[177]

Myasthenia gravis should be distinguished from the Lambert–Eaton syndrome, a clinically somewhat similar condition that is frequently associated with pulmonary small cell carcinoma and that is also immune related[155] (see Chapter 7).

The treatment of myasthenia includes thymectomy, regardless of the presence or absence of thymoma.[149] This indication also applies to cases that began in childhood,[181] and probably also to those with only ocular symptoms.[170] Unless the tumor is very large, the operation can usually be carried out through a transcervical route. Symptomatic improvement is more likely if the thymus is the site of follicular hyperplasia than if it is normal or involved by thymoma.[168] The long-term results of the operation are somewhat related to the duration and severity of the myasthenic symptoms but not to the age of the patient; however, substantial differences in this regard exist among the various published series.[152,162,163,168] Persistence of symptoms has been attributed to residual thymic tissue with lymphoid hyperplasia.[167]

The fact that myasthenia gravis is one of the few autoimmune diseases in which the target autoantigen has been characterized brings hope that specific immunotherapy against it may eventually be developed.[172]

Other associated diseases

In addition to myasthenia gravis, thymoma has been found to be associated with a large number of systemic disorders, nearly all of which are immune mediated. These include hypogammaglobulinemia (12% of the cases), erythroid hypoplasia (5%),[186] and, more rarely, white blood cell aplasia,[182] myositis, myocarditis, dermatomyositis, lupus erythematosus, rheumatoid arthritis, scleroderma, Sjögren's disease, multiple myeloma, Kaposi's sarcoma,[193] subacute motor neuronopathy,[198] inappropriate antidiuretic hormone secretion,[190] bullous dermatoses, hyperglobulinemic purpura, mucocutaneous candidiasis,[187,194] graft-versus-host-like colitis,[188] autoimmune enteropathy,[192] peripheral T-cell lymphocytosis[185,191,196] (some proved to be the result of an aberrant T-cell oligoclone in the thymoma[183]), T-cell chronic lymphocytic leukemia,[199] and T-cell lymphoblastic lymphoma/leukemia.[184] In addition, it has been claimed that patients with thymoma have an increased incidence of malignant tumors, including lymphoma.[195,197] Most of the thymomas associated with erythroid hypoplasia have been said to be largely composed of spindle cells (type A thymomas), but a recent study on the subject with a critical review of the literature did not show a strong correlation with a particular histologic type.[189]

Pathologic features; electron microscopic, histochemical, immunohistochemical and molecular genetic features

Grossly, the typical thymoma is largely or entirely solid, yellowish gray, and separated in lobules by connective tissue septa[237,251,262] (Figs 8.13 and 8.14). In approximately 80% of cases, the tumor is well encapsulated and can be removed with ease. In the remainder, infiltration of surrounding structures is noted at surgery. Most clinically evident tumors are large, but widespread performance of coronary bypass surgery has led to the discovery of a large number of small, sometimes microscopic thymomas.[254] Foci of necrosis and cystic degeneration are common, particularly among larger tumors. Sometimes the entire tumor undergoes prominent cystic, necrotic

and hemorrhagic changes, many sections being needed to identify residual diagnostic areas (Fig. 8.15).[247] Predominantly cystic thymomas should be distinguished from multilocular thymic cysts (which can coexist with thymoma, see p. 464) and other thymic neoplasms prone to undergo cystic changes.[271]

Microscopically, the majority of thymomas are composed of a mixture of neoplastic epithelial cells and non-neoplastic lymphocytes, the proportion among them varying widely from case to case and in different lobules of the same tumor[258,260,262] (Figs 8.16 to 8.22). The epithelial cells may have a round–polygonal ("plump"), stellate, or spindle oval shape (Figs 8.16 and 8.19). The nuclei are vesicular and of smooth contour; the nucleolus may be conspicuous, particularly when the nuclei are round or polygonal (see p. 477). The lymphocytes may appear mature (inactive) or show varying degrees of "activation" manifested by a larger nuclear size, open chromatin pattern, visible nucleolus, identifiable cytoplasmic rim,

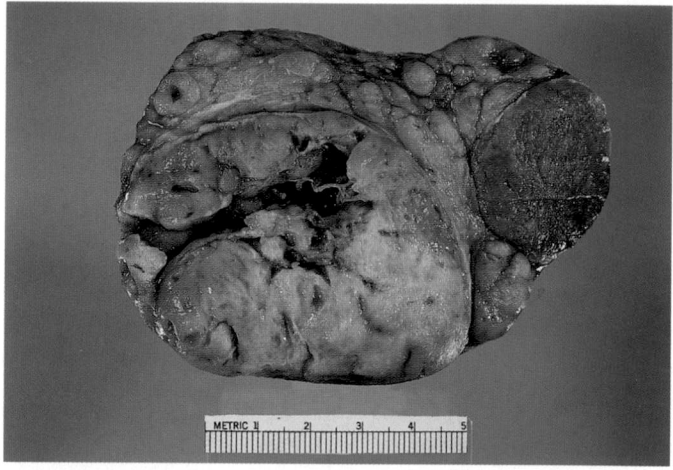

Fig. 8.13 Gross appearance of a thymoma showing distinct multinodularity. There is focal cystic change in the larger nodule.

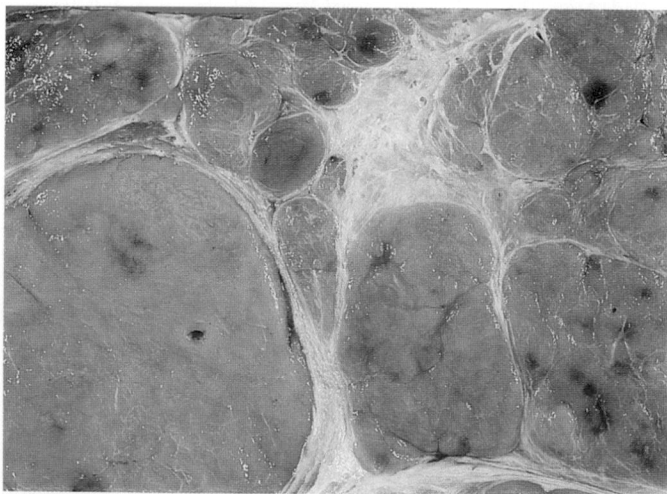

Fig. 8.14 Close-up of the cut surface of thymoma. Note the sharp lobulation induced by the fibrous bands. The pointed ends of some of the nodules are particularly typical of this entity.

and mitotic activity; however, they should not appear convoluted or cleaved. Thymomas with a sizable component of epithelial cells often show one or more features suggestive of organoid differentiation, which correlate with the various subtypes (see p. 476). These include perivascular spaces containing lymphocytes, proteinaceous fluid, red blood cells, foamy macrophages, or fibrous tissue (Fig. 8.20); rosettes without central lumina; glandlike formations within the tumor or, more often, in the tumor capsule; true glandular structures (an

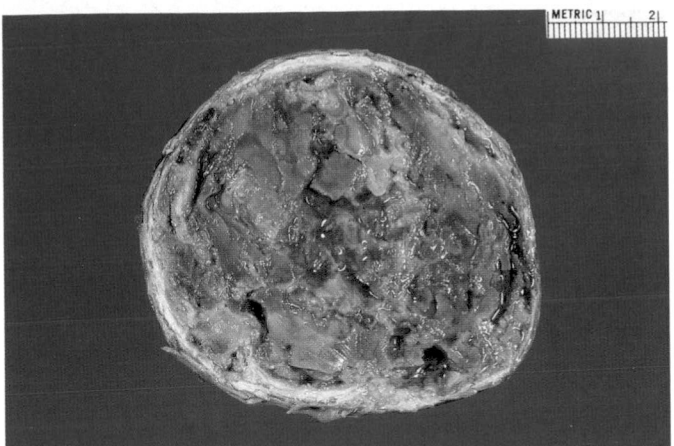

Fig. 8.15 Thymoma with extensive necrosis and cystic degeneration. Only one of many microscopic sections showed residual neoplasm. This lesion is likely to be misdiagnosed as a thymic cyst.

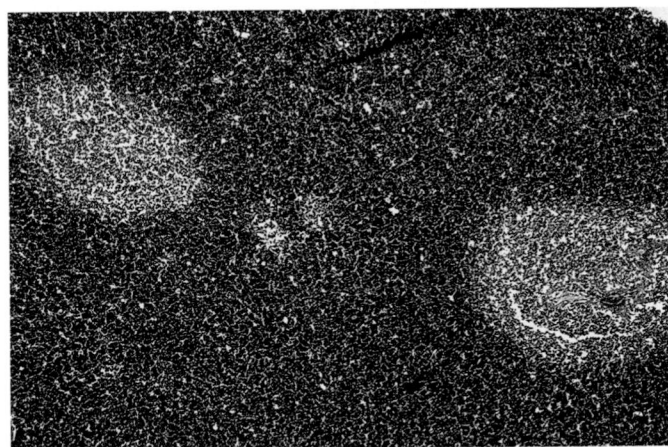

Fig. 8.18 Type B1 thymoma with prominent foci of medullary differentiation.

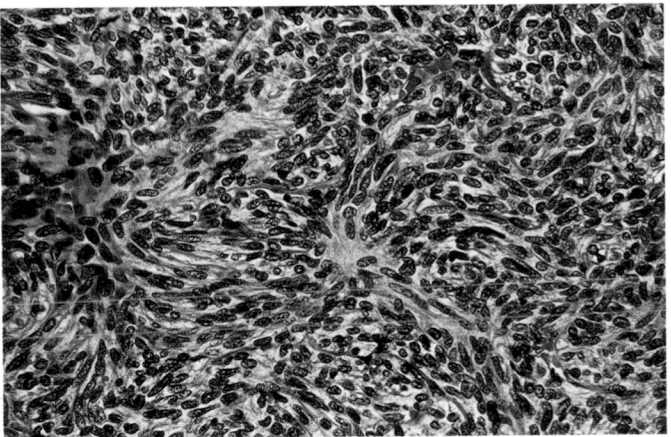

Fig. 8.16 Type A (spindle, medullary) thymoma. The pseudomesenchymal appearance of the tumor is striking.

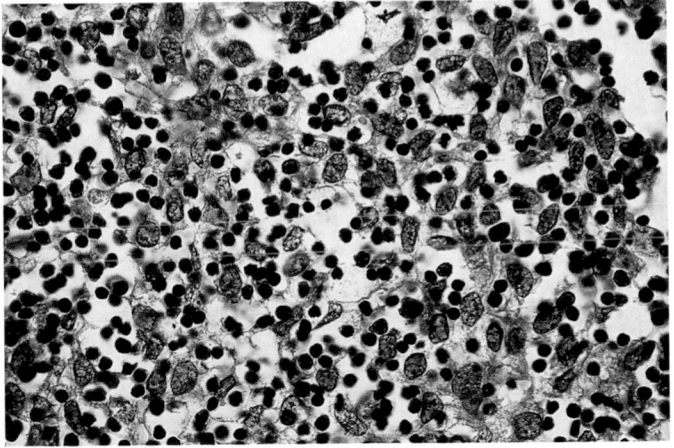

Fig. 8.19 Type B2 thymoma. There is an even proportion of neoplastic epithelial cells and non-neoplastic lymphocytes.

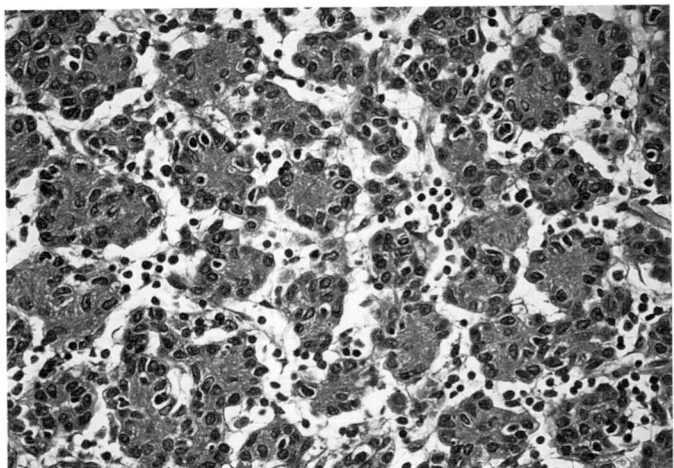

Fig. 8.17 Type A thymoma with prominent rosette formation. Notice the absence of a central lumen in the rosettes. This tumor should not be confused with thymic carcinoid.

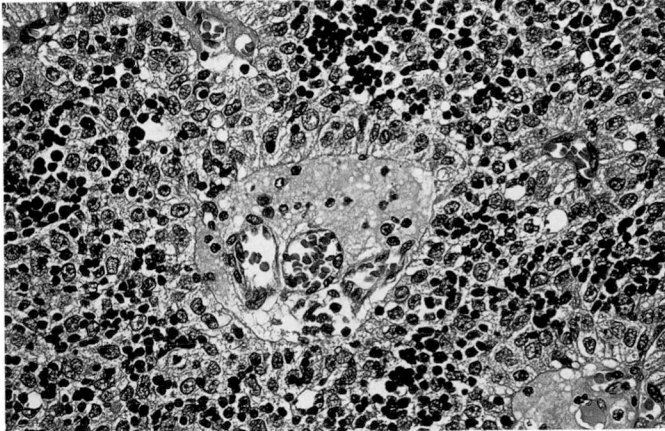

Fig. 8.20 Perivascular space in type B2 thymoma. The space is occupied by a proteinaceous fluid and lymphocytes.

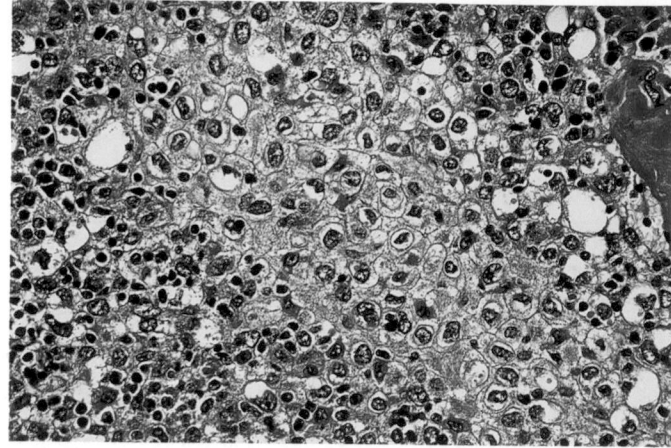

Fig. 8.21 Type B3 thymoma. This tumor, which is predominantly composed of slightly atypical neoplastic thymic epithelial cells, is also known as squamoid thymoma, atypical thymoma, and well-differentiated (organotypic) thymic carcinoma.

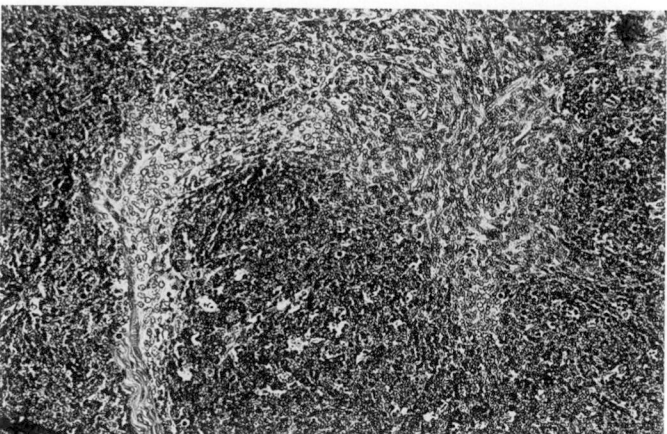

Fig. 8.22 Type AB (mixed) thymoma. The type A areas can be easily confused with hypercellular septa. This is one of the most common thymoma subtypes.

exceptional event); and whorls suggestive of abortive Hassall's corpuscle formation.[250,251,260] Well-formed Hassall's corpuscles are occasionally found within thymomas, but their presence in large numbers is usually an indication of preexisting structures surrounded by a tumor and is actually more common in other neoplasms (such as malignant lymphoma of the thymus) than in thymoma. Presence of rosette-like structures with *well-defined lumina* should suggest a diagnosis of thymic carcinoid rather than thymoma. In lymphocyte-rich (type B1, see later section) thymomas, it is common to find round, lighter foci of medullary differentiation, an important clue to the diagnosis (Fig. 8.18). Other helpful diagnostic features of thymoma are the thick, often calcified fibrous capsule, the lobular arrangement induced by these fibrous bands, the sharp interphase between tumor lobules and fibrous tracts, and the angular shape of some of the lobules. Vascularization may be prominent and may result in a mistaken diagnosis of hemangiopericytoma. Microcystic and pseudopapillary formations may be focally prominent. Sclerosis may be very extensive, possibly as a manifestation of tumor regression.[226] Exceptionally, there is a massive plasma cell infiltrate[248] or deposition of amyloid.[230]

By electron microscopy, the neoplastic epithelial cells exhibit branching tonofilaments, complex desmosomes, elongated cell processes, and basal lamina[238,239] (Fig. 8.23).

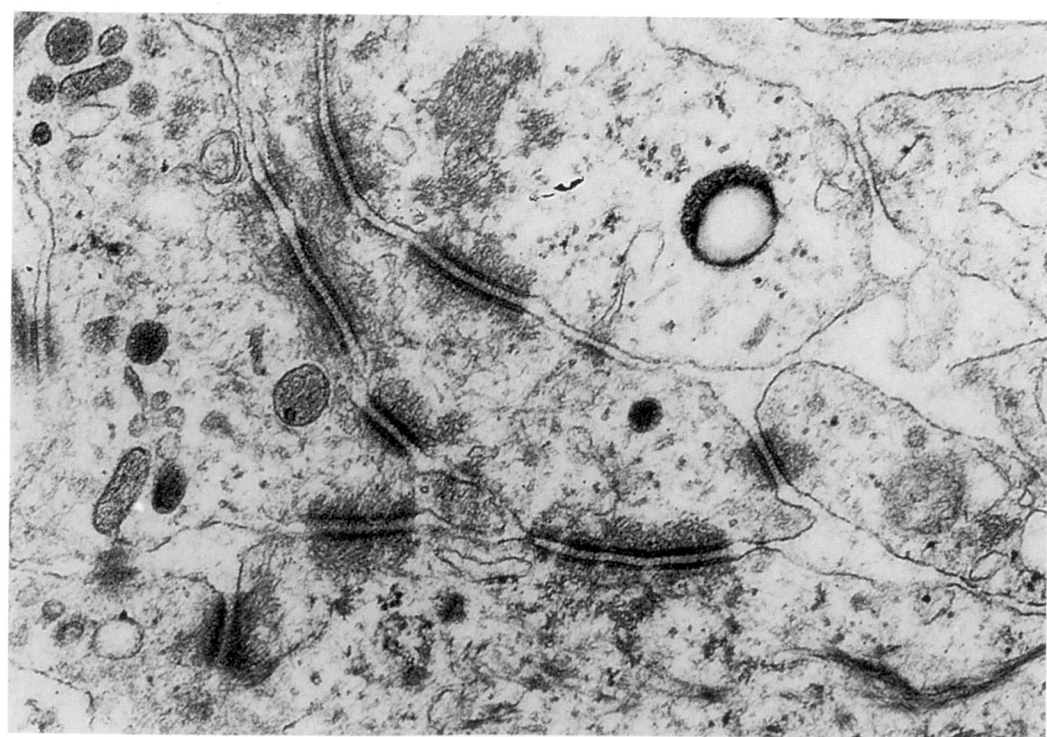

Fig. 8.23 Numerous desmosomes and tonofibrils in tumor cells indicate epithelial origin of a thymoma composed of spindle cells. (Uranyl acetate–lead citrate; ×54,500; from Levine GD, Bensch KG. Epithelial nature of spindle cell thymoma. An ultrastructural study. Cancer 1972, **30**: 500–511)

These characteristics have proved historically useful in the segregation of thymoma from other anterior mediastinal tumors, such as thymic carcinoid, malignant lymphoma, seminoma, and solitary fibrous tumor[212,239] (Table 8.1).

Immunohistochemically, the epithelial cells of thymoma exhibit reactivity for keratin, epithelial membrane antigen (EMA), and carcinoembryonic antigen (CEA)[201,244,263,264] (Fig. 8.24). The types of keratin expressed vary according to the thymoma subtype.[227] The EMA positivity is usually restricted either to the glandlike formations of spindle thymomas or to the tumors predominantly composed of round or polygonal cells.[210] Thymomas have also been found to express the tissue blood group O (H) and peanut agglutinin receptor antigens,[280] MHC class II molecules,[205] p63 (particularly in isoporm ΔN-p63α)[204a] epidermal and nerve growth factor receptors,[253] growth hormone,[234] metallothionein,[231] and the viral protein p19.[244] In addition, they react for A_2B_5 and Leu7, two antibodies that recognize neuroendocrine cells.[244] French[211,265] and Japanese[214] groups have claimed to detect reactivity for the thymic hormones thymulin and thymosin α-1, a controversial finding that needs to be investigated further in terms of frequency and specificity.

Markers that are present only in thymic carcinomas (type C thymomas) but not in conventional (types A, AB, and B) thymomas are discussed on p. 473.

Stains for basement membrane material, such as laminin or type IV collagen, show abundant deposition around individual tumor cells in spindle-shaped tumors, and paucity of this material in those made up of stellate or round or polygonal cells.[243]

The lymphocytes of thymoma are of T-cell derivation, except for those located in lymphoid follicles (whether the patients have myasthenia gravis or not).[224] Most of these T lymphocytes do not have the enzymatic and immunohistochemical phenotype of mature (peripheral) T cells but rather of immature thymocytes.[233,252,281] As such, they are reactive for CD99 and CD1a.[206,256] Many of

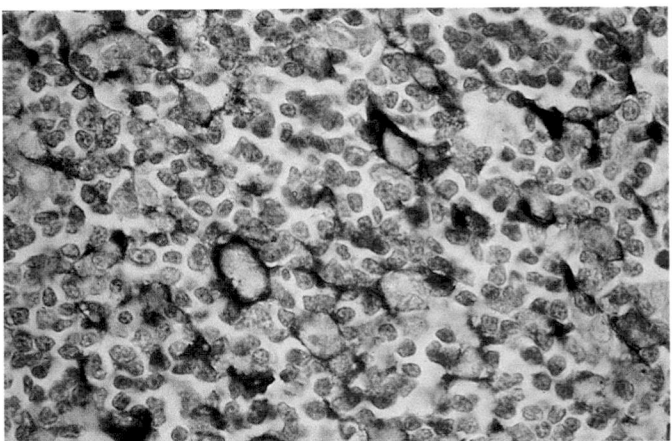

Fig. 8.24 Type B1 (lymphocyte-rich) thymoma stained for keratin. The cytoplasm and cell processes of the neoplastic epithelial cells are strongly immunoreactive for this marker.

them are also positive for Ki-67, in keeping with their "stimulated" status.[204] A close correlation has been found between the morphologic features of the more organoid thymomas and the phenotype of the lymphocytes. In the more lymphocyte-rich areas, the lymphocytes have the features of cortical (very immature) thymocytes; in areas of medullary differentiation they acquire features of medullary (less immature) thymocytes. It should be pointed out that *both* the lymphocytes of thymoma and those of lymphoblastic lymphoma usually exhibit an immature T phenotype, and therefore cell marker studies cannot be used to separate these two disorders. Instead, it has been shown that the lymphocytes of thymoma do not show evidence of clonality at the molecular level, even if this can be simulated by the presence of a polyclonal incomplete rearrangement of the T-cell receptor gene.[220,255] This finding not only provides another criterion for distinguishing the two entities but also offers corroborating evidence for the non-neoplastic nature of the lymphocytes of thymoma. Incidentally, the number of these non-neoplastic lymphocytes will be greatly decreased in patients who have been treated preoperatively with corticosteroids.[275]

In addition to epithelial cells and lymphocytes, thymomas often contain an important population of S-100 protein-positive cells, presumably non-neoplastic and of interdigitating reticulum cell nature.[223,235,261] Kondo et al.[222] found that their number and distribution correlated with the microscopic type of thymoma but not with invasiveness. Interestingly, there is also a population of interdigitating cells (designated as "asteroid cells") located in the medullary portion of the more organoid thymomas, that react immunohistochemically for the B-cell marker CD20.[276] Even more peculiar (and potentially misleading from a diagnostic standpoint) is the fact that the latter marker sometimes also reacts with some of the neoplastic epithelial cells of the thymoma, as evidenced by the coexpression of keratin by these cells.[203]

Cytogenetically, the most frequent aberrations found in thymoma are located on chromosome 6, half of them occurring in region 6q25.2.[219,284] The type and frequency of these aberrations vary among the thymoma subtypes, suggesting that these tumors may develop along different pathways.[285]

Coexpression of bcl-2 and p53 is seen in the majority of thymomas, and seems to be stronger in the clinically aggressive tumors[202,208,277] (see p. 473). There is also common expression of Fas antigen, another apoptosis-related marker.[273]

Thymic carcinoma is defined as a thymic epithelial tumor (i.e., a thymoma) exhibiting clearcut cytologic features of malignancy[257,279] (Fig. 8.25). Despite its rarity, it displays a relatively large variety of microscopic patterns, described in the following text. As a group, they differ from all other types of thymomas in the following respects: (1) they are very rarely associated with

Table 8.1 Differential features of tumors of the anterior mediastinum*

Features	Thymoma*	Large cell lymphoma	Lymphoblastic lymphoma	Thymic Hodgkin's lymphoma	Thymic seminoma	Thymic carcinoid
Patterns (low-power observation)	Sharply defined, angular lobules; Fibrous bands and capsule; Mottling and trabeculation (caused by epithelial–lymphocyte admixture)	Diffuse growth; Variable fibrosis with occasional compartmentalizing sclerotic pattern; Residual cystic thymus	Diffuse growth or pseudonodular pattern (both in lymph nodes and in thymus)	Extensive fibrosis with rounded lobules of tumor; Prominent cysts seen at low power	Subdivided by fine fibrous trabeculae into variable-sized compartments	Ribbons, festoons, punctate calcified necrosis producing discrete and rounded masses of tumor
Nuclei	Often fine chromatin contrasting with well-defined nuclear membrane; Usually inconspicuous nucleoli; great variation, including spindle shape; Epithelial mitoses usually rare	Vesicular with prominent nucleoli; Marked folding of nuclei ("cloverleaf"); Variable chromatin pattern; Mitotic figures variable (usually readily found)	Even chromatin ("dusky" at low power); Scant inconspicuous nucleoli; Numerous mitotic figures	Cytologic features—those of nodular sclerosing Hodgkin's lymphoma complicated by admixture with thymic epithelium and cysts	Coarse chromatin; marked prominence of nucleoli, variable numbers of mitotic figures	Rounded nuclei with sharp stippling chromatin; Variable number of mitotic figures (note spindle cell variant)
Cytoplasm	Great variation from scant to squamoid to squamous; Intracytoplasmic cysts (emperipolesis); Glandlike spaces	Variable, occasionally abundant and rich in RNA (methyl green–pyronine positive)	Scant	Lacunar cells often prominent	Marked retraction of cytoplasm; often glycogen-rich	Polyhedral cells with finely granular eosinophilic cytoplasm; True gland formation
Associated features	Germinal centers in surrounding thymus (in cases of myasthenia gravis); Incorporation of non-neoplastic thymus (13%)	Residual lymphocytes often form tight perivascular cuffs; Necrosis frequent; Markedly invasive	Residual Hassall's corpuscles		Germinal centers, epithelioid and giant cells	
Electron microscopy	Well-formed desmosomes; Bundles of tonofilaments	Nuclear blebs; Absence of epithelial features	Nuclear blebs; Fine chromatin; Absence of epithelial features	Absence of epithelial characteristics in Reed–Sternberg cells	Even chromatin; Prominent nucleoli; Glycogen-rich; Scant desmosomes; Only rare tonofilaments	Dense-core granules; Desmosomes inconspicuous or poorly formed; Tonofilaments only rarely prominent
Immunohisto-chemistry	Keratin	B-lymphocyte markers	T-lymphocyte markers	CD15, CD30	PLAS, CD117	Chromogranin, synaptophysin

Slightly modified from Levine GD, Rosai J. Thymic hyperplasia and neoplasia. A review of current concepts. Hum Pathol 1978, **9**: 495–515.
*Nuclear and cytoplasmic features refer only to epithelium.

myasthenia gravis or any of the other immune-mediated systemic diseases listed on p. 468; (2) they generally lack all of the ancillary features of thymoma seen with one or another of the other types, such as perivascular spaces, foci of medullary differentiation, abortive Hassall's corpuscles, rosettes, or glandlike spaces; and (3) they lack immature T lymphocytes. Lymphocytes may be present and even numerous, but they exhibit the phenotype of mature T or (rarely) B cells. In other words, thymic carcinomas lack all of the morphologic and functional attributes of the other thymoma types, allowing for the rare occurrence of intermediate or hybrid forms (Fig. 8.26). Their appearance is instead similar to and sometimes indistinguishable from that of corresponding carcinoma types in other organs, and their specific identification as thymic neoplasms can therefore be difficult or impossible. The diagnosis is often one of exclusion, in the presence of a malignant epithelial tumor located in the thymic region in the absence of disease in the lung or any other organ. There are some immunostains, however, that can be of great assistance in the identification of the two major subtypes of thymic carcinomas (see below). The first is CD5 (a receptor molecule that signals cell growth in T cells), which is present in the majority of thymic carcinomas but absent in other types of thymomas and in carcinomas of nonthymic origin.[225,274] Another is CD70, a member of the tumor necrosis factor family that mediates the interaction between B and T lymphocytes and which is again present in most thymic carcinomas but not in other thymomas.[216] Yet another is TTF-1, which stains a high percentage of lung carcinomas but not thymic carcinomas. Furthermore, thymic carcinomas have a higher expression of p53 and a stronger immunoreactivity of bcl-2 than thymomas.[252a] It should also be noted that the majority of thymic carcinomas—in striking contrast with the other thymoma types—exhibit immunohistochemical evidence of focal (and sometimes extensive) neuroendocrine differentiation (Fig. 8.27).[215,228,232]

The following microscopic types of thymic carcinoma have been recognized by the WHO Committee for the Histologic Typing of Tumors of the Thymus[259]:

Epidermoid keratinizing (squamous cell) carcinoma. This form is rich in atypical epithelial cells, many of which undergo keratinization[229,266] (Fig. 8.28). The appearance is very similar to that of squamous cell carcinoma at other sites. However, a lobular pattern of growth is generally maintained, and the tumor lobules are even more widely separated from each other by fibrous bands than in the other thymoma types[270] (Fig. 8.29). Before a diagnosis of primary squamous cell carcinoma of the thymus is made, the alternative possibility of metastatic carcinoma (particularly from the lung) should always be considered.

Epidermoid nonkeratinizing carcinoma. The overall appearance is similar to the tumors in the previous category, but the lobulation is less developed and there are no overt signs of keratinization.

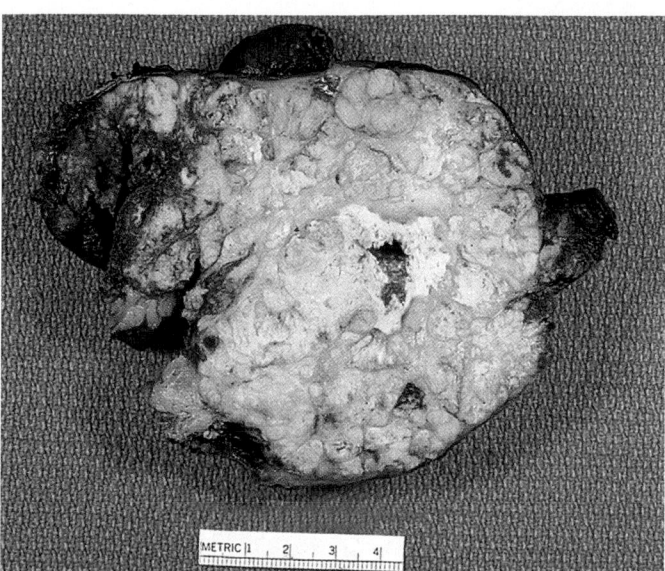

Fig. 8.25 Gross appearance of thymic carcinoma (type C thymoma). The tumor is invasive and shows foci of necrosis.

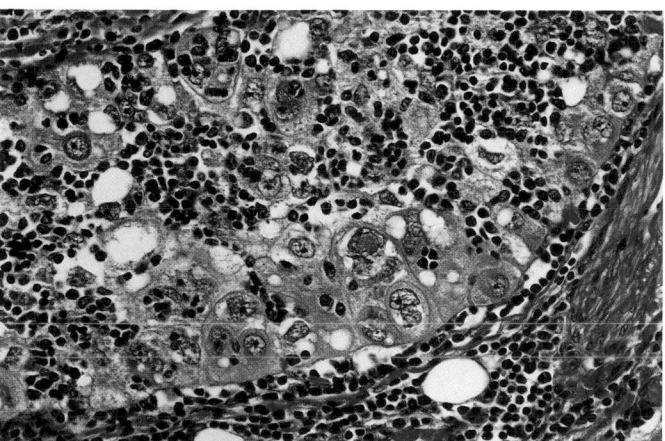

Fig. 8.26 Thymic tumor bridging the gap between thymoma and thymic carcinoma. The degree of atypia in the neoplastic cell is such as to justify a diagnosis of thymic carcinoma (type C thymoma), but the overall configuration of the tumor and the phenotype of the lymphocytes were those of conventional thymoma.

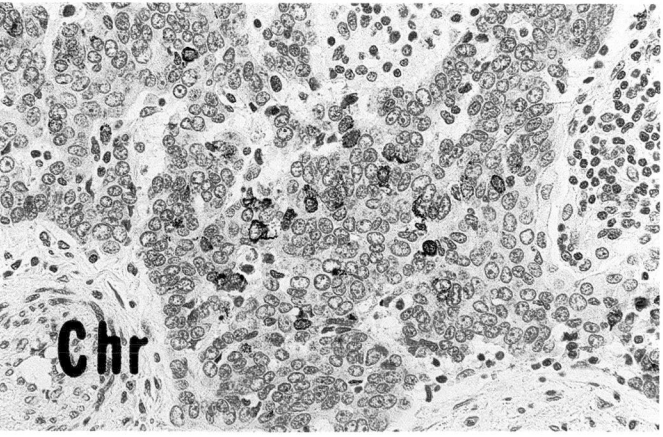

Fig. 8.27 Chromogranin reactivity in some tumor cells of thymic carcinoma (type C thymoma). This is a common finding in this subtype, as opposed to types A, AB, and B thymomas.

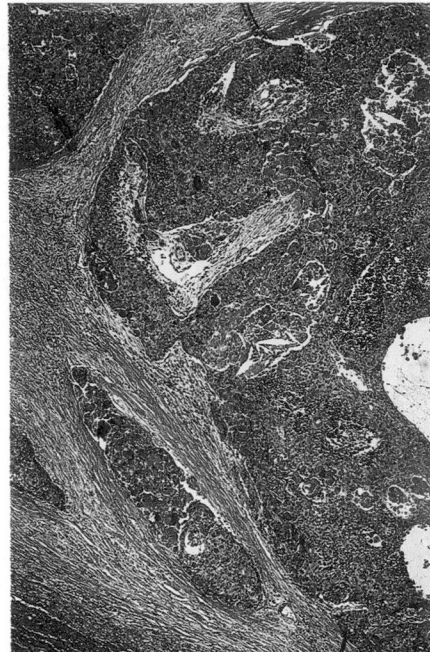

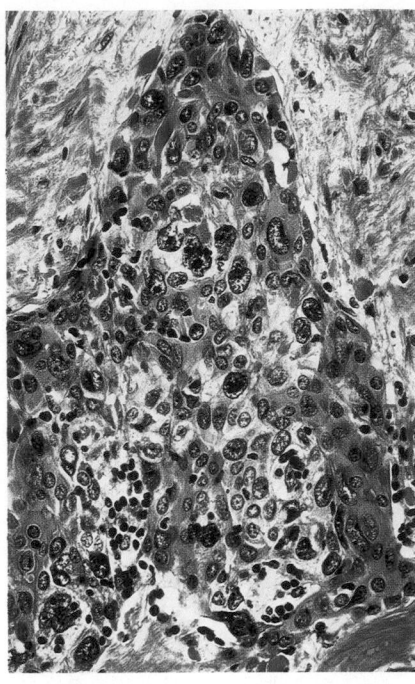

Fig. 8.28 A and **B**, Low-power and high-power appearances of thymic carcinoma of keratinizing squamous type. Note the distinct lobulation.

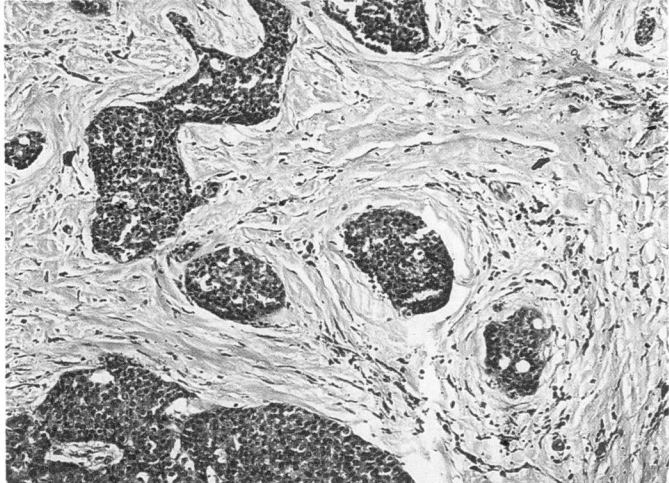

Fig. 8.29 Low-power view of thymic carcinoma (type C thymoma). The tumor lobules are more widely separated by fibrous tissue and smaller than in the conventional thymoma.

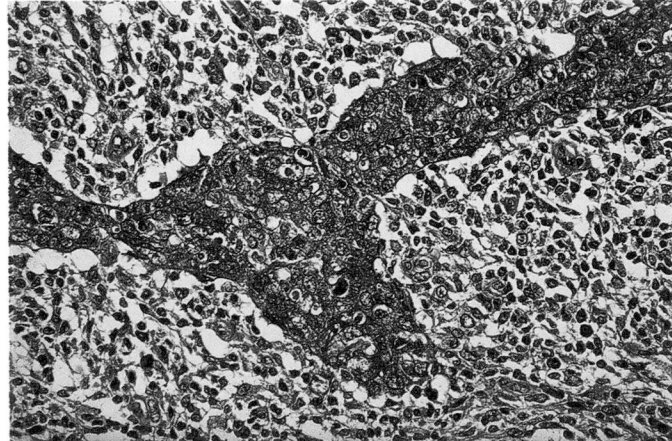

Fig. 8.30 Nonkeratinizing undifferentiated type of thymic carcinoma. The tumor has a lymphoepithelioma-like quality.

Lymphoepithelioma-like carcinoma. The appearance of the tumor approaches, and sometimes becomes indistinguishable from, that of so-called "lymphoepithelioma" of the tonsil and nasopharynx. Large, deeply acidophilic nucleoli that are sharply outlined and perfectly round are the hallmark of this neoplasm, which is also characterized by a "syncytial" appearance (Fig. 8.30). Keratinization and intercellular bridges are absent; however, the tumor cells are consistently immunoreactive for keratin. The lymphocytes of this tumor, which can be very numerous, have the phenotype of mature peripheral T cells rather than the immature thymocytic phenotype seen in ordinary thymoma. The finding of the Epstein–Barr virus (EBV) genome in several (but not all)

cases of this entity suggests that the similarity with nasopharyngeal carcinoma extends beyond the morphologic parameters.[209,240,241] Evidence of EBV is consistently absent from other thymoma types, despite initial reports to the contrary.[200,218,282]

Sarcomatoid carcinoma (carcinosarcoma). This cytologically malignant tumor simulates a mesenchymal neoplasm by virtue of its diffuse pattern of growth and the prominent spindling of tumor cells. The diagnosis is made by finding, somewhere in the tumor, foci of epithelial appearance[267] or evidence of epithelial differentiation in the spindle cells immunohistochemically or ultrastructurally (Fig. 8.31). Some authors draw a distinction between sarcomatoid or spindle cell carcinoma on one side and carcinosarcoma on the other,[268] but we regard the exercise just as futile as in other organs, in the sense that

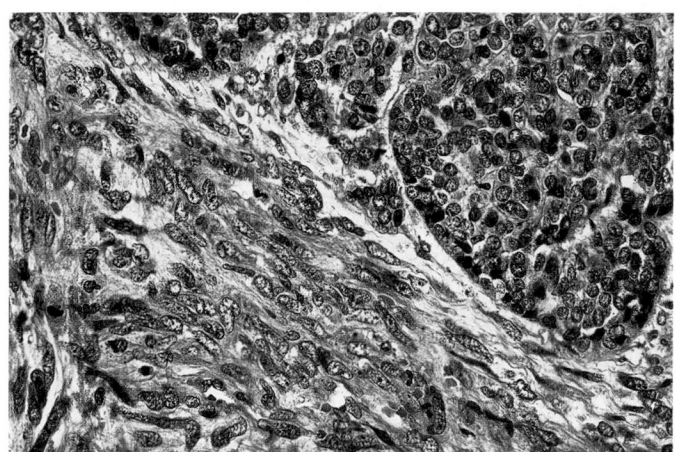

Fig. 8.31 Sarcomatoid carcinoma of thymus. Because of the sharp segregation of the carcinomatous and the sarcoma-like components, tumors with this appearance are often called carcinosarcomas.

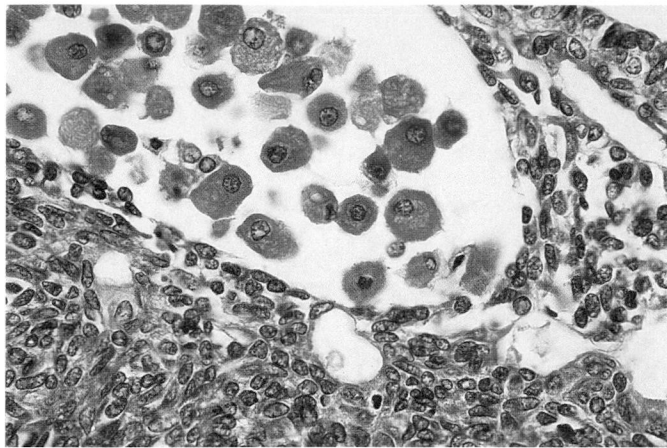

Fig. 8.32 Thymoma with clusters of myoid cells showing abundant eosinophilic cytoplasm. These cells were strongly immunoreactive for myoglobin.

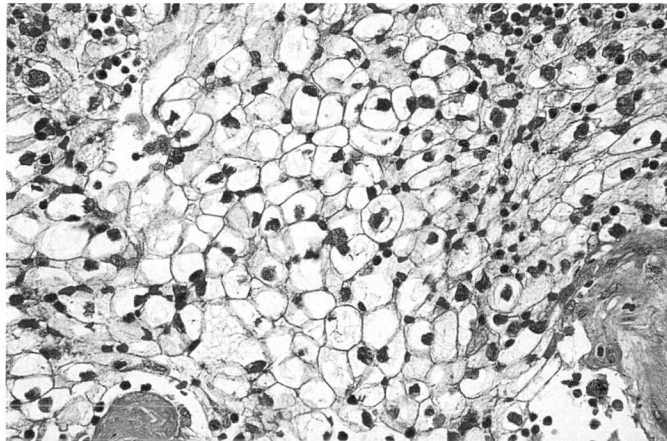

Fig. 8.33 Thymic carcinoma of clear cell type. This tumor needs to be distinguished from metastatic carcinoma, particularly from the kidney.

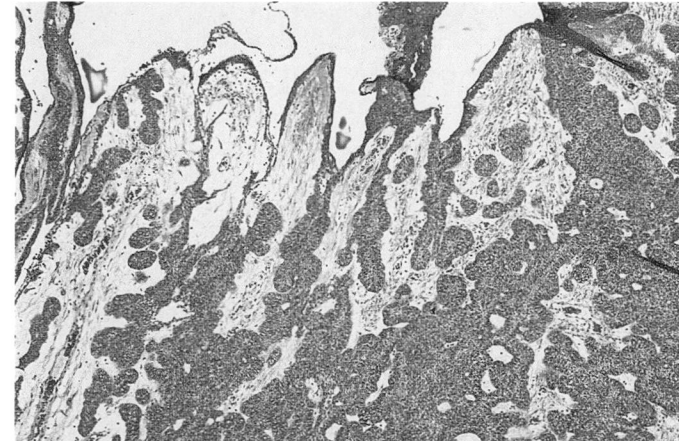

Fig. 8.34 Thymic carcinoma of basaloid type. The tumor islands are connected with the epithelium lining a cystic cavity.

both types represent carcinomas in which a component of the tumor has undergone a "phenotypical switch"; if the switch is less than complete, the appearance will be that of a sarcomatoid or spindle cell carcinoma; if complete, the result will be a carcinosarcoma. The sarcoma-like areas may include foci of cartilaginous and skeletal muscle differentiation.[207] Parenthetically, skeletal muscle ("myoid") differentiation has also been described in benign thymomas[245,249] (Fig. 8.32). The differential diagnosis of sarcomatoid carcinoma includes germ cell tumors and malignant schwannoma ("triton tumor"). It also includes a low-grade thymic tumor reported as *thymoma with pseudosarcomatous stroma* by one group[269] and as *low-grade metaplastic thymic carcinoma* by another.[283] It is characterized by a biphasic epithelial and spindle cell morphology, with absence of significant atypia in both components. All of the reported patients have been cured by surgical excision. We agree with one group about the fact that this tumor should be placed among the thymomas (rather than with the thymic carcinomas) but we side with the other group concerning the probable epithelial nature of the spindle cell component. Actually, the appearance and interplay of the two components is very reminiscent of that seen in ectopic hamartomatous thymoma, of which this lesion may represent the "orthotopic" counterpart.

Clear cell carcinoma. In this rare variant, the presence of large amounts of glycogen-rich, clear cytoplasm in the tumor cells results in a striking resemblance with renal cell carcinoma[213,267,278] (Fig. 8.33).

Basaloid carcinoma. This tumor is formed by well-defined epithelial islands with prominent peripheral palisading.[217,221] It may present as a mural nodule in what otherwise looks like a squamous-lined thymic cyst[267] (Fig. 8.34).

Mucoepidermoid carcinoma. Areas of squamous and mucin-producing glandular differentiation alternate in this neoplasm. Some of the mucin may become extracellular and elicit an inflammatory reaction[246,267,272] (Fig. 8.35).

Papillary carcinoma. This tumor resembles papillary thyroid carcinoma by virtue of the complex arborizing

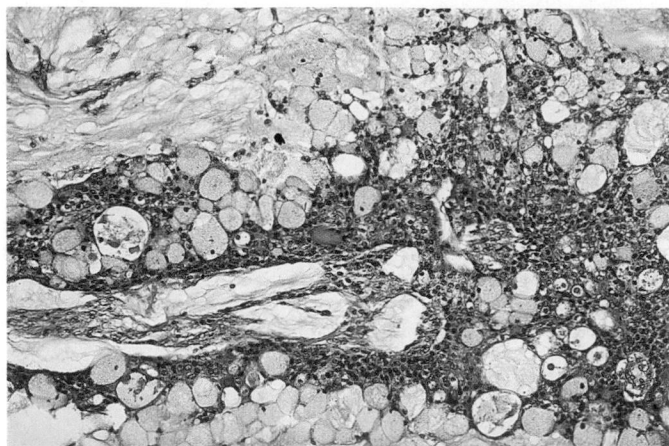

Fig. 8.35 Thymic carcinoma of mucoepidermoid type.

structure and the presence of psammoma bodies.[204a] However, it lacks optically clear nuclei, it is positive for CD5, and it shows no reactivity for thyroglobulin or TTF-1.[242] Most of the reported cases have arisen from type A (spindle cell, medullary) thymomas.[242]

Mucinous adenocarcinoma. This is the latest variety of thymic carcinoma that has been described at the time of this writing.[204b]

Small cell carcinoma and small cell–squamous cell carcinoma. These are discussed on p. 483.

Undifferentiated (anaplastic) carcinoma. This tumor shows no detectable differentiation in any specific direction and tends to exhibit considerable pleomorphism. The more undifferentiated the neoplasm, the more seriously one should consider alternative possibilities, especially large cell malignant lymphoma (see p. 491) and germ cell tumors (see p. 485). In regard to the latter, we have seen several cases of an upper mediastinal tumor in young adults that we have interpreted as *undifferentiated thymic carcinoma with germ cell-like features*, analogous to those that have been reported in the lung and other organs.

Several cases of thymic carcinoma have been described with the same chromosomal translocation (15;19), suggesting that this may represent a nonrandom event.[236]

In terms of relative frequency, the first two categories (squamous cell carcinoma and nonkeratinizing carcinoma) compose over 90% of the cases.

Classification

There has been much controversy concerning the best choice for the classification of thymic tumors. Among the two most influential proposals, the first is the descriptive scheme originally proposed by Lattes et al.[291,292] and adopted by Bernatz et al.[286] Once slight modifications are made resulting from the exclusion of minor types and of thymic tumors no longer regarded as thymomas, this proposal lists four categories[293]:

1 Predominantly spindle cell thymoma
2 Predominantly lymphocytic thymoma
3 Predominantly epithelial thymoma
4 Predominantly mixed thymoma.

The second scheme, which is based on morphofunctional principles, is the brainchild of Müller-Hermelink and his co-workers,[300,301] and comprises the following types:

1 Medullary thymoma
2 Mixed thymoma
3 Predominantly cortical (organoid) thymoma
4 Cortical thymoma
5 Well-differentiated thymic carcinoma.

It should be noted that none of these schemes includes any of the types of thymic carcinoma listed in the preceding section, the potentially misleading terminology used for the fifth tumor type in the Müller-Hermelink scheme notwithstanding.[289]

The WHO Committee for the Histologic Typing of Thymic Tumors[303] opted for a new scheme that incorporates the salient points of the two existing classifications but also takes into account two important factors. The first is that the thymus is unique in that it can be viewed as two different organs: the active, functional gland of the fetus and infant, and the inactive, "postmature" structure of adult life. The other is the presence, as an expression of differentiation, of a non-neoplastic lymphocytic component in the tumors composed of functional thymic tissue. For these, the general rules of tumor pathology apply. The better differentiated tumors (lymphocyte-rich or predominantly cortical types) recapitulate the structure of the normal organ almost to perfection, in terms of both cortical and medullary regions. Progression in these tumors composed of functional thymic tissue is manifested by an increase in the number of neoplastic epithelial cells, an increasing degree of atypia of these cells, and a corresponding decrease in the non-neoplastic lymphocytic component.

The WHO scheme consists of a combination of letters and numbers, assigned according to the following criteria:

1 The thymomas are divided into two major types depending on whether the neoplastic epithelial cells and their nuclei have a spindle/oval shape (designated as *type A*), or whether these cells have a dendritic or plump ("epithelioid") appearance (designated as *type B*). Tumors combining these two morphologies are designated as *type AB*.
2 Type B thymomas are further subdivided on the basis of the proportional increase (in relation to the lymphocytes) and emergence of atypia of the neoplastic epithelial cells into three subtypes, respectively designated as *B1*, *B2*, and *B3*.

Thymic carcinomas remain named as such. However, they are regarded in the WHO scheme as an additional subtype of thymoma (type C thymoma), a decision supported by the existence of hybrid and combined forms.[304,305]

Combinations of thymomas other than AB occur. For these cases, a term such as "combined thymoma" can be used, followed by a listing of the various components and their relative amounts. The reader may associate the various letters proposed in the WHO scheme with the various tumor patterns by mnemonically assuming that "A" stands for atrophic (i.e. the effete spindle thymic cell of adult life), "B" for bioactive (i.e. the biologically active organ of the fetus and infant), and "C" for carcinoma.

The subtypes of thymomas included in the WHO classification, the corresponding terms in the two preceding schemes, their definition, and a few comments follow.

Type A thymoma (spindle cell; medullary). *A tumor composed of a population of neoplastic thymic epithelial cells having a spindle/oval shape, lacking nuclear atypia, and accompanied by few or no non-neoplastic lymphocytes* (Figs 8.16 and 8.17).

The appearance of this tumor can simulate that of a mesenchymal neoplasm, but the immunohistochemical and ultrastructural features are clearly those of an epithelial tissue. Rosette-like formations (without a central lumen), foci with a storiform pattern of growth, and glandlike formations may be present, the latter often located within or immediately beneath the tumor capsule. Many of the features of the cells of this tumor are reminiscent of the cells seen in the atrophic thymus of adult life, some of which happen to be located in the subcapsular (rather than medullary) region.

There are exceptionally rare thymomas composed of spindle cells but exhibiting nuclear hyperchromasia, pleomorphism, mitotic activity, and/or necrosis. It is not clear whether they should be regarded as atypical or poorly differentiated forms of type A thymomas, as "spindle cell variants" of type B3 thymomas, or as sarcomatoid (spindle cell) thymic carcinomas. Clues to their recognition include a prominent reticulin fiber network among individual tumor cells and a lack or paucity of palisading cells around perivascular spaces.

An interesting variant of type A thymoma, described as micronodular thymoma, is characterized by a micronodular pattern of growth and florid lymphoid follicular hyperplasia of the stroma.[306] The lymphocytes are of B-cell type and therefore the tumor does not qualify as a type AB thymoma despite the dual cellular composition.[298,308]

Type AB thymoma (mixed). *A tumor in which foci having the features of type A thymoma are admixed with foci rich in lymphocytes* (Fig. 8.22).

The segregation of the two patterns can be sharp or indistinct, and there is a wide range in the relative amount of the two components. In particular, type A areas can be extremely scant.

Type B1 thymoma (lymphocyte-rich; lymphocytic; predominantly cortical; organoid). *A tumor that resembles the normal functional thymus in that it combines large expanses having an appearance practically indistinguishable from normal thymic cortex with areas resembling thymic medulla* (Fig. 8.18).

The resemblance between this tumor type and the normal active thymus is such that the distinction between the two may be impossible on high-power examination.[299]

Type B2 thymoma (cortical). *A tumor in which the neoplastic epithelial component appears as scattered plump cells with vesicular nuclei and distinct nucleoli among a heavy population of lymphocytes. Perivascular spaces are common and sometimes very prominent. A perivascular arrangement of tumor cells resulting in a palisading effect may be seen* (Figs 8.19 and 8.20).

The cytoplasm of the tumor cells tends to be abundant and the shape of the cells round or polygonal, this feature having led to the alternative designation (large) polygonal cell thymoma. Like B1 thymoma, type B2 thymoma is lymphocyte rich (albeit to a lesser degree), resulting in a mixed lymphocyte–epithelial pattern in some cases.

Type B3 thymoma (epithelial; atypical; squamoid; well-differentiated thymic carcinoma). *A type of thymoma predominantly composed of epithelial cells having a round or polygonal shape and exhibiting no or mild atypia. They are admixed with a minor component of lymphocytes, resulting in a sheetlike growth of the neoplastic epithelial cells* (Fig. 8.21).

This thymoma type has been traditionally known as epithelial, a term that is accurate but somewhat misleading since it implies that the other types of thymoma are not. Another term that has been suggested for it is atypical, but this is also somewhat inaccurate in view of the fact that the degree of atypia present in it may not be greater than that seen in type B2 thymoma, from which it is distinguished primarily on the basis of the proportionally larger number of epithelial cells. A further proposal is that of well-differentiated thymic carcinoma, which is potentially confusing because of the fact that in most articles on the subject and in most classification schemes this tumor is included with the thymomas rather than with the thymic carcinomas. Yet another proposal is that of squamoid thymoma because of the common presence of squamoid or squamous features in the tumor cells. However, this is neither a constant nor an exclusive feature of this tumor type.

Thymic carcinoma (type C thymoma). *A thymic tumor exhibiting clearcut cytologic atypia and a set of cytoarchitectural features no longer specific to the thymus (as for types A, AB, and B thymomas), but rather analogous to those seen in carcinomas of other organs* (Figs 8.27 and 8.34).

The various microscopic types of thymic carcinoma have been discussed in a preceding section.

• • •

Like all tumor classifications, the WHO scheme for thymomas is anything but perfect. It is affected by the site and size of the sample studied in view of the morphologic variations that can exist within the same tumor,[288,294] and limited by our very incomplete knowledge of the functioning and molecular underpinnings of the normal and neoplastic thymic epithelial cells.[295,302] Yet it provides an opportunity for achieving uniformity among workers in the field and is showing very promising results in terms of reproducibility and clinical significance,[287,296,297] which need to be further tested. This being the case, it is difficult to be enthusiastic about the introduction of alternative schemes at this juncture.[290,307]

Staging

Traditionally, thymomas of any type (other than thymic carcinomas) that appear totally encapsulated have been regarded as benign, whereas those of similar microscopic types but exhibiting evidence of aggressiveness in the form of local invasion, pleural or pericardial implants, or distant metastases have been designated as malignant[313,320] (Figs 8.36 and 8.37). This pragmatic approach does not differ substantially from that used, for instance, for follicular neoplasms of the thyroid gland and has proved equally effective in predicting prognosis. Because it relies so heavily on the presence and, to some extent, on the degree of invasion, it blends with the "clinical" staging system proposed by Masaoka et al.[314] for thymomas in 1981:

I   Macroscopically completely encapsulated and microscopically no capsular invasion
II 1 Macroscopic invasion into surrounding fatty tissue or mediastinal pleura, *or*
   2 Microscopic invasion into capsule
III   Macroscopic invasion into neighboring organ, i.e., pericardium, great vessels, or lung
IVa   Pleural or pericardial dissemination
IVb   Lymphogenous or hematogenous metastasis.

In turn, this scheme has been incorporated with some modifications into the following TNM staging system proposed by Yamakawa et al.[319,322]:

T factor

T1   Macroscopically completely encapsulated and microscopically no capsular invasion
T2   Macroscopically adhesion or invasion into surrounding fatty tissue or mediastinal pleura, or microscopic invasion into capsule
T3   Invasion into neighboring organs, such as pericardium, great vessels, and lung
T4   Pleural or pericardial dissemination

N factor

N0   No lymph node metastasis
N1   Metastasis to anterior mediastinal lymph nodes
N2   Metastasis to intrathoracic lymph nodes except anterior mediastinal lymph nodes
N3   Metastasis to extrathoracic lymph nodes

M factor

M0   No hematogenous metastasis
M1   Hematogenous metastasis.

When comparing the latter staging system with the traditional evaluation of thymomas based on the presence or absence of invasion, it becomes apparent that stage T1 corresponds to "benign" thymoma and all other stages to "malignant" thymoma. This scheme, although substantially correct, is somewhat misleading because stage T2 thymomas (included with the malignant thymomas) are much closer prognostically to stage T1 (benign) than stage T3 tumors.[311] It might therefore be preferable to diagnose thymomas according to the types listed in the previous section, followed by a descriptive equivalent of the staging system (if it can be determined from the specimen), as follows:

Fig. 8.36 Minimal invasion of the mediastinal fat beyond the thick fibrous capsule of a thymoma.

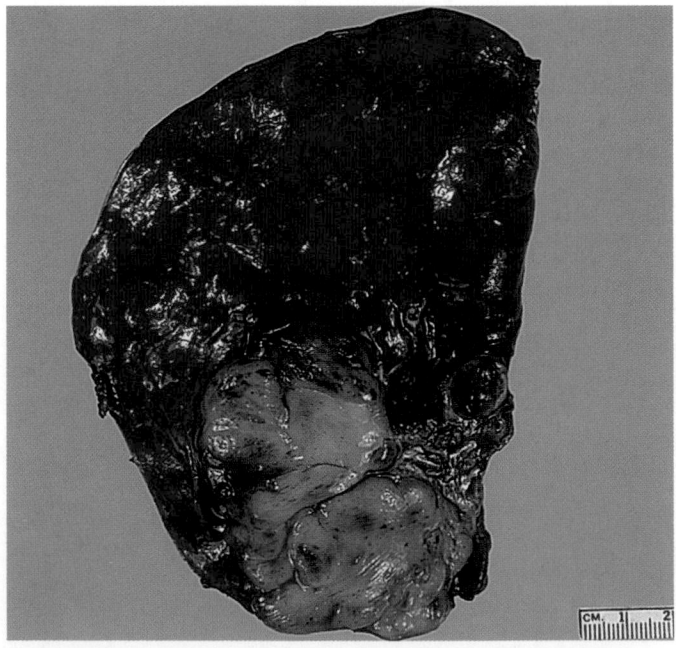

Fig. 8.37 Gross appearance of malignant thymoma invading lung.

1 Encapsulated (equivalent to stage T1)
2 Minimally invasive (equivalent to stage T2) (Fig. 8.36)
3 Widely invasive and/or with pleural or pericardial implants (equivalent to stages T3 and T4) (Fig. 8.37)
4 Metastatic (equivalent to stages N1, N2, and M1).

A recent review of thymomas treated at the National Cancer Institute at Milan, Italy, has led to the proposal of a new staging system that seems to predict survival better than the Masaoka system or its TNM version.[309]

Overall, about 70% to 80% of thymomas are encapsulated. Direct local invasion (first into the capsule and mediastinal fat and later into adjacent structures such as lung) or implants into the pleural or pericardial surfaces are considerably more common events in thymoma than distant metastases. When local invasion is extensive, it is already apparent to the surgeon at the time of thoracotomy. It is therefore important for the pathologist to know the surgical findings while remembering that fibrous adhesions resulting from secondary inflammatory, necrotic, and multilocular cystic changes can give the false impression that the tumor is invasive. Minimal invasion refers to complete capsular breaks or tumor islands in the mediastinal fat. The presence of large nerves surrounded by tumor also represents indirect evidence of invasion (sometimes the only such evidence present on the case). Distant metastases, which are exceptional, have been documented in mediastinal and cervical lymph nodes, lung, liver, bone (particularly spine), ovary (we have seen three examples), and other sites.[310,321] Usually, these distant metastases develop months or years after an invasive thymoma has been detected and treated but sometimes are noted at presentation and exceptionally represent the first clinical manifestation of the disease.

There is a close relationship between the microscopic subtype of thymoma and the likelihood of invasion, as follows[315]:

A<AB<B1<B2<B3<C

It is, however, important to point out that *any* thymoma type can be associated with the presence of direct extension, pleural or pericardial implants, or distant metastases (Fig. 8.38).

To date, special techniques such as morphometry, nuclear proliferation markers, nucleolar organizer regions, and ploidy analysis have failed to separate consistently encapsulated from invasive and/or metastatic tumors, although some differences among them have been noted.[312,316–318]

Treatment

The primary treatment of thymoma is surgical excision.[333] For the entirely encapsulated thymomas that have been removed *in toto*, no additional therapy is necessary, regardless of their microscopic type; however, if there is any question about the possibility of residual tumor, postoperative radiation therapy should be con-

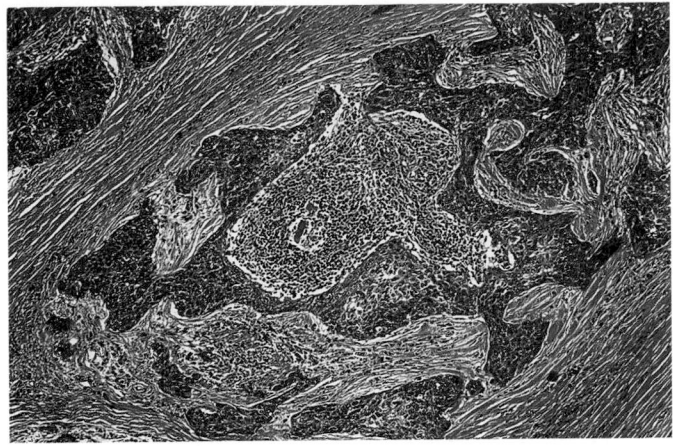
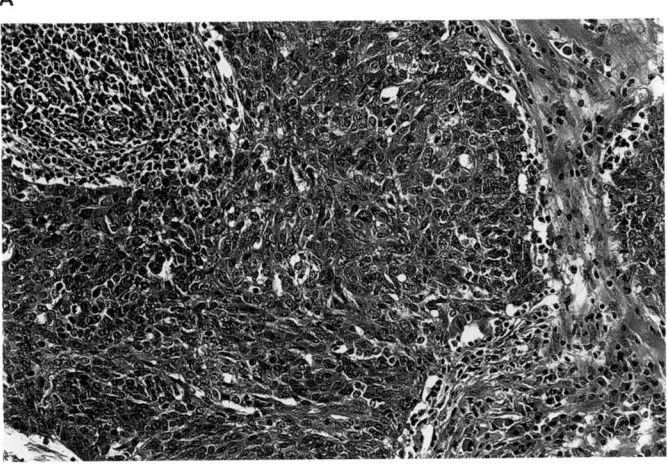

Fig. 8.38 A and **B**, This tumor had the morphologic features of a type A (spindle cell, medullary) thymoma, yet it was widely invasive.

sidered for tumors other than types A or AB (unless they are extensively invasive, which is very rarely the case).

For the other types of thymoma associated with gross invasion or implants, excision should be supplemented with radiation therapy.[334] There is only minimal information in the literature as to whether postoperative radiation therapy is also needed in thymomas that exhibit only minimal invasion,[328] but the tendency has been to recommend it.[324–327] When distant metastases are present, chemotherapy has been added; combination regimens containing *cis*-platinum have shown the best results.[323,329,331,332,335]

Thymic carcinomas of epidermoid (keratinizing or nonkeratinizing) or lymphoepithelioma-like types are treated with surgery plus radiation therapy, with chemotherapy added in cases of massive local disease or distant spread.[330]

Prognosis

The prognosis of thymoma is dependent upon the following factors:

Stage. This remains the single most important prognostic determinant, regardless of the system used. The prognosis of fully encapsulated thymoma after complete surgical excision is excellent. Recurrence has been found in 2% to 10% of cases depending on the series.[339,343,345] These local recurrences are still amenable to surgical removal.[350]

In the case of invasive tumors, the prognosis correlates with the degree of invasion, as measured by the staging system. Thus, the prognosis of minimally invasive (stage T2) thymomas is not significantly different from that of encapsulated tumors, but it drops markedly for the tumors showing gross invasion or implants and even more for the few cases associated with distant metastases.[338,346,351]

The importance of the stage also applies to thymic carcinoma.[344]

Microscopic type. There is a definite relationship between the subtype of thymoma (whatever the classification system used) and prognosis. This fact was already very evident in the large series from the Mayo Clinic reported by Lewis et al.[343] This point should be strongly emphasized in the light of subsequent publications on the subject. The reason why the usefulness of the microscopic subdivision of thymoma along these lines was minimized by Lewis et al.[343] and other authors[342] is that it is contained in and largely superseded by the staging system. Three independent studies that we have recently completed comprise three different series of thymoma patients. One deals with patients treated at Memorial Sloan-Kettering Cancer Center,[338] one with personal consultation cases,[337] and the third with patients seen at the National Cancer Institute of Milan, Italy.[336] The results of these three series, which were notably similar, confirmed the following:

1 The microscopic type of thymoma shows a close correlation with prognosis, according to this scheme of increasing clinical aggressiveness:

$$A < AB < B1 < B2 < B3 < C$$

2 There is also a very close relationship between microscopic type and stage. As a result, if the tumor stage is taken into account, the prognostic value of the microscopic type drops considerably, almost to the point of clinical insignificance.[338a] As far as thymic carcinoma is concerned, the behavior is very aggressive for the epidermoid nonkeratinizing carcinoma, lymphoepithelioma-like carcinoma, sarcomatoid carcinoma, clear cell carcinoma, and undifferentiated (anaplastic) carcinoma; intermediate for the epidermoid keratinizing carcinoma; and relatively indolent for the rare mucoepidermoid, basaloid, and papillary carcinomas.[341,343,348,352]

Completeness of excision. This is an important prognostic parameter, which is obviously related to the tumor stage[338,346,351] and which also applies to thymic carcinoma.[338a,344]

Myasthenia gravis. As already indicated, the presence or absence of myasthenic symptoms has lost much of the prognostic significance it had in the past.[345,351]

Proliferation index. The Ki-67 labeling index correlates with stage and microscopic type but it does not seem to constitute an independent prognostic factor.[347,353]

DNA ploidy. This is again related to stage and type but under multivariate analysis it fails to attain independent significance.[340]

The prognosis of thymic carcinoma depends largely on the microscopic subtype. It is very aggressive for the nonkeratinizing carcinoma (including the lymphoepithelioma-like tumors), sarcomatoid carcinoma, clear cell carcinoma, and undifferentiated (anaplastic) carcinoma; intermediate for the squamous cell carcinoma; and relatively indolent for the rare mucoepidermoid and basaloid carcinomas.[341,343,348,349,352]

Cervical tumors of thymic or related branchial pouch derivation

As mentioned previously, *ectopic thymic tissue* and *unilocular thymic cysts* can be found in the lateral aspects of the neck as a result of a malformation related to the third or possibly fourth branchial pouch (see pp. 464 and 465). In addition, the following neoplasms can develop in a similar location and on a presumably similar histogenetic basis (Table 8.2):

1 **Ectopic (cervical) thymoma.** The microscopic appearance of this tumor is not noticeably different from that of its orthotopic mediastinal counterpart. A striking and unexplained predilection for the female gender is present. All of the reported cases have behaved in a benign fashion.[355]

2 **Ectopic hamartomatous thymoma.** The location of this lesion, which shares features of a hamartomatous and a neoplastic process, is the supraclavicular–suprasternal area.[360,367,370] Most patients are males, in striking contrast with the previous entity. The bulk of the mass is composed of epithelial cells that are extremely spindle-shaped and mesenchymal-like; this finding often results in a misdiagnosis of a schwannian or fibroblastic neoplasm.[365] However, ultrastructural examination or keratin immunostaining reveals their epithelial nature. Atypia, necrosis, and mitotic figures are absent. The other component (which can be very focal) is represented by solid squamous nests, thin anastomosing cords (sometimes composed of clear cells,[363] and epithelial-lined cysts (Fig. 8.39). Islands of mature fat and clusters of small lymphocytes may also be present. This tumor, which may reach a huge size, does not seem to have a mediastinal counterpart. The behavior is benign, but exceptional cases with a superimposed carcinoma are on record.[364]

3 **Spindle epithelial tumor with thymus-like elements (SETTLE).** Most cases of this rare neoplasm have been found in adolescents or young adults and have been located in or around the thyroid.[355] Microscopically, a

Table 8.2 Salient features of tumors in the neck showing thymic or related branchial pouch differentiation

Tumor	Gender	Mean age (yr)	Anatomic location	Major histologic features	Behavior
Ectopic hamartomatous thymoma	M>F	49.9	Supraclavicular or suprasternal soft tissue	Circumscribed; haphazard admixture of bland-looking spindle (epithelial) cells, solid and cystic epithelial islands (commonly squamous and glandular), and mature fat cells	Benign: *No recurrence or metastasis* after excision
Ectopic cervical thymoma	M<F	42.7	Soft tissue of neck, often in a juxtathyroid location, or sometimes inside thyroid	Similar to mediastinal thymomas; encapsulated or invasive; jig-saw puzzle—like lobules; mixture of pale epithelial cells (plump or spindled) and lymphocytes	Most pursue a benign course with *no recurrence;* exceptionally, metastasis can occur
SETTLE	M = F (about the same)	15	Thyroid gland	Encapsulated or infiltrative; highly cellular tumor; merging of compact or reticulated spindle (epithelial) cells with glandular elements; mucous glands often present; component of lymphocytes lacking	Protracted clinical course, with a propensity to develop *delayed distant metastasis*
CASTLE	M<F	48.5	Thyroid gland (usually lower pole) and surrounding soft tissue, or soft tissues of the neck	Lymphoepithelioma-like carcinoma that may show foci of squamous differentiation; lobulation; pushing margins; lymphocytic infiltration often present	Generally indolent tumor that can *recur after long intervals; regional lymph node metastasis* occurs in about half of the cases; occasional cases pursue a more aggressive course

From Chan JK, Rosai J. Tumors of the neck showing thymic or related branchial pouch differentiation. A unifying concept. Hum Pathol 1991, **22**: 349–367.

biphasic pattern resulting from a predominant spindle cell component (more cellular than in the previous type and mitotically active) and a mucin-secreting, occasionally cystic glandular component is present (Fig. 8.40).[368] The appearance is somewhat reminiscent of synovial sarcoma, particularly when the spindle cell component predominates to the near exclusion of the glandular element.[356] Some of the reported cases have shown more prominent mitotic activity and focal necrosis.[361] Immunohistochemically and ultrastructurally, both tumor components have an epithelial phenotype.[368] At the molecular cases, Ki-*ras* gene mutation has been detected in an example of this entity.[369a] The natural history is characterized by a tendency for late (measured in years or decades) distant metastases.[355,357,362]

4 Carcinoma with thymus-like elements (CASTLE). This tumor also tends to be located within or around the thyroid, to the point that most of the reported cases

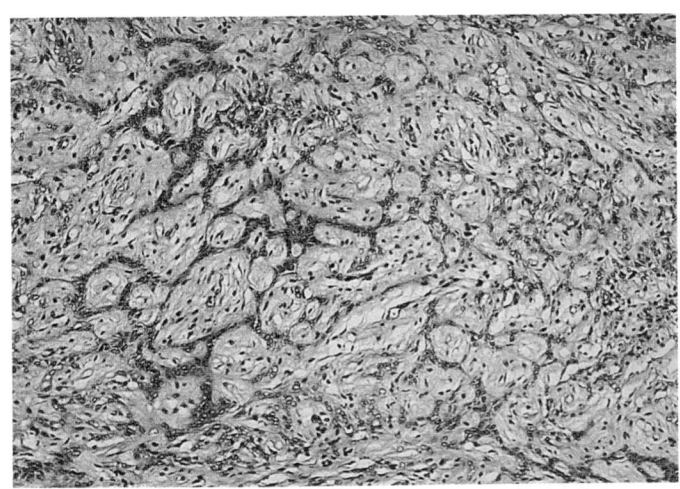

Fig. 8.39 Ectopic hamartomatous thymoma. Thin anastomosing strands of epithelial cells merge with spindle foci having a mesenchyme-like appearance.

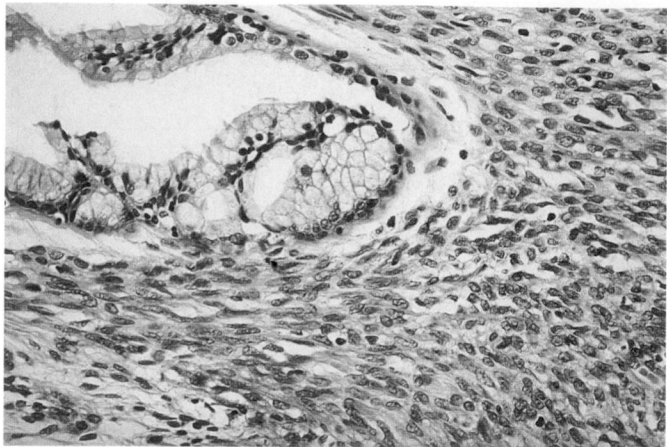

A

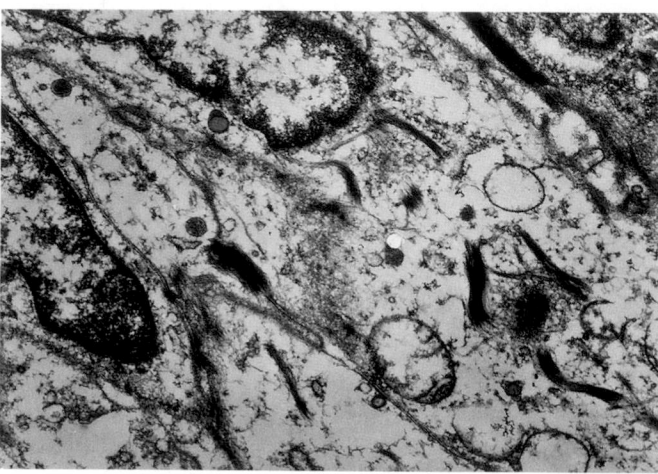

B

Fig. 8.40 A, SETTLE. Spindle epithelial cells of mesenchyme-like appearance surround a well-differentiated gland lined by mucin-producing epithelium. **B,** Electron micrograph of SETTLE. Portion of a cluster of spindle-shaped epithelial cells that are joined by well-formed desmosomes. Note the tonofilament bundles in the cytoplasm. (× 26,000; courtesy of Dr. Robert A. Erlandson, Memorial Sloan-Kettering Cancer Center)

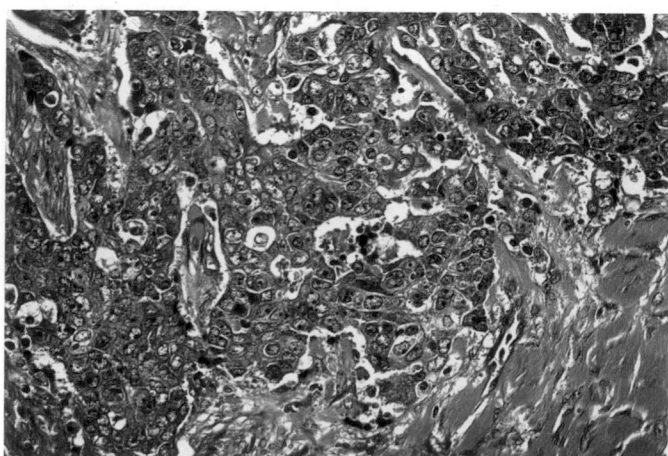

Fig. 8.41 CASTLE. The morphologic appearance is similar to that of thymic carcinoma (type C thymoma), of which it probably represents its ectopic counterpart.

were originally thought to represent squamous cell or undifferentiated carcinomas of this organ.[369] Their microscopic appearance is indistinguishable from that of thymic carcinoma (Fig. 8.41), of which it can be regarded as its ectopic (cervical) equivalent. Support for the thymic rather than thyroidal origin of CASTLE is provided by its immunoreactivity for CD5, bcl-2 and mcl-1 (all of them being markers associated with thymic carcinoma) and negativity for TTF-1.[354,358,359] The tumor has a tendency for late local recurrences, but its behavior is rather indolent, certainly more so than that of undifferentiated thyroid carcinoma.[355,362,366]

Neuroendocrine tumors

The thymus is the site of several types of neuroendocrine neoplasm, many of which were previously misinterpreted as variants of thymoma.[390,398] The gamut of neuroendocrine tumors that can develop in the thymus is basically the same as for the lung, the only difference being the relative frequencies of the various types.[387] Thus, whereas most neuroendocrine tumors of the lung fall into the two extremes (typical carcinoid and small cell carcinoma), those of the thymus tend to fall into an intermediate category (atypical carcinoid).

Carcinoid tumor of the thymus is a malignant neoplasm that often invades locally and metastasizes distantly, sometimes after a long interval; in one series, the incidence of distant metastases was 73%.[397] Well-circumscribed tumors, however, are often cured by local excision.[390] Thymic carcinoid usually lacks endocrine manifestations, and we have yet to see a case accompanied by the carcinoid syndrome. However, in one third of the cases it is associated with Cushing's syndrome or other distant manifestations[392,397]; it seems apparent that all of the reported cases of thymomas associated with Cushing's syndrome are, in reality, examples of thymic carcinoids.[374,393]

Thymic carcinoid can be associated with carcinoid tumor of other sites, such as bronchus or ileum. It can also occur as a component of multiple endocrine neoplasia (MEN) type I or IIa[391,392] or *formes frustes* of these syndromes.[396] In these patients and in those with Cushing's syndrome, the tumor tends to run a more aggressive clinical course.[391] It has also been described in patients with neurofibromatosis type I.[382]

Grossly, thymic carcinoid is solid, usually well-circumscribed but not encapsulated, and lacks the distinct lobulations of thymoma (Fig. 8.42). It tends to be highly vascularized and it may be frankly hemorrhagic.[384]

Microscopically, thymic carcinoid tumor exhibits ribbon and festoon formation, rosette-like glands with central lumina, "balls" of cells with central necrosis and calcification, marked vascularization, and frequent lymphatic and blood vessel invasion (Figs 8.43 and 8.44). Lymphocytes, perivascular spaces, and other features of thymoma are absent. The tumor cells have a more

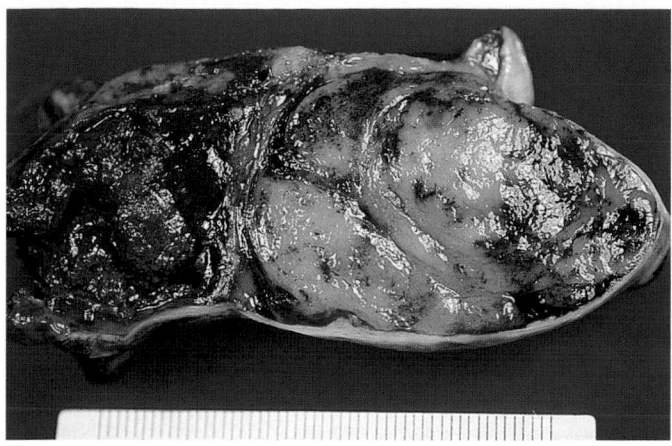

Fig. 8.42 Gross appearance of thymic carcinoid. Notice the fleshy appearance and the extensive areas of hemorrhage.

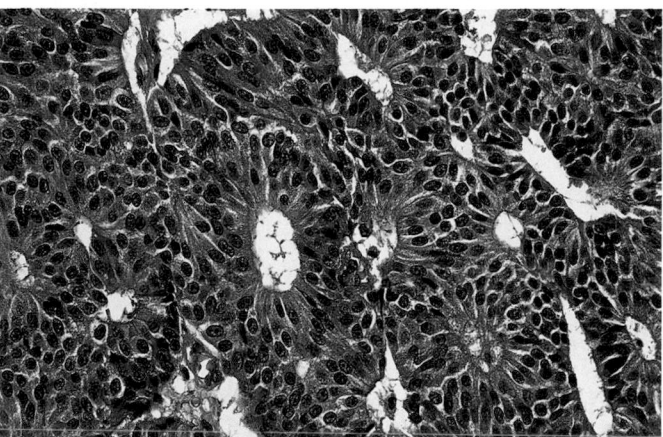

Fig. 8.43 Well-differentiated architectural and cytologic appearance of thymic carcinoid. Ribbons and rosettes are evident.

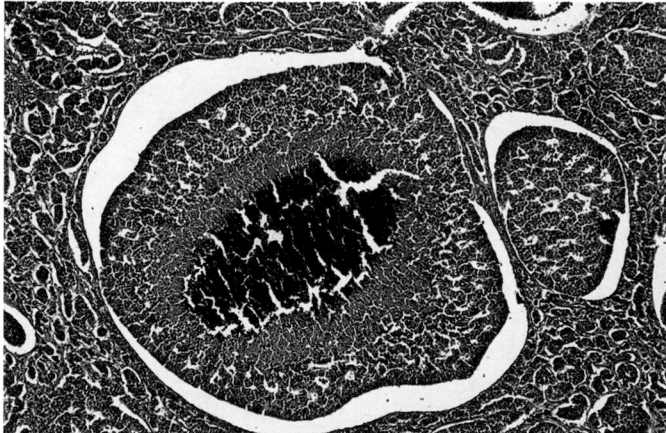

Fig. 8.44 Thymic carcinoid. The tumor nests show characteristic central necrosis with calcification.

granular cytoplasm than those of thymoma, the nuclear chromatin is slightly coarser, and mitotic activity is frequent. In this regard, it should be noted that if one were to apply to thymic carcinoids the criteria currently used for the homonymous bronchial lesion, most of them would fall into the category of *atypical* carcinoid

tumor.[373,375,395] This probably explains the fact that as a group, thymic carcinoid is a more aggressive neoplasm than bronchial carcinoid, in which the atypical form represents a minority. Some carcinoid tumors are characterized by cells with a prominent oncocytic cytoplasm.[386]

Special techniques are very useful for confirmation of a diagnosis of thymic carcinoid. The tumor cells are argyrophilic, although not argentaffin. Electron microscopy shows short interdigitating cell processes, focal basal lamina, scanty junctional processes, and practically no complex desmosomes or tonofilaments. The cytoplasm contains many dense-core granules and sometimes perinuclear whorls of microfilaments[392,400] (Fig. 8.45). Immunohistochemically, there is reactivity for keratin, neuron-specific enolase, chromogranin, and other general endocrine markers. In addition, the tumors associated with Cushing's syndrome show positivity for adrenocorticotropic hormone (ACTH). Other substances detected in this tumor include serotonin, somatostatin, cholecystokinin, neurotensin, and metenkephalin.[371,376,389,400]

Morphologic variants of thymic carcinoid tumor include lesions with a spindle cell pattern[381,383] (Fig. 8.46) and pigmented (melanin-containing) tumors.[379] There are also tumors containing amyloid and calcitonin and therefore analogous to medullary thyroid carcinoma.[392] Finally, there are carcinoid tumors accompanied by a high-grade sarcomatoid component.[378,388]

Small cell neuroendocrine carcinoma of the thymus has an appearance indistinguishable from that of its considerably more common pulmonary counterpart[392,399] (Fig. 8.47). Because of this very fact, a diagnosis of primary small cell neuroendocrine carcinoma of the thymus can only be entertained when the alternative of a mediastinal metastasis of a pulmonary neoplasm has been ruled out. As in the lung, thymic tumors have been described having an admixture of small cell neuroendocrine carcinoma and squamous cell carcinoma.[394] There are also cases combining features of carcinoid tumor and small cell carcinoma in the same lesion.[385]

Large cell neuroendocrine carcinoma, defined according to the criteria applied to pulmonary neoplasms, has been seen in the thymus, albeit only exceptionally.[372]

It is important to point out the difference that exists between all of the above tumors, generically embraced into the neuroendocrine category, and the otherwise conventional thymic carcinomas (type C thymomas) that show some evidence of neuroendocrine differentiation on immunohistochemical grounds (see p. 473).[380] Here too the situation at hand is analogous to that operating in the lung.

It should also be mentioned that not all thymic tumors showing neural differentiation are neuroendocrine carcinomas (see thymic neuroblastoma, p. 494), and that not all mediastinal neuroendocrine carcinomas are of thymic origin.[377]

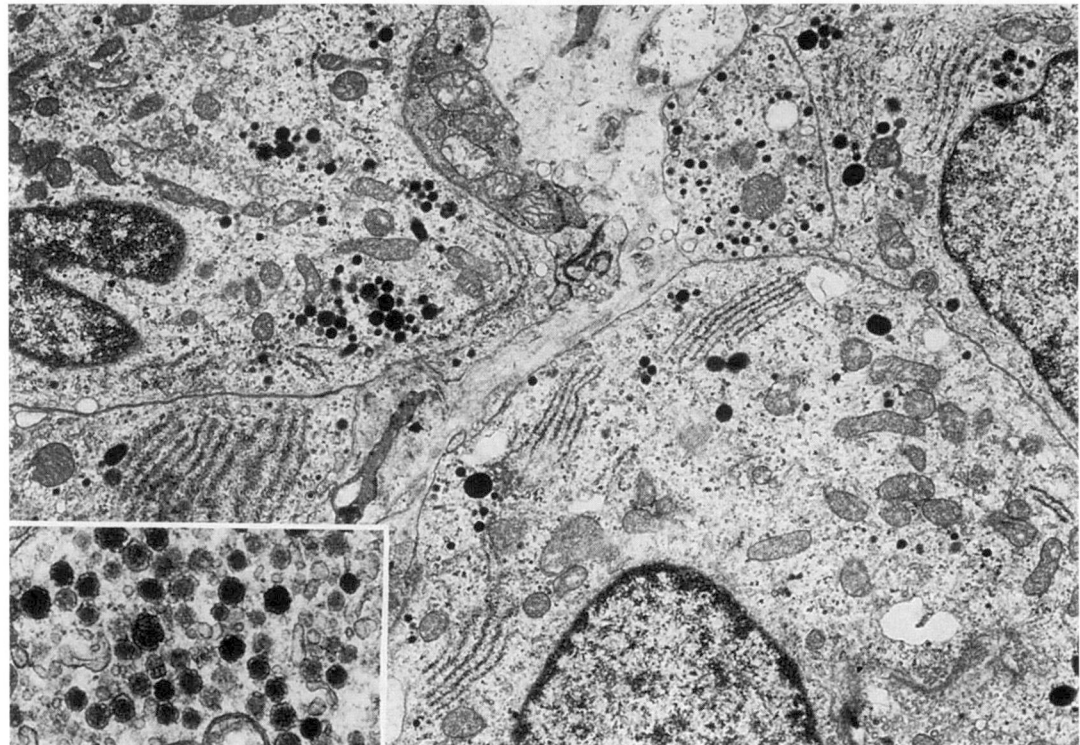

Fig. 8.45 Thymic carcinoid tumor characterized by dense-core secretory granules that separate this neoplasm from other thymic tumors. These cells also have prominent rough endoplasmic reticulum, Golgi apparatus, and scattered mitochondria. **Inset,** Note uniform, membrane-bound, dense-core granules with peripheral halo. (×7450; inset ×25,270)

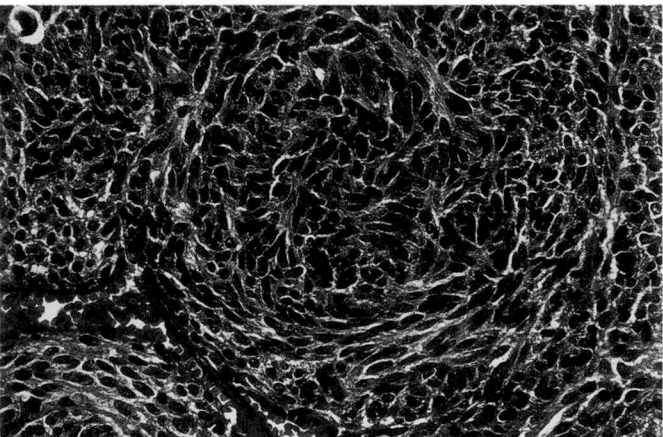

Fig. 8.46 Thymic carcinoid of spindle cell type. This tumor is easily confused with a type A (spindle cell) thymoma.

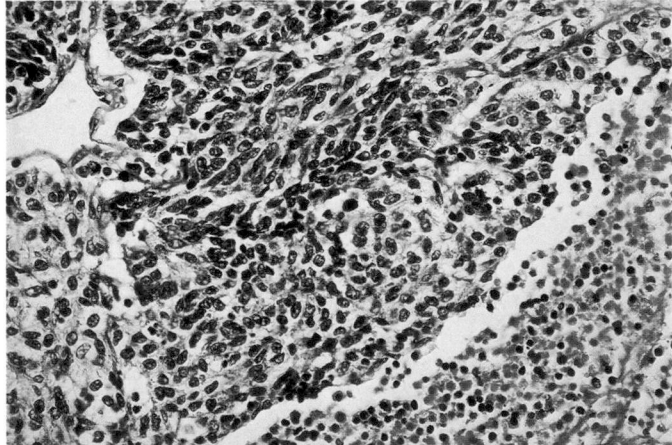

Fig. 8.47 Small cell neuroendocrine carcinoma of the thymus. The tumor cells are elongated, with darkly staining nuclei and scanty cytoplasm. There is extensive necrosis.

Stromal and other tumors

Thymolipoma is an encapsulated benign thymic lesion that can attain a huge size and can simulate radiographically cardiomegaly or pulmonary sequestration.[408] It is questionable whether it represents a true neoplastic process. The majority of the cases are asymptomatic, but isolated instances of association with myasthenia gravis, aplastic anemia, and Graves' disease are on record.[412] Their appearance on CT scan and MRI is characteristic.[410] Grossly, the lesion has the appearance of a lipoma except for the focal presence of whitish solid areas. Microscopically, there is an admixture in various proportions of mature adipose tissue and unremarkable thymic tissue (Fig. 8.48). The amount of the latter is well in excess of that normally expected for the patient's age. One case was reported in which myoid cells were present.[405] Others have shown an abundance of fibroconnective tissue ("thymofibrolipomas"),[409] or vessels ("thymohemangiolipoma").[411] There has also been a case of thymolipoma harboring a small thymoma.[402]

We and others have seen cases of low-grade malignant mesenchymal tumors seemingly arising from the thymic stroma that we interpreted as **thymic stromal sarcomas**[404,406,407] (Fig. 8.49). Their microscopic appearance is variable, but well-differentiated liposarcoma is the predominant component ("thymoliposarcoma").

Other stromal tumors that have been described in the thymus include *osteosarcoma* (allegedly arising in an ectopic hamartomatous organ),[413] and a *kaposiform hemangioendothelioma* in an infant.[414]

Malignant melanoma has been seen presenting as an apparently primary thymic mass.[401,403] Parenthetically, metastatic tumors to the thymus are exceptional.

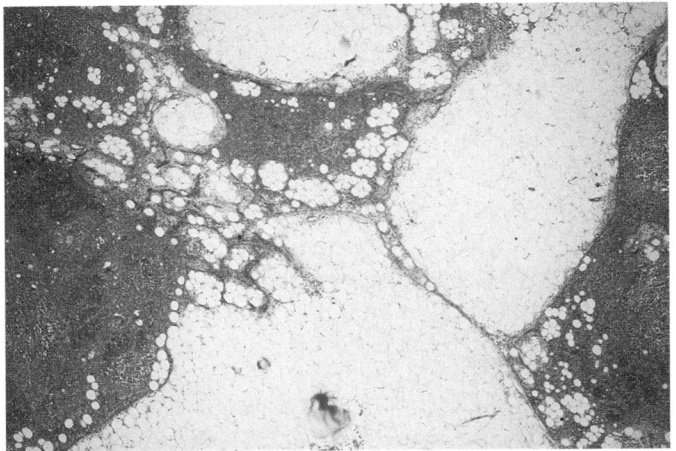

Fig. 8.48 Thymolipoma. The lesion is composed of an admixture of mature adipose tissue and microscopically normal thymus.

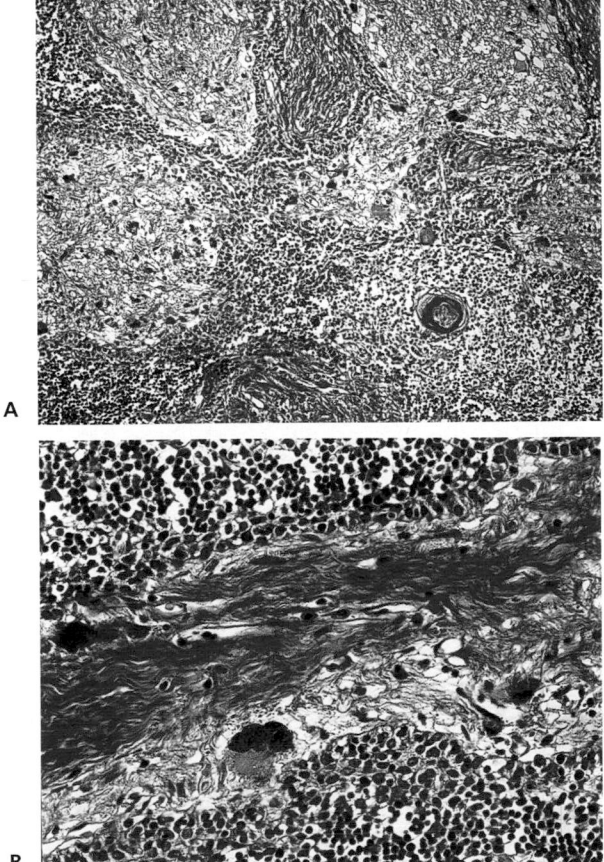

Fig. 8.49 A and **B**, Thymic stromal sarcoma with features consistent with sclerosing form of liposarcoma. Bizarre tumor cells are seen in the stroma of the thymic lobules, in close approximation to the parenchymal component.

Germ cell tumors

Germ cell tumors account for approximately 20% of the mediastinal tumors and cysts. Their histogenesis is controversial, but a primary origin from extragonadal germ cells is favored.[462,474] In this context, it should be pointed out that the mediastinal location of germ cell tumors is specifically related to the thymus gland, even if normal germ cells in this organ have yet to be conclusively demonstrated and their possible function—if indeed they are present—remains an enigma.[420,427] The thymic connection of germ cell tumors is also evident by the fact that, when small, they are found totally encased within this organ.[444] However, they seem to have no histogenetic relationship with true thymoma and should not be labeled as such. The possibility of any mediastinal germ cell tumor representing a metastasis from a testicular or ovarian primary lesion should always be investigated, although in the presence of a single upper mediastinal tumor with no evidence of retroperitoneal involvement the chances of this being the case are remote.[458,461]

This is in striking contrast with retroperitoneal germ cell tumors, as shown in the series of Daugaard et al.[423]; these authors found testicular intratubular germ cell neoplasia in 42% of 39 patients with retroperitoneal germ cell tumors but in none of 8 patients with mediastinal tumors.[423] Chaganti et al.[420] have revived the theory of the testicular origin of mediastinal germ cell tumors on the basis of the similarities in cytogenetic alterations, but all other available evidence suggests otherwise.

Some cases of mediastinal germ cell tumors have occurred in association with Klinefelter's syndrome; it has been estimated that the incidence of this syndrome among patients with mediastinal germ cell neoplasms is 30 to 40 times that seen in the general population.[430,438,446]

A definite relationship exists between the patient's sex and the incidence of the various mediastinal germ cell tumors. Seminoma (germinoma), for all practical purposes, affects only males; we have yet to see a convincing case in a female. Embryonal carcinoma, endodermal sinus tumor, teratocarcinoma, and choriocarcinoma show a great male predilection, but unquestionable cases in females have been reported.[429,463] Mature cystic teratoma affects both sexes equally.[424]

Seminoma (germinoma) of the mediastinum arises almost always within the thymus but—as already stated—should be regarded as a germ cell tumor rather than a true thymoma (Fig. 8.50). The morphologic appearance is identical to that of its testicular counterpart at the light microscopic, immunohistochemical, and ultrastructural level[444,469] (Figs 8.51 to 8.53). Conversely, they are somewhat different in their K-*ras* sequence and p53 immunostain profile.[460] Perhaps related to the latter is the fact that a greater percentage of mediastinal than gonadal seminomas show a degree of atypicality and

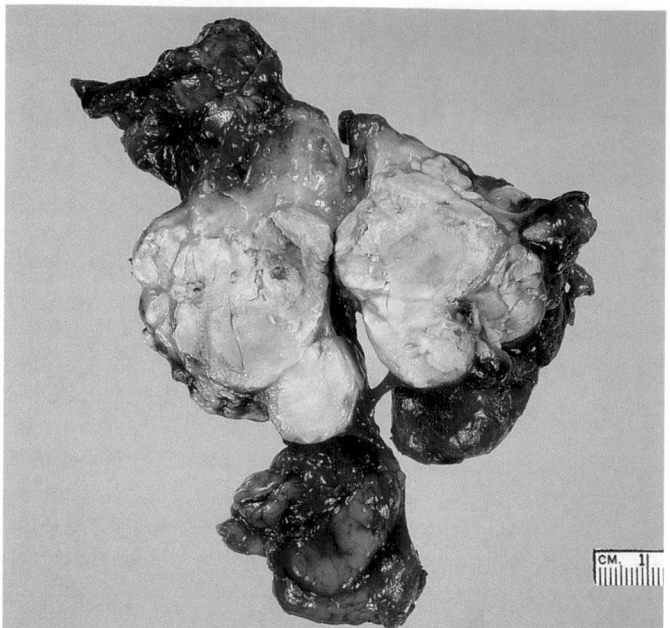

Fig. 8.50 Seminoma of thymus. The tumor is solid and homogeneous, with no necrosis. Residual thymic tissue is seen at the periphery.

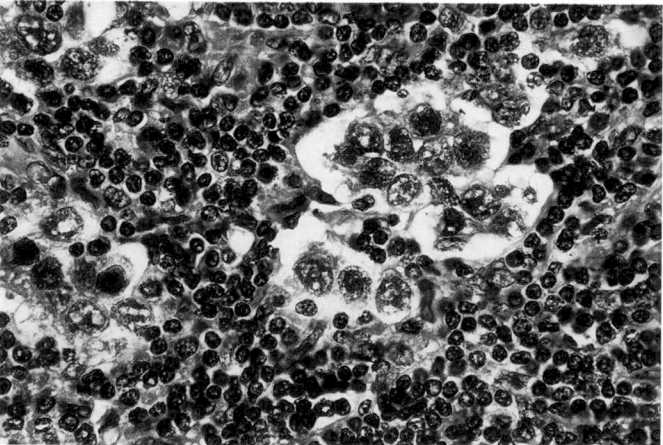

Fig. 8.51 Seminoma of thymus showing compact nests of large tumor cells surrounded by lymphocyte-rich fibrous septa.

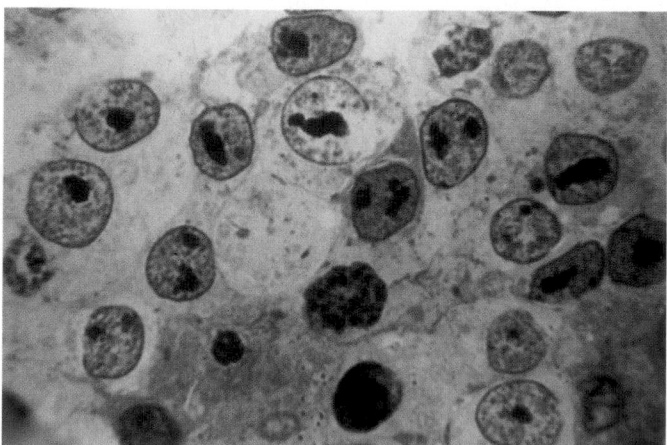

Fig. 8.52 This semi-thin section shows particularly well the multiple prominent nucleoli with ragged edges that are typical of seminoma.

mitotic activity that places them in the category of *anaplastic seminoma*, even if it is not clear whether this carries any prognostic significance. The differential diagnosis of mediastinal seminoma includes thymoma and large cell lymphoma. The presence of fibrous septa infiltrated by lymphocytes and plasma cells, epithelioid granulomas, numerous germinal centers, large amounts of cytoplasmic glycogen, and an irregular, skein-like nucleolus favors a diagnosis of seminoma. The true nature of the lesion may be obscured by the presence of a very prominent granulomatous reaction, reactive follicular hyperplasia, epithelium-lined cystic formations of thymic origin ("multilocular thymic cyst"), and fibrosis[416] (Fig. 8.54). Seminomas are immunoreactive for placental alkaline phosphatase, CD117, and often CD57(Leu7), but they are negative for CD45 and usually negative or only focally positive for keratin when using routinely processed material.[453] Mutations of c-kit are common, similar to those seen in their testicular counterparts.[459a] One should be careful not to misinterpret entrapped thymic epithelial cells as neoplastic elements (Fig. 8.55). The primary treatment is with radiation therapy, and the prognosis is very good.[417,442,464,469a] In the series of Shantz et al.,[464] one patient died after resection, but the 16 with adequate follow-up were alive and well. In the series of Bush et al.,[417] the 10-year actuarial survival rate was 69%.

Mature cystic teratoma is the most common type of mediastinal germ cell neoplasm. It usually becomes clinically apparent in early adult life. It may grow to a large size and has a distinct, sharply delineated wall that often becomes calcified.[461] The cut surface is predominantly cystic (Fig. 8.56). Adherence to surrounding structures is common. If the sebaceous material within it escapes, a prominent xanthogranulomatous inflammatory reaction follows. Perforation into the tracheobronchial tree may occur, and the patient coughs up sebaceous oily material and hair.

The microscopic appearance resembles that of the more common mature cystic teratoma of ovary. The cysts are lined by stratified squamous epithelium and contain sebaceous glands and hair follicles. Other common components are neural tissue, gastrointestinal tract, cartilage, and respiratory structures. Pancreatic tissue is particularly frequent in this location[467]; it may be accompanied by islet cell elements and result in hypoglycemia. It has been suggested that the dense adhesions often found in this tumor may be the result of pancreatic enzyme secretion.[466] The prognosis for mature teratoma is excellent.[469a]

Immature teratoma is defined, as in other sites, as a germ cell tumor similar to mature teratoma but also containing immature epithelial, mesenchymal, or neural elements without a component of embryonal carcinoma; the number of cases reported in the mediastinum is too small to know what to expect in terms of behavior.[419] This condition should be distinguished both from terato-

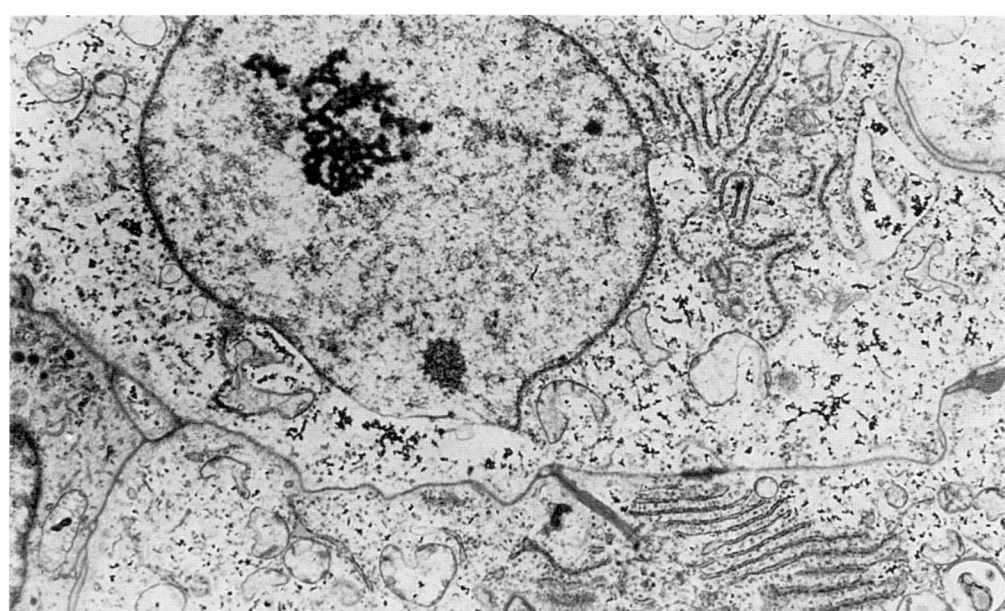

Fig. 8.53 Ultrastructural appearance of tumor cells in seminoma of thymus. (Uranyl acetate–lead citrate; ×8800; from Levine GD. Primary thymic seminoma. A neoplasm ultrastructurally similar to testicular seminoma and distinct from epithelial thymoma. Cancer 1973, **31**: 729–741)

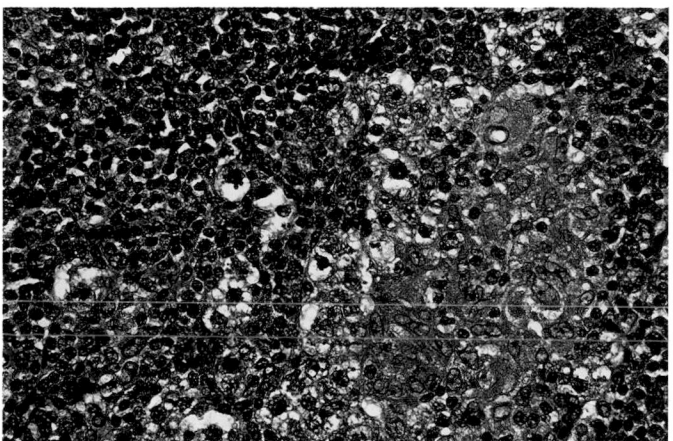

Fig. 8.54 Seminoma of thymus. The associated granulomatous response can obscure the true nature of the lesion.

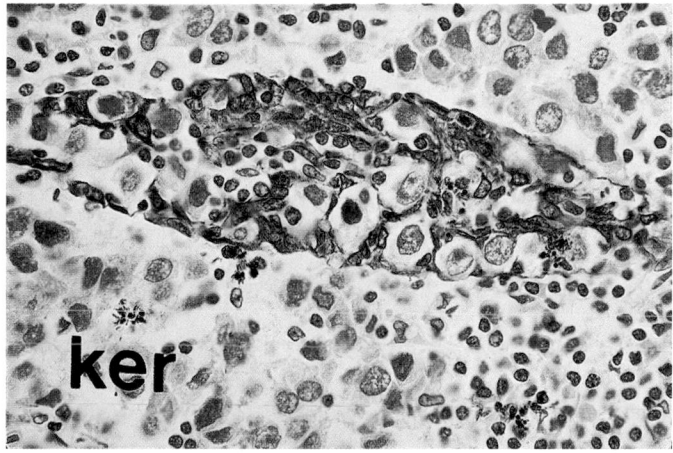

Fig. 8.55 Infiltration and entrapment of thymic epithelium by seminoma cells, as seen with the keratin immunostain.

carcinoma (see later section) and from malignant transformation of mature cystic teratoma, the latter being a very rare event (see below).

Embryonal carcinoma is an invasive, highly necrotic neoplasm. Its microscopic appearance is, by definition, poorly differentiated. Immunohistochemically, there is reactivity for keratin, PLAP, CD30, and CD57 (Leu7). It is very important for the pathologist to consider the possibility of germ cell tumor in the presence of a poorly differentiated malignant neoplasm of the mediastinum, especially if the patient is a young male, instead of automatically relegating it to the category of "undifferentiated malignant tumor;" otherwise one might be denying the patient the opportunity of remission or cure with current chemotherapeutic regimens.[426,431,433,457,469a]

Yolk sac tumor (endodermal sac tumor) may occur admixed with other germ cell elements or (more rarely) as a pure neoplasm[472] (Fig. 8.57). Yolk sac elements are

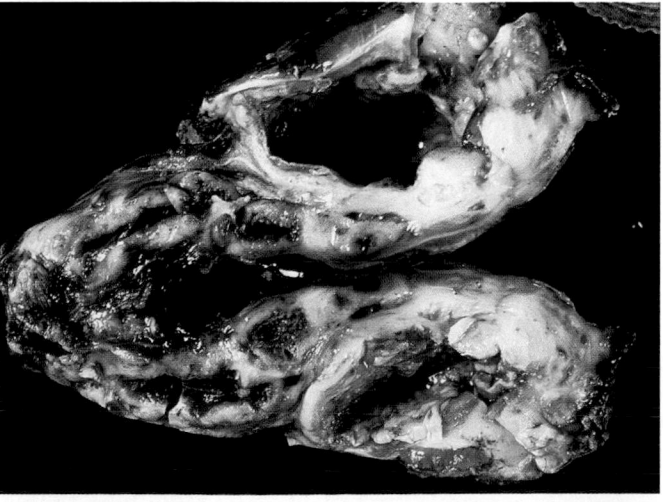

Fig. 8.56 Mature cystic teratoma with prominent cystic component. This tumor contained abundant pancreatic tissue, some of which was heavily inflamed.

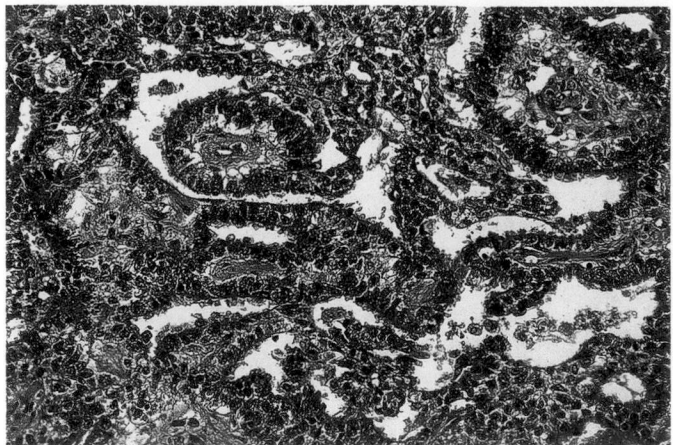

Fig. 8.57 Yolk sac tumor of mediastinum, with well-developed Schiller–Duval bodies.

said to be more common in mediastinal than in testicular neoplasms.[470] Mediastinal yolk sac tumors may have prominent spindle cell features,[449] contain a hepatoid component,[451] or be accompanied by secondary multilocular cystic changes in the adjacent non-neoplastic thymus.[450] The prognosis of pure endodermal sinus tumor is very poor,[437] although the few tumors in this category that are found to be encapsulated have a better outlook.[455]

Teratocarcinoma, defined as the combination of embryonal carcinoma and teratoma (mature and/or immature), comprises about 5% of all mediastinal germ cell tumors. It grows rapidly and infiltrates widely. Grossly, areas of hemorrhage and necrosis are present (Fig. 8.58). Microscopically, areas of embryonal carcinoma alternate with mature foci, with an abundance of foci of intermediate differentiation.

Choriocarcinoma of the mediastinum occurs, for the most part, in the third decade of life.[432,448,465,475] It is often

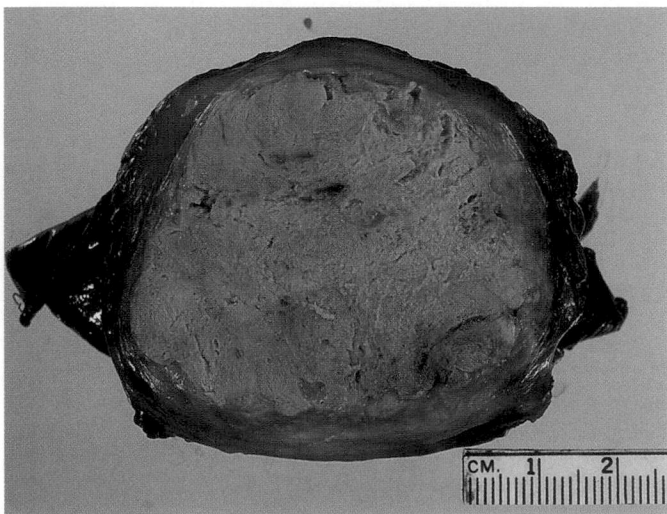

Fig. 8.58 Nonseminomatous germ cell tumor of the mediastinum of teratocarcinoma type that has undergone massive necrosis.

associated with gynecomastia and invariably accompanied by elevated serum levels of human chorionic gonadotropin (hCG). The prognosis is extremely poor.[448] The occurrence of choriocarcinoma as a primary lesion in the mediastinum has been accepted after several classical studies described cases in which serial sections of both testes showed no abnormalities.[440,445] It should be emphasized, however, that it is in choriocarcinoma, more than any other germ cell tumor, that the possibility of an occult testicular primary lesion exists because of the tendency for this tumor type to be very small and even regressed ("burnt out") at the time that the metastases develop. The case of testicular choriocarcinoma measuring only 2 mm in diameter reported by Greenwood et al.[432] is highly illustrative in this regard. The distinction, however, is mainly of academic interest inasmuch as the treatment (systemic chemotherapy) and the prognosis are similar regardless of whether an occult testicular tumor is identified or not.

Malignant nonseminomatous germ cell tumors are accompanied by serum elevation of hCG and/or AFP in about 90% of the patients, but these markers are usually negative in pure seminoma.[436]

As in other extragonadal locations and in the gonads, admixtures of various types of germ cell tumors are common.[422,452] These tumors are collectively referred to as *mixed germ cell tumors*, but it is important to describe accurately the components present. One such combination is that of seminomatous and nonseminomatous elements.[434]

A cytogenetic aberration of germ cell tumors that is seen in over 80% of the cases, regardless of microscopic type or whether the tumor is primary or metastatic, is the presence of i(12p), i.e., a gain of 12p, usually in the form of an isochromosome.[435,464] This determination, which is of great diagnostic utility in this context (particularly for the differential diagnosis between embryonal carcinoma and undifferentiated carcinoma of pulmonary or thymic origin), can now be carried out by comparative genomic hybridization analysis or interphase chromosome painting of formalin-fixed, paraffin-embedded material.[415,468]

As a group, nonseminomatous germ cell tumors of mediastinum do not respond as well to chemotherapy as their microscopically similar testicular counterparts; relapses occur more frequently and patient survival is worse.[443,470,471]

A particularly ominous complication of nonseminomatous germ cell tumors of the mediastinum is the occasional development of a somatic-type malignant tumor, such as adenocarcinoma, neuroendocrine tumors,[441] angiosarcoma, or rhabdomyosarcoma.[447,454,473] Mediastinal germ cell tumors seem to be more prone to this event than gonadal neoplasms, particularly for the sarcomas exhibiting skeletal muscle differentiation.[418] The prognostically unfavorable aspect of this development is that these somatic-type malignancies do not respond to germ cell-type chemotherapeutic protocols the way that conventional germ cell tumors do.[428]

The rare but well-documented development of hematologic neoplasia in this context can be viewed pathogenetically as another manifestation of this phenomenon.[425] It may take the form of acute leukemia or systemic mast cell disease,[421,456] and is particularly common in tumors having a yolk sac component.[430,459] The detection in these hematopoietic elements of i(12p) (a cytogenetic marker of germ cell tumors) indicates that these cells originate from the germ cell tumor rather than representing a therapy-induced malignancy from the host bone marrow.[439]

Malignant lymphoma

Malignant lymphoma can present as an anterior, superior, or middle mediastinal mass, in this order of frequency.[479–481] It represents the most common primary neoplasm of the middle portion of the mediastinum. It may appear in this area as a manifestation of a disseminated process, or it may present as a primary mediastinal disease.[477,481] The diagnosis can be suspected on clinicoradiographic grounds, and sometimes it can be confirmed with fine needle aspiration biopsy or a small tissue biopsy obtained through a suprasternal collar incision.[476] However, in most instances a formal thoracotomy is needed to establish a precise diagnosis.

The majority of malignant lymphomas presenting as primary mediastinal neoplasms fall into the four categories discussed in the following sections.[478,480] The general features of these lymphomas are discussed in Chapter 22; only those pertaining specifically to their mediastinal location will be mentioned here.

Hodgkin's lymphoma

Mediastinal Hodgkin's lymphoma can involve primarily the thymus or the lymph nodes or both sites.[486] Most patients are young adults, and there is a predilection for females. The disease may present with local pressure symptoms (dyspnea, cough, chest pain) or be found incidentally in a chest x-ray examination. Exceptional cases of thymic Hodgkin's lymphoma have been seen in association with myasthenia gravis[490] and with erythroid hypoplasia.[491] Primary Hodgkin's lymphoma of the mediastinum is nearly always of nodular sclerosis type. When affecting the nodes, its gross and microscopic appearance is similar to that seen elsewhere. When involving the thymus, it is usually sharply outlined and sometimes surrounded by a thick capsule not too dissimilar from that of a thymoma. The nodules may be multiple (a very rare event in true thymoma), and residual thymic tissue is usually identified. The consistency is hard, and the cut surface is vaguely or distinctly nodular (Fig. 8.59). It is not uncommon to find within the mass variously sized cysts containing clear or grumous fluid. Occasionally, the entire lesion has a gross appearance indistinguishable from that of a benign thymic cyst.[493] This is the result of a peculiar cystic and proliferative reaction of the thymic epithelium, which we have designated as multilocular thymic cyst (see p. 464).

The low-power appearance may resemble that of true thymoma by virtue of the presence of cellular nodules encircled by fibrous bands. In thymoma, however, the interphase between the fibrous strands and the

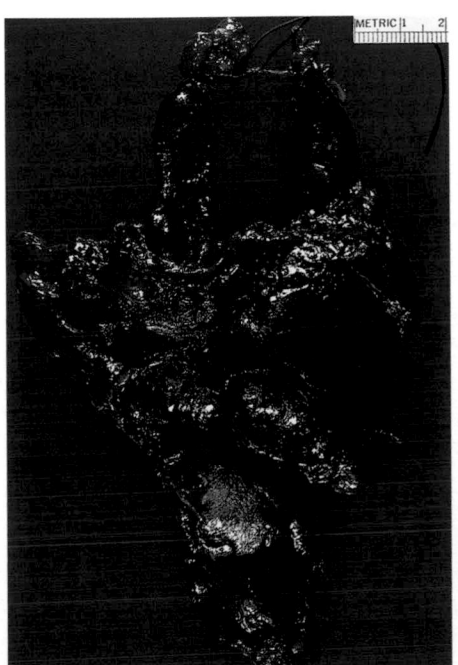
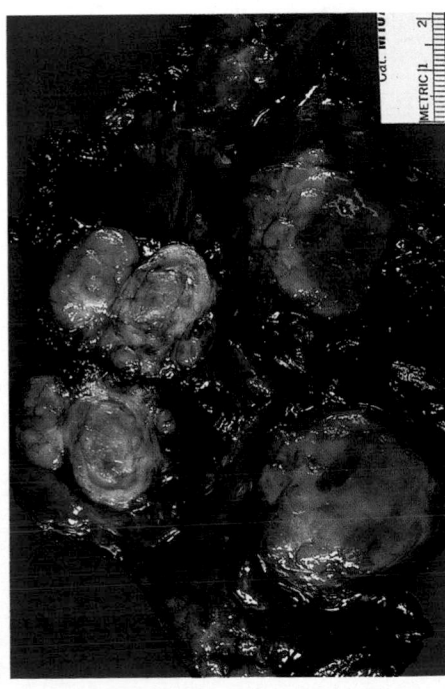

Fig. 8.59 A and **B**, Outer aspect and cut surface of nodular sclerosis Hodgkin's lymphoma of thymus showing characteristic multinodular involvement of the organ.

neoplastic nodules is usually sharper, and the contour of the nodules tends to be angular rather than round[489] (Fig. 8.60). The infiltrate of Hodgkin's lymphoma tends to be polymorphic, with lymphocytes, plasma cells, eosinophils, histiocytes, and the elements that provide

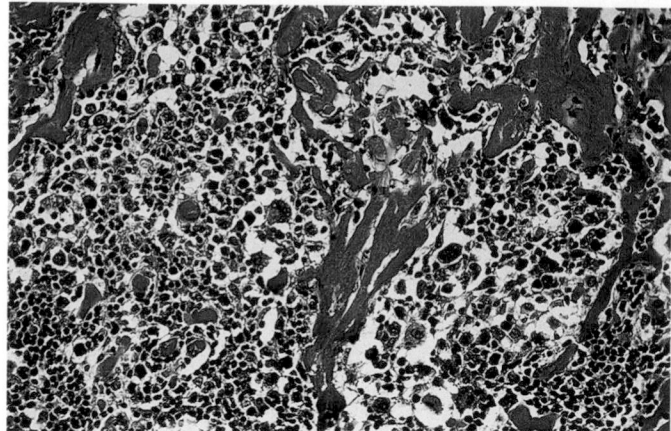

Fig. 8.60 Nodular sclerosis Hodgkin's lymphoma of thymus. Note the nodular character of the process, the intense intra- and internodular fibrosis, and the polymorphic nature of the infiltrate.

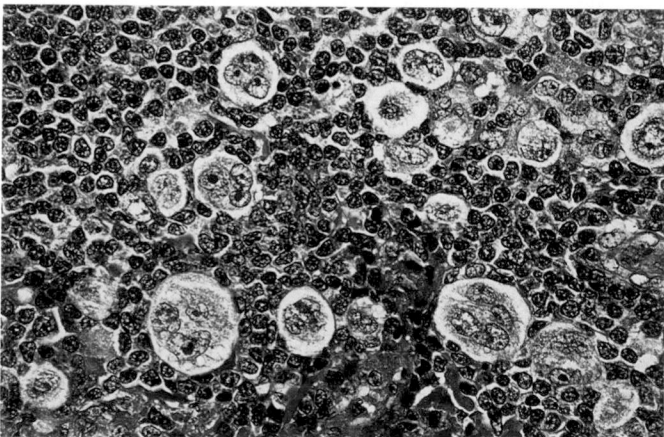

Fig. 8.61 High-power view of Hodgkin's lymphoma of thymus, showing numerous lacunar cells.

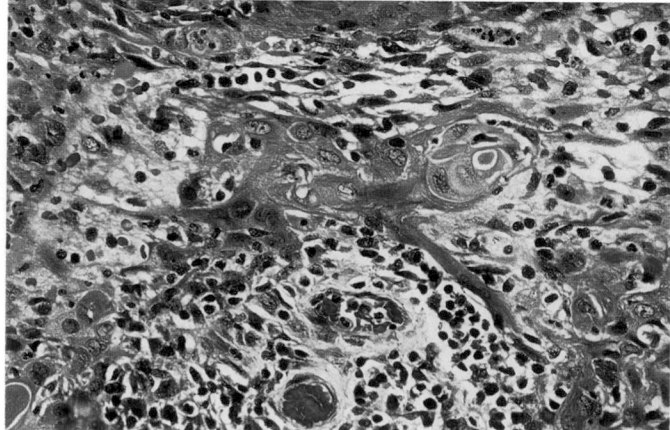

Fig. 8.62 Hodgkin's lymphoma of thymus accompanied by reactive hyperplasia of the entrapped thymic epithelium, which can simulate a thymic carcinoma of squamous type.

the diagnosis, i.e., Reed–Sternberg cells, their mononuclear variants, and lacunar cells (Fig. 8.61). These are often seen in intimate association with epithelial-lined cysts, Hassall's corpuscles, and isolated thymic epithelial cells (Fig. 8.62). This feature has led in the past to a misinterpretation of the lesion as a "granulomatous" thymoma.[484,485,492] The fact that the thymus is the only extranodal site in which Hodgkin's lymphoma occurs frequently and the intimate relationship that the Reed–Sternberg cells and other lymphoid elements bear with the thymic epithelium suggest the existence of a pathogenetic mechanism that ought to be explored. Immunohistochemical stains for CD15 or CD30 and keratin sharply delineate the lymphoid neoplastic and epithelial reactive components, respectively. Another confusing pattern results from the arrangement of these cells in compact and rather monomorphic clusters, often surrounding foci of necrosis ("syncytial type" of Hodgkin's lymphoma, see Chapter 21). These foci may simulate non-Hodgkin's lymphoma, germ cell tumor, and carcinoma. Conversely, some foci—especially at the periphery—may show only a nonspecific chronic inflammatory infiltrate and fibrosis and be misdiagnosed as sclerosing mediastinitis. In some instances, the disease is accompanied by the formation of lymphoid follicles with prominent germinal centers, so a mistaken diagnosis of Castleman's disease may result. In cases of this sort, if there is a strong radiographic suspicion of malignancy, a new biopsy from a more centrally located area should be requested. An important differential diagnostic point about the fibrosis is that in addition to wide bands, it also manifests itself as a fine network that entraps small groups of cells or even individual cells, this resulting in a blurring of the boundaries of the nodules. This is not a feature of thymoma, although it can also be seen in large cell lymphoma.

The prognosis of mediastinal Hodgkin's lymphoma is similar whether the neoplasm involves the thymus, the mediastinal lymph nodes, or both.[486] The disease seldom spreads subdiaphragmatically in the absence of supraclavicular lymph node involvement.

The primary treatment is radiation therapy,[488] although it may be appropriate to precede this by surgical excision if the lesion found at operation is of a well-circumscribed nature.[483,494] Chemotherapy is added to "unfavorable" early stages and to advanced stages. Sometimes, the aforementioned multilocular thymic cystic formations develop after the administration of radiation therapy and may simulate radiographically tumor relapse.[482,487]

Lymphoblastic lymphoma

Lymphoblastic lymphoma has a particular predilection for the thymic region. It is usually of immature T-cell type (hence the recommended T-precursor lymphoblastic lymphoma/leukemia terminology in the REAL/

WHO classification), but a certain degree of phenotypic heterogeneity occurs.[496,496a] Some cases have been found to be of pre-T-cell type,[501] others of natural killer cell phenotype,[497] and still others of B-cell lineage.[502] Its typical presentation is in the form of acute respiratory distress in an adolescent, sometimes requiring emergency radiation therapy.[499,500] Males are more commonly affected than females. The disease is usually restricted to the supradiaphragmatic region, with frequent involvement of cervical, supraclavicular, and axillary nodes but sparing of peripheral blood or bone marrow. Grossly, the tumor is generally solid, soft, and nonencapsulated. Some preservation of the thymic shape can be appreciated in early cases. Microscopically, the infiltrate involves the thymic parenchyma and can be confused with a lymphocyte-rich (type B1) thymoma. However, the lymphocytes are atypical, with a very fine chromatin pattern, frequent nuclear convolutions (hence the older term *convoluted cell lymphoma*), numerous mitotic figures, and equally numerous necrotic cells (Fig. 8.63). Their "blastic" appearance is indistinguishable from that seen in the cells of acute lymphoblastic leukemia. There is usually extension into the perithymic fat, and blood vessel invasion is frequent (Fig. 8.64). Residual thymic lobules and Hassall's corpuscles that have been expanded and infiltrated by the lymphoma cells should not be misinterpreted as evidence of thymoma (Fig. 8.65). It also should be remembered that true thymomas in children are exceptional. Fibrosis and formation of multilocular thymic cysts can be seen in thymic lymphoblastic lymphoma, but both phenomena are distinctly less common than in Hodgkin's lymphoma. Occasionally, there is a scattering of eosinophils, and we have seen a case accompanied by focal granulomatous reaction. Necrosis can be very extensive, whether spontaneous or induced by radiation or steroid therapy, to the extent that the entire biopsy may show only necrotic lymphoma tissue. Under these circumstances, if the clinicoradiographic features

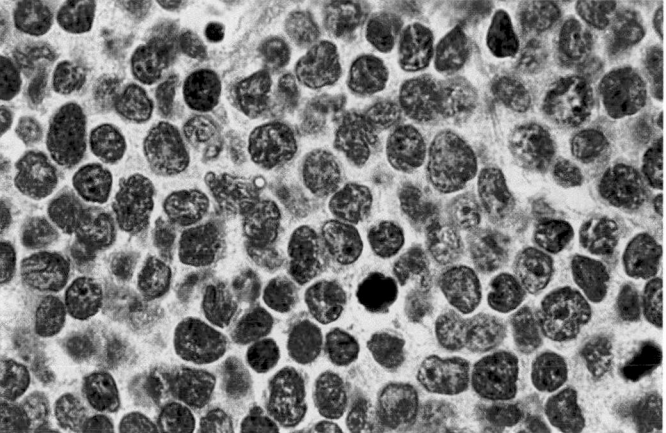

Fig. 8.63 High-power view of lymphoblastic lymphoma of thymus, showing delicate convolutions of the nuclear membrane of the tumor cells.

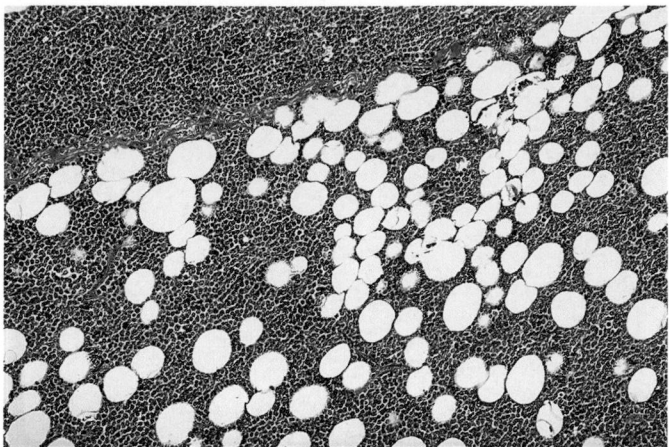

Fig. 8.64 Diffuse infiltration of mediastinal fat by lymphoblastic lymphoma.

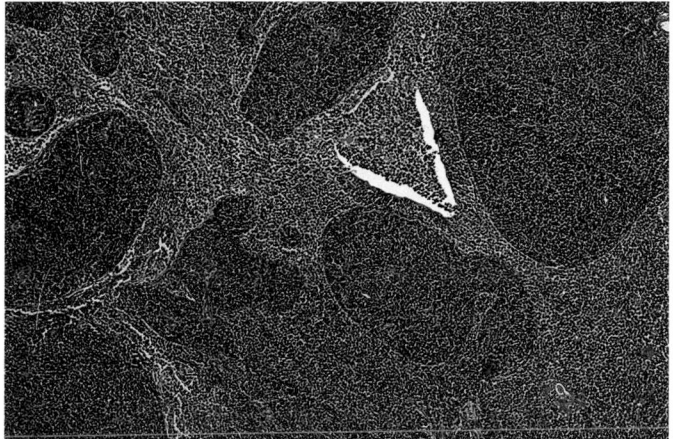

Fig. 8.65 Infiltration and expansion of thymic lobules by lymphoblastic lymphoma.

are compatible, the possibility of lymphoblastic lymphoma should be suspected, and a new biopsy should be requested.

A few cases of lymphoblastic lymphoma apparently developing from the lymphocytic component of lymphocyte-rich (type B1) thymomas have been reported.[495,498]

Large cell lymphoma

Mediastinal large cell lymphoma can present as a mass in the thymus with or without lymph node involvement. Most patients are young adult females, and presentation with superior vena caval syndrome is frequent.[503–505,518,520,525] The tumor has grossly invasive features: extension into pericardium, pleura, lung, sternum, and chest wall is common.[515,520] The consistency is generally firm, and there are frequent foci of necrosis (Fig. 8.66). Microscopically, a sometimes striking feature is the presence of wide bands of fibrosis, which results in compartmentalization of the tumor cells (Fig. 8.67) and a microscopic appearance that simulates an epithelial, germ cell, or neuroendocrine neoplasm.[520] Other reasons for the frequent misdiagnosis of this tumor

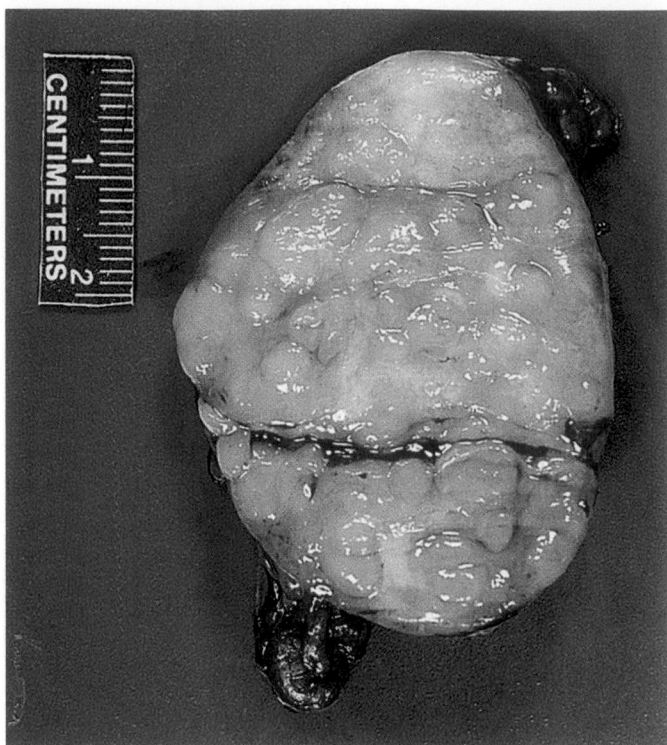

Fig. 8.66 Gross appearance of large cell lymphoma with sclerosis of the thymus. There is distinct nodularity induced by the fibrous strands. This appearance is not too dissimilar from that of nodular sclerosis Hodgkin's lymphoma.

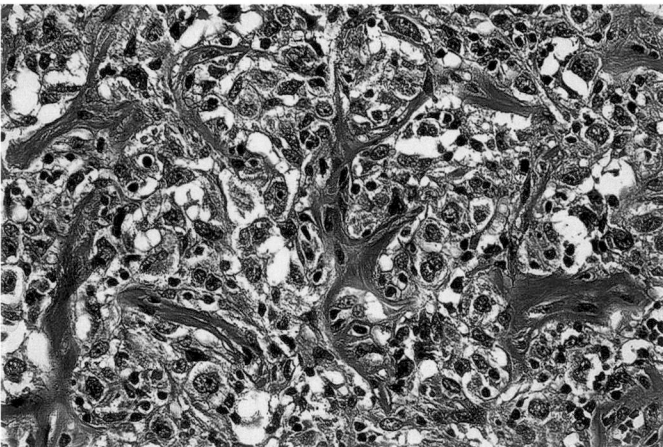

Fig. 8.67 Large B-cell lymphoma of thymus with extensive fibrosis and nodularity.

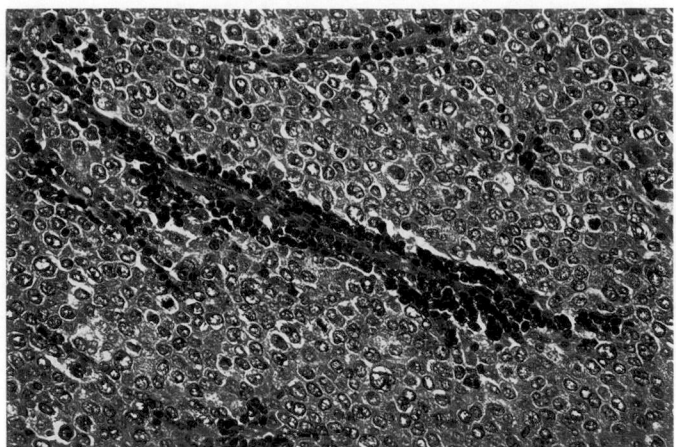

Fig. 8.68 Perivascular cuffing by small non-neoplastic lymphocytes in large B-cell lymphoma. The formations should not be confused with the perivascular spaces of thymoma.

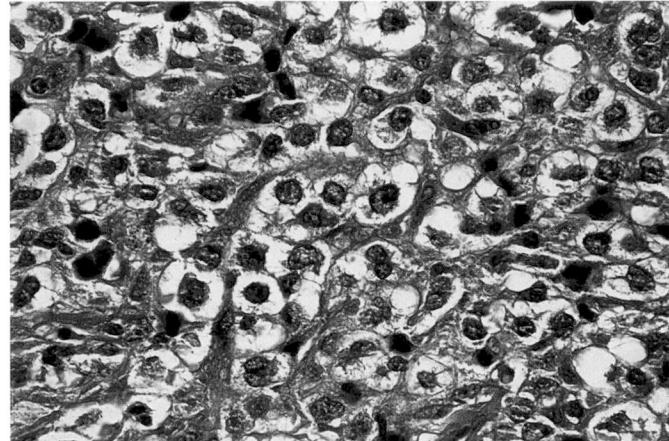

Fig. 8.69 Artifactual cytoplasmic clearing in a case of large B-cell lymphoma which has been formal-fixed.

include the following: perivascular collections of lymphocytes (which may be misinterpreted as the perivascular spaces of thymoma) (Fig. 8.68); artifactual clearing of the cytoplasm induced by formalin fixation (not present in B5 or Zenker's fixed material) (Fig. 8.69); presence of a large number of reactive T cells[510]; and entrapment of thymic epithelium.[508,520] The last feature can also create problems when the tumor is examined ultrastructurally or when immunostained for keratin.[520] Parenthetically, another immunohistochemical pitfall is represented by lysozyme and other histiocytic markers, in the sense that the sometimes abundant reactive histiocytic population may lead to a mistaken diagnosis of true histiocytic lymphoma.

A diagnosis of large cell lymphoma should be favored in the presence of tumor cells with large, vesicular, irregularly shaped nuclei (indented, kidney-shaped, polylobated); entrapment of intrathymic and perithymic fat; invasion of blood vessel wall, pleura, or lung; and the fact that the fibrosis is manifested not only in the form of wide hyaline bands but also as a fine network that entraps individual cells.[519] In some cases, the cellular pleomorphism is extreme.[523] Exceptionally, the tumor cells show tropism for germinal centers.[522] The diagnosis may be suspected on the basis of fine needle aspiration material.[521] Immunohistochemical reactivity for CD45 is invariably found. The large majority of the tumors are of B-cell nature,[504,506,517,520,528] but T-cell malignancies are also represented.[527] Close to 70% of the cases also express CD30.[512] They have also been found to express bcl-6 and CD10, suggesting a derivation from germinal center cells.[509,520a] The peculiar morphologic, immunohistochemical, and molecular attributes of mediastinal large cell lymphoma are significantly different from those of large B-cell lymphoma at other sites.[526] It has been postulated that it represents a distinct type of lymphoma, possibly arising from a subset of intrathymic lymphoid cells ("asteroid B-cells"),[508,511] and that MAL (an integral membrane protein located in glycolipid-enriched membrane microdomains, called lipid rafts) is a distinct molecular marker for this tumor.[507a] It should be kept in mind that in young females with a clinically and microscopically malignant mediastinal tumor in which the differential diagnosis is among malignant thymoma, seminoma (germinoma), and large cell malignant lymphoma, the correct diagnosis will be the latter entity in the large majority of cases.

Large cell malignant lymphoma of mediastinum is usually restricted to the intrathoracic region at the time of initial presentation. An excellent response to radiation therapy and chemotherapy is the rule,[505,516] but in some instances the tumor recurs within the chest and spreads to other sites, including peripheral lymph nodes and central nervous system.[507,514] The presence of pleural effusion at presentation is associated with poor outcome.[513] We have been impressed by the high frequency with which the kidneys have been found to be involved in recurrent disease,[520,524] and wonder whether some "homing" mechanism is involved analogous to that hypothesized for MALT lymphoma.

Marginal zone B-cell lymphoma

In recent years there have been increasingly frequent reports of cases of marginal zone B-cell lymphomas involving the thymus, particularly from Asian countries.[529] A marked predilection for females has been noted, and many of the patients had a history of Sjögren's disease[534,535] or rheumatoid arthritis.[536] Some of the cases have been associated with lymph node[530] or gastric involvement.[532]

Microscopically, the tumors are predominantly composed of small lymphocytes with a variable admixture of monocytoid cells and plasma cells (Fig. 8.70). Prominent lymphoepithelial lesions are present, and there may be cystic formations.[529] Indeed, the presence in otherwise typical thymic lymphoid hyperplasia (of the type seen in association with collagen–vascular diseases) of sheets of centrocyte-like B cells disrupting the cytokeratin-positive medullary epithelial network should suggest the possibility of lymphoma, even if molecular analysis may be necessary to confirm the diagnosis.[533]

Notably, most cases of MALT-type thymic lymphoma express an IgA phenotype (in striking contrast with the IgM phenotype observed with this tumor type at other sites) and lack the *API2–MALT1* gene fusion that has been described in MALT-type lymphomas elsewhere.[529] The clinical course is usually indolent; however, as with marginal zone B-cell lymphomas at other sites, there may be transformation to a large cell lymphoma.[531]

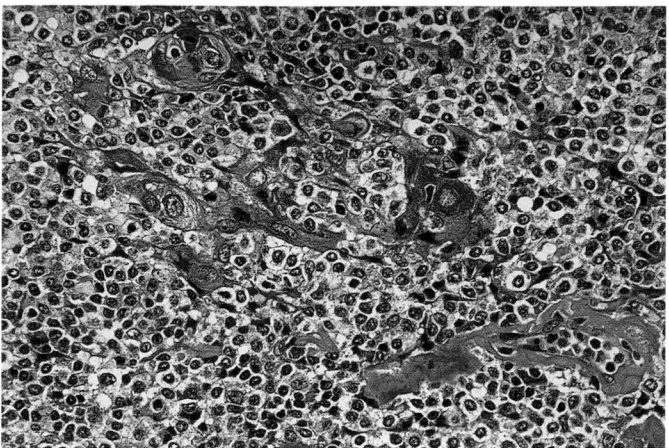

Fig. 8.70 Malignant lymphoma of marginal zone type involving the thymus. The tumor cells surround and distort Hassall's corpuscles. (Courtesy of Dr. John Chan, Hong Kong)

Other hematolymphoid conditions

Combined lymphomas of various types have been observed in this location. A type that we have seen with inordinately high frequency is that comprised by large B-cell lymphoma with sclerosis and nodular sclerosis Hodgkin's lymphoma, each component exhibiting its distinctive phenotype. The frequency of the association, the blending of the two components one sometimes observes, and the several clinicopathologic features they share (predilection for young females, tendency to induce sclerosis) suggest that these two processes are histogenetically and pathogenetically related. Support for this hypothesis comes from a molecular study carried out in one such combined case, in which the results suggested an origin of the tumor from a common precursor in which a secondary molecular event gave rise to two different clonally related lymphomas.[537]

Anaplastic large cell lymphoma can also present as a primary mediastinal mass.[539,548] The main differential diagnostic criteria are the same as for lymph nodes and other sites (see Chapter 21).

Granulocytic sarcoma (chloroma, myeloblastoma)[541,544] can present initially as a mediastinal mass and be mistaken for malignant lymphoma on microscopic grounds.

Plasmacytoma has been reported as a mediastinal mass, preceding the onset of multiple myeloma.[545]

Castleman's disease (giant lymph node hyperplasia) has a special predilection for the mediastinum. Before its recognition as an entity, it was often confused with thymoma because the hyalinized germinal centers that constitute the hallmark of the hyaline vascular form of this disease were misinterpreted as Hassall's corpuscles.[543] It usually involves mediastinal nodes, but exceptionally it may be located within the thymus.[542] Surgical removal of a unicentric mass of the hyaline vascular type of this disease (which is by far the most

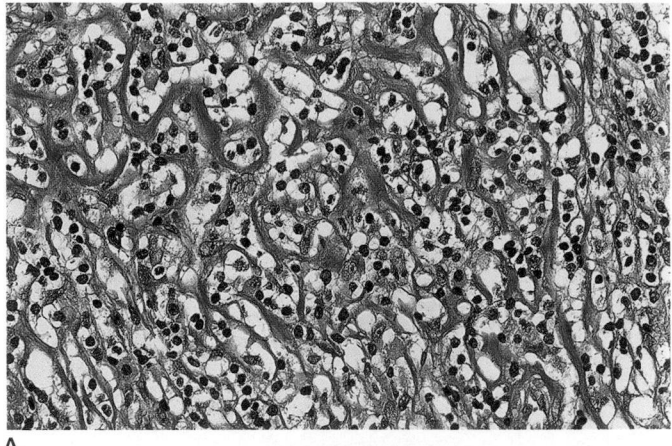

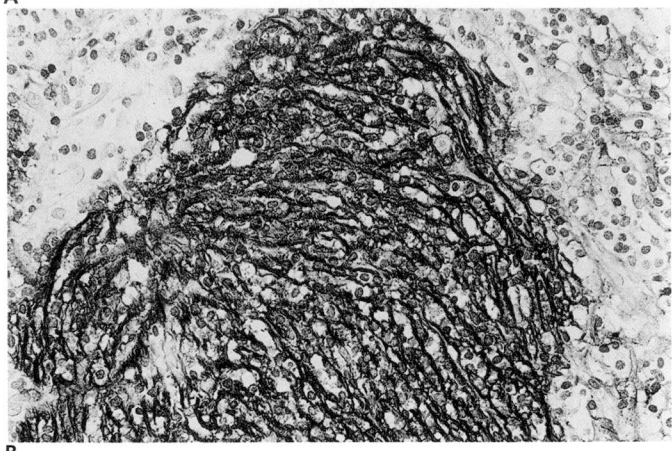

Fig. 8.71 A and **B**, H&E appearance and CD21 immunoreactivity of dendritic follicular cell tumor of mediastinum. The biphasic pattern resulting from the presence of numerous non-neoplastic lymphocytes can elicit a mistaken diagnosis of thymoma.

common) is curative.[538] This disorder is discussed more thoroughly in Chapter 21.

Extramedullary hematopoiesis may present as a large, solitary mediastinal mass, usually located along the paravertebral column. The primary disease in most patients is hereditary spherocytosis or thalassemia.[547] Myelolipoma is a microscopically similar process but it usually lacks evidence of a background hematologic disorder.[546]

Follicular dendritic cell tumor can present as a primary mediastinal mass arising from either lymph nodes or thymus[540] (Fig. 8.71). It is listed in this section because of the functional relationship of the cells of this tumor with the lymphoid system, but its behavior and response to therapy are more in keeping with a sarcoma.

Neurogenic tumors

Neurogenic tumors make up a high proportion of the posterior mediastinal neoplasms, in both adults and children, but they can also occur in other compartments.[549,552] The two major categories are tumors of the *sympathetic*

nervous system and tumors of *peripheral nerve sheath*. A definite relationship between age and the relative incidence of these tumors exists.[551] In a series of 160 cases,[550] the majority of the tumors occurring in patients younger than the age of 10 years belonged to the sympathetic nervous system category, and all of those in patients younger than 1 year of age were neuroblastomas or ganglioneuroblastomas. Most ganglioneuromas, paragangliomas, and tumors of nerve sheath origin were seen after the age of 20 years.

Radiographically, most tumors of the sympathetic nervous system have an elongated tapered appearance, whereas benign tumors of nerve sheath origin are round and well circumscribed.[550]

Tumors of sympathetic nervous system

The general features of these tumors are discussed in Chapter 16. The main difference between the mediastinal and retroperitoneal (particularly adrenal) tumors is the greater degree of differentiation seen in the former. Thus **neuroblastoma** is rather unusual in this location, appearing as an infiltrative mass with areas of necrosis and calcification, usually high in the posterior mediastinum and seen almost exclusively in children, although notable exceptions occur.[561] Most of the mediastinal tumors of this group in children are examples of **ganglioneuroblastoma**, a tumor that has an intermediate degree of differentiation and that is related to differentiating neuroblastoma and immature ganglioneuroma[553,560] (see Chapter 16). Grossly, it tends to be better circumscribed than the neuroblastoma and is sometimes surrounded by a well-formed capsule.

It should be mentioned that some neuroblastomas and ganglioneuroblastomas are located in the anterosuperior mediastinum (in close relationship with the thymus) rather than in the usual posterior location.[559] Curiously, some of these cases have been associated with inappropriate secretion of antidiuretic hormone (Fig. 8.72).[554,555]

Ganglioneuroma occurs in older children and in adults and is the most common of the three tumors.[558,562] Grossly, it forms a smooth, well-encapsulated mass, usually in the posterior portion of the mediastinum. The consistency is soft, and the cut surface is yellowish gray; it may contain cystic areas and fatty degeneration, but fresh necrosis is generally absent (Fig. 8.73). Microscopically, an admixture of mature ganglion cells and spindle cells, which could be viewed either as Schwann cells or satellite cells, is present. The ganglion cells may have several nuclei and are often arranged in clusters. Focal collections of lymphocytes are often present; they should not be confused with the immature cells of ganglioneuroblastoma. These tumors can be multiple and can occur in different locations, with various degrees of differentiation.

The survival rate in patients with tumors of the sympathetic nervous system is directly related to the degree

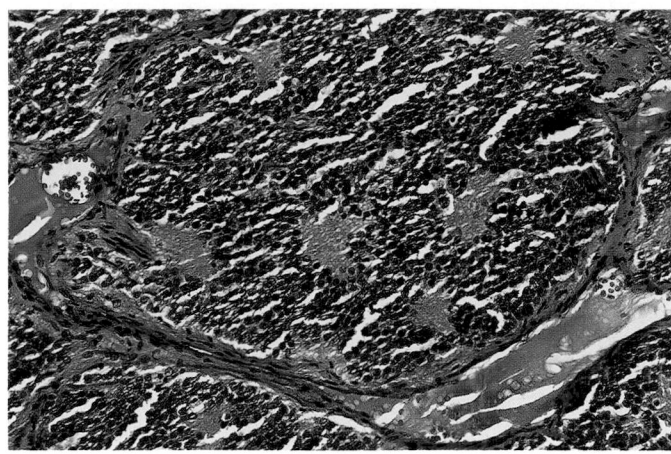

Fig. 8.72 Neuroblastoma of mediastinum with prominent rosettes in an adult patient. These tumors can be associated with inadequate secretion of ADH.

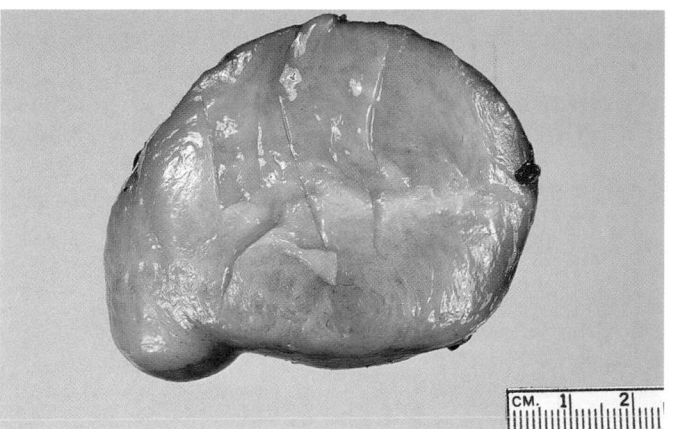

Fig. 8.73 Mediastinal ganglioneuroma. The tumor is solid, yellowish, and homogeneous.

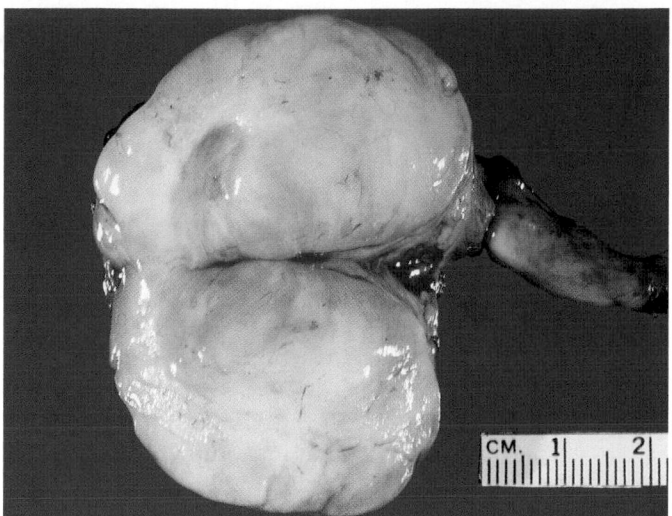

Fig. 8.74 Mediastinal neurofibroma. The tumor is attached to a large nerve trunk.

of differentiation of the tumor. As already stated, thoracic neoplasms tend to be better differentiated than their retroperitoneal (particularly adrenal) counterparts; this probably explains why as a group they are associated with a better prognosis.[556,563] Relapses in the central nervous system have occurred in some cases of intrathoracic neuroblastoma.[557] Adequate excision effects cure in all patients with ganglioneuromas. The prognosis in patients with ganglioneuroblastomas that contain both elements is somewhat unpredictable, but cure is achieved in most instances.[553] As expected, the prognosis in neuroblastoma is the least favorable for the entire group.

Tumors of peripheral nerves

The three major tumors in this category are schwannoma, neurofibroma, and malignant peripheral nerve sheath tumor (MPNST)[567–569] (Fig. 8.74). The general features of these tumors are discussed in Chapter 25. It is interesting to note that whereas neurofibroma in most other locations is a nonencapsulated tumor, in the mediastinum it is often surrounded by a complete fibrous capsule, perhaps because of the large size that it can

reach at this site. Therefore the presence of encapsulation cannot be used as a distinguishing feature between the two types of benign peripheral nerve tumor.

Another feature common to these neoplasms, perhaps again the result of their sometimes unduly large size, is the high frequency of regressive change within them, such as fatty degeneration, hemorrhage, and cystic formation. Some can become completely cystic, and their recognition may be difficult. Schwannomas exhibiting prominent cystic and other regressive changes have been described as "ancient," under the assumption that they have been present for a very long time.[564] Indeed, most benign peripheral nerve sheath tumors are asymptomatic and are discovered incidentally on chest x-ray examinations. Some schwannomas can be very cellular, somewhat pleomorphic, and mitotically active and thus be confused with sarcoma.[566,570] The prognosis for both schwannoma and neurofibroma is excellent, excision being curative in nearly every instance.

MPNST of mediastinum may arise *de novo* or, more commonly, in the setting of neurofibromatosis type I.[564,565] In the initial stages of the malignant transformation of a neurofibroma the change may be barely perceptible microscopically, the only suggestion being some slight increase in cellularity. With outspoken malignant change, the tumor cells become bizarre, and it may then be impossible to recognize the malignant tumor as originating from a preexisting neurofibroma. In these instances, the presence of neurofibromatosis, previous biopsy, or the presence of other neurofibromas may suggest the diagnosis.

Some mediastinal MPNST have areas of glandular differentiation or rhabdomyoblastic features (so-called "triton tumor"). The prognosis, which is generally poor, seems to be related to resection status, tumor, size, and tumor grade.[565]

Other neurogenic tumors

Two types of central nervous system-related neoplasm that can exceptionally present as primary (usually posterior) mediastinal neoplasms are **ependymoma**[571,573] and **meningioma**[572]; the latter, which may have its origin in the stellate ganglion, is closely related to and sometimes indistinguishable from perineurioma.

Tumors of paraganglia

Most mediastinal paragangliomas occur in association with the aorticopulmonary paraganglia and therefore occur in the anterosuperior mediastinum close to the base of the heart. Others arise from mediastinal aorticosympathetic paraganglia and occur posteriorly, along the costovertebral sulcus. Their morphologic appearance is identical to paragangliomas in other locations, such as the carotid body (see Chapter 16). A few have been pigmented.[575]

The majority of these tumors are nonfunctioning. Some, however (particularly when related to the sympathetic system), can result in hypertension and are sometimes referred to as extra-adrenal pheochromocytomas.[577] However, it is now agreed to reserve the designation of pheochromocytomas for paragangliomas located in the adrenal medulla, whether they are functioning or not.

Some mediastinal paragangliomas have occurred as a component of the so-called "Carney triad," together with pulmonary hamartomas and gastrointestinal malignant stromal tumors.[574]

Traditionally, mediastinal paragangliomas have been regarded as generally benign in nature. However, a critical long-term follow-up study of 35 reported cases revealed that the tumor had behaved in an aggressive fashion in 16 (46%), resulting in important morbidity and sometimes in death.[578] Subsequent experience with this tumor has confirmed these findings.[576]

Mesenchymal tumors

The list of microscopic types of mediastinal neoplasms of soft tissue is long despite their rarity.[600,609]

Lipoma is one of the most common benign mesenchymal neoplasms of the mediastinum. It is often very large and located just above the diaphragm. Occasionally, it extends into both pleural cavities, making complete removal difficult.[600] The presence of thymic tissue should be sought in mediastinal lipomas to rule out a diagnosis of thymolipoma (see p. 484). The differential diagnosis also includes *lipomatosis*, a diffuse accumulation of mature adipose tissue that may occur in association with obesity, Cushing's disease, or steroid therapy,[593] and

which can lead to a "sabre sheath" tracheal deformity radiographically.[594]

Other benign adipose tissue tumors of the mediastinum include *lipoblastoma* and *lipoblastomatosis* of infancy,[586] *hibernoma*,[579] and *angiolipoma*.[596]

Lymphangioma is another common mediastinal neoplasm (Fig. 8.75). Most cases are seen in the anterosuperior mediastinum of children, often in continuity with a cervical component.[583] *Lymphangiomyoma* and *lymphangiomyomatosis* occur exclusively in females, the distinction among the two depending on their circumscribed versus infiltrative pattern of growth, respectively (see Chapter 25).

Hemangioma in adults is usually of the cavernous variety (Fig. 8.76). Microscopically, it is composed of dilated vessels lined by attenuated endothelium, separated by fine septa. Foci of thrombosis, calcification, and cholesterol granulomas may be present. Excision is usually curative.[608] In children, the hemangiomas may have a very cellular appearance (benign hemangioendotheliomas).[581] **Glomus tumors** have been described in the mediastinum, some of them having

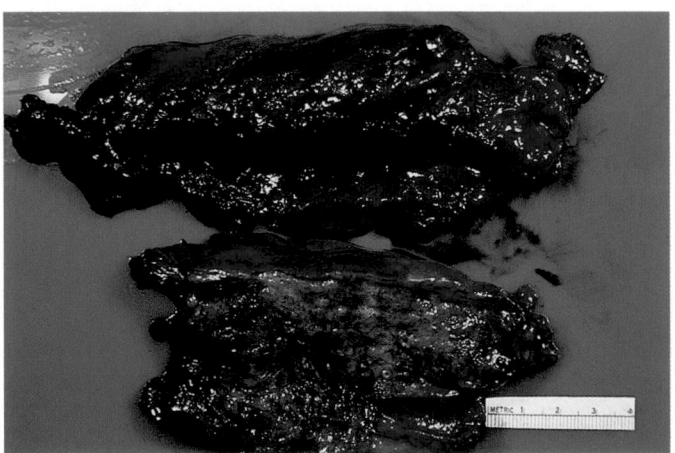

Fig. 8.75 Lymphangioma of mediastinum. The tumor has a multicystic appearance which is similar to that of multilocular thymic cyst.

Fig. 8.76 Hemangioma of mediastinum. The tumor is formed of large tortuous vessels.

atypical features.[598,592] **Hemangiopericytomas** probably occur in this location, but most anterosuperior mediastinal tumors with a hemangiopericytoma-like pattern are well-vascularized thymomas or solitary fibrous tumors (see the following section). Another vascular tumor that can occur in the mediastinum is **epithelioid hemangioendothelioma**[606,609,610]; curiously, some of these tumors have been accompanied by osteoclast-like multinucleated giant cells, a feature almost never seen in epithelioid hemangioendotheliomas at other sites.[597,611] **Angiosarcoma** also occurs[590]; in such cases, the possibility of the lesion having arisen against a background of a germ cell tumor should be investigated by thorough sampling.[598]

Leiomyoma, sometimes arising from vascular trunks, has been reported in approximately 10 instances.[602]

Rhabdomyoma has been seen in the mediastinum in connection with the thymus (see p. 475) but also independently from it.[602a]

Solitary fibrous tumor of the mediastinum is the mediastinal equivalent of solitary fibrous tumor of the pleura (formerly known as solitary fibrous mesothelioma).[591,613] It is possible that some of these tumors grow into the mediastinum from the medial pleura, but we think that most originate from the mediastinal (including thymic) stroma. Their microscopic appearance and immunohistochemical profile are similar to those of their pleural counterpart, but a higher proportion of the reported cases have run an aggressive clinical course[613] (Fig. 8.77).

Liposarcoma predominates among the malignant mesenchymal neoplasms[595,603] (Fig. 8.78). Sometimes it is seen in conjunction with liposarcoma of thigh or retroperitoneum as a manifestation of multicentric disease.[580] Some mediastinal liposarcomas containing thymic tissue can be viewed as thymic stromal sarcomas with a liposarcomatous component and as possible counterparts of thymolipomas (i.e., as thymoliposarcomas).[595]

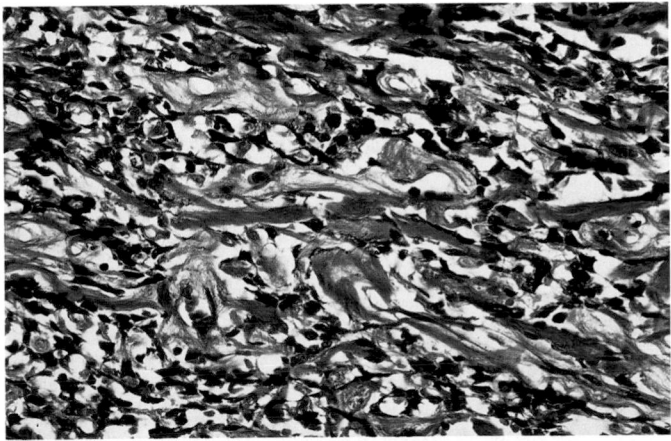

Fig. 8.77 Solitary fibrous tumor of mediastinum. The alternation of hyper- and hypocellular areas is typical of this entity.

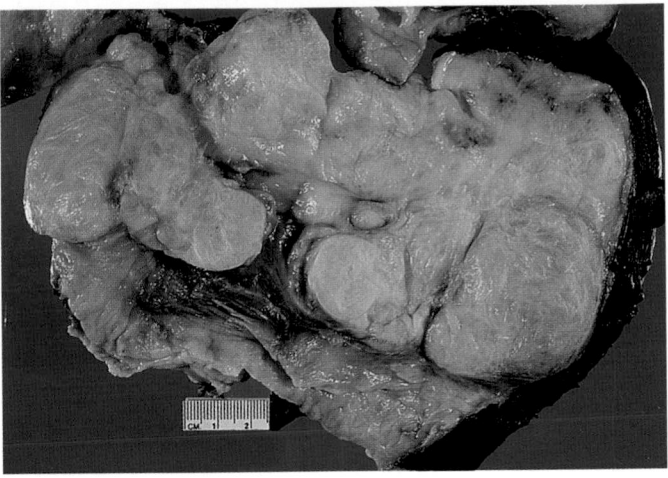

Fig 8.78 Gross appearance of a well-differentiated liposarcoma (atypical lipomatous tumor) of mediastinum.

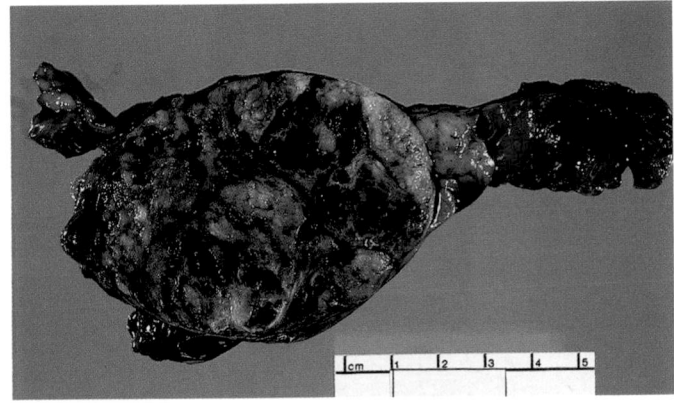

Fig. 8.79 Gross appearance of a primary synovial sarcoma of mediastinum.

Synovial sarcoma can present as a primary mediastinal neoplasm, its morphologic appearance being the same as that of the most common type occurring in the extremities[612] (Fig. 8.79). Both biphasic and monophasic types occur.

Other malignant mesenchymal tumors that have been observed in the mediastinum include **fibrosarcoma,**[601] **leiomyosarcoma,**[599,604] **rhabdomyosarcoma** (unassociated with germ cell, thymic, or peripheral nerve elements),[582,607] **chondrosarcoma**[605] (including the mesenchymal variety[585]), **alveolar soft part sarcoma,**[587] **giant cell tumor of soft parts,**[588] **malignant mesenchymoma,** and **malignant fibrous histiocytoma.**[584]

Metastatic tumors

Some tumors metastatic to the mediastinum can mimic clinically and radiographically a primary mediastinal neoplasm. Small cell undifferentiated carcinoma of the lung is the most notorious example, often appearing as a huge mediastinal mass in the presence of a small,

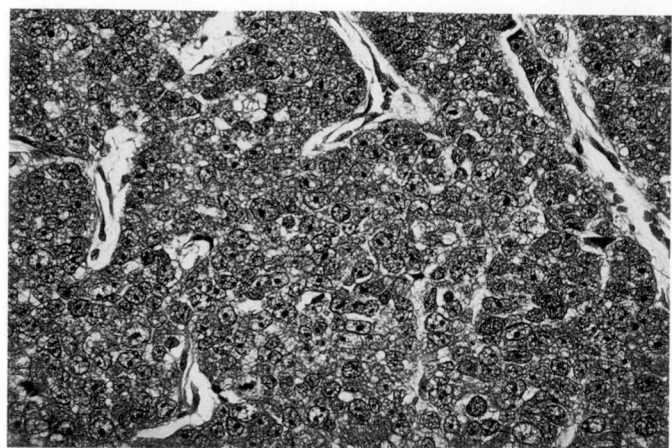

Fig. 8.80 Mediastinal metastasis of prostatic adenocarcinoma. This tumor was initially misdiagnosed as a thymic carcinoma.

radiographically undetectable bronchial lesion. Other types of lung carcinoma may produce a similar picture, by either direct extension or nodal metastases.

Direct mediastinal extension can also occur with tumors of the esophagus, pleura, chest wall, vertebra, or trachea. Other tumors that can metastasize to the mediastinum and be confused with primary neoplasms—sometimes even at the microscopic level—are carcinomas of the breast, thyroid, nasopharynx, larynx, kidney, and prostate; testicular germ cell tumors; and malignant melanoma.[614–616] Two such tumor types that we have seen initially misinterpreted as thymic carcinomas were metastatic prostatic carcinoma and metastatic malignant melanoma (Fig. 8.80). Since most of these tumors are located, at least initially, in mediastinal lymph nodes, they are usually centered in the middle mediastinum (where most lymph nodes are situated), and they may exhibit a residual nodal component at their periphery.

References

Generalities

1 Azarow KS, Pearl RH, Zurcher R, Edwards FH, Cohen AJ. Primary mediastinal masses. A comparison of adult and pediatric populations. J Thorac Cardiovasc Surg 1993, **106:** 67–72.

2 Blegvad S, Lippert H, Simper LB, Dybdahl H. Mediastinal tumours. A report of 129 cases. Scand J Thorac Cardiovasc Surg 1990, **24:** 39–42.

3 Cohen AJ, Thompson L, Edwards FH, Bellamy RF. Primary cysts and tumors of the mediastinum. Ann Thorac Surg 1991, **51:** 378–384.

4 Ingram L, Rivera GK, Shapiro DN. Superior vena cava syndrome associated with childhood malignancy. Analysis of 24 cases. Med Pediatr Oncol 1990, **18:** 476–481.

5 Mahajan V, Strimlan V, Van Ordstrand HS, Loop FD. Benign superior vena cava syndrome. Chest 1975, **68:** 32–35.

6 Marshall ME, Trump DL. Acquired extrinsic pulmonic stenosis caused by mediastinal tumors. Cancer 1982, **49:** 1496–1499.

7 Oldham HN Jr, Sabiston DC Jr. Primary tumors and cysts of the mediastinum. Monogr Surg Sci 1967, **4:** 243–279.

8 Parish JM, Marschke PF Jr, Dines DE, Lee RE. Etiologic considerations in superior vena cava syndrome. Mayo Clin Proc 1981, **56:** 407–413.

9 Ringertz N, Lidholm SO. Mediastinal tumors and cysts. J Thorac Surg 1956, **31:** 458–487.

10 Schechter MM. The superior vena cava syndrome. Am J Med Sci 1954, **227:** 46–56.

11 Simpson I, Campbell PE. Mediastinal masses in childhood. A review from a paediatric pathologist's point of view. Prog Pediatr Surg 1991, **27:** 92–126.

12 Sterrett G, Whitaker D, Glancy J. Fine-needle aspiration of lung, mediastinum, and chest wall. A clinicopathologic exercise. Pathol Annu 1982, **17**(Pt 2): 197–228.

13 Wychulis AR, Payne WS, Clagett OT, Woolner LB. Surgical treatment of mediastinal tumors. A 40-year experience. J Thorac Cardiovasc Surg 1971, **62:** 379–392.

Inflammatory diseases

14 Cogan MIC. Necrotizing mediastinitis secondary to descending cervical cellulitis. Oral Surg Oral Med Oral Pathol 1973, **36:** 307–320.

15 Crotty TB, Colby TV, Gay PC, Pisani RJ. Desmoplastic malignant mesothelioma masquerading as sclerosing mediastinitis. A diagnostic dilemma. Hum Pathol 1992, **23:** 79–82.

16 Dines DE, Payne WS, Bernatz PE, Pairolero PC. Mediastinal granuloma and fibrosing mediastinitis. Chest 1979, **75:** 320–324.

17 Domart Y, Trouillet JL, Fagon JY, Chastre J, Brun-Vezinet F, Gibert C. Incidence and morbidity of cytomegaloviral infection in patients with mediastinitis following cardiac surgery. Chest 1990, **97:** 18–22.

18 Dreyfuss D, Djedaini K, Bidault-Lapomme C, Coste F. Nontraumatic acute anterior mediastinitis in two HIV-positive heroin addicts. Chest 1992, **101:** 583–585.

19 Ferguson TB, Burford TH. Mediastinal granuloma. A 15-year experience. Ann Thorac Surg 1965, **1:** 125–141.

20 Flieder DB, Suster S, Moran CA. Idiopathic fibroinflammatory (fibrosing/sclerosing) lesions of the mediastinum: a study of 30 cases with emphasis on morphologic heterogeneity. Mod Pathol 1999, **12:** 257–264.

21 Goodwin RA, Nickell JA, Des Prez RM. Mediastinal fibrosis complicating healed primary histoplasmosis and tuberculosis. Medicine (Baltimore) 1972, **51:** 227–246.

22 Lalwani AK, Kaplan MJ. Mediastinal and thoracic complications of necrotizing fasciitis of the head and neck. Head Neck 1991, **13:** 531–539.

23 Light AM. Idiopathic fibrosis of mediastinum. A discussion of three cases and review of the literature. J Clin Pathol 1978, **31:** 78–88.

24 Magee JF, Wright JL, Dodek A, Tutassaura H. Mediastinal and retroperitoneal fibrosis with fibrotic pulmonary nodules. A case report. Histopathology 1985, **9:** 995–999.

25 Mitchell IM, Saunders HR, Maher O, Lennox SC, Walker DR. Surgical treatment of idiopathic mediastinal fibrosis. Report of five cases. Thorax 1986, **41:** 210–214.

26 Mitchinson MJ. The pathology of idiopathic retroperitoneal fibrosis. J Clin Pathol 1970, **23:** 681–689.

27 Payne WS, Larson RH. Acute mediastinitis. Surg Clin North Am 1969, **49:** 999–1009.

28 Rankin RS, Wescott JL. Superior vena cava syndrome caused by *Nocardia* mediastinitis. Am Rev Respir Dis 1973, **108:** 361–363.

29 Salyer JM, Harrison HN, Winn DF Jr, Taylor RR. Chronic fibrous mediastinitis and superior vena caval obstruction due to histoplasmosis. Dis Chest 1959, **35:** 364–377.

30 Schowengerdt CG, Suyemoto R, Main FB. Granulomatous and fibrous mediastinitis. A review and analysis of 180 cases. J Thorac Cardiovasc Surg 1969, **57:** 365–379.

31 Strimlan CV, Dines DE, Payne WS. Mediastinal granuloma. Mayo Clin Proc 1975, **50:** 702–705.

Cysts (other than thymic)
Pericardial (coelomic) cysts

32 Lillie WI, McDonald JR, Clagett OT. Pericardial celomic cysts and pericardial diverticula. A concept of etiology and report of cases. J Thorac Surg 1950, **20**: 494–504.

33 Wick MR. Mediastinal cysts and intrathoracic thyroid tumors. Semin Diagn Pathol 1990, **7**: 285–294.

Foregut cysts

34 Abell MR. Mediastinal cysts. Arch Pathol 1956, **61**: 360–379.

35 Chitale AR. Gastric cyst of the mediastinum. A distinct clinicopathological entity. J Pediatr 1969, **75**: 104–110.

36 Chuang MT, Barba FA, Kaneko M, Teirstein AS. Adenocarcinoma arising in an intrathoracic duplication cyst of foregut origin. A case report with review of the literature. Cancer 1981, **47**: 1887–1890.

37 Crombleholme TM, deLorimier AA, Adzick NS, Longaker MT, Harrison MR, Cox KL, Heyman MB. Mediastinal pancreatic pseudocysts in children. J Pediatr Surg 1990, **25**: 843–845.

38 Eraklis AJ, Griscom NT, McGovern JB. Bronchogenic cysts of the mediastinum in infancy. N Engl J Med 1969, **281**: 1150–1155.

39 Johnston RH Jr, Owensby LC, Vargas GM, Garcia-Rinaldi R. Pancreatic pseudocyst of the mediastinum. Ann Thorac Surg 1986, **41**: 210–212.

40 Olsen JB, Clemmensen O, Andersen K. Adenocarcinoma arising in a foregut cyst of the mediastinum. Ann Thorac Surg 1991, **51**: 497–499.

41 Perez-Ordonez B, Wesson DE, Smith CR, Asa SL. A pancreatic cyst of the anterior mediastinum. Mod Pathol 1996, **9**: 210–214.

42 Salyer DC, Salyer WR, Eggleston JC. Benign developmental cysts of the mediastinum. Arch Pathol 1977, **101**: 136–139.

43 Simpson I, Campbell PE. Mediastinal masses in childhood. A review from a paediatric pathologist's point of view. Prog Pediatr Surg 1991, **27**: 92–126.

44 St-Georges R, Deslauriers J, Duranceau A, Vaillancourt R, Deschamps C, Beauchamp G, Pagè A, Brisson J. Clinical spectrum of bronchogenic cysts of the mediastinum and lung in the adult. Ann Thorac Surg 1991, **52**: 6–13.

45 Wick MR. Mediastinal cysts and intrathoracic thyroid tumors. Semin Diagn Pathol 1990, **7**: 285–294.

Other cysts

46 Mori M, Kidogawa H, Isoshima K. Thoracic duct cyst in the mediastinum. Thorax 1992, **47**: 325–326.

47 Sambrook Gowar FJ. Mediastinal thoracic duct cyst. Thorax 1978, **33**: 800–802.

Thyroid and parathyroid lesions

48 Allo MD, Thompson NW. Rationale for the operative management of substernal goiters. Surgery 1983, **94**: 969–977.

49 Hofbauer LC, Spitzweg C, Arnholdt H, Landgraf R, Heufelder AE. Mediastinal parathyroid tumor: giant adenoma or carcinoma? Endocr Pathol 1997, **8**: 161–166.

50 Katlic MR, Wang C, Grillo HC. Substernal goiter. Ann Thorac Surg 1985, **39**: 391–399.

51 Murphy MN, Glennon PG, Diocee MS, Wick MR, Cavers DJ. Nonsecretory parathyroid carcinoma of the mediastinum. Light microscopic, immunocytochemical, and ultrastructural features of a case, and review of the literature. Cancer 1986, **58**: 2468–2476.

52 Schlinkert RT, Whitaker MD, Argueta R. Resection of select mediastinal parathyroid adenomas through an anterior mediastinotomy. Mayo Clin Proc 1991, **66**: 1110–1113.

53 Shields TW, Immerman SC. Mediastinal parathyroid cysts revisited. Ann Thorac Surg 1999, **67**: 581–590.

54 Wick MR. Mediastinal cysts and intrathoracic thyroid tumors. Semin Diagn Pathol 1990, **7**: 285–294.

Thymus
Normal anatomy

55 Anderson G, Jenkinson EJ. Lymphostromal interactions in thymic development and function. Nat Rev Immunol 2001, **1**: 31–40.

56 Barthélémy H, Pelletier M, Landry D, Lafontaine M, Perreault C, Tautu C, Montplaisir S. Demonstration of OKT6 antigen on human thymic dendritic cells in culture. Lab Invest 1986, **55**: 540–545.

57 Dourov N. Thymic atrophy and immune deficiency in malnutrition. In Müller-Hermelink HK (ed.): Current topics in pathology. The human thymus. Histophysiology and pathology, vol. 75. New York, 1986, Springer-Verlag, pp. 127–150.

58 Flores KG, Li J, Hale LP. B cells in epithelial and perivascular compartments of human adult thymus. Hum Pathol 2001, **32**: 926–934.

59 Fukai I, Funato Y, Mizuno T, Hashimoto T, Masaoka A. Distribution of thymic tissue in the mediastinal adipose tissue. J Thorac Cardiovasc Surg 1991, **101**: 1099–1102.

60 Goldstein G, Mackay IR. The human thymus. St. Louis, 1969, Warren H. Green.

61 Gutierrez JC, Palacios R. Heterogeneity of thymic epithelial cells in promoting T-lymphocyte differentiation in vivo. Proc Natl Acad Sci U S A 1991, **88**: 642–646.

62 Haynes BF, Sempowski GD, Wells AF, Hale LP. The human thymus during aging. Immunol Res 2000, **22**: 253–261.

63 Hsu S-M, Jaffe ES. Phenotypic expression of T lymphocytes in thymus and peripheral lymphoid tissues. Am J Pathol 1985, **121**: 69–78.

64 Janossy G, Bofill M, Trejdosiewicz LK, Willcox HNA, Chilosi M. Cellular differentiation of lymphoid subpopulations and their microenvironments in the human thymus. In Müller-Hermelink HK (ed.): Current topics in pathology. The human thymus. Histophysiology and pathology, vol. 75. New York, 1986, Springer-Verlag, pp. 89–125.

65 Kendall MD, Van de Wijngaert FP, Schuurman H-J, Rademakers LHPM, Kater L. Heterogeneity of the human thymus epithelial microenvironment at the ultrastructural level. In Klause GCB (ed.): Microenvironments in the lymphoid system. Advances in experimental medicine and biology, vol. 186. New York, 1985, Plenum Press.

66 Kuo T-t. Cytokeratin profiles of the thymus and thymomas: histogenetic correlations and proposal for a histological classification of thymomas. Histopathology 2000, **36**: 403–414.

67 Masunaga A, Sugawara I, Nakamura H, Yoshitake T, Itoyama S. Cytokeratin expression in normal human thymus at different ages. Pathol Int 1997, **47**: 842–847.

68 Parker JR, Ro JY, Ordonez NG. Benign nevus cell aggregates in the thymus: a case report. Mod Pathol 1999, **12**: 329–332.

69 Rosai J, Parkash V, Reuter VE. The origin of mediastinal germ cell tumors in men. Int J Surg Pathol 1994, **2**: 73–78.

70 Sharp JG, Crouse DA, Purtilo DT. Ontogeny and regulation of the immune system. Arch Pathol Lab Med 1987, **111**: 1106–1113.

71 Smith SM, Ossa-Gomez LJ. A quantitative histologic comparison of the thymus in 100 healthy and diseased adults. Am J Clin Pathol 1981, **76**: 657–665.

72 Steinmann GG. Changes in the human thymus during aging. In Müller-Hermelink HK (ed.): Current topics in pathology. The human thymus. Histophysiology and pathology, vol. 75. New York, 1986, Springer-Verlag, pp. 43–88.

73 Suster S, Rosai J. Thymus. In Sternberg SS (ed.): Histology for pathologists, ed. 2. Philadelphia, 1997, Lippincott-Raven, pp. 687–706.

74 Szabo P, Weksler ME. Is thymosin alpha 1 a thymic hormone? Clin Immunol Immunopathol 1992, **65**: 195–200.

75 Van Ewjik W. Immunohistology of lymphoid and non-lymphoid cells in the thymus in relation to T lymphocyte differentiation. Am J Anat 1984, **170**: 311–330.

76 von Gaudecker B. The development of the human thymus microenvironment. In Müller-Hermelink HK (ed.): Current topics in pathology. The human thymus. Histophysiology and pathology, vol. 75. New York, 1986, Springer-Verlag, pp. 1–41.

77 Wakkach A, Poea S, Chastre E, Gespach C, Lecerf F, De La Porte S, Tzartos S, Coulombe A, Berrih-Aknin S. Establishment of a human thymic myoid cell line. Phenotypic and functional characteristics. Am J Pathol 1999, 155: 1229–1240.

78 Watt SM, Thomas JA, Edwards AJ, Murdoch SJ, Horton MA. Adhesion receptors are differentially expressed on developing thymocytes and epithelium in human thymus. Exp Hematol 1992, 20: 1101–1111.

Primary immunodeficiencies

79 Berry CL, Thompson EN. Clinico-pathological study of thymic dysplasia. Arch Dis Child 1968, 43: 579–584.

80 Borzy MS, Schulte-Wissermann H, Gilbert E, Horowtiz SD, Pellett J, Hong R. Thymic morphology in immunodeficiency diseases. Results of thymic biopsies. Clin Immunol Immunopathol 1979, 12: 31–51.

81 Huber J, Zegers BJ, Schuurman HJ. Pathology of congenital immunodeficiencies. Semin Diagn Pathol 1992, 9: 31–62.

82 Nezelof C. Pathology of the thymus in immunodeficiency states. Curr Top Pathol 1986, 75: 151–177.

83 Nezelof C. Thymic pathology in primary and secondary immunodeficiencies. Histopathology 1992, 21: 499–511.

84 Van Baarlen J, Schuurman H-J, Huber J. Acute thymus involution in infancy and childhood: A reliable marker for duration of acute illness. Human Pathol 1988, 19: 1155–1160.

Cysts

85 Bleger RC, McAdams AJ. Thymic cysts. Arch Pathol 1966, 82: 535–541.

86 Dyer NH. Cystic thymomas and thymic cysts. A review. Thorax 1967, 22: 408–421.

87 Leong AS-Y, Brown JH. Malignant transformation in a thymic cyst. Am J Surg Pathol 1984, 8: 471–475.

88 Louis DN, Vickery AL Jr, Rosai J, Wang CA. Multiple branchial cleft-like cysts in Hashimoto's thyroiditis. Am J Surg Pathol 1989, 13: 45–49.

89 Michal M, Havliček F. Pseudo-epitheliomatous hyperplasia in thymic cysts. Histopathology 1991, 19: 281–282.

90 Mishalani SH, Lones MA, Said JW. Multilocular thymic cyst. A novel thymic lesion associated with human immunodeficiency virus infection. Arch Pathol Lab Med 1995, 119: 467–470.

91 Pannell TL, Jolles H. Adult cystic mediastinal lymphangioma simulating a thymic cyst. J Thorac Imaging 1991, 7: 86–89.

92 Ratnesar P. Unilateral cervical thymic cyst. J Laryngol Otol 1971, 85: 293–298.

93 Shier KT. The thymus according to Schambacher. Medullary ducts and reticular epithelium of thymus and thymomas. Cancer 1981, 48: 1183–1199.

94 Suster S, Barbuto D, Carlson G, Rosai J. Multilocular thymic cysts with pseudoepitheliomatous hyperplasia. Hum Pathol 1991, 22: 455–460.

95 Suster S, Rosai J. Multilocular thymic cyst. An acquired reactive process. Study of 18 cases. Am J Surg Pathol 1991, 15: 388–398.

96 Suster S, Rosai J. Cystic thymomas. A clinicopathologic study of ten cases. Cancer 1992, 69: 92–97.

Other non-neoplastic diseases

97 Askin FB, McCann BG, Kuhn C. Reactive eosinophilic pleuritis. A lesion to be distinguished from pulmonary eosinophilic granuloma. Arch Pathol Lab Med 1977, 101: 187–191.

98 Balcom RJ, Hakanson DO, Werner A, Gordon LP. Massive thymic hyperplasia in an infant with Beckwith-Wiedemann syndrome. Arch Pathol Lab Med 1985, 109: 153–155.

99 Bale PM, Sotelo-Avila C. Maldescent of the thymus. 34 necropsy and 10 surgical cases, including 7 thymuses medial to the mandible. Pediatr Pathol 1993, 13: 181–190.

100 Bofill M, Janossy G, Willcox N, Chilosi M, Trejdosiewicz LK, Newsom-Davis J. Microenvironments in the normal thymus and the thymus in myasthenia gravis. Am J Pathol 1985, 119: 462–473.

101 Bramwell NH, Burns BF. Histiocytosis X of the thymus in association with myasthenia gravis. Am J Clin Pathol 1986, 86: 224–227.

102 Carmosino L, DiBenedetto A, Feffer S. Thymic hyperplasia following successful chemotherapy. A report of two cases and review of the literature. Cancer 1985, 56: 1526–1528.

102a Drut R, Galliani C. Thymic tissue in the skin: a clue to the diagnosis of the branchio-oculo-facial syndrome: report of two cases. Int J Surg Path 2003, 11: 25–28.

103 Gilcrease MZ, Rajan B, Ostrowski ML, Ramzy I, Schwartz MR. Localized thymic Langerhans' cell histiocytosis and its relationship with myasthenia gravis: immunohistochemical, ultrastructural, and cytometric studies. Arch Pathol Lab Med 1997, 121: 134–138.

104 Gómez-Román JJ, Val-Bernal JF. Histioeosinophilic granuloma of the thymus. Arch Pathol Lab Med 1997, 121: 921–922.

105 Havliček F, Rosai J. Histioeosinophilic granulomas in the thymuses of 29 myasthenic patients. A complication of pneumomediastinum. Hum Pathol 1984, 15: 1137–1144.

106 Jessurun J, Azevedo M, Saldana M. Allergic angiitis and granulomatosis (Churg-Strauss syndrome). A report of a case with massive thymic involvement in a nonasthmatic patient. Hum Pathol 1986, 17: 637–639.

107 Joshi VV, Oleske JM, Saad S, Gadol C, Connor E, Bobila R, Minnefor AB. Thymus biopsy in children with acquired immunodeficiency syndrome. Arch Pathol Lab Med 1986, 110: 837–842.

108 Karcher DS, Pearson CE, Butler WM, Hurwitz MA, Cassell PF. Giant lymph node hyperplasia involving the thymus with associated nephrotic syndrome and myelofibrosis. Am J Clin Pathol 1982, 77: 100–104.

109 Katz SM, Chatten J, Bishop HC, Rosenblum H. Massive thymic enlargement. Report of a case of gross thymic hyperplasia in a child. Am J Clin Pathol 1977, 63: 786–790.

110 Kornstein MJ, Brooks JJ, Anderson AO, Levinson AI, Lisak RP, Zweiman B. The immunohistology of the thymus in myasthenia gravis. Am J Pathol 1984, 117: 184–194.

111 Kourtis AP, Abramowsky C, Ibegbu C, Kobrynski L. Enlargement of the thymus in a child with chronic granulomatous disease receiving interferon gamma therapy. Arch Pathol Lab Med 1998, 122: 562–565.

112 Lau HT, Barlow BA, Gandhi RP. Ectopic thymus presenting as neck mass. J Pediatr Surg 1984, 19: 197.

113 Linder J. The thymus gland in secondary immunodeficiency. Arch Pathol Lab Med 1987, 111: 1118–1122.

114 Löning T, Caselitz J, Otto HF. The epithelial framework of the thymus in normal and pathological conditions. Virchows Arch [A] 1981, 392: 7–20.

115 Okabe H. Thymologic lymph follicles. A histopathological study of 1,356 autopsy cases. Acta Pathol Jpn 1966, 16: 109–130.

116 Pendlebury SC, Boyages S, Koutts J, Boyages J. Thymic hyperplasia associated with Hodgkin disease and thyrotoxicosis. Cancer 1992, 70: 1985–1987.

117 Prevot S, Audouin J, Andre-Bougaran J, Griffais R, Le Tourneau A, Fournier JG, Diebold J. Thymic pseudotumorous enlargement due to follicular hyperplasia in a human immunodeficiency virus sero-positive patient. Immunohistochemical and molecular biological study of viral infected cells. Am J Clin Pathol 1992, 97: 420–425.

118 Seemayer TA, Laroche AC, Russo P, Malebranche R, Arnoux E, Guérin J-M, Pierre G, Dupuy J-M, Gartner JG, Lapp WS, Spira TJ,

Elie R. Precocious thymic involution manifest by epithelial injury in the acquired immune deficiency syndrome. Hum Pathol 1984, **15:** 469–474.

119 Siegal GP, Dehner LP, Rosai J. Histiocytosis X (Langerhans' cell granulomatosis) of the thymus. A clinicopathologic study of four childhood cases. Am J Surg Pathol 1985, **9:** 117–124.

120 Wakely P, Suster S. Langerhans' cell histiocytosis of the thymus associated with multilocular thymic cyst. Hum Pathol 2000, **31:** 1532–1534.

121 Wekerle H, Müller-Hermelink HK. The thymus in myasthenia gravis. In Müller-Hermelink HK (ed.): Current topics in pathology. The human thymus. Histophysiology and pathology, vol. 75. New York, 1986, Springer-Verlag, pp. 179–206.

122 Wolff M, Rosai J, Wright DH. Sebaceous glands within the thymus. Report of three cases. Hum Pathol 1984, **15:** 341–343.

Thymoma

General features

123 Attanoos RL, Galateau-Salle F, Gibbs AR, Muller S, Ghandour F, Dojcinov SD. Primary thymic epithelial tumours of the pleura mimicking malignant mesothelioma. Histopathology 2002, **41:** 42–49.

124 Chatten J, Katz SM. Thymoma in a 12-year-old boy. Cancer 1976, **37:** 953–957.

125 Chhieng DC, Rose D, Ludwig ME, Zakowski MF. Cytology of thymomas: Emphasis on morphology and correlation with histologic subtypes. Cancer Cytopathol 2000, **90:** 24–32.

126 Dahlgren S, Sandstedt B, Sundström C. Fine needle aspiration cytology of thymic tumors. Acta Cytol [Baltimore] 1983, **27:** 1–6.

127 Dehner LP, Martin SA, Sumner HW. Thymus related tumors and tumor-like lesions in childhood with rapid clinical progression and death. Hum Pathol 1977, **8:** 53–66.

128 Furman WL, Buckley PJ, Green AA, Stokes DC, Chien LT. Thymoma and myasthenia gravis in a 4-year-old child. Case report and review of the literature. Cancer 1985, **56:** 2703–2706.

129 Fushimi H, Tanio Y, Kotoh K. Ectopic thymoma mimicking diffuse pleural mesothelioma: a case report. Hum Pathol 1998, **29:** 409–410.

130 Green WR, Pressoir R, Gumbs RV, Warner O, Naab T, Qayumi M. Intrapulmonary thymoma. Arch Pathol Lab Med 1987, **111:** 1074–1076.

131 Groisman GM, Ben-Izhak O, Best LA. Thymoma with foci of medullary differentiation in an 11-year-old-boy. Arch Pathol Lab Med 1994, **118:** 653–655.

132 Kaplinsky C, Mor C, Cohen IJ, Goshen Y, Yaniv I, Tamary H, Jaber L, Stark B, Stern S, Zaizov R. Childhood malignant thymoma: Clinical, therapeutic, and immunohistochemical considerations. Pediatr Hematol Oncol 1992, **9:** 261–268.

133 Keen SJ, Libshitz HI. Thymic lesions. Experience with computed tomography in 24 patients. Cancer 1987, **59:** 1520–1523.

134 Kung I, Loke SL, So SY, Lam WK, Mok CK, Khin MA. Intrapulmonary thymoma. Report of two cases. Thorax 1985, **40:** 471–474.

135 Levine GD, Rosai J. Thymic hyperplasia and neoplasia. A review of current concepts. Hum Pathol 1978, **9:** 495–515.

136 Martin JME, Randhawa G, Temple WJ. Cervical thymoma. Arch Pathol Lab Med 1986, **110:** 354–357.

137 Mirra M, Zanella M, Bussani R, Falconieri G. Intrapericardial thymoma: report of two incidental autopsy cases and review of the literature. Arch Pathol Lab Med 1997, **121:** 59–63.

138 Moran CA, Travis WD, Rosado-de-Christenson M, Koss MN, Rosai J. Thymomas presenting as pleural tumors. Report of eight cases. Am J Surg Pathol 1992, **16:** 138–144.

139 Müller-Hermelink HK, Marino M, Palestro G. Pathology of thymic epithelial tumors. In Müller-Hermelink HK (ed.): Current topics in pathology. The human thymus. Histophysiology and pathology, vol. 75. New York, 1986, Springer-Verlag, pp. 207–268.

140 Pescarmona E, Giardini R, Brisigotti M, Callea F, Pisacane A, Baroni CD. Thymoma in childhood. A clinicopathological study of five cases. Histopathology 1992, **21:** 65–68.

141 Ramon y Cajal S, Suster S. Primary thymic epithelial neoplasms in children. Am J Surg Pathol 1991, **15:** 466–474.

141a Srivastava A, Padilla O, Alroy J, Ucci A, Pilichowska M, Daley B, Wolfe HT. Primary intrapulmonary spindle cell thymoma with marked granulomatous reaction: report of a case with review of literature. Int J Surg Pathol (in press, 2004).

142 Tao L-C, Pearson FG, Cooper JD, Sanders DE, Weisbrod G, Donat EE. Cytopathology of thymoma. Acta Cytol (Baltimore) 1984, **28:** 165–170.

143 Wick MR, Scheithauer BW, Dines DE. Thymic neoplasia in two male siblings. Mayo Clin Proc 1982, **57:** 653–656.

144 Yamashita H, Murakami N, Noguchi S, Noguchi A, Yokoyama S, Moriuchi A, Nakayama I. Cervical thymoma and incidence of cervical thymus. Acta Pathol Jpn 1983, **33:** 189–194.

Myasthenia gravis

145 Alpert LI, Papatestas A, Kark A, Osserman RS, Osserman K. A histologic reappraisal of the thymus in myasthenia gravis. A correlative study of thymic pathology and response to thymectomy. Arch Pathol 1971, **91:** 55–61.

146 Azer MS, Zikria E, Ford WB. Myasthenia gravis appearing after removal of a thymoma. Report of a case and review of the literature. Am Surg 1971, **37:** 109–113.

147 Butler WM, Diehl LF, Taylor HG, Weltz MD. Metastatic thymoma with myasthenia gravis. Complete remission with combination chemotherapy. Cancer 1982, **50:** 419–422.

148 Dardenne M, Savino W, Bach J-F. Thymomatous epithelial cells and skeletal muscle share a common epitope defined by a monoclonal antibody. Am J Pathol 1987, **126:** 194–198.

149 Drachman DB, McIntosh KR, Reim J, Balar L. Strategies for treatment of myasthenia gravis. Ann NY Acad Sci 1993, **681:** 515–528.

150 Eimoto T, Kusano T, Ando K, Kikuchi M, Shirakusa T, Kawanami S. Nonneoplastic and nonhyperplastic thymus in myasthenia gravis. An immunohistochemical study with double immunoenzymatic labeling of basement membrane and cellular components. Am J Clin Pathol 1990, **94:** 36–43.

151 Emilie D, Crevon MC, Cohen-Kaminsky S, Peuchmaur M, Devergne O, Berrih-Aknin S, Galanaud P. In situ production of interleukins in hyperplastic thymus from myasthenia gravis patients. Hum Pathol 1991, **22:** 461–468.

152 Genkins G, Papatestas AE, Horowitz SH, Kornfeld P. Studies in myasthenia gravis. Early thymectomy. Electrophysiologic and pathologic correlations. Am J Med 1975, **58:** 517–524.

153 Geuder KI, Marx A, Witzemann V, Schalke B, Kirchner T, Müller-Hermelink HK. Genomic organization and lack of transcription of the nicotinic acetylcholine receptor subunit genes in myasthenia gravis-associated thymoma. Lab Invest 1992, **66:** 452–458.

154 Gilhus NE, Aarli JA, Christensson B, Matre R. Rabbit antiserum to a citric acid extract of human skeletal muscle staining thymomas from myasthenia gravis patients. J Neuroimmunol 1984, **7:** 55–64.

155 Kim YI, Neher E. IgG from patients with Lambert-Eaton syndrome blocks voltage-dependent calcium channels. Science 1988, **239:** 405–408.

156 Kirchner T, Tzartos S, Hoppe F, Schalke B, Wekerle H, Müller-Hermelink HK. Pathogenesis of myasthenia gravis. Acetylcholine receptor-related antigenic determinants in tumor-free thymuses and thymic epithelial tumors. Am J Pathol 1988, **130:** 268–280.

157 Koeda T. Immunopathological study related to myoglobin in myasthenic and non-myasthenic thymuses. Acta Pathol Jpn 1986, **36:** 209–223.

158 Lewis JE, Wick MR, Scheithauer BW, Bernatz PE, Taylor WF. Thymoma. A clinicopathologic review. Cancer 1987, **60:** 2727–2743.

159 Marx A, O'Connor R, Geuder KI, Hoppe F, Schalke B, Tzartos S, Kalies I, Kirchner T, Müller-Hermelink HK. Characterization of a protein with an acetylcholine receptor epitope from myasthenia gravis-associated thymomas. Lab Invest 1990, **62:** 279–286.

160 Marx A, Wilisch A, Schultz A, Gattenlohner S, Nenninger R, Müller-Hermelink HK. Pathogenesis of myasthenia gravis. Virchows Arch 1997, **430:** 355–364.

161 Meinl E, Klinkert WEF, Wekerle H. The thymus in myasthenia gravis. Changes typical for the human disease are absent in experimental autoimmune myasthenia gravis of the Lewis rat. Am J Pathol 1991, **139:** 995–1008.

162 Monden Y, Nakahara K, Fujii Y, Hashimoto J, Ohno K, Masaoka A, Kawashima Y. Myasthenia gravis in elderly patients. Ann Thorac Surg 1985, **39:** 433–440.

163 Monden Y, Nakahara K, Kagotani K, Fujii Y, Masaoka A, Kawashima Y. Myasthenia gravis with thymoma. Analysis of and postoperative prognosis for 65 patients with thymomatous myasthenia gravis. Ann Thorac Surg 1984, **38:** 46–52.

164 Monden Y, Nakahara K, Nanjo S, Fujii Y, Matsumura A, Masaoka A, Kawashima Y. Invasive thymoma with myasthenia gravis. Cancer 1984, **54:** 2513–2518.

165 Monden Y, Uyama T, Nakahara K, Fujii Y, Hashimoto J, Ohno K, Masaoka A, Kawashima Y. Clinical characteristics and prognosis of myasthenia gravis with other autoimmune diseases. Ann Thorac Surg 1984, **41:** 189–192.

166 Namba T, Brunner NG. Myasthenia gravis in patients with thymoma, with particular reference to onset after thymectomy. Medicine (Baltimore) 1978, **57:** 411–433.

167 Rosenberg M, Jauregui WO, De Vega ME, Herrera MR, Roncoroni AJ. Recurrence of thymic hyperplasia after thymectomy in myasthenia gravis. Its importance as a cause of failure of surgical treatment. Am J Med 1983, **74:** 78–82.

168 Scadding GK, Havard CWH, Lange MJ, Domb I. The long-term experience of thymectomy for myasthenia gravis. J Neurol Neurosurg Psychiatry 1985, **48:** 401–406.

169 Schluep M, Willcox N, Vincent A, Dhoot GK, Newsom-Davis J. Acetylcholine receptors in human thymic myoid cells in situ. An immunohistological study. Ann Neurol 1987, **22:** 212–222.

170 Schumm F, Wiethölter H, Fateh-Moghadam A, Dichgans J. Thymectomy in myasthenia with pure ocular symptoms. J Neurol Neurosurg Psychiatry 1985, **48:** 332–337.

171 Slater G, Papatestas AE, Genkins G, Kornfeld P, Horowitz SH, Bender A. Thymomas in patients with myasthenia gravis. Ann Surg 1978, **188:** 171–174.

172 Steinman L, Mantegazza R. Prospects for specific immunotherapy in myasthenia gravis. FASEB J 1990, **4:** 2726–2731.

173 Vincent A. Immunology of acetylcholine receptors in relation to myasthenia gravis. Physiol Rev 1980, **60:** 756–824.

174 Vincent A. Timeline: Unravelling the pathogenesis of myasthenia gravis. Nat Rev Immunol 2002, **2:** 797–804.

175 Wekerle H, Ketelsen U-P. Intrathymic pathogenesis and dual genetic control of myasthenia gravis. Lancet 1977, **1:** 678–680.

176 Wekerle H, Müller-Hermelink HK. The thymus in myasthenia gravis. In Müller-Hermelink HK (ed.): Current topics in pathology. The human thymus. Histophysiology and pathology, vol. 75. New York, 1986, Springer-Verlag.

177 Weltfriend S, David M, Ginzburg A, Sandbank M. Generalized hair follicle hamartoma. The third case report in association with myasthenia gravis. Am J Dermatopathol 1987, **9:** 428–432.

178 Wilkins EW Jr, Edmunds LH Jr, Castleman B. Cases of thymoma at the Massachusetts General Hospital. J Thorac Cardiovasc Surg 1966, **52:** 322–330.

179 Willcox N, Schluep M, Ritter MA, Schuurman HJ, Newsom-Davis J, Christensson B. Myasthenic and nonmyasthenic thymoma. An expansion of a minor cortical epithelial cell subset? Am J Pathol 1987, **127:** 447–460.

180 Williams CL, Hay JE, Huiatt TW, Lennon VA. Paraneoplastic IgG striational autoantibodies produced by clonal thymic B cells and in serum of patients with myasthenia gravis and thymoma react with titin. Lab Invest 1992, **66:** 331–336.

181 Youssef S. Thymectomy for myasthenia gravis in children. J Pediatr Surg 1983, **18:** 537–541.

Other associated diseases

182 Ackland SP, Bur ME, Adler SS, Robertson M, Baron JM. White blood cell aplasia associated with thymoma. Am J Clin Pathol 1988, **89:** 260–263.

183 De Jong D, Richel DJ, Schenkeveld C, Boerrigter L, Van't Veer LJ. Oligoclonal peripheral T-cell lymphocytosis as a result of aberrant T-cell development in cortical thymoma. Diagn Mol Pathol 1997, **6:** 244–248.

184 Friedman HD, Inman DA, Hutchison RE, Poiez BJ. Concurrent invasive thymoma and T-cell lymphoblastic leukemia and lymphoma. A case report with necropsy findings and literature review of thymoma and associated hematologic neoplasm. Am J Clin Pathol 1994, **101:** 432–437.

185 Griffin JD, Aisenberg AC, Long JC. Lymphocytic thymoma associated with T-cell lymphocytosis. Am J Med 1978, **64:** 1075–1079.

186 Hirst E, Robertson TT. The syndrome of thymoma and erythroblastopenic anemia. A review of 56 cases including 3 case reports. Medicine (Baltimore) 1967, **46:** 225–264.

187 Kirkpatrick CH, Windhorst DB. Mucocutaneous candidiasis and thymoma. Am J Med 1979, **66:** 939–945.

188 Kornacki S, Hansen FC III, Lazenby A. Graft-versus-host-like colitis associated with malignant thymoma. Am J Surg Pathol 1994, **19:** 224–228.

189 Kuo T-t, Shis L-Y. Histologic types of thymoma associated with pure red cell aplasia: a study of five cases including a composite tumor of organoid thymoma associated with an unusual lipofibroadenoma. Int J Surg Pathol 2001, **9:** 29–35.

190 Levin L, Sealy R, Barron J. Syndrome of inappropriate antidiuretic hormone secretion following cis-dichlorodiammineplatinum II in a patient with malignant thymoma. Cancer 1982, **50:** 2279–2282.

191 Lishner M, Ravid M, Shapira J, Radnay J, Amiel A, Leytin V, Shapiro C, Klein A. Delta-T-lymphocytosis in a patient with thymoma. Cancer 1994, **74:** 2924–2929.

192 Mais DD, Mulhall BP, Adolphson KR, Yamamoto K. Thymoma-associated autoimmune enteropathy. A report of two cases. Am J Clin Pathol 1999, **112:** 810–815.

193 Moysset I, Lloreta J, Miguel A, Vadell C, Ribalta T, Estrach T, Serrano S. Thymoma associated with CD4+ lymphopenia, cytomegalovirus infection, and Kaposi's sarcoma. Hum Pathol 1997, **28:** 1211–1213.

194 Palestine RF, Su WPD, Liesegang TJ. Late-onset chronic mucocutaneous and ocular candidiasis and malignant thymoma. Arch Dermatol 1983, **119:** 580–586.

195 Skinnider LF, Alexander S, Horsman D. Concurrent thymoma and lymphoma. A report of two cases. Hum Pathol 1982, **13:** 163–166.

196 Smith GP, Perkins SL, Segal GH, Kjeldsberg CR. T-cell lymphocytosis associated with invasive thymomas. Am J Clin Pathol 1994, **102:** 447–453.

197 Souadjian JV, Silverstein MN, Titus JL. Thymoma and cancer. Cancer 1968, **22:** 1221–1225.

198 Stoll DB, Lublin F, Brodovsky H, Laucius F, Patchefsky A, Cooper H. Association of subacute motor neuronopathy with thymoma. Cancer 1984, **54:** 770–772.

199 Thomas J, De Wolf-Peeters C, Tricot G, Bekaert J, Broeckaert-van Orshoven A. T-cell chronic lymphocytic leukemia in a patient

with invasive thymoma in remission with chemotherapy. Cancer 1983, **52:** 313–317.

Pathologic, electron microscopic, histochemical, immunohistochemical and molecular genetic features

200 Chan JKC, Yip TTC, Tsang WYW, Seneviratne S, Poon YF, Wong CSC, Ma VWS. Lack of evidence of pathogenetic role of Epstein-Barr virus in thymic lymphoid hyperplasia and thymomas in the Chinese population of Hong Kong. Int J Surg Pathol 1994, **2:** 17–22.

201 Chan WC, Zaatari GS, Tabei S, Bibb M, Brynes RK. Thymoma. An immunohistochemical study. Am J Clin Pathol 1984, **82:** 160–166.

202 Chen F-F, Yan J-J, Jin Y-T, Su I-J. Detection of bcl-2 and p53 in thymoma: Expression of bcl-2 as a reliable marker of tumor aggressiveness. Hum Pathol 1996, **27:** 1089–1092.

203 Chilosi M, Castelli P, Martignoni G, Pizzolo G, Montresor E, Facchetti F, Truini M, Mombello A, Lestani M, Scarpa A, Menestrina F. Neoplastic epithelial cells in a subset of human thymomas express the B-cell associated CD20 antigen. Am J Surg Pathol 1992, **16:** 988–997.

204 Chilosi M, Iannucci A, Menestrina F, Lestani M, Scarpa A, Bonetti F, Fiore-Donati L, Dipasquale B, Pizzolo G, Palestro G, Tridente G, Janossy G. Immunohistochemical evidence of active thymocyte proliferation in thymoma. Am J Pathol 1987, **128:** 464–470.

204a Chilosi M, Zamò A, Brighenti A, Malpeli G, Montagna L, Piccoli P, Pedron S, Lestani M, Inghirami G, Scarpa A, Doglioni C, Menestrina F. Constitutive expression of ΔN-p63α isoform in human thymus and thymic epithelial tumours. Virchows Arch 2003, **443:** 175–183.

204b Choi WWL, Lui YH, Lau WH, Crowley P, Khan A, Chan JKC. Adenocarcinoma of the thymus: report of two cases, including a previously undescribed mucinous subtype. Am J Surg Pathol 2003, **27:** 124–130.

205 Datta MW, Shahsafei A, Nadler LM, Freeman GJ, Dorfman DM. Expression of MHC class II-associated invariant chain (li; CD74) in thymic epithelial neoplasms. Appl Immunohistochem Mol Morphol 2000, **8:** 210–215.

206 Dorfman DM, Pinkus GS. CD99 (p30/32^{MIC2}) immunoreactivity in the diagnosis of thymic neoplasms and mediastinal lymphoproliferative disorders: A study of paraffin sections using monoclonal antibody 013. Appl Immunohistochem 1996, **4:** 34–42.

207 Eimoto T, Kitaoka M, Ogawa H, Niwa H, Murase T, Tateyama H, Inagaki H, Soji T, Wang HJ. Thymic sarcomatoid carcinoma with skeletal muscle differentiation: report of two cases, one with cytogenetic analysis. Histopathology 2002, **40:** 46–57.

208 Engel P, Francis D, Graem N. Expression of bcl-2 in fetal thymus, thymomas and thymic carcinomas. Association with p53 expression and review of the literature. APMIS 1998, **106:** 449–455.

209 Fujii T, Kawai T, Saito K, Fukushima K, Hasegawa T, Tokunaga M, Yokoyama T. EBER-1 expression in thymic carcinoma. Acta Pathol Jpn 1993, **43:** 107–110.

210 Fukai I, Masaoka A, Hashimoto T, Yamakawa Y, Mizuno T, Tanamura O. The distribution of epithelial membrane antigen in thymic epithelial neoplasms. Cancer 1992, **70:** 2077–2081.

211 Giraud F, Fabien N, Auger C, Girod C, Loire R, Monier JC. Human epithelial thymic tumours. Heterogeneity in immunostaining of epithelial cell markers and thymic hormones. Thymus 1990, **15:** 15–29.

212 Hammond EH, Flinner RL. The diagnosis of thymoma. A review. Ultrastruct Pathol 1991, **15:** 419–438.

213 Hasserjian RP, Klimstra DS, Rosai J. Carcinoma of the thymus with clear-cell features. Report of eight cases and review of the literature. Am J Surg Pathol 1995, **19:** 305–310.

214 Hirokawa K, Utsuyama M, Moriizumi E, Hashimoto T, Masaoka A, Goldstein AL. Immunohistochemical studies in human thymomas. Localization of thymosin and various cell markers. Virchows Arch B (Cell Pathol) 1988, **55:** 371–380.

215 Hishima T, Fukayama M, Hayashi Y, Fujii T, Arai K, Shiozawa Y, Funata N, Koike M. Neuroendocrine differentiation in thymic epithelial tumors with special reference to thymic carcinoma and atypical thymoma. Hum Pathol 1998, **29:** 330–338.

216 Hishima T, Fukayama M, Hayashi Y, Fujii T, Ooba T, Funata N, Koike M. CD70 expression in thymic carcinoma. Am J Surg Pathol 2000, **24:** 742–746.

217 Iezzoni JC, Nass LB. Thymic basaloid carcinoma: A case report and review of the literature. Mod Pathol 1996, **9:** 21–25.

218 Inghirami G, Chilosi M, Knowles DM. Western thymomas lack Epstein-Barr virus by Southern blotting analysis and by polymerase chain reaction. Am J Pathol 1990, **136:** 1429–1436.

219 Inoue M, Marx A, Zettl A, Strobel P, Muller-Hermelink HK, Starostik P. Chromosome 6 suffers frequent and multiple aberrations in thymoma. Am J Pathol 2002, **161:** 1507–1513.

220 Katzin WE, Fishleder AJ, Linden MD, Tubbs RR. Immunoglobulin and T-cell receptor genes in thymomas. Genotypic evidence supporting the nonneoplastic nature of the lymphocytic component. Hum Pathol 1988, **19:** 323–328.

221 Kawashima O, Kamiyoshihara M, Sakata S, Kurihara T, Ishikawa S, Morishita Y. Basaloid carcinoma of the thymus. Ann Thorac Surg 1999, **68:** 1863–1865.

222 Kondo K, Mukai K, Sato Y, Matsuno Y, Shimosato Y, Monden Y. An immunohistochemical study of thymic epithelial tumors. III. The distribution of interdigitating reticulum cells and S-100 beta-positive small lymphocytes. Am J Surg Pathol 1990, **14:** 1139–1147.

223 Kornstein MJ, Hoxie JA, Levinson AI, Brooks JJ. Immunohistology of human thymomas. Arch Pathol Lab Med 1985, **109:** 460–463.

224 Kornstein MJ, Kay S. B cells in thymomas. Mod Pathol 1990, 3: 61–63.

225 Kornstein MJ, Rosai J. CD5 labeling of thymic carcinomas and other nonlymphoid neoplasms. Am J Clin Pathol 1998, **109:** 722–726.

226 Kuo T. Sclerosing thymoma. A possible phenomenon of regression. Histopathology 1994, **25:** 319–322.

227 Kuo T-t. Cytokeratin profiles of the thymus and thymomas: histogenetic correlations and proposal for a histological classification of thymomas. Histopathology 2000, **36:** 403–414.

228 Kuo T-t. Frequent presence of neuroendocrine small cells in thymic carcinoma: a light microscopic and immunohistochemical study. Histopathology 2000, **37:** 19–26.

229 Kuo T-t, Chang J-P, Lin F-J, Wu W-C, Chang C-H. Thymic carcinomas: Histopathological varieties and immunohistochemical study. Am J Surg Pathol 1990, **14:** 24–34.

230 Kuo T-T, Lee M-C. Amyloid production in a thymoma. Surg Pathol 1991, **4:** 69–74.

231 Kuo T-t, Lo SK. Immunohistochemical metallothionein expression in thymoma: correlation with histologic types and cellular origin. Histopathology 1997, **30:** 243–248.

232 Lauriola L, Erlandson RA, Rosai J. Neuroendocrine differentiation is a common feature of thymic carcinoma. Am J Surg Pathol 1998, **22:** 1059–1066.

233 Lauriola L, Maggiano N, Marino M, Carbone A, Piantelli M, Musiani P. Human thymoma. Immunologic characteristics of the lymphocytic component. Cancer 1981, **48:** 1992–1995.

234 Lauriola L, Maggiano N, Serra FG, Nori S, Tardio ML, Capelli A, Piantelli M, Ranelletti FO. Immunohistochemical and in situ hybridization detection of growth-hormone-producing cells in human thymoma. Am J Pathol 1997, **151:** 55–61.

235 Lauriola L, Michetti F, Stolfi VM, Tallini G, Cocchia D. Detection by S-100 immunolabelling of interdigitating reticulum cells in human thymomas. Virchows Arch (Cell Pathol) 1984, **45:** 187–195.

236 Lee ACW, Kwong Y-I, Fu KH, Chan GCF, Ma L, Lau Y-I. Disseminated mediastinal carcinoma with chromosomal translocation (15;19). Cancer 1993, **72**: 2273–2276.

237 LeGolvan DP, Abell MR. Thymomas. Cancer 1977, **39**: 2142–2157.

238 Levine GD, Bensch KG. Epithelial nature of spindle-cell thymoma. An ultrastructural study. Cancer 1972, **30**: 500–511.

239 Levine GD, Rosai J, Bearman RM, Polliack A. The fine structure of thymoma, with emphasis on its differential diagnosis. A study of ten cases. Am J Pathol 1975, **81**: 49–66.

240 Leyvraz S, Henle W, Chahinian AP, Perlman C, Klein G, Gordon RE, Rosenblum M, Holland JF. Association of Epstein-Barr virus with thymic carcinoma. N Engl J Med 1985, **312**: 1296–1299.

241 Mann RB, Wu T-C, MacMahon EM, Ling Y, Charache P, Ambinder RF. In situ localization of Epstein-Barr virus in thymic carcinoma. Mod Pathol 1992, **5**: 363–366.

242 Matsuno Y, Morozumi N, Hirohashi S, Shimosato Y, Rosai J. Papillary carcinoma of the thymus: report of four cases of a new microscopic type of thymic carcinoma. Am J Surg Pathol 1998, **22**: 873–880.

243 Mizuno T, Hashimoto T, Masaoka A. Distribution of fibronectin and laminin in human thymoma. Cancer 1990, **65**: 1367–1374.

244 Mokhtar N, Hsu S-M, Lad RP, Haynes BF, Jaffe ES. Thymoma. Lymphoid and epithelial components mirror the phenotype of normal thymus. Hum Pathol 1984, **15**: 378–384.

245 Moran C, Koss M. Rhabdomyomatous thymoma. Am J Surg Pathol 1993, **17**: 633–636.

246 Moran CA, Suster S. Mucoepidermoid carcinomas of the thymus. A clinicopathologic study of six cases. Am J Surg Pathol 1995, **19**: 826–834.

247 Moran CA, Suster S. Thymoma with prominent cystic and hemorrhagic changes and areas of necrosis and infarction: a clinicopathologic study of 25 cases. Am J Surg Pathol 2001, **25**: 1086–1090.

248 Moran CA, Suster S, Koss MN. Plasma cell-rich thymoma. Am J Clin Pathol 1994, **102**: 199–201.

249 Murakami S, Shamoto M, Miura K, Takeuchi J. A thymic tumor with massive proliferation of myoid cells. Acta Pathol Jpn 1984, **34**: 1375–1383.

250 Osborne B, Mackay B, Battifora H. Thymoma. A clinicopathologic study of 23 cases. Pathol Annu 1985, **20**(Pt 2): 289–315.

251 Otto HF. Pathologie des thymus. New York, 1984, Springer-Verlag.

252 Palestro G, Valente G, Botto Micca F, Novero D, Arisio R. Detection and distribution of alfa-naphthyl acetate esterase activity in thymocytes of normal, myasthenic thymus and thymoma. Histochemical and cytochemical study in relation to E-Rosetting. Virchows Arch (Cell Pathol) 1980, **35**: 33–43.

252a Pan C-C, Chen P C-H, Wang L-S, Lee J-Y, Chiang H. Expression of apoptosis-related markers and HER-2/*neu* in thymic epithelial tumours. Histopathology 2003, **43**: 165–172.

253 Pescarmona E, Pisacane A, Pignatelli E, Baroni CD. Expression of epidermal and nerve growth factor receptors in human thymus and thymomas. Histopathology 1993, **23**: 39–44.

254 Pescarmona E, Rosati S, Pisacane A, Rendina E, Venuta F, Baroni CD. Microscopic thymoma. Histological evidence of multifocal cortical and medullary origin. Histopathology 1992, **20**: 263–266.

255 Pizer ES, McGrath SD, Hruban RH, Drachman DB, Bulkley GB, Zehnbauer BA. Partial T-cell receptor gene rearrangement. A source of pseudo-clonal populations in thymomas and other thymic tissues. Am J Clin Pathol 1996, **105**: 262–267.

256 Pomplun S, Wotherspoon AC, Shah G, Goldstraw P, Ladas G, Nicholson AG. Immunohistochemical markers in the differentiation of thymic and pulmonary neoplasms. Histopathology 2002, **40**: 152–158.

257 Ritter JH, Wick MR. Primary carcinomas of the thymus gland. Semin Diagn Pathol 1999, **16**: 18–31.

258 Rosai J. The pathology of thymic neoplasia. International Academy of Pathology Monograph No. 29. Baltimore, 1987, Williams & Wilkins.

259 Rosai J. Histological typing of tumours of the thymus. Berlin, 1999, Springer.

260 Rosai J, Levine GD. Tumors of the thymus. In Atlas of tumor pathology, series 2, fascicle 13. Washington D.C., 1975, Armed Forces Institute of Pathology.

261 Ruco LP, Pisacane A, Pomponi D, Stopacciaro A, Pescarmona E, Rendina EA, Santoni A, Boraschi D, Tagliabue A, Uccini S. Macrophages and interdigitating reticulum cells in normal human thymus and thymomas: Immunoreactivity of interleukin-1 alpha, interleukin-1 beta and tumour necrosis factor alpha. Histopathology 1990, **17**: 291–299.

262 Salyer WR, Eggleston JC. Thymoma. A clinical and pathological study of 65 cases. Cancer 1976, **37**: 229–249.

263 Sato Y, Watanabe S, Mukai K, Kodama T, Upton MP, Goto M, Shimosato Y. An immunohistochemical study of thymic epithelial tumors. Am J Surg Pathol 1986, **10**: 862–870.

264 Savino W, Durand D, Dardenne M. Immunohistochemical evidence for the expression of the carcinoembryonic antigen by human thymic epithelial cells in vitro and in neoplastic conditions. Am J Pathol 1985, **121**: 418–425.

265 Savino W, Manganella G, Verley J-M, Wolff A, Berrih S, Levasseur P, Binet J-P, Dardenne M, Bach J-F. Thymoma epithelial cells secrete thymic hormone but do not express class II antigens of the major histocompatibility complex. J Clin Invest 1985, **76**: 1140–1146.

266 Shimosato Y, Kameya T, Nagai K, Suemasu K. Squamous cell carcinoma of the thymus. An analysis of eight cases. Am J Surg Pathol 1977, **1**: 109–121.

267 Snover DC, Levine GD, Rosai J. Thymic carcinoma. Five distinctive histologic variants. Am J Surg Pathol 1982, **6**: 451–470.

268 Suster S, Moran CA. Spindle cell thymic carcinoma: clinicopathologic and immunohistochemical study of a distinctive variant of primary thymic epithelial neoplasm. Am J Surg Pathol 1999, **23**: 691–700.

269 Suster S, Moran CA, Chan JK. Thymoma with pseudosarcomatous stroma: report of an unusual histologic variant of thymic epithelial neoplasm that may simulate carcinosarcoma. Am J Surg Pathol 1997, **21**: 1316–1323.

270 Suster S, Rosai J. Thymic carcinoma. A clinicopathologic study of 60 cases. Cancer 1991, **67**: 1025–1032.

271 Suster S, Rosai J. Cystic thymomas. A clinicopathologic study of ten cases. Cancer 1992, **69**: 92–97.

272 Tanaka M, Shimokawa R, Matsubara O, Aoki N, Kamiyama R, Kasuga T, Hatakeyama S. Mucoepidermoid carcinoma of the thymic region. Acta Pathol Jpn 1982, **32**: 703–712.

273 Tateyama H, Eimoto T, Tada T, Inagaki H, Hattori H, Takino H. Apoptosis, bcl-2 protein, and Fas antigen in thymic epithelial tumors. Mod Pathol 1997, **10**: 983–991.

274 Tateyama H, Eimoto T, Tada T, Hattori H, Murase T, Takino H. Immunoreactivity of a new CD5 antibody with normal epithelium and malignant tumors including thymic carcinoma. Am J Clin Pathol 1999, **111**: 235–240.

275 Tateyama H, Takahashi E, Saito Y, Fukai I, Fujii Y, Niwa H, Eimoto T. Histopathologic changes of thymoma preoperatively treated with corticosteroids. Virchows Arch 2001, **438**: 238–247.

276 Taubenberger JK, Jaffe ES, Medeiros LJ. Thymoma with abundant L26-positive "asteroid" cells. A case report with an analysis of normal thymus and thymoma specimens. Arch Pathol Lab Med 1991, **115**: 1254–1257.

277 Weirich G, Schneider P, Fellbaum C, Brauch H, Nathrath W, Scholz M, Präuer H, Höfler H. p53 alterations in thymic epithelial tumours. Virchows Arch 1997, **431**: 17–23.

278 Wick MR, Ritter JH, Humphrey PA, Nappi O. Clear cell neoplasms of the endocrine system and thymus. Semin Diagn Pathol 1997, **14**: 183–202.

279 Wick MR, Scheithauer BW, Weiland LH, Bernatz PE. Primary thymic carcinomas. Am J Surg Pathol 1982, **6**: 613–630.

280 Wiley EL, Nosal JM, Freeman RG. Immunohistochemical demonstration of H antigen, peanut agglutinin receptor, and saphora japonica receptor expression in infant thymuses and thymic neoplasias. Am J Clin Pathol 1990, **93**: 44–48.

281 Woda BA, Bain K, Salm TV. The phenotype of lymphocytes in a thymoma as studied with monoclonal antibodies. Clin Immunol Immunopathol 1984, **30**: 197–201.

282 Wu T-C, Kuo T-T. Study of Epstein-Barr virus early RNA1 (EBER1) expression by in situ hybridization in thymic epithelial tumors of Chinese patients in Taiwan. Hum Pathol 1993, **24**: 235–238.

283 Yoneda S, Marx A, Heimann S, Shirakusa T, Kikuchi M, Muller-Hermelink HK. Low-grade metaplastic carcinoma of the thymus. Histopathology 1999, **35**: 19–30.

284 Zettl A, Strobel P, Wagner K, Katzenberger T, Ott G, Rosenwald A, Peters K, Krein A, Semik M, Muller-Hermelink HK, Marx A. Recurrent genetic aberrations in thymoma and thymic carcinoma. Am J Pathol 2000, **157**: 257–266.

285 Zhou R, Zettl A, Strobel P, Wagner K, Muller-Hermelink HK, Zhang S, Marx A, Starostik P. Thymic epithelial tumors can develop along two different pathogenetic pathways. Am J Pathol 2001, **159**: 1853–1860.

Classification

286 Bernatz PE, Harrison EG, Glagett OT. Thymoma. A clinicopathologic study. J Thorac Cardiovasc Surg 1961, **42**: 424–444.

287 Chen G, Marx A, Wen-Hu, Yong J, Puppe B, Stroebel P, Mueller Hermelink HK. New WHO histologic classification predicts prognosis of thymic epithelial tumors: a clinicopathologic study of 200 thymoma cases from China. Cancer 2002, **95**: 420–429.

288 Eimoto T, Teshima K, Shirakusa T, Takeshita M, Okamura H, Naito H, Mitsui T, Kikuchi I. Heterogeneity of epithelial cells and reactive components in thymomas. An ultrastructural and immunohistochemical study. Ultrastruct Pathol 1986, **10**: 157–173.

289 Kirchner T, Schalke B, Buchwald J, Ritter M, Marx A, Müller-Hermelink HK. Well-differentiated thymic carcinoma. An organotypical low-grade carcinoma with relationship to cortical thymoma. Am J Surg Pathol 1992, **16**: 1153–1169.

290 Kuo T-t. Classification of thymic epithelial neoplasms: a controversial issue coming to an end? J Cell Mol Med 2001, **5**: 442–448.

291 Lattes R. Thymoma and other tumors of the thymus. An analysis of 107 cases. Cancer 1962, **15**: 1224–1260.

292 Lattes R, Jonas S. The pathological and clinical features in eighty cases of thymoma. Bull N Y Acad Med 1957, **33**: 145–147.

293 Lewis JE, Wick MR, Scheithauer BW, Bernatz PE, Taylor WF. Thymoma. A clinicopathologic review. Cancer 1987, **60**: 2727–2743.

294 Moran CA, Suster S. On the histologic heterogeneity of thymic epithelial neoplasms. Impact of sampling in subtyping and classification of thymomas. Am J Clin Pathol 2000, **114**: 760–766.

295 Muller-Hermelink HK, Marx A. Towards a histogenetic classification of thymic epithelial tumours? Histopathology 2000, **36**: 466–469.

296 Okumura M, Miyoshi S, Fujii Y, Takeuchi Y, Shiono H, Inoue M, Fukuhara K, Kadota Y, Tateyama H, Eimoto T, Matsuda H. Clinical and functional significance of WHO classification on human thymic epithelial neoplasms: a study of 146 consecutive tumors. Am J Surg Pathol 2001, **25**: 103–110.

297 Okumura M, Ohta M, Tateyama H, Nakagawa K, Matsumura A, Maeda H, Tada H, Eimoto T, Matsuda H, Masaoka A. The World Health Organization histologic classification system reflects the oncologic behavior of thymoma: a clinical study of 273 patients. Cancer 2002, **94**: 624–632.

298 Pan C-C, Chen WY, Chiang H. Spindle cell and mixed spindle/lymphocytic thymomas: an integrated clinicopathologic and immunohistochemical study of 81 cases. Am J Surg Pathol 2001, **25**: 111–120.

299 Pescarmona E, Pisacane A, Rendina EA, Ricci C, Ruco LP, Baroni CD. Organoid thymoma. A well-differentiated variant with distinctive clinicopathologic features. Histopathology 1991, **18**: 161–164.

300 Quintanilla-Martinez L, Wilkins E, Ferry J, Harris N. Thymoma—morphologic subclassification correlates with invasiveness and immunohistologic features. A study of 122 cases. Hum Pathol 1993, **24**: 958–969.

301 Quintanilla-Martinez L, Wilkins EW Jr., Choi N, Efird J, Hug E, Harris NL. Thymoma. Histologic subclassification is an independent prognostic factor. Cancer 1994, **74**: 606–617.

302 Rieker RJ, Hoegel J, Morres-Hauf A, Hoffman WJ, Blaeker H, Penzel R, Otto HF. Histologic classification of thymic epithelial tumors: comparison of established classification schemes. Int J Cancer 2002, **98**: 900–906.

303 Rosai J. Histological typing of tumours of the thymus. Berlin, 1999, Springer.

304 Suarez Vilela D, Salas Valien JS, Gonzalez Moran MA, Izquierdo Garcia F, Riera Velasco JR. Thymic carcinoma associated with a spindle cell thymoma. An immunohistochemical study. Histopathology 1992, **21**: 263–268.

305 Suster S, Moran CA. Primary thymic epithelial neoplasms showing combined features of thymoma and thymic carcinoma: A clinicopathologic study of 22 cases. Am J Surg Pathol 1996, **20**: 1469–1480.

306 Suster S, Moran CA. Micronodular thymoma with lymphoid B-cell hyperplasia: clinicopathologic and immunohistochemical study of eighteen cases of a distinctive morphologic variant of thymic epithelial neoplasm. Am J Surg Pathol 1999, **23**: 955–962.

307 Suster S, Moran CA. Thymoma, atypical thymoma, and thymic carcinoma. A novel conceptual approach to the classification of thymic epithelial neoplasm. Am J Clin Pathol 1999, **111**: 826–833.

308 Tateyama H, Saito Y, Fujii Y, Okumura M, Nakamura K, Tada H, Yasumitsu T, Eimoto T. The spectrum of micronodular thymic epithelial tumours with lymphoid B-cell hyperplasia. Histopathology 2001, **38**: 519–527.

Staging

309 Bedini AV, Andreani SM, Tavecchio L, Fabbri A, Giardini R, Camerini T, Bufalino R, Rosai J. Proposal of a novel TNM-based system to stage thymic epithelial tumors according to the World Health Organization pathologic classification (submitted for publication).

310 Guillan RA, Zelman S, Smalley RL, Iglesias PA. Malignant thymoma associated with myasthenia gravis, and evidence of extrathoracic metastases. An analysis of published cases and report of a case. Cancer 1971, **27**: 823–830.

311 Koga K, Matsuno Y, Noguchi M, Mukai K, Asamura H, Goya T, Shimosato Y. A review of 79 thymomas. Modification of staging system and reappraisal of conventional division into invasive and non-invasive thymoma. Pathol Int 1994, **44**: 359–367.

312 Kuo T-T, Lo S-K. DNA flow cytometric study of thymic epithelial tumors with evaluation of its usefulness in the pathologic classification. Hum Pathol 1993, **24**: 746–749.

313 Levine GD, Rosai J. Thymic hyperplasia and neoplasia. A review of current concepts. Hum Pathol 1978, **9**: 495–515.

314 Masaoka A, Monden Y, Nakahara K, Tanoika T. Follow-up study of thymomas with special reference to their clinical stage. Cancer 1981, **48**: 2485–2492.

315 Okumura M, Miyoshi S, Fujii Y, Takeuchi Y, Shiono H, Inoue M, Fukuhara K, Kadota Y, Tateyama H, Eimoto T, Matsuda H. Clinical and functional significance of WHO classification on human thymic epithelial neoplasms: a study of 146 consecutive tumors. Am J Surg Pathol 2001, **25**: 103–110.

316 Pich A, Chiarle R, Chiusa L, Palestro G. Argyrophilic nucleolar organizer region counts predict survival in thymoma. Cancer 1994, **74**: 1568–1574.

317 Pollack A, El-Naggar AK, Cox JD, Ro JY, Sahin A, Komaki R. Thymoma. The prognostic significance of flow cytometric DNA analysis. Cancer 1992, **69**: 1702–1709.

318 Tateyama H, Mizuno T, Tada T, Eimoto T, Hashimoto T, Masaoka A. Thymic epithelial tumours. Evaluation of malignant grade by quantification of proliferating cell nuclear antigen and nucleolar organizer regions. Virchows Arch [A] 1993, **422**: 265–269.

319 Tsuchiya R, Koga K, Matsuno Y, Mukai K, Shimosato Y. Thymic carcinoma. Proposal for pathological TNM and staging. Pathol Int 1994, **44**: 505–512.

320 Walker AN, Mills SE, Fechner RE. Thymomas and thymic carcinomas. Semin Diagn Pathol 1990, **7**: 250–265.

321 Wick MR, Nichols WC, Ingle JN, Bruckman JE, Okazaki H. Malignant, predominantly lymphocytic thymoma with central and peripheral nervous system metastases. Cancer 1981, **47**: 2036–2043.

322 Yamakawa Y, Masaoka A, Hashimoto T, Niwa H, Mizuno T, Fujii Y, Nakahara K. A tentative tumor-node-metastasis classification of thymoma. Cancer 1991, **68**: 1984–1987.

Treatment

323 Carlson RW, Dorfman RF, Sikic BI. Successful treatment of metastatic thymic carcinoma with cisplatin, vinblastine, bleomycin, and etoposide chemotherapy. Cancer 1990, **66**: 2092–2094.

324 Cooper JD. Current therapy for thymoma. Chest 1993, **103** (4 Suppl): 334S–336S.

325 Curran WJ Jr, Kornstein MJ, Brooks JJ, Turrisi AT III. Invasive thymoma. The role of mediastinal irradiation following complete or incomplete surgical resection. J Clin Oncol 1988, **6**: 1722–1727.

326 Gripp S, Hilgers K, Wurm R, Schmitt G. Thymoma: prognostic factors and treatment outcomes. Cancer 1998, **83**: 1495–1503.

327 Haniuda M, Morimoto M, Nishimura H, Kobayashi OM, Yamanda T, Lida F. Adjuvant radiotherapy after complete resection of thymoma. Ann Thorac Surg 1992, **54**: 311–315.

328 Hejna M, Haberi I, Raderer M. Nonsurgical management of malignant thymoma. Cancer 1999, **85**: 1871–1884.

329 Loehrer PJ Sr, Chen M, Kim KM, Aisner SC, Einhorn LH, Livingston R, Johnson D. Cisplatin, doxorubicin, and cyclophosphamide plus thoracic radiation therapy for limited-stage unresectable thymoma: an intergroup trial. J Clin Oncol 1997, **15**: 3093–3099.

330 Ogawa K, Toita T, Uno T, Fuwa N, Kakinohana Y, Kamata M, Koja K, Kinjo T, Adachi G, Murayama S. Treatment and prognosis of thymic carcinoma: a retrospective analysis of 40 cases. Cancer 2002, **94**: 3115–3119.

331 Ogawa K, Uno T, Toita T, Onishi H, Yoshida H, Kakinohana Y, Adachi G, Itami J, Ito H, Murayama S. Postoperative radiotherapy for patients with completely resected thymoma: a multi-institutional, retrospective review of 103 patients. Cancer 2002, **94**: 1405–1413.

332 Park HS, Shin DM, Lee JS, Komaki R, Pollack A, Putnam JB, Cox JD, Hong WK. Thymoma. A retrospective study of 87 cases. Cancer 1994, **73**: 2491–2498.

333 Thomas CR Jr, Wright CD, Loehrer PJ Sr. Thymoma: state of the art. J Clin Oncol 1999, **17**: 2280–2289.

334 Uematsu M, Kondo M. A proposal for treatment of invasive thymoma. Cancer 1986, **58**: 1979–1985.

335 Weide LG, Ulbright TM, Loehrer PJ Sr, Williams SD. Thymic carcinoma. A distinct clinical entity responsive to chemotherapy. Cancer 1993, **71**: 1219–1223.

Prognosis

336 Bedini AV, Andreani SM, Tavecchio L, Fabbri A, Giardini R, Camerini T, Bufalino R, Rosai J. Proposal of a novel TNM-based system to stage thymic epithelial tumors according to the World Health Organization pathologic classification (submitted for publication).

337 Begg CB, Cramer LD, Venkatraman ES, Rosai J. Comparing tumour staging and grading systems: a case study and a review of the issues, using thymoma as a model. Statist Med 2000; **19**: 1997–2014.

338 Blumberg D, Weksler B, Delgado R, Rosai J, Bains MS, Ginsberg RJ, Martini N, McCormack PM, Rusch V, Burt M. Thymoma. A multivariate analysis of factors predicting survival. Ann Thorac Surg 1995, **60**: 908–913.

338a Chalabreysse L, Roy P, Cordier JF, Loire R, Gamondes JP, Thivolet-Bejui F. Correlation of the WHO scheme for the classification of thymic epithelial neoplasms with prognosis:a retrospective study of 90 tumors. Am J Surg Pathol 2002, **26**: 1605–1611.

339 Fechner RE. Recurrence of noninvasive thymomas. Report of four cases and review of the literature. Cancer 1969, **23**: 1423–1427.

340 Gripp S, Hilgers K, Ploem-Zaaijer JJ, Hartmann A, Schmitt G. Prognostic significance of DNA cytometry in thymoma. J Cancer Res Clin Oncol 2000, **126**: 280–284.

341 Kuo T-T, Chang J-P, Lin F-J, Chang C-H. Thymic carcinomas. Histopathological varieties and immunohistochemical study. Am J Surg Pathol 1990, **14**: 24–34.

342 Lattes R. Thymoma and other tumors of the thymus. An analysis of 107 cases. Cancer 1962, **15**: 1224–1260.

343 Lewis JE, Wick MR, Scheithauer BW, Bernatz PE, Taylor WF. Thymoma. A clinicopathologic review. Cancer 1987, **60**: 2727–2743.

344 Liu H-C, Hsu W-H, Chen Y-J, Chan Y-J, Wu Y-C, Huang B-S, Huang M-H. Primary thymic carcinoma. Ann Thorac Surg 2002, **73**: 1076–1081.

345 Maggi G, Giaccone G, Donadio M, Ciuffreda L, Dalesio O, Leria G, Trifletti G, Casadio C, Palestro G, Mancuso M, Calciati A. Thymomas. A review of 169 cases, with particular reference to results of surgical treatment. Cancer 1986, **58**: 765–776.

346 Masaoka A, Monden Y, Nakahara K, Tanioka T. Follow-up study of thymomas with special reference to their clinical stages. Cancer 1981, **48**: 2485–2492.

347 Pan C-C, Ho M-T, Chen WY-K, Huang C-W, Chiang H. Ki67 labelling index correlates with stage and histology but not significantly with prognosis in thymoma. Histopathology 1998, **33**: 453–458.

348 Suster S, Rosai J. Thymic carcinoma. A clinicopathologic study of 60 cases. Cancer 1991, **67**: 1025–1032.

349 Truong LD, Mody DR, Cagle PT, Jackson York GL, Schwartz MR, Wheeler TM. Thymic carcinoma. A clinicopathologic study of 13 cases. Am J Surg Pathol 1990, **14**: 151–166.

350 Urgesi A, Monetti U, Rossi G, Ricardi U, Maggi G, Sannazzari GL. Aggressive treatment of intrathoracic recurrences of thymoma. Radiother Oncol 1992, **24**: 221–225.

351 Verley JM, Hollmann KH. Thymoma. A comparative study of clinical stages, histologic features, and survival in 200 cases. Cancer 1985, **55**: 1074–1086.

352 Wick MR, Scheithauer BW, Weiland LH, Bernatz PE. Primary thymic carcinomas. Am J Surg Pathol 1982, **6**: 613–630.

353 Yang W-I, Efird JG, Quintanilla-Martinez L, Choi N, Harris NL. Cell kinetic study of thymic epithelial tumors using PCNA (PC-10) and Ki-67 (MIB-1) antibodies. Hum Pathol 1996, **27**: 70–76.

Cervical tumors of thymic or related branchial pouch derivation

354 Berezowski K, Grimes MM, Gal A, Kornstein MJ. CD5 immunoreactivity of epithelial cells in thymic carcinoma and CASTLE using paraffin-embedded tissue. Am J Clin Pathol 1996, **106**: 483–486.

355 Chan JK, Rosai J. Tumors of the neck showing thymic or related

branchial pouch differentiation. A unifying concept. Hum Pathol 1991, **22**: 349–367.

356 Chetty R, Goetsch S, Nayler S, Cooper K. Spindle epithelial tumour with thymus-like element (SETTLE): the predominantly monophasic variant. Histopathology 1998, **33**: 71–74.

357 Cheuk W, Jacobson AA, Chan JK. Spindle epithelial tumor with thymus-like differentiation (SETTLE): a distinctive malignant thyroid neoplasm with significant metastatic potential. Mod Pathol 2000, **13**: 1150–1155.

358 Dorfman DM, Shahsafaei A, Miyauchi A. Intrathyroidal epithelial thymoma (ITET)/carcinoma showing thymus-like differentiation (CASTLE) exhibits CD5 immunoreactivity: new evidence for thymic differentiation. Histopathology 1998, **32**: 104–109.

359 Dorfman DM, Shahsafaei A, Miyauchi A. Immunohistochemical staining for bcl-2 and mcl-1 in intrathyroidal epithelial thymoma (ITET)/carcinoma showing thymus-like differentiation (CASTLE) and cervical thymic carcinoma. Mod Pathol 1998, **11**: 989–994.

360 Fetsch JF, Weiss SW. Ectopic hamartomatous thymoma: Clinicopathologic, immunohistochemical, and histogenetic considerations in four new cases. Hum Pathol 1990, **21**: 662–668.

361 Kirby PA, Ellison WA, Thomas PA. Spindle epithelial tumor with thymus-like differentiation (SETTLE) of thyroid with prominent mitotic activity and focal necrosis. Am J Surg Pathol 1999, **23**: 712–716.

362 Li Volsi VA. Branchial and thymic remnants in the thyroid and cervical region. An explanation for unusual tumors and microscopic curiosities (Editorial). Endocr Pathol 1993, **4**: 115–119.

363 Michal M, Mukensnabl R. Clear cell epithelial cords in an ectopic hamartomatous thymoma. Histopathology 1999, **35**: 89–90.

364 Michal M, Neubauer L, Fakan F. Carcinoma arising in ectopic hamartomatous thymoma—an ultrastructural study. Pathol Res Pract 1996, **192**: 610–618.

365 Michal M, Zamecnik M, Gogora M, Mukensnabl P, Neubauer L. Pitfalls in the diagnosis of ectopic hamartomatous thymoma. Histopathology 1996, **29**: 549–556.

366 Mizukami Y, Kurumaya H, Yamada T, Minato H, Nonomura A, Noguchi M, Matsubara F. Thymic carcinoma involving the thyroid gland. Report of two cases. Hum Pathol 1995, **26**: 576–579.

367 Rosai J, Limas C, Husband EM. Ectopic hamartomatous thymoma. A distinctive benign lesion of lower neck. Am J Surg Pathol 1984, **8**: 501–513.

368 Su L, Beals T, Bernacki EG, Giordano TJ. Spindle epithelial tumor with thymus-like differentiation: a case report with cytologic, histologic, immunohistologic, and ultrastructural findings. Mod Pathol 1997, **10**: 510–514.

369 Watanabe I, Tezuka F, Yamaguchi M, Sagawa J, Kaise N. Thymic carcinoma of the thyroid. Pathol Int 1996, **46**: 450–456.

369a Xu B, Hirokawa M, Yosimoto K, Miki H, Takahashi M, Kuma S, Sano T. Spindle epithelial tumor with thymus-like differentiation of the thyroid: a case report with pathological and molecular genetics study. Hum Pathol 2003, **34**: 190–193.

370 Zhao C, Yamada T, Kuramochi S, Yamazaki K, Mukai M, Kameyama K, Hata J. Two cases of ectopic hamartomatous thymoma. Virchows Arch 2000, **437**: 643–647.

Neuroendocrine tumors

371 Baker J, Holdaway IM, Jagusch M, Kerr AR, Donald RA, Pullan PT. Ectopic secretion of ACTH and met-enkephalin from a thymic carcinoid. J Endocrinol Invest 1982, **5**: 33–37.

372 Chetty R, Batitiang S, Govender D. Large cell neuroendocrine carcinoma of the thymus. Histopathology 1997, **31**: 274–276.

373 Fukai I, Masoaka A, Fujii Y, Yamakawa Y, Yokoyama T, Murase T, Eimoto T. Thymic neuroendocrine tumor (thymic carcinoid): a clinicopathologic study in 15 patients. Ann Thorac Surg 1999, **67**: 208–211.

374 Gartner L, Voorhess M. Adrenocorticotropic hormone-producing thymic carcinoid in a teenager. Cancer 1993, **71**: 106–111.

375 Goto K, Kodama T, Matsuno Y, Yokose T, Asamura H, Kamiya N, Shimosato Y. Clinicopathologic and DNA cytometric analysis of carcinoid tumors of the thymus. Mod Pathol 2001, **14**: 985–994.

376 Herbst WM, Kummer W, Hofmann W, Otto H, Heym C. Carcinoid tumors of the thymus. An immunohistochemical study. Cancer 1987, **60**: 2465–2470.

377 Horie Y, Kato M. Neuroendocrine carcinoma of the posterior mediastinum: a possible primary lesion. Arch Pathol Lab Med 1999, **123**: 933–936.

378 Kuo TT. Carcinoid tumor of the thymus with divergent sarcomatoid differentiation. Report of a case with histogenetic consideration. Hum Pathol 1994, **25**: 319–323.

379 Kuo T-t. Pigmented spindle cell carcinoid tumour of the thymus with ectopic adrenocorticotropic hormone secretion: report of a rare variant and differential diagnosis of mediastinal spindle cell neoplasms. Histopathology 2002, **40**: 159–165.

380 Lauriola L, Erlandson RA, Rosai J. Neuroendocrine differentiation is a common feature of thymic carcinoma. Am J Surg Pathol 1998, **22**: 1059–1066.

381 Levine GD, Rosai J. A spindle cell variant of thymic carcinoid tumor. A clinical, histologic, and fine structural study with emphasis on its distinction from spindle cell thymoma. Arch Pathol 1976, **100**: 293–300.

382 Mathew P, Roberts J, Zwischenberger J, Haque AK. Mediastinal atypical carcinoid and neurofibromatosis type 1. Arch Pathol Lab Med 2000, **124**: 319–321.

383 Moran CA, Suster S. Spindle-cell neuroendocrine carcinomas of the thymus (spindle-cell thymic carcinoid): a clinicopathologic and immunohistochemical study of seven cases. Mod Pathol 1999, **12**: 587–591.

384 Moran CA, Suster S. Angiomatoid neuroendocrine tumor of the thymus: report of a distinctive morphological variant of neuroendocrine tumor of the thymus resembling a vascular neoplasm. Hum Pathol 1999, **30**: 635–639.

385 Moran CA, Suster S. Thymic neuroendocrine carcinomas with combined features ranging from well-differentiated (carcinoid) to small cell carcinoma. A clinicopathologic and immunohistochemical study of 11 cases. Am J Clin Pathol 2000, **113**: 345–350.

386 Moran CA, Suster S. Primary neuroendocrine carcinoma (thymic carcinoid) of the thymus with prominent oncocytic features: a clinicopathologic study of 22 cases. Mod Pathol 2000, **13**: 489–494.

387 Moran CA, Suster S. Neuroendocrine carcinoma (carcinoid tumor) of the thymus. A clinicopathologic analysis of 80 cases. Am J Clin Pathol 2000, **114**: 100–110.

388 Paties C, Zangrandi A, Vassallo G, Rindi G, Solcia E. Multidirectional carcinoma of the thymus with neuroendocrine and sarcomatoid components and carcinoid syndrome. Pathol Res Pract 1991, **187**: 170–177.

389 Penman E, Wass JAH, Besser GM, Rees LH. Somatostatin secretion by lung and thymic tumours. Clin Endocrinol 1980, **13**: 613–620.

390 Rosai J, Higa E. Mediastinal endocrine neoplasm, of probable thymic origin, related to carcinoid tumor. Clinicopathologic study of 8 cases. Cancer 1972, **29**: 1061–1074.

391 Rosai J, Higa E, Davie JM. Mediastinal endocrine neoplasm in patients with multiple endocrine adenomatosis. A previously unrecognized association. Cancer 1972, **29**: 1075–1083.

392 Rosai J, Levine G, Weber WR, Higa E. Carcinoid tumors and oat cell carcinomas of the thymus. Pathol Annu 1976, **11**: 201–226.

393 Salyer WR, Salyer DC, Eggleston JC. Carcinoid tumors of the thymus. Cancer 1976, **37**: 958–973.

394 Snover DC, Levine GD, Rosai J. Thymic carcinoma. Five distinctive histological variants. Am J Surg Pathol 1982, **6**: 451–470.

395 Valli M, Fabris GA, Dewar A, Chikte S, Fisher C, Corrin B, Sheppard MN. Atypical carcinoid tumour of the thymus. A study of eight cases. Histopathology 1994, **24**: 371–375.

396 Vener JD, Zuckerbraun L, Goodman D. Carcinoid tumor of the thymus associated with a parathyroid adenoma. Arch Otolaryngol 1982, **108**: 324–326.

397 Wick MR, Carney JA, Bernatz PE, Brown LR. Primary mediastinal carcinoid tumors. Am J Surg Pathol 1982, **6**: 195–205.

398 Wick MR, Rosai J. Neuroendocrine neoplasms of the mediastinum. Semin Diagn Pathol 1991, **8**: 35–51.

399 Wick MR, Scheithauer BW. Oat-cell carcinoma of the thymus. Cancer 1982, **49**: 1652–1657.

400 Wick MR, Scheithauer BW. Thymic carcinoid. A histologic, immunohistochemical and ultrastructural study of 12 cases. Cancer 1984, **53**: 475–484.

Stromal and other tumors

401 Alli PM, Crain BJ, Heitmiller R, Argani P. Malignant melanoma presenting as an intrathymic tumor: a primary thymic melanoma. Arch Pathol Lab Med 2000, **124**: 130–134.

402 Argani P, De Chiocca IC, Rosai J. Thymoma arising with a thymolipoma. Histopathology 1998, **32**: 573–574.

403 Fushimi H, Kotoh K, Watanabe D, Tanio Y, Ogawa T, Miyoshi S. Malignant melanoma in the thymus. Am J Surg Pathol 2000, **24**: 1305–1308.

404 Havlíček F, Rosai J. A sarcoma of thymic stroma with features of liposarcoma. Am J Clin Pathol 1984, **82**: 217–224.

405 Iseki M, Tsuda N, Kishikawa M, Shimada O, Hayashi T, Kawahara K, Tomita M. Thymolipoma with striated myoid cells. Histological, immunohistochemical, and ultrastructural study. Am J Surg Pathol 1990, **14**: 395–398.

406 Jones H, Yaman M, Penn C, Clarke T. Primary stromal sarcoma of the thymus with areas of liposarcoma. Histopathology 1993, **23**: 81–82.

407 Klimstra DS, Moran CA, Perino G, Koss MN, Rosai J. Liposarcoma of the anterior mediastinum and thymus. A clinicopathologic study of 28 cases. Am J Surg Pathol 1995, **19**: 782–791.

408 Moran CA, Rosado-de-Christenson M, Suster S. Thymolipoma. Clinicopathologic review of 33 cases. Mod Pathol 1995, **8**: 741–744.

409 Moran CA, Zeren H, Koss MN. Thymofibrolipoma. A histologic variant of thymolipoma. Arch Pathol Lab Med 1994, **118**: 281–282.

410 Nishimura O, Naito Y, Noguchi Y, Matsuoka S, Takenaka K. Thymolipoma. A report of three cases. Jpn J Surg 1990, **20**: 234–237.

411 Ogino S, Franks TJ, Deuber H, Koss MN. Thymohemangiolipoma, a rare histologic variant of thymolipoma: a case report and review of the literature. Ann Diagn Pathol 2000, **4**: 236–239.

412 Otto HF, Löning TH, Lachenmayer L, Janzen RW Ch, Gürtler KF, Fischer K. Thymolipoma in association with myasthenia gravis. Cancer 1982, **50**: 1623–1628.

413 Valderrama E, Kahn LB, Wind E. Extraskeletal osteosarcoma arising in an ectopic hamartomatous thymus. Report of a case and review of the literature. Cancer 1983, **51**: 1132–1137.

414 Wilken JJ, Meier FA, Kornstein MJ. Kaposiform hemangioendothelioma of the thymus. Arch Pathol Lab Med 2000, **124**: 1542–1544.

Germ cell tumors

415 Blough RI, Heerema NA, Ulbright TM, Smolarek TA, Roth LM, Einhorn LH. Interphase chromosome painting of paraffin-embedded tissues in the differential diagnosis of possible germ cell tumors. Mod Pathol 1998, **11**: 634–641.

416 Burns BF, McCaughey WTE. Unusual thymic seminomas. Arch Pathol Lab Med 1986, **110**: 539–541.

417 Bush SE, Martinez A, Bagshaw MA. Primary mediastinal seminoma. Cancer 1981, **48**: 1877–1882.

418 Caballero C, Gomez S, Matias-Guiu X, Prat J. Rhabdomyosarcomas developing in association with mediastinal germ cell tumours. Virchows Arch [A] 1992, **420**: 539–543.

419 Carter D, Bibro MC, Touloukian RJ. Benign clinical behavior of immature mediastinal teratoma in infancy and childhood. Report of two cases and review of the literature. Cancer 1982, **49**: 398–402.

420 Chaganti RS, Rodriguez E, Mathew S. Origin of adult male mediastinal germ-cell tumours. Lancet 1994, **343**: 1130–1132.

421 Chariot P, Monnet I, Gaulard P, Abd-Alsamad I, Ruffié P, De Cremoux H. Systemic mastocytosis following mediastinal germ cell tumor. An association confirmed. Hum Pathol 1993, **24**: 111–112.

422 Cox JD. Primary malignant germ cell tumors of the mediastinum. A study of 24 cases. Cancer 1975, **36**: 1162–1168.

423 Daugaard G, Rřth M, von der Maase H, Skakkebaek NE. Management of extragonadal germ-cell tumors and the significance of bilateral testicular biopsies. Ann Oncol 1992, **4**: 283–289.

424 Dehner LP. Germ cell tumors of the mediastinum. Semin Diagn Pathol 1990, **7**: 266–284.

425 Dement SH. Association between mediastinal germ cell tumors and hematologic malignancies. An update. Hum Pathol 1990, **21**: 699–703.

426 Fox RM, Woods RL, Tattersall MHN, McGovern VJ. Undifferentiated carcinoma in young men. The atypical teratoma syndrome. Lancet 1979, **1**: 1316–1318.

427 Friedman NB. The function of the primordial germ cell in extragonadal tissues. Int J Androl 1987, **10**: 43–49.

428 Gonzalez-Vela JL, Savage PD, Manivel JC, Torkelson JL, Kennedy BJ. Poor prognosis of mediastinal germ cell cancers containing sarcomatous components. Cancer 1990, **66**: 1114–1116.

429 Gooneratne S, Keh P, Sreekanth S, Recant W, Talerman A. Anterior mediastinal endodermal sinus (yolk sac) tumor in a female infant. Cancer 1985, **56**: 1430–1433.

430 Govender D, Pillay SV. Mediastinal immature teratoma with yolk sac tumor and myelomonocytic leukemia associated with Klinefelter's syndrome. Int J Surg Pathol 2002, **10**: 157–162.

431 Greco FA, Oldham RK, Fer MF. The extragonadal germ cell cancer syndrome. Semin Oncol 1982, **9**: 448–455.

432 Greenwood SM, Goodman JR, Schneider G, Forman BH, Kress SG, Gelb AF. Choriocarcinoma in a man—the relationship of gynecomastia to chorionic somatomammotropin and estrogens. Am J Med 1971, **51**: 416–422.

433 Hainsworth JD, Greco FA. Poorly differentiated carcinoma and germ cell tumors. Hematol Oncol Clin North Am 1991, **5**: 1223–1231.

434 Hurt RD, Bruckman JE, Farrow GM, Bernatz PE, Hahn RG, Earle JD. Primary anterior mediastinal seminoma. Cancer 1982, **49**: 1658–1663.

435 Ilson DH, Bosl GJ, Motzer R, Dmitrovsky E, Chaganti RS. Genetic analysis of germ cell tumors. Current progress and future prospects. Hematol Oncol Clin North Am 1991, **5**: 1271–1283.

436 Irie T, Watanabe H, Kawaoi A, Takeuchi J. Alpha-fetoprotein (AFP), human chorionic gonadotropin (HCG), and carcinoembryonic antigen (CEA) demonstrated in the immature glands of mediastinal teratocarcinoma. A case report. Cancer 1982, **50**: 1160–1165.

437 Kuzur ME, Cobleigh MA, Greco FA, Einhorn LH, Oldham RK. Endodermal sinus tumor of the mediastinum. Cancer 1982, **50**: 766–774.

438 Lachman MF, Kim K, Koo B-C. Mediastinal teratoma associated with Klinefelter's syndrome. Arch Pathol Lab Med 1986, **110**: 1067–1071.

439 Ladanyi M, Samaniego F, Reuter VE, Motzer RJ, Jhanwar SC, Bosl GJ, Chaganti RS. Cytogenetic and immunohistochemical

evidence for the germ cell origin of a subset of acute leukemias associated with mediastinal germ cell tumors. J Natl Cancer Inst 1990, **82**: 221–227.

440 Laipply TC, Shipley RA. Extragenital choriocarcinoma in the male. Am J Pathol 1945, **21**: 921–933.

441 Lancaster K, Liang C, Myers JC, McCabe KM. Goblet cell carcinoid arising in a mature teratoma of the mediastinum. Am J Surg Pathol 1997, **21**: 109–113.

442 Lee YM, Jackson SM. Primary seminoma of the mediastinum. Cancer Control Agency of British Columbia experience. Cancer 1985, **55**: 450–452.

443 Lemariè E, Assouline PS, Diot P, Regnard JF, Levasseur P, Droz JP, Ruffiè P. Primary mediastinal germ cell tumors. Results of a French retrospective study. Chest 1992, **102**: 1477–1483.

444 Levine GD. Primary thymic seminoma. A neoplasm ultrastructurally similar to testicular seminoma and distinct from epithelial thymoma. Cancer 1973, **31**: 729–741.

445 Luna MA, Valenzuela-Tamril J. Germ cell tumors of the mediastinum. Post-mortem findings. Am J Clin Pathol 1976, **65**: 450–454.

446 McNeil MM, Leong AS-Y, Sage RE. Primary mediastinal embryonal carcinoma in association with Klinefelter's syndrome. Cancer 1981, **47**: 343–345.

447 Manivel C, Wick MR, Abenoza P, Rosai J. The occurrence of sarcomatous components in primary mediastinal germ cell tumors. Am J Surg Pathol 1986, **10**: 711–717.

448 Moran CA, Suster S. Primary mediastinal choriocarcinomas: a clinicopathologic and immunohistochemical study of eight cases. Am J Surg Pathol 1997, **21**: 1007–1012.

449 Moran CA, Suster S. Yolk sac tumors of the mediastinum with prominent spindle cell features: a clinicopathologic study of three cases. Am J Surg Pathol 1997, **21**: 1173–1177.

450 Moran CA, Suster S. Mediastinal yolk sac tumors associated with prominent multilocular cystic changes of thymic epithelium: a clinicopathologic and immunohistochemical study of five cases. Mod Pathol 1997, **10**: 800–803.

451 Moran CA, Suster S. Hepatoid yolk sac tumors of the mediastinum: a clinicopathologic and immunohistochemical study of four cases. Am J Surg Pathol 1997, **21**: 1210–1214.

452 Moran CA, Suster S, Koss MN. Primary germ cell tumors of the mediastinum: III. Yolk sac tumor, embryonal carcinoma, choriocarcinoma, and combined nonteratomatous germ cell tumors of the mediastinum—A clinicopathologic and immunohistochemical study of 64 cases. Cancer 1997, **80**: 699–707.

453 Moran CA, Suster S, Przygodzki RM, Koss MN. Primary germ cell tumors of the mediastinum: II. Mediastinal seminomas—A clinicopathologic and immunohistochemical study of 120 cases. Cancer 1997, **80**: 691–698.

454 Morinaga S, Nomori H, Kobayashi R, Atsumi Y. Well-differentiated adenocarcinoma arising from mature cystic teratoma of the mediastinum (teratoma with malignant transformation). Report of a surgical case. Am J Clin Pathol 1994, **101**: 531–534.

455 Mukai K, Adams WR. Yolk sac tumor of the anterior mediastinum. Am J Surg Pathol 1979, **3**: 77–83.

456 Nichols CR, Roth BJ, Heerema N, Griep J, Tricot G. Hematologic neoplasia associated with primary mediastinal germ-cell tumors. N Engl J Med 1990, **322**: 1425–1429.

457 Nichols CR, Saxman S, Williams SD, Loehrer PJ, Miller ME, Wright C, Einhorn LH. Primary mediastinal nonseminomatous germ cell tumors. A modern single institution experience. Cancer 1990, **65**: 1641–1646.

458 Oberman HA, Libcke JH. Malignant germinal neoplasms of the mediastinum. Cancer 1964, **17**: 498–507.

459 Orazi A, Neiman RS, Ulbright TM, Heerema NA, John K, Nichols CR. Hematopoietic precursor cells within the yolk sac tumor component are the source of secondary hematopoietic malignancies in patients with mediastinal germ cell tumors. Cancer 1993, **71**: 3873–3881.

459a Przygodzki R, Hubbs A, Zhao FQ, O'Leary TJ. Primary mediastinal seminomas: evidence of single and multiple KIT mutations. Lab Invest 2003, **82**: 1369–1375.

460 Przygodzki RM, Moran CA, Suster S, Khan MA, Swalsky PA, Bakker A, Koss MN, Finkelstein SD. Primary mediastinal and testicular seminomas: A comparison of K-ras-2 gene sequence and p53 immunoperoxidase analysis of 26 cases. Hum Pathol 1996, **27**: 975–979.

461 Rosado-de-Christenson ML, Templeton PA, Moran CA. From the archives of AFIP. Mediastinal germ cell tumors: Radiologic and pathologic correlation. Radiographics 1992, **12**: 1013–1030.

462 Rosai J, Parkash V, Reuter VE. The origin of mediastinal germ cell tumors in men. Int J Surg Pathol 1994, **2**: 73–78.

463 Sandhaus L, Strom RL, Mukai K. Primary embryonal-choriocarcinoma of the mediastinum in a woman. A case report with immunohistochemical study. Am J Clin Pathol 1981, **75**: 573–578.

464 Shantz A, Sewall W, Castleman B. Mediastinal germinoma. A study of 21 cases with an excellent prognosis. Cancer 1972, **30**: 1189–1194.

465 Sickels EA, Belliveau RE, Wiernik PH. Primary mediastinal choriocarcinoma in the male. Cancer 1974, **33**: 1196–1203.

466 Southgate J, Slade PR. Teratodermoid cyst of the mediastinum with pancreatic enzyme secretion. Thorax 1982, **37**: 476–477.

467 Suda K, Mizuguchi K, Hebisawa A, Wakabayashi T, Saito S. Pancreatic tissue in teratoma. Arch Pathol Lab Med 1984, **108**: 835–837.

468 Summersgill B, Goker H, Osin P, Huddart R, Horwich A, Fisher C, Shipley J. Establishing germ cell origin of undifferentiated tumors by identifying gain of 12p material using comparative genomic hybridization analysis of paraffin-embedded samples. Diagn Mol Pathol 1998, **7**: 260–266.

469 Suster S, Moran CA, Dominguez-Malagon H, Quevedo-Blanco P. Germ cell tumors of the mediastinum and testis: a comparative immunohistochemical study of 120 cases. Hum Pathol 1998, **29**: 737–742.

469a Takeda S, Miyoshi S, Ohta M, Minami M, Masaoka A, Matsuda H. Primary germ cell tumors in the mediastinum: a 50-year experience at a single Japanese institution. Cancer 2003, **97**: 367–376.

470 Toner GC, Geller NL, Lin SY, Bosl GJ. Extragonadal and poor risk nonseminomatous germ cell tumors. Survival and prognostic features. Cancer 1991, **67**: 2049–2057.

471 Toner GC, Panicek DM, Heelan RT, Geller NL, Lin SY, Bajorin D, Motzer RJ, Scher HI, Herr HW, Morse MJ. Adjunctive surgery after chemotherapy for nonseminomatous germ cell tumors. Recommendations for patient selection. J Clin Oncol 1990, **8**: 1683–1694.

472 Truong LD, Harris L, Mattioli C, Hawkins E, Lee A, Wheeler T, Lane M. Endodermal sinus tumor of the mediastinum. A report of seven cases and review of the literature. Cancer 1986, **58**: 730–739.

473 Ulbright TM, Loehrer PJ, Roth LM, Einhorn LH, Williams SD, Clark SA. The development of non-germ cell malignancies within germ cell tumors. A clinicopathologic study of 11 cases. Cancer 1984, **54**: 1824–1833.

474 Weidner N. Germ-cell tumors of the mediastinum. Semin Diagn Pathol 1999, **16**: 42–50.

475 Wenger ME, Dines DE, Ahmann DL, Good CA. Primary mediastinal choriocarcinoma. Mayo Clin Proc 1968, **43**: 570–575.

Malignant lymphoma

476 Bonfiglio TA, Dvoretsky PM, Piscioli F, dePapp EW, Patten SF Jr. Fine needle aspiration biopsy in the evaluation of

lymphoreticular tumors of the thorax. Acta Cytol (Baltimore) 1985, **29**: 548–553.

477 Lichtenstein AK, Levine A, Taylor CT, Boswell W, Rossman S, Feinstein DI, Lukes RJ. Primary mediastinal lymphoma in adults. Am J Med 1980, **68**: 509–514.

478 Payne CM, Grogan TM, Spier CM. Lymphomas of the mediastinum. Ultrastruct Pathol 1991, **15**: 439–474.

479 Simpson I, Campbell PE. Mediastinal masses in childhood. A review from a paediatric pathologist's point of view. Prog Pediatr Surg 1991, **27**: 92–126.

480 Strickler JG, Kurtin PJ. Mediastinal lymphoma. Semin Diagn Pathol 1991, **8**: 2–13.

481 Van Heerden JA, Harrison EG Jr, Bernatz PE, Kiely JM. Mediastinal malignant lymphoma. Chest 1970, **57**: 518–529.

Hodgkin's lymphoma

482 Baron RL, Sagel SS, Baglan RJ. Thymic cysts following radiation therapy for Hodgkin disease. Radiology 1981, **141**: 593–597.

483 Burke WA, Burford TH, Dorfman RE. Hodgkin's disease in the mediastinum. J Thorac Cardiovasc Surg 1967, **3**: 287–296.

484 Fechner RE. Hodgkin's disease of the thymus. Cancer 1969, **23**: 16–23.

485 Katz A, Lattes R. Granulomatous thymoma or Hodgkin's disease of thymus? A clinical and histologic study and a re-evaluation. Cancer 1969, **23**: 1–15.

486 Keller AR, Castleman B. Hodgkin's disease of the thymus gland. Cancer 1974, **33**: 1615–1623.

487 Kim HC, Nosher J, Haas A, Sweeney W, Lewis R. Cystic degeneration of thymic Hodgkin's disease following radiation therapy. Cancer 1985, **55**: 354–356.

488 Maity A, Goldwein JW, Lange B, D'Angio GJ. Mediastinal masses in children with Hodgkin's disease. An analysis of the Children's Hospital of Philadelphia and the Hospital of the University of Pennsylvania experience. Cancer 1992, **69**: 2755–2760.

489 Nickels J, Franssila K, Hjelt L. Thymoma and Hodgkin's disease of the thymus. Acta Pathol Microbiol Scand [A] 1973, **81**: 1–5.

490 Null JA, LiVolsi VA, Glenn WWL. Hodgkin's disease of the thymus (granulomatous thymoma) and myasthenia gravis. A unique association. Am J Clin Pathol 1977, **67**: 521–525.

491 Remigio PA. Granulomatous thymoma associated with erythroid hypoplasia. Am J Clin Pathol 1971, **55**: 68–72.

492 Rosai J. Lowenhaupt's embryology-based classification of thymic tumors and the concept of granulomatous thymoma. Cancer 1998, **82**: 1209–1216.

493 Smith PLC, Jobling C, Rees A. Hodgkin's disease in a large thymic cyst in a child. Thorax 1983, **38**: 392–393.

494 Van Heerden JA, Harrison EG Jr, Bernatz PE, Kiely JM. Mediastinal malignant lymphoma. Chest 1970, **57**: 518–529.

Lymphoblastic lymphoma

495 Adams JE. Leukemogenic thymoma. Report of a unique case. Am J Clin Pathol 1963, **40**: 173–182.

496 Ha K, Minden M, Hozumi N, Gelfand EW. Phenotypic heterogenity at the DNA level in childhood leukemia with a mediastinal mass. Cancer 1985, **56**: 509–513.

496a Karube K, Ohshima K, Tsuchiya T, Yamaguchi T, Suefuji H, Suzumiya J, Harada M, Kikuchi M. Non-B, Non-T neoplasms with lymphoblast morphology. Further clarification and classification. Am J Surg Pathol 2003, **27**: 1366–1374.

497 Koita H, Suzumiya J, Ohshima K, Takeshita M, Kimura N, Kikuchi M, Koono M. Lymphoblastic lymphoma expressing natural killer cell phenotype with involvement of the mediastinum and nasal cavity. Am J Surg Pathol 1997, **21**: 242–248.

498 Macon WR, Rynalski TH, Swerdlow SH, Cousar JB. T-cell lymphoblastic leukemia/lymphoma presenting in a recurrent thymoma. Mod Pathol 1991, **4**: 524–528.

499 Nathwani BN, Kim H, Rappaport H. Malignant lymphoma, lymphoblastic. Cancer 1976, **38**: 964–983.

500 Picozzi VJ, Coleman CN. Lymphoblastic lymphoma. Semin Oncol 1990, **17**: 96–103.

501 Quintanilla-Martinez L, Zukerberg LR, Harris NL. Prethymic adult lymphoblastic lymphoma. A clinicopathologic and immunohistochemical analysis. Am J Surg Pathol 1992, **16**: 1075–1084.

502 Soslow RA, Baergen RN, Warnke RA. B-Lineage lymphoblastic lymphoma is a clinicopathologic entity distinct from other histologically similar aggressive lymphomas with blastic morphology. Cancer 1999, **85**: 2648–2654.

Large cell lymphoma

503 Abou-Elella AA, Weisenburger DD, Vose JM, Kollath JP, Lynch JC, Bast MA, Bierman PJ, Greiner TC, Chan WC, Armitage JO. Primary mediastinal large B-cell lymphoma: a clinicopathologic study of 43 patients from the Nebraska Lymphoma Study Group. J Clin Oncol 1999, **17**: 784–790.

504 Addis BJ, Isaacson PG. Large cell lymphoma of the mediastinum. A B-cell tumor of probable thymic origin. Histopathology 1986, **10**: 379–390.

505 Aisenberg AC. Primary large cell lymphoma of the mediastinum. Semin Oncol 1999, **26**: 251–258.

506 Al-Sharabati M, Chittal S, Duga-Neulat I, Laurent G, Mazerolles C, Al-Saati T, Brousset P, Delsol G. Primary anterior mediastinal B-cell lymphoma. A clinicopathologic and immunohistochemical study of 16 cases. Cancer 1991, **67**: 2579–2587.

507 Bishop PC, Wilson WH, Pearson D, Janik J, Jaffe ES, Elwood PC. CNS involvement in primary mediastinal large B-cell lymphoma. J Clin Oncol 1999, **17**: 2479–2485.

507a Copie-Bergman C, Plonquet A, Alonso M, Boulland ML, Marquet J, Divine M, Möller P, Leroy K, Gaulard P. MAL expression in lymphoid cells: further evidence for MAL as a distinct molecular marker of primary mediastinal large B-cell lymphomas. Mod Pathol 2002, **15**: 1172–1180.

508 Davis RE, Dorfman RF, Warnke RA. Primary large-cell lymphoma of the thymus. A diffuse B-cell neoplasm presenting as primary mediastinal lymphoma. Hum Pathol 1990, **21**: 1262–1268.

509 de Leval L, Ferry JA, Falini B, Shipp M, Harris NL. Expression of bcl-6 and CD10 in primary mediastinal large B-cell lymphoma: evidence for derivation from germinal center B cells? Am J Surg Pathol 2001, **25**: 1277–1282.

510 Dunphy CH, Babich AD, Borson RA. Primary mediastinal large cell lymphoma with sclerosis containing a large number of T-cells: differential diagnosis. AIMM 1999, **7**: 48–51.

511 Eichelmann A, Koretz K, Mechtersheimer G, Möller P. Adhesion receptor profile of thymic B-cell lymphoma. Am J Pathol 1992, **141**: 729–741.

512 Higgins JP, Warnke RA. CD30 expression is common in mediastinal large B-cell lymphoma. Am J Clin Pathol 1999, **112**: 241–247.

513 Kirn D, Mauch P, Shaffer K, Pinkus G, Shipp MA, Kaplan WD, Tung N, Wheeler C, Beard CJ, Canellos GP. Large-cell and immunoblastic lymphoma of the mediastinum. Prognostic factors and treatment outcome in 57 patients. J Clin Oncol 1993, **11**: 1336–1343.

514 Lazzarino M, Orlandi E, Paulli M, Strater J, Klersy C, Gianelli U, Gargantini L, Rousset MT, Gambacorta M, Morra E, Lavabre-Bertrand T, Magrini U, Manegold C, Bernasconi C, Moller P. Treatment outcome and prognostic factors for primary mediastinal (thymic) B-cell lymphoma: A multicenter study of 106 patients. J Clin Oncol 1997, **15**: 1646–1653.

515 Levitt LJ, Aisenberg AC, Harris NL, Linggood RM, Poppema S. Primary non-Hodgkin's lymphoma of the mediastinum. Cancer 1982, **50**: 2486–2492.

516 Lones MA, Perkins SL, Sposto R, Kadin ME, Kjeldsberg CR, Wilson JF, Cairo MS. Large-cell lymphoma arising in the mediastinum in children and adolescents is associated with an excellent outcome: a children's cancer group report. J Clin Oncol 2000, **18**: 3845–3853.

517 Menestrina F, Chilosi M, Bonetti F, Lestani M, Scarpa A, Novelli P, Doglioni C, Todeschini G, Ambrosetti A, Fiore-Donati L. Mediastinal large-cell lymphoma of B-type, with sclerosis. Histopathological and immunohistochemical study of eight cases. Histopathology 1986, **10**: 589–600.

518 Miller JB, Variakojis D, Bitran JD, Sweet DL, Kinzie JJ, Golomb HM, Ultmann JE. Diffuse histiocytic lymphoma with sclerosis. A clinicopathologic entity frequently causing superior venacaval obstruction. Cancer 1981, **47**: 748–756.

519 Paulli M, Strater J, Gianelli U, Rousset M-T, Gambacorta M, Orlandi E, Kiersy C, Lavabre-Bertrand T, Morra E, Manegold C, Lazzarino M, Magrini U, Moller P. Mediastinal B-cell lymphoma: a study of its histomorphologic spectrum based on 109 cases. Hum Pathol 1999, **30**: 178–187.

520 Perrone T, Frizzera G, Rosai J. Mediastinal diffuse large-cell lymphoma with sclerosis. A clinicopathologic study of 60 cases. Am J Surg Pathol 1986, **10**: 176–191.

520a Pileri SA, Gaidano G, Zinzani PL, Falini B, Gaulard P, Zucca E, Pieri F, Berra E, Sabattini E, Ascani S, Piccioli M, Johnson P, Giardini R, Pescarmona E, Novero D, Piccaluga PP, Marafioti T, Alonso MA, Cavalli F. Primary mediastinal B-cell lymphoma: high frequency of BCL-6 mutations and consistent expression of the transcription factors OCT-2, BOB.1, and PU.1 in the absence of immunoglobulins. Am J Pathol 2003, **162**: 243–253.

521 Silverman JF, Raab SS, Park HK. Fine-needle aspiration cytology of primary large-cell lymphoma of the mediastinum. Cytomorphologic findings with potential pitfalls in diagnosis. Diagn Cytopathol 1993, **9**: 209–214.

522 Suster S. Large cell lymphoma of the mediastinum with marked tropism for germinal centers. Cancer 1992, **69**: 2910–2916.

523 Suster S, Moran CA. Pleomorphic large cell lymphomas of the mediastinum. Am J Surg Pathol 1996, **20**: 224–232.

524 Todeschini G, Ambrosetti A, Meneghini V, Pizzolo G, Menestrina F, Chilosi M, Benedetti F, Veneri D, Cetto GL, Perona G. Mediastinal large-B-cell lymphoma with sclerosis. A clinical study of 21 patients. J Clin Oncol 1990, **8**: 804–808.

525 Trump DL, Mann RB. Diffuse large cell and undifferentiated lymphomas with prominent mediastinal involvement. A poor prognostic subset of patients with non-Hodgkin's lymphoma. Cancer 1982, **50**: 277–282.

526 Tsang P, Cesarman E, Chadburn A, Liu Y-F, Knowles DM. Molecular characterization of primary mediastinal B cell lymphoma. Am J Pathol 1996, **148**: 2017–2025.

527 Waldron JA Jr, Dohring EJ, Farber LR. Primary large cell lymphomas of the mediastinum. An analysis of 20 cases. Semin Diagn Pathol 1985, **2**: 281–295.

528 Yousem SA, Weiss LM, Warnke RA. Primary mediastinal non-Hodgkin's lymphomas. A morphologic and immunologic study of 19 cases. Am J Clin Pathol 1985, **83**: 676–680.

Marginal zone B-cell lymphoma

529 Inagaki H, Chan JK, Ng JW, Okabe M, Yoshino T, Okamoto M, Ogawa H, Matsushita H, Yokose T, Matsuno Y, Nakamura N, Nagasaka T, Ueda R, Eimoto T, Nakamura S. Primary thymic extranodal marginal-zone B-cell lymphoma of mucosa-associated lymphoid tissue type exhibits distinctive clinicopathological and molecular features. Am J Pathol 2002, **160**: 1435–1443.

530 Isaacson PG, Chan JKC, Tang C, Addis BJ. Low-grade B-cell lymphoma of mucosa-associated lymphoid tissue arising in the thymus. A thymic lymphoma mimicking myoepithelial sialadenitis. Am J Surg Pathol 1990, **14**: 342–351.

531 Lorsbach RB, Pinkus GS, Shahsafaei A, Dorfman DM. Primary marginal zone lymphoma of the thymus. Am J Clin Pathol 2000, **113**: 784–791.

532 Nagasaka T, Lai R, Harada T, Chen Y-Y, Chen W-G, Arber DA, Weiss LM. Coexisting thymic and gastric lymphomas of mucosa-associated lymphoid tissues in a patient with Sjogren syndrome. Arch Pathol Lab Med 2000, **124**: 770–773.

533 Parrens M, Dubus P, Danjoux M, Jougon J, Brousset P, Velly JF, De Mascarel A, Merlio JP. Mucosa-associated lymphoid tissue of the thymus. Hyperplasia vs lymphoma. Am J Clin Pathol 2002, **117**: 51–56.

534 Takagi N, Nakamura S, Yamamoto K, Kunishima K, Takagi I, Suyama M, Shinoda M, Sugiura T, Oyama A, Suzuki H, Koshikawa T, Kontani K, Ueda R, Takahashii T, Ariyoshi Y, Suchi T. Malignant lymphoma of mucosa-associated lymphoid tissue arising in the thymus of a patient with Sjögren's syndrome. Cancer 1992, **69**: 1347–1355.

535 Yamasaki S, Matsushita H, Tanimura S, Nakatani T, Hara S, Endo Y, Hara M. B-cell lymphoma of mucosa-associated lymphoid tissue of the thymus: a report of two cases with a background of Sjogren's syndrome and monoclonal gammopathy. Am J Surg Pathol 1998, **29**: 1021–1024.

536 Yokose T, Kodama T, Matsuno Y, Shimosato Y, Nishimura M, Mukai K. Low-grade B cell lymphoma of mucosa-associated lymphoid tissue in the thymus of a patient with rheumatoid arthritis. Pathol Int 1998, **48**: 74–81.

Other hematolymphoid conditions

537 Bellan C, Lazzi S, Zazzi M, Lalinga AV, Palummo N, Galieni P, Marafioti T, Tonini T, Cinti C, Leoncini L, Pileri SA, Tosi P. Immunoglobulin gene rearrangement analysis in composite Hodgkin disease and large B-cell lymphoma: Evidence for receptor revision of immunoglobulin heavy chain variable region genes in Hodgkin-Reed-Sternberg cells? Diagn Mod Pathol 2002, **11**: 2–8.

538 Bowne WB, Lewis JJ, Filippa DA, Niesvizky R, Brooks AD, Burt ME, Brennan MF. The management of unicentric and multicentric Castleman's disease. A report of 16 cases and a review of the literature. Cancer 1999, **85**: 706–717.

539 Clavio M, Rossi E, Truini M, Carrara P, Ravetti JL, Spriano M, Vimercati AR, Santini G, Canepa L, Pierri I, Celesti L, Miglino M, Castellaneta A, Damasio E, Gobbi M. Anaplastic large cell lymphoma: a clinicopathologic study of 53 patients. Leuk Lymphoma 1996, **22**: 319–327.

540 Fassina A, Marino F, Poletti A, Rea F, Pennelli N, Ninfo V. Follicular dendritic cell tumor of the mediastinum. Ann Diagn Pathol 2001, **5**: 361–367.

541 Hishima T, Fukayama M, Hayashi Y, Shiozawa Y, Funata N, Sakamaki H, Koike M. Granulocytic sarcoma of the thymus in a nonleukaemic patient. Virchows Arch 1999, **435**: 447–451.

542 Karcher DS, Pearson CE, Butler WM, Hurwitz MA, Cassell PF. Giant lymph node hyperplasia involving the thymus with associated nephrotic syndrome and myelofibrosis. Am J Clin Pathol 1982, **77**: 100–104.

543 Keller AR, Hochholzer L, Castleman B. Hyaline-vascular and plasma-cell types of giant lymph node hyperplasia of mediastinum and other locations. Cancer 1972, **29**: 670–683.

544 McCluggage WG, Boyd HK, Jones FG, Mayne EE, Bharucha H. Mediastinal granulocytic sarcoma: a report of two cases. Arch Pathol Lab Med 1998, **122**: 545–547.

545 Moran CA, Suster S, Fishback NF, Koss MN. Extramedullary plasmacytomas presenting as mediastinal mass. Clinicopathologic study of two cases preceding the onset of multiple myeloma. Mod Pathol 1995, **8**: 257–259.

546 Strimlan CV, Khasnabis S. Primary mediastinal myelolipoma. Cleve Clin J Med 1993, **60**: 69–71.

547 Verani R, Olson J, Moake JL. Intrathoracic extramedullary

hematopoiesis. Report of a case in a patient with sickle-cell disease-β-thalassemia. Am J Clin Pathol 1980, **73**: 133–138.

548 Williams DM, Hobson R, Imeson J, Gerrard M, McCarthy K, Pinkerton CR, The United Kingdom Children's Cancer Study Group. Anaplastic large cell lymphoma in childhood: analysis of 72 patients treated on The United Kingdom Children's Cancer Study Group chemotherapy regimens. Br J Haematol 2002, **117**: 812–820.

Neurogenic tumors

549 Perez CA, Vietti T, Ackerman LV, Eagleton MD, Powers WE. Tumors of the sympathetic nervous system in children. An appraisal of treatment and results. Radiology 1967, **88**: 750–760.

550 Reed JC, Hallet KK, Feigin DS. Neural tumors of the thorax. Subject review from the AFIP. Radiology 1978, **126**: 9–17.

551 Simpson I, Campbell PE. Mediastinal masses in childhood. A review from a paediatric pathologist's point of view. Prog Pediatr Surg 1991, **27**: 92–126.

552 Talerman A, Gratama S. Primary ganglioneuroblastoma of the anterior mediastinum in a 61-year-old woman. Histopathology 1983, **7**: 967–975.

Tumors of sympathetic nervous system

553 Adam A, Hochholzer L. Ganglioneuroblastoma of the posterior mediastinum. A clinicopathologic review of 80 cases. Cancer 1981, **47**: 373–381.

554 Argani P, Erlandson R, Rosai J. Thymic neuroblastoma in adults. Report of three cases with special emphasis on its association with the syndrome of inappropriate secretion of antidiuretic hormone. Am J Clin Pathol 1997, **108**: 537–543.

555 Asada Y, Marutsuka K, Mitsukawa T, Kuribayashi T, Taniguchi S, Sumiyoshi A. Ganglioneuroblastoma of the thymus: An adult case with the syndrome of inappropriate secretion of antidiuretic hormone. Hum Pathol 1996, **27**: 506–509.

556 Carachi R, Campbell PE, Kent M. Thoracic neural crest tumors. A clinical review. Cancer 1983, **51**: 949–954.

557 Kellie SJ, Hayes FA, Bowman L, Kovnar EH, Langston J, Jenkins JJ III, Pao WJ, Ducos R, Green AA. Primary extracranial neuroblastoma with central nervous system metastases. Characterization by clinicopathologic findings and neuroimaging. Cancer 1991, **68**: 1999–2006.

558 King RM, Telander RL, Smithson WA, Banks PM, Han M-T. Primary mediastinal tumors in children. J Pediatr Surg 1982, **17**: 512–520.

559 Nagashima Y, Miyagi Y, Tanaka Y, Miyashita A, Shigematsu S, Aoki I, Nakatani Y, Misugi K. Adult ganglioneuroblastoma of the anterior mediastinum. Pathol Res Pract 1997, **193**: 727–732.

560 Saenz NC, Schnitzer JJ, Eraklis AE, Hendren WH, Grier HE, Macklis RM, Shamberger RC. Posterior mediastinal masses. J Pediatr Surg 1993, **28**: 172–176.

561 Salter JE Jr, Gibson D, Ordóñez NG, Mackay B. Neuroblastoma of the anterior mediastinum in an 80-year-old woman. Ultrastruct Pathol 1995, **19**: 305–310.

562 Simpson I, Campbell PE. Mediastinal masses in childhood. A review from a paediatric pathologist's point of view. Prog Pediatr Surg 1991, **27**: 92–126.

563 Young DG. Thoracic neuroblastoma/ganglioneuroma. J Pediatr Surg 1983, **18**: 37–41.

Tumors of peripheral nerves

564 Ackerman LV, Taylor FH. Neurogenous tumors within the thorax. A clinical pathologic evaluation of forty-eight cases. Cancer 1951, **4**: 669–691.

565 Kourea HP, Bilsky MH, Leung DHY, Lewis JJ, Woodruff JM. Subdiaphragmatic and intrathoracic paraspinal malignant peripheral nerve sheath tumors: a clinicopathologic study of 25 patients and 26 tumors. Cancer 1998, **82**: 2191–2203.

566 Lodding P, Kindblom LG, Angervall L, Stenman G. Cellular schwannoma. A clinicopathologic study of 29 cases. Virchows Arch [A] 1990, **416**: 237–248.

567 Marchevsky AM. Mediastinal tumors of peripheral nervous system origin. Semin Diagn Pathol 1999, **16**: 65–78.

568 Oberman HA, Abell MR. Neurogenous neoplasms of the mediastinum. Cancer 1960, **13**: 882–898.

569 Reed JC, Hallet KK, Feigin DS. Neural tumors of the thorax. Subject review from the AFIP. Radiology 1978, **126**: 9–17.

570 White W, Shiu MH, Rosenblum MK, Erlandson RA, Woodruff JM. Cellular schwannoma. A clinicopathologic study of 57 patients and 58 tumors. Cancer 1990, **66**: 1266–1275.

Other neurogenic tumors

571 Doglioni C, Bontempini L, Iuzzolino P, Furlan G, Rosai J. Ependymoma of the mediastinum. Arch Pathol Lab Med 1988, **112**: 194–196.

572 Falleni M, Roz E, Dessy E, Del Curto B, Braidotti P, Gianelli U, Pietra GG. Primary intrathoracic meningioma: histopathological, immunohistochemical and ultrastructural study of two cases. Virchows Arch 2001, **439**: 196–200.

573 Wilson RW, Moran CA. Primary ependymoma of the mediastinum: a clinicopathologic study of three cases. Ann Diagn Pathol 1998, **2**: 293–300.

Tumors of paraganglia

574 Blei E, Gonzalez-Crussi F. The intriguing nature of gastric tumors in Carney's triad. Cancer 1992, **69**: 292–300.

575 Hofmann WJ, Wockel W, Thetter O, Otto HF. Melanotic paraganglioma of the posterior mediastinum. Virchows Arch 1995, **425**: 641–646.

576 Odze R, Begin LR. Malignant paraganglioma of the posterior mediastinum. A case report and review of the literature. Cancer 1990, **65**: 564–569.

577 Ogawa J, Inoue H, Koide S, Kawada S, Shohtsu A, Hata J. Functioning paraganglioma in the posterior mediastinum. Ann Thorac Surg 1982, **33**: 507–510.

578 Olson JL, Salyer WR. Mediastinal paragangliomas (aortic body tumor). A report of four cases and a review of the literature. Cancer 1978, **41**: 2405–2412.

Mesenchymal tumors

579 Ahn C, Harvey JC. Mediastinal hibernoma, a rare tumor. Ann Thorac Surg 1990, **50**: 828–830.

580 Alho A, Eeg Larsen T. A case of multifocal liposarcoma? Acta Orthop Scand 1992, **63**: 98–99.

581 Awotwi JD, Zusman J, Waring WW, Beckerman RC. Benign hemangioendothelioma—a rare type of posterior mediastinal mass in children. J Pediatr Surg 1983, **18**: 581–584.

582 Begin LR, Schurch W, Lacoste J, Hiscott J, Melnychuk DA. Glycogen-rich clear cell rhabdomyosarcoma of the mediastinum. Potential diagnostic pitfall. Am J Surg Pathol 1994, **18**: 302–308.

583 Brown LR, Reiman HM, Rosenow EC III, Gloviczki PM, Divertie MB. Intrathoracic lymphangioma. Mayo Clin Proc 1986, **61**: 882–892.

584 Chen W, Chan CW, Mok CK. Malignant fibrous histiocytoma of the mediastinum. Cancer 1982, **50**: 797–800.

585 Chetty R. Extraskeletal mesenchymal chondrosarcoma of the mediastinum. Histopathology 1990, **17**: 261–263.

586 Dudgeon DL, Haller JA Jr. Pediatric lipoblastomatosis. Two unusual cases. Surgery 1984, **95**: 371–373.

587 Flieder DB, Moran CA, Suster S. Primary alveolar soft-part sarcoma of the mediastinum: a clinicopathological and immunohistochemical study of two cases. Histopathology 1997, **31**: 469–473.

588 Fu K, Moran CA, Suster S. Primary mediastinal giant cell tumors: a clinicopathologic and immunohistochemical study of two cases. Ann Diagn Pathol 2002, **6**: 100–105.

589 Gaertner EM, Steinberg DM, Huber M, Hayashi T, Tsuda N, Askin FB, Bell SW, Nguyen B, Colby TV, Nishimura SL, Miettinen M, Travis WD. Pulmonary and mediastinal glomus tumors—report of five cases including a pulmonary glomangiosarcoma: a clinicopathologic study with literature review. Am J Surg Pathol 2000, **24**: 1105–1114.

590 Gibbs AR, Johnson NF, Giddings JC, Powell DEB, Jasani B. Primary angiosarcoma of the mediastinum. Light and electron microscopic demonstration of factor VIII-related antigen in neoplastic cells. Hum Pathol 1984, **15**: 687–691.

591 Goodlad JR, Fletcher CD. Solitary fibrous tumour arising at unusual sites. Analysis of a series. Histopathology 1991, **19**: 515–522.

592 Hirose T, Hasegawa T, Seki K, Yang P, Sano T, Morizumi H, Tsuyuguchi M. Atypical glomus tumor in the mediastinum: A case report with immunohistochemical and ultrastructural studies. Ultrastruct Pathol 1996, **20**: 451–456.

593 Homer MJ, Wechsler RJ, Carter BL. Mediastinal lipomatosis. CT confirmation of a normal variant. Radiology 1978, **128**: 657–661.

594 Hoskins MC, Evans RA, King SJ, Gishen P. "Sabre sheath" trachea with mediastinal lipomatosis mimicking a mediastinal tumour. Clin Radiol 1991, **44**: 417–418.

595 Klimstra DS, Moran CA, Perino G, Koss MN, Rosai J. Liposarcoma of the anterior mediastinum and thymus. A clinicopathologic study of 28 cases. Am J Surg Pathol 1995, **19**: 782–791.

596 Kline ME, Patel BU, Agosti SJ. Noninfiltrating angiolipoma of the mediastinum. Radiology 1990, **175**: 737–738.

597 Lamovec J, Sobel HJ, Zidar A, Jerman J. Epithelioid hemangioendothelioma of the anterior mediastinum with osteoclast-like giant cells. Am J Clin Pathol 1990, **93**: 813–817.

598 Manivel C, Wick MR, Abenoza P, Rosai J. The occurrence of sarcomatous components in primary mediastinal germ cell tumors. Am J Surg Pathol 1986, **10**: 711–717.

599 Moran CA, Suster S, Perino G, Kaneko M, Koss MN. Malignant smooth muscle tumors presenting as mediastinal soft tissue masses. A clinicopathologic study of 10 cases. Cancer 1994, **74**: 2251–2260.

600 Pachter MR, Lattes R. Mesenchymal tumors of the mediastinum. Cancer 1963, **16**: 74–94; 95–107; 108–117.

601 Pescarmona E, Remotti D, Marzullo A, Faraggiana T, Muda AO, Baroni CD. Fibrosarcoma of the thymic region. A case report. Tumori 1991, **77**: 363–366.

602 Shaffer K, Pugatch RD, Sugarbaker DJ. Primary mediastinal leiomyoma. Ann Thorac Surg 1990, **50**: 301–302.

602a Sidhu J, Nicolas MM, Taylor W. Mediastinal rhabdomyoma: a case report and review of the literature. Int J Surg Pathol 2002, **10**: 313–318.

603 Standerfer RJ, Armistead SH, Paneth M. Liposarcoma of the mediastinum. Report of two cases and review of the literature. Thorax 1981, **36**: 693–694.

604 Sunderrajan EV, Luger AM, Rosenholtz MJ, Maltby JD. Leiomyosarcoma in the mediastinum presenting as superior vena cava syndrome. Cancer 1984, **53**: 2553–2556.

605 Suster S, Moran CA. Malignant cartilaginous tumors of the mediastinum: clinicopathological study of six cases presenting as extraskeletal soft tissue masses. Hum Pathol 1997, **28**: 588–594.

606 Suster S, Moran CA, Koss MN. Epithelioid hemangioendothelioma of the anterior mediastinum. Clinicopathologic, immunohistochemical, and ultrastructural analysis of 12 cases. Am J Surg Pathol 1994, **18**: 871–881.

607 Suster S, Moran CA, Koss MN. Rhabdomyosarcomas of the anterior mediastinum. Report of four cases unassociated with germ cell, teratomatous, or thymic carcinomatous components. Hum Pathol 1994, **25**: 349–356.

608 Svane H, Ottosen P. Cavernous haemangioma of the mediastinum. A rare tumor form. Acta Chir Scand 1960, **118**: 405–408.

609 Swanson PE. Soft tissue neoplasms of the mediastinum. Semin Diagn Pathol 1991, **8**: 14–34.

610 Toursarkissian B, O'Connor WN, Dillon ML. Mediastinal epithelioid hemangioendothelioma. Ann Thorac Surg 1990, **49**: 680–685.

611 Weidner N. Atypical tumor of the mediastinum. Epithelioid hemangioendothelioma containing metaplastic bone and osteoclastlike giant cells. Ultrastruct Pathol 1991, **15**: 481–488.

612 Witkin GB, Rosai J. A biphasic tumor of the mediastinum with features of synovial sarcoma. A report of four cases. Am J Surg Pathol 1989, **13**: 490–499.

613 Witkin GB, Rosai J. Solitary fibrous tumor of the mediastinum. A report of 14 cases. Am J Surg Pathol 1989, **13**: 547–557.

Metastatic tumors

614 Daly BD, Leung SF, Cheung H, Metreweli C. Thoracic metastases from carcinoma of the nasopharynx. High frequency of hilar and mediastinal lymphadenopathy. AJR Am J Roentgenol 1993, **160**: 241–244.

615 Lindell MM, Doubleday LC, Von Eschenbach AC, Libshitz HI. Mediastinal metastases from prostatic carcinoma. J Urol 1982, **128**: 331–334.

616 McLoud TC, Kalisher L, Stark P, Green R. Intrathoracic lymph node metastases from extrathoracic neoplasms. AJR Am J Roentgenol 1978, **131**: 403–407.

9 Thyroid gland

Normal anatomy

The thyroid *anlage* appears in the embryo as a midline structure at the site corresponding to the foramen cecum of the adult tongue. From here, it descends as a component of the thyroglossal duct along the midline to reach its final position in the mid neck.[12] Later, the hyoid bone is formed from the second branchial arch. The thyroglossal duct is usually situated anteriorly to this bone and is divided by it into a suprahyoid and an infrahyoid portion. In the normal course of events, the thyroglossal duct is obliterated and disappears, leaving as a vestige the pyramidal lobe in about 40% of normal individuals.[36] At the same time, the thyroid *anlage* expands laterally to form the thyroid lobes. Microscopically, cords and plates of follicular cells are formed by the ninth week, small follicular lumina appear by the tenth week, and colloid secretion becomes evident by the twelfth week. By the fourteenth week, the gland consists of well-developed follicles lined by follicular cells and containing thyroglobulin-positive colloid in the lumen.

The normal adult thyroid gland is composed of two lobes joined by the isthmus, which lies across the trachea anteriorly, below the level of the cricoid cartilage. It is endowed with a rich lymphatic network that coalesces in the subcapsular region to give rise to collecting trunks that drain into the following nodes: (1) pericapsular; (2) internal jugular chain; (3) pretracheal, paratracheal, and prelaryngeal (the pretracheal node located near the isthmus is sometimes referred to as the Delphian node); (4) recurrent laryngeal nerve chain; and (5) retropharyngeal and retroesophageal. The anterosuperior mediastinal nodes are secondary to the recurrent laryngeal nerve chain and pretracheal groups, but studies have shown that dye injected into the thyroid isthmus can also drain directly into them.[8]

Microscopically, the thyroid gland is made up of round or oval follicles that vary considerably in size, with an average diameter of 200 μm. They are lined by a single layer of follicular cells whose shape ranges from flattened to low columnar depending on their degree of activity.[5a] The cytoplasm has a pale acidophilic or amphophilic staining quality; the greater the activity of the cell, the greater its amount. Follicular cells with abundant granular acidophilic cytoplasm are referred to as Hürthle cells (a misnomer), Askanazy's cells, oxyphilic cells, or oncocytes. Ultrastructurally, this granularity is due to the accumulation of mitochondria. They can be detected immunohistochemically with antibodies directed against mitochondrial enzymes.[29]

The proliferative activity of follicular cells is related to age, being highest in the prenatal group and lowest in adults.[31a]

The main ultrastructural features of follicular cells are abundant granular endoplasmic reticulum, a well-developed Golgi apparatus, lysosomes (particularly numerous in actively secreting cells, and mainly located toward the apical side), and numerous microvilli in the luminal border.[16] The intraluminal colloid is pale staining with scalloped borders in follicles with active secretory function and densely eosinophilic in inactive ones. In old age, it tends to be broken up in globular formations. It is variably PAS positive and alcianophilic, depending on the types and relative amounts of carbohydrate components present.[31] Birefringent calcium oxalate crystals may be found, their number increasing with age.[15,30] Their presence is of practical utility in distinguishing thyroid from parathyroid tissue (which lacks them), particularly at the time of frozen section.[13] Collections of small follicles protruding into the lumen of larger follicles are commonly seen in actively secret-

ing glands; they are sometimes referred to as *Sanderson's polsters*.

Immunohistochemically, reactivity for thyroglobulin, triiodothyronine (T3), and thyroxine (T4) is found both in the colloid and in the cytoplasm of the follicular cells.[21,34] Thyroglobulin is the most useful of these markers, especially when it is searched for with monoclonal antibodies.[17,34] A lesser degree of reactivity is found in Hürthle cells. Thyroid transcription factor 1 (TTF-1) has quickly emerged as an extremely useful marker for thyroid follicular cells and tumors composed of them.[14] The only other tissue in which it is expressed with any frequency is the alveolar epithelium of the lung.[19]

Follicular cells are also positive for low-molecular-weight keratin, epithelial membrane antigen (EMA), and vimentin.[3] They are said to possess receptors for estrogen and progesterone.[26] The follicles rest on a basement membrane that is immunoreactive for laminin and type IV collagen.[23]

The other major epithelial component of the thyroid gland is represented by neuroendocrine cells known as C cells or parafollicular cells. The latter term is a misnomer, because immunohistochemical and ultrastructural studies have shown that they occupy a predominantly and perhaps exclusively intrafollicular position. These cells are of presumed neural crest derivation and reach the thyroid via the ultimobranchial body (see below). Because of this fact, C cells are restricted to the middle and upper thirds of the lateral lobes along their central axes. The number of C cells varies according to age; they are more numerous in infancy and old age than in adults. Most adult glands contain no more than 10 C cells in a low-power microscopic field. In old age, they may form nodular aggregates.[27]

Ultrastructurally, C cells contain numerous dense-core granules of neurosecretory type.[9] They are argyrophilic with the Grimelius reaction; metachromatic with toluidine blue; positive for lead hematoxylin; and immunoreactive for calcitonin, katacalcin, calcitonin gene-related peptide, neuron-specific enolase, chromogranins A and B, secretogranin II, and synaptophysin[32] (Fig. 9.1). They are also immunoreactive for carcinoembryonic antigen (CEA), although less so than their neoplastic counterparts in medullary carcinoma.[35]

Solid cell nests (*rests*) are thought to represent remnants of the ultimobranchial body, which in turn is derived from the branchial cleft pouch complex IV–V.[4,10,20,28] They measure 0.1 mm on average and can be detected in almost 90% of neonatal thyroid glands[1] (Fig. 9.2). They are mainly composed of polygonal or oval cells admixed with occasional clear cells. Small glandular lumina containing a mucinous secretion are often present,[11,25] the nests thus acquiring a combined solid and cystic appearance. An increased number of C cells may be seen around the nests, in keeping with the well-known relationship that these cells have with the ultimobranchial

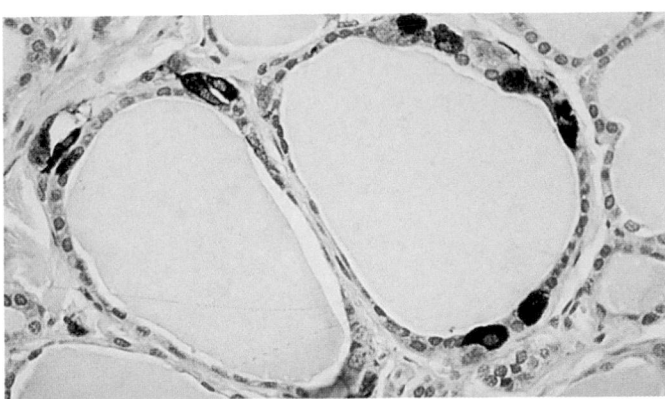

Fig. 9.1 Immunoreactivity for calcitonin in thyroid C cells. This is from a case of C cell hyperplasia.

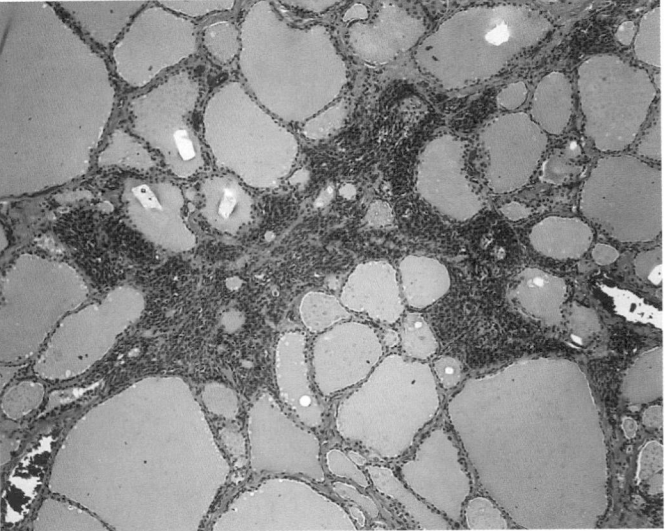

Fig. 9.2 Solid cell rest. The irregular branching shape of the nodule is characteristic.

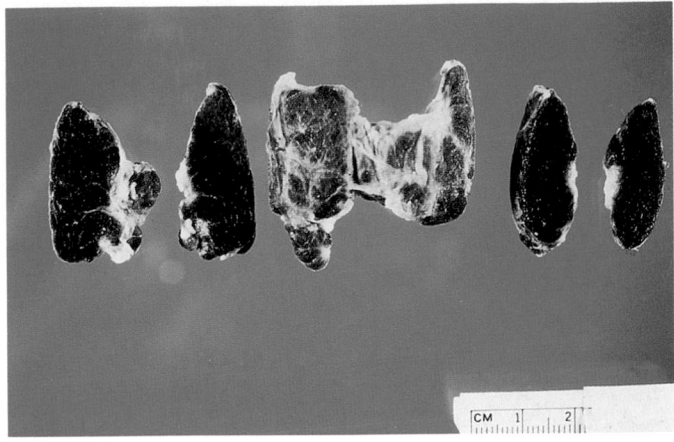

Fig. 9.3 Black thyroid following amiodarone therapy. (Courtesy of Dr. Maria Merino, Bethesda, MD)

plasm of follicular cells in old age, a process that may become massive after the administration of some medications, such as minocycline.[2,18] When intense, it is appreciable grossly and it is referred to as *melanosis thyroidi* or—less pompously—as *black thyroid*[2,37] (Fig. 9.3).

Congenital abnormalities

Thyroglossal duct anomalies are the result of a localized persistence of the thyroglossal duct. This may be in the form of a sinus tract connected either to the foramen cecum or to the suprasternal notch or in the form of a blind tubular structure.[40] It may be accompanied by a cystic dilatation, thought to be the result of secretion from the lining cells. When the cystic changes are prominent, the abnormality is designated as a *thyroglossal duct cyst*. Its usual location is the midline of the neck, in the region of the hyoid bone[40] (Fig. 9.4). Microscopically, the cyst is lined by pseudostratified ciliated or squamous epithelium. Mucous glands and thyroid follicles are commonly seen in the subjacent stroma. Secondary inflammation is common, particularly in cases accompanied by a sinus tract.[64] As a result, the epithelial lining may be partially absent, and the stroma may be infiltrated by inflammatory cells.

Most cases are clinically evident during childhood, but others become apparent only later in life.[63] The treatment is surgical removal. To minimize recurrence, it is important to include in the excision the middle third of the hyoid bone and the entire length of any sinus tract that might be present.[46]

The thyroid tissue present in these anomalies can undergo malignant transformation, usually in the form of papillary carcinoma.[46a,48,51,66] The prognosis is excellent after surgical removal, which does not need to include the thyroid gland. Other tumor types have been described, including Hürthle cell carcinoma[38] and undifferentiated (anaplastic) carcinoma.[56]

body. Ultrastructurally, there are microfollicular structures, intracytoplasmic microvacuoles, and ciliated cells, in addition to lymphoid cells.[22] Immunohistochemically, there is a strong expression of p63.[30a]

Solid cell nests need to be distinguished from metaplastic follicles, foci of nodular C-cell hyperplasia, and papillary microcarcinoma.

Focal collections of lymphocytes are seen at autopsy in the thyroid of about one half of females and one fourth of males; this finding is regarded as a subclinical manifestation of focal lymphocytic thyroiditis.[24]

Morphologic variations in the anatomy of the thyroid having no clinical significance include:

1 Adipose metaplasia of the interfollicular stroma.[33]
2 Intrathyroidal islands of mature cartilage, presumably of branchial pouch derivation (see p. 519).
3 Intrathyroidal islands of ectopic thymus.[6,7]
4 Intrathyroidal parathyroid.
5 Intrathyroidal bundles of skeletal muscle.
6 Intrathyroidal salivary gland tissue.[5]
7 Accumulation of melanin-like pigment in the cyto-

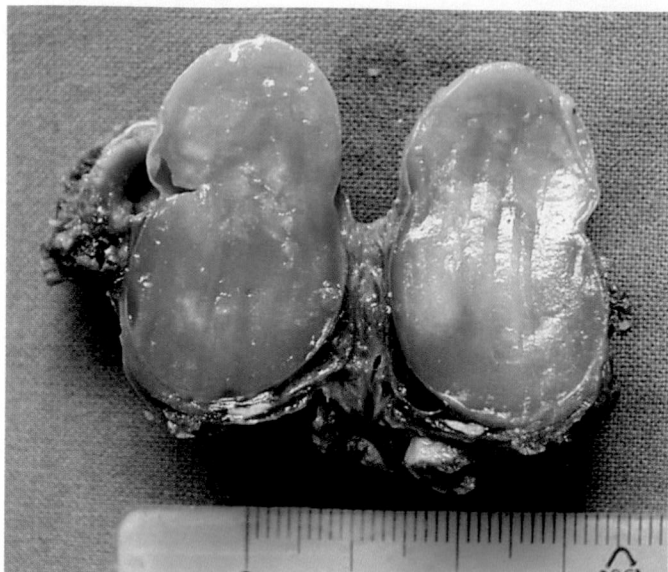

Fig. 9.4 Thyroglossal duct cyst. The content of the cyst is gelatinous.

Heterotopic thyroid tissue can be found not only as a component of thyroglossal duct cyst but anywhere along the course of the thyroglossal duct, sometimes as the sole abnormality (Fig. 9.5). The most frequent location is the base of the tongue, where it may result in difficulty in swallowing and respiratory obstruction, which in a few cases has proved fatal. At a microscopic (subclinical) level, lingual thyroid is found in 10% of normal individuals.[59] This heterotopic thyroid does not differ microscopically from that seen in the main gland. Sometimes a capsule is formed around it; in other instances, the follicles grow between the skeletal muscle of the tongue, a feature that may simulate invasion by tumor. In 70% of patients with grossly evident lingual thyroid there is absence of the normal thyroid gland. Therefore, removal of the heterotopic thyroid tissue will lead to hypothyroidism, requiring subsequent medical replacement therapy.

Other sites of heterotopic thyroid tissue are the anterior tongue, submandibular region, larynx, trachea, mediastinum (usually superior but sometimes posterior), and heart.[39,49,57] The common denominator in all these sites is their location in or close to the midline, the large majority being found in the so-called *Wölfler's area*, described by anatomists as an isosceles triangle with the edge of the mandible at its base and the concavity of the aortic arch at its apex. The possible occurrence of heterotopic thyroid tissue in cervical nodes is discussed on p. 562.

More distant locations in which heterotopic thyroid tissue has been reported include the region of the porta hepatis,[60] adrenal gland,[62] and—last but not least—the ovary and other sites as a component of a teratoma (*struma ovarii* being the most spectacular example) (see Chapter 19).

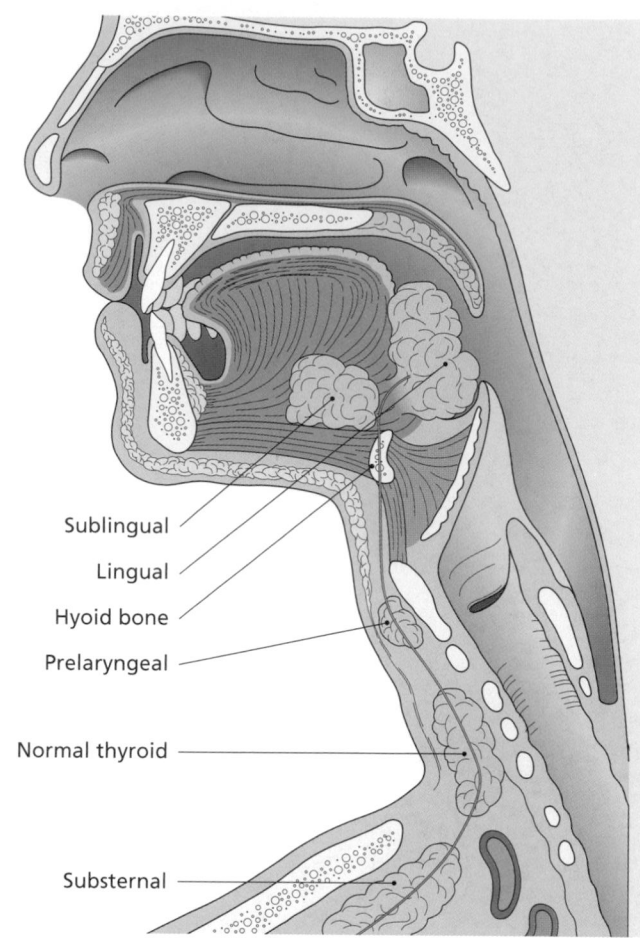

Sublingual

Lingual

Hyoid bone

Prelaryngeal

Normal thyroid

Substernal

Fig. 9.5 Distribution of heterotopic thyroid tissue. (From Lemmon WT, Paschal GW Jr. Lingual thyroid. Am J Surg 1941, **52**: 82–85)

Heterotopic thyroid tissue in any of these locations is subject to the same diseases that can affect the main gland, including inflammation, hyperplasia, and tumors. Thus several cases of follicular carcinoma arising from lingual thyroid have been reported.[45]

Branchial pouch anomalies are not directly related to the thyroid but are discussed here because of their close proximity to the gland.[67] They may present as a patent fistula, a simple sinus, a blind cyst, or an island of cartilage[42,53] (Fig. 9.6). They are located in the anterolateral region of the neck, their exact position depending on the specific branchial cleft involved. Those related to the *first pouch* appear in the preauricular area or beneath the posterior half of the mandible and may be connected to the external auditory canal. Those related to the *second pouch* appear just anterior to the sternocleidomastoid muscle in the mid neck and may have an open tract communicating with the pharynx near the superior fold of the tonsil.[52] Those related to the *third and fourth pouches* are typically found in the lower neck, in a suprasternal or supraclavicular location. Some of these have been mislabeled as bronchogenic cysts in the past.[43,61]

The lining of these cysts and fistulous tracts is usually squamous epithelium, but columnar ciliated epithelium

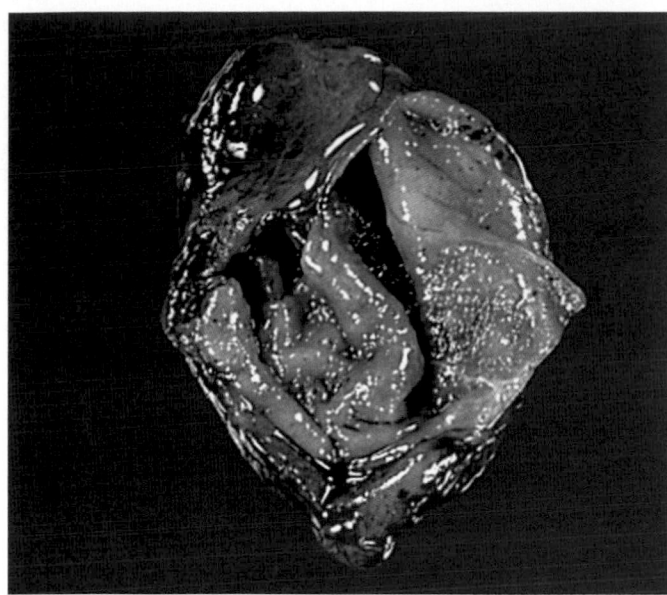

Fig. 9.6 Branchial cleft cyst that has been partially opened to expose the inner surface, which is rendered irregular by the presence of innumerable hyperplastic lymphoid follicles.

is also common. Abundant lymphoid tissue, often with germinal centers, is observed beneath. Cysts located in the lower neck may also contain mucinous, seromucinous, and sebaceous glands.[43,61] Secondary infection may complicate the microscopic picture. Squamous cell carcinomas arising in a branchial cleft cyst probably exist, but they are exceptionally rare.[41] Any cystic mass in the lateral neck containing squamous cell carcinoma must be considered a lymph node metastasis with cystic degeneration until proved otherwise, and a search for the primary tumor should be instituted, particularly in the upper aerodigestive tract.[44,55] Sites notorious for harboring small occult primary tumors include tonsil and posterior tonsillar pillar, retromolar tongue, and nasopharynx.

Similar comments pertain to the relationship of branchial cleft cysts and papillary carcinomas of thyroid type. Perhaps there exist cases of this tumor type arising in the ectopic thyroid tissue of branchial cleft cysts,[54] but there is no question that the overwhelming majority of the cystic lesions in the lateral neck containing a recognizable focus of papillary thyroid carcinoma represent lymph node metastases from a thyroid primary that have undergone secondary cystic change (see p. 540).

Branchial pouch-related structures are found within the thyroid in the form of the already mentioned solid cell rests (a remnant of the ultimobranchial body or branchial pouch complex IV–V), and—less commonly—in the form of heterotopic cartilage (sharply outlined and often kidney-shaped[47]), thymic tissue, parathyroid glands, or epithelial-lined cysts with or without an associated lymphoid component.[65] Most of the latter—sometimes designated as lymphoepithelial cysts—are seen in

glands affected by Hashimoto's thyroiditis (see p. 520), but they can also be found in its absence.[58] Exceptionally, perithyroidal epithelial cysts have been found to contain pancreatic tissue in their wall, as representatives of foregut remnants.[50]

Parenthetically, the presence of normal, cystic, or neoplastic thymic tissue in the neck should also be viewed as the expression of branchial pouch-derived anomalies (see Chapter 8).

Dyshormonogenetic goiter is discussed on p. 524.

Thyroiditis

Acute thyroiditis

Acute thyroiditis is usually of infectious nature.[71,74,76] It may be associated with acute infections of the upper aerodigestive tract (e.g., pharyngitis, tonsillitis), generalized sepsis, or major trauma to the neck with an open wound.[68] It tends to affect the malnourished infant, the debilitated elderly, and the immunocompromised patient. *Streptococcus haemolyticus, Staphylococcus aureus,* and *Pneumococcus* are the organisms most commonly responsible.[71,76] Other causes include gram-negative bacteria, fungi (particularly *Candida*), and *Pneumocystis*.[70] Viral infection is rare, but several cases of cytomegalovirus infection of the thyroid in patients with AIDS have been documented.[69]

Morphologically, the main changes in acute thyroiditis are those of neutrophilic infiltration and tissue necrosis. Nonsuppurative and suppurative forms exist, the latter sometimes evolving into an abscess. The interesting observation has been made that a large number of cases of recurrent acute suppurative thyroiditis (especially when left-sided) are secondary to the presence of a pyriform sinus fistula.[72,73,75] The best method to confirm the diagnosis is fine needle biopsy with smear cytologic examination and cultures. The presence of a pyriform sinus fistula can be established by barium meal.[72]

Medical treatment of acute thyroiditis is usually effective, but abscesses need to be drained surgically. Cases associated with pyriform sinus fistula are best treated by fistulectomy.[72]

Granulomatous (de Quervain's) thyroiditis

Granulomatous thyroiditis, also known as de Quervain's or subacute thyroiditis, typically presents in middle-aged women with sore throat, painful deglutition, and marked tenderness on palpation in the thyroid region, often associated with fever and malaise.[79] Once the initial process has subsided, pressure symptoms and/or mild hypothyroidism may develop. However, in the majority of cases there is complete resolution. Because of the sometimes asymmetric involvement of the gland, the disease may be clinically confused with carcinoma.

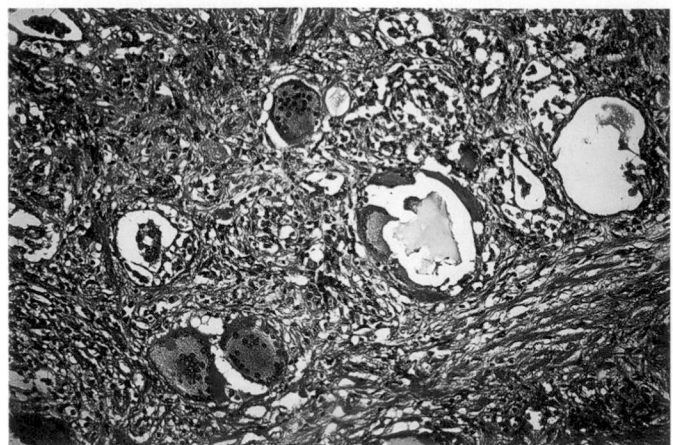

Fig. 9.7 Granulomatous thyroiditis showing multiple granulomas centered in thyroid follicles.

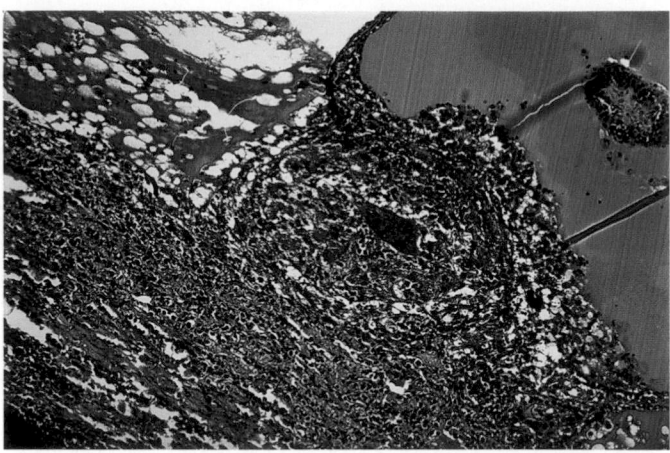

Fig. 9.8 So-called "palpation thyroiditis." This is a common incidental finding.

Elevated serum levels of T4 and T3 in combination with complete suppression of ^{131}I uptake are typical of the initial phase of this disease, which has been found to be associated with the HLA-B35 haplotype.[77]

Grossly, the process usually involves the entire gland, but the enlargement is often asymmetric. In a typical case, the gland is enlarged to approximately twice its normal size. In the advanced stage, the involved areas are firm. In contrast to Riedel's thyroiditis, there is usually little or no adherence to the surrounding structures.

Microscopically, areas of marked inflammation and granulomas containing foreign body giant cells are present. It is characteristic for these granulomas to surround follicles and for the multinucleated giant cells (most of which are of histiocytic nature) to engulf colloid (Fig. 9.7). The granulomas are not very distinct, and caseation necrosis is consistently absent. Areas of fibrosis are also seen, usually in a patchy distribution. Different stages of the same process may be seen in the same gland.[80] Strong immunoreactivity for CA19-9 is found in the late stage of the disease, whereas positivity for CEA in the center of the granuloma is a feature of the acute stage.[78]

The etiology is not known. Although the disease often follows an infection of the upper aerodigestive tract, the thyroiditis itself is of nonbacterial nature. A viral etiology has been often suggested on clinical and epidemiologic grounds but not conclusively proved.[81]

Other granulomatous inflammations

Palpation thyroiditis is the term that has been proposed for a relatively common, clinically insignificant, and grossly inconspicuous thyroid process (also known as multifocal granulomatous folliculitis) in which collections of histiocytes (some of them foamy), lymphocytes, and a few multinucleated giant cells are seen within the lumen of scattered thyroid follicles (Fig. 9.8).[82] In some of these follicles, the inflammatory infiltrate disrupts the epithelium and extends into the perifollicular region.

These changes bear no relationship to granulomatous (de Quervain's) thyroiditis. Rather, they seem to be the result of minor trauma to the gland, sometimes spontaneous and sometimes thought to be induced by vigorous palpation on physical examination, hence the term palpation thyroiditis.

Tuberculosis as a primary clinical manifestation within the thyroid gland is a pathologic curiosity.[91] In disseminated miliary tuberculosis, it is common for an occasional tubercle to occur within the gland. It is also possible for tuberculosis of cervical lymph nodes or larynx to involve the thyroid gland secondarily. Many of the cases diagnosed in the past as tuberculosis of the thyroid were actually examples of granulomatous (de Quervain's) thyroiditis.

Sarcoidosis may involve the thyroid in the form of interstitial (rather than follicle-centered) noncaseating granulomas in patients with systemic disease.[85] Occasionally it manifests initially as a thyroid mass.[90]

Mycoses of various types have been described, most of them occurring in immunocompromised hosts.[83,84,86–88,92] In many of these cases, the tissue changes are characterized by necrosis and acute inflammation rather than granuloma formation.

Postoperative necrotizing granulomas, vaguely simulating rheumatoid nodules and morphologically similar to those more commonly seen in the prostate and bladder, have been observed within the thyroid.[89]

Autoimmune (lymphocytic and Hashimoto's) thyroiditis

It is now widely accepted that the thyroid diseases traditionally known as lymphocytic thyroiditis and Hashimoto's thyroiditis represent different phases or manifestations of an organ-specific immune-mediated inflammatory disorder generically designated as autoimmune thyroiditis and characterized functionally by the production of autoantibodies that alter thyroid function.[103,109,120a,123] Some authors use the terms lymphocytic and Hashimoto's thyroiditis synonymously.[125] It is further believed that autoimmune thyroiditis is one of the two major forms in which autoimmune thyroid disease may manifest, the other being Graves' disease (p. 525). In favor of this interpretation is the existence of cases sharing features of both diseases (sometimes designated by the picturesque term *hashitoxicosis*), suggesting that one may evolve into the other.[106,131] According to this interpretation, there is an immune-mediated insult that leads initially to diffuse or nodular hyperactivity of the gland and eventually to exhaustion atrophy, manifested by diffuse oxyphilia of the follicular epithelium.[129] Rarely the sequence is reversed, in the sense that Hashimoto's disease with hypothyroidism is followed by Graves' disease.[126]

The mechanisms leading to autoimmune thyroiditis are of both humoral and cellular nature.[98,101,102,130] Circulating autoantibodies exist against thyroglobulin and other follicular cell antigens, notably thyrotropin (TSH) receptors.[123] However, it has been suggested that the initial factor resulting in autoimmune thyroiditis is an organ-specific defect in suppressor T lymphocytes.[93] The possible role of aberrant HLA-DR antigen expression on the membrane of the follicular cells remains controversial,[93,97] and no convincing linkage of autoimmune thyroid disease to HLA has been found.[95,122] The available evidence suggests that autoimmune thyroiditis is under the influence of multiple genes, is multifactorial, and is therefore of variable penetrance.

Morphologically, the common denominator of autoimmune thyroid disease in general and autoimmune thyroiditis in particular is the presence of *extensive lymphocytic infiltration of the gland associated with germinal center formation*. It is the appearance of the intervening follicles that determines the category to which a given case belongs: Graves' disease when the follicles are diffusely hyperplastic, lymphocytic thyroiditis when they are relatively normal, and Hashimoto's thyroiditis when they are lined by follicular cells showing extensive oncocytic change. A good correlation exists between the morphologic appearance of the follicular epithelium and the thyroid function.[115,116]

Lymphocytic thyroiditis, thus defined, has been more commonly diagnosed in children, often on the basis of a needle biopsy procedure.[105,133] It has also been referred to as the "juvenile form" of lymphocytic/autoimmune thyroiditis.[105] Patients usually present with asymptomatic goiter, often of short duration. Cases associated with transient thyroid hyperactivity have been described as *painless* or *silent thyroiditis with hyperthyroidism*.[119]

In contrast to Graves' disease, the radioactive iodine uptake in lymphocytic thyroiditis is generally low.[104] Grossly, the gland is diffusely enlarged and of increased consistency, with a solid, white, vaguely nodular cut surface. Microscopically, lymphocytic nodules with germinal centers are seen scattered in the interstitium. The follicles are generally unremarkable, but some may show atrophy and/or oncocytic change.

Hashimoto's thyroiditis, also known as struma lymphomatosa, is predominantly a disease of women over 40 years of age. It presents as diffuse firm thyroid enlargement, sometimes accompanied by signs of tracheal or esophageal compression. Initially the disease may be accompanied by mild hyperthyroidism and later by hypothyroidism.[121] At surgery, the thyroid gland is easily separated from other structures. The fascial attachment between the thyroid gland and the tracheal wall is, at times, slightly thickened, but there is no strong fixation. Because of the firm character of the lesion, it may be confused with carcinoma, but the diffuse involvement without fixation to the surrounding structures should be strong evidence against it.

Grossly, the typical case shows diffuse enlargement of the gland. However, in some instances, one lobe is more enlarged than the other, and in others the disease has a distinctly multinodular quality. The consistency is firm but not stony hard as in Riedel's thyroiditis. There is no extension of the process outside the gland. The cut surface is friable, vaguely or distinctly nodular, yellowish gray, and greatly resembles a hyperplastic lymph node (Fig. 9.9). Colloid is not clearly discernible. Necrosis and calcification are absent.

Microscopically, the two main abnormalities are lymphocytic infiltration of the stroma and oxyphilic change of the follicular epithelium (Fig. 9.10). The lymphoid tissue is distributed within and around the lobules, and it invariably exhibits large follicles with prominent germinal centers. Plasma cells, histiocytes, and scattered intrafollicular multinucleated giant cells can be present. Ultrastructurally, some of these giant cells have been found to be of epithelial derivation, but most are of histiocytic nature.[112] The lymphoplasmacytic population has been found to be polyclonal by immunohistochemical and gene rearrangement techniques.[96,108,113]

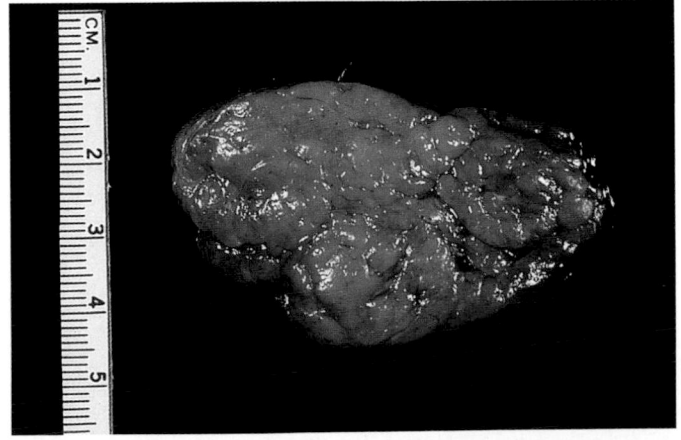

Fig. 9.9 Cut surface of thyroid involved by Hashimoto's thyroiditis. The appearance is reminiscent of a hyperplastic lymph node.

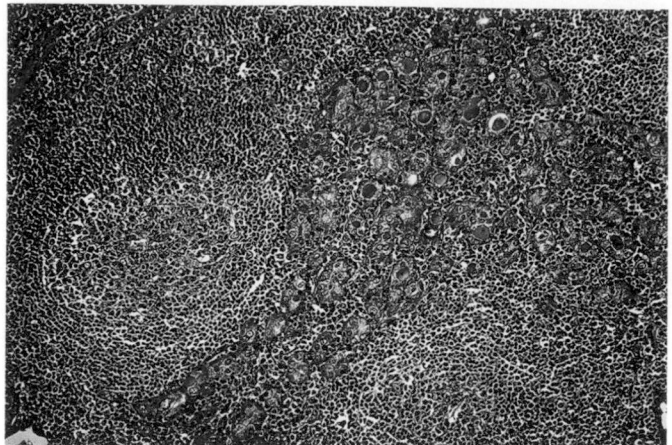

Fig. 9.10 Hashimoto's thyroiditis showing lymphoid follicles with prominent germinal centers and oncocytic follicular epithelium.

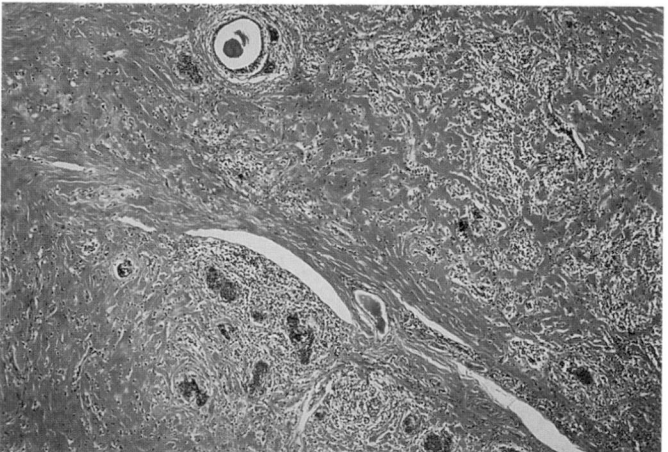

Fig. 9.11 Hashimoto's thyroiditis with extensive fibrosis, atrophy of follicular epithelium, and squamous metaplasia.

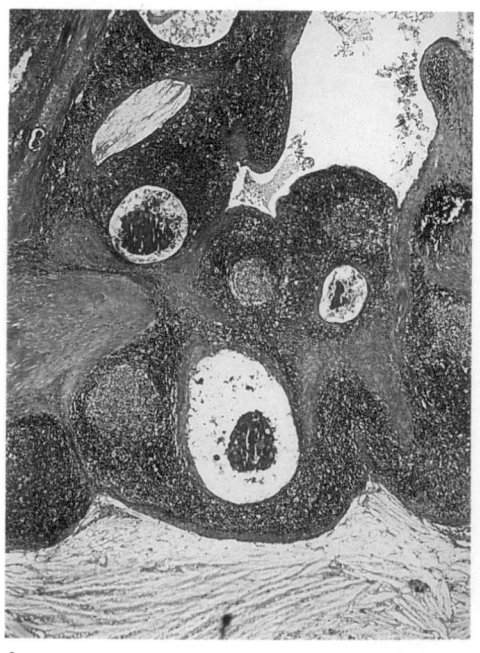

A

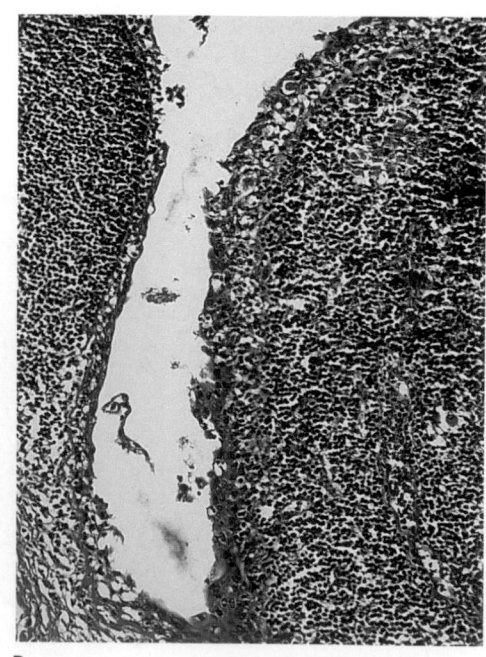

B

The thyroid follicles are small and atrophic. Most or all of them are lined by variably sized Hürthle cells. The nuclei of these cells may show enlargement and hyperchromasia or, conversely, an optically clear appearance and overlapping quality reminiscent of that seen in papillary carcinoma. Immunohistochemically, the follicular cells of autoimmune thyroiditis show greater reactivity for keratin (particularly the high-molecular-weight types), S-100 protein, HLA-DR, and *N*-acetyl-α-D-galactosamine than the corresponding normal cells, their immunohistochemical profile thus resembling that of the cells of papillary carcinoma.[109] Biochemically, the oncocytic cells of Hashimoto's thyroiditis have defects of cytochrome-c oxidase and deletions of mitochondrial DNA.[117]

Squamous nests, thought to arise from metaplasia of follicular cells, are common and can reach sizable proportions (Fig. 9.11). Rarely, large cysts lined by squamous epithelium and bordered by a row of lymphoid follicles are seen, their appearance being highly reminiscent of branchial cleft cysts[114] (Fig. 9.12). Parenthetically, similar cysts can also be seen in the absence of thyroiditis.[94]

In the typical case of Hashimoto's thyroiditis, connective tissue is scanty, with slight or moderate thickening of the interlobular septa. In the *fibrous variant* of this disease, which comprises about 12% of all cases, fibrosis is more extensive. In contrast to Riedel's thyroiditis, this fibrosis is of dense hyaline type (instead of the active proliferative fibrosis seen in the latter) and does not extend beyond the thyroid capsule. In this regard, it should be remembered that Hashimoto's and Riedel's thyroiditis can exceptionally coexist (see p. 523).

The fibrous variant of Hashimoto's thyroiditis can also be confused with carcinoma when the fibrosis is

Fig. 9.12 A and B, Hashimoto's thyroiditis with branchial cleft-like cysts. In the high-power microphotograph on the right one can appreciate the infiltration by the lymphocytes of the lining epithelium.

associated with epithelial islands showing squamous metaplasia.[110] Clinically, this variant is characterized by a very firm goiter (often with sudden enlargement), severe pressure symptoms, physical signs suggestive of cancer, and markedly elevated tanned red cell antibody titer to thyroglobulin.[110]

Although Hashimoto's thyroiditis typically exhibits a diffuse appearance both grossly and microscopically, cases do occur in which a distinct nodularity is evident, the epithelial component of the nodules having a hyperplastic quality. This could be interpreted as the combination of Hashimoto's thyroiditis and nodular hyperplasia, but in all likelihood the two abnormalities are pathogenetically related. A term such as *nodular Hashimoto's thyroiditis* would therefore seem more appropriate to designate this relatively common occurrence. A variation on the theme is represented by the Hashimoto's thyroiditis in which one or more distinct hyperplastic ("dominant") nodules exclusively composed of Hürthle cells having either a follicular or a solid configuration are present.

Occasionally, Hashimoto's thyroiditis is seen in association with a lymphocytic inflammation in other organs, presumably also on an autoimmune basis. This includes lymphocytic adrenalitis (the combination being known as *Schmidt's syndrome*)[99] and lymphocytic interstitial pneumonitis.[111]

Complications of Hashimoto's thyroiditis include malignant lymphoma and leukemia[107] (see p. 564), papillary carcinoma (see p. 532), and Hürthle cell neoplasms (see p. 544). Because all three of these conditions evolve gradually from a setting of hyperplasia of the respective cell component, their early identification may be extremely difficult. This probably explains the remarkable difference in the reported figures for these complications, particularly the latter two.[100,120,127] In this regard, the occurrence of sometimes striking nuclear clearing and overlapping in the follicular cells of Hashimoto's thyroiditis is of interest; one wonders whether this might not represent a precursor (preneoplastic) stage of papillary carcinoma. This clinically and conceptually important question needs to be re-evaluated after the astonishing claim made by two independent laboratories to the effect that thyroid glands affected by Hashimoto's thyroiditis *in the absence of morphologically recognizable papillary carcinoma* exhibit evidence of *RET/PTC* rearrangement (of the type seen in papillary carcinoma) in close to 95% of the cases.[124,135] In turn, this has led to the proposal by one of these groups[135] that all these thyroid glands should be considered as being affected by papillary carcinoma even if there is none to be seen microscopically. This seems to us a very dangerous approach from a clinical standpoint and a violent departure from the biologic definition of what constitutes the malignant neoplastic state. The fact that a third group has obtained totally opposite molecular results[118] calls for an even greater degree of caution in the interpretation and clinical application of these startling data.

Medullary carcinoma has also been described in thyroid glands with Hashimoto's thyroiditis, but the occurrence is probably coincidental.[132]

The treatment of Hashimoto's thyroiditis depends on its severity. In mild cases no therapy is needed. In some, thyroid hormone is given to relieve hypothyroidism. In still others, surgery in the form of subtotal thyroidectomy is performed because of large size and/or pressure symptoms. Some cases of Hashimoto's thyroiditis are treated surgically simply because they are clinically confused with a neoplastic process.[128]

Riedel's thyroiditis

Riedel's thyroiditis, also known as Riedel's struma, fibrous thyroiditis, and invasive thyroiditis, is an extremely rare disorder that affects adult and elderly patients and shows a slight predilection for females.[140,141] Clinically, it presents with ill-defined thyroid enlargement often associated with profound dyspnea. The lesion, which is extremely firm, binds the soft tissues of the neck in an iron collar and may compress the trachea to a slitlike state. Clinically, it is often thought to be carcinoma. In contrast to granulomatous thyroiditis, it is not preceded by an acute inflammatory process or by tenderness of the thyroid gland. The regional lymph nodes are not involved. Grossly, the process is asymmetric and involves only localized areas of the thyroid gland. The affected portion is stony hard and cuts with great resistance. Dense fibrous tracts extend from the thyroid capsule into adjacent muscle so that at surgery the tissue planes are obliterated. On cross section, areas with complete obliteration of the architecture alternate with others having a nearly normal appearance.

Microscopically, fibrous tissue that is frequently extensively hyalinized completely replaces the area of the gland involved (Fig. 9.13). Skeletal muscle cells in the

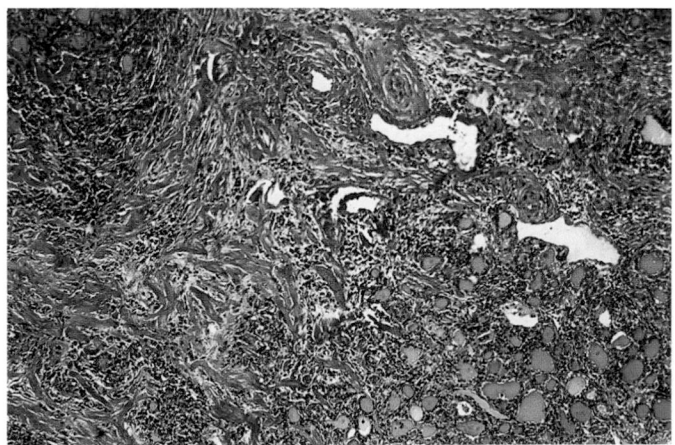

Fig. 9.13 Riedel's thyroiditis showing sclerosis, chronic inflammation, and parenchymal atrophy.

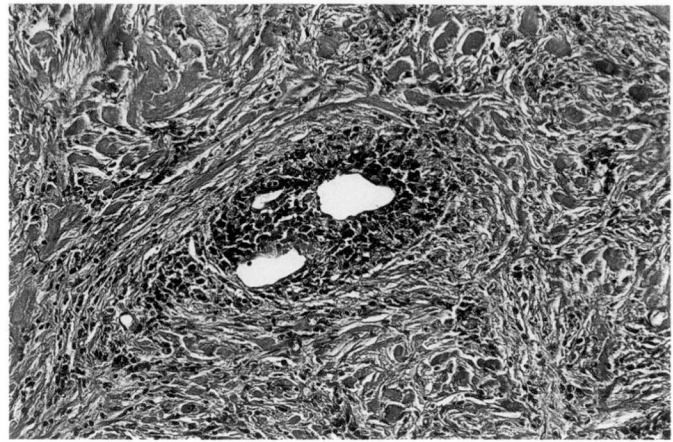

Fig. 9.14 Inflammation of a vein in Riedel's thyroiditis.

immediate area are often directly infiltrated by this connective tissue. Giant cells are absent. The inflammation present is patchy and of mononuclear type, with a predominance of lymphocytes and plasma cells. IgA-producing cells are abundant among the latter.[138] Collections of eosinophils may also be present. Medium-sized veins encased by the fibrosis may show inflammation of their wall, an important diagnostic feature[138] (Fig. 9.14). The main differential diagnosis is with the fibrous form of Hashimoto's thyroiditis, which is limited to the thyroid, distinctly lobulated, and accompanied by extensive oxyphilic changes of the follicular epithelium.

Riedel's thyroiditis is not related to Hashimoto's or granulomatous thyroiditis, despite earlier claims to the contrary and the existence of isolated instances in which the two diseases coexist.[136,139] It represents instead a manifestation of the group of idiopathic disorders generically known as *inflammatory fibrosclerosis*. As such, it may be seen coexisting with mediastinal or retroperitoneal fibrosis, sclerosing cholangitis, or inflammatory pseudotumor of the orbit.[137]

Steroid therapy has been effective in some cases, but most patients need surgical intervention to relieve the compression symptoms and to rule out the presence of carcinoma. The resection is quite difficult because no plane of cleavage exists. Adjoining muscle must be cut, and large veins may be torn. The incidence of postoperative hypothyroidism is very low.

Hyperplasia

Hyperplastic disorders of the thyroid have been classified on the basis of their presumed mechanism of production, morphologic features, and clinical manifestations. In practice, three major forms of thyroid hyperplasia are recognized by combining these criteria (Table 9.1).

Dyshormonogenetic goiter

There are several types of goiter resulting from enzyme defects in hormone synthesis.[143,152] These include lack of responsiveness to TSH, defects in iodide transport, defects in organification, defects in coupling, abnormalities of thyroglobulin synthesis and secretion, defects in deiodinase, abnormalities in the transport of thyroid hormone, and others.[150] The genetic mutations responsible for these various defects are being currently unraveled.[148]

Grossly, the gland is enlarged and multinodular (Fig. 9.15). Microscopically, the most common alteration consists of hypercellular nodules exhibiting a variety of architectural appearances, with a predominance of solid and microfollicular patterns[146,147] (Fig. 9.16). In some cases there are papillary and insular formations. Fibrosis is a common finding, in some instances resulting in irregularities at the edge of the nodules that can simulate capsular invasion. Other common features include marked nuclear atypia and minimal amounts of colloid. A diagnostically important feature is the fact that the nuclear atypia (in the form of bizarre hyperchromatic nuclei) is present mainly in the tissue *between* the hyperplastic nodules rather than in the nodules themselves.[147]

Table 9.1 Major types of thyroid hyperplastic disorders

Name	Mechanism	Pathology	Functional status
Dyshormonogenetic goiter	Genetically determined error in thyroid hormone metabolism	Nodular or (less frequently) diffuse hyperplasia	Hypothyroid
Graves' disease	Autoimmune	Diffuse hyperplasia	Hyperthyroid
Nodular hyperplasia			
Endemic goiter	Iodine deficiency	Nodular hyperplasia (preceded by a transient phase of diffuse hyperplasia)	Usually euthyroid; sometimes hypothyroid
Sporadic goiter	Unknown	Nodular hyperplasia	Usually euthyroid; sometimes hyperthyroid or hypothyroid

Fig. 9.15 Dyshormonogenetic goiter. Gross appearance. Note the multinodular quality and the hemorrhagic changes in the larger nodules. (Courtesy of Dr. Michael Kashgarian, New Haven, CT)

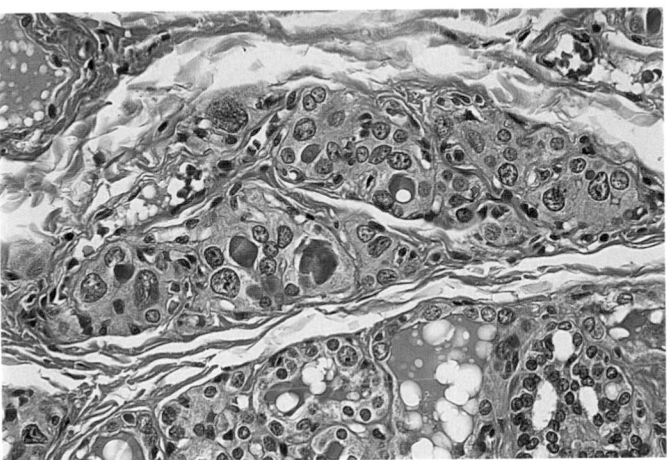

Fig. 9.16 Dyshormonogenetic goiter. Microscopic appearance. The follicles are hyperplastic and lined by follicular cells with marked nuclear pleomorphism.

Mitotic figures are often seen, presumably as a result of the continuous thyrotropin stimulation.[151]

The suggestion has been made that there is some correlation between the specific molecular defect and the morphologic appearance of the gland.[144,149,153]

Cases of thyroid carcinoma have been reported in patients with dyshormonogenetic goiter, but the number of well-documented cases is very low.[145] Most have been of follicular type, and others have been incidental papillary microcarcinomas.[147] Because dyshormonogenetic goiter is commonly associated with pleomorphism, hypercellularity, and mitotic activity of the follicular epithelium, one should be particularly strict with the criteria for the diagnosis of follicular carcinoma in this setting. Specifically, nothing short of clearcut capsular or blood vessel invasion should be accepted.[154] Cases of follicular adenomas after T4 replacement therapy have also been reported.[142]

Graves' disease (diffuse toxic goiter)

Graves' disease (also known as Basedow's disease, thyrotoxicosis, diffuse toxic goiter, and exophthalmic goiter) typically presents in young adult females with muscle weakness, weight loss, exophthalmos, irritability, tachycardia, goiter, and often a great increase of appetite. Atrial fibrillation may occur. Late clinical manifestations are localized pretibial myxedema and so-called "thyroid acropachy"; the latter is characterized by swelling of the extremities and clubbing of fingers and toes resulting from periosteal new bone formation.[173]

Graves' disease can also occur in children, in whom it constitutes the most common cause of hyperthyroidism.[183]

Laboratory tests show elevation of bound T4, free T4, or bound T3 levels and increased radioactive iodine uptake in the presence of TSH levels of less than 0.1 mU/L. A variant characterized by increased serum levels of T3 in the presence of therapy-induced low levels of T4 has been described as T3-predominant Graves' disease.[179]

Grossly, the gland shows a mild to moderate symmetric diffuse enlargement. It is succulent and reddish and has the consistency of pancreatic tissue (Fig. 9.17). The cut surface is uniformly gray or red depending on the degree of vascularity (Fig. 9.18). In longstanding cases, the gland appears friable and dull yellow.

Microscopically, the follicles are markedly hyperplastic, with prominent papillary infolding that may cause confusion with papillary carcinoma[177] (Fig. 9.19). The lining epithelium is columnar, with basally located normochromatic or hyperchromatic nuclei and a clear, sometimes microvacuolated cytoplasm that may contain fat and glycogen. These features are said to be even more prominent in T3-predominant Graves' disease.[179] A variable number of oxyphilic cells may be present, indicating that the disease may be evolving toward Hashimoto's thyroiditis. The colloid is pale and finely vacuolated,

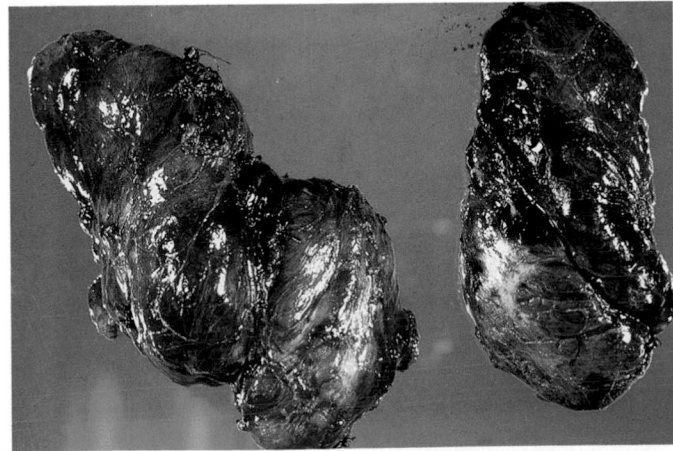

Fig. 9.17 Outer aspect of diffuse thyroid hyperplasia in a patient with Graves' disease. The gland is diffusely swollen and hyperemic.

with prominent scalloping where it abuts the epithelium. The stroma contains aggregates of lymphoid tissue with germinal center formation (Fig. 9.20). Immunohistochemically, most of these lymphocytes are of the T-cell type, the cytotoxic-suppressor subtype predominating in

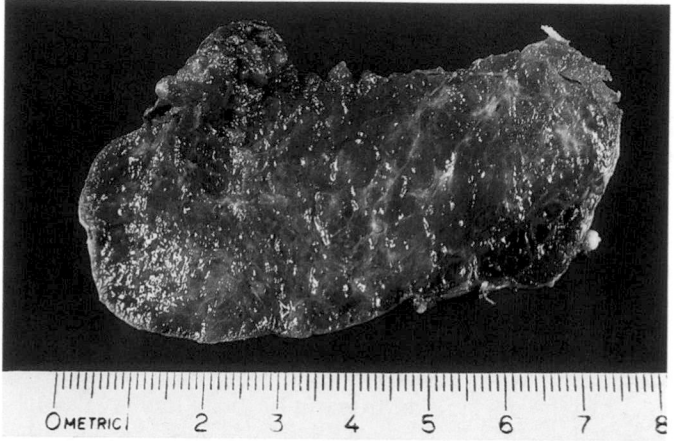

Fig. 9.18 Cut surface of thyroid gland with diffuse hyperplasia, showing a hyperemic "juicy" appearance.

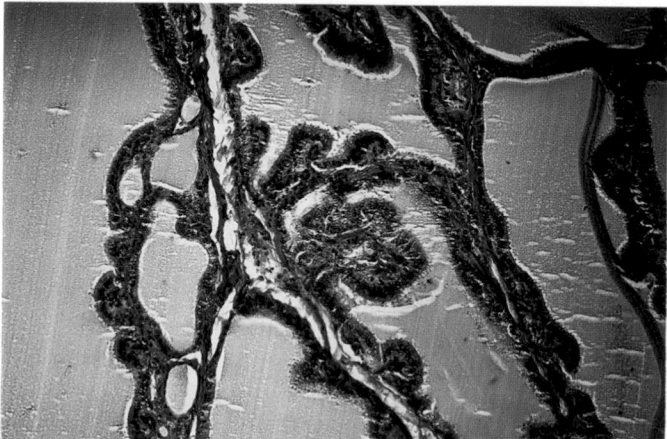

Fig. 9.19 Hyperplastic papillae protruding into dilated follicles in diffuse hyperplasia.

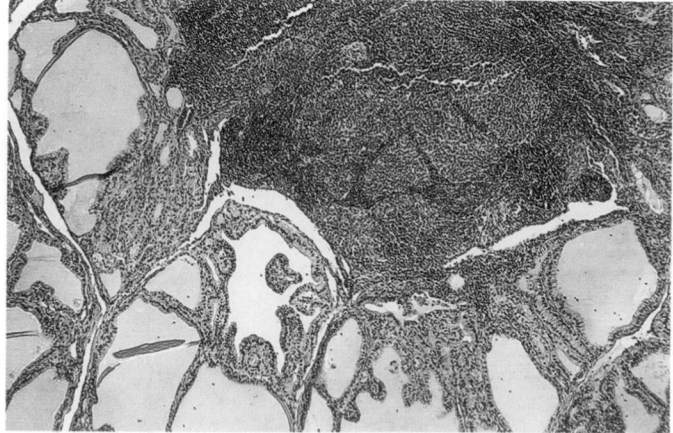

Fig. 9.20 Lymphoid follicles with germinal centers and hyperplastic thyroid follicles in diffuse hyperplasia. Note the pale-staining quality of the colloid.

the follicles and the helper-induced subtype in the interstitium.[170] Mild fibrosis is present in longstanding cases. Hyperplastic follicles may be seen outside the thyroid gland, sometimes growing into the skeletal muscle of the neck. This may represent extrathyroid extension of the hyperplastic process or—more likely—the expression of hyperplasia in ectopic thyroid follicles, which in the normal situation are so small and scanty as to pass undetected.[167] Whatever the mechanism for their development, they should not be interpreted as evidence of malignancy.

Controversy still exists as to whether there is an increase in the incidence of thyroid carcinoma in patients with Graves' disease, but the numbers are such as not to influence the selection of therapy for Graves' disease in the absence of palpable thyroid nodules.[171] Not surprisingly, incidental carcinomas have been found in the pathologic examination of thyroid glands removed for hyperthyroidism, their incidence varying from 1% to 9% in the reported series.[163] However, these figures are no higher than those reported in otherwise normal glands. Nearly all of those cases have been small papillary carcinomas without clinical significance.

The treatment of Graves' disease may consist of antithyroid drugs such as propylthiouracil, methimazole (thiamazole), and carbimazole; destruction of the gland with radioactive iodine; or subtotal thyroidectomy.[156,162,164,178] The latter operation provides the specimen most commonly seen by the pathologist in this disorder. It should be noted that the microscopic changes previously described are rarely seen in their pristine state in these organs because of the changes that supervene as a result of therapy with antithyroid drugs and iodine or beta-blockers, which are given routinely in the preoperative period. The glandular enlargement and the lymphoid infiltrate persist, but most of the hyperplastic changes in the follicles regress.[161,177] However, thorough sampling will usually reveal residual foci of hyperplasia. After surgery, the thyroid remnant regenerates so that a euthyroid status can be maintained in most of the patients, especially if the amount of thyroid tissue left is about 5 g on each side.[155] The greater the lymphocytic infiltration and the larger the number of oxyphilic cells in the operative specimen, the greater the chance that myxedema will develop postoperatively.[168]

Glands treated with radioactive iodine show initially nuclear abnormalities, dissolution of some of the follicles, and vascular alterations. In later stages, nodularity, oncocytic changes, follicular atrophy, and fibrosis occur.[159,165,172] As a consequence, the long-term incidence of hypothyroidism is very high with this therapy.[178] It should be noted that none of these therapies improves the exophthalmos associated with hyperthyroidism: rather, in some instances they have been found to worsen it.

Graves' disease is currently included among the autoimmune thyroid diseases, together with Hashimoto's thyroiditis and idiopathic myxedema.[180] TSH is not involved in the pathogenesis. Graves' disease is thought to be initiated by IgG antibodies directed against specific domains of the TSH receptor.[160,181] One such class is known as thyroid-stimulating immunoglobulin (TSI) and another as thyrotropin-binding inhibitor immunoglobulin (TBII). Antithyroid peroxidase autoantibodies are also consistently present.[158,175] The occurrence of an immune attack on the thyroid follicle is also evident on electron microscopic examination, which demonstrates deposits consistent with immune complexes in the follicular basement membrane.[174] How this autoimmune process relates to the well-known clinical fact that thyrotoxicosis often arises after a psychologic stress remains a mystery.[182] An increased incidence of Graves' disease after irradiation to the neck for lesions such as Hodgkin's lymphoma has also been observed.[166] In addition, cases of Graves' disease have been reported in association with true thymic hyperplasia.[169]

Graves' disease is only one of the many disorders—although by far the most common—that can lead to clinically evident thyroid hyperfunction (i.e., thyrotoxicosis). Other causes are "toxic" follicular adenoma (see p. 529), "toxic" sporadic (nodular) goiter (see next section), inappropriate TSH secretion, trophoblastic tumors, various types of thyroiditis associated with hormone leakage, struma ovarii, and iatrogenic causes.[157] An example of the latter is *amiodarone-associated thyrotoxicosis*. Amiodarone is a cardiac antiarrhythmic and antianginal agent that contains 37% iodine by weight. The morphologic changes in the thyroid include degenerative and destructive follicular lesions, involutional changes, and fibrosis.[176]

Nodular hyperplasia

Nodular hyperplasia (nodular or multinodular goiter, adenomatoid goiter, adenomatous hyperplasia) is the most common thyroid disease. In the form traditionally known as **endemic goiter**, the disease is due to low iodine content of the water and soil, and it can be largely prevented by the addition of iodine to common salt.[191,204] The deficiency in thyroid hormone production induced by the iodine deficiency leads to increase in TSH secretion, which results initially in a hyperactive thyroid with tall follicular epithelium and small amounts of colloid (so-called *parenchymatous goiter*) and later in follicular atrophy with massive storage of colloid, with or without nodularity (so-called *diffuse* or *nodular colloid goiter*). In these endemic areas, the frequency of the disease at post mortem examination is virtually 100%.

In the form known as **sporadic (nodular) goiter**, which is the most common seen in the US, the pathogenesis remains unknown.[189] Mild dietary deficiency of iodine, slight impairment of hormone synthesis, increased iodide clearance by the kidneys, presence of thyroid-stimulating immunoglobulins, and increased production of insulin-like growth factor I have been var-iously suggested.[186,197,201] Some cases are associated with lymphocytic or Hashimoto's thyroiditis and can be viewed as the nodular forms of these immune-mediated inflammatory diseases (see p. 522). In most patients with nodular hyperplasia, the blood levels of thyrotropin are not elevated. The incidence of the disease in the general adult population is 3% to 5% clinically and about 50% at autopsy.[198,203]

Clinically, most patients are euthyroid and when first seen have a multinodular gland that may become very large, cause tracheal obstruction, and produce considerable disfigurement. In cases with a single, firm, dominant nodule, the clinical distinction from a true neoplasm becomes impossible. Hemorrhage within a nodule can cause sudden enlargement and pain. A small proportion of patients initially have clinical signs of hyperthyroidism, but the exophthalmos of Graves' disease does not occur.

Some cases of thyroid nodular hyperplasia are located substernally and enter in the differential diagnosis of superior mediastinal tumors (see Chapter 8). The morphologic changes are similar to those of the nodular form of endemic goiter. As in the latter, the degree of thyroid nodularity is directly related to the duration of the disease.[185]

Grossly, the thyroid is enlarged, and its shape is distorted, one lobe being frequently larger than the other (Fig. 9.21). The thyroid capsule may be stretched but is intact. On cross section, multiple nodules are seen, some surrounded by a partial or complete capsule. Secondary changes in the form of hemorrhage, calcification, and cystic degeneration are common. Microscopically, there is a wide range of appearances. Some nodules are composed of huge follicles lined by flattened epithelium, others are extremely cellular and hyperplastic, and still others are composed predominantly or exclusively of Hürthle cells (Fig. 9.22). Some of the dilated follicles have a conglomerate of small active follicles at one pole (so-called *Sanderson's polsters*) (Fig. 9.23). Others have

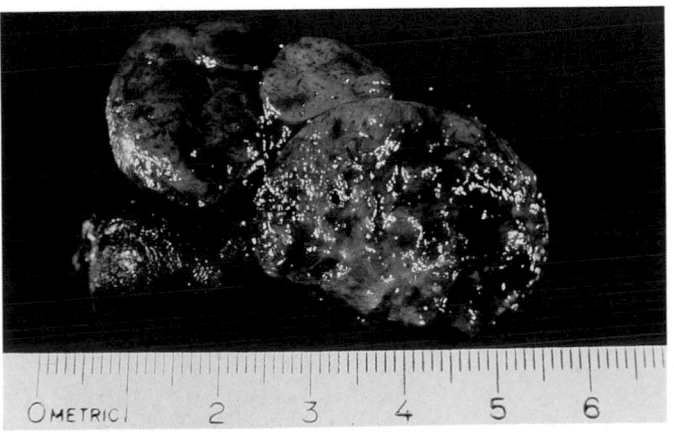

Fig. 9.21 Nodular hyperplasia of thyroid gland, with secondary cystic and hemorrhagic areas.

papillary projections facing the lumen of a cystic follicle, a feature that may lead to confusion with papillary carcinoma (Fig. 9.24).

It is not unusual to find, within a nodule predominantly composed of large dilated follicles, sharply outlined solid or microfollicular clusters of follicular

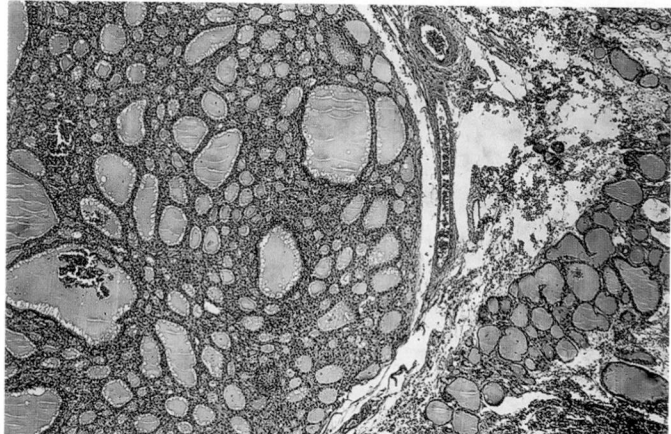

Fig. 9.22 Low-power appearance of nodular hyperplasia. The hyperplastic nodules lack a capsule.

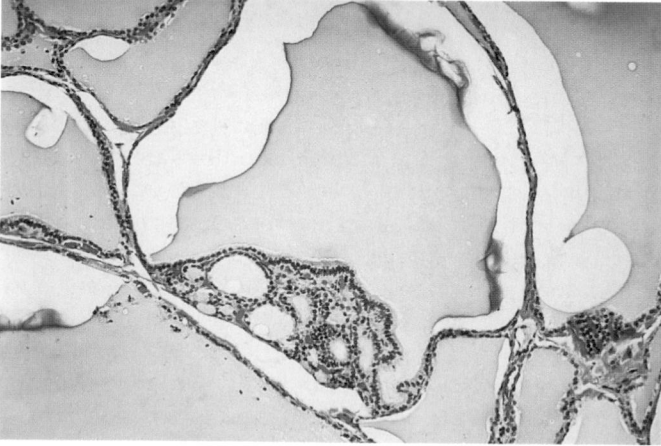

Fig. 9.23 Nodular hyperplasia showing so-called "Sanderson's polster."

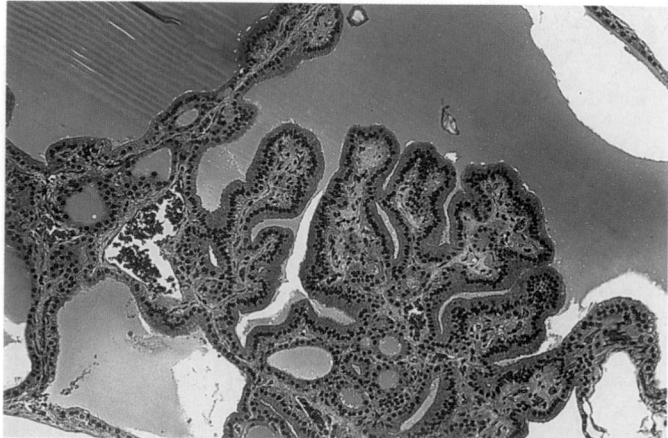

Fig. 9.24 Nodular hyperplasia with benign papillary formations protruding toward the center of a cystically dilated follicle.

cells. It has been suggested that nodular goiters grow by episodic replication of these clusters, which have been referred to as *foci of secondary proliferation* and which have been found to express immunohistochemically the *p21* proto-oncogene product.[200] The proliferative activity of the nodules can be estimated by immunostaining the sections with MIB-1.[196]

Rupture of follicles leads to a granulomatous reaction to the colloid, with appearance of histiocytes and foreign body-type giant cells. Areas of fresh and old hemorrhage, coarse fibrous trabeculation, and foci of calcification are common. Occasionally, osseous metaplasia is seen. Greatly thickened vessels with calcified media may be present at the periphery. A variable number of chronic inflammatory cells are present in the stroma in many of the cases, indicating the coexistence of chronic thyroiditis; the larger their number, the higher the chances of postoperative hypothyroidism.[192,193] The presence of highly atypical nuclei in a case of nodular hyperplasia should raise the possibility of previous exposure to radioactive substances if present in the nodule themselves, and of dyshormonogenetic goiter if present between the nodules (see p. 524). It is not possible to predict on the basis of the morphologic appearance whether the patient has clinical or laboratory evidence of hyperthyroidism.

The differential diagnosis between a dominant nodule from a case of nodular hyperplasia and a true adenoma is based on a set of admittedly arbitrary criteria. The adenoma is usually single, is totally surrounded by a capsule, is dissimilar from the remaining parenchyma, compresses the adjacent tissue, and is composed mainly of follicles that are smaller than those of the normal gland. The lesion of nodular hyperplasia is almost always one of many nodules, its encapsulation is incomplete, the follicular size is variable, some or all of the follicles are larger than those in the surrounding gland, and there is no compression of the adjacent parenchyma. In some cases, the distinction becomes impossible, inasmuch as lesions with the morphologic features of adenoma may be multiple and/or occur in a setting of nodular hyperplasia.

The initial clonality study done in both humans and experimental animals gave the expected and reassuring results, i.e., that the lesions of nodular hyperplasia were polyclonal whereas follicular adenomas were monoclonal.[195,202] Alas, the situation is much more complicated. More recent studies have shown that a significant proportion of the "dominant" nodules of nodular hyperplasia are monoclonal, whereas a smaller but still significant percentage of lesions morphologically consistent with follicular adenomas are polyclonal.[184,187,188]

A longstanding and still unresolved issue is whether nodular hyperplasia is associated with an increased incidence of carcinoma, particularly of the follicular type.[190] Suffice it to say that if such an increase really exists, it is small enough to be disregarded for practical purposes.

Mild asymptomatic cases of nodular hyperplasia require no treatment. Suppressive medical therapy with exogenous thyroid hormones is only moderately effective. If the enlargement is such that disfigurement or pressure symptoms develop, bilateral subtotal thyroidectomy is performed.[194,199]

Tumors

The majority of clinically apparent thyroid neoplasms are primary and epithelial. Traditionally, they have been divided into adenomas and carcinomas, the latter group incorporating the medullary carcinomas together with the more common lesions composed of follicular cells. From a histogenetic/differentiation standpoint, it is preferable to divide thyroid neoplasms into three major categories, depending on the cell types involved, and subdivide them into the various benign and malignant categories:

1 Tumors exhibiting follicular cell differentiation
2 Tumors exhibiting C-cell differentiation
3 Tumors exhibiting follicular and C-cell differentiation.

Lesions in the first category comprise more than 95% of the cases, the remainder being largely made up by tumors in the second category.[205]

Epithelial tumors—specific types

Follicular adenoma

Follicular adenoma is defined as a benign encapsulated tumor that shows evidence of follicular cell differentiation. It is the most common thyroid neoplasm. Most patients are euthyroid adults who initially have a thyroid lump, which on scan is usually "cold," sometimes "cool" or "warm," and only rarely "hot." Many patients with thyroid adenomas have elevated circulating levels of thyroglobulin,[231] but few of the tumors are associated with clinical hyperthyroidism (so-called *toxic adenomas*).[226,229] It has been suggested that these autonomously functioning tumors are more common in regions with iodine deficiency.[206]

The belief that follicular adenomas, because of their presumed neoplastic nature, have a clonal origin has been supported by studies involving analysis of the X chromosomes, both in mice[232] and in humans.[218,227]

Adenomas are almost always solitary (except when occurring in genetically determined syndromes, see below). They are characteristically surrounded by a generally thin capsule that is grossly and microscopically complete (Figs 9.25 and 9.26). The architectural and cytologic features are different from those of the surrounding gland, which usually shows signs of compression. Adenomas may exhibit a variety of patterns, singly or in combination: normofollicular (simple), macrofol-

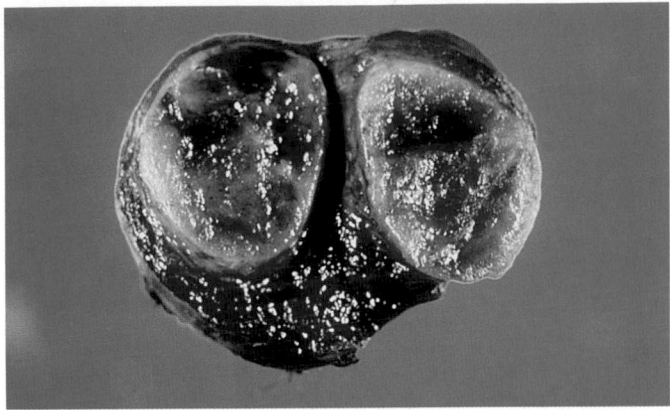

A

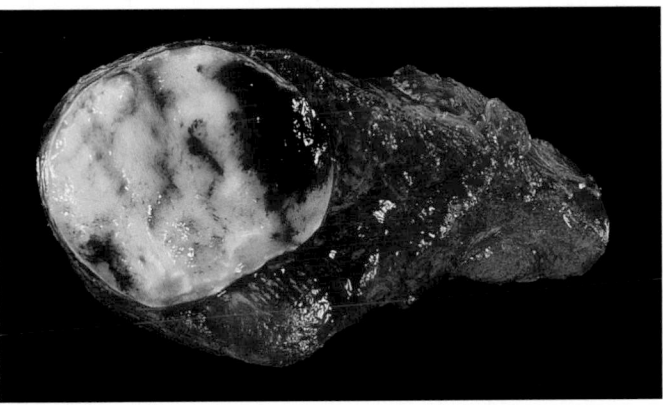

B

Fig. 9.25 A and **B**, Gross appearance of two follicular adenomas. Both tumors show focal hemorrhagic areas.

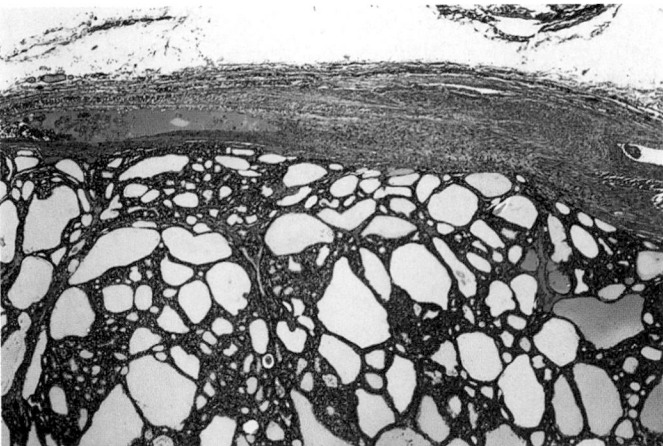

Fig. 9.26 Intact fibrous capsule around a follicular adenoma.

licular (colloid), microfollicular (fetal), and trabecular/solid (embryonal) (Fig. 9.27). Although the morphologic differences among these various patterns may be striking, they have no apparent clinical significance. Mitoses are rare or absent in the follicular adenomas. They are not necessarily indicators of malignancy, but when they are present in appreciable numbers one should sample and examine the specimen with particular care. Secondary degenerative changes such as hemorrhage,

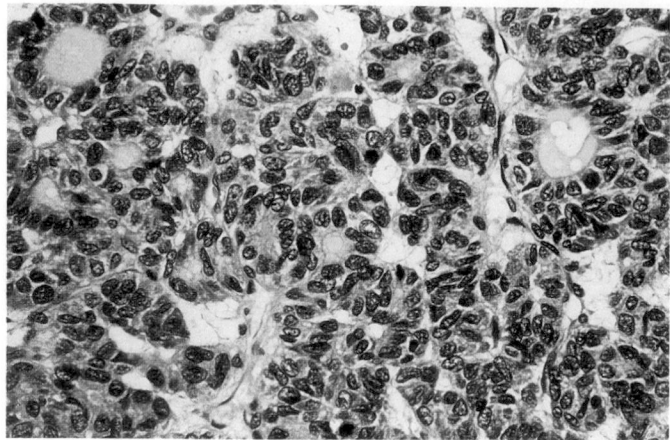

Fig. 9.27 Microfollicular pattern of growth in a follicular adenoma.

edema, fibrosis, calcification, bone formation, and cystic degeneration are common, especially among the larger tumors. Sometimes the vessels in the capsule of adenomas (and also at the periphery of hyperplastic nodules) show prominent focal thickenings of their wall, which have been referred to as *muscular cushions*.[230] Adenomas may exhibit papillary or pseudopapillary structures, which may prompt confusion with papillary carcinoma. Some authors have referred to these tumors as papillary adenoma, a term that should be replaced by that of *follicular adenomas with papillary architecture*.[224] The differential diagnosis, which includes hyperplastic nodules and encapsulated papillary carcinomas, is discussed on p. 536.

Some correlation exists between the microscopic appearance of a follicular adenoma and its activity as judged by the scan appearance.[207,214] In general, hyperfunctioning (hot) adenomas are more cellular and their cells have more abundant cytoplasm (and therefore a decreased nucleocytoplasmic ratio) than nonfunctioning (cold) tumors. However, the range of morphologic appearances that hot thyroid nodules can exhibit is wide, including less well differentiated and oncocytic patterns. It should also be remembered that hot thyroid nodules are usually but *not always benign*.[215]

The enzyme histochemical and immunohistochemical profile of adenomas mirrors that of the normal follicle.[208] There is reactivity for low-molecular-weight keratin and thyroglobulin in the cytoplasm and for laminin and other basement membrane components around the follicles.[225] DNA aneuploidy has been found by flow cytometry in about a quarter of follicular adenomas and seems to be slightly more common in the cellular types. This is an indicator neither of clinical malignancy nor of increased possibility of tumor recurrence. Thus DNA ploidy analysis does not seem to add to the prognostic prediction after a properly performed microscopic examination.[219,220,228,234]

No consistent abnormalities in oncogenes have been found in follicular adenomas.[221] Cytogenetically, preliminary results suggest the existence of frequent abnormalities in the terminal region of the long arm of chromosome 19.[209]

Patients with the genetically determined Cowden's disease have a variety of thyroid abnormalities, of which multiple follicular adenomas is the most common, often associated with hyperplastic nodules.[216]

Several variants of follicular adenoma have been described. *Hürthle cell adenoma* is discussed on p. 544, and

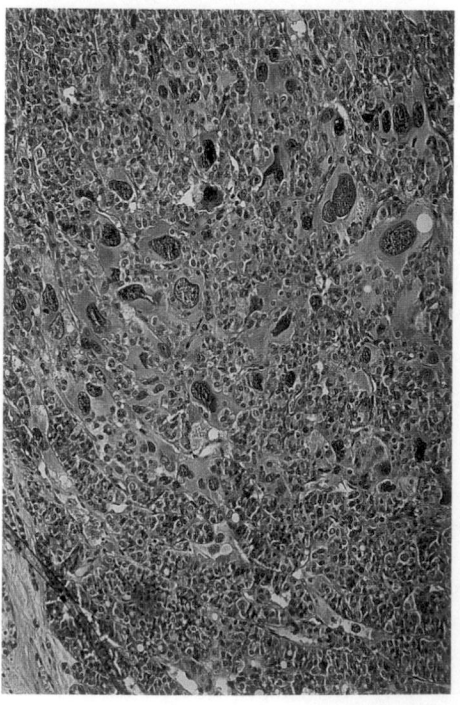

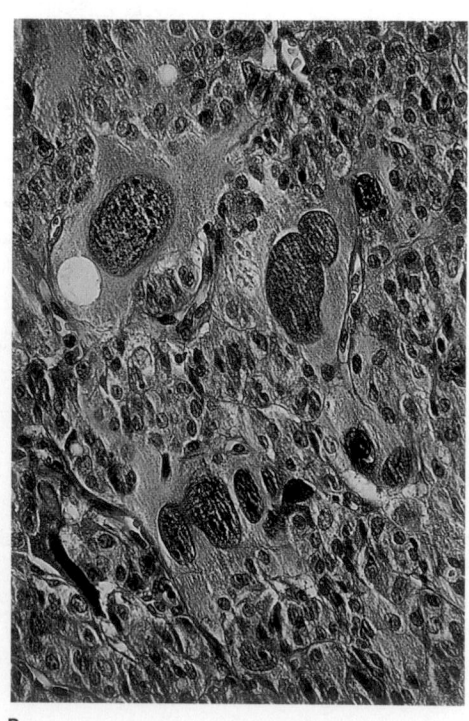

Fig. 9.28 A and **B**, Low- and high-power views of follicular adenoma with bizarre nuclei. This feature is not a sign of malignancy and is analogous to that seen in many other endocrine tumors.

hyalinizing trabecular adenoma in the subsection that follows. The term *atypical adenoma* has been proposed for adenomas with pronounced cellular proliferation and less regular cytoarchitectural patterns but still lacking evidence of capsular or blood vessel invasion.[210,217,223]

Adenoma with bizarre nuclei is characterized by the presence of huge hyperchromatic nuclei, usually in clusters, unaccompanied by other features of malignancy (Fig. 9.28). This phenomenon is analogous to that seen in parathyroid adenomas and other endocrine neoplasms.

Other rare types of follicular adenoma are those with clear cell changes (including the signet ring, mucin-producing, and lipid-rich types; see p. 547), adenomas with adipose metaplasia of the stroma (so-called *adeno-lipomas*),[212] adenomas with cartilaginous metaplasia (so-called *adenochondromas*),[233] and adenomas with massive deposition of cytoplasmic black pigment following minocycline therapy (so-called *black adenomas*).[222]

The differential diagnosis of follicular adenoma includes a dominant nodule of nodular hyperplasia, minimally invasive follicular carcinoma, and the follicular variant of papillary carcinoma. Some follicular adenomas may also be confused with vascular tumors because of their high vascularization.

The standard therapy for follicular adenoma is removal by lobectomy. Enucleation of the adenoma should not be attempted. Suppression of the nodule with levothyroxine and treatment of the toxic adenoma with ^{131}I have been used, but the results have generally been less than satisfactory.[211,213]

Hyalinizing trabecular adenoma and related lesions

Hyalinizing trabecular adenoma (HTA) is the term given to a peculiar type of adenoma exhibiting a prominent trabecular arrangement and an equally prominent hyaline appearance (Fig. 9.29). The latter is present both in the cytoplasm of the tumor cells (as the result of the accumulation of intermediate filaments) and in the extracellular space (as the result of heavy deposition of hyalinized collagen fibers and basement membrane material). The trabeculae can be straight or curved, resulting in curious organoid formations (Fig. 9.30). The pattern of growth may simulate that of paraganglioma and medullary carcinoma, whereas the presence of nuclear grooves and psammoma bodies may suggest papillary carcinoma, particularly in material from fine needle aspiration[235] (Fig. 9.31). Another supposedly distinct morphologic feature of HTA is the so-called *cytoplasmic yellow body*, which is a round, pale yellow cytoplasmic inclusion body in a paranuclear location having a refractile quality.[251]

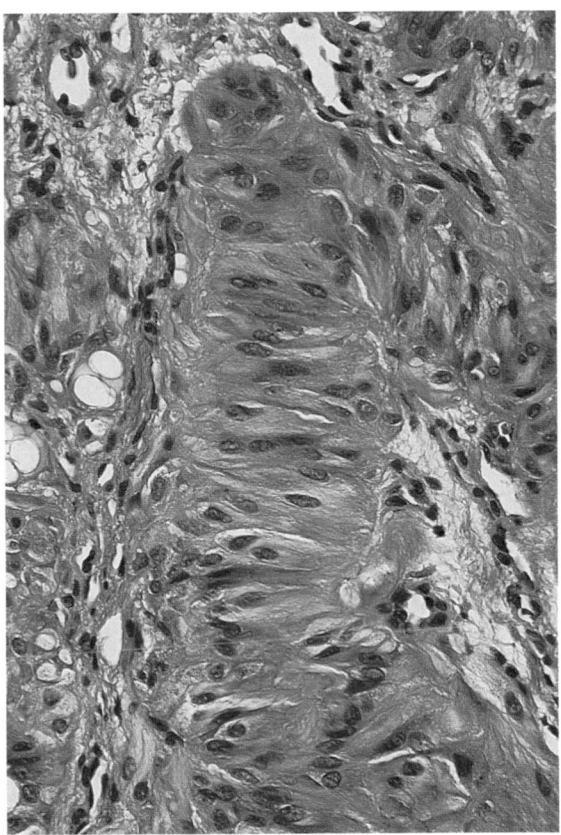

Fig. 9.30 Hyalinizing trabecular adenoma. A wide trabecula is seen in the center of the picture, with the tumor cells arranged perpendicularly to the longest axis.

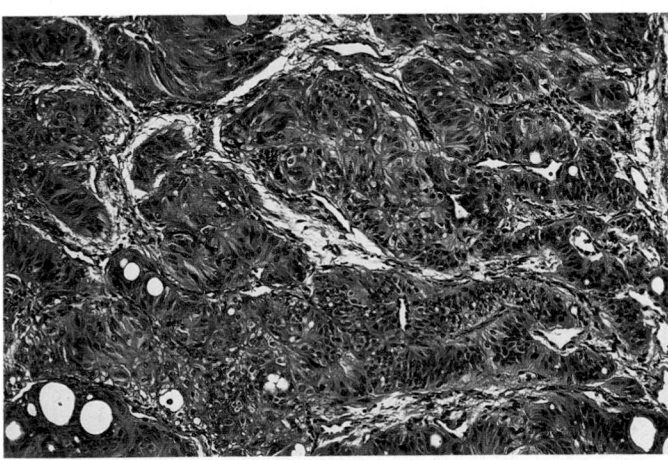

Fig. 9.29 Low-power view of hyalinizing trabecular adenoma.

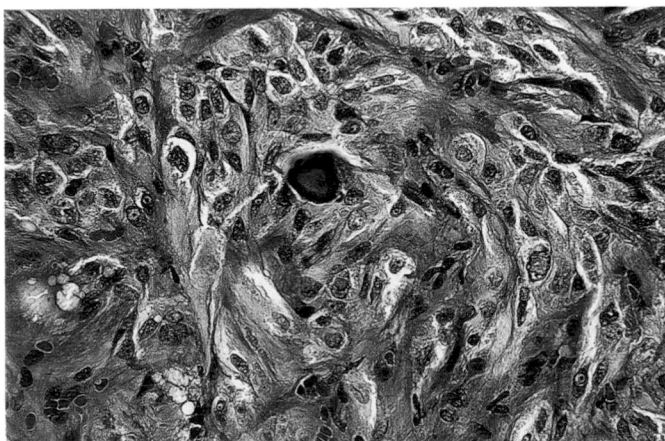

Fig. 9.31 Psammoma body formation in hyalinizing trabecular adenoma.

Immunohistochemically, HTAs show consistent positivity for thyroglobulin and focal and inconstant reactivity for neuroendocrine markers such as neuron-specific enolase (NSE) and neurotensin.[241] They also show a peculiar and as yet unexplained cell membrane and cytoplasmic (instead of nuclear) immunoreactivity with at least some of the monoclonal antibodies used to detect MIB-1.[239] Immunostains for type IV collagen show heavy deposition of this basement membrane material around the tumor cells (partially explaining their "hyaline" appearance) and—surprisingly—in the nuclear pseudo-inclusions. This phenomenon, which has also been documented at an ultrastructural level, suggests a deregulation of the secretory pathways of this molecule.[242,243]

Considerable controversy has arisen as to whether HTA is a distinct entity or a pattern of growth that can be present in a variety of thyroid lesions, the latter being the view currently favored.[249] Thus, it is now accepted that the "HTA pattern" can be seen as a microscopic incidental finding in nodular hyperplasia,[236,245] and in neoplasms accompanied by capsular and/or vascular invasion, which have therefore been designated as *hyalinizing trabecular carcinomas*.[247,248] Even more controversial and intriguing is the apparent pathogenetic link between HTA and papillary carcinoma, which manifests itself by:

1 The common presence in HTA of morphologic features traditionally associated with papillary carcinoma, such as nuclear grooves and pseudoinclusions and psammoma bodies.
2 The immunohistochemical expression of similar types of stratified epithelial-type keratins[238] (a claim which has been contested).[240]
3 The occurrence of HTAs having foci of typical papillary carcinoma within their substance.
4 The occasional occurrence of cervical lymph node metastases of papillary carcinoma having an HTA-like pattern.[244]
5 The detection in HTA of *RET/PTC* mutations with a frequency similar to or even higher than that seen in papillary carcinoma.[237,250]

On the basis of this combined evidence, it has been suggested that HTA is yet another morphologic variant of papillary carcinoma (the hyalinizing trabecular variant, so to speak).[237,238] This may well be the case, but from a practical standpoint the fact remains that a solitary encapsulated thyroid lesion fulfilling all of the morphologic criteria listed in the original article[235] will behave in a benign fashion in nearly every instance.[246]

Papillary carcinoma

General features

Papillary carcinoma is the most common type of thyroid malignancy.[255] Females are more affected than males. It can present in any age group, the mean age at the time of initial diagnosis being approximately 40 years. Papillary carcinoma accounts for more than 90% of thyroid malignancies in children. In 5% to 10% of the cases, there is a history of irradiation exposure to the neck, and the nonneoplastic gland may show nuclear aberrations as a result. There is convincing evidence for an increase in the incidence of papillary carcinoma in Hashimoto's thyroiditis, but the wide variation in the figures quoted suggests that the diagnostic criteria vary just as widely.[254] Whether the frequency of papillary carcinoma is increased in Graves' disease remains a controversial subject.[253]

Almost all patients have clinically evident disease in the neck when they are first seen. In one large series, disease was localized to the thyroid gland in 67% of cases, thyroid and lymph nodes in 13%, and lymph nodes alone in 20%.[252]

Gross features

The size of the primary tumor ranges from microscopic to huge. A very high proportion of thyroid cancers measuring less than 1 cm in diameter are of papillary type. Grossly, most cases are solid, whitish, firm, and clearly invasive; fewer than 10% are surrounded by a complete capsule[256] (Figs 9.32 and 9.33). Marked cystic changes are

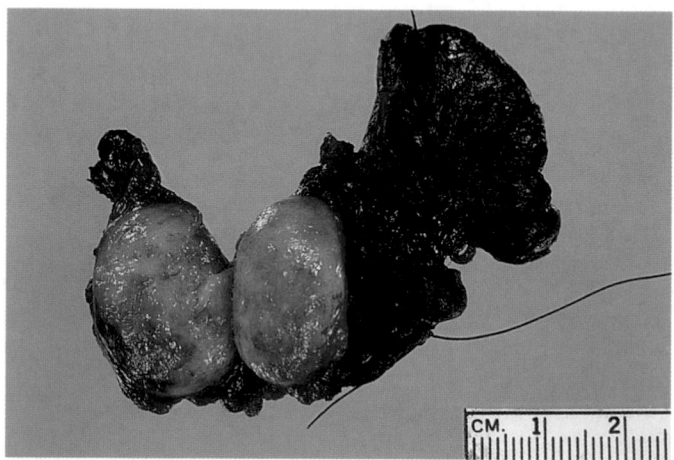

Fig. 9.32 Gross appearance of a papillary carcinoma.

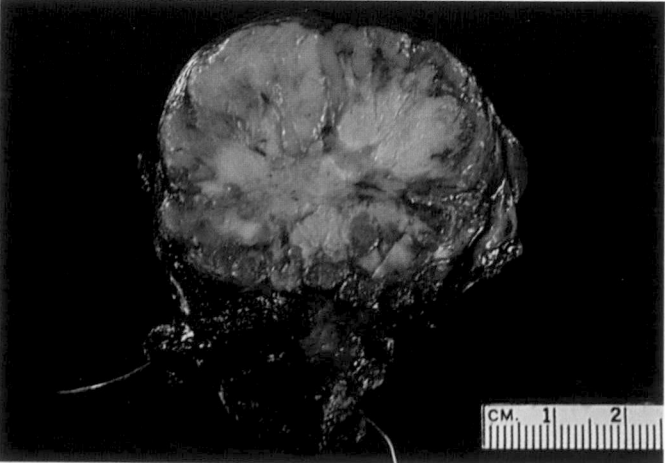

Fig. 9.33 Gross appearance of a papillary carcinoma. The tumor shown exhibits a central area of fibrosis.

seen in about 10% of cases. Sometimes papillary formations are evident to the naked eye.

Microscopic features

Microscopically, the typical papillary carcinoma contains numerous true papillae, an easily recognizable feature which—as one would have deduced—was the one originally chosen to name the tumor.[257,274,277] The papillae are usually complex, branching, and randomly oriented, with a central fibrovascular core and a single or stratified lining of cuboidal cells (Fig. 9.34). The stroma of the papillae may be edematous or hyaline, and it may contain lymphocytes, foamy macrophages, hemosiderin, or—exceptionally—adipose tissue. These papillae are nearly always associated with the formation of follicles, the ratio between the two components varying greatly from case to case. The follicles tend to be irregularly shaped, often tubular and branching. Tumors with a combination of papillary and follicular structures have the biologic behavior of papillary carcinoma and should therefore be classified as such instead of as mixed carcinomas.

With increasing experience, it became evident that the cells of papillary carcinoma have characteristic nuclear features. These have acquired so much relevance that currently the diagnosis of papillary carcinoma is dependent upon their presence rather than a papillary architecture, which may be minor or altogether absent (see under Variants).

These nuclear features consist of:

1 Ground glass (optically clear) nuclei, which often have a large size and an overlapping quality[261] (Fig. 9.35A). The nucleolus is usually inconspicuous and pushed against the nuclear membrane, which appears thickened. This change is present in sections obtained from paraffin-embedded material regardless of the fixative used but is less apparent or absent altogether in frozen sections or cytology material. It is particularly prominent in tissue fixed in high concentrations of

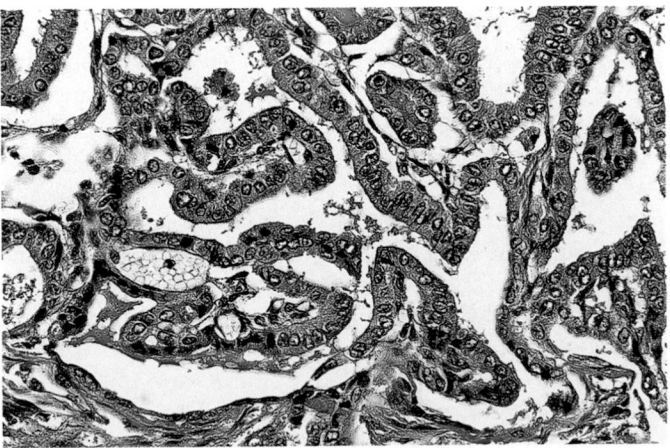

Fig. 9.34 Complex branching papillae in classic papillary carcinoma.

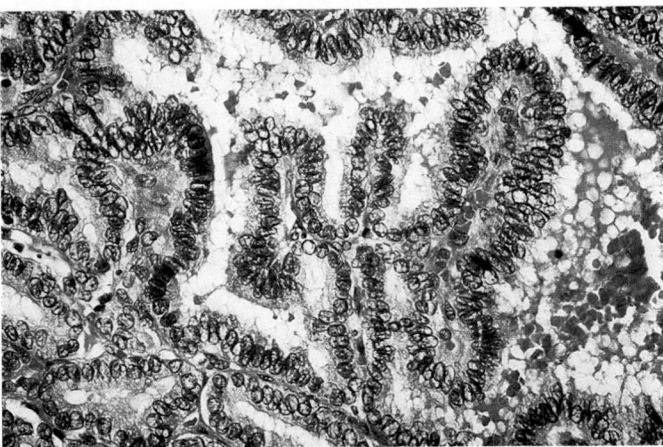

A

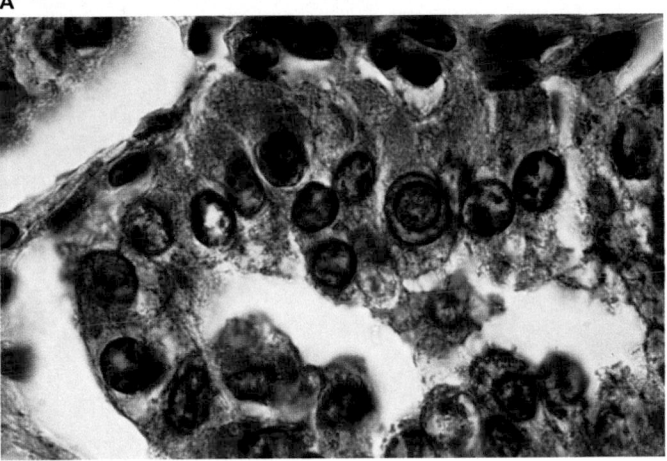

B

Fig. 9.35 A and **B**, Nuclear features of papillary carcinoma: **A**, optically clear nuclei; **B**, nuclear pseudoinclusions.

formalin.[269] The mechanism of its formation has not yet been ascertained.[256a]

2 Nuclear pseudoinclusions. These represent invaginations of the cytoplasm and appear as sharply outlined acidophilic formations[263] (Fig. 9.35B). In contrast to the ground glass feature, the pseudoinclusions are also readily apparent in specimens from frozen section and aspirations. They have been shown to react immunohistochemically for β-catenin and sometimes for type IV collagen.[270a]

3 Nuclear grooves. These tend to occur in oval or spindle nuclei, are usually arranged along the longest nuclear axis, and represent—like the pseudoinclusions—the morphologic expression of infoldings of a redundant nuclear membrane.[258,260]

4 Nuclear microfilaments. A few cases have been described in which the nuclear clearing is due to the accumulation of fine threadlike fibrils.[278]

Mitoses are very scanty or absent.[267] Over half of the cases show extensive fibrosis, usually in the form of sharply outlined bands traversing the tumor; the appearance of this fibrosis may range from sclerohyaline to highly cellular (Fig. 9.36).

Psammoma bodies are seen in approximately half of the cases. They may be located in the papillary stalk, in the fibrous stroma, or between tumor cells in solid foci (Fig. 9.37A). Their presence strongly suggests the diagnosis of papillary carcinoma, inasmuch as their occurrence in other thyroid lesions is exceptional[270];

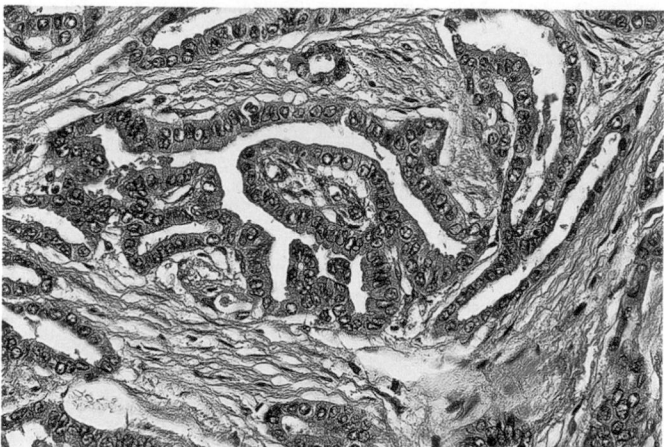

Fig. 9.36 Desmoplastic stromal reaction in papillary carcinoma.

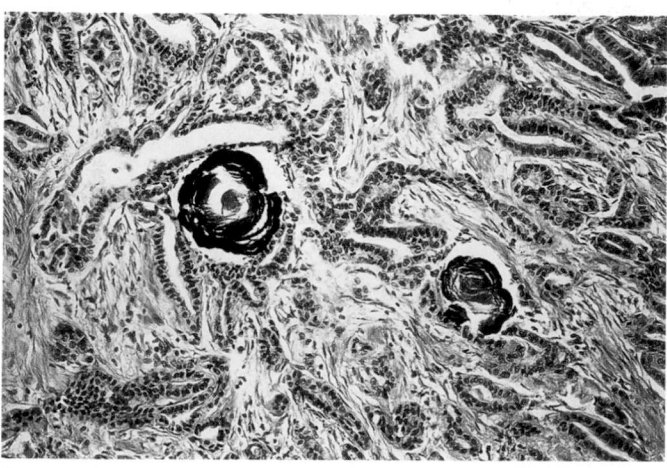

A

B

Fig. 9.37 A and **B**, Psammoma body formation in papillary carcinoma: **A**, within the stroma of the primary tumor; **B**, beneath the capsule of a cervical lymph node, without identifiable tumor cells.

Klinck and Winship[266] found them only once in a review of 2153 benign thyroids. Thus they represent a very important clue to the diagnosis not only in paraffin sections, but also in frozen sections, cytology preparations, and—if numerous enough—roentgenograms.[268] If they are present in what is otherwise normal thyroid tissue or lymph nodes from the neck, the chances are high that a papillary carcinoma is present in the immediate vicinity[262a,266] (Fig. 9.37B). These laminated basophilic structures stain for mucin, calcium, and iron and appear to arise from necrosis of individual tumor cells, which occasionally may be seen at their very center.[259,264] Osteopontin produced by macrophages is said to be involved in their development.[275] Psammoma bodies should be distinguished from other forms of calcification and from the intraluminal foci of inspissated secretion often seen in Hürthle cell tumors.[257]

Areas with a solid/trabecular pattern of growth are present in 20% of the cases and foci of squamous metaplasia in a similar number; these two patterns often merge and are probably related.[257] According to some authors, the prominence of solid/trabecular formations places the tumor in a poorly differentiated category (see p. 549).

Occasionally, papillary carcinomas are seen to contain a bland-looking spindle cell component; this clinically insignificant metaplastic change (recognizable because of its blending with more typical epithelial cells and its immunoreactivity for thyroglobulin and TTF-1) should not be confused with a mesenchymal neoplasm or with the anaplastic transformation of a papillary carcinoma.[276]

Lymphocytic infiltration of the stroma is seen in a fourth of cases; it is not clear whether this represents a reaction to the tumor or the expression of preexisting thyroiditis.[273] Many tumors also exhibit a heavy infiltrate of S-100 protein-positive dendritic/Langerhans' cells and lysozyme-positive histiocytes.[272] Scattered multinucleated giant cells may be present, probably representing a response to leakage of colloid.[262]

Multiple microscopic foci of tumor are found in about 20% of cases if a few random sections are taken and in over 75% if step sections of the entire gland are examined.[265,271] Controversy still exists as to whether this represents multicentricity or intrathyroidal lymphatic permeation, but probably both mechanisms operate. Blood vessel invasion is found in only 5% of cases.

Electron microscopic features

Ultrastructurally, the most distinctive feature of the cells of papillary carcinoma is the highly indented nuclear membrane, with formation of pseudoinclusions and multilobation.[279,280,282] Changes in distribution of chromatin and ribonucleoprotein, and a special type of nuclear body have been observed.[281] The cytoplasm is rich in mitochondria, lysosomes, and intermediate filaments. The apical surface exhibits microvillous differentiation. The abnormal intracellular and extracellular deposition of basement membrane material (of lesser degree but otherwise similar to that seen in hyalinizing trabecular carcinoma) is very evident at the ultrastructural level.[283]

Histochemical and immunohistochemical features

Immunohistochemically, the cells of papillary carcinoma are reactive for pan-keratin stains.[319] Their usual profile is CK7+/CK20–.[288] Of potentially greater diagnostic importance is the fact that the cells of this tumor stain for cytokeratin 19 and for the high-molecular-weight keratin demonstrated with 34βE12.[286,290,295,305,308,314] Reactivity for thyroglobulin and TTF-1 is the rule, although the intensity for the latter is generally less than in follicular neoplasms.[288] There is also positivity for S-100 protein[311,315]; vimentin (in the same tumor cells that express keratin)[289,296]; EMA; CEA (occasionally); CA-125 (in about half of the cases)[303]; HBME-1[313]; involucrin[299]; galectin-3[287,297,302]; CD15[298,313]; CD57[304]; α_1-antichymotrypsin[306,317]; ICAM1[320]; HER2/*neu*[322]; insulin-like growth factor 1[312]; cMet/hepatocyte growth factor receptor[316]; midkine[301]; ghrelin[322a]; promyelocytic leukemia protein[323]; ceruloplasmin[321]; and estrogen receptors.[292] The expression of the *RET* oncogene product is discussed in the next section.

The luminal surface of the tumor cells is covered by a glycoproteinaceous material that reacts positively with mucin stains (such as Alcian blue) and EMA.[284,285,291] This blood group antigen-related material includes the above mentioned CEA and other so-called "oncofetal antigens."[294,300] Laminin and type IV collagen are demonstrable immunohistochemically at the interface of the tumor with the stroma.[307] The colloid produced by the neoplastic follicles of papillary carcinoma seems to contain molecularly abnormal forms of thyroglobulin, as already suggested by its peculiar staining pattern on H&E and supported by biochemical studies[319a] and proteomic/postproteomic characterization.[311a]

The practical question, of course, is how useful this numerically impressive array of immunostains is in the differential diagnosis of papillary carcinoma. One situation is the papillary neoplasm located in a lymph node or some other extrathyroidal site in which one needs to establish whether the tumor is of thyroid nature or not. The role played here by thyroglobulin and TTF-1 is crucial, these being two of the most specific markers in existence (in the case of TTF-1, shared with the pulmonary epithelium). The other, considerably more complex situation, is the use of immunostains for the differential diagnosis of papillary thyroid carcinoma from other benign and malignant thyroid lesions. Here, unfortunately, most if not all stains fall short of the mark in one important respect, which is rarely mentioned in the many articles touting their utility. It is true that the immunohistochemical profile of papillary carcinoma is very different from that of normal follicles, follicular

neoplasms, and the benign papillae of Graves' disease and nodular hyperplasias. Specifically, the benign papillae of the latter lesions are generally negative for keratin 19 and 34βE12, whereas they show higher labeling for p27kip1, a cyclin-dependent kinase inhibitory protein.[293] However, the profile of papillary thyroid carcinoma cells is very similar to that exhibited by the follicular cells in Hashimoto's thyroiditis, a fact that should be taken into account in the differential diagnosis between the two entities and before making a claim about the "specificity" of a given antibody for papillary carcinoma.[285a,309,310,318,321a]

Molecular genetic features

The cardinal molecular alteration in papillary thyroid carcinoma is an alteration of *RET*.[329,334,336] This is a proto-oncogene located on chromosome 10q11.2 that encodes a transmembrane receptor with tyrosine kinase activity. This alteration is not a germline point mutation (as is the case in familial medullary carcinoma, see p. 556), but one or another of several somatic rearrangements, the most important of which are designated as *RET/PTC1*, *RET/PTC3*, and *RET/PTC2* (listed in order of decreasing frequency). It has been claimed that this aberration is specific for the papillary carcinoma histotype[335,339]; that it represents a very early carcinogenic event (as witnessed by its detection in papillary microcarcinoma)[328]; that it correlates with the presence of the typical nuclear changes of this tumor[331] and that it is directly responsible for them[330]; that it correlates with the tumor subtype (*RET/PTC1* with the classic and diffuse sclerosing types, and *RET/PTC3* with the follicular/solid and tall cell variants—see next section)[325,340]; that tumors with *RET* rearrangements tend to be more indolent and not to progress toward less differentiated forms[341,343]; and that introduction of this oncogene to transgenic mice induces the formation of papillary thyroid carcinomas in them.[333] These are high claims indeed, which when taken together constitute powerful evidence of the pivotal role that molecular discoveries play in unraveling thyroid carcinogenesis. There are, however, discordant notes in this enthralling story. To wit:

1 The incidence of *RET/PTC* rearrangements in the reported series of papillary carcinoma has ranged from less than 3% to over 80%, and it is as yet unclear whether these wide discrepancies are due to racial, environmental, or technical factors.

2 There have been two independent reports (recently challenged) describing *RET/PTC* rearrangements in over 90% of thyroid glands with Hashimoto's thyroiditis *without* morphologic evidence of papillary carcinoma (see p. XXX).

3 Lately, *RET/PTC* rearrangements have been found in a high proportion of cases of Hürthle cell tumors without papillary carcinoma features.[291a]

4 There is considerable skepticism about the reliability of immunohistochemical techniques in detecting

expression of the *RET* product in papillary carcinoma, at least with the use of commercially available antibodies.[327]

This body of evidence is somewhat disturbing, to say the least, and a clear indicator that additional research is needed before making too many diagnostic, prognostic, and therapeutic assumptions on the basis of these molecular findings.

Other genetic alterations found in papillary carcinoma involve the gene *NTRK1* (formerly *trek*) located on chromosome 1,[342] point mutations in *ras*,[326,332] (said to be more common in the follicular variant, see below)[343a] and lack of expression of the *Rb* gene.[324] Expression of the sodium iodide symporter is also reduced.[337]

Karyotypically, the most frequent alteration in papillary carcinoma is represented by chromosome 10q rearrangements with breakpoints at 10q11.2 (at the site of the *RET* oncogene), but many other structural abnormalities have been described.[338]

Variants

The following morphologic variants of papillary carcinoma have been described.[358]

1 **Papillary microcarcinoma**. This is defined as a papillary carcinoma measuring 1 cm or less in diameter (Figs 9.38 and 9.39). Most cases have a stellate configuration and correspond to the lesions formerly known as occult sclerosing carcinoma or nonencapsulated sclerosing tumor,[374,377,384] whereas others show partial or near total encapsulation, with or without tumor outside the capsule.[380,399] Its microscopic features and the LOH mutational profile so far investigated are not different from those of their larger counterpart.[379a] Papillary microcarcinoma is an extremely common incidental finding (25% or more, depending on the thoroughness of the examination) in thyroid glands removed for other reasons and in population-based autopsy studies.[352,375,408] In contrast to its clinically evident counterpart, papillary micro-

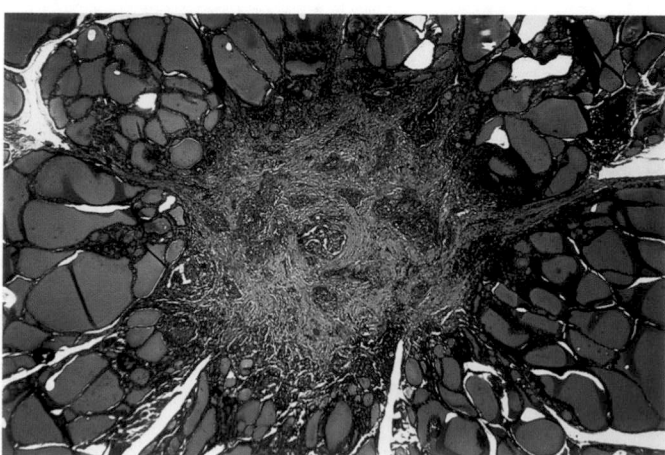

Fig. 9.38 Typical stellate appearance of papillary microcarcinoma.

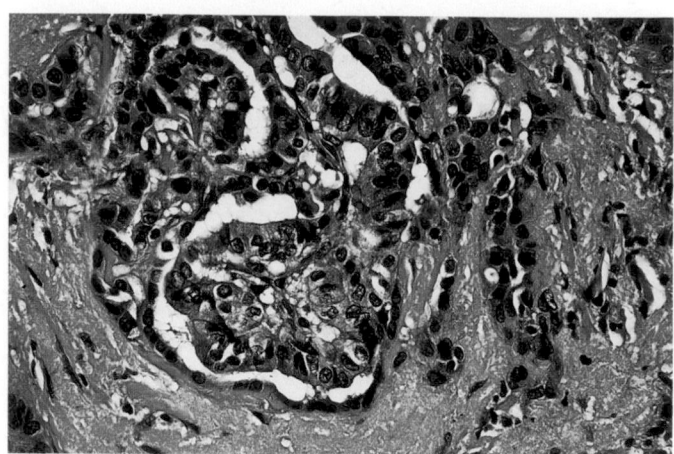

Fig. 9.39 On high power, the appearance of papillary microcarcinoma is not different from that of its larger counterpart.

carcinoma seems to be more common in males than females.[369] Despite its small size, the tumor can sometimes be identified in fine needle aspiration specimens.[409] It may be associated with cervical node metastases,[395] but distant metastases are exceptionally rare,[402] and the prognosis is generally excellent.[374] However, since our experience with the Chernobyl-related cases suggests that this clinical insignificance cannot necessarily be assumed in tumors in children, we have proposed that the existing definition of papillary microcarcinoma *be reserved* only for tumors in adults.[407] A parallel proposal, made at a thyroid cancer meeting in Porto and colloquially referred to as "the Porto proposal", is that of avoiding the term "carcinoma" for this tumor when occurring in adults in its typical form, and to replace for the term *papillary microtumor*.[394a]

2 **Encapsulated variant**. This is defined as a papillary carcinoma *totally* surrounded by a capsule. It may still be associated with nodal metastases, but the incidence of distant metastases or tumor death is nearly zero.[366,396] The cytoarchitectural (and particularly nuclear) features of this variant are the same as for the conventional invasive type. This lesion should be distinguished from the hyperplastic nodule with central cystic degeneration and papillary or pseudopapillary fronds in the wall (Figs 9.40 and 9.41). In contrast to papillary carcinomas, these lesions are hot on thyroid scan and are characterized microscopically by a pale, vacuolated colloid. The papillary areas are largely limited to the area facing the cystic cavity. The follicular cells tend to be low columnar, with basally located normochromatic or hyperchromatic nuclei (instead of the centrally located, optically clear nuclei of papillary carcinoma). Immunohistochemically, these benign cells do not stain for high-molecular-weight keratin (such as that demonstrated with the AE1 antibody) or S-100 protein and do not show a

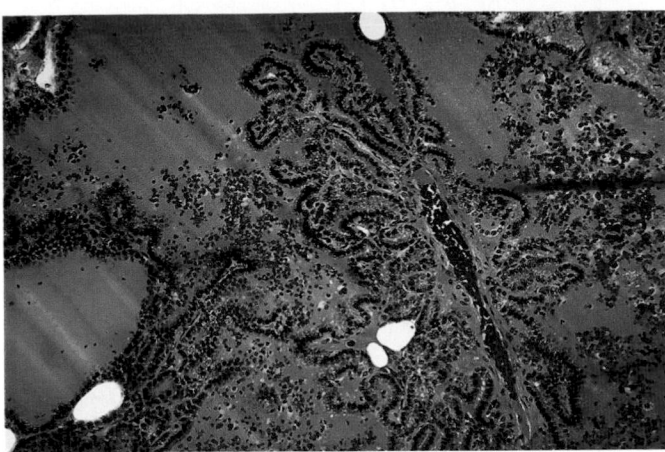

Fig. 9.40 The benign papillary formations of nodular hyperplasia point toward the center of the cystically dilated follicles.

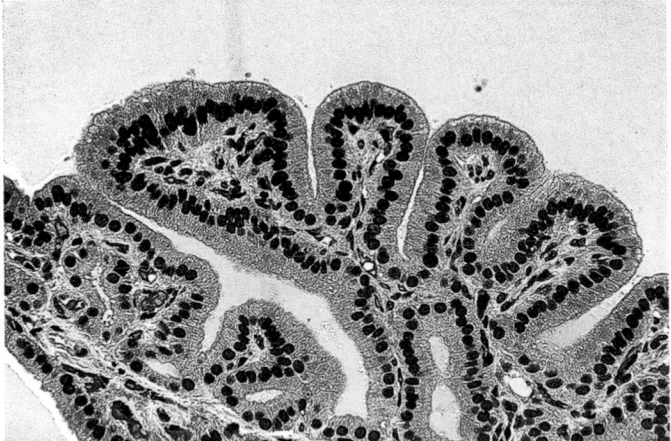

Fig. 9.41 Benign papillary formations lined by columnar cells with basally located round normochromatic nuclei. The cytoplasm has a pale basophilic quality.

coating of the luminal surface with Alcian blue or EMA-positive material.[379]

3 **Follicular variant**. This is a papillary carcinoma composed entirely or almost entirely of follicles (Fig. 9.42).[362,395,403] The diagnosis is largely based on the presence of the set of nuclear features classically associated with papillary carcinoma (see p. 533). Supportive features for the diagnosis are an invasive pattern of growth, fibrous trabeculation (particularly at the tumor periphery), psammoma bodies, strongly eosinophilic colloid with scalloped edges, and the presence of abortive papillae. The behavior of these *invasive* tumors is analogous to that of conventional papillary carcinoma[409a], particularly in regard to the high incidence of nodal metastases.[356,364] Interestingly, these metastases usually exhibit better developed papillary formations.

The follicular variant of papillary carcinoma can be viewed as the balanced result of two opposing biologic properties of the tumor cell: differentiation in the form of secretory activity (thereby making colloid-filled follicles), and proliferation. When one of these forces predominates over the other, two further variants emerge:

3A *Solid variant*. This tumor, particularly common in children, results when proliferation predominates over secretion. It is characterized by solid nests of generally round shape that can be viewed as filled-up follicles (Fig. 9.43). It is distinguished from insular carcinoma and other forms of poorly differentiated carcinoma because the nuclear features remain those of papillary carcinoma. This distinction is of great importance, because the behavior of this tumor is essentially that of papillary carcinoma (or perhaps only a little worse) but notably different from that of the truly poorly differentiated neoplasms.[391]

3B *Macrofollicular variant*. This can be viewed as the opposite of the solid variant, in the sense that the secretory activity is such as to result in large dilated follicles, so that the tumor resembles not so much a follicular neoplasm as a hyperplastic nodule[345,390] (Fig. 9.44). The requirements for inclusion of this lesion in the papillary carcinoma family should be, if

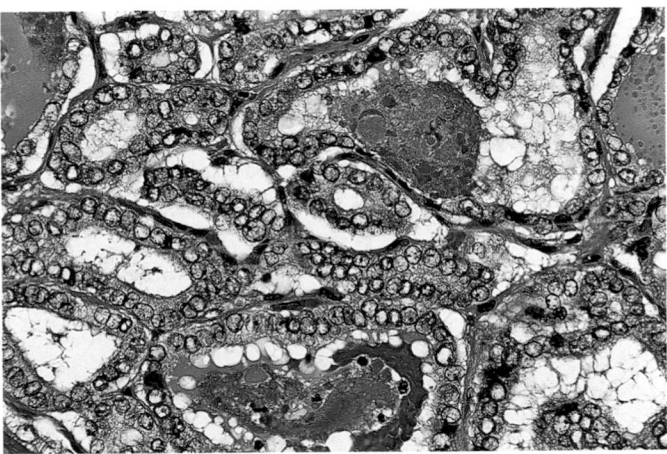

Fig. 9.42 Follicular variant of papillary carcinoma. Note the clear overlapping nuclei.

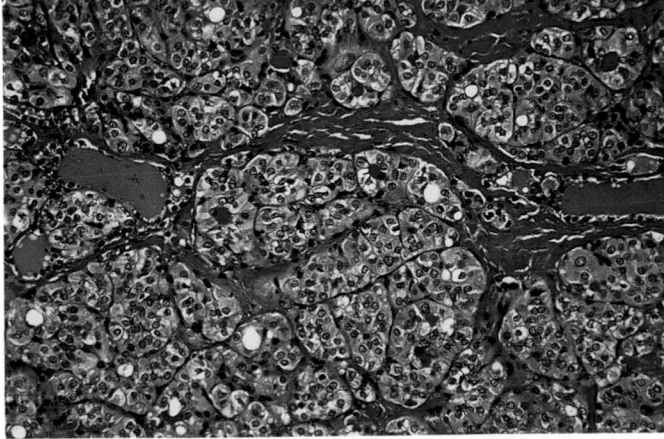

Fig. 9.43 Solid variant of papillary carcinoma. The nests are separated by fibrohyaline strands.

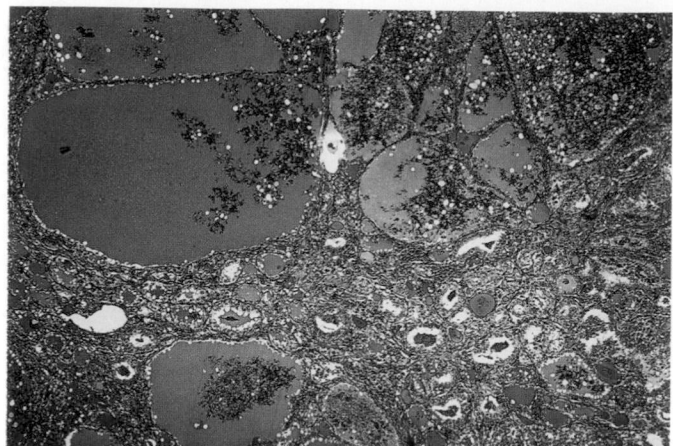

Fig. 9.44 So-called "macrofollicular variant" of papillary carcinoma. This lesion simulates nodular hyperplasia. The nuclear features that allow the diagnosis cannot be seen at this magnification.

anything, even more stringent than for the "conventional" follicular variant.

There are two additional twists in the follicular variant saga, this time depending on the nature of the tumor boundaries, taking as the standard the lesion that presents as a single invasive mass:

3C *Diffuse (multinodular) variant.* In this very unusual form, most of a thyroid lobe or sometimes both lobes are diffusely involved by the tumor growth, which is difficult to recognize because of its very diffuseness.[382]

3D *Encapsulated follicular variant.* This tumor type, which has become the single most common source of consultation material in thyroid pathology and the subject of considerable controversy, can be defined as a neoplasm surrounded by a capsule and having the cytoarchitectural features of papillary carcinoma, especially as far as the nuclei are concerned. It is also referred to as *Lindsay's tumor.* As in the case of the follicular neoplasms, there may or may not be evidence of capsular and/or blood vessel invasion. To make a diagnosis of this variant, the nuclear alterations should be widespread and well developed, and some supportive features (such as intratumoral sharply defined fibrohyaline bands, elongated and branching follicles, abortive follicles, and dense eosinophilic colloid) should be present.[348,349,359,394] The problem, of course, is what to do when they are not (Fig. 9.45). It is possible that lesions in which the nuclear changes are focal or "incomplete" represent an early development of papillary carcinoma in a preexisting benign lesion, as suggested by the fact that in microdissection experiments the *RET/PTC* rearrangements are restricted to these foci.[372] However, it is abundantly clear that such lesions will be cured by a conservative operation in nearly every instance. On the basis of this observation and with the purpose of avoiding all the responses that the term *carcinoma* induces in the

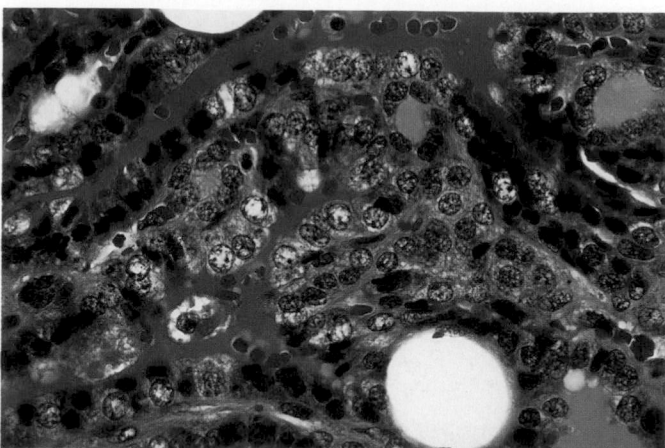

A

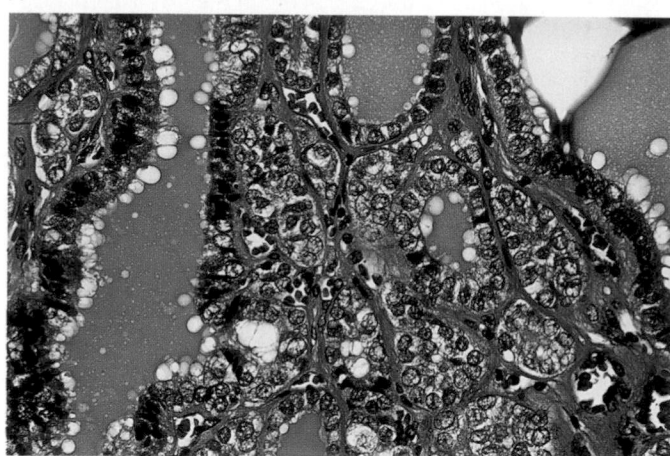

B

Fig. 9.45 A and **B,** Vesicular nuclei in benign follicular nodules. This change, which was focal, is not sufficient to diagnose this lesion as a papillary carcinoma.

surgeon and the patient, a group of pathologists interested in thyroid tumors (the author included) proposed that the following terminology be adopted, fully aware of the subjectivity and arbitrariness behind the decision as to whether a certain morphologic change is "obvious," "questionable," or "absent":

For lesions having *obvious* nuclear changes: **Papillary thyroid carcinoma, follicular variant**, regardless of the status of the capsule.

For lesions having *questionable* nuclear changes:
- **Well-differentiated carcinoma, NOS,** if there is definite capsular invasion.
- **Well-differentiated tumor of uncertain malignant potential (WDT-UMP),** if capsular invasion is questionable or absent.

The terminology proposed for tumors lacking nuclear changes is discussed in the section on follicular carcinoma (p. 543).

4 **Diffuse sclerosing variant.** This variant is characterized by diffuse involvement of one or both thyroid lobes, dense sclerosis, abundant psammoma bodies, extensive solid foci, squamous metaplasia, and heavy lymphocytic infiltration, and extensive lymph vessel permeation (Figs 9.46 and 9.47). Clinically, it may be misdiagnosed as Hashimoto's thyroiditis. Nodal metastases are nearly always present, lung metastases are common, multiple brain metastases may supervene, and the disease-free survival rate is lower than for conventional papillary carcinoma.[355,361,371,381,402a,405]

5 **Oncocytic (oxyphilic) variant.** In this variant, the nuclear features remain those of papillary carcinoma but the cytoplasm is abundant and has a granular oxyphilic quality.[351] The pattern of growth may be papillary or follicular, and the tumor may be encapsulated or invasive, this resulting in a bewildering number of possible combinations: oncocytic, encapsulated oncocytic, oncocytic follicular, and encapsulated oncocytic follicular variants. A further variation on the theme is the tumor having a papillary architecture, typical nuclear features, oncocytic cytoplasm, and a heavy lymphocytic infiltrate in the stroma of the papillae, resulting in an appearance reminiscent of Warthin's tumor of salivary glands.[346] Warthin-like tumor of the thyroid has been found to express *RET/PTC* (as a further link with papillary carcinoma[363]), and to be associated with a generally excellent prognosis.[347,386] Both oncocytic and Warthin-like papillary carcinomas are said to differ from classic papillary carcinomas regarding the expression of Rb protein and E2F-1 transcription factor.[345a]

Perhaps at this point it is worth reminding the reader that a *sine qua non* for including a tumor in *any* of these subsets of papillary carcinoma is the presence of the nuclear features of the papillary family of neoplasms.

6 **Tall cell and columnar cell carcinoma.** The *tall cell* variant is a type of papillary carcinoma characterized by papillae lined by a single layer of "tall" cells (the height being at least twice the width) and an abundant acidophilic, quasi-oncocytic cytoplasm (Fig. 9.48).[400] These features should be present in at least half of the tumor for it to be placed in this category. The pattern of growth is usually highly papillary. The nuclei usually lack the optically clear appearance, grooves, and pseudoinclusions seen in papillary carcinoma and all of its other variants, and therefore it has been questioned whether columnar cell carcinoma is really a variant of papillary carcinoma, as opposed to a different tumor type despite its highly papillary architecture. There may be an extensive lymphocytic infiltration of the stroma.[393] CD15 and CEA-like material (the latter demonstrated with antibody Zc23) are present more often than in conventional papillary carcinoma.[392] There is also a greater expression of the oncogene c-net.[390a] This variant

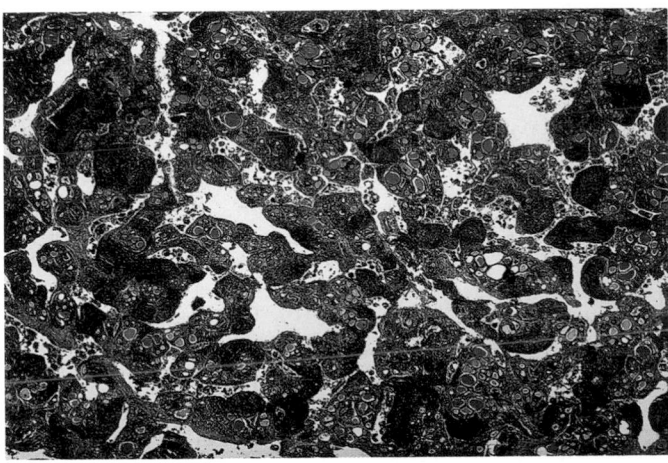

Fig. 9.46 Diffuse sclerosing variant of papillary carcinoma. Note the diffuse pattern of growth, the heavy lymphocytic infiltrate, and the sclerosis.

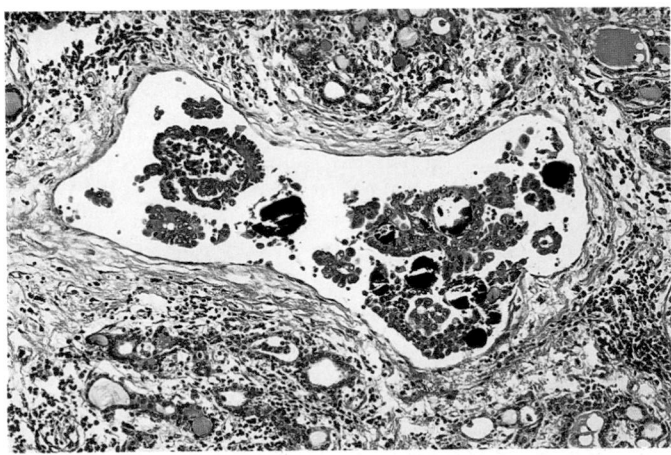

Fig. 9.47 Prominent permeation of intrathyroid lymph vessels in diffuse sclerosing papillary carcinoma. Psammoma bodies are evident.

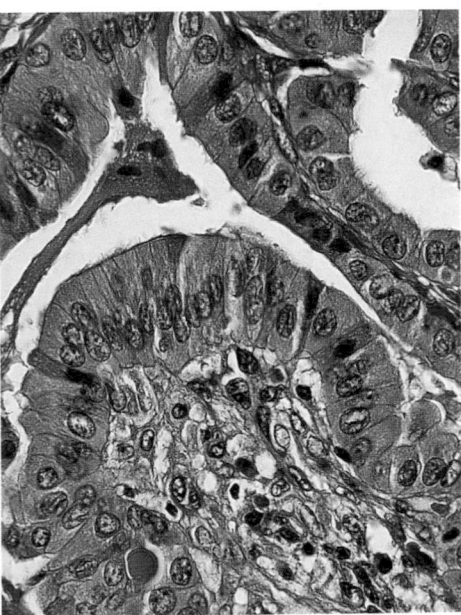

Fig. 9.48 Tall cell variant of papillary carcinoma. Note the abundant granular acidophilic cytoplasm with oncocyte-like features.

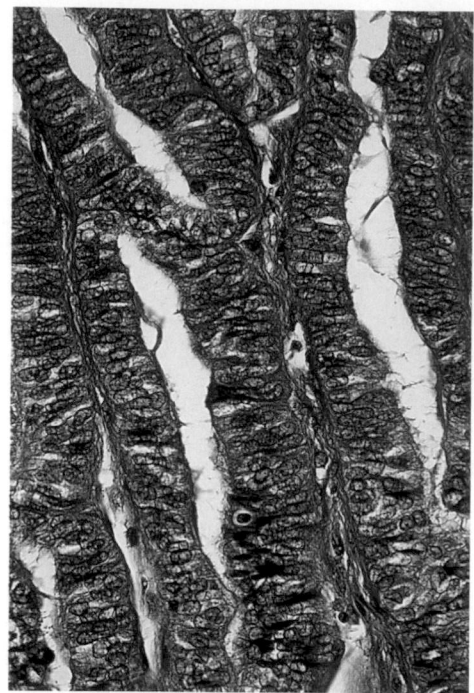

Fig. 9.49 Columnar cell variant of papillary carcinoma. The papillae are lined by a pseudostratified layer of spindle tumor cells.

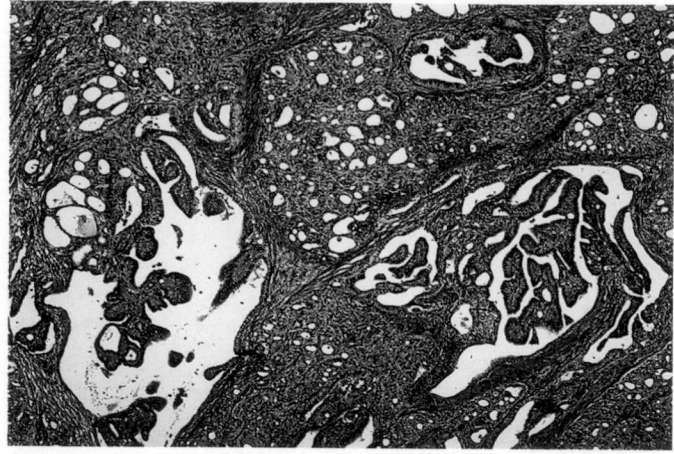

A

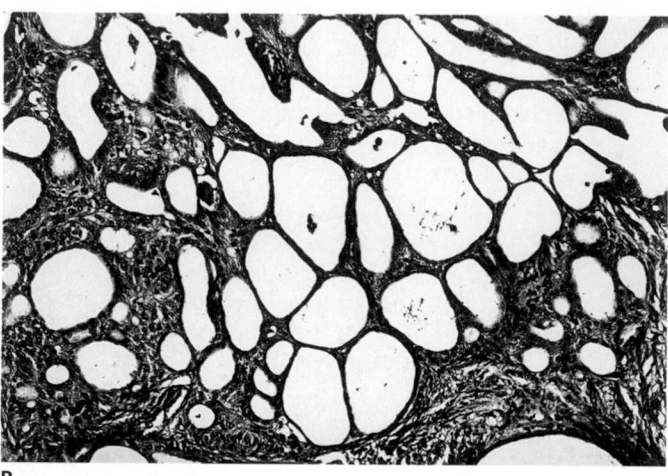

B

Fig. 9.50 A and **B**, Cribriform–morular variant of papillary carcinoma. The cribriform quality of the tumor is particularly well appreciated in **B**.

tends to affect older patients more often than the conventional form, extrathyroidal extension is more common, and the clinical course is said to be more aggressive.[370,376,383,392] In the *columnar cell carcinoma*, there is prominent stratification, and the cytoplasm is clear (sometimes with subnuclear vacuolization, reminiscent of early secretory endometrium) rather than acidophilic[350,365,373,388,399] (Fig. 9.49). Mitotic figures can be found, and the MIB-1 is relatively high.[378,385] The initial reports of this entity indicated a very poor prognosis, but more recent larger series have shown that—once again—the outcome is largely predicated by tumor stage[368,406]; specifically, encapsulated columnar cell carcinomas are associated with a favorable course.[367]

Occasional cases of papillary carcinoma have been seen in which tall and columnar cells coexist.[344,398]

7   **Cribriform–morular variant**. As the name indicates, this variant is characterized by the presence of a cribriform pattern of growth and morular formations (Fig. 9.50). Immunohistochemical staining for β-catenin shows strong nuclear-cytoplasmic staining, in contrast to the cell membrane staining of normal thyroid.[407b] Some of the cases are sporadic, whereas others are seen as part of a genetically determined syndrome that includes colonic adenomatous polyposis.[353] Most of the syndrome-associated cases that have been studied genetically have shown *germline* mutations of the *APC* gene and *somatic RET/PTC* rearrangement.[357,401] They also show evidence of alterations of the Wnt signaling pathway, as detected immunohistochemically.[407a] Interestingly, a sporadic case of this tumor type has been shown to have *somatic* mutation of the *APC* gene.[354]

8   **Papillary carcinoma with exuberant nodular fasciitis-like stroma**. In this variant, the prominence of the stromal reaction of the tumor may obscure the neoplastic epithelial component.[360,387] As a result, a biopsy may be misinterpreted as nodular fasciitis, fibromatosis, or some other proliferative stromal condition.[389,404] In some foci, the interplay of this stromal component with the tumor results in a fibroadenoma-like appearance.[360]

Spread and metastases

Extrathyroidal extension into the soft tissues of the neck is found in about one fourth of cases, and it may extend to the parathyroid glands.[410,411,413b] Involvement of cervical lymph nodes is very common (particularly in young patients), and it may be the first manifestation of the disease. The nodal metastases have a tendency to undergo cystic changes (Fig. 9.51) (see p. 519). These metastases may not be clinically apparent because of their small size

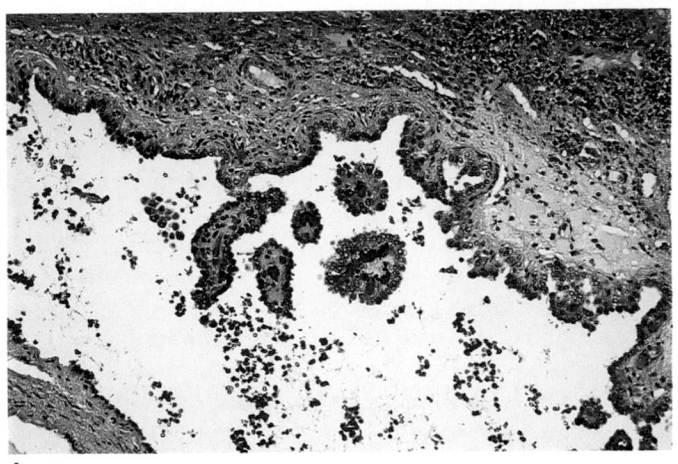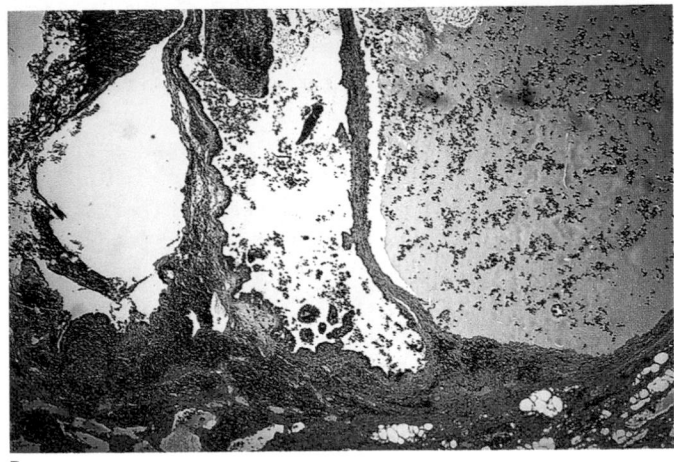

A

B

Fig. 9.51 A and **B**, Papillary thyroid carcinoma metastatic to cervical lymph node. The tumor has undergone marked cystic degeneration, simulating on low power (**A**) the appearance of a branchial cleft cyst. Small papillary formations are seen focally (**B**).

and also because their consistency may not differ from that of a normal node. In a study of 67 patients with clinically negative nodes, 41 (61%) had metastatic tumor on microscopic examination.[412]

Blood-borne metastases are less frequent than with other thyroid carcinomas, but they also occur; the most common site is the lung, but they can also develop in bones, the central nervous system, and other organs.[410,413a] The lung metastases can have a miliary micronodular pattern detectable only on ^{131}I scintiscan, or they can be rounded and macronodular.[413]

Treatment

This is discussed together with the other epithelial tumors of the thyroid gland (see p. 564).

Prognosis

The overall outcome of patients with papillary carcinoma is excellent, not significantly different from that of the general population.[422,428] Factors relating to prognosis are the following:

1 *Age.* This is of great importance. Nearly all the deaths from papillary carcinomas occur when the tumor manifests itself after the age of 40 years.[418,420,437a]

2 *Sex.* Females are said to have a better prognosis than males, although in some series the difference has not been significant.[420]

3 *Extrathyroidal extension.* This feature adversely affects the prognosis in a very significant fashion.[420,437] Parenthetically, this feature and several others included in this listing have been incorporated into the staging system for thyroid carcinoma, which—as in most other sites—has proved to be a powerful prognostic predictor.[417,419,426]

4 *Microscopic variants* (see p. 536).

5 *History of previous irradiation.* Despite previous statements to the contrary, the prognosis of tumors in which this antecedent is present does not seem to differ significantly from the others.[413c]

6 *Tumor size.* A rough inverse correlation is present between tumor size and prognosis.

7 *Capsule and margins.* Tumors that are encapsulated and/or have pushing margins have a better outcome than the others.[420,427,429]

8 *Multicentricity.* Patients in whom this is a prominent feature have a greater incidence of metastasis and a lesser chance of disease-free survival.[420]

9 *Distant metastases.* Metastases to lung have an adverse influence on prognosis; this influence is even greater for distant metastases in other sites, such as the skeletal system.[420,433]

10 *Poorly differentiated, squamous, or anaplastic foci.* These features have a markedly detrimental effect on prognosis.[423] Fortunately, they are present in fewer than 5% of the cases.[420,431]

11 *Grading.* This parameter, which is intertwined with the above, bears a definite relationship with prognosis that we feel has been underestimated.[415,435] However, it needs to be clearly defined in terms of criteria (necrosis, mitotic activity, etc.) and properly standardized for it to reach its full potential.

12 *EMA and Leu-M1 positivity.* It has been claimed that tumors showing immunoreactivity for EMA and Leu-M1 are associated with a more aggressive clinical course.[434,438]

13 *DNA ploidy.* Some studies have shown a good correlation between aneuploidy and aggressive behavior in papillary carcinoma, but it is not yet clear whether this provides information not already obtainable from the listed clinical and morphologic parameters.[421,425]

14 *Rb protein.* The pRB expression level is said to be a reliable predictor of recurrence.[432]

15 *Circulating tumor cells.* Presence of circulating tumor cells (as determined with an RT-PCR assay for thyroglobulin mRNA) seems to be associated with a higher likelihood of metastatic disease but it is not

clear whether this procedure will play a practical role in clinical management.[416,436]

16 Factors not generally found to correlate with prognosis are relative proportion of papillae and follicles; presence or amount of fibrosis; presence or amount of squamous metaplasia or psammoma bodies; and microvessel density.[414] The presence of cervical node metastases does not seem to worsen the prognosis,[424] but extracapsular extension is said to be an indicator of a greater likelihood of distant metastases and poor prognosis.[439] Apparently, this statement even applies to papillary microcarcinoma.[440] The effect of the type of therapy on prognosis remains controversial,[430] but we[420] and others have found little if any relation between the two parameters (see p. 564).

Follicular carcinoma

Follicular carcinoma could be defined in a generic sense as any malignant thyroid tumor exhibiting evidence of follicular cell differentiation. However, we prefer not to include in this category the follicular variant of papillary carcinoma (see p. 537), Hürthle cell carcinoma (see p. 544), poorly differentiated (insular) carcinoma (see p. 549), and the exceptionally rare mixed medullary–follicular carcinoma (see p. 558). When thus categorized, follicular carcinoma becomes a relatively rare neoplasm whose identification largely depends on the presence of invasion of the capsule, blood vessels, or adjacent thyroid.[447] It shares with papillary carcinoma the same predilection for females, but it occurs, on average, in patients who are a decade older. Its microscopic appearance is extremely variable, ranging from well-formed follicles to a predominantly solid growth pattern. Poorly formed follicles, cribriform areas, or trabecular formations may be present, sometimes in combination. Focal or extensive cytoplasmic clear changes can occur. Mitotic activity and nuclear atypia are usually seen but may be entirely lacking. Psammoma bodies are absent, and squamous metaplasia is exceptionally rare.

Immunohistochemically, follicular carcinomas are reactive for thyroglobulin, TTF-1, low-molecular-weight keratin, EMA, and basement membrane components such as laminin and type IV collagen.[456,473] Their reactivity for these and other markers is not significantly different from that of follicular adenomas, this also applying to their lectin-binding pattern and ultrastructural appearance.[454,466] They can also react for many of the markers that were listed in the preceding section on papillary carcinoma, although generally in a lesser percentage of the cases and with a lesser degree of intensity.

The incidence of *ras* point mutation has been found to be much higher for follicular carcinoma than for papillary carcinoma (53% versus 17%)[475]; it has been suggested that this difference may be related to the known differences in epidemiology, pathology, and clinical behavior between the two tumors.[463,474] A genetic abnormality recently detected in a subset of follicular carcinomas is the t(2;3)(q13;q25) translocation, resulting in the *PAX8–PPAR* gamma 1 fusion.[457,452a] It has been said that the follicular carcinomas with PPARgamma rearrangement tend to have vascular invasion and solid/nested histology.[447a]

Depending on its degree of invasiveness, follicular carcinoma has been subdivided into a minimally invasive and a widely invasive form.

Minimally invasive follicular carcinoma is a grossly encapsulated tumor, often with a solid and fleshy cut surface. The pattern of growth usually resembles that of an adenoma of embryonal, fetal, or atypical type. Indeed, it has been suggested that some of the cases represent malignant transformation of an adenoma. Since the diagnosis of malignancy depends entirely on the demonstration of blood vessel and/or capsular invasion, one should be very strict about these criteria (Fig. 9.52). The blood vessel invasion is almost never evident grossly. Microscopically, the vessels should be of venous caliber, be located in or immediately outside the capsule (rather than within the tumor), and contain one or more clusters of tumor cells attached to the wall and protruding into the lumen. Often, the intravascular tumor masses are covered by endothelium, in a fashion similar to that of an ordinary thrombus. We have found elastic tissue stains of only limited use in identifying these vessels. Immunohistochemical stains for actin are more likely to be positive, but often these peculiar capsular vessels lack an elastic muscular layer altogether, despite their relatively large size. Search for endothelial markers—such as CD31, factor VIII-related antigen, and *Ulex europaeus*—is more rewarding.[449,450,467] Of these, we prefer CD31 because it is less labile than the others and almost as

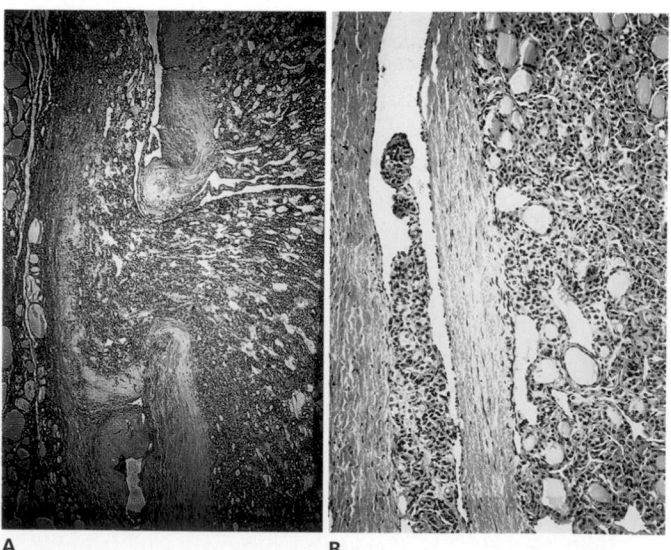

A　　　　　　　B

Fig. 9.52 Capsular (**A**) and vascular (**B**) invasion in minimally invasive follicular carcinoma.

specific under the circumstances. Interruption of the capsule must be full thickness for the process to qualify as capsular invasion.[451] After it has violated a narrow segment of the capsule, it is common for the tumor to expand in a mushroom-like fashion in the adjacent area. As a result, a tangential section might show a tumor nodule outside the main mass, separated from it by an intact capsule, deeper sections being necessary to demonstrate the focus of capsular rupture. Another interesting phenomenon is the occasional formation of a second (or even a third) capsule in the advancing edge of the tumor that has already violated the original capsule.

Foci of capsular invasion should be distinguished from capsular rupture resulting from a fine needle aspiration procedure. The latter should be suspected when the area in question has a fissure-like quality, contains foci of recent or old hemorrhage, and exhibits florid stromal reparative changes. Another mimic is represented by the pseudoinvasion resulting from herniation of tumor tissue when the section for histology has been taken perpendicularly to a previous capsule cut made by the surgeon or pathologist on the fresh specimen; to avoid this trap, it is better to disregard the areas at the very edge of the section, in which the tumor appears to be coating an abrupt cross section of the capsule. A mimic of vascular invasion is represented by the sometimes extremely florid proliferation of endothelial and smooth muscle cells of capsular vessels, which may even acquire a Kaposi's-like appearance; this peculiar change can also be seen in follicular adenomas, but with a much lower frequency[441,470] (Fig. 9.53).

It follows from the previous comments that thorough sampling of encapsulated follicular lesions is of paramount importance[446,459] (see Appendix B). Evans[445] has made the interesting observation, confirmed by others,[476] that the capsule of follicular carcinoma tends to be thicker and more irregular than that of adenoma. A common problem is the handling of well-differentiated follicular neoplasm in which capsular interruption is "incomplete," in the sense of involving only the inner half or being represented by tumor islands embedded within, a situation in which there is considerable interobserver variability.[451a] The group of thyroid pathologists mentioned in the preceding section[472] recommended the adoption of the following terminology for this situation:

- For tumors showing *definite* capsular invasion: **Follicular carcinoma**.
- For tumors showing *questionable* capsular invasion: **Follicular tumor of uncertain malignant potential (FT-UMP)** if papillary carcinoma-type nuclear changes are *absent*, and **well-differentiated tumor of uncertain malignant potential (WDT-UMP)** if those nuclear changes are *questionable*.

Widely invasive follicular carcinoma is the high-risk counterpart of the minimally invasive subtype.[444a] It shows widespread infiltration of blood vessels and/or adjacent thyroid tissue. It often lacks encapsulation altogether. In our experience, many of these tumors are poorly differentiated carcinomas at the cytoarchitectural level (see p. 549). It has been suggested that grossly encapsulated tumors showing *extensive* blood vessel invasion (4 vessels or more) should be placed in this category because of their similar natural history.

It seems to us that a clinically more significant division of follicular carcinoma is one that will take into account the following considerations:

1 There are two major categories, of widely different prognostic import: the encapsulated tumors, in which one has to look for invasion; and the widely invasive tumors, in which one has a look for a capsule;
2 Among the former, there are marked prognostic differences among those that show invasion of **only** the capsule, and those that show vascular invasion, with or without capsular invasion;

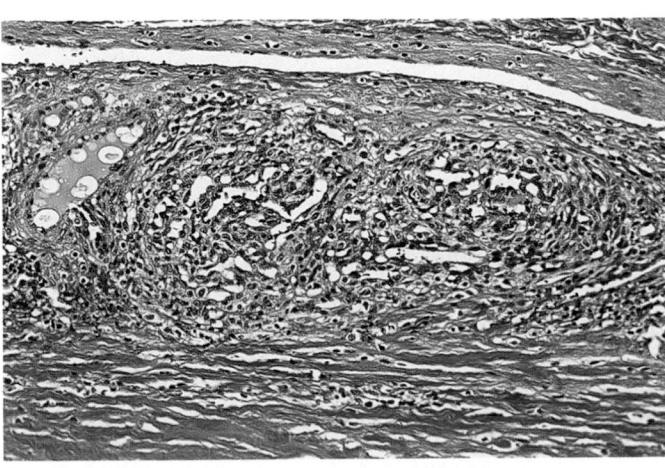
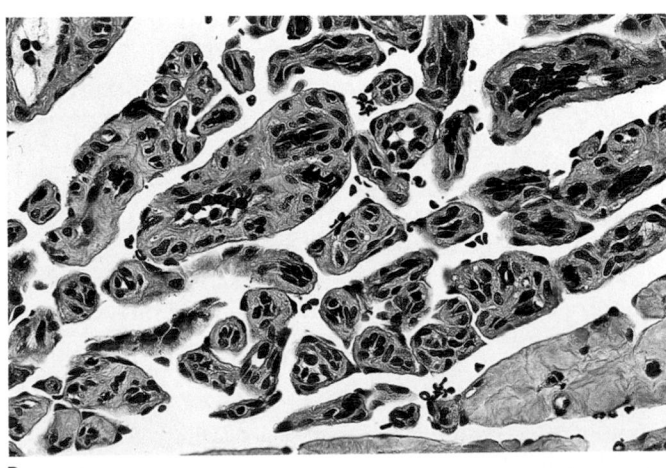

A

B

Fig. 9.53 A and **B**, Reactive vascular proliferation in the capsule of a follicular neoplasm. On high power (**B**), the lesion has a papillary configuration.

3 Among those with vascular invasion, there is a prognostic difference depending on the number of vessels involved.

The classification in question, which represents a departure from the classic scheme and which we offer for the consideration of the readers, is the following:

Follicular carcinoma
  Encapsulated
    With capsular invasion only
    With limited (<4) vascular invasion
    With extensive (≥4) vascular invasion
  Widely invasive

* * *

In contrast to papillary carcinomas, follicular carcinomas of either subtype are almost always solitary and practically never occult. Metastases are usually blood-borne (particularly to lung and bones) rather than to regional nodes.[460,469] The skeletal metastases are usually multicentric but have a predilection for the shoulder girdle, sternum, skull, and iliac bone.[462,465] Sometimes they pulsate because of their vascularity, a feature they share with metastatic renal cell carcinoma. These metastases have a strong affinity for radioiodine and—curiously—may exhibit a better differentiated appearance than the primary tumor, to the point of looking like normal thyroid as an expression of terminal differentiation (so-called "metastasizing adenoma," "malignant adenoma," or "metastasizing goiter"). The majority, however, have poorly differentiated features, at least at the architectural level.[469] Thyroglobulin and/or TTF-1 staining is essential in confirming the thyroid origin of a metastatic tumor. These metastases are common in the widely invasive type, occur in fewer than 5% of the minimally invasive tumors *with* blood vessel invasion, and develop in fewer than 1% of the tumors diagnosed as carcinoma *only* on the basis of minimal capsular invasion.[443,453,458] Whether DNA evaluation will provide information of diagnostic or prognostic significance for this group of tumors still needs to be determined, but on the whole the results to date are not very encouraging.[452,455,464] Genotyping for allelic loss after microdissection is also being tried, with interesting preliminary results.[451b]

As expected, the prognosis of follicular carcinoma is directly related to the degree of encapsulation, hence the important distinction between minimally invasive and widely invasive types.[442,461] Among the former, those showing *only* capsular invasion (without blood vessel invasion) result in metastases in an infinitesimal number of cases.[443,448,453,468,471] We have already indicated the proposal—to which we strongly adhere—not to call carcinomas those tumors in which the evidence of capsular invasion is questionable.[472] As a matter of fact, we are personally inclined to extend that designation even to tumors in which that invasion is complete *as long as*: (1)

there is no blood vessel invasion; (2) the nuclear features of papillary carcinoma are absent; (3) the tumor is well differentiated throughout, both at an architectural and cytologic level.[444]

The reciprocal situation, in which we also have taken a position slightly different from the current consensus, concerns the follicular neoplasm without evidence of capsular or blood vessel invasion but with sufficient cytoarchitectural abnormalities (in the form of solid/trabecular pattern of growth, mitotic activity, necrosis, etc.) to indicate that it represents a *noninvasive follicular carcinoma*.

Among clearly invasive tumors, the prognosis correlates with the degree of architectural and cytologic differentiation, a concept which merges with those of grading of thyroid carcinoma and the existence of a poorly differentiated category (see p. 549).

Hürthle cell (oncocytic) tumors
The oncocyte
Since the presence of oncocytes is the common denominator for all the tumors included in this section, it seems appropriate to begin with a description of these cells, which in the thyroid (as already indicated on p. 516) are usually but inaccurately designated as Hürthle cells. Their cytoplasmic granularity is due to the accumulation of mitochondria, many of which show a variety of morphologic abnormalities both on transmission and scanning electron microscopy[478,484,490] (Fig. 9.54). It is well to remember that the granularity should have a deeply eosinophilic quality in H&E-stained sections; otherwise, alternative possibilities such as (oncocytic) medullary carcinoma should be considered. Secondary clearing is not uncommon, usually due to mitochondrial swelling. We view the "tall cell" that defines a subtype of papillary carcinoma (see p. 539) as a variant of the oncocyte, a concept supported by the existence of combined tall cell–oncocytic tumors.[479] Immunohistochemically, oncocytes show reactivity for thyroglobulin (although to a lesser degree than nononcocytic follicular cells), mitochondrial antigens, glucose transporter 4 (GLUT 4), and keratin.[489,491] Regarding the latter, CK14 is emerging as a selective marker for these cells.[492] Oncocytes are also immunoreactive to CEA, S-100 protein and—surprisingly—HMB-45[477,482]; some of these reactivities may not be specific, inasmuch as oncocytes tend to show a sometimes intense spurious stain with a large variety of markers. Neoplastic oncocytes show a decrease or loss of *bcl*-2 expression, suggesting that this represents an early event in tumorigenesis.[483,488]

Not surprisingly, the total amount of mitochondrial DNA (mDNA) is increased in Hürthle cell tumors.[494] This is accompanied by mDNA somatic mutations, in the form of point mutations and large deletions.[485,486] A particularly frequent alteration is the so-called "mDNA common deletion," which is, however, not specific for

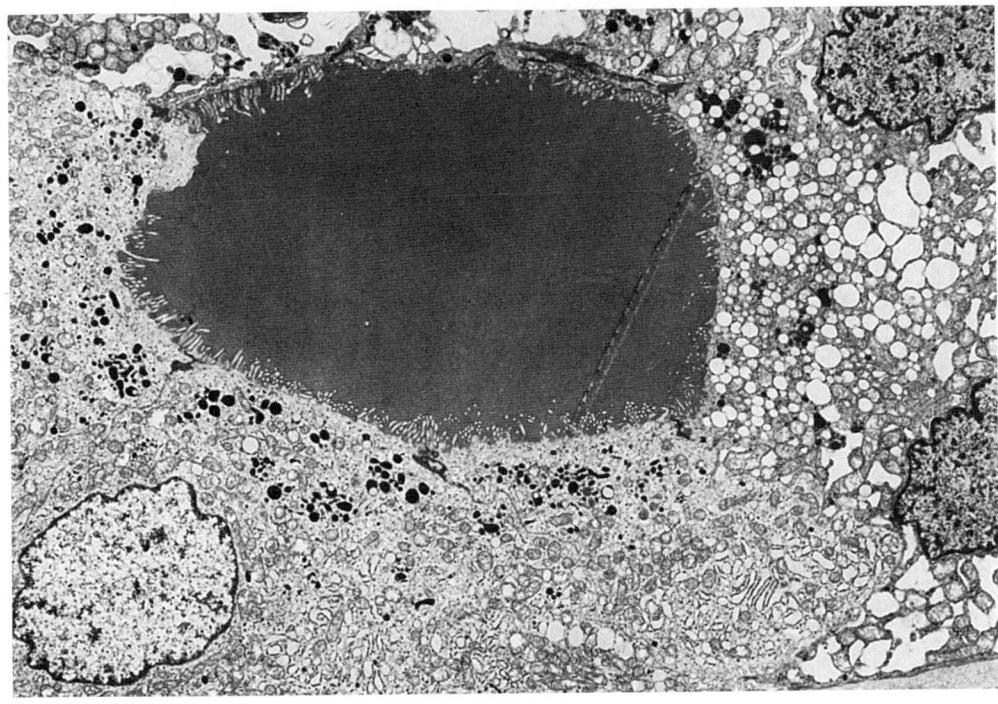

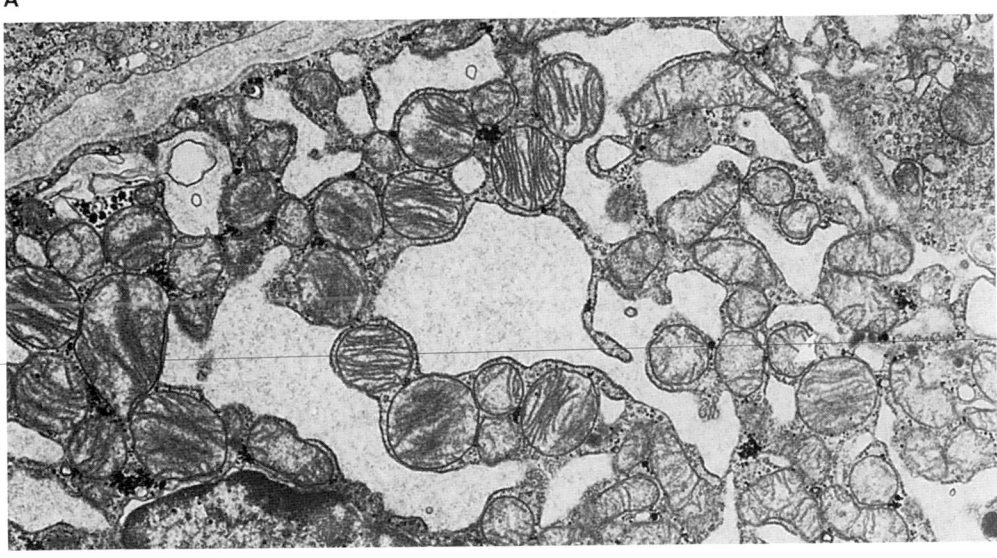

Fig. 9.54 Hürthle cell tumor of thyroid gland. **A,** The cytoplasm is packed with mitochondria. Secretory product is located toward the lumen, which is filled with colloid. **B,** Variably sized mitochondria with prominent cristae. (**A,** ×3840; **B,** ×11,230)

these tumors.[485] Alterations of chromosomal DNA are also frequent, including allelic losses in various chromosomes, particularly 22 and 10,[481,487,494] as well as multiple chromosomal gains.[493]

A somewhat disturbing observation that was recently made concerns the fact that neoplastic (but not hyperplastic) Hürthle cells frequently exhibit the same type of *RET/PTC* oncogene activation that characterizes papillary carcinoma and which has long been regarded as being restricted to the latter tumor type.[480]

Clinicopathologic features

Tumors included in this category are those composed exclusively or predominantly (over 75%) of follicular cells exhibiting oncocytic features. Some authors (includ-

ing the World Health Organization Committee for the Histological Typing of Thyroid Tumors) do not view these tumors as a distinct type and place them in one of the existing tumor categories (i.e., follicular or papillary), depending on their pattern of growth. We think that their morphologic features and natural history are distinctive enough for them to be regarded as a special group.[502,511,521]

Most patients are adults, and there is a predominance of females. Grossly, the tumors are characteristically solid, tan, and well vascularized (Fig. 9.55). Most are well encapsulated throughout; the invasive tumors tend to grow into the parenchyma in a multinodular fashion that can be very deceptive in that it can be underinterpreted as nodular hyperplasia. Microscopically, the pattern of growth may be follicular, trabecular/solid, or papillary.

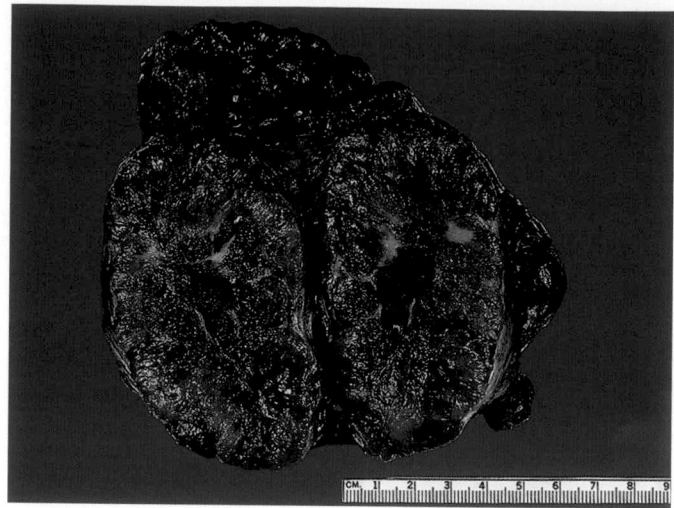

Fig. 9.55 Gross appearance of Hürthle cell carcinoma. The cut surface shows a tan color and a necrotic hemorrhagic center.

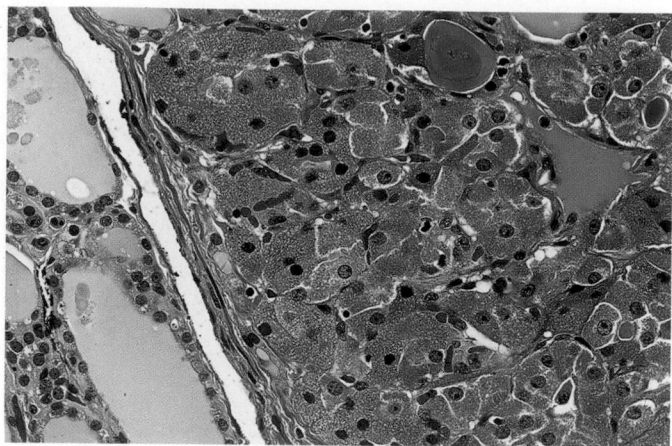

Fig. 9.56 Hürthle cell adenoma showing follicular pattern of growth and intact thin capsule.

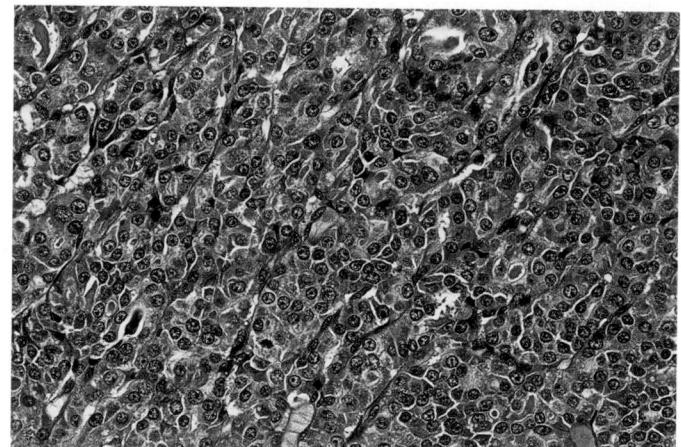

Fig. 9.57 Hürthle cell carcinoma with a predominantly solid pattern of growth. Other sections showed capsular invasion.

The former is by far the most common. The follicles, when large, are separated by long and thin fibrovascular septa that simulate papillae when cut tangentially. Another diagnostic trap is the presence of inspissated intraluminal colloid with concentric laminations, having an appearance similar to that of the psammoma bodies associated with papillary carcinoma, from which they are distinguished because of their location. The nuclei may show pleomorphism and prominent nucleoli, with occurrence of isolated bizarre forms, these not being features of malignancy by themselves. Immuno-histochemically, there is reactivity for thyroglobulin, although in lesser degree than in conventional follicular lesions. Positivity for CEA, S-100 protein, and—surprisingly—HMB-45 protein has also been described.[495,509] At the molecular level, overexpression of the E2F-1 transcription factor (an effector in the retinoblastoma pathway and also involved in apoptosis) has been documented.[522a]

We believe that Hürthle cell tumors with follicular or solid/trabecular patterns—which constitute the large majority—should be evaluated and diagnosed using criteria analogous to those used for follicular neoplasms of non-Hürthle cell types; that is, capsular and/or blood vessel invasion should be used as the main criterion for malignancy. We do not adhere to the extreme view (no longer held by its original proponents) that all Hürthle cell neoplasms are to be regarded as malignant or potentially malignant.[512] Actually, the majority behave in a benign fashion and are properly designated as *Hürthle cell adenoma*[499–502] (Fig. 9.56). Tumors with clearcut capsular and/or blood vessel invasion are designated as *Hürthle cell carcinoma*. As a group, the carcinomas occur in an older age group, show a lesser degree of female predominance, are larger, and tend to have a solid/trabecular rather than a follicular pattern of growth (Fig. 9.57). The cells of carcinoma are often smaller than those of

adenoma and have a higher nucleocytoplasmic ratio, a feature also noticeable on cytologic examination. In the presence of any of these features, the search for capsular and/or vascular invasion should be particularly thorough (Fig. 9.58). We and others have used terms such as *Hürthle cell neoplasm* or *atypical Hürthle cell adenoma* for the tumors that exhibit one or more of these features but lack unequivocal signs of malignancy.[516] In our experience and that of others, these tumors practically never metastasize, and it is therefore safe to treat them as adenomas.[503] Whether special procedures such as galectin-3 immunostaining will help in achieving a sharper separation remains to be proven.[514]

At the other end of the spectrum are the Hürthle cell carcinomas that are highly invasive, with a predominantly or exclusively solid/trabecular pattern of growth, and mitotically active; these are to be placed in a poorly differentiated category and regarded as high-risk tumors.[515]

Another problem associated with oncocytic thyroid tumors is related to their tendency to undergo massive infarct-type necrosis, often following fine needle aspiration. This phenomenon, which is analogous to that seen

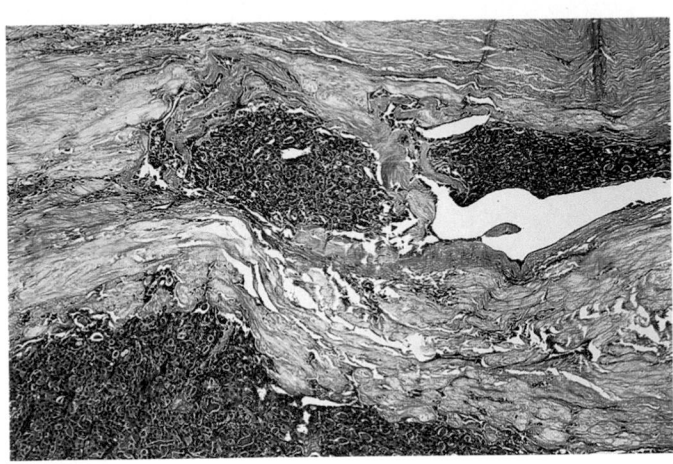

Fig. 9.58 Hürthle cell carcinoma. Same case as Fig. 9.57, showing marked blood vessel invasion.

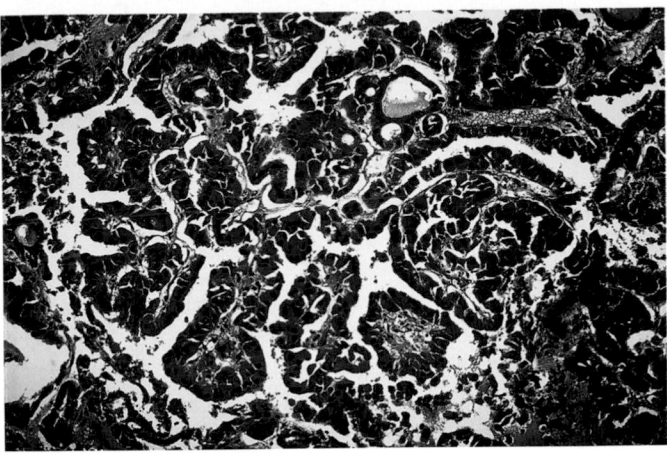

Fig. 9.59 Hürthle cell neoplasm with a papillary pattern of growth. The nuclear features of the papillary family of neoplasms are absent, and therefore this tumor should not be classified as a papillary carcinoma.

in oncocytic tumors at other sites and which is probably the consequence of the great sensitivity of oncocytes to ischemia, can render the identification of the tumor difficult or impossible. However, the shadows of the tumor cells can sometimes still be discerned by simply lowering the microscope condenser, and there can be a surprising retention of immunohistochemical markers, particularly keratin.[510] It is important to realize that under these circumstances the capsule can become very irregular and entrap within its substance thyroid follicles with "regenerative" or "reactive" atypia, including some nuclear clearing and overlapping; these changes should not be overinterpreted as carcinoma.

Hürthle cell adenomas are almost always cured by excision. The carcinomas are rather aggressive neoplasms, with a 5-year mortality rate ranging between 20% and 40%.[506,507] This may be at least partially due to the inclusion of the just mentioned poorly differentiated types. When Hürthle cell carcinomas and follicular carcinomas are stratified according to extent of invasion and degree of differentiation, the behavioral differences among them tend to disappear.[504] Metastases occur mainly in lungs and bone and less commonly in cervical nodes.[517,523] Older patient age, large tumor size, extrathyroidal extension and metastases represent unfavorable prognostic factors[522a]; in contrast to papillary carcinoma, the latter applies not only to distant metastases but also to regional lymph node involvement.[520] Analysis of DNA ploidy may prove of some prognostic significance; preliminary observations have shown a high incidence of invasive growth in aneuploid tumors.[498,505,518] Proliferative activity is higher in the carcinomas than in the adenomas, but the differences are not substantial enough for this parameter to have much diagnostic or prognostic utility.[503,513,522]

A difficult diagnostic problem is represented by the rare Hürthle cell tumors composed entirely of papillae (as opposed to the more common pseudopapillary formations previously mentioned).[497,519] Those that have the

nuclear features of papillary carcinoma should be placed in the latter category, as already indicated. Those that do not should be handled as follicular tumors (Fig. 9.59). In other words, malignancy should be largely based on the presence of capsular and/or vascular invasion. In our experience, those tumors that were encapsulated have behaved in a benign fashion,[496] whereas those that were invasive have behaved in an aggressive fashion, perhaps more so than conventional papillary carcinomas.[508]

Clear cell tumors

Clear cell changes can occur in thyroid neoplasms of various microscopic types and as a consequence of a variety of mechanisms, which include cytoplasmic vesicles (of mitochondrial, reticulum endoplasmic, or Golgi origin[524,531]) and accumulation of glycogen, lipid, thyroglobulin, or "mucin" (Fig. 9.60). The natural history of these tumors is determined by their basic nature rather than the presence of, degree of, or reason for cytoplasmic clearing

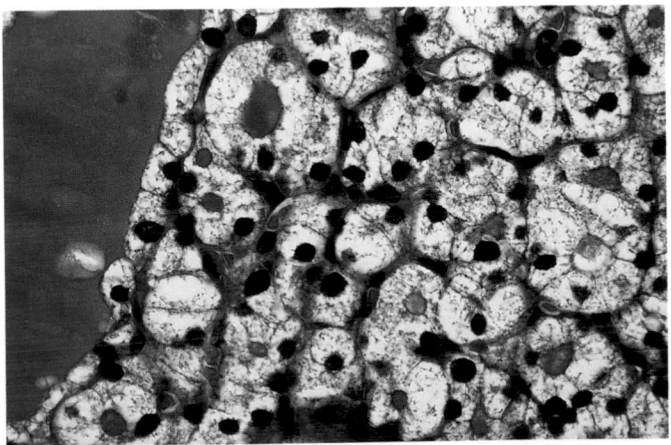

Fig. 9.60 Follicular neoplasm with cytoplasmic clear change. The clearing has a finely granular quality.

in them. Therefore *clear cell carcinoma* should not be viewed as a specific tumor type.[524,533]

The neoplasm most prone to undergo secondary clear cell changes is Hürthle cell tumor, this being the result of vesicular swelling of mitochondria[524] (Fig. 9.61). The oxyphilic and clear cell changes may be seen in cells facing each other or even in different regions of the same cell[526] (Fig. 9.62). Clear cell changes can also occur in

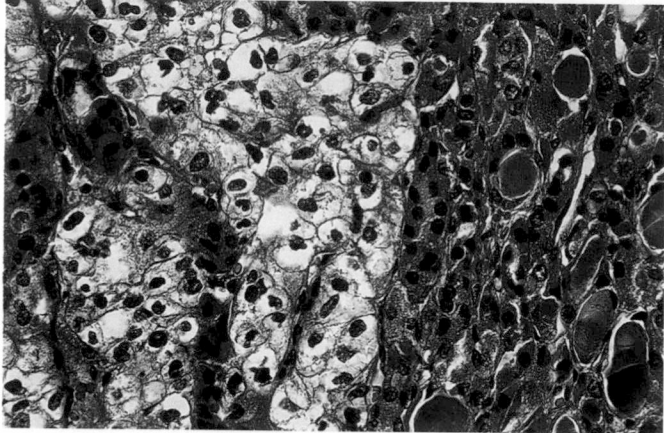

Fig. 9.61 Hürthle cell neoplasm with focal cytoplasmic clear change.

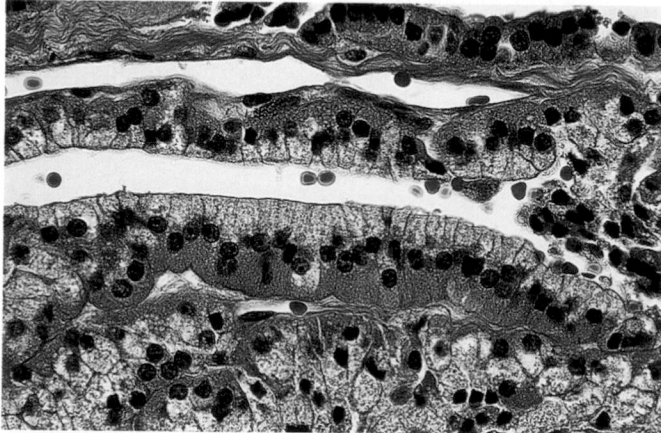

Fig. 9.62 Hürthle cell neoplasm showing oncocytic features in the basal half of the tumor cells and clearing of the apical half.

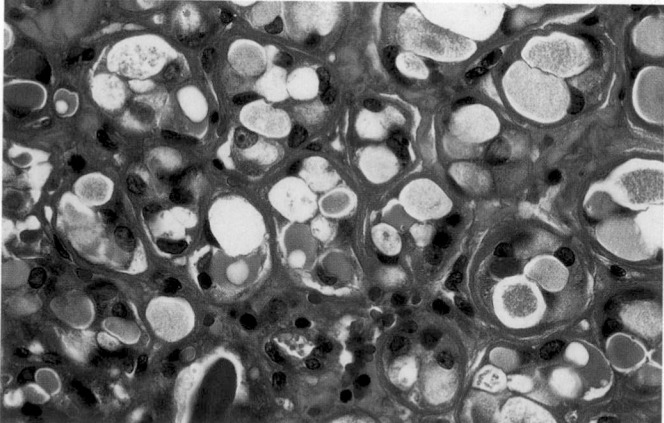

Fig. 9.63 So-called signet ring adenoma, resulting from intracytoplasmic accumulation of thyroglobulin.

follicular adenomas and carcinomas (usually because of vesicles of either mitochondrial or granular endoplasmic reticulum derivation),[530] papillary carcinoma (usually because of glycogen accumulation),[537] undifferentiated carcinoma (also the result of glycogen overload), and—exceptionally—medullary carcinoma.[528] Except for the latter, thyroglobulin stain is usually positive in these neoplasms, although sometimes in a focal and faint fashion.[524,525] Although the presence of clear cell change in a follicular neoplasm per se is not an indication of malignancy, it occurs more frequently in carcinomas than in adenomas and should therefore be viewed with suspicion when encountered.

A peculiar variant of thyroid tumor with clear cell changes is the *signet ring type,* in which the formation of variously sized cytoplasmic vacuoles results in a configuration reminiscent of signet ring cells or lipoblasts (Fig. 9.63). Most of these signet ring neoplasms are adenomas, but carcinomas with this appearance also occur.[529,534] Immunohistochemically, the vacuoles contain intracellular thyroglobulin.[524] The stroma is usually heavily hyalinized and with punctate calcification, suggesting that the signet ring change may be of degenerative nature and the expression of an arrest of folliculogenesis.[529] Some of this material has been found to react positively with mucin stains.[532]

Another rare form of clear cell change is that seen in the *lipid-rich cell adenoma,* in which the cytoplasmic vacuolization is due to the accumulation of neutral fat.[535,536]

The main differential diagnosis of primary thyroid tumors with clear cells is with parathyroid neoplasms and metastatic renal cell carcinoma[524,533] (see p. 568). When struggling with this problem, the pathologist should keep in mind the fact that both of the lesions can be intrathyroidal, whereas thyroid clear cell tumors can occur in ectopic locations.[527]

It should also be noted that cytoplasmic clear cell changes can also occur in non-neoplastic thyroid disorders, including Hashimoto's thyroiditis and dyshormonogenetic goiter.[524]

Squamous cell, mucinous, and related tumors

Squamous cells can be found in the thyroid as a result of persistence of thyroglossal duct or structures derived from the branchial pouch (such as thymic epithelium) or as an expression of squamous metaplasia in Hashimoto's thyroiditis, papillary carcinoma, or other conditions.[550] Pure **squamous cell carcinomas** are exceptional.[547,549] Some have been associated with leukocytosis and hypercalcemia.[557] Most high-grade thyroid tumors with squamous foci blend with areas of undifferentiated (anaplastic) carcinoma and are generally placed in the latter category because of their similar natural history.[541] Indeed, many of them are seen to develop from papillary carcinoma in a fashion analogous to that of undifferentiated carcinoma.[555] It has been suggested that the tall cell variant of papillary carcinoma has a particular tendency to evolve into the spindle cell type of squamous cell carcinoma.[540]

In the presence of an obvious squamous cell carcinoma involving the thyroid, the possibility should also be considered of secondary direct involvement from a tumor of larynx or trachea or a metastasis from lung or other sites.

Mucoepidermoid carcinoma has been described as a low-grade thyroid neoplasm combining foci of squamous change with mucin production and lacking immunoreactivity for thyroglobulin[544,548,552,560] (Fig. 9.64). It has been postulated that these tumors originate from solid cell nests, which in turn are thought to be of ultimobranchial body derivation.[546,556] The clinical features of the reported cases and the presence in some of these tumors of ground glass nuclei and psammoma bodies suggest that they may represent instead papillary carcinomas with an extreme degree of squamous and mucinous metaplasia. Indeed, cases of papillary carcinoma with prominent mucoepidermoid features have been described.[539] Furthermore, their P-cadherin neo-expression and the marked abnormalities of the E-cadherin/catenins complex are similar to those seen in another subtype of papillary carcinoma associated with severe squamous metaplastic changes, i.e., the diffuse sclerosing variant.[559]

A distinctive variant of this tumor is represented by the **sclerosing mucoepidermoid carcinoma with eosinophilia**.[538,542] This tumor arises in thyroid glands affected by Hashimoto's thyroiditis, often of the fibrous type (Fig. 9.65). Microscopically, strands and nests of squamous tumor cells with mild to moderate pleomorphism are seen infiltrating a dense fibrohyaline stroma. Foci of definite squamous differentiation and mucin secretion are often present, sometimes admixed with

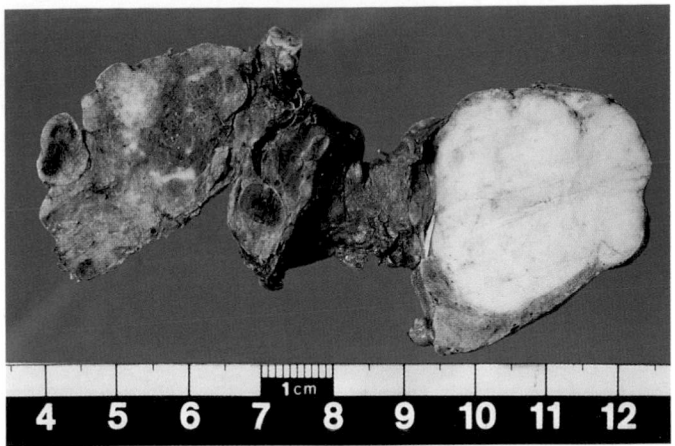

Fig. 9.65 Sclerosing mucoepidermoid carcinoma with eosinophilia occurring in a thyroid gland affected by Hashimoto's thyroiditis. The neoplasm, which almost entirely replaces a lobe, has a well-circumscribed quality. (Courtesy of Dr. Josie Zaroway, Edmonton, Canada)

mucin secretion. There is a constant and often striking infiltration by eosinophils, which tend to congregate around the more atypical tumor cells, thus helping to locate them on low-power examination (Fig. 9.66). Some of these features can be appreciated in fine needle aspiration material.[545] In retrospect, the term *sclerosing squamoid tumor with eosinophilia* that we had originally used describes more accurately the morphologic appearance of this tumor. Immunohistochemically, there is strong reactivity for keratin, but only focally if at all for TTF-1, and usually none for thyroglobulin. The clinical course is generally indolent, but cases with distant metastases and aggressive behavior have been reported.[561] The lymph node metastases may simulate microscopically Hodgkin's lymphoma.[563]

A few cases of **mucinous carcinoma** lacking a squamous component and exhibiting varying degrees of differentiation have been described.[553,562] In this regard, it is pertinent to note that the thyroglobulin molecule contains variable amounts of carbohydrates that may result in some degree of alcianophilia.[558]

Another rare entity occurring in or around the thyroid that may exhibit squamous differentiation is the malignant neoplasm we have chosen to designate as *carcinoma showing thymus-like differentiation* (CASTLE).[543] This tumor (of which a cystic variant has been described[554]) could be viewed as an ectopic thymic carcinoma.[551] It is described in more detail in Chapter 8, together with other tumors showing thymic or related branchial pouch differentiation that can occur in the neck, often in close anatomic relationship with the thyroid gland.[543]

Poorly differentiated carcinoma

In the traditional scheme of thyroid neoplasia, malignant tumors of follicular cells are divided into a well-differentiated type, composed of papillary and follicular

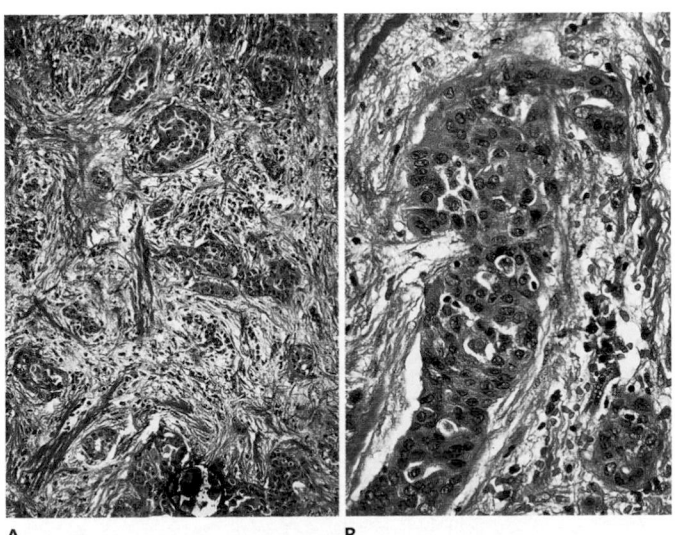

A   B

Fig. 9.64 A and **B**, Mucoepidermoid carcinoma of thyroid. (Slide courtesy of Dr. K. Franssila, Helsinki)

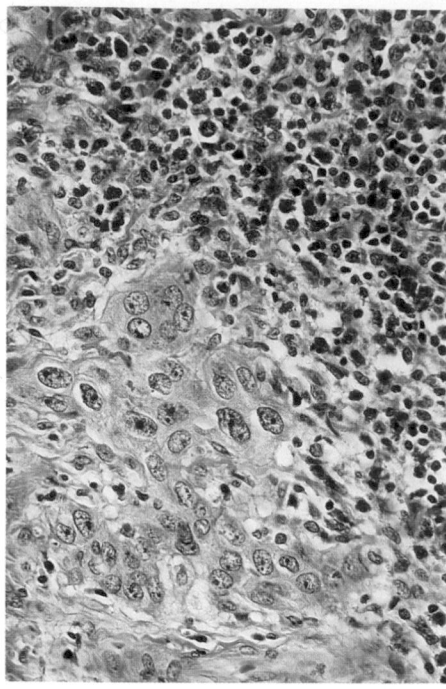

A

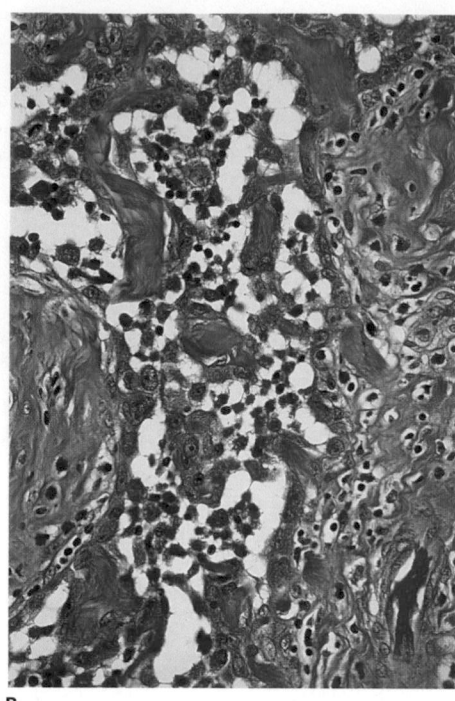

B

Fig. 9.66 A and **B,** Sclerosing mucoepidermoid carcinoma with eosinophilia. **A,** The pattern of growth is solid and squamoid and is associated with a massive eosinophilic infiltration. **B,** The formation of tissue spaces results in a pseudovascular appearance.

carcinoma, and an undifferentiated or anaplastic type. There is, however, a group of tumors that fall in between these two extremes, in terms of both morphologic appearance and behavior.[568,581] We have identified one such type under the descriptive name of **insular carcinoma**.[568] The tumor occurs in an older group than the well-differentiated tumors (although it can also occur in adolescents[570]), and is usually grossly invasive (although it can also be encapsulated). Microscopically, the distinguishing features are a nesting ("insular") pattern of growth, solid to microfollicular arrangement, small uniform tumor cells, variable mitotic activity, and fresh tumor necrosis resulting in a peritheliomatous pattern (Figs 9.67 to 9.69). Some of the so-called "compact" types of undifferentiated small cell carcinoma of older publications probably belong to this category. The insu-

lar pattern may result in a mistaken diagnosis of medullary carcinoma. Immunohistochemically, there is reactivity for thyroglobulin and TTF-1 but not for calcitonin (Fig. 9.70). However, there is often focal reactivity for neuroendocrine markers.[584] These tumors have been found to express bcl-2 in over 80% of cases, in contrast with the rarity of this event in undifferentiated (anaplastic) carcinoma; p53 may also be expressed but is restricted to the foci of infiltrative growth.[577,579]

The cytologic features as seen in fine needle aspiration include high cellularity, necrotic background, low grade of atypia, nests, trabeculae and microfollicles, and cytoplasmic vacuoles.[569,578] In contrast to undifferentiated carcinoma, poorly differentiated tumors usually concentrate radioiodine, a feature that can be used for diagnostic and therapeutic purposes.[571,575] The behavior

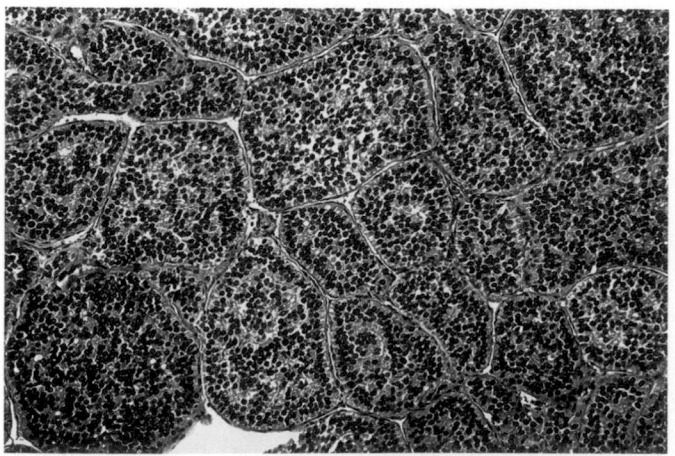

Fig. 9.67 Low-power view of poorly differentiated thyroid carcinoma, showing a well-developed insular pattern.

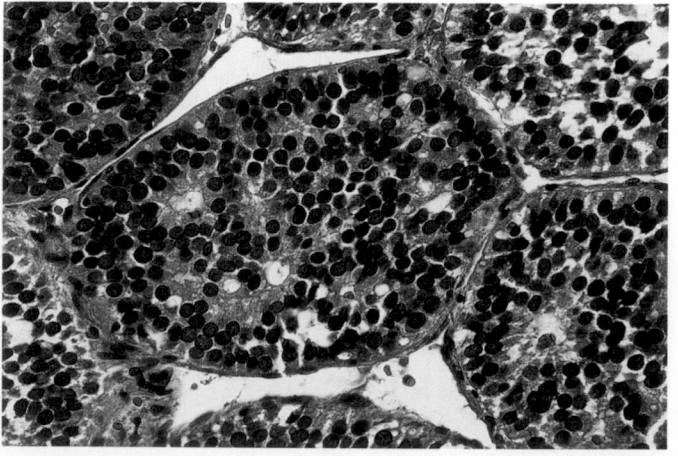

Fig. 9.68 On high power, the cells of insular carcinoma show round, medium-sized nuclei with a smooth contour and hyperchromasia.

is generally aggressive, with a high incidence of both nodal and blood-borne metastases.[568,574,576a] The unfavorable effect on prognosis of the insular pattern is not as pronounced when the tumor is largely encapsulated or when this pattern occurs as a focal change in an otherwise well-differentiated tumor.[566,583,587a]

Insular carcinoma, which is probably analogous to Langhans' *wuchernde Struma*, has a peculiar geographic distribution, in the sense that it seems to be more common in some parts of Europe and South America than in the United States. It is probable that most of these tumors represent poorly differentiated forms of follicular carcinoma.[580] Others, however, are clearly poorly differentiated forms of papillary carcinoma; indeed, some of our cases coexisted with or were preceded by typical papillary carcinomas.[568] From a prognostic standpoint, the route by which they may have originated is less significant than the fact that they are poorly differentiated tumors.[564]

Other authors have also proposed the existence of poorly differentiated tumors, although using more inclusive morphologic criteria.[585,586] French authors[567,587] designate as "less differentiated" those follicular carcinomas exhibiting a trabecular pattern of growth (Fig. 9.71); Japanese authors[573,582] include in their category of poorly differentiated those follicular *or* papillary carcinomas showing solid, trabecular, and/or scirrhous patterns. Similarly, Italian authors[575] have identified a group of thyroid carcinomas having insular, trabecular, and/or solid features and placed them into a poorly differentiated category characterized by a high incidence of recurrence and metastases; they likened the tumor cells of these cases to the "primordial" follicular cells present in the early stages of thyroid development. Furthermore, and as already mentioned, thyroid tumors in the oncocytic (Hürthle cell) category can have poorly differentiated features and behave accordingly.[576]

An extremely unusual variation on the theme is the poorly differentiated carcinoma that has a rhabdoid phenotype.[565]

The existence of a group of thyroid carcinomas situated in between well-differentiated and anaplastic neoplasms is supported by a variety of biochemical markers, including p27kip1 (a cyclin-dependent kinase

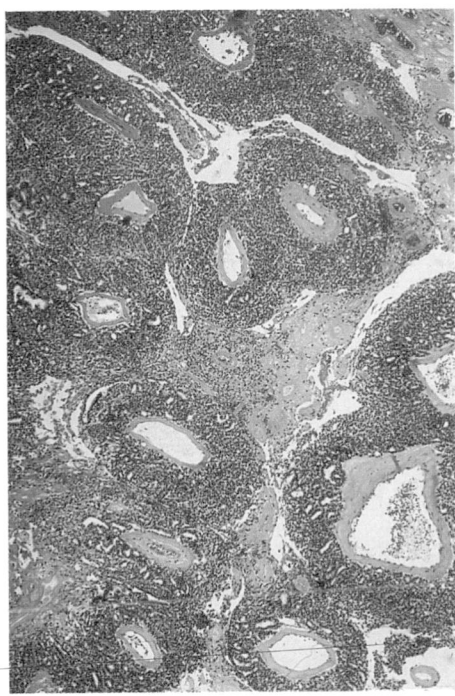

Fig. 9.69 Poorly differentiated (insular) carcinoma. The peritheliomatous pattern of growth results from necrosis associated with preservation of the tumor cells that are closer to nutrient vessels.

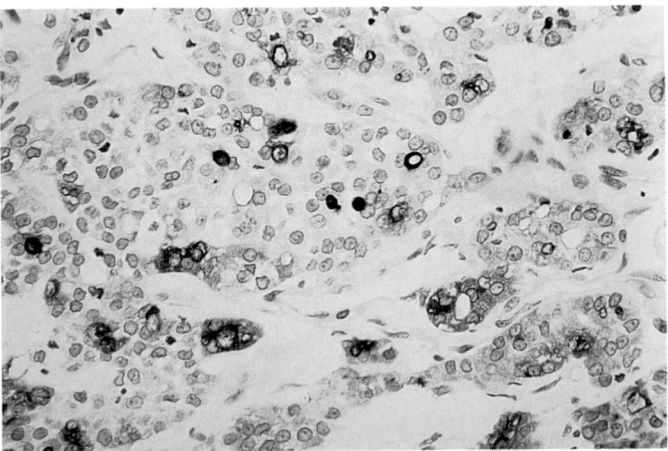

Fig. 9.70 Poorly differentiated (insular) carcinoma of thyroid showing immunoreactivity for thyroglobulin.

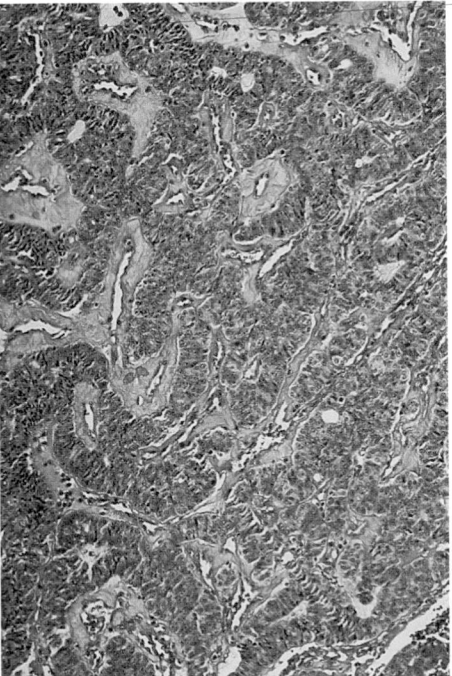

Fig. 9.71 Poorly differentiated carcinoma showing trabecular pattern of growth rather than insular formations.

inhibitor), MIB-1, and the reciprocal relationship that exists between bcl-2 and Bax (two proteins involved in cell death).[572]

Undifferentiated carcinoma

Undifferentiated (anaplastic) carcinoma usually presents in elderly patients as a rapidly growing mass associated with hoarseness, dysphagia, and dyspnea.[593] Extrathyroidal extension is encountered at the time of initial presentation in most of the cases. Grossly, a highly necrotic and hemorrhagic solid tumor mass is seen replacing large portions of the organ (Fig. 9.72).

Microscopically, the term undifferentiated or anaplastic carcinoma is used in the thyroid gland in connection with two major categories that sometimes coexist. The first is undifferentiated in the sense that it does not make follicles, papillae, or even trabeculae or nests, but the tumor still retains an unmistakable epithelial appearance on morphologic and immunohistochemical grounds. This pattern, which is referred to as **squamoid**, may blend with clearcut foci of keratinization.[593] A very unusual subset of this tumor type has a lymphoepithelioma-like appearance, but it does not seem to be related to the Epstein–Barr virus.[597,619]

The second category is actually composed of two patterns which are often seen together and which are sometimes grouped under the qualifier of *sarcomatoid*: **spindle cell** and **giant cell** (Figs 9.73 and 9.74). They may exhibit a fascicular or storiform pattern of growth, heavy neutrophilic infiltration, prominent vascularization, and cartilaginous/osseous metaplasia.[590] As a result, their appearance may closely simulate a large variety of soft tissue sarcomas, particularly malignant fibrous histiocytoma (including the inflammatory and myxoid variants),

angiosarcoma, malignant hemangiopericytoma, and fibrosarcoma.[593] Osteoclast-like multinucleated giant cells may be present, giving the tumor an appearance reminiscent of giant cell tumor of bone or soft tissues.[602] As in similar tumors in other organs these osteoclast-like giant cells are probably non-neoplastic but rather reactive cells of monocytic/histiocytic lineage derived from mononuclear cells through the mechanism of cell fusion.[600,615] Another variation on the theme of the spindle cell form of undifferentiated carcinoma is the *paucicellular variant*, which mimics Riedel's thyroiditis because of the extreme degree of fibrosis and hyalinization, and which is recognized because of the scattered atypia, areas of necrosis, vascular invasion, vascular permeation, and positivity for epithelial markers.[592,623]

It should be kept in mind that the majority of sarcoma-like tumors of the thyroid are, histogenetically speaking, undifferentiated carcinomas. Common and diagnostically useful features are palisading at the necrotic edges and tendency for the tumor cells to invade the wall of veins, replacing the normal smooth muscle. Ultrastructural examination will reveal markers suggestive of epithelial differentiation in about half of the cases.[593,606,613]

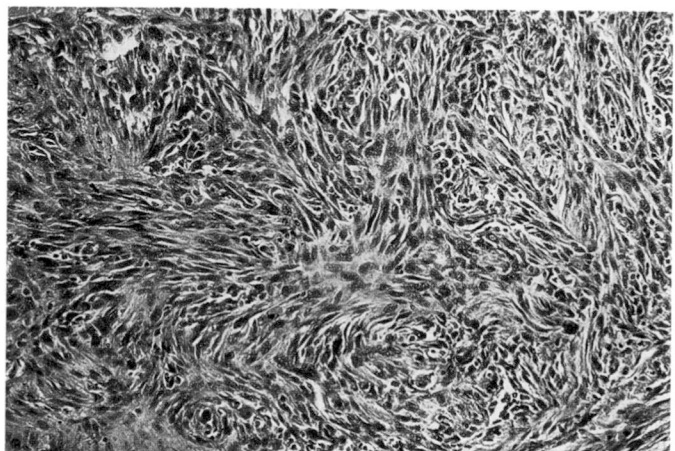

Fig. 9.73 Anaplastic carcinoma of the spindle cell type.

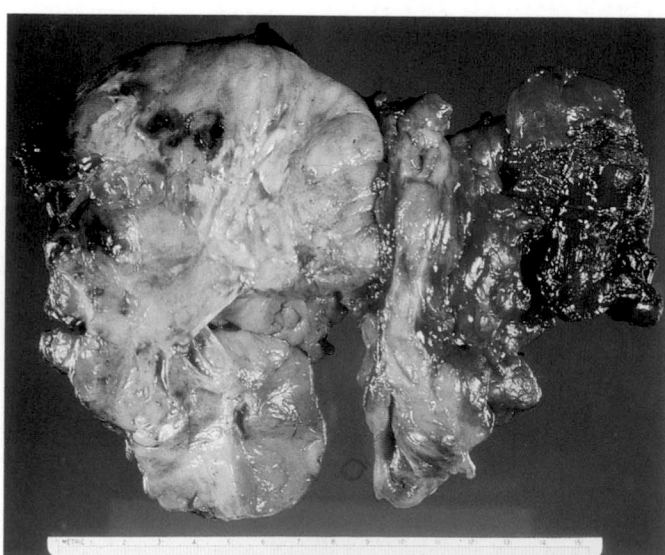

Fig. 9.72 Undifferentiated carcinoma of the thyroid entirely replacing the gland and extending into the surrounding skeletal muscle.

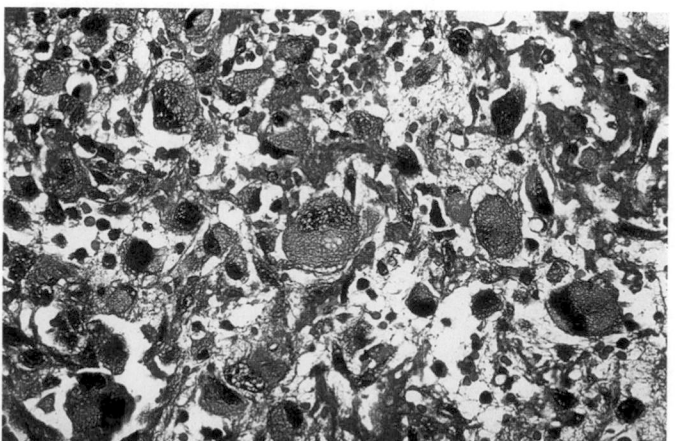

Fig. 9.74 Anaplastic carcinoma of giant cell type.

Immunohistochemically, the most useful marker is keratin, which will be found to be expressed in 50% to 100% of cases, according to the different series.[593,603,608,610] Vimentin is consistently present in the spindle cell component, there is scattered stromal (basement membrane-related) reactivity for laminin,[611] and focal EMA and CEA positivity may be found, especially in the squamoid type.[593] We and others have been generally unable to detect thyroglobulin in the truly undifferentiated cases[593,617] but other authors have apparently been more successful, even in metastatic foci[588,596,603,608,625] (Fig. 9.75). False-positive results may result from entrapment of normal thyroid, residual foci of better differentiated tumor, or diffusion of thyroglobulin from destroyed normal follicles into the tumor cells. Better results are allegedly obtained by searching for thyroglobulin mRNA by in situ hybridization.[616] As far as TTF-1 is concerned, this also is generally negative at the immunohistochemical level in undifferentiated carcinoma,[609] but in our hands it was detectable in a small percentage of cases, particularly those with a squamoid pattern.

Most if not all undifferentiated thyroid carcinomas arise as a result of anaplastic transformation of a pre-existing well-differentiated tumor, usually papillary carcinoma (Fig. 9.76) but also follicular carcinoma, Hürthle cell carcinoma, and insular carcinoma.[599,601] A variation on the theme is represented by the already mentioned spindle cell squamous cell carcinoma developing from the tall cell variant of papillary carcinoma.[591] In most instances, the anaplastic transformation takes place in the primary tumor, but it can also occur in a metastatic focus. Thorough sampling may be necessary to detect the residual well-differentiated component.[604] It is likely that the sharply outlined sclerohyaline nodules present within undifferentiated carcinoma represent the burnt-out residue of such components.[593,594] Mutations of the *p53* gene have been found in a high percentage of undifferentiated carcinomas, leading to immunohistochemically detectable accumulation of the protein product in the cytoplasm[620]; interestingly, the fact that these mutations were not present in the residual papillary component suggests that they occurred *after* the development of the papillary carcinoma and that they played a role in the progression of this tumor.[598,605,612] At the cytogenetic level, recurrent aberrations of chromosomes 5 and 8 have been detected.[624]

In older classifications of undifferentiated carcinoma, a small cell type with either a diffuse or compact pattern of growth was often included. It has become apparent that nearly all of the former are in reality malignant lymphomas and that the majority of the latter represent small cell variants of medullary carcinomas or insular carcinomas. Therefore the use of the term "small cell thyroid carcinoma" without a qualifier should be discouraged.[593,618]

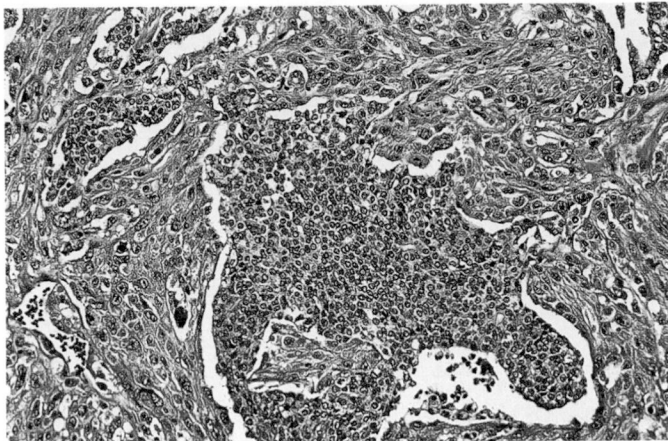

A

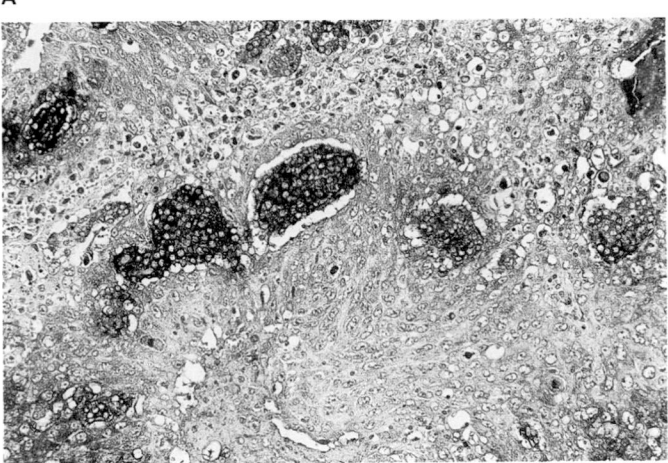

B

Fig. 9.75 A and **B,** Combined poorly differentiated and anaplastic thyroid carcinoma. Immunoreactivity for thyroglobulin is restricted to the poorly differentiated areas (**B**).

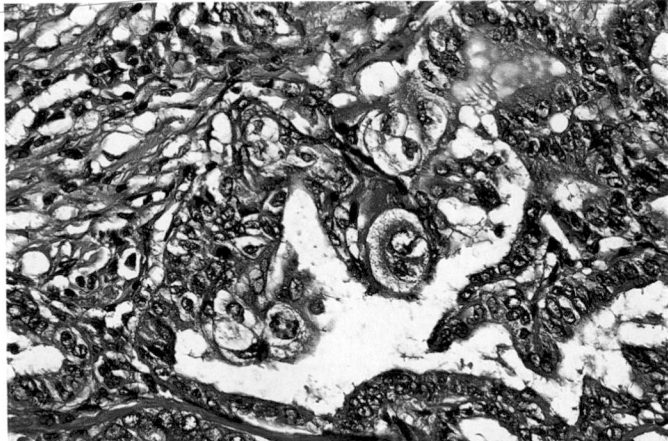

Fig. 9.76 Anaplastic thyroid carcinoma showing residual papillary carcinoma.

The evolution of all types of undifferentiated thyroid carcinoma is very rapid, with massive growth in the neck and infiltration of the ribbon muscles, esophagus, trachea, skin, and even contiguous bones. Nodal and distant metastases are also common.[614] The mortality rate is over 95%, the mean survival is less than 6 months, and the immediate cause of death is usually involvement of vital structures in the neck.[593,622] There is a slightly better chance of cure for patients in whom the undifferentiated component is only a focal change in an otherwise well-differentiated neoplasm.[589,595] Isolated successes have been obtained with a combination of surgery, radiation therapy, and chemotherapy.[607,621]

Medullary carcinoma and related neuroendocrine lesions

Medullary carcinoma

Morphologic features

Medullary carcinoma is the original and still the preferred term for a distinctive type of thyroid malignancy composed of C (parafollicular) cells; it has also been described as solid carcinoma, hyaline carcinoma, and C-cell carcinoma.[634] Grossly, the typical tumor is solid, firm, and nonencapsulated but relatively well circumscribed and has a gray to yellowish cut surface (Fig. 9.77). When the greatest diameter of the tumor is 1 cm or less (in analogy with the policy used with papillary carcinoma), the tumor is referred to as *medullary microcarcinoma*.[630] Exceptionally, the tumor is enveloped by a continuous fibrous capsule. This should be interpreted as an encapsulated medullary carcinoma and not as a medullary adenoma (see later section). Most tumors are located in the midportion or upper half of the gland, corresponding to a greater concentration of C cells in this region. Microscopically, the classic presentation is represented by a solid proliferation of round to polygonal cells of granular amphophilic cytoplasm and medium-sized nucleus, separated by a highly vascular stroma, hyalinized collagen, and amyloid[626] (Fig. 9.78). Coarse calcification is common and can be prominent enough to be detected radiographically.

The number of cytoarchitectural variations on this theme is very large. The pattern of growth can be carcinoid-like, paraganglioma-like, trabecular, glandular (tubular and follicular), or pseudopapillary[632,633,635,642] (Fig. 9.79). The stroma may be scanty, hemorrhagic, ossified, or edematous. The amyloid deposition may be widespread, limited to small psammomatoid concretions, or altogether absent. Sometimes this amyloid elicits a florid foreign body-type giant cell reaction. True psammoma bodies may be present. A heavy neutrophilic infiltrate is occasionally seen (so-called "inflammatory type"). The tumor cells may be plasmacytoid (because of nuclear peripheralization), spindle shaped, oncocytic, squamoid, or squamous, or exhibit bizarre features (so-called "anaplastic" or "giant cell" type, not to be equated with bona fide undifferentiated carcinoma).[637,641] The oncocytic variety is particularly treacherous because of its uncanny resemblance to oncocytic (Hürthle cell) neoplasms of follicular cell derivation[627] (Fig. 9.80). The diagnosis of medullary carcinoma should be suspected if

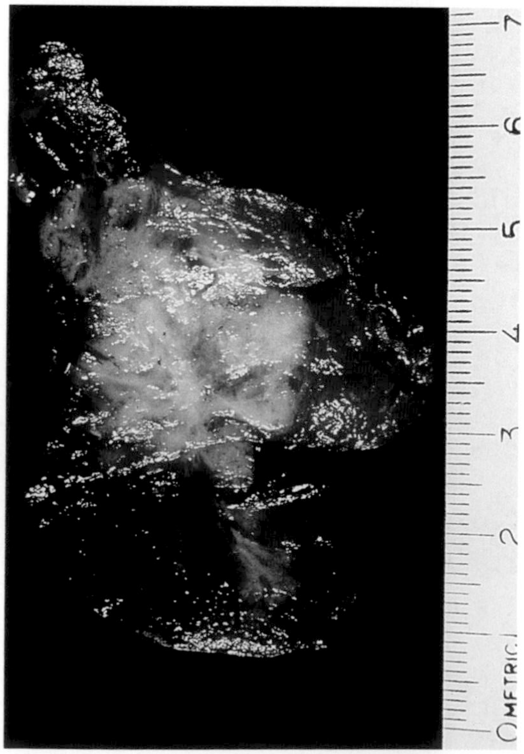

Fig. 9.77 Medullary carcinoma. Gross appearance of the tumor. Note its unencapsulated quality, solid appearance, and yellowish tan color.

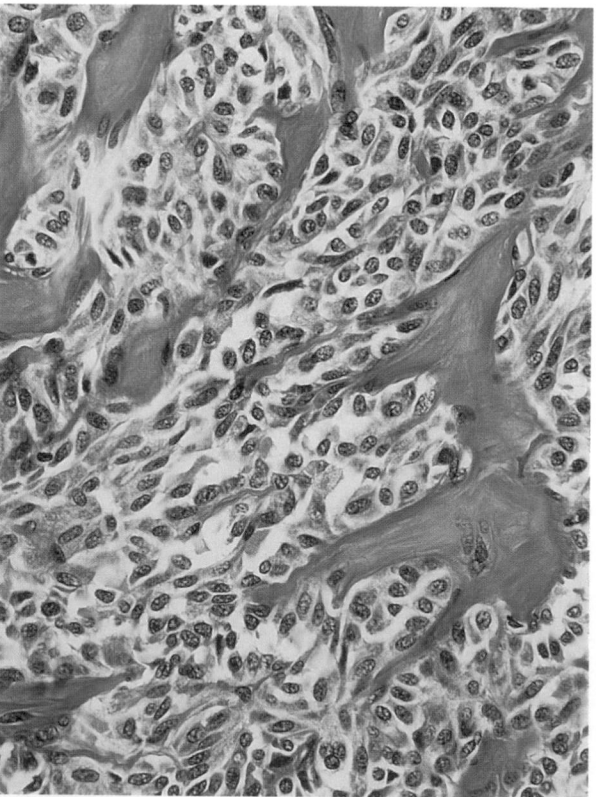

Fig. 9.78 Medullary carcinoma. Low-power microscopic view showing solid pattern of growth and deposition of amyloid.

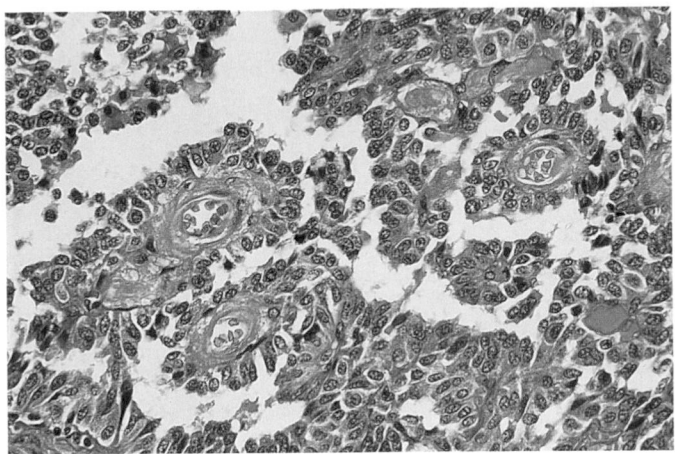

Fig. 9.79 Medullary carcinoma with pseudopapillary pattern of growth resulting from lack of cohesiveness of tumor cells.

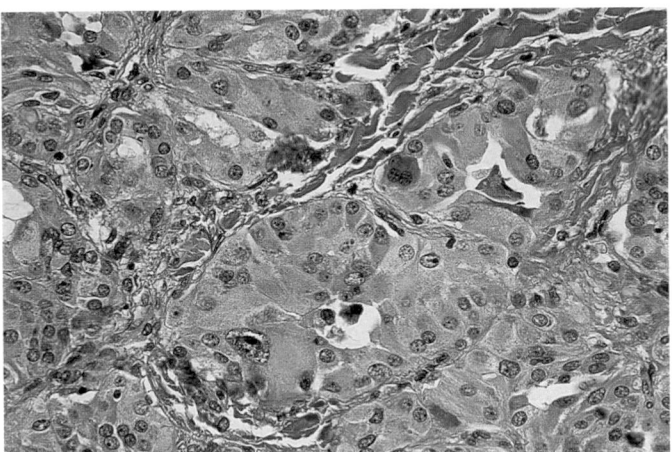

Fig. 9.80 Medullary carcinoma of oncocytic type. The appearance closely simulates that of Hürthle cell carcinoma. Clues to the diagnosis are represented by the amphophilic (rather than eosinophilic) staining quality of the cytoplasm and the prominent fibrous septation. This tumor was strongly immunoreactive for calcitonin.

the oncocytic cells are amphophilic rather than brightly eosinophilic and/or if the tumor is divided into nests by sharply outlined fibrous bands. Other unusual varieties of medullary carcinoma include a true papillary form,[638] a type exhibiting mucinous features (mucinous or amphicrine medullary carcinoma),[629] a clear cell variant,[639] a small cell type resembling the homonymous lung tumor, another small cell type with features resembling neuroblastoma,[631] and a pigmented (melanin-producing) variant.[636,640]

Cytologic features

In fine needle aspiration preparations, medullary carcinoma is characterized by eccentric nuclei, "neuroendocrine-type" chromatin, inconspicuous nucleoli, binucleated and multinucleated cells, ill-defined cell borders, and a clean background.[643,644] Sometimes the amyloid material can be identified (Fig. 9.81).

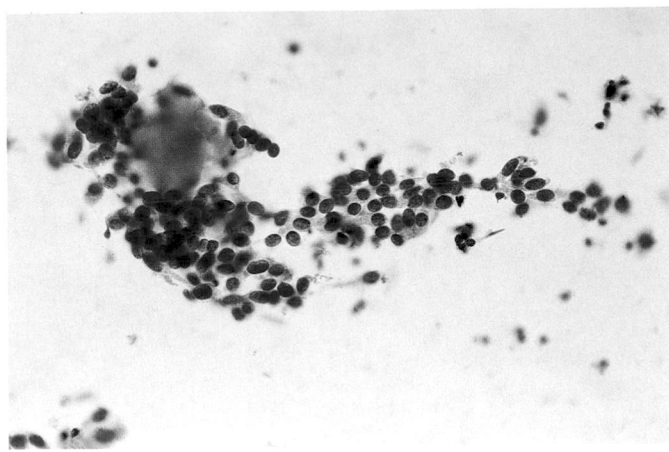

Fig. 9.81 Cytologic appearance of medullary carcinoma. The nuclei have clumped chromatin. An amorphous material compatible with amyloid is present.

Electron microscopic, histochemical, and immunohistochemical features

Ultrastructurally, cytoplasmic dense-core secretory granules are invariably present. A variability in their sizes has been detected, suggesting the existence of multiple endocrine cell types in this tumor.[646] These granules are usually argyrophilic with the Grimelius stain, especially if the tissue has been fixed in Bouin's fluid.[653] Mucin stains are often positive.[675]

Immunohistochemically, the tumor cells are reactive for epithelial markers such as keratin; general thyroid markers such as TTF-1; pan-endocrine markers such as NSE; chromogranin A, B, and C (the latter also known as secretogranin II); synaptophysin; opioid peptides; and—most important—the specific product of C cells, i.e., calcitonin[655,656,665,667] (Fig. 9.82). They are also consistently positive for CEA and generally negative for thyroglobulin.[649,650,660,668] Other products that have been detected in medullary carcinoma include somatostatin, adrenocorticotropic hormone (ACTH), calcitonin gene-related peptide, serotonin, melanocyte-stimulating hormone (MSH), prostaglandins, bombesin, gastrin-releasing peptide, substance P, L-dopa decarboxylase, histaminase, glucagon, insulin, human chorionic gonadotropin, the polysialic acid of the neural cell adhesion molecule, galectin-3, hepatocyte growth factor and its receptor, matrix metalloproteinases, prohormone convertases, and progesterone receptors (but virtually no estrogen receptors).[647,648,651,652,654,657–659,661–664,669–672,674]

Medullary carcinoma cells also express bcl-2 and c-myc, but not Bax or p53.[673]

Conceptually, synthesis by medullary carcinoma of the various peptide hormones listed above points to a histogenetic relationship of this neoplasm with carcinoid tumors of other organs, and it raises the possibility that what is now considered a single entity may well represent a family of related but eventually separable "neuroendocrine" neoplasms. Along these lines, there

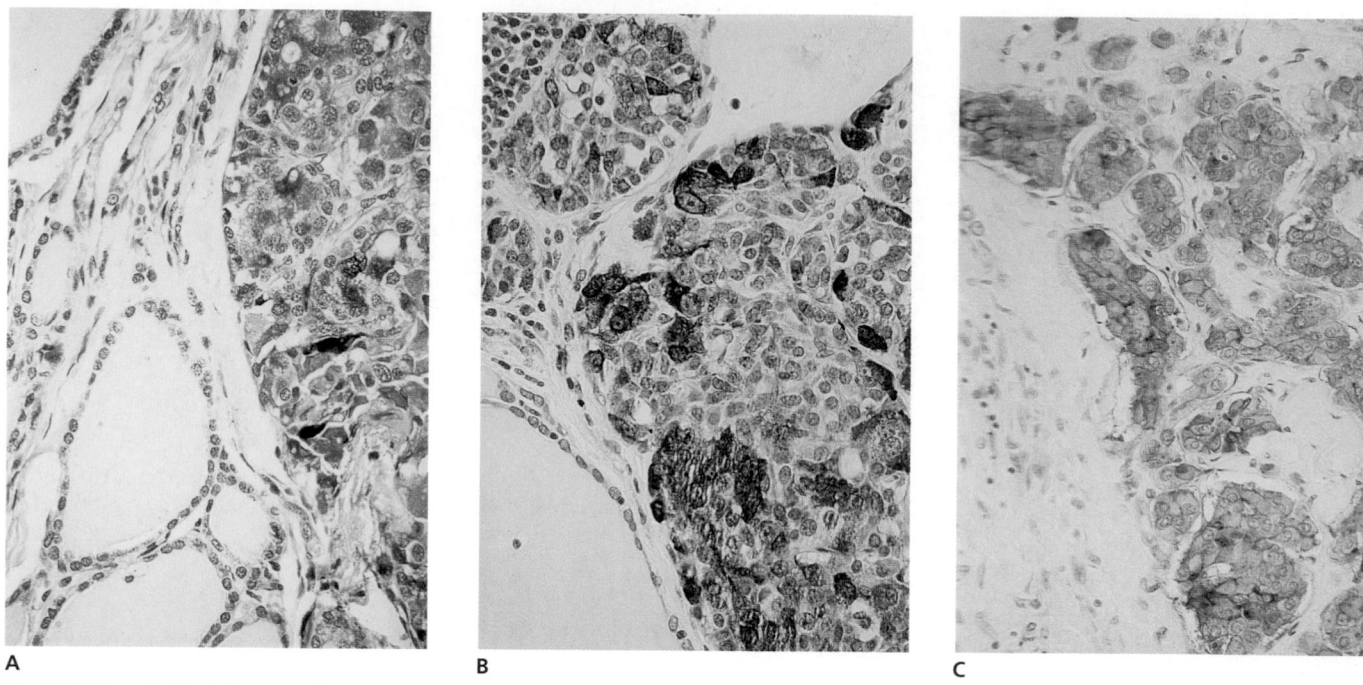

Fig. 9.82 A to **C**, Medullary carcinoma showing immunocytochemical positivity for calcitonin (**A**), chromogranin (**B**), and CEA (**C**).

are cases of thyroid carcinoma with a distinctly neuroendocrine pattern of growth that are devoid of amyloid, negative for calcitonin and thyroglobulin, and positive for neuron-specific enolase and chromogranin. Whether these tumors should be viewed as poorly differentiated ("calcitonin-free" or "atypical") variants of medullary carcinoma that have lost the capacity to produce calcitonin or whether they should be considered as separate "neuroendocrine carcinomas" analogous to those seen in many other organs is not clear.[666]

The amyloid of medullary carcinoma reacts with the generic stains for this substance and has a typical microfibrillary appearance ultrastructurally (Fig. 9.83). It also shows reactivity for calcitonin, suggesting that its production may be related to the secretion or degradation of this hormone.[645]

Familial medullary carcinoma and C-cell hyperplasia

Two forms of medullary carcinoma exist: sporadic and familial. The *sporadic* form comprises about 80% of the cases, affects adult individuals (mean age, 45 years) and is almost always solitary.[686,689] It presents as a thyroid mass that is cold on thyroid scan: in some cases, it is accompanied by intractable diarrhea or Cushing's syndrome.[681,692] Only rarely is it clinically occult.[696]

The *familial* form becomes clinically apparent in a young age group (mean age, 35 years), is often multiple and bilateral, and is invariably accompanied by C-cell hyperplasia in the residual gland. An increasing number of cases are diagnosed when measuring 1 cm or less, i.e., at the stage of medullary microcarcinomas.[684,685] Almost all cases of medullary thyroid carcinomas occurring in children belong to this type, which is inherited as an

autosomal dominant trait of virtually complete penetrance. In many cases, it represents a component of multiple endocrine neoplasia type IIA (MEN IIA) or type IIB (MEN IIB), particularly the former[678,679] (see Chapter 15). The gene involved in the development of this tumor is *RET*, located on chromosome 10q11.2, which is affected in the form of various activating *germline* mutations.[687,694] In families with familial medullary carcinoma and MEN IIA, these mutations are in one of the six codons for *CYS* in exons 10 and 11 (609, 611, 618, 620, 630, and 634). Codon mutation in exon 11 is by far the most common genetic abnormality in MEN IIA families, accounting for 85% of the kindred. Families with MEN IIB usually have mutations at codon 918 in exon 16. Mutations in codons 768 and 804 are more common in cases of familiar medullary carcinoma not associated with MEN, whereas mutations of codon 634 are associated statistically with pheochromocytoma. It should be mentioned here that *RET* mutations have also been detected in sporadic medullary carcinomas, particularly at codon 918[687]; in contrast to the familial and MEN-related cases, these mutations are *somatic*, i.e., found only in the tumor cells.

Regarding the clinical relevance of these genetic abnormalities, there is agreement that total thyroidectomy should be performed in patients older than 6 years who have a *RET* germline mutation.[687] The development of medullary carcinoma is clearly age-related, a fact that guides the decision concerning the timing for the prophylactic thyroidectomy.[686a]

C-cell hyperplasia is the precursor lesion of all these familial syndromes. Its typical location is in the central part of the lateral lobes. It may be diffuse or nodular, and the C cells may be seen in an interfollicular or intrafollic-

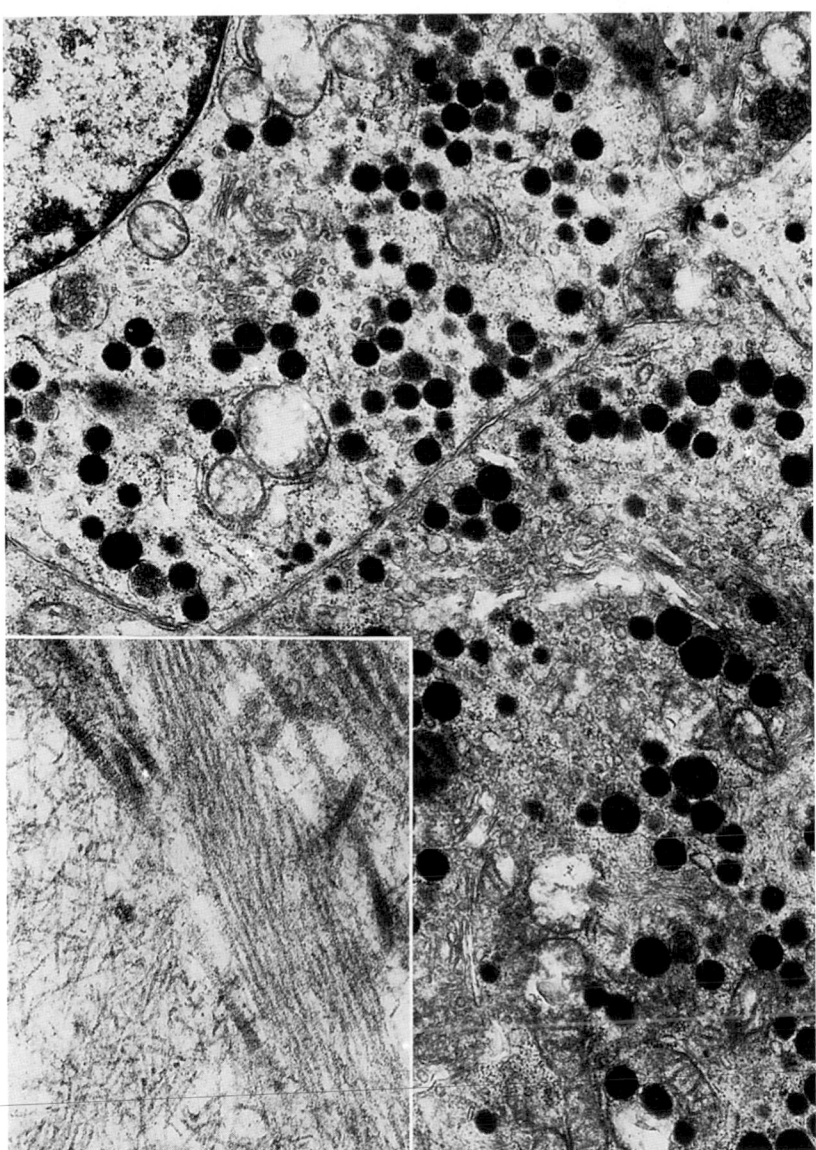

Fig. 9.83 Portions of two cells from medullary carcinoma of thyroid gland showing multiple dense secretory granules in the cytoplasm. Each granule is surrounded by a single membrane, and the dense central portion is separated from it by a clear zone. Inset shows both oriented and randomly placed amyloid filaments and may be contrasted with larger banded collagen fibers. (Courtesy of Dr. J.S. Meyer, St Louis)

ular location. The arbitrary figure of more than six cells per thyroid follicle has been suggested as an indicator of C-cell hyperplasia.[678] Because of the extreme difficulty in establishing a clear definition of C-cell hyperplasia based on cell count it is probably wise to regard the *nodular* form as the only definite precursor for the hereditary type of medullary carcinoma.

As a rule, the hyperplastic C cells exhibit greater CEA immunoreactivity than normal C cells and greater calcitonin immunoreactivity than the cells of medullary carcinoma. The differential diagnosis of this preneoplastic disorder includes on one hand early medullary carcinoma (microcarcinoma) and on the other the reactive or physiologic C-cell hyperplasias that can be seen in a variety of conditions. Medullary carcinoma is recognized because of the nesting expansile pattern, the destruction of the follicular basement membrane, and the diminished intensity of calcitonin immunostaining.[682] Reactive or physiologic C-cell hyperplasias have been described in the immediate periphery of thyroid neoplasms of various microscopic types[676,691] and in association with lymphocytic thyroiditis[677,680] and secondary hyperparathyroidism.[693] All of these conditions should be distinguished from the normal clusters of C cells seen in relation to solid cell nests[683] (see p. 516).

Patients with thyroid C hyperplasia have elevated serum levels of calcitonin and CEA[695]; in addition, patients with medullary carcinoma also have elevated levels of chromogranin A.[688]

Spread and metastases

Medullary carcinoma invades locally and gives rise to metastases in cervical and mediastinal lymph nodes and also in distant organs, particularly lung, liver, and skeletal system.[697] They appear to be more common in sporadic and MEN-IIb-associated tumors than in MEN-IIa-associated neoplasms.[698] These metastases may be the first manifestation of the disease and be a source of confusion to the pathologist.[700] Microscopically, they tend to resemble the primary tumor and—as a result—usually contain amyloid. The resemblance also applies to their immunohistochemical reactivity, although notable discrepancies occur.[699]

Treatment and prognosis

The primary treatment of medullary carcinoma is surgical, in the form of total thyroidectomy (particularly important for the familial form because of the multicentricity and C-cell hyperplasia) and cervical lymphadenectomy. Local recurrence supervenes in about 35% of patients, and the 5-year survival rate varies between 70% and 80%.[703,706,712] The tumor is not particularly responsive to radioactive iodine, external radiation therapy, or chemotherapy.

Good prognostic factors are young age, female sex, occurrence in a familial setting, tumor size, and tumor confinement to the gland.[701,703,712,713] The poorer prognosis of sporadic cases may be caused by the patients' older age at detection and more advanced tumor stage at diagnosis.[709,714] Microscopically, a greater degree of aggressiveness should be expected of tumors with high mitotic activity, necrosis, squamous pattern, and/or of the small cell type.[705] It has been claimed that poor immunohistochemical reactivity for calcitonin is an indicator of poor prognosis, particularly if coupled with increased reactivity for CEA.[705,707,710,711] Calcitonin production is related to the degree of tumor differentiation, whereas the content of calcitonin messenger RNA as detected by in situ hybridization is not, this discrepancy suggesting a defect in synthesis or storage of the peptide.[702] Other immunohistochemical markers (such as somatostatin and opioid peptides) have not proved to have an independent prognostic value in multivariate analysis.[714,715]

Flow cytometric studies have shown that about one third of medullary carcinomas are aneuploid; these tumors have a more aggressive clinical course, but the differences become nonsignificant in a multivariate analysis.[704,708] Persistent or recurrent elevation of serum calcitonin after surgery is a reliable indicator of tumor persistence or relapse.

Other neuroendocrine tumors

Medullary (C-cell) adenoma has been suggested as a diagnosis for the rare totally encapsulated forms of C-cell tumors, but it is probably more accurate to regard them as encapsulated variants of medullary carcinoma.[718] The differential diagnosis includes hyalinizing trabecular carcinoma.[722]

Mixed medullary–follicular carcinoma is a controversial entity in which the morphologic features of medullary carcinoma (together with immunoreactivity for calcitonin) coexist with those of a follicular neoplasm (together with immunoreactivity for thyroglobulin).[720,731] Some of the reported cases have been familial.[728]

Sufficient evidence has been advanced to validate the existence of this entity,[729] with the added perplexing observation that the two components are not derived from a single progenitor cell.[733] In any event, it should be kept in mind that most cases in which the diagnosis of mixed medullary–follicular carcinoma has been entertained represent either medullary carcinomas with entrapped follicles and/or secondary incorporation of thyroglobulin by the medullary carcinoma cells or medullary carcinomas with a glandular (tubular and follicular) pattern of growth (see p. 554).

Mixed medullary–papillary carcinoma represents the even more unusual combination of calcitonin-positive medullary carcinoma and thyroglobulin-positive papillary carcinoma, the latter areas having typical ground glass nuclei.[716,724,725] This should be distinguished from the more common event of separate medullary and papillary thyroid carcinoma in the same gland which may collide with each other,[730] and the even more bizarre phenomenon of a mixed medullary–follicular carcinoma colliding with a papillary carcinoma.[732]

Paraganglioma can occur adjacent to or within the thyroid, sometimes in association with carotid body tumors.[721,723] The differential diagnosis with medullary carcinoma and follicular adenoma can be very difficult, particularly with the former (Fig. 9.84). Paraganglioma reacts immunohistochemically for pan-endocrine markers such as chromogranin and opioid peptides but is negative for calcitonin, thyroglobulin, TTF-1, and keratin. A particularly useful (although neither constant nor pathognomonic) feature is the presence of S-100 protein-positive sustentacular cells at the periphery of the *Zellballen*[717] (Fig. 9.85). All but one of the reported cases have been cured by surgical excision.[727]

Small cell (neuroendocrine) carcinoma morphologically identical to the homonymous lung tumor has been described in the thyroid. Some of these tumors are calcitonin positive and are therefore regarded as small cell variants of medullary carcinoma. Those that are calcitonin negative probably represent the most undifferenti-

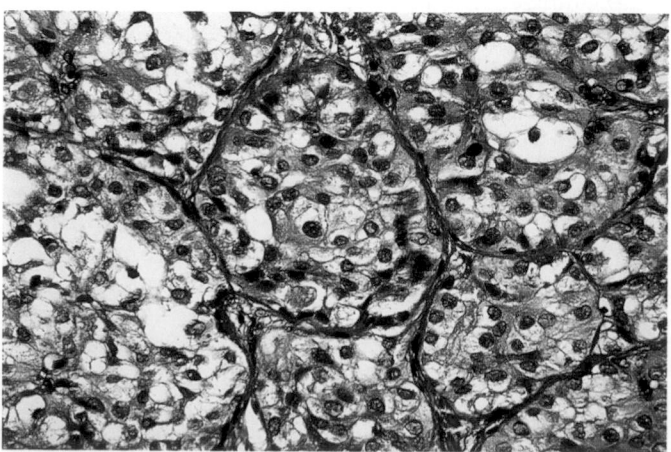

Fig. 9.84 Thyroid paraganglioma showing well-formed "Zellballen."

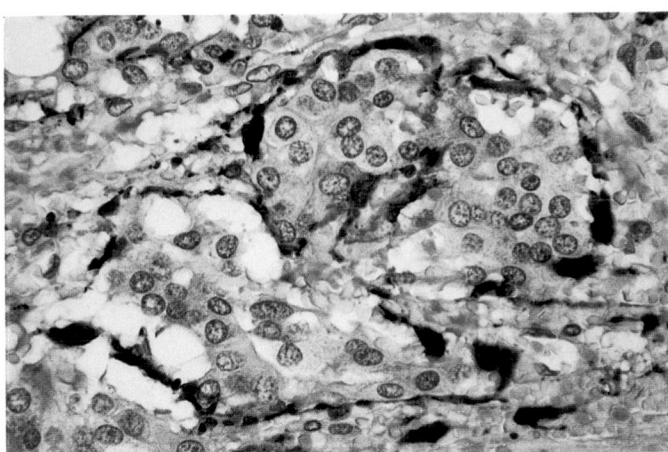

Fig. 9.85 S100 protein-positive sustentacular cells at the periphery of the Zellballen in paraganglioma of thyroid.

ated members of the spectrum; their behavior is extremely aggressive.[719]

Metastatic neuroendocrine tumors of various types (such as carcinoid tumor of lung) can metastasize to the thyroid gland and simulate a medullary carcinoma.[726]

Epithelial tumors—general features

Geographic distribution

Most series have shown a statistical correlation between iodine deficiency and an increased incidence of thyroid carcinoma of both follicular and undifferentiated types.[734–737,740] Because of difficulties in clinical detection related to the background disease, the tumors tend to be more advanced at the time of diagnosis than in nonendemic areas.[741] Shi et al.[742] made the interesting observation that the incidence of *ras* oncogene mutations is significantly higher in thyroid tumors from iodine-deficient areas, suggesting that the dietary iodine may be the modulating agent for these mutations. Whether the introduction of iodized salt actually results in a decrease in the incidence of thyroid cancer in these areas remains controversial.[739]

Papillary carcinoma is the predominant type in areas without iodine deficiency, and its frequency is said to be increased in regions with high iodine uptake.[743] No major differences seem to exist in the incidence of the various microscopic types of thyroid carcinoma between the West and the East.[738]

Thyroid neoplasia in childhood

Most thyroid tumors developing in childhood are benign and are examples of either follicular adenoma or nodular hyperplasia. However, the proportion of carcinomas is much higher than that seen in adults, to the point of surpassing the benign processes in some series.[748] Among the malignancies, papillary carcinoma comprises the overwhelming majority of the cases, followed by the familial form of medullary carcinoma and Hürthle cell

neoplasms.[746] In older series there is also an important representation of follicular carcinomas, but most of those would probably be regarded at present as follicular variants of papillary carcinomas.[749,751] Poorly differentiated carcinomas are very rare in this age group, and undifferentiated carcinomas are practically nonexistent.

The papillary carcinomas occurring in children tend to have solid and/or squamous areas and are associated with a high frequency of cervical node metastases.[744,750] The overall prognosis is excellent, but occasional aggressive and even lethal cases are on record[747]; the few such tumors that we had the opportunity to review personally contained microscopically poorly differentiated areas. Some of these children give a history of previous radiation exposure to the neck[745] (see next section).

Thyroid neoplasia and radiation exposure

Exposure of the thyroid gland to low-dose therapeutic radiation (administered for thymic enlargement, tonsillar hypertrophy, or acne to about one million patients in the United States) can result in a number of abnormalities later in life.[754] The most common of them are of a *benign* nature—a fact to remember—and consist of nodular hyperplasia, lymphocytic thyroiditis, and fibrosis.[756,758,764] There is also an unquestionable increase in the incidence of carcinoma in this population, the large majority of the tumors being of the papillary type.[757,761] Of patients in this population who have thyroid operations, the incidence of carcinoma ranges from 20% to over 50%.[752,767] Despite earlier statements to the contrary, there is no convincing evidence that these tumors behave differently from others. The quoted incidences of multicentricity and nodal metastases have been high, but the long-term prognosis has been very good.

Parenthetically, tumors from other structures of the neck can also develop in individuals with radiation exposure to the area; these include salivary gland, parathyroid, osseous, and neural neoplasms.[762,763] This obviously indicates the need for a continuous surveillance of this population.

High-dose radiation to the neck region, such as that administered for Hodgkin's lymphoma, can also result in thyroid carcinoma and other abnormalities of the gland.[753,760] There is also conclusive evidence that thyroid carcinoma (particularly of the papillary type) occurs with a much increased incidence in populations accidentally exposed to high radiation doses, such as that resulting from the highly publicized nuclear accident of Chernobyl.[755,759,765] In many of these instances the clinical records on these populations before the accident are too scanty to enable precise determination of the magnitude of the risk, but the fact that there is substantial increased risk in the Chernobyl population can no longer be doubted. A very interesting pattern has emerged from the analysis of these cases. Short latent period tumors have a significantly higher proportion of *architecturally less differentiated components* (solid and trabecular) and are more aggressive than long latent period tumors, suggesting that successive waves of carcinoma are occurring in the exposed population. On the other hand, the *type* of differentiation is linked to age at exposure rather than to the latent period, in the sense that a follicular pattern is more common in children exposed at a young age, and a papillary pattern is more frequent in children exposed at a later age.[766]

Association with other conditions

Cases of thyroid carcinoma of *nonmedullary* types (particularly of the papillary variety) have been reported in a familial setting[770,776]; in patients with ataxia–telangiectasia[778] and acromegaly[768]; and in association with parathyroid tumors,[773] paragangliomas of the carotid body, and familial colonic polyposis,[772,779] including Gardner's syndrome.[769] As already indicated, the thyroid tumors developing in the latter group of patients have a distinctive appearance[771] (see p. 540). Cases have also been described in patients with MEN I.[774,775] A candidate susceptibility gene for familial nonmedullary thyroid carcinoma has been localized to chromosome 2q21.[777]

Evaluation of the solitary thyroid nodule

The most common thyroid problem facing the surgeon and the pathologist is the evaluation of the patient with an apparently single thyroid mass.[788,791] The magnitude of the problem is obvious from the fact that about 4% of the population of the United States between the ages of 30 and 60 years have one or more palpable nodules. These are four times more common in females than in males. Because the majority of these nodules are benign and most are not even neoplastic, the goal is to be selective in the cases taken to surgery while at the same time including most of the carcinomas in this group. Factors to consider when making this difficult selection process are the following:

1 *Age.* The incidence of malignancy is higher in children and the elderly than in young or middle-aged adults.[780,782]
2 *Sex.* The incidence of malignancy is higher in males.[780]
3 *Hashimoto's thyroiditis.* The likelihood of malignancy for a nodule present in Hashimoto's thyroiditis is roughly the same as for that occurring in a normal gland.
4 *Neck irradiation.* The likelihood of malignancy is higher if there is a history of irradiation to the neck in infancy.[782]
5 *Number.* Solitary nodules are more likely to be malignant than multiple ones. It should be kept in mind, however, that approximately one third of the nodules thought to be solitary on palpation are shown to be multiple on scan and an even higher number on pathologic examination.
6 *Rate of growth.* Most adenomas are very slow growing, but this is also true for most papillary or minimally invasive follicular carcinomas. Rapid enlargement of a longstanding nodule may signify an undifferenti-

ated (anaplastic) transformation or simply the development of hemorrhage within the nodule.
7 *Associated ipsilateral adenopathy.* This is the strongest clinical indicator of malignancy if present.
8 *Function.* Nodules that are hyperfunctioning ("toxic") at the clinical level and/or hot on thyroid scintiscan are less likely to be malignant than the others.
9 *Ultrasonography.* Cystic nodules are less likely to be malignant than solid ones. These nodules are usually found to be hypofunctioning by isotopic imaging study.[783,792]
10 *Computed tomography (CT) and magnetic resonance imaging (MRI).* The role of these two techniques in thyroid disease is relatively limited.[785] MRI is said to be superior to CT for the evaluation of metastatic, retrotracheal, or mediastinal lesions.[793]
11 *Serum thyroglobulin levels.* These levels are often elevated in patients with papillary and follicular carcinoma (particularly the latter), whereas they remain normal in patients with medullary or undifferentiated carcinoma. However, because a similar elevation can also accompany follicular adenoma, this measurement cannot be used to distinguish benign from malignant tumors before surgery. This technique is particularly useful in monitoring patients after removal of a papillary or follicular carcinoma, especially if the excision was followed by radioactive iodine therapy. As a matter of fact, it has been stated that repeated total-body scans can be omitted in patients with such tumors if the serum thyroglobulin levels are undetectable, unless a strong clinical indication exists.[784,790,794]
12 *Needle biopsy.* In experienced hands, this technique provides the best means of determining the likelihood of malignancy of a thyroid nodule short of surgical excision and pathologic examination[781,786,789] (see later section).

To put these various clinical criteria in perspective, it should be mentioned that even when the nodule is solitary, solid, and cold on scintiscan, it will prove malignant in no more than 10% to 20% of the cases and that as many as one third of the thyroid nodules disappear spontaneously if left untreated.[787]

Needle biopsy and fine needle aspiration

Core needle biopsy has been used extensively in a few institutions in the United States and abroad but has failed to gain widespread acceptance.[821] It is particularly helpful in diffuse diseases such as Hashimoto's thyroiditis and in confirming the diagnosis of an advanced malignant neoplasm.[834] Most authors have been reluctant to use this technique in the evaluation of the single thyroid nodule not only because of the small but definite risk of complications (bleeding, nerve injury, tracheal perforation, tumor implantation),[814] but also because of the fact that the differential diagnosis between a benign and malignant follicular lesion is usually impossible with this technique. This is hardly surprising, inasmuch as the two main histologic criteria of malignancy (i.e., capsular and vascular invasion) will not be apparent in most needle biopsies.

Fine needle aspiration (FNA) has become instead, in a matter of few years, an extremely popular technique for the evaluation of solitary thyroid nodules. Its appeal is obvious: It is quick and inexpensive, it can be carried out in the physician's office, and the risk of complications (including tumor implantation) is minimal.[804,808,823,828] Furthermore, the material is suitable for immunohistochemical evaluation.[799,825,831] Published results claim a sensitivity and specificity of over 90%, leading some authors to recommend FNA as the initial test in the evaluation of any thyroid nodule.[795,800,809,830] Most papillary carcinomas and other types of malignancy other than follicular carcinoma can be identified with ease.[803,807,817,822] The same is true for the various types of thyroiditis.[805] The main difficulty, as in the case of the core needle biopsy, resides in the identification of well-differentiated follicular carcinoma, a task that may be impossible with this method in view of the nature of the diagnostic criteria required.[798,801,824] In most instances, the cytology report will be one of the following three[827]:

1 *Probably benign nodule*, when the material is composed largely of colloid, histiocytes, and a few normal-looking follicular cells. This will be an indication for a conservative approach unless the clinical data suggest otherwise.[826]

2 *Follicular neoplasm*, when cellularity is higher than that found in the usual hyperplastic nodule but the nuclear features of papillary carcinoma are absent (Fig. 9.86). The diagnosis of Hürthle cell neoplasm usually falls into this category.[816] The presence of highly hyperchromatic nuclei, microfollicular or solid pattern, scanty colloid, and necrotic debris suggests the presence of a poorly differentiated carcinoma.[813,832] The diagnosis of

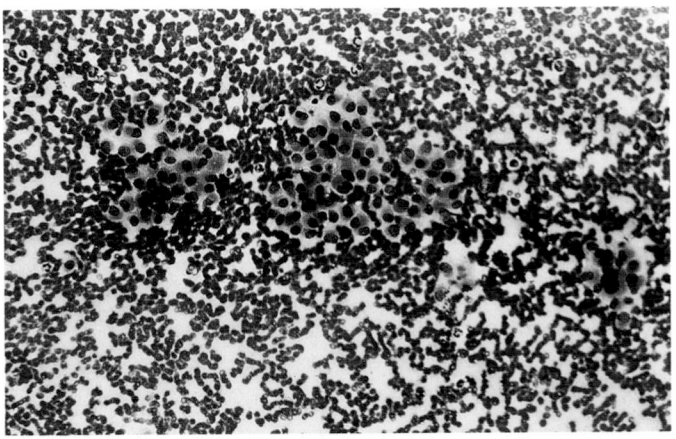

Fig. 9.86 Cytologic appearance of papillary carcinoma, showing characteristic nuclear changes.

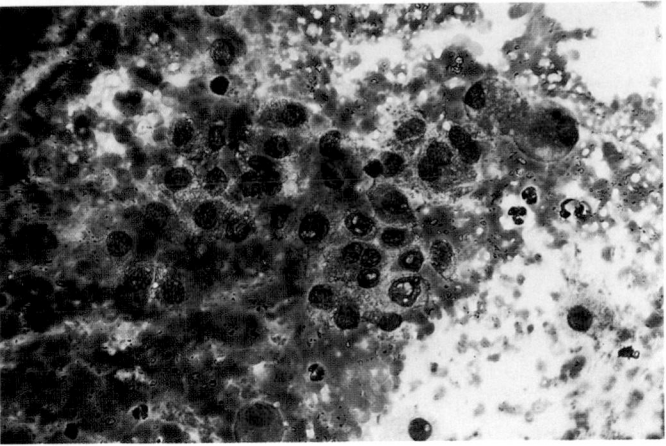

Fig. 9.87 Cytologic appearance of follicular neoplasm. This hypercellular quality is an indication for surgical excision.

follicular neoplasm is an indication for removal of the nodule unless this is contraindicated for medical reasons.[802,806,829]

3 *Papillary carcinoma*, when the characteristic cytoarchitectural features of this tumor type are present, such as papillary fronds, psammoma bodies, nuclear pseudoinclusions, and nuclear grooves (Fig. 9.87). It should be remembered that the ground glass nuclear feature is usually not apparent in cytologic preparations even when prominent in the tissue sections from the same case, that nuclear pseudoinclusions are not pathognomonic of papillary carcinoma, and that cystic degeneration of the tumor may obscure the cell details.[810,820] Concerning the follicular variant of papillary carcinoma, the nuclear changes should be particularly well developed and extensive, in keeping with the conservative diagnostic approach recommended in this situation (see p. 564).[796,811] In both the classic and the follicular variants of this tumor the colloid often exhibits a peculiar streaking and smearing effect that has been compared with that of bubble gum. The cytologic diagnosis of papillary carcinoma is obviously an indication for therapeutic intervention, even if the occasional surgical specimen may show only a papillary *micro*carcinoma (i.e., a lesion for which the need for surgery is debatable).[812]

The performance of FNA may result in partial or complete infarction of the tumor, with only a thin rim of tissue preserved at the periphery[797]; this complication is particularly common with Hürthle cell tumors,[815] and it may result in transient elevation of the serum levels of thyroglobulin.[819] Hemorrhage and thrombosis can also develop, with the secondary organization and recanalization sometimes leading to pseudoangiosarcomatous papillary endothelial hyperplastic changes.[798,833] Another complication of the procedure when carried out in cystic lesions has been the development of transient thyrotoxicosis.[818]

Frozen section

The pathologist is often asked to perform a frozen section at the time of exploration of a thyroid mass.[839] The specimen may be from an area of extrathyroidal invasion by carcinoma or from a metastatic cervical node. In these instances, the diagnosis is usually obvious, although Riedel's thyroiditis (p. 523), extrathyroidal growth in diffuse hyperplasia (p. 526), and sequestered thyroid nodule (see next section) represent important diagnostic pitfalls.[841] The most common specimen received for frozen section is a lobectomy carried out because of a nodule. A few of these will be found to be examples of granulomatous thyroiditis, Hashimoto's thyroiditis, or malignant lymphoma, each of which may manifest as an apparently single nodule on physical examination. However, in the majority of the cases the differential diagnosis will be between a dominant nodule of nodular hyperplasia, adenoma, and carcinoma.[836] An experienced pathologist should have no problem in identifying most cases of undifferentiated carcinomas, poorly differentiated carcinomas, widely invasive follicular carcinomas, conventional papillary carcinomas, or medullary carcinomas. The most difficult problem resides in the distinction between a dominant nodule of nodular hyperplasia, follicular adenoma, minimally invasive follicular carcinoma, and the variant of papillary carcinoma that is both follicular and encapsulated. These considerations also apply to the encapsulated Hürthle cell neoplasms. Capsular and/or blood vessel invasion may not be evident in the samples chosen for frozen sections but become obvious later in the more thorough sampling of permanent sections.[840,842,843] The ground glass nuclear feature that is one of the most distinctive features of papillary carcinoma may not show up at all in the frozen section. *For these reasons, the surgeon should accept the fact that a certain percentage of well-differentiated carcinomas will not be identifiable on frozen section examination regardless of the experience and astuteness of the pathologist.* This apparent deficiency does not create serious therapeutic problems because, in our opinion, most if not all of the lesions listed in this paragraph are effectively treated by lobectomy or—at the most—subtotal thyroidectomy. With the increase in popularity in the performance of fine needle aspirations, the number of cases in which the surgical planning depends on frozen section results has diminished considerably.[837,838] Parenthetically, the performance of a cytologic preparation at the time of the frozen section has proved to be a very useful diagnostic adjunct.[835,844]

Presence of thyroid tissue outside gland

There are several circumstances in which normal or abnormal thyroid tissue may be found in the neck outside the confines of the thyroid gland:

1 Ectopic thyroid tissue resulting from faulty embryogenesis. Thyroglossal duct cyst and lingual thyroid are the most common examples (see p. 517).

2 Presence of hyperplastic thyroid tissue outside the gland in Graves' disease (see p. 526).

3 Mechanical implantation of thyroid tissue in the neck as a result of surgical intervention or accidental trauma. In the former instance, suture material may be seen adjacent to the thyroid tissue.

4 So-called *sequestered thyroid nodule*. This phenomenon, also known as parasitic or accessory nodule, refers to the occurrence of a peripherally located thyroid nodule in which either the anatomic connection with the main gland is lost or this connection is missed by the surgeon, the process being somewhat analogous to that of parasitic uterine leiomyoma.[846,853] The nodule is usually an expression of nodular hyperplasia or nodular Hashimoto's thyroiditis, less commonly of diffuse hyperplasia (Graves' disease).[852] The diagnosis requires that the tissue reside in the same fascial plane as the thyroid gland, that it be unassociated with lymph nodes, and that it exhibit the same or similar histologic appearance as the main gland, whenever the latter is available. Sequestration also occurs (and may actually be more common) in thyroid nodular hyperplasia located in the mediastinum. The fact that the sequestered nodule is subject to the same morphologic alterations as the main gland may lead to significant interpretive problems in Hashimoto's thyroiditis, in which the combination of nuclear atypia (as part of the oncocytic alteration) and heavy lymphoid infiltration (as part of the thyroiditis) may result in an appearance closely simulating a lymph nodal structure containing metastatic tumor (Fig. 9.88). It has been suggested that clonal analysis might help in this situation, under the assumption that hyperplastic lesions would be expected to be polyclonal whereas carcinomas ought to be clonal,[849] but we think it would be premature to rely on this assessment at this stage of our knowledge.

5 Thyroid tissue within cervical lymph nodes. The determination of the significance of this finding in the presence of an apparently normal thyroid gland can be a very difficult exercise. This phenomenon accounts for most cases of the condition formerly called *lateral aberrant thyroid*.[845] It is now generally accepted that this may be the result of two unrelated processes and that microscopic examination permits their separation in the majority of the instances.[851]

Most cases represent metastases of clinically undetected thyroid carcinomas, nearly always of the papillary variety. It should be emphasized that detection of the primary neoplasm may require extremely careful microscopic study with embedding of the entire thyroid gland and cutting of the blocks at various levels.[854] The metastatic deposits may replace most of the node, although a peripheral rim of residual lymphoid tissue can usually be found. Secondary cystic changes can be so prominent as to simulate the appearance of a branchial cleft cyst (see Fig. 9.51). The smaller foci of

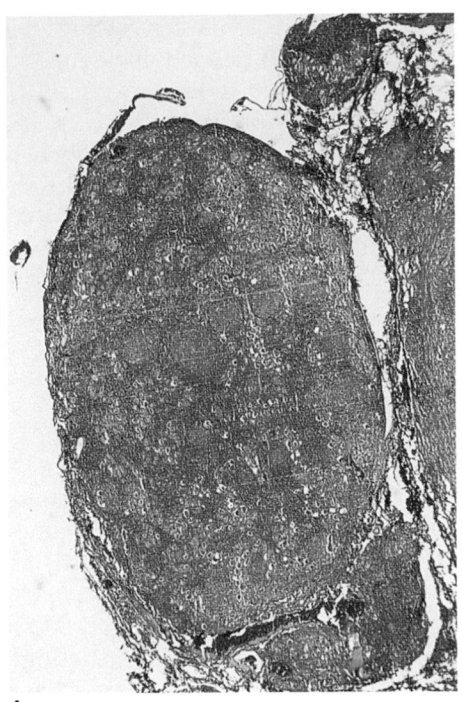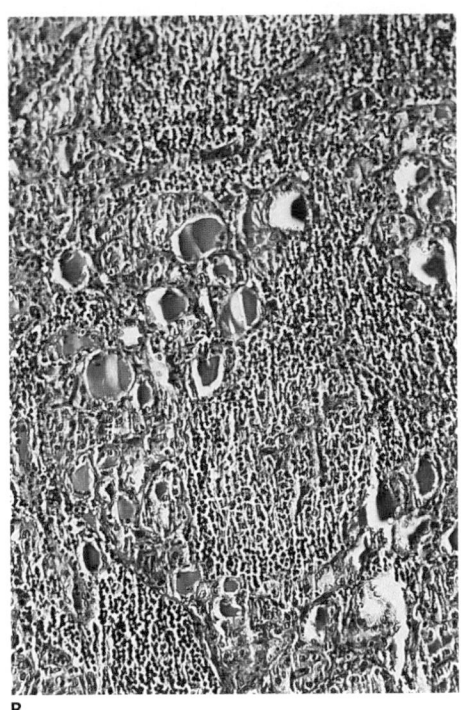

A   B

Fig. 9.88 So-called sequestered thyroid nodule occurring in association with a gland involved by Hashimoto's thyroiditis. The combination of oxyphilic change and germinal center formation in the sequestered nodule results in an appearance that can be confused with thyroid carcinoma metastatic to a lymph node.

metastatic tumor are frequently located within sinuses. The pattern of growth may be so well differentiated as to simulate normal thyroid tissue. However, close inspection will usually reveal the presence of one or more of the cytoarchitectural features of papillary carcinoma, such as small papillae, psammoma bodies, follicles with darkly staining colloid, and the characteristic nuclear changes of this tumor type.

The second situation is the occurrence of normal follicles within nodes, a concept that was originally proposed by Frantz et al.[845] and that some authors still have difficulty in accepting. The best evidence in its favor is the study performed by Meyer and Steinberg.[850] These authors serially sectioned cervical lymph nodes from 106 autopsies and found thyroid tissue in five of them. Serial section of the whole thyroid gland in these cases failed to reveal carcinoma, except for a probably unrelated microscopic papillary carcinoma in the contralateral lobe of one case. In these instances, the ectopic thyroid tissue typically presents as a small conglomerate of follicles lacking all the attributes of papillary carcinoma and limited to the periphery of one or two nodes (Fig. 9.89). Any thyroid tissue replacing most of the node and/or involving several nodes is likely to be metastatic carcinoma.

A point worth making despite its apparent obviousness is that not all metastatic papillary carcinomas with psammoma bodies in cervical lymph node originate in the thyroid. We and others have seen cases in which a thoroughly studied specimen of total thyroidectomy failed to reveal tumor in the gland.[848] The possibility of the carcinoma being extrathyroidal (e.g., salivary gland, lung, ovary, and even thymus) should

be particularly considered for those tumors lacking the classic nuclear features of papillary thyroid carcinoma and devoid of thyroglobulin immunoreactivity.

6 Thyroid as a component of teratoma. Thyroid tissue may be seen as one of the many components of teratoma, particularly those located in the ovary. This thyroid tissue may appear normal, hyperplastic, or—exceptionally—neoplastic. Ovarian teratomas composed predominantly or exclusively of thyroid tissue are referred to as *struma ovarii* (see Chapter 19). Before accepting any tissue located in an unusual place as representing thyroid, one should keep in mind that a thyroid-like appearance can result from cystically dilated glands of one type or another whenever their epithelium flattens and the intraluminal secretion inspissates.[847] Struma ovarii should also be distin-

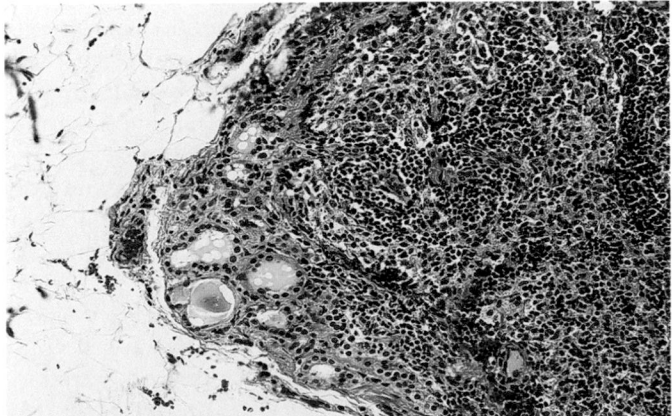

Fig. 9.89 Ectopic thyroid follicles in lymph node. The follicles are scanty, centered in the lymph node capsule, and devoid of structural and cytologic abnormalities.

guished from the exceptional thyroid carcinoma that metastasizes to the ovary.[855]

Treatment

The treatment of most types of thyroid tumors is surgical. In cases in which the nodule is limited to one lobe, lobectomy (with or without isthmusectomy) is usually done as the first approach, with subsequent therapy depending on the nature of the nodule. Nodulectomy is no longer an accepted form of therapy for these lesions. Lobectomy is adequate therapy for follicular adenoma, including Hürthle cell adenoma. We and others believe that lobectomy or—at the most—subtotal thyroidectomy also constitutes adequate therapy for most minimally invasive follicular carcinomas (including minimally invasive Hürthle cell carcinomas) and papillary carcinomas, since it achieves very similar results without the high risk of complications associated with the more radical procedures.[857,859,861,866,869,878–880,882,885] However, the issue remains highly controversial, with several groups recommending total thyroidectomy followed by the administration of radioactive iodine for these patients.[858,868,874,875] As a matter of fact, this remains the most common form of therapy for differentiated thyroid carcinoma both in the United States and Europe.[870,871]

Some authors justify their preference for total thyroidectomy by showing a high incidence of residual tumor in specimens from "completion thyroidectomy" done for either papillary or follicular carcinoma[863,864,876]; however, an analogous argument used years ago to justify the performance of radical neck dissections in thyroid papillary carcinoma is no longer considered valid. We are of the opinion that total thyroidectomy should be reserved for the high-risk group of papillary carcinomas,[857,869] widely invasive follicular carcinomas (including widely invasive Hürthle cell carcinomas), poorly differentiated carcinomas, and medullary carcinomas (particularly those arising in a familial setting). Radical surgery should also be carried out in undifferentiated carcinoma whenever feasible, but most of these tumors are found inoperable.

Radical neck dissection is recommended in cases of medullary carcinoma but no longer in papillary carcinoma.[872] In cases of the latter tumor in which obvious nodal metastases are present, these are removed without performing a formal *en bloc* lymphadenectomy.

Suppression of thyroid function is carried out routinely by the exogenous administration of thyroid hormone in cases of papillary and follicular carcinoma, although the need for this procedure has been questioned.[856]

Another controversial aspect of the therapy regards the postoperative administration of radioactive iodine. Some authors recommend it routinely for both papillary and follicular carcinoma.[873,874,878] We[857] and others[860,862,885] have not found convincing evidence that its prophylactic administration is indicated, even accepting the fact that its effectiveness in the presence of detectable metastases

is unquestioned[881] and that there is no convincing evidence that its use leads to an increased incidence of second primary tumors.[867]

External radiation therapy is of limited use in the treatment of thyroid malignancy; its main indication is for incompletely excised tumors, which is usually the result of extensive extrathyroidal tumor growth.[865,883,884]

The prognosis following these various forms of therapy is discussed under the different microscopic types. The postoperative monitoring of patients with tumors arising from follicular cells is done with physical examination, chest x-ray studies, radioiodine scan, and measurements of serum thyroglobulin levels.[877]

Prognosis

Most of the clinical and pathologic factors that relate to prognosis have been discussed with the specific tumor types. In general terms, the most important are the patient's age (very significant), patient's sex (less so), tumor microscopic type, tumor microscopic grade (to a large extent already included in the microscopic typing), and tumor stage.[886,889,891,893] These and other factors have been sometimes combined in rather complex prognostic indices.[892,894] Cady et al.[887] group their patients with well-differentiated (papillary or follicular) carcinomas into two categories having strikingly different survival rates: low-risk (comprising men under 40 years of age and women under 50 years) and high-risk (the others). We confirmed their findings for papillary carcinomas and found that the prognostic difference is even more striking if the low-risk group includes women 60 years and under.[888] The large majority of deaths from thyroid carcinomas result from undifferentiated, poorly differentiated, Hürthle cell, and medullary tumors. It should be realized that, in many series, several of these tumor types are included among the follicular carcinomas.[890]

Lymphoid tumors and tumorlike conditions

Most cases of primary **malignant lymphoma** of the thyroid are seen in adult or elderly females.[918] The thyroid enlargement is often rapid and can lead to symptoms of tracheal or laryngeal compression.[903,920] Most patients are euthyroid, and the tumor presents as one or more cold nodules on thyroid scan.[906] Grossly, the tumor shows a solid white cut surface with a fish-flesh appearance.

Microscopically, the majority of the cases are of diffuse large B-cell type[900,903] (Fig. 9.90). Sclerosis may be focally prominent. The second largest category is that of the low-grade lymphomas composed of small or "intermediate" lymphocytes, having either a diffuse or a nodular (follicular) pattern of growth[901] ("marginal zone B-cell lymphomas").[905] Many of these tumors exhibit focal plasmacytoid features,[904] and a few are composed of signet

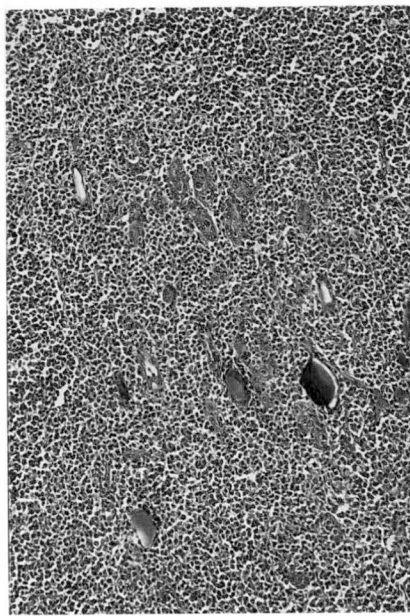 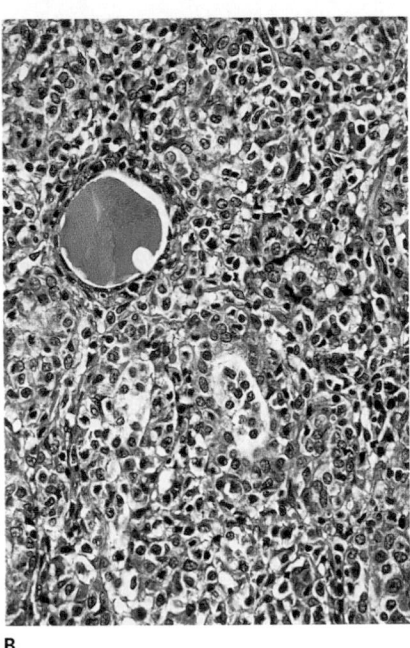

A   **B**

Fig. 9.90 A and **B**, Malignant lymphoma of thyroid. **A**, Low-power view showing a diffuse pattern of growth. **B**, Medium-power view showing tumor cells surrounding lymphoid follicles. One of the follicles shows "packing" of the lumen by lymphoid cells, a feature of diagnostic significance.

ring cells.[896] It has been proposed that both of these major thyroid lymphoma types belong to the MALT-type category despite a follicular architecture in about one quarter of the cases. This architecture is thought to be the result of colonization of the follicles by the tumor cells.[897,900,905] This is supported by the fact that large cell lymphomas often show an associated low-grade MALT-type component,[924] and that some show a marginal zone distribution of the tumor cells.[910] True follicle center lymphomas of the thyroid are exceptional.[905]

Immunohistochemically, all types of thyroid lymphomas exhibit consistent positivity for CD45, and nearly all of them show markers indicative of B-cell derivation,[907,916] whereas primary thyroid T-cell lymphomas are vanishingly rare.[895] An important diagnostic finding is the packing of follicular lumina by lymphoid cells ("lymphoepithelial lesions"), a feature usually not present in thyroiditis.[904] The differential diagnosis includes the small cell variant of medullary carcinoma and insular carcinoma, and it may require the use of immunohistochemistry.[928]

A very high proportion of primary thyroid lymphomas arise in a background of lymphocytic or Hashimoto's thyroiditis, this association representing one of the better documented examples of the pathogenetic link between immunoproliferation and autoimmune disease.[899,921] Accordingly, most of the patients have positive serum tests for antithyroid antibodies.[900] The Epstein–Barr virus does not seem to play a major pathogenetic role.[912]

The tumor may be restricted to the thyroid, may spread to the soft tissues by direct extension, or may involve the regional nodes. The prognosis is better for intrathyroid tumors than for those that have extended beyond the thyroid capsule,[929] and for marginal zone B-cell lymphomas than for diffuse large B-cell lym-

phomas.[905] Most treatment failures result from distant recurrences.[909] It is not uncommon for this recurrence to be located in the gastrointestinal tract.[927]

The treatment of thyroid lymphoma usually includes thyroidectomy followed by adjuvant therapy that varies depending on the lymphoma subtype[898]; in cases with extrathyroidal involvement, surgical debulking does not seem to be necessary before the administration of adjuvant therapy.[919]

Primary thyroid lymphoma should be distinguished from systemic lymphoma with thyroid involvement, a rather unusual event.

Plasmacytoma of thyroid can be seen as a component of widespread myeloma or as the only manifestation of the disease.[923] Immunoglobulin abnormalities may be present in the serum.[917] The term should be restricted to tumors entirely composed of plasma cells of various degrees of maturity; tumors with a lymphoid component should be placed in the malignant lymphoma category.[902] Plasmacytoma should also be distinguished from *plasma cell granuloma*, a non-neoplastic condition in which a polyclonal infiltrate of mature plasma cells is seen admixed with other inflammatory cells in a fibrotic background.[911]

Hodgkin's lymphoma involving primarily the thyroid is extremely rare, but its occurrence has been documented. Most of the cases have been of the nodular sclerosis type, and some have shown concomitant involvement of cervical lymph nodes[908] (Fig. 9.91).

Langerhans' cell histiocytosis (histiocytosis X, eosinophilic granuloma) can involve the thyroid gland as an isolated event[925,926] (Fig. 9.92). Practically all reported cases have occurred against a background of lymphocytic/Hashimoto's thyroiditis, and some have also involved the adjacent parathyroid glands.[930] A different

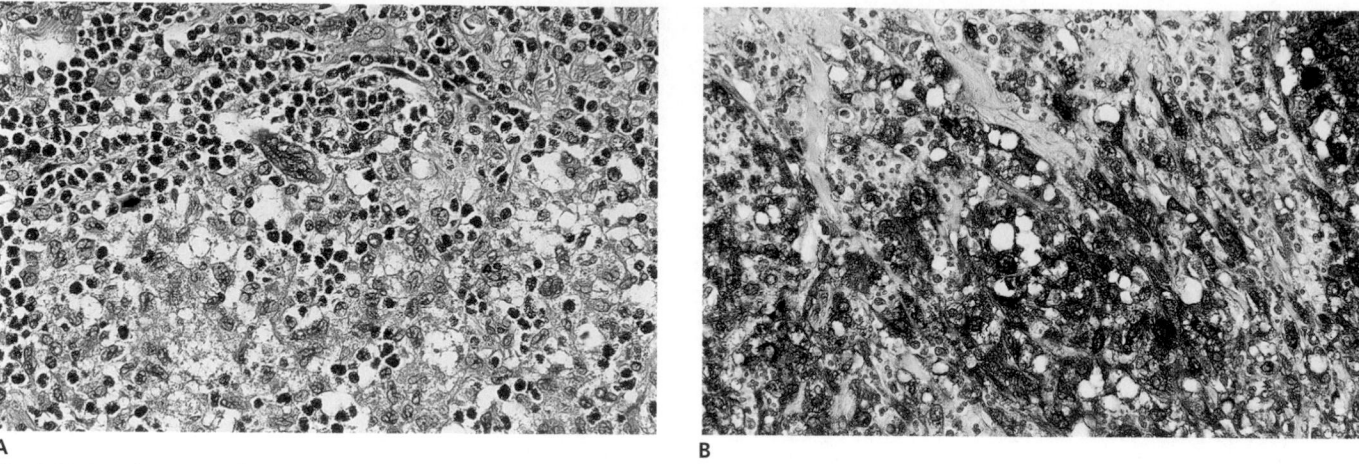

Fig. 9.91 A and **B**, Langerhans' cell histiocytosis involving the thyroid gland. **A**, Infiltrate composed of Langerhans' cells and eosinophils. **B**, S-100 protein immunoreactivity of Langerhans' cells.

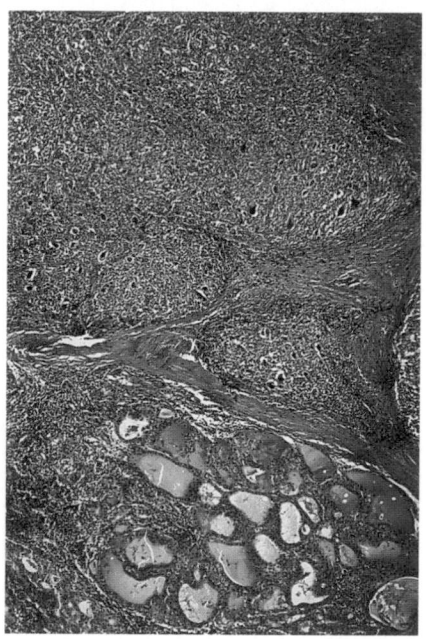 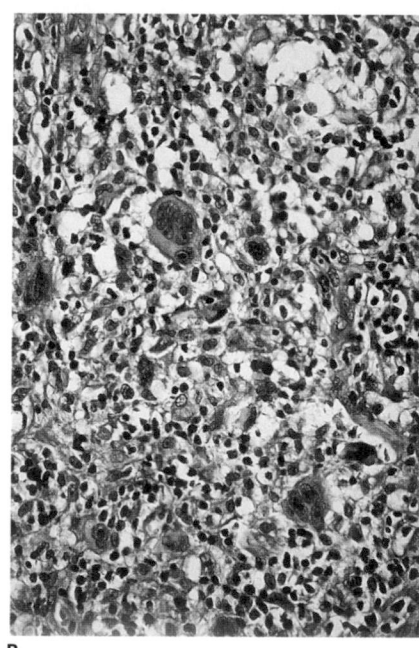

Fig. 9.92 A and **B**, Hodgkin's lymphoma involving the thyroid gland. **A**, Low-power view showing a nodular pattern of growth. **B**, High-power view showing a polymorphic infiltrate containing Reed–Sternberg cells. (Courtesy of Dr. Juan Jose Segura, San Jose, Costa Rica)

phenomenon is that of Langerhans' cell histiocytosis in lymph nodes draining papillary thyroid carcinoma.

Rosai–Dorfman disease (sinus histiocytosis with massive lymphadenopathy) can also involve the thyroid gland, either as an isolated event or as a component of multisystem disease.[913]

Extramedullary hematopoiesis has been observed within the substance of thyroid nodules in patients with myelofibrosis (agnogenic myeloid metaplasia).[914,915,922]

Mesenchymal tumors

Benign mesenchymal tumors of thyroid are exceptional. Isolated cases of *lipoma, hemangioma,*[935,950] *lymphangioma,*[937] *leiomyoma,*[931,959] *schwannoma,*[931,955] and *solitary fibrous tumor* have been reported, the latter with an increasing frequency.[934,941,951] While on the subject of hemangioma, we

thought of mentioning here the strange phenomenon by which severe hypothyroidism can accompany infantile hemangioma of liver and other sites as a result of degradation of thyroid hormone in the tumor tissue by type 3 iodothyronine deiodinase activity.[939]

Sarcomas of various microscopic types have been reported in the thyroid, usually in the form of individual case reports. These include *fibrosarcoma,*[953] *liposarcoma,*[932] *leiomyosarcoma,*[940,956] *chondrosarcoma,*[958] *osteosarcoma,*[948] and *malignant peripheral nerve sheath tumor.*[947,955] Some of the leiomyosarcomas have occurred in a setting of immunodeficiency in association with the Epstein–Barr virus.[959] It should be remembered that most sarcoma-like thyroid tumors are examples of the spindle or giant cell types of undifferentiated carcinoma[953] (see p. 552).

Controversy still exists about the frequency and very existence of thyroid *angiosarcoma*, most examples of which have been reported from Switzerland and other

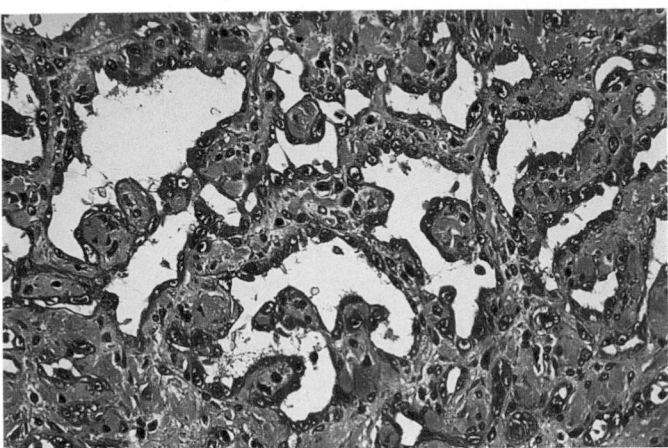

Fig. 9.93 Angiosarcoma of the thyroid. The tumor is well differentiated and composed of anastomosing vascular channels lined by somewhat epithelioid endothelial cells.

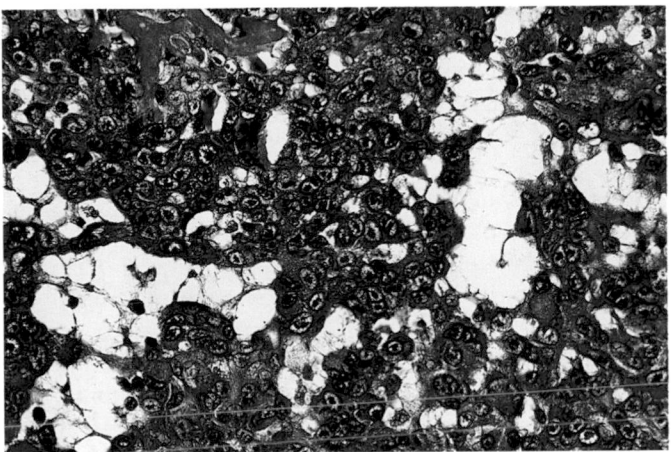

Fig. 9.94 Epithelioid angiosarcoma of thyroid. Note the prominent nucleoli.

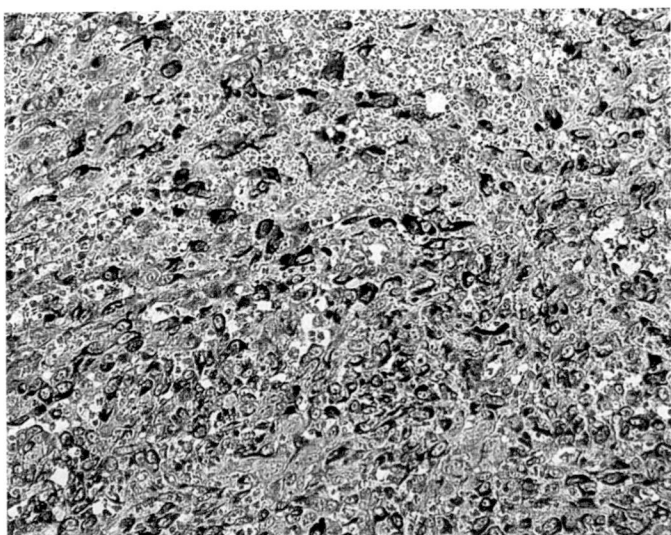

Fig. 9.95 Keratin immunoreactivity in thyroid angiosarcoma. There was also positivity for endothelial markers.

mountainous regions. There is no question that some of these neoplasms exhibit all the attributes of angiosarcoma, such as anastomosing vascular channels, Weibel–Palade bodies on ultrastructural examination, immunoreactivity for FVIII-related antigen and other endothelial cell markers, and tendency to produce hemorrhagic pleuropulmonary metastases[933,949,952,957] (Fig. 9.93). Some of the tumors we have studied have shown, together with a typical angiosarcomatous architecture and immunoreactivity for endothelial markers, an epithelioid morphology, accompanied by marked nucleolar prominence and immunoreactivity for keratin[936,943] (Figs 9.94 and 9.95). We have interpreted these lesions (some of which have occurred in non-Alpine areas[944]) as keratin-positive epithelioid angiosarcomas, in analogy to similar lesions we and others have seen in other sites, such as skin, bone, and uterine corpus.[938,960] Other authors prefer to regard these and related tumors as anaplastic carcinomas, the apparent discrepancy being due to the perennial issue of presumed histogenesis versus phenotype.[942,945,946] Most cases of this tumor type have arisen in glands with nodular hyperplasia, and the evolution has been almost uniformly fatal.

Low-grade malignant examples of endothelial vascular tumor in the category of *epithelioid hemangioendothelioma* have also been reported.[954]

Other primary tumors and tumorlike conditions

Teratomas of thyroid usually occur in infants or children.[968] The large majority of the cases have been cystic and benign. They can lead to obstruction of the airway, necessitating emergency surgery because of their location in the mid neck and the huge size that they can attain.[969]

The few thyroid teratomas that have been described in adults have been malignant[961]; some of the reported cases and several that we have personally observed had a very primitive neuroepithelial component with rosette formations associated with islands of well-differentiated cartilage.[963,968] We have reinterpreted another group of reported cases[966] as representing neoplasms showing thymic or related branchial pouch differentiation[962] (see Chapter 8).

Parathyroid tumors can occur within the thyroid gland and create problems of differential diagnosis with follicular neoplasms. They are further described in Chapter 10.

Amyloidosis can involve the thyroid as part of a systemic disease or as a localized primary *amyloid tumor* ("amyloid goiter").[964,967] The lesion may be unilateral or bilateral and is commonly associated with a foreign body-type reaction. The amyloid deposits are often accompanied by mature adipose tissue.

Malakoplakia has been described involving the thyroid and mimicking a malignant neoplasm clinically.[965]

Thymic and branchial pouch-derived tumors can involve the thyroid gland and simulate primary thyroid neoplasms; they are discussed in Chapter 8.

Metastatic tumors

Direct extension into the thyroid may occur in carcinomas of pharynx, larynx, trachea, or esophagus, as well as from metastatic lesions from adjacent cervical lymph nodes.[980] The majority of these tumors are of squamous cell type; therefore the possibility of secondary invasion should be considered when such a tumor type is encountered in a thyroid specimen, especially if the tumor is relatively well differentiated.

Blood-borne metastases are found in the thyroid at autopsy in about 10% of patients dying of malignant tumors; the most common sites for the primary tumor are skin (melanoma) (39%), breast (21%), kidney (12%), and lung (11%)[979] (Fig. 9.96). These metastases can be solitary (most commonly), multiple, or diffuse.[974] Some of these metastases are found in preexisting thyroid lesions, such as follicular neoplasms or papillary carcinoma of either the classical or follicular variant type.[970,976,978]

It is rare for metastases to the thyroid to simulate clinically a primary thyroid neoplasm.[973,977] The outstanding exception is renal cell carcinoma, which can present as a thyroid mass in the absence of renal symptoms years or decades after the removal of the primary tumor.[971,972] The differential diagnosis is with primary thyroid tumors with clear cell features (see p. 547). Features favoring the diagnosis of metastatic renal cell carcinoma are multiplicity of the nodules, optically clear (as opposed to finely granular) cytoplasm, sinusoidal-type blood vessels, intraluminal fresh hemorrhage, and a large amount of cytoplasmic glycogen and fat[971,972a] (Fig. 9.97). Immunohistochemical stains for thyroglobulin and TTF-

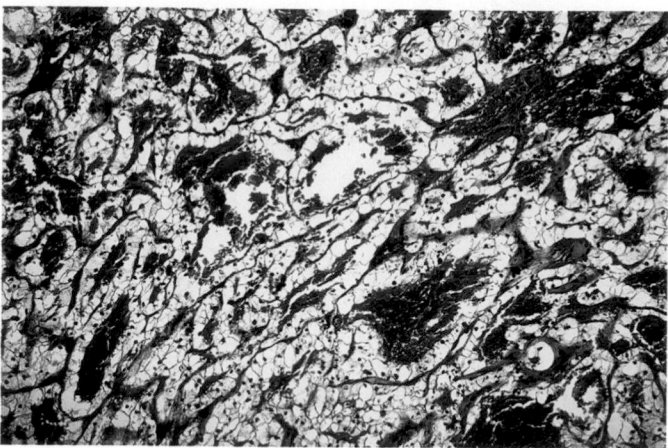

Fig. 9.97 Renal cell carcinoma of clear cell type metastatic to thyroid. Note the blood-filled glands.

1 are also helpful, but one should be aware of the fact that diffusion of the former marker from entrapped follicles may occur, with subsequent nonspecific absorption by neighboring tumor cells[971] (see Chapter 3). If material from the primary renal tumor is available, a molecular comparison with the thyroid clear cell neoplasm can also be helpful.[975]

For adenocarcinomas of other types, mucin stains are also of some use. Although exceptions certainly occur (see p. 549), the presence of intracytoplasmic mucin of an epithelial type in a malignant tumor located within the thyroid gland points toward a metastatic origin. Similarly, the presence of mucin in a metastatic tumor of unknown source makes very unlikely the possibility that the primary is in the thyroid gland. This traditional approach has been complemented and to a large extent superseded by immunohistochemical evaluation for markers such as thyroglobulin, TTF-1, CEA, and the various keratins.

The fact that neuroendocrine carcinomas can exceptionally metastasize to the thyroid and simulate a thyroid primary tumor (particularly medullary carcinoma) has already been mentioned.

References

Normal anatomy

1 Beckner ME, Schultz JJ, Richardson T. Solid and cystic ultimobranchial body remnants in the thyroid. Arch Pathol Lab Med 1990, **114:** 1049–1052.

2 Bell CD, Kovacs K, Horvath E, Rotondo F. Histologic, immunohistochemical, and ultrastructural findings in a case of minocycline-associated "black-thyroid". Endocr Pathol 2002, **12:** 443–451.

3 Bulley ID, Gatter KC, Hertet A, Mason DY. Expression of intermediate filament proteins in normal and diseased thyroid glands. J Clin Pathol 1987, **40:** 136–142.

4 Cameselle-Teijeiro J, Varela-Duran J, Sambade C, Villanueva JP, Varela-Nunez R, Sobrinho-Simões M. Solid cell nests of the thyroid. Light microscopy and immunohistochemical profile. Hum Pathol 1994, **25:** 684–693.

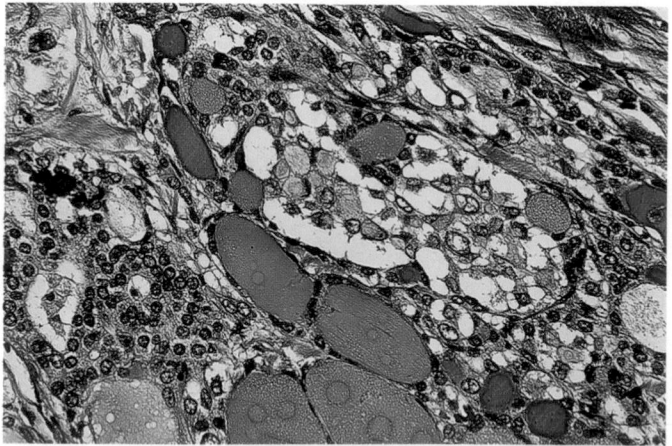

Fig. 9.96 Lobular carcinoma of the breast with signet ring features metastatic to thyroid.

5 Cameselle-Tejeiro J, Varela-Duran J. Intrathyroid salivary gland-type tissue in multinodular goiter. Virchows Arch 1994 **425:** 331–334.

5a Carcangiu ML. Thyroid. In Sternberg S (ed.): Histology for pathologists ed. 2, Philadelphia, 1997, Lippincott-Raven, 1075–1092.

6 Carpenter JL, Emery GR. Inclusions in the human thyroid. J Anat 1976, **122:** 77–89.

7 Chan JK, Rosai J. Tumors of the neck showing thymic or related branchial pouch differentiation. A unifying concept. Hum Pathol 1991, **22:** 349–367.

8 Crile G Jr. The fallacy of the conventional radical neck dissection for papillary carcinoma of the thyroid. Ann Surg 1957, **145:** 317–320.

9 DeLellis RA, Wolfe HJ. The pathobiology of the human calcitonin (C)-cell. A review. Pathol Annu 1981, 16(Pt 2): 25–52.

10 Harach HR. Solid cell nests in the thyroid. J Pathol 1988, **155:** 191–200.

11 Harach HR. Thyroglobulin in human thyroid follicles with acid mucin. J Pathol 1991, **164:** 261–263.

12 Hoyes AD, Kershaw DR. Anatomy and development of the thyroid gland. Ear Nose Throat J 1985, **64:** 318–333.

13 Isotalo PA, Lloyd RV. Presence of birefringent crystals is useful in distinguishing thyroid from parathyroid gland tissues. Am J Surg Pathol 2002, **26:** 813–814.

14 Katoh R, Kawaoi A, Miyagi E, Li X, Suzuki K, Nakamura Y, Kakudo K. Thyroid transcription factor-1 in normal, hyperplastic, and neoplastic follicular thyroid cells examined by immunohistochemistry and nonradioactive in situ hybridization. Mod Pathol 2000, **13:** 570–576.

15 Katoh R, Kawaoi A, Muramatsu A, Hemmi A, Suzuki K. Birefringent (calcium oxalate) crystals in thyroid diseases. A clinicopathological study with possible implications for differential diagnosis. Am J Surg Pathol 1993, **17:** 698–705.

16 Klinck GH, Oertel JE, Winship T. Ultrastructure of normal human thyroid. Lab Invest 1970, **22:** 2–22.

17 Kurata A, Ohta K, Mine M, Fukuda T, Ikari N, Kanazawa H, Matsunaga M, Izumi M, Nagataki S. Monoclonal antihuman thyroglobulin antibodies. J Clin Endocrinol Metab 1984, **59:** 573–579.

18 Landas SK, Schelper RL, Tio FO, Turner JW, Moore KC, Bennett-Gray J. Black thyroid syndrome. Exaggeration of a normal process? Am J Clin Pathol 1986, **85:** 411–418.

19 Lau SK, Luthringer DJ, Eisen RN. Thyroid transcription factor-1: a review. AIMM 2002, **10:** 97–102.

20 LiVolsi VA, Merino MJ. Squamous cells in the human thyroid gland. Am J Surg Pathol 1978, **2:** 133–140.

21 LiVolsi VA. The utility of some modern techniques in understanding thyroid pathology. Endocr Pathol 1990, **1:** 68–84.

22 Martin V, Martin L, Viennet G, Hergel M, Carbillet JP, Fellmann D. Ultrastructural features of "solid cell nest" of the human thyroid gland: a study of 8 cases. Ultrastruct Pathol 2000, **24:** 1–8.

23 Miettinen M, Virtanen I. Expression of laminin in thyroid gland and thyroid tumors. An immunohistologic study. Int J Cancer 1984, **34:** 27–30.

24 Mitchell JD, Kirkham N, Machin D. Focal lymphocytic thyroiditis in Southampton. J Pathol 1984, **144:** 269–273.

25 Mizukami Y, Nonomura A, Michigishi T, Noguchi M, Hashimoto T, Nakamura S, Ishizaki T. Solid cell nests of the thyroid. A histologic and immunohistochemical study. Am J Clin Pathol 1994, **101:** 186–191.

26 Money SR, Muss W, Thelmo WL, Boeckl O, Pimpl W, Kaindl H, Sungler P, Kirwin J, Waclawicek H, Jaffe B, Pertshuk LP. Immunocytochemical localization of estrogen and progesterone receptors in human thyroid. Surgery 1989, **106:** 975–979.

27 O'Toole K, Fenoglio-Preiser C, Pushparaj N. Endocrine changes associated with the human aging process. III. Effect of age on the number of calcitonin immunoreactive cells in the thyroid gland. Hum Pathol 1985, **16:** 991–1000.

28 Ozaki O, Ito K, Sugino K, Yasuda K, Yamashita T, Toshima K. Solid cell nests of the thyroid gland. Virchows Arch [A] 1991, **418:** 201–205.

29 Papotti M, Gugliotta P, Forte G, Bussolati G. Immunocytochemical identification of oxyphilic mitochondrion-rich cells. Appl Immunohistochem 1994, **2:** 261–267.

30 Reid JD, Choi C-H, Oldroyd NO. Calcium oxalate crystals in the thyroid. Their identification, prevalence, origin, and possible significance. Am J Clin Pathol 1987, **87:** 443–454.

30a Reis-Filho J, Preto A, Soares P, Ricardo S, Cameselle-Teijeiro J, Sobrinho-Simões M. P63 expression in solid cell nests of the thyroid: further evidence for a stem cell origin. Mod Pathol 2003, **16:** 43–48.

31 Rigaud C, Bogomoletz WV. "Mucin secreting" and "mucinous" primary thyroid carcinomas. Pitfalls in mucin histochemistry applied to thyroid tumours. J Clin Pathol 1987, **40:** 890–895.

31a Saad A, Bove KE, Stanek J, Medvedovic M, Nikoforov YE. Proliferative activity of thyroid follicular cells in different age groups and its correlation with the risk of radiation-induced thyroid cancer. (Abstract) Mod Pathol 2003, **16:** 7a–8a.

32 Schmid KW, Kirchmair R, Ladurner D, Fischer-Colbrie R, Bocker W. Immunohistochemical comparison of chromogranins A and B and secretogranin II with calcitonin and calcitonin gene-related peptide expression in normal, hyperplastic and neoplastic C-cells of the human thyroid. Histopathology 1992, **21:** 225–232.

33 Schroder S, Bocker W. Lipomatous lesions of the thyroid gland. A review. Appl Pathol 1985, **3:** 140–149.

34 Stanta G, Carcangiu ML, Rosai J. The biochemical and immunohistochemical profile of thyroid neoplasia. Pathol Annu 1988, 23(Pt 1): 129–157.

35 Stevenson JC. The structure and function of calcitonin. Invest Cell Pathol 1980, **3:** 187–193.

36 Sugiyama S. The embryology of the human thyroid gland including ultimobranchial body and others related. Ergeb Anat Entwicklungsgesch 1971, **44:** 3–111.

37 Veinot JP, Ghadially FN. Melanosis thyroidi. Ultrastruct Pathol 1998, **22:** 401–406.

Congenital abnormalities

38 Adler M, Freeman JL. Hürthle cell carcinoma of the thyroglossal duct. Head Neck 1991, **10:** 446–449.

39 Aguirre A, de la Piedra M, Ruiz R, Portilla J. Ectopic thyroid tissue in the submandibular region. Oral Surg Oral Med Oral Pathol 1991, **71:** 73–76.

40 Allard RHB. The thyroglossal cyst. Head Neck Surg 1982, **5:** 134–146.

41 Bernstein A, Scardino PT, Tomaszewki M-M, Cohen MH. Carcinoma arising in a branchial cleft cyst. Cancer 1976, **37:** 2417–2422.

42 Bhaskar SN, Bernier JL. Histogenesis of branchial cysts. A report of 468 cases. Am J Pathol 1959, **35:** 407–423.

43 Coleman WR, Homer RS, Kaplan RP. Branchial cleft heterotopia of the lower neck. J Cutan Pathol 1989, **16:** 353–358.

44 Compagno J, Hyams VJ, Safavian M. Does branchiogenic carcinoma really exist? Arch Pathol Lab Med 1976, **100:** 311–314.

45 Diaz-Arias AA, Bickel JT, Loy TS, Croll GH, Puckett CL, Havey AD. Follicular carcinoma with clear cell change arising in lingual thyroid. Oral Surg Oral Med Oral Pathol 1992, **74:** 206–211.

46 Ein SH, Shandling B, Stephens CA, Mancer K. The problem of recurrent thyroglossal duct remnants. J Pediatr Surg 1984, **19:** 437–439.

46a Falconieri G, Libera DD, Zanella M. Papillary thyroid carcinoma of the thyroglossal duct cyst. Int J Surg Pathol 2001, **9:** 65–71.

47 Finkle HI, Goldman RL. Heterotopic cartilage in the thyroid. Arch Pathol 1973, **95:** 48–49.

48 Joseph TJ, Komorowski RA. Thyroglossal duct carcinoma. Hum Pathol 1975, **6**: 717–729.

49 Kantelip B, Lusson JR, DeRiberolles C, Lamaison D, Bailly P. Intracardiac ectopic thyroid. Hum Pathol 1986, **17**: 1293–1296.

50 Langlois NE, Krukowski ZH, Miller ID. Pancreatic tissue in a lateral cervical cyst attached to the thyroid gland—a presumed foregut remnant. Histopathology 1997, **31**: 378–380.

51 LiVolsi VA, Perzin KH, Savetsky L. Carcinoma arising in median ectopic thyroid (including thyroglossal duct tissue). Cancer 1974, **34**: 1303–1315.

52 Lyall D, Stahl WM Jr. Lateral cervical cysts, sinuses, and fistulas of congenital origin. Int Abstr Surg 1956, **102**: 417–434.

53 Maran AGD, Buchanan DR. Branchial cysts, sinuses and fistulae. Clin Otolaryngol 1978, **3**: 77–92.

54 Matsumoto K, Watanabe Y, Asano G. Thyroid papillary carcinoma arising in ectopic thyroid tissue within a branchial cleft cyst. Pathol Int 1999, **49**: 444–446.

55 Micheau C, Cachin Y, Caillou B. Cystic metastases in the neck revealing occult carcinoma of the tonsil. A report of six cases. Cancer 1974, **33**: 228–233.

56 Nussbaum M, Buchwald RP, Ribner A, Mori K, Litwins J. Anaplastic carcinoma arising from median ectopic thyroid (thyroglossal duct remnant). Cancer 1981, **48**: 2724–2728.

57 Osammor JY, Bulman CH, Blewitt RW. Intralaryngotracheal thyroid. J Laryngol Otol 1990, **104**: 733–736.

58 Ryska A, Vokurka J, Michal M, Ludvikova M. Intrathyroidal lymphoepithelial cyst. A report of two cases not associated with Hashimoto's thyroiditis. Pathol Res Pract 1997, **193**: 777–781.

59 Sauk JJ Jr. Ectopic lingual thyroid. J Pathol 1970, **102**: 239–243.

60 Sekine S, Nagata M, Hamada H, Watanabe T. Heterotopic thyroid tissue at the porta hepatis in a fetus with trisomy 18. Virchows Arch 2000, **436**: 498–501.

61 Shareef DS, Salm R. Ectopic vestigial lesions of the neck and shoulders. J Clin Pathol 1981, **34**: 1155–1162.

62 Shiraishi T, Imai H, Fukutome K, Watanabe M, Yatani R. Ectopic thyroid in the adrenal gland. Hum Pathol 1999, **30**: 105–108.

63 Solomon JR, Rangecroft L. Thyroglossal-duct lesions in childhood. J Pediatr Surg 1984, **19**: 555–561.

64 Soucy P, Penning J. The clinical relevance of certain observations on the histology of the thyroglossal tract. J Pediatr Surg 1984, **19**: 506–509.

65 Streutker CJ, Murray D, Kovacs K, Higgins HP. Epithelial cyst of thyroid. Endocr Pathol 1997, **8**: 75–80.

66 Weiss SD, Orlich CC. Primary papillary carcinoma of a thyroglossal duct cyst. Report of a case and literature review. Br J Surg 1991, **78**: 87–89.

67 Wilson DB. Embryonic development of the head and neck. Part 2. The branchial region. Head Neck Surg 1979, **2**: 59–66.

Thyroiditis
Acute thyroiditis

68 Berger SA, Zonszein J, Villamena P, Mittman N. Infectious diseases of the thyroid gland. Rev Infect Dis 1983, **5**: 108–122.

69 Frank TS, LiVolsi VA, Connor AM. Cytomegalovirus infection of the thyroid in immunocompromised adults. Yale J Biol Med 1987, **60**: 1–8.

70 Guttler R, Singer PA, Axline SG, Greaves TS, McGill JJ. *Pneumocystis carinii* thyroiditis. Report of three cases and review of the literature. Arch Intern Med 1993, **153**: 393–396.

71 Hazard JB. Thyroiditis. A review. Am J Clin Pathol 1955, **25**: 289–298, 399–426.

72 Miyauchi A, Matsuzuka F, Kuma K, Takai S. Piriform sinus fistula. An underlying abnormality common in patients with acute suppurative thyroiditis. World J Surg 1990, **14**: 400–405.

73 Rossiter JL, Topf P. Acute suppurative thyroiditis with bilateral piriform sinus fistulae. Otolaryngol Head Neck Surg 1991, **105**: 625–628.

74 Singer PA. Thyroiditis. Acute, subacute and chronic. Med Clin North Am 1991, **75**: 61–77.

75 Skuza K, Rapaport R, Fieldman R, Goldstein S, Marquis J. Recurrent acute suppurative thyroiditis. J Otolaryngol 1991, **20**: 126–129.

76 Volpé R. Etiology, pathogenesis, and clinical aspects of thyroiditis. Pathol Annu 1978, **13**(Pt 2): 399–413.

Granulomatous (de Quervain's) thyroiditis

77 Ngulassy S, Hnilica P, Buc M, Guman M, Hirschova V, Stefanovic J. Subacute (de Quervain's) thyroiditis: association with HLA Bw35 antigen and abnormalities of the complement system, immunoglobuins and other serum proteins. J Clin Endocrinol Metab 1977, **45**: 270–274.

78 Schmid KW, Ofner C, Ramsauer T, Hittmair A, Tötsch M, Ladurner D, Böcker W. CA 19-9 expression in subacute (de Quervain's) thyroiditis. An immunohistochemical study. Mod Pathol 1992, **5**: 268–272.

79 Singer PA. Thyroiditis. Acute, subacute and chronic. Med Clin North Am 1991, **75**: 61–77.

80 Stein AA, Hernandez I, McClintock JC. Subacute granulomatous thyroiditis. Ann Surg 1961, **153**: 149–156.

81 Volpé R. Etiology, pathogenesis, and clinical aspects of thyroiditis. Pathol Annu 1978, **13**(Pt 2): 399–413.

Other granulomatous inflammations

82 Carney JA, Moore SB, Northcutt RC, Woolner LB, Stillwell GK. Palpation thyroiditis (multifocal granulomatous folliculitis). Am J Clin Pathol 1975, **64**: 639–647.

83 Dan M, Garcia A, von Westrap C. Primary actinomycosis of the thyroid mimicking carcinoma. J Otolaryngol 1984, **13**: 109–112.

84 Kakudo K, Kanokogi M, Mitsunobu M, Sawada K, Uematsu K, Noguchi T, Fujita S. Acute mycotic thyroiditis. Acta Pathol Jpn 1983, **33**: 147–151.

85 Karlish AJ, MacGregor GA. Sarcoidosis, thyroiditis and Addison's disease. Lancet 1970, **2**: 330–333.

86 Leers WD, Dussault J, Mullens JE, Volpé R, Arthurs K. Suppurative thyroiditis. An unusual case caused by *Actinomyces naeslundi*. Can Med Assoc J 1969, **101**: 714–718.

87 Lima MA, Freitas LL, Montandon C, Filho DC, Silva-Vergara ML. The thyroid in acquired immunodeficiency syndrome. Endocr Pathol 1998, **9**: 217–224.

88 Loeb JM, Livermore BM, Wofsy D. Coccidioidomycosis of the thyroid. Ann Intern Med 1979, **91**: 409–412.

89 Manson CM, Cross P, De Sousa B. Post-operative necrotizing granulomas of the thyroid. Histopathology 1992, **21**: 392–393.

90 Mizukami Y, Nonomura A, Michigishi T, Ohmura K, Matsubara S, Noguchi M. Sarcoidosis of the thyroid gland manifested initially as thyroid tumor. Pathol Res Pract 1994, **190**: 1201–1205.

91 Sachs MK, Dickinson G, Amazon K. Tuberculous adenitis of the thyroid mimicking subacute thyroiditis. Am J Med 1988, **85**: 573–575.

92 Szporn AH, Tepper S, Watson CW. Disseminated cryptococcosis presenting as thyroiditis. Acta Cytol 1985, **29**: 449–453.

Autoimmune (lymphocytic and Hashimoto's) thyroiditis

93 Aichinger G, Fill H, Wick G. In situ immune complexes, lymphocyte subpopulations, and HLA-DR-positive epithelial cells in Hashimoto thyroiditis. Lab Invest 1985, **52**: 132–140.

94 Apel RL, Asa SL, Chalvardjian A, Li Volsi VA. Intrathyroidal lymphoepithelial cysts of probable branchial origin. Hum Pathol 1994, **25**: 1238–1242.

95 Barbesino G, Chiovato L. The genetics of Hashimoto's disease. Endocrinol Metab Clin North Am 2000, **29**: 357–374.

96 Ben-Ezra J, Wu A, Sheibani K. Hashimoto's thyroiditis lacks detectable clonal immunoglobulin and T cell receptor gene rearrangements. Hum Pathol 1988, **19**: 1444–1448.

97 Bottazzo GF, Pujol-Borrell R, Hanafusa T, Feldmann M. Role of aberrant HLA-DR expression and antigen presentation in induction of endocrine autoimmunity. Lancet 1983, 2: 1115–1119.

98 Burek CL, Rose NR. Cell-mediated immunity in autoimmune thyroid disease. Hum Pathol 1986, 17: 246–253.

99 Carpenter CCJ, Solomon H, Silverberg SG, Bledsoe T, Northcutt RC, Klinenberg JR, Bennett IL, Harvey AM. Schmidt's syndrome (thyroid and adrenal insufficiency). A review of the literature and a report of fifteen new cases including ten instances of coexistent diabetes mellitus. Medicine (Baltimore) 1964, 43: 153–180.

100 Dailey ME, Lindsay S, Skahen R. Relation of thyroid neoplasms to Hashimoto's disease of the thyroid gland. Arch Surg 1955, 70: 291–297.

101 Davies TF, Kendler DL. Mechanisms of human autoimmune thyroid disease. Monogr Pathol 1993, 35: 103–117.

102 Davies TF, Martin A, Concepcion ES, Graves P, Cohen L, Ben-Nun A. Evidence of limited variability of antigen receptors on intrathyroidal T cells in autoimmune thyroid disease. N Engl J Med 1991, 325: 238–244.

103 Dayan CM, Daniels GH. Chronic autoimmune thyroiditis. N Engl J Med 1996, 335: 99–107.

104 Gluck FB, Nusynowitz ML, Plymate S. Chronic lymphocytic thyroiditis, thyrotoxicosis, and low radioactive iodine uptake. Report of four cases. N Engl J Med 1975, 293: 624–628.

105 Greenberg AH, Czernichow P, Hung W, Shelley W, Winship T, Blizzard RM. Juvenile chronic lymphocytic thyroiditis. Clinical, laboratory and histological correlations. J Clin Endocrinol Metab 1970, 30: 293–301.

106 Hirota Y, Tamai H, Hayashi Y, Matsubayashi S, Matsuzuka F, Kuma K, Kumagai F, Nagataki S. Thyroid function and histology in forty-five patients with hyperthyroid Graves' disease in clinical remission more than ten years after thionamide drug treatment. J Clin Endocrinol Metab 1986, 62: 165–169.

107 Holm L-E, Blomgren H, Löwhagen T. Cancer risks in patients with chronic lymphocytic thyroiditis. N Engl J Med 1985, 312: 601–604.

108 Hsi ED, Singleton TP, Svoboda SM, Schnitzer B, Ross CW. Characterization of the lymphoid infiltrate in Hashimoto thyroiditis by immunohistochemistry and polymerase chain reaction for immunoglobulin heavy chain gene rearrangement. Am J Clin Pathol 1998, 110: 327–333.

109 Huang W, Kukes GD. Hashimoto's thyroiditis: an organ-specific autoimmune disease – pathogenesis and recent developments. Lab Invest 1999, 79: 1175–1180.

110 Katz SM, Vickery AL. The fibrous variant of Hashimoto's thyroiditis. Hum Pathol 1974, 5: 161–170.

111 Khardori R, Eagleton LE, Soler NG, McConnachie PR. Lymphocytic interstitial pneumonitis in autoimmune thyroid disease. Am J Med 1991, 90: 649–652.

112 Knecht H, Hedinger Chr E. Ultrastructural findings in Hashimoto's thyroiditis and focal lymphocytic thyroiditis with reference to giant cell formation. Histopathology 1982, 6: 511–538.

113 Knecht H, Saremaslani P, Hedinger Chr E. Immunohistological findings in Hashimoto's thyroiditis, focal lymphocytic thyroiditis and thyroiditis de Quervain. Comparative study. Virchows Arch [A] 1981, 393: 215–231.

114 Louis DN, Vickery AL Jr, Rosai J, Wang CA. Multiple branchial cleft-like cysts in Hashimoto's thyroiditis. Am J Surg Pathol 1989, 13: 45–49.

115 Mizukami Y, Michigishi T, Kawato M, Sato T, Nonomura A, Hashimoto T, Matsubara F. Chronic thyroiditis. Thyroid function and histologic correlations in 601 cases. Hum Pathol 1992, 23: 980–988.

116 Mizukami Y, Michigishi T, Nonomura A, Nakamura S, Ishizaki T. Pathology of chronic thyroiditis. A new clinically relevant classification. Pathol Annu 1994, 29(Pt 1): 135–158.

117 Muller-Hocker J, Jacob U, Seibel P. Hashimoto thyroiditis is associated with defects of cytochrome-c oxidase in oxyphil Askanazy cells and with the common deletion (4,977) of mitochondrial DNA. Ultrastruct Pathol 1998, 22: 91–100.

118 Nikiforova MN, Caudill CM, Biddinger P, Nikiforov YE. Prevalence of RET/PTC rearrangements in Hashimoto's thyroiditis and papillary thyroid carcinomas. Int J Surg Pathol 2001, 10: 15–22.

119 Nikolai TF, Brosseau J, Kettrick MA, Roberts R, Beltaos E. Lymphocytic thyroiditis with spontaneously resolving hyperthyroidism (silent thyroiditis). Arch Intern Med 1980, 140: 478–482.

120 Okayasu I. The relationship of lymphocytic thyroiditis to the development of thyroid carcinoma. Endocr Pathol 1997, 8: 225–230.

120a Pearce EN, Farwell AP, Braverman LE. Thyroiditis. N Engl J Med 2003, 348: 2646–2655.

121 Rapoport B. Pathophysiology of Hashimoto's thyroiditis and hypothyroidism. Annu Rev Med 1991, 42: 91–96.

122 Roman SH, Greenberg D, Rubinstein P, Wallenstein S, Davies TF. Genetics of autoimmune thyroid disease. Lack of evidence for linkage to HLA within families. J Clin Endocrinol Metab 1992, 74: 496–503.

123 Saravanan P, Dayan CM. Thyroid autoantibodies. Endocrinol Metab Clin North Am 2001, 30: 315–337.

124 Sheils OM, O'Leary JJ, Uhlmann V, Lattich K, Sweeney EC. Ret/PTC-1 activation in Hashimoto thyroiditis. Int J Surg Pathol 2000, 8: 185–189.

125 Singer PA. Thyroiditis. Acute, subacute and chronic. Med Clin North Am 1991, 75: 61–77.

126 Takasu N, Yamada T, Sato A, Nakagawa M, Komiya I, Nagasawa Y, Asawa T. Graves' disease following hypothyroidism due to Hashimoto's disease. Studies of eight cases. Clin Endocrinol 1990, 33: 687–698.

127 Tamimi DM. The association between chronic lymphocytic thyroiditis and thyroid tumors. Int J Surg Pathol 2002, 10: 141–146.

128 Thomas CG Jr, Rutledge RG. Surgical intervention in chronic (Hashimoto's) thyroiditis. Ann Surg 1981, 193: 769–776.

129 Volpé R. Etiology, pathogenesis, and clinical aspects of thyroiditis. Pathol Annu 1978, 13(Pt 2): 399–413.

130 Volpé R (ed.). Autoimmunity and endocrine disease. New York, 1985, Marcel Dekker, pp. 109–285.

131 Volpé R, Farid NR, Von Westarp C, Row VV. The pathogenesis of Graves' disease and Hashimoto's thyroiditis. Clin Endocrinol 1974, 3: 239–261.

132 Weiss LM, Weinberg DS, Warhof MJ. Medullary carcinoma arising in a thyroid with Hashimoto's disease. J Clin Pathol 1983, 80: 534–538.

133 Weitzman JJ, Ling SM, Kaplan SA, Reed GB, Costin G, Landing BH. Percutaneous needle biopsy of goiter in childhood. J Pediatr Surg 1970, 5: 251–255.

134 Wick MR, Sawyer MD. Antigenic alteration in autoimmune thyroid diseases. Arch Pathol Lab Med 1989, 113: 77–81.

135 Wirtschafter A, Schmidt R, Rosen D, Kundu N, Santoro M, Fusco A, Multhaupt H, Atkins JP, Rosen MR, Keane WM, Rothstein JL. Expression of the RET/PTC fusion gene as a marker for papillary carcinoma in Hashimoto's thyroiditis. Laryngoscope 1997, 107: 95–100.

Riedel's thyroiditis

136 Baloch ZW, Feldman MD, LiVolsi VA. Combined Riedel's disease and fibrosing Hashimoto's thyroiditis: A report of three cases with two showing coexisting papillary carcinoma. Endocr Pathol 2000, 11: 157–163.

137 Comings DE, Skubi KB, Van Eyes J, Motulsky AG. Familial multifocal fibrosclerosis. Ann Intern Med 1967, 66: 884–892.

138 Harach HR, Williams ED. Fibrous thyroiditis. An immunopathological study. Histopathology 1983, 7: 739–751.

139 Julie C, Vieillefond A, Desligneres S, Schaison G, Grunfeld J, Franc B. Hashimoto's thyroiditis associated with Riedel's thyroiditis and retroperitoneal fibrosis. Pathol Res Pract 1997, **193**: 573–577.

140 Schwaegerle SM, Bauer TW, Esselstyn CB. Riedel's thyroiditis. Am J Clin Pathol 1988, **90**: 715–722.

141 Woolner LB, McConaher WM, Beahrs OH. Invasive fibrous thyroiditis. J Clin Endocrinol Metab 1957, **17**: 201–220.

Hyperplasia
Dyshormonogenetic goiter

142 Alabbasy AJ, Delbridge L, Eckstein R, Cowell C, Silink M. Microfollicular thyroid adenoma and congenital goitrous hypothyroidism. Arch Dis Child 1992, **67**: 1294–1295.

143 Batsakis JG, Nishiyama RH, Schmidt RW. Sporadic goiter syndrome. A clinicopathologic analysis. Am J Clin Pathol 1963, **39**: 241–251.

144 Camargo RYA, Gross JL, Silveiro SP, Knobel M, Medeiros-Neto G. Pathological findings in dyshormonogenetic goiter with defective iodide transport. Endocr Pathol 1998, **9**: 225–234.

145 Cooper DS, Axelrod L, DeGroot LJ, Vickery AL Jr, Maloof F. Congenital goiter and the development of metastatic follicular carcinoma with evidence for a leak of nonhormonal iodide. Clinical, pathological, kinetic, and biochemical studies and a review of the literature. J Clin Endocrinol Metab 1981, **52**: 294–306.

146 Fadda G, Baloch ZW, LiVolsi VA. Dyshormonogenetic goiter pathology. Int J Surg Pathol 1999, **7**: 125–132.

147 Ghossein RA, Rosai J, Heffess C. Dyshormonogenetic goiter: A clinicopathologic study of 56 cases. Endocr Pathol 1997, **8**: 283–292.

148 Kopp P, van Sande J, Parma J, Duprez L, Gerber H, Joss E, Jameson JL, Dumont JE, Vassart G. Congenital hyperthyroidism caused by a mutation in the thyrotropin-receptor gene. N Engl J Med 1995, **332**: 150–160.

149 Kennedy JS. The pathology of dyshormonogenetic goiter. J Pathol 1969, **99**: 251–264.

150 Lever EG, Medeiros-Neto GA, De Groot LJ. Inherited disorders of thyroid metabolism. Endocr Rev 1983, **4**: 213–239.

151 Matos PS, Bisi H, Medeiros-Neto G. Dyshormonogenetic goiter: a morphological and immunohistochemical study. Endocr Pathol 1994, **5**: 59–65.

152 Moore GH. The thyroid in sporadic goitrous cretinism. Arch Pathol 1962, **74**: 35–46.

153 Rego KG, Billerbeck AE, Targovnik HM, Santos CL, Alkmin MG, Barbosa S, Camargo R, Medeiros-Neto G. Clinical, pathological, and molecular studies of two families with iodide organification defect. Endocr Pathol 1997, **8**: 37–47.

154 Vickery AL. The diagnosis of malignancy in dyshormonogenetic goitre. Clin Endocrinol Metab 1981, **10**: 317–335.

Graves' disease (diffuse toxic goiter)

155 Bradley EL III, Liechty RD. Modified subtotal thyroidectomy for Graves' disease. A two-institution study. Surgery 1983, **94**: 955–958.

156 Caruso DR, Mazzaferri EL. Intervention in Graves' disease. Choosing among imperfect but effective treatment options. Postgrad Med 1992, **92**: 117–124, 128–129, 133–134.

157 Cavalieri RR, Gerard SK. Unusual types of thyrotoxicosis. Adv Intern Med 1991, **36**: 271–286.

158 Chardes T, Chapal N, Bresson D, Bes C, Giudicelli V, Lefranc MP, Peraldi-Roux S. The human anti-thyroid peroxidase autoantibody repertoire in Graves' and Hashimoto's autoimmune thyroid diseases. Immunogenetics 2002, **54**: 141–157.

159 Curran RC, Eckert H, Wilson GM. The thyroid gland after treatment of hyperthyroidism by partial thyroidectomy or iodine 131. J Pathol Bacteriol 1958, **76**: 541–560.

160 Davies T, Marians R, Latif R. The TSH receptor reveals itself. J Clin Invest 2002, **110**: 209–217.

161 Eggen PC, Seljelid R. The histological appearance of hyperfunctioning thyroids following various pre-operative treatments. Acta Pathol Microbiol Scand [A] 1973, **81**: 16–20.

162 Falk SA. The management of hyperthyroidism. A surgeon's perspective. Otolaryngol Clin North Am 1990, **23**: 361–380.

163 Farbota LM, Calandra DB, Lawrence AM, Paloyan E. Thyroid carcinoma in Graves' disease. Surgery 1985, **98**: 1148–1152.

164 Farrar JJ, Toft AD. Iodine-131 treatment of hyperthyroidism. Current issues. Clin Endocrinol 1991, **35**: 207–212.

165 Friedman NB, Catz B. The reactions of euthyroid and hyperthyroid glands to radioactive iodine. Arch Pathol Lab Med 1996, **120**: 660–661.

166 Hancock SL, Cox RS, McDougall IR. Thyroid diseases after treatment of Hodgkin's disease. N Engl J Med 1991, **325**: 599–605.

167 Hanson GA, Komorowski RA, Cerletty JM, Wilson SD. Thyroid gland morphology in young adults. Normal subjects versus those with prior low-dose neck irradiation in childhood. Surgery 1983, **96**: 984–988.

168 Hargreaves AW, Garner A. The significance of lymphocytic infiltration of the thyroid gland in thyrotoxicosis. Br J Surg 1968, **55**: 543–545.

169 Judd R, Bueso-Ramos C. Combined true thymic hyperplasia and lymphoid hyperplasia in Graves' disease. Pediatr Pathol 1990, **10**: 829–836.

170 Margolick JB, Hsu S-M, Volkman DJ, Burman KD, Fauci AS. Immunohistochemical characterization of intrathyroid lymphocytes in Graves' disease. Interstitial and intraepithelial populations. Am J Med 1984, **76**: 815–821.

171 Mazzaferri EL. Thyroid cancer and Graves' disease (editorial). J Clin Endocrinol Metab 1990, **70**: 826–829.

172 Mizukami Y, Michigishi T, Nonomura A, Hashimoto T, Moguchi M, Ohmura K, Matsubara F. Histologic changes in Graves' thyroid gland after ^{131}I therapy for hyperthyroidism. Acta Pathol Jpn 1992, **42**: 419–426.

173 Nixon DW, Samols E. Acral changes associated with thyroid diseases. JAMA 1970, **212**: 1175–1181.

174 Pfaltz M, Hedinger CE. Abnormal basement membrane structures in autoimmune thyroid disease. Lab Invest 1966, **55**: 531–539.

175 Smith BR. Thyroid autoantibodies. Scand J Clin Lab Invest Suppl 2001, **235**: 45–52.

176 Smyrk TC, Goellner JR, Brennan MD, Carney JA. Pathology of the thyroid in amiodarone-associated thyrotoxicosis. Am J Surg Pathol 1987, **11**: 197–204.

177 Spjut HJ, Warren WD, Ackerman LV. A clinical-pathologic study of 76 cases of recurrent Graves' disease, toxic (nonexophthalmic) goiter, and non-toxic goiter. Am J Clin Pathol 1957, **27**: 367–392.

178 Sridama V, McCormick M, Kaplan EL, Fauchet R, DeGroot LJ. Long-term follow-up study of compensated low-dose ^{131}I therapy for Graves' disease. N Engl J Med 1984, **311**: 426–432.

179 Takamatso J, Takeda K, Katayama S, Sakane S, Morita S, Kuma K, Ohsawa N. Epithelial hyperplasia and decreased colloid content of the thyroid gland in triiodothyronine-predominant Graves' disease. J Clin Endocrinol Metab 1992, **75**: 1145–1150.

180 Weetman AP. Graves' disease. N Engl J Med 2000, **343**: 1236–1248.

181 Wilkin TJ. Receptor autoimmunity in endocrine disorders. N Engl J Med 1990, **323**: 1318–1324.

182 Winsa B, Adami HO, Bergstron R, Gamstedt A, Dahlberg PA, Adamson Û, Jansson R, Karlsson A. Stressful life events and Graves' disease. Lancet 1991, **338**: 1475–1479.

183 Zimmerman D, Gan-Gaisano M. Hyperthyroidism in children and adolescents. Pediatr Clin North Am 1990, **37**: 1273–1295.

Nodular hyperplasia

184 Baloch ZW, LiVolsi VA. Clonality in thyroid nodules: the hyperplasia–neoplasia sequence. Endocr Pathol 1998, **9**: 287–292.

185 Berghout A, Wiersinga WM, Smits NJ, Touber JL.

Interrelationships between age, thyroid volume, thyroid nodularity, and thyroid function in patients with sporadic nontoxic goiter. Am J Med 1990, **89:** 602–608.

186 Brown RS, Pohl SL, Jackson IMD, Reichlin S. Do thyroid-stimulating immunoglobulins cause non-toxic and toxic multinodular goitre? Lancet 1978, **1:** 904–906.

187 Chung DH, Kang GH, Kim WH, Ro JY. Clonal analysis of a solitary follicular nodule of the thyroid with the polymerase chain reaction method. Mod Pathol 1999, **12:** 265–271.

188 DeLellis RA, Tischler AS. Clonality of endocrine proliferative lesions: a critical reappraisal. Endocr Pathol 1998, **9:** 281–286.

189 Derwahl M, Studer H. Nodular goiter and goiter nodules: Where iodine deficiency falls short of explaining the facts. Exp Clin Endocrinol Diabetes 2001, **109:** 250–260.

190 Doniach I. Etiological consideration of thyroid carcinoma. In Smithers D (ed.): Tumors of the thyroid gland. Monographs on neoplastic disease at various sites, vol. 6. Edinburgh, 1970, E. & S. Livingstone.

191 Gaitan E, Nelson NC, Poole GV. Endemic goiter and endemic thyroid disorders. World J Surg 1991, **15:** 205–215.

192 Greene R. Lymphadenoid change in the thyroid gland and its relation to postoperative hypothyroidism. Mem Soc Endocrinol 1953, **1:** 16–20.

193 Hargreaves AW, Garner A. The significance of lymphocytic infiltration of the thyroid gland in thyrotoxicosis. Br J Surg 1968, **55:** 543–545.

194 Hermus AR, Huysmans DA. Treatment of benign nodular thyroid disease. N Engl J Med 1998, **338:** 1438–1447.

195 Hicks DG, LiVolsi VA, Neidich JA, Puck JM, Kant JA. Clonal analysis of solitary follicular nodules in the thyroid. Am J Pathol 1990, **137:** 553–562.

196 Katoh R, Bray CE, Suzuki K, Komiyama A, Hemmi A, Kawaoi A, Oyama T, Sugai T, Sugai T, Sasou S. Growth activity in hyperplastic and neoplastic human thyroid determined by an immunohistochemical staining procedure using monoclonal antibody MIB-1. Hum Pathol 1995, **26:** 139–146.

197 Maiorano E, Ambrosi A, Giorgino R, Fersini M, Pollice L, Ciampolillo A. Insulin-like growth factor 1 (IGF-1) in multinodular goiters. A possible pathogenetic factor. Pathol Res Pract 1994, **190:** 1012–1016.

198 Mortensen JD, Woolner LB, Bennett WA. Gross and microscopic findings in clinically normal thyroid glands. J Clin Endocrinol Metab 1955, **15:** 1270–1280.

199 Sugenoya A, Masuda H, Komatsu M, Yokoyama S, Shimizu T, Fujimori M, Kobayashi S, Iida F. Adenomatous goitre. Therapeutic strategy, postoperative outcome, and study of epidermal growth factor receptor. Br J Surg 1992, **79:** 404–406.

200 Studer H, Gerber H, Zbaeren J, Peter HJ. Histomorphological and immunohistochemical evidence that human nodular goiters grow by episodic replication of multiple clusters of thyroid follicular cells. J Clin Endocrinol Metab 1992, **75:** 1151–1158.

201 Studer H, Ramelli F. Simple goiter and its variants. Euthyroid and hyperthyroid multinodular goiters. Endocr Rev 1982, **3:** 40–61.

202 Thomas GA, Williams D, Williams ED. The clonal origin of thyroid nodules and adenomas. Am J Pathol 1989, **134:** 141–147.

203 Tunbridge WMG, Evered DC, Hall R, Appleton D, Brewis M, Clark F, Evans JG. The spectrum of thyroid disease in a community. The Whickham survey. Clin Endocrinol 1977, **7:** 481–493.

204 Woeber KA. Iodine and thyroid disease. Med Clin North Am 1991, **75:** 169–178.

Tumors

205 Zampi G, Carcangiu ML, Rosai J (eds). Thyroid tumor pathology. Proceedings of an international workshop, San Miniato, Italy, October 1984. Semin Diagn Pathol 1985, **2:** 87–146.

Follicular adenoma

206 Belfiore A, Sava L, Runello F, Tomaselli L, Vigneri R. Solitary autonomously functioning thyroid nodules and iodine deficiency. J Clin Endocrinol Metab 1983, **56:** 283–287.

207 Campbell WL, Santiago HE, Perzin KH, Johnson PM. The autonomous thyroid nodule. Correlation of scan appearance and histopathology. Radiology 1973, **107:** 133–138.

208 Cohen MB, Miller TR, Beckstead JH. Enzyme histochemistry and thyroid neoplasia. Am J Clin Pathol 1986, **85:** 668–673.

209 Dal Cin P, Sneyers W, Aly MS, Segers A, Ostijn F, Van Damme B, Van Den Berghe H. Involvement of 19q13 in follicular thyroid adenoma. Cancer Genet Cytogenet 1992, **60:** 99–101.

210 Fukunaga M, Shinozaki N, Endo Y, Ushigome S. Atypical adenoma of the thyroid. A clinico-pathologic and flow cytometric DNA study in comparison with other follicular neoplasms. Acta Pathol Jpn 1992, **42:** 632–638.

211 Gharib H, James EM, Charboneau JW, Naessens JM, Offord KP, Gorman CA. Suppressive therapy with levothyroxine for solitary thyroid nodules. A double-blind controlled clinical study. N Engl J Med 1987, **317:** 70–75.

212 Gnepp DR, Ogorzalek JM, Heffess CS. Fat-containing lesions of the thyroid gland. Am J Surg Pathol 1989, **13:** 605–612.

213 Goldstein R, Hart IR. Follow-up of solitary autonomous thyroid nodules treated with [131]I. N Engl J Med 1983, **309:** 1473–1476.

214 Hamburger JI. Solitary autonomously functioning thyroid lesions. Diagnosis, clinical features and pathogenetic considerations. Am J Med 1975, **58:** 740–748.

215 Harach HR, Sanchez SS, Williams ED. Pathology of the autonomously functioning (hot) thyroid nodule. Ann Diagn Pathol 2002, **6:** 10–19.

216 Harach HR, Soubeyran I, Brown A, Bonneau D, Longy M. Thyroid pathologic findings in patients with Cowden disease. Ann Diagn Pathol 1999, **3:** 331–340.

217 Hazard JB, Kenyon R. Atypical adenoma of the thyroid. Arch Pathol 1954, **58:** 554–563.

218 Hicks DG, LiVolsi VA, Neidich JA, Puck JM, Kant JA. Clonal analysis of solitary follicular nodules in the thyroid. Am J Pathol 1990, **137:** 553–562.

219 Hostetter AL, Hrafnkelsson J, Wingren SO, Enestrom S, Nordenskjöld B. A comparative study of DNA cytometry methods for benign and malignant thyroid tissue. Am J Clin Pathol 1988, **89:** 760–763.

220 Hruban RH, Huvos AG, Traganos F, Reuter V, Lieberman PH, Melamed MR. Follicular neoplasms of the thyroid in men older than 50 years of age. A DNA flow cytometric study. Am J Clin Pathol 1990, **94:** 527–532.

221 Karga H, Lee JK, Vickery AL Jr, Thor A, Gaz RD, Jameson JL. Ras oncogene mutations in benign and malignant thyroid neoplasms. J Clin Endocrinol Metab 1991, **73:** 832–836.

222 Koren R, Bernheim J, Schachter P, Schwartz A, Siegel A, Gal R. Black thyroid adenoma: Clinical, histochemical, and ultrastructural features. AIMM 2000, **8:** 80–84.

223 Lang W, Georgii A, Stauch G, Kienzle E. The differentiation of atypical adenomas and encapsulated follicular carcinomas in the thyroid gland. Virchows Arch [A] 1980, **385:** 125–141.

224 Mai KT, Landry DC, Thomas J, Burns BF, Commons AS, Yazdi HM, Odell PF. Follicular adenoma with papillary architecture: a lesion mimicking papillary thyroid carcinoma. Histopathology 2001, **39:** 25–32.

225 Miettinen M, Virtanen I. Expression of laminin in thyroid gland and thyroid tumors. An immunohistologic study. Int J Cancer 1984, **34:** 27–30.

226 Mizukami Y, Michigishi T, Nonomura A, Yokoyama K, Noguchi M, Hashimoto T, Nakamura S, Ishizaki T. Autonomously functioning (hot) nodule of the thyroid gland. A clinical and histopathologic study of 17 cases. Am J Clin Pathol 1994, **101:** 29–35.

227 Namba H, Matsuo K, Fagin JA. Clonal composition of benign and malignant human thyroid tumors. J Clin Invest 1990, **86:** 120–125.

228 Oyama T, Vickery AL Jr, Preffer FI, Colvin RB. A comparative study of flow cytometry and histopathological findings in thyroid follicular carcinomas and adenomas. Hum Pathol 1994, **25:** 271–275.

229 Panke TW, Croxson MS, Parker JW, Carriere DP, Rosoff L Sr, Warner NE. Triiodothyronine-secreting (toxic) adenoma of the thyroid gland. Light and electron microscopic characteristics. Cancer 1978, **41:** 528–537.

230 Sapino A, Cassoni P, Papotti M, Bussolati G. Muscular cushions of the vessel wall at the periphery of thyroid nodules. Mod Pathol 1999, **12:** 879–884.

231 Shlossberg AH, Jacobson JC, Ibbertson HK. Serum thyroglobulin in the diagnosis and management of thyroid carcinoma. Clin Endocrinol 1979, **10:** 17–27.

232 Thomas GA, Williams D, Williams ED. The clonal origin of thyroid nodules and adenomas. Am J Pathol 1989, **134:** 141–147.

233 Visoná A, Pea M, Bozzola L, Stracca-Pansa V, Meli S. Follicular adenoma of the thyroid gland with extensive chondroid metaplasia. Histopathology 1991, **18:** 278–279.

234 Zedenius J, Auer G, Backdahl M, Falkmer U, Grimelius L, Lundell G, Wallin G. Follicular tumors of the thyroid gland. Diagnosis, clinical aspects and nuclear DNA analysis. World J Surg 1992, **16:** 589–594.

Hyalinizing trabecular adenoma and related lesions

235 Carney JA, Ryan J, Goellner JR. Hyalinizing trabecular adenoma of the thyroid gland. Am J Surg Pathol 1987, **11:** 583–591.

236 Chan JK, Tse CCH, Chiu HS. Hyalinizing trabecular adenoma-like lesion in multinodular goitre. Histopathology 1990, **16:** 611–614.

237 Cheung CC, Boerner SL, MacMillan CM, Ramyar L, Asa SL. Hyalinizing trabecular tumor of the thyroid: a variant of papillary carcinoma proved by molecular genetics. Am J Surg Pathol 2000, **24:** 1622–1626.

238 Fonseca E, Nesland JM, Sobrinho-Simões M. Expression of stratified epithelial-type cytokeratins in hyalinizing trabecular adenomas supports their relationship with papillary carcinomas of the thyroid. Histopathology 1997, **31:** 330–335.

239 Hirokawa M, Carney JA. Cell membrane and cytoplasmic staining for MIB-1 in hyalinizing trabecular adenoma of the thyroid gland. Am J Surg Pathol 2000, **24:** 575–578.

240 Hirokawa M, Carney JA, Ohtsuki Y. Hyalinizing trabecular adenoma and papillary carcinoma of the thyroid gland express different cytokeratin patterns. Am J Surg Pathol 2000, **24:** 877–881.

241 Katoh R, Jasani B, Williams ED. Hyalinizing trabecular adenoma of the thyroid. A report of three cases with immunohistochemical and ultrastructural studies. Histopathology 1989, **15:** 211–224.

242 Katoh R, Kakudo K, Kawaoi A. Accumulated basement membrane material in hyalinizing trabecular tumors of the thyroid. Mod Pathol 1999, **12:** 1057–1061.

243 Li M, Carcangiu ML, Rosai J. Abnormal intracellular and extracellular distribution of basement membrane material in papillary carcinoma and hyalinizing trabecular tumors of the thyroid: implication for deregulation of secretory pathways. Hum Pathol 1997, **28:** 1366–1372.

244 Li M, Rosai J, Carcangiu ML. Hyalinizing trabecular adenoma of the thyroid. A distinct tumor type or a pattern of growth? Evaluation of 28 cases (abstract). Mod Pathol 1995, **8:** 54A.

245 Libbey NP, Hemstreet MK, Butmarc JR, Tibbetts LM, Tucci JR. Paraganglioma-like adenomas of the thyroid (PLAT): incidental lesions with unusual features in a patient with nodular goiter. Endocr Pathol 1997, **8:** 143–151.

246 LiVolsi VA. Hyalinizing trabecular tumor of the thyroid: adenoma, carcinoma, or neoplasm of uncertain malignant potential. Am J Surg Pathol 2000, **24:** 1683–1684.

247 McCluggage WG, Sloan JM. Hyalinizing trabecular carcinoma of thyroid gland. Histopathology 1996, **28:** 357–362.

248 Molberg K, Albores-Saavedra J. Hyalinizing trabecular carcinoma of the thyroid gland. Hum Pathol 1994, **25:** 192–197.

249 Papotti M, Riella P, Montemurro F, Pietribiasi F, Bussolati G. Immunophenotypic heterogeneity of hyalinizing trabecular tumours of the thyroid. Histopathology 1997, **31:** 525–533.

250 Papotti M, Volante M, Giuliano A, Fassina A, Fusco A, Bussolati G, Santoro M, Chiappetta G. RET/PTC activation in hyalinizing trabecular tumors of the thyroid. Am J Surg Pathol 2000, **24:** 1615–1621.

251 Rothenberg HJ, Goellner JR, Carney JA. Hyalinizing trabecular adenoma of the thyroid gland: recognition and characterization of its cytoplasmic yellow body. Am J Surg Pathol 1999, **23:** 118–125.

Papillary carcinoma
General features

252 Carcangiu ML, Zampi G, Pupi A, Castagnoli A, Rosai J. Papillary carcinoma of the thyroid. A clinicopathologic study of 241 cases treated at the University of Florence, Italy. Cancer 1985, **55:** 805–828.

253 Farbota LM, Calandra DB, Lawrence AM, Paloyan E. Thyroid carcinoma in Graves' disease. Surgery 1985, **98:** 1148–1152.

254 Ott RA, Calandra DB, McCall A, Shah KH, Lawrence AM, Paloyan E. The incidence of thyroid carcinoma in patients with Hashimoto's thyroiditis and solitary cold nodules. Surgery 1985, **98:** 1202–1206.

255 Schlumberger MJ. Papillary and follicular thyroid carcinoma. N Engl J Med 1998, **338:** 297–306.

Gross features

256 Carcangiu ML, Zampi G, Pupi A, Castagnoli A, Rosai J. Papillary carcinoma of the thyroid. A clinicopathologic study of 241 cases treated at the University of Florence, Italy. Cancer 1985, **55:** 805–828.

Microscopic features

256a Baloch ZW, LiVolsi VA. Etiology and significance of the "optically clear nucleus". Endo Pathol 2002, **13:** 289–299.

257 Carcangiu ML, Zampi G, Rosai J. Papillary thyroid carcinoma. A study of its many morphologic expressions and clinical correlates. Pathol Annu 1985, **20**(Pt 1): 1–44.

258 Chan JKC, Saw D. The grooved nucleus. A useful diagnostic criterion of papillary carcinoma of the thyroid. Am J Surg Pathol 1986, **10:** 672–679.

259 Chan JKC, Tse CCH. Mucin production in metastatic papillary carcinoma of the thyroid. Hum Pathol 1988, **19:** 195–200.

260 Deligeorgi-Politi H. Nuclear crease as a cytodiagnostic feature of papillary thyroid carcinoma in fine-needle aspiration biopsies. Diagn Cytopathol 1987, **3:** 307–310.

261 Gray A, Doniach I. Morphology of the nuclei of papillary carcinoma of the thyroid. Br J Cancer 1969, **23:** 49–51.

262 Guiter GE, DeLellis RA. Multinucleate giant cells in papillary thyroid carcinoma. A morphologic and immunohistochemical study. Am J Clin Pathol 1996, **106:** 765–768.

262a Hunt JL, Barnes EL. Non-tumor-associated psammoma bodies in the thyroid. Am J Clin Pathol 2003, **119:** 90–94.

263 Johannessen JV, Gould VE, Jao W. The fine structure of human thyroid cancer. Hum Pathol 1978, **9:** 385–400.

264 Johannessen JV, Sobrinho-Simões M. The origin and significance of thyroid psammoma bodies. Lab Invest 1980, **43:** 287–296.

265 Katoh R, Sasaki J, Kurihara H, Suzuki K, Iida Y, Kawaoi A. Multiple thyroid involvement (intraglandular metastasis) in papillary thyroid carcinoma. A clinicopathologic study of 105 consecutive patients. Cancer 1992, **70:** 1585–1590.

266 Klinck GH, Winship T. Psammoma bodies and thyroid cancer. Cancer 1959, **12**: 656–662.

267 Lee TK, Myers RT, Marshall RB, Bond MG, Kardon B. The significance of mitotic rate. A retrospective study of 127 thyroid carcinomas. Hum Pathol 1985, **16**: 1042–1046.

268 Margolin FR, Winfield J, Steinbach HL. Patterns of thyroid calcifications. Roentgenologic-histologic study of excised specimens. Invest Radiol 1967, **2**: 208–212.

269 Naganuma H, Murayama H, Ohtani N, Takaya K, Mori K, Sakai N, Kakudo K. Optically clear nuclei in papillary carcinoma of the thyroid: demonstration of one of the fixation artifacts and its practical usefulness. Pathol Int 2000, **50**: 113–118.

270 Patchefsky AS, Hoch WS. Psammoma bodies in diffuse toxic goiter. Am J Clin Pathol 1972, **57**: 551–556.

270a Rezk SA, Fischer AF, Nelson V, Thein M, Byrnes RK, Khan A. Beta-catenin expression in papillary thyroid carcinoma: potential role in nuclear envelope changes. (Abstract). Mod Pathol 2003, **16**: 109a.

271 Russell WO, Ibanez ML, Clark RL, White EC. Thyroid carcinoma. Classification, intraglandular dissemination and clinicopathological study based upon whole organ sections of 80 glands. Cancer 1963, **16**: 1425–1460.

272 Schröder S, Schwarz W, Rehpenning W, Loning T, Bocker W. Dendritic/Langerhans cells and prognosis in patients with papillary thyroid carcinomas. Immunocytochemical study of 106 thyroid neoplasms correlated to follow-up data. Am J Clin Pathol 1988, **89**: 295–300.

273 Selzer G, Kahn LB, Albertyn L. Primary malignant tumors of the thyroid gland. A clinicopathologic study of 254 cases. Cancer 1977, **40**: 1501–1510.

274 Tscholl-Ducommun J, Hedinger CE. Papillary thyroid carcinomas. Morphology and prognosis. Virchows Arch [A] 1982, **396**: 19–39.

275 Tunio GM, Hirota S, Nomura S, Kitamura Y. Possible relation of osteopontin to development of psammoma bodies in human papillary thyroid cancer. Arch Pathol Lab Med 1998, **122**: 1087–1090.

276 Vergilio JA, Baloch ZW, LiVolsi VA. Spindle cell metaplasia of the thyroid arising in association with papillary carcinoma and follicular adenoma. Am J Clin Pathol 2002, **117**: 199–204.

277 Vickery AL Jr. Thyroid papillary carcinoma. Am J Surg Pathol 1983, **7**: 797–807.

278 Yamashita T, Hosoda Y, Kameyama K, Aiba M, Ito K, Fujimoto Y. Peculiar nuclear clearing composed of microfilaments in papillary carcinoma of the thyroid. Cancer 1992, **70**: 2923–2928.

Electron microscopic features

279 Albores-Saavedra J, Altamirano-Dimas M, Alcorta-Anguizola B, Smith M. Fine structure of human papillary thyroid carcinoma. Cancer 1971, **28**: 763–774.

280 Beaumont A, Ben Othman S, Fragu P. The fine structure of papillary carcinoma of the thyroid. Histopathology 1981, **5**: 377–388.

281 Echeverria OM, Hernandez-Pando R, Vazquez-Nin GH. Ultrastructural, cytochemical, and immunocytochemical study of nuclei and cytoskeleton of thyroid papillary carcinoma cells. Ultrastruct Pathol 1998, **22**: 185–197.

282 Johannessen JV, Gould VE, Jao W. The fine structure of human thyroid cancer. Hum Pathol 1978, **9**: 385–400.

283 Li M, Carcangiu ML, Rosai J. Abnormal intracellular and extracellular distribution of basement membrane material in papillary carcinoma and hyalinizing trabecular tumors of the thyroid: implication for deregulation of secretory pathways. Hum Pathol 1997, **28**: 1366–1372.

Histochemical and immunohistochemical features

284 Alves P, Soares P, Fonseca E, Sobrinho-Simões M. Papillary thyroid carcinoma overexpresses fully and underglycosylated mucins together with native and sialylated simple mucin antigens and histo-blood group antigens. Endocr Pathol 1999, **10**: 315–324.

285 Alves P, Soares P, Rossi S, Fonseca E, Sobrinho-Simões M. Clinicopathologic and prognostic significance of the expression of mucins, simple mucin antigens, and histo-blood group antigens in papillary thyroid carcinoma. Endocr Pathol 1999, **10**: 305–315.

285a Arif S, Blanes A, Diaz-Cano SJ. Hashimoto's thyroiditis shares features with early papillary thyroid carcinoma. Histopathology 2002, **41**: 357–362.

286 Baloch ZW, Abraham S, Roberts S, LiVolsi VA. Differential expression of cytokeratins in follicular variant of papillary carcinoma: an immunohistochemical study and its diagnostic utility. Hum Pathol 1999, **30**: 1166–1171.

287 Beesley MF, McLaren KM. Cytokeratin 19 and galectin-3 immunohistochemistry in the differential diagnosis of solitary thyroid nodules. Histopathology 2002, **41**: 236–243.

288 Bejarano PA, Nikiforov YE, Swenson ES, Biddinger PW. Thyroid transcription factor-1, thyroglobulin, cytokeratin 7, and cytokeratin 20 in thyroid neoplasms. AIMM 2000, **8**: 189–194.

289 Buley ID, Gatter KC, Heryet A, Mason DY. Expression of intermediate filament proteins in normal and diseased thyroid glands. J Clin Pathol 1987, **40**: 136–142.

290 Cheung CC, Ezzat S, Freeman JL, Rones IB, Asa SL. Immunohistochemical diagnosis of papillary thyroid carcinoma. Mod Pathol 2001, **14**: 338–342.

290a Chow S-M, Law SCK, Chan JK, Au S-K, Yau S, Lau W-H. Papillary microcarcinoma of the thyroid – prognostic significance of lymph node metastasis and multifocality. Cancer 2003, **40**: 31–40.

291 Damiani S, Fratamico F, Lapertosa G, Dina R, Eusebi V. Alcian blue and epithelial membrane antigen are useful markers in differentiating benign from malignant papillae in thyroid lesions. Virchows Arch [A] 1991, **419**: 131–135.

292 Diaz NM, Mazoujian G, Wick MR. Estrogen-receptor protein in thyroid neoplasms. An immunohistochemical analysis of papillary carcinoma, follicular carcinoma, and follicular adenoma. Arch Pathol Lab Med 1991, **115**: 1203–1207.

293 Erickson LA, Yousef OM, Jin L, Lohse CM, Pankratz VS, Lloyd RV. p27kip1 expression distinguishes papillary hyperplasia in Graves' disease from papillary thyroid carcinoma. Mod Pathol 2000, **13**: 1014–1019.

294 Fonseca E, Castanhas S, Sobrinho-Simões M. Carbohydrate antigens as oncofetal antigens in papillary carcinoma of the thyroid gland. Endocr Pathol 1997, **8**: 301–303.

295 Fonseca E, Nesland JM, Hoie J, Sobrinho-Simões M. Pattern of expression of intermediate cytokeratin filaments in the thyroid gland: an immunohistochemical study of simple and stratified epithelial-type cytokeratins. Virchows Arch 1997, **430**: 239–245.

296 Henzen-Logmans SC, Mullink H, Ramaekers FCS, Tadema T, Meijer CJLM. Expression of cytokeratins and vimentin in epithelial cells of normal and pathologic thyroid tissue. Virchows Arch [A] 1987, **410**: 347–354.

297 Herrmann ME, LiVolsi VA, Pasha TL, Roberts SA, Wojcik EM, Baloch ZW. Immunohistochemical expression of galectin-3 in benign and malignant thyroid lesions. Arch Pathol Lab Med 2002, **126**: 710–713.

298 Imamura Y, Fukuda M. CD15(C3D-1) immunoreactivity in normal, benign, and malignant thyroid lesions. Appl Immunohistochem 1998, **6**: 181–186.

299 Jennings TA, Boguniewicz AB, Sheehan CE, Figge J. Involucrin selectively stains papillary thyroid carcinoma. Appl Immunohistochem 1998, **6**: 55–61.

300 Kamoshida S, Ogane N, Yasuda M, Muramatsu T, Bessho T, Kajiwara H, Osamura RY. Immunohistochemical study of type-1 blood antigen expression in thyroid tumors: the significance for papillary carcinomas. Mod Pathol 2000, **13**: 736–741.

301 Kato M, Maeta H, Kato S, Shinozawa T, Terada T. Immunohistochemical and in situ hybridization analyses of midkine expression in thyroid papillary carcinoma. Mod Pathol 2000, **13:** 1060–1065.

302 Kawachi K, Matsushita Y, Yonezawa S, Nakano S, Shirao K, Natsugoe S, Sueyoshi K, Aikou T, Sato E. Galectin-3 expression in various thyroid neoplasms and its possible role in metastasis formation. Hum Pathol 2000, **31:** 428–433.

303 Keen CE, Szakacs S, Okon E, Rubin JS, Bryant BM. CA125 and thyroglobulin staining in papillary carcinomas of thyroid and ovarian origin is not completely specific for site of origin. Histopathology 1999, **34:** 113–117.

304 Khan A, Baker SP, Patwardhan NA, Pullman JM. CD57 (leu-7) expression is helpful in diagnosis of the follicular variant of papillary thyroid carcinoma. Virchows Arch 1998, **432:** 427–432.

305 Kragsterman B, Grimelius L, Wallin G, Werga P, Johansson H. Cytokeratin 19 expression in papillary thyroid carcinoma. Appl Immunohistochem 1999, **7:** 186–192.

306 Lai ML, Rizzo N, Liguori C, Zucca G, Faa G. Alpha-1-antichymotrypsin immunoreactivity in papillary carcinoma of the thyroid gland. Histopathology 1998, **33:** 332–336.

307 Li M, Carcangiu ML, Rosai J. Abnormal intracellular and extracellular distribution of basement membrane material in papillary carcinoma and hyalinizing trabecular tumors of the thyroid: implication for deregulation of secretory pathways. Hum Pathol 1997, **28:** 1366–1372.

308 Liberman E, Weidner N. Papillary and follicular neoplasms of the thyroid gland: Differential immunohistochemical staining with high-molecular-weight keratin and involucrin. AIMM 2000, **8:** 42–48.

309 LiVolsi VA, Baloch ZW. Determining the diagnosis and prognosis of thyroid neoplasms: Do special studies help? Hum Pathol 1999, **30:** 885–886.

310 Lloyd RV. Distinguishing benign from malignant thyroid lesions: galectin 3 as the latest candidate. Endocr Pathol 2001, **12:** 255–257.

311 McLaren KM, Cossar DW. The immunohistochemical localization of S100 in the diagnosis of papillary carcinoma of the thyroid. Hum Pathol 1996, **27:** 633–636.

311a Magro G, Perissinotto D, Schiappacassi M, Goletz S, Otto A, Müller E-C, Bisceglia M, Brown G, Ellis T, Grasso S, Colombatti A, Perris R. Proteomic and postproteomic characterization of keratin sulphate-glycanated isoforms of thyroglobulin and transferring uniquely elaborated by papillary thyroid carcinomas. Am J Pathol 2003, **163:** 183–196.

312 Maiorano E, Caimpolillo A, Viale G, Maisonneuve P, Ambrosi A, Triggiani V, Marra E, Perlino E. Insulin-like growth factor 1 expression in thyroid tumors. AIMM 2000, **8:** 110–119.

313 Miettinen M, Kärkkäinen P. Differential reactivity of HBME-1 and CD15 antibodies in benign and malignant thyroid tumours. Preferential reactivity with malignant tumours. Virchows Arch 1996, **429:** 213–219.

314 Miettinen M, Kovatich AJ, Kärkkäinen P. Keratin subsets in papillary and follicular thyroid lesions. A paraffin section analysis with diagnostic implications. Virchows Arch 1997, **431:** 407–413.

315 Nishimura R, Yokose T, Mukai K. S-100 protein is a differentiation marker in thyroid carcinoma of follicular cell origin: An immunohistochemical study. Pathol Int 1997, **47:** 673–679.

316 Oyama T, Ichimura E, Sano T, Kashiwabara K, Fukuda T, Nakajima T. c-Met expression of thyroid tissue with special reference to papillary carcinoma. Pathol Int 1998, **48:** 763–768.

317 Poblete MT, Nualart F, Del Pozo M, Perez JA, Figueroa CD. Alpha₁-antitrypsin expression in human thyroid papillary carcinoma. Am J Surg Pathol 1996, **20:** 956–963.

318 Sahoo S, Hoda SA, Rosai J, DeLellis R. Cytokeratin 19 immunoreactivity in the diagnosis of papillary thyroid carcinoma. A note of caution. Am J Clin Pathol 2001, **116:** 696–702.

319 Schelfhout LJ, Van Muijen GN, Fleuren GH. Expression of keratin 19 distinguishes papillary thyroid carcinoma from follicular carcinomas and follicular thyroid adenoma. Am J Clin Pathol 1989, **92:** 654–658.

319a Stanta G, Carcangiu ML, Rosai J. The biochemical and immunohistochemical profile of thyroid neoplasia. Pathol Annu 1988, **23**(Pt 1)**:** 129–157.

320 Tanda F, Cossu A, Bosincu L, Manca A, Ibba M, Massarelli G. Intracellular adhesion molecule-1 (ICAM-1) immunoreactivity in well-differentiated thyroid papillary carcinomas. Mod Pathol 1996, **9:** 53–56.

321 Tuccari G, Barresi G. Immunohistochemical demonstration of ceruloplasmin in follicular adenomas and thyroid carcinomas. Histopathology 1987, **11:** 723–731.

321a Unger P, Ewart M, Wang BY, Gan L, Kohtz S, Burstein DE. Expression of p63 in papillary thyroid carcinoma and in Hashimoto's thyroiditis: a pathobiologic link? Hum Pathol 2003, **34:** 764–769.

322 Utrilla JC, Martin-Lacave I, San Martin MV, Fernandez-Santos JM, Galera-Davidson H. Expression of c-erbB-2 oncoprotein in human thyroid tumours. Histopathology 1999, **34:** 60–65.

322a Volante M, Allia E, Fulcheri PC, Ghigo E, Muccioli G, Papotti M. Ghrelin in fetal thyroid and follicular tumors and cell lines. Am J Pathol 2003, **162:** 645–654.

323 Yu E, Lee KW, Lee HJ. Expression of promyelocytic leukaemia protein in thyroid neoplasms. Histopathology 2000, **37:** 302–308.

Molecular genetic features

324 Anwar F, Emond MJ, Schmidt RA, Hwang HC, Bronner MP. Retinoblastoma expression in thyroid neoplasms. Mod Pathol 2000, **13:** 562–569.

325 Basolo F, Giannini R, Monaco C, Melillo RM, Carlomagno F, Pancrazi M, Salvatore G, Chiappetta G, Pacini F, Elisei R, Miccoli P, Pinchera A, Fusco A, Santoro M. Potent mitogenicity of the RET/PTC3 oncogene correlates with its prevalence in tall-cell variant of papillary thyroid carcinoma. Am J Pathol 2002, **160:** 247–254.

326 Capella G, Matias-Guiu X, Ampudia X, de Leiva A, Perucho M, Prat J. Ras oncogene mutations in thyroid tumors: polymerase chain reaction-restriction-fragment-length polymorphism analysis from paraffin-embedded tissues. Diagn Mod Pathol 1996, **5:** 45–52.

327 Cerilli LA, Mills SE, Rumpel CA, Dudley TH, Moskaluk CA. Interpretation of RET immunostaining in follicular lesions of the thyroid. Am J Clin Pathol 2002, **118:** 186–193.

328 Corvi R, Martinez-Alfaro M, Harach HR, Zini M, Papotti M, Romeo G. Frequent RET rearrangements in thyroid papillary microcarcinoma detected by interphase fluorescence in situ hybridization. Lab Invest 2001, **81:** 1639–1645.

329 Eng C. Seminars in medicine of the Beth Israel Hospital, Boston. RET proto-oncogene in the development of human cancer. J Clin Oncol 1999, **17:** 380–393.

330 Fischer AH, Bond JA, Taysavang P, Battles OE, Wynford-Thomas D. Papillary thyroid carcinoma oncogene (RET/PTC) alters the nuclear envelope and chromatin structure. Am J Pathol 1998, **153:** 1443–1450.

331 Fusco A, Chiappetta G, Hui P, Garcia-Rostan G, Golden L, Kinder BK, Dillon DA, Giuliano A, Cirafici AM, Santoro M, Rosai J, Tallini G. Assessment of RET/PTC oncogene activation and clonality in thyroid nodules with incomplete morphological evidence of papillary carcinoma: a search for the early precursors of papillary cancer. Am J Pathol 2002, **160:** 2157–2167.

332 Goretzki PE, Lyons J, Stacy-Phipps S, Rosenau W, Demeure M, Clark OH, McCormick F, Roher HD, Bourne HR. Mutational activation of RAS and GSP oncogenes in differentiated thyroid

cancer and their biological implications. World J Surg 1992, **16:** 576–581.

333 Jhiang SM, Cho JY, Furminger TL, Sagartz JE, Tong Q, Capen CC, Mazzaferri EL. Thyroid carcinomas in RET/PTC transgenic mice. Recent Results Cancer Res 1998, **154:** 265–270.

334 Komminoth P. RET proto-oncogene and thyroid cancer. Endocr Pathol 1997, **8:** 235–239.

335 Lam AK, Montone KT, Nolan KA, LiVolsi VA. RET oncogene activation in papillary thyroid carcinoma: prevalence and implication on the histological parameters. Hum Pathol 1998, **29:** 565–568.

336 Nikoforov YE. RET/PTC rearrangement in thyroid tumors. Endocr Pathol 2002, **13:** 3–16.

337 Ringel MD, Anderson J, Souza SL, Burch HB, Tambascia M, Shriver CD, Tuttle RM. Expression of the sodium iodide symporter and thyroglobulin genes are reduced in papillary thyroid cancer. Mod Pathol 2001, **14:** 289–296.

338 Roque L, Nunes VM, Ribeiro C, Martins C, Soares J. Karyotypic characterization of papillary thyroid carcinomas. Cancer 2001, **92:** 2529–2538.

339 Santoro M, Carlomagno F, Hay ID, Herrmann MA, Grieco M, Melillo R, Pierotti MA, Bongarzone I, Della Porta G, Berger N. Ret oncogene activation in human thyroid neoplasms is restricted to the papillary cancer subtype. J Clin Invest 1992, **89:** 1517–1522.

340 Santoro M, Thomas GA, Vecchio G, Williams GH, Fusco A, Chiappetta G, Pozcharskaya V, Bogdanova TI, Demidchik EP, Cherstvoy ED, Voscoboinik L, Tronko ND, Carss A, Bunnell H, Tonnachera M, Parma J, Dumont JE, Keller G, Hofler H, Williams ED. Gene rearrangement and Chernobyl related thyroid cancers. Br J Cancer 2000, **82:** 315–322.

341 Soares P, Fonseca E, Wynford-Thomas D, Sobrinho-Simões M. Sporadic ret-rearranged papillary carcinoma of the thyroid: a subset of slow growing, less aggressive thyroid neoplasms? J Pathol 1998, **185:** 71–78.

342 Sozzi G, Bongarzone I, Miozzo M, Cariani CT, Mondellini P, Calderone C, Pilotti S, Pierotti MA, Della Porta G. Cytogenetic and molecular genetic characterization of papillary thyroid carcinomas. Genes Chromosomes Cancer 1992, **5:** 212–218.

343 Tallini G, Santoro M, Helie M, Carlomagno F, Salvatore G, Chiapetta G, Carcangiu ML, Fusco A. RET/PTC oncogene activation defines a subset of papillary thyroid carcinomas lacking evidence of progression to poorly differentiated or undifferentiated tumor phenotypes. Clin Cancer Res 1998, **4:** 287–294.

343a Zhu Z, Gandhi M, Nikiforova MN, Fischer AH, Nikiforov YE. Molecular profile and clinical-pathologic features of the follicular variant of papillary thyroid carcinoma. Am J Clin Pathol 2003, **120:** 71–77.

Variants

344 Akslen LA, Varhaug JE. Thyroid carcinoma with mixed tall-cell and columnar-cell features. Am J Clin Pathol 1990, **94:** 442–445.

345 Albores-Saavedra J, Gould E, Vardaman C, Vuitch F. The macrofollicular variant of papillary thyroid carcinoma. A study of 17 cases. Hum Pathol 1991, **22:** 1195–1205.

345a Anwar F. The phenotype of Hurthle and Warthin-like papillary thyroid carcinomas is distinct from classic papillary carcinoma as to the expression of retinoblastoma protein and E2F-1 transcription factor. Appl Immunohistochem Mol Morphol 2003, **11:** 20–27.

346 Apel RL, Asa SL, LiVolsi VA. Papillary Hürthle cell carcinoma with lymphocytic stroma. "Warthin-like tumor" of the thyroid. Am J Surg Pathol 1995, **19:** 810–814.

347 Baloch ZW, LaVolsi VA. Warthin-like papillary carcinoma of the thyroid. Arch Pathol Lab Med 2000, **124:** 1192–1195.

348 Baloch ZW, LiVolsi VA. Follicular-patterned lesions of the thyroid. The bane of the pathologist. Am J Clin Pathol 2002, **117:** 143–150.

349 Bell CD, Coire C, Treger T, Volpe R, Baumal R, Fornasier VL. The 'dark nucleus' and disruptions of follicular architecture: possible new histological aids for the diagnosis of the follicular variant of papillary carcinoma of the thyroid. Histopathology 2001, **39:** 33–42.

350 Berends D, Mouthaan PJ. Columnar-cell carcinoma of the thyroid. Histopathology 1992, **20:** 360–362.

351 Berho M, Suster S. The oncocytic variant of papillary carcinoma of the thyroid: a clinicopathologic study of 15 cases. Hum Pathol 1997, **28:** 47–53.

352 Bondeson L, Ljungberg O. Occult papillary thyroid carcinoma in the young and the aged. Cancer 1984, **53:** 1790–1791.

353 Cameselle-Teijeiro J, Chan JK. Cribriform-morular variant of papillary carcinoma: a distinctive variant representing the sporadic counterpart of familial adenomatous polyposis-associated thyroid carcinoma? Mod Pathol 1999, **12:** 400–411.

354 Cameselle-Teijeiro J, Ruiz-Ponte C, Loidi L, Suarez-Penaranda J, Baltar J, Sobrinho-Simões M. Somatic but not germline mutation of the APC gene in a case of cribriform–morular variant of papillary thyroid carcinoma. Am J Clin Pathol 2001, **115:** 486–493.

355 Carcangiu ML, Bianchi S. Diffuse sclerosing variant of papillary thyroid carcinoma. Clinicopathologic study of 15 cases. Am J Surg Pathol 1989, **13:** 1041–1049.

356 Carcangiu ML, Zampi G, Pupi A, Castagnoli A, Rosai J. Papillary carcinoma of the thyroid. A clinicopathologic study of 241 cases treated at the University of Florence, Italy. Cancer 1985, **55:** 805–828.

357 Cetta F, Pelizzo MR, Curia MC, Barbarisi A. Genetics and clinicopathological findings in thyroid carcinomas associated with familial adenomatous polyposis. Am J Pathol 1999, **155:** 7–9.

358 Chan JK. Papillary carcinoma of thyroid. Classical and variants. Histol Histopathol 1990, **5:** 241–257.

359 Chan JKC. Strict criteria should be applied in the diagnosis of encapsulated follicular variant of papillary thyroid carcinoma. Am J Clin Pathol 2002, **117:** 16–18.

360 Chan JK, Carcangiu ML, Rosai J. Papillary carcinoma of thyroid with exuberant nodular fasciitis-like stroma. Report of three cases. Am J Clin Pathol 1991, **95:** 309–314.

361 Chan JKC, Tsui MS, Tse CH. Diffuse sclerosing variant of papillary carcinoma of the thyroid. A histological and immunohistochemical study of three cases. Histopathology 1987, **11:** 191–201.

362 Chen KTK, Rosai J. Follicular variant of thyroid papillary carcinoma. A clinicopathologic study of six cases. Am J Surg Pathol 1977, **1:** 123–130.

363 D'Antonio A, De Chiara A, Santoro M, Chiapetta G, Losito NS. Warthin-like tumour of the thyroid gland: RET/PTC expression indicates it is a variant of papillary carcinoma. Histopathology 2000, **36:** 493–498.

364 Evans HL. Follicular neoplasms of the thyroid. Cancer 1984, **54:** 535–540.

365 Evans HL. Columnar-cell carcinoma of the thyroid. A report of two cases of an aggressive variant of thyroid carcinoma. Am J Clin Pathol 1986, **85:** 77–80.

366 Evans HL. Encapsulated papillary neoplasms of the thyroid. A study of 14 cases followed for a minimum of 10 years. Am J Surg Pathol 1987, **11:** 592–597.

367 Evans HL. Encapsulated columnar-cell neoplasms of the thyroid. A report of four cases suggesting a favorable prognosis. Am J Surg Pathol 1996, **20:** 1205–1211.

368 Ferreiro JA, Hay ID, Lloyd RV. Columnar cell carcinoma of the thyroid: report of three additional cases. Hum Pathol 1996, **27:** 1156–1160.

369 Fink A, Tomlinson G, Freeman JL, Rosen IB, Asa SL. Occult micropapillary carcinoma associated with benign follicular

thyroid disease and unrelated thyroid neoplasms. Mod Pathol 1996, **9**: 816–820.

370 Flint A, Davenport RD, Lloyd RV. The tall cell variant of papillary carcinoma of the thyroid gland. Comparison with the common form of papillary carcinoma by DNA and morphometric analysis. Arch Pathol Lab Med 1991, **115**: 169–171.

371 Fujimoto Y, Obara T, Ito Y, Kodama T, Aiba M, Yamaguchi K. Diffuse sclerosing variant of papillary carcinoma of the thyroid. Clinical importance, surgical treatment, and follow-up study. Cancer 1990, **66**: 2306–2312.

372 Fusco A, Chiappetta G, Hui P, Garcia-Rostan G, Golden L, Kinder BK, Dillon DA, Giuliano A, Cirafici AM, Santoro M, Rosai J, Tallini G. Assessment of RET/PTC oncogene activation and clonality in thyroid nodules with incomplete morphological evidence of papillary carcinoma: a search for the early precursors of papillary cancer. Am J Pathol 2002, **160**: 2157–2167.

373 Gaertner EM, Davidson M, Wenig BM. The columnar cell variant of thyroid papillary carcinoma. Case report and discussion of an unusually aggressive thyroid papillary carcinoma. Am J Surg Pathol 1995, **19**: 940–947.

374 Ha ID, Grant CS, van Heerden JA, Goellner JR, Ebersold JR, Bergstralh EJ. Papillary thyroid microcarcinoma. A study of 535 cases observed in a 50-year period. Surgery 1992, **112**: 1139–1146.

375 Harach HR, Franssila KO, Wasenius V-M. Occult papillary carcinoma of the thyroid. A "normal" finding in Finland. A systematic autopsy study. Cancer 1985, **56**: 531–538.

376 Hawk WA, Hazard JB. The many appearances of papillary carcinoma of the thyroid. Cleve Clin Q 1976, **43**: 207–216.

377 Hazard JB. Small papillary carcinoma of the thyroid. A study with special reference to so-called nonencapsulated sclerosing tumor. Lab Invest 1960, **9**: 86–97.

378 Hirokawa M, Shimizu M, Fukuya T, Manabe T, Sonoo H. Columnar cell carcinoma of the thyroid: MIB-1 immunoreactivity as a prognostic factor. Endocr Pathol 1998, **9**: 31–34.

379 Hoda SA, Reed RJ. S-100 protein immunoreactivity differentiates follicular from papillary neoplasms of thyroid (abstract). Lab Invest 1993, **6**: 38A.

379a Hunt JL, LiVolsi VA, Baloch ZW, Barnes EL, Swalsky PA, Niehouse L, Finkelstein SD. Microscopic papillary thyroid carcinoma compared with clinical carcinomas by loss of heterozygosity mutational profile. Am J Surg Pathol 2003, **27**: 159–166.

380 Iida F, Sugenoya A, Muramatsu A. Clinical and pathologic properties of small differentiated carcinomas of the thyroid gland. World J Surg 1991, **15**: 511–515.

381 Imamura Y, Kasahara Y, Fukuda M. Multiple brain metastases from a diffuse sclerosing variant of papillary carcinoma of the thyroid. Endocr Pathol 2000, **11**: 97–108.

382 Ivanova R, Soares P, Castro P, Sobrinho-Simões M. Diffuse (or multinodular) follicular variant of papillary thyroid carcinoma: a clinicopathologic and immunohistochemical analysis of ten cases of an aggressive form of differentiated thyroid carcinoma. Virchows Arch 2002, **440**: 418–424.

383 Johnson TL, Lloyd RV, Thompson NW, Beierwaltes WH, Sisson JC. Prognostic implications of the tall cell variant of papillary thyroid carcinoma. Am J Surg Pathol 1988, **12**: 22–27.

384 Klinck GH, Winship T. Occult sclerosing carcinoma of the thyroid. Cancer 1955, **8**: 701–706.

385 Lloyd RV, Ferreiro JA, Jin L, Sebo TJ. TGFB, TGFB receptors, Ki-67, and p27Kip1 expression in papillary thyroid carcinomas. Endocr Pathol 1997, **8**: 293–300.

386 Ludvikovà M, Ryska A, Korabecnà M, Rydlovà M, Michal M. Oncocytic papillary carcinoma with lymphoid stroma (Warthin-like tumour) of the thyroid: a distinct entity with favourable prognosis. Histopathology 2001, **39**: 17–24.

387 Michal M, Chlumska A, Fakan F. Papillary carcinoma of the thyroid with exuberant nodule fasciitis-like stroma. Histopathology 1992, **21**: 577–579.

388 Mizukami Y, Nonomura A, Michigishi T, Noguchi M, Nakamura S, Hashimoto T. Columnar cell carcinoma of the thyroid gland. A case report and review of the literature. Hum Pathol 1994, **25**: 1098–1101.

389 Naganuma H, Iwama N, Nakumura Y, Ohtani N, Ohtani H, Takaya K, Sakai N. Papillary carcinoma of the thyroid gland forming a myofibroblastic nodular tumor: report of two cases and review of the literature. Pathol Int 2002, **52**: 54–58.

390 Nakamura T, Moriyama S-I, Nariya S, Sano K, Shirota H, Kato R. Macrofollicular variant of papillary thyroid carcinoma. Pathol Int 1998, **48**: 467–470.

390a Nardone HC, Ziober AF, LiVolsi VA, Mandel SJ, Baloch ZW, Weber RS, Mick R, Ziober BL. c-Met expression in tall cell variant papillary carcinoma of the thyroid. Cancer 2003, **98**: 1386–1393.

391 Nikiforov YE, Erickson LA, Nikiforova MN, Caudill CM, Lloyd RV. Solid variant of papillary thyroid carcinoma: incidence, clinical-pathologic characteristics, molecular analysis, and biologic behavior. Am J Surg Pathol 2001, **25**: 1478–1484.

392 Ostrowski ML, Merino MJ. Tall cell variant of papillary thyroid carcinoma: A reassessment and immunohistochemical study with comparison to the usual type of papillary carcinoma of the thyroid. Am J Surg Pathol 1996, **20**: 964–974.

393 Ozaki O, Ito K, Mimura T, Sugino K, Hosoda Y. Papillary carcinoma of the thyroid: Tall-cell variant with extensive lymphocyte infiltration. Am J Surg Pathol 1996, **20**: 695–698.

394 Renshaw AA, Gould EW. Why there is the tendency to "overdiagnose" the follicular variant of papillary thyroid carcinoma. Am J Clin Pathol 2002, **117**: 19–21.

394a Rosai J, LiVolsi AV, Sobrinho-Simoes M, Williams ED. Renaming papillary microcarcinoma of the thyroid gland: the Porto proposal. Int J Surg Pathol 2003, **11**: 249–251.

395 Rosai J, Zampi G, Carcangiu ML. Papillary carcinoma of the thyroid. A discussion of its several morphologic expressions, with particular emphasis on the follicular variant. Am J Surg Pathol 1983, **7**: 809–817.

396 Schröder S, Böcker W, Dralle H, Kortman K-B, Stern C. The encapsulated papillary carcinoma of the thyroid. A morphologic subtype of the papillary thyroid carcinoma. Cancer 1984, **54**: 90–93.

397 Schröder S, Pfannschmidt N, Böcker W, Muller HW, De Heer K. Histopathologic types and clinical behaviour of occult papillary carcinoma of the thyroid. Pathol Res Pract 1984, **179**: 81–87.

398 Shimizu M, Hirokawa M, Manabe T. Tall cell variant of papillary thyroid carcinoma with foci of columnar cell component. Virchows Arch 1999, **434**: 173–175.

399 Sobrinho-Simões M, Nesland JM, Johannessen JV. Columnar-cell carcinoma. Another variant of poorly differentiated carcinoma of the thyroid. Am J Clin Pathol 1988, **89**: 264–267.

400 Sobrinho-Simões M, Sambade C, Nesland JM, Johannessen JV. Tall cell papillary carcinoma. Am J Surg Pathol 1989, **13**: 79–80.

401 Soravia C, Sugg SL, Berk T, Mitri A, Cheng H, Gallinger S, Cohen Z, Asa SL, Bapat BV. Familial adenomatous polyposis-associated thyroid cancer. A clinical, pathological, and molecular genetics study. Am J Pathol 1999, **154**: 127–135.

402 Strate SM, Lee EL, Childers JH. Occult papillary carcinoma of the thyroid with distant metastases. Cancer 1984, **54**: 1093–1100.

402a Thompson LDR, Wieneke JA, Heffess CS. Diffuse sclerosing papillary thyroid carcinoma: a clinicopathologic and immunophenotype analysis of 22 cases. (Abstract) Mod Pathol 2003, **16**: 110a.

403 Tielens ET, Sherman SI, Hruban RH, Ladenson PW. Follicular variant of papillary thyroid carcinoma. A clinicopathologic study. Cancer 1994, **73**: 424–431.

404 Toti P, Tanganelli P, Schurfeld K, Stumpo M, Barbagli L, Vatti R,

Luzi P. Scarring in papillary carcinoma of the thyroid: report of two new cases with exuberant nodular fasciitis-like stroma. Histopathology 1999, **35**: 418–422.

405 Vickery AL Jr, Carcangiu ML, Johannessen JV, Sobrinho-Simões M. Papillary carcinoma. Semin Diagn Pathol 1985, **2**: 90–100.

406 Wenig BM, Thompson LD, Adair CF, Shmookler B, Heffess CS. Thyroid papillary carcinoma of columnar cell type: a clinicopathologic study of 16 cases. Cancer 1998, **82**: 740–753.

407 Williams ED (on behalf of the Chernobyl Pathologists Group). Guest editorial. Two proposals regarding the terminology of thyroid tumors. Int J Surg Pathol 2000, **8**: 181–183.

407a Wu T-T, Abraham SC, Park SJ, Cang HK, Argani P. Cribriform-morular variant of papillary thyroid carcinoma: evidence for alterations of the Wnt signaling pathway in familial adenomatous polyposis-associated but not sporadic neoplasms. (Abstract) Mod Pathol 2003, **16**: 111a.

407b Xu B, Yoshimoto K, Miyauchi A, Juma S, Mizusawa N, Hirokawa Sano T. Cribriform-morular variant of papillary thyroid carcinoma pathological and molecular genetic study with evidence of frequent somatic mutations in exon 3 of the beta-catenin gene. J Pathol 2003, **199**: 58–67.

408 Yamamoto Y, Maeda T, Izumi K, Otsuka H. Occult papillary carcinoma of the thyroid. A study of 408 autopsy cases. Cancer 1990, **65**: 1173–1179.

409 Yang GC, LiVolsi VA, Baloch ZW. Thyroid microcarcinoma: fine-needle aspiration diagnosis and histologic follow-up. Int J Surg Pathol 2002, **10**: 133–139.

409a Zidan J, Karen D, Stein M, Rosenblatt E, Basher W, Kuten A. Pure versus follicular variant of papillary thyroid carcinoma. Cancer 2003, **97**: 1181–1185.

Spread and metastases

410 Carcangiu ML, Zampi G, Pupi A, Castagnoli A, Rosai J. Papillary carcinoma of the thyroid. A clinicopathologic study of 241 cases treated at the University of Florence, Italy. Cancer 1985, **55**: 805–828.

411 Cody HS III, Shah JP. Locally invasive, well-differentiated thyroid cancer. Am J Surg 1981, **142**: 480–483.

412 Frazell EL, Foote FW Jr. Papillary thyroid carcinoma. Pathological findings in cases with and without clinical evidence of cervical node involvement. Cancer 1955, **8**: 1165–1166.

413 Hoie J, Stenwig AE, Kullmann G, Lindegaard M. Distant metastases in papillary thyroid cancer. A review of 91 patients. Cancer 1988, **61**: 1–6.

413a McWilliams RR, Giannini C, Hay ID, Atkinson JL, Stafford SL, Buckner JC. Management of brain metastases from thyroid carcinoma. Cancer 2003, **98**: 356–362.

413b Tang W, Kakudo K, Nakamura Y, Nakamura M, Mori I, Morita S, Miyauchi A. Parathyroid gland involvement by papillary carcinoma of the thyroid gland. Arch Pathol Lab Med 2002, **126**: 1511–1514.

Prognosis

413c Acharya S, Sarafoglou K, LaQuaglia M, Lindsley S, Gerald W, Wollner N, Tan C, Sklar C. Thyroid neoplasms after therapeutic radiation for malignancies during childhood or adolescence. Cancer 2003, **97**: 2397–2403.

414 Akslen LA, LiVolsi VA. Increased angiogenesis in papillary thyroid carcinoma but lack of prognostic importance. Hum Pathol **31**: 439–442.

415 Akslen LA, LiVolsi VA. Prognostic significance of histologic grading compared with subclassification of papillary thyroid carcinoma. Cancer 2000, **88**: 1902–1908.

416 Bellantone R, Lombardi CP, Bossola M, Ferrante A, Princi P, Boscherini M, Maussier L, Salvatori M, Rufini V, Reale F, Romano L, Tallini G, Zelano G, Pontecorvi A. Validity of thyroglobulin mRNA assay in peripheral blood of postoperative thyroid carcinoma patients in predicting tumor recurrences varies according to the histologic type: results of a prospective study. Cancer 2001, **92**: 2273–2279.

417 Bouchard C. Follow-up of patients with thyroid carcinoma. N Engl J Med 1997, **337**: 928–930.

418 Cady B. Papillary carcinoma of the thyroid. Semin Surg Oncol 1991, **7**: 81–86.

419 Cady B. Staging in thyroid carcinoma. Cancer 1998, **83**: 844–847.

420 Carcangiu ML, Zampi G, Pupi A, Castagnoli A, Rosai J. Papillary carcinoma of the thyroid. A clinicopathologic study of 241 cases treated at the University of Florence, Italy. Cancer 1985, **55**: 805–828.

421 Cohn K, Bäckdahl M, Forsslund G, Auer G, Lundell G, Löwhagen T, Tallroth E, Willems J-S, Zetterberg A, Granberg P-O. Prognostic value of nuclear DNA content in papillary thyroid carcinoma. World J Surg 1984, **8**: 474–480.

422 DeGroot LJ, Kaplan EL, McCormick M, Straus FH. Natural history, treatment, and course of papillary thyroid carcinoma. J Clin Endocrinol Metab 1990, **71**: 414–424.

423 Gilliland FD, Hunt WC, Morris DM, Key CR. Prognostic factors for thyroid carcinoma. A population-based study of 15,698 cases from the surveillance, epidemiology and end results (SEER) program, 1973–1991. Cancer 1997, **79**: 564–573.

424 Grebe SK, Hay ID. Thyroid cancer nodal metastases: biological significance and therapeutic considerations. Surg Oncol Clin North Am 1996, **5**: 43–63.

425 Joensuu H, Klemi P, Eerola E, Tuominen J. Influence of cellular DNA content on survival in differentiated thyroid cancer. Cancer 1986, **58**: 2462–2467.

426 Lerch H, Schober O, Kuwert T, Saur HB. Survival of differentiated thyroid carcinoma studied in 500 patients. J Clin Oncol 1997, **15**: 2067–2075.

427 LiVolsi V. Papillary neoplasms of the thyroid. Pathologic and prognostic features. Am J Clin Pathol 1992, **97**: 426–434.

428 McConahey WM, Hay ID, Woolner LB, Van Heerden JA, Taylor WF. Papillary thyroid cancer treated at the Mayo Clinic, 1946 through 1970. Initial manifestations, pathologic findings, therapy, and outcome. Mayo Clin Proc 1986, **61**: 978–996.

429 Mai KT, Perkins DG, Yazdi HM, Commons AS, Thomas J, Meban S. Infiltrating papillary thyroid carcinoma: review of 134 cases of papillary carcinoma. Arch Pathol Lab Med 1998, **122**: 166–171.

430 Mazzaferri EL, Young RL. Papillary thyroid carcinoma. A 10 year follow-up report of the impact of therapy in 576 patients. Am J Med 1980, **70**: 511–518.

431 Motoyama T, Watanabe H. Simultaneous squamous cell carcinoma and papillary adenocarcinoma of the thyroid gland. Hum Pathol 1983, **14**: 1009–1010.

432 Omura K, Nagasato A, Kanehira E, Kinsen H, Amaya S, Kimura K, Kajita T, Nosaki Y, Mizukami Y, Nonomura A, Watanabe Y. Retinoblastoma protein and proliferating-cell nuclear antigen expression as predictors of recurrence in well-differentiated papillary thyroid carcinoma. J Clin Oncol 1997, **15**: 3458–3463.

433 Schlumberger M, Tubiana M, De Vathaire F, Hill C, Gardet P, Travagli J-P, Fragu P, Lumbroso J, Caillou B, Parmentier C. Long-term results of treatment of 283 patients with lung and bone metastases from differentiated thyroid carcinoma. J Clin Endocrinol Metab 1986, **63**: 960–967.

434 Schröder S, Schwarz W, Rehpenning W, Löning Th, Böcker W. Prognostic significance of Leu-M1 immunostaining in papillary carcinomas of the thyroid gland. Virchows Arch [A] 1987, **411**: 435–439.

435 Sobrinho-Simões M. Hail to the histologic grading of papillary thyroid carcinoma? Cancer 2000, **88**: 1766–1768.

436 Tallini G, Ghossein RA, Emanuel J, Gill J, Kinder B, Dimich AB, Costa J, Robbins R, Burrow GN, Rosai J. Detection of thyroglobulin, thyroid peroxidase, and RET/PTC1 mRNA transcripts in the peripheral blood of patients with thyroid disease. J Clin Oncol 1998, **16**: 1158–1166.

437 Torres J, Volpato RD, Power EG, Lopez EC, Dominguez ME, Maira JL, Ugarte JA, Martinez VC. Thyroid cancer. Survival in 148 cases followed for 10 years or more. Cancer 1985, **56:** 2298–2304.

437a Vini L, Hyer SL, Marshall J, A'Hern R, Harmer C. Long-term results in elderly patients with differentiated thyroid carcinoma. Cancer 2003, **97:** 2736–2742.

438 Yamamoto Y, Izumi K, Otsuka H. An immunohistochemical study of epithelial membrane antigen, cytokeratin, and vimentin in papillary thyroid carcinoma. Recognition of lethal and favorable prognostic types. Cancer 1992, **70:** 2326–2633.

439 Yamashita H, Noguchi S, Murakami N, Kawamoto H, Watanabe S. Extracapsular invasion of lymph node metastasis is an indicator of distant metastasis and poor prognosis in patients with thyroid papillary carcinoma. Cancer 1997, **80:** 2268–2272.

440 Yamashita H, Noguchi S, Murakami N, Toda M, Uchino S, Watanabe S, Kawamoto H. Extracapsular invasion of lymph node metastasis: a good indicator of disease recurrence and poor prognosis in patients with thyroid microcarcinoma. Cancer 1999, **86:** 842–849.

Follicular carcinoma

441 Baloch ZW, LiVolsi VA. Intravascular Kaposi's-like spindle cell proliferation of the capsular vessels of follicular-derived thyroid carcinomas. Mod Pathol 1998, **11:** 995–998.

442 Brennan MD, Bergstralh EJ, van Heerden JA, McConahey WM. Follicular thyroid cancer treated at the Mayo Clinic, 1946 through 1970. Initial manifestations, pathologic findings, therapy, and outcome. Mayo Clin Proc 1991, **66:** 11–22.

443 Cady B, Rossi R, Silverman M, Wool M. Further evidence of the validity of risk group definition in differentiated thyroid carcinoma. Surgery 1985, **98:** 1171–1178.

444 Carcangiu ML. Minimally invasive follicular carcinoma. Endocr Pathol 1997, **8:** 231–234.

444a Collini P, Sampietro G, Rosai J, Pilotti S. Minimally invasive (encapsulated) follicular carcinoma of the thyroid gland is the low-risk counterpart of widely invasive follicular carcinoma but not of insular carcinoma. Virchows Arch 2003, **442:** 71–76.

445 Evans HL. Follicular neoplasms of the thyroid. A study of 44 cases followed for a minimum of 10 years, with emphasis on differential diagnosis. Cancer 1984, **54:** 535–540.

446 Fonseca E, Sobrinho-Simões M. Diagnostic problems in differentiated carcinomas of the thyroid. Pathol Res Pract 1995, **191:** 318–331.

447 Franssila KO, Ackerman LV, Brown CL, Hedinger CE. Follicular carcinoma. Semin Diagn Pathol 1985, **2:** 101–122.

447a French CA, Alexander EK, Cibas ES, Nose V, Laguette J, Faquin W, Garer J, Moore F Jr., Fletcher JA, Larsen PR, Kroll TG. Genetic and biological subgroups of low-stage follicular thyroid cancer. Am J Pathol 2003, **162:** 1053–1060.

448 Goldstein NS, Czako P, Neill JS. Metastatic minimally invasive (encapsulated) follicular and Hurthle cell thyroid carcinoma. Mod Pathol 2000, **13:** 123–130.

449 González-Cámpora R, Montero C, Marin-Lacave I, Galera H. Demonstration of vascular endothelium in thyroid carcinomas using *Ulex europaeus* I agglutinin. Histopathology 1986, **10:** 261–266.

450 Harach HR, Jasani B, Williams ED. Factor VIII as a marker of endothelial cells in follicular carcinoma of the thyroid. J Clin Pathol 1983, **36:** 1050–1054.

451 Heffess CS, Thompson LD. Minimally invasive follicular thyroid carcinoma. Endocr Pathol 2001, **12:** 417–422.

451a Hirokawa M, Carney JA, Goellner JR, DeLellis RA, Heffess CS, Katoh R, Tsujimoto M, Kakudo K. Observer variation of encapsulated follicular lesions of the thyroid gland. Am J Surg Pathol 2002, **16:** 1508–1514.

451b Hunt JL, LiVolsi VA, Baloch ZW, Swalsky PA, Bakker A, Sasatomi E, Finkelstein S, Barnes L. A novel microdissection and genotyping of follicular-derived thyroid tumors to predict aggressiveness. Hum Pathol 2003, **34:** 375–380.

452 Hruban RH, Huvos AG, Traganos F, Reuter V, Lieberman PH, Melamed MR. Follicular neoplasms of the thyroid in men older than 50 years of age. A DNA flow cytometric study. Am J Clin Pathol 1990, **94:** 527–532.

452a Nikiforova MN, Lynch RA, Biddinger PW, Tallini G, Kroll TG, Nikiforov YE. PAX8-PARγ rearrangement, RAS mutations, and galectin-3 and HBME-1 immunoreactivity in follicular tumors of the thyroid: evidence for two distinct molecular pathways in the development of follicular carcinoma. (Abstract) Mod Pathol 2003, **16:** 107a.

453 Iida F. Surgical significance of capsule invasion of adenoma of the thyroid. Surg Gynecol Obstet 1977, **144:** 710–712.

454 Johannessen JV, Sobrinho-Simões M. Well differentiated thyroid tumors. Problems in diagnosis and understanding. Pathol Annu 1983, **18**(Pt 1): 255–285.

455 Jonasson JG, Hrafnkelsson J. Nuclear DNA analysis and prognosis in carcinoma of the thyroid gland. A nationwide study in Iceland on carcinomas diagnosed 1955–1990. Virchows Arch 1994, **425:** 349–356.

456 Kendall CH, Sanderson PR, Cope J, Talbot IC. Follicular thyroid tumours. A study of laminin and type IV collagen in basement membrane and endothelium. J Clin Pathol 1985, **38:** 1100–1105.

457 Kroll TG, Sarraf P, Pecciarini L, Chen CJ, Mueller E, Spiegelman BM, Fletcher JA. PAX8-PPAR gamma1 fusion oncogene in human thyroid carcinoma. Science 2000, **289:** 1357–1360.

458 Lang W, Choritz H, Hundeshagen H. Risk factors in follicular thyroid carcinomas. A retrospective follow-up study covering a 14-year period with emphasis on morphological findings. Am J Surg Pathol 1986, **10:** 246–255.

459 Lang W, Georgii A, Stauch G, Kienzle E. The differentiation of atypical adenomas and encapsulated follicular carcinomas in the thyroid gland. Virchows Arch [A] 1980, **385:** 125–141.

460 Massin J-P, Savoie J-C, Garnier H, Guiraudon G, Leger FA, Bacourt F. Pulmonary metastases in differentiated thyroid carcinoma. Study of 58 cases with implications for the primary tumor treatment. Cancer 1984, **53:** 982–992.

461 Muellner-Gaertner HW, Brzac HT, Rehpenning W. Prognostic indices for tumor relapse and tumor mortality in follicular thyroid carcinoma. Cancer 1991, **67:** 1903–1911.

462 Nagamine Y, Suzuki J, Katakura R, Yoshimoto T, Matoba N, Takaya K. Skull metastasis of thyroid carcinoma. Study of 12 cases. J Neurosurg 1985, **63:** 526–531.

463 Oyama T, Suzuki T, Hara F, Lino Y, Ishida T, Sakamoto A, Nakajima T. N-*ras* mutation of thyroid tumor with special reference to the follicular type. Pathol Int 1995, **45:** 45–50.

464 Oyama T, Vickery AL Jr, Preffer FI, Colvin RB. A comparative study of flow cytometry and histopathologic findings in thyroid follicular carcinomas and adenomas. Hum Pathol 1994, **25:** 271–275.

465 Pittas AG, Adler M, Fazzari M, Tickoo S, Rosai J, Larson SM, Robbins RJ. Bone metastases from thyroid carcinoma: clinical characteristics and prognostic variables in one hundred forty-six patients. Thyroid 2000, **10:** 261–268.

466 Sobrinho-Simões M, Damjanov I. Lectin histochemistry of papillary and follicular carcinoma of the thyroid gland. Arch Pathol Lab Med 1986, **110:** 722–729.

467 Stephenson TJ, Griffiths DWR, Mills PM. Comparison of *Ulex europaeus* I lectin binding and factor VIII-related antigen as markers of vascular endothelium in follicular carcinoma of the thyroid. Histopathology 1986, **10:** 251–260.

468 Thompson LD, Wieneke JA, Paal E, Frommelt RA, Adair CF, Heffess CS. A clinicopathologic study of minimally invasive follicular carcinoma of the thyroid gland with a review of the english literature. Cancer 2001, **91:** 505–524.

469 Tickoo SK, Pittas AG, Adler M, Fazzari M, Larson S, Robbins RJ,

Rosai J. Bone metastases from thyroid carcinoma: a histopathologic study with clinical correlates. Arch Pathol Lab Med 2000, **124**: 1440–1447.

470 Tse LL, Chan I, Chan JK. Capsular intravascular endothelial hyperplasia: a peculiar form of vasoproliferative lesion associated with thyroid carcinoma. Histopathology 2001, **39**: 463–468.

471 van Heerden JA, Hay ID, Goellner JR, Salomao D, Ebersold JR, Bergstralh EJ, Grant CS. Follicular thyroid carcinoma with capsular invasion alone. A non-threatening malignancy. Surgery 1992, **112**: 1130–1136.

472 Williams ED (on behalf of the Chernobyl Pathologists Group). Two proposals regarding the terminology of thyroid tumors. Int J Surg Pathol 2000, **8**: 181–184.

473 Wilson NW, Pameakian H, Richardson TC, Stokoe MR, Makin CA, Heyderman E. Epithelial markers in thyroid carcinoma. An immunoperoxidase study. Histopathology 1986, **10**: 815–829.

474 Wright PA, Lemoine NR, Mayall ES, Wyllie FS, Hughes D, Williams ED, Wynford-Thomas D. Papillary and follicular thyroid carcinomas show a different pattern of *ras* oncogenes mutation. Br J Cancer 1989, **60**: 576–577.

475 Wyllie FS, Lemoine NR, Williams ED, Wynford-Thomas D. Structure and expression of nuclear oncogenes in multi-stage thyroid tumorigenesis. Br J Cancer 1989, **60**: 561–565.

476 Yamashina M. Follicular neoplasms of the thyroid. Total circumferential evaluation of the fibrous capsule. Am J Surg Pathol 1992, **16**: 392–400.

Hürthle cell (oncocytic) tumors

The oncocyte

477 Abu-Alfa AK, Straus FH, Montag AG. An immunohistochemical study of thyroid Hürthle cells and their neoplasms. The roles of S-100 and HMB-45 proteins. Mod Pathol 1994, **7**: 529–532.

478 Ambu R, Riva A, Lai ML, Loffredo F, Riva FT, Tandler B. Scanning electron microscopy of the interior of cells in Hürthle cell tumors. Ultrastruct Pathol 2000, **24**: 211–219.

479 Baloch ZW, Mandel S, LiVolsi VA. Combined tall cell carcinoma and Hürthle cell carcinoma (collision tumor) of the thyroid. Arch Pathol Lab Med 2001, **125**: 541–543.

480 Chiappetta G, Toti P, Cetta F, Giuliano A, Pentimalli F, Amendola I, Lazzi S, Monaco M, Mazzuchelli L, Tosi P, Santoro M, Fusco A. The RET/PTC oncogene is frequently activated in oncocytic thyroid tumors (Hürthle cell adenomas and carcinomas), but not in oncocytic hyperplastic lesions. J Clin Endocrinol Metab 2002, **87**: 364–369.

481 Erickson LA, Jalal SM, Goellner JR, Law ME, Harwood A, Jin L, Roche PC, Lloyd RV. Analysis of Hürthle cell neoplasms of the thyroid by interphase fluorescence in situ hybridization. Am J Surg Pathol 2001, **25**: 911–917.

482 Johnson TL, Lloyd RV, Burney RE, Thompson NW. Hürthle cell thyroid tumors. An immunohistochemical study. Cancer 1987, **59**: 107–112.

483 Kohli A, Baker SP, Patwardhan NA, Khan A. Expression of bcl-2 and p53 in oncocytic (Hürthle cell) tumors of the thyroid: an immunohistochemical study. Endocr Pathol 1998, **9**: 117–124.

484 Lloreta-Trull J, Serrano S. Biology and pathology of the mitochondrion. Ultrastruct Pathol 1998, **22**: 357–367.

485 Maximo V, Soares P, Lima J, Cameselle-Teijeiro J, Sobrinho-Simões M. Mitochondrial DNA somatic mutations (point mutations and large deletions) and mitochondrial DNA variants in human thyroid pathology: a study with emphasis on Hürthle cell tumors. Am J Pathol 2002, **160**: 1857–1865.

486 Maximo V, Sobrinho-Simões M. Hürthle cell tumours of the thyroid. A review with emphasis on mitochondrial abnormalities with clinical relevance. Virchows Arch 2000, **437**: 107–115.

487 Mazzucchelli L, Burckhardt E, Hirsiger H, Kappeler A, Laissue JA. Interphase cytogenetics in oncocytic adenomas and carcinomas of the thyroid. Hum Pathol 2000, **31**: 854–859.

488 Muller-Hocker J. Immunoreactivity of p53, Ki-67, and Bcl-2 in oncocytic adenomas and carcinomas of the thyroid gland. Hum Pathol 1999, **30**: 926–933.

489 Muller-Hocker J, Schafer A, Strowitzki T. Glucose transporter 4(GLUT 4) is highly expressed in mitochondria-rich oxyphil cells. Appl Immunohistochem 1998, **6**: 224–227.

490 Nesland JM, Sobrinho-Simões MA, Holm R, Sambade MC, Johannessen JV. Hürthle-cell lesions of the thyroid. A combined study using transmission electron microscopy, scanning electron microscopy and immunocytochemistry. Ultrastruct Pathol 1985, **8**: 269–290.

491 Papotti M, Gugliotta P, Forte G, Bussolati G. Immunocytochemical identification of oxyphilic mitochondrion-rich cells. Appl Immunohistochem 1994, **2**: 261–267.

492 Santeusanio G, D'Alfonso V, Iafrate E, Colantoni A, Liberati F, Giusto SL, Gown AM. Antibodies to cytokeratin 14 specifically identify oncocytes (Hürthle cells) in thyroid lesions and tumors. Appl Immunohistochem 1997, **5**: 223–228.

493 Tallini G, Hsueh A, Liu S, Garcia-Rostan G, Speicher MR, Ward DC. Frequent chromosomal DNA unbalance in thyroid oncocytic (Hürthle cell) neoplasms detected by comparative genomic hybridization. Lab Invest 1999, **79**: 547–555.

494 Tallini G, Ladanyi M, Rosai J, Jhanwar SC. Analysis of nuclear and mitochondrial DNA alterations in thyroid and renal oncocytic tumors. Cytogenet Cell Genet 1994, **66**: 253–259.

Clinicopathologic features

495 Abu-Alfa AK, Straus FH, Montag AG. An immunohistochemical study of thyroid Hürthle cells and their neoplasms. The roles of S-100 and HMB-45 proteins. Mod Pathol 1994, **7**: 529–532.

496 Barbuto D, Carcangiu ML, Rosai J. Papillary Hürthle cell neoplasms of the thyroid gland. A study of 20 cases (abstract). Mod Pathol 1990, **3**: 7A.

497 Beckner ME, Heffess CS, Oertel JE. Oxyphilic papillary thyroid carcinomas. Am J Clin Pathol 1995, **103**: 280–287.

498 Bondeson L, Azavedo E, Bondeson A-G, Caspersson T, Ljungberg O. Nuclear DNA content and behavior of oxyphil thyroid tumors. Cancer 1986, **58**: 672–675.

499 Bondeson L, Bondeson A-G, Ljungberg O, Tibblin S. Oxyphil tumors of the thyroid. Follow-up of 42 surgical cases. Ann Surg 1981, **194**: 677–680.

500 Bronner MP, LiVolsi VA. Oxyphilic (Askanazy/Hürthle cell) tumors of the thyroid. Microscopic features predict biologic behavior. Surg Pathol 1988, **1**: 137–150.

501 Caplan RH, Abellera M, Kisken WA. Hürthle cell tumors of the thyroid gland. A clinicopathologic review and long-term follow-up. JAMA 1984, **251**: 3114–3117.

502 Carcangiu ML, Bianchi S, Savino D, Voynick IM, Rosai J. Follicular Hürthle cell tumors of the thyroid gland. Cancer 1991, **68**: 1944–1953.

503 Erickson LA, Jin L, Goellner JR, Lohse C, Pankratz VS, Zukerberg LR, Thompson GB, van Heerden JA, Grant CS, Lloyd RV. Pathologic features, proliferative activity, and cyclin D1 expression in Hürthle cell neoplasms of the thyroid. Mod Pathol 2000, **13**: 186–192.

504 Evans HL, Vassilopoulou-Sellin R. Follicular and Hürthle cell carcinomas of the thyroid: a comparative study. Am J Surg Pathol 1998, **22**: 1512–1520.

505 Flint A, Davenport RD, Lloyd RV, Beckwith AL, Thompson NW. Cytophotometric measurements of Hürthle cell tumors of the thyroid gland. Correlation with pathologic features and clinical behavior. Cancer 1988, **61**: 110–113.

506 Gundry SR, Burney RE, Thompson NW, Lloyd R. Total thyroidectomy for Hürthle cell neoplasm of the thyroid. Arch Surg 1983, **118**: 529–532.

507 Har-El G, Hadar T, Segal K, Levy R, Sidi J. Hürthle cell carcinoma of the thyroid gland. A tumor of moderate malignancy. Cancer 1986, **57**: 1613–1617.

508 Herrera MF, Hay ID, Wu PS, Goellner JR, Ryan JJ, Ebersold JR, Bergstrahl EJ, Grant CS. Hürthle cell (oxyphilic) papillary thyroid carcinoma. A variant with more aggressive biologic behavior. World J Surg 1992, **16:** 669–674.

509 Johnson TL, Lloyd RV, Burney RE, Thompson NW. Hürthle cell thyroid tumors. An immunohistochemical study. Cancer 1987, **59:** 107–112.

510 Judkins AR, Roberts SA, LiVolsi VA. Utility of immunohistochemistry in the evaluation of necrotic thyroid tumors. Hum Pathol 1999, **30:** 1373–1376.

511 Lloyd RV. Oncocytic tumors of the thyroid gland. Adv Anat Pathol 1997, **4:** 306–310.

511a Lopez-Penabad L, Chiu AC, Hoff AO, Schultz P, Gaztambide S, Ordoñez NG, Sherman SI. Prognostic factors in patients with Hürthle cell neoplasms of the thyroid. Cancer 2003, **97:** 1186–1194.

512 McLeod MK, Thompson NW. Hürthle cell neoplasms of the thyroid. Otolaryngol Clin North Am 1990, **23:** 441–452.

513 Maynes LJ, Hutzler MJ, Patwardhan NA, Wang S, Khan A. Cell cycle regulatory proteins p27(kip)1, cyclins D1 and E and proliferative activity in oncocytic (Hürthle cell) lesions of the thyroid. Endocr Pathol 2000, **11:** 331–340.

514 Nascimento MC, Bisi H, Alves VA, Longatto-Filho A, Kanamura CT, Medeiros-Neto G. Differential reactivity for galectin-3 in Hürthle cell adenomas and carcinomas. Endocr Pathol 2001, **12:** 275–279.

515 Papotti M, Torchio B, Grassi L, Favero A, Bussolati G. Poorly differentiated oxyphilic (Hürthle cell) carcinomas of the thyroid. Am J Surg Pathol 1996, **20:** 686–694.

516 Rosai J, Carcangiu ML. Pathology of thyroid tumors. Some recent and old questions. Hum Pathol 1984, **15:** 1008–1012.

517 Samaan NA, Schultz PN, Haynie TP, Ordonez NG. Pulmonary metastasis of differentiated thyroid carcinoma. Treatment results in 101 patients. J Clin Endocrinol Metab 1985, **65:** 376–380.

518 Schark C, Fulton N, Yashiro T, Stanislav G, Jacoby R, Straus FH II, Dytch H, Bibbo M, Kaplan EL. The value of measurement of ras oncogenes and nuclear DNA analysis in the diagnosis of Hürthle cell tumors of the thyroid. World J Surg 1992, **16:** 745–751.

519 Sobrinho-Simões MA, Nesland JM, Holm R, Sambade MC, Johannessen JV. Hürthle cell and mitochondrion-rich papillary carcinomas of the thyroid gland. An ultrastructural and immunocytochemical study. Ultrastruct Pathol 1985, **8:** 131–142.

520 Stojadinovic A, Ghossein RA, Hoos A, Urist MJ, Spiro RH, Shah JP, Brennan MF, Shaha AR, Singh B. Hürthle cell carcinoma: critical histopathologic appraisal. J Clin Pathol 2001, **19:** 2616–2625.

521 Tallini G, Carcangiu ML, Rosai J. Oncocytic neoplasms of the thyroid gland. Acta Pathol Jpn 1992, **42:** 305–315.

522 Tretiakova MS, Papotti M, Bussolati G. Proliferative activity of oxyphilic (Hürthle) cells in reactive and neoplastic thyroid lesions. Endocr Pathol 1999, **10:** 173–180.

522a Volante M, Croce S, Pecchioni C, Papotti M. E2F-1 transcription factor is overexpressed in oxyphilic thyroid tumors. Mod Pathol 2002, **15:** 1038–1043.

523 Watson RG, Brennan MD, Goellner JR, van Heerden JA, McConahey WM, Taylor WF. Invasive Hürthle cell carcinoma of the thyroid. Natural history and management. Mayo Clin Proc 1984, **59:** 851–855.

Clear cell tumors

524 Carcangiu ML, Sibley RK, Rosai J. Clear cell change in primary thyroid tumors. A study of 38 cases. Am J Surg Pathol 1985, **9:** 705–722.

525 Civantos F, Albores-Saavedra J, Nadji M, Morales AR. Clear cell variant of thyroid carcinoma. Am J Surg Pathol 1984, **8:** 187–192.

526 Dickersin GR, Vickery AL Jr, Smith SB. Papillary carcinoma of the thyroid, oxyphil cell type, "clear cell" variant. A light- and electro-microscopic study. Am J Surg Pathol 1980, **4:** 501–509.

527 Giri D, Gultekin SH, Ward RF, Hurley JR, Hoda SA. Clear-cell follicular adenoma of ectopic thyroid in the submandibular region. Endocr Pathol 1998, **9:** 347–352.

528 Landon G, Ordóñez NG. Clear cell variant of medullary carcinoma of the thyroid. Hum Pathol 1985, **16:** 844–847.

529 Mendelsohn G. Signet-cell-simulating microfollicular adenoma of the thyroid. Am J Surg Pathol 1984, **8:** 705–708.

530 Mochizuki M, Saito K, Kanazawa K. Benign follicular thyroid nodule composed of signet-ring-like cells with PAS-negative thyroglobulin accumulation in dilated rough endoplasmic reticulum. Acta Pathol Jpn 1992, **42:** 111–114.

531 Nishimura R, Nogushi M, Tsujimoto M, Noro H, Kido T, Nakahara M, Nakao K. Thyroid clear cell adenoma with marked dilatation of membranous structures: electron-microscopic study. Ultrastruct Pathol 2001, **25:** 361–366.

532 Rigaud C, Peltier F, Bogomoletz WV. Mucin producing microfollicular adenoma of the thyroid. J Clin Pathol 1985, **38:** 277–280.

533 Schröder S, Böcker W. Clear-cell carcinomas of thyroid gland. A clinicopathological study of 13 cases. Histopathology 1986, **10:** 75–89.

534 Schröder S, Böcker W. Signet-ring-cell thyroid tumors. Follicle cell tumors with arrest of folliculogenesis. Am J Surg Pathol 1985, **9:** 619–629.

535 Schröder S, Hüsselmann H, Böcker W. Lipid-rich cell adenoma of the thyroid gland. Report of a peculiar thyroid tumour. Virchows Arch [A] 1984, **404:** 105–108.

536 Tóth K, Péter I, Kremmer T, Sugár J. Lipid-rich cell thyroid adenoma. Histopathology with comparative lipid analysis. Virchows Arch [A] 1990, **417:** 273–276.

537 Variakojis D, Getz ML, Paloyan E, Straus FH II. Papillary clear cell carcinoma of the thyroid gland. Hum Pathol 1975, **6:** 384–390.

Squamous cell, mucinous, and related tumors

538 Baloch ZW, Solomon AC, LiVolsi VA. Primary mucoepidermoid carcinoma and sclerosing mucoepidermoid carcinoma with eosinophilia of the thyroid gland: a report of nine cases. Mod Pathol 2000, **13:** 802–807.

539 Bondeson L, Bondeson AG, Thompson NW. Papillary carcinoma of the thyroid with mucoepidermoid features. Am J Clin Pathol 1991, **95:** 175–179.

540 Bronner MP, LiVolsi VA. Spindle cell squamous carcinoma of the thyroid. An unusual anaplastic tumor associated with tall cell papillary cancer. Mod Pathol 1991, **4:** 630–643.

541 Carcangiu ML, Steeper T, Zampi G, Rosai J. Anaplastic thyroid carcinoma. A study of 70 cases. Am J Clin Pathol 1985, **83:** 135–158.

542 Chan JK, Albores-Saavedra J, Battifora H, Carcangiu ML, Rosai J. Sclerosing mucoepidermoid thyroid carcinoma with eosinophilia. A distinctive low-grade malignancy arising from the metaplastic follicles of Hashimoto's thyroiditis. Am J Surg Pathol 1991, **15:** 438–448.

543 Chan JK, Rosai J. Tumors of the neck showing thymic or related branchial pouch differentiation. A unifying concept. Hum Pathol 1991, **22:** 349–367.

544 Franssila KO, Harach HR, Wasenius V-M. Mucoepidermoid carcinoma of the thyroid. Histopathology 1984, **8:** 847–860.

545 Geisinger KR, Steffee CH, McGee RS, Woodruff RD, Buss DH. The cytomorphologic features of sclerosing mucoepidermoid carcinoma of the thyroid gland with eosinophilia. Am J Clin Pathol 1998, **109:** 294–301.

546 Harach HR, Vujanic GM, Jasani B. Ultimobranchial body nests in human fetal thyroid. An autopsy, histological, and immunohistochemical study in relation to solid cell nests and mucoepidermoid carcinoma of the thyroid. J Pathol 1993, **169:** 465–469.

547 Huang T-Y, Assor D. Primary squamous cell carcinoma of the thyroid gland. A report of four cases. Am J Clin Pathol 1971, **55**: 93–98.

548 Katoh R, Sugai T, Ono S, Takayama K, Tomichi N, Kurihara H, Takamatsu M. Mucoepidermoid carcinoma of the thyroid gland. Cancer 1990, **65**: 2020–2027.

549 Lam K-Y, Lo X-Y, Liu MC. Primary squamous cell carcinoma of the thyroid gland: an entity with aggressive clinical behaviour and distinctive cytokeratin expression profiles. Histopathology 2001, **39**: 279–286.

550 LiVolsi VA, Merino MJ. Squamous cells in the human thyroid gland. Am J Surg Pathol 1978, **2**: 133–140.

551 Miyauchi A, Kuma K, Matsuzuka F, Matsubayashi S, Kobayashi A, Tamai H, Katayama S. Intrathyroidal epithelial thymoma. An entity distinct from squamous cell carcinoma of the thyroid. World J Surg 1985, **9**: 128–135.

552 Mizukami Y, Matsubara F, Hashimoto T, Haratake J, Terahata S, Noguchi M, Hirose K. Primary mucoepidermoid carcinoma in the thyroid gland. A case report including an ultrastructural and biochemical study. Cancer 1984, **53**: 1741–1745.

553 Mizukami Y, Nakajima H, Annen Y, Michigishi T, Nonomura A, Nakamura S. Mucin-producing poorly differentiated adenocarcinoma of the thyroid. A case report. Pathol Res Pract 1993, **189**: 608–611.

554 Morikawa Y, Ishihara Y, Kawano I, Matsuura N, Kaname A, Kakudo K. Cystic squamous cell carcinoma of the thyroid. A possible new subgroup of intrathyroidal epithelial thymoma. Endocr Pathol 1995, **6**: 77–81.

555 Motoyama T, Watanabe H. Simultaneous squamous cell carcinoma and papillary adenocarcinoma of the thyroid gland. Hum Pathol 1983, **14**: 1009–1010.

556 Ozaki O, Ito K, Sugino K, Yasuda K, Yamashita T, Toshima K. Solid cell nests of the thyroid gland. Precursor of mucoepidermoid carcinoma? World J Surg 1992, **16**: 685–688.

557 Riddle PE, Dincsoy HP. Primary squamous cell carcinoma of the thyroid associated with leukocytosis and hypercalcemia. Arch Pathol Lab Med 1987, **111**: 373–374.

558 Rigaud C, Bogomoletz WV. "Mucin secreting" and "mucinous" primary thyroid carcinomas. Pitfalls in mucin histochemistry applied to thyroid tumours. J Clin Pathol 1987, **40**: 890–895.

559 Rocha AS, Soares P, Machado JC, Maximo V, Fonseca E, Franssila K, Sobrinho-Simões M. Mucoepidermoid carcinoma of the thyroid: a tumour histotype characterised by P-cadherin neoexpression and marked abnormalities of E-cadherin/catenins complex. Virchows Arch 2002, **440**: 498–504.

560 Sambade C, Franssila K, Basilio-de-Oliveira CA, Sobrinho-Simões M. Mucoepidermoid carcinoma of the thyroid revisited. Surg Pathol 1990, **3**: 271–280.

561 Sim SJ, Ro JY, Ordonez NG, Cleary KR, Ayala AG. Sclerosing mucoepidermoid carcinoma with eosinophilia of the thyroid: report of two patients, one with distant metastasis, and review of the literature. Hum Pathol 1997, **28**: 1091–1096.

562 Sobrinho-Simões MA, Nesland JM, Johannessen JV. A mucin-producing tumor in the thyroid gland. Ultrastruct Pathol 1985, **9**: 277–281.

563 Solomon AC, Baloch ZW, Salhany KE, Mandel S, Weber RS, LiVolsi VA. Thyroid sclerosing mucoepidermoid carcinoma with eosinophilia: mimic of Hodgkin disease in nodal metastases. Arch Pathol Lab Med 2000, **124**: 446–449.

Poorly differentiated carcinoma

564 Akslen LA, LiVolsi VA. Poorly differentiated thyroid carcinoma—it is important. Am J Surg Pathol 2000, **24**: 310–313.

565 Albores-Saavedra J, Sharma S. Poorly differentiated follicular thyroid carcinoma with rhabdoid phenotype: a clinicopathologic, immunohistochemical and electron microscopic study of two cases. Mod Pathol 2001, **14**: 98–104.

566 Albores-Saavedra J, Housini I, Vuitch F, Snyder WH III. Macrofollicular variant of papillary thyroid carcinoma with minor insular component. Cancer 1997, **80**: 1110–1116.

567 Cabanne F, Gérard-Marchant R, Heimann R, Williams ED. Tumeurs malignes du corps thyroïde. Problémes de diagnostic histopathologique. A propos de 692 lésions recueillies par le groupe coopérateur des cancers du corps thyroïde de l'OERTC. Ann Anat Pathol (Paris) 1974, **19**: 129–148.

568 Carcangiu ML, Zampi G, Rosai J. Poorly differentiated ("insular") thyroid carcinoma. A reinterpretation of Langhans' "wuchernde Struma." Am J Surg Pathol 1984, **8**: 655–668.

569 Guiter GE, Auger M, Ali SZ, Allen EA, Zakowski MF. Cytopathology of insular carcinoma of the thyroid. Cancer Cytopathol 1999, **87**: 196–202.

570 Hassoun AA, Hay ID, Goellner JR, Zimmerman D. Insular thyroid carcinoma in adolescents: A potentially lethal endocrine malignancy. Cancer 1997, **79**: 1044–1048.

571 Justin EP, Seabold JE, Robinson RA, Walker WP, Gurll NJ, Hawes DR. Insular carcinoma. A distinct thyroid carcinoma with associated iodine-131 localization. J Nucl Med 1991, **32**: 1358–1363.

572 Manetto V, Lorenzini R, Cordon-Cardo C, Krajewski S, Rosai J, Reed JC, Eusebi V. Bcl-2 and Bax expression in thyroid tumours. An immunohistochemical and western blot analysis. Virchows Arch 1997, **430**: 125–130.

573 Mizukami Y, Noguchi M, Michigishi T, Nonomura A, Hashimoto T, Otakes S, Nakamura S, Matsubara F. Papillary thyroid carcinoma in Kanazawa, Japan. Prognostic significance of histological subtypes. Histopathology 1992, **20**: 243–250.

574 Nishida T, Katayama SI, Tsujimoto M, Nakamura JI, Matsuda H. Clinicopathological significance of poorly differentiated thyroid carcinoma. Am J Surg Pathol 1999, **23**: 205–211.

575 Papotti M, Botto Micca F, Favero A, Palestini N, Bussolati G. Poorly differentiated thyroid carcinomas with primordial cell component. A group of aggressive lesions sharing insular, trabecular, and solid patterns. Am J Surg Pathol 1993, **17**: 291–301.

576 Papotti M, Torchio B, Grassi L, Favero A, Bussolati G. Poorly differentiated oxyphilic (Hürthle cell) carcinomas of the thyroid. Am J Surg Pathol 1996, **20**: 686–694.

576a Pelligriti G, Giufrrida D, Scollo C, Vigneri R, Regaluto C, Squatrito S, Belfiore A. Long-term outcome of patients with insular carcinoma of the thyroid. Cancer 2002, **95**: 2076–2085.

577 Pestereli HE, Ogus M, Oren N, Karpuzoglu G, Kerpuzoglu T. Bcl-2 and p53 expression in insular and in well-differentiated thyroid carcinomas with an insular pattern. Endocr Pathol 2001, **12**: 301–305.

578 Pietribiasi F, Sapino A, Papotti M, Bussolati G. Cytologic features of poorly differentiated "insular" carcinoma of the thyroid, as revealed by fine-needle aspiration biopsy. Am J Clin Pathol 1990, **94**: 687–692.

579 Pilotti S, Collini P, Del Bo R, Cattoretti G, Pierotti MA, Rilke F. A novel panel of antibodies that segregates immunocytochemically poorly differentiated carcinoma from undifferentiated carcinoma of the thyroid gland. Am J Surg Pathol 1994, **18**: 1054–1064.

580 Pilotti S, Collini P, Mariani L, Placucci M, Bongarzone I, Vigneri P, Cipriani S, Falcetta F, Miceli R, Pierotti MA, Rilke F. Insular carcinoma: a distinct de novo entity among follicular carcinomas of the thyroid gland. Am J Surg Pathol 1997, **21**: 1466–1473.

581 Rosai J, Saxén EA, Woolner L. Undifferentiated and poorly differentiated carcinoma. Semin Diagn Pathol 1985, **2**: 123–136.

582 Sakamoto A, Kasai N, Sugano H. Poorly differentiated carcinoma of the thyroid. A clinicopathologic entity for a high risk group of papillary and follicular carcinomas. Cancer 1983, **52**: 1849–1855.

583 Sasaki A, Daa T, Kashima K, Yokoyama S, Nakayama I, Noguchi S. Insular component as a risk factor of thyroid carcinoma. Pathol Int 1996, **46**: 939–946.

584   Satoh F, Umemura S, Yasuda M, Osamura RY. Neuroendocrine marker expression in thyroid epithelial tumors. Endocr Pathol 2001, **12**: 291–299.

585   Sobrinho-Simões M. Poorly differentiated carcinomas of the thyroid. Endocr Pathol 1996, **7**: 99–102.

586   Sobrinho-Simões M, Sambade C, Fonseca E, Soares P. Poorly differentiated carcinomas of the thyroid gland: a review of the clinicopathologic features of a series of 28 cases of a heterogeneous, clinically aggressive group of thyroid tumors. Int J Surg Pathol 2002, **10**: 123–131.

587   Tubiana M, Schlumberger M, Rougier P, Laplanche A, Benhamou E, Gardet P, Caillou B, Travagli J-P, Parmentier C. Long-term results and prognostic factors in patients with differentiated thyroid carcinoma. Cancer 1985, **55**: 794–804.

587a Volant M, Landolfi S, Codegone A, Palestini N, Dalmasso P, Papotti M. Clinico-pathological correlation in 154 thyroid carcinomas with poorly differentiated features. (Abstract) Mod Pathol 2003, **16**: 111a.

Undifferentiated carcinoma

588   Albores-Saavedra J, Nadji M, Civantos F, Morales AR. Thyroglobulin in carcinoma of the thyroid. An immunohistochemical study. Hum Pathol 1983, **14**: 62–66.

589   Aldinger KA, Samaan NA, Ibanez M, Hills CS Jr. Anaplastic carcinoma of the thyroid. A review of 84 cases of spindle and giant cell carcinoma of the thyroid. Cancer 1978, **41**: 2267–2275.

590   Blasius S, Edel G, Grunert J, Bocker W, Schmid KW. Anaplastic thyroid carcinoma with osteosarcomatous differentiation. Pathol Res Pract 1994, **190**: 507–510.

591   Bronner MP, LiVolsi VA. Spindle cell squamous carcinoma of the thyroid. An unusual anaplastic tumor associated with tall cell papillary cancer. Mod Pathol 1991, **4**: 637–643.

592   Canos JC, Serrano A, Matias-Guiu X. Paucicellular variant of anaplastic thyroid carcinoma: a report of two cases. Endocr Pathol 2001, **12**: 157–161.

593   Carcangiu ML, Steeper T, Zampi G, Rosai J. Anaplastic thyroid carcinoma. A study of 70 cases. Am J Clin Pathol 1985, **83**: 135–158.

594   Chetty R, Mills A, LiVolsi V. Anaplastic carcinoma of the thyroid with sclerohyaline nodules. Endocr Pathol 1993, **4**: 110–114.

595   Demeter JG, De Jong SA, Lawrence AM, Paloyan E. Anaplastic thyroid carcinoma. Risk factors and outcome. Surgery 1991, **110**: 956–961.

596   De Micco C, Ruf J, Carayon P, Christian M-A, Henry J-F, Toga M. Immunohistochemical study of thyroglobulin in thyroid carcinomas with monoclonal antibodies. Cancer 1987, **59**: 471–476.

597   Dominguez-Malagon H, Flores-Flores G, Vilchis JJ. Lymphoepithelioma-like anaplastic thyroid carcinoma: report of a case not related to Epstein-Barr virus. Ann Diagn Pathol 2001, **5**: 21–24.

598   Fagin JA, Matsuo K, Karmakar A, Chen DL, Tang SH, Koeffler HP. High prevalence of mutation of the p53 gene in poorly differentiated human thyroid carcinomas. J Clin Invest 1993, **91**: 179–184.

599   Fisher ER, Gregorio R, Shoemaker R, Horvat B, Hubay C. The derivation of so-called "giant-cell" and "spindle-cell" undifferentiated thyroidal neoplasms. Am J Clin Pathol 1974, **61**: 680–689.

600   Gaffey MJ, Lack EE, Christ ML, Weiss LM. Anaplastic thyroid carcinoma with osteoclast-like giant cells. A clinicopathologic, immunohistochemical, and ultrastructural study. Am J Surg Pathol 1991, **15**: 160–168.

601   Harada T, Ito K, Shimaoka K, Hosoda Y, Yakumaru K. Fatal thyroid carcinoma. Anaplastic transformation of adenocarcinoma. Cancer 1977, **39**: 2588–2596.

602   Hashimoto H, Koga S, Watanabe H, Enjoji M. Undifferentiated carcinoma of the thyroid gland with osteoclast-like giant cells. Acta Pathol Jpn 1980, **30**: 323–334.

603   Hurlimann J, Gardiol D, Scazziga B. Immunohistology of anaplastic thyroid carcinoma. A study of 43 cases. Histopathology 1987, **11**: 567–580.

604   Hutter RVP, Tollefsen HR, DeCosse JJ, Foote FW Jr, Frazell EL. Spindle and giant cell metaplasia in papillary carcinoma of the thyroid. Am J Surg 1965, **110**: 660–668.

605   Ito T, Seyama T, Mizuno T, Tsuyama N, Hayashi T, Hayashi Y, Dohi K, Nakamura N, Akiyama M. Unique association of p53 mutations with undifferentiated but not with differentiated carcinomas of the thyroid gland. Cancer Res 1992, **52**: 1369–1371.

606   Johannessen JV, Gould VE, Jao W. The fine structure of human thyroid cancer. Hum Pathol 1978, **9**: 385–400.

607   Kim JH, Leeper RD. Treatment of anaplastic giant and spindle cell carcinoma of the thyroid gland with combination adriamycin and radiation therapy. Cancer 1983, **52**: 954–957.

608   LiVolsi VA, Brooks JJ, Arendash-Durand B. Anaplastic thyroid tumors. Immunohistology. Am J Clin Pathol 1987, **87**: 434–442.

609   Miettinen M, Franssila KO. Variable expression of keratins and nearly uniform lack of thyroid transcription factor 1 in thyroid anaplastic carcinoma. Hum Pathol 2000, **31**: 1139–1145.

610   Miettinen M, Franssila K, Kehto V-P, Paasivuo R, Virtanen I. Expression of intermediate filament proteins in thyroid gland and thyroid tumors. Lab Invest 1984, **50**: 262–270.

611   Miettinen M, Virtanen I. Expression of laminin in thyroid gland and thyroid tumors. An immunohistologic study. Int J Cancer 1984, **34**: 27–30.

612   Nakamura T, Yana I, Kobayashi T, Shin E, Karakawa K, Fujita S, Miya A, Mori T, Nishisho I, Takai S. p53 gene mutations associated with anaplastic transformation of human thyroid carcinomas. Jpn J Cancer Res 1992, **83**: 1293–1298.

613   Newland JR, Mackay B, Hill CS Jr, Hickey RC. Anaplastic thyroid carcinoma. An ultrastructural study of 10 cases. Ultrastruct Pathol 1981, **2**: 121–129.

614   Nishiyama RH, Dunn EL, Thompson NW. Anaplastic spindle-cell and giant-cell tumors of the thyroid gland. Cancer 1972, **30**: 113–127.

615   Ordóñez NG, el-Naggar AK, Hickey RC, Samaan NA. Anaplastic thyroid carcinoma. Immunocytochemical study of 32 cases. Am J Clin Pathol 1991, **96**: 15–24.

616   Papotti M, Volante M, Negro F, Eusebi V, Bussolati G. Thyroglobulin mRNA expression helps to distinguish anaplastic carcinoma from angiosarcoma of the thyroid. Virchows Arch 2000, **437**: 635–642.

617   Ryff-de Lèche A, Staub JJ, Kohler-Faden R, Müller-Brand J, Heitz PU. Thyroglobulin production by malignant thyroid tumors. An immunocytochemical and radioimmunoassay study. Cancer 1986, **57**: 1145–1153.

618   Schmid KW, Kroll M, Hofstadter F, Ladurner D. Small cell carcinoma of the thyroid. A reclassification of cases originally diagnosed as small cell carcinomas of the thyroid. Pathol Res Pract 1986, **181**: 540–543.

619   Shek TW, Luk IS, Ng IO, Lo CY. Lymphoepithelioma-like carcinoma of the thyroid gland: Lack of evidence of association with Epstein-Barr virus. Hum Pathol 1996, **27**: 851–853.

620   Soares P, Cameselle-Teijeiro J, Sobrinho-Simões M. Immunohistochemical detection of p53 in differentiated, poorly differentiated and undifferentiated carcinomas of the thyroid. Histopathology 1994, **24**: 205–210.

621   Spanos GA, Wolk D, Desner MR, Khan A, Platt N, Khafif RA, Cortes EP. Preoperative chemotherapy for giant cell carcinoma of the thyroid. Cancer 1982, **50**: 2252–2256.

622   Venkatesh YS, Ordóñez NG, Schultz PN, Hickey RC, Goepfert H, Samaan NA. Anaplastic carcinoma of the thyroid. A clinicopathologic study of 121 cases. Cancer 1990, **66**: 321–330.

623   Wan SK, Chan JK, Tang SK. Paucicellular variant of anaplastic

thyroid carcinoma. A mimic of Riedel's thyroiditis. Am J Clin Pathol 1996, **105**: 388–393.

624 Wilkens L, Benten D, Tchinda J, Brabant G, Potter E, Dralle H, Wasielewski R. Aberrations of chromosomes 5 and 8 as recurrent cytogenetic events in anaplastic carcinoma of the thyroid as detected by fluorescence in situ hybridisation and comparative genomic hybridisation. Virchows Arch 2000, **436**: 312–318.

625 Wilson NW, Pambakian H, Richardson TC, Stokoe MR, Makin CA, Heyderman E. Epithelial markers in thyroid carcinoma. An immunoperoxidase study. Histopathology 1986, **10**: 815–829.

Medullary carcinoma and related neuroendocrine lesions
Morphologic features

626 Chong GC, Beahrs OH, Sizemore GW, Woolner LH. Medullary carcinoma of the thyroid gland. Cancer 1975, **35**: 695–704.

627 Dominguez-Malagon H, Delgado-Chavez R, Torres-Najera M, Gould E, Albores-Saavedra J. Oxyphil and squamous variants of medullary thyroid carcinoma. Cancer 1989, **63**: 1183–1188.

628 Dominguez-Malagon H, Macias-Martinez V, Molina-Cardenas H, Suster S. Amphicrine medullary carcinoma of the thyroid with luminal differentiation: report of an immunohistochemical and ultrastructural study. Ultrastruct Pathol 1997, **21**: 569–574.

629 Golouh R, Us-Krasovec M, Auersperg M, Jancar J, Bondi A, Eusebi V. Amphicrine – composite calcitonin and mucin-producing – carcinoma of the thyroid. Ultrastruct Pathol 1985, **8**: 197–206.

630 Guyetant S, Dupre F, Bigorgne JC, Franc B, Dutrieux-Berger N, Lecomte-Houcke M, Patey M, Caillou B, Viennet G, Guerin O, Saint-Andre JP. Medullary thyroid microcarcinoma: a clinicopathologic retrospective of 38 patients with no prior familial disease. Hum Pathol 1999, **30**: 957–963.

631 Harach H, Bergholm U. Small cell variant of medullary carcinoma of the thyroid with neuroblastoma-like features. Histopathology 1992, **21**: 378–379.

632 Harach HR, Bergholm U. Medullary carcinoma of the thyroid with carcinoid-like features. J Clin Pathol 1993, **46**: 113–117.

633 Harach HR, Williams ED. Glandular (tubular and follicular) variants of medullary carcinoma of the thyroid. Histopathology 1983, **7**: 83–97.

634 Hazard JB, Hawk WA, Crile G Jr. Medullary (solid) carcinoma of the thyroid. A clinicopathologic entity. J Clin Endocrinol Metab 1959, **19**: 152–161.

635 Horvath E, Kovacs K, Ross RC. Medullary cancer of the thyroid gland and its possible relations to carcinoids. An ultrastructural study. Virchows Arch [A] 1972, **356**: 281–292.

636 Ikeda T, Satoh M, Azuma K, Sawada N, Mori M. Medullary thyroid carcinoma with a paraganglioma-like pattern and melanin production: a case report with ultrastructural and immunohistochemical studies. Arch Pathol Lab Med 1998, **122**: 555–558.

637 Kakudo K, Miyauchi A, Ogihara T, Takai SI, Kitamura H, Kosaki G, Kumahara Y. Medullary carcinoma of the thyroid. Giant cell type. Arch Pathol Lab Med 1978, **102**: 445–447.

638 Kakudo K, Miyauchi A, Takai S, Katayama S, Kuma K, Kitamura H. C cell carcinoma of the thyroid. Papillary type. Acta Pathol Jpn 1979, **29**: 653–659.

639 Landon G, Ordóñez NG. Clear cell variant of medullary carcinoma of the thyroid. Hum Pathol 1985, **16**: 844–847.

640 Marcus JN, Dise CA, LiVolsi VA. Melanin production in a medullary thyroid carcinoma. Cancer 1982, **49**: 2518–2526.

641 Mendelsohn G, Bigner SH, Eggleston JC, Baylin SB, Wells SA Jr. Anaplastic variants of medullary thyroid carcinoma. Am J Surg Pathol 1980, **4**: 333–341.

642 Papotti M, Sambataro D, Pecchioni C, Bussolati G. The pathology of medullary carcinoma of the thyroid: Review of the literature and personal experience on 62 cases. Endocr Pathol 1996, **7**: 1–20.

Cytologic features

643 Forrest CH, Frost FA, de Boer WB, Spagnolo DV, Whitaker D, Sterrett B. Medullary carcinoma of the thyroid: accuracy of diagnosis of fine-needle aspiration cytology. Cancer Cytopathol 1998, **84**: 295–302.

644 Green I, Ali SZ, Allen EA, Zakowski MF. A spectrum of cytomorphologic variations in medullary thyroid carcinoma. Fine-needle aspiration findings in 19 cases. Cancer Cytopathol 1997, **81**: 40–44.

Electron microscopic, histochemical, and immunohistochemical features

645 Butler M, Khan S. Immunoreactive calcitonin in amyloid fibrils of medullary carcinoma of the thyroid gland. An immunogold staining technique. Arch Pathol Lab Med 1986, **110**: 647–649.

646 Capella C, Bordi C, Monga G, Buffa R, Fontana P, Bonfanti S, Bussolati G, Solcia E. Multiple endocrine cell types in thyroid medullary carcinoma. Evidence for calcitonin, somatostatin, ACTH, 5HT and small granule cells. Virchows Arch [A] 1978, **377**: 111–128.

647 Colomer A, Martinez-Mas JV, Matias-Guiu X, Llorens A, Cabezas R, Prat J, Garcia-Ameijeiras A. Sex-steroid hormone receptors in human medullary thyroid carcinoma. Mod Pathol 1996, **9**: 68–72.

648 Cvejic D, Savin S, Golubovic S, Paunovic I, Tatic S, Havelka M. Galectin-3 and carcinoembryonic antigen expression in medullary thyroid carcinoma: possible relation to tumour progression. Histopathology 2001, **37**: 530–535.

649 Dasovic-Knezevic M, Bormer O, Holm R, Hoie J, Sobrinho-Simões M, Nesland JM. Carcinoembryonic antigen in medullary thyroid carcinoma. An immunohistochemical study applying six novel monoclonal antibodies. Mod Pathol 1989, **2**: 610–617.

650 De Micco C, Chapel F, Dor A, Garcia S, Ruf J, Carayon P, Henry J, Lebreuil G. Thyroglobulin in medullary thyroid carcinoma. Immunohistochemical study with polyclonal and monoclonal antibodies. Hum Pathol 1993, **24**: 256–262.

651 Engbaek F. Serotonin (5-hydroxytryptamine) in medullary thyroid carcinoma with or without pheochromocytoma. Eur J Cancer Clin Oncol 1985, **21**: 469–473.

652 Ghatei MA, Springall DR, Nicholl CG, Polak JM, Bloom SR. Gastrin-releasing peptide-like immunoreactivity in medullary thyroid carcinoma. Am J Clin Pathol 1985, **84**: 581–586.

653 Harach HR, Wilander E, Grimelius L, Bergholm U, Westermark P, Falkmer S. Chromogranin A immunoreactivity compared with argyrophilia, calcitonin immunoreactivity, and amyloid as tumour markers in the histopathological diagnosis of medullary (C-cell) thyroid carcinoma. Pathol Res Pract 1992, **188**: 123–130.

654 Holm R, Sobrinho-Simões M, Nesland JM, Gould VE, Johannessen JV. Medullary carcinoma of the thyroid gland. An immunocytochemical study. Ultrastruct Pathol 1985, **8**: 25–41.

655 Katoh R, Miyagi E, Nakamura N, Li X, Suzuki K, Kakudo K, Kobayashi M, Kawaoi A. Expression of thyroid transcription factor (TTF-1) in human C cells and medullary thyroid carcinoma. Hum Pathol 2000, **31**: 386–393.

656 Kimura N, Nakazato Y, Nagura H, Sasano N. Expression of intermediate filaments in neuroendocrine tumors. Arch Pathol Lab Med 1990, **114**: 506–510.

657 Komminoth P, Roth J, Saremaslani P, Matias-Guiu X, Wolfe HJ, Heitz PU. Polysialic acid of the neural cell adhesion molecule in the human thyroid. A marker for medullary thyroid carcinoma and primary C-cell hyperplasia. An immunohistochemical study of 79 thyroid lesions. Am J Surg Pathol 1994, **18**: 339–411.

658 Krisch K, Krisch I, Horvat G, Neuhold N, Ulrich W, Srikanta S. The value of immunohistochemistry in medullary thyroid carcinoma. A systemic study of 30 cases. Histopathology 1985, **9**: 1077–1089.

659 Lippmann SM, Mendelsohn G, Trump DL, Wells SA Jr, Baylin SB. The prognostic and biologic significance of cellular

heterogeneity in medullary thyroid carcinoma. A study of calcitonin, L-DOPA decarboxylase, and histaminase. J Clin Endocrinol Metab 1982, **54:** 233–240.

660 Lloyd RV, Sisson JC, Marangos PJ. Calcitonin, carcinoembryonic antigen and neuron-specific enolase in medullary thyroid carcinoma. An immunohistochemical study. Cancer 1983, **51:** 2234–2239.

661 Matsubayashi S, Yanaihara C, Ohkubo M, Fukata S, Hayashi Y, Tamai H, Nakagawa T, Miyauchi A, Kuma K, Abe K. Gastrin-releasing peptide immunoreactivity in medullary thyroid carcinoma. Cancer 1984, **53:** 2472–2477.

662 Mendelsohn G, Eggleston JC, Weisburger WR, Gann DS, Baylin SB. Calcitonin and histaminase in C-cell hyperplasia and medullary thyroid carcinoma. A light microscopic and immunohistochemical study. Am J Pathol 1978, **92:** 35–52.

663 Papotti M, Olivero M, Volante M, Negro F, Prat M, Comoglio PM, DiRenzo MF. Expression of hepatocyte growth factor (HGF) and its receptor (MET) in medullary carcinoma of the thyroid. Endocr Pathol 2000, **11:** 19–30.

664 Reubi JC, Chayvialle JA, Franc B, Cohen R, Calmettes C, Modigliani E. Somatostatin receptors and somatostatin content in medullary thyroid carcinomas. Lab Invest 1991, **64:** 567–573.

665 Roth KA, Bensch KG, Hoffman AR. Characterization of opioid peptides in human thyroid medullary carcinoma. Cancer 1987, **59:** 1594–1598.

666 Schmid KW, Ensinger C. "A typical" medullary thyroid carcinoma with little or no calcitonin expression. Virchows Arch 1998, **433:** 209–215.

667 Schmid K, Kirchmai R, Ladurner D, Fischer-Colbrie R, Bocker W. Immunohistochemical comparison of chromogranins A and B and secretogranin II with calcitonin and calcitonin gene-related peptide expression in normal, hyperplastic and neoplastic C-cells of the human thyroid. Histopathology 1992, **21:** 225–232.

668 Schröder S, Klöppel G. Carcinoembryonic antigen and nonspecific cross-reacting antigen in thyroid cancer. An immunocytochemical antigen in thyroid cancer. An immunocytochemical study using polyclonal and monoclonal antibodies. Am J Surg Pathol 1987, **11:** 100–108.

669 Sikri KL, Varndell IM, Hamid QA, Wilson BS, Kameya T, Ponder BAJ, Lloyd RV, Bloom SR, Polak JM. Medullary carcinoma of the thyroid. An immunocytochemical and histochemical study of 25 cases using eight separate markers. Cancer 1985, **56:** 2481–2491.

670 Tomita T. Matrix metalloproteinases and tissue inhibitors of metalloproteinases in thyroid C-cells and medullary thyroid carcinomas. Histopathology 1997, **31:** 150–156.

671 Tomita T. Immunocytochemical localization of prohormone convertase 1/3 and 2 in thyroid C-cells and medullary thyroid carcinomas. Endocr Pathol 2000, **11:** 165–172.

672 Uribe M, Grimes M, Fenoglio-Preiser CM, Feind C. Medullary carcinoma of the thyroid gland. Clinical, pathological, and immunohistochemical features with review of the literature. Am J Surg Pathol 1985, **9:** 577–594.

673 Wang D-G, Liu W-H, Johnston CF, Sloan JM, Buchanan KD. Bcl-2 and c-Myc, but not Bax and p53, are expressed during human medullary thyroid tumorigenesis. Am J Pathol 1998, **152:** 1407–1413.

674 Wurzel JM, Kourides IA, Brooks JSJ. Medullary carcinomas of the thyroid contain immunoreactive human chorionic gonadotropin alpha subunit. Horm Metab Res 1984, **16:** 677.

675 Zaatari GS, Saigo PE, Huvos AG. Mucin production in medullary carcinoma of the thyroid. Arch Pathol Lab Med 1983, **107:** 70–74.

Familial medullary carcinoma and C-cell hyperplasia

676 Albores-Saavedra J, Monforte H, Nadji M, Morales AR. C-cell hyperplasia in thyroid tissue adjacent to follicular cell tumors. Hum Pathol 1988, **19:** 795–799.

677 Biddinger PW, Brennan MF, Rosen PP. Symptomatic C-cell hyperplasia associated with chronic lymphocytic thyroiditis. Am J Surg Pathol 1991, **15:** 599–604.

678 Bigner S, Mendelsohn G, Wells SA Jr, Cox EB, Baylin SB, Eggleston JC. Medullary carcinoma of the thyroid in the multiple endocrine neoplasia IIA syndrome. Am J Surg Pathol 1981, **5:** 459–472.

679 Eng C. The RET proto-oncogene in multiple endocrine neoplasia type 2 and Hirschsprung's disease. N Engl J Med 1996, **335:** 943–951.

680 Guyetant S, Wion-Barbot N, Rousselet MC, Franc B, Bigorgne JC, Saint-Andre JP. C-cell hyperplasia associated with chronic lymphocytic thyroiditis. A retrospective quantitative study of 112 cases. Hum Pathol 1994, **25:** 514–521.

681 Hijazi YM, Nieman LK, Medeiros LJ. Medullary carcinoma of the thyroid as a cause of Cushing's syndrome. A case with ectopic adrenocorticotropin secretion characterized by double enzyme immunostaining. Hum Pathol 1992, **23:** 592–596.

682 Hinze R, Holzhausen HJ, Gimm O, Dralle H, Rath FW. Primary hereditary medullary thyroid carcinoma – C-cell morphology and correlation with preoperative calcitonin levels. Virchows Arch 1998, **433:** 203–208.

683 Janzer RC, Weber E, Hedinger C. The relation between solid cell nests and C-cells of the thyroid gland. Cell Tissue Res 1979, **197:** 285–312.

684 Kaserer K, Scheuba C, Neuhold N, Weinhausel A, Haas OA, Vierhapper H, Niederle B. Sporadic versus familial medullary thyroid microcarcinoma: a histopathologic study of 50 consecutive patients. Am J Surg Pathol 2001, **25:** 1245–1251.

685 Krueger JE, Maitra A, Albores-Saavedra J. Inherited medullary microcarcinoma of the thyroid: A study of 11 cases. Am J Surg Pathol 2000, **24:** 853–858.

686 Ljungberg O. On medullary carcinoma of the thyroid. Acta Pathol Microbiol Scand [A] 1972, **231**(Suppl): 1–57.

686a Machens A, Niccoli-Sire P, Hoegel J, Frank-Raue K, van Vroonhoven TJ, Roeher H-D, Wahl RA, Lamesch P, Raue F, Conte-Devoix B, Dralle H. Early malignant progression of hereditary medullary thyroid cancer. N Engl J Med 2003, **349:** 1517–1525.

687 Matias-Guiu X. RET protooncogene analysis in diagnosis of medullary thyroid carcinoma and multiple endocrine neoplasia type II. Adv Anat Pathol 1998, **5:** 196–201.

688 O'Connor DT, Deftos LJ. Secretion of chromogranin A by peptide-producing endocrine neoplasms. N Engl J Med 1986, **314:** 1145–1151.

689 Raue F, Kotzerke J, Reinwein D, Schröder S, Röher HD, Deckart H, Höfer R, Ritter M, Seif F, Buhr H, Beyer J, Schober O, Becker W, Neumann H, Calvi J, Winter J, Vogt H, and the German Medullary Thyroid Carcinoma Study Group. Prognostic factors in medullary thyroid carcinoma. Evaluation of 741 patients from the German Medullary Thyroid Carcinoma Register. Clin Invest 1993, **71:** 7–12.

690 Santeusanio G, Iafrate E, Partenzi A, Mauriello A, Autelitano F, Spagnoli LG. A critical reassessment of the concept of C-cell hyperplasia of the thyroid: a quantitative immunohistochemical study. Appl Immunohistochem 1997, **5:** 160–172.

691 Scopsi L, Di Palma S, Ferrari C, Holst JJ, Rehfeld JF, Rike F. C-cell hyperplasia accompanying thyroid diseases other than medullary carcinoma: An immunohistochemical study by means of antibodies to calcitonin and somatostatin. Mod Pathol 1991, **4:** 297–304.

692 Steinfeld CM, Moertel CG, Woolner LB. Diarrhea and medullary carcinoma of the thyroid. Cancer 1973, **31:** 1237–1239.

693 Tomita T, Millard DM. C-cell hyperplasia in secondary hyperparathyroidism. Histopathology 1992, **21:** 469–474.

694 Tsukada T, Yamaguchi K, Kameya T. The MEN1 gene and associated diseases: an update. Endocr Pathol 2001, **12:** 259–273.

695 Wells SA Jr, Baylin SB, Leight GS, Dale JK, Dilley WG, Earndon

JR. The importance of early diagnosis in patients with hereditary medullary thyroid carcinoma. Ann Surg 1982, **195:** 595–599.

696 White IL, Vimadalal SD, Catz B, Van de Velde R, La Gange T. Occult medullary carcinoma of thyroid. An unusual clinical and pathologic presentation. Cancer 1981, **47:** 1364–1368.

Spread and metastases

697 Fletcher JR. Medullary (solid) carcinoma of the thyroid gland. A review of 249 cases. Arch Surg 1970, **100:** 257–262.

698 Kakudo K, Carney JA, Sizemore GW. Medullary carcinoma of thyroid. Biologic behavior of the sporadic and familial neoplasm. Cancer 1985, **55:** 2818–2821.

699 Ruppert JM, Eggleston JC, DeBustros A, Baylin SB. Disseminated calcitonin-poor medullary thyroid carcinoma in a patient with calcitonin-rich primary tumor. Am J Surg Pathol 1986, **10:** 513–518.

700 Sweeney EC, McDonnell L, O'Brien C. Medullary carcinoma of the thyroid presenting as tumours of the pharynx and larynx. Histopathology 1981, **5:** 263–275.

Treatment and prognosis

701 Bergholm U, Bergstrom R, Ekbom A. Long term follow-up of patients with medullary carcinoma of the thyroid. Cancer 1997, **79:** 132–138.

702 Boultwood J, Wynford-Thomas D, Richards GP, Craig RK, Williams ED. In-situ analysis of calcitonin and CGRP expression in medullary thyroid carcinoma. Clin Endocrinol 1990, **33:** 381–390.

703 Chong GC, Beahrs OH, Sizemore GW, Woolner LH. Medullary carcinoma of the thyroid gland. Cancer 1975, **35:** 695–704.

704 el-Naggar AK, Ordóñez NG, McLemore D, Schultz P, Hickey RC, Samaan N. Clinicopathologic and flow cytometric DNA study of medullary thyroid carcinoma. Surgery 1990, **108:** 981–985.

705 Franc B, Rosenberg-Bourgin M, Caillou B, Dutrieux-Berger N, Floquet J, Houcke-Lecomte M, Justrabo E, Lange F, Labat-Moleur F, Le Bodic MF, Patey M, Beauchet A, Saint-Andre JP, Hejblum G, Viennett G. Medullary thyroid carcinoma: search for histological predictors of survival (109 proband cases analysis). Hum Pathol 1998, **29:** 1078–1084.

706 Gharib H, McConahey W, Tiegs R, Bergstralh E, Goellner J, Grant C, van Heerden J, Sizemore G, Hay I. Medullary thyroid carcinoma. Clinicopathologic features and long-term follow-up of 65 patients treated during 1946 through 1970. Mayo Clin Proc 1992, **67:** 934–940.

707 Mendelsohn G, Wells SA Jr, Baylin SB. Relationship of tissue carcinoembryonic antigen and calcitonin to tumor virulence in medullary thyroid carcinoma. An immunohistochemical study in early, localized, and virulent disseminated stages of disease. Cancer 1984, **54:** 657–662.

708 Pyke CM, Hay ID, Goellner JR, Bergstralh EJ, van Heerden JA, Grant CS. Prognostic significance of calcitonin immunoreactivity, amyloid staining, and flow cytometric DNA measurements in medullary thyroid carcinoma. Surgery 1991, **110:** 964–970.

709 Raue F, Kotzerke J, Reinwein D, Schröder S, Röher HD, Deckart H, Höfer R, Ritter M, Seif F, Buhr H, Beyer J, Schober O, Becker W, Neumann H, Calvi J, Winter J, Vogt H, and the German Medullary Thyroid Carcinoma Study Group. Prognostic factors in medullary thyroid carcinoma. Evaluation of 741 patients from the German Medullary Thyroid Carcinoma Register. Clin Invest 1993, **71:** 7–12.

710 Saad MF, Fritsche HA Jr, Samaan NA. Diagnostic and prognostic values of carcinoembryonic antigen in medullary carcinoma of the thyroid. J Clin Endocrinol Metab 1984, **58:** 889–894.

711 Saad MF, Ordóñez NG, Guido JJ, Samaan NA. The prognostic value of calcitonin immunostaining in medullary carcinoma of the thyroid. J Clin Endocrinol Metab 1984, **59:** 850–856.

712 Saad MF, Ordóñez NG, Rashid RK, Guido JJ, Hill CS Jr, Hickey RC, Samaan NA. Medullary carcinoma of the thyroid. A study of the clinical features and prognostic factors in 161 patients. Medicine (Baltimore) 1984, **63:** 319–342.

713 Schröder S, Böcker W, Baisch H, Bürk CG, Arps H, Meiners I, Kastendieck H, Heitz PU, Klöppel G. Prognostic factors in medullary thyroid carcinomas. Survival in relation to age, sex, stage, histology, immunocytochemistry, and DNA content. Cancer 1988, **61:** 806–816.

714 Scopsi L, Sampietro G, Boracchi P, Del Bo R, Gullo M, Placucci M, Pilotti S. Multivariate analysis of prognostic factors in sporadic medullary carcinoma of the thyroid: A retrospective study of 109 consecutive patients. Cancer 1996, **78:** 2173–2183.

715 Scopsi L, Sampietro G, Boracchi P, Pilotti S. A critical appraisal of the prognostic utility of four separate immunocytochemical markers (somatostatin, gastrin-releasing peptide, neuropeptide Y, and opioid peptides) in sporadic medullary thyroid carcinoma. Appl Immunohistochem 1997, **5:** 23–28.

Other neuroendocrine tumors

716 Apel RL, Alpert LC, Rizzo A, LiVolsi VA, Asa SL. A metastasizing composite carcinoma of the thyroid with distinct medullary and papillary components. Arch Pathol Lab Med 1994, **118:** 1143–1147.

717 Collina G, Maiorana A, Fano RA, Cesinaro AM, Trentini GP. Medullary carcinoma of the thyroid gland with sustentacular cell-like cells in a patient with multiple endocrine neoplasia, type IIA. Report of a case with ultrastructural and immunohistochemical studies. Arch Pathol Lab Med 1994, **118:** 1041–1044.

718 Driman D, Murray D, Kovacs K, Stefaneanu L, Higgins HP. Encapsulated medullary carcinoma of the thyroid. A morphologic study including immunocytochemistry, electron microscopy, flow cytometry, and in situ hybridization. Am J Surg Pathol 1991, **15:** 1089–1095.

719 Eusebi V, Damiani S, Riva C, Lloyd RV, Capella C. Calcitonin free oat-cell carcinoma of the thyroid gland. Virchows Arch [A] 1990, **417:** 267–271.

720 Holm R, Sobrinho-Simões M, Nesland JM, Sambade C, Johannessen JV. Medullary thyroid carcinoma with thyroglobulin immunoreactivity. A special entity? Lab Invest 1987, **57:** 258–268.

721 Hughes JH, El-Mofty S, Sessions D, Liapis H. Primary intrathyroidal paraganglioma with metachronous carotid body tumor: report of a case and review of the literature. Pathol Res Pract 1997, **193:** 791–796.

722 Huss LJ, Mendelsohn G. Medullary carcinoma of the thyroid gland. An encapsulated variant resembling the hyalinizing trabecular (paraganglioma-like) adenoma of thyroid. Mod Pathol 1990, **3:** 581–585.

723 LaGuette J, Matias-Guiu X, Rosai J. Thyroid paraganglioma: a clinicopathologic and immunohistochemical study of three cases. Am J Surg Pathol 1997, **21:** 748–753.

724 Lax SF, Beham A, Kronberger-Schonecker D, Langsteger W, Denk H. Coexistence of papillary and medullary carcinoma of the thyroid gland – mixed or collision tumour? Clinicopathological analysis of three cases. Virchows Arch 1994, **424:** 441–447.

725 Matias-Guiu X, Caixas A, Costa I, Cabezas R, Prat J. Compound medullary-papillary carcinoma of the thyroid. True mixed tumour. Histopathology 1994, **25:** 183–184.

726 Matias-Guiu X, LaGuette J, Puras-Gil AM, Rosai J. Metastatic neuroendocrine tumors to the thyroid gland mimicking medullary carcinoma: A pathologic and immunohistochemical study of six cases. Am J Surg Pathol 1997, **21:** 754–762.

727 Mitsudo SM, Grajower MM, Balbi H, Silver C. Malignant paraganglioma of the thyroid gland. Arch Pathol Lab Med 1987, **111:** 378–380.

728 Mizukami Y, Michigishi T, Nonomura A, Nakamura S, Noguchi M, Hashimoto T, Itoh N. Mixed medullary-follicular carcinoma

of the thyroid occurring in familial form. Histopathology 1993, **22:** 284–287.

729 Papotti M, Negro F, Carney JA, Bussolati G, Lloyd RV. Mixed medullary-follicular carcinoma of the thyroid. A morphological, immunohistochemical and in situ hybridization analysis of 11 cases. Virchows Arch 1997, **430:** 397–405.

730 Pastolero GC, Coire CI, Asa SL. Concurrent medullary and papillary carcinomas of the thyroid with lymph node metastases: A collision phenomenon. Am J Surg Pathol 1996, **20:** 245–250.

731 Pfaltz M, Hedinger Chr E, Mühlethaler JP. Mixed medullary and follicular carcinoma of the thyroid. Virchows Arch [A] 1983, **400:** 53–59.

732 Shimizu M, Hirokawa M, LiVolsi VA, Mizukami Y, Harada T, Itoh T, Manabe T. Combined "mixed medullary-follicular" and "papillary" carcinoma of the thyroid with lymph node metastasis. Endocr Pathol 2000, **11:** 353–358.

733 Volante M, Papotti M, Roth J, Saremaslani P, Speel EJ, Lloyd RV, Carney JA, Heitz PU, Bussolati G, Komminoth P. Mixed medullary-follicular thyroid carcinoma. Molecular evidence for a dual origin of tumor components. Am J Pathol 1999, **155:** 1499–1509.

Epithelial tumors—general features

Geographic distribution

734 Cuello C, Correa P, Eisenberg H. Geographic pathology of thyroid carcinoma. Cancer 1969, **23:** 230–239.

735 Franssila K, Saxén E, Teppo L, Bjarnason O, Tulinius H, Normann T, Ringertz N. Incidence of different morphological types of thyroid cancer in the nordic countries. Acta Pathol Microbiol Scand [A] 1981, **89:** 49–55.

736 Hedinger Chr E. Geographic pathology of thyroid disease. Pathol Res Pract 1981, **171:** 285–292.

737 Hofstädter F. Frequency and morphology of malignant tumors of the thyroid before and after the introduction of iodine-prophylaxis. Virchows Arch [A] 1980, **385:** 263–270.

738 Nakamura S, Nakamura K, Mizukami Y. Thyroid carcinoma in Japan and the west: similarities and differences. Endocr Pathol 1996, **7:** 251–263.

739 Pendergrast WJ, Milmore BK, Marcus SC. Thyroid cancer and thyrotoxicosis in the United States. Their relation to endemic goiter. J Chronic Dis 1961, **13:** 22–38.

740 Pettersson B, Adami HO, Wilander E, Coleman MP. Trends in thyroid cancer incidence in Sweden, 1958–1981, by histopathologic type. Int J Cancer 1991, **48:** 28–33.

741 Sarda AK, Kapur MM. Thyroid carcinoma. A report of 205 cases from an area with endemic goitre. Acta Oncol 1990, **29:** 863–867.

742 Shi YF, Zou MJ, Schmidt H, Juhasz F, Stensky V, Robb D, Farid NR. High rates of *ras* codon 61 mutation in thyroid tumors in an iodine-deficient area. Cancer Res 1991, **51:** 2690–2693.

743 Williams ED, Doniach I, Bjarnason O, Michie W. Thyroid cancer in an iodine rich area. A histopathological study. Cancer 1977, **39:** 215–222.

Thyroid neoplasia in childhood

744 Farahati J, Bucsky P, Parlowsky T, Mader U, Reiners C. Characteristics of differentiated thyroid carcinoma in children and adolescents with respect to age, gender, and histology. Cancer 1997, **80:** 2156–2162.

745 Harness JK, Thompson NW, McLeod MK, Pasieka JL, Fukuuchi A. Differentiated thyroid carcinoma in children and adolescents. World J Surg 1992, **16:** 547–553.

746 Hayles AB, Kennedy RLJ, Beahrs OH, Woolner LB. Carcinoma of the thyroid gland in children. Am J Dis Child 1955, **90:** 705–715.

747 Mizukami Y, Michigishi T, Nonomura A, Hashimoto T, Noguchi M, Matsubara F, Watanabe K. Carcinoma of the thyroid at a young age – a review of 23 patients. Histopathology 1992, **20:** 63–66.

748 Raju U, Kini S. Neoplasms of thyroid follicular epithelium in children and adolescents (abstract). Lab Invest 1988, **58:** 8P.

749 Root AW. Cancer of the thyroid in childhood and adolescence. Am J Med Sci 1963, **246:** 734–749.

750 Samuel AM, Sharma SM. Differentiated thyroid carcinomas in children and adolescents. Cancer 1991, **67:** 2186–2190.

751 Winship T, Rosvoll RV. Childhood thyroid carcinoma. Cancer 1961, **14:** 734–743.

Thyroid neoplasia and radiation exposure

752 Calandra DB, Shah KH, Lawrence AM, Paloyan E. Total thyroidectomy in irradiated patients. A twenty-year experience in 206 patients. Ann Surg 1985, **202:** 356–360.

753 Carr RF, LiVolsi VA. Morphologic changes in the thyroid after irradiation for Hodgkin's and non-Hodgkin's lymphoma. Cancer 1989, **64:** 825–829.

754 De Jong SA, Demeter JG, Jarosz H, Lawrence AM, Paloyan E. Thyroid carcinoma and hyperparathyroidism after radiation therapy for adolescent acne vulgaris. Surgery 1991, **110:** 691–695.

755 Furmanchuk AW, Averkin JI, Egloff B, Ruchti C, Abelin T, Schäppi W, Korotkevich EA. Pathomorphological findings in thyroid cancers of children from the Republic of Belarus. A study of 86 cases occurring between 1986 ("post-Chernobyl") and 1991. Histopathology 1992, **21:** 401–408.

756 Hanson GA, Komorowski RA, Cerletty JM, Wilson SD. Thyroid gland morphology in young adults. Normal subjects versus those with prior low-dose neck irradiation in childhood. Surgery 1983, **96:** 984–988.

757 Hempelmann LH, Hall WJ, Phillips M, Cooper RA, Ames WR. Neoplasms in persons treated with x-rays in infancy. Fourth survey in 20 years. J Natl Cancer Inst 1975, **55:** 519–530.

758 Komorowski RA, Hanson GA. Morphologic changes in the thyroid following low-dose childhood radiation. Arch Pathol Lab Med 1977, **101:** 36–39.

759 Nikiforov YE, Gnepp DR. Pathomorphology of thyroid gland lesions associated with radiation exposure: The Chernobyl experience and review of the literature. Adv Anat Pathol 1999, **6:** 78–91.

760 Satran L, Sklar C, Dehner L, Kim T, Nesbit M. Thyroid neoplasm after high-dose radiotherapy. Am J Pediatr Hematol Oncol 1983, **5:** 307–309.

761 Schneider AB, Pinsky S, Bekerman C, Ryo UY. Characteristics of 108 thyroid cancers detected by screening in a population with a history of head and neck irradiation. Cancer 1980, **46:** 1218–1227.

762 Schneider AB, Shore-Freedman E, Ryo UY, Bekerman C, Favus M, Pinsky S. Radiation-induced tumors of the head and neck following childhood irradiation. Prospective studies. Medicine (Baltimore) 1985, **64:** 1–15.

763 Schneider AB, Shore-Freedman E, Weinstein RA. Radiation-induced thyroid and other head and neck tumors. Occurrence of multiple tumors and analysis of risk factors. J Clin Endocrinol Metab 1986, **63:** 107–112.

764 Spitalnik PF, Straus FH II. Patterns of human thyroid parenchymal reaction following low-dose childhood irradiation. Cancer 1978, **41:** 1098–1105.

765 Tronko MD, Bogdanova TI, Komissarenko IV, Epstein OV, Oliynyk V, Kovalenko A, Likhtarev IA, Kairo I, Peters SB, LiVolsi VA. Thyroid carcinoma in children and adolescents in Ukraine after the Chernobyl nuclear accident: statistical data and clinicomorphologic characteristics. Cancer 1999, **86:** 149–156.

766 Williams ED. Morphology, aggressiveness and latency of thyroid carcinoma. Lancet, in press.

767 Wilson SD, Komorowski R, Cerletty J, Majewski JT, Hooper M. Radiation-associated thyroid tumors. Extent of operation and pathology technique influence the apparent incidence of carcinoma. Surgery 1983, **94:** 663–669.

Association with other conditions

768 Barzilay J, Heatley GJ, Cushing GW. Benign and malignant tumors in patients with acromegaly. Arch Intern Med 1991, **151:** 1629–1632.

769 Bell B, Mazzaferri EL. Familial adenomatous polyposis (Gardner's syndrome) and thyroid carcinoma. A case report and review of the literature. Dig Dis Sci 1993, **38:** 185–190.

770 Harach HR. Familial nonmedullary thyroid neoplasia. Endocr Pathol 2001, **12:** 97–112.

771 Harach HR, Williams GT, Williams ED. Familial adenomatous polyposis associated thyroid carcinoma. A distinct type of follicular cell neoplasm. Histopathology 1994, **25:** 549–562.

772 Harned RK, Buck JL, Olmsted WW, Moser RP, Ros PR. Extracolonic manifestations of the familial adenomatous polyposis syndromes. Am J Roentgenol 1991, **156:** 481–485.

773 Hedman I, Tisell L-E. Associated hyperparathyroidism and nonmedullary thyroid carcinoma. The etiologic role of radiation. Surgery 1984, **95:** 392–397.

774 Ishikawa Y, Sugano H, Matsumoto T, Furuichi Y, Miller RW, Goto M. Unusual features of thyroid carcinomas in Japanese patients with Werner syndrome and possible genotype-phenotype relations to cell type and race. Cancer 1999, **85:** 1345–1352.

775 Lever EG, Refetoff S, Straus FH II, Nguyen M, Kaplan EL. Coexisting thyroid and parathyroid disease – Are they related? Surgery 1983, **94:** 893–900.

776 Lote K, Andersen K, Nordal E, Brennhovd IO. Familial occurrence of papillary thyroid carcinoma. Cancer 1980, **46:** 1291–1297.

777 McKay JD, Lesueur F, Jonard L, Patore A, Williamson J, Hoffman L, Burgess J, Duffield A, Papotti M, Stark M, Sobol H, Maes B, Murat A, Kaariainen H, Bertholon-Gregoire M, Zini M, Rossing MA, Toubert ME, Bonichon F, Cavarec M, Bernard AM, Boneu A, Leprat F, Haas O, Lasset C, Schlumberger M, Canzian F, Goldgar DE, Romeo G. Localization of a susceptibility gene for familial nonmedullary thyroid carcinoma to chromosome 2q21. Am J Hum Genet 2001, **69:** 440–446.

778 Narita T, Takagi K. Ataxia-telangiectasia with dysgerminoma of right ovary, papillary carcinoma of thyroid, and adenocarcinoma of pancreas. Cancer 1984, **54:** 1113–1116.

779 Plail RO, Bussey HJR, Glazer G, Thomson JPS. Adenomatous polyposis. An association with carcinoma of the thyroid. Br J Surg 1987, **74:** 377–380.

Evaluation of the solitary thyroid nodule

780 Belfiore A, La Rosa GL, La Porta GA, Giuffrida D, Milazzo G, Lupo L, Regalbuto C, Vigneri R. Cancer risk in patients with cold thyroid nodules. Relevance of iodine intake, sex, age, and multinodularity. Am J Med 1992, **93:** 363–369.

781 Clark OH. Fine-needle aspiration biopsy and management of thyroid tumors. Am J Clin Pathol 1997, **108:** S22–S25.

782 Davis NL, Gordon M, Germann E, Robins RE, McGregor GI. Clinical parameters predictive of malignancy of thyroid follicular neoplasms. Am J Surg 1991, **161:** 567–569.

783 de los Santos ET, Keyhani-Rofagha S, Cunningham JJ, Mazzaferri EL. Cystic thyroid nodules. The dilemma of malignant lesions. Arch Intern Med 1990, **150:** 1422–1427.

784 Ericsson UB, Tegler L, Lennquist S, Christensen SB, Stahl E, Thorell JI. Serum thyroglobulin in differentiated thyroid carcinoma. Acta Chir Scand 1984, **150:** 367–375.

785 Friedman M, Toriumi DM, Mafee MF. Diagnostic imaging techniques in thyroid cancer. Am J Surg 1988, **155:** 215–223.

786 Greenspan FS. The role of fine-needle aspiration biopsy in the management of palpable thyroid nodules. Am J Clin Pathol 1997, **108:** S26–S30.

787 Kuma K, Matsuzuka F, Kobayashi A, Hirai K, Morita S, Miyauchi A, Katayama S, Sugawara M. Outcome of long standing solitary thyroid nodules. World J Surg 1992, **16:** 583–587.

788 Mazzaferri EL. Management of a solitary thyroid nodule. N Engl J Med 1993, **328:** 553–559.

789 Oertel YC. Fine-needle aspiration in the evaluation of thyroid neoplasms. Endocr Pathol 1997, **8:** 215–224.

790 Ramanna L, Waxman AD, Brachman MB, Sensel N, Tanasescu DE, Berman DS, Catz B, Braunstein GD. Correlation of thyroglobulin measurements and radioiodine scans in the follow-up of patients with differentiated thyroid cancer. Cancer 1985, **55:** 1525–1529.

791 Ridgway EC. Clinician's evaluation of a solitary thyroid nodule. J Clin Endocrinol Metab 1992, **74:** 231–235.

792 Ross DS. Evaluation of the thyroid nodule. J Nucl Med 1991, **32:** 2181–2192.

793 Shulkin BI, Shapiro B. The role of imaging tests in the diagnosis of thyroid carcinoma. Endocrinol Metab Clin North Am 1990, **19:** 523–544.

794 van Herle AJ, Uller RP. Elevated serum thyroglobulin. A marker of metastases in differentiated thyroid carcinomas. J Clin Invest 1975, **56:** 272–277.

Needle biopsy and fine needle aspiration

795 Amrikachi M, Ramzy I, Rubenfeld S, Wheeler TM. Accuracy of fine-needle aspiration of thyroid. Arch Pathol Lab Med 2001, **125:** 484–488.

796 Baloch ZW, Gupta PK, Yu GH, Sack MJ, LiVolsi VA. Follicular variant of papillary carcinoma. Cytologic and histologic correlation. Am J Clin Pathol 1999, **111:** 216–222.

797 Baloch ZW, LiVolsi VA. Post fine-needle aspiration histologic alterations of thyroid revisited. Am J Clin Pathol 1999, **112:** 311–316.

798 Brennan MD, Bergstralh EJ, Van Heerden JA, McConahey WM. Follicular thyroid cancer treated at the Mayo Clinic, 1946 through 1970. Initial manifestations, pathologic findings, therapy, and outcome. Mayo Clin Proc 1991, **66:** 11–22.

799 Chhieng DC, Ross JS, McKenna BJ. CD44 immunostaining of thyroid fine-needle aspirates differentiates thyroid papillary carcinoma from other lesions with nuclear grooves and inclusions. Cancer Cytopathol 1997, **81:** 157–162.

800 Cramer H. Fine-needle aspiration cytology of the thyroid: an appraisal. Cancer Cytopathol 2000, **90:** 325–329.

801 Damiani S, Dina R, Eusebi V. Cytologic grading of aggressive and nonaggressive variants of papillary thyroid carcinoma. Am J Clin Pathol 1994, **101:** 651–655.

802 De Jong SA, Demeter JG, Castelli M, Jarosz H, Barbato A, Brooks MH, Brathwaite S, Emanuele MA, Lawrence AM, Paloyan E. Follicular cell predominance in the cytologic examination of dominant thyroid nodules indicates a sixty percent incidence of neoplasia. Surgery 1990, **108:** 794–799.

803 Droese M. Cytological aspiration biopsy of the thyroid gland. Stuttgart, 1980, E.K. Schattauer Verlag.

804 Frable WJ, Frable MA. Fine-needle aspiration biopsy of the thyroid. Histopathologic and clinical correlations. In Fenoglio CM, Wolff M (eds): Progress in surgical pathology, vol. 1. New York, 1980, Masson Publishing USA, pp. 105–118.

805 Friedman M, Shimaoka K, Rao U, Tsukada Y, Gavigan M, Tamura K. Diagnosis of chronic lymphocytic thyroiditis (nodular presentation) by needle aspiration. Acta Cytol (Baltimore) 1981, **25:** 513–522.

806 Gardner H, Ducatman B, Wang H. Predictive value of fine-needle aspiration of the thyroid in the classification of follicular lesions. Cancer 1993, **71:** 2598–2603.

807 Geddie WR, Bedard YC, Strawbridge HTG. Medullary carcinoma of the thyroid in fine-needle aspiration biopsies. Am J Clin Pathol 1984, **82:** 552–558.

808 Gharib H. Fine-needle aspiration biopsy of thyroid nodules.

Advantages, limitations, and effect. Mayo Clin Proc 1994, **69:** 44–49.

809 Giard RW, Hermans J. Use and accuracy of fine-needle aspiration cytology in histologically proven thyroid carcinoma: an audit using a National Pathology Database. Cancer Cytopathol 2000, **90:** 330–334.

810 Goellner JR, Johnson DA. Cytology of cystic papillary carcinoma of the thyroid. Acta Cytol (Baltimore) 1982, **26:** 797–799.

811 Goodell WM, Saboorian MH, Ashfaq R. Fine-needle aspiration diagnosis of the follicular variant of papillary carcinoma. Cancer Cytopathol 1998, **84:** 349–354.

812 Harach HR, Saravia Day E, Zusman SB. Occult papillary microcarcinoma of the thyroid – A potential pitfall of fine needle aspiration cytology? J Clin Pathol 1991, **44:** 205–207.

813 Harach HR, Zusman SB. Necrotic debris in thyroid aspirates. A feature of follicular carcinoma of the thyroid. Cytopathology 1992, **3:** 359–364.

814 Hawk WA, Crile G Jr, Hazard JB, Barrett DL. Needle biopsy of thyroid gland. Surg Gynecol Obstet 1966, **122:** 1053–1065.

815 Kini SR, Miller JM, Abrash MP, Gaba A, Johnson T. Post fine needle aspiration biopsy infarction in thyroid nodules (abstract). Lab Invest 1988, **58:** 48A.

816 Kini SR, Miller JM, Hamburger JI. Cytopathology of Hürthle cell lesions of the thyroid gland by fine needle aspiration. Acta Cytol (Baltimore) 1981, **25:** 647–652.

817 Kini SR, Miller JM, Hamburger JI, Smith MJ. Cytopathologic features of medullary carcinoma of the thyroid. Arch Pathol Lab Med 1984, **108:** 156–159.

818 Kobayashi A, Kuma K, Matsuzuka F, Hirai K, Fukata S, Sugawara M. Thyrotoxicosis after needle aspiration of thyroid cyst. J Clin Endocrinol Metab 1992, **75:** 21–24.

819 Lever EG, Refetoff S, Scherberg NH, Carr K. The influence of percutaneous fine needle aspiration on serum thyroglobulin. J Clin Endocrinol Metab 1983, **56:** 26–29.

820 Lew W, Orell S, Henderson DW. Intranuclear vacuoles in nonpapillary carcinoma of the thyroid. A report of three cases. Acta Cytol (Baltimore) 1984, **28:** 581–586.

821 Lo Gerfo P, Colacchio T, Caushaj F, Weber C, Feind C. Comparison of fine-needle and coarse-needle biopsies in evaluating thyroid nodules. Surgery 1982, **92:** 835–838.

822 Miller JM, Hamburger JI, Kini SR. The needle biopsy diagnosis of papillary thyroid carcinoma. Cancer 1981, **48:** 989–993.

823 Miller JM, Kini SR, Hamburger JI. Needle biopsy of the thyroid. New York, 1983, Praeger, p. 171.

824 Miller JM, Kini SR, Hamburger JI. The diagnosis of malignant follicular neoplasms of the thyroid by needle biopsy. Cancer 1985, **55:** 2812–2817.

825 Nasser SM, Pitman MB, Pilch BZ, Faquin WC. Fine-needle aspiration biopsy of papillary thyroid carcinoma: diagnostic utility of cytokeratin 19 immunostaining. Cancer Cytopathol 2000, **90:** 307–311.

826 Oertel YC, Oertel JE. Diagnosis of benign thyroid lesions: fine-needle aspiration and histopathologic correlation. Ann Diagn Pathol 1998, **2:** 250–263.

827 Papanicolaou Society of Cytopathology Task Force on Standards of Practice. Guidelines of the Papanicolaou Society of Cytopathology for the examination of fine-needle aspiration specimens from thyroid nodules. Mod Pathol 1996, **9:** 710–715.

828 Piromalli D, Martelli G, Del Prato I, Collini P, Pilotti S. The role of fine needle aspiration in the diagnosis of thyroid nodules. Analysis of 795 consecutive cases. J Surg Oncol 1992, **50:** 247–250.

829 Poller DN, Ibrahim AK, Cummings MH, Mikel JJ, Boote D, Perry M. Fine-needle aspiration of the thyroid: importance of an indeterminate diagnostic category. Cancer Cytopathol 2000, **90:** 239–244.

830 Ravetto C, Colombo L, Dottorini ME. Usefulness of fine-needle

aspiration in the diagnosis of thyroid carcinoma: a retrospective study in 37,895 patients. Cancer Cytopathol 2000, **90:** 357–363.

831 Sack MJ, Astengo-Osuna C, Lin BT, Battifora H, LiVolsi VA. HBME-1 immunostaining in thyroid fine-needle aspirations: a useful marker in the diagnosis of carcinoma. Mod Pathol 1997, **10:** 668–674.

832 Stroni M, Collini P, Cantaboni A. Fine needle aspiration cytology of insular thyroid carcinoma. A report of four cases. Acta Cytol 1992, **36:** 435–439.

833 Tsang K, Duggan M. Vascular proliferation of the thyroid. A complication of fine needle aspiration. Arch Pathol Lab Med 1992, **116:** 1040–1042.

834 Vickery AL Jr. Needle biopsy pathology. Clin Endocrinol Metab 1981, **10:** 275–293.

Frozen section

835 Basolo F, Baloch ZW, Baldanzi A, Miccoli P, LiVolsi VA. Usefulness of ultrafast Papanicolaou-stained scrape preparations in intraoperative management of thyroid lesions. Mod Pathol 1999, **12:** 653–657.

836 Bronner MP, Hamilton R, LiVolsi VA. Utility of frozen section analysis on follicular lesions of the thyroid. Endocr Pathol 1994, **5:** 154–161.

837 Hamburger JI, Hamburger SW. Declining role of frozen section in surgical planning for thyroid nodules. Surgery 1986, **98:** 307–312.

838 Hundahl SA, Cady B, Cunningham MP, Mazzaferri E, McKee RF, Rosai J, Shah JP, Fremgen AM, Stewart AK, Holzer S. Initial results from a prospective cohort study of 5583 cases of thyroid carcinoma treated in the United States during 1996. U.S and German Thyroid Cancer Study Group. An American College of Surgeons Commission on Cancer Patient Care Evaluation Study. Cancer 2000, **89:** 202–217.

839 Kraemer BB. Frozen section diagnosis and the thyroid. Semin Diagn Pathol 1987, **4:** 169–189.

840 Leteurtre E, Leroy X, Pattou F, Wacrenier A, Carnaille B, Proye C, Lecomte-Houcke M. Why do frozen sections have limited value in encapsulated or minimally invasive follicular carcinoma of the thyroid? Am J Clin Pathol 2001, **115:** 370–374.

841 Rosai J, Carcangiu ML. Pitfalls in the diagnosis of thyroid tumors. Pathol Res Pract 1987, **182:** 169–179.

842 Rosen Y, Rosenblatt P, Saltzman E. Intraoperative pathologic diagnosis of thyroid neoplasms. Report on experience with 504 specimens. Cancer 1990, **66:** 2001–2006.

843 Shaha AR, DiMaio T, Webber C, Jaffe BM. Intraoperative decision making during thyroid surgery based on the results of preoperative needle biopsy and frozen section. Surgery 1990, **108:** 964–967.

844 Tworek JA, Giordano TJ, Michael CW. Comparison of intraoperative cytology with frozen sections in the diagnosis of thyroid lesions. Am J Clin Pathol 1998, **110:** 456–461.

Presence of thyroid tissue outside gland

845 Frantz VK, Forsythe R, Hanford JM, Rogers WM. Lateral aberrant thyroids. Ann Surg 1942, **115:** 161–183.

846 Hathaway BM. Innocuous accessory thyroid nodules. Arch Surg 1965, **90:** 222–227.

847 Heffner DK. Low-grade adenocarcinoma of probable endolymphatic sac origin. A clinicopathologic study of 20 cases. Cancer 1989, **64:** 2292–2302.

848 Homan MR, Gharib H, Goellner JR. Metastatic papillary cancer of the neck. A diagnostic dilemma. Head Neck 1992, **14:** 113–118.

849 Kakudo K, Shan L, Nakamura Y, Inoue D, Koshiyama H, Sato H. Clonal analysis helps to differentiate aberrant thyroid tissue from thyroid carcinoma. Hum Pathol 1998, **29:** 187–190.

850 Meyer JS, Steinberg LS. Microscopically benign thyroid follicles in cervical lymph nodes. Serial section study of lymph node

inclusions and entire thyroid gland in 5 cases. Cancer 1969, **24**: 302–311.

851 Roth LM. Inclusions of non-neoplastic thyroid tissue within cervical lymph nodes. Cancer 1965, **18**: 105–111.

852 Shimizu M, Hirokawa M, Manabe T. Parasitic nodule of the thyroid in a patient with Graves' disease. Virchows Arch 1999, **434**: 241–244.

853 Sisson JC, Schmidt RW, Beierwaltes WH. Sequestered nodular goiter. N Engl J Med 1964, **270**: 927–932.

854 Wozencraft P, Foote FW Jr, Frazell EL. Occult carcinomas of the thyroid. Their bearings on the concept of lateral aberrant thyroid cancer. Cancer 1948, **1**: 574–583.

855 Young RH, Jackson A, Wells M. Ovarian metastasis from thyroid carcinoma 12 years after partial thyroidectomy mimicking struma ovarii. Report of a case. Int J Gynecol Pathol 1994, **13**: 181–185.

Treatment

856 Cady B, Cohn K, Rossi RL, Sedgwick CE, Meissner WA, Werber J, Gelman RS. The effect of thyroid hormone administration upon survival in patients with differentiated thyroid carcinoma. Surgery 1983, **94**: 978–983.

857 Carcangiu ML, Zampi G, Pupi A, Castagnoli A, Rosai J. Papillary carcinoma of the thyroid. A clinicopathologic study of 241 cases treated at the University of Florence, Italy. Cancer 1985, **55**: 805–828.

858 Clark OH. Total thyroidectomy. The treatment of choice for patients with differentiated thyroid cancer. Ann Surg 1982, **196**: 361–370.

859 Cohn KH, Bäckdahl M, Forsslund G, Auer G, Zetterberg A, Lundell G, Granberg P-O, Löwhagen T, Willems J-S, Cady B. Biologic considerations and operative strategy in papillary thyroid carcinoma. Arguments against the routine performance of total thyroidectomy. Surgery 1984, **96**: 957–971.

860 Crile G Jr. Changing end results in patients with papillary carcinoma of the thyroid. Surg Gynecol Obstet 1971, **132**: 460–468.

861 Crile G Jr, Antunez AR, Esselstyn CB, Hawk WA, Skillern PG. The advantages of subtotal thyroidectomy and suppression of TSH in the primary treatment of papillary carcinoma of the thyroid. Cancer 1985, **55**: 2691–2697.

862 Davis NL, Gordon M, Germann E, McGregor GI, Robins RE. Efficacy of 131I ablation following thyroidectomy in patients with invasive follicular thyroid cancer. Am J Surg 1992, **163**: 472–475.

863 DeGroot LJ, Kaplan EL. Second operations for "completion" of thyroidectomy in treatment of differentiated thyroid cancer. Surgery 1991, **110**: 936–939.

864 De Jong SA, Demeter JG, Lawrence AM, Paloyan E. Necessity and safety of completion thyroidectomy for differentiated thyroid carcinoma. Surgery 1992, **112**: 734–737.

865 Farahati J, Reiners C, Stuschke M, Muller SP, Stuben G, Sauerwein W, Sack H. Differentiated thyroid cancer. Impact of adjuvant external radiotherapy in patients with perithyroidal tumor infiltration (Stage pT4). Cancer 1996, **77**: 172–180.

866 Friedman M, Pacella BL Jr. Total versus subtotal thyroidectomy. Arguments, approaches, and recommendations. Otolaryngol Clin North Am 1990, **23**: 413–427.

867 Hall P, Holm LE, Lundell G, Ruden BI. Tumors after radiotherapy for thyroid cancer. A case-control study within a cohort of thyroid cancer patients. Acta Oncol 1992, **31**: 403–407.

868 Harness JK, Thompson NW, McLeod MK, Eckhauser FE, Lloyd RV. Follicular carcinoma of the thyroid gland. Trends and treatment. Surgery 1984, **96**: 972–980.

869 Hay ID, Grant CS, Taylor WF, McConahey WM. Ipsilateral lobectomy versus bilateral lobar resection in papillary thyroid carcinoma. A retrospective analysis of surgical outcome using a novel prognostic scoring system. Surgery 1987, **102**: 1088–1095.

870 Holzer S, Reiners C, Mann K, Bamberg M, Rothmund M, Dudeck J, Stewart AK, Hundahl SA. Patterns of care for patients with primary differentiated carcinoma of the thyroid gland treated in Germany during 1996. U.S. and German Thyroid Cancer Group. Cancer 2000, **89**: 192–201.

871 Hundahl S, Fleming ID, Fremgen AM, Menck HR. The National Cancer Data Base Report on 53,856 cases of thyroid carcinoma treated in the U.S. 1985–1995. Cancer 1998, **83**: 2638–2648.

872 Hutter RVP, Frazell EL, Foote FW Jr. Elective radical neck dissection. An assessment of its use in the management of papillary thyroid cancer. CA 1970, **20**: 87–93.

873 Maheshwari YK, Hill CS Jr, Haynie TP III, Hickey RC, Samaan NA. 131I therapy in differentiated thyroid carcinoma. M.D. Anderson Hospital experience. Cancer 1981, **47**: 664–671.

874 Mazzaferri EL, Young RL. Papillary thyroid carcinoma. A 10 year follow-up report of the impact of therapy in 576 patients. Am J Med 1981, **70**: 511–518.

875 Mazzaferri EL, Young RL, Oertel JE, Kemmerer WT, Page CP. Papillary thyroid carcinoma. The impact of therapy in 576 patients. Medicine (Baltimore) 1977, **56**: 171–196.

876 Pasieka JL, Thompson NW, McLeod MK, Burney RE, Macha M. The incidence of bilateral well-differentiated thyroid cancer found at completion thyroidectomy. World J Surg 1992, **16**: 711–716.

877 Ramanna L, Waxman AD, Brachman MB, Sensel N, Tanasescu DE, Berman DS, Catz B, Braunstein GD. Correlation of thyroglobulin measurements and radioiodine scans in the follow-up of patients with differentiated thyroid cancer. Cancer 1985, **55**: 1525–1529.

878 Samaan NA, Schultz PN, Hickey RC, Goepfert H, Haynie TP, Johnston DA, Ordonez NG. The results of various modalities of treatment of well differentiated thyroid carcinomas. A retrospective review of 1599 patients. J Clin Endocrinol Metab 1992, **75**: 714–720.

879 Schroder DM, Chambors A, France CJ. Operative strategy for thyroid cancer. Is total thyroidectomy worth the price? Cancer 1986, **58**: 2320–2328.

880 Shaha AR. The National Cancer Data Base Report on thyroid carcinoma: reflections of practice patterns. Cancer 1998, **83**: 2434–2436.

881 Sisson JC, Giordano TJ, Jamadar DA, Kazerooni EA, Shapiro B, Gross MD, Zempel SA, Spaulding SA. 131-i treatment of micronodular pulmonary metastases from papillary thyroid carcinoma. Cancer 1996, **78**: 2184–2192.

882 Starnes HF, Brooks DC, Pinkus GS, Brooks JR. Surgery for thyroid carcinoma. Cancer 1985, **55**: 1376–1381.

883 Tsang RW, Brierley JD, Simpson WJ, Panzarella T, Gospodarowicz MK, Sutcliffe SB. The effects of surgery, radioiodine, and external radiation therapy on the clinical outcome of patients with differentiated thyroid carcinoma. Cancer 1998, **82**: 375–388.

884 Tubiana M, Haddad E, Schlumberger M, Hill C, Rougier P, Sarrazin D. External radiotherapy in thyroid cancers. Cancer 1985, **55**: 2062–2071.

885 Vickery AL Jr, Wang C-A, Walker AM. Treatment of intrathyroidal papillary carcinoma of the thyroid. Cancer 1987, **60**: 2587–2595.

Prognosis

886 Akslen LA, Haldorsen T, Thoresen SO, Glattre E. Survival and causes of death in thyroid cancer. A population-based study of 2479 cases from Norway. Cancer Res 1991, **51**: 1234–1241.

887 Cady B, Rossi R, Silverman M, Wool M. Further evidence of the validity of risk group definition in differentiated thyroid carcinoma. Surgery 1985, **98**: 1171–1178.

888 Carcangiu ML, Zampi G, Pupi A, Castagnoli A, Rosai J. Papillary carcinoma of the thyroid. A clinicopathologic study of 241 cases treated at the University of Florence, Italy. Cancer 1985, **55**: 805–828.

889 Cunningham JP, Duda RB, Recant W, Chmiel JS, Sylvester JA, Fremgen A. Survival discriminants for differentiated thyroid cancer. Am J Surg 1990, **160**: 344–347.

890 Heitz P, Moser H, Staub JJ. Thyroid cancer. A study of 573 thyroid tumors and 161 autopsy cases observed over a thirty-year period. Cancer 1976, **37**: 2329–2337.

891 Ito J, Noguchi S, Murakami N, Noguchi A. Factors affecting the prognosis of patients with carcinoma of the thyroid. Surg Gynecol Obstet 1980, **150**: 539–544.

892 Pasieka JL, Zedenius J, Auer G, Grimelius L, Hoög A, Lundell G, Wallin G, Bäckdahl M. Addition of nuclear DNA content to the AMES risk-group classification for papillary thyroid cancer. Surgery 1992, **112**: 1154–1159.

893 Shah JP, Loree TR, Dharker D, Strong EW, Begg C, Vlamis V. Prognostic factors in differentiated carcinoma of the thyroid gland. Am J Surg 1992, **164**: 658–661.

894 Tennvall J, Biörklund A, Möller T, Ranstam J, Åkerman M. Is the EORTC prognostic index of thyroid cancer valid in differentiated thyroid carcinoma? Retrospective multivariate analysis of differentiated thyroid carcinoma with long follow-up. Cancer 1986, **57**: 1405–1414.

Lymphoid tumors and tumorlike conditions

895 Abdul-Rahman ZH, Gogas HJ, Tooze JA, Anderson B, Mansi J, Sacks NP, Finlayson CJ. T-cell lymphoma in Hashimoto's thyroiditis. Histopathology 1996, **29**: 455–459.

896 Allevato PA, Kini SR, Rebuck JW, Miller JM, Hamburger JI. Signet ring cell lymphoma of the thyroid. A case report. Hum Pathol 1985, **16**: 1066–1068.

897 Anscombe AM, Wright DH. Primary malignant lymphoma of the thyroid – a tumor of mucosa-associated lymphoid tissue. Review of seventy-six cases. Histopathology 1985, **9**: 81–97.

898 Ansell SM, Grant CS, Habermann TM. Primary thyroid lymphoma. Semin Oncol 1999, **26**: 316–323.

899 Aozasa K. Hashimoto's thyroiditis as a risk factor of thyroid lymphoma. Acta Pathol Jpn 1990, **40**: 459–468.

900 Aozasa K, Inoue A, Tajima K, Miyauchi A, Matsuzuka F, Kuma K. Malignant lymphomas of the thyroid gland. Analysis of 79 patients with emphasis on histologic prognostic factors. Cancer 1986, **58**: 100–104.

901 Aozasa K, Inoue A, Yoshimura H, Katagiri S, Katayama S, Matsuzuka F, Yonezawa T. Intermediate lymphocytic lymphoma of the thyroid. An immunologic and immunohistologic study. Cancer 1986, **57**: 1762–1767.

902 Aozasa K, Inoue A, Yoshimura H, Miyauchi A, Matsuzuka F, Kuma K. Plasmacytoma of the thyroid gland. Cancer 1986, **58**: 105–110.

903 Burke JS, Butler JJ, Fuller LM. Malignant lymphomas of the thyroid. A clinical pathologic study of 35 patients including ultrastructural observations. Cancer 1977, **39**: 1587–1602.

904 Compagno J, Oertel JE. Malignant lymphoma and other lymphoproliferative disorders of the thyroid gland. A clinicopathologic study of 245 cases. Am J Clin Pathol 1980, **74**: 1–11.

905 Derringer GA, Thompson LD, Frommelt RA, Bijwaard KE, Heffess CS, Abbondanzo SL. Malignant lymphoma of the thyroid gland: A clinicopathologic study of 108 cases. Am J Surg Pathol 2000, **24**: 623–639.

906 Devine RM, Edis AJ, Banks PM. Primary lymphoma of the thyroid. A review of the Mayo Clinic experience through 1978. World J Surg 1981, **5**: 33–38.

907 Fauré P, Chittal S, Woodman-Memeteau W, Caveriviere P, Gorguet B, Voigt J-J, Delsol G. Diagnostic features of primary malignant lymphomas of the thyroid with monoclonal antibodies. Cancer 1988, **61**: 1852–1861.

908 Feigin GA, Buss DH, Paschal B, Woodruff RD, Myers RT. Hodgkin's disease manifested as a thyroid nodule. Hum Pathol 1982, **13**: 774–776.

909 Ha CS, Shadle KM, Medeiros LJ, Wilder RB, Hess MA, Cabanillas F, Cox JD. Localized non-Hodgkin lymphoma involving the thyroid gland. Cancer 2001, **91**: 629–635.

910 Higgins JP, Warnke RA. Large B-cell lymphoma of thyroid. Two cases with a marginal zone distribution of the neoplastic cells. Am J Clin Pathol 2000, **114**: 264–270.

911 Holck S. Plasma cell granuloma of the thyroid. Cancer 1981, **48**: 830–832.

912 Lam KY, Lo CY, Kwong DL, Lee J, Srivastava G. Malignant lymphoma of the thyroid. A 30-year clinicopathologic experience and an evaluation of the presence of Epstein-Barr virus. Am J Clin Pathol 1999, **112**: 263–270.

913 Larkin DFP, Dervan PA, Munnelly J, Finucane J. Sinus histiocytosis with massive lymphadenopathy simulating subacute thyroiditis. Hum Pathol 1986, **17**: 321–324.

914 Lazzi S, Als C, Mazzucchelli L, Kraft R, Kappeler A, Laissue J. Extensive extramedullary hematopoiesis in a thyroid nodule. Mod Pathol 1996, **9**: 1062–1065.

915 Leoni F, Fabbri R, Pascarella A, Marrani C, Nozzoli C, Ciolli S, Marchetti G, Rossi Ferrini P. Extramedullary haematopoiesis in thyroid multinodular goitre preceding clinical evidence of agnogenic myeloid metaplasia. Histopathology 1996, **28**: 559–561.

916 Mizukami Y, Michigishi T, Nonomura A, Nakamura S, Hashimoto T, Katsuda S, Otake S, Matsubara F. Primary lymphoma of the thyroid. A clinical, histological and immunohistochemical study of 20 cases. Histopathology 1990, **17**: 201–209.

917 Ottó S, Péter I, Végh S, Juhos E, Besznyák I. Gamma-chain heavy-chain disease with primary thyroid plasmacytoma. Arch Pathol Lab Med 1986, **110**: 893–896.

918 Pedersen RK, Pedersen NT. Primary non-Hodgkin's lymphoma of the thyroid gland: a population based study. Histopathology 1996, **28**: 25–32.

919 Pyke CM, Grant CS, Habermann TM, Kurtin PJ, van Heerden JA, Bergstralh EJ, Kunselman A, Hay ID. Non-Hodgkin's lymphoma of the thyroid. Is more than one biopsy necessary? World J Surg 1992, **16**: 604–609.

920 Rasbach DA, Mondschein MS, Harris NL, Kaufman DS, Wang C-A. Malignant lymphoma of the thyroid gland. A clinical and pathologic study of twenty cases. Surgery 1985, **98**: 1166–1170.

921 Santana V, Rose NR. Neoplastic lymphoproliferation in autoimmune disease. An updated review. Clin Immunol Immunopathol 1992, **63**: 205–213.

922 Schmid C, Beham A, Seewann HL. Extramedullary haematopoiesis in the thyroid gland. Histopathology 1989, **15**: 423–425.

923 Shimaoka K, Gailani S, Tsukada Y, Barcos M. Plasma cell neoplasm involving the thyroid. Cancer 1978, **41**: 1140–1146.

924 Skacel M, Ross CW, Hsi ED. A reassessment of primary thyroid lymphoma: high grade MALT-type lymphoma as a distinct subtype of diffuse large B-cell lymphoma. Histopathology 2000, **37**: 10–18.

925 Thompson LD, Wenig BM, Adair CF, Smith BC, Heffess CS. Langerhans cell histiocytosis of the thyroid: A series of seven cases and a review of the literature. Mod Pathol 1996, **9**: 145–149.

926 Tsang WY, Lau MF, Chan JK. Incidental Langerhans' cell histiocytosis of the thyroid. Histopathology 1994, **24**: 397–399.

927 Williams ED. Malignant lymphoma of the thyroid. Clin Endocrinol Metab 1981, **10**: 379–389.

928 Wolf BC, Sheahan K, DeCoste D, Wariakojis D, Alpern HD, Haselow RE. Immunohistochemical analysis of small cell tumors of the thyroid gland. An Eastern Cooperative Oncology Group study. Hum Pathol 1992, **23**: 1252–1261.

929 Woolner LB, McConahey WM, Beahrs OH, Black BM. Primary malignant lymphoma of the thyroid. Review of forty six cases. Am J Surg 1966, **111**: 502–523.

930 Yap WM, Chuah KL, Tan PH. Langerhans cell histiocytosis

involving the thyroid and parathyroid glands. Mod Pathol 2001, **14:** 111–115.

Mesenchymal tumors

931 Andrion A, Bellis D, Delsedime L, Bussolati G, Mazzucco G. Leiomyoma and neurilemoma. Report of two unusual non-epithelial tumors of the thyroid gland. Virchows Arch [A] 1988, **413:** 367–372.

932 Andrion A, Gaglio A, Dogliani N, Bosco E, Mazzucco G. Liposarcoma of the thyroid gland. Fine-needle aspiration cytology, immunohistology, and ultrastructure. Am J Clin Pathol 1991, **95:** 675–679.

933 Beer TW. Malignant thyroid haemangioendothelioma in a non-endemic goitrous region, with immunohistochemical evidence of a vascular origin. Histopathology 1992, **20:** 539–541.

934 Cameselle-Teijeiro J, Varela-Duran J, Fonseca E, Villanueva JP, Sobrinho-Simões M. Solitary fibrous tumor of the thyroid. Am J Clin Pathol 1994, **101:** 535–538.

935 Clarke MR, Boppana S. Hemangioma of the thyroid gland in an adolescent with chronic lymphocytic thyroiditis and adenomatous hyperplasia. Endocr Pathol 1998, **9:** 185–190.

936 Eusebi V, Carcangiu ML, Dina R, Rosai J. Keratin-positive epithelioid angiosarcoma of thyroid. A report of four cases. Am J Surg Pathol 1990, **14:** 737–747.

937 Gardner DF, Frable WJ. Primary lymphangioma of the thyroid gland. Arch Pathol Lab Med 1989, **113:** 1084–1085.

938 Gray MH, Rosenberg AE, Dickersin GR, Bhan HK. Cytokeratin expression in epithelioid vascular neoplasms. Hum Pathol 1990, **21:** 212–217.

939 Huang SA, Tu HM, Harney JW, Venihaki M, Butte AJ, Kozakewich HP, Fishman SJ, Larsen PR. Severe hypothyroidism caused by type 3 iodothyronine deiodinase in infantile hemangiomas. N Engl J Med 2000, **343:** 185–189.

940 Iida Y, Katoh R, Yoshioka M, Oyama T, Kawaoi A. Primary leiomyosarcoma of the thyroid gland. Acta Pathol Jpn 1993, **43:** 71–75.

941 Kie JH, Kim JY, Park YN, Lee MK, Yang WI, Park JS. Solitary fibrous tumour of the thyroid. Histopathology 1997, **30:** 365–368.

942 Krisch K, Holzner JH, Kokoschka R, Jakesz R, Niederle B, Roka R. Hemangioendothelioma of the thyroid gland – True endothelioma or anaplastic carcinoma? Pathol Res Pract 1980, **170:** 230–242.

943 Lamovec J, Zidar A, Zidanik B. Epithelioid angiosarcoma of the thyroid gland. Report of two cases. Arch Pathol Lab Med 1994, **118:** 642–646.

944 Maiorana A, Collina G, Cesinaro AM, Fano RA, Eusebi V. Epithelioid angiosarcoma of the thyroid. Clinicopathological analysis of seven cases from non-Alpine areas. Virchows Arch 1996, **429:** 131–138.

945 Mills SE, Gaffey MJ, Watts JC, Swanson PE, Wick MR, Li Volsi VA, Nappi O, Weiss LM. Angiomatoid carcinoma and "angiosarcoma" of the thyroid gland. A spectrum of endothelial differentiation. Am J Clin Pathol 1994, **102:** 322–330.

946 Mills SE, Stallings RG, Austin MB. Angiomatoid carcinoma of the thyroid gland. Anaplastic carcinoma with follicular and medullary features mimicking angiosarcoma. Am J Clin Pathol 1986, **86:** 674–678.

947 Naruse T, Koike A, Suzumura K, Matsumoto K, Inamura Y, Saiguse J. Malignant "triton" tumor in the thyroid – A case report. Jpn J Surg 1991, **21:** 466–470.

948 Ohbu M, Kameya T, Wada C, Okudaira M, Furusawa S, Furukawa K, Takahashi H-O. Primary osteogenic sarcoma of the thyroid gland. A case report. Surg Pathol 1989, **2:** 67–72.

949 Pfaltz M, Hedinger Chr E, Saremaslani P, Egloff B. Malignant hemangioendothelioma of the thyroid and factor VIII-related antigen. Virchows Arch [A] 1983, **401:** 177–184.

950 Pickleman JR, Lee JF, Strauss FH II, Paloyan E. Thyroid hemangioma. Am J Surg 1975, **129:** 331–336.

951 Rodriguez I, Ayala E, Caballero C, De Miguel C, Matias-Giui X, Cubilla AL, Rosai J. Solitary fibrous tumor of the thyroid gland: report of seven cases. Am J Surg Pathol 2001, **25:** 1424–1428.

952 Ruchti C, Gerber HA, Schaffner T. Factor VIII-related antigen in malignant hemangioendothelioma of the thyroid. Additional evidence for the endothelial origin of this tumor. Am J Clin Pathol 1984, **82:** 474–480.

953 Shin W, Aftalion B, Hotchkiss E, Schenkman R, Berkman J. Ultrastructure of a primary fibrosarcoma of the human thyroid gland. Cancer 1979, **44:** 584–591.

954 Siddiqui MT, Evans HL, Ro JY, Ayala AG. Epithelioid haemangioendothelioma of the thyroid gland: a case report and review of the literature. Histopathology 1998, **32:** 473–476.

955 Thompson LD, Wenig BM, Adair CF, Heffess CS. Peripheral nerve sheath tumors of the thyroid gland: a series of four cases and a review of the literature. Endocr Pathol 1996, **7:** 309–318.

956 Thompson LD, Wenig BM, Adair CF, Shmookler BM, Heffess CS. Primary smooth muscle tumors of the thyroid gland. Cancer 1997, **79:** 579–587.

957 Tötsch M, Dobler G, Feichtinger H, Sandbichler P, Ladurner D, Schmid KW. Malignant hemangioendothelioma of the thyroid. Its immunohistochemical discrimination from undifferentiated thyroid carcinoma. Am J Surg Pathol 1990, **14:** 69–74.

958 Tseleni-Balafouta S, Arvanitis D, Kakaviatos N, Paraskevakou H. Primary myxoid chondrosarcoma of the thyroid gland. Arch Pathol Lab Med 1988, **112:** 94–96.

959 Tulbah A, Al-Dayel F, Fawaz I, Rosai J. Epstein-Barr virus-associated leiomyosarcoma of the thyroid in a child with congenital immunodeficiency: A case report. Am J Surg Pathol 1999, **23:** 473–476.

960 van Haelst UJ, Pruszczynski M, ten Cate LN, Mravunac M. Ultrastructural and immunohistochemical study of epithelioid hemangioendothelioma of bone. Coexpression of epithelial and endothelial markers. Ultrastruct Pathol 1990, **14:** 141–149.

Other primary tumors and tumorlike conditions

961 Bowker C, Whittaker R. Malignant teratoma of the thyroid. Case report and literature review of thyroid teratoma in adults. Histopathology 1992, **21:** 81–83.

962 Chan JK, Rosai J. Tumors of the neck showing thymic or related branchial pouch differentiation: A unifying concept. Hum Pathol 1991, **22:** 349–367.

963 Craver RD, Lipscomb JT, Suskind D, Velez MC. Malignant teratoma of the thyroid with primitive neuroepithelial and mesenchymal sarcomatous components. Ann Diagn Pathol 2001, **5:** 285–292.

964 Kanoh T, Shimada H, Uchino H, Matsumura K. Amyloid goiter with hypothyroidism. Arch Pathol Lab Med 1989, **113:** 542–544.

965 Katoh R, Ishizaki T, Tomichi N, Yagawa K, Kurihara H. Malacoplakia of the thyroid gland. Am J Clin Pathol 1989, **92:** 813–820.

966 Kingsley DP, Elton A, Bennett MH. Malignant teratoma of the thyroid. Case report and review of the literature. Br J Cancer 1968, **22:** 7–11.

967 Moriuchi A, Yokoyama S, Kashima K, Andoh T, Nakayama I, Noguchi S. Localized primary amyloid tumor of the thyroid developing in the course of Hashimoto's thyroiditis. Acta Pathol Jpn 1992, **42:** 210–216.

968 Thompson LD, Rosai J, Heffess CS. Primary thyroid teratomas: a clinicopathologic study of 30 cases. Cancer 2000, **88:** 1149–1158.

969 Zerella JT, Finberg FJ. Obstruction of the neonatal airway from teratomas. Surg Gynecol Obstet 1990, **170:** 126–131.

Metastatic tumors

970 Baloch ZW, LiVolsi VA. Tumor-to tumor metastasis to follicular variant of papillary carcinoma of thyroid. Arch Pathol Lab Med 1999, **123:** 703–706.

971 Carcangiu ML, Sibley RK, Rosai J. Clear cell change in primary thyroid tumors. A study of 38 cases. Am J Surg Pathol 1985, **9**: 705–722.

972 Green LK, Ro JY, Mackay B, Ayala AG, Luna MA. Renal cell carcinoma metastatic to the thyroid. Cancer 1989, **63**: 1810–1815.

972a Heffess CS, Wenig BM, Thompson LD. Metastatic renal cell carcinoma to the thyroid gland. Cancer 2002, **95**: 1869–1878.

973 Horace KI. Cancer metastatic to the thyroid. A diagnostic problem. Mayo Clin Proc 1984, **59**: 856–859.

974 Lam KY, Lo CY. Metastatic tumors of the thyroid gland: a study of 79 cases in Chinese patients. Arch Pathol Lab Med 1998, **122**: 37–41.

975 Matias-Guiu X, Garcia A, Curell R, Prat J. Renal cell carcinoma metastatic to the thyroid gland: a comparative molecular study between the primary and the metastatic tumor. Endocr Pathol 1998, **9**: 255–260.

976 Mizukami Y, Saito K, Nonomura A, Michigishi T, Hashimoto T, Nakanuma Y, Matsubara F, Takasakura E. Lung carcinoma metastatic to microfollicular adenoma of the thyroid. A case report. Acta Pathol Jpn 1990, **40**: 602–608.

977 Nakhjavani MK, Gharib H, Goellner JR, van Heerden JA. Metastasis to the thyroid gland: a report of 43 cases. Cancer 1997, **79**: 574–578.

978 Ro JY, Guerrieri C, el-Naggar AK, Ordóñez NG, Sorge JG, Ayala AG. Carcinomas metastatic to follicular adenomas of the thyroid gland. Report of two cases. Arch Pathol Lab Med 1994, **118**: 551–556.

979 Shimaoka K, Sokal JE, Pickren JW. Metastatic neoplasms in the thyroid gland. Pathological and clinical findings. Cancer 1962, **15**: 557–565.

980 Zirkin HJ, Tovi F. Tracheal carcinoma presenting as a thyroid tumor. J Surg Oncol 1984, **26**: 268–271.

10 Parathyroid glands

Normal gross anatomy and embryology

The parathyroid glands, the last major organ to be recognized in humans, were discovered in 1880 by Ivar Sandstrom, a Swedish medical student, as recounted by Aidan Carney in his delightful essay on the subject.[2]

Normally, there are four oval, resilient parathyroid glands, each averaging $4 \times 3 \times 1.5$ mm. In rare cases, more than four glands are present. In their classic study of 527 autopsy cases, Gilmour and Martin[4] reported two instances in which there were six glands (0.2%) and 31 in which there were five (5.2%). Variations in the weights of the normal glands were studied by the same authors,[4] who found that in 189 cases the mean weight of all four glands was 117.6 ± 4 mg in men and 131.3 ± 5.8 mg in women. The color varies from reddish brown to light tan to yellow, depending on fat content, which in turn depends on age, nutrition, and activity of the individual.

The parathyroid glands are arranged in two pairs. The upper pair arises from the fourth branchial cleft and descends into the neck with the thyroid gland during embryonic life. The lower pair arises from the third branchial cleft and descends into the neck with the thymus. Normally, the upper pair is located on the middle third of the posterolateral border of the thyroid gland, and the lower pair is close to the lower pole of the thyroid gland, close to the inferior thyroid artery. It has been pointed out that the parathyroid glands usually have a symmetric distribution—when one superior parathyroid gland is located in one place, the opposite parathyroid gland will be in the contralateral mirror image of that space.[1]

The vascular supply of the lower parathyroid glands comes from branches of the inferior thyroid arteries. This supply is usually independent, a circumstance that may be helpful in locating abnormally placed glands. If one of these arteries is ligated, infarction of the parathyroid gland may result. Faulty migration of the glands during embryonic life may result in anomalous positions. The upper glands may be found inside the carotid sheath or behind the cervical or thoracic esophagus. The lower glands may continue their descent with the thymus into the anterior portion of the mediastinum.[3] They may also be located inside the thyroid gland (0.2%),[5] in the pharynx,[6] or within the vagus nerve[7]; when in the last location, they have sometimes been mistaken for paraganglia. Interestingly, they can also be found within true paraganglia in the neck.[8] Wang[9] has pointed out that despite the wide distribution patterns that parathyroid glands may exhibit, these fall into an orderly scheme and can be uncovered by the experienced surgeon in the great majority of cases.

Normal histology

In the past a rigid division of cell types has been applied to the normal parathyroid gland; however, evidence suggests that this organ is made up of but one basic cell type, the **chief cell**, and that all the other cells that have been described represent morphologic variations of the former that reflect differences in physiologic activity.[20a,21]

The chief cell measures 6 to 8 μm in diameter and has a centrally located nucleus and a moderate amount of pale granular cytoplasm. Ultrastructurally, there are variable amounts of glycogen particles and secretory droplets, an inverse relationship being present in the amount of these two components.[21] Parathormone (PTH) and PTH-related protein secretion can be demonstrated immunohistochemically.[14,19,20] There is also cytoplasmic reactivity for various types of keratin and for chromogranin A but not for vimentin, glial fibrillary acidic protein, neurofilament, or chromogranin B.[16,22]

Bjerneroth et al.[10] have developed a monoclonal anti-parathyroid antibody (E11) that reacts with a high-molecular-weight protein on the surface of chief cells which mediates calcium regulation of PTH release; this antibody is said to stain the normal gland strongly and consistently but the hyperfunctioning gland only weakly and heterogeneously.

The **oxyphil cell** has a more abundant cytoplasm, which is deeply granular and acidophilic. Ultrastructurally, there are many mitochondria but few secretory granules. A rich content of oxidative enzymes can be demonstrated histochemically, although the ratio of enzyme content per mitochondria seems to be decreased.[17] These oxyphilic cells are often present in the form of nodular collections. **Transitional oxyphil cells** have an appearance that is intermediate between chief cells and oxyphil cells. The **water-clear cell** is characterized by abundant optically clear cytoplasm and sharply defined cell membranes. **Transitional water-clear cells** have an appearance that is intermediate between chief cells and water-clear cells. Both types of transitional cells are more common in hyperfunctioning than in normal glands.

The frequency distribution of the different cells varies with the age of the patient. Until puberty, the gland is composed wholly of chief cells that contain cytoplasmic glycogen but not fat. The latter appears in these cells as very fine droplets soon after puberty at about the same time that the oxyphil cells appear. They appear first singly, then in pairs, and, after 40 years of age, in the form of sharply outlined but not encapsulated islands, which may be large.

After puberty, mature adipose tissue appears in the stroma and increases in amount until about 40 years of age, remaining relatively constant thereafter. Whereas the average percentage of stromal fat cell in the adult parathyroid is about 40%, the variations in the amount of fat present (while the parenchymal cell content remains relatively constant) make it very difficult to distinguish a normal from an abnormal parathyroid solely on the basis of stromal fat content.[13,18] In a classic study, Gilmour[12] had already shown in 1947 that small parathyroid glands in adult individuals are the result of a decreased amount of stromal fat rather than parenchymal cell mass.

A few follicles and cysts of varying sizes are observed in about half of parathyroid glands after puberty. They may be filled with granular and cellular debris or with a dark blue-staining, finely granular material that is morphologically indistinguishable from thyroid colloid.[11] This material, which sometimes is positive with amyloid stains, is thought to result from a conformational change in the stored PTH polypeptide.[15] When these follicles are present, the distinction between thyroid and parathyroid tissue may become difficult. The presence of sizable amounts of cytoplasmic glycogen favors a parathyroid nature. Conversely, the presence of birefringent crystals of calcium oxalate (easily detectable with polarized light) favors thyroid, a feature to remember at the time of frozen section.[13] If doubts persist, immunohistochemical stains for thyroglobulin, TTF-1, PTH, and chromogranin should dispel them.[19]

Normal physiology

The parathyroid glands mediate their endocrine function through the production of PTH.[25] There are several forms of circulating PTH. The relationship among them is not clear, but it is known that the structural requirements for the biologic activity reside in the first 34 amino acid residues.[27,28] The chief cells are most critically sensitive to calcium concentrations in vivo and in vitro.[23] Roth and Raisz[30] demonstrated marked ultrastructural changes corresponding to enhanced production of PTH secretion when calcium concentration is reduced. These active cells contain abundant secretory granules, a prominent Golgi apparatus, and very little glycogen. Under conditions of elevated calcium concentration, the cells are nearly devoid of secretion, have an inconspicuous Golgi apparatus, and contain abundant glycogen.

The most important physiologic actions of PTH are increased renal excretion of phosphate, increased renal tubular reabsorption of calcium, increased intestinal absorption of calcium, and direct effects in bone. The latter are mainly manifested by an increased in the number of osteoclasts and an apparent increase in their phagocytic activity, with a resulting resorption of bone tissue.

The mechanism of action of PTH in the receptor tissues involves activating specific receptors located on osteoblastic and renal tubular cells. In these tissues, PTH stimulates multiple intracellular signals, including cyclic adenosine monophosphate (cAMP), inositol phosphate, and calcium; it also activates protein kinases A and C.[24,26,29]

Adenoma

Generalities and gross features

Parathyroid adenomas occur in women and men in a ratio of 3:1. They can develop at almost any age, but most occur in patients in the fourth decade. A few cases have been reported in children,[33] and some have been seen after radiation therapy to the head and neck region.[35] The large majority are single. Cases of double or triple adenomas exist,[31,37,38] but some of them would be reinterpreted today as examples of chief cell hyperplasia. Their size and weight vary greatly, with the majority being too small to allow detection on palpation of the neck. Some may be recognizable only microscopically ("microadenomas").[32] Adenomas are usually oval, may show slight lobulation, and are surrounded by a thin connective tissue capsule. On section, they are often grayish brown (Fig. 10.1). Foci of hemorrhage, calcification, and cystic change may occur. In terms of location, about 75% involve one of the inferior glands, 15% involve one of the superior glands, and 10% occur in anomalous positions (Fig. 10.2). Of the latter, 70% are in the mediastinum, 20% within the thyroid gland,[34a] and the remainder in the soft tissues behind the esophagus or—in rare cases—the esophageal wall itself.[34,36]

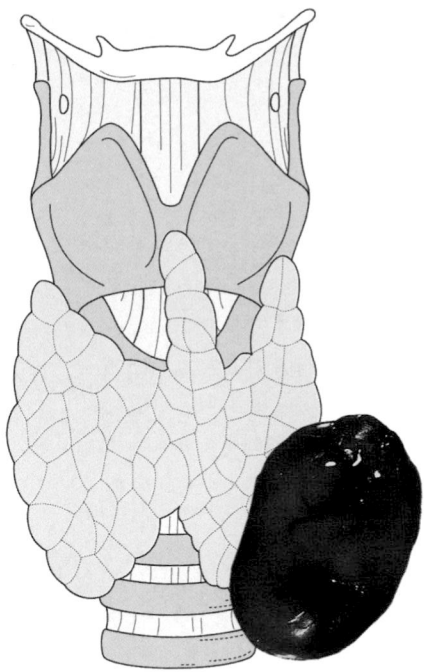

Fig. 10.2 Parathyroid adenoma arising from the left lower parathyroid gland.

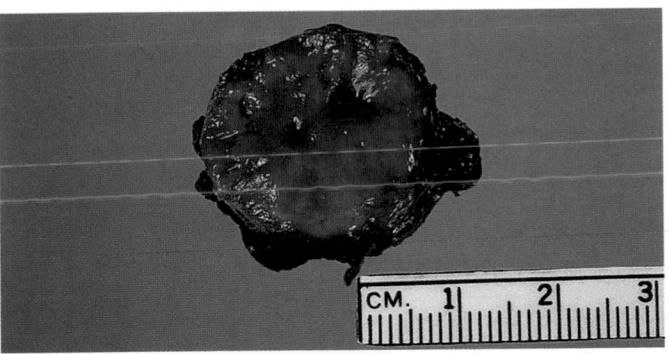

A

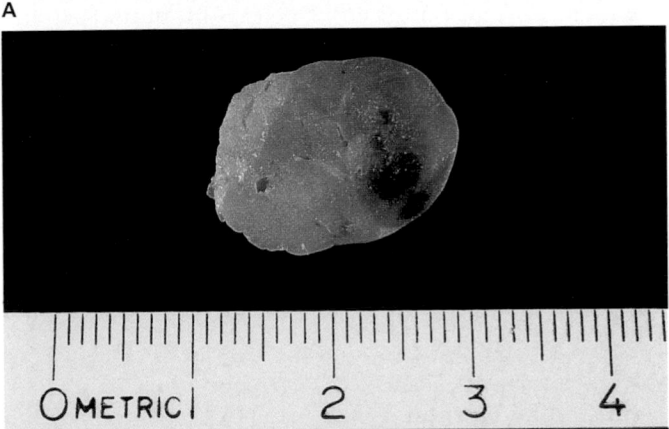

B

Fig. 10.1 A and **B.** Gross appearance of two parathyroid adenomas. Note the roundish shape, the homogeneous appearance interrupted by a few foci of fresh hemorrhagic or cystic changes, and the brown to yellowish color.

Microscopic features

Microscopically, the tumor is encapsulated and very cellular (Fig. 10.3). A rim of compressed non-neoplastic parathyroid tissue can be identified in about 60% of cases. The adenoma itself may be composed of any of the various cell types that make up the normal parathyroid gland, but chief cells usually predominate.[39] Combinations of chief cells, oxyphil cells, water-clear cells, and transitional elements are common. Variation in nuclear size may be conspicuous, with the presence of tumor cells with isolated or clustered huge hyperchromatic nuclei (Fig. 10.4). The presence of these nuclei does not indicate malignancy; as a matter of fact, they are seen more commonly in benign than in malignant tumors. Mitoses are usually absent, but occasional ones may be found (see p. 602). The pattern of growth is generally diffuse, but it may be nesting, follicular, or pseudopapillary[40] (Fig. 10.5). The follicles may contain a colloid-like material. This material sometimes stains for amyloid, as in the normal gland.[43] The presence of follicular structures may closely simulate the appearance of thyroid. Presence of birefringent crystals is a good clue for the identification of the latter. Occasionally, prominent clusters of mature lymphocytes of B and T cell type (sometimes admixed with plasma cells) are seen scattered throughout the tumor[42] (Fig. 10.6). This may be accompanied by degenerative changes in the tumor cells. It is important not to overdiagnose this inconsequential microscopic finding, which may or may not have an autoimmune pathogenesis, as a lymphomatous infiltrate.[41,44]

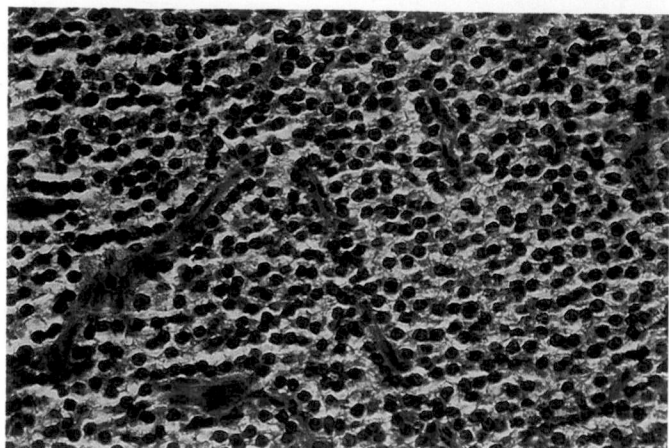

Fig. 10.3 Parathyroid adenoma. The tumor is hypercellular, homogeneous, and well vascularized.

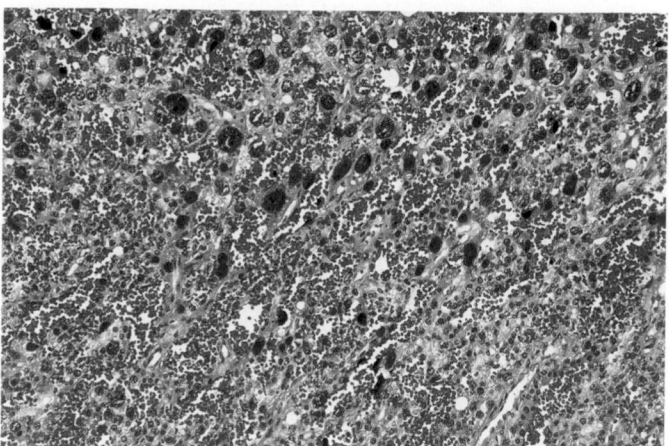

Fig. 10.4 Parathyroid adenoma with clusters of bizarre nuclei. This feature is not an indication of malignancy.

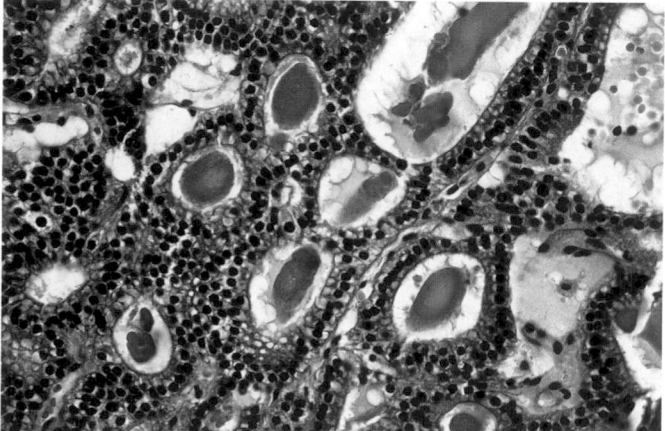

Fig. 10.5 Parathyroid adenoma with follicular structures containing a colloid-like material simulating thyroid.

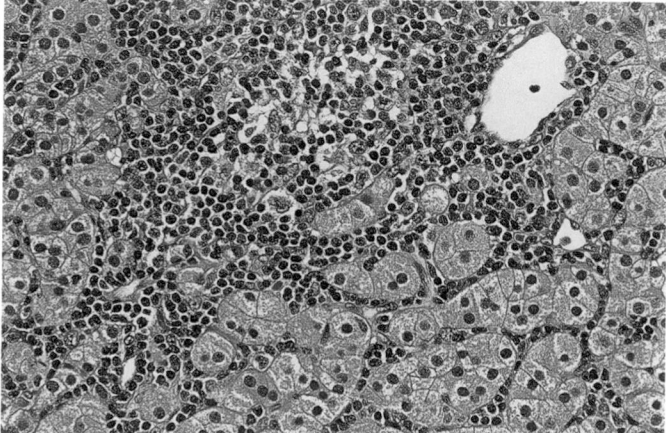

Fig. 10.6 Heavy lymphocytic infiltrate within a parathyroid adenoma.

In the typical case of parathyroid adenoma, the other parathyroid glands have a normal or atrophic appearance. Indeed, the presence of a *microscopically normal second gland* is thought to represent the best evidence that a given parathyroid lesion is an adenoma rather than chief cell hyperplasia.

Electron microscopic features

The ultrastructural appearance of the tumor cells is indicative of hyperfunction and not substantially different from that seen in primary or secondary chief cell hyperplasia. Secretory granules, prominent Golgi apparatus, abundant cisternae of granular endoplasmic reticulum, annulate lamellae, numerous ribosomes, and interdigitating cytoplasmic membranes are the main features[45] (Fig. 10.7). In contrast to normal chief cells, large quantities of glycogen and secretory vacuoles can be seen simultaneously.

Histochemical and immunohistochemical features

Immunohistochemically, there is reactivity for PTH and various types of keratin.[47] The intensity of the PTH staining tends to be weaker in the adenoma than in the peripheral rim of residual normal gland.[48] The adenoma cells express neurofilament, an intermediate filament not found in normal parathyroid cells.[47] Immunoreactivity for neuron-specific enolase, chromogranin, a number of peptide hormones, and opioid peptides has also been encountered.[46,49,50]

Molecular genetic features

Several genetic abnormalities have been detected in parathyroid adenomas, but each of these accounts for only a minority of the lesions. They include loss of heterozygosity at 1p36.3 (30 to 40% of the cases), 11q13 (20 to 40%, corresponding to the *menin* gene), 6q22–23 (30%), 11p (27%, corresponding to the PTH gene), 9p (16%), and 3qcen–3q21 (10%, corresponding to the calcium-sensing receptor gene).[53] It should be pointed out that the alterations of the *menin* gene in parathyroid adenomas are not limited to the germline mutations seen in the context of MEN I but can also be present in some cases of sporadic adenomas as an expression of a somatic event.[52,58]

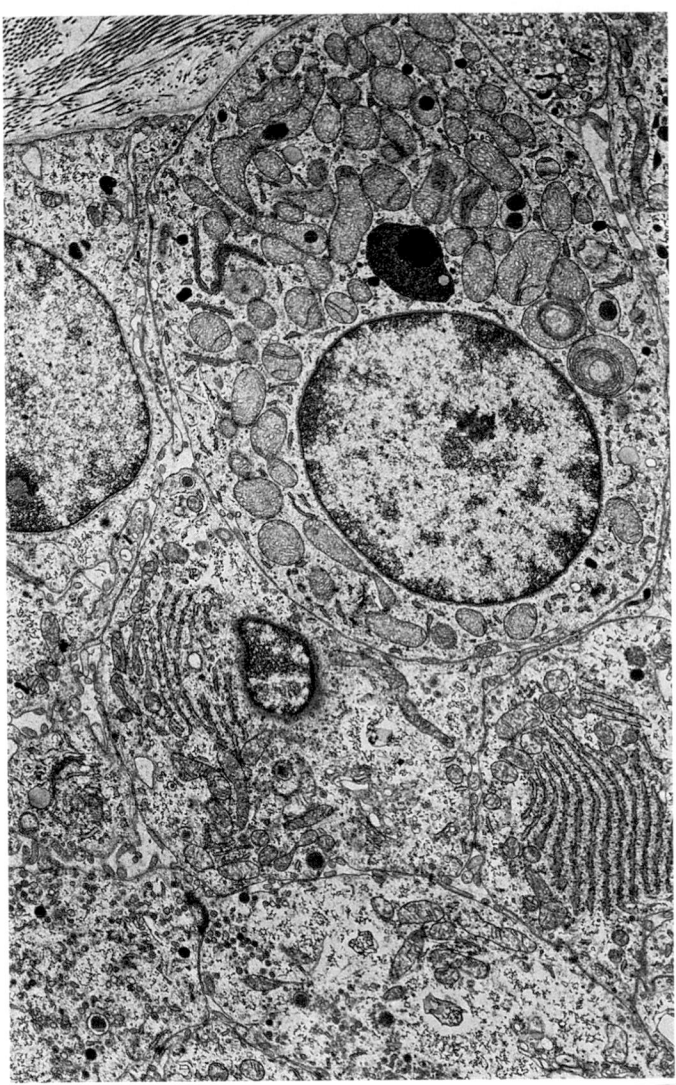

Fig. 10.7 Electron micrograph of parathyroid adenoma. An oncocytic (oxyphilic) cell with numerous mitochondria (lower right) and chief cells with attached cisternae of rough endoplasmic reticulum and diffuse glycogen are illustrated. Dense-core endosecretory granules are primarily located in the ectoplasm. (×9300) (Courtesy of Dr. Robert E. Erlandon, Memorial Sloan-Kettering Cancer Center.)

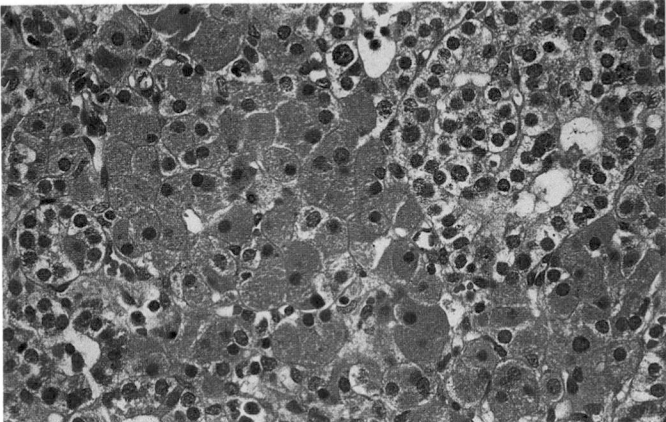

Fig. 10.8 Parathyroid adenoma composed of an admixture of chief cells and oncocytic cells.

Overexpression of p53 is present in a minority of parathyroid adenomas (as well as in carcinomas) but practically never in secondary hyperplasias.[54]

It has been proposed that the phenotype p27(+)bcl-2(+)ki-67(−)mdm2(+) is unique to nonmalignant tumors.[59a]

It was hoped that clonality studies would have clarified once and for all the vexing problem of the differential diagnosis between parathyroid adenoma/carcinoma and primary/secondary chief cell hyperplasia, under the assumption that only the former group should be clonal. Alas, the opposite has happened. Adenomas have been found to be generally clonal (despite early claims to the contrary); however, this has also often been the case for parathyroid lesions having the clinical and morphologic features of primary or secondary hyperplasia *as long as a nodular component is present in them*.[55,57,59] If to this observation we add the fact that serious issues have been raised about the techniques used to determine clonality and the realization that *clonality does not equate to neoplasia*, it becomes evident that the issue is far from settled.[51,56]

Adenoma variants

Oxyphil adenoma is a term that should be restricted to parathyroid adenomas composed entirely or almost entirely of oxyphil cells, in as much as a component of oxyphil cells can be found in many adenomas[60] (Fig. 10.8). When thus defined, most oxyphil adenomas are nonfunctioning; however, cases associated with hyperparathyroidism have been reported, with secretion of PTH and proparathormone being documented ultrastructurally, immunohistochemically, and biochemically.[61,65,66,69] The main ultrastructural feature of these cells is the packing of the cytoplasm by mitochondria.

Lipoadenoma is an unusual morphologic variant of parathyroid adenoma in which the glandular elements are associated with abundant mature adipose tissue. This lesion also has been reported as parathyroid lipohyperplasia, parathyroid hamartoma, and parathyroid adenoma with myxoid stroma.[64,67,68] Most cases are functioning.[62,63]

Chief cell hyperplasia

Chief cell hyperplasia, a condition accompanied by increased production of PTH, can be primary or secondary to impairment of renal function or chronic malabsorption.

Primary chief cell hyperplasia is a constant finding in patients with multiple endocrine neoplasia (MEN) types I and IIa.[81] In contrast, patients with MEN type IIb exhibit normal parathyroid histology during childhood and only a minimal degree of chief cell hyperplasia (consistent with absence of normal involution) during adulthood.[77]

In a *classic* case of primary chief cell hyperplasia, all glands are enlarged (sometimes weighing 10 g or more) and have a tan to reddish color.[70,78] The superior glands tend to be larger than the inferior ones, but the difference is not as striking as with water-clear cell hyperplasia. In other instances, only one gland is visibly enlarged and nodular, whereas the others are nearly normal in size. This latter variant can be confused grossly with an adenoma and is therefore referred to as *pseudoadenomatous*. In still other cases (designated as *occult*) all four glands appear normal in size to the surgeon but appear hyperplastic on histologic examination.[72]

Microscopically, the predominant element is the chief cell, but other cell types are also present in most instances. The pattern of growth may be diffuse or nodular, the former being more common among young patients and the latter in the elderly (Fig. 10.9). Glands with nodular chief cell hyperplasia tend to be asymmetric, with a variable cellular arrangement and a high proportion of oxyphil cells.[86] Fibrous septa, acinar formations, and cells with giant hyperchromatic nuclei may be present.[70] The ultrastructural features are qualitatively similar to those seen in adenoma and are indicative of a hyperfunctioning state. Their presence may establish the hyperplastic state of a gland that is debatable by light microscopy.[71]

Exceptionally, innumerable microscopic foci of hyperplastic parathyroid tissue are found in the neck in association with primary chief cell hyperplasia of the four glands, in the absence of previous surgery. This phenomenon, called *parathyromatosis*, may be responsible for some cases of recurrent hyperparathyroidism after technically successful surgical therapy.[79] Another rare entity is that of chief cell hyperplasia associated with *chronic parathyroiditis*, interpreted by some as a possible parathyroid equivalent of Hashimoto's thyroiditis.[74]

Hyperplastic parathyroid glands surgically transplanted in the forearm as part of the surgical treatment of hyperparathyroidism and which need to be excised because of recurrence of the hyperparathyroidism can exhibit morphologic features which, if present in the orthotopic situation, would have strongly suggested malignancy, such as significant mitotic activity, fibrous strands, and infiltration of the skeletal muscle. In addition to constituting a diagnostic pitfall, this remarkable experiment of nature perhaps tells us something important about the role that the interplay between epithelial cells and stroma has in the development of the morphologic features that we associate with the malignant phenotype[85] (Fig. 10.10) (see p. 602).

In **secondary chief cell hyperplasia**, all gradations are seen. At one end is the normal-sized gland that is recognized as hyperplastic only because of its tan to reddish color and the microscopic hypercellularity; at the other, there is the gland measuring up to 2 cm and weighing up

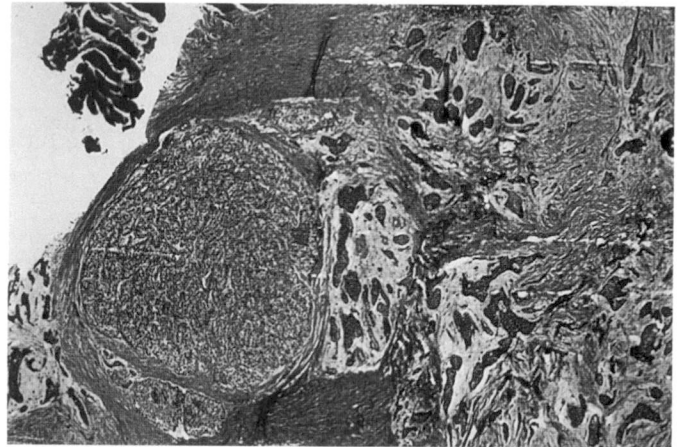

A

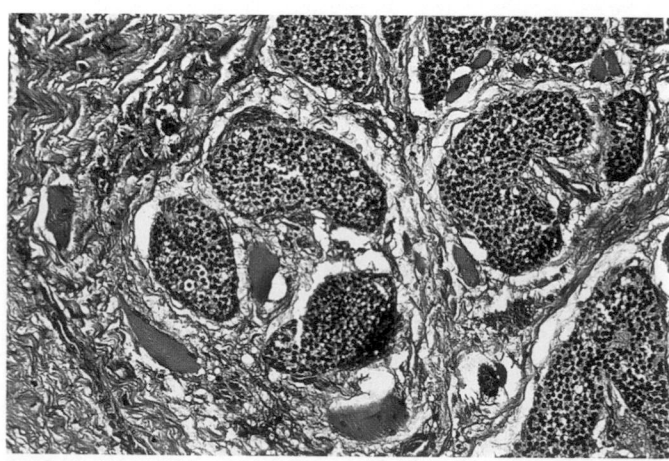

B

Fig. 10.10 A and **B**. Parathyroid gland with chief cell hyperplasia that has been surgically transplanted into the forearm. The clusters of hyperplastic chief cells infiltrate the skeletal muscle, thus simulating carcinoma.

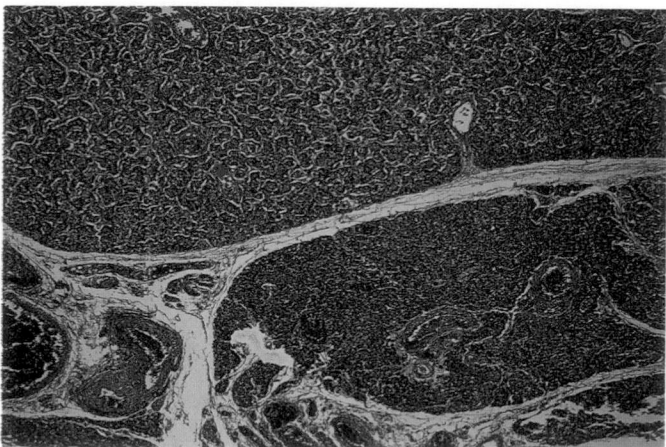

Fig. 10.9 Chief cell hyperplasia with multinodular pattern of growth.

to 6 g. In general, there is an inverse correlation between the size of the glands and the mean serum calcium level.[84] Microscopically, chief cells predominate, but there may also be increased numbers of oxyphil and transitional oxyphil cells that form nodular collections.

The distinction between primary and secondary chief cell hyperplasia cannot be made on morphologic grounds with any certainty.[83] As a rule, nodularity, fibrous septation, acinar formation, and giant nuclei are more prominent in the primary form, whereas the number of oxyphil cells is higher in the secondary form. However, in the final analysis, the differential diagnosis is made on the basis of the clinical and laboratory findings.[70] Another difficult and more pressing problem is the morphologic distinction between chief cell hyperplasia and adenoma. Size, shape, color, consistency, the cell types present, and their relative frequency are of no help in this regard. Presence of a marked degree of nuclear pleomorphism is said to favor adenoma, but the overlap with hyperplasia is too pronounced for this to represent an absolute criterion.[80] The degree of proliferative activity (as measured by PC10 and Ki-67 immunostains) is also similar in adenoma and chief cell hyperplasia, the most intense foci in both instances being present in the form of nodular collections.[82] The presence of a rim of normal parenchyma around the mass and the identification of at least a normal parathyroid gland are the only definite criteria by which a diagnosis of adenoma can be made over that of chief cell hyperplasia, but these criteria may be difficult to evaluate. It may well be, as Black and Utley[73] suggested many years ago, that adenoma and chief cell hyperplasia merely represent different morphologic manifestations of the same process.

As already indicated, flow cytometric DNA determinations and molecular genetic techniques have considerably blurred the formerly rigid distinctions between these processes.[75,76] However, it still seems worthwhile for practical reasons to attempt a distinction between adenoma and chief cell hyperplasia on morphologic grounds, using the criteria previously outlined.

Water-clear cell hyperplasia

In contrast to chief cell hyperplasia, water-clear cell hyperplasia shows no familial incidence and is not associated with multiple endocrine neoplasia. It is characterized by extreme enlargement of all parathyroid tissue so that the total weight of the glands may exceed 100 g. Strangely, this disorder (which made up a significant proportion of cases of primary hyperparathyroidism in older series) has all but disappeared in recent times, the reason being unknown.[87,91] Occasional cases are still being reported, one of them associated with a similar vacuolated clear cell appearance in the submaxillary gland.[88]

Grossly, the superior glands are distinctly larger than the inferior. Moreover, glands may coalesce so that two glands appear as one. They are soft and have a typical chocolate brown color (Fig. 10.11). Cysts and hemorrhages have been observed. Another common gross feature is the formation of pseudopods that may extend a considerable distance from the main mass of the gland. A close correlation exists between the weight of the parathyroid tissue and the severity of the symptoms.

Microscopically, the most characteristic feature is the presence of cells with optically clear cytoplasm throughout the lesion. These cells vary markedly in size, from some no larger than normal parathyroid cells to others that measure up to 40 μm (Fig. 10.12). Thus there is a combination of hyperplasia and hypertrophy. In most regions, the cytoplasm of the cell is water-clear, but in some cells small eosinophilic granules are present. High-power examination of thin sections reveals that the clarity of the cytoplasm is the result of a conglomerate of spherical clear vacuoles surrounded by thin portions of eosinophilic cytoplasmic material. This is confirmed by ultrastructural examination, which reveals numerous membrane-bound vacuoles, 0.2 to 2 μm in diameter, presumably derived from the Golgi apparatus.[90]

The nuclei average 6 to 7 μm and are basally oriented, a very distinctive feature. Although their size may vary, giant forms are not seen.

The pattern of growth may be alveolar (pseudoglandular) or compact. The connective tissue is delicate and

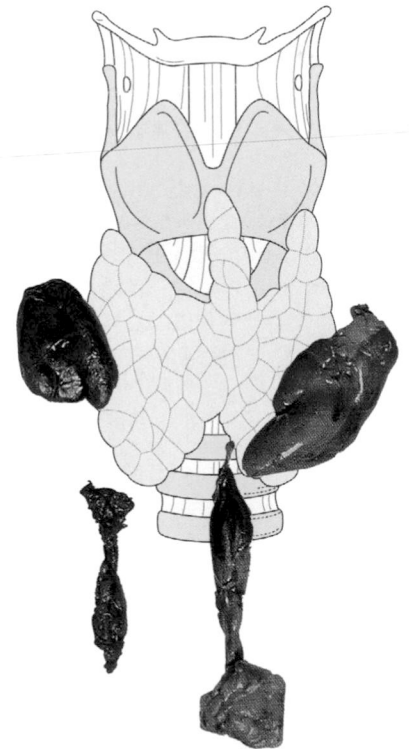

Fig. 10.11 Water-clear cell hyperplasia. Note the chocolate brown color, the pseudopods, and the greater involvement of the upper glands. (Redrawn from Castleman B. Tumors of the parathyroid glands. Atlas of tumor pathology, series 1, fascicle 15. Washington D.C., 1952.)

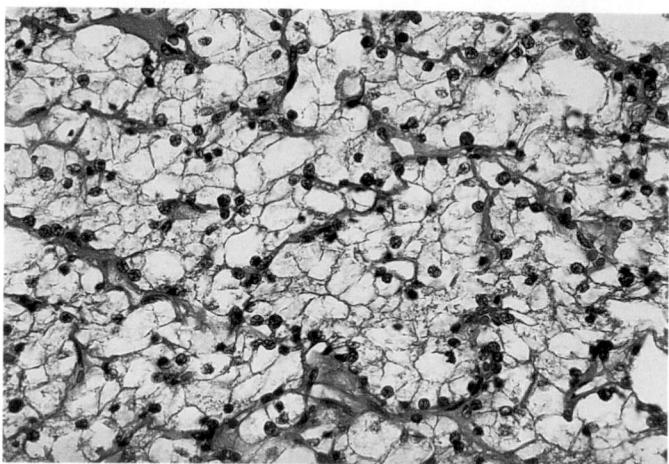

Fig. 10.12 Water-clear cell hyperplasia. The cells are very large, optically clear, and have sharply outlined cell membranes.

sparse for the most part, but in some areas it may be dense. A chief cell component is occasionally present.

It is not clear (no pun intended) whether the exceptionally rare case exhibiting water-clear cell changes in two glands represents double adenomas or asymmetric forms of water-clear hyperplasia.[89]

Carcinoma

Parathyroid carcinoma typically presents with hyperparathyroidism; in an old series, skeletal disease was present in 73% of the patients and renal disease in 26%.[104] A few convincing nonfunctioning cases are on record, and these are said to be more aggressive.[92] The absence of function may be caused by the lack of conversion of the preparathormone to the biologically active compound.[93] Parathyroid carcinoma may coexist with chief cell hyperplasia,[98,102] and with adenoma,[117] the former sometimes seen in a familial setting.[119]

Clinical features suggestive of parathyroid carcinoma in a hyperparathyroid patient include very high values of serum calcium or PTH, a palpable cervical mass, vocal cord paralysis, and recurrence of hyperparathyroidism a short time after surgery.[96,115,116,122] Some patients present with parathyroid crises.[113] At operation, a parathyroid tumor should be suspected of being carcinoma if it is hard, surrounded by a dense fibrous reaction, and adherent to or infiltrating adjacent structures.

Microscopically, carcinomas differ from adenomas mainly because of their trabecular arrangement, dense fibrous bands (present in 90% of the cases), spindle shape of the tumor cells, presence of mitotic figures (in 81%), capsular invasion (in 67%), and blood vessel invasion (in 12%)[101,114] (Figs 10.13 and 10.14). Some caveats are in order. A certain degree of fibrous banding can also occur in adenoma and in chief cell hyperplasia, particularly the primary form of the latter. Nests of tumor cells may be

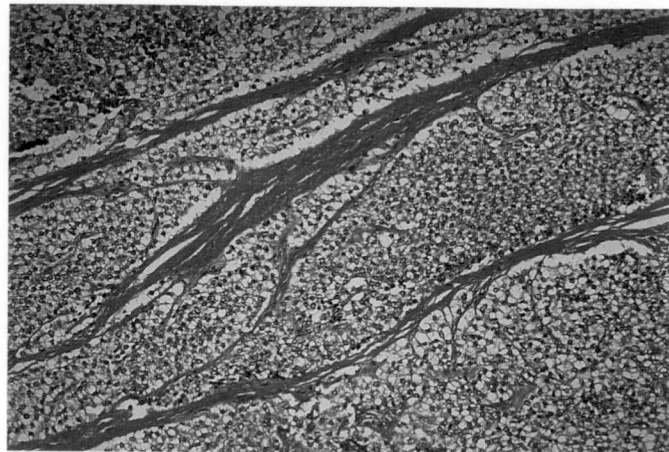

A

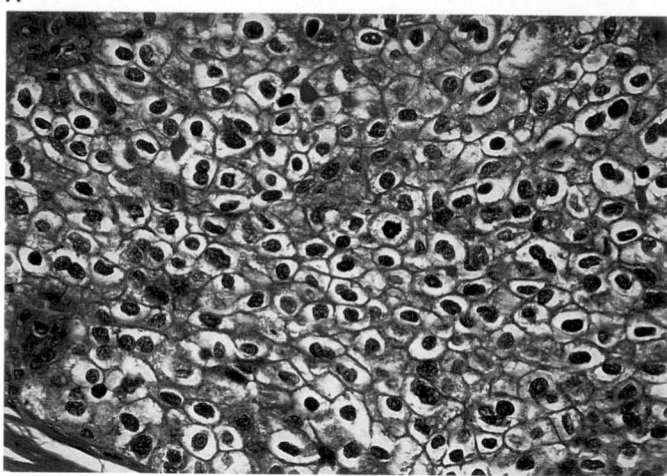

B

Fig. 10.13 Parathyroid carcinoma. **A,** Sharply outlined fibrous bands incompletely dividing the tumor into lobules. **B,** Mitotic features.

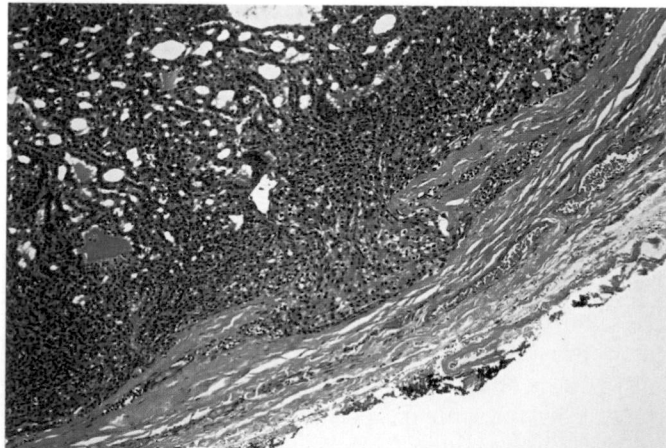

Fig. 10.14 Parathyroid carcinoma with capsular and possible capsular invasion.

present within the capsule of a benign tumor. For tumor in a vein to be of significance, it must be attached to the wall. The presence of an occasional mitotic figure in a parathyroid lesion does not necessarily indicate that the lesion in question is a carcinoma. Snover and Foucar[118] found mitoses by exhaustive search in 71% of adenomas and 80% of the chief cell hyperplasias that they examined. It is also important to be certain that the mitoses are in the tumor cells rather than in the endothelial cells of the prominent hyperplastic blood vessels that so commonly accompany these tumors.

In rare cases, parathyroid carcinoma is composed of oxyphil cells.[99,111] In contrast to parathyroid chief cell adenomas, these tumors are usually negative for CK14. They also tend to express a higher Ki-67 labeling index and a lower p27 index than their benign counterparts.[99] If the parathyroid origin of the tumor is questionable—particularly in the absence of function—immunochemical demonstration of PTH should be carried out.[112]

Special techniques can be of some help in the differential diagnosis between parathyroid adenomas and carcinoma. A significantly increased mean AgNOR number has been found in carcinomatous glands when compared with benign (normal, hyperplastic, or adenomatous) glands.[95,107,121] Ki-67 expression is significantly higher in carcinomas than in adenomas and hyperplasias.[100,123] Overexpression of cyclin D1 occurs in over 90% of the carcinomas but in less than 40% of the adenomas.[124] DNA ploidy studies have shown that significant statistical differences exist between carcinomas and adenomas and that among the former the presence of aneuploidy is associated with a more aggressive clinical course.[94,103,105,109,110] Kytola et al.[108] found "highly significant differences" by comparative genomic hybridization (CGH) between parathyroid carcinomas and adenomas, but there were no alterations that were specific for one or the other. Allelic loss of the Rb gene (detected genetically or through absence of the Rb product immunohistochemically) occurs in a variable proportion of carcinomas or otherwise "aggressive" parathyroid tumors but only exceptionally in adenomas.[97,120,123] Finally, somatic and germ-line mutations of the HRPT2 gene (which codes for the protein parafibromin and is responsible for the hereditary hyperparathyroidism and jaw tumors syndrome, see p. 605) have been found in a high percentage of parathyroid carcinoma cases.[115a]

In a follow-up of 43 patients with parathyroid carcinoma reported by Holmes et al.,[104] it was found that 30 (65%) of the patients were dead, 5 were living with persistent tumor, and 8 were living without evidence of recurrent disease. Of 39 patients studied by Schantz and Castleman,[114] 41% were alive and well, 13% were alive with disease, and 46% were dead of carcinoma. Local recurrence within the first 2 years after surgery was found to be an ominous prognostic sign. Among 286 cases of parathyroid carcinoma collected in the US National Cancer Data Base, neither tumor size nor lymph node status was found to be a significant prognostic factor. Overall relative survival at 5 years and 10 years was 85.5% and 49.1%, respectively.[106]

Other lesions

Parathyroid cysts usually arise from the inferior glands but can be located in the upper region of the neck or in the mediastinum.[125,130] In most cases they cause no symptoms other than those related to pressure. Their mean diameter is 4 cm.[125] They are lined by cuboidal or low columnar epithelial cells and contain parathyroid tissue in their wall. Heterotopic salivary gland tissue can be found around the cyst.[126]

The cyst fluid contains assayable PTH.[131] The few reported cases of parathyroid cysts associated with hyperparathyroidism most likely represent adenomas with cystic degeneration.[129]

Amyloidosis often involves the parathyroid gland, in both primary and "reactive" forms of the disease.[127]

Langerhans' cell histiocytosis (histiocytosis X; eosinophilic granuloma) involving simultaneously the parathyroid and thyroid glands has been reported.[132]

Hemangioma of the parathyroid gland has been described in two patients with hyperparathyroidism, but it is likely that the vascular tumor was simply an incidental finding.[128]

Metastatic carcinoma to the parathyroid glands is very rare, but papillary thyroid carcinoma can invade them in continuity with the main tumor.[131a]

Hyperparathyroidism

The term **hyperparathyroidism** is applied to any condition associated with the persistent production of parathyroid hormone. It is divided into primary, secondary, and tertiary, according to the presumed mechanism of production.

Primary hyperparathyroidism

In primary hyperparathyroidism, there is no evidence of previous parathyroid stimulation by chronic renal or intestinal disease. The pathologic changes in the gland may be those of adenoma, chief cell hyperplasia, carcinoma, or water-clear cell hyperplasia. Carcinoma constitutes less than 4% of cases, and water-clear cell hyperplasia has essentially disappeared; therefore the large majority of cases are caused by either adenoma or chief cell hyperplasia.[138] An interesting argument has developed over the years about the relative incidence of these two processes. Traditionally, adenoma had been regarded as the more frequent of the two. A series of articles written during the 1960s and 1970s[135,140,147] challenged that view and proposed that chief cell hyperplasia was actually the most common pathologic change. In retrospect, it seems that these conclusions may have been influenced by the inclusion of many familial cases (which tend to show hyperplasia, see following discussion), by a perhaps liberal interpretation of minimal hyperplastic changes in the other glands, and by the fact that chief cell hyperplasia and adenoma are truly interrelated and merging processes. Be that as it may, the pendulum is now back to its original position, with adenoma being held responsible for over 80% of the cases.

Primary hyperparathyroidism is said to be present in 2.5 per 1000 individuals. It is usually seen in adults but can also be found in children.[149] When seen in a familial setting, the abnormality is usually chief cell hyperplasia, although exceptions occur.[133] It may also be seen, again in a familial form, as a component of MEN types I or IIb[134,137] (see Chapter 15). In this syndrome, the parathyroid change is practically always chief cell hyperplasia, perhaps humorally induced.[136] In MEN type IIb, it is not uncommon for the surgeon to find parathyroid chief cell hyperplasia and medullary carcinoma of the thyroid gland during the same exploration. In about 10% of the cases of sporadic primary hyperparathyroidism not associated with MEN, a nonmedullary thyroid carcinoma—usually of the papillary type—is found incidentally at operation.[143] Whether this represents more than a fortuitous association remains to be determined. An association between primary hyperparathyroidism and sarcoidosis also has been encountered.[153] Finally, a definite increase in the incidence of hyperparathyroidism after irradiation to the neck has been documented.[146,151]

The typical case of primary hyperparathyroidism is biochemically characterized by hypercalcemia, hypophosphatemia, lowering of the renal phosphate threshold, hypercalciuria, elevated levels of immunoreactive PTH, elevated concentrations of 1,25-dihydroxyvitamin D, and enhanced excretion of nephrogenous cyclic AMP. Another associated, albeit inconstant, chemical finding is elevation of the serum alkaline phosphatase level. Although hypercalcemia has traditionally been one of the most constant biochemical markers of parathyroid hyperfunction, well-documented instances of normocalcemic primary hyperparathyroidism do exist.[152] In a series of 84 patients with this variant, parathyroid adenomas were found in 19, chief cell hyperplasia in 39, and normal parathyroid glands in 26; no morphologic differences were detected between patients in this group and patients with conventional primary hyperparathyroidism associated with hypercalcemia.[139]

According to the clinical presentation, patients with primary hyperparathyroidism have been traditionally classified into (1) those with osseous manifestations, (2) those with renal manifestations, and (3) those with neither of the foregoing. At present, there is a predominance of the latter group, referred to as "occult" or "asymptomatic."[150,152]

The **skeletal changes** of hyperparathyroidism are always generalized, although they may appear localized clinically or radiographically. The initial lesions show merely a decrease in bone density. In time, they may become very extensive and lead to deformities and fractures. The full-blown osseous manifestations of hyperparathyroidism have been traditionally known as osteitis fibrosa cystica or Recklinghausen's disease (not to be confused with neurofibromatosis, which also carries this eponym) (Figs 10.15 to 10.17). The seemingly localized lesions are those more likely to be misinterpreted. They present radiographically as expansile, multilocular masses. The jaw is the preferred location, and this may be the first clinical manifestation of the disease. Grossly, there is an alternation of solid and cystic areas; the latter often have a brown color because of the accumulation of abundant hemosiderin, hence the term *brown tumor* sometimes used for them. Microscopically, there is a combination of osteoblastic and osteoclastic activity, often associated with cyst formation and clusters of hemosiderin-laden macrophages. It is this combination of findings that should suggest the diagnosis (Fig. 10.18).

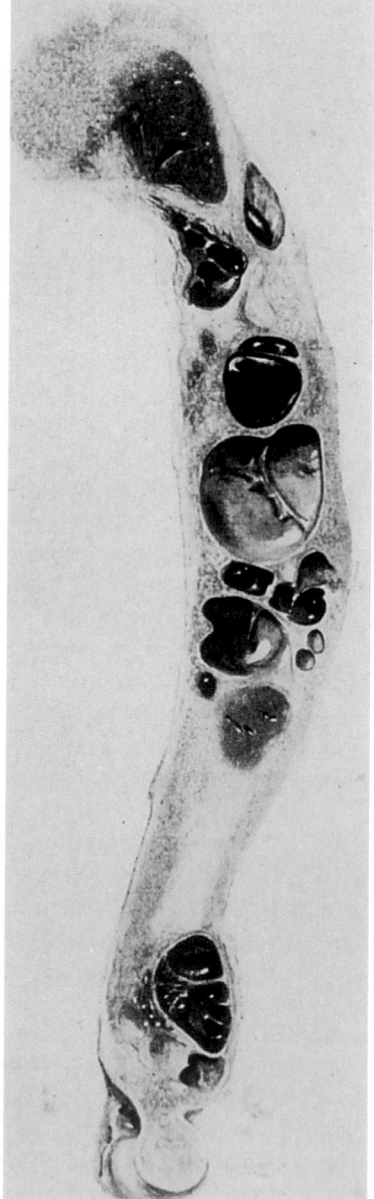

Fig. 10.15 Historical example of extreme osteitis fibrosa cystica. Note deformity of bone with numerous cysts and brown tumors. (From Hunter D, Turnbull HN. Hyperparathyroidism. Generalized osteitis fibrosa, with observations upon bones, parathyroid tumors, and normal parathyroid glands. Br J Surg 1931, **19:** 203–284.)

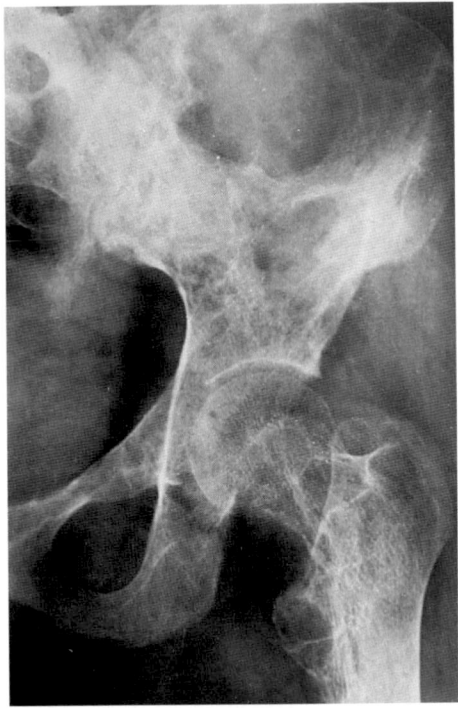 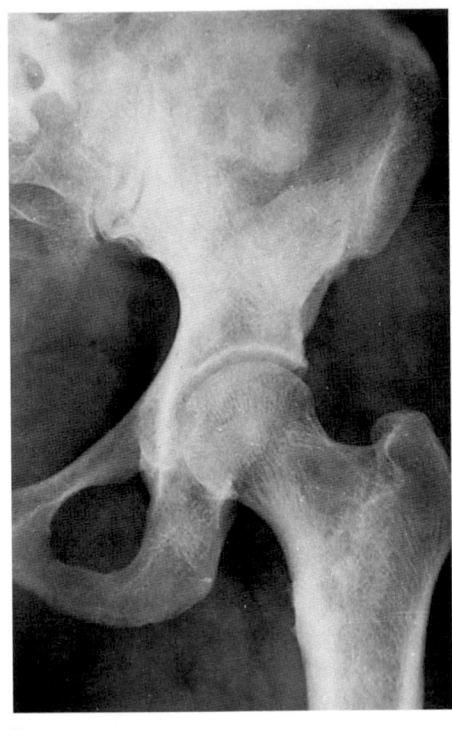

A   B

Fig. 10.16 A, Extensive changes in bones of pelvis and femur caused by functioning parathyroid adenoma. **B,** Same pelvis and femur 8 years after removal of adenoma. Note complete reversion to normal. (From Black BK, Ackerman LV. Tumors of the parathyroid. A review of twenty-three cases. Cancer 1950, **3:** 415–444.)

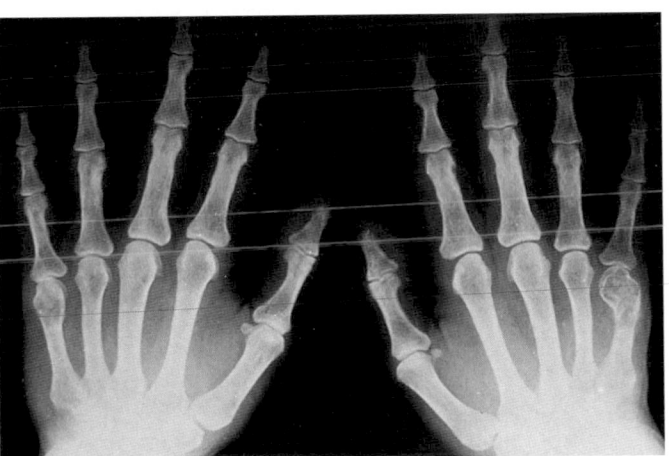 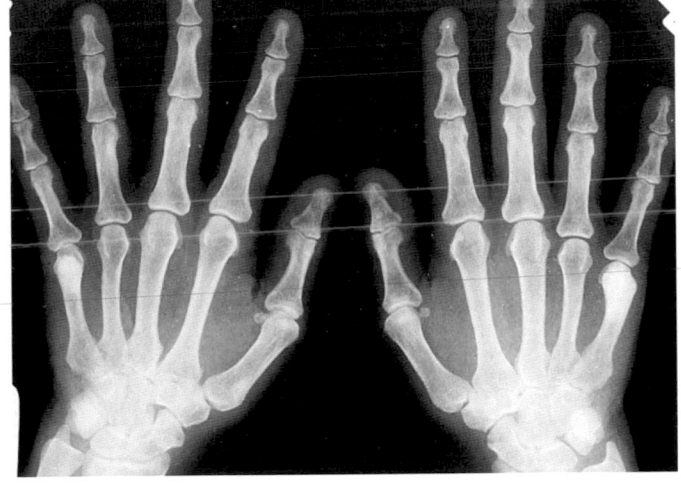

A   B

Fig. 10.17 A, Cystic changes and cortical alterations in bones of hands of patient with functioning parathyroid adenoma. **B,** Dramatic change evident 9 months after removal of adenoma.

The differential diagnosis with central giant cell reparative granuloma may be impossible on morphologic grounds because both lesions have a predilection for the jaw and their microscopic appearances are essentially the same; therefore the distinction is based on laboratory findings. The other differential diagnosis is with giant cell tumor, with which brown tumor has often been confused in the past. In giant cell tumor, the osteoclasts are more evenly spaced, the stromal cells are plumper, and osteoblastic activity is less conspicuous.

The existence should be mentioned here of an extremely rare syndrome known as *hereditary hyperparathyroidism and jaw tumors*, linked to the *HRPT2* gene

at locus 1q21–23 (and therefore different from other MEN syndromes), which can be accompanied by Wilms' tumor and other renal abnormalities. The parathyroid pathology may take the form of chief cell hyperplasia, adenoma, or carcinoma.[142,145]

Removal of the hyperfunctioning gland is usually followed by a spectacular reversal of the bone changes, sometimes in a remarkably short time; however, some of the cystic lesions may persist indefinitely (Figs 10.16 and 10.17).

The **renal changes** of primary hyperparathyroidism include renal stones, nephrocalcinosis, polyuria, polydipsia, and impairment of renal function. It is now

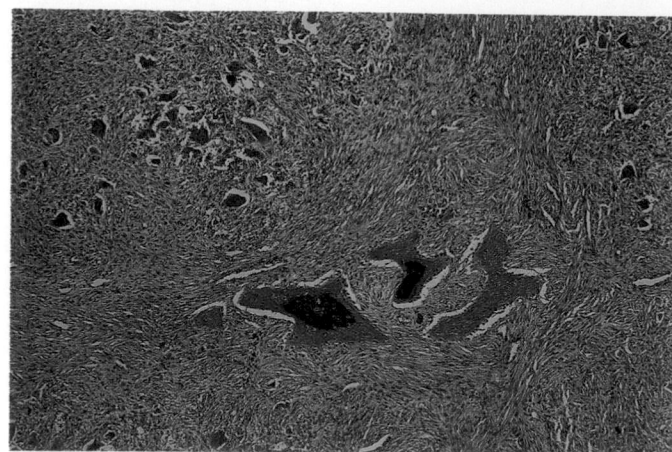

Fig. 10.18 Bone changes in hyperparathyroidism. There is marked resorption of bone trabeculae and clustering of osteoclasts.

recognized that renal stones are the most common clinical manifestation of hyperparathyroidism.[148] These renal lesions are frequently associated with hypertension. In contrast to the skeletal changes, the renal abnormalities may still progress after the removal of the parathyroid lesion.

Other manifestations of hyperparathyroidism include hypertension, peptic ulcer, acute and chronic pancreatitis, and mental disturbances. The peptic ulcer is usually in the duodenum and is more common in males[141]; it often heals after removal of the hyperfunctioning gland.

Rarely, acute gastrointestinal, cardiovascular, or central nervous system symptoms develop because of very high serum calcium levels. This condition, designated as **parathyroid crisis,** is fatal unless the offending gland or glands are rapidly excised.[144]

Secondary hyperparathyroidism

Secondary hyperparathyroidism occurs as a consequence of chronic renal disease or intestinal malabsorption, usually the former. The renal insufficiency leads to elevation of the serum phosphorus level and reciprocal decrease of serum calcium concentrations, with the resulting stimulation of the parathyroid glands.[154] Vitamin D resistance is a characteristic feature of advanced renal disease and also may play a role by contributing to reduced serum calcium concentrations.[155] Determinations of circulating PTH levels have shown these to be roughly proportional to the severity of renal failure. These levels are higher in renal failure than in any form of primary hyperparathyroidism.

The bone changes are qualitatively similar to those seen in primary hyperparathyroidism. They are usually milder, but sometimes extensive changes with cyst formation occur.[157] *Cutaneous calciphylaxis* is an uncommon and potentially lethal disorder characterized by progressive cutaneous vascular calcification. It is mainly seen in the setting of renal failure-associated hyper-

parathyroidism. Microscopically, the mural vascular calcification is often associated with skin ulceration and calcifying septal panniculitis.[156]

The parathyroid abnormality in secondary hyperparathyroidism is **chief cell hyperplasia** of generally diffuse but sometimes nodular type.

C-cell hyperplasia in the thyroid gland has been found in patients with secondary hyperparathyroidism, supposedly as a compensatory mechanism.[158]

"Tertiary" hyperparathyroidism

The term **"tertiary" hyperparathyroidism** is applied to cases of hyperparathyroidism secondary to chronic renal disease or intestinal malabsorption, in which one or more of the stimulated parathyroid glands seem to become autonomous.[162] This phenomenon, which is also referred to as **nonsuppressible, autonomous,** or **refractory** hyperparathyroidism, is usually detected after correction of the renal disease by hemodialysis or homotransplantation.[165] Follow-up studies seem to indicate that if enough time is given, the parathyroid glands will revert to a normal state in the large majority of cases.[161,164]

Morphologically, the changes in the parathyroid gland are those of chief cell hyperplasia, the main difference with the ordinary case of **suppressible** secondary hyperparathyroidism being a greater tendency to nodularity and heterogeneity, in the sense of the nodular components having a higher percentage of oxyphilic cells and acinar cell arrangements, and showing a marked variability of PTH immunoreactivity (Fig. 10.19).[163,166,167] Sometimes an entire nodule is made up of oxyphilic cells.[167] Even when the hyperplastic changes remain diffuse, the nuclear size has been shown by morphometry to be larger than that of secondary hyperplasia and approaching that of adenoma.[160] It has been demonstrated that the presence of a nodular pattern of growth (especially if coupled with a high Ki-67 fraction) is associated with a higher risk of recurrence of the hyperparathyroidism.[159] These nodules have a high prevalence

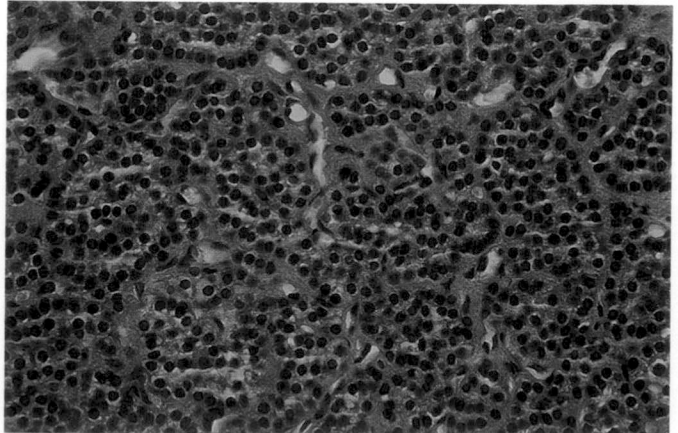

Fig. 10.19 Tertiary hyperparathyroidism. The changes are indistinguishable from those of primary chief cell hyperplasia.

of p53 expression immunohistochemically.[166] In extreme cases, one of these nodules will acquire an appearance that is indistinguishable from that of a true adenoma. However, the finding of allelic losses at chromosomes 7p, 18q, and 2 suggests that its molecular pathways are different from those of the ordinary adenoma.[168]

Differential diagnosis

Primary hyperparathyroidism must be distinguished clinically from a relatively large number of conditions associated with hypercalcemia. These include sarcoidosis, hyperthyroidism, multiple myeloma, milk–alkali syndrome, vitamin D and vitamin A intoxication, familial hypercalcemic hypocalciuria, and humoral hypercalcemia of malignancy.

Familial hypocalciuric hypercalcemia should be suspected in young patients with a presumptive diagnosis of hyperparathyroidism, especially if there is a family history.[173,177] Determination of the calcium:creatinine clearance ratio is the traditional test to identify this disorder. Heterozygous inactivating mutations of calcium-sensing receptor are found in about two thirds of the patients.[173a] Microscopically, the parathyroid glands may appear normal or exhibit a mild degree of chief cell hyperplasia, sometimes with a prominent clear cell component.[189] In other instances they show features of lipohyperplasia.[173a]

Humoral hypercalcemia of malignancy. Nonparathyroid tumors may induce hypercalcemia by producing widespread metastases in the skeletal system. In addition, symptoms and signs suggestive of hyperparathyroidism may be seen in malignant tumors of nonparathyroid origin in the absence of significant osseous metastases.[181,185] This condition is sometimes referred to as pseudohyperparathyroidism. Renal cell carcinoma and squamous cell carcinoma of the lung account for 60% of cases.[176] The parathyroid glands appear morphologically normal or only minimally hyperplastic,[172,186] but the serum biochemical parameters clearly indicate a state of suppressed parathyroid function. The mechanism for the hypercalcemia has been found to be the secretion by the tumor cells of a peptide with a partial homology to PTH, known as PTH-related peptide or PTH-related protein.[171,187,188] This peptide, which competes with PTH for receptor sites, can be detected in the tumor tissue and in the serum.[169,183] Expression of this peptide has been demonstrated in carcinomas of various sites,[175,180,182] its presence not always correlating with the serum calcium level.[174] It has also been detected in normal and abnormal parathyroid glands,[170,178] reactive human bile ductules,[184] and normal cells of the central nervous system.[190] In parathyroid adenoma, there can be co-secretion of PTH and PTH-related peptide via a regulated pathway in the secretory granules.[179]

Therapy

The surgeon embarking on therapy for hyperparathyroidism should have a thorough knowledge of parathyroid physiology and of the variations in the appearance and anatomic locations of the parathyroid glands[225,226] as well as the tumors arising from them. Wang[225] reoperated on 112 patients for persistent hyperparathyroidism after surgery. In cervical reexplorations, the missing glands were most frequently found in the posterosuperior portion of mediastinum at the thoracic inlet (38%); in mediastinal reexplorations, they were found in the anteroposterior portion of the mediastinum (67%). Wang estimated that the reasons for the initial unsuccessful surgery were (1) lack of knowledge by the surgeon of the normal location of the glands and the way they may be displaced when diseased; (2) misdiagnosis of cases of chief cell hyperplasia as adenomas, resulting in insufficient surgery; and (3) technical incompetence. The importance of the first factor was highlighted by a study in which it was found that in almost half of 71 cases of chief cell hyperplasia there was an abnormality in the number and/or location of the glands.[208]

Several techniques have been used to localize the abnormal gland preoperatively. These include ultrasonography, CT scan, radioactive scan, and selective venous catheterization, the latter being the most sensitive.[194] These techniques have been found to be particularly useful in cases of recurrent hyperparathyroidism.

Surgical identification of *all four* parathyroid glands remains the most widely used approach,[207,212] although controversy persists.[209,224] If a thorough examination of the neck reveals only three normal parathyroid glands, some authors advocate the performance of a hemithyroidectomy on the side of the missing gland, since 2% of all adenomas are found in this location.[203,217] If this also proves negative, sternotomy and mediastinal exploration should be considered 2 or 3 weeks later. The majority of the mediastinal parathyroid adenomas can be removed from the neck through a low collar thyroid incision.[210,215,219] If all four identified glands appear normal, the possibility should be considered of an abnormal fifth (supernumerary) gland being present, whether in the neck or—more commonly—in the mediastinum.[216] Roth et al.[213] devised a useful flow sheet for the surgeon who undertakes surgery for primary hyperparathyroidism as well as for the pathologist who will assist him.

Adenomas are adequately treated by local excision of the tumor.[214] It is imperative *to excise or biopsy at least one other parathyroid gland* to rule out the possibility of chief cell hyperplasia.

Primary chief cell hyperplasia and the exceptionally rare water-clear cell hyperplasia are conventionally treated by subtotal parathyroidectomy, as defined by total excision of three glands and partial excision of the fourth, leaving 30 to 50 mg of viable tissue.[227]

Some surgeons have recommended the performance of the latter procedure as the routine treatment for primary hyperparathyroidism regardless of the underlying abnormality, in view of the difficulty that sometimes exists in distinguishing chief cell hyperplasia from adenoma.[211] We do not subscribe to this extreme form of treatment, not only because of the increased risk of hypoparathyroidism, but also because it represents unnecessarily radical surgery in most cases. Many large recent series document the fact that the patient with a *single* enlarged parathyroid gland is adequately treated by removal of that gland plus an additional one for diagnostic purposes. This procedure is nearly 100% effective if the enlarged gland is the site of an adenoma and is also effective in a good number of cases on a long-term basis if the patient has a "pseudoadenomatous" form of chief cell hyperplasia *as long as the other glands are identified and are found to be normal in size*. The reason seems to be that even if the other glands have microscopic chief cell hyperplasia, the degree of this hyperplasia is such as to be of functional insignificance in the large majority of the cases.[191,192,196,198] In other words, the *amount* of abnormal parathyroid tissue removed and left in place seems to represent the most important determinant of outcome.

An alternative approach to the treatment of primary or secondary chief cell hyperplasia has been the performance of total parathyroidectomy with autotransplantation of parathyroid tissue into the forearm muscle.[205,218] The transplanted tissue may regrow briskly and lead to recurrence of the hyperparathyroidism.[199,223] The hyperplastic gland may infiltrate the skeletal muscle, simulating a malignant process. The danger of overdiagnosis under these circumstances is made greater by the fact that mitoses can be easily found in this tissue even if absent in the original lesion (see p. 600).

Parathyroid carcinoma is best treated by excision of the tumor and surrounding soft tissues and removal of the ipsilateral lateral thyroid lobe; the indication for ipsilateral node dissection remains controversial.[195,206,221,228] Surgical resection of isolated metastases is justified because of its marked palliative effect.[200]

The large majority of patients with secondary and "tertiary" hyperparathyroidism respond well to medical treatment[193,202]; however, if bone lesions are severe and if the hypercalcemia is excessive, subtotal parathyroidectomy may become necessary.

It is not clear whether asymptomatic individuals who are found to have mild hypercalcemia (less than 11 mg/dl) on routine screening should be operated on.[197,201,204] A group of such patients was followed on a long-term basis to determine their outcome. At the end of a 10-year period, 26% of the patients had had surgery because of increased serum calcium levels, decreased renal function, renal stones, psychologic considerations, or bone disease; the authors were unable to define criteria that would predict which patients with asymptomatic hyperparathyroidism would eventually require surgery.[220] A more recent study drew very similar conclusions, in the sense that one quarter of the asymptomatic patients who did not undergo surgery had progression of the disease.[222]

Frozen section

The main role of the pathologist at the time of surgery, as pedestrian as this may sound, is to determine by frozen section whether a given nodule taken by the surgeon from the neck is, in reality, parathyroid tissue, since nodules of thyroid gland, small lymph nodes, aberrant thymic tissue, and even fat may be mistaken grossly for parathyroid tissue.[241,244] This determination has an accuracy rate of over 99%.[246] With experience, this determination can also be made in imprints stained with polychrome methylene blue, a technique that saves considerable surgical time.[236,244a,245]

As far as the pathologist providing a specific diagnosis is concerned, most cases of carcinoma and water-clear cell hyperplasia should be identifiable by frozen section, particularly if the carcinoma has invaded local tissues; however, this comprises a very small proportion of cases. The two most common—and unfortunately most difficult—situations faced by the pathologist are to decide whether a gland is normal or abnormal and, if abnormal, whether it is involved by chief cell hyperplasia or adenoma. The differential features between these two entities have already been discussed on p. 601. Suffice it to say that if the pathologist is given a single gland, such a distinction will be impossible in most instances.

In regard to the decision about whether a small gland is normal or hyperplastic, estimation of the amount of stromal fat has been used, but the value of this determination is very questionable.[230,235,237,242] Some residual fat can be present in hyperplastic glands; conversely, parathyroid glands of young patients may have a very small amount. Furthermore, the distribution of stromal fat varies considerably from area to area; therefore the validity of a subjective evaluation of a few microscopic sections is highly unreliable, as studies using image-analysis techniques have shown.[239] The presence of distinct nodularity and/or more than occasional acinar formations is a feature favoring a diagnosis of hyperplasia.[229]

The performance of stains for lipid (such as Sudan IV, oil red O, or osmium carmine) has been recommended, the rationale being that the chief cells of a normal or suppressed gland have cytoplasmic lipid droplets, whereas those of adenoma or chief cell hyperplasia do not.[231,234,238,240,243] Although there is an undeniable inverse relationship between functional activity and fat content, the number of discordant results is high enough to call for caution in its interpretation.[232,233,241]

References

Normal gross anatomy and embryology

1   Akerström G, Malmacus J, Bergström R. Surgical anatomy of human parathyroid glands. Surgery 1984, **95:** 14–21.

2   Carney JA. The glandulae parathyroideae of Ivar Sandstrom: Contributions from two continents. Am J Surg Pathol 1996, **20:** 1123–1144.

3   Conn JM, Goncalves MA, Mansour KA, McGarity WC. The mediastinal parathyroid. Am Surg 1991, **57:** 62–66.

4   Gilmour JR, Martin WJ. The weight of the parathyroid glands. J Pathol Bacteriol 1937, **44:** 431–462.

5   Harach HR, Vujanic GM. Intrathyroidal parathyroid. Pediatr Pathol 1993, **13:** 71–74.

6   Herrold KM, Rabson AS, Ketcham AS. Aberrant parathyroid gland in pharyngeal submucosa. Arch Pathol 1962, **73:** 60–62.

7   Lack EE, Delay S, Linnoila RI. Ectopic parathyroid tissue within the vagus nerve: Incidence and possible clinical significance. Arch Pathol Lab Med 1962, **112:** 304–306.

8   Michal M. Ectopic parathyroid within a neck paraganglion. Histopathology 1993, **22:** 85–87.

9   Wang C. The anatomic basis of parathyroid surgery. Ann Surg 1976, **183:** 271–275.

Normal histology

10 Bjerneroth G, Juhlin C, Grimelius L, Rastad J, Akerström G. Improvement in histological diagnosis of primary hyperparathyroidism with a monoclonal anti-parathyroid antibody. Endocrinol Pathol 1992, **3:** 83–92.

11 Boquist L. Follicles in human parathyroid glands. Lab Invest 1973, **28:** 313–320.

12 Gilmour JR. The parathyroid glands and skeleton in renal diseases. London, 1947, Oxford University Press.

13 Grimelius L, Bondeson L. Histopathological diagnosis of parathyroid diseases. Path Res Pract 1995, **191:** 353–365.

13a Isotalo PA, Lloyd RV. Presence of birefringent crystals is useful in distinguishing thyroid from parathyroid gland tissues (letter to the editor). Am J Surg Pathol 2002, **26:** 813–814.

14 Hellman P, Bjerneroth G, Juhlin C, Ridefelt P, Rastad J, Akerström G, Juppner H. Immunohistochemical evidence of parathyroid hormone-related protein in human parathyroid tissue. Endocrinol Pathol 1990, **1:** 172–176.

15 Lieberman A, DeLellis RA. Intrafollicular amyloid in normal parathyroid glands. Arch Pathol 1973, **95:** 422–423.

16 Miettinen M, Clark R, Lehto V-P, Virtanen I, Damjanov I. Intermediate-filament proteins in parathyroid glands and parathyroid adenomas. Arch Pathol Lab Med 1985, **109:** 986–989.

17 Muller-Hocker J. Random cytochrome-C-oxidase deficiency of oxyphil cell nodules in the parathyroid gland. Pathol Res Pract 1992, **188:** 701–706.

18 Obara T, Fujimoto Y, Aiba M. Stromal fat content of the parathyroid gland. Endocrinol Jpn 1990, **37:** 901–905.

19 Ordoñez NG, Ibanñez ML, Samaan NA, Hickey RC. Immunoperoxidase study of uncommon parathyroid tumors, Report of two cases of nonfunctioning parathyroid carcinoma and one intrathyroid parathyroid tumor-producing amyloid. Am J Surg Pathol 1983, **7:** 535–542.

20 Pesce C, Tobia F, Carli F, Antoniotti G. The sites of hormone storage in normal and diseased parathyroid glands. A silver impregnation and immunohistochemical study. Histopathology 1989, **15:** 157–166.

20a Roth SI, Abu-Jawdeh G. Parathyroid Glands. In Sternberg S (ed.): Histology for pathologists, 2 ed. Philadelphia, 1997, Lippincott-Raven Publishers: 1093–1106.

21 Roth SI, Capen CC. Ultrastructural and functional correlations of the parathyroid gland. Int Rev Exp Pathol 1974, **13:** 161–221.

22 Schmid KW, Hittmair A, Ladurner D, Sandbichler P, Gasser R, Tötsch M. Chromogranin A and B in parathyroid tissue of cases of primary hyperparathyroidism. An immunohistochemical study. Virchows Arch [A] 1991, **418:** 295–299.

Normal physiology

23 Akerström G, Rastad J, Ljunghall S, Ridefelt P, Juhlin C, Gylfe E. Cellular physiology and pathophysiology of the parathyroid glands. World J Surg 1991, **15:** 672–680.

24 Bilezikian JP, Marcus R, Levine MA. The parathyroids: basic and clinical concepts, ed. 2. San Diego, 2001, Academic Press.

25 Habener JF, Rosenblatt M, Potts JT Jr. Parathyroid hormones. Biochemical aspects of biosynthesis, secretion, action, and metabolism. Physiol Rev 1984, **64:** 985–1053.

26 LiVolsi VA, DeLellis RA (eds). Pathobiology of the parathyroid and thyroid glands. Baltimore, 1993, Williams & Wilkins.

27 Martin KJ, Hruska KA, Freitag JJ, Klahr S, Slatopolsky E: The peripheral metabolism of parathyroid hormone. N Engl J Med 1979, **301:** 1092–1098.

28 Marx SJ. Hyperparathyroid and hypoparathyroid disorders. N Engl J Med 2000, **343:** 1863–1875.

29 Rosenblatt M, Kronenberg HM, Potts JT Jr. Parathyroid hormone. Physiology, chemistry, biosynthesis, secretion, metabolism and mode of action. In DeGroot LJ (ed.): Endocrinology, vol. 2, ed. 2. Philadelphia, 1989, W.B. Saunders.

30 Roth SI, Raisz LG. The course and reversibility of the calcium effect on the ultrastructure of the rat parathyroid gland in organ culture. Lab Invest 1966, **15:** 1187–1211.

Adenoma

Generalities and gross features

31 Attie JN, Auguste LJ. Multiple parathyroid adenomas: Report of thirty-three cases. Surgery 1990, **108:** 1014–1019.

32 Liechty RD, Teter A, Suba EJ. The tiny parathyroid adenoma. Surgery 1986, **100:** 1048–1052.

33 Nolan RB, Hayles AB, Woolner LB. Adenoma of the parathyroid gland in children. Report of case and brief review of the literature. Am J Dis Child 1960, **99:** 622–627.

34 Norris EH. Parathyroid adenoma. Study of 322 cases. Int Abstr Surg 1947, **84:** 1–41. In Surg Gynecol Obstet, Jan. 1947.

34a Pitsilos SA, Weber R, Baloch Z, LiVolsi A. Ectopic parathyroid adenoma initially suspected to be a thyroid lesion. Arch Pathol Lab Med 2002, **126:** 1541.

35 Schachner SH, Hall A. Parathyroid adenoma and previous head-and-neck irradiation. Ann Intern Med 1978, **88:** 804.

36 Sloane JA, Moody HC. Parathyroid adenoma in submucosa of esophagus. Arch Pathol Lab Med 1978, **102:** 242–243.

37 Verdonk CA, Edis AJ. Parathyroid "double adenomas. " Fact or fiction? Surgery 1981, **90:** 523–526.

38 Woolner LB, Keating FR Jr, Black BM. Tumors and hyperplasia of the parathyroid glands. A review of the pathological findings in 140 cases of primary hyperparathyroidism. Cancer 1952, **5:** 1069–1088.

Microscopic features

39 Carney JA. Pathology of hyperparathyroidism: A practical approach. Monogr Pathol 1993, **35:** 34–62.

40 Ho K-J. Papillary parathyroid adenoma: A rare occurrence and its importance in differentiation from papillary carcinoma of the thyroid. Arch Pathol Lab Med 1996, **120:** 883–884.

41 Lam K-Y, Chan AC-L, Lo C-Y. Parathyroid adenomas with pronounced lymphocytic infiltration: No evidence of autoimmune pathogenesis. Endocrine Pathol 2000, **11:** 77–84.

42 Lawton TJ, Feldman M, LiVolsi V. Lymphocytic infiltrates in solitary parathyroid adenomas. Int J Surg Pathol 1998, **6:** 5–10.

43 Leedham PW, Pollock DJ. Intrafollicular amyloid in primary hyperparathyroidism. J Clin Pathol 1970, **23:** 811–818.

44 Veress B, Nordenstrom J. Lymphocytic infiltration and

destruction of parathyroid adenomas. A possible tumour-specific autoimmune reaction in two cases of primary hyperparathyroidism. Case reports. Histopathology 1994, **25:** 373–378.

Electron microscopic features

45 Faccini JM. The ultrastructure of parathyroid glands removed from patients with primary hyperparathyroidism. A report of 40 cases, including four carcinomata. J Pathol 1970, **102:** 189–199.

Histochemical and immunohistochemical features

46 Bostwick DG, Null WE, Holmes D, Weber E, Barchas JD, Bensch KG. Expression of opioid peptides in tumors. N Engl J Med 1987, **317:** 1439–1443.

47 Miettinen M, Clark R, Lehto V-P, Virtanen I, Damjanov I. Intermediate-filament proteins in parathyroid glands and parathyroid adenomas. Arch Pathol Lab Med 1985, **109:** 986–989.

48 Tomita T. Immunocytochemical staining patterns for parathyroid hormone and chromogranin in parathyroid hyperplasia, adenoma and carcinoma. Endocr Pathol 1999, **10:** 145–156.

49 Weber CJ, Marangos PJ, Richardson S, LoGerfo P, Hardy MA, Feind C, Reemtsma K. Presence of neuron-specific enolase and somatostatin in human parathyroid tissues. Surgery 1985, **98:** 1008–1012.

50 Weiler R, Fischer-Colbrie R, Schmid KW, Feichtinger H, Bussolati G, Grimelius L, Krisch K, Kerl H, O'Connor D, Winkler H. Immunological studies on the occurrence and properties of chromogranin A and B and secretogranin II in endocrine tumors. Am J Surg Pathol 1988, **12:** 877–884.

Molecular genetic features

51 DeLellis RA, Tischler AS. Clonality of endocrine proliferative lesions: a critical reappraisal. Endocr Pathol 1998, **9:** 281–286.

52 Heppner C, Kester MB, Agarwal SK, Debelenko LV, Emmert-Buck MR, Guru SC, Manickam P, Olufemi SE, Skarulis MC, Doppman JL, Alexander RH, Kim YS, Saggar SK, Lubensky IA, Zhuang Z, Liotta LA, Chandrasekharappa SC, Collins FS, Spiegel AM, Burns AL, Marx SJ. Somatic mutation of the MEN1 gene in parathyroid tumors. Nat Genet 1997, **16:** 375–378.

53 Kakudo K, Shan L. Recent advances in the molecular pathology of hyperparathyroidism. Endocr Pathol 1999, **10:** 3–14.

54 Kishikawa S, Shan L, Ogihara K, Utsunomiya H, Nakamura M, Nakamura Y, Naito A, Kakudo K. Overexpression and genetic abnormality of p53 in parathyroid adenomas. Pathol Int 1999, **49:** 853–857.

55 Koshiishi N, Chong JM, Fukasawa T, Ikeno R, Tanaka A, Kanazawa K, Ogura M, Ebuchi M, Takizawa T, Funata N, Fukuyama M. Microsatellite instability and loss of heterozygosity in primary and secondary proliferative lesions of the parathyroid gland. Lab Invest 1999, **79:** 1051–1058.

56 Sanjuan X, Bryant BR, Sobel ME, Merino MJ. Clonality analysis of benign parathyroid lesions by human androgen receptor (HUMARA) gene assay. Endocr Pathol 1998, **9:** 293–300.

57 Shan L, Nakamura M, Nakamura Y, Inoue D, Morimoto S, Yokoi T, Kakudo K. Comparative analysis of clonality and pathology in primary and secondary hyperparathyroidism. Virchows Arch 1997, **430:** 247–252.

58 Shan L, Nakamura M, Nakamura Y, Yokoi T, Tsujimoto M, Arima R, Kameya T, Kakudo K. Somatic mutations of multiple endocrine neoplasia type 1 gene in the sporadic endocrine tumors. Lab Invest 1998, **78:** 471–475.

59 Shan L, Yang Q, Nakamura Y, Nakamura M, Miyauchi A, Tsujimoto M, Nakatani Y, Wakasa K, Mori I, Kakudo K. Frequent loss of heterozygosity at 1p36.3 and p73 abnormality in parathyroid adenomas. Mod Pathol 2001, **14:** 273–278.

59a Stojadinovic A, Hoos A, Nissan A, Dudas M, Cordon-Cardo C, Shaha A, Brennan M, Singh B, Ghossein R. Parathyroid

neoplasms: clinical, histopathological, and tissue microarray-based molecular analysis. Hum Pathol 2003, **34:** 54–64.

Adenoma variants

60 Baloch ZW, LiVolsi VA. Oncocytic lesions of the neuroendocrine system. Semin Diagn Pathol 1999, **16:** 190–199.

61 Bedetti CD, Dekker A, Watson CG. Functioning oxyphil cell adenoma of the parathyroid gland. A clinicopathologic study of ten patients with hyperparathyroidism. Hum Pathol 1984, **15:** 1121–1126.

62 Daroca PJ Jr, Landau RL, Reed RJ, Kappelman MD. Functioning lipoadenoma of the parathyroid gland. Arch Pathol Lab Med 1977, **101:** 28–30.

63 Ducatman BS, Wilkerson SY, Brown JA. Functioning parathyroid lipoadenoma. Report of a case diagnosed by intraoperative touch preparations. Arch Pathol Lab Med 1986, **110:** 645–647.

64 Legolvan DP, Moore BP, Nishiyama RH. Parathyroid hamartoma. Report of two cases and review of the literature. Am J Clin Pathol 1977, **67:** 31–35.

65 Ordoñez NG, Ibañez ML, Mackay B, Samaan NA, Hickey RC. Functioning oxyphil cell adenomas of parathyroid gland. Immunoperoxidase evidence of hormonal activity in oxyphil cells. Am J Clin Pathol 1982, **78:** 681–689.

66 Poole GV, Albertson DA, Marshall RB, Myers RT. Oxyphil cell adenoma and hyperparathyroidism. Surgery 1982, **92:** 799–805.

67 Straus FH II, Kaplan EL, Nishiyama RH, Bigos ST. Five cases of parathyroid lipohyperplasia. Surgery 1983, **94:** 901–905.

68 Weiland LH, Garrison RC, ReMine WH, Scholz DA. Lipoadenoma of the parathyroid gland. Am J Surg Pathol 1978, **2:** 3–7.

69 Woolpert HR, Vickery AL Jr, Wang C-A. Functioning oxyphil cell adenomas of the parathyroid gland. A study of 15 cases. Am J Surg Pathol 1989, **13:** 500–504.

Chief cell hyperplasia

70 Adams PH, Chalmers TM, Peters N, Rack JH, Truscott B McN. Primary chief cell hyperplasia of the parathyroid glands. Ann Intern Med 1965, **63:** 454–467.

71 Black WC III. Correlative light and electron microscopy in primary hyperparathyroidism. Arch Pathol 1969, **88:** 225–241.

72 Black WC III, Haff RC. The surgical pathology of parathyroid chief cell hyperplasia. Am J Clin Pathol 1970, **53:** 565–579.

73 Black WC III, Utley JR. The differential diagnosis of parathyroid adenoma and chief cell hyperplasia. Am J Clin Pathol 1968, **49:** 761–775.

74 Bondeson A-G, Bondeson L, Ljungberg O. Chronic parathyroiditis associated with parathyroid hyperplasia and hyperparathyroidism. Am J Surg Pathol 1984, **8:** 211–215.

75 Bonjer HJ, Bruining HA, Birkenhager JC, Nishiyama RH, Jones MA, Bagwell CB. Single and multigland disease in the primary hyperparathyroidism. Clinical follow-up, histopathology, and flow cytometric DNA analysis. World J Surg 1992, **16:** 737–743.

76 Bowlby LS, DeBault LE, Abraham SR. Flow cytometric DNA analysis of parathyroid glands. Relationship between nuclear DNA and pathologic classifications. Am J Pathol 1987, **128:** 338–344.

77 Carney JA, Roth SI, Heath H III, Sizemore GW, Hayles AB. The parathyroid glands in multiple endocrine neoplasia type 2b. Am J Pathol 1980, **99:** 387–398.

78 Castleman B, Schantz A, Roth SI. Parathyroid hyperplasia in primary hyperparathyroidism. A review of 85 cases. Cancer 1976, **38:** 1668–1675.

79 Fitko R, Roth SI, Hines JR, Rose DM, Cahill E. Parathyromatosis in hyperparathyroidism. Hum Pathol 1990, **21:** 234–237.

80 Grimelius L, Johansson H. Parathyroid histopathology. Endocr Pathol 1996, **7:** 165–172.

81 Harach HR, Jasani B. Parathyroid hyperplasia in multiple

endocrine neoplasia type 1. A pathological and immunohistochemical reappraisal. Histopathology 1992, **20:** 305–313.

82 Loda M, Lipman J, Cukor B, Bur M, Kwan P, De Lellis RA. Nodular foci in parathyroid adenomas and hyperplasias. An immunohistochemical analysis of proliferative activity. Hum Pathol 1994, **25:** 1050–1056.

83 Roth SI. Pathology of the parathyroids in hyperparathyroidism. Arch Pathol 1962, **73:** 495–510.

84 Roth SI, Marshall RB. Pathology and ultrastructure of the human parathyroid glands in chronic renal failure. Arch Intern Med 1969, **124:** 397–407.

85 Sonnenschein C, Soto AM. The society of cells: cancer and control of cell proliferation. Oxford, 1999, Bios Scientific Publishers; New York, 1999, Springer-Verlag.

86 Tominaga Y, Grimelius L, Johansson H, Rudberg C, Johansson H, Ljunghall S, Bergström R, Rastad J, Akerström G. Histological and clinical features of non-familial primary parathyroid hyperplasia. Pathol Res Pract 1992, **188:** 115–122.

Water-clear cell hyperplasia

87 Castleman B, Schantz A, Roth SI. Parathyroid hyperplasia in primary hyperparathyroidism. A review of 85 cases. Cancer 1976, **38:** 1668–1675.

88 Dorado AE, Hensley G, Castleman B. Water clear cell hyperplasia of parathyroid. Autopsy report of a case with supernumerary glands. Cancer 1976, **38:** 1676–1683.

89 Kuhel WI, Gonzales D, Hoda SA, Pan L, Chiu A, Giri D, DeLellis RA. Synchronous water-clear cell double parathyroid adenomas: a hitherto uncharacterized entity? Arch Pathol Lab Med 2001, **125:** 256–259.

90 Roth SI. The ultrastructure of primary water-clear cell hyperplasia of the parathyroid glands. Am J Pathol 1970, **61:** 233–240.

91 Tominaga Y, Grimelius L, Johansson H, Rudberg C, Johansson H, Ljunghall S, Bergstrom R, Rastad J, Akerström G. Histological and clinical features of non-familial primary parathyroid hyperplasia. Pathol Res Pract 1992, **188:** 115–122.

Carcinoma

92 Aldinger KA, Hickey RC, Ibanez ML, Samaan NA. Parathyroid carcinoma. A clinical study of seven cases of functioning and two cases of nonfunctioning parathyroid cancer. Cancer 1982, **49:** 388–397.

93 Baba H, Kishihara M, Tohmon M, Fukase M, Kizaki T, Okada S, Matsuzuka F, Kobayashi A, Kuma K, Fujita T. Identification of parathyroid hormone messenger ribonucleic acid in an apparently nonfunctioning parathyroid carcinoma transformed from a parathyroid carcinoma with hyperparathyroidism. J Clin Endocrinol Metab 1986, **62:** 247–252.

94 Bondeson L, Sandelin K, Grimelius L. Histopathological variables and DNA cytometry in parathyroid carcinoma. Am J Surg Pathol 1993, **17:** 820–829.

95 Boquist LL. Nucleolar organizer regions in normal, hyperplastic and neoplastic parathyroid glands. Virchows Arch [A] 1990, **417:** 237–241.

96 Cohn K, Silverman M, Corrado J, Sedgewick C. Parathyroid carcinoma. The Lahey Clinic experience. Surgery 1985, **98:** 1095–1100.

97 Cryns VL, Thor A, Xu HJ, Hu SX, Wierman ME, Vickery AL Jr, Benedict WF, Arnold A. Loss of the retinoblastoma tumor-suppressor gene in parathyroid carcinoma. N Engl J Med 1994, **330:** 757–761.

98 Dinnen JS, Greenwood RH, Jones JH, Walker DA, Williams ED. Parathyroid carcinoma in familial hyperparathyroidism. J Clin Pathol 1977, **30:** 966–975.

99 Erickson LA, Jin L, Papotti M, Lloyd RV. Oxyphil parathyroid

carcinomas: a clinicopathologic and immunohistochemical study of 10 cases. Am J Surg Pathol 2002, **26:** 344–349.

100 Erickson LA, Jin L, Wollan P, Thompson GB, van Heerden JA, Lloyd RV. Parathyroid hyperplasia, adenomas, and carcinomas: differential expression of p27Kip1 protein. Am J Surg Pathol 1999, **23:** 288–295.

101 Evans HL. Criteria for diagnosis of parathyroid carcinoma. A critical study. Surg Pathol 1991, **4:** 244–265.

102 Haghighi P, Astarita RW, Wepsic T, Wolf PL. Concurrent primary parathyroid hyperplasia and parathyroid carcinoma. Arch Pathol Lab Med 1983, **107:** 349–350.

103 Harlow S, Roth SI, Bauer K, Marshall RB. Flow cytometric DNA analysis of normal and parathyroid glands. Mod Pathol 1991, **4:** 310–315.

104 Holmes EC, Morton DL, Ketcham AS. Parathyroid carcinoma. A collective review. Ann Surg 1969, **169:** 631–640.

105 Howard S, Anderson C, Diels W, Gerres K, Garcia B. Nuclear DNA density of parathyroid lesions. Pathol Res Pract 1992, **188:** 497–499.

106 Hundahl SA, Fleming ID, Fremgen AM, Menck HR. Two hundred eighty-six cases of parathyroid carcinoma treated in the U.S. between 1985-1995: a National Cancer Data Base report. The American College of Surgeons Commission on Cancer and the American Cancer Society. Cancer 1999, **86:** 538–544.

107 Kanematsu E, Matsui H, Deguchi T, Yamamoto O, Korematsu M, Kobayashi A, Nezasa SI, Yamamoto N, Takeuchi T, Tanaka T, Kawada Y. Significance of AgNOR counts for distinguishing carcinoma from adenoma and hyperplasia in parathyroid gland. Hum Pathol 1997, **28:** 421–427.

108 Kytola S, Farnebo F, Obara T, Isola J, Grimelius L, Farnebo LO, Sandelin K, Larsson C. Patterns of chromosomal imbalances in parathyroid carcinomas. Am J Pathol 2000, **157:** 579–586.

109 Mallette L. DNA quantitation in the study of parathyroid lesions. A review. Am J Clin Pathol 1992, **98:** 305–311.

110 Obara T, Fujimoto Y, Hirayama A, Kanaji Y, Ito Y, Kodama T, Agata T. Flow cytometric DNA analysis of parathyroid tumors with special reference to its diagnostic and prognostic value in parathyroid carcinoma. Cancer 1990, **65:** 1789–1793.

111 Obara T, Fujimoto Y, Yamaguchi K, Takanashi R, Kino I, Sasaki Y. Parathyroid carcinoma of the oxyphil cell type. A report of two cases, light and electron microscopic study. Cancer 1985, **55:** 1482–1489.

112 Ordóñez NG, Ibañez ML, Samaan NA, Hickey RC. Immunoperoxidase study of uncommon parathyroid tumors. Report of two cases of nonfunctioning parathyroid carcinoma and one intrathyroid parathyroid tumor-producing amyloid. Am J Surg Pathol 1983, **7:** 535–542.

113 Palnaes Hansen C, Lau Pedersen M, Christensen L. Diagnosis, treatment and outcome of parathyroid cancer. A report of eight patients. Eur J Surg 1991, **157:** 517–520.

114 Schantz A, Castleman B. Parathyroid carcinoma. Cancer 1973, **31:** 600–605.

115 Shane E, Bilezikian JP. Parathyroid carcinoma. A review of 62 patients. Endocr Rev 1982, **3:** 218–226.

115a Shattuck TM, Välimäki S, Obara T, Gaz RD, Clark OH, Shoback D, Wierman ME, Tojo K, Robbins CM, Carpten JD, Farnebo L-O, Larsson C, Arnold A. Somatic and germ-line mutations of the HRPT2 gene in sporadic parathyroid carcinoma. N Engl J Med 2003, **349:** 1722–1729.

116 Shortell CK, Andrus CH, Philips CE Jr, Schwartz SI. Carcinoma of the parathyroid gland. A 30-year experience. Surgery 1991, **110:** 704–708.

117 Smith JF, Coombs RRH. Histological diagnosis of carcinoma of the parathyroid gland. J Clin Pathol 1984, **37:** 1370–1378.

118 Snover DC, Foucar K. Mitotic activity in benign parathyroid disease. Am J Clin Pathol 1981, **75:** 345–347.

119 Streeten EA, Weinstein LS, Norton JA, Mulvihill JJ, White BJ,

Friedman EM, Jaffe G, Brandi ML, Stewart K, Zimering MB. Studies in a kindred with parathyroid carcinoma. J Clin Endocrinol Metab 1992, **75**: 362–366.

120 Szijan I, Orlow I, Dalamon V, Vergani P, Danilowicz K, Mezzadri N, Cordon-Cardo C, Bruno OD. Alterations in the retinoblastoma pathway of cell cycle control in parathyroid tumors. Oncol Rep 2000, **7**: 421–425.

121 Tuccari G, Abbona GC, Giuffre G, Papotti M, Gasparri G, Barresi G, Bussolati G. AgNOR quantity as a prognostic tool in hyperplastic and neoplastic parathyroid glands. Virchows Archiv 2000, **437**: 298–303.

122 Van Heerden JA, Weiland LH, ReMine H, Walls JT, Purnell DC. Cancer of the parathyroid glands. Arch Surg 1979, **114**: 475–480.

123 Vargas MP, Vargas HI, Kleiner DE, Merino MJ. The role of prognostic markers (MiB-1, RB, and bcl-2) in the diagnosis of parathyroid tumors. Mod Pathol 1997, **10**: 12–17.

124 Vasef MA, Brynes RK, Sturm M, Bromley C, Robinson RA. Expression of cyclin D1 in parathyroid carcinomas, adenomas and hyperplasias: a paraffin immunohistochemical study. Mod Pathol 1999, **12**: 412–416.

Other lesions

125 Calandra DB, Shah KH, Prinz RA, Sullivan H, Hofmann C, Oslapas R, Ernst K, Lawrence AM, Paloyan E. Parathyroid cysts. A report of eleven cases including two associated with hyperparathyroid crisis. Surgery 1984, **94**: 887–892.

126 Carney JA. Salivary heterotopia, cysts, and parathyroid gland: Branchial pouch derivatives and remnants. Am J Surg Pathol 2000, **24**: 837–845.

127 Ellis HA, Mawhinney WHB. Parathyroid amyloidosis. Arch Pathol Lab Med 1984, **108**: 689–690.

128 Merino MJ, Chuaqui R, Fernandez P. Parathyroid hemangioma: a report of two cases. Endocr Pathol 1996, **7**: 319–322.

129 Rogers LA, Fetter BF, Peete WPJ. Parathyroid cyst and cystic degeneration of parathyroid adenoma. Arch Pathol 1969, **88**: 476–479.

130 Shields TW, Immerman SC. Mediastinal parathyroid cysts revisited. Ann Thorac Surg 1999, **67**: 581–590.

131 Silverman JF, Khazanie PG, Norris HT, Fore WW. Parathyroid hormone (PTH) assay of parathyroid cysts examined by fine-needle aspiration biopsy. Am J Clin Pathol 1986, **86**: 776–780.

131a Tang W, Kakudo K, Nakamura Y, Nakamura M, Mori I, Morita S, Miyauchi A. Parathyroid gland involvement by papillary carcinoma of the thyroid gland. Arch Pathol Lab Med 2002, **126**: 1511–1514.

132 Yap WM, Chuah KL, Tan PH. Langerhans cell histiocytosis involving the thyroid and parathyroid glands. Mod Pathol 2001, **14**: 111–115.

Hyperparathyroidism

Primary hyperparathyroidism

133 Allo M, Thompson NW. Familial hyperparathyroidism caused by solitary adenomas. Surgery 1982, **92**: 486–490.

134 Ballard HS, Frame B, Hartsock RJ. Familial multiple endocrine adenoma-peptic ulcer complex. Medicine (Baltimore) 1964, **43**: 481–516.

135 Black WC III, Utley JR. The differential diagnosis of parathyroid adenoma and chief cell hyperplasia. Am J Clin Pathol 1968, **49**: 761–775.

136 Brandi ML, Aurbach GD, Fitzpatrick LA, Quarto R, Spiegel AM, Bliziotes MM, Norton JA, Doppman JL, Marx SJ. Parathyroid mitogenic activity in plasma from patients with familial multiple endocrine neoplasia type I. N Engl J Med 1986, **314**: 1287–1293.

137 Cutler RE, Reiss E, Ackerman LV. Familial hyperparathyroidism. A kindred involving eleven cases with a discussion of primary chief cell hyperplasia. N Engl J Med 1964, **270**: 859–865.

138 Ghandur-Mnaymneh L, Kimura N. The parathyroid adenoma. A histopathologic definition with a study of 172 cases of primary hyperparathyroidism. Am J Pathol 1984, **115**: 70–83.

139 Grimelius L, Ejerblad S, Johansson H, Werner I. Parathyroid adenomas and glands in normocalcemic hyperparathyroidism. A light microscopic study. Am J Pathol 1976, **83**: 475–484.

140 Haff RC, Black WC III, Ballinger WF II. Primary hyperparathyroidism. Changing clinical, surgical and pathological aspects. Ann Surg 1970, **171**: 85–92.

141 Hellström J, Ivemark BI. Primary hyperparathyroidism. Clinical and structural findings in 138 cases. Acta Chir Scand 1962, **294**(suppl): 1–113.

142 Kakudo K, Shan L. Recent advances in the molecular pathology of hyperparathyroidism. Endocr Pathol 1999, **10**: 3–14.

143 LiVolsi VA, Feind CR. Parathyroid adenoma and nonmedullary thyroid carcinoma. Cancer 1976, **38**: 1391–1393.

144 MacLeod WAJ, Holloway CK. Hyperparathyroid crisis. A collective review. Ann Surg 1967, **166**: 1012–1015.

145 Marx SJ. Hyperparathyroid and hypoparathyroid disorders. N Engl J Med 2000, **343**: 1863–1875.

146 Netelenbos C, Lips P, Van Der Meer C. Hyperparathyroidism following irradiation of benign diseases of the head and neck. Cancer 1983, **52**: 458–461.

147 Paloyan E, Lawrence AM. The rationale for subtotal parathyroidectomy. In Varco RL, Delaney JP (eds): Controversy in surgery. Philadelphia, 1976, W.B. Saunders.

148 Pyrah LN, Hodgkinson A, Anderson CK. Critical review. Primary hyperparathyroidism. Br J Surg 1966, **53**: 245–316.

149 Rapaport D, Ziv Y, Rubin M, Huminer D, Dintsman M. Primary hyperparathyroidism in children. J Pediatr Surg 1986, **21**: 395–397.

150 Silverberg SJ, Shane E, Jacobs TP, Siris E, Bilezikian JP. A 10-year prospective study of primary hyperparathyroidism with or without parathyroid surgery. N Engl J Med 1999, **341**: 1249–1255.

151 Tisell L-E, Carlsson S, Fjalling M, Hansson G, Lindberg S, Lundberg L-M, Oden A. Hyperparathyroidism subsequent to neck irradiation. Risk factors. Cancer 1985, **56**: 1529–1533.

152 Wills MR. Normocalcaemic primary hyperparathyroidism. Lancet 1971, **1**: 849–853.

153 Winnacker JL, Becker KL, Friedlander M, Higgins GA Jr, Moore CF. Sarcoidosis and hyperparathyroidism. Am J Med 1969, **46**: 305–312.

Secondary hyperparathyroidism

154 Breslau NA. Update on secondary forms of hyperparathyroidism. Am J Med Sci 1987, **294**: 120–131.

155 Bricker NS, Slatopolsky E, Reiss E, Avioli LV. Calcium, phosphorus, and bone in renal disease and transplantation. Arch Intern Med 1969, **123**: 543–553.

156 Essary LR, Wick MR. Cutaneous calciphylaxis: an underrecognized clinicopathologic entity. Am J Clin Pathol 2000, **113**: 280–287.

157 Morgan AD, Maclagan NF. Renal disease in hyperparathyroidism. Am J Pathol 1954, **30**: 1141–1168.

158 Tomita T, Millard DM. C-cell hyperplasia in secondary hyperparathyroidism. Histopathology 1992, **21**: 469–474.

"Tertiary" hyperparathyroidism

159 Abbona C, Papotti M, Gasparri G, Bussolati G. Recurrence in parathyroid hyperplasias owing to secondary hyperparathyroidism is predicted by morphological patterns and proliferative activity values. Endocr Pathol 1996, **7**: 55–62.

160 Banerjee SS, Faragher B, Hasleton PS. Nuclear diameter in parathyroid disease. J Clin Pathol 1983, **36**: 143–148.

161 Black WC III, Slatopolsky E, Elkan I, Hoffsten P. Parathyroid morphology in suppressible and nonsuppressible renal hyperparathyroidism. Lab Invest 1970, **23**: 497–509.

162 Davies DR, Dent CE, Watson L. Tertiary hyperparathyroidism. Br Med J 1968, **3**: 395–399.

163 Harach HR, Jasani B. Parathyroid hyperplasia in tertiary hyperparathyroidism. A pathological and immunohistochemical reappraisal. Histopathology 1992, **21**: 513–519.

164 Johnson JW, Hattner RS, Hampers CL, Bernstein DS, Merrill JP, Sherwood LM. Secondary hyperparathyroidism in chronic renal failure. Effects of renal homotransplantation. JAMA 1971, **215**: 478–480.

165 McIntosh DA, Peterson EW, McPhaul JJ Jr. Autonomy of parathyroid function after renal homotransplantation. Ann Intern Med 1966, **65**: 900–907.

166 Martin LNC, Kayath MJ, Vieira JGH, Nose-Alberti V. Parathyroid glands in uraemic patients with refractory hyperparathyroidism: histopathology and p53 protein expression analysis. Histopathology 1998, **33**: 46–51.

167 Misonou J, Ishikura H, Aizawa M, Ohira S. Functioning oxyphil cell adenoma in a patient with secondary hyperparathyroidism. Acta Pathol Jpn 1987, **37**: 1357–1366.

168 Nagy A, Chudek J, Kovacs G. Accumulation of allelic changes at chromosomes 7p, 18q, and 2 in parathyroid lesions of uremic patients. Lab Invest 2001, **81**: 527–533.

Differential diagnosis

169 Burtis WJ, Brady TG, Orloff JJ, Ersback JB, Warrell RP, Olson BR, Wu TL, Mitnick ME, Broadus AE, Stewart AF. Immunochemical characterization of circulating parathyroid hormone-related protein in patients with humoral hypercalcemia of cancer. N Engl J Med 1990, **322**: 1106–1112.

170 Docherty HM, Ratcliffe WA, Heath DA, Docherty K. Expression of parathyroid hormone-related protein in abnormal human parathyroids. J Endocrinol 1991, **129**: 431–438.

171 Drucker DJ. Parathyroid hormone-like peptide. Endocrinol Pathol 1991, **2**: 4–11.

172 Dufour DR, Marx SJ, Spiegel AM. Parathyroid gland morphology in nonparathyroid hormone-mediated hypercalcemia. Am J Surg Pathol 1985, **9**: 43–51.

173 Falko JM, Maeder MC, Conway C, Mazzaferri EL, Skillman TG. Primary hyperparathyroidism. Analysis of 220 patients with special emphasis on familial hypocalciuric hypercalcemia. Heart Lung 1984, **13**: 124–131.

173a Fukumoto S, Chikatsu N, Okazaki R, Takeuchi Y, Tamura Y, Murakami T, Obara T, Fujita T. Inactivating mutations of calcium-sensing receptor results in parathyroid lipohyperplasia. Diagn Mol Pathol 2001, **10**: 242–247.

174 Gotoh A, Kitazawa S, Mizuno Y, Takenaka A, Arakawa S, Matsumoto O, Kitazawa R, Fujimori T, Maeda S, Kamidono S. Common expression of parathyroid hormone-related protein and no correlation of calcium level in renal cell carcinomas. Cancer 1993, **71**: 2803–2806.

175 Kitazawa S, Fukase M, Kitazawa R, Takenaka A, Gotoh A, Fujita T, Maeda S. Immunohistologic evaluation of parathyroid hormone-related protein in human lung cancer and normal tissue with newly developed monoclonal antibody. Cancer 1991, **67**: 984–989.

176 Lafferty FW. Pseudohyperparathyroidism. Medicine (Baltimore) 1966, **45**: 247–260.

177 Marx SJ, Spiegel AM, Levine MA, Rizzoli RE, Lasker RD, Santora AC, Downs RW Jr, Aurbach GD. Familial hypocalciuric hypercalcemia. The relation to primary parathyroid hyperplasia. N Engl J Med 1982, **307**: 416–426.

178 Matsushita H, Hara M, Nakazawa H, Shishiba Y, Matuhasi T. The presence of immunoreactive parathyroid hormone-related protein in parathyroid adenoma cells. Acta Pathol Jpn 1992, **42**: 35–41.

179 Matsushita H, Usui M, Hara M, Shishiba Y, Nakazawa H, Honda K, Torigoe K, Kohno K, Kurimoto M. Co-secretion of parathyroid hormone and parathyroid-hormone-related protein via a regulated pathway in human parathyroid adenoma cells. Am J Pathol 1997, **150**: 861–871.

180 Miraliakbari B, Asa S, Boudreau S. Parathyroid hormone-like peptide in pancreatic endocrine carcinoma and adenocarcinoma associated with hypercalcemia. Hum Pathol 1992, **23**: 884–887.

181 Mundy GR. Pathophysiology of cancer-associated hypercalcemia. Semin Oncol 1990, **17**: 10–15.

182 Rankin W, Grill V, Martin TJ. Parathyroid hormone-related protein and hypercalcemia. Cancer 1997, **80**: 1564–1571.

183 Roskams R, Desmet V. Parathyroid-hormone-related peptides. A new class of multifunctional proteins. Am J Surg Pathol 1997, **150**: 779–785.

184 Roskams T, Campos R, Drucker D, Desmet V. Reactive human bile ductules express parathyroid hormone-related peptide. Histopathology 1993, **23**: 11–20.

185 Rosol T, Capen C. Mechanisms of cancer-induced hypercalcemia. Lab Invest 1992, **67**: 680–702.

186 Sharp CF Jr, Rude RK, Terry R, Singer FR. Abnormal bone and parathyroid histology in carcinoma patients with pseudohyperparathyroidism. Cancer 1982, **49**: 1449–1455.

187 Singer FR. Pathogenesis of hypercalcemia of malignancy. Semin Oncol 1991, **18**: 4–10.

188 Strewler GJ. The physiology of parathyroid hormone-related protein. N Engl J Med 2000, **342**: 177–185.

189 Thorgeirsson U, Costa J, Marx SJ. The parathyroid glands in familial hypocalciuric hypercalcemia. Hum Pathol 1981, **12**: 229–237.

190 Weir EC, Brines ML, Ikeda K, Burtis WJ, Broadus AE, Robbins RJ. Parathyroid hormone-related peptide gene is expressed in the mammalian central nervous system. Proc Natl Acad Sci USA 1990, **87**: 108–112.

Therapy

191 Attie JN, Wise L, Mir R, Ackerman LV. The rationale against routine subtotal parathyroidectomy for primary hyperparathyroidism. Am J Surg 1978, **136**: 437–444.

192 Badder EM, Graham WP III, Harrison TS. Functional insignificance of microscopic parathyroid hyperplasia. Surg Gynecol Obstet 1977, **145**: 863–868.

193 Bricker NS, Slatopolsky E, Reiss E, Avioli LV. Calcium, phosphorus, and bone in renal disease and transplantation. Arch Intern Med 1969, **123**: 543–553.

194 Clark OH, Okerlund MD, Moss AA, Stark D, Norman D, Newton TH, Duh QY, Arnaud CD, Harris S, Gooding GAW. Localization studies in patients with persistent or recurrent hyperparathyroidism. Surgery 1985, **98**: 1083–1094.

195 Cohn K, Silverman M, Corrado J, Sedgewick C. Parathyroid carcinoma. The Lahey Clinic experience. Surgery 1985, **98**: 1095–1100.

196 Cooke TJC, Boey JH, Sweeney EC, Gilbert JM, Taylor S. Parathyroidectomy. Extent of resection and late results. Br J Surg 1977, **64**: 153–157.

197 Corlew DS, Bryda SL, Bradley EL, DiGirolamo M. Observations on the course of untreated primary hyperparathyroidism. Surgery 1985, **98**: 1064–1071.

198 Edis AJ, Beahrs OH, van Heerden JA, Akwari OE. "Conservative" versus "liberal" approach to parathyroid neck exploration. Surgery 1977, **82**: 466–473.

199 Ellis HA. Fate of long-term parathyroid autografts in patients with chronic renal failure treated by parathyroidectomy. A histopathological study of autografts, parathyroid glands and bone. Histopathology 1988, **13**: 289–310.

200 Flye MW, Brennan MF. Surgical resection of metastatic parathyroid carcinoma. Ann Surg 1981, **193**: 429–435.

201 Gaz RD, Wang C. Management of asymptomatic hyperparathyroidism. Am J Surg 1984, **147**: 124–131.

202 Goldsmith RS, Furszyfer J, Johnson WJ, Fournier AE, Arnaud CD. Control of secondary hyperparathyroidism during long-term hemodialysis. Am J Med 1971, **50**: 692–699.

203 Goodman ML, Egdahl RH, Kemp A, Carey LC.

Hyperparathyroidism from intrathyroid parathyroid adenomas. Arch Pathol 1969, **87:** 418–422.

204 Graham JJ, Harding PE, Hoare LL, Thomas DW, Wise PH. Asymptomatic hyperparathyroidism. An assessment of operative intervention. Br J Surg 1980, **67:** 115–118.

205 Herrera M, Grant C, van Heerden JA, Fitzpatrick LA. Parathyroid autotransplantation. Arch Surg 1992, **127:** 825–829.

206 Holmes EC, Morton DL, Ketcham AS. Parathyroid carcinoma. A collective review. Ann Surg 1969, **169:** 631–640.

207 Kaplan EL, Yashiro T, Salti G. Primary hyperthyroidism in the 1990s. Choice of surgical procedures for this disease. Ann Surg 1992, **215:** 300–317.

208 Liechty RD, Weil R III. Parathyroid anatomy in hyperplasia. Arch Surg 1992, **127:** 813–815.

209 Morioka WT. Trends in primary hyperparathyroidism surgery. Laryngoscope 1992, **102:** 422–425.

210 Nathaniels EK, Nathaniels AM, Wang C. Mediastinal parathyroid tumors. A clinical and pathological study of 84 cases. Ann Surg 1970, **171:** 165–170.

211 Paloyan E, Lawrence AM. The rationale for subtotal parathyroidectomy. In Varco RL, Delaney JP (eds): Controversy in surgery. Philadelphia, 1976, WB Saunders.

212 Proye CA, Carnaille B, Bizard JP, Quievreux JL, Lecomte-Houcke M. Multiglandular disease in seemingly sporadic primary hyperparathyroidism revisited: Where are we in the early 1990s? A plea against unilateral parathyroid exploration. Surgery 1992, **112:** 1118–1122.

213 Roth SI, Wang C, Potts JT Jr. The team approach to primary hyperparathyroidism. Hum Pathol 1975, **6:** 645–648.

214 Rudberg C, Akerström G, Palmér M, Ljunghall S, Adami HO, Johansson H, Grimelius L, Thorén L, Bergström R. Late results of operation for primary hyperparathyroidism in 441 patients. Surgery 1986, **99:** 643–651.

215 Russell CF, Edis AJ, Scholz DA, Sheedy PF, van Heerden JA. Mediastinal parathyroid tumors. Experience with 38 tumors requiring mediastinotomy for removal. Ann Surg 1981, **193:** 805–809.

216 Russell CF, Grant CS, van Heerden JA. Hyperfunctioning supernumerary parathyroid glands. An occasional cause of hyperparathyroidism. Mayo Clin Proc 1982, **57:** 121–124.

217 Sawasy J, Medelsohn F, Sirota RL, Taxy JB. The intrathyroidal hyperfunctioning parathyroid gland. Mod Pathol 1989, **2:** 652–657.

218 Saxe A. Parathyroid transplantation. A review. Surgery 1984, **95:** 507–526.

219 Schlinkert RT, Whitaker MD, Argueta R. Resection of select mediastinal parathyroid adenomas through an anterior mediastinotomy. Mayo Clin Proc 1991, **66:** 1110–1113.

220 Scholz DA, Purnell DC. Asymptomatic primary hyperparathyroidism. 10-year prospective study. Mayo Clin Proc 1981, **56:** 473–478.

221 Shaha AR, Shah JP. Parathyroid carcinoma: a diagnostic and therapeutic challenge. Cancer 1999, **86:** 378–380.

222 Silverberg SJ, Shane E, Jacobs TP, Siris E, Bilezikian JP. A 10-year prospective study of primary hyperparathyroidism with or without parathyroid surgery. N Engl J Med 1999, **341:** 1249–1255.

223 Tanaka Y, Seo H, Tominga Y, Funahashi H, Matsui N, Takagi H. Factors related to the recurrent hyperfunction of autografts after total parathyroidectomy in patients with severe secondary hyperparathyroidism. Surg Today 1993, **23:** 220–227.

224 Tibblin S, Bondeson A-G, Bondeson L, Ljungberg O. Surgical strategy in hyperparathyroidism due to solitary adenoma. Ann Surg 1984, **200:** 776–784.

225 Wang C. Parathyroid re-exploration. A clinical and pathological study of 112 cases. Ann Surg 1977, **186:** 140–145.

226 Wang C. Surgical management of primary hyperparathyroidism. Curr Probl Surg 1985, **22:** 1–50.

227 Wang C, Castleman B, Cope O. Surgical management of hyperparathyroidism due to primary hyperplasia. A clinical and pathologic study of 104 cases. Ann Surg 1982, **195:** 384–392.

228 Wang C, Gaz RD. Natural history of parathyroid carcinoma. Diagnosis, treatment, and results. Am J Surg 1985, **149:** 522–527.

Frozen section

229 Akerström G, Rudberg C, Grimelius L, Bergstrom R, Johansson H, Ljunghall S, Rastad J. Histologic parathyroid abnormalities in an autopsy series. Hum Pathol 1986, **17:** 520–527.

230 Allen TB, Thorburn KM. The oxyphil cell in abnormal parathyroid glands. A study of 114 cases. Arch Pathol Lab Med 1981, **105:** 421–427.

231 Bondeson A-G, Bondeson L, Ljungberg O, Tibblin S. Fat staining in parathyroid disease. Diagnostic value and impact on surgical strategy. Clinicopathologic analysis of 191 cases. Hum Pathol 1985, **16:** 1255–1263.

232 Clarke MR, Hoover WW, Carty SE, Dekker A, Worsey MJ, Barnes EL, Watson CG. Atypical fat staining patterns in hyperparathyroidism. Int J Surg Pathol 1996, **3:** 163–168.

233 Dekker A, Watson CG, Barnes EL Jr. The pathologic assessment of primary hyperparathyroidism and its impact on therapy. A prospective evaluation of 50 cases with oil-red-O stain. Ann Surg 1979, **190:** 671–675.

234 Dufour DR, Durkowski C. Sudan IV stain. Its limitations in evaluating parathyroid functional status. Arch Pathol Lab Med 1982, **106:** 224–227.

235 Dufour DR, Wilkerson SY. The normal parathyroid revisited. Percentage of stromal fat. Hum Pathol 1982, **13:** 717–721.

236 Geelhoed GW, Silverberg SG. Intraoperative imprints for the identification of parathyroid tissue. Surgery 1984, **96:** 1124–1130.

237 Ghandur-Mnaymneh L, Cassady J, Hajianpour MA, Paz J, Reiss E. The parathyroid gland in health and disease. Am J Pathol 1986, **125:** 292–299.

238 Grimelius L, Johansson H. Parathyroid histopathology. Endocr Pathol 1996, **7:** 165–172.

239 Grimelius L, Akerström G, Johansson H, Lundqvist H. Estimation of parenchymal cell content of human parathyroid glands using the image analyzing computer technique. Am J Pathol 1978, **93:** 793–800.

240 Grimelius L, Akerström G, Bodeson L, Juhlin C, Johansson H, Ljunghall S, Rastad J. The role of the pathologist in diagnosis and surgical decision making in hyperparathyroidism. World J Surg 1991, **15:** 698–705.

241 Li Volsi VA, Hamilton R. Intraoperative assessment of parathyroid gland pathology. A common view from the surgeon and the pathologist. Am J Clin Pathol 1994, **102:** 365–373.

242 Saffos RO, Rhatigan RM, Urgulu S. The normal parathyroid and the borderline with early hyperplasia. A light microscopic study. Histopathology 1984, **8:** 407–422.

243 Sasano H, Geelhoed GW, Silverberg SG. Intraoperative cytologic evaluation of lipid in the diagnosis of parathyroid adenoma. Am J Surg Pathol 1988, **12:** 282–286.

244 Saxe AW, Baier R, Tesluk H, Toreson W. The role of the pathologist in the surgical treatment of hyperparathyroidism. Surg Gynecol Obstet 1985, **161:** 101–105.

244a Shidham V, Asma Z, Rao N, Chavan A, Machhi J, Almagro U, Komorowski R. Intraoperative cytology increases the diagnostic accuracy of frozen sections for the confirmation of various tissues in the parathyroid region. Am J Clin Pathol 2002, **118:** 895–902.

245 Silverberg SG. Imprints in the intraoperative evaluation of parathyroid disease. Arch Pathol 1975, **99:** 375–378.

246 Westra WH, Pritchett DD, Udelsman R. Intraoperative confirmation of parathyroid tissue during parathyroid exploration: a retrospective evaluation of the frozen section. Am J Surg Pathol 1998, **22:** 538–544.

11 Gastrointestinal tract

Esophagus
Small bowel
Large bowel
Stomach
Appendix
Anus

Esophagus

Normal anatomy

The esophagus is a muscular tubular structure that measures approximately 25 cm in adult individuals and extends from the cricopharyngeal muscle, which forms the upper esophageal sphincter (at the level of the sixth cervical vertebra, about 15 to 18 cm from the incisors), to the lower esophageal sphincter, which forms the gastroesophageal junction (several centimeters below the diaphragm). The lower esophageal sphincter is usually described as being 40 cm from the incisors, but this is subject to considerable individual variation.

The esophagus is lined by a mucosa of nonkeratinized stratified squamous epithelial type. The basal layer is one to four cells thick and does not exceed 15% of the total epithelial thickness except in the most distal esophagus.[1,5] Melanocytes and neuroendocrine cells may be found in this layer.[4] The lamina propria is made up of loose connective tissue that in the distal portion of the organ contains mucous glands referred to as (esophageal) cardiac glands. The esophageal muscularis mucosae is rather thick compared with other portions of the gastrointestinal tract, especially in the distal portion.[2]

The submucosa contains mucosal glands distributed throughout the esophagus; their ducts, which open into the esophageal lumen, sometimes are found to be cystically dilated and surrounded by lymphoid collections. The esophageal muscularis propria consists of an admixture of striated and smooth muscle in the upper quarter and exclusively smooth muscle in the rest of the organ.[3] The esophagus lacks a serosal layer, except for its most distal portion. The autonomic nervous plexuses are represented by the Meissner's plexus in the submucosa (very sparse) and the Auerbach (myenteric) plexus in the muscularis propria (denser in the distal portion).

The upper third of the esophagus drains into the cervical nodes, the middle third into the paraesophageal and paratracheal mediastinal nodes, and the lower third into the nodes around the aorta and celiac axis.

Atresia and related anomalies

The esophagus of a 3-week-old embryo is an annular constriction between the pharynx and stomach. With growth of the lung beds and elongation of the neck, it

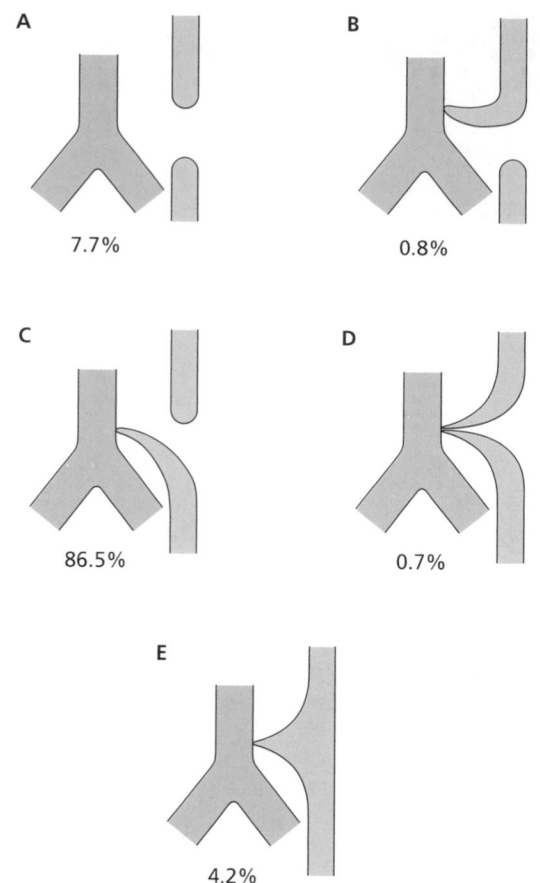

A 7.7%

B 0.8%

C 86.5%

D 0.7%

E 4.2%

Fig. 11.1 Types of tracheoesophageal anomalies and their relative frequencies. (Adapted from Holder TM, Ashcraft KW. Esophageal atresia and tracheoesophageal fistula. Ann Thorac Surg 1970, 9: 445–467)

becomes tubular. At first, the cephalad portions of the esophagus and trachea form a single channel. Later, a septum grows in and separates them.

Five major types of tracheoesophageal anomalies have been described as a result of failures in the process just described[8] (Fig. 11.1). The most common, referred to as type C, is esophageal atresia with fistula between the lower portion of the esophagus and the respiratory tree.[7,9,11] In this type, the hypertrophied and dilated upper portion of the esophagus ends blindly at a variable distance below the larynx, whereas the lower portion communicates with the trachea (usually about 0.5 cm above the bifurcation) or the right main stem bronchus. Striated muscle is present in the upper portion of the esophagus but not in the lower, which instead may contain cartilaginous rings near its fistulous end. Tracheomalacia, abnormalities of the Auerbach plexus, and cardiovascular anomalies can be seen in association with tracheoesophageal fistula.[11,12]

There also can be defects of the esophagus alone, such as congenital narrowing, stenosis, or an occluding diaphragm of mucous membrane.[6] Successful surgical repair can be accomplished for most of these abnormalities.[9,10,12]

Heterotopia

Heterotopic gastric mucosa can occur at any point in the esophagus but appears most frequently in the post-cricoid region.[20] It has been detected in approximately 4% of patients who undergo esophagoscopic examinations as a circular, flat, orange to red area, sometimes referred to as the "inlet patch."[15] Rarely, it results in a filling defect in the mid-portion of the esophagus (Fig. 11.2). It is usually asymptomatic, but it may produce dysphagia and simulate clinically and radiographically a malignant neoplasm.

Grossly, the surface has an appearance similar to that of orthotopic normal gastric mucosa. It is sharply delineated, and the border with the normal stratified epithelium is apparent. At times, ulceration occurs.

Microscopically, this gastric mucosa is usually made up of gastric glands of cardiac–fundic type, with mucous glands admixed with fundic gland elements (Fig. 11.3). Goblet cells may be present. There is often an extensive inflammatory reaction that may induce reactive proliferation and architectural distortion of the glands and lead to a mistaken diagnosis of malignancy. True instances of adenocarcinoma of the upper esophagus in heterotopic gastric mucosa have been described, in which normal lining squamous epithelium was present both proximal and distal to the lesion.[13,14]

Heterotopic pancreatic tissue in the form of acinar structures and/or Langerhans' islands can occur in the gastroesophageal junction; most of the reported cases have been in children and young adults[19] (Fig. 11.4).

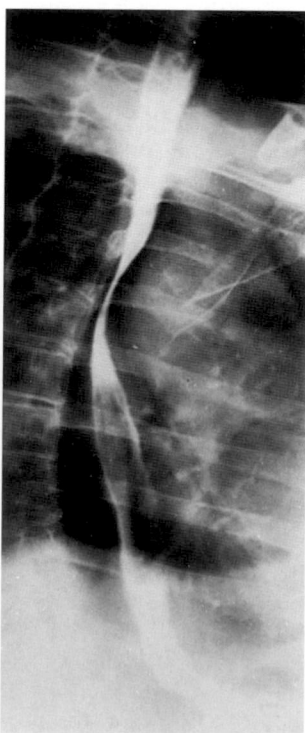

Fig. 11.2 Heterotopic gastric mucosa resulting in a smooth filling defect with compression in the mid portion of the esophagus.

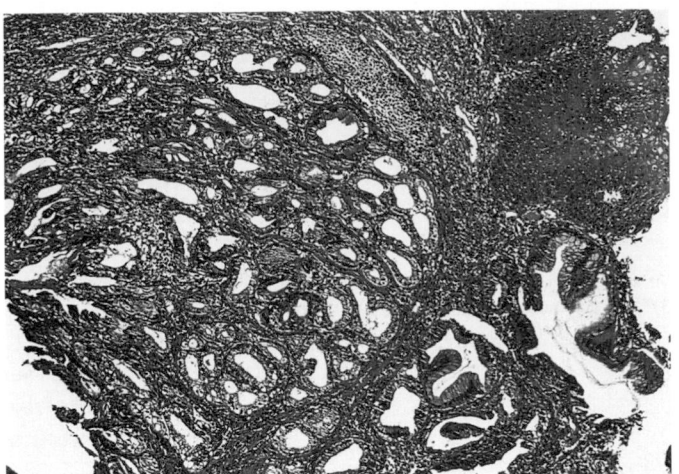

Fig. 11.3 Heterotopic gastric mucosa in the esophagus. There is some degree of inflammation and reactive epithelial changes.

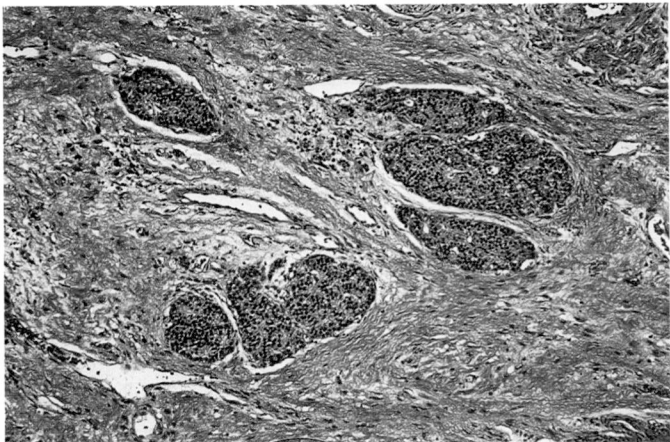

Fig. 11.4 Heterotopic pancreas in the gastroesophageal junction, mainly represented by Langerhans' islets.

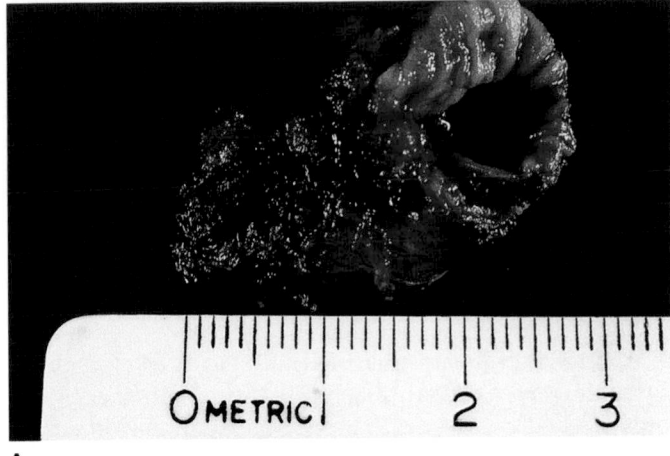

A

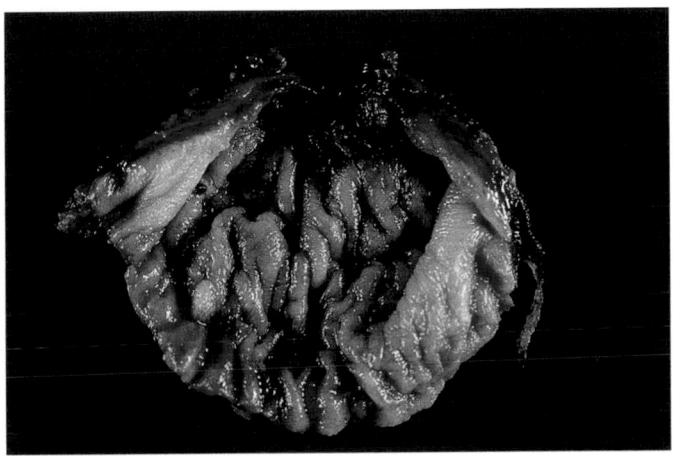

B

Fig. 11.5 A and **B,** Outer aspect and inner surface of Zenker's diverticulum.

Heterotopic sebaceous glands are rarely seen in the midportion or distal portion of the esophagus.[16,17,18]

Diverticula

The diverticula appearing in the upper portion of the esophagus (Zenker's diverticula) are the result of outpouching of esophageal mucosa at points of weakness in the wall of the esophagus at the junction with the pharynx (Fig. 11.5). They are more properly designated as pharyngoesophageal and are classified as **pulsion diverticula**. They occur at this point because of the relationship between the inferior constrictor muscle and the obliquely passing fibers of the cricopharyngeal muscles as they descend on the posterior wall of the esophagus to become longitudinal.

In the lower third of the esophagus and in the region of the hilum of the lung, inflammatory lymph nodes (usually tuberculous) become firmly attached to the esophagus and produce **traction diverticula**.

Just above the diaphragm, so-called **epiphrenic** diverticula of the pulsion variety occur rarely.[24] These outpouchings contain mucosa, submucosa, and often muscularis mucosae. They are lined by squamous epithelium and may be associated with considerable inflammation. Complications include obstruction, aspiration pneumonia and lung abscess, infection with perforation and mediastinitis, hemorrhage, and even malignancy. Carcinomas can arise within esophageal diverticula of both the pharyngoesophageal and epiphrenic varieties;[27,28] in one series the incidence of malignancy in pharyngoesophageal diverticula was 0.3%.[31] The indications for surgical removal of esophageal diverticula (particularly of the epiphrenic type) remain controversial.[21,22] Zenker's diverticula can be effectively treated endoscopically with CO_2 laser under microscopic control.[30]

An altogether different type of esophageal diverticular process has been designated **diffuse intramural esophageal (pseudo) diverticulosis**.[23] Dysphagia may be the presenting symptom. Roentgenography and endoscopy reveal innumerable 1- to 3-mm flask-shaped diverticula, with a pinpoint mouth, more numerous in the upper third of the organ. The lining is predominantly squamous. A short stricture is usually present in the region. It has been suggested that these formations represent cystically dilated ducts of submucosal glands and, therefore, are not a true diverticular process.[25,29] The pathogenesis is undetermined, but underlying motor abnormalities of the esophagus have been implicated.[26]

Cysts

Esophageal cysts are classified into *inclusion cysts* (lined by squamous or columnar epithelium, sometimes ciliated), *retention cysts* or mucoceles (arising from cystic dilatation of submucosal glands), and *developmental cysts* (of esophageal, bronchial, or gastric origin)[32,33] (Fig. 11.6). Their microscopic distinction may be very difficult. Cases of squamous cell carcinoma or adenocarcinoma arising in these cysts have been reported.[34,35]

Rings and webs

Esophageal shadows with a configuration resembling rings and webs are often described by radiologists in patients complaining of dysphagia. Those located in the upper esophagus of women and associated with iron-deficiency anemia are a component of the Plummer–Vinson or Paterson–Kelly syndrome, in which an increased incidence of carcinoma has been described. Those located in the lower esophagus are commonly referred as Schatzki's, esophagogastric, or lower esophageal rings.[39] The nature of the morphologic structure behind these shadows has been unclear because of the lack of correlative roentgenographic and microscopic studies. Goyal et al.[37] attempted to correct this deficiency

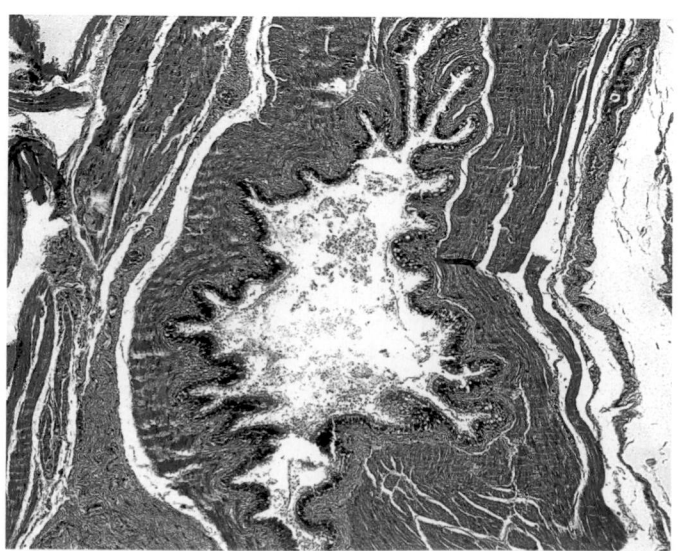

Fig. 11.6 Esophageal cyst lined by ciliated columnar mucosa.

by examining 100 autopsy specimens both radiographically and microscopically. They found two structurally different types of rings, which could be separated on radiographic examination. Nine were formed by a transverse circumferential fold of the mucosa; they were located at the squamocolumnar junction and produced a thin, weblike shadow on radiographs. Five were formed by a localized annular thickening of the muscle; they were proximal to the site of the mucosal ring, were covered by squamous epithelium, and produced a wide constriction when examined radiographically.

Clements et al.,[36] in a similar study, have shown that the cervical esophageal (pharyngoesophageal) webs also represent transverse folds of normal mucosa and submucosa.

The treatment of esophageal webs includes endoscopic dilatation and surgical myomectomy.[38,40]

Achalasia and related motor disorders

Achalasia (cardiospasm; megaesophagus) is due to a failure of the cardiac mechanism to open when peristaltic waves conveying food through the esophagus reach it. It is usually seen in adults, but it can also occur in children.[58] Some of the patients are affected by the Allgrove (Triple A) syndrome, in which the achalasia is combined with addisonianism and alacrima.[53a] A nearly complete loss of myenteric ganglion cells is present in the lower third of the esophagus in nearly all cases; this loss is in the middle third in about 20% of the cases.[46,49] This is often associated with the presence of degenerative changes in the remaining ganglion cells.[41] Secondary changes include inflammation within myenteric nerves, replacement of these nerves by collagen, muscular hypertrophy, and chronic inflammation (with prominent germinal centers).[49] This inflammatory infiltrate is predominantly composed of CD3+ T cells, the majority of which also stain for CD8.[42] In longstanding cases, the mucosa shows marked squamous metaplasia and an increased incidence of p53 immunoreactivity, some of these changes probably being of precancerous nature (see below).[54]

The pathogenesis remains unknown. At present, the hypothesis that achalasia is an inflammatory immune-mediated disease is favored, but the responsible antigen remains unknown.[62]

In the early stages, achalasia is reversible. With the passage of time, however, chronic inflammation and ulceration supervene, and fibrotic stricture results. Esophagomyotomy and pneumatic dilatation remain the major treatment modalities.[43,45] Rarely, carcinoma develops in association with longstanding achalasia.[50,53,60] The risk has been estimated to be increased 33-fold.[57] Wychulis et al.[63] observed 7 cases in a group of 1318 patients. Achalasia had been present for an average of 28 years before the diagnosis of carcinoma. The tumors arose at all levels of the esophagus but were more common in the middle third. Microscopically, most of these tumors are squamous cell carcinomas, but other types also occur.[61] They may develop years following the performance of a myotomy for the achalasia.

Cricopharyngeal dysphagia (cricopharyngeal achalasia, cricopharyngeal spasm) is a well-recognized entity with prominent clinical symptoms but only meager microscopic findings, represented by degeneration and regeneration of the fibers of the cricopharyngeal muscle, accompanied by interstitial fibrosis.[44,59]

Chagas' disease, an endemic parasitosis of South America, can be associated with alterations of Auerbach's plexus and megaesophagus.[47]

Pseudoachalasia is an esophageal motor disorder usually associated with malignancy, the clinical, radiographic and manometric features of which are very similar to those of achalasia. The most common microscopic finding, which is in keeping with its presumed pathogenesis, is neoplastic infiltration of the myenteric plexus.[55]

Giant muscular hypertrophy (diffuse spasm; corkscrew esophagus; diffuse leiomyomatosis) is a motor disorder of the esophagus characterized clinically by dysphagia and pain and pathologically by focal or diffuse hypertrophy of the muscular layer, up to a thickness of 1 cm.[51] Surgical therapy is not as successful in this disease as in achalasia.[48] Some cases of this disorder have been reported in association with an Alport-like nephropathy[56]; others have been found to be accompanied by genetic alterations similar to those seen in leiomyomas.[52]

Lye strictures

Lye strictures of the esophagus are most common at the level of bifurcation of the trachea. The mean age of the patients at the time of lye ingestion is about 6 years. Once the lesion is well established, the only method of cure is surgical resection.[65,66] Carcinoma of the esophagus may develop at the site.[64] The mean latent time is about 40 years; the later in life the lye is ingested, the shorter the interval. These tumors tend to be located at the level of the tracheal bifurcation.[67]

Reflux esophagitis

As the name indicates, this form of esophagitis (also known as gastroesophageal reflux disease) is the result of reflux of gastroduodenal contents into the esophagus. It is often associated with a sliding hiatal hernia, although it should be stressed that it is the reflux and not the hernia that causes the abnormality.[85] It has been suggested

that vagal nerve dysfunction may be important in the pathogenesis of this disorder.[75] Esophageal reflux and the complications arising from it have also been described as a result of scleroderma[81] and Zollinger–Ellison syndrome.[80]

Esophageal reflux is accompanied by regurgitation, heartburn, pain, and dysphagia. Grossly, severe lesions appear markedly hyperemic (Fig. 11.7). The early microscopic lesions consist of epithelial hyperplasia and infiltration by neutrophils and eosinophils, sometimes accompanied by focal epithelial necrosis.[72,76,78,79,82] The papillary height of the lamina propria and the degree of basal cell proliferation are substantially higher than in the control subjects, as estimated subjectively and corroborated with morphometric techniques.[70,74] Dilated and congested venules are seen high up in the top of the lengthened papillae between the epithelial layers.[73,77] According to Brown et al.,[72] intraepithelial eosinophils are the most frequent abnormality; in their series, they were noted in over half of the cases and correlated best with the gross endoscopic features. However, Tummala et al.[88] have shown that in human volunteers without evidence of esophageal reflux, occasional eosinophils are found in one third of the esophageal biopsies; therefore, they are not by themselves a reliable criterion in the evaluation of this disorder.

Cells with irregular nuclear contours can be seen amid the epithelial elements in reflux esophagitis; they represent reactive T lymphocytes and are a component of the inflammatory response.[90]

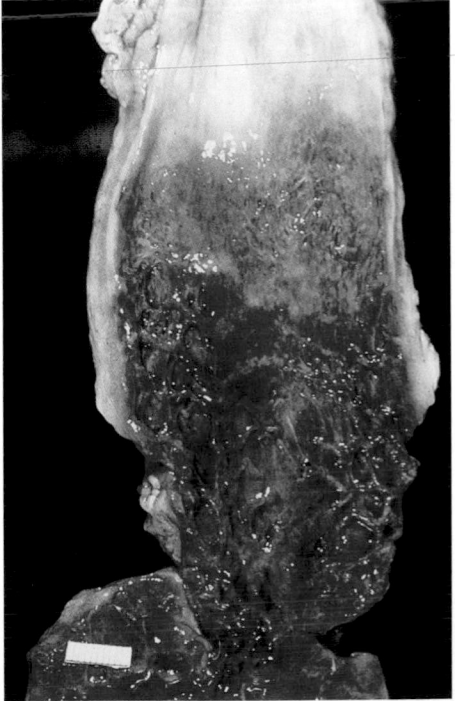

Fig. 11.7 Gross appearance of a severe case of reflux esophagitis. Marked hyperemia with focal hemorrhage is present in the area of reflux.

Reflux esophagitis may progress to superficial ulceration, spread of inflammation to the wall, and circumferential fibrosis with stricture formation and fixation to the surrounding structures[83,91] (Fig. 11.8). Sometimes a lesion develops in this background that has gross and microscopic features identical to those of a gastric ulcer ("Barrett's ulcer"), as demonstrated in several classic studies carried out in the 1940s and 1950s.[68,69,71] It is often large, oval, and well circumscribed, with elevated borders and deep craters, and it may result in massive bleeding or perforation. Microscopic examination of the short tubular segment distal to the ulcer, anatomically resembling the esophagus, shows the segment to be lined by gastric mucosa.[87] As such, this is to be regarded as an expression of Barrett's esophagus, an alteration associated with reflux esophagitis that is discussed in the next section. Occasionally, the inflammatory reaction associated with the esophagitis may be of such a degree as to result in a pseudolymphomatous appearance.[84]

Depending on the severity of the symptoms, reflux esophagitis can be treated medically (with motility-promoting drugs, H_2-receptor antagonists, or gastric proton-transport system-inhibiting drugs) or surgically.[86,89] All of the various operations that have been devised for this disorder (such as fundoplication at various angles or posterior gastropexy) involve the reduction of the hiatal hernia (often present) coupled with the construction of a valve mechanism to reestablish gastroesophageal competence.[89]

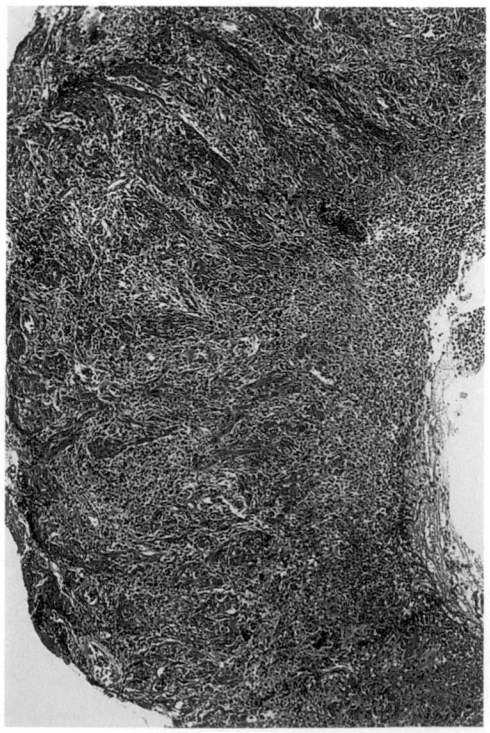

Fig. 11.8 Severe microscopic changes of reflux esophagitis featuring ulceration and extensive inflammation.

Barrett's esophagus

The occurrence of specialized columnar epithelium (as defined below) lining a segment of distal esophagus above the level of the lower esophageal sphincter is referred to as *Barrett's esophagus*.[140,142,143] The large majority of the patients are adults. However, it has also been reported in children, sometimes in association with cystic fibrosis (a condition known to induce gastroesophageal reflux) and following chemotherapy.[102,103,113,114] A genetic predisposition to develop Barrett's esophagus has been detected.[104] It has been debated for years whether Barrett's esophagus represents a congenital or an acquired abnormality,[115] and whether this segment should be regarded as belonging to the esophagus because of its shape and mobility or to the stomach because of its lining. Lack of a precise definition on the nature and location of the gastroesophageal junction and the microscopic variations at this junction have clouded the issue.[98,123,139,145] Most clinical and experimental evidence, however, indicates that this change is acquired and the result of ulceration and subsequent re-epithelization by columnar cells of what originally was esophageal squamous mucosa.[96,111,133] As such, it could be viewed as a reversed expression of the much more common phenomenon of squamous metaplasia of the glandular portion of the uterine cervix. In both instances, the attempt of the organism—viewed from a teleologic standpoint—is to replace the injured area with a type of epithelium that is better equipped to cope with the existing local conditions. In Barrett's esophagus, the ulceration is nearly always induced by gastroesophageal reflux and is said to occur in 10% of patients with this condition. The ultimate origin of the columnar cells remains uncertain; theoretically, they could arise from migration of gastric mucosa or (more likely) as a result of a phenotypic switch of undifferentiated elements in the stem cell mucosal population.[97,144]

This columnar epithelial extension may be circumferential or in the form of finger-like projections or islands. The microscopic definition of the type of mucosa that needs to be present above the level of the lower esophageal sphincter to qualify as Barrett's esophagus has changed over the years and has yet to be entirely satisfactory. Until recently, any type of glandular mucosa present (atrophic fundal type, cardiac or junctional type, or specialized columnar) qualified. At present, only the specialized columnar type does. This is regarded as a form of incomplete intestinal metaplasia exhibiting a villiform surface and crypts, with a mixed population of columnar, goblet, Paneth, and endocrine cells[107,122] (Fig. 11.9). Of these changes, which are age related,[135] the presence of goblet cells is the most significant for the diagnosis of the condition, a fact emphasized by the dictum "No goblets, no Barrett's."[92] This restriction is somewhat questionable, given that the presence of

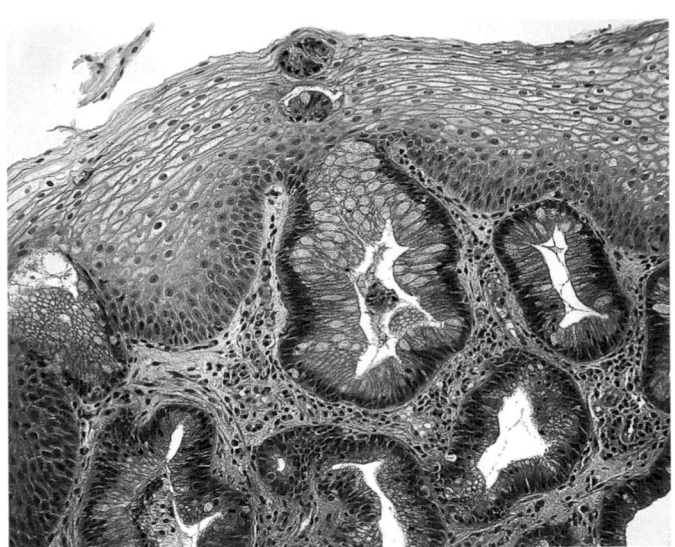

Fig. 11.9 Barrett's esophagus with complete intestinal metaplasia.

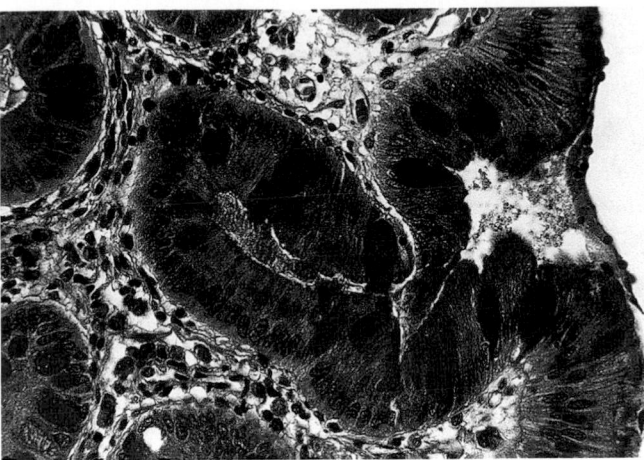

Fig. 11.10 Barrett's esophagus featuring secretion of acidic mucin, as demonstrated with Alcian blue staining at pH 2.5.

cardiac mucosa or fundal-type mucosa in the distal esophagus is indicative of abnormal acid exposure[99] and that there is a non-goblet cell population in Barrett's esophagus with clearcut features of intestinal epithelium.[100,126] A further and much more questionable requirement that has been incorporated into the definition of Barrett's esophagus by the Practice Parameters Committee of the American College of Gastroenterologists is that this change "can be recognized at endoscopy."[138] It would seem to us that the biologic significance of incomplete intestinal metaplasia of the lower esophagus should be the same even if the endoscopist were unable to recognize it, and we can all think of various reasons why that may happen.[131]

It has been suggested that a precursor lesion of Barrett's esophagus (i.e., an early or intermediate stage of columnar metaplasia) is represented by multilayered epithelium having morphologic and ultrastructural features of both squamous and columnar epithelium.[106]

Barrett's esophagus has been further subdivided into *long-segment* (the classic form, in which the changes involve 3 cm or more of the esophagus) and *short-segment* (less than 3 cm). For practical purposes, these two artificially defined types are managed similarly.[125]

At the histochemical level, most of the mucin present in specialized columnar epithelium is of neutral type, but in over 70% of the cases there are also sialomucins and sulfomucins[119,120,132] (Fig. 11.10). The intestinal type of differentiation is also evidenced by the common presence of the intestinal-type mucin MUC2, in addition to gastrin-type mucins (MUC5AC, MUC6) and TFF peptides (TFF1 and TFF2)[101,149] and by the presence of the Cdx2 protein, as detected immunohistochemically.[132a] Endocrine cells are demonstrated by argyrophilic stains in 90% of the biopsies, irrespective of the type of epithelium; 5-hydroxytryptamine (serotonin), somatostatin, secretin, and pancreatic polypeptide have been detected immunohis-

tochemically in them.[110] It should be remembered that intestinal metaplasia can also occur in the gastric cardia in the absence of Barrett's esophagus.[108,109,128] It has been suggested that this condition can be distinguished from Barrett's esophagus on the basis of the immunohistochemical keratin profile (superficial CK20 staining and strong CK7 staining of both superficial and deep glands in Barrett's esophagus).[127,147] However, other studies have failed to confirm this claim.[105,124]

The diagnosis of Barrett's esophagus is usually first suggested by the barium swallow. Manometric examinations, intraesophageal pH monitoring, and other techniques are useful as supporting evidence, but confirmation of the diagnosis requires endoscopic examination and biopsy. Of course, it is essential that the biopsy be taken above the lower esophageal sphincter.

Helicobacter pylori may be found in Barrett's mucosa,[129,136,148] but apparently only when also present in the stomach, thus providing additional evidence for the presence of reflux in this condition. Barrett's esophagus can rarely be accompanied by pancreatic metaplasia[117] and osseous metaplasia[112] (see also under Heterotopia, p. 616). A reduplication of the muscularis mucosae is another frequent finding.[146]

The main complications of Barrett's esophagus are the same as for reflux esophagitis (i.e., peptic ulcer, stricture, bleeding), plus the development of dysplasia and adenocarcinoma[118]; the latter is discussed in the next section. The initial treatment for Barrett's esophagus in the absence of dysplastic changes is in the form of acid suppression (omeprazole), laser, and photodynamic therapy.[93,150] If this fails, an operation is usually performed, in the form of esophagogastroplasty, fundoplication, or posterior gastropexy. The indications for surgery remain controversial.[130,137] The main parameters that are used to influence the decision are failure of medical therapy, the length of the Barrett's epithelium,[116,122] and the presence of dysplastic changes as detected with a variety of techniques.

The latter are discussed in the next section. There is controversy as to how often these procedures will result in microscopic regression of the changes, but most studies suggest that this phenomenon does indeed occur, with partial or total squamous re-epithelization of the metaplastic columnar epithelium.[94,95,134,141] Residual glandular mucosa, sometimes exhibiting dysplastic features, is still frequently found within the squamous epithelium.[94]

Dysplasia and carcinoma in situ in Barrett's esophagus

One of the most important complications that can supervene in Barrett's esophagus is carcinoma, which is nearly always accompanied and preceded by dysplasia.[162,169a] The dysplasia, which nearly always arises in area of incomplete intestinal metaplasia,[210] should be distinguished from the reactive hyperplasia seen secondary to inflammatory injury and should be graded according to its severity.[170,202] The diagnostic categories remain those agreed upon at the 1988 consensus conference for grading dysplasia in Barrett's esophagus,[168,190,202] which are the following:

- **Negative for dysplasia**: The architecture is within normal limits. The nuclei do not vary greatly in size or shape and are located basally. The nucleocytoplasmic ratio is not increased (Fig. 11.11A). The nuclear envelope is generally smooth. Nucleoli are not markedly enlarged. Focal nuclear stratification is acceptable, as are small numbers of "dystrophic" goblet cells, the apical aspect of which does not communicate with the luminal surface. Greater nuclear alterations are acceptable when associated with evidence of inflammation, erosion, or ulceration (Fig. 11.11B). Numbers of abnormal-appearing mitoses are variable. Apical cytoplasmic mucus is usually present but may be reduced or absent in inflammation.
- **Indefinite for dysplasia (IND)**: The architecture may be moderately distorted. Nuclear abnormalities are less marked than those seen in dysplasia. Other features that may lead to a diagnosis of IND include more numerous dystrophic goblet cells, more extensive nuclear stratification, diminished or absent mucus production, increased cytoplasmic basophilia, and increased mitoses (Fig. 11.11C). The diagnosis of IND should be limited to cases in which the changes are too marked for negative but not sufficient for the diagnosis of dysplasia.
- **Positive for low-grade dysplasia (LGD) or high-grade dysplasia (HGD)**: The diagnosis of LGD or HGD is based on the severity of both architectural and cytologic criteria that suggest neoplastic transformation of the columnar epithelium. Although either architectural or cytologic abnormalities may predominate, HGD is diagnosed if either one is sufficiently prominent. Architectural abnormalities may include

budded, branched, crowded, or irregularly shaped glands; papillary extensions into gland lumina; and villiform configuration of the mucosal surface (Fig. 11.11D,E,F). Nuclear features may include marked variation in size and shape, nuclear and/or nucleolar enlargement, increased nucleocytoplasmic ratio, hyperchromatism, and increased numbers of abnormal mitoses. Nuclear alterations are especially noteworthy if they involve the mucosal surface. Diagnostic features easily recognizable at low power are cytoplasmic basophilia with loss of mucus and excessive nuclear stratification, often extending from the epithelial basement membrane to the luminal surface.

- **Intramucosal carcinoma**: Intramucosal carcinoma is defined as carcinoma that has penetrated through the basement membrane of the glands into the lamina propria but has not yet invaded through the muscularis mucosae into the submucosa. Most biopsy specimens will not be deep enough to rule out submucosal invasion.

In some cases of dysplasia, the polypoid architecture of the lesion and the crowding and stratification of the hyperchromatic nuclei are similar to those seen in adenomas of the large bowel,[183,196,224] whereas other cases resemble the pattern of dysplasia seen in the large bowel as a complication of ulcerative colitis[204,215]; it has been suggested that carcinoma is associated more often with the latter pattern.[175,204]

Dysplasia, as thus defined, is found in Barrett's esophagus in the absence of carcinoma in 5% to 10% of the cases and in association with carcinoma in 68% to 100% of the cases.[153,163,172,192,204,215] Confirmation of the diagnosis requires endoscopic biopsy (ideally combined with endoscopic mapping[154]), but its initial detection is possible by cytology and with flow cytometry.[169,173,205,216] The risk for the development of invasive carcinoma in patients with dysplasia in Barrett's esophagus is certainly increased, at least for the high-grade type.[184] The magnitude of this risk remains to be determined,[220] but it is estimated to be 30- to 40-fold higher than in the general population.[160,219] The molecular alterations that have been detected in the course of the dysplasia–adenocarcinoma sequence are listed on p. 624.

The treatment of dysplasia in Barrett's esophagus ranges from close monitoring to surgical excision depending on a variety of factors, such as—first and foremost—the degree of the dysplasia,[189,203] but also correlation of endoscopic and biopsy findings,[185] and the combination of DNA ploidy and biopsy findings.[201] Whether p53 protein overexpression, clonal cytogenetic abnormalities, c-*erb*B-2 oncoprotein overexpression, or amplification of the *EGFR* gene will play a significant role in this difficult decision remains to be determined.[151,158,191,199,200]

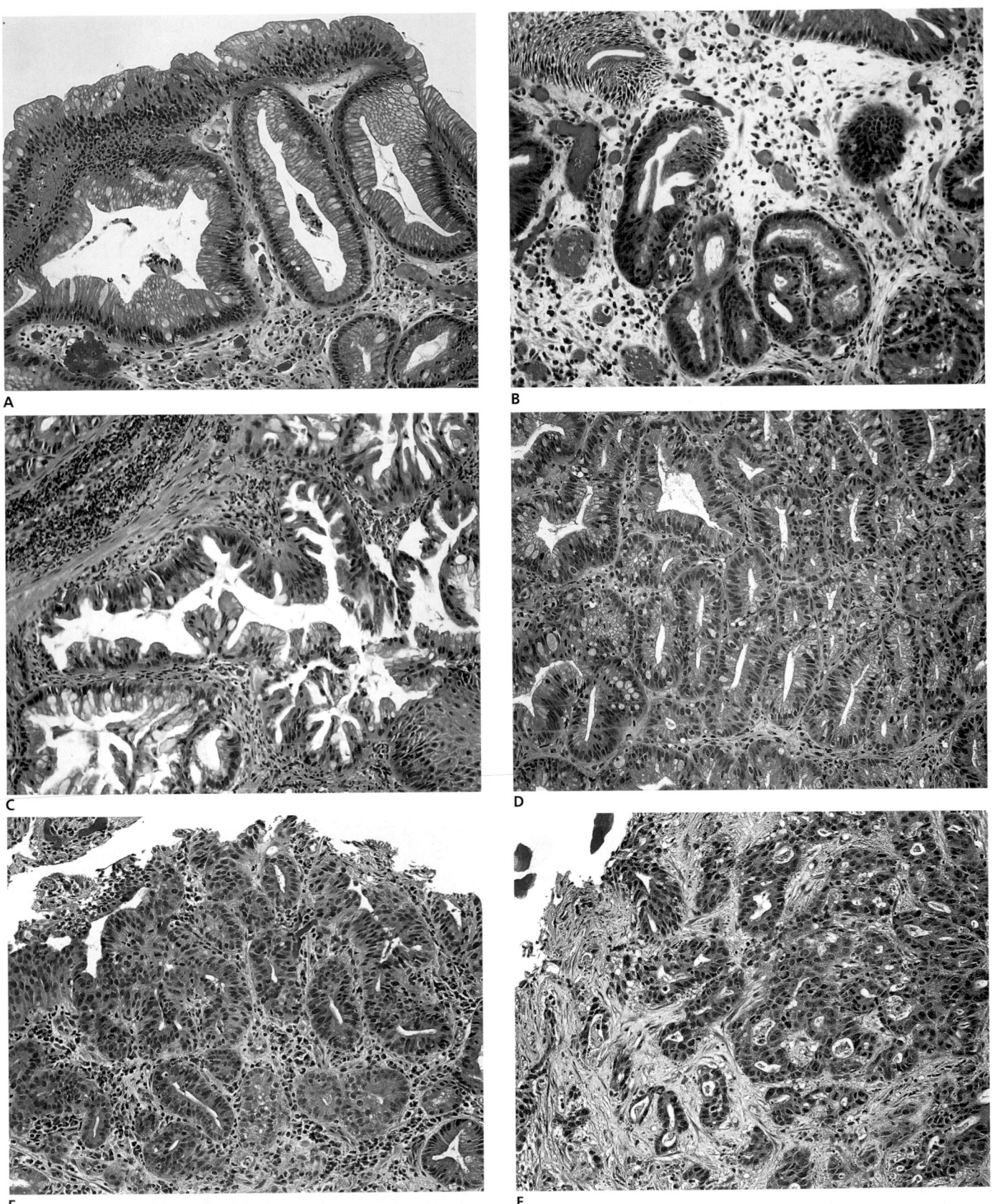

Fig. 11.11 A, Barrett's esophagus negative for dysplasia. **B**, Barrett's esophagus with chronic inflammation and glandular reactive atypia, but negative for dysplasia. **C**, Barrett's esophagus with glandular changes judged "indefinite for dysplasia." **D**, Barrett's esophagus with low-grade dysplasia. **E**, Barrett's esophagus with high-grade dysplasia/carcinoma in situ. **F**, Barrett's esophagus with intramucosal carcinoma. The entire tumor was above the muscularis mucosae.

Adenocarcinoma arising in Barrett's esophagus. Invasive carcinoma developing in Barrett's esophagus is nearly always of the adenocarcinoma type.[174,177] Some of the reported cases have been in children.[178] It has been estimated that Barrett-associated adenocarcinoma accounts for 5% to 10% of all esophageal cancers.[172] The main features used to suggest an origin for an adenocarcinoma in this region from a Barrett's esophagus are the association with a dysplastic or nondysplastic Barrett's mucosa and the location of more than half of the tumor mass in the esophagus. The likelihood of development of high-grade dysplasia and early invasive carcinoma in Barrett's esophagus seems to be the same along the entire length of the abnormality.[188] Adenocarcinomas of the gastroesophageal junction have essentially similar morphologic, immunohistochemically, and epidemiologic features whether an associated Barrett's metaplasia can be detected in the specimen or not.[167,167a,177,180,186,223] The tumor may be multicentric and is often far advanced at the time of diagnosis, with extension into the wall and nodal metastases.[218] Most patients are white males, and the average age at diagnosis is 57 years.[165,219,222] Microscopically, a wide range of glandular differentiation exists, sometimes in the same tumor.[152,195] Architecturally and immunohistochemically, these tumors resemble their gastric counterparts,[213] including the common presence of a variable component of neuroendocrine cells.[176]

Many molecular alterations have been identified in specimens of Barrett's esophagus containing lesions within the dysplasia–adenocarcinoma sequence.[156,179,206,232] These include mutation and overexpression of p53,[155] various apoptosis-related proteins,[226] myc amplification,[214] mutations of beta-catenin and other alterations of the cadherin/catenin membrane complex,[164,231] LOH and microsatellite instability,[232] and expression of CD44.[181] These changes seem to be similar in the long-segment and short-segment forms of the disease[193]; instead, there are significant differences in metastatic Barrett's adenocarcinoma and related lymph node metastases when compared with nonmetastatic Barrett's adenocarcinoma.[228]

Surgical resection is the primary treatment, sometimes combined with preoperative chemotherapy and radiation therapy.[221,229] The extent of the resection depends on several factors, including the extent of the in situ component if present.[227]

The prognosis of adenocarcinoma in Barrett's esophagus is poor, with a 5-year survival rate of 14.5% in one of the largest published series.[212] Stage by stage, this prognosis seems to be similar to that of conventional squamous cell carcinoma of the esophagus.[182,207] The preeminent prognostic factor, as in so many other sites, is tumor stage, particularly in relation to the lymph node status.[225] In addition, it has been claimed that Her-2/*neu* amplification and beta-catenin abnormal expression are related to prognosis.[159,194]

Other malignant tumors arising in Barrett's esophagus. Unusual types of malignancy arising in Barrett's esophagus include adenosquamous carcinoma, squamous cell carcinoma, sarcomatoid carcinoma (carcinosarcoma), various types of neuroendocrine carcinoma, choriocarcinoma, and yolk sac tumor, sometimes alone and sometimes in association with adenocarcinoma.[161,166,187,208,209,211,217,218,230]

Other types of esophagitis

Herpes simplex esophagitis is a frequent autopsy finding in immunosuppressed hosts and is being detected with increasing frequency.[235,247,248] It can also occur in immunocompetent individuals. It may be symptomatic or result in odynophagia, retrosternal chest pain, and fever.[239] The diagnosis should be suspected in the presence of "volcano ulcers" at endoscopy and discrete, diffusely scattered, shallow ulcers on double-contrast esophagogram.[235,252] Microscopically, inflammation, ulcerations, and Cowdry type A inclusions are the hallmarks of the disease, but the latter are not always identifiable[246] (Fig. 11.12). Multinucleated epithelial cells constitute another classic morphologic feature of herpes esophagitis; however, it should be noted that similar multinucleated cells can be seen in esophagitis of other etiologies as a nonspecific regenerative response to injury.[253] Aggregates of large (CD68+) mononuclear cells with convoluted nuclei adjacent to the inflamed epithelium constitute an important diagnostic clue.[240]

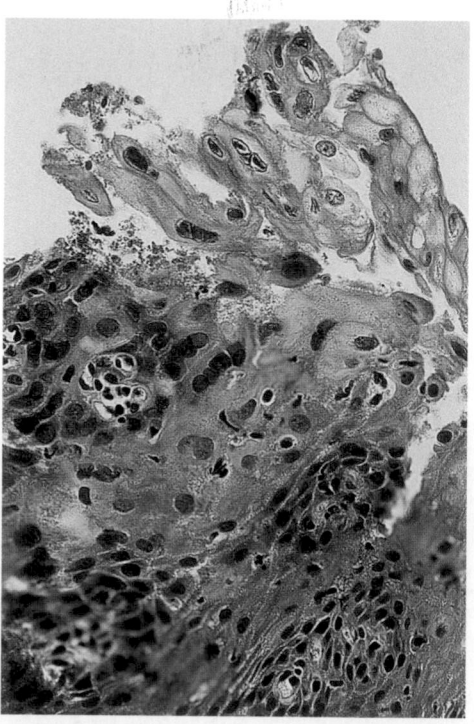

Fig. 11.12 Herpes simplex esophagitis. Several typical intranuclear eosinophilic inclusions are seen in the squamous epithelium.

Cytomegalovirus (CMV) esophagitis is also on the rise because of its predilection for immunocompromised patients.[244] Its endoscopic appearance is similar to that of herpes esophagitis. Microscopically, the diagnosis is made by finding the typical large cells with basophilic cytoplasm and large oval, basophilic intranuclear inclusions. These can also be detected in cytologic preparations.[254]

Candida esophagitis can complicate the ulcers of herpes or CMV esophagitis or appear in the absence of viral infection, usually in immunosuppressed individuals.[244] It may also be seen secondary to esophageal stricture or in children as mucocutaneous candidiasis, an expression of an immunologic deficiency.[251] The diagnosis can be made by brush cytology[258] (Fig. 11.13).

AIDS-related chronic idiopathic esophageal ulceration is characterized by the presence of large, undermined ulcers with severe acute inflammation.[257] No evidence of herpes simplex, CMV, fungi, or tumors has been found, and the startling suggestion has been made that the ulcers are the direct result of the HIV itself.[243]

Crohn's disease can involve the esophagus, usually in association with gastric and/or intestinal disease.[238,241]

Idiopathic eosinophilic esophagitis has been described as an unusual variant of the family of presumably allergic eosinophilic disorders that can involve any portion of the gastrointestinal tract.[245,255] This very rare condition should be distinguished from the much more common eosinophilic infiltration of esophageal mucosa seen in patients with reflux (see p. 619).

Other types of esophagitis include those caused by tuberculosis,[236] blastomycosis,[249] Behçet's disease,[250] drugs (including iron medication, which can lead to erosions[234]), allergic reactions (particularly in children[256]), irradiation, and ingestion of corrosive chemicals.[237]

Primarily dermatologic diseases that can involve the esophagus include scleroderma, pemphigus vulgaris, lichen planus,[233] and epidermolysis bullosa.[242] Inflammation and sometimes perforation of the esophagus may result from instrumentation, intubation, or the ingestion of foreign bodies.[237]

Squamous cell carcinoma

General and clinical features

Squamous cell carcinoma of the esophagus occurs more frequently in men over 50 years of age. It is relatively common in China and other Oriental countries and is the most common tumor of the alimentary tract in the African Bantus.[272,276] In the United States, it is distinctly less common than carcinoma of the large bowel,[283] but there are some regions with increased rates.[260] Smoking and alcohol are two important and well-known risk factors.[279] In Western countries, there has been a recent epidemiologic switch from esophageal squamous cell carcinoma associated with tobacco and alcohol to Barrett-related adenocarcinoma.[265,282] The tumor has also been reported in association with lye strictures, achalasia, Plummer–Vinson syndrome, diverticula, celiac sprue, tylosis (an autosomal dominant disorder characterized by hyperkeratosis of palms and soles),[259] and history of previous irradiation (see respective sections in this chapter). Some authors have also found an increased incidence of esophagitis[264,268,274] and a history of previous gastrectomy[270] in patients with esophageal squamous cell carcinoma.

Cases of carcinoma have been reported following irradiation to the area.[266] Another known association is with squamous cell carcinoma in other sites, particularly the oropharynx and larynx[267]; in one autopsy series, this combination was found in 12% of the cases.[271] Tumor multicentricity in the esophagus is a rare event, but it may occur either synchronously or metachronously.[261] Sometimes, esophageal squamous cell carcinoma is seen together with gastric adenocarcinoma.[273,277] The main symptom of esophageal carcinoma is dysphagia. This is related to the local spread of the tumor and is usually the expression of advanced disease. A few cases of esophageal carcinoma have been reported in association with humoral hypercalcemia.[278]

It has been suggested that human papilloma virus (HPV) plays an etiologic role in esophageal carcinogenesis.[262] Studies searching for DNA sequences of HPV in esophageal squamous cell carcinomas have given widely divergent results, with a tendency for low prevalence in North American cases.[262,269,275,280,281]

Morphologic features and local spread

Squamous cell carcinoma can occur in any portion of the esophagus but is most common in the middle and lower

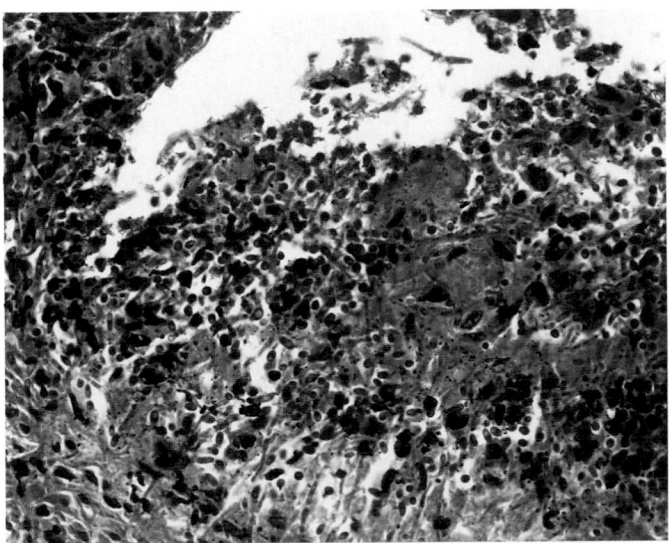

Fig. 11.13 Esophageal candidiasis. Numerous fungal organisms are seen covering a widely ulcerated surface. The Candida spores should not be confused with *Histoplasma capsulatum*.

thirds in areas of normal anatomic constrictions[286,292] (Fig. 11.14). Grossly, the tumor usually is circumferential, often ulcerated, with sharply demarcated margins. Polypoid forms occur,[291] but are much less common than with adenocarcinoma.[292] On cut section, a grayish white tumor is seen to invade part or all of the muscular wall, from which it may extend into the surrounding soft tis-sues and trachea. Intraluminal growth also occurs and may eventually lead to total obstruction. Distally located tumors often invade the stomach.[296] Submucosal spread, not appreciable grossly, is also common, sometimes up to 5 cm or more beyond the gross margins of the tumor.[285] Intraepithelial spread is even more frequent, with or without involvement of the glandular ducts.[288,295] Blood

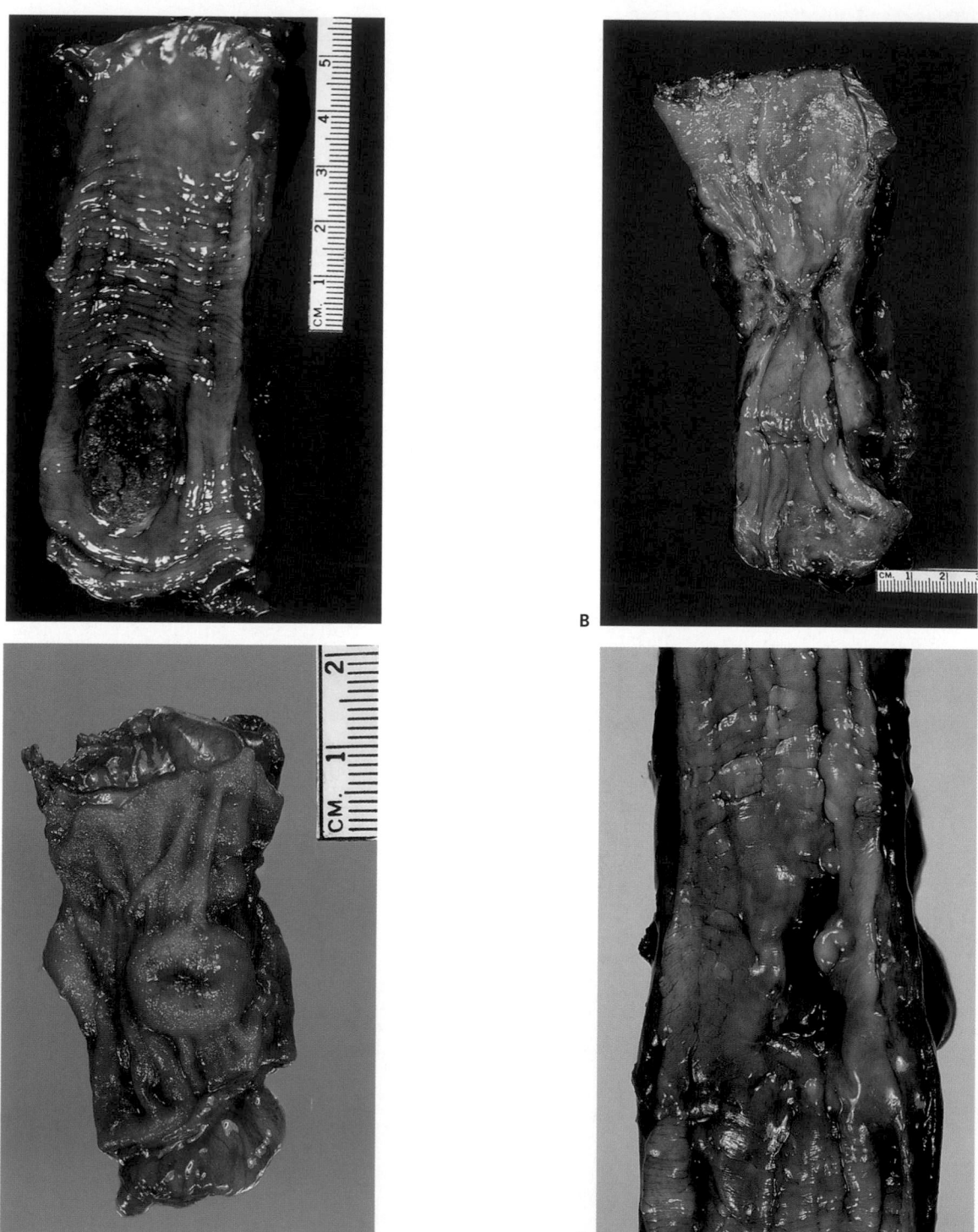

Fig. 11.14 Various gross appearances of esophageal squamous cell carcinoma. **A,** Cake-like exophytic mass. **B,** Circumferential constricting region. **C,** Elevated round nodule with central ulceration. **D,** Widely invasive lesion with deep ulceration.

therapy or chemotherapy.[301] Deletion of the expected A, B, or H blood group antigens has been found in about one quarter of the cases, regardless of their depth of invasion.[318] A similar proportion of cases are immunoreactive for B72.3, a marker directed against the Sialyl-Tn antigen (which is not expressed in normal epithelium and only very rarely in dysplastic epithelium).[304] Some poorly differentiated carcinomas react for human chorionic gonadotrophin (hCG), even in the absence of morphologically demonstrable trophoblastic differentiation.[319] Production of basement membrane components such as laminin and type IV collagen correlates with the degree of differentiation of the tumor.[307]

DNA studies have shown that two thirds to three fourths of the cases have an aneuploid pattern and that this correlates with a higher grading and a higher incidence of nodal metastases.[306,311] Poor microscopic differentiation is associated with a high DNA ploidy on microspectrophotometric determination.[316] Heterogeneity in DNA ploidy in the same case is frequent, whether comparing the primary tumor with its metastasis or comparing different areas of the primary tumor.[312,320]

Mutations and/or overexpression of p53 have been found in a high proportion of esophageal carcinomas and have led to the belief that p53 abnormalities are common genetic events in the pathogenesis of this tumor,[302,303,313,315,321] also because of their presence in early and premalignant lesions.[300,310,322] Instead, mutations of the *APC* (adenomatous polyposis coli) gene have not been found.[309]

Epidermal growth factor receptor (EGFR) has been measured immunohistochemically and by binding assay; it is found to be strongly expressed in most of the cases.[308,324]

Cyclin D1 is overexpressed in a high number of cases of esophageal squamous cell carcinoma (and also of esophageal adenocarcinoma).[299,305,314]

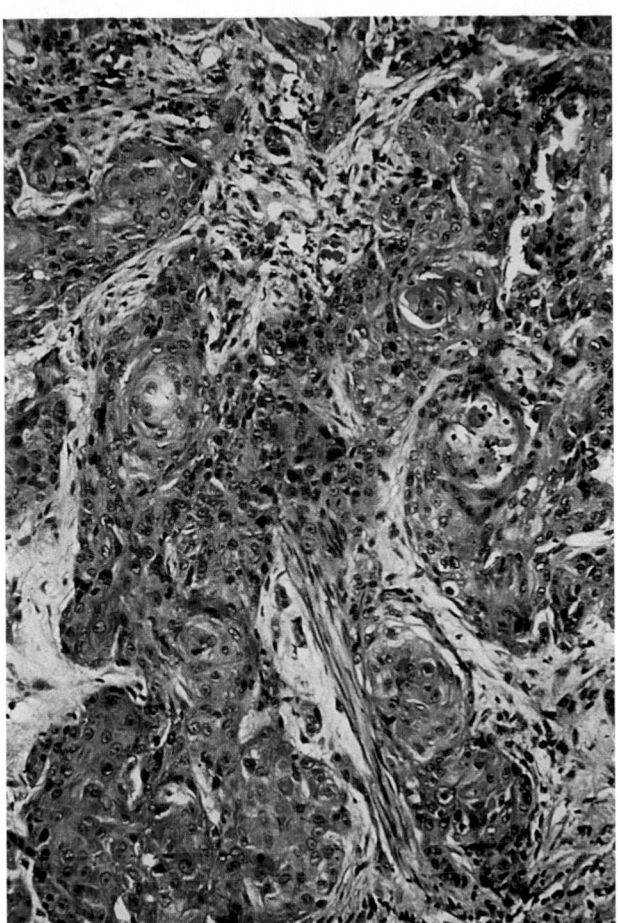

Fig. 11.15 Low-power microscopic view of an invasive, moderately well differentiated squamous cell carcinoma of the esophagus.

vessel invasion is present in three fourths of the cases.[298] In some cases, separate tumor nodules are seen in the wall of the esophagus or stomach (so-called "intramural metastases").[293]

Microscopically, the degree of squamous differentiation is variable, but most tumors are well or moderately differentiated (Fig. 11.15). Occasionally, lack of cohesiveness of tumor cells results in a pseudoglandular configuration.[284] With extensive search or ultrastructural examination, true glandular and/or mucus-secreting components are found focally in one fifth of the cases[287,290,294]; when these are extensive, the tumors are designated *adenosquamous carcinomas*. The occasional presence of an intraepithelial component with the appearance of *Paget's disease* has also been described.[289,298]

Immunohistochemical and molecular genetic features

Esophageal squamous cell carcinomas are invariably immunoreactive for keratins, the reaction patterns being related to the degree of differentiation of the tumor.[317,323] Some tumors also express vimentin, and a few are focally immunoreactive for neurofilaments. The incidence of the latter phenomenon is said to be higher after radiation

In situ and superficial squamous cell carcinoma and related lesions

Dysplasia and *carcinoma in situ* (CIS) of the esophagus (esophageal intraepithelial neoplasia; EIN) are being recognized with increasing frequency, particularly in regions of the world with a high incidence of invasive esophageal carcinoma.[325,330,344] A probably related finding is the fact that biopsies taken in asymptomatic individuals in these high-risk groups have shown an increased degree of epithelial proliferation by tritiated thymidine labeling.[338] The risk factors for esophageal CIS and dysplasia are the same as for the invasive tumors[347] (see p. 625). As in other sites, CIS can be the only lesion present or may simply represent the peripheral (and presumably preexisting) component of an invasive carcinoma, the latter being the most common situation. CIS has been found at the periphery of an invasive tumor in 30% of the cases, the incidence being much higher when no preoperative irradiation has been given and when the main lesion is superficial[336]; sometimes the in situ lesion is found anatomically separate from the main tumor and associated with foci of dysplasia, supporting the concept of a field effect.[325,336,337,348] The malignant change can extend into the ducts of the submucosal glands, in a fashion analogous to endocervical gland involvement by cervical CIS.[346] Occasionally, the dysplastic or malignant cells exhibit a pagetoid pattern of growth, which can be very extensive.[329,333]

(Intra) mucosal carcinoma is the term employed for the carcinomas that do not invade beyond the lamina propria, *superficial (or microinvasive) carcinoma* for those that do not invade beyond the submucosa, and *superficial(ly) spreading carcinoma* for those tumors having a lateral intramucosal spread of at least 2 cm beyond the invasive lesion.[341,342,349] The term *early carcinoma* is sometimes used as a synonym for some of the lesions just described (particularly superficial carcinoma),[331] but its use is discouraged because of the unproven assumption it connotes. As the tumor proceeds to invade beyond the mucosa, there tends to be an increase in its proliferative index and in the overexpression of p53.[335] Grossly, superficial carcinomas have been arbitrarily divided into flat, coarse, verrucous, polypoid, and ulcerating infiltrating.[328] The more polypoid the lesion, the more likely that it will be found to invade the submucosa and that it will be associated with lymph node metastases.[327,332,339,345] The incidence of multicentricity for these superficial lesions is very high.[326,340] The incidence of nodal metastases is zero for CIS and virtually zero for intramucosal carcinomas; it ranges from over 20% to almost 50% in the cases with submucosal invasion, depending on the series.[332,334,349] Consequently, it is not surprising that whereas the 5-year survival rate is practically 100% for CIS or (intra)mucosal carcinoma, it drops to 50% for the superficial carcinomas.[343]

Metastases

The abundant lymphatic supply of the esophagus is responsible for the high frequency of lymph node metastases in the periesophageal area, below the diaphragm, and upward into the cervical nodes.[350,354] These nodal metastases occur early in the course of the disease and are the main reason for treatment failure. In a series of 40 patients without evidence of metastatic disease by conventional techniques, laparotomy with celiac lymph node biopsy showed involvement in 40%.[352] However, it should be pointed out that in small carcinomas confined to the esophageal wall, the lymph node metastasis is solitary in almost half of the cases.[353] Metastases to distant organs are also frequent, particularly to liver, lung, and adrenal glands.[351] The tumor may also metastasize to the submucosa of the stomach, probably through the submucosal lymphatic plexus.[355]

Cytology

Exfoliative cytology in experienced hands is an extremely accurate technique for the evaluation of esophageal lesions, particularly those of the lower third.[359,362] For many years, it was clearly superior to radiography or endoscopy.[361] However, since the introduction of the flexible fiberoptic endoscope, the diagnostic accuracy of direct-vision biopsy has become as high as that of cytology.[357] Prolla et al.[363] compared the results of direct-vision endoscopic biopsy with brush cytology performed in 183 patients with proven carcinoma of the esophagus and stomach: 95% were diagnosed correctly by cytology and 79% by biopsy. The combined biopsy and cytology approach provided a positive diagnosis in 95%. In the experience of Kasugai et al.[358] with 116 cases of esophageal carcinoma, the diagnostic accuracy was 97% for brush cytology using a fiberscope, 90% for direct-vision biopsy, and 99% for combined cytology and biopsy.

Diagnostic cytology is particularly rewarding in countries with a high incidence of esophageal carcinoma, such as China or South Africa.[360,364] Positive results have been obtained in asymptomatic patients with negative radiographs. Surgical resection has shown in situ or superficially invasive lesions, often with multiple foci of origin. A high percentage of these patients have survived for 5 years.[356]

Treatment

Traditionally, radiation therapy has been the most common form of treatment for carcinoma of the upper two thirds of the esophagus, and surgery (in the form of esophagogastrectomy) the usual approach for carcinoma of the lower third.[365,369,382,383,384] The current approach favors combined modalities consisting of preoperative radiation therapy (intracavitary or external beam) followed by surgery[372,385] or the combination of chemotherapy and radiation therapy, with or without surgery.[374,377]

There is apparently no relation between the degree of response to chemotherapy by the tumor and its degree of differentiation.[367] The overall results with any of these combination therapies remain disappointingly poor.[366,375,378,380]

Earlam and Cunha-Melo[368] reviewed data from 83,783 patients with squamous cell carcinoma of the esophagus reported in 122 articles. Of these, 58% were explored, and 39% had the tumor resected; 13% died in the hospital. Of the 26% leaving the hospital with the tumor excised, 18% survived for 1 year, 9% for 2 years, and 4% for 5 years. The operative mortality, still inordinately high, is mainly due to pyothorax, pulmonary complications, suture leak, and hemorrhage.[370,371,376]

In inoperable cases, considerable palliation can still be achieved by well-planned irradiation.[373,379,381]

Prognosis

As already stated in the preceding section, the overall prognosis for esophageal squamous cell carcinoma is very poor, the median survival after diagnosis being less than 1 year.[403] Factors thought to influence survival are the following:[396]

1 *Sex*. In several series, females have fared better than males.[412]

2 *Stage*. As for most other sites, this factor is of paramount importance[224,395] (see Appendix C). In situ and (intra) mucosal carcinomas are nearly always curable, and the cure rate is significantly higher for superficial carcinomas than for deeper tumors[397a] (see p. 628). Among cases with nodal involvement, those with two or more positive nodes do worse than those with a single metastasis.[409]

3 *Lymph node metastases*. Naturally, this parameter is included in the staging system. Among node-positive cases, cases with two or more involved nodes do worse than those with a single metastasis.[391,409] The prognostic value of micrometastases detected immunohistochemically is still uncertain.[392,394] Parenthetically, expression of bcl-2 in the primary tumor has been found to be associated with an increased likelihood of nodal metastases.[402]

4 *Tumor length*. Data from the SEER program have indicated that tumor length is an independent predictor of mortality when controlling for depth of invasion in patients with localized disease.[391]

5 *Microscopic grade*. The importance of this parameter is controversial but, on the whole, not substantial. Some studies have shown a more favorable prognosis for the better differentiated tumors, but grade loses most of its significance in multivariate analyses.[389,406]

6 *Other microscopic findings*. In one study,[389] vascular or lymphatic invasion and marked tumor necrosis were associated with a worse prognosis, whereas peritumoral fibrosis and lymphocytic reaction to the tumor were associated with a better prognosis; however, only the latter parameter reached statistical significance. The prognostic value of lymph vessel invasion has been confirmed by other studies.[387,411] It has also been claimed that tumor vascularity correlates with prognosis.[410]

7 *Surgical margins*. Involvement of the circumferential surgical margins is associated with a high probability of local recurrence.[407]

8 *DNA ploidy and proliferation indices*. A correlation between aneuploidy and either survival or time to recurrence has been found in several studies (including some that performed a multivariate analysis)[386,388,398,399] but not in others.[390,404,406] AgNOR counts have been said to correlate with probability of recurrence in superficial carcinomas[397] and with overall prognosis.[400]

9 *Epidermal growth factor receptor (EGFR)*. Overexpression of EGFR has been found to correlate with grade, lymph node status, and poor prognosis.[401,413] Tumors expressing elevations in both EGFR and TGF-α seem to have an especially aggressive behavior.[393]

10 *p53*. Patients whose tumors have overexpressed and/or mutated p53 have a worse survival rate than the others.[405,408]

Other types of carcinoma

Sarcomatoid carcinoma (pseudosarcoma; carcinosarcoma; spindle cell carcinoma; polypoid carcinoma) usually presents as a large polypoid neoplasm[431,439] (Fig. 11.16). The epithelial-appearing component can be very inconspicuous and is usually limited to a few areas of in situ or superficially invasive carcinoma. Its appearance is usually that of a squamous cell carcinoma of either conventional type or the basaloid variety (Figs 11.17 and 11.18). The bulk of the tumor has a pleomorphic sarcoma-like appearance (Fig. 11.21). It usually resembles malignant fibrous histiocytoma of soft tissues, and sometimes it exhibits focal differentiation toward cartilage, bone, or skeletal muscle.[432,433] Most evidence suggests that this component is also of epithelial derivation, and that all of the morphologically diverse tumor components have the same clonal origin.[418,429,434,451] Ultrastructurally, *some* of these sarcoma-like cells in *some* of the tumors retain epithelial markers, such as desmosomes and tonofibrils (Fig. 11.19). Most others have the appearance of myofibroblasts or other mesenchymal cells.[442,447] Immunohistochemically, keratin can be consistently demonstrated in the epithelial-appearing component and, in a high proportion of cases, also in some of the sarcoma-like cells. The latter also exhibit

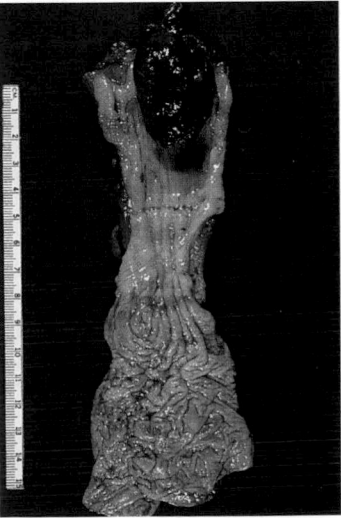

Fig. 11.16 Gross appearance of sarcomatoid carcinoma of esophagus. The tumor has a characteristic large size and polypoid shape. The cardioesophageal junction is in the middle, and the stomach is at the bottom of the specimen.

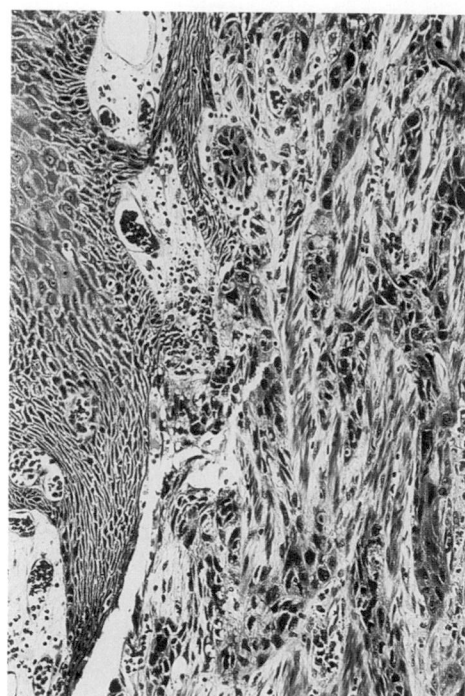

Fig. 11.17 Sarcomatoid carcinoma of esophagus. Areas of well-differentiated squamous cell carcinoma merge with a spindle cell component having a fascicular pattern of growth.

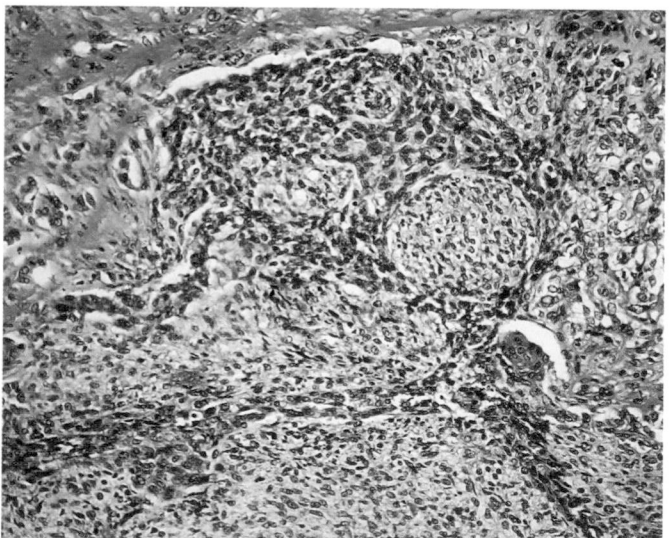

Fig. 11.18 Sarcomatoid carcinoma of esophagus. In this case, the carcinomatous component has a basaloid appearance.

strong reactivity for vimentin and, occasionally, for actin and desmin[441] but are negative for S-100 protein except for areas of cartilaginous metaplasia.[474,475] The epithelial component may exhibit focal neuroendocrine features as a sign of multidirectional differentiation.[440,459] The sarcoma-like component has a higher proliferative index and higher aneuploidy than the morphologically identifiable carcinomatous component, these properties giving it a growth advantage and probably explaining its dominance.[444] There is a constant overexpression of p53, as

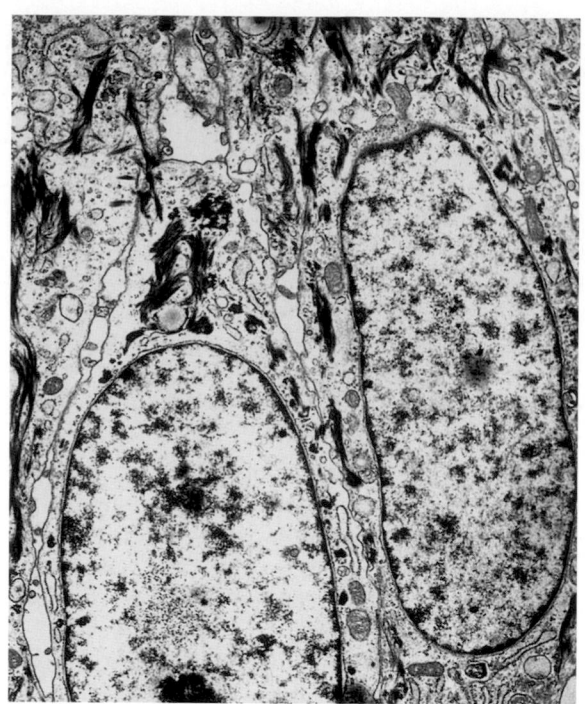

Fig. 11.19 Electron micrograph of sarcomatoid carcinoma of esophagus. The spindle-shaped tumor cells contain conspicuous cytoplasmic tonofibrils and are joined by an occasional desmosome. (×7000; courtesy of Dr. Robert A. Erlandson, Memorial Sloan-Kettering Cancer Institute)

there is in conventional squamous cell carcinoma of this organ.[416] Metastases or recurrences supervene in about 20% of the patients undergoing surgery, and the overall survival rate is in the neighborhood of 50%.[457] The nodal metastases usually contain epithelial elements alone or a mixture of epithelial and spindle elements; occasionally, the entire metastatic focus is made up of the spindle cell element, giving further credence to the interpretation that this component is indeed neoplastic and not a stromal reaction to the tumor.[449] Occasionally the metaplastic foci are seen only at a metastatic site.[471]

Verrucous carcinoma, morphologically identical to its more common counterpart in the oral cavity, has been described in the esophagus.[415,453] It is grossly polypoid and well differentiated throughout microscopically. Despite these features and its inability to metastasize, the mortality associated with this tumor in this particular location is high.[419]

Adenocarcinoma of the esophagus can arise from Barrett's metaplastic mucosa (discussed on p. 624), from a focus of heterotopic gastric mucosa (see p. 616), or—theoretically—from esophageal glands.[440a] Adenocarcinomas make up about 10% of esophageal cancers, but their relative frequency seems to be on the rise in the United States.[473] A very small proportion of primary esophageal adenocarcinomas have *signet ring cell* features[425]; in these cases, esophageal extension of a gastric carcinoma should be ruled out. Other esophageal adenocarcinomas are accompanied by pagetoid spread in the lining squamous epithelium.[440a] Still others exhibit focal or extensive rhabdoid features.[415a]

Adenosquamous carcinoma shows evidence of both squamous and glandular differentiation.[420] For all practical purposes, this rare high-grade tumor should be equated with the conventional squamous cell carcinoma. It should be distinguished from both the low-grade **mucoepidermoid carcinoma**, possibly arising in salivary-type submucosal esophageal glands[428,476] and the equally rare **collision tumor**, represented by a merging of two originally separate neoplasms (i.e., squamous cell carcinoma and adenocarcinoma).[448,465]

Basaloid (squamous cell) carcinoma is the currently preferred term for a highly malignant esophageal neoplasm often misdiagnosed as adenoid cystic carcinoma.[424,463] Although this tumor has been viewed as the esophageal counterpart of adenoid cystic carcinoma of the salivary glands, it exhibits both morphologic and behavioral differences from the latter. It should be regarded primarily as a squamous cell tumor exhibiting focal and sometimes extensive differentiation toward primitive glandular structures.[430] Peripheral palisading, round glandular lumina, and abundant basal lamina material deposition are the most important features[466] (Fig. 11.20). Immunohistochemically, there is a predominant expression of keratins 14 and 19 at the periphery of the basaloid nests.[414] Multipotential differentiation may be present in the form of neuroendocrine and/or sarcomatoid features.[426] Bcl-2 expression and c-myc amplification are frequent.[462] The behavior is extremely aggressive.[417] Similar tumors occur in the oral cavity, pharynx, larynx, and anal canal.[472]

Small cell carcinoma (small cell neuroendocrine carcinoma; anaplastic small cell carcinoma) is a highly malignant esophageal tumor having morphologic features very similar to those of its pulmonary counterpart.[454] Grossly, it usually exhibits a fungating pattern of growth.[450] Occasionally, multiple foci are found.[460] Microscopically, small cells with dark nuclei of round or oval shape and very scanty cytoplasm are seen growing in a predominantly diffuse fashion. As in small cell carcinoma of the lung, there may be rosette formation and focal mucin secretion. Argyrophilic granules can be demonstrated by the Sevier-Munger or Grimelius technique, and dense-core granules are consistently found by electron microscopy.[450,458] The diagnosis can be made by cytologic examination.[333] Some cases have been associated with ACTH and 5-HT production.[438,469] Some tumors, presumably less differentiated, lack these ultrastructural and histochemical markers but are otherwise identical morphologically and behaviorally.[422,467] The prognosis is very poor; most patients die within 1 year with generalized metastases.[423,443,445,452,456,461] This tumor probably arises from the same multipotent epithelial basal cells that give rise to conventional squamous cell

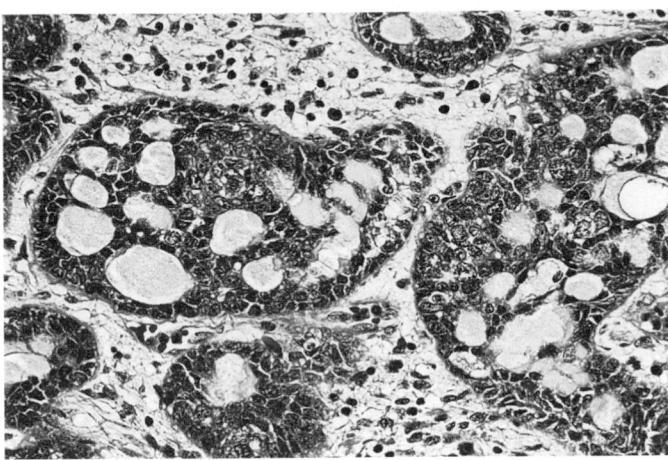

A

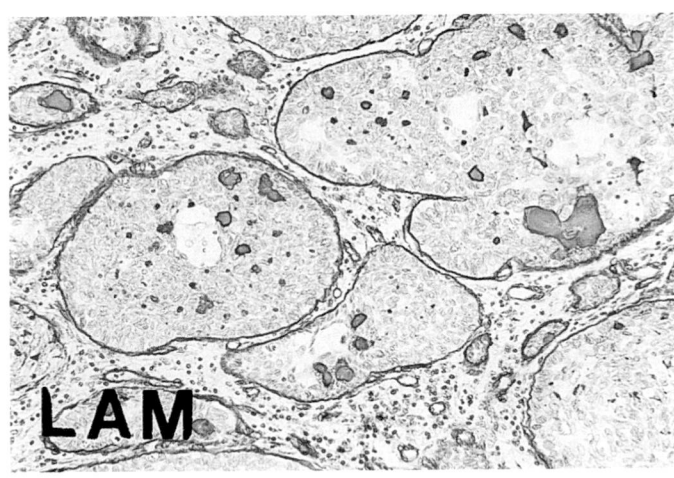

B

Fig. 11.20 Basaloid (squamous cell) carcinoma. **A,** In this area the tumor has an appearance that resembles that of adenoid cystic carcinoma. **B,** Immunocytochemical staining for laminin showing heavy deposition of basal membrane material around the tumor nests and within the "cylinders."

carcinoma.[435] Supporting this contention is the fact that it may be found closely intermingled with in situ or invasive squamous cell carcinoma.[427,454,464]

Small cell carcinoma should be clearly separated from the much better differentiated **carcinoid tumor**.[421,468] The latter neoplasm, which is vanishingly rare in this location, probably arises from the endocrine cells ordinarily present in the normal esophageal mucosa.[470] Its gross appearance tends to be polypoid. Some of the cases have been seen as an incidental finding in association with adenocarcinoma arising against the background of Barrett's esophagus.[436] **Atypical carcinoid tumor** of the esophagus has also been described, the diagnostic criteria for the identification being the same as for its pulmonary counterpart.[446]

Lymphoepithelioma-like carcinoma has been reported in the esophagus; as in other sites, it has been found to contain EBV DNA.[455]

Smooth muscle tumors and GIST-type stromal tumors

Leiomyomas are the most common benign tumors of the esophagus.[484] In careful autopsy cases, the frequency of this lesion has been found to be almost 8%.[485] Half of the surgically excised cases are asymptomatic; dysphagia and vague thoracic pain are the main complaints in the others.[483] The majority arise from the inner circular muscle and are more common in the distal third.[485] Multiple leiomyomas occur and need to be distinguished from giant muscular hypertrophy (see p. 619) although they share the same underlying molecular pathogenesis.[478] Some of the cases of multiple tumors have occurred in association with leiomyomas of lung and uterus in patients with multiple endocrine neoplasia type 1 (MEN-1).[480] Grossly, leiomyomas form well-defined masses in the esophageal wall and have a solid, grayish white appearance on cross section (Fig. 11.21). When they grow intraluminally, they encroach on the mucosa and appear as sessile or pedunculated polyps. Ulceration of the overlying mucosa is a rare event, in contrast to its common occurrence in gastric leiomyomas.

Microscopically, leiomyomas have the usual characteristics of a benign smooth muscle tumor. Local resection or enucleation is usually successful.

Leiomyosarcomas are quite unusual in the esophagus, in contrast to the lower gastrointestinal tract.[477] Grossly, they may be indistinguishable from leiomyoma, although they tend to be larger and softer and often are

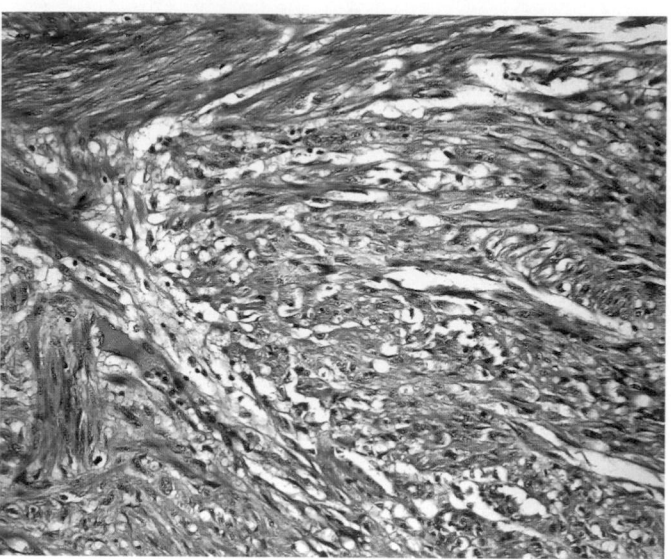

Fig. 11.22 Malignant gastrointestinal stromal tumor (GIST) of esophagus. (Courtesy of Dr. Fabio Facchetti, Brescia, Italy)

associated with areas of hemorrhage and necrosis.[482] The presence of a large number of mitotic figures is the main microscopic criterion by which they are separated from their benign counterpart (Fig. 11.22).

GIST-type stromal tumors also occur in the esophagus, although their relative frequency is considerably lower than in the stomach or bowel. As in the latter locations, they are characteristically positive for CD117 and CD34, with an occasional additional immunoreactivity for actin.[481] At the genetic level, they usually show mutations in exon 11 of *c-kit*, as do their gastrointestinal counterparts. Microscopically, some exhibit an epithelioid morphology. A few show phenotypic features indicating neural differentiation analogous to gastrointestinal autonomic nerve (GAN) tumors.[479] As a group, the behavior of esophageal stromal tumors is aggressive, particularly for the large-sized and/or mitotically active tumors.[481]

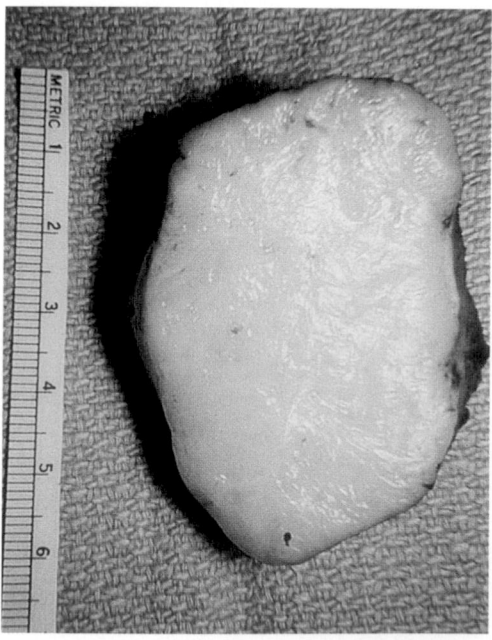

Fig. 11.21 Gross appearance of leiomyoma of the esophagus. The sharply circumscribed tumor has a white color and elastic consistency.

Other tumors and tumorlike conditions

Glycogenic acanthosis appears grossly as multiple, uniformly sized, oval or round white elevations measuring usually less than 1 cm. Traditionally, these have been equated with "leukoplakia," but, microscopically, they show no resemblance to the lesions so designated in the oral cavity and other sites. Instead, they represent areas of focal thickening of the epithelium resulting from a marked increase in cytoplasmic glycogen.[521] The proposal has been made that these formations may be related to gastroesophageal reflux.[528] Glycogenic acanthosis needs to be distinguished at the gross level from epidermization, an exceptionally rare event in which the esophageal mucosa acquires epidermis-like features.[512]

Amyloidosis in its localized form (so-called "amyloid tumor") can present as an intramural esophageal mass; exceptionally, it may result in perforation and hematemesis.

Sclerotherapy for bleeding esophageal varices may be complicated by superficial and deep mucosal ulceration, extensive fibrosis, and sometimes the formation of hematomas.[496,519]

Squamous papillomas rarely occur in the esophagus.[500] Winkler et al.[530] detected in some of these papillomas and in smaller esophageal lesions that they called *focal epithelial hyperplasia* evidence of human papilloma virus infection, on both microscopic and immunohistochemical grounds. These findings have been duplicated by some authors[513] but not by others.[490,491]

Benign fibrovascular polyps (inflammatory fibrous polyps) of the esophagus usually are pedunculated and solitary. They may attain huge dimensions.[526] Patients present with dysphagia and sometimes with intermittent regurgitation of a fleshy mass in the mouth. Death from asphyxia can result from laryngeal impaction. Most of the 53 cases reviewed by Jang et al.[505] occurred in adults, and approximately 85% were located in the upper third of the esophagus. Microscopically, they are composed of fibrous tissue and numerous blood vessels, with stromal edema and occasional lymphocytic infiltration.[531] The overlying mucosa often is ulcerated. These polyps most likely represent a reactive condition. Local excision is curative.[506]

Hyperplastic polyps of the esophagus and gastroesophageal junction are characterized by hyperplastic epithelium of foveolar and/or squamous type accompanied by stromal inflammation. They are usually associated with (and probably the result of) recent esophageal ulcers and erosive esophagitis.[486]

Granular cell tumors have been described in the esophagus, as either solitary or multiple nodules; sometimes they are associated with similar lesions in the stomach.[494,529] As in other sites, they can induce a pseudoepitheliomatous hyperplasia of the overlying epithelium. Their pattern of growth can be deceptively invasive.[493] A malignant example has also been recorded.[514]

Other benign esophageal tumors that have been exceptionally reported include *lobular capillary hemangioma*,[515] *neurofibroma*,[522] *schwannoma*,[518] (including the plexiform variety[492a]), *hemangiopericytoma*,[489] a peculiar benign *pigmented tumor* probably of neural origin,[488] and an equally peculiar *serous cystadenoma*.[527]

Carcinoid tumors are discussed on p. 631.

Malignant melanoma as an expression of a primary esophageal neoplasm has been fully documented.[495] The tumor can be located at any level in the esophagus, but it has a predilection for the lower third.[511] Grossly, the tumor is usually large and has a prominent polypoid appearance[507] (Fig. 11.23). Microscopically, epithelioid, spindle-cell, and pleomorphic areas may be seen singly or in combination. The amount of melanin produced is highly variable. Immunohistochemically, S-100 protein and HMB-45 positivity are the rule.[495,524] The search for a lateral intraepidermal component ("junctional activity") should be made in order to confirm the primary nature of the tumor (Fig. 11.24). In some cases, the melanoma has

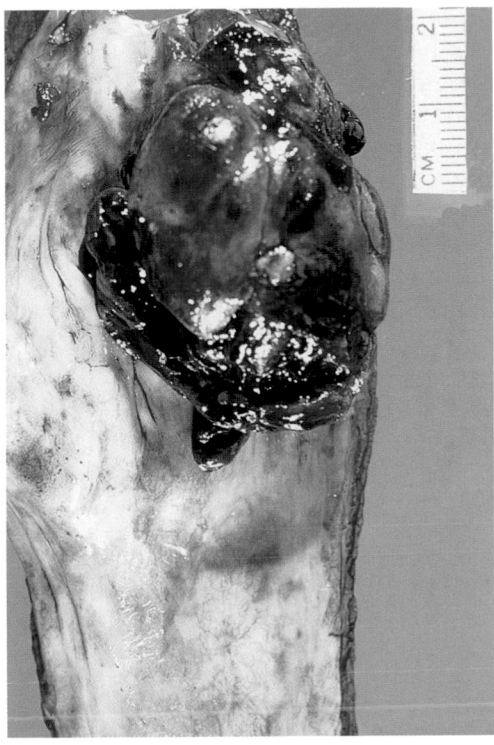

Fig. 11.23 Malignant melanoma of esophagus. The tumor has a characteristic polypoid appearance and is partially ulcerated. The dark color is the combined result of melanin deposition and hemorrhage within the tumor.

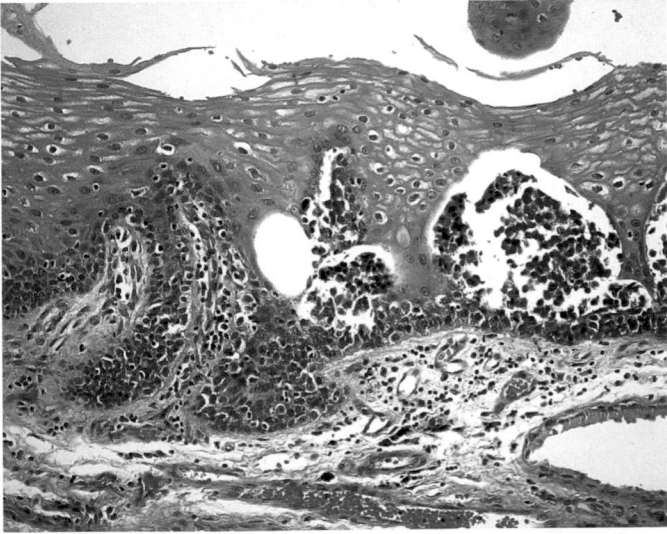

Fig. 11.24 Primary malignant melanoma of esophagus. There is a prominent intraepithelial component, with formation of large tumor nests.

been associated with focal or diffuse melanosis of the esophageal mucosa.[502,517] The prognosis is exceedingly poor.

Non-Hodgkin's malignant lymphoma[509,525] and **plasmacytoma**[487] occasionally present with dysphagia because of diffuse esophageal involvement. Some of the lymphoma cases have occurred in HIV-infected patients,[520] and at least one of them has been thought to be of true histiocytic type.[523] The esophageal wall can also be the site of leukemic infiltration,[497] Hodgkin's lymphoma[498] and focal lymphoid hyperplasia.[499]

Malignant mesenchymal neoplasms other than of smooth muscle origin have been occasionally reported, such as *osteosarcoma*,[510] *rhabdomyosarcoma*,[492] *synovial sarcoma*,[516] Ewing's sarcoma/PNET,[508] and *malignant peripheral nerve sheath tumor with skeletal metaplasia* (so-called "triton tumor").[516]

Metastatic carcinoma in the esophagus usually represents extension from pulmonary, laryngeal, gastric, or thyroid tumors, either directly or via periesophageal nodes.[503] Rarely, blood-borne metastases occur from carcinomas of distant sites, such as prostate,[501] endometrium,[532] or breast.[504] Achalasia may be simulated clinically.[504]

References

Normal anatomy

1   DeNardi FG, Riddell RH. Esophagus. In Sternberg S (ed.): Histology for pathologists, 2nd. Ed., Philadelphia, Lippincott-Raven Publishers, 1997, pp. 461–480.
2   Geboes K, Desmet K. Histology of the esophagus. In vander Reis L (ed.): Frontier gastrointestinal research, vol 3. Basel, 1978, Karger.
3   Meyer GW, Austin RM, Brady CE III, Castell DO. Muscle anatomy of the human esophagus. J Clin Gastroenterol 1986, **8:** 131–134.
4   Tateishi R, Taniguchi H, Wada A, Horai T, Taniguchi K. Argyrophil cells and melanocytes in esophageal mucosa. Arch Pathol 1974, **98:** 87–89.
5   Weinstein WM, Bogoch ER, Bowes KL. The normal human esophageal mucosa. A histological reappraisal. Gastroenterology 1975, **68:** 40–44.

Atresia and related anomalies

6   Aprigliano F. Esophageal stenosis in children. Ann Otol Rhinol Laryngol 1980, **89:** 391–396.
7   Holden MP, Wooler GH. Tracheooesophageal fistula and oesophageal atresia. Results of 30 years' experience. Thorax 1970, **25:** 406–412.
8   Holder TM, Ashcraft KW. Esophageal atresia and tracheoesophageal fistula. Ann Thorac Surg 1970, **9:** 445–467.
9   Holder TM, Cloud DT, Lewis JE Jr, Pilling GP IV. Esophageal atresia and tracheoesophageal fistula. A survey of its members by the Surgical Section of the American Academy of Pediatrics. Pediatrics 1964, **34:** 542–549.
10 Manning PB, Morgan RA, Coran AG, Wesley JR, Polley TZ Jr, Behrendt DM, Kirsch MM, Sloan HE. Fifty years' experience with esophageal atresia and tracheoesophageal fistula. Beginning with Cameron Haight's first operation in 1935. Ann Surg 1986, **204:** 446–453.
11 Nakazato Y, Landing BH, Wells TR. Abnormal Auerbach plexus in the esophagus and stomach of patients with esophageal atresia and tracheoesophageal fistula. J Pediatr Surg 1986, **21:** 831–837.
12 Spitz L, Kiely E, Brereton RJ. Esophageal atresia. Five year experience with 148 cases. J Pediatr Surg 1987, **22:** 103–108.

Heterotopia

13 Chatelain D, De Lajarte-Thirouard AS, Tiret E, Flejou JF. Adenocarcinoma of the upper esophagus arising in heterotopic gastric mucosa: common pathogenesis with Barrett's adenocarcinoma? Virchows Arch 2002, **441:** 406–411.
14 Christensen WN, Sternberg SS. Adenocarcinoma of the upper esophagus arising in ectopic gastric mucosa. Two case reports and review of the literature. Am J Surg Pathol 1987, **11:** 397–402.
15 Jabbari M, Goresky CA, Lough J, Yaffe C, Daly D, Côté C. The inlet patch. Heterotopic gastric mucosa in the upper esophagus. Gastroenterology 1985, **89:** 352–356.
16 Marcial MA, Villafana M. Esophageal ectopic sebaceous glands. Endoscopic and histologic findings. Gastrointest Endosc 1994, **40:** 630–632.
17 Merino MJ, Brand M, LiVolsi VA, McCallum RW. Sebaceous glands in the esophagus diagnosed in a clinical setting. Arch Pathol Lab Med 1982, **106:** 47–48.
18 Nakanishi Y, Ochial A, Shimoda T, Yamaguchi H, Tachimori Y, Kato H, Watanabe H, Hirohashi S. Heterotopic sebaceous glands in the esophagus: histopathological and immunohistochemical study of resected esophagus. Pathol Int 1999, **49:** 364–368.
19 Popiolek D, Kahn E, Markowitz J, Daum F. Prevalence and pathogenesis of pancreatic acinar tissue at the gastroesophageal junction in children and young adults. Arch Pathol Lab Med 2000, **124:** 1165–1167.
20 Variend S, Howat AJ. Upper eosophageal gastric heterotopia. A prospective necropsy study in children. J Clin Pathol 1988, **41:** 742–745.

Diverticula

21 Altorki NK, Sunagawa M, Skinner DB. Thoracic esophageal diverticula. Why is operation necessary? J Thorac Cardiovasc Surg 1993, **105:** 260–264.
22 Benacci JC, Deschamps C, Trastek VF, Allen MS, Daly RC, Pairolero PC. Epiphrenic diverticulum. Results of surgical treatment. Ann Thorac Surg 1993, **55:** 1109–1113.
23 Graham DY, Goyal RK, Sparkman J, Cogan ME, Pogonowska MJ. Diffuse intramural esophageal diverticulosis. Gastroenterology 1975, **68:** 781–785.
24 Janes RM. Diverticula of the lower thoracic esophagus. Ann Surg 1946, **124:** 637–652.
25 Levine MS, Moolten DN, Herlinger H, Laufer I. Esophageal intramural pseudodiverticulosis. A reevaluation. AJR 1986, **147:** 1165–1170.
26 Murney RG Jr, Linne JH, Curtis J. High-amplitude peristaltic contractions in a patient with esophageal intramural pseudodiverticulosis. Dig Dis Sci 1983, **28:** 843–847.
27 Philippakis M, Karkanias GG, Sakorafas GH. Carcinoma within an epiphrenic diverticulum. Case report. Eur J Surg 1991, **157:** 617–618.
28 Pierce WS, Johnson J. Squamous cell carcinoma in a pharyngoesophageal diverticulum. Cancer 1969, **24:** 1068–1070.
29 Umlas J, Sakhuja R. The pathology of esophageal intramural pseudodiverticulosis. Am J Clin Pathol 1976, **65:** 314–320.
30 Wouters B, van Overbeek JJ. Endoscopic treatment of the hypopharyngeal (Zenker's) diverticulum. Hepatogastroenterology 1992, **39:** 105–108.
31 Wychulis AR, Gunnlaugsson GH, Claggett OT. Carcinoma occurring in pharyngoesophageal diverticulum. Report of three cases. Surgery 1969, **66:** 976–979.

Cysts

32 Akiyama S, Sakamoto J, Suyama M, Imaizumi M, Ichihashi H, Kondo T. Esophageal cyst. A case report and a review of the literature. Jpn J Surg 1980, **10:** 338–342.

33 Harvell JD, Macho JR, Klein HZ. Isolated intra-abdominal esophageal cyst: case report and review of the literature. Am J Surg Pathol 1996, **20**: 476–479.

34 McGregor DH, Mills G, Boudet RA. Intramural squamous cell carcinoma of the esophagus. Cancer 1976, **37**: 1556–1561.

35 Olsen JB, Clemmensen O, Andersen K. Adenocarcinoma arising in a foregut cyst of the mediastinum. Ann Thorac Surg 1991, **51**: 497–499.

Rings and webs

36 Clements JL Jr, Cox GW, Torres WE, Weens HS. Cervical esophageal webs. A roentgen-anatomic correlation. Observations on the pharyngoesophagus. Am J Roentgenol Radium Ther Nucl Med 1974, **121**: 221–231.

37 Goyal RK, Bauer JL, Spiro HM. The nature and location of lower esophageal ring. N Engl J Med 1971, **284**: 1175–1180.

38 Guelrud M, Villasmil L, Mendez R. Late results in patients with Schatzki ring treated by endoscopic electrosurgical incision of the ring. Gastrointest Endosc 1987, **33**: 96–98.

39 Johnson AC, Lester PD, Johnson S, Sudarsanam D, Dunn D. Esophagogastric ring. Why and when we see it, and what it implies. A radiologic-pathologic correlation. South Med J 1992, **85**: 946–952.

40 Lindgren S. Endoscopic dilatation and surgical myectomy of symptomatic cervical esophageal webs. Dysphagia 1991, **6**: 235–238.

Achalasia and related motor disorders

41 Adams CWM, Brain RHF, Trounce JR. Ganglion cells in achalasia of the cardia. Virchows Arch [A] 1976, **372**: 75–79.

42 Clark SB, Rice TW, Tubbs RR, Richter JE, Goldblum JR. The nature of the myenteric infiltrate in achalasia: an immunohistochemical analysis. Am J Surg Pathol 2000, **24**: 1153–1158.

43 Cohen S. Motor disorders of the esophagus. N Engl J Med 1979, **301**: 184–192.

44 Cruse JP, Edwards DAW, Smith JF, Wyllie JH. The pathology of a cricopharyngeal dysphagia. Histopathology 1979, **3**: 223–232.

45 Csendes A. Results of surgical treatment of achalasia of the esophagus. Hepatogastroenterology 1991, **38**: 474–480.

46 Csendes A, Smok G, Braghetto I, Gonzalez P, Henriquez A, Csendes P, Pizurno D. Histological studies of Auerbach's plexuses of the oesophagus, stomach, jejunum, and colon in patients with achalasia of the oesophagus. Correlation with gastric acid secretion, presence of parietal cells and gastric emptying of solids. Gut 1992, **33**: 150–154.

47 Dantas RO. Idiopathic achalasia and Chagasic megaesophagus. J Clin Gastroenterol 1988, **10**: 13–15.

48 Ferguson TB, Woodbury JD, Roper CL, Burford TH. Giant muscular hypertrophy of the esophagus. Ann Thorac Surg 1969, **8**: 209–218.

49 Goldblum JR, Whyte RI, Orringer MB, Appelman HD. Achalasia. A morphologic study of 42 resected specimens. Am J Surg Pathol 1994, **18**: 327–337.

50 Hankins JR, McLaughlin JS. The association of carcinoma of the esophagus with achalasia. J Thorac Cardiovasc Surg 1975, **69**: 355–360.

51 Heald J, Moussalli H, Hasleton PS. Diffuse leiomyomatosis of the oesophagus. Histopathology 1986, **10**: 755–759.

52 Heidet L, Boye E, Cai Y, Sado Y, Zhang X, Flejou JF, Fekete F, Ninomiya Y, Gubler MC, Antignac C. Somatic deletion of the 5′ ends of both the COL4A5 and COL4A6 genes in a sporadic leiomyoma of the esophagus. Am J Pathol 1998, **152**: 673–678.

53 Just-Viera JO, Haight C. Achalasia and carcinoma of the esophagus. Surg Gynecol Obstet 1969, **128**: 1081–1095.

53a Khelif K, De Laet M-H, Chaouchi B, Segers V, Vanderwinden J-M. Achalasia of the cardia in Allgrove's (Triple A) Syndrome. Am J Surg Pathol 2003, **27**: 667–672.

54 Lehman MB, Clark SB, Ormsby AH, Rice TW, Richer JE, Goldblum JR. Squamous mucosal alterations in esophagectomy specimens from patients with end-stage achalasia. Am J Surg Pathol 2001, **25**: 1413–1418.

55 Liu W, Fackler W, Rice TW, Richter JE, Achkar E, Goldblum JR. The pathogenesis of pseudoachalasia: a clinicopathologic study of 13 cases of a rare entity. Am J Surg Pathol 2002, **26**: 784–788.

56 Lonsdale RN, Roberts PF, Vaughan R, Thiru S. Familial oesophageal leiomyomatosis and nephropathy. Histopathology 1992, **20**: 127–133.

57 Meijssen MA, Tilanus HW, van Blankenstein M, Hop WC, Ong GL. Achalasia complicated by oesophageal squamous cell carcinoma. A prospective study in 195 patients. Gut 1992, **33**: 155–158.

58 Nihoul-Fekete C, Bawab F, Lortat-Jacob S, Arhan P. Achalasia of the esophagus in childhood. Surgical treatment in 35 cases, with special reference to familial cases and glucocorticoid deficiency association. Hepatogastroenterology 1991, **38**: 510–513.

59 Palmer ED. Disorders of the cricopharyngeus muscle. A review. Gastroenterology 1976, **71**: 510–519.

60 Peracchia A, Segalin A, Bardini R, Ruol A, Bonavina L, Baessato M. Esophageal carcinoma and achalasia. Prevalence, incidence and results of treatment. Hepatogastroenterology 1991, **38**: 514–516.

61 Proctor DD, Fraser JL, Mangano MM, Calkins DR, Rosenberg SJ. Small cell carcinoma of the esophagus in a patient with longstanding primary achalasia. Am J Gastroenterol 1992, **87**: 664–667.

62 Raymond L, Lach B, Shamji FM. Inflammatory aetiology of primary oesophageal achalasia: an immunohistochemical and ultrastructural study of Auerbach's plexus. Histopathology 1999, **35**: 445–453.

63 Wychulis AR, Woolam GL, Andersen HA, Ellis FH Jr. Achalasia and carcinoma of the esophagus. JAMA 1971, **215**: 1638–1641.

Lye strictures

64 Appelqvist P, Salmo M. Lye corrosion carcinoma of the esophagus. A review of 63 cases. Cancer 1980, **45**: 2655–2658.

65 Bosher LH Jr, Burford TH, Ackerman LV. The pathology of experimentally produced lye burns and strictures of the esophagus. J Thorac Surg 1951, **21**: 483–489.

66 Burford T, Webb WR, Ackerman LV. Caustic burns of the esophagus and their surgical management. Ann Surg 1953, **138**: 453–460.

67 Isolauri J, Markkula H. Lye ingestion and carcinoma of the esophagus. Acta Chir Scand 1989, **155**: 269–271.

Reflux esophagitis

68 Allison PR. Peptic ulcer of the esophagus. Thorax 1948, **3**: 20–42.

69 Barrett NR. Chronic peptic ulcer of the oesophagus and "oesophagitis." Br J Surg 1950, **38**: 175–182.

70 Behar J, Sheahan DC. Histologic abnormalities in reflux esophagitis. Arch Pathol 1975, **99**: 387–391.

71 Belsey R. Peptic ulcer of the esophagus. Ann R Coll Surg Engl 1954, **14**: 303–322.

72 Brown LF, Goldman H, Antonioli DA. Intraepithelial eosinophils in endoscopic biopsies of adults with reflux esophagitis. Am J Surg Pathol 1984, **8**: 899–905.

73 Collins BJ, Elliott H, Sloan JM, McFarland RJ, Love AHG. Oesophageal histology in reflux oesophagitis. J Clin Pathol 1985, **38**: 1265–1272.

74 Collins JSA, Watt PCH, Hamilton PW, Collins BJ, Sloan JM, Elliott H, Love AHG. Assessment of oesophagitis by histology and morphometry. Histopathology 1989, **14**: 381–390.

75 Cunningham KM, Horowitz M, Riddell PS, Maddern GJ, Myers JC, Holloway RH, Wishart JM, Jamieson GG. Relations among autonomic nerve dysfunction, oesophageal motility, and gastric

emptying in gastro-oesophageal reflux disease. Gut 1991, **32**: 1436–1440.

75a Esposito S, Valente G, Zavallone A, Guidali P, Rapa A, Oderda G. Histological score of cells with irregular nuclear contours for the diagnosis of reflux esophagitis in children. Hum Pathol 2004, (in press).

76 Fierson HF Jr. Histological criteria for the diagnosis of reflux esophagitis. Pathol Annu 1992, **27**(Pt 1): 87–104.

77 Geboes K, Desmet V, Vantrappen G. Esophageal histology in the early stage of gastroesophageal reflux letter. Arch Pathol Lab Med 1979, **103**: 205.

78 Haber MM, Lopez I. Reflux gastritis in gastroesophageal reflux disease: a histopathological study. Ann Diagn Pathol 1999, **3**: 281–286.

79 Ismail-Beigi F, Horton PF, Pope CE II. Histological consequences of gastroesophageal reflux in man. Gastroenterology 1970, **58**: 163–174.

80 Karl TR, Pindyck F, Sicular A. Zollinger-Ellison syndrome with esophagitis and Barrett Mucosa. Am J Gastroenterol 1983, **78**: 611–614.

81 McKinley M, Sherlock P. Barrett's esophagus with adenocarcinoma in scleroderma. Am J Gastroenterol 1984, **79**: 438–440.

82 Riddell RH. The biopsy diagnosis of gastroesophageal reflux disease, "carditis," and Barrett's esophagus, and sequelae of therapy. Am J Surg Pathol 1996, **20**: S31–50.

83 Sandry RJ. Pathology of reflux esophagitis. In Skinner DB, Belsey RHR, Hendrix TR, Zuidema GD (eds.): Gastroesophageal reflux in hiatal hernia. Boston, 1972, Little, Brown, & Co.

84 Sheahan DG, West AB. Focal lymphoid hyperplasia (pseudolymphoma) of the esophagus. Am J Surg Pathol 1985, **9**: 141–147.

85 Skinner DB. Pathophysiology of gastroesophageal reflux. Ann Surg 1985, **202**: 546–556.

86 Spechler SJ, Department of Veterans Affairs Gastroesophageal Reflux Disease Study Group. Comparison of medical and surgical therapy for complicated gastroesophageal reflux disease in veterans. N Engl J Med 1992, **326**: 786–792.

87 Trier JS. Morphology of the epithelium of the distal esophagus in patients with midesophageal peptic strictures. Gastroenterology 1970, **58**: 444–461.

88 Tummala V, Barwick KW, Sontag SJ, Vlahcevic RZ, McCallum RW. The significance of intraepithelial eosinophils in the histologic diagnosis of gastroesophageal reflux. Am J Clin Pathol 1987, **87**: 43–48.

89 Tytgat GNJ, Bianchi Porro G, Feussner H, Pace F, Richter JE, Siewert JR. Longterm strategy for the treatment of gastro-oesophageal reflux disease. Gastroenterol Int 1991, **4**: 21–32.

90 Wang HH, Mangano MM, Antonioli DA. Evaluation of T-lymphocytes in esophageal mucosal biopsies. Mod Pathol 1994, **7**: 55–58.

91 Yardley JH. Biopsy findings in low-grade reflux esophagitis. In Skinner DB, Belsey RHR, Hendrix TR, Zuidema GD (eds.): Gastroesophageal reflux and hiatal hernia. Boston, 1972, Little, Brown, & Co.

Barrett's esophagus

92 Batts KP. Barrett esophagus—more steps forward (editorial). Hum Pathol 2001, **32**: 357–359.

93 Biddlestone LR, Barham CP, Wilkinson SP, Barr H, Shepherd NA. The histopathology of treated Barrett's esophagus: squamous reepithelialization after acid suppression and laser and photodynamic therapy. Am J Surg Pathol 1998, **22**: 239–245.

94 Biddlestone LR, Bailey TA, Whittles CE, Shepherd NA. The clinical and molecular pathology of Barrett's oesophagus. Progress in pathology 2001, **5**: 57–80.

95 Brand DL, Ylvisaker JT, Gelfand M, Pope CE II. Regression of columnar esophageal (Barrett's) epithelium after antireflux surgery. N Engl J Med 1980, **302**: 844–848.

96 Bremner CG, Lynch VP, Ellis FH Jr. Barrett's esophagus. Congenital or acquired? An experimental study of esophageal mucosal regeneration in the dog. Surgery 1970, **68**: 209–216.

97 Chandrasoma PT, Der R, Dalton P, Kobayashi G, Ma Y, Peters J, Demeester T. Distribution and significance of epithelial types in columnar-lined esophagus. Am J Surg Pathol 2001, **25**: 1188–1193.

98 Chandrasoma PT, Der R, Ma Y, Dalton P, Taira M. Histology of the gastroesophageal junction: an autopsy study. Am J Surg Pathol 2000, **24**: 402–409.

99 Chandrasoma PT, Lokuhetty DM, Deemester TR, Bremner CG, Peters JH, Oberg S, Groshen S. Definition of histopathologic changes in gastroesophageal reflux disease. Am J Surg Pathol 2000, **24**: 344–351.

100 Chaves P, Cardoso P, De Almeida JC, Pereira AD, Leitao CN, Soares J. Non-goblet cell population of Barrett's esophagus: an immunohistochemical demonstration of intestinal differentiation. Hum Pathol 1999, **30**: 1291–1295.

101 Chinyama CN, Marshall RE, Owen WJ, Mason RC, Kothari D, Wilkinson ML, Sanderson JD. Expression of MUC1 and MUC2 mucin gene products in Barrett's metaplasia, dysplasia and adenocarcinoma: an immunopathological study with clinical correlation. Histopathology 1999, **35**: 517–524.

102 Dahms BB, Greco MA, Strandjord SE, Rothstein FC. Barrett's esophagus in three children after antileukemia chemotherapy. Cancer 1987, **60**: 2896–2900.

103 Dahms BB, Rothstein FC. Barrett's esophagus in children. A consequence of chronic gastroesophageal reflux. Gastroenterology 1984, **86**: 318–323.

104 Fahmy N, King JF. Barrett's esophagus. An acquired condition with genetic predisposition. Am J Gastroenterol 1993, **88**: 1262–1265.

105 Glickman JN, Wang HH, Das KM, Goyal RK, Spechler SJ, Antonioli D, Odze RD. Phenotype of Barrett's esophagus and intestinal metaplasia of the distal esophagus and gastroesophageal junction: an immunohistochemical study of cytokeratins 7 and 20, Das-1 and 45M1. Am J Surg Pathol 2001, **25**: 87–94.

106 Glickman JN, Chen YY, Wang HH, Antonioli DA, Odze RD. Phenotypic characteristics of a distinctive multilayered epithelium suggests that it is a precursor in the development of Barrett's esophagus. Am J Surg Pathol 2001, **25**: 569–578.

107 Goldblum JR. The significance and etiology of intestinal metaplasia of the esophagogastric junction. Ann Diagn Pathol 2002, **6**: 67–73.

108 Goldstein NS. Gastric cardia intestinal metaplasia: biopsy follow-up of 85 patients. Mod Pathol 2000, **13**: 1072–1079.

109 Goldstein NS, Karim R. Gastric cardia inflammation and intestinal metaplasia: associations with reflux esophagitis and Helicobacter pylori. Mod Pathol 1999, **12**: 1017–1024.

110 Griffin M, Sweeney EC. The relationship of endocrine cells, dysplasia and carcinoembryonic antigen in Barrett's mucosa to adenocarcinoma of the oesophagus. Histopathology 1987, **11**: 53–62.

111 Hamilton SR, Yardley JA. Regeneration of cardiac type mucosa and acquisition of Barrett mucosa after esophagogastrostomy. Gastroenterology 1977, **72**: 669–675.

112 Haque S, Eisen RN, West AB. Heterotopic bone formation in the gastrointestinal tract. Arch Pathol Lab Med 1996, **120**: 666–670.

113 Hassall E, Israel DM, Davidson AG, Wong LT. Barrett's esophagus in children with cystic fibrosis. Not a coincidental association. Am J Gastroenterol 1993, **88**: 1934–1938.

114 Hassall E, Weinstein WM, Ament ME. Barrett's esophagus in childhood. Gastroenterology 1985, **89**: 1331–1337.

115 Heitmann P, Csendes A, Strauszer T. Esophageal strictures and low esophagus lined with columnar epithelium. Am J Dig Dis 1971, **16**: 307–320.

116 Iftikhar SY, James PD, Steele RJ, Hardcastle JD, Atkinson M.

Length of Barrett's oesophagus. An important factor in the development of dysplasia and adenocarcinoma. Gut 1992, **33**: 1155–1158.

117 Krishnamurthy S, Dayal Y. Pancreatic metaplasia in Barrett's esophagus. An immunohistochemical study. Am J Surg Pathol 1995, **19**: 1172–1180.

118 Lagergren J, Bergstrom R, Lindgren A, Nyren O. Symptomatic gastroesophageal reflux as a risk factor for esophageal adenocarcinoma. N Engl J Med 1999, **340**: 825–831.

119 Lapertosa G, Baracchini P, Fulcheri E. Mucin histochemical analysis in the interpretation of Barrett's esophagus. Results of a multicenter study. The Operative Group for the Study of Esophageal Anatomy and Histology, Genoa, Italy. Am J Clin Pathol 1992, **98**: 5–7.

120 Lee RG. Mucins in Barrett's esophagus. A histochemical study. Am J Clin Pathol 1984, **81**: 500–503.

121 Levine DS, Rubin CE, Reid BJ, Haggitt RC. Specialized metaplastic columnar epithelium in Barrett's esophagus. A comparative transmission electron microscopic study. Lab Invest 1989, **60**: 418–432.

122 Menke-Pluymers MB, Hop WC, Dees J, van Blankenstein M, Tilanus HW. Risk factors for the development of an adenocarcinoma in columnar-lined (Barrett) esophagus. The Rotterdam Esophageal Tumor Study Group. Cancer 1993, **72**: 1155–1158.

123 Mittal RK, Balaban DH. The esophagogastric junction. N Engl J Med 1997, **336**: 924–932.

124 Mohammed IA, Streutker CJ, Riddel RH. Utilization of cytokeratins 7 and 20 does not differentiate between Barrett's esophagus and gastric cardiac intestinal metaplasia. Mod Pathol 2002, **15**: 611–616.

125 Nobukawa B, Abraham SC, Gill J, Hietmiller RF, Wu TT. Clinicopathologic and molecular analysis of high grade dysplasia and early adenocarcinoma in short- versus long-segment Barrett esophagus. Hum Pathol 2001, **32**: 447–454.

126 Offner FA, Lewin KJ, Weinstein WM. Metaplastic columnar cells in Barrett's esophagus: a common and neglected cell type. Hum Pathol 1996, **27**: 885–889.

127 Ormsby AH, Goldblum JR, Rice TW, Richter JE, Falk GW, Vaezi MF, Gramlich TL. Cytokeratin subsets can reliably distinguish Barrett's esophagus from intestinal metaplasia of the stomach. Hum Pathol 1999, **30**: 288–294.

128 Ormsby A, Kilgore SP, Goldblum JR, Richter JE, Rice TW, Gramlich TL. The location and frequency of intestinal metaplasia at the esophagogastric junction in 223 consecutive autopsies: implications for patient treatment and preventive strategies in Barrett's esophagus. Mod Pathol 2000, **13**: 614–620.

129 Paull G, Yardley JH. Gastric and esophageal *Campylobacter pylori* in patients with Barrett's esophagus. Gastroenterology 1988, **95**: 216–218.

130 Pera M, Trastek VF, Carpenter HA, Allen MS, Deschamps C, Pairolero PC. Barrett's esophagus with high-grade dysplasia. An indication for esophagectomy? Ann Thorac Surg 1992, **54**: 199–204.

131 Petras RE, Sivak MV Jr, Rice TW. Barrett's esophagus. A review of the pathologist's role in diagnosis and management. Pathol Annu 1991, **26**(Pt 2): 1–32.

132 Peuchmaur M, Potet F, Goldfain D. Mucin histochemistry of the columnar epithelium of the oesophagus (Barrett's oesophagus). A prospective biopsy study. J Clin Pathol 1984, **37**: 607–610.

132a Phillips RW, Frierson HF, Moskaluk CA. Cdx2 as a marker of epithelial intestinal differentiation in the esophagus. Am J Surg Pathol 2003, **27**: 1442–1447.

133 Phillips RW, Wong RK. Barrett's esophagus. Natural history, incidence, etiology, and complications. Gastroenterol Clin North Am 1991, **20**: 791–816.

134 Pope CE II. Regression of Barrett's epithelium. In Spechler SJ,

Goyal RK (eds.): Barrett's esophagus. Pathophysiology, diagnosis, and management. New York, 1985, Elsevier Science, pp. 224–229.

135 Qualman SJ, Murray RD, McClung HJ, Lucas J. Intestinal metaplasia is age related in Barrett's esophagus. Arch Pathol Lab Med 1990, **114**: 1236–1240.

136 Quddus MR, Henley JD, Sulaiman RA, Palumbo TC, Gnepp DR. Helicobacter pylori infection and adenocarcinoma arising in Barrett's esophagus. Hum Pathol 1997, **28**: 1007–1009.

137 Rusch VW, Levine DS, Haggitt R, Reid BJ. The management of high grade dysplasia and early cancer in Barrett's esophagus. A multidisciplinary problem. Cancer 1994, **74**: 1225–1229.

138 Sampliner RE. Practice guidelines on the diagnosis, surveillance, and therapy of Barrett's esophagus. Am J Gastroenterol 1998, **93**: 1028–1031.

139 Sarbia M, Donner A, Gabbert HE. Histopathology of the gastroesophageal junction: a study on 36 operation specimens. Am J Surg Pathol 2002, **26**: 1207–1212.

140 Sjogren RW Jr, Johnson LF. Barrett's esophagus. A review. Am J Med 1983, **74**: 313–321.

141 Skinner DB, Walther BC, Riddell RH, Schmidt H, Iascone C, DeMeester TR. Barrett's esophagus. Ann Surg 1983, **198**: 554–566.

142 Splechler SJ. Barrett's esophagus. N Engl Med 2002, **346**: 836–842.

143 Stein HJ, Siewert JR. Barrett's esophagus. Pathogenesis, epidemiology, functional abnormalities, malignant degeneration, and surgical management. Dysphagia 1993, **8**: 276–288.

144 Suo Z, Nesland JM. Barrett's esophagus: intestinal metaplasia or phenotypic shift of undifferentiated elements in the stem cells. Ultrastruct Pathol 2002, **26**: 53–54.

145 Takubo K. Squamous metaplasia with reserve cell hyperplasia in the esophagogastric junction zone. Acta Pathol Jpn 1981, **31**: 349–359.

146 Takubo K, Sasajima K, Yamashita K, Tanaka Y, Fujita K. Double muscularis mucosae in Barrett's esophagus. Hum Pathol 1991, **22**: 1158–1161.

147 Taniere P, Borghi-Scoazec G, Saurin JC, Lombert-Bohas C, Boulez J, Berger F, Hainaut P, Scoazec JY. Cytokeratin expression in adenocarcinomas of the esophagogastric junction: a comparative study of adenocarcinomas of the distal esophagus and of the proximal stomach. Am J Surg Pathol 2002, **26**: 1203–1221.

148 Torrado J, Ruiz B, Garay J, Asenjo JL, Tovar JA, Cosme A, Correa P. Blood-group phenotypes, sulfomucins, and Helicobacter pylori in Barrett's esophagus. Am J Surg Pathol 1997, **21**: 1023–1029.

149 Warson C, Van De Bovenkamp JH, Korteland-van Male AM, Buller HA, Einerhand AW, Ectors NL, Dekker J. Barrett's esophagus is characterized by expression of gastric-type mucins (MUC5AC, MUC6) and TFF peptides (TFF1 and TFF2), but the risk of carcinoma development may be indicated by the intestinal-type mucin MUC2. Hum Pathol 2002, **33**: 660–668.

150 Williamson WA, Ellis FH Jr, Gibb SP, Aretz HT. Barrett's ulcer. A surgical disease? J Thorac Cardiovasc Surg 1992, **103**: 2–6.

Dysplasia and carcinoma in situ in Barrett's esophagus; Adenocarcinoma arising in Barrett's esophagus

151 al-Kasspooles M, Moore JH, Orringer MB, Beer DG. Amplification and overexpression of the EGFR and erbB-2 genes in human esophageal adenocarcinomas. Int J Cancer 1993, **54**: 213–219.

152 Banner BF, Memoli VA, Warren WH, Gould VE. Carcinoma with multidirectional differentiation arising in Barrett's esophagus. Ultrastruct Pathol 1983, **4**: 205–217.

153 Berenson MM, Riddell RH, Skinner DB, Freston JW. Malignant transformation of esophageal columnar epithelium. Cancer 1978, **41**: 554–561.

154 Bhargava P, Eisen GM, Holterman DA, Azumi N, Hartmann DP, Hanfelt JJ, Benjamin SB, Lippman ME, Montgomery EA. Endoscopic mapping and surrogate markers for better

surveillance in Barrett esophagus. A study of 700 biopsy specimens. Am J Clin Pathol 2000, **114**: 552–563.

155 Bian YS, Osterheld MC, Bosman FT, Benhattar J, Fontilliet C. p53 gene mutation and protein accumulation during neoplastic progression in Barrett's esophagus. Mod Pathol 2001, **14**: 397–403.

156 Biddlestone LR, Bailey TA, Whittles CE, Shepherd NA. The clinical and molecular pathology of Barrett's oesophagus. Progress in pathology 2001, **5**: 57–80.

157 Blot WJ, Devesa SS, Kneller RW, Fraumeni JF Jr. Rising incidence of adenocarcinoma of the esophagus and gastric cardia. JAMA 1991, **265**: 1287–1289.

158 Blount PL, Ramel S, Raskind WH, Haggitt RC, Sanchez CA, Dean PJ, Rabinovitch PS, Reid BJ. 17p allelic deletions and p53 protein overexpression in Barrett's adenocarcinoma. Cancer Res 1991, **51**: 5482–5486.

159 Brien TP, Odze RD, Sheehan CE, Mc Kenna BJ, Ross JS. HER-2/neu gene amplification by FISH predicts poor survival in Barrett's esophagus associated adenocarcinoma. Hum Pathol 2000, **31**: 35–39.

160 Cameron AJ, Ott BJ, Payne WS. The incidence of adenocarcinoma in columnarlined (Barrett's) esophagus. N Engl J Med 1985, **313**: 857–859.

161 Cary NR, Barron DJ, McGoldrick JP, Wells FC. Combined oesophageal adenocarcinoma and carcinoid in Barrett's oesophagitis. Potential role of enterochromaffin-like cells in oesophageal malignancy. Thorax 1993, **48**: 404–405.

162 Chejfec G. Atypias, dysplasias, and neoplasias of the esophagus and stomach. Semin Diagn Pathol 1985, **2**: 31–41.

163 Cho KJ, Hunter TB, Whitehouse WM. The columnar-lined lower esophagus and its association with adenocarcinoma of the esophagus. Radiology 1975, **115**: 563–586.

164 Choi YW, Heath EI, Heitmiller R, Forastiere AA, Wu TT. Mutations in beta-catenin and APC genes are uncommon in esophageal and esophagogastric junction adenocarcinomas. Mod Pathol 2000, **13**: 1055–1059.

165 Duhaylongsod FG, Wolfe WG. Barrett's esophagus and adenocarcinoma of the esophagus and gastroesophageal junction. J Thorac Cardiovasc Surg 1991, **102**: 36–41.

166 Dworak O, Koerfgen HP. Carcinosarcoma in Barrett's oesophagus. A case report with immunohistological examination. Virchows Arch [A] 1993, **422**: 423–426.

167 Fein R, Kelsen DP, Geller N, Bains M, McCormack P, Brennan MF. Adenocarcinoma of the esophagus and gastroesophageal junction. Prognostic factors and results of therapy. Cancer 1985, **56**: 2512–2518.

167a Flucke U, Steinborn E, Dries V, Mönig, Schneider PM, Thiel J, Hölscher AH, Dienes HP, Baldus SE. Immunoreactivity of cytokeratins (CK7, CK20) and mucin peptide core antigens (MUC1, MUC2, MUC5AC) in adenocarcinomas, normal and metaplastic tissues of the distal oesophagus, oesophago-gastric junction and proximal stomach. Histopathology 2003, **43**: 127–134.

168 Geboes K, Van Eyken P. The diagnosis of dysplasia and malignancy in Barrett's esophagus. Histopathology 2000, **37**: 99–107.

169 Geisinger KR, Teot LA, Richter JE. A comparative cytopathologic and histologic study of atypia, dysplasia, and adenocarcinoma in Barrett's esophagus. Cancer 1992, **69**: 8–16.

169a Goldblum JR. Barrett's esophagus and Barrett's-related dysplasia. Mod Pathol 2003, **16**: 316–324.

170 Goldblum JR, Lauwers GY. Dysplasia arising in Barrett's esophagus: diagnostic pitfalls and natural history. Semin Diagn Pathol 2002, **19**: 12–19.

171 Haggitt RC. Barrett's esophagus, dysplasia, and adenocarcinoma. Hum Pathol 1994, **25**: 982–993.

172 Haggitt RC, Dean PJ. Adenocarcinoma in Barrett's epithelium. In Spechler SJ, Goyal RK (eds.): Barrett's esophagus.

Pathophysiology, diagnosis, and management. New York, 1985, Elsevier Science, pp. 153–166.

173 Haggitt RC, Reid BJ, Rabinovitch PS, Rubin CE. Barrett's esophagus. Correlation between mucin histochemistry, flow cytometry, and histologic diagnosis for predicting increased cancer risk. Am J Pathol 1988, **131**: 53–61.

174 Haggitt RC, Tryzelaar J, Ellis FH, Colcher H. Adenocarcinoma complicating columnar epithelium-lined (Barrett's) esophagus. Am J Clin Pathol 1978, **70**: 1–5.

175 Hamilton SR, Smith RRL. The relationship between columnar epithelial dysplasia and invasive adenocarcinoma arising in Barrett's esophagus. Am J Clin Pathol 1987, **87**: 301–312.

176 Hamilton K, Chiappori A, Olson S, Sawyers J, Johnson D, Washington K. Prevalence and prognostic significance of neuroendocrine cells in esophageal adenocarcinoma. Mod Pathol 2000, **13**: 475–481.

177 Harle IA, Finley RJ, Belsheim M, Bondy DC, Booth M, Lloyd D, McDonald JWD, Sullivan S, Valberg LS, Watson WC, Frei JV, Slinger R, Troster M, Meads GE, Duff JH. Management of adenocarcinoma in a columnar-lined esophagus. Ann Thorac Surg 1985, **60**: 330–336.

178 Hassall E, Dimmick JE, Magee JF. Adenocarcinoma in childhood Barrett's esophagus. Case documentation and the need for surveillance in children. Am J Gastroenterol 1993, **88**: 282–288.

179 Jankowski JA, Wright NA, Melter SJ, Triadafilopoulos G, Geboes K, Casson AG, Kerr D, Young LS. Molecular evolution of the metaplasia-dysplasia-adenocarcinoma sequence in the esophagus. Am J Pathol 1999, **154**: 965–973.

180 Kalish RJ, Clancy PE, Orringer MB, Appelman HD. Clinical, epidemiologic, and morphologic comparison between adenocarcinomas arising in Barrett's esophageal mucosa and in the gastric cardia. Gastroenterology 1984, **86**: 461–467.

180a Koppert LB, Wijnhoven Bas PL, Tilanus HW, Stijnen T, van Dekken H, Dinjens WNM. Neuroendocrine cells in Barrett's mucosa and adenocarcinomas of the gastro-esophageal junction. Int J Surg Pathol. (in press, 2004).

181 Lagorce-Pages C, Paraf F, Dubois S, Belghiti J, Flejou JF. Expression of CD44 in premalignant and malignant Barrett's oesophagus. Histopathology 1998, **32**: 7–14.

182 Law SY, Fok M, Cheng SW, Wong J. A comparison of outcome after resection for squamous cell carcinomas and adenocarcinomas of the esophagus and cardia. Surg Gynecol Obstet 1992, **175**: 107–112.

183 Lee RG. Adenomas arising in Barrett's esophagus. Am J Clin Pathol 1986, **85**: 629–632.

184 Lee RG. Dysplasia in Barrett's esophagus. A clinicopathologic study of six patients. Am J Surg Pathol 1985, **9**: 845–852.

185 Levine DS, Haggitt RC, Blount PL, Rabinovitch PS, Rusch VW, Reid BJ. An endoscopic biopsy protocol can differentiate high-grade dysplasia from early adenocarcinoma in Barrett's esophagus. Gastroenterology 1993, **105**: 40–50.

186 MacDonald WC, MacDonald JB. Adenocarcinoma of the esophagus and/or gastric cardia. Cancer 1987, **60**: 1094–1098.

187 Matea M, Koga S, Kimura A. Simultaneous superficial squamous cell carcinoma of the esophagus and early gastric adenocarcinoma. Hepatogastroenterology 1991, **38**: 554–556.

188 McArdle JE, Lewin KJ, Randall G, Weinstein W. Distribution of dysplasias and early invasive carcinoma in Barrett's esophagus. Hum Pathol 1992, **23**: 479–482.

189 Montgomery E, Goldblum JR, Greenson JK, Haber MM, Lamps LW, Lauwers GY, Lazerby AJ, Lewin DN, Robert ME, Washington K, Zahrak ML, Hart J. Dysplasia as a predictive marker for invasive carcinoma in Barrett esophagus: a follow-up study based on 138 cases from a diagnostic variability study. Hum Pathol 2001, **32**: 379–388.

190 Montgomery E, Bronner MP, Goldblum JR, Greenson JK, Haber

MM, Hart J, Lamps LW, Lauwers GY, Lazenby AJ, Lewin DN, Robert ME, Toledano AY, Shyr Y, Washington K. Reproducibility of the diagnosis of dysplasia in Barrett Esophagus: a reaffirmation. Hum Pathol 2001, **32**: 368–378.

191 Nakamura T, Nekarda H, Hoelscher AH, Bollschweiler E, Harbec N, Becker K, Siewert JR. Prognostic value of DNA ploidy and c-*erb*B-2 oncoprotein overexpression in adenocarcinoma of Barrett's esophagus. Cancer 1994, **73**: 1785–1794.

192 Neal AP, Savary M, Ozzello L. Columnar-lined lower esophagus. An acquired lesion with malignant predisposition. J Thorac Cardiovasc Surg 1975, **70**: 826–835.

193 Nobukawa B, Abraham SC, Gill J, Hietmiller RF, Wu TT. Clinicopathologic and molecular analysis of high grade Dysplasia and early adenocarcinoma in short- versus long-segment Barrett esophagus. Hum Pathol 2001, **32**: 447–454.

194 Osterheld MC, Bian YS, Bosman FT, Bernhattar J, Fontoilliet C. Beta-catenin expression and its association with prognostic factors in adenocarcinoma developed in Barrett esophagus. Am J Clin Pathol 2002, **117**: 451–456.

195 Paraf F, Fléjou J-F, Pignon J-P, Fékété F, Potet F. Surgical pathology of adenocarcinoma arising in Barrett's esophagus. Am J Surg Pathol 1995, **19**: 183–191.

196 Paraf F, Flejou JF, Potet F, Molas G, Fekete F. Adenomas arising in Barrett's esophagus with adenocarcinoma. Report of three cases. Pathol Res Pract 1992, **188**: 1028–1032.

197 Pera M, Cameron AJ, Trastek VF, Carpenter HA, Zinsmeister AR. Increasing incidence of adenocarcinoma of the esophagus and esophagogastric junction. Gastroenterology 1993, **104**: 510–513.

198 Potet F, Flejou JF, Gervaz H, Paraf F. Adenocarcinoma of the lower esophagus and the esophagogastric junction. Semin Diagn Pathol 1991, **8**: 126–136.

199 Ramel S, Reid BJ, Sanchez CA, Blount PL, Levine DS, Neshat K, Haggitt RC, Dean PJ, Thor K, Rabinovitch PS. Evaluation of p53 protein expression in Barrett's esophagus by two-parameter flow cytometry. Gastroenterology 1992, **102**: 1220–1228.

200 Raskind WH, Norwood T, Levine DS, Haggitt RC, Rabinovitch PS, Reid BJ. Persistent clonal areas and clonal expansion in Barrett's esophagus. Cancer Res 1992, **52**: 2946–2950.

201 Reid BJ, Blount PL, Rubin CE, Levine DS, Haggitt RC, Rabinovitch PS. Flow-cytometric and histological progression to malignancy in Barrett's esophagus. Prospective endoscopic surveillance of a cohort. Gastroenterology 1992, **102**: 1212–1219.

202 Reid BJ, Haggitt RC, Rubin CE, Roth G, Surawicz CM, Van Belle G, Lewin K, Weinstein WM, Antonioli DA, Goldman H, MacDonald W, Owen D. Observer variation in the diagnosis of dysplasia in Barrett's esophagus. Hum Pathol 1988, **19**: 166–178.

203 Rice TW, Falk GW, Achkar E, Petras RE. Surgical management of high-grade dysplasia in Barrett's esophagus. Am J Gastroenterol 1993, **88**: 1832–1836.

204 Riddell RH. Dysplasia and regression in Barrett's epithelium. In Spechler SJ, Goyal RK (eds.): Barrett's esophagus. Pathophysiology, diagnosis, and management. New York, 1985, Elsevier Science, pp. 143–152.

205 Robey SS, Hamilton SR, Gupta PK, Erozan YS. Diagnostic value of cytopathology in Barrett esophagus and associated carcinoma. Am J Clin Pathol 1988, **89**: 493–498.

206 Romagnoli S, Roncalli M, Graziani D, Cassani B, Roz E, Bonavina L, Peracchia A, Bosari S, Coggi G. Molecular alterations of Barrett's esophagus on microdissected endoscopic biopsies. Lab Invest 2001, **81**: 241–247.

207 Rosenberg JC, Budev H, Edwards RC, Singal S, Steiger Z, Sundareson AS. Analysis of adenocarcinoma in Barrett's esophagus utilizing a staging system. Cancer 1985, **55**: 1353–1360.

208 Rosengard AM, Hamilton SR. Squamous carcinoma of the esophagus in patients with Barrett esophagus. Mod Pathol 1989, **2**: 2–7.

209 Rosty C, Prevot S, Tiret E, Wendum D, De Saint-Maur PP. Adenocarcinosarcoma in Barrett's esophagus: report of a case. Int J Surg Pathol 1996, **4**: 43–48.

210 Rual A, Parenti A, Zaninotto G, Merigliano S, Costantini M, Cagol M, Alfieri R, Bonavina L, Peracchia A, Ancona E. Intestinal metaplasia is the probable common precursor of adenocarcinoma in Barrett esophagus and adenocarcinoma of gastric cardia. Cancer 2000, **88**: 2520–2528.

211 Rubio CA, Aberg B. Barrett's mucosa in conjunction with squamous carcinoma of the esophagus. Cancer 1991, **68**: 583–586.

212 Sanfey H, Hamilton SR, Smith RRL, Cameron JL. Carcinoma arising in Barrett's esophagus. Surg Gynecol Obstet 1985, **161**: 570–574.

213 Sarbia M, Borchard F, Hengels KJ. Histogenetical investigations on adenocarcinomas of the esophagogastric junction. An immunohistochemical study. Pathol Res Pract 1993, **189**: 530–535.

214 Sarbia M, Arjumand J, Wolter M, Reifenberger G, Heep H, Gabbert HE. Frequent c-myc amplification in high-grade dysplasia and adenocarcinoma in Barrett esophagus. Am J Clin Pathol 2001, **115**: 835–840.

215 Schmidt HG, Riddell RH, Walther B, Skinner DB, Riemann JF. Dysplasia in Barrett's esophagus. Cancer Res Clin Oncol 1985, **110**: 145–152.

216 Shurbaji MS, Erozan YS. The cytopathologic diagnosis of esophageal adenocarcinoma. Acta Cytol 1991, **35**: 189–194.

217 Slavin J, Pitson G, Dowling JP. Neuroendocrine carcinoma arising in Barrett's esophagus. Int J Surg Pathol 1994, **2**: 43–46.

218 Smith RRL, Hamilton SR, Boitnott JK, Rogers EL. The spectrum of carcinoma arising in Barrett's esophagus. A clinicopathologic study of 26 patients. Am J Surg Pathol 1984, **8**: 563–573.

219 Spechler SJ, Goyal RK. Barrett's esophagus. N Engl J Med 1986, **315**: 362–371.

220 Spechler SJ, Robbins AH, Rubins HB, Vincent ME, Heeren T, Doos WG, Colton T, Schimmel EM. Adenocarcinoma and Barrett's esophagus. An overrated risk? Gastroenterology 1984, **87**: 927–933.

221 Stewart JR, Hoff SJ, Johnson DH, Murray MJ, Butler DR, Elkins CC, Sharp KW, Merrill WH, Sawyers JL. Improved survival with neoadjuvant therapy and resection for adenocarcinoma of the esophagus. Ann Surg 1993, **218**: 571–576.

222 Streitz JM Jr, Ellis FH Jr, Gibb SP, Balogh K, Watkins E Jr. Adenocarcinoma in Barrett's esophagus. A clinicopathologic study of 65 cases. Ann Surg 1991, **213**: 122–125.

223 Thompson JJ, Zinsser KR, Enterline HT. Barrett's metaplasia and adenocarcinoma of the esophagus and gastroesophageal junction. Hum Pathol 1983, **14**: 42–61.

224 Thurberg BL, Duray PH, Odze RD. Polypoid dysplasia in Barrett's esophagus: a clinicopathologic, immunohistochemical, and molecular study of five cases. Hum Pathol 1999, **30**: 745–752.

225 Torres CM, Turner JR, Wang HH, Richards W, Sugarbaker D, Shahsafaei A, Odze RD. Pathologic prognostic factors in Barrett's-associated adenocarcinoma. A follow-up study of 96 patients. Cancer 1999, **85**: 520–528.

226 Van Der Woude CJ, Jansen PL, Tiebosch AT, Beuving A, Homan M, Kleibeuker JH, Moshage H. Expression of apoptosis-related proteins in Barrett's metaplasia-dysplasia-carcinoma sequence: a switch to a more resistant phenotype. Hum Pathol 2002, **33**: 686–692.

227 Van Sandick JW, Van Lanschot JB, Ten Kate FJ, Offerhaus GJ, Fockens P, Tytgat GN, Obertop H. Pathology of early invasive adenocarcinoma of the esophagus or esophagogastric junction: implications for therapeutic decision making. Cancer 2000, **88**: 2429–2437.

228 Walch AK, Zitzelsberger HF, Bink K, Hutzler P, Bruch J, Braselmann H, Aubele MM, Mueller J, Stein H, Silewert JR, Hofler H, Werner M. Molecular genetic changes in metastatic primary Barrett's adenocarcinoma and related lymph node

metastases: comparison with nonmetastatic Barrett's adenocarcinoma. Mod Pathol 2000, **13**: 814–824.

229 Walsh TN, Noonan N, Hollywood D, Kelly A, Keeling N, Hennessy TP. A comparison of multimodal therapy and surgery for esophageal adenocarcinoma. N Engl J Med 1996, **335**: 462–467.

230 Wasan HS, Schofield JB, Krausz T, Sikora K, Waxman J. Combined choriocarcinoma and yolk sac tumor arising in Barrett's esophagus. Cancer 1994, **73**: 514–517.

231 Washington K, Chiappori A, Hamilton K, Shyr Y, Blanke C, Johnson D, Sawyers J, Beauchamp D. Expression of beta-catenin, alpha-catenin, and E-cadherin in Barrett's esophagus and esophageal adenocarcinomas. Mod Pathol 1998, **11**: 805–913.

232 Yanagi M, Keller G, Mueller J, Walch A, Werner M, Stein HJ, Siewert JR, Hofler H. Comparison of loss of heterozygosity and microsatellite instability in adenocarcinomas of the distal esophagus and proximal stomach. Virchows Arch 2000, **437**: 605–610.

Other types of esophagitis

233 Abraham SC, Ravich WJ, Anhalt GJ, Yardley JH, Wu TT. Esophageal lichen planus: case report and review of the literature. Am J Surg Pathol 2000, **24**: 1678–1682.

234 Abraham SC, Yardley JH, Wu TT. Erosive injury to the upper gastrointestinal tract in patients receiving iron medication: an underrecognized entity. Am J Surg Pathol 1999, **23**: 1241–1247.

235 Agha FP, Lee HH, Nostrant TT. Herpetic esophagitis. A diagnostic challenge in immunocompromised patients. Am J Gastroenterol 1986, **81**: 246–253.

236 Dow CJ. Oesophageal tuberculosis. Four cases. Gut 1981, **22**: 234–236.

237 Enterline H, Thompson J. Pathology of the esophagus. New York, 1984, Springer-Verlag.

238 Freedman PG, Dieterich DT, Balthazar EJ. Crohn's disease of the esophagus. Case report and review of the literature. Am J Gastroenterol 1984, **79**: 835–838.

239 Galbraith JC, Shafran SD. Herpes simplex esophagitis in the immunocompetent patient. Report of four cases and review. Clin Infect Dis 1992, **14**: 894–901.

240 Greenson JK, Beschorner WE, Boitnott JK, Yardley JH. Prominent mononuclear cell infiltrate is characteristic of herpes esophagitis. Hum Pathol 1991, **22**: 541–549.

241 Haggitt RC, Meissner WA. Crohn's disease of the upper gastrointestinal tract. Am J Clin Pathol 1973, **59**: 613–622.

242 Kaneko F, Mori M, Tsukinaga I, Miura Y. Pemphigus vulgaris of esophageal mucosa. Arch Dermatol 1985, **121**: 272–273.

243 Kotler DP, Reka S, Orenstein JM, Fox CH. Chronic idiopathic esophageal ulceration in the acquired immunodeficiency syndrome. Characterization and treatment with corticosteroids. J Clin Gastroenterol 1992, **15**: 284–290.

244 Laine L, Bonacini M, Sattler F, Young T, Sherrod A. Cytomegalovirus and *Candida* esophagitis in patients with AIDS. J Acquir Immune Defic Syndr 1992, **5**: 605–609.

245 Lee RG. Marked eosinophilia in esophageal mucosal biopsies. Am J Surg Pathol 1985, **9**: 475–479.

246 McBane RD, Gross JB Jr. Herpes esophagitis. Clinical syndrome, endoscopic appearance, and diagnosis in 23 patients. Gastrointest Endosc 1991, **37**: 600–603.

247 McDonald GB, Sharma P, Hackman RC, Meyers JD, Thomas ED. Esophageal infections in immunosuppressed patients after marrow transplantation. Gastroenterology 1985, **88**: 1111–1117.

248 McKay JS, Day DW. Herpes simplex oesophagitis. Histopathology 1983, **7**: 409–420.

249 McKenzie R, Khakoo R. Blastomycosis of the esophagus presenting with gastrointestinal bleeding. Gastroenterology 1985, **88**: 1271–1273.

250 Mori S, Yoshihira A, Kawamura H, Takeuchi A, Hashimoto T, Inaba G. Esophageal involvement in Behcet's disease. Am J Gastroenterol 1983, **78**: 548–553.

251 Orringer MB, Sloan H. Monilial esophagitis. An increasingly frequent cause of esophageal stenosis. Ann Thorac Surg 1978, **26**: 364–374.

252 Shortsleeve MJ, Levine MS. Herpes esophagitis in otherwise healthy patients. Clinical and radiographic findings. Radiology 1992, **182**: 859–861.

253 Singh SP, Odze RD. Multinucleated epithelial giant cell changes in esophagitis: a clinicopathologic study of 14 cases. Am J Surg Pathol 1998, **22**: 93–99.

254 Teot LA, Ducatman BS, Geisinger KR. Cytologic diagnosis of cytomegaloviral esophagitis. A report of three acquired immunodeficiency syndrome-related cases. Acta Cytol 1993, **37**: 93–96.

255 Vitellas KM, Bennett WF, Bova JG, Johnston JC, Caldwell JH, Mayle JE. Idiopathic eosinophilic esophagitis. Radiology 1993, **186**: 789–793.

256 Walsh SV, Antonioli DA, Goldman H, Fox VL, Bousvaros A, Leichtner AM, Furuta GT. Allergic esophagitis in children: a clinicopathologic entity. Am J Surg Pathol 1999, **23**: 390–396.

257 Wilcox CM, Zaki SR, Coffield LM, Greer PW, Schwartz DA. Evaluation of idiopathic esophageal ulceration for human immunodeficiency virus. Mod Pathol 1995, **8**: 568–572.

258 Young JA, Elias E. Gastro-oesophageal candidiasis. Diagnosis by brush cytology. J Clin Pathol 1985, **38**: 293–296.

Squamous cell carcinoma

General and clinical features

259 Ashworth MT, Nash JR, Ellis A, Day DW. Abnormalities of differentiation and maturation in the oesophageal squamous epithelium of patients with tylosis. Morphological features. Histopathology 1991, **19**: 303–310.

260 Blot WJ. Esophageal cancer trends and risk factors. Semin Oncol 1994, **21**: 403–410.

261 Burkett FE, Johnson RL. Carcinoma of the esophagus twelve years after curative resection for carcinoma of the esophagus. Cancer 1983, **51**: 2237–2331.

262 Chang F, Syrjanen S, Wang L, Syrjanen K. Infectious agents in the etiology of esophageal cancer. Gastroenterology 1992, **103**: 1336–1348.

263 Chen B, Yin H, Dhurandhar N. Detection of human papillomavirus DNA in esophageal squamous cell carcinomas by the polymerase chain reaction using general consensus primers. Hum Pathol 1994, **25**: 920–923.

264 Crespi M, Muñoz N, Grassi A, Qiong S, Jing WK, Jien LJ. Precursor lesions of oesophageal cancer in a low-risk population in China. Comparison with high-risk populations. Int J Cancer 1984, **34**: 599–602.

265 Devesa SS, Blot WJ, Fraumeni JF Jr. Changing patterns in the incidence of esophageal and gastric carcinoma in the United States. Cancer 1998, **83**: 2049–2053.

266 Goffman TE, McKeen EA, Curtis RE, Schein PS. Esophageal carcinoma following irradiation for breast cancer. Cancer 1983, **52**: 1808–1809.

267 Kuwano H, Mortia M, Tsutsui S, Kido Y, Morei M, Sugimachi K. Comparison of characteristics of esophageal squamous cell carcinoma associated with head and neck cancer and those with gastric cancer. J Surg Oncol 1991, **46**: 107–109.

268 Kuylenstierna R, Munck-Wikland E. Esophagitis and cancer of the esophagus. Cancer 1985, **56**: 837–839.

269 Lam KY, He D, Ma L, Zhang D, Ngan HY, Wan TS, Tsao SW. Presence of human papillomavirus in esophageal squamous cell carcinoma of Hong Kong Chinese and its relationship with p53 gene mutation. Hum Pathol 1997, **28**: 657–663.

270 Maeta M, Koga S, Andachi H, Yoshioka H, Wakatsuki T. Esophageal cancer developed after gastrectomy. Surgery 1986, **95**: 87–91.

271 Mandard AM, Chasle J, Marnay J, Villedieu B, Bianco C, Roussel A, Elie H, Vernhes JC. Autopsy findings in 111 cases of esophageal cancer. Cancer 1981, **48**: 329–335.

272 Mannell A, Murray W. Oesophageal cancer in South Africa. A review of 1926 cases. Cancer 1989, **64**: 2604–2608.

273 Matsuura H, Morita M, Tsutsui S, Kido Y, Mori M. Esophageal carcinoma is frequently accompanied with early gastric carcinoma. Int Surg 1992, **77**: 69–71.

274 Oettlé GJ, Paterson AC, Leiman G, Segal I. Esophagitis in a population at risk for esophageal carcinoma. Cancer 1986, **57**: 2222–2229.

275 Poljak M, Cerar A, Seme K. Human papillomavirus infection in esophageal carcinomas: a study of 121 lesions using multiple broad-spectrum polymerase chain reactions and literature review. Hum Pathol 1998, **29**: 266–271.

276 Schottenfeld D. Epidemiology of cancer of the esophagus. Semin Oncol 1984, **11**: 92–100.

277 Souquet J-C, Berger F, Bonvoisin S, Partensky C, Boulez J, Descos F, Lambert R. Esophageal squamous cell carcinoma associated with gastric adenocarcinoma. Cancer 1989, **63**: 786–790.

278 Stephens RL, Hansen HH, Muggia FM. Hypercalcemia in epidermoid tumors of the head and neck and esophagus. Cancer 1973, **31**: 1487–1491.

279 Sugimachi K, Sumiyoshi K, Nozoe T, Yasuda M, Watanabe M, Kitamura K, Tsutsui S, Mori M, Kuwano H. Carcinogenesis and histogenesis of esophageal carcinoma. Cancer 1995, **75**: 1440–1445.

280 Suzuk L, Noffsinger AE, Hui YZ, Fenoglio-Preiser CM. Detection of human papillomavirus in esophageal squamous cell carcinoma. Cancer 1996, **78**: 704–710.

281 Turner JR, Shen LH, Crum CP, Dean PJ, Odze RD. Low prevalence of human papillomavirus infection in esophageal squamous cell carcinomas from North America: analysis by a highly sensitive and specific polymerase chain reaction-based approach. Hum Pathol 1997, **28**: 174–178.

282 Vizcaino AP, Moreno V, Lamber R, Parkin DM. Time trends incidence of both major histologic types of esophageal carcinomas in selected countries, 1973-1995. Int J Cancer 2002, **99**: 860–868.

283 Yang PC, Davis S. Incidence of cancer of the esophagus in the U.S. by histologic type. Cancer 1988, **61**: 612–617.

Morphologic features and local spread

284 Drut R. Acantholytic squamous-cell carcinoma of the esophagus. Patología 1977, **15**: 81–90.

285 Fukuzumi N. Intramural spread of esophageal carcinoma. Surg Pathol 1994, **5**: 269–294.

286 Gunnlaugsson Gh, Wychulis AR, Roland C, Ellis FH Jr. Analysis of the records of 1,657 patients with carcinoma of the esophagus and cardia of the stomach. Surg Gynecol Obstet 1970, **130**: 997–1005.

287 Kuwano H, Ueo H, Sugimachi K, Inokuchi K, Toyoshima S, Enjoji M. Glandular or mucus-secreting components in squamous cell carcinoma of the esophagus. Cancer 1985, **56**: 514–518.

288 Mandard AM, Marnay J, Gignoux M, Segol P, Blanc L, Ollivier JM, Borel B, Mandard JC. Cancer of the esophagus and associated lesions. Detailed pathologic study of 100 esophagectomy specimens. Hum Pathol 1984, **15**: 660–669.

289 Matsukuma S, Aida S, Shima S, Tamai S. Paget's disease of the esophagus. A case report with review of the literature. Am J Surg Pathol 1995, **19**: 948–955.

290 Newman J, Antonakopoulos GN, Darnton SJ, Matthews HR. The ultrastructure of oesophageal carcinomas. Multidirectional differentiation. A transmission electron microscopic study of 43 cases. J Pathol 1992, **167**: 193–198.

291 Sasajima K, Takai A, Taniguchi Y, Yamashita K, Hao K, Takubo K, Onda M. Polypoid squamous cell carcinoma of the esophagus. Cancer 1989, **64**: 94–97.

292 Sons HU, Borchard F. Esophageal cancer. Autopsy findings in 171 cases. Arch Pathol Lab Med 1984, **108**: 983–988.

293 Takubo K, Sasajima K, Yamashita K, Tanaka Y, Fujita K. Prognostic significance of intramural metastasis in patients with esophageal carcinoma. Cancer 1990, **65**: 1816–1819.

294 Takubo K, Sasajima K, Yamashita K, Tanaka Y, Fujita K, Mafune K, Wang Q-H. Morphological heterogeneity of esophageal carcinoma. Acta Pathol Jpn 1989, **39**: 180–189.

295 Takubo K, Takai A, Takayama S, Sasajima K, Yamashita K, Fujita K. Intraductal spread of esophageal squamous cell carcinoma. Cancer 1987, **59**: 1751–1757.

296 Tanner NC, Smithers DW (eds.): Tumours of the oesophagus. In Smithers DW (general ed.): Neoplastic disease at various sites, vol IV. London, 1961, E & S Livingstone.

297 Theunissen PH, Borchard F, Poortvliet DC. Histopathological evaluation of oesophageal carcinoma. The significance of venous invasion. Br J Surg 1991, **78**: 930–932.

298 Yates DR, Ross LG. Paget's disease of the esophageal epithelium. Arch Pathol 1968, **86**: 447–452.

Immunohistochemical and molecular genetic features

299 Arber N, Gammon MD, Hibshoosh H, Britton JA, Zhang Y, Schonberg JB, Roterdam H, Fabian I, Hold PR, Weinstein IB. Overexpression of cyclin D1 occurs in both squamous carcinomas and adenocarcinomas of the esophagus and in adenocarcinomas in the stomach. Hum Pathol 1999, **30**: 1087–1092.

300 Coggi G, Bosari S, Roncalli M, Graziani D, Bossi P, Viale G, Buffa R, Ferrero S, Piazza M, Blandamura S, Segalin A, Bonavina L, Peracchia. p53 protein accumulation and p53 gene mutation in esophageal carcinoma: a molecular and immunohistochemical study with clinicopathologic correlation. Cancer 1997, **79**: 425–432.

301 Fischer H-P, Wallner F, Maier H, Weber K, Osborn M, Altmannsberger M. Coexpression of intermediate filaments in squamous cell carcinomas of upper aerodigestive tract before and after radiation and chemotherapy. Lab Invest 1989, **61**: 433–439.

302 Hollstein MC, Metcalf RA, Welsh JA, Montesano R, Harris CC. Frequent mutation of the p53 gene in human esophageal cancer. Proc Natl Acad Sci U S A 1990, **87**: 9958–9961.

303 Huang Y, Meltzer SJ, Yin J, Tong Y, Chang EH, Srivastava S, McDaniel T, Boynton RF, Zou ZQ. Altered messenger RNA and unique mutational profiles of p53 and Rb in human esophageal carcinomas. Cancer Res 1993, **53**: 1889–1894.

304 Ikeda Y, Kuwano H, Baba K, Ikebe M, Matushima T, Adachi Y, Mori M, Sugimachi K. Expression of Sialyl-Tn antigens in normal squamous epithelium, dysplasia, and squamous cell carcinoma in the esophagus. Cancer Res 1993, **53**: 1706–1708.

305 Jiang W, Khan SM, Tomita N, Zhang YJ, Lu SH, Weinstein IB. Amplification and expression of the human cyclin D gene in esophageal cancer. Cancer Res 1992, **52**: 2980–2983.

306 Kaketani K, Saito T, Kobayashi M. Flow cytometric analysis of nuclear DNA content in esophageal cancer. Aneuploidy as an index for highly malignant potential. Cancer 1989, **64**: 887–891.

307 Mori M, Shimono R, Kido A, Kuwano H, Akazawa K, Sugimachi K. Distribution of basement membrane antigens in human esophageal lesions. An immunohistochemical study. Int J Cancer 1991, **47**: 839–842.

308 Mukaida H, Toi M, Hirai T, Yamashita Y, Toge T. Clinical significance of the expression of epidermal growth factor and its receptor in esophageal cancer. Cancer 1991, **68**: 142–148.

309 Ogasawara S, Maesawa C, Tamura G, Satodate R. Lack of mutations of the adenomatous polyposis coli gene in oesophageal and gastric carcinomas. Virchows Arch 1994, **424**: 607–611.

310 Parenti AR, Rugge M, Shiao YH, Ruol A, Ancona E, Bozzola L, Ninto V. bcl-2 and p53 immunophenotypes in pre-invasive, early and advanced oesophageal squamous cancer. Histopathology 1997, **31**: 430–435.

311 Ruol A, Segalin A, Panozzo M, Stephens JK, Dalla Palma P, Skinner DB, Peracchia A, Little AG. Flow cytometric DNA analysis of squamous cell carcinoma of the esophagus. Cancer 1990, **65**: 1185–1188.

312 Sasaki K, Murakami T, Murakami T, Nakamura M. Intratumoral heterogeneity in DNA ploidy of esophageal squamous cell carcinomas. Cancer 1991, **68**: 2403–2406.

313 Sasano H, Goukon Y, Nishihara T, Nagura H. In situ hybridization and immunohistochemistry of p53 tumor suppressor gene in human esophageal carcinoma. Am J Pathol 1992, **141**: 545–550.

314 Sheyn I, Noffsinger AE, Heffelfinger S, Davis B, Miller MA, Fenoglio-Preiser CM. Amplification and expression of cyclin D1 gene in anal and esophageal squamous cell carcinomas. Hum Pathol 1997, **28**: 270–276.

315 Stemmermann G, Heffelfinger SC, Noffsinger A, Hui YZ, Miller MA, Fenoglio-Presser CM. The molecular biology of esophageal and gastric cancer and their precursors. Oncogenes, tumor suppressor genes, and growth factors. Hum Pathol 1994, **25**: 968–981.

316 Sugimachi K, Koga Y, Mori M, Huang GJ, Yang K, Zhang RG. Comparative data on cytophotometric DNA in malignant lesions of the esophagus in the Chinese and Japanese. Cancer 1987, **59**: 1947–1950.

317 Takahashi H, Shikata N, Senzaki H, Shintaku M, Tsubura A. Immunohistochemical staining patterns of keratins in normal oesaphageal epithelium and carcinoma of the oesophagus. Histopathology 1995, **26**: 45–50.

318 Tauchi K, Kakudo K, Machimura T, Makuuchi H, Mitomi T. Immunohistochemical studies of blood group-related antigens in human superficial esophageal carcinomas. Cancer 1991, **67**: 3042–3050.

319 Trias I, Campo E, Benasco C, Palacin A, Cardesa A. Human chorionic gonadotropin in esophageal carcinomas. An immunohistochemical study. Pathol Res Pract 1991, **187**: 503–507.

320 Tsutsui S, Kuwano H, Mori M, Matsuura H, Sugimachi K. A flow cytometric analysis of DNA content in primary and metastatic lesions of esophageal squamous cell carcinoma. Cancer 1992, **70**: 2586–2591.

321 Wang LD, Hong JY, Qiu SL, Gao H, Yang CS. Accumulation of p53 protein in human esophageal precancerous lesions. A possible early biomarker for carcinogenesis. Cancer Res 1993, **53**: 1783–1787.

322 Wang LD, Zhou Q, Hong JY, Qui SL, Yang CS. p53 protein accumulation and gene mutations in multifocal esophageal precancerous lesions from symptom free subjects in a high incidence area for esophageal carcinoma in Henan, China. Cancer 1996, **77**: 1244–1249.

323 Yang K, Lipkin M. AEI cytokeratin reaction patterns in different differentiation states of squamous cell carcinoma of the esophagus. Am J Clin Pathol 1990, **94**: 261–269.

324 Yano H, Shiozaki K, Kobayashi K, Yano T, Tahara H, Tamura S, Mori T. Immunohistologic detection of the epidermal growth factor receptor in human esophageal squamous cell carcinoma. Cancer 1991, **67**: 91–98.

In situ and superficial squamous cell carcinoma and related lesions

325 Ackerman LV, Weinstein IB, Kaplan HS, other members of Delegation. Cancer of the esophagus. In Kaplan HS, Tsuchitani PJ (eds.): Cancer in China. New York, 1978, Alan R Liss, pp. 111–136.

326 Anani PA, Gardiol D, Savary M, Monnier P. An extensive morphological and comparative study of clinically early and obvious squamous cell carcinoma of the esophagus. Pathol Res Pract 1991, **187**: 214–219.

327 Araki K, Ohno S, Egashira A, Saeki H, Kawaguchi H, Sugimachi K. Pathologic features of superficial esophageal squamous cell carcinoma with lymph node and distal metastasis. Cancer 2002, **94**: 570–575.

328 Bogomoletz WV, Molas G, Gayet B, Potet F. Superficial squamous cell carcinoma of the esophagus. A report of 76 cases and review of the literature. Am J Surg Pathol 1989, **13**: 535–546.

329 Chu P, Stagias J, West AB, Traube M. Diffuse pagetoid squamous cell carcinoma in situ of the esophagus: a case report. Cancer 1997, **79**: 1865–1870.

330 Dry SM, Lewin KJ. Esophageal squamous dysplasia. Semin Diagn Pathol 2002, **19**: 2–11.

331 Goseki N, Koike M, Yoshida M. Histopathologic characteristics of early stage esophageal carcinoma. A comparative study with gastric carcinoma. Cancer 1992, **69**: 1088–1093.

332 Haruma K, Tokutomi T, Tsuda T, Yoshihara M, Sumii K, Kajiyama G. Superficial esophageal carcinoma. A report of 27 cases in Japan. Am J Gastroenterol 1991, **86**: 1723–1728.

333 Hurlimann J, Gardiol D. Immunohistochemistry of dysplasias and carcinomas of the esophageal epithelium. Pathol Res Pract 1989, **184**: 567–576.

334 Kato H, Tachimori Y, Watanabe H, Yamaguchi H, Ishikawa T, Itabashi M. Superficial esophageal carcinoma. Surgical treatment and the results. Cancer 1990, **66**: 2319–2323.

335 Kawamura T, Goseki N, Koike M, Takizawa T, Endo M. Acceleration of proliferative activity of esophageal squamous cell carcinoma with invasion beyond the mucosa: immunohistochemical analysis of Ki-67 and p53 antigen in relation to histopathologic findings. Cancer 1996, **77**: 843–849.

336 Kuwano H, Matsuda H, Matsuoka H, Kai H, Okudaira Y, Sugimachi K. Intraepithelial carcinoma concomitant with esophageal squamous cell carcinoma. Cancer 1987, **59**: 783–787.

337 Kuwano H, Morita M, Mastuda H, Mori M, Sugimachi K. Histopathologic findings of minute foci of squamous cell carcinoma in the human esophagus. Cancer 1991, **68**: 2617–2620.

338 Muñoz N, Lipkin M, Crespi M, Wahrendorf J, Grassi A, Shih-Hsien L. Proliferative abnormalities of the oesophageal epithelium of Chinese populations at high and low risk for oesophageal cancer. Int J Cancer 1985, **36**: 187–189.

339 Ohashi K, Momma K, Yamada Y, Yoshida M, Horiguchi S, Matsubayashi J, Shimizu S, Moriyama S, Hishima T, Funata N, Takizawa T, Koike M. Vertical and horizontal growth features of superficial esophageal squamous cell carcinomas: histopathological evaluation of endoscopically resected specimens. Virchows Arch 2002, **441**: 350–357.

340 Pesko P, Rakic S, Milicevic M, Bulajic P, Gerzic Z. Prevalence and clinicopathologic features of multiple squamous cell carcinoma of the esophagus. Cancer 1994, **73**: 2687–2690.

341 Rubio CA, Lie F-S, Zhao H-Z. Histological classification of intraepithelial neoplasias and microinvasive squamous carcinoma of the esophagus. Am J Surg Pathol 1989, **13**: 685–690.

342 Soga J, Tanaka O, Sasaki K, Kawaguchi M, Muto T. Superficial spreading carcinoma of the esophagus. Cancer 1982, **50**: 1641–1645.

343 Sugimachi K, Ikebe M, Kitamura K, Toh Y, Matsuda H, Kuwano H. Long-term results of esophagectomy for early esophageal carcinoma. Hepatogastroenterology 1993, **40**: 203–206.

344 Sugimachi K, Sumiyoshi K, Nozoe T, Yasuda M, Watanabe M, Kitamura K, Tsutsui S, Mori M, Kuwano H. Carcinogenesis and histogenesis of esophageal carcinoma. Cancer 1995, **75**: 1440–1445.

345 Tajima Y, Nakanishi Y, Ochial A, Tachimori Y, Kato H, Watanabe H, Yamaguchi H, Yoshimura K, Kusano M, Simoda T. Histopathologic findings predicting lymph node metastasis and prognosis of patients with superficial esophageal carcinomas: analysis of 240 surgically resected tumors. Cancer 2000, **88**: 1285–1293.

346 Tajima Y, Nakanishi Y, Tachimori Y, Kato H, Watanabe H, Yamaguchi H, Yoshimura K, Kusano M, Shimoda T. Significance

of involvement by squamous cell carcinoma of the ducts of esophageal submucosal glands: analysis of 201 surgically resected superficial squamous cell carcinoma. Cancer 2000, **89:** 248–254.

347 Takiyama W, Moriwaki S, Mandai K, Takashima S. Dysplasia in the human esophagus. Clinicopathological study of 500 esophagi at autopsy. Jpn J Clin Oncol 1992, **22:** 250–255.

348 Ushigome S, Spjut HJ, Noon GP. Extensive dysplasia and carcinoma in situ of esophageal epithelium. Cancer 1967, **20:** 1023–1029.

349 Yoshinaka H, Shimazu H, Fukumoto T, Baba M. Superficial esophageal carcinoma. A clinicopathological review of 59 cases. Am J Gastroenterol 1991, **86:** 1413–1418.

Metastases

350 Akiyama H, Tsurumaru M, Kawamura T, Ono Y. Principles of surgical treatment for carcinoma of the esophagus. Analysis of lymph node involvement. Ann Surg 1981, **194:** 438–446.

351 Anderson LL, Lad TE. Autopsy findings in squamous-cell carcinoma of the esophagus. Cancer 1982, **50:** 1587–1590.

352 Guernsey JM, Knudsen DF. Abdominal exploration in the evaluation of patients with carcinoma of the thoracic esophagus. J Thorac Cardiovasc Surg 1970, **59:** 62–66.

353 Matsubara T, Ueda M, Kaisaki S, Kuroda J, Uchida C, Kokudo N, Takahashi T, Nakajima T, Yanagisawa A. Localization of initial lymph node metastasis from carcinoma of the thoracic esophagus. Cancer 2000, **89:** 1869–1873.

354 Nishimaki T, Tanaka O, Suzuki T, Aizawa K, Hatakeyama K, Muto T. Patterns of lymphatic spread in thoracic esophageal cancer. Cancer 1994, **74:** 4–11.

355 Saito T, Iizuka T, Kato H, Watanabe H. Esophageal carcinoma metastatic to the stomach. A clinicopathologic study of 35 cases. Cancer 1985, **56:** 2235–2241.

Cytology

356 Ackerman LV, Weinstein IB, Kaplan HS, other members of Delegation. Cancer of the esophagus. In Kaplan HS, Tsuchitani PJ (eds.): Cancer in China. New York, 1978, Alan R Liss, pp. 111–136.

357 Goldman H, Antonioli DA. Mucosal biopsy of the esophagus, stomach, and proximal duodenum. Hum Pathol 1982, **13:** 423–448.

358 Kasugai T, Kobayashi S, Kuno N. Endoscopic cytology of the esophagus, stomach and pancreas. Acta Cytol (Baltimore) 1978, **22:** 327–330.

359 Koss LG. Cytologic diagnosis of oral, esophageal, and peripheral lung cancer. J Cell Biochem Suppl 1993, **17F:** 66–81.

360 Lazarus C, Jaskiewicz K, Sumeruk RA, Nainkin J. Brush cytology technique in the detection of oesophageal carcinoma in the asymptomatic, high risk subject. A pilot survey. Cytopathology 1992, **3:** 291–296.

361 MacDonald WC, Brandburg LL, Taniguchi L, Rubin CE. Esophageal exfoliative cytology. Ann Intern Med 1963, **59:** 332–337.

362 O'Donoghue J, Waldron R, Gough D, McCabe J, Kerin M, McGuire M, Horgan PG, Given HF. An analysis of the diagnostic accuracy of endoscopic biopsy and cytology in the detection of oesophageal malignancy. Eur J Surg Oncol 1992, **18:** 332–334.

363 Prolla JC, Reilly RW, Kirsner JB, Cockerham L. Direct vision endoscopic cytology and biopsy in the diagnosis of esophageal and gastric tumors. Current experience. Acta Cytol (Baltimore) 1977, **21:** 399–402.

364 Shen O, Liu SF, Dawsey SM, Cao J, Zhou B, Wang DY, Cao SG, Zhao HZ, Li GY, Taylor PR, et al. Cytologic screening for esophageal cancer. Results from 12,877 subjects from a high-risk population in China. Int J Cancer 1993, **54:** 185–188.

Treatment

365 Berry B, Miller RR, Luoma A, Nelems B, Hay J, Flores AD. Pathologic findings in total esophagectomy specimens after intracavitary and external-beam radiotherapy. Cancer 1989, **64:** 1833–1837.

366 Bosset JF, Gignoux M, Triboulet JP, Tiret E, Mantion G, Elias D, Lozach P, Ollier JC, Pavy JJ, Mercier M, Sahmoud T. Chemoradiotherapy followed by surgery compared with surgery alone in squamous-cell cancer of the esophagus. N Engl J Med 1997, **337:** 161–167.

367 Darnton SJ, Allen SM, Edwards CW, Matthews HR. Histopathological findings in oesophageal carcinoma with and without preoperative chemotherapy. J Clin Pathol 1993, **46:** 51–55.

368 Earlam R, Cunha-Melo JR. Oesophageal squamous cell carcinoma. I. A critical review of surgery. Br J Surg 1980, **67:** 381–390.

369 Ellis FH Jr. Treatment of carcinoma of the esophagus or cardia. Mayo Clin Proc 1989, **64:** 945–955.

370 Galandiuk S, Hermann RE, Cosgrove DM, Gassman JJ. Cancer of the esophagus. The Cleveland Clinic experience. Ann Surg 1986, **203:** 101–108.

371 Giuli R, Sancho-Garnier H. Diagnostic, therapeutic, and prognostic features of cancers of the esophagus. Results of the international prospective study conducted by the OESO group (790 patients). Surgery 1986, **99:** 614–622.

372 Hambraeus GM, Mercke CE, Hammar E, Landberg TG, Wang-Andersen W. Surgery alone or combined with radiation therapy in esophageal carcinoma. Cancer 1981, **48:** 63–68.

373 Hancock SL, Glatstein E. Radiation therapy of esophageal cancer. Semin Oncol 1984, **11:** 144.

374 Herskovic A, Martz K, al-Sarraf M, Leichman L, Brindle J, Vaitkevicius V, Cooper J, Byhardt R, Davis L, Emami B. Combined chemotherapy and radiotherapy compared with radiotherapy alone in patients with cancer of the esophagus. N Engl J Med 1992, **326:** 1593–1598.

375 Ilson DH, Kelson DP. Chemotherapy in esophageal cancer. Anticancer Drugs 1993, **4:** 287–299.

376 Isono K, Onoda S, Ishikawa T, Sato H, Nakayama K. Studies on the causes of deaths from esophageal carcinoma. Cancer 1982, **49:** 2173–2179.

377 Kelsen DP, Ahuja R, Hopfan S, Bains MS, Kosloff C, Martini N, McCormack P, Golbey RB. Combined modality therapy of esophageal carcinoma. Cancer 1981, **48:** 131–137.

378 Kelsen DP, Ginsberg R, Pajak TK, Shehan DG, Gunderson L, Mortimer J, Estes N, Haller DG, Ajani J, Kocha W, Minsky BD, Roth JA. Chemotherapy followed by surgery compared with surgery alone for localized esophageal cancer. N Engl Med 1998, **339:** 1979–1984.

379 Marcial VA, Tomé JM, Ubiñas J, Bosch A, Correa JN. The role of radiation therapy in esophageal cancer. Radiology 1966, **87:** 231–239.

380 Medical Research Council Oesophageal Cancer Working Group. Surgical resection with or without preoperative chemotherapy in oesophageal cancer: a randomised controlled trial. Lancet 2002, **359:** 1727–1733.

381 Pearson JG. The value of radiotherapy in the management of squamous oesophageal cancer. Br J Surg 1971, **58:** 794–798.

382 Pearson JG. The present status and future potential of radiotherapy in the management of esophageal cancer. Cancer 1977, **39:** 882–890.

383 Roth JA, Putnam JB Jr. Surgery for cancer of the esophagus. Semin Oncol 1994, **21:** 453–461.

384 Skinner DB. Surgical treatment for esophageal carcinoma. Semin Oncol 1984, **11:** 136–143.

385 van Andel JG, Dees J, Dijkhuis CM, Fokkens W, van Houten H, de Jong PC, van Woerkom-Eykenboom WM. Carcinoma of the esophagus. Results of treatment. Ann Surg 1979, **190:** 684–689.

Prognosis

386 Bottger T, Storkel S, Stockle M, Wahl W, Jugenheimer M, Effenberger-Kim O, Vinh T, Junginger T. DNA image cytometry. A prognostic tool in squamous cell carcinoma of the esophagus? Cancer 1991, **67**: 2290–2294.

387 Brucher BL, Stein HJ, Werner M, Siewert JR. Lymphatic vessel invasion is an independent prognostic factor in patients with a primary resected tumor with esophageal squamous cell carcinoma. Cancer 2001, **92**: 2228–2233.

388 Doki Y, Shiozaki H, Tahara H, Kobayashi K, Miyata M, Oka H, Iihara K, Mori T. Prognostic value of DNA ploidy in squamous cell carcinoma of esophagus. Analyzed with improved flow cytometric measurement. Cancer 1993, **72**: 1813–1818.

389 Edwards JM, Hillier VF, Lawson RAM, et al. Squamous carcinoma of the oesophagus. Histological criteria and their prognostic significance. Br J Cancer 1989, **59**: 429–433.

390 Edwards JM, Jones DJ, Wilkes SJL, et al. Ploidy as a prognostic indicator in oesophageal squamous carcinoma and its relationship to various histological criteria. J Pathol 1989, **159**: 35–41.

391 Eloubeidi MA, Desmond R, Arguedas MR, Reed CE, Wilcox CM. Prognostic factors for the survival of patients with esophageal carcinoma in the U.S.: the importance of tumor length and lymph node status. Cancer 2002, **95**: 1434–1443.

392 Glickman JN, Torres C, Wang HH, turner JR, Shahsafaei A, Richards WG, Sugarbaker DJ, Odze RD. The prognostic significance of lymph node micrometastasis in patients with esophageal carcinoma. Cancer 1999, **85**: 769–778.

393 Iihara K, Shiozaki H, Tahara H, Kobayashi K, Inoue M, Tamura S, Miyata M, Oka H, Doki Y, Mori T. Prognostic significance of transforming growth factoralpha in human esophageal carcinoma. Implication for the autocrine proliferation. Cancer 1993, **71**: 2902–2909.

394 Izbicki JR, Hosch SB, Pichlmeier U, Rehders A, Bush C, Niendorf A, Passlick B, Broelsch CE, Pantel K. Prognostic value of immunohistochemically identifiable tumor cells in lymph nodes of patients with completely resected esophageal cancer. N Engl J Med 1997, **337**: 1188–1194.

395 Kato H, Tachimori Y, Watanabe H, Iizuka T. Evaluation of the new (1987) TNM classification for thoracic esophageal tumors. Int J Cancer 1993, **53**: 220–223.

396 Klimstra DS. Pathologic prognostic factors in esophageal carcinoma. Semin Oncol 1994, **21**: 425–430.

397 Maesawa C, Masuda T, Tamura G, Satodate R, Ishida K, Saito K. Prognostic assessment of superficial squamous cell carcinoma of the esophagus using karyometric analysis and nucleolar organizer regions. J Surg Oncol 1992, **51**: 164–168.

397a Mariette C, Balon J-M, Piessen G, Fabre S, Van Seuningen I, Triboulet J-P. Pattern of recurrence following complete resection of esophageal carcinoma and factors predictive of recurrent disease. Cancer 2003, **97**: 1616–1623.

398 Matsuura H, Kuwano H, Morita M, Tsutsui S, Kido Y, Mori M, Sugimachi K. Predicting recurrence time of esophageal carcinoma through assessment of histologic factors and DNA ploidy. Cancer 1991, **67**: 1406–1411.

399 Matsuura H, Sugimachi K, Ueo H, Kuwano H, Koga Y, Okamura T. Malignant potentiality of squamous cell carcinoma of the esophagus predictable by DNA analysis. Cancer 1986, **57**: 1810–1814.

400 Morita M, Kuwano H, Matsuda H, Moriguchi S, Sugimachi K. Prognostic significance of argyrophilic nucleolar organizer regions in esophageal carcinoma. Cancer Res 1991, **51**: 5339–5341.

401 Mukaida H, Toi M, Hirai T, Yamashita Y, Toge T. Clinical significance of the expression of epidermal growth factor and its receptor in esophageal cancer. Cancer 1991, **68**: 142–148.

402 Ohbu M, Seagusa M, Kobauashi N, Tsukamoto H, Mieno H, Kakita A, Okayasu I. Expression of bcl-2 protein in esophageal

squamous cell carcinoma and its association with lymph node metastasis. Cancer 1997, **79**: 1287–1293.

403 Oliver SE, Robertson CS, Logan RF. Oesophageal cancer. A population-based study of survival after treatment. Br J Surg 1992, **79**: 1321–1325.

404 Patil P, Redkar A, Patel SG, Krishnamurthy S, Mistry RC, Deshpande RK, Mittra I, Desai PB. Prognosis of operable squamous cell carcinoma of the esophagus. Relationship with clinicopathologic features and DNA ploidy. Cancer 1993, **72**: 20–24.

405 Ribeiro V Jr, Finkelstein SD, Safatie-Ribeiro AV, Landreneau RJ, Clarke MR, Bakker A, Swalsky PA, Gooding WE, Posner MC. p53 sequence analysis predicts treatment response and outcome of patients with esophageal carcinoma. Cancer 1998, **83**: 7–18.

406 Robey-Cafferty SS, el-Naggar AK, Sahin AA, Bruner JM, Ro JY, Cleary KR. Prognostic factors in esophageal squamous carcinoma. A study of histologic features, blood group expression, and DNA ploidy. Am J Clin Pathol 1991, **95**: 844–849.

407 Sagar PM, Johnston D, McMahon MJ, Dixon MF, Quirke P. Significance of circumferential resection margin involvement after oesophagectomy for cancer. Br J Surg 1993, **80**: 1386–1388.

408 Shimaya K, Shiozaki H, Inoue M, Tahara H, Monden T, Shimano T, Mori T. Significance of p53 expression as a prognostic factor in oesophageal squamous cell carcinoma. Virchows Arch [A] 1993, **422**: 271–276.

409 Skinner DB, Little AG, Ferguson MK, Soriano A, Staszak VM. Selection of operation for esophageal cancer based on staging. Ann Surg 1986, **204**: 391–401.

410 Tanigawa N, Matsumura M, Amaya H, Kitaoka A, Shimomatsuya T, Lu C, Muraoka T, Tanaka T. Tumor vascularity correlates with the prognosis of patients with esophageal squamous cell carcinoma. Cancer 1997, **79**: 220–225.

411 Torres CM, Wang HH, Turner JR, Richards W, Sugarbaker D, Shahsafaei A, Odze RD. Pathologic prognostic factors in esophageal squamous cell carcinoma: a follow-up study of 74 patients with or without preoperative chemoradiation therapy. Mod Pathol 1999, **12**: 961–968.

412 Utsumi Y, Nakamura T, Nagasue N, Kubota H, Morikawa S. Role of estrogen receptors in the growth of human esophageal carcinoma. Cancer 1989, **64**: 88–93.

413 Yano H, Shiozaki H, Kobayashi K, Yano T, Tahara H, Tamura S, Mori T. Immunohistologic detection of the epidermal growth factor receptor in human esophageal squamous cell carcinoma. Cancer 1991, **67**: 91–98.

Other types of carcinoma

414 Abe K, Sasano H, Itakura Y, Nishihira T, Mori S, Nagura H. Basaloid-squamous carcinoma of the esophagus: a clinicopathologic, DNA ploidy, and immunohistochemical study of seven cases. Am J Surg Pathol 1996, **20**: 453–461.

415 Agha FP, Weatherbee L, Sams JS. Verrucous carcinoma of the esophagus. Am J Gastroenterol 1984, **79**: 844–849.

415a Amrikachi M, Ro JY, Ordonez NG, Ayala AG. Adenocarcinomas of the gastrointestinal tract with prominent rhabdoid features. Ann of Diagn Pathol 2002, **6**: 357–363.

416 Ansari-Lari MA, Hoque MO, Califano J, Westra WH. Immunohistochemical p53 expression patterns in sarcomatoid carcinomas of the upper respiratory tract. Am J Surg Pathol 2002, **26**: 1024–1031.

417 Banks ER, Frierson HF Jr, Mills SE, George E, Zarbo RJ, Swanson PE. Basaloid squamous cell carcinoma of the head and neck. A clinicopathologic and immunohistochemical study of 40 cases. Am J Surg Pathol 1992, **16**: 939–946.

418 Battifora H. Spindle cell carcinoma. Ultrastructural evidence of squamous origin and collagen production by the tumor cells. Cancer 1976, **37**: 2275–2282.

419 Biemond P, ten Kate FJ, van Blankenstein M. Esophageal

verrucous carcinoma. Histologically a low-grade malignancy but clinically a fatal disease. J Clin Gastroenterol 1991, 13: 102–107.

420 Bombi JA, Riverola A, Bordas JM, Cardesa A. Adenosquamous carcinoma of the esophagus. A case report. Pathol Res Pract 1991, 187: 514–519.

421 Brenner S, Heimlich H, Widman M. Carcinoid of esophagus. NY State J Med 1969, 69: 1337–1339.

422 Briggs JC, Ibrahim NBN. Oat cell carcinoma of the oesophagus. A clinicopathological study of 23 cases. Histopathology 1983, 7: 261–277.

423 Casas F, Ferrer F, Farrus B, Casals J, Biete A. Primary small cell carcinoma of the esophagus: a review of the literature with emphasis on therapy and prognosis. Cancer 1997, 80: 1366–1372.

424 Cerar A, Jutersek A, Vidmar S. Adenoid cystic carcinoma of the esophagus. A clinicopathologic study of three cases. Cancer 1991, 67: 2159–2164.

425 Chejfec G, Jablokow VR, Gould VE. Linitis plastica carcinoma of the esophagus. Cancer 1983, 51: 2139–2143.

426 Cho KJ, Jang JJ, Lee SS, Zo JI. Basaloid squamous carcinoma of the oesophagus: a distinct neoplasm with multipotential differentiation. Histopathology 2000, 36: 331–340.

427 Cook MG, Eusebi V, Betts CM. Oat-cell carcinoma of the oesophagus. A recently recognized entity. J Clin Pathol 1976, 29: 1068–1073.

428 Drut R. Carcinoma mucoepidermoide del esofago. Presentación de dos casos y revisión de la literatura. Patología 1977, 15: 163–169.

429 Du Boulay CEH, Isaacson P. Carcinoma of the oesophagus with spindle cell features. Histopathology 1981, 5: 403–414.

430 Epstein JI, Sears DL, Tucker RS, Eagan JW Jr. Carcinoma of the esophagus with adenoid cystic differentiation. Cancer 1984, 53: 1131–1136.

431 Gal AA, Martin SE, Kernen JA, Patterson MJ. Esophageal carcinoma with prominent spindle cells. Cancer 1987, 60: 2244–2250.

432 Guarino M, Reale D, Micoli G, Forloni B. Carcinosarcoma of the oesophagus with rhabdomyoblastic differentiation. Histopathology 1993, 22: 493–498.

433 Hanada M, Nakano K, Ii Y, Yamashita H. Carcinosarcoma of the esophagus with osseous and cartilaginous production. A combined study of keratin immunohistochemistry and electron microscopy. Acta Pathol Jpn 1984, 34: 669–678.

434 Handra-Luca A, Terris B, Couvelard A, Molas G, Degott C, Flejou JF. Spindle cell squamous carcinoma of the oesophagus: an analysis of 17 cases, with new immunohistochemical evidence for a clonal origin. Histopathology 2001, 39: 125–132.

435 Ho K-J, Herrera GA, Jones JM, Alexander CB. Small cell carcinoma of the esophagus. Evidence for a unified histogenesis. Hum Pathol 1984, 15: 460–468.

436 Hoang MP, Hobbs CM, Sobin LH, Albores-Saavedra J. Carcinoid tumor of the esophagus: a clinicopathologic study of four cases. Am J Surg Pathol 2002, 26: 517–522.

437 Hoda SA, Hajdu SI. Small cell carcinoma of the esophagus. Cytology and immunohistology in four cases. Acta Cytol 1992, 36: 113–120.

438 Horai T, Nishihara H, Tateishi R, Matsuda M, Hattori S. Oat-cell carcinoma of the lung simultaneously producing ACTH and serotonin. J Clin Endocrinol Metab 1973, 37: 212–219.

439 Iezzoni J, Mills SF. Sarcomatoid carcinomas (carcinosarcomas) of the gastrointestinal tract. A review. Semin Diagn Pathol 1993, 10: 176–187.

440 Kanamoto A, Nakanishi Y, Ochiai A, Shimoda T, Yamaguchi H, Tachimori Y, Kato H, Watanabe H. A case of small polypoid esophageal carcinoma with multidirectional differentiation, including neuroendocrine, squamous, ciliated glandular, and sarcomatous component. Arch Pathol Lab Med 2000, 124: 1685–1687.

440a Haleem A, Kfoury H, Al Juboury M, Al Husseini H. Paget's

disease of the oesophagus associated with mucous gland carcinoma of the lower oesophagus. Histopathology 2003, 42: 61–65.

441 Kimura N, Tezuka F, Ono I, Ishioka K, Sasano N. Myogenic expression in esophageal polypoid tumors. Arch Pathol Lab Med 1989, 113: 1159–1165.

442 Lagacé R, Schurch W, Seemayer TA. Carcinome polypoïde pseudosarcomateux. Histogènese. Evidence d'une réponse myofibroblastique. Ann Pathol 1981, 1: 27–37.

443 Lam KY, Law S, Tung PH, Wong J. Esophageal small cell carcinomas: clinicopathologic parameters, p53 overexpression, proliferation marker and their impact on pathogenesis. Arch Pathol Lab Med 2000, 124: 228–233.

444 Lauwers GY, Grant LD, Scott GV, Carr NJ, Sobin LH. Spindle cell squamous carcinoma of the esophagus: analysis of ploidy and tumor proliferative activity in a series of 13 cases. Hum Pathol 1998, 29: 863–868.

445 Law SY, Fok M, Lam KY, Loke SL, Ma LT, Wong J. Small cell carcinoma of the esophagus. Cancer 1994, 73: 2894–2899.

446 Lindberg GM, Molberg KH, Vuitch F, Albores-Saavedra J. Atypical carcinoid of the esophagus: a case report and review of the literature. Cancer 1997, 79: 1476–1481.

447 Linder J, Stein RB, Roggli VL, Vollmer RT, Croker BP, Postlethwait RW, Shelburne JD. Polypoid tumor of the esophagus. Hum Pathol 1987, 18: 692–700.

448 Majmudar B, Dillard R, Susann PW. Collision carcinoma of the gastric cardia. Hum Pathol 1978, 9: 471–473.

449 Martin MR, Kahn LB. So-called pseudosarcoma of the esophagus. Nodal metastases of the spindle cell element. Arch Pathol Lab Med 1977, 101: 604–609.

450 Matsusaka T, Watanabe H, Enjoji M. Anaplastic carcinoma of the esophagus. Report of three cases and their histogenetic consideration. Cancer 1976, 37: 1352–1358.

451 Matsusaka T, Watanabe H, Enjoji M. Pseudosarcoma and carcinosarcoma of the esophagus. Cancer 1976, 37: 1546–1555.

452 Medgyesy DC, Wolff RA, Putnam JB Jr, Ajani JA. Small cell carcinoma of the esophagus: the University of Texas M.D. Anderson cancer center experience and literature review. Cancer 2000, 88: 262–267.

453 Minielly JA, Harrison EG Jr, Fontana RS, Payne WS. Verrucous squamous cell carcinoma of the esophagus. Cancer 1967, 20: 2078–2087.

454 Mori M, Matsukuma A, Adachi Y, Miyagahara T, Matsuda H, Kuwano H, Sugimachi K, Enjoji M. Small cell carcinoma of the esophagus. Cancer 1989, 63: 564–573.

455 Mori M, Watanabe M, Tanaka S, Mimori K, Kuwano H, Sugimachi K. Epstein-Barr virus-associated carcinomas of the esophagus and stomach. Arch Pathol Lab Med 1994, 118: 998–1001.

456 Nichols GL, Kelsen DP. Small cell carcinoma of the esophagus. The Memorial Hospital experience 1970 to 1987. Cancer 1989, 64: 1531–1533.

457 Osamura RY, Shimamura K, Hata J, Tamaoki N, Watanabe K, Kubota M, Yamazaki S, Mitomi T. Polypoid carcinoma of the esophagus. A unifying term for "carcinosarcoma" and "pseudosarcoma." Am J Surg Pathol 1978, 2: 201–208.

458 Reyes CV, Chejfec G, Jao W, Gould VE. Neuroendocrine carcinomas of the esophagus. Ultrastruct Pathol 1980, 1: 367–376.

459 Robertson NJ, Rahamim J, Smith ME. Carcinosarcoma of the oesophagus showing neuroendocrine, squamous and glandular differentiation. Histopathology 1997, 31: 263–266.

460 Rosenthal SN, Lemkin JA. Multiple small cell carcinomas of the esophagus. Cancer 1983, 51: 1944–1946.

461 Sabanathan S, Graham GP, Salama FD. Primary oat cell carcinoma of the oesophagus. Thorax 1986, 41: 318–321.

462 Sarbia M, Loberg C, Wolter M, Arjumand J, Heep H, Reifenberger G, Gabbert HE. Expression of bcl-2 and

amplification of c-myc are frequent in basaloid squamous cell carcinomas of the esophagus. Am J Pathol 1999, **155**: 1027–1032.

463 Sarbia M, Verreet P, Bittinger F, Dutkowski P, Heep H, Willers R, Gabbert HE. Basaloid squamous cell carcinoma of the esophagus: diagnosis and prognosis. Cancer 1997, **79**: 1871–1878.

464 Sato T, Mukai M, Ando N, Tashiro Y, Iri H, Abe O, Watanabe Y. Small cell carcinoma (non-oat cell type) of the esophagus concomitant with invasive squamous cell carcinoma and carcinoma in situ. A case report. Cancer 1986, **57**: 328–332.

465 Spagnolo DV, Heenan PJ. Collision carcinoma at the esophagogastric junction. Report of two cases. Cancer 1980, **46**: 2702–2708.

466 Takubo K, Mafune K, Tanaka Y, Miyama T, Fujita K. Basaloid-squamous carcinoma of the esophagus with marked deposition of basement membrane substance. Acta Pathol Jpn 1991, **41**: 59–64.

467 Takubo K, Nakamura K-I, Sawabe M, Arai T, Esaki Y, Miyashita M, Mafune K, Tanaka Y, Sasajima K. Primary undifferentiated small cell carcinoma of the esophagus. Hum Pathol 1999, **30**: 216–221.

468 Tanoue S, Shimoda T, Suzuki M, Ikegami M, Ishikawa E, Sano T. Anaplastic carcinoma of the esophagus. Acta Pathol Jpn 1983, **33**: 831–841.

469 Tateishi R, Taniguchi K, Horai T, Iwanaga T, Taniguchi H, Kabuto T, Sano M, Ishiguro S, Wada A. Argyrophil cell carcinoma (apudoma) of the esophagus. A histopathologic entity. Virchows Arch [A] 1976, **371**: 283–294.

470 Tateishi R, Taniguchi H, Wada A, Horai T, Taniguchi K. Argyrophil cells and melanocytes in esophageal mucosa. Arch Pathol 1974, **98**: 87–89.

471 Terada N, Yamamoto R, Ishiguro S, Hata K, Sawada M, Hiramatsu Y, Hioki K, Kitamura Y. Squamous cell carcinoma of the esophagus with cartilaginous metaplasia at metastatic lesions. Acta Pathol Jpn 1990, **40**: 435–441.

472 Wain SL, Kier R, Vollmer RT, Bossen EH. Basaloid-squamous carcinoma of the tongue, hypopharynx, and larynx. Report of 10 cases. Hum Pathol 1986, **17**: 1158–1166.

473 Wang HH, Antonioli DA, Goldman H. Comparative features of esophageal and gastric adenocarcinomas. Recent changes in type and frequency. Hum Pathol 1986, **17**: 482–487.

474 Wang ZY, Itabashi M, Hirota T, Watanabe H, Kato H. Immunohistochemical study of the histogenesis of esophageal carcinosarcoma. Jpn J Clin Oncol 1992, **22**: 377–386.

475 Weidner N. Sarcomatoid carcinoma of the upper aerodigestive tract. Semin Diagn Pathol 1987, **4**: 157–168.

476 Woodard BH, Shelburn JD, Vollmer RT, Postlethwait RW. Mucoepidermoid carcinoma of the esophagus. A case report. Hum Pathol 1978, **9**: 352–354.

Smooth muscle tumors and GIST-type stromal tumors

477 Athanasoulis CA, Aral IM. Leiomyosarcoma of the esophagus. Gastroenterology 1968, **54**: 271–274.

478 Heidet L, Boye E, Cai Y, Sado Y, Zhang X, Flejou JF, Fekete F, Ninomiya Y, Gubler MC, Antignac C. Somatic deletion of the 5′ ends of both the COL4A5 and COL4A6 genes in a sporadic leiomyoma of the esophagus. Am J Pathol 1998, **152**: 673–678.

479 Lam KY, Law SY, Chu KM, Ma LT. Gastrointestinal autonomic nerve tumor of the esophagus: a clinicopathologic, immunohistochemical, ultrastructural study of a case and review of the literature. Cancer 1996, **78**: 1651–1659.

480 McKeeby JL, Li X, Zhuang Z, Vortmeyer AO, Huang S, Pirner M, Skarulis MC, James-Newton L, Marx SJ, Lubensky IA. Multiple leiomyomas of the esophagus, lung, and uterus in multiple endocrine neoplasia type 1. Am J Pathol 2001, **159**: 1121–1127.

481 Miettinen M, Sarlomo-Rikala M, Sobin LH, Lasota J. Esophageal stromal tumors; a clinicopathologic, immunohistochemical, and molecular genetic study of 17 cases and comparison with esophageal leiomyomas and leiomyosarcomas. Am J Surg Pathol 2000, **24**: 211–222.

482 Rainer WG, Brus R. Leiomyosarcoma of the esophagus. Review of the literature and report of 3 cases. Surgery 1965, **50**: 343–350.

483 Seremetis MG, Lyons WS, deGuzman VC, Peabody JW Jr. Leiomyomata of the esophagus. An analysis of 838 cases. Cancer 1976, **38**: 2166–2177.

484 Solomon MP, Rosenblum H, Rosato FE. Leiomyoma of the esophagus. Ann Surg 1984, **199**: 246–248.

485 Takubo K, Nakagawa H, Tsuchiya S, Mitomo Y, Sasajima K, Shirota A. Seedling leiomyoma of the esophagus and esophagogastric junction zone. Hum Pathol 1981, **12**: 1006–1010.

Other tumors and tumorlike conditions

486 Abraham SC, Singh VK, Yardley JH, Wu TT. Hyperplastic polyps of the esophagus and esophagogastric junction: histologic and clinicopathologic findings. Am J Surg Pathol 2001, **25**: 1180–1187.

487 Ahmed N, Ramos S, Sika J, LeVeen HH, Piccone VA. Primary extramedullary esophageal plasmacytoma. First case report. Cancer 1976, **38**: 943–947.

488 Assor D. A melanocytic tumor of the esophagus. Cancer 1975, **35**: 1438–1443.

489 Burke JS, Ranchod M. Hemangiopericytoma of the esophagus. Hum Pathol 1981, **12**: 96–97.

490 Carr NJ, Bratthauer GL, Lichy JH, Taubenberger JK, Monihan JM, Sobin LH. Squamous cell papillomas of the esophagus. A study of 23 lesions for human papillomavirus by in situ hybridization and the polymerase chain reaction. Hum Pathol 1994, **25**: 536–540.

491 Chang F, Janatuinen E, Pikkarainen P, Syrjanen S, Syrjanen K. Esophageal squamous cell papillomas. Failure to detect human papillomavirus DNA by in situ hybridization and polymerase chain reaction. Scand J Gastroenterol 1991, **26**: 535–543.

492 Chetty R, Learmonth GM, Price SK, Taylor DA. Primary oesophageal rhabdomyosarcoma. Cytopathology 1991, **2**: 103–108.

492a Cokelaere K, Sciot R, Geboes K. Esophageal plexiform schwannoma. Int J Surg Pathol 2000, **8**: 353–357.

493 David O, Jakate S. Multifocal granular cell tumor of the esophagus and proximal stomach with infiltrative pattern: a case report and review of the literature. Arch Pathol Lab Med 1999, **123**: 967–973.

494 de S Coutinho DS, Soga J, Yoshikawa T, Miyashita K, Tanaka O, Sasaki K, Muto T, Shimizu T. Granular cell tumors of the esophagus. A report of two cases and review of the literature. Am J Gastroenterol 1985, **80**: 758–762.

495 DiCostanzo DP, Urmacher C. Primary malignant melanoma of the esophagus. Am J Surg Pathol 1987, **11**: 46–52.

496 Evans DMD, Jones DB, Cleary BK, Smith PM. Oesophageal varices treated by sclerotherapy. A histopathological study. Gut 1982, **23**: 615–620.

497 Fulp SR, Nestock BR, Powell BL, Evans JK, Geisinger KR, Gilliam JH III. Leukemic infiltration of the esophagus. Cancer 1993, **71**: 112–116.

498 Gelb AB, Medeiros LJ, Chen YY, Weiss LM, Weidner N. Hodgkin's disease of the esophagus. Am J Clin Pathol 1997, **108**: 593–598.

499 Gervaz E, Potet F, Mahe R, Lemasson G. Focal lymphoid hyperplasia of the oesophagus. Report of a case. Histopathology 1992, **21**: 187–190.

500 Goldman H, Antonioli DA. Mucosal biopsy of the esophagus, stomach, and proximal duodenum. Hum Pathol 1982, **13**: 423–448.

501 Gore RM, Sparberg M. Metastatic carcinoma of the prostate to the esophagus. Am J Gastroenterol 1982, **77**: 358–359.

502 Guzman RP, Wightman R, Ravinsky E, Unruh HW. Primary malignant melanoma of the esophagus with diffuse melanocytic atypia and melanoma in situ. Am J Clin Pathol 1990, **92**: 802–804.

503 Hale RJ, Merchant W, Hasleton PS. Polypoidal intra-oesophageal

thyroid carcinoma. A rare cause of dysphagia. Histopathology 1990, **17**: 475–476.

504 Herrera JL. Case report. Esophageal metastasis from breast carcinoma presenting as achalasia. Am J Med Sci 1992, **303**: 321–323.

505 Jang GC, Clouse ME, Fleischner FG. Fibrovascular polyp. A benign intraluminal tumor of the esophagus. Radiology 1969, **92**: 1196–1200.

506 LiVolsi VA, Perzin KH. Inflammatory pseudotumors (inflammatory fibrous polyps) of the esophagus. A clinicopathologic study. Am J Dig Dis 1975, **20**: 475–481.

507 Ludwig ME, Shaw R, de Suto-Nagy G. Primary malignant melanoma of the esophagus. Cancer 1981, **48**: 2528–2534.

508 Maesawa C, Lijima S, Sato N, Yoshinori N, Suzuki M, Tarusawa M, Ishida K, Tamura G, Saito K, Masuda T. Esophageal extraskeletal Ewing's sarcoma. Hum Pathol 2002, **33**: 130–132.

509 Matsuura H, Saito R, Nakajima S, Yoshihara W, Enomoto T. Non-Hodgkin's lymphoma of the esophagus. Am J Gastroenterol 1985, **80**: 941–946.

510 McIntyre M, Webb JN, Browning GCP. Osteosarcoma of the esophagus. Hum Pathol 1982, **13**: 680–682.

511 Mills SE, Cooper PH. Malignant melanoma of the digestive system. Pathol Annu 1983, **18**(Pt 2): 1–26.

512 Nakanishi Y, Ochiai A, Shimoda T, Yamaguchi H, Tachimori Y, Kato H, Watanabe H, Hirohashi S. Epidermization in the esophageal mucosa: unusual epithelial changes clearly detected by Lugol's staining. Am J Surg Pathol 1997, **21**: 605–609.

513 Odze R, Antonioli D, Shocket D, Noble-Topham S, Goldman H, Upton M. Esophageal squamous papillomas. A clinicopathologic study of 38 lesions and analysis for human papillomavirus by the polymerase chain reaction. Am J Surg Pathol 1993, **17**: 803–812.

514 Ohmori T, Arita N, Uraga N, Tabei R, Tani M, Okamura H. Malignant granular cell tumor of the esophagus. A case report with light and electron microscopic, histochemical, and immunohistochemical study. Acta Pathol Jpn 1987, **37**: 775–783.

515 Okumura T, Tanoue S, Chiba K, Tanaka S. Lobular capillary hemangioma of the esophagus. A case report and review of the literature. Acta Pathol Jpn 1983, **33**: 1303–1308.

516 Perch SJ, Soffen EM, Whittington R, Brooks JJ. Esophageal sarcomas. J Surg Oncol 1991, **48**: 194–198.

517 Piccone VA, Klopstock R, LeVeen HH, Sika J. Primary malignant melanoma of the esophagus associated with melanosis of the entire esophagus. First case report. J Thorac Cardiovasc Surg 1970, **59**: 865–870.

518 Prevot S, Bienvenu L, Vaillant JC, De Sain-Maur PP. Benign schwannoma of the digestive tract: a clinicopathologic and immunohistochemical study of five cases, including a case of esophageal tumor. Am J Surg Pathol 1999, **23**: 431–436.

519 Pushpanathan C, Idikio H. Pathological findings in the esophagus after endoscopic sclerotherapy for variceal bleeding. Am J Gastroenterol 1986, **81**: 9–13.

520 Radin DR. Primary esophageal lymphoma in AIDS. Abdom Imaging 1993, **18**: 223–224.

521 Rywlin AM, Ortega R. Glyogenic acanthosis of the esophagus. Arch Pathol 1970, **90**: 439–443.

522 Saitoh K, Nasu M, Kamiyama R, Hatakeyama S, Maruyama M, Tsuruta K, Takeshita K. Solitary neurofibroma of the esophagus. Acta Pathol Jpn 1985, **35**: 527–531.

523 Seo IS, Henley JD, Min KW, Yum MN. True histiocytic lymphoma of the esophagus in an HIV-positive patient: an ultrastructural and immunohistochemical study. Ultrastruct Pathol 1999, **23**: 333–339.

524 Symmans WF, Grimes MM. Malignant melanoma of the esophagus. Histologic variants and immunohistochemical findings in four cases. Surg Pathol 1991, **4**: 222–234.

525 Taal BG, Van Heerde P, Somers R. Isolated primary oesophageal involvement by lymphoma. A rare cause of dysphagia. Two case histories and a review of other published data. Gut 1993, **34**: 994–998.

526 Totten RS, Stout AP, Humphreys GH II, Moore RL. Benign tumors and cysts of the esophagus. J Thorac Surg 1953, **25**: 606–622.

527 Tsutsumi M, Mizumoto K, Tsujiuchi T, Maruyama H, Koizumi M, Inagaki T, Toyokawa M, Konishi Y. Serous cystadenoma of the esophagus. Acta Pathol Jpn 1990, **40**: 153–155.

528 Vadva MD, Triadafilopoulos G. Glycogenic acanthosis of the esophagus and gastroesophageal reflux. J Clin Gastroenterol 1993, **17**: 79–83.

529 Vuyk HD, Snow GB, Tiwari RM, van Velzen D, Veldhuizen RW. Granular cell tumor of the proximal esophagus. A rare disease. Cancer 1985, **55**: 445–449.

530 Winkler B, Capo V, Reumann W, Ma A, La Porta R, Reilly S, Green PMR, Richart RM, Crum CP. Human papillomavirus infection of the esophagus. A clinicopathologic study with demonstration of papillomavirus antigen by the immunoperoxidase technique. Cancer 1985, **55**: 149–155.

531 Wolf BC, Khettry U, Leonardi HK, Neptune WB, Bhattacharyya AK, Legg MA. Benign lesions mimicking malignant tumors of the esophagus. Hum Pathol 1988, **19**: 148–154.

532 Zarian LP, Berliner L, Redmond P. Metastatic endometrial carcinoma to the esophagus. Am J Gastroenterol 1983, **78**: 9–11.

Stomach

Normal anatomy

The stomach is divided grossly into the following regions: cardia, fundus, corpus or body, pyloric antrum, and pylorus. These show some correspondence to (but should not be equated with) the three major microscopic types of gastric mucosa: cardiac, fundic, and pyloric (antral), which exhibit transitional areas in between.[3,6] All of the gastric glands have two major components: foveola (crypt, pit) and secretory portion (adenomere). The foveolae represent the most important area for the genesis of gastric carcinoma, in particular the layer of generative cells located at their base.[6,7] The differences among the various types of gastric mucosa depend on the relative proportions between foveolae and secretory portions and the microscopic composition of the latter. Cardiac and pyloric glands are similar: foveolae occupy the upper half, and branching mucus-secreting glands occupy the lower half. Looser packing of the glands and the presence of occasional cysts in cardiac glands are the only two minor microscopic differences that exist with the pyloric glands. The cytoplasm of the pyloric cells can be bubbly, vacuolated, granular, or glassy.[9] Subnuclear vacuolization of mucous cells sometimes occurs and should not be misinterpreted as an expression of metaplasia.[16] Similarly, pyloric cells with glassy cytoplasm

occurring in cohesive clusters should not be confused with signet ring adenocarcinoma.[10] Ciliated cells are sometimes found in the pyloric area; they are more common in the Japanese and are regarded by some as an expression of metaplasia.[12,17] Parenthetically, several other geographic differences have been noted in the histologic characteristics of the gastric mucosa.[11]

The fundic (oxyntic, acidopeptic) glands are characterized by foveolae that occupy only one fourth of the thickness, and straight glands of composite cell distribution, which includes chief (zymogenic) cells, parietal (acid-secreting) cells, endocrine cells, and mucous neck cells. Immunohistochemical and in situ hybridization studies have shown production of pepsinogen I in both chief and mucous neck cells (but not in the pyloric region, which features instead production of pepsinogen II).[1,13]

The mucin secreted by the gastric mucosa is almost entirely of neutral type and therefore is positive for PAS but negative for Alcian blue and Mayer's mucicarmine; however, the normal mucous neck cells may produce small amounts of sialomucin and sulfomucin.[2] At the immunohistochemical level, the foveolar epithelium expresses MUC1 and MUC5AC, and the glands express MUC6. Regarding Lewis antigen, the foveolar epithelium expresses type-1 chain antigens Le(a) and Le(b), whereas the glands express type-2 chain antigens Le(x) and Le(y).[14]

At least 16 types of endocrine–paracrine cells have been identified in the gastrointestinal mucosa, and many of them occur in the stomach.[4,5,8,15] In the pyloric mucosa, approximately 50% of the endocrine cells are G cells (gastrin producing), 30% are enterochromaffin (EC) cells (5-HT [serotonin] producing), and 15% are D cells (somatostatin producing). In the fundic mucosa, the predominant endocrine cell is the EC-like (ECL) cell (histamine storing); there are also a few X cells (of unknown secretory product) and EC cells. ECL cells are thought to play a key role in the mechanism of gastric acid secretion as controlled by gastrin stimulation. Their functional and proliferative activities are strongly stimulated by gastrin.[15]

The other two components of the mucosa are the lamina propria and the muscularis mucosae. The latter is formed of an inner circular and an outer longitudinal layer; it is continuous with thin fascicles of smooth muscle that go up inside the lamina propria to reach beneath the surface epithelium.

The other layers of the stomach are the same as for the rest of the gastrointestinal tract (i.e., submucosa, muscularis externa [propria], and serosa). The submucosa consists of loose connective tissue with numerous elastic fibers; it contains plexuses of arteries, veins, lymph vessels, and Meissner's nerve plexus. The muscularis externa is composed of three layers: outer longitudinal, inner circular, and innermost oblique. The inner circular layer forms the pyloric sphincter at the gastroduodenal junction. The Auerbach (myenteric) plexus is located between the circular and longitudinal layers of the muscularis externa. The interstitial cells of Cajal are discussed on p. 677 in connection with their alleged relationship with the neoplasms known as GISTs (gastrointestinal stromal tumors), as well as on p. 648.

The blood supply of the stomach originates from the celiac axis, hepatic artery, and splenic artery. The lymph vessels drain into four major areas, according to the following scheme:

1 Cardia and most of lesser curvature: left gastric nodes
2 Pylorus and distal lesser curvature: right gastric and hepatic nodes
3 Proximal portion of the greater curvature: pancreaticosplenic nodes in the splenic hilum
4 Distal portion of greater curvature: right gastroepiploic nodes in greater omentum and pyloric nodes at the head of the pancreas.

Heterotopic tissues

Heterotopic pancreas can present clinically as a gastric mass or be discovered incidentally at autopsy or at laparotomy.[27,28] Exceptionally, it has been found to cause hemorrhage in the newborn.[29] Grossly, it may form a hemispheric mass, a symmetric cone, or a short cylindric nipple-like projection. In the last instance, one or more ducts are usually seen emptying on the gastric lumen; this feature constitutes an important diagnostic sign radiographically (Fig. 11.25). Approximately 85% of these lesions occur in the submucosa and most of the others in the muscular layer. Most are located in the antrum (61%) or pylorus (24%).[27] Grossly, the cut surface looks like normal pancreas except for the occasional occurrence of cystic structures. Microscopically, pancreatic acini and ducts are always present, but islets are seen in only one third of the cases. Mucocele-like changes may be seen.[24] Calcification may be present.[25] Some cases of intramural gastric carcinoma are said to have arisen in these heterotopic tissues.[19,21,26]

An altogether different phenomenon is represented by the **pancreatic metaplasia** of gastric mucosa, thought to arise from "erroneous differentiation" of primitive epithelium (Fig. 11.26).[30,31] These cells, which can be

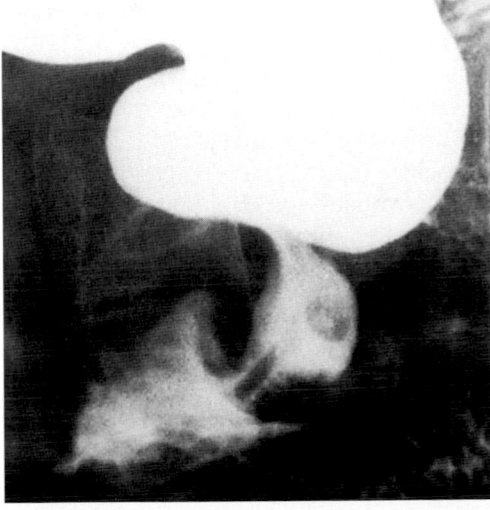

Fig. 11.25 Heterotopic pancreatic tissue presenting radiographically as a small, round nodule with central umbilication in antrum.

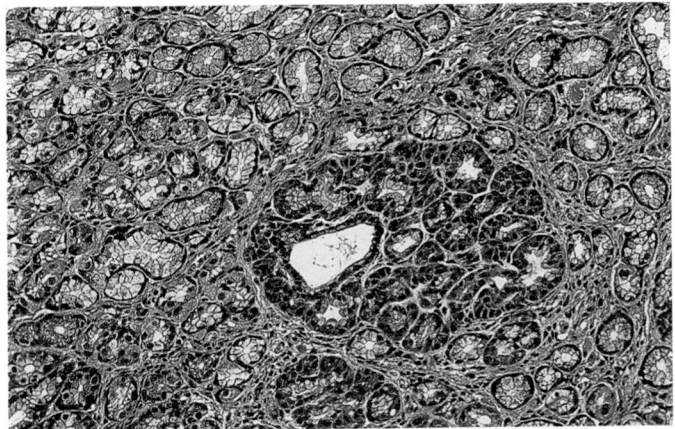

Fig. 11.26 Island of exocrine pancreatic tissue composed of acini within gastric mucosa.

found in adults and in children,[23] are immunohistochemically reactive for pancreatic lipase and trypsinogen[18,31]; they also contain amylase, but not as frequently or abundantly as the heterotopic glands. There is also occasional positivity for PP and other peptide hormones.[31]

The lesion described as **gastric adenomyoma** is closely related to heterotopic pancreas. It is probably a hamartoma rather than a true neoplasm, the usual components being large ducts, Brunner's glands, and prominent smooth muscle bundles.[20] Like conventional heterotopic pancreas, it has occasionally been found to undergo malignant transformation.[22]

Hypertrophic pyloric stenosis

Hypertrophic pyloric stenosis is one of the most common congenital anomalies, but its incidence is decreasing, suggesting that environmental factors are of importance in this disorder.[36] Most patients are males, and the most common age of onset is between 3 and 12 weeks. The gross appearance is that of a greatly thickened pyloric muscle, which occludes the pyloric channel and partially obstructs the gastric outflow. The etiology and pathogenesis remain obscure; a ganglion dysfunction similar to that of esophageal achalasia has been postulated. There is increasing evidence that the smooth muscle cells of the gastric wall are not properly innervated,[39] and that the phasic and tonic contractile activity in the gastroduodenal junction of these patients is not coordinated with the antral contractions.[37] A possible pathogenetic role of the interstitial cells of Cajal has been postulated.[40,41] The operation of choice for decades has been the Fredet–Ramstedt pyloromyotomy, which basically consists of a linear incision through the hypertrophic muscle, leaving the mucosa intact. At present, this procedure is usually performed endoscopically.[34] Usually no tissue is resected in this procedure. The few microscopic studies that have been done on this condition have shown no alterations of note.[32]

Hypertrophy of the pylorus in the adult is a rare condition. Approximately 80% of the cases have occurred in males. Clinically and radiographically, a tumor may be suspected and the stomach resected. Grossly and microscopically, all that is found is hypertrophy of the pyloric circular muscle fibers that ends abruptly at the duodenum, sometimes accompanied by a mild degree of fibrosis.[42] Chronic gastritis is usually present.[33,35,43]

The presence of pyloric hypertrophy in an adult in the absence of another gastric abnormality occurs only exceptionally.[38] Although it is possible that some of the cases represent a persistence of the infantile form into adult life, in most instances the process is probably secondary to antral gastritis or peptic ulcer of the pyloric channel, which may have healed by the time of surgery. It is also well to remember that the gross appearance of pyloric hypertrophy can be simulated by the diffuse form of gastric adenocarcinoma traditionally known as linitis plastica.

Chronic gastritis

The incidence and natural history of chronic gastritis has been greatly clarified by the systematic use of endoscopic gastric biopsy.[63,70,102] The two main features of this disease are infiltration of the lamina propria by inflammatory cells and atrophy of the glandular epithelium. Plasma cells and lymphocytes (with occasional formation of follicles) predominate among the inflammatory cells, but eosinophils and neutrophils may also be present. If the inflammatory infiltrate is limited to the foveolar region and unaccompanied by glandular atrophy, the condition is designated as **chronic superficial gastritis**. Subtle epithelial abnormalities seen in this form include a reduced amount of cytoplasmic mucin, nuclear and nucleolar enlargement, and some increase in foveolar mitoses. When the inflammation is more extensive and accompanied by glandular atrophy, the condition is termed **chronic atrophic gastritis** and is further categorized as *mild, moderate, or severe* by roughly estimating the thickness of the glandular portion in relation to the thickness of the whole mucosa.[99,100] Naturally, a properly oriented biopsy containing muscularis mucosae is needed to make this estimation. Glandular atrophy is also manifested by an increase in the distance between the individual glands and the condensation of reticulin fibers in the lamina propria.[60] If thinning of the mucosa is seen in the absence of inflammatory changes, the condition is designated **gastric atrophy**, acknowledging the fact that in most cases this probably represents the end stage of a chronic atrophic gastritis. Increasing degrees of atrophy are commonly associated with cystic dilatation of glands and metaplasia. In rare cases of (auto)immune gastritis (see below), the atrophy may have a patchy quality, resulting in a pseudopolypoid appearance of the oxyntic mucosa.[73a]

Two types of **metaplastic changes** can occur in chronic gastritis, often in combination: pyloric metaplasia of the fundic mucosa and intestinal metaplasia.[89]

In *pyloric metaplasia*, there is a replacement of the fundic-type glands by mucus-secreting glands. This is a gradual process that proceeds as a front along the fundic–pyloric junction and moves proximally toward the cardia. *Intestinal metaplasia* refers to the progressive replacement of the gastric mucosa by epithelium having the light and electron microscopic features of intestinal epithelium of either small or large bowel type, including goblet cells, absorptive (brush border) cells, Paneth cells, and a variety of endocrine cells.[46,76,90] Ciliated cells may also be present.[96] Intestinal metaplasia has been further divided into *complete (type I)* and *incomplete (type II)* types. In complete metaplasia, the gastric mucosa changes to a pattern nearly identical to that of small bowel epithelium, with the development of villi and crypts in the most advanced cases. In incomplete metaplasia, absorptive cells are absent, whereas columnar cells with the appearance of gastric foveolar cells are retained.[45,75,81] Histochemically, the predominant mucin present in complete intestinal metaplasia is sialomucin, with small amounts of sulfomucins and/or neutral mucins; in the incomplete form, there may be predominance of either neutral mucins (type IIA) or sulfomucins (type IIB).[68] Immunohistochemically, type I intestinal metaplasia is characterized by MUC2 intestinal-type mucin and a correspondingly decreased or absent expression of MUC1, MUC5AC and MUC6. In type II metaplasia there is, as expected, a coexpression of MUC2 and the mucins normally expressed in the stomach.[84] Intestinal metaplasia is also accompanied by increased immunoreactivity for the secretory component of immunoglobulins[98] and for the T (Thomsen–Friedenreich) antigen, the latter indicating aberrant mucin glycosylation.[48] Curiously, glands with intestinal metaplasia are also consistently immunoreactive for hepatocyte antigen (Hep-Par-1).[49a]

The relationship between intestinal metaplasia of the stomach and *Helicobacter pylori* is of interest. *H. pylori* is usually absent in foci of type I intestinal metaplasia but often present in type II foci, i.e., those in which some gastric features are retained.[78] Type IIB intestinal metaplasia is said to show a closer association with intestinal-type gastric carcinoma than the other types,[58,67,83] but the results in the literature have been conflicting.[74]

Nonspecific chronic gastritis is a very common disease. Its prevalence in the US population is unknown, but series from unselected populations in Europe and Japan have shown that its incidence increases with age, and that it is present in more than half of the individuals over the age of 60 years.[72,87] Most patients with mild forms of gastritis are asymptomatic.

Endoscopically and grossly, well-developed atrophic gastritis and gastric atrophy produce a thin, smooth mucosa with undue prominence of submucosal vessels. There is an excellent correlation between the degree of gastric atrophy as estimated by endoscopic biopsy and the results of acid secretory tests. Conversely, the correlation of histology with symptomatology, radiology, and gastroscopy is poor.[78a]

Chronic gastritis has been divided into two types having similar histologic features (as already described) but a presumed different pathogenesis. The first type, which is less common, is designated as *type A* or *immune*.[56,92] It usually affects the fundus in a diffuse manner, spares the antrum, and is associated with antibodies to parietal cells, hypochlorhydria or achlorhydria, and high serum gastrin levels. The alpha and beta subunits of the gastric proton pump have been identified as the major molecular target of this presumed autoimmune disease, which may evolve into pernicious anemia.[91,95]

The other type, by far the more frequent, begins in the antrum and progresses proximally so that the fundic–pyloric border rises up gradually.[51] This is referred to as *type B* or *nonimmune gastritis*.[92] In some classification schemes, this has been further subdivided into a form restricted to the antrum and associated with hyperchlorhydria and often duodenal peptic ulceration (*hypersecretory gastritis*) and a form that involves both antrum and fundus in an initially patchy and eventually diffuse distribution (*environmental gastritis*).[50,70,71]

Chronic atrophic gastritis is usually present in cases of gastric carcinoma, and in general its severity is proportional to the extent of the tumor. Most cases of gastric peptic ulcer are associated with antral and fundic gastritis, whereas in duodenal ulcer the gastritis, if present at all, is restricted to the antrum. The incidence and extent of intestinal metaplasia are greatest in stomachs removed for carcinoma, least in those with duodenal ulcer, and intermediate in cases of gastric ulcer.[77]

The pathogenesis of type B chronic gastritis is complex and probably multifactorial. Factors known to be statistically associated with this disorder include alcohol, tobacco, duodenal reflux (reflux gastritis), allergy to foods, and various drugs (particularly anti-inflammatory agents).[57,79,88]

The most important advance in the field of chronic gastritis and other gastric diseases (peptic ulcer, carcinoma, and malignant lymphoma) has been the awareness of the crucial role played by *H. pylori*.[47,85,86,93,101,104] This organism, formerly known as *Campylobacter pylori*, is a curved spirochete-like bacterium, of which two major genotypes exist.[94] This organism colonizes the gastric mucosa (particularly the antrum and cardia) in a variety of ways: free in mucus, surface adhesion, and intercellularly.[49] Cases with intracellular colonization show the greatest degree of epithelial damage.[49] These changes include disintegration and loss of apical mucus with formation of epithelial pits and—less frequently—erosions and ulcerations.[66] The presumed main mechanisms for these alterations are motility and urease activity by the organism.[54,64] There is also a relation between *H. pylori* infection and prevalence of lymphoid follicles[55,61] (see p. 681).

Medical therapy can lead to eradication of the organism and a regression of the inflammatory changes in the mucosa.[52,62]

H. pylori can be recognized in routine hematoxylin–eosin stains, and in most instances that is all that is needed. However, if the density of the organism is low, its detection can be greatly facilitated by the performance of special stains, which include Giemsa, Warthin–Starry or Steiner silver stains (Fig. 11.27),[59,73] the Alcian yellow–toluidine blue method, Genta stain, or immunohistochemistry.[44] No clear advantage of one over the others has been demonstrated[69,97]; in our department we have adopted the immunohistochemical method. Polymerase chain reaction (PCR) techniques are also available.[65,82,98a]

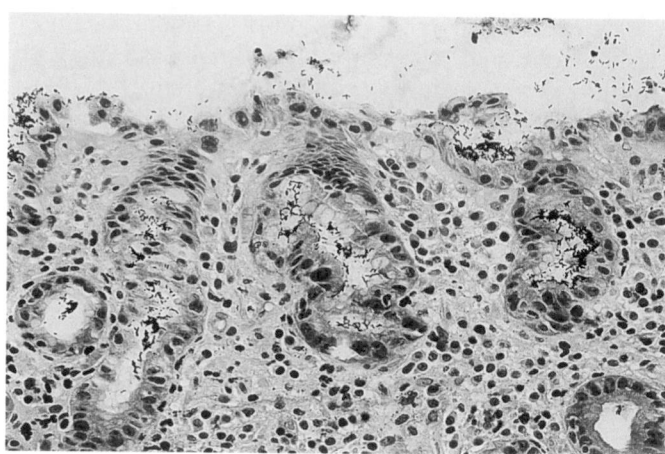

Fig. 11.27 *Helicobacter pylori* organisms demonstrated with silver stain.

With the use of these techniques, *H. pylori* has been found in 90% of patients with chronic gastritis, 95% with duodenal ulcer disease, 70% with gastric ulcer, and 50% with gastric carcinoma.[103]

In 1991, a system was proposed for the comprehensive microscopic reporting of gastritis. This method, referred to as "the Sydney system"[80] and upgraded in 1994,[53] recommends the following:

1. For antral and corpus biopsies to be assessed separately
2. For gastritis to be classified into
   Acute
   Chronic
   Special (e.g., lymphocytic, granulomatous)
3. For the following variables to be graded
   H: pylori
   Chronic inflammation
   Neutrophils (as a sign of activity)
   Atrophy
   Intestinal metaplasia
4. A concluding summary is to be provided, indicating the etiology (if known), topography (antrum, corpus, or pangastritis), and morphology (including all variables).

Other types of gastritis

Acute gastritis may result from the ingestion of alcohol, salicylates, and other anti-inflammatory drugs, or by the reflux of bile salts. Endoscopic biopsies, rarely taken in this condition, may show hyperemia, focal fresh hemorrhage, focal necrosis of surface and foveolar cells, and neutrophilic infiltration of the foveolar and glandular lumina.[115]

Acute infectious nonbacterial gastroenteritis (a common condition induced by the Norwalk agent) is not associated with a histologically detectable gastric mucosal lesion, at least in its usual mild form.[138]

Hemorrhagic gastritis is an acute life-threatening condition usually engrafted on a background of chronic gastritis.[140] Alcoholism, anti-inflammatory drugs, and stress have been implicated as precipitating factors.[112] Some cases have been attributed to cytomegalovirus (CMV) infection.[128] The appearance of the stomach at surgery is characterized by multiple areas of hemorrhage throughout the entire mucosa (Fig. 11.28). The microscopic appearance is not as dramatic as the surgical findings would anticipate. In some cases, multiple superficial erosions are found (and the term *erosive gastritis* is therefore used), but in many others the only abnormality seen in the biopsy is a chronic atrophic gastritis, with perhaps some extravasation of blood in the lamina propria. In Lulu and Dragstedt's series,[121] the overall mortality was 55%. They advocated vagotomy and high subtotal gastrectomy as the treatment of choice. The diffuse gastric condition, often seen as a complication of portal hypertension and sometimes leading to severe hemorrhage, is often reported as a form of hemorrhagic gastritis, but the microscopic changes are more consistent with mucosal vascular ectasia ("congestive gastropathy"), with secondary and usually mild inflammatory changes.[122]

Collagenous gastritis is an exceptionally rare condition which—like its more common colonic counterpart—is characterized by a thick subepithelial collagen band associated with a mucosal inflammatory infiltrate.[134] The reported pediatric cases have presented with severe anemia and have been limited to the stomach, whereas those in adults have been usually associated with collagenous colitis.[120]

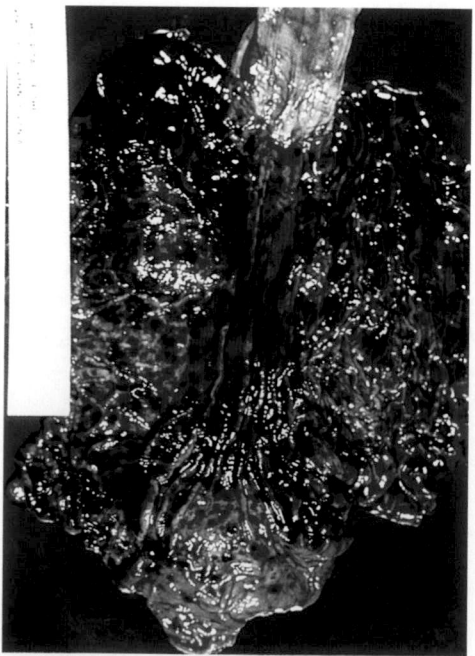

Fig. 11.28 Gross appearance of hemorrhagic gastritis as seen at autopsy. The entire gastric mucosa is involved by fresh hemorrhage.

Lymphocytic gastritis is a term not to be used for any chronic gastritis having a predominant small lymphocytic component (most chronic gastritides do), but rather for a condition resembling celiac disease and lymphocytic colitis.[137] Indeed, most cases are associated with celiac disease, although others may be related to *H. pylori* infection. Microscopically, the condition is characterized by lymphocytosis of foveolar and surface epithelium (intraepithelial lymphocytosis).[142]

Allergic gastroenteritis presents in a gastric biopsy as infiltration of the lamina propria by eosinophils, which in severe cases is diffuse and accompanied by degenerative and regenerative changes of the surface and foveolar epithelium.[116]

Diffuse eosinophilic gastroenteritis involves the distal portion of the stomach and proximal portion of the duodenum and can cause pyloric obstruction.[119,124] It may be associated with allergic phenomena and extreme peripheral eosinophilia.[129] Microscopically, edema and diffuse infiltration by eosinophils are prominent. Necrotizing angiitis has been observed in some cases.[123] The lesion probably represents in most cases a local reaction to ingested allergens. Ashby et al.[106] concluded that many of their cases were secondary to infestation by *Eustoma rotundatum*, a parasite of the North Sea herring. In other instances, the disease may be a manifestation of a collagen–vascular disease, such as scleroderma, polymyositis, or polyarteritis.[110] Diffuse eosinophilic gastroenteritis should be distinguished from other disorders in which eosinophils may be numerous, such as inflammatory fibroid polyp (see p. 659), malignant lymphoma, and even carcinoma. There is no evidence that diffuse eosinophilic gastroenteritis and inflammatory fibroid polyp are related conditions.

Granulomatous gastritis can be caused by tuberculosis,[111] mycosis,[111] sarcoidosis,[132] or Crohn's disease,[109,126,141] or may be part of a vasculitis syndrome.[127] When the cause of the inflammation remains unknown, the term *idiopathic granulomatous gastritis* is used, but with the understanding that this is not a specific entity; indeed, most such cases probably represent examples of gastric involvement by Crohn's disease or sarcoidosis.[131]

Syphilis of the stomach, now extremely rare but still encountered, begins as an erosive or ulcerative lesion in the pyloric portion.[108,114] In later stages, the stomach is shrunken and fibrotic, with a leather bottle appearance that simulates radiographically and grossly linitis plastica.[139] Microscopically, there is ulceration, chronic inflammation rich in plasma cells, and fibrosis; endarteritis obliterans may also be present. Other cases may show a heavy lymphoid infiltrate.[107,117] Treponemal DNA has been isolated from some of these cases by PCR.[118]

Malakoplakia can present as a focal gastric lesion. As in other sites, the disease is characterized microscopically by a predominantly histiocytic inflammatory infiltrate containing Michaelis–Gutmann bodies.[113,125]

Cytomegalovirus infection has been diagnosed in gastric biopsies of bone marrow transplant recipients and other immunocompromised patients; the finding is indicative of generalized disease.[133] It may be complicated by perforation and fistula formation.[105] Its diagnosis may require immunocytochemistry or in situ hybridization.[130]

Cryptococcosis is another infectious disease that has been observed in the stomach and other portions of the digestive tract in susceptible individuals.[135]

Bacillary angiomatosis can involve the stomach of HIV-infected individuals and result in severe hematemesis.[109a]

Graft-versus-host disease following allogeneic bone marrow transplantation manifests in the stomach with subtle microscopic findings, including apoptosis and gland destruction, sparse inflammatory infiltrate, and granular eosinophilic debris in dilated glands. The latter is a very specific but relatively insensitive marker. In its absence, the differential diagnosis with CMV infection may not be possible.[136]

Peptic and other benign ulcers

Peptic ulcer can occur wherever mucosa is bathed by gastric secretion. This includes the stomach, duodenum, lower third of esophagus, margin of a gastrojejunostomy, and Meckel's diverticulum with ectopic gastric mucosa. Acid peptic digestion is the ultimate cause for ulceration, but the mechanism(s) that render the mucosa susceptible to this digestion are just as important for the pathogenesis.

Duodenal ulcers (which are more common than gastric ulcers, although their relative incidence seems to be decreasing) are classically associated with acid hypersecretion, but most patients with gastric ulcer secrete either low normal or below normal amounts of acid. Thus it would seem that the initial event in gastric ulcer is mucosal injury, which renders it more susceptible to acid peptic damage. This injury may be mediated in some instances by reflux of bile and pancreatic juice and is manifested anatomically by the presence of gastritis, an almost invariable finding in patients with peptic ulcer disease. In recent years, considerable evidence has accumulated suggesting that *H. pylori* plays a crucial role in the pathogenesis of this disease.[145,150,158,161,164] The risk for the development of a peptic ulcer is approximately 10-fold higher in patients with nonatrophic *H. pylori*-positive gastritis than in those with a normal stomach, and the risk is increased further (twofold to threefold) when there is antral atrophy. Instead, the presence of corpus atrophy decreases the incidence of ulcer (to practically zero levels when the atrophy is complete).[160]

Acute gastric ulcer is a common finding at autopsy and is usually a terminal event (Fig. 11.29). It may also be

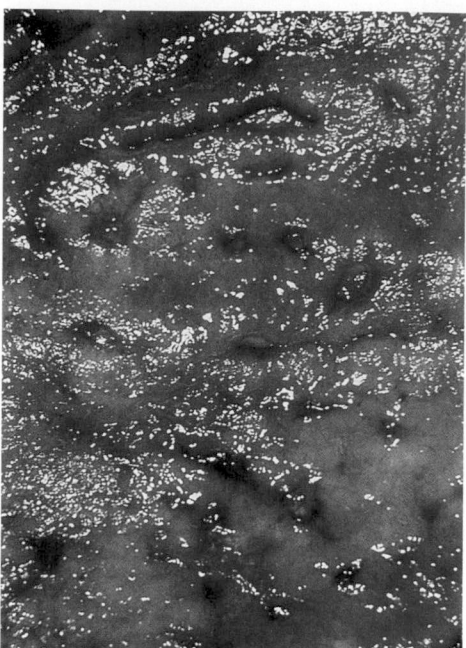

Fig. 11.29 Multiple acute ulcers of the stomach, occurring in a chronically debilitated patient. Microscopically, there was very little fibrous reaction in the ulcer bed.

seen during life in any debilitating illness, in sepsis, following surgery or trauma (*stress ulcer*), in patients with central nervous system injury or disease (*Cushing's ulcer*), as a complication of long-term steroid therapy (*steroid ulcer*), in association with aspirin ingestion, in patients with extensive burns (*Curling's ulcer*), as a complication of radiation therapy or hepatic arterial chemotherapy, and following the introduction of tubes into the stomach.[144,149,155,156,159,163] Marked epithelial atypia may be present in the gastric lesions resulting from hepatic arterial infusion chemotherapy.[148,154] If the ulcer involves only the mucosa (a process usually designated as *erosion*), it can heal completely; however, if part of the muscle is destroyed, it is replaced by fibrotic tissue, leaving a depressed pit. Any of these ulcers, if deep enough, may perforate; this complication is particularly common in ulcers induced by radiation therapy.

Chronic peptic ulcer always occurs in an achlorhydric zone of mucosa (i.e., an area of stomach lined by pyloric-type mucosa). Up to 95% of the ulcers are located on the lesser curvature (so-called *Magenstrasse*) near the incisura angularis; however, since chronic gastritis is accompanied by antral metaplasia of the fundal mucosa that advances proximally from the pylorus, peptic ulcer can be found anywhere in the stomach, although it is always surrounded by antral-type mucosa.

The average age at the time of diagnosis is 50 years, but the disease can occur in any age group, including children. A male predilection exists but seems to be decreasing. Approximately 5% of ulcers are multiple. The radiographic diagnosis is approximately 95% accu-

rate, but atypical cases cannot be distinguished with certainty from carcinoma. Although some controversy persists, most authors believe that ulcers of giant size (over 3 cm), or those located in the greater curvature, do not indicate a high likelihood of malignancy as formerly believed. The diagnosis of peptic ulcer has been greatly facilitated by the use of fiberoptic gastroscopy, which allows the endoscopist to have a direct view of the ulcer, to photograph it, and to obtain biopsies from the edges; multiple (about 10) biopsies are recommended for the standard-size ulcer.

Grossly, an active lesion is sharply delineated, usually oval or round but sometimes linear, with converging mucosal folds extending to its margin (Fig. 11.30A). The proximal margin tends to have overhanging edges, whereas the distal margin usually has sloping borders (Fig. 11.30B). On section, there is undermining of the edges (especially on the proximal side) and complete replacement of the muscle wall by grayish white fibrous tissue. On the serosal side, there may be subserosal fibrosis and inflammatory enlargement of the regional lymph

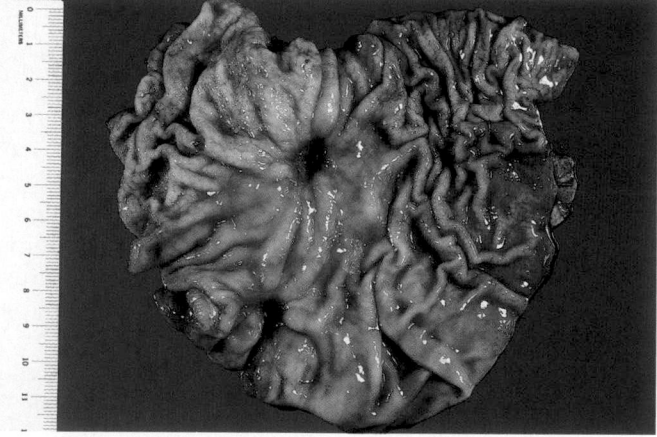

A

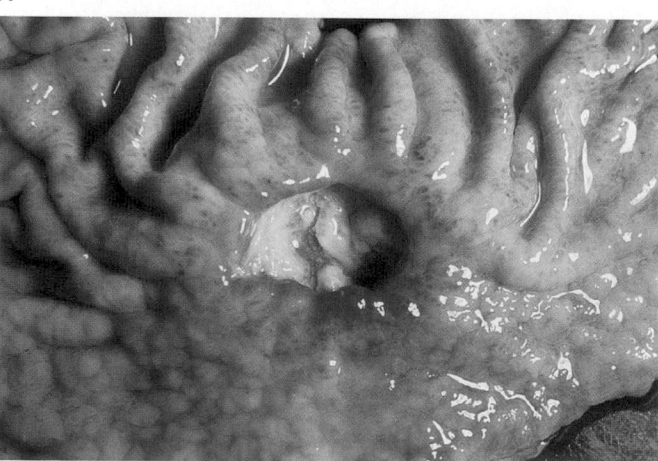

B

Fig. 11.30 A, Typical gross appearance of chronic peptic ulcer of stomach. **B,** Sharply delimited chronic peptic ulcer with converging folds of mucosa in the upper half. The ulcer bed is covered by fibrinopurulent exudate.

nodes. Prominent marginal nodularity about the ulcer should suggest the presence of carcinoma; however, it should be remembered that it may be impossible to distinguish grossly a peptic ulcer from an ulcerated carcinoma. As a matter of fact, approximately 10% to 15% of gastric carcinomas appear, grossly, to be benign ulcers.

Microscopically, an active, well-developed, chronic peptic ulcer will show four more or less distinct layers: (1) a surface coat of purulent exudate, bacteria, and necrotic debris; (2) fibrinoid necrosis; (3) granulation tissue; and (4) fibrosis replacing the muscle wall and extending into the subserosa (Fig. 11.31). At the edges, the muscularis mucosae is seen to fuse with the muscularis externa. Other common features in the ulcer bed include thickening of vessels caused by subendothelial fibrous proliferation and hypertrophy of nerve bundles; both of these changes are probably secondary events. The necrotic surface may show superimposed infection by *Candida albicans*.[152]

As already stated, the mucosa surrounding the ulcer is of pyloric type, including a component of gastrin (and somatostatin) immunoreactive cells.[151] In cases infected with *H. pylori*, a typical constellation of morphologic changes (loss of the apical portion and dropout of epithelial cells, epithelial pits, erosions, and cellular tufts) is seen at the ulcer edge.[146]

Peptic ulcers can be classified according to their shape and size (round-oval, giant, linear), activity (open ulcers or ulcer scars), depth of penetration (submucosa, muscularis externa, or beyond), or a combination of these criteria.[157]

In the healing process of a peptic ulcer, regenerating epithelium grows over the surface. Any epithelium growing above an area where the muscularis mucosae is interrupted is to be regarded as regenerating. This epithelium often exhibits features of intestinal metaplasia and may contain chief and parietal cells when the ulcer is located in the fundic area[157]; the presence of

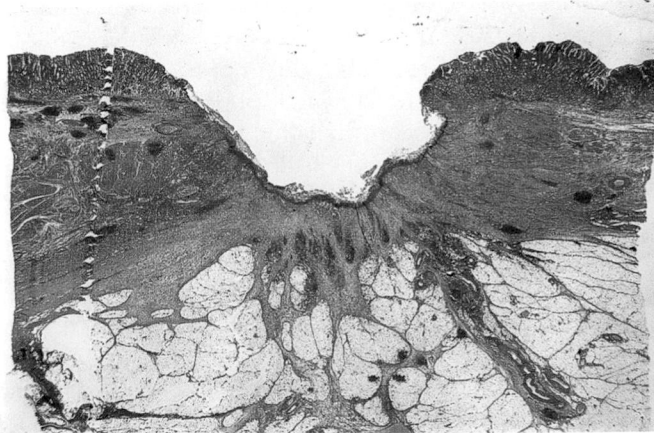

Fig. 11.31 Whole mount view of chronic peptic ulcer. The external muscle layer has been totally destroyed. Note the overhanging mucosa on one edge and the sloping mucosa on the other.

irregularities in its deep portion should not be misinterpreted as carcinoma. The danger of overdiagnosis is particularly great in the ulcers caused by arterial infusion chemotherapy because of the marked epithelial atypia that may be present.[163] The problem of possible malignant transformation of peptic ulcer is discussed later (see p. 669).

The medical treatment of gastric ulcer consists of antacids and/or H₂-blockers.[153,162] The usual criterion for adequate healing is a reduction in crater size of at least 50% over a 6- to 8-week period of intensive medical management. Failure to pass this test, development of complications (hemorrhage, perforation, obstruction), and recurrence of the ulcer are indications for surgery. Giant ulcer size (over 3 cm) is another quoted indication, although medical therapy can also be successful in these cases.[143] It should be remembered that as many as 15% of gastric carcinomas may pass the "healing test" and that some benign ulcers may actually enlarge during the test. The surgical procedures in general use for peptic ulcer are subtotal gastric resection without vagotomy, truncal vagotomy and drainage (either gastroenterostomy or pyloroplasty), and truncal vagotomy plus antrectomy. When a portion of stomach is removed, continuity is reestablished through a gastroduodenostomy (Billroth I) or gastrojejunostomy (Billroth II). The long-term results of surgery are good to excellent in over 80% of the patients.[147]

Other non-neoplastic lesions

Duplication of the stomach, a very rare anomaly, presents as a unilocular or multilocular cyst lined by gastric mucosa.[166] It may communicate with the lumen of the normal stomach; usually it does not, the result being distention with fluid causing obstruction and a palpable mass.[172,185]

Diverticula occur for the most part in a juxtacardiac position and are probably the result of anatomically weak areas. The remaining lesions can occur anywhere else in the stomach and are commonly associated with an acquired disease, such as peptic ulcer.[169,189]

Cysts may be found in a mucosal or submucosal location.[192] Intramucosal cysts, which are the most common, have been classified into various types according to their lining; they appear to be associated with intestinal metaplasia.[188] Submucosal cysts have also been designated as *gastritis cystica profunda*[171] (Fig. 11.32). Both of these are said to be more common in patients with gastric carcinoma.[175,177,196] Although some may be an expression of heterotopia,[195] it seems likely that the majority are acquired.[175]

Bezoars are foreign bodies in the stomach and are occasionally seen as surgical specimens (Fig. 11.33). The great majority fall into two categories: *trichobezoar*,

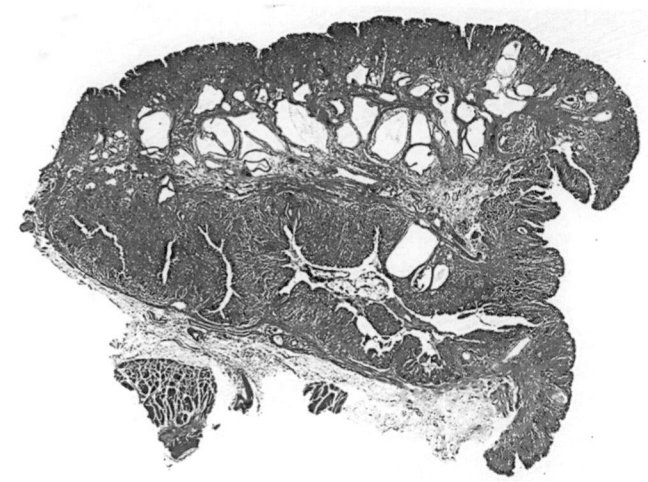

Fig. 11.32 Whole mount view of gastritis cystica profunda.

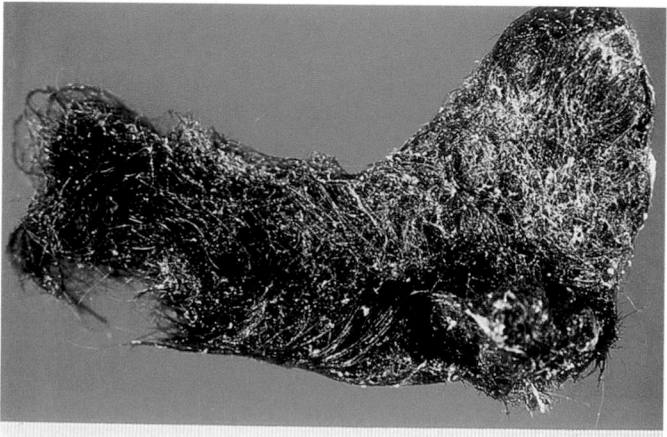

Fig. 11.33 Huge trichobezoar removed from the stomach. The tangled mass of hair looks like a mold of the gastric cavity.

composed of hair, and *phytobezoar*, composed of vegetable matter.[174] More than 85% of the latter are caused by ingestion of unripened persimmons.[168] Factors favoring the development of bezoars include lack of teeth, vagotomy, and obstructing lesions of the gastric outlet.[165]

Aneurysms of gastric vessels (Dieulafoy's disease; caliber-persistent artery) are thought to be of malformative rather than degenerative origin.[182,183] They are usually single, located in the submucosa, usually high on the lesser curvature, and characterized by a large tortuous vessel surmounted by a small defect in the overlying mucosa.[183] Amyloid may deposit in the vessel wall.[194] When the lesion perforates, massive and sometimes fatal hemorrhage may result.[181]

Gastric antral vascular ectasia (GAVA or "watermelon stomach") has been described as an acquired vascular disease of the stomach that may result in blood loss and iron deficiency anemia. Endoscopically, one sees parallel red stripes at the crest of the mucosal folds in the antrum, resembling the stripes of a watermelon. Cases have also been described located at the cardia.[190] The

microscopic changes on gastric biopsy are minimal and consist of an increase in the number and caliber of vessels, fibrin thrombi, and fibromuscular hyperplasia.[191,193] It remains to be seen whether this is a real entity.

Xanthoma (xanthelasma) of the stomach appears as a small yellow intramucosal lesion characterized by the accumulation of neutral fat in foamy histiocytes in the lamina propria. This clinically insignificant lesion, which seems to be relatively common in Japan and was described many years ago by German pathologists as *Lipoidinsel der Magenschleinhaut*, should not be confused microscopically with early carcinoma or signet ring carcinoma, lesions with which it may coexist.[178,187]

Other rare non-neoplastic gastric disorders include **pseudoxanthoma elasticum** (which can result in severe hemorrhage),[167] **elastofibroma** (accompanied by similar lesions in their usual soft tissue location),[170] **mucosal calcinosis** (secondary to the administration of aluminum-containing antacids or sucralfate therapy in organ transplant patients),[173] **hyalinization** (severe hyaline thickening of the submucosa),[180,186] **amyloidosis** (diffuse or localized, sometimes complicated by bleeding),[176] **barium granuloma** (developing in the gastric wall following radiographic examination),[179] and isolated **Langerhans' cell histiocytosis** (histiocytosis X).[184]

Polyps

The nomenclature of gastric polyps is confusing, one of the reasons being that in the past they have often been regarded as analogous to colorectal polyps in microscopic appearance and natural history.[236] This is unfortunate because most types of gastric polyps do not have an exact counterpart in the large bowel.[241]

Hyperplastic polyps (also known as regenerative, inflammatory, hyperplasiogenic, hamartomatous, and types I and II polyps of Japanese authors) comprise approximately 75% of all gastric polyps.[238] Use of the term *hamartomatous polyp* for these lesions should be discouraged because it elicits confusion with the different type of polyp seen as a component of the Peutz–Jeghers syndrome. The term hyperplastic polyp is preferable, but it should be emphasized that this lesion is morphologically very different from the lesion so named in the large bowel. Gastric hyperplastic polyps tend to occur against the background of hypochlorhydria, low levels of pepsinogen I, hypergastrinemia, chronic gastritis, and gastric atrophy.[200,210] They are randomly distributed in the stomach, generally small, sessile, and multiple, with a smooth or slightly lobulated contour (Fig. 11.34A). Microscopically, they show elongation, tortuosity, and dilatation (often cystic) of the gastric foveolae, with a component of pyloric or—less commonly—fundic type of glands in the deeper portion. The stroma, usually prominent, is characterized by edema, patchy fibrosis, inflammatory cells, and scattered smooth muscle bundles from the muscularis mucosae (Fig. 11.34B). Exceptionally, collections of foamy macrophages (not to be confused with signet ring cells) are present. Epithelial atypia is either absent or minimal, of a regenerative type, and limited to the tips of the foveolae. In the presence of significant focal atypia, the diagnosis of a mixed (hyperplastic and neoplastic) polyp should be considered (see later discussion). Some authors separate hyperplastic from inflammatory polyps on the basis of relative amounts of glandular and stromal changes, but the presence of a continuous spectrum suggests that these are different stages of the same process.[227] Rarely, atypical reactive cells appear in the stroma and simulate a malignant process.[204,246]

The gastric lesion designated by Menétrier as *polyadenomes polypeux* (see next section) probably corresponds to multiple hyperplastic polyps.[233] The polypoid lesion

sometimes developing on the gastric side of gastroenterostomy stomas may also have a microscopic appearance similar to that of a hyperplastic polyp, except for its more diffuse nature; adenomatous and dysplastic changes can also occur at this site.[206,249]

Hyperplastic polyps have been found to coexist frequently with carcinoma elsewhere in the stomach,[235,251] but these figures are biased, since most of the specimens studied had been removed because of carcinoma. The incidence of gastric carcinoma developing after endoscopic removal of hyperplastic polyps is low and probably more related to the atrophic gastritis that often accompanies the polyp than to the polyp itself; in a study from Germany with up to 7 years' follow-up, this incidence was only 1.4%.[245]

As the name indicates, hyperplastic polyps have traditionally been regarded as non-neoplastic processes; however, they share some molecular alterations with the adenomatous lesions described below. Furthermore, they may undergo progression to dysplastic and carcinomatous changes, although the likelihood of this occurring remains much lower than for their adenomatous counterparts.[237,240] Malignant transformation is accompanied by increased proliferative activity and p53 expression.[237,262]

Adenomas (types III and IV polyps of Japanese authors) are usually antral in location, generally single and large, and either sessile or pedunculated (Fig. 11.35). Microscopically, they are composed of *dysplastic* glands with pseudostratified epithelium showing nuclear abnormalities and high mitotic count.[238,251] They have been further subdivided into gastric-type and intestinal-type depending on the nature of the glandular epithelium.[197] The intestinal-type adenomas, which are the most common, are analogous in appearance and natural history to those in the colorectum and are thought to arise on the basis of intestinal metaplasia.[217] Like their large bowel counterparts, they can be divided into adenomatous polyps (tubular adenomas), villoglandular polyps

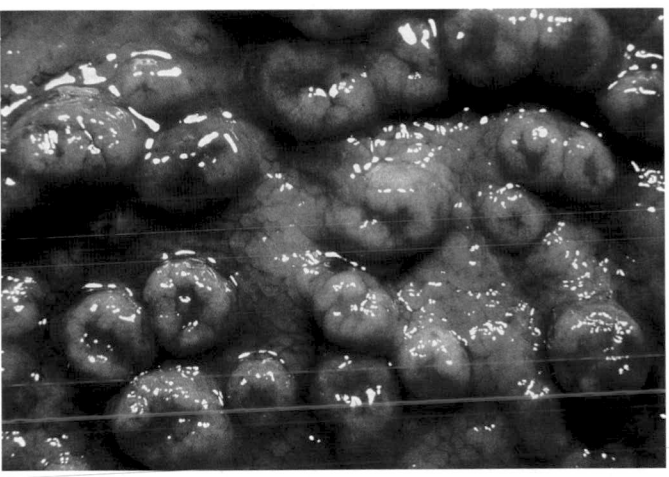

A

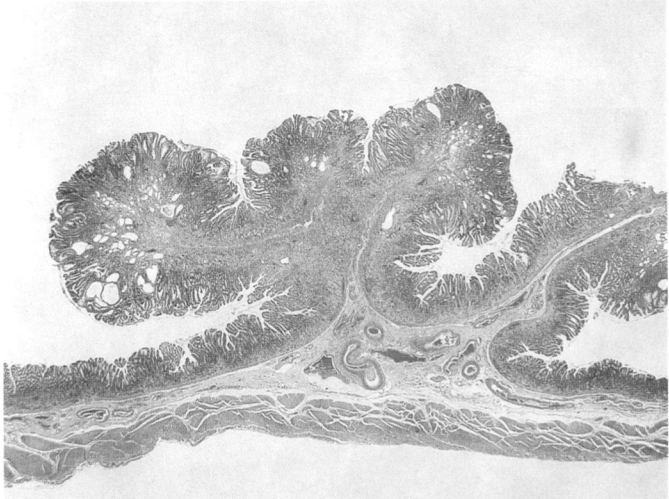

B

Fig. 11.34 A, Gross appearance of gastric polyps of hyperplastic type. Many of the lesions show central umbilication. **B,** Low-power microscopic view of gastric polyps of hyperplastic type. The cystic dilatation of the glands is more evident on the left side.

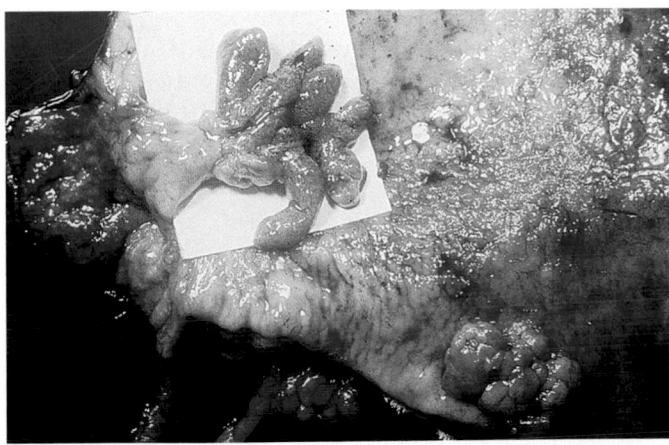

Fig. 11.35 Gross appearance of gastric adenomatous polyps. The larger lesion is a tangle of fingerlike projections.

(tubulovillous or tubulopapillary adenomas), and villous adenomas (papillary adenomas)[219,234] (Fig. 11.36). Adenomatous polyps appear grossly as elevated lesions with a flat surface. Microscopically, they show a characteristic two-layered structure, with dysplastic epithelium on top and cystically dilated glands devoid of dysplasia beneath. Scattered endocrine cells—most of them immunoreactive for 5-HT—are common. Lysozyme-containing Paneth cells may also be present and exceptionally may be the predominant element.[243] A few of these polyps appear as shallow mucosal depressions rather than elevations; these are referred to as *depressed adenomas*.[218,261] Villous adenomas have a lesser representation of endocrine cells than adenomatous polyps. CEA reactivity and overexpression of p53 are commonly found in all types of adenomas, particularly in the cytologically most atypical areas.[217,226] Many of these polyps have been described in stomachs that have been removed because of an independent carcinoma, but a selection bias is obviously operating[251]; however, there is no question that the two processes are related and that the polyps themselves can undergo malignant transformation, along lines similar to those of their colorectal counterparts[203,221,222,229] (Fig. 11.37). The exact incidence of this complication is not known, but it seems to be relatively low. In a series from Germany with up to 7 years' follow-up, it was 3.4%.[245] According to some authors, the tendency for malignant transformation is higher for the intestinal-type than for the gastric-type adenomas[197] despite the fact that the molecular alterations that have been detected in these two polyp types are similar.[198a]

Mixed (hyperplastic and adenomatous) polyps are also recognized. These should be distinguished from the already mentioned and much more common regenerative changes commonly seen focally at the surface of hyperplastic polyps.[212]

All of the previously described polyps express HLA-DR antigen more commonly than nonpolypoid gastric mucosa.[258]

Fundic gland polyps (fundic gland hyperplasia, hamartomatous cystic polyps, polyps with fundic glandular cysts) present as multiple small (average size 2.3 mm) polypoid projections in the gastric fundus or body.[224,232,252] Their distinguishing microscopic feature is the presence of microcysts lined by fundic epithelium, including oxyphilic cells; the overlying foveolae are usually shortened.[205,228,247] There is also an increase in the smooth muscle content, often in a pericystic distribution.[242] These polyps can occur in a sporadic form or present in patients with the Zollinger–Ellison syndrome, those on long-term treatment with proton pump inhibitor, and those affected by colonic polyposis.[201] In the latter instance, they are more likely to show focal dysplastic changes than otherwise.[199,260] It has been proposed that the key molecular alteration in sporadic fundic gland polyps is an activating mutation of the β-catenin gene.[198]

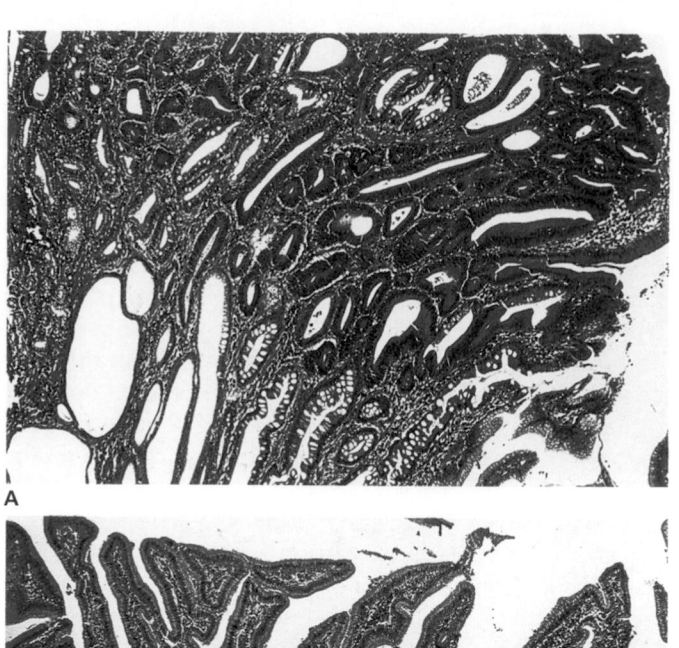

Fig. 11.36 A, Adenomatous polyp. **B**, Villous adenoma (From Oota K, Sobin LH: Histological typing of gastric and oesophageal tumours, Geneva, World Health Organization, 1977.

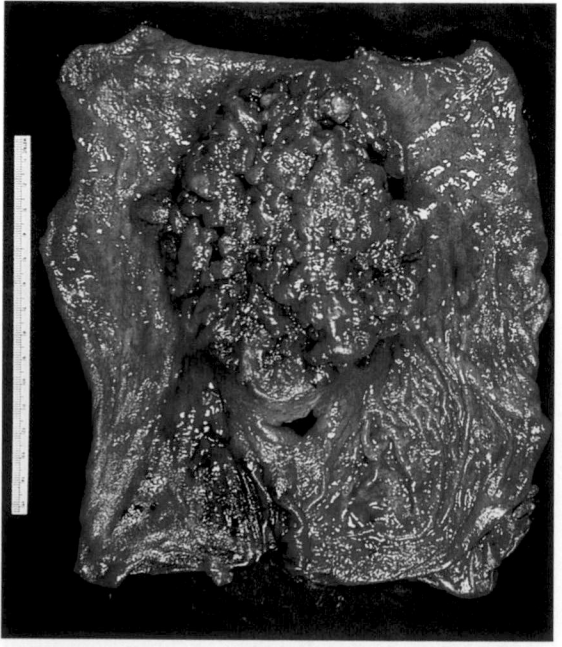

Fig. 11.37 Large villous adenoma of the stomach containing areas of adenocarcinoma. The tumor was located near the cardia.

Other types of gastric epithelial polypoid lesions that have been described include *foveolar* or *focal hyperplasia* (which arises against an early background of atrophic gastritis and perhaps represents an early stage of hyperplastic polyp[209]), *antral gland hyperplasia* (probably analogous to so-called "pyloric gland adenoma"[256a]), the *hamartomatous polyp* associated with Peutz–Jeghers syndrome, and *retention (juvenile) polyps*.[248]

It should be stated that polyps of different types can coexist in the same stomach and that occasional lesions cannot be properly placed in a specific category, especially if the only material available is a small biopsy specimen.

Polyposis syndromes of the gastrointestinal tract often involve the stomach. In familial colonic polyposis and related Gardner's syndrome, gastric involvement occurs in over 50% of the cases; the gastric polyps can be adenomatous, hyperplastic, or of the fundic gland hyperplasia type.[202,214,216,248,255,257] As stated above, fundic gland polyps in these patients tend to show dysplastic features; they also display the somatic gene alterations associated with colonic polyposis.[198] It should be noted that, although fundic gland polyps are particularly common in familial polyposis, they are not specific for this disorder, as previously claimed. They also occur in association with so-called "hereditary flat adenoma syndrome" and in the absence of either of these conditions.[231,254] Other gastric tumors described in familial colonic polyposis are adenocarcinoma and carcinoid tumor.[255,257] In Peutz–Jeghers syndrome, hamartomatous gastric polyps have been found in approximately 20% of the cases (sometimes accompanied by an adenomatous component) and gastric adenocarcinomas occasionally.[207,215] In generalized juvenile polyposis and the related Cronkhite–Canada syndrome, the incidence of gastric retention (juvenile) polyps is very high,[230] and there have been occasional cases of gastric adenocarcinoma.[244] Cowden's syndrome (multiple hamartoma syndrome) can also be accompanied by small sessile gastric polyps, most of which seem to be of the hyperplastic type.[248]

Inflammatory fibroid polyp of the stomach is the currently preferred term for a non-neoplastic lesion previously described under names such as eosinophilic granuloma, inflammatory pseudotumor, granuloblastoma, neurofibroma, and hemangiopericytoma.[220] It is frequently associated with hypochlorhydria or achlorhydria and is usually located in the antrum.[213] Radiographically and endoscopically, it presents as a sessile or pedunculated mass.[208] Grossly, it is elevated and sessile (Fig. 11.38). Microscopically, this lesion is centered in the submucosa and is characterized by vascular and fibroblastic proliferation (often in a whorl-like arrangement around blood vessels) and a polymorphic inflammatory response, usually dominated by eosinophils (Fig. 11.39). Ultrastructurally, many of the proliferating cells have a myofibroblastic appearance, in keeping with its presumed reactive nature.[239] Immunohistochemically, the

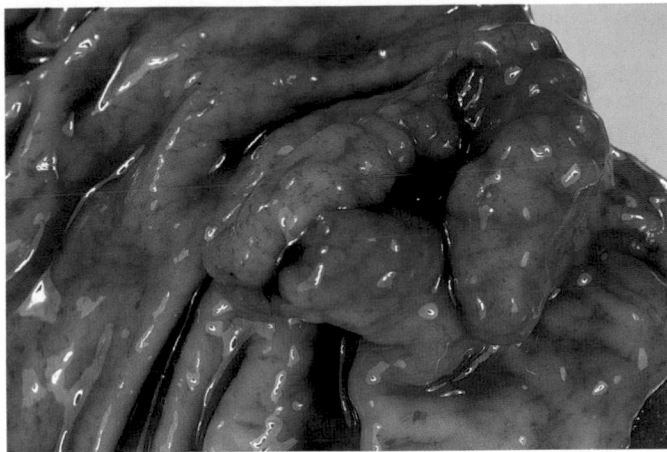

Fig. 11.38 Gross appearance of inflammatory fibroid polyp of stomach. The surface has a knobbly appearance.

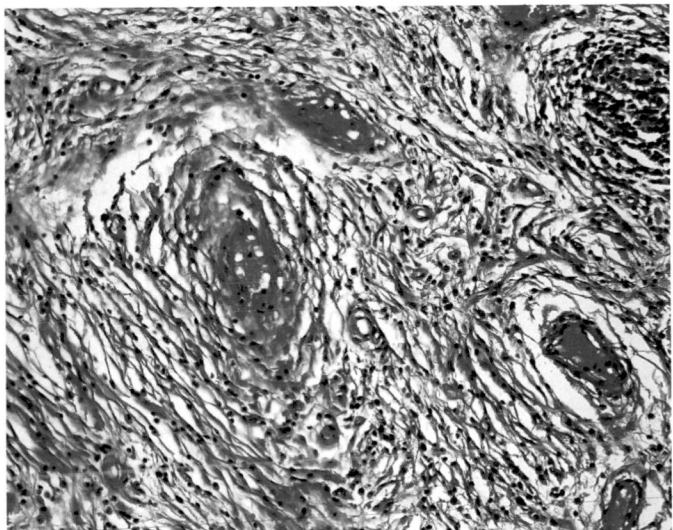

Fig. 11.39 Inflammatory fibroid polyp of stomach. Characteristic features include concentric fibrosis around vessels, scattering of eosinophils, and lymphoid nodules.

spindle cells are reactive for vimentin, CD34, and bcl-2 and, sometimes, for actin and various histiocytic markers.[211,223,225,256,259] Endothelial cells are also well represented.[253] Local excision (sometimes in the form of endoscopic removal) is the treatment of choice, and the evolution is benign.[250]

Menétrier's disease and Zollinger–Ellison syndrome

In 1888, Menétrier described two different gastric diseases under the common term *polyadenomes*.[269,270] The first, *polyadenomes polypeux*, is probably equivalent to multiple hyperplastic polyps (see p. 657). The second, *polyadenomes en nappe*, is the form to which the term **Menétrier's disease** is usually restricted at present. It is also known as hypertrophic or hyperplastic gastropathy, giant hypertrophic gastritis, and giant hypertrophy of gastric rugae. It is accompanied by hypochlorhydria or achlorhydria and often by impressive hypoproteinemia. Chronicity and severity are the rule in adults, but in the few reported pediatric cases the disease has usually been self-limited.[268] Radiographically, endoscopically, and grossly, the condition can be confused with malignant lymphoma and carcinoma. It is often centered along the greater curvature of the stomach and is characterized grossly by markedly hypertrophic rugae resembling cerebral convolutions. The transition between normal and diseased mucosa is always abrupt (Fig. 11.40). In the typical form of the disease, there is diffuse involvement of the fundic portion, with sparing of the antrum. In the localized form, there is a well-circumscribed cerebroid mass either in the fundus or the antrum.[273] Microscopically, there is a striking *foveolar hyperplasia*, accompanied by tortuosity, some degree of cystic dilatation, and extension into the base of the glands and sometimes even beyond the muscularis mucosae (Fig. 11.41). The glandular component is diminished, and the stroma is edematous and inflamed.[267] It should be mentioned here that many cases diagnosed by radiologists and gastroscopists as hypertrophic gastritis do not show the diagnostic morphologic features of Menétrier's disease but rather a chronic gastritis with prominent lymphocytic infiltration and varying degrees of glandular atrophy ("hypertrophic lymphocytic gastritis").[275] The relationship between the latter disorder (sometimes designated as "varioliform gastritis" by endoscopists)

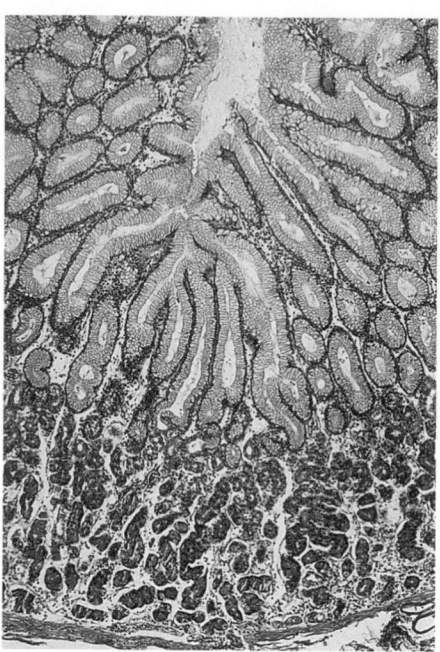

Fig. 11.41 Microscopic appearance of Menétrier's disease. There is marked hyperplasia of the crypts accompanied by mild atrophy of the underlying secretory mucosa.

and the fully developed Menétrier's disease is not clear.[265]

Carcinoma may develop in a stomach affected by Menétrier's disease, but the incidence does not seem higher than that seen in ordinary atrophic gastritis.[266,271]

Zollinger–Ellison syndrome may be accompanied by gastric changes radiographically and grossly similar to those of Menétrier's disease; however, microscopic examination will reveal hyperplasia primarily affecting the *secretory* rather than the foveolar portion of the fundic gland, even if the latter may also participate (Fig. 11.42). This hyperplasia mainly involves the parietal cells, but there may also be an increase in the number of ECL cells, both of these phenomena presumably resulting from gastrin stimulation.[264] In some of these patients, the Zollinger–Ellison syndrome is part of multiple endocrine neoplasia. We have seen several cases of this syndrome associated with multicentric carcinoid tumors, mainly located in the fundus and composed of ECL cells (see p. 673).

Other abnormalities of the gastric mucosa that can be seen in patients with Zollinger–Ellison syndrome include fundic gland polyps (see p. 658) and intramucosal cysts, the latter probably being a precursor of the former.[263]

The occurrence of gastric lesions with morphologic features similar to those seen in the Zollinger–Ellison syndrome but without hypergastrinemia (some of them associated with protein loss and others with gastric adenocarcinoma) suggests the existence of clinicopathologic variations among these poorly understood disorders.[267,272,274]

Fig. 11.40 Gross appearance of Menétrier's disease. The entire fundic mucosa is involved by an exuberant proliferative change. Note the sharp edge of the lesion at the junction of fundic with antral mucosa.

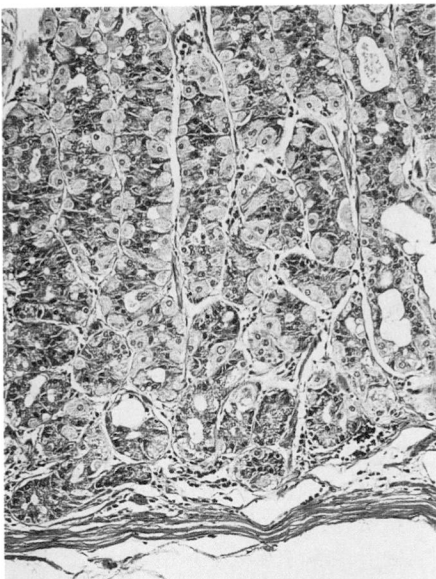

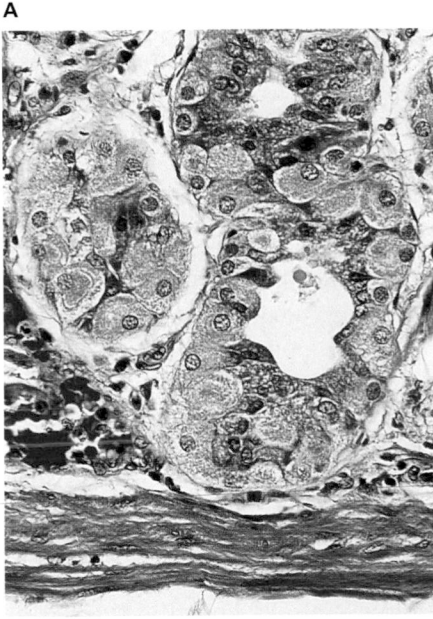

Fig. 11.42 A and **B**, Medium- and high-power views of gastric mucosa in a patient with Zollinger–Ellison syndrome. Note the large increase in the number of parietal cells.

Dysplasia

It is now widely acknowledged that most carcinomas of the stomach are accompanied—and often preceded—by a phase of **dysplasia**; therefore, the recognition of dysplasia in biopsy specimens is of great importance in giving warning of the possibility of a coexisting carcinoma and in indicating that the patient may be at a higher risk for the subsequent development of gastric cancer. Dysplasia should be clearly separated from the **regenerative hyperplasia** that often occurs in areas of mucosal injury, such as gastritis and peptic ulceration.

Regenerative hyperplasia can be divided into simple and atypical. In *simple* hyperplasia, the cells are immature, with basophilic cytoplasm, hyperchromatic nuclei, and reduced or absent mucus secretion. These cells are uniform in size and shape, with basally or centrally located nuclei arranged in a row; pseudostratification is slight or absent. Maturation and differentiation toward the surface are present. There may also be glandular dilatation and some degree of intraglandular papillary growth. In *atypical* hyperplasia, there is more pseudostratification and compression and less maturation and differentiation, but the cytologic features are not substantially different. There is usually an accompanying inflammatory reaction, sometimes intense, and focal erosive changes are common. A particularly atypical form of reactive hyperplasia is that reported following chemoradiotherapy for esophageal carcinoma.[276]

In **dysplasia**, there is increased cell proliferation accompanied by abnormalities in cell size, configuration, and orientation. Mucus secretion is reduced or absent, and there is an increase in the nucleocytoplasmic ratio, loss of nuclear polarity, and pseudostratification. Mitoses are numerous, and some of them are atypical.[291] These cellular abnormalities are accompanied by architectural derangement of the glands, resulting in cellular crowding, intraluminal folding, and glandular budding and branching. Sometimes the appearance is reminiscent of the mucosa lining colonic polyps.[286] Many systems have been proposed for the grading of dysplasia,[283,290] but most commonly used at present is the one that divides them into two categories: low-grade and high-grade.[284,287,289] High-grade dysplasia is regarded as synonymous with carcinoma in situ (CIS) and must be distinguished from intramucosal carcinoma, in which the process has broken through the basement membrane (p. 669). These concepts have been incorporated into the recommendation made by several pathology groups[288,292,296] that gastric biopsies be grouped for reporting purposes into the following categories:

1 Negative for dysplasia
2 Indefinite for dysplasia
3 Low-grade dysplasia
4 High-grade dysplasia/carcinoma in situ
5 Intramucosal carcinoma
6 Invasive carcinoma.

The risk for invasive carcinoma is small for low-grade dysplasia and considerable for high-grade dysplasia/CIS, to the extent that the performance of a gastrectomy should be considered whenever the latter change is found.[278–281,293,295]

It remains to be seen whether evaluation of cell proliferation markers, AgNOR counts, or morphometric analysis will provide a more objective and useful way of evaluating these abnormalities.[277,282,285,297] In one study, positive nuclear staining for the product of p53 was obtained in 36% of the cases of dysplasia studied, the figure rising to 64% in the cases with severe changes.[294] Other authors have shown that microsatellite stability (a molecular change usually absent in gastric intestinal metaplasia without dysplasia) can develop during this sequence.[282a] It is hoped that the unraveling of the molecular basis of the dysplasia–carcinoma sequence will eventually generate markers with powerful prognostic and predictive values.[298]

Carcinoma

General features

The pathogenesis of gastric carcinoma is closely related to environmental factors.[324] Its incidence has markedly decreased in some countries, such as the United States and England,[305,307,309,341] but it remains inordinately high in others, such as Japan, Chile, and Italy.[325] However, there is increasing evidence that a genetic predisposition may also play an important role in at least a subset of patients (see p. 665).[317]

Classifications of gastric carcinoma
Bormann, 1926[343]
Type I (polypoid)
Type II (fungating)
Type III (ulcerated)
Type IV (infiltrative)
Stout (Atlas of Tumor Pathology), 1953[368]
Fungating
Penetrating
Spreading
Superficial spreading
Linitis plastica
No special type
Lauren, 1965[359]
Intestinal
Diffuse
Ming, 1977[362]
Expanding
Infiltrative
Japanese Society for Gastric Cancer, 1981[356]
Papillary
Tubular
Poorly differentiated
Mucinous
Signet ring
World Health Organization, 2000[370]
Adenocarcinoma
intestinal type
diffuse type
Papillary adenocarcinoma
Tubular adenocarcinoma
Mucinous adenocarcinoma
Signet-ring cell carcinoma
Adenosquamous carcinoma
Squamous cell carcinoma
Small cell carcinoma
Undifferentiated carcinoma
Others

Most patients are over 50 years of age,[308] but cases in younger individuals and even children are on record.[310,329,337,339]

Practically all gastric carcinomas arise from the generative or basal cells of the foveolae,[336] in most instances on a background of chronic atrophic gastritis with intestinal metaplasia and preceded by various stages of dysplasia, CIS, and superficial carcinoma.[300,313] Some cases have been said to originate in heterotopic pancreatic tissue or other epithelium-lined submucosal cysts in the gastric wall,[316,326] but this is an exceptional event (see pp. 649 and 655).

Gastric carcinoma is accompanied by hypochlorhydria in 85% to 90% of the cases, and it has been shown that hypochlorhydria may precede gastric cancer by several years. It has been postulated that high intragastric pH promotes the growth of bacteria that reduce dietary nitrate to nitrite and then convert dietary amines, in the presence of this nitrite, into carcinogenic N-nitroso compounds.[312] The coexistence of chronic atrophic gastritis and carcinoma is common, but the etiopathogenic link between the two and the relative risk for malignancy in the former condition remain controversial.[304,315,323,330,331] The same could be said for pernicious anemia; the rate of carcinoma development, although statistically increased, is not high enough to justify surveillance in asymptomatic patients.[327]

Lately, *H. pylori* has been implicated as an important etiologic factor in gastric carcinoma through its role in the development of chronic gastritis.[306,318,322,340]

It has been postulated that the tumor characterized by the epidemiologic and sequential features described above represents one type of gastric carcinoma, albeit the most common one; it has been referred to as *intestinal-type adenocarcinoma* by Lauren[319] (see p. 663). The other, designated as the *diffuse type*, does not show these associations and seems to be less related to environmental influences.[332,334] Thus it has been shown that in high-risk areas the intestinal-type carcinoma predominates; furthermore, when a population shows a decline in the incidence of gastric cancer, the fall is primarily in that microscopic type.[299,303,304,320]

Other factors thought to be involved in the pathogenesis of gastric cancer are gastric polyps, Menétrier's disease, gastric peptic ulcer, and gastric stump (see respective sections in this chapter).

Cases of gastric carcinoma in young patients following irradiation and chemotherapy for other malignancies have been reported.[301] On occasion, gastric adenocarcinoma is seen together with esophageal squamous cell carcinoma.[333]

Some cases of gastric adenocarcinomas are EBV related, the incidence varying from 6% to 7% in Japan and Europe, to 16% in the United States.[321,328,338] EBV presence is higher in men than in women,[328] and higher in some countries than in others.[302,314] It is the rule in tumors with a lymphoepithelioma-like appearance (see p. 667). When present, it seems to be an early event independent of bcl-2 expression and p53 accumulation.[311,335]

Morphologic features and classification

There is wide variation in the gross appearance of carcinoma of the stomach. Many intermediate stages exist between the two extremes represented by the fungating tumor growing mainly into the lumen and the flat, ulcerated, and deeply invasive tumor growing through the wall of the stomach[346,368] (Figs 11.43 and 11.44). Borrman[343] based his time-honored gross classification of gastric carcinoma into four types on the relative proportions of exophytic and endophytic components. Carcinomas located in the fundic area are more likely to have invaded the submucosa and beyond at the time of surgery than those located in the pyloric area.[371] Depending on the relative amounts of mucin secreted and desmoplastic reaction elicited, the tumors may have a fleshy, fibrous, or gelatinous gross appearance. In terms of location, any area of the stomach can be affected: anterior and posterior walls, lesser curvature, and greater curvature (in that order of frequency).[372] Multiple tumors are found in approximately 6% of the cases.[348,358]

The non-neoplastic mucosa adjacent to the carcinoma is often thickened, a feature that may result in false-negative endoscopic biopsies and that has been attributed to production of epidermal growth factor by the tumor.[360] Microscopically, nearly all gastric carcinomas are of the adenocarcinoma type and are composed of one or more of the following four major cell types: foveolar, mucopeptic, intestinal columnar, and goblet cell.[350] As already indicated, two major categories exist, which have been designated *intestinal* (53%) and *diffuse* (33%) by Lauren[359]; the remainder are heterogeneous in composition.[349]

Intestinal-type adenocarcinomas are thought to arise from metaplastic epithelium, an assumption supported by electron microscopic and immunohistochemical studies.[363] Their degree of differentiation ranges widely and correlates inversely with tumor size.[354] In the better differentiated tumors, most of the cells are columnar and mucin secreting (Fig. 11.45). On occasions, the tumor is so well differentiated as to simulate a complete-type intestinal metaplasia.[347] Poorly differentiated variants have a predominantly solid pattern.[364] Exceptionally, the better differentiated tumor cells are ciliated.[345] The amount of mucin production is highly variable; when abundant, it is often accompanied by calcification. Sometimes, metaplastic ossification is present either in the primary tumor or the metastasis. Scattered endocrine cells may be demonstrated with silver or immunohistochemical stains (see p. 666). The occurrence of easily identifiable Paneth cells is less common but has been well documented.[352] Exceptionally, they represent the predominant element of the tumor.[357,365] On occasion the stroma of the tumor is heavily infiltrated by neutrophils or histiocytes (Fig. 11.46).[367]

Diffuse-type adenocarcinomas are best represented by the tumor type classically known as *linitis plastica* and currently designated as *signet ring (adeno)carcinoma*. It

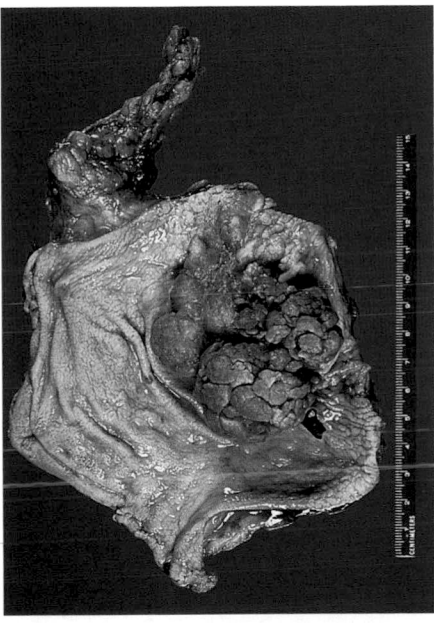

Fig. 11.43 Gross appearance of gastric adenocarcinoma of polypoid type.

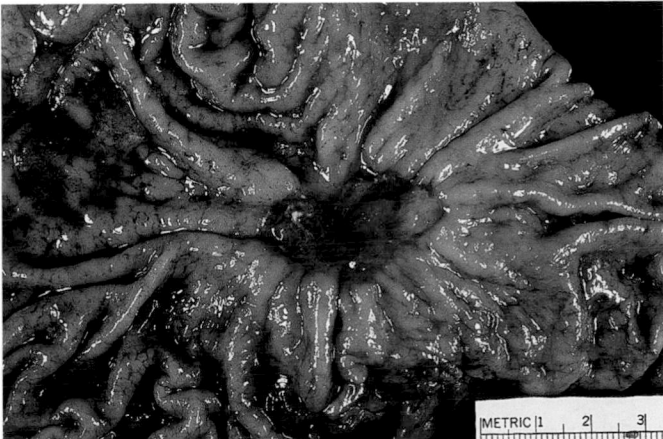

Fig. 11.44 Gross appearance of gastric adenocarcinoma of ulcerative type showing marked resemblance to chronic peptic ulcer (compare with Fig. 11.30).

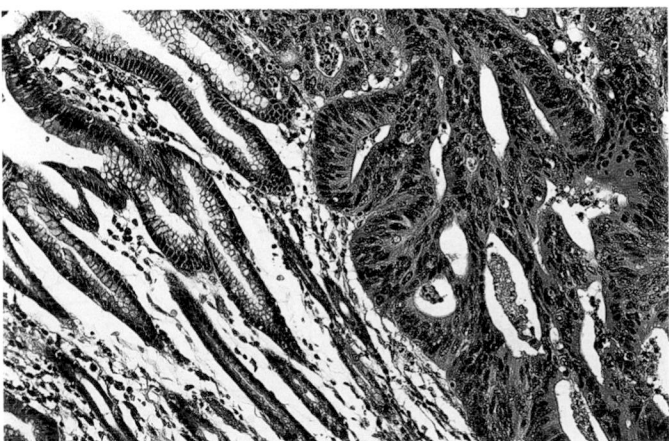

Fig. 11.45 Gastric adenocarcinoma of intestinal type.

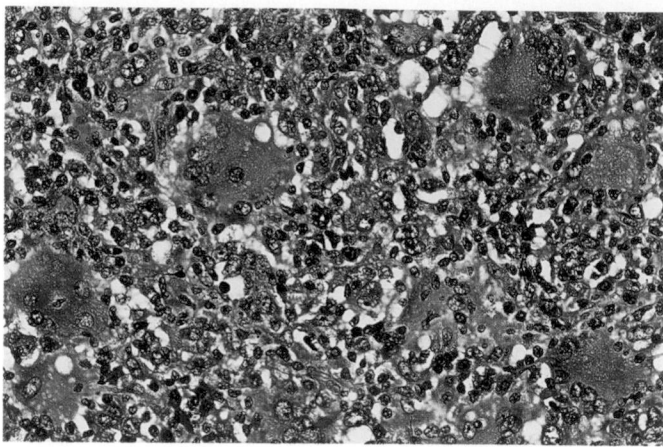

Fig. 11.46 Gastric adenocarcinoma accompanied by marked histiocytic reaction.

intramucosal type of signet ring carcinoma occurs,[373] in many cases of this entity the mucosa is less affected than the deeper layers. Glandular formations are rare, and most tumor cells grow individually (Fig. 11.48). Most of the mucin produced is intracytoplasmic, resulting in the typical signet ring appearance (Fig. 11.49). Pools of extracellular mucin may also be present, but as long as signet ring cells are evident this tumor should be categorized as signet ring carcinoma rather than mucinous (mucoid) carcinoma (see p. 666).

There are few malignant tumors in the human body that are more likely to be missed on microscopic examination than this type of gastric cancer. Over the years, we have seen specimens from stomach wall, lymph nodes, omentum, mesentery, pelvic peritoneum, and ovary that were initially misinterpreted as a benign process because of the inconspicuousness of the tumor cells and the marked degree of inflammatory and desmoplastic reaction. The tumor may also closely simulate malignant

represents a disproportionately high percentage of cases of gastric cancers occurring in the young,[351,361,369] and its *relative* incidence seems to be on the rise in the United States.[342] The gross alterations usually begin in the prepyloric area. Pyloric obstruction often develops, as the wall of the stomach becomes thickened and rigid (Fig. 11.47). Sections of the wall show marked submucosal fibrosis, with or without mucosal ulceration. The muscle is hypertrophic and segmented by the presence of thin, parallel, grayish white, longitudinal lines that give it a comb-like appearance. These lines are continuous with foci of subserosal thickening.

Microscopically, a diffuse growth of malignant cells is seen, associated with extensive fibrosis and inflammation. Often the entire wall is involved. Although an

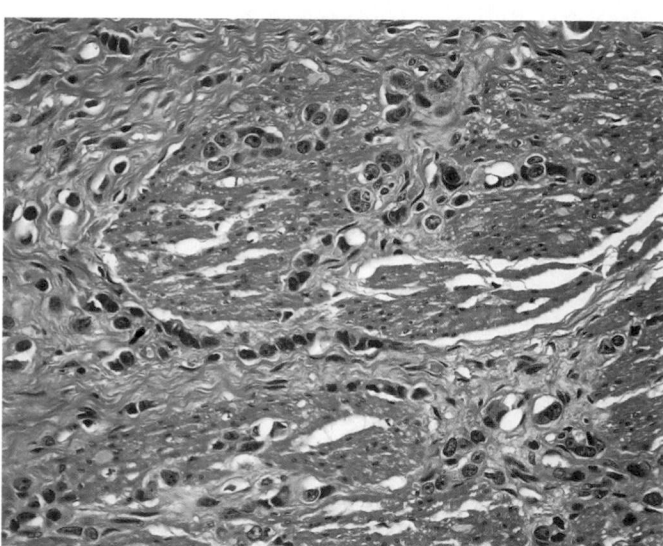

Fig. 11.48 Diffuse type of gastric adenocarcinoma. An Indian file pattern of infiltration of the muscularis externa can be appreciated.

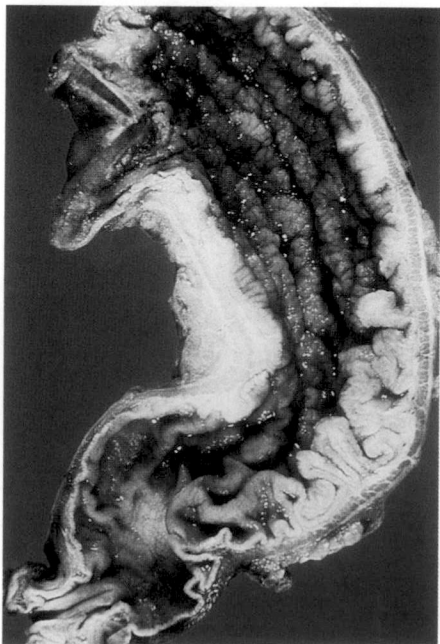

Fig. 11.47 Typical gross appearance of diffuse carcinoma of so-called "linitis plastica" type. Practically the entire wall of the stomach is involved by tumor. Note the prominence of rugal folds.

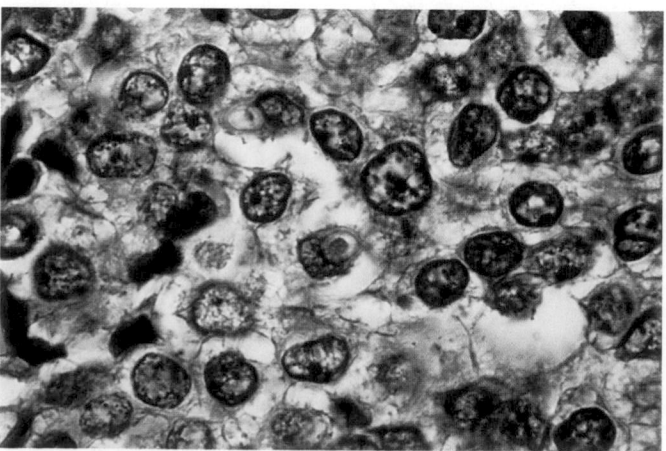

Fig. 11.49 Intracytoplasmic mucin droplet, as shown with Mayer's mucicarmine stain.

lymphoma because of its diffuse pattern of growth and the round shape of the cells and their nuclei.

The most important classifications that have been proposed for gastric carcinoma, including the one already mentioned, are listed in the box.

The differential diagnosis of gastric carcinoma in a biopsy specimen includes severe dysplasia and a variety of reactive or otherwise non-neoplastic conditions that may simulate malignancy—such as bizarre epithelial atypia associated with chemotherapy or radiochemotherapy,[344,366] degenerative changes associated with erosion and regeneration (characterized by a striking background eosinophilia),[355] plump reactive mesenchymal cells related to granulation tissue,[355] cohesive clusters of pyloric cells with glassy cytoplasm (see p. 648), polyvinylpyrrolidone storage disease,[353] and gastric "xanthoma" (see p. 656). The three latter conditions resemble the cytologic features of signet ring carcinoma.

Histochemical, immunohistochemical, and electron microscopic features

The secretory product of most gastric adenocarcinomas (especially those of intestinal type) is an acid mucosubstance, easily detected with Mayer's mucicarmine, Alcian blue or colloidal iron stains and having features analogous to those of intestinal-type mucins.[387,390] Various alterations of the syalidation of these mucins occur and can be detected histochemically or immunohistochemically.[414] The mucin secreted by the diffuse-type carcinoma and present within the cytoplasm of the signet ring cell is of either acidic or neutral type, the latter predominating in some of the cases.[377]

At the immunohistochemical level, the main mucin types expressed are MUC1 for the intestinal type, MUC5AC for the diffuse type, and MUC2 for the mucinous type (see below).[382,386] There is also an interesting relationship between mucin type and tumor location, in the sense that MUC5AC is prevalent with carcinoma of the antrum whereas MUC2 is expressed in greater amounts with carcinoma of the cardia.[396]

In terms of other immunomarkers, reactivity of gastric adenocarcinoma cells for keratin, epithelial membrane antigen, and CEA is the rule.[393] The keratins present are usually of the simple epithelium type (low molecular weight), but sometimes those seen in normal squamous epithelia (such as CK13 and 16) are also detected.[388] The CK7/CK20 expression patterns of gastric carcinoma vary considerably; on the whole, approximately 70% of the cases are CK7+ and 20% are CK20+.[395] In some cases (particularly of the diffuse type) there is coexpression of keratin and vimentin.[407] Markers indicative of specific gastric differentiation include gastric proteases such as pepsinogen I, pepsinogen II, and chymosin.[380,404,408]

Immunoreactivity for MI (a mucin antigen) and cathepsins D and E (an aspartic proteinase) is seen in most of the cases as an expression of differentiation toward foveolar cells.[381,392]

The reactivity that has been detected for lysozyme in approximately one third of gastric carcinomas may be an abortive expression of Paneth cell differentiation.[375,401] Immunohistochemical positivity for α_1-antitrypsin, α_1-antichymotrypsin, and α_2-macroglobulin is also common, particularly in advanced tumors.[402] Reactivity to hCG is found in scattered tumor cells in approximately 10% to 50% of the cases, depending on the series[384,389,412]; the microscopic appearance of these tumors is usually not different from others, and therefore this phenomenon should not be equated with the rare entity of gastric choriocarcinoma, whether pure or associated with adenocarcinoma (see p. 685).

Other substances that have been detected immunohistochemically in the cells of gastric carcinoma are pancreatic secretory trypsin inhibitor (PSTI),[383] lactoferrin,[406] hormone receptors,[385,411] hormone receptor-related proteins p52 and ERD5,[376] epidermal growth factor (EGF) and EGF receptor (suggesting the presence of an autocrine mechanism for the tumor growth),[400] immunoglobulin and secretory component,[403] villin (a cytoskeletal protein associated with the axial microfilament bundles of the microvilli of the brush border),[374] α-catenin (an undercoat protein of specialized cell junctions),[391] the enzymes superoxide dismutase and aromatase,[394,398] the CDw75 antigen (a sialylated carbohydrate component of mucin),[378] CD44 (a cell-adhesion molecule),[409] placental alkaline phosphatase,[410] HLA-DR antigen (especially in intestinal-type carcinoma),[405] and PTH-related protein (especially in cases showing heterotopic ossification, either in the primary lesion or in the metastases).[413] Basement membrane components such as laminin and type IV collagen are much more commonly expressed by intestinal than by diffuse types of carcinoma.[379]

AgNOR counts are higher in adenocarcinoma than in dysplasia, but there is a considerable overlap in the values.[397,399]

Molecular genetic features

DNA ploidy studies have shown a much higher incidence of aneuploidy in intestinal than in diffuse-type tumors.[433]

Germline truncating mutations of the E-cadherin gene have been found in families with hereditary cancer of the diffuse type. The penetrant susceptibility is so high as to have led some authors to propose prophylactic gastrectomy for these individuals.[419,422] Somatic mutations of this gene have been found in approximately 30% of sporadic diffuse-type carcinomas but not in intestinal-type tumors.[416,430] A closely related aberration is loss of β-catenin, which is bound to cadherin as a complex that regulates cell-to-cell adhesion.[439]

Microsatellite instability (MSI) is found in approximately 20% of gastric carcinomas in the United States.[424,436]

Tumors with this feature tend to have a phenotype characterized by older age, antral location, polypoid gross appearance, intestinal subtype, lower incidence of nodal metastases, and lower stage.[427]

Accumulation of p53 has been detected in close to 50% of the cases.[421] It occurs primarily in intestinal-type tumors and in advanced stages of mixed glandular and diffuse types.[423,429]

Somatic mutations of the *APC* gene are present in only 4% of gastric adenocarcinomas, in contrast to an incidence of 76% in adenomas or flat dysplasia.[428] These startling results suggest that *APC* mutations do not play a significant role in the progression from adenoma to carcinoma.

The *ras* p21 product is overexpressed in dysplasia, intestinal metaplasia, and adenocarcinoma of both major microscopic types.[417,435]

A minority of tumors (5% to 15% in most of the series) show membrane immunostaining for *c-erbB-2* protein.[420,431,438]

Loss of p16 (the *CDKN2A* gene product) is seen in roughly a quarter of gastric carcinomas; it is most common in tumors located in the body and those associated with EBV.[434]

Apoptosis-regulating proteins (such as bcl-2 and Bax) are more commonly expressed in intestinal-type than in diffuse-type gastric carcinomas.[425,426]

Loss of Fhit expression is common in diffuse-type carcinoma and in the ovarian metastases that can result from it (Krukenberg tumor).[418]

Overexpression of cyclin D1 occurs frequently in gastric adenocarcinoma (as it does in adenocarcinoma and squamous cell carcinoma of the esophagus).[415] In the stomach, this phenomenon is more frequent with the intestinal-type tumors.[415]

Upregulation of telomerase is a frequent event in gastric carcinoma, and it may play a role in its development.[432,437]

Other microscopic types

Neuroendocrine differentiation can be seen in a wide range of gastric neoplasms, which differ greatly among themselves both in morphologic and in behavioral features.[445] Although admixtures and overlaps occur, most of the gastric tumors with neuroendocrine differentiation can be placed into one of the following categories:

1 Well-differentiated and slow-growing **well-differentiated neuroendocrine tumors** (traditionally known as carcinoid tumors), composed of any of the neuroendocrine cells of the gastric mucosa (see p. 672).
2 Tumors with obvious morphologic features of neuroendocrine differentiation (trabeculae, rosettes, insulae; dense-core secretory granules ultrastructurally; immunoreactivity for NSE and other neuroendocrine markers) but equally obvious atypical morphologic features (marked invasiveness, necrosis, mitotic activity). These tumors have been variously called *atypical carcinoid tumors, neuroendocrine carcinomas,* and (lately) *large cell neuroendocrine carcinomas.*[462,482,487] This is probably a heterogeneous group, which probably explains the differences in prognosis depending on the series. When the tumor has features analogous to those of large cell neuroendocrine carcinoma of the lung, the prognosis is poor.[462]
3 **Small cell carcinomas** that are morphologically analogous to their more common pulmonary counterpart and characterized by a very aggressive clinical course.[462]
4 Otherwise typical **adenocarcinomas** of either diffuse or intestinal type (particularly the former), having cells that exhibit argyrophilia or some other phenotypical attribute of neuroendocrine cells.[446,459,489] Rarely, the neuroendocrine cells can be recognized at the H&E level because of the fact that their granules are brightly eosinophilic, thus resembling those of Paneth cells.[460] These tumors do not behave differently from ordinary adenocarcinomas. By performing dual chromogranin A and PCNA staining, Ooi et al.[475] concluded that the neuroendocrine cells in these tumors represent terminally differentiated elements that do not replicate.

Most of the gastric tumors described in the literature as *neuroendocrine carcinomas* belong to the second and third categories. Admixtures occur, particularly between the third and fourth types.[450,469] Adenocarcinomas (including "early" carcinomas) occurring concurrently but independently from carcinoid tumors have also been described.[443,492,493]

Adenosquamous and **squamous cell carcinomas** comprise less than 1% of all gastric carcinomas.[448,467] Only cases surrounded on all sides by gastric mucosa can be accepted, particularly for the pure squamous cell carcinomas. Those also involving the lower end of the esophagus should be interpreted as primary esophageal carcinomas with gastric extension. The behavior of gastric adenosquamous carcinomas is largely determined by the degree of differentiation of the glandular component, which varies widely.[467] Careful sectioning of tumors originally thought to be squamous cell carcinomas will show a minute glandular component in most of them.[468]

Mucinous (mucoid; gelatinous; colloid) carcinoma is characterized by prominent glandular formations and abundant mucin deposition, nearly all of which is extracellular (Figs 11.50 and 11.51). The mucin secreted by this tumor is a distinct *O*-acylated form of sialomucin which is immunoreactive for MUC2.[483,485] The prognosis is better than that of signet ring carcinoma, but not significantly different from that of ordinary adenocarcinoma, except perhaps when the *entire* tumor is of mucinous type.[440,447]

Hepatoid adenocarcinoma is a recently described type of gastric carcinoma having both glandular and

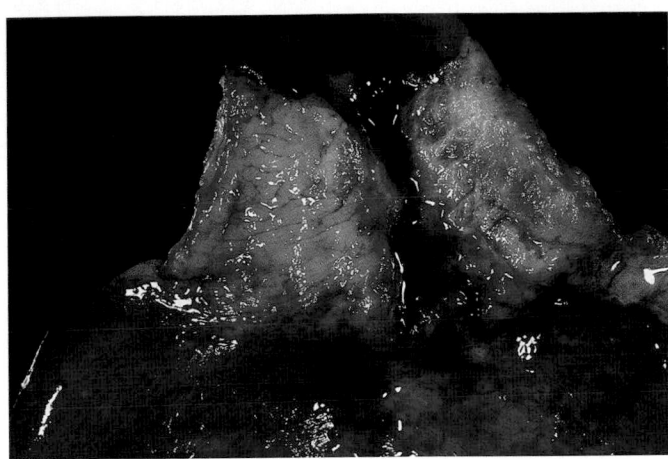

Fig. 11.50 Gross appearance of mucinous carcinoma of the stomach. The cut surface has a homogeneous gelatinous appearance.

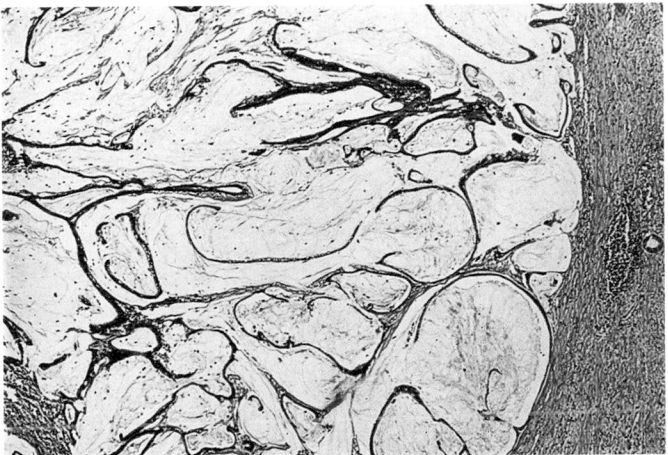

Fig. 11.51 Microscopic appearance of mucinous carcinoma of the stomach. In contrast to diffuse carcinoma, most of the mucin is located extracellularly.

hepatocellular differentiation, with frequent admixtures between the two components.[455,479] There is also a tubulopapillary pattern with clear cells, which has been interpreted as representing enteroblastic differentiation.[464] As a group, these tumors are characterized by a nodular or massive pattern of growth, presence of abundant cytoplasmic glycogen and hyaline globules, extensive venous invasion, and poor prognosis. Sometimes this venous permeation extends to the omental and mesenteric vessels in a fashion resembling that of hepatocellular carcinoma.[456] The exceptional occurrence of a neuroendocrine component has been recorded.[478] A "canalicular" pattern of staining is seen with polyclonal CEA. Immunoreactivity for Hep-Par-1 is the rule,[461] and positivity for AFP is present in about half of the cases.[471] These tumors should be distinguished from otherwise typical gastric adenocarcinomas (without morphologically recognizable hepatoid features), which are immunoreactive for AFP.[470,471,476]

Parietal gland (oncocytic) carcinoma is yet another newly recognized variant of gastric carcinoma.[449,488] The tumor grows in a glandular or solid fashion (to the point of simulating lymphoma) and is composed of cells with abundant eosinophilic granular (oncocytic) cytoplasm that stains for PTAH and Luxol fast blue[481] (Fig. 11.52). The most distinctive features are seen ultrastructurally— abundant mitochondria, tubulovesicles, intracellular canaliculi, and intercellular lumina filled with undulating microvilli. It is possible that immunohistochemical evaluation of gastric tumors with parietal cell antibodies obtained from patients with type A gastritis will allow the detection of this cell type in future cases.[490] Occasionally, focal parietal cell differentiation is seen in an otherwise typical intestinal-type adenocarcinoma.[451]

Lymphoepithelioma-like carcinoma (undifferentiated carcinoma with intense lymphoid infiltration) resembles morphologically the homonymous tumor of the upper respiratory tract; the presence of EBV has been documented in most of the cases.[465,474,477,484] This tumor is probably related (or at least very similar morphologically) to the type that has been described as gastric (medullary) carcinoma with lymphocytic infiltration,[441,466,472] which shows a similarly strong relationship with EBV.[452,463] It should be commented here that EBV is also found in a certain percentage of gastric adenocarcinomas of conventional microscopic types (see p. 662).[454,494] Lymphocyte-rich gastric carcinoma has also been found to be associated with microsatellite instability.[453a]

Sarcomatoid carcinoma (carcinosarcoma) is a tumor of dual composition, with epithelial elements (usually glandular) intermingling with a sarcoma-like spindle cell component.[442,458,480] The sarcomatoid component may contain heterologous elements such as skeletal muscle and bone,[473] and the epithelial component may contain

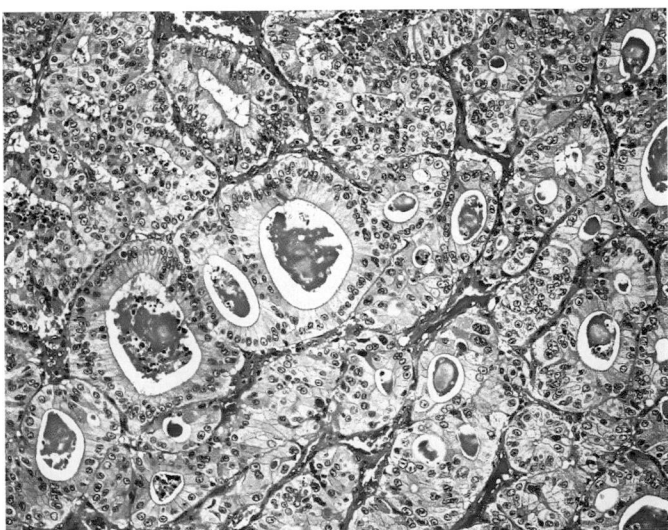

Fig. 11.52 So-called "parietal cell carcinoma" of stomach. The cytoplasm of the tumor cells has an oncocyte-like quality.

neuroendocrine cells.[453] This tumor type is much less common in the stomach than in the esophagus.

A variant of this tumor in which the epithelial component appears benign has been designated as *adenosarcoma*, in accordance with the terminology used under these circumstances in the female genital tract.[457]

(Adeno)carcinoma with rhabdoid features is a very rare form of gastric carcinoma that grows in a solid fashion and is characterized by the presence of eosinophilic inclusion-like cytoplasmic material displacing and indenting the nucleus of the tumor cells.[491] These neoplasms coexpress keratin and vimentin; they run a very aggressive course, as tumors with a rhabdoid phenotype usually do wherever they occur.[444]

Gastric carcinoma with osteoclast-like giant cells has a solid or cribriform pattern of growth and a scattering of multinucleated cells that exhibit histiocytic markers.[486]

Diagnosis—biopsy and cytology

Symptoms from gastric carcinoma usually indicate advanced disease. If the tumor is located in the cardiac or pyloric areas, it may produce obstruction relatively early; otherwise the symptoms are vague and nonspecific, consisting of dyspepsia, weight loss, and anemia. Sometimes, the first sign of gastric carcinoma is the detection of a nodal, hepatic, or pulmonary metastasis. Isolated nodal metastasis in the left supraclavicular region is sometimes referred to as Trousseau's sign or Virchow's node.

Radiographic examination of the stomach will demonstrate the lesion in most cases, but in approximately 10% it will be impossible to determine whether it is benign or malignant.

In countries with a high incidence of gastric carcinoma, particularly Japan, the increased use of mass screening, endoscopy, cytology, and biopsy has resulted in the identification of a large percentage (up to a third) of early cases, with a corresponding increase in survival rates[500,501,505,507] (see p. 669).

The technique traditionally used for cytologic examination of the stomach has been vigorous lavage by saline or Ringer's solution in patients who had been prepared with overnight fasting, proper hydration, and overnight suction in the presence of gastric obstruction to ensure a completely empty stomach at the time of the test. This method has provided very accurate results over the years for symptomatic patients, as good as or better than with the use of mucolytic agents or abrasive methods[498,506]; however, this rather involved procedure precludes its use as a general screening method for unselected patients. Furthermore, even in high-risk patients, such as those with pernicious anemia or low hydrochloric acid levels, the results of screening tests have been disappointing.[495,504] MacDonald et al.[504] screened 500 patients with these conditions and found only 3 cases of carcinoma, only one of which was potentially curable.

With the introduction of the flexible fiberoptic gastroscope, the results of direct-vision gastric biopsy and brush cytology have improved dramatically[496,499,508] (Figs 11.53 to 11.55) In 63 patients with carcinoma of the stomach studied by Kasugai et al.,[503] the accuracy was 78% for direct-vision cytology, 85% for biopsy, and 94%

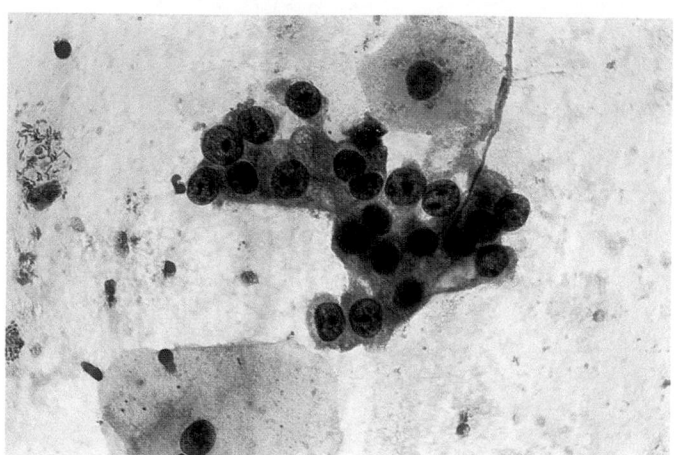

Fig. 11.53 Cytologic appearance of reactive (reparative) atypia.

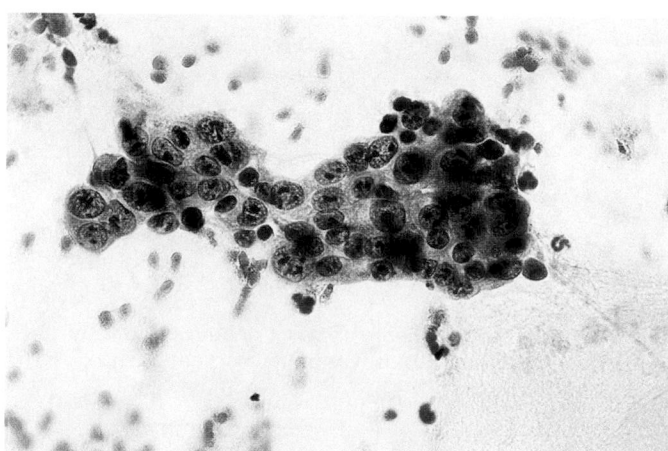

Fig. 11.54 Cytologic appearance of intestinal-type gastric adenocarcinoma.

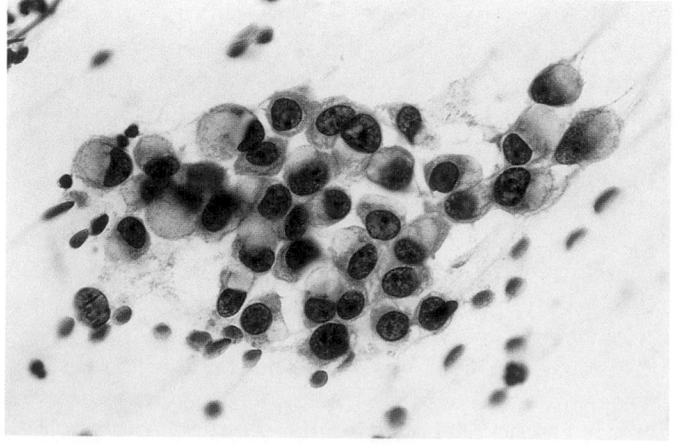

Fig. 11.55 Cytologic appearance of diffuse-type gastric adenocarcinoma.

for both used in combination. In 119 patients with carcinomas of the cardia, a positive diagnosis was obtained by cytology in 78%, by biopsy in 73%, and by both in 89%. The same authors obtained extremely high accuracy (96%) by gastric lavage cytology under direct vision in 512 patients with gastric carcinoma, both in early (95%) and in advanced (97%) cases. Yamada et al.[509] described an improved selective chymotrypsin lavage method under fluoroscopy. This method was applied to 420 selected patients suspected of having small carcinomas on radioscopy and/or endoscopy. In 16 patients, small (<1 cm) and "point" (<0.3 cm) tumors were found by combined cytology and biopsy.

False-negative diagnoses with biopsy specimens are most often seen with the ulcerating types and are inversely related to the number of specimens obtained.[502] There is also a greater rate of false-negative results with diffuse compared with intestinal-type carcinomas, a finding not surprising in view of the predominantly submucosal distribution of this tumor (see p. 673). The suggestion has been made that immunocytochemical staining for *ras* oncogene p21 may prove of utility in the cytologic diagnosis of gastric carcinoma.[497]

Relationship with peptic ulcer

The possibility of malignant transformation of gastric peptic ulcer has been argued for years. Stout,[538] G(tm)m(tm)ri,[516] and others accepted it, whereas equally prominent authorities such as Mallory[524] and Palmer[529] denied it. It seems to us that the problem should be analyzed from two different perspectives.

The first approach is pathogenetic and can be proposed in the following way: Are there any pathologic criteria by which a gastric carcinoma can be assumed to have arisen from a peptic ulcer? Malignant tumors with central ulceration without steep overhanging margins, with neoplastic cells at the base, and with preservation of the muscle should be considered primary ulcerating carcinomas. The presence of carcinoma on both margins of an ulcer is also suggestive that the ulceration is secondary to the neoplasm. The main problem of interpretation resides with lesions having all the typical features of chronic peptic ulcer in which carcinoma is found *in only one margin* after subserial sectioning of the lesion. In these cases, did the carcinoma arise from the mucosa at one edge of the ulcer, or did the ulcer arise because of the carcinoma in an area of diminished resistance? There is simply no way to answer this question with the data presently available.

The second approach dealing with a possible relationship is a practical one and regards the management of patients with symptoms and radiographic signs suggestive of peptic ulcer. Fortunately, there is now enough information to satisfactorily answer the three basic questions in this regard[518]:

1 How reliable are the diagnostic methods in distinguishing a benign peptic ulcer from a carcinoma? The differential diagnosis between peptic ulcer and ulcerated carcinoma by radiographic examination is subject to error.[526] In a published series of patients with lesions diagnosed radiographically as benign who were subsequently operated on, carcinoma was found in 6% to 15%[518]; however, by combining radiographic, endoscopic, and pathologic (biopsy and/or cytology) techniques, the degree of accuracy in making this distinction approaches 100%.

2 Of patients with a clinical and radiographic diagnosis of peptic ulcer who have been treated medically, how many will later be found to have gastric cancer? In three series, the incidence was found to be 1.1% (5 out of 473 patients, followed for ≥10 years),[518] 1.8% (2 out of 111 patients, followed for ≥5 years),[520] and 1.8% (8 out of 452 patients, followed for ≥3 years).[514]

3 Is the risk of developing gastric carcinoma greater among patients who have had surgical treatment for benign peptic ulcer than among the general population? This remains a controversial question.[523,525,537] The incidence of gastric carcinoma in this group has been variously reported as higher than,[512–515,527,530,535] similar to, or even lower than[518,521,534,539] the frequency of gastric carcinoma in the general population. The tumors are almost always of adenocarcinoma type,[519] but a few cases of squamous cell carcinomas and malignant lymphoma have also been reported.[531] Chronic atrophic gastritis with intestinal metaplasia and some degree of atypia is common in the gastric stump, especially in the anastomotic area,[510,511,528,533,535,536] and this has been said to be responsible for the alleged increase in incidence of carcinoma; however, it should be concluded that if there is indeed an increased risk in these patients, it must be very small. Thus it would not seem that prophylactic endoscopic examination of these patients is indicated.[517] Interestingly, some of the carcinomas that have developed at the site of old gastrojejunostomy stomas have been associated with prominent polypoid cystic mucosal changes of hyperplastic type (see p. 656). The carcinomas themselves are not significantly different from those developing in the intact stomach.[532]

Parenthetically, it should be mentioned that the coexistence of *duodenal* peptic ulcer and gastric carcinoma is very rare, to the extent that the presence of an active duodenal ulcer has been thought to protect against the development of gastric carcinoma; however, cases showing this combination certainly occur, and the natural history of the gastric carcinoma developing under these circumstances is not significantly different from others.[522]

So-called "early" carcinoma

"Early" gastric carcinoma is defined by the Japanese authors as a carcinoma confined to the mucosa or to the mucosa and submucosa (not extending into the muscularis externa), regardless of the status of the regional lymph nodes (Fig. 11.56).[545,550,551,565,575] The name is inaccurate because the concept is not related to size or duration of the lesion but exclusively to depth of penetration. Other terms that have been used for this entity include *surface, superficial, superficial spreading*, and *microinvasive cancer*.[546,549] They have been further subdivided into *minute* and *small*, depending on the size (≤5 mm or 6 to 10 mm in greatest diameter, respectively).[563,572] The form limited to the mucosa, known as *intramucosal carcinoma*, needs to be separated from severe dysplasia–CIS (as discussed on p. 661). This is based on the presence of invasion through the glandular basement membrane into the lamina propria, a determination that is admittedly not always easy to make.

Most cases of early carcinoma are of Lauren's intestinal type, but early forms of diffuse carcinoma (composed almost entirely of signet ring cells) and of mucinous carcinoma also exist[542,577] (see p. 666). The degree of microscopic differentiation varies widely. The better differentiated types are more vascularized and show a higher association with *H. pylori* than the poorly differentiated tumors.[541,573] The deep mucosal component underlying the carcinoma often shows cystic dilatation of the glands.[570] Histochemically, these tumors may have an intestinal or a gastric or an intestinal phenotype, like their larger counterpart.[554,559] Early carcinoma can coexist with peptic ulcer, pseudolymphoma, and carcinoid tumor.[540,543]

The relative incidence of early carcinoma is clearly related to the magnitude of the diagnostic efforts of fiberoptic gastroscopy and double-contrast barium meal examination, which, when combined with histologic-cytologic evaluation, allows diagnosis of lesions measuring 5 mm or less in diameter.[552,567] In Japan, the proportion of early carcinoma cases has risen from 5.7% in the early 1920s to 45% in the late 1990s.[545,556,561] Variations in gross appearance of early carcinoma at endoscopy mirror those of its larger counterpart—protruding or type I (polypoid, nodular, or villous), superficial or type II (elevated, flat, or depressed), and excavated or type III. Combinations are common.[562,566] Most cases are located in the distal third of the stomach, but they also occur at the gastric cardia[560,564]; multicentricity is seen in approximately 10% of the cases, although the reported incidence varies widely.[544,545,553] Genetic studies suggest that these lesions are truly multicentric, supporting the theory of field cancerization.[555] Abnormalities in DNA ploidy are just as common in early as in advanced carcinomas.[558] In one series, aneuploidy was more common in the diffuse than in the intestinal type,[548] but another series showed just the opposite.[547]

On the average, lymph node metastases are seen in approximately 5% of the intramucosal tumors and in 10% to 20% of those invading the submucosa[546,569]; the incidence seems higher in those tumors that invade the submucosa in an expansile fashion with complete destruction of the muscularis mucosae.[557]

The 5-year survival rate following resection is between 80% and 95% and remains remarkably high even when nodal metastases are present.[546] The incidence of local recurrence is very low.[571] It is also related to lymph vessel invasion, ulceration, and tumor size.[576] As expected, the prognosis of early gastric carcinomas with focal invasion of the muscle layer is intermediate between that of the truly superficial tumors and the obviously invasive ones.[568] The natural evolution of cases not treated by gastrectomy is to progress to advanced carcinoma.[574]

Spread

Distal carcinomas of the stomach invade the duodenum in a high percentage of cases.[593] Similarly, carcinomas of the proximal stomach often involve the esophagus (to the point that a distinction between them and the tumors arising from Barrett's esophagus is not always possible) and induce reactive changes in the adjacent esophageal epithelium.[589] The presence of serosal spread is more common, and its extent is greater in tumors with an infiltrative pattern of growth than in the expanding types.[578] Local extension also occurs in the omentum, colon, pancreas, and spleen. The rich mucosal and submucosal (Borrman's) lymphatic plexus of the stomach is often invaded; from here, the tumor can spread to perigastric, periaortic, and celiac axis-related lymph nodes.[587] Tumors of the distal third show a high incidence of involvement of hepatoduodenal nodes.[592] The presence of mucosal lymphangiectasia has been found to be statistically associated with the presence of regional lymph node metastases.[588] Invasion of the blood vessel walls by the tumor ("*vasculitis carcinomatosa*") can also occur.[591]

The incidence of detectable lymph node metastases is influenced by the method used to search for them; it is

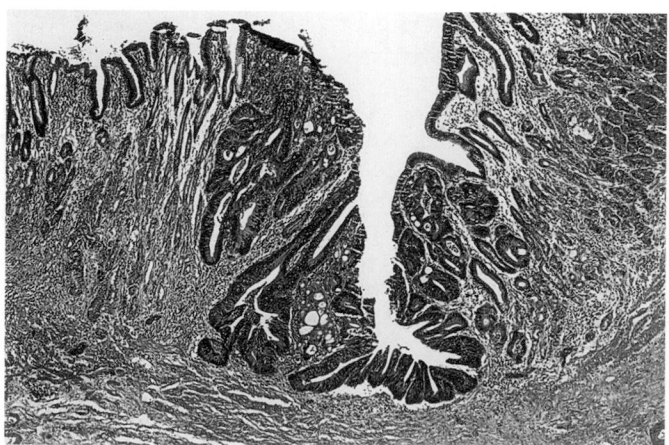

Fig. 11.56 "Early" gastric carcinoma limited to the mucosal layer of the organ.

significantly higher when a comprehensive fat-clearing method is employed[579] or if the microscopic sections are evaluated immunohistochemically for keratin.[583,585] Tumor cells can also permeate diffusely the lymphatic plexus of the bowel, more often at the level of the upper duodenum but sometimes down into the distal ileum and even the large bowel; the latter feature is seen almost exclusively in carcinomas of the diffuse type.[582] The most frequent sites of distant metastases are liver (often found unexpectedly at operation), peritoneum, lung, adrenal gland, and ovary. Bilateral ovarian metastases from gastric carcinoma constitute the majority of the cases referred to as *Krukenberg's tumor*. Metastases can also develop in the uterine body and cervix.[584]

The diffuse type of gastric carcinoma shows a wider pattern of dissemination than the intestinal type, with more frequent involvement of peritoneum, lungs, and ovary.[580,581] On the other hand, liver metastases are more common with intestinal-type tumors, particularly if they are highly cellular ("medullary").[581,586] Occasionally, the liver metastases grow in a diffuse intrasinusoidal pattern and lead to hepatic failure.[590]

Treatment

The standard treatment for gastric carcinoma is gastrectomy, the extent of surgery being largely dependent on the extent of tumor and status of the rest of the mucosa.[597,603] In the United States, the resectability rate remains much lower than in Japan.[596,600] The operations most commonly performed are subtotal gastrectomy, radical subtotal gastrectomy, and total gastrectomy. These are often accompanied by splenectomy, but there is no evidence that this increases survival figures.[599] There is also no convincing evidence that extended lymph node dissection, as advocated by some Japanese surgeons, significantly increases survival.[595] The operative mortality following total gastrectomy is low, but the morbidity remains high. This operation is most often performed for carcinomas located at the cardia or high on the lesser curvature. For most of the others, subtotal resections are most popular because of the lower morbidity, despite occasional tumor recurrence in the gastric stump.[601,602] Gastric carcinoma responds little to radiation therapy and is also relatively unresponsive to chemotherapy.[594,598]

Frozen section

The need for frozen section in a gastric ulcer of debatable nature depends a great deal on its location. If it is situated in the midportion of the distal half of the stomach and no evidence of neoplastic spread beyond the stomach exists, it is probably better to perform a resection directly, without gastrotomy and biopsy, since the extent of the excision will not differ significantly regardless of whether the lesion is benign or malignant. If the lesion is located instead in the cardiac region, not only are the chances of its being malignant increased, but the type of surgical therapy will vary considerably according to the nature of the process; therefore, frozen section biopsy is indicated, despite the theoretic possibility of tumor spread. Frozen sections may also be performed at the edge of perforated ulcers, surgical margins, enlarged regional nodes, and liver nodules or peritoneal implants.

Diagnosis of diffuse carcinoma is one of the most difficult problems that the surgical pathologist will ever encounter in frozen section material. The small size of the tumor cells, lack or inconspicuousness of glandular formations, and marked inflammatory and fibroblastic reaction that accompany this neoplasm all combine to render its determination a very difficult one.

Prognosis

The prognosis for gastric carcinoma in the United States remains disappointingly poor. The overall survival rate for all patients admitted is between 4% and 13%.[607,617,631,636] The rate is substantially better in countries such as Japan and England.[636,647] In a series of 10,000 consecutive cases from Fukuoka, Japan, the 5-year survival rates were 46% for advanced carcinoma and 89% for "early" carcinoma.[637] Possible explanations for these striking figures include a greater frequency of superficial carcinomas, a more meticulous pathologic examination of the specimens, the performance of extended nodal dissection, and intrinsic differences in the growth patterns of the tumors.[638] Different criteria in the differential diagnosis between severe dysplasia and carcinoma between Japanese and Western authors may also account for some of the differences.[636]

The prognosis for gastric carcinoma has been found to be related to several other factors:

1 *Patient's age.* Gastric carcinomas in the young have traditionally been associated with a grim prognosis, this being the result of both delay in diagnosis and a higher percentage of diffuse cases in this age group.[619,649]

2 *Tumor stage.* As in most other sites, this parameter is of the greatest significance.[626] One of the features that it incorporates is the depth of invasion, for the deeper the penetration, the greater the chance of metastases.[642,652,654a] However, depth of invasion is significantly associated with survival independently of lymph node status.[620] This feature is directly related to the gross appearance of the tumors—polypoid, largely intraluminal neoplasms have a much lower incidence of metastases than those growing primarily within the wall.[608] In tumors with serosal involvement, there seems to be a relationship between prognosis and the surface area of serosal invasion.[625]

3 *Location within the stomach.* In 80% of the 5-year survivors, the lesion is in the distal half of the stomach.

In a series of 1497 cases reported by Dupont et al.,[617] there were practically no long-term survivors among those with lesions of the cardia, fundus, or esophagogastric junction.

4 *Tumor margins.* The presence of a pushing or expanding border is a favorable prognostic sign, whereas diffuse infiltration is associated with a decreased survival rate.[621,634,639,645,653] Consequently, prognosis for the expanding type of gastric carcinoma in Ming's classification is better than for the infiltrative type.[635]

5 *Tumor size.* Small tumor size is associated with a better prognosis, but this is closely linked to the depth of penetration.[637]

6 *Microscopic type and grading.* The intestinal-type tumors in Lauren's classification behave relatively better than the diffuse types.[604,614,635,646] Within each category, very little correlation has in general been found between microscopic grading and prognosis once the special types of gastric carcinoma have been excluded. However, the claim has been made that a new grading system that combines intracellular mucin content and tubular differentiation (Goseki's grading) is significantly related to survival.[615] Another proposed grouping of gastric carcinomas for prognostic purposes is the following, listed in decreasing order of malignancy: high grade (adenosquamous, anaplastic, and small cell neuroendocrine); diffuse and mixed; cohesive (glandular and solid).[612]

7 *Inflammatory reaction.* The finding of a cellular infiltrate at the interface between the tumor and normal tissue, often associated with degenerative changes in the tumor, is a good prognostic sign.[644,653] This has also been claimed for the presence of abundant S-100 protein-positive Langerhans' cells in advanced carcinomas.[650]

8 *Perineurial invasion.* In one series of ≥T2 gastric carcinomas, tumors showing perineurial invasion had a poorer prognosis than negative cases.[648]

9 *Surgical margins.* When carcinoma is found at the limit of the excision, early recurrence is to be expected.[637]

10 *Regional lymph node involvement.* If lymph nodes are found to be negative on a thorough pathologic examination, over 50% of the patients may be expected to survive for 5 years. With nodal involvement, the figure drops to less than 10%.[610,621] The number of nodes involved is more important prognostically than nodal stage.[622] There is some evidence that the presence of immunohistochemically detected micrometastases may also carry some prognostic significance.[630,654]

11 *Type of surgery.* In one large series, subtotal gastrectomy was the procedure performed most frequently, but radical subtotal gastrectomy resulted in the best survival (22.1%).[617] In another series, radical lym-

phadenectomy led to better survival than standard lymphadenectomy.[641]

12 *DNA ploidy and cell proliferation.* The results of several series suggest that determination of DNA ploidy with flow cytometry and determination of rate of cell proliferation with a variety of markers (p105, PC10) may be a reliable indicator of prognosis in gastric carcinoma.[623,624,627–629,632]

13 *c-erbB-2 protein.* Overexpression of *c-erbB*-2 protein in gastric carcinoma was found to be an independent indicator of poor prognosis.[606,609,640,651]

14 *p53 protein.* In one series from England, gastric carcinomas overexpressing the product of the *p53* gene (57% of the cases) were associated with a decreased survival,[633] but in a series from Germany in which the incidence of p53 overexpression was exactly the same, no such relationship was found.[618]

15 *Cathepsins.* Increasing levels of cathepsin D detection by immunohistochemistry have been associated with a poorer survival.[605] Along the same lines, high expression of cathepsins B and L has been found to be related to a greater tumor capacity for invasion and metastases.[616]

16 *p27Kip1 expression.* Immunohistochemical detection of this cyclin-dependent kinase inhibitor is said to be an indicator of reduced survival.[643]

17 *Fhit.* Preliminary studies seem to indicate that loss of Fhit protein is an indicator of poor prognosis.[611]

18 *T antigen.* Expression of this precursor of the blood MN system is said to correlate with depth of invasion and metastatic spread in gastric carcinoma.[613]

Well-differentiated neuroendocrine tumors ("carcinoid tumors")

Discussed in this section are all the well-differentiated neoplasms composed of any of the cells of the diffuse (neuro)endocrine system, of which several types are known to occur in the normal stomach of humans.[657,676] Traditionally, these well-differentiated neuroendocrine tumors (WDNETs) have been known as *carcinoid tumors,*[674] and at present the two terms are often used interchangeably.[692] This can be a source of confusion, since some authors like to restrict the term carcinoid tumor to the subtype of WDNETs composed of serotonin-containing argentaffin cells. In this section we have, therefore, chosen to avoid the term carcinoid tumor except for the latter subtype (which is extremely rare in the stomach) and have used instead the generic term WDNET.

Grossly, gastric WDNETs tend to be small, sharply outlined, and covered by a flattened mucosa.[674] Occasionally, they have the appearance of gastric polyps.[667] Microscopically, the predominant pattern of growth may be microglandular, trabecular, or—rarely—insular (Fig. 11.57). The nuclei are regular and normochromatic, mitoses are scanty, necrosis is usually absent, and vascularization is florid. Exceptionally, the cytoplasm has a clear appearance.[678,684] Focal mucin positivity may be present. Immunohistochemically, there is consistent positivity for neuron-specific enolase, chromogranin, synaptophysin, and keratin (Fig. 11.58). Ultrastructurally, dense-core secretory granules are found in the cytoplasm, usually in abundance. The rate of growth of these tumors is very slow.

The histogenetic diversity of WDNETs of the stomach is already indicated by the wide variety of products that these tumors have been found to secrete, such as 5-hydroxytryptophan (serotonin), epinephrine, norepinephrine, somatostatin, VIP, PP, YY peptide, secretogranin, ACTH, β-MSH, and α_1-antitrypsin.[668,671,675,680,685–688,690,691,693,694]

A combined morphologic, ultrastructural, and immunohistochemical approach has allowed the identification of

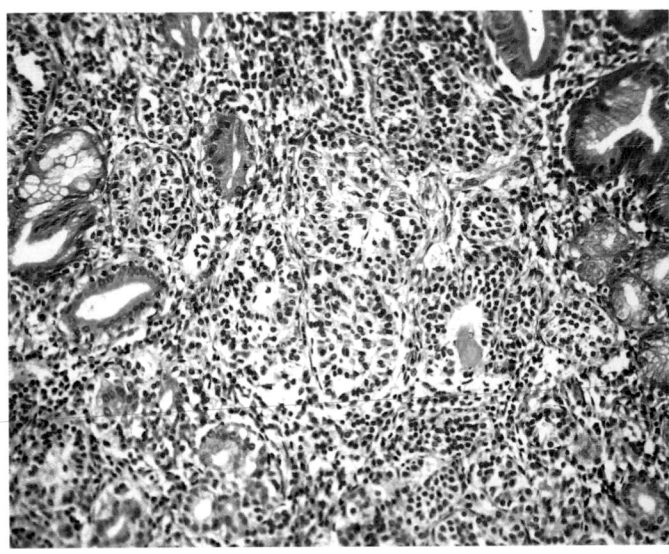

Fig. 11.57 Small carcinoid tumor of the stomach composed of enterochromaffin-like cells.

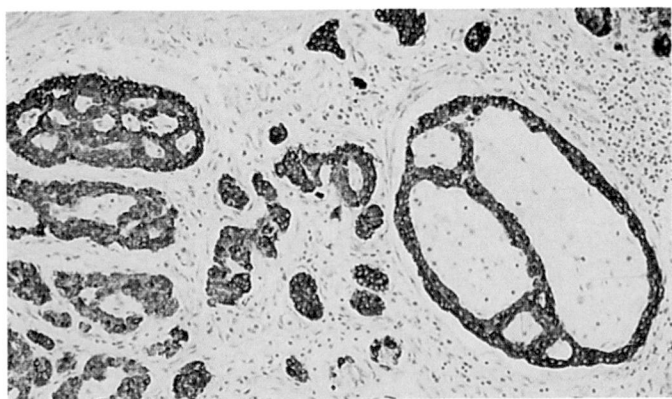

Fig. 11.58 Carcinoid tumor of stomach immunostained for chromogranin.

at least two definite subtypes of gastric WDNETs. The first is a tumor composed of **G-cells** (gastrinoma), analogous to its most common pancreatic or duodenal counterpart; this is usually solitary, located in the antrum, non-argentaffin and non-argyrophilic, immunoreactive for gastrin, and sometimes associated with peptic ulcer.[673] Parenthetically, gastric G-cell tumor should be clearly separated from the disputed entity of *primary G-cell hyperplasia*, in which an increased number of G-cells in the antrum is accompanied by hyper-gastrinemia and an ulcerogenic syndrome resembling the Zollinger–Ellison syndrome.[677]

The second form, which constitutes by far the most common type of gastric WDNET, is composed of **enterochromaffin-like (ECL) cells**.[687,693] These lesions are usually multiple, often polypoid, and distributed throughout the fundus. They are non-argentaffin but strongly argyrophilic, nonreactive for any of the standard gastroduodenopancreatic hormones, and accompanied by diffuse hyperplasia of similar argyrophilic cells in the surrounding mucosa.[655,656] Various types of smooth muscle proliferation may be present, possibly as a response to the production of basic fibroblastic growth factor.[657] These tumors and hyperplasias usually occur on a background of atrophic gastritis with intestinal metaplasia, with or without pernicious anemia.[664,679,691] The gastritis is usually of type A (immune) with a low incidence of *H. pylori* colonization.[670] The tumors have also been seen in association with the Zollinger–Ellison syndrome, either alone or as a component of MEN type I.[662,681,690] Since the common denominator for these disorders is hypergastrinemia, and since gastrin is known to have a trophic influence on ECL cells, it has been postulated that these tumors are the direct result of the combined continuous stimulation by gastrin and a predisposing genetic background.[659,683] On the basis of these observations, it has been proposed that ECL cell tumors of the stomach be divided into three types: type I, associated with chronic atrophic gastritis; type II, associated with MEN I; and type III, sporadic. Loss of heterozygosity of 11q13 (where the *MEN-1* gene is located) has been detected in nearly all cases of type II ECL cell tumors; interestingly, a high frequency of this genetic alteration has also been found in type I but not in type III tumors.[666]

Regression of type I and type II lesions has been documented following the performance of antrectomy and normalization of serum gastrin levels,[669,672] suggesting that some of them may represent nodular hyperplasias of ECL cells rather than true neoplasms. Indeed, an almost continuous spectrum exists between the clearly hyperplastic and the clearly neoplastic proliferation, making the dividing line between the two processes an arbitrary one. The figure of 0.5 mm has been suggested as the dividing line between WDNETs and their precursors.[663]

Although no peptide secretory product has yet been identified in ECL tumor cells, it is known that they store histamine[695] and that histamine-producing WDNETs composed of argyrophilic ECL-like cells are very common in the stomach of the South African rodent, *Mastomys (Praomys) natalensis*.

In terms of natural history, most WDNETs of the stomach grow very slowly. Metastases, if they occur, are usually restricted to regional lymph nodes and liver, and their presence does not preclude long-term survival.[674,696,697] This favorable outcome applies particularly to types I and II ECL cell tumors, although exceptions occur.[660] Conversely, the rare type III (sporadic) ECL cell tumors tend to run a more aggressive clinical course.[661,665,688,693] In terms of morphologic criteria, the main features that relate to prognosis are invasion or metastases, angioinvasion, tumor size, and mitotic and/or Ki-67 index.[682,689]

Neuroendocrine tumors with atypical histologic features and adenocarcinomas with focal endocrine features are discussed in the section on gastric carcinoma (see p. 666).

Stromal tumors (GISTs and related lesions)

Histogenetic considerations; microscopic, immunohistochemical, electron microscopic, and molecular genetic features

Stromal tumors constitute the majority of primary nonepithelial neoplasms of the stomach.[704] They are members of a larger family that can also involve the small bowel, other portions of the digestive tract, omentum, mesentery, and retroperitoneum, and which are collectively designated as *gastrointestinal stromal tumors*

(GISTs).[741] The general features of this complex group and their peculiarities as they pertain to their gastric location are discussed here, whereas the features connected with the other sites are dealt with in the respective sections.

GISTs show a remarkable variability in their differentiation pathways. This has resulted in a considerable degree of confusion in their interpretation, which, if anything, has exacerbated recently. For many years, they were all regarded as being basically of smooth muscle nature and designated as leiomyomas and leiomyosarcomas when composed of spindle cells, and as benign or malignant leiomyoblastomas (or epithelioid leiomyomas and leiomyosarcomas, respectively) when composed of epithelioid cells.[744] The many immunohistochemical and ultrastructural studies that have been carried out by numerous authors in recent times have shown a much more complex picture.[706] Acknowledging the fact that additional work needs to be done to fully understand these neoplasms and taking into account all the provisos discussed below, it would seem that they can be roughly divided into four major categories on the basis of their phenotypic features:

1. Tumors showing differentiation toward smooth muscle cells, as evidenced immunohistochemically by the expression of smooth muscle actin, desmin, calponin, caldesmon and/or myosin, and ultrastructurally by the presence of pinocytotic vesicles, subplasmalemmal dense patches, and cytoplasmic microfilaments with focal densities[706,714,718,723,724,730,732,747,751,764,769,770] (Fig. 11.59). These tumors constitute by far the largest category. Theoretically, they could arise from the muscularis propria, muscularis mucosae, or vessel-related smooth muscle cells.

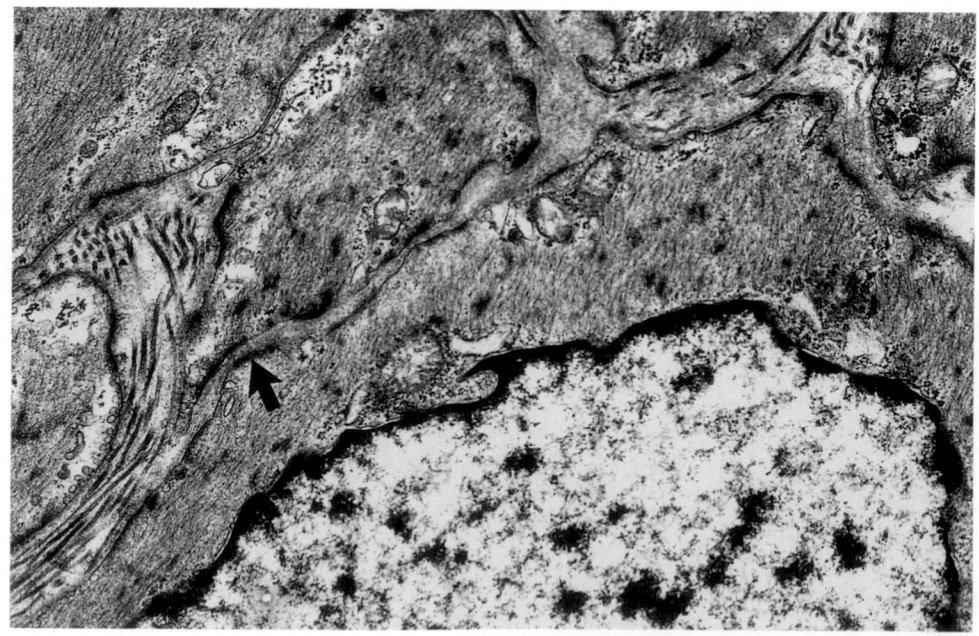

Fig. 11.59 Electron micrograph of GIST showing smooth muscle differentiation. Portions of neoplastic smooth muscle cells containing numerous actin microfilaments with interspersed fusiform densities are seen. Electron-dense membrane attachment plaques (arrow) are prominent. (×21,300; courtesy of Dr. Robert A. Erlandson, Memorial Sloan-Kettering Cancer Center)

2 Tumors showing apparent differentiation toward neural elements, mainly determined by the presence on ultrastructural examination of neural-like features, such as long cytoplasmic processes resembling axons joined by primitive cell junctions, scattered microtubules consistent with neurotubules, and dense-core neurosecretory-type granules (Fig. 11.60). These features have been likened to those of neural cells in the autonomic myenteric plexus and the tumors have been consequently designated as *gastrointestinal autonomic nerve tumors (GANTs), myenteric plexus tumors,* or *plexosarcomas*.[705,712,719,738,754,766] Significantly, immunohistochemical support for this interpretation has been meager, in the sense that neural/neuroendocrine markers such as neurofilaments, chromogranin, synaptophysin and Hu have been generally absent, and that the only markers in this category showing consistently positive results have been the less specific neuron-specific enolase, Leu7, and S-100 protein.[714,716,726] These tumors, which by definition lack markers of smooth muscle differentiation, constitute the second largest category. What relation they may have with the exceptional reported cases of gastric schwannoma (see p. 685) is not clear.[702,740] Suffice it to say that, as a group, GANTs show ultrastructural features consistent with neuronal rather than schwannian derivation, whereas at a histochemical level they show features more in keeping with a central or peripheral schwannian/glial line, such as S-100 protein and GFAP.[746]

3 Tumors showing dual differentiation toward smooth muscle and neural elements, defined according to the criteria previously listed. These are the less common members of this family.

4 Tumors lacking differentiation toward either cell type, even after exhaustive immunohistochemical and ultrastructural probing. Some authors use the term GIST in a restricted sense only for this particular group, which is almost as unusual as the third. Interestingly, a high percentage of tumors in this "uncommitted" category show immunoreactivity for CD34.[733,735,736]

For some of the tumors in the first category, smooth muscle features are already clearly identifiable at the hematoxylin–eosin level, in that they look similar to their counterparts in the uterus, esophagus, rectum, and other sites. This is usually the case with the small and sometimes multiple minute subserosal neoplasms found incidentally at autopsy or in stomachs removed for other reasons.[728] For many of the clinically apparent tumors (and for the hypercellular small tumors[734]), the prediction concerning to which of the four categories they will belong is instead notoriously difficult to make. Spindle tumor cells with acidophilic fibrillary cytoplasm and the presence of cytoplasmic vacuoles at both ends of the nucleus should suggest smooth muscle differentiation (Fig. 11.61). An epithelioid appearance is also more likely to be associated with evidence of smooth muscle differentiation, but many exceptions occur. This epithelioid morphology is defined by the presence of round to polygonal cells with a central nucleus and a usually abundant acidophilic or clear cytoplasm,[701,739,758,761] the latter thought to be an artifact of fixation[742,748] (Fig. 11.62). Tumors with features of neural differentiation are generally composed of spindle (but sometimes epithelioid) cells growing in the form of fascicles, palisades, and whorls. Deposition of amorphous eosinophilic extra-

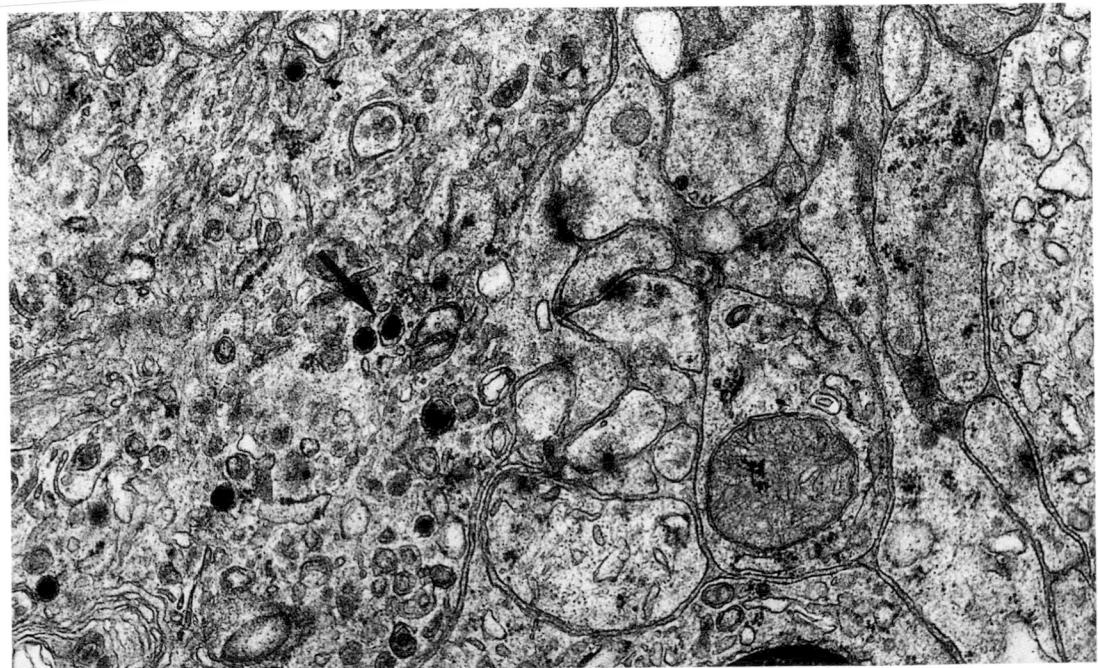

Fig. 11.60 Electron micrograph of GIST showing neural differentiation. Dense core neurosecretory granules (arrow) and complex cell processes are seen joined by rudimentary cell junctions (right center). (×73,200; courtesy of Dr. Robert A. Erlandson, Memorial Sloan-Kettering Cancer Center)

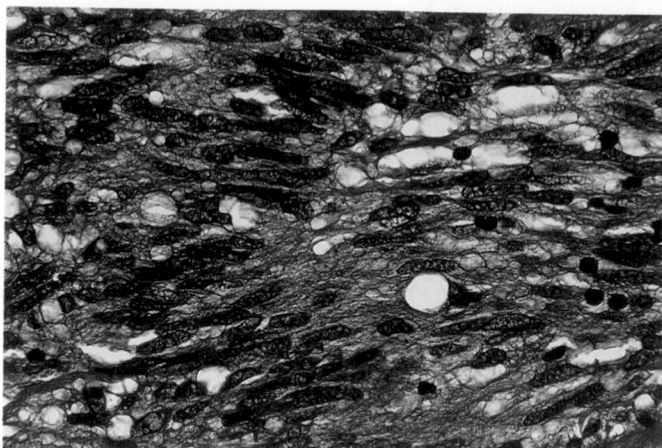

Fig. 11.61 GIST showing characteristic cytoplasmic vacuoles indenting the nuclear poles.

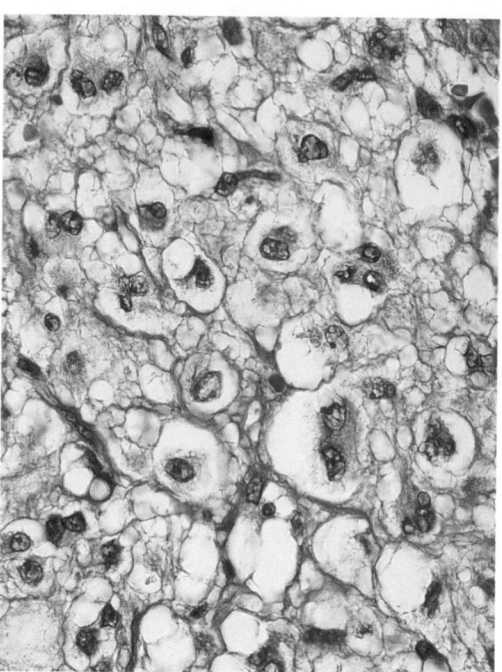

A

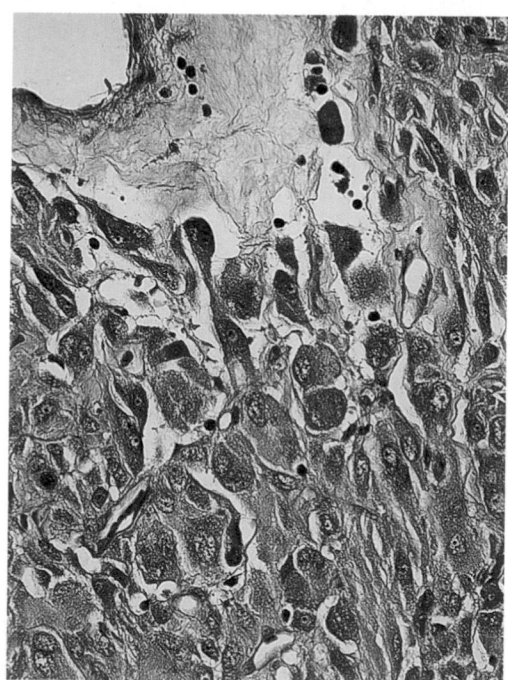

B

Fig. 11.62 Microscopic appearance of GIST. **A,** The tumor cells have a round epithelioid appearance, clear cytoplasm, and well-defined cell membranes. This corresponds to the pattern that has been traditionally designated as leiomyoblastoma. **B,** In this case the cells are also epithelioid but more pleomorphic and with deeply acidophilic cytoplasm. This tumor had features of smooth muscle differentiation at the immunohistochemical level.

cellular collections of abnormal collagen (immunoreactive for type VI) referred to as *skenoid (skeinoid) fibers* is generally associated with neural differentiation, but it can also be seen in tumors with smooth muscle-type or dual differentiation[711,725,729,763] (Fig. 11.63). Features such as degree of cellularity, large cells with bizarre hyperchromatic nuclei, marked diffuse vascularity, and nuclear palisading are of no help in determining the line of differentiation (Fig. 11.64). Conventional special stains such as Masson's trichrome or Mallory's phosphotungstic acid–hematoxylin are also uninformative as a rule. In the final analysis, the subcategorization of most of these tumors is largely dependent on the results provided by the special studies previously enumerated.

Additional morphologic variations that have been described (some related to the subtypes above listed and some apparently independent from them) include a prominent myxoid matrix (Fig. 11.65),[760] signet ring cell features (a variation on the theme of cytoplasmic clearing),[708,759] granular cell changes,[773] oncocytic cytoplasmic features (described in the GANT-type tumors),[703] aneurone cell features (as seen ultrastructurally),[756] crystalloid formation (associated with schwannian differentiation),[771] heavy inflammatory infiltrate,[755] tumor giant cells (Fig. 11.66), and osteoclast-like giant cells.[721] At the immunohistochemical level, in addition to the differentiation markers related to the lines of differentiation above listed,[762] there may be occasional reactivity for keratin and for *tau* (a microtubule-associated protein).[699]

The most important advance that has occurred in the field has been the discovery that the overwhelming majority of GISTs are accompanied by a somatic mutation of CD117 (c-*kit*), a tyrosine kinase receptor normally expressed by the interstitial cells of Cajal, mast cells, and germ cells.[700,710,713,749] This mutation occurs independently from age of the patient at diagnosis, anatomic site of the tumor,[737] size, line of differentiation, or cytologic features (except for a claim that it is more common in spindle than in epithelioid cell tumors[768]). This mutation, primarily at exon 11, rarely at exons 9 and 13, and occasionally at other sites,[698,722] results in a ligand-independent activation of the receptor, which in turn leads to its detection at the immunohistochemical level[745] (Fig. 11.67). This has

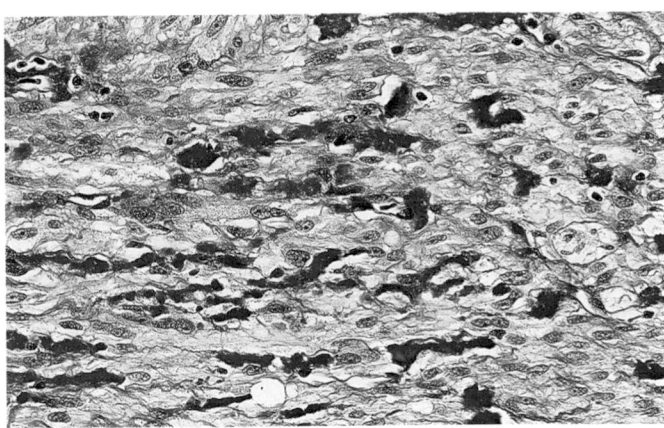

Fig. 11.63 So-called "skenoid fibers" highlighted by the PAS stain.

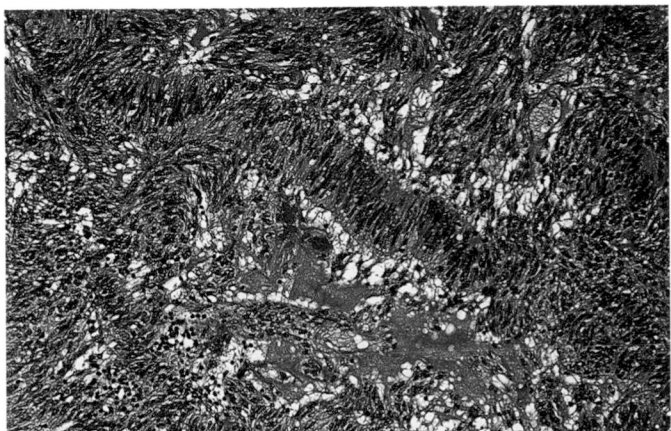

Fig. 11.64 GIST showing prominent palisading. This feature is not necessarily indicative of neural differentiation.

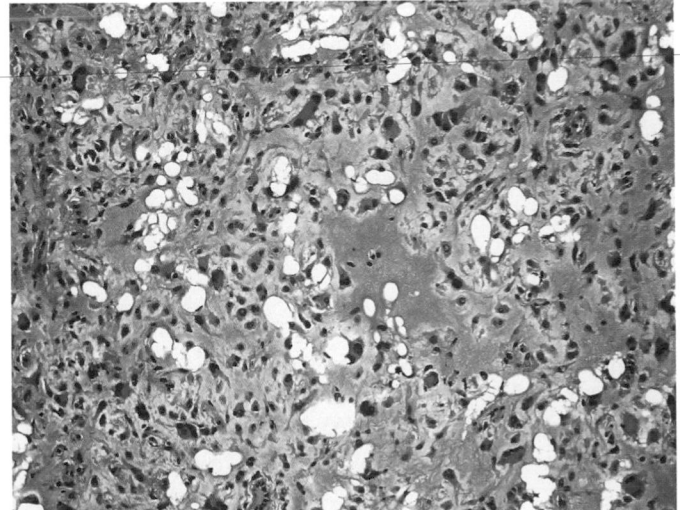

Fig. 11.65 GIST with abundant myxoid matrix separating the individual tumor cells.

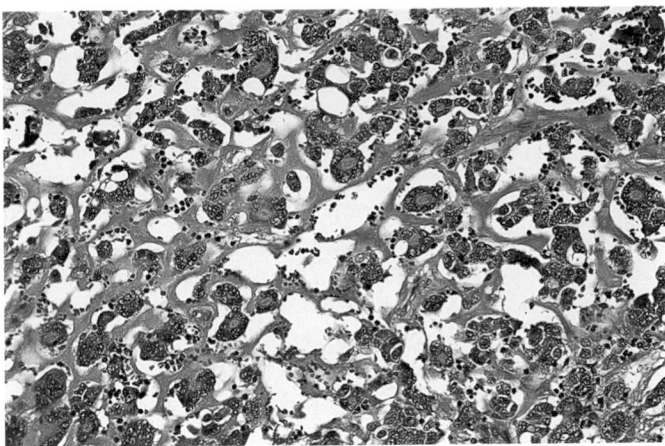

Fig. 11.66 GIST containing numerous multinucleated tumor giant cells.

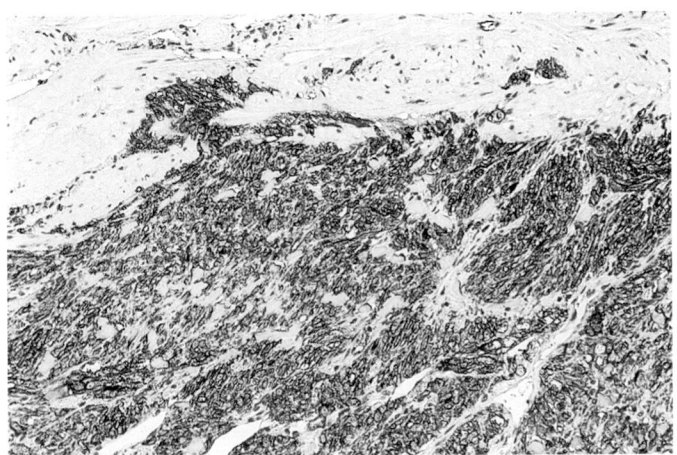

Fig. 11.67 Strong CD117 immunoreactivity in a GIST.

provided a very useful tool for the confirmation of the diagnosis of GIST tumor, in the sense that such a diagnosis should be questioned when faced with a CD117-negative tumor, while a diagnosis other than GIST should be questioned when encountering a mesenchymal tumor that is strongly positive for CD117.[715,731,750] Alas, it has also led to some rather questionable statements concerning the histogenetic and predictive conclusions one may draw from this occurrence. We feel that the following caveats are in order:

1 *Cell of origin.* The interstitial cell of Cajal is a mesodermally derived cell located in the wall of the gastrointestinal tract and thought to function as a "pacemaker cell" in the transmission of the stimuli leading to the coordinated contraction of smooth muscle (see p. 650). Since this cell normally expresses CD117, it was assumed that the CD117 positivity exhibited by GIST (plus some alleged ultrastructural similarities) was evidence of origin from that cell type.[743,757] Indeed, the picturesque term *gastrointestinal pacemaker cell tumor* was coined for it.[717,752,753] The argument is flawed for the reason that the CD117 expression by GIST is due—as indicated above—to an altogether different mechanism, i.e., a gain-of-function mutation. The link between GIST and the interstitial cell of Cajal on the basis of their alleged shared reactivity for CD34 has not fared better, following the

realization that the normal CD34+ cells in the gastric wall are not the cells of Cajal but rather fibroblasts adjacent to them.[765] It is our impression that all attempts to *rigidly* subdivide GISTs along histogenetic lines (i.e., muscular, neural, Cajal cell, schwannian, fibrous, etc.) are ill conceived, whether based on ultrastructural, immunohistochemical, or combined grounds.[707,720,746,767,772] Rather, we believe that there is a wide range of differentiation among these tumors along several lines, either simply or combined.

We wonder whether this may not be the manifestation at the neoplastic level of the phenotypical and functional potentialities of the normal stromal cells, in the sense that some differentiate toward a primarily contractile function and others (such as the Cajal interstitial cells) toward a neural-like transmitting ("pacemaker") function. According to this line of reasoning, tumors differentiating along the former line would appear more smooth muscle-like, whereas the latter would acquire neural-like features. It is of interest in this regard that the sites along the digestive tract where the contractile force of the stromal cells is most expressed—esophagus and rectum—is where stromal tumors show the most obvious evidence of smooth muscle differentiation, whereas the segment where coordinated activity along a long stretch is more needed—the small bowel—is the area in which the more neural-looking (GANT-type) tumors are found.

2 *Defining criteria for the diagnosis of GIST.* Some authors now make CD117 positivity an absolute requirement for the definition of GIST. This seems to us a questionable premise, as are nearly all proposals to define an entity on the basis of a single marker. We believe that the rare tumors having all of the morphologic and other phenotypic features of GIST, which for one reason or another do not stain for CD117, should still be diagnosed as GISTs,[727] and that tumors that are outside the morphologic range of GIST (which, as already noted, is wide indeed) should not be designated as GIST simply because they are CD117+. Along those lines, the most convincing pattern of CD117 positivity is one featuring a *membrane component* in addition to a cytoplasmic one. Mesenchymal tumors other than GIST that may stain for CD117 (such as fibromatosis) tend to show *only* cytoplasmic staining with a coarse granular pattern.

3 *Molecular significance of CD117 immunoreactivity.* The presence of CD117 immunoreactivity in a tumor (GIST or otherwise) does not necessarily indicate that a mutation of the gene is present. Conversely, a CD117 mutation can exist in the absence of the immunohistochemically detectable marker.

Microscopic differential diagnosis

Knowing the wide morphologic spectrum of GISTs, one is not overly surprised that the differential diagnosis of this entity is so large. Depending on the tumor location and the microscopic features, it includes solitary fibrous tumor, fibromatosis, inflammatory fibroid tumor, glomus tumor, schwannoma, leiomyoma/leiomyosarcoma, and even malignant lymphoma and carcinoma. Fibromatosis (desmoid tumor) is particularly likely to be misdiagnosed as GIST because it can extensively involve the gastrointestinal wall and exhibit CD117 immunoreactivity (although the latter tends to be exclusively cytoplasmic and not on the cell membrane).[778] To make matters even more complicated, sometimes fibromatosis develops postoperatively in patients treated for GIST. Nuclear positivity for β-catenin for fibromatosis is said to be of help in this differential.[774] Solitary fibrous tumor shares CD34 positivity with GIST but is negative for CD117.[777] The differential diagnosis of GIST with leiomyoma/leiomyosarcoma and schwannoma becomes cloudy because of the smooth muscle and/or neural features that GIST can exhibit. A simple-minded but effective approach to the problem is to designate as leiomyomas/leiomyosarcomas or schwannomas the tumors having the typical morphologic and immunohistochemical features of the respective tumor types (as we know them from other locations) if they lack CD117 immunoreactivity.[775] The differences that have been found in the DNA patterns of GISTs, leiomyomas and schwannomas support the policy of separating these tumors from each other whenever feasible.[776]

General, clinical, and gross features

Some cases of GIST have occurred in patients with Recklinghausen's disease,[784,795] their microscopic appearance not being necessarily more neural-like than others. Other cases have developed in the context of the Carney triad, which also includes pulmonary chondroma and extra-adrenal paragangliomas.[780,781,794,796] These tumors are characteristically multiple and have an epithelioid morphology. A familial syndrome characterized by paraganglioma and gastric GIST different from the Carney triad has also been described.[782]

GISTs with neural-like features (so-called "GANTs") sometimes present as multiple tumors throughout the gastrointestinal tract in the familial setting of small intestinal neuronal dysplasia.[791] In these cases, there is a germline mutation of the CD117 gene.[787,790]

Exceptionally, gastric GISTs are found coincidentally with anatomically separate epithelial tumors of the stomach.[789]

Clinically, most GISTs occur in adults, but they have also been described in children and neonates.[779,788] Those seen in children are often clinically malignant.[786,793,797] The most common symptoms associated with gastric GISTs are abdominal pain and melena.[783]

In terms of location, most clinically apparent GISTs of the stomach are located in the pars media (40%), followed by the antrum (25%).[792] Although 20% occur near

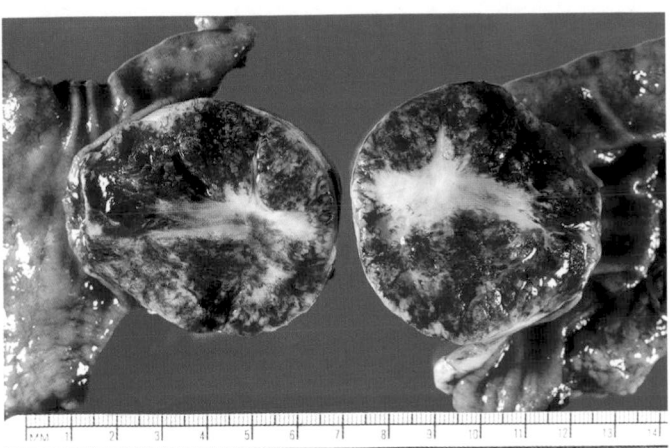

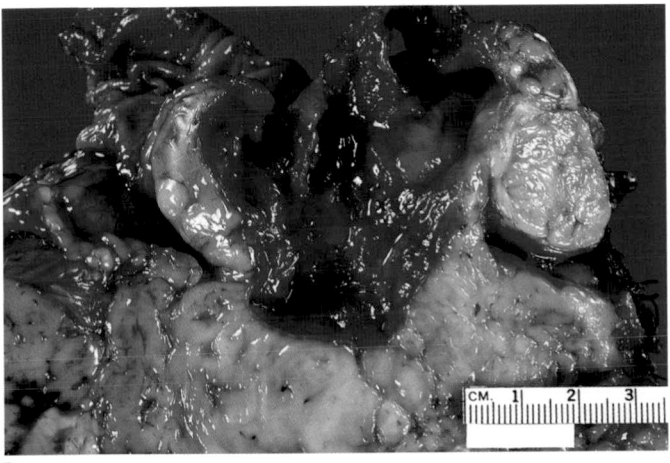

Fig. 11.68 Gross appearance of GIST. **A,** This example is polypoid and has a large central scar. **B,** This example shows a deep, large ulceration, a common complication of this entity. (Courtesy of Dr. RA Cooke, Brisbane, Australia; from Cooke RA, Stewart B: Colour Atlas of Anatomical Pathology. Edinburgh, Churchill Livingstone, 2004).

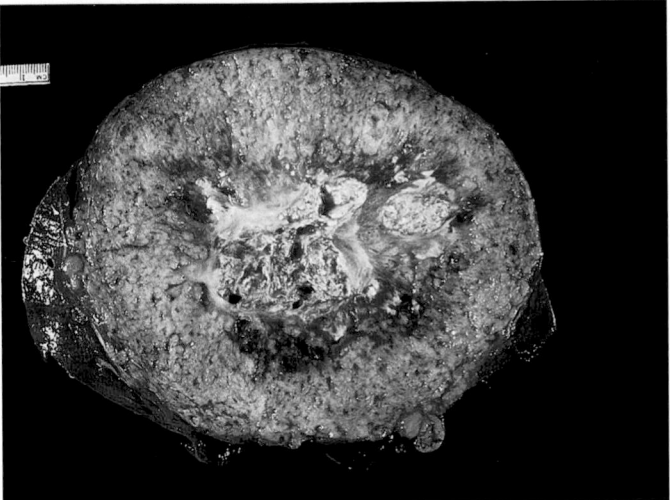

Fig. 11.69 Gross appearance of liver metastasis from GIST.

the pylorus, obstruction is rare. Approximately 60% are submucosal and grow toward the lumen, where they make a smooth projection (Fig. 11.68A). In time, central ulceration may occur (more commonly with the clinically malignant tumors) and may penetrate deeply into the tumor mass and result in hematemesis (Fig. 11.68B). The smooth outline of the tumor and the central niche result in a highly characteristic radiographic appearance. Approximately 30% of the tumors are subserosal, and the other 10% are intramural. Grossly, they tend to be well circumscribed and have a smooth, lobulated, or whorled-silk appearance on cut section. An hourglass defect may occur at the cardia or pylorus if the tumor encircles the stomach. Prominent fibrohyaline areas may be present, and they may undergo calcification.[785]

Spread and metastases

The most common sites of metastases of malignant GISTs are the liver, peritoneum, and lungs[798,799] (Fig. 11.69). These metastases can develop as long as 30 years after the removal of the primary tumor.

Treatment

The primary treatment of GIST consists of excision of the tumor with a good margin of normal tissue. Depending on the site and size of the tumor, this may involve a partial, subtotal, or total gastrectomy. Simple enucleation of the tumor should be discouraged. Wide resection of lymph node areas is not indicated because of the extreme rarity of lymph node metastases. The type and extent of the operation are more dependent on the tumor size and location than its subtyping according to line of differentiation.

A remarkable development in the treatment of GISTs has been the discovery that these tumors are exquisitely sensitive to the action of the tyrosine kinase inhibitor imatinib mesylate (STI571; Gleevac; Glivec),[800,801] a response that is dependent upon the presence and type of CD117 mutation. This has led to some of the most spectacular results ever obtained with the medical therapy of solid tumors, even if the initial total regression is sometimes followed by a recurrence in the form of a tumor that has acquired resistance to the drug through an additional mutation. In terms of the relation between response to this drug and information obtainable from the tumor tissue, pathologists should be aware that a GIST-type morphology is a better predictor of response (since it is usually associated with a CD117 mutation) than immunoreactivity for CD117 (which may or may not be associated with mutation).

Prognosis

In an old series in which GISTs of the stomach were classified as leiomyosarcomas, the overall 5-year survival rate was 56%.[829]

It has been known for a long time that the standard criteria of tumor size, mitotic activity, hypercellularity, necrosis, and hemorrhage relate to prognosis in these tumors.[804,805,812,831] Of these, mitotic count has been proved to be a particularly powerful prognostic predictor (although perhaps not nearly as good as for uterine smooth muscle tumors), despite the admittedly imprecise way in which it is measured.[825,830,833] Some authors have selected the combination of tumor size and mitotic activity to divide these tumors into risk categories,[802,816] and recently a group of pathologists has adopted this approach in their consensus proposal,[814] which is shown in Table 11.1.

One of the most attractive features of this proposal is that, following the lead of Franquemont,[816] it avoids the deceptively facile but not very scientific distinction between "benign" and "malignant" and groups the tumors instead by risk category, which is in reality all that the pathologist can do (not an insignificant contribution).

As expected, there is a good correlation between mitotic count and PCNA index, and between PCNA or Ki-67 (MIB-1) index and prognosis.[819,826] There is no good evidence that measuring proliferative activity with these immunodetectable markers improves accuracy over mitotic count.

A statistical relationship exists between tumor site and clinical malignancy, in the sense that in the stomach the tumors with favorable outcome outnumber the others, whereas the reverse is true in the intestine.[810,822]

For the gastric tumors composed of epithelioid cells (the old epithelioid leiomyosarcomas), features predicting aggressive behavior are location in the proximal anterior wall (rather than the antropyloric region), small tumor cell size (very important), alveolar arrangement, and paucity of reticulin fibers.[803]

There also seems to be a relation between clinical malignancy and pattern of differentiation,[816] although it is not clear how independent this feature is from the criteria of tumor size and mitoses. Tumors which tend to behave in an aggressive fashion are those exhibiting neural-type differentiation (GANs; although not those containing numerous skenoid fibers), tumors featuring *dual* smooth muscle and neural differentiation, and tumors exhibiting *neither*, i.e., those positive only for vimentin.[817] A poor outcome has also been associated with loss of CD44 expression.[813]

It has been claimed that determination of DNA ploidy by flow cytometry can provide information of prognostic value.[806,807,809,815,821,827,832] There also seems to be a relationship between prognosis and the following parameters: apoptosis (as measured with the TUNEL technique and bcl-2 staining),[808] loss of heterozygosity at 1p36,[823] a high level of "secondary" cytogenetic aberrations,[818] telomerase activity,[828] and c-myc expression.[824]

As far as a possible relationship between the type of CD117 mutation and malignancy is concerned, early claims that such a relationship existed have not been substantiated.[811,820] (The determination of presence and type of CD117 mutation is, however, important as a predictor of medical response, as already discussed).

Lymphoid tumors and tumorlike conditions

Primary malignant lymphoma of the stomach makes up only a small percentage of all malignant tumors of this organ, but there is evidence that its incidence is increasing. Nearly all of the cases are of non-Hodgkin's type and the large majority are of B-cell derivation.[836,838,839,841,844] As such, they show monotypic expression of immunoglobulin and rearrangement of the immunoglobulin gene.[843] For practical purposes, they can be divided into two large categories: (1) low-grade lymphomas, composed of small lymphoid cells, and (2) intermediate/high-grade lymphomas, composed of large cells. Mixed small cell–large cell lymphomas also occur, but they constitute a distinct minority of the cases.[846]

Occasionally, gastric lymphoma of one type or another is seen adjacent to an adenocarcinoma, as an expression of collision tumor.[840,842,845] In other instances, the lymphoma precedes a carcinoma by several years, raising the possibility that the latter might have been related to the therapy for the former.[834,847] In still others, the carcinoma appears following the diagnosis and treatment of a gastric lymphoma.[835] In some of the cases the carcinoma has been of the lymphoepithelioma type.[837]

The MALT concept

Mucosa-associated lymphoid tissue (MALT) is the term proposed by Isaacson et al.[849,858,859] for the component of the immune system that has evolved to protect the freely permeable surface of the gastrointestinal tract and other mucosal membranes directly exposed to the external

Table 11.1 Risk categories for GISTs based on tumor size and mitotic activity (HPF, high-power fields). From Fletcher CDM et al.[814]

Risk	Size (cm)*	Mitotic count (per 50 HPF)†
Very low	<2	<5
Low	2–5	<5
Intermediate	<5	6–10
	5–10	<5
High	>5	>5
	>10	Any
	Any	>10

*Size represents the single largest dimension. Admittedly this may vary somewhat before and after fixation and between observers. There is a general but poorly defined sense that perhaps the size threshold for aggressive behavior should be 1–2 cm less in the small bowel than elsewhere.

† Ideally mitotic count should be standardized according to surface area examined (based on size of high-power fields), but there are no agreed definitions in this regard. Despite inevitable subjectivity in recognition of mitoses and variability in the area of high-power fields, such mitotic counts still prove useful.

environment. This comprises lymphoid nodules (which in the ileum form the Peyer's patches), lymphocytes and plasma cells in the lamina propria, and intraepithelial lymphocytes. The corollary of this concept is that this immune compartment has distinctive morphofunctional features, and that this is also true of the lymphomas arising from it ("MALTomas").[856] One such feature is their propensity to involve other mucosal sites when they spread, which has been explained by the normal homing pattern of MALT lymphocytes[861]; as part of this scheme, a particular tendency of lymphoma of Waldeyer's ring to develop following gastrointestinal lymphoma has been detected.[868]

Originally the concept was applied primarily to small lymphocytic low-grade lesions, but it has now been expanded to include some intermediate/high-grade (large cell) lesions, on the basis of their occasional coexistence, immunohistochemical and molecular similarities, and clonal link.[851,863,867] Another interesting corollary of this concept relates to the possible pathogenesis of gastric lymphoma. It has been postulated that *H. pylori* infection provides the necessary background in which this tumor develops,[850,866,870] and it has been pointed out that there is idiotype identity between MALT-type lymphoma and the inflammatory component,[854] that the lymphoma cells may be antigen-responsive,[857,869] and that the lymphoma may regress following eradication of *H. pylori* infection.[865,872]

As attractive as the concept is from a conceptual standpoint, it suffers from several drawbacks. The first, which may be only temporary, relates to the fact that no specific morphologic, immunohistochemical, or molecular features (except possibly for the t(11;18) translocation) have yet been associated with either the normal MALT-related cells or their tumors. It is rather the combination of markers (particularly the reactivity for CD19, CD20, and CD20 coupled with negativity for CD5, CD10, and CD23) that is said to be characteristic.[848,852,860] The second is that the concept now embraces, both in the stomach and in the small bowel, tumors with such a variety of appearances and behaviors as to lack a precise clinical connotation unless the term is used with the proper qualifier. As a matter of fact, one could argue that since virtually all of the lymphoid cells present in the normal stomach are part of the MALT system (including lymphoid follicles), it follows that *any* tumor arising from them could be regarded as a MALToma regardless of its appearance. Indeed, some hematopathologists would accept as a MALT-type lesion any lymphoma that lacks features of any other lymphoma type.[855]

The fourth and perhaps more important issue—both on conceptual and clinical grounds—is whether a well-differentiated lymphocytic population in a *H. pylori*-infected stomach, which has a remarkably indolent clinical course and which may even disappear following eradication of the microorganism, deserves to be regarded as a lymphoma, i.e., a malignant tumor, because of the fact that it is clonal,[862,864] bearing in mind that monoclonality is a common finding in the lymphoid follicles of gastritis.[871] Genta expressed this feeling very sharply in his witty and thoughtful editorial entitled "*Le lymphoma imaginaire.*"[853]

Low-grade lymphomas

Low-grade lymphomas comprise about half of the cases. They usually occur in individuals over the age of 50 years. Some of the cases have occurred in immunosuppressed patients.[883,890] The clinical symptoms often simulate those of gastritis or benign peptic ulcer. Grossly, advanced cases present as giant convolutions mimicking hypertrophic gastritis or gastric polyps.[894] Microscopically, there may be transmural involvement. Most cases are located in the distal half of the stomach, but the pylorus is involved only rarely. Multicentricity is common, as supported by molecular studies; with progression, dominant clones appear which disseminate throughout the organ.[882,892,893]

Microscopically, most of these low-grade tumors are of the so-called "MALT type"[882] (Figs 11.70 and 11.71). It is common for them to exhibit focal or extensive plasmacytoid differentiation, to the point that some of these tumors have been designated (inaccurately, in our opinion) plasmacytomas. It is better to reserve the latter term for the neoplasms *entirely composed* of mature and immature plasma cells, which are exceptional in this location.[878] Dutcher bodies (true intranuclear eosinophilic inclusions made up of immunoglobulin) can be encountered in these lymphomas, and they are of great diagnostic significance. Despite the high frequency of plasmacytoid features, it is extremely rare for these tumors to be associated with the presence of an M protein in the serum. An

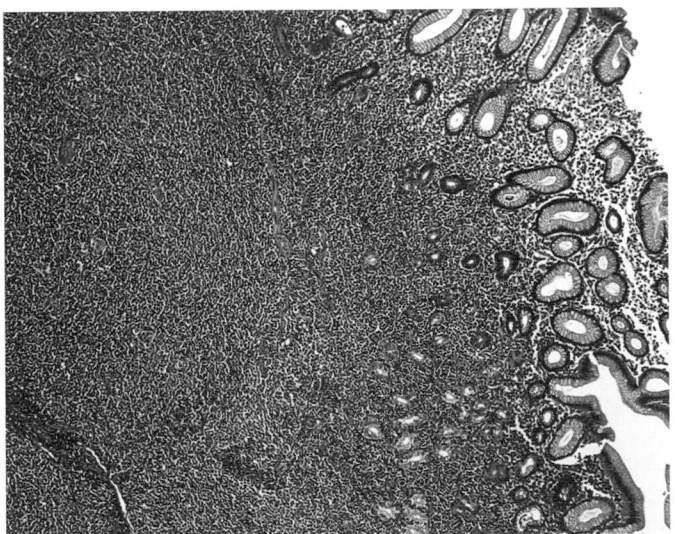

Fig. 11.70 MALT-type malignant lymphoma of stomach involving mucosa and submucosa.

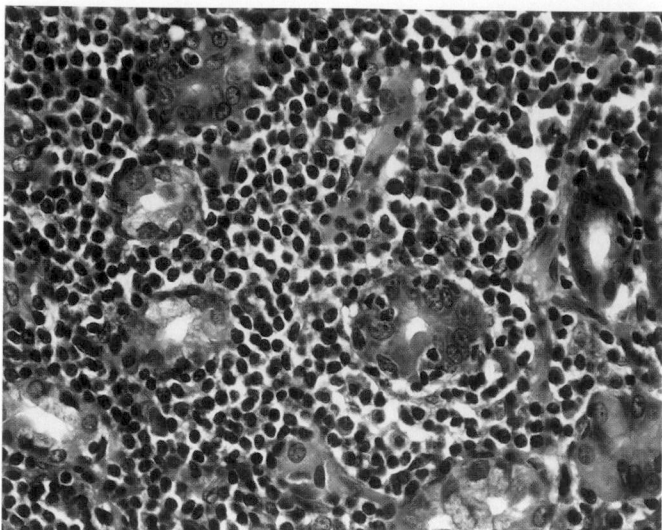

Fig. 11.71 High-power view of mucosal involvement by MALT-type lymphoma. A few of the neoplastic lymphocytes are seen within the glandular epithelium.

important diagnostic sign is the infiltration of the glandular epithelium by the neoplastic lymphocytes, resulting in so-called "lymphoepithelial lesions."

A smaller proportion of low-grade lymphomas are of follicular type; these are composed of small cleaved cells and have a follicular pattern of growth.[885] Yet others are thought to represent mantle cell lymphomas.[877] A variation on the theme of low-grade lymphoma is represented by the rare cases in which the tumor cells have a signet ring configuration because of intracellular accumulation of immunoglobulin, thus simulating a signet ring carcinoma.[881,895]

The main microscopic differential diagnosis of low-grade lymphoma is with chronic inflammatory conditions, including reactive lymphoid hyperplasia and plasma cell granuloma (see later discussion). The most important features in favor of lymphoma are the presence of lymphoepithelial lesions, Dutcher bodies, and cytologic atypia.[887,896]

At the molecular level, low-grade MALT-type lymphoma often shows microsatellite instability, allelic imbalance, and trisomies, particularly of chromosome 3; the latter can be detected by fluorescence in situ hybridization (FISH) in paraffin-embedded material.[875] Approximately half of the cases have the *AP12–MLT* fusion, the result of the t(11;18) translocation, an abnormality that is absent in all other types of gastric lymphoma.[874]

The PCR reaction has been used to demonstrate clonality in paraffin-embedded endoscopic biopsy specimens,[873,876,888] but great caution should be exercised in its interpretation, in the sense that the presence of a clonal lymphocytic population does not imply the existence of a malignant tumor.[880]

Table 11.2 Grading system indicating the degree of certainty of the diagnosis of MALT-type lymphoma. From Wotherspoon AC et al.[892]

Grade 0 (Normal)	Scattered plasma cells in lamina propria. No lymphoid follicles.
Grade 1 (Chronic active gastritis)	Small clusters of lymphocytes in lamina propria. No lymphoid follicles. No LELs.
Grade 2 (Chronic active gastritis with florid lymphoid follicle formation)	Prominent lymphoid follicles with surrounding mantle zone and plasma cells. No LELs.
Grade 3 (Suspicious lymphoid infiltrate in lamina propria, probably reactive)	Lymphoid follicles surrounded by small lymphocytes that infiltrate diffusely in lamina propria and occasionally into epithelium.
Grade 4 (Suspicious lymphoid infiltrate in lamina propria, probably lymphoma)	Lymphoid follicles surrounded by CCL cells that infiltrate diffusely in lamina propria and into epithelium in small groups.
Grade 5 (Low-grade B-cell lymphoma of MALT)	Presence of dense diffuse infiltrate of CCL cells in lamina propria with prominent LELs.

It needs to be recognized that, in many instances, it will not be possible to determine with certainty in a gastric biopsy whether one is dealing with a chronic gastritis or a lymphoma. Wotherspoon et al.[891] devised a very useful grading system by which to indicate the degree of certainty of the diagnosis (Table 11.2).

Low-grade lymphoma is characterized by a very slow clinical evolution, a tendency to remain localized for a long time, and a propensity to involve other mucosal sites when spreading.[879,889] Furthermore, MALT-type gastric lymphoma may coexist with a microscopically similar tumor in the thymus.[886] Regional lymph node involvement is much less frequent than in large cell lymphoma.[884] The treatment is dependent on the stage: extended field radiation therapy for stage I and a combination of radiation therapy and chemotherapy for stages II and III. Approximately 70% of patients with stage I disease are cured.

Lymphoid hyperplasia and plasma cell granuloma

Pseudolymphoma of the stomach is a condition traditionally regarded as of inflammatory nature, although it is notoriously difficult to distinguish from lymphoma radiographically, grossly, and microscopically.[900,904] It presents in most cases in association with a gastric ulceration or erosion and is accompanied by extensive fibrosis.[901,903] Microscopically, the features favoring a diagnosis of pseudolymphoma are said to be the presence of clearly reactive germinal centers throughout the lesion, a mixed population of inflammatory cells (including mature lymphocytes and plasma cells), proliferation of blood vessels, and a polyclonal pattern of immunoglobulin stain.[905] Occasionally, the lymphoid nodules present in the lesion have the morphologic features of progressively transformed germinal centers[901] or of those seen in giant lymph node hyperplasia (Castleman's disease).

Although, as mentioned earlier, pseudolymphoma has been viewed as a reactive condition, thought to arise in most cases as an exaggerated inflammatory reaction to peptic ulcer, the presence in some cases of monotypic cytoplasmic immunoglobulin,[899,908] the occasional coexistence with obvious malignant lymphoma,[906] and the fact that some patients with this lesion have subsequently developed blatant gastric lymphoma[898,910] indicate the need for caution in the interpretation of this process (particularly in its nodular form) and the necessity for careful follow-up of these patients. Indeed, some authors have recommended that the term gastric pseudolymphoma be abandoned, in that cases given this appellation in the past fall into three categories: low-grade malignant lymphoma of MALT type (the large majority); reactive lymphoid hyperplasia; and "atypical lymphoid infiltrate" (to be used for cases of borderline or indeterminate nature).[897]

Plasma cell granuloma is a localized reactive condition rich in plasma cells that should be distinguished from plasmacytoma and from malignant lymphoma with plasmacytoid differentiation.[902,907] The plasma cells are mature and accompanied by other inflammatory elements and fibrosis. Immunoglobulin production is polyclonal. Some of these cases have occurred in association with gastric carcinoma.[909]

A

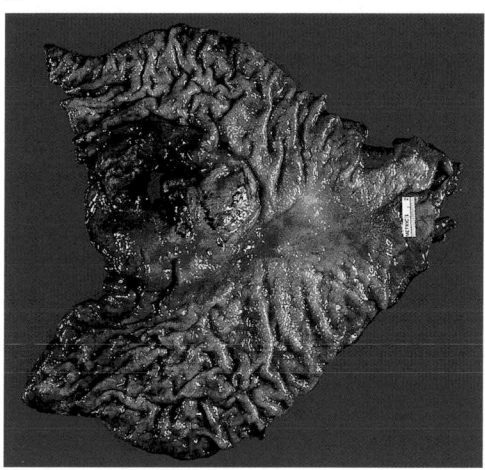

B

Fig. 11.72 A, Large cell lymphoma of stomach presenting as a large, ulcerated mass. **B**, Large cell lymphoma of stomach presenting grossly as a large polypoid mass with central ulceration.

Intermediate/high-grade (large cell) lymphomas

Intermediate/high-grade lymphomas are usually seen in patients over the age of 50 years, but the age range is wider than for low-grade tumors. Patients may have a large palpable mass and still be in excellent physical condition. Grossly, the tumor usually appears as a large lobulated (sometimes polypoid) mass. Superficial or deep ulceration is common (Fig. 11.72). The gross or radiographic distinction from carcinoma may be very difficult. Like the low-grade form, it has a predilection for the distal half of the stomach, with a tendency to spare the pylorus. Full-thickness invasion of the gastric wall, direct extension to adjacent organs, and involvement of regional and retroperitoneal nodes develop late in the course of the disease. At times, free perforation into the abdominal cavity occurs.

Large cell lymphoma of the stomach constitutes a heterogeneous category.[915] Most cases are now included in the MALT-type family because of the presence of lymphoepithelial lesions and/or the coexistence of a low-grade MALT-type component, the remainder being de novo lymphomas belonging to several different categories.[922,925,937] A high proportion of large cell lymphomas of the stomach express bcl-6 (in contrast to low-grade lymphomas), whether they are thought to be of MALT type or not.[931]

Some cases of large cell lymphoma of the stomach seen in a setting of immunosuppression (i.e., transplant recipients) and inflammatory bowel disease have been shown to be EBV positive.[921,924] These tumors seem distinct from MALT-type lymphoma and consistently show overexpression of p53.[912]

Microscopically, most cases of gastric large cell lymphoma are composed of cells resembling large noncleaved cells (centroblasts) but with a slightly more abundant cytoplasm, sometimes resulting in a plasmablastic or immunoblastic appearance (Fig. 11.73). Multinucleated cell forms vaguely resembling Reed–Sternberg cells may be present. The phenotypical features are those of B cells.

Many of these tumors have been misinterpreted as "histiocytic" in the past, first on the basis of their

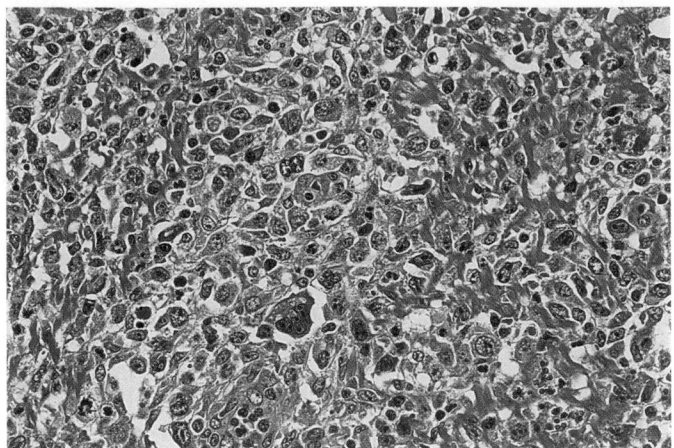

Fig. 11.73 High-power view of a large cell lymphoma of the stomach with transmural involvement. The pleomorphism and the presence of multinucleated giant cells may induce confusion with Hodgkin's lymphoma.

morphologic appearance and more recently because of possible overinterpretation of immunohistochemical stains for lysozyme and other "histiocytic" markers.[920,929]

The main microscopic differential diagnosis of large cell lymphoma is with undifferentiated carcinoma. Features favoring a diagnosis of lymphoma are the lack of continuity between epithelium and tumor cells, lack of suggestion of an acinar pattern, and preservation of muscularis mucosae fibers. If uncertainties remain, they can be eliminated in nearly every instance with the performance of mucin stains and immunocytochemical evaluation of lymphoid markers, keratin, and CEA.[914]

The diagnosis of large cell lymphoma can also be made with cytology, the detection rate being between 40% and 60%.[932,936] Following a biopsy or cytologic diagnosis of large cell lymphoma, exploratory laparotomy with gastric resection and surgical staging is indicated.[916,919] Controversy still exists as to whether postoperative radiation therapy and/or chemotherapy should be given in cases of apparently limited disease, but most authors recommend a combination of radiation therapy and chemotherapy for all stages.[913,930,935,939] The tumor may also be treated with radiation therapy following a biopsy diagnosis, but danger of gastric perforation exists if the tumor involvement is transmural. Distant disease is the most common form of treatment failure.[933]

The prognosis for gastric large cell lymphoma is substantially better than for gastric carcinoma. The overall 5-year disease-free survival rate is approximately 60%[911,926,928] and is directly related to the stage of the tumor.[934] Favorable prognostic signs are small tumor size, superficial mural invasion, presence of low-grade MALT-type areas, and absence of regional lymph node involvement.[911,917,918,927,933] Some large cell lymphomas run an unusually aggressive course.[948] Tumors located in the lesser curvature are said to have a significantly worse prognosis than those located elsewhere.[935] It has been

suggested that determination of DNA content may provide information of prognostic utility.[923]

Other types of lymphoma and related conditions

Anaplastic large cell (Ki-1) lymphomas have been described as primary gastric neoplasms.[947,950]

True histiocytic lymphoma probably exists, although—as already indicated—most cases so designated in the past were in reality large cell lymphomas. A case has been reported associated with low-grade MALT-type lymphoma.[940]

Plasmacytoma and **multiple myeloma** can involve the stomach,[943] but before making this diagnosis one should rule out the more likely possibility of a malignant lymphoma with plasmacytoid features.

Peripheral T-cell lymphoma has been described by Japanese authors, sometimes in association with HTLV-1.[944,948,949]

Hodgkin's lymphoma of the stomach also occurs but is extremely rare[942,946]; most cases so designated in the past are examples of non-Hodgkin's lymphoma.

Granulocytic sarcoma can occasionally present initially as a gastric tumor in the absence of bone marrow involvement and be confused with malignant lymphoma or carcinoma.[941]

Langerhans' cell histiocytosis is rarely encountered in the stomach, either as an isolated lesion or in association with disease elsewhere.[945,952] Exceptionally, this infiltrate (which is typically immunoreactive for S-100 protein and CD1a) has malignant cytologic features.[951]

Other tumors

Glomus tumors have been described in the stomach.[955] In fact, for some peculiar reason the stomach is one of the most common extracutaneous sites for this tumor. There is a strong female predominance.[971] Microscopically, the tumors are composed of clear epithelioid cells arranged around dilated vessels (Fig. 11.74A,B). By electron microscopy, the cytoplasm is packed with myofilaments exhibiting focal condensations.[968] Immunohistochemically, glomus tumors are reactive for actin and calponin, and are surrounded by abundant basement membrane material as demonstrated by type IV collagen and laminin stains. They are negative for desmin, S-100 protein and—significantly—CD117 (c-kit).[971] The behavior of this tumor is almost universally benign, but a case has been reported showing multicentricity and extensive intravascular spread,[965] and another resulted in the patient's death from liver metastases.[971]

Lipomas arise within the gastric wall and may protrude into the lumen, resulting in a typical filling defect on radiographic examination.[978] Sometimes they mimic peptic ulcer in their clinical presentation.

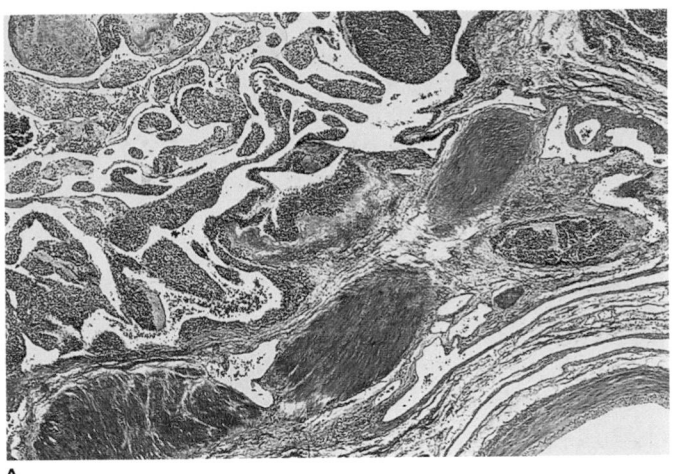
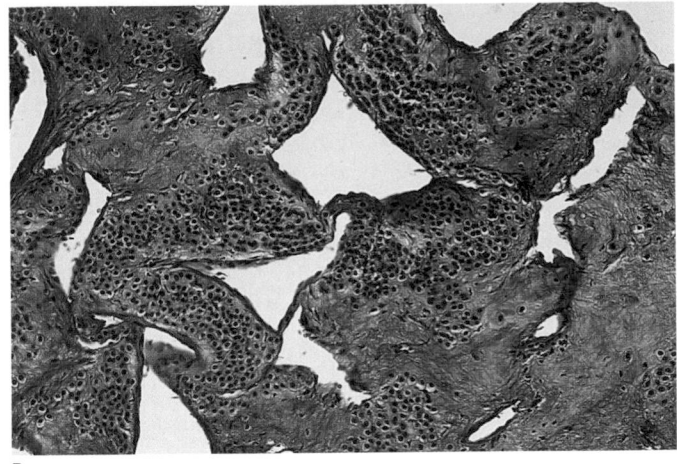

Fig. 11.74 Two cases of glomus tumor of the stomach. The small size of the round epithelioid cells and the intimate relationship with blood vessels with dilated lumina are characteristic.

Granular cell tumors can occur beneath the gastric mucosa: they can be either solitary or multiple and can be associated with similar tumors in other portions of the gastrointestinal tract.[967]

Peripheral nerve sheath tumors can occur in the stomach and need to be distinguished from GISTs and other neural neoplasms. They include *schwannoma* (occasionally pigmented[958]) and *neurofibroma*. Some of these tumors have developed in patients with Recklinghausen's disease. At the molecular level, gastric schwannomas appear to be different not only from GISTs but also from conventional schwannomas of soft tissues.[968a]

Other mesenchymal tumors are extremely rare. *Fibromas* and *myxofibromas* have been reported,[966] but most cases so designated are probably examples of other types of mesenchymal neoplasms with secondary regressive changes. *Benign fibrous histiocytoma* of the stomach can be associated with severe anemia.[954] *Inflammatory myofibroblastic tumor* can involve the stomach and needs to be distinguished from inflammatory fibroid polyp.[970] *Malignant fibrous histiocytoma,*[979] *rhabdomyosarcoma,*[961] *synovial sarcoma,*[957] *alveolar soft part sarcoma,*[981] *follicular dendritic cell sarcoma,*[964] *clear cell sarcoma (soft tissue type),*[973,982] and *malignant rhabdoid tumor*[975] have all been reported in the stomach. The latter probably does not represent a specific entity but rather a phenotype that can be exhibited by several different tumor types, including carcinoma (see p. 668).

Germ cell-type tumors can occur in the stomach, the two most common forms being *choriocarcinoma* and *yolk sac tumor* (Figs 11.75A,B and 11.76). Either can present in a pure form, admixed with each other, or associated with conventional adenocarcinoma.[962,972,977,980] The choriocarcinomas show immunohistochemical evidence of

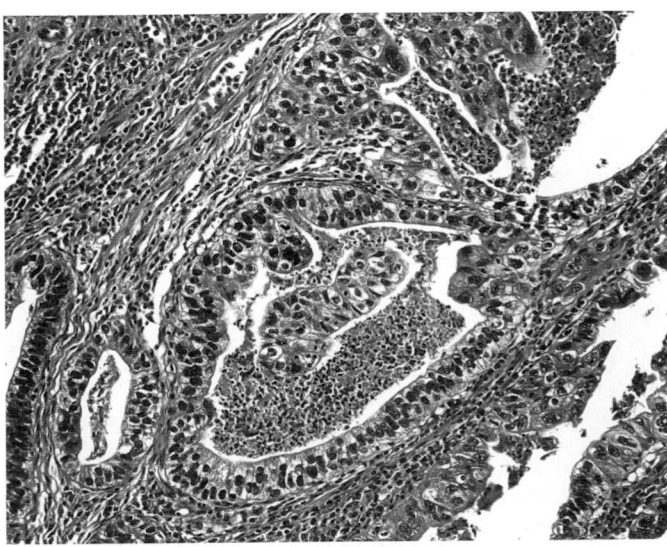
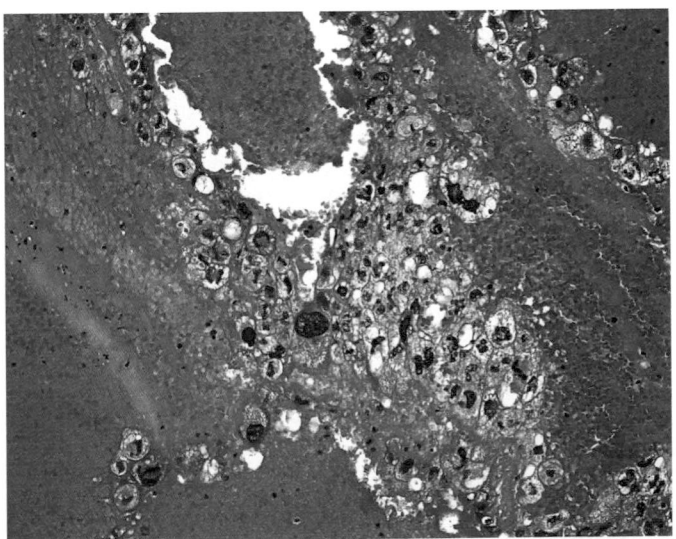

Fig. 11.75 A and **B,** Mixed adenocarcinoma and choriocarcinoma of stomach. **A,** Adenocarcinomatous portion. **B,** Choriocarcinomatous portion surrounded by massive hemorrhage.

hCG production and can be associated with elevated serum levels of this marker.[976,980] The tumors combined with adenocarcinoma (some of which have arisen in a gastric stump) have been shown to belong to the same clone (Fig. 11.75A,B).[974] Molecular genetic studies in primary gastric choriocarcinoma have shown aberrations usually associated with gastric adenocarcinomas combined with others commonly seen with gestational choriocarcinoma, suggesting that this tumor represents an alternative differentiation pathway of adenocarcinoma.[969]

Metastatic carcinoma may develop in the stomach from any widely disseminated neoplasm, particularly from the breast and lung.[959,963] Endoscopically, some of these lesions have been described as having a characteristic volcano-like ulcerative appearance.[963] Metastases to the stomach from lobular carcinoma of the stomach can look indistinguishable from the primary diffuse carcinoma of this organ ("linitis plastica")[960] (Fig. 11.77). It has been said that, in the United States (considering the high frequency of breast carcinoma and the low frequency of gastric carcinoma), the occurrence of a linitis plastica-type appearance in the stomach is more likely to be due to metastatic mammary lobular carcinoma than to a primary tumor of this organ. The presence of tumor cells with a bulls-eye appearance (indicative of intracellular lumina) and immunoreactivity for hormone receptors favor metastatic breast carcinoma, whereas positivity for keratin 20 favors a gastric primary.

Another malignancy that may metastasize to the stomach as part of its systemic spread is malignant melanoma[953]; it may simulate microscopically a variety of other lesions, including malignant lymphoma.[956]

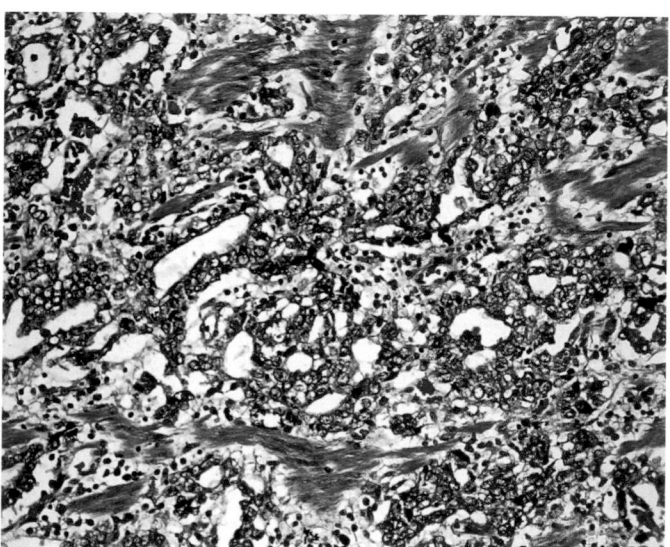

Fig. 11.76 Yolk sac tumor of stomach. It was associated with a high elevation of serum AFP levels.

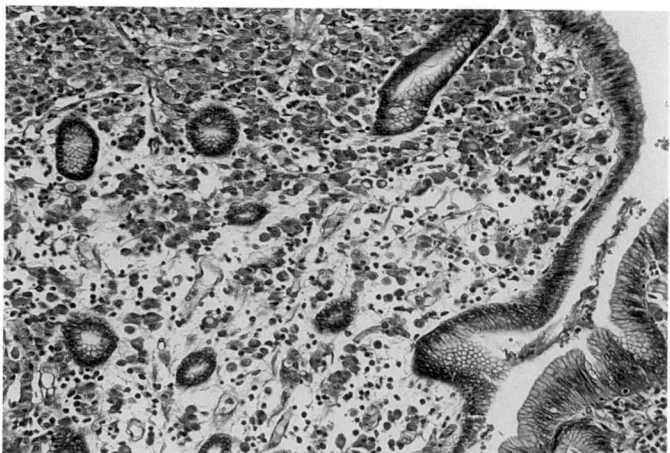

Fig. 11.77 Lobular carcinoma of the breast metastatic to stomach. The tumor cells grow in a diffuse fashion in the lamina propria, mimicking the pattern of growth of primary diffuse carcinoma of the stomach. Some of the cells have a signet ring appearance.

References

Normal anatomy

1 Cornaggia M, Capella C, Riva C, Finzi G, Solcia E. Electron immunocytochemical localization of pepsinogen I (PgI) in chief cells, mucous-neck cells and transitional mucous-neck/chief cells of the human fundic mucosa. Histochemistry 1986, **85**: 5–11.

2 Filipe MI. Mucins in the gastro-intestinal epithelium. A review. Invest Cell Pathol 1979, **2**: 195–216.

3 Joske RA, Finckh ES, Wood IJ. Gastric biopsy. A study of 1,000 consecutive successful gastric biopsies. Q J Med 1955, **95**: 269–294.

4 Lechago J. Endocrine cells of the gastrointestinal tract and their pathology. Part 2. Pathol Annu 1978, **13**: 329–350.

5 Lewin KJ. The endocrine cells of the gastrointestinal tract. The normal endocrine cells and their hyperplasias. Part 1. Pathol Annu 1986, **21**: 1–27.

6 Owen DA. Normal histology of the stomach. Am J Surg Pathol 1986, **10**: 48–61.

7 Owen DA. Stomach. In Sternberg S (ed.): Histology for pathologists, ed. 2. Philadelphia, 1997, Lippincott-Raven, pp. 481–494.

8 Rubin W, Ross LL, Sleisenger MJ, Jeffries GH. The normal human gastric epithelia. A fine structural study. Lab Invest 1968, **19**: 598–626.

9 Rubio CA. Five types of pyloric cells in the antral mucosa of the stomach. Pathol Res Pract 1992, **188**: 157–161.

10 Rubio C, Hirota T, Itabashi M, Hirohashi S, Kato Y. A possible error in the interpretation of gastric carcinoma. Jpn J Cancer Res 1991, **82**: 1354–1355.

11 Rubio CA, Jessurum J, de Ruiz PA. Geographic variations in the histologic characteristics of the gastric mucosa. Am J Clin Pathol 1991, **96**: 330–333.

12 Rubio CA, Stemmermann GN, Hayashi T. Ciliated gastric cells among Japanese living in Hawaii. Jpn J Cancer Res 1991, **82**: 86–89.

13 Sano J, Miki K, Ichinose M, Kimura M, Kurokawa K, Aida T, Ishizaki M, Asano G, Masugi Y, Wong RNS, Takahashi K. In situ localization of pepsinogens I and II mRNA in human gastric mucosa. Acta Pathol Jpn 1989, **39**: 765–771.

14 Silva E, Teixeira A, David L, Carneiro F, Reis CA, Sobrinho-Simoes J, Serpa J, Veerman E, Bolscher J, Sobrinho-Simoes M. Mucins as key molecules for the classification of intestinal metaplasia of the stomach. Virchows Arch 2002, **440**: 311–317.

15 Solcia E, Rindi G, Silini E, Villani L. Enterochromaffin-like (ECL) cells and their growths. Relationships to gastrin, reduced acid

secretion and gastritis. Baillieres Clin Gastroenterol 1993, **7:** 149–165.

16 Thompson IW, Day DW, Wright NA. Subnuclear vacuolated mucous cells. A novel abnormality of simple mucin-secreting cells of nonspecialized gastric mucosa and Brunner's glands. Histopathology 1987, **11:** 1067–1081.

17 Torikata C, Mukai M. Pathology of ciliated metaplasia of the human stomach. Pathol Annu 1992, **27**(Pt 2): 187–212.

Heterotopic tissues

18 Doglioni C, Laurino L, Dei Tos AP, De Boni M, Franzin G, Braidotti P, Viale G. Pancreatic (acinar) metaplasia of the gastric mucosa. Histology, ultrastructure, immunocytochemistry, and clinicopathologic correlations of 101 cases. Am J Surg Pathol 1993, **17:** 1134–1143.

19 Goldfarb WB, Bennett D, Monafo W. Carcinoma in heterotopic gastric pancreas. Ann Surg 1963, **158:** 56–58.

20 Hui Y-Z, Qian-Xin G. Adenomyoma of the stomach presenting as an antral polyp. Histopathology 1990, **16:** 99–101.

21 Jeng KS, Yang KC, Kuo SH. Malignant degeneration of heterotopic pancreas. Gastrointest Endosc 1991, **37:** 196–198.

22 Kneafsey PD, Demetrick DJ. Malignant transformation in a pyloric adenomyoma. A case report. Histopathology 1992, **20:** 433–435.

23 Krishnamurthy S, Integlia MJ, Grand RJ, Dayal Y. Pancreatic acinar cell clusters in pediatric gastric mucosa. Am J Surg Pathol 1998, **22:** 100–105.

24 Nopajaroonsri C. Mucus retention in heterotopic pancreas of the gastric antrum. A lesion mimicking mucinous carcinoma. Am J Surg Pathol 1994, **18:** 953–957.

25 Oka R, Okai T, Kitakata H, Ohta T. Heterotopic pancreas with calcification: a lesion mimicking leiomyosarcoma of the stomach. Gastrointest Endosc 2002, **56:** 939–942.

26 Osanai M, Miyokawa N, Tamaki T, Yonekawa M, Kawamura A, Sawada N. Adenocarcinoma arising in gastric heterotopic pancreas: clinicopathological and immunohistochemical study with genetic analysis of a case. Pathol Int 2001, **51:** 549–554.

27 Palmer ED. Benign intramural tumors of the stomach. A review with special reference to gross pathology. Medicine (Baltimore) 1951, **30:** 81–181.

28 Tanaka K, Tsunoda T, Eto T, Yamada M, Tajima Y, Shimogama H, Yamaguchi T, Matsuo S, Izawa K. Diagnosis and management of heterotopic pancreas. Int Surg 1993, **78:** 32–35.

29 Ueno S, Ishida H, Hayashi A, Kamagata S, Morikawa M. Heterotopic pancreas as a rare cause of gastrointestinal hemorrhage in the newborn. Report of a case. Surg Today 1993, **23:** 269–272.

30 Wang HH, Zeroogian JM, Spechler SJ, Goyal RK, Antonioli DA. Prevalence and significance of pancreatic acinar metaplasia at the gastroesophageal junction. Am J Surg Pathol 1996, **20:** 1507–1510.

31 Yamagiwa H, Onishi N, Nishii M. Heterotopic pancreas of the stomach. Histogenesis and immunohistochemistry. Acta Pathol Jpn 1992, **42:** 249–254.

Hypertrophic pyloric stenosis

32 Batcup G, Spitz L. A histopathological study of gastric mucosal biopsies in infantile hypertrophic pyloric stenosis. J Clin Pathol 1979, **32:** 625–628.

33 Bateson EM, Talerman A, Walrond ER. Radiological and pathological observations in a series of seventeen cases of hypertrophic pyloric stenosis of adults. Br J Radiol 1969, **42:** 1–8.

34 Downey EC Jr. Laparoscopic pyloromyotomy. Semin Pediatr Surg 1998,**7:** 220–224.

35 Du Plessis DJ. Primary hypertrophic pyloric stenosis in the adult. Br J Surg 1966, **53:** 485–492.

36 Hedback G, Abrahamsson K, Husberg B, Granholm T, Oden A. The epidemiology of infantile hypertrophic pyloric stenosis in Sweden 1987-1996. Arch Dis Child 2001, **85:** 379–381.

37 Kawahara H, Imura K, Yagi M, Kubota A, Okada A. Motor abnormality in the gastroduodenal junction in patients with infantile hypertrophic pyloric stenosis. J Pediatr Surg 2001, **36:** 1641–1645.

38 Lumsden K, Truelove SC. Primary hypertrophic pyloric stenosis in the adult. Br J Radiol 1955, **31:** 261–266.

39 Ohshiro K, Puri P. Pathogenesis of infantile hypertrophic pyloric stenosis: recent progress. Pediatr Surg Int 1998, **13:** 243–252.

40 Vanderwinden JM. Role of interstitial cells of Cajal and their relationship with the enteric nervous system. Eur J Morphol 1999, **37:** 250–256.

41 Vanderwinden JM, Rumessen JJ. Interstitial cells of Cajal in human gut and gastrointestinal disease. Microsc Res Tech 1999, **47:** 344–360.

42 Van Roggen JG, Van Krieken JH. Adult hypertrophic pyloric stenosis: case report and review. J Clin Pathol 1998, **51:** 479–480.

43 Wellman KF, Kagan A, Fang H. Hypertrophic pyloric stenosis in adults. Gastroenterology 1964, **46:** 601–608.

Chronic gastritis

44 Anim JT, Al-Sobkie N, Prasad A, John B, Sharma PN, Al-Hamar I. Assessment of different methods for staining Helicobacter pylori in endoscopic gastric biopsies. Acta Histochem 2000, **102:** 129–137.

45 Barwick KW. Chronic gastritis. The pathologist's role. Part 2. Pathol Annu 1987, **22:** 223–251.

46 Bordi C, Gabrielli M, Missale G. Pathological changes of endocrine cells in chronic atrophic gastritis. An ultrastructural study on peroral gastric biopsy specimens. Arch Pathol Lab Med 1978, **102:** 129–135.

47 Buck GE, Gourley WK, Lee WK, Subramanyam K, Latimer JM, DiNuzzo AR. Relation of *Campylobacter pyloridis* to gastritis and peptic ulcer. J Infect Dis 1986, **153:** 664–669.

48 Carneiro F, Santos L, David L, Dabelsteen E, Clausen H, Sobrinho-Simoes M. T (Thomsen-Friedenreich) antigen and other simple mucin-type carbohydrate antigens in precursor lesions of gastric carcinoma. Histopathology 1994, **24:** 105–113.

49 Chan WY, Hui PK, Leung KM, Thomas TM. Modes of *Helicobacter* colonization and gastric epithelial damage. Histopathology 1992, **21:** 521–528.

49a Chu PG, Jiang Z, Weiss LM. Hepatocyte antigen as a marker of intestinal metaplasia. Am J Surg Pathol 2003, **27:** 952–959.

50 Correa P. The epidemiology and pathogenesis of chronic gastritis. Three etiologic entities. Fron Gastointest Res 1980, **6:** 98–108.

51 Correa P. Clinical implications of recent developments in gastric carcinoma pathology and epidemiology. Semin Oncol 1985, **12:** 2–10.

52 Di Napoli A, Petrino R, Boero M, Bellis D, Chiandussi L. Quantitative assessment of histological changes in chronic gastritis after eradication of *Helicobacter pylori*. J Clin Pathol 1992, **45:** 796–798.

53 Dixon MF, Genta RM, Yardley JH, Correa P. Classification and grading of gastritis: the updated Sydney system, International Workshop on the Histopathology of Gastritis, Houston 1994. Am J Surg Pathol 1996, **20:** 1161–1181.

54 Dunn BE. Pathogenic mechanisms of *Helicobacter pylori*. Gastroenterol Clin North Am 1993, **22:** 43–57.

55 Eidt S, Stolte M. Prevalence of lymphoid follicles and aggregates in *Helicobacter pylori* gastritis in antral and body mucosa. J Clin Pathol 1993, **46:** 832–835.

56 Eidt S, Oberhuber G, Schneider A, Stolte M. The histopathological spectrum of type A gastritis. Pathol Res Pract 1996, **192:** 101–106.

57 El-Zimaity HM, Genta RM, Graham DY. Histological features do not define NSAID-induced gastritis. Hum Pathol 1996, **27:** 1348–1354.

58 Filipe MI, Potet F, Bogomoletz WV, Dawson PA, Fabiani B, Chauveinc P, Fenzy A, Gazzard B, Goldfain D, Zeegen R. Incomplete sulphomucin-secreting intestinal metaplasia for gastric cancer. Preliminary data from a prospective study from three centres. Gut 1985, **26:** 1319–1326.

59 Garvey W, Fathi A, Bigelow F. Modified Steiner for the demonstration of spirochetes. J Histotechnol 1985, **8:** 15–17.

60 Genta RM. Recognising atrophy: another step toward a classification of gastritis. Am J Surg Pathol 1996, **20:** S23–S30.

61 Genta RM, Hamner HW, Graham DY. Gastric lymphoid follicles in *Helicobacter pylori* infection. Frequency, distribution, and response to triple therapy. Hum Pathol 1993, **24:** 577–583.

62 Genta RM, Lew GM, Graham DY. Changes in the gastric mucosa following eradication of *Helicobacter pylori*. Mod Pathol 1993, **6:** 281–289.

63 Goldman H, Antonioli DA. Mucosal biopsy of the esophagus, stomach, and proximal duodenum. Hum Pathol 1982, **13:** 423–448.

64 Halter F, Hurlimann S, Inauen W. Pathophysiology and clinical relevance of *Helicobacter pylori*. Yale J Biol Med 1992, **65:** 625–638.

65 Ho SA, Hoyle JA, Lewis FA, Secker AD, Cross D, Mapstone NP, Dixon MF, Wyatt JI, Tompkins DS, Taylor GR. Direct polymerase chain reaction test for detection of *Helicobacter pylori* in humans and animals. J Clin Microbiol 1991, **29:** 2543–2549.

66 Hui PK, Chan WY, Cheung PS, Chan JK, Ng CS. Pathologic changes of gastric mucosa colonized by *Helicobacter pylori*. Hum Pathol 1992, **23:** 1314–1315.

67 Iida F, Kusama J. Gastric carcinoma and intestinal metaplasia. Significance of types of intestinal metaplasia upon development of gastric carcinoma. Cancer 1982, **50:** 2854–2858.

68 Jass JR, Filipe MI. The mucin profiles of normal gastric mucosa, intestinal metaplasia and its variants and gastric carcinoma. Histochem J 1981, **13:** 931–939.

69 Jhala N, Lechago S, Lechago J, Younes M. Is immunostaining for Helicobacter pylori superior to the special stain thiazine in detecting small numbers of H. pylori in gastric biopsies? Appl Immunohistochem Mol Morphol 2002, **10:** 82–84.

70 Joske RA, Finckh ES, Wood IJ. Gastric biopsy. A study of 1,000 consecutive successful gastric biopsies. Q J Med 1955, **95:** 269–294.

71 Kekki M, Villako K. Dynamic behavior of gastritis in various populations and subpopulations. Ann Clin Res 1981, **13:** 119–122.

72 Kimura K. Chronological transition of the fundic pyloric border determined by stepwise biopsy of the lesser and greater curvatures of the stomach. Cancer 1972, **63:** 584–592.

73 Kolts BE, Joseph B, Achem SR, Bianchi T, Monteiro C. *Helicobacter pylori* detection. A quality and cost analysis. Am J Gastroenterol 1993, **88:** 650–655.

73a Krasinskas AM, Abraham SC, Metz DC, Furth EE. Oxyntic mucosa pseudopolyps. Am J Surg Pathol 2003, **27:** 236–241.

74 Matsukuma A, Mori M, Enjoji M. Sulphomucin-secreting intestinal metaplasia in the human gastric mucosa. An association with intestinal-type gastric carcinoma. Cancer 1990, **66:** 689–694.

75 Matsukura N, Suzuki K, Kawachi T, Aoyagi M, Sugimura T, Kitaoka H, Numajiri H, Shirota A, Itabashi M, Hirota T. Distribution of marker enzymes and mucin in intestinal metaplasia in human stomach and relation of complete and incomplete types of intestinal metaplasia to minute gastric carcinoma. J Natl Cancer Inst 1980, **65:** 231–240.

76 Mingazzini P, Carlei F, Malchiodi-Albedi F, Lezoche E, Covotta A, Speranza V, Polak JM. Endocrine cells in intestinal metaplasia of the stomach. J Pathol 1984, **144:** 171–178.

77 Morson BC. Intestinal metaplasia of the gastric mucosa. Br J Cancer 1955, **9:** 365–376.

78 Ota H, Katsuyama T, Nakajima S, El-Zimaity H, Kim JG, Graham DY, Genta RM. Intestinal metaplasia with adherent Helicobacter

pylori: a hybrid epithelium with both gastric and intestinal features. Hum Pathol 1998, **29:** 846–850.

78a Owen DA. Gastritis and carditis. Mod Pathol 2003, **16:** 325–341.

79 Parl FF, Lev R, Thomas E, Pitchumoni CS. Histologic and morphometric study of chronic gastritis in alcoholic patients. Hum Pathol 1979, **10:** 45–56.

80 Price AB. The Sydney System. Histological division. J Gastroenterol Hepatol 1991, **6:** 209–222.

81 Rothery GA, Day DW. Intestinal metaplasia in endoscopic biopsy specimens of gastric mucosa. J Clin Pathol 1985, **38:** 613–621.

82 Scholte GH, van Doorn LJ, Quint WG, Lindeman J. Polymerase chain reaction for the detection of Helicobacter pylori in formaldehyde-sublimate fixed, paraffin-embedded gastric biopsies. Diagn Mod Pathol 1997, **6:** 238–243.

83 Segura DI, Montero C. Histochemical characterization of different types of intestinal metaplasia in gastric mucosa. Cancer 1983, **52:** 498–503.

84 Silva E, Teixeira A, David L, Carneiro F, Reis CA, Sobrinho-Simoes J, Serpa J, Veerman E, Bolscher J, Sobrinho-Simoes M. Mucins as key molecules for the classification of intestinal metaplasia of the stomach. Virchows Arch 2002, **440:** 311–317.

85 Sipponen P. *Helicobacter pylori*. A cohort phenomenon. Am J Surg Pathol 1995, **19:** S30–S36.

86 Sipponen P, Kekki M, Siurala M. The Sydney System. Epidemiology and natural history of chronic gastritis. J Gastroenterol Hepatol 1991, **6:** 244–251.

87 Siurala M, Isokoski M, Varis K, Kekki M. Prevalence of gastritis in a rural population. Bioptic study of subjects selected at random. Scand J Gastroenterol 1968, **3:** 211–223.

88 Sobala GM, O'Connor HJ, Dewar EP, King RF, Axon AT, Dixon MF. Bile reflux and intestinal metaplasia in gastric mucosa. J Clin Pathol 1993, **46:** 235–240.

89 Stemmermann GN. Intestinal metaplasia of the stomach. A status report. Cancer 1994, **74:** 556–564.

90 Stockton M, McColl I. Comparative electron microscopic features of normal intermediate and metaplastic pyloric epithelium. Histopathology 1983, **7:** 859–871.

91 Strickland RG. The Sydney System. Auto-immune gastritis. J Gastroenterol Hepatol 1991, **6:** 238–243.

92 Strickland RG, MacKay IR. A reappraisal of the nature and significance of chronic atrophic gastritis. Am J Dig Dis 1973, **18:** 426–440.

93 Suerbaum S, Michetti P. Helicobacter pylori infection. N Engl J Med 2002, **347:** 1175–1186.

94 Tham KT, Peek RM Jr, Atherton JC, Cover TL, Perez-Perez GI, Shyr Y, Blaser MJ. Helicobacter pylori genotypes, host factors, and gastric mucosal histopathology in peptic ulcer disease. Hum Pathol 2001, **32:** 264–273.

95 Toh BH, van Driel IR, Gleeson PA. Autoimmune gastritis. Tolerance and autoimmunity to the gastric H +/K+ ATPase (proton pump). Autoimmunity 1992, **13:** 165–172.

96 Torikata C, Mukai M, Kawakita H. Ciliated cells in the human gastric mucosa. Acta Pathol Jpn 1990, **40:** 98–106.

97 Toulaymat M, Marconi S, Garb J, Otis C, Nash S. Endoscopic biopsy pathology of Helicobacter pylori gastritis: comparison of bacterial detection by immunohistochemistry and Genta stain. Arch Pathol Lab Med 1999, **123:** 778–781.

98 Tsutsumi YT, Nagura H, Watanabe K. Immune aspects of intestinal metaplasia of the stomach. An immunohistochemical study. Virchows Arch [A] 1984, **403:** 345–359.

98a Versalovic J. Pathology and diagnostic strategies. Helicobacter pylori. Am J Clin Pathol 2003, **119:** 403–412.

99 Whitehead R. Gastritis. Clinical and pathological aspects. In Truelove SC, Jewell DP (eds): Topics in gastroenterology. Oxford, 1973, Blackwell Scientific Publications, pp. 45–57, Chapter 4.

100 Whitehead R, Truelove SC, Gear MWL. The histological

diagnosis of chronic gastritis in fibreoptic gastroscope biopsy specimens. J Clin Pathol 1972, **25:** 1–11.

101 Wu ML, Lewin KJ. Understanding Helicobacter pylori. Hum Pathol 2001, **32:** 247–249.

102 Wyatt J. Routine reporting of non-neoplastic gastric biopsies. In Kirkham N, Lemoine NR (eds): Progress in pathology, vol. 5. London, 2001, GMM, pp. 121–134.

103 Wyatt JI. Gastritis and its relation to gastric carcinogenesis. Semin Diagn Pathol 1991, **8:** 137–148.

104 Wyatt JI. Histopathology of gastroduodenal inflammation. The impact of *Helicobacter pylori*. Histopathology 1995, **26:** 1–15.

Other types of gastritis

105 Aqel NM, Tanner P, Drury A, Francis ND, Henry K. Cytomegalovirus gastritis with perforation and gastrocolic fistula formation. Histopathology 1991, **18:** 165–168.

106 Ashby BS, Appleton PJ, Dawson I. Eosinophilic granuloma of gastro-intestinal tract caused by herring parasite, *Eustoma rotundatum*. Br Med J 1964, **1:** 1141–1145.

107 Atten MJ, Attar BM, Teopengco E, Nadimpalli V. Gastric syphilis: a disease with multiple manifestations. Am J Gastroenterol 1994, **89:** 2227–2229.

108 Butz WC, Watts JC, Rosales-Quintana S, Hicklin MD. Erosive gastritis as a manifestation of secondary syphilis. Am J Clin Pathol 1975, **63:** 895–900.

109 Cary ER, Tremaine WJ, Banks PM, Nagorney DM. Isolated Crohn's disease of the stomach. Mayo Clin Proc 1989, **64:** 776–779.

109a Chetty R, Sabaratnam RM. Upper gastrointestinal bacillary angiomatosis causing hematemesis: a case report. Int J Surg Pathol 2003, **11:** 241–244.

110 DeSchryver-Kecskemeti K, Clouse RE. A previously unrecognized subgroup of "eosinophilic gastroenteritis." Association with connective tissue diseases. Am J Surg Pathol 1984, **8:** 171–180.

111 Ectors NL, Dixon MF, Geboes KJ, Rutgeerts PJ, Desmet VJ, Vantrappen GR. Granulomatous gastritis. A morphological and diagnostic approach. Histopathology 1993, **23:** 55–61.

112 Editorial. Erosive gastritis. Br Med J 1974, **2:** 211–212.

113 Flint A, Murad TM. Malakoplakia and malakoplakia like lesions of the upper gastrointestinal tract. Ultrastruct Pathol 1984, **7:** 167–176.

114 Fyfe B, Poppiti R, Lubin J, Robinson M. Gastric syphilis: primary diagnosis by gastric biopsy. Report of four cases. Arch Pathol Lab Med 1993, **117:** 820–823.

115 Goldman H, Antonioli DA. Mucosal biopsy of the esophagus, stomach and proximal duodenum. Hum Pathol 1982, **13:** 423–448.

116 Goldman H, Proujansky R. Allergic proctitis and gastroenteritis in children. Clinical and mucosal biopsy features in 53 cases. Am J Surg Pathol 1986, **10:** 75–86.

117 Greenstein DB, Wilcox CM, Schwartz DA. Gastric syphilis. Report of seven cases and review of the literature. J Clin Gastroenterol 1994, **18:** 4–9.

118 Inagaki H, Kawai T, Miyata M, Nagaya S, Tateyama H, Eimoto T. Gastric syphilis: polymerase chain reaction detection of treponemal DNA in pseudolymphomatous lesions. Hum Pathol 1996, **27:** 761–765.

119 Johnstone JM, Morson BC. Eosinophilic gastroenteritis. Histopathology 1978, **2:** 335–348.

120 Lagorce-Pages C, Fabiani B, Bouvier R, Scoazec JY, Durand L, Flejou JF. Collagenous gastritis: a report of six cases. Am J Surg Pathol 2001, **25:** 1174–1179.

121 Lulu DJ, Dragstedt LR II. Massive bleeding due to acute hemorrhagic gastritis. Arch Surg 1970, **101:** 550–554.

122 McCormack TT, Sims J, Eyre-Brook I, Kennedy H, Goepel J, Johnson AG, Triger DR. Gastric lesions in portal hypertension. Inflammatory gastritis or congestive gastropathy? Gut 1985, **26:** 1226–1232.

123 McCune WS, Gusack M, Newman W. Eosinophilic gastroduodenitis with pyloric obstruction. Ann Surg 1955, **142:** 510–518.

124 McNabb PC, Fleming CR, Higgins JA, Davis GL. Transmural eosinophilic gastroenteritis with ascites. Mayo Clin Proc 1979, **54:** 119–122.

125 Nakabayashi H, Ito T, Izutsu K, Yatani R, Ishida K. Malakoplakia of the stomach. Report of a case and review of the literature. Arch Pathol Lab Med 1978, **102:** 136–139.

126 Oberhuber G, Hirsch M, Stolte M. High incidence of upper gastrointestinal tract involvement in Crohn's disease. Virchows Arch 1998, **432:** 49–52.

127 O'Donovan C, Murray J, Staunton H, Doyle JS, Leader M. Granulomatous gastritis. Part of a vasculitic syndrome. Hum Pathol 1991, **22:** 1057–1058.

128 Ruiz AR Jr, Borum ML. Cytomegalovirus hemorrhagic gastritis. AIDS Patient Care STDS 2001, **15:** 1–5.

129 Salmon PR, Paulley JW. Eosinophilic granuloma of the gastro-intestinal tract. Gut 1967, **8:** 8–14.

130 Schwartz D, Wilcox CM. Atypical cytomegalovirus inclusions in gastrointestinal biopsy specimens from patients with the acquired immunodeficiency syndrome. Diagnostic role of in situ nucleic acid hybridization. Hum Pathol 1992, **23:** 1019–1026.

131 Shapiro JL, Goldblum JR, Petras RE. A clinicopathologic study of 42 patients with granulomatous gastritis: is there really an "idiopathic" granulomatous gastritis? Am J Surg Pathol 1996, **20:** 462–470.

132 Sirak HD. Boeck's sarcoid of the stomach simulating linitis plastica. Arch Surg 1954, **69:** 769–776.

133 Strayer DS, Phillips GB, Barker KH, Winokur T, DeSchryver-Kecskemeti K. Gastric cytomegalovirus infection in bone marrow transplant patients. An indication of generalized disease. Cancer 1981, **48:** 1478–1483.

134 Vesoulis Z, Lozanski G, Ravichandran P, Esber E. Collagenous gastritis: a case report, morphologic evaluation, and review. Mod Pathol 2000, **13:** 591–596.

135 Washington K, Gottfried MR, Wilson ML. Gastrointestinal cryptococcosis. Mod Pathol 1991, **4:** 707–711.

136 Washington K, Bentley RC, Green A, Olson J, Treem WR, Krigman HR. Gastric graft-versus-host disease: a blinded histologic study. Am J Surg Pathol 1997, **21:** 1037–1046.

137 Weinstein WM. Emerging gastritides. Curr Gastroenterol Rep 2001, **3:** 523–527.

138 Widerlite L, Trier JS, Blacklow NR, Schreiber S. Structure of the gastric mucosa in acute infectious nonbacterial gastroenteritis. Gastroenterology 1975, **68:** 425–430.

139 Williams C, Kimmelstiel P. Syphilis of the stomach. JAMA 1940, **115:** 578–582.

140 Winawer SJ, Bejar J, McCray RS, Zamcheck N. Hemorrhagic gastritis. Importance of associated chronic gastritis. Arch Intern Med 1971, **127:** 120–131.

141 Wright CL, Riddell RH. Histology of the stomach and duodenum in Crohn's disease. Am J Surg Pathol 1998, **22:** 383–390.

142 Wu TT, Hamilton SR. Lymphocytic gastritis: association with etiology and topology. Am J Surg Pathol 1999, **23:** 153–158.

Peptic and other benign ulcers

143 Barragry TP, Blatchford JW III, O'Connor AM. Giant gastric ulcers. A review of 49 cases. Ann Surg 1986, **203:** 255–259.

144 Börsch G, Schmidt G. What's new in steroid and nonsteroid drug effects on gastroduodenal mucosa? Pathol Res Pract 1985, **180:** 437–444.

145 Chan FK, Leung WK. Peptic-ulcer disease. Lancet 2002, **360:** 933–941.

146 Chan WY, Hui PK, Chan JK, Cheung PS, Ng CS, Sham CH, Gwi E. Epithelial damage by *Helicobacter pylori* in gastric ulcers. Histopathology 1991, **19:** 47–53.

147 Davis Z, Verheyden CN, Van Heerden JA. The surgically treated chronic gastric ulcer. An extended followup. Ann Surg 1977, **185:** 205–209.

148 Doria MI Jr, Doria LK, Faintuch J, Levin B. Gastric mucosal injury after hepatic arterial infusion chemotherapy with floxuridine. A clinical and pathologic study. Cancer 1994, **73:** 2042–2047.

149 Fitts CD, Cathcart RS III, Artz CP, Spicer SS. Acute gastrointestinal tract ulceration. Cushing's ulcer, steroid ulcer, Curling's ulcer and stress ulcer. Am Surg 1971, **37:** 218–223.

150 Flier JS. Pathogenesis of peptic ulcer and implications for therapy. N Engl J Med 1990, **322:** 909–916.

151 Hacker GW, Bernatzky G, Graf AH, Holbling N, Stilianu L, Payreder MH, Miller K, Thurner J, Adam H. Gastrin – and somatostatin – immunoreactive cells of the antral mucosa in patients with duodenal or gastric ulcers. Pathol Res Pract 1991, **186:** 723–731.

152 Katzenstein AL, Maksem J. Candidal infection of gastric ulcers. Am J Clin Pathol 1979, **71:** 137–141.

153 Kelly KA, Malagelada JR. Medical and surgical treatment of chronic gastric ulcer. Clin Gastroenterol 1984, **13:** 621–634.

154 Kwee WS, Wils JA, Schlangen J, Nuyens CM, Arends JW. Gastric epithelial atypia complicating hepatic arterial infusion chemotherapy. Histopathology 1994, **24:** 151–154.

155 Langman MJS. Epidemiological evidence for the association of aspirin and acute gastrointestinal bleeding. Gut 1970, **11:** 627–634.

156 Nash S. Benign lesions of the gastrointestinal tract that may be misdiagnosed as malignant tumors. Semin Diagn Pathol 1990, **7:** 102–114.

157 Oohara T, Tohma H, Aono G, Ukawa S, Kondo Y. Intestinal metaplasia of the regenerative epithelia in 549 gastric ulcers. Hum Pathol 1983, **14:** 1066–1071.

158 Peterson WL. *Helicobacter pylori* and peptic ulcer disease. N Engl J Med 1991, **324:** 1043–1048.

159 Pruitt BA Jr, Foley FD, Moncriff JA. Curling's ulcer. A clinical-pathology study of 323 cases. Am Surg 1970, **172:** 523–539.

160 Sipponen P, Hyvarinen H. Role of *Helicobacter pylori* in the pathogenesis of gastritis, peptic ulcer and gastric cancer. Scand J Gastroenterol Suppl 1993, **196:** 3–6.

161 Suerbaum S, Michetti P. Helicobacter pylori infection. N Engl J Med 2002, **347:** 1175–1186.

162 Walan A, Bader J-P, Classen M, Lamers CBHW, Piper DW, Rutgersson K, Eriksson S. Effect of omeprazole and ranitidine on ulcer healing and relapse rates in patients with benign gastric ulcer. N Engl J Med 1989, **320:** 69–75.

163 Weidner N, Smith JG, LaVanway JM. Peptic ulceration with marked epithelial atypia following hepatic arterial infusion chemotherapy. A lesion initially misinterpreted as carcinoma. Am J Surg Pathol 1983, **7:** 261–268.

164 Wu ML, Lewin KJ. Understanding Helicobacter pylori. Hum Pathol 2001, **32:** 247–249.

Other non-neoplastic lesions

165 Buchholz RR, Haisten AS. Phytobezoars following gastric surgery for duodenal ulcer. Surg Clin North Am 1972, **52:** 341–352.

166 Carachi R, Azmy A. Foregut duplications. Pediatr Surg Int 2002, **18:** 371–374.

167 Cunningham JR, Lippman SM, Renie WA, Francomano CA, Maumenee IH, Pyeritz RE. Pseudoxanthoma elasticum. Treatment of gastrointestinal hemorrhage by arterial embolization and observations on autosomal dominant inheritance. Johns Hopkins Med J 1980, **147:** 168–173.

168 Delia CW. Phytobezoars (diospyrobezoars). A clinicopathologic correlation and review of six cases. Arch Surg 1961, **82:** 579–583.

169 Eells RW, Simril WA. Gastric diverticula. Report of thirty-one cases. Am J Roentgenol Radium Ther Nucl Med 1952, **68:** 8–14.

170 Enjoji M, Sumiyoshi K, Sueyoshi K. Elastofibromatous lesion of the stomach in a patient with elastofibroma dorsi. Am J Surg Pathol 1985, **9:** 233–237.

171 Franzin G, Novelli P. Gastritis cystica profunda. Histopathology 1981, **5:** 535–547.

172 Goon CD. Duplication of the stomach with extension into the chest. Am Surg 1953, **19:** 721–727.

173 Greenson J, Trinidad S, Pfeil S, Brainard J, McBride T, Colijn H, Tesi R, Lucas J. Gastric mucosal calcinosis. Calcified aluminum phosphate deposits secondary to aluminum-containing antacids or sucralfate therapy in organ transplant patients. Am J Surg Pathol 1993, **17:** 45–50.

174 Holloway WD, Lee SP, Nicholson GI. The composition and dissolution of phytobezoars. Arch Pathol Lab Med 1980, **104:** 159–161.

175 Iwanaga T, Koyama H, Takahashi Y, Taniguchi H, Wada A. Diffuse submucosal cysts and carcinoma of the stomach. Cancer 1975, **36:** 606–614.

176 Jensen K, Raynor S, Rose SG, Bailey ST, Schenken JR. Amyloid tumors of the gastrointestinal tract. A report of two cases and review of the literature. Am J Gastroenterol 1985, **80:** 784–786.

177 Kato Y, Sugano H, Rubio CA. Classification of intramucosal cysts of the stomach. Histopathology 1983, **7:** 931–938.

178 Ludvikova M, Michal M, Datková D. Gastric xanthelasma associated with diffuse signet ring carcinoma. A potential diagnostic problem. Histopathology 1994, **25:** 581–582.

179 Marek J, Jurek K. Comparative light microscopical and x-ray microanalysis study of barium granuloma. Pathol Res Pract 1981, **171:** 293–302.

180 McGregor DH, Haque AU. Gastric hyalinization associated with peptic ulceration. Arch Pathol Lab Med 1982, **106:** 472–475.

181 Millard M. Fatal rupture of gastric aneurysm. Arch Pathol 1955, **59:** 363–371.

182 Molnár P, Mik̕- T. Multiple arterial caliber persistence resulting in hematomas and fatal rupture of the gastric wall. Am J Surg Pathol 1982, **6:** 83–86.

183 Mower GA, Whitehead R. Gastric hemorrhage due to ruptured arteriovenous malformation (Dieulafoy's disease). Pathology 1986, **18:** 54–57.

184 Nihei K, Terashima K, Aoyama K, Imai Y, Sato H. Benign histiocytosis X of stomach. Previously undescribed lesion. Acta Pathol Jpn 1983, **33:** 577–588.

185 Parker BC, Guthrie J, France NE, Atwell JD. Gastric duplications in infancy. J Pediatr Surg 1972, **7:** 294–298.

186 Parrott NR, Sunter JP, Taylor RMR, Johnston IDA. Gastric hyalinization presenting in life and mimicking gastric cancer. Arch Pathol Lab Med 1986, **110:** 155–156.

187 Pieterse AS, Rowland R, Labrooy JT. Gastric xanthomas. Pathology 1985, **17:** 455–457.

188 Rubio CA. Intramucosal gastric cysts simulating submucosal cysts. Pathol Res Pract 1989, **184:** 418–421.

189 Schweiger F, Noonan JS. An unusual case of gastric diverticulosis. Am J Gastroenterol 1991, **86:** 1817–1819.

190 Stotzer PO, Willen R, Kilander AF. Watermelon stomach: not only an antral disease. Gastrointest Endosc 2002, **55:** 897–900.

191 Suit PF, Petras RE, Bauer TW, Petrini JL Jr. Gastric antral vascular ectasia. A histologic and morphometric study of "the watermelon stomach." Am J Surg Pathol 1987, **11:** 750–757.

192 Sung ME. Histopathological study of mucosal and submucosal cysts of stomach. Acta Pathol Jpn 1991, **41:** 31–40.

193 Tanaka T, Mori Y, Morishita Y, Kojima T, Kawamori T, Amano K, Ichihara M, Tarao M, Gotoh A, Mori H. Gastric antral vascular ectasia. Hum Pathol 1991, **22:** 1053–1055.

194 Walley VM. Amyloid deposition in a gastric arteriovenous malformation. Arch Pathol Lab Med 1986, **110:** 69–71.

195 Yamagiwa H, Matsuzaki O, Ishihara A, Yoshimura H. Heterotopic gastric glands in the submucosa of the stomach. Acta Pathol Jpn 1979, **29:** 347–350.

196 Zhu FG, Deng XJ, Cheng NJ. Intramucosal cysts in gastric mucosa adjacent to carcinoma and peptic ulcer. A histochemical study. Histopathology 1987, **11**: 631–638.

Polyps

197 Abraham SC, Montgomery EA, Singh VK, Yardley JH, Wu TT. Gastric adenomas: intestinal-type and gastric-type adenomas differ in the risk of adenocarcinoma and presence of background mucosal pathology. Am J Surg Pathol 2002, **26**: 1276–1285.

198 Abraham SC, Nobukawa B, Giardiello FM, Hamilton SR, Wu TT. Sporadic fundic gland polyps arising through activating mutations in the beta-catenin gene. Am J Pathol 2001, **158**: 1005–1010.

198a Abraham SC, Park SJ, Lee H, Mugartegui L, Wu T-T. Genetic alterations in gastric adenomas of intestinal and faveolar phenotypes. Mod Pathol 2003, **16**: 786–795.

199 Abraham SC, Park SJ, Mugartegui L, Hamilton SR, Wu TT. Sporadic fundic gland polyps with epithelial dysplasia: evidence for preferential targeting for mutations in the adenomatous polyposis coli gene. Am J Pathol 2002, **161**: 1735–1742.

200 Abraham SC, Singh VK, Yardley JH, Wu TT. Hyperplastic polyps of the stomach: associations with histologic patterns of gastritis and gastric atrophy. Am J Surg Pathol 2001, **25**: 500–507.

201 Choudhry U, Boyce HW Jr, Coppola D. Proton pump inhibitor-associated gastric polyps. A retrospective analysis of their frequency, and endoscopic, histologic, and ultrastructural characteristics. Am J Clin Pathol 1998, **110**: 615–621.

202 Church JM, McGannon E, Hull-Boiner S, Sivak MV, Van Stolk R, Jagelman DG, Fazio VW, Oakley JR, Lavery IC, Milsom JW. Gastroduodenal polyps in patients with familial adenomatous polyposis. Dis Colon Rectum 1992, **35**: 1170–1173.

203 Cristallini EG, Ascani S, Bolis GB. Association between histologic type of polyp and carcinoma in the stomach. Gastrointest Endosc 1992, **38**: 481–484.

204 Dirschmid K, Walser J, Hügel H. Pseudomalignant erosion in hyperplastic gastric polyps. Cancer 1984, **54**: 2290–2293.

205 Elster K. Histologic classification of gastric polyps. Curr Top Pathol 1976, **63**: 77–93.

206 Griffel B, Engleberg M, Reiss R, Saba H. Multiple polypoid cystic gastritis in old gastroenteric stoma. Arch Pathol 1974, **97**: 316–318.

207 Halbert RE. Peutz-Jeghers syndrome with metastasizing gastric adenocarcinoma. Report of a case. Arch Pathol Lab Med 1982, **106**: 517–520.

208 Harned RK, Buck JL, Shekitka KM. Inflammatory fibroid polyps of the gastrointestinal tract. Radiologic evaluation. Radiology 1992, **183**: 863–866.

209 Haruma K, Sumii K, Yoshihara M, Watanabe C, Kajiyama G. Gastric mucosa in female patients with fundic glandular polyps. J Clin Gastroenterol 1991, **13**: 565–569.

210 Haruma K, Yoshihara M, Sumii K, Tari A, Watanabe C, Kodoi A, Kajiyama G. Gastric acid secretion, serum pepsinogen I, and serum gastrin in Japanese with gastric hyperplastic polyps or polypoid-type early gastric carcinoma. Scand J Gastroenterol 1993, **28**: 633–637.

211 Hasegawa T, Yang P, Kagawa N, Hirose T, Sano T. CD34 expression by inflammatory fibroid polyps of the stomach. Mod Pathol 1997, **10**: 451–456.

212 Hattori T. Morphological range of hyperplastic polyps and carcinomas arising in hyperplastic polyps of the stomach. J Clin Pathol 1985, **38**: 622–630.

213 Helwig EB, Ranier A. Inflammatory fibroid polyps of the stomach. Surg Gynecol Obstet 1953, **96**: 355–367.

214 Hizawa K, Iida M, Matsumoto T, Aoyagi K, Yao T, Fujishima M. Natural history of fundic gland polyposis without familial adenomatosis coli. Follow-up observations in 31 patients. Radiology 1993, **189**: 429–432.

215 Hizawa K, Iida M, Matsumoto T, Kohrogi N, Yao T, Fujishima M. Neoplastic transformation arising in Peutz-Jeghers polyposis. Dis Colon Rectum 1993, **36**: 953–957.

216 Iida M, Yao T, Itoh H, Watanabe H, Matsui T, Iwashita A, Fujishima M. Natural history of gastric adenomas in patients with familial adenomatosis coli/Gardner's syndrome. Cancer 1988, **61**: 605–611.

217 Ito H, Hata J, Yokozaki H, Nakatani H, Oda N, Tahara E. Tubular adenoma of the human stomach. An immunohistochemical analysis of gut hormones, serotonin, carcinoembryonic antigen, secretory component, and lysozyme. Cancer 1986, **58**: 2264–2272.

218 Ito H, Yasui W, Yoshida K, Nakayama H, Tahara E. Depressed tubular adenoma of the stomach. Pathological and immunohistochemical features. Histopathology 1990, **17**: 419–426.

219 Ito H, Yokozaki H, Ito M, Tahara E. Papillary adenoma of the stomach. Arch Pathol Lab Med 1989, **113**: 1030–1034.

220 Johnstone JM, Morson BC. Inflammatory fibroid polyp of the gastrointestinal tract. Histopathology 1978, **2**: 349–361.

221 Kamiya T, Morishita T, Asakura H, Miura S, Munakata Y, Tsuchiya M. Longterm follow-up study of gastric adenoma and its relation to gastric protruded carcinoma. Cancer 1982, **50**: 2496–2503.

222 Kim HS, Woo DK, Bae SI, Kim Y, Kim WH. Microsatellite instability in the adenoma-carcinoma sequence of the stomach. Lab Invest 2000, **80**: 57–64.

223 Kim MK, Higgins J, Cho EY, Ko YH, Oh YL. Expression of CD34, bcl-2, and Kit in inflammatory fibroid polyps of the gastrointestinal tract. Appl Immunohistochem Mol Morphol 2000, **8**: 147–153.

224 Kinoshita Y, Tojo M, Yano T, Kitajima N, Itoh T, Nishiyama K, Inatome T, Fukuzaki H, Watanabe M, Chiba T. Incidence of fundic gland polyps in patients without familial adenomatous polyposis. Gastrointest Endosc 1993, **39**: 161–163.

225 Kolodziejczyk P, Yao T, Tsuneyoshi M. Inflammatory fibroid polyp of the stomach. A special reference to an immunohistochemical profile of 42 cases. Am J Surg Pathol 1993, **17**: 1159–1168.

226 Lauwers GY, Wahl SJ, Melamed J, Rojas-Corona RR. p53 expression in pre-cancerous gastric lesions. An immunohistochemical study of PAb 1801 monoclonal antibody on adenomatous and hyperplastic gastric polyps. Am J Gastroenterol 1993, **88**: 1916–1919.

227 Laxén F, Sipponen P, Ihamäki T, Hakkiluoto A, Dortscheva A. Gastric polyps. Their morphological and endoscopical characteristics and relation to gastric carcinoma. Acta Pathol Microbiol Immunol Scand A 1982, **90**: 221–228.

228 Lee RG, Burt RW. The histopathology of fundic gland polyps of the stomach. Am J Clin Pathol 1986, **86**: 498–503.

229 Lee J-H, Abraham SC, Kim H-S, Nam J-H, Choi C, Lee M-C, Park C-S, Juhng S-W, Rashid A, Hamilton SR, Wu T-T. Inverse relationship between APC gene mutation gastric adenomas and development of adenocarcinoma. Am J Pathol 2002, **161**: 611–618.

230 Lipper S, Kahn LB. Superficial cystic gastritis with alopecia. A forme fruste of the Cronkhite-Canada syndrome. Arch Pathol Lab Med 1977, **101**: 432–436.

231 Lynch HT, Smyrk TC, Lanspa SJ, Jenkins JX, Lynch PM, Cavalieri J, Lynch JF. Upper gastrointestinal manifestations in families with hereditary flat adenoma syndrome. Cancer 1993, **71**: 2709–2714.

232 Marcial MA, Villafana M, Hernandez-Denton J, Colon-Pagan JR. Fundic gland polyps: prevalence and clinicopathologic features. Am J Gastroenterol 1993, **88**: 1711–1713.

233 Menétrier P. Des polyadenomes gastriques et de leures rapports avec le cancer de l'estomac. Arch Physiol Norm Pathol 1888, **1**: 32–55, 236–262, Pl. III.

234 Miller JH, Gisvold JJ, Weiland LH, Mellrath DC. Upper gastrointestinal tract villous tumors. AJR 1980, **134**: 933–936.

235 Ming SC, Goldman H. Gastric polyps. Histogenetic classification and its relation to carcinoma. Cancer 1965, **18**: 721–726.

236 Monaco AP, Roth SI, Castleman B, Welch CE. Adenomatous polyps of the stomach. A clinical and pathological study of one hundred and fifty-three cases. Cancer 1962, **15**: 456–467.

237 Murakami K, Mitomi H, Yamashita K, Tanabe S, Saigenji K, Okayasu I. P53, but not c-Ki-ras, mutation and down-regulation of p21WAF1/CIP1 and cyclin D1 are associated with malignant transformation in gastric hyperplastic polyps. Am J Clin Pathol 2001, **115**: 224–234.

238 Nakamura T, Nakano G-I. Histopathological classification and malignant change in gastric polyps. J Clin Pathol 1985, **38**: 754–764.

239 Navas-Palacios JJ, Colina-Ruizdelgado F, Sanchez-Larrea MD, Cortes-Cansino J. Inflammatory fibroid polyps of the gastrointestinal tract. An immunohistochemical and electron microscopic study. Cancer 1983, **51**: 1682–1690.

240 Nogueira AM, Carneiro F, Seruca R, Cirnes L, Viega I, Machado JC, Sobrinho-Simoes M. Microsatellite instability in hyperplastic and adenomatous polyps of the stomach. Cancer 1999, **86**: 1649–1656.

241 Oberhuber G, Stolte M. Gastric polyps: an update of their pathology and biological significance. Virchows Arch 2000, **437**: 581–590.

242 Odze RD, Marcial MA, Antonioli D. Gastric fundic gland polyps: a morphological study including mucin histochemistry, stereometry, and MIB-1 immunohistochemistry. Hum Pathol 1996, **27**: 896–903.

243 Rubio CA. Paneth cell adenoma of the stomach. Am J Surg Pathol 1989, **13**: 325–328.

244 Sassatelli R, Bertoni G, Serra L, Bedogni G, Ponz de Leon M. Generalized juvenile polyposis with mixed pattern and gastric cancer. Gastroenterology 1993, **104**: 910–915.

245 Seifert E, Gail K, Weismuller J. Gastric polypectomy. Long term results (survey of 23 centres in Germany). Endoscopy 1983, **15**: 8–11.

246 Shekitka KM, Helwig EB. Deceptive bizarre stromal cells in polyps and ulcers of the gastrointestinal tract. Cancer 1991, **67**: 2111–2117.

247 Sipponen P, Laxén F, Seppälä K. Cystic "hamartomatous" gastric polyps. A disorder of oxyntic glands. Histopathology 1983, **7**: 729–737.

248 Snover DC. Benign epithelial polyps of the stomach. Pathol Annu 1985, **20**(Pt 1): 303–329.

249 Stemmermann GN, Hayashi T. Hyperplastic polyps of the gastric mucosa adjacent of gastroenterostomy stomas. Am J Clin Pathol 1979, **71**: 341–345.

250 Tada S, Iida M, Yao T, Matsui T, Kuwano Y, Hasuda S, Fujishima M. Endoscopic removal of inflammatory fibroid polyps of the stomach. Am J Gastroenterol 1991, **86**: 1247–1250.

251 Tomasulo J. Gastric polyps. Histologic types and their relationship to gastric carcinoma. Cancer 1971, **27**: 1346–1355.

252 Torbenson M, Lee J-H, Cruz-Correa M, Ravich W, Rastgar K, Abraham SC, Wu TT. Sporadic fundic gland polyposis: a clinical, histological, and molecular analysis. Mod Pathol 2002, **15**: 718–723.

253 Trillo AA, Rowden G. The histogenesis of inflammatory fibroid polyps of the gastrointestinal tract. Histopathology 1991, **19**: 431–436.

254 Tsuchikame N, Ishimaru Y, Ohshima S, Takahashi M. Three familial cases of fundic gland polyposis without polyposis coli. Virchows Arch [A] 1993, **422**: 337–340.

255 Utsunomiya J, Maki T, Iwama T, Hamaguchi E, Aoki M. Gastric lesion of familial polyposis coli. Cancer 1974, **34**: 745–754.

256 van de Rijn M, Hendrickson MR, Rouse RV. An immunohistochemical study of inflammatory fibroid polyps of the gastrointestinal tract. Appl Immunohistochem 1994, **211**: 54–59.

256a Vieth M, Kushima R, Borchard F, Stolte M. Pyloric gland adenoma: a clinico-pathological analysis of 90 cases. Virchows Arch 2003, **442**: 317–321.

257 Watanabe H, Enjoji M, Yao T, Ohsato K. Gastric lesions in familial adenomatosis coli. Their incidence and histologic analysis. Hum Pathol 1978, **9**: 269–283.

258 Wee A, Teh M, Raju GC. Expression of HLA-DR antigen in different histological types of gastric polyp. J Clin Pathol 1992, **45**: 509–512.

259 Wille P, Borchard F. Fibroid polyps of intestinal tract are inflammatory-reactive proliferations of CD34-positive perivascular cells. Histopathology 1998, **32**: 498–502.

260 Wu TT, Kornacki S, Rashid A, Yardley JH, Hamilton SR. Dysplasia and dysregulation of proliferation of foveolar and surface epithelia of fundic gland polyps from patients with familial adenomatous polyposis. Am J Surg Pathol 1998, **22**: 293–298.

261 Xuan ZX, Ambe K, Enjoji M. Depressed adenoma of the stomach, revisited. Histologic, histochemical, and immunohistochemical profiles. Cancer 1991, **67**: 2382–2389.

262 Yao T, Kajiwara M, Kuroiwa S, Iwashita A, Oya M, Kabashima A, Tsuneyoshi M. Malignant transformation of gastric hyperplastic polyps: alteration of phenotypes, proliferative activity, and p53 expression. Hum Pathol 2002, **33**: 1016–1022.

Menétrier's disease and Zollinger–Ellison syndrome

263 Aprile MR, Azzoni C, Gibril F, Jensen RT, Bordi C. Intramucosal cysts in gastric body of patients with Zollinger-Ellison syndrome. Hum Pathol 2000, **31**: 140–148.

264 Delle Fave G, Marignani M, Corleto VD, Angeletti S, D'Ambra G, Ferraro G, D'Adda T, Azzoni C, Jensen RT, Annibale B, Bordi C. Progression of gastric enterochromaffin-like cells growth in Zollinger-Ellison syndrome and atrophic body gastritis patients. Dig Liver Dis 2002, **34**: 270–278.

265 Haot J, Bogomoletz WV, Jouret A, Mainguet P. Menétrier's disease with lymphocytic gastritis: an unusual association with possible pathogenic implications. Hum Pathol 1991, **22**: 379–386.

266 Hsu CT, Ito M, Kawase Y, Sekine I, Ohmagari T, Hashimoto S. Early gastric cancer arising from localized Menétrier's disease. Gastroenterol Jpn 1991, **26**: 213–217.

267 Komorowski RA, Caya JG. Hyperplastic gastropathy. Clinicopathologic correlation. Am J Surg Pathol 1991, **15**: 577–585.

268 Kraut JR, Powell R, Hruby MA, Lloyd-Still JD. Menétrier's disease in childhood. Report of two cases and a review of the literature. J Pediatr Surg 1981, **16**: 707–711.

269 Menétrier P. Des polyadenomes gastriques et de leures rapports avec le cancer de l'estomac. Arch Physiol Norm Pathol 1888, **1**: 32–55, 236–262, Pl III.

270 Palmer ED. What Menétrier really said. Gastrointest Endosc 1968, **15**: 83–90.

271 Scharschmidt BF. The natural history of hypertropic gastropathy (Menétrier's disease). Report of a case with 16 year follow-up and review of 120 cases from the literature. Am J Med 1977, **63**: 644–652.

272 Solcia E, Capella C, Buffa R, et al. Pathology of the Zollinger-Ellison syndrome. In Fenoglio CM, Wolff M (eds): Progress in surgical pathology, vol. 1. New York, 1980, Masson, pp. 119–134.

273 Stamm B. Localized hyperplastic gastropathy of the mucous cell- and mixed cell-type (localized Menétrier's Disease): a report of 11 patients. Am J Surg Pathol 1997, **21**: 1334–1342.

274 Stamm B, Saremaslani P. Coincidence of fundic glandular hyperplasia and carcinoma of the stomach. Cancer 1989, **63**: 354–359.

275 Wolfsen HC, Carpenter HA, Talley NJ. Menétrier's disease. A form of hypertrophic gastropathy or gastritis? Gastroenterology 1993, **104**: 1310–1319.

Dysplasia

276 Brien TP, Farraye FA, Odze RD. Gastric dysplasia-like epithelial atypia associated with chemoradiotherapy for esophageal cancer: a clinicopathologic and immunohistochemical study of 15 cases. Mod Pathol 2001, **14:** 389–396.

277 Burke AP, Sobin LH, Shekitka KM, Avallone FA. Correlation of nucleolar organizer regions and glandular dysplasia of the stomach and esophagus. Mod Pathol 1990, **3:** 357–360.

278 Burke AP, Sobin LH, Shekitka KM, Helwig EB. Dysplasia of the stomach and Barrett esophagus. A follow-up study. Mod Pathol 1991, **4:** 336–341.

279 Di Gregorio C, Morandi P, Fante R, De Gaetani C. Gastric dysplasia. A follow-up study. Am J Gastroenterol 1993, **88:** 1714–1719.

280 Farinati F, Rugge M, DiMario F, Valiante F, Baffa R. Early and advanced gastric cancer in the follow-up of moderate and severe gastric dysplasia patients. A prospective study. Endoscopy 1993, **25:** 261–264.

281 Fertitta AM, Comin U, Terruzzi V, Minoli G, Zambelli A, Cannatelli G, Bodini P, Bertoli G, Negri R, Brunati S. Clinical significance of gastric dysplasia. A multicenter follow-up study. Gastrointestinal Endoscopic Pathology Study. Endoscopy 1993, **25:** 265–268.

282 Filipe MI, Mendes R, Lane DP, Morris RW. Assessment of proliferating cell nuclear antigen expression in precursor stages of gastric carcinoma using the PC10 antibody to PCNA. Histopathology 1993, **22:** 349–354.

282a Garay J, Bravo JC, Correa P, Schneider BG. Infrequency of microsatellite instability in complete and incomplete gastric intestinal metaplasia. Hum Pathol 2004 (in press).

283 Goldstein NS, Lewin KJ. Gastric epithelial dysplasia and adenoma: historical review and histological criteria for grading. Hum Pathol 1997, **28:** 127–133.

284 Grundmann E. Classification and clinical consequences of precancerous lesions in the digestive and respiratory tracts. Acta Pathol Jpn 1983, **33:** 195–217.

285 Jarvis LR, Whitehead R. Morphometric analysis of gastric dysplasia. J Pathol 1985, **147:** 133–138.

286 Jass JR. A classification of gastric dysplasia. Histopathology 1983, **7:** 181–193.

287 Ming S-C, Bajtai A, Correa P, Elster K, Jarvi OH, Munoz N, Nagayo T, Stemmerman GN. Gastric dysplasia. Significance and pathologic criteria. Cancer 1984, **54:** 1794–1801.

288 Misdraji J, Lauwers GY. Gastric epithelial dysplasia. Semin Diagn Pathol 2002, **19:** 20–30.

289 Morson BC, Sobin LH, Grundmann E, Johansen A, Nagoya T, Serck-Hanssen A. Precancerous conditions and epithelial dysplasia in the stomach. J Clin Pathol 1980, **33:** 711–721.

290 Riddell RH, Iwafuchi M. Problems arising from Eastern and Western classification systems for gastrointestinal dysplasia and carcinoma: are they resolvable? Histopathology 1998, **33:** 197–202.

291 Rubio CA, Hirota T, Itabashi T. Atypical mitoses in elevated dysplasias of the stomach. Pathol Res Pract 1985, **180:** 372–376.

292 Rugge M, Correa P, Dixon MF, Hattori T, Leandro G, Lewin K, Riddell RH, Sipponen P, Watanabe H. Gastric dysplasia: the Padova International Classification. Am J Surg Pathol 2000, **24:** 167–176.

293 Rugge M, Farinati F, DiMario F, Baffa R, Valiante F, Cardin F. Gastric epithelial dysplasia. A prospective multicenter follow-up study from the Interdisciplinary Group on Gastric Epithelial Dysplasia. Hum Pathol 1991, **22:** 1002–1008.

294 Rugge M, Shiao YH, Correa P, Baffa R, DiMario F. Immunohistochemical evidence of p53 overexpression in gastric epithelial dysplasia. Cancer Epidemiol Biomarkers Prev 1992, **1:** 551–554.

295 Saraga E-P, Gardiol D, Costa J. Gastric dysplasia. A histological follow-up study. Am J Surg Pathol 1987, **11:** 788–796.

296 Schlemper RJ, Riddell RH, Kato Y, Borchard F, Cooper HS, Dawse SM, Dixon MF, Fenoglio-Preiser CM, Flejou JF, Geboes K, Hattori T, Hirota T, Itabashi M, Iwafuchi M, Iwashita A, Kim YI, Kirchner T, Klimpfinger M, Koike M, Lauwers GY, Lewin KJ, Oberhuber G, Offner F, Price AB, Rubio CA, Shimizu M, Shimoda T, Sipponen P, Solcia E, Stolte M, Watanabe H, Yamabe H. The Vienna classification of gastrointestinal epithelial neoplasia. Gut 2000, **47:** 251–255.

297 Tosi P, Baak J, Luzi P, Miracco C, Lio R, Barbini P. Morphometric distinction of low- and high-grade dysplasias in gastric biopsies. Hum Pathol 1989, **20:** 839–844.

298 Zukerberg L. The molecular basis of dysplasia. Semin Diagn Pathol 2002, **19:** 48–53.

Carcinoma

General features

299 Antonioli DA. Precursors of gastric carcinoma. A critical review with a brief description of early (curable) gastric cancer. Hum Pathol 1994, **25:** 994–1005.

300 Bronner MP. Gastric cancer and intestinal metaplasia. Hum Pathol 1999, **30:** 733.

301 Brumback RA, Gerber JE, Hicks DG, Strauchen JA. Adenocarcinoma of the stomach following irradiation and chemotherapy of lymphoma in young patients. Cancer 1984, **54:** 994–998.

302 Chapel F, Fabiani B, Davi F, Raphael M, Tepper M, Champault G, Guettier C. Epstein-Barr virus and gastric carcinoma in Western patients: comparison of pathological parameters and p53 expression in EBV-positive and negative tumours. Histopathology 2000, **36:** 252–261.

303 Correa P. Clinical implications of recent developments in gastric carcinoma pathology and epidemiology. Semin Oncol 1985, **12:** 2–10.

304 Correa P. Human gastric carcinogenesis. A multistep and multifactorial process. First American Cancer Society Award Lecture on Cancer Epidemiology and Prevention. Cancer Res 1992, **15:** 6735–6740.

305 Correa P. The epidemiology of gastric cancer. World J Surg 1991, **15:** 228–234.

306 Correa P. *Helicobacter pylori* and gastric carcinogenesis. Am J Surg Pathol 1995, **19:** S37–S43.

307 Devesa SS, Blot WJ, Fraumeni JF Jr. Changing patterns in the incidence of esophageal and gastric carcinoma in the United States. Cancer 1998, **83:** 2049–2053.

308 Dupont JB Jr, Lee JR, Burton GR, Cohn I Jr. Adenocarcinoma of the stomach. Review of 1,497 cases. Cancer 1978, **41:** 941–947.

309 Fuchs CS, Mayer RJ. Gastric carcinoma. N Engl J Med 1995, **333:** 32–41.

310 Grabiec J, Owen DA. Carcinoma of the stomach in young persons. Cancer 1985, **56:** 388–396.

311 Gulley ML, Pulitzer DR, Eagan PA, Schneider BG. Epstein-Barr virus infection is an early event in gastric carcinogenesis and is independent of bcl-2 expression and p53 accumulation. Hum Pathol 1996, **27:** 20–27.

312 Hall CN, Darkin D, Brimblecombe R, Cook AJ, Kirkham JS, Northfield TC. Evaluation of the nitrosamine hypothesis of gastric carcinogenesis in precancerous conditions. Gut 1986, **27:** 491–498.

313 Hattori T. Development of adenocarcinomas in the stomach. Cancer 1986, **57:** 1528–1534.

314 Herrera-Goepfert R, Reyes E, Hernandez-Avila M, Mohar A, Shinkura R, Fujiyama C, Akiba S, Eizuru Y, Harada Y, Tokunaga M. Epstein-Barr virus-associated gastric carcinoma in Mexico: analysis of 135 consecutive gastrectomies in two hospitals. Mod Pathol 1999, **12:** 873–878.

315 Hill MJ. Etiology of gastric carcinoma. Clin Oncol 1984, **3:** 237–249.

316 Iwanaga T, Koyama H, Takahashi Y, Taniguchi H, Wada A. Diffuse submucosal cysts and carcinoma of the stomach. Cancer 1975, **36**: 606–614.

317 Keller G. Hereditary aspects of gastric cancer. Pathologica 2002, **94**: 229–233.

318 Koshida Y, Koizumi W, Sasabe M, Katoh Y, Okayasu I. Association of Helicobacter pylori-dependent gastritis with gastric carcinomas in young Japanese patients: histopathological comparison of diffuse and intestinal type cancer cases. Histopathology 2000, **37**: 124–130.

319 Lauren P. The two histological main types of gastric carcinoma. Diffuse and so-called intestinal type carcinoma. Acta Pathol Microbiol Scand 1965, **64**: 31–49.

320 Lauren PA, Nevalainen TJ. Epidemiology of intestinal and diffuse types of gastric carcinoma. A time-trend study in Finland with comparison between studies from high- and low-risk areas. Cancer 1993, **71**: 2926–2933.

321 Leoncini L, Vindigni C, Megha T, Funto I, Pacenti L, Musaro M, Renieri A, Seri M, Anagnostopoulos J, Tosi P. Epstein-Barr virus and gastric cancer. Data and unanswered questions. Int J Cancer 1993, **53**: 898–901.

322 Loffeld RJLF, Willems I, Flendrig JA, Arends JW. *Helicobacter pylori* and gastric carcinoma. Histopathology 1990, **17**: 537–541.

323 Murayama Y, Kikuchi M, Enjoji M, Morita N, Haraguchi Y. Changes in gastric mucosa that antedate gastric carcinoma. Cancer 1990, **66**: 2017–2026.

324 Neugut AI, Hayek M, Howe G. Epidemiology of gastric cancer. Semin Oncol 1996, **23**: 281–291.

325 Noguchi Y, Yoshikawa T, Tsuburaya A, Motohashi H, Karpeh MS, Brennan MF. Is gastric carcinoma different between Japan and the United States? Cancer 2000, **89**: 2237–2246.

326 Pillay I, Petrelli M. Diffuse cystic glandular malformation of the stomach associated with adenocarcinoma. Case report and review of the literature. Cancer 1976, **38**: 915–920.

327 Schafer LW, Larson DE, Melton LJ III, Higgins JA, Zinsmeister AR. Risk of development of gastric carcinoma in patients with pernicious anemia. A population-based study in Rochester, Minnesota. Mayo Clin Proc 1985, **60**: 444–448.

328 Shibata D, Weiss LM. Epstein-Barr virus-associated gastric adenocarcinoma. Am J Pathol 1992, **140**: 769–774.

329 Siegel SM, Hays DM, Romansky S, Issacs H. Carcinoma of the stomach in childhood. Cancer 1976, **38**: 1781–1784.

330 Sipponen P, Kekki M, Haapakoski J, Ihamäki T, Siurala M. Gastric cancer risk in chronic atrophic gastritis. Statistical calcualtions of cross-sectional data. Int J Cancer 1985, **35**: 173–177.

331 Sipponen P, Kekki M, Siurala M. Atrophic chronic gastritis and intestinal metaplasia in gastric carcinoma. Comparison with a representative population sample. Cancer 1983, **52**: 1062–1068.

332 Solcia E, Fiocca R, Luinetti O, Villani L, Padovan L, Calistri D, Ranzani GN, Chiaravalli A, Capella C. Intestinal and diffuse gastric cancers arise in a different background of Helicobacter pylori gastritis through different gene involvement. Am J Surg Pathol 1996, **20**: S8–S22.

333 Souquet JC, Berger F, Bonvoisin S, Partensky C, Boulez J, Descos F, Lambert R. Esophageal squamous cell carcinoma associated with gastric adenocarcinoma. Cancer 1989, **63**: 786–790.

334 Stemmermann GN, Nomura AM, Kolonel LN, Goodman MT, Wilkens LR. Gastric carcinoma: pathology findings in a multiethnic population. Cancer 2002, **95**: 744–750.

335 Takano Y, Kato Y, Saegusa M, Mori S, Shiota M, Masuda M, Mikami T, Okayasu I. The role of the Epstein-Barr virus in the oncogenesis of EBV(+) gastric carcinomas. Virchows Arch 1999, **434**: 17–22.

336 Taki K, Kuwabara N. Studies of histogenesis of the gastric carcinoma using minute cancers. Pathol Res Pract 1981, **172**: 176–190.

337 Theuer CP, Kurosaki T, Taylor TH, Anton-Culver H. Unique features of gastric carcinomas in the young: a population-based analysis. Cancer 1998, **83**: 25–33.

338 Tokunaga M, Land CE, Uemura Y, Tokudome T, Tanaka S, Sato E. Epstein Barr virus in gastric carcinoma. Am J Pathol 1993, **143**: 1250–1254.

339 Tso PL, Bringaze WL III, Dauterive AH, Correa P, Cohn I Jr. Gastric carcinoma in the young. Cancer 1987, **59**: 1362–1365.

340 Uemura N, Okamoto S, Yamamoto S, Matsumura N, Yamaguchi S, Yamakido M, Taniyama K, Sasaki N, Schlemper RJ. Helicobacter pylori infection and the development of gastric cancer. N Engl J Med 2001, **345**: 784–839.

341 Whitehead R, Skinner JM, Heenan PJ. Incidence of carcinoma of stomach and tumour type. Br J Cancer 1974, **30**: 370–372.

Morphologic features and classification

342 Antonioli DA, Goldman H. Changes in the location and type of gastric adenocarcinoma. Cancer 1982, **50**: 775–781.

343 Borrman R. Geschwülste des Magens und Duodenums. In Henske F, Lubarsch O (eds): Handbuch der Speziellen Pathologischen Antomie und Histologie. Berlin, 1926, Julius Springer.

344 Brien TP, Farraye FA, Odze RD. Gastric dysplasia-like epithelial atypia associated with chemoradiotherapy for esophageal cancer: a clinicopathologic and immunohistochemical study of 15 cases. Mod Pathol 2001, **14**: 389–396.

345 Chan WY, Hui PK, Leung KM, Robertson CS, Chung SC. Gastric adenocarcinoma with ciliated tumor cells. Hum Pathol 1993, **24**: 1107–1113.

346 Correa P. Pathology of gastric cancer. Clin Oncol 1984, **3**: 251–257.

347 Endoh Y, Tamura G, Motoyama T, Ajioka Y, Watanabe H. Well-differentiated adenocarcinoma mimicking complete-type intestinal metaplasia in the stomach. Hum Pathol 1999, **30**: 826–832.

348 Esaki Y, Hirokawa K, Yamashiro M. Multiple gastric cancers in the aged with special reference to intramucosal cancers. Cancer 1987, **59**: 560–565.

349 Fenoglio-Preiser CM, Noffsinger AE, Belli J, Stemmermann GM. Pathologic and phenotypic features of gastric cancer. Semin Oncol 1996, **23**: 292–306.

350 Fiocca R, Villani L, Tenti P, Solcia E, Cornaggia M, Frigerio B, Capella C. Characterization of four main cell types in gastric cancer. Foveolar, mucopeptic, intestinal columnar and goblet cells. An histopathologic, histochemical and ultrastructural study of "early" and "advanced" tumours. Pathol Res Pract 1987, **182**: 308–325.

351 Grabiec J, Owen DA. Carcinoma of the stomach in young persons. Cancer 1985, **56**: 388–396.

352 Heitz PU, Wegmann W. Identification of neoplastic Paneth cells in an adenocarcinoma of the stomach using lysozyme as a marker and electron microscopy. Virchows Arch [A] 1980, **386**: 107–116.

353 Hewan-Lowe K, Hammers Y, Lyons JM, Wilcox CM. Polyvinylpyrrolidone storage disease: a source of error in the diagnosis of signet ring cell gastric adenocarcinoma. Ultrastruct Pathol 1994, **18**: 271–278.

354 Ikeda Y, Mori M, Kamakura T, Haraguchi Y, Saku M, Sugimachi K. Increased incidence of undifferentiated type of gastric cancer with tumor progression in 912 patients with early gastric cancer and 1245 with advanced gastric cancer. Cancer 1994, **73**: 2459–2463.

355 Isaacson P. Biopsy appearances easily mistaken for malignancy in gastrointestinal endoscopy. Histopathology 1982, **6**: 377–389.

356 Kaibara N, Kimura O, Nishidoi H, Makino M, Kawasumi H, Koga S. High incidence of liver metastasis in gastric cancer with medullary growth pattern. J Surg Oncol 1985, **28**: 195–198.

357 Kazzaz BA, Eulderink F. Paneth cell-rich carcinoma of the stomach. Histopathology 1989, **15**: 303–311.

358 Kosaka T, Miwa K, Yonemura Y, Urade M, Ishida T, Takegawa S, Kamata T, Ooyama S, Maeda K, Sugiyama K, Fujimura T, Hasegawa H, Yamaguchi A, Miyazaki I. A clinicopathologic study on multiple gastric cancers with special reference to distal gastrectomy. Cancer 1990, **65**: 2602–2605.

359 Lauren P. The two histological main types of gastric carcinoma. Diffuse and so-called intestinal type carcinoma. Acta Pathol Microbiol Scand 1965, **64**: 31–49.

360 Lee EY, Wang TC, Clouse RE, DeSchryver-Kecskemeti K. Mucosal thickening adjacent to gastric malignancy. Association with epidermal growth factor. Mod Pathol 1989, **2**: 397.

361 Maehara Y, Sakaguchi Y, Moriguchi S, Orita H, Korenaga D, Kohnoe S, Sugimachi K. Signet ring cell carcinoma of the stomach. Cancer 1992, **69**: 1645–1650.

362 Ming SC. Gastric carcinoma. A pathobiological classification. Cancer 1977, **39**: 2475–2485.

363 Ming SC, Goldman H, Freiman DG. Intestinal metaplasia and histogenesis of carcinoma in human stomachs. Light and electron microscopic study. Cancer 1967, **20**: 1418–1429.

364 Murayama H, Imai T, Kikuchi J. Solid carcinomas of the stomach. A combined histochemical, light and electron microscopy study. Cancer 1983, **51**: 1673–1681.

365 Ooi A, Nakanishi I, Itoh T, Ueda H, Mai M. Predominant Paneth cell differentiation in an intestinal type gastric cancer. Pathol Res Pract 1991, **187**: 220–225.

366 Petras RE, Hart WR, Bukowski RM. Gastric epithelial atypia associated with hepatic arterial infusion chemotherapy. Its distinction from early gastric carcinoma. Cancer 1985, **56**: 745–750.

367 Rice AJ, Griffiths AP, Martin IG, Dixon MF. Gastric carcinoma with prominent neutrophil infiltration. Histopathology 2000, **37**: 289–290.

368 Stout AP. Tumors of the stomach. In Atlas of tumor pathology, section VI, fascicle 21, Washington, D.C., 1953, Armed Forces Institute of Pathology.

369 Tso PL, Bringaze WL III, Dauterive AH, Correa P, Cohn I Jr. Gastric carcinoma in the young. Cancer 1987, **59**: 1362–1365.

370 World Health Organization. Classification of Tumors of the Digestive System. Hamilton S, Aaltouen R, (eds). Lyon, IARC Press, 2000, p. 38.

371 Yamada Y, Kato Y. Greater tendency for submucosal invasion in fundic area gastric carcinomas than those arising in the pyloric area. Cancer 1989, **63**: 1757–1760.

372 Yamagiwa H, Yoshimura H, Tomiyama H, Onishi T, Matsuzaki O. Clinicopathological study of gastric cancers in the greater curvature. Acta Pathol Jpn 1984, **34**: 519–527.

373 Yamashina M. A variant of early gastric carcinoma. Histologic and histochemical studies of early signet ring cell carcinomas discovered beneath preserved surface epithelium. Cancer 1986, **58**: 1333–1339.

Histochemical, immunohistochemical, and electron microscopic features

374 Bacchi CE, Gown AM. Distribution and pattern of expression of villin, a gastrointestinal-associated cytoskeletal protein, in human carcinomas. A study employing paraffin-embedded tissue. Lab Invest 1991, **64**: 418–424.

375 Capella C, Cornaggia M, Usellini L, Bordi C, Bondi A, Cook MG, Eusebi V. Neoplastic cells containing lysozyme in gastric carcinomas. Pathology 1984, **16**: 87–92.

376 Chaubert P, Bouzourene H, Saraga E. Estrogen and progesterone receptors and pS2 and ERD5 antigens in gastric carcinomas from the European population. Mod Pathol 1996, **9**: 189–193.

377 Cook HC. Neutral mucin content of gastric carcinomas as a diagnostic aid in the identification of secondary deposits. Histopathology 1982, **6**: 591–599.

378 David L, Nesland JM, Funderud S, Sobrinho-Simoes M. CDw75 antigen expression in human gastric carcinoma and adjacent mucosa. Cancer 1993, **72**: 1522–1527.

379 David L, Nesland JM, Holm R, Sobrinho-Simoes M. Expression of laminin, collagen IV, fibronectin, and type IV collagenase in gastric carcinoma. An immunohistochemical study of 87 patients. Cancer 1994, **73**: 518–527.

380 Fiocca R, Cornaggia M, Villani L, Capella C, Solcia E, Samloff IM. Expression of pepsinogen II in gastric cancer. Its relationship to local invasion and lymph node metastases. Cancer 1988, **61**: 956–962.

381 Fiocca R, Villani L, Tenti P, Cornaggia M, Finzi G, Riva C, Capella C, Bara J. Samloff IM, Solcia E. The foveolar cell component of gastric cancer. Hum Pathol 1990, **21**: 260–270.

382 Gurbuz Y, Kahlke V, Kloppel G. How do gastric carcinoma classification systems relate to mucin expression patterns? An immunohistochemical analysis in a series of advanced gastric carcinomas. Virchows Arch 2002, **440**: 505–511.

383 Higashiyama M, Monden T, Ogawa M, Matsuura N, Murotani M, Kawasaki Y, Tomita N, Murata A, Shimano T, Mori T. Immunohistochemical study on pancreatic secretory trypsin inhibitor (PSTI) in gastric carcinomas. Am J Clin Pathol 1990, **93**: 8–13.

384 Ito H, Tahara E. Human chorionic gonadotropin in human gastric carcinoma. A retrospective immunohistochemical study. Acta Pathol Jpn 1983, **33**: 287–296.

385 Kojima O, Takahashi T, Kawakami S, Uehara Y, Matsui M. Localization of estrogen receptors in gastric cancer using immunohistochemical staining of monoclonal antibody. Cancer 1991, **67**: 2401–2406.

386 Lee HS, Lee HK, Kim HS, Yang HK, Kim YI, Kim WH. MUC1, MUC2, MUC5AC, and MUC6 expressions in gastric carcinomas: their roles as prognostic indicators. Cancer 2001, **92**: 1427–1434.

387 Lev R. The mucin histochemistry of normal and neoplastic gastric mucosa. Lab Invest 1965, **14**: 2080–2100.

388 Levy R, Czernobilsky B, Geiger B. Cytokeratin polypeptide in gastrointestinal adenocarcinoma displaying squamous differentiation. Hum Pathol 1992, **23**: 695–702.

389 Louhimo J, Nordling S, Alfthan H, von Boguslawski K, Stenman UH, Haglund C. Specific staining of human chorionic gonadotropin beta in benign and malignant gastrointestinal tissues with monoclonal antibodies. Histopathology 2001, **38**: 418–424.

390 Ma J, De Boer WGRM, Nayman J. Intestinal mucinous substances in gastric intestinal metaplasia and carcinoma studied by immunofluorescence. Cancer 1982, **49**: 1664–1667.

391 Matsui S, Shiozaki H, Inoue M, Tamura S, Doki Y, Kadowski T, Iwazawa T, Shimaya K, Nagafuchi A, Tsukita S, Mori T. Immunohistochemical evaluation of alpha-catenin expression in human gastric cancer. Virchows Arch 1994, **424**: 375–381.

392 Matsuo K, Kobayashi I, Tsukuba T, Kiyoshima T, Ishibashi Y, Miyoshi A, Yamamoto K, Sakai H. Immunohistochemical localization of cathepsins D and E in human gastric cancer: a possible correlation with local invasive and metastatic activities of carcinoma cells. Hum Pathol 1996, **27**: 184–190.

393 Nielsen K, Teglbjaerg PS. Carcino-embryonic antigen (CEA) in gastric adenocarcinomas Morphologic patterns and their relationship to a histogenetic classification. Acta Pathol Microbiol Immunol Scand A 1982, **90**: 393–396.

394 Oka S, Ogino K, Houbara T, Yoshimura S, Okazaki Y, Takemoto T, Kato N, Iida Y, Uda T. An immunohistochemical study of copper, zinc-containing superoxide dismutase detected by a monoclonal antibody in gastric mucosa and gastric cancer. Histopathology 1990, **17**: 231–236.

395 Park SY, Kim HS, Hong EK, Kim WH. Expression of cytokeratins 7 and 20 in primary carcinomas of the stomach and colorectum and their value in the differential diagnosis of metastatic carcinomas to the ovary. Hum Pathol 2002, **33**: 1078–1085.

396 Pinto-De-Sousa J, David L, Reis CA, Gomes R, Silva L, Pimenta A. Mucins MUC1, MUC2, MUC5AC and MUC6 expression in the evaluation of differentiation and clinico-biological behaviour of gastric carcinoma. Virchows Arch 2002, **440**: 304–310.

397 Rosa J, Mehta A, Filipe MI. Nucleolar organizer regions in gastric carcinoma and its precursor stages. Histopathology 1990, **16**: 265–269.

398 Saitoh Y, Sasano H, Naganuma H, Ohtani H, Sasano N, Ohuchi A, Matsuno S. De novo expression of aromatase in gastric carcinoma. Light and electron microscopic immunohistochemical and immunoblot study. Pathol Res Pract 1992, **188**: 53–60.

399 Suarez V, Newman J, Hiley C, Crocker J, Collins M. The value of NOR numbers in neoplastic and non-neoplastic epithelium of the stomach. Histopathology 1989, **14**: 61–66.

400 Sugiyama K, Yonemura Y, Miyazaki I. Immunohistochemical study of epidermal growth factor and epidermal growth factor receptor in gastric carcinoma. Cancer 1989, **63**: 1557–1561.

401 Tahara E, Ito H, Shimamoto F, Iwamoto T, Nakagami K, Niimoto H. Lysozyme in human gastric carcinoma. A retrospective immunohistochemical study. Histopathology 1982, **6**: 409–421.

402 Tahara E, Ito H, Taniyama K, Yokozaki H, Hata J. Alpha 1-antitrypsin, alpha 1-antichymotrypsin, and alpha2-macroglobulin in human gastric carcinomas. A retrospective immunohistochemical study. Hum Pathol 1984, **15**: 957–964.

403 Takemura K, Hirokawa K, Esaki Y, Mishima Y. Distribution of immunoglobulins and secretory component in gastric cancer of the aged. Cancer 1990, **66**: 2168–2173.

404 Tatematsu M, Ichinose M, Miki K, Hasegawa R, Kato T, Ito N. Gastric and intestinal phenotypic expression of human stomach cancers as revealed by pepsinogen immunohistochemistry and mucin histochemistry. Acta Pathol Jpn 1990, **40**: 494–504.

405 Teh M, Lee YS. HLA-DR antigen expression in intestinal-type and diffuse-type gastric carcinoma. Cancer 1992, **69**: 1104–1107.

406 Tuccari G, Barresi G, Arena F, Inferrera C. Immunocytochemical detection of lactoferrin in human gastric carcinomas and adenomas. Arch Pathol Lab Med 1989, **113**: 912–915.

407 Utsunomiya T, Yao T, Masuda K, Tsuneyoshi M. Vimentin-positive adenocarcinomas of the stomach: co-expression of vimentin and cytokeratin. Histopathology 1996, **29**: 507–516.

408 Warner TF, Donnelly WJ, Hafez GR, Renwick B, Engstrand D, Barsness L. Immunocytochemical evidence of gastric proteases in adenocarcinoma of the stomach. Cancer 1986, **58**: 1328–1332.

409 Washington K, Gottfried MR, Telen MJ. Expression of the cell adhesion molecule CD44 in gastric adenocarcinomas. Hum Pathol 1994, **25**: 1043–1049.

410 Watanabe H, Tokuyama H, Ohta H, Satomura Y, Okai T, Ooi A, Mai M, Sawabu N. Expression of placental alkaline phosphatase in gastric and colorectal cancers. An immunohistochemical study using the prepared monoclonal antibody. Cancer 1990, **66**: 2575–2582.

411 Wu C-W, Chi C-W, Chang T-J, Lui W-Y, P'eng F-K. Sex hormone receptors in gastric cancer. Cancer 1990, **65**: 1396–1400.

412 Yakeishi I, Mori M, Enjoji M. Distribution of β-human chorionic gonadotropin-positive cells in noncancerous gastric mucosa and in malignant gastric tumors. Cancer 1990, **66**: 695–701.

413 Yamamura-Idei Y, Kitazawa S, Kitazawa R, Fujimori T, Chiba T, Maeda S. Parathyroid hormone-related protein in gastric cancers with heterotopic ossification. Cancer 1993, **72**: 1849–1852.

414 Yamashita Y, Chung YS, Horie R, Kannagi R, Sowa M. Alterations in gastric mucin with malignant transformation. Novel pathway for mucin synthesis. JNCI 1995, **87**: 441–446.

Molecular genetic features

415 Arber N, Gammon MD, Hibshoosh H, Britton JA, Zhang Y, Schonberg JB, Roterdam H, Fabian I, Holt PR, Weinstein IB. Overexpression of cyclin D1 occurs in both squamous carcinomas and adenocarcinomas of the esophagus and in adenocarcinomas of the stomach. Hum Pathol 1999, **30**: 1087–1092.

416 Ascano JJ, Frierson H Jr, Moskaluk CA, Harper JC, Roviello F, Jackson CE, El-Rifai W, Vindigni C, Tosi P, Powell S. Inactivation of the E-cadherin gene in sporadic diffuse-type gastric cancer. Mod Pathol 2001, **14**: 942–949.

417 Carneiro F, David L, Sunkel C, Lopes C, Sobrinho-Simoes M. Immunohistochemical analysis of ras oncogene p21 product in human gastric carcinomas and their adjacent mucosas. Pathol Res Pract 1992, **188**: 263–272.

418 Chang YT, Wu MS, Chang CJ, Huang PH, Hsu SM, Lin JT. Preferential loss of fhit expression in signet-ring cell and Krukenberg subtypes of gastric cancer. Lab Invest 2002, **82**: 1201–1208.

419 Chun YS, Lindor NM, Smyrk TC, Petersen BT, Burgart LJ, Guilford PJ, Donohue JH. Germline E-cadherin gene mutations: is prophylactic total gastrectomy indicated? Cancer 2001, **92**: 181–187.

420 David L, Seruca R, Nesland JM, Soares P, Sansonetty F, Holm R, Borresen AL, Sobrinho-Simoes M. C-erbB-2 expression in primary gastric carcinomas and their metastases. Mod Pathol 1992, **5**: 384–390.

421 Fukunaga M, Monden T, Nakanishi H, Ohue M, Fukuda K, Tomita N, Shimano T, Mori T. Immunohistochemical study of p53 in gastric carcinoma. Am J Clin Pathol 1994, **101**: 177–180.

422 Huntsman DG, Carneiro F, Lewis FR, MacLeod PM, Hayashi A, Monaghan KG, Maung R, Seruca R, Jackson CE, Caldas C. Early gastric cancer in young, asymptomatic carriers of germ-line E-cadherin mutations. N Engl J Med 2001, **344**: 1904–1909.

423 Hurlimann J, Saraga EP. Expression of p53 protein in gastric carcinomas. Association with histologic type and prognosis. Am J Surg Pathol 1994, **18**: 1247–1253.

424 Kang GH, Yoon GS, Lee HK, Kwon YM, Ro JY. Clinicopathologic characteristics of replication error-positive gastric carcinoma. Mod Pathol 1999, **12**: 15–20.

425 Krajewska M, Fenoglio-Preiser CM, Krajewski S, Song K, Macdonald JS, Stemmerman G, Reed JC. Immunohistochemical analysis of Bcl-2 family proteins in adenocarcinomas of the stomach. Am J Pathol 1996, **149**: 1449–1457.

426 Lauwers GY, Scott GV, Karpeh MS. Immunohistochemical evaluation of bcl-2 protein expression in gastric adenocarcinomas. Cancer 1995, **75**: 2209–2213.

427 Lee HS, Choi SI, Lee HK, Kim HS, Yang HK, Kang GH, Kim YI, Lee BL, Kim WH. Distinct clinical features and outcomes of gastric cancers with microsatellite instability. Mod Pathol 2002, **15**: 632–640.

428 Lee JH, Abraham SC, Kim HS, Nam JH, Choi C, Lee MC, Park CS, Juhng SW, Rashid A, Hamilton SR, Wu TT. Inverse relationship between APC gene mutation in gastric adenomas and development of adenocarcinoma. Am J Pathol 2002, **161**: 611–618.

429 Luinetti O, Fiocca R, Villani L, Alberizzi P, Ranzani GN, Solcia E. Genetic pattern, histological structure, and cellular phenotype in early and advanced gastric cancers: evidence for structure-related genetic subsets and for loss of glandular structure during progression of some tumors. Hum Pathol 1998, **29**: 702–709.

430 Machado JC, Carneiro F, Beck S, Rossi S, Lopes J, Taveira-Gomes A, Cardoso-Oliveira M. E-cadherin expression is correlated with the isolated cell-diffuse histotype and with features of biological aggressiveness of gastric carcinoma. Int J Surg Pathol 1998, **6**: 135–144.

431 Mizutani T, Onda M, Tokunaga A, Yamanaka N, Sugisaki Y. Relationship of C-erbB-2 protein expression and gene amplification to invasion and metastasis in human gastric cancer. Cancer 1993, **72**: 2083–2088.

432 Rathi A, Hur K, Gazdar AF, Bae JS, Jang JJ, Kim DY. Telomerase RNA expression during progression of gastric cancer. Hum Pathol 1999, **30**: 1302–1308.

433 Saal K, Vollmers HP, Muller J, Kohler J, Hohn H, Muller-Hermelink HK. Cytogenetic differences between intestinal and diffuse types of human gastric carcinoma. Virchows Arch [Cell Pathol] 1993, **64**: 145–150.

434 Schneider BG, Gulley ML, Eagan P, Bravo JC, Mera R, Geradts J. Loss of p16/CDKN2A tumor suppressor protein in gastric adenocarcinoma is associated with Epstein-Barr virus and anatomic location in the body of the stomach. Hum Pathol 2000, **31**: 45–50.

435 Teh M, Lee YS. An immunohistochemical study of *ras* oncoprotein expression in gastric carcinoma. Cancer 1993, **72**: 1846–1848.

436 Theuer CP, Campbell BS, Peel DJ, Lin F, Carpenter P, Ziogas A, Butler JA. Microsatellite instability in Japanese vs European American patients with gastric cancer. Arch Surg 2002, **137**: 960–965.

437 Yao J, Park SY, Kang SJ, Kim BK, Shim SI, Kang CS. Expression of telomerase activity, human telomerase RNA, and telomerase reverse transcriptase in gastric adenocarcinomas. Mod Pathol 2003, **16**: 700–707.

438 Yonemura Y, Ninomiya I, Ohoyama S, Kimura H, Yamaguchi A, Fushida S, Kosaka T, Miwa K, Miyazaki I, Endou Y. Expression of c-*erb*B-2 oncoprotein in gastric carcinoma. Immunoreactivity for c-*erb*B-2 protein is an independent indicator of poor short-term prognosis in patients with gastric carcinoma. Cancer 1991, **67**: 2914–2918.

439 Zhou YN, Xu CP, Han B, Li M, Qiao L, Fang DC, Yang JM. Expression of E-cadherin and beta-catenin in gastric carcinoma and its correlation with the clinicopathological features and patient survival. World J Gastroenterol 2002, **8**: 987–993.

Other microscopic types

440 Adachi Y, Mori M, Kido A, Shimono R, Maehara Y, Sugimachi K. A clinico-pathologic study of mucinous gastric carcinoma. Cancer 1992, **15**: 866–871.

441 Adachi Y, Mori M, Maehara Y, Sugimachi K. Poorly differentiated medullary carcinoma of the stomach. Cancer 1992, **70**: 1462–1466.

442 Aiba M, Hirayama A, Suzuki T, Hamano K, Nomura K. Carcinosarcoma of the stomach. Report of a case with review of the literature of gastrectomized patients. Surg Pathol 1991, **4**: 75–83.

443 Ambe K, Mori M, Enjoji M. Early gastric carcinoma with multiple endocrine cell micronests. Am J Surg Pathol 1987, **11**: 310–315.

444 Amrikachi M, Ro JY, Ordonez NG, Ayala AG. Adenocarcinomas of the gastrointestinal tract with prominent rhabdoid features. Ann Diagn Pathol 2002, **6**: 357–363.

445 Blumenfeld W, Chandhoke DK, Sagerman P, Turi GK. Neuroendocrine differentiation in gastric adenocarcinomas: an immunohistochemical study. Arch Pathol Lab Med 1996, **120**: 478–481.

446 Bonar SF, Sweeney EC. The prevalence, prognostic significance and hormonal content of endocrine cells in gastric cancer. Histopathology 1986, **10**: 53–63.

447 Brander WL, Needham PRG, Morgan AD. Indolent mucoid carcinoma of stomach. J Clin Pathol 1974, **27**: 536–541.

448 Callery CD, Sanders MM, Pratt S, Turnbull AD. Squamous cell carcinoma of the stomach. A study of four patients with comments on histogenesis. J Surg Oncol 1985, **29**: 166–172.

449 Capella C, Frigerio B, Cornaggia M, Solcia E, Pinzon-Trujillo Y, Chejfec G. Gastric parietal cell carcinoma. A newly recognized entity. Light microscopic and ultrastructural features. Histopathology 1984, **8**: 813–824.

450 Caruso ML, Pilato FP, D'Adda T, Baggi MT, Fucci L, Valentini AM, Lacatena M, Bordi C. Composite carcinoid-adenocarcinoma of the stomach associated with multiple gastric carcinoids and nonantral gastric atrophy. Cancer 1989, **64**: 1534–1539.

451 Caruso RA, Fabiano V, Rigoli L, Inferrera A. Focal parietal cell differentiation in a well-differentiated (intestinal-type) early gastric cancer. Ultrastruct Pathol 2000, **24**: 417–422.

452 Chang MS, Kim WH, Kim CW, Kim YI. Epstein-Barr virus in gastric carcinomas with lymphoid stroma. Histopathology 2000, **37**: 309–315.

453 Cruz JJ, Paz JI, Cordero M, Martin J, del Mar Abad M. Carcinosarcoma of the stomach with endocrine differentiation. A case report. Tumori 1991, **77**: 355–357.

453a Grogg KL, Lohse CM, Pankratz S, Halling KC, Smyrk TC. Lymphocyte-rich gastric cancer: associations with Epstein-Barr virus, microsatellite instability, histology, and survival. Mod Pathol 2003, **16**: 641–651.

454 Harn H-J, Chang J-Y, Wang M-W, Ho L-I, Lee H-S, Chiang J-H, Lee W-H. Epstein-Barr virus-associated gastric adenocarcinoma in Taiwan. Hum Pathol 1995, **26**: 267–271.

455 Ishikura H, Kirimoto K, Shamoto M, Miyamoto Y, Yamagiwa H, Itoh T, Aizawa M. Hepatoid adenocarcinomas of the stomach. An analysis of seven cases. Cancer 1986, **58**: 119–126.

456 Ishikura H, Kishimoto T, Andachi H, Kakuta Y, Yoshiki T. Gastrointestinal hepatoid adenocarcinoma: venous permeation and mimicry of hepatocellular carcinoma, a report of four cases. Histopathology 1997, **31**: 47–54.

457 Kallakury BV, Bui HX, Del Rosario A, Wallace J, Solis OG, Ross JS. Primary gastric adenosarcoma. Arch Pathol Lab Med 1993, **117**: 299–301.

458 Kida Y, Miyauchi K, Takano Y. Gastric adenocarcinoma with differentiation to sarcomatous components associated with monoclonal Epstein-Barr virus infection and LMP-I expression. Virchows Archiv [A] 1993, **423**: 383–388.

459 Kubo T, Watanabe H. Neoplastic argentaffin cells in gastric and intestinal carcinomas. Cancer 1971, **27**: 447–454.

460 Kuwashima Y, Nakamura T, Sawabe M, Kanno J, Kitagawa M, Matsubara O, Kasuga T. Neoplastic argentaffin cells with intracytoplasmic eosinophilic granules in a gastric adenocarcinoma. Acta Pathol Jpn 1991, **41**: 905–910.

461 Maitra A, Murakata LA, Albores-Saavedra J. Immunoreactivity for hepatocyte paraffin 1 antibody in hepatoid adenocarcinomas of the gastrointestinal tract. Am J Clin Pathol 2001, **115**: 689–694.

462 Matsui K, Jin XM, Kitagawa M, Miwa A. Clinicopathologic features of neuroendocrine carcinomas of the stomach: appraisal of small cell and large cell variants. Arch Pathol Lab Med 1998, **122**: 1010–1017.

463 Matsunou H, Konishi F, Hori H, Ikeda T, Sasaki K, Hirose Y, Yamamichi N. Characteristics of Epstein-Barr virus-associated gastric carcinoma with lymphoid stroma in Japan. Cancer 1996, **77**: 1998–2004.

464 Matsunou H, Konishi F, Jalal REA, Yamamichi N, Mukawa A. Alpha-fetoprotein-producing gastric carcinoma with enteroblastic differentiation. Cancer 1994, **73**: 534–540.

465 Min KW, Holmquist S, Peiper SC, O'Leary TJ. Poorly differentiated adenocarcinoma with lymphoid stroma (lymphoepithelioma-like carcinomas) of the stomach. Report of three cases with Epstein-Barr virus genome demonstrated by the polymerase chain reaction. Am J Clin Pathol 1991, **96**: 219–227.

466 Minamoto T, Mai M, Watanabe K, Ooi A, Kitamura T, Takahashi Y, Ueda H, Ogino T, Nakanishi I. Medullary carcinoma with lymphocytic infiltration of the stomach. Clinicopathologic study of 27 cases and immunohistochemical analysis of the subpopulations of infiltrating lymphocytes in the tumor. Cancer 1990, **66**: 945–952.

467 Mori M, Iwashita A, Enjoji M. Adenosquamous carcinoma of the stomach. A clinicopathologic analysis of 28 cases. Cancer 1986, **57**: 333–339.

468 Mori M, Iwashita A, Enjoji M. Squamous cell carcinoma of the stomach. Report of three cases. Am J Gastroenterol 1986, **81**: 339–342.

469 Morishita Y, Tanaka T, Kato K, Kawamori T, Amano K, Funato T, Tarao M, Mori H. Gastric collision tumor (carcinoid and adenocarcinoma) with gastritis cystica profunda. Arch Pathol Lab Med 1991, **115**: 1006–1010.

470 Motoyama T, Aizawa K, Watanabe H, Fukase M, Saito K. 2-Fetoprotein producing gastric carcinomas. A comparative study of three different subtypes. Acta Pathol Jpn 1993, **43**: 654–661.

471 Nagai E, Ueyama T, Yao T, Tsuneyoshi M. Hepatoid adenocarcinoma of the stomach. A clinicopathologic and immunohistochemical analysis. Cancer 1993, **72**: 1827–1835.

472 Nakamura S, Ueki T, Yao T, Ueyama T, Tsuneyoshi M. Epstein-Barr virus in gastric carcinoma with lymphoid stroma. Special reference to its detection by the polymerase chain reaction and in situ hybridization in 99 tumors, including a morphologic analysis. Cancer 1994, **73**: 2239–2249.

473 Nakayama Y, Murayana H, Iwasaki H, Iwanaga S, Kikuchi M, Ikeda S, Okada M, Iizuka Y, Iwashita A. Gastric carcinosarcoma (sarcomatoid carcinoma) with rhabdomyoblastic and osteoblastic differentiation. Pathol Int 1997, **47**: 557–563.

474 Oda K, Tamaru J, Takenouchi T, Mikata A, Nunomura M, Saitoh N, Sarashina H, Nakajima N. Association of Epstein-Barr virus with gastric carcinoma with lymphoid stroma. Am J Pathol 1993, **143**: 1063–1071.

475 Ooi A, Hayashi H, Katsuda S, Nakanishi I. Gastric carcinoma cells with endocrine differentiation show no evidence of proliferation. Hum Pathol 1993, **24**: 114–115.

476 Ooi A, Nakanishi I, Sakamoto N, Tsukada Y, Takahashi Y, Minamoto T, Mai M. Alpha-fetoprotein (AFP)-producing gastric carcinoma. Is it hepatoid differentiation? Cancer 1990, **65**: 1741–1747.

477 Pittaluga S, Loke S, So K, Cheung K, Ma L. Clonal Epstein-Barr virus in lymphoepithelioma-like carcinoma of the stomach; demonstration of viral genome by in situ hybridization and Southern blot analysis. Mod Pathol 1992, **5**: 661–664.

478 Rassidakis GZ, Delladetsima JK, Letsos SP, Polyzos A, Yannopoulos A. Hepatoid adenocarcinoma of the stomach with extensive neuroendocrine differentiation and a coexisting carcinoid tumour. Histopathology 1998, **33**: 186–188.

479 Roberts CC, Colby TV, Batts KP. Carcinoma of the stomach with hepatocyte differentiation (hepatoid adenocarcinoma). Mayo Clin Proc 1997, **72**: 1154–1160.

480 Robey-Cafferty SS, Grignon DJ, Ro JY, Cleary KR, Ayala AG, Ordonez NG, Mackay B. Sarcomatoid carcinoma of the stomach. A report of three cases with immunohistochemical and ultrastructural observations. Cancer 1990, **65**: 1601–1606.

481 Robey-Cafferty SS, Ro JY, McKee EG. Gastric parietal cell carcinoma with an unusual, lymphoma-like histologic appearance: report of a case. Mod Pathol 1989, **2**: 536–540.

482 Rogers LW, Murphy RC. Gastric carcinoid and gastric carcinoma. Am J Surg Pathol 1979, **3**: 195–202.

483 Saez C, Japon MA, Poveda MA, Segura DI. Mucinous (colloid) adenocarcinomas secrete distinct O-acylated forms of sialomucins: a histochemical study of gastric, colorectal and breast adenocarcinomas. Histopathology 2001, **39**: 554–560.

484 Shibata D, Tokunaga M, Uemura Y, Sato E, Tanaka S, Weiss LM. Association of Epstein-Barr virus with undifferentiated gastric carcinomas with intense lymphoid infiltration. Am J Pathol 1991, **139**: 469–474.

485 Silva E, Teixeira A, David L, Carneiro F, Reis CA, Sobrinho-Simoes J, Serpa J, Veerman E, Bolscher J, Sobrinho-Simoes M. Mucins as key molecules for the classification of intestinal metaplasia of the stomach. Virchows Arch 2002, **440**: 311–317.

486 Stracca-Pansa V, Menegon A, Donisi PM, Bozzola L, Fedeli F, Quarto F, Nappi O, Pettinato G. Gastric carcinoma with osteoclast-like giant cells. Report of four cases. Am J Clin Pathol 1995, **103**: 453–459.

487 Sweeney EC, McDonnell LM. Atypical gastric carcinoids. Histopathology 1980, **4**: 215–224.

488 Tabuko K, Honma N, Sawabe M, Arai T, Izumiyama-Shimomura N, Kammori M, Sasajima K, Esaki Y. Oncocytic adenocarcinoma of the stomach: parietal cell carcinoma. Am J Surg Pathol 2002, **26**: 458–465.

489 Tahara E, Ito H, Nakagami K, Shimamoto F, Yamamoto M, Sumii K. Scirrhous argyrophil cell carcinoma of the stomach with multiple production of polypeptide hormones, amine, CEA, lysozyme, and HCG. Cancer 1982, **49**: 1904–1915.

490 Tsutsumi Y, Hara M. Application of parietal cell autoantibody to histopathological studies. Acta Pathol Jpn 1985, **35**: 823–829.

491 Ueyama T, Nagai E, Yao T, Tsuneyoshi M. Vimentin-positive gastric carcinomas with rhabdoid features. A clinicopathologic and immunohistochemical study. Am J Surg Pathol 1993, **17**: 813–819.

492 Ulich TR, Kollin M, Lewin KJ. Composite gastric carcinoma. Report of a tumor of the carcinoma-carcinoid spectrum. Arch Pathol Lab Med 1988, **112**: 91–93.

493 Yamashina M, Flinner RA. Concurrent occurrence of adenocarcinoma and carcinoid tumor in the stomach. A composite tumor or collision tumors? Am J Clin Pathol 1985, **83**: 233–236.

494 Yuen ST, Chung LP, Leung SY, Luk IS, Chan SY, Ho J. In situ detection of Epstein-Barr virus in gastric and colorectal adenocarcinomas. Am J Surg Pathol 1994, **18**: 1158–1163.

Diagnosis—biopsy and cytology

495 Boon TH, Schade ROK, Middleton GD, Reece M. An attempt at presymptomatic diagnosis of gastric carcinoma in pernicious anaemia. Gut 1964, **5**: 269–270.

496 Chambers LA, Clark WE II. The endoscopic diagnosis of gastroesophageal malignancy. A cytologic review. Acta Cytol Baltimore 1986, **30**: 110–114.

497 Czerniak B, Herz F, Koss LG, Schlom J. ras Oncogene p21 as a tumor marker in the cytodiagnosis of gastric and colonic carcinomas. Cancer 1987, **60**: 2432–2436.

498 Foushee JHS, Kalnins ZA, Dixon FR, Girsh S, Morehead RP, O'Brien TF, Pribor H, Tattory C. Gastric cytology. Evaluation of methods and results in 1,670 cases. Acta Cytol Baltimore 1969, **13**: 339–406.

499 Gupta RK, Rogers KE. Endoscopic cytology and biopsy in the diagnosis of gastroesophageal malignancy. Acta Cytol Baltimore 1983, **27**: 17–22.

500 Halvorsen RA Jr, Yee J, McCormick VD. Diagnosis and staging of gastric cancer. Semin Oncol 1996, **23**: 325–335.

501 Iishi H, Yamamoto R, Tatsuta M, Okuda S. Evaluation of fine-needle aspiration biopsy under direct vision gastrofiberscopy in diagnosis of diffusely infiltrative carcinoma of the stomach. Cancer 1986, **57**: 1365–1369.

502 Jorde R, Østensen H, Bostad LH, Burhol PG, Langmark FT. Cancer detection in biopsy specimens taken from different types of gastric lesions. Cancer 1986, **58**: 376–382.

503 Kasugai T, Kobayashi S, Kuno N. Endoscopic cytology of the esophagus, stomach and pancreas. Acta Cytol Baltimore 1978, **22**: 327–330.

504 MacDonald WC, Brandborg LL, Taniguchi L, Beh JE, Rubin CE. Exfoliative cytologic screening for gastric cancer. Cancer 1964, **17**: 163–169.

505 Nagata T, Ikeda M, Nakayama F. Changing state of gastric cancer in Japan. Histologic perspective of the past 76 years. Am J Surg 1983, **145**: 226–233.

506 Schade ROK. Gastric cytology. Principles, methods and results. London, 1960, Edward Arnold, Ltd., pp. 38–40.

507 Shiratori Y, Nakagawa S, Kikuchi A, Ishii M, Ueno M, Miyashita T, Sakurai T, Negami J, Suzuki T, Sato I. Significance of a gastric mass screening survey. Am J Gastroenterol 1985, **80**: 831–835.

508 Tatsuta M, Iishi H, Okuda S, Oshima A, Taniguchi H. Prospective evaluation of diagnostic accuracy of gastrofiberscopic biopsy in diagnosis of gastric cancer. Cancer 1989, **63**: 1415–1420.

509 Yamada T, Murochisa B, Muto Y, Okubo H, Okamoto K, Doi K, Fujimori I. Point, minute and small cancers of the stomach at the early developmental stage detected by improved chymotrypsin lavage method for diagnostic cytology. Acta Cytol Baltimore 1978, **22**: 460–469.

Relationship with peptic ulcer

510 Bedossa P, Lemaigre G, Martin ED. Histochemical study of mucosubstances in carcinoma of the gastric remnant. Cancer 1987, **60**: 2224–2227.

511 Bogomoletz WV, Potet F, Barge J, Molas G, Qizilbash AH. Pathological features and mucin histochemistry of primary gastric stump carcinoma associated with gastritis cystica polyposa. A study of six cases. Am J Surg Pathol 1985, **9**: 401–410.

512 Côté R, Dockerty MB, Cain JC. Cancer of the stomach after gastric resection for peptic ulcer. Surg Gynecol Obstet 1958, **107**: 200–204.

513 Domellof L, Janunger K-G. The risk for gastric carcinoma after partial gastrectomy. Am J Surg 1977, **134**: 581–584.

514 Eckardt VF, Giessler W, Kanzler G, Bernhard G. Does endoscopic follow-up improve the outcome of patients with benign gastric ulcers and gastric cancer? Cancer 1992, **70**: 2741–2742.

515 Giarelli L, Melato M, Stanta G, Bucconi S, Manconi R. Gastric resection. A cause of high frequency of gastric carcinoma. Cancer 1983, **52**: 1113–1116.

516 Gômôri G. Carcinoma arising from chronic gastric ulcer. Surg Gynecol Obstet 1933, **57**: 439–450.

517 Graem N, Fischer AB, Beck H. Dysplasia and carcinoma in the Billroth II resected stomach. 27–35 years postoperatively. Acta Pathol Microbiol Immunol Scand A 1984, **92**: 185–188.

518 Ihre BJE, Barr H, Havermark G. Ulcer-cancer of the stomach. A follow-up study of 473 cases of gastric ulcer. Gastroenterologia (Basel) 1964, **102**: 78–91.

519 Ikeguchi M, Kondou A, Shibata S, Yamashiro H, Tsujitani S, Maeta M, Kaibara N. Clinicopathologic differences between carcinoma in the gastric remnant stump after distal partial gastrectomy for benign gastroduodenal lesions and primary carcinoma in the upper third of the stomach. Cancer 1994, **73**: 15–21.

520 Jordan S. The relationship of gastric ulcer to gastric carcinoma. Cancer 1950, **3**: 515–552.

521 Krag E. Long-term prognosis in medically treated peptic ulcer. A clinical, radiographical and statistical follow-up study. Acta Med Scand 1966, **180**: 657–670.

522 Lewis JH, Woods M III. Gastric carcinoma in patients with unoperated duodenal ulcer disease. Am J Gastroenterol 1982, **77**: 368–373.

523 MacDonald WC, Owen DA. Gastric carcinoma after surgical treatment of peptic ulcer: an analysis of morphologic features and a comparison with cancer in the nonoperated stomach. Cancer 2001, **91**: 1732–1738.

524 Mallory TB. Carcinoma in situ of the stomach and its bearing on the histogenesis of malignant ulcers. Arch Pathol 1940, **30**: 348–362.

525 Melato M, Laurino L. Gastric stump. A malignancy promotor? (letter to the editor). Am J Surg Pathol 1990, **14**: 596–597.

526 Nelson SW. The discovery of gastric ulcers and the differentiated diagnosis between benignancy and malignancy. Radiol Clin North Am 1969, **7**: 5–25.

527 Nicholls JC. Carcinoma of the stomach following partial gastrectomy for benign gastroduodenal lesions. Br J Surg 1974, **61**: 244–249.

528 Offerhaus GJA, Stadt VD, Huibregtse K, Tersmette AC, Tytgat GNJ. The mucosa of the gastric remnant harboring malignancy. Histologic findings in the biopsy specimens of 504 asymptomatic patients 15 to 46 years after partial gastrectomy with emphasis on nonmalignant lesions. Cancer 1989, **64**: 698–703.

529 Palmer WL. Benign and malignant gastric ulcers. Their relation and clinical differentiation. Ann Intern Med 1939, **13**: 317–338.

530 Picton TD, Owen DA, MacDonald WC. Comparison of esophagocardiac and more distal gastric cancer in patients with prior ulcer surgery. Cancer 1993, **71**: 5–8.

531 Ruck P, Wehrmann M, Campbell M, Horny H-P, Breucha G, Kaiserling E. Squamous cell carcinoma of the gastric stump. A case report and review of the literature. Am J Surg Pathol 1989, **13**: 317–324.

532 Safatle-Ribeiro AV, Ribeiro U Jr, Reynolds JC, Gama-Rodrigues JJ, Iriya K, Kim R, Bakker A, Swalsky PA, Pinotti HW, Finkelstein SD. Morphologic, histologic, and molecular similarities between adenocarcinomas arising in the gastric stump and the intact stomach. Cancer 1996, **78**: 2288–2299.

533 Savage A, Jones S. Histological appearances of the gastric mucosa 15–27 years after partial gastrectomy. J Clin Pathol 1979, **32**: 179–186.

534 Schafer LW, Larson DE, Melton LJ III, Higgins JA, Ilstrup DM. The risk of gastric carcinoma after surgical treatment for benign ulcer disease. A population-based study of Olmsted County, Minnesota. N Engl J Med 1983, **309**: 1210–1213.

535 Schrumpf E, Stadaas J, Myren J, Serck-Hanssen A, Aune S, Osnes M. Mucosal changes in the gastric stump 20–25 years after partial gastrectomy. Lancet 1977, **2**: 467–469.

536 Stael von Holstein C, Hammar E, Eriksson S, Huldt B. Clinical significance of dysplasia in gastric remnant biopsy specimens. Cancer 1993, **72**: 1532–1535.

537 Stalsberg H, Taksdal S. Stomach cancer following gastric surgery for benign conditions. Lancet 1971, **2**: 1175–1177.

538 Stout AP. The relationship of gastric ulcer to gastric carcinoma. Cancer 1950, **3**: 515–552.

539 Tokudome S, Kono S, Ikeda M, Kuratsune M, Sano C, Inokuchi K, Kodama Y, Ichimiya H, Nakayama F, Kaibara N, Koga S, Yamada H, Ikejiri T, Oka N, Tsurumaru H. A prospective study of primary gastric stump cancer following partial gastrectomy for benign gastroduodenal diseases. Cancer Res 1984, **44**: 2208–2212.

So-called "early" carcinoma

540 Adachi Y, Mori M, Enjoji M, Saku M. Coexistence of pseudolymphoma and early carcinoma in the stomach. Arch Pathol Lab Med 1986, **110**: 1080–1082.

541 Adachi Y, Mori M, Enjoji M, Sugimachi K. Microvascular architecture of early gastric carcinoma. Microvascular-histopathologic correlates. Cancer 1993, **72**: 32–36.

542 Adachi Y, Yasuda K, Inomata M, Shiraishi N, Kitano S, Sugimachi K. Clinicopathologic study of early-stage mucinous gastric carcinoma. Cancer 2001, **91**: 698–703.

543 Ambe K, Mori M, Enjoji M. Early gastric carcinoma with multiple endocrine cell micronests. Am J Surg Pathol 1987, **11**: 310–315.

544 Bearzi I, Ranaldi R. Multifocal early gastric cancer. Morphology and histogenesis. Pathol Res Pract 1986, **181**: 144–147.

545 Bogomoletz WV. Early gastric cancer. Am J Surg Pathol 1984, **8**: 381–391.

546 Bragg DG, Seaman WB, Lattes R. Roentgenologic and pathologic aspects of superficial spreading carcinoma of the stomach. Am J Roentgenol Radium Ther Nucl Med 1967, **101**: 437–446.

547 Brito MJ, Filipe MI, Williams GT, Thompson H, Ormerod MG, Titley J. DNA ploidy in early gastric carcinoma (T1). A flow cytometric study of 100 European cases. Gut 1993, **34**: 230–234.

548 Czerniak B, Herz F, Koss LG. DNA distribution patterns in early gastric carcinomas. A Feulgen cytometric study of gastric brush smears. Cancer 1987, **59**: 113–117.

549 Golden R, Stout AP. Superficial spreading carcinoma of the

stomach. Am J Roentgenol Radium Ther Nucl Med 1948, **59**: 157–167.

550 Grigioni WF, D'Errico A, Milani M, Villanacci V, Avellini C, Miglioli M, Mattioli S, Biasco G, Barbara L, Possati L. Early gastric cancer. Clinico-pathological analysis of 125 cases of early gastric cancer (EGC). Acta Pathol Jpn 1984, **34**: 979–989.

551 Grundmann E, Schlake W. Histological classification of gastric cancer from initial to advanced stages. Pathol Res Pract 1982, **173**: 260–274.

552 Iishi H, Tatsuta M, Okuda S. Endoscopic diagnosis of minute gastric cancer of less than 5 mm in diameter. Cancer 1985, **56**: 655–659.

553 Isozaki H, Okajima K, Hu X, Fujii K, Sako S. Multiple early gastric carcinomas: clinicopathologic features and histogenesis. Cancer 1996, **78**: 2078–2086.

554 Kabashima A, Yao T, Sugimachi K, Tsuneyoshi M. Gastric or intestinal phenotypic expression in the carcinomas and background mucosa of multiple early gastric carcinomas. Histopathology 2000, **37**: 513–522.

555 Kang GH, Kim CJ, Kim WH, Kang YK, Kim HO, Kim YI. Genetic evidence for the multicentric origin of synchronous multiple gastric carcinoma. Lab Invest 1997, **76**: 407–417.

556 Kitamura K, Yamaguchi T, Sawai K, Nishida S, Yamamoto K, Okamoto K, Taniguchi H, Hagiwara A, Takahashi T. Chronologic changes in the clinicopathologic findings and survival of gastric cancer patients. J Clin Oncol 1997, **15**: 3471–3480.

557 Kodama Y, Inokuchi K, Soejima K, Matsusaka T, Okamura T. Growth patterns and prognosis in early gastric carcinoma. Superficially spreading and penetrating growth types. Cancer 1983, **51**: 320–326.

558 Korenaga D, Mori M, Okamura T, Sugimachi K, Enjoji M. DNA ploidy in clinical malignant gastric lesions less than 5 mm in diameter. Cancer 1986, **58**: 2542–2545.

559 Koseki K, Takizawa T, Koike M, Ito M, Nihei Z, Sugihara K. Distinction of differentiated type early gastric carcinoma with gastric type mucin expression. Cancer 2000, **89**: 724–732.

560 Maehara Y, Okuyama T, Oshiro T, Baba H, Anai H, Akazawa K, Sugimachi K. Early carcinoma of the stomach. Surg Gynecol Obstet 1993, **177**: 593–597.

561 Maruyama M, Takeshita K, Endo M, Deakin M, Moossa A. Clinicopathological study of gastric carcinoma in high- and low-mortality countries: comparison between Japan and the United States. Gastric Cancer 1998, **1**: 64–70.

562 Mori M, Adachi Y, Kakeji Y, Korenaga D, Sugimachi K, Motooka M, Ooiwa T. Superficial flat-type early carcinoma of the stomach. Cancer 1992, **69**: 306–313.

563 Mori M, Enjoji M, Sugimachi K. Histopathologic features of minute and small human gastric adenocarcinomas. Arch Pathol Lab Med 1989, **113**: 926–931.

564 Mori M, Kitagawa S, Iida M, Sakurai T, Enjoji M, Sugimachi K, Ooiwa T. Early carcinoma of the gastric cardia. A clinicopathologic study of 21 cases. Cancer 1987, **59**: 1758–1766.

565 O'Brien MJ, Burakoff R, Robbins EA, Golding RM, Zamchek N, Gottlieb LS. Early gastric cancer. Clinicopathologic study. Am J Med 1985, **78**: 195–202.

566 Ohta H, Noguchi Y, Takagi K, Nishi M, Kajitani T, Kato Y. Early gastric carcinoma with special reference to macroscopic classification. Cancer 1987, **60**: 1099–1106.

567 Oohara T, Aono G, Ukawa S, Takezoe K, Johjima Y, Kurosaka H, Asakura R, Tohma H. Clinical diagnosis of minute gastric cancer less than 5 mm in diameter. Cancer 1984, **53**: 162–165.

568 Osterheld MC, Laurini R, Saraga E. Early gastric carcinoma with focal advanced cancer: a particular subtype of gastric carcinoma. Hum Pathol 1998, **29**: 815–819.

569 Oya M, Yao T, Nagai E, Tsuneyoshi M. Metastasizing intramucosal gastric carcinomas. Well differentiated type and proliferative activity using proliferative cell nuclear antigen and Ki-67. Cancer 1995, **75**: 926–935.

570 Rubio CA, Slezak P, Øhman U, Emas S. The histological classification of early gastric ulcer (micro-invasive carcinoma of the stomach). Acta Pathol Microbiol Immunol Scand A 1982, **90**: 311–316.

571 Sano T, Sasako M, Kinoshita T, Maruyama K. Recurrence of early gastric cancer. Follow-up of 1475 patients and review of the Japanese literature. Cancer 1993, **72**: 3174–3178.

572 Sasaki I, Yao T, Nawata H, Tsuneyoshi M. Minute gastric carcinoma of differentiated type with special reference to the significance of intestinal metaplasia, proliferative zone, and p53 protein during tumor development. Cancer 1999, **85**: 1719–1729.

573 Tatsuta M, Iishi H, Okuda S, Taniguchi H, Yokota Y. The association of *Helicobacter pylori* with differentiated-type early gastric cancer. Cancer 1993, **72**: 1841–1845.

574 Tsukuma H, Mishima T, Oshima A. Prospective study of "early" gastric cancer. Int J Cancer 1983, **31**: 421–426.

575 Xuan ZX, Ueyema T, Yao T, Tsuneyoshi M. Time trends of early gastric carcinoma. A clinicopathologic analysis of 2846 cases. Cancer 1993, **72**: 2889–2894.

576 Yamao T, Shirao K, Ono H, Kondo H, Saito D, Yamaguchi H, Sasako M, Sano T, Ochiai A, Yoshida S. Risk factors for lymph node metastasis from intramucosal gastric carcinoma. Cancer 1996, **77**: 602–606.

577 Yamashina M. A variant of early gastric carcinoma. Histologic and histochemical studies of early signet ring cell carcinomas discovered beneath preserved surface epithelium. Cancer 1986, **58**: 1333–1339.

Spread

578 Baba H, Korenaga D, Haraguchi M, Okamura T, Saito A, Watanabe A, Sugimachi K. Width of serosal invasion and prognosis in advanced human gastric cancer with special reference to the mode of tumor invasion. Cancer 1989, **64**: 2482–2486.

579 Candela FC, Urmacher C, Brennan MF. Comparison of the conventional method of lymph node staging with a comprehensive fat-clearing method for gastric adenocarcinoma. Cancer 1990, **66**: 1828–1832.

580 Duarte I, Llanos O. Patterns of metastases in intestinal and diffuse types of carcinoma of the stomach. Hum Pathol 1981, **12**: 237–242.

581 Esaki Y, Hirayama R, Hirokawa K. A comparison of patterns of metastasis in gastric cancer by histologic type and age. Cancer 1990, **65**: 2086–2090.

582 Fernet P, Azar HA, Stout AP. Intramural (tubal) spread of linitis plastica along the alimentary tract. Gastroenterology 1965, **48**: 419–424.

583 Fukagawa T, Sasako M, Mann GB, Sano T, Katai H, Maruyama K, Nakanishi Y, Shimoda T. Immunohistochemically detected micrometastases of the lymph nodes in patients with gastric carcinoma. Cancer 2001, **92**: 753–760.

584 Imachi M, Tsukamoto N, Amagase H, Shigematsu T, Amada S, Nakano H. Metastatic adenocarcinoma to the uterine cervix from gastric cancer. A clinicopathologic analysis of 16 cases. Cancer 1993, **71**: 3472–3477.

585 Ishida K, Katsuyama T, Sugiyama A, Kawasaki S. Immunohistochemical evaluation of lymph node micrometastases from gastric carcinomas. Cancer 1997, **79**: 1069–1076.

586 Kaibara N, Kimura O, Nishidoi H, Makino M, Kawasumi H, Koga S. High incidence of liver metastasis in gastric cancer with medullary growth pattern. J Surg Oncol 1985, **28**: 195–198.

587 Lehnert T, Erlandson RA, Decosse JJ. Lymph and blood capillaries of the human gastric mucosa. A morphologic basis for metastasis in early gastric carcinoma. Gastroenterology 1985, **89**: 939–950.

588 Mak KL, Hui PK, Chan WY, Leung KM. Mucosal

lymphangiectasia in gastric adenocarcinoma. Arch Pathol Lab Med 1996, **120:** 78–80.

589 Okamura T, Korenaga D, Saito A, Baba H, Sugimachi K. Reactive changes in the esophageal epithelium and predictability of survival for patients with adenocarcinoma of the upper third of the stomach. Cancer 1989, **63:** 769–773.

590 Sawabe M, Kato Y, Ohashi I, Kitagawa T. Diffuse intrasinusoidal metastasis of gastric carcinoma to the liver leading to fulminant hepatic failure. A case report. Cancer 1990, **65:** 169–173.

591 Sweeney S, Utzschneider R, Fraire AE. Vasculitis carcinomatosa occurring in association with adenocarcinoma of the stomach. Ann Diagn Pathol 1998, **2:** 247–249.

592 Wu CW, Hsieh MJ, Lo SS, Tsay SH, Lui WY, P'eng FK. Lymph node metastasis from carcinoma of the distal one-third of the stomach. Cancer 1994, **73:** 3109–3114.

593 Zinninger MM. Extension of gastric cancer in the intramural lymphatics and its relation to gastrectomy. Am Surg 1954, **20:** 920–927.

Treatment

594 Ajani JA, Ota DM, Jessup JM, Ames FC, McBride C, Boddie A, Levin B, Jackson DE, Roh M, Hohn D. Resectable gastric carcinoma. An evaluation of preoperative and postoperative chemotherapy. Cancer 1991, **68:** 1501–1506.

595 Bonenkamp JJ, Hermans J, Sasako M, van de Velde CJ. Extended lymph-node dissection for gastric cancer. Dutch Gastric Cancer Group. N Engl J Med 1999, **340:** 908–914.

596 Brennan MF, Karpeh MS Jr. Surgery for gastric cancer: the American view. Semin Oncol 1996, **23:** 352–359.

597 Douglass HO Jr, Nava HR. Gastric adenocarcinoma. Management of the primary disease. Semin Oncol 1985, **12:** 32–45.

598 Imanaga H, Nakazato H. Results of surgery for gastric cancer and effect of adjuvant mitomycin C on cancer recurrence. World J Surg 1977, **1:** 213–220.

599 Maehara Y, Moriguchi S, Yoshida M, Takahashi I, Korenaga D, Sugimachi K. Splenectomy does not correlate with length of survival in patients undergoing curative total gastrectomy for gastric carcinoma. Univariate and multivariate analyses. Cancer 1991, **67:** 3006–3009.

600 Maruyama M, Takeshita K, Endo M, Deakin M, Moossa A. Clinicopathological study of gastric carcinoma in high- and low-mortality countries: comparison between Japan and the United States. Gastric Cancer 1998, **1:** 64–70.

601 Matsusaka T, Kodama Y, Soejima K, Miyazaki M, Yoshimura K, Sugimachi K, Inokuchi K. Recurrence in early gastric cancer. A pathologic evaluation. Cancer 1980, **46:** 168–172.

602 McNeer G, VanderBerg H, Donn FY, Bowden L. A critical evaluation of subtotal gastrectomy for the cure of cancer of the stomach. Ann Surg 1951, **134:** 2–7.

603 Schein PS, Smith FP, Woolley PV, Ahlgren JD. Current management of advanced and locally unresectable gastric carcinoma. Cancer 1982, **50:** 2590–2597.

Prognosis

604 Adachi Y, Yasuda K, Inomata M, Sato K, Shiraishi N, Kitano S. Pathology and prognosis of gastric carcinoma: well versus poorly differentiated type. Cancer 2000, **89:** 1418–1424.

605 Allgayer H, Babic R, Grützner KU, Beyer BC, Tarabichi A, Schildberg FW, Heiss MM. An immunohistochemical assessment of cathepsin D in gastric carcinoma: its impact on clinical prognosis. Cancer 1997, **80:** 179–187.

606 Allgayer H, Babic R, Gruetzner KU, Tarabichi A, Schildberg FW, Heiss MM. c-erbB-2 is of independent prognostic relevance in gastric cancer and is associated with the expression of tumor-associated protease systems. J Clin Oncol 2000, **18:** 2201–2209.

607 Bizer LS. Adenocarcinoma of the stomach. Current results of treatment. Cancer 1983, **51:** 743–745.

608 Borrman R. Geschwulste des Magens und Duodenums. In Henke F, Lubarsch O (eds): Handbuch der Speziellen pathologischen Anatomie und Histologie. Berlin, 1926, Julius Springer, pp. IV-L, 864–871.

609 Brien TP, Depowski PL, Sheehan CE, Ross JS, McKenna BJ. Prognostic factors in gastric cancer. Mod Pathol 1998, **11:** 870–877.

610 Bucholtz TW, Welch CE, Malt RA. Clinical correlates of resectability and survival in gastric carcinoma. Ann Surg 1978, **188:** 711–720.

611 Capuzzi D, Santoro E, Hauck WW, Kovatich AJ, Rosato FE, Baffa R, Hubner K, McCue PA. Fhit expression in gastric adenocarcinoma: correlation with disease stage and survival. Cancer 2000, **88:** 24–34.

612 Chiaravalli AM, Cornaggia M, Furlan D, Capella C, Fiocca R, Tagliabue G, Klersy C, Solcia E. The role of histological investigation in prognostic evaluation of advanced gastric cancer. Analysis of histological structure and molecular changes compared with invasive pattern and stage. Virchows Arch 2001, **439:** 158–169.

613 Chung YS, Yamashita Y, Kato Y, Nakata B, Sawada T, Sowa M. Prognostic significance of T antigen expression in patients with gastric carcinoma. Cancer 1996, **77:** 1768–1773.

614 Davessar K, Pezzullo JC, Kessimian N, Hale JH, Jauregui HO. Gastric adenocarcinoma. Prognostic significance of several pathologic parameters and histologic classifications. Hum Pathol 1990, **21:** 325–332.

615 Dixon MF, Martin IG, Sue-ling HM, Wyatt JI, Quirke P, Johnston D. Goseki grading in gastric cancer. Comparison with existing systems of grading and its reproducibility. Histopathology 1994, **25:** 309–316.

616 Dohchin A, Suzuki J, Seki H, Masutani M, Shiroto H, Kawakami Y. Immunostained cathepsins B and L correlate with depth of invasion and different metastatic pathways in early stage gastric carcinoma. Cancer 2000, **89:** 482–487.

617 Dupont JB Jr, Lee JR, Burton GR, Cohn I Jr. Adenocarcinoma of the stomach. Review of 1,497 cases. Cancer 1978, **41:** 941–947.

618 Gabbert HE, Müller W, Schneiders A, Meier S, Hommel G. The relationship of p53 expression to the prognosis of 418 patients with gastric carcinoma. Cancer 1995, **76:** 720–726.

619 Grabiec J, Owen DA. Carcinoma of the stomach in young persons. Cancer 1985, **56:** 388–396.

620 Harrison JC, Dean PJ, Vander Zwaag R, el-Zeky F, Wruble LD. Adenocarcinoma of the stomach with invasion limited to the muscularis propria. Hum Pathol 1991, **22:** 111–117.

621 Hawley PR, Westerholm P, Morson BC. Pathology and prognosis of carcinoma of the stomach. Br J Surg 1970, **57:** 877–883.

622 Ichikura T, Tomimatsu S, Okusa Y, Uefuji K, Tamakuma S. Comparison of the prognostic significance between the number of metastatic lymph nodes and nodal stage based on their location in patients with gastric cancer. J Clin Oncol 1993, **11:** 1894–1900.

623 Inokuchi K, Kodama Y, Sasaki O, Kamegawa T, Okamura T. Differentiation of growth patterns of early gastric carcinoma determined by cytophotometric DNA analysis. Cancer 1983, **51:** 1138–1141.

624 Jain S, Filipe MI, Hall PA, Waseem N, Lane DP, Levison DA. Prognostic value of proliferating cell nuclear antigen in gastric carcinoma. J Clin Pathol 1991, **44:** 655–659.

625 Kaibara N, Iitsuka Y, Kimura A, Kobayashi Y, Hirooka Y, Nishihoi H, Koga S. Relationship between area of serosal invasion and prognosis in patients with gastric carcinoma. Cancer 1987, **60:** 136–139.

626 Katai H, Yoshimura K, Maruyama K, Sasako M, Sano T. Evaluation of the new International Union Against Cancer TNM staging for gastric carcinoma. Cancer 2000, **88:** 1796–1800.

627 Kimura H, Yonemura Y. Flow cytometric analysis of nuclear

DNA content in advanced gastric cancer and its relationship with prognosis. Cancer 1991, **67**: 2588–2593.

628 Kimura H, Yonemura Y, Epstein AL. Flow cytometric quantitation of the proliferation-associated nuclear antigen p105 and DNA content in advanced gastric cancers. Cancer 1991, **68**: 2175–2180.

629 Korenaga D, Okamura T, Sugimachi K, Inokuchi K. Prognostic study of intramucosal carcinoma of the stomach with DNA aneuploidy. Jpn J Surg 1985, **15**: 443–448.

630 Lee E, Chae Y, Kim I, Choi J, Yeom B, Leong AS. Prognostic relevance of immunohistochemically detected lymph node micrometastasis in patients with gastric carcinoma. Cancer 2002, **94**: 2867–2873.

631 Lumpkin WM, Crow RL Jr, Hernandez CM, Cohn I Jr. Carcinoma of stomach. Review of 1,035 cases. Ann Surg 1964, **159**: 919–931.

632 Maeda K, Chung Y, Onoda N, Kato Y, Nitta A, Arimoto Y, Yamada N, Kondo Y, Sowa M. Proliferating cell nuclear antigen labeling index of preoperative biopsy specimens in gastric carcinoma with special reference to prognosis. Cancer 1994, **73**: 528–533.

633 Martin HM, Filipe MI, Morris RW, Lane DP, Silvestre F. p53 Expression and prognosis in gastric carcinoma. Int J Cancer 1992, **50**: 859–862.

634 Monafo WW Jr, Krause GL Jr, Guerra Medina J. Carcinoma of the stomach. Morphological characteristics affecting survival. Arch Surg 1962, **85**: 754–762.

635 Moutinho Ribeiro M, Sarmento JA, Sobrinho Simões MA, Bastos J. Prognostic significance of Lauren and Ming classifications and other pathologic parameters in gastric carcinoma. Cancer 1981, **47**: 780–784.

636 Nagata T, Ikeda M, Nakayama F. Changing state of gastric cancer in Japan. Histologic perspective of the past 76 years. Am J Surg 1983, **145**: 226–233.

637 Nakamura K, Ueyama T, Yao T, Xuan ZX, Ambe K, Adachi Y, Yakeishi Y, Matsukuma A, Enjoji M. Pathology and prognosis of gastric carcinoma. Findings in 10,000 patients who underwent primary gastrectomy. Cancer 1992, **70**: 1030–1037.

638 Noguchi Y, Imada T, Matsumoto A, Coit DG, Brennan MF: Radical surgery for gastric cancer. A review of the Japanese experience. Cancer 1989, **64**: 2053–2062.

639 Pagnini CA, Rugge M. Advanced gastric cancer and prognosis. Virchows Arch [A] 1985, **406**: 213–221.

640 Pinto-De-Sousa J, David L, Almeida R, Leitao D, Preto JR, Seixas M, Pimenta A. c-*erb* B-2 expression is associated with tumor location and venous invasion and influences survival of patients with gastric carcinoma. Int J Surg Pathol 2002, **10**: 247–256.

641 Roder JD, Bottcher K, Siewert JR, Busch R, Hermanek P, Meyer HJ. Prognostic factors in gastric carcinoma. Results of the German Gastric Carcinoma Study 1992. Cancer 1993, **72**: 2089–2097.

642 Serlin O, Keehn RJ, Higgins GA Jr, Harrower HW, Mendeloff GL. Factors related to survival following resection for gastric carcinoma. Analysis of 903 cases. Cancer 1977, **40**: 1318–1329.

643 Sgambato A, Migaldi M, Leocata P, Ventura L, Criscuolo M, Di Giacomo C, Capelli G, Cittadini A, De Gaetani C. Loss of p27 KIP1 expression is a strong independent prognostic factor of reduced survival in N0 gastric carcinomas. Cancer 2000, **89**: 2247–2257.

644 Songun I, van de Velde CJ, Arends JW, Blok P, Grond AJ, Offerhaus GJ, Hermans J, van Krieken JH. Classification of gastric carcinoma using the Goseki system provides prognostic information additional to TNM staging. Cancer 1999, **85**: 2114–2118.

645 Steiner PE, Maimon SN, Palmer WL, Kirsner JB. Gastric cancer. Morphologic factors in five-year survival after gastrectomy. Am J Pathol 1948, **24**: 947–969.

646 Stemmermann GN, Brown C. A survival study of intestinal and diffuse types of gastric carcinoma. Cancer 1974, **33**: 1190–1195.

647 Sue-Ling HM, Johnston D, Martin IG, Dixon MF, Lansdown MR, McMahon MJ, Axon AT. Gastric cancer. A curable disease in Britain. Br Med J 1993, **307**: 591–596.

648 Tanaka A, Watanabe T, Okuno K, Yasutomi M. Perineural invasion as a predictor of recurrence of gastric cancer. Cancer 1994, **73**: 550–555.

649 Tso PL, Bringaze WL III, Dauterive AH, Correa P, Cohn I Jr. Gastric carcinoma in the young. Cancer 1987, **59**: 1362–1365.

650 Tsujitani S, Kakeji Y, Watanabe A, Kohnoe S, Maehara Y, Sugimachi K. Infiltration of dendritic cells in relation to tumor invasion and lymph node metastasis in human gastric cancer. Cancer 1990, **66**: 2012–2016.

651 Uchino S, Tsuda H, Maruyama K, Kinoshita T, Sasako M, Saito T, Kobayashi M, Hirohashi S. Overexpression of c-*erb*B-2 protein in gastric cancer. Its correlation with long-term survival of patients. Cancer 1993, **72**: 3179–3184.

652 Wang LS, Wu CW, Hsieh MJ, Fahn HJ, Huang MH, Chien KY. Lymph node metastasis in patients with adenocarcinoma of gastric cardia. Cancer 1993, **71**: 1948–1953.

653 Watanabe H, Enjoji M, Imai T. Gastric carcinoma with lymphoid stroma. Its morphologic characteristics and prognostic correlations. Cancer 1976, **38**: 232–243.

654 Yasuda K, Adachi Y, Shiraishi N, Inomata M, Takeuchi H, Kitano S. Prognostic effect of lymph node micrometastasis in patients with histologically node-negative gastric cancer. Ann Surg Oncol 2002, **9**: 771–774.

654a Yasuda K, Shiraishi N, Suematsu T, Yamaguchi K, Adachi Y, Kitano S. Rate of detection of lymph node metastasis is correlated with the depth of submucosal invasion in early stage gastric carcinoma. Cancer 1999, **85**: 2119–2123.

Well-differentiated neuroendocrine tumors ("carcinoid tumors")

655 Black WC, Haffner HE. Diffuse hyperplasia of gastric argyrophil cells and multiple carcinoid tumors. A histochemical and ultrastructural study. Cancer 1968, **21**: 1080–1099.

656 Borch K, Renvall H, Kullman E, Wilander E. Gastric carcinoid associated with the syndrome of hypergastrinemic atrophic gastritis. A prospective analysis of 11 cases. Am J Surg Pathol 1987, **11**: 435–444.

657 Bordi C. Endocrine tumors of the stomach. Pathol Res Pract 1995, **191**: 373–380.

658 Bordi C, Caruana P, D'Adda T, Azzoni C. Smooth muscle cell abnormalities associated with gastric ECL cell carcinoids. Endocr Pathol 1995, **6**: 103–113.

659 Bordi C, D'Adda T, Azzoni C, Pilato FP, Caruana P. Hypergastrinemia and gastric enterochromaffin-like cells. Am J Surg Pathol 1995, **19**: S8–S19.

660 Bordi C, Falchetti A, Azzoni C, D'Adda T, Canavese G, Guariglia A, Santini D, Tomassetti P, Brandi ML. Aggressive forms of gastric neuroendocrine tumors in multiple endocrine neoplasia type I. Am J Surg Pathol 1997, **21**: 1075–1082.

661 Bordi C, Yu JY, Baggi MT, Davoli C, Pilato FP, Baruzzi G, Gardini G, Zamboni G, Franzin G, Papotti M. Gastric carcinoids and their precursor lesions. A histologic and immunohistochemical study of 23 cases. Cancer 1991, **67**: 663–672.

662 Cadiot G, Lehy T, Mignon M. Gastric endocrine cell proliferation and fundic argyrophil carcinoid tumors in patients with the Zollinger-Ellison syndrome. Acta Oncol 1993, **32**: 135–140.

663 Capella C, Heitz PU, Höfler H, Solcia E, Klöppel G. Revised classification of neuroendocrine tumors of the lung, pancreas and gut. Virchows Archiv 1995, **425**: 547–560.

664 Carney JA, Go VLW, Fairbanks VF, Moore SB, Alport EC, Nora FE. The syndrome of gastric argyrophil carcinoid tumors and nonantral gastric atrophy. Ann Intern Med 1983, **99**: 761–766.

665 D'Adda T, Azzoni C, Franze A, Bordi C. Malignant

enterochromaffin-like cell carcinoid of the gastric stump. An ultrastructural study. Ultrastruct Pathol 1991, **15**: 257–265.

666 D'Adda T, Keller G, Bordi C, Hofler H. Loss of heterozygosity in 11q13-14 regions in gastric neuroendocrine tumors not associated with multiple endocrine neoplasia type 1 syndrome. Lab Invest 1999, **79**: 671–677.

667 DeSchryver-Kecskemeti K, Clouse RE, Kraus FT. Surgical pathology of gastric and duodenal neuroendocrine tumors masquerading clinically as common polyps. Semin Diagn Pathol 1984, **1**: 5–12.

668 Hirata Y, Sakamoto N, Yamamoto H, Matsukura S, Imura H, Okada S. Gastric carcinoid with ectopic production of ACTH and β-MSH. Cancer 1976, **37**: 377–385.

669 Hirschowitz BI, Griffith J, Pellegrin D, Cummings OW. Rapid regression of enterochromaffin-like cell gastric carcinoids in pernicious anemia after antrectomy. Gastroenterology 1992, **102**: 1409–1418.

670 Itsuno M, Watanabe H, Iwafuchi M, Ito S, Yanaihara N, Sato K, Kikuchi M, Akiyama N. Multiple carcinoids and endocrine cell micronests in type A gastritis. Their morphology, histogenesis, and natural history. Cancer 1989, **63**: 881–890.

671 Iwafuchi M, Watanabe H, Ishihara N, Shimoda T, Iwashita A, Ito S. Peptide YY immunoreactive cells in gastrointestinal carcinoids. Immunohistochemical and ultrastructural studies of 60 tumors. Hum Pathol 1986, **17**: 291–296.

672 Kern SE, Yardley JH, Lazenby AJ, Boitnott JK, Yang VW, Bayless TM, Sitzmann JV. Reversal by antrectomy of endocrine cell hyperplasia in the gastric body in pernicious anemia. A morphometric study. Mod Pathol 1990, **3**: 561–566.

673 Larraza O, Rojas ME, Rosai J, Albores Saavedra J. G cell tumor of the stomach associated with peptic ulcer, chronic atrophic gastritis and diffuse lymphocytic thyroiditis. Rev Invest Clin Mex 1980, **32**: 303–310.

674 Lattes R, Grossi C. Carcinoid tumors of the stomach. Cancer 1956, **9**: 698–711.

675 Le Gall F, Vallet VS, Thomas D, de Monti M, Duval J, Ramee MP. Immunohistochemical study of secretogranin II in 62 neuroendocrine tumors of the digestive tract and of the pancreas in comparison with other granins. Pathol Res Pract 1997, **193**: 179–185.

676 Lewin KJ. The endocrine cells of the gastrointestinal tract. The normal endocrine cells and their hyperplasias. Pathol Annu 1986, **21**(Pt 1): 1–27.

677 Lewin KJ, Yang K, Ulich T, Elashoff JD, Walsh J. Primary gastrin cell hyperplasia. Report of five cases and a review of the literature. Am J Surg Pathol 1984, **8**: 821–832.

678 Luk IS, Bhuta S, Lewin KJ. Clear cell carcinoid tumor of stomach: a variant mimicking gastric xanthelasma. Arch Pathol Lab Med 1997, **121**: 1100–1103.

679 Mendelsohn G, De La Monte S, Dunn JL, Yardley JH. Gastric carcinoid tumors, endocrine cell hyperplasia, and associated intestinal metaplasia. Histologic, histochemical, and immunohistochemical findings. Cancer 1987, **60**: 1022–1031.

680 Mertz H, Vyberg M, Paulsen SM, Teglbjaerg PS. Immunohistochemical detection of neuroendocrine markers in tumors of the lungs and gastrointestinal tract. Appl Immunohistochem 1998, **6**: 175–180.

681 Mignon M, Lehy T, Bonnefond A, Ruszniewski P, Labeille D, Bonfils S. Development of gastric argyrophil carcinoid tumors in a case of Zollinger-Ellison syndrome with primary hyperparathyroidism during long-term antisecretory treatment. Cancer 1987, **59**: 1959–1962.

682 Moyana TN, Xiang J, Senthilsevan A, Kulaga A. The spectrum of neuroendocrine differentiation among gastrointestinal carcinoids: importance of histologic grading, MIB-1, p53, and bcl-2 immunoreactivity. Arch Pathol Lab Med 2000, **124**: 570–576.

683 Müller J, Kirchner T, Müller-Hermelink HK. Gastric endocrine

684 Ordonez NG, Mackay B, el-Naggar A, Bannayan GA, Duncan J. Clear cell carcinoid tumour of the stomach. Histopathology 1993, **22**: 190–193.

685 Papotti M, Bongiovanni M, Volante M, Allia E, Landolfi S, Helboe L, Schindler M, Cole SL, Bussolati G. Expression of somatostatin receptor types 1-5 in 81 cases of gastrointestinal and pancreatic endocrine tumors. A correlative immunohistochemical and reverse-transcriptase polymerase chain reaction analysis. Virchows Arch 2002, **440**: 461–475.

686 Ray MB, Geboes K, Callea F, Desmet VJ. Alpha-I-antitrypsin immunoreactivity in gastric carcinoid. Histopathology 1982, **6**: 289–297.

687 Rindi G. Clinicopathologic aspects of gastric neuroendocrine tumors. Am J Surg Pathol 1995, **19**: S20–S29.

688 Rindi G, Luinetti O, Cornaggia M, Capella C, Solcia E. Three subtypes of gastric argyrophil carcinoid and the gastric neuroendocrine carcinoma. A clinicopathologic study. Gastroenterology 1993, **105**: 1264–1266.

689 Rindi G, Zaaoni C, La Rosa S, Klersy C, Paolotti D, Rappel S, Stolte M, Capella C, Bordi C, Solcia E. ECL cell tumor and poorly differentiated endocrine carcinoma of the stomach: prognostic evaluation by pathological analysis. Gastroenterology 1999, **116**: 532–542.

690 Solcia E, Capella C, Fiocca R, Rindi G, Rosai J. Gastric argyrophil carcinoidosis in patients with Zollinger-Ellison syndrome due to type 1 multiple endocrine neoplasia. A newly recognized association. Am J Surg Pathol 1990, **14**: 503–513.

691 Solcia E, Fioccia R, Villani L, Luinetti O, Capella C. Hyperplastic, dysplastic, and neoplastic enterochromaffin-like-cell proliferations of the gastric mucosa. Classification and histogenesis. Am J Surg Pathol 1995, **19**: S1–S7.

692 Solcia E, Kloppel G, Sobin LH (eds). Histological typing of endocrine tumours, ed. 2. International Histological Classification of Tumours. World Health Organization, Berlin, 2000, Springer.

693 Solcia R, Rindi G, Silini E, Villani L. Enterochromaffin-like (ECL) cells and their growths. Relationships to gastrin, reduced acid secretion and gastritis. Baillieres Clin Gastroenterol 1993, **7**: 149–165.

694 Solt J, Kádas I, Polak JM, Németh A, Bloom SR, Rauth J, Horváth L. A pancreatic-polypeptide-producing tumor of the stomach. Cancer 1984, **54**: 1101–1104.

695 Sundler F, Eriksson B, Grimelius L, Hakanson R, Lonroth H, Lundell L. Histamine in gastric carcinoid tumors. Immunocytochemical evidence. Endocr Pathol 1992, **3**: 23–27.

696 Thomas RM, Baybick JH, Elsayed AM, Sobin LH. Gastric carcinoids. An immunohistochemical and clinicopathologic study of 104 patients. Cancer 1994, **73**: 2053–2058.

697 Thompson GB, van Heerden JA, Martin JK, Schutt AJ, Ilstrup DM, Carney JA. Carcinoid tumors of the gastrointestinal tract. Presentation, management, and prognosis. Surgery 1985, **98**: 1054–1063.

Stromal tumors (GISTs and related lesions)

Histogenetic considerations; microscopic, immunohistochemical, electron microscopic, and molecular genetic features

698 Andersson J, Sjogren H, Meis-Kindblom JM, Stenman G, Aman P, Kindblom LG. The complexity of KIT gene mutations and chromosome rearrangements and their clinical correlation in gastrointestinal stromal (pacemaker cell) tumors. Am J Pathol 2002, **160**: 15–22.

699 Chambonnière ML, Mosnier-Damet M, Mosnier JF. Expression of microtubule-associated protein tau by gastrointestinal stromal tumors. Hum Pathol 2001, **32**: 1166–1173.

700 Corless CL, McGreevey L, Haley A, Town A, Heinrich MC. KIT

mutations are common in incidental gastrointestinal stromal tumors one centimeter or less in size. Am J Pathol 2002, **160:** 1567–1572.

701 Cornog JL Jr. Gastric leiomyoblastoma. A clinical and ultrastructural study. Cancer 1974, **34:** 711–719.

702 Daimuru Y, Kido H, Hashimoto H, Enjoji M. Benign schwannoma of the gastrointestinal tract. A clinicopathologic and immunohistochemical study. Hum Pathol 1988, **19:** 257–264.

703 Damiani S, Pasquinelli G, Eusebi V. GANT-like gastrointestinal pacemaker cell tumours with oncocytic features. Virchows Arch 1999, **435:** 143–150.

704 Dei Tos AP. The reappraisal of gastrointestinal stromal tumors: from Stout to the KIT revolution. Virchows Arch 2003, **442:** 421–428.

705 Donner LR. Gastrointestinal autonomic nerve tumor: a common type of gastrointestinal stromal neoplasm. Ultrastruct Pathol 1997, **21:** 419–424.

706 Erlandson RA, Klimstra DS, Woodruff JM. Subclassification of gastrointestinal stromal tumors based on evaluation by electron microscopy and immunohistochemistry. Ultrastruct Pathol 1996, **20:** 373–394.

707 Eyden B, Chorneyko KA, Shanks JH, Menasce LP, Banerjee SS. Contribution of electron microscopy to understanding cellular differentiation in mesenchymal tumors of the gastrointestinal tract: a study of 82 tumors. Ultrastruct Pathol 2002, **26:** 269–285.

708 Ferrer MD, Lloreta J, Corominas JM, Ribalta T, Iglesias M, Serrano S. Signet ring epithelioid stromal tumor of the small intestine. Ultrastruct Pathol 1999, **23:** 45–50.

709 Greenson JK. Gastrointestinal stromal tumors and other mesenchymal lesions to the gut. Mod Pathol 2003, **16:** 366–375.

710 Heinrich MC, Rubin BP, Longley B, Fletcher JA. Biology and genetic aspects of gastrointestinal stromal tumors: Kit activation and cytogenetic alterations. Hum Pathol 2002, **33:** 484–495.

711 Hemmi A, Komiyama A, Ohno S, Fujii Y, Terada N, Katoh R, Yokoyama A, Kawaoi A. Autonomic nerve tumour with skeinoid fibres: ultrastructure of skeinoid fibres examined by quick-freezing and deep-etching method. Virchows Arch 1999, **434:** 267–276.

712 Herrera GA, Cerezo L, Jones JE, Sack J, Grizzle WE, Pollack J, Lott RL. Gastrointestinal autonomic nerve tumors. Arch Pathol Lab Med 1989, **113:** 846–853.

713 Hirota S, Isozaki K, Moriyama Y, Hashimoto K, Nishida T, Ishiguro S, Kawano K, Hanada M, Kurata A, Takeda M, Muhammad Tunio GM, Matsuzawa Y, Kanakura Y, Shinomura Y, Kitamura Y. Gain-of-function mutations of c-kit in human gastrointestinal stromal tumors. Science 1998, **279:** 577–580.

714 Hjermstad BM, Sobin LH, Helwig EB. Stromal tumors of the gastrointestinal tract. Myogenic or neurogenic? Am J Surg Pathol 1987, **11:** 383–386.

715 Hornick JL, Fletcher CDM. Immunohistochemical staining for KIT (CD117) in soft tissue sarcomas is very limited in distribution. Am J Clin Pathol 2002, **117:** 188–193.

716 Hurlimann J, Gardiol D. Gastrointestinal stromal tumours. An immunohistochemical study of 165 cases. Histopathology 1991, **19:** 311–320.

717 Kindblom LG, Remotti HE, Aldenborg F, Meis-Kindblom JM. Gastrointestinal pacemaker cell tumor (GIPACT): gastrointestinal stromal tumors show phenotypic characteristics of the interstitial cells of Cajal. Am J Pathol 1998, **152:** 1259–1269.

718 Knapp RH, Wick MR, Goellner JR. Leiomyoblastomas and their relationship to other smooth-muscle tumors of the gastrointestinal tract. An electron-microscopic study. Am J Surg Pathol 1984, **8:** 449–461.

719 Lauwers GY, Erlandson RA, Casper ES, Brennan MF, Woodruff JM. Gastrointestinal autonomic nerve tumors. A clinicopathological, immunohistochemical, and ultrastructural

study of 12 cases. Am J Surg Pathol 1993, **17:** 887–897.

720 Lee JR, Joshi V, Griffin JW Jr, Lasota J, Miettinen M. Gastrointestinal autonomic nerve tumor: immunohistochemical and molecular identity with gastrointestinal stromal tumor. Am J Surg Pathol 2001, **25:** 979–987.

721 Leung KM, Wong S, Chow TC, Lee KC. A malignant gastrointestinal stromal tumor with osteoclast-like giant cells. Arch Pathol Lab Med 2002, **126:** 972–974.

722 Lux ML, Rubin BP, Biase TL, Chen CJ, Maclure T, Demetri G, Xiao S, Singer S, Fletcher CDM, Fletcher JA. KIT extracellular and kinase domain mutations in gastrointestinal stromal tumors. Am J Pathol 2000, **156:** 791–795.

723 Ma CK, Amin MB, Kintanar E, Linden MD, Zarbo RJ. Immunohistologic characterization of gastrointestinal stromal tumors: a study of 82 cases compared with 11 cases of leiomyomas. Mod Pathol 1993, **6:** 139–144.

724 Mackay B, Ro J, Floyd C, Ordoñez NG. Ultrastructural observations on smooth muscle tumors. Ultrastruct Pathol 1987, **11:** 593–607.

725 Matsukuma S, Doi M, Suzuki M, Ikegawa K, Sato K, Kuwabara N. Numerous eosinophilic globules (skeinoid fibers) in a duodenal stromal tumor: an exceptional case showing smooth muscle differentiation. Pathol Int 1997, **47:** 789–793.

726 Mazur MT, Clark HB. Gastric stromal tumors. Reappraisal of histogenesis. Am J Surg Pathol 1983, **7:** 507–519.

727 Medeiros F, Duensing A, Hornick JL, Oliveria AM, Fletcher JA, Fletcher CDM. KIT negative gastrointestinal stromal tumors (Abstract). Mod Pathol 2003, **16:** 128A.

728 Meissner WA. Leiomyoma of the stomach. Arch Pathol 1944, **38:** 207–209.

729 Mentzel T, Katenkamp D. Gastrointestinal stromal tumour with skeinoid fibres and bidirectional immunohistochemical differentiation. Histopathology 1996, **29:** 175–177.

730 Miettinen M. Gastrointestinal stromal tumors. An immunohistochemical study of cellular differentiation. Am J Clin Pathol 1988, **89:** 601–610.

731 Miettinen M, Sobin LH, Sarlomo-Rikala M. Immunohistochemical spectrum of GISTs at different sites and their differential diagnosis with a reference to CD117 (KIT). Mod Pathol 2000, **13:** 1134–1142.

732 Miettinen M, Sarlomo-Rikala M, Kovatich AJ, Lasota J. Calponin and h-caldesmon in soft tissue tumors: consistent h-caldesmon immunoreactivity in gastrointestinal stromal tumors indicates traits of smooth muscle differentiation. Mod Pathol 1999, **12:** 756–762.

733 Miettinen M, Virolainen M, Maarit-Sarlomo-Rikala. Gastrointestinal stromal tumors. Value of CD34 antigen in their identification and separation from true leiomyomas and schwannomas. Am J Surg Pathol 1995, **19:** 207–216.

734 Mikami T, Terada T, Nakamura K, Okayasu I. The gastric hypercellular microleiomyoma as a precursor lesion for clinical gastrointestinal stromal tumors. Hum Pathol 1997, **28:** 1355–1360.

735 Mikhael AI, Bacchi CE, Zarbo RJ, Ma CK, Gown AM. CD34 expression in stromal tumors of the gastrointestinal tract. Appl Immunohistochem 1994, **2:** 89–93.

736 Monihan JM, Carr NJ, Sobin LH. CD 34 immunoexpression in stromal tumours of the gastrointestinal tract and in mesenteric fibromatoses. Histopathology 1994, **25:** 469–473.

737 Patel R, Goldblum JR, Antonescu CR. Mutational analysis of c-kit in extragastrointestinal stromal tumors (EGIST): a molecular study of six cases. (Abstract) Mod Pathol 2003, **16:** 18A–19A.

738 Perez-Atayde AR, Shamberger RC, Kozakewich HW. Neuroectodermal differentiation of the gastrointestinal tumors in the Carney triad. An ultrastructural and immunohistochemical study. Am J Surg Pathol 1993, **17:** 706–714.

739 Pizzimbono CA, Higa E, Wise L. Leiomyoblastoma of the lesser

sac. Case report and review of the literature. Am Surg 1973, **39**: 692–699.

740 Prevot S, Bienvenu L, Vaillant JC, de Sain-Maur PP. Benign schwannoma of the digestive tract: a clinicopathologic and immunohistochemical study of five cases, including a case of esophageal tumor. Am J Surg Pathol 1999, **23**: 431–436.

741 Reith JD, Goldblum JR, Lyles RH, Weiss SW. Extragastrointestinal (soft tissue) stromal tumors: an analysis of 48 cases with emphasis on histologic predictors of outcome. Mod Pathol 2000, **13**: 577–585.

742 Ritter JH, Mills SE, Gaffey MJ, Nappi O, Wick MR. Clear cell tumors of the alimentary tract and abdominal cavity. Semin Diagn Pathol 1997, **14**: 213–219.

743 Robinson TL, Sircar K, Hewlett BR, Chorneyko K, Riddel RH, Huizinga JD. Gastrointestinal stromal tumors may originate from a subset of CD34-positive interstitial cells of Cajal. Am J Pathol 2000, **156**: 1157–1163.

744 Rosai J. GIST: an update. Int J Surg Pathol 2003, **11**: 177–186.

745 Rubin BP, Fletcher JA, Fletcher CDM. Molecular insights into the histogenesis and pathogenesis of gastrointestinal stromal tumors. Int J Surg Pathol 2000, **8**: 5–11.

746 Rudolph P, Chiaravalli AM, Pauser U, Oschlies I, Hillemanns M, Gobbo M, Marichal M, Eusebi V, Hofler H, Capella C, Klopper G. Gastrointestinal mesenchymal tumors – immunophenotypic classification and survival analysis. Virchows Arch 2002, **441**: 238–248.

747 Sakurai S, Fukasawa T, Chong JM, Tanaka A, Fukayama M. Embryonic form of smooth muscle myosin heavy chain (SMemb/MHC-B) in gastrointestinal stromal tumor and interstitial cells of Cajal. Am J Pathol 1999, **154**: 23–28.

748 Salazar H, Totten RS. Leiomyoblastoma of the stomach. An ultrastructural study. Cancer 1970, **25**: 176–185.

749 Sandberg AA, Bridge JA. Updates on the cytogenetics and molecular genetics of bone soft tissue tumors: gastrointestinal stromal tumors. Cancer Genet Cytogenet 2002, **135**: 1–22.

750 Sarlomo-Rikala M, Kovatich AJ, Barusevicius A, Miettinen M. CD117: a sensitive marker for gastrointestinal stromal tumors that is more specific than CD34. Mod Pathol 1998, **11**: 728–734.

751 Saul SH, Rast ML, Brooks JJ. The immunohistochemistry of gastrointestinal stromal tumors. Evidence supporting an origin from smooth muscle. Am J Surg Pathol 1987, **11**: 464–473.

752 Schmid S, Wegmann W. Gastrointestinal pacemaker cell tumor: clinicopathological, immunohistochemical, and ultrastructural study with special reference to c-kit receptor antibody. Virchows Arch 2000, **436**: 234–242.

753 Seidal T, Edvardsson H. Expression of c-kit (CD117) and Ki67 provides information about the possible cell origin and clinical course of gastrointestinal stromal tumours. Histopathology 1999, **34**: 416–424.

754 Shanks JH, Harris M, Banerjee SS, Eyden BP. Gastrointestinal autonomic nerve tumours: a report of nine cases. Histopathology 1996, **29**: 112–121.

755 Shek TW, Luk IS, Loong F, Ip P, Ma L. Inflammatory cell-rich gastrointestinal autonomic nerve tumor: an expansion of its histologic spectrum. Am J Surg Pathol 1996, **20**: 325–331.

756 Shia J, Erlandson RA, Antonescu CR. Metastatic epithelioid gastrointestinal stromal tumor: yet another tumor with anemone cell features. Ultrastructural Pathol 2003, **27**: 95–100.

757 Sircar K, Hewlett BR, Huizinga JD, Chorneyko K, Berezin I, Riddell RH. Interstitial cells of Cajal as precursors of gastrointestinal stromal tumors. Am J Surg Pathol 1999, **23**: 377–389.

758 Stout AP. Bizarre smooth muscle tumors of the stomach. Cancer 1962, **15**: 400–409.

759 Suster S, Fletcher CDM. Gastrointestinal stromal tumors with prominent signet-ring cell features. Mod Pathol 1996, **9**: 609–613.

760 Suster S, Sorace D, Moran CA. Gastrointestinal stromal tumors with prominent myxoid matrix. Clinicopathologic, immunohistochemical, and ultrastructural study of nine cases of a distinctive morphologic variant of myogenic stromal tumor. Am J Surg Pathol 1995, **19**: 59–70.

761 Tallquist G, Salmela H, Lindstrom BL. Leiomyoblastoma of the stomach. A clinicopathological study of 10 cases. Acta Pathol Microbiol Scand 1967, **17**: 194–202.

762 Tazawa K, Tsukada K, Makuuchi H, Tsutsumi Y. An immunohistochemical and clinicopathologic study of gastrointestinal stromal tumors. Pathol Int 2000, **49**: 786–798.

763 Tsutsumi Y, Tazawa K, Shibuya M. Type VI collagen immunoreactivity in skeinoid fibers in small intestinal stromal tumors. Pathol Int 1999, **49**: 836–839.

764 Ueyama T, Guo KJ, Hashimoto H, Daimaru Y, Enjoji M. A clinicopathologic and immunohistochemical study of gastrointestinal stromal tumors. Cancer 1992, **69**: 947–955.

765 Vanderwinden JM, Rumessen JJ, De Laet MH, Vanderhaeghen JJ, Schiffmann SN. CD34+ cells in human intestine are fibroblasts adjacent to but distinct from interstitial cells of Cajal. Lab Invest 1999, **79**: 59–65.

766 Walker P, Dvorak AM. Gastrointestinal autonomic nerve (GAN) tumor. Ultrastructural evidence for a newly recognized entity. Arch Pathol Lab Med 1986, **110**: 309–316.

767 Wang L, Vargas H, French SW. Cellular origin of gastrointestinal stromal tumors: a study of 27 cases. Arch Pathol Lab Med 2000, **124**: 1471–1475.

768 Wardelmann E, Neidt I, Bierhoff E, Speidel N, Manegold C, Fischer H-P, Pfeifer U, Pietsch T. c-kit mutations in gastrointestinal stromal tumors occur preferentially in the spindle rather than in the epithelioid cell variant. Mod Pathol 2002, **15**: 125–136.

769 Weiss RA, Mackay B. Malignant smooth muscle tumors of the gastrointestinal tract. An ultrastructural study of 20 cases. Ultrastruct Pathol 1981, **2**: 231–240.

770 Welsh RA, Meyer AT. Ultrastructure of gastric leiomyoma. Arch Pathol 1969, **87**: 71–81.

771 Yagihashi N, Kaimori M, Katayama Y, Yagihashi S. Crystalloid formation in gastrointestinal schwannoma. Hum Pathol 1997, **28**: 304–308.

772 Yantiss RK, Rosenberg AE, Selig MK, Nielsen GP. Gastrointestinal stromal tumors: an ultrastructural study. Int J Surg Pathol 2002, **10**: 101–113.

773 Yao T, Aoyagi K, Hizawa K, Kimura Y, Tsuneyoshi M. Gastric epithelioid stromal tumor (leiomyoma) with granular changes. Int J Surg Pathol 1996, **4**: 37–42.

Microscopic differential diagnosis

774 Montgomery E, Torbenson MS, Kaushal M, Fisher C, Abraham SC. Beta-catenin immunohistochemistry separates mesenteric fibromatosis from gastrointestinal stromal tumor and sclerosing mesenteritis. Am J Surg Pathol 2002, **26**: 1296–1301.

775 Plaat BE, Hollema H, Molenaar WM, Broers GH, Pijpe J, Mastik MF, Hoekstra HJ, van den Berg E, Scheper RJ, van der Graaf WT. Soft tissue leiomyosarcomas and malignant gastrointestinal stromal tumors: differences in clinical outcome and expression of multidrug resistance proteins. J Clin Oncol 2000, **18**: 3211–3220.

776 Sarlomo-Rikala M, El-Rifai W, Lahtinen T, Andersson LC, Miettinen M, Knuutila S. Different patterns of DNA copy number changes in gastrointestinal stromal tumors, leiomyomas, and schwannomas. Hum Pathol 1998, **29**: 476–481.

777 Shidham VB, Chivukula M, Gubta D, Rao RN, Komorowski R. Immunohistochemical comparison of gastrointestinal stromal tumor and solitary fibrous tumor. Arch Pathol Lab Med 2002, **126**: 1189–1192.

778 Yantiss RK, Spiro IJ, Compton CC, Rosenberg AE. Gastrointestinal stromal tumor versus intra-abdominal

fibromatosis of the bowel wall: a clinically important differential diagnosis. Am J Surg Pathol 2000, **24**: 947–957.

General, clinical, and gross features

779 Bates AW, Feakins RM, Scheimberg I. Congenital gastrointestinal stromal tumour is morphologically indistinguishable from the adult form, but does not express CD117 and carries a favourable prognosis. Histopathology 2000, **37**: 316–322.

780 Carney JA. The triad of gastric epithelioid leiomyosarcoma, pulmonary chondroma, and functioning extra-adrenal paraganglioma. A five-year review. Medicine (Baltimore) 1983, **62**: 159–169.

781 Carney JA. Gastric stromal sarcoma, pulmonary chondroma, and extra-adrenal paraganglioma (Carney Triad): natural history, adrenocortical component, and possible familial occurrence. Mayo Clin Proc 1999, **74**: 543–552.

782 Carney JA, Stratakis CA. Familial paraganglioma and gastric stromal sarcoma: a new syndrome distinct from the Carney triad. Am J Med Genet 2002, **108**: 132–139.

783 Farrugia G, Kim CH, Grant CS, Zinsmeister AR. Leiomyosarcoma of the stomach. Determinants of long-term survival. Mayo Clin Proc 1992, **67**: 533–536.

784 Fuller CE, Williams GT. Gastrointestinal manifestations of type 1 neurofibromatosis (von Recklinghausen's disease). Histopathology 1991, **19**: 1–11.

785 Golden T, Stout AP. Smooth muscle tumors of the gastrointestinal tract and retroperitoneal tissues. Surg Gynecol Obstet 1941, **73**: 784–810.

786 Hamazoe R, Shimizu N, Nishidoi H, Maeta M, Koga S. Gastric leiomyoblastoma in childhood. J Pediatr Surg 1991, **26**: 225–227.

787 Hirota S, Okazaki T, Kitamura Y, O'Brien P, Kapusta L, Dardick I. Cause of familial and multiple gastrointestinal autonomic nerve tumors with hyperplasia of interstitial cells of Cajal is germline mutation of the c-kit gene. Am J Surg Pathol 2000, **24**: 326–327.

788 Kerr JZ, Hicks MJ, Nuchtern JG, Saldivar V, Heim-Hall J, Shah S, Kelly DR, Cain WS, Chintagumpala MM. Gastrointestinal autonomic nerve tumors in the pediatric population. A report of four cases and a review of the literature. Cancer 1999, **85**: 220–230.

789 Maiorana A, Fante R, Cesinaro A, Fano R. Synchronous occurrence of epithelial and stromal tumors in the stomach: a report of 6 cases. Arch Pathol Lab Med 2000, **124**: 682–686.

790 Nishida T, Hirota S, Taniguchi M, Hashimoto K, Isozaki K, Nakamura H, Kanakura Y, Tanaka T, Takabayashi A, Matsuda H, Kitamura Y. Familial gastrointestinal stromal tumours with germline mutation of the KIT gene. Nat Genet 1998, **19**: 323–324.

791 O'Brien P, Kapusta L, Dardick I, Axler J, Gnidec A. Multiple familial gastrointestinal autonomic nerve tumors and small intestinal neuronal dysplasia. Am J Surg Pathol 1999, **23**: 198–204.

792 Palmer ED. Benign intramural tumors of the stomach. A review with special reference to gross pathology. Medicine (Baltimore) 1951, **30**: 81–181.

793 Persson S, Kindblom LG, Angervall L, Tisell LE. Metastasizing gastric epithelioid leiomyosarcomas (leiomyoblastomas) in young individuals with long-term survival. Cancer 1992, **70**: 721–732.

794 Raafat F, Salman WD, Roberts K, Ingram L, Rees R, Mann JR. Carney's triad. Gastric leiomyosarcoma, pulmonary chondroma and extra-adrenal paraganglioma in young females. Histopathology 1986, **10**: 1325–1333.

795 Schaldenbrand JD, Appelman HD. Solitary solid stromal gastrointestinal tumors in von Recklinghausen's disease with minimal smooth muscle differentiation. Hum Pathol 1984, **15**: 229–232.

796 Wick MR, Ruebner BH, Carney JA. Gastric tumors in patients with pulmonary chondroma or extra-adrenal paraganglioma. An ultrastructural study. Arch Pathol Lab Med 1981, **105**: 527–531.

797 Wurlitzer FP, Mares AJ, Isaacs H Jr, Handling BH, Woolley MM. Smooth muscle tumors of the stomach in childhood and adolescence. J Pediatr Surg 1973, **8**: 421–427.

Spread and metastases

798 Ng EH, Pollock RE, Romsdahl MM. Prognostic implications of patterns of failure for gastrointestinal leiomyosarcomas. Cancer 1992, **69**: 1334–1341.

799 Salmela H. Smooth muscle tumours of the stomach. A clinical study of 112 cases. Acta Chir Scand 1968, **134**: 384–391.

Treatment

800 De Matteo RP, Heinrich MC, El-Rifai WM, Demetri G. Clinical management of gastrointestinal stromal tumors: before and after STI-571. Hum Pathol 2002, **33**: 466–477.

801 Demetri GD, von Mehren M, Blanke CD, Van den Abbele A, Eisenberg B, Roberts PJ, Heinrich MC, Tuveson DA, Singer S, Janicek M, Fletcher JA, Silverman SG, Silberman SL, Capdeville R, Kiese B, Peng B, Dimitrijevic S, Druker BJ, Corless C, Fletcher CD, Joensuu H. Efficacy and safety of imatinib mesylate in advanced gastrointestinal stromal tumors. N Engl J Med 2002, **347**: 472–480.

Prognosis

802 Amin MB, Ma CK, Linden MD, Kubus JJ, Zarbo RJ. Prognostic value of proliferating cell nuclear antigen index in gastric stromal tumors. Correlation with mitotic count and clinical outcome. Am J Clin Pathol 1993, **100**: 428–432.

803 Appelman HD, Helwig EB. Gastric epithelioid leiomyoma and leiomyosarcoma (leiomyoblastoma). Cancer 1976, **38**: 709–728.

804 Appelman HD, Helwig EB. Sarcomas of the stomach. Am J Clin Pathol 1977, **67**: 2–10.

805 Appelman H, Helwig EB. Cellular leiomyomas of the stomach in 49 patients. Arch Pathol Lab Med 1977, **101**: 373–377.

806 Carillo R, Candia A, Rodriquez-Peralto JL, Caz V. Prognostic significance of DNA ploidy and proliferative index (MIB-1 index) in gastrointestinal stromal tumors. Hum Pathol 1997, **28**: 160–165.

807 Cooper PN, Quirke P, Hardy GJ, Dixon MF. A flow cytometric, clinical, and histological study of stromal neoplasms of the gastrointestinal tract. Am J Surg Pathol 1992, **16**: 163–170.

808 Cunningham RE, Abbondanzo SL, Chu WS, Emory TS, Sobin LH, O'Leary TJ. Apoptosis, bcl-2 expression, and p53 expression in gastrointestinal stromal/smooth muscle tumors. Appl Immunohistochem Mol Morphol 2001, **9**: 19–23.

809 El-Naggar AK, Ro JY, McLemore D, Garnsey L, Ordonez N, MacKay B. Gastrointestinal stromal tumors. DNA flow-cytometric study of 58 patients with at least five years of follow-up. Mod Pathol 1989, **2**: 511–515.

810 Emory TS, Sobin LH, Lukes L, Lee DH, O'Leary TJ. Prognosis of gastrointestinal smooth-muscle (stromal) tumors: dependence on anatomic site. Am J Surg Pathol 1999, **23**: 82–87.

811 Ernst SI, Hubbs AE, Przygodzki RM, Emory TS, Sobin LH, O'Leary TJ. KIT mutation portends poor prognosis in gastrointestinal stromal/smooth muscle tumors. Lab Invest 1998, **78**: 1633–1636.

812 Evans HL. Smooth muscle tumors of the gastrointestinal tract. A study of 56 cases followed for a minimum of 10 years. Cancer 1985, **56**: 2242–2250.

813 Fisher C, Deasel R, Abraham SC, Amr SS, Sheikh SS, Chadburn A, Montgomery E. CD44 loss in gastric stromal tumors as a prognostic marker. (Abstract) Mod Pathol 2003, **16**: 12A.

814 Fletcher CDM, Berman JJ, Corless C, Gorstein F, Lasota J, Longley BJ, Miettinen M, O'Leary TJ, Remotti H, Rubin BP, Shmookler B, Sobin LH, Weiss SW. Diagnosis of gastrointestinal stromal tumors: a consensus approach. Hum Pathol 2000, **33**: 459–465; Int J Surg Pathol 2002, **10**: 81–90.

815 Flint A, Appelman HD, Beckwith AL. DNA analysis of gastric

stromal neoplasms: correlation with pathologic features. Surg Pathol 1989, **2**: 117–124.

816 Franquemont DW. Differentiation and risk assessment of gastrointestinal stromal tumors. Am J Clin Pathol 1995, **103**: 41–47.

817 Franquemont DW, Frierson HF Jr. Muscle differentiation and clinicopathologic features of gastrointestinal stromal tumors. Am J Surg Pathol 1992, **16**: 947–954.

818 Gunawan B, Bergmann F, Hoer J, Langer C, Schumpelick V, Becker H, Fuzesi L. Biological and clinical significance of cytogenetic abnormalities in low-risk and high-risk gastrointestinal stromal tumors. Hum Pathol 2002, **33**: 316–321.

819 Hasegawa T, Matsuno Y, Shimoda T, Hirohashi S. Gastrointestinal stromal tumor: consistent CD117 immunostaining for diagnosis, and prognostic classification based on tumor size and MIB-1 grade. Hum Pathol 2002, **33**: 669–676.

820 Lasota J, Jasinski M, Sarlomo-Rikala M, Miettinen M. Mutations in exon 11 of c-kit occur preferentially in malignant versus benign gastrointestinal stromal tumors and do not occur in leiomyomas or leiomyosarcomas. Am J Pathol 1999, **154**: 53–60.

821 Lerma E, Oliva E, Tugues D, Prat J. Stromal tumours of the gastrointestinal tract. A clinicopathological and ploidy analysis of 33 cases. Virchows Arch 1994, **424**: 19–24.

822 Miettinen M, El-Rifai W, Sobin LH, Lasota J. Evaluation of malignancy and prognosis of gastrointestinal stromal tumors: a review. Hum Pathol 2002, **33**: 478–483.

823 O'Leary T, Ernst S, Przygodzki R, Emory T, Sobin L. Loss of heterozygosity at 1p36 predicts poor prognosis in gastrointestinal stromal/smooth muscle tumors. Lab Invest 1999, **79**: 1461–1467.

824 Panizo-Santos A, Sola I, Vega F, de Alava E, Lozano MD, Iodate MA, Pardo-Mindán J. Predicting metastatic risk of gastrointestinal stromal tumors: role of cell proliferation and cell cycle regulatory proteins. Int J Surg Pathol 2000, **8**: 133–144.

825 Ranchod M, Kempson RL. Smooth muscle tumors of the gastrointestinal tract and retroperitoneum. A pathologic analysis of 100 cases. Cancer 1977, **39**: 255–262.

826 Ray R, Tahan SR, Andrews C, Goldman H. Stromal tumors of the stomach. Prognostic value of the PCNA index. Mod Pathol 1994, **7**: 26–30.

827 Rudolph P, Gloeckner K, Parwaresch R, Harms D, Schmidt D. Immunophenotype, proliferation, DNA ploidy, and biological behavior of gastrointestinal stromal tumors: a multivariate clinicopathologic study. Hum Pathol 1998, **29**: 791–800.

828 Sakurai S, Fukayama M, Kaizaki Y, Saito K, Kanazawa K, Kitamura M, Iwasaki Y, Hishima T, Hayashi Y, Koike M. Telomerase activity in gastrointestinal stromal tumors. Cancer 1998, **83**: 2060–2066.

829 Shiu MH, Farr GH, Papachristou DN, Hajdu SI. Myosarcomas of the stomach. Natural history, prognostic factors and management. Cancer 1982, **49**: 177–187.

830 Tornoczky T, Kalman E, Hegedus G, Horvath OP, Sapi Z, Antal L, Jakso P, Pajor L. High mitotic index associated with poor prognosis in gastrointestinal autonomic nerve tumour. Histopathology, 1999, **35**: 121–128.

831 Trupiano JK, Stewart RE, Misick C, Appelman HD, Goldblum JR. Gastric stromal tumors: a clinicopathologic study of 77 cases with correlation of features with non aggressive and aggressive clinical behaviors. Am J Surg Pathol 2002, **26**: 705–714.

832 Tsushima K, Rainwater LM, Goellner JR, van Heerden JA, Lieber MM. Leiomyosarcomas and benign smooth muscle tumors of the stomach. Nuclear DNA patterns studied by flow cytometry. Mayo Clin Proc 1987, **62**: 275–280.

833 Wong NACS, Young R, Malcomson RDG, Nayer AG, Jamieson LA, Save VE, Carey FA, Brewster DH, Han C, Al-Nafussi A. Prognostic indicators for gastrointestinal stromal tumors: a clinicopathological and immunohistochemical study of 108 resected cases of the stomach. Histopathology 2003, **43**: 118–126.

Lymphoid tumors and tumorlike conditions

834 Appelman HD, Hirsch SD, Schnitzer B, Coon WW. Clinicopathologic overview of gastrointestinal lymphomas. Am J Surg Pathol 1985, **9**: 71–83.

835 Baron BW, Bitter MA, Baron JM, Bostwick DG. Gastric adenocarcinoma after gastric lymphoma. Cancer 1987, **60**: 1876–1882.

836 Chan JK. Gastrointestinal lymphomas: an overview with emphasis on new findings and diagnostic problems. Semin Diagn Pathol 1996, **13**: 260–296.

837 Greiner A, Kirchner T, Ott G, Marx A, Fischbach W, Muller-Hermelink HK. Occurrence of multiple lymphoepithelioma-like carcinomas and MALT-type lymphoma in the stomach: detection of EBV in carcinomas but not in lymphoma. Histopathology 1996, **29**: 51–56.

838 Grody WW, Weiss LM, Warnke RA, Magidson JG, Hu E, Lewin KJ. Gastrointestinal lymphomas. Immunohistochemical studies on the cell of origin. Am J Surg Pathol 1985, **9**: 328–337.

839 Hsi ED, Eisbruch A, Greenson JK, Singleton TP, Ross CW, Schnitzer B. Classification of primary gastric lymphomas according to histologic features. Am J Surg Pathol 1998, **22**: 17–27.

840 Ioachim HL, Hajdu C, Giancotti FR, Dorsett B. Lymphoid proliferations and lymphomas associated with gastric metaplasia, dysplasia, and carcinoma. Hum Pathol 1999, **30**: 833–842.

841 Isaacson PG, Spencer J, Finn T. Primary B-cell gastric lymphoma. Hum Pathol 1986, **17**: 72–82.

842 Kane EP, Weingarten LA, Payson BA, Mori K, Sarlin JG. Synchronous ulcerating adenocarcinoma and malignant lymphoma of the stomach. Am J Gastroenterol 1982, **77**: 461–463.

843 Kossakowska A, Eyton-Jones S, Urbanski S. Immunoglobulin and T-cell receptor gene rearrangements in lesions of mucosa-associated lymphoid tissue. Diagn Mol Pathol 1993, **2**: 233–240.

844 Lewin KJ, Ranchod M, Dorfman RF. Lymphomas of the gastrointestinal tract. A study of 117 cases presenting with gastrointestinal disease. Cancer 1978, **42**: 693–707.

845 Nakamura S, Aoyagi K, Iwanaga S, Yao T, Tsuneyoshi M, Fujishima M. Synchronous and metachronous primary gastric lymphoma and adenocarcinoma: a clinicopathologic study of 12 patients. Cancer 1997, **79**: 1077–1085.

846 Papadimitriou CS, Papacharalampous NX, Kittas C. Primary gastrointestinal malignant lymphomas. A morphologic and immunohistochemical study. Cancer 1985, **55**: 870–879.

847 Shani A, Schutt AJ, Weiland LH. Primary gastric malignant lymphoma followed by gastric adenocarcinoma. Report of 4 cases and review of the literature. Cancer 1978, **42**: 2039–2044.

The MALT concept

848 Arends JE, Bot FJ, Gisbertz IAM, Schouten HC. Expression of CD10, CD75 and CD43 in MALT lymphoma and their usefulness in discriminating MALT lymphoma from follicular lymphoma and chronic gastritis. Histopathology 1999, **35**: 209–215.

849 Banks PM, Isaacson PG. Malt lymphomas in 1997. Where do we stand? Am J Clin Pathol 1999, **111**: S75–S83.

850 Bouzourene H, Haefliger T, Delacretaz F, Saraga E. The role of Helicobacter pylori in primary gastric MALT lymphoma. Histopathology 1999, **34**: 118–123.

851 Chan JKC, Ng CS, Isaacson PG. Relationship between high-grade lymphoma and low-grade B-cell mucosa-associated lymphoid tissue lymphoma (MALToma) of the stomach. Am J Pathol 1990, **136**: 1153–1164.

852 Dorfman DM, Pinkus GS. Utility of immunophenotypic studies in the diagnosis of low-grade lymphoma of mucosa-associated lymphoid tissue (MALT) and other low-grade non-Hodgkin's lymphomas of extranodal sites. Appl Immunohistochem 1995, **3**: 160–167.

853 Genta RM. Le lymphome imaginaire (editorial). Hum Pathol 1998, **29**: 769–770.

854 Greiner A, Marx A, Heesemann J, Leebmann J, Schmausser B, Muller-Hermelink HK. Idiotype identity in a MALT-type lymphoma and B cells in *Helicobacter pylori* associated chronic gastritis. Lab Invest 1994, **70**: 572–578.

855 Harris NL, Isaacson PG. What are the criteria for distinguishing MALT from non-MALT lymphoma at extranodal sites? Am J Clin Pathol 1999, **111**(Suppl): S126–S132.

856 Hussell T, Isaacson P, Crabtree J, Dogan A, Spencer J. Immunoglobulin specificity of low grade B cell gastrointestinal lymphoma of mucosa-associated lymphoid tissue (MALT) type. Am J Pathol 1993, **142**: 285–292.

857 Hussell T, Isaacson PG, Crabtree JE, Spencer J. The response of cells from low-grade B-cell gastric lymphomas of mucosa-associated lymphoid tissue to *Helicobacter pylori*. Lancet 1993, **342**: 571–574.

858 Isaacson P, Wright DH. Malignant lymphoma of mucosa-associated lymphoid tissue. A distinctive type of B-cell lymphoma. Cancer 1983, **52**: 1410–1416.

859 Isaacson PG. Gastrointestinal lymphoma. Hum Pathol 1994, **25**: 1020–1029.

860 Kroft SH, Hsi ED, Ross CW, Schnitzer B, Singleton TP. Evaluation of CD23 expression in paraffin-embedded gastric lymphomas of mucosa-associated lymphoid tissue. Mod Pathol 1998, **11**: 967–970.

861 Krol AD, Hermans J, Kramer MH, Kluin PM, Kluin-Nelemans HC, Blok P, Heering KJ, Noordijk EM, van Krieken JH. Gastric lymphomas compared with lymph node lymphomas in a population-based registry differ in stage distribution and dissemination patterns but not in patient survival. Cancer 1997, **79**: 390–397.

862 Miyamoto M, Haruma K, Hiyama T, Kamada T, Masuda H, Shimamoto F, Inoue K, Chayama K. High incidence of B-cell monoclonality in follicular gastritis: a possible association between follicular gastritis and MALT lymphoma. Virchows Arch 2002, **440**: 376–380.

863 Montalbán C, Manzanal A, Castrillo JM, Escribano L, Bellas C. Low grade gastric B-cell MALT lymphoma progressing into high grade lymphoma. Clonal identity of the two stages of the tumour, unusual bone involvement and leukaemic dissemination. Histopathology 1995, **27**: 89–91.

864 Nakamura S, Aoyagi K, Furuse M, Suekane H, Matsumoto T, Yao T, Sakai Y, Fuchigami T, Yamamoto I, Tsuneyoshi M, Fujishima M. B-cell monoclonality precedes the development of gastric MALT lymphoma in Helicobacter pylori-associated chronic gastritis. Am J Pathol 1998, **152**: 1271–1279.

865 Ohashi S, Segawa K, Okamura S, Urano H, Kanamori S, Ishikawa H, Hara K, Hukutomi A, Shirai K, Maeda M. A clinicopathologic study of gastric mucosa-associated lymphoid tissue lymphoma. Cancer 2000, **88**: 2210–2219.

866 Parsonnet J, Hansen S, Rodriguez L, Gelb AB, Warnke RA, Jellum E, Orentreich N, Vogelman JH, Friedman GD. *Helicobacter pylori* infection and gastric lymphoma. N Engl J Med 1994, **330**: 1267–1271.

867 Peng H, Du M, Diss TC, Isaacson PG, Pan L. Genetic evidence for a clonal link between low and high-grade components in gastric MALT B-cell lymphoma. Histopathology 1997, **30**: 425–429.

868 Ree HJ, Rege VB, Knisley RE, Thayer WR, D'Amico RP, Song JY, Crowley JP. Malignant lymphoma of Waldeyer's following gastrointestinal lymphoma. Cancer 1980, **46**: 1528–1535.

869 Wotherspoon AC, Doglioni C, Diss TC, Pan L, Moschini A, de Boni M, Isaacson PG. Regression of primary low-grade B-cell gastric lymphoma of mucosa-associated lymphoid tissue type after eradication of *Helicobacter pylori*. Lancet 1993, **342**: 575–577.

870 Wotherspoon AC, Ortiz-Hidalgo C, Falzon MR, Isaacson PG. *Helicobacter pylori*-associated gastritis and primary B-cell gastric lymphoma. Lancet 1992, **339**: 745–746.

871 Wündisch T, Neubauer A, Stolte M, Ritter M, Thiede C. B-cell monoclonality is associated with lymphoid follicles in gastritis. Am J Surg Pathol 2003, **27**: 882–887.

872 Yamashita H, Watanabe H, Ajioka Y, Nishikura K, Maruta K, Fujino MA. When can complete regression of low-grade gastric lymphoma of mucosa-associated lymphoid tissue be predicted after Helicobacter pylori eradication? Histopathology 2000, **37**: 131–140.

Low-grade lymphomas

873 Aiello A, Giardini R, Tondini C, Balzarotti M, Diss T, Peng H, Delia D, Pilotti S. PCR-based clonality analysis: a reliable method for the diagnosis and follow-up monitoring of conservatively treated gastric B-cell MALT lymphomas? Histopathology 1999, **34**: 326–330.

874 Baens M, Maes B, Steyls A, Geboes K, Marynen P, De Wolf-Peeters C. The product of the t(11;18), an AP12-MLT fusion, marks nearly half of the gastric MALT type lymphomas without large cell proliferation. Am J Pathol 2000, **156**: 1433–1439.

875 Blanco R, Lyda M, Davis B, Kraus M, Fenoglio-Preiser C. Trisomy 3 in gastric lymphomas of extranodal marginal zone B-cell (mucosa-associated lymphoid tissue) origin demonstrated by FISH in intact paraffin tissue sections. Hum Pathol 1999, **30**: 706–711.

876 El-Zimaity HM, El-Zaatari FA, Dore MP, Oweiss S, Gutierrez O, Yuksul M, Ramchatesingh J, Graham DY. The differential diagnosis of early gastric mucosa-associated lymphoma: polymerase chain reaction and paraffin section immunotyping. Mod Pathol 1999, **12**: 885–893.

877 Fraga M, Lloret E, Sanchez-Verde L, Orradre JL, Campo E, Bosch F, Piris MA. Mucosal mantle cell (centrocytic) lymphomas. Histopathology 1995, **26**: 413–422.

878 Funakoshi N, Kanoh T, Kobayashi Y, Miyake T, Uchino H, Ochi K. IgM-producing gastric plasmacytoma. Cancer 1984, **54**: 638–643.

879 Fung CY, Grossbard ML, Linggood RM, Younger J, Flieder A, Harris NL, Graeme-Cook F. Mucosa-associated lymphoid tissue lymphoma of the stomach. Long term outcome after local treatment. Cancer 1999, **85**: 9–17.

880 Genta RM. Le lymphome imaginaire (editorial). Hum Pathol 1998, **29**: 769–770.

881 Hernandez JA, Sheehan WW. Lymphomas of the mucosa-associated lymphoid tissue. Signet ring cell lymphomas presenting in mucosal lymphoid organs. Cancer 1985, **55**: 592–597.

882 Hoshida Y, Kusakabe H, Furukawa H, Kasugai T, Miwa H, Ishiguro S, Aozasa K. Reassessment of gastric lymphoma in light of the concept of mucosa-associated lymphoid tissue lymphoma: analysis of 53 patients. Cancer 1997, **80**: 1151–1159.

883 Hsi ED, Singleton TP, Swinnen L, Dunphy CH, Alkan S. Mucosa-associated lymphoid tissue-type lymphomas occurring in post-transplantation patients. Am J Surg Pathol 2000, **24**: 100–106.

884 Ko YH, Han JJ, Noh JH, Ree HJ. Lymph nodes in gastric B-cell lymphoma: pattern of involvement and early histological changes. Histopathology 2002, **40**: 497–504.

885 Lebrun D, Kamel O, Cleary M, Dorfman R, Warnke R. Follicular lymphomas of the gastrointestinal tract. Pathologic features in 31 cases and BCL-2 oncogenic protein expression. Am J Pathol 1992, **140**: 1327–1335.

886 Nagasaka T, Lai R, Harada T, Chen YY, Chen WG, Arber DA, Weiss LM. Coexisting thymic and gastric lymphomas of mucosa-associated lymphoid tissues in a patient with Sjogren syndrome. Arch Pathol Lab Med 2000, **124**: 770–773.

887 Papadaki L, Wotherspoon AC, Isaacson PG. The lymphoepithelial lesion of gastric low-grade B-cell lymphoma of mucosa-associated lymphoid tissue (MALT). An ultrastructural study. Histopathology 1992, **21**: 415–421.

888 Sukpanichnant S, Vnencak-Jones CL, McCurley TL. Determination of B-cell clonality in paraffin-embedded endoscopic biopsy specimens of abnormal lymphocytic infiltrates and gastrointestinal lymphoma by polymerase chain reaction. Am J Clin Pathol 1994, **102**: 299–305.

889 Thieblemont C, Bastion Y, Berger F, Rieux C, Salles G, Dumontet C, Felman P, Coiffier B. Mucosa-associated lymphoid tissue gastrointestinal and nongastrointestinal lymphoma behavior: analysis of 108 patients. J Clin Oncol 1997, **15**: 1624–1630.

890 Wotherspoon AC, Diss TC, Pan L, Singh N, Whelan J, Isaacson PG. Low grade gastric B-cell lymphoma of mucosa associated lymphoid tissue in immunocompromised patients. Histopathology 1996, **28**: 129–134.

891 Wotherspoon AC, Doglioni C, Diss TC, Pan L, Moschini A, de Boni M, Isaacson PG. Regression of primary low-grade B-cell gastric lymphoma of mucosa-associated lymphoid tissue type after eradication of *Helicobacter pylori*. Lancet 1993, **342**: 575–577.

892 Wotherspoon AC, Doglioni C, Isaacson PG. Low-grade gastric B-cell lymphoma of mucosa-associated lymphoid tissue (MALT). A multifocal disease. Histopathology 1992, **20**: 29–34.

893 Yamauchi A, Tomita Y, Miwa H, Sakamoto H, Sugiyama H, Aozasa K. Clonal evolution of gastric lymphoma of mucosa-associated lymphoid tissue type. Mod Pathol 2001, **14**: 957–962.

894 Yokoi T, Nakamura T, Kasugai K, Yatabe Y, Fujita M, Kuroda M, Akaza K, Nomura C, Hamajima E, Suchi T, Seto M, Hara K, Nakamura S. Primary low-grade gastric mucosa-associated lymphoid tissue (MALT) lymphoma with polypoid appearance. Polypoid gastric MALT lymphoma: a clinicopathologic study of eight cases. Pathol Int 1999, **49**: 702–709.

895 Zamboni G, Franzin G, Scarpa A, Bonetti F, Pea M, Mariuzzi GM, Menestrina F. Carcinoma-like signet-ring cells in gastric mucosa-associated lymphoid tissue (MALT) lymphoma. Am J Surg Pathol 1996, **20**: 588–598.

896 Zukerberg LR, Ferry JA, Southern JF, Harris NL. Lymphoid infiltrates of the stomach. Evaluation of histologic criteria for the diagnosis of low-grade gastric lymphoma on endoscopic biopsy specimens. Am J Surg Pathol 1990, **14**: 1087–1990.

Lymphoid hyperplasia and plasma cell granuloma

897 Abbondanzo SL, Sobin LH. Gastric "pseudolymphoma": a retrospective morphologic and immunophenotypic study of 97 cases. Cancer 1997, **79**: 1656–1663.

898 Brooks JJ, Enterline HT. Gastric pseudolymphoma. Its three subtypes and relation to lymphoma. Cancer 1983, **51**: 476–486.

899 Eimoto T, Futami K, Naito H, Takeshita M, Kikuchi M. Gastric pseudolymphoma with monotypic cytoplasmic immunoglobulin. Cancer 1985, **55**: 788–793.

900 Faris TD, Saltzstein SL. Gastric lymphoid hyperplasia. A lesion confused with lymphosarcoma. Cancer 1964, **17**: 207–212.

901 Hyjek E, Kelényi G. Pseudolymphomas of the stomach. A lesion characterized by progressively transformed germinal centres. Histopathology 1982, **6**: 61–68.

902 Isaacson P, Buchanan R, Mepham BL. Plasma cell granuloma of the stomach. Hum Pathol 1978, **9**: 355–358.

903 Perez CA, Dorfman RF. Benign lymphoid hyperplasia of the stomach and duodenum. Radiology 1966, **87**: 505–510.

904 Ranchod M, Lewin KJ, Dorfman RF. Lymphoid hyperplasia of the gastrointestinal tract. A study of 26 cases and review of the literature. Am J Surg Pathol 1978, **2**: 383–400.

905 Saraga P, Hurlimann J, Ozzello L. Lymphomas and pseudolymphomas of the alimentary tract. An immunohistochemical study with clinicopathologic correlations. Hum Pathol 1981, **12**: 713–723.

906 Scoazec J-Y, Brousse N, Potet F, Jeulain J-F. Focal malignant lymphoma in gastric pseudolymphoma. Histologic and immunohistochemical study of a case. Cancer 1986, **57**: 1330–1336.

907 Soga J, Saito K, Suski N, Sukai T. Plasma cell granuloma of the stomach. Cancer 1970, **25**: 618–625.

908 Spencer J, Diss TC, Isaacson PG. Primary B cell gastric lymphoma. A genotypic analysis. Am J Pathol 1989, **135**: 557–564.

909 Tada T, Wakabayashi T, Kishimoto H. Plasma cell granuloma of the stomach. A report of a case associated with gastric cancer. Cancer 1984, **54**: 541–544.

910 Wolf JA Jr, Spjut HJ. Focal lymphoid hyperplasia of the stomach preceding gastric lymphoma. Case report and review of the literature. Cancer 1981, **48**: 2518–2523.

Intermediate/high-grade (large cell) lymphomas

911 Brooks JJ, Enterline HT. Primary gastric lymphomas. A clinicopathologic study of 58 cases with long-term follow-up and literature review. Cancer 1983, **51**: 701–711.

912 Chan WY, Chan EK, Chow JH. Epstein-Barr virus-associated gastric lymphomas are distinct from mucosa-associated lymphoid tissue-type lymphomas: genetic abnormalities of p53 gene. Diagn Mol Pathol 2001, **10**: 153–160.

913 Crump M, Gospodarowicz M, Shepherd FA. Lymphoma of the gastrointestinal tract. Semin Oncol 1999, **26**: 324–337.

914 Dean PJ, Moinuddin SM, Emerson LD. Application of anti-leukocyte common antigen and anti-cytokeratin antibodies to the biopsy diagnosis of gastric large cell lymphoma. Hum Pathol 1987, **18**: 918–923.

915 De Wolf-Peeters C, Achten R. The histogenesis of large cell gastric lymphomas. Histopathology 1999, **34**: 71–75.

916 Dragosics B, Bauer P, Radaszkiewicz T. Primary gastrointestinal non-Hodgkin's lymphomas. A retrospective clinicopathologic study of 150 cases. Cancer 1985, **55**: 1060–1073.

917 Ferreri AJ, Freschi M, Dell'Oro S, Viale E, Villa E, Ponzoni M. Prognostic significance of the histopathologic recognition of low- and high-grade components in stage I-II B-cell gastric lymphomas. Am J Surg Pathol 2001, **25**: 95–102.

918 Filippa DA, Lieberman PH, Weingrad DN, Decosse JJ, Bretsky SS. Primary lymphomas of the gastrointestinal tract. Analysis of prognostic factors with emphasis on histological type. Am J Surg Pathol 1983, **7**: 363–372.

919 Gobbi PG, Dionigi P, Barbieri F, Corbella F, Bertoloni D, Grignani G, Jemos V, Pieresca G, Ascari E. The role of surgery in the multimodal treatment of primary gastric non-Hodgkin's lymphomas. A report of 76 cases and review of the literature. Cancer 1990, **65**: 2528–2536.

920 Grody WW, Weiss LM, Warnke RA, Magidson JG, Hu E, Lewin KJ. Gastrointestinal lymphomas. Immunohistochemical studies on the cell of origin. Am J Surg Pathol 1985, **9**: 328–337.

921 Guettier C, Hamilton-Dutoit S, Guillemain R, Farge D, Amrein C, Vulser C, Hofman P, Carpentier A, Diebold J. Primary gastrointestinal malignant lymphomas associated with Epstein-Barr virus after heart transplantation. Histopathology 1992, **20**: 21–28.

922 Hatano B, Ohshima K, Tsuchiya T, Yamaguchi T, Kawasaki C, Kikuchi M. Clinicopathological features of gastric B-cell lymphoma: a series of 317 cases. Pathol Int 2002, **52**: 677–682.

923 Joensuu H, Söderström K-O, Klemi PJ, Eerola E. Nuclear DNA content and its prognostic value in lymphoma of the stomach. Cancer 1987, **60**: 3042–3048.

924 Kumar S, Fend F, Quintanilla-Martinez L, Kingma DW, Sorbara L, Raffeld M, Banks PM, Jaffe ES. Epstein-Barr virus-positive primary gastrointestinal Hodgkin's disease: association with inflammatory bowel disease and immunosuppression. Am J Surg Pathol 2000, **24**: 66–73.

925 Kwon MS, Go JH, Choi JS, Lee SS, Ko YH, Rhee JC, Ree HJ. Critical evaluation of Bcl-6 protein expression in diffuse large B-cell lymphoma of the stomach and small intestine. Am J Surg Pathol 2003, **27**: 790–798.

926 Lewin KJ, Ranchod M, Dorfman RF. Lymphomas of the

gastrointestinal tract. A study of 117 cases presenting with gastrointestinal disease. Cancer 1978, **42**: 693–707.

927 Lim FE, Hartman AS, Tan EGC, Cady B, Meissner WA. Factors in the prognosis of gastric lymphoma. Cancer 1977, **39**: 1715–1720.

928 Maor MH, Maddux B, Osborne BM, Fuller LM, Sullivan JA, Nelson RS, Martin RG, Libshitz HI, Velasquez WS, Bennett RW. Stages IE and IIE non-Hodgkin's lymphomas of the stomach. Comparison of treatment modalities. Cancer 1984, **54**: 2330–2337.

929 Mir R, Kahn LB, Selzer G. Immunohistochemistry of primary gastrointestinal lymphomas. A study of 76 cases. Histopathology 1986, **10**: 391–403.

930 Mittal B, Wasserman TH, Griffith RC. Non-Hodgkin's lymphoma of the stomach. Am J Gastroenterol 1983, **78**: 780–787.

931 Omonishi K, Yoshino T, Sakuma I, Kobayashi K, Moriyama M, Akagi T. bcl-6 protein is identified in high-grade but not low-grade mucosa-associated lymphoid tissue lymphomas of the stomach. Mod Pathol 1998, **11**: 181–185.

932 Prolla JC, Kobayashi S, Krisner JB. Cytology of malignant lymphomas of the stomach. Acta Cytol Baltimore 1970, **14**: 291–296.

933 Shimm DS, Dosoretz DE, Anderson T, Linggood RM, Harris NL, Wang CC. Primary gastric lymphoma. An analysis with emphasis on prognostic factors and radiation therapy. Cancer 1983, **52**: 2044–2048.

934 Shimodaira M, Tsukamoto Y, Niwa Y, Goto H, Hase S, Hayakawa T, Nagasaka T. A proposed staging system for primary gastric lymphoma. Cancer 1994, **73**: 2709–2715.

935 Shiu MH, Karas M, Nisce L, Lee BJ, Filippa DA, Lieberman PH. Management of primary gastric lymphoma. Ann Surg 1982, **195**: 196–202.

936 Taebel DW, Prolla JC, Kirsner JB. Exfoliative cytology in the diagnosis of stomach cancer. Ann Intern Med 1965, **63**: 1018–1026.

937 Takeshita M, Iwashita A, Kurihara K, Ikejiri K, Higashi H, Udoh T, Kikuchi M. Histologic and immunohistologic findings and prognosis of 40 cases of gastric large B-cell lymphoma. Am J Surg Pathol 2000, **24**: 1641–1649.

938 van Krieken JHJM, Medeiros LJ, Pals ST, Raffeld M, Kluin PM. Diffuse aggressive B-cell lymphomas of the gastrointestinal tract. An immunophenotypic and gene rearrangement analysis of 22 cases. Am J Clin Pathol 1992, **97**: 170–178.

939 Weingrad DN, Decosse JJ, Sherlock P, Straus D, Lieberman PH, Filippa DA. Primary gastrointestinal lymphoma. A 30-year review. Cancer 1982, **49**: 1258–1265.

Other types of lymphoma and related conditions

940 Alvaro T, Bosch R, Salvado MT, Piris MA. True histiocytic lymphoma of the stomach associated with low-grade B-cell mucosa-associated lymphoid tissue (Malt)-type lymphoma. Am J Surg Pathol 1996, **20**: 1406–1411.

941 Brugo EA, Marshall RB, Riberi AM, Pautasso OE. Preleukemic granulocytic sarcomas of the gastrointestinal tract. Am J Clin Pathol 1977, **68**: 616–621.

942 Devaney K, Jaffe ES. The surgical pathology of gastrointestinal Hodgkin's disease. Am J Clin Pathol 1991, **95**: 794–801.

943 Griffiths AP, Shepherd NA, Beddall A, Williams JG. Gastrointestinal tumour masses due to multiple myeloma: a pathological mimic of malignant lymphoma. Histopathology 1997, **31**: 318–323.

944 Isaacson PG. Gastrointestinal lymphomas of T- and B-cell types. Mod Pathol 1999, **12**: 151–158.

945 Iwafuchi M, Watanabe H, Shiratsuka M. Primary benign histiocytosis X of the stomach. A report of a case showing spontaneous remission after 5 1/2 years. Am J Surg Pathol 1990, **14**: 489–496.

946 Mori N, Yatabe Y, Narita M, Hayakawa S, Ishido T, Kikuchi M, Asai J. Primary gastric Hodgkin's disease. Morphologic,

immunohistochemical, and immunogenetic analyses. Arch Pathol Lab Med 1995, **119**: 163–166.

947 Paulli M, Rosso R, Kindl S, Boveri E, Bonoldi E, Stracca V, Motta T, Arrigoni G, Lazzarino M, Menestrina F, Magrini U. Primary gastric CD30 (Ki-1)-positive large cell non-Hodgkin's lymphomas. A clinicopathologic analysis of six cases. Cancer 1994, **73**: 541–549.

948 Sakata H, Fujimoto K, Iwakiri R, Mizuguchi M, Koyama T, Sakai T, Inoue E, Tokunaga O, Shimamoto Y. Gastric lesions in 76 patients with adult T-cell leukaemia/lymphoma: endoscopic evaluation. Cancer 1996, **78**: 396–402.

949 Shimada-Hiratsuka M, Fukayama M, Hayashi Y, Ushijima T, Suzuki M, Hishima T, Funata N, Koike M, Watanabe T. Primary gastric T-cell lymphoma with and without human T-lymphotropic virus type 1. Cancer 1997, **80**: 292–303.

950 Taccagni G, Terreni M, Rovere E, Villa E, Cantaboni A. Anaplastic large cell Ki-1 lymphoma of the stomach with villopodial projections. an immunocytochemical and ultrastructural study and review of the literature. Ultrastruct Pathol 1992, **16**: 291–302.

951 Terracciano L, Kocher T, Cathomas G, Bubendorf L, Lehmann FS. Langerhans cell histiocytosis of the stomach with atypical morphological features. Pathol Int 1999, **49**: 553–556.

952 Wada R, Yahihashi S, Konta R, Ueda T, Izumiyama T. Gastric polyposis caused by multifocal histiocytosis X. Gut 1992, **33**: 994–996.

Other tumors

953 Adair C, Ro JY, Sahin AA, El-Naggar AK, Ordoñez N, Ayala A. Malignant melanoma metastatic to gastrointestinal tract. A clinicopathologic study. Int J Surg Pathol 1994, **2**: 3–10.

954 Alerte F. Xanthofibroma of the stomach. Report of a case with severe secondary hypochromic anemia. Arch Pathol 1963, **75**: 99–104.

955 Appelman HD, Helwig FB. Glomus tumors of the stomach. Cancer 1969, **23**: 203–213.

956 Attanoos R, Griffiths D. Metastatic small cell melanoma to the stomach mimicking primary gastric lymphoma. Histopathology 1992, **21**: 173–174.

957 Billings SD, Meisner LF, Cummings OW, Tejada E. Synovial sarcoma of the upper digestive tract: a report of two cases with demonstration of the X;18 translocation by fluorescence in situ hybridization. Mod Pathol 2000, **13**: 68–76.

958 Burns DK, Silva FG, Forde KA, Mount PM, Clark HB. Primary melanocytic schwannoma of the stomach. Evidence of dual melanocytic and schwannian differentiation in an extra-axial site in a patient without neurofibromatosis. Cancer 1983, **52**: 1432–1441.

959 Choi SH, Sheehan FR, Pickren JW. Metastatic involvement of the stomach by breast cancer. Cancer 1964, **17**: 791–797.

960 Cohn M, Middleton L, Valero V, Sahin A, UT. Gastrointestinal metastases of carcinoma of the breast. (Abstract) Mod Pathol 2003, **16**: 26A.

961 Fox KR, Moussa SM, Mitre RJ, Zidar BL, Raves JJ. Clinical and pathologic features of primary gastric rhabdomyosarcoma. Cancer 1990, **66**: 772–778.

962 Garcia RL, Ghali VS. Gastric choriocarcinoma and yolk sac tumor in a man. Observations about its possible origin. Hum Pathol 1985, **16**: 955–958.

963 Green LK. Hematogenous metastases to the stomach. A review of 67 cases. Cancer 1990, **65**: 1596–1600.

964 Han JH, Kim SH, Noh SH, Lee YC, Kim HG, Yang WI. Follicular dendritic cell sarcoma presenting as a submucosal tumor of the stomach. Arch Pathol Lab Med 2000, **124**: 1693–1696.

965 Haque S, Modlin IM, West AB. Multiple glomus tumors of the stomach with intravascular spread. Am J Surg Pathol 1992, **16**: 291–299.

966 Hull MT, Jesseph JE. Ultrastructure of gastric myxofibroma with intracytoplasmic collagen. Ultrastruct Pathol 1982, **3:** 25–30.

967 Johnston J, Helwig EB. Granular cell tumors of the gastrointestinal tract and perianal region. A study of 74 cases. Dig Dis Sci 1981, **26:** 807–816.

968 Kanwar YS, Manaligod JR. Glomus tumor of the stomach. An ultrastructural study. Arch Pathol 1975, **99:** 392–397.

968a Lasota J, Wasag B, Dansonka-Mieszkowska A, Karcz D, Millward CL, Rys J, Stachura J, Sobin LH, Miettinen M. Evaluation of *NF2* and *NF1* tumor suppressor genes in distinctive gastrointestinal nerve sheath tumors traditionally diagnosed as benign schwannomas: a study of 20 cases. Lab Invest 203, **83:** 1361–1371.

969 Liu AY, Chan WY, Ng EK, Zhang X, Li BC, Chow JH, Chung SC. Gastric choriocarcinoma shows characteristics of adenocarcinoma and gestational choriocarcinoma: a comparative genomic hybridization and fluorescence in situ hybridization study. Diagn Mol Pathol 2001, **10:** 161–165.

970 Makhlouf HR, Sobin LH. Inflammatory myofibroblastic tumors (inflammatory pseudotumors) of the gastrointestinal tract: how closely are they related to inflammatory fibroid polyps? Hum Pathol 2002, **33:** 307–315.

971 Miettinen M, Paal E, Lasota J, Sobin JH. Gastrointestinal glomus tumors: a clinicopathologic, immunohistochemical, and molecular genetic study of 32 cases. Am J Surg Pathol 2002, **26:** 301–311.

972 Motoyama T, Saito K, Iwafuchi M, Watanabe H. Endodermal sinus tumor of the stomach. Acta Pathol Jpn 1985, **35:** 497–505.

973 Pauwels P, Debiec-Rychter M, Sciot R, Vlasveld T, den Butter B, Hagemeijer A, Hogendoorn PCW. Clear cell sarcoma of the stomach. Histopathology 2002, **41:** 526–530.

974 Puglisi F, Damante G, Pizzolitto S, Mariuzzi L, Guerra S, Pellizzari L, Binotto F, Beltrami CA. Combined yolk sac tumor and adenocarcinoma in a gastric stump: molecular evidence of clonality. Cancer 1999, **85:** 1910–1916.

975 Read HS, Webb JN, Macintyre IM. Malignant rhabdoid tumour of stomach. Histopathology 1997, **29:** 474–477.

976 Saigo PE, Brigati DJ, Sternberg SS, Rosen PP, Turnbull AD. Primary gastric choriocarcinoma. An immunohistological study. Am J Surg Pathol 1981, **5:** 333–342.

977 Suzuki T, Kimura N, Shizawa S, Yabuki N, Yamaki T, Sasano H, Nagura H. Yolk sac tumor of the stomach with an adenocarcinomatous component: a case report with immunohistochemical analysis. Pathol Int 1999, **49:** 557–562.

978 Turkington RW. Gastric lipoma. Report of a case and review of the literature. Am J Dig Dis 1965, **10:** 719–726.

979 Wright JR Jr, Kyriakos M, DeSchryver-Kecskemeti K. Malignant fibrous histiocytoma of the stomach. A report and review of malignant fibrohistiocytic tumors of the alimentary tract. Arch Pathol Lab Med 1988, **112:** 251–258.

980 Wurzel J, Brooks JJ. Primary gastric choriocarcinoma. Immunohistochemistry, postmortem documentation, and hormonal effects in a postmenopausal female. Cancer 1981, **48:** 2756–2761.

981 Yagihashi S, Yagihashi N, Hase Y, Nagai K, Alguacil-Garcia A. Primary alveolar soft-part sarcoma of stomach. Am J Surg Pathol 1991, **15:** 399–406.

982 Zambrano E, Reyes-Mugica M, Franchi A, Rosai J. An osteoclast-rich tumor of the gastrointestinal tract with features resembling clear cell sarcoma of soft parts: reports of 6 cases of a GIST simulator. Int J Surg Pathol 2003, **11:** 75–81.

Small bowel

Normal anatomy

The small bowel is divided into three portions: duodenum (approximately 25 cm in length, largely retroperitoneal, and fixed), jejunum (approximately 40% of the mobile small bowel), and ileum (corresponding to the distal 60%). The ligament of Treitz is the anatomic landmark for the duodenojejunal junction, at which site the bowel becomes unfixed and wrapped in a mesentery.

The inner side of the small bowel is characterized by the presence of transverse mucosal folds known as *valvulae conniventes* (a double misnomer) or *Kerckring's folds*. They are prominent in the proximal jejunum and flat or absent in the terminal ileum. Another characteristic feature of this region is represented by *Peyer's patches*, which are seen in the antimesenteric side of the terminal ileum. Their shape is oval, with the long axis parallel to that of the bowel. They represent lymphoid follicles and are more prominent in young individuals.

The small bowel ends at the ileocecal valve, a two-lip structure in which lymphoid tissue—and sometimes adult adipose tissue—tends to accumulate.

Microscopically, the small bowel is composed of four layers: mucosa, submucosa, muscularis externa, and serosa. The mucosa is lined by villi, which are short and stubby (sometimes leaf-like) in the duodenum, very tall in the jejunum, and of intermediate height in the ileum. The mucosa is made up of epithelium, lamina propria, and muscularis mucosae. The villous epithelium is composed of an admixture of tall columnar absorptive cells (enterocytes) and goblet cells (more numerous in the ileum).[10]

The *crypts of Lieberkuhn* comprise the lower 20% of the epithelium and represent its proliferative zone. They are surrounded by a pericrypt fibroblast sheath and are composed of multipotential stem cells (often exhibiting mitoses, about 1 or 2 per crypt), Paneth cells (with large cytoplasmic acidophilic granules containing a variety of digestive enzymes and lysozyme), scattered goblet cells, and (neuro)endocrine cells, of which the *Kultschitsky (argentaffin, basigranular)* cell is the better known representative. The stem cells are the progenitors of all the cell types located in the intestinal mucosa, including those just mentioned. The sum total of the neuroendocrine cells (also known as APUD cells) constitutes the so-called "diffuse endocrine system", a concept brilliantly postulated by Feyrter many decades ago. Functionally speaking, most of these cells are actually paracrine rather than endocrine, in that their action is exerted at a local level. They were thought to be of neural crest origin, but many independent studies (particularly those carried out by LeDouarin with the quail–chick chimera model) have shown that they are endodermally derived,[1] at least in mammals.[9] The qualifier "neuroendocrine" can however be retained for them on functional/phenotypical grounds.[11]

The lamina propria is composed of a loose connective tissue matrix. It contains lymphocytes, plasma cells, and occasionally eosinophils, macrophages, mast cells, and neutrophils. It also has blood vessels, lymph (lacteal) vessels, and numerous nerves. CD38 (a type of transmembrane glycoprotein involved in signaling and adhesion) has been found to stain the human lymph (lacteal) vessels, but not the lymph vessels of other organs.[4]

The submucosa consists of connective tissue, blood vessels, lymphatics, and the *submucosal (Meissner's) neural plexus*. In the duodenum (particularly the first two portions), it also contains numerous mucus-secreting glands known as *Brunner's glands*.

The muscularis externa (propria) is made up of an inner circular and an outer longitudinal layer, with the *myenteric (Auerbach's) plexus* located between. This plexus is composed of ganglion cells, satellite cells (similar but not identical to Schwann cells), and perineurial fibroblasts.[2,3,5,6] In addition, there is the "interstitial cell," described by Cajal in 1893 and interpreted by him as a primitive neural cell featuring several long anastomosing processes. These cells are intercalated between the ganglion cells and the effector smooth muscle cells and function as a gastroenteric "pacemaker" system.[12,13] Their physiological development depends upon signaling via the c-kit receptor pathway.[15] They are normally immunoreactive for this molecule, as demonstrated with CD117, a fact that has linked them with the histogenesis of GIST (see p. 734). Instead, they are negative for CD34, despite early claims to the contrary.[14] Their ultrastructural appearance is varied, ranging from smooth muscle-like to fibroblast-like; significantly, they lack neural features.[7,8a]

The interstitial cells of Cajal originate from the same mesodermal precursors that give rise to smooth muscle cells, and not from the neural crest.[8,16] Therefore, these cells should not be regarded as neural, a widespread misconception.

The serosa is covered by a single layer of attenuated mesothelium, separated from the muscularis by a normally thin layer of loose connective tissue.

The duodenum drains its lymph vessels into the portal and pyloric lymph nodes, the jejunum and proximal ileum into the nodes located in the mesentery and around the superior mesenteric artery, and the terminal ileum into the ileocolic nodes.

Congenital defects

Heterotopic pancreas

Heterotopic pancreas consists mainly of ducts and acini, usually without islet tissue. The duodenum is the most common location (particularly in the region of the ampulla of Vater),[18] but it can also occur in the jejunum and (very rarely) in the ileum.

Two lesions that are probably pathogenetically related to heterotopic pancreas are the tumorlike processes that have been described as *adenomyoma*[20] and *myoepithelial hamartoma*.[22] They are composed of exocrine-type ducts and bundles of smooth muscle, with or without an acinar cell component. Other types of small bowel hamartomas are discussed on p. 738. Blockage of the duct can occur where it empties into the intestinal tract, and this blockage can cause cystic dilatation, infection, and fat necrosis.[19] Heterotopic pancreas is subject to any of the pathologic changes seen in the orthotopic organ, including acute pancreatitis, (neuro)endocrine tumors, and adenocarcinoma.[21] It has also been suggested that the rare duodenal wall cysts may be derived from the ductal component of ectopic pancreas.[23]

Heterotopic gastric mucosa

Foci of heterotopic gastric mucosa may present as discrete small nodules or sessile polyps in the duodenum. Microscopically, the mucosa is of fundic type, with chief and parietal cells.[24,26,28] It may undergo hyperplastic and adenomatous changes,[25,27] and it should be distinguished from pyloric gland metaplasia.

Duplication, atresia, and related defects

Duplication and atresia of the gastrointestinal tract occur much more often in the small bowel (particularly ileum) than in the stomach or colon. Duodenal duplication (very rare) needs to be distinguished from the more common choledochocele.

Intestinal duplication may be spherical (more common) or tubular and is usually incomplete, with a common muscular wall between the normal and the duplicate segments. The lumen of the duplicated segment sometimes communicates with the lumen of the bowel, and occasionally with the main pancreatic duct.[37] In other instances, the duplicated segment is totally independent and hangs free on its own mesentery. Exceptionally, it may be found within the substance of the liver.[35] Secondary inflammatory changes may supervene. The treatment is surgical.[38] Since the duplication cannot be separated in most cases from the adjacent normal bowel, the treatment usually involves resection of the entire duplication and the segment of normal bowel attached to it or resection of the wall of the duplication that is not part of the wall of the normal bowel. Several cases of malignancy have been reported as developing within the duplicated bowel.[29]

Intestinal atresia can involve any portion of the small bowel.[30,32,39] It is characterized by an obliteration of the bowel lumen and its replacement by a fibrous cord that connects the proximal and distal segments (Fig. 11.78). Specific subtypes include apple-peel atresia, multiple intestinal atresia with short-gut syndrome, and proximal jejunal atresia with megaduodenum.[39] Traditionally, intestinal atresia has been regarded as an embryologic defect. Currently, the interpretation that the disease is the result of in utero mechanical injury to the vascular system of the bowel is favored.[36] This may result from intussusception, volvulus, or incarceration. A causal relationship between the use of methylene blue in second-trimester amniocentesis and the occurrence of jejunal atresia has been suggested.[40]

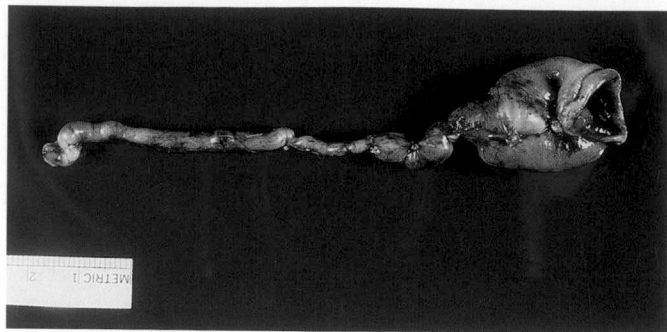

Fig. 11.78 Long atretic segment of small bowel of congenital nature.

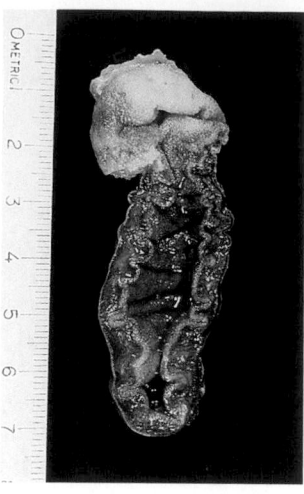

Fig. 11.79 Meckel's diverticulum showing marked passive congestion resulting from mechanical venous obstruction.

Complications include perforation, meconium peritonitis, and—as a rare late occurrence—brown bowel syndrome[41] (see p. 727).

Congenital defects in the intestinal musculature can result in neonatal intestinal perforation.[33,34] As in the case of congenital atresia, there is some controversy about whether this lesion is truly congenital or the result of intrauterine ischemia.[34] The existence of cases showing concurrence of these two abnormalities speaks in favor of a common pathogenesis.[31]

Meckel's diverticulum and related vitelline duct abnormalities

Early in fetal life, the intestine communicates with the yolk sac. By the fourth week, the opening has gradually narrowed to form a tubular structure known as the *vitelline* or *omphalomesenteric duct*. At the 7-mm stage, the vitelline duct normally is obliterated by atrophy and forms a fibrous cord connecting the umbilicus and bowel. This band is subsequently absorbed.

Failure of all or part of the vitelline duct to become obliterated accounts for the various types of vitelline duct abnormalities.[55]

Persistent fibrous cord presents as a solid round cord of fibrous appearance, one end of which is attached to the umbilicus. The other end may be attached to the bowel wall, to the tip of a Meckel's diverticulum, or to the mesentery.

Enteroumbilical fistula is the consequence of a persistent patency of the entire vitelline duct.

Meckel's diverticulum is the result of persistence of the proximal portion of the vitelline duct. It is found in 2% of the population and is more frequent in males (63%).[50,56] Approximately 30% of patients have other congenital abnormalities, including tracheoesophageal fistula.[44] The usual location in the adult is approximately 80 cm proximal to the ileocecal valve. It is always on the outer mesenteric border—an important diagnostic sign—and it varies in length from less than 1 to 8 cm (Fig. 11.79). The lining is predominantly of small intestinal type, identical to that of the adjacent bowel; however, gastric, duodenal, or colonic mucosa may also be found,

usually near the tip.[43] Pancreatic tissue may also be present.[54]

The complications of Meckel's diverticulum include perforation, vesicodiverticular fistula,[46] ulceration, hemorrhage, intussusception, intestinal obstruction from attached bands, and tumors[48,35] (Figs 11.80 and 11.81). The ulceration is of peptic type, caused by acid secretion from the ectopic gastric mucosa, and is usually in the adjacent ileum rather than in the Meckel's diverticulum itself. It may result in massive hemorrhage, particularly in children. *Helicobacter pylori* does not seem to be involved in the pathogenesis.[47] Among the neoplasms, carcinoid tumor predominates, either alone[51,57] or—rarely—associated with carcinoid tumors of similar histologic appearance in the small bowel.[52] Other tumors include villous adenoma, adenocarcinoma, GIST, leiomyoma, leiomyosarcoma, and malignant melanoma.[42,45,49] Because of all these potential complications, Meckel's diverticula should be removed whenever encountered incidentally at surgery.

Other diverticula

Duodenal diverticula occur in 1% to 2% of all individuals. Most are solitary and located in the second portion; they can attain a large size and produce obstructive jaundice, pancreatitis, duodenal obstruction, fistulas, hemorrhage, and perforation.[61] Some of them project into the lumen like a polyp.[60] Most penetrate the pancreas along the embryologic fusion line of the ventral and dorsal components.[67] Microscopically, up to half of them show aggregates of foamy macrophages in the submucosa.[64]

Jejunal diverticula are found in 0.3% to 1.4% of post mortem examinations. Most of them affect the upper portion of the jejunum and are characteristically located along the mesenteric border[65,66] (Fig. 11.82). They are often multiple, and their wall is thin, with a decreased number of smooth muscle fibers. They tend to be associated with diverticula elsewhere in the gastrointestinal

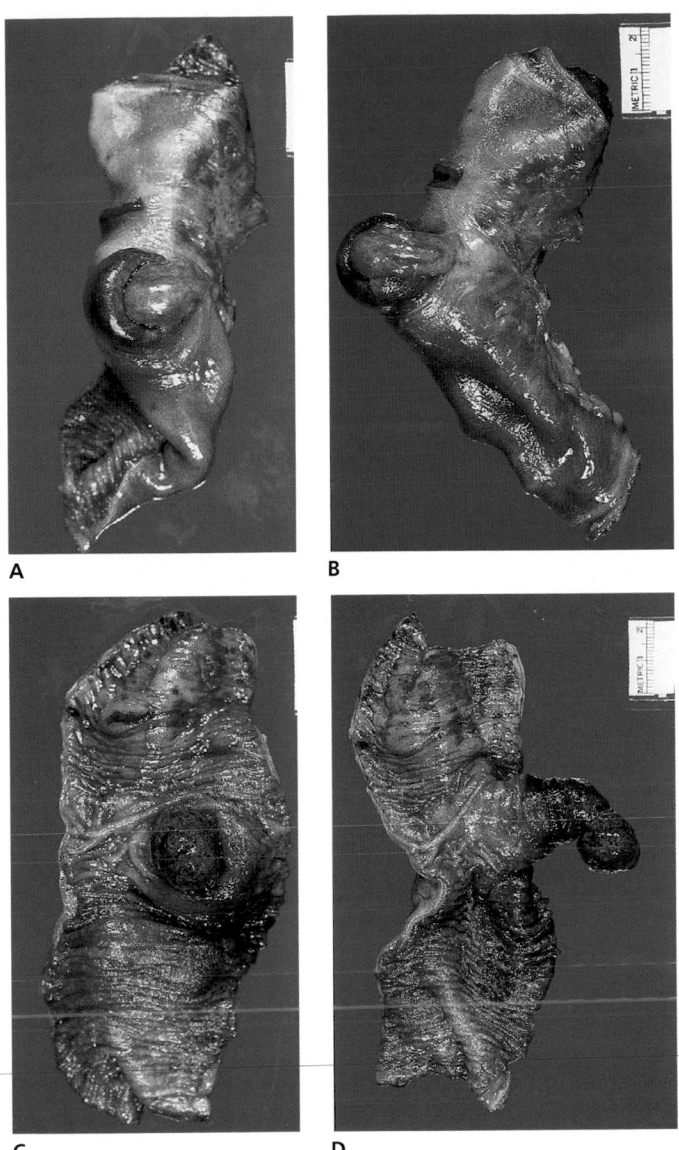

A B

C D

Fig. 11.80 A to **D**, Meckel's diverticulum that has undergone intussusception, as seen from the serosal side (**A**, **B**) and the mucosal side (**C**, **D**).

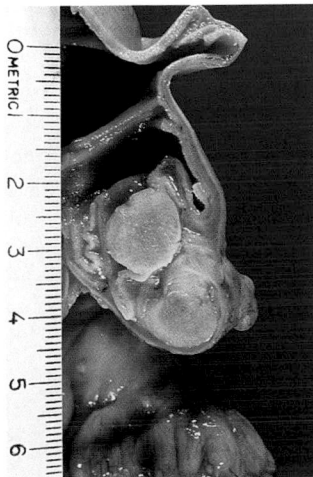

Fig. 11.81 Meckel's diverticulum complicated by the development of a carcinoid tumor, the cut surface of which has a characteristic yellow color after formalin fixation.

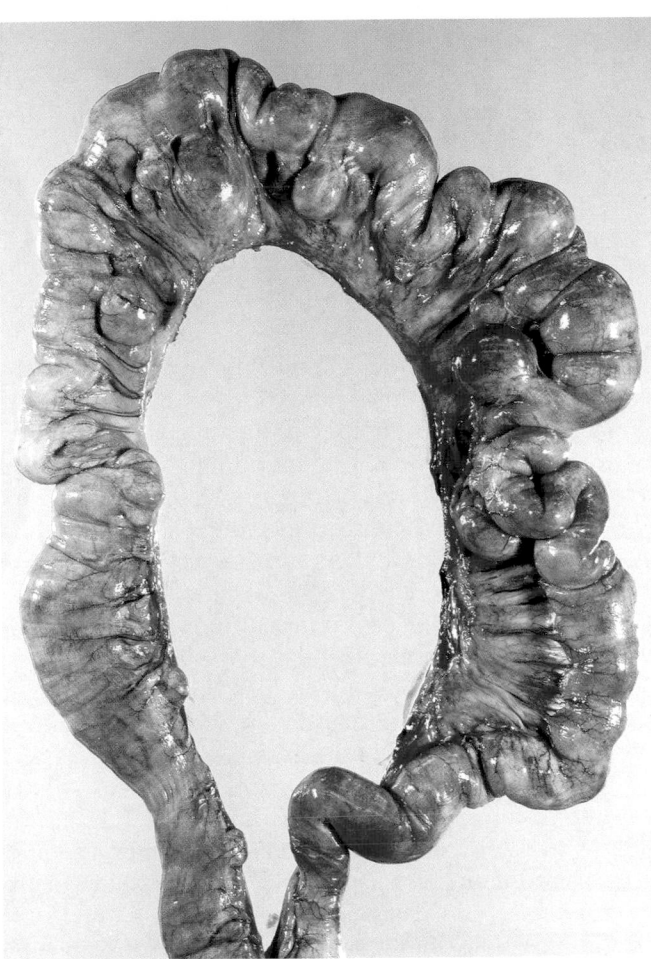

Fig. 11.82 Multiple jejunal diverticula. They are typically located along the antimesenteric border. (Courtesy of Dr. RA Cooke, Brisbane, Australia; from Cooke RA, Stewart B: Colour Atlas of Anatomical Pathology. Edinburgh, Churchill Livingstone, 2004).

tract. Some jejunal diverticula are congenital and may contain ectopic pancreatic tissue at their base; most are thought to be acquired, perhaps resulting from a defect in the muscle wall or myenteric plexus.[62] The majority are asymptomatic, but some may lead to hemorrhage, perforation, abscess formation, intramural gas cyst formation, obstruction caused by enterolith formation, or metabolic disturbances, such as vitamin B_{12} deficiency and malabsorption.[58,59,63,68] Many of these symptoms, which are typically intermittent, are thought to be caused by bacterial overgrowth in these diverticula.

Other congenital defects

Hirschsprung's disease, when involving the whole colon, may extend to the small intestine. The form is associated with a high mortality, the most common complication being enterocolitis.[70]

Ehlers–Danlos syndrome, a congenital defect affecting collagen fibers throughout the body, may result in serious intestinal complications, such as spontaneous perforation and massive bleeding.[69]

Malabsorption

The development of flexible peroral biopsy tubes has made it possible to biopsy the mucosa of the small intestine with a minimum of discomfort or risk. When the tube has reached the desired level, a tuft of mucous membrane is drawn into it by negative pressure. A small full-thickness mucosal biopsy can then be taken.[130] The incidence of serious complications, such as bleeding or perforation, is negligible.

Two basic requirements should be met to obtain the maximum possible information from a small bowel biopsy. Since the morphology of the mucosa shows normal regional variations, it is important that biopsies be taken from approximately the same area in all patients. This is achieved by fluoroscopic control. The standard site of biopsy is a point slightly distal to the ligament of Treitz. Once the biopsy is obtained, it should be placed quickly on a flat surface, mucosal side up, preferably with the aid of a dissecting microscope. Filter paper and Gelfoam are commonly used for this purpose. The mucosal appearance under the dissecting microscope can be recorded as part of the gross description. The five basic patterns are (1) villous or finger-like, (2) villous, leaf-like or tongue-like, (3) convoluted or cerebroid, (4) mosaic, and (5) flat. The information obtained is somewhat useful and gives a preliminary assessment of the mucosal state, but it should never replace an accurate light microscopic examination. More important, the handling of the mucosa during this procedure should be extremely gentle. Wiping away of adherent mucus should not be attempted.[153]

The tissue is fixed in formalin with the filter paper or Gelfoam attached to it to prevent curling. The filter paper should be removed during any one of the subsequent steps, whereas Gelfoam can be embedded in the paraffin block attached to the tissue. It is imperative that sections be cut at right angles to the mucosal surface.[87]

Small bowel biopsy is of the utmost importance in the evaluation of malabsorption, a syndrome that can result from a large variety of organic and functional disorders, of which celiac disease is the most important.[80]

Celiac disease (celiac sprue, nontropical sprue, gluten-sensitive enteropathy), is a condition characterized in its fully developed state by a totally flat mucosa, a dramatic clinical and morphologic response to the removal of gluten from the diet, and relapse when gluten is reintroduced.[77,84,98,138] The clinical manifestations can be extremely varied.[92a]

Grossly, the duodenal folds appear to be reduced or absent, an important diagnostic clue on endoscopic examination.[117] Microscopically, the villi are atrophic or absent, but the overall thickness of the mucosa is essentially normal (Fig. 11.83). This is accompanied by an increase in the number of lymphocytes, immunoglobulin-containing plasma cells in the lamina propria, accumulation of large fat globules in the surface epithelium,[145] and immunohistochemical absence of α_1-antitrypsin in the crypts.[124] There is an increase in the number of intraepithelial T-lymphocytes, a clue to the diagnosis in specimens in which villous atrophy may not be evident[72a,96,117b]; interestingly, in pediatric cases these intraepithelial lymphocytes have also been detected in the gastric and esophageal mucosa.[72] There is also an increase in the number of mitoses in the epithelium,[138] and hyperplasia of 5-hydroxytryptamine-containing neuroendocrine cells.[120] The epithelial cells have been shown to have a shortened life span.[137,144]

Drut et al.[87] have proposed grading the severity of the changes by estimating the villous/crypt (V/C) ratio, which is 2.5 or more in the normal mucosa. The grades were defined as follows: Grade 1: 2–2.5; Grade 2: 1–2, Grade 3: 1–0.5; and Grade 4: less than 0.5. In their series, celiac disease was consistently associated with grades 3 and 4, which reverted to normal or grade 1 after introduction of a gluten-free diet.

It should be emphasized that villous atrophy is not pathognomonic of celiac disease. According to Rubin et al.[136] the same appearance can be seen in dermatitis herpetiformis, kwashiorkor, and severe cases of tropical sprue. Weinstein et al.[150] have further segregated from classic celiac disease a type characterized by increased deposition of eosinophilic hyaline material within the lamina propria, which they have designated as *collagenous sprue*. Whether this is a specific entity or merely a morphologic variant of celiac disease is not clear at the present time.

The pathogenesis of celiac disease is related to inappropriate intestinal T-cell activation in HLA-DQ2-positive individuals triggered by antigenic peptides from wheat gluten or prolamins from barley and

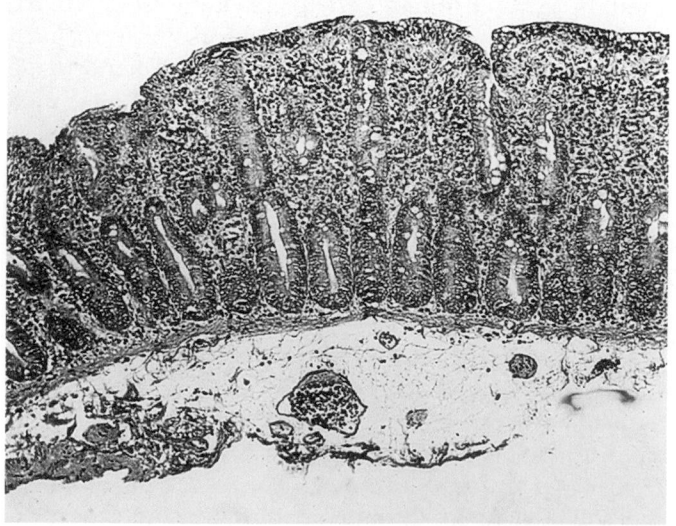

Fig. 11.83 Jejunal mucosa in celiac disease. It is totally flat and devoid of villi, but its height is not decreased.

rye.[77,108,111,112,115,116,117a] Circulating antibodies directed against gliadin (the toxic moiety of gluten) are present. A 33-mer peptide has been isolated that is thought to be the primary initiator of the inflammatory response.[140]

A well-documented, albeit rare, complication of celiac disease is the development of *intestinal malignant lymphoma*.[100,143] The development of this complication must be suspected in patients with a long history of celiac disease who develop reversal of the response to gluten withdrawal accompanied by fever, weight loss, abdominal pain, finger clubbing, bowel ulcerations, or a sustained rise in serum IgA levels. In one series of cases with this complication, the mean duration of the celiac disease was 28 years.[99]

Grossly, cases with full-blown lymphoma tend to involve the small bowel in a widespread, patchy fashion, causing ulceration, stricture formation, and perforation.[123] Microscopically, the process is gradual, beginning as a mixed cell infiltrate in the lamina propria with increasing numbers of atypical large lymphoid cells and ending as a large cell lymphoma[152] (Fig. 11.84A). Atypical binucleated or multinucleated cells may be present and lead to a mistaken diagnosis of Hodgkin's lymphoma (Fig. 11.84B). Although formerly thought to be a histiocytic malignancy,[101] it is now known that this complication of celiac disease represents a T-cell malignancy (perhaps arising from the intraepithelial subpopulation of these cells). The phenotype is that of cytotoxic T cells,[82] and the condition is usually referred to as *enteropathy-associated T-cell lymphoma*.[120,142] There is a high frequency of genetic aberrations,[74a] and the presence of the Epstein–Barr virus (EBV) genome has been documented in a minority of the cases.[81,127,148] The clinical course is aggressive and the prognosis is poor, in part due to the often delayed diagnosis.[93]

Another reported complication of celiac disease is *chronic nonspecific ulcerative duodenojejunoileitis*,[118] which is characterized by abdominal pain and fever on the background of a malabsorption syndrome. Most instances of this condition probably represent the initial stage of the malignant lymphoid process just described,[153] as supported by the fact that the lymphocytic population is clonal.[73] This comment also applies to cases diagnosed as refractory sprue, which are defined as (usually severe) malabsorption disorders that are refractory to a gluten-free diet.[78,121] In a review of 10 cases with this disorder, Robert at al.[134] found subcryptal chronic inflammation in all, and features of collagenous sprue in half; one patient developed lymphoma. According to de Serre et al.[128] refractory sprue can be distinguished immunohistochemically from celiac disease because of the presence in the former of abnormal intraepithelial T lymphocytes expressing a cytoplasmic CD3 chain (CD3c), lacking surface CD3 and CD8, and showing TCR-γ gene rearrangement.

Yet another rare complication of adult celiac disease is the development of *carcinoma*, usually in the jejunum but sometimes in the ileum, duodenum, or esophagus.[92,126,131] The jejunal tumor is usually solitary and of adenocarcinomatous type.[125]

Tropical sprue is an altogether different condition.[104,105,150] It has a definite geographic distribution, is relatively unaffected by gluten ingestion, and responds to folic acid, vitamin B$_{12}$, and tetracycline.[97] The morphologic changes are nonspecific. The large majority of cases show *partial* villous atrophy, although examples of both normal mucosa and total villous atrophy have been reported.[90] The favored interpretation at present is that tropical sprue is of bacterial etiology, with or without the additive effects of fat. Features in favor of this interpreta-

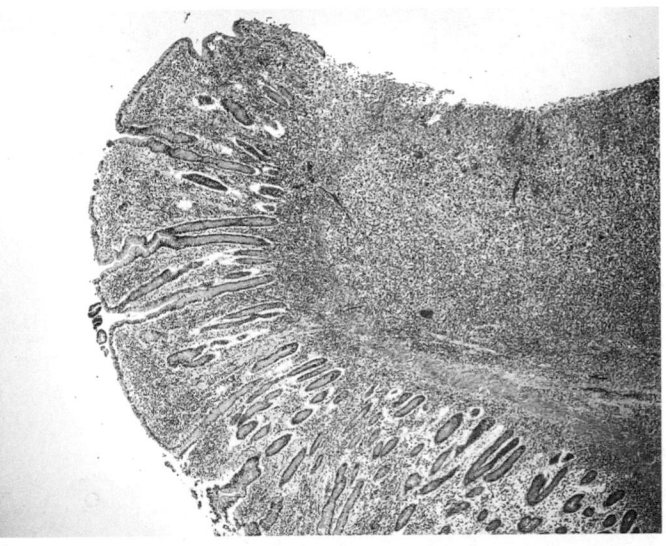

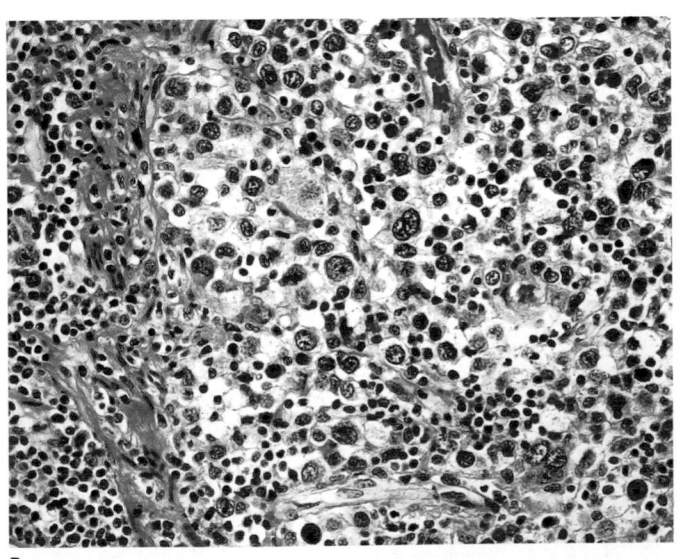

A **B**

Fig. 11.84 A and **B,** Celiac disease complicated by the development of malignant lymphoma. **A,** Low-power view showing flat mucosa on the left and lymphoma on the right. **B,** High-power view of the lymphoma, showing a high degree of pleomorphism.

tion are the isolation of enterotoxigenic coliform bacilli, the endemic nature of the disease (and the fact that it may affect visitors to areas where it is endemic), and the well-known response to antibiotics.

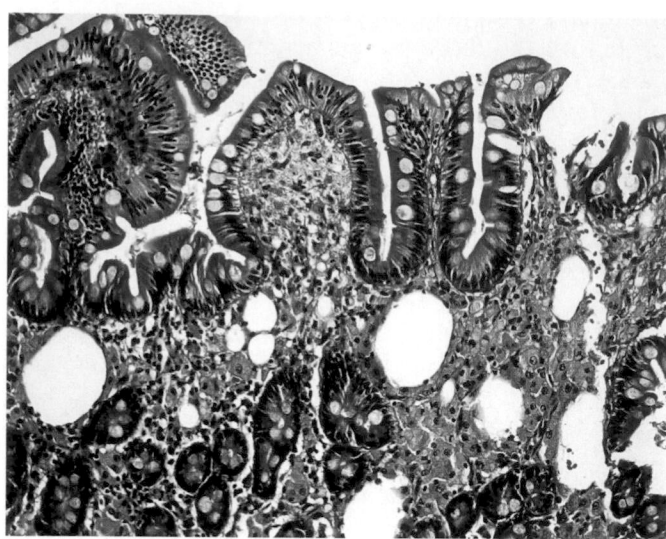

Fig. 11.85 Jejunal mucosa in Whipple's disease. The lamina propria is packed with histiocytes and empty round spaces. The latter contained lipid material that has been extracted during tissue processing.

Whipple's disease (intestinal lipodystrophy) has a very typical appearance in a jejunal biopsy. Large macrophages are seen crowding the lamina propria, distorting the villi, and alternating with empty spaces[146] (Fig. 11.85). Occasionally, the disease is restricted to the submucosa and can, therefore, be missed in a mucosal biopsy.[107] The cytoplasm of the histiocytes contains large amounts of a diastase-resistant, PAS-positive material. This is due to the presence of bacilliform bodies, which also occur in the lumen, between the epithelial cells, and in macrophages. They have been well demonstrated by electron microscopy[75,115] (Fig. 11.86) and immunohistochemistry,[74,109a] and there have been some successful attempts at culturing.[132] This organism, which has been named *Tropheryma whippelii*, has been identified by sequencing the largest part of a bacterial 16S ribosomal DNA, followed by PCR amplification.[86,133] Ultrastructure and immunohistochemistry are useful not only in demonstrating the presence of the diagnostic microorganisms but also in evaluating the adequacy of therapy and in identifying early reactivation of the disease.[74,83,119] The response to antibiotic therapy is good, although relapses are common.[79,103]

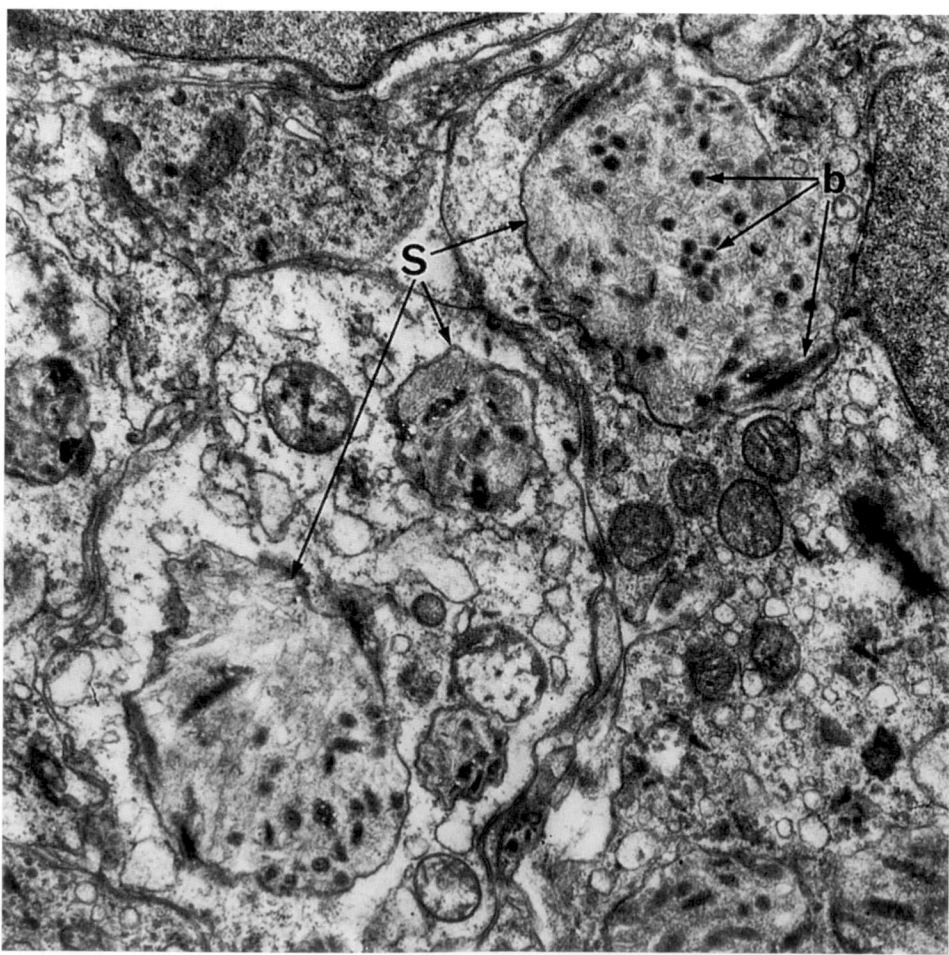

Fig. 11.86 Electron micrograph of macrophage in submucosa of small intestine in Whipple's disease. Cytoplasm contains membrane-limited sacs (S) that are filled with dense spherical and rod-shaped bodies (b) intermixed with fine membranous profiles. These rods have been shown to be the organisms responsible for the disease. (×15,000)

The disease is not restricted to the bowel. Macrophages of identical appearance have been identified in the rest of the alimentary tract, regional and peripheral lymph nodes, heart, lung, liver, spleen, adrenal glands, nervous system, and several other sites[91,94] (Fig. 11.87). The round empty spaces, which may be surrounded by giant cells and are also present in mesenteric lymph nodes, are seen to contain neutral fat by special stains. The diagnosis can be suggested in fine needle aspiration specimens.[139] However, it should be remembered that a similar change (although not accompanied by PAS-positive macrophages) is often seen in intra-abdominal lymph nodes of normal individuals, probably secondary to the ingestion of mineral oil.[76] Small bowel biopsy remains the best way to diagnose Whipple's disease. An important differential diagnosis is the AIDS enteropathy caused by *Mycobacterium avium-intracellulare*[114] (see p. 724.

Biopsy of peripheral lymph nodes can be suggestive of the disease if the typical macrophages are present but is not pathognomonic.[113] Immunohistochemistry and PCR have been successfully used in these circumstances to confirm the diagnosis.[71,109] The interpretation of rectal biopsies is hampered by the fact that mucin-containing macrophages ("muciphages") present in the lamina propria of 10% of normal individuals have a strong resemblance to the histiocytes of Whipple's disease, at least at a light microscopic level.[89] Whether Whipple's disease represents a specific disease caused by a unique bacterium capable of intracellular survival and replication or a common organism in a host with impaired immunity remains to be determined.[85] In connection to the latter, Ector et al.[88] have shown abnormal phagocytic capacity, increased numbers of intraepithelial lymphocytes, a decreased CD4+/CD8+ cell ratio, and an increased IgM/IgA ratio in the plasma cells of the lamina propria. A few cases of extraintestinal malignant lymphoma have been reported in patients with Whipple's disease.[95]

Other diseases associated with malabsorption in which small bowel biopsy may be of value include **abetalipoproteinemia** (acanthocytosis), in which the apical villous cytoplasm shows striking vacuolation as a result of inability to synthesize β-lipoprotein[102] (Fig. 11.88); **agammaglobulinemic sprue,** characterized by total absence of plasma cells in the lamina propria[106]; **intestinal lymphangiectasia**, in which a protein-losing enteropathy develops probably as a result of the entrance of protein-rich fluid into the extracellular space of the lamina propria from the dilated lymphatic channels and subsequent drainage into the gut lumen[147]; **amyloidosis; scleroderma**[110]; and **parasitic infestation,** such as giardiasis,[135,154] hookworm disease,[141] strongyloidiasis,[154] and capillariasis.[151]

Pena and Whitehead[129] studied the small bowel morphology in different types of **disaccharide deficiencies**. They found no detectable abnormality in isolated lactase deficiency. Whenever morphologic changes are present, *all* the disaccharidases measured (i.e., lactase, maltases, and sucrase) were found to be depressed.

A

B

Fig. 11.87 A and **B,** Outer aspect and cut surface of mesenteric lymph nodes massively involved by Whipple's disease.

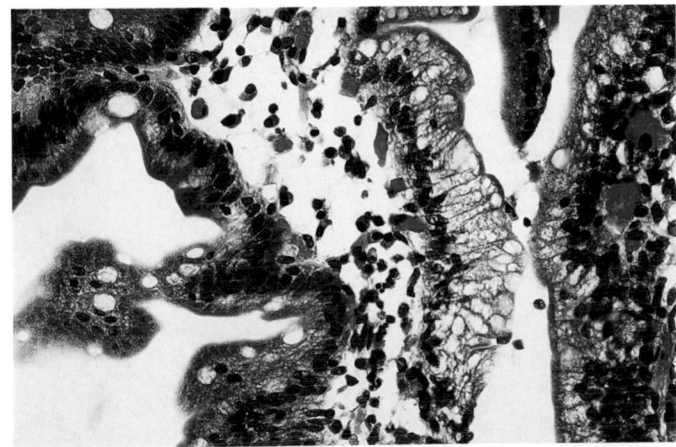

Fig. 11.88 Marked cytoplasmic vacuolization of the glandular epithelium of small bowel in abetalipoproteinemia.

Ulcers

Duodenal peptic ulcer remains a very common disease, although its incidence seems to be decreasing.[167] *H. pylori* is currently regarded as the most important factor in its pathogenesis, which is also related to the interplay of aggressive factors (gastric juice eroding and digesting its way into the mucosa) and defensive factors (bicarbonate and intact epithelium).[160,165] Gastric acid hypersecretion is the rule in these patients. Thus a preserved fundic mucosa in the stomach is a prerequisite for the formation of duodenal peptic ulcer.

Grossly, duodenal peptic ulcer is usually single and within 2 cm of the pylorus (Fig. 11.89), although it may also occur in the second portion of the duodenum. When the ulcer is in the latter position, it may be the source of upper abdominal pain and bleeding, yet not be discernible radiographically. When duodenal ulcers are multiple and randomly distributed in the proximal and distal portions of the duodenum, the possibility of Zollinger–Ellison syndrome should be ruled out. Another important cause of non-*H. pylori*-related duodenal ulcer is nonsteroidal anti-inflammatory drug usage.[162]

Peptic ulcer has well-defined margins sharply set off from the surrounding mucosa. Most of its microscopic features are analogous to those of its gastric counterpart (see p. 653). Gastric metaplasia is common, as documented by light microscopy, mucin histochemistry, and electron microscopy.[157] At times, a large vessel with an open lumen may be seen at the base of the ulcer. Fibrosis of a healed ulcer may produce secondary diverticula and considerable shortening of the duodenum. Chronic duodenitis is regularly present.[161] Peptic ulcer of the duodenum does not become malignant.

With the widespread use of H$_2$-receptor antagonists, proton pump inhibitors, and *H. pylori* eradication, the number of cases of duodenal ulcers requiring surgical

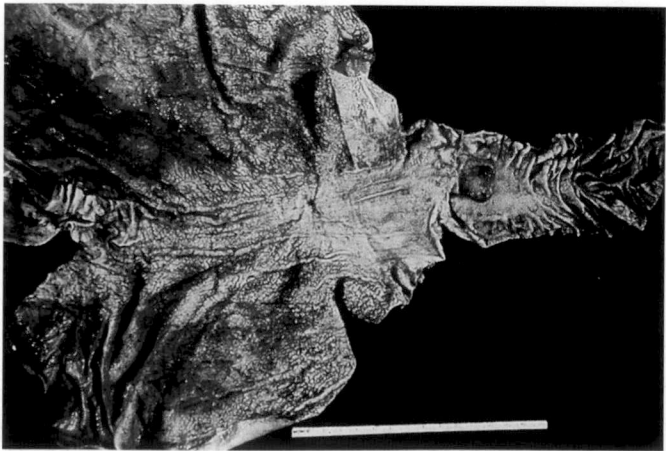

Fig. 11.89 Duodenal peptic ulcer, characteristically located in the first portion of the organ.

intervention has markedly decreased. The refractory ulcers tend to occur in younger patients, to be larger, and to be associated with more severe duodenitis.[163] Indications for surgery are complications, such as hemorrhage, perforation, and obstruction, and lack of response to medical therapy.[168] The two standard surgical techniques currently performed are vagotomy with antrectomy and gastroenterostomy, and vagotomy with pyloroplasty. The gastric resection may not include the ulcer, and only in a few instances is complete excision of the ulcer performed.

Marginal ulcer is a type of peptic ulcer that appears at the site of a gastrojejunostomy opening. Although the ulcer may be at the stoma itself, in most instances it is located on the jejunum at some distance from the opening. It was a common complication at the time when gastroenterostomy for duodenal peptic ulcer was being done without a concomitant gastric resection. It is still seen, although rarely, following gastroenteroanastomosis with gastric resection (Billroth II operation) for duodenal ulcer, especially if the entire antrum is not removed or if the afferent jejunal loop is of excessive length.[159] Occasionally, marginal ulcer develops following gastric resection for peptic ulcer or carcinoma of the stomach.

Small bowel ulcer not related to gastroduodenal pathology is an uncommon lesion. Grossly, a transverse area of ulceration is seen surrounded by congestion, hemorrhage, or edema. Obstruction, perforation, and hemorrhage are the most common presenting signs. Microscopically, the changes are nonspecific. Many of the cases in the early 1960s were due to the ingestion of enteric-coated tablets of potassium chloride.[155] With that medication off the market, most of the ulcers seen today are "idiopathic." Diseases to be considered in the differential diagnosis include congenital abnormalities, mechanical disorders, vascular occlusions,[164,166] specific inflammations, radiation effect, celiac disease, endometriosis, and tumors.[158] As is sometimes the case with peptic ulcers, idiopathic ulcers of the small bowel can be accompanied by a prominent lymphocytic and histiocytic reaction, which can be confused with malignant lymphoma.[156]

Vascular diseases

The consequences of mesenteric vascular occlusion are discussed in Chapter 26, but a few points regarding small bowel changes will be made here. These changes can closely mimic Crohn's disease, both clinically and radiographically.[184] They range from complete gangrene to foci of mucosal ulceration, accompanied by extensive submucosal edema.[172,185,186] Perforation may develop. Healing may lead to severe stenosis. The vascular alterations in the bowel that lead to these complications are usually the result of atherosclerosis, but they can also be secondary to postoperative adhesions from radiation therapy (see p. 726), rheumatoid arthritis,[177] periarteritis nodosa,[169] giant cell arteritis,[180] thromboangiitis obliterans,[175] oral contraceptives,[178] cocaine ingestion,[171] amyloidosis,[179] infection by viruses,[183] or infection by fungi.[170] Phlebitis may be seen in the absence of arteritis, in which case there is little risk of systemic involvement.[169,173,182] Depending on the predominance of a given morphologic alteration, terms such as *lymphocytic, granulomatous* and *necrotizing phlebitis* have been used, but all of these conditions are probably pathogenetically related. This may also apply to some of the cases reported as *myointimal venous hyperplasia* and *veno-occlusive disease of small bowel*.[181] Anticoagulant therapy can be complicated by the development of massive hemorrhage in the wall of the small and large bowel.[174,176]

Crohn's disease

Crohn's disease occurs with equal frequency in both sexes.[228] Most patients are in their twenties or thirties,[216] but the disease can first manifest at any age, including childhood[193,252] and old age.[200] White individuals of Anglo-Saxon extraction are more susceptible to the disease, the incidence of which seems to be increasing.[224] The etiology remains unknown. A tendency for familial clustering has been noted,[232] suggesting a perhaps HLA-DR determined genetic predisposition to an as yet undetermined exogenous factor.[238,240,244,247] Various types of mycobacteria (particularly *M. paratuberculosis*), *E. coli*, *Yersinia*, streptococcus, and viruses (including measles) have been implicated, but the causative agent remains elusive.[191,203,219a,230,257,261,264,269] The idea currently favored is that Crohn's disease results from immune and other inflammatory responses initiated by a stimulation of the luminal flora or their products, a notion that on the whole remains disappointingly vague.[244] Cases have been reported in females in association with endometriosis.[194a]

Grossly, the ileum is the usual site of the disease, although any portion of the small bowel can be involved. As a matter of fact, Crohn's disease can affect any segment of the digestive tract, including the oral cavity, minor salivary glands, esophagus, stomach, duodenum, large bowel, and anus.[202,233,236,243,258,272] Large bowel involvement is discussed later in this chapter.

In a series of 297 cases of Crohn's disease studied by Morson,[233] 66% of the cases were restricted to the small bowel, 17% were restricted to the large bowel, and 17% had involvement of both segments. In more recent series, in only one third of the cases have lesions been limited to the small bowel.

Crohn's disease can also involve sites outside the alimentary system, such as the skin (particularly around ileostomy or colostomy stomas),[262] vulva,[196] bone and joints,[235] skeletal muscle,[227] larynx, and spleen. The overall incidence of extraintestinal involvement is about 25%.[248] Nonspecific complications of the disease include arthritis, hydronephrosis, osteoporosis, amyloidosis, hidradenitis suppurativa, pyoderma gangrenosum, and various ocular disorders.[187,208,255]

Grossly, in the early stages of the disease the involved small bowel has a soggy feeling. The mucosa is reddish purple, and it may show pinpoint erosions known as "aphthoid ulcers" (Fig. 11.90). In later stages, ulceration becomes prominent. These ulcers are linear or serpiginous and often have a longitudinal disposition, arranged in parallel and connected by short transverse ulcerations.[246] Rarely, the mucosa has a polypoid configuration because of granulation tissue formation or nodular lymphangiectasia.[214,273] The gross changes in the wall evolve from edema to fibrosis, with marked narrowing of the lumen accompanied by dilatation and hypertrophy of the proximal segment (Figs 11.91 to 11.94). At this stage, the impression on palpation has been imaginatively likened to an eel in rigor mortis. The serosa may be focally or diffusely thickened; rarely, it is found to have multiple ("miliary") white nodules composed of either lymphoid aggregates or granulomas.[195] The mesentery becomes fibrosed and shortened, resulting in a corrugated bowel contour and piling up of mesenteric fat. Regional lymph nodes are moderately enlarged.

Two of the most distinctive features of Crohn's disease, partially alluded to, are the predilection for the terminal portion of the small bowel and the often segmental nature of the process, with sharply outlined foci separated by seemingly normal bowel ("skip areas"). However, on occasion, the disease involves the entire length of the small bowel (diffuse jejunoileitis).[263]

Local complications of Crohn's disease include the development of intramural abscesses and the formation of fistulas connecting the small bowel with other loops of small bowel or with large bowel, abdominal wall, or bladder.[237] At times, free perforation occurs.[231,267]

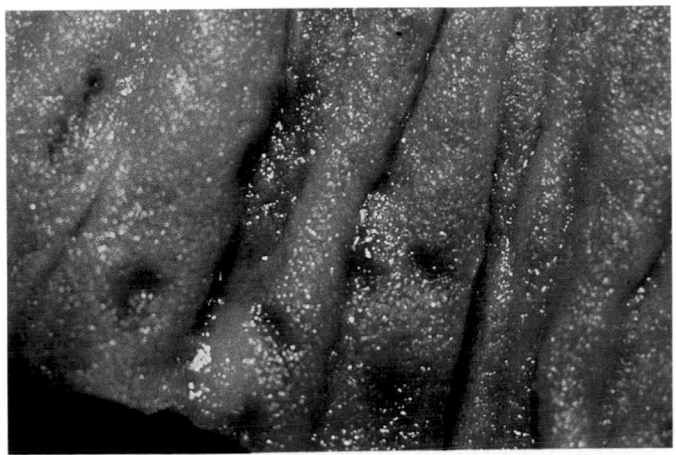

Fig. 11.90 So-called "aphthoid ulcers," an early feature of Crohn's disease.

Microscopically, submucosal lymphedema is one of the earliest changes. This is accompanied by lymphoid hyperplasia in the lamina propria and submucosa and a scattering of chronic inflammatory cells, including plasma cells (including some binucleated forms), lymphocytes, eosinophils, histiocytes (some containing prominent lysosomal inclusions),[266] and mast cells.[198,239]

The ulcerations are often seen to begin at the very top of the lymphoid follicles and are preceded by epithelial patchy necrosis, as detected by light microscopy[197] or ultrastructural examination.[222] It has been suggested that they have a vascular pathogenesis.[256]

The most typical ulcers are referred to as *fissures*. These are seen in approximately 30% of the cases and are

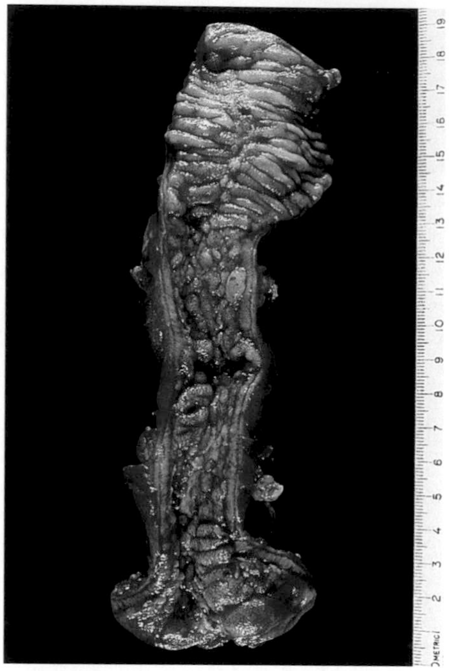

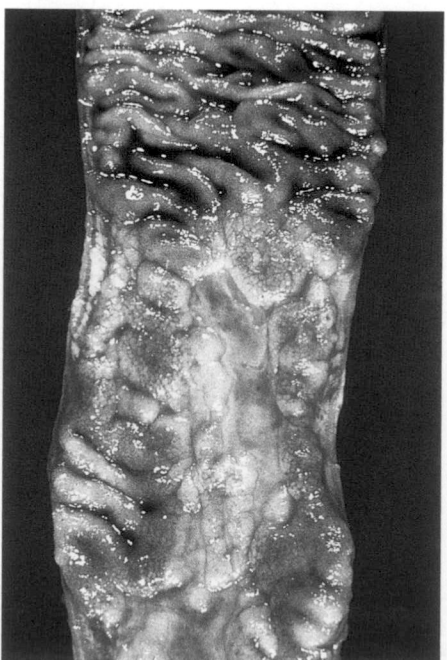

Fig. 11.91 Gross appearance of Crohn's disease. Note the segmental nature of the inflammation, and rigidity of the wall, and flattening of the mucosa are characteristic.

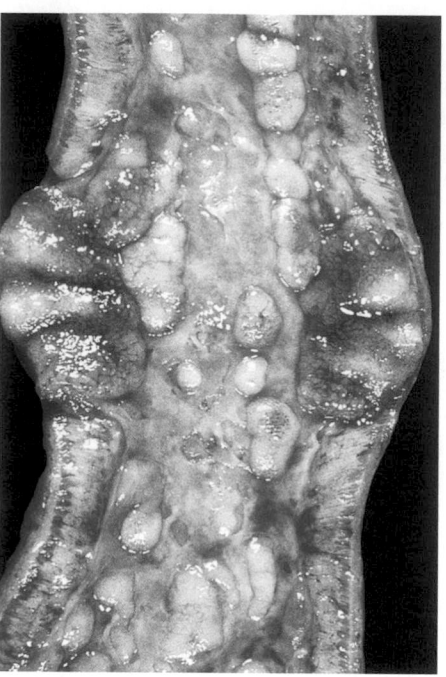

Fig. 11.93 Gross appearance of Crohn's disease. The combination of ulceration and elevated remnants of mucosa results in a typical cobblestone appearance.

Fig. 11.92 Gross appearance of Crohn's disease. There is a sharp demarcation between the involved and the uninvolved areas.

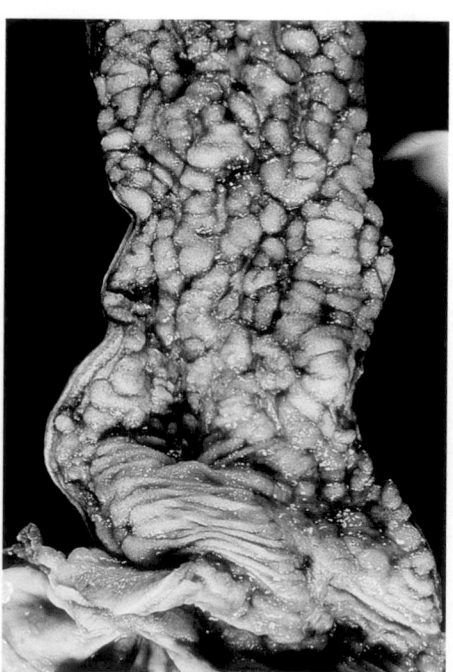

Fig. 11.94 Gross appearance of Crohn's disease. Another example of cobblestone appearance.

defined as slitlike formations with sharp edges and narrow lumina, arranged perpendicularly to the mucosa and extending deeply into the submucosa and even the muscularis externa (Fig. 11.95). The nonulcerated mucosa usually shows a combination of atrophy and regenerative hyperplasia. Foci of pyloric metaplasia may also be present.[249,251]

In well-developed Crohn's disease, there is nearly always microscopic evidence of *transmural involvement*, although the changes are much more severe in the submucosa and subserosa than in the muscularis externa (Fig. 11.96). There are edema, lymphatic dilatation, hyperemia, hyperplasia of the muscularis mucosae, and fibrosis.[220,249] The hyperemia is usually of mild to moderate degree. The inflammatory changes can involve the walls of veins and arteries.[206] There is an increase in the number of smooth muscle fibers in the submucosa ("obliterative muscularization"), a change that may contribute to the development of obstruction.[219] Along these lines, it has been found that tenascin (an extracellular matrix protein involved in the morphogenesis of muscle

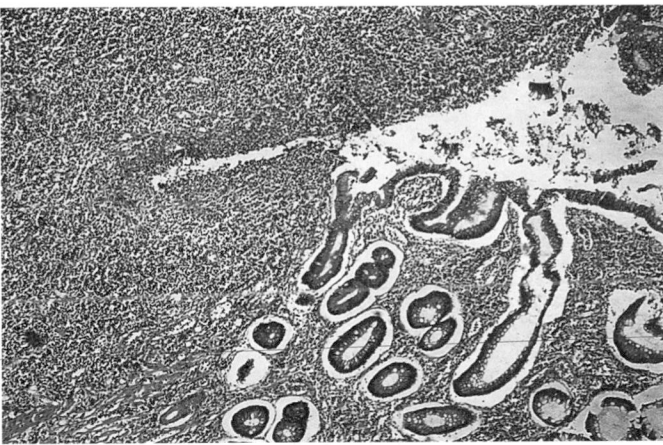

Fig. 11.95 Crohn's disease showing marked inflammatory changes and the formation of a fissure.

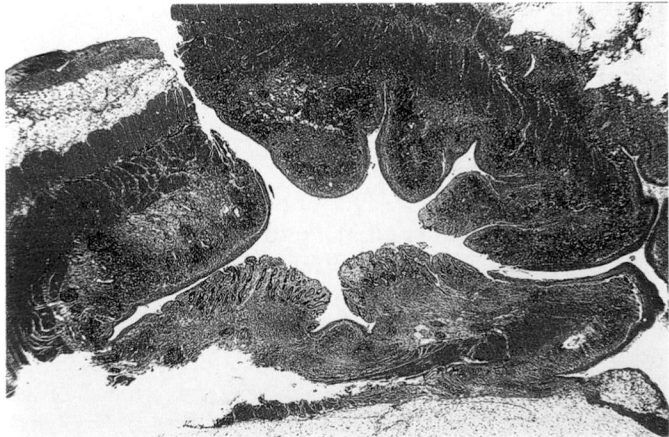

Fig. 11.96 Whole mount specimen of Crohn's disease showing transmural inflammation with predominance of the inflammation in the mucosa and submucosa.

tissue and wound healing) is strongly expressed, especially in areas of stricture.[205] The submucosal and myenteric nerve plexuses are often prominent, and electron microscopy has shown severe and extensive axonal necrosis,[199] but these are generally regarded as representing secondary phenomena related to the intense inflammation. Exceptionally, cystically dilated glands are seen in the wall of the bowel, an abnormality known as *enteritis cystica profunda*.[201]

Another important microscopic change of Crohn's disease, seen in approximately 60% of the cases, is the presence of *granulomas*. These have been described as sarcoid-like and are often seen to arise from within the centers of the lymphoid follicles. They are largely composed of epithelioid cells and multinucleated giant cells, with necrosis being usually absent or limited to a small central area.[259] If necrosis is extensive, the alternative possibility of tuberculosis and other infectious processes should be ruled out with the appropriate techniques. The granulomas of Crohn's disease may be found anywhere in the wall of the bowel (including serosa), in the regional lymph nodes (which also show sinusal dilatation and lymphoid hyperplasia), and at any other site of involvement. Only a minority of these granulomas are related to vessel walls, a feature that has been regarded by some as evidence of granulomatous vasculitis.[223]

Of all the microscopic features just described, those with greater diagnostic significance are transmural involvement, fissures, and granulomas. It should be noted, however, that a superficial variant of the disease exists in which the inflammation is limited to the mucosa and submucosa,[225] and that granulomas indistinguishable from those of Crohn's disease can be seen in many other conditions, particularly tuberculosis, yersiniosis, and (in the large bowel) complicated diverticular disease.[259]

Crohn's disease has an undulating, yet progressive course. Complete regression is rare. Occasionally this disorder is complicated by the development of small bowel carcinoma, most of the reported cases being of adenocarcinoma type and located in the ileum.[194,229,253] Sometimes the tumors are very small and detected only at the time of pathologic examination.[265] Some have been identified at the in situ stage, in association with hyperplastic dysplastic changes of the adjacent mucosa.[215,234,242,260] The carcinomas always develop in inflamed portions of bowel; in approximately one third of the cases they have arisen in a surgically bypassed segment.[204] Mixed adenocarcinoma–carcinoid tumors, pure carcinoid tumors, anaplastic carcinomas, carcinosarcomas, and malignant lymphomas (including Hodgkin's lymphoma) have also been reported.[189,212,213,217,241,250,268]

The initial treatment of Crohn's disease is medical (immunosuppression, elemental diet, total parenteral nutrition); however, because of the limitations and hazards of these therapies, surgical intervention is often needed.[187] Operation is indicated in the presence of partial or complete intestinal obstruction, internal or external fistulas, perforation with abscess, hemorrhage, and intractability despite medical management.

Specific surgical procedures to be used in these patients should be individualized; however, resection of the involved small bowel seems preferable to bypass procedures when the condition of the patient is not critical, unless there is extensive disease with several stenotic segments. The reason for this is that bypass surgery is associated with the highest reoperation rate.[226] The initial location of the disease also influences the prognosis after surgery, the risk of recurrence being higher in ileocolonic disease than in pure ileal or colonic disease.[209,221,270] Recurrence rates are the lowest in patients with the longest preoperative duration of the disease.[254] Following ileocolectomy, recurrence is much more likely to develop in the ileum adjacent to the colon than the distal ileum in the blind pouch.[190]

In general, the type and extent of the pathologic features bear little relationship to prognosis.[210] No statistical relationship has been found between involvement of the surgical margins as determined by frozen section at the time of surgery and recrudescence.[211,218] Claims have been made that the presence of granulomas is associated with a better prognosis,[207] at least for Crohn's disease of the large bowel,[192] but no statistically significant differences have been detected between the two groups.[272]

AIDS-related inflammatory diseases

The small bowel is the site of numerous types of abnormalities in HIV-infected and other immunocompromised patients,[282,288] and small bowel biopsy is very helpful in the diagnostic evaluation.[275] Some of the disorders are neoplastic (such as Kaposi's sarcoma, malignant lymphoma, and smooth muscle tumors), and these are discussed in the respective sections. Most are of an infectious nature and are listed here. It should be commented that occasionally some of these disorders are seen in individuals without evidence of immunodeficiency. Conversely, AIDS patients may obviously be affected by some of the other infectious diseases discussed in this chapter, such as tuberculosis. The generic term **AIDS enteropathy** is sometimes used by clinicians to cover all of the non-neoplastic small bowel disorders that can develop in patients with advanced HIV infection,[274,278,282] and the term *diarrheogenic bacterial enteritis* has been proposed for bacterial infections (such as *E. coli*) that result in diarrhea.[284]

CMV duodenitis can present with ulcer-type symptoms or bleeding.[291]

Atypical mycobacteriosis produced by *M. avium-intracellulare* may result in an appearance similar to Whipple's disease (Fig. 11.97). The lamina propria of the

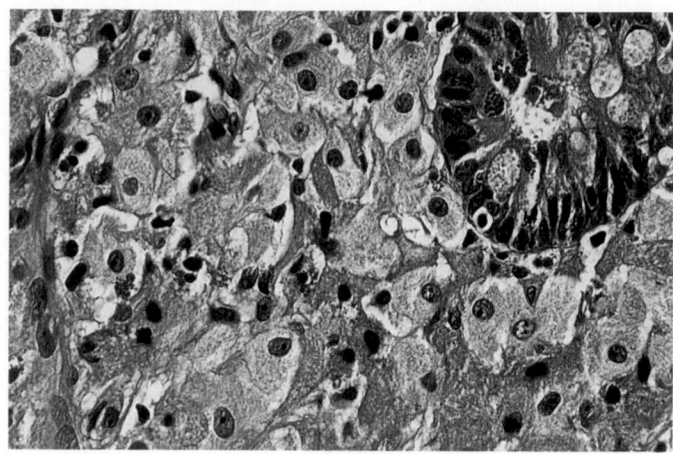

A

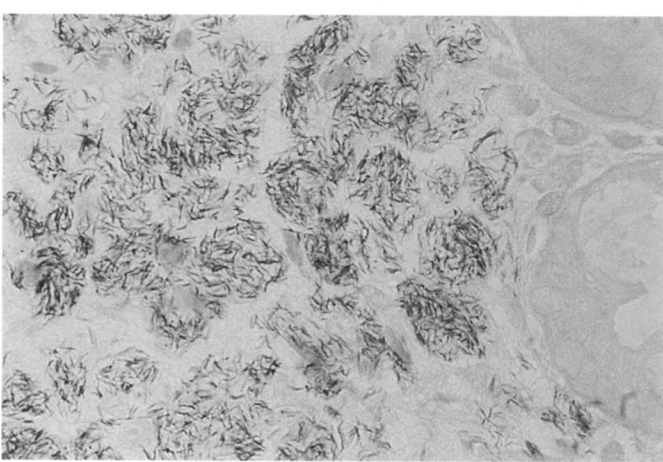

B

Fig. 11.97 A, Small bowel biopsy in an HIV-infected patient, showing packing of the lamina propria by histiocytes similar to those seen in Whipple's disease. **B**, Acid-fast stain from the same case showing innumerable *Mycobacterium avium-intracellulare* organisms.

bowel and the regional lymph nodes are infiltrated by plump, foamy, PAS-positive macrophages containing a myriad of organisms.[114,279,287]

Cryptosporidiosis is the result of infestation by a coccidial protozoan, *Cryptosporidium*. In sections, the organisms appear as 2 to 5 μm basophilic spherical structures attached to the luminal surface of the epithelium (Fig. 11.98A). Their appearance can be simulated by cellular debris or mucin. The organisms stain well with Giemsa, silver methenamine, and PAS, but are not acid fast (Fig. 11.98B). Their ultrastructural appearance is characteristic. They do not result in identifiable light microscopic changes in the mucosa,[280,281,290] except for cases with massive infection.[276]

Microsporidiosis is another AIDS-related small bowel disorder caused by an obligate intracellular protozoan.[289] The organism, *Enterocytozoon bieneusi*, is best demonstrated by electron microscopic examination but can also be detected with Giemsa and other special stains.[277,286]

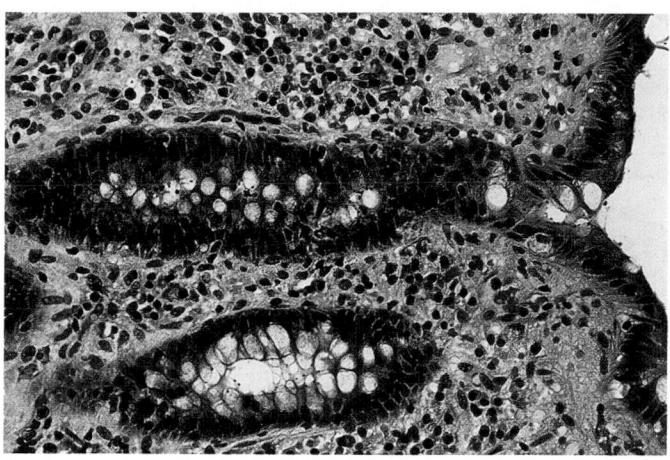

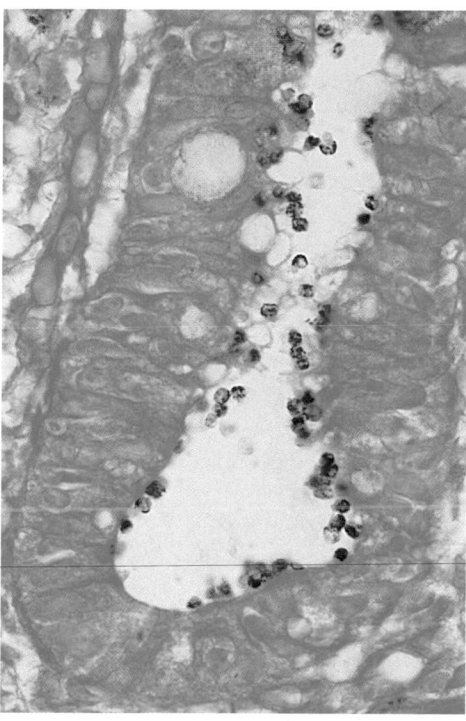

Fig. 11.98 Hematoxylin–eosin (**A**) and silver stain (of small bowel) (**B**) of intestinal cryptosporidiosis in an HIV-infected patient.

Other organisms belonging to the phylum Microspora have been identified in the same setting. The area of digestive tract most heavily parasitized is the jejunum.[285] Exceptionally, systemic dissemination occurs.[283] Morphologic changes in the affected mucosa are minimal or absent.

Other inflammatory diseases

Duodenitis is a common finding in patients with dyspepsia, the microscopic appearance correlating well with the endoscopic findings.[306] Mild cases show increased numbers of plasma cells, edema, and some degree of intraepithelial neutrophilic infiltration; more severe cases are accompanied by a more pronounced neutrophilic response and villous atrophy but a decreased number of plasma cells.[299] Since the evaluation of the milder changes is difficult and subjective, the smart suggestion has been made to use as control a biopsy of endoscopically normal mucosa from the lower duodenum taken at the same time.[304] Gastric metaplasia of the duodenum is more common in patients with duodenitis than in those with normal endoscopic findings, although the incidence of this finding shows some geographic variation.[302] *H. pylori* is often found in this setting, and is probably directly involved in the pathogenesis of the duodenitis.[293,296,316]

Acute (phlegmonous) jejunitis is an obscure entity of unknown etiology that occurs with equal frequency in men and women past 55 years of age.[295] Most of the reported cases have been from Scandinavian countries.[308] Grossly, the involved loop of bowel is sharply demarcated. The inflammation is mainly in the mucosa, but there may be pus on the serosal surface. The bowel wall is edematous and slightly distended. This process may also involve the jejunum or duodenum. Microscopically, there is frequently a widespread lymphangitis and regional lymphadenitis, accompanied by lymph node enlargement. The mesentery has a somewhat glassy appearance. Abscesses between folds of the mesentery have been observed.

Ulcerative jejunitis is discussed in connection with celiac disease (see p. 717).

Tuberculosis of the small bowel, still frequent in some parts of the world,[292,301] can be confused with Crohn's disease on both gross and microscopic examination.[305] In contrast with Crohn's disease, tuberculous ulcers are multiple and circumferential rather than linear and serpiginous.[312] Destruction of the muscularis externa is common. Microscopically, the tuberculous granulomas tend to be confluent and often have a caseous center and a peripheral lymphocytic ring. Obviously, special stains for acid-fast bacilli are in order whenever this differential diagnosis is entertained.

Sarcoidosis may involve the small bowel as part of disseminated disease, but the occurrence is exceptional.[307] The large majority of cases containing sarcoid-like granulomas in the bowel wall or mesenteric lymph nodes are the result of Crohn's disease.

Giardiasis may result in malabsorption (see earlier discussion) and chronic diarrhea,[309] and may be associated with nodular lymphoid hyperplasia (see p. 737). The mucosa is usually intact, but there may be blunting of villi and an increased number of inflammatory cells. The organisms have a teardrop shape, with paired nuclei ("owl-eye" appearance) and a central longitudinal axostyle.[310]

Yersiniosis results from infection by the gram-negative bacillus *Yersinia enterocolitica*. It may manifest as ulcerative enteritis, enterocolitis, acute appendicitis, and/or mesenteric lymphadenitis. The small bowel changes resemble somewhat those of typhoid fever. Elongated ulcerations with underlying lymphoid hyperplasia are seen together with small punctate aphthoid ulcers.[298] Colonies of gram-negative bacteria are seen beneath the ulcers, and there is an abundance of neutrophils at the ulcer base, two features of importance in the differential diagnosis with typhoid fever.[298,300] Although the microscopic appearance is suggestive, the correct diagnosis depends on proper identification of the organism in cultures from stool, lymph nodes, blood, or peritoneal fluid.[294]

Intestinal spirochetosis is seen microscopically as prominent colonization of the brush-border of the small bowel mucosa by spirochetes (Fig. 11.99A). The organisms are best visualized with Giemsa or Steiner stains (Fig. 11.99B). The symptoms are mild, there is usually not an associated colitis, and most affected individuals are immunocompetent.[292a]

Necrotizing enterocolitis, a disease predominantly affecting premature infants, is discussed on p. 792.

Eosinophilic enteritis and **gastroenteritis** often are accompanied by marked peripheral eosinophilia and

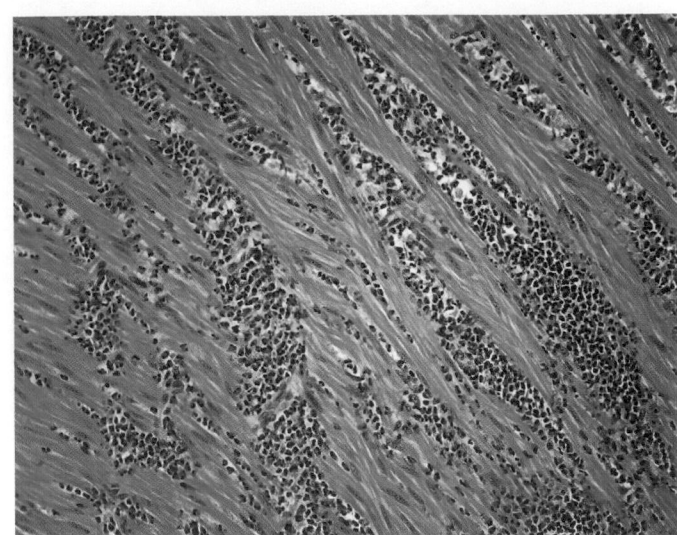

Fig. 11.100 Heavy infiltration of the small bowel muscle wall by mature eosinophils in eosinophilic enteritis. The mucosa was only minimally involved.

allergic symptoms. The gastrointestinal manifestations include nausea, vomiting, diarrhea, pain, steatorrhea, and protein-losing enteropathy. Morphologically, the main change is a diffuse eosinophilic infiltration of the intestinal wall, accompanied by other inflammatory cells, increased vascularity, and in some cases, necrotizing granulomas and vasculitis[308] (Fig. 11.100). The involvement may be predominantly in the muscle or subserosa; in the latter instance, it is often associated with eosinophilic peritonitis and ascites. Some cases are the result of parasitic infestation (such as *Ancylostoma caninum* or *Anisakis*[313,315]) and others are secondary to collagen vascular disease,[297] but the pathogenesis of most remains obscure.[308]

Ulcerative colitis usually spares the small bowel entirely, but some cases are associated with ileitis, jejunitis, and even diffuse duodenitis[314]; there may also be ileal involvement in **lymphocytic** and **collagenous colitis**.[301a,303]

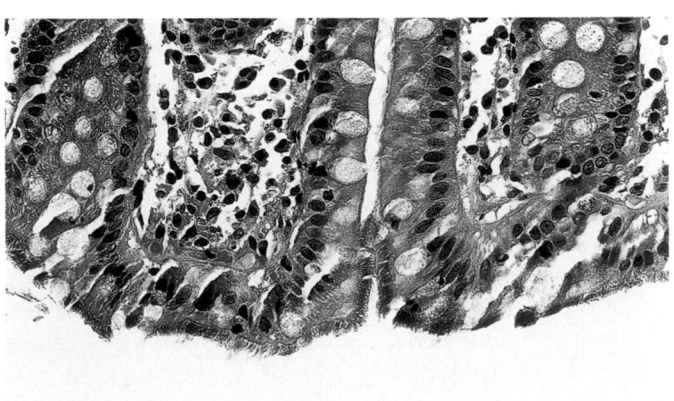

A

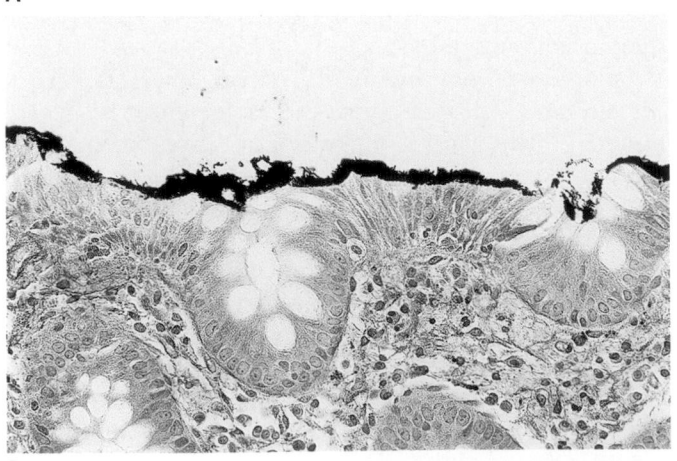

B

Fig. 11.99 A and **B**, Hematoxylin–eosin and modified Steiner's silver stain in a case of intestinal spirochetosis.

Irradiation effect

Radiation therapy of malignant tumors within the peritoneal cavity may cause damage to the intestinal tract, the amount of which depends on many factors.[320] Damage occurs most frequently in patients treated for carcinoma of the cervix, but there is an increased number of cases in children who had been treated for Wilms' tumor, malignant lymphoma, or other tumors.[318] Symptoms usually appear years after the radiation. Grossly, the small bowel appears thickened. The wall may be partially replaced by fibrous tissue, particularly in the submucosa. This is often accompanied by mucosal ulceration.[322]

There is a close correlation between the elapsed time interval between irradiation and surgery and the morphologic changes present.[320] Early irradiation effect is manifested by an increased production of mucus and by nuclear changes in the lining epithelium. Later, submucosal edema that may be completely reversible occurs. If the damage is severe, fibrosis of the muscular wall and ulceration develop. Vascular changes are prominent; they are characterized by subendothelial accumulation of lipid-laden macrophages, calcification, and thrombosis.[319,321] Operative resection of the affected segment of bowel is often needed.[317]

Frozen section is a reliable method of determining the degree of radiation damage and assessing whether or not the ends of the intestine can be expected to heal after resection and anastomosis.

Intussusception

In intussusception, a length of intestine (the intussuscipiens) literally swallows part of the bowel just proximal to it. This swallowed portion (the intussusceptum) is drawn down within the intussuscipiens until it can go no farther because of traction of the mesentery (Fig. 11.101). The specimen has a curved sausage-like form, with concavity toward the root of the mesentery. Increasing traction and compression shut off circulation to the intussusceptum so that it becomes necrotic and sloughs. The upper ends of the intussuscipiens and the intussusceptum may become firmly united. In exceptional instances, the result has been spontaneous cure in the form of a naturally occurring equivalent of a surgical end-to-end anastomosis.

Most cases of intussusception are seen during the first 5 years of life, with over one half occurring during the first year. This is probably related to the fact that the amount of lymphoid tissue in the ileocecal region and the degree of projection of the valve into the cecum are at their maximum during this period and that both decrease substantially after the second year.[326] There is

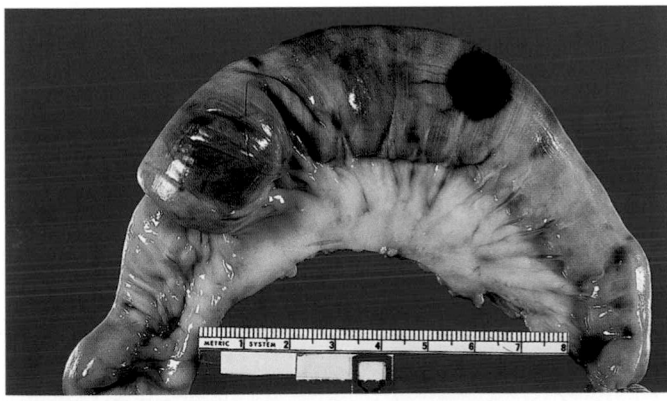

Fig. 11.101 Outer aspect of small bowel in intussusception.

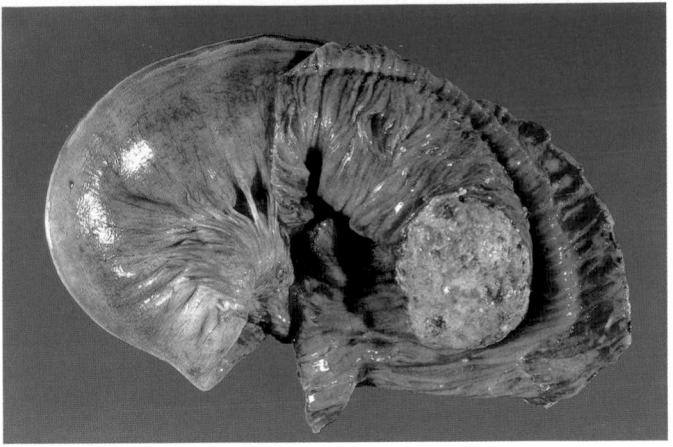

Fig. 11.102 Intussusception of small bowel caused by an adenocarcinoma. The tumor, located at the tip of the intussusceptum, is ulcerated and necrotic.

now general agreement that the lymphoid hyperplasia precedes and is often the cause of the intussusception rather than the result, although secondary inflammatory changes certainly occur. This lymphoid hyperplasia, which is limited to the mucosa and submucosa, is probably of viral etiology in many instances, as indicated by the finding of intranuclear inclusion bodies in one third of the cases[328] and the fact that viruses (particularly adenoviruses) have often been isolated from these children.[323,323a,325] Several cases of intussusception caused by lymphoid hyperplasia in AIDS patients have been reported.[324]

In early uncomplicated cases, a barium enema may be used to reduce the intussusception. Surgery is otherwise needed. If performed early enough, manual reduction of the intussusception is possible; resection is necessary when reduction is not feasible. Mortality is directly related to the time that elapses between onset and surgery. In children, there is a rapid rise in mortality after the second day.

In older children and in adults, intussusception is frequently the result of a pedunculated intraluminal tumor such as lipoma, smooth muscle tumor/GIST, or inflammatory fibroid polyp (Fig. 11.102). A CT scan is most useful in making the diagnosis of intussusception in adult patients.[327]

Other non-neoplastic diseases

Brown bowel syndrome is characterized by a prominent brown discoloration of the bowel wall, grossly evident from the serosal side and on cut section, and often associated with malabsorption. Microscopically, large amounts of lipofuscin granules are seen in the cytoplasm of smooth muscle cells. The pathogenesis is unknown, but the suggestion that it may be caused by vitamin E deficiency has been advanced[332]; a primary abnormality of smooth muscle mitochondria has also been postulated.[329]

Amyloidosis may involve the vessels or the stroma of the small bowel, either as part of generalized disease or—rarely—as a localized finding.[333,334] In the latter instance, it may lead to intestinal obstruction.[331]

Graft-versus-host disease following bone marrow transplantation affects primarily the skin, gastrointestinal tract, and liver. Involvement of the small bowel is manifested clinically by diarrhea and microscopically by a variety of changes, of which single epithelial cell necrosis is the most consistent.[335]

Microvillous inclusion disease (familial microvillous atrophy) is a disorder of the intestinal brush border that results in intractable secretory diarrhea in infants. The diagnosis has been based on the presence of microvillous inclusions at the ultrastructural level. Recently, it has been shown that immunohistochemical staining for CD10 (a membrane-associated neutral peptidase) is highly suggestive of the disease by showing a cytoplasmic pattern (as opposed to the normal linear brush border staining).[330]

Tumors

Benign epithelial tumors

So-called **Brunner's gland adenoma** (polypoid hamartoma; brunneroma) is characterized by a nodular proliferation of histologically normal Brunner's glands, accompanied by ducts and scattered stromal elements (Fig. 11.103). It may be accompanied by ciliated cysts and adipose tissue.[338] It can be focal, multifocal, or diffuse. It is probably not a true neoplasm but rather an expression

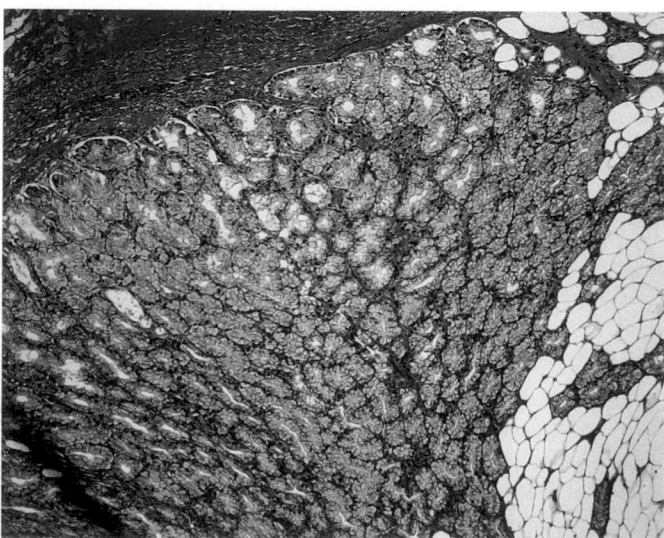

Fig. 11.103 So-called "Brunner's gland adenoma." A compact collection of microscopically normal Brunner's glands is interspersed with lobules of mature fat.

of nodular hyperplasia or hamartoma.[361] The most common location is the posterior wall of the duodenum at the junction between the first and second portions. It can be associated with duodenitis and erosions, and be the cause of melena or duodenal obstruction.[353,360]

Adenomas similar to those of the large bowel can develop in the small bowel, but their frequency is minuscule.[357] The duodenum and jejunum are involved more often than the ileum. They can be single or multiple, pedunculated or sessile, and they can have the microscopic appearance of an adenomatous polyp (tubular adenoma), a villoglandular polyp (tubulovillous adenoma), or a villous adenoma.[341,354] Malignant transformation can occur in them; as for their colorectal counterparts, the incidence of this complication is greater if the lesions are villous, large, and/or multiple. Villous adenomas of the duodenum have been reported with increasing frequency in recent years, undoubtedly as a result of the widespread use of endoscopy. Many of them are located at the level of the ampulla of Vater and are further discussed in Chapter 15. Their morphologic appearance and natural history are entirely similar to those of villous adenomas of large bowel: they are often large and sessile, with a tendency to recur and a high incidence of malignant transformation.[350,357] Thorough sampling at endoscopy is of importance for detection of the latter.[336]

Some of the small bowel adenomas develop in patients with multiple colonic polyposis; a few of them have been reported in the duodenum and have been of the so-called "depressed" type.[352] Others have been reported in the ileal patch following ileocystoplasty.[348,349]

Hamartomatous polyps of the jejunoileum are usually seen as a component of the *Peutz–Jeghers syndrome*. This is a familial disorder transmitted as a mendelian autosomal dominant trait with variable degrees of penetrance.[337,345] Similar polyps can also be present in the stomach, duodenum, and large bowel, and the patients have a typical pigmentation of the lips, oral mucosa, digits, palms, and soles. Grossly, these polyps do not differ from the usual adenomatous polyp, but microscopically they are very different. The glands are supported by broad bands of smooth muscle fibers, which are thick in the center of the lesion and thinner on the periphery[344] (Fig. 11.104). The intimate intermingling of glands and smooth muscle fibers may simulate the appearance of invasion and lead to a mistaken diagnosis of carcinoma.[355]

Several types of epithelial cells are present, as demonstrated by light and electron microscopy.[343] Columnar and goblet cells predominate in the superficial portion, whereas Paneth and endocrine cells are seen at the base next to the muscular framework. This microscopic architecture is similar for polyps occurring elsewhere in the gastrointestinal tract, but the cytologic composition depends on the location.[345] Sometimes the goblet cells are sloughed off secondarily to intussusception and assume

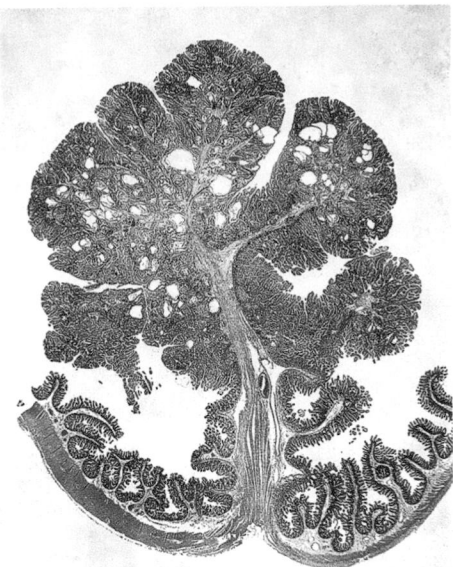

A

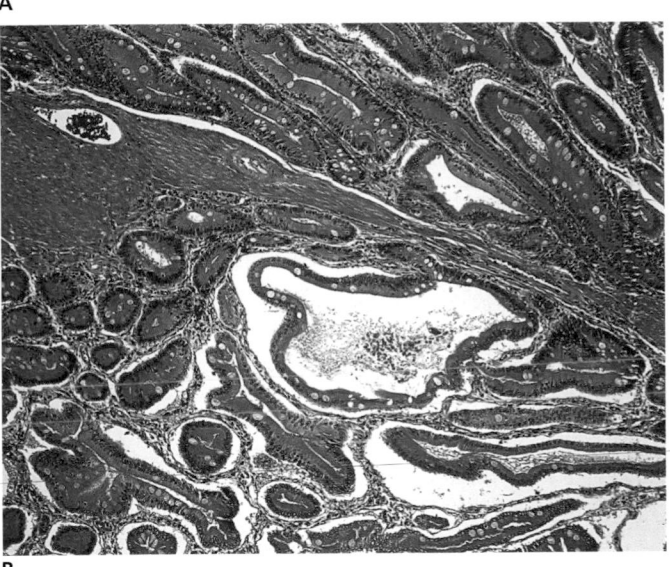

B

Fig. 11.104 A and **B**, Hamartomatous polyp of small bowel in Peutz–Jeghers syndrome. **A**, Whole mount view. **B**, Higher-power view, showing dilated glands devoid of atypia separated by bundles of smooth muscle.

a signet ring cell appearance that can be mistaken for malignancy.[340]

Some hamartomatous polyps occur in the absence of the other features of the syndrome. Some are associated with mucosal glands and mucinous cysts deeply embedded in the submucosa or beyond, a change sometimes designated as *enteritis cystica profunda*,[351,362] and which represents another source of misdiagnosis.[359] Several cases of adenocarcinoma of the gastrointestinal tract have been reported in patients with Peutz–Jeghers syndrome. They have been located in the stomach, small bowel, or large bowel.[346,347] The prognosis has been poor, probably because of the lateness of the diagnosis.[342] In some of these cases, the invasive carcinoma has been seen to coexist with areas of carcinoma in situ and adenomatous change.[356,358] Patients with Peutz–Jeghers syndrome may also develop the distinctive ovarian neoplasm known as sex-cord tumor with annular tubules (see Chapter 19), so-called "adenoma malignum of uterine cervix" (see Chapter 19), ovarian mucinous tumors, breast carcinoma (often bilateral), and other types of malignancy.[339,363]

Adenocarcinoma

Adenocarcinoma of the small bowel is 40 to 60 times less common than its counterpart in the large bowel. Most patients are elderly, and there is no sex predilection.[365,366] It can develop in any segment but is more common in the upper portions.[372,375,377] Approximately 40% to 50% of the cases occur in the duodenum; an increasing number of cases in this location are being reported with the use of fiberoptic endoscopy.[381,382] Most cases of duodenal carcinomas arise from the mucosa in the region of the ampulla and are discussed in Chapter 15, in the section on carcinoma of the periampullary region exclusive of the pancreas.

Adenocarcinoma of small bowel has been described in hereditary nonpolyposis colorectal carcinoma syndrome,[380] Peutz–Jeghers syndrome (see p. 728), Recklinghausen's disease,[370] bowel duplication,[364] Crohn's disease (see p. 723), at ileostomy sites,[367,373] in surgically bypassed duodenum,[378] in the jejunal limb of a Roux-en-Y esophago-jejunostomy,[374] and in the ileal segment of a defunctionalized ileocystoplasty.[384]

Duodenal carcinoma tends to have a papillary configuration and is, therefore, amenable to brush cytologic diagnosis.[369] Those lesions located more distally usually have a napkin-ring appearance and produce partial intestinal obstruction with marked dilatation of the proximal bowel; approximately 20% have a predominantly polypoid or fungating appearance, perhaps caused in some instances by their origins in preexisting adenomatous polyps or villous adenomas.[372] Occasionally these carcinomas present as multiple tumors[385] or in association with primary malignant neoplasms in other sites.[368,383]

Microscopically, these tumors are usually moderately well differentiated adenocarcinomas. Mucin production and CEA reactivity are the rule[371]; there may also be immunoreactivity for lysozyme, suggesting focal differentiation toward Paneth cells.[379] Immunohistochemical expression of COX-2, sPLA2 and cPLA2 is common, the pattern being similar to that of large bowel adenocarcinoma.[385a] In addition, it is common to find a scattering of endocrine cells, particularly in tumors located in the ileum. These cells are positive for chromogranin and 5-HT and may also show immunoreactivity for a variety of peptide hormones, including somatostatin, YY peptide, neurotensin, glucagon, and glycentin.[376] Ultrastructurally, there may be a prominent development of microvilli.[386]

At the time of diagnosis, the majority of the tumors have extended deeply into the wall and may have already metastasized to regional lymph nodes. The prognosis mainly depends on the presence or absence of regional lymph node involvement. In one series,[372] 88% of the patients with positive nodes died of tumors, contrasted with 45% of those with negative nodes.

Other types of carcinoma

Small cell neuroendocrine carcinoma is a rare type of small bowel malignancy composed of small, round, or oval cells with scanty cytoplasm and hyperchromatic nucleus. The appearance is very similar to that of pulmonary small cell carcinoma. As in the latter, dense-core granules of neurosecretory type can be identified ultrastructurally and neuroendocrine markers immunohistochemically.[393] These tumors can present in a pure form or mixed with ordinary adenocarcinoma. They are deeply invasive, highly prone to metastasize, and associated with a very poor prognosis.

Adenosquamous carcinoma has been reported on a few occasions, with either the glandular or the squamous component predominating.[389,391]

Anaplastic (sarcomatoid) carcinoma is composed of highly bizarre tumor cells, some of them multinucleated, with abundant cytoplasm and no signs of glandular differentiation. The behavior is extremely aggressive.[387,388,390,392]

Carcinoid tumors and related endocrine tumors

General and clinical features

Carcinoid tumor is the generic term traditionally applied to low-grade malignant neoplasms originating from the diffuse endocrine system outside of the pancreas and the thyroid C-cell.[398,405,410] It is now acknowledged that they represent a group of related neoplasms rather than a single pathologic entity.[403,409] This stems from the fact that the digestive tract in general and the small bowel in particular contain a large number of endocrine types, any of which can be represented in these neoplasms, singly or in combination.[395,403,404] The most common form of carcinoid tumor is known as classical or insular; this is the type usually referred to when the designation "carcinoid tumor" is used for a neoplasm of the small bowel without a qualifier. It comprises approximately one third of all neoplasms of this organ.[400]

The majority of carcinoid tumors of small bowel occur in adults, but they have also been documented in children.[397] Most are located in the ileum (including Meckel's diverticulum), followed in frequency by the jejunum and distal duodenum.[396,406] They have also been described in small bowel affected by celiac disease[399] and Crohn's disease,[407] in bowel duplication,[408] and in association with Recklinghausen's disease[401] and with inflammatory polyps.[394] Carcinoid tumors of the small bowel are multiple in 15% to 35% of the cases[411a] and are sometimes

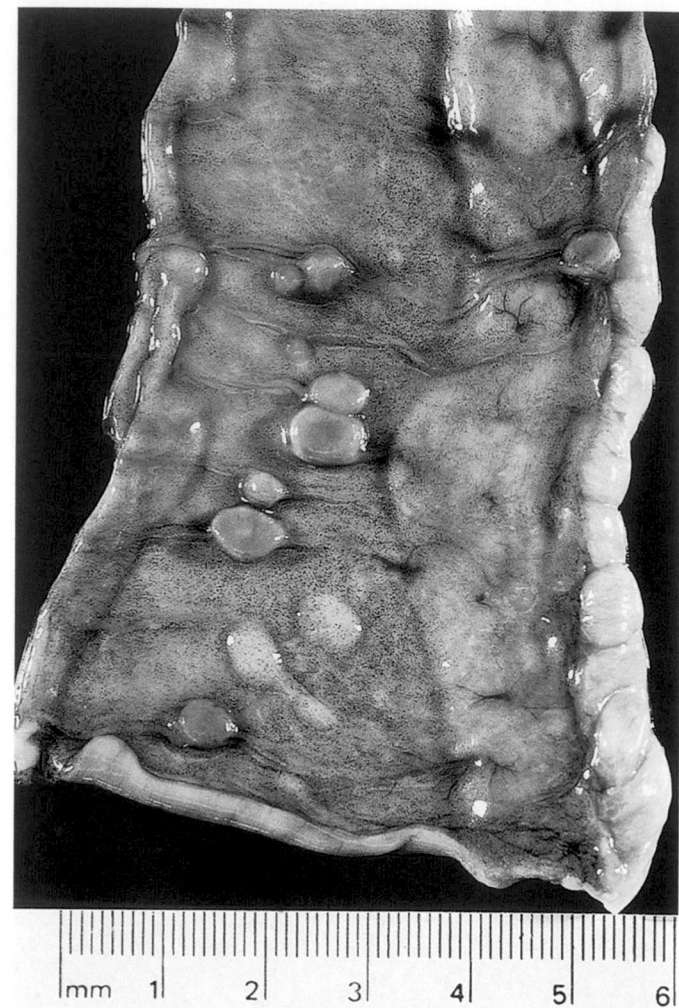

Fig. 11.105 Multiple carcinoid tumors of small bowel presenting as small sessile polyps. (Courtesy of Dr. RA Cooke, Brisbane, Australia; from Cooke RA, Stewart B: Colour Atlas of Anatomical Pathology. Edinburgh, Churchill Livingstone, 2004).

associated with malignant gastrointestinal tumors of other microscopic types[402] or with tumors of endocrine differentiation in other locations[411] (Fig. 11.105).

Morphologic features

Grossly, the mucosa is often intact over the tumor. Infiltration of the submucosa is the rule, and extension into the muscularis externa is common (Figs 11.106 to 11.108). The tumor invasion and the accompanying fibrosis may "buckle" the bowel wall. Following formalin fixation, the tumor acquires a bright yellow color that is not evident in the fresh state. Microscopically, the pattern is that of solid nests of monotonous-appearing cells with small, round nuclei; a moderate amount of finely granular cytoplasm; and fine nucleoli (Fig. 11.109). Peripheral palisading is common. The nesting pattern is accentuated by artifactual retraction from the stroma. Mitotic figures are scanty. Tumor emboli in lymph vessels are

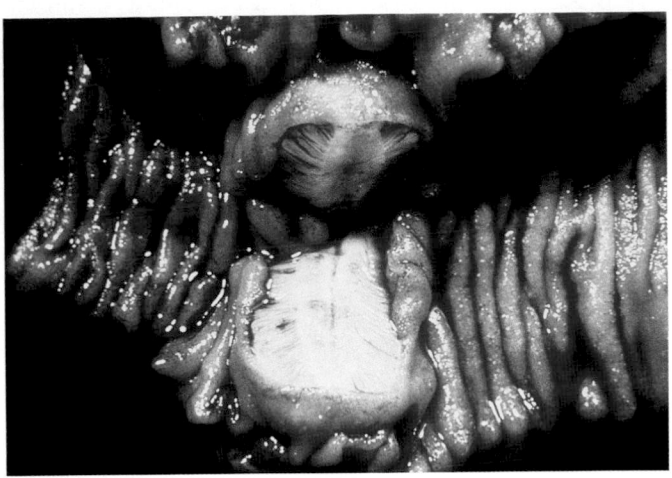

Fig. 11.106 Cut surface of carcinoid tumor of the ileum. The tumor is solid, yellowish, and accompanied by marked thickening of the muscularis externa.

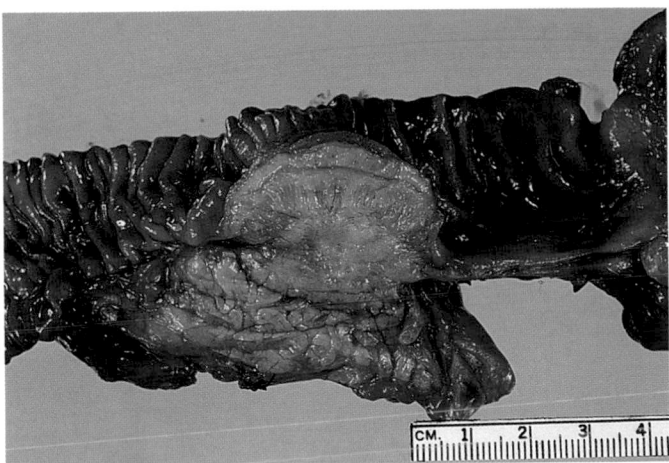

Fig. 11.107 Large carcinoid tumor of duodenum. This lesion was composed of D cells (somatostatin-secreting).

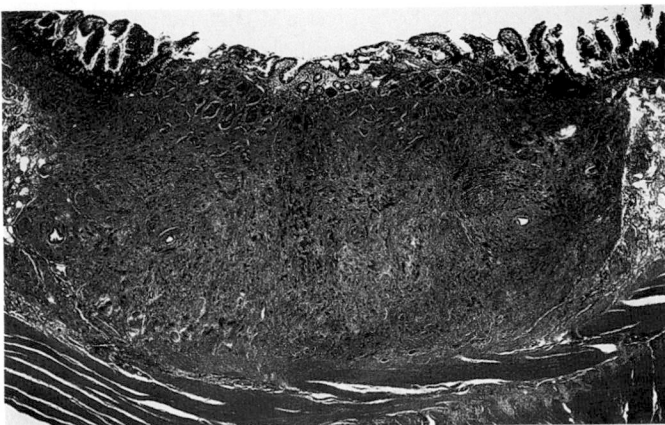

Fig. 11.108 Panoramic view of ileal carcinoid tumor showing full thickness involvement with a largely preserved mucosa.

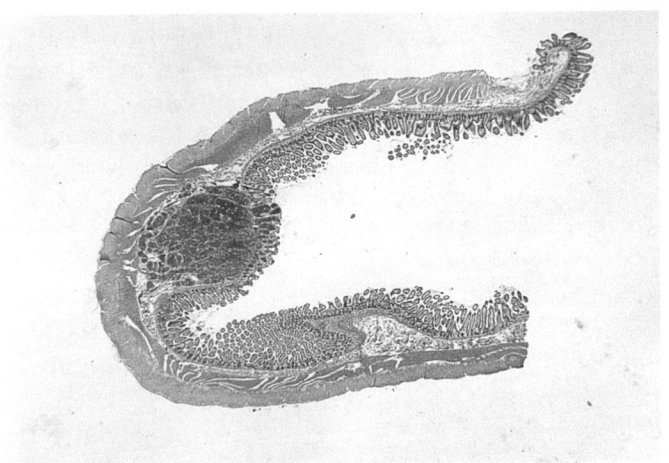

A

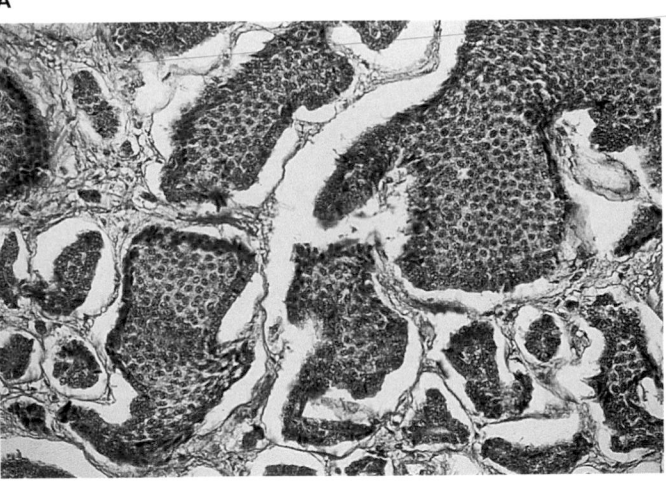

B

Fig. 11.109 A and B, Carcinoid tumor of small bowel. A, Panoramic view showing submucosal nodule. B, Closer view. Note the nesting (insular) pattern of growth.

often seen. It is also common to find tumor cells within submucosal nerves.

The mucosa surrounding the carcinoid tumor may show highly vascular polypoid formations that can simulate Crohn's disease[414]; the change has been attributed by some authors to the secretion of a transforming growth factor by the tumor cells[413] and interpreted by others as a nonspecific reaction secondary to mucosal prolapse.[412]

Microscopic types

Many variations exist within the basic theme just described. Trabecular and glandular (tubular) formations may be present, the latter sometimes containing intraluminal mucin. Carcinoid tumors with a predominantly glandular pattern are referred to as *adenocarcinoids* and are further subdivided into tubular and signet ring types.[418] On occasion, features of endocrine and exocrine secretion can be seen in the same cell (so-called

"amphicrine cell").[416,417] The existence of these and other variations has led to the division of carcinoid tumors into several types largely based on their patterns of growth: A, B, C, D, and E,[420] or insular, trabecular, glandular, undifferentiated, and mixed,[419] these various types correlating with behavioral differences; however, most of these varieties are much less common than in the appendix. Sometimes a typical carcinoid pattern is seen in association with an adenocarcinomatous pattern, whether in the primary tumor or in metastases. Furthermore, Carstens et al.[415] reported an intestinal tumor with the light microscopic features of a carcinoid tumor (but negative with silver stains) that had electron microscopic features (cytoplasmic filaments, fibrils, and caveolae) similar to those of the intestinal caveolated cell.

Histochemical, immunohistochemical, and electron microscopic features

The distinctive phenotypic profile of classic carcinoid tumor can be demonstrated by a variety of special techniques. At the histochemical level, the tumor is argentaffin (and therefore also argyrophilic), positive for the diazo reaction, and generally negative for mucin stains (Fig. 11.110). Ultrastructurally, there are numerous dense-core pleomorphic secretory granules scattered throughout the cytoplasm.[426] Immunohistochemically, there is reactivity indicative of both epithelial and neuroendocrine differentiation. The first is manifested by keratin and—in the tumors with a glandular component—by apical or luminal CEA.[437,440,452] Among the keratins, CK7 is expressed in almost 10% of the cases, and CK20 in approximately 25%.[423] The second property is brought forward by a series of "pan-endocrine" markers, such as neuron-specific enolase, chromogranin, synaptophysin, Leu7, and PGP 9.5.[435,443–445,448]

5-Hydroxytryptamine can be demonstrated immunohistochemically or through formalin-induced fluorescence, both in sections and in smears.[451] A variety of peptide hormones has also been demonstrated in these tumors. These include substance P (by far the most common), gastrin, somatostatin (and somatostatin receptors), glucagon, glycentin, pancreatic polypeptide, bombesin, gastrin-releasing peptide (GRP), and growth hormone-releasing factor (GRF).[422,424,432,436,440,442,449,450,453] Peptide YY is found only rarely, in contrast to its consistent presence in rectal carcinoids.[427,447] Neurofilaments are usually absent.[438] There is also consistent lack of reactivity for TTF-1, in contrast to pulmonary carcinoid.[423] Other substances that have been detected in gastrointestinal carcinoid tumors include calbindin-D28K (a calcium-binding protein expressed by some neural and neuroendocrine cells),[428] villin,[454] and myosin XVA (a member of the myosin super-family).[431] Staining for S-100 protein is negative, in contrast to the usual positivity encountered in carcinoid tumors of the appendix; this may be related to the alleged difference in the origin of these tumors: endocrine cells from Lieberkuhn's crypts for the carcinoid tumors of small bowel and subepithelial endocrine cells related to nerves for those in the appendix.[433,434] Curiously, some carcinoid tumors have also been found to be

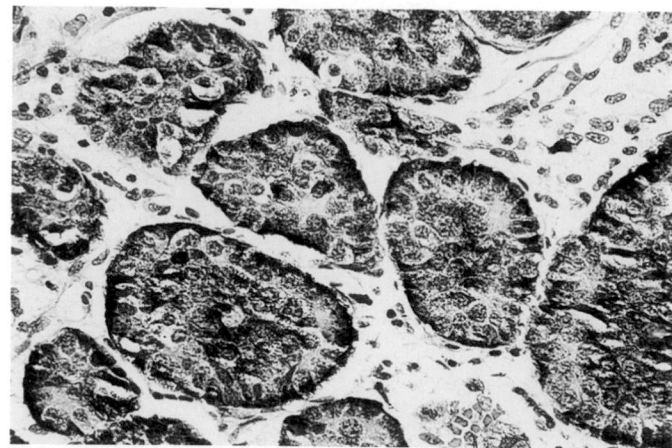

A

B

Fig. 11.110 Carcinoid tumor of small bowel. **A**, Argentaffin reaction (Fontana–Masson). **B**, Argyrophil reaction (Sevier–Munger).

immunoreactive for prostatic acid phosphatase,[446] but this is less common in ileal than in rectal carcinoid tumors.[421]

Several growth factors and their receptors have been detected in carcinoids of small bowel, and the suggestion has been made that they participate in the autocrine modulation of the tumor growth.[429,430,441]

Most of the metastatic foci react immunohistochemically in a fashion identical to that of the primary tumor, but some produce either additional or fewer hormones.[453] Some of the aforementioned substances (5-HT, chromogranin, substance P, and—rarely—neuron-specific enolase) can be elevated in the serum of these patients and thus serve as circulatory markers for these tumors.[425]

The non-neoplastic mucosa of a small bowel bearing one or more carcinoid tumors may show hyperplasia of endocrine cells, although this is not nearly as common or as prominent as with some types of carcinoid tumors of the stomach.[439]

Molecular genetic features

Aneuploidy is present in over half of the ileal carcinoid tumors, this feature being possibly related to prognosis.[456]

Loss of heterozygosity at the *MEN-1* gene locus site on 11q is usually absent in jejunoileal carcinoid tumors, suggesting that the *MEN-1* gene is not involved in their pathogenesis.[455]

Immunoreactivity for p53 is rare in carcinoid tumors,[458] but said to be more frequent in the metastasizing lesions.[457]

Spread and metastases

Classic carcinoid tumors are low-grade malignant neoplasms that have a slow growth rate but also are highly invasive and have metastasizing properties.[460,461] Metastases occur most commonly in the regional lymph nodes and liver but are also seen in other sites, such as bone, skin, and thyroid.[462] The liver metastases are usually multiple and solid but occasionally have a prominent cystic component.[459]

Treatment and prognosis

The primary treatment of carcinoid is wide surgical removal of the primary tumor and its lymphatic drainage. Solitary liver metastases are also amenable to surgical excision. Because of the propensity for multiplicity and association with other gastrointestinal tumors, a thorough exploration of the abdominal cavity is indicated.

The overall 5-year relative survival rate of small bowel carcinoid is between 50% and 65%,[465] with a marked difference existing between the patients in whom the tumors are confined to the wall (85% 5-year survival) and those in whom the lesion invades the serosa or beyond (5% 5-year survival).[468] Tumor size correlates with prognosis, but classification schemes that divide these tumors into benign and low-grade malignant depending on size must be viewed as arbitrary at best.[463] CEA expression is said to correlate with a more aggressive course.[464,466] Resection of the primary tumor is worthwhile even in the presence of extensive liver metastasis because prolonged survival is possible under these circumstances.[467]

Carcinoid syndrome

Carcinoid tumor may be associated with the *carcinoid syndrome*.[470,474] Nearly all of the reported cases of this syndrome have occurred in tumors that have metastasized to the liver, presumably because of the liver's capacity to inactivate biologically active substances released into the portal circulation; however, exceptions occur.[471] The syndrome is characterized by cyanosis of the face and anterior part of the chest, intermittent hypertension, palpitation, and frequent watery stools. Traditionally, it has been assumed that the syndrome was due to 5-HT, an indolamine regularly secreted by the tumor cells and easily detectable in the urine in the form of its catabolite 5-hydroxyindolacetic acid; however, there is little relation between the serum levels of this marker and the occurrence of the syndrome, especially in regard to its vasodilatation component. Other substances known to be secreted by carcinoid tumor—such as tachykinins, prostaglandins, and histamine—have been postulated.[473,476,480] It is also apparent that the cells of carcinoid tumor must secrete some substance that elicits the deposition of extracellular connective tissue around the tumor and sometimes at a distance. Manifestations of this phenomenon include extensive fibrosclerosis, often seen in the tumor itself; fibrosclerosis of the right-sided cardiac valves that results in so-called "carcinoid heart disease"[479]; obliterative elastic sclerosis of mesenteric blood vessels that may lead to small bowel gangrene[469,478]; and dermal sclerosis that results in scleroderma-like lesions.[472] A few carcinoid tumors have resulted in spontaneous hypoglycemia,[475] apparently because of insulin production by the tumor cells.[477]

Duodenal endocrine tumors

Endoscopically, duodenal endocrine tumors appear as smooth, round elevations, usually measuring between 5 and 20 mm in diameter but occasionally larger[492] (see Fig. 11.107). Microscopically, they rarely have the features of classic carcinoids as described in the previous section. Many of the reported cases have been composed of either G- or D-cells, as demonstrated by their immunoreactivity for gastrin and somatostatin, respectively.[481–484,487] The G-cell tumors (gastrinomas) may be associated with Zollinger–Ellison syndrome and MEN type I,[495,497] whereas D-cell tumors (somatostatinomas) are usually hormonally silent at the clinical level.[496] A high percentage of duodenal tumors predominantly composed of D-cells have occurred in black patients with Recklinghausen's disease.[486,489,498] Immunohistochemistry is needed to identify conclusively the specific cell types; however, the nature of these tumors can already be suspected in routinely stained sections by the fact that both of them tend to have a well-developed glandular component and that D-cell tumors have, in addition, numerous psammoma bodies, usually located within glandular lumina.[488,491,493] It should be noted, however, that psammoma bodies are not specific for D-cell tumors; they can also be seen in carcinoid tumors of other types and in B-cell tumors of the pancreas.[490] Exceptionally, duodenal endocrine tumors are of pancreatic B-cell type.[494]

Metastases were present in 21% of the duodenal endocrine tumors studied by Burke et al.,[485] and three of the patients died of metastatic disease. There is a relationship between tumor size and incidence of metastasis, at least for the D-cell tumors.[496]

Gangliocytic paraganglioma

Gangliocytic paraganglioma (nonchromaffin paraganglioma; paraganglioneuroma) is a morphologically distinct tumor occurring almost exclusively in the second portion of the duodenum, usually in proximity to the ampulla of Vater[500,508,515] (Fig. 11.111). A few cases have been reported at a more distal location, including the jejunoileum[512] and appendix.[516] Occasionally the lesion is multiple[507] or seen in association with Recklinghausen's disease and carcinoid tumors.[509,514] Most lesions are small, pedunculated, and submucosal, with frequent ulceration of the overlying mucosa and bleeding. The microscopic appearance is distinctive, with no exact counterpart elsewhere in the body. Three cell components are present: (1) endocrine cells with a carcinoid-like appearance arranged in compact nests and trabeculae containing dense-core granules ultrastructurally and exhibiting immunoreactivity for a variety of markers, particularly pancreatic polypeptide (PP); (2)

isolated ganglion cells, immunoreactive for neuron-specific enolase and other neural markers; and (3) spindle-shaped Schwann cells and/or sustentacular cells, immunoreactive for S-100 protein[499,501,503,510,511,513] (Fig. 11.112). Somatostatin may be present in both ganglion cells and endocrine cells.[504] In one series, three of six cases contained amyloid.[512] The peculiar location of this tumor, its highly organoid arrangement, and the striking predominance of PP cells suggest that this lesion may represent a hamartomatous process derived from the ventral primordium of the pancreas.[511] Nearly all cases published so far have followed a benign clinical course, but isolated instances associated with lymph node metastases are on record.[502,505,506]

Gastrointestinal stromal tumors and related tumors

The general considerations concerning gastrointestinal stromal tumors (GISTs) and related lesions are discussed in the chapter on the stomach (p. 674) and will not be repeated here.

Among small bowel tumors reported as leiomyosarcoma in the pre-GIST era, 10% were located in the duodenum, 37% in the jejunum, and 53% in the ileum.[534] As in the stomach, the small bowel tumors may show a variety of differentiation patterns.[524] The ratio is different, however, in the sense that there is a greater incidence of tumors with neural-type features (especially for those located in the duodenum and jejunum) (Fig. 11.113). In particular, GISTs containing so-called "skenoid fibers" are characteristically in this location. Also in analogy with the stomach, some relationship exists between these differentiation patterns and the clinicopathologic features. Thus, multiple stromal nodules involving both small and large bowel are always obviously muscular in

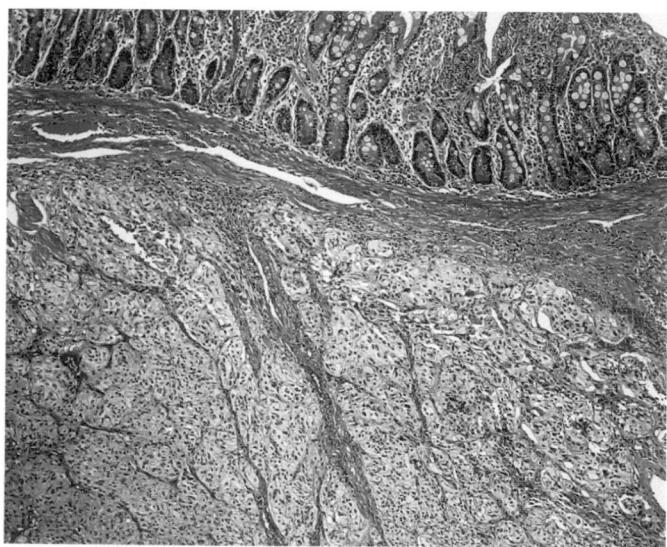

Fig. 11.111 Gangliocytic paraganglioma of duodenum centered in the submucosa, separated from the normal mucosa by a preserved muscularis mucosae.

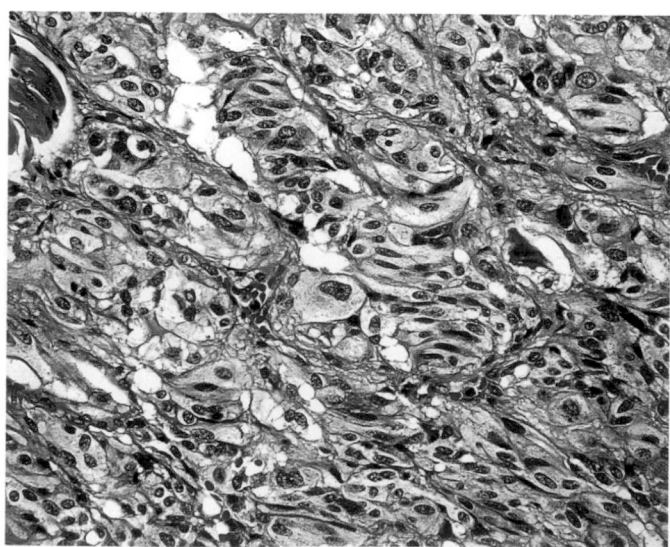

Fig. 11.112 Gangliocytic paraganglioma of duodenum showing a trabecular pattern of growth and scattered ganglion-like cells.

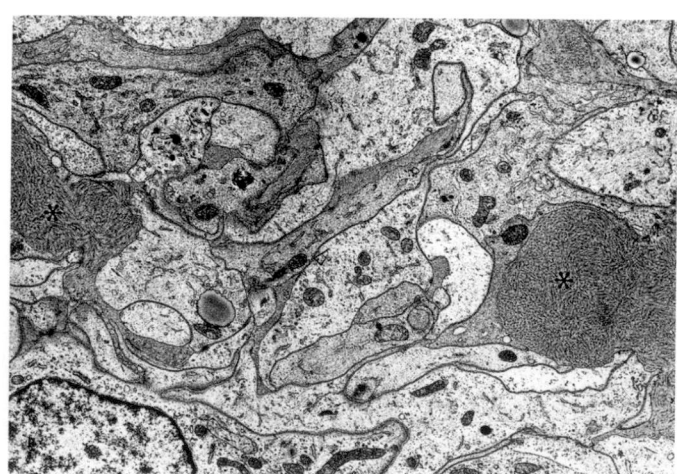

Fig. 11.113 GIST with neural differentiation (so-called "GANT") of ileum. Neuritic processes containing occasional dense-core neurosecretory-type granules and skenoid collagen fibers (asterisks) are illustrated. (×11,100; courtesy of Dr. Robert A. Erlandson, Memorial Sloan-Kettering Cancer Center)

nature ("leiomyomatosis").[532] The percentage of tumors with epithelioid morphology is smaller than in GISTs located in the stomach.[533]

The subdivision into risk categories is based on criteria similar to those used for their gastric counterparts. Among GISTs of the duodenum, those composed of large cells and having an organoid pattern are predictably low risk, whereas highly cellular tumors with small cells and little or no organoid pattern are high risk.[520,525a,531] It should also be kept in mind that the percentage of clinically malignant cases is higher in GISTs of small bowel than in those for the stomach.

Malignant GISTs of small bowel may invade adjacent structures such as the pancreas by direct extension.[530] They also tend to invade the bloodstream and metastasize distantly.[517,526] Staging, microscopic grading, and DNA ploidy have been shown to correlate with prognosis.[518,519,529,530] Of 20 patients diagnosed by Ranchod and Kempson[528] as leiomyosarcoma in the pre-GIST era, 15 developed metastases (usually to the liver and peritoneum), and 4 others developed intra-abdominal tumor with prominent retroperitoneal spread; only one patient was found to be alive and free of disease at the time of the last follow-up.

Cases of multiple GISTs of small bowel have been reported in association with Recklinghausen's disease and neuronal intestinal dysplasia.[521,522,523,527]

Stromal tumors occurring in the AIDS-affected population have definite smooth muscle features and often exhibit a close microscopic relationship with vessel walls, suggesting an origin from them. They are CD117 negative and should be segregated from GISTs.[525]

Malignant lymphoma and related disorders

Important criteria used to classify malignant lymphomas involving the small bowel include (1) their presumed primary versus systemic nature, (2) their cell lineage (B cell or T cell), and (3) the presence and type of an associated and/or predisposing condition.[546]

Although the gastrointestinal tract is the most common site of primary extranodal lymphoma,[535,547,556] the possibility of disease being present elsewhere should always be investigated, inasmuch as 10% of patients with non-Hodgkin's lymphomas have involvement of some part of the gastrointestinal tract at the time of initial evaluation.[574] The discussion below deals with the primary types of intestinal lymphomas.

T-cell malignant lymphomas represent, in most instances, a complication of longstanding celiac sprue or related malabsorption syndrome.[543,544] Some of these T-cell lymphomas are CD56 positive, have angiocentric qualities, and are associated with EBV, but there is controversy as to whether they should be regarded as analogous to the natural killer-cell lymphomas of the sinonasal region.[545,548,571,597] These are referred to as *enteropathy-associated T-cell lymphomas* and are discussed

on p. 717. T-cell lymphomas of the small bowel unassociated with malabsorption also occur.[543,544] Some of these T-cell lymphomas (whether related to malabsorption or not) are associated with an intense eosinophilic infiltration that may obscure the diagnosis.[590]

B-cell malignant lymphomas may present in a variety of forms.[568a] The large majority of these tumors are thought to arise from mucosa-associated lymphoid tissue (MALT; i.e., the component of the immune system that is believed to function as a protective mechanism for the freely permeable surface of the gastrointestinal tract).[542,565,567]

Most B-cell lymphomas of the small bowel are solitary. The ileum is more commonly affected, followed by the jejunum and duodenum.[579] Grossly, they can show a diffusely infiltrating mass with a garden hose appearance, a bulky tumor mass with extensive ulceration, or a predominantly polypoid growth (Figs 11.115 and 11.116). The regional lymph nodes are involved in approximately half of the patients with bowel lymphoma. In the series of Lewin et al.[574] the 2-year actuarial survival was 42%, lower than for malignant lymphomas of the stomach or rectum. The survival rate is related both to histologic typing and clinical staging.[549]

A distinct type of B-cell lymphoma of small bowel thought to be a special form of MALT lymphoma is known as **immunoproliferative small intestinal disease** (IPSID), Mediterranean lymphoma,[567,582] and Middle Eastern lymphoma.[564,582,589] It is relatively common among non-European Jews, Arabs in the Middle East, and the black population of South Africa.[568] Patients often have a short history of diarrhea and malabsorption, but the mucosa is not completely flat in most cases. Biopsies of the bowel and regional lymph nodes in the low-grade form of this disease (by far the most common)

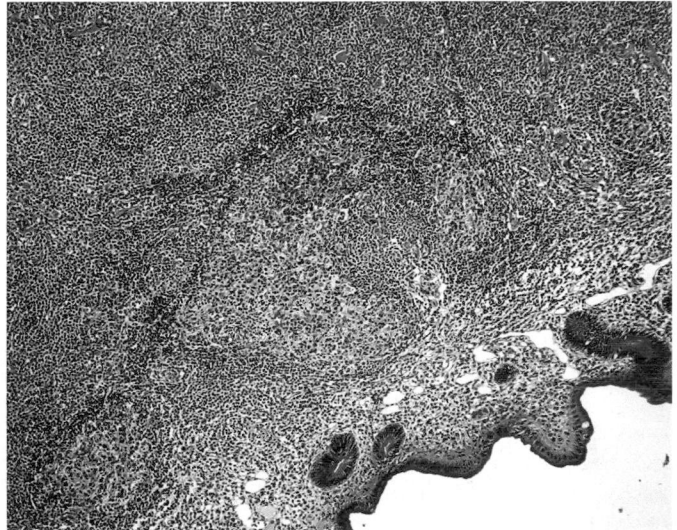

Fig. 11.114 MALT-type malignant lymphoma of small bowel. Note the colonization of the germinal centers by the tumor cells.

Fig. 11.115 Gross appearance of malignant lymphoma involving the ileum in a diffuse fashion and resulting in prominence of the transverse mucosal folds.

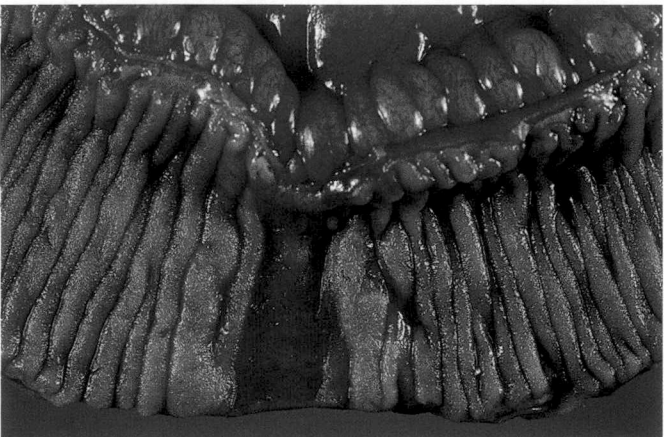

Fig. 11.116 Malignant lymphoma of small bowel presenting as a circumferential ulcerated lesion that resulted in stenosis.

show a heavy lymphoplasmacytic infiltration by cells that appear mature or only slightly immature at both the light and electron microscopic levels.[573,587] This is associated with the presence of monoclonal alpha heavy chains of immunoglobulins in their cytoplasm,[563,585] as well as in the serum and urine—hence the alternative designation "alpha chain disease." Light chains may also be detected.[566] It has been speculated that this lymphoplasmacytic infiltration is originally reactive in nature and that it represents a response to a continuous antigenic stimulus of possible infectious nature. The initially polyclonal nature of the proliferation and the fact that some cases have responded to tetracycline supports this contention.[537]

In the high-grade form of the disease, which is usually preceded and accompanied by the low-grade form, the microscopic appearance of the tumor is that of highly pleomorphic large cell lymphoma with immunoblastic and plasmacellular features, to the point that it has also been designated (*malignant*) *plasmacytoma*. Pangalis and Rappaport[584] have shown that the large tumor cells exhibit an immunocytochemical staining for alpha chain

similar to that of the small cell lymphoplasmacytic component, suggesting that they represent a clone of highly malignant elements that originate from it. A prominent "starry sky" pattern may be present, as well as intense follicular lymphoid hyperplasia.[555,582]

The diagnosis of immunoproliferative small intestinal disease can usually be made by endoscopic biopsy, especially if areas with an infiltrating pattern are sampled.[557] The involvement centers in the distal portions of the duodenum and the upper jejunum. Grossly, the presence of diffusely thickened folds with small nodules or discrete tumor growths heralds the emergence of a high-grade malignancy, which proves rapidly fatal in most instances.

Low-grade B-cell lymphoma of so-called "MALT type" (other than IPSID) is not as common in the small bowel as it is in the stomach. Its gross, microscopic, and immunohistochemical features are similar to those of its gastric counterpart[580] (see p. 680). The key features are the predominance of small lymphoid cells (centrocyte-like or monocytoid B cells), the formation of lymphoepithelial lesions, and the presence of reactive follicles (Fig. 11.114). The clinical course is generally very indolent.[593] The *high-grade* form of this tumor may be seen in association with the low-grade form or in its absence. This is a **large cell lymphoma of large cell type**, often associated with plasmacytoid forms. The latter feature can be so pronounced as to have led some authors to regard such lesions as plasma cell tumors.[559] Another problem is represented by the frequent occurrence of multinucleated tumor cells vaguely resembling Reed–Sternberg cells and leading to a mistaken diagnosis of Hodgkin's lymphoma.

Follicular lymphoma (follicle center cell lymphoma) of small bowel is another form of B-cell malignancy which has a predilection for the terminal ileum[572,592] but which can also occur in the jejunum or duodenum.[599] Some of these cases present grossly as innumerable small polypoid masses throughout the bowel, a condition known as lymphomatoid polyposis. The 14:18 translocation that is typical of this lymphoma type has been detected by PCR in routinely processed tissue.[591] Immunoglobulin gene analysis suggests that follicular lymphoma of small bowel arises from local antigen-responsive ("antigen-experienced") B cells.[538a]

Mantle cell lymphoma has rarely been described in the bowel. Its morphologic distinction from the other low-grade B-cell lymphomas previously described can be very difficult. Its gross presentation may be in the form of multiple lymphoid polyps similar to those seen with follicular lymphoma.[558,583]

Burkitt's lymphoma is usually seen in children; the ileum and ileocecal valve are most often involved.[594] This tumor is relatively common in the Middle East and Algeria.

Hodgkin's lymphoma is extremely rare. Only two

cases were found by Lewin et al.[574] in a review of 117 lymphomas of the gastrointestinal tract. The large majority of cases so diagnosed in the past are examples of non-Hodgkin's lymphoma of either B- or T-cell type.

Anaplastic large cell lymphoma can present as a primary lesion of the small bowel; most of the reported cases have been of T-cell lineage.[541]

Multiple myeloma can involve the bowel as a manifestation of systemic extramedullary disease.[552] As already mentioned, most cases reported in the past as plasmacytomas at this site would be placed in other categories at present.

Clinical variations on the theme of intestinal malignant lymphoma include those developing in AIDS or other immunocompromised hosts[551] (including heart transplant recipients[554]), those complicating Crohn's disease[570] (see p. 723), and those coexisting with adenocarcinoma (although probably not causally related).[598]

Pathologic variations include the highly unusual signet ring[561] and myxoid forms,[550] the former simulating metastatic signet ring carcinoma and the latter resembling a soft tissue sarcoma.

Post-transplant lymphoproliferative disorders can exhibit predominant involvement of the small bowel. As in other sites, the appearance of the lymphoid cells ranges from polymorphic to monomorphic, and the population may be polyclonal or monoclonal.[581]

True histiocytic lymphomas seem to occur in the small bowel, in the sense of the tumor cells having morphologic *and* immunohistochemical markers of histiocytes and/or dendritic cells and lacking the markers of lymphoid cells[577,578]; curiously, their appearance is somewhat reminiscent of Rosai–Dorfman disease. It should be remembered that most of the large cell tumors that have been regarded in the past as histiocytic on morphologic grounds and on the basis of their alleged immunohistochemical positivity for lysozyme and α_1-antitrypsin, have been shown to be of B-cell origin.[553]

Follicular dendritic cell tumor can present as a primary mass in the small bowel.[562]

Granulocytic sarcoma can present initially as a small bowel mass, preceding the development of acute granulocytic leukemia.[539] This condition may be simulated by bacterial infection, since macrophages that have phagocytosed large numbers of bacteria may appear strongly positive with the Leder stain.[569]

Lymphoid hyperplasia is a focal reactive process, also known as *pseudolymphoma* (a term which is probably better avoided).[586,596] The ileocecal region is the most common location.[588] The variety leading to intussusception in young children has been discussed previously (see p. 727). In other cases (*nodular lymphoid hyperplasia*) the entire small bowel is studded with well-circumscribed nodes of lymphoid tissue. *Giardia lamblia* is often present in the latter condition, and some of the patients

have low or absent IgA and IgM levels, decreased IgG level, susceptibility to infection, and diarrhea with or without steatorrhea.[560,586,595] In children, this condition is often associated with viral infection.[538] The presence of highly reactive germinal centers, numerous cell types, prominent vascularity, and polyclonality as determined immunohistochemically are the most important features in the differential diagnosis with malignant lymphoma.[576] It has become apparent in recent years that many lesions designated as lymphoid hyperplasia in the past on purely morphologic grounds represent instead low-grade malignant lymphomas.[540] This is almost certainly the case for many of the lesions interpreted as nodular lymphoid hyperplasia seen in association with an obvious lymphoma,[575] and it may also apply to at least some of the "pseudolymphomas" characterized by a pleomorphic infiltrate containing atypical cells.[536]

Other tumors and tumorlike conditions

Endometriosis may result in a mass-like effect and cause obstruction[646] (Fig. 11.117). Microscopically, endometrial

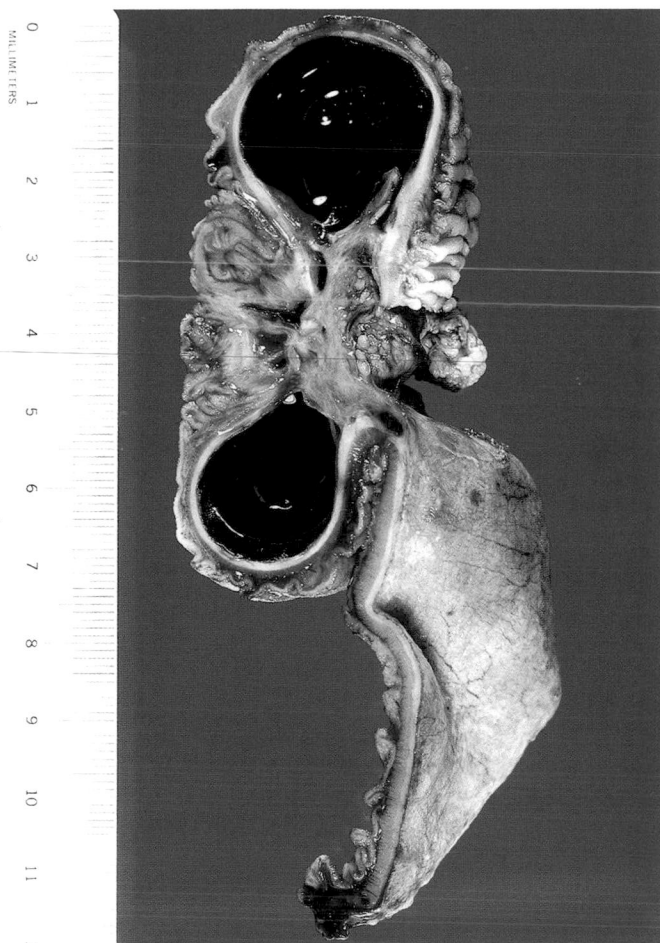

Fig. 11.117 Large blood-filled cystic lesion in the wall of the small bowel due to endometriosis. There is also hyperplasia of smooth muscle, a very common finding. (Courtesy of Dr. RA Cooke, Brisbane, Australia; from Cooke RA, Stewart B: Colour Atlas of Anatomical Pathology. Edinburgh, Churchill Livingstone, 2004).

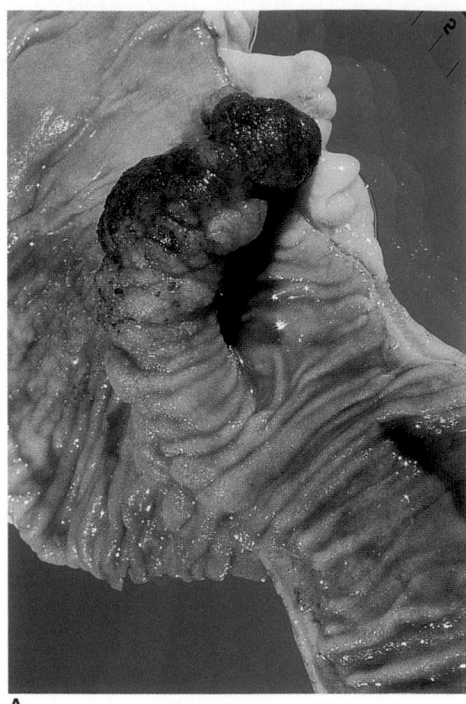

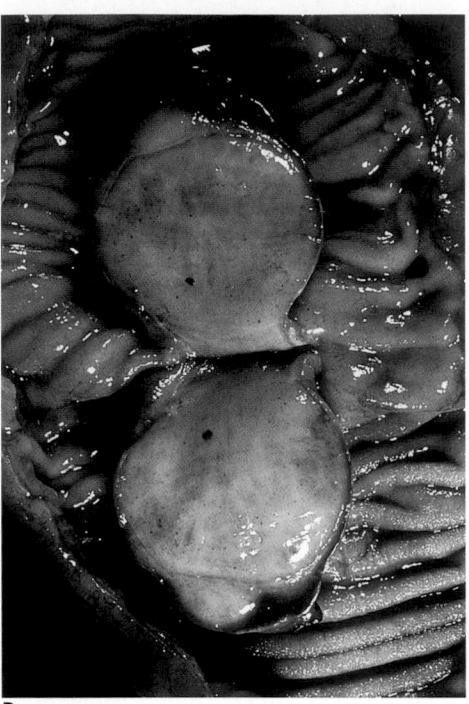

A

B

Fig. 11.118 A and **B**, Gross appearance of inflammatory fibroid polyp.

glands and stroma, foci of fresh and old hemorrhage, and bundles of hypertrophic smooth muscle (which may constitute the bulk of the process) are seen.[604] These endometriotic foci may exceptionally undergo malignant transformation in the form of endometrioid carcinoma, müllerian adenosarcoma, and endometrial (endometrioid) stromal sarcoma.[647] *Endocervicosis* is a related müllerian-type process in which the metaplastic mucosa has the appearance of endocervix rather than endometrium.[605] As already mentioned (see p. 721), endometriosis can be seen in association with Crohn's disease.

Neuromuscular and vascular hamartoma of the small bowel is a submucosally-based proliferation of mature vessels, nerves, and smooth muscle fibers that can cause obstruction.[613] It has been suggested that this process may be related to so-called *diaphragm disease* and caused by the intake of nonsteroidal anti-inflammatory drugs.[607]

Inflammatory fibroid polyp (inflammatory pseudotumor) appears grossly as a localized submucosal sessile polypoid mass[619,636] (Fig. 11.118). The process occasionally extends to the entire thickness of the wall. Despite some microscopic similarities, this entity is probably unrelated to eosinophilic enteritis. The appearance of this intestinal polyp is also similar to that of the homonymous gastric lesion, except that the neural-like features commonly seen in the latter are less prominent (see p. 659) (Fig. 11.119). By electron microscopy, the principal mesenchymal cell has the features of a myofibroblast. Immunohistochemically, there is consistent positivity for CD34, in keeping with the assumption that this lesion is primarily composed of primitive perivascular cells.[643] There is also positivity for bcl-2 and CD117 (c-kit).[624] The

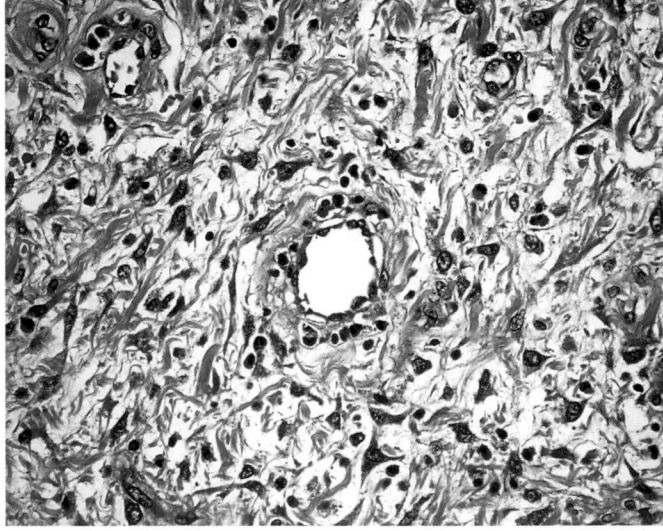

Fig. 11.119 Inflammatory fibroid polyp showing myofibroblast-like cells, eosinophils, and other inflammatory cells in a sclerotic background.

latter differs from that of GISTs in that it has a coarsely granular cytoplasmic quality without membrane accentuation. There is also a sometimes prominent histiocytic population.[638] Inflammatory fibroid polyp (a clearly benign condition) should be distinguished from inflammatory pseudotumor, the nosologic position of which remains controversial.[626] The lesion is benign, and the pathogenesis is unknown.[636] Multiple and recurrent cases in a familial setting have been described.[602] Obstruction and intussusception are two well-known complications of this entity.[630]

Lipomas of the small bowel are characteristically centered in the submucosa.[628,641] Grossly, they are bright yellow, round, encapsulated tumors that bulge upward into the mucosa surface (Fig. 11.120). They have a very characteristic radiographic appearance.[618] The large majority are solitary. Approximately 5% are multiple; these should be distinguished from the rare condition known as *lipomatosis*, in which a segment of bowel (on occasions the entire organ) is infiltrated by mature fat, sometimes in association with diverticulosis or intussusception.[606] Complications of lipoma include ulceration and intussusception.

Benign vascular tumors and tumorlike conditions of various types occur in the small bowel. *Hemangiomas* may be single or multiple and may be associated with similar lesions in other organs.[603,635] They may bleed or perforate. Grossly, the lesions are soft, elevated, reddish, and not well defined. The midjejunum is the most common location, but they can also occur in the duodenum and other sites. Microscopically, cavernous hemangioma is the most common variety. *Lymphangiomas* often occur, particularly in children, in association with similar tumors in other sites[617] (Figs 11.121 and 11.122). They should be distinguished from the *lymphatic cysts (lacteal cysts)* commonly seen as an incidental finding in the elderly.[600]

In *hereditary telangiectasia* there are vascular lesions of the mucous membrane and skin. These lesions are multiple, and severe gastrointestinal hemorrhage can occur from them. Smith et al.[637] reported 159 patients, 21 of whom had significant hemorrhage. Demonstration of these lesions at surgery is difficult, and surgical resection is usually not successful.

There are isolated case reports of glomus tumors and hemangiopericytomas;[616] most of the latter would probably be designated solitary fibrous tumors at present.

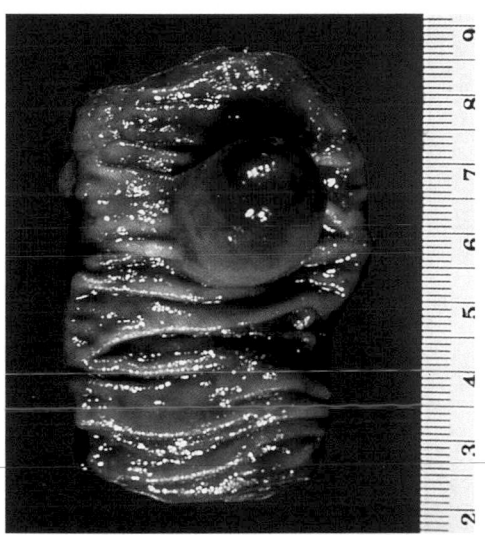

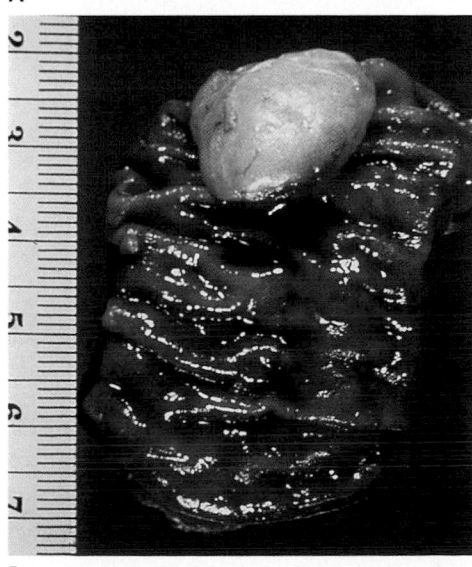

Fig. 11.120 Outer aspect (**A**) and cut surface (**B**) of lipoma of small bowel.

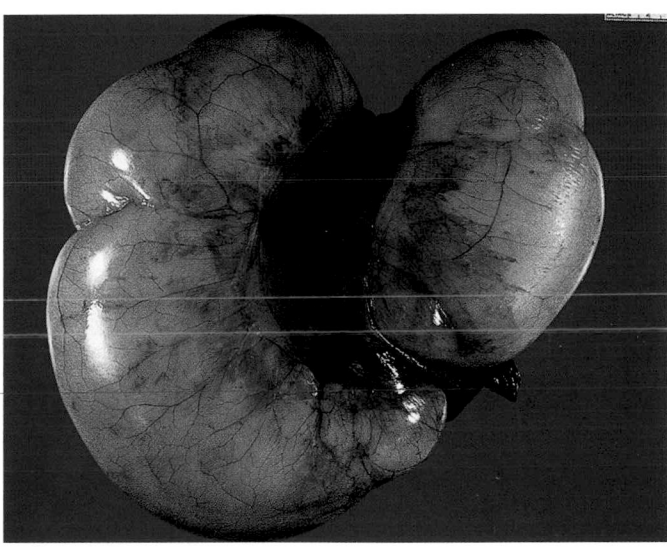

Fig. 11.121 Lymphangioma involving small bowel and adjacent mesentery.

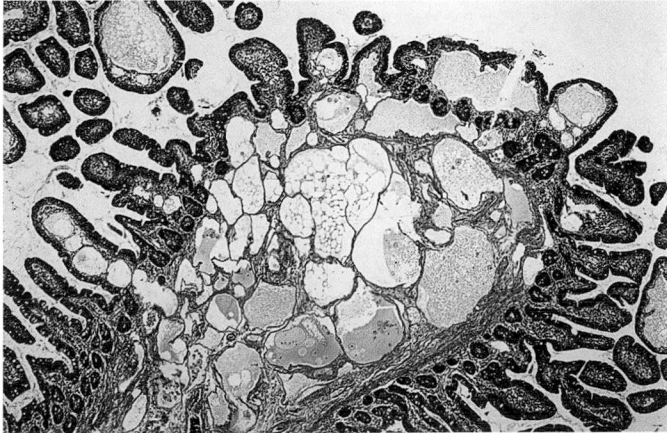

Fig. 11.122 Low-power appearance of lymphangioma showing predominantly submucosal involvement.

Neurofibroma and **ganglioneuroma** may occur as isolated neoplasms or as components of Recklinghausen's disease or multiple endocrine neoplasia[634] (Fig. 11.123). It should be mentioned here that gastrointestinal involvement in Recklinghausen's disease may manifest in a variety of ways: hyperplasia of the submucosal and myenteric nerve plexuses, mucosal ganglioneuromatosis, GISTs showing varying degrees of neural or smooth muscle differentiation, somatostatin-rich endocrine tumor of the duodenum, adenocarcinoma with (and perhaps without) neuroendocrine features, and gangliocytic paraganglioma.[614]

Congenital fibromatosis may result in a solitary intestinal mass, leading to intestinal obstruction in the neonate.[615]

Primary malignant tumors other than those already described include *Kaposi's sarcoma* (characteristically multiple), *angiosarcoma* (also with a tendency to multiplicity and sometimes showing epithelioid features[610,631,645]), *liposarcoma, fibrosarcoma, malignant peripheral nerve sheath tumor, extraskeletal osteosarcoma, malignant mesenchymoma, primary choriocarcinoma, Ewing sarcoma/PNET*[623a], and *malignant rhabdoid tumor*.[608,625,627,632,633,639]

We have seen six cases of a primary small bowel neoplasm characterized by a monotonous population of medium-sized round-to-oval cells with focally clear cytoplasm admixed with osteoclast-like multinucleated cells (Fig. 11.124). The mononuclear tumor cells were strongly positive for S-100 protein and negative for Mart-1, HMB-45, and CD117 (c-kit). One of the cases showed at the cytogenetic level the t(11;22)(q13;q12) translocation. We believe that these lesions—of which isolated cases had been previously reported[611,612]—represent a tumor entity related to *clear cell sarcoma of soft parts* and separate from GIST.[648] This tumor should not be confused with the renal-type clear cell sarcoma, of which one case has been described in the terminal ileum.[622] It should also be noted that there are occasional case reports of malignant melanoma of conventional type allegedly primary in the small bowel.[621]

Metastatic tumors can involve the small bowel, often in the form of multiple polypoid tumors. The lesions may result in obstruction or perforation, necessitating palliative resection.[609,640,644] The most common types of primary tumor are malignant melanoma, carcinoma from lung, breast and ovary, and choriocarcinoma[601,620,629] (Figs 11.125 and 11.126). The melanomas can present radiographically as intraluminal masses, ulcerated lesions, diffuse infiltration of the wall, or implants.[623] Patients with multiple metastases of melanoma usually die within 1 year following palliative surgery, but an occasional long-term survivor will be found among those with isolated metastases.[642]

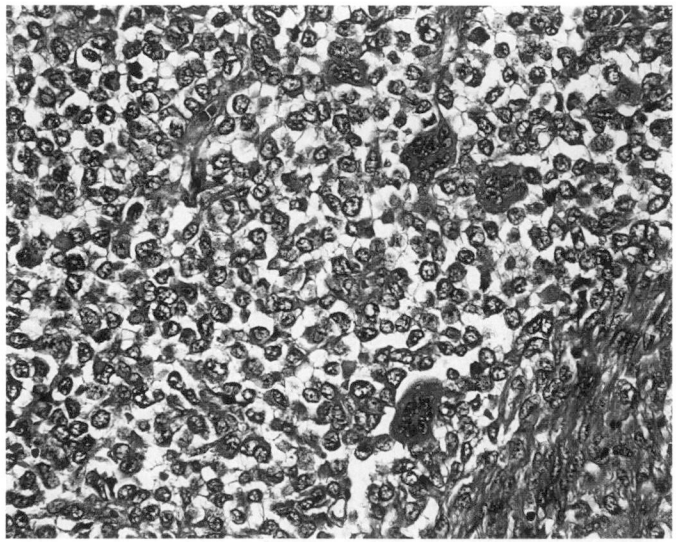

Fig. 11.124 Tumor with morphologic and cytogenetic features of soft tissue-type clear cell sarcoma involving the small bowel. The presence of scattered osteoclast-like multinucleated giant cells has been a constant feature of the cases reported in this location.

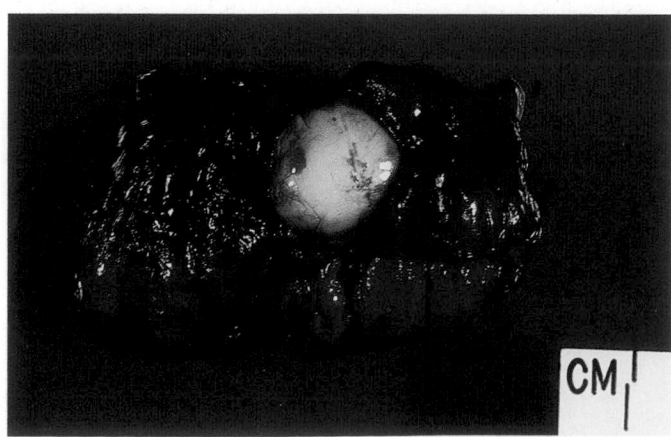

Fig. 11.123 Neurofibroma of small bowel showing a characteristic white, glistening cut surface.

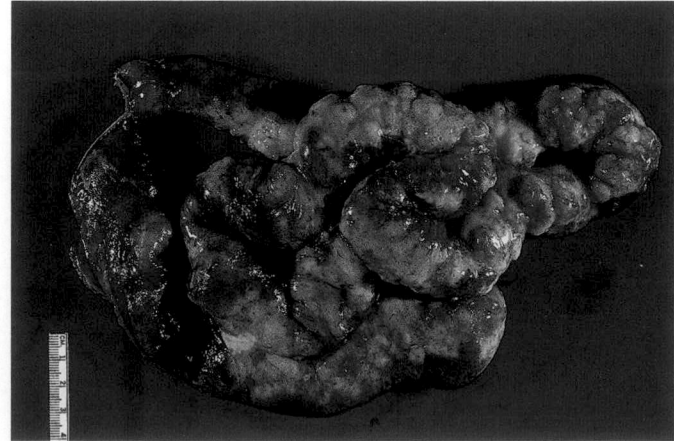

Fig. 11.125 Extensive involvement of the small bowel serosa by a serous papillary adenocarcinoma of ovarian origin.

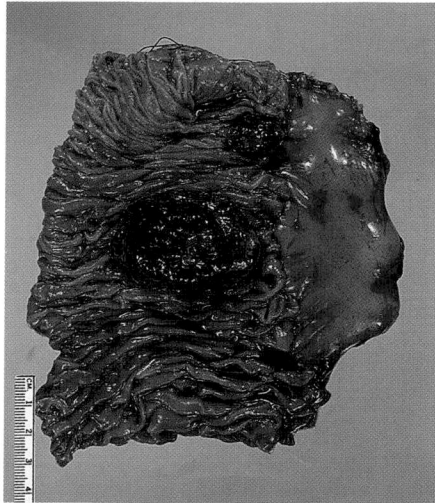

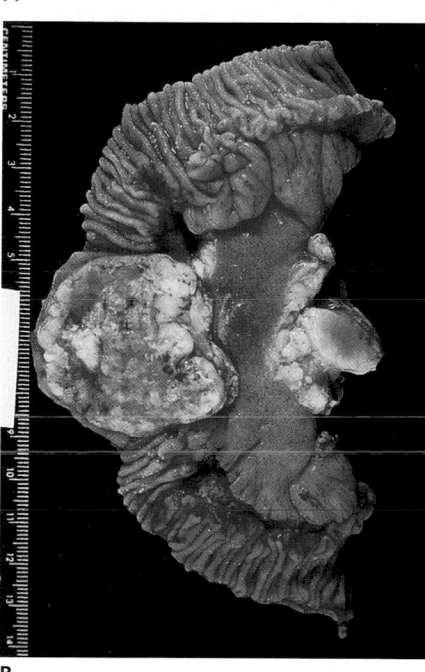

Fig. 11.126 Malignant melanoma metastatic to small bowel. The tumor shown in **A** was deeply pigmented, whereas that illustrated in **B** was amelanotic.

References

Normal anatomy

1 Andrew A, Kramer B, Rawdon BB. The origin of gut and pancreatic neuroendocrine (APUD) cells – the last word? J Pathol 1998, **186:** 117–118.

2 Del Rio Hortega P, Polak M, Prado J. Investigaciones sobre la neuroglía de los ganglios sensitivos. Arch Histol Norm Patol (B Aires) 1942, **1:** 233–275.

3 Dulac C, Le Douarin NM. Phenotypic plasticity of Schwann cells and enteric glial cells in response to the microenvironment. Proc Natl Acad Sci U S A 1991, **88:** 6358–6362.

4 Farstad IN, Malavasi F, Haraldsen G, Huitfeldt HS, Brondtzeg P. CD38 is a marker of human lacteals. Virchows Arch 2002, **441:** 605–613.

5 Furness JB, Costa M. The enteric nervous system. New York, 1987, Churchill-Livingstone.

6 Goyal RK, Hirano I. The enteric nervous system. N Engl J Med 1996, **334:** 1106–1115.

7 Komuro T, Seki K, Horiguchi K. Ultrastructural characterization of the interstitial cells of Cajal. Arch Histol Cytol 1999, **62:** 295–316.

8 Lecoin L, Gabella G, Le Douarin N. Origin of the c-kit-positive interstitial cells in the avian bowel. Development 1996, **122:** 725–733.

8a Min K-W, Seo IS. Interstitial cells of Cajal in the human small intestine: immunochemical and ultrastructural study. Ultrastruct Path 2003, **27:** 67–78.

9 Rosai J. An evolutionary view of neuroendocrine cells and their tumors. Int J Surg Pathol 2001, **9:** 87–92.

10 Segal GH, Petras RE. Small intestine. In Sternberg, S (ed.): Histology for pathologists, ed. 2. Philadelphia, 1997, Lippincott-Raven, pp. 495–518.

11 Skipper M, Lewis J. Getting to the guts of enteroendocrine differentiation. Nat Genet 2000, **24:** 3–4.

12 Takayama I, Horiguchi K, Daigo Y, Mine T, Fujino MA, Ohno S. The interstitial cells of Cajal and a gastroenteric pacemaker system. Arch Histol Cytol 2002, **65:** 1–26.

13 Thuneberg L. Interstitial cells of Cajal. Intestinal pacemaker cells? Adv Anat Embryol Cell Biol 1982, **71:** 1–130.

14 Vanderwinden JM, Rumessen JJ, De Laet MH, Vanderhaeghen JJ, Schiffmann SN. CD34 immunoreactivity and interstitial cells of Cajal in the human and mouse gastrointestinal tract. Cell Tissue Res 2000, **302:** 145–153.

15 Ward SM, Sanders KM. Physiology and pathophysiology of the interstitial cell of Cajal: from bench to bedside. I. Functional development and plasticity of interstitial cells of Cajal networks. Am J Physiol Gastrointest Liver Physiol 2001, **281:** 602–611.

16 Young HM. Embryological origin of interstitial cells of Cajal. Microsc Res Tech 1999, **47:** 303–308.

Congenital defects
Heterotopic pancreas

17 Castro Barbosa JJ, Dockerty MB, Waugh JM. Pancreatic heterotopia. Surg Gynecol Obstet 1946, **82:** 527–542.

18 Chan JK. Gastrointestinal lymphomas: an overview with emphasis on new findings and diagnostic problems. Semin Diagn Pathol 1996, **13:** 260–296.

19 Flejou JF, Potet F, Molas G, Bernades P, Amouyal P, Fekete F. Cystic dystrophy of the gastric and duodenal wall developing in heterotopic pancreas. An unrecognised entity. Gut 1993, **34:** 343–347.

20 Gal R, Rath-Wolfson L, Ginzberg M, Kessler E. Adenomyomas of the small intestine. Histopathology 1991, **18:** 369–371.

21 Makhlouf HR, Almeida JL, Sobin LH. Carcinoma in jejunal pancreatic heterotopia. Arch Pathol Lab Med 1999, **123:** 707–711.

22 Ryan A, Lafnitzegger JR, Lin DH, Jakate S, Staren ED. Myoepithelial hamartoma of the duodenal wall. Virchows Arch 1998, **432:** 191–194.

23 Suda K, Takase M, Shiono S, Yamasaki S, Nobulkawa B, Kasamaki S, Arakawa A, Suzuki F. Duodenal wall cysts may be derived from a ductal component of ectopic pancreatic tissue. Histopathology 2002, **41:** 351–356.

Heterotopic gastric mucosa

24 Franzin G, Musola R, Negi A, Mencarelli R, Fratton A. Heterotopic gastric (fundic) mucosa in the duodenum. Endoscopy 1982, **14:** 166–167.

25 Kushima R, Ruthlein HJ, Stolte M, Bamba M, Hattori T, Borchard F. 'Pyloric gland-type adenoma' arising in heterotopic gastric mucosa of the duodenum, with dysplastic progression of the gastric type. Virchows Arch 1999, **435:** 452–457.

26 Lessels AM, Martin DF. Heterotopic gastric mucosa in the duodenum. J Clin Pathol 1982, **35:** 591–595.

27 Russin V, Krevsky B, Caroline DF, Tang C-K, Ming S-C. Mixed hyperplastic and adenomatous polyp arising from ectopic gastric mucosa of the duodenum. Arch Pathol Lab Med 1986, **110:** 556–558.

28 Spiller RC, Shousha S, Barrison IG. Heterotopic gastric tissue in the duodenum. A report of eight cases. Dig Dis Sci 1982, **27:** 880–883.

Duplication, atresia, and related defects

29 Adair HM, Trowell JE. Squamous cell carcinoma arising in a duplication of the small bowel. J Pathol 1981, **133:** 25–31.

30 Akhtar J, Guiney EJ. Congenital duodenal obstruction. Br J Surg 1992, **79:** 133–135.

31 Alvarez SP, Greco MA, Genieser NB. Small intestinal atresia and segmental absence of muscle coats. Hum Pathol 1982, **13:** 948–951.

32 Grosfeld JL, Rescorla FJ. Duodenal atresia and stenosis. Reassessment of treatment and outcome based on antenatal diagnosis, pathologic variance, and long-term follow-up. World J Surg 1993, **17:** 301–309.

33 Izraeli S, Freud E, Mor C, Litwin A, Zer M, Merlob P. Neonatal intestinal perforation due to congenital defects in the intestinal muscularis. Eur J Pediatr 1992, **151:** 300–303.

34 Litwin A, Avidor I, Schujman E, Grunebaum M, Wilunsky E, Wolloch Y, Reisner SH. Neonatal intestinal perforation caused by congenital defects of the intestinal musculature. Am J Clin Pathol 1984, **81:** 77–80.

35 Seidman JD, Yale-Loehr AJ, Beaver B, Sun CC. Alimentary duplication presenting as an hepatic cyst in a neonate. Am J Surg Pathol 1991, **15:** 695–698.

36 Smith DW. Recognizable patterns of human malformation. Genetic, embryologic, and clinical aspects, ed. 3. Philadelphia, 1982, W.B. Saunders.

37 Stern LE, Warner BW. Gastrointestinal duplications. Semin Pediatr Surg 2000, **9:** 135–140.

38 Stringer MD, Spitz L, Abel R, Kiely E, Drake DP, Agrawal M, Stark Y, Brereton RJ. Management of alimentary tract duplication in children. Br J Surg 1995, **82:** 74–78.

39 Touloukian RJ. Diagnosis and treatment of jejunoileal atresia. World J Surg 1993, **17:** 310–317.

40 van der Pol JG, Wolf H, Boer K, Treffers PE, Leschot NJ, Hey HA, Vos A. Jejunal atresia related to the use of methylene blue in genetic amniocentesis in twins. Br J Obstet Gynaecol 1992, **99:** 141–143.

41 Ward HC, Leake J, Milla PJ, Spitz L. Brown bowel syndrome. A late complication of intestinal atresia. J Pediatr Surg 1992, **27:** 1593–1595.

Meckel's diverticulum and related vitelline duct abnormalities

42 Bloch T, Tejada E, Brodhecker C. Malignant melanoma in Meckel's diverticulum. Am J Clin Pathol 1986, **86:** 231–234.

43 Cserni G. Gastric pathology in Meckel's diverticulum. Review of cases resected between 1965 and 1995. Am J Clin Pathol 1996, **106:** 782–785.

44 Ford EG, Woolley MM. Tracheoesophageal fistula associated with perforated Meckel's diverticulum. J Pediatr Surg 1992, **27:** 1223–1224.

45 Haugen OA, Pegg CS, Kyle J. Leiomyosarcoma of Meckel's diverticulum. Cancer 1970, **26:** 929–934.

46 Hudson HM II, Millham FH, Dennis R. Vesico-diverticular fistula. A rare complication of Meckel's diverticulum. Am Surg 1992, **58:** 784–786.

47 Kumar S, Small P, Nawroz I, Mohammed R. *Helicobacter pylori* and Meckel's diverticulum. J R Coll Surg Edinb 1991, **36:** 225–226.

48 Kusumoto H, Yoshida M, Takahashi I, Anai H, Maehara Y, Sugimachi K. Complications and diagnosis of Meckel's diverticulum in 776 patients. Am J Surg 1992, **164:** 382–383.

49 Kusumoto H, Yoshitake H, Mochida K, Kumashiro R, Sano C, Inutsuka S. Adenocarcinoma in Meckel's diverticulum. Report of a case and review of 30 cases in the English and Japanese literature. Am J Gastroenterol 1992, **87:** 910–913.

50 Mackey WC, Dineen P. A fifty year experience with Meckel's diverticulum. Surg Gynecol Obstet 1983, **156:** 56–64.

51 Nies C, Zielke A, Hasse C, Ruschoff J, Rothmund M. Carcinoid tumors of Meckel's diverticula. Report of two cases and review of the literature. Dis Colon Rectum 1992, **35:** 589–596.

52 Ohmori T, Okada K, Arita N, Tabei R. Multiple ileal carcinoids and appendiceal endocrine carcinoma in association with Meckel's diverticulum. A histochemical and immunohistochemical study. Arch Pathol Lab Med 1994, **118:** 283–288.

53 Pfalzgraf RR, Zumwalt RE, Kenny MR. Mesodiverticular band and sudden death in children. A report of two cases. Arch Pathol Lab Med 1988, **112:** 182–184.

54 Söderlund S. Meckel's diverticulum. A clinical and histologic study. Acta Chir Scand Suppl 1959, **248:** 1–233.

55 Steck WD, Helwig EB. Cutaneous remnants of the omphalomesenteric duct. Arch Dermatol 1964, **90:** 463–470.

56 St-Vil D, Brandt ML, Panic S, Bensoussan AL, Blanchard H. Meckel's diverticulum in children. A 20-year review. J Pediatr Surg 1991, **26:** 1289–1292.

57 Weitzner S. Carcinoid of Meckel's diverticulum. Report of a case and review of the literature. Cancer 1969, **23:** 1436–1440.

Other diverticula

58 Ahlman H, Bjorck S, Jonsson O, Gamklou R. Perforated jejunal diverticula. A report on two cases. Acta Chir Scand 1980, **146:** 79–80.

59 Cooke WT, Cox EV, Fone DJ, Meynell MJ, Gaddie R. The clinical and metabolic significance of jejunal diverticula. Gut 1963, **4:** 115–131.

60 Fleming CR, Newcomer AD, Stephens DH, Carlson HC. Intraluminal duodenal diverticulum. Report of two cases and review of the literature. Mayo Clin Proc 1975, **50:** 244–248.

61 Juler JL, List JW, Stemmer EA, Connolly JE. Duodenal diverticulitis. Arch Surg 1969, **99:** 572–578.

62 Krishnamurthy S, Kelly MM, Rohrmann CA, Schuffler MD. Jejunal diverticulosis. A heterogenous disorder caused by a variety of abnormalities of smooth muscle or myenteric plexus. Gastroenterology 1983, **85:** 538–547.

63 Lopez PV, Welch JP. Enterolith intestinal obstruction owing to acquired and congenital diverticulosis. Report of two cases and review of the literature. Dis Colon Rectum 1991, **34:** 941–944.

64 Matsukuma S, Suda K. Foamy cell aggregation in duodenal diverticula. Histopathology 1996, **29:** 271–274.

65 Meagher AP, Porter AJ, Rowland R, Ma G, Hoffmann DC. Jejunal diverticulosis. Aust N Z J Surg 1993, **63:** 360–366.

66 Palder SB, Frey CB. Jejunal diverticulosis. Arch Surg 1988, **123:** 889–894.

67 Suda K, Mizuguchi K, Matsumoto M. A histopathological study on the etiology of duodenal diverticulum related to the fusion of the pancreatic anlage. Am J Gastroenterol 1983, **78:** 335–338.

68 Zakhour HD, Clark RG. Intramural gas cysts in a case of diverticular disease of the jejunum. Histopathology 1982, **6:** 363–369.

Other congenital defects

69 Beighton PH, Murdoch JL, Votteler T. Gastrointestinal complications of the Ehlers-Danlos syndrome. Gut 1969, **10:** 1004–1008.

70 Walker AW, Kempson RL, Ternberg JL. Aganglionosis of the small intestine. Surgery 1966, **60:** 449–457.

Malabsorption

71 Alkan S, Beals TF, Schnitzer B. Primary diagnosis of whipple disease manifesting as lymphadenopathy. Use of polymerase

chain reaction for detection of tropheryma whippelii. Am J Clin Pathol 2001, **116**: 898–904.

72 Alsaigh N, Odze R, Goldman H, Antonioli D, Ott MJ, Leichtner A. Gastric and esophageal intraepithelial lymphocytes in pediatric celiac disease. Am J Surg Pathol 1996, **20**: 865–870.

72a Antonioli DA. Celiac disease: a progress report. Mod Pathol 2003, **16**: 342–346.

73 Ashton-Key M, Diss TC, Pan L, Du MQ, Isaacson PG. Molecular analysis of T-cell clonality in ulcerative jejunitis and enteropathy-associated T-cell lymphoma. Am J Pathol 1997, **151**: 493–498.

74 Baisden BL, Lepidi H, Raoult D, Argani P, Yardley JH, Dumler JS. Diagnosis of Whipple disease by immunohistochemical analysis. A sensitive and specific method for the detection of Tropheryma whipplei (the Whipple bacillus) in paraffin-embedded tissue. Am J Clin Pathol 2002, **118**: 742–748.

74a Baumgärtner AK, Zettl A, Chott A, Ott G, Müller-Hermelink HK, Starostik P. High frequency of genetic aberrations in enteropathy-type T-cell lymphoma. Lab Invest 2003, **83**: 1509–1516.

75 Bhagavan BS, Hofkin GA, Cochran BA. Whipple's disease. Morphologic and immunofluorescence characterization of bacterial antigens. Hum Pathol 1981, **12**: 930–936.

76 Boitnott JK, Margolis S. Mineral oil in human tissues. Part II. Oil droplets in lymph nodes of the porta hepatis. Bull Hopkins Hosp 1966, **118**: 414–422.

77 Cardenas A, Kelly CP. Celiac sprue. Semin Gastrointest Dis. 2002, **13**: 232–244.

78 Cellier C, Delabesse E, Helmer C, Patey N, Matuchansky C, Jabri B, Macintyre E, Cerf-Bensussan N, Brousse N. Refractory sprue, celiac disease, and enteropathy-associated T-cell lymphoma. French Coeliac Disease Study Group. Lancet 2000, **356**: 203–208.

79 Comer GM, Brandt LJ, Abissi CJ. Whipple's disease. A review. Am J Gastroenterol 1983, **78**: 107–114.

80 Cuvelier C, Demetter P, Mielants H, Veys EM, DeVos M. Interpretation of ileal biopsies: morphological features in normal and diseased mucosa. Histopathology 2001, **38**: 1–12.

81 De Bruin PC, Jiwa NM, Oudejans JJ, Radaszkiewicz T, Meijer CJLM. Epstein-Barr virus in primary gastrointestinal T cell lymphomas. Association with gluten-sensitive enteropathy, pathological features, and immunophenotype. Am J Pathol 1995, **146**: 861–867.

82 De Bruin PC, Connolly CE, Oudejans JJ, Kummer JA, Jansen W, McCarthy CF, Meijer CJL. Enteropathy-associated T-cell lymphomas have a cytotoxic T-cell phenotype. Histopathology 1997, **31**: 313–317.

83 Denholm RB, Mills PR, More IAR. Electron microscopy in the long-term follow-up of Whipple's disease. Effect of antibiotics. Am J Surg Pathol 1981, **5**: 507–516.

84 DeSchryver K. Biopsies of small intestine. St Louis, 1995, Mosby.

85 Dobbins WO. Whipple's disease. Springfield, Ill, 1987, Charles C Thomas.

86 Dobbins WO III. The diagnosis of Whipple's disease (editorial). N Engl J Med 1995, **332**: 390–392.

87 Drut R, Rua EC. The histopathology of pediatric celiac disease: order must prevail out of chaos. Int J Surg Path 2001, **9**: 261–264.

88 Ectors N, Geboes K, De Vos R, Heidbuchel H, Rutgeerts P, Desmet V, Vantrappen G. Whipple's disease. A histological, immunocytochemical and electron microscopic study of the immune response in the small intestinal mucosa. Histopathology 1992, **21**: 1–12.

89 Ekuan JH, Hill RB Jr. Colonic histiocytosis. Clinical and pathological evaluation. Gastroenterology 1968, **55**: 619–625.

90 England N. Intestinal pathology of tropical sprue. Am J Clin Nutr 1966, **21**: 962–975.

91 Enzinger FM, Helwig EB. Whipple's disease. A review of the literature and report of fifteen patients. Virchows Arch [A] 1963, **336**: 238–269.

92 Farrell DJ, Shrimankar J, Griffin SM. Duodenal adenocarcinoma complicating coeliac disease. Histopathology 1991, **19**: 285–287.

92a Fasano A. Celiac disease – how to handle a clinical chameleon. New Engl J Med 2003, **348**: 2568–2570.

93 Gale J, Simmonds PD, Mead GM, Sweetenham JW, Wright DH. Enteropathy type intestinal T-cell lymphoma: clinical features and treatment of 31 patients in a single center. J Clin Oncol 2000, **18**: 795–803.

94 Gerard A, Sarrot-Reynauld F, Liozon E, Cathebras P, Besson G, Robin C, Vighetto A, Mosnier JF, Durieu I, Vital Durand D, Rousse H. Neurologic presentation of Whipple disease: report of 12 cases and review of the literature. Medicine (Baltimore) 2002, **81**: 443–457.

95 Gillen CD, Coddington R, Monteith PG, Taylor RH. Extraintestinal lymphoma in association with Whipple's disease. Gut 1993, **34**: 1627–1629.

96 Goldstein NS, Underhill J. Morphologic features suggestive of gluten sensitivity in architecturally normal duodenal biopsy specimens. Am J Clin Pathol 2001, **116**: 63–71.

97 Guerra R, Wheby MS, Bayless TM. Long-term antibiotic therapy in tropical sprue. Ann Intern Med 1965, **63**: 619–634.

98 Halter SA, Greene HL, Helinek G. Gluten-sensitive enteropathy. Sequence of villous regrowth as viewed by scanning electron microscopy. Hum Pathol 1982, **13**: 811–818.

99 Harris OD, Cooke WT, Thompson H, Waterhouse JAH. Malignancy in adult coeliac disease and idiopathic steatorrhoea. Am J Med 1967, **42**: 899–912.

100 Holmes GK. Coeliac disease and malignancy. Dig Liver Dis 2002, **34**: 229–237.

101 Isaacson P, Jones DB, Sworn MJ, Wright DH. Malignant histiocytosis of the intestine. Report of three cases with immunological and cytochemical analysis. J Clin Pathol 1982, **35**: 510–516.

102 Isselbacher KJ, Scheig R, Plotkin GR, Caulfield JB. Congenital β lipoprotein deficiency. An hereditary disorder involving a defect in the absorption and transport of lipids. Medicine (Baltimore) 1964, **43**: 347–361.

103 Keinath RD, Merrell DE, Vlietstra R, Dobbins WO III. Antibiotic treatment and relapse in Whipple's disease. Long-term followup of 88 patients. Gastroenterology 1985, **88**: 1867–1873.

104 Klipstein FA. Tropical sprue in travelers and expatriates living abroad. Gastroenterology 1981, **80**: 590–600.

105 Klipstein FA, Baker SJ. Regarding the definition of tropical sprue. Gastroenterology 1970, **58**: 717–721.

106 Kopp WL, Trier JS, Stiehm ER, Foroozan P. "Acquired" agammaglobulinemia with defective delayed hypersensitivity. Ann Intern Med 1968, **69**: 309–317.

107 Kuhajda FP, Belitsos NJ, Keren DF, Hutchins GM. A submucosal variant of Whipple's disease. Gastroenterology 1982, **82**: 46–50.

108 Kumar PJ. The enigma of celiac disease. Gastroenterology 1985, **89**: 214–216.

109 Lepidi H, Costedoat N, Piette JC, Harle JR, Raoult D. Immunohistological detection of Tropheryma whipplei (Whipple bacillus) in lymph nodes. Am J Med 2002, **113**: 334–336.

109a Lepidi H, Fenollar F, Gerolami R, Mege J-L, Bonzi M-F, Chappuis M, Sahel J, Raoult D. Whipple's disease: immunospecific and quantitative immunohistochemical study of intestinal biopsy specimens. Hum Pathol 2003, **34**: 589–596.

110 Levinson JD, Kirsner JB. Infiltrative diseases of the small bowel and malabsorption. Am J Dig Dis 1970, **15**: 741–766.

111 Lundin KE, Scott H, Hansen T, Paulsen G, Halstensen TS, Fausa O, Thorsby E, Sollid LM. Gliadin-specific, HLA-DQ(alpha 1*0501, beta 1*0201) restricted T cells isolated from the small intestinal mucosa of celiac disease patients. J Exp Med 1993, **178**: 187–196.

112 MacDermott RP. Cell-mediated immunity in gastrointestinal disease. Hum Pathol 1986, **17**: 219–233.

113 Maizell H, Ruffin JM, Dobbins WO III. Whipple's disease. A review of 19 patients from one hospital and a review of the literature since 1950. Medicine Baltimore 1970, **49**: 175–205.

114 Maliha GM, Hepps KS, Maia DM, Gentry KR, Fraire AE, Goodgame RW. Whipple's disease can mimic chronic AIDS enteropathy. Am J Gastroenterol 1991, **86**: 79–81.

115 Marsh MN (ed.). Immunopathology of the small intestine. New York, 1987, John Wiley & Sons.

116 Marsh MN. Gluten, major histocompatibility complex, and the small intestine. A molecular and immunobiologic approach to the spectrum of gluten sensitivity ("celiac sprue"). Gastroenterology 1992, **102**: 330–354.

117 McIntyre AS, Ng DP, Smith JA, Amoah J, Long RG. The endoscopic appearance of duodenal folds is predictive of untreated adult celiac disease. Gastrointest Endosc 1992, **38**: 148–151.

117a McManus R, Kelleher D. Celiac disease – the villain unmasked? New Engl J Med 2003, **348**: 2573–2574.

117b Mino M, Lauwers GY. Role of lymphocytic immunophenotyping in the diagnosis of gluten-sensitive enteropathy with preserved villous architecture. Am J Surg Pathol 2003, **27**: 1237–1242.

118 Modigliani R, Poitras P, Galian A, Messing B, Guyet-Rousset P, Libeskind M, Piel-Desruisseaux JL, Rambaud JC. Chronic non-specific ulcerative duodenojejunoileitis. Report of four cases. Gut 1979, **20**: 318–328.

119 Morningstar WA. Whipple's disease. An example of the value of the electron microscope in diagnosis, follow-up, and correlation of pathologic process. Hum Pathol 1975, **6**: 443–454.

120 Moyana TN, Shukoor S. Gastrointestinal endocrine cell hyperplasia in celiac disease. A selective proliferative process of serotonergic cells. Mod Pathol 1991, **4**: 419–423.

121 Mulder CJ, Wahab PJ, Moshaver B, Meijer JW. Refractory coeliac disease: a window between coelic disease and enteropathy associated T-cell lymphoma. Scand J Gastroenterol Suppl 2000, **232**: 32–37.

122 Murray A, Cuevas EC, Jones DB, Wright DH. Study of the immunohistochemistry and T cell clonality of enteropathy-associated T cell lymphoma. Am J Pathol 1995, **146**: 509–519.

123 Nash JRG, Gradwell E, Day DW. Large-cell intestinal lymphoma occurring in coeliac disease. Morphological and immunohistochemical features. Histopathology 1986, **10**: 195–205.

124 Nielsen K. Coeliac disease. Alpha-1-antitrypsin contents in jejunal mucosa before and after gluten-free diet. Histopathology 1984, **8**: 759–764.

125 Nielsen SNJ, Wold LE. Adenocarcinoma of jejunum in association with nontropical sprue. Arch Pathol Lab Med 1986, **110**: 822–824.

126 O'Brien CJ, Saverymuttu S, Hodgson HJF, Evans DJ. Coeliac disease, adenocarcinoma of jejunum and in situ squamous carcinoma of oesophagus. J Clin Pathol 1983, **36**: 62–67.

127 Pan L, Diss TC, Peng H, Lu Q, Wotherspoon AC, Thomas JA, Isaacson PG. Epstein-Barr virus (EBV) in enteropathy-associated T-cell lymphoma (EATL). J Pathol 1993, **170**: 137–143.

128 Patey-Mariaud de Serre N, Cellier C, Jabri B, Delabesse E, Verkarre V, Roche B, Lavergne A, Briere J, Mauvieux L, Leborgne M, Barbier JP, Modigliani R, Matuchansky C, Macintyre E, Cerf-Bensussan N, Brousse N. Distinction between coeliac disease and refractory sprue: a simple immunohistochemical method. Histopathology 2000, **37**: 70–77.

129 Peña AS, Whitehead R. Quoted by Whitehead.[153]

130 Perera DR, Weinstein WM, Rubin CE. Small intestinal biopsy. Hum Pathol 1975, **6**: 157–217.

131 Petreshock EP, Pessah M, Menachemi E. Adenocarcinoma of the jejunum associated with nontropical sprue. Am J Dig Dis 1975, **20**: 796–799.

132 Raoult D, Birg ML, La Scola B, Fournier PE, Enea M, Lepidi H, Roux V, Piette JC, Vandenesch F, Vital-Durand D, Marrie TJ. Cultivation of the bacillus of Whipple's disease. N Engl J Med 2000, **342**: 620–625.

133 Relman DA, Schmidt TM, MacDermott RP, Falkow S.

Identification of the uncultured bacillus of Whipple's disease. N Engl J Med 1992, **327**: 293–301.

134 Robert ME, Ament ME, Weinstein WM. The histologic spectrum and clinical outcome of refractory and unclassified sprue. Am J Surg Pathol 2000, **24**: 676–687.

135 Rosekrans PCM, Lindeman J, Meijer CJLM. Quantitative histological and immunohistological findings in jejunal biopsy specimens in giardiasis. Virchows Arch [A] 1981, **393**: 145–151.

136 Rubin CE, Eidelman S, Weinstein WM. Sprue by any other name. Gastroenterology 1970, **58**: 409–413.

137 Rubin W, Ross LL, Sleisenger MH, Weser E. An electron microscopic study of adult celiac disease. Lab Invest 1966, **15**: 1720–1747.

138 Rubio CA, Theorell M, Befrits R, Uribe A. The characteristics of mitotic figures in jejunal mucosa of patients with celiac disease. Am J Clin Pathol 1992, **98**: 575–578.

139 Saleh H, Williams TM, Mimda JM, Gupta PK. Whipple's disease involving the mesenteric lymph nodes diagnosed by fine-needle aspiration. Diagn Cytopathol 1992, **8**: 177–180.

140 Shan L, Molberg O, Parrot I, Hausch F, Filiz F, Gray GM, Sollid LM, Khosla C. Structural basis for gluten intolerance in celiac sprue. Science 2002, **297**: 2275–2279.

141 Sheehy TW, Meroney WH, Cox RS, Soler JE. Hookworm disease and malabsorption. Gastroenterology 1962, **42**: 148–156.

142 Spencer J, Cerf-Bensussan N, Jarry A, Brousse N, Guy-Grand D, Krajewski AS, Isaacson PG. Enteropathy associated T cell lymphoma (malignant histiocytosis of the intestine) is recognized by a monoclonal antibody (HML1) that defines a membrane molecule on human mucosal lymphocytes. Am J Pathol 1988, **132**: 1–5.

143 Thompson H. Necropsy studies on adult coeliac disease. J Clin Pathol 1974, **27**: 710–721.

144 Trier JS, Browning TH. Epithelial-cell renewal in cultured duodenal biopsies in celiac sprue. N Engl J Med 1970, **283**: 1245–1250.

145 Variend S, Placzek M, Raafat F, Walker-Smith JA. Small intestinal mucosal fat in childhood enteropathies. J Clin Pathol 1984, **37**: 373–377.

146 Von Herbay A, Maiwald M, Ditton HJ, Otto HF. Histology of intestinal Whipple's disease revisited. A study of 48 patients. Virchows Arch 1997, **429**: 335–343.

147 Waldmann TA. Protein-losing enteropathy. Gastroenterology 1966, **50**: 422–443.

148 Walsh SV, Egan LJ, Connolly CE, Stevens FM, Egan EL, McCarthy CF. Enteropathy-associated T-cell lymphoma in the West of Ireland. Low-frequency of Epstein-Barr virus in these tumors. Mod Pathol 1995, **8**: 753–757.

149 Weinstein WM, Saunders DR, Tytgat GN, Rubin CE. Collagenous sprue. An unrecognized type of malabsorption. N Engl J Med 1970, **283**: 1297–1301.

150 Westergaard H. The sprue syndromes. Am J Med Sci 1985, **290**: 249–262.

151 Whalen GE, Rosenberg EB, Strickland GT, Gutman RA, Cross JH, Watten RH, Uylangeo C, Dizou JJ. Intestinal capillariasis. A new disease in man. Lancet 1969, **1**: 13–16.

152 Whitehead R. Primary lymphadenopathy complicating idiopathic steatorrhoea. Gut 1968, **9**: 569–575.

153 Whitehead R. The interpretation and significance of morphological abnormalities in jejunal biopsies. J Clin Pathol 1971, **24**(Suppl 5): 108–124.

154 Yardley JH, Takano J, Hendrix TR. Epithelial and other mucosal lesions of the jejunum in giardiasis. Jejunal biopsy studies. Bull Hopkins Hosp 1964, **115**: 389–406.

Ulcers

155 Allen AC, Boley SJ, Schultz L, Schwartz S. Potassium-induced lesions of the small bowel. JAMA 1965, **193**: 85–90.

156 Artinian B, Lough JO, Palmer JD. Idiopathic ulcer of small bowel with pseudolymphomatous reactions. A clinicopathological study of six cases. Arch Pathol 1971, **91:** 327–333.

157 Bode G, Malfertheiner P, Mader U, Stanescu A, Ditschuneit H. Fine structure of active and healed duodenal ulcer. Am J Gastroenterol 1991, **86:** 179–186.

158 Davies DR, Brightmore T. Idiopathic and drug-induced ulceration of the small intestine. Br J Surg 1970, **57:** 134–139.

159 Dean ACB, Mason MK. The distribution of pyloric mucosa in partial gastrectomy specimens. Gut 1964, **5:** 64–67.

160 Madsen JE, Vetvik K, Aase S. *Helicobacter*-associated duodenitis and gastric metaplasia in duodenal ulcer patients. APMIS 1991, **99:** 997–1000.

161 McCallum RW, Singh D, Wollman J. Endoscopic and histologic correlations of the duodenal bulb. Arch Pathol Lab Med 1979, **103:** 169–172.

162 Quan C, Talley NJ. Management of peptic ulcer disease not related to Helicobacter pylori or NSAIDs. Am J Gastroenterol 2002, **97:** 2950–2961.

163 Pounder RE. Duodenal ulcers that will not heal. Gut 1984, **25:** 697–702.

164 Raf LE. Ischaemic stenosis of the small intestine. Acta Clin Scand 1969, **135:** 253–259.

165 Saita H, Murakami M, Yoo JK, Teramura S, Dekigai H, Takahashi Y, Kita T. Link between *Helicobacter pylori*-associated gastritis and duodenal ulcer. Dig Dis Sci 1993, **38:** 117–122.

166 Saito K, Shimizu H, Yokoyama T, Kawata K, Matsumura T, Morioka Y. Annular ulcer of the stagnant ileum. A clinicopathological study on the morphogenesis. Acta Pathol Jpn 1983, **33:** 257–263.

167 Szabo S. Pathogenesis of duodenal ulcer disease. Lab Invest 1984, **51:** 121–147.

168 Thompson JC, Wiener I. Evaluation of surgical treatment for duodenal ulcer. Acute and long-term effects. Clin Gastroenterol 1984, **13:** 569–600.

Vascular diseases

169 Burke AP, Sobin LH, Virmani R. Localized vasculitis of the gastrointestinal tract. Am J Surg Pathol 1995, **19:** 338–349.

170 Cohen R, Heffner JE. Bowel infarction as the initial manifestation of disseminated aspergillosis. Chest 1992, **101:** 877–879.

171 Endress C, Gray DG, Wollschlaeger G. Bowel ischemia and perforation after cocaine use. AJR 1992, **159:** 73–75.

172 Feurle GE, Haag B. Acute small bowel ischemia without transmural infarction. Z Gastroenterol 1991, **29:** 349–352.

173 Flaherty MJ, Lie JT, Haggitt RC. Mesenteric inflammatory veno-occlusive disease. A seldom recognized cause of intestinal ischemia. Am J Surg Pathol 1994, **18:** 779–784.

174 Gilbert AE, Jorgenson NC. Small bowel obstruction due to hemorrhage secondary to anticoagulant therapy. Am J Surg 1960, **99:** 945–948.

175 Kempezinski RF, Clark SM, Blebea J, Koelliker DD, Fenoglio-Presier C. Intestinal ischemia secondary to thromboangiitis obliterans. Ann Vasc Surg 1993, **7:** 354–358.

176 Levine S, Whelan TJ Jr. Small bowel infarction due to intramural hematoma during anticoagulant therapy. Arch Surg 1967, **95:** 245–248.

177 McCurley TL, Collins RD. Intestinal infarction in rheumatoid arthritis. Three cases due to unusual obliterative vascular lesions. Arch Pathol Lab Med 1984, **108:** 125–128.

178 Ottinger LW. Mesenteric ischemia. N Engl J Med 1982, **307:** 535–537.

179 Oweity T, West AB, Stokes MB. Necrotizing angiitis of the small intestine related to AA-amyloidosis: a novel association. Int J Surg Pathol 2001, **9:** 149–154.

180 Phelan MJ, Kok K, Burrow C, Thompson RN. Small bowel infarction in association with giant cell arteritis. Br J Rheumatol 1993, **32:** 63–65.

181 Saraga E, Bouzourenne H. Enterocolic (lymphocytic) phlebitis: a rare cause of intestinal ischemic necrosis: a series of six patients and review of the literature. Am J Surg Pathol 2000, **24:** 824–829.

182 Shah IA, Lewin KL, Iqbal J, Mukherjee R. Veno-occlusive disease of the small bowel: an entity in search of identity. Arch Pathol Lab Med 1996, **120:** 872–875.

183 Shintaku M, Inoue N, Sasaki M, Izuno Y, Ueda Y, Ikehara S. Cytomegalovirus vasculitis accompanied by an exuberant fibroblastic reaction in the intestine of an AIDS patient. Acta Pathol Jpn 1991, **41:** 900–904.

184 Wang CC, Reeves JD. Mesenteric vascular disease. Am J Roentgenol Radium Ther Nucl Med 1960, **83:** 895–908.

185 Whitehead R. The pathology of ischemia of the intestines. Pathol Annu 1976, **11:** 1–52.

186 Williams LF Jr. Vascular insufficiency of the intestines. Gastroenterology 1971, **61:** 757–777.

Crohn's disease

187 Attanoos RL, Appleton MA, Hughes LE, Ansell ID, Douglas-Jones AG, Williams GT. Granulomatous hidradenitis suppurativa and cutaneous Crohn's disease. Histopathology 1993, **23:** 111–115.

188 Aufses AH Jr. The surgery of granulomatous inflammatory bowel disease. In Current problems in surgery. Chicago, 1983, Year Book Medical Publishers.

189 Brown I, Schofield JB, MacLennan KA, Tagart RE. Primary non-Hodgkin's lymphoma in ileal Crohn's disease. Eur J Surg Oncol 1992, **18:** 627–631.

190 Cameron JL, Hamilton SR, Coleman J, Sitzmann JV, Bayless TM. Patterns of ileal recurrence in Crohn's disease. A prospective randomized study. Ann Surg 1992, **215:** 546–551.

191 Cartun RW, Van Kruiningen HJ, Pedersen CA, Berman MM. An immunocytochemical search for infectious agents in Crohn's disease. Mod Pathol 1993, **6:** 212–219.

192 Chambers TJ, Morson BC. The granuloma in Crohn's disease. Gut 1979, **20:** 269–274.

193 Chong SKF, Blackshaw AJ, Boyle S, Williams CB, Walker-Smith JA. Histological diagnosis of chronic inflammatory bowel disease in childhood. Gut 1985, **326:** 55–59.

194 Collier PE, Turowski P, Diamond DL. Small intestinal adenocarcinoma complicating regional enteritis. Cancer 1985, **55:** 516–521.

194a Craninx M, D'Haens G, Cokelaere K, Baert F, Pennickx F, D'Hoore A, Ectors N, Rutgeerts P, Geboes K. Crohn's disease and intestinal endometriosis: an intriguing coexistence. Eur J Gastroenterol Hepatol 2000, **12:** 217–221.

195 Daum F, Boley SJ, Cohen MI. Miliary Crohn's disease. Gastroenterology 1974, **67:** 527–530.

196 Devroede G, Schlaeder G, Sanchez G, Haddad H. Crohn's disease of the vulva. Am J Clin Pathol 1975, **63:** 348–358.

197 Dourmashkin RR, Davies H, Wells C, Shah D, Price A, O'Morain C, Levi J. Epithelial patchy necrosis in Crohn's disease. Hum Pathol 1983, **14:** 643–648.

198 Dvorak AM, Monahan RA. Crohn's disease—mast cell quantitation using one micron plastic sections for light microscopic study. Part I. Pathol Annu 1983, **18:** 181–190.

199 Dvorak AM, Silen W. Differentiation between Crohn's disease and other inflammatory conditions by electron microscopy. Ann Surg 1985, **201:** 53–63.

200 Fabricius PJ, Gyde SN, Shouler P, Keighley MRB, Alexander-Williams J, Allan RN. Crohn's disease in the elderly. Gut 1985, **26:** 461–465.

201 Faul SH, Wong LK, Zinsser KR. Enteritis cystica profunda. Association with Crohn's disease. Hum Pathol 1986, **17:** 600–603.

202 Fielding JF, Toye DKM, Benton DC, Cooke WT. Crohn's disease of the stomach and duodenum. Gut 1970, **11:** 1001–1006.

203 Frank TS, Cook SM. Analysis of paraffin sections of Crohn's

disease for mycobacterium paratuberculosis using polymerase chain reaction. Mod Pathol 1996, **9**: 32–35.

204 Fresko D, Lazarus SS, Dotan J, Reingold M. Early presentation of carcinoma of the small bowel in Crohn's disease ("Crohn's carcinoma"). Case reports and review of the literature. Gastroenterology 1982, **82**: 783–789.

205 Geboes K, El-Zine MY, Dalle I, El-Haddad S, Rutgeerts P, Van Eyken P. Tenascin and strictures in inflammatory bowel disease: an immunohistochemical study. Int J Surg Pathol 2001, **9**: 281–286.

206 Geller SA, Cohen A. Arterial inflammatory-cell infiltration in Crohn's disease. Arch Pathol Lab Med 1983, **107**: 473–475.

207 Glass RE, Baker WNW. Role of the granuloma in recurrent Crohn's disease. Gut 1976, **17**: 75–77.

208 Greenstein AJ, Janowitz HD, Sacher DB. The extraintestinal complications of Crohn's disease and ulcerative colitis. A study of 700 patients. Medicine (Baltimore) 1976, **55**: 401–412.

209 Greenstein AJ, Sachar DB, Pasternack BS, Janowitz HD. Reoperation and recurrence in Crohn's colitis and ileocolitis. Crude and cumulative rates. N Engl J Med 1975, **293**: 685–690.

210 Gump FE, Sakellariadis P, Wolff M, Broell JR. Clinical-pathological investigation of regional enteritis as a guide to prognosis. Ann Surg 1972, **176**: 233–242.

211 Hamilton SR. Pathologic features of Crohn's disease associated with recrudescence after resection. Pathol Annu 1983, **18**(Pt 1): 191–203.

212 Hawker PC, Gyde SN, Thompson H, Allan RN. Adenocarcinoma of the small intestine complicating Crohn's disease. Gut 1982, **23**: 188–193.

213 Hock YL, Scott KW, Grace RH. Mixed adenocarcinoma/carcinoid tumour of large bowel in a patient with Crohn's disease. J Clin Pathol 1993, **46**: 183–185.

214 Kahn E, Daum F. Pseudopolyps of the small intestine in Crohn's disease. Hum Pathol 1984, **15**: 84–86.

215 Kilgore SP, Sigel JE, Goldblum JR. Hyperplastic-like mucosal change in Crohn's disease: an unusual form of dysplasia? Mod Pathol 2000, **13**: 797–801.

216 Kirsner JB, Shorter RG. Recent developments in nonspecific inflammatory bowel disease. N Engl J Med 1982, **306**: 837–848.

217 Kortbeek J, Kelly JK, Preshaw RM. Carcinoid tumors and inflammatory bowel disease. J Surg Oncol 1992, **49**: 122–126.

218 Kotanagi H, Kramer K, Fazio VW, Petras RE. Do microscopic abnormalities at resection margins correlate with increased anastomotic recurrence in Crohn's disease? Dis Colon Rectum 1991, **34**: 909–916.

219 Koukoulis G, Ke Y, Henley JD, Cummings OW. Obliterative muscularization of the small bowel submucosa in crohn disease: a possible mechanism of small bowel obstruction. Arch Pathol Lab Med 2001, **125**: 1331–1334.

219a Lamps LW, Madhusudhan KT, Havens JM, Greenson JK, Bronner MP, Chiles MC, Dean PJ, Scott MA. Pathogenic *Yersinia* DNA is detected in bowel and mesenteric lymph nodes from patients with Crohn's disease. Int J Surg Pathol 2003, **27**: 220–227.

220 Lee EY, Stenson WF, DeSchryver-Kecskemeti K. Thickening of muscularis mucosae in Crohn's disease. Mod Pathol 1991, **4**: 87–90.

221 Lock MR, Farmer RG, Fazio VW, Jagelman DG, Lavery IC, Weakley FL. Recurrence and reoperation for Crohn's disease. The role of disease location in prognosis. N Engl J Med 1981, **304**: 1586–1588.

222 Marin ML, Geller SA, Greenstein AJ, Marin RH, Gordon RE, Aufses AH Jr. Ultrastructural pathology of Crohn's disease. Correlated transmission electron microscopy, scanning electron microscopy, and freeze fracture studies. Am J Gastroenterol 1983, **78**: 355–364.

223 Matson AP, Van Kruiningen HJ, West AB, Cartun RW, Colombel J-F, Cortot A. The relationship of granulomas to blood vessels in intestinal Crohn's disease. Mod Pathol 1995, **8**: 680–685.

224 Mayberry JF. Epidemiological aspects of Crohn's disease. A review of the literature. Gut 1984, **25**: 886–899.

225 McQuillan AC, Appelman HD. Superficial Crohn's disease. A study of 10 patients. Surg Pathol 1989, **2**: 231–240.

226 Mekhjian HS, Switz DM, Watts HD, Deren JJ, Katon RM, Beman FM. National Cooperative Crohn's Disease Study. Factors determining recurrence of Crohn's disease after surgery. Gastroenterology 1979, **77**: 907–913.

227 Menard DB, Haddad H, Blain JG, Beaudry R, Devroede G, Massé S. Granulomatous myositis and myopathy associated with Crohn's colitis. N Engl J Med 1976, **295**: 818–819.

228 Michelassi F, Balestracci T, Chappell R, Block GE. Primary and recurrent Crohn's disease. Experience with 1379 patients. Ann Surg 1991, **214**: 230–238.

229 Michelassi F, Testa G, Pomidor WJ, Lashner BA, Block GE. Adenocarcinoma complicating Crohn's disease. Dis Colon Rectum 1993, **36**: 654–661.

230 Mishina D, Katsel P, Brown ST, Gilberts ECA, Greenstein RJ. On the etiology of Crohn disease. Proc Natl Acad Sci U S A 1996, **93**: 9816–9820.

231 Mogadam M, Priest RJ. Necrotizing enteritis in Crohn's disease of the small bowel. Gastroenterology 1969, **56**: 337–341.

232 Monsen U, Bernell O, Johansson C, Hellers G. Prevalence of inflammatory bowel disease among relatives of patients with Crohn's disease. Scand J Gastroenterol 1991, **26**: 302–306.

233 Morson B. Crohn's disease. Lecture 2. Trans Med Soc Lond 1970, **86**: 177–192.

234 Noffsinger A, Unger B, Fenoglio-Preiser CM. Increased cell proliferation characterizes Crohn's disease. Mod Pathol 1998, **11**: 1198–1203.

235 Nugent FW, Glaser D, Fernandez-Herlihy L. Crohn's colitis associated with granulomatous disease. N Engl J Med 1976, **294**: 262–263.

236 Oberhuber G, Hirsch M, Stolte M. High incidence of upper gastrointestinal tract involvement in Crohn's disease. Virchows Arch 1998, **432**: 49–52.

237 Oberhuber G, Stangl PC, Vogelsang H, Schober E, Herbst F, Gasche C. Significant association of strictures and internal fistula formation in Crohn's disease. Virchows Arch 2000, **437**: 293–297.

238 Oberhuber G, Puspok A, Peck-Radosavlevic M, Kutilek M, Lamprecht A, Chott A, Vogelsang H, Stolte M. Aberrant esophageal HLA-DR expression in a high percentage of patients with Crohn's disease. Am J Surg Pathol 1999, **23**: 970–976.

239 Otto HF, Gebbers J-O. Electron microscopic, ultracytochemical and immunohistological observations in Crohn's disease of the ileum and colon. Virchows Arch [A] 1981, **391**: 189–205.

240 Pavli P, Gibson PR. Pathogenic factors in inflammatory bowel disease. Part 2. Crohn's disease. Dig Dis 1992, **10**: 72–84.

241 Perosio PM, Brooks JJ, Saul SH, Haller DG. Primary intestinal lymphoma in Crohn's disease. Minute tumor with a fatal outcome. Am J Gastroenterol 1992, **87**: 894–898.

242 Perzin KH, Peterson M, Castiglione CL, Fenoglio CM, Wolff M. Intramucosal carcinoma of the small intestine arising in regional enteritis (Crohn's disease). Report of a case studied for carcinoembryonic antigen and review of the literature. Cancer 1984, **54**: 151–162.

243 Plauth M, Jenss H, Meyle J. Oral manifestations of Crohn's disease. An analysis of 79 cases. J Clin Gastroenterol 1991, **13**: 29–37.

244 Polodsky DK. Inflammatory bowel disease. N Engl J Med 1991, **325**: 928–937 and 1008–1016.

245 Podolsky DK. Inflammatory bowel disease. N Engl J Med 2002, **347**: 417–429.

246 Price AB, Morson BC. Inflammatory bowel disease. The surgical pathology of Crohn's disease and ulcerative colitis. Hum Pathol 1975, **6**: 7–29.

247 Probert CS, Jayanthi V, Hughes AO, Thompson JR, Wicks AC, Mayberry JF. Prevalence and family risk of ulcerative colitis and

Crohn's disease. An epidemiological study among Europeans and south Asians in Leicestershire. Gut 1993, **34:** 1547–1551.

248 Rankin GB, Watts D, Melnyk CS, Kelley ML Jr. National Cooperative Crohn's Disease Study. Extraintestinal manifestations and perianal complications. Gastroenterology 1979, **77:** 914–920.

249 Rappaport H, Bourgoyne FH, Smetana HF. The pathology of regional enteritis. Milit Surg 1951, **109:** 463–502.

250 Ribeiro MB, Greenstein AJ, Heimann TM, Yamazaki Y, Aufses AH Jr. Adenocarcinoma of the small intestine in Crohn's disease. Surg Gynecol Obstet 1991, **173:** 343–349.

251 Roberts IS, Stoddart RW. Ulcer-associated cell lineage ("pyloric metaplasia") in Crohn's disease. A lectin histochemical study. J Pathol 1993, **171:** 13–19.

252 Rubin S, Lambie RW, Chapman J. Regional ileitis in childhood. Am J Dis Child 1967, **114:** 106–110.

253 Rubio CA, Befritz R, Poppen B, Svenberg T, Slezak P. Crohn's disease and adenocarcinoma of the intestinal tract. Report of four cases. Dis Colon Rectum 1991, **34:** 174–180.

254 Sachar DB, Wolfson DM, Greenstein AJ, Goldberg J, Styezynski R, Janowitz HD. Risk factors for postoperative recurrence of Crohn's disease. Gastroenterology 1983, **85:** 917–921.

255 Salmon JF, Wright JP, Murray AD. Ocular inflammation in Crohn's disease. Ophthalmology 1991, **98:** 480–484.

256 Sankey EA, Dhillon AP, Anthony A, Wakefield AJ, Sim R, More L, Hudson M, Sawyerr AM, Pounder RE. Early mucosal changes in Crohn's disease. Gut 1993, **34:** 375–381.

257 Sarsfield P, Jones DB, Wright DH. Accessory cells in Crohn's disease of the terminal ileum. Histopathology 1996, **28:** 213–219.

258 Schnitt SJ, Antonioli DA, Jaffe B, Peppercorn MA. Granulomatous inflammation of minor salivary gland ducts. A new oral manifestation of Crohn's disease. Hum Pathol 1987, **18:** 405–407.

259 Shepherd NA. Granulomas in the diagnosis of intestinal Crohn's disease: a myth exploded? Histopathology 2002, **41:** 166–168.

260 Simpson S, Traube J, Riddell RH. The histologic appearance of dysplasia (precarcinomatous change) in Crohn's disease of the small and large intestine. Gastroenterology 1981, **81:** 492–501.

261 Stainsby KJ, Lowes JR, Allan RN, Ibbotson JP. Antibodies to *Mycobacterium paratuberculosis* and nine species of environmental mycobacteria in Crohn's disease and control subjects. Gut 1993, **34:** 371–374.

262 Sutphen JL, Cooper PH, Mackel SE, Nelson DL. Metastatic cutaneous Crohn's disease. Gastroenterology 1984, **86:** 941–944.

263 Tan WC, Allan RN. Diffuse jejunoileitis of Crohn's disease. Gut 1993, **34:** 1374–1378.

264 Tanaka K, Wilks M, Coates PJ, Farthing MJ, Walker-Smith JA, Tabaqchali S. *Mycobacterium paratuberculosis* and Crohn's disease. Gut 1991, **32:** 43–45.

265 Thompson EM, Clayden G, Price AB. Cancer in Crohn's disease – an "occult" malignancy. Histopathology 1983, **7:** 365–376.

266 Thyberg J, Graf W, Klingenström P. Intestinal fine structure in Crohn's disease. Lysosomal inclusions in epithelial cells and macrophages. Virchows Arch [A] 1981, **391:** 141–152.

267 Tonelli F, Ficari F. Pathological features of Crohn's disease determining perforation. J Clin Gastroenterol 1991, **13:** 226–230.

268 Vanbockrijck M, Cabooter M, Casselman J, Vanvuchelen J, Van Hoof A, Michielssen P. Primary Hodgkin disease of the ileum complicating Crohn disease. Cancer 1993, **72:** 1784–1789.

269 Wakefield AJ, Pittilo RM, Sim R, Cosby SL, Stephenson JR, Dhillon AP, Pounder RE. Evidence of persistent measles virus infection in Crohn's disease. J Med Virol 1993, **39:** 345–353.

270 Whelan G, Farmer RG, Fazio VW, Goormastic M. Recurrence after surgery in Crohn's disease. Relationship to location of disease (clinical pattern) and surgical indication. Gastroenterology 1985, **88:** 1826–1833.

271 Wolfson DM, Sachar DB, Cohen A, Goldberg J, Styczynski R,

Greenstein AJ, Gelernt IM, Janowitz HD. Granulomas do not affect postoperative recurrence rates in Crohn's disease. Gastroenterology 1982, **83:** 405–409.

272 Wright CL, Riddell RH. Histology of the stomach and duodenum in Crohn's disease. Am J Surg Pathol 1998, **22:** 383–390.

273 Zalev AH, Gardiner GW. Crohn's disease of the small intestine with polypoid configuration. Gastrointest Radiol 1991, **16:** 18–20.

AIDS-related inflammatory diseases

274 Church DL, Sutherland LR, Gill MJ, Visser ND, Kelly JK. Absence of an association between enteric parasites in the manifestations and pathogenesis of HIV enteropathy in gay men. Scand J Infect Dis 1992, **24:** 567–575.

275 Cranston RD, Anton PA, McGowan IM. Gastrointestinal mucosal biopsy in HIV disease and AIDS. Gastrointest Endosc Clin N Am 2000, **10:** 637–667.

276 Genta RM, Chappell CL, White AC Jr, Kimball KT, Goodgame RW. Duodenal morphology and intensity of infection in AIDS-related intestinal cryptosporidiosis. Gastroenterology 1993, **105:** 1769–1775.

277 Giang TT, Kotler DP, Garro ML, Orenstein JM. Tissue diagnosis of intestinal microsporidiosis using the chromotrope-2R modified trichrome stain. Arch Pathol Lab Med 1993, **117:** 1249–1251.

278 Greenson JK, Belitsos PC, Yardley JH, Bartlett JG. AIDS enteropathy. Occult enteric infections and duodenal mucosal alterations in chronic diarrhea. Ann Intern Med 1991, **114:** 366–372.

279 Grillin JS, Urmacher C, West R, Shike M. Disseminated *Mycobacterium avium-intracellulare* infection in acquired immunodeficiency syndrome mimicking Whipple's disease. Gastroenterology 1983, **85:** 1187–1191.

280 Guarda LA, Stein SA, Cleary KA, Ordonez NG. Human cryptosporidiosis in the acquired immunodeficiency syndrome. Arch Pathol Lab Med 1983, **107:** 562–566.

281 Lefkowitch JH, Krumholz S, Feng-Chen K-C, Griffin P, Despommier D, Brasitus TA. Cryptosporidiosis of the human small intestine. A light and electron microscopic study. Hum Pathol 1984, **15:** 746–752.

282 Nannini EC, Okhuysen PC. HIV1 and the gut in the era of highly active antiretroviral therapy. Curr Gastroenterol Rep 2002, **4:** 392–398.

283 Orenstein JM, Dieterich DT, Kotler DP. Systemic dissemination by a newly recognized intestinal microsporidia species in AIDS. AIDS 1992, **6:** 1143–1150.

284 Orenstein JM, Kotler DP. Diarrheogenic bacterial enteritis in acquired immune deficiency syndrome. A light and electron microscopy study of 52 cases. Hum Pathol 1995, **26:** 481–492.

285 Orenstein JM, Tenner M, Cali A, Kotler DP. A microsporidian previously undescribed in humans, infecting enterocytes and macrophages, and associated with diarrhea in an acquired immunodeficiency syndrome patient. Hum Pathol 1992, **23:** 722–728.

286 Peacock CS, Blanshard C, Tovey DG, Ellis DS, Gazzard BG. Histological diagnosis of intestinal microsporidiosis in patients with AIDS. J Clin Pathol 1991, **44:** 558–563.

287 Roth RI, Owen RL, Keren DF. AIDS with *Mycobacterium avium-intracellulare* lesions resembling those of Whipple's disease. N Engl J Med 1983, **309:** 1324–1325.

288 Rotterdam H, Tsang P. Gastrointestinal disease in the immunocompromised patient. Hum Pathol 1994, **25:** 1123–1140.

289 Shadduck JA, Orenstein JM. Comparative pathology of microsporidiosis. Arch Pathol Lab Med 1993, **117:** 1215–1219.

290 Soave R, Danner RL, Honig CL, Ma P, Hart CC, Nash T, Roberts RB. Cryptosporidiosis in homosexual men. Ann Intern Med 1984, **100:** 504–511.

291 Wilcox CM, Schwartz DA. Symptomatic CMV duodenitis. An important clinical problem in AIDS. J Clin Gastroenterol 1992, **14:** 293–297.

Other inflammatory diseases

292 Ahmed FB. Tuberculous enteritis. Br Med J 1996, **313**: 215–217.

292a Alsaigh N, Fogt F. Intestinal spirochetosis: clinicopathological features with review of the literature. Colorectal Dis 2002, **4**: 97–100.

293 Andersen LP, Holck S, Elsborg L, Justesen T. The *Helicobacter (Campylobacter) pylori*-colonized duodenal mucosa and gastric metaplasia. APMIS (Denmark) 1991, **99**: 244–248.

294 Bradford WD, Noce PS, Gutman LT. Pathologic features of enteric infection with *Yersinia enterocolitica*. Arch Pathol 1974, **98**: 17–22.

295 Brynjulfsen BC. Jejunitis acuta – ileitis regionalis acuta. Acta Chir Scand 1948, **96**: 361–388.

296 Crabtree JE, Shallcross TM, Wyatt JI, Taylor JD, Heatley RV, Rathbone BJ, Losowsky MS. Mucosal humoral immune response to *Helicobacter pylori* in patients with duodenitis. Dig Dis Sci 1991, **36**: 1266–1273.

297 DeSchryver-Kecskemeti K, Clouse RE. A previously unrecognized subgroup of "eosinophilic gastroenteritis." Association with connective tissue diseases. Am J Surg Pathol 1984, **8**: 171–180.

298 Gleason TH, Patterson SD. The pathology of *Yersinia enterocolitica* ileocolitis. Am J Surg Pathol 1982, **6**: 347–355.

299 Jenkins D, Goodall A, Gillet FR, Scott BB. Defining duodenitis. Quantitative histological study of mucosal responses and their correlations. J Clin Pathol 1985, **38**: 1119–1126.

300 Kraus MD, Amatya B, Kimula Y. Histopathology of typhoid enteritis: morphologic and immunophenotypic findings. Mod Pathol 1999, **12**: 949–955.

301 Marshall JB. Tuberculosis of the gastrointestinal tract and peritoneum. Am J Gastroenterol 1993, **88**: 989–999.

301a Padmanabhan V, Callas PW, Li SC, Trainer TD. Histopathological features of the terminal ileum in lymphocytic and collagenous colitis: a study of 32 cases and review of literature. Mod Pathol 2003, **16**: 115–119.

302 Recavarren-Arce S, Leon-Barua R, Cok J, Rodriguez C, Berendson R, Gilman RH, Ramirez-Ramos A, Watanabe J. Low prevalence of gastric metaplasia in the duodenal mucosa in Peru. J Clin Gastroenterol 1992, **15**: 296–301.

303 Sapp H, Ithamukkala S, Brien TP, Ayata G, Shaz B, Dorfman DM, Wang HH, Antonioli DA, Farraye FA, Odze RD. The terminal ileum is affected in patients with lymphocytic or collagenous colitis. Am J Surg Pathol 2002, **26**: 1484–1492.

304 Schmitz-Moormann P, Pittner PM, Reichmann L, Massarat S. Quantitative histological study of duodenitis in biopsies. Pathol Res Pract 1984, **178**: 499–507.

305 Schulze K, Warner HA, Murray D. Intestinal tuberculosis. Experience at a Canadian teaching institution. Am J Med 1977, **63**: 735–745.

306 Shousha S, Spiller RC, Parkins RA. The endoscopically abnormal duodenum in patients with dyspepsia. Biopsy findings in 60 cases. Histopathology 1983, **7**: 23–34.

307 Sprague R, Harper P, McClain S, Trainer T, Beeken W. Disseminated gastrointestinal sarcoidosis. Case report and review of the literature. Gastroenterology 1984, **87**: 421–425.

308 Suen KC, Burton JD. The spectrum of eosinophilic infiltration of the gastrointestinal tract and its relationship to other disorders of angiitis and granulomatosis. Hum Pathol 1979, **10**: 31–43.

309 Sullivan PB, Marsh MN, Phillips MB, Dewit O, Neale G, Cevallos AM, Yamson P, Farthing MJ. Prevalence and treatment of giardiasis in chronic diarrhoea and malnutrition. Arch Dis Child 1991, **66**: 304–306.

310 Sun T. The diagnosis of giardiasis. Am J Surg Pathol 1980, **4**: 265–271.

311 Svane S. Acute phlegmonous jejunitis and viridans streptococcal peritonitis associated with bronchial carcinoma. Scand J Infect Dis 2000, **32**: 421–422.

312 Tandon HD, Prakash A. Pathology of intestinal tuberculosis and its distinction from Crohn's disease. Gut 1972, **13**: 260–269.

313 Tuñon T, Zozaya E, Tabar AI, Dorronsoro MLG, Gomez B, Valenti C. Eosinophilic enteritis due to anisakis: a call for pathologists' attention. Int J Surg Pathol 1997, **5**: 69–76.

314 Valdez R, Appleman HD, Bronner MP, Greenson JK. Diffuse duodenitis associated with ulcerative colitis. Am J Surg Pathol 2000, **24**: 1407–1413.

315 Walker NI, Croese J, Clouston AD, Loukas A, Prociv P. Eosinophilic enteritis in Northeastern Australia. Pathology, association with *Ancylostoma caninum*, and implications. Am J Surg Pathol 1995, **19**: 328–337.

316 Wyatt J. Histopathology of gastroduodenal inflammation. The impact of *Helicobacter pylori*. Histopathology 1995, **26**: 1–16.

Irradiation effect

317 Cross MJ, Frazee RC. Surgical treatment of radiation enteritis. Am Surg 1992, **58**: 132–135.

318 Donaldson SS, Jundt S, Ricour C, Sarrazin D, Lemerle J, Schweisguth O. Radiation enteritis in children. A retrospective review, clinicopathologic correlation, and dietary management. Cancer 1975, **35**: 1167–1178.

319 Hasleton PS, Carr N, Schofield PF. Vascular changes in radiation bowel disease. Histopathology 1985, **9**: 517–534.

320 Oya M, Yao T, Tsuneyoshi M. Chronic irradiation enteritis: its correlation with the elapsed time interval and morphological changes. Hum Pathol 1996, **27**: 774–781.

321 Perkins DE, Spjut JH. Intestinal stenosis following radiation therapy. Am J Roentgenol Radium Ther Nucl Med 1962, **88**: 953–966.

322 Sugg WL, Lawler WH, Ackerman LV, Butcher HR Jr. Operative therapy for severe irradiational injury in the enteral and urinary tracts. Ann Surg 1963, **157**: 62–70.

Intussusception

323 Bell TM, Steyn JH. Viruses in lymph nodes of children with mesenteric adenitis and intussusception. Br Med J 1962, **1**: 700–702.

323a Guarner J, de Leon-Bojorge B, Lopez-Corella E, Ferebee-Harris T, Gooding L, Garnett LC, Shieh W-J, Dawson J, Erdman D, Zaki SR. Intestinal intussusception associated with adenovirus infection in Mexican children. Am J Clin Pathol 2003, **120**: 845–850.

324 Meyerson S, Desai TK, Polidori G, Raval MF, Ehrinpreis MN. A case of intussusception and lymphoid hyperplasia in a patient with AIDS. Am J Gastroenterol 1993, **88**: 303–306.

325 Montgomery EA, Popek EJ. Intussusception, adenovirus, and children. A brief reaffirmation. Hum Pathol 1994, **25**: 169–174.

326 Sarason EL, Prior JT, Prowda RL. Recurrent intussusception associated with hypertrophy of Peyer's patches. N Engl J Med 1955, **253**: 905–908.

327 Takeuchi K, Tsuzuki Y, Ando T, Sekihara M, Hara T, Kori T, Kuwano H. The diagnosis and treatment of adult intussusception. J Clin Gastroenterol 2003, **36**: 18–21.

328 Yunis EJ, Atchison RW, Michaels RH, DeCicco FA. Adenovirus and ileocecal intussusception. Lab Invest 1975, **33**: 347–351.

Other non-neoplastic diseases

329 Foster CS. The brown bowel syndrome. A possible smooth muscle mitochondrial myopathy? Histopathology 1979, **3**: 1–17.

330 Groisman GM, Amar M, Livne E. CD10: a valuable tool for the light microscopic diagnosis of microvillous inclusion disease (familial microvillous atrophy). Am J Surg Pathol 2002, **26**: 902–907.

331 Hamaya K, Kitamura M, Doi K. Primary amyloid tumors of the jejunum producing intestinal obstruction. Acta Pathol Jpn 1989, **39**: 207–211.

332 Hosler JP, Kimmel KK, Moeller DD. The "brown bowel syndrome." A case report. Am J Gastroenterol 1982, **77**: 854–855.

333 Johnson DH, Guthrie TH, Tedesco FJ, Griffin JW, Anthony HF Jr.

Amyloidosis masquerading as inflammatory bowel disease with a mass lesion simulating a malignancy. Am J Gastroenterol 1982, **77:** 141–145.

334 Smith TR, Cho KC. Small intestine amyloidosis producing a stippled punctate mucosal pattern. Radiological-pathological correlation. Am J Gastroenterol 1986, **81:** 477–479.

335 Snover DC, Weisdorf SA, Vercellotti GM, Rank B, Hutton S, McGlave P. A histopathologic study of gastric and small intestinal graft-versus-host disease following allogeneic bone marrow transplantation. Hum Pathol 1985, **16:** 387–392.

Tumors

Benign epithelial tumors

336 Blackman E, Nash SV. Diagnosis of duodenal and ampullary epithelial neoplasms by endoscopic biopsy. A clinicopathologic and immunohistochemical study. Hum Pathol 1985, **16:** 901–910.

337 Buck JL, Harned RK, Lichtenstein JE, Sobin LH. Peutz-Jeghers syndrome. Radiographics 1992, **12:** 365–378.

338 Chatelain D, Maillet E, Boyer L, Checkouri G, Mourra N, Flejou JF. Brunner gland hamartoma with predominant adipose tissue and ciliated cysts. Arch Pathol Lab Med 2002, **126:** 734–735.

339 Chen KTK. Female genital tract tumors in Peutz-Jeghers syndrome. Hum Pathol 1986, **17:** 858–861.

340 Chen KTK. Benign signet-ring cell aggregates in Peutz-Jeghers polyps. A diagnostic pitfall. Surg Pathol 1989, **2:** 335–338.

341 Cooperman M, Clausen KP, Hecht C, Lucas JG, Keith LM. Villous adenomas of the duodenum. Gastroenterology 1978, **74:** 1295–1297.

342 Dozois RR, Judd ES, Dahlin DC, Bartholomew LG. The Peutz-Jeghers syndrome. Is there a predisposition to the development of intestinal malignancy? Arch Surg 1969, **98:** 509–517.

343 Estrada R, Spjut HJ. Hamartomatous polyps in Peutz-Jeghers syndrome. A light histochemical, and electron-microscopic study. Am J Surg Pathol 1983, **7:** 747–754.

344 Fulcheri E, Baracchini P, Pagani A, Lapertosa G, Bussolati G. Significance of the smooth muscle cell component in Peutz-Jeghers and juvenile polyps. Hum Pathol 1991, **22:** 1136–1140.

345 Haggitt RC, Reid BJ. Hereditary gastrointestinal polyposis syndromes. Am J Surg Pathol 1986, **10:** 871–887.

346 Halbert RE. Peutz-Jeghers syndrome with metastasizing gastric adenocarcinoma. Report of a case. Arch Pathol Lab Med 1982, **106:** 517–520.

347 Hizawa K, Iida M, Matsumoto T, Kohrogi N, Yao T, Fujishima M. Neoplastic transformation arising in Peutz-Jeghers polyposis. Dis Colon Rectum 1993, **36:** 953–957.

348 Iseki M, Tsuda N, Hayashi T, Tamaru N, Anami M, Matsuya F, Tagawa Y, Toriyama K, Itakura H. Multifocal villous adenomas of the anastomotic area following ileocystoplasty: a case report and literature review. J Urol Pathol 2000, **12:** 29–38.

349 King PH, Osborn DE, Mackay EH. Tubulovillous adenoma arising 30 years after ileocystoplasty. J Clin Pathol 1992, **45:** 928–929.

350 Komorowski RA, Cohen EB. Villous tumors of the duodenum. A clinicopathologic study. Cancer 1981, **47:** 1377–1386.

351 Kyriakos M, Condon SC. Enteritis cystica profunda. Am J Clin Pathol 1978, **69:** 77–85.

352 Matsumoto T, Iida M, Nakamura S, Hizawa K, Mizuno M, Yao T, Tsuneyoshi M, Fujishima M. Depressed adenoma of the duodenum in patients with familial adenomatous polyposis: endoscopic and immunohistochemical features. Cancer 1999, **86:** 1414–1420.

353 Merine D, Jones B, Ghahremani GG, Hamilton SR, Bayless TM. Hyperplasia of Brunner glands. The spectrum of its radiographic manifestations. Gastrointest Radiol 1991, **16:** 104–108.

354 Miller JH, Gisvold JJ, Weiland LH, McIlrath DC. Upper gastrointestinal tract. Villous tumors. AJR 1980, **134:** 933–936.

355 Morson BC. Some peculiarities in the histology of intestinal polyps. Dis Colon Rectum 1962, **5:** 337–344.

356 Narita T, Eto T, Ito T. Peutz-Jeghers syndrome with adenomas and adenocarcinomas in colonic polyps. Am J Surg Pathol 1987, **11:** 76–81.

357 Perzin KH, Bridge MF. Adenomas of the small intestine. A clinicopathologic review of 51 cases and a study of their relationship to carcinoma. Cancer 1981, **48:** 799–819.

358 Perzin KH, Bridge MF. Adenomatous and carcinomatous changes in hamartomatous polyps of the small intestine (Peutz-Jeghers syndrome). Report of a case and review of the literature. Cancer 1982, **49:** 971–983.

359 Petersen VC, Sheehan AL, Bryan CP, Armstrong CP, Sheperd NA. Misplacement of dysplastic epithelium in Peutz-Jeghers polyps: the ultimate diagnostic pitfall? Am J Surg Pathol 2000, **24:** 34–39.

360 ReMine WH, Brown PW Jr, Gomes MMR, Harrison EG Jr. Polypoid hamartomas of Brunner's glands. Report of six surgical cases. Arch Surg 1970, **100:** 313–316.

361 Rüfenacht H, Kasper M, Heitz PU, Streule K, Harder F. "Brunneroma." Hamartoma or tumor? Pathol Res Pract 1986, **181:** 107–109.

362 Spjut HJ, Helgason AH, Trabanino JG II. Jejunitis cystica profunda in a hamartomatous polyp. Report of a case. Am J Surg Pathol 1987, **11:** 328–332.

363 Trau H, Schewach-Millet M, Fisher BK, Tsur H. Peutz-Jeghers syndrome and bilateral breast carcinoma. Cancer 1982, **50:** 788–792.

Adenocarcinoma

364 Adair HM, Trowell JE. Squamous cell carcinoma arising in a duplication of the small bowel. J Pathol 1981, **133:** 25–31.

365 Adler SN, Lyon DT, Sullivan PD. Adenocarcinoma of the small bowel. Clinical features, similarity to regional enteritis, and analysis of 338 documented cases. Am J Gastroenterol 1982, **77:** 326–330.

366 Arai T, Murata T, Sawabe M, Takubo K, Esaki Y. Primary adenocarcinoma of the duodenum in the elderly: clinicopathological and immunohistochemical study of 17 cases. Pathol Int 1999, **49:** 23–29.

367 Baciewicz F, Sparberg M, Lawrence JB, Potichá SM. Adenocarcinoma of an ileostomy site with skin invasion. A case report. Gastroenterology 1983, **84:** 168–170.

368 Barclay THC, Schapira DV. Malignant tumors of the small intestine. Cancer 1983, **51:** 878–881.

369 Bardales RH, Stanley MW, Simpson DD, Baker SJ, Steele CT, Schaefer RF, Powers CN. Diagnostic value of brush cytology in the diagnosis of duodenal, biliary, and ampullary neoplasms. Am J Clin Pathol 1998, **109:** 540–548.

370 Benharroch D, Sion-Vardi N, Goldstein J. Neurofibromatosis involving the small bowel associated with adenocarcinoma of the ileum with a neuroendocrine component. Pathol Res Pract 1992, **188:** 959–963.

371 Blackman E, Nash SV. Diagnosis of duodenal and ampullary epithelial neoplasms by endoscopic biopsy. A clinicopathologic and immunohistochemical study. Hum Pathol 1985, **16:** 901–910.

372 Bridge MF, Perzin KH. Primary adenocarcinoma of the jejunum and ileum. A clinicopathologic study. Cancer 1975, **36:** 1876–1887.

373 Cuesta MA, Donner R. Adenocarcinoma arising at an ileostomy site. Report of a case. Cancer 1976, **37:** 949–952.

374 Guadagni S, Catarci M, Ventura T, Leocata P, Carboni M. Primary adenocarcinoma arising in the jejunal limb of a Roux-en-Y esophagojejunostomy. A case report. Jpn J Clin Oncol 1993, **23:** 59–63.

375 Howe JR, Karnell LH, Menck HR, Scott-Conner C. The American College of Surgeons Commission on Cancer and the American Cancer Society. Adenocarcinoma of the small bowel: review of the National Cancer Data Base, 1985-1995. Cancer 1999, **86:** 2693–2706.

376 Iwafuchi M, Watanabe H, Ishihara N, Enjoji M, Iwashita A, Yanaihara N, Ito S. Neoplastic endocrine cells in carcinomas of the small intestine. Histochemical and immunohistochemical studies of 24 tumors. Hum Pathol 1987, **18:** 185–194.

377 Lien G-S, Mori M, Enjoji M. Primary carcinoma of the small intestine. A clinicopathologic and immunohistochemical study. Cancer 1988, **61**: 316–323.

378 Lipper S, Graves GV Jr. Villous adenocarcinoma arising in the bypassed duodenum 18 years after a Billroth II subtotal gastrectomy. Report of a case and review of the literature. Am J Gastroenterol 1985, **80**: 174–176.

379 Lundqvist M, Wilander E. Exocrine and endocrine cell differentiation in small intestinal adenocarcinomas. Acta Pathol Microbiol Immunol Scand A 1983, **91**: 469–474.

380 Rodriguez-Bigas MA, Vasen HF, Lynch HT, Watson P, Myrhoj T, Jarvinen HJ, Mecklin JP, Macrae F, S.John DJ, Bertario L, Fidalgo P, Madlensky L, Rozen P. International Collaborative Group on HNPCC. Characteristics of small bowel carcinoma in hereditary nonpolyposis colorectal carcinoma. Cancer 1998, **83**: 240–244.

381 Rudan N, Nola P, Popovic S. Primary adenocarcinoma of the duodenum. Report of two cases. Cancer 1984, **54**: 1105–1109.

382 Spira IA, Ghazi A, Wolff WI. Primary adenocarcinoma of the duodenum. Cancer 1977, **39**: 1721–1726.

383 Stemmermann GN, Goodman MT, Nomura AM. Adenocarcinoma of the proximal small intestine. A marker for familial and multicentric cancer? Cancer 1992, **70**: 2766–2771.

384 Takahashi A, Tsukamoto TD, Kumamoto Y, Sato Y, Shibuya A, Sato M. Adenocarcinoma arising in the ileal segment of a defunctionalized ileocystoplasty. Hinyokika Kiyo 1993, **39**: 753–755.

385 Wagner KM, Thompson J, Herlinger H, Caroline D. Thirteen primary adenocarcinomas of the ileum and appendix. A case report. Cancer 1982, **49**: 797–801.

385a Wendum D, Svrcek M, Rigau V, Boëlle P-Y, Sebbagh N, Parc R, Masliah J, Trugnan G, Fléjou J-F. COX-2, inflammatory secreted PLA2, and cytoplasmic PLA2 protein expression in small bowel adenocarcinomas compared with colorectal adenocarcinomas. Mod Pathol 2003, **16**: 130–136.

386 Yamashina M. Primary adenocarcinoma of the small intestine with emphasis on microvillous differentiation. Acta Pathol Jpn 1987, **37**: 1061–1070.

Other types of carcinoma

387 Bak M, Teglbjaerg PS. Pleomorphic (giant cell) carcinoma of the intestine. An immunohistochemical and electron microscopic study. Cancer 1989, **64**: 2557–2564.

388 Fukuda T, Kamishima T, Ohnishi Y, Suzuki T. Sarcomatoid carcinoma of the small intestine: histologic, immunohistochemical and ultrastructural features of three cases and its differential diagnosis. Pathol Int 1996, **46**: 682–688.

389 Griesser GH, Schumacher U, Elfeldt R, Horny H-P. Adenosquamous carcinoma of the ileum. Report of a case and review of the literature. Virchows Arch [A] 1985, **406**: 483–487.

390 Jones EA, Flejou JF, Molas G, Potet F. Pleomorphic carcinoma of the small bowel. The limitations of immunohistochemical specificity. Pathol Res Pract 1991, **187**: 235–240.

391 Ngo N, Villamil C, Macauley W, Cole SR. Adenosquamous carcinoma of the small intestine: report of a case and review of the literature. Arch Pathol Lab Med 1999, **123**: 739–742.

392 Robey-Cafferty SS, Silva EG, Cleary KR. Anaplastic and sarcomatoid carcinoma of the small intestine. Hum Pathol 1989, **20**: 858–863.

393 Swanson PE, Dykoski D, Wick MR, Snover DC. Primary duodenal small-cell neuroendocrine carcinoma with production of vasoactive intestinal polypeptide. Arch Pathol Lab Med 1986, **110**: 317–320.

Carcinoid tumors and related endocrine tumors
General and clinical features

394 Allibone RO, Hoffman J, Gosney JR, Helliwell TR. Granulation tissue polyposis associated with carcinoid tumours of the small intestine. Histopathology 1993, **22**: 475–480.

395 Bordi C, D'Adda T, Assoni C, Canavese G, Brandi ML. Gastrointestinal endocrine tumors: recent developments. Endocr Pathol 1998, **9**: 99–116.

396 Burke AP, Thomas RM, Elsayed AM, Sobin L. Carcinoids of the jejunum and ileum: an immunohistochemical and clinicopathologic study of 167 cases. Cancer 1997, **79**: 1086–1093.

397 Chow CW, Sane S, Campbell PE, Carter RF. Malignant carcinoid tumors in children. Cancer 1982, **49**: 802–811.

398 DeLellis RA, Dayal Y, Wolfe HJ. Carcinoid tumors. Changing concepts and new perspectives. Am J Surg Pathol 1984, **8**: 295–300.

399 Gardiner GW, Van Patter T, Murray D. Atypical carcinoid tumor of the small bowel complicating celiac disease. Cancer 1985, **56**: 2716–2722.

400 Godwin JD II. Carcinoid tumors. An analysis of 2837 cases. Cancer 1975, **36**: 560–569.

401 Hough DR, Chan A, Davidson H. Von Recklinghausen's disease associated with gastrointestinal carcinoid tumors. Cancer 1983, **51**: 2206–2208.

402 Kuiper DH, Gracie WA Jr, Pollard HM. Twenty years of gastrointestinal carcinoids. Cancer 1970, **25**: 1424–1430.

403 Lewin KJ. The endocrine cells of the gastrointestinal tract. The normal endocrine cells and their hyperplasias. Pathol Annu 1986, **21**(Pt 1): 1–27.

404 Lewin KJ, Ulich T, Yang K, Layfield L. The endocrine cells of the gastrointestinal tract tumors. Pathol Annu 1986, **21**(Pt 2): 181–215.

405 Lloyd RV. Overview of neuroendocrine cells and tumors. Endocr Pathol 1996, **7**: 323–328.

406 Modlin IM, Lye KD, Kidd M. A 5-decade analysis of 13,715 carcinoid tumors. Cancer 2003, **97**: 934–959.

407 Sigel JE, Goldblum JR. Neuroendocrine neoplasms arising in inflammatory bowel disease: a report of 14 cases. Mod Pathol 1998, **11**: 537–542.

408 Smith JHF, Hope PG. Carcinoid tumor arising in a cystic duplication of the small bowel. Arch Pathol Lab Med 1985, **109**: 95–96.

409 Solcia E, Capella C, Buffa R, Usellini L, Fiocca R, Sessa F, Tortora O. The contribution of immunohistochemistry to the diagnosis of neuroendocrine tumors. Semin Diagn Pathol 1984, **2**: 285–296.

410 Solcia E, Fiocca R, Rindi G, Villani L, Luinetti O, Burrell M, Bosi F, Silini E. Endocrine tumors of the small and large intestine. Pathol Res Pract 1995, **191**: 366–372.

411 Wick MR, Stanley M, Cherwitz DL, Savage JE. Concomitant neuropeptide-producing endometrial carcinomas and ileal carcinoid tumors. Am J Clin Pathol 1986, **85**: 406–410.

411a Yantiss RK, Odze RD, Farraye FA, Rosenberg AE. Solitary versus multiple carcinoid tumors of the ileum. Am J Surg Pathol 2003, **27**: 811–817.

Morphologic features

412 Abrahams NA, Vesoulis Z, Petras RE. Angiogenic polypoid proliferation adjacent to ileal carcinoid tumors: a non-specific finding related to mucosal prolapse. Mod Pathol 2001, **14**: 821–827.

413 Cai YC, Barnard G, Hiestand L, Woda B, Colby J, Banner B. Florid angiogenesis in mucosa surrounding an ileal carcinoid tumor expressing transforming growth factor alpha. Am J Surg Pathol 1997, **21**: 1373–1377.

414 Vesoulis Z, Abrahams N, Becker J, Slezak F. Carcinoid-related angiomatous polyposis simulating Crohn disease. Arch Pathol Lab Med 2000, **124**: 450–454.

Microscopic types

415 Carstens PHB, Broghamer WL Jr, Hire D. Malignant fibrillo-caveolated cell carcinoma of the human intestinal tract. Hum Pathol 1976, **7**: 505–517.

416 Chejfec G, Capella C, Solcia E, Jao W, Gould VE. Amphicrine cells, dysplasias, and neoplasias. Cancer 1985, **56**: 2683–2690.

417 DeLellis RA, Tischler AS, Wolfe HJ. Multidirectional differentiation in neuroendocrine neoplasms. J Histochem Cytochem 1984, **32**: 899–904.

418 Höfler H, Klöppel G, Heitz PU. Combined production of mucus, amines and peptides by goblet-cell carcinoids of the appendix and ileum. Pathol Res Pract 1984, **178**: 555–561.

419 Johnson LA, Lavin P, Moertel CG, Weiland L, Dayal Y, Doos WG, Geller SA, Cooper HS, Nime F, Massé S, Simson IW, Sumner H, Fölsch E, Engstrom P. Carcinoids. The association of histologic growth pattern and survival. Cancer 1983, **51**: 882–889.

420 Soga J. Carcinoids. Their changing concepts and a new histologic classification. In Fujita T (ed.): Gastro-entero-pancreatic endocrine system. Stuttgart, 1974, Thieme.

Histochemical, immunohistochemical, and electron microscopic features

421 Azumi N, Traweek ST, Battifora H. Prostatic acid phosphatase in carcinoid tumors. Immunohistochemical and immunoblot studies. Am J Surg Pathol 1991, **15**: 785–790.

422 Bostwick DG, Roth KA, Barchas JD, Bensch KG. Gastrin-releasing peptide immunoreactivity in intestinal carcinoids. Am J Clin Pathol 1984, **82**: 428–431.

423 Cai YC, Banner B, Glickman J, Odze RD. Cytokeratin 7 and 20 and thyroid transcription factor 1 can help distinguish pulmonary from gastrointestinal carcinoid and pancreatic endocrine tumors. Hum Pathol 2001, **32**: 1087–1093.

424 Capella C, Heitz PU, Höfler H, Solcia E, Klöppel G. Revised classification of neuroendocrine tumors of the lung, pancreas and gut. Virchows Arch 1995, **425**: 547–560.

425 Emson PC, Gilbert RFT, Martensson H, Nobin A. Elevated concentrations of substance P and 5-HT in plasma in patients with carcinoid tumors. Cancer 1984, **54**: 715–718.

426 Hammond EH, Yowell RL, Flinner RL. Neuroendocrine carcinomas: role of immunocytochemistry and electron microscopy. Hum Pathol 1998, **29**: 1367–1371.

427 Iwafuchi M, Watanabe H, Ishihara N, Shimoda T, Iwashita A, Ito S. Peptide YY immunoreactive cells in gastrointestinal carcinoids. Immunohistochemical and ultrastructural studies of 60 tumors. Hum Pathol 1986, **17**: 291–296.

428 Katsetos CD, Jami MM, Krishna L, Jackson R, Patchefsky AS, Cooper HS. Novel immunohistochemical localization of 28,000 molecular-weight (Mr) calcium binding protein (calbindin-D28k) in enterochromaffin cells of the human appendix and neuroendocrine tumors (carcinoids and small-cell carcinomas) of the midgut and foregut. Arch Pathol Lab Med 1994, **118**: 633–639.

429 Krishnamurthy S, Dayal Y. Immunohistochemical expression of transforming growth factor alpha and epidermal growth factor receptor in gastrointestinal carcinoids. Am J Surg Pathol 1997, **21**: 327–333.

430 La Rosa S, Uccella S, Erba S, Capella C, Sessa F. Immunohistochemical detection of fibroblast growth factor receptors in normal endocrine cells and related tumors of the digestive system. Appl Immunohistochem Mol Morphol 2001, **9**: 319–328.

431 La Rosa S, Capella C, Lloyd RV. Localization of myosin XVA in endocrine tumor of gut and pancreas. Endocr Pathol 2002, **13**: 29–37.

432 Lundqvist M, Wilander E. Somatostatin-like immunoreactivity in mid-gut carcinoids. Acta Pathol Microbiol Scand A 1981, **89**: 335–337.

433 Lundqvist M, Wilander E. Subepithelial neuroendocrine cells and carcinoid tumours of the human small intestine and appendix. A comparative immunohistochemical study with regard to serotonin, neuron-specific enolase and S-100 protein reactivity. J Pathol 1986, **148**: 141–147.

434 Lundqvist M, Wilander E. A study of the histopathogenesis of carcinoid tumors of the small intestine and appendix. Cancer 1987, **60**: 201–206.

435 Martin JME, Maung RT. Differential immunohistochemical reactions of carcinoid tumors. Hum Pathol 1987, **18**: 941–945.

436 Mertz H, Vyberg M, Paulsen SM, Teglbjaerg PS. Immunohistochemical detection of neuroendocrine markers in tumors of the lungs and gastrointestinal tract. Appl Immunohistochem 1998, **6**: 175–180.

437 Miettinen M, Lehto V-P, Dahl D, Virtanen I. Varying expression of cytokeratin and neurofilaments in neuroendocrine tumors of human gastrointestinal tract. Lab Invest 1985, **52**: 429–436.

438 Mooney EE, Casey M, Dervan PA. Intermediate filament expression in carcinoid tumors. Ir J Med Sci 1991, **160**: 339–341.

439 Moyana TN, Satkunam N. A comparative immunohistochemical study of jejunoileal and appendiceal carcinoids. Implications for histogenesis and pathogenesis. Cancer 1992, **70**: 1081–1088.

440 Nash SV, Said JW. Gastroenteropancreatic neuroendocrine tumors. A histochemical and immunohistochemical study of epithelial (keratin proteins, carcinoembryonic antigen) and neuroendocrine (neuron-specific enolase, bombesin and chromogranin) markers in foregut, midgut, and hindgut tumors. Am J Clin Pathol 1986, **86**: 415–422.

441 Nilsson O, Wangberg B, McRae A, Dahlstrom A, Ahlman H. Growth factors and carcinoid tumours. Acta Oncol 1993, **32**: 115–124.

442 Papotti M, Bongiovanni M, Volante M, Allia E, Landolfi S, Helboe L, Schindler M, Cole SL, Bussolati G. Expression of somatostatin receptor types 1-5 in 81 cases of gastrointestinal and pancreatic endocrine tumors. A correlative immunohistochemical and reverse-transcriptase polymerase chain reaction analysis. Virchows Arch 2002, **440**: 461–475.

443 Portela-Gomes GM, Grimelius L, Johansson H, Wilander E, Stridsberg M. Cromogranin A in human neuroendocrine tumors: an immunohistochemical study with region-specific antibodies. Am J Surg Pathol 2001, **25**: 1261–1267.

444 Rode J, Dhillon AP, Doran JF, Jackson P, Thompson RJ. PGP 9.5, a new marker for human neuroendocrine tumors. Histopathology 1985, **9**: 147–158.

445 Simpson S, Vinik AI, Marangos PJ, Lloyd RV. Immunohistochemical localization of neuron-specific enolase in gastroenteropancreatic neuroendocrine tumors. Correlation with tissue and serum levels of neuron-specific enolase. Cancer 1984, **54**: 1364–1369.

446 Sobin LH, Hjermstad BM, Sesterhenn IA, Helwig EB. Prostatic acid phosphatase activity in carcinoid tumors. Cancer 1986, **58**: 136–138.

447 Takatoh H, Iwamoto H, Ikezu M, Katoh N, Ito S, Kaneko H. Immunohistochemical demonstration of peptide YY in gastrointestinal endocrine tumors. Acta Pathol Jpn 1987, **37**: 737–746.

448 Walts AE, Said JW, Shintaku IP, Lloyd RV. Chromogranin as a marker of neuroendocrine cells in cytologic material—an immunocytochemical study. Am J Clin Pathol 1985, **84**: 273–277.

449 Wick MR. Immunohistology of neuroendocrine and neurectodermal tumors. Semin Diagn Pathol 2000, **17**: 194–203.

450 Wilander E, El-Salhy M. Immuno-cyto-chemical staining of mid-gut carcinoid tumours with sequence-specific gastrin antisera. Acta Pathol Microbiol Scand A 1981, **89**: 247–250.

451 Wilander E, Lundqvist M, El-Salhy M. Serotonin in fore-gut carcinoids. A survey of 60 cases with regard to silver stains, formalin-induced fluorescence and serotonin immunocytochemistry. J Pathol 1985, **145**: 251–258.

452 Wilander E, Scheibenpflug L. Cytokeratin expression in small intestinal and appendiceal carcinoids. A basis for classification. Acta Oncol 1993, **32**: 131–134.

453 Yang K, Ulich T, Cheng L, Lewin KJ. The neuroendocrine

products of intestinal carcinoids. An immunoperoxidase study of 35 carcinoid tumors stained for serotonin and eight polypeptide hormones. Cancer 1983, **51**: 1918–1926.

454 Zhang PJ, Harris KR, Alobeid B, Bros JJ. Immunoexpression of villin in neuroendocrine tumors and its diagnostic implications. Arch Pathol Lab Med 1999, **123**: 812–816.

Molecular genetic features

455 D'Adda T, Pizzi S, Azzoni C, Bottarelli L, Crafa P, Pasquali C, Davoli C, Corleto VD, Fave GD, Bordi C. Different patterns of 11q allelic losses in digestive endocrine tumors. Hum Pathol 2002, **33**: 322–329.

456 Goolsby CL, Punyarit P, Mehl PJ, Rao MS. Flow cytometric DNA analysis of carcinoid tumors of the ileum and appendix. Hum Pathol 1992, **23**: 1340–1343.

457 Moyana TN, Xiang J, Senthilsevan A, Kulaga A. The spectrum of neuroendocrine differentiation among gastrointestinal carcinoids: importance of histologic grading, MIB-1, p53, and bcl-2 immunoreactivity. Arch Pathol Lab Med 2000, **124**: 570–576.

458 Weckstrom P, Hedrum A, Makridis C, Akerstrom G, Rastad J, Scheibenpflug L, Uhlen M, Juhlin C, Wilander E. Midgut carcinoids and solid carcinomas of the intestine: differences in endocrine markers and p53 mutations. Endocr Pathol 1996, **7**: 273–280.

Spread and metastases

459 Dent GA, Feldman JM. Pseudocystic liver metastases in patients with carcinoid tumors. Report of three cases. Am J Clin Pathol 1984, **82**: 275–279.

460 Lechago J. Gastrointestinal neuroendocrine cell proliferations. Hum Pathol 1994, **25**: 1114–1122.

461 Modlin IM, Sandor A. An analysis of 8305 cases of carcinoid tumors. Cancer 1997, **79**: 813–829.

462 Rodriguez G, Villamizar R. Carcinoid tumor with skin metastasis. Am J Dermatopathol 1992, **14**: 263–269.

Treatment and prognosis

463 Capella C, Heitz Pu, Höfler H, Solcia E, Klöppel G. Revised classification of neuroendoerine tumors of the lung, pancreas and gut. Virchows Arch 1995, **425**: 547–560.

464 Federspiel BH, Burke AP, Shekitka KM, Sobin LH. Carcinoembryonic antigen and carcinoids of the gastrointestinal tract. Mod Pathol 1990, **3**: 586–590.

465 Godwin JD II. Carcinoid tumors. An analysis of 2837 cases. Cancer 1975, **36**: 560–569.

466 Hayashi H, Nakagawa M, Kitagawa S, Yamada T, Ishida K, Kurumaya H. Immunohistochemical analysis of gastrointestinal carcinoids. Gastroenterol Jpn 1993, **28**: 483–490.

467 Moertel CG, Sauer WG, Dockerty MB, Baggenstoss AH. Life history of the carcinoid tumor of the small intestine. Cancer 1961, **14**: 901–912.

468 Zakariai YM, Quan SHQ, Hajdu SI. Carcinoid tumors of the gastrointestinal tract. Cancer 1975, **35**: 588–591.

Carcinoid syndrome

469 Anthony PP. Gangrene of the small intestine—a complication of argentaffin carcinoma. Br J Surg 1970, **57**: 118–122.

470 Feldman JM. Carcinoid tumors and syndrome. Semin Oncol 1987, **14**: 237–246.

471 Feldman JM, Jones RS. Carcinoid syndrome from gastrointestinal carcinoids without liver metastasis. Ann Surg 1982, **196**: 33–37.

472 Fries JF, Lindgren JA, Bull JM. Scleroderma-like lesions and the carcinoid syndrome. Arch Intern Med 1973, **131**: 550–553.

473 Ganim RB, Norton JA. Recent advances in carcinoid pathogenesis, diagnosis and management. Surg Oncol 2000, **9**: 173–179.

474 Kuwada SK. Carcinoid tumors. Semin Gastrointest Dis 2000, **11**: 157–161.

475 Modhi G, Nicolis G. Hypoglycemia associated with carcinoid tumors. A case report and review of the literature. Cancer 1984, **53**: 1804–1806.

476 Oates JA. The carcinoid syndrome. N Engl J Med 1986, **315**: 702–703.

477 Pelletier G, Cortot A, Launay J-M, Debons-Guillemain M-C, Nemeth J, Le Charpentier Y, Celerier M, Modigliani R. Serotonin-secreting and insulin secreting ileal carcinoid tumor and the use of in vitro culture of tumoral cells. Cancer 1984, **54**: 319–322.

478 Qizilbash AH. Carcinoid tumors, vascular elastosis, and ischemic disease of the small intestine. Dis Colon Rectum 1977, **20**: 554–560.

479 Quaedvlieg PF, Lamers CB, Taal BG. Carcinoid heart disease: an update. Scand J Gastroenterol Suppl 2002, **236**: 66–71.

480 Sandler M, Williams ED, Karim SMM. The occurrence of prostaglandins in amine-peptide-secreting tumours. In Mantegazza P, Horton EW (eds.): Prostaglandins, peptides and amines. London and New York, 1969, Academic Press Inc.

Duodenal endocrine tumors

481 Alumets J, Ekelund G, Hakanson R, Ljundberg O, Ljungquist U, Sundler F, Tibblin S. Jejunal endocrine tumour composed of somatostatin and gastrin cells and associated with duodenal ulcer disease. Virchows Arch [A] 1978, **378**: 17–22.

482 Attanoos R, Williams GT. Epithelial and neuroendocrine tumors of the duodenum. Semin Diagn Pathol 1991, **8**: 149–162.

483 Bisceglia M, Giordano M, Bosman C. Argyrophil-negative G-cell duodenal carcinoid. Am J Gastroenterol 1992, **87**: 534–537.

484 Burke AP, Federspiel BH, Sobin LH, Shekitka KM, Helwig EB. Carcinoids of the duodenum. A histologic and immunohistochemical study of 65 tumors. Am J Surg Pathol 1989, **13**: 828–837.

485 Burke AP, Sobin LH, Federspiel BH, Shekitka KM, Helwig EB. Carcinoid tumors of the duodenum. A clinicopathologic study of 99 cases. Arch Pathol Lab Med 1990, **114**: 700–704.

486 Burke AP, Sobin LH, Shekitka KM, Federspiel BH, Helwig EB. Somatostatin-producing duodenal carcinoids in patients with von Recklinghausen's neurofibromatosis. A predilection for black patients. Cancer 1990, **65**: 1591–1595.

487 Capella C, Riva C, Rindi G, Sessa F, Usellini L, Chiaravalli A, Carnevali L, Solcia E. Histopathology, hormone products, and clinicopathological profile of endocrine tumors of the upper small intestine. A study of 44 cases. Endocr Pathol 1991, **2**: 92–110.

488 Dayal Y, Doos WG, O'Brien MJ, Nunnemacher G, DeLellis RA, Wolfe HJ. Psammomatous somatostatinomas of the duodenum. Am J Surg Pathol 1983, **7**: 653–665.

489 Dayal Y, Tallberg KA, Nunnemacher G, DeLellis RA, Wolfe HJ. Duodenal carcinoids in patients with and without neurofibromatosis. A comparative study. Am J Surg Pathol 1986, **10**: 348–357.

490 Greider MH, DeSchryver-Kecskemeti K, Kraus FT. Psammoma bodies in endocrine tumors of the gastroenteropancreatic axis. A rather common occurrence. Semin Diagn Pathol 1984, **1**: 19–29.

491 Griffiths DFR, Jasani B, Newman GR, Williams ED, Williams GT. Glandular duodenal carcinoid – a somatostatin rich tumor with neuroendocrine associations. J Clin Pathol 1984, **37**: 163–169.

492 Hirakawa K, Iida M, Matsui T, Matsumoto T, Nakao Y, Yao T, Fuchigami T, Fujishima M. Endoscopic findings in carcinoid tumor of the duodenum. Am J Gastroenterol 1991, **86**: 603–605.

493 Marcial MA, Pinkus GS, Skarin A, Hinrichs HR, Warhol MJ. Ampullary somatostatinoma. Psammomatous variant of gastrointestinal carcinoid tumor – an immunohistochemical and ultrastructural study. Report of a case and review of the literature. Am J Clin Pathol 1983, **80**: 755–761.

494 Miyazaki K, Funakoshi A, Nishihara S, Wasada T, Koga A, Ibayashi H. Aberrant insulinoma in the duodenum. Gastroenterology 1986, **90**: 1280–1285.

495 Pipeleers-Marichal M, Somers G, Willems G, Foulis A, Imrie C, Bishop AL, Polak JM, Häck WH, Stamm B, Heitz PU, Klöppel G. Gastrinomas in the duodenums of patients with multiple endocrine neoplasia type 1 and the Zollinger-Ellison syndrome. N Engl J Med 1990, **322**: 723–727.

496 Tanaka S, Yamasaki S, Matsushita H, Osawa Y, Kurosaki A, Takeuchi K, Hoshihara Y, Doi T, Watanabe G, Kawaminami K. Duodenal somatostatinoma: a case report and review of 31 cases with special reference to the relationship between tumor size and metastasis. Pathol Int 2000, **50**: 146–152.

497 Vesoulis Z, Petras RE. Duodenal microgastrinoma producing the Zollinger Ellison syndrome. Arch Pathol Lab Med 1985, **109**: 40–42.

498 Yoshida A, Hatanaka S, Ohi Y, Umekita Y, Yoshida H. Von Recklinghausen's disease associated with somatostatin-rich duodenal carcinoid (somatostatinoma) medullary thyroid carcinoma and diffuse adrenal medullary hyperplasia. Acta Pathol Jpn 1991, **41**: 847–856.

Gangliocytic paraganglioma

499 Altavilla G, Chiarelli S, Fassina A. Duodenal periampullary gangliocytic paraganglioma: report of two cases with immunohistochemical and ultrastructural study. Ultrastruct Pathol 2001, **25**: 137–145.

500 Burke AP, Helwig EB. Gangliocytic paraganglioma. Am J Clin Pathol 1989, **92**: 1–9.

501 Collina G, Maiorana A, Trentini GP. Duodenal gangliocytic paraganglioma. Case report with immunohistochemical study on the expression of keratin polypeptides. Histopathology 1991, **19**: 476–478.

502 Dookhan DB, Miettinen M, Finkel G, Gibas Z. Recurrent duodenal gangliocytic paraganglioma with lymph node metastases. Histopathology 1993, **22**: 399–401.

503 Guarda LA, Ordóñez NG, del Junco GW, Luna MA. Gangliocytic paraganglioma of the duodenum. An immunocytochemical study. Am J Gastroenterol 1983, **78**: 794–798.

504 Hamid QA, Bishop AE, Rode J, Dhillon AP, Rosenberg BF, Reed RJ, Sibley RK, Polak JM. Duodenal gangliocytic paragangliomas. A study of 10 cases with immunocytochemical neuroendocrine markers. Hum Pathol 1986, **17**: 1151–1157.

505 Hashimoto S, Kawasaki S, Matsuzawa K, Harada H, Makuuchi M. Gangliocytic paraganglioma of the papilla of Vater with regional lymph node metastasis. Am J Gastroenterol 1992, **87**: 1216–1218.

506 Inai K, Kobuke T, Yonehara S, Tokuoka S. Duodenal gangliocytic paraganglioma with lymph node metastasis in a 17-year old boy. Cancer 1989, **63**: 2540–2545.

507 Kawaguchi K, Takizawa T, Koike M, Tabata I, Goseki N. Multiple paraganglioneuromas. Virchows Arch [A] 1985, **406**: 373–380.

508 Kepes JJ, Zacharias DL. Gangliocytic paragangliomas of the duodenum. Report of two cases with light and electron microscopic examination. Cancer 1971, **27**: 61–70.

509 Kheir SM, Halpern NB. Paraganglioma of the duodenum in association with congenital neurofibromatosis. Possible relationship. Cancer 1984, **53**: 2491–2496.

510 Min KW. Gangliocytic paraganglioma of the duodenum: report of a case with immunocytochemical and ultrastructural investigation. Ultrastruct Pathol 1997, **21**: 587–595.

511 Perrone T, Sibley RK, Rosai J. Duodenal gangliocytic paraganglioma. An immunohistochemical and ultrastructural study and a hypothesis concerning its origin. Am J Surg Pathol 1985, **9**: 31–41.

512 Reed RJ, Daroca PJ Jr, Harkin JC. Gangliocytic paraganglioma. Am J Surg Pathol 1977, **1**: 207–216.

513 Scheithauer BW, Nora FE, Lechago J, Wick MR, Crawford BG, Weiland LH, Carney JA. Duodenal gangliocytic paraganglioma. Clinicopathologic and immunocytochemical study of 11 cases. Am J Clin Pathol 1986, **86**: 559–565.

514 Stephens M, Williams GT, Jasani B, Williams ED. Synchronous duodenal neuroendocrine tumours in von Recklinghausen's disease. A case report of coexisting gangliocytic paraganglioma and somatostatin-rich glandular carcinoid. Histopathology 1987, **11**: 1331–1340.

515 Taylor HB, Helwig EB. Benign nonchromaffin paragangliomas of the duodenum. Virchows Arch [A] 1962, **335**: 356–366.

516 Van Eeden S, Offerhaus GJ, Peterse HL, Dingemans KP, Blaauwgeers HLG. Gangliocytic paraganglioma of the appendix. Histopathology 2000, **36**: 47–49.

Gastrointestinal stromal tumors and related tumors

517 Brainard JA, Goldblum JR. Stromal tumors of the jejunum and ileum: a clinicopathologic study of 39 cases. Am J Surg Pathol 1997, **21**: 407–416.

518 Cooper PN, Quirke P, Hardy GJ, Dixon MF. A flow cytometric, clinical, and histological study of stromal neoplasms of the gastrointestinal tract. Am J Surg Pathol 1992, **16**: 163–170.

519 Cunningham RE, Federspiel BH, McCarthy WF, Sobin LH, O'Leary TJ. Predicting prognosis of gastrointestinal smooth muscle tumors. Role of clinical and histologic evaluation, flow cytometry, and image cytometry. Am J Surg Pathol 1993, **17**: 588–594.

520 Goldblum JR, Appelman HD. Stromal tumors of the duodenum. A histologic and immunohistochemical study of 20 cases. Am J Surg Pathol 1995, **19**: 71–80.

521 Handra-Luca A, Fléjou JF, Molas G, Sauvanet A, Belghiti J, Degott C, Terris B. Familial multiple gastrointestinal stromal tumours with associated abnormalities of the myenteric plexus layer and skeinoid fibres. Histopathology 2001, **39**: 359–363.

522 Ishida T, Wada I, Horiuchi H, Oka T, Machinami R. Multiple small intestinal stromal tumors with skeinoid fibers in association with neurofibromatosis 1 (von Recklinghausen's disease). Pathol Int 1996, **46**: 689–695.

523 Jeng YM, Mao TL, Hsu WM. Congenital interstitial cell of Cajal hyperplasia with neuronal intestinal dysplasia. Am J Surg Pathol 2000, **24**: 1568–1572.

524 Ma CK, Peralta MN, Amin MB, Linden MD, Dekovich AA, Kubus JJ, Zarbo RJ. Small intestinal stromal tumors. A clinicopathologic study of 20 cases with immunohistochemical assessment of cell differentiation and the prognostic role of proliferation antigens. Am J Clin Pathol 1997, **108**: 641–651.

525 McClain KL, Leach CT, Jenson HB, Joshi W, Pollock BH, Parmley RT, DiCarlo FJ, Chadwick EG, Murphy SB. Association of Epstein-Barr virus with leiomyosarcomas in young people with AIDS. N Engl J Med 1995, **332**: 12–18.

525a Miettinen M, Kopczynski J, Makhlouf HR, Sarlomo-Rikala M, Gyorffy H, Burke A, Sobin LH, Lasota J. Gastrointestinal stromal tumors, intramural leiomyomas, and leiomyosarcomas in the duodenum. Am J Surg Pathol 2003, **27**: 625–641.

526 Ng EH, Pollock RE, Munsell MF, Atkinson EN, Romsdahl MM. Prognostic factors influencing survival in gastrointestinal leiomyosarcomas. Implications for surgical management and staging. Ann Surg 1992, **215**: 68–77.

527 O'Brien P, Kapusta L, Dardick I, Axler J, Gnidec A. Multiple familial gastrointestinal autonomic nerve tumors and small intestinal neuronal dysplasia. Am J Surg Pathol 1999, **23**: 198–204.

528 Ranchod M, Kempson RL. Smooth muscle tumors of the gastrointestinal tract and retroperitoneum. A pathologic analysis of 100 cases. Cancer 1977, **39**: 255–262.

529 Ricci A Jr, Ciccarelli O, Cartun RW, Newcomb P. A clinicopathologic and immunohistochemical study of 16 patients with small intestinal leiomyosarcoma. Limited utility of immunophenotyping. Cancer 1987, **60**: 1790–1799.

530 Shiu MH, Farr GH, Egeli RA, Quan SHG, Hajdu SI. Myosarcomas of the small and large intestine. A clinicopathologic study. J Surg Oncol 1983, **24**: 67–72.

531 Tworek JA, Appelman HD, Singleton TP, Greenson JK. Stromal tumors of the jejunum and ileum. Mod Pathol 1997, **10**: 200–209.

532 Vallaeys JH, Cuvelier CA, Bekaert L, Roels H. Combined leiomyomatosis of the small intestine and colon. Arch Pathol Lab Med 1993, **116**: 281–283.

533 Weiss RA, Mackay B. Malignant smooth muscle tumors of the gastrointestinal tract. An ultrastructural study of 20 cases. J Ultrastruct Pathol 1981, **2**: 231–240.

534 Wilson JM, Melvin DB, Gray GF, Thorbjarnarson B. Primary malignancies of the small bowel. A report of 96 cases and review of the literature. Ann Surg 1974, **180**: 175–179.

Malignant lymphoma and related disorders

535 Appelman HD, Hirsch SD, Schnitzer B, Coon WW. Clinicopathologic overview of gastrointestinal lymphomas. Am J Surg Pathol 1985, **9**: 71–83.

536 Artinian B, Lough JO, Palmer JD. Idiopathic ulcer of small bowel with pseudolymphomatous reactions. A clinicopathological study of six cases. Arch Pathol 1971, **91**: 327–333.

537 Asselah F, Slavin G, Sowter G, Asselah H. Immunoproliferative small intestinal disease in Algerians. Part I. Light microscopic and immunochemical studies. Cancer 1983, **52**: 227–237.

538 Atwell JD, Burge D, Wright D. Nodular lymphoid hyperplasia of the intestinal tract in infancy and childhood. J Pediatr Surg 1985, **20**: 25–29.

538a Bende RJ, Smit LA, Bossenbroek JG, Aarts WM, Spaargaren M, De Leval L, Boeckxstaens GEE, Pals ST, Van Noesel CJM. Primary follicular lymphoma of the small intestine. Am J Pathol 2003, **162**: 105–113.

539 Brugo EA, Larkin E, Molina-Escobar J, Costanzi J. Primary granulocytic sarcoma of the small bowel. Cancer 1975, **35**: 1333–1340.

540 Burke JS, Sheibani K, Nathwani BN, Winberg CD, Rappaport H. Monoclonal small (well-differentiated) lymphocytic proliferations of the gastrointestinal tract resembling lymphoid hyperplasia. A neoplasm of uncertain malignant potential. Hum Pathol 1987, **18**: 1238–1245.

541 Carey MJ, Medeiros LJ, Roepke JE, Kjeldsberg CR, Elenitoba-Johnson KS. Primary anaplastic large cell lymphoma of the small intestine. Am J Clin Pathol 1999, **112**: 696–701.

542 Chan JK. Gastrointestinal lymphomas: an overview with emphasis on new findings and diagnostic problems. Semin Diagn Pathol 1996, **13**: 260–296.

543 Chott A, Dragosics B, Radaszkiewicz T. Peripheral T-cell lymphomas of the intestine. Am J Pathol 1992, **141**: 1361–1371.

544 Chott A, Vesely M, Simonitsch I, Mosberger I, Hanak H. Classification of intestinal T-cell neoplasms and their differential diagnosis. Am J Clin Pathol 1999, **111**: S68–S74.

545 Chott A, Haedicke W, Mosberger I, Fodinger M, Winkler K, Mannhalter C, Muller-Hermelink HK. Most CD56+ intestinal lymphomas are CD8+CD5– T-cell lymphomas of monomorphic small to medium size histology. Am J Pathol 1998, **153**: 1483–1490.

546 Crump M, Gospodarowicz M, Shepherd FA. Lymphoma of the gastrointestinal tract. Semin Oncol 1999, **26**: 324–337.

547 Domizio P, Owen RA, Shepherd NA, Talbot IC, Norton AJ. Primary lymphoma of the small intestine. A clinicopathological study of 119 cases. Am J Surg Pathol 1993, **17**: 429–442.

548 Drut R, Drut RM. Primary angiocentric T-cell intestinal lymphoma with Epstein-Barr virus in a 5-year-old boy. Int J Surg Pathol 2001, **9**: 163–168.

549 Filippa DA, Lieberman PH, Weingrad DN, Decosse JJ, Bretsky SS. Primary lymphomas of the gastrointestinal tract. Analysis of prognostic factors with emphasis on histological type. Am J Surg Pathol 1983, **7**: 363–372.

550 Fung DT, Chan JK, Tse CC, Sze WM. Myxoid change in malignant lymphoma. Pathogenetic considerations. Arch Pathol Lab Med 1992, **116**: 103–105.

551 Gonzalez-Vitale JC, Gomez LG, Goldblum RM, Goldman AS, Patterson M. Immunoblastic lymphoma of small intestine complicating late-onset immunodeficiency. Cancer 1982, **49**: 445–449.

552 Griffiths AP, Shepherd NA, Beddall A, Williams JG. Gastrointestinal tumour masses due to multiple myeloma: a pathological mimic of malignant lymphoma. Histopathology 1997, **31**: 318–323.

553 Grody WW, Weiss LM, Warnke RA, Magidson JG, Hu E, Lewin KJ. Gastrointestinal lymphomas. Immunohistochemical studies on the cell of origin. Am J Surg Pathol 1985, **9**: 328–337.

554 Guettier C, Hamilton-Dutoit S, Guillemain R, Farge D, Amrein C, Vulser C, Hofman P, Carpentier A, Diebold J. Primary gastrointestinal malignant lymphomas associated with Epstein-Barr virus after heart transplantation. Histopathology 1992, **20**: 21–28.

555 Haghighi P, Kharazmi A, Gerami C, Haghshenass M, Abadi P, Omidi H, Mostafavi N. Primary upper small intestinal lymphoma and alpha-chain disease. Report of 10 cases emphasizing pathological aspects. Am J Surg Pathol 1978, **2**: 147–157.

556 Hall PA, Levison DA. Malignant lymphoma in the gastrointestinal tract. Semin Diagn Pathol 1991, **8**: 163–177.

557 Halphen M, Najjar T, Jaafoura H, Cammoun M, groupe Trufali. Diagnostic value of upper intestinal fiber endoscopy in primary small intestinal lymphoma. A prospective study by the Tunisian-French Intestinal Lymphoma Group. Cancer 1986, **58**: 2140–2145.

558 Hashimoto Y, Nakamura N, Kuze T, Ono N, Abe M. Multiple lymphomatous polyposis of the gastrointestinal tract is a heterogenous group that includes mantle cell lymphoma and follicular lymphoma: analysis of somatic mutation of immunoglobulin heavy chain gene variable region. Hum Pathol 1999, **30**: 581–587.

559 Henry K, Farrer-Brown G. Primary lymphomas of the gastrointestinal tract. Part I. Plasma cell tumors. Histopathology 1977, **1**: 53–76.

560 Hermans PE, Huizenga KA, Hoffman HN, Brown AL, Markowitz H. Dysgammaglobulinemia associated with nodular lymphoid hyperplasia of the small intestine. Am J Med 1966, **40**: 78–89.

561 Hernandez JA, Sheehan WW. Lymphomas of the mucosa-associated lymphoid tissue. Signet ring cell lymphomas presenting in mucosal lymphoid organs. Cancer 1985, **55**: 592–597.

562 Holowood K, Stamp G, Zouvani J, Fletcher CDM. Extranodal follicular dendritic cell sarcoma of the gastrointestinal tract. Morphologic, immunohistochemical and ultrastructural analysis of two cases. Am J Clin Pathol 1995, **103**: 90–97.

563 Isaacson P. Middle East lymphoma and α-chain disease. An immunohistochemical study. Am J Surg Pathol 1979, **3**: 431–441.

564 Isaacson PG. Middle Eastern intestinal lymphoma. Semin Diagn Pathol 1985, **2**: 210–223.

565 Isaacson PG. Gastrointestinal lymphoma. Hum Pathol 1994, **25**: 1020–1029.

566 Isaacson PG, Price SK. Light chains in Mediterranean lymphoma. J Clin Pathol 1985, **38**: 601–607.

567 Isaacson PG. Gastrointestinal lymphomas of T- and B-cell types. Mod Pathol 1999, **12**: 151–158.

568 Khojasteh A, Haghshenass M, Haghighi P. Immunoproliferative small intestinal disease. A "third-world lesion." N Engl J Med 1983, **308**: 1401–1405.

568a Kohno S, Ohshima K, Yoneda S, Kodama T, Shirakusa T, Kikuchi M. Clinicopathological analysis of 143 primary malignant lymphomas in the small and large intestines based on the new WHO classification. Histopathology 2003, **43**: 135–143.

569 Kraemer BB, Foucar K, Osborne B, Butler JJ. Bacterial infection simulating granulocytic sarcoma of the small bowel. Am J Clin Pathol 1981, **76**: 227–231.

570 Kwee WS, Wils JAMJ, van den Tweel JG. Malignant lymphoma,

immunoblastic with plasmacytic differentiation, complicating Crohn's disease. Histopathology 1985, **9**: 1115–1120.

571 Lavergne A, Brocheriou I, Delfau MH, Copie-Bergman C, Houdart R, Gaulard PH. Primary intestinal gamma-delta T-cell lymphoma with evidence of Epstein-Barr virus. Histopathology 1998, **32**: 271–276.

572 LeBrun DP, Kamel OW, Cleary ML, Dorfman RF, Warnke RA. Follicular lymphomas of the gastrointestinal tract. Pathologic features in 31 cases and bcl-2 oncogenic protein expression. Am J Pathol 1992, **140**: 1327–1335.

573 Lewin KJ, Kahn LB, Novis BH. Primary intestinal lymphoma of "Western" and "Mediterranean" type, alpha chain disease and massive plasma cell infiltration. A comparative study of 37 cases. Cancer 1976, **38**: 2511–2528.

574 Lewin KJ, Ranchod M, Dorfman RF. Lymphomas of the gastrointestinal tract. A study of 117 cases presenting with gastrointestinal disease. Cancer 1978, **42**: 693–707.

575 Matuchansky C, Touchard G, Lemaire M, Babin P, Demeocq F, Fonck Y, Meyer M, Preud'homme J-L. Malignant lymphoma of the small bowel associated with diffuse nodular lymphoid hyperplasia. N Engl J Med 1985, **313**: 166–171.

576 McDonald GB, Schuffler MD, Kadin ME, Tytgat GNJ. Intestinal pseudoobstruction caused by diffuse lymphoid infiltration of the small intestine. Gastroenterology 1985, **89**: 882–889.

577 Miettinen M, Fletcher CD, Lasota J. True histiocytic lymphoma of small intestine. Analysis of two S-100 protein-positive cases with features of interdigitating reticulum cell sarcoma. Am J Clin Pathol 1993, **100**: 285–292.

578 Milchgrub S, Kamel OW, Wiley E, Vuitch F, Cleary ML, Warnke RA. Malignant histiocytic neoplasms of the small intestine. Am J Surg Pathol 1992, **16**: 11–20.

579 Najem AZ, Porcaro JL, Rush BF Jr. Primary non-Hodgkin's lymphoma of the duodenum. Case report and literature review. Cancer 1984, **54**: 895–898.

580 Nakamura S, Matsumoto T, Takeshita M, Kurahara K, Yao T, Tsuneyoshi M, Iida M, Fujishima M. A clinicopathologic study of primary small intestine lymphoma: prognostic significance of mucosa-associated lymphoid tissue-derived lymphoma. Cancer 2000, **88**: 286–294.

581 Nalesnik MA. Involvement of the gastrointestinal tract by Epstein-Barr virus-associated posttransplant lymphoproliferative disorders. Am J Surg Pathol 1990, **14**(Suppl 1): 92–100.

582 Nassar VH, Salem PA, Shahid MJ, Alami SY, Balikian JB, Salem AA, Nasrallah SM. "Mediterranean abdominal lymphoma" or immunoproliferative small intestinal disease. Part II. Pathological aspects. Cancer 1978, **41**: 1340–1354.

583 O'Briain DS, Kennedy MJ, Daly PA, O'Briain AA, Tanner WA, Rogers P, Lawlor E. Multiple lymphomatous polyposis of the gastrointestinal tract. A clinicopathologically distinctive form of non-Hodgkin's lymphoma of B-cell centrocytic type. Am J Surg Pathol 1989, **13**: 691–699.

584 Pangalis GA, Rappaport H. Common clonal origin of lymphoplasmacytic proliferation and immunoblastic lymphoma and intestinal alpha-chain disease. Lancet 1977, **2**: 880.

585 Price SK. Immunoproliferative small intestinal disease. A study of 13 cases with alpha heavy-chain disease. Histopathology 1990, **17**: 7–17.

586 Ranchod M, Lewin KJ, Dorfman RF. Lymphoid hyperplasia of the gastrointestinal tract. A study of 26 cases and review of the literature. Am J Surg Pathol 1978, **2**: 383–400.

587 Rappaport H, Ramot B, Hulu N, Park JK. The pathology of so-called Mediterranean abdominal lymphoma with malabsorption. Cancer 1972, **29**: 1502–1514.

588 Rubin A, Isaacson PG. Florid reactive lymphoid hyperplasia of the terminal ileum in adults. A condition bearing a close resemblance to low-grade malignant lymphoma. Histopathology 1990, **17**: 19–26.

589 Salem P, El-Hashimi L, Anaissie E, Geha S, Habboubi N, Ibrahim N, Khalyl M, Allam C. Primary small intestinal lymphoma in adults. A comparative study of IPSID versus non-IPSID in the Middle East. Cancer 1987, **59**: 1670–1676.

590 Shepherd NA, Blackshaw AJ, Hall PA, Bostad L, Coates PJ, Lowe DG, Levison DA, Morson BC, Stansfeld AG. Malignant lymphoma with eosinophilia of the gastrointestinal tract. Histopathology 1987, **11**: 115–130.

591 Shepherd NA, McCarthy KP, Hall PA. 14; 18 translocation in primary intestinal lymphoma. Detection by polymerase chain reaction in routinely processed tissue. Histopathology 1991, **18**: 415–419.

592 Shia J, Teruya-Feldstein, Pan D, Hegde A, Klimstra DS, Chaganti RSK, Qin J, Portlock CS, Filippa DA. Primary follicular lymphoma of the gastrointestinal tract: a clinical and pathologic study of 26 cases. Am J Surg Pathol 2002, **26**: 216–224.

593 Thieblemont C, Bastion Y, Berger F, Rieux C, Salles G, Dumontet C, Felman P, Coiffier B. Mucosa-associated lymphoid tissue gastrointestinal and nongastrointestinal lymphoma behavior: analysis of 108 patients. J Clin Oncol 1997, **15**: 1624–1630.

594 Van Krieken JH, Medeiros LP, Pals ST, Raffeld M, Kluin PM. Diffuse aggressive B-cell lymphomas of the gastrointestinal tract. An immunophenotypic and gene rearrangement analysis of 22 cases. Am J Clin Pathol 1992, **97**: 170–178.

595 Ward H, Jalan KN, Maitra TK, Agarwal SK, Mahalanabis D. Small intestinal nodular lymphoid hyperplasia in patients with giardiasis and normal serum immunoglobulins. Gut 1983, **24**: 120–126.

596 Weaver DK, Batsakis JG. Pseudolymphomas of the small intestine. Am J Gastroenterol 1965, **44**: 374–381.

597 Weiss RL, Lazarus KH, Macon WR, Gulley ML, Kjeldsberg CR. Natural killer-like T-cell lymphoma in the small intestine of a child without evidence of enteropathy. Am J Surg Pathol 1997, **21**: 964–969.

598 Williamson RCN, Welch CE, Malt RA. Adenocarcinoma and lymphoma of the small intestine. Distribution and etiologic associations. Ann Surg 1983, **197**: 172–178.

599 Yoshino T, Miyake K, Ichimura K, Mannami T, Ohara N, Hamazaki S, Akagi T. Increased incidence of follicular lymphoma in the duodenum. Am J Surg Pathol 2000, **24**: 688–693.

Other tumors and tumorlike conditions

600 Aase S, Gundersen R. Submucous lymphatic cysts of the small intestine. An autopsy study. Acta Pathol Microbiol Immunol Scand A 1983, **91**: 191–194.

601 Adair C, Ro JY, Sahin AA, El-Naggar AK, Ordóñez NG, Ayala AG. Malignant melanoma metastatic to gastrointestinal tract. A clinicopathologic study. Int J Surg Pathol 1994, **2**: 3–10.

602 Allibone RO, Nanson JK, Anthony PP. Multiple and recurrent inflammatory fibroid polyps in a Devon family ("Devon polyposis syndrome"). An update. Gut 1992, **33**: 1004–1005.

603 Boyle L, Lack EE. Solitary cavernous hemangioma of small intestine. Case report and literature review. Arch Pathol Lab Med 1993, **117**: 939–941.

604 Cappell MS, Friedman D, Mikhail N. Endometriosis of the terminal ileum simulating the clinical, roentgenographic, and surgical findings in Crohn's disease. Am J Gastroenterol 1991, **86**: 1057–1062.

605 Chen KT. Endocervicosis of the small intestine. Int J Surg Pathol 2002, **10**: 65–67.

606 Climie ARW, Wylin RF. Small intestinal lipomatosis. Arch Pathol Lab Med 1981, **105**: 40–42.

607 Cortina G, Wren S, Armstrong B, Lewin K, Fajardo L. Clinical and pathologic overlap in nonsteroidal anti-inflammatory drug-related small bowel diaphragm disease and the neuromuscular and vascular hamartoma of the small bowel. Am J Surg Pathol 1999, **23**: 1414–1417.

608 Damiani S, Nappi O, Eusebi V. Primary rhabdomyosarcoma of the ileum in an adult. Arch Pathol Lab Med 1991, **115**: 235–238.

609 de Castro CA, Dockerty MB, Mayo CW. Metastatic tumors of the small intestine. Surg Gynecol Obstet 1957, **105**: 159–165.

610 Delvaux V, Sciot R, Neuville B, Moerman P, Peeters M, Filez L, Van Beckvoort D, Ectors N, Geboes K. Multifocal epithelioid angiosarcoma of the small intestine. Virchows Arch 2000, **437**: 90–94.

611 Donner LR, Trompler RA, Dobin S. Clear cell sarcoma of the ileum: the crucial role of cytogenetics for the diagnosis. Am J Surg Pathol 1998, **22**: 121–124.

612 Ekfors TO, Kujari H, Isomaki M. Clear cell sarcoma of tendons and aponeuroses (malignant melanoma of soft parts) in the duodenum. The first visceral case. Histopathology 1993, **22**: 255–259.

613 Fernando SS, McGovern VJ. Neuromuscular and vascular hamartoma of small bowel. Gut 1982, **23**: 1008–1012.

614 Fuller CE, Williams GT. Gastrointestinal manifestations of type 1 neurofibromatosis (von Recklinghausen's disease). Histopathology 1991, **19**: 1–11.

615 Gonzalez-Crussi F, Noronha R. Solitary intestinal fibromatosis in the newborn. Rare cause of neonatal intestinal obstruction. Arch Pathol Lab Med 1985, **109**: 97–99.

616 Hamilton CW, Shelburne JD, Bossen EH, Lowe JE. A glomus tumor of the jejunum masquerading as a carcinoid tumor. Hum Pathol 1982, **13**: 859–861.

617 Hanagiri T, Baba M, Shimabukuro T, Hashimoto M, Takemoto H, Inoue A, Sugitani A, Shirakusa T. Lymphangioma in the small intestine. Report of a case and review of the Japanese literature. Surg Today 1992, **22**: 363–367.

618 Hurwitz MM, Redleaf PD, Williams HJ, Edwards JE. Lipomas of the gastrointestinal tract. An analysis of 72 tumors. AJR 1967, **99**: 84–89.

619 Johnstone JM, Morson BC. Inflammatory fibroid polyp of the gastrointestinal tract. Histopathology 1978, **2**: 349–361.

620 Jorge E, Harvey HA, Simmonds MA, Lipton A, Joehl RJ. Symptomatic malignant melanoma of the gastrointestinal tract. Operative treatment and survival. Ann Surg 1985, **193**: 328–331.

621 Kadivar TF, Vanek VW, Krishnan EU. Primary malignant melanoma of the small bowel. A case study. Am Surg 1992, **58**: 418–422.

622 Kataoka Y, Shimada H, Sugimoto T, Mine H, Hachitanda Y, Doi Y, Sawada T, Weeks DA. Congenital sarcoma in the terminal ileum histologically resembling clear cell sarcoma of the kidney. A case report with an immunohistochemical study. Hum Pathol 1993, **24**: 1026–1030.

623 Kawashima A, Fishman EK, Kuhlman JE, Schuchter LM. CT of malignant melanoma. Patterns of small bowel and mesenteric involvement. J Comput Assist Tomogr 1991, **15**: 570–574.

623a Kie J-H, Lee M-K, Kim C-J, Lee K, Kwon K-W, Yang W-I. Primary Ewing's sarcoma of the duodenum. A case report. Int J Surg Pathol 2003, **11**: 331–337.

624 Kim MK, Higgins J, Cho EY, Ko YH, Oh YL. Expression of CD34, bcl-2, and Kit in inflammatory fibroid polyps of the gastrointestinal tract. Appl Immunohistochem Mol Morphol 2000, **8**: 147–153.

625 Lee JR, Chamberlain CR, Gerrity RG, McKee EM, Gadacz TR, Rao RN. Malignant rhabdoid tumor of the duodenum. Ann Diagn Pathol 1998, **2**: 25–30.

626 Makhlouf HR, Sobin LH. Inflammatory myofibroblastic tumors (inflammatory pseudotumors) of the gastrointestinal tract: how closely are they related to inflammatory fibroid polyps? Hum Pathol 2002, **33**: 307–315.

627 Matthews TH, Heaton GE, Christopherson WM. Primary duodenal choriocarcinoma. Arch Pathol Lab Med 1986, **110**: 550–552.

628 Mayo CW, Pagtalunan RJG, Brown CJ. Lipoma of the alimentary tract. Surgery 1963, **53**: 598–603.

629 McNeill PM, Wagman LD, Neifeld JP. Small bowel metastases from primary carcinoma of the lung. Cancer 1987, **59**: 1486–1489.

630 Nkanza NK, King M, Hutt MSR. Intussusception due to inflammatory fibroid polyps of the ileum. A report of 12 cases from Africa. Br J Surg 1980, **67**: 271–274.

631 Ordóñez NG, del Junco GW, Ayala AG, Ahmed N. Angiosarcoma of the small intestine. An immunoperoxidase study. Am J Gastroenterol 1983, **78**: 218–221.

632 Papadopoulos T, Kirchner T, Bergmann M, Muller-Hermelink HK. Primary liposarcoma of the jejunum. Pathol Res Pract 1990, **186**: 803–808.

633 Sato N, Zaloudek C, Geelhoed GW, Orenstein JM. Malignant mesenchymoma of the small intestine. Arch Pathol Lab Med 1984, **108**: 164–167.

634 Shekitka KM, Sobin LH. Ganglioneuromas of the gastrointestinal tract. Relation to von Recklinghausen disease and other multiple tumor syndromes. Am J Surg Pathol 1994, **18**: 250–257.

635 Shepherd JA. Angiomatous conditions of the gastrointestinal tract. Br J Surg 1953, **40**: 409–421.

636 Shimer GR, Helwig EB. Inflammatory fibroid polyps of the intestine. Am J Clin Pathol 1984, **81**: 708–714.

637 Smith CR Jr, Bartholomew LG, Cain JC. Hereditary hemorrhagic telangiectasia and gastrointestinal hemorrhage. Gastroenterology 1963, **44**: 1–6.

638 van de Rijn M, Hendrickson MR, Rouse RV. An immunohistochemical study of inflammatory fibroid polyps of the gastrointestinal tract. Appl Immunohistochem 1994, **2**: 54–59.

639 Vartanian RK, O'Connell JX, Holden JK, MacFarlane J, Owen DA. Primary jejunal well-differentiated liposarcoma (atypical lipomatous tumor) with leiomyosarcomatous dedifferentiation. Int J Surg Pathol 1996, **4**: 29–36.

640 Washington K, McDonagh D. Secondary tumors of the gastrointestinal tract. Surgical pathologic findings and comparison with autopsy survey. Mod Pathol 1995, **8**: 427–433.

641 Weisberg T, Feldman M Sr. Lipomas of the gastrointestinal tract. Am J Clin Pathol 1955, **25**: 272–281.

642 Willbanks OL, Fogelman MJ. Gastrointestinal melanosarcoma. Am J Surg 1970, **120**: 602–606.

643 Wille P, Borchard F. Fibroid polyps of intestinal tract are inflammatory-reactive proliferations of CD34-positive perivascular cells. Histopathology 1998, **32**: 498–502.

644 Winchester DP, Merrill JR, Victor TA, Scanlon EF. Small bowel perforation secondary to metastatic carcinoma of the lung. Cancer 1977, **40**: 410–415.

645 Wolov RB, Sato N, Azumi N, Lack EE. Intra-abdominal angiosarcomatosis. Report of two cases after pelvic irradiation. Cancer 1991, **67**: 2275–2279.

646 Yantiss RK, Clement PB, Young RH. Endometriosis of the intestinal tract: a study of 44 cases of a disease that may cause diverse challenges in clinical and pathologic evaluation. Am J Surg Pathol 2001, **25**: 445–454.

647 Yantiss RK, Clement PB, Young RH. Neoplastic and preneoplastic changes in gastrointestinal endometriosis: a study of 17 cases. Am J Surg Pathol 2000, **24**: 513–524.

648 Zambrano E, Reyes-Mugica M, Franchi A, Rosai J. An osteoclast-rich tumor of the gastrointestinal tract with features resembling clear cell sarcoma of soft parts: reports of 6 cases of a GIST simulator. Int J Surg Pathol 2003, **11**: 75–81.

Appendix

Normal anatomy

The appendix in humans is a rudimentary structure with no obvious function. It arises from the medial wall of the cecum and averages 6 to 7 cm in length and 0.7 cm in greatest diameter. The position of the appendix varies considerably; it may lie posterior to the cecum or ascending colon (its most common site), in the pericolic gutter, in front or behind the terminal ileum, on the psoas muscle, or in the subhepatic region.[2]

The mucosa of the appendix is similar to that of the large bowel, except for a greater representation of lymphoid tissue (which is particularly prominent during adolescence). Grossly, it has a yellowish tint. Foci of fresh hemorrhage are usually attributable to surgical trauma. Microscopically, the epithelium contains absorptive cells, goblet cells, neuroendocrine cells (mainly of Kultschitsky type and located at the base), and very few Paneth cells.[4] Additional neuroendocrine cells may be detected with chromogranin or related stains within the lamina propria, unconnected with the glands, and in close association with nerves (see p. 768). Occasionally, these neuroendocrine cells are identifiable on routinely stained sections because of the presence of bright eosinophilic cytoplasmic granules, not to be confused with those of Paneth cells.[3] Most of the plasma cells present in the lamina propria are IgA producing. The submucosal, muscular, and serosal layers are qualitatively similar to their counterparts in the rest of the lower intestinal tract. Grossly, the serosa is smooth, glistening, and transparent. Hyperemia of surface vessels is usually related to surgical trauma. The mesoappendix, which is largely made up of adipose tissue, contains the appendiceal vessels. Very infrequently, one or more small lymph nodes are found within it; these drain to the pericolic and superior mesenteric nodes.

Obliteration of the tip of the appendix is a frequent finding, the mechanism of which is not well understood. Some view it as a normal aging process and others as a sequela of a resolved acute appendicitis.[1] The opposite phenomenon is represented by a moderate dilatation of the lumen, an inconsequential process usually accompanied by some mucosal atrophy and sometimes dignified with the term *appendiceal ectasia*. This is not to be called mucocele or—worse—to be regarded as a mucinous neoplasm (see p. 762).

Acute appendicitis

Epidemiology and pathogenesis

Acute appendicitis is predominantly a disease of the Western world. It is particularly common in Great Britain and the United States and very rare in Asia and Africa. In the United States, it is more common among Caucasians than among blacks or Orientals.[12] The difference has been explained on the basis of a dietary variance, the highest risk occurring when the diet is reduced in bulk, with diminished cellulose and a high protein intake.[7]

Despite some recent challenges,[8] there is a wide belief that many and perhaps most cases of acute appendicitis develop as a result of obstruction, the resulting secretion under pressure impairing the resistance of the appendiceal mucosa to invasion by microorganisms, as shown by Wagensteen's pioneer studies in humans[17] and by experimental animal models. Mucosal injury develops in one area, ulceration occurs, and the inflammation spreads from that point.[9,11,16] An obstructed appendix that was previously normal is more susceptible to infection than one affected by fibrous obliteration of the lumen. The most common cause of obstruction is a fecalith, but it may be a foreign body, a true calculus, a gallstone, a tumor of the cecum, or a primary tumor of the appendix.[6,10,14,19] In children from the age of 10 years to young adults, diffuse lymphoid hyperplasia is another cause of obstruction.[13] Nonobstructive appendicitis can be secondary to a generalized infection, usually of viral etiology.[15]

Cases of appendicitis in AIDS patients do not differ significantly from those seen in immunocompetent individuals, except for a lesser tendency to have an elevation of the white blood cell count.[5,18]

Clinical features

Acute appendicitis is seen most frequently in young men but can occur in either sex and at any age. When it occurs in young children[27,30] and in the elderly[31,33] it is more likely to be mishandled because of failure to consider the diagnosis and because the clinical findings are often atypical. The usual presentation of acute appendicitis is with periumbilical colicky pain and vomiting, with the pain later localizing in the right lower abdominal quadrant. These symptoms are often accompanied by fever, leukocytosis, an elevated erythrosedimentation rate, and C-reactive protein.[32] If perforation of the appendix occurs, there may be temporary relief of pain followed by signs of acute peritonitis. The accuracy of the clinical diagnosis is approximately 80%.[24] False-positive diagnoses are twice as common in females as in males. The conditions most closely mimicking appendicitis are mesenteric lymphadenitis, gynecologic lesions, acute diverticulitis, Meckel's diverticulitis, infarction of the greater omentum, and chemotherapy-induced typhlitis as seen in children with leukemia and other malignancies.[21,22,24] The diagnosis of acute appendicitis is supported by the demonstration of a mass effect on the cecum and nonfilling of the appendix on barium enema, but these radiographic changes are not entirely specific.[23]

Unenhanced CT is an accurate imaging technique for the initial examination of these patients,[25,26] whereas the practical value of ultrasonography is controversial.[20,28,29] Peritoneal aspiration is "positive" (in the sense of showing acute inflammatory cells and some mesothelial hyperplasia) in over 70% of the cases.[34]

Pathologic features

Grossly, an appendix with well-developed acute inflammation shows a fibrinous or purulent coating of the serosa, with engorgement of the vessels (Fig. 11.127). The mucosa shows areas of ulceration against a markedly hyperemic background. Obstruction of the lumen by a fecalith or some other agent is found in approximately one fourth to one third of the cases.[37] Microscopically, the changes range from minimal focal inflammation to total necrosis of the appendiceal wall, the degree of abnormalities being partially dependent on the interval between the onset of symptoms and the operation (Fig. 11.128). In early lesions, neutrophils appear at the base of the crypt adjacent to a small defect in the epithelium. After this inflammatory process reaches the submucosa, it spreads quickly to the remaining appendix.[44] In advanced stages, the mucosa is absent, and the wall is necrotic. Thrombosed vessels are seen in one fourth of cases.[42]

Clusters of neutrophils in the lumen should stimulate a search for evidence of mucosal inflammation, but they are not diagnostic of acute appendicitis by themselves.

The various stages of acute appendicitis are sometimes designated as *acute focal, acute suppurative, gangrenous*

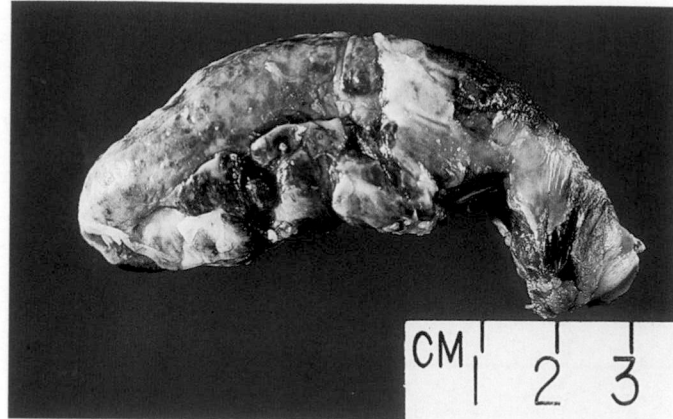

Fig. 11.127 Outer aspect of appendix involved by acute inflammation. A thick purulent coating is seen together with marked hyperemia of the serosa.

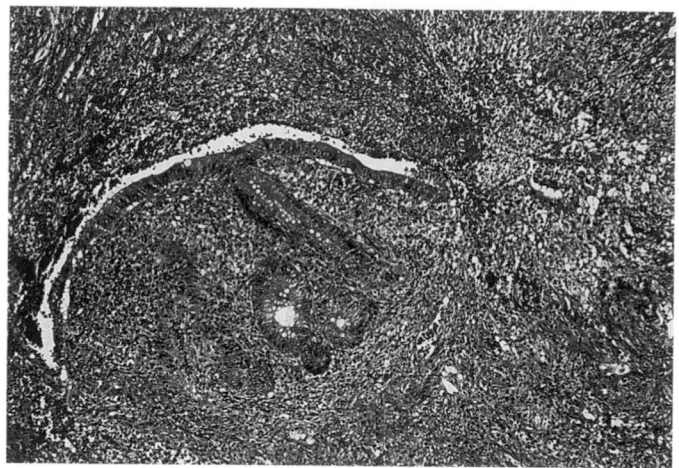

Fig. 11.128 Acute appendicitis with massive inflammatory infiltrate, extensive ulceration, and hemorrhage. An island of heavily inflamed residual mucosa is seen in the center.

(phlegmonous), and *perforative*. The type of inflammatory infiltrate and the likelihood of recovering bacteria from the appendiceal tissue and peritoneal fluid differ among these various stages.[35,47] Anaerobic bacteria are found in over half of the cases, perhaps as secondary colonizers.[45] Cases having a prominent histiocytic component with clusters of xanthoma-type cells are referred to as *xanthogranulomatous appendicitis*.[36] This is regarded as an unusual healing pattern of appendicitis, in contrast to the conventional pattern, which may feature an intraluminal cord of granulation tissue.[38]

There is close correlation between the gross and microscopic findings in acute appendicitis. In a classic study, Therkelsen[46] reviewed 154 organs with microscopic evidence of acute appendicitis; grossly, evidence of inflammation was evident in 125, equivocal in 25, and absent in 4. The notion that there is a form of acute appendicitis that is microscopically normal and that it can be identified only through the expression of "inflammatory markers" (such as cyclooxygenase 1 and 2, prostaglandin E)[41] appears to us a very dubious proposition.

The most common complication of acute appendicitis is perforation, which may lead to diffuse peritonitis or to the formation of a periappendiceal abscess or fibrous induration ("ligneous perityphlitis") (Fig. 11.129).[43] This condition, which may clinically simulate a neoplasm, is usually located in the right iliac fossa lateral to the cecum (Fig. 11.130) but can occur in other sites, depending on

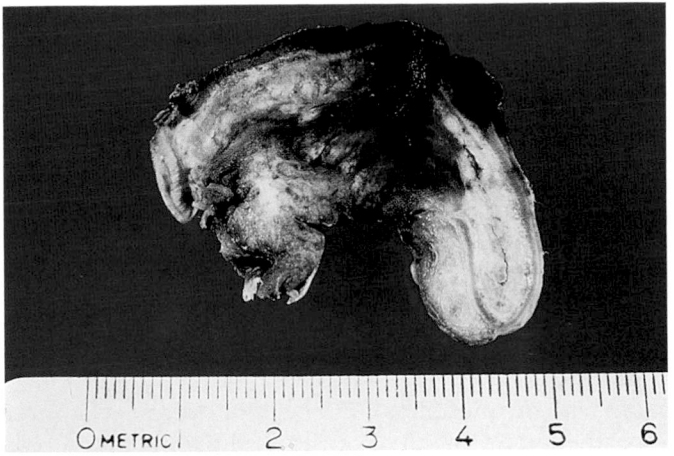

Fig. 11.129 Rupture of appendix secondary to transmural acute appendicitis.

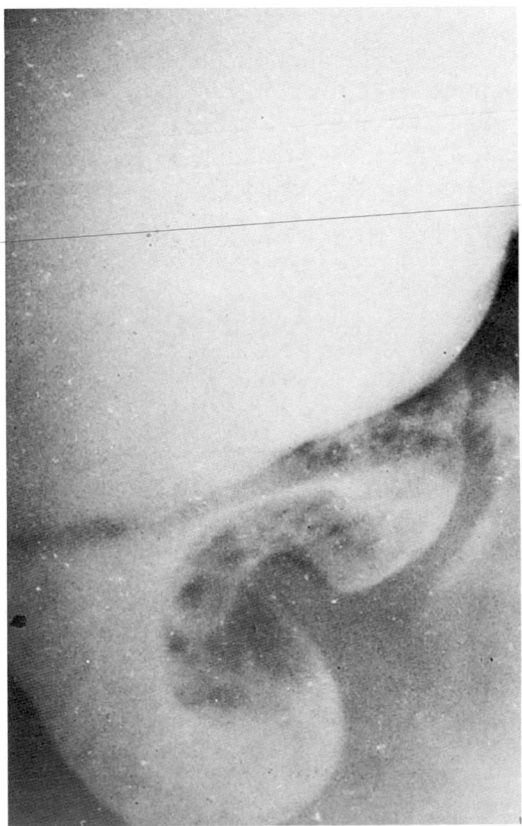

Fig. 11.130 Detailed view of a defect in the ileocecal area in a case of acute appendicitis resulting in a mass effect. The lesion was misinterpreted as carcinoma and was radically removed.

the original location of the appendix (see p. 758). This abscess may perforate into the cecum, ileum, or rectum or even open onto the skin surface. Appendicitis with perforation can also result in infertility in women because of obstruction of the fallopian tubes.[39] Another serious complication is the spread of the inflammation via the ileocolic, upper mesenteric, and portal veins to the liver, with formation of "pylephlebitic" abscesses in the latter.

Periappendicitis refers to acute or chronic inflammation of the appendiceal serosa (Fig. 11.131).[40] It is invariably present in the advanced stages of appendicitis, but it can also be seen in the absence of a primary inflammation of this organ, as a result of spread of an inflammatory process from another site, such as the female adnexa.[40] In the presence of periappendicitis, evidence of mucosal involvement should be thoroughly sought; if none is found, the diagnosis given should be that of periappendicitis rather than appendicitis, the implication being that the primary site of the inflammation is probably located elsewhere. In order not to overdiagnose this condition, it should be remembered that surgical manipulation may induce a neutrophilic infiltrate in the serosa.

Treatment

In 1886, Reginald H. Fitz (arguably the first American surgical pathologist) demonstrated that the appendix was the origin of the mysterious and often fatal inflammation of the right iliac fossa previously known as *perityphlitis*.[50] Three years later, McBurney emphasized the importance of accurate early diagnosis and prompt surgical intervention. By 1900, the mortality rate had already fallen to 35%.[48,51] During the next three decades,

Fig. 11.131 Acute periappendicitis. The serosa of the appendix is markedly edematous and has a coating of neutrophils at the surface. These changes may be seen, as in this case, as a result of the serosal extension of an acute appendicitis. However, they can be present in the absence of mucosal changes, in which case they may represent extension of inflammation from another intra-abdominal organ.

it was further reduced to 5% as a result of better awareness on the part of the patient and the physician concerning the symptoms and signs of acute appendicitis, the need for early surgical intervention, and the dangers of catharsis and morphine for undiagnosed abdominal pain.

In the following 25 years, a combination of improved surgical technique, better preoperative and postoperative care, advances in anesthesiology, and the development of effective antibacterial agents led to further declines in mortality to a fraction of 1%. The later reduction in risk was accomplished mainly in three classes of patients: those with perforation and peritonitis, the very young, and the very old.[49]

Chronic appendicitis

The existence of primary chronic appendicitis as a pathologic or clinical entity has been greatly disputed. Its symptoms and signs are as vague and shadowy as its pathology. Just because vague preoperative symptoms disappear following appendectomy is not necessarily evidence that the symptoms were in any way related to the appendix. The anatomic structure of appendices commonly removed under the diagnosis of chronic appendicitis shows no variation from the appendices of individuals suffering from no abdominal complaint whatsoever. Unfortunately, in some laboratories the pathologist is a willing accomplice to the surgeon who is liberal in the clinical diagnosis of chronic appendicitis. These pathologists never call an appendix normal. Rough handling and clamping of the appendix may produce mucosal hemorrhage and engorgement of serosal vessels. Normally, there may be collections of lymphocytes in the muscular wall of the appendix, and a rare plasma cell or eosinophil may be seen in the mucosa. Fibrous obliteration of the appendiceal tip, whatever its pathogenesis, does not cause symptoms. Finally, residual changes may be found in appendices that were the site of the acute appendicitis that subsided in the past. If gangrene occurred, only a stump of the appendix may remain. In other instances in which an inflammatory process has destroyed the muscle, fibrous replacement is present. If the original process was superficial and confined to the mucosa and submucosa, no changes will be found. Many cases clinically diagnosed as chronic appendicitis represent *recurrent* acute appendicitis, the pathologic findings depending on whether the appendectomy was performed during an acute attack or between bouts. Along these lines, the finding of a significant increase in neural fibers, Schwann cells, and enlarged ganglia in cases of clinically acute appendicitis may be indicative of repeated bouts of inflammation.[52]

Other inflammatory processes

Oxyuriasis is found in approximately 3% of the appendices removed in the United States. The parasite, known as *Oxyuris (Enterobius) vermicularis*, is most often found in the appendices of children between the ages of 7 and 11 years. The infestation is not a causal agent of appendicitis, although it may simulate its symptoms; it is more commonly seen in otherwise normal appendices than in these involved by acute appendicitis.[87] The parasite wanders widely and frequently invades the lower female genital tract. From there, it may reach the peritoneal cavity by ascending along the uterus and fallopian tubes. Granulomas caused by this organism have been observed in the endometrium, fallopian tubes, ovaries, mesentery, and mesoappendix.[86]

Eosinophilic appendicitis is characterized by a diffuse eosinophilic infiltration or by the presence of appendiceal granulomas composed of epithelioid cells, fibroblasts, and a large number of eosinophils having necrotic centers and surrounded by diffuse eosinophilic infiltration (Fig. 11.132). These changes have been correlated with the presence of *Strongyloides stercoralis* in stool examinations[82]; the larva of the organism is found only exceptionally within the granulomas.[74]

Schistosomiasis can involve the appendix, but its possible role in the pathogenesis of acute appendicitis remains controversial.[57,79]

H. pylori organisms were found by an immunohistochemical technique in 3 out of 116 appendectomy specimens studied by van Spreeuwel et al.[85] The histologic changes present in these appendices were similar to those seen in colonic biopsies from patients with *H. pylori* colitis (see section on large bowel).

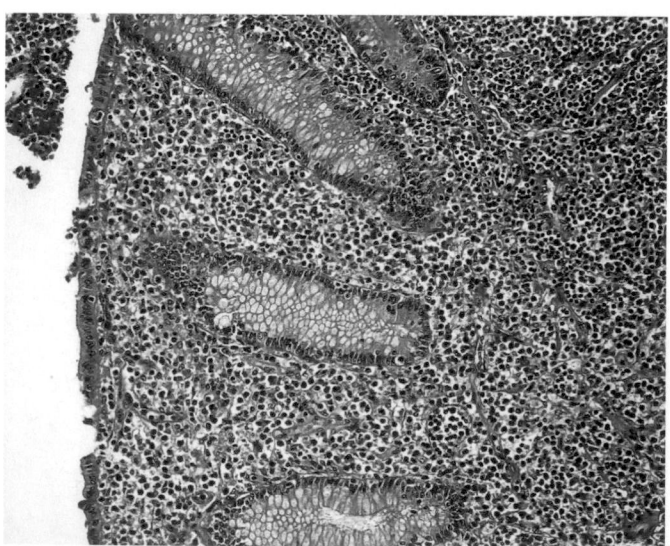

Fig.11.132 Intense eosinophilic appendicitis. This was secondary to infestation by *Angiostrongylus costaricensis*.

Acute necrotizing arteritis may be found in the vessels of the appendix. In most cases the disease is restricted to the appendix, but a minority of patients will develop systemic disease.[56,71]

Measles can be accompanied by appendicitis during its prodromal stage. Microscopic examination shows marked lymphoid hyperplasia with the presence of multinucleated giant cells of the Warthin–Finkeldey type ("polykaryocytes"), similar to those seen in the tonsil[63] (Fig. 11.133). An astute pathologist can thus tell the patient's physician that the child is about to break out into the characteristic rash of measles.[62] At a later stage there can be a suppurative component.[77]

Infectious mononucleosis can also be accompanied by marked hyperplasia of the appendiceal lymphoid tissue, with marked expansion of the lamina propria by a mixed proliferation of small lymphoid cells and immunoblasts, some of the latter resembling Reed–Sternberg cells.[75]

Ulcerative colitis involves the appendix in approximately 50% of cases. This is almost always in continuity with cecal disease, but sometimes "skip" lesions occur.[58,64,67,80]

Crohn's disease can involve the appendix and simulate clinically acute appendicitis (Fig. 11.134).[66,76,81] As a matter of fact, a good number of patients with Crohn's disease give a history of previous appendectomy; however, patients whose removed appendices show granulomatous changes suggestive of Crohn's disease very rarely develop disease in other portions of the gastrointestinal tract.[53,54] It has therefore been concluded that so-called "Crohn's disease limited to the appendix" is a form of *idiopathic granulomatous appendicitis* that is nosologically unrelated to true Crohn's disease in the majority of the cases,[54] and that in some instances the granuloma may have developed in an ordinary acute

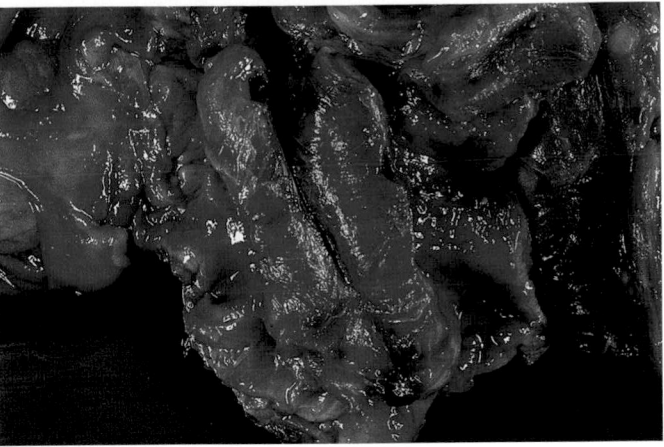

Fig. 11.134 Severe appendiceal involvement by Crohn's disease, in continuity with ileal and colonic involvement.

appendicitis simply because of the fact that the operation was delayed (so-called "interval appendectomy").[64a] It has been said that the more numerous the granulomas in the appendix the less likely that there will be conventional Crohn's disease in the ileum,[61] but the correlation is not very good. Therefore, follow-up is necessary in all of these cases.[65]

Sarcoidosis is responsible for a few of the reported cases of granulomatous inflammation of the appendix.[84]

Yersiniosis (produced by *Yersinia enterocolitica*) may result in appendiceal granulomas; these show central necrosis and formation of microabscesses with scanty Langerhans' giant cells. A positive culture, serologic test, or PCR identification of the organism is necessary to confirm the diagnosis.[55,68,83]

CMV appendicitis has been reported in HIV-infected patients.[60,73]

Rosai–Dorfman disease can exceptionally involve the appendix as an isolated event or in association with involvement of other portions of the gastrointestinal tract.[69]

Invasive candidiasis has been reported to result in granulomatous appendicitis in immunosuppressed patients.[72]

Other rare infections of the appendix include **amebiasis**[69] and **cryptosporidiosis**.[78]

Tumors

Mucinous tumors and tumorlike conditions (including so-called "mucocele")

In the appendiceal disease traditionally designated as *mucocele*, the appendix shows localized or diffuse globular enlargement. The lumen is dilated and contains large amounts of glairy mucus. In the past, it has been assumed that these changes were secondary to proximal obstruction of the lumen. Cheng's experimental model[90]

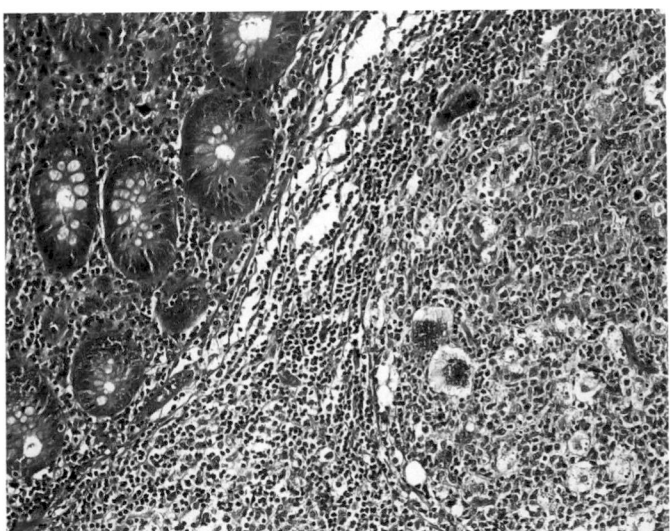

Fig. 11.133 Warthin–Finkeldey multinucleated giant cells in the appendix of a child with measles.

is often quoted in this regard. In reality, all he showed is that if the lumen of the rabbit "appendix" is surgically occluded, dilatation of the distal portion with flattening of the epithelium and accumulation of mucus results, and that if the mucus is transplanted to the rabbit peritoneum, it acts as foreign material and in time is absorbed.

In our opinion, the term *mucocele* is to be avoided because it tells nothing about the underlying cause for the mucinous accumulation, which ranges from a hyperplastic to a malignant process.[98] It would be equivalent to use the term "hematocele" for any blood-containing lesion, regardless of whether the underlying lesion was a hematoma, a cavernous hemangioma, an angiomatoid malignant fibrous histiocytoma, or an angiosarcoma. Few people still use the term mucocele for appendiceal lesions, but unfortunately some authors have brought back this terminology at other sites, such as breast and pancreas. In those sites, as in the appendix, *mucocele is not an entity*. What matters is the nature of the underlying lesion, not the fact that abundant mucin is being produced by it.

In the appendix, there are a few instances in which this gross appearance is the result of occlusion of the lumen by endometriosis, carcinoid tumor, or some other process.[94] The epithelium is flat, atrophic, and devoid of any atypical features. In cystic fibrosis, the "mucocele" is due to the accumulation of inspissated mucus. In other cases, a localized focus of **mucosal hyperplasia** is seen, the appearance being indistinguishable from that of a hyperplastic colorectal polyp[89,98,111] (Fig. 11.135). The remaining cases, which represent most of the lesions included under the generic designation "mucocele," have morphologic, histochemical, and ultrastructural features of true mucinous neoplasms.[98,100,112] The distinction between the hyperplastic and neoplastic cases is in general quite easy, although examples exist that combine features of both.[98,125]

The large majority of these mucinous neoplasms are benign (i.e., **mucinous cystadenomas**) (Fig. 11.136). They are lined by *atypical* mucinous epithelium with at least some areas of papillary configuration (Fig. 11.137). It is possible, and indeed likely, that some of these lesions begin as adenomatous polyps, villoglandular polyps, or villous adenomas[97,124] and that the progressive accumulation of mucus in the cavity eventually obliterates the diagnostic features of these entities.[93,112] However, to designate all of these lesions as villous adenomas—as some authors have suggested—is too much of an assumption, ignores the several differences that exist between these appendiceal lesions and conventional villous adenomas of the large bowel, and represents an inaccurate description of the morphologic features of the typical case.

Secondary changes in mucinous cystadenomas include thinning of the wall, extensive ulceration, and

calcification. The last may be evident radiographically. As a result of increased intraluminal pressure, mucus may penetrate into the wall (through a process analogous to that of diverticulosis[101]), reach the serosa, and appear as a peri-appendicular or retroperitoneal mass

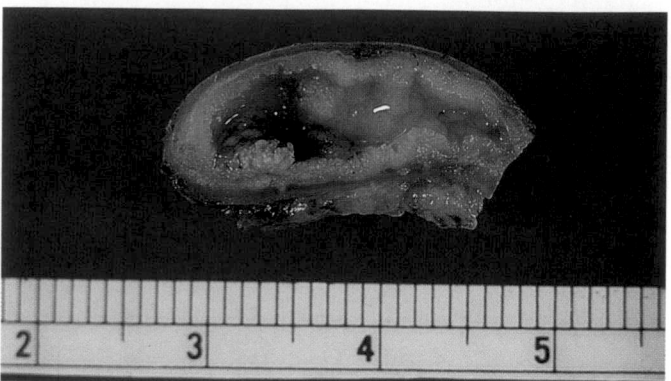

A

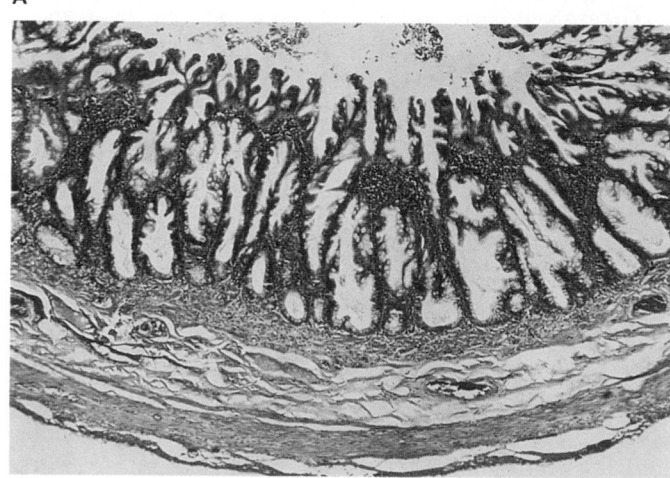

B

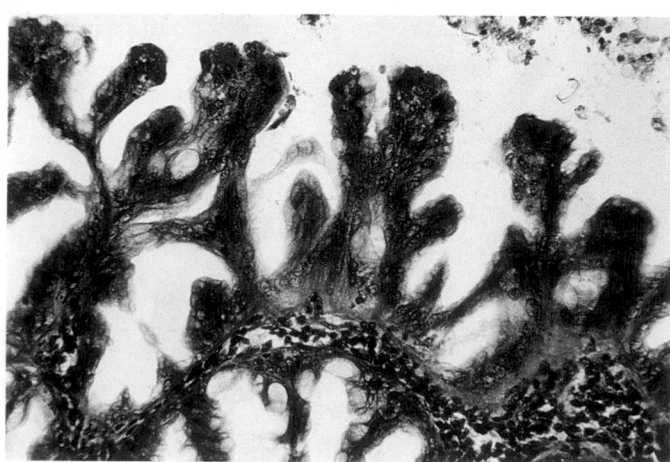

C

Fig. 11.135 A, Gross appearance of appendiceal mucosal hyperplasia. The lumen is mildly dilated and occupied by mucinous material. There is moderate thickening of the mucosa, which is accentuated near the tip. This was an incidental finding. **B,** Low-power microscopic view of mucosal hyperplasia. The features are analogous to those of hyperplastic polyp of large bowel. **C,** The superficial portion shows a typical micropapillary configuration.

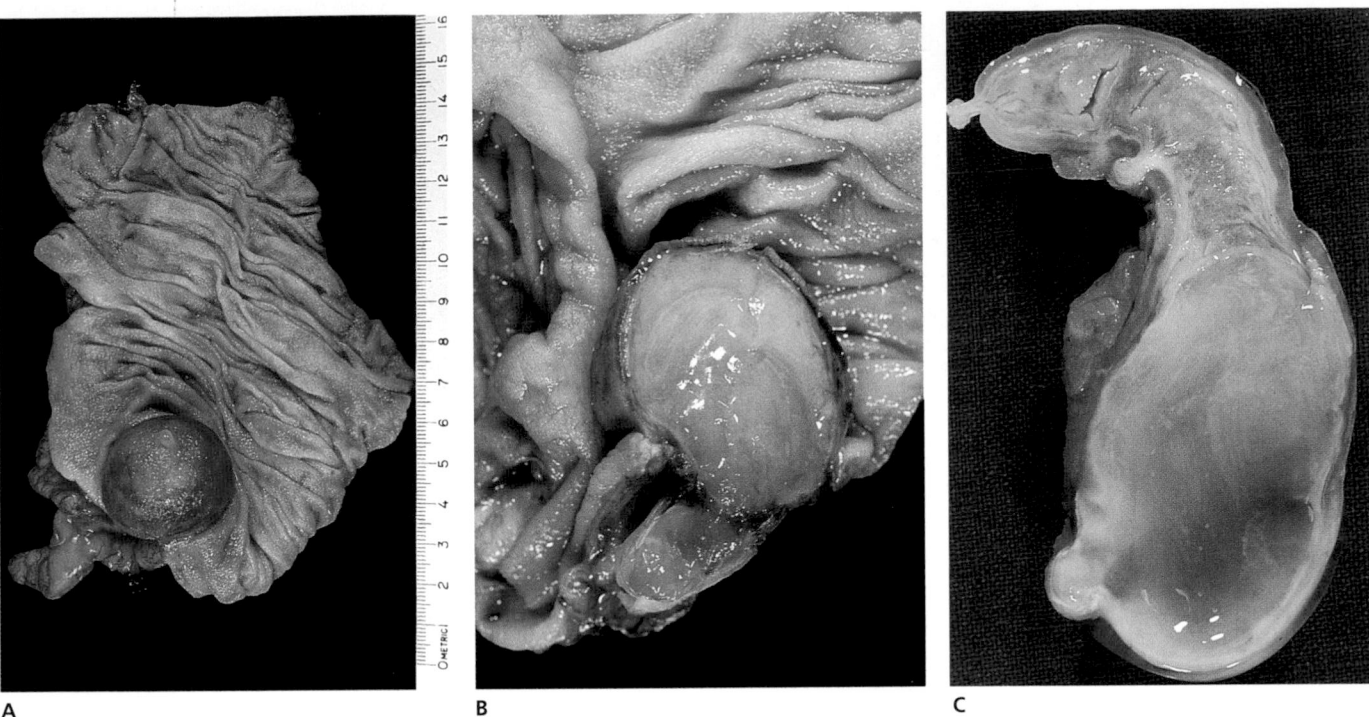

Fig. 11.136 A, Gross appearance of mucinous cystadenoma of appendix covered by cecal mucosa and protruding into the cecum. **B,** Cut surface of the same tumor showing cystically dilated lumen filled with thick mucin. **C,** Mucinous cystadenoma involving the proximal half of the appendix and associated with diverticular formation.

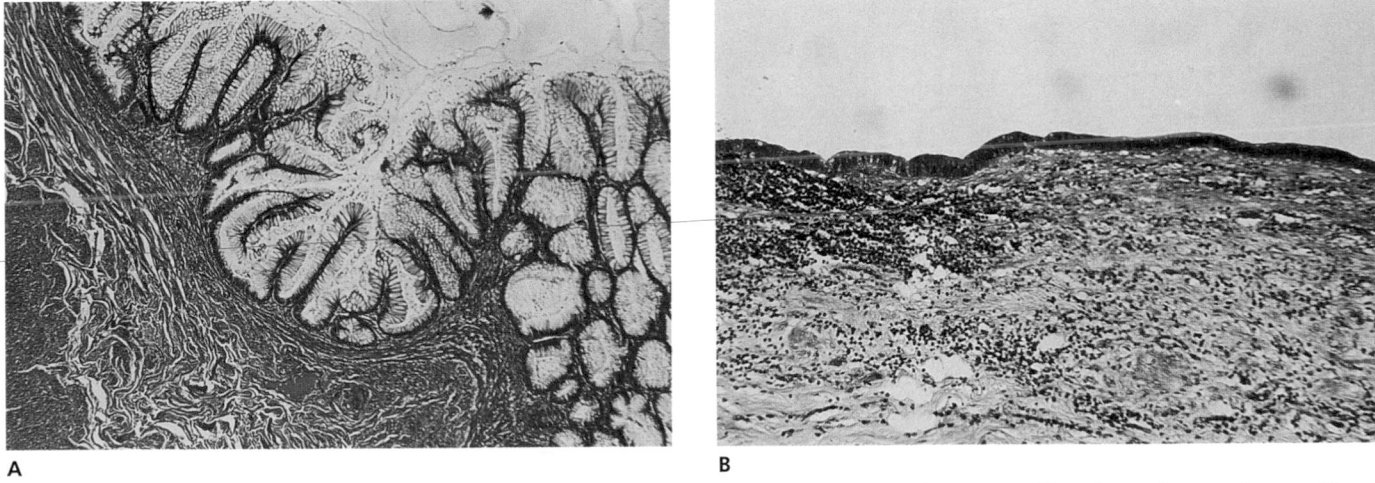

Fig. 11.137 Microscopic appearance of mucinous cystadenoma of appendix. The tumor in **A** shows a proliferative and somewhat papillary configuration, whereas that illustrated in **B** is flat and accompanied by atrophy, fibrosis, and chronic inflammation of the underlying wall.

at operation (Fig. 11.138). Removal of the appendix is curative, even in the presence of the latter complication. A certain proportion of these cases are associated with ovarian mucinous cystadenoma of strikingly similar microscopic appearance.[117,129] There is also a high association with synchronous or metachronous neoplasms elsewhere in the colon.[98,126]

The malignant counterpart (i.e., **mucinous cystadenocarcinoma**) has the same gross appearance and many microscopic features in common with the benign form[99] (Fig. 11.139), and it may be associated with a similar independent lesion of the ovary. We have used two crite-

ria for malignancy in these lesions: (1) the identification of invasion of the appendiceal wall by obviously malignant glands and (2) clearly identifiable epithelial cells (whether atypical or not) in the peritoneal mucinous deposits, when these are present (Fig. 11.140). One could argue about the appropriateness of naming these appendiceal neoplasms in one way or another depending on the findings at another site (i.e., the peritoneal cavity), but there is no question that from a prognostic standpoint the distinction is of great importance.[98,102,104] One should also comment that, were one to use the terminology currently applied to mucinous tumors of the ovary

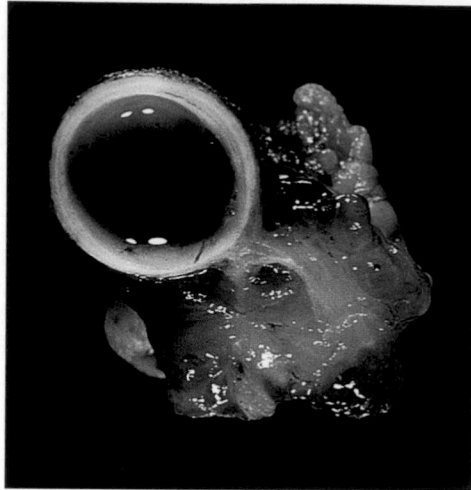

Fig. 11.138 Mucinous cystadenoma of appendix associated with spillage of mucin in the periappendiceal area. Microscopically, there were no epithelial cells within the mucinous pools.

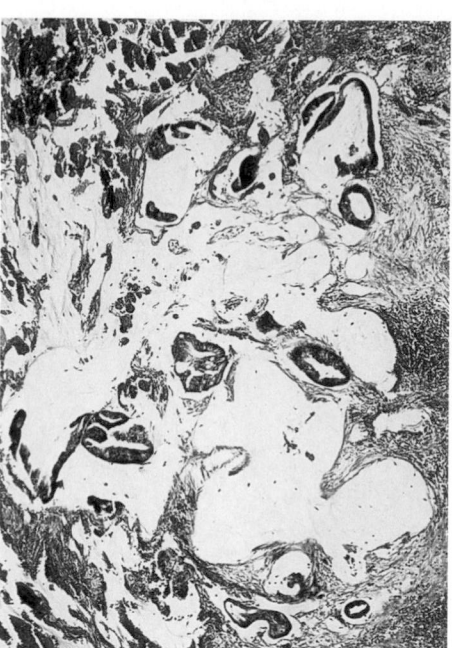

Fig. 11.140 Pseudomyxoma peritonei. The diagnosis is made by the presence of well-differentiated glandular epithelium, admixed with extracellular mucin.

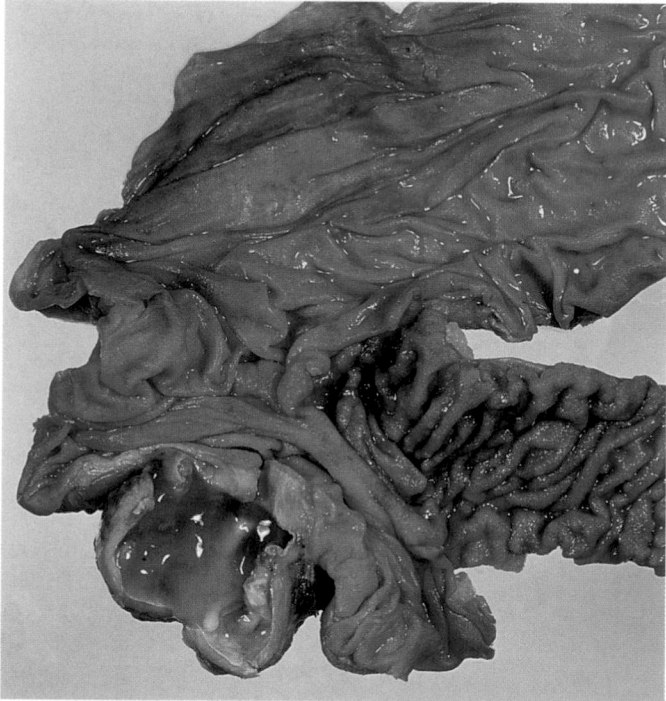

Fig. 11.139 Mucinous cystadenocarcinoma of appendix. The tumor is grossly indistinguishable from a mucinous cystadenoma.

for these appendiceal tumors, many would fit into a *borderline* category. Indeed, they have been designated as *borderline mucinous neoplasms* by some authors.[116] Others have proposed calling them *low-grade mucinous neoplasms (LAMNs)* when well differentiated and noninvasive, and *mucinous adenocarcinomas (MACAs)* when highly atypical and/or invasive.[104]

It should also be mentioned that proliferative mucinous lesions of the appendix (including mucosal hyperplasia) can be seen in association with adenocarcinomas of the large bowel.[98,128]

At the molecular genetic level, frequent loss of 18q has been found in mucinous (as well as in nonmucinous) appendiceal adenocarcinomas.[103a]

Pseudomyxoma peritonei

The presence of mucin within the peritoneal cavity has been classically referred to as **pseudomyxoma peritonei**.[103,118] We believe that this designation should be reserved for those cases in which the condition is widespread (rather than limited to a small pool of mucin around the appendix) and in which epithelial tumor cells are identifiable microscopically. Actually, these two features often go together. When thus defined, this process forms gelatinous nodules and in time may cause the death of the patient through infection or intestinal obstruction by invasion of the surrounding structures such as the bladder, abdominal wall, and intestine. It may also involve the outer aspect of the spleen[95] and extend through the diaphragm to produce *pseudomyxoma pleurii*.[106] It can also result in the formation of pedunculated peritoneal surface polyps.[121] Finally, it can extend into inguinal and other hernia sacs; as a matter of fact, it is not rare for the disease to be first diagnosed on histologic examination of the contents of a herniorrhaphy operation.[96,130]

Sometimes a mucinous tumor of the appendix coexists with a morphologically similar tumor in the ovary, usually with, but sometimes without, associated pseudomyxoma peritonei.[117,129] The ovarian tumors are bilateral in a minority of the cases; when unilateral, they tend to be right sided. The ovarian and appendiceal lesions are usually synchronous, but one can appear many years after the removal of the other.[107] Some authors[110,129] have taken the view that the ovarian tumors represent secondary deposits from the appendiceal neoplasms. Others favor an independent origin of the ovarian and appendiceal lesions[117,122] (see Chapter 19). Although the argument is not entirely settled,[91] it is fair to say that the bulk of the immunohistochemical and ultrastructural evidence favors the hypothesis that the ovarian tumor is an implant/metastasis from the appendiceal neoplasm.[92,113,114,123] A similar conclusion has been drawn for the exceptional cases in which the well-differentiated mucinous epithelium is seen to line the endometrium and endocervix, supposedly having reached those sites through a transtubal route.[105]

Microscopically, the bulk of the mass in pseudomyxoma peritonei is composed of extracellular mucin accompanied by hyperemia, fibrosis, and mesothelial reaction. Also present (and necessary for the diagnosis) are strips of generally extremely well-differentiated mucin-producing tumor cells.

The term *adenomucinosis* has been proposed for this extremely well-differentiated form of disease, reserving the term *peritoneal mucinous carcinomatosis* for those cases in which the cytoarchitectural atypia is greater.[115] Although the distinction is of prognostic significance, it should be realized that these refer to different grades of malignancy, and that the overwhelming majority of cases of pseudomyxoma peritonei belong to the first category.

An interesting aspect of this disease is the mechanism behind the accumulation of extracellular mucin. It has been recently reported that pseudomyxoma is characterized by the production of MUC2, a gel-forming mucin that is known to form strong bonds with the stroma and is thought to have tumor suppressor activities.[88,108] The other factor that is pathogenetically responsible for the extracellular accumulation of mucin is an alteration in cell polarity, so that the secreted glycoproteins are expressed predominantly in the stroma-facing surfaces of the tumor cells. This is in contrast to ordinary adenocarcinomas, in which these substances are either on the luminal surfaces in well-differentiated areas or dispersed throughout the cytoplasm in the poorly differentiated areas. It has even been suggested that alterations in cell polarity may affect the regulation of cell proliferation and thus cause tumors.[109]

The current treatment for pseudomyxoma peritonei consists of surgical removal of as much of the tumor as possible ("cytoreduction") combined with intraperitoneal chemotherapy.[119,120] The prognosis is dependent upon the bulk of disease and the microscopic degree of differentiation.[115,127]

Adenocarcinoma

It is not uncommon for large carcinomas of the cecum to secondarily involve the base of the appendix. These tumors are sometimes erroneously assumed to be of primary appendiceal origin.

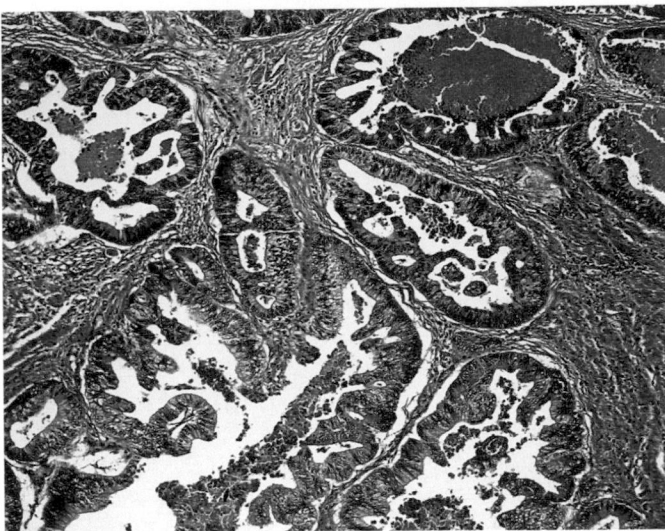

Fig. 11.141 Well-differentiated appendiceal adenocarcinoma of intestinal type.

Primary adenocarcinoma of the appendix is a rarity after one eliminates the mucinous cystadenocarcinoma and the carcinoid tumors associated with the production of glands and mucin (adenocarcinoids) (see respective sections).[131,134,137] It can be located in any part of the appendix. The symptoms resemble acute appendicitis; actually, inflammation is often found in addition to the carcinoma.[139] The microscopic appearance is essentially the same as that of colorectal adenocarcinoma and is indeed referred to as colonic type[135,136] (Fig. 11.141). Right hemicolectomy is the treatment of choice except for very superficial tumors of well-differentiated nature that can be cured by simple appendectomy.[138] Dukes' staging system correlates with prognosis as well as it does in the colorectum.[139]

An exceptionally rare type of primary appendiceal tumor is the **signet ring** or linitis plastica type of carcinoma.[136] This needs to be distinguished from a metastasis of a gastric or mammary tumor and from goblet cell carcinoid tumor (see the following discussion). Signet ring carcinomas have more extensive mucosal involvement, more nuclear atypia, and a more complex and irregular invasive pattern than mucinous carcinoid tumors, and they lack features of neuroendocrine differentiation ultrastructurally and immunohistochemically. Another difference may be the preservation of E-cadherin and β-catenin in goblet cell carcinoid and their loss in pure signet ring adenocarcinoma.[133]

Interestingly (and somewhat surprisingly) the genetic alterations in terms of microsatellite instability, p53 overexpression and k-*ras* mutations between colonic-type adenocarcinoma and mucinous (cyst)adenocarcinoma are practically the same.[132]

Carcinoid tumor

Carcinoid tumors are found in about 1 of every 300 routine appendectomies[168] and represent the most common tumor of the appendix.[167a] The peak incidence is in the third and fourth decades of life, but they can occur in any age group, including children.[176] In most of the cases they are incidental findings, but they may be found associated with acute appendicitis as a result of obstruction of the lumen. Of the 144 cases reported by Moertel et al.,[168] 71% were located in the tip of the appendix, 22% in the body, and 7% in the base; 70% of the lesions were less than 1 cm in diameter, and only two measured 2 cm or more. Grossly, the tumors are firm, grayish white, and fairly well circumscribed but not encapsulated (Fig. 11.142). They acquire a characteristic yellow color after formalin fixation. Those located at the tip often result in a typical "bell clapper" configuration.

Microscopically, carcinoid tumors of the appendix can be divided into several categories. The *classic* (insular) type is formed by solid nests of small monotonous cells with occasional acinar or rosette formation[178] (Fig. 11.143). Mitoses are exceedingly rare. A peculiar retraction of the tumor periphery from the stroma is evident. Some of the cells are found within intra-appendiceal nerves, a feature that may be related to their histogenesis.[149,151,161] Invasion of muscle and lymph vessels is the rule, and spread to the peritoneal surface is not rare. The tumor cells are argentaffin; argyrophilic; positive for the diazo reaction; filled with pleomorphic dense-core secretory granules on ultrastructural examination; and immunohistochemically reactive for neuron-specific enolase, chromogranin, protein gene product 9.5, 5-HT, calbindin-D28k, and (inconstantly) a variety of peptide hormones, including somatostatin, substance P, peptide YY, and glucagon.[142,155,158] Keratin staining tends to be weaker than in ileal carcinoids.[183] The tumor cells are intimately associated with a population of S-100 protein-positive Schwann-like cells.[149] Most of these tumors have

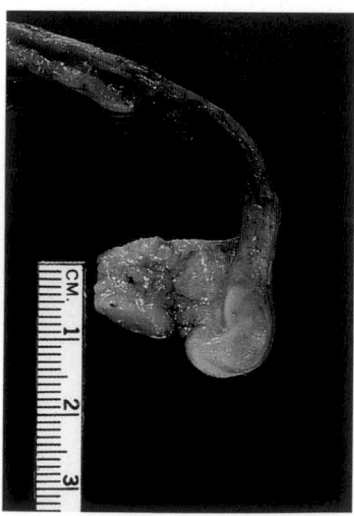

Fig. 11.142 Gross appearance of carcinoid tumor of the appendix. The tumor has a solid appearance and a whitish color and is characteristically located in the tip. Microscopically, it was of the classic (insular) type.

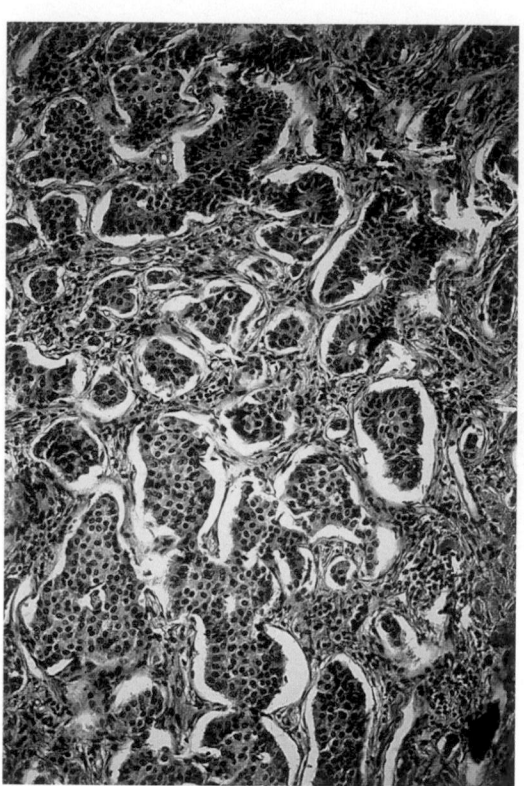

Fig. 11.143 Carcinoid tumor of classic type.

a diploid DNA pattern on flow cytometry examination.[150]

The other types of carcinoid tumor feature glandular formations and are therefore designated as adenocarcinoids or carcinoids with glandular differentiation. A subtype, referred to as *tubular type adenocarcinoid* by Warkel et al.,[182] which is often misdiagnosed as primary or metastatic adenocarcinoma, is characterized by glandular formation without solid nests[146] (Fig. 11.144). Mucin is usually present.[149] The argentaffin reaction is positive in 75% of the cases and the argyrophilic reaction in 89%.[182] The lack of mitoses and atypia, orderly arrangement, and origin at the base of the glands with an otherwise normal mucosa should suggest the diagnosis. On occasion, the cytoplasmic granules of these cells are large and acidophilic, simulating those of Paneth cells, a feature also sometimes exhibited by normal Kulchitsky cells.[166] These tumors often secrete glucagon, as shown by immunohistochemistry and in situ hybridization.[142,177] They are also immunoreactive for immunoglobulin A.[149]

It is not rare for carcinoid tumors of either the classic or (more rarely) the tubular type to be found in the tip of obliterated appendices, often as an incidental microscopic finding. The nodules are sometimes so small that one wonders whether it is correct to regard all of them as neoplasms, as opposed to a nodular hyperplasia of neuroendocrine cells, analogous to the "tumorlets" seen in bronchiectatic lungs and the islet cell hyperplasia found in the chronically inflamed pancreas.

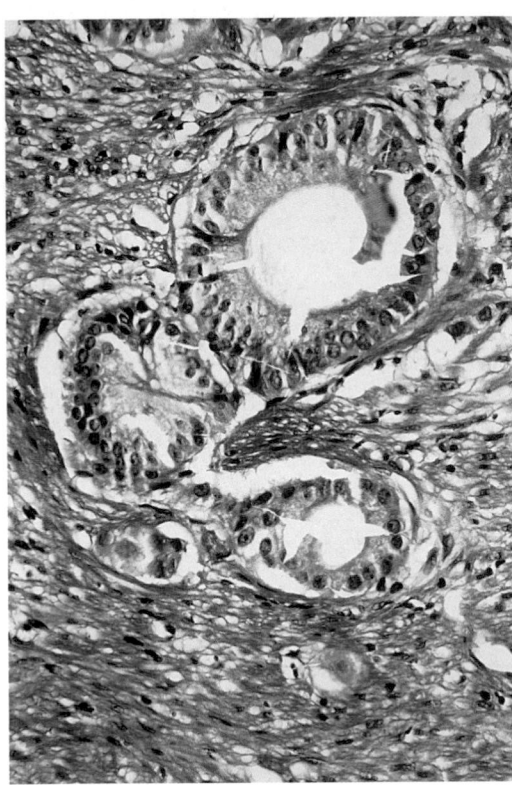

Fig. 11.144 Adenocarcinoid tumor of tubular type.

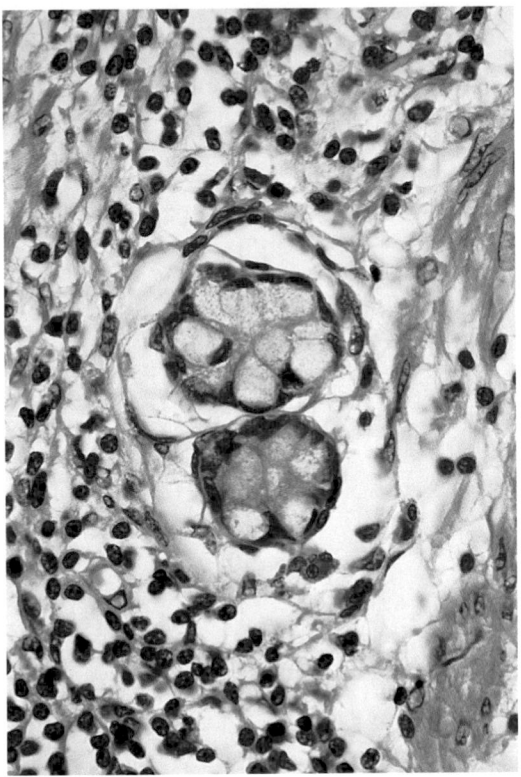

Fig. 11.145 Adenocarcinoid tumor of goblet cell type.

Another subtype of carcinoid with glandular differentiation has been variously called *goblet cell carcinoid*,[141,144,157,179] *goblet cell type adenocarcinoid*,[182] *mucinous carcinoid tumor*,[160] *microglandular carcinoma*,[184] and *crypt cell carcinoma*.[154] Grossly, it may be found in any portion of the appendix and appears as an area of whitish, sometimes mucoid induration without dilatation of the lumen; acute appendicitis is a common complication. Microscopically, and like the other two carcinoid types, it is characterized by predominantly submucosal growth. Extension into the muscle and serosa is common, but the mucosa is characteristically spared, except for areas of apparent connection between tumor nests and the base of the crypts. The tumor itself is formed by small uniform nests of signet ring cells, often arranged in a microglandular fashion and sometimes accompanied by extracellular mucus (Fig. 11.145). A component of lysozyme-positive cells with features of Paneth cells may also be present,[154] as well as foci resembling Brunner glands.[182] Mucicarmine and CEA stains are consistently positive, and argyrophil stains show cytoplasmic granules in approximately 88% of the cases[159,182] (Fig. 11.146). Electron microscopic studies have shown mucin droplets and neurosecretory type granules, some of them probably located in the same cell ("amphicrine cells").[140,145,174] The morphologic, immunohistochemical, and ultrastructural features of this type of carcinoid tumor indicate that all the cells normally present in the crypt of Lieberkuhn may be represented in it, hence the alternative term *crypt cell carcinoma*.[154] As a

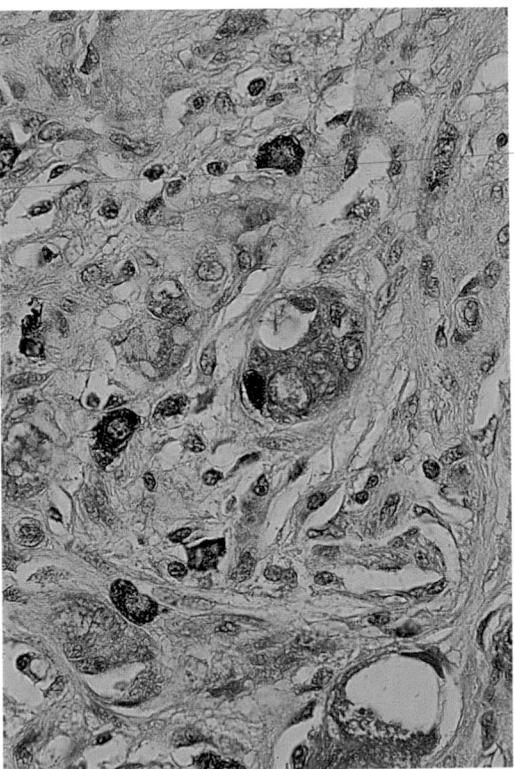

Fig. 11.146 Adenocarcinoid tumor of goblet cell type showing dual positivity for Mayer's mucicarmine (pink) and chromogranin (brown). Some of the chromogranin-positive cells are located within the glands, whereas others appear as isolated elements surrounded by cellular stroma.

matter of fact, small crypt-like structures are often present in it.[143]

At the molecular level, p53 mutations were found in one series in 25% of goblet cell carcinoid tumors and in 44% of typical carcinoid tumors, whereas k-*ras* mutations were not detected in either type.[172]

There is little question that the cells of classic carcinoid tumor have morphologic, immunohistochemical, and ultrastructural features similar to those of the Kultschitsky cells normally located at the base of Lieberkuhn's glands, but there is still debate over whether this tumor arises from these cells or from similar cells located in the lamina propria and submucosa in close association with nerves. In the latter situation, discrete units known as *subepithelial neuroendocrine complexes* are formed, which were first identified by Masson.[149,161,164,167,170,173]

Carcinoid syndrome secondary to appendiceal carcinoid tumor is extremely rare and is almost always related to the presence of liver metastases.[163] Occasionally, appendiceal carcinoids are found to secrete ACTH and to result in a clinical picture of Cushing's syndrome.[156] Five (4.2%) of the patients with carcinoid tumor in the series reported by Moertel et al.[168] had an associated carcinoid of the ileum, and 19 (13%) had a second primary cancer.

The behavior of most classic and tubular carcinoid tumors is very indolent. Metastatic spread is unusual, often limited to the regional lymph nodes and usually restricted to tumors greater than 2 cm in diameter, allowing for the occasional exception.[162] Most authors agree that simple appendectomy is adequate therapy for carcinoid tumors measuring less than 1 cm (even if associated with mesoappendix infiltration) and that right hemicolectomy is indicated for the rare tumors measuring more than 2 cm.[148,168,169,175,175a] The treatment of carcinoid tumors measuring 1 to 2 cm remains controversial,[175,180] with a tendency for a more radical approach in young patients.[175,180] The behavior of mucinous carcinoid tumor is much more aggressive than that of the other two types, particularly if the tumor has transmural involvement

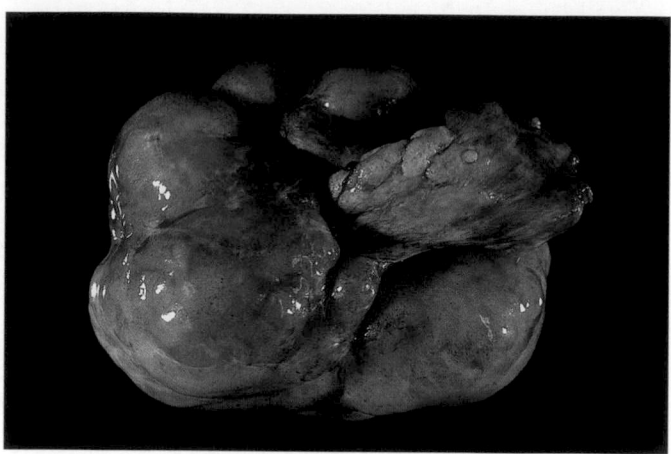

Fig. 11.148 Ovarian metastasis of appendiceal adenocarcinoid tumor of goblet cell type. Sometimes this constitutes the initial presentation of this tumor type.

(Fig. 11.147), if it has extended into the cecum at the time of the operation, and if it contains signet ring cells or single-file structures on microscopic examination (in which case Burke et al.[143] use the term *mixed carcinoid-adenocarcinoma* for it). Metastases have been documented in 8% to 20% of the cases.[147,171,179,182,184] They are particularly common in the ovary, where they can acquire the features of Krukenberg tumor[152,153,165] (Fig. 11.148). Because of this, the performance of a right hemicolectomy is usually recommended for this tumor type, especially if it has spread beyond the appendix and/or shows a high mitotic count.[182]

Before leaving the subject of neuroendocrine tumors of the appendix, it should be mentioned that a case interpreted as a primary *gangliocytic paraganglioma* of this organ has been reported.[181]

Other lesions

Heterotopic gastric and **esophageal tissue** have been described within the appendix.[190]

Melanosis of appendix refers to the presence of melanin-like pigment in lamina propria macrophages. It is analogous to the homonymous large bowel condition and is relatively common at the microscopic level both in the pediatric and in the adult population.[192,207]

Endometriosis, endosalpingiosis, and **ectopic decidual reaction** ("deciduosis") are sometimes seen as incidental findings beneath the serosa[186,202,211]; exceptionally, endometriosis may result in appendiceal rupture. As in other sites, it can be accompanied by mucinous epithelium ("endocervicosis") and/or atypical/dysplastic changes.[197] Appendiceal endometriosis can also lead to obstruction of the lumen with a mucocele-like distal dilatation.[189]

Diverticula of the appendix are usually multiple (Fig. 11.149). They are of the "false" type, arising in a weak

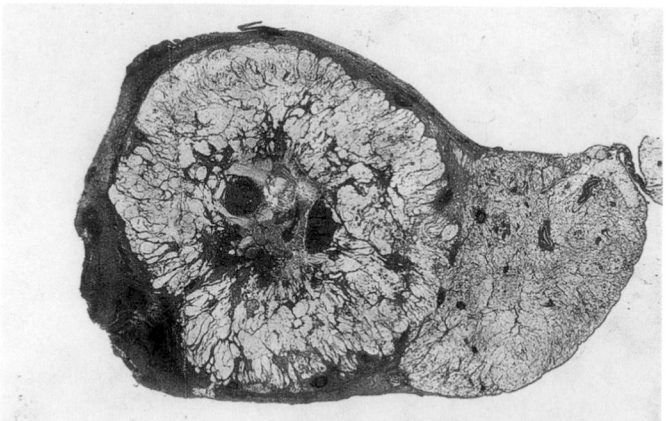

Fig. 11.147 Adenocarcinoid tumor of goblet cell type showing transmural involvement and massive mucin production.

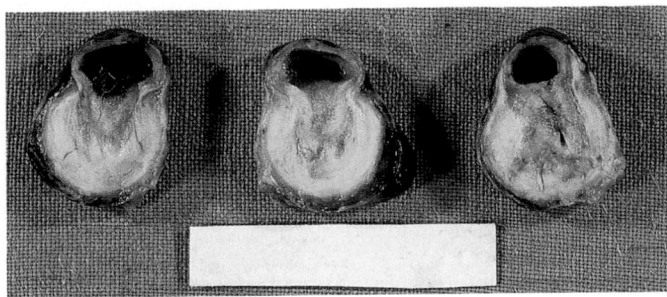

Fig. 11.149 Cross sections of appendix affected by diverticulosis.

area as a result of increased intraluminal pressure. Diverticulitis may occur, resulting in a clinical picture indistinguishable from that of acute appendicitis.[188,206] Diverticulosis of the appendix may have diverse etiologies[199]; it is relatively common in patients with cystic fibrosis, presumably as a result of increased intraluminal pressure produced by the inspissated mucus.[191]

Inverted appendiceal stump from a previous appendectomy may appear as a filling defect in the cecum on barium examination and simulate a neoplasm.

Intussusception (invagination) of the appendix into the cecal lumen may develop spontaneously; it may be of the entire appendix or, more commonly, of only the base.[194,196] The underlying cause is often lymphoid hyperplasia.

Inflammatory fibroid tumor similar to that more commonly seen in the small bowel can involve the appendix.[201]

Granular cell tumor can involve the appendiceal wall.[195] In approximately 5% of appendectomy specimens, single or clustered granular cells with an appearance similar to those of granular cell tumor are found in the wall[193]; these seem to represent altered smooth muscle cells rather than Schwann cells.[209]

Paraganglioma located in the mesoappendix has been described.[187]

Neuroma (neurogenous hyperplasia) of the appendix presenting with the gross appearance of fibrous obliteration was thoroughly described by Masson over 50 years ago[198,199] (Fig. 11.150); recent immunohistochemical and ultrastructural studies have confirmed the correctness of his interpretation.[204,210] Endocrine cells are often found within the hypertrophied nerve bundles, and these may well be the cells of origin for carcinoid tumor.

Neurofibroma and **schwannoma** of the appendix or mesoappendix has been reported, the latter either as a solitary lesion or as a component of Recklinghausen's disease.[203]

Angiomyolipoma has been reported in the appendix, the appearance being that of the so-called *epithelioid monotypic variety* of this tumor type.[205]

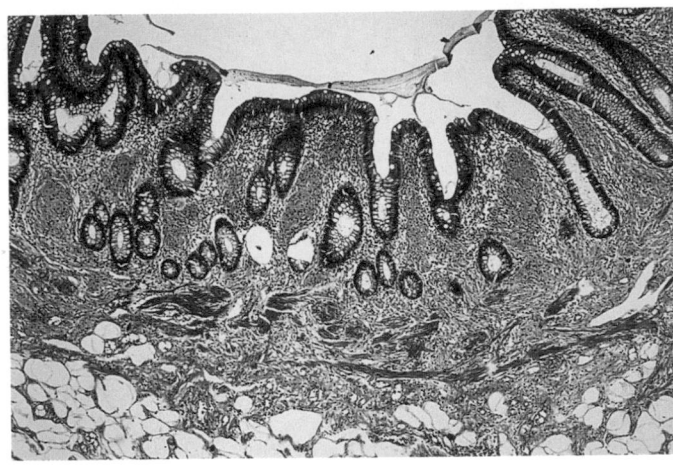

A

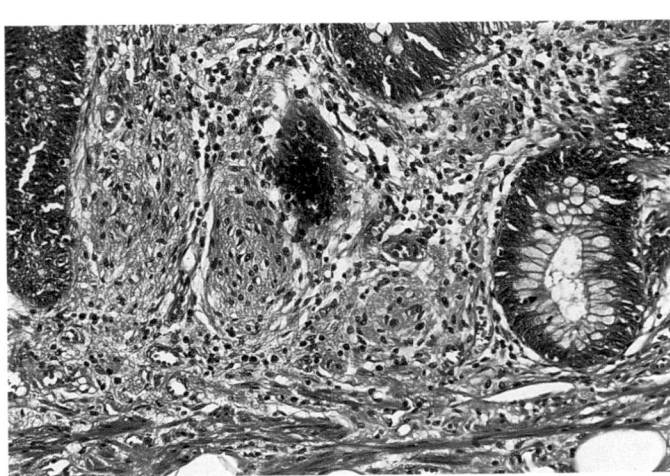

B

Fig. 11.150 A and **B,** Low- and high-power view of neuroma (neurogenous hyperplasia) of appendix. The proliferating spindle cells shown in these photographs were strongly immunoreactive for S-100 protein.

GIST can rarely involve the appendix as a primary site; most of the reported cases have featured skenoid fibers.[201] There have also been isolated reports of appendiceal **leiomyosarcoma** in HIV-infected patients.[201]

Malignant lymphoma can involve the appendix; cases of Burkitt's lymphoma have been seen in children presenting with the clinical picture of appendicitis.[208]

Kaposi's sarcoma involving the appendix of HIV-infected individuals and resulting in acute appendicitis has been reported.[212]

Metastases to the appendix usually originate in carcinomas of the gastrointestinal tract, breast, or female genital tract[185] (Fig. 11.151).

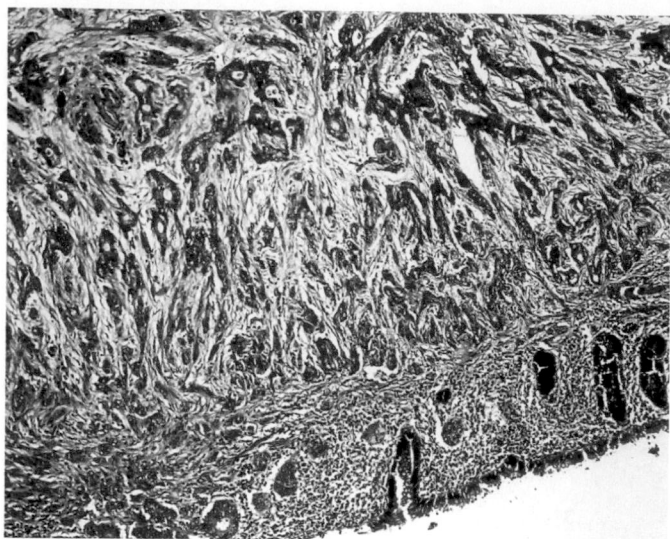

Fig. 11.151 Carcinoma of breast metastatic to appendix, covered by slightly atrophic mucosa.

References

Normal anatomy

1 Andreou P, Blain S, Du Boulay CE. A histopathological study of the appendix at autopsy and after surgical resection. Histopathology 1990, **17**: 427–431.
2 Guidry SP, Poole GV. The anatomy of appendicitis. Am Surg 1994, **60**: 68–71.
3 Millikin PD. Eosinophilic argentaffin cells in the human appendix. Arch Pathol 1974, **98**: 393–395.
4 Segal GH, Petras RE. Vermiform appendix. In Sternberg S (ed.): Histology for pathologists, ed. 2. Philadelphia, 1997, Lippincott-Raven, pp. 539–550.

Acute appendicitis
Epidemiology and pathogenesis

5 Binderow SR, Shaked AA. Acute appendicitis in patients with AIDS/HIV infection. Am J Surg 1991, **162**: 9–12.
6 Bizer LS. Acute appendicitis is rarely the initial presentation of cecal cancer in an elderly patient. J Surg Oncol 1993, **54**: 45–46.
7 Burkitt DP. The aetiology of appendicitis. Br J Surg 1971, **58**: 695–699.
8 Carr NJ. The pathology of acute appendicitis. Ann Diagn Pathol 2000, **4**: 46–58.
9 Dymock RB. Pathological changes in the appendix. A review of 1000 cases. Pathology 1977, **9**: 331–339.
10 Forbes GB, Lloyd-Davies RW. Calculous disease of the vermiform appendix. Gut 1966, **7**: 583–592.
11 Gray GF Jr, Wackym PA. Surgical pathology of the vermiform appendix. Part 2. Pathol Annu 1986, **21**: 111–144.
12 Luckmann R, Davis P. The epidemiology of acute appendicitis in California. Racial, gender, and seasonal variation. Epidemiology 1991, **2**: 323–330.
13 Nathans AA, Merenstein H, Brown SS. Lymphoid hyperplasia of the appendix. Pediatrics 1955, **12**: 516–524.
14 Peltokallio P. Acute appendicitis associated with carcinoma of the colon. Dis Colon Rectum 1966, **9**: 453–456.
15 Reif RM. Viral appendicitis. Hum Pathol 1981, **12**: 193–196.
16 Sisson RG, Ahlvin RC, Harlow MC. Superficial mucosal ulceration and the pathogenesis of acute appendicitis in childhood. Am J Surg 1971, **122**: 378–380.
17 Wangensteen OH, Dennis C. Experimental proof of the obstructive origin of appendicitis in man. Ann Surg 1939, **110**: 629–647.
18 Whitney TM, Macho JR, Russell TR, Bossart KJ, Heer FW, Schecter WP. Appendicitis in acquired immunodeficiency syndrome. Am J Surg 1992, **164**: 467–470.
19 Zarabi M, LaBach JP. Ganglioneuroma causing acute appendicitis. Hum Pathol 1982, **13**: 1143–1146.

Clinical features

20 Albiston E. The role of radiological imaging in the diagnosis of acute appendicitis. Can J Gastroenterol 2002, **16**: 451–463.
21 Alecce AA, Sullivan SG, Ashworth W. Spontaneous idiopathic segmental infarction of the omentum. Ann Surg 1955, **142**: 316–320.
22 Angel CA, Rao BN, Wrenn E Jr, Lobe TE, Kumar AP. Acute appendicitis in children with leukemia and other malignancies. Still a diagnostic dilemma. J Pediatr Surg 1992, **27**: 476–479.
23 Fedyshin P, Kelvin FM, Rice RP. Nonspecificity of barium enema findings in acute appendicitis. Am J Radiol 1984, **143**: 99–102.
24 Gilmore OJA, Browett JP, Griffin PH, Ross IK, Brodribb AJM, Cooke TJC, Higgs MJ, Williamson RCN. Appendicitis and mimicking conditions. A prospective study. Lancet 1975, **2**: 421–424.
25 Hershko DD, Sroka G, Bahouth H, Ghersin E, Mahajna A, Krausz MM. The role of selective computed tomography in the diagnosis and management of suspected acute appendicitis. Am Surg 2002, **68**: 1003–1007.
26 Malone AJ Jr, Wolf CR, Malmed AS, Melliere BF. Diagnosis of acute appendicitis. Value of unenhanced CT. AJR Am J Roentgenol 1993, **160**: 763–766.
27 Marrero RR Jr, Barnwell S, Hoover EL. Appendicitis in children. A continuing clinical challenge. J Natl Med Assoc 1992, **84**: 850–852.
28 Ooms HW, Koumans RK, Ho Kang You PJ, Puylaert JB. Ultrasonography in the diagnosis of acute appendicitis. Br J Surg 1991, **78**: 315–318.
29 Puig S, Hormann M, Rebhandl W, Felder-Puig R, Prokop M, Paya K. US as a primary diagnostic tool in relation to negative appendectomy: six years experience. Radiology 2003, **226**: 101–104.
30 Reynolds SL. Missed appendicitis in a pediatric emergency department. Pediatr Emerg Care 1993, **9**: 1–3.
31 Thorbjarnarson B, Loehr WJ. Acute appendicitis in patients over the age of sixty. Surg Gynecol Obstet 1967, **125**: 1277–1280.
32 van Dieijen-Visser MP, Go PM, Brombacher PJ. The value of laboratory tests in patients suspected of acute appendicitis. Eur J Clin Chem Clin Biochem 1991, **29**: 749–752.
33 Williams JS, Hale HW Jr. Acute appendicitis in the elderly. Review of 83 cases. Ann Surg 1965, **162**: 208–212.
34 Young VK, Caldwell MT, Watson RG. Correlation of peritoneal aspiration cytology with acute appendicitis. Ir J Med Sci 1993, **162**: 306–308.

Pathologic features

35 Baron EJ, Bennion R, Thompson J, Strong C, Summanen P, McTeague M, Finegold SM. A microbiological comparison between acute and complicated appendicitis. Clin Infect Dis 1992, **14**: 227–231.
36 Birch PJ, Richmond I, Bennett MK. Xanthogranulomatous appendicitis. Histopathology 1993, **22**: 597–598.
37 Butler C. Surgical pathology of acute appendicitis. Hum Pathol 1981, **12**: 870–878.
38 Carr NJ, Montgomery E. Patterns of healing in the appendix. The morphologic changes in resolving primary acute appendicitis and a comparison with Crohn's disease. Int J Surg Pathol 1994, **2**: 23–30.

39 Mueller BA, Daling JR, Moore DE, Weiss NS, Spadoni LR, Stadel BV, Soules MR. Appendectomy and the risk of tubal infertility. N Engl J Med 1986, **315:** 1506–1508.

40 Mukherjee A, Schlenker E, LaMasters T, Johnson M, Brunz J, Thomas E. Periappendicitis: is it a clinical entity? Am Surg 2002, **68:** 913–916.

41 Nemeth L, Reen DJ, O'Briain DS, McDermott M, Puri P. Evidence of an inflammatory pathologic condition in "normal" appendices following emergency appendectomy. Arch Pathol Lab Med 2001, **125:** 759–764.

42 Remington JH, McDonald JR. Vascular thrombosis in acute appendicitis. Surgery 1948, **24:** 787–792.

43 Rex JC, Harrison EG Jr, Priestley JT. Appendicitis and ligneous perityphlitis. Arch Surg 1961, **82:** 735–745.

44 Sisson RG, Ahlvin RC, Harlow MC. Superficial mucosal ulceration and the pathogenesis of acute appendicitis in childhood. Am J Surg 1971, **122:** 378–380.

45 Thadepalli H, Mandal AK, Chuah SK, Lou MA. Bacteriology of the appendix and the ileum in health and in appendicitis. Am Surg 1991, **57:** 317–322.

46 Therkelsen F. On histologic diagnosis of appendicitis. Acta Chir Scand 1948, **94**(Suppl 108): 1–48.

47 Tsuji M, Puri P, Reen DJ. Characterization of the local inflammatory response in appendicitis. J Pediatr Gastroenterol Nutr 1993, **16:** 43–48.

Treatment

48 Berry J Jr, Malt RA. Appendicitis near its centenary. Ann Surg 1984, **200:** 567–575.

49 Maxwell JM, Ragland JJ. Appendicitis. Improvements in diagnosis and treatment. Am Surg 1991, **57:** 282–285.

50 Scully RE, Vickery AL. Surgical pathology at the hospitals of Harvard Medical School. In Rosai J (ed.): Guiding the Surgeon's Hand. The history of American Surgical Pathology. Washington D.C., 1997, American Registry of Pathology, pp. 88–89.

51 Williams GR. A history of appendicitis. With anecdotes illustrating its importance. Ann Surg 1983, **197:** 495–506.

Chronic appendicitis

52 Xiong S, Puri P, Nemeth L, O'Briain DS, Reen DJ. Neuronal hypertrophy in acute appendicitis. Arch Pathol Lab Med 2000, **124:** 1429–1433.

Other inflammatory processes

53 Allen DC, Biggart JD. Granulomatous disease in the vermiform appendix. J Clin Pathol 1983, **36:** 632–638.

54 Ariel I, Vinograd I, Hershlag A, Olsha O, Argov S, Klausner JM, Rabau MY, Freund U, Rosenmann E. Crohn's disease isolated to the appendix. Truths and fallacies. Hum Pathol 1986, **17:** 1116–1121.

55 Bennion RS, Thompson JE Jr, Gil J, Schmit PJ. The role of *Yersinia enterocolitica* in appendicitis in the southwestern United States. Am Surg 1991, **57:** 766–768.

56 Burke AP, Sobin LH, Virmani R. Localized vasculitis of the gastrointestinal tract. Am J Surg Pathol 1995, **19:** 338–349.

57 Collins DC. 71,000 human appendix specimens. A final report, summarizing forty years' study. Am J Proctol 1963, **14:** 265–281.

58 Cullinane DC, Schultz SC, Zellos L, Holt RW. Sarcoidosis manifesting as acute appendicitis: report of a case. Dis Colon Rectum 1997, **40:** 109–111.

59 Davison AM, Dixon MF. The appendix as a "skip lesion" in ulcerative colitis. Histopathology 1990, **16:** 93–95.

60 Dieterich DT, Kim MH, McMeeding A, Rotterdam H. Cytomegalovirus appendicitis in a patient with acquired immunodeficiency syndrome. Am J Gastroenterol 1991, **86:** 904–906.

61 Dudley TH Jr, Dean PJ. Idiopathic granulomatous appendicitis, or Crohn's disease of the appendix revisited. Hum Pathol 1993, **24:** 595–601.

62 Galloway WH. Appendicitis in the course of measles. Br Med J 1957, **2:** 1412–1414.

63 Gaulier A, Sabatier P, Prevot S, Fournier JG. Do measles early giant cells result from fusion of non-infected cells? An immunohistochemical and in situ hybridization study in a case of morbillous appendicitis. Virchows Arch [A] 1991, **419:** 245–249.

64 Goldblum JR, Appelman HD. Appendiceal involvement in ulcerative colitis. Mod Pathol 1992, **5:** 607–610.

64a Guo G, Greenson JK. Histopathology of interval (delayed) appendectomy specimens. Am J Surg Pathol 2003, **27:** 1147–1151.

65 Huang JC, Appelman HD. Another look at chronic appendicitis resembling Crohn's disease. Mod Pathol 1996, **9:** 975–981.

66 Kahn E, Markowitz J, Daum F. The appendix in inflammatory bowel disease in children. Mod Pathol 1992, **5:** 380–383.

67 Kroft SH, Stryker SJ, Rao MS. Appendiceal involvement as a skip lesion in ulcerative colitis. Mod Pathol 1994, **7:** 912–914.

68 Lamps LW, Madhusudhan KT, Greenson JK, Pierce RH, Massoll NA, Chiles MC, Dean PJ, Scott MA. The role of Yersinia enterocolitica and Yersinia pseudotuberculosis in granulomatous appendicitis: a histologic and molecular study. Am J Surg Pathol 2001, **25:** 508–515.

69 Lauwers GY, Perez-Atayde A, Dorfman RF, Rosai J. The digestive system manifestations of Rosai-Dorfman disease (sinus histiocytosis with massive lymphadenopathy): review of 11 cases. Hum Pathol 2000, **31:** 380–385.

70 Malik AK, Hanum N, Yip CH. Acute isolated amoebic appendicitis. Histopathology 1994, **24:** 87–88.

71 Moyana TN. Necrotizing arteritis of the vermiform appendix. A clinicopathologic study of 12 cases. Arch Pathol Lab Med 1988, **112:** 738–741.

72 Moyana TN, Kulaga A, Xiang J. Granulomatous appendicitis in acute myeloblastic leukaemia: expanding the clinicopathologic spectrum of invasive candidiasis. Arch Pathol Lab Med 1996, **120:** 203–205.

73 Neumayer LA, Makar R, Ampel NM, Zukoski CF. Cytomegalovirus appendicitis in a patient with human immunodeficiency virus infection. Case report and review of the literature. Arch Surg 1993, **128:** 467–468.

74 Noodleman JS. Eosinophilic appendicitis. Demonstration of *Strongyloides stercoralis* as a causative agent. Arch Pathol Lab Med 1981, **105:** 148–149.

75 O'Brien A, O'Briain DS. Infectious mononucleosis. Appendiceal lymphoid tissue involvement parallels characteristic lymph node changes. Arch Pathol Lab Med 1985, **109:** 680–682.

76 Oren R, Rachmilewitz D. Preoperative clues to Crohn's disease in suspected, acute appendicitis. Report of 12 cases and review of the literature. J Clin Gastroenterol 1992, **15:** 306–310.

77 Paik SY, Oh JT, Choi YJ, Know KW, Yang WI. Measles-related appendicitis: differing histologic findings according to the stage. Arch Pathol Lab Med 2002, **126:** 82–84.

78 Ramsden K, Freeth M. Cryptosporidial infection presenting as an acute appendicitis. Histopathology 1989, **14:** 209–211.

79 Satti MB, Tamimi DM, Sohaibani MA, Quorain AA. Appendicular schistosomiasis. A cause of clinical acute appendicitis? J Clin Pathol 1987, **40:** 424–428.

80 Scott IS, Sheaff M, Coumbe A, Freakins RM, Rampton DS. Appendiceal inflammation in ulcerative colitis. Histopathology 1998, **33:** 168–173.

81 Stangl PC, Herbst F, Birner P, Oberhuber G. Crohn's disease of the appendix. Virchows Arch 2002, **440:** 397–403.

82 Stemmerman GN. Eosinophilic granuloma of the appendix. A study of its relation to *Strongyloides* infestation. Am J Clin Pathol 1961, **36:** 524–531.

83 Timmcke AE. Granulomatous appendicitis. Is it Crohn's disease? Report of a case and review of the literature. Am J Gastroenterol 1986, **81**: 283–287.

84 Tinker MA, Viswanathan B, Laufer H, Margolis IB. Acute appendicitis and pernicious anemia as complications of gastrointestinal sarcoidosis. Am J Gastroenterol 1984, **79**: 868–872.

85 van Spreeuwel JP, Lindeman J, Bax R, Elbers HJR, Sybrandy R, Meijer CJLM. *Campylobacter*-associated appendicitis. Prevalence and clinicopathologic features. Pathol Annu 1987, **22**(Pt 1): 55–65.

86 Vinuela A, Fernandez-Rojo F, Martinez-Merino A. *Oxyuris* granulomas of pelvic peritoneum and appendicular wall. Histopathology 1979, **3**: 69–77.

87 Wiebe BM. Appendicitis and *Enterobius vermicularis*. Scand J Gastroenterol 1991, **26**: 336–338.

Tumors

Mucinous tumors and tumorlike conditions (including so-called "mucocele"); pseudomyxoma peritonei

88 Adsay NV, Merati K, Nassar H, Shia J, Sarkar F, Pierson CR, Cheng JD, Visscher DW, Hruban RH, Klimstra DS. Pathogenesis of colloid carcinoma of exocrine organs. Coupling of gel-forming mucin (MUC2) production with altered cell polarity and abnormal cell-stroma interaction may be the key factor in the morphogenesis and indolent behavior of colloid carcinoma in the breast and pancreas. Am J Surg Pathol 2003, **27**: 571–578.

89 Carr NJ, Sobin LH. Unusual tumors of the appendix and pseudomyxoma peritonei. Semin Diagn Pathol 1996, **13**: 314–325.

90 Cheng KK. An experimental study of mucocele of the appendix and pseudomyxoma peritonei. J Pathol Bacteriol 1940, **61**: 217–225.

91 Chuaqui RF, Zhuang Z, Emmert-Buck MR, Bryant BR, Nogales F, Tavassoli FA, Merino MJ. Genetic analysis of synchronous mucinous tumors of the ovary and appendix. Hum Pathol 1996, **27**: 165–171.

92 Cuatrecasas M, Matias-Guiu X, Prat J. Synchronous mucinous tumors of the appendix and the ovary associated with pseudomyxoma peritonei: A clinicopathologic study of six cases with comparative analysis of c-Ki-ras mutations. Am J Surg Pathol 1996, **20**: 739–746.

93 Darby AJ, Doctor A. Villous papilloma of the appendix associated with mucocoele and intussusception. Postgrad Med J 1974, **50**: 650–654.

94 Driman DK, Melega DE, Vilos GA, Plewes EA. Mucocele of the appendix secondary to endometriosis. Report of two cases, one with localized pseudomyxoma peritonei. Am J Clin Pathol 2000, **113**: 860–864.

95 Du Plessis DG, Louw JA, Wranz PA. Mucinous epithelial cysts of the spleen associated with pseudomyxoma peritonei. Histopathology 1999, **35**: 551–557.

96 Esquivel J, Sugarbaker PH. Pseudomyxoma peritonei in a hernia sac: analysis of 20 patients in whom mucoid fluid was found during a hernia repair. Eur J Surg Oncol 2001, **27**: 54–58.

97 Hameed K. Villous adenoma of the vermiform appendix with Cushing's syndrome. Ultrastructural study of a case. Cancer 1971, **27**: 681–686.

98 Higa E, Rosai J, Pizzimbono CA, Wise L. Mucosal hyperplasia, mucinous cystadenoma and mucinous cystadenocarcinoma of the appendix. A reevaluation of appendiceal "mucocele." Cancer 1973, **32**: 1525–1541.

99 Hilsabeck JR, Judd ES Jr, Woolner LB. Carcinoma of the vermiform appendix. Surg Clin North Am 1951, **31**: 995–1011.

100 Klemi PJ, Nevalainen TJ, Aho AJ. The histogenesis of mucinous cystadenoma of the appendix. Arch Pathol 1980, **104**: 162–163.

101 Lamps LW, Gray GF, Dilday BR, Washington MK. The coexistence of low-grade mucinous neoplasms of the appendix

and appendiceal diverticula: a possible role in the pathogenesis of pseudomyxoma peritonei. Mod Pathol 2000, **13**: 495–501.

102 Landen S, Bertrand C, Maddern GJ, Herman D, Pourbaix A, de Neve A, Schmitz A. Appendiceal mucoceles and pseudomyxoma peritonei. Surg Gynecol Obstet 1992, **175**: 401–404.

103 Little JM, Halliday JP, Glenn DC. Pseudomyxoma peritonei. Lancet 1969, **2**: 659–663.

103a Maru DM, Canada A, Rashid A, Wu TT, Cleary KC, Hamilton SR. Frequent 18q loss in appendiceal mucinous and non-mucinous adenocarcinoma. (Abstract) Mod Pathol 2003, **16**: 127a.

104 Misdraji J, Yantiss RK, Graeme-Cook FM, Balis UJ, Young RH. Appendiceal mucinous neoplasms: a clinicopathological analysis of 107 cases. Am J Surg Pathol 2003, **27**: 1089–1103.

105 Moore WF, Bentley RC, Kim KR, Olatidoye B, Gray SR, Robboy SJ. Goblet-cell mucinous epithelium lining the endometrium and endocervix: evidence of a metastasis from an appendiceal primary tumor through the use of cytokeratin-7 and -20 immunostains. Int J Gynecol Pathol 1998, **17**: 363–367.

106 Mortman KD, Sugarbaker PA, Shmookler BM, DeGuzman VC, Soberman MS. Pulmonary metastases in pseudomyxoma peritonei syndrome. Ann Thorac Surg 1997, **64**: 1434–1436.

107 Nogales FF, Caballero T, Fernandez PL, Linares J, Ruiz-Avila I. Pseudomyxoma peritonei et ovarii associated with sequential ovarian and appendicular tumors and acromegaly. Gynecol Oncol 1991, **40**: 78–80.

108 O'Connell JT, Tomlinson JS, Roberts AA, McGonigle KF, Barsky SH. Pseudomyxoma peritonei is a disease of MUC2-expressing goblet cells. Am J Pathol 2002, **161**: 551–564.

109 Peifer M. Travel bulletin – traffic jams cause tumors. Science 2000, **289**: 67–69.

110 Prayson RA, Hart WR, Petras RE. Pseudomyxoma peritonei. A clinicopathologic study of 19 cases with emphasis on site of origin and nature of associated ovarian tumors. Am J Surg Pathol 1994, **18**: 591–603.

111 Qizilbash AH. Hyperplastic (metaplastic) polyps of the appendix. Report of 19 cases. Arch Pathol 1974, **97**: 385–388.

112 Qizilbash AH. Mucoceles of the appendix. Their relationship to hyperplastic polyps, mucinous cystadenomas, and cystadenocarcinomas. Arch Pathol 1975, **99**: 548–555.

113 Ronnett BM, Kurman RJ, Shmookler BM, Sugarbaker PH, Young RH. The morphologic spectrum of ovarian metastases of appendiceal adenocarcinomas: a clinicopathologic and immunohistochemical analysis of tumors often misinterpreted as primary ovarian tumors or metastatic tumors from other gastrointestinal sites. Am J Surg Pathol 1997, **21**: 1144–1155.

114 Ronnett BM, Shmookler BM, Diener-West M, Sugarbaker PH, Kurman RJ. Immunohistochemical evidence supporting the appendiceal origin of pseudomyxoma peritonei in women. Int J Gynecol Pathol 1997, **16**: 1–9.

115 Ronnett BM, Yan H, Kurman RJ, Shmookler BM, Wu L, Sugarbaker PH. Patients with pseudomyxoma peritonei associated with disseminated peritoneal adenomucinosis have a significantly more favorable prognosis than patients with peritoneal mucinous carcinomatosis. Cancer 2001, **92**: 85–91.

116 Schwartz MR. Mucoceles and epithelial tumors of the appendix: a new look at nomenclature and prognostic factors. Adv Anat Pathol 1996, **3**: 355–361.

117 Seidman JD, Elsayed AM, Sobin LH, Tavassoli FA. Association of mucinous tumors of the ovary and appendix. A clinicopathologic study of 25 cases. Am J Surg Pathol 1993, **17**: 22–34.

118 Smith JW, Kemeny N, Caldwell C, Banner P, Sigurdson E, Huvos A. Pseudomyxoma peritonei of appendiceal origin. The Memorial Sloan-Kettering Cancer Center experience. Cancer 1992, **70**: 396–401.

119 Sugarbaker PH. Cytoreduction including total gastrectomy for pseudomyxoma peritonei. Br J Surg 2002, **89**: 208–212.

120 Sugarbaker PH, Chang D. Results of treatment of 385 patients with peritoneal surface spread of appendiceal malignancy. Ann Surg Oncol 1999, **6**: 727–731.

121 Sugarbaker PH, Yan H, Shmookler B. Pedunculated peritoneal surface polyps in pseudomyxoma peritonei syndrome. Histopathology 2001, **39**: 525–528.

122 Sumithran E, Susil BJ. Concomitant mucinous tumors of appendix and ovary. Result of a neoplastic field change? Cancer 1992, **70**: 2980–2983.

123 Szych C, Staebler A, Connolly DC, Wu R, Cho KR, Ronnett BM. Molecular genetic evidence supporting the clonality and appendiceal origin of pseudomyxoma peritonei in women. Am J Pathol 1999, **154**: 1849–1855.

124 Williams GR, du Boulay CE, Roche WR. Benign epithelial neoplasms of the appendix. Classification and clinical associations. Histopathology 1992, **21**: 447–451.

125 Williams RA, Whitehead R. Non-carcinoid epithelial tumours of the appendix – a proposed classification. Pathology 1986, **18**: 50–53.

126 Wolff M, Ahmed N. Epithelial neoplasms of the vermiform appendix (exclusive of carcinoid). Part II. Cystadenomas, papillary adenomas, and adenomatous polyps of the appendix. Cancer 1976, **37**: 2511–2522.

127 Yan H, Pestieau SR, Shmookler BM, Sugarbaker PH. Histopathologic analysis in 46 patients with pseudomyxoma peritonei syndrome: failure versus success with a second-look operation. Mod Pathol 2001, **14**: 164–171.

128 Younes M, Katikaneni PR, Lechago J. Association between mucosal hyperplasia of the appendix and adenocarcinoma of the colon. Histopathology 1995, **26**: 33–37.

129 Young RH, Gilks CB, Scully RE. Mucinous tumors of the appendix associated with mucinous tumors of the ovary and pseudomyxoma peritonei. A clinicopathological analysis of 22 cases supporting an origin in the appendix. Am J Surg Pathol 1991, **15**: 415–429.

130 Young RH, Rosenberg AE, Clement PB. Mucin deposits within inguinal hernia sacs: a presenting finding of low-grade mucinous cystic tumors of the appendix. A report of two cases and a review of the literature. Mod Pathol 1997, **10**: 1228–1232.

Adenocarcinoma

131 Carr NJ, McCarthy WF, Sobin LH. Epithelial noncarcinoid tumors and tumor-like lesions of the appendix. A clinicopathologic study of 184 patients with a multivariate analysis of prognostic factors. Cancer 1995, **75**: 757–768.

132 Kabbani W, Houlihan PS, Luthra R, Hamilton SR, Rashid A. Mucinous and nonmucinous appendiceal adenocarcinomas: different clinicopathological features but similar genetic alterations. Mod Pathol 2002, **15**: 599–605.

133 Li CC, Hirokawa M, Qian ZR, Xu B, Sano T. Expression of E-cadherin, beta-catenin, and Ki-57 in goblet cell carcinoids of the appendix: an immunohistochemical study with clinical correlation. Endocr Pathol 2002, **13**: 47–58.

134 Mauritzen K. Primary adenocarcinoma of the appendix. Report of sixteen cases. Acta Chir Scand 1958, **115**: 447–456.

135 McCusker ME, Cotè TR, Clegg LX, Sobin LH. Primary malignant neoplasms of the appendix: a population-based study from the surveillance, epidemiology and end-result program, 1973–1998. Cancer 2002, **94**: 3307–3312.

136 Qizilbash AH. Primary adenocarcinoma of the appendix. A clinicopathological study of 11 cases. Arch Pathol 1975, **99**: 556–562.

137 Sieracki JC, Tesluck H. Primary adenocarcinoma of vermiform appendix. Cancer 1956, **9**: 997–1011.

138 Steinberg M, Cohn I Jr. Primary adenocarcinoma of the appendix. Surgery 1967, **61**: 644–660.

139 Wolff M, Ahmed N. Epithelial neoplasms of the vermiform appendix (exclusive of carcinoid). Part I. Adenocarcinoma of the appendix. Cancer 1976, **37**: 2493–2510.

Carcinoid tumor

140 Abt AB, Carter SL. Goblet cell carcinoid of the appendix. An ultrastructural and histochemical study. Arch Pathol Lab Med 1976, **100**: 301–306.

141 Anderson NH, Somerville JE, Johnston CF, Hayes DM, Buchanan KD, Sloan JM. Appendiceal goblet cell carcinoids. A clinicopathological and immunohistochemical study. Histopathology 1991, **18**: 61–65.

142 Burke AP, Sobin LH, Federspiel BH, Shekitka KM. Appendiceal carcinoids. Correlation of histology and immunohistochemistry. Mod Pathol 1989, **2**: 630–637.

143 Burke AP, Sobin LH, Federspiel BH, Shekitka KM, Helwig EB. Goblet cell carcinoids and related tumors of the vermiform appendix. Am J Clin Pathol 1990, **94**: 27–35.

144 Chen V. Goblet cell carcinoid tumors of the appendix. Arch Pathol Lab Med 1979, **103**: 180–182.

145 Cooper PH, Warkel RL. Ultrastructure of the goblet cell type of adenocarcinoma of the appendix. Cancer 1978, **42**: 2687–2695.

146 Dische FE. Argentaffin and non-argentaffin carcinoid tumours of the appendix. J Clin Pathol 1968, **21**: 60–66.

147 Edmonds P, Merino MJ, LiVolsi VA, Duray PH. Adenocarcinoid (mucinous carcinoid) of the appendix. Gastroenterology 1984, **86**: 302–309.

148 Glasser CM, Bhagavan BS. Carcinoid tumors of the appendix. Arch Pathol Lab Med 1980, **104**: 272–275.

149 Goddard MJ, Lonsdale RN. The histogenesis of appendiceal carcinoid tumours. Histopathology 1992, **20**: 345–349.

150 Goolsby CL, Punyarit P, Mehl PJ, Rao MS. Flow cytometric DNA analysis of carcinoid tumors of the ileum and appendix. Hum Pathol 1992, **23**: 1340–1343.

151 Hirose T, Sano T, Hizawa K. Ultrastructural study on an appendiceal carcinoid tumor showing intra-nerve fiber growth. Acta Pathol Jpn 1986, **36**: 123–131.

152 Hirschfield LS, Kahn LB, Winkler B, Bochner RZ, Gibstein AA. Adenocarcinoid of the appendix presenting as bilateral Krukenberg's tumor of the ovaries. Immunohistochemical and ultrastructural studies and literature review. Arch Pathol Lab Med 1985, **109**: 930–933.

153 Ikeda E, Tsutsumi Y, Yoshida H, Yanagi K. Goblet cell carcinoid of the vermiform appendix with ovarian metastasis mimicking mucinous cystadenocarcinoma. Acta Pathol Jpn 1991, **41**: 455–460.

154 Isaacson P. Crypt cell carcinoma of the appendix (so-called adenocarcinoid tumor). Am J Surg Pathol 1981, **5**: 213–224.

155 Iwafuchi M, Watanabe H, Kijima H, Ajioka Y, Shimoda T, Iwashita A, Ito S. Immunohistochemical and ultrastructural studies of twelve argentaffin and six argyrophil carcinoids of the appendix vermiformis. Hum Pathol 1990, **21**: 773–780.

156 Johnston WH, Waisman J. Carcinoid tumor of the vermiform appendix with Cushing's syndrome. Cancer 1971, **27**: 681–686.

157 Kanthan R, Saxena A, Kanthan SC. Goblet cell carcinoids of the appendix: immunophenotype and ultrastructural study. Arch Pathol Lab Med 2001, **125**: 386–390.

158 Katsetos CD, Jami MM, Krishna L, Jackson R, Patchefsky AS, Cooper HS. Novel immunohistochemical localization of 28,000 molecular-weight (Mr) calcium binding protein (calbindin-D28k) in enterochromaffin cells of the human appendix and neuroendocrine tumors (carcinoids and small-cell carcinomas) of the midgut and foregut. Arch Pathol Lab Med 1994, **118**: 633–639.

159 Klappenbach RS, Kurman RJ, Sinclair CF, James LP. Composite carcinoma-carcinoid tumors of the gastrointestinal tract. A morphologic, histochemical, and immunocytochemical study. Am J Clin Pathol 1985, **84**: 137–143.

160 Klein HZ. Mucinous carcinoid tumor of the vermiform appendix. Cancer 1974, **33**: 770–777.

161 Lundqvist M, Wilander E. A study of the histopathogenesis of carcinoid tumors of the small intestine and appendix. Cancer 1987, **60**: 201–206.

162 MacGillivray DC, Heaton RB, Rushin JM, Cruess DF. Distant metastasis from a carcinoid tumor of the appendix less than one centimeter in size. Surgery 1992, **111**: 466–471.

163 Markgraf WH, Dunn TM. Appendiceal carcinoid with carcinoid syndrome. Am J Surg 1964, **107**: 730–732.

164 Masson P. Carcinoids (argentaffin-cell tumors) and nerve hyperplasia of the appendicular mucosa. Am J Pathol 1928, **4**: 181–211.

165 Merino MJ, Edmonds P, LiVolsi V. Appendiceal carcinoma metastatic to the ovaries and mimicking primary ovarian tumors. Int J Gynecol Pathol 1985, **4**: 110–120.

166 Millikin PD. Eosinophilic argentaffin cells in the human appendix. Arch Pathol 1974, **98**: 393–395.

167 Millikin PD. Extraepithelial enterochromaffin cells and Schwann cells in the human appendix. Arch Pathol Lab Med 1983, **107**: 189–194.

167a Modlin IM, Lye KD, Kidd M. A 5-decade analysis of 13,715 carcinoid tumors. Cancer 2003, **97**: 934–959.

168 Moertel CG, Dockerty MB, Judd ES. Carcinoid tumors of the vermiform appendix. Cancer 1968, **21**: 270–278.

169 Moertel CG, Weiland LH, Nagorney DM, Dockerty MB. Carcinoid tumor of the appendix. Treatment and prognosis. N Engl J Med 1987, **317**: 1699–1701.

170 Moyana TN, Satkunam N. A comparative immunohistochemical study of jejunoileal and appendiceal carcinoids. Implications for histogenesis and pathogenesis. Cancer 1992, **70**: 1081–1088.

171 Olsson B, Ljungberg O. Adenocarcinoid of the vermiform appendix. Virchows Arch [A] 1980, **386**: 201–210.

172 Ramnani DM, Wistuba II, Behrens C, Gazdar AF, Sobin LH, Albores-Saavedra J. K-ras and p53 mutations in the pathogenesis of classical and goblet cell carcinoids of the appendix. Cancer 1999, **86**: 14–21.

173 Rode J, Dhillon AP, Papadaki L, Griffiths D. Neurosecretory cells of the lamina propria of the appendix and their possible relationship to the carcinoids. Histopathology 1982, **6**: 69–79.

174 Rodriguez FH Jr, Sarma DP, Lunseth JH. Goblet cell carcinoid of the appendix. Hum Pathol 1982, **13**: 286–288.

175 Roggo A, Wood WC, Ottinger LW. Carcinoid tumors of the appendix. Ann Surg 1993, **217**: 285–390.

175a Rossi G, Valli R, Bertolini F, Sighinolfi P, Losi L, Cavazza A, Rivasi F, Luppi G. Does mesoappendix infiltration predict a worse prognosis in incidental neuroendocrine tumors of the appendix? Am J Clin Pathol 2003, **120**: 706–711.

176 Ryden SE, Drake RM, Franciosi RA. Carcinoid tumors of the appendix in children. Cancer 1975, **36**: 1538–1542.

177 Shaw PA, Pringle JH. The demonstration of a subset of carcinoid tumours of the appendix by in situ hybridization using synthetic probes to proglucagon mRNA. J Pathol 1992, **167**: 375–380.

178 Soga J, Tazawa K. Pathologic analysis of carcinoids. Histologic re-evaluation of 62 cases. Cancer 1971, **28**: 990–998.

179 Subbuswamy SG, Gibbs NM, Ross CF, Morson BC. Goblet cell carcinoid of the appendix. Cancer 1974, **34**: 338–344.

180 Syracuse DC, Perzin KH, Price JB, Wiedel PD, Mesa-Tejada R. Carcinoid tumors of the appendix. Mesoappendiceal extension and nodal metastases. Ann Surg 1979, **190**: 58–63.

181 Van Eeden S, Offerhaus GJ, Peterse HL, Dingemans KP, Blaauwgeers HL. Gangliocytic paraganglioma of the appendix. Histopathology 2000, **36**: 47–49.

182 Warkel RL, Cooper PH, Helwig EB. Adenocarcinoid, a mucin-producing carcinoid tumor of the appendix. A study of 39 cases. Cancer 1978, **42**: 2781–2793.

183 Wilander E, Scheibenpflug L. Cytokeratin expression in small intestinal and appendiceal carcinoids. A basis for classification. Acta Oncol 1993, **32**: 131–134.

184 Wolff M, Ahmed N. Epithelial neoplasms of the vermiform appendix (exclusive of carcinoid). Part I. Adenocarcinoma of the appendix. Cancer 1976, **37**: 2493–2510.

Other lesions

185 Bolker H, Shapiro AL. Appendiceal metastasis in carcinoma of the breast. NY State J Med 1940, **40**: 219–220.

186 Cajigas A, Axiotis CA. Endosalpingiosis of the vermiform appendix. Int J Gynecol Pathol 1990, **9**: 291–295.

187 Clark DE, Stocks JF, Wilkis JL. Mesoappendiceal paraganglioma. Am J Gastroenterol 1985, **80**: 340–342.

188 Deschenes L, Couture J, Garneau R. Diverticulitis of the appendix. Report of sixty-one cases. Am J Surg 1971, **121**: 706–709.

189 Driman DK, Melega DE, Vilos GA, Plewes EA. Mucocele of the appendix secondary to endometriosis, report of two cases one with localized pseudomyxoma peritonei. Am J Clin Pathol 2000, **113**: 860–864.

190 Droga BW, Levine S, Baker JJ. Heterotopic gastric and esophageal tissue in the vermiform appendix. Am J Clin Pathol 1963, **40**: 190–193.

191 George, DH. Diverticulosis of the vermiform appendix in patients with cystic fibrosis. Hum Pathol 1987, **18**: 75–79.

192 Graf NS, Arbuckle S. Melanosis of the appendix: common in the paediatric age group. Histopathology 2001, **39**: 243–249.

193 Hausman R. Granular cells in musculature of appendix. Arch Pathol 1963, **75**: 360–372.

194 Jevon JP, Daya D, Qizilbash AH. Intussusception of the appendix. A report of four cases and review of the literature. Arch Pathol Lab Med 1992, **116**: 960–964.

195 Johnston J, Helwig EB. Granular cell tumors of the gastrointestinal tract and perianal region. A study of 74 cases. Dig Dis Sci 1981, **26**: 807–816.

196 Lauwers GY, Prendergast NC, Wahl SJ, Bagchi S. Invagination of vermiform appendix. Dig Dis Sci 1993, **38**: 565–568.

197 Mai KT, Burns BF. Development of dysplastic mucinous epithelium from endometriosis of the appendix. Histopathology 1999, **35**: 368–372.

198 Masson P. Carcinoids (argentaffin-cell tumors) and nerve hyperplasia of the appendicular mucosa. Am J Pathol 1928, **4**: 181–211.

199 Medlicott SAC, Urbansi SJ. Acquired diverticulosis of the vermiform appendix: a disease of multiple etiologies. Int J Surg Pathol 1998, **6**: 23–28.

200 Michalany J, Galindo W. Classification of neuromas of the appendix. Beitr Pathol Bd 1973, **150**: 213–228.

201 Miettinen M, Sobin LH. Gastrointestinal stromal tumors in the appendix: a clinicopathologic and immunohistochemical study of four cases. Am J Surg Pathol 2001, **25**: 1433–1437.

202 Nielsen M, Lykke J, Thomsen JL. Endometriosis of the vermiform appendix. Acta Pathol Microbiol Immunol Scand (A) 1983, **91**: 253–256.

203 Olsen BS. Giant appendicular neurofibroma. A light and immunohistochemical study. Histopathology 1987, **11**: 851–855.

204 Olsen BS, Holck S. Neurogenous hyperplasia leading to appendiceal obliteration. An immunohistochemical study of 237 cases. Histopathology 1987, **11**: 843–849.

205 Prasad ML, Keating JP, Teoh HH, McCarthy SW, Battifora H, Wasef E, Rosai J. Pleomorphic angiomyolipoma of digestive tract: a heretofore unrecognized entity. Int J Surg Pathol 2000, **8**: 67–72.

206 Rabinovitch J. Diverticulosis and diverticulitis of the vermiform appendix. Ann Surg 1962, **155**: 434–440.

207 Rutty GN, Shaw PA. Melanosis of the appendix: prevalence,

distribution and review of the pathogenesis of 47 cases. Histopathology 1997, **30**: 319–323.

208 Sin IC, Ling E-T. Prentice RSA. Burkitt's lymphoma of the appendix. Report of two cases. Hum Pathol 1980, **11**: 465–470.

209 Sobel HJ, Marquet E, Schwarz R. Granular degeneration of appendiceal smooth muscle. Arch Pathol 1971, **92**: 427–432.

210 Stanley MW, Cherwitz D, Hagen K, Snover DC. Neuromas of the appendix. A light-microscopic, immunohistochemical and electron-microscopic study of 20 cases. Am J Surg Pathol 1986, **10**: 801–815.

211 Suster S, Moran CA. Deciduosis of the appendix. Am J Gastroenterol 1990, **85**: 841–845.

212 Zebrowska G, Walsh NM. Human immunodeficiency virus-related Kaposi's sarcoma of the appendix and acute appendicitis. Report of a case and review of the literature. Arch Pathol Lab Med 1991, **115**: 1157–1160.

Large bowel

Normal anatomy

The large bowel comprises the terminal 1 to 1.5 m of the gastrointestinal tract and is divided into the following regions: cecum, ascending (right) colon, transverse colon, descending (left) colon, sigmoid colon, and rectum. The hepatic flexure is at the junction of the ascending and transverse colon, and the splenic flexure is at the junction of the transverse and descending colon. The rectum forms the distal 8 to 15 cm of extraperitoneal large bowel that lies within the pelvis and ends at the anal canal.

The large bowel wall is composed of four layers: mucosa, submucosa, muscularis externa (propria), and serosa (or, in the rectum, perimuscular tissues). The mucosa has three components: epithelium, lamina propria, and muscularis mucosae. The mucosal surface is covered by a single layer of low columnar to cuboidal epithelium into which the crypts of Lieberkuhn open, either on the surface itself (the majority) or onto the innominate grooves.[22] This surface epithelium is composed of absorptive cells (with basally located nuclei, mucin-negative acidophilic cytoplasm, and luminally directed apical striated borders) and goblet cells (which synthesize, store, and secrete mucin granules). Lymphocytes and occasional eosinophils may be present between the surface epithelial cells, which rest on a continuous thin basement membrane.[5,18] The crypts have a tubular, test tube-like shape, and are arranged parallel to each other. Branching of these glands occurs very rarely; its presence is usually an indication of quiescent inflammatory disease. It should be distinguished from the cloverleaf-like structure resulting from the opening of several crypts into a single innominate groove.[10,11]

The crypt epithelium contains mature absorptive cells and goblet cells similar to those in the surface epithelium, but in addition it features immature and undifferentiated precursor cells, endocrine cells, and Paneth cells. Both precursor and endocrine cells predominate at the base of the crypts.[12] As for the small intestine, the precursor cells are the progenitors of all other types of epithelial mucosal cells.[4] Paneth cells, identified by their numerous eosinophilic secretory granules (much larger than those of endocrine cells), contain lysozyme, epidermal growth factor, and other substances. They are normally present only in the cecum and proximal right colon; their occurrence elsewhere in the colon is a sign of metaplasia, usually secondary to chronic inflammation.[20]

Immunohistochemically, the epithelial cells of the normal colonic mucosa contain keratins 8, 18, and 19; immunoreactivity for the latter increases as the cells progress up the crypt toward the surface.[15]

The lamina propria contains a few lymphocytes (both T and B cells) plasma cells, histiocytes, and mast cells scattered in a network of collagen fibers, smooth muscle bundles, vessels, and nerves.[2,9] *Lymphoglandular complexes* ("microbursae") are normal structures formed by deep crypt epithelium surrounded by lymphoid follicles that extend from the mucosa through the muscularis mucosae into the submucosa.[8,16] The *pericryptal fibroblast sheath* is a collection of fibroblasts or myofibroblasts located around the crypts and at the most superficial portion of the lamina propria.[7]

The macrophages in the lamina propria may contain brown pigment consisting of hemosiderin (usually as the result of prior mucosal hemorrhages) or "pseudomelanin" (as the consequence of ingestion of anthracene-type laxatives).[6] The latter condition, if extensive enough to be detectable grossly, is referred to as *melanosis coli*.[19,21] Macrophages containing mucin ("muciphages") are a normal finding and should not be confused with the cells of Whipple's disease.[1,14] When grouping in clusters, they have been dignified with the name *colonic histiocytosis*, but they are not the manifestation of a disease entity. Rather, they are probably the expression of a previous unimportant local injury.[3,17] Histochemically they may contain neutral or acidic mucin, mainly of the sialomucin type.[3]

The lamina propria vessels consist of capillaries (regularly distributed) and lymph vessels (limited to the region immediately above the muscularis mucosae).

The submucosa is composed of loose connective tissue having cell constituents similar to the lamina propria.[13] It also contains the submucosal plexus of Meissner. The muscularis externa (propria) includes a circular inner layer and a longitudinal outer layer, with the myenteric plexus of Auerbach lying between them. The serosa is composed of a single layer of flattened to cuboidal mesothelial cells and the subjacent fibroelastic tissue.

Interstitial cells of Cajal are present scattered throughout the wall, as they are in other portions of the gastrointestinal tract.

The large bowel is supplied by branches of the superior mesenteric artery (from cecum to splenic flexure) and the inferior mesenteric artery (distal to the splenic flexure). The lower portion of the rectum is irrigated by the middle and inferior rectal arteries, which are branches of the internal iliac arteries.

The lymphatic drainage of the colon is mainly through the mesentery into the paracolic groups of lymph nodes located along the marginal vascular arcades. Subsequent stations are the intermediate nodal groups (more proximal, at the level of major arterial branches), the central or principal lymph nodes (adjacent to the superior and inferior mesenteric arteries), and the entire para-aortic chain. The lymphatic drainage of the rectum is toward the inferior mesenteric artery nodes, the superior hemorrhoidal chain, and the hypogastric and common iliac nodes.

Hirschsprung's disease and related disorders

Hirschsprung's disease is a frequent congenital disorder (1 in 5000 newborns) that results from lack of coordinated propulsive movement of the distal portion of the large bowel resulting from loss of intrinsic inhibitory innervation.[48] This is caused by the absence of parasympathetic ganglion cells in the intramural and submucosal plexuses, which in turn may be caused by either failure of migration from the neural crest or by immune-mediated neuronal necrosis[50,57,79] (Fig. 11.152). It is diagnosed during the first year of life in most patients, but it may

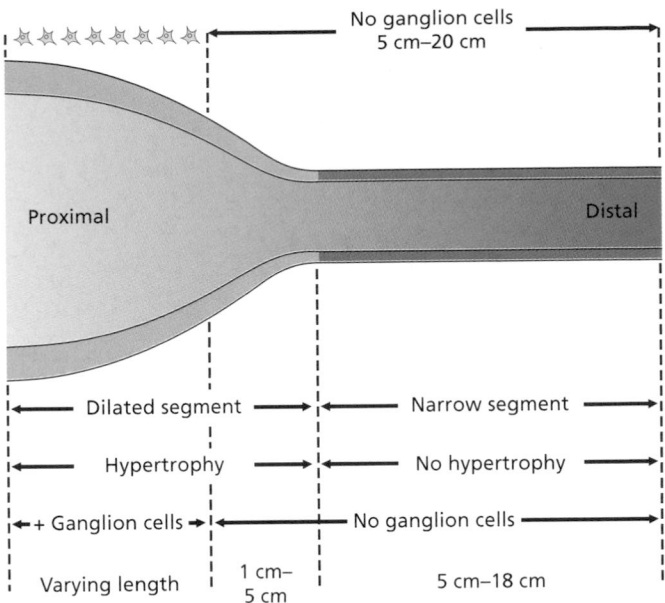

Fig. 11.152 Schematic diagram of gross and microscopic changes in 15 cases of Hirschsprung's disease.

present later, occasionally even in adulthood.[34] Approximately 80% of the patients are male; 10% have Down's syndrome, and another 5% have other serious neurologic abnormalities.[67,71] Cases have also been associated with intestinal atresia[52] and anorectal malformations.[84] Familial cases have been described.[39,60,73] Hirschsprung's disease is currently regarded as a genetic disorder with a complex pattern of inheritance. As many as eight genes appear to be involved, with the *RET* proto-oncogene apparently playing a major role.[25,38,76]

The symptoms usually begin shortly after birth, with abdominal gaseous distention, delayed meconium passage, and tight anus. With the passage of time, the large bowel proximal to the lesion undergoes dilatation of the lumen and hypertrophy of the muscular wall, whereas the diseased segment appears grossly normal (Fig. 11.153). Mucosal prolapse may be seen at the junction between the ganglionic and aganglionic bowel, particularly in older patients.[32] The most important complications are acute intestinal obstruction and enterocolitis.[46,51,64]

Microscopically, the hallmark of the disease is the *absence* of ganglion cells (aganglionosis) in *both* plexuses of a segment of bowel.[29,57,86] This is associated with the presence of hypertrophied, disorganized, nonmyelinated nerve fibers of both adrenergic and nonadrenergic type in the aganglionic segment,[53] which apparently fail to properly innervate the muscle layers of the bowel.[88] There may also be an altered distribution of the interstitial cells of Cajal,[65] fibromuscular dysplasia in the arteries located in the transitional zone between the aganglionic and the dilated segments,[77] and hyperplasia of lymphoglandular complexes (the latter as an expression of secondary diversion colitis).[37]

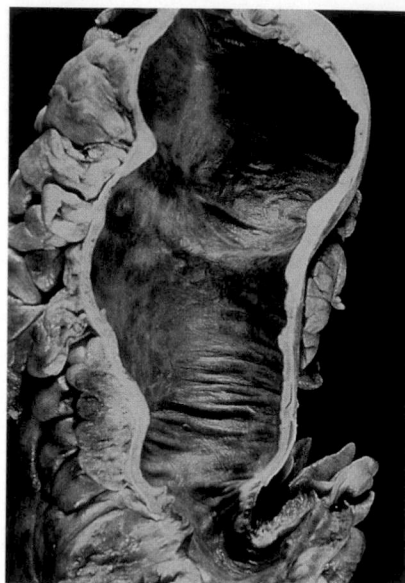

Fig. 11.153 Gross specimen of Hirschsprung's disease. The proximally dilated segment of bowel has been resected.

Depending on the extent and location of the aganglionic segment, several forms of the disease have been recognized:

1 *Classic form.* The aganglionic segment begins in the distal colorectum and extends for a considerable distance in the adjoining proximal dilated bowel.
2 *Short-segment form.* The aganglionic segment involves the rectum and rectosigmoid for a distance of only a few centimeters.
3 *Ultra-short form.* In this variant, the aganglionic segment is so narrow that the diagnosis can be missed if the biopsy is taken too high.[82]
4 *Long-segment form.* Here the abnormality is more extensive, involving most or all of the large bowel, and occasionally extending even to the small bowel.[28,45,61] These patients present with symptoms of intestinal obstruction without megacolon.
5 *Zonal colonic aganglionosis.* Only a short segment of bowel is involved. In contrast to all other forms, in this variant the ganglion cells are present not only above but also *below* the aganglionic segment.[49,55]

The traditional approach to morphologic documentation of Hirschsprung's disease is the biopsy procedure described by Swenson et al.,[75] in which a full-thickness segment of the muscular wall of the rectum is excised and examined for the presence of ganglion cells in the myenteric plexus. Since ganglion cells are normally scanty near the internal anal sphincter, the standard guideline is that the biopsy should be taken at a point 2 cm above the anal valve in infants and 3 cm in older children,[24,85] even if some authors believe that biopsies taken at 1 to 1.5 cm from the anal valves may also be adequate.[82] The pres-

ence of squamous or transitional epithelium in a specimen indicates that the site of the biopsy is too low. This procedure is highly accurate, but it requires technical skill and general anesthesia, and it may lead to complications. For these reasons, the alternatives of diagnosing Hirschsprung's disease with "suction" or mucosal rectal biopsies are now frequently employed.[26,43] These are based on the premise that the limit of aganglionosis in Hirschsprung's disease coincides closely in the submucosal and myenteric plexus, as shown by the careful microscopic mapping studies of Gherardi.[40] The ganglion cells of the submucosal plexus are smaller and more irregularly distributed than are those located intermuscularly, and their identification requires expertise, patience, and the performance of serial sections in the biopsy obtained. Another abnormality that ought to be looked for is the presence of large (40 μm or greater) submucosal nerve trunks, since they correlate closely with the absence of ganglion cells.[59] Yunis et al.[90] found that in experienced hands it is a simple and effective method for the exclusion of Hirschsprung's disease. These biopsies also can be evaluated for acetylcholinesterase activity, which is markedly increased throughout the lamina propria and muscularis mucosae in patients with this disorder.[27,47,58] The increase can be detected by both histochemical stains and biochemical analysis, the former being the more practical of the two[31,62] (Fig. 11.154). In problematic cases, it has been stated that the determination of the acetylcholinesterase–butyryl-cholinesterase ratio may be helpful.[30] Two groups of immunohistochemical techniques represent additional tools for the diagnosis of this disorder. One is represented by neuron-specific enolase, PGP 9.5, neurofilaments, microtubule-associated ("Tau") protein, antisynaptic vesicles 171 B.5, Neu N, and cathepsin D (which highlight the presence of hypertrophied nerve fibers and the absence of ganglion cells); the other is represented by S-100 protein (which shows absence of the normal periganglionic satellite cells and accentuates the enlarged nerve bundles).[23,35,41,68,78,80,83,87,89] These changes are accompanied by an increase in the number of mucosal endocrine cells.[72]

The ganglion cells present in the proximal segment, and that appear normal by both H&E and the generic neuronal stains already listed above, may still fail to react for colonic neuropeptides such as VIP, GAL, SP, NPY, CGRP, and Met-ENR. It has been suggested that these abnormalities of enteric innervation may be responsible for the unsatisfactory postoperative results seen in approximately 20% of the cases.[66]

Another interesting recent finding is the marked elevation of class II major histocompatibility antigens in the aganglionic area (not present in patients with chronic constipation resulting from other causes), suggesting an underlying autoimmune mechanism for the disease.[42]

Frozen section is routinely used for documenting the absence of ganglion cells and determining the level of

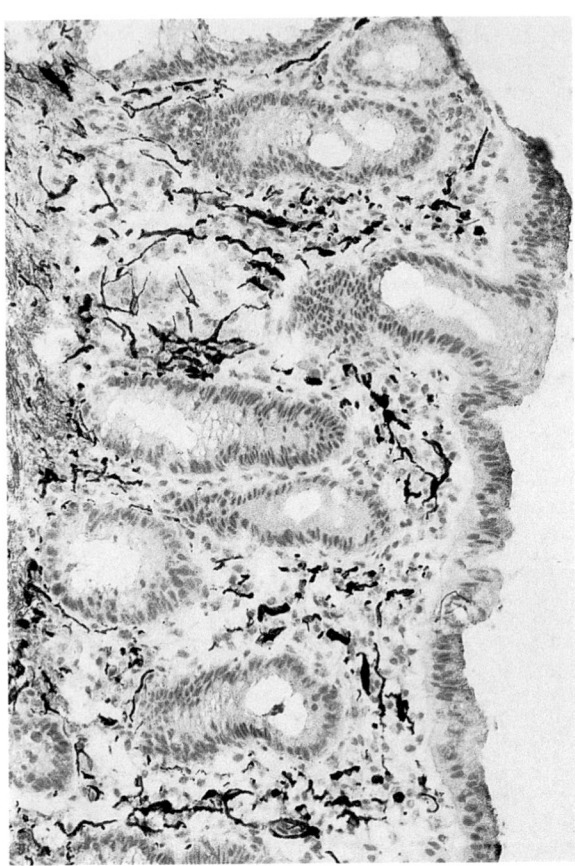

Fig. 11.154 Colonic mucosa stained for acetylcholinesterase from a patient with Hirschsprung's disease. There is a marked increase in the number of nerve fibers in the lamina propria.

aganglionic bowel in conventional Hirschsprung's disease.

Intestinal neuronal dysplasia (neuronal colonic dysplasia, hyperganglionosis) is another controversial entity or entities included in the vague group of disorders generically designated as pseudo-Hirschsprung's disease.[63] Hyperplasia of the myenteric nerves is accompanied by giant ganglia, isolated ganglion cells in the submucosa, and an increase in acetylcholinesterase staining[69]; it has been described in association with Recklinghausen's disease and multiple endocrine neoplasia.[29,74] As several authors have pointed out,[54] the entity is far from well defined, and its diagnosis should be reserved for the rare florid cases that occur in the absence of associated obstruction or other known entities and should be made only if multiple biopsies, including ample submucosa or transmural sections (preferably the latter), are available.[70]

Megacolon can also result from **cytomegalovirus (CMV) infection** and **Chagas' disease** as the result of acquired abnormalities of the neural plexus.[36,81]

Chronic idiopathic intestinal pseudo-obstruction is a syndrome in which symptoms of intestinal obstruction are present in the absence of mechanical obstruction. It has been attributed to an abnormal physiology of the bowel propulsive system. Loss of CD117-positive (presumably Cajal's interstitial cells) and CD34-positive cells has been found in a subset of these cases.[74a]

Diverticulosis

Most cases of diverticulosis are acquired and occur in patients over the age of 40 years. Clinical evidence of diverticulosis is seen in slightly over 10% of the individuals in this age group, but surgical complications develop in only 10% of them. Naturally, the incidence of diverticulosis at autopsy is higher; in a study from Australia, 45% of 200 examined large bowels had diverticula.[104] There have been scattered reports of diverticula occurring in children, in young patients with Marfan's or Ehlers–Danlos syndrome, and in association with polycystic kidney disease.[91]

Diverticulosis shows a remarkable geographic difference in its frequency. It is common in North America, Europe, and Australia but unusual in Asia, Africa, and parts of South America. The main protective factor seems to be a high-residue diet, although the evidence is not conclusive.[97,118] This type of diet is thought to act by diminishing the degree of colonic segmentation, which is the mechanism responsible for mucosal herniation.[112] The disease is characteristically multiple and preferentially involves the left side of the colon. In the previously mentioned autopsy study from Australia,[104] the sigmoid colon was affected in 99% of the specimens. This was the only area of involvement in 41% of the cases; in 30%, the

transection of the bowel at surgery. This procedure is facilitated if the surgeon gives the pathologist a rectangular piece of the entire muscular wall, so that the tissue can be properly oriented. For frozen section evaluation to be reliable, the piece examined should be at least 4 mm long, and multiple serial sections should be taken. Even under these ideal circumstances it should be understood that the inaccuracy rate is relatively high, significantly more so than for frozen section diagnoses in general.[56]

The most common operations for the treatment of Hirschsprung's disease are Swenson's proctectomy with pull-through of ganglionic bowel to the anus, the Duhamel side-to-side anastomosis of ganglionic bowel with the aganglionic rectal stump, and the Soave endorectal pull-through, in which the rectal mucosa is stripped away and the ganglionic bowel brought down to the anus.[44,71]

Occasionally, successfully operated patients again develop obstructive symptoms and are found to have aganglionosis in pulled-through bowel that had previously been shown to be ganglionated.[33]

Hypoganglionosis is a disputed entity in which there is a deficiency rather than an absence of ganglion cells.[86] It should be remembered that hypoganglionosis is usually present at the junction between normal and

disease had spread to the descending colon; in 4%, to the transverse colon; and in 16%, to the entire colon. The rectum is only rarely affected. The distribution of the disease is different in patients from the Far East, in whom there is a greater frequency of right-sided involvement.[108,117]

As seen radiographically and grossly, the diverticula are located on the mesenteric and lateral aspects of the bowel (Figs 11.155 and 11.156). They have a flask-like shape and may be filled with feces or mucin. Some extend into the appendices epiploicae and bulge over the serosa, but they may still be difficult to recognize at the time of surgery in obese persons. The muscular wall of the bowel always appears abnormal in the area of diverticulosis. The teniae are prominent, with an almost cartilaginous look. The circular layer is also thickened, with a corrugated appearance corresponding to interdigitating processes of the muscle.[104,110] Microscopically, the diverticulum lacks a muscle layer except for residual bundles of muscularis mucosae (Fig. 11.157). The adjacent bowel, including the myenteric plexus, shows no appreciable abnormalities. Polypoid prolapsing mucosal folds may occur, probably resulting from a combination of venous congestion and mucosal redundancy caused by the spastic contraction of the muscle coat.[105]

Cecal diverticula may be of two types.[94] One, usually multiple, is similar in all aspects to diverticula of the left colon and is often associated with them. The other, thought to be congenital, is solitary and unassociated with diverticular disease elsewhere; it is usually located on the medial wall of the cecum near the ileocecal valve and contains an external muscle layer.[106]

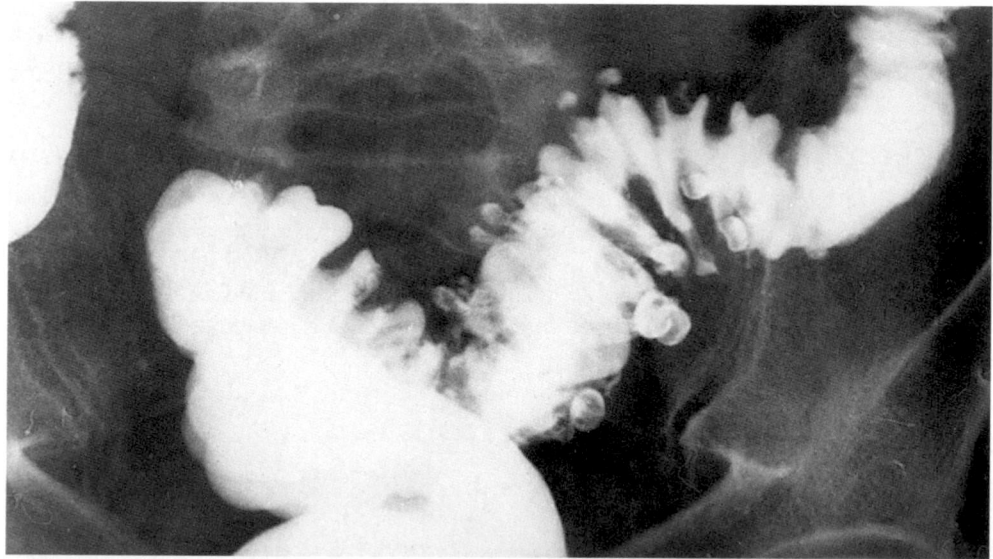

Fig. 11.155 Classic radiographic appearance of diverticulosis.

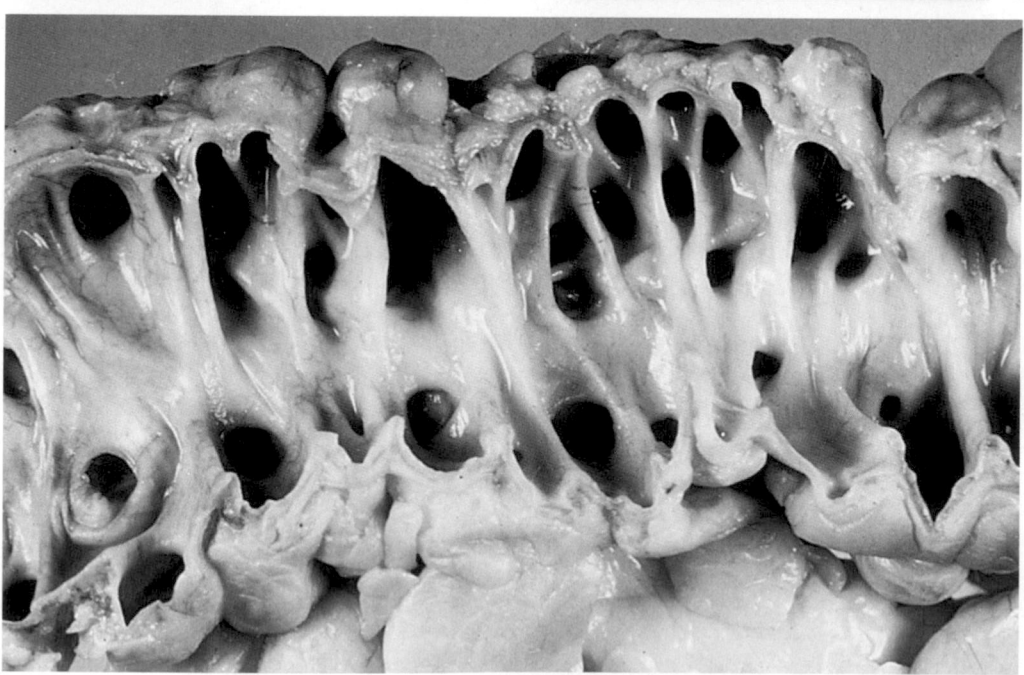

Fig. 11.156 Extensive diverticulosis of sigmoid colon with segmentation and shortening of bowel. Openings of diverticula can be seen clearly. Circular muscle is thick and corrugated.

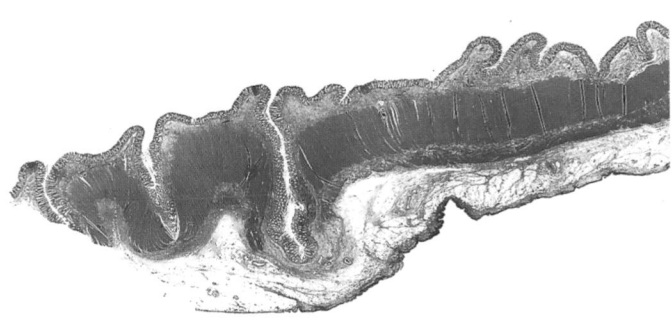

Fig. 11.157 Whole mount of colon with diverticular disease.

The main complications of diverticulosis are hemorrhage, perforation, and diverticulitis.[116] The bleeding, which may be massive, results from rupture of one of the colonic nutrient vessels that run on the side of the diverticulum.[93] Arteriographic and microangiographic techniques have shown a characteristic asymmetric rupture of the vessel toward the lumen of the diverticulum precisely at its dome or antimesenteric margin.[109]

Perforation of the diverticulum may lead to a pericolic or pericecal abscess, which in later stages evolves into an indurated mass that may be confused with carcinoma clinically and radiographically[111] (Fig. 11.158). The abscess may drain into bladder or adjacent bowel and result in a fistulous formation ("dissecting diverticulitis"), producing a double tracking effect on x-ray studies. Rarely, this fistulous tract may extend into the perineum,

scrotum, buttocks, hip, or even lower extremities.[114] Acute free perforation into the abdominal cavity is rare. Sometimes the release of mucin contained within the diverticula results in a pericolic mucocele-like formation.

Diverticulitis manifests radiographically with sawtoothed serrations and a narrowed lumen. It may resemble carcinoma, but the segment involved is usually longer and the mucosa is intact. Microscopically, there is acute or chronic inflammation in—but mainly around—the base of the diverticulum (Fig. 11.159). Sometimes there is a granulomatous inflammation around the diverticulum that can simulate Crohn's disease.[95,100] On other occasions there is a chronic colitis limited to sigmoid colons harboring diverticula that would be most difficult to distinguish from idiopathic inflammatory bowel disease in the absence of clinical and endoscopic data.[99,107] The inflammation can spread into the mesentery and result in panniculitis, not to be confused with the group of conditions known as inflammatory fibrosclerosis.[92]

Pain, a common symptom of diverticular disease, may be secondary to these inflammatory changes; however, it may also be present in the absence of diverticulitis and is probably induced by the muscle abnormalities. Parenthetically, chronic corticosteroid therapy may lead to free perforation of the colon and closely simulate the picture of diverticulosis with diverticulitis.[119] Exceptionally, a polyp or carcinoma is found contained within a diverticulum.[113]

Surgical resection is being performed more frequently in patients with complications of diverticulitis such as

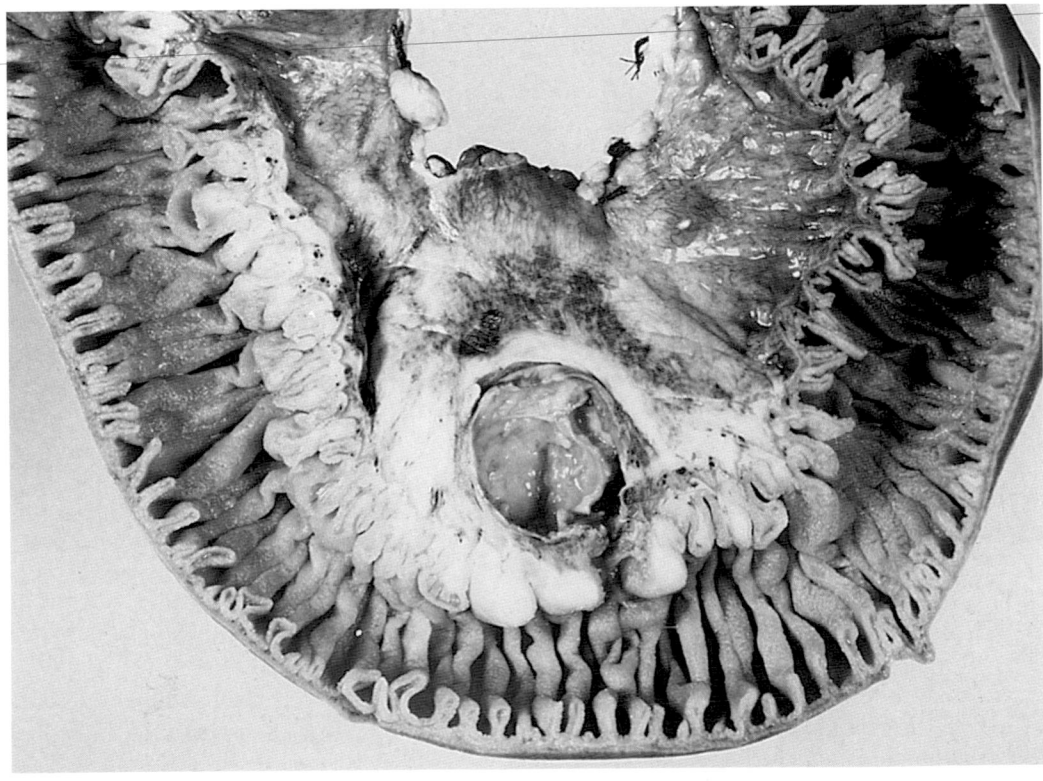

Fig. 11.158 In this colon with extensive diverticulosis, one of the diverticula perforated and formed a large inflammatory mass in the mesentery.

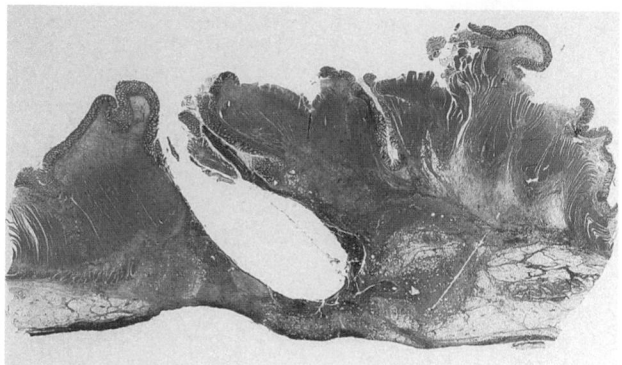

Fig. 11.159 Whole-mount view of colonic diverticulosis. One of the diverticula shows marked chronic peridiverticulitis. Note hypertrophy of the muscle wall.

perforation, obstruction, and hemorrhage.[101,102,115] The wisdom of prompt resection for patients with free diverticular perforation and spreading peritonitis has been repeatedly shown.[96,103] Not surprisingly, morbidity and mortality rates are higher in these instances than when resections are performed for uncomplicated acute diverticulitis.[98] Other indications for surgery are repeated attacks of diverticulitis while on a good medical regimen and the development of urinary symptoms. The latter may be the manifestation of an impending sigmoid–vesical fistula.

Colitis

The term *inflammatory bowel disease*—sometimes preceded by the qualifier *idiopathic*—is employed for a group of inflammatory disorders thought to be the result of inappropriate activation of the mucosal immune system driven by the presence of normal luminal flora.[120] The two main representatives are ulcerative colitis and Crohn's disease (granulomatous colitis). As discussed later, it is still not clear whether these are two different diseases or part of a continuum.

Ulcerative colitis

Ulcerative colitis occurs with equal frequency in both sexes. It appears most often in patients between 20 and 30 years of age, with a second peak between 70 and 80 years; however, it can occur at any age, including in childhood.[131,134,140,161] The etiology remains unknown. There is increasing evidence that susceptibility is inherited, although the genetic contribution does not seem to be as important as for Crohn's disease. The duration is usually prolonged, with many remissions and exacerbations; nutritional deficiencies and anemia are common accompanying features.[169]

Ulcerative colitis is characteristically a left-sided disease, which usually begins in the rectosigmoid area. In some cases, it remains localized to the rectum (ulcerative

proctitis[132]), but in most instances it spreads proximally, sometimes to involve the entire colon (pancolitis).

The gross appearance of the lesions varies with the stage of the disease[158] (Fig. 11.160). In the acute form, the mucosal surface of the bowel is wet and glaring from blood and mucus, and petechial hemorrhages are often seen. Various-sized ulcers of irregular configuration then appear. Some of these ulcers undermine the mucosa so that mucosal bridges with an underlying inflammatory infiltrate develop. Extensive longitudinal ulcers, especially if connected by transverse ulcers, are *not* a feature of ulcerative colitis but rather of granulomatous colitis. Elevated sessile reddish nodules, known as *pseudopolyps*, are often seen in an otherwise flat surface (Fig. 11.161). They are typically small and multiple. Rarely, they may have a filiform configuration; sometimes they attain a giant size, thus raising the clinical and radiographic suspicion of carcinoma.[148]

In the more advanced stages of the process, the entire bowel becomes fibrotic, narrowed, and shortened. The cicatricial stenosis associated with an inflammatory mass may result in an erroneous clinical and radiographic diagnosis of carcinoma. If the colon has become defunctionalized with an ileostomy or colostomy before the colectomy, it may show extreme narrowing of the lumen, great atrophy of all the components of the wall, and a marked increase in pericolic fat. However, in the quiescent stage the ulceration is absent, the mucosa is atrophic, and there may be extensive submucosal fat deposition. In some of these cases, the mucosa may appear grossly normal.

Microscopically, ulcerative colitis is primarily a mucosal and submucosal disease.[184] In the acute phase, there is an increase in the number of inflammatory cells in the lamina propria.[137] Crypt abscesses (i.e., collections of neutrophils in the glandular lumen) appear; these are preceded by accumulation of these cells at the base of the crypts[136] (Fig. 11.162). This leads to a progressive destruction of the glands, which show a marked decrease in cytoplasmic mucus and irregular shapes, resulting from a combination of atrophic and regenerative changes.[143] These regenerative changes are also manifested by nuclear enlargement and increased mitotic activity; the latter is no longer limited to the lower portion of the crypts, as in the normal mucosa, a feature also apparent by special techniques.[133,146] The decrease in total mucin is accompanied by an alteration in a particular species of mucin, a feature that has led some authors to postulate a specific mucin defect.[150] Paneth cells, usually absent beyond the cecum in normal individuals, appear as an expression of metaplasia.[182] Parenthetically, Paneth cells can also be encountered in other inflammatory and neoplastic disorders of the large bowel.[178]

The stromal inflammatory infiltrate of ulcerative colitis is composed of neutrophils, lymphocytes (many of which are activated T lymphocytes[141]), plasma cells, a

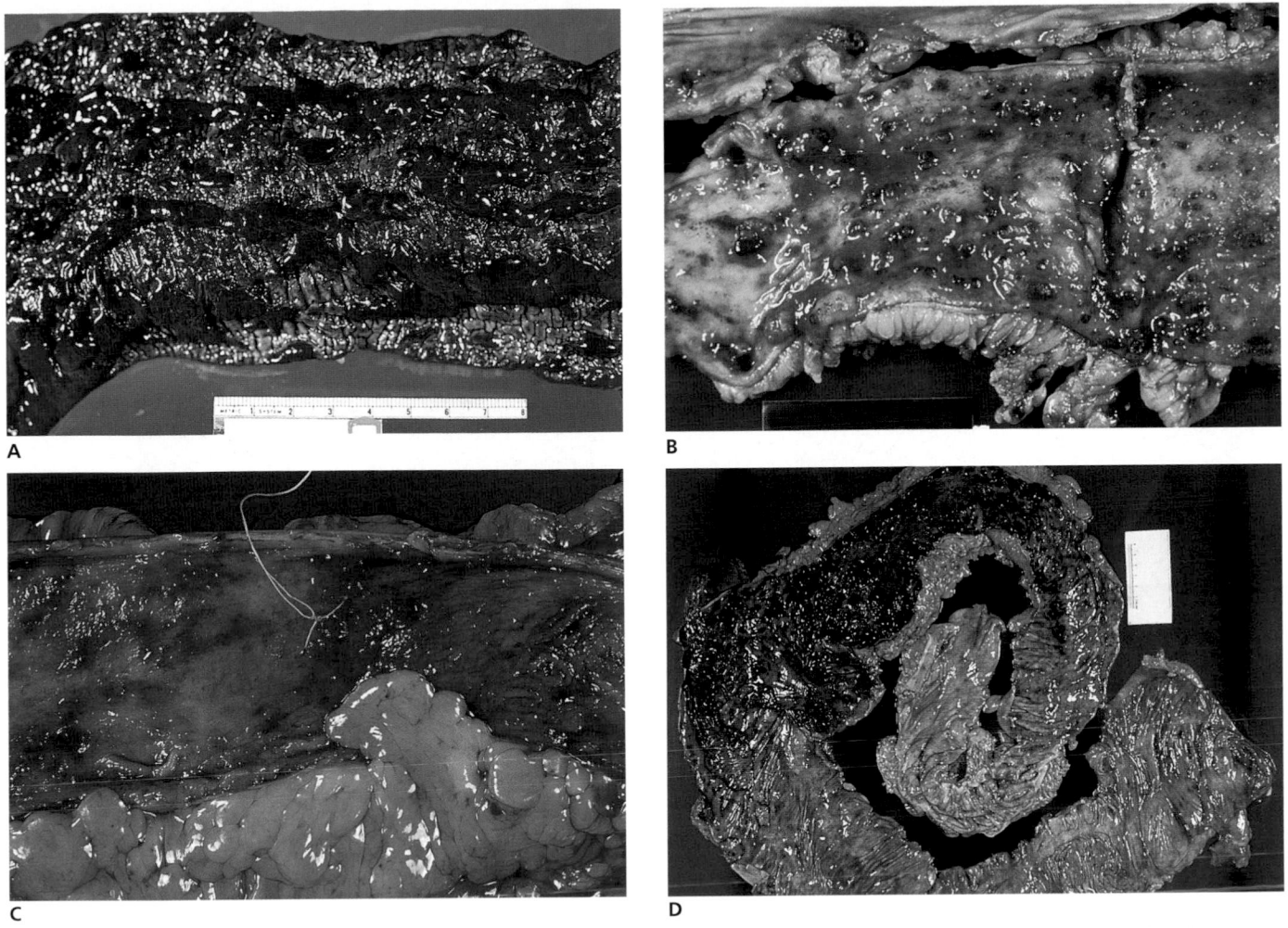

Fig. 11.160 A to **D,** Various gross appearances of ulcerative colitis. **A,** Acute form with marked hyperemia. **B,** Chronic form, showing mucosal ulceration with residual foci of elevated and hyperemic mucosa. **C,** Late stage, showing total mucosal atrophy. **D,** Case complicated with toxic megacolon.

few histiocytes and other "accessory" cells, scattered eosinophils, and mast cells.[125,162,180] As a rule, granulomas containing epithelioid and multinucleated giant cells are absent, this being an important criterion in the differential diagnosis with Crohn's disease. However, crypt-associated intramucosal granulomas may supervene in ulcerative colitis as a result of crypt rupture.[129,159] The plasma cells represent a polyclonal population of IgG-, IgM-, and IgA-producing cells.[149] Mast cells are said to accumulate at the line of demarcation between normal and abnormal mucosa.[151] The infiltrate may be accompanied by numerous lymphoid follicles, particularly in the rectum, and may lead to marked distortion of the crypts.[171] Blood vessels are dilated, and mucosal capillary thrombi may be seen.[128] The inflammation may remain above the muscularis mucosae or extend into the submucosa. The ulcers are covered by nonspecific granulation tissue. The pseudopolyps are also largely composed of granulation tissue mixed with inflamed and hyperemic mucosa. Occasionally, prominent reactive stromal cells are present in these pseudopolyps, a feature

that should not be confused with malignancy.[145,168] In some instances, the mucosal regeneration acquires a villous configuration reminiscent of small bowel mucosa.[157] Depending on the stage of the disease, the submucosa may appear normal or inflamed, hyperemic, infiltrated by fat, or fibrosed; sometimes it contains glands that have herniated through gaps in the muscularis mucosae, which often appears hypertrophic.[122,130,173] In approximately 10% of cases, the submucosal arteries show features of endarteritis obliterans, with or without thrombosis. The muscularis mucosae may appear reduplicated.[177] The muscularis externa is usually normal or slightly hypertrophic, and there may be minor subserosal fibrosis.

As already stated, in the quiescent or resolving stage of the disease, the mucosa may appear grossly normal, with nearly total restoration of the mucin content. However, subtle microscopic abnormalities will be detected in the form of branching and irregular glands (rather than parallel, evenly spaced glands), a gap between the base of the crypts and the muscularis

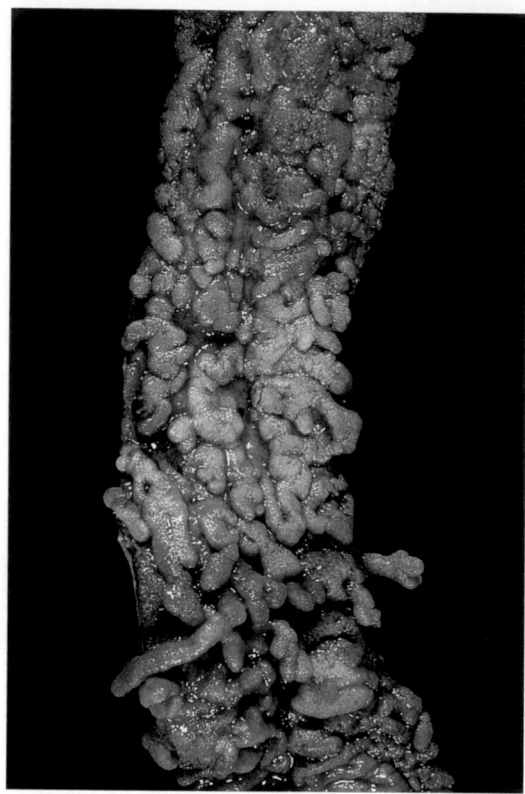

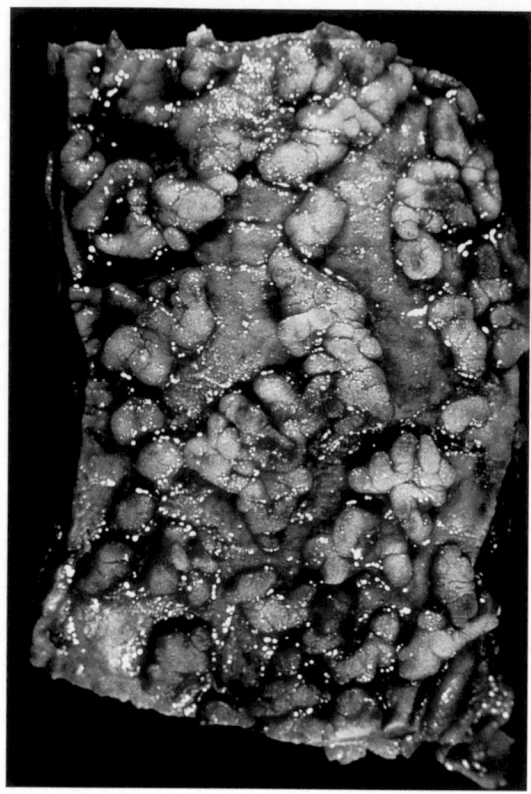

A

B

Fig. 11.161 A and **B**, Pseudopolyps in ulcerative colitis.

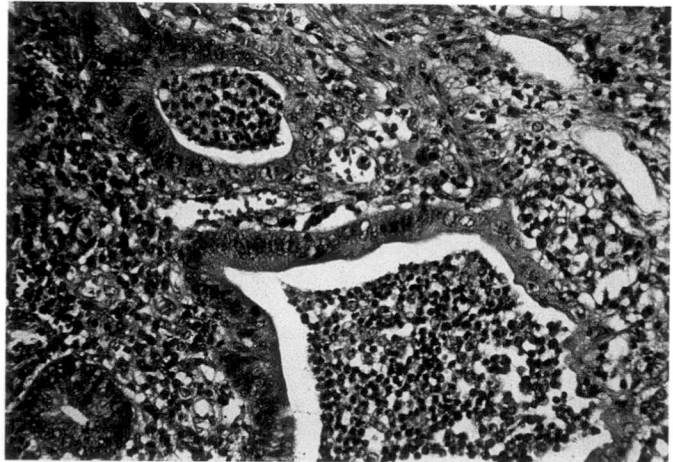

Fig. 11.162 Ulcerative colitis featuring crypt abscesses.

mucosae, the appearance of Paneth cells, hyperplasia of endocrine cells, the presence of more than occasional neutrophils, and islands of lipocytes in the lamina propria.[127,171] If the rectal biopsy of a patient with colitis is *microscopically* normal, the diagnosis of ulcerative colitis is unlikely.[165] However, it is well to remember that these changes can be very mild,[154] particularly if the patient is a child[160] and/or if steroid or 5-aminosalicylic acid enemas have been administered.[167] In known instances of ulcerative colitis, the biopsy may demonstrate a microscopically active process before clinical relapse occurs.

Ulcerative colitis can spread to other portions of the gastrointestinal tract. The ileum is involved in approximately one third of the cases. This involvement (sometimes referred to as *backwash ileitis*) is superficial, of little clinical importance, and always in continuity with the colonic disease; it rarely spreads more than 10 cm from the ileocecal valve and may be accompanied by dilatation of the lumen (in striking contrast to the typical stenosis of Crohn's disease). Rare cases of diffuse duodenitis in ulcerative colitis patients have been described.[179]

Interestingly, the ileal stoma of proctocolectomized patients may develop colonic metaplasia and ulcerative colitis-like lesions, including inflammatory polyps.[124] Similar changes have been described in pelvic ileal reservoirs (ileal pouches) constructed in patients with ulcerative colitis (post-colectomy pouchitis).[176] In turn, the defunctioned rectum may show changes that can simulate granulomatous colitis; these are thought to result from a combination of defunctioning and of active ulcerative colitis.[181]

The appendix is affected in 20% to 60% of cases; this may occur in continuity with adjacent involved cecum or as a skip lesion.[135, 175] In the anal canal, there is often involvement of the glandular epithelium,[123] and sometimes there are hyperplastic changes of the transitional mucosa. Anal lesions are seen in 10% of cases; they may consist of midline dorsal fissures, skin excoriations, acute perianal and ischiorectal abscesses, or rectovaginal fistulas.

Some patients with ulcerative colitis have associated liver disease. This may consist of fatty infiltration, abscess, cirrhosis, sclerosing cholangitis, pericholangitis, and—rarely—carcinoma of the biliary tract.[126,142,144,164,170] Patients in whom the latter complication occurs are younger than those developing carcinoma de novo.[172] The mean duration of colitis before the onset of biliary symptoms from carcinoma is almost 20 years.[121]

Other distant manifestations of ulcerative colitis include arthritis, uveitis, pyoderma gangrenosum, and limited forms of Wegener's granulomatosis.[147] These are usually limited to patients with extensive colonic involvement and appear only exceptionally in those with disease limited to the rectum.

Local complications of ulcerative colitis are perforation with peritonitis and abscess, toxic megacolon (Fig. 11.163), venous thrombosis (most often in the iliac vein), and carcinoma. The latter complication is discussed in the next section.

Fig. 11.163 Ulcerative colitis complicated by toxic megacolon. (Courtesy of Dr. Fabio Facchetti, Brescia, Italy)

Table 11.3 Differences between ulcerative colitis and Crohn's disease (granulomatous colitis)

Features	Ulcerative colitis	Crohn's disease
Clinical		
Rectal bleeding	Common	Inconspicuous
Abdominal mass	Practically never	10%–15%
Abdominal pain	Usually left-sided	Usually right-sided
Sigmoidoscopy	Abnormal in 95%	Abnormal in less than 50%
Free perforation	12%	4%
Colon carcinoma	5%–10%	Very rare
Anal complications	Rare; minor	75%; fissures, fistulas, ulceration
Response to steroid therapy	75%	25%
Results of surgery	Very good	Fair
Ileostomy dysfunction	Rare	Common
Radiographic		
Sparing of rectum	Exceptional	90%
Involvement of ileum	Rare; dilated ("backwash ileitis")	Common; constricted
Strictures	Absent	Often present
Skip areas	Absent	Common
Internal fistulas	Absent	May be present
Longitudinal and transverse ulcers	Exceptional	Common
Fissuring	Absent	Common
Thumbprinting	Absent	Common
Morphologic		
Distribution of involvement	Diffuse; predominantly left-sided; mucosal and submucosal	Focal; predominantly right-sided transmural
Mucosal atrophy and regeneration	Marked	Minimal
Cytoplasmic mucin	Diminished	Preserved
Lymphoid aggregates	Rare	Common
Edema	Minimal	Marked
Hyperemia	May be extreme	Minimal
Granulomas	Absent	Present in 60%
Fissuring	Absent	Present
Crypt abscesses	Common	Rare
Rectal involvement	Practically always	50%
Ileal involvement	Minimal; dilated not more than 10 cm	50%; constricted; transmural inflammation
Lymph nodes	Reactive hyperplasia	May contain granulomas

The main differential diagnosis of ulcerative colitis is with colorectal Crohn's disease (granulomatous colitis) (see p. 788) and nonspecific bacterial colitis (see p. 791). For many years, the presence of a chronic inflammatory disease of the large bowel not attributed to a specific organism was equivalent to a diagnosis of ulcerative colitis. It is now apparent that many of these cases actually represent examples of Crohn's disease involving the colon. The clinical, radiographic, and morphologic differences between these two diseases have now been clearly delineated (Table 11.3). It also has become apparent that in approximately 15% of cases features of both conditions are present and the differential diagnosis becomes impossible. The term *indeterminate colitis* has been proposed under these circumstances.[156,166a] On long-term follow-up, very few of these patients eventually develop features of Crohn's disease.[183] Patients with indeterminate colitis seem predisposed to perineal complications following ileal pouch–anal anastomosis.[155]

The occurrence of these transitional or indeterminate cases, the occasional coexistence of typical Crohn's disease of the small bowel and ulcerative colitis of the large bowel in the same patient, the development of Crohn's disease-like complications in patients with ulcerative colitis after proctocolectomy and ileal pouch–anal anastomosis,[139] and the occurrence of both diseases in the same family[152] suggest that perhaps the distinction between these two entities has been too rigidly drawn.[138,174] In any event, there are enough clinical and pathologic differences in the majority of the cases to justify a separation that has prognostic and therapeutic implications.

The treatment of ulcerative colitis, depending on its extent, severity, and duration, includes local or systemic steroid therapy and total colectomy.

Carcinoma and dysplasia in ulcerative colitis

The incidence of carcinoma of the large bowel is markedly increased in patients with ulcerative colitis.[210,218,257] The overall incidence of this complication in older series ranged between 5% and 10%,[203,211] but the current rate is closer to 2%.[232] This represents only 1% of all cases of colorectal carcinoma in the general population.[232] The risk of carcinoma is higher when the entire colon is involved; when the disease is continuous, unremitting, and of long standing (over 10 years),[203] and when the disease begins in childhood.[206,219,250] In a series of 396 cases of ulcerative colitis in children reported by Devroede et al.,[201] carcinoma developed in 3% by 10 years, in 23% by 20 years, and in 43% by 35 years after the onset of ulcerative colitis. Pericholangitis and sclerosing cholangitis are also risk factors for dysplasia and carcinoma.[202]

Early workers emphasized the atypical gross appearance of the carcinoma developing in ulcerative colitis, its more even distribution in the large bowel, its frequent multiplicity (10% to 20% of the cases), its tendency to occur in younger persons, and the fact that the site of origin is almost always a flat rather than a polypoid mucosa.[200,211,230] Carcinoma may also develop in the rectal stump following ileorectal anastomosis.[207,215]

The earliest gross change is often represented by a thick mucosa with a finely nodular or velvety surface configuration.[231] Microscopically, most of these tumors are adenocarcinomas of varying degrees of differentiation; however, the proportion of poorly differentiated and mucinous carcinomas is higher than for the tumors arising in an uninflamed mucosa[230] (Fig. 11.164). It has been traditionally assumed that carcinomas developing on the basis of ulcerative colitis carry an ominous prognosis; however, in several series with control subjects from a population without colitis matched by stage and microscopic grade, no difference in survival between the two groups has been found.[216,220,242,249] The apparent discrepancy may result from the fact that in the ulcerative colitis group there tends to be a higher proportion of inoperable and high-grade tumors.[242]

The development of adenocarcinoma is always accompanied—and probably always preceded—by dysplastic changes of the colorectal mucosa, as first described by Morson and Pang.[233] These dysplastic changes, which tend to occur in flat atrophic mucosa, should be distinguished from the more common ones resulting from regeneration atypia.[212] As a rule, the diagnosis of dysplasia should not be made in areas of active inflammation. The evaluation of these changes is difficult and somewhat subjective,[228] but when properly done, it has been successful in identifying a population at high risk for developing colorectal carcinoma.[260] The presence of dysplastic changes does not necessarily indicate that the patient harbors an invasive carcinoma elsewhere in

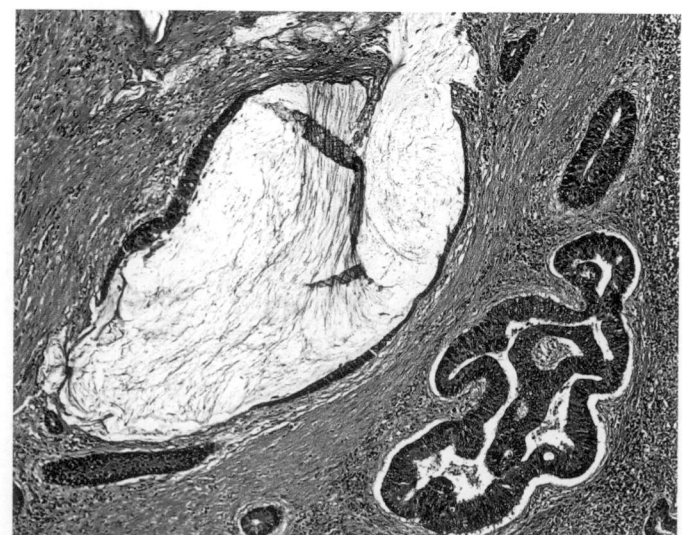

Fig. 11.164 Adenocarcinoma with mucinous features arising in a colon affected by ulcerative colitis. This is a common tumor subtype in this particular setting.

the bowel[199] as the original report had claimed.[233] Furthermore, the absence of such changes does not guarantee that the patient is free of carcinoma proximally, although it makes this possibility unlikely.[186,203] Multiple rectal biopsies are recommended for the detection of the dysplasia[237,241] (Fig. 11.165). A standardized classification of dysplasia has been recommended,[240] using the following terminology:

1 Negative for dysplasia
2 Indefinite for dysplasia, probably negative
3 Indefinite for dysplasia, unknown
4 Indefinite for dysplasia, probably positive
5 Positive for dysplasia, low grade
6 Positive for dysplasia, high grade

The reader is referred to the original publication for a detailed definition of these categories.[240] Whether morphometric analysis will improve the accuracy of this evaluation remains to be determined.[187,217]

The implications for patient management are to continue regular follow-up in categories 1 and 2, to institute short-term follow-up in categories 3 and 4, and to consider colectomy for category 6 following confirmation of the diagnosis. For category 5, the recommendation is either to institute short-term follow-up or to consider colectomy following confirmation of the diagnosis, especially if a gross lesion is present. The importance of the detection of gross lesions endoscopically was emphasized by this and other studies for the detection of dysplasia or frank carcinoma. These lesions may be in the form of polypoid, elevated, nodular or villous formations, ulcers, or strictures.[193,239,253]

At an immunohistochemical level, the dysplastic changes are associated with a relative excess of sialomucin production,[204,205,209] higher reactivity for CEA,[185,238] appearance of cytoplasmic staining for sucrase-isomaltase (which shows only membrane staining in inflammatory and regenerative mucosa),[188] decreased

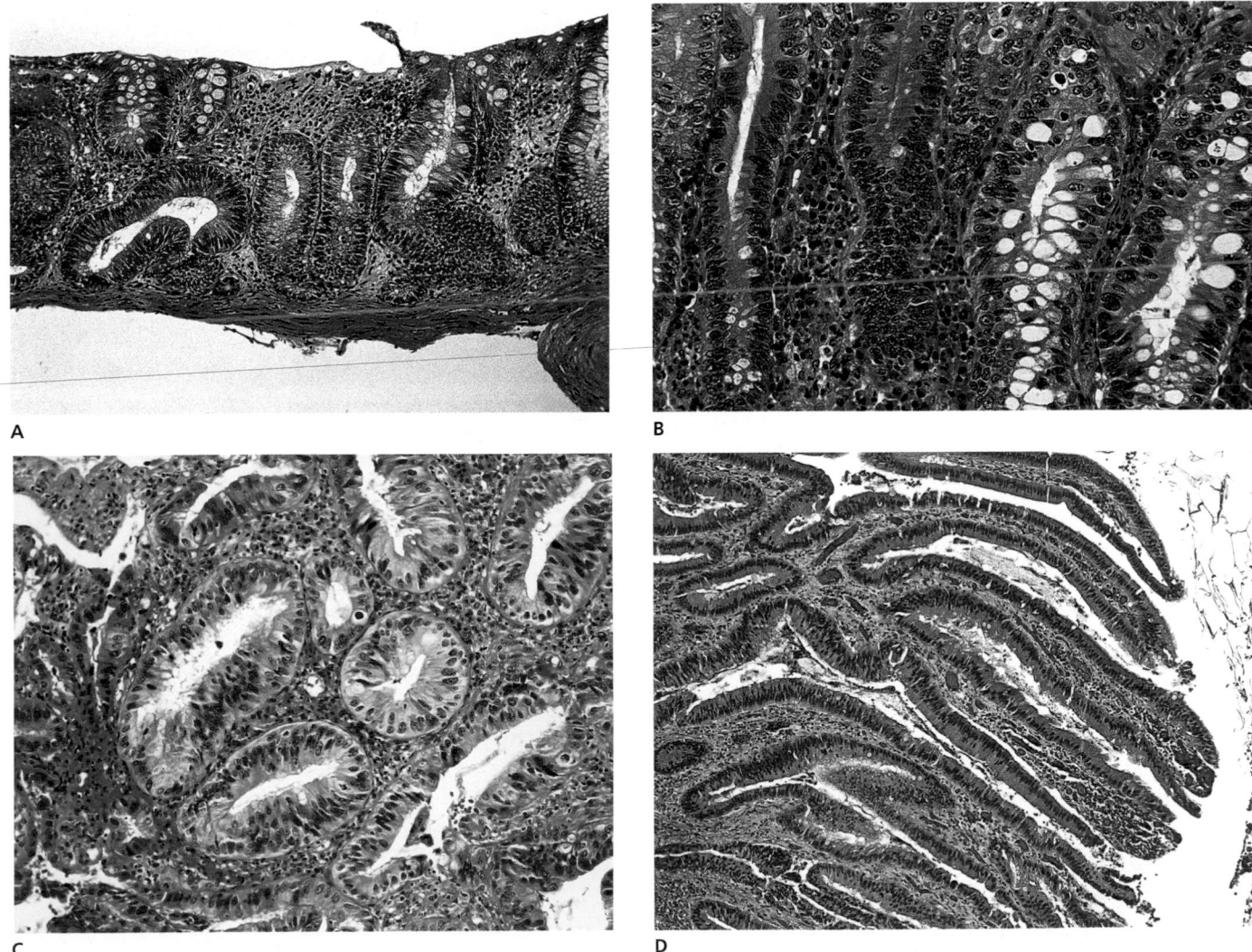

Fig. 11.165 A to **D**, Dysplasia in ulcerative colitis. **A**, Indefinite for dysplasia. **B**, Low-grade dysplasia. **C**, High-grade dysplasia. **D**, Dysplasia with papillary features.

staining for the secretory component of immuno-globulin,[185] abnormalities in lectin binding,[198] strong immunoreactivity for p53,[189,255,258] and MIB-1 (Ki-67) staining above the basal two thirds of the crypt.[258] Structural alterations have been identified by scanning electron microscopy,[247] and abnormalities of DNA content have been detected by flow cytometry.[223,224,323] At the molecular level, the aberrations encountered in the dysplastic glands have included *p53* mutations,[192,214,235,261] K-*ras* mutations,[194,195,225] and microsatellite instability.[225] The latter has been found to represent an early event in the progression pathway from ulcerative colitis to carcinoma.[256] It has also been found that ulcerative colitis patients with dysplasia and/or carcinoma have a much greater degree of genomic instability *in both their dysplastic and non-dysplastic mucosa* than those lacking morphologic features of dysplasia/carcinoma.[195a]

An interesting issue is whether the immunohistochemical and molecular alterations of the dysplastic lesions in ulcerative colitis (and therefore the mechanisms leading to its appearance and progression) are the same as or different from those operating in colorectal adenomas (which, of course, can be present in patients with ulcerative colitis).[234,254] Although the results from the various groups are not always congruent, a consensus is beginning to build that the flat dysplastic lesions in ulcerative colitis patients show many substantial differences to de novo colorectal adenomas, whereas the polypoid dysplastic lesions in the same patients are very similar if not identical to the de novo lesions.[190,208,236]

The presence of these immunohistochemical or molecular alterations may be helpful in confirming the presence of dysplasia and eventually contribute to its grading, but at the present time this determination is largely based on the appearance of the epithelium in routinely stained sections. The surveillance protocols that have been devised for patients with ulcerative colitis, recommended to be started after 8 to 10 years of extensive colitis and after 15 years of left-sided colitis, depend on skill and experience with endoscopic and microscopic features on the part of the gastroenterologist and pathologist, respectively.[222,230,232,243,259] Whether this close surveillance will prove beneficial remains to be seen.[191,196,197,245] It needs to be emphasized in this regard that the absence of dysplasia in a colorectal biopsy does not exclude the possibility of the patient developing adenocarcinoma in the future.[251,252]

Other colorectal malignancies that have occurred in association with ulcerative colitis are *neuroendocrine neoplasms* (microcarcinoids, atypical carcinoids, and small cell neuroendocrine carcinomas)[226,227,229,244,248] and *malignant lymphoma*.[213,246]

Crohn's disease (granulomatous colitis)

Crohn's disease, originally described as a small bowel disorder, is now known to involve the large bowel in

approximately 40% of all cases, with or without a concomitant ileal component.

The etiology remains undetermined. Susceptibility to the disease is inherited, suggesting a genetic contribution to its development.[279] The possibility of a bacterial infection—mycobacterial or otherwise—is brought up periodically,[263] but definite proof of an infectious agent has not been forthcoming. Another possibility to consider is that Crohn's disease of the large bowel may not be a distinct entity but rather a pattern of reaction resulting from a variety of causes, including vascular disorders. It has been suggested that at least some of the cases of Crohn's disease in the elderly have a vascular pathogenesis.[270,291,296]

Grossly, segmental distribution of the lesions (with "skip" areas that can be demonstrated radiographically) and preference for the right side of the colon are two important diagnostic features.[274] Other gross findings of significance include stricture formation, fissuring, a cobblestone appearance, transmural involvement, and fat wrapping (Fig. 11.166).[292] The ulcers are linear, serpigi-

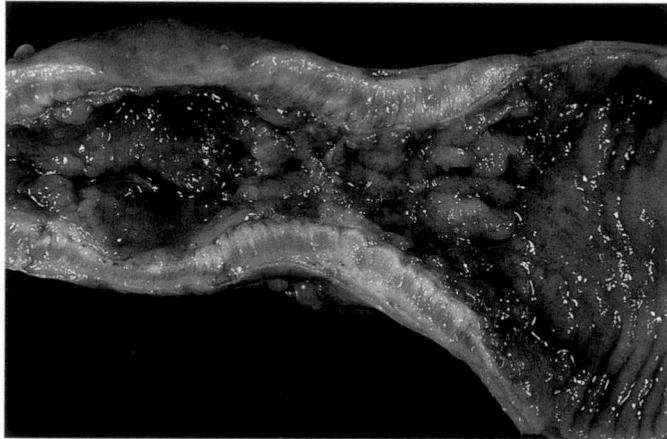

A

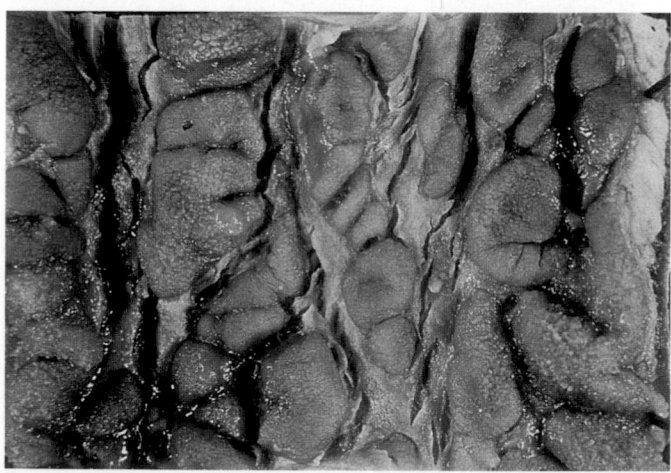

B

Fig. 11.166 A and **B**, Gross appearance of Crohn's disease of large bowel. **A**, Segmental involvement with transmural spread. The appearance is very similar to that seen in the small bowel in the same condition. **B**, Typical cobblestone appearance.

nous, and discontinuous, with an intervening normal or edematous (but not markedly abnormal) mucosa. Often, they run longitudinally for long distances and are connected by short transversal ulcers (Fig. 11.167). Healing of this process leads to long rail-track scars. Sometimes, pseudopolyps (of the usual filiform or giant type) and mural bridging lesions may develop, similar to those seen in ulcerative colitis.[262,272,280,283] The microscopic appearance of Crohn's disease in the large bowel is not qualitatively different from that seen in the small bowel. Fissures, noncaseating sarcoid-like granulomas (present in 40% to 60% of cases), and transmural involvement are typical (Fig. 11.168). The mucosa has a relatively normal appearance and retains a significant amount of mucus, even in areas immediately adjacent to ulcerations. Immunoglobulin-producing plasma cells are distinctly less common than in ulcerative colitis.[289] The presence of a well-defined focus of inflammatory cells surrounded by noninflamed and histologically normal mucosa is particularly suggestive of Crohn's disease, as is the predominance of inflammatory infiltrate deep into the mucosa and extending into the submucosa ("disproportionate inflammation"). However, on occasions the disease is superficial (i.e., limited to the mucosa and submucosa); in these instances, the cobblestone pattern is more diffuse and more finely nodular than is seen in classic Crohn's disease.[276]

The main features to look for in an endoscopic biopsy are granulomas, preservation of the goblet cell population, and maintenance of the architecture of the glands.[285] Serial sections may be necessary to demonstrate the granulomas, which are associated with the severity of the inflammation.[278,287,288,295] A rectal biopsy may be normal or show minor nonspecific changes.[282,286] As a matter of fact, a normal rectal biopsy in a definite case of colitis strongly favors Crohn's disease over ulcerative colitis.[282] If a colon involved by Crohn's disease contains diverticula, the inflammatory process often spreads to them.[277] In such cases, the differential diagnosis with diverticulitis and peridiverticulitis may become very difficult (see p. 779).

The ileum is involved in approximately 50% of cases of Crohn's disease of the large bowel.[282] Anal lesions are seen in 75% of cases and may present as chronic fissures, fistulas, and ulceration. They can be the first clinical manifestation of Crohn's disease and are recognized microscopically by the presence of granulomas.[267] These should not be confused with the foreign-body granulomas often seen in nonspecific anal fistulas. The regional lymph nodes are often enlarged. Microscopically, they do not differ significantly from those in patients with ulcerative colitis, except for the occasional presence of granulomas.[294]

One of the most common complications of Crohn's disease is the formation of fistulas, arising on the basis of fissuring. Although perianal fistulas can be seen in both Crohn's disease and ulcerative colitis, internal fistulas are virtually pathognomonic of the former.

Other complications of Crohn's disease include skin ulceration (of perianal skin, around colostomies and ileostomies, and elsewhere) and toxic megacolon.[268] In a series of 615 patients with Crohn's disease studied at the Cleveland Clinic,[266] the overall incidence of toxic megacolon was 4%. No cases were found when the disease was limited to the small bowel, but megacolon developed in 2% of patients with ileocolic disease and in 11% when the disease was limited to the colon. It should be pointed out that if the bowel is removed at the time when a toxic megacolon has developed, it may be impossible to distinguish the nature of the underlying disease.[281] Specifically, the criterion of transmural inflammation as a differential diagnostic point loses its significance. Examination of biopsies taken during the quiescent phase may be needed to resolve the difficulty.[281]

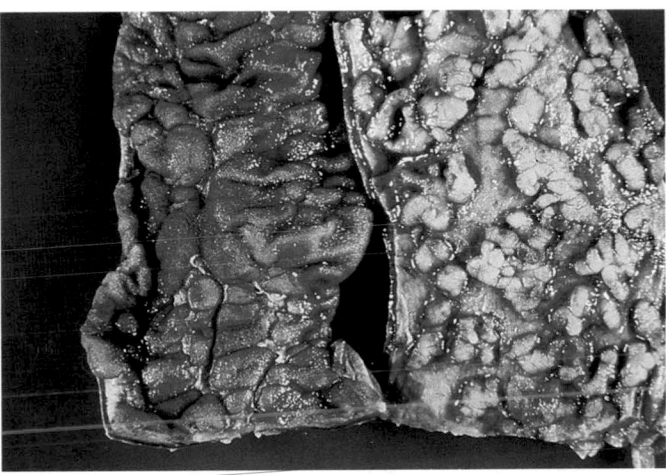

Fig. 11.167 Comparison between the pseudopolyps of ulcerative colitis (left), and the cobblestone pattern of Crohn's disease (right).

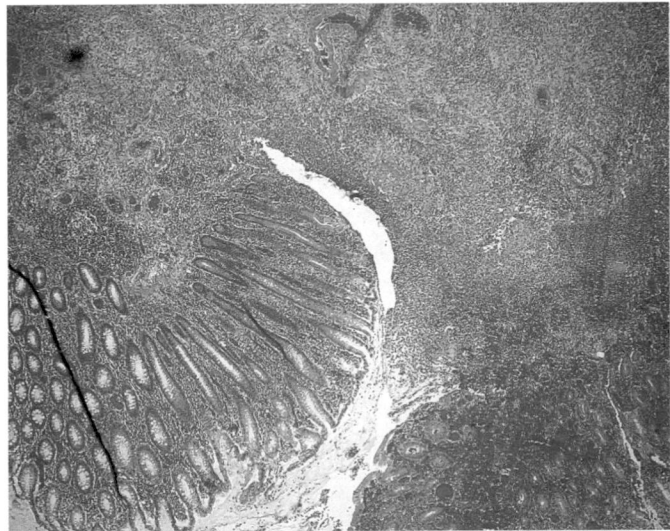

Fig. 11.168 Prominent fissuring in Crohn's disease of large bowel.

The other important complication of Crohn's disease is the development of large bowel carcinoma. Although the incidence is much lower than for ulcerative colitis, there is no longer any doubt that the risk is substantially higher than for the normal population.[265,269,271] As in ulcerative colitis, the malignancy can be difficult to identify grossly,[297] and it can also be accompanied and/or preceded by dysplastic changes of the colonic mucosa.[264,290,293,299] The criteria for the recognition and nomenclature of the dysplasia are the same in both conditions.[284] The associated immunohistochemical and DNA ploidy abnormalities are also similar.[275] In addition, it has been suggested that a peculiar mucosal change resembling colorectal hyperplastic polyps that is sometimes found in large bowels affected by Crohn's disease may be another form of dysplasia characteristic of this setting.[273]

The majority of patients with Crohn's disease of the large bowel eventually require surgical excision of the disease; the decision as to which operation to perform depends on the extent and site of the disease, the presence of perianal involvement, and the age of the patient.[279,298]

Ischemic and obstructive colitis

Ischemic colitis (colonic ischemia) has often been confused in the past with Crohn's disease and ulcerative colitis, and to some extent it still is. Most of the cases occur in patients over 50 years of age, and the usual predisposing factors are arteriosclerosis, diabetes, and vascular surgery.[300,306,310,313] It has also been seen in younger patients in association with collagen-vascular diseases (i.e., scleroderma and rheumatoid arthritis), Wegener's granulomatosis,[307] idiopathic lymphocytic phlebitis,[315,316,319] amyloidosis,[318] and as a complication of birth control pill use.[303,308] Arteriosclerosis may lead to ischemic colitis by intrinsic obstruction of colonic vessels or by atheromatous embolism[312] (Fig. 11.169). The process usually manifests itself by sudden onset of bleeding and abdominal pain. It is a segmental disease, the splenic flexure being the classic site of involvement because of its relative paucity of blood supply; however, other sites, including the rectum, can be involved. Morson[311] has described three morphologic variants: infarct, transient ischemia, and ischemic stricture (Fig. 11.170). The last is more likely to be seen as a surgical specimen. The typical radiographic signs are gas within the bowel wall and "thumbprinting."[314] Radiographic, endoscopic, and intraoperative confusion with carcinoma may occur.[302] Grossly, pseudopolyps may be present in addition to the ulcerations and the fibrosis.[302] Microscopically, there is ulceration covered by granulation tissue, which extends into the submucosa and surrounds individual smooth muscle fibers of the muscularis mucosae. Hemosiderin is abundant. Hyaline thrombi can be seen in the lumen of small vessels.

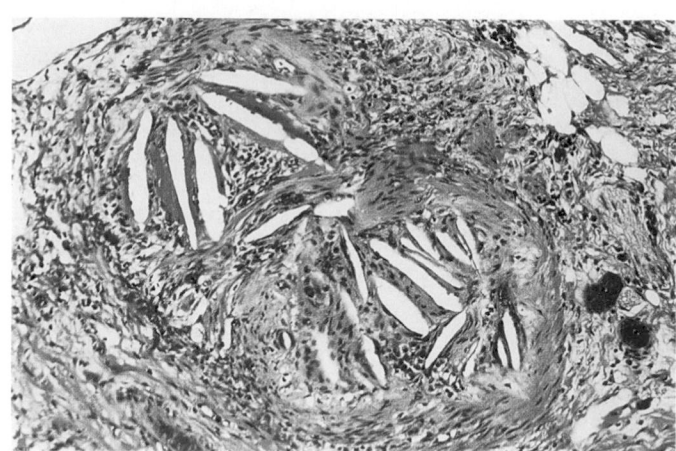

Fig. 11.169 Cholesterol emboli in mesenteric vessels which resulted in ischemic colitis.

Fig. 11.170 Ischemic colitis. The lesion is typically located in the splenic flexure. The mucosa is markedly hyperemic and covered by a fibrinopurulent exudate. (Courtesy of Dr. RA Cooke, Brisbane, Australia; from Cooke RA, Stewart B: Colour Atlas of Anatomical Pathology. Edinburgh, Churchill Livingstone, 2004).

Fissures, lymphoid follicles, and granulomas are absent, but crypt abscesses may be seen.[301] Microscopic features suggestive of ischemic necrosis are full-thickness mucosal necrosis in the acute stage, and hyalinization of the lamina propria, hemorrhage, and atrophic microcrypts in the healed phase.[304] Two changes that can result in overdiagnosis are represented by atypical reactive changes mimicking dysplasia,[320] and isolated goblet cells simulating neoplastic signet ring cells ("signet ring cell change").[305,319a]

The main differential diagnosis is with Crohn's disease. Although the latter may be seen in any age group, it should be remembered that ischemic colitis is the most common form of colitis in the elderly.[301]

Aggressive management is of crucial importance to minimize the damage to the ischemic colon. Surgical intervention is indicated if there is evidence of peritonitis, transmural infarction, or perforation.[300]

Obstructive colitis is the term given to an inflammatory and often ulcerative disorder of the colon occurring proximal to an obstructing lesion, which is usually an adenocarcinoma.[309,317] Grossly, the changes may be represented by small circumscribed ulcers or confluent circumferential lesions. These are always separated from the distal obstructing lesion by a segment of colon that may measure anywhere from 2.5 to 35 cm.[317] Microscopically, there is granulation tissue involving the mucosa and submucosa, occasionally extending to the muscularis propria. Many of these features suggest that obstructive colitis is a type of ischemic colitis.

Other types of colitis

Nonspecific bacterial colitis (acute self-limited colitis; acute infectious-type colitis) is a self-limited diarrheal illness thought to be caused by infectious agents, particularly *Campylobacter, Salmonella*, and *Shigella*; however, in over half of the cases the etiology remains undetermined.[404] Microscopically, there is inflammatory infiltration of the lamina propria, edema, hyperemia, and hemorrhage; the changes may be indistinguishable from those of an early stage of ulcerative colitis,[336,433,434] and a follow-up biopsy may be necessary to separate the two.[341,344] Infections by *Salmonella* and *Shigella* organisms are particularly well known for their capacity to simulate ulcerative colitis clinically and radiographically.[322] The microscopic appearance varies from nonspecific edematous and inflammatory changes to severe cases exhibiting crypt abscesses, extensive necrosis and hemorrhage, and microthrombi.[401] *Escherichia coli* has a tendency to cause acute hemorrhagic colitis,[334,338] with microscopic changes in the biopsy ranging from normal to those of an infectious-type colitis.[379,380] Acute inflammation out of proportion to chronic inflammation should suggest an infective etiology. Conversely, crypt distortion and plasma cell infiltration in the basal portion of the mucosa favor a diagnosis of ulcerative colitis.[391,427] The distinction between the two conditions is easier if the biopsy is taken within the first 4 days from the onset of symptoms.[363,404]

Allergic colitis and **proctitis** are related to foods (particularly cows' milk) and are seen more commonly in infants and children.[405,444] They present with rectal bleeding, sometimes accompanied by diarrhea. The main microscopic abnormalities on rectal biopsy are mucosal edema and eosinophilic infiltration. The eosinophils tend to aggregate around lymphoid nodules; others are located within crypt abscesses and among bundles of muscularis mucosae.[365,431,446]

Collagenous colitis usually presents clinically in middle-aged women as chronic watery diarrhea. Endoscopic and radiographic studies are often normal. Microscopically, the disease is characterized by collagen deposition beneath the surface epithelium, this homogeneous hyaline layer reaching a thickness of 10 μm or more[429] (Fig. 11.171). This alteration can be patchy and should not be the only criterion on which the diagnosis is based.[392,429] It is said to be better developed in the transverse portion of the colon.[406] The mucosa shows evidence of focal or diffuse injury and infiltration by lymphocytes and other inflammatory cells.[329,374,380] Lymphocytes and neutrophils may be present in the crypts, and there is an increased number of inflammatory cells in the lamina propria. The basal lamina located over the thickened collagen is normal.[353] Immunostaining for tenascin shows prominent subepithelial reactivity and supports the diagnosis.[321] Recently, a pseudomembranous form of collagenous colitis has been described.[449a]

An immune pathogenesis and a relationship with celiac disease have been postulated.[323,374] It has been further suggested that nonsteroidal anti-inflammatory drugs may play an etiologic role in some of these cases.[362,416] The clinical course is rather benign, and microscopic resolution may occur.[335,354,382] One case has been reported in association with colonic carcinoma.[359]

Lymphocytic (microscopic) colitis is closely related to collagenous colitis.[328,373,442] There are occasional transitions between these two disorders, which have been grouped by some under the term "watery diarrhea–colitis syndrome."[420] The main microscopic differences between the two are the absence of a thickened collagenous layer and the prominence of intraepithelial lymphocytes in lymphocytic colitis.[364,393] Changes morphologically indistinguishable from lymphocytic colitis have been consistently found in large bowel biopsies of patients with celiac disease, further suggesting a pathogenetic relationship between these disorders.[447]

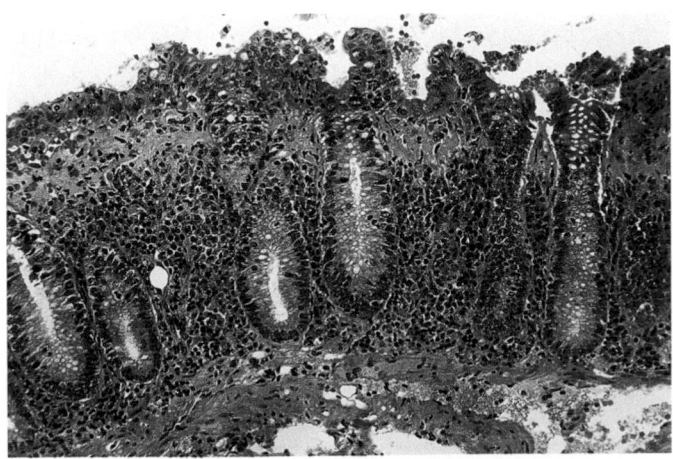

Fig. 11.171 Collagenous colitis. A thick layer of hyalinized collagen is seen beneath the surface epithelium.

The terminal ileum may be involved in cases of collagenous or lymphocytic colitis.[419] Recently, a subtype of lymphocytic (microscopic) colitis containing scattered multinucleated giant cells in the subepithelial region has been described.[397]

It is still unclear whether lymphocytic colitis is a specific entity or not. It has been suggested that it represents a heterogeneous group as far as etiology is concerned.[441] In some instances, the microscopic features of lymphocytic colitis have been seen in patients later found to have Crohn's disease.[366] The matter is complicated by the fact that in some cases of collagenous/lymphocytic colitis there may be crypt irregularities, neutrophilic cryptitis, and crypt abscesses.[325] Finally, it should be mentioned that colonic biopsies taken in patients with *Brainerd's diarrhea* (a chronic watery diarrhea of unknown etiology characterized by acute onset and prolonged duration) show a microscopic appearance similar to that of lymphocytic colitis but usually lacking surface degenerative changes.[332]

Focal active colitis refers to the presence in a large bowel biopsy of focal crypt and surface epithelial injury by neutrophils associated with increase of inflammatory cells in the lamina propria. It represents a pattern of reaction rather than a specific diagnosis; most cases correlate clinically with infectious-type colitis but sometimes focal active colitis is a harbinger of Crohn's disease, particularly in children.[368,436,447a]

Pseudomembranous colitis is thought to be due in most instances to a toxin produced by *Clostridium difficile*.[350,360,412] A substantial number of cases have been associated with the use of the antibiotics lincomycin and clindamycin,[414] and a few cases have been described following resection for Hirschsprung's disease.[326] It has also been suggested that some cases are part of the spectrum of collagenous colitis (see p. 791). Florid cases of this condition are difficult to distinguish from ulcerative colitis and Crohn's disease on clinical and radiographic grounds.[402] Acute abdomen may be the presenting manifestation.[432] The thickening of the wall can be appreciated by CT and sonographic techniques.[343,352] Grossly, discrete yellow–white mucosal plaques are seen (Fig. 11.172). The microscopic distinguishing feature is a "focal explosive mucosal lesion" characterized by the presence of a mushroom-like mass of mucus and neutrophils attached to the surface of the mucosal glands.[367,426] The mucosa immediately adjacent to these changes is remarkably normal. The wall may show massive edema, probably resulting from vascular injury.[423] Intramucosal signet ring cells may be present and potentially be overinterpreted as malignant[340,421] (see p. 815). Emergency surgery may be needed for complications, including colonic perforation and toxic colitis.[339,438]

Diversion colitis is an inflammatory bowel disorder resulting from diversion of the fecal stream by ileostomy or colostomy. The pathogenesis is unknown, but the removal of short-chain fatty acids present in the fecal stream is suspected to play an important role.[345] The

Fig. 11.172 Pseudomembranous colitis. There are multiple, discrete white plaques of purulent exudate on the mucosal surface. The patient was taking ampicillin. (Courtesy of Dr. RA Cooke, Brisbane, Australia; from Cooke RA, Stewart B: Colour Atlas of Anatomical Pathology. Edinburgh, Churchill Livingstone, 2004).

disease occurs in adults as well as in children.[437] The abnormalities range from minimal mucosal friability to gross ulcerations.[351] Microscopically, the most common changes are mild-to-moderate chronic inflammation in the lamina propria, crypt abscesses, and follicular lymphoid hyperplasia.[361] Aphthous ulcers are present in the most severe cases.[369,386,398] Of all these changes, lymphoid follicular hyperplasia is the most common and prominent.[449] These abnormalities quickly revert after reanastomosis.

Neonatal necrotizing enterocolitis is a condition primarily affecting infants who either are premature or have had exchange transfusions.[383] A few cases have followed thrombosis of the abdominal aorta,[375,388] suggesting that ischemia is an important risk factor. The condition may also be seen as a complication of Hirschsprung's disease (see p. 777). Most cases begin in the first week of life and are manifested by abdominal distention, the disappearance of bowel sounds, and the passage of small amounts of blood-stained stool.[418,425] The area of maximal involvement is the terminal ileum and ascending colon. The mucosa becomes necrotic and may partially slough off. Small submucosal gas-filled cysts are often present (Fig. 11.173); these can be seen radiographically and represent an important diagnostic sign.[411] Bowel perforation may occur. In these cases, resection of the perforated and necrotic bowel is indicated.[445]

Ecchymotic colitis is the name sometimes given to a condition seen in neonates and leading to isolated rectal bleeding. It is characterized endoscopically by ecchymotic mucosal lesions, and microscopically by a predominantly neutrophilic inflammation, foci of hemorrhage, and sometimes foci of pneumatosis. The etiology is unknown.[333]

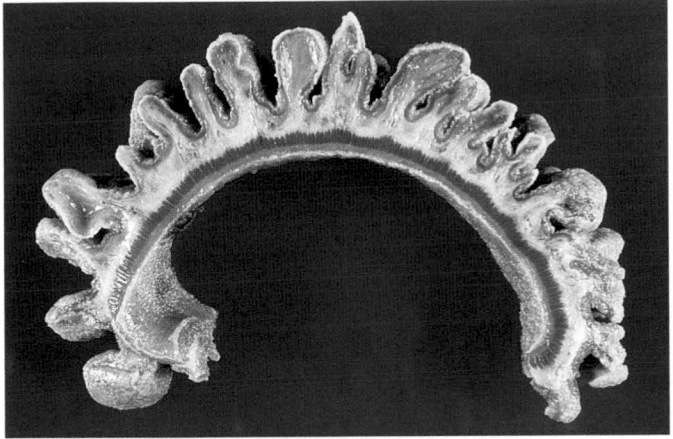

A

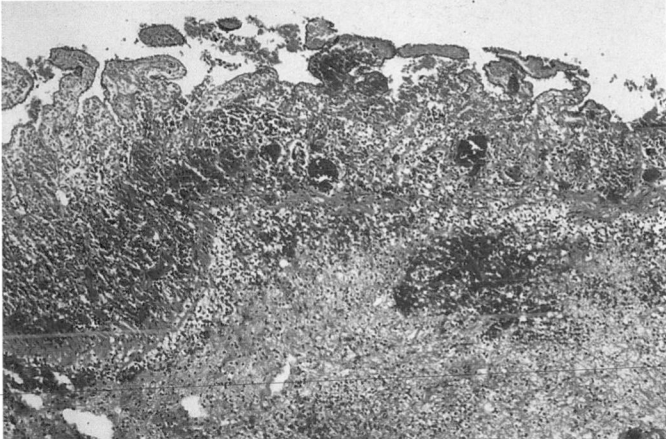

B

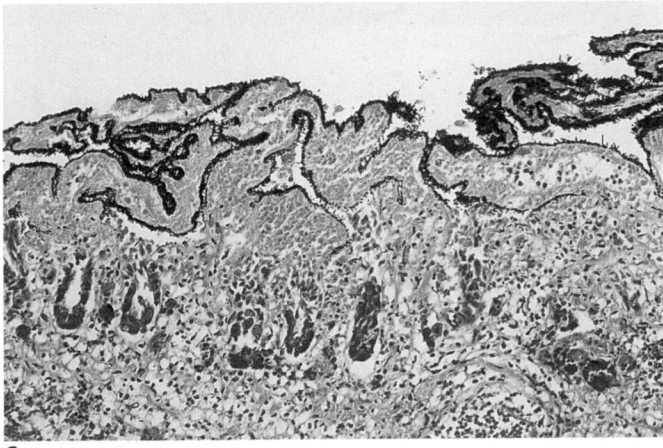

C

Fig. 11.173 A to **C,** Necrotizing enterocolitis. **A,** Gross appearance. The mucosa is necrotic. Numerous small gas-filled cysts are present in the wall. **B,** Low-power microscopic appearance showing extensive ulceration, necrosis, and hemorrhage. **C,** Gram stain showing coating of the ulcerated surface by *Enteritis necroticans* organisms.

Amebic colitis can closely simulate ulcerative colitis or Crohn's disease on clinical grounds.[409] The classic sigmoidoscopic appearance is that of discrete areas of ulceration covered by exudate, with normal intervening mucosa; however, many cases depart from this description. Amebiasis may involve any part of the bowel, but it has a predilection for the cecum and ascending colon (Fig. 11.174). In many cases the entire large bowel is involved, and there may even be extension into the terminal ileum.[331,368a] Perforation occurs in 5% to 10% of the cases. The microscopic appearance of a rectal biopsy is rather nonspecific, although the relative paucity of inflammatory cells beneath the ulcer and the flask shape of the ulcer itself should alert the pathologist to the diagnosis. The confirmation rests on the identification of trophozoites of *Entamoeba histolytica*. They can be seen in hematoxylin–eosin slides, although the inexperienced observer may confuse them with macrophages (and vice versa). Typically, the parasites are surrounded by an artifactually clear space.[384] They are round or ovoid, measure 6 to 40 nm in diameter, and contain an abundant cytoplasm with a distinctive vacuolated appearance and relatively small, perfectly round nuclei with prominent nuclear borders and a central karyosome. Erythrocytosis by the trophozoites is usually present and can be easily demonstrated with Heidenhain's iron hematoxylin staining. The organisms can also be demonstrated with PAS and with immunoperoxidase stains, both in sections and in smears.[385,400,410,413]

Tuberculosis may involve the gastrointestinal tract in the presence of minimal pulmonary disease.[346,377,407] The

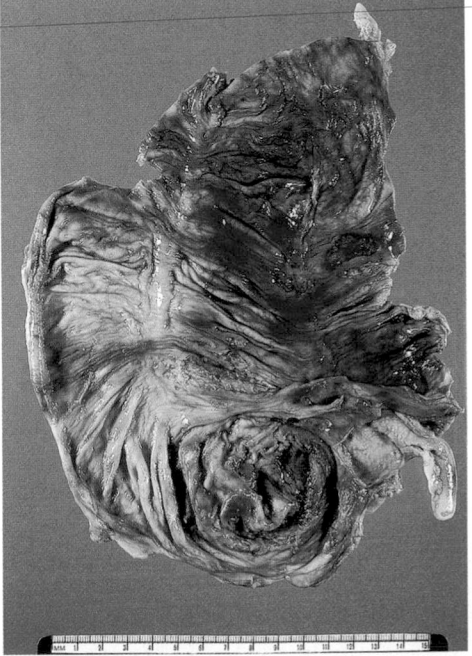

Fig. 11.174 Amebic colitis. Multiple, undermined ulcers are present in the cecum and ascending colon. (Courtesy of Dr. RA Cooke, Brisbane, Australia; from Cooke RA, Stewart B: Colour Atlas of Anatomical Pathology. Edinburgh, Churchill Livingstone, 2004).

usual location is the ileocecal area, and a mass can be palpated in approximately half of the cases ("tuberculoma").[371] Grossly, there is ulceration with diffuse fibrosis extending through the wall, causing stenosis and obstruction. Coexistent tuberculous peritonitis is seen in only a few of the cases. Microscopically, typical granulomas are usually present, accompanied by ulceration and extensive desmoplasia. The granulomas can be caseating, noncaseating, suppurative, or fibrous (healed).[356] Vasculitis may be present.[399] In some instances, a nonspecific, diffuse, chronic inflammation with fibrosis without granulomas is seen focally or—

very rarely—as the sole pattern.[356] Demonstration of acid-fast bacilli, either by stain of the sections or by culture, is needed to establish a diagnosis. It should be remembered that the large majority of cases of granulomatous disease of the ileocecal area seen in the United States and western Europe represent examples of Crohn's disease[394]; features favoring tuberculosis over Crohn's disease are caseation and coalescence of the granulomas.[430] Most patients with secondary ulcerating tuberculosis of the colon can be treated medically; surgery, sometimes in the form of ileocolectomy, is reserved for the large cecal tuberculomas.

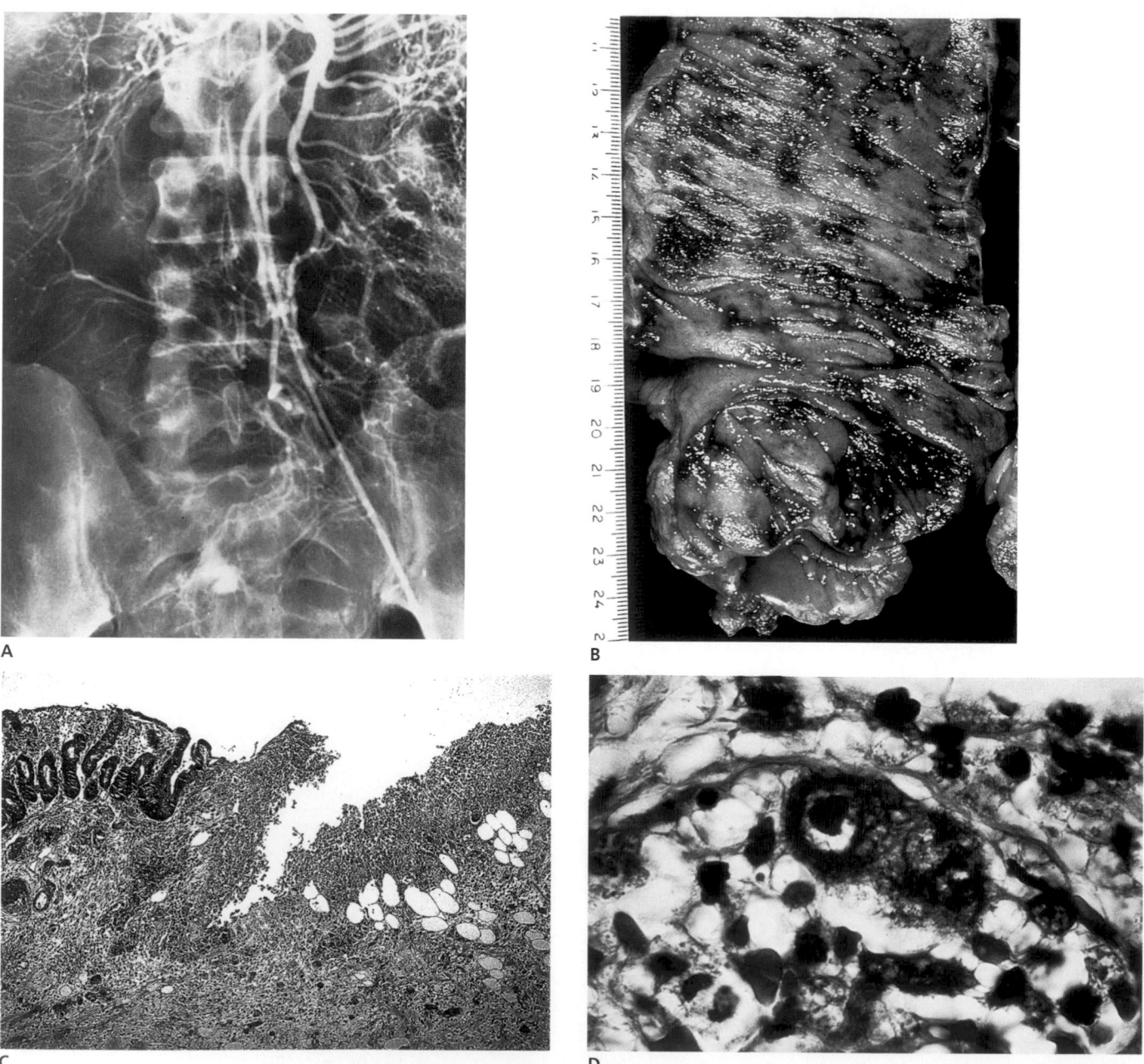

Fig. 11.175 A to **D**, Cytomegalovirus infection of large bowel in a renal transplant recipient. **A**, Arteriogram showing site of bleeding in cecum. **B**, Gross appearance of resected specimen showing numerous superficial ulcerations. **C**, Microscopic section showing inflammation and ulcerations. **D**, High-power view of infected cell with huge intranuclear inclusion.

Cytomegalovirus colitis is seen with increased frequency in immunocompromised patients, such as transplant recipients and individuals affected by AIDS.[342,348,387,390,403,428] The disease has a predilection for the ileocecal area; it may be accompanied by extensive ulceration and sometimes a discrete mass.[415] Inclusion bodies are found mainly in cells located in the wall or lining the lumen of submucosal vessels showing features of vasculitis, but they may also be seen in fibroblasts and epithelial cells.[355] The diagnosis can be confirmed immunohistochemically[355] (Figs 11.175 and 11.176). Surgical resection may be necessary in cases resulting in massive hemorrhage.

HIV-infected patients may also develop colitis caused by *Pneumocystis*,[327] *Histoplasma*,[337] adenovirus,[372,488] and *Toxoplasma*.[408,422] In addition, it has been suggested that HIV itself may be responsible for some cases of chronic colitis in this population.[370]

Behçet's colitis (i.e., the colitis associated with Behçet's syndrome) is characterized by multiple ulcers of various sizes, shapes, and depths involving any portion of the large bowel and is accompanied by lymphocytic vasculitis of the submucosal veins[381,396]; it may closely resemble the appearance of Crohn's disease.[395]

Graft-versus-host disease (GVHD), occurring in patients who have received bone marrow allografts, manifests in the gastrointestinal tract primarily as colitis.[424] Microscopically, there is focal crypt epithelial cell apoptosis, a feature that is thought to signify cell-mediated cytolysis.[330,347,358,417] Crypt abscesses may also be present. Severe disease may lead to loss of crypts, sloughing of the mucosa, and formation of inflammatory polyps.[357,424] In the chronic phase there is architectural distortion (villiform surface with crypt branching and atrophy) similar to that seen in idiopathic inflammatory bowel disease.[324] The histology of acute GVHD can be simulated by cytoreductive agents and viral infections, particularly CMV. Similar changes are also seen in patients with AIDS, the pathogenesis being presumably related to immune rather than infectious factors.[389,443]

Typhlitis is a colitis centered in or restricted to the cecum. Most of the reported cases have been seen in patients with acute leukemia. The etiology can be bacterial or fungal.[378]

Neutropenic colitis is a rare complication of chemotherapy administered for hematologic malignancies and—less commonly—solid tumors.[349] Full-thickness involvement of the bowel wall may lead to perforation and require surgery.[435,439]

Toxic megacolon may result from several of the previously mentioned types of colitis, although the incidence of this complication is much less than in ulcerative colitis.[376]

Other non-neoplastic lesions

Colonic atresia is much less common than atresia of the small bowel; it is treated surgically with segmental resection and anastomosis.[487]

Heterotopic gastric epithelium and **salivary gland tissue** may be rarely found in the rectum.[508] The lesions present clinically as a sessile polypoid mass.[498]

Neuronal storage diseases of various types are accompanied by changes in the ganglion cells of the submucosal and myenteric plexuses, so that the conditions may be diagnosed by rectal biopsy.[454,470,486]

Melanosis coli is the name given to a condition in which macrophages filled with a lipofuscin-like pigment ("pseudomelanin") are found within the lamina propria (Fig. 11.177).[465] If they are numerous enough, the mucosa acquires a brown-to-black color (Fig. 11.178A). Interestingly, adenomatous polyps that may be present

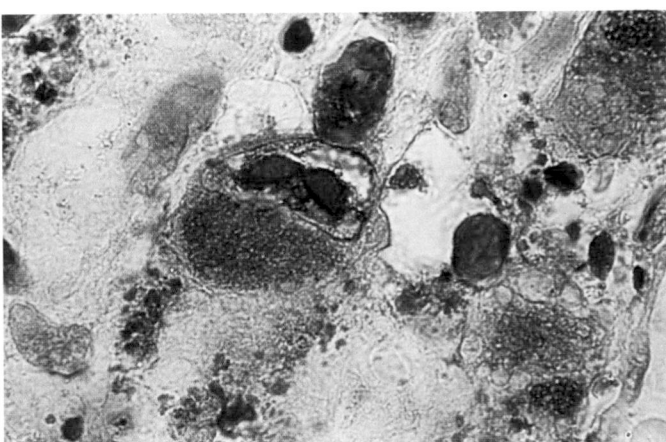

Fig. 11.176 Cytomegalovirus colitis in an immunosuppressed patient. This immunoperoxidase stain shows both nuclear and cytoplasmic positivity.

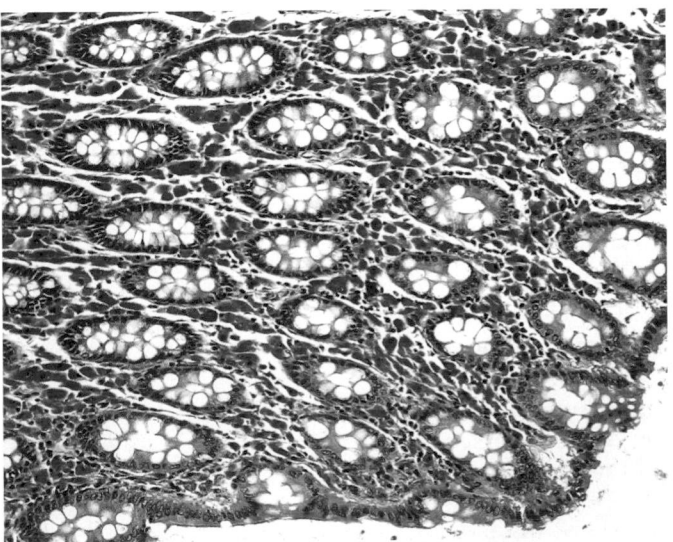

Fig. 11.177 Melanosis coli. Pigment-containing macrophages pack the lamina propria.

A

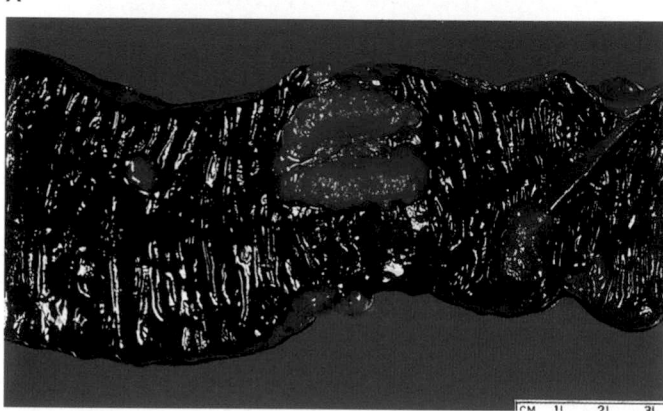

B

Fig. 11.178 A and **B**, Gross appearance of melanosis coli. The disease begins sharply at the level of the ileocecal valve (**A**). Interestingly, the carcinoma and polyps present in the second specimen (**B**) are not involved by the melanosis. **B**, Large bowel diffusely involved by melanosis coli. There is also a carcinoma (center) as well as several adenomatous polyps. The neoplastic lesions are not involved by the melanosis.

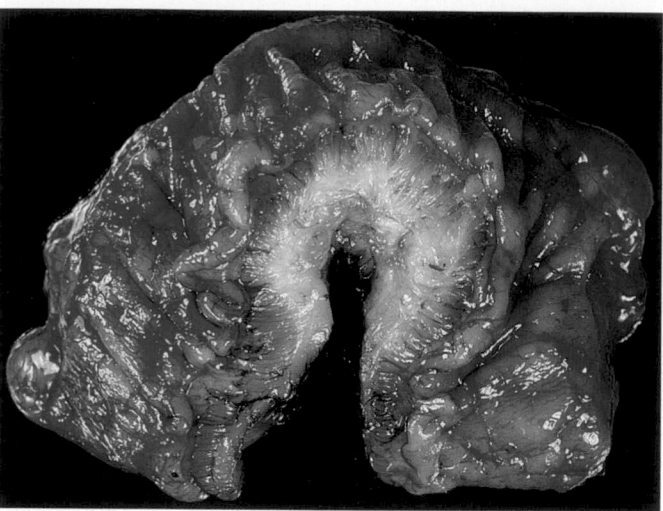

Fig. 11.179 Endometriosis of large bowel showing thickening of the wall associated with muscle hyperplasia, resulting in partial obstruction.

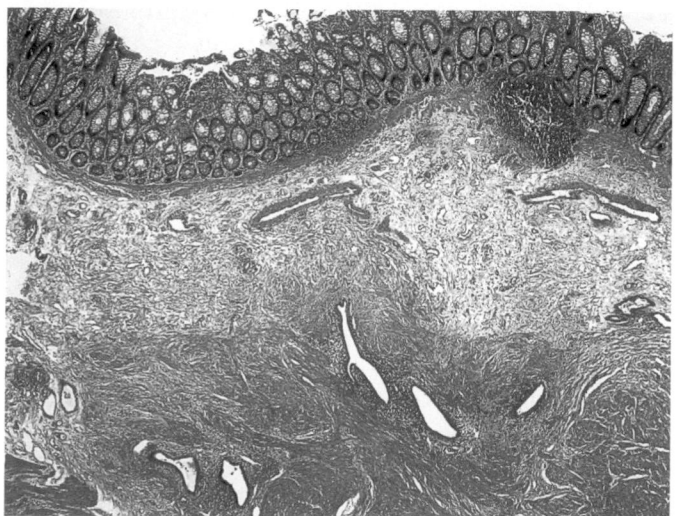

A

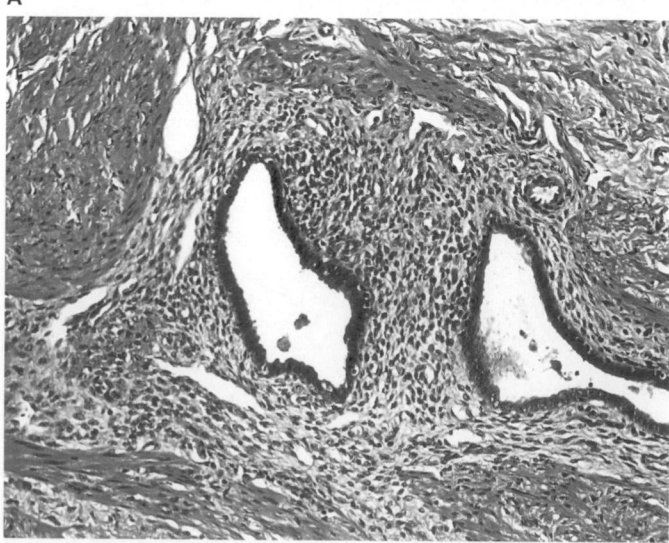

B

Fig. 11.180 A and **B**, Endometriosis of large bowel. The disease is located deeply in the wall, and is composed of endometrial glands and stroma.

in such a mucosa do not show any pigmentation (Fig. 11.178B). Melanosis coli has been associated with the ingestion of anthraceneline laxatives,[499,503] but it can also be seen in patients without this history. Increased apoptosis seems to be the pathogenetic mechanism responsible for the change.[456]

It should be mentioned here that other pigments sometimes seen in specimens from this region include the India ink and methylene blue used as endoscopic tattoo agents.[472]

Endometriosis may involve the wall of the large bowel, induce secondary smooth muscle hypertrophy, and result in almost complete obstruction[511] (Fig. 11.179). Microscopically, endometrial glands and stroma are seen surrounded by proliferated smooth muscle and clusters of hemosiderin-laden macrophages (Fig. 11.180). The overlying epithelium may show various types of inflammatory and ulcerative changes that may simulate inflammatory bowel disease or solitary rectal ulcer syndrome in a biopsy specimen.[455,473] On occasion, there is coexistent lymph node involvement.[469]

Neoplastic transformation can supervene in these endometriotic foci, usually in the form of endometrioid adenocarcinoma but also müllerian adenosarcoma and endometrial stromal sarcoma.[451,483,495,510] Sometimes these changes are accompanied or preceded by atypical hyperplasia or carcinoma in situ.[510]

Amyloidosis can involve the large bowel and be diagnosed on rectal biopsy.[463] The results are comparable to those obtained by renal biopsy and better than those achieved by liver biopsy. It is important for the specimen to include the submucosa, for this can be the only place of amyloid deposition.[471] If the amyloid deposition is mainly beneath the epithelium, the appearance may simulate that of collagenous colitis.[467] Occasionally, amyloid deposition results in ischemic changes in the colon (see p. 790).

Volvulus of the large bowel is a rare cause of acute abdominal obstruction.[466] Approximately 25% to 40% of cases occur in the cecum.[481] Prompt surgical intervention is imperative. Gangrene is found in approximately 25% of cases at the time of exploration and is a definite indication for resection.

Malakoplakia can involve the colon diffusely[485,502] (Fig. 11.181). Most of the patients are adults, but cases in infants have been described.[494] Malakoplakia can occur as a complication of ulcerative colitis[478] and of paracoccidioidomycosis,[488] and as a focal change in the stroma of adenomatous polyps (see p. 801). It can also be found in association with adenocarcinoma.[490]

Barium granulomas of the rectum and perirectal tissues can occur following barium enema. Barium escapes through a break in the mucosa produced by infection, tumor, foreign body, or trauma and provokes a granulomatous reaction. The crystals are easily visible under polarized light.[452]

Radiation changes in the colon and rectum can be accompanied by bizarre cellular changes in the epithelium of the crypts. Inflammation is also present, even with the formation of crypt abscesses; eosinophils may be numerous.[464,476,506] These acute changes usually subside within 1 to 2 months. Late changes include arterial stenosis due to the subendothelial accumulation of macrophages (Fig. 11.182). Severe radiation changes include ulceration, necrosis, hemorrhage, and perforation[489] (Fig. 11.183). In rare instances, glandular atypia develops, from which a postradiation adenocarcinoma may arise.[492]

Solitary cecal ulcers have an unknown etiology, and their microscopic appearance is nonspecific.[455,479]

Pneumatosis cystoides intestinalis occurring in infants is usually seen as a component of necrotizing enterocolitis and often has a fatal outcome.[507] Exceptionally, it occurs in

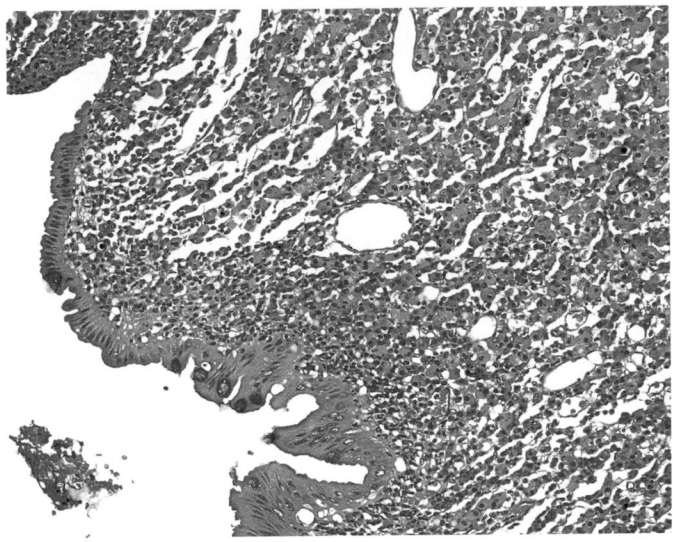

A

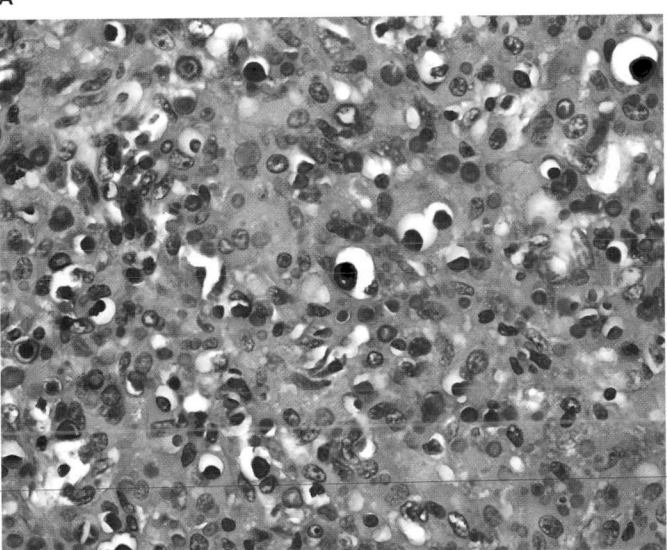

B

Fig. 11.181 A and **B**, Malakoplakia. **A**, Low-power view showing packing of the lamina propria by an inflammatory infiltrate rich in histiocytes. **B**, High-power view showing numerous histiocytes, some containing Michaelis–Gutmann bodies.

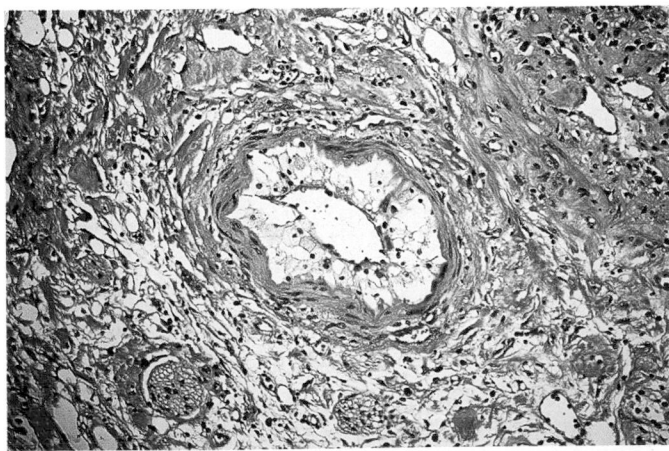

Fig. 11.182 Subendothelial accumulation of foamy macrophages in a vessel in radiation colitis.

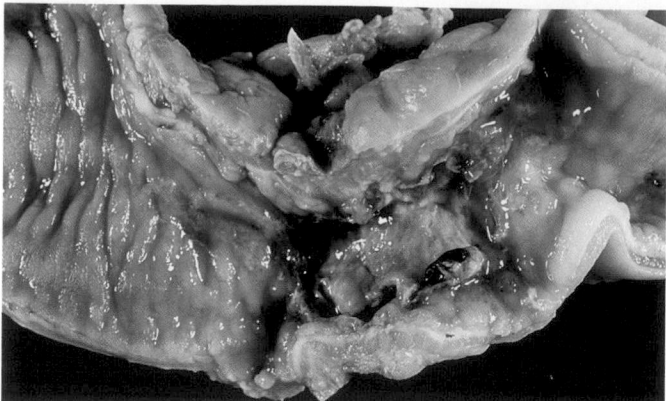

Fig. 11.183 Radiation colitis resulting in thickening of the wall, ulceration, and perforation.

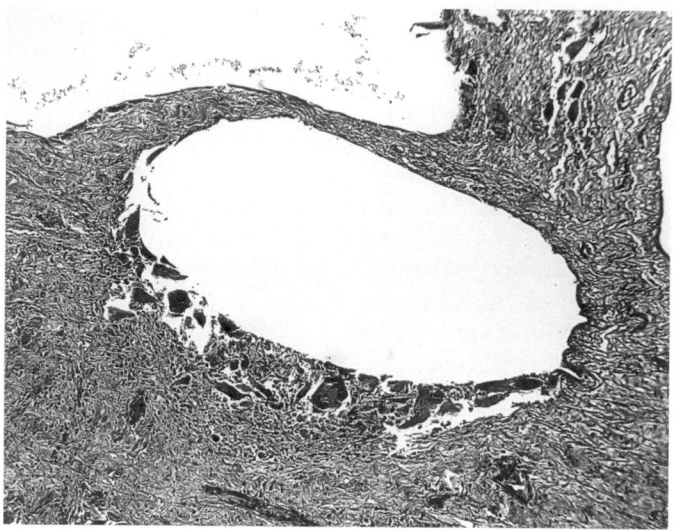

Fig. 11.185 Pneumatosis cystoides intestinalis. The cysts are partially lined by multinucleated giant cells.

association with cystic fibrosis.[509] In adults (mean age, 56 years), it may present as an idiopathic finding or in association with mechanical intestinal obstruction, chronic lung disease, or scleroderma.[496] When not associated with other abnormalities, it follows a chronic and indolent clinical course, although in some instances it may produce signs of intestinal obstruction and lead to an incorrect radiographic diagnosis of carcinoma. Grossly, polypoid grapelike masses formed by submucosal gas-filled cysts protrude through the mucosa (Fig. 11.184). Microscopically, the cysts are lined by multinucleated giant cells (Fig. 11.185). The overlying mucosa may show cryptitis, crypt abscesses, chronic inflammation, and granulomas (i.e., changes that may mimic inflammatory bowel disease, particularly Crohn's disease).[501] It is believed that the gas is generated in the lumen or within inflamed crypts, from where it penetrates through the muscularis mucosae to accumulate in the form of submucosal cysts.[484] Some authors have suggested a lymphatic origin for the cysts, but this seems unlikely.[468]

The peculiar condition described as *mucosal pseudolipomatosis* may represent a lesion related to pneumatosis in which the gas-filled cysts are extremely small and limited to the lamina propria of the mucosa, resulting in an endoscopic appearance that simulates lipomatosis.[497]

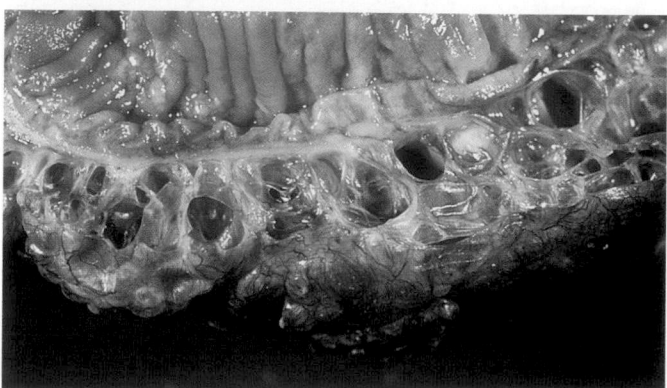

Fig. 11.184 Pneumatosis cystoides intestinalis in a patient with scleroderma.

Colitis cystica profunda is a non-neoplastic condition characterized by the presence of intramural mucus-containing cysts in the colon and rectum. It may present as a single polypoid mass or involve extensive areas of the bowel.[450,459] The localized form, also known as *hamartomatous inverted polyp*,[450] is typically located in the rectum, 5 to 12 cm from the anal margin. It presents as a plaque, nodule, or polyp and is associated with chronic proctitis.[505] This form may be related to solitary rectal ulcer (see below).

The diffuse form is in most cases the result of inflammation and ulceration of the bowel, as seen in ulcerative colitis, Crohn's disease, or irradiation change[480]; the ulceration provides the means by which mucosa can extend along granulation tracts and thus form lakes of mucus in the submucosa. This disease may be mistaken for a mucinous carcinoma of the rectum or rectosigmoid[493]; however, the mucin production in colitis cystica profunda is not accompanied by epithelial atypia and only rarely extends beyond the submucosa.

Solitary rectal ulcer (sometimes referred to as "solitary ulcer syndrome" or benign idiopathic recurrent rectal ulceration [BIRRU]) presents as a solitary ulcerated or polypoid lesion located 4 to 18 cm from the anal margin, often in association with mucosal prolapse.[460,491] The usual symptoms are the passage of blood and mucus via the rectum, an alteration in bowel habits, and pain.[460] Microscopically, there is a very superficial and irregular mucosal ulceration, hyperplasia of the crypts (some of which have a peculiar diamond shape), a tendency toward villous configuration, obliteration of the lamina propria by fibroblasts, elastin, and smooth muscle cells from the muscularis mucosae, a reduction in the number of lymphocytes and plasma cells, and thickening of the muscularis mucosae with splaying of its fibers[461,491,504] (Fig. 11.186). In chronic cases, changes analogous to those

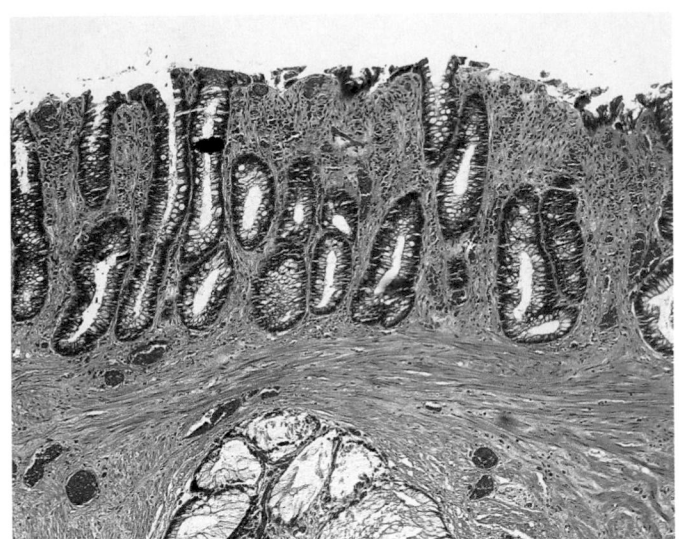

Fig. 11.186 So-called "solitary rectal ulcer." The glands are distorted by prominent fibrosis of the lamina propria. The muscularis mucosae is thickened, and there is some glandular displacement in the submucosa.

of colitis cystica profunda may occur.[500] Indeed, it is likely that the above described localized form of colitis cystica profunda (hamartomatous inverted polyp) and so-called "inflammatory cloacogenic polyp" are variations on the same pathogenetic theme. It has been proposed that solitary rectal ulcer is the result of the descending perineal syndrome in most cases, and the term *mucosal prolapse syndrome* has been suggested as a unifying concept for this and related disorders[453,458]; however, in some cases, there is no evidence of rectal prolapse.[462,491]

It is important to be aware of the fact that morphologic alterations consistent with solitary rectal ulcer can be seen overlying primary and metastatic carcinomas as a secondary event.[476]

Rosai–Dorfman disease can involve the large bowel; this is an exceptional event, usually associated with other extranodal manifestations of the disease.[474]

Fibrosing colonopathy is a rare condition seen in patients with cystic fibrosis who have been treated with high-strength enzyme replacement. Morphologically, the affected colon has a cobblestone appearance, submucosal fibrosis, thickening of the muscularis externa and chronic mucosal inflammation.[482]

Tumors

Epithelial polyps

The colorectal polyps included in this discussion are those of epithelial origin, which represent the large majority. They can be divided into several distinct categories, acknowledging the existence of transitional forms.[529]

Adenomatous polyps (tubular adenomas) are distrib-

uted rather regularly throughout the large bowel, with 40% found in the right colon, 40% in the left colon, and 20% in the rectum.[515,590] They are found at autopsy in approximately 30% to 35% of adult individuals, their frequency rising with age.[668] Blacks have a lower prevalence than whites, and a predominance of right-sided lesions.[618] A familial predisposition has been detected and found to result from an inherited autosomal dominant gene for susceptibility.[528] Most polyps are asymptomatic, but they may result in bleeding from twisting or vascular obstruction.[650] If large enough, they may cause changes in bowel habits or intussusception. Grossly, most measure under 1 cm in diameter. They may be sessile or pedunculated and single or multiple (Fig. 11.187). When multiple, they have a tendency to cluster.[546] When pedunculated, they may have a short or a long stalk attached by a narrow base. When sessile, they may be protruding, flat, or depressed (in which case the term "polyp" is a misnomer, but so is adenoma).[591,672] Flat and depressed lesions are being described with increasing frequency, particularly by Japanese authors using the high-magnification chromoscopic endoscopy technique.[576a] Knob-like projections are frequently seen on the surface of these tumors, whether sessile or pedunculated. Microscopically, there is an increase in the number of glands and cells per unit area compared to the normal mucosa. The cells are crowded, contain enlarged hyperchromatic nuclei, and have an increased number of mitoses, some of which may be atypical[572,633] (Figs 11.188 and 11.189). Despite early statements to the contrary, there are no consistent morphologic differences between polypoid, flat, and depressed adenomas.[638,677] Mucin production is highly variable but usually decreased. The basement membrane is not thickened. The changes first affect the superficial portion of the glands, a fact substantiated by in vivo incorporation of tritiated thymidine.[536] Obvious nuclear and cytoplasmic alterations, such as abnormal secretory droplets, are evident at the electron microscopic level.[610] Immunohistochemically, increased CEA staining is seen, particularly in the highly atypical areas.[577] Various types of keratin are expressed, the pattern being similar to that seen in adenocarcinoma.[553] Aneuploidy can be detected by flow cytometry in approximately 35% of adenomatous polyps[562,611]; p53 overexpression is found in a minority of cases; and bcl-2 immunoreactivity is present in virtually all cases.[525,587]

Focal areas of villous configuration are not infrequent in adenomatous polyps.[555,655] Fung and Goldman[555] found them in 35% of 67 polyps by careful examination of multiple sections taken with the guidance of a dissecting microscope. The incidence was related to the size of the polyp, reaching 76% in lesions larger than 1 cm in diameter. Polyps in which the adenomatous and villous components are present in approximately equal amounts are referred to as *villoglandular polyps, tubulovillous adenomas*, or *papillary adenomas*[627]; the last term should be

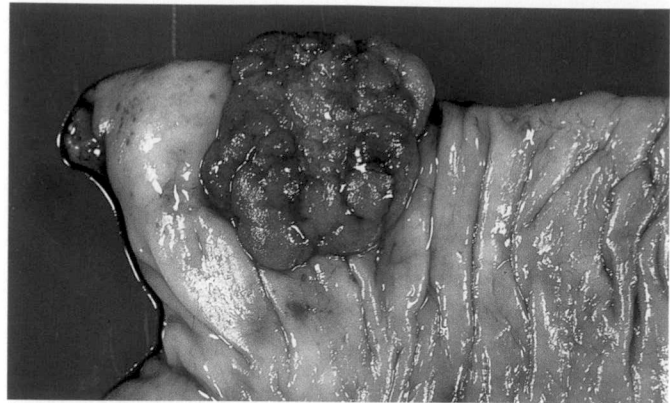

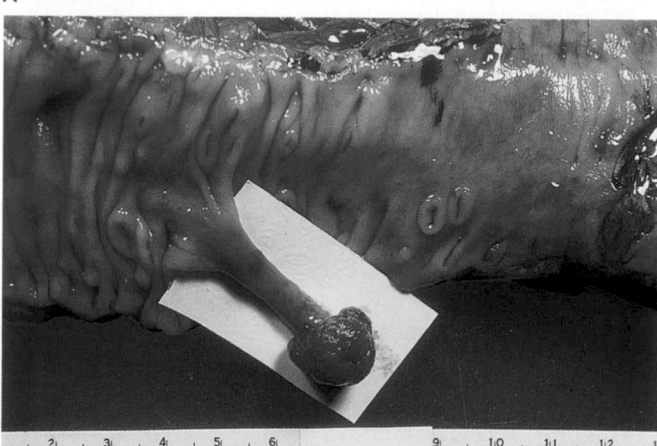

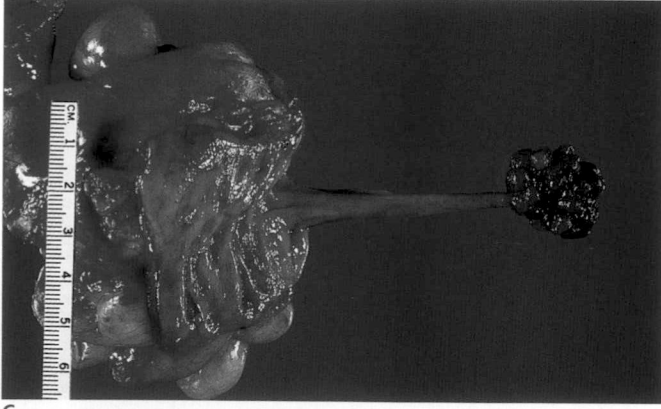

Fig. 11.187 A to **C**, Various gross appearances of adenomatous villoglandular polyps. **A**, Sessile polyp. **B** and **C**, Pedunculated polyps.

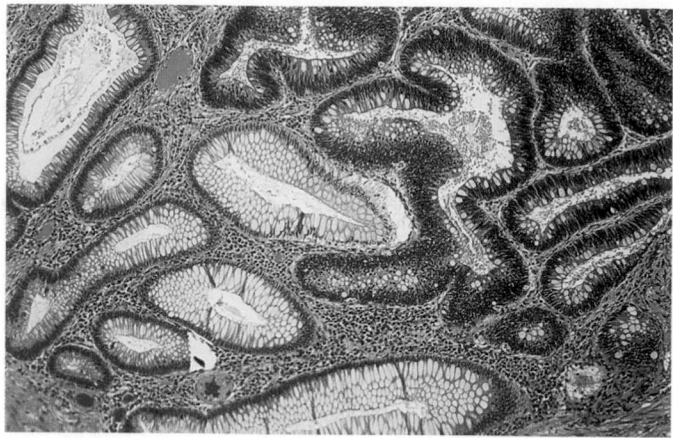

Fig. 11.188 Adenomatous polyp showing marked contrast between the dysplastic glands of the polyp and adjacent normal glands.

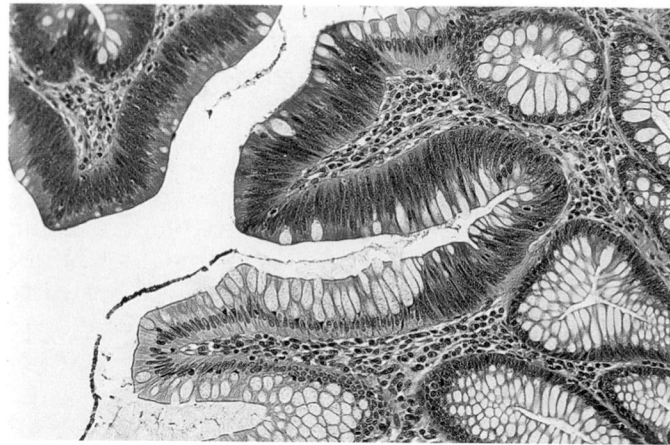

Fig. 11.189 In this portion of the adenomatous polyp the dysplastic changes are sharply segregated from the normal goblet cells.

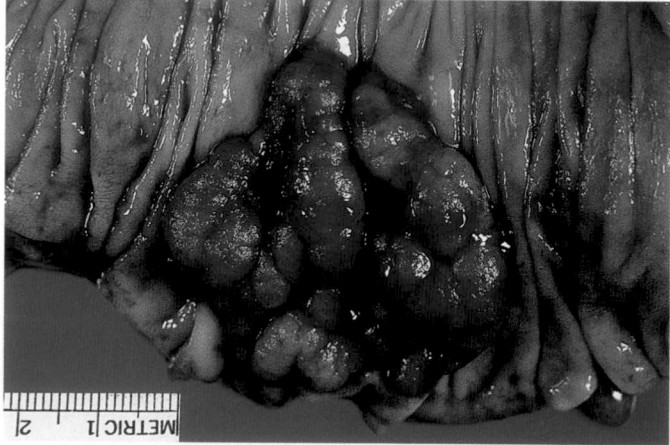

Fig. 11.190 Gross appearance of villoglandular polyp.

avoided because of its possible confusion with villous adenoma (Figs 11.190 and 11.191).

The degree of atypia seen in adenomatous polyps is related to increasing age, number of polyps per patient, size of the polyps, and presence of villous changes.[590] It can be graded into mild, moderate, and severe; the latter is equivalent to carcinoma in situ.

Sometimes, clusters of atypical glands in an adenomatous or villoglandular polyp are seen beneath the muscularis mucosae and may lead to a mistaken diagnosis of malignant transformation.[560] This is not an uncommon event; as a matter of fact, it may be more prevalent than true malignant transformation. The features that allow its recognition are as follows[612]: (1) the cytologic features of the misplaced glands are similar to those in the surface; (2) the glands are surrounded by inflamed loose stroma and scattered bundles of muscularis mucosae, instead of the desmoplastic reaction

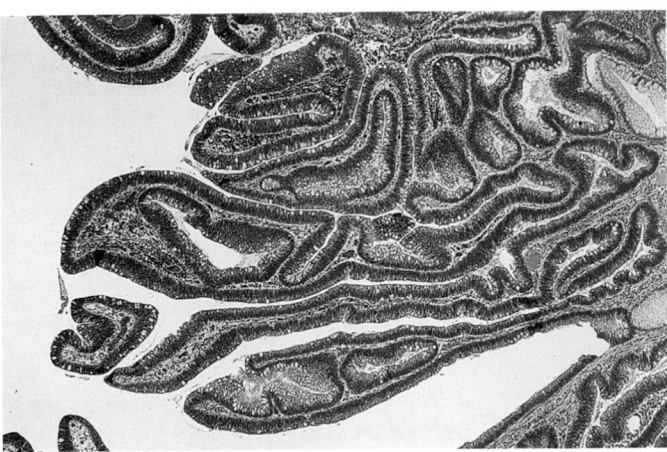

Fig. 11.191 Microscopic appearance of villoglandular polyp. There is an admixture of villous and glandular structures.

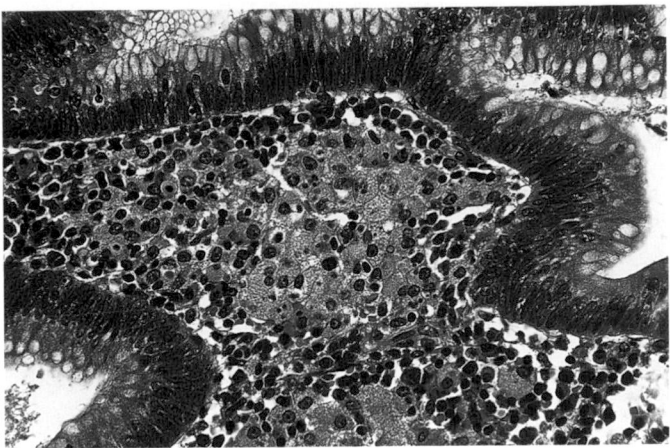

Fig. 11.193 Malakoplakia within the stroma of an adenomatous polyp, a most unusual event.

associated with carcinoma; and (3) there are abundant hemosiderin granules around the neoplastic glands (Fig. 11.192). Some of the glands may become cystic, rupture, and result in the formation of mucin lakes. The overall appearance is reminiscent of, and probably pathogenetically analogous to, the localized form of colitis cystica profunda. Muto et al.[612] believe that this pseudocarcinomatous invasion is the result of repeated twisting of the stalk of the polyp. Support for this interpretation comes from the observation that similar changes have been observed as a result of the biopsy procedure.[544] A mild to moderate degree of inflammatory infiltrate may be found in the stroma of the polyp.[517,520]

Rarely, adenomatous polyps may exhibit morular formation (with biotin-containing optically clear nuclei),[516,639,640] focal squamous metaplasia,[513] cytoplasmic clear cell changes,[545] a minor component of Paneth cells,[661] and a population of endocrine (Grimelius-positive) cells.[518] Less frequent phenomena are the occurrence of focal malakoplakia in the stroma of the polyp[629] (Fig. 11.193),

the development of osseous metaplasia,[564] or the presence of metastases from another site within the polyp.[670]

"Aberrant crypts" were originally described in experimental animals exposed to colonic carcinogens and were identified by methylene blue stains of whole-mount preparations. Similar structures have been identified in humans. Microscopically, the crypts are enlarged and hyperplastic; they often show foci of dysplasia.[543,648] They may represent the earliest identifiable "adenomatous" change, and the alternative term "microadenoma" has been proposed for them.[624,630] They seem to be more numerous in colons harboring a carcinoma than in those devoid of malignancy.[614,616,647] Not surprisingly, they are regarded as possible precursors of cancer, especially when large and/or with dysplastic foci.[653]

The standard treatment for adenomatous and villoglandular polyps is polypectomy, followed by repeated colonoscopy[593,671]; the incidence of development of new polyps in a group with a mean follow-up time of 26 months was 30%.[615]

Familial polyposis of the large bowel (polyposis coli) must be segregated from the sporadic adenomatous polyps, despite the fact that the microscopic appearance of the individual lesions is indistinguishable by either light or electron microscopic criteria.[541,567] This inherited defect is an autosomal mendelian dominant characteristic with a high degree of penetrance.[530,635,637] The responsible gene (APC) has been localized to chromosome 5q21.[522,596] An alternative genetic mechanism is a germ-line mutation of the base-excision repair gene MYH.[647a] The tumors in familial polyposis become manifest much earlier than the usual adenomatous polyp, usually in the second decade of life.[526a] A PCR technique has been developed for the presymptomatic diagnosis of this disorder.[514,609,623]

Radiographically and grossly, the bowel is studded with polyps ranging from very slight elevations of the

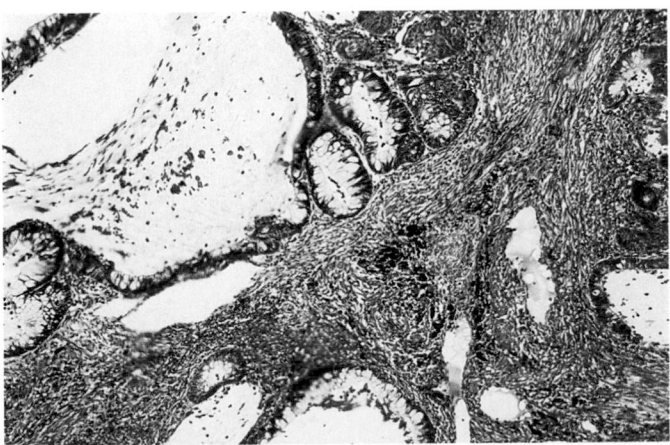

Fig. 11.192 Pseudoinvasion in an adenomatous polyp. The fibrosis, focal collections of hemosiderin-laden macrophages, and the cystic dilatation of glands are clues to the diagnosis.

normal mucosa to relatively large masses (Figs 11.194 and 11.195). Flat and depressed adenomas also occur.[592] The presence of several adenomatous polyps in a patient does not necessarily indicate the presence of familial polyposis. A minimum of 100 polyps needs to be present before such a diagnosis can be justified on morphologic grounds. Actually, in most examples of this condition the number of polyps is in the thousands. Microautoradiographic studies in patients with familial polyposis have shown persistence of DNA synthesis (as evidenced by the incorporation of tritiated thymidine) in the epithelial cells lining the polyps and also in the surface cells of the intervening flat mucosa.[542,598] Similarly, ornithine decarboxylase, an enzyme essential for intestinal mucosal proliferation, has been found to be elevated in both the polyps and the intervening flat mucosa.[601]

K-*ras* mutations are found in approximately one fourth of these polyps, the frequency being similar to that seen in sporadic cases.[526] These mutations are also increased in the morphologically normal mucosa.[531] Cytogenetically, polyps from patients with familial polyposis tend to have fewer structural abnormalities than sporadic adenomatous polyps; numerical abnormalities are the most common chromosomal abnormality in both conditions.[561]

Familial polyposis can involve other portions of the gastrointestinal tract, such as stomach and small bowel.[626,678] It should be remembered, however, that most polypoid lesions of the ileum seen in patients with this disorder represent foci of lymphoid hyperplasia,[573,637] and that many of the gastric lesions in these same patients are fundic gland polyps.[512,673]

If familial polyposis is left untreated, one or more carcinomas of the large bowel will develop in nearly every instance.[579] Malignant change is suggested by fixation or ulceration of the surface (Fig. 11.196). Carcinomas arising in a background of familial polyposis occur on the average some 20 years earlier than the ordinary colorectal carcinomas, most of them becoming manifest in the early thirties; therefore, prophylactic colectomy must be performed at 20 to 25 years of age, at the latest.[580] If the surgery performed is an abdominal colectomy with ileoproctostomy to preserve the anal function, a close monitoring of the rectal stump is indicated because of the possibility of development of polyps and carcinoma in it.

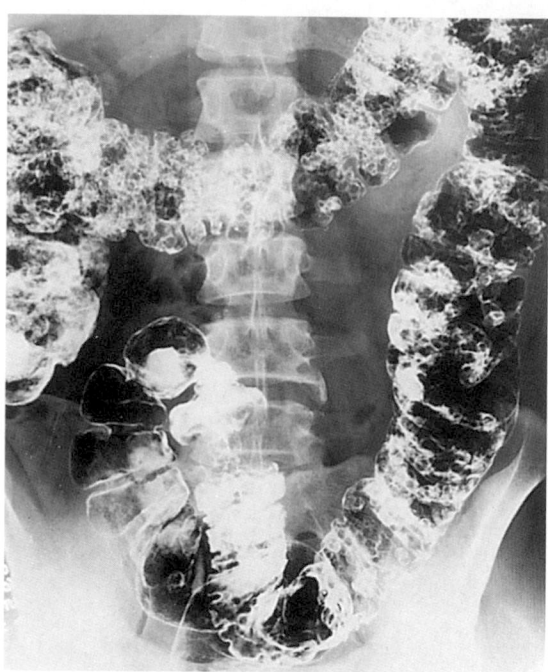

Fig. 11.194 Familial polyposis involving the entire bowel.

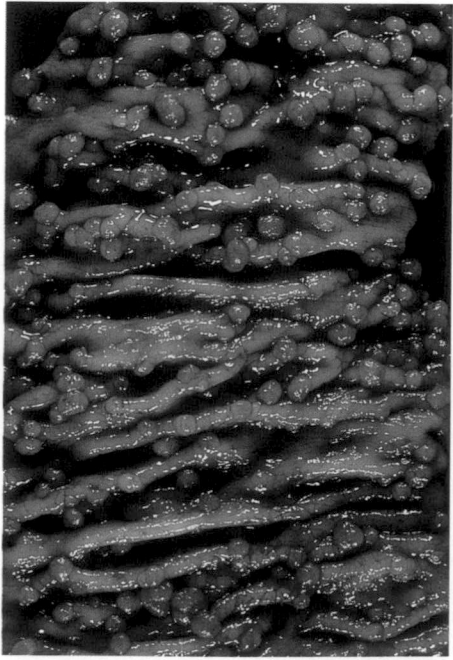

Fig. 11.195 Gross appearance of familial polyposis. The entire large bowel was involved. Note the fact that practically all of the polyps are small and sessile.

Fig. 11.196 Familial colonic polyposis with associated adenocarcinoma.

Actually, the incidence of this complication is so high in some series (up to 59% of patients followed for 23 years after surgery) that some surgeons favor the initial performance of a proctocolectomy, if acceptable to the patient.[663]

Carcinomas developing in other organs, such as the gallbladder, pancreas, thyroid, and adrenal gland, have also been reported in this disorder.[524,559,619] The thyroid carcinomas developing in these patients have a distinct microscopic appearance characterized by cribriform and morular formations.[569]

Gardner's syndrome is a related familial condition in which adenomatous polyps of the large bowel are seen associated with multiple osteomas of the skull and mandible, multiple keratinous cysts of the skin, and soft tissue neoplasms, especially fibromatosis.[556,644] Most of the fibromatoses are intra-abdominal and develop following surgical intervention.[620] These lesions show coexistence of somatic and germline mutations of the *APC* gene, suggesting that inactivation of both alleles of this gene is involved in their development.[608] Because of the variable degree of penetrance, only one of the extracolonic manifestations may be present, such as fibromatosis.[583] Adenomatous polyps may also be present in the small bowel and stomach. The potential for development of large bowel carcinoma appears to be as high as for familial polyposis. In addition, patients with this syndrome can develop carcinomas of the small bowel, particularly in the periampullary area.[604] The recommended treatment for the colorectal component of Gardner's syndrome is similar to that of familial polyposis.[664]

Turcot's syndrome is the name given to the odd combination of colorectal adenomatous polyps and brain tumors, usually of glioblastoma type.[547,578,597,605,643] This is an entity distinct from familial polyposis, with a recessive pattern of inheritance.[656] This syndrome can result from two distinct types of germlike defects: mutations of the *APC* gene or mutation of a mismatch-repair gene.[568]

Other described associations of familial polyposis are with hepatoblastoma,[589] multiple endocrine neoplasia,[621,642] and nasopharyngeal angiofibroma.[558]

In the variant of familial polyposis known as *hereditary flat adenoma syndrome*, the polyps are flat rather than elevated, they usually number less than 100, and they exhibit a right-sided predominance.[603] The chromosomal abnormality is in the same locus as in ordinary familial polyposis,[603] and the affected individuals may develop the same types of upper gastrointestinal tract lesions.[602]

Villous adenoma (villous papilloma) is a distinctive, relatively infrequent type of polyp that, in most cases, presents as a single mass in the rectum or rectosigmoid of older patients, sometimes associated with fluid and electrolyte depletion.[628,651] With continuous growth the tumor may completely encircle the bowel. The consistency is so soft that the lesion can be missed completely on digital examination.[625] It has papillary villous projections and is usually attached by a wide base (Fig. 11.197), less than 10% of cases being pedunculated; therefore, if a biopsy of a polypoid lesion having a definite stalk shows villous areas, the most likely diagnosis is that of villoglandular polyp. Microscopically, the villous projections ramify through a long, papillary, crown-like growth

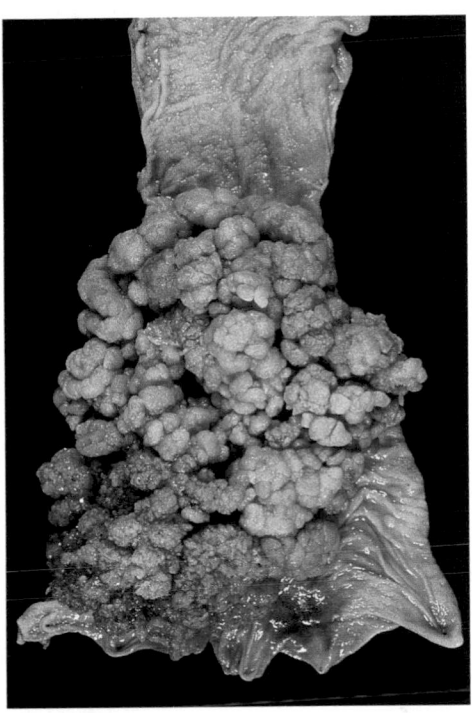

A

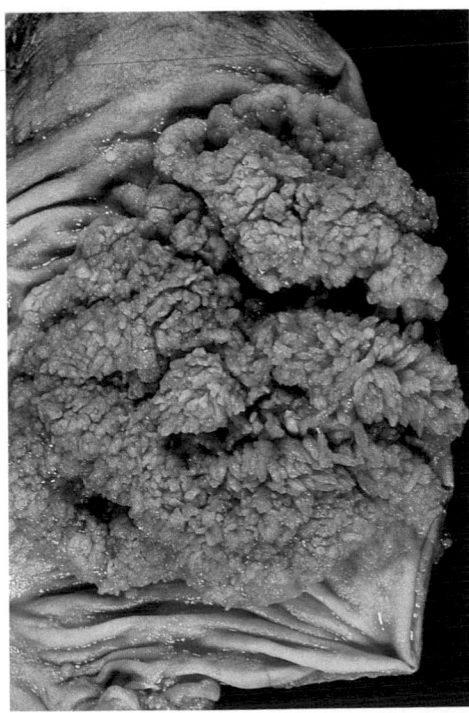

B

Fig. 11.197 Gross appearance of villous adenoma. The lesion is characteristically large and flat and has an arborescent architecture.

(Fig. 11.198). The pattern of mucin and CEA reactivity is similar to that seen in adenomatous polyps.[577] In time, a high percentage of these lesions become malignant, the recorded incidence ranging from 29% to 70%[516,665,666] (Figs 11.199 and 11.200). On rectal palpation, the area of carcinoma has a firmer consistency than the surrounding adenoma; therefore, it is important to biopsy any indurated areas in villous adenomas. Local excision is the treatment of choice in the absence of carcinoma, but sometimes an abdominoperineal resection is needed because of the huge size of the lesion.[665]

Hyperplastic (metaplastic) polyps are characteristically sessile and of small size, rarely exceeding 5 mm in diameter; however, they may be pedunculated and/or large, up to several centimeters[548,594,669] (Fig. 11.1201). If a careful gross examination of the colonic mucosa is made, hyperplastic polyps will be found in 30% to 50% of adult individuals.[533] Microscopically, elongated glands with intraluminal infoldings are seen, resulting in a saw-toothed configuration (Fig. 11.202). Mitotic activity is increased only at the base, paralleling the pattern of the normal mucosa and showing a striking contrast with the pattern of adenomatous polyps and villous adenomas.[667] Elsewhere, the epithelial cells have an inconspicuous basal nucleus and abundant cytoplasm filled with mucin. The basement membrane beneath the surface epithelium is thickened, a change that can be easily appreciated on hematoxylin–eosin-stained sections. The surface epithelium has a micropapillary appearance and is often infiltrated by "nuclear dust." Paneth cells are present in approximately 8% of cases. With increasing size of the polyp, alterations in architecture and differentiation appear, accompanied by increased secretion of CEA,

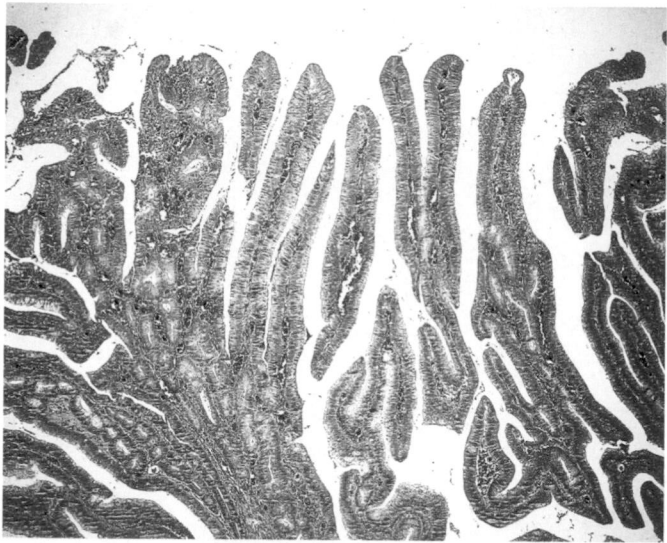

Fig. 11.198 Low-power microscopic appearance of villous adenoma. Long villi are arranged in parallel, perpendicularly to the mucosa.

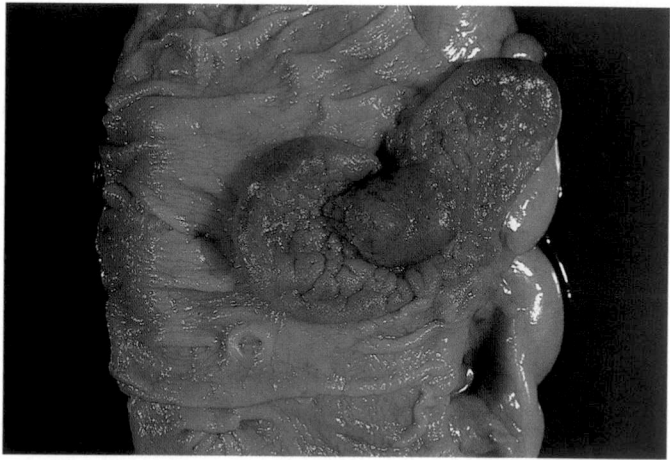

A

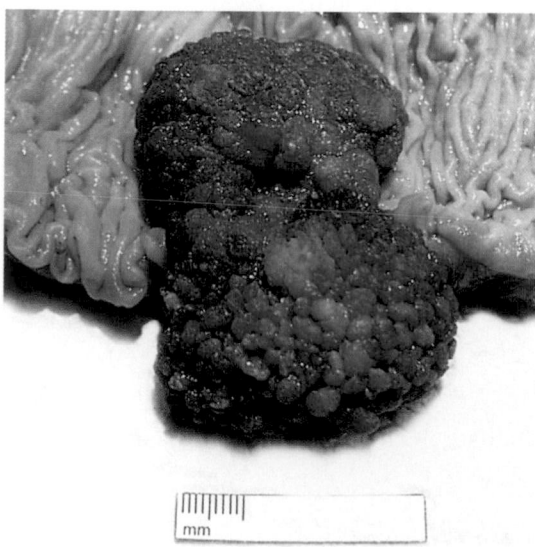

Fig. 11.199 Large villous adenoma with an ulcerated adenocarcinoma in its center. (Courtesy of Dr. Facchetti, Brescia, Italy)

B

Fig. 11.200 A and **B**, Large bowel polyp complicated by the development of an adenocarcinoma, as seen grossly (**A**) and on the whole mount (**B**).

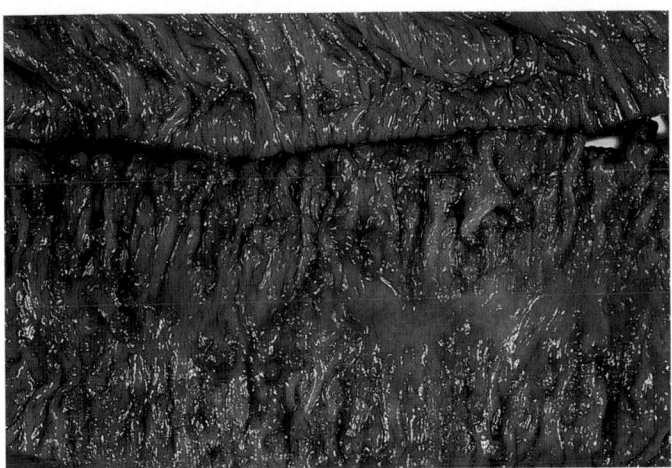

Fig. 11.201 Gross appearance of multiple hyperplastic polyps. The lesions are characteristically small, sessile, and pale.

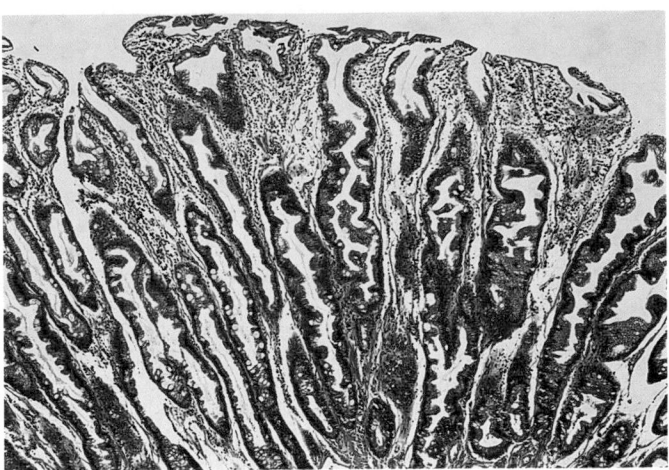

Fig. 11.202 Microscopic appearance of hyperplastic polyp. The individual glands show a typical serration of their mid portion.

changes in blood group antigen expression,[537] reduced secretion of sialomucins,[581] and the appearance of focal adenomatous changes.[548,551]

Mixed hyperplastic–adenomatous polyps are characterized by a prominent sawtoothed appearance, to the point that the alternative term "serrated adenoma" has been suggested for them.[600,617a,519a] Their mucin histochemistry, Ki-67, p53 and bcl-2 expression are indeed intermediate between those of pure adenomatous and hyperplastic polyps.[585,634] Some subtle morphologic differences have been found between right-sided and left-sided serrated adenomas, and the latter have been further subdivided into three groups.[657] Because of the presence of adenoma-like areas with abnormal proliferation, these hybrid lesions are thought to have a malignant potential.[180a] From a genetic standpoint these polyps appear to be heterogeneous.[549,641] It has been suggested that the serrated appearance is due to an inhibition of apoptosis.[654]

A variant of hyperplastic polyp, known as *inverted*, which is more frequent in the right colon, is characterized by an endophytic pattern of growth and penetration of the muscularis mucosae.[645,649,675] Another variant is characterized by surface differentiation toward absorptive enterocytes, mimicking the histology of normal small bowel mucosa.[677]

Pure hyperplastic polyps do not become malignant; however, carcinomas have been found containing residual adenomatous and hyperplastic epithelium.[538,658,662] Furthermore, in patients with the **multiple hyperplastic polyposis syndrome**, these polyps tend to be large and sometimes accompanied by adenocarcinoma.[521,526a,669]

As the name indicates, hyperplastic polyps have been traditionally regarded as proliferative but not neoplastic processes. They have acquired greater significance lately because of the finding that they seem to show a statistical association with colorectal carcinoma, especially in the latter situation.[595] Specifically, it has been suggested that hyperplastic polyps (and serrated adenomas) may be associated with colorectal cancers featuring DNA microsatellite instability.[582]

Juvenile (retention) polyp is the most frequent colonic polyp seen in children, but approximately one third of the cases occur in adults.[631] Traditionally, it has been described as single and located in the rectosigmoid area[571]; however, increased use of endoscopy has shown that in many cases there is more than one polyp present and that a high proportion of them occur proximal to the sigmoid colon.[539,606] The lesion usually presents with rectal bleeding; autoamputation is common, the polyp being sloughed off and passed per rectum.

Grossly, juvenile polyp has a granular, red surface and a cystic, lattice-like appearance on cross section (Fig. 11.203). Microscopically, ulceration covered by granulation tissue is often seen at the surface. Beneath, there are cystically dilated glands filled with mucus, devoid of atypical features, and separated by an inflamed and edematous stroma (Fig. 11.204). Hyperplastic mucosal changes are present in approximately 20% of cases. As the name indicates, juvenile (retention) polyps have not been traditionally regarded as neoplastic.[550,576,617] However, the occasional presence in them of foci of severe dysplasia/CIS and of genetic alterations (such as k-*ras* mutations) raises some questions as to their true nature.[534,535,674]

Rarely, multiple polyps of this type are seen throughout the bowel (Fig. 11.205). This condition, known as **multiple juvenile polyposis**, can be life threatening[526a,566,660] and associated with the development of adenomatous polyps and adenocarcinoma of the large bowel, duodenum, stomach, or pancreas.[563,565,579,632,652] Some of the polyps in this disorder have combined juvenile and adenomatous features.[552,607] Cases have been reported associated with neurofibromatous proliferation.[622] The genetic defect in juvenile polyposis has been found to be inherited inactivating mutations of the *SMAD4* or *BMPR1A* genes, this inactivation being limited to the stromal cells.[659]

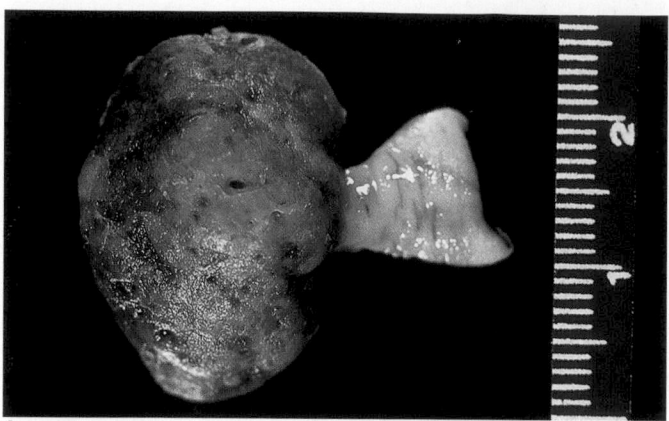

A

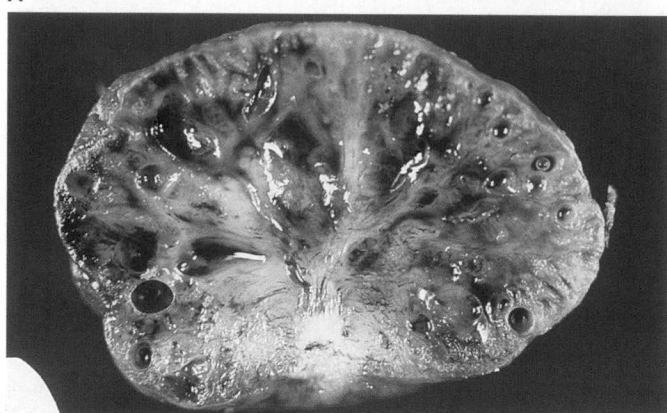

B

Fig. 11.203 A and **B**, Outer aspect and cut surface of juvenile (retention) polyp. Note the ulcerated, highly hyperemic surface (**A**), and the cystically dilated glands in an edematous stroma (**B**). (Courtesy of Dr. RA Cooke, Brisbane, Australia; from Cooke RA, Stewart B: Colour Atlas of Anatomical Pathology. Edinburgh, Churchill Livingstone, 2004).

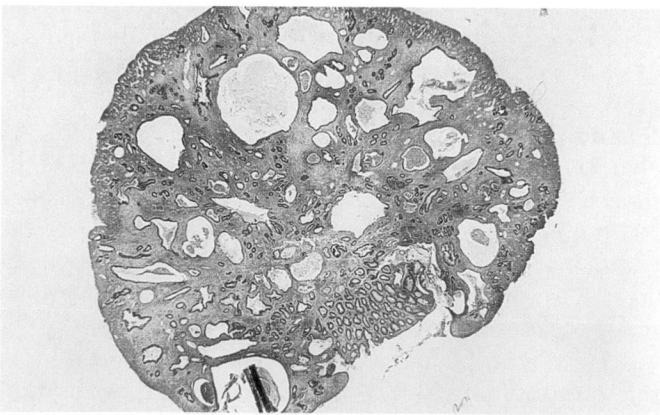

Fig. 11.204 Whole-mount view of a juvenile (retention) polyp.

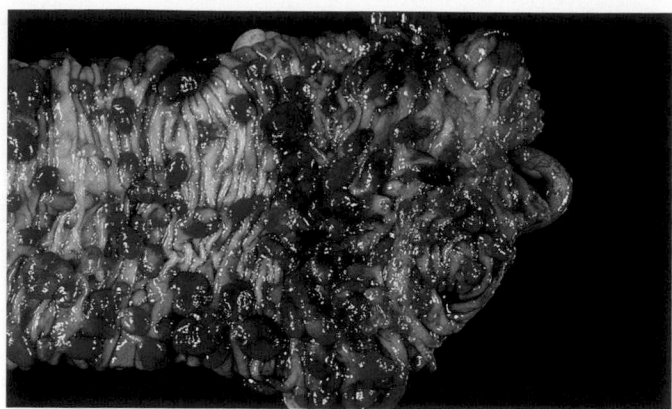

Fig. 11.205 Juvenile polyposis. The markedly hyperemic quality is a characteristic feature of these lesions.

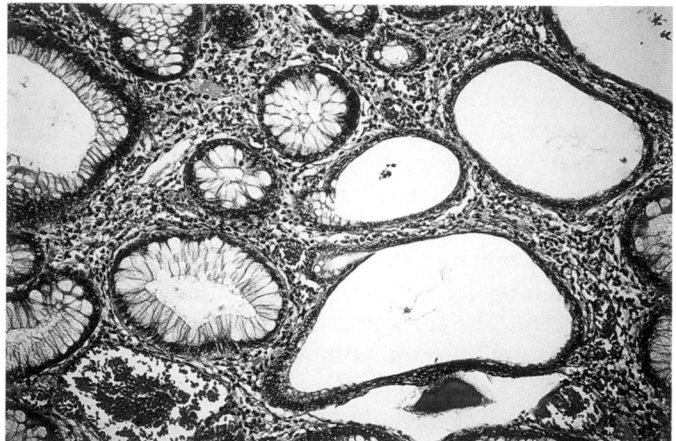

Fig. 11.206 Colonic polyps in a patient with Cronkhite–Canada syndrome. The appearance is that of juvenile (retention) polyps.

In **Cronkhite–Canada syndrome**, a nonhereditary disorder, multiple colorectal polyps of the juvenile type are associated with ectodermal changes (alopecia, nail atrophy, and hyperpigmentation)[540,588,636] (Fig. 11.206). The polyps associated with this syndrome are less commonly pedunculated than other juvenile polyps.[527] Adenomatous changes and colorectal carcinoma may also develop in these patients.[557,586] Another lesion with some morphologic resemblance to retention polyp (but mixed with elements of adenomatous polyp) is the polypoid change sometimes developing at the site of a ureterosigmoidostomy.

Peutz–Jeghers polyps have microscopic features similar to those seen in the small bowel in this syndrome. Lack of atypia, disorganization of glands, the occurrence of several cell types (including Paneth cells), and the presence of smooth muscle fibers from the muscularis mucosae (which give the lesion a "hamartomatous" appearance) are the most important features[554] (Fig. 11.207). This pattern of glandular disorganization and epithelial misplacement simulating invasion should not be confused with malignancy[523,662]; however, it should also be recognized that patients with this syndrome may also have adenomatous polyps with a marked degree of atypia and that some of these patients may develop colorectal adenocarcinoma.[574,575,613] The Peutz–Jeghers syndrome is due to mutations of the *LKB1* gene.[519]

Cowden's syndrome (multiple hamartoma syndrome) is an autosomal dominant illness characterized by mucocutaneous stigmata (facial trichilemmomas, acral keratoses, and oral mucosal papillomas), colorectal

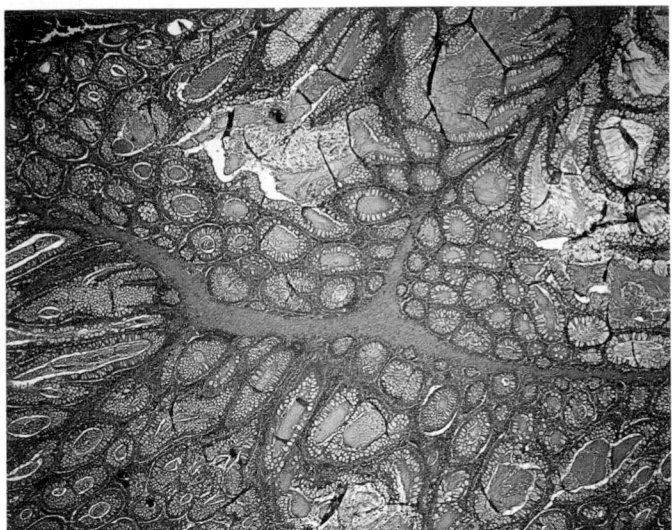

Fig. 11.207 Peutz–Jeghers polyp. Note the lack of dysplasia, the mucous hypersecretion, and the ramifying bundles of smooth muscle.

polyps, and an increased incidence of malignancy in various sites. The polyps have hamartomatous features, with disorganization and proliferation of the muscularis mucosae, but they differ microscopically from the polyps of Peutz–Jeghers syndrome.[532,567]

Transitional polyp is the name that has been proposed for a small polypoid colorectal lesion characterized by elongated and widened crypts and enlarged goblet cells with increased mucin production[570]; the appearance is similar to that often seen in the mucosa adjacent to carcinomas and other tumors.

Relationship with carcinoma and treatment

One can hardly think of a subject in tumor pathology that has been more controversial over the years than that of the precancerous nature of colorectal epithelial polyps.[679,686,703,726,730,745] Needless to say, the issue is a complex one. Yet some well-documented facts are known that provide us with guidelines to tackle the problem:

1 The rate of malignant transformation of *solitary* hyperplastic polyps (which represent the large majority of epithelial colonic polyps), retention polyps, and the polyps of Peutz–Jeghers is negligible.

2 Patients with any type of polyposis syndrome are at increased risk for the development of large bowel carcinoma. This incidence is extremely high (nearly 100%) in familial polyposis and Gardner's syndrome; it is lower, but still increased, in patients with Peutz–Jeghers syndrome, juvenile polyposis, and hyperplastic polyposis. This is clearly related to the fact that any of these polyposis syndromes can be accompanied by the development of adenomatous changes in some of the polyps. As already indicated, patients with familial polyposis are also at an increased risk for duodenal and ampullary adenocarcinoma.[733]

3 Villous adenomas can become malignant, and they do so in a *high* proportion of cases (29% to 70%).

4 Adenomatous polyps *can* undergo malignant transformation. Every pathologist with experience has seen adenomatous polyps with focal carcinoma in them. This statement also applies to flat adenomas and villoglandular polyps, which for the purposes of this discussion, will be included with the adenomatous polyps.[752]

5 *Not all* adenomatous polyps become malignant, at least not during the normal life span of an individual. If that were the case, and knowing the frequency of adenomatous polyps in the general population, the incidence of carcinoma should be at least 20 times higher than it actually is. Similarly, patients with familial polyposis (who have literally thousands of adenomatous polyps) who carry the disease in the large bowel for 20 or more years should develop not one or even several colorectal carcinomas but hundreds of them. The most important issue from a practical standpoint is the likelihood of an adenomatous polyp becoming malignant during a reasonable life span. If we were to assume that all colorectal carcinomas arise on the basis of polyps (an assumption that has yet to be proved) and compare the rate of adenomatous polyps to carcinoma in the general population, we come up with a figure of approximately 5%. Percentages lower than this are usually given in series that list the number of cases in which a focal carcinoma was found in an adenomatous polyp on pathologic examination, but this is understandable because these polyps are examined at only one point in time during their natural history. It also seems well established that the larger and more villous a polyp is, the greater the likelihood that it will contain focal carcinoma.[708]

6 There is overwhelming evidence for a parallelism between adenomatous polyps and colonic carcinoma. Epidemiologic studies have shown that populations that have high incidence of polyps also have a high incidence of carcinomas and vice versa.[683,688,694] Large bowels with carcinomas have a higher incidence of polyps elsewhere in the specimen than those without carcinoma.[698] Adenomatous polyps are a good epidemiologic indicator of colon carcinoma risk. The morphologic, histochemical (mucin stains), immunochemical (CEA, blood group substances), flow cytometric, nuclear morphometric, and ultrastructural features of adenocarcinomas, and the most atypical areas of adenomatous polyps are extremely similar.[682,684,691,692,709,729,732,742,750,760]

7 The malignant transformation of polyps (so-called "adenoma–carcinoma sequence") has been carefully documented with chemically induced colorectal tumors in animals,[714,725] and it has become a paradigm of the process of malignant transformation of

epithelial tissue. This has been made possible by the demonstration that the morphologic progression from adenomatous polyp with mild to moderate to severe atypia ("carcinoma in situ") to invasive and metastatic carcinoma is accompanied by (and presumably caused by) a series of molecular alterations (Fig. 11.208).[687,701,711,712,718] These alterations include the mutational activation of oncogenes and the inactivation of tumor-suppressor genes. It is thought that mutations in at least four or five genes are required to produce a fully malignant phenotype. These include activational mutation of the *ras* oncogene (found in approximately 50% of colorectal carcinomas and in a similar percentage of adenomatous polyps with moderate or severe atypia), mutations of the *p53* gene (located on chromosome 17),[681,715] deletion of the *dcc* ("*d*eleted in *c*olonic *c*arcinoma") gene (located on chromosome 18),[700] and possibly mutations of the *mcc* ("*m*utated in *c*olonic *c*arcinoma") gene (located on chromosome 5).[720] An additional (and very early) change is a mutation of the *apc* (*a*denomatous *p*olyposis *c*oli) gene (located on chromosome 5).[713,735]

As fundamental as this work is for our understanding of neoplastic progression and as confirmation of the multistep theory of carcinogenesis, it may be appropriate to point out the following:

a None of the genetic alterations just described is a universal feature in sporadic adenomatous polyps.[717]

b These alterations, when present, do not always occur in the sequence indicated in Fig. 11.208.[685]

c These alterations do not result in the transformation of a benign tumor into a malignant one, as the terms adenoma and carcinoma imply. In our opinion, adenomatous polyps, villoglandular polyps, and villous adenomas are *not* adenomas (i.e., benign neoplasms of glandular tissue). They represent instead localized areas of epithelial dysplasia or atypical hyperplasia that have a tendency to protrude on the surface of the bowel (i.e., to become polypoid). From that point of view, the term adenomatous polyp (i.e., a protruding lesion that resembles an adenoma but is not) is a less inaccurate term than tubular adenoma, which firmly places this lesion into the erroneous category of a benign neoplasm.

8 Colonoscopic polypectomy results in a lower-than-expected incidence of colorectal carcinoma in the population subjected to that procedure, providing support to the current practice of searching for and removing adenomatous polyps.[754]

9 There is evidence suggesting that some colorectal carcinomas arise de novo rather than on the basis of preexisting polyps.[740] Contrary to others' experience,[697,730] we have rarely found residual adenomatous epithelium at the edge of a carcinoma.[744] This has been the case even for extremely minute carcinomas (as small as 3 mm in diameter[743]) for which the interpretation that the malignant growth has totally overrun the polyp is hardly tenable. If anything, the existence of these cases seems to indicate that colonic carcinomas can arise from flat mucosa.[696,728,734,738,751] Furthermore, the distribution of polyps and carcinomas in the colon differs.[716] Finally, there is the important and controversial issue as to whether patients with isolated small polyps have a higher incidence of carcinoma of the large bowel or not. Most large series show a slight increase, whether the polyps are large or small.[724,736,741] Interestingly, siblings and parents of patients with adenomatous polyps appear to be at an increased risk for colorectal cancer.[756]

These are the facts as we see them. Using this information, we can begin to address the main practical questions that arise in the management of patients with colorectal polyps. First of all, there is no difficulty in the treatment of solitary juvenile polyps. Simple removal is sufficient. At the other extreme, since all untreated patients with familial polyposis eventually develop carcinoma of the colon, colectomy is indicated even though the patient is young.[746] Depending on the number of polyps in the rectum, the operation may consist of a total colectomy with colostomy or a colectomy with ileorectal anastomosis.[731] Use of the nonsteroidal anti-inflammatory drug sulindac[757] and oral calcium[749] has been found

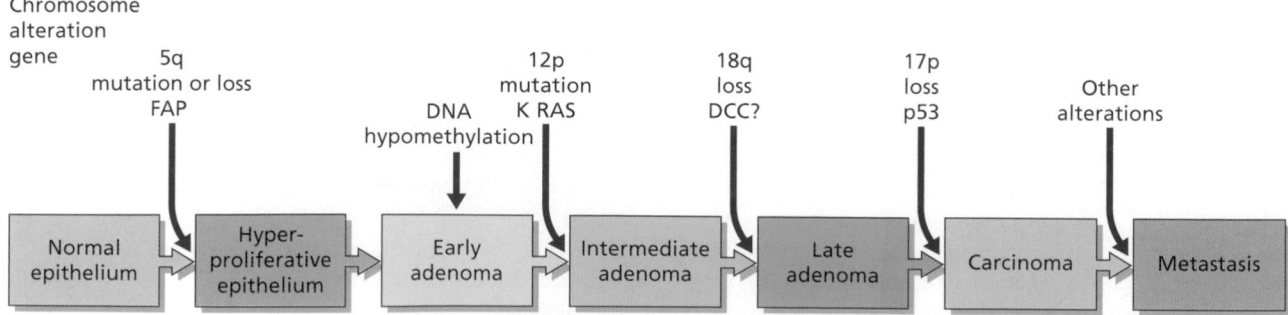

Fig. 11.208 Diagrammatic representation of morphologic and molecular events in colorectal tumorigenesis. (From Fearon ER, Vogelstein B. A genetic model for colorectal tumorigenesis. Cell 1990, **61**: 759–767)

to reduce the number and size of adenomatous polyps in this disorder, but its effect is incomplete, and it is therefore unlikely to replace colectomy as primary therapy.[707]

Villous adenomas should be removed in toto, preferably in one piece. This allows a proper orientation of the specimen, so that in the presence of focal carcinoma the extent of the tumor can be assessed. This determination is of great importance in deciding whether further surgery is indicated.

The solitary adenomatous polyp located under the reach of the rectosigmoidoscope is routinely removed endoscopically. Following such therapy, the long-term risk of a subsequent carcinoma is so low that the recommendation has been made for an interval of at least 3 years to be allowed before follow-up colonoscopy[755]; others have even questioned the need of surveillance after polypectomy.[680,719]

The main difficulty resides in treating the patient with an isolated adenomatous polyp located higher up in the large bowel, although the advent of the fiberoptic scope has revolutionized the approach to these lesions.[753,758,759] Since this technique has become available, the indication is for any polypoid lesion anywhere in the large bowel to be removed as soon as it is detected, unless obvious contraindications exist.[708] This avoids the periodic radiographic examinations needed if the polyp is left in situ and the laparotomy that was once necessary to excise the proximally located lesions; however, it has not made things easier for the pathologist. The specimens obtained with this method are often fragmented and difficult to orient. When a focal carcinoma is present in a polyp, it may be impossible to decide whether invasion of the stalk has occurred. We have seen cases in which a small biopsy taken from the tip of a polypoid colonic lesion was correctly diagnosed microscopically as carcinoma, but examination of the subsequent colectomy specimen showed only an adenomatous polyp with focal carcinoma with a noninvolved stalk.

When several polyps are present, the patient can be safely managed by removing these polyps individually rather than performing a partial or total colectomy.

If a proximally located lesion is large, a small endoscopic biopsy may fail to detect the area of malignant transformation if present; therefore such a lesion is best treated by anterior resection of a segment of bowel.

What should be the treatment for a patient in whom an area of carcinoma is found in an otherwise typical adenomatous polyp? To answer this question, one needs to realize that there are three distinct stages of the process that can be recognized pathologically and that bear a direct relationship to the therapeutic approach:[693]

1 The carcinomatous glands may be present only in the mucosa and lamina propria above the muscularis mucosae ("carcinoma in situ"; Fig. 11.209).
2 They may extend beyond the muscularis mucosae but

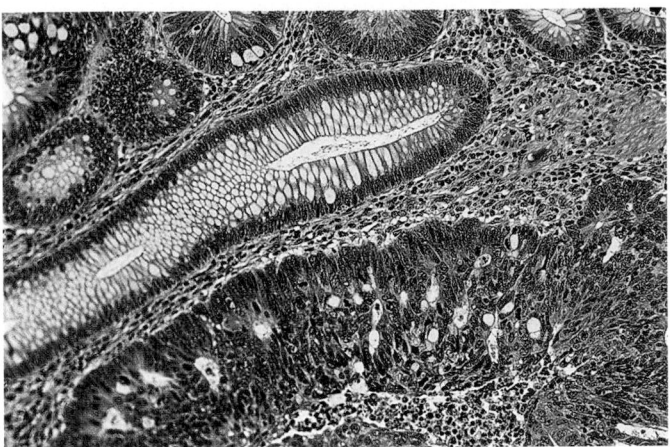

Fig. 11.209 Adenomatous polyp with adenocarcinoma entirely located above the muscularis mucosae.

not invade the stalk of the polyp ("focal carcinoma"; Fig. 11.210).
3 They may extend to the base of the stalk or beyond ("focal carcinoma with stalk invasion"); in some of these cases, the tumor is seen to extend to the margin of resection, which is identified in a properly oriented specimen by the typical diathermy effect.

The first situation, which is recognized by an architectural pattern of back-to-back glands with total loss of polarity and lack of intervening stroma, has *never* been found associated with lymph node metastases. This may be so because in the lamina propria of the large bowel—in contrast to that of the small bowel—the lymph vessels are limited to the area immediately above the muscularis mucosae.[702] It is obvious that under these circumstances, nothing other than a simple polypectomy needs to be done.[706] Some prominent pathologists have even questioned whether the diagnosis of carcinoma should be given at all under these circumstances. We use for such

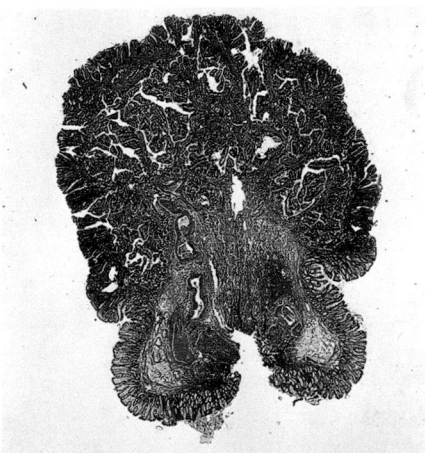

Fig. 11.210 Adenomatous polyp with focal carcinoma invading the stroma but with free stalk and negative surgical margins. Polypectomy is nearly always curative in cases with these features.

cases the term **severe dysplasia/CIS**, to be consistent with the terminology employed for analogous situations in other portions of the gastrointestinal tract. Since every adenomatous polyp, by definition, shows some degree of dysplasia, we use the foregoing description *only* for those polyps that fulfill the morphologic criteria for CIS.

The second situation ("focal carcinoma" with free stalk) can result in lymph node metastases[721,747], but the incidence is so low (less than 1%) that a simple polypectomy seems again the logical therapy for this lesion.[704,722,727] An exception to this approach is the rare lesion that is undifferentiated, with signet ring features, accompanied by obvious vascular invasion.[690,695,705,739,748]

Once invasion of the stalk has occurred (the third situation), the possibility of lymph node metastases, although still relatively low, is probably high enough to justify a formal bowel resection. This indication becomes more definite when the carcinoma is found in the submucosa of the underlying colonic wall and/or when it is present at the surgical margin.[695,710,723,737]

It is unlikely that total agreement in this field will be achieved in the near future. Indeed, articles appear periodically advocating a more aggressive surgical intervention, based on highly questionable figures.[689] In the meantime, we believe that following the rather conservative recommendations presented herein will help avoid subjecting patients with colorectal polyps to unnecessarily radical, costly, and potentially dangerous procedures. Obviously, a thorough pathologic evaluation is of paramount importance in this determination.[699]

Carcinoma

General features

Carcinoma of the large bowel is common in Northwest Europe, North America, and other Anglo-Saxon areas and low in Africa, Asia, and some parts of South America.[762,764] In the United States, it is by far the most common and most curable carcinoma of the gastrointestinal tract. There is some evidence of a further increase in its occurrence, particularly in young blacks.[779] Males and females are affected equally. The mean age of incidence is 62 years.

The cause and pathogenesis of colorectal carcinoma are related to both environmental and genetic factors.[778,787] The former are largely dietary, particularly in terms of fats and animal protein; they are related to their influence on the intestinal microflora and ultimately on the chemical composition of the intraluminal content.[766,770] Specifically, there is a close association between beef consumption, the ingestion of large amounts of animal fat, and the incidence of bowel carcinoma; however, the issue is complex, and the precise nature of the relationship is far from established.[785]

The genetic factor manifests itself in a variety of ways. The most obvious is the high predisposition for colorectal carcinoma in patients with familial polyposis (nearly 100% by age 50 years) and in those with the hereditary nonpolyposis colorectal cancer syndrome or *Lynch syndrome* (50% risk to a first-degree relative of an affected patient in the direct genetic lineage).[767,770a,771,774] Patients with Lynch syndrome, which is due to germline mutations in genes responsible for repair of DNA mismatches, are also at an increased risk for other malignant tumors such as cholangiocarcinoma.[777,786]

A variation on the theme of Lynch syndrome is represented by colorectal carcinoma-prone families who have right-sided flat adenomas. The number of polyps is intermediate between that in familial polyposis and that in classic Lynch syndrome; the carcinomas, most of which are also right sided, occur at a later age than in the other two conditions.[772] In *Torre–Muir syndrome*, the colorectal tumor (which is often multiple) is associated with multiple sebaceous tumors and keratoacanthomas.[761]

In familial colorectal carcinoma (defined by the presence of two or more first-degree relatives with this tumor), the risk for first-degree relatives of affected individuals is increased threefold.[773] Mutant alleles of the H-*ras*-1 minisatellite may predispose to this condition.[768,776,781]

The debated issues of the relationship between epithelial polyps and colorectal carcinoma and the sequence of molecular alterations that have been detected in these lesions have already been discussed. Patients with inflammatory bowel disease (particularly ulcerative colitis) have a definite predisposition to colorectal carcinoma, but they make up only a small percentage of the patients with large bowel carcinoma in the general population. Some cases of colorectal carcinomas have been seen as a late complication of pelvic irradiation, usually for carcinoma of the cervix.[763,782] A few others have been reported as arising at ureteral implantation sites.[783,784] Parenthetically, transitional cell carcinomas, undifferentiated carcinomas, and polyps of juvenile and/or adenomatous type can also occur at this juncture.[765,769,780] Interestingly, these changes are preceded by abnormal patterns of colonic mucin secretion.[775]

Clinical features

Carcinomas of the large bowel may present with rectal bleeding, changes in bowel habits (such as diarrhea alternating with constipation), anemia resulting from chronic blood loss, and vague abdominal pain. Intestinal obstruction is common when the tumor is situated in the left colon and rare for tumors in the cecum or ascending colon. One of four cecal carcinomas will present with signs suggestive of appendicitis. Perforation may rarely occur, either at the site of the carcinoma or in the cecum as a result of distention caused by an obstructing rectosigmoid carcinoma. The endoscopic appearance is usually characteristic, but some inflammatory lesions may simulate carcinoma, and some undifferentiated carcinomas may have an innocent appearance.

Unfortunately, the previously mentioned symptoms are often indicative of advanced disease; therefore, many attempts have been made over the years to detect tumors at an earlier stage.[800,803] One such procedure is the performance of appropriately timed proctosigmoidoscopic examinations of both men and women over 40 years of age; such examinations should detect approximately 50% of cases.[789,791,792,796] Whether routine examination of the entire large bowel with the fiberscope will prove rewarding as a screening method remains to be seen. Routine barium enemas are too expensive and not entirely without risk, although they are certainly indicated (preferably with air contrast) in any patient with symptoms. Guaiac stool examination for occult blood also has proved to be an efficient and inexpensive way of detecting cases of early, asymptomatic carcinoma.[790,798] In one study, the 13-year cumulative mortality from colorectal carcinoma was decreased by 33%.[793]

Carcinoembryonic antigen (CEA) is a glycocalix-related antigen that has been detected in the serum of 72% to 97% of patients with colorectal carcinoma.[799,805] It disappears after resection of the tumor and reappears in the event of recurrence or metastases. Higher values are found in tumors that have spread beyond the bowel wall, in poorly differentiated neoplasms, and in tumors associated with blood vessel, lymphatic, and perineural invasion.[804] Elevated circulating levels of CEA also occur in carcinomas of the stomach, pancreas, breast, and prostate gland. Serum CEA is practically never elevated in normal individuals, but high values can be found in patients with chronic liver or renal disease.[804] Unfortunately, the test is often negative during the early stages of colorectal carcinoma and is, therefore, not a good screening procedure. Its main utility has been in the monitoring of therapy, in the early detection of metastases, and as an indicator for second-look surgery.[788,794]

CEA can also be detected in the tumor tissue by immunocytochemistry, radioimmunometric assay, or enzyme immunometric assay; its ability to discriminate between normal and carcinomatous tissue is higher than that of CA-199, CA-125, and CA-195, these being other antigens that have been found to be associated with colorectal carcinoma.[795,802]

A novel and very promising screening approach is that of searching for mutations of the *ras* and *APC* genes in the stools; unfortunately, the test does not distinguish polyps from carcinoma.[797,801]

Site and gross features

Approximately 50% of all carcinomas occur in the rectosigmoid area, although their relative incidence seems to be decreasing,[816] in the sense that a shift in location toward the proximal colon during the past few decades has been noted.[807] Some interesting correlations between certain clinical features and the anatomic subsite of the tumor have been made.[809] Right-sided tumors are said to be more common in the elderly,[818] in blacks,[821] and in patients with diverticular disease.[819] Multicentric carcinomas are found in 3% to 6% of the cases.[811,813]

Grossly, most colorectal carcinomas can be described as either polypoid or ulcerative/infiltrating[808] (Fig. 11.211). The former presents as a bulky mass with well-defined, rolled margins and a sharp dividing line with the normal bowel. The latter has a less elevated surface and is centrally ulcerated. A particular variant of this tumor type is referred to as "flat" or "depressed" carcinoma and is thought to arise de novo rather than through malignant transformation of an adenoma.[814,815] These flat carcinomas have a greater tendency for deep stromal invasion with lymphovascular permeation than the more common polypoid types.[820]

In general, there is good correspondence between the gross and the microscopic margins of the tumor. Extensive lateral superficial spread of the type often seen in the stomach is very rare in colorectal tumors but it does occur.[822] Retrograde intramural spread occurs in less than 5% of cases.[806,817] On cross section, grayish white tissue is seen replacing the bowel wall. The edges may be well demarcated or with finger-like projections extending from the main mass. Highly mucinous tumors have a gelatinous, glaring appearance, and layers of mucus may separate the layers of bowel wall.

Important features to evaluate at the time of gross inspection are whether the tumor is confined to the wall or whether it has extended to the pericolic tissues, whether gross invasion of veins is present,[810] and whether the remainder of the colon shows other carcinomas or polyps of any type.

Microscopic features

The usual malignant tumor of the large bowel is a well-to-moderately differentiated adenocarcinoma secreting variable amounts of mucin (Fig. 11.212). The tumor cells represent a combination of columnar and goblet cells, with occasional participation of endocrine cells (see p. 815) and the exceptional occurrence of Paneth cells.[835] The carcinoma consistently elicits an inflammatory and desmoplastic reaction, which is particularly prominent at the edge of the tumor. Most of the inflammatory cells are T lymphocytes,[828] but B lymphocytes, plasma cells, histiocytes, and dendritic cells positive for S-100 protein may also be present.[823] Occasionally there are numerous eosinophils, a feature thought to be due to interleukin-5 production.[837]

The tumor may be seen invading all the layers of the bowel and extending into the pericolic fat, permeating perineurial spaces, and invading veins. The latter feature, which is of prognostic significance, can be better appreciated with stains for elastic fibers (Verhoeff–van Gieson) or for smooth muscle actin (with immunohistochemical techniques).[824] Rarely, the tumor stroma may exhibit metaplastic bone formation.[826]

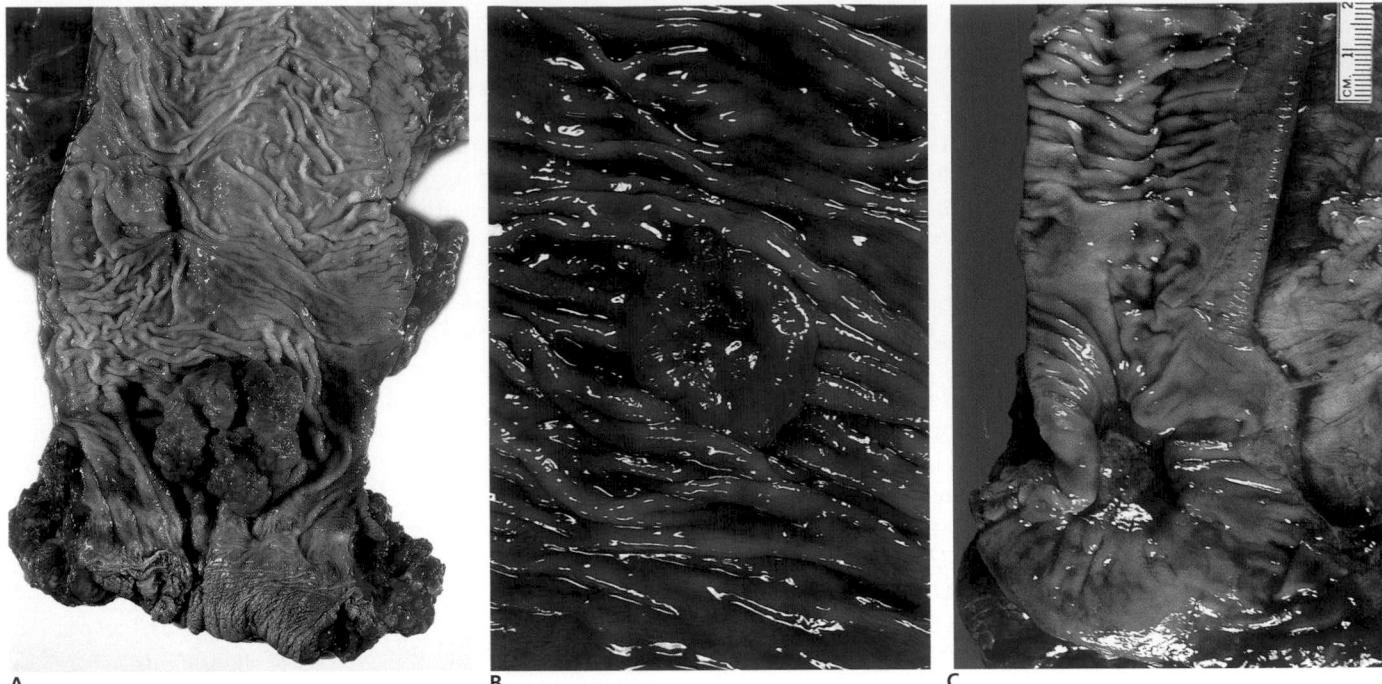

Fig. 11.211 A to C, Various gross appearances of adenocarcinoma of large bowel. **A,** Polypoid pattern of growth in a rectal lesion. **B,** Cake-like configuration with central ulceration. **C,** Deeply penetrating and ulcerated tumor. (Courtesy of Dr. RA Cooke, Brisbane, Australia; from Cooke RA, Stewart B: Colour Atlas of Anatomical Pathology. Edinburgh, Churchill Livingstone, 2004).

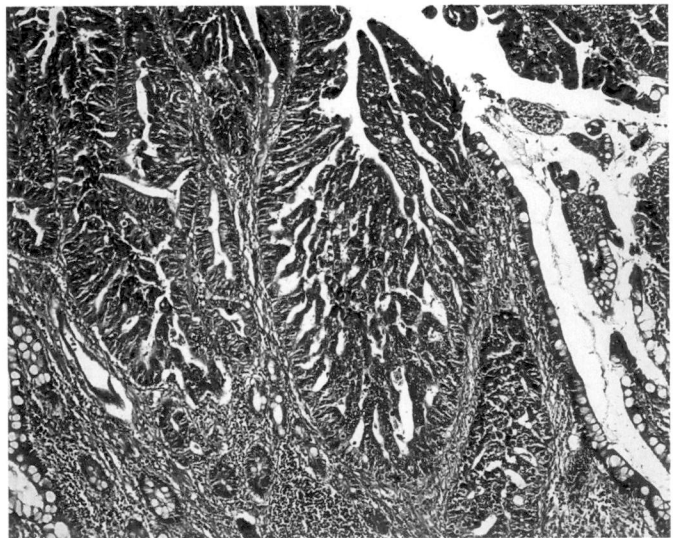

Fig. 11.212 Moderately differentiated colonic adenocarcinoma.

The edge of the tumor may show foci of a residual polyp, but it is more common to see at this site a hyperplastic change in the glands, which appear taller, more tortuous, and with more goblet cells than the normal mucosa.[833] This change, which is accompanied by histochemically detectable alterations in mucin secretion,[832] has been referred to as *transitional mucosa*.[825,830] This is probably a reactive change, inasmuch as it can also occur at the edge of other tumors (such as malignant lymphoma and metastatic carcinoma) and non-neoplastic conditions, including anastomotic sites.[827,829,831,834,836]

Histochemical, immunohistochemical, and electron microscopic features

Histochemically, the large majority of colorectal carcinomas are positive for mucin stains. Culling et al.[848] have devised a modification of the PAS technique that preferentially stains mucin of the lower intestinal tract. The stain is usually negative in adenocarcinomas of other sites, but unfortunately, it will also stain tumors of intestinal type in those locations, thus diminishing its diagnostic utility. Immunohistochemically, the main mucin protein cores expressed by conventional adenocarcinoma of large bowel are MUC1 and MUC3 (as opposed as MUC2 in the mucinous carcinoma).[845] In contrast to pancreatobiliary carcinoma, there is usually no expression of MUC5AC.[869a]

Colorectal adenocarcinomas are invariably positive for keratin.[851] A common pattern is represented by positivity for keratin 20 and negativity for keratin 7, whereas the reverse is extremely rare; this fact is of great significance in the differential diagnosis between colorectal adenocarcinomas and adenocarcinomas of other sites, such as lung and ovary.[841,857,859] However, aberrant patterns of immunoreactivity can be found in poorly differentiated carcinomas.[886a] Reactivity for CEA is also the rule; as a matter of fact, failure to demonstrate CEA in an adenocarcinoma makes a colorectal origin unlikely.[862] The positivity for this marker is equally distributed throughout the cell surface in most cases, as opposed to the polar distribution seen in normal mucosa and in the better differentiated tumors.[838,855] There is good correlation of the immunohistologic pattern with the serum levels but not with tumor staging or degree of differentiation.[852,860,863] A variety of monoclonal antibodies to different epitopes of the CEA molecule are available. Of these, the ones that recognize epitopes of group 1 or 2 have been found to have the greatest degree of sensitivity and specificity.[850] However, no evidence has yet been offered for the existence of site-specific CEA species.[866]

CDX2 is a recently cloned caudal-type homeobox gene which encodes a transcription factor that plays an important role in the proliferation and differentiation of intestinal epithelial cells. It has been found by immunohistochemistry in the overwhelming majority of colorectal carcinomas, but also in primary mucinous carcinomas of ovary and bladder.[856a,868a]

Tumor-associated glycoprotein (TAG-72), recognized by monoclonal antibody B72.3, is present not only in 100% of invasive colorectal carcinomas but also in the majority of hyperplastic and adenomatous polyps and even in normal mucosa; however, the frequency of reactivity and the pattern of expression vary depending on the condition.[858]

Another tumor-associated antigen, designated large external antigen (LEA), has been identified in the tumor tissue and sera of colorectal carcinoma cases.[842] Carcinomas of the large bowel often show loss of blood group isoantigens and of HLA A, B, and C expression, particularly if poorly differentiated.[849,861] Correspondingly, these tumors acquire reactivity for blood group substance H.[846,865] Immunoreactivity for the secretory component of immunoglobulin is seen in approximately half of cases and is particularly strong in the well-differentiated tumors.[839]

Blood group antigens in the same synthetic pathway may be coexpressed in the same cell; antigens of different protein backbones are occasionally expressed in the same cell but in different subcellular compartments.[847]

Abnormalities in lectin binding have been described, reflecting increased sialylation of cell surface glycoproteins as a result of the de novo expression of a specific type of sialyl-transferase.[864]

Another marker consistently expressed by colorectal carcinoma regardless of differentiation is villin, a cytoskeletal protein associated with the axial microfilament bundles of brush border microvilli.[840] Increased expression of cathepsin B (a lysosomal cysteine proteinase) is also a feature of these tumors, particularly in advanced stages of the disease.[842]

Calretinin can be expressed by a minority of colorectal adenocarcinomas (especially the undifferentiated ones), a fact to be remembered in the differential diagnosis with mesothelioma.[853]

A high percentage of colorectal carcinomas have shown immunohistochemical reactivity for hCG[844,854]; this seems particularly common in mucinous and poorly differentiated tumors.[844] Placental alkaline phosphatase (PLAP) has been detected in approximately 10% of all colorectal carcinomas.[868] Estrogen and progesterone receptors are usually absent or are present in a small minority of tumor cells.[867,869]

Ultrastructurally, a constant feature of colorectal carcinoma is the presence of prominent collections of microfilaments running perpendicular to the cell membrane and entering the brush border[858] (Fig. 11.213). This feature, although helpful, is not diagnostic. It can also be found in intestinal-type carcinomas of the stomach, small bowel, gallbladder, and pancreas.

Molecular genetic features

The identification of several types of familial carcinoma of the large bowel has led to the discovery of some of the genetic alterations associated with (and presumably pathogenetically responsible for) these tumors.[887,894] It was subsequently shown that somatic mutations of these genes also occur in sporadic colorectal cancer.[883,886,893] The most important of these genes are *APC*, mismatch repair genes, *p53*, k-*ras*, and *DCC*.[870] These have already discussed briefly in the section on epithelial polyps and their relationship to carcinoma. The model still standing for colonic carcinogenesis is that proposed by Vogelstein and his colleagues in the late 1980s, but it has become increasingly obvious that many variations exist and that not all colorectal cancers follow the same genetic pathway during carcinogenesis. Specifically, DNA mismatch repair deficiencies with resulting microsatellite instability (MSI) has been found to be an important alternate pathway, present in approximately 15% of cases; it operates in hereditary nonpolyposis colorectal carcinomas[876,879,890] and is possibly a marker for the cancers arising from hyperplastic polyps and serrated adenomas.[882]

Tumors associated with microsatellite instability tend to be mucinous or poorly differentiated, with a prominent host response, a circumscribed growth pattern, and right-sided location. In one study, presence of tumor-infiltrating lymphocytes was found to be the best histological predictor of microsatellite instability.[880a,899a] It has been further pointed out that differences may exist depending on the specific type of mismatch repair gene involved.[900a]

Another group of molecules thought to play an important role in the pathogenesis of colorectal carcinomas is that of E-cadherin and catenins.[875,877,900] Beta-catenin is associated with APC protein and is dysregulated at all stages of the adenoma–carcinoma sequence.[871,872] The expression of E-cadherin and α-catenin in colorectal carcinoma correlates with local invasion and metastases.[880] Mutations of *p53* have been detected by molecular techniques in the majority of colorectal carcinomas[897] and have been correlated with an overexpression of the protein coded by the abnormal gene, as detected immunohistochemically.[899] Approximately half of the tumors show positive staining; these do not seem to differ from the others in terms of site, differentiation, or

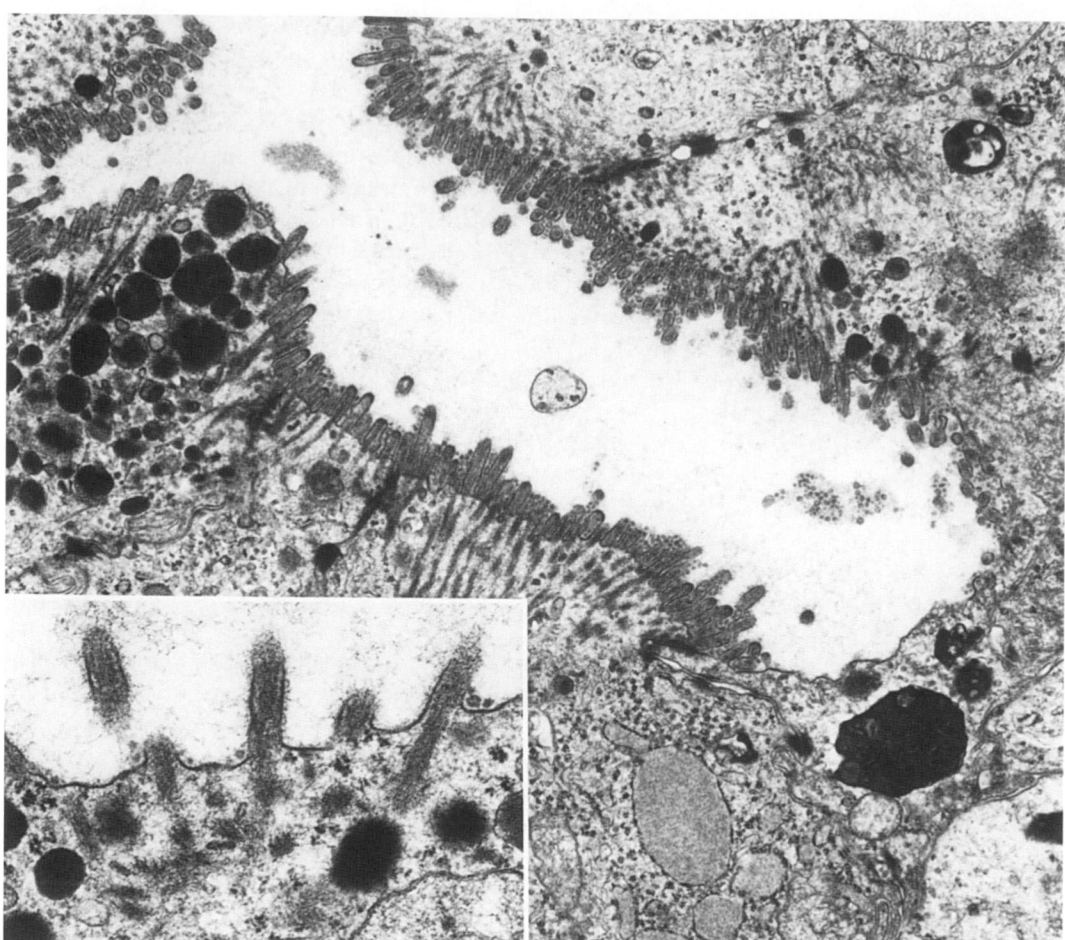

Fig. 11.213 Adenocarcinoma of colon with true lumen formation and mucin secretory product. Prominent collections of microfilaments that are related to brush border are characteristic of adenocarcinoma of colon and intestinal-type cancers of other organs. Inset, Microfilaments entering border and mucin secretory product. (×11,230; inset ×25,270)

DNA ploidy.[881,896] As expected, the "transitional" mucosa present between the edge of the carcinoma and the normal mucosa is uniformly negative for this marker.[873]

Mutations of the *ras* oncogene have been found in a minority of colorectal carcinomas, particularly those in the metastatic group[878,892] (see p. 820). Expression of this gene, which is said to influence the morphogenesis of early cancers,[888] can be detected immunohistochemically in histologic and cytogenetic preparations.[874,884]

Deletion of the von Hippel–Lindau gene has been detected in a high proportion of colorectal adenocarcinoma cases.[901] Enhanced expression of the c-*myc* oncogene occurs in approximately 90% of colorectal carcinomas.[891] The increased proliferative activity of colorectal carcinoma has been measured by S-phase determination, staining for Ki-67 or PCNA, AgNOR counts, and simple mitotic counts.[883,889,895,898] None of these determinations correlates very closely with the microscopic grade, and they may carry prognostic implications of their own.

Other microscopic types

Mucinous carcinoma is a special type of colorectal carcinoma in which large lakes of extracellular mucin are formed, mixed with collections of tumor cells[947] (Fig. 11.214). By definition, these mucinous foci should constitute at least half of the tumor mass.[911] In some cases there

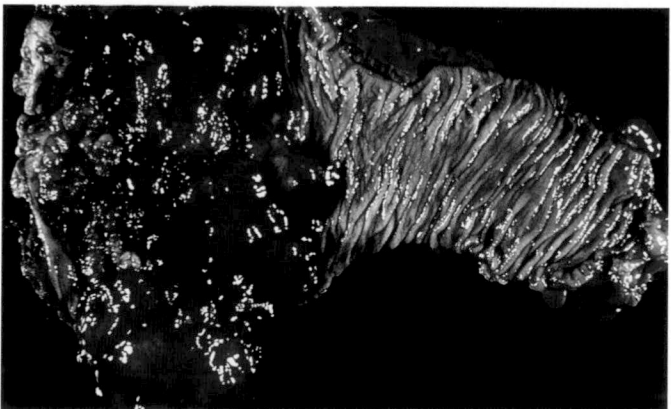

Fig. 11.214 Mucinous adenocarcinoma of the rectum. The tumor is extremely large and has a glaring quality.

is an admixture of extracellular and intracellular mucin formation, the latter resulting in signet ring configuration.[911] These tumors secrete distinct *O*-acylated forms of mucin containing the MUC-2 protein core.[924,945] They usually have an exophytic shape and should not be equated to the pure signet ring carcinomas described later.[912] Mucinous tumors comprise 15% of colorectal carcinomas and occur most commonly in the rectum. In a series of 132 cases reported by Symonds and Vickery,[956] 31% were associated with villous adenomas, 7% with ulcerative colitis, 8% with colitis, and 5% with prior pelvic irradiation. Mucinous carcinomas are also more frequently associated with adenomas elsewhere in the colorectum than are conventional adenocarcinomas[955] and tend to present at a more advanced stage.[960] Their prognosis is somewhat worse than for the conventional type of adenocarcinoma, at least when they are located in the rectum and/or if they are stage B lesions.[911,921,944]

Signet ring carcinoma (linitis plastica-type carcinoma) is a rare form of colorectal malignancy that usually affects young patients. Like its more common gastric counterpart, it usually presents grossly as a diffuse infiltration of the wall,[917,934] although it has also been described arising in an adenomatous polyp[923] (Fig. 11.215). Microscopically, the tumor grows in a diffuse fashion, with little if any glandular formation.[902,951] Most or all of the mucin is intracellular, in contrast to the pattern seen in mucinous carcinoma. This intracellular accumulation of mucin results in displacement of the nucleus and a typical signet ring configuration of the cells. Metastases tend to develop in lymph nodes, the peritoneal surface, and the ovary rather than the liver. The pattern of spread is mainly in the form of peritoneal dissemination, and the prognosis is extremely poor.[903,936] The possibility of the colorectal lesion representing a metastasis from a gastric or mammary primary lesion should always be investigated before a diagnosis of primary signet ring carcinoma is made.[905,953] Immunohistochemically, a CK7–/CK20+ profile favors a large bowel primary, whereas CK7+/CK20– favors a metastasis.[918] Care should be exercised in distinguishing signet ring carcinoma from the benign signet ring change that may accompany pseudomembranous colitis and other inflammatory conditions.[957a]

Basaloid (cloacogenic) carcinoma similar to its counterpart in the anal canal has been reported on a few occasions in the colorectum, as proximally as the splenic flexure.[922,937]

Clear cell carcinoma is not a specific entity but rather a minor morphologic variant of adenocarcinoma in

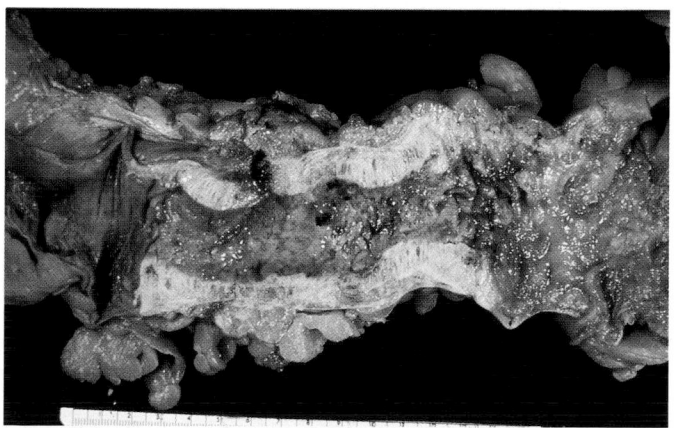

Fig. 11.215 Gross appearance of signet ring carcinoma. This tumor type is highly malignant, narrows the lumen, and has a pebbly mucosal surface and thickened muscular wall.

which the accumulation of glycogen results in a clear appearance of the cytoplasm.[931]

Hepatoid adenocarcinoma can arise in the colon, the appearance being similar to that of its more common gastric counterpart (see p. 666).[929]

Medullary (solid, poorly differentiated) adenocarcinoma usually presents in the cecum or right colon of females. Some cytoarchitectural features suggest neuroendocrine differentiation, but neuroendocrine markers are negative. The behavior is not nearly as aggressive as the morphologic appearance might have suggested.[930,954] Genetically, they are characterized by microsatellite instability.[933,943]

Anaplastic (spindle and giant cell, sarcomatoid) carcinoma should be clearly separated from the above. Its appearance is similar to that of its counterpart in many other organs and its behavior is very aggressive.[942,943,949]

Squamous differentiation may be present in colorectal carcinoma; this is more common in cecal neoplasms but may be seen in any other area of the large bowel.[914,928] In most instances, the squamous component is associated with glandular elements (*adenosquamous carcinoma*) but occasionally it is seen in a pure form (*squamous cell carcinoma*). One such case developed in a duplication of the colon,[927] and another led to hypercalcemia through the production of a parathyroid-like substance.[909] An association has been noted between squamous changes in colorectal carcinoma and ulcerative colitis. It has been postulated that some of these squamous tumors may arise from areas of squamous differentiation in preexisting adenomatous polyps.[959] For the squamous tumors located in the low rectum, the alternative possibility of upward extension or submucosal metastasis from a carcinoma of the anal canal should be considered.

Trophoblastic differentiation can occur focally in colorectal adenocarcinoma, as it does in tumors of stomach and gallbladder.[932] hCG can be demonstrated immunohistochemically in the tumor cells.[941] Occasionally the entire tumor has the appearance of a choriocarcinoma[939] or of a *glassy cell carcinoma*.[904] This phenomenon should be distinguished from the more common finding of hCG positivity in morphologically conventional adenocarcinomas.

Endocrine differentiation may manifest itself in a variety of ways, as it does elsewhere in the gastrointestinal tract:

1 As *scattered endocrine cells* in otherwise typical adenocarcinomas (particularly of the mucinous type), a feature that does not seem to independently influence the prognosis or natural history of these tumors.[906,915,952,957] This occurs in 15% to 50% of all adenocarcinomas, as detected immunohistochemically or by hybridization procedures for neuroendocrine markers such as chromogranin.[940] This phenomenon seems to be more frequent after chemotherapy and radiotherapy, a fact

which suggests that it might be induced by these treatment modalities.[950]

2　In the form of tumors with a *mixed composition*, in which typical adenocarcinoma intermingles with a component exhibiting clear-cut endocrine differentiation.[925,926] The existence of these tumors is explained by assuming an origin from endodermally derived multipotential cells located at the base of the crypts, which during the course of neoplastic transformation undergo differentiation along several different pathways.[913] As in other organs, neuroendocrine differentiation can be a component of a multidirectional differentiation, which also includes glandular (exocrine) and squamous components.[938]

3　In the form of tumors showing throughout the appearance of a *neuroendocrine carcinoma* but having a more organoid appearance and being composed of larger cells than the small cell carcinomas described later.[916] These tumors have been variously called the intermediate variant of small cell neuroendocrine carcinoma, atypical carcinoid (a term better to avoid in this situation), and high-grade neuroendocrine carcinoma.

4　In the form of *small cell (neuroendocrine) carcinoma*, a tumor having a microscopic appearance similar to that of its pulmonary homonym.[910,948] Most of the cases are located in the right colon.[907] Electron microscopy usually reveals a few dense-core secretory granules in the cytoplasm, and immunohistochemical techniques may show positivity for neuron-specific enolase and other endocrine markers such as synaptophysin.[920,958] The entire tumor may have this appearance, or there may be foci of glandular differentiation, with or without mucin production.[919] Squamous differentiation may also be present.[907] Some of these small cell carcinomas arise on the basis of an adenoma, usually of villous type[935,946] (Fig. 11.216). The prognosis is poor, with early metastases to lymph nodes and liver.[907]

5　In the form of typical *carcinoid tumors*. These are discussed on p. 821.

Rhabdoid features can be seen in adenocarcinoma of the cecum and other portions of the large bowel[908]; as in other sites, they are harbingers of aggressive behavior.

Biopsy

A positive biopsy should always be obtained before radical surgery for colorectal carcinoma is undertaken. In large lesions, it is advisable to perform several biopsies from diverse areas; those from the center may show only granulation tissue, and those from the very periphery may contain only hyperplastic (so-called "transitional") colonic epithelium. Lesions below the peritoneal reflection should be removed in toto wherever possible to facilitate their orientation for section by the pathologist. Most adenocarcinomas are diagnosed easily, the main problems being presented by the better differentiated tumors and—paradoxically—the highly malignant

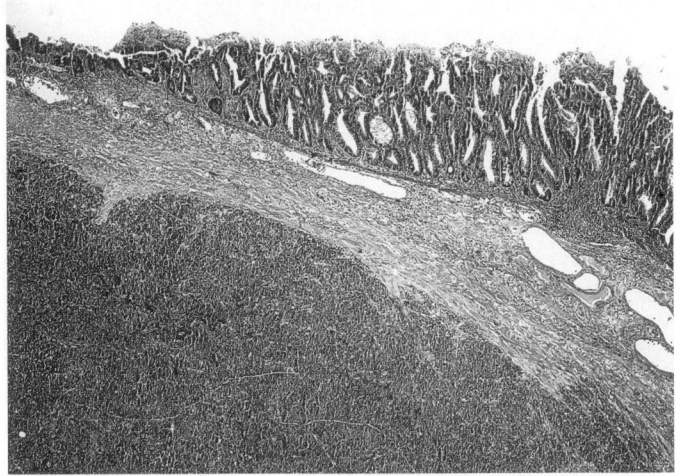

A

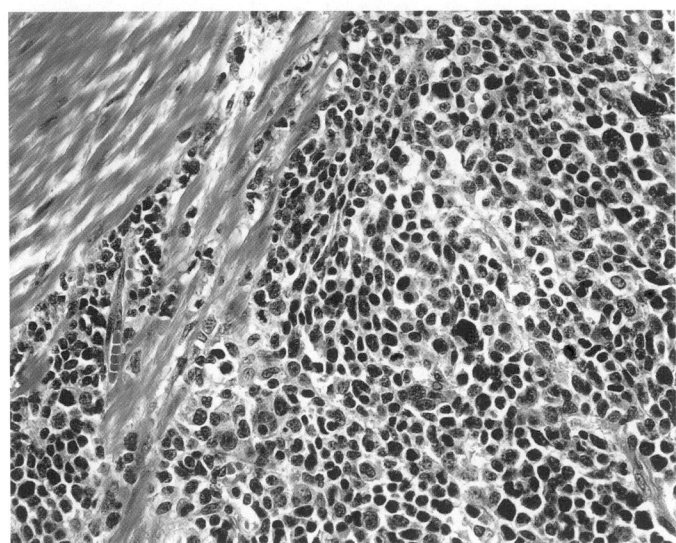

B

Fig. 11.216 A and **B**, Villous adenoma complicated by the development of a small cell neuroendocrine carcinoma. The high-power view (**B**) shows a predominant population of small cells, with scattered larger elements.

signet ring carcinomas in which only a few tumor cells may be present. A sometimes more difficult (but just as critical) determination once a carcinoma has been recognized is to ascertain its position and extent. Obviously, the significance of the finding is markedly different if the fragment of tissue with adenocarcinoma was taken from the tip of a pedunculated polyp or from the side of a large ulcerated mass. Close communication with the endoscopist and surgeon, intact biopsy of an adequate size and depth, and proper orientation of the specimen are essential requisites for this determination.

For rectal tumors, it has been advised to biopsy the submucosal invasive tumor front, in that the morphologic features seen in it allow an estimate of the local tumor spread.[961]

Cytology

Cytology is unquestionably an accurate way of diagnosing colorectal carcinoma but until now has proved of little practical value. Raskin and Pleticka[963] studied 87 patients with carcinoma and correctly identified the malignancy in 70 (80%); the incidence of false positives in 438 patients was 0.45%. However, the technique employed to obtain the specimen—which involves extensive cleansing of the colon followed by a diagnostic enema with manipulation of the patient—has led to an unenthusiastic response from clinicians.

Low-lying rectal lesions can be easily sampled.[964] Brush cytology can also be performed via the fiberoptic scope. It is a sensitive technique, perhaps even more so than endoscopic biopsy,[962,965] but it has not yet found widespread acceptance.

Staging and grading

In 1937 Dukes[968,969] proposed his famous staging system for rectal carcinomas that also can be applied to carcinomas of the colon. It is still widely used in one form or another because of its direct relationship with prognosis. Stage A tumors involve the wall of the bowel only, stage B tumors extend through the wall, and stage C tumors have lymph node metastases. A common misconception exists—one that received a lot of publicity some years ago in connection with the colonic tumor of a very prominent citizen[977]—that carcinomas which have invaded the muscular layer of the bowel become automatically Dukes' stage B tumors. If the serosa of the bowel (or the perimuscular fat if the tumor is below the peritoneal reflection) has not been reached, the tumor is still a Dukes' stage A carcinoma. Part of the problem resides in the fact that several modifications have been proposed to this simple and effective scheme, the first by Dukes himself when he subdivided stage C carcinomas into those where only the regional nodes were positive (C1) and those where the nodes at the point of the mesenteric blood vessel ligature were involved (C2).[977] Later, a stage D category was added by others to indicate the presence of distant metastases.[977]

A different staging system was proposed in 1954 by Astler and Coller,[966] based on a previous scheme by Kirklin et al.[976] This system, although useful by itself, has created considerable confusion because it is often misinterpreted as relating to the Dukes' system. It classifies the tumors into stages A (limited to the mucosa), B1 (involving the muscularis externa but not penetrating it), B2 (penetrating through the muscularis externa), C1 (confined to the bowel wall but with nodal metastases), and C2 (penetrating through the wall and with nodal metastases).

An additional staging system, more detailed but not necessarily more prognostically accurate than the Dukes' classification, has been proposed by the American Joint Committee on Cancer (AJCC) and the Union Internationale Contre Le Cancer (UICC) by grouping the various TNM components.[967,973]

Yet another system for staging colorectal carcinoma has been proposed by Jass et al.[974]; in this scheme, peritumoral lymphocytic infiltration ("Crohn's like") and tumor growth pattern are introduced as significant indicators of prognosis.[971,974]

In a study of 745 cases of rectal carcinoma staged according to the first three methods, it was found that the Dukes' staging method is the simplest and most consistent algorithm related to prognosis; the only modification it might require to further enhance its value is the subdivision of C cases according to the criteria of Astler and Coller rather than those proposed by Dukes himself.[970]

Recently, endorectal ultrasonography has been employed to increase the accuracy of the staging of rectal carcinomas, both in terms of depth of rectal wall involvement and the presence of regional lymphadenopathy.[972,975]

A common source of argument among pathologists, regardless of the staging system used, is the exact definition of stage B tumors in locations where a peritoneal surface is present. We believe that the requirement of identification of tumor cells *at the surface* is unrealistic, in view of the fact that invasive tumors are nearly always surrounded by a layer of desmoplastic stroma.[979] The absence of an identifiable layer of smooth muscle fibers from the muscularis externa between the tumor and the serosal surface suffices to place the tumor into this category.

Microscopically, colorectal carcinomas can be graded into I (well differentiated), II (moderately differentiated), and III (poorly differentiated). Although this is a worthwhile exercise because of its correlation with prognosis, it suffers from all the drawbacks of a subjective evaluation, especially when performed in biopsy material.[974,978]

Spread and metastases

The most common sites of metastatic involvement of colorectal carcinoma are regional lymph nodes and liver. Lymph node metastases are more common in the tumors showing poorly differentiated areas and a highly infiltrative pattern of growth.[992] If there is tumor present in the lymph nodes, it is necessary to examine the tissue in the immediate vicinity of nodes, for tumor frequently extends beyond the lymph node capsule to invade surrounding veins.

Because of the great prognostic significance of lymph node metastases, it is imperative that the search for lymph nodes be thorough, whether done in the fresh or fixed specimen, with or without clearing. Sometimes, the metastases will be present only in lymph nodes measuring 1 or 2 mm.[981] It has been estimated that the minimum number of nodes recovered from a surgical specimen of colorectal carcinoma should be 14 or 15.[986,998] In a series of 50 consecutive cases of rectal carcinoma excised at the National Cancer Institute of Milan, Andreola et al.[980] found an average of 36 nodes per patient by meticulous manual dissection without clearing.

Lymph node micrometastases can be searched by step H&E sections, immunohistochemistry for keratin and other markers, and PCR techniques for CK19/20 or mutated k-*ras*[982,988,995]; their possible prognostic significance is discussed on p. 820.

Sometimes isolated tumor nodules are found in a perineural, perivascular, or intravascular location beyond the muscularis propria. These are referred to as *pericolonic tumor deposits (PTDs)* and should be distinguished from lymph node metastases.[987]

Liver metastases are more common in the tumors showing evidence of blood vessel invasion.[989] Other relatively common metastatic sites include peritoneum, lung, and ovaries. The incidence of ovarian metastases is high enough to justify the performance of a prophylactic bilateral oophorectomy in a postmenopausal woman at the time of resection of the colorectal tumor. Rare metastatic sites include central nervous system, bone, testis, uterus, and oral cavity.[985,991,994] Some of the metastases from colorectal adenocarcinoma can closely simulate primary tumors of the respective organs. This is particularly true for the ovary, in which the metastasis can be misdiagnosed as a primary endometrioid (including the secretory variant) or clear cell carcinoma.[983,997,999] Immunohistochemical and molecular studies can be helpful in this differential.[984,990] Secondary invasion of the bladder can simulate a primary tumor of this organ,[996] and intrabiliary growth in the liver may mimic a primary neoplasm of the biliary tract.[993]

Treatment

The standard therapy for colorectal carcinoma is surgical resection, the type of surgery depending on the site of the tumor.[1000,1007,1030] For carcinoma of the cecum or ascending colon, ileocolectomy is the treatment of choice. Tumors located below the peritoneal reflection have been traditionally treated by an abdominoperineal resection,[1009] but the experience at the National Cancer Institute of Milan and other centers has shown that sphincter-preserving procedures are very effective if the cases are carefully selected.[1002,1019] Carcinomas located in other areas of the large bowel are treated by anterior resection, the extent of the operation being such as to remove the potentially involved lymph nodes. An extensive resection of the tumor may cure certain patients who would die of carcinoma after less radical surgery.[1010] Local recurrence sometimes develops at the anastomotic line, from tumor cells apparently implanted on the raw surface at the time of operation. Surgical techniques for minimizing this occurrence have been devised.[1006,1014] The current resectability rate for colorectal carcinoma is 92%, and the operative mortality for resections for cure is 2%. Regular endoscopic examinations in the first year after surgery are important for the detection of potentially curable recurrences.[1004]

Fulguration, endoscopic transrectal resection, and full-thickness local excision are acceptable alternative procedures for rectal carcinomas if the tumor is small, superficial, and well differentiated[1008,1015,1018,1028] and/or if the patient is a poor candidate for abdominoperineal resection.[1024] If a specimen from a local resection shows extensive tumor "budding," microacinar structures, undifferentiated cells and/or blood vessel invasion, the chances of lymph node metastases are higher and adjuvant treatment should be considered.[1013]

The role of preoperative or postoperative irradiation and/or chemotherapy for operable carcinoma of the large bowel (particularly rectum) has been investigated in several centers.[1012,1021,1022,1025,1027,1031] In one study, a slight improvement in survival was noted following postoperative irradiation in Dukes' C but not in Dukes' B tumors.[1003] In two others, it was shown that combined postoperative chemotherapy and radiation therapy to the pelvis decrease the likelihood of local recurrence and prolong survival in rectal carcinomas.[1020,1023]

Finally, two large European studies have shown improved survival with preoperative radiation therapy combined with total mesorectal excision.[1017]

Isolated (and sometimes even multiple) distant metastases to liver and other organs can benefit from surgical excision; long-term survival has been obtained in some of these cases.[1001,1011]

Prognosis

The 5-year crude survival rate after curative resection for colorectal carcinoma ranges between 40% and 60% in most large series.[1060,1082,1097] Local recurrence and/or regional lymph node metastases occur in over 90% of the failure cases, and they represent the only site of tumor in about half of them.[1043,1064,1099,1104,1105] A total of 71% of the recurrences are evident within the first 2 years and 91% by 5 years.[1063]

The prognosis of colorectal carcinoma is related to a number of clinical and pathologic parameters given in the list below.[1043a]

It is to be noted that these are not listed in order of significance but rather following the order in which

---

Category I
Well supported by the literature, generally used in patient management and of sufficient importance to modify TNM stage groups

Category IIA
Extensively studied biologically and/or clinically. Prognostic value for therapy, sufficient to be noted in pathology report

Category IIB
Well studied but not sufficiently established for Category I or IIA

Category III
Not yet established to meet criteria for Category I or II

Category IV
Studied and shows no consistent prognostic significance

these features were discussed in the preceding sections. It should be apparent to the reader that it is extremely difficult to judge the relative worth of these determinations, as many if not most of the studies are not conclusive by statistical standards and the results and conclusions from different series often clash with each other. At a Consensus Conference of the Colorectal Working Group of the American Joint Committee on Cancer Prognostic Factors,[1044] a brave attempt was made to divide these factors into categories depending on their perceived practical value, according to the scheme in the box above. Whenever indicated, the category assigned by this group to the items listed below is indicated in parentheses.

1 **Age.** Tumors occurring in very young and very old patients are associated with a poor prognosis.[1063] In the first group, this probably results from a combination of factors: greater delay in diagnosis leading to more advanced stages, greater proportion of cases arising in ulcerative colitis, and greater number of signet ring and mucinous tumors.[994,1094,1102,1109] Age is said to play a more important role in rectal than in colonic tumors.[1117]

2 **Sex.** The prognosis is significantly better for females than for males.[1063]

3 **CEA serum levels.** Elevated serum CEA levels >5.0 ng/ml have been shown to have an adverse impact on prognosis that is independent of tumor stage[1067,1079] (AJC category 1).

4 **Tumor location.** This factor remains controversial. In one large study, lesions located in the left colon had the most favorable prognosis, whereas those situated in the sigmoid colon and rectum had the worst outcome.[1105] In another series, the diagnostic significance of tumor location was found to be minimal.[1113] A third study, with long-term follow-up, showed a greater propensity of left-sided lesions for late recurrences.[1051]

5 **Tumor multiplicity.** The survival rate for patients with synchronous or metachronous malignancies of the large bowel is similar to that for patients with solitary colorectal carcinoma.[1072]

6 **Local extent.** The prognosis is excellent if focal microscopic carcinoma is discovered incidentally in a polyp, and in general if the tumor is restricted to the mucosa and submucosa. Among tumors that have metastasized to regional lymph nodes, the prognosis is worse for those that, in addition, have extended beyond the bowel wall.

7 **Tumor size.** Although a correlation between size of the tumor and prognosis exists,[1114] there are too many exceptions for this to be a reliable prognostic indicator.[1124] Along the same lines, there is little relation between the size of the tumor and the incidence of nodal metastases[1123] (AJC category III).

8 **Tumor edge.** Advanced colorectal carcinomas with a nonpolypoid edge seem to have a worse prognosis than polypoid tumors[1058] (AJC category III).

9 **Obstruction.** This feature has been found to be an indicator of a worsened prognosis independent of Dukes' staging in some series[1063,1113,1125] but not in others.[1074]

10 **Perforation.** Perforation resulting from extensive tumor invasion of the bowel wall is linked to a poor prognosis.[1113] In the series of Welch and Donaldson,[1121] there were essentially no cures once free perforation into the peritoneal cavity had occurred.

11 **Tumor margin and inflammatory reaction.** Carcinomas having pushing margins and an inflammatory infiltrate at the interphase between the tumor and the neighboring tissue (made up of plasma cells and lymphocytes and associated with degenerative changes within the tumor) have a better prognosis than those lacking these features[1088,1112] (AJC category IIA). Sometimes this infiltrate resembles that of Crohn's disease. The favorable prognostic connotation of this finding has been noted,[1061] to the point of having been incorporated into one staging system[1066] (AJC category IIB). It has been claimed that infiltration of the tumor stroma by eosinophils[1100] and dendritic cells positive for S-100 protein[1033] are features associated with an improved prognosis. Conversely, the presence of four or more mast cells ×30 oil immersion fields was found in one series to correlate with a lower overall survival rate.[1055]

12 **Vascular invasion.** When vein invasion is present, the 5-year survival decreases markedly.[1075,1086,1096,1116] This feature is of more prognostic significance when it involves extramural vessels than when it is located within the bowel wall.[1048,1076] Lymph vessel invasion is of lesser import than blood vessel invasion, but it represents an adverse prognostic factor when present extensively in patients with stage III disease[1110] (AJC category IIA).

13 **Perineurial invasion.** Perineurial invasion is usually a sign of advanced disease and tends to be accompanied by other unfavorable pathologic findings (AJC category IIA).

14 **Surgical margins.** Tumor involvement of the radial margin (as defined by adventitial soft tissue margin of a nonperitonealized surface) in rectal carcinoma may be the single most critical factor in predicting local recurrence in rectal carcinoma[1032] (AJC category IIA). In addition, the risk of local recurrence in rectal adenocarcinoma after total mesorectal resection is higher if the tumor is less than 2 mm from the circumferential margin.[1089]

15 **Tumor thickness.** Measurement of the tumor thickness in the "central depressed area" of the tumor is said to correlate with incidence of lymph node and liver metastases and with prognosis.[1068]

16 **Microscopic tumor type**. Mucinous carcinoma, signet ring carcinoma, and anaplastic carcinoma have a worse prognosis than the ordinary type of adenocarcinoma, whereas medullary carcinoma is said to be associated with an improved outcome (*AJC category IIB*).

17 **Acinar morphology**. A microacinar pattern of growth is associated with poor prognosis but does not represent an independent prognostic factor.[1122]

18 **Presence of neuroendocrine cells**. There are discrepant data in the literature as to whether the presence of a neuroendocrine cell component as determined immunohistochemically carries prognostic implications (*AJC category III*).[1047,1054,1057,1060a,1106a,1081]

19 **Tumor angiogenesis**. Several independent studies have concluded that tumor angiogenesis predicts recurrence and is associated with decreased survival in colorectal carcinoma[1037,1053,1080,1115] (*AJC category III*).

20 **Mucin-related antigens**. Colorectal carcinomas that express the mucin-associated antigens sialyl-Tn and sialyl-Lewis(*x*) antigen have been said to run a more aggressive clinical course.[1070,1090] In a recent study, MUC1 and sialyl-Lewis(*x*) immunoreactive tumors had a higher incidence of tumor progression, and MUC1 was an independent prognostic factor[1036] (*AJC category III*).

21 **HLA-DR expression**. In one series, patients with tumors having strong HLA-DR expression showed the best survival, even within the same Dukes' stage.[1034] In another, downregulation of HLA-A expression was found to correlate with a better prognosis.[1085a]

22 **hCG expression**. Despite some early claims to the contrary, immunoreactivity for hCG has not been found to represent an adverse prognostic indicator in colorectal adenocarcinoma.[1045]

23 **Bcl-2 protein expression**. It has been stated that immunohistochemical expression of bcl-2 is associated with an improved prognosis[1077] (*AJC category IIB*).

24 **DNA ploidy**. Flow cytometric determinations have been found to relate to the Dukes' stage microscopic grade of differentiation and tumor progression.[1052,1107,1108,1118] The tumors are generally homogeneous in their DNA pattern, and several studies have shown a correlation between aneuploidy and risk of recurrence of survival, particularly in rectal tumors.[1035,1059,1103] However, whether the technique has prognostic value independently from staging remains doubtful.[1038,1046,1056,1119,1128]

25 **Cell proliferation**. Determination of S-phase fraction has shown a relation with survival rate in some studies[1039] but not in others.

26 **Allelic loss of chromosome 18q**. This karyotypic alteration has a strongly negative prognostic significance in colorectal carcinoma[1071,1095] (*AJC category IIB*).

Along the same lines, retention of 18q alleles in microsatellite-stable tumors points to a favorable outcome after adjuvant chemotherapy for stage III colonic carcinoma.[1120]

27 **TGF-β_1 mutations**. Mutations of the gene for the type II receptor for TGF-β_1 in cancers with high levels of microsatellite instability are a favorable prognostic feature.[1120]

28 **Oncogene expression**. K-*ras* mutation at certain codon sites has been found to be much more common in patients with recurrent disease[1041] (*AJC category IIB*). This is also true for overexpression of the *ras* p21 protein as detected immunohistochemically.[1087]

In one study, tumors overexpressing p53 had a greater relative risk of resulting in a patient's death than the others, despite the fact that there was no correlation between p53 expression and histologic grade or stage.[1127] In several others, p53 overexpression was found to be an independent predictor of survival[1040,1042,1127] (*AJC category IIB*). Expression of the c-*myc* oncogene has been found to correlate with the degree of differentiation of the tumor.[1111]

Presence of microsatellite instability in the tumor appears to predict improved patient survival[1065,1106]; in one study, patients with stage II-III colonic carcinoma with microsatellite-stable or nearly stable tumors benefited from fluororacil-based adjuvant chemotherapy, whereas those with tumors exhibiting high-frequency microsatellite instability did not.[1102a] Overexpression of thymidylate synthase mRNA or protein is associated with a poor prognosis and resistance to chemotherapy.[1126] Lack of p27 expression (a cell cycle inhibitor with a potential tumor suppressor function) is associated with a poor prognosis[1083] (*AJC category IIB*).

Telomerase-negative stage II colorectal carcinomas have been found to correlate with poor prognosis.[1073]

29 **Lymph node involvement**. Once the tumor has spread to the lymph nodes, the 5-year survival rate drops sharply (*AJC category I, as part of the staging*). The location and extent of lymph node involvement are also significant. Cures are very rare when nodes other than those in the immediate vicinity of the tumor are involved.[1069,1092] Involvement of the apical node is a particularly ominous feature.[1085,1093] The greater the number of lymph nodes involved, the worse the prognosis. In one study,[1112] if more than 6 lymph nodes contained metastatic carcinoma, less than 10% of the patients survived more than 5 years. If more than 16 mesenteric lymph nodes contained carcinoma, all patients died within the 5-year period. The former extent of involvement was not observed in carcinomas less than 2 cm in greatest diameter, and the latter extent of involvement was not observed in carcinomas less than 3 cm in diameter.

Within these parameters, there was correlation between degree of lymph node involvement and size of tumor. It has been claimed that nodal micrometastases detected only immunohistochemically or molecularly (with a RT-PCR technique for CEA) are also associated with a decreased survival,[1062,1078] but independent verifications of these claims are needed (AJC category III).

30 **Pattern of lymph node reaction.** It has been shown that patients with colorectal carcinoma in whom the regional lymph nodes show morphologic evidence of a cell-mediated immune response (manifested by an increased number of paracortical immunoblasts and/or sinus histiocytosis) survive longer than those patients whose nodes do not show these changes.[1098]

32 **Staging.** The staging systems, which represent a combination of the criteria of local extent (and lymph node involvement) have proved to be a powerful way of predicting the prognosis of patients with colorectal carcinoma, whether one uses the original scheme proposed by Dukes or any of the modifications that have been subsequently advanced[1114] (AJC category I).

32 **Microscopic grade.** There is a definite relationship between the microscopic grade of the tumor and its prognosis,[1049,1050,1063,1091] especially if the tumors are stratified into two rather than three or five categories (low-grade and high-grade) (AJC category IIA). It has been suggested that the grade assigned to a tumor should be determined by the worst pattern rather than the predominant one.[1101]

Carcinoid tumor

Carcinoid tumors can occur in any portion of the large bowel but are more common in the rectum. Those located in the colon tend to be large, extend deeply through the wall of the bowel, and involve the regional lymph nodes. In the rectum, they are often located in the anterior or lateral wall. Their shape is rounded, and ulceration is usually lacking. Of the 147 cases of rectal carcinoid tumor examined by Caldarola et al.,[1131] 105 measured less than 0.5 cm in diameter. Only 3 were associated with lymph node metastases, and all of these were larger than 2 cm in diameter. A similarly close correlation between tumor size and probability of nodal metastases has been found in more recent series.[1140] Rectal carcinoids have been reported in bowels affected by ulcerative colitis[1135] or Crohn's disease[1137]; under these circumstances, they tend to be multicentric and often atypical.[1144] They have also been reported in association with ovarian carcinoid,[1155] and together with an adenomatous component as an expression of a collision tumor.[1141] Colorectal carcinoid tumor is practically never associated with the carcinoid syndrome. Grossly, it may appear as a flat and slightly depressed plaque or as a polypoid lesion.[1143] One of its most distinctive features is the yellow color that it

acquires after formalin fixation. Microscopically, invasion of the stroma by small uniform cells growing in a ribbon or festoon fashion is seen (Fig. 11.217). This may be associated with crypt cell proliferative micronests (presumably the precursor lesion).[1142,1146] A minor tubular and/or acinar component associated with mucin production may also be present.[1129] These tumors are consistently argyrophil but usually not argentaffin.[1132,1149] However, several examples of argentaffin rectal carcinoid tumors are on record.[1132,1156] Immunocytochemically, they stain for the panendocrine markers (neuron-specific enolase, chromogranin, synaptophysin) and for a variety of peptide hormones.[1132] Somatostatin, glucagon, substance P, and peptide YY are the ones most commonly represented, but gastrin/cholecystokinin, calcitonin, pancreatic polypeptide, and motilin have also been demonstrated in some cases.[1136,1147–1149,1153,1154] Many of the tumors are polyhormonal.[1147] The presence of peptides of the glucagon-glycentin and of the PP-PYY families is of particular interest because of their usual absence in carcinoid tumors at other sites.[1130,1138,1151] Rectal carcinoid tumors have also often been found to exhibit immunoreactivity for CEA,[1132] human chorionic gonadotropin,[1133,1134] and prostatic acid phosphatase.[1132,1150] The latter, whether real or the result of a cross-reaction, is of practical importance because metastatic prostatic carcinoma may enter in the differential diagnosis with carcinoid tumor; the distinction is made because the latter is consistently negative for prostate specific antigen.[1150]

Rectal carcinoid tumors smaller than 2 cm and limited to the mucosa or submucosa are best treated by local excision; those of larger size and/or exhibiting invasion of the muscularis externa are usually treated by radical surgery, in view of their propensity for lymph node involvement,[1131,1139,1146] even if the assumed survival

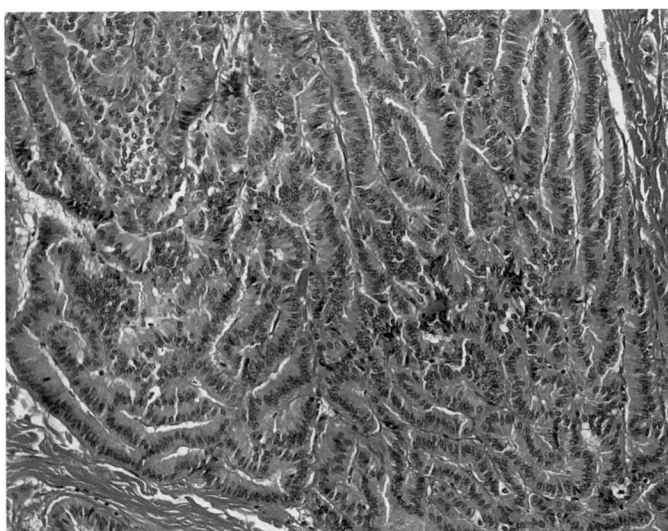

Fig. 11.217 Rectal carcinoid tumor. The trabecular arrangement is typical of well-differentiated neuroendocrine tumors of this location.

advantage of extensive surgery over local excision has been questioned.[1140] In one study, all of the 19 nonmetastasizing carcinoid tumors showed a diploid pattern by flow cytometry, whereas all three metastasizing tumors were aneuploid.[1152] If this remarkable correlation is confirmed, DNA ploidy analysis may become important in this situation to decide on the extent of the operation.

Malignant lymphoma and related lesions

Malignant lymphomas are less frequently found in the large bowel than in the small bowel or stomach.[1167a] Those located in the ileocecal region are discussed on p. 734. Some of the cases of large bowel lymphoma have been seen in immunosuppressed patients (HIV-infected or transplant recipients) or in patients with ulcerative colitis.[1160,1163,1166,1176,1178] These tumors can occur at any level of the colorectum.[1166,1182] They may produce prominent mucosal folds, prominent ulceration, a large mass, or a solitary polyp, or multiple small polyps distributed throughout the colorectum that may also extend to the small bowel ("lymphomatous polyposis").[1167,1170,1175,1180]

The regional lymph nodes are involved in approximately half of the cases.

Colorectal malignant lymphomas are nearly always of non-Hodgkin's type.[1167a] Most of the low-grade tumors are thought to belong to the MALT-type category. They often show evidence of plasmacytic differentiation; when this is extensive and associated with abundant immunoglobulin production (and occasionally also with amyloid deposits), the designation of plasmacytoma was sometimes used in the past for them.[1161]

Other reported types of colorectal lymphoma include mantle cell lymphoma[1172] (Fig. 11.218), anaplastic large cell lymphoma[1179] (one occurring at the site of an ileocolonic anastomosis[1159]), AILD-like lymphoma,[1173] and Hodgkin's lymphoma.[1181]

Some cases of colorectal lymphoma present in the form of innumerable small polyps ("lymphomatous polyposis"); it was initially thought that this presentation was more common with mantle cell lymphoma,[1169,1170] but it has also been documented with follicle center cell lymphoma,[1174] MALT-type lymphoma,[1183] and large cell lymphoma.[1162]

Lymphoid polyps of benign (reactive) nature are sometimes found in the rectal area.[1177] They have also been designated as *lymphoid hyperplasia, pseudolymphoma,* and *"rectal tonsil."* They appear as soft, superficial polyps usually covered by an intact, gray, smooth mucosa. The patient may complain of a mass, bleeding, or prolapse. In Helwig and Hanson's series,[1164] 40 were single, and 25 were multiple. Microscopically, these lesions are located in the submucosa and are made up of lymphoid tissue with follicle formation, a lobular pattern, and germinal centers. They may distort the muscularis mucosae and even extend to the muscularis externa. In a superficial or small biopsy, they can be

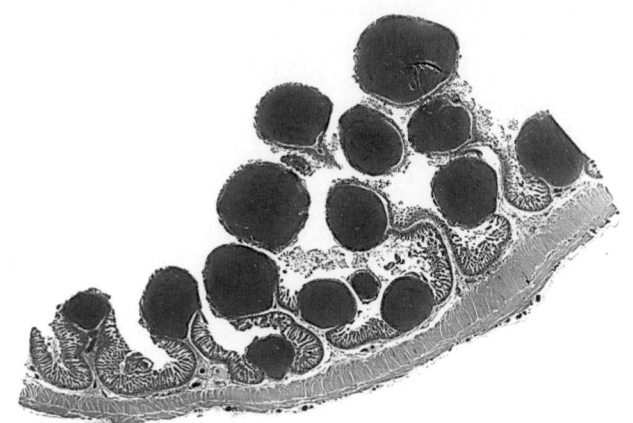

A

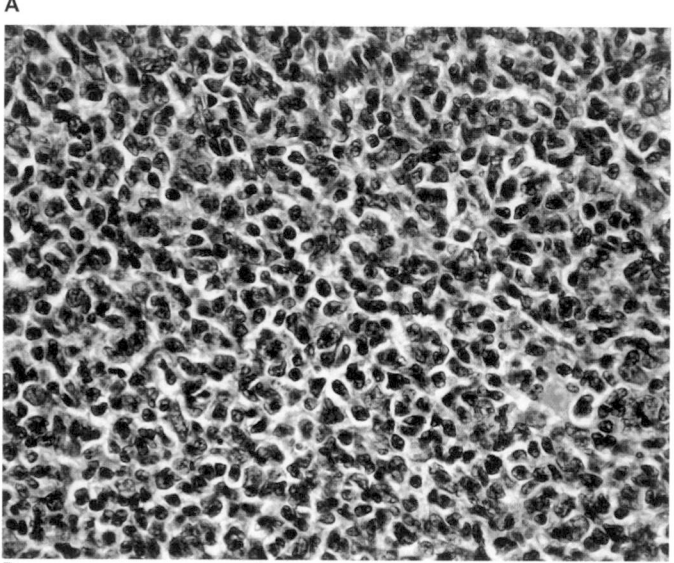

B

Fig. 11.218 A and **B,** Mantle cell lymphoma of large bowel resulting in so-called "lymphomatous polyposis." On high power (**B**), the tumor cells show irregularity of their nuclear contours.

incorrectly diagnosed as malignant lymphoma. Local excision is curative.

Langerhans' cell histiocytosis (histiocytosis X) can involve the gastrointestinal tract and be diagnosed by rectal biopsy.[1171]

Other hematolymphoid disorders that have been reported to involve the colorectal region include *true histiocytic lymphoma,*[1158] *dendritic follicular cell tumor,*[1157] and *mast cell sarcoma.*[1168]

Gastrointestinal stromal tumors and related tumors

The general features of GISTs are discussed in the Stomach chapter (p. 674) and will not be repeated here. In the large bowel, the ratio between GISTs (as currently defined on the basis of their immunoreactivity for CD34 and particularly CD117, regardless of whether they coexpress actin or not) and smooth muscle tumors (negative for both CD34 and CD117 and positive for actin and/or desmin) is different from the small bowel. GISTs still predominate, but the number of tumor-exhibiting clear-cut evidence of smooth muscle differentiation and lacking CD34 and CD117 immunoreactivity is greater.[1184,1185] The latter group includes the *leiomyosarcomas*, which tend to be polypoid and apparently associated with a better prognosis than GISTs[1184] and the superficial *leiomyomas* arising from the muscularis mucosae.[1186] These superficial leiomyomas are small, sharply circumscribed, and lack mitotic activity and necrosis. They also generally lack atypia, although occasional examples containing bizarre hyperchromatic nuclei ("symplasmic leiomyomas") are on record.[1186] A few of the leiomyosarcomas have been found to contain scattered osteoclast-like multinucleated giant cells, similar to those seen with a greater frequency in the uterus.[1188]

The prognostic criteria among the GISTs/leiomyosarcomas are similar to those in other locations of the gastrointestinal tract[1184,1185,1189] (see p. 674).

Tumors with the morphologic features of schwannoma occur in the colon and rectum.[1187] They most commonly present as polypoid masses. Immunohistochemically, they are reactive for S-100 protein, p75, type IV collagen and GFAP, and negative for CD117. A few are of the plexiform or epithelioid varieties.[1187]

Other tumors and tumorlike conditions

Tumorlike conditions include the *inflammatory myoglandular polyp*, a solitary pedunculated polypoid lesion of the left (especially sigmoid) colon, characterized by submucosal granulation tissue, proliferation of smooth muscle, and hyperplastic glands with occasional cystic dilatation.[1213]

Another tumorlike condition is represented by the *bizarre stromal cells* sometimes present in polyps and ulcers of the gastrointestinal tract; they are characterized by a pyramidal shape and a strongly basophilic cytoplasm. They represent reactive myofibroblastic cells and should not be confused with malignant cells.[1220]

Yet another pseudomalignant condition is the *florid vascular proliferation* that can result secondary to intussusception and muscular prolapse and which can be overdiagnosed as angiosarcoma.[1190]

Dermoid cyst has been recorded in the cecal region.[1234]

Vascular ectasias of the right colon are being increasingly recognized as an important cause of lower intestinal bleeding in the elderly. They have also been designated as angiomas, angiodysplasias, and arteriovenous malformations, these various names reflecting the uncertainty about their nature.[1192,1209,1215] An acquired pathogenesis seems likely for most cases. They have been reported in association with aortic stenosis[1230] and von Willebrand disease[1195] and are sometimes found to contain cholesterol emboli. The lesions are often small, multiple, and easily demonstrated by arteriography but may be difficult to identify in a colonic biopsy or after

they have collapsed following colectomy[1224]; injection with silicone rubber or other compounds followed by clearing of the specimen shows them dramatically[1226] (Fig. 11.219). These lesions should be distinguished from the *colonic varices* that may be seen as a complication of portal hypertension.[1228]

Hemangiomas rarely involve the large bowel. Most are of the cavernous type and may be multicentric.[1207] Others are of cellular type and occur in infants.[1202] *Pyogenic granulomas* (lobular capillary hemangiomas) also occur.[1236]

Lipomas of the large bowel are rare; they are invariably submucosal and therefore may intussuscept[1200] (Figs 11.220 and 11.221). Lipomas can also present in the form of multiple polyps in the colon.[1219] Some may exhibit atypical stromal cells and simulate malignancy.[1222] **Lipomatosis** of the ileocecal valve or other portions of the colon may be mistaken radiographically for a tumor.[1237]

Smooth muscle tumors are usually located in the rectum, where they tend to be small and benign.[1225] Those situated higher up in the colon have a higher incidence of malignancy.[1201,1203,1217] As in other sites of the gastrointestinal tract, tumor size is a good predictor of behavior.[1211] Occasionally, these tumors are multiple and associated with similar tumors in the small bowel.[1227,1238]

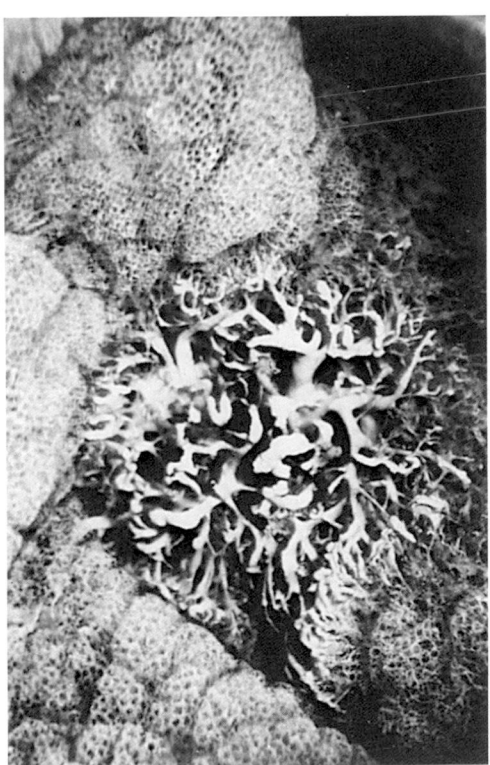

Fig. 11.219 Angiodysplasia of colonic mucosa demonstrated by silicone rubber injection and clearing of specimen. (Reprinted, by permission, from Case Records of the Massachusetts General Hospital—Weekly Clinicopathologic Exercises: Case 36-1974. N Engl J Med 1974, **291**: 569–575)

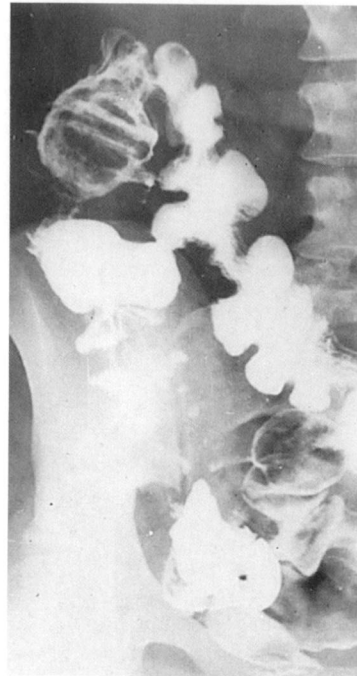

Fig. 11.220 Filling defect caused by lipoma. The appearance is highly characteristic.

A

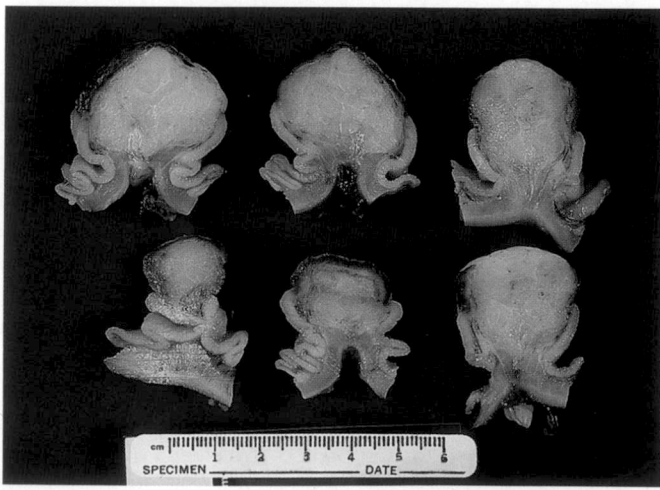

B

Fig. 11.221 A and **B**, Lipoma of colon, as seen from the mucosal surface and on cross section.

Diffuse ganglioneuromatosis can occur in association with Recklinghausen's disease,[1198,1221] with multiple endocrine neoplasia type IIB, or in the absence of either condition (Fig. 11.222).[1194] Most of these cases appear to arise from the neural plexuses in the bowel wall (transmural type), but others with a predominantly mucosal distribution (mucosal type) have been reported, sometimes in association with juvenile polyps, adenomatous polyps, and/or adenocarcinoma.[1193,1208,1223,1232]

Lymphangioleiomyomatosis can involve the colon in a diffuse fashion and be confused with leiomyomatosis[1199]; HMB-45 immunoreactivity is a key to the diagnosis.

Angiomyolipoma is a related tumor of HMB-45-positive smooth muscle cells that can occur in the large bowel, both in its conventional and epithelioid forms.[1205,1216]

Melanoma of the anorectal region is discussed on p. 865. Suffice it to say here that most cases of melanomas located in the lower rectum represent upward extensions or metastases of tumors originating in the anal canal.[1214]

Kaposi's sarcoma can involve the large bowel; occasionally, the disease may initially present with intestinal symptoms and simulate the appearance of ulcerative colitis, particularly in AIDS patients.[1218,1231]

Angiosarcoma can present as a solitary or multicentric mass; as in other sites, it may exceptionally develop from the granulation tissue that surrounds a foreign body.[1191] These tumors can be of the conventional or the epithelioid variety.[1229]

Other primary malignant tumors of the large bowel, all of them exceptionally rare, include *malignant fibrous histiocytoma*,[1212] *liposarcoma*,[1204] *carcinosarcoma*,[1233] *malignant rhabdoid tumor*,[1235] and *malignant giant cell tumor*.[1196] *Xanthogranuloma* has also been reported in this region.[1210]

Metastatic tumors occur as a part of a disseminated process. These tumors form disk-like areas in which there is a central area of ulceration; the normal mucosa

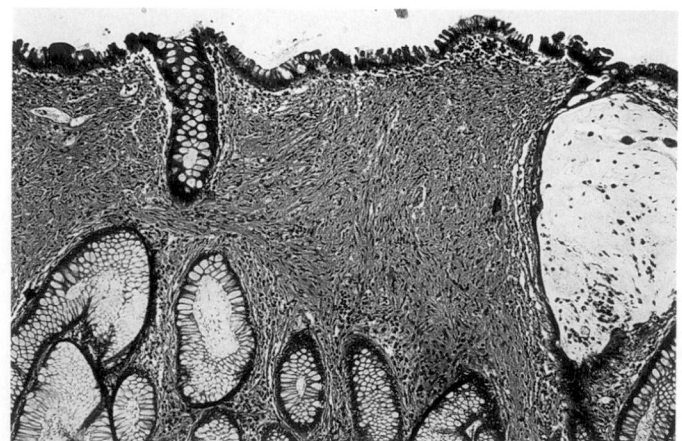

Fig. 11.222 Colonic ganglioneuromatosis. Tangled fascicles of Schwann-like spindle cells expand the lamina propria.

extends to the ulcer, giving indirect evidence that the metastatic focus began in the submucosa. This phenomenon is particularly common in malignant melanoma and primary carcinoma of the lung. Our most exotic case was the metastasis of a renal cell carcinoma to an intestinal carcinoid tumor, grossly simulating an adenomatous polyp.

Prostatic carcinoma can extend into the rectum and simulate a primary rectal neoplasm.[1197] Metastatic malignant mesothelioma has been seen presenting as multiple colonic polyps.[1206]

References

Normal anatomy

1 Azzopardi JG, Evans DJ. Mucoprotein-containing histiocytes (muciphages) in the rectum. J Clin Pathol 1966, **19**: 368–374.

2 Bartnik W, ReMine SG, Chiba M, Thayer WR, Shorter RG. Isolation and characterization of colonic intraepithelial and lamina propria lymphocytes. Gastroenterology 1980, **78**: 976–985.

3 Bejarano PA, Aranda-Michel J, Fenoglio-Preiser C. Histochemical and immunohistochemical characterization of foamy histiocytes (muciphages and xanthelasma) of the rectum. Am J Surg Pathol 2000, **24**: 1009–1015.

4 Cheng H, Leblond CP. Origin, differentiation and renewal of the four main epithelial cell types in the mouse small intestine. Part V. Unitarian theory of the origin of the four epithelial cell types. Am J Anat 1974, **141**: 537–561.

5 Filipe MI. Mucins in the human gastrointestinal epithelium. A review. Invest Cell Pathol 1979, **2**: 195–216.

6 Ghadially FN, Walley VM. Pigments of the gastrointestinal tract. A comparison of light microscopic and electron microscopic findings. Ultrastruct Pathol 1995, **19**: 213–220.

7 Kaye GI, Pascal RR, Lane N. The colonic pericryptal fibroblast sheath. Replication, migration, and cytodifferentiation of a mesenchymal cell system in adult tissue. III. Replication and differentiation in human hyperplastic and adenomatous polyps. Gastroenterology 1971, **60**: 515–536.

8 Kealy WF. Colonic lymphoid-glandular complex (microbursa). Nature and morphology. J Clin Pathol 1976, **29**: 241–244.

9 Leonard RCF, MacLennan ICM. Distribution of plasma cells in normal rectal mucosa. J Clin Pathol 1982, **35**: 820–823.

10 Levine DS, Haggitt RC. Normal histology of the colon. Am J Surg Pathol 1989, **13**: 966–984.

11 Levine DS, Haggitt RC. Colon. In Sternberg S (ed.): Histology for pathologists, ed. 2. Philadelphia, 1997, Lippincott-Raven, pp. 519–538.

12 Lewin KJ. The endocrine cells of the gastrointestinal tract. The normal endocrine cells and their hyperplasias. Pathol Annu 1986, **21**(Pt 1): 1–27.

13 Lord MG, Valies P, Broughton AC. A morphologic study of the submucosa of the large intestine. Surg Gynecol Obstet 1977, **145**: 55–60.

14 Lou TY, Teplitz C, Thayer WR. Ultrastructural morphogenesis of colonic PAS-positive macrophages ("colonic histiocytosis"). Hum Pathol 1971, **2**: 421–439.

15 McKinley M, Listrom MB, Fenoglio-Preiser CM. Cytokeratin 19. A potential marker of colonic differentiation. Surg Pathol 1990, **3**: 107–114.

16 O'Leary AD, Sweeney EC. Lymphoglandular complexes of the colon. Structure and distribution. Histopathology 1986, **10**: 267–283.

17 Salto-Tellez M, Price AB, Shepherd NA. The significance of muciphages in otherwise normal colorectal biopsies. What is the significance of muciphages in colorectal biopsies? Histopathology 2000, **36**: 556–562.

18 Shamsuddin AM, Phelps PC, Trump BF. Human large intestinal epithelium. Light microscopy, histochemistry, and ultrastructure. Hum Pathol 1982, **13**: 790–803.

19 Steer HW, Colin-Jones DG. Melanosis coli. Studies of the toxic effects of irritant purgatives. J Pathol 1975, **115**: 199–205.

20 Symonds DA. Paneth cell metaplasia in diseases of the colon and rectum. Arch Pathol 1974, **97**: 343–347.

21 Walker NI, Bennett RE, Axelsen RA. Melanosis coli. A consequence of anthraquinone-induced apoptosis of colonic epithelial cells. Am J Pathol 1988, **131**: 465–476.

22 Williams I. Innominate grooves in the surface of mucosa. Radiology 1965, **84**: 877–880.

Hirschsprung's disease and related disorders

23 Abu-Alfa AK, Kuan SF, West AB, Reyes-Mugica M. Cathepsin D in intestinal ganglion cells: a potential aid to diagnosis in suspected Hirschsprung's disease. Am J Surg Pathol 1997, **21**: 201–205.

24 Aldridge RT, Campbell PE. Ganglion cell distribution in the normal rectum and anal canal. A basis for the diagnosis of Hirschsprung's disease by anorectal biopsy. J Pediatr Surg 1968, **3**: 475–490.

25 Amiel J, Lyonnet S. Hirschsprung disease, associated syndromes, and genetics: a review. J Med Genet 2001, **38**: 729–739.

26 Ariel I, Vinograd I, Lernau OZ, Nissan S, Rosenmann E. Rectal mucosal biopsy in aganglionosis and allied conditions. Hum Pathol 1983, **14**: 991–995.

27 Barr LC, Booth J, Filipe MI, Lawson JON. Clinical evaluation of the histochemical diagnosis of Hirschsprung's disease. Gut 1985, **26**: 393–399.

28 Bickler SW, Harrison MW, Campbell TJ, Campbell JR. Long-segment Hirschsprung's disease. Arch Surg 1992, **127**: 1047–1050.

29 Blisard KS, Kleinman R. Hirschsprung's disease. A clinical and pathologic overview. Hum Pathol 1986, **17**: 1189–1191.

30 Causse E, Vaysse P, Fabre J, Valdiguie P, Thouvenot J-P. The diagnostic value of acetylcholinesterase/butyrylcholinesterase ratio in Hirschsprung's disease. Am J Clin Pathol 1987, **88**: 477–480.

31 Challa VR, Moran JR, Turner CS, Lyerly AD. Histologic diagnosis of Hirschsprung's disease. The value of concurrent hematoxylin and eosin and cholinesterase staining of rectal biopsies. Am J Clin Pathol 1987, **88**: 324–328.

32 Chetty R, Govender D. Mucosal prolapse changes in Hirschsprung's disease. Histopathology 1997, **30**: 324–327.

33 Cohen MC, Moore SW, Neveling U, Kaschula RO. Acquired aganglionosis following surgery for Hirschsprung's disease. A report of five cases during a 33-year experience with pull-through procedures. Histopathology 1993, **22**: 163–168.

34 Crocker NL, Messmer JM. Adult Hirschsprung's disease. Clin Radiol 1991, **44**: 257–259.

35 Deguchi E, Iwai N, Goto Y, Yanagihara J, Fushiki S. An immunohistochemical study of neurofilament and microtubule-associated Tau protein in the enteric innervation in Hirschsprung's disease. J Pediatr Surg 1993, **28**: 886–890.

36 Dimmick JE, Bove KE. Cytomegalovirus infection of the bowel in infancy. Pathogenetic and diagnostic significance. Pediatr Pathol 1984, **2**: 95–102.

37 Drut R, Drut RM. Hyperplasia of lymphoglandular complexes in colon segments in Hirschsprung's disease. A form of diversion colitis. Pediatr Pathol 1992, **12**: 575–581.

38 Eng C. Seminars in medicine of the Beth Israel Hospital, Boston. The RET proto-oncogene in multiple endocrine neoplasia type 2 and Hirschsprung's disease. N Engl J Med 1996, **335**: 943–951.

39 Engum SA, Petrites M, Rescorla FJ, Grosfeld JL, Morrison AM, Engles D. Familial Hirschsprung's disease. 20 cases in 12 kindreds. J Pediatr Surg 1993, **28**: 1286–1290.

40 Gherardi GJ. Pathology of the ganglionic-aganglionic junction in congenital megacolon. Arch Pathol 1960, **69:** 520–523.

41 Hall CL, Lampert PW. Immunohistochemistry as an aid in the diagnosis of Hirschsprung's disease. Am J Clin Pathol 1985, **83:** 177–181.

42 Hirobe S, Doody DP, Ryan DP, Kim SH, Donahoe PK. Ectopic class II major histocompatibility antigens in Hirschsprung's disease and neuronal intestinal dysplasia. J Pediatr Surg 1992, **27:** 357–362.

43 Hirose R, Hirata Y, Yamada T, Kawana T, Taguchi T, Suita S. The simple technique of rectal mucosal biopsy for the diagnosis of Hirschsprung's disease. J Pediatr Surg 1993, **28:** 942–944.

44 Ikeda K, Goto S. Diagnosis and treatment of Hirschsprung's disease in Japan. An analysis of 1628 patients. Ann Surg 1984, **199:** 400–405.

45 Ikeda K, Goto S. Total colonic aganglionosis with or without small bowel involvement. An analysis of 137 patients. J Pediatr Surg 1986, **21:** 319–322.

46 Imamura A, Puri P, O'Briain DS, Reen DJ. Mucosal immune defence mechanisms in enterocolitis complicating Hirschsprung's disease. Gut 1992, **33:** 801–806.

47 Ito Y, Tatekawa I, Nishiyama F, Hirano H. Ultrastructural localization of acetylcholinesterase activity in Hirschsprung's disease. Arch Pathol Lab Med 1987, **111:** 161–165.

48 Johanson JF, Carney JA, Go VL, Koch TR. Segmental distribution of colonic neuropeptides in Hirschsprung's disease. Regul Pept 1991, **36:** 59–69.

49 Kadair RG, Sims JE, Critchfield CF. Zonal colonic hypoganglionosis. JAMA 1977, **238:** 1838–1840.

50 Kapur RP. Contemporary approaches toward understanding the pathogenesis of Hirschsprung disease. Pediatr Pathol 1993, **13:** 83–100.

51 Klein MD, Philippart AI. Hirschsprung's disease. Three decades' experience at a single institution. J Pediatr Surg 1993, **28:** 1291–1294.

52 Lally KP, Chwals WJ, Weitzman JJ, Black T, Singh S. Hirschsprung's disease. A possible cause of anastomotic failure following repair of intestinal atresia. J Pediatr Surg 1992, **27:** 469–470.

53 Larsson LT, Malmfors G, Ekblad E, Ekman R, Sundler F. NPY hyperinnervation in Hirschsprung's disease. Both adrenergic and nonadrenergic fibers contribute. J Pediatr Surg 1991, **26:** 1207–1214.

54 Lumb PD, Moore L. Back to the drawing board. Intestinal neuronal dysplasia type B: not a histological entity yet. Virchows Arch 1998, **432:** 99–102.

55 MacMahon RA, Moore CCM, Cussen LJ. Hirschsprung-like syndromes in patients with normal ganglion cells on suction rectal biopsy. J Pediatr Surg 1981, **16:** 835–839.

56 Maia DM. The reliability of frozen-section diagnosis in pathologic evaluation of Hirschsprung's disease. Am J Surg Pathol 2000, **24:** 1675–1677.

57 Meier-Ruge W. Hirschsprung's disease. Its aetiology, pathogenesis and differential diagnosis. In Grundmann E, Kirsten WH (eds.): Current topics in pathology, vol. 59. New York, 1974, Springer-Verlag.

58 Meier-Ruge W, Lutterbeck PM, Herzog B, Morger R, Moser R, Schärli A. Acetylcholinesterase activity in suction biopsies of the rectum in the diagnosis of Hirschsprung's disease. J Pediatr Surg 1972, **7:** 11–17.

59 Monforte-Munoz H, Gonzalez-Gomez I, Rowland JM, Landing BH. Increased submucosal nerve trunk caliber in aganglionosis: a "positive" and objective finding in suction biopsies and segmental resections in Hirschsprung's disease. Arch Pathol Lab Med 1998, **122:** 721–725.

60 Moore SW, Rode H, Millar AJ, Albertyn R, Cywes S. Familial aspects of Hirschsprung's disease. Eur J Pediatr Surg 1991, **1:** 97–101.

61 N-Fékété C, Ricour C, Martelli H, Lortat Jacob S, Pellerin D. Total colonic aganglionosis (with or without ileal involvement). A review of 27 cases. J Pediatr Surg 1986, **21:** 251–254.

62 Patrick WJA, Besley GTN, Smith II. Histochemical diagnosis of Hirschsprung's disease and a comparison of the histochemical and biochemical activity of acetylcholinesterase in rectal mucosal biopsies. J Clin Pathol 1980, **33:** 336–343.

63 Qualman SJ, Murray R. Aganglionosis and related disorders. Hum Pathol 1994, **25:** 1141–1149.

64 Rescorla FJ, Morrison AM, Engles D, West KW, Grosfeld JL. Hirschsprung's disease. Evaluation of mortality and long-term function in 260 cases. Arch Surg 1992, **127:** 934–941.

65 Rolle U, Piasecza Piotrowska A, Nemeth L, Puri P. Altered distribution of interstitial cells of Cajal in Hirschsprung disease. Arch Pathol Lab Med 2002, **126:** 928–933.

66 Romanska HM, Bishop AE, Brereton RJ, Spitz L, Polak JM. Immunocytochemistry for neuronal markers shows deficiencies in conventional histology in the treatment of Hirschsprung's disease. J Pediatr Surg 1993, **28:** 1059–1062.

67 Ryan ET, Ecker JL, Christakis NA, Folkman J. Hirschsprung's disease. Associated abnormalities and demography. J Pediatr Surg 1992, **27:** 76–81.

68 Sams VR, Bobrow LG, Happerfield L, Keeling J. Evaluation of PGP 9.5 in the diagnosis of Hirschsprung's disease. J Pathol 1992, **168:** 55–58.

69 Schärli AF, Meier-Ruge W. Localized and disseminated forms of neuronal intestinal dysplasia mimicking Hirschsprung's disease. J Pediatr Surg 1981, **16:** 164–170.

70 Schofield DE, Yunis EJ. What is intestinal neuronal dysplasia? Pathol Annu 1992, **27**(Pt 1): 249–262.

71 Sieber WK. Hirschsprung's disease. In Welch KJ, Randolph JG, Ravitch MM (eds.): Pediatric surgery, ed. 4. Chicago, 1986, Year Book Medical Publishers.

72 Soeda J, O'Briain DS, Puri P. Mucosal neuroendocrine cell abnormalities in the colon of patients with Hirschsprung's disease. J Pediatr Surg 1992, **27:** 823–827.

73 Stannard VA, Fowler C, Robinson L, Besner G, Glick PL, Allen JE, Jewett TC, Cooney DR. Familial Hirschsprung's disease. Report of autosomal dominant and probable recessive X-linked kindreds. J Pediatr Surg 1991, **26:** 591–594.

74 Staple TW, McAlister WH, Anderson MS. Plexiform neurofibromatosis of the colon simulating Hirschsprung's disease. Am J Roentgenol Radium Ther Nucl Med 1964, **91:** 840–845.

74a Streutker CJ, Huizinga JD, Campbell F, Ho J, Riddell RH. Loss of CD117 (c-kit)- and CD34-positive ICC and associated CD34-positive fibroblasts defines a subpopulation of chronic intestinal pseudo-obstruction. Am J Surg Pathol 2003, **27:** 228–235.

75 Swenson O, Fisher JH, MacMahon HE. Rectal biopsy as an aid in the diagnosis of Hirschsprung's disease. N Engl J Med 1955, **253:** 632–635.

76 Swenson O. Hirschsprung's disease: a review. Pediatrics 2002, **109:** 914–918.

77 Taguchi T, Tanaka K, Ikeda K. Fibromuscular dysplasia of arteries in Hirschsprung's disease. Gastroenterology 1985, **88:** 1099–1103.

78 Taguchi T, Tanaka K, Ikeda K. Immunohistochemical study of neuron specific enolase and S-100 protein in Hirschsprung's disease. Virchows Arch [A] 1985, **405:** 399–409.

79 Tam PKH, Lister J. Development profile of neuron-specific enolase in human gut and its implications in Hirschsprung's disease. Gastroenterology 1986, **90:** 1901–1906.

80 Tam PK, Owen G. An immunohistochemical study of neuronal microtubule-associated proteins in Hirschsprung's disease. Hum Pathol 1993, **24:** 424–431.

81 Tam PK, Quint WG, van Velzen D. Hirschsprung's disease. A viral etiology? Pediatr Pathol 1992, **12:** 807–810.

82 Venugopal S, Mancer K, Shandling B. The validity of rectal biopsy in relation to morphology and distribution of ganglion cells. J Pediatr Surg 1981, **16**: 433–437.

83 Vinores SA, May E. Neuron-specific enolase as an immunohistochemical tool for the diagnosis of Hirschsprung's disease. Am J Surg Pathol 1985, **9**: 281–285.

84 Watanatittan S, Suwatanaviroj A, Limprutithum T, Rattanasuwan T. Association of Hirschsprung's disease and anorectal malformation. J Pediatr Surg 1991, **26**: 192–195.

85 Weinberg AG. The anorectal myenteric plexus. Its relation to hypoganglionosis of the colon. Am J Clin Pathol 1970, **54**: 637–642.

86 Weinberg AG. Hirschsprung's disease. A pathologist's view. In Rosenberg HS, Bolande RP (eds.): Perspectives in pediatric pathology, vol. 2. Chicago, 1975, Year Book Medical Publishers.

87 Yamataka A, Miyano T, Okazaki T, Nishiye H. Correlation between extrinsic nerve fibers and synapses in the muscle layers of bowels affected by Hirschsprung's disease. J Pediatr Surg 1992, **27**: 1213–1216.

88 Yamataka A, Miyano T, Urao M, Nishiye H. Hirschsprung's disease. Diagnosis using monoclonal antibody 171B5. J Pediatr Surg 1992, **27**: 820–822.

89 Yang S, Donner LR. Detection of ganglion cells in the colonic plexuses by immunostaining for neuron-specific marker NeuN: an aid for the diagnosis of Hirschsprung disease. Appl Immunohistochem Mol Morphol 2002, **10**: 218–220.

90 Yunis EJ, Dibbins AW, Sherman FE. Rectal suction biopsy in the diagnosis of Hirschsprung's disease in infants. Arch Pathol Lab Med 1976, **100**: 329–333.

Diverticulosis

91 Almy TP, Howell DA. Diverticular disease of the colon. N Engl J Med 1980, **302**: 324–331.

92 Bak M. Nodular intra-abdominal panniculitis: an accompaniment of colorectal carcinoma and diverticular disease. Histopathology 1996, **29**: 21–27.

93 Bateman AC, Beer TW, Bass PS, Odurny A, Gallagher PJ. Massive arterial haemorrhage from the lower gastrointestinal tract. Histopathology 1996, **29**: 225–231.

94 Bova JG, Hopens TA, Goldstein HM. Diverticulitis of the right colon. Dig Dis Sci 1984, **29**: 150–156.

95 Burroughs SH, Bowrey DJ, Morris-Stiff GJ, Williams GT. Granulomatous inflammation in sigmoid diverticulitis: two diseases or one? Histopathology 1998, **33**: 349–353.

96 Eng K, Ranson JHC, Localio SA. Resection of the perforated segment. A significant advance in treatment of diverticulitis with free perforation or abscess. Am J Surg 1977, **133**: 67–72.

97 Fisher N, Berry CS, Fearn T, Gregory JA, Hardy J. Cereal dietary fiber consumption and diverticular disease. A lifespan study in rats. Am J Clin Nutr 1985, **42**: 788–804.

98 Giffin JM, Butcher HR Jr, Ackerman LV. The surgical management of colonic diverticulitis. Arch Surg 1967, **94**: 619–626.

99 Goldstein NS, Ahmad E. Histology of the mucosa in sigmoid colon specimens with diverticular disease. Observations for the interpretation of sigmoid colonoscopic biopsy specimens. Am J Clin Pathol 1997, **107**: 438–444.

100 Goldstein NS, Leon-Armin C, Mani A. Crohn's colitis-like changes in sigmoid diverticulitis specimens is usually an idiosyncratic inflammatory response to the diverticulosis rather than Crohn's colitis. Am J Surg Pathol 2000, **24**: 668–675.

101 Gouge TH, Coppa GF, Eng K, Ranson JHC, Localio SA. Management of diverticulitis of the ascending colon. Ten years' experience. Am J Surg 1983, **145**: 387–391.

102 Hackford AW, Veidenheimer MC. Diverticular disease of the colon. Current concepts and management. Surg Clin North Am 1985, **65**: 347–363.

103 Himal HS, Ashby DB, Duignan JP, Richardson DM, Miller SL, MacLean LD. Management of perforating diverticulitis of the colon. Surg Gynecol Obstet 1977, **144**: 225–226.

104 Hughes LE. Portmortem survey of diverticular disease of the colon. Part I. Diverticulosis and diverticulitis. Part II. The muscular abnormality in the sigmoid colon. Gut 1969, **10**: 336–351.

105 Kelly JK. Polypoid prolapsing mucosal folds in diverticular disease. Am J Surg Pathol 1991, **15**: 871–878.

106 Magness LJ, Sanfelippo PM, van Heerden JA, Judd ES. Diverticular disease of the right colon. Surg Gynecol Obstet 1975, **140**: 30–32.

107 Makapugay LM, Dean PJ. Diverticular disease-associated chronic colitis. Am J Surg Pathol 1996, **20**: 94–102.

108 Markham NI, Li AK. Diverticulitis of the right colon – experience from Hong Kong. Gut 1992, **33**: 547–549.

109 Meyers MA, Alonso DR, Gray GF, Baier JW. Pathogenesis of bleeding colonic diverticulosis. Gastroenterology 1976, **71**: 577–583.

110 Morson BC. The muscle abnormality in diverticular disease of the colon. Proc R Soc Med 1963, **56**: 798–800.

111 Nicholas ER, Frymark WB, Raffensperger JR. Acute cecal diverticulitis. Report of 25 cases. JAMA 1962, **182**: 157–160.

112 Painter NS, Burkitt DP. Diverticular disease of the colon. A deficiency disease of Western civilization. Br Med J 1971, **2**: 450–454.

113 Prescott RJ, Haboubi NY, Dunaway DJ, Kiff ES. Carcinoma arising in a diverticulum of sigmoid colon. Histopathology 1992, **21**: 387–389.

114 Ravo B, Khan SA, Ger R, Mishrick A, Soroff HS. Unusual extraperitoneal presentations of diverticulitis. Am J Gastroenterol 1985, **80**: 346–351.

115 Smirniotis V, Tsoutsos D, Fotopoulos A, Pissiotis AC. Perforated diverticulitis. A surgical dilemma. Int Surg 1992, **77**: 44–47.

116 Sorger K, Wacks MR. Exsanguinating arterial bleeding associated with diverticulating disease of the colon. Arch Surg 1971, **102**: 9–14.

117 Sugihara K, Muto T, Morioka T, Asano A, Yamamoto T. Diverticular disease of the colon in Japan. A review of 615 cases. Dis Colon Rectum 1984, **27**: 531–537.

118 Talbot JM. Role of dietary fiber in diverticular disease and colon cancer. Fed Proc 1981, **40**: 2337–2342.

119 Warshaw AL, Welch JP, Ottinger LW. Acute perforation of the colon associated with chronic corticosteroid therapy. Am J Surg 1976, **131**: 442–446.

Colitis

120 Podolsky DK. Inflammatory bowel disease. N Engl J Med 2002, **347**: 417–429.

Ulcerative colitis

121 Akwari OE, Van Heerden JA, Foulk WT, Baggenstoss AH. Cancer of the bile ducts associated with ulcerative colitis. Ann Surg 1975, **181**: 303–309.

122 Allen DC, Biggart JD. Misplaced epithelium in ulcerative colitis and Crohn's disease of the colon and its relationship to malignant mucosal changes. Histopathology 1986, **10**: 37–52.

123 Ambroze WL Jr, Pemberton JH, Dozois RR, Carpenter HA, O'Rourke JS, Ilstrup DM. The histological pattern and pathological involvement of the anal transition zone in patients with ulcerative colitis. Gastroenterology 1993, **104**: 514–518.

124 Berman JJ, Ullah A. Colonic metaplasia of ileostomies. Biological significance for ulcerative colitis patients following total colectomy. Am J Surg Pathol 1989, **13**: 955–960.

125 Bischoff SC, Wedemeyer J, Herrmann A, Meier PN, Trautwein C, Cetin Y, Maschek H, Stolte M, Gebel M, Manns MP. Quantitative assessment of intestinal eosinophils and mast cells in inflammatory bowel disease. Histopathology 1996, **28**: 1–13.

126 Broome U, Lindberg G, Lofberg R. Primary sclerosing cholangitis in ulcerative colitis – a risk factor for the development of dysplasia and DNA aneuploidy? Gastroenterology 1992, **102:** 1877–1880.

127 Chambers TJ, Morson BC. Large bowel biopsy in the differential diagnosis of inflammatory bowel disease. Invest Cell Pathol 1980, **3:** 159–173.

128 Dhillon AP, Anthony A, Sim R, Wakefield AJ, Sankey EA, Hudson M, Allison MC, Pounder RE. Mucosal capillary thrombi in rectal biopsies. Histopathology 1992, **21:** 127–133.

129 Dundas SA, Dutton J, Skipworth P. Reliability of rectal biopsy in distinguishing between chronic inflammatory bowel disease and acute self-limiting colitis. Histopathology 1997, **31:** 60–66.

130 Dyson JL. Herniation of mucosal epithelium into the submucosa in chronic ulcerative colitis. J Clin Pathol 1975, **38:** 189–194.

131 Farmer RG, Easley KA, Rankin GB. Clinical patterns, natural history, and progression of ulcerative colitis. A long-term follow-up of 1116 patients. Dig Dis Sci 1993, **38:** 1137–1146.

132 Folley JH. Ulcerative proctitis. N Engl J Med 1970, **282:** 1362–1364.

133 Franklin WA, McDonald GB, Stein HO, Gatter KC, Jewell DP, Clarke LC, Mason DY. Immunohistologic demonstration of abnormal colonic crypt cell kinetics in ulcerative colitis. Hum Pathol 1985, **16:** 1129–1132.

134 Garland CF, Lilienfeld AM, Mendeloff AI, Markowitz JA, Terrell KB, Garland FC. Incidence rates of ulcerative colitis and Crohn's disease in fifteen areas of the United States. Gastroenterology 1981, **81:** 1115–1124.

135 Goldblum JR, Appelman HD. Appendiceal involvement in ulcerative colitis. Mod Pathol 1992, **5:** 607–610.

136 Goldman H. Colonic mucosal biopsy in inflammatory bowel disease. Surg Pathol 1991, **4:** 3–24.

137 Goldman H, Antonioli DA. Mucosal biopsy of the rectum, colon, and distal ileum. Hum Pathol 1982, **13:** 981–1012.

138 Goldman J, Hinrichs R, Glotzer DJ, Gardner RC, Zeitzel L. Ulcerative versus granulomatous colitis. Lab Invest 1970, **22:** 497–498.

139 Goldstein NS, Sanford WW, Bodzin JH. Crohn's-like complications in patients with ulcerative colitis after total proctocolectomy and ileal pouch-anal anastomosis. Am J Surg Pathol 1997, **21:** 1343–1353.

140 Gryboski JD. Ulcerative colitis in children 10 years old or younger. J Pediatr Gastroenterol Nutr 1993, **17:** 24–31.

141 Haruta J, Kusugami K, Kuroiwa A, Ina K, Shinoda M, Morise K, Iokawa H, Morita M, Ishihara A, Sarai S. Phenotypic and functional analysis of lamina propria mononuclear cells from colonoscopic biopsy specimens in patients with ulcerative colitis. Am J Gastroenterol 1992, **87:** 448–454.

142 Haworth AC, Manley PN, Groll A, Pace R. Bile duct carcinoma and biliary tract dysplasia in chronic ulcerative colitis. Arch Pathol Lab Med 1989, **113:** 434–436.

143 Hellstrom HR, Fisher ER. Estimation of mucosal mucin as an aid in the differentiation of Crohn's disease of the colon and chronic ulcerative colitis. Am J Clin Pathol 1967, **48:** 259–268.

144 Herzog K, Goldblum JR. Gallbladder adenocarcinoma and acalculous chronic lymphoplasmacytic cholecystitis associated with ulcerative colitis corrected. Mod Pathol 1996, **9:** 194–198.

145 Jessurun J, Paplanus SH, Nagle RB, Hamilton SR, Yardley JH, Tripp M. Pseudosarcomatous changes in inflammatory pseudopolyps of the colon. Arch Pathol Lab Med 1986, **110:** 833–836.

146 Kanemitsu T, Koike A, Yamamoto S. Study of the cell proliferation kinetics in ulcerative colitis, adenomatous polyps, and cancer. Cancer 1985, **56:** 1094–1098.

147 Kedziora JA, Wolff M, Chang J. Limited form of Wegener's granulomatosis in ulcerative colitis. Am J Roentgenol Radium Ther Nucl Med 1975, **125:** 127–133.

148 Kelly JK, Langevin JM, Price LM, Hershfield NB, Share S, Blustein P. Giant and symptomatic inflammatory polyps of the colon in idiopathic inflammatory bowel disease. Am J Surg Pathol 1986, **10:** 420–428.

149 Keren DF, Appelman HD, Dobbins WO III, Wells JJ, Whisenant B, Foley J, Dieterle R, Geisinger K. Correlation of histopathologic evidence of disease activity with the presence of immunoglobulin-containing cells in the colons of patients with inflammatory bowel disease. Hum Pathol 1984, **15:** 757–763.

150 Kim YS, Byrd JC. Ulcerative colitis. A specific mucin defect? Gastroenterology 1984, **87:** 1193–1195.

151 King T, Biddle W, Bhatia P, Moore J, Miner PB Jr. Colonic mucosal mast cell distribution at line of demarcation of active ulcerative colitis. Dig Dis Sci 1992, **37:** 490–495.

152 Kirsner JB. Ulcerative colitis; mysterious, multiplex, and menacing. J Chronic Dis 1971, **23:** 681–684.

153 Kjeldsen J. Treatment of ulcerative colitis with high doses of oral prednisolone. The rate of remission, the need for surgery, and the effect of prolonging the treatment. Scand J Gastroenterol 1993, **28:** 821–826.

154 Kleer CG, Appelman HD. Ulcerative colitis: patterns of involvement in colorectal biopsies and changes with time. Am J Surg Pathol 1998, **22:** 983–989.

155 Koltun WA, Schoetz DJ Jr, Roberts PL, Murray JJ, Coller JA, Veidenheimer MC. Indeterminate colitis predisposes to perineal complications after ileal pouch-anal anastomosis. Dis Colon Rectum 1991, **34:** 857–860.

156 Lee KS, Medline A, Shockey S. Indeterminate colitis in the spectrum of inflammatory bowel disease. Arch Pathol Lab Med 1979, **103:** 173–176.

157 Lee RG. Villous regeneration in ulcerative colitis. Arch Pathol Lab Med 1987, **111:** 276–278.

158 Lennard-Jones JE, Ritchie JK, Hilde W, Spicer CC. Assessment of severity in colitis. Gut 1975, **16:** 579–584.

159 Mahadeva U, Martin JP, Patel NK, Price AB. Granulomatous ulcerative colitis: a re-appraisal of the mucosal granuloma in the distinction of Crohn's disease from ulcerative colitis. Histopathology 2002, **41:** 50–55.

160 Markowitz J, Kahn E, Grancher K, Hyams J, Treem W, Daum F. Atypical rectosigmoid histology in children with newly diagnosed ulcerative colitis. Am J Gastroenterol 1993, **88:** 2034–2037.

161 Mayberry JS. Some aspects of the epidemiology of ulcerative colitis. Gut 1985, **26:** 968–974.

162 McAuley RL, Sommers SC. Mast cells in nonspecific ulcerative colitis. Am J Dig Dis 1961, **6:** 233–236.

163 McLeod RS. Chronic ulcerative colitis. Traditional surgical techniques. Surg Clin North Am 1993, **73:** 891–908.

164 Morowitz DA, Glagov S, Dordal E, Kirsner JB. Carcinoma of the biliary tract complicating chronic ulcerative colitis. Cancer 1971, **27:** 356–361.

165 Morson B. Current concepts of colitis. Lecture 1. Trans Med Soc Lond 1970, **86:** 159–176.

166 Morson B. Crohn's disease. Lecture 2. Trans Med Soc Lond 1970, **86:** 177–192.

166a Odze R. Diagnostic problems and advances in inflammatory bowel disease. Mod Pathol 2003, **16:** 347–358.

167 Odze R, Antonioli D, Peppercorn M, Goldman H. Effect of topical 5-aminosalicylic acid (5-ASA) therapy on rectal mucosal biopsy morphology in chronic ulcerative colitis. Am J Surg Pathol 1993, **17:** 869–875.

168 Pitt MA, Knox WF, Haboubi NY. Multinucleated stromal giant cells of the colonic lamina propria in ulcerative colitis. J Clin Pathol 1993, **46:** 874–875.

169 Podolsky DK. Inflammatory bowel disease. N Engl J Med 1991, **325:** 928–937, 1008–1016.

170 Rasmussen HH, Fallingborg J, Mortensen PB, Freund L,

Tage-Jensen U, Kruse V, Rasmussen SN. Primary sclerosing cholangitis in patients with ulcerative colitis. Scand J Gastroenterol 1992, **27**: 732–736.

171 Riddell RH, Goldman H, Ransohoff DF, Appelman HD, Fenoglio CM, Haggitt RC, Ahren C, Correa P, Hamilton SR, Morson BC, Sommers SC, Yardley JH. Dysplasia in inflammatory bowel disease. Standardized classification with provisional clinical applications. Hum Pathol 1983, **14**: 931–968.

172 Ritchie JK, Allan RM, Macartney J, Thompson H, Hawley PR, Cooke WT. Biliary tract carcinoma associated with ulcerative colitis. Q J Med 1974, **43**: 263–279.

173 Rubio CA. Ectopic colonic mucosa in ulcerative colitis and in Crohn's disease of the colon. Dis Colon Rectum 1984, **27**: 182–186.

174 Schachter H, Goldstein MJ, Rappaport H, Fennessy JJ, Kirsner JB. Ulcerative and "granulomatous" colitis – validity of differential diagnostic criteria. A study of 100 patients treated by total colectomy. Ann Intern Med 1970, **72**: 841–851.

175 Scott IS, Sheaff M, Coumbe A, Feakins RM, Rampton DS. Appendiceal inflammation in ulcerative colitis. Histopathology 1998, **33**: 168–173.

176 Shepherd NA, Healey CJ, Warren BF, Richman PI, Thomson WH, Wilkinson SP. Distribution of mucosal pathology and an assessment of colonic phenotypic change in the pelvic ileal reservoir. Gut 1993, **34**: 101–105.

177 Soundy VC, Davies SE, Warren BF. The double muscularis mucosa in ulcerative colitis: is it all new? Histopathology 1998, **32**: 484–485.

178 Symonds DA. Paneth cell metaplasia in diseases of the colon and rectum. Arch Pathol 1974, **97**: 343–347.

179 Valdez R, Appelman HD, Bronner MP, Greenson JK. Diffuse duodenitis associated with ulcerative colitis. Am J Surg Pathol 2000, **24**: 1407–1413.

180 Waraich T, Sarsfield P, Wright DH. The accessory cell populations in ulcerative colitis: a comparison between the colon and appendix in colitis and acute appendicitis. Hum Pathol 1997, **28**: 297–303.

181 Warren BF, Shepherd NA, Bartolo DC, Bradfield JW. Pathology of the defunctioned rectum in ulcerative colitis. Gut 1993, **34**: 514–516.

182 Watson AJ, Roy AD. Paneth cells in the large intestine in ulcerative colitis. J Pathol Bacteriol 1960, **80**: 309–316.

183 Wells AD, McMillan I, Price AB, Ritchie JK, Nicholls RJ. Natural history of indeterminate colitis. Br J Surg 1991, **78**: 179–181.

184 Whitehead R. Mucosal biopsy of the gastrointestinal tract. In Bennington JL (consulting ed): Major problems in pathology, vol. 3, ed. 3. Philadelphia, 1985, W.B. Saunders.

Carcinoma and dysplasia in ulcerative colitis

185 Allen DC, Biggart JD, Orchin JC, Foster H. An immunoperoxidase study of epithelial marker antigens in ulcerative colitis with dysplasia and carcinoma. J Clin Pathol 1985, **38**: 18–29.

186 Allen DC, Biggart JD, Pyper PC. Large bowel mucosal dysplasia and carcinoma in ulcerative colitis. J Clin Pathol 1985, **38**: 30–43.

187 Allen DC, Hamilton PW, Watt PCH, Biggart JD. Morphometrical analysis in ulcerative colitis with dysplasia and carcinoma. Histopathology 1987, **11**: 913–926.

188 Andrews CW Jr, O'Hara CJ, Goldman H, Mercurio AM, Silverman ML, Steele GD Jr. Sucrase-isomaltase expression in chronic ulcerative colitis and dysplasia. Hum Pathol 1992, **23**: 774–779.

189 Arai N, Mitomi H, Ohtani Y, Igarashi M, Kakita A, Okayasu I. Enhanced epithelial cell turnover associated with p53 accumulation and high p21$^{WAF?CIP!}$ expression in ulcerative colitis. Mod Pathol 1999, **12**: 604–611.

190 Aust DE, Willenbucher RF, Terdiman JP, Ferrell LD, Chang CG, Moore DH II, Molinaro-Clark A, Baretton GB, Loehrs U,

Waldman FM. Chromosomal alterations in ulcerative colitis-related and sporadic colorectal cancers by comparative genomic hybridization. Hum Pathol 2000, **31**: 109–114.

191 Bernstein CN, Shanahan F, Weinstein WM. Are we telling patients the truth about surveillance colonoscopy in ulcerative colitis? Lancet 1994, **343**: 71–74.

192 Burmer GC, Rabinovitch PS, Haggitt RC, Crispin DA, Brentnall TA, Kolli VR, Stevens AC, Rubin CE. Neoplastic progression in ulcerative colitis. Histology, DNA content, and loss of a p53 allele. Gastroenterology 1992, **103**: 1602–1610.

193 Butt JH, Konishi F, Morson BC, Lennard-Jones JE, Ritchie JK. Macroscopic lesions and dysplasia and carcinoma complicating ulcerative colitis. Dig Dis Sci 1983, **28**: 18–26.

194 Chaubert P, Benhattar J, Saraga E, Costa J. K-*ras* mutations and p53 alterations in neoplastic and nonneoplastic lesions associated with longstanding ulcerative colitis. Am J Pathol 1994, **144**: 767–775.

195 Chen J, Compton C, Cheng E, Fromowitz F, Viola MV. c-Ki-*ras* mutations in dysplastic fields and cancers in ulcerative colitis. Gastroenterology 1992, **102**: 1983–1987.

195a Chen R, Ravinovitch PS, Crispin DA, Emond MJ, Koprowicz KM, Bronner MP, Brentnall TA. DNA fingerprinting abnormalities can distinguish ulcerative colitis patients with dysplasia and cancer from those who are dysplasia/cancer-free. Am J Surg Pathol 2003, **162**: 665–672.

196 Choi PM, Nugent FW, Schoetz DJ Jr, Silverman ML, Haggitt RC. Colonoscopic surveillance reduces mortality from colorectal cancer in ulcerative colitis. Gastroenterology 1993, **105**: 418–424.

197 Collins RH Jr, Feldman N, Fordtran JS. Colon cancer, dysplasia, and surveillance in patients with ulcerative colitis. A critical review. N Engl J Med 1987, **316**: 1654–1658.

198 Compton CC. Premalignancy in chronic ulcerative colitis. Lectin binding as a diagnostic adjuvant. Hum Pathol 1989, **20**: 407–409.

199 Cook MG, Goligher JC. Carcinoma and epithelial dysplasia complicating ulcerative colitis. Gastroenterology 1975, **68**: 1127–1136.

200 Counsell PB, Dukes CE. The association of chronic ulcerative colitis and carcinoma of the rectum and colon. Br J Surg 1952, **39**: 485–495.

201 Devroede GJ, Taylor WF, Sauer WG, Jackman RJ, Stickler GB. Cancer risk and life expectancy of children with ulcerative colitis. N Engl J Med 1971, **285**: 17–52.

202 D'Haens GR, Lashner BA, Hanauer SB. Pericholangitis and sclerosing cholangitis are risk factors for dysplasia and cancer in ulcerative colitis. Am J Gastroenterol 1993, **88**: 1174–1178.

203 Dukes CE, Lockhart-Mummery HE. Practical points in the pathology and surgical treatment of ulcerative colitis. A critical review. Br J Surg 1957, **45**: 25–36.

204 Ehsannulah M, Filipe MI, Gazzard B. Mucin secretion in inflammatory bowel disease. Correlation with disease activity and dysplasia. Gut 1982, **23**: 485–489.

205 Ehsannulah M, Morgan MN, Filipe MI, Gazzard B. Sialomucins in the assessment of dysplasia and cancer-risk patients with ulcerative colitis treated with colectomy and ileo-rectal anastomosis. Histopathology 1985, **9**: 223–235.

206 Ekbom A, Helmick C, Zack M, Adami HO. Ulcerative colitis and colorectal cancer. A population-based study. N Engl J Med 1990, **323**: 1228–1233.

207 Filipe MI, Edwards MR, Ehsannulah M. A prospective study of dysplasia and carcinoma in the rectal biopsies and rectal stump of eight patients following ileorectal anastomosis in ulcerative colitis. Histopathology 1985, **9**: 1139–1153.

208 Fogt F, Urbanski SJ, Sanders ME, Furth EE, Zimmerman RL, Deren JJ, Noffsinger AE, Vortmeyer AO, Hartmann CJ, Odze RL, Brown CA. Distinction between dysplasia-associated lesion or mass (DALM) and adenoma in patients with ulcerative colitis. Hum Pathol 2000, **31**: 288–291.

209 Fozard JBJ, Dixon MF, Axon ATR, Giles GR. Lectin and mucin histochemistry as an aid to cancer surveillance in ulcerative colitis. Histopathology 1987, **11**: 385–394.

210 Fujii S, Fujimori T, Kashida H. Ulcerative colitis-associated neoplasia. Pathol Int 2002, **52**: 195–203.

211 Goldgraber MB, Humphreys EM, Kirsner JB, Palmer WL. Carcinoma and ulcerative colitis. Gastroenterology 1958, **34**: 809–839.

212 Greenson JK. Dysplasia in inflammatory bowel disease. Semin Diagn Pathol 2002, **19**: 31–37.

213 Greenstein AJ, Mullin GE, Strauchen JA, Heimann T, Janowitz HD, Aufses AH Jr, Sachar DB. Lymphoma in inflammatory bowel disease. Cancer 1992, **69**: 1119–1123.

214 Greenwald BD, Harpaz N, Yin J, Huang Y, Tong Y, Brown VL, McDaniel T, Newkirk C, Resau JH, Meltzer SJ. Loss of heterozygosity affecting the p53, Rb, and mcc/apc tumor suppressor gene loci in dysplastic and cancerous ulcerative colitis. Cancer Res 1992, **52**: 741–745.

215 Grundfest AF, Fazio V, Weiss RA, Jagelman D, Lavery I, Weakley FL, Turnbull RB Jr. The risk of cancer following colectomy and ileorectal anastomosis for extensive mucosal ulcerative colitis. Ann Surg 1981, **193**: 9–14.

216 Gyde SN, Prior P, Thompson H, Waterhouse JAH, Allan RN. Survival of patients with colorectal cancer complicating ulcerative colitis. Gut 1984, **25**: 228–231.

217 Hamilton PW, Allen DC, Watt PC. A combination of cytological and architectural morphometry in assessing regenerative hyperplasia and dysplasia in ulcerative colitis. Histopathology 1990, **17**: 59–68.

218 Harpaz N, Talbot IC. Colorectal cancer in idiopathic inflammatory bowel disease. Semin Diagn Pathol 1996, **13**: 339–357.

219 Langholz E, Munkholm P, Davidsen M, Binder V. Colorectal cancer risk and mortality in patients with ulcerative colitis. Gastroenterology 1992, **103**: 1444–1451.

220 Lavery IC, Chiulli RA, Jagelman DG, Fazio VW, Weakley FL. Survival with carcinoma arising in mucosal ulcerative colitis. Ann Surg 1982, **195**: 508–512.

221 Lennard-Jones JE, Morson BC, Ritchie JK, Shove DC, Williams CB. Cancer in colitis. Assessment of the individual risk by clinical and histological criteria. Gastroenterology 1977, **73**: 1280–1289.

222 Lennard-Jones JE, Ritchie JK, Morson BC, Williams CB. Cancer surveillance in ulcerative colitis. Experience over 15 years. Lancet 1983, **2**: 149–152.

223 Levine DS, Rabinovitch PS, Haggitt RC, Blount PL, Dean PJ, Rubin CE, Reid BJ. Distribution of aneuploid cell populations in ulcerative colitis with dysplasia or cancer. Gastroenterology 1991, **101**: 1198–1210.

224 Lofberg R, Brostrom O, Karlen P, Ost A, Tribukait B. DNA aneuploidy in ulcerative colitis. Reproducibility, topographic distribution, and relation to dysplasia. Gastroenterology 1992, **102**: 1149–1154.

225 Lyda MH, Noffsinger A, Belli J, Fenoglio-Preiser CM. Microsatellite instability and K-ras mutations in patients with ulcerative colitis. Hum Pathol 2000, **31**: 665–671.

226 Lyss AP, Thompson JJ, Glick JH. Adenocarcinoid tumor of the colon arising in preexisting ulcerative colitis. Cancer 1981, **48**: 833–839.

227 McNeely B, Owen DA, Pezim M. Multiple microcarcinoids arising in chronic ulcerative colitis. Am J Clin Pathol 1992, **98**: 112–116.

228 Melville DM, Jass JR, Morson BC, Pollock DJ, Richman PI, Shepherd NA, Ritchie JK, Love SB, Lennard-Jones JE. Observer study of the grading of dysplasia in ulcerative colitis. Comparison with clinical outcome. Hum Pathol 1989, **20**: 1008–1014.

229 Miller RR, Sumner HW. Argyrophilic cell hyperplasia and an atypical carcinoid tumor in chronic ulcerative colitis. Cancer 1982, **50**: 2920–2925.

230 Mir-Madjlessi SH, Farmer RG, Easley KA, Beck GJ. Colorectal and extra-colonic malignancy in ulcerative colitis. Cancer 1986, **58**: 1569–1574.

231 Morson BC. Current concepts of colitis. Lecture 1. Trans Med Soc Lond 1970, **86**: 159–176.

232 Morson BC. Precancer and cancer in inflammatory bowel disease. Pathology 1985, **17**: 173–180.

233 Morson BC, Pang LSC. Rectal biopsy as an aid to cancer control in ulcerative colitis. Gut 1967, **8**: 423–434.

234 Mueller JD, Bethke B, Stolte M. Colorectal de novo carcinoma: a review of its diagnosis histopathology, molecular biology, and clinical relevance. Virchows Arch 2002, **440**: 453–460.

235 Noffsinger AE, Belli JM, Miller MA, Fenoglio-Preiser CM. A unique basal pattern of p53 expression in ulcerative colitis is associated with mutation in the p53 gene. Histopathology 2001, **39**: 482–492.

236 Odze RD, Brown CA, Hartmann CJ, Noffsinger AE, Fogt F. Genetic alterations in chronic ulcerative colitis-associated adenoma-like DALMs are similar to non-colitic sporadic adenomas. Am J Surg Pathol 2000, **24**: 1209–1216.

237 Pascal RR. Dysplasia and early carcinoma in inflammatory bowel disease and colorectal adenomas. Hum Pathol 1994, **25**: 1160–1171.

238 Pavelic ZP, Pavelic L, Pavelic K, Genta RM, Ray MB, Dvornik G, Scukanec-Spoljar M, Peacock JS. Expression of carcinoembryonic antigen in ulcerative colitis, tubular adenomas and hyperplastic polyps. Correlations with the degree of dysplasia. Anticancer Res 1991, **11**: 1671–1675.

239 Ransohoff DF, Riddell RH, Levin B. Ulcerative colitis and colonic cancer. Problems in assessing the diagnostic usefulness of mucosal dysplasia. Dis Colon Rectum 1985, **28**: 383–388.

240 Riddell RH, Goldman H, Ransohoff DF, Appelman HD, Fenoglio CM, Haggitt RC, Ahren C, Correa P, Hamilton SR, Morson BC, Sommers SC, Yardley JH. Dysplasia in inflammatory bowel disease. Standardized classification with provisional clinical applications. Hum Pathol 1983, **14**: 931–968.

241 Riddell RH, Morson BC. Value of sigmoidoscopy and biopsy in detection of carcinoma and premalignant change in ulcerative colitis. Gut 1979, **20**: 575–580.

242 Ritchie JK, Hawley PR, Lennard-Jones JE. Prognosis of carcinoma in ulcerative colitis. Gut 1981, **22**: 752–755.

243 Rosenstock E, Farmer RG, Petras R, Sivak MV Jr, Rankin GB, Sullivan BH. Surveillance for colonic carcinoma in ulcerative colitis. Gastroenterology 1985, **89**: 1342–1346.

244 Rubin A, Pandya PP. Small cell neuroendocrine carcinoma of the rectum associated with chronic ulcerative colitis. Histopathology 1990, **16**: 95–97.

245 Sachar DB. Clinical and colonoscopic surveillance in ulcerative colitis. Are we saving colons or saving lives? Gastroenterology 1993, **105**: 588–597.

246 Shepherd NA, Hall PA, Williams GT, Codling BW, Jones EL, Levison DA, Morson BC. Primary malignant lymphoma of the large intestine complicating chronic inflammatory bowel disease. Histopathology 1989, **15**: 325–337.

247 Shields HM, Bates ML, Goldman H, Zuckerman GR, Mills BA, Best CJ, Bair FA, Goran DA, DeSchryver-Kecskemeti K. Scanning electron microscopic appearance of chronic ulcerative colitis with and without dysplasia. Gastroenterology 1985, **89**: 62–72.

248 Sigel JE, Goldblum JR. Neuroendocrine neoplasms arising in inflammatory bowel disease: a report of 14 cases. Mod Pathol 1998, **11**: 537–542.

249 Sugita A, Greenstein AJ, Ribeiro MB, Sachar DB, Bodian C, Panday AK, Szporn A, Pozner J, Heimann T, Palmer M, et al. Survival with colorectal cancer in ulcerative colitis. A study of 102 cases. Ann Surg 1993, **218**: 189–195.

250 Sugita A, Sachar DB, Bodian C, Ribeiro MB, Aufses AH Jr, Greenstein AJ. Colorectal cancer in ulcerative colitis. Influence of anatomical extent and age at onset on colitis-cancer interval. Gut 1991, **32:** 167–169.

251 Taylor BA, Pemberton JH, Carpenter HA, Levin KE, Schroeder KW, Welling DR, Spencer MP, Zinsmeister AR. Dysplasia in chronic ulcerative colitis. Implications for colonoscopic surveillance. Dis Colon Rectum 1992, **35:** 950–956.

252 Thomas DM, Filipe MI, Smedley FH. Dysplasia and carcinoma in the rectal stump of total colitis who have undergone colectomy and ileo-rectal anastomosis. Histopathology 1989, **14:** 289–298.

253 Torres C, Antonioli D, Odze RD. Polypoid dysplasia and adenomas in inflammatory bowel disease: a clinical, pathologic, and follow-up study of 89 polyps from 59 patients. Am J Surg Pathol 1998, **22:** 275–284.

254 Urbanski SJ, Fogt F. Dysplasia in chronic ulcerative colitis: a molecular approach to its differential diagnosis. Int J Surg Pathol 2000, **8:** 11–16.

255 Walsh SV, Loda M, Torres CM, Antonioli D, Odze RD. p53 and beta catenin expression in chronic ulcerative colitis-associated polypoid dysplasia and sporadic adenomas: an immunohistochemical study. Am J Surg Pathol 1999, **23:** 963–969.

256 Willenbucher RF, Aust DE, Chang CG, Zelman SJ, Ferrell LD, Moore DH II, Waldman FM. Genomic instability is an early event during the progression pathway of ulcerative-colitis-related neoplasia. Am J Pathol 1999, **154:** 1825–1830.

257 Wong NA, Harrison DJ. Review. Colorectal neoplasia in ulcerative colitis – recent advances. Histopathology 2001, **39:** 221–234.

258 Wong NA, Mayer NJ, MacKell S, Gilmour HM, Harrison DJ. Immunohistochemical assessment of Ki67 and p53 expression assists the diagnosis and grading of ulcerative colitis-related dysplasia. Histopathology 2000, **37:** 108–114.

259 Woolrich AJ, Da Silva MD, Korelitz BI. Surveillance in the routine management of ulcerative colitis. The predictive value of low-grade dysplasia. Gastroenterology 1992, **103:** 431–438.

260 Yardley JH, Keren DF. "Precancer" lesions in ulcerative colitis. A retrospective study of rectal biopsy and colectomy specimens. Cancer 1974, **34:** 835–844.

261 Yin J, Harpaz N, Tong Y, Huang Y, Laurin J, Greenwald BD, Hontanosas M, Newkirk C, Meltzer SJ. p53 point mutations in dysplastic and cancerous ulcerative colitis lesions. Gastroenterology 1993, **104:** 1633–1639.

Crohn's disease (granulomatous colitis)

262 Buchanan WM, Fyfe AHB. Giant pseudopolyposis in granulomatous colitis. J Pathol 1979, **127:** 51–54.

263 Chiodini RJ, Van Kruiningen HT, Thayer WR, Merkal RS, Coutu JA. Possible role of mycobacteria in inflammatory bowel disease. Part I. An unclassified *Mycobacterium* species isolated from patients with Crohn's disease. Dig Dis Sci 1984, **29:** 1073–1079.

264 Craft CF, Mendelsohn G, Cooper HS, Yardley JH. Colonic "precancer" in Crohn's disease. Gastroenterology 1981, **80:** 578–584.

265 Farmer RG, Hawk WA, Turnbull RB Jr. Carcinoma associated with mucosal ulcerative colitis and with transmural colitis and enteritis (Crohn's disease). Cancer 1971, **28:** 289–292.

266 Farmer RG, Hawk WA, Turnbull RB Jr. Clinical patterns in Crohn's disease. A statistical study of 1615 cases. Gastroenterology 1975, **68:** 627–635.

267 Gray BK, Lockhart-Mummery HE, Morson BC. Crohn's disease of the anal region. Gut 1965, **6:** 515–524.

268 Greenstein AJ, Janowitz HD, Sachar DB. The extraintestinal complications of Crohn's disease and ulcerative colitis. A study of 700 patients. Medicine (Baltimore) 1976, **55:** 401–412.

269 Hamilton SR. Colorectal carcinoma in patients with Crohn's disease. Gastroenterology 1985, **89:** 398–407.

270 Hoffman WA, Rosenberg MA. Granulomatous colitis in the elderly. Am J Gastroenterol 1972, **58:** 508–518.

271 Jones JH. Colonic cancer and Crohn's disease. Gut 1969, **10:** 651–654.

272 Kelly JK, Langevin J, Price LM, Hershfield NB, Share S, Blustein P. Giant and symptomatic inflammatory polyps of the colon in idiopathic inflammatory bowel disease. Am J Surg Pathol 1986, **10:** 420–428.

273 Kilgore SP, Sigel JE, Goldblum JR. Hyperplastic-like mucosal change in Crohn's disease: an unusual form of dysplasia? Mod Pathol 2000, **13:** 797–801.

274 Lockhart-Mummery HE, Morson BC. Crohn's disease of the large intestine. Gut 1964, **5:** 493–509.

275 Lofberg R, Brostrom O, Karlen P, Ost A, Tribukait B. Carcinoma and DNA aneuploidy in Crohn's colitis – a histological and flow cytometric study. Gut 1991, **32:** 900–904.

276 McQuillan AC, Appelman HD. Superficial Crohn's disease. A study of 10 patients. Surg Pathol 1989, **2:** 231–240.

277 Meyers MA, Alonso DR, Morson BC, Bartram C. Pathogenesis of diverticulitis complicating granulomatous colitis. Gastroenterology 1978, **74:** 24–31.

278 Petri M, Poulsen SS, Christensen K, Jarnum S. The incidence of granulomas in serial sections of rectal biopsies from patients with Crohn's disease. Acta Pathol Microbiol Immunol Scand (A) 1982, **90:** 145–147.

279 Podolsky DK. Inflammatory bowel disease. N Engl J Med 2002, **347:** 417–429.

280 Poller DN, Armitage NC. Mural bridging lesions in colonic Crohn's disease. Arch Pathol Lab Med 1993, **117:** 550–552.

281 Price AB. Overlap in the spectrum of non-specific inflammatory bowel disease – "colitis indeterminate." J Clin Pathol 1978, **31:** 567–577.

282 Price AB, Morson BC. Inflammatory bowel disease. The surgical pathology of Crohn's disease and ulcerative colitis. Hum Pathol 1975, **6:** 7–29.

283 Renison DM, Forouhar FA, Levine JB, Breiter JR. Filiform polyposis of the colon presenting as massive hemorrhage. An uncommon complication of Crohn's disease. Am J Gastroenterol 1983, **78:** 413–416.

284 Riddell RH, Goldman H, Ransohoff DF, Appelman HD, Fenoglio CM, Haggitt RC, Ahren C, Correa P, Hamilton SR, Morson BC, Sommers SC, Yardley JH. Dysplasia in inflammatory bowel disease. Standardized classification with provisional clinical applications. Hum Pathol 1983, **14:** 931–968.

285 Rotterdam H, Korelitz BI, Sommers SC. Microgranulomas in grossly normal rectal mucosa in Crohn's disease. Am J Clin Pathol 1977, **67:** 550–554.

286 Schmitz-Moormann P, Himmelmann G-W, Brandes J-W. Relationships between clinical data and histology of the large bowel in Crohn's disease and ulcerative colitis. Part I, Pathol Annu 1985, **20:** 281–301.

287 Schmitz-Moormann P, Pittner PM, Malchow H, Brandes JW. The granuloma in Crohn's disease. A bioptical study. Pathol Res Pract 1984, **178:** 467–476.

288 Schmitz-Moormann P, Pittner PM, Sangmeister M. Probability of detecting a granuloma in a colorectal biopsy of Crohn's disease. Pathol Res Pract 1984, **178:** 227–229.

289 Schneider H-M, Loos M, Storkel S, Gross M. Immunohistological differential diagnosis of inflammatory colonic diseases. Histopathology 1984, **8:** 583–588.

290 Shamsuddin AKM, Phillips RM. Preneoplastic and neoplastic changes in colonic mucosa in Crohn's disease. Arch Pathol Lab Med 1981, **105:** 283–286.

291 Shapiro PA, Peppercorn MA, Antonioli DA, Joffe N, Goldman H. Crohn's disease in the elderly. Am J Gastroenterol 1981, **76:** 132–137.

292 Sheehan AL, Warren BF, Gear MW, Shepherd NA. Fat-wrapping

in Crohn's disease. Pathological basis and relevance to surgical practice. Br J Surg 1992, **79**: 955–958.

293 Sigel JE, Petras RE, Lashner BA, Fazio VW, Goldblum JR. Intestinal adenocarcinoma in Crohn's disease: a report of 30 cases with a focus on coexisting dysplasia. Am J Surg Pathol 1999, **23**: 651–655.

294 Skinner JM, Whitehead R. A morphological assessment of immunoreactivity in colonic Crohn's disease and ulcerative colitis by a study of the lymph nodes. J Clin Pathol 1974, **27**: 202–206.

295 Surawicz CM, Meisel JL, Ylvisaker T, Saunders DR, Rubin CE. Rectal biopsy in the diagnosis of Crohn's disease. Value of multiple biopsies and serial sectioning. Gastroenterology 1981, **81**: 66–71.

296 Tchirkow G, Lavery IC, Fazio VW. Crohn's disease in the elderly. Dis Colon Rectum 1983, **26**: 177–181.

297 Thompson EM, Clayden G, Price AB. Cancer in Crohn's disease. An "occult" malignancy. Histopathology 1983, **7**: 365–376.

298 Tjandra JJ, Fazio VW. Surgery for Crohn's colitis. Int Surg 1992, **77**: 9–14.

299 Warren R, Barwick KW. Crohn's colitis with carcinoma and dysplasia. Report of a case and review of 100 small and large bowel resections for Crohn's disease to detect incidence of dysplasia. Am J Surg Pathol 1983, **7**: 151–159.

Ischemic and obstructive colitis

300 Bower TC. Ischemic colitis. Surg Clin North Am 1993, **73**: 1037–1053.

301 Brandt L, Boley S, Goldberg L, Mitsudo S, Berman A. Colitis in the elderly. A reappraisal. Am J Gastroenterol 1981, **76**: 239–245.

302 Brandt LJ, Katz HJ, Wolf EL, Mitsudo S, Boley SJ. Simulation of colonic carcinoma by ischemia. Gastroenterology 1985, **88**: 1137–1142.

303 Deana DG, Dean PJ. Reversible ischemic colitis in young women. Association with oral contraceptive use. Am J Surg Pathol 1995, **19**: 454–462.

304 Dignan CR, Greenson JK. Can ischemic colitis be differentiated from C difficile colitis in biopsy specimens? Am J Surg Pathol 1997, **21**: 706–710.

305 Galli C. Signet ring cells in ischemic ileitis. Int J Surg Pathol 2000, **8**: 239.

306 Gillespie IE. Intestinal ischaemia. Gut 1985, **26**: 653–655.

307 Haworth SJ, Pusey CD. Severe intestinal involvement in Wegener's granulomatosis. Gut 1984, **25**: 1296–1300.

308 Kilpatrick ZM, Silverman JF, Betancourt E, Farman J, Lawson JP. Vascular occlusion of the colon and oral contraceptives. Possible relation. N Engl J Med 1968, **278**: 438–440.

309 Levine TS, Price AB. Obstructive enterocolitis. A clinico-pathological discussion. Histopathology 1994, **25**: 57–64.

310 Longo WE, Ballantyne GH, Gusberg RJ. Ischemic colitis. Patterns and prognosis. Dis Colon Rectum 1992, **35**: 726–730.

311 Morson BC. Ischaemic colitis. Postgrad Med J 1968, **44**: 665–666.

312 O'Briain DS, Jeffers M, Kay EW, Hourihane DO. Bleeding due to colorectal atheroembolism. Diagnosis by biopsy of adenomatous polyps or of ischemic ulcer. Am J Surg Pathol 1991, **15**: 1078–1082.

313 Parish KL, Chapman WC, Williams LF Jr. Ischemic colitis. An ever-changing spectrum? Am Surg 1991, **57**: 118–121.

314 Robson NK, Khan SM, Rawlinson J, Dewbury KC. Ischaemic colitis. Clinical, radiological and pathological correlation in three cases. Clin Radiol 1992, **46**: 337–339.

315 Saraga E, Bouzourenne H. Enterocolic (lymphocytic) phlebitis: a rare cause of intestinal ischemic necrosis: a series of six patients and review of the literature. Am J Surg Pathol 2000, **24**: 824–829.

316 Saraga EP, Costa J. Idiopathic entero-colic lymphocytic phlebitis. A cause of ischemic intestinal necrosis. Am J Surg Pathol 1989, **13**: 303–308.

317 Toner M, Condell D, O'Briain DS. Obstructive colitis. Ulceroinflammatory lesions occurring proximal to colonic obstruction. Am J Surg Pathol 1990, **14**: 719–728.

318 Trinh TD, Jones B, Fishman EK. Amyloidosis of the colon presenting as ischemic colitis. A case report and review of the literature. Gastrointest Radiol 1991, **16**: 133–136.

319 Tuppy H, Haidenthaler A, Schandalik R, Oberhuber G. Idiopathic enterocolic lymphocytic phlebitis: a rare cause of ischemic colitis. Mod Pathol 2000, **13**: 897–899.

319a Weinrach DM, Wang K, Ramirez J, Keh P, Rao MS. Signet ring cell change versus signet ring cell carcinoma: a comparative morphological and immunohistochemical analysis. (Abstract) Mod Pathol 2003, **16**: 136a.

320 Zhang S, Ashraf M, Schinella R. Ischemic colitis with atypical reactive changes that mimic dysplasia (pseudodysplasia). Arch Pathol Lab Med 2001, **125**: 224–227.

Other types of colitis

321 Anagnostopoulos I, Schuppan D, Riecken EO, Gross UM, Stein H. Tenascin labelling in colorectal biopsies: a useful marker in the diagnosis of collagenous colitis. Histopathology 1999, **34**: 425–431.

322 Anand BS, Malhotra V, Bhattacharya SK, Datta P, Datta D, Sen D, Bhattacharya MK, Mukherjee PP, Pal SC. Rectal histology in acute bacillary dysentery. Gastroenterology 1986, **90**: 654–660.

323 Armes J, Gee DC, Macrae FA, Schroeder W, Bhathal PS. Collagenous colitis: jejunal and colorectal pathology. J Clin Pathol 1992, **45**: 784–787.

324 Asplund S, Gramlich TL. Chronic mucosal changes of the colon in graft-versus-host disease. Mod Pathol 1998, **11**: 513–515.

325 Ayata G, Ithamukkala S, Sapp H, Shaz BH, Brien TP, Wang HH, Antonioli DA, Farraye FA, Odze RD. Prevalence and significance of inflammatory bowel disease-like morphologic features in collagenous and lymphocytic colitis. Am J Surg Pathol 2002, **26**: 1414–1423.

326 Bagwell CE, Langham MR Jr, Mahaffey SM, Talbert JL, Shandling B. Pseudomembranous colitis following resection for Hirschsprung's disease. J Pediatr Surg 1992, **27**: 1261–1264.

327 Bellomo AR, Perlman DC, Kaminsky DL, Brettholz EM, Sarlin JG. Pneumocystis colitis in a patient with the acquired immunodeficiency syndrome. Am J Gastroenterol 1992, **87**: 759–761.

328 Bogomoletz WV. Collagenous, microscopic and lymphocytic colitis. An evolving concept. Virchows Arch 1994, **424**: 573–579.

329 Bogomoletz WV, Flejou JF. Newly recognized forms of colitis. Collagenous colitis, microscopic (lymphocytic) colitis, and lymphoid follicular proctitis. Semin Diagn Pathol 1991, **8**: 178–189.

330 Bombi JA, Nadal A, Carreras E, Ramírez J, Muñoz J, Rozman C, Cardesa A. Assessment of histopathologic changes in the colonic biopsy in acute graftversus-host disease. Am J Clin Pathol 1995, **103**: 690–695.

331 Brandt H, Perez-Tamayo R. Pathology of human amebiasis. Hum Pathol 1970, **1**: 351–385.

332 Bryant DA, Mintz ED, Puhr ND, Griffin PM, Petras RE. Colonic epithelial lymphocytosis associated with an epidemic of chronic diarrhoea. Am J Surg Pathol 1996, **20**: 1102–1109.

333 Canioni D, Pauliat S, Gaillard JL, Mougenot JF, Bompard Y, Berche P, Schmitz J, Brousse N. Histopathology and microbiology of isolated rectal bleeding in neonates: the so-called "ecchymotic colitis". Histopathology 1997, **30**: 472–477.

334 Cantey JR. Infectious diarrhea. Pathogenesis and risk factors. Am J Med 1985, **78**: 65–75.

335 Carpenter HA, Tremaine WJ, Batts KP, Czaja AJ. Sequential histologic evaluations in collagenous colitis. Correlations with disease behavior and sampling strategy. Dig Dis Sci 1992, **37**: 1903–1909.

336 Choudari CP, Mathan M, Rajah DP, Raghavan R, Mathan VI. A correlative study of etiology, clinical features and rectal mucosal pathology in adults with acute infectious diarrhea in southern India. Pathology 1985, **37:** 443–450.

337 Clarkston WK, Bonacini M, Peterson I. Colitis due to *Histoplasma capsulatum* in the acquired immune deficiency syndrome. Am J Gastroenterol 1991, **86:** 913–916.

338 Cohen MB, Giannella RA. Hemorrhagic colitis associated with *Escherichia coli* O157:H7. Adv Intern Med 1992, **37:** 173–195.

339 Counihan TC, Roberts PL. Pseudomembranous colitis. Surg Clin North Am 1993, **73:** 1063–1074.

340 Damiani S, Campidelli C. Pseudomembranous colitis with signet-ring cells. Histopathology 2002, **41:** 176–177.

341 Dickinson RJ, Gilmour HM, McClelland DBL. Rectal biopsy in patients presenting to an infectious disease unit with diarrhoeal disease. Gut 1979, **20:** 141–148.

342 Dieterich DT, Rahmin M. Cytomegalovirus colitis in AIDS. Presentation in 44 patients and a review of the literature. J Acquir Immune Defic Syndr 4 (Suppl) 1991, **1:** S29–S35.

343 Downey DB, Wilson SR. Pseudomembranous colitis. Sonographic features. Radiology 1991, **180:** 61–64.

344 Dundas SA, Dutton J, Skipworth P. Reliability of rectal biopsy in distinguishing between chronic inflammatory bowel disease and acute self-limiting colitis. Histopathology 1997, **31:** 60–66.

345 Edwards CM, George B, Warren B. Diversion colitis – new light through old windows. Histopathology 1999, **34:** 1–5.

346 Ehsannulah M, Isaacs A, Filipe MI, Gazzard BG. Tuberculosis presenting as inflammatory bowel disease. Report of two cases. Dis Colon Rectum 1984, **27:** 134–136.

347 Epstein RJ, McDonald GB, Sale GE, Shulman HM, Thomas ED. The diagnostic accuracy of the rectal biopsy in acute graft-versus-host disease. A prospective study of thirteen patients. Gastroenterology 1980, **78:** 764–771.

348 Esforzado N, Poch E, Almirall J, Bombi JA, Lopez-Pedret J, Revert L. Cytomegalovirus colitis in chronic renal failure. Clin Nephrol 1993, **39:** 275–278.

349 Ettinghausen SE. Collagenous colitis, eosinophilic colitis, and neutropenic colitis. Surg Clin North Am 1993, **73:** 993–1016.

350 Fekety R, Shah AB. Diagnosis and treatment of *Clostridium difficile* colitis. JAMA 1993, **269:** 71–75.

351 Ferguson CM, Siegel RJ. A prospective evaluation of diversion colitis. Am Surg 1991, **57:** 46–49.

352 Fishman EK, Kavuru M, Jones B, Kuhlman JE, Merine DS, Lillimoe KD, Siegelman SS. Pseudomembraneous colitis. CT evaluation of 26 cases. Radiology 1991, **180:** 57–60.

353 Flejou JF, Grimaud JA, Molas G, Baviera E, Patet F. Collagenous colitis. Ultrastructural study and collagen immunotyping of four cases. Arch Pathol Lab Med 1984, **108:** 977–982.

354 Foerster A, Fausa O. Collagenous colitis. Pathol Res Pract 1985, **180:** 99–104.

355 Foucar E, Mukai K, Foucar K, Sutherland DER, Van Buren CT. Colon ulceration in lethal cytomegalovirus infection. Am J Clin Pathol 1981, **76:** 788–801.

356 Gaffney EF, Condell D, Majmudar B, Nolan N, McDonald GSA, Griffin M, Sweeney EC. Modification of caecal lymphoid tissue and relationship to granuloma formation in sporadic ileocaecal tuberculosis. Histopathology 1987, **11:** 691–704.

357 Galati JS, Wisecarver JL, Quigley EM. Inflammatory polyps as a manifestation of intestinal graft versus host disease. Gastrointest Endosc 1993, **39:** 719–722.

358 Gallucci BB, Sale GE, McDonald GB, Epstein R, Shulman HM, Thomas ED. The fine structure of human rectal epithelium in acute graft-versus-host disease. Am J Surg Pathol 1982, **6:** 293–305.

359 Gardiner GW, Goldberg R, Currie D, Murray D. Colonic carcinoma associated with an abnormal collagen table. Collagenous colitis. Cancer 1984, **54:** 2973–2977.

360 George RH, Symonds JM, Dimock F, Brown JD, Arabi Y, Shinagawa N, Keighley MRB, Alexander-Williams J, Burden DW. Identification of *Clostridium difficile* as a cause of pseudomembranous colitis. Br Med J 1978, **1:** 695.

361 Geraghty JM, Talbot IC. Diversion colitis. Histological features in the colon and rectum after defunctioning colostomy. Gut 1991, **32:** 1020–1023.

362 Gibson GR, Whitacre EB, Ricotti CA. Colitis induced by nonsteroidal antiinflammatory drugs. Report of four cases and review of the literature. Arch Intern Med 1992, **152:** 625–632.

363 Goldman H. Acute versus chronic colitis. How and when to distinguish by biopsy. Gastroenterology 1984, **86:** 199–201.

364 Goldman H. Interpretation of large intestinal mucosal biopsy specimens. Hum Pathol 1994, **25:** 1150–1159.

365 Goldman H, Proujansky R. Allergic proctitis and gastroenteritis in children. Clinical and mucosal biopsy features in 53 cases. Am J Surg Pathol 1986, **10:** 75–86.

366 Goldstein NS, Gyorfi T. Focal lymphocytic colitis and collagenous colitis: patterns of Crohn's colitis? Am J Surg Pathol 1999, **23:** 1075–1081.

367 Goulston SJM, McGovern VJ. Pseudomembranous colitis. Gut 1965, **6:** 207–212.

368 Greenson JK, Stern RA, Carpenter SL, Barnett JL. The clinical significance of focal active colitis. Hum Pathol 1997, **28:** 729–733.

368a Haque R, Huston CD, Hughes M, Houpt E, Petri WA. Amebiasis. N Engl J Med 2003, **348:** 1565–1573.

369 Haque S, Eisen RN, West AB. The morphologic features of diversion colitis. Studies of a pediatric population with no other disease of the intestinal mucosa. Hum Pathol 1993, **24:** 211–219.

370 Hing MC, Goldschmidt C, Mathijs JM, Cunningham AL, Cooper DA. Chronic colitis associated with human immunodeficiency virus infection. Med J Aust 1992, **156:** 683–687.

371 Howell JS, Knapton PJ. Ileo-caecal tuberculosis. Gut 1964, **5:** 524–529.

372 Janoff EN, Orenstein JM, Manischewitz JF, Smith PD. Adenovirus colitis in the acquired immunodeficiency syndrome. Gastroenterology 1991, **100:** 976–979.

373 Jawhari A, Talbot IC. Microscopic, lymphocytic and collagenous colitis. Histopathology 1996, **29:** 101–110.

374 Jessurun J, Yardley JH, Giardiello FM, Hamilton SR, Bayless TM. Chronic colitis with thickening of the subepithelial collagen layer (collagenous colitis). Histopathologic findings in 15 patients. Hum Pathol 1987, **18:** 839–848.

375 Joshi VV, Draper DA, Bates RD III. Neonatal necrotizing enterocolitis. Occurrence secondary to thrombosis of abdominal aorta following umbilical arterial catheterization. Arch Pathol 1975, **99:** 540–543.

376 Kalkay MN, Ayanian ZS, Lehaf EA, Baldi A. *Campylobacter*-induced toxic megacolon. Am J Gastroenterol 1983, **78:** 557–559.

377 Kasulke RJ, Anderson WJ, Gupta SK, Gliedman ML. Primary tuberculous enterocolitis. Report of three cases and review of the literature. Arch Surg 1981, **116:** 110–113.

378 Katz JA, Wagner ML, Gresik MV, Mahoney DH, Fernbach DJ. Typhilitis. An 18-year experience and postmortem review. Cancer 1990, **65:** 1041–1047.

379 Kelly J, Oryshak A, Wenetsek M, Grabiec J, Handy S. The colonic pathology of *Escherichia coli* 0157:H7 infection. Am J Surg Pathol 1990, **14:** 87–92.

380 Kelly JK, Pai CH, Jadusingh IH, Macinnis ML, Shaffer EA, Hershfield NB. The histopathology of rectosigmoid biopsies from adults with bloody diarrhea due to verotoxin-producing *Escherichia coli*. Am J Clin Pathol 1987, **88:** 78–82.

381 Kim HJ, Piao Z, Kim H. Pathologic features of recurrent intestinal Behcet's disease. Int J Surg Pathol 1997, **5:** 11–18.

382 Kingham JGC, Levison DA, Morson BC, Dawson AM. Collagenous colitis. Gut 1986, **27:** 570–577.

383 Kliegman RM, Fanaroff AA. Necrotizing enterocolitis. N Engl J Med 1984, **310:** 1093–1103.

384 Knight R. Hepatic amebiasis. Semin Liver Dis 1984, **4**: 277–292.

385 Kobayashi TK, Koretoh O, Kamachi M, Watanabe S, Ishigooka S, Matsushita I, Sawaragi I. Cytologic demonstration of *Entamoeba histolytica* using immunoperoxidase techniques. Report of two cases. Acta Cytol (Baltimore) 1985, **29**: 414–418.

386 Komorowski RA. Histologic spectrum of diversion colitis. Am J Surg Pathol 1990, **14**: 548–554.

387 Komorowski RA, Cohen EB, Kauffman HM, Adams MB. Gastrointestinal complications in renal transplant recipients. Am J Clin Pathol 1986, **86**: 161–167.

388 Kosloske AM. Necrotizing enterocolitis in the neonate. Surg Gynecol Obstet 1979, **148**: 259–269.

389 Kotler DP, Weaver SC, Terzakis JA. Ultrastructural features of epithelial cell degeneration in rectal crypts of patients with AIDS. Am J Surg Pathol 1986, **10**: 531–538.

390 Kraus MD, Feran-Doza M, Garcia-Moliner ML, Antin J, Odze RD. Cytomegalovirus infection in the colon of bone marrow transplantation patients. Mod Pathol 1998, **11**: 29–36.

391 Kumar NB, Nostrant TT, Appelman HD. The histopathologic spectrum of acute self-limited colitis (acute infectious-type colitis). Am J Surg Pathol 1982, **6**: 523–529.

392 Lazenby AJ, Yardley JH, Giardiello FM, Bayless TM. Pitfalls in the diagnosis of collagenous colitis. Experience with 75 cases from a registry of collagenous colitis at the Johns Hopkins Hospital. Hum Pathol 1990, **21**: 905–910.

393 Lazenby AJ, Yardley JH, Giardiello FM, Jessurun J, Bayless TM. Lymphocytic ("microscopic") colitis. A comparative histopathologic study with particular reference to collagenous colitis. Hum Pathol 1989, **20**: 18–28.

394 Lee FD, Roy AD. Ileo-caecal granulomata. Gut 1964, **5**: 517–523.

395 Lee RG. The colitis of Behçet's syndrome. Am J Surg Pathol 1986, **10**: 888–893.

396 Leonard N, Palazzo J, Jameson J, Denman AM, Talbot IC, Price AB. Behcet's colitis has distinctive pathological features. Int J Surg Pathol 1998, **6**: 1–4.

397 Libbrecht L, Croes R, Ectors N, Staels F, Geboes K. Microscopic colitis with giant cells. Histopathology 2002, **40**: 335–338.

398 Ma CK, Gottlieb C, Haas PA. Diversion colitis. A clinicopathologic study of 21 cases. Hum Pathol 1990, **21**: 429–436.

399 Mapstone NP, Dixon MF. Vasculitis in ileocaecal tuberculosis. Similarities to Crohn's disease. Histopathology 1992, **21**: 477–479.

400 McAllister TA. Diagnosis of amoebic colitis on routine biopsies from rectum and sigmoid colon. Br Med J 1962, **1**: 362–364.

401 McGovern VJ, Savutin LJ. Pathology of salmonella colitis. Am J Surg Pathol 1979, **3**: 483–490.

402 Medline A, Shin DH, Medline NM. Pseudomembranous colitis associated with antibiotics. Hum Pathol 1976, **7**: 693–703.

403 Meiselman MS, Cello JP, Margaretten W. Cytomegalovirus colitis. Report of the clinical, endoscopic, and pathologic findings in two patients with the acquired immune deficiency syndrome. Gastroenterology 1985, **88**: 171–175.

404 Nostrant TT, Kumar NB, Appelman HD. Histopathology differentiates acute self-limited colitis from ulcerative colitis. Gastroenterology 1987, **92**: 318–328.

405 Odze RD, Bines J, Leichtner AM, Goldman H, Antonioli DA. Allergic proctocolitis in infants. A prospective clinicopathologic biopsy study. Hum Pathol 1993, **24**: 668–674.

406 Offner FA, Jao RV, Lewin KJ, Havelec L, Weinstein WM. Collagenous colitis: a study of the distribution of morphological abnormalities and their histological detection. Hum Pathol 1999, **30**: 451–457.

407 Palmer KR, Patil DH, Basran GS, Riordan JF, Silk DBA. Abdominal tuberculosis in urban Britain. A common disease. Gut 1985, **26**: 1296–1305.

408 Pauwels A, Meyohas MC, Eliaszewicz M, Legendre C, Mougeot G, Frottier J. *Toxoplasma* colitis in the acquired immunodeficiency syndrome. Am J Gastroenterol 1992, **87**: 518–519.

409 Pittman FE, Hashimi WK, Pittman JC. Studies of human amebiasis. Part 1. Clinical and laboratory findings in eight cases of acute amebic colitis. Gastroenterology 1973, **65**: 581–587.

410 Pittman FE, Hennigar GR. Sigmoidoscopic and colonic mucosal biopsy findings in amebic colitis. Arch Pathol 1974, **97**: 155–158.

411 Pochaczevsky R, Kassner EG. Necrotizing enterocolitis in infancy. Am J Roentgenol Radium Ther Nucl Med 1971, **113**: 283–296.

412 Pothoulakis C, La Mont JT. *Clostridium difficile* colitis and diarrhea. Gastroenterol Clin North Am 1993, **22**: 623–637.

413 Prathap K, Gilman R. The histopathology of acute intestinal amebiasis. Am J Pathol 1970, **60**: 229–245.

414 Price AB, Davies DR. Pseudomembranous colitis. J Clin Pathol 1977, **30**: 1–12.

415 Rich JD, Crawford JM, Kazanjian SN, Kazanjian PH. Discrete gastrointestinal mass lesions caused by cytomegalovirus in patients with AIDS. Report of three cases and review. Clin Infect Dis 1992, **5**: 609–614.

416 Riddell RH, Tanaka M, Mazzoleni G. Non-steroidal anti-inflammatory drugs as a possible cause of collagenous colitis. A case-control study. Gut 1992, **33**: 683–686.

417 Sale GE, Shulman HM, McDonald GB, Thomas ED. Gastrointestinal graft-versus-host disease in man. A clinicopathologic study of the rectal biopsy. Am J Surg Pathol 1979, **3**: 291–299.

418 Santulli TV, Schullinger JN, Heird WC, Gongaware RD, Wigger J, Barlow B, Blanc WA, Berdon WE. Acute necrotizing enterocolitis in infancy. A review of 64 cases. Pediatrics 1975, **55**: 376–387.

419 Sapp H, Ithamukkala S, Brien TP, Ayata G, Shaz B, Dorfman DM, Wang HH, Antonioli DA, Farraye FA, Odze RD. The terminal ileum is affected in patients with lymphocytic or collagenous colitis. Am J Surg Pathol 2002, **26**: 1484–1492.

420 Saul SH. The watery diarrhea-colitis syndrome. A review of collagenous and microscopic/lymphocytic colitis. Int J Surg Pathol 1993, **1**: 65–82.

421 Schiffman R. Signet-ring cells associated with pseudomembranous colitis. Am J Surg Pathol 1996, **20**: 599–602.

422 Schmitt SL, Wexner SD. Bacterial, fungal, parasitic, and viral colitis. Surg Clin North Am 1993, **73**: 1055–1062.

423 Schnitt SJ, Antonioli DA, Goldman H. Massive mural edema in severe pseudomembranous colitis. Arch Pathol Lab Med 1983, **107**: 211–213.

424 Snover DC. Graft-versus-host disease of the gastrointestinal tract. Am J Surg Pathol 1990, **14**(Suppl 1): 101–108.

425 Stevenson JK, Graham CB, Oliver TK Jr, Goldenberg VE. Neonatal necrotizing enterocolitis. A report of twenty-one cases with fourteen survivors. Am J Surg 1969, **118**: 260–272.

426 Sumner HW, Tedesco FJ. Rectal biopsy in clindamycin-associated colitis. An analysis of 23 cases. Arch Pathol 1975, **99**: 237–241.

427 Surawicz CM, Belic L. Rectal biopsy helps to distinguish acute self-limited colitis from idiopathic inflammatory bowel disease. Gastroenterology 1984, **86**: 104–113.

428 Sutherland DER, Chan FY, Foucar E, Simmons PL, Howard RJ, Najarian JS. The bleeding cecal ulcer in transplant patients. Surgery 1979, **86**: 386–398.

429 Tanaka M, Mazzoleni G, Riddell RH. Distribution of collagenous colitis. Utility of flexible sigmoidoscopy. Gut 1992, **33**: 65–70.

430 Tandon HD, Prakash A. Pathology of intestinal tuberculosis and its distinction from Crohn's disease. Gut 1972, **13**: 260–269.

431 Thomas DW, Talley NJ, Mahnovski V, Haight M, Sinatra FR. Rectal mucosal major basic protein in infants with dietary protein-induced colitis. Ann Allergy 1993, **71**: 66–69.

432 Triadafilopoulos G, Hallstone AE. Acute abdomen as the first presentation of pseudomembranous colitis. Gastroenterology 1991, **101**: 685–691.

433 Van Spreeuwel JP, Duursma GC, Meijer CJLM, Bax R, Rosekrans PCM, Lindeman J. *Campylobacter* colitis. Histological, immunohistochemical, and ultrastructural findings. Gut 1985, **26**: 945–951.

434 Vesterby A, Baandrup U, Jacobsen NO, Albertsen K. *Campylobacter* enterocolitis. An important differential diagnosis in ulcerative colitis. Acta Pathol Microbiol Immunol Scand (A) 1983, **91**: 31–33.

435 Vohra R, Prescott RJ, Banerjee SS, Wilkinson PM, Schofield PF. Management of neutropenic colitis. Surg Oncol 1992, **1**: 11–15.

436 Volk EE, Shapiro BD, Easley KA, Goldblum JR. The clinical significance of a biopsy-based diagnosis of focal active colitis: a clinicopathologic study of 31 cases. Mod Pathol 1998, **11**: 789–794.

437 Vujanic GM, Dojcinov SD. Diversion colitis in children: an iatrogenic appendix vermiformis? Histopathology 2000, **36**: 41–46.

438 Waddell TK, McLeod RS, Rotstein OD, Cohen Z. Surgical management of fulminant pseudomembranous colitis. Can J Surg 1992, **35**: 555–559.

439 Wade DS, Nava HR, Douglass HO Jr. Neutropenic enterocolitis. Clinical diagnosis and treatment. Cancer 1992, **69**: 17–23.

440 Wang KK, Perrault J, Carpenter HA, Schroeder KW, Tremaine WJ. Collagenous colitis. A clinicopathologic correlation. Mayo Clin Proc 1987, **62**: 665–671.

441 Wang N, Dumot JA, Achkar E, Easley KA, Petras RE, Goldblum JR. Colonic epithelial lymphocytosis without a thickened subepithelial collagen table: a clinicopathologic study of 40 cases supporting a heterogeneous entity. Am J Surg Pathol 1999, **23**: 1068–1074.

442 Warren BF, Edwards CM, Travis SP. "Microscopic colitis": classification and terminology. Histopathology 2002, **40**: 374–376.

443 Weber JR Jr, Dobbins WO III. The intestinal and rectal epithelial lymphocyte in AIDS. An electron-microscope study. Am J Surg Pathol 1986, **10**: 627–639.

444 Whitehead R. Forms of colitis. A review of recent developments. Pathology 1985, **17**: 204–208.

445 Wilson SE, Woolley MM. Primary necrotizing enterocolitis in infants. Arch Surg 1969, **99**: 563–566.

446 Winter HS, Antonioli DA, Fukagawa N, Marcial M, Goldman H. Allergy-related proctocolitis in infants. Diagnostic usefulness of rectal biopsy. Mod Pathol 1990, **3**: 5–10.

447 Wolber R, Owen D, Freeman H. Colonic lymphocytosis in patients with celiac sprue. Hum Pathol 1990, **21**: 1092–1096.

447a Xin W, Brown PI, Greenson JK. The clinical significance of focal active colitis in pediatric patients. Am J Surg Pathol 2003, **27**: 1134–1138.

448 Yan Z, Nguyen S, Poles M, Melamed J, Scholes JV. Adenovirus colitis in human immunodeficiency virus infection: an underdiagnosed entity. Am J Surg Pathol 1998, **22**: 1101–1106.

449 Yeong ML, Bethwaite PB, Prasad J, Isbister WH. Lymphoid follicular hyperplasia – a distinctive feature of diversion colitis. Histopathology 1991, **19**: 55–61.

449a Yuan S, Reyes V, Bronner MP. Pseudomembranous collagenous colitis. Am J Surg Pathol 2003, **27**: 1375–1379.

Other non-neoplastic lesions

450 Allen MS Jr. Hamartomatous inverted polyps of the rectum. Cancer 1966, **19**: 257–265.

451 Amano S, Yamada N. Endometrioid carcinoma arising from endometriosis of the sigmoid colon. A case report. Hum Pathol 1981, **12**: 845–848.

452 Beddoe H, Kaye S, Kaye S. Barium granuloma of the rectum. Report of case. JAMA 1954, **154**: 747–748.

453 Bogomoletz WV. Solitary rectal ulcer syndrome. Mucosal prolapse syndrome. Pathol Annu 1992, **27**(Pt 1): 75–86.

454 Brett EM, Berry CL. Value of rectal biopsy in pediatric neurology. Report of 165 biopsies. Br Med J 1967, **3**: 400–403.

455 Brodey PA, Hill RP, Baron S. Benign ulceration of the cecum. Radiology 1977, **122**: 323–327.

456 Byers RJ, Marsh P, Parkinson D, Haboubi NY. Melanosis coli is associated with an increase in colonic epithelial apoptosis and not with laxative use. Histopathology 1997, **30**: 160–164.

457 Daya D, O'Connell G, DeNardi F. Rectal endometriosis mimicking solitary rectal ulcer syndrome. Mod Pathol 1995, **8**: 599–602.

457a Downs-Kelly E, Hoschar AP, Prayson RA. Salivary gland heterotopia in the rectum. Ann Diagn Pathol 2003, **7**: 124–126.

458 Du Boulay CE, Fairbrother J, Isaacson PG. Mucosal prolapse syndrome. A unifying concept for solitary ulcer syndrome and related disorders. J Clin Pathol 1983, **36**: 1264–1268.

459 Epstein SE, Ascari WQ, Albow RC, Seaman WB, Lattes R. Colitis cystica profunda. Am J Clin Pathol 1966, **45**: 186–201.

460 Ford MJ, Anderson JR, Gilmour HM, Holt S, Sircus W, Heading RC. Clinical spectrum of "solitary ulcer" of the rectum. Gastroenterology 1983, **84**: 1533–1540.

461 Franzin G, Scarpa A, Dina R, Novelli P. "Transitional" and hyperplastic-metaplastic mucosa occurring in solitary ulcer of the rectum. Histopathology 1981, **5**: 527–533.

462 Gad A. Benign idiopathic recurrent rectal ulceration (BIRRU). Scand J Gastroenterol 1979, **54**(Suppl): 111–113.

463 Gafni J, Sohar E. Rectal biopsy for the diagnosis of amyloidosis. Am J Med Sci 1960, **240**: 332–336.

464 Gelfand MD, Tepper M, Katz LA, Binder HJ, Vesner R, Flock MH. Acute irradiation proctitis in man. Development of eosinophilic crypt abscesses. Gastroenterology 1968, **54**: 401–411.

465 Ghadially FN, Walley VM. Melanoses of the gastrointestinal tract. Histopathology 1994, **25**: 197–207.

466 Grodsinsky C, Ponka JL. Volvulus of the colon. Dis Colon Rectum 1977, **20**: 314–324.

467 Groisman GM, Lachter J, Vlodavsky E. Amyloid colitis mimicking collagenous colitis. Histopathology 1997, **31**: 201–202.

468 Haboubi NY, Honan RP, Hasleton PS, Ali HH, Anfield C, Hobbiss J, Schofield PF. Pneumatosis coli. A case report with ultrastructural study. Histopathology 1984, **8**: 145–155.

469 Insabato L, Pettinato G. Endometriosis of the bowel with lymph node involvement – a report of three cases and review of the literature. Pathol Res Pract 1996, **192**: 957–961.

470 Kamoshita S, Landing BH. Distribution of lesions in myenteric plexus and gastrointestinal mucosa in lipidoses and other neurologic disorders of children. Am J Clin Pathol 1968, **49**: 312–318.

471 Kyle RA, Spencer RJ, Dahlin DC. Value of rectal biopsy in the diagnosis of primary systemic amyloidosis. Am J Med Sci 1966, **251**: 501–506.

472 Lane KL, Vallera R, Washington K, Gottfried MR. Endoscopic tattoo agents in the colon: tissue responses and clinical implications. Am J Surg Pathol 1996, **20**: 1266–1270.

473 Langlois NE, Park KG, Keenan RA. Mucosal changes in the large bowel with endometriosis. A possible cause of misdiagnosis of colitis? Hum Pathol 1994, **25**: 1030–1034.

474 Lauwers GY, Perez-Atayde A, Dorfman RF, Rosai J. The digestive system manifestations of Rosai-Dorfman disease (sinus histiocytosis with massive lymphadenopathy): Review of 11 cases. Hum Pathol 2000, **31**: 380–385.

475 Leupin N, Curschmann J, Kranzbuhler H, Mauer CA, Laissue JA, Mazzucchelli L. Acute radiation colitis in patients treated with short-term preoperative radiotherapy for rectal cancer. Am J Surg Pathol 2002, **26**: 498–504.

476 Li SC, Hamilton SR. Malignant tumors in the rectum simulating solitary rectal ulcer syndrome in endoscopic biopsy specimens. Am J Surg Pathol 1998, **22**: 106–112.

477 Lobert PF, Appelman HD. Inflammatory cloacogenic polyp. A unique inflammatory lesion of the anal transition zone. Am J Surg Pathol 1981, **5**: 761–766.

478 MacKay EH. Malakoplakia in ulcerative colitis. Arch Pathol Lab Med 1978, **102**: 140–145.

479 Madigan R, Morson BC. Solitary ulcer of the rectum. Gut 1969, **10**: 871–881.

480 Magidson JG, Lewin KJ. Diffuse colitis cystica profunda. Report of a case. Am J Surg Pathol 1981, **5**: 393–399.

481 O'Mara CS, Wilson TH Jr, Stonesifer GL, Cameron JL. Cecal volvulus. Analysis of 50 patients with long-term follow-up. Ann Surg 1979, **189**: 724–731.

482 Pawel BR, de Chadarevian JP, Franco ME. The pathology of fibrosing colonopathy of cystic fibrosis: a study of 12 cases and review of the literature. Hum Pathol 1997, **28**: 395–399.

483 Petersen VC, Underwood JC, Wells M, Shepherd NA. Primary endometrioid adenocarcinomas of the large intestine arising in colorectal endometriosis. Histopathology 2002, **40**: 171–176.

484 Pieterse AS, Leong AS-Y. Rowland R. The mucosal changes and pathogenesis of pneumatosis cystoides intestinalis. Hum Pathol 1985, **16**: 683–688.

485 Ranchod M, Kahn LB. Malakoplakia of the gastrointestinal tract. Arch Pathol 1972, **94**: 90–97.

486 Rapola J, Santavuori P, Savilahti E. Suction biopsy of rectal mucosa in the diagnosis of infantile and juvenile types of neuronal ceroid lipofuscinoses. Hum Pathol 1984, **15**: 352–360.

487 Rescorla FJ, Grosfeld JL. Intestinal atresia and stenosis. Analysis of survival in 120 cases. Surgery 1985, **98**: 668–676.

488 Rocha N, Suguiama EH, Maia D, Costa H, Coelho KI, Franco M. Intestinal malakoplakia associated with paracoccidioidomycosis: a new association. Histopathology 1997, **30**: 79–83.

489 Roswit B, Malsky SJ, Reid CB. Severe radiation injuries of the stomach, small intestine, colon, and rectum. Am J Roentgenol Radium Ther Nucl Med 1972, **114**: 460–475.

490 Sandmeier D, Guillou L. Malakoplakia and adenocarcinoma of the caecum. A rare association. J Clin Pathol 1993, **46**: 959–960.

491 Saul SH. Inflammatory cloacogenic polyp. Relationship to solitary rectal ulcer syndrome/mucosal prolapse and other bowel disorders. Hum Pathol 1987, **18**: 1120–1125.

492 Shamsuddin AKM, Elias EG. Rectal mucosa. Malignant and premalignant changes after radiation therapy. Arch Pathol Lab Med 1981, **105**: 150–151.

493 Silver H, Stolar J. Distinguishing features of well-differentiated mucinous adenocarcinoma of the rectum and colitis cystica profunda. Am J Clin Pathol 1969, **51**: 493–500.

494 Sinclair-Smith C, Kahn LB, Cywes S. Malacoplakia in childhood. Case report with ultrastructural observations and review of the literature. Arch Pathol 1975, **99**: 198–203.

495 Slavin RE, Krum R, Van Dinh T. Endometriosis-associated intestinal tumors: a clinical and pathologic study of 6 cases and review of the literature. Hum Pathol 2000, **31**: 456–463.

496 Smith BH, Welter LH. Pneumatosis intestinalis. Am J Clin Pathol 1967, **48**: 455–465.

497 Snover DC, Sandstad J, Hutton S. Mucosal pseudolipomatosis of the colon. Am J Clin Pathol 1985, **84**: 575–580.

498 Srinivasan R, Loewenstine H, Mayle JE. Sessile polypoid gastric heterotopia of rectum: a report of 2 cases and review of the literature. Arch Pathol Lab Med 1999, **123**: 222–224.

499 Steer HW, Colin-Jones DG. Melanosis coli. Studies of the toxic effects of irritant purgatives. J Pathol 1975, **115**: 199–205.

500 Stuart M. Proctitis cystica profunda. Incidence, etiology, and treatment. Dis Colon Rectum 1984, **27**: 153–156.

501 Suarez V, Chesner IM, Price AB, Newman J. Pneumatosis cystoides intestinalis. Histological mucosal changes mimicking inflammatory bowel disease. Arch Pathol Lab Med 1989, **113**: 898–901.

502 Terner JY, Lattes R. Malakoplakia of colon and retroperitoneum. Am J Clin Pathol 1965, **44**: 20–31.

503 Walker NI, Bennett RE, Axelsen RA. Melanosis coli. A consequence of anthraquinone-induced apoptosis of colonic epithelial cells. Am J Pathol 1988, **131**: 465–476.

504 Warren BF, Dankwa EK, Davies JD. "Diamond-shaped" crypts and mucosal elastin. Helpful diagnostic features in biopsies of rectal prolapse. Histopathology 1990, **17**: 129–134.

505 Wayte DM, Helwig EB. Colitis cystica profunda. Am J Clin Pathol 1967, **48**: 159–169.

506 Weisbrot IM, Liber AF, Gordon BS. The effects of therapeutic radiation on colonic mucosa. Cancer 1975, **36**: 931–940.

507 Wilson SE, Woolley MM. Primary necrotizing enterocolitis in infants. Arch Surg 1969, **99**: 563–566.

508 Wolff M. Heterotopic gastric epithelium in the rectum. A report of three new cases with a review of 87 cases of gastric heterotopia in the alimentary canal. Am J Clin Pathol 1971, **55**: 604–616.

509 Wood RE, Herman CJ, Johnson KW, di Sant'Agnese PA. Pneumatosis coli in cystic fibrosis. Clinical, radiological, and pathological features. Am J Dis Child 1975, **129**: 246–248.

510 Yantiss RK, Clement PB, Young RH. Neoplastic and preneoplastic changes in gastrointestinal endometriosis: a study of 17 cases. Am J Surg Pathol 2000, **24**: 513–524.

511 Yantiss RK, Clement PB, Young RH. Endometriosis of the intestinal tract: a study of 44 cases of a disease that may cause diverse challenges in clinical and pathologic evaluation. Am J Surg Pathol 2001, **25**: 445–454.

Tumors

Epithelial polyps

512 Abraham SC, Nobukawa B, Giardiello FM, Hamilton SR, Wu TT. Fundic gland polyps in familial adenomatous polyposis. Neoplasms with frequent somatic adenomatous polyposis coli gene alterations. Am J Pathol 2000, **157**: 747–754.

513 Almagro UA, Pintar K, Zellmer RB. Squamous metaplasia in colorectal polyps. Cancer 1984, **53**: 2679–2682.

514 Ando H, Miyoshi Y, Nagase H, Baba S, Nakamura Y. Detection of 12 germ-line mutations in the adenomatous polyposis coli gene by polymerase chain reaction. Gastroenterology 1993, **104**: 989–993.

515 Arminski TC, McLean DW. Incidence and distribution of adenomatous polyps of the colon and rectum based on 1,000 autopsy examinations. Dis Colon Rectum 1964, **7**: 249–261.

516 Bacon HE, Eisenberg SW. Papillary adenoma or villous tumor of the rectum and colon. Ann Surg 1971, **174**: 1002–1008.

517 Banner BF, Sonmez-Alpan E, Yousem SA. An immunophenotypic study of the inflammatory cell populations in colon adenomas and carcinomas. Mod Pathol 1993, **6**: 295–301.

518 Bansal M, Fenoglio CM, Robboy SJ, West King D. Are metaplasias in colorectal adenomas truly metaplasias? Am J Pathol 1984, **115**: 253–265.

519 Bardeesy N, Sinha M, Hezel AF, Signoretti S, Hathaway NA, Sharpless NE, Loda M, Carrasco DR, DePinho RA. Loss of the Lkb1 tumour suppressor provokes intestinal polyposis but resistance to transformation. Nature 2002, **419**: 162–166.

519a Bariol C, Hawkins NJ, Turner JJ, Meagher AP, Williams DB, Ward RL. Histopathological and clinical evaluation of serrated adenomas of the colon and rectum. Mod Pathol 2003, **16**: 417–423.

520 Bedossa P, Poynard T, Bacci J, Naveau S, Lemaigre G, Chaput JC, Martin E. Expression of histocompatibility antigens and characterization of the lymphocyte infiltrate in hyperplastic polyps of the large bowel. Hum Pathol 1990, **21**: 319–324.

521 Bengoechea O, Martínez-Peñuela JM, Larrínaga B, Valerdi J, Borda F. Hyperplastic polyposis of the colorectum and adenocarcinoma in a 24-year-old man. Am J Surg Pathol 1987, **11**: 323–327.

522 Bodmer WF, Bailey CJ, Bodmer J, Bussey HJR, Ellis A, Gorman P, Lucibello FC, Murday VA, Rider SH, Scambler P, Sheer D, Solomon E, Spurr NK. Localization of the gene for familial adenomatous polyposis on chromosome 5. Nature 1987, **328**: 614–616.

523 Bolwell JS, James PD. Peutz-Jeghers syndrome with pseudoinvasion of hamartomatous polyps and multiple epithelial neoplasms. Histopathology 1979, **3**: 39–50.

524 Bombi JA, Rives A, Astudillo E, Pera C, Cardesa A. Polyposis coli associated with adenocarcinoma of the gallbladder. Report of a case. Cancer 1984, **53**: 2561–2563.

525 Bosari S, Moneghini L, Graziani D, Lee AKC, Murray JJ, Coggi G, Viale G. bcl-2 oncoprotein in colorectal hyperplastic polyps, adenomas, and adenocarcinomas. Hum Pathol 1995, **26**: 534–540.

526 Boughdady IS, Kinsella AR, Haboubi NY, Schofield PF. K-*ras* gene mutation in colorectal adenomas and carcinomas from familial adenomatous polyposis patients. Surg Oncol 1992, **1**: 269–274.

526a Bronner MP. Gastrointestinal inherited polyposis syndromes. Mod Pathol 2003, **16**: 359–365.

527 Burke AP, Sobin LH. The pathology of Cronkhite-Canada polyps. A comparison to juvenile polyposis. Am J Surg Pathol 1989, **13**: 940–946.

528 Burt RW, Bishop DT, Cannon LA, Dowdle MA, Lee RG, Skolnick MH. Dominant inheritance of adenomatous colonic polyps and colorectal cancer. N Engl J Med 1985, **312**: 1540–1544.

529 Bussey HJR. Gastrointestinal polyposis. Gut 1970, **11**: 970–978.

530 Bussey HJR. Familial polyposis coli. Baltimore, 1975, Johns Hopkins University Press.

531 Campbell F, Geraghty JM, Appleton MAC, Williams ED, Williams GT. Increased stem cell somatic mutation in the non-neoplastic colorectal mucosa of patients with familial adenomatous polyposis. Hum Pathol 1998, **29**: 1531–1535.

532 Carlson GJ, Nivatvongs S, Snover DC. Colorectal polyps in Cowden's disease (multiple hamartoma syndrome). Am J Surg Pathol 1984, **8**: 763–770.

533 Chapman I. Adenomatous polypi of large intestine. Incidence and distribution. Ann Surg 1963, **157**: 223–226.

534 Cleary K. Juvenile polyp – A premalignant lesion? Adv Anat Pathol 1998, **5**: 95–98.

535 Coffin CM, Dehner LP. What is a juvenile polyp? An analysis based on 21 patients with solitary and multiple polyps. Arch Pathol Lab Med 1996, **120**: 1032–1038.

536 Cole JW, McKalen A. Studies on the morphogenesis of adenomatous polyps in the human colon. Cancer 1963, **16**: 998–1002.

537 Cooper HS, Marshall C, Ruggerio F, Steplewski Z. Hyperplastic polyps of the colon and rectum. An immunohistochemical study with monoclonal antibodies against blood groups antigens (sialosyl = Le^a, Le^b, Le^x, Le^y, A, B, H). Lab Invest 1987, **57**: 421–428.

538 Cooper HS, Patchefsky AS, Marks G. Adenomatous and carcinomatous changes within hyperplastic colon epithelium. Dis Colon Rectum 1979, **22**: 152–156.

539 Dajani YF, Kamal MF. Colorectal juvenile polyps. An epidemiological and histopathological study of 144 cases in Jordanians. Histopathology 1984, **8**: 765–779.

540 Daniel ES, Ludwig SL, Lewin KJ, Ruprecht RM, Rajacich GM, Schwabe AD. The Cronkhite-Canada syndrome. An analysis of clinical and pathologic features and therapy in 55 patients. Medicine (Baltimore) 1982, **61**: 293–309.

541 Dawson PA, Filipe MI, Bussey HJR. Ultrastructural features of the colonic epithelium in familial polyposis coli. Histopathology 1977, **1**: 105–113.

542 Deschner EE, Lipkin M. Proliferative patterns in colonic mucosa in familial polyposis. Cancer 1975, **35**: 413–418.

543 Di Gregorio C, Losi L, Fante R, Modica S, Ghidoni M, Pedroni M, Tamassia MG, Gafa L, Ponz De Leon M, Roncucci L. Histology of aberrant crypt foci in the human colon. Histopathology 1997, **30**: 328–334.

544 Dirschmid K, Kiesler J, Mathis G, Beller S, Stoss F, Schobel B. Epithelial misplacement after biopsy of colorectal adenomas. Am J Surg Pathol 1993, **17**: 1262–1265.

545 Domoto H, Terahata S, Senoh A, Sato K, Aida S, Tamai S. Clear cell change in colorectal adenomas: its incidence and histological characteristics. Histopathology 1999, **34**: 250–256.

546 Eide TJ, Schweder T. Clustering of adenomas in the large intestine. Gut 1984, **25**: 1262–1267.

547 Erbe RW. Current concepts in genetics. Inherited gastrointestinal-polyposis syndromes. N Engl J Med 1976, **394**: 1101–1104.

548 Estrada RG, Spjut HJ. Hyperplastic polyps of the large bowel. Am J Surg Pathol 1980, **4**: 127–133.

549 Fogt F, Brien T, Brown CA, Hartmann CJ, Zimmerman RL, Odze RD. Genetic alterations in serrated adenomas: comparison to conventional adenomas and hyperplastic polyps. Hum Pathol 2002, **33**: 87–91.

550 Franzin G, Zamboni G, Dina R, Scarpa A, Fratton A. Juvenile and inflammatory polyps of the colon. A histological and histochemical study. Histopathology 1983, **7**: 719–728.

551 Franzin G, Zamboni G, Scarpa A, Dina R, Iannuci A, Novelli P. Hyperplastic (metaplastic) polyps of the colon. A histologic and histochemical study. Am J Surg Pathol 1984, **8**: 687–698.

552 Friedman CJ, Fechner RE. A solitary juvenile polyp with hyperplastic and adenomatous glands. Dig Dis Sci 1982, **27**: 946–948.

553 Fujisaki J, Shimoda T. Expression of cytokeratin subtypes in colorectal mucosa, adenoma, and carcinoma. Gastroenterol Jpn 1993, **28**: 647–656.

554 Fulcheri E, Baracchini P, Pagani A, Lapertosa G, Bussolati G. Significance of the smooth muscle cell component in Peutz-Jeghers and juvenile polyps. Hum Pathol 1991, **22**: 1136–1140.

555 Fung CH, Goldman H. The incidence and significance of villous change in adenomatous polyps. Am J Clin Pathol 1970, **53**: 21–25.

556 Gardner EJ. Follow-up study of a family group exhibiting dominant inheritance for a syndrome including intestinal polyps, osteomas, fibromas, and epidermal cysts. Am J Hum Genet 1962, **14**: 375–389.

557 Giardiello FM, Hamilton SR, Kern SE, Offerhaus GJ, Green PA, Celano P, Krush AJ, Booker SV. Colorectal neoplasia in juvenile polyposis or juvenile polyps. Arch Dis Child 1991, **66**: 971–975.

558 Giardiello FM, Hamilton SR, Krush AJ, Offerhaus JA, Booker SV, Petersen GM. Nasopharyngeal angiofibroma in patients with familial adenomatous polyposis. Gastroenterology 1993, **105**: 1550–1552.

559 Giardiello FM, Offerhaus GJ, Lee DH, Krush AJ, Tersmette AC, Booker SV, Kelley NC, Hamilton SR. Increased risk of thyroid and pancreatic carcinoma in familial adenomatous polyposis. Gut 1993, **34**: 1394–1396.

560 Greene FL. Epithelial misplacement in adenomatous polyps of the colon and rectum. Cancer 1974, **33**: 206–217.

561 Griffin CA, Lazar S, Hamilton SR, Giardiello FM, Long P, Krush AJ, Booker SV. Cytogenetic analysis of intestinal polyps in polyposis syndromes: comparison with sporadic colorectal adenomas. Cancer Genet Cytogenet 1993, **67**: 14–20.

562 Griffioen G, Cornelisse CJ, Verspaget HW, Sier CF, Eulderink F, Bosman FT, Lamers CB. Association of aneuploidy in index adenomas with metachronous colorectal adenoma development and a comparison. Cancer 1992, **70**: 2035–2043.

563 Grigioni WF, Alampi G, Martinelli G, Piccaluga A. Atypical juvenile polyposis. Histopathology 1981, **5**: 361–376.

564 Groisman GM, Benkov KJ, Adsay V, Dische MR. Osseous metaplasia in benign colorectal polyps. Arch Pathol Lab Med 1994, **118**: 64–65.

565 Grotsky HW, Rickert RR, Smith WD, Newsome JF. Familial juvenile polyposis coli. A clinical and pathologic study of a large kindred. Gastroenterology 1982, **82**: 494–501.

566 Haggitt RC, Pitcock JA. Familial juvenile polyposis of the colon. Cancer 1970, **26**: 1232–1238.

567 Haggitt RC, Reid BJ. Hereditary gastrointestinal polyposis syndromes. Am J Surg Pathol 1986, **10**: 871–887.

568 Hamilton SR, Liu B, Parsons RE, Papadopoulos N, Jen J, Powell SM, Krush AJ, Berk T, Cohen Z, Tetu B, Burger C, Wood PA, Taqui F, Booker SV, Petersen GM, Offerhaus GJA, Tersmette AC, Giardiello FM, Vogelstein B, Kinzler KW. The molecular basis of Turcot's syndrome. N Engl J Med 1995, 332: 839–847.

569 Harach HR, Williams GT, Williams ED. Familial adenomatous polyposis associated thyroid carcinoma. A distinct type of follicular cell neoplasm. Histopathology 1994, 25: 549–561.

570 Heillmann KL, Schmidbauer G, Schyma G. The transitional polyp of the colorectal mucosa. Pathol Res Pract 1987, 182: 690–693.

571 Helwig EB. Adenomas of the large intestine in children. Am J Dis Child 1946, 72: 289–295.

572 Helwig EB. The evolution of adenomas of the large intestine and their relation to carcinoma. Surg Gynecol Obstet 1947, 84: 36–49.

573 Helwig EB, Hanson J. Lymphoid polyps (benign lymphoma) and malignant lymphoma of the rectum and anus. Surg Gynecol Obstet 1951, 92: 233–243.

574 Hizawa K, Iida M, Matsumoto T, Kohrogi N, Kinoshita H, Yao T, Fujishima M. Cancer in Peutz-Jeghers syndrome. Cancer 1993, 72: 2777–2781.

575 Hizawa K, Iida M, Matsumoto T, Kohrogi N, Yao T, Fujishima M. Neoplastic transformation arising in Peutz-Jeghers polyposis. Dis Colon Rectum 1993, 36: 953–957.

576 Horrilleno EG, Eckert C, Ackerman LV. Polyps of the rectum and colon in children. Cancer 1957, 10: 1210–1220.

576a Hurlstone DP, Brown S, Cross SS. The role of flat and depressed colorectal lesions in colorectal carcinogenesis: new insights from clinicopatholical findings in high-magnification chromoscopic colonoscopy. Histopathology 2003, 43: 413–426.

577 Isaacson P, LeVann HP. The demonstration of carcinoembryonic antigen in colorectal carcinoma and colonic polyps using an immunoperoxidase technique. Cancer 1976, 38: 1348–1356.

578 Itoh H, Hirata K, Ohsato K. Turcot's syndrome and familial adenomatous polyposis associated with brain tumor. Review of related literature. Int J Colorectal Dis 1993, 8: 87–94.

579 Järvinen H, Franssila KO. Familial juvenile polyposis coli. Increased risk of colorectal cancer. Gut 1984, 25: 792–800.

580 Järvinen HJ. Time and type of prophylactic surgery for familial adenomatosis coli. Ann Surg 1985, 202: 93–97.

580a Jass JR. Serrated adenoma of the colorectum. Am J Surg Pathol 2003, 162: 705–708.

581 Jass JR, Filipe MI, Abbas S, Falcon CAJ, Wilson Y, Lovell D. A morphologic and histochemical study of metaplastic polyps of the colorectum. Cancer 1984, 53: 510–515.

582 Jass JR, Young J, Leggett BA. Hyperplastic polyps and DNA microsatellite unstable cancers of the colorectum. Histopathology 2000, 37: 295–301.

583 Jones IT, Jagelman DG, Fazio VW, Lavery IC, Weakley FL, McGannon E. Desmoid tumors in familial polyposis coli. Ann Surg 1986, 204: 94–97.

584 Jones MA, Hebert JC, Trainer TD. Juvenile polyp with intramucosal carcinoma. Arch Pathol Lab Med 1987, 111: 200–201.

585 Kang M, Mitomi H, Sada M, Tokumitsu Y, Takahashi Y, Igarashi M, Katsumata T, Okayasu I. Ki-67, p53, and Bcl-2 expression of serrated adenomas of the colon. Am J Surg Pathol 1997, 21: 417–423.

586 Katayama Y, Kimura M, Konn M. Cronkhite-Canada syndrome associated with a rectal cancer and adenomatous changes in colonic polyps. Am J Surg Pathol 1985, 9: 65–71.

587 Kawasaki Y, Monden T, Morimoto H, Murotani M, Miyoshi Y, Kobayashi T, Shimano T, Mori T. Immunohistochemical study of p53 expression in microwave-fixed, paraffin-embedded sections of colorectal carcinoma and adenoma. Am J Clin Pathol 1992, 97: 244–249.

588 Kindblom L-G, Angervall L, Santesson B, Selander S. Cronkhite-Canada syndrome. Case report. Cancer 1977, 39: 2651–2657.

589 Kingston JE, Herbert A, Draper GJ, Mann JR. Association between hepatoblastoma and polyposis coli. Arch Dis Child 1983, 58: 959–962.

590 Konishi F, Morson BC. Pathology of colorectal adenomas. A colonoscopic survey. J Clin Pathol 1982, 35: 830–841.

591 Kubota O, Kino I. Minute adenomas of the depressed type in familial adenomatous polyposis of the colon. A pathway to ordinary polypoid adenomas. Cancer 1993, 72: 1159–1164.

592 Kubota O, Kino I. Depressed adenomas of the colon in familial adenomatous polyposis. Histology, immunohistochemical detection of proliferating cell nuclear antigen (PCNA), and analysis of the background mucosa. Am J Surg Pathol 1995, 19: 318–327.

593 Lambert R, Sobin LH, Waye JD, Stalder GA. The management of patients with colorectal adenomas. CA 1984, 34: 167–176.

594 Lane N, Kaplan H, Pascal RR. Minute adenomatous and hyperplastic polyps of the colon. Divergent patterns of epithelial growth with specific associated mes enchymal changes; contrasting roles in the pathogenesis of carcinoma. Gastroenterology 1971, 60: 537–551.

595 Leggett BA, Devereaux B, Biden K, Searle J, Young J, Jass J. Hyperplastic polyposis: association with colorectal cancer. Am J Surg Pathol 2001, 25: 177–184.

596 Leppert M, Dobbs M, Scambler P, O'Connell P, Nakamura Y, Stauffer D, Woodward S, Burt R, Hughes J, Gardner E, Lathrop M, Wasmuth J, Lalouel J-M, White R. The gene for familial polyposis coli maps to the long arm of chromosome 5. Science 1987, 238: 1411–1413.

597 Lewis JH, Ginsberg AL, Toomey KE. Turcot's syndrome. Evidence for autosomal 15 dominant inheritance. Cancer 1983, 51: 524–528.

598 Lipkin M, Blattner WA, Gardner EJ, Burt RW, Lynch H, Deschner E, Winawer S, Fraumeni JF Jr. Classification and risk assessment of individuals with familial polyposis, Gardner's syndrome, and familial non-polyposis colon cancer from [³H]thymidine labeling patterns in colonic epithelial cells. Cancer Res 1984, 44: 4201–4207.

599 Lipper S, Kahn LB, Sandler RS, Varma V. Multiple juvenile polyposis. A study of the pathogenesis of juvenile polyps and their relationship to colonic adenomas. Hum Pathol 1981, 12: 804–813.

600 Longacre TA, Fenoglio-Preiser CM. Mixed hyperplastic adenomatous polyps/serrated adenomas. A distinct form of colorectal neoplasia. Am J Surg Pathol 1990, 14: 524–537.

601 Luk GD, Baylin SB. Ornithine decarboxylase as a biologic marker in familial colonic polyposis. N Engl J Med 1984, 311: 80–83.

602 Lynch HT, Smyrk TC, Lanspa SJ, Jenkins JX, Lynch PM, Cavalieri J, Lynch JF. Upper gastrointestinal manifestations in families with hereditary flat adenoma syndrome. Cancer 1993, 71: 2709–2714.

603 Lynch HT, Smyrk TC, Watson P, Lanspa SJ, Lynch PM, Jenkins JX, Rouse J, Cavalieri J, Howard L, Lynch J. Hereditary flat adenoma syndrome. A variant of familial adenomatous polyposis? Dis Colon Rectum 1992, 35: 411–421.

604 MacDonald JM, David WC, Crago HR, Berk AD. Gardner's syndrome and periampullary malignancy. Am J Surg 1967, 113: 425–430.

605 Mastronardi L, Ferrante L, Lunardi P, Cervoni L, Fortuna A. Association between neuroepithelial tumor and multiple intestinal polyposis (Turcot's syndrome). Report of a case and critical analysis of the literature. Neurosurgery 1991, 28: 449–452.

606 Mestre JR. The changing pattern of juvenile polyps. Am J Gastroenterol 1986, 81: 312–314.

607 Mills SE, Fechner RE. Unusual adenomatous polyps in juvenile polyposis coli. Am J Surg Pathol 1982, 6: 177–183.

608 Miyaki M, Konishi M, Kikuchi-Yanoshita R, Enomoto M, Tanaka K, Takahashi H, Muraoka M, Mori T, Konishi F, Iwama T. Coexistence of somatic and germ-line mutations of APC gene in

desmoid tumors from patients with familial adenomatous polyposis. Cancer Res 1993, **53:** 5079–5082.

609 Miyoshi Y, Ando H, Nagase H, Nishisho I, Horii A, Miki Y, Mori T, Utsunomiya J, Baba S, Petersen G, et al. Germ-line mutations of the APC gene in 53 familial adenomatous polyposis patients. Proc Natl Acad Sci U S A 1992, **89:** 4452–4456.

610 Mughal S, Filipe MI, Jass JR. A comparative ultrastructural study of hyperplastic and adenomatous polyps, incidental and in association with colorectal cancer. Cancer 1981, **48:** 2746–2755.

611 Murad T, Bauer K, Scarpelli DG. Histopathologic and flow cytometric analysis of adenomatous colonic polyps. Arch Pathol Lab Med 1989, **113:** 1003–1008.

612 Muto T, Bussey HJR, Morson BC. Pseudo-carcinomatous invasion in adenomatous polyps of the colon and rectum. J Clin Pathol 1973, **26:** 25–31.

613 Narita T, Eto T, Ito T. Peutz-Jeghers syndrome with adenomas and adenocarcinomas in colonic polyps. Am J Surg Pathol 1987, **11:** 76–81.

614 Nascimbeni R, Villanacci V, Mariani PM, De Betta E, Ghirardi M, Donato F, Salerni B. Aberrant crypt foci in the hyman colon: frequency and histologic patterns in patients with colorectal cancer or diverticular disease. Am J Surg Pathol 1999, **23:** 1256–1263.

615 Neugut AI, Johnsen CM, Forde KA, Treat MR. Recurrence rates for colorectal polyps. Cancer 1985, **55:** 1586–1589.

616 Nucci MR, Robinson CR, Longo P, Campbell P, Hamilton SR. Phenotypic and genotypic characteristics of aberrant crypt foci in human colorectal mucosa. Hum Pathol 1997, **28:** 1396–1407.

617 Nugent KP, Talbot IC, Hodgson SV, Phillips RK. Solitary juvenile polyps. Not a marker for subsequent malignancy. Gastroenterology 1993, **105:** 698–700.

617a Oh K, Redson M, Odze RD. Clinical, pathologic and immunohistochemical characteristics of colonic mixed hyperplastic/adenomatous polyps suggests that they are a precursor to serrated adenomas. (Abstract) Mod Pathol 2003, **16:** 129–130a.

618 Offerhaus GJ, Giardiello FM, Tersmette KW, Mulder JW, Tersmette AC, Moore GW, Hamilton SR. Ethnic differences in the anatomical location of colorectal adenomatous polyps. Int J Cancer 1991, **49:** 641–644.

619 Painter TA, Jagelman DG. Adrenal adenomas and adrenal carcinomas in association with hereditary adenomatosis of the colon and rectum. Cancer 1985, **55:** 2001–2004.

620 Penna C, Tiret E, Parc R, Sfairi A, Kartheuser A, Hannoun L, Nordinger B. Operation and abdominal desmoid tumors in familial adenomatous polyposis. Surg Gynecol Obstet 1993, **177:** 263–268.

621 Perkins JT, Blackstone MO, Riddell RH. Adenomatous polyposis coli and multiple endocrine neoplasia type 2b. A pathogenetic relationship. Cancer 1985, **55:** 375–381.

622 Pham BN, Villanueva RP. Ganglioneuromatous proliferation associated with juvenile polyposis coli. Arch Pathol Lab Med 1989, **113:** 91–94.

623 Powell SM, Petersen GM, Krush AJ, Booker S, Jen J, Giardiello FM, Hamilton SR, Vogelstein B, Kinzler KW. Molecular diagnosis of familial adenomatous polyposis. N Engl J Med 1993, **329:** 1982–1987.

624 Pretlow TP, Barrow BJ, Ashton WS, O'Riordan MA, Pretlow TG, Jurcisek JA, Stellato TA. Aberrant crypts. Putative preneoplastic foci in human colonic mucosa. Cancer Res 1991, **51:** 1564–1567.

625 Ramirez RF, Culp CE, Jackman RJ, Dockerty MB. Villous tumors of the lower part of the large bowel. JAMA 1965, **194:** 121–125.

626 Ranzi T, Castagnone D, Velio P, Bianchi P, Polli EE. Gastric and duodenal polyps in familial polyposis coli. Gut 1981, **22:** 363–367.

627 Reissenweber N, Gualco G, Zrdao G, Velazquez S, Kliche I, Fosman E, Almeida E. The interrelationship between tubular and papillary sectors of tubulo-villous colorectal adenomas: comparative morphometric analysis and evaluation of cell proliferation. Hum Pathol 1998, **29:** 431–437.

628 Rickert RR. Papillary adenoma of the large intestine: a historical perspective. Cancer 1998, **83:** 825–829.

629 Robert J, Lagace R, Delage C. Malakoplakia of the colon associated with a villous adenoma. Report of a case. Dis Colon Rectum 1974, **17:** 668–671.

630 Roncucci L, Stamp D, Meline A, Cullen JB, Bruce WR. Identification and quantification of aberrant crypt foci and microadenomas in the human colon. Hum Pathol 1991, **22:** 387–394.

631 Roth SI, Helwig EB. Juvenile polyps of the colon and rectum. Cancer 1963, **16:** 468–479.

632 Rozen P, Baratz M. Familial juvenile colonic polyposis with associated colon cancer. Cancer 1982, **49:** 1500–1503.

633 Rubio CA. Atypical mitoses in colorectal adenomas. Pathol Res Pract 1991, **187:** 508–513.

634 Rubio CA, Slezak P, Rodensjo M. Differences in the distribution of acidic mucins between flat tubular adenomas and flat serrated adenomas of the colorectal mucosa. In Vivo 1996, **10:** 383–388.

635 Rustgi AK. Hereditary gastrointestinal polyposis and nonpolyposis syndromes. N Engl J Med 1994, **331:** 1694–1702.

636 Ruymann FB. Juvenile polyps with cachexia. Report of an infant and comparison with Cronkhite-Canada syndrome in adults. Gastroenterology 1969, **57:** 431–438.

637 Sachatello CR. Familial polyposis of the colon. A four-decade follow-up. Cancer 1971, **28:** 581–587.

638 Samowitz WS, Burt RL. The nonspecificity of histological findings reported for flat adenomas. Hum Pathol 1995, **26:** 571–573.

639 Sarlin JG, Mori K. Morules in epithelial tumors of the colon and rectum. Am J Surg Pathol 1984, **8:** 281–285.

640 Sasaki A, Yokoyama S, Arita T, Inomata M, Kashima K, Nakayama I. Morules with biotin-containing optically clear nuclei in colonic tubular adenoma. Am J Surg Pathol 1999, **23:** 226–341.

641 Sawyer EJ, Cerar A, Hanby AM, Gorman P, Arends M, Talbot IC, Tomlinson IP. Molecular characteristics of serrated adenomas of the colorectum. Gut 2002, **51:** 200–206.

642 Schneider NR, Cubilla AL, Chaganti RSK. Association of endocrine neoplasia with multiple polyposis of the colon. Cancer 1983, **51:** 1171–1175.

643 Schröder S, Moehrs D, von Weltzien J, Winkler R, Otto HF. The Turcot syndrome. Report of an additional case and review of the literature. Dis Colon Rectum 1983, **26:** 533–538.

644 Schuchardt WA Jr, Ponsky JL. Familial polyposis and Gardner's syndrome. Surg Gynecol Obstet 1979, **148:** 97–103.

645 Shepherd NA. Inverted hyperplastic polyposis of the colon. J Clin Pathol 1993, **46:** 56–60.

646 Shepherd NA, Bussey HJR, Jass JR. Epithelial misplacement in Peutz-Jeghers polyps. A diagnostic pitfall. Am J Surg Pathol 1987, **11:** 743–749.

647 Shpitz B, Bornstein Y, Mekori Y, Cohen R, Kaufman Z, Neufeld D, Galkin M, Bernheim J. Aberrant crypt foci in human colons: distribution and histomorphologic characteristics. Hum Pathol 1998, **29:** 469–475.

647a Sieber OM, Lipton L, Crabtree M, Heinimann K, Fidalgo P, Phillips RKS, Bisgaard M-L, Orntoft TF, Aaltonen LA, Hodgson SV, Thomas HJW, Tomlinson IPM. Multiple colorectal adenomas, classic adenomatous polyposis, and germ-line mutations in MYH. N Engl J Med 2003, **348:** 791–799.

648 Siu IM, Pretlow TG, Amini SB, Pretlow TP. Identification of dysplasia in human colonic aberrant crypt foci. Am J Pathol 1997, **150:** 1805–1813.

649 Sobin LH. Inverted hyperplastic polyps of the colon. Am J Surg Pathol 1985, **9:** 265–272.

650 Sobin LH. The histopathology of bleeding from polyps and carcinomas of the large intestine. Cancer 1985, **55:** 577–581.

651 Solomon SS, Moran JM, Nabseth DC. Villous adenoma of rectosigmoid accompanied by electrolyte depletion. JAMA 1965, **194**: 117–122.

652 Stemper TJ, Kent TH, Sommers RW. Juvenile polyposis and gastrointestinal carcinoma. A study of a kindred. Ann Intern Med 1975, **83**: 639–646.

653 Takayama T, Katsuki S, Takahashi Y, Ohi M, Nojiri S, Sakamaki S, Kato J, Kogawa K, Miyake H, Niitsu Y. Aberrant crypt foci of the colon as precursors of adenoma and cancer. N Engl J Med 1998, **339**: 1277–1284.

654 Tateyama H, Li W, Takahashi E, Miura Y, Sugiura H, Eimoto T. Apoptosis index and apoptosis-related antigen expression in serrated adenoma of the colorectum: the saw-toothed structure may be related to inhibition of apoptosis. Am J Surg Pathol 2002, **26**: 249–256.

655 Thompson JJ, Enterline HT. The macroscopic appearance of colorectal polyps. Cancer 1981, **48**: 151–160.

656 Tops CM, Vasen HF, van Berge Henegouwen G, Simoons PP, van de Klift HM, van Leeuwen SJ, Breukel C, Fodde R, den Hartog Jager FC, Nagengast FM, et al. Genetic evidence that Turcot syndrome is not allelic to familial adenomatous polyposis. Am J Med Genet 1992, **43**: 888–893.

657 Torlakovic E, Skovlund E, Snover DC, Torlakovic G, Nesland JM. Morphologic reappraisal of serrated colorectal polyps. Am J Surg Pathol 2003, **27**: 65–81.

658 Urbanski SJ, Kossakowska AE, Marcon N, Bruce WR. Mixed hyperplastic adenomatous polpys. An underdiagnosed entity. Report of a case of adenocarcinoma arising within a mixed hyperplastic adenomatous polyp. Am J Surg Pathol 1984, **8**: 551–556.

659 Van Der Weyden L, Jonkers J, Bradley A. Stuck at first base. Nature 2002, **419**: 127–128.

660 Veale AMO, McColl I, Bussey HJR, Morson BC. Juvenile polyposis coli. J Med Genet 1969, **3**: 1–76.

661 Wada R, Miwa H, Abe H, Santo RM, Kitamura S, Kuwabara N, Suda K, Kondo K, Yamada S, Hamada T, et al. Incidence of Paneth cells in minute tubular adenomas and adenocarcinomas of the large bowel. Acta Pathol Jpn 1992, **42**: 579–584.

662 Warner AS, Glick ME, Fogt F. Multiple large hyperplastic polyps of the colon coincident with adenocarcinoma. Am J Gastroenterol 1994, **89**: 123–125.

663 Watne AL, Carrier JM, Durham JP, Hrabovsky EE, Chang W. The occurrence of carcinoma of the rectum following ileoproctostomy for familial polyposis. Ann Surg 1983, **197**: 550–554.

664 Watne AL, Lai H-Y, Carrier J, Coppula W. The diagnosis and surgical treatment of patients with Gardner's syndrome. Surgery 1977, **82**: 327–333.

665 Welch JP, Welch CE. Villous adenomas of the colorectum. Am J Surg 1976, **131**: 185–191.

666 Wheat MW Jr, Ackerman LV. Villous adenomas of the large intestine. Clinicopathologic evaluation of 50 cases of villous adenomas with emphasis on treatment. Ann Surg 1958, **147**: 476–487.

667 Wiebecke B, Brandts A, Eder M. Epithelial proliferation and morphogenesis of hyperplastic adenomatous and villous polyps of the human colon. Virchows Arch [A] 1974, **364**: 35–49.

668 Williams AR, Balasooriya BAW, Day DW. Polyps and cancer of the large bowel. A necropsy study in Liverpool. Gut 1982, **23**: 835–842.

669 Williams GT, Arthur JF, Bussey HJR, Morson BC. Metaplastic polyps and polyposis of the colorectum. Histopathology 1980, **4**: 155–170.

670 Wiltz O, O'Toole K, Fenoglio CM. Breast carcinoma metastatic to a solitary adenomatous polyp in the colon. Arch Pathol Lab Med 1984, **108**: 318–320.

671 Winawer SJ, Stewart ET, Zauber AG, Bond JH, Ansel H, Waye JD, Hall D, Hamlin JA, Schapiro M, O'Brien MJ, Sternberg SS, Gottlieb LS. A comparison of colonoscopy and double-contrast barium enema for surveillance after polypectomy. A National Polyp Study Work Group. N Engl J Med 2000, **342**: 1766–1772.

672 Wolber RA, Owen DA. Flat adenomas of the colon. Hum Pathol 1991, **22**: 70–74.

673 Wu TT, Kornacki S, Rashid A, Yardley JH, Hamilton SR. Dysplasia and dysregulation of proliferation in foveolar and surface epithelia of fundic gland polyps from patients with familial adenomatous polyposis. Am J Surg Pathol 1998, **22**: 293–298.

674 Wu TT, Rezai B, Rashid A, Luce MC, Cayouette MC, Kim C, Sani N, Mishra L, Moskaluk CA, Yardley JH, Hamilton SR. Genetic alterations and epithelial dysplasia in juvenile polyposis syndrome and sporadic juvenile polyps. Am J Pathol 1997, **150**: 939–947.

675 Yantiss RK, Goldman H, Odze RD. Hyperplastic polyp with epithelial misplacement (inverted hyperplastic polyp): a clinicopathologic and immunohistochemical study of 19 cases. Mod Pathol 2001, **14**: 869–875.

676 Yao T, Tada S, Tsuneyoshi M. Colorectal counterpart of gastric depressed adenoma. A comparison with flat and polypoid adenomas with special reference to the development of pericryptal fibroblasts. Am J Surg Pathol 1994, **18**: 559–568.

677 Yokoo H, Usman I, Wheaton S, Kampmeier PA. Colorectal polyps with extensive absorptive enterocyte differentiation. Histologically distinct variant of hyperplastic polyps. Arch Pathol Lab Med 1999, **123**: 404–410.

678 Yonemoto RH, Slayback JB, Byron RL Jr, Rosen RB. Familial polyposis of the entire gastrointestinal tract. Arch Surg 1969, **99**: 427–434.

Relationship with carcinoma and treatment

679 Ackerman LV. Malignant potential of polypoid lesions of the large intestine. Trans Stud Coll Phys Phila 1964, **32**: 5–14.

680 Atkin WS, Morson BC, Cuzick J. Long-term risk of colorectal cancer after excision of rectosigmoid adenomas. N Engl J Med 1992, **326**: 658–662.

681 Baker SJ, Fearon ER, Nigro JM, Hamilton SR, Preisinger AC, Jessup JM, Van Tuinen P, Ledbetter DH, Barker DF, Nakamura YH, White R, Vogelstein B. Chromosome 17 deletions and p53 gene mutations in colorectal carcinomas. Science 1989, **244**: 217–221.

682 Banner BF, Chacho MS, Roseman DL, Coon JS. Multiparameter flow cytometric analysis of colon polyps. Am J Clin Pathol 1987, **87**: 313–318.

683 Bat L, Pines A, Ron E, Rosenblum Y, Niv Y, Shemesh E. Colorectal adenomatous polyps and carcinoma in Ashkenazi and non-Ashkenazi Jews in Israel. Cancer 1986, **58**: 1167–1171.

684 Boland CR, Montgomery CK, Kim YS. A cancer-associated mucin alteration in benign colonic polyps. Gastroenterology 1982, **82**: 664–672.

685 Boland CR, Sato J, Appelman HD, Bresalier RS, Feinberg AP. Microallelotyping defines the sequence and tempo of allelic losses at tumour suppressor gene loci during colorectal cancer progression. Nat Med 1995, **1**: 902–909.

686 Castleman B, Krikstein HI. Do adenomatous polyps of the colon become malignant? N Engl J Med 1962, **267**: 469–475.

687 Cho KR, Vogelstein B. Genetic alterations in the adenoma-carcinoma sequence. Cancer 1992, **70**: 1727–1731.

688 Clark JC, Collan Y, Eide TJ, Estève J, Ewen S, Gibbs NM, Jensen OM, Koskela E, MacLennan R, Simpson JG, Stalsberg H, Zaridze DG. Prevalence of polyps in an autopsy series from areas with varying incidence of large-bowel cancer. Int J Cancer 1985, **36**: 179–186.

689 Colacchio TA, Forde KA, Scantlebury VP. Endoscopic polypectomy. Inadequate treatment for invasive colorectal carcinoma. Ann Surg 1981, **194**: 704–707.

690 Cooper HS. Surgical pathology of endoscopically removed malignant polyps of the colon and rectum. Am J Surg Pathol 1983, **7**: 613–623.

691 Cooper HS, Reuter VE. Peanut lectin-binding sites in polyps of the colon and rectum. Lab Invest 1983, **49**: 655–661.

692 Cooper HS, Cox J, Patchevsky AS. Immunohistologic study of blood group substances in polyps of the distal colon. Expression of a fetal antigen. Am J Clin Pathol 1980, **73**: 345–350.

693 Cooper HS, Deppisch LM, Kahn EI, Lev R, Manley PN, Pascal RR, Qizilbash AH, Rickert RR, Silverman JF, Wirman JA. Pathology of the malignant colorectal polyp. Hum Pathol 1998, **29**: 15–26.

694 Correa P, Strong JP, Reif A, Johnson WD. The epidemiology of colorectal polyps. Prevalence in New Orleans and international comparisons. Cancer 1977, **39**: 2258–2264.

695 Coverlizza S, Risio M, Ferrari A, Fenoglio-Preiser CM, Rossini FP. Colorectal adenomas containing invasive carcinoma. Pathologic assessment of lymph node metastatic potential. Cancer 1989, **64**: 1937–1947.

696 Crawford BE, Stromeyer FW. Small nonpolypoid carcinomas of the large intestine. Cancer 1983, **51**: 1760–1763.

697 Eide TJ. Remnants of adenomas in colorectal carcinomas. Cancer 1983, **51**: 1866–1872.

698 Eide TJ. Prevalence and morphological features of adenomas of the large intestine in individuals with and without colorectal carcinoma. Histopathology 1986, **10**: 111–118.

699 Euscher ED, Niemann TH, Lucas JG, Kurokawa AM, Frankel WL. Large colorectal adenomas: an approach to pathologic evaluation. Am J Clin Pathol 2001, **116**: 336–340.

700 Fearon ER, Cho KR, Nigro JM, Kern SE, Simons JW, Ruppert JM, Hamilton SR, Preisinger AC, Thomas G, Kinzler KW, Vogelstein B. Identification of a chromosome 18q gene that is altered in colorectal cancers. Science 1990, **247**: 49–56.

701 Fearon ER, Vogelstein B. A genetic model for colorectal tumorigenesis. Cell 1990, **61**: 759–767.

702 Fenoglio CM, Kaye GI, Lane N. Distribution of human colonic lymphatics in normal, hyperplastic, and adenomatous tissue. Its relationship to metastasis from small carcinomas in pedunculated adenomas, with two case reports. Gastroenterology 1973, **64**: 51–66.

703 Fenoglio CM, Lane N. The anatomical precursor of colorectal carcinoma. Cancer 1974, **34**: 819–823.

704 Frei JV. Endoscopic large bowel polypectomy. Adequate treatment of some completely removed, minimally invasive lesions. Am J Surg Pathol 1985, **9**: 355–359.

705 Fried GM, Hreno A, Duguid WP, Hampson LG. Rational management of malignant colon polyps based on long-term follow-up. Surgery 1984, **96**: 815–822.

706 Fucini C, Wolff BG, Spencer RJ. An appraisal of endoscopic removal of malignant colonic polyps. Mayo Clin Proc 1986, **61**: 123–126.

707 Giardiello FM, Hamilton SR, Krush AJ, Piantadosi S, Hylind LM, Celano P, Booker SV, Robinson CR, Offerhaus GJ. Treatment of colonic and rectal adenomas with sulindac in familial adenomatous polyposis. N Engl J Med 1993, **328**: 1313–1316.

708 Gillespie PE, Chambers TJ, Chan KW, Doronzo F, Morson BC, Williams CB. Colonic adenomas. A colonoscopic survey. Gut 1979, **20**: 240–245.

709 Griffioen G, Bosman FT, Verspaget HW, de Bruin PA, Biemond I, Lamers CB. Mucin profiles and potential for malignancy of human colorectal adenomatous polyps. Cancer 1989, **63**: 1587–1591.

710 Haggitt RC, Glotzbach RE, Soffer EE, Wruble LD. Prognostic factors in colorectal carcinomas arising in adenomas. Implications for lesions removed by endoscopic polypectomy. Gastroenterology 1985, **89**: 328–336.

711 Hamilton SR. Molecular genetics of colorectal carcinoma. Cancer 1992, **70**: 1216–1221.

712 Hamilton SR. The adenoma-adenocarcinoma sequence in the large bowel. Variations on a theme. J Cell Biochem Suppl 1992, **16G**: 41–46.

713 Heppner Goss KH, Groden J. Biology of the adenomatous polyposis coli tumor suppressor. J Clin Oncol 2000, **18**: 1967–1979.

714 Hermanek PJ Jr, Giedl J. The adenoma-carcinoma sequence in AMMN-induced colonic tumors of the rat. Pathol Res Pract 1984, **178**: 548–554.

715 Hosaka S, Aoki Y, Akamatsu T, Nakamura N, Hosaka N, Kiyosawa K. Detection of genetic alterations in the p53 suppressor gene and the K-ras oncogene among different grades of dysplasia in patients with colorectal adenomas. Cancer 2002, **94**: 219–227.

716 Hultborn KA. The causal relationship between benign epithelial tumors and adenocarcinoma of the colon and rectum. Acta Radiol 1954, **113**: 1–71.

717 Ichii S, Takeda S, Horii A, Nakatsuru S, Miyoshi Y, Emi M, Fujiwara Y, Koyama K, Furuyama J, Utsunomiya J, et al. Detailed analysis of genetic alterations in colorectal tumors from patients with and without familial adenomatous polyposis (FAP). Oncogene 1993, **8**: 2399–2405.

718 Iino H, Fukayama M, Maeda Y, Koike M, Mori T, Takahashi T, Kikuchi-Yanoshita R, Miyaki M, Mizuno S, Watanabe S. Molecular genetics for clinical management of colorectal carcinoma. 17p, 18q, and 22q loss of heterozygosity and decreased DCC expression are correlated with the metastatic potential. Cancer 1994, **73**: 1324–1331.

719 Jorgensen OD, Kronborg O, Fenger C. The Funen Adenoma Follow-up Study. Incidence and death from colorectal carcinoma in an adenoma surveillance program. Scand J Gastroenterol 1993, **28**: 869–874.

720 Kinzler KW, Nilbert MC, Vogelstein B, Bryan TM, Levy DB, Smith KJ, Preisinger AC, Hamilton SR, Hedge P, Markham A, et al. Identification of a gene located at chromosome 5q21 that is mutated in colorectal cancers. Science 1991, **251**: 1366–1370.

721 Kraus FT. Pedunculated adenomatous polyp with carcinoma in the tip and metastasis to lymph nodes. Dis Colon Rectum 1965, **8**: 283–286.

722 Kyzer S, Begin LR, Gordon PH, Mitmaker B. The care of patients with colorectal polyps that contain invasive adenocarcinoma. Endoscopic polypectomy or colectomy? Cancer 1992, **70**: 2044–2050.

723 Lipper S, Kahn LB, Ackerman LV. The significance of microscopic invasive cancer in endoscopically removed polyps of the large bowel. A clinicopathologic study of 51 cases. Cancer 1983, **52**: 1691–1699.

724 Lotfi AM, Spencer RJ, Ilstrup DM, Melton LJ III. Colorectal polyps and the risk of subsequent carcinoma. Mayo Clin Proc 1986, **61**: 337–343.

725 Madara JL, Harte P, Deasy J, Ross D, Lahey S, Steele G Jr. Evidence for an adenoma-carcinoma sequence in dimethylhydrazine-induced neoplasms of rat intestinal epithelium. Am J Pathol 1983, **110**: 230–235.

726 Morson BC. The pathogenesis of colorectal cancer. In Bennington JL (consulting ed.): Major problems in pathology, vol. 10. Philadelphia, 1978, W.B. Saunders.

727 Morson BC, Whiteway JE, Jones EA, Macrae FA, Williams CB. Histopathology and prognosis of malignant colorectal polyps treated by endoscopic polypectomy. Gut 1984, **25**: 437–444.

728 Mueller JD, Bethke B, Stolte M. Colorectal de novo carcinoma: a review of its diagnosis, histopathology, molecular biology, and clinical relevance. Virchows Arch 2002, **440**: 453–460.

729 Mulder JW, Offerhaus GJ, de Feyter EP, Floyd JJ, Kern SE, Vogelstein B, Hamilton SR. The relationship of quantitative nuclear morphology to molecular genetic alterations in the adenoma-carcinoma sequence of the large bowel. Am J Pathol 1992, **141**: 797–804.

730 Muto T, Bussey HJR, Morson BC. The evolution of cancer of the colon and rectum. Cancer 1975, **36**: 2251–2270.

731 Nugent KP, Spigelman AD, Phillips RK. Life expectancy after colectomy and ileorectal anastomosis for familial adenomatous polyposis. Dis Colon Rectum 1993, **36**: 1059–1062.

732 Offerhaus GJ, De Feyter EP, Cornelisse CJ, Tersmette KW, Floyd J, Kern SE, Vogelstein B, Hamilton SR. The relationship of DNA aneuploidy to molecular genetic alterations in colorectal carcinoma. Gastroenterology 1992, **102**: 1612–1619.

733 Offerhaus GJ, Giardiello FM, Krush AJ, Booker SV, Tersmette AC, Kelley NC, Hamilton SR. The risk of upper gastrointestinal cancer in familial adenomatous polyposis. Gastroenterology 1992, **102**: 1980–1982.

734 Owen DA. Flat adenoma, flat carcinoma, and de novo carcinoma of the colon. Cancer 1996, **77**: 3–6.

735 Powell SM, Zilz N, Beazer-Barclay Y, Bryan TM, Hamilton SR, Thibodeau SN, Vogelstein B, Kinzler KW. APC mutations occur early during colorectal tumorigenesis. Nature 1992, **359**: 235–237.

736 Read TE, Read JD, Butterly LF. Importance of adenomas 5 mm or less in diameter that are detected by sigmoidoscopy. N Engl J Med 1997, **336**: 8–12.

737 Riddell RH. Hands off "cancerous" large bowel polyps. Gastroenterology 1985, **89**: 432–441.

738 Shamsuddin AM, Kato Y, Kunishima N, Sugano H, Trump BF. Carcinoma *in situ* in nonpolypoid mucosa of the large intestine. Report of a case with significance in strategies for early detection. Cancer 1985, **56**: 2849–2854.

739 Shatney CH, Lober PH, Gilbertsen VA, Sosin H. The treatment of pedunculated adenomatous colorectal polyps with focal cancer. Surg Gynecol Obstet 1974, **139**: 845–850.

740 Shimoda T, Ikegami M, Fujisaki J, Matsui T, Aizawa S, Ishikawa E. Early colorectal carcinoma with special reference to its development de novo. Cancer 1989, **64**: 1138–1146.

741 Simons BD, Morrison AS, Lev R, Verhoek-Oftedahl W. Relationship of polyps to cancer of the large intestine. J Natl Cancer Inst 1992, **84**: 962–966.

742 Skinner JM, Whitehead R. Tumor-associated antigens in polyps and carcinoma of the human large bowel. Cancer 1981, **47**: 1241–1245.

743 Spjut HJ, Frankel NB, Appel MF. The small carcinoma of the large bowel. Am J Surg Pathol 1979, **3**: 39–46.

744 Spratt JS Jr, Ackerman LV. Small primary adenocarcinomas of the colon and rectum. JAMA 1962, **179**: 337–346.

745 Spratt JS Jr, Moyer C, Ackerman LV. Relationship of polyps of the colon to colonic cancer. Ann Surg 1958, **148**: 682–698.

746 Spratt JS Jr, Watson FR. The rationale of practice for polypoid lesions of the colon. Cancer 1971, **28**: 153–159.

747 Stamm B, Ristivojevic B. Small pedunculated tubular adenoma of the colon with carcinoma restricted to the head, invasion of lymphatics and widespread metastases. Case report and review of the literature. Virchows Arch [A] 1983, **402**: 83–89.

748 Tandon M, Sostek M, Klein MA. Focus of signet ring cell carcinoma in an adenoma of the sigmoid colon. Arch Pathol Lab Med 1999, **123**: 957–959.

749 Thomas MG, Thomson JP, Williamson RC. Oral calcium inhibits rectal epithelial proliferation in familial adenomatous polyposis. Br J Surg 1993, **80**: 499–501.

750 van den Ingh HF, Bara J, Cornelisse CJ, Nap M. Aneuploidy and expression of gastric-associated mucus antigens M[1] and CEA in colorectal adenomas. Am J Clin Pathol 1987, **87**: 174–179.

751 Wada R, Matsukuma S, Abe H, Kuwabara N, Suda K, Arakawa A, Kitamura S. Histopathological studies of superficial-type early colorectal carcinoma. Cancer 1996, **77**: 44–50.

752 Watanabe T, Muto T, Sawada T, Miyaki M. Flat adenoma as a precursor of colorectal carcinoma in hereditary nonpolyposis colorectal carcinoma. Cancer 1996, **77**: 627–634.

753 Williams C, Muto T, Rutter KRP. Removal of polyps with fibreoptic colonoscope. A new approach to colonic polypectomy. Br Med J 1973, **1**: 451–452.

754 Winawer SJ, Zauber AG, Ho MN, O'Brien MJ, Gottlieb LS, Sternberg SS, Waye JD, Schapiro M, Bond JH, Panish JF, Ackroyd F, Shike M, Kurtz RC, Hornsby-Lewis L, Gerdes H, Stewart ET, and the National Polyp Study Workgroup. Prevention of colorectal cancer by colonoscopic polypectomy. N Engl J Med 1993, **329**: 1977–1981.

755 Winawer SJ, Zauber AG, O'Brien MJ, Ho MN, Gottlieb L, Sternberg SS, Waye JD, Bond J, Schapiro M, Stewart ET, et al. Randomized comparison of surveillance intervals after colonoscopic removal of newly diagnosed adenomatous polyps. The National Polyp Study Workgroup. N Engl J Med 1993, **328**: 901–906.

756 Winawer SJ, Zauber AG, Gerdes H, O'Brien MJ, Gottlieb LS, Sternberg SS, Bond JH, Waye JD, Schapiro M, Panish JF, Kurtz RC, Shike M, Ackroyd FW, Stewart ET, Skolnick M, Bishop DT. Risk of colorectal cancer in the families of patients with adenomatous polyps. National Polyp Study Work Group. N Engl J Med 1996, **334**: 82–87.

757 Winde G, Gumbinger HG, Osswald H, Kemper F, Bunte H. The NSAID sulindac reverses rectal adenomas in colectomized patients with familial adenomatous polyposis. Clinical results of a dose-finding study on rectal sulindac administration. Int J Colorectal Dis 1993, **8**: 13–17.

758 Wolff WI, Shinya H. Polypectomy via the fiberoptic colonoscope. Removal of neoplasms beyond reach of the sigmoidoscope. N Engl J Med 1973, **288**: 329–332.

759 Wolff WI, Shinya H. Endoscopic polypectomy. Therapeutic and clinicopathologic aspects. Cancer 1975, **36**: 683–690.

760 Zotter S, Lossnitzer A, Hageman PC, Delemarre JFM, Hilkens J, Hilgers J. Immunohistochemical localization of the epithelial marker MAM-6 in invasive malignancies and highly dysplastic adenomas of the large intestine. Lab Invest 1987, **57**: 193–199.

Carcinoma

General features

761 Alessi E, Brambilla L, Luporini G, Mosca L, Bevilacqua G. Multiple sebaceous tumors and carcinomas of the colon. Torre syndrome. Cancer 1985, **55**: 2566–2574.

762 Berg JW, Howell MA. The geographic pathology of bowel cancer. Cancer 1974, **34**: 807–814.

763 Black WC, Ackerman LV. Carcinoma of the large intestine as a late complication of pelvic radiotherapy. Clin Radiol 1965, **16**: 278–281.

764 Boyle P, Zaridze DG, Smans M. Descriptive epidemiology of colorectal cancer. Int J Cancer 1985, **36**: 9–18.

765 Cipolla R, Garcia RL. Colonic polyps and adenocarcinoma complicating ureterosigmoidostomy. Report of a case. Am J Gastroenterol 1984, **79**: 453–457.

766 Hill MJ. Bacteria and the etiology of colonic cancer. Cancer 1974, **34**: 815–818.

767 Jass JR. Diagnosis of hereditary non-polyposis colorectal cancer. Histopathology 1998, **32**: 491–497.

768 Krontiris TG, Devlin B, Karp DD, Robert NJ, Risch N. An association between the risk of cancer and mutations in the HRAS1 minisatellite locus. N Engl J Med 1993, **329**: 517–523.

769 Lasser A, Acosta AE. Colonic neoplasms complicating ureterosigmoidostomy. Cancer 1975, **35**: 1218–1222.

770 Levin B. Nutrition and colorectal cancer. Cancer 1992, **70**: 1723–1726.

770a Lynch HT, de la Chapelle A. Hereditary colorectal cancer. N Engl J Med 2003, **348**: 919–932.

771 Lynch HT, Kimberling W, Albano WA, Lynch JF, Biscone K, Schuelke GS, Sandberg AA, Lipkin M, Deschner EE, Mikol YB, Elston RC, Bailey-Wilson JE, Danes BS. Hereditary nonpolyposis

colorectal cancer (Lynch syndromes I and II). Part I. Clinical description of resource. Cancer 1985, **56**: 934–938.

772 Lynch HT, Smyrk TC, Lanspa SJ, Lynch PM, Watson P, Strayhorn PC, Bronson EK, Lynch JF, Priluck IA, Appelman HD. Phenotypic variation in colorectal adenoma/cancer expression in two families. Hereditary flat adenoma syndrome. Cancer 1990, **66**: 909–915.

773 Lynch HT, Watson P, Smyrk TC, Lanspa SJ, Borna BM, Boland CR, Lynch JF, Cavalieri RJ, Leppert M, White R, et al. Colon cancer genetics. Cancer 1992, **70**: 1300–1312.

774 Lynch HT, Smyrk TC. Hereditary colorectal cancer. Semin Oncol 1999, **26**: 478–484.

775 Marcheggiano A, Iannoni C, Pallone F, Frieri G, Gallucci M, Caprilli R. Abnormal patterns of colonic mucin secretion after ureterosigmoidostomy. Hum Pathol 1984, **15**: 647–650.

776 Marra G, Boland CR. Hereditary nonpolyposis colorectal cancer. The syndrome, the genes, and historical perspectives. J Natl Cancer Inst 1995, **87**: 1114–1125.

777 Mecklin JP, Jarvinen HJ, Virolainen M. The association between cholangiocarcinoma and hereditary nonpolyposis colorectal carcinoma. Cancer 1992, **69**: 1112–1114.

778 Mendeloff AI. Dietary fiber and the gastrointestinal tract. Critical assessment. In Beek JE (ed.): Developments in digestive diseases. Philadelphia, 1979, Lea & Febiger.

779 Mills SE, Allen MS Jr. Colorectal carcinoma in the first decades of life. Am J Surg Pathol 1979, **3**: 443–448.

780 O'Higgins N, Digney J, Duff FA, Kelly DG. Three polypoid colorectal tumours associated with different types of ureterocolic implantation. Br J Urol 1981, **53**: 278–279.

781 Peltomaki P, Aaltonen LA, Sistonen P, Pykkanen L, Mecklin JP, Jarvinen H, Green JS, Jass JR, Weber JL, Leach FS, et al. Genetic mapping of a locus predisposing to human colorectal cancer. Science 1993, **260**: 810–812.

782 Qizilbash AH. Radiation-induced carcinoma of the rectum. A late complication of pelvic irradiation. Arch Pathol 1974, **98**: 118–121.

783 Rivard J-Y, Bedard A, Dionne L. Colonic neoplasm following ureterosigmoidostomy. J Urol 1975, **113**: 781–786.

784 Schipper H, Decter A. Carcinoma of the colon arising at ureteral implant sites despite early external diversion. Pathogenetic and clinical implications. Cancer 1981, **47**: 2062–2065.

785 Stemmermann GN, Nomura AMY, Heilbrun LK. Dietary fat and the risk of colorectal cancer. Cancer Res 1984, **44**: 4633–4637.

786 Watson P, Lynch HT. Extracolonic cancer in hereditary nonpolyposis colorectal cancer. Cancer 1993, **71**: 677–685.

787 Weisburger JH. Causes, relevant mechanisms, and prevention of large bowel cancer. Semin Oncol 1991, **18**: 316–336.

Clinical features

788 American Society of Clinical Oncology. Clinical practice guidelines for the use of tumor markers in breast and colorectal cancer. Adopted on May 17, 1966 by the American Society of Clinical Oncology. J Clin Oncol 1996, **14**: 2843–2877.

789 Gilbertsen VA. Proctosigmoidoscopy and polypectomy in reducing the incidence of rectal cancer. Cancer 1974, **34**: 936–939.

790 Gilbertsen VA, McHugh R, Schuman L, Williams SE. The earlier detection of colorectal cancers. A preliminary report of the results of the occult blood study. Cancer 1980, **45**: 2889–2901.

791 Gilbertsen VA, Nelms JM. The prevention of invasive cancer of the rectum. Cancer 1978, **41**: 1137–1139.

792 Levin B. Colorectal cancer screening. Cancer 1993, **72**: 1056–1060.

793 Mandel JS, Bond JH, Church TR, Snover DC, Broadley GM, Schuman LM, Ederer F, For the Minnesota Colon Cancer Control Study. Reducing mortality from colorectal cancer by screening for fecal occult blood. N Engl J Med 1993, **328**: 1365–1371.

794 Minton JP, Hoehn JL, Gerber DM, Horsley JS, Connolly DP, Salwan F, Fletcher WS, Cruz AB Jr, Gatchell FG, Oviedo M,

Meyer KK, Leffall LD Jr, Berk RS, Stewart PA, Kurucz SE. Results of a 400-patient carcinoembryonic antigen second-look colorectal cancer study. Cancer 1985, **55**: 1284–1290.

795 Quentmeier A, Möller P, Schwarz V, Abel U, Schlag P. Carcinoembryonic antigen, CA 19–9, and CA 125 in normal and carcinomatous human colorectal tissue. Cancer 1987, **60**: 2261–2266.

796 Selby JV, Friedman GD, Quesenberry CP Jr, Weiss NE. A case-control study of screening sigmoidoscopy and mortality from colorectal cancer. N Engl J Med 1992, **326**: 653–657.

797 Sidransky D, Tokino T, Hamilton SR, Kinzler KW, Levin B, Frost P, Vogelstein B. Identification of *ras* oncogene mutations in the stool of patients with curable colorectal tumors. Science 1992, **256**: 102–105.

798 Thomas WM, Pye G, Hardcastle JD, Walker AR. Screening for colorectal carcinoma. An analysis of the sensitivity of haemoccult. Br J Surg 1992, **79**: 833–835.

799 Thompson DMP, Krupey J, Freedman SO, Gold P. The radioimmunoassay of circulating carcinoembryonic antigen of the human digestive system. Proc Natl Acad Sci U S A 1969, **64**: 161–167.

800 Toribara NW, Sleisenger MH. Screening for colorectal cancer. N Engl J Med 1995, **332**: 861–867.

801 Traverso G, Shuber A, Levin B, Johnson C, Olsson L, Schoetz DJ Jr, Hamilton SR, Boynton K, Kinzler KW, Vogelstein B. Detection of APC mutations in fecal DNA from patients with colorectal tumors. N Engl J Med 2002, **346**: 311–320.

802 van der Schouw YT, Verbeek AL, Wobbes T, Segers MF, Thomas CM. Comparison of four serum tumour markers in the diagnosis of colorectal carcinoma. Br J Cancer 1992, **66**: 148–154.

803 Winawer S, Schottenfeld D, Sherlock P. Screening for colorectal cancer. The issues. Gastroenterology 1985, **88**: 841–844.

804 Zamcheck N, Doos WG, Prudente R, Lurie BB, Gottlieb LS. Prognostic factors in colon carcinoma. Correlation of serum carcinoembryonic antigen level and tumor histopathology. Hum Pathol 1975, **6**: 31–45.

805 Zamcheck N, Moore TL, Dhar P, Kupchik H. Immunologic diagnosis and prognosis of human digestive-tract cancer. Carcinoembryonic antigens. N Engl J Med 1972, **286**: 83–86.

Site and gross features

806 Black WA, Waugh JM. The intramural extension of carcinoma of the descending colon, sigmoid, and recto-sigmoid. Surg Gynecol Obstet 1948, **87**: 457–464.

807 Cady B, Stone MD, Wayne J. Continuing trends in the prevalence of right-sided lesions among colorectal carcinomas. Arch Surg 1993, **128**: 505–509.

808 Cooper HS, Slemmer JR. Surgical pathology of carcinoma of the colon and rectum. Semin Oncol 1991, **18**: 367–380.

809 Dubrow R, Bernstein J, Holford TR. Age-period-cohort modelling of large-bowel-cancer incidence by anatomic sub-site and sex in Connecticut. Int J Cancer 1993, **53**: 907–913.

810 Dukes CE. Cancer of the rectum. An analysis of 1,000 cases. J Pathol Bacteriol 1940, **50**: 527–539.

811 Ekelund GR. Multiple carcinomas of the colon and rectum. Cancer 1974, **33**: 1630–1634.

812 George SM, Makinen MJ, Jernvall P, Makela J, Vihko P, Karttunen TJ. Classification of advanced colorectal carcinomas by tumor edge morphology: evidence for different pathogenesis and significance of polypoid and nonpolypoid tumors. Cancer 2000, **89**: 1901–1909.

813 Greenstein AJ, Slater G, Heimann TM, Sachar DB, Aufses AH Jr. A comparison of multiple synchronous colorectal cancer in ulcerative colitis, familial polyposis coli, and *de novo* cancer. Ann Surg 1986, **203**: 123–128.

814 Iishi H, Tatsuta M, Tsutsui S, Imanishi K, Otani T, Okuda S, Ishiguro S, Taniguchi H. Early depressed adenocarcinoma of the large intestine. Cancer 1992, **69**: 2406–2410.

815 Kuramoto S, Oohara T. Flat early cancers of the large intestine. Cancer 1989, **64**: 950–955.

816 Netscher DT, Larson GM. Colon cancer. The left to right shift and its implications. Surg Gastroenterol 1983, **2**: 13–18.

817 Quer RE, Dahlin DC, Mayo CW. Retrograde intramural spread of carcinoma of the rectum and rectosigmoid. A microscopic study. Surg Gynecol Obstet 1953, **96**: 24–30.

818 Slater G, Papatestas AE, Tartter PI, Mulvihill M, Aufses AH Jr. Age distribution of right- and left-sided colorectal cancers. Am J Gastroenterol 1982, **77**: 63–66.

819 Stefansson T, Ekbom A, Sparen P, Pahlman L. Increased risk of left sided colon cancer in patients with diverticular disease. Gut 1993, **34**: 499–502.

820 Tada S, Yao T, Iida M, Koga H, Hizawa K, Fujishima M. A clinicopathologic study of small flat colorectal carcinoma. Cancer 1994, **74**: 2430–2435.

821 Thomas CR Jr, Jarosz R, Evans N. Racial differences in the anatomical distribution of colon cancer. Arch Surg 1992, **127**: 1241–1245.

822 Yasuda K, Ajioka Y, Watanabe H, Matsuda K, Kitano S. Morphogenesis and development of superficial spreading tumor of the colon and rectum. Pathol Int 1997, **47**: 769–774.

Microscopic features

823 Ambe K, Mori M, Enjoji M. S-100 protein-positive dendritic cells in colorectal adenocarcinomas. Distribution and relation to the clinical prognosis. Cancer 1989, **63**: 496–503.

824 Bellis D, Marci V, Monga G. Light microscopic and immunohistochemical evaluation of vascular neural invasion in colorectal cancer. Pathol Res Pract 1993, **189**: 443–447.

825 Dawson PA, Filipe MI. An ultrastructural and histochemical study of the mucous membrane adjacent to and remote from carcinoma of the colon. Cancer 1976, **37**: 2388–2398.

826 Dukes CE. Ossification in rectal cancer. Proc R Soc Med 1939, **32**: 1489–1494.

827 Franzin G, Grigioni WF, Dina R, Scarpa A, Zamboni G. Mucin secretion and morphological changes of the mucosa in non-neoplastic diseases of the colon. Histopathology 1983, **7**: 707–718.

828 Horny H-P, Horst H-A. Lymphoreticular infiltrates in adenocarcinoma of the large intestine. Pathol Res Pract 1987, **182**: 222–227.

829 Isaacson P, Atwood PRA. Failure to demonstrate specificity of the morphological and histochemical changes in mucosa adjacent to colonic carcinoma (transitional mucosa). J Clin Pathol 1979, **32**: 214–218.

830 Lev R, Lance P, Camara P. Histochemical and morphologic studies of mucosa bordering rectosigmoid carcinomas. Comparisons with normal, diseased, and malignant colonic epithelium. Hum Pathol 1985, **16**: 151–161.

831 Listinsky CM, Riddell RH. Patterns of mucin secretion in neoplastic and non-neoplastic diseases of the colon. Hum Pathol 1981, **12**: 923–929.

832 Robey-Cafferty SS, Ro JY, Ordóñez NG, Cleary KR. Transitional mucosa of colon. A morphological, histochemical, and immunohistochemical study. Arch Pathol Lab Med 1990, **114**: 72–75.

833 Saffos RO, Rhatigan RM. Benign (nonpolypoid) mucosal changes adjacent to carcinomas of the colon. A light microscopic study of 20 cases. Hum Pathol 1977, **8**: 441–449.

834 Sawady J, Friedman MI, Katin WE, Mendselsohn G. Role of the transitional mucosa of the colon in differentiating primary adenocarcinoma from carcinomas metastatic to the colon. An immunohistochemical study. Am J Surg Pathol 1991, **15**: 136–144.

835 Shousha S. Paneth cell-rich papillary adenocarcinoma and a mucoid adenocarcinoma occurring synchronously in colon. A light and electron microscopic study. Histopathology 1979, **3**: 489–501.

836 Sunter JP, Higgs MJ, Cowan WK. Mucosal abnormalities at the anastomosis site in patients who have had intestinal resection for colonic cancer. J Clin Pathol 1985, **38**: 385–389.

837 Tajima K, Yamakawa M, Inaba Y, Katagiri T, Sasaki H. Cellular localization of interleukin-5 expression in rectal carcinoma with eosinophilia. Hum Pathol 1998, **29**: 1024–1027.

Histochemical, immunohistochemical, and electron microscopic features

838 Ahnen DJ, Nakane PK, Brown WR. Ultrastructural localization of carcinoembryonic antigen in normal intestine and colon cancer. Abnormal distribution of CEA on the surfaces of colon cancer cells. Cancer 1982, **49**: 2077–2090.

839 Arends JW, Wiggers T, Thijs CT, Verstijnen C, Swaen GJV, Bosman FT. The value of secretory component (SC) immunoreactivity in diagnosis and prognosis of colorectal carcinomas. Am J Clin Pathol 1984, **82**: 267–274.

840 Bacchi CE, Gown AM. Distribution and pattern of expression of villin, a gastrointestinal-associated cytoskeletal protein, in human carcinomas. A study employing paraffin-embedded tissue. Lab Invest 1991, **64**: 418–424.

841 Berezowski K, Stastny JF, Kornstein MJ. Cytokeratins 7 and 20 and carcinoembryonic antigen in ovarian and colonic carcinoma. Mod Pathol 1996, **9**: 426–429.

842 Bleday R, Song J, Walker ES, Salcedo BF, Thomas P, Wilson RE, Chen LB, Steele G Jr. Characterization of a new monoclonal antibody to a cell surface antigen on colorectal cancer and fetal gut tissues. Cancer 1986, **57**: 433–440.

843 Campo E, Muñoz J, Miquei R, Palacín A, Cardesa A, Sloane BF, Emmert-Buck MR. Cathepsin B expression in colorectal carcinomas correlates with tumor progression and shortened patient survival. Am J Pathol 1994, **145**: 301–309.

844 Campo E, Palacín A, Benasco C, Quesada E, Cardesa A. Human chorionic gonadotropin in colorectal carcinoma. An immunohistochemical study. Cancer 1987, **59**: 1611–1616.

845 Cao Y, Schlag PM, Karsten U. Immunodetection of epithelial mucin (MUC1, MUC3) and mucin-associated glycotopes (TF, Tn, and sialosyl-Tn) in benign and malignant lesions of colonic epithelium: apolar localization corresponds to malignant transformation. Virchows Arch 1997, **431**: 159–166.

846 Compton C, Wyatt R, Konugres A, Ehrenthal D, Durda P. Immunohistochemical studies of blood group substance H in colorectal tumors using a monoclonal antibody. Cancer 1987, **59**: 118–127.

847 Cooper HS, Malecha MJ, Bass C, Fagel PL, Steplewski Z. Expression of blood group antigens H-2, Le(y) and sialylated-Le(a) in human colorectal carcinoma. An immunohistochemical study using double-labelling techniques. Am J Pathol 1991, **138**: 103–110.

848 Culling CFA, Reid PE, Burton JD, Dunn WL. A histochemical method of differentiating lower gastrointestinal tract mucin from other mucins in primary or metastatic tumours. J Clin Pathol 1975, **28**: 656–658.

849 Ernst C, Thurin J, Atkinson B, Wurzel H, Herlyn M, Stromberg N, Civin C, Koprowski H. Monoclonal antibody localization of A and B isoantigens in normal and malignant fixed human tissues. Am J Pathol 1984, **117**: 451–461.

850 Esteban JM, Paxton R, Mehta P, Battifora H, Shively JE. Sensitivity and specificity of Gold types 1 to 5 anti-carcinoembryonic antigen monoclonal antibodies. Immunohistologic characterization in colorectal cancer and normal tissues. Hum Pathol 1993, **24**: 322–328.

851 Garin Chesa P, Rettig WJ, Melamed MR. Expression of cytokeratins in normal and neoplastic colonic epithelial cells. Implications for cellular differentiation and carcinogenesis. Am J Surg Pathol 1986, **10**: 829–835.

852 Goslin R, O'Brien MJ, Steele G, Mayer R, Wilson R, Corson JM,

Zamcheck N. Correlation of plasma CEA and CEA tissue staining in poorly differentiated colorectal cancer. Am J Med 1981, **71:** 246–253.

853 Gotzos V, Wintergerst ES, Musy JP, Spichtin HP, Genton CY. Selective distribution of calretinin in adenocarcinomas of the human colon and adjacent tissues. Am J Surg Pathol 1999, **23:** 701–711.

854 Hainsworth JD, Greco FA. Human chorionic gonadotropin production by colon carcinoma. Biochemical heterogeneity and identification of a chemotherapy-sensitive cell subpopulation. Cancer 1985, **56:** 1337–1340.

855 Hamada Y, Yamamura M, Hioki K, Yamamoto M, Nagura H, Watanabe K. Immunohistochemical study of carcinoembryonic antigen in patients with colorectal cancer. Correlation with plasma carcinoembryonic antigen levels. Cancer 1985, **55:** 136–141.

856 Hickey WF, Seiler MW. Ultrastructural markers of colonic adenocarcinoma. Cancer 1981, **47:** 140–145.

856a Kaimaktchiev V, Dimhofer S, Sauter G, Korcheva V, Mirlacher M, Loda M, Corless CL. Selective staining of gastrointestinal adenocarcinomas by the homeobox intestinal differentiation factor CDX2. (Abstract) Mod Pathol 2003, **16:** 123A.

857 Lagendijk JH, Mullink H, Van Diest PJ, Meijer GA, Meijer CJL. Tracing the origin of adenocarcinomas with unknown primary using immunohistochemistry: differential diagnosis between colonic and ovarian carcinomas as primary sites. Hum Pathol 1998, **29:** 491–497.

858 Listrom MB, Little JV, McKinley M, Fenoglio-Preiser CM. Immunoreactivity of tumor-associated glycoprotein (TAG-72) in normal, hyperplastic, and neoplastic colon. Hum Pathol 1989, **20:** 994–1000.

859 Loy TS, Calaluce RD. Utility of cytokeratin immunostaining in separating pulmonary adenocarcinomas from colonic adenocarcinomas. Am J Clin Pathol 1994, **102:** 764–767.

860 Midiri G, Amanti C, Benedetti M, Campisi C, Santeusanio G, Castagna G, Peronace L, Di Tondo U, Di Paola M, Pascal RR. CEA tissue staining in colorectal cancer patients. A way to improve the usefulness of serial serum CEA evaluation. Cancer 1985, **55:** 2624–2629.

861 Momburg F, Degener T, Bacchus E, Moldenhauer G, Hömmerling GJ, Möller P. Loss of HLA-A, B, C and de novo expression of HLA-D in colorectal cancer. Int J Cancer 1986, **37:** 179–184.

862 O'Brien MJ, Zamsheck N, Burke B, Kirkham S, Saravis C, Gottlieb LS. Immunocytochemical localization of carcinoembryonic antigen in benign and malignant colo-rectal tissues. Assessment of diagnostic value. Am J Clin Pathol 1981, **75:** 283–290.

863 Pihl E, McNaughton J, Ma J, Ward HA, Nairn RC. Immunohistological patterns of carcinoembryonic antigen in colorectal carcinoma. Correlation with staging and blood levels. Pathology 1980, **12:** 7–13.

864 Sata T, Roth J, Zuber C, Stamm B, Heitz PU. Expression of alpha 2,6-linked sialic acid residues in neoplastic but not in normal human colonic mucosa. A lectin-gold cytochemical study with *Sambucus nigra* and *Maackia amurensis* lectins. Am J Pathol 1991, **139:** 1435–1448.

865 Schoentag R, Williams V, Kuhns W. The distribution of blood group substance H and CEA in colorectal carcinoma. Cancer 1984, **53:** 503–509.

866 Sheahan K, O'Brien MJ, Burke B, Dervan PA, O'Keane JC, Gottlieb LS, Zamcheck N. Differential reactivities of carcinoembryonic antigen (CEA) and CEA-related monoclonal and polyclonal antibodies in common epithelial malignancies. Am J Clin Pathol 1990, **94:** 157–164.

867 Slattery ML, Samowitz WS, Holden JA. Estrogen and progesterone receptors in colon tumors. Am J Clin Pathol 2000, **113:** 364–368.

868 Watanabe H, Tokuyama H, Ohta H, Satomura Y, Okai T, Ooi A, Mai M, Sawabu N. Expression of placental alkaline phosphatase in gastric and colorectal cancers. An immunohistochemical study using the prepared monoclonal antibody. Cancer 1990, **66:** 2575–2582.

868a Werling RW, Yaziji H, Bacchi CE, Gown AM. CDX2, a highly sensitive and specific marker of adenocarcinomas of intestinal origin. Am J Surg Pathol 2003, **27:** 303–310.

869 Witte D, Chirala M, Younes A, Li Y, Younes M. Estrogen receptor beta is expressed in human colorectal adenocarcinoma. Hum Pathol 2001, **32:** 940–944.

869a Zhang H, Maitra A, Tabacka P, Wilentz RE, Hruban RH, Adsay NV. Differential MUC1, MUC2 and MUC5AC expression in colorectal, ampullary and pancreatobiliary carcinomas: potential biologic and diagnostic implications. (Abstract) Mod Pathol 2003, **16:** 138A.

Molecular genetic features

870 Bosman FT. Molecular pathology of colorectal cancer. Cytogenet Cell Genet 1999, **86:** 112–117.

871 Brabletz T, Jung A, Reu S, Prozner M, Hlubek F, Kunz-Schughart LA, Knuechel R, Kirchner T. Variable beta-catenin expression in colorectal cancers indicates tumors progression driven by the tumor environment. Proc Natl Acad Sci USA 2001, **98:** 10356–10361.

872 Brabletz T, Jung A, Kirchner T. Beta-catenin and the morphogenesis of colorectal cancer. Virchows Arch 2002, **441:** 1–11.

873 Connelly JH, Bruner JM, Robey-Cafferty SS, Sahin A. p53 protein expression in transitional mucosa and adenocarcinomas of the colorectum. Mod Pathol 1992, **5:** 537–539.

874 Czerniak B, Herz F, Koss LG, Schlom J. *ras* oncogene p21 as a tumor marker in the cytodiagnosis of gastric and colonic carcinomas. Cancer 1987, **60:** 2432–2436.

875 Dorudi S, Sheffield JP, Poulson R, Northover JM, Hart IR. E-cadherin expression in colorectal cancer. An immunocytochemical and in situ hybridization study. Am J Pathol 1993, **142:** 981–986.

876 Edmonston TB, Cuesta KH, Burkholder S, Barusevicius V, Rose D, Kovatich AJ, Boman B, Fry R, Fishel R, Palazzo JP. Colorectal carcinomas with high microsatellite instability: defining a distinct immunologic and molecular entity with respect to prognostic markers. Hum Pathol 2000, **31:** 1506–1514.

877 El-Baharawy MA, Poulsom R, Jeffery R, Talbot I, Alison MR. The expression of E-cadherin and catenins in sporadic colorectal carcinoma. Hum Pathol 2001, **32:** 1216–1224.

878 Finkelstein SD, Sayegh R, Christensen S, Swalsky PA. Genotypic classification of colorectal adenocarcinoma. Biologic behavior correlates with K-*ras*-2 mutation type. Cancer 1993, **71:** 3827–3838.

879 Gafà R, Maestri I, Matteuzzi M, Santini A, Ferretti S, Cavazzini L, Lanza G. Sporadic colorectal adenocarcinomas with high-frequency microsatellite instability. Cancer 2000, **89:** 2025–2037.

880 Gofuku J, Shiozaki H, Tsujinaka T, Inoue M, Tamura S, Doki Y, Matsui S, Tsukita S, Kikkawa N, Monden M. Expression of E-cadherin and alpha-catenin in patients with colorectal carcinoma. Correlation with cancer invasion and metastasis. Am J Clin Pathol 1999, **111:** 29–37.

880a Greenson JK, Bonner JD, Ben-Yzhak O, Cohen HI, Miselevich I, Resnick MB, Trougouboff P, Tomsho LD, Kim E, Low M, Almog R, Rennert G, Gruber SB. Phenotype of microsatellite unstable colorectal carcinomas. Am J Surg Pathol 2003, **27:** 563–570.

881 Hanski C, Bornhoeft G, Shimoda T, Hanski ML, Lane DP, Stein H, Riecken EO. Expression of p53 protein in invasive colorectal carcinomas of different histologic types. Cancer 1992, **70:** 2772–2777.

882 Hawkins NJ, Ward RL. Sporadic colorectal cancer with microsatellite instability and their possible origin in hyperplastic

polyps and serrated adenomas. J Natl Cancer Inst 2001, **93:** 1307–1313.

883 Ilyas M, Tomlinson IP. Genetic pathways in colorectal cancer. Histopathology 1996, **28:** 389–399.

884 Jansson DS, Radosevich JA, Carney WP, Rosen ST, Schlom J, Staren ED, Hyser MJ, Gould VE. An immunohistochemical analysis of *ras* oncogene expression in epithelial neoplasms of the colon. Cancer 1990, **65:** 1329–1337.

885 Johnston PG, O'Brien MJ, Dervan PA, Carney DN. Immunohistochemical analysis of cell kinetic parameters in colonic adenocarcinomas, adenomas, and normal mucosa. Hum Pathol 1989, **20:** 696–700.

886 Jothy S, Flanders TY, Nowacki PM. New developments in the molecular pathology of human colon cancer relevance to pathogenesis and diagnosis. Adv Anat Pathol 1996, **3:** 343–350.

886a Kende AI, Carr NJ, Sobin LH. Expression of cytokeratins 7 and 20 in carcinomas of the gastrointestinal tract. Histopathology 2003, **42:** 137–140.

887 Kinzler KW, Vogelstein B. Lessons from hereditary colorectal cancer. Cell 1996, **87:** 159–170.

888 Kobayashi M, Watanabe H, Ajioka Y, Honma T, Asakura H. Effect of K-ras mutation on morphogenesis of colorectal adenomas and early cancers: relationship to distribution of proliferating cells. Hum Pathol 1996, **27:** 1042–1049.

889 Linden MD, Ma CK, Kubus J, Brown RD, Zarbo RJ. Ki-67 and proliferating cell nuclear antigen tumor proliferative indices in DNA diploid colorectal adenocarcinomas. Correlation with histopathologic characteristics and cell cycle analysis with two-color DNA flow cytometry. Am J Clin Pathol 1993, **100:** 206–212.

890 Loukola A, Salovaara R, Kristo P, Moisio A-L, Kaariainen H, Ahtola H, Eskelinen M, Harkonen N, Julkunen R, Kangas E, Ojala S, Tulikoura J, Valkamo E, Jarvinen H, Mecklin JP, de la Chapelle A, Aaltonen LA. Microsatellite instability in adenomas as a marker for hereditary nonpolyposis colorectal cancer. Am J Pathol 1999, **155:** 1849–1853.

891 Matsumura T, Dohi K, Takanashi A, Ito H, Tahara E. Alteration and enhanced expression of the c-*myc* oncogene in human colorectal carcinomas. Pathol Res Pract 1990, **186:** 205–211.

892 Meyers FJ, Gumerlock PH, Kokoris SP, deVere White RW, McCormick F. Human bladder and colon carcinomas contain activated *ras* p21. Cancer 1989, **63:** 2177–2181.

893 Mueller E, Vieth M, Stolte M, Mueller J. The differentiation of true adenomas from colitis-associated dysplasia in ulcerative colitis: a comparative immunohistochemical study. Hum Pathol 1999, **30:** 898–905.

894 Parsons R. Molecular genetics and hereditary cancer: hereditary nonpolyposis colorectal carcinoma as a model. Cancer 1997, **80:** 533–536.

895 Porschen R, Lohe B, Hengels K-J, Borchard F. Assessment of cell proliferation in colorectal carcinomas using the monoclonal antibody Ki-67. Correlation with pathohistologic criteria and influence of irradiation. Cancer 1989, **64:** 2501–2505.

896 Purdie CA, O'Grady J, Piris J, Wylie AH, Bird CC. p53 expression in colorectal tumors. Am J Pathol 1991, **138:** 807–813.

897 Rodrigues NR, Rowan A, Smith MEF, Kerr IB, Bodmer WF, Gannon JV, Lane DP. p53 mutations in colorectal cancer. Proc Natl Acad Sci U S A 1990, **87:** 7555–7559.

898 Rüschoff J, Bittinger A, Neumann K, Schmitz-Moormann P. Prognostic significance of nucleolar organizing regions (NORs) in carcinomas of the sigmoid colon and rectum. Pathol Res Pract 1990, **186:** 85–91.

899 Sasaki A, Yokoyama S, Arita T, Inomata M, Kashima K, Nakayama I. Morules with biotin-containing optically clear nuclei in colonic tubular adenoma. Am J Surg Pathol 1999, **23:** 226–341.

899a Shia J, Ellis NA, Paty PB, Nash GM, Qin J, Offit K, Zhang X-M, Markowitz AJ, Nafa K, Guillem JG, Wong D, Gerald WL, Klimstra DS. Am J Surg Pathol 2003, **27:** 1407–1417.

900 Wong NA, Pignatelli M. Beta-catenin – a linchpin in colorectal carcinogenesis? Am J Pathol 2002, **160:** 389–401.

900a Wright CL, Stewart ID. Histopathology and mismatch repair status of 458 consecutive colorectal carcinomas. Am J Surg Pathol 2003, **27:** 1393–1406.

901 Zhuang Z, Emmert-Buck MR, Roth MJ, Gnarra J, Linehan WM, Liotta LA, Lubensky IA. Von-Hippel Lindau disease gene deletion detected in microdissected sporadic human colon carcinoma specimens. Hum Pathol 1996, **27:** 152–156.

Other microscopic types

902 Almagro UA. Primary signet-ring carcinoma of the colon. Cancer 1983, **52:** 1453–1457.

903 Amorn Y, Knight WA Jr. Primary linitis plastica of the colon. Report of two cases and review of the literature. Cancer 1978, **41:** 2420–2425.

904 Aru A, Rasmussen LA, Federspiel B, Horn T. Glassy cell carcinoma of the colon with human chorionic gonadotropin-production: a case report with immunohistochemical and ultrastructural analysis. Am J Surg Pathol 1996, **20:** 187–192.

905 Balthazar EJ, Rosenberg HD, Davidian MM. Primary and metastatic scirrhous carcinoma of the rectum. Am J Roentgenol 1979, **132:** 711–715.

906 Bosman FT. Neuroendocrine cells in colonic tumors. Mod Pathol 1992, **5:** 312–314.

907 Burke AB, Shekitka KM, Sobin LH. Small cell carcinomas of the large intestine. Am J Clin Pathol 1991, **95:** 315–321.

908 Chetty R, Bhathal PS. Caecal adenocarcinoma with rhabdoid phenotype. An immunohistochemical and ultrastructural analysis. Virchows Arch [A] 1993, **422:** 179–182.

909 Chevinsky AH, Berelowitz M, Hoover HC Jr. Adenosquamous carcinoma of the colon presenting with hypercalcemia. Cancer 1987, **60:** 1111–1116.

910 Clery AP, Dockerty MB, Waugh JM. Small-cell carcinoma of the colon and rectum. A clinicopathologic study. Arch Surg 1961, **83:** 164–172.

911 Connelly JH, Robey-Cafferty SS, Cleary KR. Mucineous carcinomas of the colon and rectum. An analysis of 62 stage B and C lesions. Arch Pathol Lab Med 1991, **115:** 1022–1025.

912 Connelly JH, Robey-Cafferty SS, el-Naggar AK, Cleary KR. Exophytic signetring cell carcinoma of the colorectum. Arch Pathol Lab Med 1991, **115:** 134–136.

913 Cox WF Jr, Pierce GB. The endodermal origin of the endocrine cells of an adenocarcinoma of the colon of the rat. Cancer 1982, **50:** 1530–1538.

914 Crissman JD. Adenosquamous and squamous cell carcinoma of the colon. Am J Surg Pathol 1978, **2:** 47–54.

915 de Bruine AP, Wiggers T, Beek C, Volovics A, von Meyenfieldt M, Arends JW, Bosman FT. Endocrine cells in colorectal adenocarcinomas. Incidence, hormone profile and prognostic relevance. Int J Cancer 1993, **54:** 765–771.

916 Gaffey MJ, Mills SE, Lack EE. Neuroendocrine carcinoma of the colon and rectum. A clinicopathologic, ultrastructural, and immunohistochemical study of 24 cases. Am J Surg Pathol 1990, **14:** 1010–1023.

917 Giacchero A, Aste H, Baracchini P, Conio M, Fulcheri E, Lapertosa G, Tanzi R. Primary signet-ring carcinoma of the large bowel. Report of nine cases. Cancer 1985, **56:** 2723–2726.

918 Goldstein NS, Long A, Kuan SF, Hart J. Colon signet ring cell adenocarcinoma: immunohistochemical characterization and comparison with gastric and typical colon adenocarcinoma. Appl Immunohistochem Mol Morphol 2000, **8:** 183–188.

919 Gould VE, Chejfec G. Neuroendocrine carcinomas of the colon. Ultrastructural and biochemical evidence of their secretory function. Am J Surg Pathol 1978, **2:** 31–38.

920 Grabowski P, Schonfelder J, Ahnert-Hilger G, Foss HD, Heine B, Schindler I, Stein H, Berger G, Zeitz M, Scherubl H. Expression of neuroendocrine markers: a signature of human undifferentiated carcinoma of the colon and rectum. Virchows Arch 2002, 441: 256–263.

921 Green JB, Timmcke AE, Mitchell WT, Hicks TC, Gathright JB Jr, Ray JE. Mucinous carcinoma – just another colon cancer? Dis Colon Rectum 1993, 36: 49–54.

922 Hall-Craggs M, Toker C. Basaloid tumor of the sigmoid colon. Hum Pathol 1982, 13: 497–500.

923 Hamazaki M, Kono S, Mimaya J, Ishihara A. Signet ring cell carcinoma in a polyp of the colon. A case report of a six-year old boy. Acta Pathol Jpn 1987, 37: 1679–1684.

924 Hara A, Saegusa M, Mitomi H, Kurihara M, Ishihara K, Hotta K, Okayasu I. Colonic mucin-carbohydrate components in colorectal tumors and their possible relationship to MUC2, p53 and DCC immunoreactivities. Pathol Res Pract 2000, 196: 159–166.

925 Hernandez FJ, Fernandez BB. Mucus-secreting colonic carcinoid tumors. Light- and electron-microscopic study of three cases. Dis Colon Rectum 1974, 17: 387–396.

926 Hernandez FJ, Reid JD. Mixed carcinoid and mucus-secreting intestinal tumors. Arch Pathol 1969, 88: 489–496.

927 Hickey WF, Corson JM. Squamous cell carcinoma arising in a duplication of the colon. Case report and literature review of squamous cell carcinoma of the colon and of malignancy complicating colonic duplication. Cancer 1981, 47: 602–609.

928 Horne BD, McCulloch CF. Squamous cell carcinoma of the cecum. A case report. Cancer 1978, 42: 1879–1882.

929 Ishikura H, Kishimoto T, Andachi H, Kakuta Y, Yoshiki T. Gastrointestinal hepatoid adenocarcinoma: venous permeation and mimicry of hepatocellular carcinoma, a report of four cases. Histopathology 1997, 31: 47–54.

930 Jessurun J, Romero-Guadarrama M, Manivel JC. Medullary adenocarcinoma of the colon: clinicopathologic study of 11 cases. Hum Pathol 1999, 30: 843–848.

931 Jewell LD, Barr JR, McCaughey WTE, Nguyen G-K, Owen DA. Clear-cell epithelial neoplasms of the large intestine. Arch Pathol Lab Med 1988, 112: 197–199.

932 Kubosawa H, Nagao K, Kondo Y, Ishige H, Inaba N. Coexistence of adenocarcinoma and choriocarcinoma in the sigmoid colon. Cancer 1984, 54: 866–868.

933 Lanza G, Gafa R, Matteuzzi M, Santini A. Medullary-type poorly differentiated adenocarcinoma of the large bowel: a distinct clinicopathologic entity characterized by microsatellite instability and improved survival. J Clin Oncol 1999, 17: 2429–2438.

934 Laufman H, Saphir O. Primary linitis plastica type of carcinoma of the colon. Arch Surg 1951, 62: 79–91.

935 Mills SE, Allen MS Jr, Cohen AR. Small-cell undifferentiated carcinoma of the colon. A clinicopathological study of five cases and their association with colonic adenomas. Am J Surg Pathol 1983, 7: 643–651.

936 Nakahara H, Ishikawa T, Itabashi M, Hirota T. Diffusely infiltrating primary colorectal carcinoma of linitis plastica and lymphangiosis types. Cancer 1992, 69: 901–906.

937 Newell KJ, Penswick JL, Driman DK. Basaloid carcinoma of the colon arising at the splenic flexure. Histopathology 2001, 38: 232–236.

938 Onishi R, Sano T, Nakamura Y, Namiuchi S, Sawada S, Ihara C, Shimatsu A. Ectopic adrenocorticotropin syndrome associated with undifferentiated carcinoma of the colon showing multidirectional neuroendocrine, exocrine, and squamous differentiation. Virchows Arch 1996, 427: 537–541.

939 Ordóñez NG, Luna MA. Choriocarcinoma of the colon. Am J Gastroenterol 1984, 79: 39–42.

940 Pagani A, Papotti M, Abbona GC, Bussolati G. Chromogranin gene expressions in colorectal adenocarcinomas. Mod Pathol 1995, 8: 626–632.

941 Park CH, Reid JR. Adenocarcinoma of the colon with choriocarcinoma in its metastases. Cancer 1980, 46: 570–575.

942 Reyes CV, Siddiqui MT. Anaplastic carcinoma of the colon: clinicopathologic study of eight cases of a poorly recognized lesion. Ann Diagn Pathol 1997, 1: 19–25.

943 Ruschoff J, Dietmaier W, Luttges J, Seitz G, Bocker T, Zirngibl H, Schlegel J, Schackert HK, Jauch KW, Hofstaedter F. Poorly differentiated colonic adenocarcinoma, medullary type. Clinical, phenotypic, and molecular characteristics. Am J Pathol 1997, 150: 1815–1825.

944 Sadahiro S, Ohmura T, Saito T, Akatsuka S. An assessment of the mucous component in carcinoma of the colon and rectum. Cancer 1989, 64: 1113–1116.

945 Saez C, Japon MA, Poveda MA, Segura DI. Mucinous (colloid) adenocarcinomas secrete distinct O-acylated forms of sialomucins: a histochemical study of gastric, colorectal and breast adenocarcinomas. Histopathology 2001, 39: 554–560.

946 Sarsfield P, Anthony PP. Small cell undifferentiated ("neuroendocrine") carcinoma of the colon. Histopathology 1990, 16: 357–363.

947 Sasaki O, Atkin WS, Jass JR. Mucinous carcinoma of the rectum. Histopathology 1987, 11: 259–272.

948 Schwartz AM, Orenstein JM. Small-cell undifferentiated carcinoma of the rectosigmoid colon. Arch Pathol Lab Med 1985, 109: 629–632.

949 Serio G, Aguzzi A. Spindle and giant cell carcinoma of the colon. Histopathology 1997, 30: 383–385.

950 Shia J, Tickoo SK, Guillem JG, Qin J, Nissan A, Hoos A, Stojadibovic A, Ruo L, Wong WD, Paty PB, Weiser MR, Minsky BD, Klimstra DS. Increased endocrine cells in treated rectal adenocarcinomas: a possible reflection of endocrine differentiation in tumor cells induced by chemotherapy and radiotherapy. Am J Surg Pathol 2002, 26: 863–872.

951 Shirouzu K, Isomoto H, Morodomi T, Ogata Y, Akagi Y, Kakegawa T. Primary linitis plastica carcinoma of the colon and rectum. Cancer 1994, 74: 1863–1868.

952 Smith DM Jr, Haggitt RC. The prevalence and prognostic significance of argyrophil cells in colorectal carcinomas. Am J Surg Pathol 1984, 8: 123–128.

953 Stevens WR, Ruiz P. Primary linitis plastica carcinoma of the colon and rectum. Mod Pathol 1989, 2: 265–269.

954 Sugao Y, Yao T, Kubo C, Tsuneyoshi M. Improved prognosis of solid-type poorly differentiated colorectal adenocarcinoma: a clinicopathological and immunohistochemical study. Histopathology 1997, 31: 123–133.

955 Sunblad AS, Paz RA. Mucinous carcinomas of the colon and rectum and their relation to polyps. Cancer 1982, 50: 2504–2509.

956 Symonds DA, Vickery AL Jr. Mucinous carcinoma of the colon and rectum. Cancer 1976, 37: 1891–1900.

957 Ulich TR, Cheng L, Glover H, Yang K, Lewin KJ. A colonic adenocarcinoma with argentaffin cells. An immunoperoxidose study demonstrating the presence of numerous neuroendocrine products. Cancer 1983, 51: 1483–1489.

957a Wang K, Weinrach D, Lal A, Musunuri S, Ramirez J, Ozer O, Keh P, Rao S. Signet-ring cell change versus signet-ring cell carcinoma. A comparative analysis. Am J Surg Pathol 2003, 27: 1429–1433.

958 Wick MR, Weatherby RP, Weiland LH. Small cell neuroendocrine carcinoma of the colon and rectum. Clinical, histologic, and ultrastructural study and immunohistochemical comparison with cloacogenic carcinoma. Hum Pathol 1987, 18: 9–21.

959 Williams GT, Blackshaw AJ, Morson BC. Squamous carcinoma of the colorectum and its genesis. J Pathol 1979, 129: 139–147.

960 Younes M, Katikaneni PR, Lechago J. The value of the preoperative mucosal biopsy in the diagnosis of colorectal mucinous adenocarcinoma. Cancer 1993, 72: 3588–3592.

Biopsy

961   Ueno H, Mochizuki H, Shinto E, Hashiguchi Y, Hase K, Talbot IC. Histologic indices in biopsy specimens for estimating the probability of extended local spread in patients with rectal carcinoma. Cancer 2002, **94**: 2882–2891.

Cytology

962   Ehya H, O'Hara BJ. Brush cytology in the diagnosis of colonic neoplasms. Cancer 1990, **66**: 1563–1567.

963   Raskin HF, Pleticka S. The cytologic diagnosis of cancer of the colon. Acta Cytol (Baltimore) 1964, **8**: 131–140.

964   Wilson MS, El Teraifi H, Schofield PF. The value of exfoliative cytology in the diagnosis of rectal malignancy. Int J Colorectal Dis 1993, **8**: 78–80.

965   Winawer SJ, Leidner SD, Hajdu SI, Sherlock P. Colonoscopic biopsy and cytology in the diagnosis of colon cancer. Cancer 1978, **42**: 2849–2853.

Staging and grading

966   Astler VB, Coller FA. The prognostic significance of direct extension of carcinoma of the colon and rectum. Ann Surg 1954, **139**: 846–851.

967   Beahrs OH. Staging of cancer of the colon and rectum. Cancer 1992, **70**: 1393–1396.

968   Dukes CE. Histologic grading of rectal carcinoma. Proc R Soc Med 1937, **30**: 371–376.

969   Dukes CE. Peculiarities in the pathology of cancer of the anorectal region. Proc R Soc Med 1946, **39**: 763–765.

970   Fisher ER, Sass R, Palekar A, Fisher B, Wolmark N, contributing National Surgical Adjuvant Breast and Bowel Projects Investigators. Dukes' classification revisited. Findings from the National Surgical Breast and Bowel Projects (Protocol R-01). Cancer 1989, **64**: 2354–2360.

971   Harrison JC, Dean PJ, el-Zeky F, Vander Zwaag R. From Dukes through Jass. Pathological prognostic indicators in rectal cancer. Hum Pathol 1994, **25**: 498–505.

972   Hawes RH. New staging techniques. Endoscopic ultrasound. Cancer 1993, **71**: 4207–4213.

973   Hutter RVP, Sobin LH. A universal staging system for cancer of the colon and rectum. Let there be light. Arch Pathol Lab Med 1986, **110**: 367–368.

974   Jass JR, Atkin WS, Cuzick J, Bussey HJR, Morson BC, Northover JMA, Todd IP. The grading of rectal cancer. Historical perspectives and a multivariate analysis of 447 cases. Histopathology 1986, **10**: 437–459.

975   Jochem RJ, Reading CC, Dozois RR, Carpenter HA, Wolff BG, Charboneau JW. Endorectal ultrasonographic staging of rectal carcinoma. Mayo Clin Proc 1990, **65**: 1571–1577.

976   Kirklin JW, Dockerty MB, Waugh JM. The role of the peritoneal reflection in the prognosis of carcinoma of the rectum and sigmoid colon. Surg Gynecol Obstet 1949, **88**: 326–331.

977   Kyriakos M. The President's cancer, the Dukes classification, and confusion. Arch Pathol Lab Med 1985, **109**: 1063–1066.

978   Thomas GDH, Dixon MF, Smeeton NC, Williams NS. Observer variation in the histological grading of rectal carcinoma. J Clin Pathol 1983, **36**: 385–391.

979   Zang Z, Cohen AM, Hajdu S, Sternberg SS, Sigurdson ER, Enker W. Serosal cytologic study to determine free mesothelial penetration of intraperitoneal colon cancer. Cancer 1992, **70**: 737–740.

Spread and metastases

980   Andreola S, Leo E, Belli F, Bufalino R, Tomasic G, Lavfarino C, Baldini MT, Meroni E. Manual dissection of adenocarcinoma of the lower third of the rectum specimens for detection of node metastases smaller than 5 mm. Cancer 1996, **77**: 607–612.

981   Andreola S, Leo E, Belli F, Gallino G, Sirizzotti G, Sampietro G. Adenocarcinoma of the lower third of the rectum: metastases in lymph nodes smaller than 5 mm and occult micrometastases: preliminary results on early tumor recurrence. Ann Surg Oncol 2001, **8**: 413–417.

982   Davidson BR, Sams VR, Styles J, Deane C, Boulos PB. Detection of occult nodal metastases in patients with colorectal carcinoma. Cancer 1990, **65**: 967–970.

983   Daya D, Nazerali L, Frank GL. Metastatic ovarian carcinoma of large intestinal origin simulating primary ovarian carcinoma. A clinicopathologic study of 25 cases. Am J Clin Pathol 1992, **97**: 751–758.

984   Dionigi A, Facco C, Tibiletti MG, Bernasconi B, Riva C, Capella C. Ovarian metastases from colorectal carcinoma. Clinicopathologic profile, immunophenotype, and karyotype analysis. Am J Clin Pathol 2000, **114**: 111–122.

985   Goldstein J, Mazor M, Leiberman JR. Primary carcinoma of the cecum with uterine metastases. Hum Pathol 1981, **12**: 1139–1140.

986   Goldstein NS. Lymph node recoveries from 2427 pT3 colorectal resection specimens spanning 45 years: recommendations for a minimum number of recovered lymph nodes based on predictive probabilities. Am J Surg Pathol 2002, **26**: 179–189.

987   Goldstein NS, Turner JR. Pericolonic tumor deposits in patients with T3N+M0 colon adenocarcinomas: markers of reduced disease free survival and intra-abdominal metastases and their implications for TNM classification. Cancer 2000, **88**: 2228–2238.

988   Gunn J, McCall JL, Yun K, Wright PA. Detection of micrometastases in colorectal cancer patients by K19 and K20 reverse-transcription polymerase chain reaction. Lab Invest 1996, **75**: 611–616.

989   Inada K, Shimokawa K, Ikeda T, Hayashi M, Azuma S. Development of liver metastasis in colorectal carcinoma. With special reference to venous invasion and basement membrane laminin. Acta Pathol Jpn 1991, **41**: 2240–2245.

990   Krebs PA, Albuquerque A, Quezado M, Bryant B, Sobel ME, Merino MJ, Otis CN. The use of microsatellite instability in the distinction between synchronous endometrial and colonic adenocarcinoma. Int J Gynecol Pathol 1999, **18**: 320–324.

991   Moore JB, Law DK, Moore EE, Dean CM. Testicular mass. An initial sign of colon carcinoma. Cancer 1982, **49**: 411–412.

992   Morodomi T, Isomoto H, Shirouzu K, Kakegawa K, Irie K, Morimatsui M. An index for estimating the probability of lymph node metastasis in rectal cancers. Lymph node metastasis and the histopathology of actively invasive regions of cancer. Cancer 1989, **63**: 539–543.

993   Riopel MA, Klimstra DS, Godellas CV, Blumgart LH, Westra WH. Intrabiliary growth of metastatic colonic adenocarcinoma: a pattern of intrahepatic spread easily confused with primary neoplasia of the biliary tract. Am J Surg Pathol 1997, **21**: 1030–1036.

994   Rusthoven JJ, Fine S, Thomas G. Adenocarcinoma of the rectum metastatic to the oral cavity. Two cases and a review of the literature. Cancer 1984, **54**: 1110–1112.

995   Sasaki M, Watanabe H, Jass JR, Ajioka Y, Kobayashi M, Hatakeyama K. Immunoperoxidase staining for cytokeratins 8 and 18 is very sensitive for detection of occult node metastasis of colorectal cancer: a comparison with genetic analysis of K-ras. Histopathology 1998, **32**: 199–208.

996   Silver SA, Epstein JI. Adenocarcinoma of the colon simulating primary urinary bladder neoplasia. A report of nine cases. Am J Surg Pathol 1993, **17**: 171–178.

997   Taal BG, Hageman PC, Delemarre JF, Bonfrer JM, den Hartog Jager FC. Metastatic ovarian or colonic cancer. A clinical challenge. Eur J Cancer 1992, **28**: 394–399.

998   Wong JH, Severino R, Honnebier MB, Tom P, Namiki TS. Number of nodes examined and staging accuracy in colorectal carcinoma. J Clin Oncol 1999, **17**: 2896–2900.

999   Young RH, Hart WR. Metastatic intestinal carcinomas

simulating primary ovarian clear cell carcinoma and secretory endometrioid carcinoma: a clinicopathologic and immunohistochemical study of five cases. Am J Surg Pathol 1998, **22**: 805–815.

Treatment

1000 Abcarian H. Operative treatment of colorectal cancer. Cancer 1992, **70**: 1350–1354.

1001 Ambiru S, Miyazaki M, Ito H, Nakagawa K, Shimizu H, Kato A, Nakamura S, Omoto H, Nakajima N. Resection of hepatic and pulmonary metastases in patients with colorectal carcinoma. Cancer 1998, **82**: 274–278.

1002 Andreola S, Leo E, Belli F, Bonfanti G, Sirizzotti G, Greco P, Valvo F, Tomasic G, Gallino FG. Adenocarcinoma of the lower third of the rectum surgically treated with a <10-mm distal clearance: preliminary results in 35 N0 patients. Ann Surg Oncol 2001, **8**: 611–615.

1003 Balslev IB, Pedersen M, Teglbjaerg PS, Hanberg-Soerensen F, Bone J, Jacobsen NO, Overgaard J, Sell A, Bertelsen K, Hage E, Fenger C, Kronborg O, Hansen L, Hoestrup H, Noergaard-Pedersen B. Postoperative radiotherapy in Dukes' B and C carcinoma of the rectum and rectosigmoid. A randomized multicenter study. Cancer 1986, **58**: 22–28.

1004 Bühler H, Seefeld U, Deyhle P, Buchmann P, Metzger U, Ammann R. Endoscopic follow-up after colorectal cancer surgery. Early detection of local recurrence? Cancer 1984, **54**: 791–793.

1005 Cady B, Stone MD. The role of surgical resection of liver metastases in colorectal carcinoma. Semin Oncol 1991, **18**: 399–406.

1006 Cole WH, McDonald GO, Roberts SS, Southwick HW. Dissemination of cancer. Prevention and therapy. New York, 1961, Appleton-Century-Crofts.

1007 Cooper HS, Slemmer JR. Surgical considerations in patients with cancer of the colon and rectum. Semin Oncol 1991, **18**: 381–387.

1008 De Cosse JJ, Wong RJ, Quan SH, Friedman NB, Sternberg SS. Conservative treatment of distal rectal cancer by local excision. Cancer 1989, **63**: 219–223.

1009 Enker WE. Designing the optimal surgery for rectal carcinoma. Cancer 1996, **78**: 1847–1850.

1010 Falterman KW, Hill CB, Markey JC, Fox JW, Cohn I Jr. Cancer of the colon, rectum, and anus. A review of 2313 cases. Cancer 1974, **34**: 951–959.

1011 Fong Y, Cohen AM, Fortner JG, Enker WE, Turnbull AD, Cilt DG, Marrero AM, Prasad M, Blumgart LH, Brennan MF. Liver resection for colorectal metastases. J Clin Oncol 1997, **15**: 938–946.

1012 Foswit B, Higgins GA, Humphrey EW, Robinette CD. Preoperative irradiation of operable adenocarcinoma of the rectum and rectosigmoid colon. Report of a randomized study. Radiology 1973, **108**: 389–395.

1013 Goldstein NS, Hart J. Histologic features associated with lymph node metastasis in stage T1 and superficial T2 rectal adenocarcinomas in abdominoperineal resection specimens. Identifying a subset of patients for whom treatment with adjuvant therapy or completion abdominoperineal resection should be considered after local excision. Am J Clin Pathol 1999, **111**: 51–58.

1014 Goligher JC, Dukes CE, Bussey HJR. Local recurrences after sphincter-saving excisions for carcinoma of the rectum and rectosigmoid. Br J Surg 1951, **39**: 199–211.

1015 Grem JL. Current treatment approaches in colorectal cancer. Semin Oncol 1991, **18**: 17–26.

1016 Higgins GA, Humphrey EW, Dwight RW, Roswit B, Lee LE Jr, Keehn RJ. Preoperative radiation and surgery for cancer of the rectum. Veterans Administration Surgical Oncology Group Trial II. Cancer 1986, **58**: 352–359.

1017 Kapiteijn E, Marijnmen CA, Nagtegaal ID, Putter H, Steup WH, Wiggers T, Rutten HJ, Pahlman L, Glimelius B, van Krieken JH, Leer JW, van de Velde CH, for the Dutch Colorectal Cancer Group. Preoperative radiotherapy combined with total mesorectal excision for resectable rectal cancer. N Engl Med 2001, **345**: 638–646.

1018 Karita M, Tada M, Okita K, Kodama T. Endoscopic therapy for early colon cancer: the strip biopsy resection technique. Gastrointest Endosc 1991, **37**: 128–132.

1019 Leo E, Belli F, Andreola S, Gallino G, Bonfanti G, Ferro F, Zingaro E, Sirizzotti G, Civelli E, Valvo F, Gios M, Brunelli C. Total rectal resection and complete mesorectum excision followed by coloendoanal anastomosis as the optimal treatment for low rectal cancer: the experience of the National Cancer Institute of Milano. Ann Surg Oncol 2000, **7**: 125–132.

1020 Mayer RJ, O'Connell MJ, Tepper JE, Wolmark N. Status of adjuvant therapy for colorectal cancer. J Natl Cancer Inst 1989, **81**: 1359–1364.

1021 Minsky BD, Cohen AM, Enker WE, Mies C. Sphincter preservation in rectal cancer by local excision and postoperative radiation therapy. Cancer 1991, **67**: 908–914.

1022 Mohiuddin M, Ahmed MM. Critical issues in the evolving management of rectal cancer. Semin Oncol 1997, **24**: 732–744.

1023 O'Connell MJ, Martenson JA, Wieand HS, Krook JE, Macdonald JS, Haller DG, Mayer RJ, Gunderson LL, Rich TA. Improving adjuvant therapy for rectal cancer by combining protracted-infusion fluorouracil with radiation therapy after curative surgery. N Engl J Med 1994, **331**: 502–507.

1024 Ottery FD, Bruskewitz RC, Weese JL. Endoscopic transrectal resection of rectal tumors. Cancer 1986, **57**: 563–566.

1025 Rosenthal SA, Yeung RS, Weese JL, Eisenberg BL, Hoffman JP, Coia LR, Hanks GE. Conservative management of extensive low-lying rectal carcinomas with transanal local excision and combined preoperative and postoperative radiation therapy. A report of a phase I–II trial. Cancer 1992, **69**: 335–341.

1026 Saclarides TJ, Krueger BL, Szeluga DJ, Warren WH, Faber LP, Economou SG. Thoracotomy for colon and rectal cancer metastases. Dis Colon Rectum 1993, **36**: 425–429.

1027 Schnall SF, Macdonald JS. Adjuvant therapy in colorectal carcinoma. Semin Oncol 1991, **18**: 560–570.

1028 Stearns MW Jr, Sternberg SS, DeCosse JJ. Treatment alternatives. Localized rectal cancer. Cancer 1984, **54**: 2691–2694.

1029 Turk PS, Wanebo HJ. Results of surgical treatment of nonhepatic recurrence of colorectal carcinoma. Cancer 1993, **71**: 4267–4277.

1030 Winawer SJ, Zauber AG, Stewart E, O'Brien MJ. The natural history of colorectal cancer. Opportunities for intervention. Cancer 1991, **67**: 1143–1149.

1031 Withers HR, Romsdahl MM. Post-operative radiotherapy for adenocarcinoma of the rectum and rectosigmoid. Int J Radiat Oncol Biol Phys 1977, **2**: 1069–1074.

Prognosis

1032 Adam IJ, Mohamdee MO, Martin IG, Scott N, Finan PJ, Johnston D, Dixon MF, Quirke P. Role of circumferential margin involvement in the local recurrence of rectal cancer. Lancet 1994, **344**: 707–711.

1033 Ambe K, Mori M, Enjoji M. S-100 protein-positive dendritic cells in colorectal adenocarcinomas. Distribution and relation to the clinical prognosis. Cancer 1989, **63**: 496–503.

1034 Anderson SN, Rognum TO, Lund E, Meling GI, Hauge S. Strong HLA-DR expression in large bowel carcinomas is associated with good prognosis. Br J Cancer 1993, **68**: 80–85.

1035 Armitage NC, Ballantyne KC, Sheffield JP, Clarke P, Evans DF, Hardcastle JD. A prospective evaluation of the effect of tumor cell DNA content on recurrence in colorectal cancer. Cancer 1991, **67**: 2599–2604.

1036 Baldus SE, Monig SP, Hanish FG, Zirbes TK, Flucke U, Oelert S, Zilkens G, Madejczik B, Thiele J, Schneider PM, Holscher AH, Dienes HP. Comparative evaluation of the prognostic value of MUC1, MUC2, sialyl-Lewis(a) and sialyl-Lewis(x) antigens in colorectal adenocarcinoma. Histopathology 2002, **40**: 440–449.

1037 Banner BF, Whitehouse R, Baker SP, Swanson RS. Tumor angiogenesis in stage II colorectal carcinoma association with survival. Am J Clin Pathol 1998, **109**: 733–737.

1038 Bauer KD, Bagwell CB, Giaretti W, Melamed M, Zarbo RJ, Witzig TE, Rabinovitch PS. Consensus review of the clinical utility of DNA flow cytometry in colorectal cancer. Cytometry 1993, **14**: 486–491.

1039 Bauer KD, Lincoln ST, Vera-Roman JM, Wallemark CB, Chmiel JS, Madurski ML, Murad T, Scarpelli DG. Prognostic implications of proliferative activity and DNA aneuploidy in colonic adenocarcinomas. Lab Invest 1987, **57**: 329–335.

1040 Belluco C, Guillem JG, Kemeny N, Huang Y, Klimstra D, Berger MF, Cohen AM. p53 nuclear protein overexpression in colorectal cancer: a dominant predictor of survival in patients with advanced hepatic metastases. J Clin Oncol 1996, **14**: 2696–2701.

1041 Benhattar J, Losi L, Chaubert P, Givel JC, Costa J. Prognostic significance of K-*ras* mutations in colorectal carcinoma. Gastroenterology 1993, **104**: 1044–1048.

1042 Bosari S, Viale G, Bossi P, Maggioni M, Coggi G, Murray JJ, Lee AK. Cyto plasmic accumulation of p53 protein. An independent prognostic indicator in colorectal adenocarcinomas. J Natl Cancer Inst 1994, **86**: 681–687.

1043 Cass AW, Million RR, Pfaff WW. Patterns of recurrence following surgery alone for adenocarcinoma of the colon and rectum. Cancer 1976, **37**: 2861–2865.

1043a Compton CC. Colorectal carcinoma: diagnostic, prognostic and molecular features. Mod Pathol 2003, **16**: 376–388.

1044 Compton C, Fenoglio-Preiser CM, Pettigrew N, Fielding LP. American Joint Committee on Cancer Prognostic Factors Consensus Conference: colorectal working group. Cancer 2000, **88**: 1739–1757.

1045 Connelly JH, Johnston DA, Bruner JM. The prognostic value of human chorionic gonadotropin expression in colorectal adenocarcinomas. An immunohistochemical study of 102 stage B2 and C2 nonmucinous adenocarcinomas. Arch Pathol Lab Med 1993, **117**: 824–826.

1046 Deans GT, Williamson K, Heatley M, Hamilton P, Arthurs K, Crockard A, Patterson CC, Rowlands BJ, Parks G, Spence RA. The role of flow cytometry in carcinoma of the colon and rectum. Surg Gynecol Obstet 1993, **177**: 377–382.

1047 de Bruine AP, Wiggers T, Beek C, Volovics A, von Meyenfieldt M, Arends JW, Bosman FT. Endocrine cells in colorectal adenocarcinomas. Incidence, hormone profile and prognostic relevance. Int J Cancer 1993, **54**: 765–771.

1048 Dirschmid K, Lang A, Mathis G, Haid A, Hansen M. Incidence of extramural venous invasion in colorectal carcinoma: findings with a new technique. Hum Pathol 1996, **27**: 1227–1230.

1049 Dukes CE. The significance of the unusual in the pathology of intestinal tumor. Ann R Coll Surg Engl 1949, **4**: 90–103.

1050 Dukes CE. The surgical pathology of rectal cancer. J Clin Pathol 1949, **2**: 95–98.

1051 Eisenberg B, DeCosse JJ, Harford F, Michalek J. Carcinoma of the colon and rectum. The natural history reviewed in 1704 patients. Cancer 1982, **49**: 1131–1134.

1052 Enblad P, Glimelius B, Bengtsson A, Pontén J, Påhlman L. DNA content in carcinoma of the rectum and rectosigmoid. Acta Pathol Microbiol Immunol Scand (A) 1985, **93**: 277–284.

1053 Engel CJ, Bennett ST, Chambers AF, Doig GS, Kerkvliet N, O'Malley FP. Tumor angiogenesis predicts recurrence in invasive colorectal cancer when controlled for Dukes staging. Am J Surg Pathol 1996, **20**: 1260–1265.

1054 Ferraro S, Buffa R, Pruneri G, Siccardi AG, Pelagi M, Lee AKC, Coggi G, Bosari S. The prevalence and clinical significance of chromogranin A and secretogranin II immunoreactivity in colorectal adenocarcinomas. Virchows Arch 1995, **426**: 587–592.

1055 Fisher ER, Paik SM, Rockette H, Jones J, Caplan R, Fisher B. Prognostic significance of eosinophils and mast cells in rectal cancer. Findings from the National Surgical Adjuvant Breast and Bowel Project (protocol R-01). Hum Pathol 1989, **20**: 159–163.

1056 Fisher ER, Siderits RH, Sass R, Fisher B. Value of assessment of ploidy in rectal cancers. Arch Pathol Lab Med 1989, **113**: 525–528.

1057 Foley EF, Gaffey MJ, Frierson HF Jr. The frequency and clinical significance of neuroendocrine cells within stage III adenocarcinomas of the colon. Arch Pathol Lab Med 1998, **122**: 912–914.

1058 George SM, Makinen MJ, Jernvall P, Makela J, Vihko P, Karttunen TJ. Classification of advanced colorectal carcinomas by tumor edge morphology: evidence for different pathogenesis and significance of polypoid and nonpolypoid tumors. Cancer 2000, **89**: 1901–1909.

1059 Giaretti W, Danova M, Geido E, Mazzini G, Sciallero S, Aste H, Scivetti P, Riccardi A, Marsano B, Merlo F, et al. Flow cytometric DNA index in the prognosis of colorectal cancer. Cancer 1991, **67**: 1921–1927.

1060 Glenn F, McSherry CK. Carcinoma of the distal large bowel – 32-year review of 1026 cases. Ann Surg 1966, **163**: 838–849.

1060a Grabowski P, Schindler I, Anagnostopoulos I, et al. Neuroendocrine differentiation is a relevant prognostic factor in stage III-IV colorectal cancer. Eur J Gastroenterol Hepatol 2001, **13**: 405–411.

1061 Graham DM, Appelman HD. Crohn's-like lymphoid reaction and colorectal carcinoma. A potential histologic prognosticator. Mod Pathol 1990, **3**: 332–335.

1062 Greenson JK, Isenhart CE, Rice R, Mojzisik C, Houchens D, Martin EW Jr. Identification of occult micrometastases in pericolic lymph nodes of Duke's B colorectal cancer patients using monoclonal antibodies against cytokeratin and CC49. Correlation with long-term survival. Cancer 1994, **73**: 563–569.

1063 Griffin MP, Bergstralh EJ, Coffey RJ, Beart RW Jr, Melton LJ III. Predictors of survival after curative resection of carcinoma of the colon and rectum. Cancer 1987, **60**: 2318–2324.

1064 Gunderson LL, Sosin H. Areas of failure found at reoperation (second or symptomatic look) following "curative surgery" for adenocarcinoma of the rectum. Clinicopathologic correlation and implications for adjuvant therapy. Cancer 1974, **34**: 1278–1292.

1065 Halling KC, French AJ, McDonnell SK, Burgart LJ, Schaid DJ, Peterson BJ, Moon-Tasson L, Mahoney MR, Sargent DJ, O'Connell MJ, Witzig TE, Farr GH Jr, Goldberg RM, Thibodeau SN. Microsatellite instability and 8p allelic imbalance in stage B2 and C colorectal cancers. J Natl Cancer Inst 1999, **91**: 1295–1303.

1066 Harrison JC, Dean PJ, el-Zeky F, Vander Zwaag R. From Dukes through Jass. Pathological prognostic indicators in rectal cancer. Hum Pathol 1994, **25**: 498–505.

1067 Harrison LE, Guillem JG, Paty P, Cohen AM. Preoperative carcinoembryonic antigen predicts outcomes in node-negative colon cancer patients: a multivariate analysis of 572 patients. J M Coll Surg 1997, **185**: 55–59.

1068 Hasebe T, Morihiro M, Sasaki S, Shimoda T, Sugitoh M, Moriya Y, Ono M, Arai T, Ochiai A. Tumor thickness is a histopathologic predictive parameter of tumor metastasis and prognosis in patients with Dukes stage C ulcerative-type colorectal carcinoma: a two hospital-based study. Cancer 2000, **89**: 35–45.

1069 Hermanek P, Altendorf A. Classification of colorectal

carcinomas with regional lymphatic metastases. Pathol Res Pract 1981, **173**: 1–11.

1070 Itzkowitz SH, Bloom EJ, Kokal WA, Modin G, Hakomori S, Kim YS. Sialosyl-Tn. A novel mucin antigen associated with prognosis in colorectal cancer patients. Cancer 1990, **66**: 1960–1966.

1071 Jen J, Kim H, Piantadosi S, Liu ZF, Levitt RC, Sistonen P, Kinzler KW, Vogelstein B, Hamilton SR. Allelic loss of chromosome 18q and prognosis in colorectal cancer. N Engl J Med 1994, **331**: 213–221.

1072 Kaibara N, Koga S, Jinnai D. Synchronous and metachronous malignancies of the colon and rectum in Japan with special reference to a coexisting early cancer. Cancer 1984, **54**: 1870–1874.

1073 Kawanishi-Tabata R, Lopez F, Fratantonio S, Kim N, Goldblum J, Tubs R, Elson P, Lavery I, Bukowski RM, Ganapathi R, Ganapathi MK. Telomerase activity in stage II colorectal carcinoma. Cancer 2002, **95**: 1834–1839.

1074 Korenaga D, Ueo H, Mochida K, Kusumoto T, Baba H, Tamura S, Moriguchi S, Sugimachi K. Prognostic factors in Japanese patients with colorectal cancer. The significance of large bowel obstruction – univariate and multivariate analyses. J Surg Oncol 1991, **47**: 188–192.

1075 Krasna MJ, Flancbaum L, Cody RP, Shneibaum S, Ari GB. Vascular and neural invasion in colorectal carcinoma. Incidence and prognostic significance. Cancer 1988, **61**: 1018–1023.

1076 Lapertosa G, Baracchini P, Fulcheri E, Tanzi R. Prognostic value of the immunocytochemical detection of extramural venous invasion in Dukes' C colorectal adenocarcinomas. A preliminary study. Am J Pathol 1989, **135**: 939–945.

1077 Leahy DT, Mulcahy HE, O'Donoghue DP, Parfrey NA. bcl-2 protein expression is associated with better prognosis in colorectal cancer. Histopathology 1999, **35**: 360–367.

1078 Liefers GJ, Cleton-Jansen AM, van de Velde CJ, Hermans J, van Krieken JH, Cornelisse CJ, Tollenaar RA. Micrometastases and survival in stage II colorectal cancer. N Engl J Med 1998, **339**: 223–228.

1079 Lindmark G, Bergstrom R, Pahlman L, Glimelius B. The association of preoperative serum tumour markers with Dukes' stage and survival in colorectal cancer. Br J Cancer 1995, **71**: 1090–1094.

1080 Lindmark G, Gerdin B, Sundberg C, Pahlman L, Bergstrom R, Glimelius B. Prognostic significance of the microvascular count in colorectal cancer. J Clin Oncol 1996, **14**: 461–466.

1081 Lloyd RV, Schroeder F, Bauman MD, Krook JE, Jin L, Goldberg RM, Farr GH Jr. Prevalence and prognostic significance of neuroendocrine differentiation in colorectal carcinomas. Endocr Pathol 1998, **9**: 35–42.

1082 Lockhart-Mummery HE, Ritchie JK, Hawley PR. The results of surgical treatment for carcinoma of the rectum at St. Mark's Hospital from 1948 to 1972. Br J Surg 1976, **63**: 673–677.

1083 Loda M, Cukor B, Tam SW, Lavin P, Fiorentino M, Draetta GF, Jessup JM, Pagano M. Increased proteasome-dependent degradation of the cyclin-dependent kinase inhibitor p27 in aggressive colorectal carcinomas. Nat Med 1997, **3**: 231–234.

1084 Lui IOL, Kung ITM, Lee JMH, Boey JH. Primary colorectal signet-ring cell carcinoma in young patients. Report of 3 cases. Pathology 1985, **17**: 31–35.

1085 Malassagne B, Valleur P, Serra J, Sarnacki S, Galian A, Hoang C, Hautefeuille P. Relationship of apical lymph node involvement to survival in resected colon carcinoma. Dis Colon Rectum 1993, **36**: 645–653.

1085a Menon AG, Morreau H, Tollenaar RAEM, Alphenaar E, van Puijenbroek M, Putter H, Janssen-Van Rijn CM, van de Velde CJH, Fleuren GJ, Kuppen PjK. Down-regulation of HLA-A expression correlates with a better prognosis in colorectal cancer patients. Lab Invest 2002, **82**: 1725–1733.

1086 Minsky BD, Mies C, Recht A, Rich TA, Chaffey JT. Resectable adenocarcinoma of the rectosigmoid and rectum. Part II. The influence of blood vessel invasion. Cancer 1988, **61**: 1417–1424.

1087 Miyahara M, Saito T, Kaketani K, Sato K, Kuwahara A, Shimoda K, Kobayashi M. Clinical significance of *ras* p21 overexpression for patients with an advanced colorectal cancer. Dis Colon Rectum 1991, **34**: 1097–1102.

1088 Nacopoulou L, Azaris P, Papacharalampous N, Davaris P. Prognostic significance of histologic host response in cancer of the large bowel. Cancer 1981, **47**: 930–936.

1089 Nagtegaal ID, Marijnen CA, Kranenbarg EK, van de Velde CJ, van Krieken JH, for the pathology review committee and the cooperative clinical investigators. Circumferential margin involvement is still an important predictor of local recurrence in rectal carcinoma: not one millimeter but two millimeters is the limit. Am J Surg Pathol 2002, **26**: 350–357.

1090 Nakamori S, Kameyama M, Imaoka S, Furukawa H, Ishikawa O, Sasaki Y, Kabuto T, Iwanaga T, Matsushita Y, Irimura T. Increased expression of sialyl Lewis^x antigen correlates with poor survival in patients with colorectal carcinoma. Clinicopathological and immunohistochemical study. Cancer Res 1993, **53**: 3632–3637.

1091 Newland RC, Chapuis PH, Pheils MT, MacPherson JG. The relationship of survival to staging and grading of colorectal carcinoma. A prospective study of 503 cases. Cancer 1981, **47**: 1424–1429.

1092 Newland RC, Chapuis PH, Smyth EJ. The prognostic value of substaging colorectal carcinoma. A prospective study of 1117 cases with standardized pathology. Cancer 1987, **60**: 852–857.

1093 Newland RC, Dent OF, Lyttle MN, Chapuis PH, Bokey EL. Pathologic determinants of survival associated with colorectal cancer with lymph node metastases. A multivariate analysis of 579 patients. Cancer 1994, **73**: 2076–2082.

1094 Odone V, Chang L, Caces J, George SL, Pratt CB. The natural history of colorectal carcinoma in adolescents. Cancer 1982, **49**: 1716–1720.

1095 Ogunbiyi OA, Goodfellow PJ, Herfarth K, Gagliardi G, Swantson PE, Birnbaum EH, Read TE, Fleshman JW, Kodner IJ, Moley JF. Confirmation that chromosome 18Q allelic loss in colon cancer is a prognostic indicator. J Clin Oncol 1998, **16**: 427–433.

1096 Ouchi K, Sugawara T, Ono H, Fujiya T, Kamiyama Y, Kakugawa Y, Mikuni J, Tateno H. Histologic features and clinical significance of venous invasion in colorectal carcinoma with hepatic metastasis. Cancer 1996, **78**: 2313–2317.

1097 Patel SC, Tovee EB, Langer B. Twenty-five years of experience with radical surgical treatment of carcinoma of the extraperitoneal rectum. Surgery 1977, **82**: 460–465.

1098 Patt DJ, Brynes RK, Vardiman JW, Coppleson LW. Mesocolic lymph node histology is an important prognostic indicator for patients with carcinoma of the sigmoid colon. An immunomorphologic study. Cancer 1975, **35**: 1388–1397.

1099 Pilipshen SJ, Heilweil M, Quan SHQ, Sternberg SS, Enker WE. Patterns of pelvic recurrence following definitive resections of rectal cancer. Cancer 1984, **53**: 1354–1362.

1100 Pretlow TP, Keith EF, Cryar AK, Bartolucci AA, Pitts AM, Pretlow TG II, Kimball PM. Boohaker EA. Eosinophil infiltration of human colonic carcinomas as a prognostic indicator. Cancer Res 1983, **43**: 2997–3000.

1101 Purdie CA, Piris J. Histopathological grade, mucinous differentiation and DNA ploidy in relation to prognosis in colorectal carcinoma. Histopathology 2000, **36**: 121–126.

1102 Rao BN, Pratt CB, Fleming ID, Dilawari RA, Green AA, Austin BA. Colon carcinoma in children and adolescents. A review of 30 cases. Cancer 1985, **55**: 1322–1326.

1102a Ribic CM, Sargent DJ, Moore MJ, Thibodeau SN, French AJ, Goldberg RM, Hamilton SR, Laurent-Puig P, Gryfe R, Shepherd

LE, Tu D, Redston M, Gallinger S. Tumor microsatellite-instability status as a predictor of benefit from fluorouracil-based adjuvant chemotherapy for colon cancer. N Engl J Med 2003, **349**: 247–257.

1103 Robey-Cafferty SS, El-Naggar AK, Grignon DJ, Cleary KR, Ro JY. Histologic parameters and DNA ploidy as predictors of survival in Stage B adenocarcinoma of colon and rectum. Mod Pathol 1990, **3**: 261–266.

1104 Russell AH, Pelton J, Reheis CE, Wisbeck WM, Tong DY, Dawson LE. Adenocarcinoma of the colon. An autopsy study with implications for new therapeutic strategies. Cancer 1985, **56**: 1446–1451.

1105 Russell AH, Tong D, Dawson LE, Wisbeck W. Adenocarcinoma of the proximal colon. Sites of initial dissemination and patterns of recurrence following surgery alone. Cancer 1984, **53**: 360–367.

1106 Sankila R, Aaltonen LA, Jarvinen HJ, Mecklin JP. Better survival rates in patients with MLH1-associated hereditary colorectal cancer. Gastroenterology 1996, **110**: 682–687.

1106a Scherübl H, Grabowski P. The chromogranin-secretogranin family. N Engl J Med 2003, **348**: 2570–2581.

1107 Scott CA, Desinan L, Avellini C, Bardus P, Rimondi G, Rizzi V, Beltrami CA. DNA index shift with disease progression in colorectal adenocarcinoma: a morphological and flow cytometric study. Hum Pathol 1998, **29**: 482–490.

1108 Scott NA, Grande JP, Weiland LH, Pemberton JH, Beart RW Jr, Lieber MM. Flow cytometric DNA patterns from colorectal cancers. How reproducible are they? Mayo Clin Proc 1987, **62**: 331–337.

1109 Sessions RT, Reiddell DJ. Cancer of the large bowel in the young adult. Am J Surg 1961, **102**: 66–69.

1110 Shirouzu K, Isomoto H, Morodomi T, Kakegawa T. Carcinomatous lymphatic permeation. Prognostic significance in patients with rectal carcinoma. A long term prospective study. Cancer 1995, **75**: 4–10.

1111 Sikora K, Chan S, Evan G, Gabra H, Markham N, Stewart J, Watson J. c-*myc* oncogene expression in colorectal cancer. Cancer 1987, **59**: 1289–1295.

1112 Spratt JS Jr. Spjut HJ. Prevalence and prognosis of individual clinical and pathologic variables associated with colorectal carcinoma. Cancer 1967, **20**: 1976–1985.

1113 Steinberg SM, Barkin JS, Kaplan RS, Stablein DM. Prognostic indicators of colon tumors. The Gastrointestinal Tumor Study Group experience. Cancer 1986, **57**: 1866–1870.

1114 Steinberg SM, Barwick KW, Stablein DM. Importance of tumor pathology and morphology in patients with surgically resected colon cancer. Findings from the Gastrointestinal Tumor Study Group. Cancer 1986, **58**: 1340–1345.

1115 Takebayashi Y, Akiyama S, Yamada K, Akiba S, Aikou T. Angiogenesis as an unfavorable prognostic factor in human colorectal carcinoma. Cancer 1996, **78**: 226–231.

1116 Talbot IC, Ritchie S, Leighton M, Hughes AO, Bussey HJR, Morson BC. Invasion of veins by carcinoma of rectum. Method of detection, histological features and significance. Histopathology 1981, **5**: 141–163.

1117 Tominaga T, Sakabe T, Koyama Y, Hamano K, Yasutomi M, Takahashi T, Kodaira S, Kato T, Ogawa N. Prognostic factors for the patients with colon or rectal carcinoma treated with resection only: five-year follow-up report. Cancer 1996, **78**: 403–408.

1118 Tribukait B, Hammarberg C, Rubio C. Ploidy and proliferation patterns in colorectal adenocarcinomas related to Dukes' classification and to histopathological differentiation. A flow-cytometric DNA study. Pathol Microbiol Immunol Scand (A) 1983, **91**: 89–95.

1119 Visscher DW, Zarbo RJ, Ma CK, Sakr WA, Crissman JD. Flow cytometric DNA and clinicopathologic analysis of Dukes' A&B colonic adenocarcinomas. A retrospective study. Mod Pathol 1990, **3**: 709–712.

1120 Watanabe T, Wu TT, Catalano PJ, Ueki T, Satriano R, Haller DG, Benson AB III, Hamilton SR. Molecular predictors of survival after adjuvant chemotherapy for colon cancer. N Engl J Med 2001, **344**: 1196–1206.

1121 Welch JP, Donaldson GA. Perforative carcinoma of the colon and rectum. Ann Surg 1974, **180**: 734–740.

1122 Whittaker MA, Carr NJ, Midwinter MJ, Badham DP, Higgins B. Acinar morphology in colorectal cancer is associated with survival but is not an independent prognostic variable. Histopathology 2000, **36**: 439–442.

1123 Wolmark N, Cruz I, Redmond CK, Fisher B, Fisher ER and contributing NSABP investigators. Tumor size and regional lymph node metastasis in colorectal cancer. A preliminary analysis from the NSABP clinical trials. Cancer 1983, **51**: 1315–1322.

1124 Wolmark N, Fisher ER, Wieand HS, Fisher B and contributing NSABP investigators. The relationship of depth of penetration and tumor size to the number of positive nodes in Dukes C colorectal cancer. Cancer 1984, **53**: 2707–2712.

1125 Wolmark N, Wieand HS, Rockette HE, Fisher B, Glass A, Lawrence W, Lerner H, Cruz AB, Volk H, Shibata H, Evans J, Prager D and other NSABP investigators. The prognostic significance of tumor location and bowel obstruction in Dukes B and C colorectal cancer. Findings from the NSABP clinical trials. Ann Surg 1987, **198**: 743–752.

1126 Yamachika T, Nakanishi H, Inada K, Tsukamoto T, Kato T, Fukushima M, Inoue M, Tatematsu M. A new prognostic factor for colorectal carcinoma, thymidylate synthase, and its therapeutic significance. Cancer 1998, **82**: 70–77.

1127 Yamaguchi A, Kurosaka Y, Fushida S, Kanno M, Yonemura Y, Miwa K, Miyazaki I. Expression of p53 protein in colorectal cancer and its relationship to short-term prognosis. Cancer 1992, **70**: 2778–2784.

1128 Zarbo RJ, Nakleh RE, Brown RD, Kubus JJ, Ma CK, Mackowiak P. Prognostic significance of DNA ploidy and proliferation in 309 colorectal carcinomas as determined by two-color multiparametric DNA flow cytometry. Cancer 1997, **79**: 2073–2086.

Carcinoid tumor

1129 Arai T, Kino I. Histochemical and ultrastructural analyses of glandular differentiation in typical carcinoid tumor of the hindgut. Pathol Int 1994, **44**: 49–56.

1130 Bordi C, D'Adda T, Assoni C, Canavese G, Brandi ML. Gastrointestinal endocrine tumors: recent developments. Endocr Pathol 1998, **9**: 99–116.

1131 Caldarola VT, Jackman RJ, Moertel CG, Dockerty MB. Carcinoid tumors of the rectum. Am J Surg 1964, **107**: 844–849.

1132 Federspiel BH, Burke AP, Sobin LH, Shekitka KM. Rectal and colonic carcinoids. A clinicopathologic study of 84 cases. Cancer 1990, **65**: 135–140.

1133 Fukayama M, Hayashi Y, Koike M. Human chorionic gonadotropin in the rectosigmoid colon. Immunohistochemical study on unbalanced distribution of subunits. Am J Pathol 1987, **127**: 83–89.

1134 Fukayama M, Hayashi Y, Shiozawa Y, Okabe S, Koike M. Human chorionic gonadotropin alpha-subunit in rectal carcinoids. Its mode of presence and the change of granule morphology. Am J Pathol 1989, **135**: 1065–1072.

1135 Gledhill A, Hall PA, Cruse JP, Pollock DJ. Enteroendocrine cell hyperplasia, carcinoid tumours and adenocarcinoma in long-standing ulcerative colitis. Histopathology 1986, **10**: 501–508.

1136 Grönstad K, Grimelius L, Ekman R, Kewenter J, Ahiman H. Disseminated rectal carcinoid tumor with production of immunoreactive motilin. Endocrinol Pathol 1992, **3**: 194–200.

1137 Hock YL, Scott KW, Grace RH. Mixed adenocarcinoma/carcinoid tumour of large bowel in a patient with Crohn's disease. J Clin Pathol 1993, **46**: 183–185.

1138 Iwafuchi M, Watanabe H, Ishihara N, Shimoda T, Iwashita A, Ito S. Peptide YY immunoreactive cells in gastrointestinal carcinoids. Immunohistochemical and ultrastructural studies of 60 tumors. Hum Pathol 1986, **17**: 291–296.

1139 Jetmore AB, Ray JE, Gathright JB Jr, McMullen KM, Hicks TC, Timmcke AE. Rectal carcinoids. The most frequent carcinoid tumor. Dis Colon Rectum 1992, **35**: 717–725.

1140 Koura AN, Giacco GG, Curley SA, Skibber JM, Feig BW, Ellis LM. Carcinoid tumors of the rectum: effect of size, histopathology, and surgical treatment on metastasis free survival. Cancer 1997, **79**: 1294–1298.

1141 Lyda MH, Fenoglio-Preiser CM. Adenoma-carcinoid tumors of the colon. Arch Pathol Lab Med 1998, **122**: 262–265.

1142 Maruyama M, Fukayama M, Koike M. A case of multiple carcinoid tumors of the rectum with extraglandular endocrine cell proliferation. Cancer 1988, **60**: 131–136.

1143 Matsui K, Iwase T, Kitagawa M. Small, polypoid-appearing carcinoid tumors of the rectum. Clinicopathologic study of 16 cases and effectiveness of endoscopic treatment. Am J Gastroenterol 1993, **88**: 1949–1953.

1144 McNeely B, Owen DA, Pezim M. Multiple microcarcinoids arising in chronic ulcerative colitis. Am J Clin Pathol 1992, **98**: 112–116.

1145 Moyana TN, Satkunam N. Crypt cell proliferative micronests in rectal carcinoids. An immunohistochemical study. Am J Surg Pathol 1993, **17**: 350–356.

1146 Naunheim KS, Zeitels J, Kaplan EL, Sugimoto J, Shen K-L, Lee C-H, Straus FH II. Rectal carcinoid tumors. Treatment and prognosis. Surgery 1983, **94**: 670–676.

1147 O'Briain DS, Dayal Y, DeLellis RA, Tischler AS, Bendon R, Wolfe HJ. Rectal carcinoids as tumors of the hindgut endocrine cells. A morphological and immunohistochemical analysis. Am J Surg Pathol 1982, **6**: 131–142.

1148 Ratzenhofer R, Gamse R, Höfler H, Auböck L, Popper H, Pohl P, Lembeck F. Substance P in an argentaffin carcinoid of the caecum. Biochemical and biological characterization. Virchows Arch [A] 1981, **392**: 21–31.

1149 Shimoda T, Ishikawa E, Sano T, Watanabe K, Ikegami M. Histopathological and immunohistochemical study of neuroendocrine tumors of the rectum. Acta Pathol Jpn 1984, **34**: 1059–1077.

1150 Sobin LH, Hjermstad BM, Sesterhenn IA, Helwig EB. Prostatic acid phosphatase activity in carcinoid tumors. Cancer 1986, **58**: 136–138.

1151 Takatoh H, Iwamoto H, Ikezu M, Katoh N, Ito S, Kaneko H. Immunohistochemical demonstration of peptide YY in gastrointestinal endocrine tumors. Acta Pathol Jpn 1987, **37**: 737–746.

1152 Tsioulias G, Muto T, Kubota Y, Masaki T, Suzuki K, Akasu T, Morioka Y. DNA ploidy pattern in rectal carcinoid tumors. Dis Colon Rectum 1991, **34**: 32–36.

1153 Wilander E, El-Salhy M, Lundqvist M, Grimelius L, Terenius L, Lundberg JM, Tatemoto K, Schwartz TW. Polypeptide YY (PYY) and pancreatic polypeptide (PP) in rectal carcinoids. An immunocytochemical study. Virchows Arch [A] 1983, **401**: 67–72.

1154 Wilander E, Portela-Gomes G, Grimelius L, Lundqvist G, Skoog V. Enteroglucagon and substance P-like immunoreactivity in argentaffin and argyrophil rectal carcinoids. Virchows Arch [Cell Pathol] 1977, **25**: 117–124.

1155 Williams RM. A light and electron microscopic study of an ovarian and rectal carcinoid. Histopathology 1979, **3**: 19–30.

1156 Yoshida A, Yano M, Fujinaga Y, Sano C, Mori H, Yoshida H, Fukunishi R. Argentaffin carcinoid tumor of the rectum. Cancer 1981, **48**: 2103–2106.

Malignant lymphoma and related lesions

1157 Chang KC, Jin YT, Chen FF, Su IJ. Follicular dendritic cell sarcoma of the colon mimicking stromal tumour. Histopathology 2001, **38**: 25–29.

1158 Chin NW, Gangi M, Fani K, De Soto-La Paix F, Papandreou C, Surapaneni RK, Landor JH. Colonic histiocytic neoplasm mimicking malignant histiocytosis and presenting as intussusception. Hum Pathol 1995, **26**: 682–686.

1159 Cooperberg MR, Fiedler PN. Ki-1 anaplastic large-cell lymphoma occurring at the site of ileocolonic anastomosis in a patient treated surgically for colonic adenocarcinoma: case report and review of the literature. Ann Diagn Pathol 2001, **5**: 162–167.

1160 DePond W, Said JW, Tasaka T, de Vos S, Kahn D, Cesarman E, Knowles DM, Koeffler HP. Kaposi's sarcoma-associated herpesvirus and human herpesvirus 8 (KSHV/HHV8)-associated lymphoma of the bowel: report of two cases in HIV-positive men with secondary effusion lymphomas. Am J Surg Pathol 1997, **21**: 719–724.

1161 Gleason TH, Hammar SP. Plasmacytoma of the colon. Case report with lambda light chain, demonstrated by immunoperoxidase studies. Cancer 1982, **50**: 130–133.

1162 Gloeckner K, Leithaeuser F, Lang W, Merz H, Feller AC. Colonic primary large cell lymphoma with marginal zone growth pattern presenting as multiple polyps. Am J Surg Pathol 1999, **23**: 1149–1153.

1163 Greenstein AJ, Mullin GE, Strauchen JA, Heimann T, Janowitz HD, Aufses AH Jr, Sachar DB. Lymphoma in inflammatory bowel disease. Cancer 1992, **69**: 1119–1123.

1164 Helwig EB, Hanson J. Lymphoid polyp (benign lymphoma) and malignant lymphoma of the rectum and anus. Surg Gynecol Obstet 1951, **92**: 233–243.

1165 Hwang WS, Yao JC, Cheng SS, Tseng HH. Primary colorectal lymphoma in Taiwan. Cancer 1992, **70**: 575–580.

1166 Ioachim HL, Antonescu C, Giancotti F, Dorsett B, Weinstein MA. EBV-associated anorectal lymphomas in patients with acquired immune deficiency syndrome. Am J Surg Pathol 1997, **21**: 997–1006.

1167 Isaacson PG, Maclennan KA, Subbuswamy SG. Multiple lymphomatous polyposis of the gastrointestinal tract. Histopathology 1984, **8**: 641–656.

1167a Kohno S, Ohshima K, Yoneda S, Kodama T, Shirakusa T, Kikuchi M. Clinicopathological analysis of 143 primary malignant lymphomas in the small and large intestines based on the new WHO classification. Histopathology 2003, **43**: 135–143.

1168 Kojima M, Nakamura S, Itoh H, Ohno Y, Masawa N, Joshita T, Suchi T. Mast cell carcoma with tissue eosinophilia arising in the ascending colon. Mod Pathol 1999, **12**: 739–743.

1169 Lavergne A, Brouland JP, Launay E, Nemeth J, Ruskone-Fourmestraux A, Galian A. Multiple lymphomatous polyposis of the gastrointestinal tract. An extensive histopathologic and immunohistochemical study of 12 cases. Cancer 1994, **74**: 3042–3050.

1170 Le Brun DP, Kamel OW, Cleary ML, Dorfman RF, Warnke RA. Follicular lymphomas of the gastrointestinal tract. Pathologic features in 31 cases and bcl-2 oncogenic protein expression. Am J Pathol 1992, **140**: 1327–1335.

1171 Lee RG, Braziel RM, Stenzel P. Gastrointestinal involvement in Langerhans cell histiocytosis (histiocytosis X). Diagnosis by rectal biopsy. Mod Pathol 1990, **3**: 154–157.

1172 McCullough JE, Kim CH, Banks PM. Mantle zone lymphoma of the colon simulating diffuse inflammatory bowel disease. Role of immunohistochemistry in establishing the diagnosis. Dig Dis Sci 1992, **37**: 934–938.

1173 Mezwa DG, Feczko PJ, Korensky T. Angioimmunoblastic

lymphadenopathy of the colon with malignant transformation. Gastrointest Radiol 1991, **16**: 348–350.

1174 Moynihan MJ, Bast MA, Chan WC, Delabie J, Wickert RS, Wu G, Weisenburger DD. Lymphomatous polyposis: a neoplasm of either follicular mantle or germinal center cell origin. Am J Surg Pathol 1996, **20**: 442–452.

1175 O'Briain DS, Kennedy MJ, Daly PA, O'Brien AAJ, Tanner WA, Rogers P, Lawlor E. Multiple lymphomatous polyposis of the gastrointestinal tract. A clinicopathologically distinctive form of non-Hodgkin's lymphoma of B-cell centrocytic type. Am J Surg Pathol 1989, **13**: 691–699.

1176 Pinkus GS, Wilson RE, Corson JM. Reticulum cell sarcoma of the colon following renal transplantation. Cancer 1974, **34**: 2103–2108.

1177 Ranchod M, Lewin KJ, Dorfman RF. Lymphoid hyperplasia of the gastrointestinal tract. A study of 26 cases and review of the literature. Am J Surg Pathol 1978, **2**: 383–400.

1178 Robert ME, Kuo FC, Longtine JA, Sklar JL, Schrock T, Weidner N. Diffuse colonic mantle cell lymphoma in a patient with presumed ulcerative colitis: detection of a precursor monoclonal lymphoid population using polymerase chain reaction and immunohistochemistry. Am J Surg Pathol 1996, **20**: 1024–1031.

1179 Ross CW, Hanson CA, Schnitzer B. CD30 (Ki-1)-positive, anaplastic large cell lymphoma mimicking gastrointestinal carcinoma. Cancer 1991, **70**: 2517–2523.

1180 Schmid C, Vazquez JJ, Diss TC, Isaacson PG. Primary B-cell mucosa-associated lymphoid tissue lymphoma presenting as a solitary colorectal polyp. Histopathology 1994, **24**: 357–362.

1181 Thomas DB, Huston BM, Lamm K, Maia D. Primary Hodgkin's disease of the sigmoid colon: a case report and review of the literature. Arch Pathol Lab Med 1997, **121**: 528–532.

1182 Van der Henle B, Taylor CR, Terry R, Lukes RJ. Presentation of malignant lymphoma in the rectum. Cancer 1982, **49**: 2602–2607.

1183 Yatabe Y, Nakamura S, Nakamura T, Seto M, Ogura M, Kimura M, Kuhara H, Kobayashi T, Taniwaki M, Morishima Y, Koshikawa T, Suchi T. Multiple polypoid lesions of primary mucosa-associated lymphoid-tissue lymphoma of colon. Histopathology 1998, **32**: 116–125.

Gastrointestinal stromal tumors and related tumors

1184 Miettinen M, Furlong M, Sarlomo-Rikala M, Burke A, Sobin LH, Lasota J. Gastrointestinal stromal tumors, intramural leiomyomas, and leiomyosarcomas in the rectum and anus: a clinicopathologic, immunohistochemical, and molecular genetic study of 144 cases. Am J Surg Pathol 2001, **25**: 1121–1133.

1185 Miettinen M, Sarlomo-Rikala M, Sobin LH, Lasota J. Gastrointestinal stromal tumors and leiomyosarcomas in the colon: a clinicopathologic, immunohistochemical, and molecular genetic study in 44 cases. Am J Surg Pathol 2000, **24**: 1339–1352.

1186 Miettinen M, Sarlomo-Rikala M, Sobin LH. Mesenchymal tumors of muscularis mucosae of colon and rectum are benign leiomyomas that should be separated from gastrointestinal stromal tumors – a clinicopathologic and immunohistochemical study of eighty-eight cases. Mod Pathol 2001, **14**: 950–956.

1187 Miettinen M, Shekitka KM, Sobin LH. Schwannomas in the colon and rectum: a clinicopathologic and immunohistochemical study of 20 cases. Am J Surg Pathol 2001, **25**: 846–855.

1188 Terada T, Endo K, Maeta H, Horie S, Otha T. Epithelioid leiomyosarcoma with osteoclast-like giant cells in the rectum. Arch Pathol Lab Med 2000, **124**: 438–440.

1189 Tworek JA, Goldblum JR, Weiss SW, Greenson JK, Appelman HD. Stromal tumors of the abdominal colon: a clinicopathologic study of 20 cases. Am J Surg Pathol 1999, **23**: 937–945.

Other tumors and tumorlike conditions

1190 Bavikatty NR, Goldblum JR, Abdul-Karim FW, Nielsen SL, Greenson JK. Florid vascular proliferation of the colon related to intussusception and mucosa prolapse: potential diagnostic confusion with angiosarcoma. Mod Pathol 2001, **14**: 1114–1118.

1191 Ben-Izhak O, Kerner H, Brenner B, Lichtig C. Angiosarcoma of the colon developing in a capsule of a foreign body. Report of a case with associated hemorrhagic diathesis. Am J Clin Pathol 1992, **97**: 416–420.

1192 Boley SJ, Sammartano R, Adams A, DiBiase A, Kleinhaus S, Sprayregen S. On the nature and etiology of vascular ectasias of the colon. Degenerative lesions of aging. Gastroenterology 1977, **72**: 650–660.

1193 d'Amore ES, Manivel JC, Pettinato G, Niehans GA, Snover DC. Intestinal ganglioneuromatosis. Mucosal and transmural types. A clinicopathologic and immunohistochemical study of six cases. Hum Pathol 1991, **22**: 276–286.

1194 DeSchryver-Kecskemeti K, Clouse RE, Goldstein MN, Gersell D, O'Neal L. Intestinal ganglioneuromatosis. A manifestation of overproduction of nerve growth factor? N Engl J Med 1983, **308**: 635–640.

1195 Duray PH, Marcal JM, LiVolsi VA, Fisher R, Scholhamer C, Brand MH. Gastrointestinal angiodysplasia. A possible component of von Willebrand's disease. Hum Pathol 1984, **15**: 539–544.

1196 Eshun-Wilson K. Malignant giant-cell tumor of the colon. Acta Pathol Microbiol Scand (A) 1973, **81**: 137–144.

1197 Fry DE, Amin M, Harbrecht PJ. Rectal obstruction secondary to carcinoma of the prostate. Ann Surg 1979, **189**: 488–492.

1198 Fuller CE, Williams GT. Gastrointestinal manifestations of type 1 neurofibromatosis (von Recklinghausen's disease). Histopathology 1991, **19**: 1–11.

1199 Goh SG, Ho JM, Chuah KL, Tan PH, Poh WT, Riddell RH. Leiomyomatosis-like lymphangioleiomyomatosis of the colon in a female with tuberous sclerosis. Mod Pathol 2001, **14**: 1141–1146.

1200 Haller JD, Roberts TW. Lipomas of the colon. Clincopathologic study of 20 cases. Surgery 1964, **55**: 773–781.

1201 Haque S, Dean PJ. Stromal neoplasms of the rectum and anal canal. Hum Pathol 1992, **23**: 762–767.

1202 Lanjewar DN, Jain P, Shiveshwarkar WS, Kirtane JM. Cellular haemangioma of caecum in a child. Histopathology 1996, **29**: 585–586.

1203 MacKenzie DA, McDonald JR, Waugh JM. Leiomyoma and leiomyosarcoma of the colon. Ann Surg 1954, **139**: 67–75.

1204 Magro G, Gurrera A, Di Cataldo A, Licata A, Vasquez E. Well differentiated lipoma-like liposarcoma of the caecum. Histopathology 2000, **36**: 378–380.

1205 Maluf H, Dieckgraefe B. Angiomyolipoma of the large intestine: report of a case. Mod Pathol 1999, **12**: 1132–1136.

1206 Masangkay AV, Susin M, Baker R, Ward R, Kahn E. Metastatic malignant mesothelioma presenting as colonic polyps. Hum Pathol 1997, **28**: 993–995.

1207 Matsuhashi N, Nakagama H, Moriya K, Ohnishi S, Gunji T, Saito T, Sugano K, Imawari M, Takaku F, Minami M, et al. Multiple diffuse hemangiomas of the large intestine. Gastroenterol Jpn 1991, **26**: 654–660.

1208 Mendelsohn G, Diamond MP. Familial ganglioneuromatous polyposis of the large bowel. Report of a family with associated juvenile polyposis. Am J Surg Pathol 1984, **8**: 515–520.

1209 Meyer CT, Troncale FJ, Galloway S, Sheahan DG. Arteriovenous malformations of the bowel. An analysis of 22 cases and a review of the literature. Medicine (Baltimore) 1981, **60**: 36–48.

1210 Morimatsu M, Shirozu K, Nakashima T, Fujimi T, Isomoto H. Xanthogranuloma of the rectum. Acta Pathol Jpn 1985, **35**: 165–171.

1211 Moyana TN, Friesen R, Tan LK. Colorectal smooth-muscle tumors. A pathobiologic study with immunohistochemistry and histomorphometry. Arch Pathol Lab Med 1991, **115:** 1016–1021.

1212 Murata I, Makiyama K, Miyazaki K, Kawamoto AS, Yoshida N, Muta K, Itsuno M, Hara K, Nakagoe T, Tomita M, et al. A case of inflammatory malignant fibrous histiocytoma of the colon. Gastroenterol Jpn 1993, **28:** 554–563.

1213 Nakamura S, Kino I, Akagi T. Inflammatory myoglandular polyps of the colon and rectum. A clinicopathological study of 32 pedunculated polyps, distinct from other types of polyps. Am J Surg Pathol 1992, **16:** 772–779.

1214 Nicholson AG, Cox PM, Marks CG, Cook MG. Primary malignant melanoma of the rectum. Histopathology 1993, **22:** 261–264.

1215 Pounder DJ, Rowland R, Pieterse AS, Freeman R, Hunter R. Angiodysplasias of the colon. J Clin Pathol 1982, **35:** 824–829.

1216 Prasad ML, Keating JP, Teoh HH, McCarthy SW, Battifora H, Wasef E, Rosai J. Pleomorphic angiomyolipoma of digestive tract: a heretofore unrecognized entity. Int J Surg Pathol 2000, **8:** 67–72.

1217 Ranchod M, Kempson RL. Smooth muscle tumors of the gastrointestinal tract and retroperitoneum. A pathologic analysis of 100 cases. Cancer 1977, **39:** 255–262.

1218 Roth JA, Schell S, Panzarino S, Coronato A. Visceral Kaposi's sarcoma presenting as colitis. Am J Surg Pathol 1978, **2:** 209–214.

1219 Santos-Briz A, Garcia JP, Gonzales C, Colina F. Lipomatous polyposis of the colon. Histopathology 2001, **38:** 81–83.

1220 Shekitka KM, Helwig EB. Deceptive bizarre stromal cells in polyps and ulcers of the gastrointestinal tract. Cancer 1991, **67:** 2111–2117.

1221 Shekitka KM, Sobin LH. Ganglioneuromas of the gastrointestinal tract. Relation to von Recklinghausen disease and other multiple tumor syndromes. Am J Surg Pathol 1994, **18:** 250–257.

1222 Snover DC. Atypical lipomas of the colon. Report of two cases with pseudomalignant features. Dis Colon Rectum 1984, **27:** 485–488.

1223 Snover DC, Weigent CE, Sumner HW. Diffuse mucosal ganglioneuromatosis of the colon associated with adenocarcinoma. Am J Clin Pathol 1981, **75:** 225–229.

1224 Stamm B, Heer M, Bühler H, Ammann R. Mucosal biopsy of vascular ectasia (angiodysplasia) of the large bowel detected during routine colonoscopic examination. Histopathology 1985, **9:** 639–646.

1225 Tarasidis G, Brown BC, Skandalakis LJ, Mackay G, Lauer RC, Gray SW, Skandalakis JE. Smooth muscle tumors of the appendix and colon. A collective review of the world literature. J Med Assoc Ga 1991, **80:** 667–683.

1226 Thelmo WL, Vetrano A, DiMaio TM, Cruz-Vetrano WP, Kim DS. Angiodysplasia of colon revisited. Pathologic demonstration without the use of intravascular injection technique. Hum Pathol 1992, **23:** 37–40.

1227 Vallaeys JH, Cuvelier CA, Bekaert L, Roels H. Combined leiomyomatosis of the small intestine and colon. Arch Pathol Lab Med 1992, **116:** 281–283.

1228 Vella-Camilleri FC, Friedrich R, Vento AO. Diffuse colonic varices. An uncommon cause of intestinal bleeding. Am J Gastroenterol 1986, **81:** 492–494.

1229 Watanabe K, Hoshi N, Suzuki T. Epithelioid angiosarcoma of the intestinal tract with endothelin-1-like immunoreactivity. Virchows Arch [A] 1993, **423:** 309–314.

1230 Weaver GA, Alpern HD, Davis JS, et al. Gastrointestinal angiodysplasia associated with aortic valve disease. Part of a spectrum of angiodysplasia of the gut. Gastroenterology 1979, **77:** 1–11.

1231 Weber JN, Carmichael DJ, Boylston A, Munro A, Whitear WP, Pinching AJ. Kaposi's sarcoma of the bowel presenting as apparent ulcerative colitis. Gut 1985, **26:** 295–300.

1232 Weidner N, Flanders DJ, Mitros FA. Mucosal ganglioneuromatosis associated with multiple colonic polyps. Am J Surg Pathol 1984, **8:** 779–786.

1233 Weidner N, Zekan P. Carcinosarcoma of the colon. Report of a unique case with light and immunohistochemical studies. Cancer 1986, **58:** 1126–1130.

1234 Wilkinson N, Cairns A, Benbow EW, Donnai P, Buckley CH. Dermoid cyst of the caecum. Histopathology 1996, **29:** 186–188.

1235 Yang AH, Chen WY, Chiang H. Malignant rhabdoid tumour of colon. Histopathology 1994, **24:** 89–91.

1236 Yao T, Nagai E, Utsunomiya T, Tsuneyoshi M. An intestinal counterpart of pyogenic granuloma of the skin. A newly proposed entity. Am J Surg Pathol 1995, **19:** 1054–1060.

1237 Yatto RP. Colonic lipomatosis. Am J Gastroenterol 1982, **77:** 436–437.

1238 Zornig C, Thoma G, Schroder S. Diffuse leiomyosarcomatosis of the colon. Cancer 1990, **65:** 570–572.

Anus

Normal anatomy

The anal canal is a tubular structure measuring 3 to 4 cm in length. It extends from the perineal skin to the lower end of the rectum and is demarcated by the proximal and distal margins of the internal sphincter muscle (Fig. 11.223).[3] The junction between the anal canal and the perineal skin is known as the *anal verge* or *Hilton's line* and is identified microscopically by the appearance of cutaneous adnexa.[10] The *pectinate (dentate) line* is located at the very center of the anal canal. The segment of anal canal located immediately below this line exhibits a number of longitudinal folds known as *anal columns (of Morgagni)*. Homologous structures in the lower rectum are designated *rectal columns (of Morgagni)*, and the depressions between them as *rectal sinuses (of Morgagni)*. The anal columns are connected at the dentate line by the *anal* or *semilunar valves (transverse plicae)*. These valves form the inner boundary of minute pockets designated as *anal crypts (of Morgagni)*.

The anal canal is lined by columnar epithelium in its upper portion and by keratinized or nonkeratinized squamous epithelium in its lower portion, which is known as *pecten*. At the interphase between the two, roughly corresponding to the pectinate line, there is a circular zone, 0.3 to 1.1 cm in width, with a glistening, wrinkled appearance made discontinuous by the presence of anal papillae.[3] This zone is lined by epithelium known as *transitional, intermediate,* or *cloacogenic*. It con-

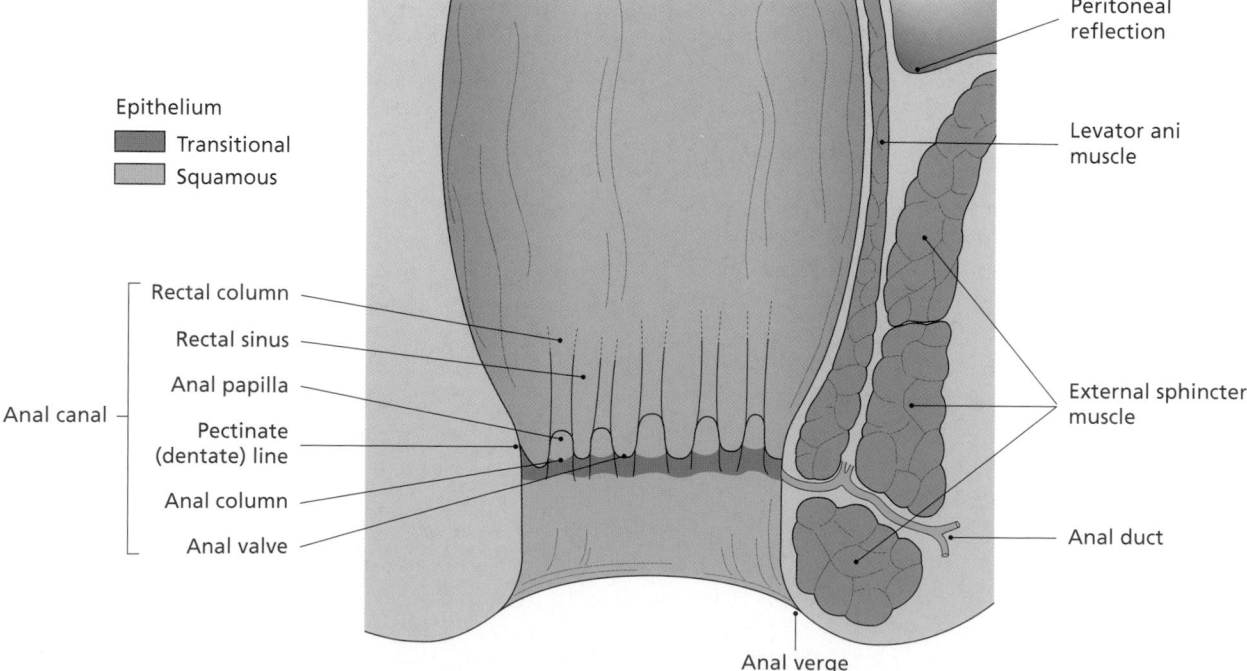

Epithelium
- ▬ Transitional
- ▬ Squamous

Labels: Rectal column · Rectal sinus · Anal papilla · Pectinate (dentate) line · Anal column · Anal valve · Anal canal · Anal verge · Peritoneal reflection · Levator ani muscle · External sphincter muscle · Anal duct

Fig. 11.223 Diagrammatic representation of normal anal structures. Most cases of anal carcinoma arise from small area of transitional epithelium.

sists of four to nine cell layers, extending from the small basal cells at the bottom to the surface cells (which can be columnar, cuboidal, or polygonal) (Fig. 11.224). It resembles bladder epithelium at the light microscopic but not at the ultrastructural level.[4] Immunohistochemically, it expresses keratins 7 and 19 but not keratin 20.[8,11] Scattered neuroendocrine cells are sometimes identified in the basilar portion of this epithelium.[5] Melanocytes are more common in the anal squamous zone than in the transitional zone.[1]

Anal papillae are toothlike, raised projections located on top of the anal columns, extending upward onto the rectum and representing ridges of squamous mucosa directly joining the rectal mucosa. Both anal crypts and papillae show marked individual variations and are occasionally absent. The *anal glands* discharge into the anal crypts through anal ducts, which can extend upward or, more commonly, downward. They penetrate the sphincters and sometimes extend into the perianal fat[6,7] (Fig. 11.225). The epithelium that lines these ducts is similar to that of the overlying transitional epithelium, including sparse mucin production characterized by scarcity or absence of *O*-acylated sialic acids.[4] Immunohistochemically, the anal glands are strongly positive for CK7 but negative for CK20, a pattern similar to that of the overlying mucosa.[8]

It has been proposed that the strip of transitional epithelium represents a vestige of the cloacal membrane; although this is indeed the case, it should be pointed out that the entire anal canal, not just the transitional zone, is a cloacal derivative. A method for the gross demonstration of this anal transitional zone using whole-mount staining with Alcian dyes has been described.[2]

The vascular supply originates from the superior, middle, and inferior rectal arteries. Individual peculiar vessels characterized by a complex convoluted appearance have been referred to as *anal glomeruli*, and the network formed by these structures has been designated as *corpus cavernosum recti*.[9]

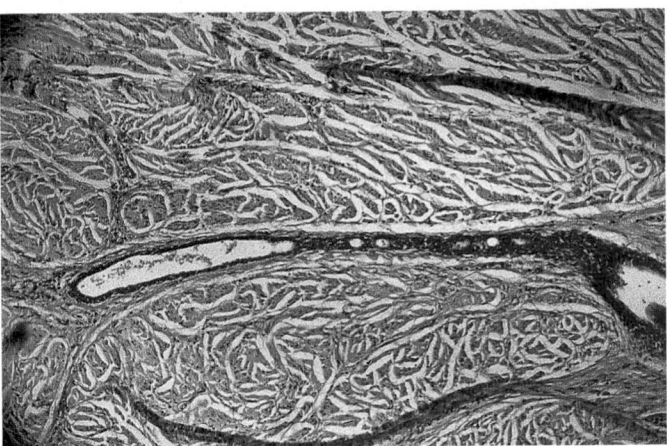

Fig. 11.225 Normal anal ducts running longitudinally through the muscle wall.

The two most important components of the anal musculature are the *internal anal sphincter* (a continuation of the circular muscle coat of the rectum) and the *external anal sphincter* (a complex triple-loop structure).

The lower part of the anal canal (below the dentate line) and the anal skin drain to the superficial inguinal nodes; the upper part has a wide draining field, which includes hypogastric, obturator, and internal iliac nodes.

Embryologic defects

Anorectal anomalies occur in approximately 1 of every 3000 to 5000 births. They are often associated with other anomalies[12] and are divided into three major types, depending on the relationship of the lower bowel to the puborectalis component of the levator ani muscle.[13–15] **High** or **supralevator anomalies** (40%) (anorectal agenesis) are characterized by an absence of the anal canal, with the rectum ending above the levator muscle. They have a serious prognosis because of severe obstruction, common association with other congenital anomalies (in the vertebrae and urinary tract), and defective innervation of the pelvic muscles. A fistulous tract from the rectum to the bladder, urethra, or vagina is often present. A complicated sacroabdominoperineal approach is needed for reconstruction. **Low** or **translevator anomalies** (40%) comprise the ectopic (perineal, vestibular, or vulvar) anus, anal stenosis, and covered anus. In these forms, obstruction is rarely severe. The pelvic innervation is normal, and associated anomalies are rare. Fistulas may or may not be present. A simple perineal operation will cure most of these patients. **Intermediate anomalies** are rare (15%). They include anal agenesis, anorectal stenoses, and anorectal membrane. An abdominoperineal approach is usually needed for reconstruction. The remaining varieties, which are quite rare (5%), include **perineal groove** and **persistent anal membrane**.

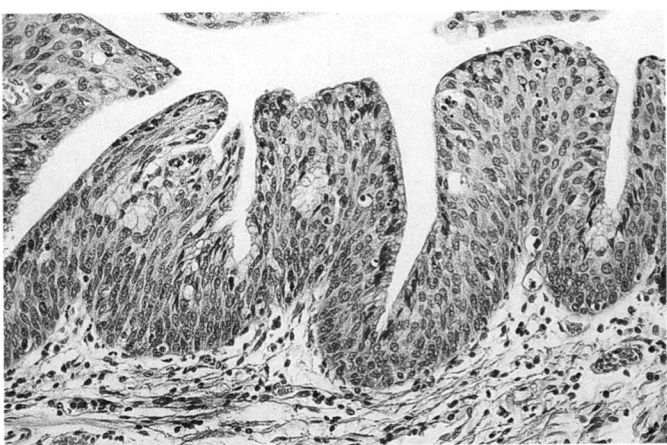

Fig. 11.224 Microscopic appearance of the normal transitional mucosa of anal canal.

Familiarity with the anatomic variants of anorectal anomalies and a thorough radiologic investigation (plain x-ray films, cystograms, and fistulograms) are essential for accurate diagnosis and therefore proper treatment. Unsuccessful surgery leads to stricture and colonic obstruction, which may eventually necessitate a permanent colostomy.

Inflammatory diseases

Anal fissure is a single linear separation of the tissues of the anal canal extending through the mucous membrane.[27] Approximately 90% of anal fissures are found at the posterior commissure overlying the bifurcation of the sphincter as it divides to circle the rectum. The microscopic appearance is nonspecific.

Anal ulcer is a chronic process, usually oval, that extends into the muscular layer. Above it is a hypertrophied papilla, and behind this papilla is an infected crypt. The ulcer has a nonspecific microscopic appearance and is surrounded by chronic edema and fibrosis.

Anal fistula is an abnormal tract having an internal opening within the anal canal, usually at the dentate line.[20] The fistulous tract may lead to the skin, or it may end blindly in the perianal soft tissues. A classification of anal fistulas into five categories on the basis of their anatomic relationships has been proposed.[28] The lining of the fistula is made of granulation tissue, although epithelium may eventually grow at either end of the tract. Most cases of anal fistulas are caused by an intersphincteric abscess originating in an anal duct[25,29] and have a nonspecific microscopic appearance. However, anal fistulas may also be a manifestation of tuberculosis,[21,26] Crohn's disease,[19,22] ulcerative colitis,[24] and actinomycosis.[18] It is important therefore that tissue obtained from an anal fistula be examined microscopically. The incidence of tuberculosis as a cause of anal fistulas dropped from 16% to less than 1% at St. Mark's Hospital (London) in a 50-year period.[26] These patients almost invariably show radiologic evidence of pulmonary tuberculosis. Fistulas caused by Crohn's disease are often complex and painless, with irregular edges and little induration.[19] The diagnosis may be suggested by the presence of noncaseating granulomas, but it is important not to confuse them with the foci of foreign body reaction sometimes seen in nonspecific fistulas. A hyperplastic appearance of the transitional epithelium of the anal canal is often noted in association with Crohn's disease and other inflammatory conditions of the region.

Granuloma inguinale is a chronic superficial ulceration caused by *Calymmatobacterium granulomatosis*, which can extend to the perianal region and which may be confused clinically with squamous cell carcinoma (Fig. 11.226). Biopsy in such cases will allow a definite diagno-

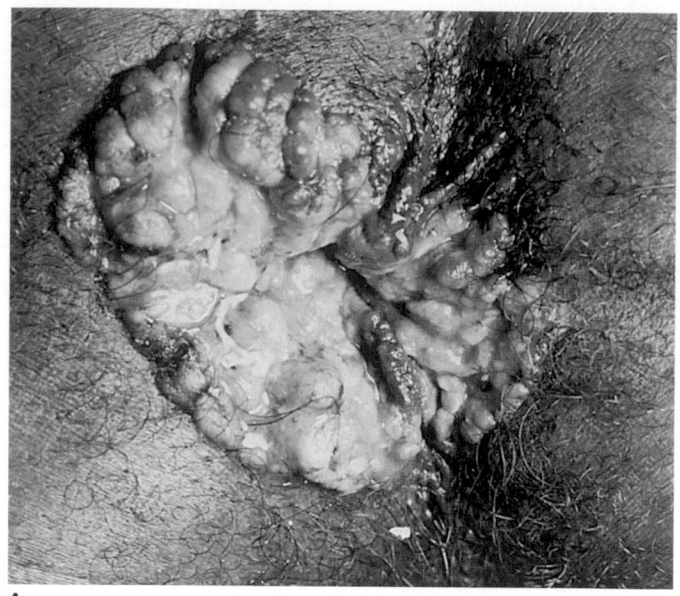

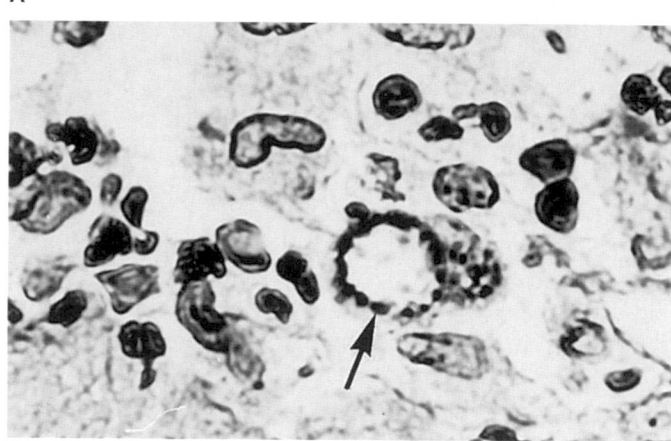

Fig. 11.226 A, Granuloma inguinale clinically simulating carcinoma. **B**, Donovan bodies (arrow) within cyst in cytoplasm of macrophage in patient with granuloma inguinale. (**B**, Warthin–Starry stain)

sis if Donovan bodies are found in Warthin–Starry or Giemsa preparations.

Lymphogranuloma venereum is a sexually transmitted disease caused by *Chlamydia trachomatis*, the incidence of which is rising. It may cause a granulomatous proctitis very similar to Crohn's disease. Microscopically, the main changes are follicular lymphohistiocytic and plasmacellular infiltrate in the wall, associated with neuromatous hyperplasia and extensive fibrosis.[17] Longstanding cases lead to rectal stricture and rectal squamous metaplasia. Occasionally, squamous cell carcinoma develops on the basis of these lesions (Fig. 11.227).

HIV-infected patients may develop a variety of inflammatory diseases of the anal region. In addition to some of those already listed in this section, they include abscesses,[16] CMV and herpes simplex perianal ulceration,[23,30] and HPV-related processes. The latter

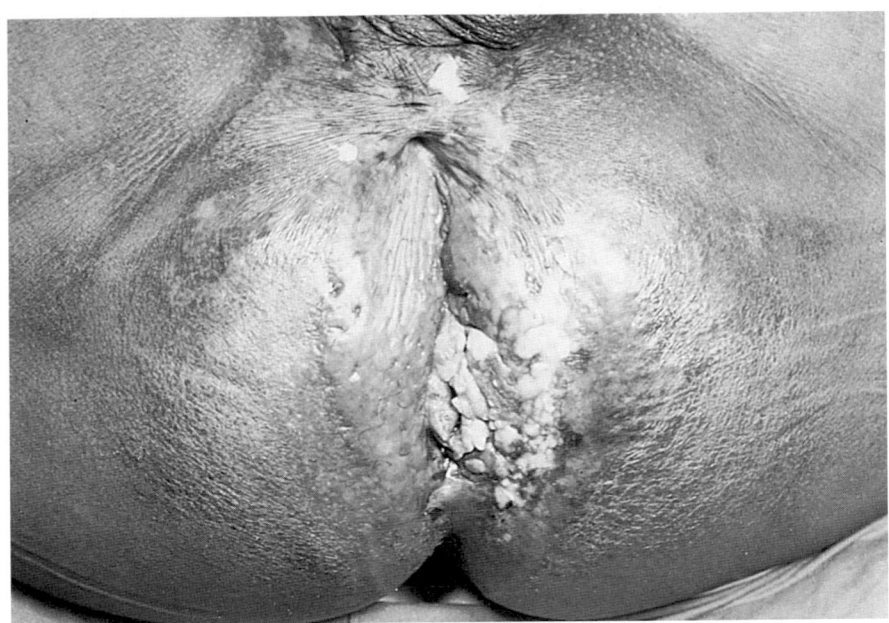

Fig. 11.227 Lymphogranuloma venereum complicated with squamous cell carcinoma. Frei test was positive.

have tumor or tumorlike qualities and are discussed on p. 860.

Hypertrophied papillae

Anal papillae can enlarge as a result of edema, inflammation, and fibrosis and protrude into the anal canal in a polypoid fashion. They are often seen immediately above anal ulcers (Fig. 11.228). Microscopically, they are lined by squamous epithelium and contain a central core of edematous and inflamed fibrovascular stroma. Their appearance is similar to that of cutaneous "fibroepithelial polyps" or "skin tags."[32] Occasionally, atypical stromal cells with large and/or multiple nuclei and stellate cytoplasmic outlines occur in them.[31,34] These cells are immunoreactive for CD34.[33] Hyalinized vessels are a frequent accompanying change.[33]

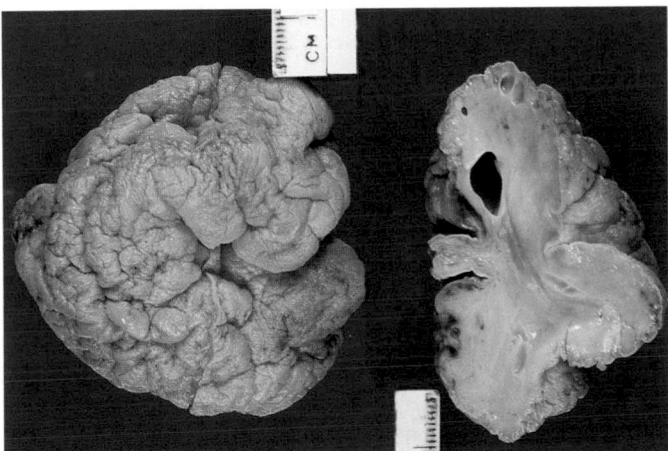

Fig. 11.228 Giant fibrous polyp of anus. This large lesion can be viewed as extremely exuberant form of hypertrophic anal papilla.

Hemorrhoids

Stasis of blood in the veins of the hemorrhoidal plexus is usually caused simply by dependency. However, pathologic processes in the drainage path of those veins may cause secondary engorgement. Therefore, the presence of hemorrhoids may be an indication of some other process such as cirrhosis of the liver with portal hypertension, carcinoma of the rectum, leiomyoma of the uterus, or pregnancy. Some authors have drawn a distinction on pathogenetic grounds between the usual hemorrhoids and the dilated (varicose) vessels seen in association with portal hypertension.[38,41] Indeed, it has been pointed out that **hemorrhoidal cushions** are a normal component of the anatomy of this region.[37a,39]

Hemorrhoids can be present either within or outside the anus. Thrombosis of these dilated veins is frequent. If the cause of venous obstruction is removed, the hemorrhoids may disappear, although in many instances resection is necessary. Inflammatory changes are secondary to surface ulceration rather than thrombosis.[40] The organization and recanalization of thrombi can lead to florid papillary endothelial hyperplasia, a process that can be overinterpreted as angiosarcoma; as a matter of fact, the original description of this process by Pierre Masson was in a hemorrhoidal vessel.

Microscopic examination of tissue submitted with the clinical diagnosis of hemorrhoids rarely may show nonspecific granulomas, tuberculosis, malignant lymphoma, koilocytotic changes, dysplasia/carcinoma in situ, invasive squamous cell carcinoma, or even malignant melanoma.[35–37,42] The latter is sometimes interpreted clinically as a thrombosed hemorrhoid because of its polypoid shape and dark brown color, a fact that renders mandatory the microscopic examination of all such specimens.

Tumors

Condyloma and other human papilloma virus-related lesions

Human papilloma virus (HPV) is associated with and probably responsible for a variety of benign and malignant proliferative anal lesions, of which **condyloma acuminatum** is the more common and better known[44,45] (Fig. 11.229). This presents as one or more papillary excrescences lined by hyperkeratotic squamous epithelium usually exhibiting variable degrees of koilocytotic changes. Sometimes the latter are absent, presumably because the viral infection has subsided.[47]

Approximately 7% to 20% of these condylomas show dysplastic changes on microscopic or cytologic examination.[43,46] The types of HPV most commonly encountered are 6, 11, 16, and 18, but types 31, 35, and 39 are also observed.[46] Condylomas and other proliferative squamous anal lesions associated with high-risk HPV infection often show overexpression of p16 and loss of Rb nuclear staining.[43a] Other lesions in which HPV participation is often found include anal dysplasia/carcinoma in situ (see next section), verrucous carcinoma/giant condyloma acuminatum of Buschke–Löwenstein (see p. 861), and squamous cell/basaloid carcinoma (see below) (i.e., practically all of the major types of squamous proliferations of this region). The HIV-infected population is particularly at risk for all of these disorders.

Dysplasia and carcinoma in situ

Morphologic changes of dysplasia and carcinoma in situ (CIS) in the anal epithelium can occur within the context of (and be confined to) a condyloma acuminatum (see previous section) or occur in a flat mucosa.[54] The anal canal is the usual location, but they can also be encountered in the perianal skin. As already indicated, sometimes they are found incidentally on microscopic examination of a hemorrhoidectomy specimen.[49] Multicentricity is common.[52]

Squamous cell CIS of this region has been traditionally equated with Bowen's disease.[53] More recently, the term *anal intraepithelial neoplasia (AIN)* has been proposed to embrace the entire range of these pathogenetically related processes (Fig. 11.230). HPV is commonly detected in these lesions, to which HIV-infected individuals are particularly at risk.[48,50] Cytologic examination is very useful for their detection.[51]

Carcinoma

General and clinical features

The incidence of anal carcinoma is increasing in both males and females.[59,60] At present, the female to male ratio is about 3:1, but it seems to be increasing.[60] Clinically, the disease presents with bleeding (50%), pain (40%; much more common than in colonic cancer), mass (25%), and pruritus (15%). Approximately 25% of the patients are asymptomatic. In some instances, the tumor develops in association with Crohn's disease,[68] lymphogranuloma venereum,[66] condyloma acuminatum (see previous section), or independent carcinomas of the lower genital tract (particularly cervix) in females.[55,63,65] There is convincing evidence that sexually transmitted infection is a cause of anal cancer[60]; in particular, a strong association has been found between anal carcinoma and receptive anal intercourse related to

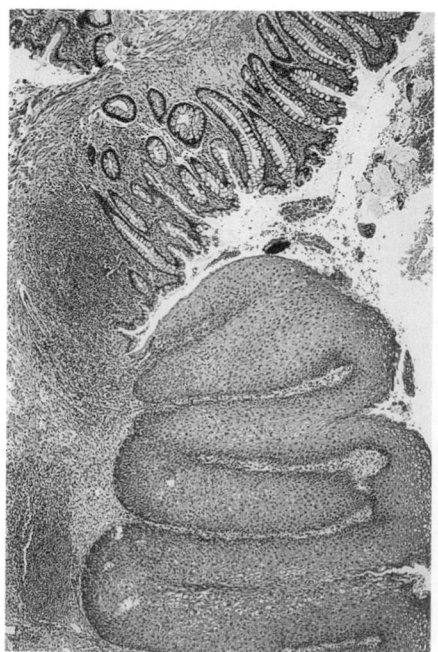

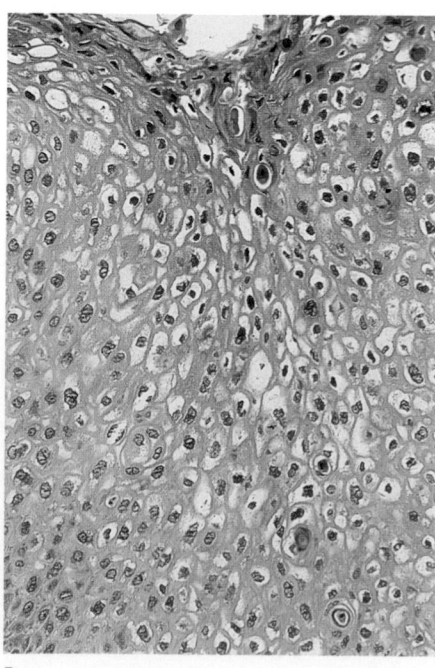

Fig. 11.229 A and **B**, Condyloma acuminatum of anus. **A**, Low-power view showing a condylomatous proliferation beginning at the squamocolumnar junction. **B**, High-power view showing koilocytotic changes.

A

B

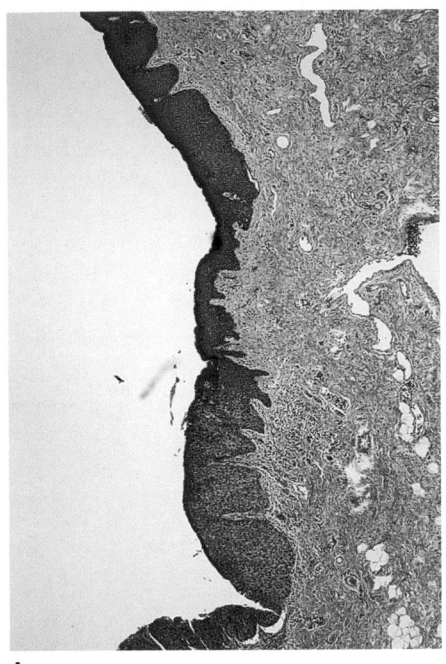
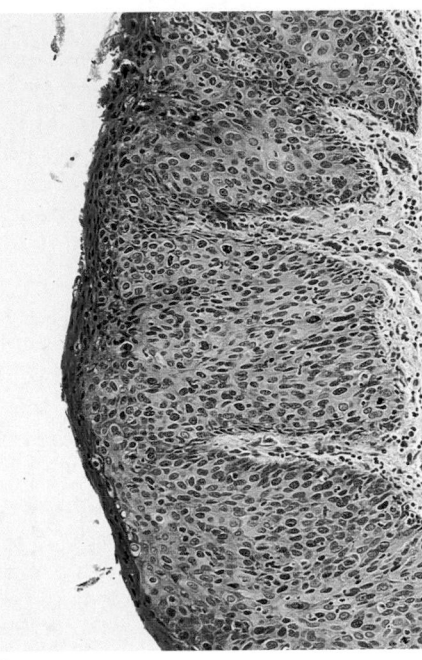

Fig. 11.230 A and **B**, Carcinoma in situ of the anus (AIN III). **A**, Low-power view showing a sharp separation between normal and abnormal mucosa. The latter is thickened and accompanied by a lymphocytic inflammatory infiltrate in the underlying stroma. **B**, High-power view showing marked atypia and increased mitotic activity throughout the epithelial layer.

A

B

homosexual behavior.[57] There is also a statistical association between anal carcinoma and smoking.[56]

HPV has been detected in anal carcinomas with a variety of techniques, including immunohistochemistry and in situ and dot blot hybridization, the incidence varying greatly depending on the technique used.[57,60,69,71] In one series, HPV DNA was found in 85% with the use of dot blot hybridization, HPV 16 being the specific subtype in 82% of the positive cases.[58] This is in stark contrast to rectal adenocarcinomas, which are invariably negative.[62] There is no significant difference in HPV positivity among the major microscopic types of anal carcinoma.[62,67,70] Instead, the presence of HPV in tumor cells is significantly associated with an increased proliferative rate and aneuploid status.[64] HPV-negative tumors occur in an older age group and are less likely to be accompanied by dysplasia/CIS of the adjacent epithelium.[62]

Morphologic features

Grossly, anal carcinoma most commonly appears near the pectinate line and grows either upward into the rectum and surrounding tissues or outward to the perianal tissues[74] (Fig. 11.231). Sometimes the tumor is located proximal to this line without encroaching on it. When this is the case, its gross appearance may be indistinguishable from that of an adenocarcinoma of the rectum,

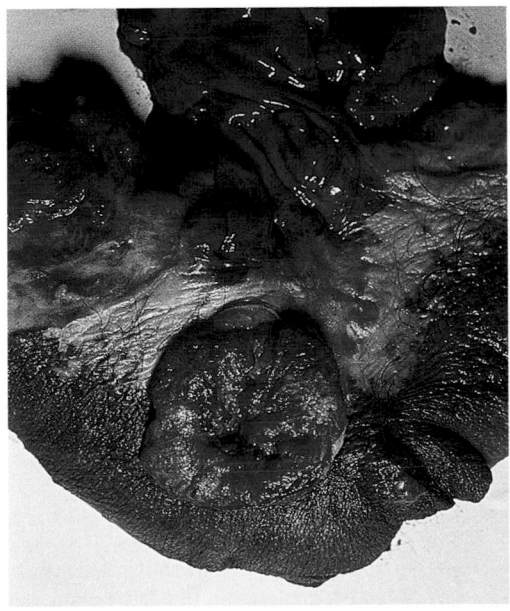
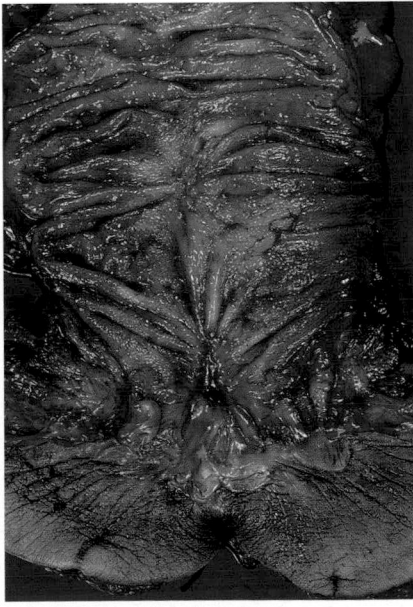

A

B

Fig. 11.231 A and **B**, Gross appearance of carcinoma of anal canal. Both tumors involve the dentate line. The tumor shown in **A** is exophytic with a central ulceration, whereas the one depicted in **B** is also ulcerated but primarily infiltrative.

and the correct diagnosis is made only after biopsy. Involvement of the perianal skin may be superficial, with only surface ulceration and slightly elevated margins. Such lesions can be mistaken for an inflammatory process. In other instances, a deeply ulcerated neoplasm with rolled edges is seen. Upward local extension may burrow beneath the overlying epithelium to ulcerate at a higher level.

The interpretation of the microscopic pathology of carcinoma of the anal canal has changed considerably in the course of the years. Traditionally, these tumors were regarded and classified as squamous cell (epidermoid) carcinomas.[72] Some years ago, it was proposed that there were two distinct types of carcinoma in this area: (1) *squamous cell* carcinoma, analogous to its counterpart elsewhere in the skin (Fig. 11.232), and (2) *cloacogenic* (transitional, basaloid) carcinoma, supposedly originating from the transitional epithelium and recapitulating the features of this zone at both a light and electron microscopic level.[76,77,80] The latter tumor, which was said to comprise approximately 20% of all anal cancers, was identified by the presence of solid tumor nests exhibiting peripheral palisading somewhat resembling that seen in cutaneous basal cell carcinoma (hence the alternative term *basaloid*) (Fig. 11.233), sometimes accompanied by foci of mucin secretion and areas of squamous differentiation.[78,81,83] With increasing experience, it became obvious that distinguishing these two tumor types is not only difficult in practice but also histogenetically unwarranted. It seems likely that we are dealing with a carcinoma that is basically of *squamous cell* nature but that manifests in various degrees a tendency toward glandular (adnexal) differentiation in a manner analogous to that sometimes seen in the tumors of the oral cavity, larynx, or esophagus currently designated as basaloid carcinomas. Indeed, if one were to be consistent in nomenclature, the preferred term for this anal tumor should be that of basaloid carcinoma. As is the case with the homonymous tumors in the upper digestive tract, these anal neoplasms exhibit a variability in their appearance. Dougherty and Evans[73] have proposed to subdivide them into five types: keratinizing, nonkeratinizing, basaloid, with mucous cysts, and pseudoadenoid cystic.

Tumors described in the past as mucoepidermoid carcinomas of the anal canal are presently incorporated into this general scheme, although whether this is justified remains to be determined. Some anal carcinomas have

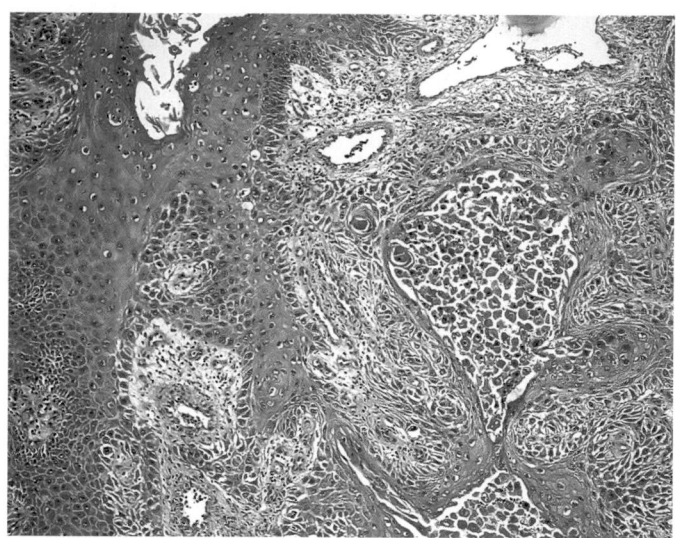

Fig. 11.232 Invasive well-differentiated squamous cell carcinoma of the anal canal.

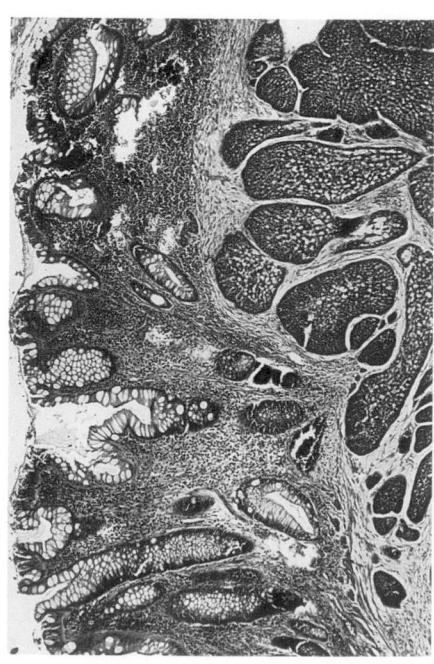

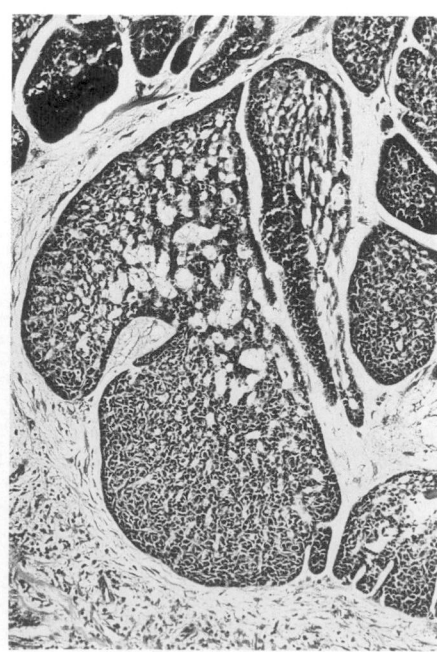

A   B

Fig. 11.233 Low-power (**A**) and medium-power (**B**) views of basaloid carcinoma of the anal canal. The appearance is analogous to that of basaloid squamous cell carcinoma of the upper aerodigestive tract.

clear cell features.[82] Others are accompanied by a massive infiltration of mature eosinophils,[79] a feature again analogous to that seen in carcinomas of other mucosal sites, particularly of squamous cell type. Foci of dysplasia and carcinoma in situ are not uncommon in the epithelium adjacent to invasive anal carcinomas.[75]

Immunohistochemical and molecular genetic features

Immunohistochemically, anal carcinomas exhibit reactivity for all cytokeratin classes, epithelial membrane antigen, CEA, and blood group isoantigens.[90] The cytokeratin polypeptides expressed are similar to those of the basal layer of anal squamous epithelium, transitional epithelium, and basal cells of anal glands.[86] Williams et al[91] found that most tumors express keratin 4, 13, 17, 18, and 19, with a minority expressing keratins 1, 10, and 7; this profile is somewhat different from that of squamous cell carcinoma of the anal margin.[84]

Search for estrogen and progesterone receptors has given negative results.[85] Intense positivity for the c-*myc* oncogene has been found in approximately 70% of the cases,[87] and p53 overexpression has been detected in over 85% of the cases.[88,89]

Spread and metastases

The local pattern of spread of this tumor up and down the anal canal has already been mentioned (p. 861). As far as lymph node metastases are concerned, stations along the rectum and in the inguinal areas can both be involved because of the dual lymphatic supply of the pectinate line.

Therapy

The traditional therapy for anal carcinomas has been abdominoperineal resection,[96,97] sometimes combined with hypogastric lymph node dissection and with posterior vaginectomy in women.[94,105] Alternative methods using radiation therapy and chemotherapy (alone or in combination) have been advocated,[92,95,98,101,106] and currently represent the preferred approach.[99,103,104] A combined approach of chemotherapy and radiation therapy followed by local resection or abdominoperineal resection is also used.[102] Local excision is adequate for small tumors.[93,105] The overall 5-year survival rate ranges from 50% to 70% in the various series,[93,100] the figures reaching 82% in the series in which a combined approach was employed.[102]

Prognosis

The prognosis of carcinoma of the anal canal is related to several parameters.

1 *Tumor stage.* The prognosis depends largely on the stage of the disease, as determined by depth of invasion and regional nodal involvement.[107,109,114] Involvement of inguinal lymph nodes is a particularly grave prognostic sign.[113]

2 *Tumor size.* Tumor size is related to stage and inversely related to prognosis.

3 *Tumor recurrence.* Tumor recurrence in the pelvic or perineal regions following abdominoperineal resection carries an ominous prognosis; instead, subsequent development of inguinal lymph node metastases is still compatible with long-term survival following the performance of an inguinal lymphadenectomy.[108,111]

4 *Microscopic type and grade.* An evaluation of the prognostic significance of the various microscopic subtypes is difficult because of the wide disparity in terminology used.[107,109,110,113]

In the series of Pang and Morson,[112] the 5-year survival rate was 90%, 60%, and 0% for well-differentiated, moderately differentiated, and poorly differentiated tumors, respectively. Since poor differentiation in this series was equated with the presence of basaloid features, these striking differences in survival could also be expressed by stating that the more basaloid the tumor, the worse the prognosis. Again, this is not substantially different from the situation in the upper digestive tract. At both sites, however, the differences are minimized when these microscopic types or subtypes are compared stage by stage.

Paget's disease

Paget's disease is a malignant glandular neoplasm having a predominant or exclusive intraepithelial location. Clinically, it presents as an erythematous, ulcerated lesion of eczematoid appearance (Fig. 11.234). Microscopically, the Paget cells are large, with an abundant pale cytoplasm, predominantly located along the epithelial basal layer (Fig. 11.235). Most of them are arranged individually, but occasionally there are nests and gland-like formations. Occasionally the tumor cells have a signet ring appearance.[119]

It would seem that Paget's disease of this region can be subdivided into two types depending on their pattern of

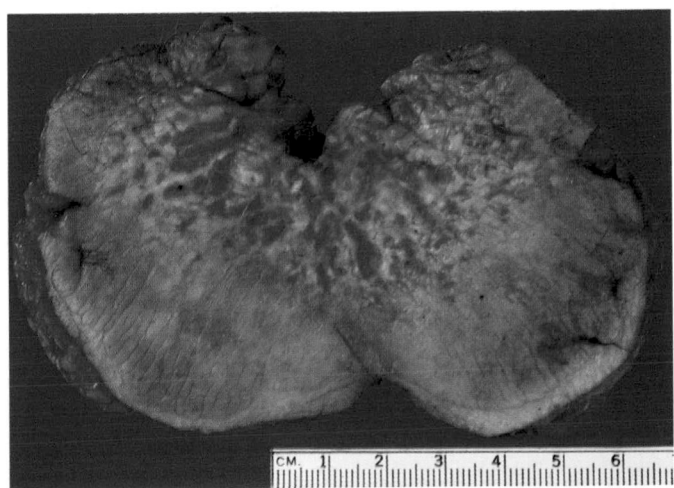

Fig. 11.234 Gross appearance of Paget's disease of the anus. The lesion is erosive and hyperemic and has ill-defined borders.

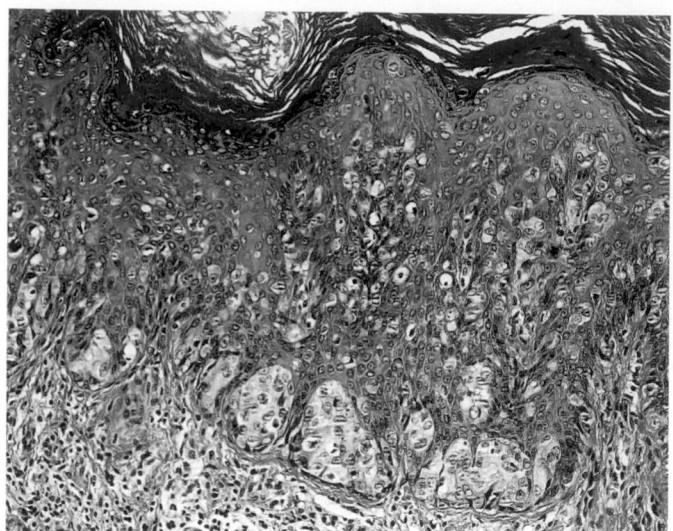

Fig. 11.235 Paget's disease of anal canal. The tumor cells are arranged individually and in nests along the basal layer.

differentiation, one resembling apocrine glands and the other resembling colorectal adenocarcinoma.[119,120,124] As a rule, the former is exclusively intraepithelial (as is its counterpart in the vulva), whereas the latter is often associated with invasive rectal adenocarcinoma.[119,122] It is likely that the apocrine type arises from multipotential epithelial cells located in the basal layer having the capacity to differentiate toward glandular cells. Along those lines, it is interesting that cells identical to those described by Toker in the nipple have been detected in the anal region.[117]

Histochemically, the cells of anogenital Paget's disease invariably contain acid mucosubstances, an important feature in the differential diagnosis with melanoma and Bowen's disease.[126,127] Immunohistochemically, they are reactive for keratin, CEA, and EMA.[121] Those differentiating toward apocrine-type epithelium are usually positive for CK7 and GCDFP-15 and negative for CK20, whereas those of colorectal type are usually positive for CK7, CK20, B72.3 and CD15, while being negative for GCDFP-15.[119,123] This pattern differs from that of ordinary colorectal adenocarcinoma unassociated with Paget's disease, in the sense that CK7 is usually negative.[125] Interestingly, the cells of extramammary Paget's disease consistently lack estrogen and progesterone receptors but frequently express androgen receptor, which has been found to be structurally altered.[116,118]

Sometimes, Paget's disease is accompanied by an atypical proliferation of the adjacent malpighian cells[115]; in most instances these probably represent a secondary reactive change, but some of the cases we have seen have led us to the conclusion that they can also be neoplastic, perhaps indicating dual differentiation of the tumor cells in a glandular and a squamous direction.

The prognosis of Paget's disease largely depends on the presence or absence of an invasive component and—

in the latter instance—whether the regional lymph nodes are involved or not.[122] Local recrudescence is very common because of the ill-defined nature of the process, its sometimes multifocal nature, and the difficulties in delimiting it grossly.

Other microscopic types

Small cell (neuroendocrine) carcinoma is a highly undifferentiated neoplasm formed by large solid nests of small hyperchromatic cells with central necrosis; their appearance is reminiscent of the pulmonary homonymous tumors. These lesions have been found to have signs of neuroendocrine differentiation ultrastructurally and immunohistochemically.[138] Their behavior is extremely aggressive. Cases of this tumor type have been reported in HIV-infected patients.[135]

Spindle cell (sarcomatoid) carcinoma is not as common here as in the upper digestive tract, but it does occur.[134] A spectacular case showing neuroendocrine and rhabdomyoblastic features has been described.[137]

Verrucous carcinoma presents as a polypoid neoplasm that is microscopically composed of extremely well differentiated squamous epithelium but that invades the underlying stroma in a pushing fashion (Fig. 11.236). This lesion is closely related if not identical to the so-called *giant condyloma acuminatum of Buschke–Löwenstein*. Actually, a continuum seems to exist between the HPV-induced condyloma acuminatum, the "giant" form of this process, and verrucous carcinoma.[130] These lesions are morphologically identical to those seen in the lower female genital tract and other sites (see Chapter 19).

Adenocarcinoma involving the anal canal usually represents a downgrowth of a rectal tumor. However, some primary malignant glandular tumors occur at this site, thought to arise from anal glands; these are characterized by the haphazard growth of small glands with scant mucin production invading the wall and lacking a mucosal component.[132]

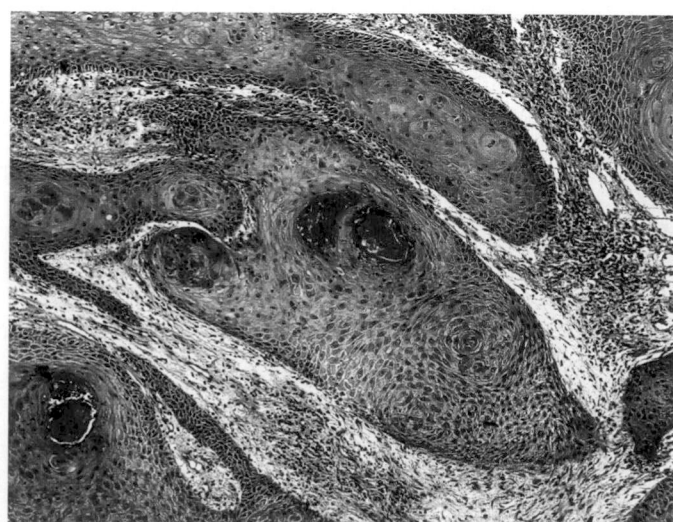

Fig. 11.236 Verrucous carcinoma of anal canal.

Mucinous (colloid) adenocarcinoma is sometimes found in the anal region, often presenting with multiple fistulous tracts and, on rare occasions, as vaginal cysts.[129] This tumor is also thought to arise from the epithelium of anal ducts, either de novo or on the basis of preexisting anal fistulas.[131,139] Jones and Morson[133] have suggested that some of these carcinomas associated with fistulas arise in congenital duplications of the distal end of the hindgut. These tumors need to be distinguished from low rectal, mucin-producing adenocarcinomas.[136]

Basal cell carcinoma can occur in the skin at the anal margin and can be cured either by local excision or by irradiation[140]; before making this diagnosis, the more likely probability of basaloid carcinoma should be considered, especially when the tumor encroaches on the anal canal. The distinction is of great importance because of the vast difference in behavior between the two tumors.[128]

Malignant melanoma

Approximately one melanoma is seen for every eight squamous cell carcinomas and one for every 250 adenocarcinomas of the anorectal region.[150,152] Rectal bleeding is the most common complaint. The typical gross appearance is that of single or multiple polypoid masses covered by a smooth surface (Fig. 11.237). In the early stages, it can simulate clinically thrombosed hemorrhoids.[147] The tumor is usually in or close to the pectinate line, from which it tends to grow toward the rectal ampulla. Sometimes it extends proximally a long way along the submucosa and emerges through the mucosa at a high point, thus simulating a primary rectal tumor.[148] Rectal bleeding, palpable mass, and pain are the most common complaints.[142] Microscopically, the tumors are usually pigmented, and two thirds show a "junctional" component with a lentiginous appearance in the adjacent mucosa[151] (Fig. 11.238). Their appearance is similar to that of melanomas of other mucosal membranes. The tumor is occasionally of the desmoplastic variety.[141] The overall prognosis, which in general is extremely poor, is directly related to tumor size and depth of invasion.[143,145,149,151] It is also said to show a correlation with cell proliferation markers.[141]

Malignant melanoma should be distinguished from the exceptionally rare adenocarcinoma of this region which contains abundant melanin in the tumor cells, perhaps through a colonization mechanism similar to that sometimes seen in breast carcinoma.[146]

Other tumors and tumorlike conditions

Ectopic prostatic tissue has been reported in the anal canal.[165]

Pseudotumors may be produced by sclerosing agents used to obliterate hemorrhoids.[153]

Langerhans' cell histiocytosis (histiocytosis X) can involve the perianal skin.[164]

Endometriosis secondary to an episiotomy scar has been found to involve the external anal sphincter.[168]

Inflammatory cloacogenic polyp is discussed in the large bowel section (see p. 776).

Keratinous cysts of epidermal type located in the anal canal are probably of the inclusion type.[155]

Sweat gland tumors of various types can arise from the apocrine glands of the region, in addition to the already mentioned Paget's disease (see p. 863). They include *hidradenoma*,[172] *fibroadenoma*,[154] and *apocrine mixed tumor* containing abundant cartilage.[157]

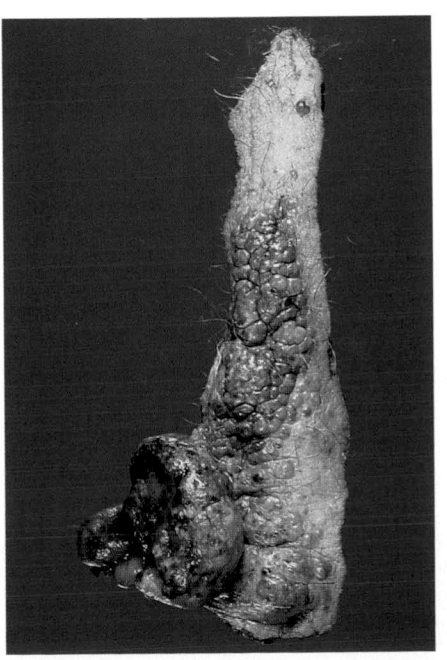

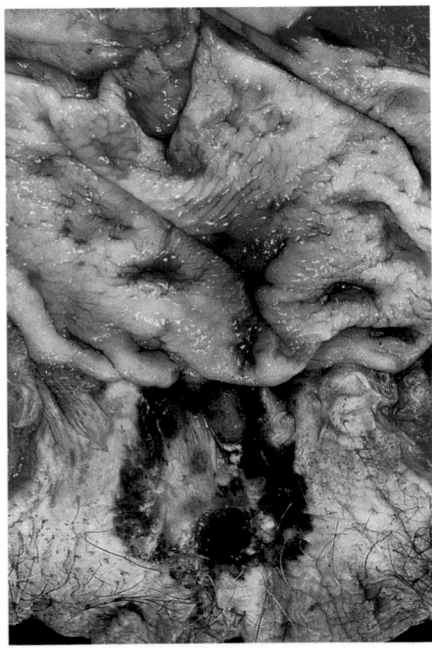

A **B**

Fig. 11.237 A, Gross appearance of malignant melanoma of the anal canal. The large size, polypoid shape, deep pigmentation, and extension into the surrounding mucosa are characteristic of this entity. **B**, Another malignant melanoma of the anal canal showing irregular edges and focally deep pigmentation.

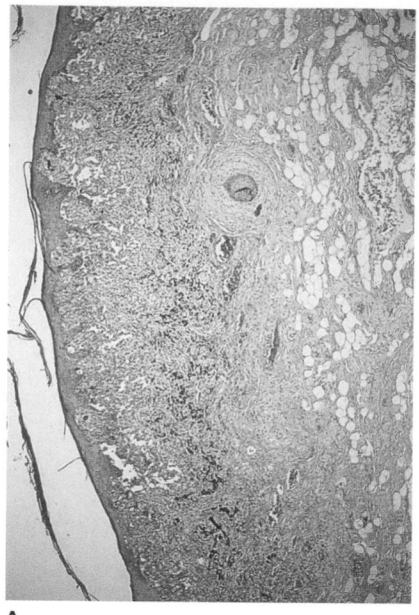

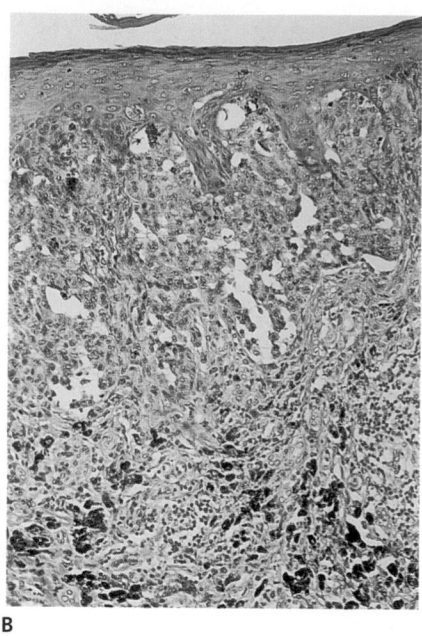

A   **B**

Fig. 11.238 A, Low-power view of malignant melanoma showing diffuse involvement along the dermoepidermal junction and a band-like infiltrate of melanin-containing macrophages. **B,** Medium-power view of malignant melanoma showing large expanses of malignant melanocytes.

Benign mesenchymal tumors are rare if one avoids labeling hypertrophied anal papillae as "fibromas."

Granular cell tumor may grow to a relatively large size and ulcerate, thus simulating clinically the appearance of a malignant tumor.[161] Cases of *cavernous hemangioma,*[170] *leiomyoma,*[156,171] and perianal *spindle cell lipoma*[166] have been reported.

Leiomyosarcoma is the most common primary malignant stromal tumor in the region.[174] Sometimes it is difficult to decide whether to classify these tumors as anal or rectal.[163,171,173]

Embryonal rhabdomyosarcoma can occur in the perianal region of infants and children[169] (Fig. 11.239). Some of these tumors are of the botryoid variety. Electron microscopy and immunohistochemistry are helpful in its recognition (Fig. 11.240).

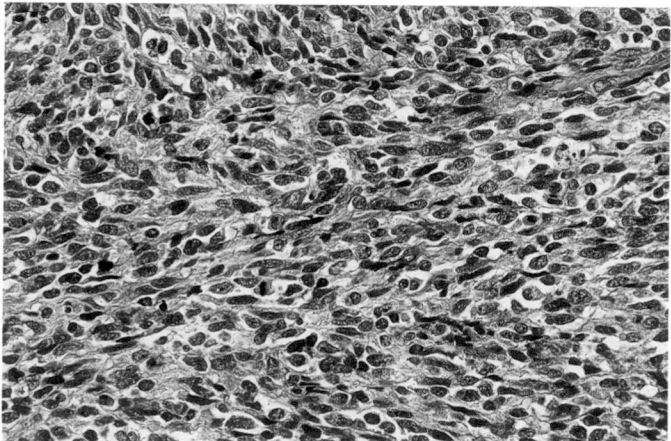

Fig. 11.239 Embryonal rhabdomyosarcoma of perianal region.

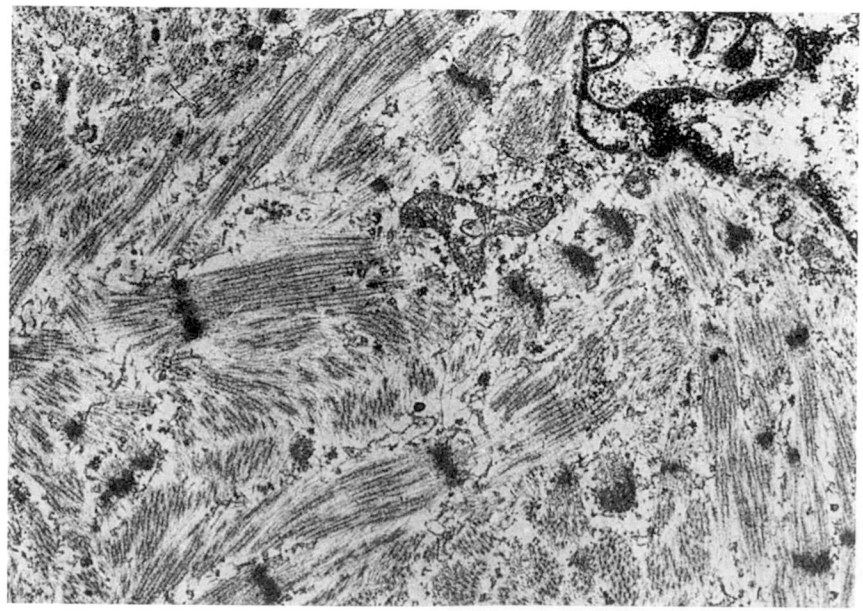

Fig. 11.240 Electron microscopic appearance of embryonal rhabdomyosarcoma arising in perianal region. There is clear-cut evidence of skeletal muscle differentiation, including the formation of Z lines. (Courtesy of Dr. J. Magidson, Brookhaven, NY)

Malignant lymphoma of the anorectal region has been observed in HIV-infected patients.[160,162] Some of these tumors have been found to be EBV-related.[158]

Metastases to the anal region often arise from rectal carcinomas. They have also been reported from distant sites such as the kidney.[167] Sometimes these metastases have been seen to develop at the site of a recently performed hemorrhoidectomy.[159]

References

Normal anatomy

1 Clemmensen OJ, Fenger C. Melanocytes in the anal canal epithelium. Histopathology 1991, **18**: 237–241.
2 Fenger C. The anal transitional zone. Acta Pathol Microbiol Scand (A) 1978, **86**: 225–230.
3 Fenger C. Anal Canal. Histology for pathologists 1997, **2**: 551–574.
4 Fenger C, Knoth M. The anal transitional zone. A scanning and transmission electron microscopic investigation of the surface epithelium. Ultrastruct Pathol 1981, **2**: 163–173.
5 Fetissof F, Dubois MP, Assan R, Arbeille-Brassart B, Baroudi A, Tharanne MJ, Jobard P. Endocrine cells in the anal canal. Virchows Arch [A] 1984, **404**: 39–47.
6 Grinvalsky HT, Helwig EB. Carcinoma of the anorectal junction. Part I. Histological considerations. Cancer 1956, **9**: 480–488.
7 Klotz RG, Pamukcoglu T, Souillard DH. Transitional cloacogenic carcinoma of the anal canal. Cancer 1967, **20**: 1727–1745.
8 Ramalingam P, Hart WR., Goldblum JR. Cytokeratin subset immunostaining in rectal adenocarcinomas and normal anal glands. Arch Pathol Lab Med 2001, **125**: 1074–1077.
9 Stelzner F, Staubesand J, Machleidt H. Das Corpus Cavernosum Recti – die Grundlage der inneren Hämorrhoiden. Langenbecks Arch Klin Chir 1962, **299**: 302–312.
10 Van der Putte SCJ. Anogenital "sweat" glands. Histology and pathology of a gland that may mimic mammary glands. Am J Dermatopathol 1991, **13**: 557–567.
11 Williams GR, Talbot IC. Keratin expression in the normal anal canal. Histopathology 1995, **26**: 39–44.

Embryologic defects

12 Cushieri A, EUROCAT Working Group. Anorectal anomalies associated with or as part of other anomalies. Am J Med Genet 2002, **110**: 122–130.
13 Louw JH, Cywes S, Cremin BJ. Anorectal malformations. Classification and clinical features. S Afr J Surg 1971, **9**: 11–20.
14 Santulli TV, Kiesewetter WB, Bill AH Jr. Anorectal anomalies. A suggested international classification. J Pediatr Surg 1970, **5**: 281–287.
15 Van der Putte SCJ. Normal and abnormal development of the anorectum. J Pediatr Surg 1986, **21**: 434–440.

Inflammatory diseases

16 Corfitsen MT, Hansen CP, Christensen TH, Kaae HH. Anorectal abscesses in immunosuppressed patients. Eur J Surg 1992, **158**: 51–53.
17 de la Monte SM, Hutchins GM. Follicular proctocolitis and neuromatous hyperplasia with lymphogranuloma venereum. Hum Pathol 1985, **16**: 1025–1032.
18 Fry GA, Martin WJ, Dearing WH, Culp CE. Primary actinomycosis of the rectum with multiple perianal and perineal fistulae. Mayo Clin Proc 1965, **40**: 296–299.
19 Gray BK, Lockhart-Mummery HE, Morson BC. Crohn's disease of the anal region. Gut 1965, **6**: 515–525.
20 Hanley PH. Anorectal abscess fistula. Surg Clin North Am 1978, **58**: 487–503.
21 Harland RW, Varkey B. Anal tuberculosis. Report of two cases and literature review. Am J Gastroenterol 1992, **87**: 1488–1491.
22 Hughes LE. Clinical classification of perianal Crohn's disease. Dis Colon Rectum 1992, **35**: 928–932.
23 Kamel PL. Cytomegalovirus-associated perianal ulcerations in AIDS. J Clin Gastroenterol 1992, **14**: 105–108.
24 Lennard-Jones JE, Lockhart-Mummery HE, Chir M, Morson BC. Clinical and pathological differentiation of Crohn's disease and proctocolitis. Gastroenterology 1968, **54**: 1162–1170.
25 Lilius HG. Fistula-in-ano. An investigation of human foetal anal ducts and intramuscular glands and a clinical study of 150 patients. Acta Chir Scand 1968, **383**(Suppl): 1–88.
26 Logan VS. Anorectal tuberculosis. Proc R Soc Med 1969, **62**: 1227–1230.
27 Madoff RD, Fleshman JW. AGA technical review on the diagnosis and care of patients with anal fissure. Gastroenterology 2003, **124**: 235–245.
28 Marks CG, Ritchie JK. Anal fistulas at St. Mark's Hospital. Br J Surg 1977, **64**: 84–91.
29 Parks AG, Morson BC. The pathogenesis of fistula-in-ano. Proc R Soc Med 1962, **55**: 751–754.
30 Puy-Montbrun T, Denis J, Ganansia R, Mathoniere F, Lemarchand N, Arnous-Dubois N. Anorectal lesions in human immunodeficiency virus-infected patients. Int J Colorectal Dis 1992, **7**: 26–30.

Hypertrophied papillae

31 Groisman GM, Amar M, Polak-Charcon S. Multinucleated stromal cells of the anal mucosa: a common finding. Histopathology 2000, **36**: 224–228.
32 Groisman GM, Polak-Charcon S. Fibroepithelial polyps of the anus: a histologic, immunohistochemical and ultrastructural study, including comparison with the normal anal subepithelial layer. Am J Surg Pathol 1998, **22**: 70–76.
33 Sakai Y, Matsukuma S. CD34+ stromal cells and hyalinized vascular changes in the anal fibroepithelial polyps. Histopathology 2002, **41**: 230–235.
34 Schinella RA. Stromal atypia in anal papillae. Dis Colon Rectum 1976, **19**: 611–613.

Hemorrhoids

35 Cataldo PA, Mac Keigan JM. The necessity of routine pathologic evaluation of hemorrhoidectomy specimens. Surg Gynecol Obstet 1992, **174**: 302–304.
36 Foust RL, Dean PJ, Stoler MH, Moinuddin SM. Intraepithelial neoplasis of the anal canal in hemorrhoidal tissue. A study of 19 cases. Hum Pathol 1991, **22**: 528–534.
37 Gordsky L. Unsuspected anal cancer discovered after minor anorectal surgery. Dis Colon Rectum 1967, **10**: 471–478.
37a Hulme-Moir M, Bartolo DC. Hemorrhoids. Gastroenterol Clin North Am 2001, **30**: 183–197.
38 Jacobs DM, Bubrick MP, Onstad GR, Hitchcock CR. The relationship of hemorrhoids to portal hypertension. Dis Colon Rectum 1980, **23**: 567–569.
39 Kuo TT, Sayers CP, Rosai J. Masson's "vegetant intravascular hemangioendothelioma"; a lesion often mistaken for angiosarcoma: study of seventeen cases located in the skin and soft tissues. Cancer 1976, **38**: 1227–1236.
40 Laurence AE, Murray AJ. Histopathology of prolapsed and thrombosed hemorrhoids. Dis Colon Rectum 1962, **5**: 56–61.
41 McCormack TT, Bailey HR, Simms JM, Johnson AG. Rectal varices are not piles. Br J Surg 1984, **71**: 163.
42 Val-Bernal JF, Pinto J. Pagetoid dyskeratosis is a frequent incidental finding in hemorrhoidal disease. Arch Pathol Lab Med 2001, **125**: 1058–1062.

Tumors

Condyloma and other human papilloma virus-related lesions

43 Law CL, Qassim M, Thompson CH, Rose BR, Grace J, Morris BJ, Cossart YE. Factors associated with clinical and sub-clinical anal human papillomavirus infection in homosexual men. Gentourin Med 1991, **67**: 92–98.

43a Lu DW, El-Mofty SK, Wang HL. Expression of p16, Rb, and p53 proteins in squamous cell carcinomas of the anorectal region harbouring human papillomavirus DNA. Mod Pathol 2003, **16**: 692–699.

44 Noffsinger A, Witte D, Fenoglio-Preiser CM. The relationship of human papillomavirus to anorectal neoplasia. Cancer 1992, **70**: 1276–1287.

45 Palefsky JM. Human papillomavirus-associated anogenital neoplasia and other solid tumors in human immunodeficiency virus-infected individuals. Curr Opin Oncol 1991, **3**: 881–885.

46 Puy-Montbrun T, Denis J, Ganansia R, Mathoniere F, Lemarchand N, Arnous-Dubois N. Anorectal lesions in human immunodeficiency virus-infected patients. Int J Colorectal Dis 1992, **7**: 26–30.

47 Rock B, Shah KV, Farmer ER. A morphologic, pathologic, and virologic study of anogenital warts in men. Arch Dermatol 1992, **128**: 495–500.

Dysplasia and carcinoma in situ

48 Fenger C. Anal neoplasia and its precursors. Facts and controversies. Semin Diagn Pathol 1991, **8**: 190–201.

49 Grodsky L. Unsuspected anal cancer discovered after minor anorectal surgery. Dis Colon Rectum 1967, **10**: 471–478.

50 Kiviat NB, Critchlow CW, Holmes KK, Kuypers J, Sayers J, Dunphy C, Surawicz C, Kirby P, Wood R, Daling JR. Association of anal dysplasia and human papillomavirus with immunosuppression and HIV infection among homosexual men. AIDS 1993, **7**: 43–49.

51 Palefsky JM, Holly EAM, Gonzales J, Lamborn K, Hollander H. Natural history of anal cytologic abnormalities and papillomavirus infection among homosexual men with group IV HIV disease. J Acquir Immune Defic Syndr 1992, **5**: 1258–1265.

52 Scholefield JH, Hickson WG, Smith JH, Rogers K, Sharp F. Anal intraepithelial neoplasia. Part of a multifocal disease process. Lancet 1992, **340**: 1271–1273.

53 Strauss RJ, Fazio VW. Bowen's disease of the anal and perianal area. Am J Surg 1979, **137**: 231–234.

54 Surawicz CM, Kirby P, Critchlow C, Sayer J, Dunphy C, Kiviat N. Anal dysplasia in homosexual men. Role of anoscopy and biopsy. Gastroenterology 1993, **105**: 658–666.

Carcinoma

General and clinical features

55 Cabrera A, Tsukada Y, Pickren JW, Moore R, Bross IDJ. Development of lower genital carcinomas in patients with anal carcinomas. A more than casual relationship. Cancer 1966, **19**: 470–480.

56 Daling JR, Sherman KJ, Hislop TG, Maden C, Mandelson MT, Beckmann AM, Weiss NS. Cigarette smoking and the risk of anogenital cancer. Am J Epidemiol 1992, **135**: 180–189.

57 Daling JR, Weiss NS, Hislop TG, Maden C, Coates RJ, Sherman KJ, Ashley RL, Beagrie M, Ryan JA, Coney L. Sexual practices, sexually transmitted diseases, and the incidence of anal cancer. N Engl J Med 1987, **317**: 973–977.

58 Duggan MA, Boras VF, Inoue M, McGregor SE. Human papillomavirus DNA in anal carcinomas. Comparison of in situ and dot blot hybridization. Am J Clin Pathol 1991, **96**: 318–325.

59 Frisch M, Melbye M, Moller H. Trends in incidence of anal cancer in Denmark. Br Med J 1993, **306**: 419–422.

60 Frisch M, Glimelius B, van den Brule AJ, Wohlfahrt J, Meijer CJ, Walboomers JM, Goldman S, Svensson C, Adami HO, Melbye M. Sexually transmitted infection as a cause of anal cancer. N Engl J Med 1997, **337**: 1350–1358.

61 Heino P, Goldman S, Lagerstedt U, Dillner J. Molecular and serological studies of human papillomavirus among patients with anal epidermoid carcinoma. Int J Cancer 1993, **53**: 377–381.

62 Higgins GD, Uzelin DM, Phillips GE, Pieterse AS, Burrell CJ. Differing characteristics of human papillomavirus RNA-positive and RNA-negative anal carcinomas. Cancer 1991, **68**: 561–567.

63 Melbye M, Sprogel P. Aetiological parallel between anal cancer and cervical cancer. Lancet 1991, **338**: 657–659.

64 Noffsinger AE, Hui YZ, Suzuk L, Yochman LK, Miller MA, Hurtubise P, Gal AA, Fenoglio-Preiser CM. The relationship of human papillomavirus to proliferation and ploidy in carcinoma of the anus. Cancer 1995, **75**: 958–967.

65 Rabkin CS, Biggar RJ, Melbye M, Curtis RE. Second primary cancers following anal and cervical carcinoma: evidence of shared etiologic factors. Am J Epidemiol 1992, **136**: 54–58.

66 Rainey R. The association of lymphogranuloma inguinale and cancer. Surgery 1954, **35**: 221–235.

67 Shroyer KR, Brookes CG, Markham NE, Shroyer AL. Detection of human papillomavirus in anorectal squamous cell carcinoma. Correlation with basaloid pattern of differentiation. Am J Clin Pathol 1995, **104**: 299–305.

68 Slater G, Greenstein A, Aufses AH Jr. Anal carcinoma in patients with Crohn's disease. Ann Surg 1984, **199**: 348–350.

69 Vincent-Salomon A, de al Rochefordiere AR, Salmon R, Validire P, Zafrani B, Sastre-Garau X. Frequent association of human papillomavirus 16 and 18 DNA with anal squamous cell and basaloid carcinoma. Mod Pathol 1996, **9**: 614–620.

70 Wolber R, Dupuis B, Thiyagaratnam P, Owen D. Anal cloacogenic and squamous carcinomas. Comparative histologic analysis using in situ hybridization for human papillomavirus DNA. Am J Surg Pathol 1990, **14**: 176–182.

71 Zaki SR, Judd R, Coffield LM, Greer P, Rolston F, Evatt BL. Human papillomavirus infection and anal carcinoma. Retrospective analysis by in situ hybridization and the polymerase chain reaction. Am J Pathol 1992, **140**: 1345–1355.

Morphologic features

72 Dillard BM, Spratt JS Jr, Ackerman LV, Butcher HR Jr. Epidermoid cancer of anal margin and canal. Review of 79 cases. Arch Surg 1963, **16**: 772–776.

73 Dougherty BG, Evans HL. Carcinoma of the anal canal. A study of 79 cases. Am J Clin Pathol 1985, **83**: 159–164.

74 Fenger C. Anal canal tumors and their precursors. Pathol Annu 1988, **23**(Pt 1): 45–46.

75 Fenger C, Nielsen VT. Precancerous changes in the anal canal epithelium in resection specimens. Acta Pathol Microbiol Immunol Scand (A) 1986, **94**: 63–69.

76 Gillespie JJ, MacKay B. Histogenesis of cloacogenic carcinoma. Fine structure of anal transitional epithelium and cloacogenic carcinoma. Hum Pathol 1978, **9**: 579–587.

77 Grinvalsky HT, Helwig EB. Carcinoma of the anorectal junction. Part I. Histological consideration. Cancer 1956, **8**: 480–488.

78 Klotz RG Jr, Pamukcoglu T, Souillard DH. Transitional cloacogenic carcinoma of the anal canal. Clinicopathologic study of three hundred and seventy-three cases. Cancer 1967, **20**: 1727–1745.

79 Lowe D, Fletcher CDM. Eosinophilia in squamous cell carcinoma of the oral cavity, external genitalia, and anus. Clinical correlations. Histopathology 1984, **8**: 627–632.

80 Morson BC, Pang LSC. Pathology of anal cancer. Proc R Soc Med 1968, **61**: 623–626.

81 Pang LSC, Morson BC. Basaloid carcinoma of the anal canal. J Clin Pathol 1967, **20**: 128–135.

82 Watson PH. Clear-cell carcinoma of the anal canal. A variant of anal transitional zone carcinoma. Hum Pathol 1990, **21:** 350–351.

83 Williams GR, Talbot IC. Anal carcinoma. A histological review. Histopathology 1994, **25:** 507–516.

Immunohistochemical and molecular genetic features

84 Behrendt GC, Hansmann ML. Carcinomas of the anal canal and anal margin differ in their expression of cadherin, cytokeratins and p53. Virchows Arch 2001, **439:** 782–786.

85 Goldman S, Skoog L, Wilking N. Immunocytochemical analysis of receptors for estrogen and progesterone in fine needle aspirates from anal epidermoid carcinoma. Dis Colon Rectum 1992, **35:** 163–165.

86 Levy R, Czernobilsky B, Geiger B. Cytokeratin polypeptide expression in a cloacogenic carcinoma and in the normal anal canal epithelium. Virchows Arch [A] 1991, **418:** 447–455.

87 Ogunbiyi OA, Scholefield JH, Rogers K, Sharp F, Smith JH, Polacarz SV. C-*myc* oncogene expression in anal squamous neoplasia. J Clin Pathol 1993, **46:** 23–27.

88 Ogunbiyi OA, Scholefield JH, Smith JH, Polacarz SV, Rogers K, Sharp F. Immunohistochemical analysis of p53 expression in anal squamous neoplasia. J Clin Pathol 1993, **46:** 507–512.

89 Walts AE, Koeffler HP, Said JW. Localization of p53 protein and human papillomavirus in anogenital squamous lesions. Immunohistochemical and in situ hybridization studies in benign, dysplastic, and malignant epithelia. Hum Pathol 1993, **24:** 1238–1242.

90 Wick MR, Weatherby RP, Weiland LH. Small cell neuroendocrine carcinoma of the colon and rectum. Clinical, histologic, and ultrastructural study and immunohistochemical comparison with cloacogenic carcinoma. Hum Pathol 1987, **18:** 9–21.

91 Williams GR, Talbot IC, Leigh IM. Keratin expression in anal carcinoma: an immunohistochemical study. Histopathology 1997, **30:** 443–450.

Therapy

92 Allal A, Kurtz JM, Pipard G, Marti MC, Miralbell R, Popowski Y, Egeli R. Chemoradiotherapy versus radiotherapy alone for anal cancer. A retrospective comparison. Int J Radiat Oncol Biol Phys 1993, **27:** 59–66.

93 Boman BM, Moertel CG, O'Connell MJ, Scott M, Weiland LH, Beart RW, Gunderson LL, Spencer RJ. Carcinoma of the anal canal. A clinical and pathologic study of 188 cases. Cancer 1984, **54:** 114–125.

94 Clark J, Petrelli N, Herrera L, Mittelman A. Epidermoid carcinoma of the anal canal. Cancer 1986, **57:** 400–406.

95 Cummings BJ, Keane TJ, O'Sullivan B, Wong CS, Catton CN. Mitomycin in anal canal carcinoma. Oncology 1993, **50:** 63–69.

96 Dillard BM, Spratt JS Jr, Ackerman LV, Butcher HR Jr. Epidermoid cancer of anal margin and canal. Review of 79 cases. Arch Surg 1963, **16:** 772–776.

97 Frost DB, Richards PC, Montague ED, Giacco GG, Martin RG. Epidermoid cancer of the anorectum. Cancer 1984, **53:** 1285–1293.

98 Johnson D, Lipsett J, Leong L, Wagman LD, Terz JJ. Carcinoma of the anus treated with primary radiation therapy and chemotherapy. Surg Gynecol Obstet 1993, **177:** 329–334.

99 Klas JV, Rothenberger DA, Wong WD, Madoff RD. Malignant tumors of the anal canal: the spectrum of disease, treatment, and outcomes. Cancer 1999, **85:** 1685–1693.

100 Klotz RG Jr, Pamukcoglu T, Souillard DH. Transitional cloacogenic carcinoma of the anal canal. Clinicopathologic study of three hundred and seventy-three cases. Cancer 1967, **20:** 1727–1745.

101 Martenson JA Jr, Gunderson LL. External radiation therapy without chemotherapy in the management of anal cancer. Cancer 1993, **71:** 1736–1740.

102 Miller EJ, Quan SH, Thaler HT. Treatment of squamous cell carcinoma of the anal canal. Cancer 1991, **67:** 2038–2041.

103 Myerson RJ, Karnell LH, Menck HR. The National Cancer Data Base report on carcinoma of the anus. Cancer 1997, **80:** 805–815.

104 Ryan DR, Compton CC, Mayer RJ. Carcinoma of the anal canal. N Engl J Med 2000, **342:** 792–800.

105 Schraut WH, Wang C-H, Dawson PJ, Block GE. Depth of invasion, location, and size of cancer of the anus dictate operative treatment. Cancer 1983, **51:** 1291–1296.

106 Touboul E, Schlienger M, Buffat L, Lefkopoulos D, Pene F, Parc R, Tiret E, Gallot D, Malafosse M, Laugier A. Epidermoid carcinoma of the anal canal. Results of curative-intent radiation therapy in a series of 270 patients. Cancer 1994, **73:** 1569–1579.

Prognosis

107 Boman BM, Moertel CG, O'Connell MJ, Scott M, Weiland LH, Beart RW, Gunderson LL, Spencer RJ. Carcinoma of the anal canal. A clinical and pathologic study of 188 cases. Cancer 1984, **54:** 114–125.

108 Dillard BM, Spratt JS Jr, Ackerman LV, Butcher HR Jr. Epidermoid cancer of anal margin and canal. Review of 79 cases. Arch Surg 1963, **16:** 772–776.

109 Dougherty BG, Evans HL. Carcinoma of the anal canal. A study of 79 cases. Am J Clin Pathol 1985, **83:** 159–164.

110 Frost DB, Richards PC, Montague ED, Giacco GG, Martin RG. Epidermoid cancer of the anorectum. Cancer 1984, **53:** 1285–1293.

111 Greenall MJ, Magill GB, Quan SHQ, DeCosse JJ. Recurrent epidermoid cancer of the anus. Cancer 1986, **57:** 1437–1441.

112 Pang LSC, Morson BC. Basaloid carcinoma of the anal canal. J Clin Pathol 1967, **20:** 128–135.

113 Schraut WH, Wang C-H, Dawson PJ, Block GE. Depth of invasion, location, and size of cancer of the anus dictate operative treatment. Cancer 1983, **51:** 1291–1296.

114 Shepherd NA, Scholefield JH, Love SB, England J, Northover JMA. Prognostic factors in anal squamous carcinoma. A multivariate analysis of clinical, pathological and flow cytometric parameters in 235 cases. Histopathology 1990, **16:** 545–556.

Paget's disease

115 Brainard J, Hart WR. Proliferative epidermal lesions associated with anogenital Paget's disease. Am J Surg Pathol 2000, **24:** 543–552.

116 Diaz de Leon E, Carcangiu ML, Prieto VG, McCue PA, Burchette JL, To G, Norris BA, Kovatich AJ, Sanchez RL, Krigman HR, Gatalica Z. Extramammary Paget's disease is characterized by the consistent lack of estrogen and progesterone receptors but frequently expresses androgen receptor. Am J Clin Pathol 2001, **113:** 572–575.

117 Eusebi V. Personal communication, 2003.

118 Fujimoto A, Takata M, Hatta N, Takehara K. Expression of structurally unaltered androgen receptor in extramammary Paget's disease. Lab Invest 2000, **80:** 1465–1471.

119 Goldblum JR, Hart WR. Perianal Paget's disease: a histologic and immunohistochemical study of 11 cases with and without associated rectal adenocarcinoma. Am J Surg Pathol 1998, **22:** 170–179.

120 Goldman S, Ihre T, Lagerstedt U, Svensson C. Perianal Paget's disease. Report of five cases. Int J Colorectal Dis 1992, **7:** 167–169.

121 Helm KF, Goellner JR, Peters MS. Immunohistochemical stains in extramammary Paget's disease. Am J Dermatopathol 1992, **14:** 402–407.

122 Helwig EB, Graham JH. Anogenital (extramammary) Paget's disease. A clinicopathological study. Cancer 1963, **16:** 387–403.

123 Miller LR, McCunniff AJ, Randall ME. An immunohistochemical study of perianal Paget's disease. Possible origins and clinical implications. Cancer 1992, **69:** 2166–2171.

124 Nowak MA, Guerrier-Kovach P, Pathan A, Campbell TE,

Deppisch LM. Perianal Paget's disease: distinguishing primary and secondary lesions using immunohistochemical studies including gross cystic disease fluid protein-15 and cytokeratin 20 expression. Arch Pathol Lab Med 1998, **122:** 1077–1081.

125 Ramalingam P, Hart WR, Goldblum JR. Cytokeratin subset immunostaining in rectal adenocarcinomas and normal anal glands. Arch Pathol Lab Med 2001, **125:** 1074–1077.

126 Wood WS, Culling CFA. Perianal Paget disease. Histochemical differentiation utilizing the borohydride-KOH-PAS reaction. Arch Pathol 1975, **99:** 442–445.

127 Yoshii N, Kitajima S, Yonezawa S, Matsukita S, Setoyama M, Kanzaki T. Expression of mucin core proteins in extramammary Paget's disease. Pathol Int 2002, **52:** 390–399.

Other microscopic types

128 Alvarez-Canas MC, Fernandez FA, Rodilla IG, Val-Bernal JF. Perianal basal cell carcinoma: a comparative histologic, immunohistochemical, and flow cytometric study with basaloid carcinoma of the anus. Am J Dermatopathol 1996, **18:** 371–379.

129 Askin FB, Muhlendorf K, Walz BJ. Mucinous carcinoma of anal duct origin presenting clinically as a vaginal cyst. Cancer 1978, **42:** 566–569.

130 Bogomoletz WV, Potet F, Molas G. Condylomata acuminata, giant condyloma acuminatum (Buschke-Loewenstein tumour) and verrucous squamous carcinoma of the perianal and anorectal region. A continuous precancerous spectrum? Histopathology 1985, **9:** 1155–1169.

131 Dukes CE, Galvin C. Colloid carcinoma arising within fistulae in the anorectal region. Ann R Coll Surg Engl 1956, **18:** 246–261.

132 Hobbs CM, Lowry MA, Owen D, Sobin LH. Anal gland carcinoma. Cancer 2001, **92:** 2045–2049.

133 Jones EA, Morson BC. Mucinous adenocarcinoma in anorectal fistulae. Histopathology 1984, **8:** 279–292.

134 Kalogeropoulos NK, Antonakopoulos GN, Agapitos MB, Papacharalampous NX. Spindle cell carcinoma (pseudosarcoma) of the anus. A light, electron microscopic and immunocytochemical study of a case. Histopathology 1985, **9:** 987–994.

135 Nakahara H, Moriya Y, Shinkai T, Hirota T. Small cell carcinoma of the anus in a human HIV carrier. Report of a case. Surg Today 1993, **23:** 85–88.

136 Prioleau PG, Allen MS Jr, Roberts T. Perianal mucinous adenocarcinoma. Cancer 1977, **39:** 1295–1299.

137 Roncaroli F, Montironi R, Feliciotti F, Losi L, Eusebi V. Sarcomatoid carcinoma of the anorectal junction with neuroendocrine and rhabdomyoblastic features. Am J Surg Pathol 1995, **19:** 217–223.

138 Wick MR, Weatherby RP, Weiland LH. Small cell neuroendocrine carcinoma of the colon and rectum. Clinical, histologic, and ultrastructural study and immunohistochemical comparison with cloagenic carcinoma. Hum Pathol 1987, **18:** 9–21.

139 Winkelman J, Grosfeld J, Bigelow B. Colloid carcinoma of anal-gland origin. Am J Clin Pathol 1964, **42:** 395–401.

140 Wittoesch JH, Woolner LB, Jackman RJ. Basal cell epithelioma and basaloid lesions of the anus. Surg Gynecol Obstet 1957, **104:** 75–80.

Malignant melanoma

141 Ackermann DM, Polk HC Jr, Schrodt GR. Desmoplastic melanoma of the anus. Hum Pathol 1985, **16:** 1277–1279.

142 Angeras U, Jönsson N, Jönsson P-E. Primary anorectal malignant melanoma. J Surg Oncol 1983, **22:** 261–264.

143 Antoniuk PM, Tjandra JJ, Webb BW, Petras RE, Milsom JW, Fazio VW. Anorectal malignant melanoma has a poor prognosis. Int J Colorectal Dis 1993, **8:** 81–86.

144 Ben-Izhak O, Bar-Chana M, Sussman L, Dobiner V, Sandbank J, Cagnano M, Cohen H, Sabo E. Ki67 antigen and PCNA

proliferation markers predict survival in anorectal malignant melanoma. Histopathology 2002, **41:** 519–525.

145 Ben-Izhak O, Levy R, Weill S, Groisman G, Cohen H, Stajerman S, Misselevich I, Nitecky S, Eidelman S, Kerner H. Anorectal malignant melanoma: a clinicopathologic study, including immunohistochemistry and DNA flow cytometry. Cancer 1997, **79:** 18–25.

146 Chumas JC, Lorelle CA. Melanotic adenocarcinoma of the anorectum. Am J Surg Pathol 1981, **5:** 711–717.

147 Felz MW, Winburn GB, Kallab AM, Lee JR. Anal melanoma: an aggressive malignancy masquerading as hemorrhoids. South Med J 2001, **94:** 880–885.

148 Mason JK, Helwig EB. Ano-rectal melanoma. Cancer 1966, **19:** 39–50.

149 Mills SE, Cooper PH. Malignant melanoma of the digestive system. Pathol Annu 1983, **18**(Pt 2): 1–26.

150 Morson BC, Volkstädt H. Malignant melanoma of the anal canal. J Clin Pathol 1963, **16:** 126–132.

151 Wanebo HJ, Woodruff JM, Farr GH, Quan SH. Anorectal melanoma. Cancer 1981, **47:** 1891–1900.

152 Weinstock MA. Epidemiology and prognosis of anorectal melanoma. Gastroenterology 1993, **104:** 174–178.

Other tumors and tumorlike conditions

153 Al-Ghnaniem R, Leather AJ, Rennie JA. Survey of methods of treatment of hemorrhoids and complications of injection sclerotherapy. Ann R Coll Surg Engl 2001, **83:** 325–328.

154 Assor D, Davis JB. Multiple apocrine fibroadenomas of the anal skin. Am J Clin Pathol 1977, **68:** 397–398.

155 Bonser GM, Raper FP, Shuchsmith HS. Epidermoid cysts in the region of the rectum and anus. A report of four cases. Br J Surg 1950, **37:** 303–306.

156 Haque S, Dean PJ. Stromal neoplasms of the rectum and anal canal. Hum Pathol 1992, **23:** 762–767.

157 Hirsch P, Helwig EB. Chondroid syringoma. Mixed tumor of skin, salivary gland type. Arch Dermatol 1961, **84:** 835–847.

158 Ioachim HL, Antonescu C, Giancotti F, Dorsett B, Weinstein MA. EBV-associated anorectal lymphomas in patients with acquired immune deficiency syndrome. Am J Surg Pathol 1997, **21:** 997–1006.

159 Isbister WH. Unusual "recurrence" sites for colorectal cancer. Dig Surg 2000, **17:** 81–83.

160 Joachim HL, Weinstein MA, Robbins RD, Sohn N, Lugo PN. Primary anorectal lymphoma. A new manifestation of the acquired immune deficiency syndrome (AIDS). Cancer 1987, **60:** 1449–1453.

161 Johnston J, Helwig EB. Granular cell tumors of the gastrointestinal tract and perianal region. A study of 74 cases. Dig Dis Sci 1981, **26:** 807–816.

162 Mehta K, Pawel BR. Human immunodeficiency virus-associated large-cell immunoblastic lymphoma presenting as a perianal abscess. Arch Pathol Lab Med 1989, **113:** 531–533.

163 Minsky BD, Cohen AM, Hajdu SI. Conservative management of anal leiomyosarcoma. Cancer 1991, **68:** 1633–1639.

164 Morales AR, Fine G, Horn RC Jr, Watson JHL. Langerhans cells in a localized lesion of the eosinophilic granuloma type. Lab Invest 1969, **20:** 412–423.

165 Morgan MB. Ectopic prostatic tissue of the anal canal. J Urol 1992, **147:** 165–166.

166 Robb JA, Jones RA. Spindle cell lipoma in a perianal location. Hum Pathol 1982, **13:** 1052.

167 Sawh RN, Borkowski J, Broaddus R. Metastatic renal cell carcinoma presenting as a hemorrhoid. Arch Pathol Lab Med 2002, **126:** 856–858.

168 Sayfan J, Benosh L, Segal M, Orda R. Endometriosis in episiotomy scar with anal sphincter involvement. Report of a case. Dis Colon Rectum 1991, **34:** 713–716.

169 Srouji MN, Donaldson MH, Chatten J, Koblenzer CS. Perianal rhabdomyosarcoma in childhood. Cancer 1976, **38**: 1008–1012.

170 Takamatsu H, Akiyama H, Noguchi H, Tahara H, Kajiya H. Endorectal pull-through operation for diffuse cavernous hemangiomatosis of the sigmoid colon, rectum and anus. Eur J Pediatr Surg 1992, **2**: 245–247.

171 Tarasidis G, Brown BC, Skandalakis LJ, Mackay G, Lauer RC, Gray SW, Skandalakis JE. Smooth muscle tumors of the rectum and anus. A collective review of the world literature. J Med Assoc Ga 1991, **80**: 685–699.

172 Teloh HA. Apocrine adenoma of the anus. Cancer 1954, **7**: 367–372.

173 Tworek JA, Goldblum JR, Weiss SW, Greenson JK, Appelman HD. Stromal tumors of the anorectum: a clinicopathologic study of 22 cases. Am J Surg Pathol 1999, **23**: 936–954.

174 Ueyama T, Hashimoto H, Tsuneyoshi M. Leioimyosarcoma of the anus. A clinicopathologic and immunohistochemical study. Int J Surg Pathol 1994, **1**: 221–226.

12 Major and minor salivary glands

Normal anatomy

Salivary gland tissue is distributed widely. The major salivary glands are the parotid, submaxillary (submandibular), and sublingual glands. The parotid gland weighs 14 to 28 g, the submaxillary gland weighs 7 to 8 g, and the sublingual gland weighs 3 g. The main duct of the parotid gland (Stensen's duct) empties into the oral cavity opposite the crown of the second maxillary molar. The ducts of both the submaxillary glands (Wharton's duct) and sublingual glands (Bartholin's duct) open in the floor of the mouth, on each side of the tongue frenulum.

The parotid gland is composed of a broad superficial lobe and a smaller deep lobe, with the facial nerve between the two lobes. Variations of this anatomy and the distribution of the facial nerve occur.[1]

Salivary gland tissue is present in many other locations, where it may give rise to inflammatory conditions, benign tumors, and malignant tumors. Its location influences, to some extent, the clinical signs and symptoms, the morphologic features, and the treatment. It is found in the lips (more in the upper than the lower lip), gingiva, floor of mouth, cheek, hard and soft palates, tongue, tonsillar areas, and oropharynx.

Microscopically, salivary glands are compound exocrine glands composed of a ductal and an acinar portion, the latter of either serous or mucinous type.[5] The parotid gland is exclusively serous, the submaxillary gland is mixed with serous predominance, and the sublingual gland is mixed with mucinous predominance. The intercalated ducts and acini represent the terminal portion of the system (ductoacinar unit). Under normal conditions, sebaceous glands are annexed to the duct system in the parotid and submaxillary glands.[5] The reserve cells of the intercalated ducts are the source of regeneration of the acinar tissue and the terminal duct system and are thought to be the progenitors (together with the closely apposed myoepithelial cells) of most salivary gland tumors.[3] However, it has been pointed out that basal and luminal cells at all levels of the duct system and even acinar cells are capable of DNA synthesis and mitosis, and therefore they all have the potential to give rise to neoplasms.[2] The myoepithelial cell component shows some differences in its immunohistochemical profile depending on its location: in the parotid gland the myoepithelial cells express mainly calponin and h-caldesmon; in the submaxillary glands they also express smooth muscle actin; and in the minor salivary glands there is an additional expression of smooth muscle myosin heavy chain.[4]

A peculiar feature of salivary gland duct epithelium is its constant immunoreactivity for prostate-specific antigen, which is also manifested in some of the tumors arising from these structures.[7] The lymphoid tissue of the region is represented by small nodes located near or within the parotid gland and by scattered lymphoid cells located in the connective tissue around the acini and ducts. The latter are thought to be part of the mucosa-associated lymphoid tissue (MALT).[6]

Heterotopia

Heterotopia of salivary gland tissue has been divided into intranodal and extranodal types.[14] The intranodal variety is the most frequent. Almost all lymph nodes located within or near the parotid gland in infants contain salivary gland tissue.[8] The finding is not as prevalent in adults but it is still very frequent. The salivary gland tissue is usually located in the medullary portion of the node and is predominantly composed of intercalated and intralobular ducts; it may also contain acini (mainly of serous type) and small ducts of immature type.[15]

Extranodal heterotopia has been divided into high and low forms, depending on its location in the head and neck region. Sites of high heterotopia include the mandible, ear, palatine tonsil, mylohyoid muscle, pituitary gland, and cerebellopontine angle; these are probably all the result of abnormalities in the embryonic migration of the salivary glands.[14] Low heterotopia is related to the branchial pouches and is found in association with cysts and sinuses in the lower neck and in the thyroid gland.[9,11,16,17] The most common location is along the medial border of the right sternomastoid muscle near the sternoclavicular joint.[17]

Heterotopic salivary tissue is subject to the same pathologic changes as its orthotopic counterpart, including cystic formation, oncocytic metaplasia, ductal hyperplasia, and neoplasms.[15] Among the latter,

Warthin's tumor is the most frequent (see p. 883 for a possible explanation of this fact), but several other benign and malignant types have been described.[10,12,13]

Sialolithiasis

Calculi may form in the major ducts of the submaxillary, sublingual, and parotid glands, sometimes in a multicentric and bilateral fashion.[24,25] They are more common in the submaxillary gland than in the parotid gland, presumably because in the former the saliva is more saturated with calcium salts[21] (Fig. 12.1). Rarely, they affect minor salivary glands.[20] Some of the stones have a foreign body or bacterial nidus. Others do not have an identifiable nidus, are laminated, and are composed of the crystalline compound carbonate apatite.[18] The formation of calculi blocks secretion and produces swelling of the distal salivary gland tissue. If ductal obstruction persists, the gland becomes inflamed and indurated as acinar tissue is destroyed. With obstructed ducts of the submaxillary and sublingual glands, marked induration can occur in the floor of the mouth that may be mistaken for neoplasm by palpation. The duct orifices become erythematous and swollen. Radiographic examination may demonstrate a radiopaque mass, and sialography will show partial or total blockage of the duct. The stones can also be demonstrated by ultrasound.[19,27] Microscopic examination of glands that have been affected by stones shows dilatation of ducts, at times squamous metaplasia of the epithelium, moderate to prominent chronic

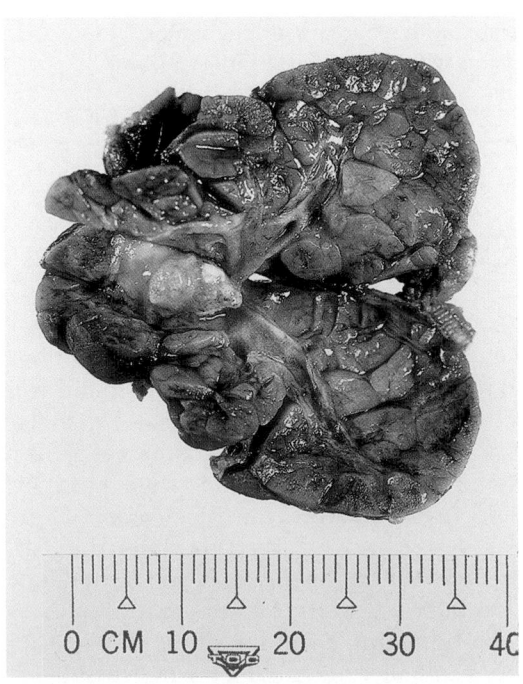

Fig. 12.1 Sialolithiasis with secondary chronic sialadenitis. A large stone is blocking a major salivary duct.

inflammation, and a variable destruction of acinar tissue. Degenerative changes in the secretory and myoepithelial cells are also apparent at the immunohistochemical and ultrastructural levels.[26]

The treatment of symptomatic sialolithiasis consists of surgical removal or disintegration of the calculus. The latter is achieved with techniques such as intracorporeal or extracorporeal shock-wave lithotripsy.[22,23]

Sialadenitis

Acute sialadenitis can be localized to one salivary gland (usually parotid or submaxillary) or be the expression of a systemic infection. *Viral* sialadenitis (rarely seen as a surgical specimen or biopsy) can be caused by paramyxovirus (mumps), Epstein–Barr virus, coxsackievirus, and influenza A and parainfluenza viruses.[30] *Acute suppurative sialadenitis* is generally caused by *Staphylococcus aureus*, *Streptococcus* species, and gram-negative bacteria. Dehydration, malnutrition, immunosuppression, and sialolithiasis are predisposing factors. Once an abscess has formed, surgical drainage may be necessary (Fig. 12.2).[30]

Chronic sialadenitis in the form of mild lymphocytic infiltration of the major salivary gland unaccompanied by clinical symptoms is relatively common. Some cases are of focal obstructive nature and are accompanied by various degrees of parenchymal atrophy, fibrosis, and microliths[33,43]; others, more common in females, are age related, have a high statistical association with rheumatoid arthritis, and are probably immune mediated.[34,39] In clinically apparent cases, sialolithiasis is the most common cause. Chronic sclerosing sialadenitis of the submandibular gland is sometimes referred to as *Kuttner's tumor*.[31,38] This disorder, which is unilateral, is characterized by a plasmacytic and lymphocytic periductal infiltrate eventually leading to encasement of

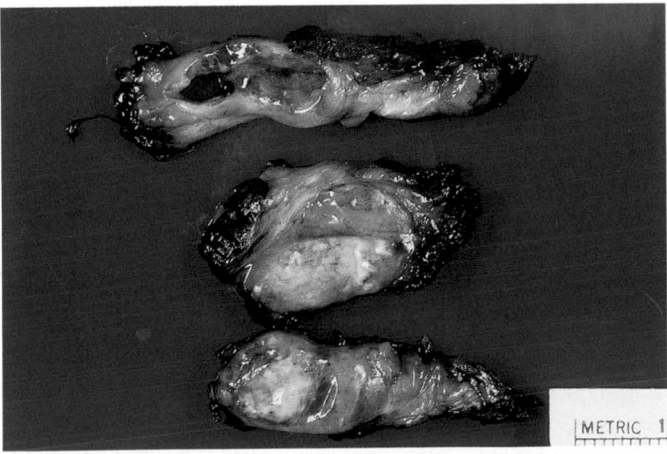

Fig. 12.2 Gross appearance of suppurative sialadenitis.

ducts in thick fibrous tissue.[37] Surgical excision may be necessary for some cases of chronic sialadenitis.[35] The lymphocytes that infiltrate the epithelial component of these lesions are mainly B cells, often characterized by a lack of bcl-2 expression.[32] However, the disease is thought to be mainly due to a T-cell immune reaction triggered by intraductal antigens.[42a]

Sclerosing polycystic adenosis is a recently described entity characterized by the presence of a discrete mass (usually in the parotid gland) formed by fibrohyaline stroma enclosing dilated and hyperplastic ductal and acinar structures. Apocrine-like metaplasia and transluminal bridges with a cribriform pattern of growth are present.[29,42] The few cases of this condition that we have seen have shown sufficient atypia of the ductal epithelial component to make us wonder whether this process is truly inflammatory, as opposed to a low-grade malignant neoplasm; other authors have expressed a similar feeling.[41] It is also possible that the disease begins as an inflammatory process and in some cases progresses to a neoplastic condition.

Granulomatous sialadenitis can result from tuberculosis, mycosis, sarcoidosis, or duct obstruction from calculi or malignant tumors.[40] In the latter instance, the granulomas result from rupture of ducts and may contain small pools of mucin.[44] A *xanthogranulomatous* variant of sialadenitis has also been described.[36] A fact to remember before making the clinical or pathologic diagnosis of parotitis is that the condition can be simulated by inflammatory processes involving intraparotid or periparotid lymph nodes.[28]

Benign lymphoepithelial cysts and HIV-related lesions

Benign lymphoepithelial cysts are lesions of the parotid or upper cervical lymph nodes characterized by multilocular cystic formations lined by glandular or squamous epithelium surrounded by a florid lymphoid hyperplasia with prominent germinal centers.[46,47,54] The cyst lining is often heavily infiltrated by lymphocytes.[49,61] We favor the interpretation that this is an acquired process resulting from the proliferation of branchial pouch-derived or analogous epithelium induced by the lymphoid hyperplasia, probably through a specific interaction between the epithelial cells and a subset of lymphocytes.[59] Other examples of this phenomenon in the head and neck area are branchial cleft cyst, the branchial cleft cystlike formations sometimes seen in Hashimoto's thyroiditis, and multilocular thymic cyst.

Warthin's tumor is another lesion in the salivary glands that could conceivably be related to this group in general and to the benign lymphoepithelial cyst in particular. This lesion is universally regarded as neoplastic (see p. 883), but could be viewed instead as an oncocytic variant of benign lymphoepithelial cyst.[59] In this regard, it is of interest that a case of Warthin's tumor has been reported in intimate connection with Hodgkin's lymphoma.[45]

Another salivary gland lesion that merits mention in this context is **HIV-associated lymphoepithelial cyst** (Fig. 12.3).[50,55] The morphologic changes in this condition include lymphoepithelial cysts similar to those previously described, solid lymphoepithelial lesions (epimyoepithelial islands) similar to those seen in Mikulicz's disease (see next section), and a combination of both.[53,55,57,60] The more prominent the combination of these changes, the more likely that HIV infection is the causative factor. Three-dimensional reconstructions have shown that the cysts arise from the intralobular duct system rather than from intraparotid lymph nodes.[51]

The lymphoid follicles of HIV-induced salivary gland disease show a prominent network of dendritic reticular cells and numerous intrafollicular CD8+ lymphocytes. The dendritic reticulum cells show a strong expression of HIV-1 major core protein and HIV-1 RNA, indicating that there is active replication of the virus within them.[52]

There are two other polycystic diseases of the salivary glands that need to be mentioned here for differential diagnosis purposes. The first is *polycystic (dysgenetic) disease*, a developmental disorder so far reported only in females and characterized by bilateral gland enlargement.[48,56,58] The other is the already mentioned *sclerosing polycystic adenosis*. One should also keep in mind that some neoplasms of salivary gland may undergo promi-

nent cystic changes. This is particularly true of mucoepidermoid carcinoma, sebaceous lymphadenoma, and occasionally, benign mixed tumor.

Mikulicz's disease and Sjögren's syndrome

Mikulicz's disease (benign lymphoepithelial lesion) most often presents as a slowly increasing and eventually striking enlargement of the salivary and lacrimal glands.[79] This enlargement is usually bilateral and symmetric, but it can also be unilateral and localized, at least at the clinical level. If an infection develops, the process may subside only to recur when the infection is gone.

Grossly, the gland is enlarged and whitish, sometimes admixed with occasional cysts (Fig. 12.4A). Microscopically, the two cardinal changes are marked lymphoid infiltration and so-called "epimyoepithelial islands".[83] This combination of findings has been used to create a synonym for the disease associated with a catchy acronym, i.e., *myoepithelial sialadenitis (MESA)*.[75] The lymphoid tissue contains numerous well-formed germinal centers and is composed of a mixed population of B and T lymphocytes, accompanied by scattered histiocytes and dendritic cells. The so-called "epimyoepithelial islands" appear as solid epithelial nests surrounded and infiltrated by lymphoid cells, which are mainly of monocytoid B type (Fig. 12.4B). A hyaline substance is

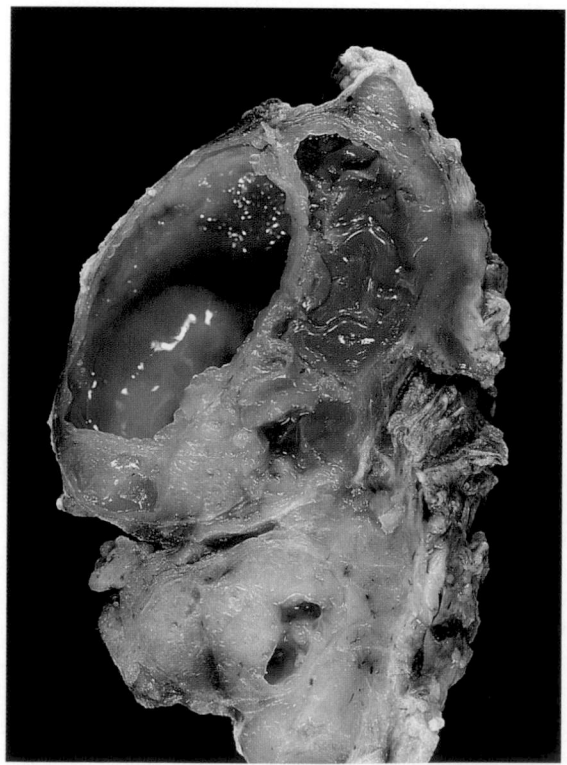

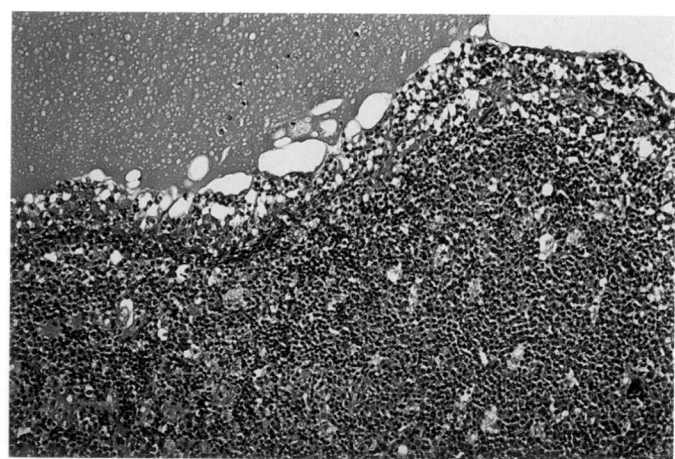

Fig. 12.3 A, Lymphoepithelial cysts in parotid gland removed from an HIV-infected patient. The solid white areas correspond to infiltration by lymphoid tissue. **B,** Lymphoepithelial cyst of parotid gland in an HIV-infected patient. Note the lymphocytic infiltration of the epithelium.

deposited between the cells, which is shown ultrastructurally to represent basement membrane material, including type IV collagen.[77,84] The nature of the cells within the islands, i.e., whether acinar or ductal, basal or myoepithelial, remains a controversial subject.[64,65,77] Current evidence suggests a lack of myoepithelial cell participation, which—if true—would make the term "epimyoepithelial islands" inaccurate, and the alternative "lymphoepithelial lesions" more appropriate.[76]

Mikulicz's disease can remain localized to the salivary gland but more often is a manifestation of a generalized

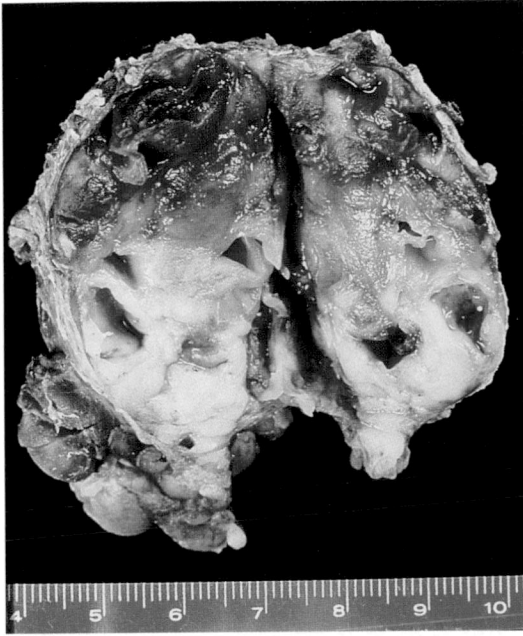

A

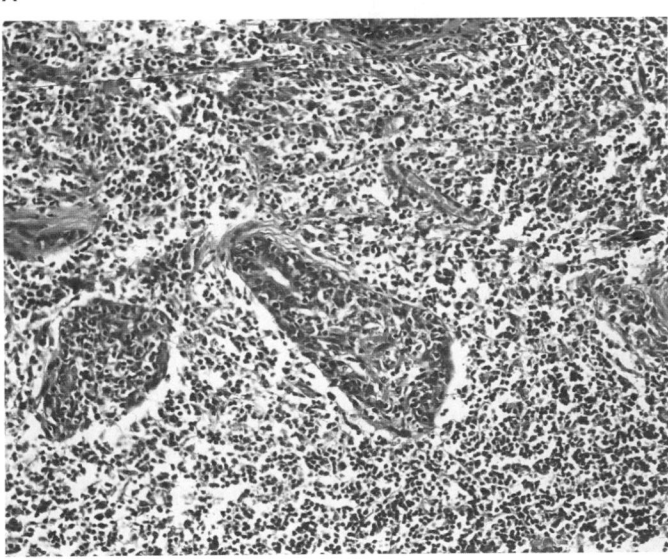

B

Fig. 12.4 A, Gross appearance of Mikulicz's disease of parotid gland. There is a combination of solid areas resulting from infiltration by lymphocytes and small cystic formations representing dilated ductal lumina. **B**, Prominent proliferation of duct epithelium in a patient with Mikulicz's disease.

symptom complex known as **Sjögren's syndrome**, the other components of which are keratoconjunctivitis, xerostomia, rheumatoid arthritis, and hypergammaglobulinemia.[72,73,82] In this condition, lymphoid infiltrates similar to those present in the major salivary glands are also seen in the lacrimal glands and minor salivary glands of the oral cavity. This fact is of diagnostic utility, in the sense that biopsy of the labial glands is often used to document the diagnosis of this condition.[63] It should be noted, however, that so-called "epimyoepithelial islands" are usually scanty or absent at these sites. Occasionally, the lymphoid infiltrates extend to other organ systems, such as lymph nodes, lung, kidney, bone marrow, skeletal muscle, skin, or liver.[67,92] Interestingly, the skin lesions may show formations similar to epimyoepithelial islands in the sweat glands.[89] Autoimmune thyroiditis and systemic vasculitis can also be seen,[88,91] and there may be amyloid deposits at various sites.[89]

The etiology of Mikulicz's disease, with or without Sjögren's syndrome, remains enigmatic. The possible role of Epstein–Barr virus is still in dispute.[68,93] The incidence of the disease is markedly increased in HIV-infected patients. As a matter of fact, there is a marked morphologic similarity (and probably a close pathogenetic relationship) between Sjögren's syndrome as seen in this population and the HIV-related changes described in the previous section. Interestingly, a chronic lymphocytic sialadenitis morphologically very similar to Mikulicz's disease occurs in HCV-related chronic liver disease.[87]

The prevalent view is that Mikulicz's disease is a systemic autoimmune process. In the typical case the lymphocyte population is polytypic, in keeping with a reactive process. However, this population may undergo small clonal expansions, detectable on Southern blots.[71,72,78,80] In some cases, these evolve into full-blown lymphomas, whether in the salivary gland or in extraglandular locations.[62,80,81] Some of these are large B-cell lymphomas (often with an immunoblastic appearance), while others are small lymphocytic lymphomas with or without plasmacytoid features (see below), and exceptional cases of Hodgkin's lymphoma and peripheral T-cell lymphoma have been reported.[66,86,90] When one of these lymphoma types develops, there is usually not much difficulty in identifying it. The vexing problem is how to interpret the usual case of Mikulicz's disease that is composed of a morphologic mature ("benign") lymphocytic population, especially if a monotypic component has been detected with molecular techniques. Is it a reactive, possibly autoimmune process with a tendency to evolve into a recognizable malignant lymphoma, or is it a malignant lymphoma already?[69,70,94] Some authors have taken the latter view and have placed Mikulicz's disease in the ever-expanding MALT category, mainly on the basis of the molecular findings. It seems to us that to label a process as malignant at a stage at which it shows neither clinical or morphologic signs of malignancy is neither conceptually nor medically sound.[75] At the present state of knowledge, it is probably wiser to restrict the diagnosis of lymphoma to those cases showing some *morphologic* evidence of such. The most important feature in this regard is the number and distribution of the monocytoid B cells. The presence of these cells outside of the lymphoepithelial lesions and especially as broad anastomosing strands is in favor of lymphoma; the same is true for sheets of plasma cells, with or without Dutcher bodies.[74,85]

The development of lymphoma in patients with Mikulicz's disease should not be confused with the entity known as *malignant lymphoepithelial lesion*. This represents a poorly differentiated carcinoma with prominent lymphoid stroma. This process, which we view as unrelated to Mikulicz's disease, is discussed on p. 896.

Irradiation effect

The submaxillary glands, which are often included in the field of irradiation for tumors of the oral cavity, swell and become firm as a result of the therapy. These changes may be mistaken clinically for metastatic carcinoma in submaxillary lymph nodes and sometimes have led to unnecessary radical surgery. Microscopic examination shows atrophy of acinar elements and chronic inflammatory cells in the stroma. The lining of the duct epithelium may show prominent squamous metaplasia. In experiments on animals, the functional effects of irradiation to the salivary glands can be demonstrated within 24 hours.[96] In human subjects, the increase in serum amylase levels has been found to be a reliable marker of an early irradiation effect to this organ, as a probable reflection of the death of serous glandular cells. However, this may not necessarily relate to the late irradiation effects previously described.[95]

Other non-neoplastic lesions

Lymphoid disorders of reactive nature can involve the intraparotid lymph nodes and be confused clinically with a primary salivary gland tumor. These include nonspecific follicular hyperplasia, healed abscesses, and granulomatous inflammations, such as those produced by cat-scratch disease.

Keratinous cysts of epidermal type have been reported in the parotid region. Perhaps these are related to the skin adnexal-type choristomatous processes that can occur at this site (see p. 897).

Amyloidosis may involve the salivary gland as part of a generalized process or as a localized pseudotumoral mass ("amyloid tumor"), and it may result in the sicca

syndrome.[102] This disorder can be diagnosed in fine needle biopsy aspiration specimens.[100]

Nodular fasciitis can present as a primary intraparotid lesion; its microscopic appearance is identical to that of its more common soft tissue counterpart.[98]

Inflammatory pseudotumor is composed of a predominant population of myofibroblasts in an edematous and inflammatory background.[103] As in other sites where this entity occurs, there is a question as to whether it may represent a neoplastic condition, hence the alternative designation of *inflammatory myofibroblastic tumor*.

Rosai–Dorfman disease (sinus histiocytosis with massive lymphadenopathy) can involve the major salivary glands, with or without accompanying lymph node enlargement.[99,101]

Adenomatous ductal hyperplasia of major salivary glands may coexist with salivary gland tumors of various types (especially epithelial–myoepithelial carcinomas) and with chronic parotitis.[104] It is composed of intercalated duct epithelium, and therefore different from the adenomatoid acinar hyperplasia found predominantly in intraoral salivary glands.[97] It has been suggested that adenomatous ductal hyperplasia may be a precursor lesion of salivary gland tumors (see next section).

Epithelial tumors

Classification

The classification of salivary gland tumors has proved a most difficult and frustrating exercise. If anything, it is even more complex than that of the somewhat related breast and sweat gland tumors. One of the major stumbling blocks is that most of the salivary gland tumors arise from—or differentiate toward—the same cell lines: epithelial (ductal or acinar) and myoepithelial. This results in a considerable overlap at all levels, compounded by the fact that each of these cells can undergo a variety of metaplastic changes (e.g., oncocytic, sebaceous, squamous, chondroid). A conceptually sound classification of salivary gland tumors is still wanting. The WHO classification stresses the distinction between benign and malignant tumors (i.e., adenomas and carcinomas).[105–107] In this chapter, a somewhat different approach has been used. The tumors have been grouped, whenever possible, according to their predominant line of differentiation; this has been followed by a discussion of the benign and malignant members within each group.

Tumors with stromal differentiation

Benign mixed tumor (pleomorphic adenoma)

Benign mixed tumor is the most common neoplasm of the salivary glands. It is most frequent in women in the fourth decade of life, but it can be seen in children and in elderly persons of either sex.[142] It is about ten times more common in the parotid than in the submaxillary gland, and it is very rare in the sublingual gland. In the parotid gland, most tumors arise within the superficial lobe, from either the tail (50%) or the anterior portion (25%). The remaining 25% arise from the deep lobe and often present as a pharyngeal mass without external evidence of tumor.[115]

Grossly, the tumor forms a rubbery, resilient mass with a bosselated surface and may grow to a large size (Fig. 12.5). The consistency depends on the relative amount of epithelial cells and stroma and the type of the latter. Although the tumor tends to be well circumscribed, small extensions can be seen protruding into the adjacent normal tissue. The appearance of the cut surface again depends on the relative proportion of epithelium and stroma. Islands of cartilage can be recognized by their glistening, translucent appearance. In rare cases, foci of mature bone are identified.

Microscopically, benign mixed tumor is frequently misdiagnosed as carcinoma by the neophyte in pathology. Its bewildering pattern, extreme cellularity, scattered bizarre tumor cells,[177] partial penetration of the capsule, and occasional occurrence of clusters of tumor cells in the vascular lumina[108] all make it very confusing. It has been pointed out that the capsule tends to be thicker and less likely to be penetrated by tumor in the lesions located in the deep lobe compared with those in the superficial lobe.[129]

The typical mixed tumor has a biphasic appearance resulting from the intimate admixture of epithelium and stroma (Figs 12.6 and 12.7). Most of the epithelial component is of a glandular nature, but foci of squamous metaplasia are common, sometimes accompanied by keratinized epithelial plugs in the lumen. The neoplastic glands have a lining composed of two cell types, the basally located cells displaying morphologic features of myoepithelial cells.[121] They may be cuboidal, flattened, clear, spindle shaped, or "hyaline"[147] (Fig. 12.6). The stroma may have a nonspecific fibromyxoid appearance, sometimes containing abundant elastic tissue[122] or extensive adipose tissue[139]; however, areas of clearcut cartilaginous differentiation are usually found.[183] This phenomenon is more common and prominent in parotid and submaxillary tumors than in those arising from minor salivary glands. There is convincing morphologic, ultrastructural, immunohistochemical and molecular evidence to suggest that these mesenchymal elements

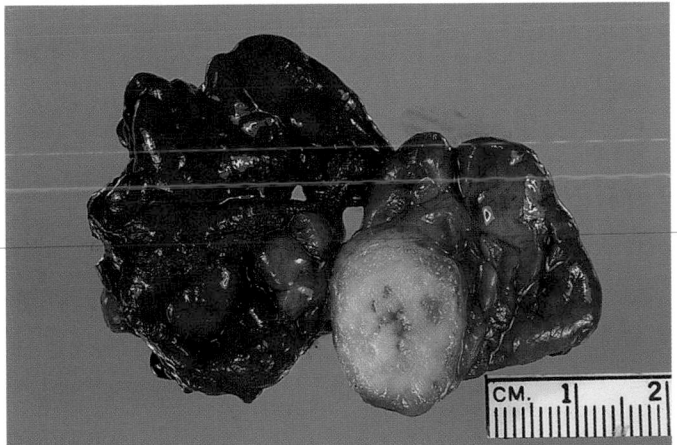

A

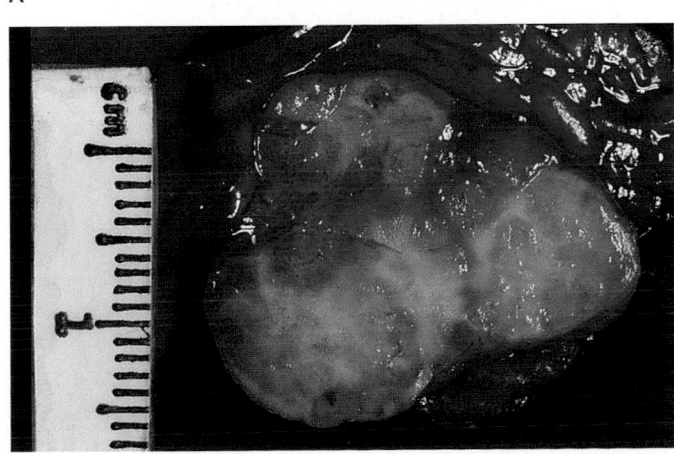

C

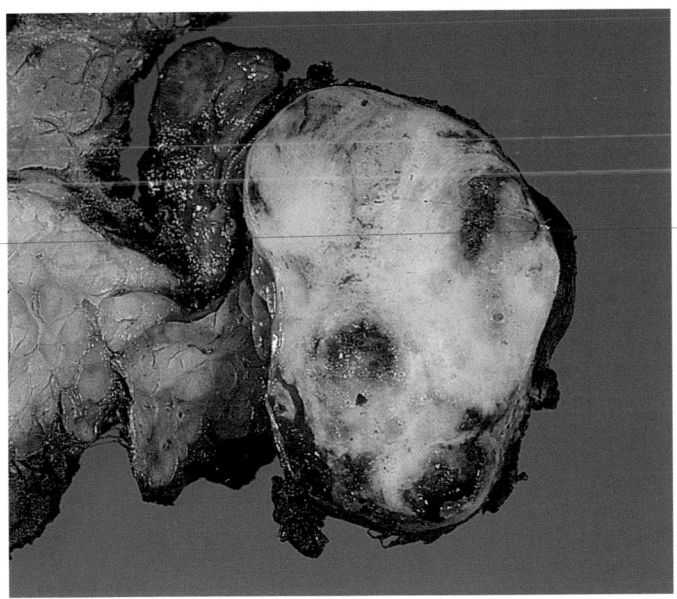

B

Fig. 12.5 A–C. Gross appearance of three benign mixed tumors of parotid gland. Note the sharply outlined character and predominantly solid cut surface. The tumors shown in **B** and **C** have a glistening surface indicative of cartilaginous differentiation.

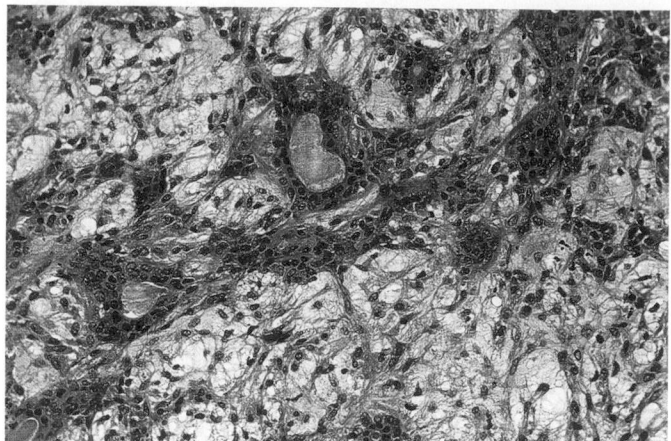

Fig. 12.6 Microscopic appearance of benign mixed tumor. Epithelial and myoepithelial cells can be easily distinguished.

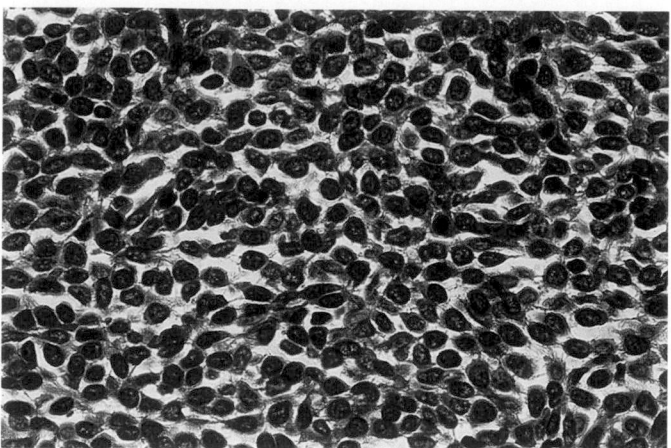

Fig. 12.8 Benign mixed tumor with a markedly hypercellular appearance.

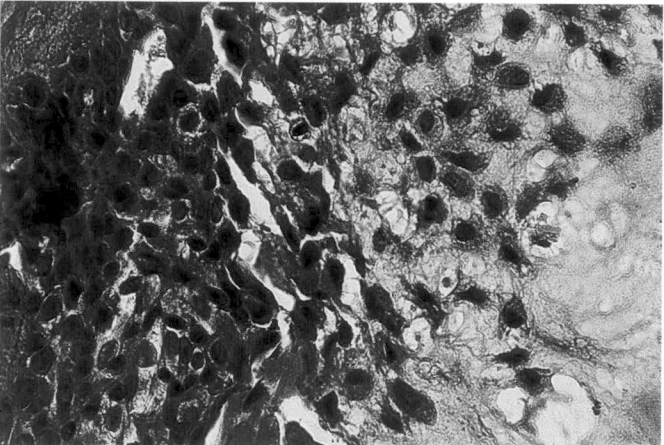

Fig. 12.7 Benign mixed tumor. The myoepithelial cells are undergoing cartilaginous metaplasia.

share the same origin as the epithelial cells,[123,146,161] and that they represent modified myoepithelial cells.[110,125] Actually, transitions between basally located myoepithelial cells and the myxochondroid cells of the stroma are often found. Ultrastructurally, a continuum of cytoplasmic features from epithelial to mesenchymal cells is also present.[120,144,152]

Two types of mucin are formed by benign mixed tumor, one of epithelial and the other of connective tissue type.[110,165] The former is characterized by its high content of neutral glycoprotein, and the latter contains both sulfated and nonsulfated glycosaminoglycans.[135,156,158] Both of these mucin types are probably secreted by cells of epithelial derivation, as shown by tissue culture and inoculation studies.[178] Other extracellular substances sometimes found in benign mixed tumors include tyrosine-rich crystalloids in the myxoid areas,[113,133] collagenous spherules,[170] calcium oxalate crystals, amyloid,[179] and intraductal birefringent crystalloids of unknown chemical composition.[134,138]

Some benign mixed tumors are extremely cellular, the

tumor cells being either round or spindle shaped (Fig. 12.8). Others may show cytologic atypia in the form of scattered large hyperchromatic nuclei (which have been shown to be polyploid).[151,180] Follow-up studies have indicated that these tumors do not behave differently from the ordinary variety. The rarity of mitotic figures and absence of necrosis aid in the differential diagnosis with true malignant neoplasms. Something similar can be said of pleomorphic adenomas with foci that superficially resemble the adenoid cystic carcinoma pattern. The presence of these foci does not influence the prognosis and therefore should be disregarded.

Immunohistochemically, the ductal epithelial component is positive for keratin, EMA, secretory component, CEA, lysozyme, α_1-antitrypsin, α_1-antichymotrypsin, lactoferrin, GCDFP-15, interleukin-6, and steroid C-21 hydroxylase.[126,131,132,141,153,155,167,174,175] Conversely, amylase is usually absent.[141] The keratins most frequently expressed are CK19 (with or without CK14) in the luminal cells of the tubular structures, and CK14 in the nonluminal peripheral cells.[162] A potential source of confusion is represented by the fact that about half of the cases of pleomorphic adenoma contain cells reactive for prostate-specific antigen (PSA) and prostate-specific acid phosphatase (PSAP).[182] The myoepithelial component is immunoreactive for keratin, actin, myosin, other smooth muscle-specific proteins, fibronectin, and S-100 protein.[119,148,163,168,176,181,188] The latter marker is also strongly expressed in the cartilaginous areas and in a subtype of the epithelial ductal cells. In the cartilaginous foci there is abundant expression of type II collagen and (pericellularly) of type IV collagen.[159] There is also expression of the bone morphogenetic proteins.[143] The immunohistochemical profile of the epithelial component is similar to that of the normal intercalated duct cells, particularly regarding the expression of lactoferrin and secretory component.[141] The demonstration in some of the tumors of glial fibrillary acidic protein and astroprotein, two glial markers, is more difficult to explain[157,172]; it has been suggested that it is the result of cross-reactivity with other intermediate filaments of similar structure and chemical composition.[109] Regardless of the reason for this occurrence, it seems to be related to the capacity of this tumor for cartilaginous differentiation, and it therefore may be useful in the differential diagnosis with adenoid cystic carcinoma and basal cell adenoma, in which such a differentiation does not occur.[160,185]

Basement membrane proteins such as type IV collagen and laminin are consistently present[127]; those related to epithelial ductular cells have a linear quality, whereas those connected with myoepithelial cells have a thicker, more "membranous" appearance.[169] Type II collagen and tenascin are expressed in connection with the chondroid areas.[145,171] The cell proliferation index is low, whether measured with Ki-67, proliferating cell nuclear antigen (PCNA), silver-staining nucleolar organizer region (AgNOR), or flow cytometry,[130,154,186] Cytogenetically, pleomorphic adenomas have been divided into three major subgroups characterized respectively by an apparently normal karyotype, rearrangement of 8q12, or rearrangements of 12q14–15.[112,173] Overexpression of p53 is rare in pleomorphic adenoma, in contrast to its malignant counterpart.[124]

The *recurrence rate* of benign mixed tumor depends almost entirely on the adequacy of the primary excision as several classic studies have conclusively demonstrated.[164] Recurrence is very high if the tumor is removed by a simple enucleation (Fig. 12.9). This is because small inconspicuous nodules attached by

threadlike filaments of neoplastic tissue may be present surrounding the main mass.[136] They may have the shape and appearance of lymph nodes and may be mistaken for nodal metastases by both the surgeon and the pathologist. If the tumor is enucleated, these small remnants will be left behind and will provide the nidus for recurrence.[128,149] Most of these recurrences will appear during the first 18 months after surgery, but others supervene over an exceedingly long period (50 years or more). Because of this, long-term follow-up is essential. It has been proposed that patients with tumor spillage at operation or residual tumor left behind should have radiation therapy immediately to minimize the possibility of recurrence.[111] Usually the microscopic pattern of the recurrent tumor exactly mimics that of the original neoplasm. Surgery for recurrent tumor often fails. In about one fourth of cases, further recurrences develop, often in the form of multiple foci.[150] The proper therapy for pleomorphic adenoma is its total surgical removal, along with a margin of normal salivary tissue that surrounds it. For the tumors located in the superficial lobe of the parotid gland, which represent the majority, the standard surgery is a superficial parotidectomy with preservation of the facial nerve. The incidence of recurrence after this procedure is almost zero, and the long-term prognosis for properly treated pleomorphic adenoma is excellent.[140]

Under rare circumstances, a benign mixed tumor of ordinary microscopic appearance will metastasize to the lymph nodes, lungs, bone, or other organs, with the metastases appearing as benign as the original tumor.[114,116,117] Some of these cases have occurred in immunologically compromised patients and have followed a rapidly aggressive clinical course.[166] Usually these metastases are preceded by one or more local recurrences.[184] Curiously, a good number of these metastases have presented as isolated masses in the kidney.[118]

It could perhaps be mentioned here that there is a totally different type of "mixed" tumor in the parotid, formed by glandular structures with sertoliform features of probable striated duct nature and mature adipose tissue; this pathologic curiosity has been referred to as *lipoadenoma*,[187] and an *oncocytic variant* of it has already been described.[137]

Malignant mixed tumor

Two major categories of malignant mixed tumor exist.[197,203] The first and more common can be viewed as a malignant transformation of a preexisting benign mixed tumor. This complication occurs in about 5% to 10% of these neoplasms.[198,199] Clinical features that suggest this event in a long-standing tumor are sudden increase in growth, pain, and facial paralysis.[194,195,200] A history of previous surgery and/or radiation therapy is often obtained. Documentation that a malignant salivary gland tumor arose from a preexistent benign mixed tumor may be difficult to obtain. The clinical history,

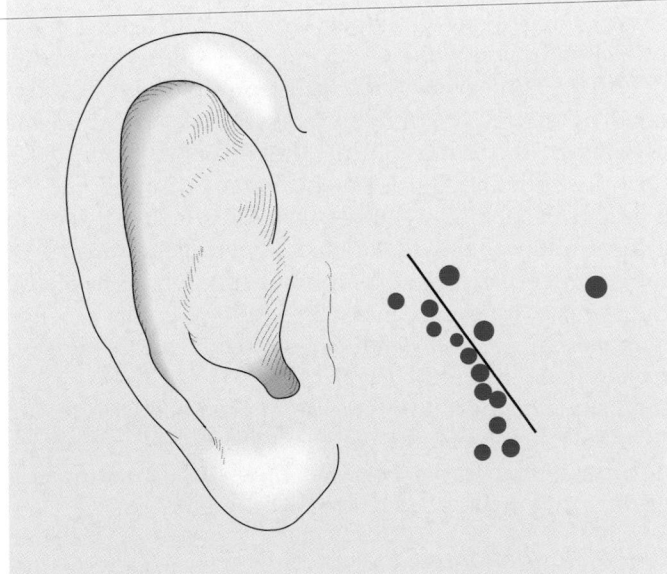

Fig. 12.9 Distribution of recurrent tumor nodules (shown as black dots) as demonstrated by careful histologic study of re-excision of benign mixed tumor of parotid gland, which at time of first operation had apparently been enucleated. Surgical scar measured 3.5 cm. (Courtesy of Dr. F. Leidler, Houston.)

although suggestive of the process, is not by itself diagnostic. It is necessary to have microscopic evidence of a previously existing benign tumor or to have benign and malignant tumor in the same neoplasm. This may require thorough sampling of the tumor. Sometimes the preexisting benign lesion is represented only by a totally hyalinized round nodule surrounded by carcinoma. Features said to indicate a greater likelihood of malignant transformation of a mixed tumor are submandibular (as opposed to parotid) location, older patient age, large tumor size, and—at the microscopic level—prominent zones of hyalinization and a moderate degree of mitotic activity.[189]

The malignant component of this tumor always has an epithelial appearance (Fig. 12.10). It has been stated that these malignant areas often assume the appearance of one of the well-recognized variants of salivary gland carcinoma (such as mucoepidermoid carcinoma or adenoid cystic carcinoma),[198] but this has rarely been the case in our experience or that of others.[190,195,196] In the series of Tortoledo et al.,[203] the malignant component was classified as salivary ductal carcinoma in 13 cases, undifferentiated carcinoma in 10, terminal duct carcinoma in 9, myoepithelial carcinoma in 3, and unclassified in 2. Most of the tumors have a poorly differentiated appearance. As a matter of fact, whenever a high-grade adenocarcinoma that is difficult to classify is found in the salivary gland, the possibility of it having arisen from a benign mixed tumor should be considered.[196] Extensive immunoreactivity for B72.3 is more common in malignant than in benign mixed tumors regardless of the subtype of the former.[192] In the malignant areas there is often overexpression of p53 (as a result of mutation) and of c-*erb*B-2.[193,205]

LiVolsi and Perzin[197] have pointed out that if the cytologically malignant foci are found entirely within a benign mixed tumor (i.e., in the form of carcinoma in situ), they are not associated with clinical malignancy.

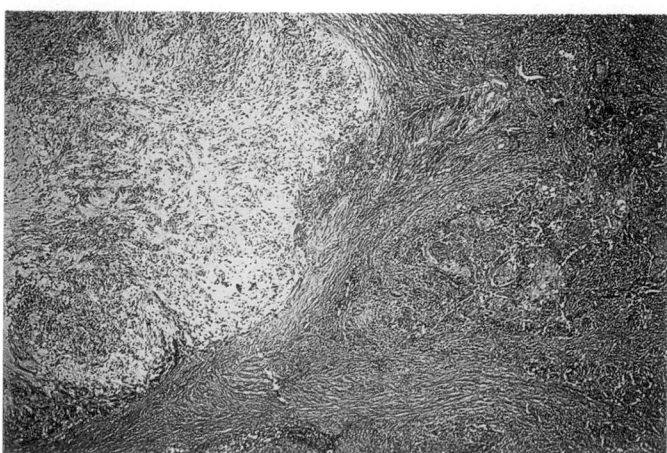

Fig. 12.10 Benign mixed tumor (left) with area of malignant transformation in the form of poorly differentiated carcinoma (right).

Only when invasion occurs beyond the capsule of the original neoplasm will the lesion behave clinically in a malignant fashion. For invasive tumors, the extent of invasion beyond the capsule is of importance. In one series, all patients whose malignant neoplasms extended for more than 8 mm beyond the capsule died of tumor.[203] Therefore the importance of thorough sampling cannot be overemphasized. The prognosis also depends on the histologic type of carcinoma, the microscopic grade (which is related to the former), and the proliferative index.[203,204]

The most common sites of metastases are regional lymph nodes, lungs, bone (especially the vertebral column), and abdominal organs.[202]

The second type of malignant mixed tumor has a biphasic composition similar to that of benign mixed tumor, but both the epithelial and the mesenchyme-like elements have a malignant appearance, the former often in the form of a ductal carcinoma and the latter in the form of chondrosarcoma. Since no preexisting benign tumor is found, the designation of *carcinoma ex pleomorphic adenoma*, which has been suggested as an alternative term for malignant mixed tumor, is inappropriate.[200] Names such as *true malignant mixed tumor* and *carcinosarcoma* have been proposed instead.[191,201,206] This is an aggressive, often rapidly lethal neoplasm.

Tumors with oxyphilic (oncocytic) change

Oncocytes or oxyphilic cells are large ductal epithelial cells with a granular, deeply eosinophilic cytoplasm crowded with mitochondria.[207] Their number in the normal salivary gland increases with age, and their secretory activity is minimal, suggesting that they are the expression of a degenerative change. However, no defects of the mitochondrial enzyme cytochrome-*c*-oxidase have been detected.[210] Sometimes one finds multiple parotid cysts lined by oncocytic epithelium, associated with tyrosine crystals in the lumen.[208] In other instances, oncocytes form well-defined clusters scattered throughout the gland. It is not clear whether these clusters represent an exaggeration of the age-related hyperplastic process or the emergence of a neoplasm, an uncertainty reflected by the terms that have been used to designate this process: *oncocytosis,*[213] *multinodular oncocytoma,*[209] and *multifocal adenomatous oncocytic hyperplasia.*[211,214]

The two major tumor types composed of oncocytes are oxyphilic adenoma and Warthin's tumor.[212,215] There are no transitional forms between these two tumors, suggesting that their pathogenesis is different.

Oxyphilic adenoma

Oxyphilic adenoma (oncocytoma; mitochondrioma) is defined as a benign tumor exclusively composed of oxyphilic cells.[222] The majority occur in the parotid but they are also well documented in the submaxillary gland.[226] In one large series, 20% of patients had either radiation therapy to the region or long-term occupational exposure.[217] Grossly, the tumor presents as a solid, well-circumscribed mass, usually small and with a characteristic tan color (Fig. 12.11). Microscopically, it is composed of large cells with round nuclei and abundant granular acidophilic cytoplasm (Fig. 12.12). Ultrastructurally, the cytoplasm is packed with mitochondria (Fig. 12.13). Some of these mitochondria contain large amounts of glycogen, and others are partitioned, suggesting division.[225] Mitotic figures are absent, and cellular transition from normal lining cells of the ducts may be seen. Occasionally, the cells undergo a clear change as a result of cystic dilatation of mitochondria. The lumen of the glandular spaces formed by these tumors may contain psammoma bodies[218] or tyrosine-rich crystals.[219] Focal collections of oncocytes may be present in the adjacent normal gland. Local excision is usually curative.[220]

Oxyphilic carcinoma (malignant oncocytoma; oncocytic adenocarcinoma) is the malignant counterpart of oxyphilic adenoma, a tumor type so rare as to represent a pathologic curiosity.[216,217,221,223,224] It is characterized by cell atypia, mitotic activity, and infiltrative growth.

Warthin's tumor

Warthin's tumor (cystadenoma lymphomatosum papilliferum) is found almost exclusively in the parotid gland.[236] Cases have also been reported in the submaxillary gland, but some of them probably arose from the mandibular extension of the parotid gland. Warthin's tumor is more common in males, and a statistical relationship with smoking has been found.[246,249] It is often multicentric and is bilateral in 10% to 15% of cases. It comprises 70% of all bilateral salivary gland neoplasms.[264] Grossly, it appears as a lobulated mass that may be fixed to the overlying skin and simulate a malignant neoplasm. On cross section, it has a typical multicystic appearance, with fluid-filled spaces separated by grayish septa of

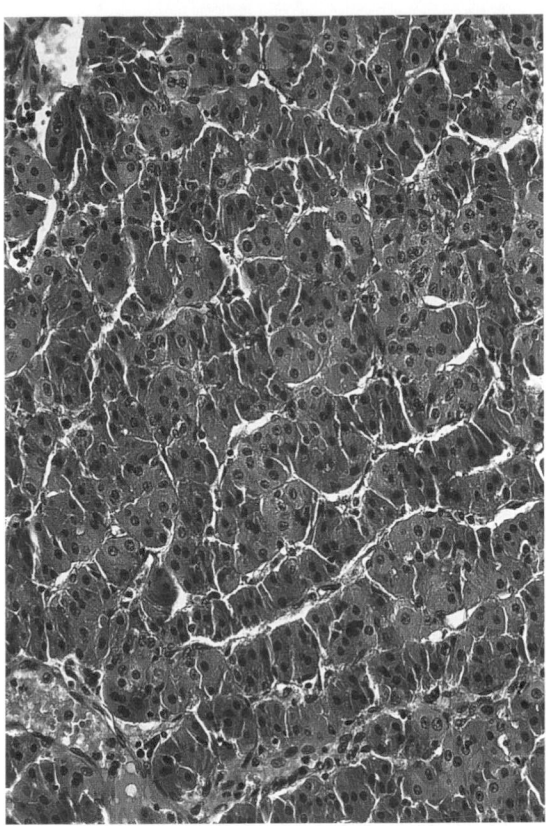

Fig. 12.12 Low-power microscopic view of oxyphilic adenoma. The pattern of growth is solid, with a suggestion of trabecular formations. The tumor cells have a uniform granular eosinophilic staining quality.

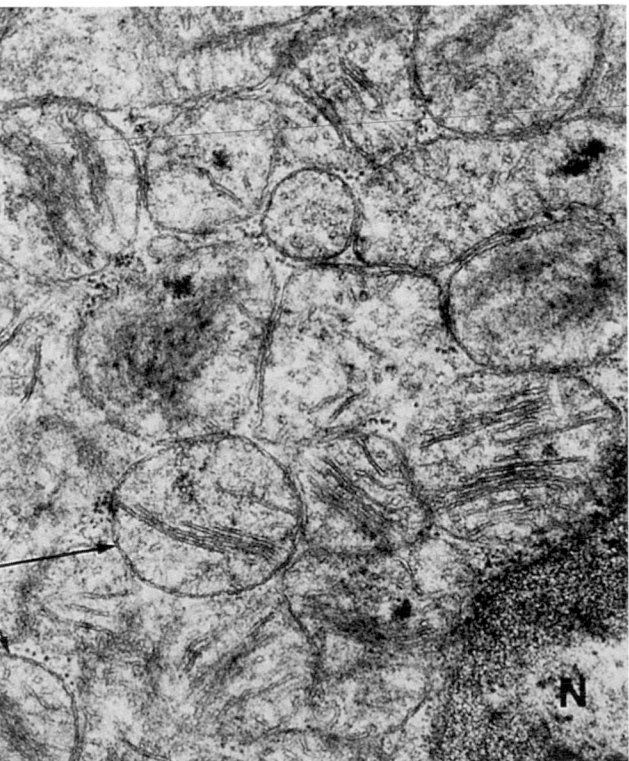

Fig. 12.13 Electron micrograph of oxyphilic adenoma showing cytoplasm packed with mitochondria (arrow). A portion of the nucleus (N) is at right. (×31,000)

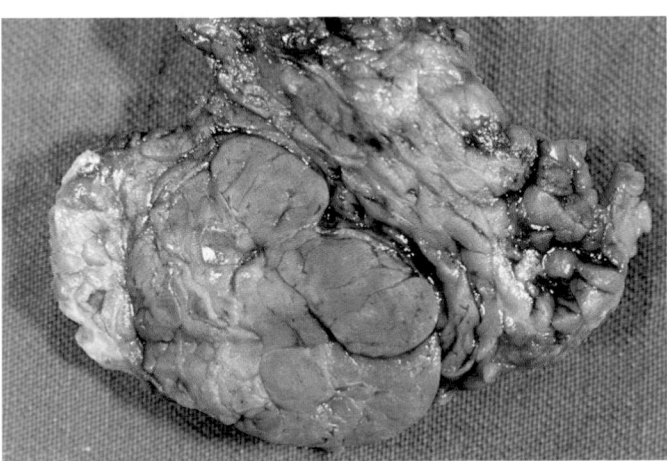

Fig. 12.11 Gross appearance of oncocytoma. The tumor is well circumscribed, solid, and light brown. (Courtesy of Dr. F. Facchetti, Brescia, Italy.)

varying thickness (Fig. 12.14). Occasionally the entire tumor undergoes necrotic changes consistent with hemorrhagic infarct.[236,254] These changes can occur spontaneously, but are more common following fine needle biopsy.[233]

Microscopically, lymphoid tissue is prominent, often with germinal centers; this has led to the time-honored suggestion that the lesion originates from excretory ducts located within intraparotid lymph nodes (Fig. 12.15).[263] This lymphoid stroma is predominantly composed of B lymphocytes,[231] but it also contains T lymphocytes, mast cells, and S-100 protein-positive dendritic cells.[230,255,260,267] The lymphocytic population is polyclonal,[245] with a predominance of IgA-producing cells.[242] Covering the surface of this lymphoid tissue are large epithelial cells with oncocytic features, similar in most respects to those seen in oxyphilic adenoma (Fig.

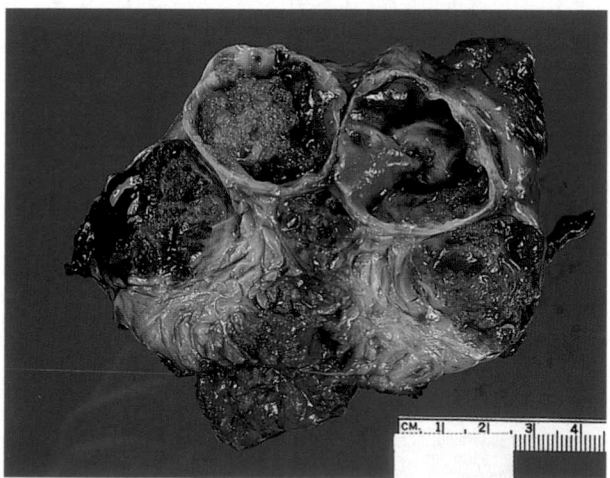

Fig. 12.14 Gross appearance of Warthin's tumor of parotid gland. The presence of multiple large cystic spaces is characteristic of this lesion.

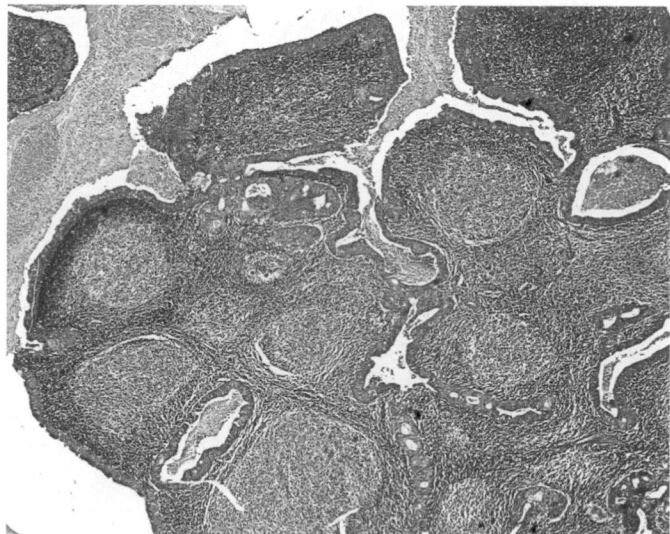

Fig. 12.15 Low-power appearance of Warthin's tumor. Germinal centers are very prominent.

12.16). These cells are arranged in two layers, with some morphologic and immunohistochemical differences between them.[243] Some of the apical cells may be ciliated.[236] These oncocytic cells are immunoreactive for keratin, secretory component, and mitochondria-associated markers, focally positive for ribonuclease, lactoferrin, CEA, and lysozyme, and negative for amylase, vimentin, and desmin (Fig. 12.17).[245,250,253,258] The keratin expressed is that typical for columnar differentiation, i.e., CK7, 8, 18, and 19.[256] Interestingly, somatostatin has also been detected in the epithelial cells of some of these tumors.[240] Mucin-secreting cells and groups of sebaceous cells may also be present.[235,238] There is no evidence for a myoepithelial cell component.[239] Occasionally, the lymphoid component is scanty or absent.[236] By electron microscopy, the cytoplasm of the granular epithelial cells is packed with mitochondria.[247] The mitochondrial partitions commonly seen ultrastructurally in oxyphilic adenoma are usually absent in Warthin's tumor; however, cup-shaped and concentric-ring forms of mitochondria occur.[244]

The cases associated with infarct-like necrosis may exhibit focal squamous metaplasia, sometimes with features analogous to those of necrotizing sialometaplasia in the oral cavity,[261,265] and are just as likely to be overinterpreted as squamous cell carcinoma.[234]

The treatment of Warthin's tumor is surgical excision; the incidence of local recurrence is extremely low.

Malignant transformation of Warthin's tumor is a rare event, but has been documented both in terms of the lymphoid component evolving into malignant lymphoma[227,229,257] and the epithelial component evolving into adenocarcinoma, mucoepidermoid carcinoma, squamous cell carcinoma, oncocytic carcinoma, and Merkel cell carcinoma.[228,232,237,251,252,262,266] Warthin's tumor is universally regarded as a true neoplasm, hence its inclusion in this section. However, we have made the suggestion that it may belong instead to the group of acquired multicystic reactive conditions of the head and neck that also includes benign lymphoepithelial cyst (see p. 875) and other lesions of branchial pouch derivation.[259] The fact that the epithelial component of this lesion has been found to be polyclonal supports this contention.[241] If this interpretation is correct, one should regard the parotid lesions having a multicystic oncocytic-lined component but lacking a lymphoid stroma (*oncocytic cystadenomas*) as belonging to a different category.[236] Sometimes the epithelium of this exceptionally rare entity shows prominent signet-ring features.[248]

Monomorphic adenoma

The term *monomorphic adenoma* was originally proposed for any benign epithelial salivary gland tumor other than benign mixed tumor (pleomorphic adenoma). It therefore includes tumors as disparate as oxyphilic adenoma, Warthin's tumor, sebaceous lymphadenoma, and basal

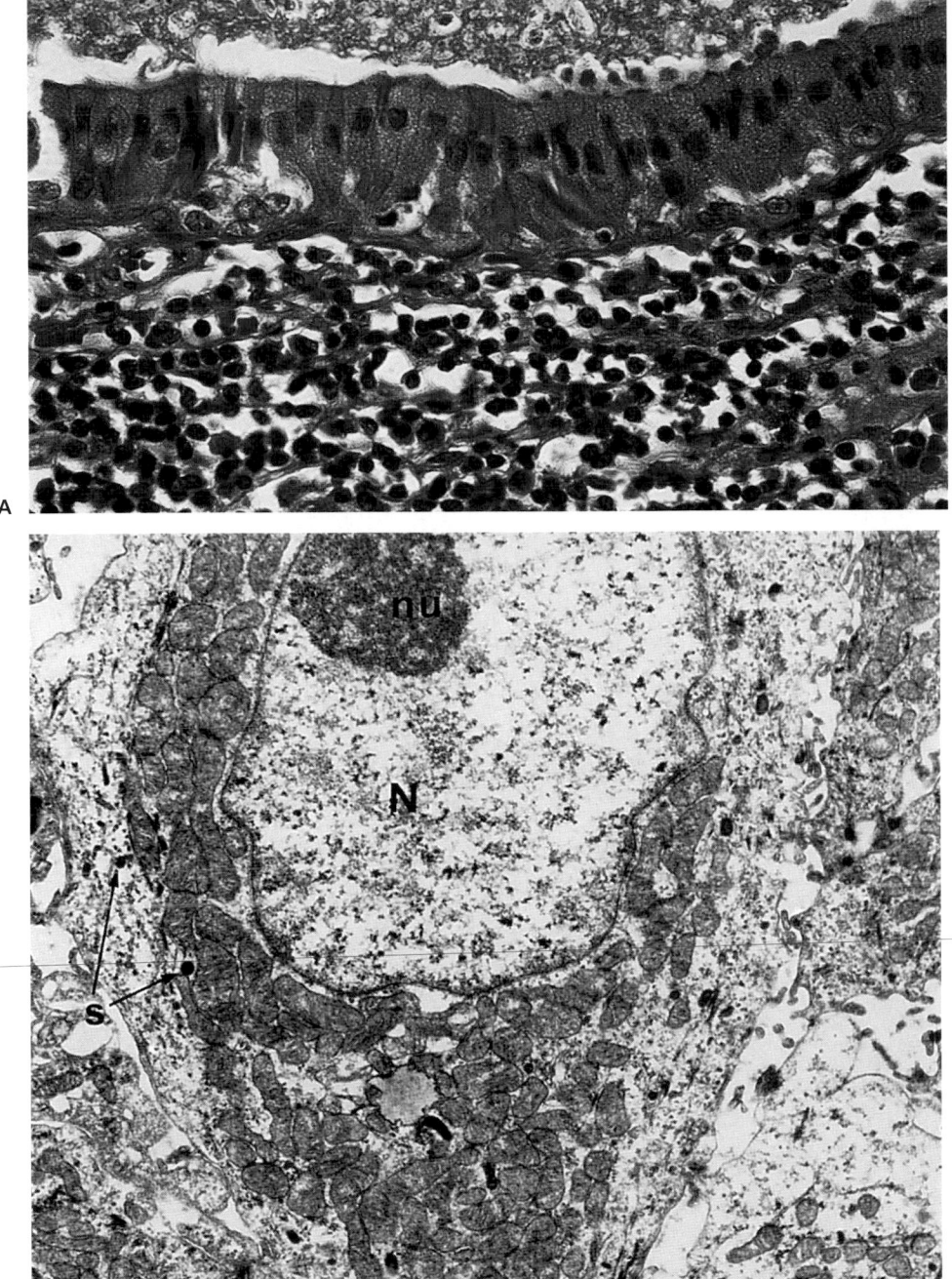

Fig. 12.16 A, High-power view of the lining of one of the cysts of Warthin's tumor. The epithelium is tall and oxyphilic, with a discontinuous layer of small cells at the base. The stroma beneath contains a monotonous lymphocytic infiltrate. B, Electron micrograph of oxyphil cells in epithelium of Warthin's tumor. The cytoplasm is packed with mitochondria, almost to the exclusion of other organelles. Unidentified dense rods and spheres (s) are scattered through the cytoplasm. The nucleus (N) and nucleolus (nu) are prominent. (×9000)

cell adenoma.[268,270] The very inclusiveness of the term when so defined, and the fact that some people have used it instead as a synonym for only one member of the group (i.e., for basal cell adenoma), has resulted in confusion. Therefore it is probably advisable to regard monomorphic adenoma not as a specific pathologic diagnosis but rather as the expression of a nosologic grouping and to name the tumors in this category according to their composition and appearance.[269] The term "monomorphic adenoma" does not appear in the new WHO classification of salivary gland tumors.[271]

Basal cell adenoma and adenocarcinoma

Basal cell adenomas usually occur in adult patients, and there is a slight predilection for females.[274] An extremely unusual congenital form has been described, which needs to be distinguished from embryoma (see p. 897).[299] Most cases occur in the parotid but a few have been

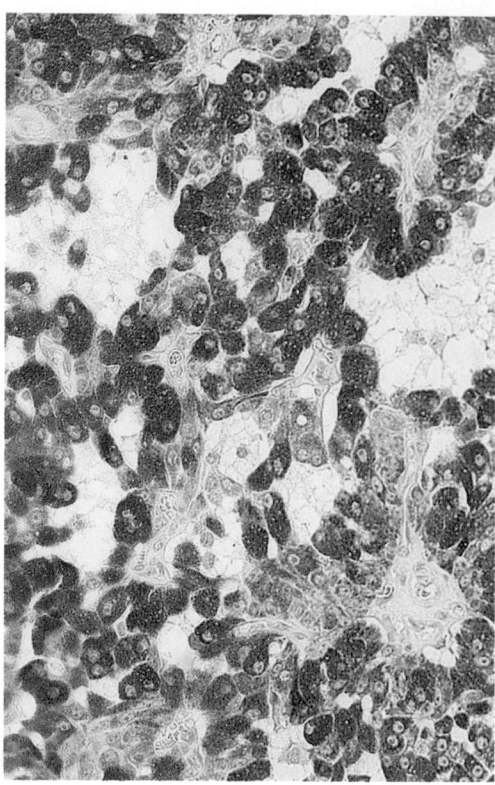

Fig. 12.17 Positive immunostaining for antimitochondrial antibody in oncocytes. (Courtesy of Dr. F. Facchetti, Brescia, Italy)

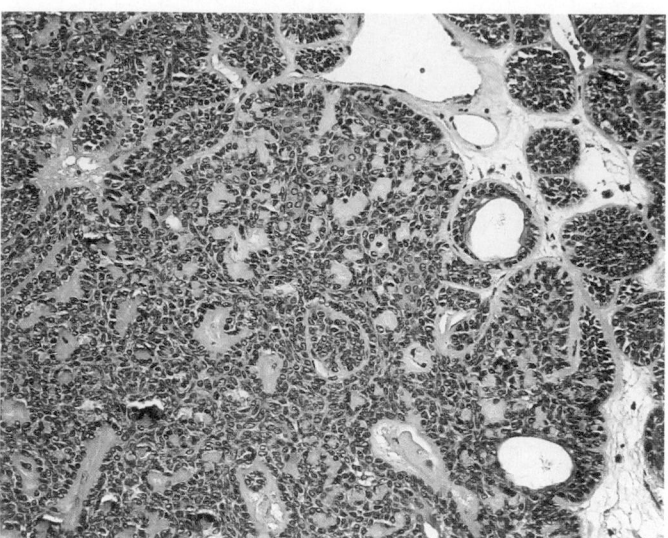

Fig. 12.18 Basal cell adenoma of parotid gland. The appearance is reminiscent of that of a skin adnexal tumor.

reported within periparotid lymph nodes.[292] Grossly, these tumors are encapsulated and often cystic; as a group, they tend to be smaller than benign mixed tumors. Microscopically, an important distinguishing feature is the palisading at the periphery of the epithelial nests, giving the tumor a "basaloid" appearance. The pattern of growth may be predominantly tubular, trabecular, or solid.[280,283,288] In a variant of the latter designated as **membranous** or **dermal analogue tumor**, there is deposition of abundant basal lamina material around and within the epithelial nests, in a pattern nearly identical to that of the cutaneous sweat gland tumor known as eccrine dermal cylindroma[272,273] (Fig. 12.18). Actually, there have been cases of multiple dermal cylindromas coexisting with multiple parotid tumors with the same microscopic appearance.[276,289,298] Furthermore, the same cytogenetic abnormality in the chromosome 16q region has been found at the two sites.[279]

Another variant of basal cell adenoma is characterized by the presence of bilayered strands or ribbons of columnar cells separated by a loose, well-vascularized stroma. This has been referred to as **canalicular adenoma** and is increasingly regarded as an entity separate from basal cell adenoma[281,288] because of its greater tendency to arise from minor salivary glands.[300] However, the frequent occurrence in this tumor of foci of basaloid cells and the equally frequent merging of canalicular and trabecular structures suggest that a sharp separation between these

entities is not always feasible.[303] Foci of acinar differentiation have been occasionally observed in basal cell adenoma, indicating that the presence of acinar cells in a salivary gland tumor is not always indicative of acinic cell carcinoma.[297]

The main differential diagnosis of basal cell adenoma is with basal cell adenocarcinoma (see later discussion), benign mixed tumor, and adenoid cystic carcinoma.[294] Basal cell carcinoma lacks the mesenchyme-like component of benign mixed tumor. In contrast to adenoid cystic carcinoma, it is encapsulated and devoid of stromal and perineurial invasion. Ultrastructural studies suggest that basal cell adenoma, like most other salivary gland tumors, derives from the intercalated portion of the duct, with a minor participation of myoepithelial cells[277,278,282,290] (Fig. 12.19). Immunohistochemically, the duct-lining cells in the tubuloglandular and trabecular areas express keratins, α_1-antichymotrypsin, CEA, and the alpha subunit of S-100 protein; the basaloid cells in the trabecular and solid areas express vimentin, actin, and the beta subunit of S-100 protein, indicative of myoepithelial cell participation.[285,301] Basal cell adenoma behaves in a benign fashion, analogous to that of benign mixed tumor, and excision is curative.

Malignant transformation of basal cell adenoma is a rare but well-documented event; the dermal analogue type is said to be particularly at risk.[275] In 6 cases of this phenomenon reported by Luna et al.,[291] the malignant component was diagnosed as adenoid cystic carcinoma in 3 and as basal cell adenocarcinoma in the other 3.

Basal cell adenocarcinoma (basaloid carcinoma) is the malignant counterpart of basal cell adenoma.[284,287,293] Like its benign counterpart, it can arise either in the major or the minor salivary glands.[286] It has a similar architecture and immunohistochemical profile,[302] but it differs by virtue of its infiltrative quality, perineurial spread, and vascular invasion, as well as a variable degree of cytologic atypia and mitotic activity. It also tends to express p53, bcl-2, and EGFR.[295] The parotid gland is the predominant site, and the peak incidence is in the sixth decade of life. Solid, membranous, trabecular, and tubular patterns of growth have been described. The aggressiveness of the tumor can be manifested by local recurrence or metastases to the lymph nodes and lung. Like its benign counterpart, it can be associated with dermal cylindromas.[284]

Basal cell adenocarcinoma should be distinguished from malignant transformation of basal cell adenoma, a phenomenon equivalent to that more commonly seen with pleomorphic adenoma.[296]

Tumors with sebaceous differentiation

Cells with a sebaceous appearance are often found within otherwise normal parotid glands. They are also found in a variety of salivary gland tumors. They are particularly common in Warthin's tumor but may also

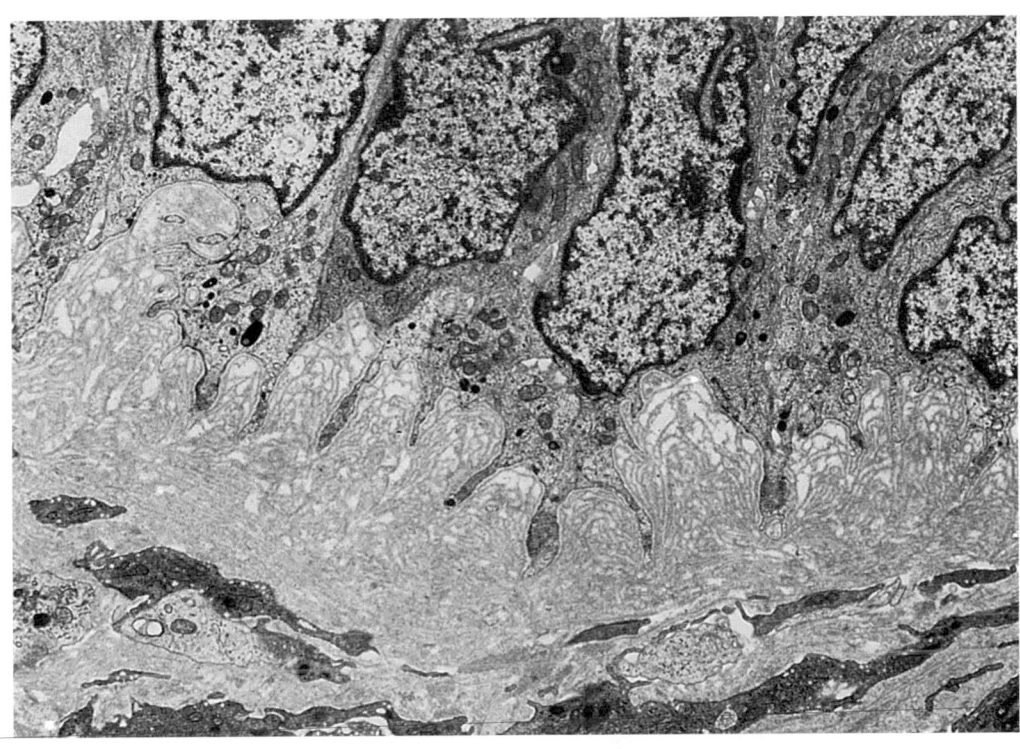

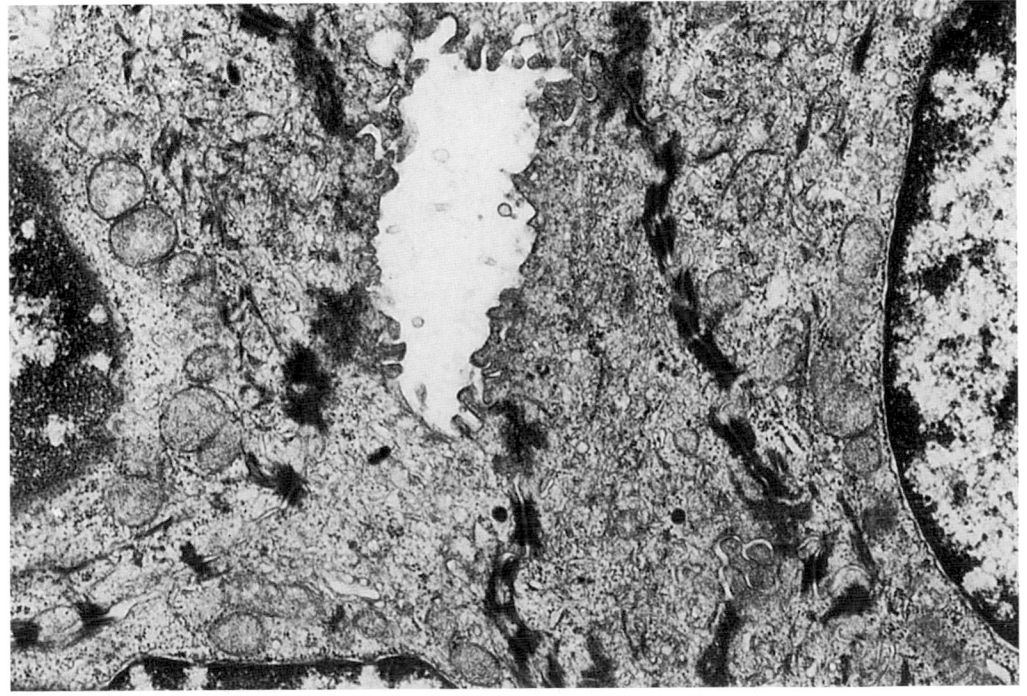

Fig. 12.19 Basal cell adenoma of parotid gland. **A,** Prominent reduplication of basal lamina is present. Cells are nondescript and are attached by numerous desmosomes. **B,** These epithelial cells contain numerous tonofilaments that are attached by desmosomes and form a true lumen. (**A,** ×5065; **B,** ×16,850)

appear in benign mixed tumor, mucoepidermoid carcinoma, and adenoid cystic carcinoma.[304,305,309] The similarities of these cells to those of cutaneous sebaceous glands are also evident on electron microscopic examination and thin-layer chromatography of the lipid material.[310]

Benign tumors with a predominant sebaceous component have been designated as **sebaceous adenoma** when pure and **sebaceous lymphadenoma** when accompanied by a prominent lymphoid stroma[306,307] (Fig. 12.20). The latter tumor may present as a unilocular cystic mass on gross inspection.[308] When the tumor contains the same admixture of epithelial glandular cells and lymphocytes but lacks sebaceous differentiation, it is simply designated as *lymphadenoma*.[566a] Rare malignant counterparts of these tumors exist; these have been called **sebaceous carcinoma** and **sebaceous lymphadenocarcinoma**, respectively.[306]

Tumors with myoepithelial differentiation

Myoepithelial cells are a component of several types of benign and malignant salivary gland tumors, particularly benign mixed tumors, adenoid cystic carcinoma, and terminal duct carcinoma.[314,324,332,346] Tumors thought to be composed exclusively of myoepithelial cells are generically referred to as **myoepitheliomas**.[350] Three major morphologic types have been identified: spindle cell, hyaline (plasmacytoid), and clear cell. However, it should be noted that combined and intermediate forms exist, that the myoepithelial nature of the hyaline cell type has been questioned,[329] and that the clear cell type has an associated (terminally differentiated) epithelial cell component.[322,327,357]

The *spindle cell type* tumors have a stromalike appearance and can be confused with lesions of fibroblasts, Schwann cells, or smooth muscle cells (Fig. 12.21).[316] In the variant known as *oncocytic myoepithelioma*, the

cytoplasm has a granular oxyphilic quality.[353] Collagen stroma is scanty, microcystic formations may be present, and various degrees of secondary myxoid change or lipomatous metaplasia of the stroma may be seen.[349,352] Collagenous crystalloids may be present.[351] Ultrastructurally and immunohistochemically, microfilaments of both actin and keratin type can be demonstrated[356] (Fig. 12.22). The *hyaline (plasmacytoid) cell type* tumors are

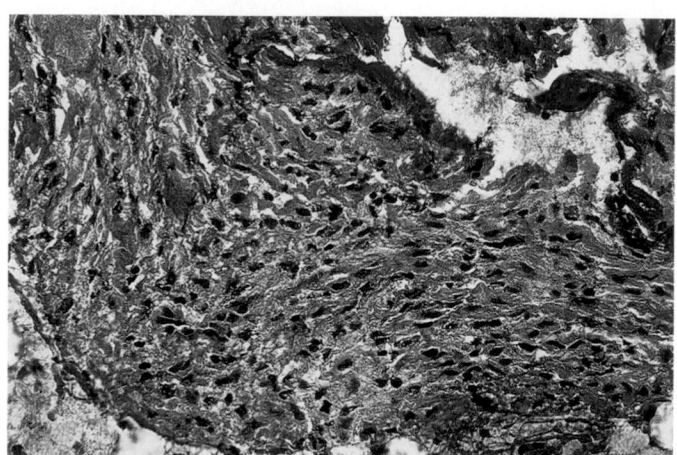

Fig. 12.21 Spindle cell myoepithelioma of parotid gland. It would be very difficult to distinguish this tumor from a soft tissue neoplasm on purely morphologic grounds.

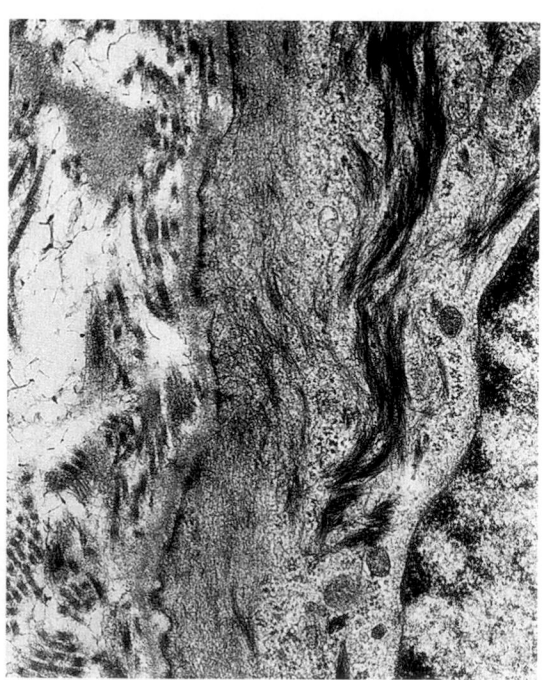

Fig. 12.22 Electron micrograph of a myoepithelioma of parotid gland. Portion of a neoplastic myoepithelial cell illustrating (left to right) extracellular space with collagen fibrils and basement membrane, electron-dense attachment plaques on the cell membrane, linear arrays of 6 nm actin microfilaments, perinuclear bundles of tonofilaments (indicative of squamous metaplasia), and a portion of the nucleus. (×22,900) (Courtesy of Dr. Robert A. Erlandson, Memorial Sloan-Kettering Cancer Center)

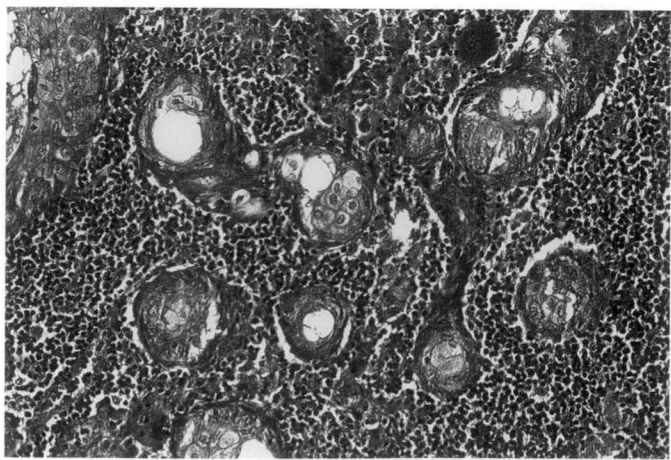

Fig. 12.20 So-called "sebaceous lymphadenoma." Ductal structures merge with well-differentiated sebaceous glands, which in turn are surrounded by a heavy lymphocytic infiltrate.

composed of cells with eccentric nuclei, some degree of pleomorphism and hyperchromasia, but scanty or no mitotic activity. The cytoplasm is abundant, with a *diffuse* eosinophilia that is very different from the fine granular quality seen in oncocytes. The cell margins are polygonal and sharply outlined (Fig. 12.23). The appearance of hyaline cells may simulate that of neoplastic plasma cells

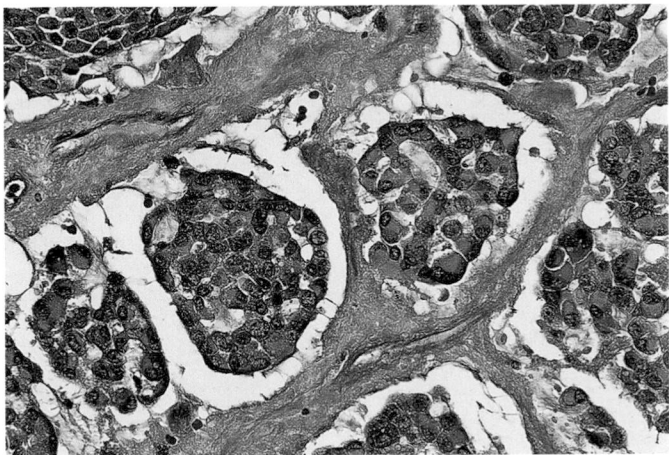

A

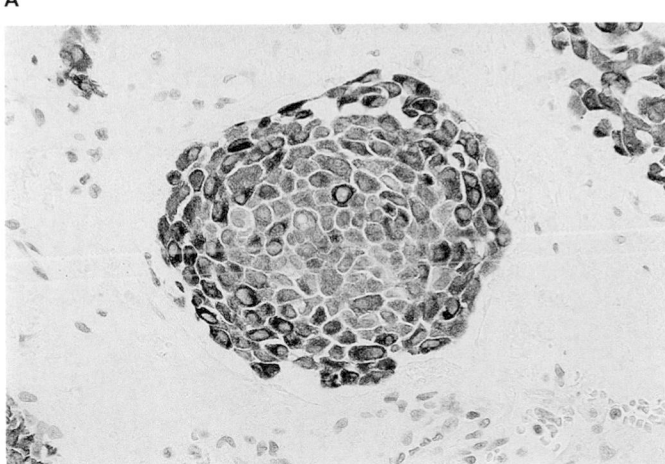

B

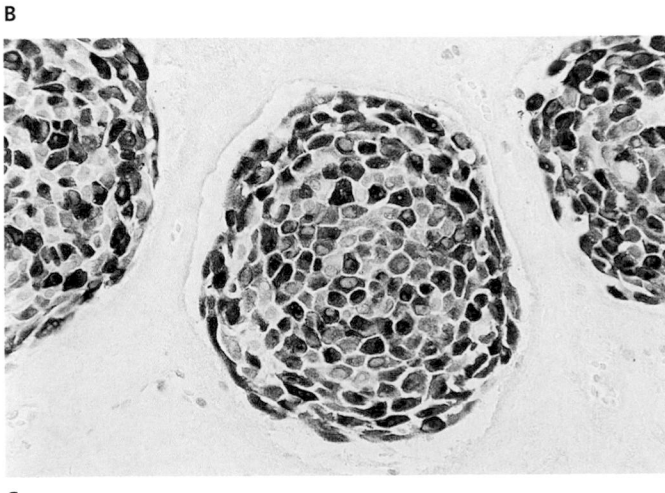

C

Fig. 12.23 Myoepithelioma composed of so-called "hyaline cells." (**A**, H&E; **B**, keratin; **C**, S-100 protein)

or even skeletal muscle cells. Ultrastructurally, their main feature is the presence of abundant, uniformly dispersed microfilaments measuring 50 to 100 Å in diameter.[354] The *clear cell type* tumors are composed of small tubules lined by a single layer of small cuboidal cells surrounded by one or more layers of prominent clear cells, with hyalinlike material in between (Fig. 12.24). These clear cells contain variable amounts of glycogen but no fat or mucin. In some areas, ductal formations are scanty, the lesion appearing as a sheet of clear cells.[339] This type has also been described as clear cell adenoma, glycogen-rich adenoma, glycogen-rich adenocarcinoma, tubular carcinoma, and epithelial–myoepithelial carcinoma.[313,318,319,321,330,340,347] An association has been described between epithelial–myoepithelial carcinoma and intercalated duct hyperplasia, and the suggestion has been made that the latter may be a precursor lesion.[317] Immunohistochemically, the neoplastic myoepithelial cells show reactivity for keratin, both forms of S-100 protein, and in some cases, vimentin, actin, and myosin.[323,331,334,338,341,344,345] In this regard, it is important to point out that many myoepitheliomas fail to react with smooth muscle actin.[333] There are differences in the immunohistochemical profile related to the myoepithelioma subtype, as well as a great deal of heterogeneity within each category.[341,342] Some of these differences may be related to regional variability in the immunohistochemical profile of normal myoepithelial cells.[328]

Most of the reported cases of spindle cell and clear cell myoepitheliomas have occurred in the parotid gland, whereas most pure examples of hyaline myoepitheliomas have been described in minor salivary glands, particularly those in the palate.[335,336]

There is a range of differentiation among these tumors, with both benign and malignant variants represented. The majority of cases with a hyaline cell morphology

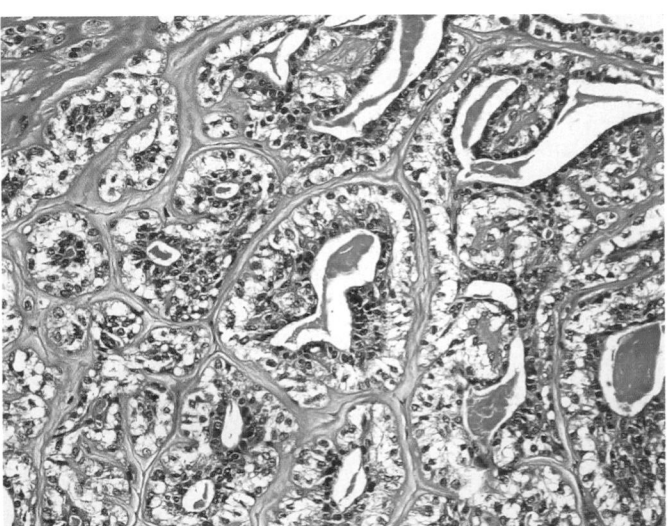

Fig. 12.24 Epithelial–myoepithelial carcinoma. The myoepithelial component is represented by the cells with clear cytoplasm.

have behaved in a benign fashion,[312] although well-documented exceptions exist.[335] Many malignant examples of the spindle cell and particularly of the clear cell types have been described.[315,320,326,343,348] In general, these have been characterized by invasive properties and cytologic atypia.[312] In some instances, a high-grade carcinomatous component is identified focally in an otherwise typical epithelial–myoepithelial carcinoma.[311] According to some authors, *all* myoepitheliomas of clear cell type should be regarded as potentially malignant.[337] Support for this contention comes from the fact that in one series of this entity there were local recurrences in 37%, lymph node metastases in 17%, distant metastases in 9%, and tumor-related deaths in 9%.[338]

These malignant myoepitheliomas can arise de novo or as a malignant transformation of a benign mixed tumor or a basal cell adenoma.[325,355]

Tumors with clear cell change

As is true in most other organs, clear cell-containing neoplasms of the salivary gland do not constitute a homogeneous or specific type.[358–360,362] In the presence of such features, the differential diagnosis should include clear cell myoepithelioma (positive for glycogen), sebaceous neoplasms (positive for fat), mucoepidermoid carcinoma (positive for mucin), acinic cell carcinoma (usually negative for all nonimmune stains), clear cell change in oncocytic tumors, and metastatic renal cell carcinoma (positive for glycogen, fat vimentin and CD10, and negative for high-molecular-weight keratin and CEA).[363,364,366] There are some malignant salivary gland tumors composed of clear cells that cannot be placed into any of those categories and for which the descriptive term *clear cell* carcinoma is used.[361,365] Most of these tumors occur in the oral cavity rather than in the major salivary glands and are accompanied by a prominent fibrohyaline stroma (hence the newly proposed term *hyalinizing clear cell carcinoma* for them).[361]

Mucoepidermoid carcinoma

Most cases of mucoepidermoid carcinoma are located in the parotid gland.[388] This lesion represents the most common malignant salivary gland tumor in children, in whom it may represent a second malignancy.[385–387] Microscopically, four cell types can be identified: mucin-producing, squamous, intermediate, and clear.[390] This tumor has been divided into low- and high-grade types.[382] The former presents grossly as a relatively well-circumscribed mass with cystic areas containing mucinous material (Fig. 12.25). Microscopically, well-differentiated mucinous cells predominate (Fig. 12.26). The high-grade variety is more solid and has a more infiltrative pattern of growth. Squamous intermediate and clear cells predominate over the mucin-producing cells. It should be pointed out that marked nuclear atypia, frequent mitoses, and extensive necrosis are not typical

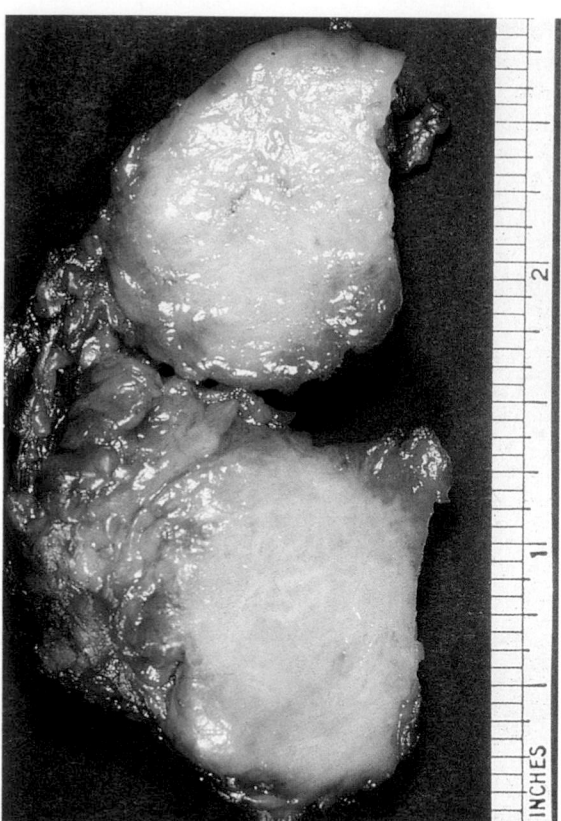

Fig. 12.25 Gross appearance of mucoepidermoid carcinoma. This particular tumor is entirely solid, without the cystic formations commonly seen in low-grade lesions.

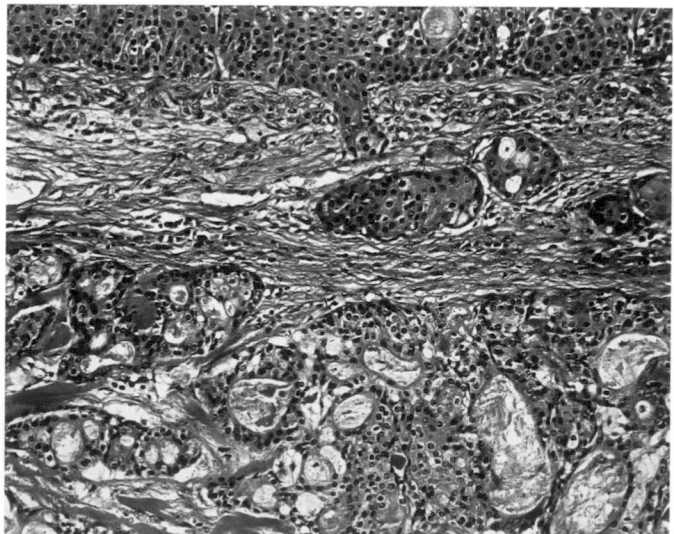

Fig. 12.26 Mucoepidermoid carcinoma. Mucous, squamous, and intermediate cells can be seen.

of mucoepidermoid carcinoma of any grade. When these features are present, the alternative possibilities of poorly differentiated adenocarcinoma and adenosquamous carcinoma should be considered.[373] A focal component of sebaceous cells is occasionally present,[381] and varying degrees of oncocytic change have been rarely reported (*oncocytic mucoepidermoid carcinoma*).[379,383] Recently, a case of mucoepidermoid carcinoma with a dedifferentiated component has been reported.[387a]

When the mucin or keratin formed by mucoepidermoid carcinoma escapes into the interstitial tissue, it causes an inflammatory reaction. Although true post-traumatic sialoceles and mucoceles certainly occur,[370] in the presence of mucin-filled cystic spaces in the parotid region the possibility of a well-differentiated mucoepidermoid carcinoma should always be ruled out by taking additional sections. Sometimes, extensive fibrosis accompanies the spillage of mucin.[369]

Ultrastructural studies of mucoepidermoid carcinoma have shown a mixed population of luminal epithelial cells and a component identified as being of myoepithelial nature.[371]

Immunohistochemically, simple mucin-type carbohydrate antigens (T, Tn, and syalosyl-Tn) have been detected in this tumor.[375] It has been pointed out that low-grade mucoepidermoid carcinoma has a characteristic profile (CK7, CK14, and mitochondrial antibodies) suggestive of striated duct differentiation.[376]

There is a marked difference in prognosis depending on the grade of the tumor, whether one uses the traditional two-tier system or the three-grade scheme proposed by the AFIP authors, which has recently gained in popularity.[368,377,378] This is based on a points system: intracystic component greater than 20%, 2 points; neural invasion, 2 points; necrosis, 3 points; 4 or more mitoses per 10 HPF, 3 points; anaplasia, 4 points. A total score between 0 and 4 defines a low-grade tumor, a score of 5 to 6 applies to an intermediate-grade tumor, and a score of 7 or more indicates a high-grade tumor.[372]

In the series reported by Jakobsson et al.[384] the determinate 5-year survival rate was 98% for the low-grade variety and 56% for the high-grade variety. Most of the latter tumors showed their malignant behavior within the first 5 years after surgery, in contrast with the continuous fall in survival rate over a 20-year period seen with adenoid cystic carcinoma and acinic cell carcinoma. In another series involving 69 cases, all but 2 of the 14 deaths and all 6 instances of distant metastases occurred in high-grade tumors, which were also associated with an increased incidence of local recurrence and regional lymph node metastases.[373] A correlation has also been found between prognosis and the following parameters: age (better in younger patients), sex (better in females), location (better in the parotid than in the submandibular gland), extraglandular extension, vascular invasion, necrosis, mitotic rate, cell proliferation as measured by MIB-1 antibody, DNA ploidy, and activation of the ERK-1/ERK-2 pathway.[367,368,374,377,380,389]

Acinic cell carcinoma

Acinic cell carcinoma comprises 1% to 3% of all salivary gland tumors. There is a male predominance and a peak incidence in the third decade of life.[391] A few familial cases have been described.[396] The majority are located in the parotid gland, but many examples in the minor salivary glands have been recorded.[392,394,414] Cases have also been seen located within intraparotid lymph nodes.[405]

Grossly, the tumor presents as an encapsulated round mass with a solid, friable, grayish-white cut surface, usually measuring less than 3 cm in diameter.[391] Occasionally it undergoes marked cystic degeneration.

The microscopic appearance shows considerable variation from case to case. The pattern of growth may be predominantly solid, microcystic, papillary–cystic, or follicular.[391] There is also marked variability in the appearance of the tumor cells. The most characteristic cell, known as acinic, has a cytoplasmic appearance (granular and basophilic), an ultrastructural morphology, and a secretory behavior pattern analogous to that of acinic cells of normal salivary glands[398,400] (Fig. 12.27). Other cell types have been designated as intercalated duct, clear, vacuolated, and nonspecific glandular.[391] When the clear cell component predominates, the tumor acquires an "hypernephroid" appearance reminiscent of renal cell carcinoma. These clear cells do not contain fat or mucin but may have variable amounts of glycogen. However, focal mucin positivity can be encountered in the papillary–cystic or follicular areas.[411] The occurrence of these cytologic and architectural variations indicates that this neoplasm differentiates in the direction of the terminal ductular–acinar unit of the salivary gland, which includes secretory acinar cells, intercalated duct cells, pluripotential reserve cells, and myoepithelial cells.[393] Lymphoid follicles with germinal centers may be prominent at the periphery of the tumor[406] and laminated concretions with the appearance of psammoma bodies may be seen within the lumina.[391] Immunohistochemically, there is positivity for keratin and also focal

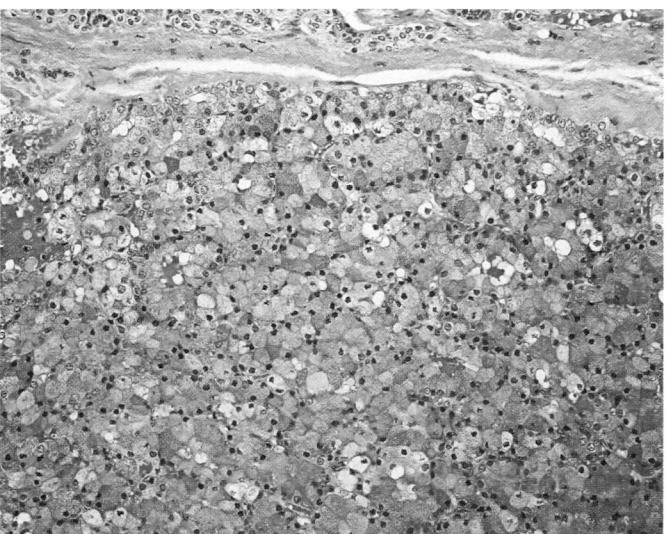

Fig. 12.27 Acinic cell carcinoma. The cells have an abundant cytoplasm filled with basophilic zymogen granules.

reactivity for amylase, α_1-antichymotrypsin, transferrin, lactoferrin, IgA, secretory component, and proline-rich protein.[412,413] A neuroendocrine component may also be present, identified by its argyrophilia, presence of dense-core granules ultrastructurally,[403] and immunoreactivity for vasoactive intestinal peptide.[401]

In a classic study of 37 cases reported by Eneroth and Jakobsson,[398] there was local recurrence in 11 cases and metastases in 7 cases; 4 recurrences were in regional lymph nodes. The determinate survival rate at 5 years was 89%, but it fell to 56% after 20 years. In a larger series reported by Ellis and Corio,[397] there was a recurrence rate of 12%, a metastatic rate of 7.8%, and a death rate of 6.1%. The regional lymph nodes are the most common site of metastases.[397]

Features of prognostic importance are pain or fixation, gross invasion, desmoplasia, cytologic atypia, increased mitotic activity, and adequacy of initial excision.[404] The latter is of particular importance.[408,409] In the series of Perzin and LiVolsi,[409] recurrent tumor was found in 14 of 15 patients treated with limited local excisions but in only 3 of 28 patients who had wide local excisions. Local recurrence was associated with an increased incidence of locally uncontrollable and metastatic disease. Neck dissection does not appear warranted unless the nodes are clinically involved.[399] The role of radiation therapy for this tumor remains controversial; most series have not shown clearcut beneficial effects.[410]

A particularly ominous but fortunately rare event in acinic cell carcinoma is the emergence of an anaplastic (dedifferentiated) component.[402] This development is associated with aneuploidy on flow cytometry, appearance of peculiar helioid inclusions at the ultrastructural level, and an accelerated clinical tempo.[395,407]

Adenoid cystic carcinoma

Adenoid cystic carcinoma (formerly known as cylindroma) is a generally slow-growing but highly malignant neoplasm with a remarkable capacity for recurrence. In the parotid gland it is less common than mucoepidermoid carcinoma and acinic cell carcinoma, but in the minor salivary glands it is the most common malignant tumor.

Grossly, it usually has a solid appearance and an infiltrative pattern of growth, although some examples can be well circumscribed. Microscopically, the typical adenoid cystic carcinoma has a pattern described as *cribriform*: nests and columns of cells of rather bland appearance are arranged concentrically around gland-like spaces ("pseudocysts") filled with homogeneous eosinophilic PAS-positive material or granular basophilic material (Figs 12.28 and 12.29). Most of these are not true glandular spaces; they represent instead extracellular cavities containing reduplicated basal lamina material and mucin produced by the tumor cells[449] (Fig. 12.30). Small true glandular lumina are also formed. Indeed, identification of *both* pseudocysts and true

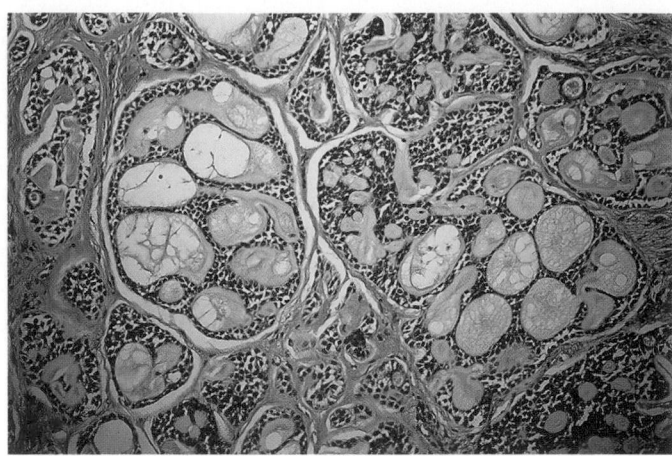

Fig. 12.28 Adenoid cystic carcinoma. Typical low-power appearance.

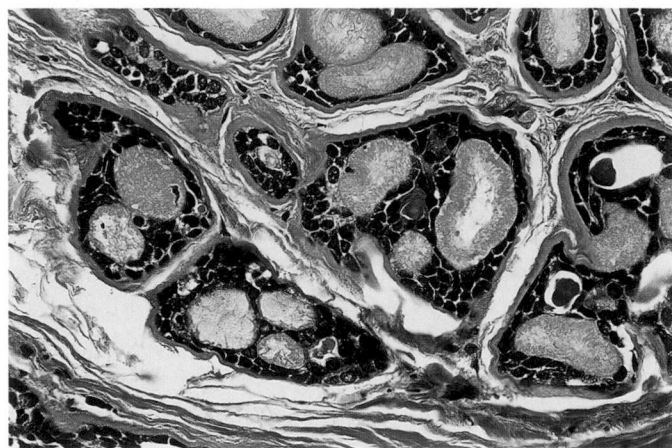

Fig. 12.29 Adenoid cystic carcinoma. Numerous "cylinders" containing a homogeneous acidophilic material can be seen.

glandular lumina is required to make a diagnosis of adenoid cystic carcinoma. This tumor has a remarkable tendency for invasion of perineurial spaces, to the degree that the diagnosis of adenoid cystic carcinoma should be questioned if an adequate sample taken from the periphery of the tumor does not exhibit this feature (Fig. 12.31). This is thought to be caused or promoted by the production of brain-derived neurotrophic factor.[433a]

Some adenoid cystic carcinomas have a predominantly *tubular* pattern of growth, whereas others are mainly *solid*.[442,445] Combined patterns of growth are common, whether in the original tumor or in the recurrences (Fig. 12.32). Adenoid cystic carcinoma can also occur in association with other tumor types, as an example of combined or hybrid tumor.[443]

The main ultrastructural features of adenoid cystic carcinoma are pseudocysts, intercellular spaces, abundant basal lamina, and true glandular lumens.[434] The cell types present combine features of intercalated ducts, myoepithelial cells, secretory cells, and pluripotential reserve cells.[422] Thus the composition of this tumor is not substantially different from that of benign mixed tumor, suggesting a similar histogenesis.[439]

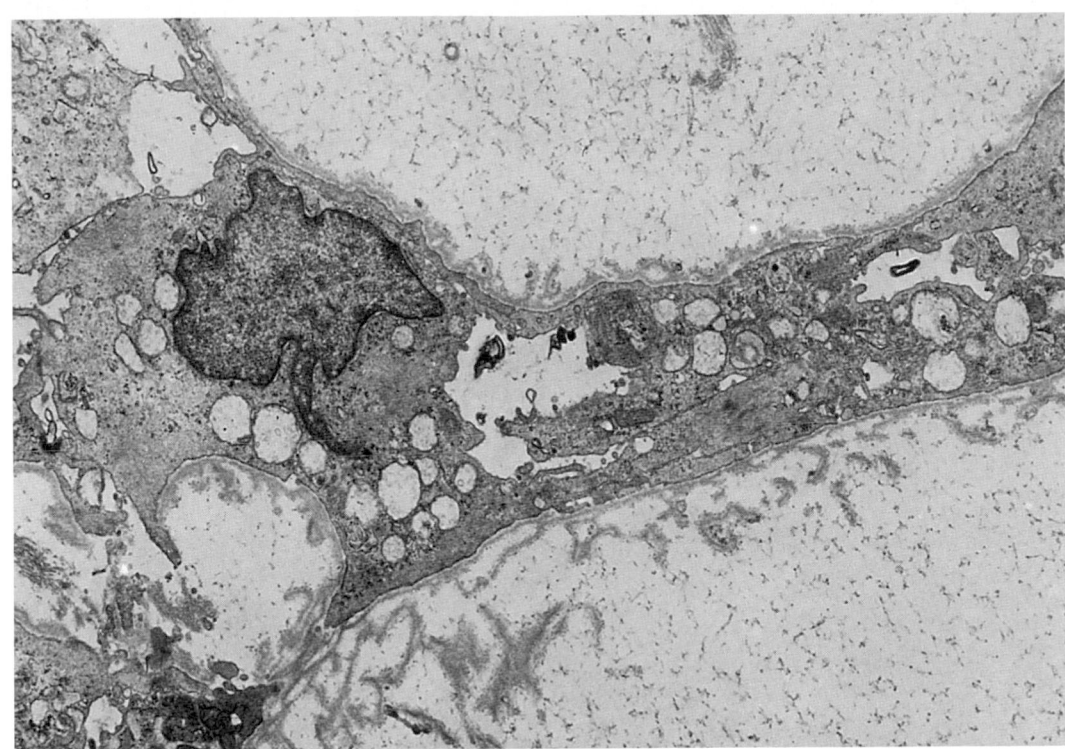

Fig. 12.30 Adenoid cystic carcinoma of oral minor salivary gland. The tumor is made up of myoepithelial cells covered by reduplicated basal lamina. False lumina are thus formed. (×7450)

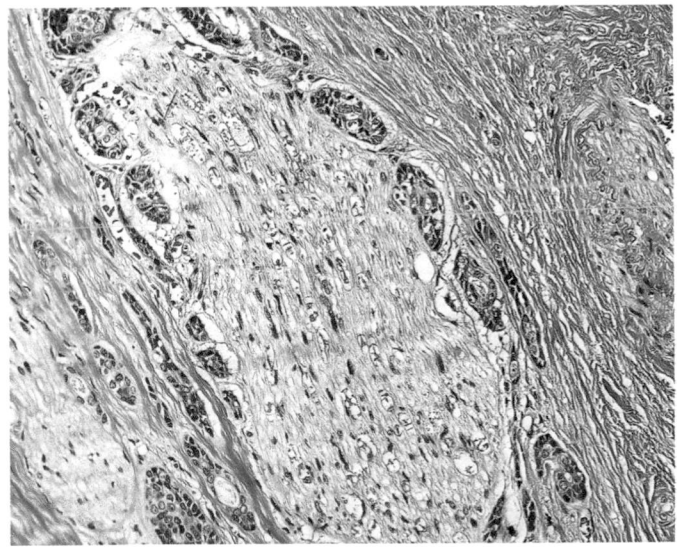

Fig. 12.31 Adenoid cystic carcinoma with prominent perineurial invasion.

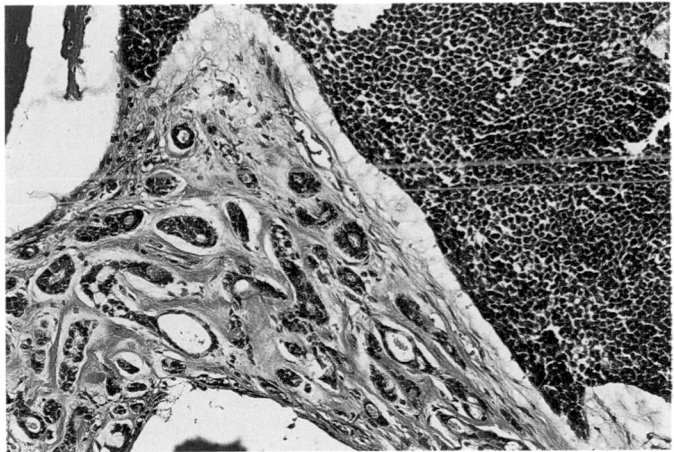

Fig. 12.32 Adenoid cystic carcinoma combining tubular and solid features.

Immunohistochemically, the tumor cells located in recognizable duct structures express a phenotype similar to that of the intercalated duct (positive for keratin, CEA, lysozyme, lactoferrin, α_1-antichymotrypsin, S-100 protein and CD117 (c-kit)), and those around pseudocysts have a phenotype suggestive of myoepithelial cell differentiation (positive for S-100 protein and actin and variably positive for keratin).[416,418,419,425,430,441] There is also strong reactivity for basement membrane components, particularly along the inner luminal surface of the pseudocysts.[450] These components include type IV collagen, laminin, their integrin ligands, heparan sulfate proteoglycan (perlecan), and entactin.[423,432,435] The basement membrane material also stains for a_1-antitrypsin.[448] Interestingly, adenoid cystic carcinomas have also been found to express hormone receptors.[440]

Cytogenetically, there is a high incidence of LOH at chromosome 6q23–35.[446] Alterations of p53 are uncommon,[433] except in dedifferentiated cases (see below). A microarray analysis has demonstrated the common expression of genes indicative of myoepithelial differentiation, transcription factors 50×4 ad AP-2y, and members of the Wnt/β-catenin signaling pathway.[428a]

The differential diagnosis with benign mixed tumor can be difficult. Unfortunately, histochemical reactions are of no help in this regard, inasmuch as they are very similar in the two neoplasms, except perhaps for a greater representation of nonsulfated glycosaminoglycans (such as hyaluronic acid) in the benign mixed tumor.[417,437] Important points to remember are that adenoid cystic carcinoma is usually invasive and is often associated with perineurial invasion and that mesenchyme-like areas and foci of squamous metaplasia are consistently absent.

Another important differential diagnosis is with polymorphous low-grade carcinoma, which is rendered easier by the realization that the latter is almost nonexistent in the *major* salivary glands. At the microscopic level, the nuclei of adenoid cystic carcinoma tend to be hyperchromatic and angulated rather than bland and uniform. Furthermore, as already stated, adenoid cystic carcinoma is usually strongly immunoreactive for CD117 (c-kit), whereas polymorphous low-grade carcinoma is either negative or shows a lesser intensity of staining.[441]

Since the prognosis of adenoid cystic carcinoma is greatly influenced by its pattern of growth, this feature has been used as a grading system.[436,438,442,447] In one series, the recurrence rate was 59% for the tubular tumors, 89% for the classic cribriform lesions, and 100% for the solid variety.[442] In another series in which a somewhat similar grading system was used, the cumulative survival rates at 15 years were 39%, 26%, and 5%, respectively.[447] The solid or anaplastic type of adenoid cystic carcinoma is associated with a higher incidence of metastases and a rapid clinical course.[426,436] A behavior just as aggressive (if not more so) is to be expected in the rare instances in which a conventional adenoid cystic carcinoma undergoes dedifferentiation,[424] an event that is accompanied by p53 gene mutation.[421] Other factors that influence the prognosis of adenoid cystic carcinoma are stage (very important), presence of tumor at the margins, anatomic site, size of the primary lesion, degree of atypia, and lymph node metastases.[442,444,447] DNA ploidy does not seem to be an important independent prognostic determinant.[427,429,432,435] Abnormalities of E-cadherin expression have been detected, and the claim has been made that reduced expression of this adhesion molecule correlates with an unfavorable prognosis.[428]

Adenoid cystic carcinomas frequently metastasize to the lungs. These metastases are usually silent, and it is not unusual to find multiple nodules in the chest x-ray film of a totally asymptomatic individual. Lymph node metastases are rare, at least at the time of the initial presentation; many of them seem to represent direct extension from the perinodal soft tissues rather than true embolic deposits.[415]

In the treatment of adenoid cystic carcinoma, a radical surgical approach should be used, no matter how well differentiated the tumor appears under the microscope.[420] Cures after tumor recurrence are very difficult to achieve. Radiation therapy is rarely curative, but it may improve results when combined with surgery,[436] and it may produce excellent temporary regression of inoperable recurrences.[431,438]

Salivary duct tumors

Salivary duct papilloma usually arises within minor salivary glands, but a few cases have been reported in the parotid.[460,464,467,471]

Salivary duct carcinoma is usually seen in elderly males, most commonly in the parotid gland but also in the submaxillary gland.[462,468,470] Microscopically, it resembles ductal carcinoma of the breast, whether comedo, solid, cribriform, papillary, mucinous, the usual invasive form, or even a sarcomatoid variety.[453,461,463,473,473a] (Fig. 12.33). In other words, it spans the same wide range of differentiation as its more common mammary counterpart, including low-grade varieties.[455,469,474] Fine needle aspiration specimens from high-grade tumors are easily recognizable, but the low-grade forms may lead to a false negative interpretation.[457,466] The immunohistochemical profile is that of a ductal-type adenocarcinoma, with expression of keratin (including CK14),[454a] HER2/neu,[473b] CEA, B72.3, and Lewis Y antigen.[452,475] It also frequently expresses androgen receptors (but usually no estrogen or progesterone receptors), GCDFP-15 (especially in the intraductal component), and prostate-specific antigen and other prostate-related markers.[458,465] The biomarker profile in terms of Her-2-neu, p53, and DNA content mirrors in general that of the corresponding type of mammary carcinoma.[459]

The high-grade invasive form of this tumor is markedly aggressive, with frequent metastases to both regional nodes and distant organs and a mortality rate of 70%.[454,470] Some cases develop on the basis of a pre-existing pleomorphic adenoma. The prognosis depends

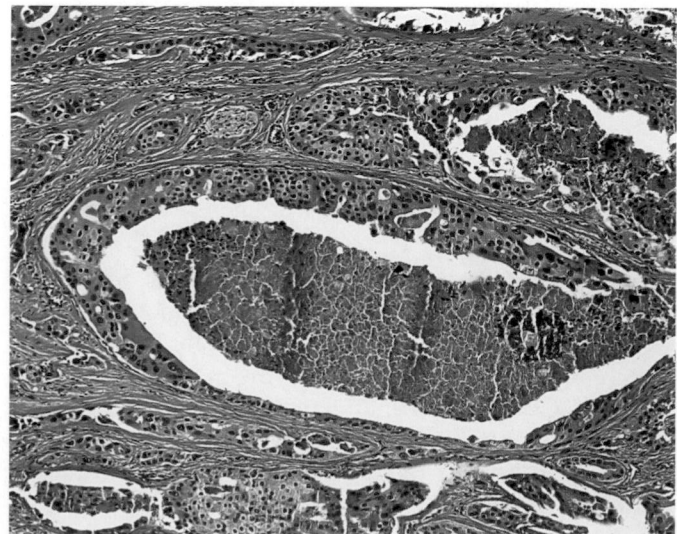

Fig. 12.33 High-grade ductal-type carcinoma of parotid gland. There is some degree of cytoplasmic apocrine-like change.

on the relative proportion of the in situ and invasive components, and on the microscopic grade of these components.[455,456] The pure intraductal tumors treated by a simple excision recur frequently, either with the same intraductal pattern or as invasive tumor.[451]

It should be pointed out that the term "salivary duct carcinoma" refers to the pattern of growth of the tumor rather than to its anatomic location. Most reported carcinomas of Stensen's duct have not been salivary duct carcinomas but rather mucoepidermoid, squamous cell, or undifferentiated carcinomas.[472]

Terminal duct carcinoma

Terminal duct carcinoma is also known as *lobular carcinoma* and *polymorphous low-grade adenocarcinoma*. It is usually restricted to the minor salivary glands of the oral cavity and is therefore discussed in Chapter 5.[477,478,481] Those occurring in the major salivary glands nearly always arise against a background of benign mixed tumor.[479,480] The main differential diagnosis is with adenoid cystic carcinoma and benign mixed tumor.[476,482]

Papillary adenocarcinoma

Papillary adenocarcinoma comprises less than 3% of all parotid tumors.[484,489] It may grow large and be accompanied by hemorrhage and necrosis. Similar cases have been described in the oral cavity.[486,488] Microscopically, the presence of well-defined papillary structures is the most important distinguishing feature. Mucin production is usually present, but there are no squamous or intermediate components (Fig. 12.34). If there is a prominent cystic component, the tumors are designated as *(papillary) cystadenocarcinomas*.[483,485] Sometimes the malignant papillary component is a focal feature in an otherwise benign-looking mucinous cystadenoma.[487] The differential diagnosis includes mucoepidermoid carcinoma, acinic cell carcinoma, and metastatic carcinoma, particularly from the thyroid. Blanck et al.[484] divided their cases into high- and low-grade varieties based on the presence or absence of stromal invasion. The former had a poor prognosis, comparable with that of adenoid cystic carcinoma, whereas the latter did not differ prognostically from low-grade mucoepidermoid carcinoma.

Squamous cell carcinoma

Most squamous cell carcinomas in the parotid region represent metastases in the intraparotid lymph nodes of tumors located in the oral cavity, some other region in the upper aerodigestive tract, or the skin.[492]

True pure squamous cell carcinomas of the salivary gland are very rare. Some represent the malignant component of a mixed tumor, and others are predominantly squamous cell types of high-grade mucoepidermoid tumors, as shown by their focal positivity for mucin stains. An in situ malignant ductal component has been occasionally encountered.[491] These tumors grow rapidly and infiltrate surrounding structures. The treatment of choice is radical surgery, but radiation therapy is also effective. The overall 5-year survival rate in a series of 18 cases from the Mayo Clinic was 50%.[490]

Small cell carcinoma and other neuroendocrine carcinomas

There are malignant tumors of the salivary gland that are entirely composed of a solid population of small cells with a darkly staining nucleus, high mitotic activity, and scanty cytoplasm.[498,504] Some of these tumors are indistinguishable from small cell carcinomas of the lung. They may be pure or associated with areas of glandular or squamous differentiation.[494,496,500,502] Ultrastructurally, dense-core granules suggestive of endocrine differentiation are found in most but not all of the cases.[497,499,504] Immunohistochemically, all of the 11 cases studied by Gnepp and Wick[495] expressed at least one neuroendocrine marker, such as Leu7, neuron-specific enolase (NSE), chromogranin, or synaptophysin. Keratin and epithelial membrane antigen (EMA) are also regularly expressed.

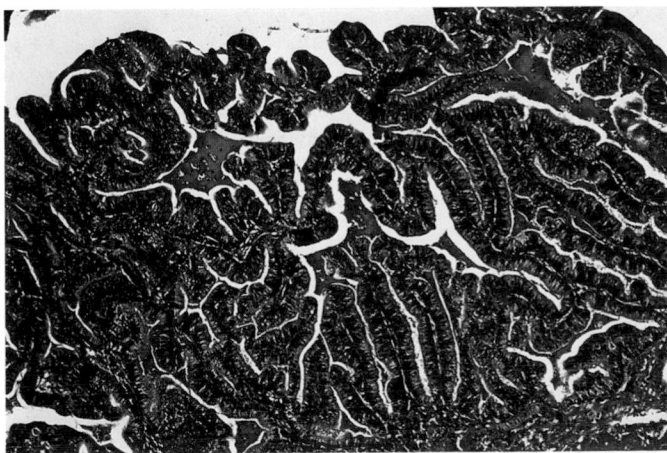

Fig. 12.34 Papillary adenocarcinoma of parotid gland.

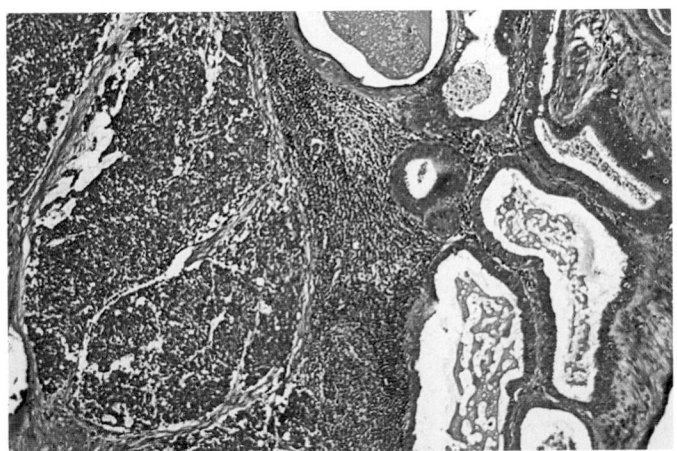

Fig. 12.35 Collision between Warthin's tumor (right) and Merkel cell carcinoma (left).

In a few instances, these tumors have been found to have features analogous to those of Merkel cell carcinoma of skin.[503] We have seen several cases, two of them associated with Warthin's tumor (Fig. 12.35).[493]

Large cell neuroendocrine carcinoma of the salivary gland has also been described, the criteria for its recognition being the same as for the homologous lung tumor.[501]

Lymphoepithelioma-like carcinoma

Lymphoepithelioma-like carcinoma is the preferred term for a type of salivary gland carcinoma that has also been reported as malignant lymphoepithelial lesion and lymphoepithelial carcinoma,[509,512,514] and which represents an important subtype of the undifferentiated carcinomas.[516] This tumor is particularly frequent among Eskimos and Chinese, in whom it may show evidence of familial clustering.[505,507,508,511,514] It presents as a unilateral mass, in either the parotid or submaxillary glands, in adult patients without any of the peripheral manifestations of Sjögren's syndrome. Its low-power appearance is reminiscent of Mikulicz's disease because of the mixture of epithelial solid islands and lymphoid tissue. However, high-power examination shows that the islands have malignant cytologic features throughout. The appearance is that of a nonkeratinizing large cell carcinoma, with occasional spindle-shaped areas, analogous by light and electron microscopy to the nasopharyngeal tumor classically known as lymphoepithelioma.[512,515] That the analogy may be more than morphologic is suggested by the fact that many of these patients have serologic evidence of Epstein–Barr virus infection,[514] and that EBV DNA has been found in the tumors by in situ hybridization and other molecular techniques.[506,510,513,517] Perineurial invasion may be present.[514] Immunohistochemically, there is strong positivity for keratin.[514] The reactive lymphoid tissue forms germinal centers and may exhibit focally a starry sky pattern. Regional lymph node metastases are very common, and distant metastases (particularly to the lung, liver, and bone) also occur.[508] Wide variations in mortality rates have been reported, but the overall outcome in the better documented cases seems to be relatively good.[514]

Other primary carcinomas

Some *adenocarcinomas* of salivary gland combine features of two histologically distinct types. They are referred to as **hybrid carcinomas**, and one of the two components is often of myoepithelial nature.[519,525] Other adenocarcinomas do not fit into any of the previously described patterns[518]; many of these are high-grade neoplasms, the malignancy of which is already obvious at the clinical level.[523] Some have a prominent *mucinous* component[526]; others grow in a *solid* or *undifferentiated* pattern throughout.[524,527] Some of these have been reported in children.[520] Some undifferentiated carcinomas are associated with a sarcoma-like component (so-called *carcinosarcomas*).[521,522]

Following the description of salivary duct carcinoma, terminal duct carcinoma, and epimyoepithelial carcinoma, the number of adenocarcinomas not otherwise specified has shrunk considerably.[518]

Endodermal sinus (yolk sac) tumor has been reported as a primary parotid neoplasm in childhood.[528]

Malignant lymphoma

Malignant lymphoma in the parotid region may arise from an intraparotid lymph node or in the gland itself. In the former instance, the histologic features and natural history of the disease are those of nodal lymphoma in general. When the salivary gland tissue is involved, this may represent the expression of disseminated involvement or, more commonly, a primary process of this organ. The large majority of primary lymphomas of salivary gland involve the parotid gland, but several cases of submaxillary gland disease are on record.[533,540] Clinically, most present as unilateral masses. The large majority of salivary gland lymphomas are of B-cell derivation. They can be composed of large cells (cleaved, noncleaved, or immunoblastic), small cells (small lymphocytic or small cleaved), or mixed.[535,540] In a series of 33 cases, 21 had a nodular pattern, and 12 were diffuse.[536] Sclerosis is a common feature, particularly among the large cell tumors.[546]

The lymphomas composed of small lymphoid cells often arise against a background of Mikulicz's disease (see p. 876). They have also been reported in transplant recipients[534] and in chronic sclerosing sialadenitis (Kuttner's tumor).[543]

Some salivary gland lymphomas are of follicular type, in the sense of having a follicular pattern of growth, being composed of cleaved cells, and featuring the 14;18 translocation.[538,539,545] Some have sclerosing features and simulate chronic sclerosing sialadenitis (Kuttner's tumor.[539a] Others—the majority—are composed of small lymphocytes and lack the above features. These tumors are currently regarded as belonging to the MALT/marginal zone type.[529,547] They are also characterized by a very slow evolution and an excellent long-term prognosis[546]; it is not unusual for recurrent disease to supervene in the contralateral parotid, skin, or in some other location a decade or more after the initial diagnosis.[532] In contrast, lymphomas composed of large cells (particularly if immunoblastic) run a rapidly progressive clinical course.[542] Cases of malignant lymphoma have also been observed in association with Warthin's tumor.[530,541] Isolated cases of **plasmacytoma** of the salivary gland have been reported, some later developing typical radiographic bone changes of multiple myeloma.[537,544]

T-cell lymphomas of salivary gland are rare but well documented.[536] These include tumors of T/natural killer cells. They may show prominent lymphoepithelial lesions, and cannot therefore be reliably distinguished from the B-cell tumors on morphologic grounds.[531]

Hodgkin's lymphoma presenting as a primary salivary gland neoplasm is very rare.[535] Most cases so diagnosed in the past would probably be reclassified today.

Other primary neoplasms

Benign vascular tumors of blood vessel and lymph vessel type (lymphangiomas) occur in the parotid gland.[565]

Capillary hemangioma of the benign (infantile) hemangioendothelioma type is the most common salivary gland tumor in infants and children.[567] It is often congenital and usually involves the parotid gland. It forms a diffuse soft mass without fixation to the overlying skin. Microscopically, it is made up of anastomosing thin-walled capillaries growing between salivary ducts and acini. The solid proliferation of endothelial cells and the presence of mitotic figures may lead to a mistaken diagnosis of malignant tumor.[556a] These lesions do not become malignant and can regress spontaneously. Some of the cases have been associated with the Kasabach–Merritt syndrome.[572]

Lipoma rarely involves the region of the parotid salivary gland.[550] It should be distinguished from *lipomatosis*, which is a diffuse nontumoral deposition of adipose tissue throughout the gland accompanied by enlargement of the organ. The latter has been seen in association with diabetes, cirrhosis, chronic alcoholism, malnutrition, and hormonal disturbances.[557] In some cases, this has been preceded by hypertrophy of the serous acinar cells, interstitial edema, and ductal atrophy, a process known as *sialosis* or *sialadenosis*.[548]

Schwannoma can arise from one of the fine radicles of the facial nerve and present clinically as a primary salivary gland tumor.[564] It is grossly encapsulated, and its microscopic appearance is similar to that of schwannomas elsewhere (see Chapter 25). Failure to recognize this neoplasm as benign may result in needless sacrifice of the facial nerve.

Rhabdomyoma often presents in the soft tissues of the submandibular area, but the gland itself is rarely affected.[568]

Solitary fibrous tumor has been reported in the parotid and in the submandibular gland.[561,563] Its morphologic appearance blends with that of hemangiopericytoma and its clinical course is similar to that of its soft tissue counterpart.[555]

Sialolipoma is a benign tumor composed of mature adipose tissue and glandular elements, which are probably entrapped.[569]

Skin adnexal-type tumors can occur within major salivary glands. These include tumors with the appearance of *pilomatrixoma*, *trichoadenoma* and *keratocystomas*[568a]; they are thought to be examples of choristomas, i.e.,

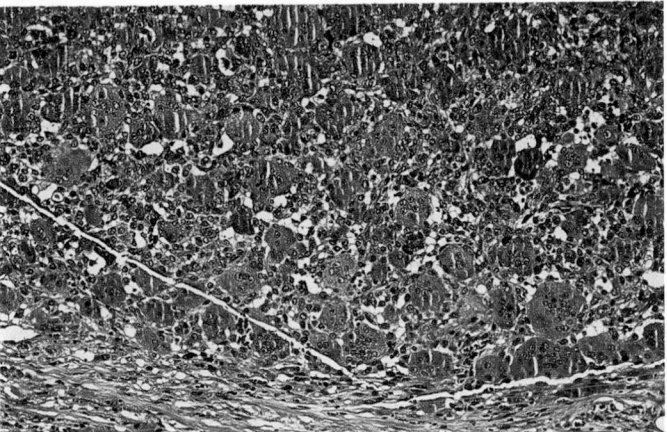

Fig. 12.36 Giant cell tumor of parotid. The appearance is very similar to the homonymous bone tumor.

malformative lesions composed of tissue not normally present in the region.[571] Others view them as true neoplasms.

Pilomatrixoma can present as an intraparotid or periparotid tumor and can be clinically confused with benign mixed tumor.

Embryoma (sialoblastoma) is a term used for a highly cellular epithelial parotid tumor of infancy with an embryonal or blastomatous appearance.[552,554,566] This tumor is probably of epithelial type and should be distinguished from the even rarer **teratoma** of salivary gland.[570] Some of the embryomas have recurred locally, and one had regional lymph node involvement.[563a]

Salivary gland anlage tumor is another congenital tumor of minor salivary gland type that has been described only in the nasopharynx[559] (see Chapter 7).

Sarcomas are very rare and need to be distinguished from epithelial, myoepithelial, and melanocytic tumors with a spindle cell pattern.[549] The types described in adults include *malignant peripheral nerve sheath tumor, fibrosarcoma, synovial sarcoma, Kaposi's sarcoma, angiosarcoma,*[560a] *Ewing's sarcoma/PNET,* and *malignant fibrous histiocytoma.*[549,553,556,558,574,575] In children, *embryonal rhabdomyosarcoma* can arise in the parotid region and secondarily invade the gland.[573]

Giant cell tumors similar to those of bone or soft tissue can occasionally develop in the salivary gland (Fig. 12.36).[551,560] The multinucleated giant cells resemble osteoclasts in all respects. In some of the reported cases, the giant cell component was associated with foci of carcinoma or "carcinosarcoma," a phenomenon similar to that observed with giant cell tumors of other organs, such as pancreas, thyroid gland, or breast.[560,562]

Metastatic tumors

Most metastatic tumors to this region are centered in intraparotid or submandibular lymph nodes.[580] As the tumor grows, it closely mimics a primary neoplasm of the salivary gland. It should be remembered that the most common tumor in the submaxillary region is a metastatic carcinoma in the submaxillary nodes rather than a primary salivary gland neoplasm. The most common types are squamous cell carcinoma (from the upper aerodigestive tract or skin) and malignant melanoma, including the desmoplastic variant of the latter.[578,581,582] Of the distant tumors metastasizing to this area, lung, kidney, and breast tumors are the most common.[576,579,580] Other reported sites include prostate and large bowel.[577,582]

General features of salivary gland tumors

Relative incidence and malignancy

Salivary gland tumors are 12 times more frequent in the parotid than in the submaxillary gland, a difference that cannot be explained on the basis of gland size alone. The majority are benign and largely represented by the benign mixed tumor.[590,600]

In a series of 2632 salivary gland tumors reported by Eneroth,[589] the incidence of malignancy was 17% for the parotid gland, 38% for the submaxillary gland, and 44% for the palate. The incidence of malignancy is highest for tumors of the sublingual gland.[590] The most common malignant tumor of the parotid gland is mucoepidermoid carcinoma, followed by undifferentiated carcinoma and acinic cell carcinoma. Adenoid cystic carcinoma comprises most submaxillary and palatal malignant salivary gland neoplasms.[586]

Most tumors of major salivary glands are unilateral and single. Bilaterality and multiplicity are common only in Warthin's tumor but can also be seen with benign mixed tumor and acinic cell carcinoma.[592]

Tumors of minor salivary glands can be found anywhere in the oral cavity, including the hard and soft palate, cheek, gingiva, tonsillar area, and tongue.[591] Their frequency seems to be roughly proportional to the amount of normal glandular tissue in this area, which may explain their marked predilection for the hard palate. They can also occur in the lip (particularly upper lip), nasal cavity and paranasal sinuses, ear, jaw, pharynx, larynx, trachea, and bronchi. Furthermore, tumors of the salivary gland type may arise from a variety of glandular structures, particularly breast and sweat glands (see Chapters 4 and 20).

Finally, salivary gland tumors of various types have been described as arising from lymph nodes located in or around the major salivary gland, presumably on the basis of ectopic salivary tissue. Warthin's tumor is by far the most common type, but examples of sebaceous lymphadenoma, benign mixed tumor, basal cell adenoma, acinic cell carcinoma, and mucoepidermoid carcinoma have also been reported.[596,599]

Little is known about the etiology of salivary gland tumors, and high-risk populations have not been identified except for the rare lymphoepithelioma-like carcinoma[583] (see p. 896). An increased incidence of benign mixed tumors and other neoplasms has been observed following therapeutic childhood irradiation,[598,601] and a possible increase in carcinomas (particularly of mucoepidermoid type) has been noted among atomic bomb survivors.[597]

A sudden, sustained, and as yet unexplained doubling in the incidence of salivary gland carcinoma has been documented in the male population of the San Francisco–Oakland area, which apparently is unrelated to the AIDS epidemic.[593]

In children, the most common salivary gland tumor is benign mixed tumor, but the proportion of malignant tumors is higher than in adults. Among the malignant neoplasms, mucoepidermoid carcinoma, adenoid cystic carcinoma, and acinic cell carcinoma are the most common.[585,587,588,594]

Clinical diagnosis

Benign tumors of the minor salivary glands usually can be distinguished from the high-grade malignant varieties on the basis of their clinical and gross characteristics. The presence of facial nerve paralysis is almost diagnostic of malignancy. These criteria do not apply for the low-grade acinic cell carcinomas and mucoepidermoid carcinomas, since their clinical presentation is usually indistinguishable from that of benign neoplasms. The reverse also may be true, although only in rare cases. Warthin's tumor, for instance, may be clinically thought to be malignant because of its adherence to the skin.

Staging

A clinical staging system using the TNM classification scheme for salivary gland tumors has been proposed. It is based on five parameters: size of the primary tumor, local extension, palpability of the regional lymph nodes, degree of suspicion of the regional lymph nodes, and the presence or absence of distant metastases (see Appendix C).[584,595]

Biopsy and cytology

Tumors of the submaxillary gland are usually treated by removal of the gland without previous biopsy. For tumors of the parotid glands, several choices are available depending on the size and location of the tumor, clinical features, and expertise of the pathologist. Tumors involving the superficial parotid lobe lacking clinical features of malignancy can be properly handled by a superficial lobectomy with frozen section, any subsequent therapy depending on the diagnosis of the frozen section. Obviously malignant tumors with skin invasion can usually be diagnosed with a small incisional biopsy and treated accordingly. Other options are core needle biopsy and fine needle aspiration. Although the former usually provides diagnostic material, the possibility of implantation along the needle track and the difficulty sometimes encountered in the differential diagnosis (particularly among adenoid cystic carcinoma, monomorphic adenoma, and benign mixed tumor) have resulted in a less than enthusiastic response from clinicians and pathologists. Instead, fine needle aspiration has been used successfully by several European institutions (particularly the Karolinska Institute in Sweden) and has now become widespread in the United States (Figs 12.37 and 12.38).[602,603,616] The overall accuracy rate has been over 90% in most reported series.[604,608,610,611,614] The fine needle aspiration procedure can induce necrotic and reparative

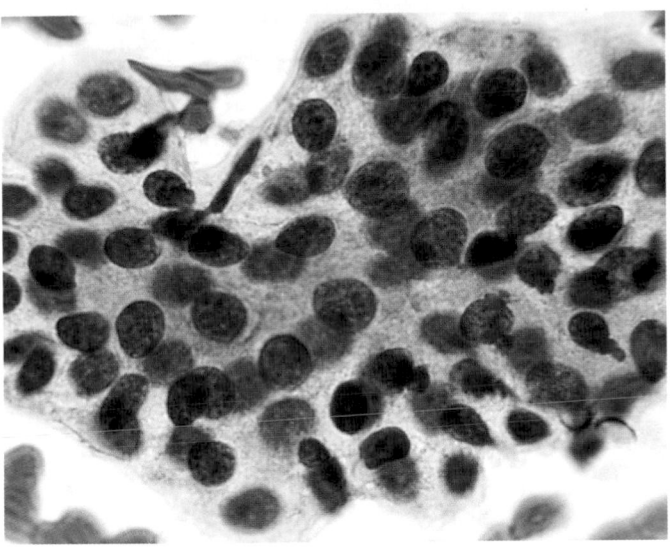

Fig. 12.38 Typical appearance of adenoid cystic carcinoma on FNA. The nuclei are small and hyperchromatic. There is a pink amorphous basement membrane-like material, which corresponds to the "cylinders" seen in the histologic sections.

changes in the tumor, particularly if composed of oncocytes[609]; however, the subsequent microscopic evaluation of the case is rarely compromised.[613]

Frozen section

Intraoperative examination of salivary gland tumors is an accurate procedure that can help the surgeon determine the extent of the surgery needed, particularly for parotid neoplasms.[605,606] Obviously, the usefulness of this procedure depends on the expertise of the pathologist in providing accurate diagnoses and the wisdom of the surgeon in applying this information.[615] The most common error with this technique is to misdiagnose a mucoepidermoid carcinoma as a benign neoplasm.[607,612]

Treatment

The extent of surgical treatment of parotid tumors is determined by their microscopic type and the anatomic peculiarities of the parotid gland, particularly its intimate relationship with the facial nerve.[619,624]

Fortunately, most parotid benign mixed tumors arise from the superficial lobe, so a superficial or partial parotidectomy with preservation of the nerve can be performed; actually, the nerve can be preserved in selected cases even if the entire gland is removed.[625]

Most low-grade malignant tumors of mucoepidermoid or acinic cell type can be treated in a similar fashion. If the carcinoma is advanced and/or high grade, total parotidectomy with sacrifice of the facial nerve is usually necessary. If there is clinical evidence of nodal involvement, this procedure needs to be coupled with radical neck dissection. Elective wide dissection should be considered in tumors that are of high grade and/or larger than 4 cm.[617]

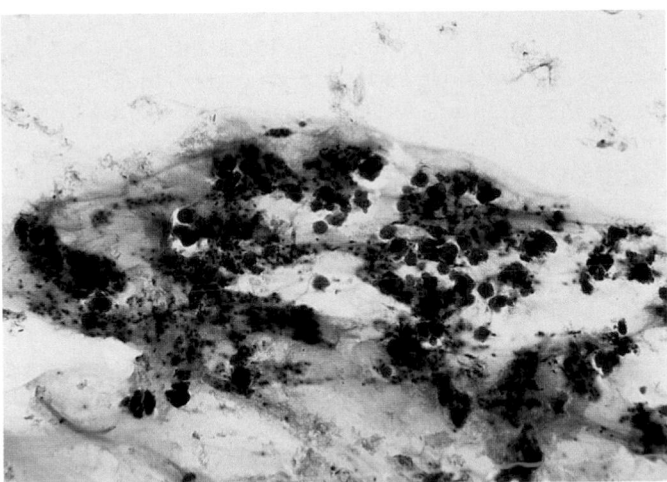

A

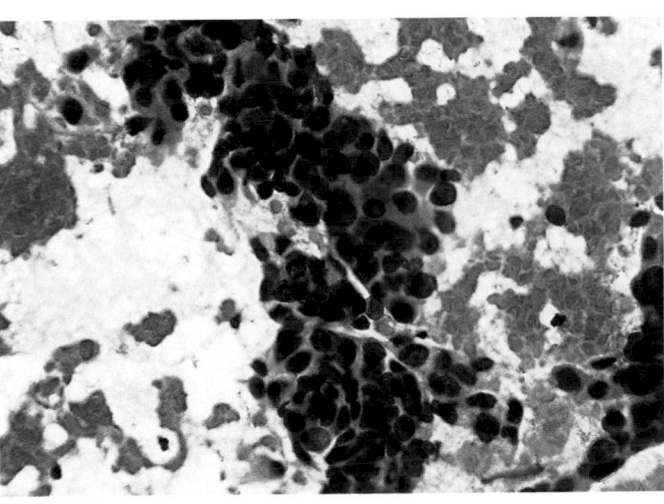

B

Fig. 12.37 A, Fine needle aspiration specimen from a benign mixed tumor of parotids. Clusters of benign-appearing epithelial cells are seen against a bluish myxoid matrix. Tyrosine-rich crystals are also present. **B,** Fine needle aspiration of mucoepidermoid carcinoma of parotid gland. Most of the cells are of the so-called "third" cell type, and some exhibit focal squamous differentiation. (**A**, Courtesy of Dr. Maureen Zakowski, Memorial Sloan-Kettering Cancer Center)

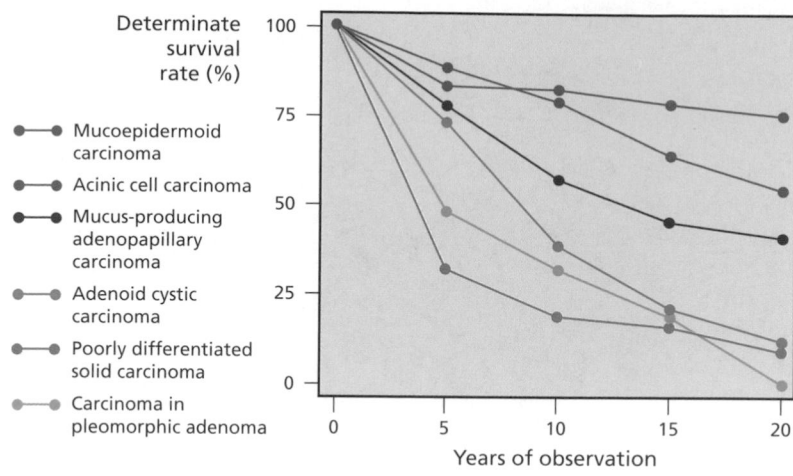

Determinate survival rate (%)

- ●━━● Mucoepidermoid carcinoma
- ●━━● Acinic cell carcinoma
- ●━━● Mucus-producing adenopapillary carcinoma
- ●━━● Adenoid cystic carcinoma
- ●━━● Poorly differentiated solid carcinoma
- ●━━● Carcinoma in pleomorphic adenoma

Years of observation

Fig. 12.39 Survival rates in malignant salivary gland tumors. (From Eneroth CM, Hamberger CA. Principles of treatment of different types of parotid tumors. Laryngoscope 1974, **84**: 1732–1740.)

The surgical treatment of submaxillary tumors, whether benign or malignant, is total removal of the gland. The recurrence rate of carcinomas of this particular gland is relatively high because of the close relation of the gland to the mandible.

Patients who develop postoperative recurrence of high-grade malignant salivary gland tumors do poorly; most have a relatively short survival, and subsequent treatment is effective in only one of four cases.

Radiation therapy has been used as the primary form of therapy in inoperable tumors and as a postoperative modality in cases selected on the basis of the microscopic type and surgical procedure.[620,622] There is evidence that this may result in a decrease in the incidence of local recurrence.[618,621,623]

Prognosis

The prognosis of salivary gland tumors is determined by the clinical staging, location, and microscopic type[629,630,633,634] (see Appendix C) (Fig. 12.39). This has led to the proposal of a prognostic score in which these various parameters are included.[638] Malignant tumors of the submaxillary gland have a higher incidence of recurrence and metastases than parotid tumors of the same type.[626,628] For adenoid cystic carcinoma, the prognosis is best when located in the palate, intermediate when in the parotid gland, and worst in the submaxillary gland. For parotid malignant tumors, the presence of facial nerve paralysis is an ominous prognostic sign. In regard to microscopic types, the prognosis is best for the low-grade variants of mucoepidermoid and acinic cell carcinoma and worst for the high-grade variants of these tumors and for adenoid cystic carcinoma, malignant mixed tumor, salivary duct carcinoma, and squamous cell carcinoma. Additional prognostic parameters are discussed in connection with the respective tumor types.

DNA ploidy analysis and AgNOR determinations have shown higher values in high-grade carcinomas (such as salivary duct carcinoma) than in low-grade carcinomas or benign mixed tumors but have not yet proved to have independent prognostic value.[631]

Amplification of c-*erb*B-2 oncogene[637] and p53 oncoprotein expression[632] have been claimed to correlate with aggressive behavior, but it is not clear that these parameters represent independent prognostic determinators.[627,635,636]

References

Normal anatomy

1 Conley J. Salivary glands and the facial nerve. New York, 1975, Grune & Stratton.
2 Dardick I, Byard RW, Carnegie JA. A review of the proliferative capacity of major salivary glands and the relationship to current concepts of neoplasia in salivary glands. Oral Surg Oral Med Oral Pathol 1990, **69**: 53–67.
3 Dardick I, van Nostrand AWP. Morphogenesis of salivary gland tumors. A prerequisite to improving classification. Pathol Annu 1987, **22**(Pt1): 1–53.
4 Foschini MP, Scarpellini F, Gown AM, Eusebi V. Differential expression of myoepithelial markers in salivary, sweat and mammary glands. Intern J Surg Pathol 2000, **8**: 29–38.
5 Martínez-Madrigal F, Bosq J, Casiraghi O. Major salivary glands. In Sternberg S (ed.): Histology for pathologists, ed. 2. Philadelphia, 1997, Lippincott-Raven Publishers, pp. 405–432.
6 Seifert G. The pathology of the salivary gland immune system. Diseases and correlations with other organ systems. Surg Pathol 1993, **5**: 161–180.
7 Tazawa K, Kurihara Y, Kamoshida S, Tsukada K, Tsutsumi Y. Localization of prostate-specific antigen-like immunoreactivity in human salivary gland and salivary gland tumors. Pathol Int 1999, **49**: 500–505.

Heterotopia

8 Brown RB, Gaillard RA, Turner JA. Significance of aberrant or heterotopic parotid gland tissue in lymph nodes. Ann Surg 1953, **138**: 850–856.
9 Carney JA. Salivary heterotopia, cysts, and the parathyroid gland: Branchial pouch derivatives and remnants. Am J Surg Pathol 2000, **24**: 837–845.
10 Evans MG, Rubin SZ. Pleomorphic adenoma arising in a salivary rest in childhood. J Pediatr Surg 1991, **26**: 1314–1315.

11 Jernstrom P, Prietto CA. Accessory parotid gland tissue at base of neck. Arch Pathol 1962, **73**: 473–480.

12 Ludmer B, Joachims HZ, Ben-Arie J, Eliachar I. Adenocarcinoma in heterotopic salivary tissue. Arch Otolaryngol 1981, **107**: 547–548.

13 Luna M, Monheit J. Salivary gland neoplasms arising in lymph nodes. A clinicopathologic analysis of 13 cases (abstract). Lab Invest 1988, **58**: 58A.

14 Martinez-Madrigal F, Bosq J, Casiraghi O. Major salivary glands. In Sternberg SS (ed.): Histology for pathologists, ed. 2. Philadelphia, 1997, Lippincott-Raven, pp. 418–419.

15 Shinohara M, Harada T, Nakamura S, Oka M, Tashiro H. Heterotopic salivary gland tissue in lymph nodes of the cervical region. Int J Oral Maxillofac Surg 1992, **21**: 166–171.

16 Singer MI, Applebaum EL, Loy KD. Heterotopic salivary gland tissue in the neck. Laryngoscope 1979, **89**: 1772–1777.

17 Youngs LA, Scoffield HH. Heterotopic salivary gland tissue in the lower neck. Arch Pathol 1967, **83**: 550–556.

Sialolithiasis

18 Blatt IM, Denning RM, Zumberge JH, Maxwell JH. Studies in sialolithiasis. Ann Otol Rhinol Laryngol 1958, **67**: 595–617.

19 Bruneton JN, Mourou MY. Ultrasound in salivary gland disease. ORL J Otorhinolaryngol Relat Spec 1993, **55**: 284–289.

20 Ho V, Currie WJ, Walker A. Sialolithiasis of minor salivary glands. Br J Oral Maxillofac Surg 1992, **30**: 273–275.

21 Husted E. Sialolithiasis. Acta Chir Scand 1953, **105**: 161–171.

22 Iro H, Waitz G, Nitsche N, Benninger J, Schneider T, Ell C. Extracorporeal piezoelectric shock-wave lithotripsy of salivary gland stones. Laryngoscope 1992, **102**: 492–494.

23 Konigsberger R, Feyh J, Goetz A, Kastenbauer E. Endoscopically-controlled electrohydraulic intracorporeal shock wave lithotripsy (EISL) of salivary stones. J Otolaryngol 1993, **22**: 12–13.

24 Lutcavage GJ, Schaberg SJ. Bilateral submandibular sialolithiasis and concurrent sialadenitis. A case report. J Oral Maxillofac Surg 1991, **49**: 1220–1222.

25 Raymond AK, Batsakis JG. Angiolithiasis and sialolithiasis in the head and neck. Ann Otol Rhinol Laryngol 1992, **101**: 455–457.

26 Shinohara M, Oka M, Yamada K, Hashimura K, Yuba K, Mori M. Immunohistochemical and electron microscopic studies of obstructive lesions in submandibular glands. J Oral Pathol Oral Med 1992, **21**: 370–375.

27 Traxler M, Schurawitzki H, Ulm C, Solar P, Blahout R, Piehslinger E, Schadlbauer E. Sonography of nonneoplastic disorders of the salivary glands. Int J Oral Maxillofac Surg 1992, **21**: 360–363.

Sialadenitis

28 Akiner MN, Saatci MR, Yilmaz O, Erekul S. Intraglandular toxoplasmosis lymphadenitis of the parotid gland. J Laryngol Otol 1991, **105**: 860–862.

29 Batsakis JG. Sclerosing polycystic adenosis: Newly recognized salivary gland lesion – A form of chronic sialadenitis? Adv Anat Pathol 1996, **3**: 298–304.

30 Brook I. Diagnosis and management of parotitis. Arch Otolaryngol Head Neck Surg 1992, **118**: 469–471.

31 Chan JK. Kuttner tumor (chronic sclerosing sialadenitis) of the submandibular gland: an underrecognized entity. Adv Anat Pathol 1998, **5**: 239–251.

32 Chetty R. HIV-associated lymphoepithelial cysts and lesions: morphological and immunohistochemical study of the lymphoid cells. Histopathology 1998, **33**: 222–229.

33 Harrison JD, Epivatianos A, Bhatia SN. Role of microliths in the aetiology of chronic submandibular sialadenitis: a clinicopathological investigation of 154 cases. Histopathology 1997, **31**: 237–251.

34 Kurashima C, Hirokawa K. Age-related increase of focal lymphocytic infiltration in the human submandibular glands. J Oral Pathol 1986, **15**: 172–178.

35 O'Brien CJ, Murrant BJ. Surgical management of chronic parotitis. Head Neck 1993, **15**: 445–449.

36 Padfield CJH, Choyce MQ, Eveson JW. Xanthogranulomatous sialadenitis. Histopathology 1993, **23**: 488–491.

37 Rásánen O, Jokinen K, Dammert K. Sclerosing inflammation of the submandibular salivary gland (Kuttner tumour). Acta Otolaryngol 1972, **74**: 297–301.

38 Seifert G. Tumour-like lesions of the salivary glands. The new WHO classification. Pathol Res Pract 1992, **188**: 836–846.

39 Seifert G. Aetiological and histological classification of sialadenitis. Pathologica 1997, **89**: 7–17.

40 Singh B, Maharaj TJ. Tuberculosis of the parotid gland. Clinically indistinguishable from a neoplasm. J Laryngol Otol 1992, **106**: 929–931.

41 Skàlovà A, Michal M, Simpson RHW, Stàrek I, Pradna J, Pfaltz M. Sclerosing polycystic adenosis of parotid gland with dysplasia and ductal carcinoma in situ. Report of three cases with immunohistochemical and ultrastructural examination. Virchows Arch 2002, **440**: 29–35.

42 Smith BC, Ellis GL, Slater LJ, Foss RD. Sclerosing polycystic adenosis of major salivary glands: A clinicopathologic analysis of nine cases. Am J Surg Pathol 1996, **20**: 161–170.

42a Tiemann M, Teymoortash A, Schrader C, Werner J, Parwaresch R, Seifert G, Klöppel G. Chronic sclerosing sialadenitis of the submandibular gland is mainly due to a T lymphocyte immune reaction. Mod Pathol 2002, **15**: 845–852.

43 Triantafyllou A, Harrison JD, Donath K. Microlithiasis in parotid sialadenosis and chronic submandibular sialadenitis is related to the microenvironment: an ultrastructural and microanalytical investigation. Histopathology 1998, **32**: 530–535.

44 Van der Walt JD, Leake J. Granulomatous sialadenitis of the major salivary glands. A clinicopathological study of 57 cases. Histopathology 1987, **11**: 131–144.

Benign lymphoepithelial cysts and HIV-related lesions

45 Badve S, Evans G, Mady S, Coppen M, Sloane J. A case of Warthin's tumor with coexistent Hodgkin's disease. Histopathology 1993, **22**: 280–281.

46 Bernier JL, Bhaskar SN. Lymphoepithelial lesions of salivary glands. Histogenesis and classification based on 186 cases. Cancer 1958, **11**: 1156–1179.

47 Cohen MN, Rao U, Shedd DP. Benign cysts of the parotid gland. J Surg Oncol 1984, **27**: 85–88.

48 Dobson CM, Ellis HA. Polycystic disease of the parotid glands. Case report of a rare entity and review of the literature. Histopathology 1987, **11**: 953–961.

49 Elliott JN, Oertel YC. Lymphoepithelial cysts of the salivary glands. Histological and cytologic features. Am J Clin Pathol 1990, **93**: 39–43.

50 Finfer MD, Schinella RA, Chiriboga LA, Rothstein SG, Persky MS, Feiner HD. Cystic lesions of the parotid gland in patients at risk for AIDS. An immunohistochemical study. Surg Pathol 1991, **4**: 35–45.

51 Ihrler S, Zietz C, Riederer A, Diebold J, Lohrs U. HIV-related parotid lymphoepithelial cysts. Immunohistochemistry and 3-D reconstruction of surgical and autopsy material with special reference to formal pathogenesis. Virchows Arch 1996, **429**: 139–148.

52 Labouyrie E, Merlio JP, Beylot-Barry M, Delord B, Vergier B, Brossard G, Lacoste D, Beylot J, Leng B, Fleury H, et al. Human immunodeficiency virus type I replication within cystic lymphoepithelial lesion of the salivary gland. Am J Clin Pathol 1993, **100**: 41–46.

53 Maiorano E, Favia F, Viale G. Lymphoepithelial cysts of salivary glands: an immunohistochemical study of HIV-related and HIV-unrelated lesions. Hum Pathol 1998, **29**: 260–265.

54 Pieterse AS, Seymour AE. Parotid cysts. An analysis of 16 cases and suggested classification. Pathology 1981, **13**: 225–234.

55 Schiodt M. HIV-associated salivary gland disease. A review. Oral Surg Oral Med Oral Pathol 1992, **73**: 164–167.

56 Seifert G, Thomsen St, Donath K. Bilateral dysgenetic polycystic parotid glands. Morphological analysis and differential diagnosis of a rare disease of the salivary glands. Virchows Arch [A] 1981, **390**: 273–288.

57 Shaha AR, Di Maio T, Webber C, Thelmo W, Jaffe BM. Benign lymphoepithelial lesions of the parotid. Am J Surg 1993, **166**: 403–406.

58 Smyth AG, Ward-Booth RP, High AS. Polycystic disease of the parotid glands. Two familial cases. Br J Oral Maxillofac Surg 1993, **31**: 38–40.

59 Suster S, Rosai J. Multilocular thymic cyst. An acquired reactive process. Study of 18 cases. Am J Surg Pathol 1991, **15**: 388–398.

60 Terry JH, Loree TR, Thomas MD, Marti JR. Major salivary gland lymphoepithelial lesions and the acquired immunodeficiency syndrome. Am J Surg 1991, **162**: 324–329.

61 Weidner N, Geisinger KR, Sterling RT, Miller TR, Yen TSB. Benign lymphoepithelial cysts of the parotid gland. A histologic, cytologic, and ultrastructural study. Am J Clin Pathol 1986, **85**: 395–401.

Mikulicz's disease and Sjögren's syndrome

62 Anderson LG, Talal N. The spectrum of benign to malignant lymphoproliferation in Sjögren's syndrome. Clin Exp Immunol 1971, **9**: 199–221.

63 Bodeutsch C, de Wilde PC, Kater L, van Houwelingen JC, van den Hoogen FH, Kruize AA, Hene RJ, van de Putte LB, Voojis GP. Quantitative immunohistochemical criteria are superior to the lymphocytic focus score criterion for the diagnosis of Sjögren's syndrome. Arthritis Rheum 1992, **35**: 1075–1087.

64 Caselitz J, Osborn M, Wustrow J, Seifert G, Weber K. Immunohistochemical investigations on the epimyoepithelial islands in lymphoepithelial lesions. Use of monoclonal keratin antibodies. Lab Invest 1986, **55**: 427–432.

65 Chaudhry AP, Cutler LS, Yamane GM, Satchidanand S, Labay G, Sunder Raj M. Light and ultrastructural features of lymphoepithelial lesions of the salivary glands in Mikulicz's disease. J Pathol 1986, **146**: 239–250.

66 Chevalier X, Gaulard P, Voisin MC, Martigny J, Farcet JP, Larget-Piet B. Peripheral T cell lymphoma with Sjögren's syndrome. A report with immunologic and genotypic studies. J Rheumatol 1991, **18**: 1744–1746.

67 Constantopoulos SH, Tsianos EV, Moutsopoulos HM. Pulmonary and gastrointestinal manifestations of Sjögren's syndrome. Rheum Dis Clin North Am 1992, **18**: 617–635.

68 Di Giuseppe JA, Wu TC, Corio RL. Analysis of Epstein-Barr virus-encoded small RNA 1 expression in benign lymphoepithelial salivary gland lesions. Mod Pathol 1994, **7**: 555–559.

69 Diss TC, Wotherspoon AC, Speight P, Pan L, Isaacson PG. B-cell monoclonality, Epstein Barr virus, and t(14; 18) in myoepithelial sialadenitis and low-grade B-cell MALT lymphoma of the parotid gland. Am J Surg Pathol 1995, **19**: 531–536.

70 Falzon M, Isaacson PG. The natural history of benign lymphoepithelial lesion of the salivary gland in which there is a monoclonal population of B cells. A report of two cases. Am J Surg Pathol 1991, **15**: 59–65.

71 Fishleder A, Tubbs R, Hesse B, Levine H. Uniform detection of immunoglobulin-gene rearrangement in benign, lymphoepithelial lesions. N Engl J Med 1987, **316**: 1118–1121.

72 Fox RI, Kang HI. Pathogenesis of Sjögren's syndrome. Rheum Dis Clin North Am 1992, **18**: 517–538.

73 Friedlaender MH. Ocular manifestations of Sjögren's syndrome. Keratoconjunctivitis sicca. Rheum Dis Clin North Am 1992, **18**: 591–608.

74 Harris NL. Lymphoid proliferations of the salivary glands. Am J Clin Pathol 1999, **111**: S94–S103.

75 Hsi ED, Siddiqui J, Schnitzer B, Alkan S, Ross CW. Analysis of immunoglobulin heavy chain gene rearrangement in myoepithelial sialadenitis by polymerase chain reaction. Am J Clin Pathol 1996, **106**: 498–503.

76 Ihrler S, Zietz C, Sendelhofert A, Riederer A, Lohrs U. Lymphoepithelial duct lesions in Sjogren-type sialadenitis. Virchows Arch 1999, **434**: 315–324.

77 Kahn LB. Benign lymphoepithelial lesion (Mikulicz's disease) of the salivary gland. An ultrastructural study. Hum Pathol 1979, **10**: 99–104.

78 Lasota J, Miettinen MM. Coexistence of different B-cell clones in consecutive lesions of low-grade MALT lymphoma of the salivary gland in Sjögren's disease. Mod Pathol 1997, **10**: 872–878.

79 MacLean H, Ironside JW, Cullen JF, Butt Z. Mikulicz syndrome and disease. 2 case reports highlighting the difference. Acta Ophthalmol 1993, **71**: 136–141.

80 McCurley TL, Collins RD, Ball E, Collins RD. Nodal and extranodal lymphoproliferative disorders in Sjögren's syndrome. A clinical and immunopathologic study. Hum Pathol 1990, **21**: 482–492.

81 Miller DG. The association of immune disease and malignant lymphoma. Ann Intern Med 1967, **66**: 507–521.

82 Molina R, Provost TT, Arnett FC, Bias WB, Hochberg MC, Wilson RW, Alexander EL. Primary Sjögren's syndrome in men. Clinical, serologic, and immunogenetic features. Am J Med 1986, **80**: 23–31.

83 Morgan WS, Castleman B. A clinicopathologic study of "Mikulicz's disease." Am J Pathol 1953, **29**: 471–503.

84 Palmer RM, Eveson JW, Gusterson BA. "Epimyoepithelial" islands in lymphoepithelial lesions. Virchows Arch [A] 1986, **408**: 603–609.

85 Quintana PG, Kapadia SB, Bahler DW, Johnson JT, Swerdlow SH. Salivary gland lymphoid infiltrates associated with lymphoepithelial lesions: a clinicopathologic, immunophenotypic, and genotypic study. Hum Pathol 1997, **28**: 850–861.

86 Schmid U, Helbron D, Lennert K. Development of malignant lymphoma in myoepithelial sialadenitis (Sjögren's syndrome). Virchows Arch [A] 1982, **395**: 11–43.

87 Scott CA, Avellini C, Desinan L, Pirisi M, Ferraccioli FG, Bardus P, Fabris C, Casatta L, Bartoli E, Beltrami CA. Chronic lymphocytic sialoadenitis in HCV-related chronic liver disease: comparison with Sjögren's syndrome. Histopathology 1997, **30**: 41–48.

88 Tsokos M, Lazarou SA, Moutsopoulos HM. Vasculitis in primary Sjögren's syndrome. Histologic classification and clinical presentation. Am J Clin Pathol 1987, **88**: 26–31.

89 van der Valk PG, Hollema H, van Voorst Vander PC, Brinker MG, Poppema S. Sjögren's syndrome with specific cutaneous manifestations and multifocal clonal T-cell populations progressing to a cutaneous pleomorphic T-cell lymphoma. Am J Clin Pathol 1989, **92**: 357–361.

90 Vivancos J, Bosch X, Grau JM, Coca A, Font J. Development of Hodgkin's disease in the course of primary Sjögren's syndrome. Br J Rheumatol 1992, **31**: 561–563.

91 Warfvinge G, Larsson A, Henricsson V, Ericsson UB, Hansen B, Manthorpe R. Salivary gland involvement in autoimmune thyroiditis, with special reference to the degree of association with Sjögren's syndrome. Oral Surg Oral Med Oral Pathol 1992, **74**: 288–293.

92 Weisbrot IM. Lymphomatoid granulomatosis of the lung, associated with a long history of benign lymphoepithelial lesions of the salivary glands and lymphoid interstitial pneumonitis. Report of a case. Am J Clin Pathol 1976, **66**: 792–801.

93 Wen S, Shimizu N, Yoshiyama H, Mizugaki Y, Shinozaki F, Takada K. Association of Epstein-Barr virus (EBV) with Sjogren's syndrome. Differential EBV expression between epithelial cells

and lymphocytes in salivary glands. Am J Pathol 1996, **149:** 1511–1517.

94 Zulman J, Jaffe R, Talal N. Evidence that the malignant lymphoma of Sjögren's syndrome is a monoclonal B-cell neoplasm. N Engl J Med 1978, **299:** 1215–1220.

Irradiation effect

95 Leslie MD, Dische S. Changes in serum and salivary amylase during radiotherapy for head and neck cancer. A comparison of conventionally fractionated radiotherapy with CHART. Radiother Oncol 1992, **24:** 27–31.

96 Nagler RM, Baum BJ, Fox PC. Acute effects of X irradiation on the function of rat salivary glands. Radiat Res 1993, **136:** 42–47.

Other non-neoplastic lesions

97 Arafat A, Brannon RB, Ellis GL. Adenomatoid hyperplasia of mucous salivary glands. Oral Surg Oral Med Oral Pathol 1981, **52:** 51–55.

98 Fischer JR, Abdul-Karim FW, Robinson RA. Intraparotid nodular fasciitis. Arch Pathol Lab Med 1989, **113:** 1276–1278.

99 Foucar E, Rosai J, Dorfman RD. Sinus histiocytosis with massive lymphoadenopathy (Rosai-Dorfman disease). Review of the entity. Semin Diagn Pathol 1990, **7:** 19–73.

100 Herold J, Nicholson AG. Fine needle aspiration cytology in the diagnosis of amyloid in the submandibular gland. Br J Oral Maxillofac Surg 1992, **30:** 393–394.

101 Juskevicius R, Finley JL. Rosai-Dorfman disease of the parotid gland: cytologic and histopathologic findings with immunohistochemical correlation. Arch Pathol Lab Med 2001, **125:** 1348–1350.

102 Myssiorek D, Alvi A, Bhuiya T. Primary salivary gland amyloidosis causing sicca syndrome. Ann Otol Rhinol Laryngol 1992, **101:** 487–490.

103 Williams SB, Foss RD, Ellis GL. Inflammatory pseudotumors of the major salivary glands. Clinicopathologic and immunohistochemical analysis of six cases. Am J Surg Pathol 1992, **16:** 896–902.

104 Yu G-Y, Donath K, Mult D. Adenomatous ductal proliferation of the salivary gland. Oral Surg Oral Med Oral Pathol Oral Radiol Endod 2001, **91:** 215–221.

Epithelial tumors
Classification

105 Seifert G, Brocheriou C, Cardesa A, Eveson JW. WHO International Histological Classification of Salivary Gland Tumors. Pathol Res Pract 1990, **186:** 555–581.

106 Seifert G, Sobin LH. The World Health Organization's Histological Classification of Salivary Gland Tumors. A commentary on the second edition. Cancer 1992, **70:** 379–385.

107 Simpson RHW. Classification of tumours of the salivary glands. Histopathology 1994, **24:** 187–191.

Tumors with stromal differentiation
Benign mixed tumor (pleomorphic adenoma)

108 Altini M, Coleman H, Kienle F. Intra-vascular tumour in pleomorphic adenomas—a report of four cases. Histopathology 1997, **31:** 55–59.

109 Anderson C, Knibbs DR, Abbott SJ, Pedersen C, Krutchkoff D. Glial fibrillary acidic protein expression in pleomorphic adenoma of salivary gland. An immunoelectron microscopic study. Ultrastruct Pathol 1990, **14:** 263–271.

110 Azzopardi JG, Smith OD. Salivary gland tumours and their mucins. J Pathol Bacteriol 1959, **77:** 131–140.

111 Barton J, Slevin NJ, Gleave EN. Radiotherapy for pleomorphic adenoma of the parotid gland. Int J Radiat Oncol Biol Phys 1992, **22:** 925–928.

112 Bullerdiek J, Wobst G, Meyer-Bolte K, Chilla R, Haubrich J, Thode B, Bartnitzke S. Cytogenetic subtyping of 220 salivary gland pleomorphic adenomas. Correlation to occurrence, histological subtype, and in vitro cellular behavior. Cancer Genet Cytogenet 1993, **65:** 27–31.

113 Chaplin AJ, Darke P, Patel S. Tyrosine-rich crystals in pleomorphic adenomas of parotid glands. J Oral Pathol 1983, **12:** 342–346.

114 Chen KTK. Metastasizing pleomorphic adenoma of the salivary gland. Cancer 1978, **42:** 2407–2411.

115 Chu W, Strawitz JG. Parapharyngeal growth of parotid tumors. Report of two cases. Arch Surg 1977, **112:** 709–711.

116 Collina G, Eusebi V, Carasoli PT. Pleomorphic adenoma with lymph-node metastases. Report of two cases. Pathol Res Pract 1989, **184:** 188–193.

117 Cresson DH, Goldsmith M, Askin FB, Reddick RL, Postma DS, Siegal GP. Metastasizing pleomorphic adenoma with myoepithelial cell predominance. Pathol Res Pract 1990, **186:** 795–800.

118 Czader M, Eberhart CG, Bhatti N, Cummings C, Westra WH. Metastasizing mixed tumor of the parotid: Initial presentation as a solitary kidney tumor and ultimate carcinomatous transformation at the primary site. Am J Surg Pathol 2000, **24:** 1159–1164.

119 Dardick I, Ostrynski VL, Ekem JK, Leung R, Burford-Mason AP. Immunohistochemical and ultrastructural correlates of muscle-actin expression in pleomorphic adenomas and myoepitheliomas based on comparison of formalin and methanol fixation. Virchows Arch [A] 1992, **421:** 95–104.

120 Dardick I, van Nostrand AWP, Jeans MTD, Rippstein P, Edwards V. Pleomorphic adenoma. II. Ultrastructural organization of "stromal" regions. Hum Pathol 1983, **14:** 798–809.

121 Dardick I, van Nostrand AWP, Phillips MJ. Histogenesis of salivary gland pleomorphic adenoma (mixed tumor) with an evaluation of the role of the myoepithelial cell. Hum Pathol 1982, **13:** 62–75.

122 David R, Buchner A. Elastosis in benign and malignant salivary gland tumors. Cancer 1980, **45:** 2301–2310.

123 Debiec-Richter M, Van Valckenborgh I, Van den Broeck C, Hagemeijer A, Van de Ven WJ, Kas K, Van Damme B, Voz ML. Histologic localization of PLAG1 (pleomorphic adenoma gene 1) in pleomorphic adenoma of the salivary gland: cytogenetic evidence of common origin of phenotypically diverse cells. Lab Invest 2001, **81:** 1289–1297.

124 Deguchi H, Hamano H, Hayashi Y. C-*myc*, *ras* p21 and p53 expression in pleomorphic adenoma and its malignant form of the human salivary glands. Acta Pathol Jpn 1993, **43:** 413–422.

125 Erlandson RA, Cardon-Cardo C, Higgins PJ. Histogenesis of benign pleomorphic adenoma (mixed tumor) of the major salivary glands. An ultrastructural and immunohistochemical study. Am J Surg Pathol 1984, **8:** 803–820.

126 Fantasia JE, Lally ET. Localization of free secretory component in pleomorphic adenomas of minor salivary gland origin. Cancer 1984, **53:** 1786–1789.

127 Felix A, Rosa JC, Fonseca I, Cidadao A, Soares J. Laminin and collagen IV in pleomorphic adenoma and carcinoma ex-pleomorphic adenoma: an immunohistochemical study. Hum Pathol 1999, **30:** 964–969.

128 Ferlito A, Baldan M, Andretta M, Blandamura S, Pesavento G, Piazza M. Implantation of parotid pleomorphic adenoma in the upper neck. ORL J Otorhinolaryngol Relat Spec 1991, **53:** 165–176.

129 Fliss DM, Rival R, Gullane P, Mock D, Freeman JL. Pleomorphic adenoma. A preliminary histopathologic comparison between tumors occurring in the deep and superficial lobes of the parotid gland. Ear Nose Throat J 1992, **71:** 254–257.

130 Fujita S, Takahashi H, Okabe H. Proliferative activity in normal salivary gland and pleomorphic adenoma. A study by argyrophilic nucleolar organizer region (AgNOR) staining. Acta Pathol Jpn 1992, **42:** 573–578.

131 Gandour-Edwards R, Kapadia SB, Gumerlock PH, Barnes L. Immunolocalization of interleukin-6 in salivary gland tumors. Hum Pathol 1995, **26**: 501–503.

132 Gusterson BA, Lucas RB, Ormerod MG. Distribution of epithelial membrane antigen in benign and malignant lesions of the salivary glands. Virchows Arch [A] 1982, **397**: 227–233.

133 Harris BR, Shipkey F. Tyrosine-rich crystalloids in neoplasms and tissues of the head and neck. Arch Pathol Lab Med 1986, **110**: 709–712.

134 Harrison JD. Ultrastructural observation of calcification in a pleomorphic adenoma of the parotid gland. Ultrastruct Pathol 1991, **15**: 185–188.

135 Harrison JD, Auger DW. Mucosubstance histochemistry of pleomorphic adenoma of parotid and submandibular salivary glands of man. Light and electron microscopy. Histochem J 1991, **23**: 293–302.

136 Henriksson G, Westrin KM, Carlsoo B, Silfversward C. Recurrent primary pleomorphic adenomas of salivary gland origin: intrasurgical rupture, histopathologic features, and pseudopodia. Cancer 1998, **82**: 617–620.

137 Hirokawa M, Shimizu M, Manabe T, Ito J, Ogawa S. Oncocytic lipoadenoma of the submandibular gland. Hum Pathol 1998, **29**: 410–412.

138 Humphrey PA, Ingram P, Tucker A, Shelburne JD. Crystalloids in salivary gland pleomorphic adenomas. Arch Pathol Lab Med 1989, **113**: 390–393.

139 Jin YT, Lian JD, Yan JJ, Hwang TZ, Tsai ST. Pleomorphic adenoma with extensive adipose content. Histopathology 1996, **28**: 87–88.

140 Kirklin JW, McDonald JR, Harrington SW, New GB. Parotid tumors. Histopathology, clinical behavior, and end results. Surg Gynecol Obstet 1951, **92**: 721–733.

141 Korsrud FR, Brandtzaeg P. Immunofluorescence study of secretory epithelial markers in pleomorphic adenomas. Virchows Arch [A] 1984, **403**: 291–300.

142 Krolls SO, Trodahl JN, Boyers RC. Salivary gland lesions in children. A survey of 430 cases. Cancer 1972, **30**: 459–469.

143 Kusafuka K, Yamaguchi A, Kayano T, Fujiwara M, Takemura T. Expression of bone morphogenetic proteins in salivary pleomorphic adenomas. Virchows Arch 1998, **432**: 247–254.

144 Lam RMY. An electron microscopic histochemical study of the histogenesis of major salivary gland pleomorphic adenoma. Ultrastruct Pathol 1985, **8**: 207–223.

145 Landini G. Immunohistochemical demonstration of type II collagen in the chondroid tissue of pleomorphic adenomas of the salivary glands. Acta Pathol Jpn 1991, **41**: 270–276.

146 Lee PS, Sabbath-Solitare M, Redondo TC, Ongcapin EH. Molecular evidence that the stromal and epithelial cells in pleomorphic adenoma of salivary gland arise from the same origin: Clonal analysis using human androgen receptor gene (HUMARA) assay. Hum Pathol 2000, **31**: 498–503.

147 Lomax-Smith JD, Azzopardi JG. The hyaline cell. A distinctive feature of "mixed" salivary tumours. Histopathology 1978, **2**: 77–92.

148 Luo M, Takagi H, Tsubone M, Ando C, Ogata K, Shrestha P, Mori M. Fibronectin expression in salivary gland pleomorphic adenoma. Arch Anat Cytol Pathol 1993, **41**: 68–74.

149 Malett KJ, Harrison MS. The recurrence of salivary gland tumours. J Laryngol Otol 1971, **85**: 439–448.

150 Maran AGD, Mackenzie IJ, Stanley RE. Recurrent pleomorphic adenomas of the parotid gland. Arch Otolaryngol 1984, **110**: 167–171.

151 Martin AR, Mantravadi J, Kotylo PK, Mullins R, Walker S, Roth LM. Proliferative activity and aneuploidy in pleomorphic adenomas of the salivary glands. Arch Pathol Lab Med 1994, **118**: 252–259.

152 Mills SE, Cooper PH. An ultrastructural study of cartilaginous zones and surrounding epithelium in mixed tumors of salivary glands and skin. Lab Invest 1981, **44**: 6–12.

153 Mori M, Sumitomo S, Iwai Y, Meenagham MA. Immunolocalization of keratins in salivary gland pleomorphic adenoma using monoclonal antibodies. Oral Surg Oral Med Oral Pathol 1986, **61**: 611–616.

154 Murakami M, Ohtani I, Hojo H, Wakasa H. Immunohistochemical evaluation with Ki-67. An application to salivary gland tumours. J Laryngol Otol 1992, **106**: 35–38.

155 Murase N, Kobayashi K, Mitani H, Mori M. Immunohistochemical localization of α 1-antitrypsin and α 1-antichymotrypsin in salivary pleomorphic adenomas. Virchows Arch [A] 1985, **408**: 107–116.

156 Nakanishi K, Kawai T, Suzuki M, Shinmei M. Glycosaminoglycans in pleomorphic adenoma and adenoid cystic carcinoma of the salivary gland. Arch Pathol Lab Med 1990, **114**: 1227–1231.

157 Nakazato Y, Ishizeki J, Takahashi K, Yamaguchi H, Kamei T, Mori T. Localization of S-100 protein and glial fibrillary acidic protein-related antigen in pleomorphic adenoma of the salivary glands. Lab Invest 1982, **46**: 621–626.

158 Nara Y, Takeuchi J, Yoshida K, Fukatsu T, Nagasaka T, Kawaguchi T, Meng N, Kikuchi H, Nakashima N. Immunohistochemical characterisation of extracellular matrix components of salivary gland tumours. Br J Cancer 1991, **64**: 307–314.

159 Neureiter D, Bohmer J, Kirchner T, Aigner T. Pleomorphic adenomas of the parotid express mesenchymal phenotypes: demonstration of matrix gene expression products characteristic of the fibroblastic and chondrocytic cell lineages. Histopathology 1999, **35**: 373–379.

160 Nishimura T, Furukawa M, Kawahara E, Miwa A. Differential diagnosis of pleomorphic adenoma by immunohistochemical means. J Laryngol Otol 1991, **105**: 1057–1060.

161 Noguchi S, Aihara T, Oshino K, Motomura K, Inaji H, Imaoka S, Koyama H. Demonstration of monoclonal origin of human parotid gland pleomorphic adenoma. Cancer 1996, **77**: 431–435.

162 Ogawa Y, Toyosawa S, Ishida T, Ijuhin N. Keratin 14 immunoreactive cells in pleomorphic adenomas and adenoid cystic carcinomas of salivary glands. Virchows Arch 2000, **437**: 58–68.

163 Palmer RM, Lucas RB, Knight J, Gusterson B. Immunocytochemical identification of cell types in pleomorphic adenoma, with particular reference to myoepithelial cells. J Pathol 1985, **146**: 213–220.

164 Patey DH, Thackray AC. The treatment of parotid tumours in the light of a pathological study of parotidectomy material. Br J Surg 1958, **45**: 477–487.

165 Quintarelli G, Robinson L. The glycosaminoglycans of salivary gland tumors. Am J Pathol 1967, **511**: 19–37.

166 Sampson BA, Jarcho JA, Winters GL. Metastasizing mixed tumor of the parotid gland: a rare tumor with unusually rapid progression in a cardiac transplant recipient. Mod Pathol 1998, **11**: 1142–1145.

167 Sasano H, Ohkubo T, Sasano N. Immunohistochemical demonstration of steroid C-21 hydroxylase in normal and neoplastic salivary glands. Cancer 1988, **61**: 750–753.

168 Savera AT, Gown AM, Zarbo RJ. Immunolocalization of three novel smooth muscle-specific proteins in salivary gland pleomorphic adenoma: assessment of the morphogenetic role of myoepithelium. Mod Pathol 1997, **10**: 1093–1100.

169 Skalova A, Leivo I. Basement membrane proteins in salivary gland tumours. Distribution of type IV collagen and laminin. Virchows Arch [A] 1992, **420**: 425–431.

170 Skalova A, Leivo I, Michal M, Saksela E. Analysis of collagen isotypes in crystalloid structures of salivary gland tumors. Hum Pathol 1992, **23**: 748–754.

171 Soini Y, Paakko P, Virtanen I, Lehto VP. Tenascin in salivary gland tumours. Virchows Arch A Pathol Anat Histopathol 1992, **421**: 217–222.

172 Stead RH, Qizilbash AH, Kontozoglou T, Daya AD, Riddell RH. An immunohistochemical study of pleomorphic adenomas of the salivary gland. Glial fibrillary acidic protein-like immunoreactivity identifies a major myoepithelial component. Hum Pathol 1988, **19**: 32–40.

173 Stenman G, Sahlin P, Mark J, Landys D. Structural alterations of the c-mos locus in benign pleomorphic adenomas with chromosome abnormalities of 8q12. Oncogene 1991, **6**: 1105–1108.

174 Su L, Morgan PR, Harrison DL, Waseem A, Lane EB. Expression of keratin mRNAs and proteins in normal salivary epithelial and pleomorphic adenomas. J Pathol 1993, **171**: 173–181.

175 Swanson PE, Pettinato G, Lillemoe TJ, Wick MR. Gross cystic disease fluid protein-15 in salivary gland tumors. Arch Pathol Lab Med 1991, **115**: 158–163.

176 Takai Y, Mori M, Dardick I, Mackay A, Leung R, Wattimena D, Christensen H, Burford-Mason A. Myofilament localization and immunoelectron microscopic detection of muscle-specific actin in neoplastic myoepithelial cells in pleomorphic adenomas and myoepitheliomas. Ultrastruct Pathol 1994, **18**: 575–592.

177 Takeda Y. An immunohistochemical study of bizarre neoplastic cells in pleomorphic adenoma: its cytological nature and proliferative activity. Pathol Int 1999, **49**: 993–999.

178 Takeuchi J, Sobue M, Yoshida M, Esaki T, Katok Y. Pleomorphic adenoma of the salivary gland. With special reference to histochemical and electron microscopic studies and biochemical analysis of glycosaminoglycans in vivo and in vitro. Cancer 1975, **36**: 1771–1789.

179 Tandler B. Amyloid in a pleomorphic adenoma of the parotid gland. Electron microscopic observations. J Oral Pathol 1981, **10**: 158–163.

180 Thunnissen FB, Peterse JL, Buchholtz P, Van der Beek JM, Bosman FT. Polyploidy in pleomorphic adenomas with cytological atypia. Cytopathology 1992, **3**: 101–109.

181 Toto PD, Hsu DJ. Product definition of pleomorphic adenoma of minor salivary glands. J Oral Pathol 1985, **14**: 818–832.

182 van Krieken JH. Prostate marker immunoreactivity in salivary gland neoplasms. A rare pitfall in immunohistochemistry. Am J Surg Pathol 1993, **17**: 410–414.

183 Welsh RA, Meyer AT. Mixed tumors of human salivary gland, histogenesis. Arch Pathol 1968, **85**: 433–447.

184 Wenig BM, Hitchcock CL, Ellis GL, Gnepp DR. Metastasizing mixed tumor of salivary glands. A clinicopathologic and flow cytometric analysis. Am J Surg Pathol 1992, **16**: 845–858.

185 Wittchow R, Landas SK. Glial fibrillary acidic protein expression in pleomorphic adenoma, chordoma, and astrocytoma. A comparison of three antibodies. Arch Pathol Lab Med 1991, **115**: 1030–1033.

186 Yang L, Hashimura K, Qin C, Shrestha P, Sumimoto S, Mori M. Immunoreactivity of proliferating cell nuclear antigen in salivary gland tumours. An assessment of growth potential. Virchows Arch [A] 1993, **422**: 481–486.

187 Yau KC, Tsang WY, Chan JK. Lipoadenoma of the parotid gland with probable striated duct differentiation. Mod Pathol 1997, **10**: 242–246.

188 Zarbo RJ, Bacchi CE, Gown AM. Muscle-specific protein expression in normal salivary glands and pleomorphic adenomas. An immunocytochemical study with biochemical confirmation. Mod Pathol 1991, **4**: 621–626.

Malignant mixed tumor

189 Auclair PL, Ellis GL. Atypical features in salivary gland mixed tumors: Their relationship to malignant transformation. Mod Pathol 1996, **9**: 652–657.

190 Batsakis JG. Carcinoma ex pleomorphic adenoma's "Big Tent" has room for low- and high-grade tumors. Adv Anat Pathol 1997, **4**: 176–178.

191 Bleiweiss IJ, Huvos AG, Lara J, Strong EW. Carcinosarcoma of the submandibular salivary gland. Immunohistochemical findings. Cancer 1992, **69**: 2031–2035.

192 Brandwein MS, Huvos AG, Patil J, Jagirdar J. Tumor-associated glycoprotein distribution detected by monoclonal antibody B72.3 in salivary neoplasia. Cancer 1992, **69**: 2623–2630.

193 Rosa JC, Fonseca I, Felix A, Soares J. Immunohistochemical study of C-erbB-2 expression in carcinoma ex-pleomorphic adenoma. Histopathology 1996, **28**: 247–252.

194 Eneroth C-M. Histological and clinical aspects of parotid tumours. Acta Otolarynol (Stockh) 1964, **191**(Suppl): 1–99.

195 Gnepp DR. Malignant mixed tumors of the salivary glands. A review. Pathol Annu 1993, **28**(Pt 1): 279–328.

196 Lewis JE, Olsen KD, Sebo TJ. Carcinoma ex pleomorphic adenoma: pathologic analysis of 73 cases. Hum Pathol 2001, **32**: 596–604.

197 LiVolsi VA, Perzin KH. Malignant mixed tumors arising in salivary glands. I. Carcinomas arising in benign mixed tumors. A clinicopathologic study. Cancer 1977, **39**: 2209–2230.

198 Moberger JG, Eneroth C-M. Malignant mixed tumors of the major salivary glands. Special reference to the histologic structure in metastases. Cancer 1968, **21**: 1198–1211.

199 Nagao K, Matsuzaki O, Saiga H, Sugano I, Shigematsu H, Kaneko T, Katoh T, Kitamura T. Histopathologic studies on carcinoma in pleomorphic adenoma of the parotid gland. Cancer 1981, **48**: 113–121.

200 Spiro RH, Huvos AG, Strong EW. Malignant mixed tumor of salivary origin. A clinicopathologic study of 146 cases. Cancer 1977, **39**: 388–396.

201 Stephen J, Batsakis JG, Luna MA, von der Heyden U, Byers RM. True malignant mixed tumors (carcinosarcoma) of salivary glands. Oral Surg Oral Med Oral Pathol 1986, **61**: 597–602.

202 Thomas WH, Coppola ED. Distant metastasis from mixed tumors of the salivary glands. Am J Surg 1965, **109**: 724–730.

203 Tortoledo ME, Luna MA, Batsakis JG. Carcinomas ex pleomorphic adenoma and malignant mixed tumors. Histomorphologic indexes. Arch Otolaryngol 1984, **110**: 172–176.

204 Xin W, Paulino AFG. Prognostic factors in malignant mixed tumors of the salivary gland: correlation of immunohistochemical markers with histologic classification. Ann Diagn Pathol 2002, **6**: 205–210.

205 Yamamoto Y, Kishimoto Y, Wistuba II, Virmani AK, Vuitch F, Gazdar AF, Albores-Saavedra J. DNA analysis at p53 locus in carcinomas arising from pleomorphic adenomas of salivary glands: Comparison of molecular study and p53 immunostaining. Pathol Int 1998, **48**: 265–272.

206 Yamashita T, Kameda N, Katayama K, Hiruta N, Nakada M, Takeda Y. True malignant mixed tumor of the submandibular gland. Acta Pathol Jpn 1990, **40**: 137–142.

Tumors with oxyphilic (oncocytic) change

207 Chang A, Harawi SJ. Oncocytes, oncocytosis, and oncocytic tumors. Pathol Annu 1992, **27**(Pt 1): 263–304.

208 Chaushu G, Buchner A, David R. Multiple oncocytic cysts with tyrosine-crystalloids in the parotid gland. Hum Pathol 1999, **30**: 237–238.

209 Ghandur-Mnaymneh L. Multinodular oncocytoma of the parotid gland. A benign lesion simulating malignancy. Hum Pathol 1984, **15**: 485–486.

210 Muller-Hocker J. Random cytochrome-C-oxidase deficiency of oxyphil cell nodules in the parathyroid gland. A mitochondrial cytopathy related to cell aging? Pathol Res Pract 1992, **188**: 701–706.

211 Palmer TJ, Gleeson MJ, Eveson JW, Cawson RA. Oncocytic adenomas and oncocytic hyperplasia of salivary glands. A

clinicopathological study of 26 cases. Histopathology 1990, **16:** 487–493.

212 Paulino AFG, Huvos AG. Oncocytic and oncocytoid tumors of the salivary glands. Semin Diagn Pathol 1999, **16:** 98–104.

213 Schwartz IS, Feldman M. Diffuse multinodular oncocytoma ("oncocytosis") of the parotid gland. Cancer 1969, **23:** 636–640.

214 Storensen M, Baunsgaard P, Frederiksen P, Haahr PA. Multifocal adenomatous oncocytic hyperplasia of the parotid gland. (Unusual clear cell variant in two female siblings.) Pathol Res Pract 1986, **181:** 254–257.

215 Tallini G. Oncocytic tumours. Virchows Arch 1998, **433:** 5–12.

Oxyphilic adenoma

216 Bazaz-Malik G, Gupta DN. Metastasizing (malignant) oncocytoma of the parotid gland. Z Krebsforsch 1968, **70:** 193–197.

217 Brandwein MS, Huvos AG. Oncocytic tumors of major salivary glands. A study of 68 cases with follow-up of 44 patients. Am J Surg Pathol 1991, **15:** 514–528.

218 Feiner HD, Goldstein S, Ittman M, Pelton K, Jacobs J. Oncocytic adenoma of the parotid gland with psammoma bodies. Arch Pathol Lab Med 1986, **110:** 640–644.

219 Gilcrease MZ, Nelson FS, Guzman-Paz M. Tyrosine-rich crystals associated with oncocytic salivary gland neoplasms. Arch Pathol Lab Med 1998, **122:** 644–649.

220 Gray SR, Cornog JL Jr, Seo IS. Oncocytic neoplasms of salivary glands. A report of fifteen cases including two malignant oncocytomas. Cancer 1976, **38:** 1306–1317.

221 Haberman RS II, Rogers WA, Haberman PH. Malignant oncocytic adenocarcinoma of the parotid gland with metastases to bone. Surg Pathol 1990, **3:** 221–226.

222 Hamperl H. Benign and malignant oncocytoma. Cancer 1962, **15:** 1019–1027.

223 Ruby SG, Kish JK. Oncocytic adenocarcinoma of minor salivary gland. An unusual glossal presentation of minor salivary gland tumor. Pathol Res Pract 1996, **192:** 856–864.

224 Sugimoto T, Wakizono S, Uemura T, Tsuneyoshi M, Enjoji M. Malignant oncocytoma of the parotid gland. A case report with an immunohistochemical and ultrastructural study. J Laryngol Otol 1993, **107:** 69–74.

225 Tandler B, Hutter RVP, Erlandson RA. Ultrastructure of oncocytoma of the parotid gland. Lab Invest 1970, **23:** 567–580.

226 Thompson LD, Wenig BM, Ellis GL. Oncocytomas of the submandibular gland: A series of 22 cases and a review of the literature. Cancer 1996, **78:** 2281–2287.

Warthin's tumor

227 Banik S, Howell JS, Wright DH. Non-Hodgkin's lymphoma arising in adenolymphoma. A report of two cases. J Pathol 1985, **146:** 167–177.

228 Bengoechea O, Sanchez F, Larrinaga B, Martinez-Penuela JM. Oncocytic adenocarcinoma arising in Warthin's tumor. Pathol Res Pract 1989, **185:** 907–911.

229 Bunker ML, Locker J. Warthin's tumor with malignant lymphoma. DNA analysis of paraffin-embedded tissue. Am J Clin Pathol 1989, **91:** 341–344.

230 Caselitz J, Salfelder A, Seifert G. Adenolymphoma. An immunohistochemical study with monoclonal antibodies against lymphocyte antigens. J Oral Pathol 1984, **13:** 438–447.

231 Cossman J, Deegan MJ, Batsakis JG. Warthin tumor. B-lymphocytes within the lymphoid infiltrate. Arch Pathol Lab Med 1977, **101:** 354–356.

232 Damjanov I, Sneff EM, Delerme AN. Squamous cell carcinoma arising in Warthin's tumor of the parotid gland. A light, electron microscopic, and immunohistochemical study. Oral Surg Oral Med Oral Pathol 1983, **55:** 286–290.

233 Di Palma S, Simpson RH, Skalova A, Michal M. Metaplastic (infarcted) Warthin's tumour of the parotid gland: a possible consequence of fine needle aspiration biopsy. Histopathology 1999, **35:** 432–438.

234 Donath K, Seifert G. Tumour-simulating squamous cell metaplasia (SCM) in necrotic areas of salivary gland tumours. Pathol Res Pract 1997, **193:** 689–693.

235 Dreyer T, Battmann A, Silberzahn J, Glanz H, Schulz A. Unusual differentiation of a combination tumor of the parotid gland. A case report. Pathol Res Pract 1993, **189:** 577–581.

236 Eveson JW, Cawson RA. Warthin's tumor (cystadenolymphoma) of salivary glands. A clinicopathologic investigation of 278 cases. Oral Surg Oral Med Oral Pathol 1986, **61:** 256–262.

237 Foschini MP, Marucci G, Eusebi V. Low-grade mucoepidermoid carcinoma of salivary glands: characteristic immunohistochemical profile and evidence of striated duct differentiation. Virchows Arch 2002, **440:** 536–542.

238 Gnepp DR. Warthin tumor exhibiting sebaceous differentiation and necrotizing sialometaplasia. Virchows Arch [A] 1981, **391:** 267–273.

239 Gustafsson H, Kjörell U, Carlsöö B. Cytoskeletal proteins in oncocytic tumors of the parotid gland. Arch Otolaryngol 1985, **111:** 99–105.

240 Hayashi Y, Saito H, Saito S, Yanagawa T, Yoshida H, Yura Y, Sato M. Immunoreactive somatostatin in Warthin's tumor. Am J Pathol 1985, **123:** 250–255.

241 Honda K, Kashima K, Daa T, Yokoyama S, Nakayama I. Clonal analysis of the epithelial component of Warthin's tumor. Hum Pathol 2000, **31:** 1377–1380.

242 Hsu S-M, Hsu P-L, Nayak RN. Warthin's tumor. An immunohistochemical study of its lymphoid stroma. Hum Pathol 1981, **12:** 251–257.

243 Hsu S-M, Raine L. Warthin's tumor. Epithelial cell differences. Am J Clin Pathol 1982, **77:** 78–81.

244 Kataoka R, Hyo Y, Hoshiya T, Miyahara H, Matsunaga T. Ultrastructural study of mitochondria in oncocytes. Ultrastruct Pathol 1991, **15:** 231–239.

245 Korsrud FR, Brandtzaeg P. Immunohistochemical characterization of cellular immunoglobulins and epithelial marker antigens in Warthin's tumor. Hum Pathol 1984, **15:** 361–367.

246 Kotwall CA. Smoking as an etiologic factor in the development of Warthin's tumor of the parotid gland. Am J Surg 1992, **164:** 646–647.

247 McGavran MH. The ultrastructure of papillary cystadenoma lymphomatosum of the parotid gland. Virchows Arch [A] 1965, **338:** 195–202.

248 Michal M, Hrabal P, Skàlovà A. Oncocytic cystadenoma of the parotid gland with prominent signet-ring cell features. Pathol Int 1998, **48:** 629–633.

249 Monk JS Jr, Church JS. Warthin's tumor. A high incidence and no sex predominance in central Pennsylvania. Arch Otolaryngol Head Neck Surg 1992, **118:** 477–478.

250 Morley DJ, Hodes JE, Calland J, Hodes ME. Immunohistochemical demonstration of ribonuclease and amylase in normal and neoplastic parotid glands. Hum Pathol 1983, **14:** 969–973.

251 Nagao T, Sugano I, Ishida Y, Tajima Y, Furuya N, Kondo Y, Nagao K. Mucoepidermoid carcinoma arising in Warthin's tumour of parotid gland: report of two cases with histopathological, ultrastructural and immunohistochemical studies. Histopathology 1998, **33:** 379–386.

252 Nakashima N, Goto K, Takeuchi J. Malignant papillary cystadenoma lymphomatosum. Light and electron microscopic study. Virchows Arch [A] 1983, **399:** 207–219.

253 Orito T, Shinohara H, Okada Y, Mori M. Heterogeneity of keratin expression in epithelial tumor cells of adenolymphoma in paraffin sections. Pathol Res Pract 1989, **184:** 600–608.

254 Patey DH, Thackray AC. Infected adenolymphomas. A new parotid syndrome. Br J Surg 1970, **57:** 569–572.

255 Ruco LP, Rosati S, Remotti D, Modesti A, Vitolo D, Baroni CD. Immunohistology of adenolymphoma (Warthin's tumour). Evidence for a role of vascularization in the organization of the lympho-epithelial structure. Histopathology 1987, **11**: 557–565.

256 Schwerer MJ, Kraft K, Baczako K, Maier H. Cytokeratin expression and epithelial differentiation in Warthin's tumour and its metaplastic (infarcted) variant. Histopathology 2001, **39**: 347–352.

257 Shikhani AH, Shikhani LT, Kuhajda FP, Allam CK. Warthin's tumor-associated neoplasms. Report of two cases and review of the literature. Ear Nose Throat J 1993, **72**: 264–269.

258 Shintaku M, Honda T. Identification of oncocytic lesions of salivary glands by anti-mitochondrial immunohistochemistry. Histopathology 1997, **31**: 408–411.

259 Suster S, Rosai J. Multilocular thymic cyst. An acquired reactive process. Study of 18 cases. Am J Surg Pathol 1991, **15**: 388–398.

260 Takahashi H, Tsuda N, Tezuka F, Okabe H. An immunoperoxidase investigation of S-100 protein in the epithelial component of Warthin's tumor. Oral Surg Oral Med Oral Pathol 1986, **62**: 57–62.

261 Taxy JB. Necrotizing squamous/mucinous metaplasia in oncocytic salivary gland tumors. A potential diagnostic problem. Am J Clin Pathol 1992, **97**: 40–45.

262 Therkildsen MH, Christensen N, Andersen LJ, Larsen S, Katholm M. Malignant Warthin's tumour. A case study. Histopathology 1992, **21**: 167–171.

263 Thompson AS, Bryant HC Jr. Histogenesis of papillary cystadenoma lymphomatosum (Warthin's tumor) of the parotid salivary gland. Am J Pathol 1950, **26**: 807–849.

264 Turnbull AD, Frazell EL. Multiple tumors of the major salivary glands. Am J Surg 1969, **118**: 787–789.

265 Weiss LM, Brodsky GL. Adenolymphoma with massive necrosis and squamous metaplasia. Acta Pathol Jpn 1984, **34**: 1469–1474.

266 Williamson JD, Simmons BH, El-Naggar A, Medeiros LJ. Mucoepidermoid carcinoma involving Warthin tumor. A report of five cases and review of the literature. Am J Clin Pathol 2000, **114**: 564–570.

267 Yamamoto H, Caselitz J, Seifert G. Cystadenolymphoma. An immunohistochemical study with special reference to IgE and mast cells. Pathol Res Pract 1985, **180**: 364–368.

Monomorphic adenoma

268 Cho KJ, Kim YI. Monomorphic adenomas of the salivary glands. A clinicopathologic study of 12 cases with immunohistochemical observation. Pathol Res Pract 1989, **184**: 614–620.

269 Gardner DG, Daley TD. The use of the terms *monomorphic adenoma, basal cell adenoma*, and *canalicular adenoma* as applied to salivary gland tumors. Oral Surg Oral Med Oral Pathol 1983, **56**: 608–615.

270 Mintz GA, Abrams AM, Melrose RJ. Monomorphic adenomas of the major and minor salivary glands. Report of twenty-one cases and review of the literature. Oral Surg Oral Med Oral Pathol 1982, **53**: 375–386.

271 Simson RHW. Classification of tumours of salivary glands. Histopathology 1994, **24**: 187–191.

Basal cell adenoma and adenocarcinoma

272 Batsakis JG. Basal cell adenoma of the parotid gland. Cancer 1972, **29**: 226–230.

273 Batsakis JG, Brannon RB. Dermal analogue tumours of major salivary glands. J Laryngol Otol 1981, **95**: 155–164.

274 Batsakis JG, Brannon RB, Sciubba JJ. Monomorphic adenomas of major salivary glands. A histologic study of 96 tumours. Clin Otolaryngol 1981, **6**: 129–143.

275 Batsakis JG, Luna MA. Basaloid salivary carcinoma. Ann Otol Rhinol Laryngol 1991, **100**(Pt 1): 785–787.

276 Batsakis JG, Luna MA, el-Naggar AK. Basaloid monomorphic adenomas. Ann Otol Rhinol Laryngol 1991, **100**: 687–690.

277 Chaudhry AP, Cutler LS, Satchidanand S, Labay G, Sunder Raj M. Ultrastructure of monomorphic adenoma (ductal type) of the minor salivary glands. Arch Otolaryngol 1983, **109**: 118–122.

278 Chaudhry AP, Cutler LS, Satchidanand S, Labay G, Sunder Raj M, Lin C-C. Monomorphic adenomas of the parotid glands. Their ultrastructure and histogenesis. Cancer 1983, **52**: 112–120.

279 Choi HR, Batsakis JG, Callender DL, Prieto VG, Luna MA, El-Naggar AK. Molecular analysis of chromosome 16q regions in dermal analogue tumors of salivary glands: a genetic link to dermal cylindroma? Am J Surg Pathol 2002, **26**: 778–783.

280 Crumpler C, Scharfenberg JC, Reed RJ. Monomorphic adenomas of salivary glands. Trabecular, tubular, canalicular, and basaloid variants. Cancer 1976, **38**: 193–200.

281 Daley TD, Gardner DG, Smout MS. Canalicular adenoma. Not a basal cell adenoma. Oral Surg Oral Med Oral Pathol 1984, **57**: 181–188.

282 Dardick I, Kahn HJ, van Nostrand AWP, Baumal R. Salivary gland monomorphic adenoma. Ultrastructural, immunoperoxidase, and histogenetic aspects. Am J Pathol 1984, **115**: 334–348.

283 Dardick I, Lytwyn A, Bourne AJ, Byard RW. Trabecular and solid-cribriform types of basal cell adenoma. A morphologic study of two cases of an unusual variant of monomorphic adenoma. Oral Surg Oral Med Oral Pathol 1992, **73**: 75–83.

284 Ellis GL, Wiscovitch JG. Basal cell adenocarcinomas of the major salivary glands. Oral Surg Oral Med Oral Pathol 1990, **69**: 461–469.

285 Ferreiro JA. Immunohistochemistry of basal cell adenoma of the major salivary glands. Histopathology 1994, **24**: 539–542.

286 Fonseca I, Soares J. Basal cell adenocarcinoma of minor salivary and seromucous glands of the head and neck region. Semin Diagn Pathol 1996, **13**: 128–137.

287 Gallimore AP, Spraggs PDR, Allen JP, Hobsley M. Basaloid carcinomas of salivary glands. Histopathology 1994, **24**: 139–144.

288 Gardner DG, Daley TD. The use of the terms *monomorphic adenoma, basal cell adenoma*, and *canalicular adenoma* as applied to salivary gland tumors. Oral Surg Oral Med Oral Pathol 1983, **56**: 608–615.

289 Herbst EW, Utz W. Multifocal dermal-type basal cell adenomas of parotid glands with co-existing dermal cylindromas. Virchows Arch [A] 1984, **403**: 95–102.

290 Jao W, Keh PC, Swerdlow MA. Ultrastructure of the basal cell adenoma of parotid gland. Cancer 1976, **37**: 1322–1333.

291 Luna MA, Batsakis JG, Tortoledo ME, del Junco GW. Carcinomas ex monomorphic adenoma of salivary glands. J Laryngol Otol 1989, **103**: 756–759.

292 Luna MA, Tortoledo ME, Allen M. Salivary dermal analogue tumors arising in lymph nodes. Cancer 1987, **59**: 1165–1169.

293 Muller S, Barner L. Basal cell adenocarcinoma of the salivary glands: Report of seven cases and review of the literature. Cancer 1996, **78**: 2471–2477.

294 Nagao K, Matsuzaki O, Saiga H, Sugano I, Shigematsu H, Kaneko T, Katoh T, Kitamura T. Histopathologic studies of basal cell adenoma of the parotid gland. Cancer 1982, **50**: 736–745.

295 Nagao T, Sugano I, Ishida Y, Hasegawa M, Matsuzaki O, Konno A, Kondo Y, Nagao K. Basal cell adenocarcinoma of the salivary glands: comparison with basal cell adenoma through assessment of cell proliferation, apoptosis, and expression of p53 and bcl-2. Cancer 1998, **82**: 439–447.

296 Nagao T, Sugano I, Ishida Y, Matsuzaki O, Konno A, Kondo Y, Nagao K. Carcinoma in basal cell adenoma of the parotid gland. Pathol Res Pract 1997, **193**: 171–178.

297 Pulitzer DR, Reed RJ, Megehee JA. Tubuloalveolar adenoma of salivary gland. Hum Pathol 1985, **16**: 641–644.

298 Reingold IM, Keasbey LE, Graham JH. Multicentric dermal-type cylindromas of the parotid glands in a patient with florid turban tumor. Cancer 1977, **40**: 1702–1710.

299 Seifert G, Donath K. The congenital basal cell adenoma of salivary glands. Contribution to the differential diagnosis of congenital salivary gland tumors. Virchows Arch 1997, **430:** 311–320.

300 Suarez P, Hammond HL, Luna MA, Stimson PG. Palatal canalicular adenoma: report of 12 cases and review of the literature. Ann Diagn Pathol 1998, **2:** 224–228.

301 Takahashi H, Fujita S, Okabe H, Tsuda N, Tezuka F. Immunohistochemical characterization of basal cell adenomas of the salivary gland. Pathol Res Pract 1991, **187:** 145–156.

302 Williams SB, Ellis GL, Auclair PL. Immunohistochemical analysis of basal cell adenocarcinoma. Oral Surg Oral Med Oral Pathol 1993, **75:** 64–69.

303 Zarbo RJ, Prasad AR, Regezi JA, Gown AM, Savera AT. Salivary gland basal cell and canalicular adenomas: immunohistochemical demonstration of myoepithelial cell participation and morphogenetic considerations. Arch Pathol Lab Med 2000, **124:** 401–405.

Tumors with sebaceous differentiation

304 Cramer SF, Gnepp DR, Kiehn CL, Levitan J. Sebaceous differentiation in adenoid cystic carcinoma of the parotid gland. Cancer 1980, **46:** 1405–1410.

305 Gnepp DR. Sebaceous neoplasms of salivary gland origin. A review. Pathol Annu 1983, **18**(Pt 1): 71–102.

306 Gnepp DR, Brannon R. Sebaceous neoplasms of salivary gland origin. Report of 21 cases. Cancer 1984, **53:** 2155–2170.

307 McGavran MH, Bauer WC, Ackerman LV. Sebaceous lymphadenoma of the parotid salivary gland. Cancer 1960, **13:** 1185–1187.

308 Merwin WH Jr, Barnes L, Myers EN. Unilocular cystic sebaceous lymphadenoma of the parotid gland. Arch Otolaryngol 1985, **111:** 273–275.

309 Rawson AJ, Horn RC Jr. Sebaceous glands and sebaceous gland-containing tumors of parotid salivary gland, with consideration of histogenesis of papillary cystadenoma lymphomatosum. Surgery 1950, **27:** 93–101.

310 Tschen JA, McGavran MH. Sebaceous lymphadenoma. Ultrastructural observations and lipid analysis. Cancer 1979, **44:** 1388–1392.

Tumors with myoepithelial differentiation

311 Alos L, Carrillo R, Ramos J, Baez JM, Mallofre C, Fernandez PL, Cardesa A. High-grade carcinoma component in epithelial-myoepithelial carcinoma of salivary glands: clinicopathological, immunohistochemical and flow-cytometric study of three cases. Virchows Arch 1999, **434:** 291–300.

312 Barnes L, Appel BN, Perez H, El-Attar AM. Myoepitheliomas of the head and neck. Case report and review. J Surg Oncol 1985, **28:** 21–28.

313 Batsakis JG, el-Naggar AK, Luna MA. Epithelial-myoepithelial carcinoma of salivary glands. Ann Otol Rhinol Laryngol 1992, **101:** 540–542.

314 Batsakis JG, El-Naggar AK. Myoepithelium in salivary and mammary neoplasms is host-friendly. Adv Anat Pathol 1999, **6:** 218–226.

315 Brocheriou C, Auriol M, de Roquancourt A, Gaulard P, Fornes P. Epithelial-myoepithelial carcinoma of the salivary glands. Study of 15 cases and review of the literature. Ann Pathol (France) 1991, **11:** 316–325.

316 Chaudhry AP, Satchidanand S, Peer R, Cutler LS. Myoepithelial cell adenoma of the parotid gland. A light and ultrastructural study. Cancer 1982, **49:** 288–293.

317 Chetty R. Intercalated duct hyperplasia: possible relationship to epithelial-myoepithelial carcinoma and hybrid tumours of salivary glands. Histopathology 2000, **37:** 260–263.

318 Cho KJ, el-Naggar AK, Ordóñez NG, Luna MA, Austin J, Batsakis JG. Epithelial-myoepithelial carcinoma of salivary glands. A clinicopathologic, DNA flow cytometric, and immunohistochemical study of Ki-67 and HER-2/neu oncogene. Am J Clin Pathol 1995, **103:** 432–437.

319 Corio RL, Sciubba JJ, Brannon RB, Batsakis JG. Epithelial-myoepithelial carcinoma of intercalated duct origin. A clinicopathologic and ultrastructural assessment of sixteen cases. Oral Surg Oral Med Oral Pathol 1982, **53:** 280–287.

320 Crissman JD, Wirman JA, Harris A. Malignant myoepithelioma of the parotid gland. Cancer 1977, **40:** 3042–3049.

321 Daley TD, Wysocki GP, Smout MS, Slinger RP. Epithelial-myoepithelial carcinoma of salivary glands. Oral Surg Oral Med Oral Pathol 1984, **57:** 512–519.

322 Dardick I, Cavell S, Boivin M, Hoppe D, Parks WR, Stinson J, Yamada S, Burns BF. Salivary gland myoepithelioma variants. Histological, ultrastructural, and immunocytological features. Virchows Arch [A] 1989, **416:** 25–42.

323 Dardick I, Ostrynski VL, Ekem JK, Leung R, Burford-Mason AP. Immunohistochemical and ultrastructural correlates of muscle-actin expression in pleomorphic adenomas and myoepitheliomas based on comparison of formalin and methanol fixation. Virchows Arch [A] 1992, **42:** 95–104.

324 Dardick I, Thomas MJ, van Nostrand AW. Myoepithelioma—new concepts of histology and classification. A light and electron microscopic study. Ultrastruct Pathol 1989, **13:** 187–224.

325 Di Palma S, Guzzo M. Malignant myoepithelioma of salivary glands. Clinicopathological features of ten cases. Virchows Arch [A] 1993, **423:** 389–396.

326 Fonseca I, Soares J. Epithelial-myoepithelial carcinoma of the salivary glands. A study of 22 cases. Virchows Arch [A] 1993, **422:** 389–396.

327 Fonseca I, Soares J. Proliferating cell nuclear antigen immunohistochemistry in epithelial-myoepithelial carcinoma of the salivary glands. Arch Pathol Lab Med 1993, **117:** 993–995.

328 Foschini MP, Scarpellini F, Gown AM, Eusebi V. Differential expression of myoepithelial markers in salivary, sweat and mammary glands. Int J Surg Pathol 2000, **8:** 29–37.

329 Franquemont DW, Mills SE. Plasmacytoid monomorphic adenoma of salivary glands. Absence of myogenous differentiation and comparison to spindle cell myoepithelioma. Am J Surg Pathol 1993, **17:** 146–153.

330 Goldman RL, Klein HZ. Glycogen-rich adenoma of the parotid gland. An uncommon benign clear-cell tumor resembling certain clear-cell carcinomas of salivary origin. Cancer 1972, **30:** 749–754.

331 Hara K, Ito M, Takeuchi J, Iijima S, Endo T, Hidaka H. Distribution of S-100b protein in normal salivary glands and salivary gland tumors. Virchows Arch [A] 1983, **401:** 237–249.

332 Hubner G, Klein HJ, Kleinsasser O, Schieffer HG. Role of myoepithelial cells in the development of salivary gland tumors. Cancer 1971, **27:** 1255–1261.

333 Jones H, Moshtael F, Simpson RH. Immunoreactivity of alpha smooth muscle actin in salivary gland tumours. A comparison with S100 protein. J Clin Pathol 1992, **45:** 938–940.

334 Kahn HJ, Baumal R, Marks A, Dardick I, van Nostrand AWP. Myoepithelial cells in salivary gland tumors. An immunohistochemical study. Arch Pathol Lab Med 1985, **109:** 190–195.

335 Kuwabara H, Uda H, Miyabe K, Saito K, Shibanushi T. Malignant plasmacytoid myoepithelioma of the palate: histological observations compared to benign predominant plasmacytoid myoepithelial cells in pleomorphic adenoma of the palate. Ultrastruct Pathol 1998, **22:** 153–160.

336 Lomax-Smith JD, Azzopardi JG. The hyaline cell. A distinctive feature of "mixed" salivary tumors. Histopathology 1978, **2:** 77–92.

337 Luna MA, Batsakis JG, Ordóñez NG, Mackay B, Tortoledo ME. Salivary gland adenocarcinomas. A clinicopathologic analysis of three distinctive types. Semin Diagn Pathol 1987, **4:** 117–135.

338 Luna MA, Ordóñez NG, Mackay B, Batsakis JG, Guillamondegui O. Salivary epithelial-myoepithelial carcinomas of intercalated ducts. A clinical, electron microscopic, and immunocytochemical study. Oral Surg Oral Med Oral Pathol 1985, **59**: 482–490.

339 Michal M, Skàlová A, Simpson RH, Rychterova V, Leivo I. Clear cell malignant myoepithelioma of the salivary glands. Histopathology 1996, **28**: 309–316.

340 Mohamed AH, Cherrick HM. Glycogen-rich adenocarcinoma of minor salivary glands. A light and electron microscopic study. Cancer 1975, **36**: 1057–1066.

341 Mori M, Ninomiya T, Okada Y, Tsukitani K. Myoepitheliomas and myoepithelial adenomas of salivary gland origin. Immunohistochemical evaluation of filament proteins, S-100 alpha and beta, glial fibrillary acidic proteins, neuron-specific enolase, and lactoferrin. Pathol Res Pract 1989, **184**: 168–178.

342 Morinaga S, Nakajima T, Shimosato Y. Normal and neoplastic myoepithelial cells in salivary glands. An immunohistochemical study. Hum Pathol 1987, **18**: 1218–1226.

343 Nagao T, Sugano I, Ishida Y, Tajima Y, Matsuzaki O, Konno A, Kondo Y, Nagao K. Salivary gland malignant myoepithelioma: a clinicopathologic and immunohistochemical study of ten cases. Cancer 1998, **83**: 1292–1299.

344 Nilsen R, Donath K. Actin containing cells in normal human salivary glands. An immunohistochemical study. Virchows Arch [A] 1981, **391**: 315–322.

345 Palmer RM. The identification of myoepithelial cells in human salivary glands. A review and comparison of light microscopical methods. J Oral Pathol 1986, **15**: 221–229.

346 Prasad AR, Savera AT, Gown AM, Zarbo RJ. The myoepithelial immunophenotype in 135 benign and malignant salivary gland tumors other than pleomorphic adenoma. Arch Pathol Lab Med 1999, **123**: 801–806.

347 Saksela E, Tarkkanen J, Wartiovaara J. Parotid clear-cell adenoma of possible myoepithelial origin. Cancer 1972, **30**: 742–748.

348 Savera AT, Sloman A, Huvos AG, Klimstra DS. Myoepithelial carcinoma of the salivary glands: A clinicopathologic study of 25 patients. Am J Surg Pathol 2000, **24**: 761–774.

349 Sciubba JJ, Brannon RB. Myoepithelioma of salivary glands. Report of 23 cases, Cancer 1982, **49**: 562–572.

350 Simpson RHW, Jones H, Beasley P. Benign myoepithelioma of the salivary glands. A true entity? Histopathology 1995, **27**: 1–9.

351 Skalova A, Michal M. Biphasic myoepithelioma of parotid gland with collagenous crystalloids. Histopathology 1994, **24**: 583–586.

352 Skàlová A, Stàrek I, Simpson RH, Kucenovà V, Dvorackovà J, Curik R, Duskova M. Spindle cell myoepithelial tumours of the parotid gland with extensive lipomatous metaplasia. A report of four cases with immunohistochemical and ultrastructural findings. Virchows Arch 2001, **439**: 762–767.

353 Skàlová A, Michal M, Ryska A, Simpson RH, Kinkor Z, Walter J, Leivo I. Oncocytic myoepithelioma and pleomorphic adenoma of the salivary glands. Virchows Arch 1999, **434**: 537–546.

354 Stromeyer FW, Haggitt RC, Nelson JF, Hardman JM. Myoepithelioma of minor salivary gland origin. Light and electron microscopical study. Arch Pathol 1975, **99**: 242–245.

355 Suzuki H, Inoue K, Fujioka Y, Ishikura H, Furuta Y, Fukuda S. Myoepithelial carcinoma with predominance of plasmacytoid cells arising in a pleomorphic adenoma of the parotid gland. Histopathology 1998, **32**: 86–87.

356 Takai Y, Mori M, Dardick I, MacKay A, Leung R, Wattimena D, Christensen H, Burford-Mason A. Myofilament localization and immunoelectron microscopic detection of muscle-specific actin in neoplastic myoepithelial cells in pleomorphic adenomas and myoepitheliomas. Ultrastruct Pathol 1994, **18**: 575–591.

357 Tanimura A, Nakamura Y, Nagayama K, Tanaka S, Hachisuka H. Myoepithelioma of the parotid gland. Report of two cases with immunohistochemical technique for S-100 protein and electron microscopic observation. Acta Pathol Jpn 1985, **35**: 409–417.

Tumors with clear cell change

358 Batsakis JG. Clear cell tumors of salivary glands. Ann Otol Rhinol Laryngol 1980, **89**(2 Pt 1): 196–197.

359 Ellis GL. Clear cell neoplasms in salivary glands: clearly a diagnostic challenge. Ann Diagn Pathol 1998, **2**: 61–78.

360 Maiorano E, Altini M, Favia G. Clear cell tumors of the salivary glands, jaws, and oral mucosa. Semin Diagn Pathol 1997, **14**: 203–212.

361 Milchgrub S, Gnepp DR, Vuitch F, Delgado R, Albores-Saavedra J. Hyalinizing clear cell carcinoma of salivary gland. Am J Surg Pathol 1994, **18**: 74–82.

362 Ogawa I, Nikai H, Takata T, Ijuhin N, Miyauchi M, Ito H, Vuhahula E. Clear cell tumors of minor salivary gland origin. An immunohistochemical and ultrastructural analysis. Oral Surg Oral Med Oral Pathol 1991, **72**: 200–207.

363 Rezende RB, Drachenberg CB, Kumar D, Blanchaert R, Ord RA, Ioffe OB, Papadimitriou JC. Differential diagnosis between monomorphic clear cell adenocarcinoma of salivary glands and renal (clear) cell carcinoma. Am J Surg Pathol 1999, **23**: 1532–1538.

364 Seifert G. Classification and differential diagnosis of clear and basal cell tumors of the salivary gland. Semin Diagn Pathol 1996, **13**: 95–103.

365 Simpson RH, Sarsfield PT, Clarke T, Babajews AV. Clear cell carcinoma of minor salivary glands. Histopathology 1990, **17**: 433–438.

366 Wang B, Brandwein M, Gordon R, Robinson R, Urken M, Zarbo RJ. Primary salivary clear cell tumors—a diagnostic approach: a clinicopathologic and immunohistochemical study of 20 patients with clear cell carcinoma, clear cell myoepithelial carcinoma, and epithelial-myoepithelial carcinoma. Arch Pathol Lab Med 2002, **126**: 676–685.

Mucoepidermoid carcinoma

367 Auclair PL, Goode RK, Ellis GL. Mucoepidermoid carcinoma of intraoral salivary glands. Evaluation and application of grading criteria in 143 cases. Cancer 1992, **69**: 2021–2030.

368 Brandwein MS, Ivanov K, Wallace DI, Hille JJ, Wang B, Fahmy A, Bodian C, Urken ML, Gnepp DR, Huvos A, Lumerman H, Mills SE. Mucoepidermoid carcinoma: a clinicopathologic study of 80 patients with special reference to histological grading. Am J Surg Pathol 2001, **25**: 835–845.

369 Chan JKC, Saw D. Sclerosing mucoepidermoid tumour of the parotid gland. Report of a case. Histopathology 1987, **11**: 203–207.

370 Cholankeril JV, Scioscia PA. Post-traumatic sialoceles and mucoceles of the salivary glands. Clin Imaging 1993, **17**: 41–45.

371 Dardick I, Daya D, Hardie J, van Nostrand AWP. Mucoepidermoid carcinoma. Ultrastructural and histogenetic aspects. J Oral Pathol 1984, **13**: 342–358.

372 Ellis GL, Auclair PL. Tumors of the salivary glands. Atlas of tumor pathology, series 3, fascicle 17. Washington D.C., 1996, Armed Forces Institute of Pathology.

373 Evans HL. Mucoepidermoid carcinoma of salivary glands. A study of 69 cases with special attention to histologic grading. Am J Clin Pathol 1984, **81**: 696–701.

374 Fonseca I, Clode AL, Soares J. Mucoepidermoid carcinoma of major and minor salivary glands. A survey of 43 cases with study of prognostic indicators. Int J Surg Pathol 1993, **1**: 3–12.

375 Fonseca I, Costa Rosa J, Felix A, Therkildsen MH, Mandel U, Soares J. Simple mucin-type carbohydrate antigens (T, Tn and sialosyl-Tn) in mucoepidermoid carcinoma of the salivary glands. Histopathology 1994, **25**: 537–544.

376 Foschini MP, Marucci G, Eusebi V. Low-grade mucoepidermoid carcinoma of salivary glands: characteristic immunohistochemical profile and evidence of striated duct differentiation. Virchows Arch 2002, **440**: 536–542.

377 Goode RK, Auclair PL, Ellis GL. Mucoepidermoid carcinoma of

the major salivary glands: clinical and histopathologic analysis of 234 cases with evaluation of grading criteria. Cancer 1998, **82:** 1217–1224.

378 Guzzo M, Andreola S, Sirizzotti G, Cantu G. Mucoepidermoid carcinoma of the salivary glands: clinicopathologic review of 108 patients treated at the national cancer institute of Milan. Ann Surg Oncol 2002, **9:** 688–695.

379 Hamed G, Shmookler BM, Ellis GL, Punja U, Feldman D. Oncocytic mucoepidermoid carcinoma of the parotid gland. Arch Pathol Lab Med 1994, **118:** 313–314.

380 Hamper K, Schimmelpenning H, Caselitz J, Arps H, Berger J, Askensten U, Auer G, Seifert G. Mucoepidermoid tumors of the salivary glands. Correlation of cytophotometrical data and prognosis. Cancer 1989, **15:** 708–717.

380a Handra-Luca A, Bilal H, Bertrand J-C, Fouret P. Extra-cellular signal-regulated ERK-1/ERK-2 pathway activation in human salivary gland mucoepidermoid carcinoma. Association to aggressive tumor behavior and tumor cell proliferation. Am J Pathol 2003, **163:** 957–967.

381 Hayes MM, Cameron RD, Jones EA. Sebaceous variant of mucoepidermoid carcinoma of the salivary gland. A case report with cytohistologic correlation. Acta Cytol 1993, **37:** 237–241.

382 Healey WV, Perzin KH, Smith L. Mucoepidermoid carcinoma of salivary gland origin. Classification, clinical-pathologic correlation, and results of treatment. Cancer 1970, **26:** 368–388.

383 Jahan-Parwar B, Huberman RM, Donovan DT, Schwartz MR, Ostrowski ML. Oncocytic mucoepidermoid carcinoma of the salivary glands. Am J Surg Pathol 1999, **23:** 523–529.

384 Jakobsson PA, Blanck C, Eneroth C-M. Mucoepidermoid carcinoma of the parotid gland. Cancer 1968, **22:** 111–124.

385 Krolls SO, Trodahl JN, Boyers RC. Salivary gland lesions in children. A survey of 430 cases. Cancer 1972, **30:** 459–469.

386 Loy TS, McLaughlin R, Odom LF, Dehner LP. Mucoepidermoid carcinoma of the parotid as a second malignant neoplasm in children. Cancer 1989, **64:** 2174–2177.

387 Luna MA, Batsakis JG, el-Naggar AK. Salivary gland tumors in children. Ann Otol Rhinol Laryngol 1991, **100:** 869–871.

387a Nagao T, Gaffey TA, Kay PA, Unni KK, Nascimento AG, Serbo TJ, Serizawa H, Minato H, Lewis JE. Dedifferentiation in low-grade mucoepidermoid carcinoma of the parotid gland. Hum Pathol 2003, **34:** 1068–1072.

388 Nascimento AG, Amaral ALP, Prado LAF, Kligerman J, Silveira TRP. Mucoepidermoid carcinoma of salivary glands. A clinicopathologic study of 46 cases. Head Neck Surg 1986, **8:** 409–417.

389 Skalova A, Lehtonen H, von Boguslawsky K, Leivo I. Prognostic significance of cell proliferation in mucoepidermoid carcinomas of the salivary gland. Clinicopathological study using MIB 1 antibody in paraffin sections. Hum Pathol 1994, **25:** 929–935.

390 Woolner LB, Pettet JR, Kirklin JW. Mucoepidermoid tumors of major salivary glands. Am J Clin Pathol 1954, **24:** 1350–1362.

Acinic cell carcinoma

391 Abrams AM, Cornyn J, Scofield HH, Hansen LS. Acinic cell adenocarcinoma of the major salivary glands. A clinicopathologic study of 77 cases. Cancer 1965, **18:** 1145–1162.

392 Batsakis JG, Chinn EK, Weimert TA, Work WP, Krause CJ. Acinic cell carcinoma. A clinicopathologic study of thirty-five cases. J Laryngol Otol 1979, **93:** 325–340.

393 Chaudhry AP, Cutler LS, Leifer C, Satchidanand S, Labay G, Yamane G. Histogenesis of acinic cell carcinoma of the major and minor salivary glands. An ultrastructural study. J Pathol 1986, **148:** 307–320.

394 Chen SY, Brannon RB, Miller AS, White DK, Hooker SP. Acinic cell adenocarcinoma of minor salivary glands. Cancer 1978, **42:** 678–685.

395 Di Palma S, Corletto V, Lavarino C, Birindelli S, Pilotti S.

Unilateral aneuploid dedifferentiated acinic cell carcinoma associated with bilateral-low grade diploid acinic cell carcinoma of the parotic gland. Virchows Arch 1999, **434:** 361–366.

396 Depowski PL, Setzen G, Chui A, Koltai PJ, Dollar J, Ross JS. Familial occurrence of acinic cell carcinoma of the parotid gland. Arch Pathol Lab Med 1999, **123:** 1118–1120.

397 Ellis GL, Corio RL. Acinic cell adenocarcinoma. A clinicopathologic analysis of 294 cases. Cancer 1983, **52:** 542–549.

398 Eneroth C-M, Jakobsson PA. Acinic cell carcinoma of the parotid gland. Cancer 1966, **19:** 1761–1772.

399 Godwin JT, Foote FW Jr, Frazell EL. Acinic cell adenocarcinoma of the parotid gland. Report of 27 cases. Am J Pathol 1954, **30:** 465–477.

400 Gustafsson H, Carlsö B, Henriksson R. Ultrastructural morphometry and secretory behavior of acinic cell carcinoma. Cancer 1985, **55:** 1706–1710.

401 Hayashi Y, Nishida T, Yoshida H, Yanagawa T, Yura Y, Sato M. Immunoreactive vasoactive intestinal polypeptide in acinic cell carcinoma of the parotid gland. Cancer 1987, **60:** 962–968.

402 Henley JD, Geary WA, Jackson CL, Wu CD, Gnepp DR. Dedifferentiated acinic cell carcinoma of the parotid gland: a distinct rarely described entity. Hum Pathol 1997, **28:** 869–872.

403 Ito K, Kakudo K, Mori I, Horiuchi M, Osamura Y. Neuroendocrine differentiation in a case of acinic cell carcinoma of the parotid gland. Acta Pathol Jpn 1990, **40:** 279–287.

404 Lewis JE, Olsen KD, Weiland LH. Acinic cell carcinoma. Clinicopathologic review. Cancer 1991, **67:** 172–179.

405 Lidang Jensen M, Kiaer H. Acinic cell carcinoma with primary presentation in an intraparotid lymph node. Pathol Res Pract 1992, **188:** 226–231.

406 Michal M, Skàlovà A, Simpson RH, Leivo I, Ryska A, Starek I. Well-differentiated acinic cell carcinoma of salivary glands associated with lymphoid stroma. Hum Pathol 1997, **28:** 595–600.

407 Nunes JF, Fonseca I, Soares J. Helioid inclusions in dedifferentiated acinic cell carcinoma of the parotid gland. Ultrastruct Pathol 1996, **20:** 443–450.

408 Oliveira P, Fonseca I, Soares J. Acinic cell carcinoma of the salivary glands. A long term follow-up study of 15 cases. Eur J Surg Oncol 1992, **18:** 7–15.

409 Perzin KH, LiVolsi VA. Acinic cell carcinomas arising in salivary glands. A clinicopathologic study. Cancer 1979, **44:** 1434–1457.

410 Spafford PD, Mintz DR, Hay J. Acinic cell carcinoma of the parotid gland. Review and management. J Otolaryngol 1991, **20:** 262–266.

411 Spiro RH, Huvos AG, Strong EW. Acinic cell carcinoma of salivary origin. A clinicopathologic study of 67 cases. Cancer 1978, **41:** 924–935.

412 Takahashi H, Fujita S, Okabe H, Tsuda N, Tezuka F. Distribution of tissue markers in acinic cell carcinomas of salivary gland. Pathol Res Pract 1992, **188:** 692–700.

413 Warner TFCS, Seo IS, Azen EA, Hafez GR, Zarling TA. Immunocytochemistry of acinic cell carcinomas and mixed tumors of salivary glands. Cancer 1985, **56:** 2221–2227.

414 Zhaeren P, Lehmann W, Widgren S. Acinic cell carcinoma of minor salivary gland origin. J Laryngol Otol 1991, **105:** 782–785.

Adenoid cystic carcinoma

415 Allen MS Jr, Marsh WL Jr. Lymph node involvement by direct extension in adenoid cystic carcinoma. Absence of classic embolic lymph node metastasis. Cancer 1976, **38:** 2017–2021.

416 Azumi N, Battifora H. The cellular composition of adenoid cystic carcinoma. An immunohistochemical study. Cancer 1987, **60:** 1589–1598.

417 Bloom GD, Carlsö B, Gustafsson H, Henriksson R. Distribution of mucosubstances in adenoid cystic carcinoma. A light and electron microscopic study. Virchows Arch [A] 1977, **375:** 1–12.

418 Caselitz J, Becker J, Seifert G, Weber K, Osborn M. Coexpression of keratin and vimentin filaments in adenoid cystic carcinomas of salivary glands. Virchow Arch [A] 1984, **403**: 337–344.

419 Caselitz J, Jaup T, Seifert G. Immunohistochemical detection of carcinoembryonic antigen (CEA) in parotid gland carcinomas. Analysis of 52 cases. Virchows Arch [A] 1981, **394**: 49–60.

420 Casler JD, Conley JJ. Surgical management of adenoid cystic carcinoma in the parotid gland. Otolaryngol Head Neck Surg 1992, **106**: 332–338.

421 Chau YP, Hongyo T, Aozasa K, Chan JK. Dedifferentiation of adenoid cystic carcinoma: report of a case implicating p53 gene mutation. Hum Pathol 2001, **32**: 1403–1406.

422 Chaudhry AP, Leifer C, Cutler LS, Satchidanand S, Labay GR, Yamane GM. Histogenesis of adenoid cystic carcinoma of the salivary glands. Light and electronmicroscopic study. Cancer 1986, **58**: 72–82.

423 Cheng J, Saku T, Okabe H, Furthmayr H. Basement membranes in adenoid cystic carcinoma. An immunohistochemical study. Cancer 1992, **69**: 2631–2640.

424 Cheuk W, Chan JK, Ngan RK. Dedifferentiation in adenoid cystic carcinoma of salivary gland: an uncommon complication associated with an accelerated clinical course. Am J Surg Pathol 1999, **23**: 465–472.

425 Chomette G, Auriol M, Vaillant JM, Kasai T, Niwa M, Mori M. An immunohistochemical study of the distribution of lysozyme, lactoferrin, alpha 1-antitrypsin and alpha 1-antichymotrypsin in salivary adenoid cystic carcinoma. Pathol Res Pract 1991, **187**: 1001–1008.

426 Eby LS, Johnson DC, Baker HW. Adenoid cystic carcinoma of the head and neck. Cancer 1972, **29**: 1160–1168.

427 Eibling DE, Johnson JT, McCoy JP Jr, Barnes EL, Syms CA, Wagner RL, Campbell J. Flow cytometric evaluation of adenoid cystic carcinoma. Correlation with histologic subtype and survival. Am J Surg 1991, **162**: 367–372.

428 Franchi A, Gallo O, Bocciolini C, Franchi L, Paglierani M, Santucci M. Reduced E-cadherin expression correlates with unfavorable prognosis in adenoid cystic carcinoma of salivary glands of the oral cavity. Am J Clin Pathol 1999, **111**: 43–50.

428a Frierson H, El-Naggar A, Welsh J, Sapinoso L, Su A, Cheng J, Saku T, Moskaluk C, Hampton G. Large scale molecular analysis identifies genes with altered expression in salivary adenoid cystic carcinoma. Am J Pathol 2002, **161**: 1315.

429 Greiner TC, Robinson RA, Maves MD. Adenoid cystic carcinoma. A clinicopathologic study with flow cytometric analysis. Am J Clin Pathol 1989, **92**: 711–720.

430 Holst VA, Marshall CE, Moskaluk CA, Frierson HF Jr. KIT protein expression and analysis of c-kit gene mutation in adenoid cystic carcinoma. Mod Pathol 1999, **12**: 956–960.

431 Hosokawa Y, Ohmori K, Kaneko M, Yamasaki M, Ahmed M, Arimoto T, Irie G. Analysis of adenoid cystic carcinoma treated by radiotherapy. Oral Surg Oral Med Oral Pathol 1992, **74**: 251–255.

432 Kimura S, Cheng J, Ida H, Hao N, Fujimori Y, Saku T. Perlecan (heparan sulfate proteoglycan) gene expression reflected in the characteristic histological architecture of salivary adenoid cystic carcinoma. Virchows Arch 2000, **437**: 122–128.

433 Kiyoshima T, Shima K, Kobayashi I, Matsuo K, Okamura K, Komatsu S, Rasul AM, Sakai H. Expression of p53 tumor suppressor gene in adenoid cystic and mucoepidermoid carcinomas of the salivary glands. Oral Oncol 2001, **37**: 315–322.

433a Kowalski P, Paulino A. Perineural invasion in adenoid cystic carcinoma: its causation/promotion by brain-derived neurotrophic factor. Hum Pathol 2002, **33**: 933–936.

434 Lawrence JB, Mazur MT. Adenoid cystic carcinoma. A comparative pathologic study of tumors in salivary gland, breast, lung, and cervix. Hum Pathol 1982, **13**: 916–924.

435 Loducca SVL, Raitz R, Araujo NS, Araujo VC. Polymorphous low-grade adenocarcinoma and adenoid cystic carcinoma;

distinct architectural composition revealed by collagen IV, laminin and their integrin ligands (alfa2beta1 and alfa3beta1). Histopathology 2000, **37**: 118–123.

436 Matsuba HM, Spector GJ, Thawley SE, Simpson JR, Mauney M, Pikul FJ. Adenoid cystic salivary gland carcinoma. A histopathologic review of treatment failure patterns. Cancer 1986, **57**: 519–524.

437 Nakanishi K, Kawai T, Suzuki M, Shinmei M. Glycosaminoglycans in pleomorphic adenoma and adenoid cystic carcinoma of the salivary gland. Arch Pathol Lab Med 1990, **114**: 1227–1231.

438 Nascimento AG, Amaral ALP, Prado LAF, Kligerman J, Silveira TRP. Adenoid cystic carcinoma of salivary glands. A study of 61 cases with clinicopathologic correlation. Cancer 1986, **57**: 312–319.

439 Orenstein JM, Dardick I, van Nostrand AWP. Ultrastructural similarities of adenoid cystic carcinoma and pleomorphic adenoma. Histopathology 1985, **9**: 623–638.

440 Ozono S, Onozuka M, Sato K, Ito Y. Immunohistochemical localization of estradiol, progesterone, and progesterone receptor in human salivary glands and salivary adenoid cystic carcinomas. Cell Struct Funct 1992, **17**: 169–175.

441 Penner CR, Folpe AL, Budnick SD. C-kit expression distinguishes salivary gland adenoid cystic carcinoma from polymorphous low-grade adenocarcinoma. Mod Pathol 2002, **15**: 687–691.

442 Perzin KH, Gullane P, Clairmont AC. Adenoid cystic carcinomas arising in salivary glands. A correlation of histologic features and clinical course. Cancer 1978, **42**: 265–282.

443 Snyder ML, Paulino AF. Hybrid carcinoma of the salivary gland: salivary duct adenocarcinoma and adenoid cystic carcinoma. Histopathology 1999, **35**: 380–383.

444 Spiro RH, Huvos AG. Stage means more than grade in adenoid cystic carcinoma. Am J Surg 1992, **164**: 623–628.

445 Spiro RH, Huvos AG, Strong EW. Adenoid cystic carcinoma of salivary origin. A clinicopathologic study of 242 cases. Am J Surg 1974, **128**: 512–520.

446 Stallmach I, Zenklusen P, Komminoth P, Schmid S, Perren A, Roos M, Jianming Z, Heitz PU, Pfaltz M. Loss of heterozygosity at chromosome 6q23-35 correlates with clinical and histologic parameters in salivary glands adenoid cystic carcinoma. Virchows Arch 2002, **440**: 77–84.

447 Szanto PA, Luna MA, Tortoledo ME, White RA. Histologic grading of adenoid cystic carcinoma of the salivary glands. Cancer 1984, **54**: 1062–1069.

448 Takahashi H, Tsuda N, Fujita S, Tazuka F, Okabe H. Immunohistochemical investigation of vimentin, neuron-specific enolase, alpha 1-antichymotrypsin and alpha 1-antitrypsin in adenoid cystic carcinoma of the salivary gland. Acta Pathol Jpn 1990, **40**: 655–664.

449 Tandler B. Ultrastructure of adenoid cystic carcinoma of salivary gland origin. Lab Invest 1971, **24**: 504–512.

450 Toida M, Takeuchi J, Hara K, Sobue M, Tsukidate K, Goto K, Nakashima N. Histochemical studies of intercellular components of salivary gland tumors with special reference to glycosaminoglycan, laminin and vascular elements. Virchows Arch [A] 1984, **403**: 15–26.

Salivary duct tumors

451 Anderson C, Muller R, Piorkowski R, Knibbs DR, Vignoti P. Intraductal carcinoma of major salivary gland. Cancer 1992, **69**: 609–614.

452 Brandwein MS, Jagirdar J, Patil J, Biller H, Kaneko M. Salivary duct carcinoma (cribriform salivary carcinoma of excretory ducts). A clinicopathologic and immunohistochemical study of 12 cases. Cancer 1990, **85**: 2307–2314.

453 Chen KTK, Hafez GR. Infiltrating salivary duct carcinoma. A clinicopathologic study of five cases. Arch Otolaryngol 1981, **107**: 37–39.

454 Colmenero Ruiz C, Patron Romero M, Martin Perez M. Salivary duct carcinoma. A report of nine cases. J Oral Maxillofac Surg 1993, **51**: 641–646.

454a Araújo V, Loducca S, Sobral A, Kowalski L, Soares F, Araújo N. Salivary duct carcinoma: cytokeratin 14 as a marker of in-situ intraductal growth. Histopathology 2002, **41**: 244–249.

455 Delgado R, Klimstra D, Albores-Saavedra J. Low grade salivary duct carcinoma. A distinctive variant with a low grade histology and a predominant intraductal growth pattern. Cancer 1996, **78**: 958–967.

456 Delgado R, Vuitch F, Albores-Saavedra J. Salivary duct carcinoma. Cancer 1993, **72**: 1503–1512.

457 Domson KK, Wakely PE Jr. Aspiration and imprint cytopathology of salivary duct carcinoma. Cancer Cytopathol 1997, **81**: 281–286.

458 Fan CY, Wang J, Barnes EL. Expression of androgen receptor and prostatic specific markers in salivary duct carcinoma: An immunohistochemical analysis of 13 cases and review of the literature. Am J Surg Pathol 2000, **24**: 579–586.

459 Felix A, El-Naggar AK, Press MF, Ordonez NG, Fonseca I, Tucker SL, Luna MA, Batsakis JG. Prognostic significance of biomarkers (c-erbB-2, p53, proliferating cell nuclear antigen, and DNA content) in salivary duct carcinoma. Hum Pathol 1996, **27**: 561–566.

460 Franklin CD, Ong TK. Ductal papilloma of the minor salivary gland. Histopathology 1991, **19**: 180–182.

461 Garland TA, Innes DJ, Fechner RE. Salivary duct carcinoma. An analysis of four cases with review of literature. Am J Clin Pathol 1984, **81**: 436–441.

462 Grenko RT, Gemryd P, Tytor M, Lundqvist P-G, Boeryd B. Salivary duct carcinoma. Histopathology 1995, **26**: 261–266.

463 Henley JD, Seo IS, Dayan D, Gnepp DR. Sarcomatoid salivary duct carcinoma of the parotid gland. Hum Pathol 2000, **31**: 208–213.

464 Ishikawa T, Imada S, Ijuhin N. Intraductal papilloma of the anterior lingual salivary gland. Case report and immunohistochemical study. Int J Oral Maxillofac Surg 1993, **22**: 116–117.

465 James GK, Pudek M, Berean KW, Diamandis EP, Archibald BL. Salivary duct carcinoma secreting prostate-specific antigen. Am J Clin Pathol 1996, **106**: 242–247.

466 Khurana KK, Pitman MB, Powers CN, Korourian S, Bardales RH, Stanley MW. Diagnostic pitfalls of aspiration cytology of salivary duct carcinoma. Cancer Cytopathol 1997, **81**: 373–379.

467 King PH, Hill J. Intraduct papilloma of parotid gland. J Clin Pathol 1993, **46**: 175–176.

468 Kumar RV, Kini L, Bhargava AK, Mukherjee G, Hazarika D, Shenoy AM, Anantha N. Salivary duct carcinoma. J Surg Oncol 1993, **54**: 193–198.

469 Lewis JE, McKinney BC, Weiland LH, Ferreiro JA, Olsen KD. Salivary duct carcinoma: Clinicopathologic and immunohistochemical review of 26 cases. Cancer 1996, **77**: 223–230.

470 Luna MA, Batsakis JG, Ordonez NG, Mackay B, Tortoledo ME. Salivary gland adenocarcinomas. A clinicopathologic analysis of three distinctive types. Semin Diagn Pathol 1987, **4**: 117–135.

471 Nagao T, Sugano I, Matsuzaki O, Hara H, Kondo Y, Nagao K. Intraductal papillary tumors of the major salivary glands: case reports of benign and malignant variants. Arch Pathol Lab Med 2000, **124**: 291–295.

472 Raymond AK, Batsakis JG. Stensen's duct carcinomas. Ann Otol Rhinol Laryngol 1991, **100**: 1035–1036.

473 Simpson RH, Clarke TJ, Sarsfield PT, Babajews AV. Salivary duct carcinoma. Histopathology 1991, **18**: 229–235.

473a Simpson RHW, Prasad AR, Lewis JE, Skálová A, David L. Mucin-rich variant of salivary duct carcinoma. A clinicopathologic and immunohistochemical study of four cases. Am J Surg Pathol 2003, **27**: 1070–1079.

473b Skálová A, Stárek I, Vanecek T, Kucerová V, Plank L, Szépe P, Di Palma S, Leivo I. Expression of HER-2.neu gene and protein in salivary duct carcinomas of parotid gland as revealed by fluorescence in-situ hybridization and immunohistochemistry. Histopathology 2003, **42**: 348–356.

474 Wick MR, Ockner DM, Mills SE, Ritter JH, Swanson PE. Homologous carcinomas of the breasts, skin, and salivary glands. A histologic and immunohistochemical comparison of ductal mammary carcinoma, ductal sweat gland carcinoma, and salivary duct carcinoma. Am J Clin Pathol 1998, **109**: 75–84.

475 Yoshihara T, Shino A, Ishii T, Kawakami M. Ultrastructural and immunohistochemical study of salivary duct carcinoma of the parotid duct. Ultrastruct Pathol 1994, **18**: 553–559.

Terminal duct carcinoma

476 Anderson C, Krutchkoff D, Pedersen C, Cartun R, Berman M. Polymorphous low-grade adenocarcinoma of minor salivary gland. A clinicopathologic and comparative immunohistochemical study. Mod Pathol 1990, **3**: 76–82.

477 Castle JT, Thompson LD, Frommelt RA, Wenig BM, Kessler H. Polymorphous low grade adenocarcinoma: a clinicopathologic study of 164 cases. Cancer 1999, **86**: 207–219.

478 Evans HL, Luna MA. Polymorphous low-grade adenocarcinoma: a study of 40 cases with long-term follow-up and an evaluation of the importance of papillary areas. Am J Surg Pathol 2000, **24**: 1319–1328.

479 George MK, Mansour P, Pahor AL. Terminal parotid duct carcinoma. J Laryngol Otol 1991, **105**: 780–781.

480 Miliauskas JR. Polymorphous low-grade (terminal duct) adenocarcinoma of the parotid gland. Histopathology 1991, **19**: 555–557.

481 Norberg L, Dardick I. The need for clinical awareness of polymorphous low-grade adenocarcinoma. A review. J Otolaryngol 1992, **21**: 149–159.

482 Simpson RH, Clarke TJ, Sarsfield PT, Gluckman PG, Babajews AV. Polymorphous low-grade adenocarcinoma of the salivary glands. A clinicopathological comparison with adenoid cystic carcinoma. Histopathology 1991, **19**: 121–129.

Papillary adenocarcinoma

483 Batsakis JG. Cystadenocarcinoma: a specific diagnosis or just another adenocarcinoma NOS? Adv Anat Pathol 1997, **4**: 252–255.

484 Blanck C, Eneroth C-M, Jakobsson PÅN. Mucus-producing adenopapillary (nonepidermoid) carcinoma of the parotid gland. Cancer 1971, **28**: 676–685.

485 Foss RD, Ellis GL, Auclair PL. Salivary gland cystadenocarcinomas. A clinicopathologic study of 57 cases. Am J Surg Pathol 1996, **20**: 1440–1447.

486 Kardos TB, Ferguson JW, McMillan MD. Mucus-producing adenopapillary carcinoma of the oral cavity. Int J Oral Maxillofac Surg 1992, **21**: 160–162.

487 Michal M, Skalova A, Mukensnabl P. Micropapillary carcinoma of the parotid gland arising in mucinous cystadenoma. Virchows Arch 2000, **437**: 465–468.

488 Mostofi R, Wood RS, Christison W, Talerman A. Low-grade papillary adenocarcinoma of minor salivary glands. Case report and literature review. Oral Surg Oral Med Oral Pathol 1992, **73**: 591–595.

489 Nagao T, Sugano I, Matsuzaki O, Hara H, Kondo Y, Nagao K. Intraductal papillary tumors of the major salivary glands: case reports of benign and malignant variants. Arch Pathol Lab Med 2000, **124**: 291–295.

Squamous cell carcinoma

490 Gaughan RK, Olsen KD, Lewis JE. Primary squamous cell carcinoma of the parotid gland. Arch Otolaryngol Head Neck Surg 1992, **118**: 798–801.

491 Leader M, Jass JR. In situ neoplasia in squamous cell carcinoma of the parotid. A case report. Histopathology 1985, **9**: 325–329.

492 Taxy JB. Squamous carcinoma in a major salivary gland: a review of the diagnostic considerations. Arch Pathol Lab Med 2001, **125**: 740–745.

Small cell carcinoma and other neuroendocrine carcinomas

493 Fornelli A, Eusebi V, Pasquinelli G, Quattrone P, Rosai J. Merkel cell carcinoma of the parotid gland associated with Warthin tumour: report of two cases. Histopathology 2001, **39**: 342–347.

494 Gnepp DR, Corio RL, Brannon RB. Small cell carcinoma of the major salivary glands. Cancer 1986, **58**: 705–714.

495 Gnepp DR, Wick MR. Small cell carcinoma of the major salivary glands. An immunohistochemical study. Cancer 1990, **66**: 185–192.

496 Hayashi Y, Nagamine S, Yanagawa T, Yoshida H, Yura Y, Azuma M, Sato M. Small cell undifferentiated carcinoma of the minor salivary gland containing exocrine, neuroendocrine, and squamous cells. Cancer 1987, **60**: 1583–1588.

497 Huntrakoon M. Neuroendocrine carcinoma of the parotid gland. A report of two cases with ultrastructural and immunohistochemical studies. Hum Pathol 1987, **18**: 1212–1217.

498 Koss LG, Spiro RH, Hajdu S. Small cell (oat cell) carcinoma of minor salivary gland origin. Cancer 1972, **30**: 737–741.

499 Kraemer BB, Mackay B, Batsakis JG. Small cell carcinomas of the parotid gland. A clinicopathologic study of three cases. Cancer 1983, **52**: 2115–2121.

500 Leipzig B, Gonzales-Vitale JC. Small cell epidermoid carcinoma of salivary glands. "Pseudo" oat cell carcinoma. Arch Otolaryngol 1982, **108**: 511–514.

501 Nagao T, Sugano I, Ishida Y, Tajima Y, Munakata S, Asoh A, Yamazaki K, Muto H, Konno A, Kondo Y, Nagao K. Primary large cell neuroendocrine carcinoma of the parotid gland: Immunohistochemical and molecular analysis of two cases. Mod Pathol 2000, **13**: 554–561.

502 Rollins CE, Yost BA, Costa MJ, Vogt PJ. Squamous differentiation in small-cell carcinoma of the parotid gland. Arch Pathol Lab Med 1995, **119**: 183–185.

503 Tanda F, Scott C, Pittaluga S, Massarelli G. Undifferentiated neuroendocrine (Merkel cell) carcinoma of the salivary glands. A light and electron microscopic study of two cases (abstract). Pathol Res Pract 1983, **178**: 167.

504 Wirman JA, Battifora HA. Small cell undifferentiated carcinoma of salivary gland origin. An ultrastructural study. Cancer 1976, **37**: 1840–1848.

Lymphoepithelioma-like carcinoma

505 Arthaud JB. Anaplastic parotid carcinoma ("malignant lymphoepithelial lesion") in seven Alaskan natives. Am J Clin Pathol 1972, **57**: 275–289.

506 Chan JKC, Yip TTC, Tsang WYW, Poon YF, Wong CSC, Ma VWS. Specific association of Epstein-Barr virus with lymphoepithelial carcinoma among tumors and tumorlike lesions of the salivary gland. Arch Pathol Lab Med 1994, **118**: 994–997.

507 Gravanis MB, Giansanti JS. Malignant histopathologic counterpart of the benign lymphoepithelial lesion. Cancer 1970, **26**: 1332–1342.

508 Hanji D, Gohao L. Malignant lymphoepithelial lesions of the salivary glands with anaplastic carcinomatous change. Report of nine cases and review of literature. Cancer 1983, **52**: 2245–2252.

509 Kott ET, Goepfert H, Ayala AG, Ordóñez NG. Lymphoepithelial carcinoma (malignant lymphoepithelial lesion) of the salivary glands. Arch Otolaryngol 1984, **110**: 50–53.

510 Kuo T-t, Tsang N-M. Salivary gland type nasopharyngeal carcinoma: a histologic, immunohistochemical, and Epstein–Barr virus study of 15 cases including a psammomatous mucoepidermoid carcinoma. Am J Surg Pathol 2001, **25**: 80–86.

511 Merrick Y, Albeck H, Nielsen NH, Hansen HS. Familial clustering of salivary gland carcinoma in Greenland. Cancer 1986, **57**: 2097–2102.

512 Nagao K, Matsuzaki O, Saiga H, Akikusa B, Sugano I, Shigematsu H, Kaneko T, Katoh T, Kitamura T, Asano Y, Okamoto M. A histopathologic study of benign and malignant lymphoepithelial lesions of the parotid gland. Cancer 1983, **52**: 1044–1052.

513 Raab-Traub N, Rajadurai P, Flynn K, Lanier AP. Epstein-Barr virus infection in carcinoma of the salivary gland. J Virol 1991, **65**: 7032–7036.

514 Saw D, Lau WH, Ho JHC, Chan JKC, Ng CS. Malignant lymphoepithelial lesion of the salivary gland. Hum Pathol 1986, **17**: 914–923.

515 Sehested M, Hainau B, Albeck H, Nielsen NH, Hansen JPH. Ultrastructural investigation of anaplastic salivary gland carcinomas in Eskimos. Cancer 1985, **55**: 2732–2736.

516 Sheen TS, Tsai CC, Ko JY, Chang YL, Hsu MM. Undifferentiated carcinoma of the major salivary glands. Cancer 1997, **80**: 357–363.

517 Tsai CC, Chen CL, Hsu HC. Expression of Epstein-Barr virus in carcinomas of major salivary glands: a strong association with lymphoepithelioma-like carcinoma. Hum Pathol 1996, **27**: 258–262.

Other primary carcinomas

518 Batsakis JG, el-Naggar AK, Luna MA. "Adenocarcinoma, not otherwise specified." A diminishing group of salivary carcinomas. Ann Otol Rhinol Laryngol 1992, **101**: 102–104.

519 Croitoru CM, Suarez PA, Luna MA. Hybrid carcinomas of salivary glands: report of 4 cases and review of the literature. Arch Pathol Lab Med 1999, **123**: 698–702.

520 Donath K, Seifert G, Lentrodt J. The embryonal carcinoma of the parotid gland. A rare example of an embryonal tumor. Virchows Arch [A] 1984, **403**: 425–440.

521 Latkovich P, Johnson RL. Carcinosarcoma of the parotid gland: report of a case with cytohistologic and immunohistochemical findings. Arch Pathol Lab Med 1998, **122**: 743–746.

522 Lopez JI, Ballestin C, Garcia-Prats MD, De Agustin P. Carcinosarcoma of the parotid gland. Immunohistochemical study of a case. Histopathology 1994, **25**: 388–390.

523 Nagao K, Matsuzaki O, Saiga H, Sugano I, Kaneko T, Katoh T, Kitamura T, Shigematsu H, Maruyama N. Histopathologic studies on adenocarcinoma of the parotid gland. Acta Pathol Jpn 1986, **36**: 337–347.

524 Nagao K, Matsuzaki O, Saiga H, Sugano I, Shigematsu H, Kaneko T, Katoh T, Kitamura T. Histopathologic studies of undifferentiated carcinoma of the parotid gland. Cancer 1982, **50**: 1572–1579.

525 Nagao T, Sugano I, Ishida Y, Asoh A, Munakata S, Yamazaki K, Konno A, Iwaya K, Shimizu T, Serizawa H, Ebihara Y. Hybrid carcinomas of the salivary glands: report of nine cases with a clinicopathologic, immunohistochemical, and *p53* gene alteration analysis. Mod Pathol 2002, **15**: 724–733.

526 Osaki T, Hirota J, Ohno A, Tatemoto Y. Mucinous adenocarcinoma of the submandibular gland. Cancer 1990, **66**: 1796–1801.

527 Takata T, Caselitz J, Seifert G. Undifferentiated tumours of salivary glands. Immunocytochemical investigations and differential diagnosis of 22 cases. Pathol Res Pract 1987, **182**: 161–168.

528 Viva E, Zorzi F, Annibale G, Stefini S, Baronchelli C, Bonetti MF. Endodermal sinus (yolk sac) tumor of the parotid gland. A case report. Int J Pediatr Otorhinolaryngol 1992, **24**: 269–274.

Malignant lymphoma

529 Abbondanzo SL. Extranodal marginal-zone B-cell lymphoma of the salivary gland. Ann Diagn Pathol 2001, **5**: 246–254.

530 Banik S, Howell JS, Wright DH. Non-Hodgkin's lymphoma

arising in adenolymphoma. A report of two cases. J Pathol 1985, **146:** 167–177.

531 Chan JK, Tsang WY, Hui PK, Ng CS, Sin VC, Khan SM, Siu LL. T- and T/natural killer-cell lymphomas of the salivary gland: a clinicopathologic, immunohistochemical and molecular study of six cases. Hum Pathol 1997, **28:** 238–245.

532 Dunphy CH, Grosso LE, Rodriquez JJ, Dunphy FR. Bilateral mucosa-associated lymphoid tissue lymphomas of parotid glands: A 13-year interval. Mod Pathol 1996, **9:** 560–565.

533 Gleeson MJ, Bennett MH, Cawson RA. Lymphomas of salivary glands. Cancer 1986, **58:** 699–704.

534 Hsi ED, Singleton TP, Swinnen L, Dunphy CH, Alkan S. Mucosa-associated lymphoid tissue-type lymphomas occurring in post-transplantation patients. Am J Surg Pathol 2000, **24:** 100–106.

535 Hyman GA, Wolff M. Malignant lymphomas of the salivary glands. Review of the literature and report of 33 new cases, including four cases associated with the lymphoepithelial lesion. Am J Clin Pathol 1976, **65:** 421–438.

536 James M, Norton AJ, Akosa AB. Primary T-cell lymphoma of submandibular salivary gland. Histopathology 1993, **22:** 83–85.

537 Kerr PD, Dort JC. Primary extramedullary plasmacytoma of the salivary glands. J Laryngol Otol 1991, **105:** 687–692.

538 Kerrigan DP, Irons J, Chen I-M. Bcl-2 gene rearrangement in salivary gland lymphoma. Am J Surg Pathol 1990, **14:** 1133–1138.

539 Kojima M, Nakamura S, Ichimura K, Shimizu K, Itoh H, Masawa N. Follicular lymphoma of the salivary gland: a clinicopathological and molecular study of six cases. Int J Surg Pathol 2001, **9:** 287–294.

539a Kojima M, Nakamura S, Itoh H, Yamane Y, Tanaka H, Sugihara S, Sakata N, Masawa N. Sclerosing variant of follicular lymphoma arising from submandibular glands and resembling "Küttner tumor". A report of 3 patients. Int J Surg Pathol 2003, **11:** 303–307.

540 Mehle ME, Kraus DH, Wood BG, Tubbs R, Tucker HM, Lavertu P. Lymphoma of the parotid gland. Laryngoscope 1993, **103:** 17–21.

541 Miller R, Yanagihara ET, Dubrow AA, Lukes RJ. Malignant lymphoma in a Warthin's tumor. Report of a case. Cancer 1982, **50:** 2948–2950.

542 Nime FA, Cooper HS, Eggleston JC. Primary malignant lymphomas of the salivary glands. Cancer 1976, **37:** 906–912.

543 Ochoa ER, Harris NL, Pilch BZ. Marginal zone B-cell lymphoma of the salivary gland arising in chronic sclerosing sialadenitis (Kuttner tumor). Am J Surg Pathol 2001, **25:** 1546–1550.

544 Pascoe HR, Dorfman RF. Extramedullary plasmacytoma of the submaxillary gland. Am J Clin Pathol 1969, **51:** 501–507.

545 Pisa EK, Pisa P, Kang HI, Fox RI. High frequency of t(14;18) translocation in salivary gland lymphomas from Sjögren's syndrome patients. J Exp Med 1991, **174:** 1245–1250.

546 Schmid U, Helbron D, Lennert K. Primary malignant lymphomas localized in salivary glands. Histopathology 1982, **6:** 673–687.

547 Takahashi H, Cheng J, Fujita S, Tsuda N, Tezuka F, Liu AR, Okabe H. Primary malignant lymphoma of the salivary gland. A tumor of mucosa-associated lymphoid tissue. J Oral Pathol Med 1992, **21:** 318–325.

Other primary neoplasms

548 Ascoli V, Albedi FM, De Blasiis R, Nardi F. Sialadenosis of the parotid gland. Report of four cases diagnosed by fine-needle aspiration cytology. Diagn Cytopathol 1993, **9:** 151–155.

549 Auclair PL, Langloss JM, Weiss SW, Corio RL. Sarcomas and sarcomatoid neoplasms of the major salivary gland regions. A clinicopathologic and immunohistochemical study of 67 cases and review of the literature. Cancer 1986, **58:** 1305–1315.

550 Baker SE, Jensen JL, Correll RW. Lipomas of the parotid gland. Oral Surg Oral Med Oral Pathol 1981, **52:** 167–171.

551 Balogh K, Wolbarsht RL, Federman M, O'Hara CJ. Carcinoma of the parotid gland with osteoclastlike giant cells. Immunohistochemical and ultrastructural observations. Arch Pathol Lab Med 1985, **109:** 756–761.

552 Batsakis JG, Frankenthaler R. Embryoma (sialoblastoma) of salivary glands. Ann Otol Rhinol Laryngol 1992, **101:** 958–960.

553 Benjamin E, Wells S, Fox H, Reeve NL, Knox F. Malignant fibrous histiocytomas of salivary glands. J Clin Pathol 1982, **35:** 946–953.

554 Brandwein M, Al-Naeif NS, Manwani D, Som P, Goldfeder L, Rothschild M, Granowetter L. Sialoblastoma: Clinicopathological/immunohistochemical study. Am J Surg Pathol 1999, **23:** 342–348.

555 Carrillo R, Rodriguez-Peralto JL, Batsakis JG, el-Naggar AK. Primary haemangiopericytomas of the parotid gland. J Laryngol Otol 1992, **106:** 659–661.

556 Castle JT, Thompson LD. Kaposi sarcoma of major salivary gland origin: A clinicopathologic series of six cases. Cancer 2000, **88:** 15–23.

556a Childers E, Furlong M, Fanburg-Smith J. Hemangioma of the salivary gland: a study of ten cases of a rarely biopsied/excised lesion. Ann Diagn Pathol 2002, **6:** 339–344.

557 Davidson D, Leibel BS, Berris B. Asymptomatic parotid gland enlargement in diabetes mellitus. Ann Intern Med 1969, **70:** 31–38.

558 Deb RA, Desai SB, Amonkar PP, Aiyer PM, Borges AM. Primary primitive neuroectodermal tumour of the parotid gland. Histopathology 1998, **33:** 375–378.

559 Dehner LP, Valbuena L, Perez-Atayde A, Reddick RL, Askin FB, Rosai J. Salivary gland anlage tumor ("congenital pleomorphic adenoma"). A clinicopathologic, immunohistochemical and ultrastructural study of nine cases. Am J Surg Pathol 1994, **18:** 25–36.

560 Eusebi V, Martin SA, Govoni E, Rosai J. Giant cell tumor of major salivary glands. Report of three cases, one occurring in association with a malignant mixed tumor. Am J Clin Pathol 1984, **81:** 666–675.

560a Fanburg-Smith J, Furlong M, Childers E. Oral and salivary gland angiosarcoma: a clinicopathologic study of 290 cases. Mod Pathol 2003, **16:** 263–271.

561 Ferreiro JA, Nascimento AG. Solitary fibrous tumour of the major salivary glands. Histopathology 1996, **28:** 261–264.

562 Grenko RT, Tytor M, Boeryd B. Giant cell tumour of the salivary gland with associated carcinosarcoma. Histopathology 1993, **23:** 594–595.

563 Guarino M, Giordano F, Pallotti F, Ponzi S. Solitary fibrous tumour of the submandibular gland. Histopathology 1998, **32:** 571–573.

563a Hsueh C, Gonzalez-Crussi F. Sialoblastoma: a case report and review of the literature on congenital epithelial tumors of salivary gland origin. Pediatr Pathol 1992, **12:** 205–214.

564 Katz AD, Passy V, Kaplan L. Neurogenous neoplasms of major nerves of face and neck. Arch Surg 1971, **103:** 51–56.

565 Livesey JR, Soames JV. Cystic lymphangioma in the adult parotid. J Laryngol Otol 1992, **106:** 566–568.

566 Luna MA. Sialoblastoma and epithelial tumors in children: their morphologic spectrum and distribution by age. Adv Anat Pathol 1999, **6:** 287–292.

566a Ma J, Chan J, Chow C, Orell S. Lymphadenoma: a report of three cases of an uncommon salivary gland neoplasm. Histopathology 2002, **41:** 342–350.

567 Mantravadi J, Roth LM, Kafrawy AH. Vascular neoplasms of the parotid gland. Parotid vascular tumors. Oral Surg Oral Med Oral Pathol 1993, **75:** 70–75.

568 Murrell GL, Barnes M, Langford FP, Kenan PD. Submandibular rhabdomyoma. Ear Nose Throat J 1992, **71:** 663–664.

568a Nagao T, Serizawa H, Iwaya K, Shimizu T, Sugano I, Ishida Y, Yamazaki K, Shimizu M, Itoh T, Konno A, Ebihara Y.

Keratocystoma of the parotid gland: a report of two cases of an unusual pathologic entity. Mod Pathol 2001, **15**: 1005–1010.

569 Nagao T, Sugano I, Ishida Y, Asoh A, Munakata S, Yamazaki K, Konno A, Kondo Y, Nagao K. Sialolipoma: a report of seven cases of a new variant of salivary gland lipoma. Histopathology 2001, **38**: 30–36.

570 Rose PE, Howard ER. Congenital teratoma of the submandibular gland. J Pediatr Surg 1982, **17**: 414–416.

571 Seifert G, Donath K, Jautzke G. Unusual choristoma of the parotid gland in a girl. A possible trichoadenoma. Virchows Arch 1999, **434**: 355–360.

572 Takato T, Komuro Y, Yonehara Y. Giant hemangioma of the parotid gland associated with Kasabach-Merritt syndrome. A case report. J Oral Maxillofac Surg 1993, **51**: 425–428.

573 Walterhouse DO, Pappo AS, Baker KS, Parham DM, Anderson JR, Donaldson SS, Paidas CN, Womer RN, Crist WM. Rhabdomyosarcoma of the parotid region occurring in childhood and adolescence: a report from the intergroup rhabdomyosarcoma study group. Cancer 2001, **92**: 3135–3146.

574 Wiley EL, Stewart D, Brown M, Albores-Saavedra J. Fibrous histiocytoma of the parotid gland. Am J Clin Pathol 1992, **97**: 512–516.

575 Yu FH, Kobos JW, Brooks JSJ. Synovial sarcoma of the parotid gland region: a case report and review of the literature. Int J Surg Pathol 1996–1997, **4**: 239–244.

Metastatic tumors

576 Brodsky G, Rabson AB. Metastasis to the submandibular gland as the initial presentation of small cell ("oat cell") lung carcinoma. Oral Surg Oral Med Oral Pathol 1984, **58**: 76–80.

577 Hrebinko R, Taylor SR, Bahnson RR. Carcinoma of prostate metastatic to parotid gland. Urology 1993, **41**: 272–273.

578 Jennings TA, Okby NT, Schroer KR, Wolf BC, Mihm MC Jr. Parotid involvement by desmoplastic melanoma. Histopathology 1996, **29**: 165–170.

579 Melnick SJ, Amazon K, Dembrow V. Metastatic renal cell carcinoma presenting as a parotid tumor: A case report with immunohistochemical findings and a review of the literature. Hum Pathol 1989, **20**: 195–197.

580 Seifert G, Hennings K, Caselitz J. Metastatic tumors to the parotid and submandibular glands. Analysis and differential diagnosis of 108 cases. Pathol Res Pract 1986, **181**: 684–692.

581 Shah JP, Kraus DH, Dubner S, Sarkar S. Patterns of regional lymph node metastases from cutaneous melanomas of the head and neck. Am J Surg 1991, **162**: 320–323.

582 Simpson RH, Skàlovà A. Metastatic carcinoma of the prostate presenting as parotid tumour. Histopathology 1997, **30**: 70–74.

General features of salivary gland tumors

Relative incidence and malignancy; Clinical diagnosis; Staging

583 Albeck H, Nielsen NH, Hansen HE, Bentzen J, Ockelmann HH, Bretlau P, Hansen HS. Epidemiology of nasopharyngeal and salivary gland carcinoma in Greenland. Arctic Med Res 1992, **51**: 189–195.

584 Baker HW. Staging of head and neck cancer. Semin Surg Oncol 1992, **8**: 73–77.

585 Baker SR, Malone B. Salivary gland malignancies in children. Cancer 1985, **55**: 1730–1736.

586 Byers RM, Jesse RH, Guillamondegui OM, Luna MA. Malignant tumors of the submaxillary gland. Am J Surg 1973, **126**: 458–463.

587 Byers RM, Piorkowski R, Luna MA. Malignant parotid tumors in patients under 20 years of age. Arch Otolaryngol 1984, **110**: 232–235.

588 Callender DL, Frankenthaler RA, Luna MA, Lee SS, Goepfert H. Salivary gland neoplasms in children. Arch Otolaryngol Head Neck Surg 1992, **118**: 472–476.

589 Eneroth C-M. Incidence and prognosis of salivary gland tumours at different sites. A study of parotid, submandibular and palatal tumours in 2632 patients. Acta Otolaryngol (Stockh) 1970, **263**: 174–178.

590 Eveson JW, Cawson RA. Salivary gland tumours. A review of 2410 cases with particular reference to histological types, site, age, and sex distribution. J Pathol 1985, **146**: 51–58.

591 Fine G, Marshall RB, Horn RC Jr. Tumors of the minor salivary glands. Cancer 1960, **13**: 653–669.

592 Gnepp DR, Schroeder W, Heffner D. Synchronous tumors arising in a single major salivary gland. Cancer 1989, **83**: 1219–1224.

593 Horn-Ross PL, West DW, Brown SR. Recent trends in the incidence of salivary gland cancer. Int J Epidemiol 1991, **20**: 628–633.

594 Krolls SO, Trodahl JN, Boyers RC. Salivary gland lesions in children. A survey of 430 cases. Cancer 1972, **30**: 459–469.

595 Levitt SH, McHugh RB, Gómez-Marin O, Hyams VJ, Soule EH, Strong EW, Sellers AH, Woods JE, Guillamondegui OM. Clinical staging system for cancer of the salivary gland. A retrospective study. Cancer 1981, **47**: 2712–2724.

596 Luna MA, Tortoledo ME, Allen M. Salivary dermal analogue tumors arising in lymph nodes. Cancer 1987, **59**: 1165–1169.

597 Saku T, Hayashi Y, Takahara O, Matsuura H, Tokunaga M, Tokuoka S, Soda M, Mabuchi K, Land CE. Salivary gland tumors among atomic bomb survivors, 1950–1987. Cancer 1997, **79**: 1465–1475.

598 Shore-Freedman E, Abrahams C, Recant W, Schneider AB. Neurilemomas and salivary gland tumors of the head and neck following childhood irradiation. Cancer 1983, **51**: 2159–2163.

599 Smith A, Winkler B, Perzin KH, Wazen J, Blitzer A. Mucoepidermoid carcinoma arising in an intraparotid lymph node. Cancer 1985, **55**: 400–403.

600 Spiro RH. Salivary neoplasms. Overview of a 35-year experience with 2,807 patients. Head Neck Surg 1986, **8**: 177–184.

601 Spitz MR, Batsakis JG. Major salivary gland carcinoma. Descriptive epidemiology and survival of 498 patients. Arch Otolaryngol 1984, **110**: 45–49.

Biopsy and cytology; Frozen section

602 Chan MK, McGuire LJ, King W, Li AK, Lee JC. Cytodiagnosis of 112 salivary gland lesions. Correlation with histologic and frozen section diagnosis. Acta Cytol 1992, **36**: 353–363.

603 Cohen MB, Reznicek MJ, Miller TR. Fine-needle aspiration biopsy of the salivary glands. Pathol Annu 1992, **27**(Pt 2): 213–245.

604 Geisinger KR, Weidner N. Aspiration cytology of salivary glands. Semin Diagn Pathol 1986, **3**: 219–226.

605 Granick MS, Erickson ER, Hanna DC. Accuracy of frozen-section diagnosis in salivary gland lesions. Head Neck Surg 1985, **7**: 465–467.

606 Heller KS, Attie JN, Dubner S. Accuracy of frozen section in the evaluation of salivary tumors. Am J Surg 1993, **166**: 424–427.

607 Hillel AD, Fee WE Jr. Evaluation of frozen section in parotid gland surgery. Arch Otolaryngol 1983, **109**: 230–232.

608 Layfield LJ, Tan P, Glasgow BJ. Fine-needle aspiration of salivary gland lesions. Comparison with frozen sections and histologic findings. Arch Pathol Lab Med 1987, **111**: 346–353.

609 Li S, Baloch ZW, Tomaszewski JE, LiVolsi VA. Worrisome histologic alterations following fine-needle aspiration of benign parotid lesions. Arch Pathol Lab Med 2000, **124**: 87–91.

610 Lussier C, Klijanienko J, Vielh P. Fine-needle aspiration of metastatic nonlymphomatous tumors to the major salivary glands: a clinicopathologic study of 40 cases cytologically diagnosed and histologically correlated. Cancer Cytopathol 2000, **90**: 350–356.

611 MacLeod CB, Frable WJ. Fine-needle aspiration biopsy of the salivary gland. Problem cases. Diagn Cytopathol 1993, **9**: 216–224.

612 Miller RH, Calcaterra TC, Paglia DE. Accuracy of frozen section diagnosis of parotid lesions. Ann Otol Rhinol Laryngol 1979, **88**: 573–576.

613 Mukunyadzi P, Bardales RH, Palmer HE, Stanley MW. Tissue effects of salivary gland fine-needle aspiration. Does this procedure preclude accurate histologic diagnosis? Am J Clin Pathol 2000, **114**: 741–745.

614 O'Dwyer P, Farrar WB, James AG, Finkelmeier W, McCabe DP. Needle aspiration biopsy of major salivary gland tumors. Its value. Cancer 1986, **57**: 554–557.

615 Rigual NR, Milley P, Loré JM Jr, Kaufman S. Accuracy of frozen-section diagnosis in salivary gland neoplasms. Head Neck Surg 1986, **8**: 442–446.

616 Zurrida S, Alasio L, Tradati N, Bartoli C, Chiesa F, Pilotti S. Fine-needle aspiration of parotid masses. Cancer 1993, **72**: 2306–2311.

Treatment

617 Armstrong JG, Harrison LB, Thaler HT, Friedlander-Klar H, Fass DE, Zelefsky MJ, Shah JP, Strong EW, Spiro RH. The indications for elective treatment of the neck in cancer of the major salivary glands. Cancer 1992, **69**: 615–619.

618 Elkon D, Colman M, Hendrickson FR. Radiation therapy in the treatment of malignant salivary gland tumors. Cancer 1978, **41**: 502–506.

619 Eneroth C-M, Hamberger CA. Principles of treatment of different types of parotid tumors. Laryngoscope 1974, **84**: 1732–1740.

620 Garden AS, Weber RS, Ang KK, Morrison WH, Matre J, Peters LJ. Postoperative radiation therapy for malignant tumors of minor salivary glands. Outcome and patterns of failure. Cancer 1994, **73**: 2563–2569.

621 Shingaki S, Ohtake K, Nomura T, Nakajima T. The role of radiotherapy in the management of salivary gland carcinomas. J Craniomaxillofac Surg 1992, **20**: 220–224.

622 Spiro IJ, Wang CC, Montgomery WW. Carcinoma of the parotid gland. Analysis of treatment results and patterns of failure after combined surgery and radiation therapy. Cancer 1993, **71**: 2699–2705.

623 Tu G, Hu Y, Jiang P, Qin D. The superiority of combined therapy (surgery and postoperative irradiation) in parotid cancer. Arch Otolaryngol 1982, **108**: 710–713.

624 Witten J, Hybert F, Hansen HS. Treatment of malignant tumors in the parotid glands. Cancer 1990, **65**: 2515–2520.

625 Yamashita T, Tomoda K, Kumazawa T. The usefulness of partial parotidectomy for benign parotid gland tumors. A retrospective study of 306 cases. Acta Otolaryngol Suppl 1993, **500**: 113–116.

Prognosis

626 Andersen LJ, Therkildsen MH, Ockelmann HH, Bentzen JD, Schiodt T, Hansen HS. Malignant epithelial tumors in the minor salivary glands, the submandibular gland, and the sublingual gland. Prognostic factors and treatment results. Cancer 1991, **68**: 2431–2437.

627 El-Naggar AK, Hurr K, Kagan J, Gillenwater A, Callender D, Luna MA, Batsakis JG. Genotypic alterations in benign and malignant salivary gland tumors: histogenetic and clinical implications. Am J Surg Pathol 1997, **21**: 691–697.

628 Eneroth C-M, Hjertman L, Moberger G. Malignant tumours of submandibular gland. Acta Otolaryngol (Stockh) 1967, **64**: 514–536.

629 Frankenthaler RA, Luna MA, Lee SS, Ang KK, Byers RM, Guillamondegui OM, Wolf P, Goepfert H. Prognostic variables in parotid gland cancer. Arch Otolaryngol Head Neck Surg 1991, **117**: 1251–1256.

630 Fu KK, Leibel SA, Levine ML, Friedlander LM, Boles R, Phillips TL. Carcinoma of the major and minor salivary glands. Analysis of treatment results and sites and causes of failures. Cancer 1977, **40**: 2882–2890.

631 Fujita S, Takahashi H, Okabe H. Nucleolar organizer regions in malignant salivary gland tumors. Acta Pathol Jpn 1992, **42**: 727–733.

632 Gallo O, Franchi A, Bianchi S, Boddi V, Giannelli E, Alajmo E. p53 oncoprotein expression in parotid gland carcinoma is associated with clinical outcome. Cancer 1995, **75**: 2037–2044.

633 Gallo O, Franchi A, Bottai GV, Fini-Storchi I, Tesi G, Boddi V. Risk factors for distant metastases from carcinoma of the parotid gland. Cancer 1997, **80**: 844–851.

634 Hickman RE, Cawson RA, Duffy SW. The prognosis of specific types of salivary gland tumors. Cancer 1984, **54**: 1620–1624.

635 Kamio N. Coexpression of p53 and c-erbB-2 proteins is associated with histological type, tumour stage, and cell proliferation in malignant salivary gland tumours. Virchows Arch 1996, **428**: 75–84.

636 Muller S, Vigneswaran N, Gansler T, Gramlich T, De Rose PB, Cohen C. c-*erb*B-2 oncoprotein expression and amplification in pleomorphic adenoma and carcinoma ex pleomorphic adenoma. Relationship to prognosis. Mod Pathol 1994, **7**: 628–632.

637 Sugano S, Mukai K, Tsuda H, Hirohashi S, Furuya S, Shimosato Y, Ebihara S, Takeyama I. Immunohistochemical study of c-erbB-2 oncoprotein overexpression in human major salivary gland carcinoma. An indicator of aggressiveness. Laryngoscope 1992, **102**: 923–927.

638 Vander Poorten VLM, Balm AJ, Hilgers FJ, Tan IB, Loftus-Coll BM, Keus RB, van Leeuwen FE, Hart AA. The development of a prognostic score for patients with parotid carcinoma. Cancer 1999, **85**: 2057–2067.

13 Liver

Valeer J. Desmet* and Juan Rosai

Non-neoplastic diseases
Tumors and tumorlike conditions

* Author of the section on "Non-neoplastic diseases."

Non-neoplastic diseases

Normal anatomy

Several structural and functional units have been proposed in the microanatomy of the liver. Of these, the most relevant for the diagnostic histopathologist are the liver lobule and the liver acinus. For several years the liver acinus[4] was the preferred concept in textbooks of pathology and hepatology, as it appeared to better explain the "bridging" type of lesions connecting afferent and efferent vascular landmarks: portal–central bridging necrosis and fibrosis. The simple liver acinus corresponds to the clump of parenchyma vascularized by a single terminal branch of the portal vein (portal venule) and hepatic artery, and drained by the neighboring terminal twigs of the hepatic vein (terminal hepatic venules). In spite of its popularity in recent years, the liver acinus did not stand the scrutiny of further detailed angioarchitectural, morphologic and histochemical investigations, and virtually all later studies support the lobular concept of liver architecture, albeit with several types of subunits.

The classical hexagonal liver lobule of Kiernan is equivalent to the more recently described secondary lobule of Matsumoto et al., which itself is composed of 6 to 8 primary lobules.[3] Whereas the acinus is centered on the "afferent" portal tract, the classical liver lobule is surrounded by (on average) 6 portal tracts and centered on a terminal twig of the hepatic vein: the centrolobular (or central) vein. The portal vein ramifications in the portal tracts give off a series of branches in the plane between adjacent portal tracts; these in turn give rise to sinusoids that drain the blood toward the center of the lobule. The lobular equivalents of the acinar zones 1, 2 and 3 are the periportal zone, midzonal area (or midlobular zone), and centrolobular area.

The liver parenchymal cell or hepatocyte is a polygonal cell with a mostly central, single nucleus. Hepatocytes are arranged in plates one cell thick (muralia) with a sinusoid on either side, thus exposing each hepatocyte to portal blood on two surfaces. Within the muralium each hepatocyte adjoins adjacent parenchymal cells with its intercellular surface. This intercellular domain of the cell membrane carries a groove (hemicanaliculus) as a girdle around the cell. The hemicanaliculi of two adjacent hepatocytes form the intercellular bile canaliculus, which is separated from the rest of the intercellular space and the blood compartment by tight junctions.

The virtual cleft between the sinusoidal lining cells and the sinusoidal domain of the hepatocyte surface is the space of Disse. The hepatic sinusoids are lined by different cell types. The sinusoidal endothelial cells are of the fenestrated type. Kupffer cells bulge out on the luminal side of the sinusoids; they are resident members of the mononuclear phagocyte system that undergo enlargement and proliferation in response to a wide variety of stimuli. Hepatic stellate cells (previously also termed Ito cells, fat-storing cells or lipocytes) are contractile perisinusoidal "pericytes" located in the space of Disse. They store vitamin A in their cytoplasmic lipid droplets and are able to switch their phenotype to myofibroblast-like cells under appropriate stimulation. They are matrix producers in normal liver and in pathologic intralobular fibrosis. Hepatic stellate cells are only identified with difficulty in routinely stained preparations; immunostaining for synaptophysin marks both resting and activated cells, and immunostaining for α-smooth muscle actin reveals activated stellate cells.[1]

Located on the inside of endothelial cells are some scattered "pit cells," which correspond to resident intrahepatic lymphocytes, to a large extent of the natural killer phenotype.

The portal tracts at the lobular periphery are composed of connective tissue, ensheathing branches of the hepatic artery, portal vein, bile duct, and lymphatics. The caliber of portal tracts and their composing structures decreases from the hilum of the liver toward its periphery. This explains why surgical liver biopsies and autopsy specimens usually contain larger portal areas than needle biopsy specimens.

Percutaneous needle biopsies may preferentially sample peripheral tissue, the microarchitectural variability of which is greater than at deeper sites within the liver. Portal dyads (with only two of the three profiles: artery, vein, and bile duct) are almost as common as portal triads in normal peripheral liver tissue.[2] However, due to the presence of more than one branch of artery, vein, or duct, the average number of profiles per portal tract is 6 ± 5. On average, one may expect two interlobular bile ducts, two hepatic arteries, and one portal vein per portal tract.[2]

Interlobular bile ducts, usually located in the center of the portal tract, are connected with the lobular canaliculi by ductules (or cholangioles). The latter are hardly visible on hematoxylin–eosin (H&E) staining but clearly revealed by cytokeratin immunostains.[5]

Liver cell plates and sinusoids have a more regular radial arrangement in the center of the lobule, whereas the periportal zone is characterized by a less regular, anastomosing network pattern of these structures.

Hepatocytes are polygonal in shape, with clearly outlined margins in H&E preparations. The cytoplasm is granular and eosinophilic, with basophilic aggregates of rough endoplasmic reticulum in a perinuclear distribution. The nucleus is centrally placed and carries one or more easily identifiable nucleoli. Mitotic figures are very rare. Hepatocytes are rich in glycogen, with diurnal and diet-related variations in amount and distribution. Glycogen accumulation in nuclei occurs as clear vacuoles, predominantly in periportal hepatocytes. This is common in childhood and may be conspicuous in some adult diseases (for example diabetes and Wilson's disease) but is not by itself of diagnostic significance. Lipofuscin occurs as fine, light brown, PAS-positive and acid-fast granules in the pericanalicular region of centrolobular hepatocytes. Stainable iron is absent or demonstrable in only scant amounts. An occasional hepatocyte in normal liver may contain fat. The perisinusoidal space of Disse is not seen in biopsy material, but appears dilated in autopsy specimens.

There is some variation in hepatic microscopic appearance with age. In neonates, extramedullary hematopoiesis may persist during the first weeks of life. In children below the age of 5 years, liver cell plates are two cells thick, whereas in adulthood twin cell plates indicate regeneration. With increasing age, there is more variation in nuclear size (anisokaryosis), somewhat more pronounced centrolobular lipofuscinosis ("wear and tear pigment"), some atrophy of centrolobular hepatocytes and correspondingly broader appearance of perivenular sinusoids, possible hyalinization of the wall of hepatic artery branches, slight infiltration of macrophages and a few lymphocytes in some (not all) portal tracts, insignificant or minimal amounts of stainable iron in hepatocytes, and thickening of the liver capsule with some fibrous extensions reaching for 1 to 2 mm into the underlying parenchyma.

Biopsy

Light microscopic examination of liver tissue remains an essential part of the diagnostic procedure and of the follow-up of the majority of liver diseases.[9] There are four primary methods to obtain a liver biopsy: the transcutaneous intercostal route (blind percutaneous needle biopsy), peritoneoscopy, open surgery, or the transvenous approach (transjugular or less often transfemoral). Various types of needle can be used: variations of the aspiration needle advocated by Menghini[21] or of the cutting type (Vim–Silverman needle, later the Tru-cut).

Aspiration needles vary in diameter from the skinny Chiba needle (0.9 mm) to 1.2 to 1.8 mm sized needles. Tru-cut needles of various sizes have become available, ranging from 1 to 2 mm. The smaller ones are mostly used with a gun, to biopsy focal lesions rapidly. CT- or ultrasound-guided fine needle aspiration is established as an effective method for diagnosing focal hepatic lesions.[15] The choice of the technique and of the needle depends on the suspected lesion (focal or diffuse) and on the presence of contraindications to the usual percutaneous approach.[9]

A surgical incisional biopsy should be performed immediately on entering the peritoneal cavity. Biopsies taken at the end of an operative procedure show surgical artifacts, amongst others so-called "surgical necroses," appearing as coagulative necrosis of single or small groups of hepatocytes surrounded and infiltrated by neutrophil polymorphs; the lesion is usually centrolobular but its extent depends on the duration of the operation and the degree of manipulation of the liver.[6] The subcapsular area is not representative of the entire organ; marked subcapsular fibrosis may coexist with minimal changes deeper in the liver.[14,23] Therefore the surgeon should perform not only an incisional biopsy but also a deeper needle biopsy.

Liver biopsy is an invasive procedure and therefore the indication and techniques should be carefully considered. Complications of percutaneous liver biopsy comprise pain, vagal reaction, perforation of diaphragm, gallbladder, or large blood vessels, and seeding of malignant cells. In large series, a mortality rate of 0.01%[22,24] has been recorded, and clinically important hemorrhage in 0.2% to 1%.[17] The diagnostic usefulness of liver biopsy changes over time. The availability of serologic tests for the etiologic diagnosis of acute viral hepatitis has reduced the need for liver biopsy in this condition.[28] The refinement of liver imaging techniques and of endoscopic retrograde cholangiopancreatography rendered largely obsolete the use of liver biopsy for the differentiation between intra- and extrahepatic cholestasis.[11,28]

However, liver histopathology remains a mainstay in the diagnostic work-up of most liver diseases. Several studies emphasized its diagnostic usefulness and impact on therapy: for the elucidation of chronic elevation of transaminase levels[16,30]; for revealing nonalcoholic liver disease in alcoholics[18]; for the diagnosis of granulomatous liver disease[8]; for the recognition of side effects of drugs[10,28]; and for the diagnosis of cirrhosis, including the incomplete septal variety,[27] and other conditions such as noncirrhotic portal hypertension.[26] A recent review discusses the usefulness of and diagnostic problems in liver histopathology.[13]

With the advent of liver transplantation, liver biopsy remains the gold standard for the diagnosis of cellular rejection[7] and for study of the principal causes of morbidity and late mortality.[19] It is indicated for the assessment of treatment results, for instance in chronic viral hepatitis[12,20] and primary biliary cirrhosis.[25] In an appreciable number of cases, the expert histopathologist may discover the presence of unsuspected liver alterations in combination with the lesions of a clinically presumed diagnosis: for instance α_1-antitrypsin deficiency in chronic viral hepatitis B or C, primary sclerosing cholangitis in genetic hemochromatosis, etc.[9]

Over the years, the accuracy and diagnostic yield of liver histopathology have been steadily increasing through expanding opportunities for immunohistochemistry and in situ hybridization. The number and type of routine stains applied will vary from one laboratory to the next. As in all diagnostic histopathology, the H&E stain is the mainstay in liver pathology. Special stains are useful for visualizing inapparent or easily overlooked features. Some pathologists favor a standard battery, others opt for a selected few and order additional stains according to need.

The strict minimum is H&E and a connective tissue stain. Very useful are Perls' stain for iron; the PAS–diastase stain for ceroid macrophages, α_1-antitrypsin inclusions, fungi, and thickened basement membranes of interlobular bile ducts; the rhodanine stain for copper (in Wilson's disease, chronic cholestasis, and copper toxicosis); Shikata's orcein stain for revealing elastic fibers (useful to differentiate old fibrosis from recent postnecrotic collapse), for hepatitis B surface antigen, and for copper-binding protein. A useful alternative to orcein is Victoria blue.

Immunohistochemical staining for "bile duct type cytokeratins" (cytokeratins 7 and 19) is extremely useful in cholestatic liver diseases, for recognizing early stages of cholate stasis, cholestatic liver cell rosettes, ductular reaction, and ductopenia.[9,29]

The diagnostic accuracy of liver histopathology depends on numerous factors, which are not always optimal in every instance and which hardly lend themselves to quantitative evaluation. Several factors relate to the biopsy specimen. Its size is important, although not in an absolute way. Since the average needle biopsy represents 1 hundred to 1 fifty thousandth of the liver organ, sampling variability and error is an obvious possibility.

A reliable diagnosis of a disease with unequal involvement of portal tracts (such as chronic hepatitis or primary biliary cirrhosis) requires a longer tissue cylinder than a condition with diffuse involvement (such as classical acute hepatitis). The diagnostic accuracy of focal lesions (e.g., granulomas, cytomegalovirus inclusions) is improved by examining multiple sections. Architectural changes (e.g., cirrhosis) are more readily appreciated in specimens obtained with the Tru-cut than with the Menghini needle. Two general statements can be made with respect to the size of the biopsy: (1) an ideal needle biopsy should be 10 to 20 mm long; and (2) the pathologist should carefully examine even inadequately sized specimens in order to assure maximum yield of information from an invasive procedure.

Factors determining accuracy which are related to the interpreter include experience, availability of clinical information, and sufficient interest in clinical hepatology. Even under optimal circumstances, an occasional biopsy may happen not to provide a final or complete diagnosis, or may even fail to give helpful information.[9]

In recent years, with the emphasis on evidence-based medicine, semiquantitative scoring systems have been proposed for the (semi)quantitation of various diagnostic features. Examples include the assessment of hepatic iron content, of liver fibrosis, and of the degree of necroinflammation and fibrosis in chronic hepatitis, primary biliary cirrhosis, alcoholic hepatitis, and nonalcoholic steatohepatitis (NASH).[9]

Although a reliable final diagnosis definitely requires knowledge of the clinical background of the patient, it is equally true that objectivity in analysis and conclusion is best served by a preceding examination without any clinical information.

Viral hepatitis

Viral hepatitis, or liver inflammation due to viral infection, may be caused by specific hepatotropic viruses (the "hepatitis viruses") and by several other viruses which mostly cause generalized infections (e.g., cytomegalovirus, Epstein–Barr virus).

Viral hepatitis caused by hepatotropic viruses

Viral hepatitis may be caused by at least five distinct viruses, belonging to entirely different families (Table 13.1). They

Table 13.1 Major hepatitis viruses

Virus	Type and family	Infection route	Disease
Hepatitis A (HAV)	RNA Hepatovirus Picornaviridae	Fecal–oral	Acute
Hepatitis B (HBV)	DNA Orthohepadnavirus Hepadnaviridae	Parenteral	Acute, chronic
Hepatitis C (HCV)	RNA virus Flaviviridae	Parenteral or sporadic	Acute, chronic
Hepatitis D (HDV)	RNA virus (related to plant viroids)	Pathogenic when combined with HBV	Acute, chronic
Hepatitis E (HEV)	RNA virus unclassified	Fecal–oral Epidemic or sporadic	Acute

Other hepatitis viruses include: hepatitis G virus (HGV or GVB-C); transfusion transmitted virus (TTV); a novel DNA virus, SEN-V; a toga-like virus sometimes referred to as hepatitis F; and a paramyxovirus causing giant cell hepatitis (see text).

have very little in common except that they affect the liver as target organ and some degree of shared epidemiology. All have a worldwide distribution.

When adequate diagnostic tests for hepatitis A (HAV) and B (HBV) became available in transfusion centers for screening of donor blood, evidence was produced for the existence of a fraction of virus-induced post-transfusion hepatitis not due to HAV or HBV, designated by the term non-A, non-B hepatitis.[37] After more than a decade of intensive research, hepatitis C virus (HCV) was discovered and found to be responsible for the majority of non-A, non-B hepatitis (Table 13.1).[31,33,43,44] Two of these viruses (HAV and HEV) are spread principally by the fecal–oral route, and three (HBV, HCV, HDV) are spread mainly by exposure to blood, although HBV is frequently spread by unprotected sex.[44]

More recently identified hepatitis viruses, of lower or still debated pathogenicity, include hepatitis G virus (HGV), transfusion-transmitted virus (TTV), and SEN virus (SEN-V). HGV can be transmitted by transfusion, but a causal relation between HGV and liver cell damage was questioned,[32] although some later studies suggested a pathogenic role of this virus.[35,40]

TTV, originally named for the initials of the patient from whom it was recovered,[39] but incidentally also fitting for "transfusion transmitted virus",[47] appears to be a widespread virus of low pathogenicity that might be responsible for a proportion of cases of non-A, non-G acute and chronic hepatitis[48] of mild severity.[38]

A strong association of SEN-V (a novel DNA virus) with transfusion-associated non-A to E hepatitis compared with controls has raised the still unproven possibility that SEN-V might be a causative agent of post-transfusion hepatitis.[49]

Other possible human hepatitis viruses comprise a togavirus-like agent implicated in fulminant hepatitis,[36] sometimes referred to as hepatitis F virus (HFV), and a paramyxovirus incriminated in some cases of giant cell hepatitis.[42]

The outcome of infection of a human being by a hepatitis virus depends on a number of variables includ-

ing viral factors (viral load, genotype, mutations, etc.), virus–host interactions, host characteristics (age, gender, general condition, life style, alcohol abuse, etc.), expression of viral proteins, nature of the host immune response, patterns of cytokines, etc., which will finally determine the histologic alterations of viral hepatitis.[33,34,41,45,46] The great multitude of factors explains the striking variability in severity, course, and complications of the disease caused by the same virus in different patients.

Acute viral hepatitis

The morphologic features of viral hepatitis have been extensively described in the past.[50–52] Although the introduction of serologic and molecular tests for hepatitis viruses has decreased the indication for liver biopsy in acute hepatitis, biopsy may still be used to confirm a diagnosis, to assess severity and evolution of the disease, and to exclude concomitant disease (e.g., alcoholic type liver damage in HCV seropositive patients). When evaluating biopsies, one should assess the type and the degree of hepatocellular damage, the characteristics of the inflammatory response, the stromal reactions, and the presence of parenchymal regeneration.

The histologic picture of acute hepatitis due to different hepatitis viruses may be sufficiently similar to cause problems in differentiation. The general changes of hepatitis are first described, followed by some characteristics specific to individual types of viruses. Acute viral hepatitis may be of varying severity—mild, moderate, severe, and fatal—which is reflected in the nature and extent of histopathologic lesions. The lesions concern the lobular parenchyma and the portal tracts. The lesions of the moderately severe form, "classical lobular hepatitis with spotty necrosis," may serve as a base for comparison with the other forms.

Typical acute viral hepatitis

Typical acute viral hepatitis with spotty necrosis is a panlobular disease, although the changes may predominate in the centrolobular region in hepatitis B and C, and in the periportal zone in hepatitis A. Hepatocellular alterations are variable. Some parenchymal cells show ballooning, with increased cell volume and pale-staining, granular cytoplasm (so-called "hydropic change") (Fig. 13.1); they probably are precursor stages of lytic necrosis or cell dropout. Other hepatocytes show shrinkage, increased eosinophilia, and nuclear pyknosis, most of them representing cells in the process of apoptosis[53,55]; they are often described as "acidophil bodies" or (incorrectly) as Councilman bodies. Apoptotic bodies may appear as a condensed shrunken cell, or as clusters of cell fragments, which may or may not contain pyknotic nuclear material; they may appear naked, or in close proximity to mononuclear inflammatory cells, or inside phagocytosing macrophages (Fig. 13.2). A mild degree of steatosis may be seen in a minority of cases with acute hepatitis from any cause. Several hepatocytes may appear in mitosis.

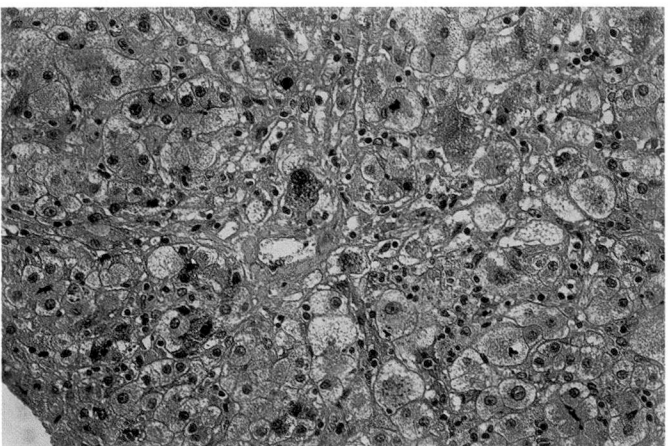

Fig. 13.1 Acute viral hepatitis B. Centrolobular area of liver lobule, characterized by liver cell pleomorphism (including ballooning of hepatocytes), some canalicular bilirubin stasis, focal liver cell loss, and mononuclear (mainly lymphocytic) inflammatory infiltration. (H&E)

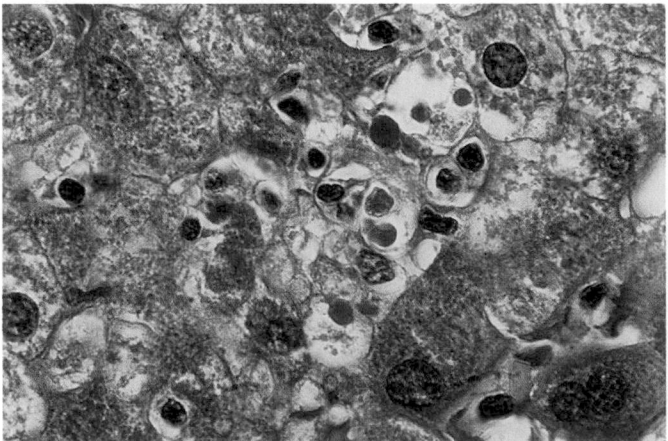

Fig. 13.2 Detail of lobular parenchyma in mild acute viral hepatitis C. Eosinophil condensation of hepatocellular cytoplasm (Mallory body-like) and rounded eosinophil fragments of apoptotic hepatocyte, with a few adjacent mononuclear inflammatory cells. (H&E)

Syncytial, multinucleated, giant hepatocytes, which are typical of neonatal hepatitis, may sometimes be found in adults as well, without truly diagnostic significance for a specific etiology.

The heterogeneous appearance of parenchymal cells (ballooning, shrinkage, apoptosis) results in liver cell pleomorphism, which, together with cell dropout and regeneration of surviving hepatocytes, leads to a loss of the normal regular liver cell plate pattern; this "lobular disarray" is a diagnostically helpful feature.

Some degree of microscopic bilirubin stasis is common in acute hepatitis; this reflects the usual, somewhat variable degree of cholestasis in the disease. The term "cholestatic hepatitis" should be reserved for patients with a clinically marked and protracted cholestasis.

The altered parenchyma is infiltrated by inflammatory cells, with predominance of mononuclear and lymphocytic cell types. The majority of lymphocytes are activated memory T cells.[57] Also, plasma cells may be found from the early stage.[54] Small clusters of lymphocytes, whether or not in close proximity to apoptotic bodies, represent foci of cytotoxic lymphocyte-mediated target cell attack, and represent the lesion indicated by the terms "focal inflammation," "focal necrosis," and "spotty necrosis."

Kupffer cells enlarge and become more prominent; they phagocytose cell debris from dying hepatocytes, which results in the intracellular accumulation of clumps of golden brown, lipid-rich "ceroid" pigment, which is best revealed in PAS–diastase stains. In the earlier stages, these "ceroid macrophages" are small and scattered as single cells; later on, they are larger and form clusters which predominate in centrolobular and midzonal areas; in still later stages, they are found migrated into the portal connective tissue. Ceroid macrophages in acute viral hepatitis may also stain for iron in some cases.

Although the lobular parenchymal lesions predominate in the acute forms of viral hepatitis, the portal tracts, or most of them, also become involved. They are the seat of mononuclear cell infiltration: lymphocytes and plasma cells, admixed with some neutrophils, eosinophils, and—especially in the later stages—pigment-laden macrophages. The cellular infiltrate usually remains confined within the portal connective tissue, with preservation of the limiting plate. In several instances, the infiltrate may spill out into the adjacent parenchyma, blurring the outline of the portal tract and resembling so-called "piecemeal necrosis" or interface hepatitis characteristic of chronic hepatitis. This renders the differentiation between acute and chronic hepatitis on purely histologic grounds quite delicate; the global histologic picture and also the clinical data should be taken into account for a final diagnosis.

An increase in ductular profiles at the portal–parenchymal interface (so-called "ductular reaction") occurs in acute hepatitis; this is very mild in classical acute lobular hepatitis and better revealed by cytokeratin 7 immunostains; the extent of ductular reaction increases with the severity of the necrotizing parenchymal lesions. Lymphocytic infiltration between and inside bile duct lining cells, and some degree of bile duct epithelial damage may occur, especially in viral hepatitis C.[56]

In the later stages of acute, self-limited hepatitis, most of the parenchymal and portal changes gradually disappear. Residual changes such as mild infiltration in some portal tracts, some focal inflammation in the lobules, a few remaining macrophages, and anisokaryosis too prominent for the patient's age, may persist for several months.

Minimal acute hepatitis

Minimal acute hepatitis is characterized by a limited degree of damage and inflammation. Slight liver cell ballooning, some apoptotic bodies, no bilirubin stasis, mild lymphocytic infiltrate, scant numbers of macrophages, and minimal infiltration in only part of the portal areas create a poorly diagnostic picture resembling so-called "nonspecific reactive hepatitis." The latter term indicates a mild degree of hepatitic changes, observed in the liver of patients with extrahepatic inflammatory disease (e.g., pneumonia).

Severe acute hepatitis, acute hepatitis with bridging necrosis

Death of larger groups of hepatocytes occurs in severely necrotizing hepatitis. This more extensive pattern of parenchymal damage is usually reflected by lytic necrosis of hepatocytes affecting contiguous parenchymal territories ("confluent necrosis"), predominantly in the microcirculatory periphery. These patterns of necrosis are best explained according to the acinar concept of liver architecture.[58]

With increasing degree of severity, the confluent necrosis wipes out the parenchyma of the periphery of acinar zone 3, resulting in centrolobular confluent necrosis. A higher degree involves the entire acinar zone 3, giving rise to dropout of parenchyma between portal tracts and central veins—bridging hepatic necrosis. Although the term bridging hepatic necrosis had originally a broader meaning,[59,60] it will be used here in the mentioned definition of acinar zone 3 necrosis or "portal–central bridging necrosis" (Fig. 13.3). A still higher degree of severity is represented by lytic necrosis of all acinar zones, resulting in panlobular and multilobular necrosis.

The necrotic bridges change in appearance over time. Freshly necrotizing bridges reveal lobular areas where the parenchyma has disappeared, without or with only little collapse of the reticulin framework. The necrotizing areas are infiltrated by mononuclear cells and some small ceroid macrophages. Later stages are characterized by collapse of the reticulin fibers, proliferation of mesenchymal cells and collagen deposition, possibly bulging of the

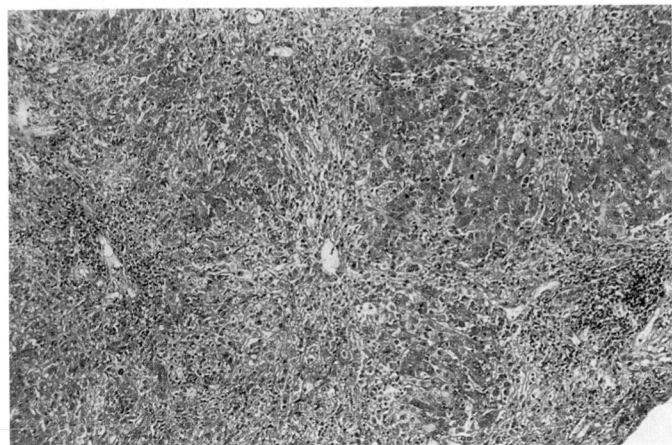

Fig. 13.3 Severe necrotizing acute viral hepatitis B. Overview of liver lobule; mild to moderate mononuclear cell infiltration in portal tracts (lower left, top, and lower right). Bridging portal–central confluent lytic necrosis, realizing a "star-shaped" area of necrosis with a centrolobular vein at its center and peripheral points reaching portal tracts. Inflammatory cells are scattered throughout the lobule. (H&E)

regenerating remaining parenchyma, and larger numbers of ceroid macrophages. Older necrotic bridges heal with fibrous scars, resulting in portal–central bridging fibrosis.

Obvious fibrosis is a characteristic of chronic rather than of acute hepatitis. Fibrous bridges in chronic hepatitis can be recognized by the fact that gradual deposition of elastic fibers takes place. Thus, bridging fibrosis of chronic hepatitis is positive on elastica stains, whereas bridges in acute hepatitis stain negative.[61] Severely necrotizing hepatitis is characterized by a higher degree of periportal ductular reaction. The areas of surviving parenchyma reveal the changes of acute hepatitis described for classical lobular hepatitis, but usually with more marked degrees of focal necrosis and bilirubin stasis.

Acute hepatitis with panlobular and multilobular necrosis (submassive liver necrosis)

Severe and very severe necrotizing hepatitis, which occurs in a minority of patients, corresponds clinically to fulminant hepatitis with acute liver failure and coma. In such patients, lytic confluent necrosis of the parenchyma extends throughout the entire liver lobule (panlobular necrosis) and affects several adjacent lobules (multilobular necrosis). Extensive confluent necrosis is usually distributed in a heterogeneous way throughout the liver organ, thus needle biopsies may not be representative.

Ductular reaction is more prominent in multilobular necrosis, and represents an attempt at regeneration by liver progenitor cells. It corresponds to so-called "atypical" ductular reaction, in which the epithelial proliferation comprises not only bile ductular cells, but also elements with a phenotype intermediate between that of cholangiocytes and hepatocytes—so-called "transitional cells".[62,63] Some of the ductules may contain inspissated bilirubin-stained concrements in cases with severe necrosis or with sepsis[64]; this lesion should not be mistaken as a sign of biliary obstruction.

In surviving patients, multilobular necrosis (or submassive necrosis) results in collapse and fibrous scarring of necrotic zones, alternating with nodular regeneration of surviving parenchymal territories.

Severe necrotizing hepatitis may have causes other than infection by hepatitis viruses: autoimmune hepatitis, adverse drug reactions, toxic liver cell necrosis, Wilson's disease. As all or most of the parenchymal cells have disappeared through lytic necrosis, there are fewer markers pointing to a particular etiology, so that it is often impossible to pinpoint the etiology on histologic grounds alone.

Causative viruses

It is not possible to histologically diagnose with certainty the etiology of acute viral hepatitis, since the main histopathologic traits of acute viral hepatitis A, B, C, D, and E are quite similar. Nevertheless, there are suggestive trends and patterns, but one has to keep in mind that the histopathologic picture may be confused by coinfection with more than one virus, or by concomitant liver disease (hepatitis of the alcoholic type, primary sclerosing cholangitis, etc.).

Acute viral hepatitis A[65,79,85,88] may reveal a picture dominated by centrolobular bilirubin stasis with only little liver cell damage and inflammation; this may be mistaken for other causes of cholestasis (e.g., drug-induced cholestasis). Particularly in adults, HAV infection may cause cholestatic hepatitis, even with some bile duct damage.[67]

In several patients the hepatitic changes show a periportal predominance, with dense, plasma cell-rich portal infiltrates. Periportal parenchymal necrosis with interruptions of canals of Hering may contribute to the cholestatic features.[85] Other patterns of hepatitis as described above are also found. Since hepatitis A may occasionally present a prolonged and polyphasic clinical course characterized by two or more relapses of rise in transaminase values, a correct diagnosis and prognosis requires serologic analysis.[90] Severely necrotizing hepatitis with multilobular necrosis is rare in HAV infection. Fibrin ring granulomas have been reported.[81,91]

Immunohistochemical staining reveals viral antigen in the cytoplasm of hepatocytes and Kupffer cells[86]; viral RNA can be located in situ by in situ hybridization.[87]

Acute viral hepatitis B. The histopathology is roughly similar to that of other forms of hepatitis[65,73,79,82] with centrolobular predominance of liver cell damage and inflammation. Lymphocytes may lie in close contact with hepatocytes (peripolesis) and even inside them (emperipolesis). Liver cell damage is apparently caused by T cell-mediated and humoral mechanisms.[69] In the

fully developed stage of acute hepatitis B, only little or no hepatitis B surface antigen (HBsAg) and hepatitis B core antigen (HBcAg) can be demonstrated immunohistochemically, consistent with the notion that acute hepatitis B is an "elimination type" of disease, resulting in eradication of the virus and assuring a self-limited course of the disease.[66] Ground glass hepatocytes are not seen in the acute form; their presence indicates chronicity of viral hepatitis B. As in other parenterally transmitted hepatitis, such as hepatitis D and C, intravenous drug abuse may be recognized by the presence of birefringent spicules of talc in portal tracts.[76,77]

Whether a chronic course can be predicted on the findings in the liver biopsy during the acute stage has caused controversy for years. A tentative conclusion is that no single lesion has predictive value in the early stage of infection. Later biopsies (after 2 months) may yield unfavorable prognostic information in the form of periportal interface hepatitis, possibly in the presence of confluent lytic (bridging) necrosis, and definitely when viral antigens (HBsAg, HBcAg) can be demonstrated in the tissue. Periportal interface hepatitis must be evaluated most carefully in order to avoid overdiagnosis of chronic liver disease.[70]

Acute viral hepatitis C. The pathologic features of acute hepatitis C are essentially those described in previous years for non-A, non-B hepatitis,[71,74,82,84] characterized by liver cell swelling, apoptosis, cholestasis, and lymphocytic intralobular infiltration. Bile duct damage and development of portal lymphoid aggregates and lymphoid follicles, the most characteristic features of hepatitis C in the chronic stage, may also occur in the acute phase.

Lymphocytic infiltration may be prominent in the sinusoids ("indian file" appearance) in the absence of noticeable parenchymal damage, resembling Epstein–Barr virus hepatitis ("mononucleosis-like" picture). Steatosis is fairly common.[73] Fulminant hepatitis with multilobular necrosis does occur, but is rare in the Western world.

Immunohistochemical demonstration of viral antigens with different antibodies was repeatedly reported, but the overall results appeared to lack specificity. The same criticism applies to in situ hybridization for HCV RNA.[78]

Acute viral hepatitis D can occur in three settings: (1) simultaneous acute hepatitis D infection and acute type B hepatitis; (2) acute hepatitis D superimposed on chronic hepatitis B; and (3) chronic hepatitis D infection superimposed on chronic hepatitis B.[83] The histologic picture of HDV hepatitis is similar to that of other forms of hepatitis, and although it tends to be more severe, it cannot be reliably distinguished histologically from hepatitis B or C.[68,75,89] Immunohistochemical staining for HDV antigens in tissue is a reliable method of documenting infection.[68,72,89]

In parts of South America and Africa, acute HDV infection has been associated with microvesicular change in hepatocytes[80]; this "spongiocytic change" or "morula cell degeneration" was attributed to accumulation of small lipid droplets in damaged hepatocytes.

Differential diagnosis

Acute hepatitis with marked cholestasis can be differentiated from obstructive forms of cholestasis by the typical necroinflammatory lobular lesions in acute hepatitis. Drug-induced hepatitis may be indistinguishable histologically from viral hepatitis (the "viral hepatitis-like form" of drug-induced liver disease); hence it follows that drug-induced liver disease should always be kept in mind when facing a hepatitis histology of doubtful etiology. Features suggestive of a drug-induced lesion comprise sharply delineated centrolobular necrosis, abundant eosinophils, and granulomas. However, absence of these features does not exclude drug hepatitis. Autoimmune hepatitis can have an acute onset, histologically similar to viral hepatitis.

Acute hepatitis of the alcoholic type is recognized by conspicuous steatosis, Mallory bodies, neutrophil satellitosis, and pericellular ("chicken-wire") fibrosis. Differentiation of acute from chronic hepatitis is generally based on the predominance of portal and periportal changes and fibrosis in the latter, whereas lobular lesions prevail in acute hepatitis. However, the distinction may be very difficult and sometimes impossible in the absence of clinical data.

Chronic (viral and other) hepatitis

Elementary lesions

Schematically, the elementary lesions that compose the histopathologic picture of chronic hepatitis comprise "spotty necrosis," confluent lytic necrosis, portal inflammation, interface hepatitis, fibrosis, and cirrhosis.[92]

"Spotty necrosis" is an older term, loosely applied to apoptosis and genuine necrosis of single hepatocytes. A more appropriate morphologic term would be "focal necroinflammation," recognizable as a small cluster of mononuclear cells (lymphocytes, possibly with histiocytes) with or without an adjacent identifiable apoptotic body or bodies. Spotty necrosis in chronic hepatitis looks the same as in acute hepatitis (Fig. 13.1). Confluent parenchymal necrosis of the lytic type, or dropout of contiguous groups of hepatocytes with denudation of the reticulin framework, occurs in more severe forms of chronic hepatitis. It usually coincides with clinical episodes of disease exacerbation.[99] As in acute hepatitis, the extent of confluent necrosis may range from focal and zonal confluent necrosis over "bridging" confluent necrosis (Fig. 13.4) to the more extensive panlobular and multilobular degrees.

Severe parenchymal necrosis is often accompanied by the development of small, glandlike clusters of surviving

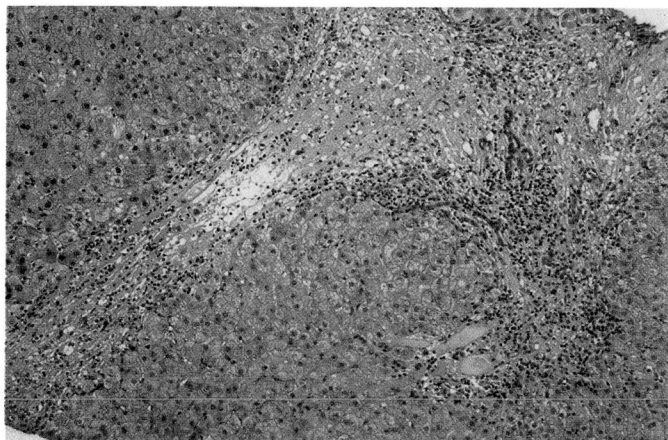

Fig. 13.4 Bridging confluent lytic necrosis in severe chronic viral hepatitis B. Inflamed portal tract "bridged" through area of necrosis with centrolobular area (lower left). The upper right part corresponds to an area of extensive lytic necrosis in phase of postnecrotic collapse of the reticulin framework and early fibrosis. (H&E)

hepatocytes within the inflamed tissue (Fig. 13.5). These "hepatitic rosettes" are usually surrounded by connective tissue and presumably represent attempts at regeneration from surviving hepatocytes in an unfavorable environment.

Portal inflammation in chronic hepatitis may be mild, moderate, or dense. It is composed of mononuclear cells, comprising mainly lymphocytes, variable numbers of plasma cells, and other mononuclear cells (histiocytes, immature lymphocytes). Lymphoid aggregates and true lymphoid follicles may develop.

Interface hepatitis was originally termed "piecemeal necrosis," referring to a periportal lesion.[96] It corresponds to the extension of the lymphocytic portal infiltrate beyond the limits of the portal tract, associated with cell death (cell by cell or "piecemeal") of hepatocytes,

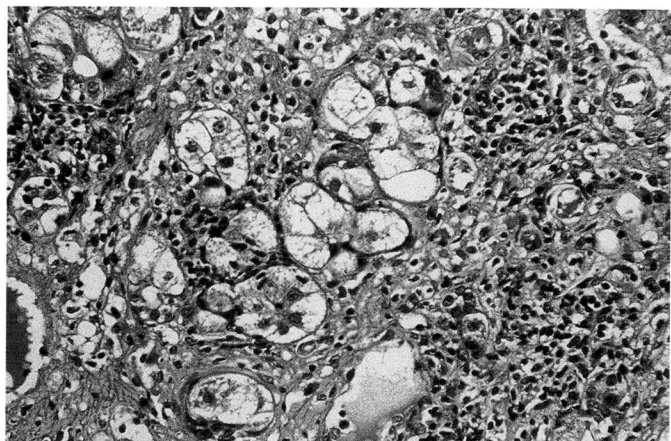

Fig. 13.5 Severe chronic viral hepatitis B. Area of multilobular lytic necrosis in phase of postnecrotic collapse and early fibrosis, with several small islands of surviving hepatocytes, appearing swollen and pale, and sometimes arranged in tubular fashion ("hepatitic-type liver cell rosettes"). (H&E)

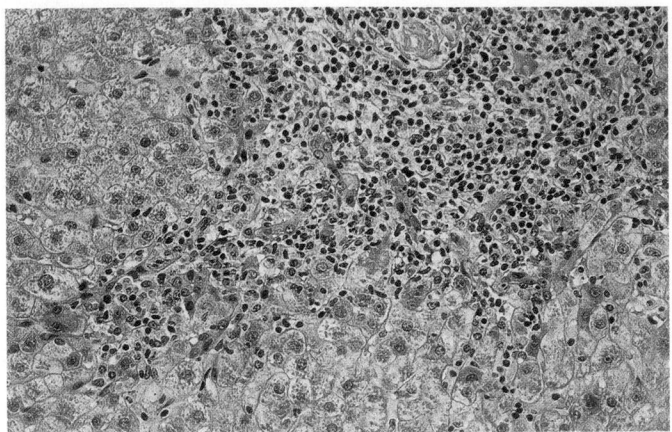

Fig. 13.6 Marked interface hepatitis ("piecemeal necrosis") in chronic viral hepatitis B. Note inflamed portal tract (upper right) and wedgelike extension of necroinflammation (towards lower left) and irregular interface between portal periphery and adjacent parenchyma all around the necroinflammatory area.

trapping of surviving hepatocytes within this inflammatory infiltrate, neoangiogenesis, and fibrosis (Fig. 13.6). Interface hepatitis is a better term, as the mode of liver cell death is apoptosis, not necrosis,[94,97,98] and the lesion is located at the interface between mesenchyme (portal tract or septum) and parenchyma. Interface hepatitis may be mild (one or a few foci around the portal perimeter without noticeable fibrous extension), or severe (with wedge-shaped extension of the necroinflammatory lesion and obvious fibrosis deep into the lobule).

Interface hepatitis is responsible for the enlargement of portal tracts with irregular outlines. The distinction should be made between true "lymphocytic piecemeal necrosis" as described above, and "biliary piecemeal necrosis" which occurs in chronic biliary disease. In the latter variety, the irregular outline of the enlarging portal tract is not due to "invading" lymphocytes, but to ductular reaction with associated neutrophil infiltration and cholate stasis of periportal hepatocytes[93] (see p. 951).

Fibrosis is progressive in the more active variants of chronic hepatitis. Intralobular fibrosis apparently results from continuous ongoing lobular necroinflammatory damage.[95]

Septal fibrosis appears as periportal, portal–portal and portal–central septa. Periportal and portal–portal septa presumably result from interface hepatitis, whereas portal–central septa seem to be sequels of portal–central (bridging) confluent necrosis.

Ongoing necroinflammation, associated with progressive fibrosis and parenchymal regeneration, eventually leads to cirrhosis. In the cirrhotic stage, the necroinflammatory changes may have subsided (inactive cirrhosis) or may continue unabated (active cirrhosis).

Classification

The introduction of needle aspiration biopsy of the liver[108] greatly contributed to the recognition of non-cirrhotic forms of chronic inflammatory liver disease. After World War II, chronic sequelae of epidemic hepatitis were described in several parts of the world.[103] A form of chronic hepatitis, apparently autoimmune in nature, was described by Waldenström in 1950.[118]

In the 1960s, chronic hepatitis was presumed to be a sequel of viral hepatitis in several patients, although a causative agent had not been identified. The autoimmune type was considered as the "classical" form of chronic active hepatitis. Because of marked semantic confusion, a simple classification of chronic hepatitis, based on histology, was proposed by a group of hepatologists and pathologists in 1968.[102] Since at that time immunosuppression was the standard treatment, to be reserved for the more "active" forms of the disease, the classification distinguished between a milder form (chronic persistent hepatitis—CPH) with a low degree of necroinflammatory activity, and more severe variants (chronic aggressive or active hepatitis—CAH) featuring higher degrees of necroinflammatory lesions. This classification of chronic hepatitis became widely accepted and was used worldwide for nearly 40 years. Although it was emphasized that CPH and CAH were not to be considered as distinct disease entities, but as variations in the degree of disease activity, this message was frequently, and with the passage of time, increasingly ignored.

Since 1968, remarkable progress has been achieved in the elucidation of the multiple etiologies of chronic hepatitis, with the discoveries of HBV, HCV, and HDV[112] (Table 13.2). A drug-induced form of chronic hepatitis was recognized in 1971[113] and is now established as a classical cause of the disease.[111] Autoimmune forms of chronic hepatitis remained a diagnostic category, with gradual refinements in clinical and serologic diagnosis.[109]

Wilson's disease was shown to resemble chronic hepatitis clinically and histologically in some cases[116,117]; the same appeared to apply to another metabolic disease, α_1-antitrypsin deficiency.[106] Piecemeal necrosis, a very important diagnostic criterion in CAH, but (incorrectly) thought by some to be pathognomonic of and synonymous with chronic hepatitis, was also observed in chronic biliary diseases such as primary biliary cirrhosis and primary sclerosing cholangitis.

Investigations into the natural course of the disease in chronic viral hepatitis B revealed successive phases of viral replication, elimination, and integration, associated successively with lesser, higher, and again decreasing

Table 13.2 Etiology of chronic hepatitis

Viral
HBV, HDV, HCV
combined infections: B+D, B+C, C+HIV, C+HGV
Autoimmune
Drug-induced
Cryptogenic

degrees of necroinflammatory disease activity.[100,101] This implied successive occurrence of CPH and CAH variants in individual patients, confusing those who considered CPH and CAH to be distinct diseases. A change of view on chronic hepatitis was indicated.[114] Most importantly, the development of more efficient treatment for viral types of chronic hepatitis (interferons and antiviral agents) urgently necessitated a revision of chronic hepatitis classification.[105,107,110,115] In 1994, two proposals for a new classification of chronic hepatitis were published.[104,119] Both are largely parallel, although the latter includes chronic biliary and metabolic diseases (which may mimic chronic hepatitis) under that heading. There appears to be general agreement to restrict the term "chronic hepatitis" to its original meaning: a clinical and pathologic syndrome with several causes and characterized by varying degrees of hepatocellular necrosis and inflammation. For lack of a better definition of chronicity, chronic hepatitis is still defined (as in 1968) as a continuing disease without improvement for at least 6 months.[104]

In order to be comprehensive and clinically useful, the new classifications consider: (1) the etiology; (2) the grade of disease activity; and (3) the stage of progression of the disease (Table 13.3).

The first question to be asked by the pathologist when classifying chronic hepatitis remains: "Is this chronic hepatitis, or another liver disease?" Several liver diseases may have clinical and histologic features resembling those of chronic hepatitis, and need to be considered in the differential diagnosis, but do not correspond to "chronic hepatitis" in its strictest sense. The second step concerns determination of the etiology (Table 13.3), which cannot be based on histology alone and requires consideration of clinical and serologic data. Histopathologic study of the liver biopsy, however, may be useful in establishing, confirming, or refining an etiologic diagnosis.

The next item corresponds to grading of disease activity, which is evaluated by clinical symptoms, by aminotransferase levels, and by histopathology of the liver biopsy. Histologically, the degree of disease activity is evaluated by considering the main components in the histopathologic picture: portal inflammation, interface hepatitis, intralobular damage and inflammation, and confluent necrosis. Several systems can be utilized to express the degree of disease activity in the liver biopsy. In daily practice, an adequate report consists of an accurate estimate of the various lesions, described as minimal, mild, moderate, or severe. For specific purposes, such as

Table 13.3 Classification of chronic hepatitis

1. Diagnosis of chronic hepatitis
2. Etiology
3. Grade of disease activity
4. Stage of disease progression

comparison of pre- and post-treatment biopsy specimens and for evaluation of therapeutic trials, semiquantitative scoring systems are indicated (see Grading and staging, below).

Staging of the disease is an attempt to place the disease of the patient into a specific segment along an assumed course or time of progression.[119] The evolutionary stage has significant prognostic and therapeutic implications. Its histologic evaluation is based on the extent of fibrosis and the development of cirrhosis. Connective tissue stains are essential for staging. As is the case for histologic grading, staging can also be expressed in classical descriptions, and is the appropriate method for daily reporting of biopsies. Again, for specific purposes, semiquantitative scoring systems can be used (see below).

Grading and staging

Several systems for semiquantitative scoring as also applied in other areas of diagnostic histopathology[127] have been proposed for semiquantitative evaluation of liver lesions in chronic hepatitis.[120–123,128,129,133,138–143,148,149] The most widely used has been the Histological Activity Index published in 1981 (the HAI or Knodell index).[141] A simple scoring system was proposed by Scheuer,[149] and found to be easily applicable and reproducible.[133]

A "modified HAI" was published as an extension of the original Knodell system, with a series of modifications attempting to overcome some of the problems that had emerged in its use[139] (Tables 13.4 and 13.5). This modified HAI has been validated for intra- and interobserver variability.[152] For the evaluation of chronic hepatitis C, the system proposed by the French METAVIR Cooperative Study Group[122,123] has been applied to very large numbers of biopsies, especially for staging purposes.[146,147]

Several papers have commented on the different scoring systems, with discussions of their advantages and disadvantages.[124,134–137,150] The conclusion is that each of the systems currently in use has strengths and weaknesses. All suffer from the problems that apply to any form of histologic scoring of liver biopsies in chronic hepatitis: lack of scientific validation, observer variation, sample variation, and etiologic differences.[135] In this era of evidence-based medicine,[132] numerical scoring of liver biopsies will continue to have a place. The pathologist engaging in semiquantitative scoring of liver biopsies should follow published advice.[122,124,135,150] Histologic scoring is less relevant in routine clinical practice, and should be reserved for special purposes: for comparing pre- and post-treatment biopsies of a single patient, as a research method for studying the course of the disease, and as a tool for use in clinical therapeutic trials.[129] The system most suitable for the purpose should be chosen, for instance for grading[151] and staging[126] for alcoholic liver disease. The system that is most appropriate for

Table 13.4 Modified Histological Activity Index grading: necroinflammatory scores[139]

	Score
A. Periportal or periseptal interface hepatitis (piecemeal necrosis)	
Absent	0
Mild (focal, few portal areas)	1
Mild/moderate (focal, most portal areas)	2
Moderate (continuous around <50% of tracts or septa)	3
Severe (continuous around >50% of tracts or septa)	4
B. Confluent necrosis	
Absent	0
Focal confluent necrosis	1
Zone 3 necrosis in some areas	2
Zone 3 necrosis in most areas	3
Zone 3 necrosis + occasional portal–central (P-C) bridging	4
Zone 3 necrosis + multiple P-C bridging	5
Panacinar or multiacinar necrosis	6
C. Focal (spotty) lytic necrosis, apoptosis and focal inflammation*	
Absent	0
One focus or less per 10 × objective	1
One to four foci per 10 × objective	2
Five to ten foci per 10 × objective	3
More than ten foci per 10 × objective	4
D. Portal inflammation	
None	0
Mild, some or all portal areas	1
Moderate, some or all portal areas	2
Moderate/marked, all portal areas	3
Marked, all portal areas	4

*Does not include diffuse sinusoidal infiltration by inflammatory cells. Maximum possible score for grading **18**
Additional features which should be noted but not scored:
Bile duct inflammation and damage
Lymphoid follicles
Steatosis, mild, moderate, or marked
Hepatocellular dysplasia, large- or small-cell
Adenomatous hyperplasia
Iron or copper overload
Intracellular inclusions (e.g. PAS-positive globules, Mallory bodies)
Immunohistochemical findings:
Information on viral antigens, lymphocyte subsets or other features, when available, should be recorded and may be semi-quantitatively expressed.
Data from Ishak K.G. et al.,[139] with permission from authors and publisher.

Table 13.5 Modified Histological Activity Index staging[139]: architectural changes, fibrosis, and cirrhosis

Change	Score
No fibrosis	0
Fibrous expansion of some portal areas, with or without short fibrous septa	1
Fibrous expansion of most portal areas, with or without short fibrous septa	2
Fibrous expansion of most portal areas with occasional portal to portal (P-P) bridging	3
Fibrous expansion of portal areas with marked bridging (portal–portal (P-P) as well as portal–central (P-C))	4
Marked bridging (P-P and/or P-C) with occasional nodules (incomplete cirrhosis)	5
Cirrhosis, probable or definite	6

Maximum possible score 6.
Additional features which should be noted but not scored:
Intra-acinar fibrosis, perivenular ("chicken wire") fibrosis.
Phlebosclerosis of terminal hepatic venules.
Data from Ishak K.G. et al.,[139] with permission from authors and publisher.

observers involved should discuss and agree on scoring criteria.[122] Assessment of larger numbers of biopsies should be performed within a relatively short space of time (in terms of weeks rather than years) to avoid drift of criteria over time.[150] Intra- and interobserver variation should be controlled. Since interobserver variation represents a problem,[132] comparison between scores generated in different centers and different series of biopsies can only be approximate, and accurate meta-analysis is not possible.[150] Mathematical operations on grading totals are inappropriate since these are derived from a variety of pathologic processes and from nonlinear scales. Comparisons should only be made between the scores generated for each separate grading component. In view of the problems associated with semiquantitative scoring, alternative methods are under investigation. The usefulness of a reliable and reproducible mathematical scoring system based on fractal geometry for quantifying the irregular pattern of liver fibrosis in chronic liver disease has been evaluated.[130] Morphometry[131] and image-analysis quantification[125,144,145] appear to be more sensitive than semiquantitative scoring in detecting smaller changes in degree of fibrosis. These newer methods are promising, but at present are restricted to specialized centers and are best used in combination with semiquantitative histologic evaluation systems.[144]

Histopathology

Chronic viral hepatitis B. During some stages of chronic infection with HBV, overload of some cellular compartments with viral antigens may be so extensive as to be recognizable by light microscopy, creating helpful diagnostic markers of disease. Two such markers are "ground glass hepatocytes" and "sanded nuclei."

clinical practice may not be the most informative for investigative work. The development of separate systems tailored to clinical use or research may be warranted.[124] The components measured should be relevant for the study, and the criteria for each score should be defined as strictly as possible.[139,150] In order to assure consistent and reliable results, scoring should be carried out by at least two observers.[122] Before beginning a study, the

"*Ground glass hepatocytes*"[201] are parenchymal liver cells with a finely granular and more pale appearance of part or all their cytoplasm; the "ground glass" area is often separated from the cell membrane by a clear halo, which is an artifact, albeit a helpful one (Fig. 13.7). The ground glass appearance is due to marked hypertrophy of the smooth endoplasmic reticulum, which displaces the cytoplasmic organelles to the periphery of the cell and which contains excess filamentous structures of HBsAg in its cisternae.[195,276]

Ground glass appearance of hepatocytes is, however, not entirely specific, and also occurs in other liver diseases (Table 13.6). Drug-induced hypertrophy of the smooth endoplasmic reticulum which predominates in centrolobular hepatocytes may mimic a "ground glass" appearance[215,218]; injury caused by alcohol aversion drugs (cyanamide) may cause a ground glass appearance, preferentially in periportal hepatocytes.[170] Fibrinogen inclusions in parenchymal cells in patients with hypofibrinogenemia ("fibrinogen storage disease") may look like ground glass hepatocytes.[172] Lafora's disease (myoclonus epilepsy)[244] and glycogenosis type IV (amylopectinosis or Anderson's disease)[160] produce similar hepatocellular changes (Table 13.6). Ground glass hepatocytes from several causes may coexist in the same biopsy.[155]

Special stains, such as Shikata's orcein stain,[265] Victoria blue,[270] and aldehyde fuchsin[263] confirm the HBsAg relationship of the ground glass appearance. Even more convincing is immunohistochemical staining with specific antibody.

Sanded nuclei[161] are hepatocellular nuclei with a finely granular, pale eosinophilic appearance of the larger central part of the nucleus, due to massive accumulation of

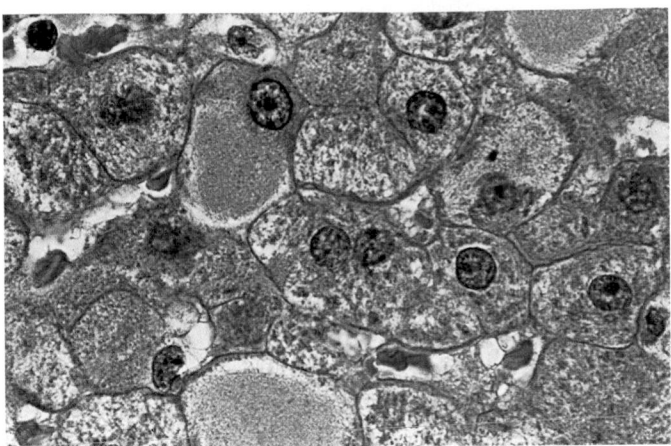

Fig. 13.7 Chronic viral hepatitis B, high magnification. Ground glass hepatocytes, characterized by more pale, eosinophilic, and homogeneous cytoplasm than surrounding normal (more granular) hepatocytes. Note (artifactual) cleft between "ground glass" cytoplasm and hepatocellular cell membrane. The first nucleated hepatocyte in the left lower corner reveals a less pronounced "ground glass" appearance (corresponding to less extensive endoplasmic reticulum hyperplasia and less massive accumulation of HBsAg). (H&E)

HBcAg. They are not easily recognized, and specific immunohistochemistry is most helpful in identifying HBcAg.

The clinical, histopathologic and immunohistochemical findings in chronic viral hepatitis B vary over time during the course of the disease.[173,185,232] During the early viral replication and immune tolerance phase, liver biopsy reveals only minimal hepatocellular damage and inflammation. Immunohistochemically, this viral replicative phase is characterized by nuclear and cytoplasmic localization of HBcAg[209] and HBeAg[176] which also

Table 13.6 Differential diagnosis of ground glass hepatocytes in nontumoral liver

Location	PAS stain	Orcein and Victoria blue	Electron microscopy	Pathologic condition
At random, single or in clusters	–	+	Hypertrophy of SER, with filamentous HBsAg	Chronic hepatitis B, especially viral integration phase (HBsAg carrier)
	+	–	Filaments in SER	Fibrinogen storage disease
Centrolobular or panlobular	–	–	Hypertrophy of SER	Drug induction
Periportal	+	–	Secondary lysosomes, disintegrating organelles, glycogen, lipid	Alcohol aversion, drug-induced injury (cyanamide)
	+	–	Fibrillar	Glycogenosis type IV (Anderson's disease)
	+	–	Aggregates of SER + glycogen	Lafora's disease

Data from Ishak,[107] with permission from author and publisher.

localizes in the liver cell membranes (Fig. 13.8).[277] HBsAg is found in the cytoplasm of some scattered hepatocytes and in the membrane of numerous parenchymal cells, revealing a honeycomb-like pattern (Fig. 13.9).[177,208]

A second phase is characterized by low viral replication and immune clearance of hepatocytes: the "viral elimination phase," associated with seroconversion from HBeAg to HBe antibody, and with disappearance of HBV DNA from the serum. Liver biopsy reveals more necroinflammatory lesions, including confluent lytic necrosis of variable extent in the more severe cases.[228] Immunostaining reveals nuclear, cytoplasmic, and membranous staining for HBcAg; HBsAg is found as weak positivity in the cytoplasm of some hepatocytes, associated with a membranous staining pattern.[173,185,208] HBeAg staining reveals nuclear and cytoplasmic localization.[230]

Some virus-replicating hepatocytes apparently escape immune elimination, leading to persistence of viral infection and integration of viral DNA into the host genome, thus realizing a third phase of "viral integration." If cirrhosis does not supervene after the more damaging "elimination phase," the liver may recover to an extent that only minimal histologic abnormalities are seen.[269] After a series of acute exacerbations[184] the liver may have developed cirrhotic changes in about 40% of patients.[173] Patients with persistent HBcAg in the liver and higher levels of HBV viremia are more likely to have more aggressive forms of disease[208] and even cirrhosis.[269] Thus, in the final integration phase, liver biopsy may reveal normal architecture, variable degrees of fibrosis, or even cirrhosis. Active replication of HBV has ceased but HBsAg is continuously produced by liver cells that contain integrated HBV genome[174] and the patient becomes an HBsAg carrier. HBsAg accumulates in clusters of hepatocytes, appearing as ground glass cells or staining in the periphery of parenchymal cells (Fig. 13.10). HBcAg is usually absent. Mild inflammation may persist for some time after loss of HBsAg in the serum[248] but substantial necroinflammation at this stage should alert for the possibility of superinfection with another virus. Some patients show ongoing inflammatory activity and interface hepatitis in the HBe antibody-positive phase, due to persistence of a special mutant of HBV characterized by deficient HBeAg synthesis.[171,239] Immunostaining then reveals cytoplasmic HBcAg.[247]

Cirrhosis present in the viral integration phase will progress slowly over 20 to 30 years, eventually with decompensation and other complications. Initially of the micronodular type, the cirrhosis becomes more macronodular,[173] and hepatocellular carcinoma may develop as a further sequela. Even in patients without cirrhosis in the integration phase (so-called "healthy HBsAg carriers") the risk for developing hepatocellular carcinoma is higher than in non-carriers.

Precancerous lesions (large cell dysplasia, small cell dysplasia, and macroregenerative nodules) may occur in

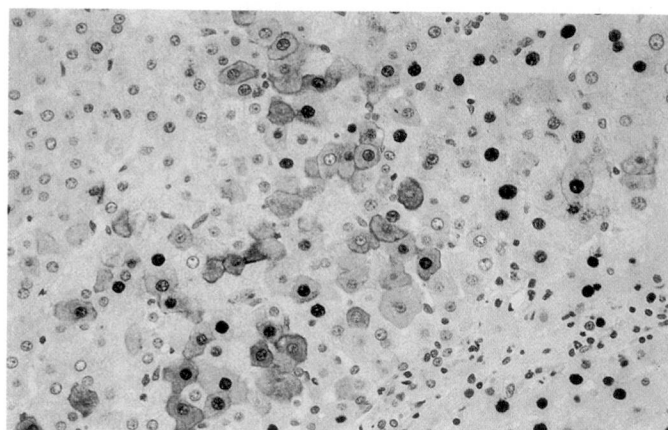

Fig. 13.8 Chronic viral hepatitis B; viral replicative phase. Hepatitis B core antigen is localized in hepatocellular nuclei and, in several hepatocytes, also in the cytoplasm and cell membrane. (Immunoperoxidase stain for HBcAg)

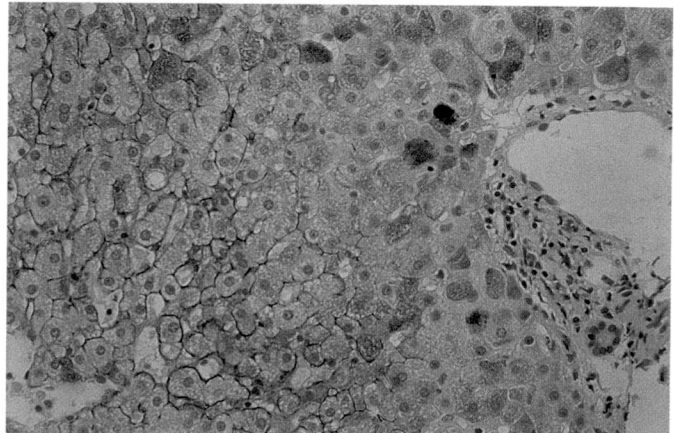

Fig. 13.9 Chronic viral hepatitis B: viral replicative phase. Hepatitis B surface antigen is localized in variable quantity in the cytoplasm and in the cell membrane of several hepatocytes. Note only mild lymphocytic infiltrate in portal tract and lobule. (Immunoperoxidase stain for HBsAg)

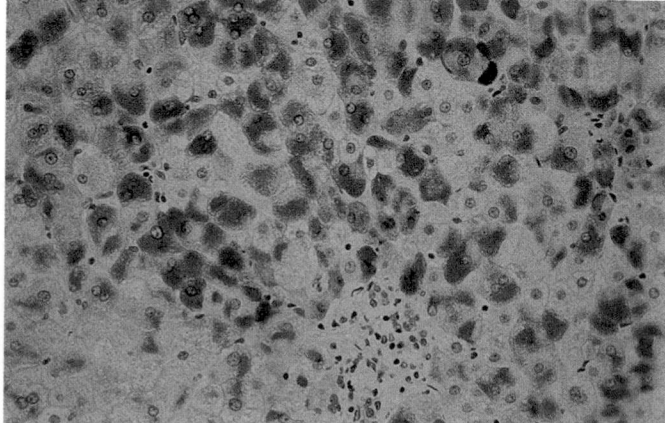

Fig. 13.10 Chronic viral hepatitis B: viral nonreplicative (integration) phase. Hepatitis B surface antigen is localized in considerable quantity in the cytoplasm of a contiguous group ("clone") of hepatocytes. Note relatively mild lymphocytic infiltrate in portal tract and lobule. The more intensely staining cells appear as "ground glass hepatocytes" on H&E staining. (Immunoperoxidase stain for HBsAg)

the precirrhotic and cirrhotic stages of chronic viral hepatitis B and C (see p. 932).

Chronic viral hepatitis B + D. Chronic hepatitis D tends to be more severe, with higher activity and risk of progression than does uncomplicated chronic hepatitis B.[191,231] Rapid progression to cirrhosis is the fate in a minority of patients with active HBV replication. More commonly, the disease evolution is slow and insidious, evolving into cirrhosis over many years.[162,253] HDV selectively suppresses HBcAg and HBeAg, but not HBsAg,[222] although it depends on low-grade HBV multiplication and release.[242]

Immunohistochemically, HDAg is found mainly in liver cell nuclei[241] which may show a sanded appearance[236] due to excess HDAg, and in the cytoplasm and membranes of hepatocytes.[268] Double immunostaining for HBV and HDV antigens often shows separate expression of HDAg versus HBsAg or HBcAg, but coexpression does occur.[220]

Chronic viral hepatitis C. HCV infection is characterized by a silent onset in most infected individuals, a high rate of viral persistence, and the potential for development of worsening chronic liver disease ranging from chronic hepatitis to cirrhosis and occasionally to hepatocellular carcinoma.[156] Retrospective studies from referral centers have tended to overestimate the progression to cirrhosis and cancer. Prospective and cohort studies, avoiding a referral bias, indicate a lower rate of progression, suggest that spontaneous viral clearance may be higher than is currently believed, and result in the conclusion that severe, life-threatening, progressive liver disease occurs in a minority (perhaps 30%) of chronically infected persons. However, the sheer magnitude of the infected population will result in a large number with severe, life-threatening disease, thus rendering HCV, with 170 million chronically infected people, a staggering worldwide problem.[156,166]

Histologically, chronic viral hepatitis C is often mild initially with little parenchymal damage (mainly focal inflammation and hepatocellular apoptosis).[254]

A carrier state with normal liver biopsy has been reported[169] whereas abnormal liver histology has been recorded in HCV RNA positive patients with normal serum alanine aminotransferase.[153] The histopathology of chronic viral hepatitis C, although not pathognomonic, is highly characteristic, and has been reviewed on several occasions.[187,189,200,271]

The histopathology is often that of a relatively mild degree of necroinflammation; there are spontaneous exacerbations,[264] reactivations after immunosuppressive therapy,[272] and relapses after interferon therapy. The portal infiltrate is rich in lymphocytes, often forming lymphoid aggregates (Fig. 13.11) and even follicles with prominent germinal centers.[158,193,196,206,219,224,237,261] Follicles are not specific for hepatitis C, and are also found in hepatitis B,[158,224] in autoimmune hepatitis,[158] and in pri-

mary biliary cirrhosis. Nevertheless, they are particularly prominent in hepatitis C.

Lesions of interlobular bile ducts have been described (Fig. 13.12), with frequencies ranging from 15%[200] to 91% of biopsies.[158] This broad variation indicates a poor consensus on the definition of "bile duct lesion." The most frequently observed bile duct lesions consist of infiltration of lymphocytes between cholangiocytes, with variable degrees of vacuolation, stratification, and crowding of the bile duct lining cells. The most pronounced bile duct lesion, originally described before HCV was discovered,[175] is characterized by swelling and polystratification of bile duct lining cells, infiltration by lymphocytes and larger mononuclear cells, and preservation of the basement membrane of the bile duct.[274] This hepatitic type of bile duct lesion needs to be differentiated from that occurring in primary biliary cirrhosis, which on occasion may be very difficult.

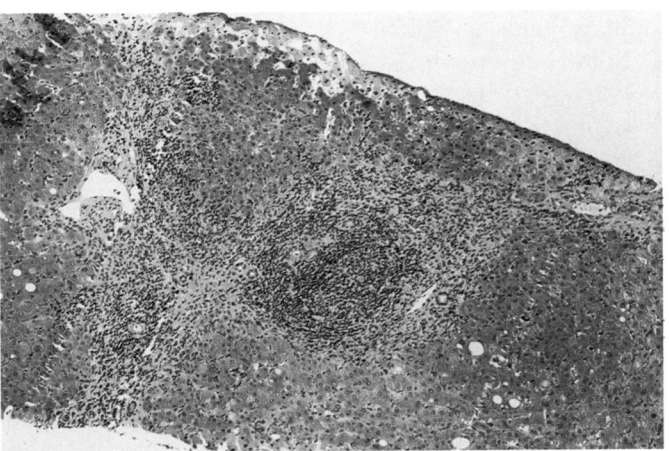

Fig. 13.11 Chronic viral hepatitis C. Low-power view of two joined portal tracts with dense mononuclear cell infiltration, forming a lymphoid aggregate and a lymph follicle. The portal–parenchymal interface is irregular (moderate degree of interface hepatitis). A few scattered macrovesicular steatosis vacuoles are visible in the lobular parenchyma. (H&E)

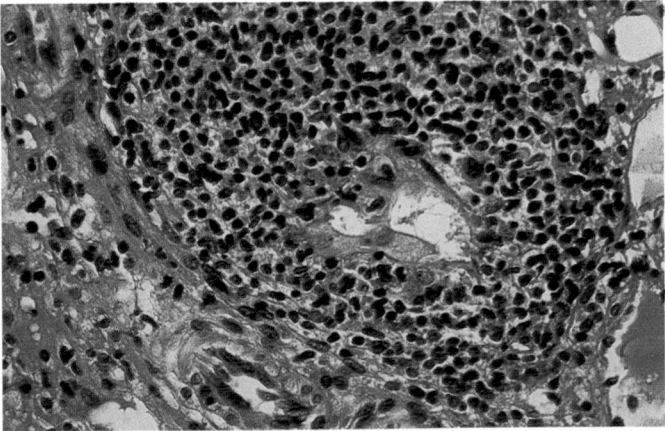

Fig. 13.12 Chronic viral hepatitis C. Detail of portal tract showing a lymph follicle containing an irregular and damaged bile duct near its center. Note the epithelial irregularity and intramural lymphocytic infiltrate. (H&E)

Lobular lesions may comprise a striking number of acidophil bodies (apoptosis). Mild to moderate steatosis, usually of the macrovesicular type, was described in frequencies ranging from 1%[200] to 72%[158] of biopsies, and appears to be mainly a viral effect,[183] especially of HCV genotype 3 (Fig. 13.13).[256]

Periportal hepatocytes may contain coarse clumps of eosinophilic cytoplasm (Mallory body-like).[210,224] The lymphocytic infiltration in the lobules may form rows along the sinusoids (indian files) resembling hepatic mononucleosis. Venous lesions resembling endotheliitis observed in cellular liver allograft rejection were also reported.[233]

A confusing lesion is the occurrence of epithelioid granulomas in a small minority (5%) of cases,[190,197,278] apparently as a transient feature.[245] The development of granulomas has been correlated with interferon-α therapy,[207] associated with good[204] as well as bad response.[258] Of course, other causes of granulomas have to be ruled out as much as possible.[197]

Some bile duct loss or a minor degree of ductopenia was reported in the late (cirrhotic) stage of chronic viral hepatitis C.[198] Epithelioid granulomas and bile duct loss are lesions which render the differentiation from primary biliary cirrhosis more difficult.

Increased amounts of hepatic iron have been reported in patients with chronic hepatitis C, even in the absence of a history of blood transfusion or alcohol abuse.[203] As iron overload was shown to impair the response to interferon therapy,[163] assessment of liver biopsies of patients with chronic hepatitis C should include a comment about the presence or absence of excess iron in hepatocytes.[202] The histopathology of chronic viral hepatitis C in children is quite similar to that in adults[216] with perhaps faster development of fibrosis.[159] The different genotypes of HCV may have some influence on the histopathologic picture, such as degree of steatosis, rate of bile duct

lesions, and disease activity.[165,235] In chronic hepatitis C patients with clinical manifestations of autoimmunity, the histology shows higher inflammatory activity, especially interface hepatitis.[182]

HCV RNA can be detected in frozen liver tissue sections by in situ hybridization. Several studies were published, but on review were found to lack sufficient specificity.[240] Immunocytochemical demonstration of viral antigens in the cytoplasm of hepatocytes has been reported in several studies. Few antibodies tried so far have given reproducible and clinically useful results in paraffin-embedded material. A recent study using antibody IGH222 (Innogenetics, Ghent, Belgium), tested on a high number of biopsies and validated by comparison with clinical, serologic, and molecular data, may be more promising (Fig. 13.14).[273]

The pathogenesis of hepatocellular damage in chronic hepatitis C is mainly immune mediated.[243] To date there are no accurate noninvasive markers of disease activity and fibrosis; liver biopsy is indicated in chronic viral hepatitis C to exclude other forms of liver pathology and to establish the stage of liver disease. The majority of patients will require a liver biopsy, which has important implications for staging of the disease, prognosis, and possibly further management options.[168,259]

Premalignant lesions in chronic viral hepatitis B and C. There is a strong association between hepatocellular carcinoma and chronic hepatitis B[257] and chronic hepatitis C.[188] The main presumed or proven premalignant lesions found in chronic hepatitis type B and C are liver cell dysplasia and macroregenerative nodules (adenomatous hyperplasia).[180] Liver cell dysplasia has been categorized into large and small cell types.[275]

Large cell dysplasia is the lesion originally described in an African population with a high incidence of hepatocellular carcinoma.[157] Such hepatocytes are enlarged;

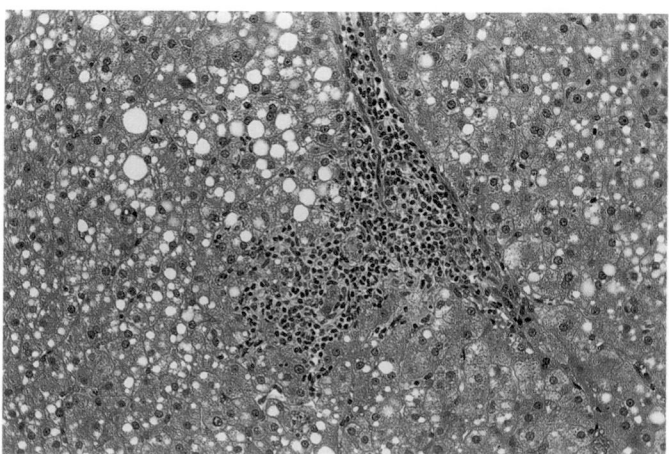

Fig. 13.13 Chronic viral hepatitis C: moderately dense portal infiltrate, focus of interface hepatitis; marked macro- and mediovesicular steatosis; occasional apoptotic body (middle left). (H&E)

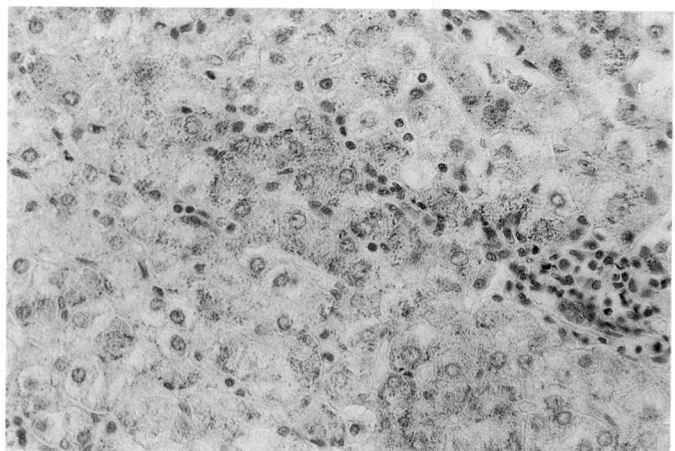

Fig. 13.14 Chronic viral hepatitis C. Viral antigen (HCV-E2), appearing as positive cytoplasmic granules, is localized in virtually every periportal hepatocyte in this case. (Immunoperoxidase "Envision" technique, using antibody IGH222—Innogenetics, Ghent, Belgium[273])

their nuclei are irregular in shape and hyperchromatic with prominent nucleoli. The nucleocytoplasmic ratio is normal or only slightly increased.[255] Large cell dysplasia is mainly found in patients with HBV and HCV infection.[223] Although these cells are apparently not direct forerunners of malignant carcinoma cells, their presence is a warning sign and an independent risk factor for development of hepatocellular carcinoma.[229]

Small dysplastic cells are smaller, with basophilic cytoplasm and a moderately increased nucleus, resulting in an increased nucleocytoplasmic ratio.[275] Small cell dysplasia has been considered by some authors to be a better precancerous candidate than the large cell variety.[205] Groups of (large-cell or small-cell) dysplastic hepatocytes less than 1 mm in diameter have been termed "dysplastic foci."[213]

A macroregenerative nodule (MRN; previously termed adenomatous hyperplasia) is an unusually large regenerative nodule of 0.8 cm or more in diameter, developing in cirrhosis and other chronic liver disease, particularly frequently in macronodular cirrhosis.[194,238] In contrast to dysplastic foci, dysplastic nodules are larger than 1 mm and are considered to be more advanced precursor lesions.[213] These nodules can be classified as low-grade or high-grade dysplastic nodules, with varying degrees of liver cell dysplasia, increased cellularity, loss of cohesiveness, pseudoacini, or focal loss of reticulin fibers.[192,238]

Autoimmune hepatitis. Several types of autoimmune hepatitis are characterized by different patterns of autoantibodies.[212] Correct diagnosis is important, as the patient may benefit from immunosuppressive therapy. The histopathology is that of chronic hepatitis in general, with some suggestive features.[182,234] Necroinflammatory activity tends to be high in untreated patients: bridging confluent necrosis, marked interface hepatitis, and hepatitic liver cell rosettes are common features.[214] Multinucleated giant hepatocytes may be found[186,221] although they also occur in other types of hepatitis.[214] The inflammatory infiltrate is mainly composed of lymphocytes, but plasma cells are a prominent component, often in clusters.[158] Lymphoid aggregates and follicles also may form, but less so than in viral hepatitis C. Immunosuppressive treatment reduces the severity of necroinflammation and fibrosis.[262] Overlap syndromes with features of both autoimmune hepatitis and biliary disease have been reported (see p. 951). This issue is confounded by the finding that bile duct lesions, even destructive ones, may occur in genuine autoimmune hepatitis.[181]

Drug-induced chronic hepatitis. This topic is described under Drug-induced liver disease (p. 938). Drug-induced chronic hepatitis is a possibility that needs always to be considered when the etiology of a chronic hepatitis is obscure.

Cryptogenic chronic hepatitis has no characteristic features pointing to a particular etiology. The activity of the disease is often mild.[199]

Histologic differential diagnosis of chronic hepatitis. In cases without interface hepatitis, the differential diagnoses to be considered include resolving acute hepatitis, nonspecific inflammation, primary biliary cirrhosis, and lymphoma. Chronic hepatitis with lobular lesions has to be distinguished from acute hepatitis. Orcein staining helps in identifying older collapse, and ground glass hepatocytes testify to chronicity in hepatitis B. Bilirubin stasis occurs much more frequently in acute than in chronic hepatitis.

Liver biopsies featuring interface hepatitis need differential diagnostic consideration of the chronic biliary diseases primary biliary cirrhosis and primary sclerosing cholangitis, Wilson's disease, α_1-antitrypsin deficiency, and lymphoma.

Alertness, special stains, and coordination with clinical information are essential for correct diagnosis.

Combined pathology in chronic hepatitis. *Combined infection with HBV and HCV* increases the severity of the histologic liver lesions.[279] Triple infection with HBV, HDV, and HCV results in severe disease in the acute superinfection stage; however, the course is relatively benign, slowly progressive, and usually dominated by HCV.[227] A comprehensive review of the role of HCV in dual and triple hepatitis virus infection has been published.[226]

Superinfection of chronic hepatitis B with HDV is usually characterized by severe activity with extensive interface hepatitis.[161,230]

Human immunodeficiency virus (HIV) infection results in reactivation of hepatitis B, with higher levels of HBV replication without an increase in necroinflammation, but more immunocytochemically demonstrable HBcAg and HBeAg.[178] Necroinflammatory activity is higher in HIV-positive than in HIV-negative patients with chronic hepatitis C, and cirrhosis is more frequent.[154]

HGV virus infection does not appear to affect the histopathologic severity and characteristics of chronic hepatitis C, suggesting a minor role of HGV infection in human liver disease.[167,266] Also, *TTV infection* was reported not to affect the clinicopathologic course of chronic hepatitis B or C and the response to interferon-α therapy.[217] Multiple hepatitis virus infection is quite common; it cannot be reliably recognized histologically,[179] but a repertoire of immunocytochemical stainings for viral antigens is helpful although not sufficient by itself.[211]

Many factors have been proposed to be associated with fibrosis in patients with chronic HCV infection. Although the strength of the association varies, these factors include male gender, advanced age, excessive alcohol use, duration of infection, human immunodeficiency virus (HIV) coinfection,[251,252,260] nonalcoholic steatohepatitis (NASH),[246] and porphyria cutanea tarda.[164]

Foci of hepatocellular hemosiderosis (iron-rich foci) have been described in a few patients with *chronic viral hepatitis C and B*, highlighting the potential for irregular iron storage in chronic viral liver disease and potential confusion with genetic hemochromatosis.[225] In an Italian study, histologically detectable iron was evident in 48% of cases with features of nonhemochromatosis iron overload.[250] Heterozygosity for hereditary hemochromatosis[267] and hepatic iron overload[249] may influence progression toward liver fibrosis.

Chronic infection with HBV and HCV may occur in patients with nonrelated liver diseases, such as primary biliary cirrhosis, primary sclerosing cholangitis, genetic hemochromatosis, and alcohol-related liver injury. The histopathologist should alert the clinician to any finding of combined disease that may hasten the progression to cirrhosis and increase the risk of hepatocellular carcinoma, as is the case in alcoholic liver disease.[202]

Hepatitis caused by "nonhepatitis" viruses

Several viruses not belonging to the group of specific "hepatitis" viruses may also induce liver inflammation, as primary disease or, more often, as part of systemic or other organ infections. Examples are cytomegalovirus (see p. 963) and Epstein–Barr virus (see p. 963), herpes virus, and adenovirus infections.

Cirrhosis

Cirrhosis is the end stage of many chronic liver diseases. Cirrhosis corresponds to diffuse hepatic fibrosis with replacement of normal lobular architecture by parenchymal nodules separated by fibrous tissue.[280] Portal–central septa linking portal tracts and central veins are an important component of cirrhosis. Cirrhosis may be strongly suspected on clinical, laboratory, and imaging parameters, but the final diagnosis requires morphologic confirmation by liver biopsy. Architectural changes are histologically best appreciated on a reticulin stain.[283]

The morphologic classification of cirrhosis is based on the size of the nodules.[280] Cirrhosis is *micronodular* if nearly all of the nodules are less than 3 mm in diameter (Fig. 13.15), and *macronodular* if greater than 3 mm in diameter (Fig. 13.16). A *mixed micro-macronodular cirrhosis* comprises approximately equal numbers of nodules greater than and less than 3 mm in diameter. The size of the nodules has some use in defining the etiology of the process, but this is relative since micronodular cirrhosis may convert into a macronodular type under circumstances more favorable for parenchymal regeneration.[285]

Nodular size is more important in determining the ease with which the **diagnosis** of cirrhosis can be made in needle biopsy specimens. Nodularity and septa may be readily evident in specimens from micronodular

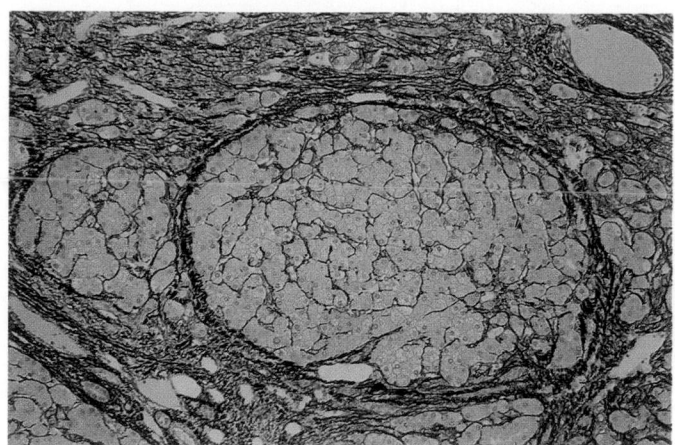

Fig. 13.15 Detail from micronodular cirrhosis. (Reticulin silver impregnation)

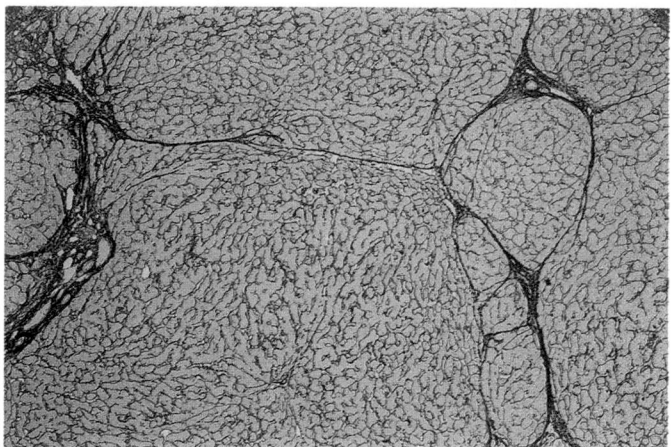

Fig. 13.16 Detail from macronodular cirrhosis. Note larger nodules, thin, fibrous septa, and irregular orientation of liver cell plates. (Reticulin silver impregnation)

cirrhosis, whereas more subtle criteria have to be relied on to arrive at more or less convincing evidence in macronodular cirrhosis. Helpful criteria in this respect include: fragmentation of the biopsy specimen (especially with slender tissue cylinders provided by thin aspiration type needles such as the Menghini needle); thin layers of connective tissue adhering to rounded edges of nodular biopsy fragments; abnormal orientation of reticulin fibers resulting from different rates of parenchymal growth in different areas; abnormal spacing of portal tracts and central veins, and excess numbers of draining veins in relation to the number of portal tracts; presence of minute and poorly formed portal tracts ("mini-portal tracts"); hepatocellular features of regeneration—double-cell plates over widespread areas, different appearance of hepatocytes in adjacent areas; liver cell dysplasia of the large cell and small cell type.

The most difficult anatomic type to recognize is *incomplete septal cirrhosis* (Fig. 13.17). This is characterized by vague nodularity, slender septa, some of which end blindly, mini-portal tracts, excess efferent veins, and

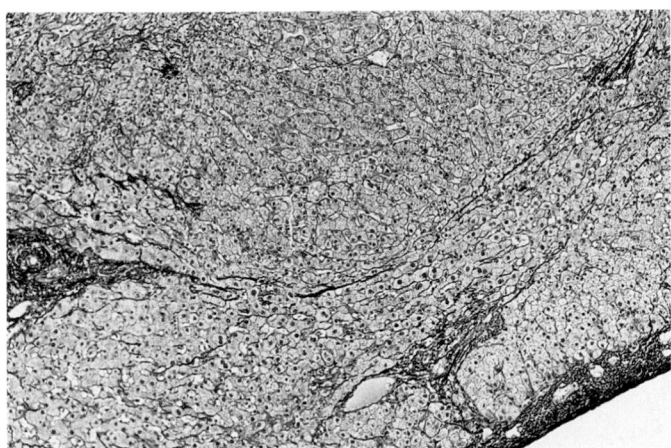

Fig. 13.17 Detail from "incomplete septal type" cirrhosis. Can be considered a macronodular variety of cirrhosis with large multilobular nodules, thin, incomplete septa, and little inflammatory activity. (Sirius red stain)

sinusoidal dilatation. There is evidence of parenchymal hyperplasia with corresponding compression of reticulin fibers in adjacent areas. Inflammation and necrosis are generally absent or minimal.[294] The diagnosis is more easy in surgical than in needle specimens. This condition forms the borderline between cirrhosis and various forms of noncirrhotic portal hypertension.[289,293] The ease with which cirrhosis is diagnosed further depends on the type of specimen (surgical or needle), the type of needle used (aspiration type, Tru-cut, or transjugular), and the quality of applied reticulin stains. In some instances, the histopathologist can only hint at the possibility of cirrhosis.

A further complicating factor is the dynamic nature of the process. Cirrhosis does not appear overnight, but may take months or years to develop. A biopsy report may have to conclude "developing cirrhosis" or "incipient cirrhosis" in spite of everyone preferring black and white decisions, which are possible in "fully developed" and "advanced" cirrhosis.

Besides confirming the presence or absence of cirrhotic architecture, its anatomic type, and **stage of development**, liver biopsy further permits assessment of the **etiology** of the liver disease, in many instances with the use of some additional stains and attention to a number of features.

The pattern of nodules and fibrosis may be helpful. Biliary cirrhosis is characterized by garland-shaped nodules, and its progressive nature is reflected in a clear halo in the nodular periphery due to edema, cholate stasis, and ductular reaction. Chronic venous outflow obstruction leads to central–central fibrous septa, and in an occasional case results in "cardiac-type cirrhosis" or cardiac sclerosis with nodules centered by normal-looking portal tracts.[288]

Ductopenia indicates "vanishing bile duct disease" as the etiology, most frequently primary biliary cirrhosis or primary sclerosing cholangitis in adults; other ductopenia syndromes predominate in children and young adults. Ductular reaction (cholangiolitis) reflects active, ongoing biliary disease.

Hepatic venous lesions (occlusion, narrowing, or recanalization) may suggest a venous outflow block as the cause of the cirrhosis, but are also found in other types of cirrhosis.[291] Steatohepatitis may still be present in cirrhotic alcohol abusers (ASH) and in teetotal patients (NASH). Cirrhosis without etiologic markers ("cryptogenic cirrhosis") may possibly result from NASH.[292]

Posthepatitic cirrhosis may still show features of activity (necroinflammation) as in precirrhotic chronic hepatitis. Ground glass hepatocytes and demonstration of HBsAg, HBcAg, HBeAg or HBxAg help in recognizing HBV infection as the cause. HCV is suggested by lymphoid aggregates and lymph follicles. Numerous plasma cells are suggestive (but not proof) of autoimmune hepatitis.

Some etiologies are identified on the finding of intracellular deposits. Genetic hemochromatosis is recognized by severe parenchymal siderosis.[284] Deposits of copper (rhodanine stain) and metallothionein (orcein stain) are found in cirrhosis of different etiologies. Perinodular copper suggests biliary disease. Positive staining of entire nodules is seen in Wilson's disease although other nodules may be negative. Abundant copper deposition is also noted in Indian childhood cirrhosis.[290] Furthermore, copper and copper-binding protein can sometimes be detected in cirrhosis of any etiology.[286]

α_1-Antitrypsin deficiency is recognized by hepatocellular inclusions of this glycoprotein; they are eosinophilic, PAS positive, and diastase resistant, and best recognized by specific immunostaining.[281]

A characteristic of cirrhotic nodular parenchyma is the variability in hepatocellular features (or "individual behavior") of individual nodules. This applies to features such as steatosis, siderosis, and ground glass hepatocytes.

The **histologic activity** of a cirrhotic liver should be noted, as it may reflect ongoing disease even in its cirrhotic stage. Activity consists of the various forms of liver cell damage and inflammation seen in the precirrhotic stage of the disease, e.g., interface hepatitis in posthepatitic cirrhosis, and steatohepatitis in cirrhotic alcoholics and patients with NASH. Inactive cirrhosis is characterized by (near) absence of necroinflammatory lesions, and a sharp delineation between the paucicellular septa and nodules. Further useful information for the clinician that can be recognized in liver biopsies of cirrhotic livers are some complications of cirrhosis. Coagulation necrosis of entire nodules or of their centers ("*nodular infarction*") is seen in hypoperfusion.[287] The *decompensation phase* of a cirrhotic liver often shows severe bilirubin stasis in a nonbiliary cirrhosis.[283] *Hepatocellular carcinoma* arises commonly in cirrhotic

Table 13.7 Differential diagnosis of cirrhosis

Disease	Diffuse involvement of the liver	Septa	Nodules
Cirrhosis	+	+	+
Nodular regenerative hyperplasia	+	−	+
Focal nodular hyperplasia	−	+	+

liver. Its putative precancerous markers and stages (macroregenerative nodules, dysplastic foci and nodules, large cell and small cell liver cell dysplasia) should be looked for and their presence reported.[282]

Cirrhosis has to be distinguished from other nodular and fibrotic conditions of the liver. The **differential diagnosis** comprises nodular regenerative hyperplasia, congenital hepatic fibrosis, and focal nodular hyperplasia (Table 13.7). The latter may closely resemble ductopenic biliary cirrhosis; such a misdiagnosis is easily avoided if information is provided (or if suspicion arises) of a focal lesion in the liver.

Drug-induced and toxic liver injury

Adverse drug reactions and toxic damage to the liver are not surprising since this organ is the main site of biotransformation of endo- and xenobiotics. More than 600 potentially hepatotoxic drugs have been identified.[308]

Recognition of drug-induced liver damage is difficult for several reasons.[295] Drug-induced liver damage may mimic any naturally occurring liver disease, and it occurs with compounds from all classes of drugs.[297,300,307] Clinical signs of a hypersensitivity reaction may not occur in all cases, and a patient's drug history is often far from reliable. It is often impossible to pinpoint the causative agent in patients on multiple drug therapy, which usually is the case in elderly patients. The same drug may cause different patterns of liver damage in different patients.[306] Hepatotoxicity may not yet have been reported for the drug in question, even when it has been on the market for a long time. The liver damaging effect may be accentuated by the concomitant administration of other pharmacologic agents.

The diagnostic histopathologist should be aware of the type of lesions most likely to be induced by drugs, and how to try to differentiate these from features not induced by drugs. It is further useful to know of specific sources of information such as recent books[301,308] and reviews.[296,298,302–304]

The distinction has been made between predictable (or intrinsic, or drug-dependent) toxicity effects on the one hand, and unpredictable (or hypersensitive, or idiosyncratic, or host-dependent) reactions on the other hand.[300]

Predictable reactions are due to the intrinsic hepatotoxicity of the molecule, are dose dependent, occur in all exposed individuals, occur with a relatively short (though variable) latent period, and are reproducible in experimental animals. Acetaminophen (paracetamol) overdose is an example. In spite of the occurrence of occasional accidents, this type of adverse reaction is not the main problem in therapeutic practice. Of more concern is the far more frequent unpredictable type of hepatic adverse drug reaction. It occurs in only a small fraction of the population exposed, there is no clear dose relationship, the latent period may be quite long (weeks or months), and it is not reproducible in experimental animals. The exceptional sensitivity to a particular drug may be based on genetically determined differences in drug metabolism ("metabolic idiosyncrasy") or to immunologically based reactions to neoantigens formed by interaction between a drug metabolite and some tissue or cell membrane component ("immuno-allergic idiosyncrasy").[299,300]

Conclusive proof of responsibility of a particular drug or combination of drugs is often impossible to obtain; re-challenge would be an effective test, but is obviously unethical. Inadvertent re-challenge may provide strong circumstantial evidence, even many years after a first episode.[305]

Drug-induced adverse reactions in the liver may cause structural and functional changes in all cellular components of the organ, and create various composite patterns, which are summarized below.

Elementary lesions

Hepatocytes

In view of the parenchymal heterogeneity in the liver lobule, with predominance of microsomal biotransformation enzymes in the centrolobular zone, it is not surprising that drug-induced effects may show a zonal distribution or predominance.

A **ground glass appearance** of hepatocytes in the centrolobular area, due to hypertrophy of the smooth endoplasmic reticulum with associated enzyme induction, is caused by a number of drugs (examples include phenobarbital, rifampin (rifampicin), and dioxin).[312] This change reflects adaptation rather than injury. Ground glass inclusions in periportal hepatocytes, resembling those in viral hepatitis B, in Lafora's disease and in glycogenosis type IV, can be induced by alcohol aversion drugs (cyanamide).[321] Such inclusions can be immunostained using a monoclonal antibody against Lafora bodies (KM279) with specificity for polyglucosan.[310]

Lipofuscinosis or increased accumulation of lipofuscin (wear-and-tear pigment) in centrolobular hepatocytes is induced by prolonged intake of some drugs such as phenacetin, aminopyrine (aminophenazone), chlorpromazine, Cascara Sagrada,[309] and by anticonvulsant therapy.[311] It has to be differentiated from the pigment accumulation in Dubin–Johnson syndrome.

Steatosis or hepatocellular fat accumulation is a frequently occurring effect of xenobiotics. *Macrovesicular steatosis* is seen with carbon tetrachloride, methotrexate, and ethanol.[320] *Microvesicular steatosis* (fine-droplet fatty change) may be associated with clinical manifestations of severe liver injury, even in the absence of overt hepatocellular necrosis. Microvesicular steatosis is caused by alcohol, intravenous tetracycline, amiodarone, valproate, and acetyl salicylate in children (Reye's syndrome), and is also seen in Jamaican vomiting sickness and in acute fatty liver of pregnancy.[317,318] It is apparently due to inhibition of mitochondrial fatty acid β-oxidation and mitochondrial dysfunction.[315] In recent years, microvesicular steatosis has also been reported with several antiviral nucleoside analogs (e.g., fialuridine).[314]

Phospholipidosis is characterized by foamy cytoplasmic vacuoles and enlargement of hepatocytes and Kupffer cells due to phospholipid accumulation. Electron microscopy reveals lamellated myeloid bodies (fingerprints) in enlarged lysosomes. The lesion is caused by Coralgil (4,4-diethylamino-ethoxy-hexestrol), perhexiline maleate, and amiodarone.[316]

Simple **drug-induced cholestasis** is histologically characterized by bland bilirubin stasis. Such "simple" or "pure" cholestasis is seen with several drugs, the prototypes being anabolic and contraceptive steroids. The mechanisms are multiple and complex.[313] Cholestatic drug reactions are the most frequent side effects. Most drugs that cause cholestasis (or cholestatic hepatitis) are substrates for several of the transporting polypeptides located on the canalicular membrane. The mechanisms of transporter inhibition are beginning to become elucidated.[319]

Hepatocellular death: apoptosis and necrosis

Severe hepatocellular injury may be potentiated and perpetuated by inflammatory mediators; cytokines and their cognate receptors may induce injury by triggering hepatocyte apoptosis and necrosis.[324] Both modes of hepatocellular death may also be induced by toxic drug metabolites and immuno-allergic hypersensitivity reactions. Hepatocellular necrosis may be variable in appearance (coagulative or lytic), in topography (centrolobular or periportal), and in extent (focal, zonal, bridging, lobular, and multilobular). With larger doses, most hepatotoxic drugs (e.g., chloroform, acetaminophen) and hepatic poisons (e.g., the mushroom *Amanita phalloides*, carbon tetrachloride) produce centrolobular necrosis, associated with ballooning and steatosis in adjacent non-necrotic parenchymal cells, and with no or little inflammatory infiltration.[322] Other chemicals (e.g., ferrous sulfate, the yellow form of inorganic phosphorus) cause periportal necrosis. Most of these agents cause fatal massive necrosis when administered in sufficient dose. In smaller doses, apoptosis of liver cells occurs, and, with time, may result in fibrosis and cirrhosis.[323]

Binucleated hepatocytes increase in number with sulindac, and **multinucleated hepatocytes** were reported in several instances of acute and chronic drug-induced hepatitis (e.g., clometacin).[325]

Hepatocellular tumors

Oral contraceptives, anabolic–androgenic steroids, and thorium dioxide are the best known causative agents of liver tumors in medical practice.[326] Oral contraceptives may be responsible for the development of benign liver cell adenoma. Whether they induce hepatocellular carcinoma is debated; apparently the risk is low. Anabolic–androgenic steroids also may induce adenomas and peliosis. Thorium dioxide (Thorotrast—used as a radiologic contrast medium between the 1920s and mid 1950s) has caused hepatocellular carcinoma, angiosarcoma, and cholangiocarcinoma.[326]

Kupffer cells are involved in storage of foreign materials and in granuloma development. Materials stored in Kupffer cells include talc and cellulose in drug addicts, silica and anthracotic pigment in coal miners, polyvinyl pyrrolidone and hydroxyethyl starch[327] from infusion of plasma expanders, silicone from prosthetic heart valve devices, and Thorotrast after administration of this contrast medium.[333]

Approximately 60 drugs—amongst them sulfonamides, methyldopa, and phenylbutazone—have been incriminated in the production of **hepatic granulomas**.[334] A special variant, the *fibrin ring granuloma* is observed in hypersensitivity to allopurinol.[338,339] *Mineral oil granulomas* are composed of lipophages and occur in portal tracts and near central veins. They have been ascribed to the absorption and deposition of mineral oil taken as a medicinal agent (laxative) or ingested as a food additive or food contaminant from food packaging,[328,341] whereas others relate them to liver steatosis.[330] Gold has been identified in lipophages and granulomas in patients who received gold therapy for rheumatoid arthritis.[337]

Periportal sinusoidal dilatation is related to oral contraceptive use, but may also be associated with inflammatory disease.[340] **Peliosis hepatis** (see p. 960) has been associated with the administration of anabolic–androgenic steroids, contraceptive steroids, and azathioprine.[342] **Angiosarcoma** has been ascribed to inorganic arsenicals, Thorotrast, anabolic–androgenic steroids, oral contraceptives, vinyl chloride, and radium therapy.[340]

Hepatic stellate cell (Ito cell) hyperplasia, corresponding to an increased number of hepatic stellate cells with prominent lipid vacuoles per unit volume of liver tissue, possibly with associated pericellular and septal fibrosis, is observed in hypervitaminosis A[335] and in patients undergoing methotrexate therapy, although to a lesser extent than once thought.[336]

Bile duct damage and ductopenia may be due to the effect of several drugs.[332] Because of the ductopenia, cholestasis of this type is usually prolonged, and may last for months and even years.[329] The mechanism may be direct toxicity to bile duct cells or immuno-allergic injury.[331] The syndrome was reported after intake of a number of drugs, including chlorpromazine, haloperidol, ajmaline, glycyrrhizin, amoxicillin, and floxacillin (flucloxacillin).[332] The differential diagnosis includes most "vanishing bile duct diseases" (see p. 948).

Vascular lesions induced by drugs may affect all intrahepatic blood vessels. *Thrombosis of hepatic veins* (Budd–Chiari syndrome) and of portal vein branches is a rare complication of contraceptive steroids. *Venoocclusive disease*, or nonthrombotic narrowing of central vein lumina by loose connective tissue, is caused by pyrrolizidine alkaloids, radiation, antineoplastic agents, and conditioning for bone marrow transplantation.[340] *Phlebosclerosis of portal vein branches* has been associated with long-term use of inorganic arsenicals (Fowler's solution), with Thorotrast, vinyl chloride, vitamin A, azathioprine, and methotrexate.[340] Thrombosis and phlebosclerosis of portal vein branches may lead to the development of nodular regenerative hyperplasia.[341] *Arteritis* due to drug hypersensitivity may affect intrahepatic branches of the hepatic artery, resulting in multifocal hemorrhagic necrosis and exceptionally rupture of the liver.[340]

Composite patterns

Drug-induced liver disease often creates histopathologic pictures that combine several elementary lesions in varying proportions. The most important are mentioned below.

Drug-induced acute hepatitis combines hepatocellular damage and death (variable in degree) with portal and parenchymal inflammation (to a variable extent). Numerous drugs of diverse classes can cause this reaction, which is of the immuno-allergic idiosyncratic type. Classical examples include isoniazid (a tuberculostatic agent), halothane (an anesthetic), and indomethacin (a nonsteroidal anti-inflammatory drug). The histopathology is virtually indistinguishable from that of acute viral hepatitis.

Drug-induced chronic hepatitis occurs in a small number of patients after prolonged or repeated exposure to some drugs. The histopathology comprises the elementary lesions of chronic hepatitis in various stages, including cirrhosis. Examples of incriminated drugs are nitrofurantoin[351] and phenytoin.[349] There are no specific histologic lesions. Even serologically, the presence of autoantibodies may cause confusion with autoimmune hepatitis.[350] The diagnosis relies on a high degree of suspicion of a possible drug etiology in the absence of viral markers, and close cooperation from clinician and patient. Diagnosis is important, since the patient may be cured by withdrawal of the drug.

Drug-induced steatohepatitis resembles acute hepatitis of the alcoholic type. It may be caused by amiodarone[348] and by parenteral nutrition.[344] Again, diagnosis requires clinical information.

Drug-induced cholestatic hepatitis features lesions of acute hepatitis combined with a moderate or marked degree of bilirubin stasis. Eosinophils may or may not be prominent in the inflammatory infiltrate. Differentiation from bile duct obstruction relies on the absence or low expression of typical obstructive features such as portal edema and neutrophil-associated ductular proliferation. Severe liver cell damage and marked inflammation are more suggestive of viral hepatitis or viral-like drug-induced acute hepatitis.

Drug-induced granulomatous hepatitis combines the features of a usually mild hepatitis with the appearance of noncaseating granulomas. When in addition some degree of bilirubin stasis and infiltration of eosinophils is noted, the histopathologic picture is virtually diagnostic for drug-induced liver disease.[346]

Diagnostic hints for the histopathologist. One should always maintain a high degree of suspicion for a drug-induced etiology, especially in elderly patients. A histopathologic picture resembling viral hepatitis, but with a disproportionately severe degree of parenchymal necrosis in relation to the patient's clinical condition, or with associated steatosis, granulomas, or infiltration by eosinophils, or with associated bile duct damage, should arouse suspicion for drug-induced disease.[343] The same applies for centrolobular necrosis sharply delineated from non-necrotic parenchyma, especially if associated with steatosis, with only mild or minimal inflammation, but with numerous ceroid macrophages.[343] Parenchymal giant cell hepatitis in adult patients, and the association of hepatocyte necrosis with venoocclusive disease should also act as an alert for a drug-induced etiology.[345] The final conclusion concerning the diagnosis of drug-induced and toxic liver damage is that it requires a sustained high degree of suspicion and alertness on the part of both the clinician and the pathologist. An impressive example is the detective story of the Epping jaundice.[347]

Steatosis and steatohepatitis

Steatosis

Steatosis (fatty liver, fatty change) corresponds to accumulation of triglycerides in the cytoplasm of hepatocytes. It is a frequent finding and represents a manifestation of reversible cell injury.[352] Steatosis is a nonspecific lesion induced by a variety of causes. The degree of lipid accumulation is variable, ranging from occasional fat droplets to diffuse deposition involving most parenchymal cells. Minor amounts of steatosis are of uncertain significance, and occur more frequently in elderly people, possibly as part of the aging process.[353] More extensive steatosis is seen in a variety of primary hepatic diseases and in several systemic conditions. Histologically, in routinely fixed tissue, steatosis is represented by cytoplasmic vacuoles as the lipid is dissolved during processing. Very small droplet steatosis may be difficult to recognize. Histochemical staining is helpful. Lipid can be demonstrated in frozen sections using oil red O, or Sudan black, or in tissue that has been postfixed in osmium tetroxide.[354] The clinical aspects of steatosis include hepatomegaly and elevated levels of serum aminotransferases, of alkaline phosphatase, and/or γ-glutamyl transpeptidase.

Patterns and distribution

Two morphologic patterns are recognized: macrovesicular and microvesicular steatosis. Both may occur together to some extent in the same biopsy specimen, suggesting that large droplets form through coalescence of small lipid vacuoles.

Macrovesicular steatosis (large droplet fatty change; Fig. 13.18) is the most common pattern, in which a single large vacuole distends the hepatocyte and displaces the nucleus to one side. Uncomplicated macrovesicular steatosis used to be regarded as a benign and potentially fully reversible lesion, but this notion has been challenged (see p. 940).[357,358] Its zonal distribution is variable. It is most often centrolobular, for instance in alcoholic liver disease, obesity, and diabetes. In more severe degrees, the steatosis may become panlobular. Steatosis in periportal zones is more commonly seen in cachexia and protein–energy malnutrition (kwashiorkor), in acquired immune deficiency syndrome (AIDS), after total parenteral nutrition, with phosphorus poisoning, and in steroid therapy. There are exceptions to the rule, however, and it is not possible to define the etiology solely on the pattern of lipid distribution in the individual case; identification of the cause requires close clinicopathologic correlation.

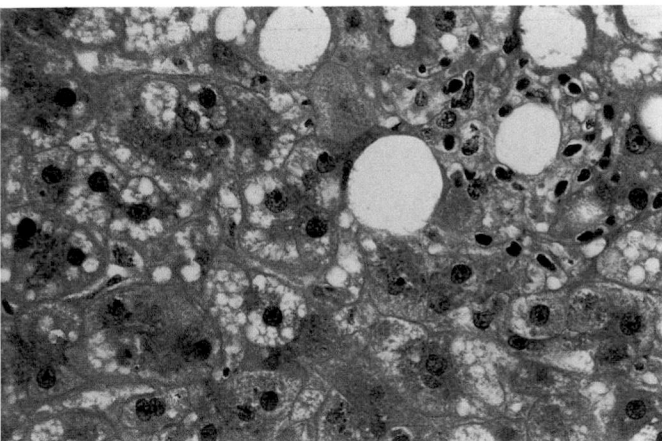

Fig. 13.18 Hepatic steatosis in patient with alcohol abuse. The picture shows a mixture of macrovesicular and microvesicular steatosis and a lipogranuloma (upper right corner). (H&E)

The pathologist should provide information on severity by indicating the approximate amount of parenchyma involved (mild: less than one third; moderate: one third to two thirds; severe: more than two thirds). Further useful information for the clinician is the finding of a mixed pattern of macro- and microvesicular steatosis because this may be of prognostic importance in relation to alcoholic liver disease.[369]

The pathogenesis of steatosis is complex. Alterations at many points of the complicated pathway of lipid metabolism can lead to accumulation of neutral fat within hepatocytes. The reader is referred to recent reviews on the topic.[359,361]

Microvesicular steatosis (small droplet fatty change; Fig. 13.18, see also Fig. 13.41) is often more difficult to recognize, and its demonstration may require histochemistry. It is generally a serious lesion associated with impairment of β-oxidation of lipids and frequently accompanied by disturbed liver function and coma.[368] The causes are multiple. The first to be recognized, more than half a century ago, was *acute fatty liver of pregnancy* (see p. 961).

Reye's syndrome occurs principally, but not exclusively, in young children; it presents clinically with an initial acute, mild viral illness, followed by vomiting, lethargy, and coma, resulting in death in about one third of patients. The steatosis is usually panlobular, with smaller droplets in centrolobular areas and somewhat larger fat vacuoles in periportal regions. There may be necrosis of periportal hepatocytes. A number of Reye's syndrome cases may be attributable to salicylate use.[364] In some children, it may be related to a preexisting inherited metabolic disorder of mitochondrial β-oxidation.[363] Many patients once thought to have Reye's syndrome have been found subsequently to have defects in fatty acid oxidation, a form of primary mitochondrial hepatopathy.[365,367]

A number of *therapeutic drugs* have been associated with the development of microvesicular steatosis: salicylates (see above for Reye's syndrome), sodium valproate, and intravenous high dose tetracycline.[362] Further causes include *ethanol* (in a small proportion of patients: alcoholic foamy degeneration), *fulminant hepatitis D* in the Amazon basin,[366] and *multiple hornet stings*.[371]

A number of *inborn errors of mitochondrial fatty acid β-oxidation* and *inherited urea cycle disorders* are responsible for microvesicular steatosis.[355]

Conditions associated with microvesicular steatosis are potentially life threatening, with impairment of liver function and effects on other tissues as well. In the event that the patient survives, there are no long-term effects on the liver.

Lipogranuloma (or fat granuloma) represents a focal response to rupture of lipid-laden hepatocytes. It contains macrophages, occasional lymphocytes, eosinophils, and sometimes giant cells (Fig. 13.18). Serial sections may be required to identify a central fat globule and to differentiate the lesion from other forms of granuloma.[356] These focal lesions can be abundant, especially in alcohol-induced steatosis; they even may be confluent. Lipogranulomas lead to focal fibrosis without great clinical significance. Fat-laden macrophages may also be located within portal tracts.[360] They must be distinguished from mineral oil granulomas, the vacuoles of which are larger and more irregular and in which there is generally more fibrosis.[370]

Focal steatosis. The improved quality and frequent application of modern imaging techniques of the liver have led to the identification of focal steatosis in some patients. Although there may be other coincident liver pathology, over 40 cases have been described in which focal fatty change was an isolated finding. The lesion is usually located under the liver capsule. Multifocal steatosis resembling metastatic liver disease radiologically has been described in AIDS.[355]

Steatohepatitis, fibrosis, and cirrhosis

The understanding of hepatic steatosis has progressed considerably in recent years. Several studies have challenged previous assertions that macrovesicular steatosis is entirely benign. They indicate that fatty liver of either alcoholic or nonalcoholic etiologies can coincide with or lead to necroinflammation and fibrosis. Surprisingly, experimental studies have implicated steatosis itself as a direct cause of more advanced pathology.[373] The mere presence of oxidizable fat within the liver is enough to trigger lipid peroxidation.[375] Nevertheless, many patients with steatosis never progress to necroinflammation or fibrosis.[372] These observations led to the "two-hit" hypothesis. In addition to steatosis (the first "hit"), the development of steatohepatitis requires the presence of some other factor(s) (second "hit").[374]

One such mechanism linking steatosis to necroinflammation and fibrosis is lipid peroxidation causing oxidative stress of the cell. Interindividual differences in the magnitude of the second hit (oxidative stress) explain the apparent individual susceptibility to the development of steatohepatitis.[374,376] Steatohepatitis occurs in chronic alcoholics (alcoholic steatohepatitis or ASH) and also in patients who do not consume alcohol (nonalcoholic steatohepatitis or NASH).

Alcoholic steatohepatitis

In its early stages, steatohepatitis affects predominantly the centrolobular zone. It usually affects all lobules and comprises a constellation of changes, which need not all be present in the individual case. The most essential features are: (1) liver cell injury reflected in ballooning of hepatocytes with or without Mallory bodies and liver cell death by necrosis and/or apoptosis[399]; (2) inflammatory infiltrates composed predominantly, though not exclusively, of neutrophil polymorphs; (3) pericellular

fibrosis (so-called "chicken-wire fibrosis") possibly accompanied by perivenular fibrosis and phlebosclerosis (Figs 13.19 and 13.20). The severity of the changes and the extent of lobular involvement vary considerably without good correlation with clinical and biochemical data. A minority of alcoholic cases are characterized by centrolobular confluent areas where parenchyma is replaced by fibrosis and central–central bridging fibrosis (originally described as "sclerosing hyaline necrosis").[383] Other, less essential features include giant mitochondria, venoocclusive lesions, and ductular metaplasia.[398] A series of reviews of the histopathology of alcoholic steatohepatitis has appeared over the years, including alternative terminologies (acute alcoholic hepatitis, acute hepatitis of the alcoholic type, alcoholic steatonecrosis, and fatty liver hepatitis).[377,381,384,387,392]

Steatosis is frequently present, and usually macrovesicular. As mentioned, a mixed macro- and microvesicular pattern carries a worse prognosis.[396] Still worse is an almost panlobular, predominantly microvesicular steatosis with canalicular bilirubin stasis (so-called "alcoholic foamy degeneration").[397]

Ballooned hepatocytes may contain so-called "Mallory bodies": homogeneous, eosinophilic, perinuclear inclusions of variable size and shape (Fig. 13.19). These are complex structures composed of aggregated hyperphosphorylated cytokeratin polypeptides (including cytokeratins 7, 18, and 19), together with ubiquitin, heat shock proteins, and tan proteins. The pathobiology of these intriguing cell inclusions is periodically reviewed.[380,386,389,390] In florid cases, Mallory bodies are easily discernible in routinely stained sections. In mild disease, they may be small and difficult to identify. Immunostaining of cytokeratins or ubiquitin is helpful. Neutrophil granulocytes often surround and even invade hepatocytes containing Mallory bodies (so-called

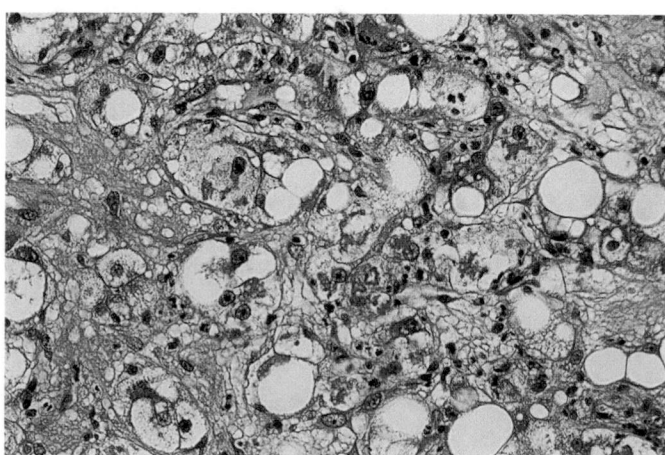

Fig. 13.19 Acute alcoholic hepatitis (ASH). Detail of centrolobular parenchyma, characterized by pericellular fibrosis, steatosis, hydropic swelling of several hepatocytes containing Mallory bodies, and neutrophils swarming around hydropic parenchymal cells (satellitosis). (H&E)

"satellitosis"). Macrophages and lymphocytes also may be found, as well as apoptotic bodies from dying hepatocytes and some degree of bilirubin stasis.

Megamitochondria appear as eosinophilic, PAS–diastase-negative, round, oval, or cigar-shaped inclusions of variable size. They can be better visualized with chromotrope–aniline blue (CAB) stain and immunohistochemistry.[385] They are not specific for alcohol-induced liver disease, but several authors found them more frequently in liver with alcohol-related fibrosis.[391]

Fibrosis is a constant feature in alcoholic steatohepatitis. It appears in different patterns. The most characteristic is pericellular (or perisinusoidal) "chickenwire" fibrosis, ensheathing pillars of hepatocytes (Fig. 13.20).[382] Its adequate identification requires collagen stains. Fibrosis also involves the central vein, resulting in thickening of its wall (perivenular fibrosis). This lesion was suggested to be a marker of future cirrhosis, but others give more prognostic importance to pericellular fibrosis.[393]

There is a strong correlation between the degree of steatosis (without steatohepatitis) and the number of activated hepatic stellate cells,[395] which can be stimulated by ethanol metabolites in the absence of necroinflammation.[379]

In several cases of alcoholic steatohepatitis, the lumen of the central veins is narrowed or occluded by subendothelial fibrosis[392] (Fig. 13.20), again requiring collagen stains for due appreciation. In later stages, fibrosis extends to the lobular periphery and necrotic bridges and fibrous septa start to link central veins with portal tracts, obscuring lobular topography and, together with parenchymal regeneration, leading to cirrhosis.[388] A semiquantitative scoring system suitable for alcoholic fibrosis has been published.[378]

Cirrhosis of alcoholic origin is of the micronodular type. Ongoing superimposed lesions of steatohepatitis

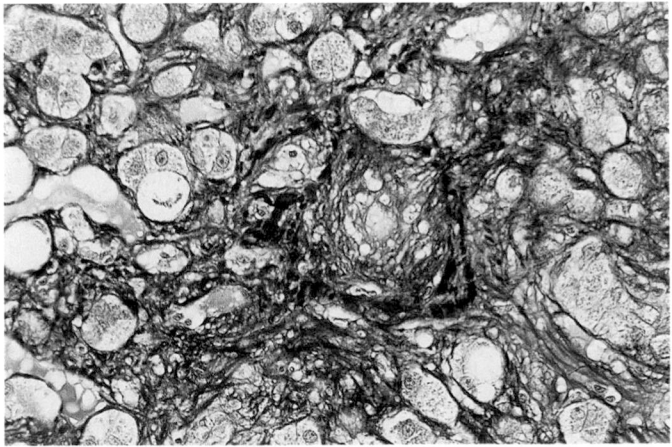

Fig. 13.20 Acute alcoholic hepatitis (ASH). Detail of centrolobular zone, showing fibrous obliteration of the centrolobular vein (veno-occlusive lesions; center) and marked pericellular ("chickenwire") fibrosis. (Sirius red stain)

worsen the prognosis[394] and suggest the etiology. In their absence, an alcoholic etiology can be suspected (but not proved) on account of the micronodular pattern, the dense fibrosis blurring the nodular edges, the steatosis, and central vein occlusions. When the patient stops alcohol intake, parenchymal regeneration improves, nodules increase in size, and all features of alcoholic etiology disappear.

Differential diagnosis of alcoholic steatohepatitis

Liver biopsy is quite useful for the diagnosis of alcoholic liver disease,[402] but differentiation from other diseases remains important. Viral hepatitis may be suspected clinically, but its liver histopathology is quite different from ASH. An incomplete picture of ASH, with only perivenular and pericellular centrolobular fibrosis, may be confused with chronic venous congestion.

Mallory bodies, neutrophils, and fibrosis are part of the histopathology of diseases unrelated to alcohol such as chronic cholestasis and Wilson's disease. *Chronic cholestatic disease* is easy to differentiate, because of the periportal predominance of the changes. *Wilson's disease* may resemble alcoholic hepatitis but is a differential diagnosis that should always be considered, especially in younger patients.

Hypervitaminosis A may cause pericellular fibrosis progressing to cirrhosis.[400] The pathologist should be alert for hepatic stellate cell hyperplasia. Hepatocellular siderosis occurs in some alcoholics and may be confused with genetic *hemochromatosis*. Difficult cases may be solved by quantitative tissue iron determination and calculation of the hepatic iron index.[401] A differential diagnosis that cannot be solved by histology alone is *nonalcoholic steatohepatitis (NASH)*, drug-induced or otherwise, because of the identical histopathology (see below).

Nonalcoholic liver disease in the alcoholic patient

Patients with a heavy alcohol intake may suffer from nonalcoholic liver diseases, amongst others cholangitis, viral hepatitis, and passive venous congestion.[409] Alcohol intake may hasten the onset of hepatic and cutaneous manifestations of *porphyria cutanea tarda*.[404] The hepatocytes contain birefringent acicular cytoplasmic inclusions[405] and usually some degree of siderosis. Chronic alcohol ingestion may also increase the risk of *acute drug-induced liver injury*, such as paracetamol-induced centrolobular necrosis.[410] Alcoholic patients undergoing *aversion therapy* with cyanamide may develop a dramatic form of ground glass change in periportal hepatocytes. The lesion may lead to cirrhosis.[413] Severe siderosis in the alcoholic patient may be the result of genuine *genetic hemochromatosis*, to be checked by iron determination and the hepatic iron index. Chronic venous congestion resulting in centrolobular fibrosis can be seen in patients with *alcoholic cardiomyopathy*.[407]

Chronic alcoholic pancreatitis may lead to stricturing of the common bile duct and cause lesions of extrahepatic bile duct obstruction with or without cholangitis.[408] Some of these patients may develop biliary cirrhosis.[403] An exclusively or predominantly periportal pattern of fibrosis should arouse suspicion of chronic pancreatitis.[411] *Chronic hepatitis* with portal tract infiltrates and interface hepatitis may be observed in alcoholics. An alcoholic etiology has been suggested,[406] but in most instances the cause is chronic viral hepatitis B, and even more often, the cause is hepatitis C.[412] *Hepatocellular carcinoma* may complicate alcoholic cirrhosis, and alcohol abuse may promote the development of this tumor in patients with chronic hepatitis C.[414]

Nonalcoholic steatohepatitis

The definable causes of nonalcoholic steatohepatitis (NASH) include jejunoileal bypass surgery, gastroplasty and other causes of rapid and profound weight loss in obese subjects, total parenteral nutrition, drugs (amiodarone, perhexiline maleate, estrogens and estrogen receptor ligands, methotrexate), occupational hepatotoxicity as reported from a petrochemical plant in Brazil,[418] copper toxicity, and disorders characterized by extreme insulin resistance. In most cases the etiopathogenesis of NASH appears multifactorial (obesity, type 2 diabetes, and hypertriglyceridemia) and the disease can be regarded as the hepatic consequence of the metabolic syndrome or cardiovascular dysmetabolic syndrome or syndrome X.[417] The disease also occurs in children.[428]

The clinical features and natural history have recently been reviewed. There is a need for consensus regarding the minimal histologic criteria necessary and the maximum amount of alcohol intake permitted to establish the diagnosis of NASH.[421] Ludwig and associates proposed a subclassification to include etiopathogenesis: primary NASH (related to obesity and insulin resistance), and secondary NASH (post bypass surgery, drugs, and toxins).[424] The histologic criteria put forth by Ludwig et al.[424] include patterns of injury that are similar to features of alcoholic injury. However, the minimal criteria for diagnosis are not agreed upon by all investigators.[419,422,423,425,429] The term "nonalcoholic fatty liver disease" (NAFLD) has been proposed as a more inclusive term that incorporates the entire spectrum of steatotic syndromes not induced by alcohol.[425] The various views were discussed in a recent review which stressed that not all of the lesions of alcoholic liver disease are present in NASH and that not all of the lesions of NASH are seen in alcoholic liver disease.[415] Further discussion of the criteria and the terminology is clearly indicated. A system for grading and staging the histologic lesions in NASH has been published by Brunt et al.[415,416]

It is of paramount importance to realize that no qualitative histologic differences exist between ASH and NASH to allow classification of an *individual case* as alcoholic or nonalcoholic on the basis of morphology alone.[415] However, when larger groups of patients are compared, alcoholics tend to develop more severe disease, whereas NASH is usually associated with more fat and nuclear glycogen, but less hepatocellular damage, inflammation and fibrosis, and fewer Mallory bodies, although progression to cirrhosis is definitely possible.[420,426]

One should be aware that the liver histology loses characteristic markers of the disease as NASH progresses, ending in cirrhosis without specific etiologic features ("cryptogenic"). A couple of studies suggested a relationship between cryptogenic cirrhosis and NASH through the shared risk factors of obesity and diabetes.[427]

Cholestasis and biliary diseases

Histopathologic liver changes of cholestasis in general

The histopathologic changes of the liver in cholestatic liver diseases can be grouped into two categories: (1) features of cholestasis in general; and (2) features characteristic of individual liver diseases. The former lesions allow the diagnostic histopathologist to solve the differential diagnostic problem *between* cholestatic and noncholestatic disorders, whereas the latter changes serve to differentiate between diseases *within* the group of cholestatic disorders.

The term cholestasis refers to an arrest, or at least a marked reduction, in bile secretion and bile flow. It may be caused by a functional secretory disturbance of the hepatic parenchymal cells[432] and/or by an obstruction at any level in the excretory pathways of bile, from the canaliculi to the papilla of Vater.[430]

Intrahepatic cholestasis refers to those conditions in which the *primary focus* is located inside the liver organ; it thus comprises diseases of the parenchymal cells and of the intrahepatic bile ducts. Some conditions combine both: for instance, progressive familial intrahepatic cholestasis type 3 combines a deficit of canalicular phospholipid transport and damage to interlobular ducts.[432]

Extrahepatic cholestasis occurs when the bile excretory block is located in larger ducts: outside the liver along the extrahepatic bile ducts (e.g., gallstones, bile duct tumors, bile duct strictures), but also in larger hilar intrahepatic ducts. Some cholestatic disorders affect both the intra- and extrahepatic segments of the biliary tree, and hence qualify as combined intra- and extrahepatic cholestasis. Examples are so-called "extrahepatic bile duct atresia" in neonates and primary sclerosing cholangitis in adults and children.

The block in bile secretion may be complete or variably incomplete. Complete cholestasis denotes a total arrest of bile secretion, with retention of bile salts and bilirubin, be it functional or obstructive. Incomplete cholestasis usually indicates an incomplete or partial obstruction of the intrahepatic and/or extrahepatic bile ducts, with retention of bile salts but not of bilirubin.

Incomplete intrahepatic cholestasis is mostly due to destructive diseases of intrahepatic bile ducts (vanishing bile duct diseases) such as primary biliary cirrhosis (PBC) and primary sclerosing cholangitis (PSC). Incomplete extrahepatic cholestasis corresponds to incomplete obstruction (narrowing or strictures) of segments of larger bile ducts.

Cholestasis may be acute or chronic. Acute cholestasis is usually complete cholestasis, corresponding to either total functional exocrine secretory failure of the hepatocytes (e.g., drug-induced cholestasis), or complete obstruction of the extrahepatic bile ducts (e.g., impacted gallstone). Chronic cholestasis indicates a cholestatic condition of longer duration (weeks, months, years), which may be complete (e.g., chronic total extrahepatic bile duct obstruction by a carcinoma of the pancreas) or variably incomplete (e.g., PBC, PSC).

Cholestasis and icterus (or jaundice) are not synonymous terms: the distinction must be made between icteric and anicteric conditions of cholestasis. Patients with incomplete cholestasis may remain anicteric for long periods. In parallel, histologic cholestasis is not characterized by the microscopically visible accumulation of the bile pigment bilirubin in liver tissue sections. This underscores the usefulness of distinguishing between bilirubin stasis and cholate stasis, which either separately or in combination may constitute a light microscopic picture of histologic cholestasis.[431]

Acute complete cholestasis

Changes occur in the lobular parenchyma and in the portal tracts. An acute disease associated with complete cholestasis is characterized by microscopically demonstrable bilirubin accumulation in the liver lobule (Fig. 13.21) which starts in the centrolobular zone; it corresponds to pigment granules in parenchymal cells (hepatocellular bilirubin stasis) and inspissated bilirubin-stained bile plugs in more or less dilated intercellular canaliculi (canalicular bilirubin stasis). Retention of detergent bile acids results in hepatocellular damage and even death (necrotic or apoptotic), leading to Kupffer cell activation. The hypertrophic Kupffer cells phagocytose the debris from dying parenchymal cells and the liberated canalicular bile plugs, resulting in Kupffer cell bilirubin stasis. The latter feature indicates a cholestatic condition of at least several days' duration.[434]

Bilirubin stasis in its various locations should not be confused with the dark brown to black deposits (in hepatocytes, canaliculi, Kupffer cells, and ductules) in liver biopsies from patients with erythropoietic protoporphyria. The latter deposits are darker brown or black and easily identified by the use of polarized light; protoporphyrin deposits have a red to yellow birefringence with a maltese cross configuration in coarser (ductular) deposits (Fig. 13.22).[433]

Acute complete cholestasis, especially in cases of extrahepatic obstructive origin, is further characterized by edema of the portal tract connective tissue, causing

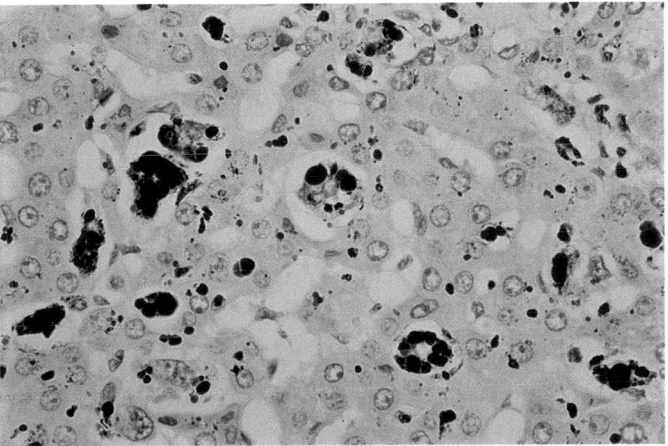

A

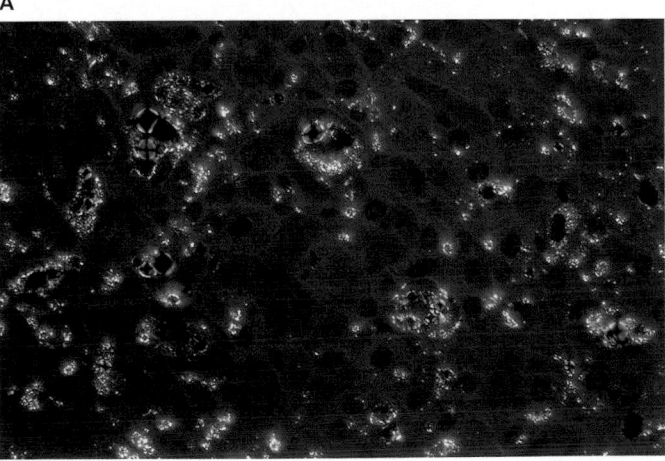

B

Fig. 13.22 Erythropoietic protoporphyria. **A,** Dark brownish-black deposits of protoporphyrin in hepatocytes, canaliculi, Kupffer cells, and ductules. (H&E) **B,** The deposits are birefringent, and show a maltese cross picture of red birefringence in the larger deposits. (Polarized light)

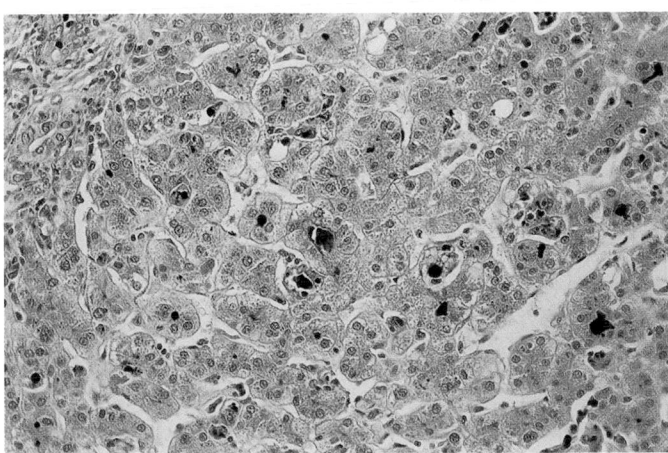

Fig. 13.21 Marked bilirubin stasis in hepatocytes, canaliculi, and Kupffer cells in neonate with extrahepatic bile duct atresia. (H&E)

some rounding of portal contours, and an incipient "ductular reaction" (described below).

Chronic complete cholestasis

The parenchymal changes in complete cholestasis of longer duration comprise a number of lesions which appear with time superimposed on the early bilirubin stasis. The latter gradually extends toward the periportal parenchyma. In most forms of chronic cholestasis lasting for weeks, some lymphocytic inflammatory infiltrate occurs in the areas with bilirubin stasis, apparently secondary to cholestatic changes. Unlike the inflammation in acute hepatitis, this infiltrate is mild and restricted to the area with bilirubin stasis. The further parenchymal, portal, and periportal alterations observed in chronic complete cholestasis also occur in chronic incomplete cholestasis, as described in the following section. The basic difference between chronic complete cholestasis and the incomplete variety consists in the absence of bilirubin stasis in the incomplete category, and the occasionally more pronounced expression of some of the other lesions in the complete variety.

Chronic incomplete cholestasis

As mentioned, bilirubin stasis (as well as clinical jaundice) is not a feature of liver diseases associated with incomplete cholestasis, except in the terminal decompensating phase of the disease or in the case of superimposed pathologic changes (e.g., drug-induced liver damage). This implies that the histopathologist has to identify the presence of a chronic cholestatic disease in the absence of what used to be regarded in the past as the most characteristic feature of cholestasis (bilirubin stasis). The histopathologic diagnosis of chronic (complete as well as incomplete) cholestasis relies on the following parenchymal, portal, and periportal alterations. The parenchymal changes include cholate stasis, cholestatic liver cell rosettes, feathery degeneration, xanthomatous cells, and bile infarcts.

Cholate stasis refers to a lesion of periportal hepatocytes (Figs 13.23 to 13.26). This hepatocellular alteration is thought to be due to the membrane-damaging effect of retained bile acids.[436] The affected hepatocytes appear swollen, pale, and coarsely granular (Fig. 13.23); they contain granules of lysosomal copper, complexed with copper-binding protein (metallothionein), which are stainable with rhodanine (copper) and orcein (metallothionein) (Figs 13.24 and 13.25). With time, Mallory bodies develop in these cells, and bilirubin inclusions also may appear in the very late stages. The earliest stages of cholate stasis may be revealed by immunostaining for cytokeratin 7, revealing a phenotypic switch to a biliary type of intermediate filament cytoskeleton in periportal hepatocytes (Fig. 13.26). With time, cytokeratin 7 expression extends with a decreasing gradient from the limiting plate toward the center of the lobule, over a distance of several cells.[448]

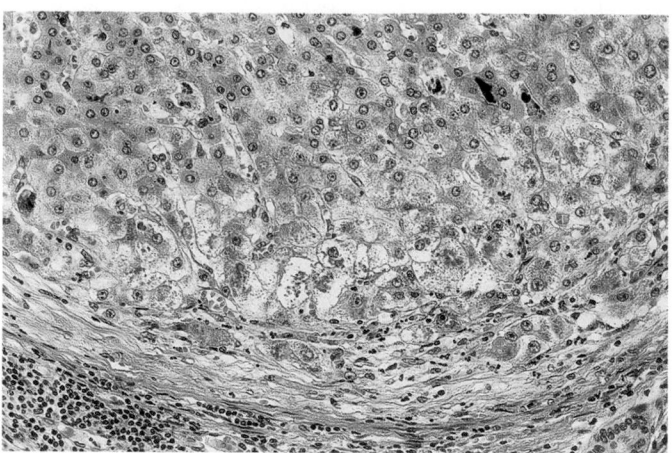

Fig. 13.23 Cholate stasis in periphery of parenchymal nodule in cirrhotic liver of patient with end stage primary sclerosing cholangitis. The hepatocytes near the fibrous septum (lower part) show hydropic swelling, clumping of the cytoplasm, and Mallory bodies. (H&E)

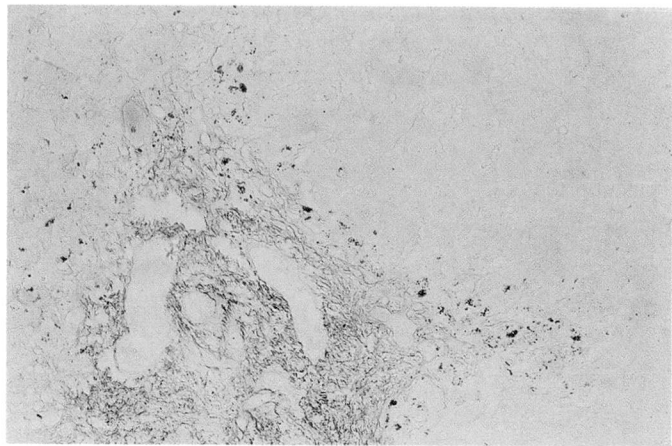

Fig. 13.24 Cholate stasis in periportal parenchyma in patient with primary sclerosing cholangitis. The picture shows orcein-positive granules in periportal hepatocytes, representing lysosomal localization of copper binding protein (metallothionein). (Orcein stain)

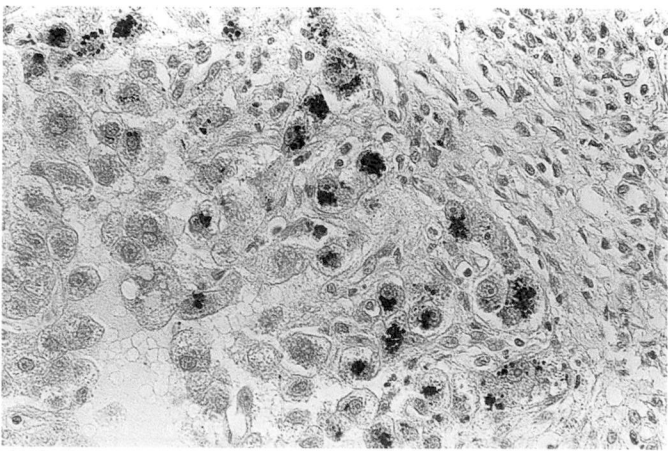

Fig. 13.25 Cholate stasis in periphery of cirrhotic nodule in patient with stage 4 primary biliary cirrhosis. Lysosomal copper–metallothionein complexes appear as red-stained granules in the copper-specific rhodanine stain.

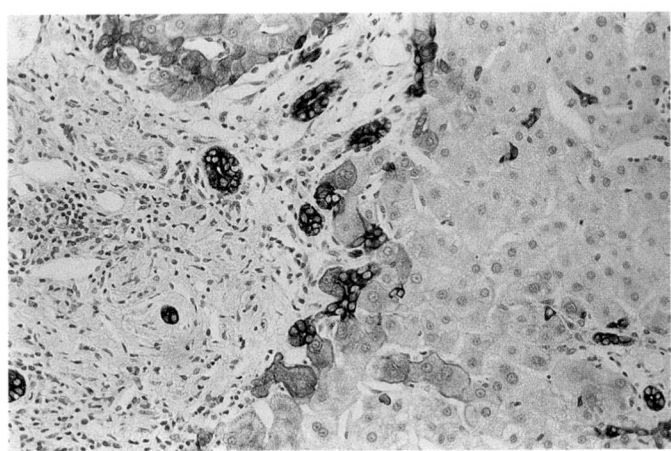

Fig. 13.26 Primary biliary cirrhosis. Detail of portal tract and surrounding parenchyma. This cytokeratin 7 immunostain highlights an increase in the number of ductular structures at the portal tract periphery; expression of cytokeratin 7 in periportal hepatocytes (early stage of cholate stasis), and a few scattered, small cytokeratin 7 positive cells at some distance from the portal tract (presumed hepatic progenitor cells). (Immunostain for cytokeratin 7)

Cholestatic liver cell rosettes[445] represent a very useful diagnostic feature in any chronic cholestatic condition. They correspond to a tubular rearrangement of the liver cell plates that are normally one cell thick. Under the light microscope, they appear as glandular or tubular structures lined by four or more hepatocytes around a central lumen. The lumen may vary greatly in diameter (Fig. 13.27A); it may appear empty, or be filled with eosinophilic or bilirubin-stained material in variable degrees of inspissation. Some or all of the lining hepatocytes may show feathery degeneration (see below) and express bile duct-type cytokeratins (cytokeratin 7 and tissue polypeptide antigen—TPA), indicating a partial shift toward a bile duct cell phenotype (Fig. 13.27B).[448–450] They should not be misinterpreted as expression of hepatocellular regeneration.

Feathery degeneration is a further lesion observed in chronic (incomplete and complete) cholestasis. It affects single cells or groups of parenchymal cells; these are characterized by hydropic swelling. There may be some bilirubin impregnation of the remaining visible cytoplasm in cases of chronic complete cholestasis.

Xanthomatous cells are a feature of longstanding incomplete and complete cholestasis. They are lipid-laden histiocytes with foamy cytoplasm, accumulating in the parenchyma but also in portal tracts, appearing singly or in clusters. They represent the tissular expression of the hyperlipidemia that accompanies chronic cholestasis.

Bile infarcts (so-called "Charcot–Gombault infarcts") are a late parenchymal lesion in severe cholestasis of long duration, mainly (but not exclusively) seen in large duct obstruction. The lesions consist of necrotic hepatocytes,

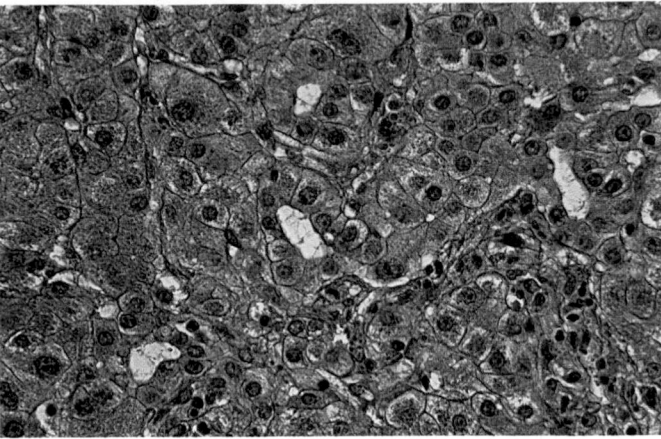

A

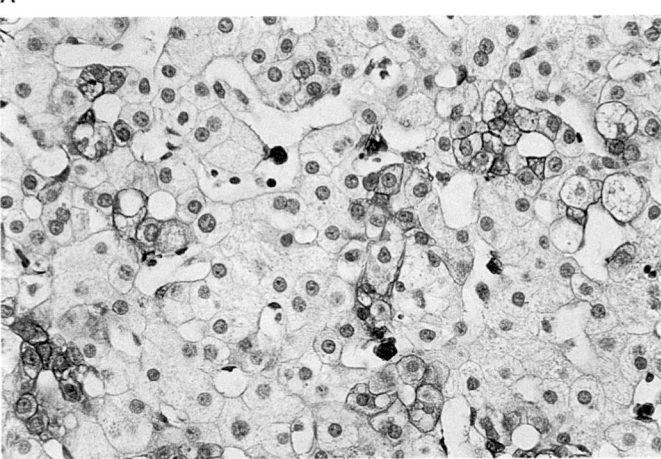

B

Fig. 13.27 Cholestatic liver cell rosettes. **A**, Liver biopsy of patient with primary sclerosing cholangitis. The involved hepatocytes appear in tubular arrangement. (H&E) **B**, Immunostaining for cytokeratin 7 reveals cholestatic liver cell rosettes to better advantage. Normal hepatocytes do not express cytokeratin 7, whereas cells in cholestatic rosettes express this intermediate filament to variable extent.

mostly in a paraportal location, possibly showing bilirubin impregnation of the central necrotic area. Bile infarcts are gradually replaced by organizing mesenchymal tissue, finally resulting in fibrous scars.

In addition to the general parenchymal features of cholestasis, two further changes usually characterize the histologic picture in **neonatal cholestatic liver diseases**: parenchymal giant cells and extramedullary hematopoiesis.

Parenchymal multinucleated giant cells result from syncytial fusion of several mononucleated hepatocytes. The number of nuclei and their location are variable. Giant cells often contain pigment granules corresponding to bilirubin, lipofuscin, hemosiderin, or a combination thereof. Giant cell transformation of parenchymal cells occurs in a variety of conditions; they are considered a nonspecific reaction of the infant's hepatocytes to various types of injury and appear to be more specific for age than disease, although they are occasionally observed in adult liver as well. Parenchymal giant cells may appear necrotic and surrounded by neutrophil polymorphs.[447]

Foci of **extramedullary hematopoiesis**, comprising clusters of erythrocyte precursor cells, myeloid precursor cells, and megakaryocytes or a combination of these, are often observed in cholestatic liver specimens of young infants. They are not a reliable criterion for differentiation between various cholestatic diseases such as biliary atresia and neonatal hepatitis.

The periportal and architectural changes of chronic incomplete and complete cholestasis comprise ductular reaction, ductular reabsorption, periductular fibrosis, biliary fibrosis, and eventually the final stage of biliary cirrhosis.

Ductular reaction is recognized as an increased number of ductular profiles in the periphery of the portal tract, gradually extending into the periportal parenchyma toward the neighboring portal tracts (in the periphery of the liver lobule), and accompanied by edema and neutrophil polymorphonuclear leukocyte infiltration (Fig. 13.28).[435] Ductular reaction in diseases with obstruction of (extrahepatic) bile ducts is mainly due to increased bile pressure,[440,446] involves elongation rather than sprouting of preexisting bile ductules,[446] and has been described as "marginal bile duct proliferation" in human liver biopsies.[444] In other cholestatic diseases, not necessarily obstructive in origin, proinflammatory cytokines may be the predominant triggers.[438,443] The cholangiocytes lining the ductules may show signs of reabsorption, reflected in vacuolization of their cytoplasm and accumulation of bilirubin and lipofuscin. The wedge-shaped periportal extension of ductular reaction with the accompanying inflammation into the periportal parenchyma, which possibly shows features of cholate stasis, results in an irregular portal–parenchymal interface, termed "biliary piecemeal necrosis."[441]

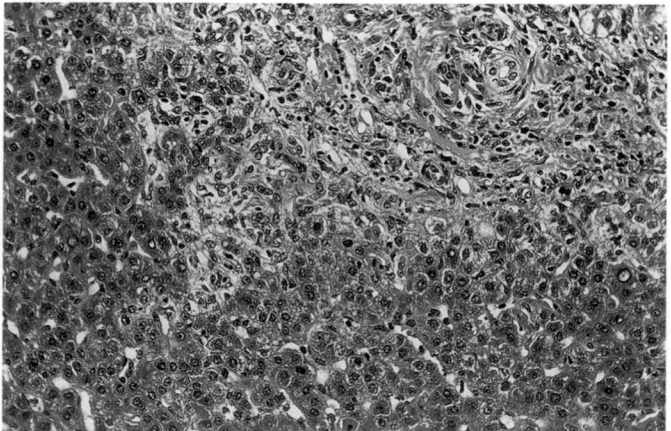

Fig. 13.28 Ductular reaction in chronic cholestasis. Liver biopsy from patient with primary sclerosing cholangitis. The picture shows a mildly inflamed portal tract (upper part) with (at 8 o'clock) a focus of "ductular reaction" composed of bile ductules, edematous stroma, and some neutrophil infiltration. (H&E)

For reasons which have not been finally elucidated, chronic states of cholestasis in some patients lack an obvious ductular reaction; this may be the case in Alagille's syndrome, some cases of primary sclerosing cholangitis, and chronic liver allograft rejection.

Ductular reaction is accompanied by periductular fibrosis. The progressive ductular reaction with periductular fibrosis eventually results in fibrous linkage of adjacent portal tracts. This stage of **biliary fibrosis** (portal–portal septal fibrosis) is a potentially reversible lesion[439] since the basic angioarchitectural pattern of the liver is preserved.[437] Biliary fibrosis as such is to be distinguished from true **biliary cirrhosis**, which represents the final stage in disturbance of the lobular architecture, characterized—like any cirrhosis—by additional portal–central fibrous septa and nodular parenchymal regeneration. Ongoing cholestasis in the stage of biliary cirrhosis is characterized by persistence of the ductular reaction with accompanying edema and periductular inflammation and fibrosis. Together with lesions of cholate stasis in the nodular periphery, this creates at low magnification the impression of a clear halo between the cirrhotic nodules and the fibrous septa. This feature indicates actively progressing disease in its cirrhotic stage.

The periportal and architectural changes of chronic cholestasis form the basis for staging in chronic cholestatic liver diseases: portal (stage 1); periportal (stage 2); septal (stage 3); and cirrhotic (stage 4).[442]

Individual cholestatic liver diseases

Cholestatic liver diseases can be subdivided in different ways: intrahepatic and extrahepatic; medical and surgical; neonatal and adult, etc. In the following section, an attempt is made to classify the disorders according to the primary focus of the disease along the pathways through which bile has to travel from its source in the hepatocytes to its destination in the gut.

It is realized that such a categorization is imperfect: in the first place, because the etiology and pathogenesis of most cholestatic liver diseases remain incompletely clarified, and second because some disorders are due to disturbance in two or more sites simultaneously. Nevertheless, a subdivision can be based on the anatomic sites that appear to bear the brunt of the lesion according to present-day insight.

Hepatocellular (parenchymal) diseases

A group of **congenital cholestatic diseases** appear to be caused by functional defects in the liver parenchymal cells.[464]

Progressive familial intrahepatic cholestasis type 1 (PFIC-1) is an autosomal recessive hereditary cholestatic syndrome, characterized by severe cholestasis in infants and children, also known as Byler's disease. It is caused by mutations of the gene *ATP8B1* (initially named *FIC-1*), encoding a P-type ATPase, which might be involved in bile salt excretion and/or the enterohepatic circulation of bile salts.[469]

Progressive familial intrahepatic cholestasis type 2 (PFIC-2) is phenotypically similar to PFIC-1, but is caused by mutations of the gene of the canalicular bile salt export pump (BSEP).[467]

Progressive familial intrahepatic cholestasis type 3 (PFIC-3) is caused by mutations of the *MDR3* gene encoding the canalicular phospholipid export pump.[463] These subtypes were recently discovered and their histopathologic documentation will require further investigation. The histopathology of these entities evolves with the chronologic evolution of the disease.

In young patients at presentation, PFIC-1 is characterized by bland bilirubin stasis, followed by slowly progressive intralobular fibrosis. On electron microscopy, the canalicular bile plugs reveal a coarsely granular texture, so-called "Byler bile."[451,452]

The histopathology of PFIC-2 in young patients corresponds to that of so-called "neonatal hepatitis," showing generalized hepatocellular unrest, parenchymal giant cell transformation, and extramedullary hematopoiesis in association with parenchymal bilirubin stasis. Later stages show faster development of fibrosis, chronic inflammation, cholate stasis, and cirrhosis.[451] On electron microscopic study the canalicular bile plugs reveal a filamentous pattern, not corresponding to "Byler bile."[452] Both PFIC-1 and PFIC-2 are characterized by (near)normal levels of γ-glutamyl transpeptidase in the serum,[452] although this enzyme activity is increased in the liver tissue.[455]

In contrast, PFIC-3 is characterized by elevated serum levels of γ-glutamyl transpeptidase.[468] Its histology, in contrast to most cases of PFIC-1 and PFIC-2, is characterized by inflammatory infiltration in portal tracts, and damage of interlobular bile ducts and ductular proliferation.[464,468] PFIC-3 corresponds to the previously recognized subgroup of patients with Byler syndrome characterized by elevated γ-glutamyl transpeptidase in the serum and ductular reaction in the liver histopathology.[456,457,462,466]

Benign recurrent intrahepatic cholestasis (BRIC) is a recurrent cholestatic disorder in children and adults, caused, like PFIC-1, by mutations of the *FIC-1* gene,[453,469] but in different regions of the gene, possibly explaining the different phenotypic appearances of PFIC-1 and BRIC. Contrasting with PFIC-1, BRIC is characterized by recurrent episodes of cholestasis that do not progress to liver cirrhosis. Nevertheless, considerable overlap may exist between the clinical presentations of PFIC-1 and BRIC, and both conditions may represent the extremes of a broad spectrum of cholestatic syndromes.[469] Histologically, BRIC is characterized by simple or bland bilirubin stasis, with bilirubin deposits in hepatocytes, canaliculi, and Kupffer cells only during the episodes of clinical cholestasis. BRIC is also known as Summerskill–Tygstrup–De Groote disease.

The metabolic disorders **galactosemia** and **hereditary fructose intolerance** show a histologic picture of severe bilirubin stasis with bile deposits in pseudoglandular tubules of hepatocytes and steatosis; the early stage is characterized by a periportal ductular reaction. **Tyrosinemia** shows a similar histopathology, with in addition parenchymal siderosis, extramedullary hematopoiesis, and foci of nodular parenchymal regeneration.[461] The diagnostic feature of **a_1-antitrypsin deficiency** is the presence of eosinophilic, PAS-positive, diastase-resistant inclusions in periportal hepatocytes, immunoreactive with specific anti-α_1-antitrypsin antibodies.[454] The entity is discussed on p. 954.

Cryptogenic neonatal cholestasis (often referred to as **neonatal giant cell hepatitis**) is histologically characterized by the elementary lesions of cholestasis, possibly parenchymal giant cells and extramedullary hematopoiesis, and sometimes some degree of parenchymal siderosis and intralobular fibrosis. It represents a heterogeneous group of neonatal cholestatic diseases of unknown origin, left over after the elucidation of a series of etiologies during recent years (e.g., α_1-antitrypsin deficiency, PFIC-1, PFIC-2, PFIC-3).[460]

Several **acquired cholestatic disorders** appear to be characterized by a predominantly hepatocellular focus of the disease. This is the case in acute viral hepatitis, alcoholic steatohepatitis (ASH) and nonalcoholic steatohepatitis (NASH), drug-induced liver disease,[458] intrahepatic cholestasis of pregnancy (see p. 962), and some forms of postoperative[459] cholestasis.

Acute venous congestion of the liver (e.g., in heart decompensation, in the Budd–Chiari syndrome) may be associated with parenchymal bilirubin stasis.[465] The associated changes are those of venous outflow block.

Ductular pathology

In some cholestatic disorders, the disease appears to focus on the ductules and canals of Hering. Most of these conditions are characterized by ductular reaction and ductular bilirubin stasis; the latter is represented by smaller or larger bilirubin-impregnated deposits or concrements in more or less dilated ductular segments. **Ductular bilirubin stasis** occurs in diverse situations, and is thought to result from damage to ductular cells with total paralysis or partial impairment of their normal secretion of bicarbonate-rich fluid. Ductular bilirubin stasis is observed in patients with massive liver cell necrosis[477]; in septicemia and endotoxic shock[470,476]; in extrahepatic bile duct atresia[473]; in total parenteral nutrition[471]; and in some patients with mucoviscidosis (cystic fibrosis).[475] In extrahepatic bile duct atresia, the ductular bilirubin deposits often appear as a string of pearls in a series of ductular dilatations.

In endotoxic shock and septicemia, the ductules may appear broadly dilated; the bilirubin concrements may show variable degrees of inspissation and admixture of

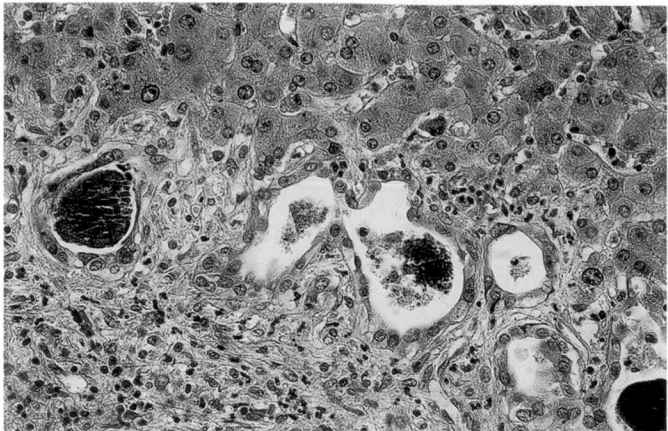

Fig. 13.29 Ductular bilirubin stasis in septicemia. The picture shows part of a portal tract (lower part), which contains (all around its periphery) numerous profiles of dilated ductules. The ductules contain bile concrements in varying degrees of inspissation; their epithelial lining shows degenerative changes and may even be necrotic; they are often accompanied by neutrophil polymorphs. (H&E)

Table 13.8 Vanishing bile duct diseases

Neonatal age
Extrahepatic bile duct atresia
Paucity of interlobular bile ducts
Syndromic
Nonsyndromic
Adult age
Primary biliary cirrhosis (PBC)
Overlap syndrome autoimmune hepatitis—PBC
Primary sclerosing cholangitis (PSC)
Overlap syndrome autoimmune hepatitis—PSC
Sarcoidosis with intrahepatic cholestasis
Idiopathic adulthood ductopenia
Chronic liver allograft rejection
Chronic graft-versus-host disease
Drug-induced ductopenia
Histiocytosis X, Hodgkin's lymphoma
Mucoviscidosis

PAS-positive material, and part or all of the lining ductular cells may appear flattened, desquamating, or necrotizing, and infiltrated with neutrophil polymorphs. The dilated ductules may appear all around the perimeter of some portal tracts (Fig. 13.29). This lesion is highly suggestive of septicemia and constitutes a prognostically ominous sign ("cholangitis lenta").[476] In view of its sinister prognosis, this finding necessitates urgent reporting to the clinician. It is presumably due to raised levels of tumor necrosis factor-α (TNF-α) and interleukin-6 (IL-6) in the presence of endotoxemia.[472,478]

In patients with cystic fibrosis (mucoviscidosis), the concrements in the dilated ductular lumina are PAS positive and diastase resistant with variable degrees of bilirubin impregnation, leaving the impression that the primary lesion consists in the accumulation of a tenacious mucoid secretion.[474]

As mentioned above, ductular deposits are also seen in erythropoietic protoporphyria, and easily diagnosed by the use of polarized light.

Ductal pathology: vanishing bile duct diseases

A number of cholestatic liver diseases are associated with progressive inflammatory destruction of intrahepatic bile ducts of a particular caliber. They are classified as vanishing bile duct disorders[496,498] and represent a vast and intriguing chapter in liver pathology (Table 13.8). They all result in reduction of the number of interlobular bile ducts, or *paucity of ducts* or *ductopenia*.

A sound morphologic diagnosis of ductopenia requires a sufficiently large biopsy specimen and quantitative evaluation of interlobular ducts. Although originally a surgical biopsy was recommended,[480] it is felt that a needle biopsy may suffice, provided the specimen contains at least five portal tracts.[514] Recognition of a missing duct is facilitated by comparing with branches of the hepatic artery; 70% to 80% of arterial branches are normally accompanied by a duct of approximately similar size near the center of the portal tract. A "widowed artery" signals a missing duct.[534] Immunostains for cytokeratin 7 (or 19) or tissue polypeptide antigen (TPA) are helpful for better visualization of interlobular ducts,[553] especially in very young children.[552] Paucity of interlobular ducts or ductopenia was originally defined as a ratio of the number of interlobular ducts to the number of portal tracts of less than 0.5. In normal children and adults this ratio lies between 0.9 and 1.8.[480]

A definition of ductopenia as a ratio of 0.5 was valid at the time of its definition in neonatal disease, but since 1975 evidence has accumulated that ductopenia in general is not a static condition but corresponds to a progressive destruction of interlobular ducts. It follows that a reduced bile duct to portal tract ratio higher than 0.5 (i.e., a less pronounced degree of ductopenia) can be considered "ductopenia," especially when, besides a few portal tracts with missing ducts, ducts with degenerative changes are also observed.[502]

The histopathology in vanishing bile duct diseases is mainly that of chronic incomplete cholestasis, with sometimes in addition features specific for the individual disease; the latter are usually most prominent in the portal tracts and concern the interlobular ducts and the surrounding portal mesenchyme.[555] One has to keep in mind that such features are not necessarily present in every biopsy specimen and do not persist throughout the entire course of the disease; and that the specificity of the histopathology decreases with advancing disease.

Vanishing bile duct diseases in the neonatal period and childhood are represented by paucity of interlobular bile ducts and by so-called "extrahepatic bile duct atresia" (see Table 13.8).

Paucity of interlobular bile ducts (PILBD) is diagnosed by calculating the bile duct to portal tract ratio as mentioned above. However, in premature infants, a ratio of less than 0.9 may be normal[515] due to the incompleteness of bile duct development at the time of birth; full development of the finest ramifications of the intrahepatic bile duct system takes an additional 4 weeks.[554] Paucity of interlobular bile ducts is subdivided according to associated clinical features into a syndromic and a nonsyndromic variety. Both categories are characterized by a nonspecific, inflammatory destruction of interlobular ducts, resulting in progressive ductopenia. Both categories are characterized by histopathologic changes of neonatal cholestasis (see p. 947).

In *syndromic paucity of interlobular bile ducts* (Alagille's syndrome or arteriohepatic dysplasia), the loss of small interlobular bile ducts is associated with a set of clinical features (abnormal facies, vertebral, cardiac, ocular, and renal abnormalities) which, according to their presence or absence, result in a complete or incomplete syndrome.[538] Destruction of ducts mostly starts after 3 months of age. Early changes do not allow prediction of the future development of fibrosis.[511]

Nonsyndromic paucity of interlobular ducts may be an isolated hepatic abnormality (idiopathic) or one component of a more complex systemic process with or without a known cause. It may be associated with α_1-antitrypsin deficiency, rubella, trisomy 21, Turner's syndrome, Byler's disease, and several other conditions. Nonsyndromic paucity constitutes the most frequent diagnosis in patients with conjugated hyperbilirubinemia in the first month of life.[514] The destruction of interlobular ducts starts early (before 3 months) and the progression is usually faster than in syndromic paucity.[511,514]

Extrahepatic bile duct atresia (EHBDA; *biliary atresia*). Despite the terminology, EHBDA is not restricted to the extrahepatic segments of the biliary system, but also affects the intrahepatic ducts. It is a panbiliary disease consisting in a progressive necroinflammatory destruction of the bile ducts with originally maximal involvement of part or all of the extrahepatic duct system. The disease may start in utero or in the perinatal period. Primary treatment consists in hepatic portoenterostomy or Kasai operation with resection of the obliterated extrahepatic ducts. The histopathology of these fibrous remnants reveals various stages of nonspecific inflammation, epithelial desquamation and necrosis, ulceration, and fibrosis.[506,507]

The search for a correlation between the number and size of the patent ducts in the porta hepatis at the time of portoenterostomy and the success of the procedure has yielded controversial results.[500] Some pediatric surgeons still insist on assessment of bile duct luminal size in frozen sections of the proximal resection margin during a Kasai procedure. Some consider the total diameter of all the prehilar structures an important prognostic parameter, with a total diameter of more than 400 μm indicating a favorable prognosis for adequate bile drainage.[547] A more recent study showed no correlation between duration of patient survival and size of the bile ducts at the resection margins.[550]

Liver biopsy remains the cornerstone in the diagnosis of EHBDA. The histopathology evolves over time, as in any extrahepatic bile duct obstruction. During the first 3 to 4 weeks, biopsy mostly reveals nonspecific bilirubin stasis, some parenchymal giant cells, and foci of extramedullary hematopoiesis. Gradually, portal edema and ductular reaction set in. The latter reaction is considered the most reliable, although not pathognomonic criterion in diagnosing extrahepatic obstruction in liver specimens.[518] The ductules often contain inspissated bile concrements. In later stages, periportal fibrosis develops, finally resulting in secondary biliary cirrhosis. Important for the differentiation from other causes of obstruction (mainly choledochal cyst in this neonatal period) are the degenerative lesions of the intrahepatic ducts, which are part of the basic sclerosing cholangitic process in EHBDA (Fig. 13.30). The ducts show irregularity of their lining cholangiocytes, which feature vacuolization, nuclear pyknosis, atrophy, and infiltration by inflammatory cells. Thickening of the basement membrane occurs, associated with progressing atrophy and disappearance of the ducts. With time, progressive ductopenia of intrahepatic ducts develops, constituting an ominous sign for the success of hepatic portoenterostomy.[547]

In about a quarter[495,543] or more[551] of the patients, the interlobular bile ducts still appear in their early embryologic shape (so-called "ductal plate malformation") (Fig. 13.31), suggesting an antenatal start of the disease associated with arrest of remodeling of the embryonic ductal plates.[499] In such patients, histology reveals an

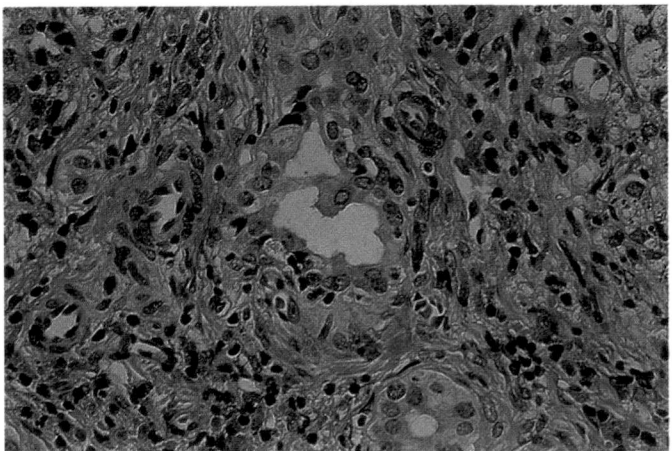

Fig. 13.30 Extrahepatic bile duct atresia (EHBDA). Detail of a portal tract in liver biopsy from neonate with EHBDA, showing mild inflammatory infiltrate, and a bile duct with irregular outline and epithelial damage: vacuolization in some cholangiocytes, apoptosis in others, and some inflammatory cells inside the basement membrane. (H&E)

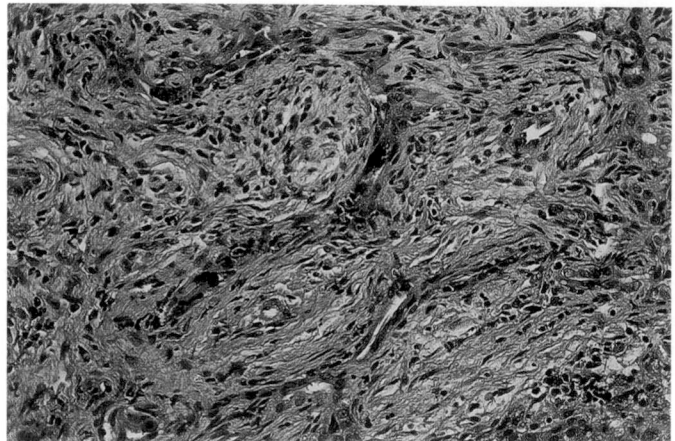

Fig. 13.31 Extrahepatic bile duct atresia (EHBDA), "early severe" type in stage of advanced fibrosis. The picture shows part of a large, fibrous portal area, with recognizable hepatic artery branches, barely visible or no portal vein branches, and bile duct structures in ductal plate configuration ("ductal plate malformation"). The lining cholangiocytes show involutional changes: flattening, shrinkage, and nuclear pyknosis. (H&E)

advanced degree of fibrosis even at the very young age of 4 weeks, justifying the term "early, severe" variant of EHBDA.

The differential diagnosis of EHBDA includes bile duct obstruction by choledochal cyst, so-called "neonatal giant cell hepatitis" (no or much less ductular reaction, more intralobular than perilobular fibrosis), chronic liver injury by parenteral nutrition, and several inborn errors of metabolism. The etiology of EHBDA remains unknown. Most probably, EHBDA is a heterogeneous disorder and represents the common phenotype of several underlying disorders.[482,549]

Vanishing bile duct diseases in adulthood comprise a number of different disorders, listed in Table 13.8.

Primary biliary cirrhosis (PBC) is considered an autoimmune disease, often associated with other autoimmune disorders. Although the proof for its autoimmune nature is strong, it is only indirect and circumstantial.[508] The basic lesion is a chronic, nonsuppurative, destructive cholangitis, possibly ending in cirrhosis.[545] The disease is nearly 10 times more frequent in females than in males, and usually has an insidious onset starting with pruritus. Characteristic for PBC is the presence of antimitochondrial antibodies (the most specific being directed against the M2 component of the pyruvate dehydrogenase complex), detectable in over 90% of patients.[508] Liver biopsy plays an important role in the diagnosis and staging of PBC.[498]

The bile duct lesion in the early stage of PBC affects ducts between 40 and 80 μm diameter, corresponding to segmental and larger interlobular ducts. The actual size of the ducts may on occasion be difficult to estimate since some of them tend to enlarge, apparently through damage to the basement membrane and reactive hyperplasia

of the lining epithelium.[537] The early lesions are focal in the liver and segmental within the duct system. The affected duct segments show epithelial swelling or eosinophil condensation, possibly stratification, and infiltration by lymphocytes and plasma cells. Damage of the basement membrane may lead to rupture of the duct. Inflammatory cells accumulate beside or around the duct. They comprise mainly lymphocytes, sometimes aggregated in a lymphoid follicle with germinal center. Plasma cells may be abundant, eosinophils quite prominent, and neutrophils may be present. Single or small clusters of epithelioid cells may participate in the infiltrate, and in some cases epithelioid granulomas develop close to or surrounding the bile duct. The florid bile duct lesion in PBC can thus be categorized as lymphocytic, pleomorphic, and granulomatous cholangitis (Fig. 13.32), the latter being the most diagnostic.[520] Smaller ducts may be surrounded by edema or fibrosis, presumably as a result of more distal obstruction.

Sampling variability means that not every liver biopsy from a patient with PBC in this stage reveals the characteristic bile duct lesions, preventing a firm histologic diagnosis. Parenchymal changes may occur even in the early stages: lobular infiltration by scattered lymphocytes and nodular regenerative hyperplasia.[493] Together with narrowing of portal vein branches,[535] this may explain the development of portal hypertension before the development of fibrosis and cirrhosis. Parenchymal lesions of chronic cholestasis are absent or minimal at his stage.

The majority of patients show histologic progression within 2 years; a minority (20%) remain histologically stable, whereas sustained regression is rare (2%).[519] Progression consists in extension beyond the limits of the portal tract, associated with increasing fibrosis and disturbance of lobular architecture. Basically two processes

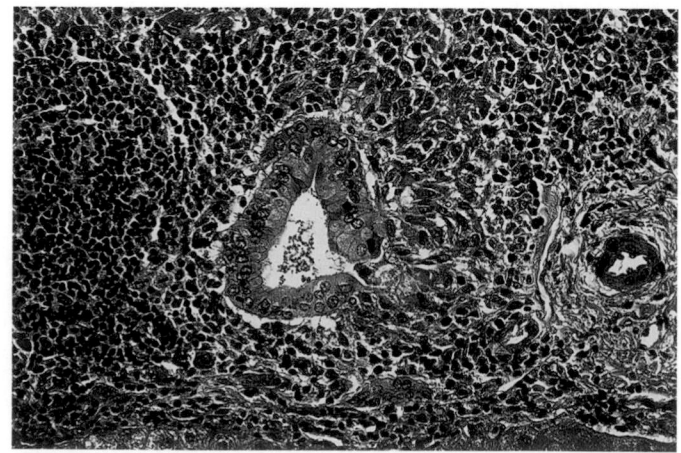

Fig. 13.32 Granulomatous cholangitis in primary biliary cirrhosis (PBC). Detail from a portal tract with dense lymphoplasmacytic infiltrate and lymphoid aggregate (left). The interlobular bile duct (center) shows a focal rupture of its cholangiocytic lining, at the site of an adjacent epithelioid granuloma. (H&E)

appear to drive the histologic progression: the periportal and architectural changes of chronic cholestasis (see p. 944), and lymphocytic interface hepatitis (piecemeal necrosis).[536,541] As in chronic hepatitis, the intralobular "invading" lymphocytes of interface hepatitis play a role in the development of septal fibrosis[531] (Fig. 13.33), and there may be a variable degree of intralobular necroinflammation.[532] Liver cell dysplasia of the large and small cell type may be present.[533] Progressive ductopenia develops.

In advanced cases, portal lymphoid aggregates mark the site of disappeared bile ducts (Fig. 13.33). The combination of cholestatic and hepatitic features results in progressive fibrosis with portal–portal septum formation, followed by additional portal–central septa.[531] When cholestatic features predominate, the eventual resulting cirrhosis is of the biliary type, whereas in cases with predominance of hepatitic features, the cirrhosis is more of the macronodular type. As may be expected, any combination of the two patterns can occur. The hepatitic-type lesions appear to be the most important for the progression of fibrosis.[494]

Several systems have been proposed for staging of PBC.[524,540,545,546] The most popular staging system, which is applicable to any vanishing bile duct disease, is that of Ludwig et al.,[524] which distinguishes four stages: portal (stage 1); periportal (stage 2); septal fibrosis (stage 3); and cirrhosis (stage 4). Staging of PBC in small needle biopsy specimens is valuable as long as it is interpreted with caution, bearing in mind that there is considerable variability in the degree of fibrosis in different parts of the liver.[505] A recent study suggested that aberrant expression of cytokeratin 7 in hepatocytes (Fig. 13.26) may be a marker for the degree of cholestasis and for progression in PBC.[557]

The differential diagnosis of PBC requires consideration of two groups of diseases: (1) for early stages,

diseases characterized by portal inflammation and bile duct damage; and (2) for later stages, chronic ductopenic diseases.

Early stage PBC requires differentiation from *chronic hepatitis*, especially viral hepatitis C. In the latter, the affected duct segment shows vacuolization and stratification of cholangiocytes, with preservation of the basement membrane.[492] Cholestatic features are absent. *Drug-induced bile duct damage* usually affects ducts of smaller caliber than those involved in PBC, and the clinical history comprises an episode of jaundice.[497] Conditions characterized by bile duct damage and granulomas comprise *fascioliasis* and *sarcoidosis*. The latter may cause real problems of differentiation, as it also may lead to ductopenia and chronic cholestatic liver disease; the final diagnosis requires consideration of the clinical context and laboratory data.

Immune cholangitis[489] or *autoimmune cholangiopathy*[483] is clinically, biochemically, and histologically very similar to PBC, but antimitochondrial antibodies are negative. The consensus at present is that this entity represents antimitochondrial antibody-negative PBC.[512] Refined techniques were recently reported to detect reactivity to recombinant mitochondrial antigens by immunoblotting in about three quarters of such patients.[529]

An autoimmune hepatitis–PBC overlap syndrome has been described in rare patients presenting with clinical, biological, and histologic features of both PBC and autoimmune hepatitis, either simultaneously or sequentially. Such cases are histologically characterized by higher degrees of the "hepatitic component" of PBC, which responds to corticosteroid therapy.[542] The significance of overlap syndromes is nuclear. Some believe that the term "overlap syndrome" reflects the current imprecision in the definition of the individual diseases, in part due to lack of understanding of their etiology.[556]

Primary sclerosing cholangitis (PSC) is one of the most common adult chronic cholestatic liver diseases. Of PSC patients, 75% are male, on average 40 years old at the time of diagnosis. PSC is typically associated with inflammatory bowel disease (70%).[481,509,527] It also occurs in children.[544] PSC is characterized by inflammation, strictures, and saccular dilatations in the biliary system; any part of the biliary tree may be involved. "Small duct PSC" corresponds to involvement of only the microscopically identifiable (septal and interlobular) ducts, previously indicated by the now obsolete term "pericholangitis."[521] The majority of PSC patients have both large and small duct PSC combined. It follows that cholangiography and microscopic examination of a liver biopsy are complementary investigations in PSC, with primary importance of cholangiography.

The histopathologic changes in the liver biopsy of patients with PSC depend on the stage of the disease and on the site of the biopsy in relation to the duct lesions caused by the disease. In portal tracts proximal to

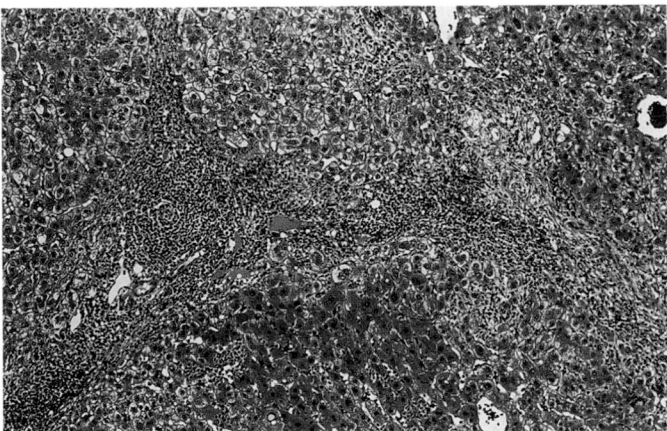

Fig. 13.33 Primary biliary cirrhosis, stage 3. The picture shows portal–portal septal fibrosis (septal stage 3), portal inflammation with lymphoid aggregate, absence of interlobular bile duct (ductopenia), and cholate stasis in periportal and periseptal parenchyma. (H&E)

strictures, only features of obstruction and cholangitis are seen.

Portal tracts affected by the primary disease show pleomorphic and fibrous–obliterative cholangitis,[520] the key lesion in PSC, characterized by onion-skin type periductal fibrosis (Fig. 13.34) with degeneration and atrophy of the epithelial lining, resulting in disappearance of the duct and its eventual replacement by a fibrous scar. Loss of ducts is more frequent in smaller portal tracts, whereas periductal fibrosis is more often seen in medium-sized tracts.[510] Periductal fibrosis is not a pathognomonic lesion as it can also be observed in other types of biliary disease, but it is a very suggestive and helpful finding. Evidently, it is not present in every stage of the disease, and is found in fewer than 40% of biopsy specimens.[520] PAS–diastase staining reveals thickening of the basement membrane around damaged ducts (Fig. 13.35) or wrinkled empty basement membranes.[503] In

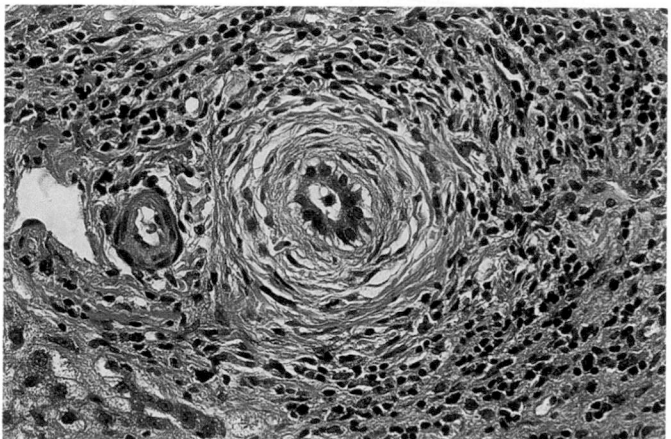

Fig. 13.34 Primary sclerosing cholangitis. Detail of portal tract with moderately dense inflammatory infiltrate (mainly lymphocytes, some eosinophils) and concentric, lamellated, periductal fibrosis ("onion skin" fibrosis) around the interlobular bile duct (center). (H&E)

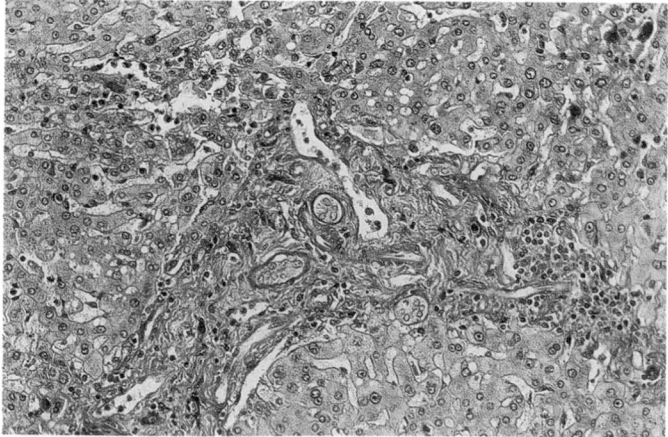

Fig. 13.35 Primary sclerosing cholangitis. Overview of portal tract and periportal parenchyma. This portal tract shows only mild inflammation; two interlobular bile ducts show clear-cut thickening of their basement membrane, a helpful diagnostic feature. (PAS–diastase stain)

some patients, the scars of the vanished bile ducts are unusually prominent, resembling keloid scars.[485,526]

In patients with longlasting and more severe disease, portal fibrosis is more marked, fibrous septa develop, and biliary cirrhosis ensues. More progressive disease is characterized by moderate to severe degrees of the lymphocytic type of interface hepatitis.[479] Other patients suffer from less severe PSC, with only mild and insignificant lesions during several years.[487]

The parenchymal changes in PSC are less striking than the portal ones and correspond to features of chronic cholestasis. Nodular regenerative hyperplasia may develop before the precirrhotic stage. Patients with PSC have an increased risk of developing cholangiocarcinoma.[488] A strong association was found between dysplasia of bile duct epithelium and cholangiocarcinoma in PSC, suggesting that biliary dysplasia might be used as a marker for current or developing malignancy.[504]

The main differential diagnoses of PSC are chronic hepatitis, PBC, and other vanishing bile duct diseases. *Chronic hepatitis* lacks periductal fibrosis, ductopenia, and cholestatic features. *Primary biliary cirrhosis* may be difficult to differentiate from PSC in the later stages. Note that epithelioid granulomas can also be found in about 4% of PSC cases, but not as part of granulomatous cholangitis.[523] Florid portal inflammation with or without lymph follicle formation favors PBC. Overlap between autoimmune hepatitis and PSC has been described.[501,516,528]

Idiopathic adulthood ductopenia is diagnosed in adults with cholestasis and ductopenia after exclusion of all other possible causes.[522,525] Familial cases[490] and asymptomatic patients[530] have been described.

Chronic liver allograft rejection is characterized by ductopenia ("ductopenic rejection") (see p. 967), as is **chronic graft-versus-host disease** (see p. 969). Drug-induced ductopenia is mentioned under drug-induced disease (see p. 937).

Finally, ductopenia is a possible sequel of sarcoidosis, histiocytosis X, Hodgkin's lymphoma, and mucoviscidosis.

Large duct obstruction (hilar and extrahepatic). A very large number of lesions, such as gallstones, bile duct strictures, and tumors, may cause complete or incomplete obstruction of the larger hilar and extrahepatic bile ducts. Acute complete obstruction induces the full clinical picture of obstructive jaundice, and histopathologically the sequence of changes already described under Acute complete cholestasis (see p. 943). Chronic complete obstruction shows all the components of chronic cholestasis (see p. 944) and eventually results in secondary biliary cirrhosis. An additional lesion which is near-pathognomonic for longstanding large duct obstruction, and which occurs in a few cases, is rupture of an interlobular duct with escape of bile into the portal connective tissue, giving rise to a *bile extravasate*, which in turn induces a foreign-body giant cell reaction. Chronic incomplete obstruction induces clinically an anicteric cholestasis, with elevated serum levels of alkaline phosphatase, 5′-nucleotidase, and γ-glutamyl transpeptidase, but no increase in serum levels of conjugated bilirubin. In parallel, histologic bilirubin stasis remains absent for long periods of time, and liver biopsy shows parenchymal and periportal features of chronic cholestasis. Examples of chronic incomplete obstruction comprise, amongst others, postoperative strictures of the common bile duct, large duct sclerosing cholangitis, cholangitis proliferans,[517] and annular pancreas.[484]

Ascending cholangitis. Incomplete bile duct obstruction predisposes to bacterial infection. In bacterial ascending cholangitis the number of neutrophils infiltrating the portal tracts is higher than in aseptic bile duct obstruction. Neutrophil polymorphs are also found in the wall and inside the lumen of portal ducts. Interlobular ducts are often more affected than larger ducts.[513]

The inflamed duct may rupture, resulting in portal abscess formation. Associated lesions include lobular abscesses and sinusoidal neutrophil infiltration, and thrombosis and thrombophlebitis of portal vein branches with the sequel of parenchymal necrosis. Bilirubin stasis is not an obligate feature.[491,548]

Ascending cholangitis may be caused by choledocholithiasis, cholecystitis, strictures of any cause, biliary parasites, cholangiocarcinoma, and Caroli's disease. In immunodeficient patients (e.g., AIDS), cholangitis is often due to cryptosporidium, cytomegalovirus, or species of microsporidia.[486,539] Persisting cholangitis may result in (secondary) biliary cirrhosis. Cholangitis easily gives rise to septicemia, in which the lesion of ductular bilirubin stasis is an important diagnostic feature (see p. 947).

Childhood disorders and disorders of metabolism

The histopathologic diagnosis of liver disease in neonates and young children requires special attention to particular lesions of diagnostic importance in this age group. Such changes include parenchymal giant cell transformation, ductular reaction, cholate stasis, ductular bilirubin stasis, ductopenia, ductal plate malformation, hepatocellular content of iron and copper, hepatocellular inclusions, and abnormal storage products in Kupffer cells.

Cholestasis and hyperbilirubinemia
Cholestatic disorders
Numerous neonatal liver diseases are associated with cholestasis, rendering "neonatal cholestasis" a particular challenge for the pathologist, as it involves differential diagnosis between extrahepatic bile duct atresia, paucity of interlobular bile ducts, biliary transporter deficiencies, disorders of bile acid metabolism, metabolic disorders, and viral infections.

Transporter deficiencies. This group comprises the congenital cholestatic disorders identified in recent years: progressive familial intrahepatic cholestasis (PFIC) types 1, 2 and 3, mentioned on p. 946; benign recurrent intrahepatic cholestasis (BRIC), described on p. 947; and cystic fibrosis (mucoviscidosis).

Disorders of bile acid metabolism. Some defects in bile acid synthesis and metabolism have been identified. These defects appear as familial and progressive infantile or late-onset cholestasis. The histopathology is not diagnostic, falling into the category of "neonatal giant cell hepatitis" or "cryptogenic neonatal cholestasis." Diagnosis rests on screening of biological fluids for abnormal bile acids by fast atom bombardment ionization mass spectrometry (FAB-MS).[558]

Extrahepatic bile duct atresia. This entity is discussed on p. 949.

Paucity of intrahepatic bile ducts. This entity is discussed on p. 949.

Hyperbilirubinemias
Gilbert's syndrome is a common form of familial unconjugated hyperbilirubinemia, with normal liver histology except for possibly slight degrees of parenchymal siderosis. The **Dubin–Johnson syndrome** is a deficiency of the canalicular multispecific organic anion transporter MRP2,[560] characterized mainly by hyperbilirubinemia of the conjugated type and absence of cholestasis. Liver biopsy reveals the presence of coarsely granular, dark brown pigment in a pericanalicular location and predominating in the centrolobular zone. The pigment resembles lipofuscin histologically and histochemically (variable PAS positivity and acid fastness). Electron microscopy may allow differentiation.[559]

Inherited metabolic disorders

Inherited metabolic defects leading to hepatic abnormalities are many and involve disorders of metabolism of porphyrin, carbohydrates, proteins and glycoproteins, amino acids, lipoproteins, lipids, and metals. Reviews in specialized books should be consulted for a full description of morphologic changes and differential diagnosis.[561]

Endoplasmic reticulum storage diseases
The endoplasmic reticulum storage diseases are a group of inborn errors of metabolism affecting secretory proteins that result in retention in the endoplasmic reticulum and deficiency of the corresponding protein in the plasma.[566] The most important is α_1-antitrypsin deficiency. Others are α_1-antichymotrypsin deficiency,

fibrinogen storage disease, and possibly antithrombin III deficiency. The storage results from a molecular abnormality of the protein, hindering its transfer through the endoplasmic reticulum.

α_1-Antitrypsin deficiency. α_1-Antitrypsin (α_1-AT) is a serum glycoprotein and protease inhibitor, the serum levels of which are increased by hormonal influences, inflammatory stimuli, and most liver diseases (acute phase reactant). More than 70 allelic variants of α_1-AT have been described.[563] The usual phenotype of the protease inhibitor (Pi) system is PiM. The most common deficiency alleles are PiZ and PiS. Liver abnormalities are mainly found in individuals carrying the Z allele. An amino acid substitution (lysine for glutamic acid at position 342) causes abnormal folding and retention of α_1-AT in the rough endoplasmic reticulum, resulting in failure of secretion and plasma deficiency.[580]

α_1-AT deficiency may be associated with neonatal cholestasis in neonates, and may also present with liver disease in adults, even in older people.[574] Periportal hepatocytes contain eosinophilic, PAS–diastase-positive globular inclusions ranging in diameter from 1 to 10 µm (Fig. 13.36). The inclusions are difficult to detect in infants less than 3 months of age. Immunostaining with polyclonal anti-α_1-AT antibody is more sensitive and more specific. Use of a specific monoclonal antibody allows identification of the PiZ gene products.[565] Immunoelectron microscopy located the globules in the endoplasmic reticulum.[571] In conditions of clinical stimulation, large areas of lobular hepatic parenchyma may be immunopositive for α_1-AT in PiMZ individuals.[568] Immunoreactive globules have further been found in several liver diseases,[564] necessitating α_1-AT phenotyping in plasma by immunodiffusion or electrophoresis for final diagnosis.

In children, the most common liver disease is neonatal cholestasis, which is seen in 11% of infants and usually resolves without therapy by 6 months of age. The histologic changes comprise parenchymal giant cells, ductular reaction, and fibrosis and in some cases also paucity of interlobular bile ducts.[575] The disease may resemble extrahepatic bile duct atresia, hence the need to screen for α_1-AT deficiency before a Kasai procedure. Evidence for hepatocellular injury in deficient children decreases until the teenage years.[582] Up to 10% of infants with α_1-AT deficiency have paucity of interlobular bile ducts, suffer from pruritus, and develop cirrhosis. Persistence of hyperbilirubinemia beyond 1 year of age heralds a poor prognosis.[573,579]

α_1-Antitrypsin deficient adults usually present with pulmonary emphysema.[577] The incidence of liver disease increases with age[576] and consists of varying degrees of fibrosis and development of cirrhosis. An increased prevalence of hepatitis B and C viral infection was found in α_1-AT deficiency and was suggested to contribute to these hepatic complications,[581,583] although in transgenic mice retention of the molecule causes liver damage per se.[569] An increased incidence of hepatocellular carcinoma has been documented in adult homozygous PiZ patients with or without cirrhosis.[570] Heterozygosity for α_1-AT Pi types appears not to be associated with an increased risk for hepatocellular or bile duct carcinoma.[562] However, heterozygosity for PiZ type bears an increased risk for chronic liver disease in middle-aged or old adults.[572]

α_1-Antichymotrypsin (α_1-ACT) deficiency has also been described in a few cases with granular α_1-ACT inclusions in periportal/periseptal hepatocytes.[570] Eosinophilic, PAS-positive globules were also described in **antithrombin deficiency**.[578]

Fibrinogen storage disease (afibrinogenemia and hypofibrinogenemia) is associated with hepatocellular inclusions which are small and irregular or large and spherical. They are weakly PAS–diastase positive, stain with phosphotungstic acid–hematoxylin, and are immunoreactive with antifibrinogen antibodies. In some patients, cirrhosis may develop.[567]

Fibropolycystic diseases

In view of their common morphologic lesion, this group of conditions is described in the section on Ductal plate malformation, p. 957.

Indian childhood cirrhosis

Indian childhood cirrhosis, originally thought to be peculiar to the Indian subcontinent, has now been reported from elsewhere, and some of these cases were Caucasians.[584–586] The disease carries a high mortality and sometimes appears familial. The pathogenesis involves genetic factors and an increased dietary copper intake (tap water, cooking utensils). Histopathology reveals hepatocellular swelling and ballooning in the early stages, with Mallory bodies and necrosis. Accumulations of neutrophils (satellitosis) may be seen and pericellular fibrosis, as in (alcoholic) steatohepatitis, but fatty change

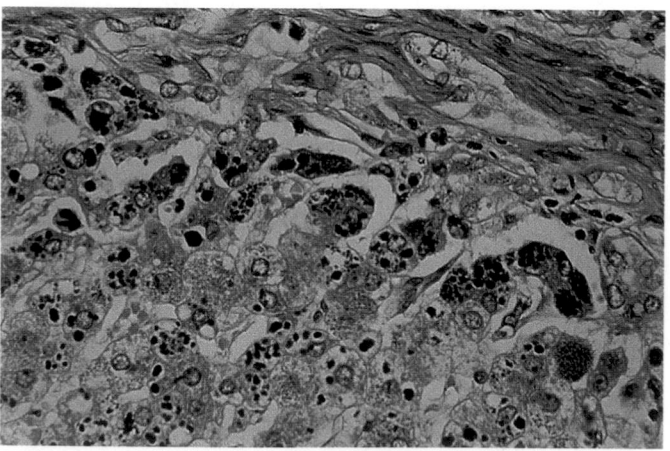

Fig. 13.36 α_1-Antitrypsin deficiency. Detail of periportal parenchyma, showing PAS-positive inclusions of varying size in the majority of periportal hepatocytes. (PAS–diastase stain)

is virtually absent. Huge amounts of copper and copper-binding protein can be demonstrated in the hepatocytes by rhodanine and orcein stains respectively.[587,588] The lesions evolve into a type of cirrhosis characterized by very small parenchymal nodules.

Disorders of copper and iron metabolism

Wilson's disease (hepatolenticular degeneration)

Wilson's disease results from tissue injury by copper overload in the liver and other organs (brain, cornea, and kidneys). It is a rare autosomal recessive disorder, the gene mutation of which is localized on chromosome 13q14–21.[589] Liver biopsy is useful in diagnosis and monitoring. Homozygous subjects have increased copper levels in the liver at a very young age, but symptoms of liver disease do not develop before the age of 5 years.[593] The disease may manifest itself as acute hepatitis, as fulminant hepatitis, as chronic hepatitis, and as cirrhosis.

Histologic liver abnormalities precede the clinical appearance of disease. In the early stage there is steatosis and sometimes lipogranulomas.[597] Lipofuscin may be strikingly abundant in periportal hepatocytes, as may glycogen vacuoles in their nuclei.[601] Kupffer cells may be laden with iron as a result of the acute hemolytic crises that frequently complicate the disease. Electron microscopy is helpful because of characteristic mitochondrial and lysosomal changes.[599] Progressive fibrosis develops with fine septa extending from portal tracts. In some patients portal tracts become infiltrated with mononuclear inflammatory cells, creating a picture indistinguishable from chronic hepatitis due to other causes.[598,600,601] In untreated patients, the disease progresses to cirrhosis. Helpful diagnostic clues include steatosis, ballooned hepatocytes, glycogenated nuclei, moderate to marked copper deposition, presence of Mallory bodies in periportal hepatocytes, lymphocytic portal and interface inflammation, and possibly occlusive venous lesions.[601] As mentioned, fulminant hepatic failure may be the first manifestation of Wilson's disease, associated with extensive parenchymal necrosis, collapse of the reticulin framework, nodular parenchymal regeneration, and development of a cirrhotic pattern.[590]

Cytochemical staining for copper and copper-binding protein may be useful in establishing the diagnosis (Fig. 13.37). Timm's silver stain appears to be the most sensitive technique.[596] However, the stains may be negative in some stages of the disease. On the other hand, copper and metallothionein may accumulate in other diseases (e.g., cholestasis, Indian childhood cirrhosis) and, furthermore, neonatal liver usually contains high levels of copper.[591] Quantitative determination of hepatic copper may

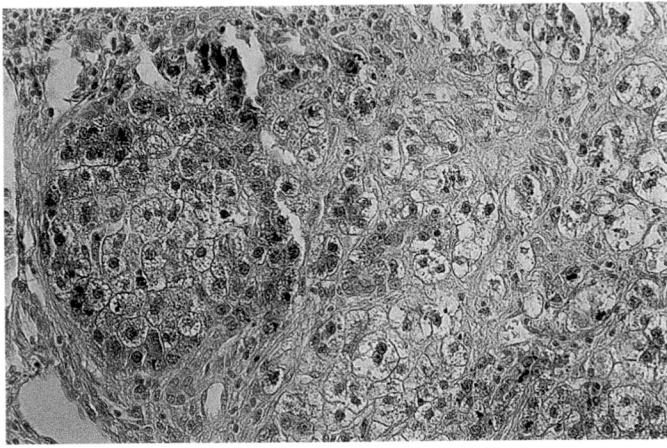

Fig. 13.37 Wilson's disease, cirrhotic stage. This rhodanine stain reveals accumulation of copper (red granules) in varying degree, most pronounced in a nodular cluster of hepatocytes (left). (Rhodanine stain)

be necessary for final diagnosis; this can be performed on routinely processed paraffin-embedded tissue.[594]

In young asymptomatic patients with Wilson's disease hepatic copper levels are high but difficult to demonstrate histochemically because of diffuse distribution in the cytoplasm of hepatocytes. Copper stains (e.g., rhodanine) reveal at most a faint cytoplasmic staining. In somewhat older patients with signs of disease, the metal is both diffusely distributed and intralysosomal, while in patients with advanced disease all the copper is confined to lysosomes,[592] resulting in a granular pattern that is more easily recognized. In the cirrhotic stage, parenchymal nodules may vary strikingly in copper content (Fig. 13.37), as they may vary for other lesions in cirrhosis due to other causes. Staining results for copper and copper-binding protein are usually equal, but may on occasion give divergent results.[595]

The great variety of possible lesions in Wilson's disease creates difficult problems for the histopathologist. It must become a habit to consider Wilson's disease in the differential diagnosis of hepatocellular disease at all ages, but especially in the young. This may save lives. Treatment (penicillamine or zinc acetate) may arrest the disease in patients and prevent its development in siblings.

Iron overload (siderosis, hemosiderosis)

The terms siderosis and hemosiderosis refer to the presence of demonstrable iron in tissues. The causes of iron overload are many: genetic hemochromatosis, siderosis secondary to chronic anemia, neonatal iron overload, blood transfusion, hemolysis, chronic renal failure, porphyria cutanea tarda, and others. It is preferable not to use the terms hemosiderosis and hemochromatosis as synonyms for iron loading, and to use the term hemochromatosis specifically to indicate genetic (or hereditary) iron overload. Faced with hepatic siderosis, the pathologist should always consider the possible presence of genetic hemochromatosis.

Siderosis is best demonstrated by the Perls' stain (using acid ferrocyanide), which gives the Prussian blue reaction with the ferric compounds ferritin and hemosiderin. Ferritin dispersed in the hyaloplasm gives a diffuse bluish tint to the cell's cytoplasm, whereas intense blue granules correspond to ferritin and hemosiderin packed together within siderosomes (or iron-laden lysosomes).[607] Evaluation of the Perls' stain requires attention to both the extent (grade or amount) of stainable iron and its distribution in different cell types of portal tract and lobule.

Iron distribution may vary according to the cause of siderosis. The siderosis is predominantly parenchymal in hemochromatosis and neonatal iron overload. Both hepatocytes and Kupffer cells store iron in thalassemia, whereas exogenous siderosis loads Kupffer cells in the first instance (Fig. 13.38). Dense Perls-positive granules are found in endothelial cells in various liver diseases, including acute hepatitis and alcoholic liver disease. Hepatocellular siderosis is always most pronounced in periportal hepatocytes. Semiquantitative assessment of stored tissue iron can be achieved in different ways. The simplest system grades from 1 (minimal) to 4 (massive deposits), with grades 2 and 3 indicating intermediate amounts.

Basset and colleagues[602] introduced the hepatic iron index (HII), representing the chemically measured hepatic iron concentration (μmol/g dry weight) divided by the patient's age in years. It enables the distinction of genetic hemochromatosis (HII of 1.9 or more) from heterozygous individuals and patients with siderosis from other causes. The hepatic iron index is based on the principle that progressively increasing hepatic iron concentration is found in homozygotes for genetic hemochromatosis, unlike what happens in heterozygotes or in patients with alcoholic siderosis.

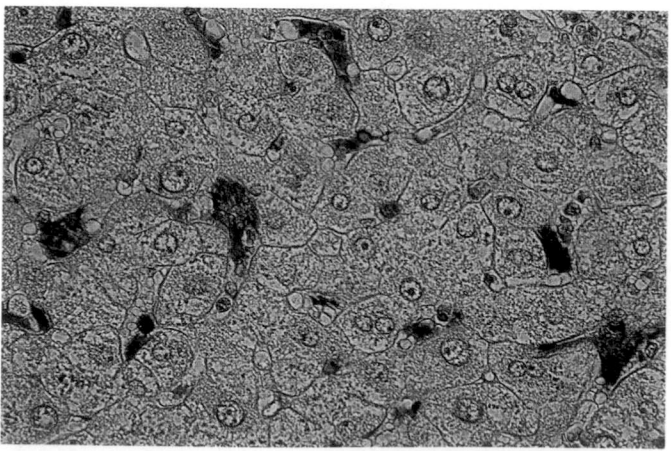

Fig. 13.38 Secondary siderosis. Hemosiderin (blue) is located exclusively in Kupffer cells, sparing the hepatocytes. (Perls' iron stain)

Deugnier et al.[603] estimated iron in hepatocytes, mesenchymal cells, cholangiocytes, blood vessels, and connective tissue, generating a score between 0 and 60. This grading system, together with the Histological Hepatic Iron Index (HHII)[604] (dividing by the age in years) is helpful in the assessment of patients with genetic hemochromatosis.

Chemical determination of tissue iron can be performed on liver tissue separated from the specimen taken for histology, or on the block deparaffinized after histopathologic study is completed. The latter procedure ensures that the tissular composition of the sample is known.[605] Since the chemically measured HII correlates well with the HHII,[604] microscopic evaluation may allow the blocked tissue to be preserved and can be used to quantitate when chemical iron determination is not possible. Computerized image analysis, which also correlates well with classical assays, represents an additional technique for assessment of siderosis.[606]

Genetic (hereditary, primary, or idiopathic) hemochromatosis

Hereditary hemochromatosis is an autosomal recessive disease and the most common inherited disorder in white Caucasians.[608] In Northern Europe, more than 90% of hemochromatosis patients are homozygous for a missense mutation (C282Y) in the *HFE* gene, located on the short arm of chromosome 6. This mutation leads to a dysregulation of intracellular iron homeostasis in enterocytes, resulting in inappropriately high iron absorption. The role of a second mutation (H63D) in the *HFE* gene is at present unclear.[615]

Homozygotes accumulate iron progressively in the liver, heart, pancreas, and other organs. The rate of accumulation varies even among homozygous subjects within the same family. The diagnosis of genetic hemochromatosis is usually based on clinical, biochemical, genetic, and histopathologic data. In recent years, genetic diagnosis has become a reality[613] although phenotypic as well as genetic diagnosis still remains important.[610]

In young homozygotes, the first abnormality is the appearance of stainable iron in periportal hepatocytes, positivity in males generally being greater than in females of the same age. Unexplained small amounts of iron in hepatocytes should always raise suspicion about a possible early stage of genetic hemochromatosis. Calculation of the (H)HII and further serum biochemistry may be of help to establish a firm diagnosis; this is highly important, because cirrhosis can be prevented by appropriate treatment both in the patient and his homozygous relatives, with return of their life expectancy to normal.[616]

With advancing age, the deposition of hemosiderin progresses toward the centrolobular area, but usually maintains a decreasing portal–central gradient. Some

Kupffer cells and an occasional portal macrophage may also become iron positive, although this involvement is greatly overwhelmed by almost exclusive parenchymal storage. The hepatocellular iron appears as pericanalicular granules representing lysosomal storage (Fig. 13.39). With progressing siderosis, fibrosis develops with expansion of portal tracts and appearance of small fibrous spurs conferring a spiked contour to portal tracts. The enlarged portal tracts carry iron-laden macrophages and there is some increase in ductular profiles, usually without marked inflammation. The cholangiocytes of ductules and interlobular ducts begin to accumulate granules of stainable iron. Some authors report the occurrence of foci of eosinophilic or lytic hepatocellular necrosis of iron-laden hepatocytes, often in close association with clusters of macrophages (so-called "sidero-necrosis").[611] The proportion of iron located outside hepatocytes versus hepatocellular iron rises progressively.

Periportal fibrosis proceeds with slender periportal septa that join portal tracts and progressively envelope the lobules, resulting in a combination of discrete parenchymal nodules and partially preserved lobules, a pattern characteristic for hemochromatosis.[617] Still further advancement of disease results in a diffuse micronodular pattern with portal-based septal fibrosis, resembling secondary biliary cirrhosis.

Excessive alcohol consumption induces a shift of hemosiderin from parenchymal to Kupffer cells and macrophages in the fibrous septa.[617] In later stages of heavy iron overload, occasional small areas can be found without or with very little parenchymal siderosis and with only some Kupffer cell iron load. Such parenchymal iron-free areas are most often seen in established cirrhosis and represent a preneoplastic lesion.[612]

Hepatocellular carcinoma occurs with an incidence of approximately 15%, predominantly in males. Tumor development is not prevented by removal of iron.[616]

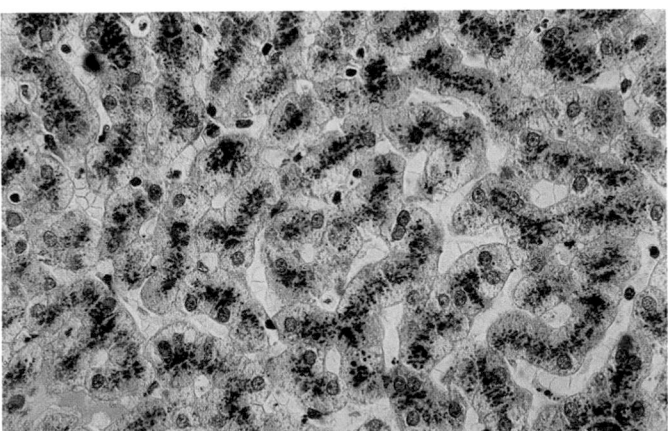

Fig. 13.39 Parenchymal siderosis in genetic hemochromatosis. Detail of lobular parenchyma showing marked parenchymal siderosis in typical lysosomal (pericanalicular) localization. There was a decreasing portal–central gradient in lobular siderosis (not shown). (Perls' iron stain)

Effective treatment with therapeutic phlebotomies results in a steady disappearance of stainable iron; the pattern of iron removal is the reverse of its accumulation, with periportal hepatocytes remaining Perls positive for longer. Most resistant to removal is iron encrusted in portal collagen. Iron removal unmasks a brown lipofuscin-resembling pigment in hepatocytes and portal mesenchyme. Heterozygosity for the hemochromatosis defect is rarely associated with liver damage due to iron alone.[609] The C282Y mutation alone only leads to mild hepatic siderosis, with the exception of H63D/C282Y compound heterozygotes.[614]

Neonatal (perinatal) iron overload (neonatal (perinatal) hemochromatosis)

Neonatal (perinatal) iron overload is a rare disease characterized by marked hepatocellular necrosis, parenchymal giant cell transformation, siderosis, fibrosis, and parenchymal nodule development during fetal life and in the perinatal period.[618] The etiology is unknown; there is no relationship with genetic hemochromatosis. Putative environmental agents are suspected to interact with one or more factors intrinsic to the developing fetal liver.[619]

Hepatic siderosis of varied etiology

The human fetal and neonatal liver often shows prominent hepatocellular siderosis, mostly in periportal hepatocytes[624]; the iron content shows a striking interindividual variability and uneven distribution throughout the liver.[623]

Hepatic siderosis is a common finding in pathologic livers of neonates.[624] Hepatic iron overload associated with fibrosis and cirrhosis occurs in patients with thalassemia and other forms of chronic anemia (often termed "secondary hemochromatosis"); in these cases, Kupffer cell and macrophage siderosis is present from the early stages. In contrast with genetic hemochromatosis, there is often more portal and lobular lymphocytic infiltration, due to transfusion-related viral hepatitis C.[625] Ingestion of excessive amounts of iron (amongst others self-medication with iron compounds; use of iron containers by South African blacks for brewing traditional beers) results in combined reticuloendothelial and hepatocellular siderosis.[621]

Some degree of hepatic siderosis is common in cirrhosis in general. There is, however, evidence that the majority of alcoholics with marked iron overload in the liver also suffer from genetic hemochromatosis.[620] In porphyria cutanea tarda, the liver histopathology is often characterized by siderosis in periportal hepatocytes which is usually mild.[622]

Fibropolycystic diseases (ductal plate malformation)

Hepatobiliary fibropolycystic diseases[630] comprise a series of congenital abnormalities involving the intrahepatic bile ducts, most of them related to an abnormal remodeling of the embryonic ductal plate.[626,627] The primitive embryonic form of the developing intrahepatic bile ducts corresponds to a double epithelial cylinder which surrounds the future portal tracts and is termed the ductal plate.[626] Progressive remodeling of the ductal plate results in the formation of mature tubular ducts located in the portal mesenchyme. Lack of such remodeling results in the persistence of the primitive embryonic pattern[627]: the ductal plate malformation (DPM).[629]

In a case of complete lack of remodeling, DPM appears in cross sections as a circular lumen containing a fibrovascular axis in its center. Incomplete remodeling results in rings of interrupted curved lamina around a central fibrovascular axis or gives rise to the image of a grossly dilated duct containing a polypoid projection.[626,627]

Modern imaging techniques of the liver allow visualization of the macroscopic abnormalities of DPM in larger branches of the intrahepatic bile duct.[628] DPM is usually associated with abnormalities in the ramification pattern of the developing portal vein, resulting in too many, too small, and too closely spaced branches ("pollard willow" pattern).[626] Two main groups of congenital diseases of intrahepatic bile ducts are characterized by DPM: a subgroup of cases with extrahepatic bile duct atresia (so-called "early severe form"; see p. 950); and diseases characterized by a variable degree of ectasia of intrahepatic bile ducts associated with more or less fibrosis—"fibrocystic" diseases.[627]

Autosomal recessive polycystic kidney disease (infantile-type polycystic disease)

The gene of autosomal recessive polycystic kidney disease (ARPKD) has been localized to chromosome 6. The renal lesions correspond to fusiform dilatation of the collecting ducts. The hepatic lesions are fairly uniform and seldom give rise to macroscopically visible cysts. Microscopically, the portal tracts may be enlarged and contain numerous, somewhat dilated bile duct profiles corresponding to incompletely remodeled ductal plates. In surviving children, the liver and kidney lesions seem to progress, with a decrease in epithelial (hepatic and renal) tubular profiles and an increase in interstitial (hepatic and renal) fibrosis.[631]

Congenital hepatic fibrosis

Congenital hepatic fibrosis (CHF) has been considered by several authors as the "juvenile" form of ARPKD.[632] This recessively inherited disorder classically presents with signs of portal hypertension in childhood, more rarely in adults. Besides the classical portal hypertensive CHF, clinical variants include cholangitic CHF, combined portal hypertensive and cholangitic CHF, and latent CHF.

Grossly, the liver is enlarged and very hard, showing a fine reticular pattern of fibrosis. The histopathologic picture varies; some cases only reveal enlarged portal

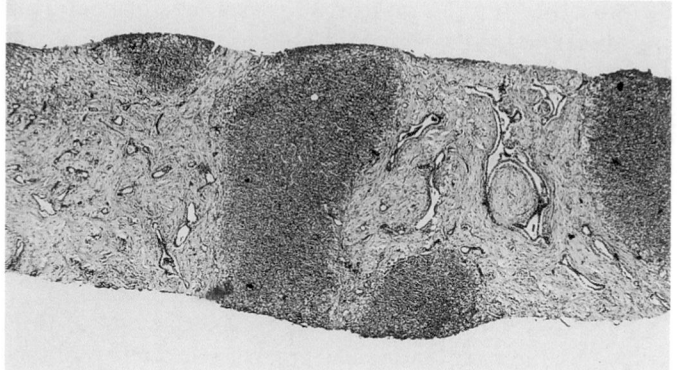

Fig. 13.40 Congenital hepatic fibrosis. Low-power view of needle biopsy specimen. Portal tracts are large and joined by portal–portal fibrous connections. Bile ducts appear in their immature, embryonic shape (ductal plate malformation). The ductal plate configuration is most easily recognized in the right half of the picture; in the left half, ductal plate remodeling is more advanced, although still incomplete. Note mature aspects of fibrous tissue and virtual absence of inflammation. (H&E)

tracts with bile ducts in ductal plate configuration, whereas others show bands of connective tissue of variable thickness that link adjacent portal tracts and contain ductal plate vestigia (Fig. 13.40). The bile duct lumina may contain inspissated bile. The portal vein branches are usually hypoplastic ("pollard willow" pattern), the hepatic artery branches instead may be numerous and conspicuous. In some cases, mild features of cholate stasis can be found. There is usually no inflammation, no necrosis, and no parenchymal regeneration.

The more fibrotic forms of CHF might be confused with biliary fibrosis and secondary biliary cirrhosis, in which the overall pattern of fibrosis may be similar; however, in the latter case the septa are inflamed, with ductular reaction at the septal–parenchymal interface, usually more marked signs of cholate stasis and bilirubin stasis, absence of ductal plate structures, and normal size of portal vein branches.

Caroli's disease (congenital dilatation of the intrahepatic bile ducts)

Caroli's disease corresponds to a congenital dilatation of the larger intrahepatic bile ducts. Two variants are recognized: a pure type characterized by only ectasia of intrahepatic bile ducts (Caroli's disease); and a combined type in which Caroli's disease is associated with lesions of congenital hepatic fibrosis (Caroli's syndrome).

Caroli's disease consists of moniliform or saccular dilatations of the larger intrahepatic bile ducts, predominantly segmental ducts. The ectasias predispose to repeated attacks of cholangitis, and complications such as intrahepatic lithiasis, amyloidosis, and cholangiocarcinoma. Patients with Caroli's syndrome have additional lesions of congenital hepatic fibrosis. The polypoid projections or cross bridges often seen in the dilated bile duct lumina attest to the ductal plate malformation nature of the lesions.[633] The duct ectasias should not be confused with the acquired cholangiectases that may occur in primary sclerosing cholangitis, but this is mainly a macroscopic or hepatic imaging topic.[634]

Von Meyenburg complex (microhamartoma)

Von Meyenburg complexes are small, often multiple nodules occurring close to portal tracts throughout the liver. They may be visible as 1 to 2 mm white nodules on the liver surface (see also p. 1005). They may occur in an otherwise normal liver, or in association with congenital hepatic fibrosis, Caroli's syndrome, or adult polycystic disease.[635]

The lesion comprises a variable number of dilated bile ducts embedded in a fibrous, sometimes hyalinizing stroma. Some profiles may contain inspissated bile, and some may reveal ductal plate malformation configurations. Von Meyenburg complexes do not normally cause symptoms and are often incidental findings, sometimes mistaken for hepatic metastases at surgery. The lesion apparently represents ductal plate malformations of smaller, more peripheral interlobular bile ducts in portal tracts with a "pollard willow" branching pattern.[636]

Autosomal dominant polycystic kidney disease (adult-type polycystic disease)

Autosomal dominant polycystic kidney disease (ADPKD) affects 1 in 400 to 1 in 1000 persons, representing the most common hereditary kidney abnormality. Liver cysts are found in most patients with ADPKD, and their prevalence increases with age. Grossly, the liver contains multiple cysts of variable diameter that are disseminated throughout the organ or—more rarely—restricted to one lobe. The cavities are lined by a biliary-type epithelium, surrounded by a fibrous capsule, and located in or close to portal tracts. The cysts contain a colorless fluid but may collapse, resembling corpora atretica in the ovary. The cysts are usually associated with von Meyenburg complexes or with congenital hepatic fibrosis. Complications are infection or rupture of the cysts. In addition to genetic factors, cyst development is further modulated by age, pregnancy, female gender, and severity of the kidney lesions.[637]

Solitary (nonparasitic) cyst

The solitary cyst may be uni- or multilocular. It is presumed to be of developmental origin. The lining consists of a single layer of flat, cuboidal, or columnar epithelium, which rarely may be ciliated[638] or squamous.

Vascular disorders

Hepatoportal sclerosis (noncirrhotic portal fibrosis, obliterative portal venopathy, noncirrhotic portal hypertension, idiopathic portal hypertension)

Portal hypertension is most often caused by cirrhosis of the liver. Other causes include noncirrhotic fibrosis of varied etiology (e.g., chronic biliary disease, chronic alcohol-induced disease, sarcoidosis, schistosomiasis), portal vein disorders (including hepatoportal sclerosis, discussed below), venous outflow obstruction, and massive liver infiltration by malignancy and amyloidosis.[652]

Hepatoportal sclerosis (HPS) is a term suggested by Mikkelsen et al. to describe fibrous intimal thickening of the portal vein or its branches in patients with noncirrhotic portal hypertension.[642] In a small number of cases the cause is identified as a toxin: arsenic,[644] vinyl chloride,[650] and cytotoxic drugs.[649] In the majority of patients, HPS is of unknown cause. HPS represents a major cause of portal hypertension in India and Japan.[647]

Needle liver biopsies are not always diagnostic. The lesions are heterogeneous in the same liver and not all abnormalities are found in the same case. The hallmarks of the disease are thrombosis/sclerosis of portal vein branches and the presence of intrahepatic aberrant vessels.[640] In macrovascular portal vein disease, eccentric intimal thickening of the portal vein suggests organized thrombosis. Smooth muscle hyperplasia of the venous media suggests arterialization of the vessel.[643] The hepatic lesions are often patchy in distribution. Microvascular portal vein disease results in a more homogeneous phlebosclerosis of smaller portal tracts.[646] Recent and old thromboembolus, with or without recanalization, may be superimposed, realizing the "obliterative portal venopathy" of the Indian authors. The vein may have completely disappeared, leaving a fibrous scar surrounded by several thin-walled vascular spaces presumably resulting from proliferating or recanalized venules[641] ("cavernous transformation"). The vascular changes are accompanied by portal and periportal fibrosis of varying extent. In areas without phlebosclerotic lesions, this fibrosis may be the only histologic abnormality. Abnormal vessels occur in the periportal area, termed megasinusoids,[641] or periportal angiomatosis,[648] or aberrant intrahepatic vessels,[645] which correspond to dilated terminal portal vein branches or inlet venules.[640] Similar thin-walled vessels occur randomly in the lobules; efferent veins may show sclerosis or dilatation.[641]

According to some, nodular regenerative hyperplasia is always present to some degree in patients with HPS; not surprisingly so, since the pathogenesis of the two entities is the same.[640] The mild to moderate incomplete septation and development of parenchymal nodules brings the morphology of HPS close to that of incomplete septal cirrhosis in the nosologic spectrum of noncirrhotic portal hypertension. Furthermore, the progression from HPS to incomplete septal cirrhosis has occasionally been noted.[639] Hepatoportal sclerosis, nodular regenerative hyperplasia, and incomplete septal cirrhosis are characterized by portal hypertension with only mild liver function abnormalities,[648] supporting the suspicion that these entities represent a spectrum of diseases in which nonuniformity of blood supply to the parenchyma plays a pathogenetic role. In some rare instances the cause of the portal hypertension is obscure: the liver histology is normal and no occlusion of portal or splenic veins can be identified (truly idiopathic portal hypertension).[651] A recent review summarizes diagnostic guidelines for the histopathologic study of liver biopsies from patients with noncirrhotic portal hypertension.[646]

Sinusoidal dilatation

Sinusoidal dilatation often shows a zonal distribution: centrolobular, periportal, or irregular. Centrolobular sinusoidal dilatation is the most common variety, with prominent involvement of the perivenous region extending to the midzonal region in more severe forms. It is an integral feature of venous outflow obstruction. It is further observed in some drug-induced lesions (including azathioprine and vitamin A toxicity), in rheumatoid arthritis, and in malignant or granulomatous diseases.[653] Periportal dilatation affects the periportal sinusoids, eventually extending more centripetally. Long-term contraceptive use is a cause,[656] as is preeclampsia and eclampsia in association with sinusoidal fibrin thrombi and periportal ischemic hepatocellular necrosis.[655] Irregular or nonzonal sinusoidal dilatation is noted in many settings, and is often of unknown causation. Of diagnostic importance is its occurrence in the vicinity of intrahepatic space-occupying lesions (granulomas, tumors, and abscesses), in this instance combined with obstructive-type periportal ductular reaction. This finding in a biopsy specimen provides evidence of a missed mass lesion and may prompt additional investigation.[654]

Peliosis hepatis

Peliosis hepatis consists in the presence of cystic blood-filled spaces in the liver parenchyma.[658] The lesions may be macroscopic or microscopic, ranging in size from less than one to several millimeters in diameter. Lesions are randomly distributed without zonal preference. The endothelial lining is often incomplete. Classification on the basis of the presence or absence of endothelium is not warranted.[661] Peliosis occurs in association with numerous different conditions including wasting diseases, malignancy, liver or renal transplantation, treatment with steroid hormones,[659] and antitumor chemotherapy.[657] The lesions may be incidental findings, but occasional cases have ruptured resulting in fatal hemoperitoneum.[660]

Venous outflow obstruction

Each case of venous outflow obstruction should be specifically defined by the location, cause, and nature of the occlusive lesion, in order to avoid inappropriate and confusing use of the term Budd–Chiari syndrome.[663] A picture of severe congestion by itself does not permit specification of the location and nature of the outflow block. In this case, the appropriate term to use is *venous outflow obstruction*.

The histopathology of venous outflow obstruction varies according to its severity and duration (acute or chronic), independent of its cause. *Acute venous outflow obstruction* is characterized by dilatation and congestion of sinusoids, predominantly in the centrolobular area. In mild congestion, the liver cell plates may be thinned. In severe cases, the hepatocytes become atrophic and may disappear, leaving a denuded framework of lining cells and perisinusoidal fibers. Severe congestion creates a hemorrhagic, blood lake-like appearance. Erythrocytes may extravasate into the space of Disse and permeate the liver cell plates, supplanting the disappeared hepatocytes,[662] a pattern obviously most visible when sinusoidal red blood cells have drained out during tissue processing.

Chronic venous outflow obstruction results in centrolobular fibrosis of variable extent. The fibrotic areas eventually join, resulting in central–central bridging fibrosis that encircles normal portal tracts and their surrounding parenchyma (so-called "reversed lobulation"). Cirrhosis can evolve in far advanced cases (termed cardiac cirrhosis).

Budd–Chiari syndrome is a clinicopathologic syndrome variously defined as hepatic vein thrombosis, noncardiac venous outflow obstruction, or venous outflow obstruction of any cause or site. Several authors use the term in its restricted sense, that is, occlusion of the larger vessels draining the liver—the major hepatic veins and their segmental branches and the inferior vena cava—usually by thrombosis. Late consequences of thromboses may take the form of fibrous webs.[665]

The microscopic lesions are those of venous outflow obstruction. The centrolobular and lobular veins may contain recent or organized thrombi, presumably extensions of thrombus in the larger veins.

With time, the fibrous lesions of chronic venous outflow obstruction develop. The surviving periportal parenchyma often shows evidence of regeneration; nodular hyperplasia and even cirrhosis may develop.[664] The liver is often unevenly affected.

Venoocclusive disease

The term venoocclusive disease (VOD) indicates the fibrous occlusion of the small branches of the hepatic vein system: centrolobular and sublobular veins. In contrast to most cases of Budd–Chiari syndrome, the outflow block can be detected in needle biopsies. The further lesions are those of acute or chronic venous outflow obstruction. The classical cause of VOD is ingestion of pyrrolizidine alkaloids[670]; this remains a hazard.[666] VOD has been described in patients with bone marrow, kidney, or liver transplantation, after liver irradiation, after tumor chemotherapy, in arsenic poisoning, and in heroin addiction.[668] Venoocclusive lesions are further observed in alcoholic liver disease[667] and in liver cirrhosis from whatever cause.[669]

Nodular regeneration

Recommendations for the classification and terminology of nodular regenerative lesions have been provided by an International Working Party.[671]

Nodular regenerative hyperplasia

Nodular regenerative hyperplasia (NRH) is defined by the presence of non-neoplastic nodules that are not delimited by fibrous septa.[677] The condition was originally considered to be rare and to accompany a limited number of disorders, such as congestive heart failure, Felty's syndrome, lymphoproliferative disorders, or a drug-induced reaction, usually associated with portal hypertension. Subsequently, attention turned to its probable etiology. Wanless et al.[677] postulated that the basic lesion is portal venous thrombosis, resulting in parenchymal atrophy and compensatory hyperplasia. Arterial lesions, particularly age-associated arteriosclerosis, also may contribute to development of the changes.[677] Nodular regenerative hyperplasia may be part of the early noncirrhotic stages of primary biliary cirrhosis[672] and may occur in livers containing metastatic or primary liver tumor.[674] Several patients with NRH have portal hypertension and elevated levels of alkaline phosphatase and γ-glutamyl transpeptidase.

The histopathologic diagnosis of NRH is easier on surgical specimens but is possible on needle biopsies.[675] The nodularity is better revealed on a reticulin stain.[673] Microscopically, NRH is characterized by nodules of hyperplastic hepatocytes arranged in plates more than one cell thick, whereas the parenchymal cells adjacent to the nodules (usually centrolobular areas) are compressed and atrophic. Portal tracts are generally located in the center of the nodules. The interface between nodules is not defined by fibrous septa, which differentiates the lesion from cirrhosis (Table 13.7). In some cases, the compressed parenchyma between the nodules shows perisinusoidal fibrosis. In general, there is no or only minimal inflammation and no evidence of liver cell damage. Vascular changes may be subtle and inconspicuous in needle biopsies. In cases with portal hypertension—but even in patients without (or possibly with a subclinical stage of portal hyperpressure)—the aberrant "paraportal shunt" vessels of noncirrhotic portal hypertension (portal phlebosclerosis) may be found.[676]

Partial nodular transformation

Partial nodular transformation (PNT) is a rare entity in which the nodules are larger than in nodular regenerative hyperplasia (NRH) and often restricted to the perihilar region. Again, portal venous thrombosis is invoked in the pathogenesis of the lesions, but in this instance situated near the porta hepatis in the larger portal vein branches.[678,679]

Focal nodular hyperplasia

Focal nodular hyperplasia (FNH) is discussed on p. 992. This nodular lesion is also thought to result from a vascular anomaly: arterial hyperplasia producing focal hyperemia resulting in nodular parenchymal hyperplasia[681] characterized by cholestatic features.[680]

Liver disease in pregnancy

Normal pregnancy does not entail specific light microscopic hepatic changes. Diseases affecting the liver in pregnancy can be subdivided into those which occur in the context of and exclusively during pregnancy and those which occur simultaneously with gestation.[682]

Liver disease unique to pregnancy

Acute fatty liver of pregnancy

Acute fatty liver of pregnancy (AFLP) is a rare but grave complication that develops in the last weeks of gestation and affects both primigravidae and multipara. It is the most serious of the pregnancy-associated diseases, but over the last couple of decades the prognosis has improved dramatically.[685] It is caused by a fatty acid transport and mitochondrial oxidation (FATMO) disorder of the fetus.[684] Affected livers are grossly yellow and frequently small, a reflection of substantial loss of parenchyma. The most characteristic microscopic feature is microvesicular steatosis, usually involving the entire liver lobule, sometimes sparing a narrow periportal rim of hepatocytes (Fig. 13.41). Hepatocytes containing very fine fat droplets of less than 1 μm diameter may not be recognized as steatotic but rather as ballooned hepatocytes on routinely stained sections. This mimics the hydropic swelling of liver cells in acute viral hepatitis and may cause problems of diagnosis in the 10% to 20% of cases in which a lymphoplasmacytic infiltrate and

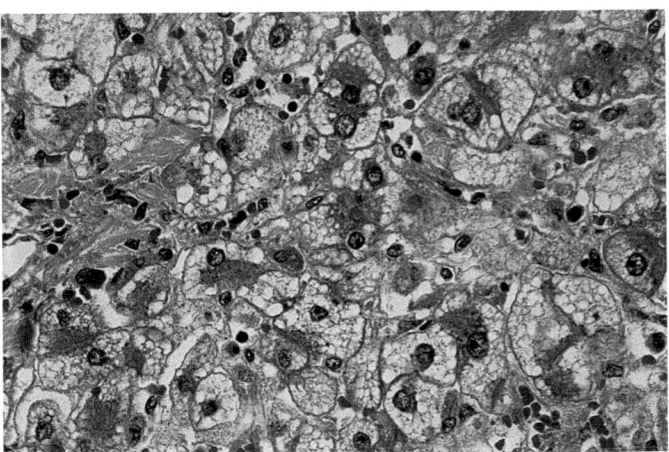

Fig. 13.41 Acute fatty liver of pregnancy. Detail of lobular parenchyma characterized by microvesicular steatosis and a small number of lymphocytes. (H&E)

acidophil bodies occur.[683,685] Histochemical fat stains on frozen sections make the diagnosis clear. Therefore, in patients with unexplained jaundice in late pregnancy, it is wise to reserve part of the biopsy specimen for frozen sectioning and oil red O staining.[686]

Fibrin thrombi are occasionally demonstrable in the hepatic sinusoids, and some patients show cholestasis, hepatocellular necrosis, extramedullary hematopoiesis, and giant mitochondria.[685,686] Termination of pregnancy and supportive care for hepatic encephalopathy and extrahepatic complications assist most patients in cure and survival. AFLP hardly ever recurs in subsequent pregnancies; exceptions are very rare.[687]

Toxemia of pregnancy (preeclampsia/eclampsia)

Preeclampsia is characterized by hypertension induced or aggravated by pregnancy, in association with proteinuria, peripheral edema, and occasional coagulation abnormalities. Convulsions and coma may follow and this stage corresponds to eclampsia.[689]

Preeclampsia develops in 5% of pregnancies, generally during the third trimester, and especially in primigravidae. The incidence is increased in patients with acute fatty liver of pregnancy.[688] Severe preeclampsia and eclampsia cause hepatocellular dysfunction reflected by elevation of serum transaminases and/or alkaline phosphatase. Macroscopically, the liver shows diffuse, fine or blotchy hemorrhages over the capsule and on the cut surface.[689,690] Endothelial injury and disruption cause intravascular coagulation. Histopathologically, fibrin thrombi are found in portal vessels and periportal sinusoids, in variable combination with hemorrhage and hepatocellular necrosis. Fibrin can be identified by phosphotungstic acid–hematoxylin (PTAH) staining or immunohistochemistry. Extensive periportal lesions may lead to liver failure, and two rare complications—rupture preceded by subcapsular hematoma and infarction of the liver—often prove fatal.[690]

HELLP syndrome

The acronym HELLP stands for hemolysis, elevated levels of liver enzymes, and low platelet count. The syndrome is exceedingly rare and occurs in preeclamptic women.[691] The characteristic lesion is periportal hemorrhage, hepatocellular necrosis, and fibrin exudate.

Intrahepatic cholestasis of pregnancy

Intrahepatic cholestasis of pregnancy (ICP) is a reversible form of cholestasis, usually occurring in late pregnancy and persisting until delivery. The incidence of ICP in Europe is approximately 10 to 150 per 10,000 pregnancies. Quality of life can be impaired by pruritus, jaundice, and fat malabsorption; the prognosis for the mother is good, but ICP may be a condition with lethal outcome for the unborn child. Heterozygote mutations of hepatobiliary transport proteins predispose to ICP.[692] In general, liver biopsy is unnecessary for diagnosis. Histopathology

reveals canalicular and hepatocellular bilirubin stasis, especially in the centrolobular area.[693,694]

Other liver disease in pregnancy

Further hepatic problems during pregnancy include intercurrent liver disease encountered during pregnancy (e.g., viral hepatitis, cholelithiasis) and preexisting liver disease in the pregnant patient.

Liver involvement in other organ and systemic diseases

This section is restricted to some more frequently observed lesions. For full coverage of the topics, the reader is referred to textbooks of hepatic pathology.

Granulomas

Epithelioid granulomas are present in 3% to 15% of liver biopsies, the incidence varying according to geographic location and method of selection of patients for biopsy.[697,704] Etiologies are diverse, and their relative proportion again depends on geographic site and case selection.[695] The cause of hepatic granulomas may remain unknown in up to half the cases even after clinical follow-up with comprehensive laboratory evaluation.[703]

A full diagnosis of hepatic granulomatous lesions requires careful histologic evaluation of the granulomas themselves and of the associated changes (e.g., hepatitis, bilirubin stasis, bile duct damage). Step sections are often helpful, and are essential when granulomatous disease is suspected but not found in the initial sections. Special techniques may be helpful, for example stains for microorganisms (Ziehl–Neelsen, silver methenamine for fungi, immunostaining for specific organisms), polarizing microscopy for inclusions, and X-ray microanalysis (e.g., for gold, barium, silicon).[695]

When not fully established, the etiologic diagnosis should be made with the clinical context in mind. From this point of view, hepatic granulomas fall into one of four groups[695]:

1 See the cause. The etiology is clear from microscopic examination, because the cause can be seen. Examples include granulomas around the ova of *Schistosoma*, and lesions with demonstrable mycobacteria after appropriate staining.

2 Know the cause, or at least the diagnosis. Correct interpretation requires knowledge of clinical data. A diagnosis of primary biliary cirrhosis can be made if granulomas and lymphoid infiltrates are found adjacent to injured bile ducts in a middle-aged female patient with pruritus, raised serum alkaline phosphatase, and positive testing for antimitochondrial antibodies.[695]

3 Suspect the diagnosis. Even in the absence of a firm etiologic conclusion, one is able to suggest a produc-

tive line of investigation based on histologic features. For instance, granulomas with plenty of eosinophils suggest drug-induced lesions or parasitosis.

4 Cause unknown. Regretfully, this is the largest group. Histology remains helpful insofar as it establishes the presence of granulomas and thus somewhat narrows the diagnostic field. As tuberculosis remains a worldwide problem, this diagnosis should always be considered among the possibilities.

Sarcoidosis. The incidence of granulomas in livers of patients with established sarcoid varies in the literature from 21% to 79%. In liver biopsies from patients with sarcoidosis and clinical evidence of hepatic disease (a discrete subset of all patients suffering from sarcoidosis) granulomatous inflammation was found in 100% in a series of biopsies referred to the Armed Forces Institute of Pathology.[696] In this study, three broad categories of abnormalities were noted besides the granulomatous inflammation: cholestatic (58%); necroinflammatory (41%); and vascular (20%). Histologic mimics of several other disorders, including primary biliary cirrhosis, primary sclerosing cholangitis, drug-induced liver disease, bile duct obstruction, and viral hepatitis were noted. Hepatic fibrosis was found in 21% of biopsies, including 6% with cirrhosis. Although these numbers may reflect referral bias, they do suggest that some patients with hepatic sarcoidosis have progressive liver disease. The epithelioid granulomas of sarcoidosis typically occur with greatest frequency in the portal and periportal areas, often in clusters. The granulomas may be of differing "ages" and typically heal with fibrosis, so that varying numbers and degrees of epithelioid cells, inflammation, giant cells, and scarring are often seen in the same biopsy. In a few cases, masses of granulomas and fibrosis may develop (sarcoidoma), raising clinical suspicion of a neoplasm.[696]

Primary biliary cirrhosis can at times be particularly difficult to differentiate from sarcoidosis since both conditions may lead to portal granulomas, bile duct injury and destruction, ductopenia, and chronic cholestasis.[700,702] Both conditions might even coexist.[698]

Some sarcoidosis patients present with predominantly portal hypertension.[705] The syndrome is due to portal granulomas and fibrosis.[706] A final diagnosis of sarcoidosis cannot be made by histopathologic study of a liver biopsy alone, due to the multiplicity of mimicking granulomatous diseases.

Fibrin-ring (or doughnut) granulomas show a distinctive ring pattern in which fibrin is deposited circumferentially within or at the margin of the granuloma, which is composed of epithelioid cells, giant cells, and neutrophils and a central fat vacuole (Fig. 13.42). Serial sectioning may be required to detect the typical "fibrin-ring" configuration.[701] Originally described in Q fever, it was also reported in allopurinol hypersensitivity,

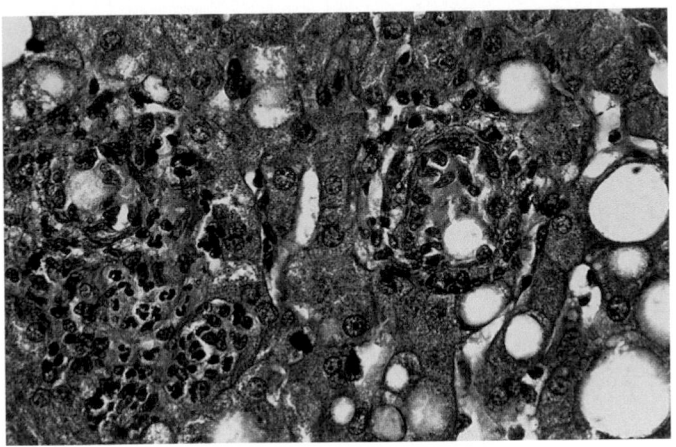

Fig. 13.42 Q fever. Detail of lobular parenchyma with some steatosis and two fibrin ring granulomas. The granuloma is composed of a central fat vacuole, a layer of histiocytes and lymphocytes, a fibrin ring, and additional accumulation of inflammatory cells. (H&E)

cytomegalovirus and Epstein–Barr virus infection, leishmaniasis, toxoplasmosis, hepatitis A, Hodgkin's lymphoma, giant cell arteritis, and systemic lupus. It has been suggested that it possibly represents a nonspecific reaction to liver injury.[699]

Lipogranulomas in steatohepatitis and **mineral oil granulomas** are discussed on pp. 939 and 940 respectively.

Cytomegalovirus infection

Cytomegalovirus (CMV) may be a cause of neonatal hepatitis, and CMV genome can be identified by polymerase chain reaction in several cases.[707] CMV is the most important cause of opportunistic hepatitis in immunodeficient patients. Typical nuclear CMV inclusions surrounded by a clear halo are easily found in symptomatic immunocompromised patients. CMV inclusions may occur in any type of hepatic cell: hepatocytes, bile duct cells, endothelial cells, and portal fibroblasts. Specific immunostains may reveal CMV antigens even in cells without inclusions,[711] but often characterized by an abnormally basophilic granular cytoplasm.[712] In situ hybridization for viral DNA can be applied, but the sensitivity of the technique has been questioned.[710] Aggregation of neutrophils in sinusoids or microabscesses may occur even near hepatocytes without evidence of CMV[712]; this is a useful diagnostic signal that should prompt a diligent search for viral inclusions or antigens.

In immunocompetent hosts, a picture resembling mononucleosis hepatitis may occur, in which portal tracts and sinusoids reveal a prominent mononuclear infiltrate composed mainly of small and large atypical lymphocytes.[709] Small aggregates of Kupffer cells, epithelioid granulomas, and fibrin-ring granulomas have been reported.[708] Hepatocellular damage is usually limited to scattered focal necroses and apoptosis.

Infectious mononucleosis

The liver is affected in over 90% of patients with infectious mononucleosis, although this is generally a clinically inapparent hepatitis. Symptomatic liver involvement develops in only 5% to 10% of patients. Histopathologically, dense mononuclear infiltrates containing large atypical lymphocytes are found in portal tracts and sinusoids. In the latter, they spread in a distinctive single-file array. This pattern needs to be distinguished from hepatic involvement by leukemia or lymphoma, but is usually less monotonous in character. Kupffer cells are hypertrophic, and epithelioid and fibrin-ring granulomas are occasionally found. Small foci of hepatocellular necrosis and acidophil bodies may be seen, but generally the parenchymal damage is not in proportion with the density of the infiltrate. Bilirubin stasis is usually absent or minimal.[713]

Acquired immune deficiency syndrome

The liver is not a primary target of human immunodeficiency virus (HIV) infection. Most of the hepatic manifestations reflect opportunistic infections, lymphoma, and Kaposi's sarcoma,[722] although Kupffer cells can serve as a reservoir for HIV.[721] Liver biopsy is an important diagnostic tool in patients with HIV infection or AIDS in whom abnormal liver function tests are found.[719] Such biopsies are prototype candidates for special investigations. A portion of the specimen should be reserved for bacterial and viral cultures. Special stains (e.g., acid fast and silver stains), immunohistochemistry, and in situ hybridization are often necessary to identify more precisely the infections and tumoral lesions in these patients. A wide spectrum of liver abnormalities may be observed in AIDS and HIV infection.[720,730]

Nonspecific changes can be found, including mild mononuclear portal infiltrate, scattered intralobular lymphocytes and apoptotic bodies, some fibrosis and ductular reaction, macrovesicular steatosis, and Kupffer cell siderosis. Sinusoidal dilatation, peliosis,[728] and bacillary peliosis[724] may be seen.

Specific infections include reactivation of past viral hepatitis B. The course of hepatitis B, delta, or C is variable in HIV-infected patients, often with a tendency for more severe progression to cirrhosis.[718,727,729] Hepatic involvement by CMV is quite common.[722,730] Other opportunistic infections and infestations involving the liver and bile ducts include *Mycobacterium avium intracellulare* and *Mycobacterium tuberculosis* infection, cryptococcosis, candidiasis, histoplasmosis, malaria, cryptosporidiosis, and microsporidiosis.[720,722,730] *Pneumocystis carinii* may cause multiple foci of eosinophilic foamy exudate similar to that seen in pulmonary infection.[725]

Granulomas may be due to mycobacterial and fungal infections, but can also be drug-induced or cryptogenic. A frequently encountered hepatic lesion is the occurrence of multiple granulomas containing *Mycobacterium avium intracellulare*, visualized to better advantage by PAS–diastase, Ziehl–Neelsen, or Gomori's methenamine silver stains.[723] The mycobacteria are packed in the foamy histiocytes that constitute the granulomas and often show a striated appearance. Small numbers or even single mycobacteria may also be present in scattered Kupffer cells.

AIDS cholangiopathy resembling sclerosing cholangitis may be due to several microorganisms that infect the biliary tree.[715] The biopsy changes resemble those of large bile duct obstruction. Cryptosporidia and microsporidia can be identified in aspirates obtained at endoscopy.[726]

Non-Hodgkin's lymphomas, especially of the Burkitt and immunoblastic types, may involve the liver, occurring as portal infiltrates or as nodular masses.[714] Hepatic involvement by **Kaposi's sarcoma** is generally unsuspected before death, but may be diagnosed on biopsy.[717] Lipid-laden perisinusoidal cells are another hepatic change reported in AIDS.[716]

Malaria

The most distinctive feature is the presence of finely granular, dark brown or black pigment (hemozoin), initially in Kupffer cells and later in portal macrophages. It is birefringent, and negative with PAS and iron stains. It resembles the artifactual formalin pigment and is likewise soluble in saturated alcoholic picric acid. It strongly resembles schistosomal pigment although it differs biochemically. Anthracotic pigment, which resembles malarial pigment, is not birefringent.[731] Additional histologic changes may include focal necrosis, steatosis, and a mild mononuclear portal infiltrate.

Total parenteral nutrition

Long-term total parenteral nutrition (TPN) may be associated with steatosis, steatohepatitis, portal and periportal fibrosis, and intrahepatic cholestasis.[735,736] The cholestatic lesions may resemble large bile duct obstruction.[732] Steatosis is the predominant lesion in adults.[735] In infants and children, cholestasis is the most frequent hepatic complication of TPN.[734] A ductular reaction after 3 weeks of TPN may progress to portal fibrosis after 90 days, and on occasion even to cirrhosis after 5 months.[733]

Amyloidosis and light chain deposition disease

Although systemic amyloidosis commonly involves the liver, it rarely gives rise to clinically evident hepatic disease. Amyloid is recognized as a homogeneous eosinophilic extracellular material (Fig. 13.43) displaying apple green birefringence after positive Congo red staining. Primary myeloma-associated (AL) amyloidosis and reactive (AA) amyloidosis cannot reliably be distinguished by the topographic distribution pattern of the deposits. Potassium permanganate treatment before Congo red staining leaves AL amyloid Congo red positive,[742] and AL amyloid stains positive in light chain immunostains.[737]

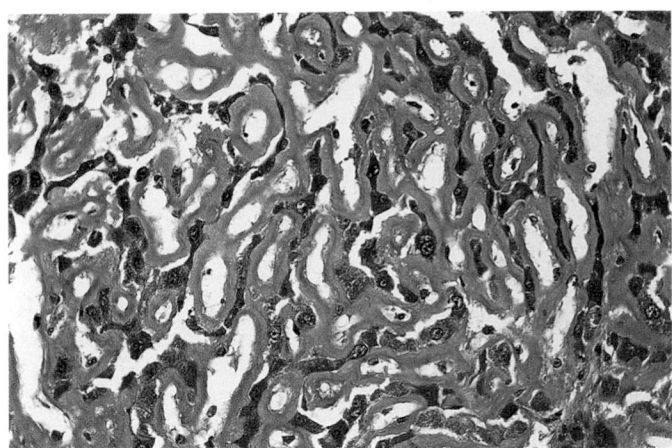

Fig. 13.43 Amyloidosis. Detail of lobular parenchyma with massive amyloid deposition in the space of Disse and corresponding marked atrophy of liver cell plates. (H&E)

Amyloid is usually deposited in the hepatic artery branches or along the sinusoids in the space of Disse, and often occurs in both locations. Perisinusoidal deposition leads to atrophy of liver cell plates and narrowing of sinusoids, occasionally resulting in intrahepatic cholestasis and portal hypertension.[739,740] Much more rarely, amyloid is found in globular deposits.[741]

Homogeneous perisinusoidal and portal depositions closely resembling amyloid are seen in hepatic involvement in **light chain deposition disease**, which usually causes renal symptoms. Immunohistochemical staining for kappa and lambda light chains permits identification of the deposits, usually kappa (Fig. 13.44). Light chain deposits are Congo red negative and show no green birefringence after Congo red staining. In exceptional cases, light chain deposition and amyloid are found in the same patient, even more rarely associated with intrahepatic cholestasis.[738]

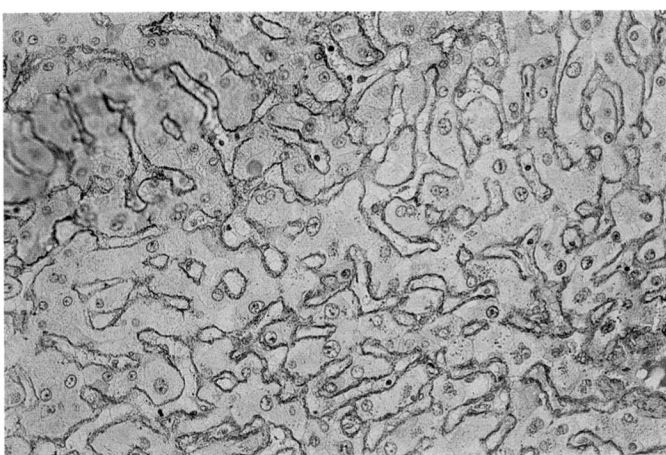

Fig. 13.44 Light chain deposition disease. Detail of lobular parenchyma with kappa chain deposition in the space of Disse. (Immunostain for kappa light chain)

Nonspecific reactive changes

Several primarily extrahepatic diseases, including febrile, inflammatory, and neoplastic conditions, especially in older patients, are associated with nonspecific reactive changes in the liver. One may find portal and lobular inflammation, steatosis, Kupffer cell hypertrophy, and even focal necrosis of hepatocytes. Clinical information is required for adequate distinction from mild chronic or residual hepatitis.[743,744]

Liver pathology in organ transplantation

Hepatic abnormalities may be associated with transplantation of the liver and of other organs.

Liver transplantation

Over the last few decades, the pathology of liver transplantation has evolved into a completely new chapter in hepatic pathology. If close clinicopathologic collaboration is essential in modern medicine in general, it is a necessity par excellence in the field of organ transplantation. In transplantation centers, the pathologist is part of the clinical care team, involved in evaluation of the patient's primary disease before possible transplantation, in identification of underlying donor liver disease (e.g., steatosis, cancer) at the time of allograft procurement, and in recognition of a wide variety of complications following transplantation.[748] As liver transplantation centers become established all over the world for the treatment of severe acute and chronic liver disease, pathologists in local hospitals may become confronted with the problems of transplant recipients during their later medical care and follow-up and need some familiarity with hepatic transplant pathology.[748]

Percutaneous liver biopsies are obtained when the clinician is warned by symptoms of deterioration of liver function. Some centers carry out biopsies, often referred to as "protocol biopsies," on a planned schedule irrespective of liver chemistry.[746,750] In experienced hands, fine needle aspiration biopsy may also yield adequate information.[749] The pathologist may be requested to exclude preexisting disease of a potential donor liver by frozen section. For instance, marked macrovesicular steatosis carries the risk of primary graft dysfunction.[745] Parenchymal involvement should be semiquantitated as absent, mild (<30%), moderate (30–60%), or marked (>60%),[745,752] since the last category is considered unsuitable for use because of the high risk of primary dysfunction of the allograft.[751,752] Microvesicular steatosis, in contrast, is not a contraindication.[747] Demonstration of a primary or metastatic malignant tumor is a contraindication.

The grafted liver is subject to all sorts of diseases affecting nontransplanted livers, and, in addition, to a multitude of other abnormalities, including preservation injury, allograft rejection, various complications (e.g., surgical mishaps, hepatic artery and portal vein thrombosis, bile duct problems such as dehiscence, leaks, necrosis, strictures, concrement formation, infection), drug reactions, opportunistic infections, recurrent disease, and post-transplant lymphoproliferative disorders.

Preservation injury

Preservation injury refers to nonimmunologic graft damage resulting from the harvesting, ischemic preservation, transportation, and reperfusion of the donor liver.[753] This injury appears early (first 2 weeks post transplant) and regresses spontaneously over several weeks.[759] For evaluation of possible preservation (ischemia/reperfusion) injury, specimens are obtained at the time of transplantation directly after revascularization of the graft (time zero biopsies).[755] Quite common are so-called "surgical necroses," as often observed in any surgical specimen,[754] consisting of clusters of neutrophils and scattered acidophil bodies (Fig. 13.45). Another preservation injury is so-called "functional cholestasis," with bilirubin stasis in hepatocytes and canaliculi.[760] This should be distinguished from cholestasis associated with acute rejection, drug toxicity, hepatitis, bile duct obstruction, or sepsis. Another aspect, possibly associated with bilirubin stasis, is hepatocellular ballooning, either diffuse or centrolobular,[756,758] which, by itself, does not carry a bad prognosis.[758] A preservation injury of higher severity due to hypoperfusion is represented by centrolobular hepatocyte necrosis. This is a differential diagnostic problem, since confluent necrosis is found in vascular complications, drug-induced injury, and—as a poor prognostic sign—in acute and chronic allograft rejection.[757]

Allograft rejection

Hepatic allograft rejection designates the injury to the transplanted liver caused by the immunologic reaction of the host. Rejection has been classified as humoral, acute (cellular), and chronic (ductopenic).[769,777] The histopathologic lesions have been well characterized.[761,765,766,770,776]

Humoral rejection (hyperacute or antibody-mediated rejection) is rare; it develops in patients with preformed or subsequently formed antibodies to an ABO blood group-incompatible donor.[764] The antibodies react with the graft vasculature and cause endothelial damage and thrombosis within the first few hours, ultimately resulting in coagulative and hemorrhagic necrosis in a few days.

Acute (cellular) rejection is the most common form of rejection with a mean incidence of about 50%.[761] It generally develops within the first 3 weeks after transplantation, and its median onset ranges between 7 and 10 days (with exceptions, of course).[778] Late presentations are usually related to decreased immunosuppression.[772] It results from a cell-mediated immune reaction directed at bile duct epithelium and the endothelium of portal and centrolobular veins.[777]

Histologically, cellular rejection is characterized by the triad of portal infiltration, bile duct damage, and endotheliitis (although the latter may be missing in some cases) (Fig. 13.46). None of these features is by itself entirely specific for rejection. The portal infiltrate consists of a mixture of inflammatory cells: small lymphocytes predominate, intermixed with larger lymphoid type cells, immunoblasts, macrophages, plasma cells, neutrophils, and eosinophils. In some cases eosinophils are abundant and represent a helpful diagnostic feature of

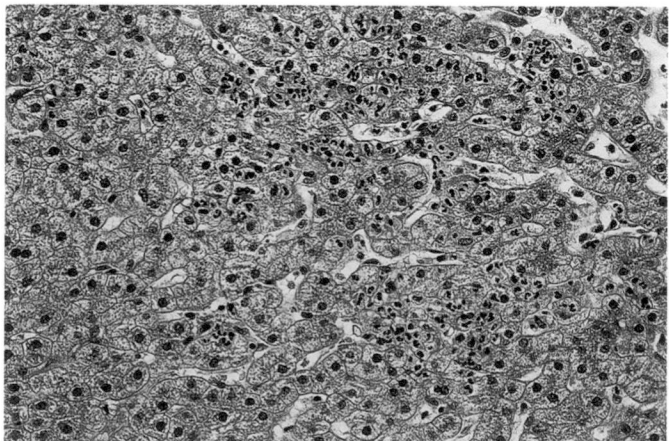

Fig. 13.45 Surgical necroses consist of focal necrosis of hepatocytes and accumulation of clusters of neutrophil polymorphs. Originally described in specimens taken at the end of abdominal surgical interventions, they are nowadays also recognized as a marker of "preservation damage" in donor livers after revascularization during liver transplantation. (H&E)

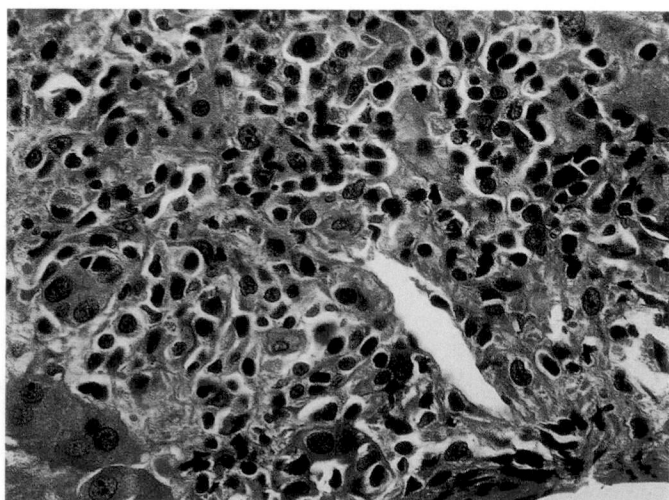

Fig. 13.46 Acute (cellular) rejection of liver allograft. Detail of portal tract showing dense mixed infiltrate (including lymphocytes, more immature lymphoid type cells, and eosinophils), mild endotheliitis (from center to lower right), and bile duct involvement (center left and center bottom). (H&E) (Courtesy of Prof. T. Roskams, Leuven)

rejection.[773] The infiltrate typically expands the portal tract, but may be focally and unevenly distributed. Occasionally, the infiltrate extends beyond the limits of the portal tract and even leads to portal–portal bridging necrosis.[763]

Endotheliitis can be present in either portal or central veins, consisting of supraendothelial and subendothelial lymphocytes, endothelial damage, and lifting off of endothelium from the underlying layers. Endotheliitis of centrolobular veins, accompanied by necrosis of centrolobular hepatocytes and periportal extension of the portal inflammatory infiltrate, is indicative of severe cellular rejection.[767] A less frequent form of cellular rejection with endothelial predominance appears as isolated central venulitis in adult and pediatric liver allograft recipients[762,771] and may result in perivenular fibrosis and a venoocclusive syndrome.[775]

Bile ducts are infiltrated by lymphocytes and lymphoid-type cells (lymphocytic cholangitis); bile duct epithelial damage is reflected in anisonucleosis, cytoplasmic vacuolization, areas of cell stratification or occasional dropout, and irregularities in duct outlines.

Several grading systems of cellular (acute) rejection have been proposed. Their rationale is to predict unfavorable clinical outcomes. A review of grading systems was updated by Batts.[761] A consensus document,[767] published by an international panel that met in Banff, Canada, recommends the grading listed in Table 13.9.

Additional features that are less consistently present include bilirubin stasis, some lobular inflammatory mononuclear infiltrate, and, in cases of severe rejection, centrolobular confluent parenchymal necrosis.

Chronic rejection. Chronic liver allograft rejection can be defined as an immunologic injury to the allograft which usually evolves from severe or persistent acute cellular rejection and results in potentially irreversible damage to the bile ducts, arteries, and terminal hepatic veins with surrounding parenchyma.[768] Terms such as "vanishing bile duct syndrome" and "ductopenic rejection" are no longer recommended, because bile duct loss is just one aspect of chronic liver allograft rejection.[769]

The clinical diagnosis of chronic rejection is suspected in a patient with a history of acute cellular rejection who develops progressive cholestasis. The final diagnosis of chronic rejection should be based on a combination of the clinical, radiological, laboratory, and histopathologic findings. Histopathologically, the minimal diagnostic criteria are: (1) the presence of bile duct atrophy/pyknosis, affecting a majority of the bile ducts, with or without bile duct loss; (2) convincing foam cell obliterative arteriopathy; or (3) bile duct loss affecting more than 50% of portal tracts. Since arteries with pathognomonic changes predominate in the hilar region and are rarely present in needle biopsy specimens, considerable significance is placed on damage and loss of small bile ducts. Obviously, other causes of ductal injury and loss should be reasonably excluded; these include biliary tract obstruction and hepatic artery thrombosis.[768]

The histopathologic changes of the liver in chronic rejection mainly affect the portal tracts and centrolobular areas. Within the portal tracts, chronic rejection reveals itself by damage followed by loss of small bile ducts and small branches of the hepatic artery (Fig. 13.47).

Early bile duct changes include uneven nuclear spacing, nuclear enlargement and hyperchromasia, and interrupted epithelial lining of ducts. Early arterial lesions consist in accumulation of subintimal, medial, and adventitial foamy macrophages, but, as mentioned, these lesions are not routinely sampled in peripheral needle biopsies. Late bile duct and arterial damage is mainly evaluated by the extent of loss of these structures. Bile duct loss is considered present when less than 80% of the portal tracts contain bile ducts; arterial loss is considered

Table 13.9 Grading of acute cellular rejection

Global assessment*	Criteria
Indeterminate	Portal inflammatory infiltrate that fails to meet the criteria for the diagnosis of acute rejection
Mild	Rejection infiltrate in a minority of the triads, generally mild, and confined within the portal spaces
Moderate	Rejection infiltrate, expanding most or all of the triads
Severe	As above for moderate, with spillover into periportal areas and moderate to severe perivenular inflammation that extends into the hepatic parenchyma and is associated with centrolobular hepatocyte necrosis

*Verbal description of mild, moderate, or severe acute rejection could also be labeled grades I, II and III respectively.
Data from Demetris et al.,[767] with permission from authors and publisher.

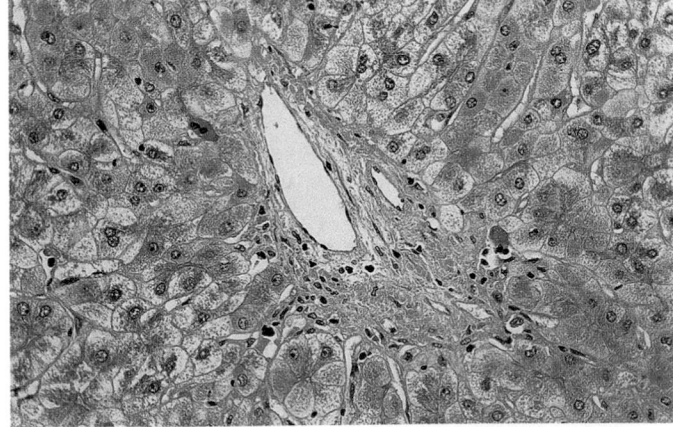

Fig. 13.47 Chronic "ductopenic" rejection of liver allograft. Portal tract without bile duct and very sparse lymphocytic infiltration. (H&E)

present when less than 77% of the portal tracts contain hepatic artery branches.[768]

The early lesions of chronic rejection in the centrolobular area are characterized by subendothelial and perivenular mononuclear inflammation of the centrolobular vein, accompanied by centrolobular hepatocyte dropout, pigment-laden macrophages, and mild perivenular fibrosis. A "transitional hepatitis," sometimes difficult to distinguish from viral hepatitis, may occur during the evolution to late stages of chronic rejection.[774] Late chronic rejection is reflected in severe (bridging) perivenular fibrosis, with at least focal central–central or central–portal bridging and occasional obliteration of terminal hepatic venules.

The features used to define chronic rejection are not uniformly present in all cases: bile duct loss can occur without arteriopathy, and vice versa, and severe (bridging) centrolobular fibrosis may be present without significant bile duct loss or obliterative arteriopathy. An individual patient may have late features of one component (e.g., bile duct loss) and early features of another component (e.g., perivenular necrosis).[768]

A working formulation for histopathologic staging and reporting of chronic liver allograft rejection has been proposed. Early chronic rejection is diagnosed if no more than one of the target structures shows late changes. An overall diagnosis of late chronic rejection requires that at least two or more of the target structures show late changes.[768]

Other complications

Bile duct strictures at the site of anastomosis or elsewhere can be a cause of graft dysfunction. The histologic features are those of any biliary obstruction. **Hepatic artery thrombosis**, alone or in combination with **portal vein thrombosis**, occurs more commonly in children. The consequences are ischemic injury (infarction) of varying extent, distribution, and age.

Infections are frequent complications. Hepatic allograft recipients, like other immunocompromised individuals, are susceptible to a wide range of bacterial, viral, fungal, and protozoal pathogens. These include cytomegalovirus and Epstein–Barr virus infections and sepsis due to gram-negative bacilli.

Drug-induced injury. Several of the drugs in the therapeutic regimen for immunosuppression are capable of causing hepatic damage. Because of the numerous confounding features, it may be difficult to incriminate a specific drug. Sinusoidal congestion and centrolobular necrosis have been observed in liver transplant patients treated with *azathioprine*.[779] *Cyclosporine* (ciclosporin) may cause canalicular bilirubin stasis, hepatocyte ballooning, and vacuolization of bile duct epithelial cells.[780]

Recurrent disease

The risk of recurrence is highest with neoplastic disorders and chronic viral hepatitis. The diagnosis of recurrent disease can be controversial on liver biopsy because some of these pre-transplant disorders have histopathologic features that overlap with those seen in rejection or post-transplant biliary stricture.

Recurrent hepatitis B may cause acute and chronic hepatitis, cirrhosis, minimal histologic changes (carrier state) and, in a minority of cases, so-called *"fibrosing cholestatic hepatitis."*[784] The latter occurs early (before 150 days),[788] is associated with rapidly progressive graft dysfunction, and is histologically characterized by perisinusoidal bands of fibrosis around plates of ductular-type epithelium, prominent bilirubin stasis, ground glass hepatocytes, hepatocellular ballooning with cell loss, and a mild mixed inflammatory reaction.[784] Fibrosing cholestatic hepatitis is associated with high viral load and occurs in other types of immunodeficiency states such HIV infection and in renal transplant patients.[783] **Co-infection by hepatitis B and D virus** as primary disease may attenuate HBV recurrence post transplantation.[792]

HCV recurrence as defined by histologic injury is almost universal. In a small group of patients graft injury is severe and may result in graft loss.[781,792,796] Differentiation from cellular rejection may require sequential biopsies and grading of lesions to document the progressive appearance of hepatitis C features.[791] A severe progressive cholestatic syndrome, reminiscent of that in recurrent HBV infection, has been reported with an incidence of 2% to 10%, apparently due to a direct viral cytopathic effect by high viral load.[782,794]

In most patients transplanted for **primary biliary cirrhosis (PBC)**, antimitochondrial antibodies persist and do not correlate with disease recurrence. Liver biopsy remains the gold standard for diagnosis of PBC recurrence.[785] Florid bile duct lesions and epithelioid granulomas are the most helpful features, although granulomatous cholangitis has also been observed in chronic viral hepatitis C.[787] Portal lymphoid aggregates and ductopenia are less helpful, as they may occur in chronic hepatitis C and in allograft rejection. Ductular reaction and progressive cholate stasis (amongst others copper deposition) are useful for diagnosis of PBC recurrence. The presence of plasma cells in the portal infiltrate has been suggested as an early marker of recurrence of PBC.[795]

The diagnosis of recurrence of **primary sclerosing cholangitis**[786] requires well-defined cholangiographic and histologic criteria,[785] since the features of PSC resemble those of complications of the transplant procedure, e.g., ischemic or anastomotic bile duct strictures.

Recurrence of **autoimmune hepatitis** is based on clinical, biochemical, serologic, and histologic criteria.[785] Portal and periportal inflammation (interface hepatitis) containing plasma cells are consistent with recurrent disease.[797]

Neoplastic disease. Malignancies after liver transplantation comprise hepatocellular carcinoma and post-transplant lymphoproliferative disease. Recurrent[790] or de novo[789,793] hepatocellular carcinoma mainly develops in recipients transplanted for chronic viral hepatitis B and C. Post-transplant lymphoproliferative disease is mostly a nodal and extranodal B-cell lymphoma as a complication of immunosuppressive treatment in transplanted patients.

Difficult diagnostic problems should be solved by close clinicopathologic collaboration. It must be kept in mind that several pathologic conditions may coexist in the liver allograft: drug toxicity, viral hepatitis, disease recurrence, and rejection are not mutually exclusive!

Bone marrow transplantation: graft-versus-host disease

Bone marrow transplantation may cause several complications, especially liver damage. The injury can be due to pre-transplant conditioning regimens, to immunosuppression-related infections, and to graft-versus-host disease (GVHD).[799,802] The histopathology of hepatic GVHD depends on the stage of evolution. **Acute hepatic GVHD**, occurring within 90 days after transplantation, is characterized by cholestasis and bile duct damage. Affected ducts show an irregular profile, epithelial atypia with nuclear pleomorphism, cytoplasmic vacuolation, cell necrosis, and possible duct destruction. Lymphocytes infiltrate the duct epithelium, although the portal inflammation is mild. Early biopsies (less than 35 days) reveal less bile duct damage and marked hepatocellular apoptosis,[801] a picture easily confused with viral hepatitis C. Other lesions include endotheliitis, siderosis, and venoocclusive disease.[800]

Chronic GVHD, although usually preceded by acute GVHD, may occur de novo in about 25% of cases, and develops more than 3 months after transplantation. Hepatic involvement consists in similar lesions as in acute GVHD, but with more severe expression: ductopenia develops.[803] Portal infiltration is dense, in some cases associated with periportal extension and interface hepatitis. Lobular changes include bilirubin stasis and apoptotic bodies. More advanced chronic GVHD is associated with ductopenia, cholate stasis, progressive periportal fibrosis, and even cirrhosis.[798,804]

Echinococcus cyst (hydatid cyst)

Hydatid disease is caused by the larval or cystic stage of echinococcus tapeworms, of which *Echinococcus granulosus* is the most frequent; the adult parasites are found in dogs and jackals in all continents.[810] After ingestion of eggs of *E. granulosus*, the eggs hatch and the larval oncospheres pass to the liver by the portal vein. Three quarters of infected individuals develop one or more hepatic cysts, which grow slowly. The typical hydatid cyst is spherical and may measure up to more than 30 cm in diameter. The majority occur in the right lobe, but they may be multiple, involving all lobes[808,809] (Fig. 13.48).

Histologic examination of the cyst wall shows an outer chitinous (or fibrous laminar) layer and an inner germinal layer. The cyst wall may be surrounded by either granulation tissue or a fibrous capsule (so-called "pericyst layer"). Calcification in the latter layer signifies that the cyst is dead. The adjacent liver parenchyma often shows pressure atrophy and a portal infiltrate in which eosinophils may be prominent. The viable cyst is filled with colorless fluid, which contains daughter cysts and brood capsules with scolices. In some patients, daughter cysts are found outside the chitinous layer of the cyst; these are referred to as extracapsular or satellite cysts.[806]

The scolices can be easily identified after macerating a portion of the germinal layer in saline solution. They have characteristic hooklets of 20 to 40 μm length.

Communication with the biliary tract and superimposed infection are frequent in echinococcosis of the liver.[807] Rupture of the cysts into the peritoneal cavity may result in a fatal anaphylactic reaction or in the formation of innumerable small granulomas grossly resembling peritoneal tuberculosis. Identification of fragments of germinal membrane or scolices in their center points to the diagnosis. Hepatic echinococcus cysts can also rupture inside the gallbladder or through the diaphragm into the pleural space and lung.

Echinococcus multilocularis is less common but causes a more aggressive clinical disease. The liver lesions appear as multilocular, necrotic, cystic cavities containing thick pasty material, not surrounded by a fibrous wall. Histologically, the irregular cysts have a laminated membrane, but no nucleated germinal membrane or protoscolices. The laminated membrane is clearly visualized

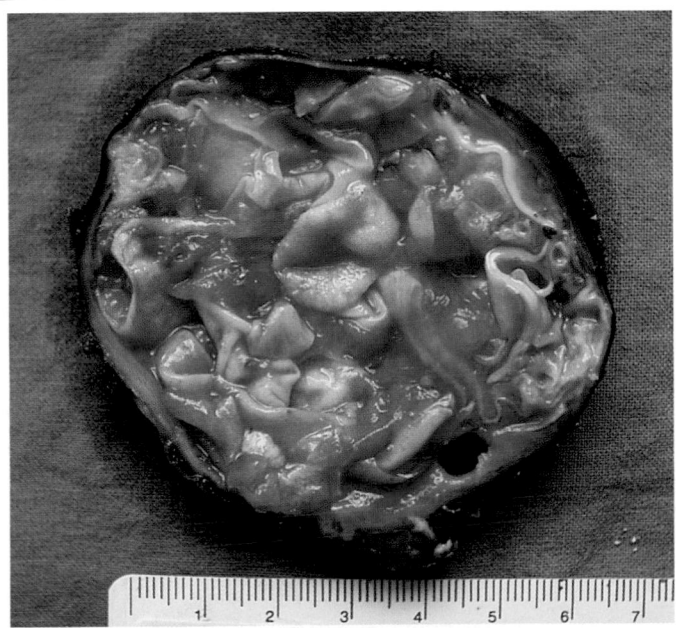

Fig. 13.48 Echinococcosis of the liver.

by the PAS stain; it is often fragmented. The lesion may be surrounded by a granulomatous reaction containing neutrophils and eosinophils, or a peripheral rim of necrosis, fibrosis, and focal calcification.[805]

ABSCESS

The incidence of hepatic abscess had been fairly stable over the past 50 years. However, the character of the disease has changed drastically during that time. In the past, hepatic abscesses often affected young adults: most were amebic (see later section) or secondary to pylephlebitis. Today, the disease in the United States is usually due to enteric bacteria and is seen either in older patients or in HIV-infected or other immunocompromised young individuals. In the latter population, an increasing number of tuberculous "abscesses" of the liver has been detected.[821,824] The incidence of culture-negative abscesses diminishes markedly when proper anaerobic cultures are obtained.[811] The mortality rate, which ranged from 30% to 80% until recently, has dropped to 10% to 20% in the more recent studies on the subject.[813,817]

Currently, the predisposing factors, in descending order of frequency, are (1) biliary tract obstruction/infection, (2) systemic bacteremia, (3) direct extension from a contiguous infection, (4) trauma (penetrating and non-penetrating), and (5) pylephlebitis.[814,826] Specific causes of hepatic abscess are secondary bacterial infection of metastatic tumor nodules, inflammatory bowel disease,[828] pancreatitis,[811] chemotherapy,[819] and dental disease.[815]

Hepatic abscesses vary considerably in size (Fig.13.49). Multiplicity of lesions is seen in about half of the pyogenic abscesses and a fourth of amebic abscesses.[818] In slightly less than half of the cases, there is communication between the abscess and the intrahepatic biliary system.[816]

Diagnostic imaging (ultrasonography, CT, MRI, and angiograpy) is useful in identifying hepatic abscesses and in distinguishing them from necrotic tumors.[812,813] Treatment of hepatic abscess includes antibiotics, aspira-

Fig. 13.50 Amebic abscesses occupying most of the right lobe of the liver. Three distinct lobules are seen. (Courtesy of Dr. RA Cooke, Brisbane, Australia; from Cooke RA, Stewart B: Colour Atlas of Anatomical Pathology. Edinburgh, Churchill Livingstone, 2004).

tion alone, drainage, and excision; the first two are rarely effective by themselves.[823,826]

Amebic abscess is usually single, most frequently right sided, and close to the liver dome[827] (Fig. 13.50). In immunocompromised patients, it has a greater tendency for multicentricity. Most cases occur in adults, but they can also develop in infants and children.[820,822] The necrotic center usually contains an odorless, pasty, chocolate brown fluid. Microscopically, the bulk of the lesion consists of necrotic material with few if any neutrophils, surrounded by a layer of fibrin, macrophages, lymphocytes, and a few fibroblasts. The abscess wall is thinner than that of bacterial liver abscess. Clusters of ameba are usually found, but extensive search may be necessary for their detection. Superinfection by bacteria may supervene, as well as extension and perforation into pleuropulmonary structures, subphrenic space, peritoneal cavity, and—less commonly—pericardial sac, bile ducts, kidney, mediastinum, chest wall, abdominal wall, and flank.[825]

HETEROTOPIA

Heterotopic (ectopic) liver tissue is a very uncommon finding. It has been described in the gallbladder, spleen, pancreas, umbilicus, adrenal gland, small intestine, lesser omentum, and lung.[830-836] This heterotopic tissue is not anatomically connected with the main liver, this constituting the most important differential feature with accessory lobe. Heterotopic supradiaphragmatic liver may be associated with cardiac anomalies.[829,831,835]

References

Normal anatomy

1 Cassiman D, Van Pelt J, De Vos R, Van Lommel F, Desmet V, Yap P, Roskams T. Synaptophysin: a novel marker for human and rat hepatic stellate cells. Am J Pathol 1999, **155**: 1831–1839.

Fig. 13.49 Large liver abscess surrounded by a thick fibrous wall.

2 Crawford AR, Lin XZ, Crawford JM. The normal adult human liver biopsy: a quantitative reference standard. Hepatology 1998, **28**: 323–331.

3 Matsumoto R, Kawakami M. The unit-concept of hepatic parenchyma – a re-examination based on angioarchitectural studies. Acta Pathol Jpn 1982, **32**: 285–314.

4 Rappaport AM, Borowy ZJ, Lougheed WM, Lotto WN. Subdivision of hexagonal liver lobules into a structural and functional unit. Role in hepatic physiology and pathology. Anat Rec 1954, **119**: 11–34.

5 Van Eyken P, Desmet VJ. Cytokeratins and the liver. Liver 1993, **13**: 113–122.

Biopsy

6 Christoffersen P, Poulsen H, Skeie E. Focal liver cell necrosis accompanied by infiltration of granulocytes arising during operation. Acta Hepatosplenol 1970, **17**: 240–245.

7 Demetris AJ, Seaberg EC, Batts KP, Ferrell L, Ludwig J, Markin R, Belle S, Detre K. Reliability and predictive value of the NIDDK liver transplant database nomenclature and grading system for cellular rejection of liver allografts. Hepatology 1995, **21**: 408–416.

8 Denk H, Scheuer PJ, Baptista A, Bianchi L, Callea F, De Groote J, Desmet VJ, Gudat F, Ishak KG, Korb G, MacSween RNM, Phillips MJ, Portmann B, Poulsen H, Schmid M, Thaler H. Guidelines for the diagnosis and interpretation of hepatic granulomas. Histopathology 1994, **25**: 209–218.

9 Desmet V, Fevery J. Liver biopsy. In Hayes PC (ed.): Baillière's Clinical Gastroenterology. International practice and research. Investigations in hepatology, vol. 9, no. 4. London, 1995, Baillière Tindall, pp. 811–828.

10 Desmet VJ. Drug-induced liver disease: pathogenetic mechanisms and histopathological lesions. Eur J Med 1993, **2**: 36–47.

11 Desmet VJ. Cholestasis: extrahepatic obstruction and secondary biliary cirrhosis. In MacSween RNM, Anthony PP, Scheuer PJ, Burt AD, Portmann BC (eds): Pathology of the liver, ed. 3. Edinburgh, 1994, Churchill Livingstone, pp. 425–476.

12 Farci P, Mandas A, Coiana A, Lai ME, Desmet V, Van Eyken P, Gibo Y, Caruso L, Scaccabarozzi S, Criscuolo D, Ryff J-C. Treatment of chronic hepatitis D with interferon alpha-2a. N Engl J Med 1994, **330**: 88–94.

13 Ferrell L. Liver pathology: cirrhosis, hepatitis, and primary liver tumors. Update and diagnostic problems. Mod Pathol 2000, **13**: 679–704.

14 Gerber MA, Thung SN. Histology of the liver. Am J Surg Pathol 1987, **11**: 709–722.

15 Glenthøj A, Sehested M, Torp-Pedersen S. Diagnostic reliability of histological and cytological fine needle biopsies from focal liver lesions. Histopathology 1989, **15**: 375–383.

16 Hay JE, Czaja AJ, Rakela J, Ludwig J. The nature of unexplained chronic aminotransferase elevations of a mild to moderate degree in asymptomatic patients. Hepatology 1989, **9**: 193–197.

17 Hederström E, Forsberg L, Floren CH, Prytz H. Liver biopsy complications monitored by ultrasound. J Hepatol 1989, **8**: 97–98.

18 Levin DM, Baker AL, Riddell RH, Rochman H, Boyer JL. Non-alcoholic liver disease: overlooked causes of liver injury in patients with heavy alcohol consumption. Am J Med 1979, **66**: 429–434.

19 Lucey MR. Editorial. Serial liver biopsies: a gateway into understanding the long-term health of the liver allograft. J Hepatol 2001, **34**: 762–763.

20 Marcellin P, Boyer N, Giostra E, Degott C, Courouce AM, Degos F, Coppere H, Cales P, Couzigou P, Benhamou JP. Recombinant human alpha-interferon in patients with chronic non-A, non-B hepatitis: a multicenter randomized controlled trial from France. Hepatology 1991, **13**: 393–397.

21 Menghini G. One second biopsy of the liver; problems of its clinical application. N Engl J Med 1970, **283**: 582–585.

22 Perrault J, McGill DB, Ott BJ, Taylor W. Liver biopsy: complications in 1000 inpatients and outpatients. Gastroenterology 1978, **74**: 103–106.

23 Petrelli M, Scheuer PJ. Variation in subcapsular liver structure and its significance in the interpretation of wedge biopsies. J Clin Pathol 1967, **20**: 743–748.

24 Piccinino F, Sagnelli E, Pasquale G, Giusti G. "Complications following percutaneous liver biopsy; a multicentre retrospective study on 68.276 biopsies". J Hepatol 1986, **2**: 165–173.

25 Poupon RE, Balkau B, Eschwège E, Poupon R, UDCA-PBC Study Group. A multicenter, controlled trial of ursodiol for the treatment of primary biliary cirrhosis. N Engl J Med 1991, **324**: 1548–1554.

26 Roskams T, Baptista A, Bianchi L, Burt A, Callea F, Denk H, De Groote J, Desmet V, Hübscher S, Ishak K, MacSween R, Portmann B, Poulsen H, Scheuer P, Terracciano L, Thaler H. Histopathology of portal hypertension. A practical guideline. Histopathology 2002, **42**: 2–13.

27 Sciot R, Staessen D, Van Damme B, Van Steenbergen W, Fevery J, De Groote J, Desmet VJ. Incomplete septal cirrhosis: histopathological aspects. Histopathology 1988, **13**: 593–603.

28 Thung SN, Schaffner F. Liver biopsy. In MacSween RNM, Anthony PP, Scheuer PJ, Burt AD, Portmann BC (eds): Pathology of the liver, ed. 3. Edinburgh, 1994, Churchill Livingstone, pp. 787–796.

29 Van Eyken P. Cytokeratin immunohistochemistry in liver histopathology. Adv Clin Pathol 2000, **4**: 201–211.

30 Van Ness M, Diehl AM. Is liver biopsy useful in the evaluation of patients with chronically elevated liver enzymes? Ann Intern Med 1989, **111**: 473–478.

Viral hepatitis

Viral hepatitis caused by hepatotropic viruses

31 Aggarwal R, Krawczynski K. Hepatitis E: an overview and recent advances in clinical and laboratory research. J Gastroenterol Hepatol 2000, **15**: 9–20.

32 Alter HJ, Nakatsuji Y, Melpolder J, Wages J, Wesley R, Shih JW-K, Kim JP. The incidence of transfusion-associated hepatitis G virus infection and its relation to liver disease. N Engl J Med 1997, **336**: 747–754.

33 Alter HJ, Seeff LB. Recovery, persistence, and sequelae in hepatitis C virus infection: a perspective on long-term outcome. Semin Liver Dis 2000, **20**: 17–35.

34 Blum HE. Hepatitis B virus: significance of naturally occurring mutants. Intervirology 1993, **35**: 40–50.

35 Chu CW, Hwang SJ, Luo JC, Wang YJ, Lu RH, Lai CR, Tsay SH, Li CP, Wu JC, Chang FY, Lee SD. Clinical, virological, immunological, and pathological significance of GB virus/C hepatitis G infection in patients with chronic hepatitis C. Hepatol Res 2001, **19**: 225–236.

36 Fagan EA, Ellis DS, Tovey GM, Lloyd G, Smith HM, Portmann B, Tan KC, Zuckerman AJ, Williams R. Toga virus-like particles in acute liver failure attributed to sporadic non-A, non-B hepatitis and recurrence after liver transplantation. J Med Virol 1992, **38**: 71–77.

37 Feinstone SM, Kapikian AZ, Purcell RH, Alter HJ, Holland PV. Transfusion-associated hepatitis not due to viral hepatitis type A or B. New Engl J Med 1975, **292**: 767–770.

38 Foschini MP, Morandi L, Macchia S, Dal Monte PR, Pession A. TTV related acute recurrent hepatitis: histological features of a case and review of the literature. Virchows Arch 2001, **439**: 752–755.

39 Ikeda H, Takasu M, Inoue K, Okamoto H, Miyakawa Y, Mayumi M. Infection with an unenveloped DNA virus (TTV) in patients with acute or chronic liver disease in unknown etiology and in

those positive for hepatitis C virus RNA. J Hepatol 1999, **30:** 205–212.

40 Moriyama M, Matsumura H, Shimizu T, Shioda A, Kaneko M, Saito H, Miyazawa K, Tanaka N, Sugitani M, Komiyama K, Arakawa Y. Hepatitis G virus coinfection influences the liver histology of patients with chronic hepatitis C. Liver 2000, **20:** 397–404.

41 Naoumov NV, Eddleston ALWF. Host immune response and variations in the virus genome: pathogenesis of liver damage caused by hepatitis B virus. Gut 1994, **35:** 1013–1017.

42 Phillips MJ, Blendis LM, Poucell S, Patterson J, Petric M, Roberts E, Levy GA, Superina RA, Greig PD, Cameron R, Langer B, Purcell RH. Syncytial giant cell hepatitis: sporadic hepatitis with distinctive pathology, severe clinical course and paramyxoviral features. N Engl J Med 1991, **324:** 455–460.

43 Purcell R. The hepatitis C virus: overview. Hepatology 1997, **26** (Suppl 1): 11S–14S.

44 Purcell R. Hepatitis viruses: changing patterns of human disease. Proc Natl Acad Sci U S A 1994, **91:** 2401–2406.

45 Rehermann B. Interaction between the hepatitis C virus and the immune system. Semin Liver Dis 2000, **20:** 127–141.

46 Schaff Z, Lotz G, Schulte-Herman R. Pathomorphological characteristics and pathogenesis of viral hepatitis. Pathol Oncol Res 1996, **2:** 132–143.

47 Simmonds P, Davidson F, Lycett C, Prescott LE, MacDonald DM, Ellender J, Yap PL, Ludlam CA, Haydon GH, Gillon J, Jarvis LM. Detection of a novel DNA virus (TTV) in blood donors and blood products. Lancet 1998, **352:** 191–195.

48 Tuveri R, Jaffredo F, Lunel F, Nalpas B, Pol S, Feray C, Marcellin P, Thibault V, Delagneau JF, Opolon P, Scarpa B, Brechot C, Thiers V. Impact of TT virus infection in acute and chronic, viral and non-viral related liver disease. J Hepatol 2000, **33:** 121–127.

49 Umemura T, Yeo AE, Sottini A, Moratto D, Tanaka Y, Wang RY, Shi JW, Donahue P, Prime D, Alter HJ. SEN virus infection and its relationship to transfusion-associated hepatitis. Hepatology 2001, **33:** 1303–1311.

Acute viral hepatitis

50 Bianchi L. Liver biopsy interpretation in hepatitis. Part II: histopathology and classification of acute and chronic viral hepatitis/differential diagnosis. Pathol Res Pract 1983, **178:** 180–213.

51 Bianchi L, De Groote J, Desmet V, Gedigk P, Korb G, Popper H, Poulsen H, Scheuer P, Schmid M, Thaler H, Wepler W. Morphological criteria in viral hepatitis. Lancet 1971, **I:** 333–337.

52 Ishak KG. Light microscopic morphology of viral hepatitis. Am J Clin Pathol 1976, **65:** 787–827.

Typical acute viral hepatitis

53 Lau JY, Xie X, Lai MM, Wu PC. Apoptosis and viral hepatitis. Semin Liver Dis 1998, **18:** 169–176.

54 Mietkiewski JM, Scheuer PJ. Immunoglobulin-containing plasma cells in acute hepatitis. Liver 1985, **5:** 84–88.

55 Schaff Z, Lotz G, Schulte-Herman R. Pathomorphological characteristics and pathogenesis of viral hepatitis. Pathol Oncol Res 1996, **2:** 132–143.

56 Schmid M, Pirovino M, Altorfer J, Gudat F, Bianchi L. Acute hepatitis non-A, non-B; are there any specific light microscopic features? Liver 1982, **2:** 61–67.

57 Volpes R, Van den Oord JJ, Desmet VJ. Memory T cells represent the predominant lymphocyte subset in acute and chronic liver inflammation. Hepatology 1991, **13:** 826–829.

Severe acute hepatitis, acute hepatitis with bridging necrosis

58 Bianchi L, De Groote J, Desmet V, Gedigk P, Korb G, Popper H, Poulsen H, Scheuer P, Schmid M, Thaler H, Wepler W. Morphological criteria in viral hepatitis. Lancet 1971, **I:** 333–337.

59 Boyer JL. Chronic hepatitis. A perspective on classification and determinants of prognosis. Gastroenterology 1976, **70:** 1161–1171.

60 Boyer JL, Klatskin G. Prognostic value of bridging. N Engl J Med 1971, **283:** 1063–1071.

61 Scheuer PJ, Maggi G. Hepatic fibrosis and collapse: histological distinction by orcein staining. Histopathology 1980, **4:** 487–490.

Acute hepatitis with panlobular and multilobular necrosis (submassive liver necrosis)

62 Desmet V, Roskams T, Van Eyken P. Ductular reaction in the liver. Path Res Pract 1995, **191:** 513–524.

63 Roskams T, Desmet V. Ductular reaction and its diagnostic significance. Semin Diagn Pathol 1998, **15:** 259–269.

64 Schmid M, Cueni B. Portal lesions in viral hepatitis with submassive hepatic necrosis. Hum Pathol 1972, **3:** 209–216.

Causative viruses

65 Abe H, Beninger PR, Ikejiri N, Setoyama H, Sata M, Tanikawa K. Light microscopic findings of liver biopsy specimens from patients with hepatitis type A and comparison with type B. Gastroenterology 1982, **82:** 938–947.

66 Bianchi L. The immunopathology of acute type B hepatitis. Springer Semin Immunopathol 1981, **3:** 421–438.

67 Corpechot C, Cadranel JF, Hoang C, Assogba U, Beaumont JL, Rogeaux O, Lunel F, Opolon P. Hépatite virale A cholestatique de l'adulte. Gastroenterol Clin Biol 1994, **18:** 743–750.

68 Craig JR, Govindarajan S, DeCock KM. Delta viral hepatitis. Histopathology and course. Pathol Annu 1986, **21** (Pt 2): 1–21.

69 Desmet V. Liver lesions in hepatitis B viral infection. Yale J Biol Med 1988, **61:** 61–83.

70 Desmet VJ. Acute viral hepatitis: Hepatitis B. In Gitnick G (ed.): Modern concepts of acute and chronic hepatitis. New York, 1989, Plenum Publishing Corporation, pp. 87–111.

71 Dienes HP, Popper H, Arnold W, Lobeck H. Histologic observations in human hepatitis non-A, non-B. Hepatology 1982, **2:** 562–571.

72 Govindarajan S, DeCock KM, Peters RL. Morphologic and immunohistochemical features of fulminant delta hepatitis. Hum Pathol 1985, **16:** 262–268.

73 Kryger P, Christoffersen P. Liver histopathology of the hepatitis A virus infection: a comparison with hepatitis type B and non-A, non-B. J Clin Pathol 1983, **36:** 650–654.

74 Lefkowitch JH, Apfelbaum TF. Non-A, non-B hepatitis: characterization of liver biopsy pathology. J Clin Gastroenterol 1989, **11:** 225–232.

75 Lok ASF, Lindsay I, Scheuer PJ, Thomas HC. Clinical and histological features of delta infection in chronic hepatitis B virus carriers. J Clin Pathol 1985, **38:** 530–533.

76 Min KW, Gyorkey F, Cain GD. Talc granulomata in liver disease in narcotic addicts. Arch Pathol 1974, **98:** 331–335.

77 Molos MA, Litton N, Schubert TT. Talc liver. J Clin Gastroenterol 1987, **9:** 198–203.

78 Negro F. Detection of hepatitis C virus RNA in liver tissue: an overview. Ital J Gastroenterol Hepatol 1998, **30:** 205–210.

79 Okuno T, Sano A, Deguchi T, Katsuma Y, Ogasawara T, Okanoue T, Takino T. Pathology of acute hepatitis A in humans. Comparison with acute hepatitis B. Am J Clin Pathol 1984, **81:** 162–169.

80 Popper H, Thung SN, Gerber MA, Hadler SC, de Monzon M, Ponzetto A, Anzola E, Rivera D, Mondolfi A, Bracho A. Histologic studies of severe delta agent infection in Venezuelan Indians. Hepatology 1983, **3:** 906–912.

81 Ruel M, Sevestre H, Henry-Biabaud E, Courouce AM, Capron JP, Erlinger S. Fibrin ring granulomas in hepatitis A. Dig Dis Sci 1992, **37:** 1915–1917.

82 Rugge M, Vanstapel MJ, Ninfo V, Realdi G, Tremolada F,

Montanari PG, Van Damme B, Fevery J, De Groote J, Desmet V. Comparative histology of acute hepatitis B and non-A, non-B in Leuven and Padova. Virchows Arch [A] 1983, **401:** 275–288.

83 Ryley NG, Heryet AR, Goldin R, Monjardino J, Saldanha J, Fleming KA. Co-expression of markers for hepatitis delta and hepatitis B viruses in human liver. Histopathology 1992, **20:** 331–337.

84 Schmid M, Cueni B. Portal lesions in viral hepatitis with submassive hepatic necrosis. Hum Pathol 1972, **3:** 209–216.

85 Sciot R, Van Damme B, Desmet VJ. Cholestatic features in hepatitis A. J Hepatol 1986, **3:** 172–181.

86 Shimizu YK, Shikata T, Beninger PR, Sata M, Setoyama H, Abe H, Tanikawa K. Detection of hepatitis A antigen in human liver. Infect Immun 1982, **36:** 320–324.

87 Taylor M, Goldin RD, Ladva S, Scheuer PJ, Thomas HC. In situ hybridization studies of hepatitis A viral RNA in patients with acute hepatitis A. J Hepatol 1994, **20:** 380–387.

88 Teixeira MR, Weller IV, Murray A, Bamber M, Thomas HC, Sherlock S, Scheuer PJ. The pathology of hepatitis A in man. Liver 1982, **2:** 53–60.

89 Verme G, Amoroso P, Lettieri G, Pierri P, David E, Sessa F, Rizzi R, Bonino F, Recchia S, Rizzetto M. A histologic study of hepatitis delta virus liver disease. Hepatology 1986, **6:** 1303–1307.

90 Villari D, Raimondo G, Attard L, Verucchi G, Spinella S, Pernice M, Rodino G. Polyphasic type A hepatitis: histological features. Infection 1993, **21:** 46–48.

91 Yamamoto T, Ishii M, Nagura H, Miyazaki Y, Miura M, Igarashi T, Toyota T. Transient hepatic fibrin-ring granulomas in a patient with acute hepatitis A. Liver 1995, **15:** 276–279.

Chronic (viral and other) hepatitis
Elementary lesions

92 Desmet V. Liver lesions in hepatitis B viral infection. Yale J Biol Med 1988, **61:** 61–83.

93 Desmet VJ. Current problems in diagnosis of biliary disease and cholestasis. Semin Liver Dis 1986, **6:** 233–245.

94 Galle PR. Apoptosis in liver disease. J Hepatol 1997, **27:** 405–412.

95 Paradis V, Mathurin P, Laurent A, Charlotte F, Vidaud M, Poynard T, Hoang C, Opolon P, Bedossa P. Histological features predictive of liver fibrosis in chronic hepatitis C infection. J Clin Pathol 1996, **49:** 998–1004.

96 Popper H, Paronetto F, Schaffner F. Immune processes in the pathogenesis of liver disease. Ann NY Acad Sci 1965, **124:** 781–799.

97 Powell LW. The nature of cell death in piecemeal necrosis: is order emerging from chaos? Hepatology 1987, **7:** 794–796.

98 Searle J, Harmon BV, Bishop CJ, Kerr JFR. The significance of cell death by apoptosis in hepatobiliary disease. J Gastroenterol Hepatol 1987, **2:** 77–96.

99 Villari D, Raimondo G, Brancatelli S, Longo G, Rodino G, Smedile V. Histological features in liver biopsy specimens of patients with acute reactivation of chronic type B hepatitis. Histopathology 1991, **18:** 73–77.

Classification

100 Chen DS. Natural history of chronic hepatitis B virus infection: new light on an old story. J Gastroenterol Hepatol 1993, **8:** 470–475.

101 Chu CM, Karayiannis P, Fowler MJF, Monjardino J, Liaw YF, Thomas HC. Natural history of chronic hepatitis B virus infection in Taiwan. Studies of hepatitis B virus DNA in serum. Hepatology 1985, **5:** 431–434.

102 De Groote J, Desmet VJ, Gedigk P, Korb G, Popper H, Poulsen H, Scheuer P, Schmid M, Thaler H, Uehlinger E, Wepler W. A classification of chronic hepatitis. Lancet 1968, **II:** 626–628.

103 Desmet VJ. Histological classification of chronic hepatitis. Acta Gastroenterol Belg 1997, **60:** 259–267.

104 Desmet VJ, Gerber M, Hoofnagle JH, Manns M, Scheuer PJ. Classification of chronic hepatitis: diagnosis, grading and staging. Hepatology 1994, **19:** 1513–1520.

105 Gerber MA. Chronic hepatitis C: the beginning of the end of a time-honored nomenclature? Hepatology 1992, **15:** 733–734.

106 Hodges JR, Millward-Sadler GH, Wright R. Chronic active hepatitis: the spectrum of disease. Lancet 1982, **1:** 550–552.

107 Ishak KG. Chronic hepatitis: morphology and nomenclature. Mod Pathol 1994, **7:** 690–713.

108 Iversen P, Roholm K. On aspiration biopsy of the liver, with remarks on its diagnostic signification. Acta Med Scand 1939, **102:** 1–16.

109 Johnson PJ, McFarlane IG, convenors, on behalf of the panel. Meeting report: International Autoimmune Hepatitis Group. Hepatology 1993, **18:** 998–1005.

110 Ludwig J. The nomenclature of chronic active hepatitis: an obituary. Gastroenterology 1993, **105:** 274–278.

111 Pessayre D, Larrey D. Acute and chronic drug-induced hepatitis. Baillières Clin Gastroenterol 1988, **2:** 385–422.

112 Purcell R. Hepatitis viruses: changing patterns of human disease. Proc Natl Acad Sci U S A 1994, **91:** 2401–2406.

113 Reynolds TB, Peters RL, Yamada S. Chronic active and lupoid hepatitis caused by a laxative, oxyphenisatin. N Engl J Med 1971, **285:** 813–820.

114 Scheuer PJ. Changing views on chronic hepatitis. Histopathology 1986, **10:** 1–4.

115 Scheuer PJ. Classification of chronic viral hepatitis: a need for reassessment. J Hepatol 1991, **13:** 372–374.

116 Scott J, Gollan JL, Samourian S, Sherlock S. Wilson's disease presenting as chronic active hepatitis. Gastroenterology 1978, **74:** 645–651.

117 Sternlieb I, Scheinberg IH. Chronic hepatitis as a first manifestation of Wilson's disease. Ann Intern Med 1972, **76:** 59–64.

118 Waldenström J. Leber, Blutproteine und Nahrungseiweisz. Bad Kissingen, 1950, Dtsch Z Verdau Stoffwechselkr, **10** (Sonderband XV Tagung): 8.

119 Working Party. Terminology of chronic hepatitis, hepatic allograft rejection, and nodular lesions of the liver: summary of recommendations developed by an international working party, supported by the World Congresses of Gastroenterology, Los Angeles, 1994. Am J Gastroenterol 1994, **89:** S177–S181.

Grading and staging

120 Batts KP, Ludwig J. Chronic hepatitis. An update on terminology and reporting. Am J Surg Pathol 1995, **19:** 1409–1417.

121 Bedossa P. Présentation d'une grille d'analyse informatisée pour le recueil des lésions histopathologiques dans l'hépatite chronique virale C. Ann Pathol 1993, **13:** 260–265.

122 Bedossa P, Bioulac-Sage P, Callard P, Chevallier M, Degott C, Deugnier Y, Fabre M, Reynes M, Voigt JJ, Zafrani ES. Intraobserver and interobserver variations in liver biopsy interpretation in patients with chronic hepatitis C. Hepatology 1994, **20:** 15–20.

123 Bedossa P, Poynard T, Group MCS. An algorithm for the grading of activity in chronic hepatitis C. Hepatology 1996, **24:** 289–293.

124 Brunt EM. Grading and staging the histopathological lesions of chronic hepatitis: the Knodell Histology Activity Index and beyond. Hepatology 2000, **31:** 241–246.

125 Caballero T, Perez-Milena A, Masseroli M, O'Valle F, Salmeron FJ, Del Moral RMG, Sanchez-Salgado G. Liver fibrosis assessment with semiquantitative indexes and image analysis quantification in sustained-responder and non-responder interferon-treated patients with chronic hepatitis C. J Hepatol 2001, **34:** 740–747.

126 Chevallier M, Guerret S, Chossegros P, Gerard F, Grimaud JA. A histological semiquantitative scoring system for evaluation of

hepatic fibrosis in needle liver biopsy specimens: comparison with morphometric studies. Hepatology 1994, **20**: 349–355.

127 Cross SS. Review. Grading and scoring in histopathology. Histopathology 1998, **33**: 99–106.

128 Demeulenaere F, Desmet VJ, Dupont E, Fiasse R, Gisselbrecht H, Heully F, Jeanpierre R, Lecompte J, Lennes G, Macinot C, Migeotte P, Pirotte J, Rauber G, Ruyters L, Van Cauwenberge H. Effects du (+)-cyanidanol-3 dans le traitement de l'hépatite chronique active. Gastroenterol Clin Biol 1981, **5**: 314–323.

129 Desmet VJ, Gerber M, Hoofnagle JH, Manns M, Scheuer PJ. Classification of chronic hepatitis: diagnosis, grading and staging. Hepatology 1994, **19**: 1513–1520.

130 Dioguardi N, Grizi F, Bossi P, Roncalli M. Fractal and spectral dimension analysis of liver fibrosis in needle biopsy specimens. Anal Quant Cytol Histol 1999, **21**: 262–266.

131 Duchatelle V, Marcellin P, Giostra E, Bregeaud L, Pouteau M, Boyer N, Auperin A, Guerret S, Erlinger S, Henin D, Degott C. Changes in liver fibrosis at the end of alpha interferon therapy and 6 to 18 months later in patients with chronic hepatitis C: quantitative assessment by a morphometric method. J Hepatol 1998, **29**: 20–28.

132 Fleming KA. Evidence-based pathology. J Pathol 1996, **179**: 127–128.

133 Goldin RD, Goldin JG, Burt AD, Dhillon PA, Hubscher S, Wyatt J, Patel N. Intra-observer and inter-observer variation in the histopathological assessment of chronic viral hepatitis. J Hepatol 1996, **25**: 649–654.

134 Hall PDL. Broadsheet number 47: Chronic hepatitis: an update with guidelines for histopathological assessment of liver biopsies. Pathology 1998, **30**: 369–380.

135 Hübscher SG. Histological grading and staging in chronic hepatitis: clinical applications and problems. J Hepatol 1998, **29**: 1015–1022.

136 Hunt N, Fleming K. Reproducibility of liver biopsy grading and staging. Liver 1999, **19**: 169–170.

137 Hytiroglou P, Thung SN, Gerber MA. Histological classification and quantitation of the severity of chronic hepatitis: keep it simple! Semin Liver Dis 1995, **15**: 414–421.

138 Ichida F, Tsuji T, Omata M, Ichida T, Inoue K, Kamimura T, Yamada G, Hino K, Yokosuka O, Suzuki H. Classification report. New Inuyama Classification: new criteria for histological assessment of chronic hepatitis. Int Hepatol Commun 1996, **6**: 112–119.

139 Ishak K, Baptista A, Bianchi L, Callea F, De Groote J, Gudat F, Denk H, Desmet V, Korb B, MacSween RNM, Phillips MJ, Portmann BG, Poulsen H, Scheuer PJ, Schmid M, Thaler H. Histological grading and staging of chronic hepatitis. J Hepatol 1995, **22**: 696–699.

140 Ishak KG. Pathologic features of chronic hepatitis: a review and update. Am J Clin Pathol 2000, **113**: 40–55.

141 Knodell RG, Ishak KG, Black WC, Chen TS, Craig R, Kaplowitz N, Kiernan TW, Wollman J. Formulation and application of a numerical scoring system for assessing histological activity in asymptomatic chronic active hepatitis. Hepatology 1981, **1**: 431–435.

142 Lok ASF, Lindsay I, Scheuer PJ, Thomas HC. Clinical and histological features of delta infection in chronic hepatitis B virus carriers. J Clin Pathol 1985, **38**: 530–533.

143 Ludwig J. The nomenclature of chronic active hepatitis: an obituary. Gastroenterology 1993, **105**: 274–278.

144 Masseroli M, Caballero T, O'Valle F, Del Moral RMG, Perez-Milena A, Del Moral RG. Automatic quantification of liver fibrosis: design and validation of a new image analysis method: comparison with semiquantitative indexes of fibrosis. J Hepatol 2000, **32**: 453–464.

145 Pilette C, Rousselet MC, Bedossa P, Chappard D, Oberti F, Rifflet H, Maiga MY, Gallois Y, Cales P. Histopathological evaluation of liver fibrosis: quantitative image analysis versus semi-

quantitative scores. Comparison with serum markers. J Hepatol 1998, **28**: 439–446.

146 Poynard T, Ratziu V, Benhamou Y, Di Martino V, Bedossa P, Opolon P. Fibrosis in patients with chronic hepatitis C: detection and significance. Semin Liver Dis 2000, **20**: 47–55.

147 Poynard T, Ratziu V, Charlotte F, Goodman Z, McHutchison J, Albrecht J. Rates and risk factors of liver fibrosis progression in patients with chronic hepatitis C. J Hepatol 2001, **34**: 730–739.

148 Reichard O, Glaumann H, Fryden A, Norkrans G, Schvarcz R, Sönnerborg A, Yun Z-B, Weiland O. Two-year biochemical, virological, and histological follow-up in patients with chronic hepatitis C responding in a sustained fashion to interferon Alfa-2b treatment. Hepatology 1995, **21**: 918–922.

149 Scheuer PJ. Classification of chronic viral hepatitis: a need for reassessment. J Hepatol 1991, **13**: 372–374.

150 Scheuer PJ. Scoring of liver biopsies: are we doing it right? Eur J Gastroenterol Hepatol 1996, **8**: 1141–1143.

151 Trinchet JC, Gerhardt MF, Balkau B, Munz C, Poupon RE. Serum bile acids and cholestasis in alcoholic hepatitis. Relationship with usual liver tests and histological features. J Hepatol 1994, **21**: 235–240.

152 Westin J, Lagging LM, Westjal R, Norkrans G, Dhillon P. Interobserver study of liver histopathology using the Ishak score in patients with chronic hepatitis C virus infection. Liver 1999, **19**: 183–187.

Histopathology

153 Alberti A, Morsica G, Chemello L, Cavalletto D, Noventa F, Pontisso P, Ruol A. Hepatitis C viraemia and liver disease in symptom-free individuals with anti-HCV. Lancet 1992, **340**: 697–698.

154 Allory Y, Charlotte F, Benhamou Y, Opolon P, Le Charpentier Y, Poynard T. Impact of human immunodeficiency virus infection on the histological features of chronic hepatitis C: a case control study. The MULTIVIRC group. Hum Pathol 2000, **31**: 69–74.

155 Alonso-Marti C, Moreno A, Barat A, Solera JC, Oliva H. Co-existence of hepatocyte ground-glass inclusions from several causes. Histopathology 1990, **16**: 304–307.

156 Alter HJ, Seeff LB. Recovery, persistence, and sequelae in hepatitis C virus infection: a perspective on long-term outcome. Semin Liver Dis 2000, **20**: 17–35.

157 Anthony PP, Vogel CL, Barker LF. Liver cell dysplasia: a premalignant condition. J Clin Pathol 1973, **26**: 217–223.

158 Bach N, Thung SN, Schaffner F. The histological features of chronic hepatitis C and autoimmune chronic hepatitis: a comparative analysis. Hepatology 1992, **15**: 572–577.

159 Badizadegan K, Jonas MJ, Ott MJ, Nelson SP, Perez-Atayde AR. Histopathology of the liver in children with chronic hepatitis C viral infection. Hepatology 1998, **28**: 1416–1423.

160 Bannayan GA, Dean WJ, Howell RR. Type IV glycogen-storage disease. Light microscopic, electron-microscopic and enzymatic study. Am J Clin Pathol 1976, **66**: 702–709.

161 Bianchi L, Gudat F. Sanded nuclei in hepatitis B. Eosinophilic inclusions in liver cell nuclei due to excess in hepatitis B core antigen formation. Lab Invest 1976, **35**: 1–5.

162 Bonino F, Negro F, Baldi M, Brunetto MR, Chiaberge E, Capalbo M, Maran E, Lavarini C, Rocca N, Rocca G. The natural history of chronic delta hepatitis. Prog Clin Biol Res 1987, **234**: 145–152.

163 Bonkovsky HL, Banner BF, Rothman AL. Iron and chronic viral hepatitis. Hepatology 1997, **25**: 759–768.

164 Bonkovsky HL, Poh-Fitzpatrick M, Pimstone M, Obando J, Di Bisceglie A, Tattrie C, Tortorelli K, LeClair P, Mercurio M, Lambrecht RW. Porphyria cutanea tarda, hepatitis C and HFE gene mutations in North America. Hepatology 1998, **27**: 1661–1699.

165 Booth JCL, Foster GR, Levine T, Thomas HC, Goldin RD. The relationship of histology to genotype in chronic HCV infection. Liver 1997, **17**: 144–151.

166 Boyer N, Marcellin P. Pathogenesis, diagnosis and management of hepatitis C. J Hepatol 2000, **32** (Suppl 1): 98–112.

167 Bralet MP, Roudot-Thoraval F, Pawlotsky JM, Bastie A, Tran Van Nhieu J, Duval J, Dhumeaux D, Zafrani ES. Histopathologic impact of GB virus C infection on chronic hepatitis C. Gastroenterology 1997, **112**: 188–192.

168 Bralet MP, Zafrani ES. Diagnosis and histologic surveillance of hepatitis C. Rev Prat 2000, **50**: 1078–1082.

169 Brillanti S, Foli M, Gaiani S, Masci C, Miglioli M, Barbara L. Persistent hepatitis C viraemia without liver disease. Lancet 1993, **341**: 464–465.

170 Bruguera M, Lamar C, Bernet M, Rodaos J. Hepatic disease associated with ground-glass inclusions in hepatocytes after cyanamide therapy. Arch Pathol Lab Med 1986, **110**: 906–910.

171 Brunetto MR, Stemler M, Schödel F, Will H, Ottobrelli A, Rizzetto M, Verme G, Bonino F. Identification of HBV variants which cannot produce precore derived HBeAg and may be responsible for severe hepatitis. Ital J Gastroenterol 1989, **21**: 151–154.

172 Callea F, De Vos R, Togni R, Tardanico R, Vanstapel MJ, Desmet VJ. Fibrinogen inclusions in liver cells: a new type of ground-glass hepatocyte. Immune light and electron microscopic characterization. Histopathology 1986, **10**: 65–73.

173 Chen DS. Natural history of chronic hepatitis B virus infection: new light on an old story. J Gastroenterol Hepatol 1993, **8**: 470–475.

174 Chen DS, Sung JL. Hepatitis Be antigen and its antibody in chronic type B hepatitis. J Gastroenterol Hepatol 1987, **2**: 255–270.

175 Christoffersen P, Poulsen H, Scheuer PJ. Abnormal bile duct epithelium in chronic aggressive hepatitis and primary biliary cirrhosis. Hum Pathol 1972, **3**: 227–235.

176 Chu CM, Liaw YF. Immunohistological study of intrahepatic expression of hepatitis B core and E antigens in chronic type B hepatitis. J Clin Pathol 1992, **45**: 791–795.

177 Chu CM, Liaw YF. Membrane staining for hepatitis B surface antigen in hepatocytes: a sensitive and specific marker of active viral replication in hepatitis B. J Clin Pathol 1995, **48**: 470–473.

178 Colin JF, Cazals-Hatem D, Loriot MA, Martinot-Peignoux M, Pham BN, Auperin A, Degott C, Benhamou JP, Erlinger S, Valla D, Marcellin P. Influence of human immunodeficiency virus infection in chronic hepatitis B in homosexual men. Hepatology 1999, **29**: 1306–1310.

179 Colombari R, Dhillon AP, Piazzola E, Tomezzoli AA, Angelini GP, Capra F, Tomba A, Scheuer PJ. Chronic hepatitis in multiple virus infection: histopathological evaluation. Histopathology 1993, **22**: 319–325.

180 Crawford JM. Pathologic assessment of liver cell dysplasia and benign liver tumors: differentiation from malignant tumors. Semin Diagn Pathol 1990, **7**: 115–128.

181 Czaja AJ, Carpenter HA. Autoimmune hepatitis with incidental histologic features of bile duct injury. Hepatology 2001, **34**: 659–665.

182 Czaja AJ, Carpenter HA. Sensitivity, specificity, and predictability of biopsy interpretations in chronic hepatitis. Gastroenterology 1993, **105**: 1824–1832.

183 Czaja AJ, Carpenter HA, Santrach PJ, Moore SB. Host- and disease-specific factors affecting steatosis in chronic hepatitis C. J Hepatol 1998, **29**: 198–206.

184 Davis GL, Hoofnagle JH. Reactivation of chronic type B hepatitis presenting as acute viral hepatitis. Ann Intern Med 1985, **102**: 762–765.

185 Desmet VJ. Immunopathology of chronic viral hepatitis. Hepatogastroenterology 1991, **38**: 14–21.

186 Devaney K, Goodman ZD, Ishak KG. Postinfantile giant-cell transformation in hepatitis. Hepatology 1992, **16**: 327–333.

187 Dhillon AP, Dusheiko GM. Pathology of hepatitis C virus infection. Histopathology 1995, **26**: 297–309.

188 DiBisceglie AM, Simpson LH, Lotze MT, Hoofnagle JH.

189 Dienes HP, Drebber U, von Both I. Liver biopsy in hepatitis C. J Hepatol 1999, **31** (Suppl 1): 43–46.

190 Emile JF, Sebagh M, Féray C, David F, Reynès M. The presence of epithelioid granulomas in hepatitis C virus-related cirrhosis. Hum Pathol 1993, **24**: 1095–1097.

191 Fattovich G, Boscaro S, Noventa F, Pornaro E, Stenico D, Alberti A, Ruol A, Realdi G. Influence of hepatitis delta virus infection on progression to cirrhosis in chronic hepatitis type B. J Infect Dis 1987, **155**: 931–935.

192 Ferrell LD, Crawford JM, Dhillon AP, Scheuer PJ, Nakanuma Y. Proposal for standardized criteria for the diagnosis of benign, borderline, and malignant hepatocellular lesions arising in chronic advanced liver disease. Am J Surg Pathol 1993, **17**: 1113–1123.

193 Freni MA, Artuso D, Gerken G, Spanti C, Marafioti T, Alessi N, Spadaro A, Ajello A, Ferrau O. Focal lymphocytic aggregates in chronic hepatitis C: occurrence, immunohistochemical characterization, and relation to markers of autoimmunity. Hepatology 1995, **22**: 389–394.

194 Furuya K, Nakamura M, Yamamoto Y, Togei K, Otsuka H. Macroregenerative nodule of the liver. A clinicopathologic study of 345 autopsy cases of chronic liver disease. Cancer 1988, **61**: 99–105.

195 Gerber MA, Hadziyannis S, Vissoulis C, Schaffner F, Paronetto F, Popper H. Electron microscopy and immuno-electronmicroscopy of cytoplasmic hepatitis B antigen in hepatocytes. Am J Pathol 1974, **75**: 489–502.

196 Gerber MA, Krawczynski K, Alter MJ, Sampliner RE, Margolis HS, the Sentinel Counties chronic non-A non-B hepatitis Study Team. Histopathology of community acquired chronic hepatitis C. Mod Pathol 1992, **5**: 483–486.

197 Goldin RD, Levine TS, Foster GR, Thomas HC. Granulomas and hepatitis C. Histopathology 1996, **28**: 265–267.

198 Goldin RD, Patel NK, Thomas HC. Hepatitic C and bile duct loss. J Clin Pathol 1996, **49**: 836–838.

199 Goldstein NS, Kodali VP, Godon SC. Histologic spectrum of cryptogenic chronic liver disease and comparison with chronic autoimmune and chronic type C hepatitis. Am J Clin Pathol 1995, **104**: 567–573.

200 Goodman ZD, Ishak KG. Histopathology of hepatitis C virus infection. Semin Liver Dis 1995, **15**: 70–81.

201 Hadziyannis S, Gerber MA, Vissoulis C, Popper H. Cytoplasmic hepatitis B antigen in "ground-glass" hepatocytes of carriers. Arch Pathol 1973, **96**: 327–330.

202 Hall PDL. Broadsheet number 47: Chronic hepatitis: an update with guidelines for histopathological assessment of liver biopsies. Pathology 1998, **30**: 369–380.

203 Haque S, Chandra B, Gerber MA, Lok ASF. Iron overload in patients with chronic hepatitis C: a clinicopathologic study. Hum Pathol 1996, **27**: 1277–1281.

204 Harada K, Minato H, Hiramatsu K, Nakanuma Y. Epithelioid cell granulomas in chronic hepatitis C: immunohistochemical character and histological marker of favourable response to interferon-α therapy. Histopathology 1998, **33**: 216–221.

205 Henmy A, Uchida T, Shikata T. Karyometric analysis of liver cell dysplasia and hepatocellular carcinoma. Evidence against precancerous nature of liver cell dysplasia. Cancer 1985, **55**: 2594–2599.

206 Hino K, Okuda M, Konishi T, Yamashita A, Kayano K, Kubota M, Yasunaga M, Fukumoto Y, Okita K. Analysis of lymphoid follicles in liver of patients with chronic hepatitis C. Liver 1992, **12**: 387–391.

207 Hoffmann RM, Jung MC, Motz R, Gössl C, Emslander HP, Zachoval R, Pape GR. Case report. Sarcoidosis associated with

interferon-α therapy for chronic hepatitis C. J Hepatol 1998, **28:** 1058–1063.

208 Hsu HC, Lai MY, Su IJ, Chen DS, Chang MH, Yang PM, Wu CY, Hsieh HC. Correlation of hepatocyte HBsAg expression with virus replication and liver pathology. Hepatology 1988, **8:** 749–754.

209 Hsu HC, Su IJ, Lai MY, Chen DS, Chang MH, Chuang SM, Sung JL. Biologic and prognostic significance of hepatocyte hepatitis B core antigen expressions in the natural course of chronic hepatitis B virus infection. J Hepatol 1987, **5:** 45–50.

210 Hu B, French SW. Mallory body and empty cell in hepatitis C. Hepatol Res 1997, **8:** 13–20.

211 Huang SN, Chen CT, Tsai SL, Liaw YF. Histopathology and pathobiology of hepatotropic virus-induced liver injury. J Gastroenterol Hepatol 1997, **12:** S195–S217.

212 International Autoimmune Hepatitis Group. International Autoimmune Hepatitis Group Report: review of criteria for diagnosis of autoimmune hepatitis. J Hepatol 1999, **31:** 929–938.

213 International Working Party. Terminology of nodular hepatocellular lesions. Hepatology 1995, **22:** 983–993.

214 Ishak KG. Pathologic features of chronic hepatitis: a review and update. Am J Clin Pathol 2000, **113:** 40–55.

215 Jezequel AM, Librari ML, Mosca P, Novel-Li G, Lorenzini I, Orlandi F. Changes induced in human liver by long-term anticonvulsant therapy. Functional and ultrastructural data. Liver 1984, **4:** 307–330.

216 Kage M, Fujisawa T, Shiraki K, Tanaka T, Fujisawa T, Kimura A, Shimamatsu K, Nakashima E, Kojiro M, Koike M, Tazawa Y, Abukawa D, Okaniwa M, Takita H, Matsui A, Hayashi T, Etou T, Terasawa S, Sugiyama K, Tajiri H, Yoden A, Kajiwara Y, Sata M, Uchimura Y. Pathology of chronic hepatitis C in children. Hepatology 1997, **26:** 771–775.

217 Kao JH, Chen W, Chen PJ, Lai MY, Chen DS. TT virus infection in patients with chronic hepatitis B or C: influence on clinical, histological and virological features. J Med Virol 2000, **60:** 387–392.

218 Klinge O, Bannasch P. The increase of smooth endoplasmatic reticulum in hepatocytes of human liver punctates. Verh Dtsch Ges Pathol 1968, **52:** 568–573.

219 Kobayashi K, Hashimoto E, Ludwig J, Hisamitsu T, Obata H. Liver biopsy features of acute hepatitis C compared with hepatitis A, B and non-A, non-B, non-C. Liver 1993, **13:** 69–73.

220 Kojima T, Callea F, Desmyter J, Sakurai I, Desmet VJ. Immuno-light and electron microscopic features of chronic hepatitis D. Liver 1990, **10:** 17–27.

221 Lau JY, Koukoulis G, Mieli-Vergani G, Portmann BC, Williams R. Syncytial giant-cell hepatitis. A specific disease entity? J Hepatol 1992, **15:** 216–219.

222 Lau JYN, Portmann BC, Alexander GJH, Williams R. Differential effect of chronic hepatitis D virus infection on intrahepatic expression of hepatitis B viral antigen. J Clin Pathol 1992, **45:** 314–318.

223 Lefkowitch JH, Apfelbaum TF. Liver cell dysplasia and hepatocellular carcinoma in non-A, non-B hepatitis. Arch Pathol Lab Med 1987, **111:** 170–173.

224 Lefkowitch JH, Schiff ER, Davis GL, Perillo RP, Lindsay K, Bodenheimer HC Jr, Balart LA, Ortego TJ, Payne J, Dienstag JL, Gibas A, Jacobson IM, Tamburro CH, Carey W, O'Brien C, Sampliner R, Van Thiel DH, Feit D, Albrecht J. Pathological diagnosis of chronic hepatitis C: a multicenter comparative study with chronic hepatitis B. Gastroenterology 1993, **104:** 595–603.

225 Lefkowitch JH, Yee HT, Sweeting J, Green PHR, Magun AM. Iron-rich foci in chronic hepatitis. Hum Pathol 1998, **29:** 116–118.

226 Liaw YF. Role of hepatitis C virus in dual and triple hepatitis virus infection. Hepatology 1995, **22:** 1101–1108.

227 Liaw YF, Tsai SL, Sheen IS, Chao M, Yeh CT, Hsieh SY, Chu CM. Clinical and virological course of chronic hepatitis B virus infection with hepatitis C and D virus markers. Am J Gastroenterol 1998, **93:** 354–359.

228 Liaw YF, Yang SS, Chen TJ, Chu CM. Acute exacerbation in hepatitis B e antigen-positive chronic type B hepatitis – a clinico-pathological study. J Hepatol 1985, **1:** 227–233.

229 Libbrecht L, Craninx M, Nevens F, Desmet V, Roskams T. Predictive value of liver cell dysplasia for development of hepatocellular carcinoma in patients with non-cirrhotic and cirrhotic chronic viral hepatitis. Histopathology 2001, **39:** 66–73.

230 Lindh M, Savage K, Rees J, Garwood L, Horal P, Norkrans G, Dhillon AP. HBeAg immunostaining of liver tissue in various stages of chronic hepatitis B. Liver 1999, **19:** 294–298.

231 Lok ASF, Lindsay I, Scheuer PJ, Thomas HC. Clinical and histological features of delta infection in chronic hepatitis B virus carriers. J Clin Pathol 1985, **38:** 530–533.

232 Lok ASF, McMahon BJ. Chronic hepatitis B. Hepatology 2001, **34:** 1225–1241.

233 Lory J, Zimmermann A. Endotheliitis-like changes in chronic hepatitis C. Histol Histopathol 1997, **12:** 359–366.

234 Meyer zum Büschenfelde KH, Dienes HP. Autoimmune hepatitis. Definition – classification – histopathology – immunopathogenesis. Virchows Arch 1996, **429:** 1–12.

235 Mihm S, Fayyazi A, Hartmann H, Ramadori G. Analysis of histopathological manifestations of chronic hepatitis C virus infection with respect to virus genotype. Hepatology 1997, **25:** 735–739.

236 Moreno A, Ramon Y, Cajal S, Marazuela M, Carreno V, Milicua JM, Cerezo E, Ciesta C, Oliva H. Sanded nuclei in delta patients. Liver 1989, **9:** 367–371.

237 Mosnier JF, Degott C, Marcellin P, Henin D, Erlinger S, Benhamou JP. The intraportal lymphoid nodule and its environment in chronic active hepatitis C: an immunohistochemical study. Hepatology 1993, **17:** 366–371.

238 Nakanuma Y, Terada T, Veda K, Terasaki S, Nonomura A, Matsui O. Adenomatous hyperplasia of the liver as a precancerous lesion. Liver 1993, **13:** 1–9.

239 Naoumov NV, Schneider R, Grötzinger T, Jung MC, Miska S, Pape GR, Will H. Precore mutant hepatitis B virus infection and liver disease. Gastroenterology 1992, **102:** 538–543.

240 Negro F. Detection of hepatitis C virus RNA in liver tissue: an overview. Ital J Gastroenterol Hepatol 1998, **30:** 205–210.

241 Negro F, Pacchioni D, Bussolati G, Bonino F. Hepatitis delta virus heterogeneity: a study by immunofluorescence. J Hepatol 1991, **13** (Suppl 4): S125–S129.

242 Negro F, Rizzetto M. Pathobiology of hepatitis delta virus. J Hepatol 1993, **17:** S149–S153.

243 Nelson DR, Lau JYN. Pathogenesis of hepatocellular damage in chronic hepatitis virus infection. Clin Liver Dis 1997, **1:** 515–528.

244 Nishimura RN, Ishak KG, Reddick R, Porter R, James S, Barranger JA. Lafora disease: diagnosis by liver biopsy. Ann Neurol 1979, **8:** 409–415.

245 Okuno T, Arai K, Matsumoto M, Shindo M. Epithelioid granulomas in chronic hepatitis C: a transient pathological feature. J Gastroenterol Hepatol 1995, **10:** 532–537.

246 Ong JP, Younossi ZM, Speer C, Olno A, Gramlich T, Boparai N. Chronic hepatitis C and superimposed nonalcoholic fatty liver disease. Liver 2001, **21:** 266–271.

247 Park YN, Han KH, Kim KS, Chung JP, Kim S, Park C. Cytoplasmic expression of hepatitis B core antigen in chronic hepatitis B virus infection: role of precore stop mutants. Liver 1999, **19:** 199–205.

248 Perillo RP, Brunt EM. Hepatic histologic and immunohistochemical changes in chronic hepatitis B after prolonged clearance of HBeAg and hepatitis B surface antigen. Ann Intern Med 1991, **115:** 113–115.

249 Piperno A, Vergani A, Malosio I, Parma L, Fossati L, Ricci A, Bovo G, Boari G, Mancia G. Hepatic iron overload in patients

with chronic viral hepatitis: role of HFE mutations. Hepatology 1998, **28**: 1105–1109.

250 Pirisi M, Scott CA, Auellini C, Toniutto P, Fabris C, Soardo G, Beltrami CA, Bartoli E. Iron deposition and progression of disease in chronic hepatitis C. Role of interface hepatitis, portal inflammation, and HFE missense mutations. Am J Clin Pathol 2000, **113**: 546–554.

251 Poynard T, Bedossa P, Opolon P. Natural history of liver fibrosis progression in patients with chronic hepatitis C. Lancet 1997, **349**: 825–832.

252 Poynard T, Ratziu V, Benhamou Y, Di Martino V, Bedossa P, Opolon P. Fibrosis in patients with chronic hepatitis C: detection and significance. Semin Liver Dis 2000, **20**: 47–55.

253 Rizzetto M, Durazzo M. Hepatitis delta (HDV) infections. Epidemiological and clinical heterogeneity. J Hepatol 1991, **13** (Suppl 4): S116–S118.

254 Roberts JM, Searle JW, Cooksley WGE. Histological patterns of prolonged hepatitis C infection. Gastroenterol Jpn 1993, **28** (Suppl 5): 37–41.

255 Roncalli M, Borzio M, Tombesi MV, Ferrari A, Servida E. A morphometric study of liver cell dysplasia. Hum Pathol 1988, **19**: 471–474.

256 Rubbia-Brandt L, Leandro G, Spahr L, Giostra E, Quadri R, Malé PJ, Negro F. Liver steatosis in chronic hepatitis C: a morphological sign suggesting infection with HCV genotype 3. Histopathology 2001, **39**: 119–124.

257 Ruiz J, Sangro B, Cuende JI, Beloqui O, Riezu-Boj JI, Herrero JI, Prieto J. Detection of hepatitis B and C viral infections in patients with hepatocellular carcinoma. Hepatology 1992, **16**: 637–641.

258 Ryan BM, McDonald GSA, Pilkington R, Kelleher D. The development of hepatic granulomas following interferon-alpha2b therapy for chronic hepatitis C infection. Eur J Gastroenterol Hepatol 1998, **10**: 349–351.

259 Saadeh S, Cammell G, Carey WD, Younossi Z, Barnes D, Easley K. The role of liver biopsy in chronic hepatitis C. Hepatology 2001, **33**: 196–200.

260 Sarbah SA, Younossi ZM. Hepatitis C: an update on the silent epidemic. J Clin Gastroenterol 2000, **30**: 125–143.

261 Scheuer PJ, Ashrafzadeh P, Sherlock S, Brown D, Duscheiko GM. The pathology of hepatitis C. Hepatology 1992, **15**: 567–571.

262 Schvarcz R, Glaumann H, Weiland O. Survival and histological resolution of fibrosis in patients with autoimmune chronic active hepatitis. J Hepatol 1993, **18**: 15–23.

263 Senba M. Staining method for hepatitis B surface antigen (HBsAg) and its mechanism. Am J Clin Pathol 1982, **77**: 312–315.

264 Sheen IS, Liaw YF, Lin DY, Chu CM. Acute exacerbations in chronic hepatitis C: a clinicopathological and prognostic study. J Hepatol 1996, **24**: 525–531.

265 Shikata T, Uzawa T, Yoshiwara N, Akatsuka T, Yamazaki S. Staining methods of Australia antigen in paraffin section – detection of cytoplasmic inclusion bodies. Jpn J Exp Med 1974, **44**: 25–36.

266 Slimane SB, Albrecht JK, Fang JW, Goodman Z, Mizokami M, Qian K, Lau JY. Clinical, virological and histological implications of GB virus C/hepatitis G virus infection in patients with chronic hepatitis C virus infection: a multicentre study based on 671 patients. J Viral Hep 2000, **7**: 51–55.

267 Smith BC, Grove J, Guzaic MA, Day CP, Daly AK, Burt AD, Bassendine MF. Heterozygosity for hereditary hemochromatosis is associated with more fibrosis in chronic hepatitis C. Hepatology 1998, **27**: 1685–1699.

268 Stöcklin E, Gudat F, Spichtin HP, von Overbeck J, Krey G, Durmuller U, Bianchi L, Stalder GA, Altorfer J, Schmid M. Die Delta-Koinfektion der Hepatitis B in der Schweiz: Histologie und Serologie von 28 Patienten. Schweiz Med Wschr 1984, **114**: 1047–1052.

269 Su IJ, Lai MY, Hsu HC, Chen DS, Yang PM, Chuang SM, Sung JL.

Diverse virological, histopathological and prognostic implications of seroconversion from hepatitis B e antigen to anti-HBe in chronic hepatitis B virus infection. J Hepatol 1986, **3**: 182–189.

270 Tanaka K, Mori W, Suwa K. Victoria blue-nuclear fast red stain for HBs antigen detection in paraffin sections. Acta Pathol Jpn 1981, **31**: 93–98.

271 Uchida T. Pathology of hepatitis C. Intervirology 1994, **37**: 126–132.

272 Vento S, Cainelli F, Mirandola F, Cosco L, Di Perri G, Solbiati M, Ferraro T, Concia E. Fulminant hepatitis on withdrawal of chemotherapy in carriers of hepatitis C virus. Lancet 1996, **347**: 92–93.

273 Verslype C, Nevens F, Depla E, Sinelli N, Clarysse G, Maertens G, van Pelt J, Fevery J, Roskams T. Hepatic immunohistochemical staining with a monoclonal antibody against HCV–E2 to evaluate antiviral therapy and reinfection of liver grafts in hepatitis C viral infection. J Hepatol 2003, **38**: 208–214.

274 Vyberg M. The hepatitis-associated bile duct lesion. Liver 1993, **13**: 289–301.

275 Watanabe S, Okita K, Harada T, Kodama T, Numa Y, Takemoto T, Takahashi T. Morphologic studies of the liver cell dysplasia. Cancer 1983, **51**: 2197–2205.

276 Yamada G, Nakane PK. Hepatitis B core and surface antigens in liver tissue. Light and electron microscopic localization by the peroxidase-labelled antibody method. Lab Invest 1977, **26**: 649–659.

277 Yamada G, Takaguchi K, Matsueda K, Nishimoto H, Takahashi M, Fujiki S, Mizuno M, Kinoyama S, Tsuji T. Immunoelectron microscopic observation of intrahepatic HBeAg in patients with chronic hepatitis B. Hepatology 1990, **12**: 133–140.

278 Yamamoto S, Iguchi Y, Ohomoto K, Mitsui Y, Shimabara M, Mikami Y. Epithelioid granuloma formation in type C chronic hepatitis: report of two cases. Hepatogastroenterology 1995, **42**: 291–293.

279 Zarski JP, Bohn B, Bastie A, Pawlotsky JM, Baud M, Bost-Bezeaux F, Tran Van Nhieu J, Seigneurin JM, Buffet C, Dhumeaux D. Characteristics of patients with dual infection by hepatitis B and C viruses. J Hepatol 1998, **28**: 27–33.

Cirrhosis

280 Anthony PP, Ishak KG, Nayak NC, Poulsen HE, Scheuer P, Sobin LH. The morphology of cirrhosis. J Clin Pathol 1978, **31**: 395–414.

281 Callea F, Brisigotti M, Faa G, Lucini L, Eriksson S. Identification of PiZ gene products in liver tissue by a monoclonal antibody specific for the Z mutant of alpha-1-antitrypsin. J Hepatol 1991, **12**: 372–376.

282 Crawford JM. Pathologic assessment of liver cell dysplasia and benign liver tumors: differentiation from malignant tumors. Semin Diagn Pathol 1990, **7**: 115–128.

283 Desmet VJ, Sciot R, Van Eyken P. Differential diagnosis and prognosis of cirrhosis: role of liver biopsy. Acta Gastroenterol Belg 1990, **53**: 198–208.

284 Deugnier Y, Turlin B, le Quilleuc D, Moirand R, Loreal O, Messner M, Meunier B, Brissot P, Launois B. A reappraisal of hepatic siderosis in patients with end-stage cirrhosis: practical implications for the diagnosis of hemochromatosis. Am J Surg Pathol 1997, **21**: 669–675.

285 Fauerhold L, Schlichting P, Christensen E, Poulsen H, Tygstrup N, Juhl E. Conversion of micronodular cirrhosis into macronodular cirrhosis. Hepatology 1983, **3**: 928–931.

286 Guarascio P, Yentis F, Cevikbas U, Portmann B, Williams R. Value of copper associated protein in diagnostic assessment of liver biopsy. J Clin Pathol 1983, **36**: 18–23.

287 Henrion J, Colin L, Schmitz A, Schapira M, Heller FR. Ischemic hepatitis in cirrhosis. Rare but lethal. J Clin Gastroenterol 1993, **16**: 35–39.

288 Lefkowitch JH, Mendez L. Morphological features of hepatic injury in cardiac disease and shock. J Hepatol 1986, **2**: 313–327.

289 Lepez JI, Sciot R, Van Damme B, Desmet VJ. Does incomplete septal cirrhosis link non-cirrhotic nodulations with cirrhosis? Histopathology 1989, **15**: 318–320.

290 Mehrotra R, Pandey RK, Nath P. Hepatic copper in Indian childhood cirrhosis. Histopathology 1981, **5**: 659–665.

291 Nakanuma Y, Ohta G, Doishita K. Quantitation and serial section observation of focal venoocclusive lesions of hepatic veins in liver cirrhosis. Virchows Arch [A] 1985, **405**: 429–438.

292 Poonawala A, Nair SP, Thulavath PJ. Prevalence of obesity and diabetes in patients with cryptogenic cirrhosis: a case-control study. Hepatology 2000, **32**: 689–692.

293 Roskams T, Baptista A, Bianchi L, Burt A, Callea F, Denk H, De Groote J, Desmet V, Hübscher S, Ishak K, MacSween R, Portmann B, Poulsen H, Scheuer P, Terracciano L, Thaler H. Histopathology of portal hypertension. A practical guideline. Histopathology 2002, **42**: 2–13.

294 Sciot R, Staessen D, Van Damme B, Van Steenbergen W, Fevery J, De Groote J, Desmet VJ. Incomplete septal cirrhosis: histopathological aspects. Histopathology 1988, **13**: 593–603.

Drug-induced and toxic liver injury

295 Benhamou J-P. Drug-induced hepatitis: clinical aspects. In Guillouzo A (ed.): Liver cells and drugs, vol. 164. 1988, Colloque INSERM/John Libbey Eurotext Ltd, Paris pp. 3–12.

296 Bénichou C. Criteria of drug-induced liver disorders. Report of an international consensus meeting. J Hepatol 1990, **11**: 272–276.

297 Bianchi L, De Groote J, Desmet V, Gedigk P, Korb G, Popper H, Poulsen H, Scheuer PJ, Schmid M, Thaler H, Wepler W. Guidelines for diagnosis of therapeutic drug-induced liver injury in liver biopsies. Lancet 1974, **II**: 854–857.

298 Bircher J. Adverse drug reactions in the differential diagnosis of GI and liver diseases. Baillières Clin Gastroenterol Edn. London, 1988, Baillière Tindall.

299 Bissell DM, Gores GT, Laskin DL, Hoofnagle JH. Drug-induced liver injury: mechanisms and test systems. Hepatology 2001, **33**: 1009–1013.

300 Desmet VJ. Drug-induced liver disease: pathogenetic mechanisms and histopathological lesions. Eur J Med 1993, **2**: 36–47.

301 Farrell GC. Drug-induced liver disease. Edinburgh, 1994, Churchill Livingstone.

302 Friis H, Andreasen PB. Drug-induced hepatic injury: an analysis of 1100 cases reported to the Danish Committee on Adverse Drug Reactions between 1978 and 1987. J Intern Med 1992, **232**: 133–138.

303 Kaplowitz N. Recent advances in drug metabolism and hepatotoxicity. Semin Liver Dis 1990, **10**: 234–338.

304 Lewis JH. Drug-induced liver disease. Med Clin North Am 2000, **84**: 1275–1311.

305 Paiva LA, Wright PJ, Koff RS. Long-term hepatic memory for hypersensitivity to nitrofurantoin. Am J Gastroenterol 1992, **87**: 891–893.

306 Pessayre D, Larrey D. Acute and chronic drug-induced hepatitis. Baillières Clin Gastroenterol 1988, **2**: 385–422.

307 Sherlock S. The spectrum of hepatotoxicity due to drugs. Lancet 1986, **2**: 440–444.

308 Stricker BHC. Drug-induced hepatic injury, ed. 2. Amsterdam, 1992, Elsevier.

Elementary lesions

Hepatocytes

309 Abrahams C, Wheatley A, Rubenstein AH, Stables D. Hepatocellular lipofuscin after excessive ingestion of analgesics. Lancet 1964, **2**: 621–622.

310 Hashimoto K, Hoshii Y, Takahashi M, Mitsuno S, Hanai N,
Watanabe Y, Ishihara T. Use of a monoclonal antibody against Lafora bodies for the immunocytochemical study of ground-glass inclusions in hepatocytes due to cyanamide. Histopathology 2001, **39**: 60–65.

311 Jezequel AM, Librari ML, Mosca P, Novel-Li G, Lorenzini I, Orlandi F. Changes induced in human liver by long-term anticonvulsant therapy. Functional and ultrastructural data. Liver 1984, **4**: 307–330.

312 Klinge O, Bannasch P. The increase of smooth endoplasmatic reticulum in hepatocytes of human liver punctates. Verh Dtsch Ges Pathol 1968, **52**: 568–573.

313 Larrey D, Erlinger S. Drug-induced cholestasis. Baillières Clin Gastroenterol 1988, **2**: 423–452.

314 McKenzie R, Fried MW, Sallie R, Conjeevaram H, Di Bisceglie AM, Park Y, Savarese B, Kleiner D, Tsokos M, Luciano C. Hepatic failure and lactic acidosis due to fialuridine (FIAU), an investigational nucleoside analogue for chronic hepatitis B. N Engl J Med 1995, **333**: 1099–1105.

315 Pessayre D, Mansouri A, Haouzi D, Fromenty B. Hepatotoxicity due to mitochondrial dysfunction. Cell Biol Toxicol 1999, **15**: 367–373.

316 Poucell S, Ireton J, Valencia-Mayoral P, Downar E, Larratt L, Patterson J, Blendis L, Phillips MJ. Amiodarone-associated phospholipidosis and fibrosis of the liver. Light, immunohistochemical and electron microscopic studies. Gastroenterology 1984, **86**: 926–936.

317 Sherlock S. Acute fatty liver of pregnancy and the microvesicular fat diseases. Gut 1983, **24**: 265–269.

318 Sokol RJ, Treem WR. Mitochondria and childhood liver diseases. J Pediatr Gastroenterol Nutr 1999, **28**: 4–16.

319 Stieger B, Fattinger K, Madon J, Kullak-Ublick GA, Meier PJ. Drug- and estrogen-induced cholestasis through inhibition of the hepatocellular bile salt export pump (Bsep) of rat liver. Gastroenterology 2000, **118**: 422–430.

320 Thaler H. Fatty change. Baillières Clin Gastroenterol 1988, **2**: 453–462.

321 Vazquez JJ, Pardo-Mindan J. Liver cell injury (bodies similar to Lafora's) in alcoholics treated with disulfiram (antabuse). Histopathology 1979, **3**: 377–384.

Hepatocellular death: apoptosis and necrosis

322 Bianchi L, De Groote J, Desmet V, Gedigk P, Korb G, Popper H, Poulsen H, Scheuer PJ, Schmid M, Thaler H, Wepler W. Guidelines for diagnosis of therapeutic drug-induced liver injury in liver biopsies. Lancet 1974, **II**: 854–857.

323 Bursch W, Oberhammer F, Schulte-Hermann R. Cell death by apoptosis and its protective role against disease. Trends Pharmacol Sci 1992, **13**: 245–251.

324 Leist M, Gantner F, Kunstle G, Wendel A. Cytokine-mediated hepatic apoptosis. Rev Physiol Biochem Pharmacol 1998, **133**: 109–155.

325 Pessayre D, Degos F, Feldmann G, Degott C, Bernuau J, Benhamou JP. Chronic active hepatitis and giant multinucleated hepatocytes in adults treated with clometacin. Digestion 1981, **22**: 66–72.

Hepatocellular tumors

326 Anthony PP. Liver tumours. Baillières Clin Gastroenterol 1988, **2**: 501–522.

327 Christidis C, Mal F, Ramos J, Senejoux A, Callard P, Navarro R, Trinchet JC, Larrey D, Beaugrand M, Guettier C. Worsening of hepatic dysfunction as a consequence of repeated hydroxyethylstarch infusions. J Hepatol 2001, **35**: 726–732.

328 Cruickshank B, Thomas MJ. Mineral oil (follicular) lipidosis. II. Histologic studies of spleen, liver, lymphnodes, and bone marrow. Hum Pathol 1984, **15**: 731–737.

329 Degott C, Feldmann G, Larrey D, Durand-Schneider AM, Grange

D, Machayekhi JP, Moreau A, Potet F, Benhamou JP. Drug-induced prolonged cholestasis in adults: a histological semiquantitative study demonstrating progressive ductopenia. Hepatology 1992, **15**: 244–251.

330 Delladetsima JK, Horn T, Poulsen H. Portal tract lipogranulomas in liver biopsies. Liver 1987, **7**: 9–17.

331 Desmet VJ. Drug-induced liver disease: pathogenetic mechanisms and histopathological lesions. Eur J Med 1993, **2**: 36–47.

332 Desmet VJ. Vanishing bile duct syndrome in drug-induced liver disease. J Hepatol 1997, **26** (Suppl 1): 31–35.

333 Ishak KG. New developments in diagnostic liver pathology. In Farber E, Phillips MJ, Kaufman N (eds): Pathogenesis of liver diseases. Baltimore, 1987, Williams and Wilkins, pp. 223–373.

334 Ishak KG, Zimmerman HJ. Drug-induced and toxic granulomatous hepatitis. Baillières Clin Gastroenterol 1988, **2**: 463–480.

335 Jorens PG, Michielsen PP, Pelckmans PA, Fevery J, Desmet VJ, Geubel AP, Rahier J, Van Maercke YM. Vitamin A abuse: development of cirrhosis despite cessation of vitamin A. A six-year clinical and histopathologic follow-up. Liver 1992, **12**: 381–386.

336 Kaplan MM. Methotrexate hepatotoxicity and the premature reporting of Mark Twain's death: both greatly exaggerated. Hepatology 1990, **12**: 784–786.

337 Mitros F, Landas S, Furst D, Labrecque D. Lipogranulomas and gold in liver in rheumatoid arthritis. Lab Invest 1986, **54**: 44A.

338 Murphy E, Griffiths MR, Hunter JA, Burt AD. Fibrin-ring granulomas: a non-specific reaction to liver injury? Histopathology 1991, **19**: 91–93.

339 Roberts ISD, Armstrong GR. Hepatic fibrin-ring granulomas (letter). Histopathology 1992, **20**: 549.

340 Valla D, Benhamou JP. Drug-induced vascular and sinusoidal lesions of the liver. Baillières Clin Gastroenterol 1988, **2**: 481–500.

341 Wanless IR, Geddie WR. Mineral oil lipogranulomata in liver and spleen. Arch Pathol Lab Med 1985, **109**: 283–286.

342 Zafrani ES, Pinaudeau Y, Dhumeaux D. Drug-induced vascular lesions of the liver. Arch Intern Med 1983, **143**: 495–502.

Composite patterns

343 Bianchi L, De Groote J, Desmet V, Gedigk P, Korb G, Popper H, Poulsen H, Scheuer PJ, Schmid M, Thaler H, Wepler W. Guidelines for diagnosis of therapeutic drug-induced liver injury in liver biopsies. Lancet 1974, **II**: 854–857.

344 Degott C, Messing B, Moreau D, Chazouilleres O, Paris R, Colombel JF, Lebrec D, Potet F, Feldmann G, Benhamou JP. Liver phospholipidosis induced by parenteral nutrition: histologic, histochemical and ultrastructural investigations. Gastroenterology 1988, **95**: 183–191.

345 Desmet VJ. Drug-induced liver disease: pathogenetic mechanisms and histopathological lesions. Eur J Med 1993, **2**: 36–47.

346 Ishak KG, Zimmerman HJ. Drug-induced and toxic granulomatous hepatitis. Baillières Clin Gastroenterol 1988, **2**: 463–480.

347 Kopelman H, Robertson MH, Saunders PG. The Epping jaundice. Br Med J 1966, **1**: 514–518.

348 Lewis JH, Mullick F, Ishak KG, Ranard RC, Ragsdale B, Perse RM, Rusnock EJ, Wolke A, Benjamin SB, Seeff LB, Zimmerman HJ. Histopathologic analysis of suspected amiodarone hepatotoxicity. Hum Pathol 1990, **21**: 59–67.

349 Roy AK, Mahoney HC, Levine RA. Phenytoin-induced chronic hepatitis. Dig Dis Sci 1993, **38**: 740–743.

350 Scully LJ, Clarke D, Barr RJ. Diclofenac induced hepatitis. Three cases with features of autoimmune chronic active hepatitis. Dig Dis Sci 1993, **38**: 744–751.

351 Stricker BH, Blok AP, Claas FH, Van Parijs GE, Desmet VJ. Hepatic injury associated with the use of nitrofurans: a clinicopathological study of 52 reported cases. Hepatology 1988, **8**: 599–606.

Steatosis and steatohepatitis

Steatosis

352 Burt AD, Mutton A, Day CP. Diagnosis and interpretation of steatosis and steatohepatitis. Semin Diagn Pathol 1998, **15**: 246–258.

353 Findor J, Perez V, Bruch Iguarta E, Giovanetti M, Fioravanti N. Structure and ultrastructure of the liver in aged persons. Acta Hepato-Gastroenterol 1973, **20**: 200–204.

354 Hall P, Gormley BM, Jarvis LR, Smith RD. A staining method for the detection and measurement of fat droplets in hepatic tissue. Pathology 1980, **12**: 605–608.

Patterns and distribution

355 Burt AD, Mutton A, Day CP. Diagnosis and interpretation of steatosis and steatohepatitis. Semin Diagn Pathol 1998, **15**: 246–258.

356 Christofferson P, Braendstrup O, Juhl E, Poulsen H. Lipogranulomas in human liver biopsies with fatty change. A morphological, biochemical and clinical investigation. Acta Pathol Microbiol Scand A 1971, **79**: 150–158.

357 Day CP, James OFW. Hepatic steatosis – innocent bystander or guilty party? Hepatology 1998, **27**: 1463–1466.

358 Day CP, James OFW. Steatohepatitis: a tale of two "hits"? Gastroenterology 1998, **114**: 842–844.

359 Day CP, Yeaman SJ. The biochemistry of alcohol-induced fatty liver. Biochim Biophys Acta 1994, **1215**: 33–48.

360 Delladetsima JK, Horn T, Poulsen H. Portal tract lipogranulomas in liver biopsies. Liver 1987, **7**: 9–17.

361 Eaton S, Record CO, Bartlett K. Multiple biochemical effects in the pathogenesis of alcoholic fatty liver. Eur J Clin Invest 1997, **27**: 719–722.

362 Fromenty B, Pessayre D. Impaired mitochondrial function in microvesicular steatosis: effects of drugs, ethanol, hormones and cytokines. J Hepatol 1997, **26**: 43–54.

363 Glasgow JFT, Middleton B, Moore R, Gray A, Hill J. The mechanism of inhibition of beta-oxidation by aspirin metabolites in skin fibroblasts from Reye's syndrome patients and controls. Biochim Biophys Acta 1999, **1454**: 115–125.

364 Hurwitz ES, Barrett MJ, Bregman D, Gunn WJ, Pinsky P, Schonberger LB, Drage JS, Kaslow RA, Burlington DB, Quinnan GV, LaMontagne JR, Fairweather WR, Dayton D, Dowdle WR. Public health service study of Reye's syndrome and medications. JAMA 1987, **257**: 1905–1911.

365 Orlowski JP. Whatever happened to Reye's syndrome? Did it really exist? Crit Care Med 1999, **27**: 1582–1587.

366 Popper H, Thung SN, Gerber MA, Hadler SC, de Monzon M, Ponzetto A, Anzola E, Rivera D, Mondolfi A, Bracho A, et al. Histologic studies of severe delta agent infection in Venezuelan Indians. Hepatology 1983, **3**: 906–912.

367 Rinaldo P. Fatty acid transport and mitochondrial oxidation disorders. Semin Liver Dis 2001, **21**: 489–500.

368 Sherlock S. Acute fatty liver of pregnancy and the microvesicular fat diseases. Gut 1983, **24**: 265–269.

369 Teli MR, Day CP, Burt AD, Bennet MK, James OF. Determinants of progression to cirrhosis or fibrosis in pure alcoholic fatty liver. Lancet 1995, **346**: 987–990.

370 Wanless IR, Geddie WR. Mineral oil lipogranulomata in liver and spleen. Arch Pathol Lab Med 1985, **109**: 283–286.

371 Weizman Z, Mussafi H, Ishay JS, Shvil Y, Goitein K, Livini N, Deckelbaum RJ. Multiple hornet stings with features of Reye's syndrome. Gastroenterology 1985, **89**: 1407–1410.

Steatohepatitis, fibrosis, and cirrhosis

372 Burt AD, Mutton A, Day CP. Diagnosis and interpretation of steatosis and steatohepatitis. Semin Diagn Pathol 1998, **15**: 246–258.

373 Day CP, James OFW. Hepatic steatosis – innocent bystander or guilty party? Hepatology 1998, **27**: 1463–1466.

374 Day CP, James OFW. Steatohepatitis: a tale of two "hits"? Gastroenterology 1998, **114**: 842–844.

375 Letteron P, Fromenty B, Terris B, Degott C, Pessayre D. Acute and chronic hepatic steatosis lead to in vivo lipid peroxidation in mice. J Hepatol 1996, **24**: 200–208.

376 Pessayre D, Berson A, Fromenty B, Mansouri A. Mitochondria in steatohepatitis. Semin Liver Dis 2001, **21**: 57–69.

Alcoholic steatohepatitis

377 Baptista A, Bianchi L, De Groote J, Desmet VJ, Gedigk P, Korb G, MacSween RNM, Popper H, Poulsen H, Schever PJ, Schmid M, Thaler H, Wepler W. Alcoholic liver disease: morphologic manifestations. Lancet 1981, **1**: 707–711.

378 Chevallier M, Guerret S, Chossegros P, Gerard F, Grimaud JA. A histological semiquantitative scoring system for evaluation of hepatic fibrosis in needle liver biopsy specimens: comparison with morphometric studies. Hepatology 1994, **20**: 349–355.

379 Day CP. Is necroinflammation a prerequisite for fibrogenesis? Hepatogastroenterology 1996, **43**: 104–120.

380 Denk H, Stumptner C, Zatloukal K. Review. Mallory bodies revisited. J Hepatol 2000, **32**: 689–702.

381 Desmet VJ. Alcoholic liver disease. Histological features and evolution. Acta Med Scand Suppl 1985, **703**: 111–126.

382 Dinges HP, Zatloukal K, Denk H, Smolle J, Mair S. Alcoholic liver disease. Parenchyma to stroma relationship in fibrosis and cirrhosis as revealed by three-dimensional reconstruction and immunohistochemistry. Am J Pathol 1992, **141**: 69–83.

383 Edmondson HA, Peters RL, Reynolds TB, Kuzma OT. Sclerosing hyaline necrosis in the liver of the chronic alcoholic. A recognizable syndrome. Ann Intern Med 1963, **59**: 646–673.

384 Fleming KA, McGee JOD. Alcoholic induced liver disease. Review article. J Clin Pathol 1984, **37**: 721–733.

385 Macchia S, Losi L, Dei Tos AP, Pasquinelli G, Di Tommaso L, Del Duca S, Roncaroli F, Dal Monte PR. Identification of mitochondria in liver biopsies: A study by immunohistochemistry, immunogold and Western blot analysis. Virchows Arch 1998, **433**: 267–273.

386 French SW. The Mallory body: structure, composition and pathogenesis. Hepatology 1981, **1**: 76–83.

387 French SW, Nash J, Shitabata P, Kachi K, Hara C, Chedid A, Mendenhall CL. Pathology of alcoholic liver disease. Semin Liver Dis 1993, **13**: 154–169.

388 Gerber MA, Popper H. Relation between central canals and portal tracts in alcoholic hepatitis. A contribution to the pathogenesis of cirrhosis in alcoholics. Hum Pathol 1972, **3**: 199–207.

389 Jensen K, Gluud C. The Mallory body: morphological, clinical and experimental studies (Part 1 of a literature survey). Hepatology 1994, **20**: 1061–1077.

390 Jensen K, Gluud C. The Mallory body: theories on development and pathological significance (Part 2 of a literature survey). Hepatology 1994, **20**: 1330–1342.

391 Junge J, Horn T, Christoffersen P. Megamitochondria as a diagnostic marker for alcohol induced centrilobular and periportal fibrosis in the liver. Virchows Arch [A] Pathol Anat Histopathol 1987, **410**: 553–558.

392 MacSween RNM, Burt AD. Histologic spectrum of alcoholic liver disease. Semin Liver Dis 1986, **6**: 221–232.

393 Nasrallah SM, Nassar VH, Galambos JT. Importance of terminal hepatic venule thickening. Arch Pathol Lab Med 1980, **104**: 84–86.

394 Orrego H, Vlake JE, Blendis LM, Medline A. Prognosis of alcoholic cirrhosis in the presence and absence of alcoholic hepatitis. Gastroenterology 1987, **92**: 208–214.

395 Reeves H, Burt AD, Wood S, Day CP. Hepatic stellate cell activation occurs in the absence of hepatitis in alcoholic liver disease and correlates with the severity of steatosis. J Hepatol 1996, **25**: 677–683.

396 Teli MR, Day CP, Burt AD, Bennet MK, James OF. Determinants of progression to cirrhosis or fibrosis in pure alcoholic fatty liver. Lancet 1995, **346**: 987–990.

397 Uchida T, Kao H, Quispe-Sjogren M, Peters RL. Alcoholic foamy degeneration – a pattern of acute alcoholic injury of the liver. Gastroenterology 1983, **84**: 683–692.

398 Uchida T, Peters RL. The nature and origin of proliferated bile ductules in alcoholic liver disease. Am J Clin Pathol 1983, **79**: 326–333.

399 Ziol M, Tepper M, Lohez M, Arcangeli G, Ganne N, Christidis C, Trinchet JC, Beaugrand M, Guillet JG, Guettier C. Clinical and biological relevance of hepatocyte apoptosis in alcoholic hepatitis. J Hepatol 2001, **34**: 254–260.

Differential diagnosis of alcoholic steatohepatitis

400 Jorens PG, Michielsen PP, Pelckmans PA, Fevery J, Desmet VJ, Geubel AP, Rahier J, Van Maercke YM. Vitamin A abuse: development of cirrhosis despite cessation of vitamin A. A six-year clinical and histopathologic follow-up. Liver 1992, **12**: 381–386.

401 Ludwig J, Batts KP, Moyer TP, Baldus WP, Fairbanks VF. Liver biopsy diagnosis of homozygous hemochromatosis: a diagnostic algorithm. Mayo Clin Proc 1993, **68**: 263–267.

402 Talley NJ, Roth A, Woods J, Hench V. Diagnostic value of liver biopsy in alcoholic liver disease. J Clin Gastroenterol 1988, **10**: 647–650.

Nonalcoholic liver disease in the alcoholic patient

403 Afroudakis A, Kaplowitz N. Liver histopathology in chronic common bile duct stenosis due to chronic alcoholic pancreatitis. Hepatology 1981, **1**: 65–72.

404 Bloomer JR. The hepatic porphyrias. Pathogenesis, manifestations and management. Gastroenterology 1976, **71**: 689–701.

405 Cortes JM, Oliva H, Paradinas FJ, Hernandez-Guio C. The pathology of the liver in porphyria cutanea tarda. Histopathology 1980, **4**: 471–485.

406 Crapper RM, Bhathal PS, Mackay IR. Chronic active hepatitis in alcoholic patients. Liver 1983, **3**: 327–337.

407 Lefkowitch JH, Fenoglio JJJ. Liver disease in alcoholic cardiomyopathy: evidence against cirrhosis. Hum Pathol 1983, **14**: 457–463.

408 Lesur G, Levy P, Flejou JF, Belghiti J, Fekete F, Bernades P. Factors predictive of liver histopathological appearance in chronic alcoholic pancreatitis with common bile duct stenosis and increased serum alkaline phosphatase. Hepatology 1993, **18**: 1078–1081.

409 Levin DM, Baker AL, Riddell RH, Rochman H, Boyer JL. Non-alcoholic liver disease: overlooked causes of liver injury in patients with heavy alcohol consumption. Am J Med 1979, **66**: 429–434.

410 Maddrey W. Hepatic effects of acetaminophen. Enhanced toxicity in alcoholics. J Clin Gastroenterol 1987, **9**: 180–185.

411 Morgan MY, Sherlock S, Scheuer PJ. Portal fibrosis in the livers of alcoholic patients. Gut 1978, **19**: 1015–1021.

412 Rosman AS, Paronetto F, Galvin K, Williams RJ, Lieber CS. Hepatitis C virus antibody in alcoholic patients. Association with the presence of portal and/or lobular hepatitis. Arch Intern Med 1993, **153**: 965–969.

413 Vazquez JJ. Ground-glass hepatocytes: light and electron microscopy. Characterization of the different types. Histopathology 1990, **5**: 379–386.

414 Yamauchi M, Nakahara M, Maezawa Y, Satoh S, Nishikawa F, Ohata M, Mizuhara Y, Hirakawa J, Nakajima H, Fujisawa K,

Toda G. Prevalence of hepatocellular carcinoma in patients with alcoholic cirrhosis and prior exposure to hepatitis C. Am J Gastroenterol 1993, **88:** 39–43.

Nonalcoholic steatohepatitis

415 Brunt EM. Nonalcoholic steatohepatitis: definition and pathology. Semin Liver Dis 2001, **21:** 3–16.

416 Brunt EM, Janney CG, Di Bisceglie AM, Neuschwander-Tetri BA, Bacon BR. Nonalcoholic steatohepatitis: a proposal for grading and staging the histological lesions. Am J Gastroenterol 1999, **94:** 2467–2474.

417 Chitturi S, Farrell GC. Etiopathogenesis of nonalcoholic steatohepatitis. Semin Liver Dis 2001, **21:** 27–41.

418 Cotrim HP, Andrade ZA, Parana R, Portugal M, Lyra LG, Freitas LA. Nonalcoholic steatohepatitis: a toxic liver disease in industrial workers. Liver 1999, **19:** 299–304.

419 Diehl AM. Nonalcoholic steatohepatitis. Semin Liver Dis 1999, **19:** 221–229.

420 Diehl AM, Goodman Z, Ishak KG. Alcohollike liver disease in nonalcoholics. A clinical and histologic comparison with alcohol-induced liver injury. Gastroenterology 1988, **95:** 1056–1062.

421 Falck-Ytter Y, Younossi ZM, Marchesini G, McCullough AJ. Clinical features and natural history of nonalcoholic steatosis syndromes. Semin Liver Dis 2001, **21:** 17–26.

422 James OF, Day CP. Non-alcoholic steatohepatitis (NASH): a disease of emerging identity and importance. J Hepatol 1998, **29:** 495–501.

423 Lee RG. Nonalcoholic steatohepatitis: tightening the morphological screws on a hepatic rambler. Hepatology 1995, **21:** 1742–1743.

424 Ludwig J, Viggiano TR, McGill DB, Oh BJ. Nonalcoholic steatohepatitis. Mayo Clinic experiences with a hitherto unnamed disease. Mayo Clin Proc 1980, **55:** 434–438.

425 Matteoni CA, Younossi AM, Gramlich T, Boparai N, Liu YC, McCullough AJ. Nonalcoholic fatty liver disease: a spectrum of clinical and pathological severity. Gastroenterology 1999, **116:** 1413–1419.

426 Pinto HC, Baptista A, Camilo ME, Valente A, Saragoca A, Carneiro de Moura M. Nonalcoholic steatohepatitis. Clinico-pathological comparison with alcoholic hepatitis in ambulatory and hospitalized patients. Dig Dis Sci 1996, **41:** 172–179.

427 Poonawala A, Nair SP, Thulavath PJ. Prevalence of obesity and diabetes in patients with cryptogenic cirrhosis: a case-control study. Hepatology 2000, **32:** 689–692.

428 Rashid M, Roberts EA. Nonalcoholic steatohepatitis in children. J Pediatr Gastroenterol Nutr 2000, **30:** 48–53.

429 Younossi ZM, Gramlich T, Liu YC, Matteoni C, Petrelli M, Goldblum J, Rybicki L, McCullough AJ. Nonalcoholic fatty liver disease: assessment of variability in pathologic interpretations. Mod Pathol 1998, **11:** 560–565.

Cholestasis and biliary diseases
Histopathologic liver changes of cholestasis in general

430 Desmet VJ. Cholestasis: extrahepatic obstruction and secondary biliary cirrhosis. In MacSween RNM, Anthony PP, Scheuer PJ, Burt AD, Portmann BC (eds): Pathology of the liver, ed. 3. Edinburgh, 1994, Churchill Livingstone, pp. 425–476.

431 Desmet VJ. Chronic cholestasis. In Hoofnagle JH, Goodman Z (eds): Liver biopsy. Interpretation for the 1990's. Thorofare, 1991, Slack Incorporated, pp. 25–38.

432 Trauner M, Meier PJ, Boyer JL. Molecular regulation of hepatocellular transport systems in cholestasis. J Hepatol 1999, **31:** 165–178.

Acute complete cholestasis

433 Bloomer JR. The liver in protoporphyria. Hepatology 1988, **8:** 402–407.

434 Desmet VJ, Roskams T. Histological features. In Bircher J, Benhamou JP, McIntyre N, Rizzetto M, Rodes J (eds): Oxford Textbook of clinical hepatology, ed. 2., vol. 1. Oxford, 1999, Oxford University Press, pp. 463–470.

Chronic incomplete cholestasis

435 Desmet V, Roskams T, Van Eyken P. Ductular reaction in the liver. Path Res Pract 1995, **191:** 513–524.

436 Desmet VJ. Current problems in diagnosis of biliary disease and cholestasis. Semin Liver Dis 1986, **6:** 233–245.

437 Desmet VJ. Cirrhosis: Aetiology and pathogenesis: cholestasis. In Boyer JL, Bianchi L (eds): Liver cirrhosis. Falk Symposium 44. Lancaster, 1987, MTP Press, pp. 101–118.

438 Desmet VJ, Roskams T, Van Eyken P. Pathology of the biliary tree in cholestasis: ductular reaction. In Manns MP, et al. (eds): Cholestatic liver diseases. Lancaster, 1998, Kluwer Academic Publishers, pp. 143–154.

439 Hammel P, Couvelard A, O'Toole D, Ratouis A, Sauvanet A, Flejou JF, Degott C. Regression of liver fibrosis after biliary drainage in patients with chronic pancreatitis and stenosis of the common bile duct. N Engl J Med 2001, **344:** 418–423.

440 James J, Lygidakis NJ, Van Eyken P, Tanka AKF, Bosch KS, Ramaekers FCS, Desmet V. Application of keratin immunocytochemistry and Sirius red staining in evaluating intrahepatic changes with acute extrahepatic cholestasis due to hepatic duct carcinoma. Hepatogastroenterology 1989, **36:** 151–155.

441 Ludwig J. New concepts in biliary cirrhosis. Semin Liver Dis 1987, **7:** 293–301.

442 Ludwig J, La Russo NF, Wiesner RH. The syndrome of primary sclerosing cholangitis. In Popper H, Schaffner F (eds): Progress in liver diseases, vol. IX. Philadelphia, 1990, W.B. Saunders, pp. 555–566.

443 Matsumoto K, Fuji H, Michalopoulos G, Fung JJ, Demetris AJ. Human biliary epithelial cells secrete and respond to cytokines and hepatocyte growth factors in vitro: interleukin-6, hepatocyte growth factor promote DNA synthesis in vitro. Hepatology 1994, **20:** 376–382.

444 Matzen P, Junge J, Christoffersen P, Poulsen H. Reproducibility and accuracy of liver biopsy findings suggestive of an obstructive cause of jaundice. In Brunner H, Thaler H (eds): Hepatology. A Festschrift for Hans Popper. New York, 1985, Raven Press, pp. 285–293.

445 Nagore N, Howe S, Scheuer PJ. The three-dimensional liver. In Popper H, Schaffner F (eds): Progress in liver diseases, vol. IX. Philadelphia, 1990, W.B. Saunders, pp. 1–10.

446 Slott PA, Liu MH, Tavoloni N. Origin, pattern and mechanism of bile duct proliferation following biliary obstruction in the rat. Gastroenterology 1990, **99:** 466–477.

447 Thaler H. Leberkrankheiten. Histopathologie. Pathophysiologie. Klinik. Berlin, 1982, Springer.

448 Van Eyken P. Cytokeratin immunohistochemistry in liver histopathology. Adv Clin Pathol 2000, **4:** 201–211.

449 Van Eyken P, Desmet VJ. Cytokeratins and the liver. Liver 1993, **13:** 113–122.

450 Van Eyken P, Sciot R, Desmet VJ. A cytokeratin immunohistochemical study of cholestatic liver disease: evidence that hepatocytes can express "bile duct-type" cytokeratins. Histopathology 1989, **15:** 125–135.

Individual cholestatic liver diseases
Hepatocellular (parenchymal) diseases

451 Alonso EM, Snover DC, Montag A, Freese DK, Whitington PF. Histologic pathology of the liver in progressive familial intrahepatic cholestasis. J Pediatr Gastroenterol Nutr 1994, **18:** 123–133.

452 Bull LN, Carlton VEH, Stricker NL, Baharloo S, De Young JA, Freimer NB, Magid MS, Kahn E, Markowitz J, Di Carlo FJ, McLoughlin L, Boyle JT, Dahms BB, Faught PR, Fitzgerald JF, Piccoli DA, Witzleben CL, O'Connell NC, Setchell KDR, Agostini RM, Kocoshis SA, Reyes J, Knisely AS. Genetic and morphological findings in progressive familial intrahepatic cholestasis (Byler Disease [PFIC-1] and Byler Syndrome): evidence for heterogeneity. Hepatology 1997, **26**: 155–164.

453 Bull LN, van Eijk MJT, Pawlikowska L, DeYoung JA, Juijn JA, Liao M, Klomp LW, Lomri N, Berger R, Scharschmidt BF, Knisely AS, Houwen RH, Freimer NB. A gene encoding a P-type ATPase mutated in two forms of hereditary cholestasis. Nat Genet 1998, **18**: 219–224.

454 Callea F, Brisigotti M, Faa G, Lucini L, Eriksson S. Identification of PiZ gene products in liver tissue by a monoclonal antibody specific for the Z mutant of alpha-1-antitrypsin. J Hepatol 1991, **12**: 372–376.

455 Chobert MN, Bernard O, Bulle F, Lemonnier A, Guellaen G, Alagille D. High hepatic gamma-glutamyltransferase (gamma-GT) activity with normal serum gamma-GT in children with progressive idiopathic cholestasis. J Hepatol 1989, **8**: 22–25.

456 de Vree JM, Jacquemin E, Sturm E, Cresteil D, Bosma PJ, Aten J, Deleuze JF, Desrochers M, Burdelski M, Bernard O, Oude-Elferink RP, Hadchouel M. Mutations in the MDR3 gene cause progressive familial intrahepatic cholestasis. Proc Natl Acad Sci U S A 1998, **95**: 282–287.

457 Deleuze JF, Jacquemin E, Dubuisson C, Cresteil D, Dumont M, Erlinger S, Bernard O, Hadchouel M. Defect of multidrug-resistance 3 gene expression in a subtype of progressive familial intrahepatic cholestasis. Hepatology 1996, **23**: 904–908.

458 Desmet VJ. Drug-induced liver disease: pathogenetic mechanisms and histopathological lesions. Eur J Med 1993, **2**: 36–47.

459 Desmet VJ. Cholestasis: extrahepatic obstruction and secondary biliary cirrhosis. In MacSween RNM, Anthony PP, Scheuer PJ, Burt AD, Portmann BC (eds): Pathology of the liver, ed. 3. Edinburgh, 1994, Churchill Livingstone, pp. 425–476.

460 Desmet VJ, Callea F. Cholestatic syndromes of infancy and childhood. In Zakim D, Boyer TD (eds): Hepatology: a textbook of liver disease, ed. 3, vol. 2. Philadelphia, 1996, W.B. Saunders, pp. 1649–1698.

461 Ishak KG, Sharp HL. Metabolic errors and liver disease. In MacSween RNM, Anthony PP, Scheuer PJ, Ishak KG, Portmann BC, Burt AD (eds): Pathology of the liver, ed. 4. Edinburgh, 2001, Churchill Livingstone.

462 Jacquemin E. Progressive familial intrahepatic cholestasis. J Gastroenterol Hepatol 1999, **14**: 594–599.

463 Jacquemin E. Role of multidrug resistance 3 deficiency in pediatric and adult liver disease: one gene for three diseases. Semin Liver Dis 2001, **21**: 551–562.

464 Jansen PLM, Müller M, Sturm E. Genes and cholestasis. Hepatology 2001, **34**: 1067–1074.

465 Nolte D. Ikterus der Leber bei chronischer Herzinsuffizienz. Virchows Arch [A] Pathol Anat Histopathol 1966, **341**: 37–42.

466 Riely CA. Familial intrahepatic cholestasis syndromes. In Suchy FJ (ed.): Liver disease in children. St. Louis, 1994, Mosby, pp. 443–459.

467 Thompson R, Strautnieks S. BSEP: function and role in progressive familial intrahepatic cholestasis. Semin Liver Dis 2001, **21**: 545–550.

468 Trauner M, Meier PJ, Boyer JL. Molecular regulation of hepatocellular transport systems in cholestasis. J Hepatol 1999, **31**: 165–178.

469 Van Mil S, Klomp LWJ, Bull LN, Houwen RHJ. FICI disease: a spectrum of intrahepatic cholestatic disorders. Semin Liver Dis 2001, **21**: 535–544.

Ductular pathology

470 Banks JG, Foulis AK, Ledingham IMA, MacSween RN. Liver function in septic shock. J Clin Pathol 1982, **35**: 1249–1252.

471 Cohen C, Olsen MM. Pediatric total parenteral nutrition: liver histopathology. Arch Pathol Lab Med 1981, **105**: 152–156.

472 Crawford JM, Boyer JL. Clinicopathology conferences: inflammation-induced cholestasis. Hepatology 1998, **28**: 253–260.

473 Desmet VJ, Callea F. Cholestatic syndromes of infancy and childhood. In Zakim D, Boyer TD (eds): Hepatology: a textbook of liver disease, ed. 3, vol. 2. Philadelphia, 1996, W.B. Saunders, pp. 1649–1698.

474 Feranchak AP, Sokol RJ. Cholangiocyte biology and cystic fibrosis liver disease. Semin Liver Dis 2001, **21**: 471–488.

475 Ishak KG, Sharp HL. Metabolic errors and liver disease. In MacSween RNM, Anthony PP, Scheuer PJ, Burt AD, Portmann BC (eds): Pathology of the liver, ed. 3. Edinburgh, 1994, Churchill Livingstone, pp. 123–218.

476 Lefkowitch JH. Bile ductular cholestasis: an ominous histopathologic sign related to sepsis and "cholangitis lenta". Hum Pathol 1982, **13**: 19–24.

477 Schmid M, Cueni B. Portal lesions in viral hepatitis with submassive hepatic necrosis. Hum Pathol 1972, **3**: 209–216.

478 Wang P, Ba ZF, Chaudry IH. Mechanisms of hepatocellular dysfunction during early sepsis. Key role of increased gene expression and release of proinflammatory cytokines Tumor Necrosis Factor and Interleukin-6. Arch Surg 1997, **132**: 364–370.

Ductal pathology: vanishing bile duct diseases

479 Aadland E, Schrumpf E, Fausa O, Elgjo K, Heilo A, Aakhus T, Gjone E. Primary sclerosing cholangitis: a long-term follow-up study. Scand J Gastroenterol 1987, **22**: 655–664.

480 Alagille D, Odièvre M, Gautier M, Dommergues JP. Hepatic ductular hypoplasia associated with characteristic facies, vertebral malformations, retarded physical, mental and sexual development and cardiac murmur. J Pediatr 1975, **86**: 63–71.

481 Angula P, Lindor KD. Primary sclerosing cholangitis. Hepatology 1999, **30**: 325–332.

482 Balistreri WF, Grand R, Hoofnagle JH, Suchy FJ, Ryckman FC, Perlmutter DH, Sokol RJ. Biliary atresia: current concepts and research directions. Hepatology 1996, **23**: 1682–1692.

483 Ben Ari Z, Dhillon AP, Sherlock S. Autoimmune cholangiopathy: part of the spectrum of autoimmune chronic active hepatitis. Hepatology 1993, **18**: 10–15.

484 Benger JR, Thompson MH. Annular pancreas and obstructive jaundice. Am J Gastroenterol 1997, **92**: 713–714.

485 Bhathal PS, Powell LW. Primary intrahepatic obliterating cholangitis: a possible variant of sclerosing cholangitis. Gut 1969, **10**: 886–893.

486 Bouche H, Housset C, Dumont J-L, Carnot F, Menu Y, Aveline B, Belghiti J, Boboc B, Erlinger S, Berthelot P, Pol S. AIDS-related cholangitis. Diagnostic features and course in 15 patients. J Hepatol 1993, **17**: 34–39.

487 Broome U, Glaumann H, Hultcrantz R. Liver histology and follow up of 68 patients with ulcerative colitis and normal liver function tests. Gut 1990, **31**: 468–472.

488 Broomé U, Olsson R, Lööf L, Bodemar G, Hultcrantz R, Danielsson A, Prytz H, Sandberg-Gertzén H, Wallerstedt S, Lindberg G. Natural history and prognostic factors in 305 Swedish patients with primary sclerosing cholangitis. Gut 1996, **38**: 610–615.

489 Brunner G, Klinge O. Ein der chronisch-destruierenden nicht-eitrigen Cholangitis ähnliches Krankheitsbild mit antinukleären Antikörpern (Immuncholangitis). Dtsch Med Wochenschr 1987, **112**: 1454–1458.

490 Burak KW, Pearson DC, Swain MG, Kelly J, Urbanski SJ, Bridges RJ. Case report. Familial idiopathic adulthood ductopenia: a report of five cases in three generations. J Hepatol 2000, **32**: 159–163.

491 Carpenter HA. Bacterial and parasitic cholangitis. Mayo Clin Proc 1998, **73**: 473–478.

492 Christoffersen P, Poulsen H, Scheuer PJ. Abnormal bile duct epithelium in chronic aggressive hepatitis and primary biliary cirrhosis. Hum Pathol 1972, **3:** 227–235.

493 Colina F, Pinedo F, Solis JA, Moreno D, Nevado M. Nodular regenerative hyperplasia of the liver in early histological stages of primary biliary cirrhosis. Gastroenterology 1992, **102:** 1319–1324.

494 Degott C, Zafrani ES, Callard P, Balkau B, Poupon RE, Poupon R. Histopathological study of primary biliary cirrhosis and the effect of ursodeoxycholic acid treatment on histology progression. Hepatology 1999, **29:** 1007–1012.

495 Desmet V, Callea F. Ductal plate malformation (DPM) in extrahepatic bile duct atresia (EHBDA). In Ohi R (ed.): Biliary atresia. Tokyo, 1991, ICOM Associates, pp. 27–31.

496 Desmet VJ. Vanishing bile duct disorders. In Boyer JL, Ockner RK (eds): Progress in liver diseases, vol. X. Philadelphia, 1992, W.B. Saunders, pp. 89–121.

497 Desmet VJ. Vanishing bile duct syndrome in drug-induced liver disease. J Hepatol 1997, **26** (Suppl 1): 31–35.

498 Desmet VJ. Histopathology of chronic cholestasis and adult ductopenic syndrome. In Lindor KD, Dickson ER (eds): Clinics in liver disease, vol. 2, no. 2. Primary biliary cirrhosis, primary sclerosing cholangitis and adult cholangiopathies. Philadelphia, 1998, W.B. Saunders, pp. 249–264.

499 Desmet VJ. Pathogenesis of ductal plate abnormalities. Mayo Clin Proc 1998, **73:** 80–89.

500 Desmet VJ, Callea F. Cholestatic syndromes of infancy and childhood. In Zakim D, Boyer TD (eds): Hepatology: a textbook of liver disease, ed. 3, vol. 2. Philadelphia, 1996, W.B. Saunders, pp. 1649–1698.

501 Domschke W, Klein R, Terracciano L-M, Jung P, Kirchner T, Berg PA, Bianchi L. Sequential occurrence of primary sclerosing cholangitis and autoimmune hepatitis type III in a patient with ulcerative colitis: a follow up study over 14 years. Liver 2000, **20:** 340–345.

502 Faa G, Van Eyken P, Demelia L, Vallebona E, Costa V, Desmet VJ. Idiopathic adulthood ductopenia presenting with chronic recurrent cholestasis. A case report. J Hepatol 1991, **12:** 14–20.

503 Fleming KA. Interlobular bile duct basement membrane thickening – a specific marker for primary sclerosing cholangitis (PSC)? J Pathol 1993, **169** (Suppl): 135A.

504 Fleming KA, Boberg KM, Glaumann H, Berrgquist A, Smith D, Clausen OPF. Biliary dysplasia as a marker of cholangiocarcinoma in primary sclerosing cholangitis. J Hepatol 2001, **34:** 360–365.

505 Garrido MC, Hubscher SG. Accuracy of staging in primary biliary cirrhosis. J Clin Pathol 1996, **49:** 556–559.

506 Gautier M, Elliot N. Extrahepatic biliary atresia. Morphological study of 98 biliary remnants. Arch Pathol Lab Med 1981, **105:** 397–402.

507 Gautier M, Jehan P, Odièvre M. Histologic study of biliary fibrous remnants in 48 cases of extra-hepatic biliary atresia: correlation with postoperative bile flow restoration. J Pediatr 1976, **89:** 704–709.

508 Gershwin ME, Ansari AA, Mackay IR, Nakanuma Y, Nishio A, Rowley MJ, Coppel RL. Primary biliary cirrhosis: an orchestrated immune response against epithelial cells. Immunol Rev 2000, **174:** 210–225.

509 Harnois D, Lindor KD. Primary sclerosing cholangitis: evolving concepts in diagnosis and treatment. Dig Dis 1997, **15:** 23–41.

510 Harrison RF, Hubscher SG. The spectrum of bile duct lesions in end-stage primary sclerosing cholangitis. Histopathology 1991, **19:** 321–327.

511 Hashida Y, Yunis EJ. Syndromatic paucity of interlobular bile ducts: hepatic histopathology of the early and endstage liver. Pediatr Pathol 1988, **8:** 1–15.

512 Heathcote EJ. Autoimmune cholangitis. In Lindor KD, Dickson ER (eds): Clinics in liver disease, vol. 2, no. 2. Primary biliary cirrhosis, primary sclerosing cholangitis and adult cholangiopathies. Philadelphia, 1998, W.B. Saunders, pp. 303–311.

513 International Group. Histopathology of the intrahepatic biliary tree. Liver 1983, **3:** 161–175.

514 Kahn E. Paucity of interlobular bile ducts. Arteriohepatic dysplasia and nonsyndromic duct paucity. In Abramowsky CR, Bernstein J, Rosenberg HS (eds): Perspectives in pediatric pathology. Transplantation pathology – hepatic morphogenesis, vol. 14. Basel, 1991, Karger, pp. 168–215.

515 Kahn E, Markowitz J, Aiges H, Daum F. Human ontogeny of the bile duct to portal space ratio. Hepatology 1989, **10:** 21–23.

516 Kaya M, Angulo P, Lindor KD. Overlap of autoimmune hepatitis and primary sclerosing cholangitis: an evaluation of a modified scoring system. J Hepatol 2000, **33:** 537–542.

517 Krukowski ZH, McPhie JL, Farquharson AGH, Matheson NA. Proliferative cholangitis (cholangitis glandularis proliferans). Br J Surg 1983, **70:** 166–171.

518 Lefkowitch JH. Biliary atresia. Mayo Clin Proc 1998, **73:** 90–95.

519 Locke GR III, Therneau TM, Ludwig J, Dickson ER, Lindor KD. Time course of histological progression in primary biliary cirrhosis. Hepatology 1996, **23:** 52–56.

520 Ludwig J. New concepts in biliary cirrhosis. Semin Liver Dis 1987, **7:** 293–301.

521 Ludwig J. Small-duct primary sclerosing cholangitis. Semin Liver Dis 1991, **11:** 11–17.

522 Ludwig J. Idiopathic adulthood ductopenia: an update. Mayo Clin Proc 1998, **73:** 285–291.

523 Ludwig J, Colina F, Poterucha JJ. Granulomas in primary sclerosing cholangitis. Liver 1995, **15:** 307–312.

524 Ludwig J, Dickson ER, McDonald GSA. Staging of chronic nonsuppurative destructive cholangitis (syndrome of primary biliary cirrhosis). Virchows Arch [A] 1978, **379:** 103–112.

525 Ludwig J, Wiesner RH, La Russo NF. Idiopathic adulthood ductopenia. A cause of chronic cholestatic liver disease and biliary cirrhosis. J Hepatol 1988, **7:** 193–199.

526 MacSween RNM, Burt AD, Haboubi NY. Unusual variant of primary sclerosing cholangitis. J Clin Pathol 1987, **40:** 541–545.

527 Martins EB, Chapman RW. Sclerosing cholangitis. Curr Opin Gastroenterol 1999, **15:** 436–441.

528 McNair AN, Moloney M, Portmann BC, Williams R, McFarlane IG. Autoimmune hepatitis overlapping with primary sclerosing cholangitis in five cases. Am J Gastroenterol 1998, **93:** 777–784.

529 Miyakawa H, Tanaka A, Kikuchi K, Matsushita M, Kitazawa E, Kawaguchi N, Fujikawa H, Gershwin ME. Detection of antimitochondrial autoantibodies in immunofluorescent AMA-negative patients with primary biliary cirrhosis using recombinant autoantigens. Hepatology 2001, **34:** 243–248.

530 Moreno A, Carreno V, Cano A, Gonzalez C. Idiopathic biliary ductopenia in adults without symptoms of liver disease. N Engl J Med 1997, **336:** 835–838.

531 Nakanuma Y. Pathology of septum formation in primary biliary cirrhosis: a histological study in the non-cirrhotic stage. Virchows Arch [A] 1991, **419:** 381–387.

532 Nakanuma Y. Necroinflammatory changes in hepatic lobules in primary biliary cirrhosis with less well-defined cholestatic changes. Hum Pathol 1993, **24:** 378–383.

533 Nakanuma Y, Hirata K. Unusual hepatocellular lesions in primary biliary cirrhosis resembling but unrelated to hepatocellular neoplasms. Virchows Arch [A] 1993, **422:** 17–23.

534 Nakanuma Y, Ohta G. Histometric and serial section observations of the intrahepatic bile ducts in primary biliary cirrhosis. Gastroenterology 1979, **76:** 1326–1332.

535 Nakanuma Y, Ohta G, Kobayashi K, Kato Y. Histological and histometric examination of the intrahepatic portal vein branches in primary biliary cirrhosis without regenerative nodules. Am J Gastroenterol 1982, **77:** 405–413.

536 Nakanuma Y, Saito K, Unoura M. Semiquantitative assessment of cholestasis and lymphocytic piecemeal necrosis in primary biliary cirrhosis: a histologic and immunohistochemical study. J Clin Gastroenterol 1990, **12**: 357–362.

537 Nakanuma Y, Tsuneyama K, Gershwin ME, Yasoshima M. Pathology and immunopathology of primary biliary cirrhosis with emphasis on bile duct lesions: recent progress. Semin Liver Dis 1995, **15**: 313–328.

538 Piccoli DA, Spinner NB. Alagille syndrome and the Jagged 1 gene. Semin Liver Dis 2001, **21**: 525–534.

539 Pol S, Romana CA, Richard S, Amouyal P, Desportes-Livage I, Carnot F, Pays JF, Berthelot P. Microsporidia infection in patients with the human immunodeficiency virus and unexplained cholangitis. N Engl J Med 1993, **328**: 95–99.

540 Popper H, Schaffner F. Nonsuppurative destructive chronic cholangitis and chronic hepatitis. In Popper H, Schaffner F (eds): Progress in liver diseases, vol. III. New York, 1970, Grune and Stratton, pp. 336–354.

541 Portmann B, Popper H, Neuberger J, Williams R. Sequential and diagnostic features in primary biliary cirrhosis based on serial histologic study in 209 patients. Gastroenterology 1985, **88**: 1777–1790.

542 Poupon R, Chazouillères O, Poupon RE. Chronic cholestatic diseases. J Hepatol 2000, **32** (Suppl 1): 129–140.

543 Raweily EA, Gibson AAM, Burt AD. Abnormalities of intrahepatic bile ducts in extrahepatic biliary atresia. Histopathology 1990, **17**: 521–527.

544 Roberts EA. Primary sclerosing cholangitis in children. J Gastroenterol Heptol 1999, **14**: 588–593.

545 Rubin E, Schaffner F, Popper H. Primary biliary cirrhosis: Chronic non-suppurative destructive cholangitis. Am J Pathol 1965, **46**: 387–407.

546 Scheuer PJ. Primary biliary cirrhosis. Proc R Soc Med 1967, **60**: 1257–1260.

547 Schweizer P. Extrahepatische Gallengangsatresie – Eine analytische Bewertung prognostischer Faktoren. Ein Beitrag zu einem rationelen Therapieansatz. Z Kinderchir 1990, **45**: 365–370.

548 Shimada H, Nihmoto S, Matsuba A, Nakagawara G. Acute cholangitis: a histopathologic study. J Clin Gastroenterol 1988, **10**: 197–200.

549 Sokol RJ, Mack C. Etiopathogenesis of biliary atresia. Semin Liver Dis 2001, **21**: 517–524.

550 Tan CE, Davenport M, Driver M, Howard ER. Does the morphology of the extrahepatic biliary remnants in biliary atresia influence survival? A review of 205 cases. J Pediatr Surg 1994, **29**: 1459–1464.

551 Terracciano LM, Cathomas G, Vecchione R, Tornillo L, Gudat F, Bianchi L. Extrahepatic bile duct atresia associated with hyperplasia of the intrahepatic bile ducts ("early severe form"): high incidence in a south-italian population. Pathol Res Pract 1995, **191**: 192.

552 Treem WR, Krzymowski GA, Cartun RW, Pedersen CA, Hyams JS, Berman M. Cytokeratin immunohistochemical examination of liver biopsies in infants with Alagille syndrome and biliary atresia. J Pediatr Gastroenterol Nutr 1992, **15**: 73–80.

553 Van Eyken P, Desmet VJ. Cytokeratins and the liver. Liver 1993, **13**: 113–122.

554 Van Eyken P, Sciot R, Callea F, Van der Steen K, Moerman P, Desmet VJ. The development of the intrahepatic bile ducts in man: a keratin-immunohistochemical study. Hepatology 1988, **8**: 1586–1595.

555 West AB, Chatila R. Differential diagnosis of bile duct injury and ductopenia. Semin Diagn Pathol 1998, **15**: 270–284.

556 Woodward J, Neuberger J. Autoimmune overlap syndromes. Hepatology 2001, **33**: 994–1002.

557 Yabushita K, Yamamoto K, Ibuki N, Okano N, Matsumura S, Okamoto R, Shimada N, Tsuji T. Aberrant expression of cytokeratin 7 as a histological marker of progression in primary biliary cirrhosis. Liver 2001, **21**: 50–55.

Childhood disorders and disorders of metabolism
Cholestasis and hyperbilirubinemia
Cholestatic disorders

558 Setchell KDR, O'Connell NC. Disorders of bile acid synthesis and metabolism: a metabolic basis for liver disease. In Suchy FJ, Sokol RJ, Balistreri WF (eds): Liver disease in children, ed. 2. Philadelphia, 2001, Lippincott Williams & Wilkins, pp. 701–733.

Hyperbilirubinemias

559 Toker C, Trevino N. Hepatic ultrastructure in chronic idiopathic jaundice. Arch Pathol 1965, **80**: 453–460.

560 Trauner M, Meier PJ, Boyer JL. Molecular pathogenesis of cholestasis. N Engl J Med 1998, **339**: 1217–1227.

Inherited metabolic disorders

561 Ishak KG, Sharp HL. Metabolic errors and liver disease. In MacSween RNM, Anthony PP, Scheuer PJ, Ishak KG, Portmann BC, Burt AD (eds): Pathology of the liver, ed. 4. Edinburgh, 2001, Churchill Livingstone.

Endoplasmic reticulum storage diseases

562 Berkowitz M, Gavalier JS, Kelly RH, Prieto J, Van Thiel DH. Lack of increased heterozygous alpha-1-antitrypsin deficiency phenotypes among patients with hepatocellular and bile duct carcinoma. Hepatology 1992, **15**: 407–410.

563 Brantly MT, Nukiwa T, Crystal RG. Molecular basis of alpha-1-antitrypsin deficiency. Am J Med 1988, **84** (Suppl 6A): 13–31.

564 Brind AM, Bassendine MF, Bennett MK, James OF. Alpha-1-antitrypsin granules in the liver – always important? Q J Med 1990, **76**: 699–709.

565 Callea F, Brisigotti M, Faa G, Lucini L, Eriksson S. Identification of PiZ gene products in liver tissue by a monoclonal antibody specific for the Z mutant of alpha-1-antitrypsin. J Hepatol 1991, **12**: 372–376.

566 Callea F, Brisigotti M, Fabretti G, Bonino F, Desmet VJ. Hepatic endoplasmic reticulum storage diseases. Liver 1992, **12**: 357–362.

567 Callea F, De Vos R, Togni R, Tardanico R, Vanstapel MJ, Desmet VJ. Fibrinogen inclusions in liver cells: a new type of ground-glass hepatocyte. Immune light and electron microscopic characterization. Histopathology 1986, **10**: 65–73.

568 Callea F, Fevery J, Massi G, Lievens C, De Groote J, Desmet VJ. Alpha-1-antitrypsin (AAT) and its stimulation in the liver of PiMZ phenotype individuals. A "recruitment-secretory block" ("R-SB") phenomenon. Liver 1984, **4**: 325–337.

569 Carlson JA, Rogers BB, Sifers RN, Finegold MJ, Clift SM, De Mayo FJ, Bullock DW, Woo SL. The accumulation of PiZ alpha-1-antitrypsin causes liver damage in transgenic mice. J Clin Invest 1989, **83**: 1183–1190.

570 Eriksson S, Carlson J, Velez R. Risk of cirrhosis and primary liver cancer in alpha-1-antitrypsin deficiency. N Engl J Med 1986, **314**: 736–739.

571 Feldman G, Bignon J, Chahinian P, Degott C, Benhamou JP. Hepatocyte ultrastructural changes in alpha-1-antitrypsin deficiency. Gastroenterology 1974, **67**: 1214–1224.

572 Fischer HP, Ortiz-Pallardo ME, Ko Y, Esch C, Zhou H. Chronic liver disease in heterozygous alpha-1-antitrypsin deficiency PiZ. J Hepatol 2000, **33**: 883–892.

573 Ibarguen E, Gros C, Savik K, Sharp HL. Liver disease in alpha-1-antitrypsin deficiency: prognostic indicators. J Pediatr 1990, **117**: 864–870.

574 Jack CIA, Evans CC. Three cases of alpha-1-antitrypsin deficiency in the elderly. Postgrad Med J 1991, **67**: 840–842.

575 Kahn E. Paucity of interlobular bile ducts. Arteriohepatic

dysplasia and nonsyndromic duct paucity. In Abramowsky CR, Bernstein J, Rosenberg HS (eds): Perspectives in pediatric pathology. Transplantation pathology—hepatic morphogenesis, vol. 14. Basel, 1991, Karger, pp. 168–215.

576 Larsson C. Natural history and life expectancy in severe alpha-1-antitrypsin deficiency PiZ. Acta Med Scand 1978, **204:** 345–351.

577 Laurell CB, Eriksson S. The electrophoretic alpha-1-globulin pattern of serum alpha-1-antitrypsin deficiency. Scand J Clin Lab Invest 1963, **15:** 132–140.

578 Mendelsohn G, Gomperts ED, Gurwitz D. Severe antithrombin III deficiency in an infant associated with multiple arterial and venous thromboses. Thromb Haemost 1976, **36:** 495–502.

579 Odièvre M, Martin JP, Hadchouel M, Alagille D. Alpha-1-antitrypsin deficiency and liver disease in children: phenotypes, manifestations and prognosis. Pediatrics 1976, **57:** 226–231.

580 Perlmutter DH. Alpha-1-antitrypsin deficiency. Semin Liver Dis 1998, **18:** 217–225.

581 Propst T, Propst A, Dietze O, Judmaier G, Braunstainer H, Vogel W. High prevalence of viral infection in adults with homozygous and heterozygous alpha-1-antitrypsin deficiency and chronic liver disease. Ann Intern Med 1992, **117:** 641–645.

582 Sveger T. Prospective study of children with alpha-1-antitrypsin deficiency: eight-year-old follow-up. J Pediatr 1989, **104:** 91–94.

583 Vogel W, Propst T, Propst A, Dietze O, Judmaier G, Braunsteiner H. Causes of liver disease in an adult population with heterozygous and homozygous alpha-1-antitryspin deficiency. Acta Paediatr 1994, **Suppl 393:** 24–26.

Indian childhood cirrhosis

584 Adamson M, Reiner B, Olson JL, Goodman Z, Plotnick L, Bernardini I, Gahl WA. Indian childhood cirrhosis in an American child. Gastroenterology 1992, **102:** 1771–1777.

585 Lefkowitch JH, Honig CL, King ME, Hagstrom JW. Hepatic copper overload and features of Indian childhood cirrhosis in an American sibship. N Engl J Med 1982, **307:** 271–277.

586 Müller-Höcker J, Meyer U, Wiebecke B, Hubner G, Eife R, Kellner M, Schramel P. Copper storage disease of the liver and chronic dietary copper intoxication in two further German infants mimicking Indian childhood cirrhosis. Pathol Res Pract 1988, **183:** 39–45.

587 Popper H, Goldfischer S, Sternlieb I, Nayak NL, Madhavan TV. Cytoplasmic copper and its toxic effects. Studies in Indian childhood cirrhosis. Lancet 1979, **1:** 1205–1208.

588 Tanner MS, Portmann B, Mowat AP, Williams R, Pandit AN, Mills CF. Increased hepatic copper concentration in Indian childhood cirrhosis. Lancet 1979, **1:** 1203–1205.

Disorders of copper and iron metabolism
Wilson's disease (hepatolenticular degeneration)

589 Bowcock AM, Farrer LA, Hebert JM, Agger M, Sternlieb I, Scheinberg IH, Buys CH, Scheffer H, Frydman M, Chajek-Saul T, Bonne-Tamir B, Cavalli-Sforza LL. Eight closely linked loci place the Wilson's disease locus within 13q14-q21. Am J Hum Genet 1988, **43:** 664–674.

590 Davies SE, Williams R, Portmann B. Hepatic morphology and histochemistry of Wilson's disease presenting as fulminant hepatic failure: a study of 11 cases. Histopathology 1989, **15:** 385–394.

591 Faa G, Ligvori C, Columbano A, Diaz G. Uneven copper distribution in the newborn liver. Hepatology 1987, **7:** 838–842.

592 Goldfischer S, Sternlieb I. Changes in the distribution of hepatic copper in relation to the progression of Wilson's disease (hepatolenticular degeneration). Am J Pathol 1968, **53:** 883–891.

593 Gollan JL, Gollan TJ. Wilson disease in 1998: genetic, diagnostic and therapeutic aspects. J Hepatol 1998, **28:** 28–36.

594 Ludwig J, Moyer TP, Rakela J. The liver biopsy diagnosis of Wilson's disease. Methods in pathology. Am J Clin Pathol 1994, **102:** 443–446.

595 Mulder TPJ, Janssens AR, Verspaget HW, Van Hattum J, Lamers CBHW. Metallotheonein concentration in the liver of patients with Wilson's disease, primary biliary cirrhosis, and liver metastasis of colorectal cancer. J Hepatol 1992, **16:** 346–350.

596 Pilloni L, Lecca S, Van Eyken P, Flore C, Demelia L, Pilleri G, Nurchi AM, Farci AM, Ambu R, Callea F, Faa G. Value of histochemical stains for copper in the diagnosis of Wilson's disease. Histopathology 1998, **33:** 28–33.

597 Scheinberg IH, Sternlieb I. Wilson's disease. Major problems in internal medicine XXIII. Philadelphia, 1984, W.B. Saunders.

598 Scott J, Gollan JL, Samourian S, Sherlock S. Wilson's disease presenting as chronic active hepatitis. Gastroenterology 1978, **74:** 645–651.

599 Sternlieb I. Fraternal concordance of types of abnormal hepatocellular mitochondria in Wilson's disease. Hepatology 1992, **16:** 728–732.

600 Sternlieb I, Scheinberg IH. Chronic hepatitis as a first manifestation of Wilson's disease. Ann Intern Med 1972, **76:** 59–64.

601 Stromeyer FW, Ishak KG. Histology of the liver in Wilson's disease: a study of 34 cases. Am J Clin Pathol 1980, **73:** 12–24.

Iron overload (siderosis, hemosiderosis)

602 Basset ML, Halliday JW, Powell LW. Value of hepatic iron measurements in early hemochromatosis and determination of the critical iron level associated with fibrosis. Hepatology 1986, **6:** 24–29.

603 Deugnier YM, Loréal O, Turlin B, Guyader D, Jouanolle H, Moirand R, Jacquelinet C, Brissot P. Liver pathology in genetic hemochromatosis: a review of 135 homozygous cases and their bioclinical correlations. Gastroenterology 1992, **102:** 2050–2059.

604 Deugnier YM, Turlin B, Powell LW, Summers KM, Moirand R, Fletcher L, Loréal O, Brissot P, Halliday JW. Differentiation between heterozygotes and homozygotes in genetic hemochromatosis by means of a histological hepatic iron index: a study of 192 cases. Hepatology 1993, **17:** 30–34.

605 Ludwig J, Batts KP, Moyer TP, Baldus WP, Fairbanks VF. Liver biopsy diagnosis of homozygous hemochromatosis: a diagnostic algorithm. Mayo Clin Proc 1993, **68:** 263–267.

606 Olynyk J, Hall P, Sallie R, Reed W, Shilkin K, Mackinnon M. Computerized measurement of iron in liver biopsies: a comparison with biochemical iron measurement. Hepatology 1990, **12:** 26–30.

607 Richter GW. The iron-loaded cell – the cytopathology of iron storage. Am J Pathol 1978, **91:** 362–404.

Genetic (hereditary, primary or idiopathic) hemochromatosis

608 Bacon BR, Powell LW, Adams PC, Kresina TF, Hoofnagle JH. Molecular medicine and hemochromatosis: at the crossroad. Gastroenterology 1999, **116:** 193–207.

609 Bulaj ZJ, Griffen LM, Jorde LB, Edwards CQ, Kushner JP. Clinical and biochemical abnormalities in people heterozygous for hemochromatosis. N Engl J Med 1996, **335:** 1799–1805.

610 Camaschella C, Fargion S, Sampietro M, Roetto A, Bosio S, Garozzo G, Arosio C, Piperno A. Inherited HFE-unrelated hemochromatosis in Italian families. Hepatology 1999, **29:** 1563–1564.

611 Deugnier YM, Loréal O, Turlin B, Guyader D, Jouanolle H, Moirand R, Jacquelinet C, Brissot P. Liver pathology in genetic hemochromatosis: a review of 135 homozygous cases and their bioclinical correlations. Gastroenterology 1992, **102:** 2050–2059.

612 Deugnier YM, Turlin B, Powell LW, Summers KM, Moirand R, Fletcher L, Loréal O, Brissot P, Halliday JW. Differentiation between heterozygotes and homozygotes in genetic

hemochromatosis by means of a histological hepatic iron index: a study of 192 cases. Hepatology 1993, **17**: 30–34.

613 EASL International Consensus Conference on Haemochromatosis. J Hepatol 2000, **33**: 485–504.

614 Höhler T, Leininger S, Köhler HH, Schirmacher P, Galle PR. Heterozygosity for the hemochromatosis gene in liver diseases – prevalence and effects on liver histology. Liver 2000, **20**: 482–486.

615 Moirand R, Jouanolle AM, Brissot P, Le Gaill JY, David V, Deugnier Y. Phenotypic expression of HFE mutations: a French study of 1110 unrelated iron-overloaded patients and relatives. Gastroenterology 1999, **116**: 372–377.

616 Niederau C, Fischer R, Sonnenberg A, Stremmel W, Trampisch HJ, Strohmeyer G. Survival and causes of death in cirrhotic and in noncirrhotic patients with primary hemochromatosis. N Engl J Med 1985, **319**: 1256–1262.

617 Powell LW, Kerr JFR. The pathology of the liver in hemochromatosis. Pathobiol Annu 1975, **5**: 317–337.

Neonatal (perinatal) iron overload (neonatal (perinatal) hemochromatosis)

618 Moerman P, Pauwels P, Vandenberghe K, Devlieger H, Fryns JP, Verresen H, Jaeken J, Lauweryns J, Eggermont E. Neonatal haemochromatosis. Histopathology 1990, **17**: 345–351.

619 Silver MM, Valberg LS, Cutz E, Lines LD, Phillips MJ. Hepatic morphology and iron quantitation in perinatal hemochromatosis. Am J Pathol 1993, **143**: 1312–1325.

Hepatic siderosis of varied etiology

620 Bassett ML, Halliday JW, Powell LW. Genetic hemochromatosis. Semin Liver Dis 1984, **4**: 217–227.

621 Bothwell TH, Abrahams C, Bradlow BA, Charlton RW. Idiopathic and Bantu hemochromatosis. Arch Pathol 1965, **79**: 163–168.

622 Cortes JM, Oliva H, Paradinas FJ, Hernandez-Guio C. The pathology of the liver in porphyria cutanea tarda. Histopathology 1980, **4**: 471–485.

623 Faa F, Sciot R, Farci AMG, Callea F, Ambu R, Congiu T, Van Eyken P, Cappai G, Marras A, Costa V, Desmet VJ. Iron concentration and distribution in the newborn liver. Liver 1994, **14**: 193–199.

624 Silver MM, Valberg LS, Cutz E, Lines LD, Phillips MJ. Hepatic morphology and iron quantitation in perinatal hemochromatosis. Am J Pathol 1993, **143**: 1312–1325.

625 Wonke B, Hoffbrand AV, Brown D, Dusheiko G. Antibody to hepatitis C virus in multiply transfused patients with thalassaemia major. J Clin Pathol 1990, **43**: 638–640.

Fibropolycystic diseases (ductal plate malformation)

626 Desmet VJ. Congenital diseases of intrahepatic bile ducts: variations on the theme "ductal plate malformation". Hepatology 1992, **16**: 1069–1083.

627 Desmet VJ. Pathogenesis of ductal plate abnormalities. Mayo Clin Proc 1998, **73**: 80–89.

628 Inui A, Fujisawa T, Suemitsu T, Fujikawa S, Ariizumi M, Kagimoto S, Kinoshita K. A case of Caroli's disease with special reference to hepatic CT and US findings. J Pediatr Gastroenterol Nutr 1992, **14**: 463–466.

629 Jørgensen MJ. The ductal plate malformation. A study of the intrahepatic bile duct lesion in infantile polycystic disease and congenital hepatic fibrosis. Acta Pathol Microbiol Scand [Suppl] 1977, **257**: 1–88.

630 Summerfield JA, Nagafuchi Y, Sherlock S, Cadafalch J, Scheuer PJ. Hepatobiliary fibropolycystic disease: a clinical and histological review of 51 patients. J Hepatol 1986, **2**: 141–156.

Autosomal recessive polycystic kidney disease

631 Premkumar A, Berdon WE, Levy J, Amodio J, Abramson SJ, Newhouse JH. The emergence of hepatic fibrosis and portal hypertension in infants and children with autosomal recessive polycystic kidney disease: initial and follow-up sonographic and radiographic findings. Pediatr Radiol 1988, **18**: 123–129.

Congenital hepatic fibrosis

632 Desmet VJ. What is congenital hepatic fibrosis? Histopathology 1992, **20**: 465–477.

Caroli's disease

633 Desmet VJ. Pathogenesis of ductal plate abnormalities. Mayo Clin Proc 1998, **73**: 80–89.

634 Ludwig J, MacCarty RL, La Russo NF, Krom RAF, Wiesner RH. Intrahepatic cholangiectases and large-duct obliteration in primary sclerosing cholangitis. Hepatology 1986, **6**: 560–568.

Von Meyenburg complex (microhamartoma)

635 Chung EB. Multiple bile duct hamartomas. Cancer 1970, **26**: 287–296.

636 Desmet VJ. Pathogenesis of ductal plate abnormalities. Mayo Clin Proc 1998, **73**: 80–89.

Autosomal dominant polycystic kidney disease

637 Gabow PA, Johnson AM, Kaehny WD, Manco-Johnson ML, Duley IT, Everson GT. Risk factors for the development of hepatic cysts in autosomal dominant polycystic kidney disease. Hepatology 1990, **11**: 1033–1037.

Solitary (nonparasitic) cyst

638 Wheeler DA, Edmondson HA. Ciliated hepatic foregut cyst. Am J Surg Pathol 1984, **8**: 467–470.

Vascular disorders

Hepatoportal sclerosis

639 Bernard PH, Le Bail B, Cransac M, Barcina MG, Carles J, Balabaud C, Bioulac-Sage P. Progression from idiopathic portal hypertension to incomplete septal cirrhosis with liver failure requiring liver transplantation. J Hepatol 1995, **22**: 495–499.

640 Bioulac-Sage P, Le Bail B, Bernard P-H, Balabaud C. Hepatoportal sclerosis. Semin Liver Dis 1995, **15**: 329–339.

641 Ludwig J, Hashimoto E, Obata H, Baldus WP. Idiopathic portal hypertension: a histopathological study of 26 Japanese cases. Histopathology 1993, **22**: 227–234.

642 Mikkelsen WP, Edmondson HA, Peters RL, Redeker AG, Reynolds TR. Extra- and intrahepatic portal hypertension without cirrhosis (hepatoportal sclerosis). Ann Surg 1965, **162**: 602–620.

643 Nakanuma Y, Hoso M, Sasaki M, Terada T, Katayanagi K, Nonomura A, Kurumaya H, Harada A, Obata H. Histopathology of the liver in non-cirrhotic portal hypertension of unknown aetiology. Histopathology 1996, **28**: 195–204.

644 Nevens F, Fevery J, Van Steenbergen W, Sciot R, Desmet V, De Groote J. Arsenic and non-cirrhotic portal hypertension. A report of eight cases. J Hepatol 1990, **11**: 80–85.

645 Ohbu M, Okudaira M, Watanabe K, Kaneko S, Takai T. Histopathological study of intrahepatic aberrant vessels in cases of non-cirrhotic portal hypertension. Hepatology 1994, **20**: 302–308.

646 Roskams T, Baptista A, Bianchi L, Burt A, Callea F, Denk H, De Groote J, Desmet V, Hübscher S, Ishak K, MacSween R, Portmann B, Poulsen H, Scheuer P, Terracciano L, Thaler H. Histopathology of portal hypertension. A practical guideline. Histopathology 2002, **42**: 2–13.

647 Sarin SK. Non-cirrhotic portal fibrosis. Gut 1989, **30**: 406–415.

648 Sciot R, Staessen D, Van Damme B, Van Steenbergen W, Fevery J, De Groote J, Desmet VJ. Incomplete septal cirrhosis: histopathological aspects. Histopathology 1988, **13**: 593–603.

649 Shepherd P, Harrison DJ. Idiopathic portal hypertension associated with cytotoxic drugs. J Clin Pathol 1990, **43**: 206–210.

650 Thomas LB, Popper H, Berk PD, Selikoff I, Falk H. Vinyl chloride-induced liver disease. From idiopathic portal hypertension (Banti's syndrome) to angiosarcomas. N Engl J Med 1975, **292**: 17–22.

651 Villeneuve JP, Huet PM, Joly JG, Marleau D, et al. Idiopathic portal hypertension. Am J Med 1997, **61**: 459–464.

652 Wanless IR. Noncirrhotic portal hypertension: recent concepts. Prog Liver Dis 1996, **14**: 265–278.

Sinusoidal dilatation

653 Bruguera M, Aranguibel F, Ros E, Rodes J. Incidence and clinical significance of sinusoidal dilatation in liver biopsies. Gastroenterology 1978, **75**: 474–478.

654 Gerber MA, Thung SN, Bodenheimer HCJ, Kapelman B, Schaffner F. Characteristic histologic triad in liver adjacent to metastatic neoplasm. Liver 1986, **6**: 85–88.

655 Rolfes DB, Ishak KG. Liver disease in toxemia of pregnancy. Am J Gastroenterol 1986, **81**: 1138–1144.

656 Winkler K, Christoffersen P. A reappraisal of Poulsen's disease (hepatic zone 1 sinusoidal dilatation). APMIS 1991, **Suppl 23**: 86–90.

Peliosis hepatis

657 Larrey D, Pessayre D. Genetic factors in hepatotoxicity. In Guillouzo A (ed.): Liver cells and drugs, vol. 164. 1988, Colloque INSERM/John Libbey Eurotext, pp. 143–152.

658 Oligny LL, Lough J. Hepatic sinusoidal ectasia. Hum Pathol 1992, **23**: 953–956.

659 Soe KL, Soe M, Gluud C. Liver pathology associated with the use of anabolic-androgenic steroids. Liver 1992, **12**: 73–79.

660 Takiff H, Brems JJ, Pockros PJ, Elliott ML. Focal hemorrhagic necrosis of the liver. A rare cause of hemoperitoneum. Dig Dis Sci 1992, **37**: 1910–1914.

661 Wold LE, Ludwig J. Peliosis hepatis: two morphologic variants? Hum Pathol 1981, **12**: 388–389.

Venous outflow obstruction

662 Kanel GC, Ucci AA, Kaplan MM, Wolfe HJ. A distinctive perivenular hepatic lesion associated with heart failure. Am J Clin Pathol 1980, **73**: 235–329.

663 Ludwig J, Hashimoto E, McGill DB, Van Heerden JA. Classification of hepatic venous outflow obstruction: ambiguous terminology of the Budd-Chiari syndrome. Mayo Clin Proc 1990, **65**: 51–55.

664 Tanaka M, Wanless IR. Pathology of the liver in Budd-Chiari syndrome: portal vein thrombosis and the histogenesis of veno-centric cirrhosis, veno-portal cirrhosis, and large regenerative nodules. Hepatology 1998, **27**: 488–496.

665 Vickers CR, West RJ, Hübscher SG, Elias E. Hepatic vein webs and resistant ascites. Diagnosis, management and implications. J Hepatol 1989, **8**: 287–293.

Venoocclusive disease

666 Bach N, Thung SN, Schaffner F. Comfrey herb tea-induced hepatic veno-occlusive disease. Am J Med 1989, **87**: 97–99.

667 Burt AD, MacSween RNM. Hepatic vein lesions in alcoholic liver disease: retrospective biopsy and necropsy study. J Clin Pathol 1986, **39**: 63–67.

668 McDonald GB, Hinds MS, Fisher LD, Schoch HG, Wolford JL, Banaji M, Hardin BJ, Shulman HM, Clift RA. Veno-occlusive disease of the liver and multiorgan failure after bone marrow transplantation: a cohort study of 355 patients. Ann Intern Med 1993, **118**: 255–267.

669 Nakanuma Y, Ohta G, Doishita K. Quantitation and serial section observation of focal venoocclusive lesions of hepatic veins in liver cirrhosis. Virchows Arch [A] 1985, **405**: 429–438.

670 Stuart KL, Bras G. Veno-occlusive disease of the liver. Q J Med 1957, **26**: 291–315.

Nodular regeneration

671 International Working Party. Terminology of nodular hepatocellular lesions. Hepatology 1995, **22**: 983–993.

Nodular regenerative hyperplasia

672 Colina F, Pinedo F, Solis JA, Moreno D, Nevado M. Nodular regenerative hyperplasia of the liver in early histological stages of primary biliary cirrhosis. Gastroenterology 1992, **102**: 1319–1324.

673 Forbes GM, Silkin KB, Reed WD. Nodular regenerative hyperplasia of the liver. The importance of combined macroscopic and microscopic findings. Med J Aust 1991, **154**: 415–417.

674 Kobayashi S, Saito K, Nakanuma Y. Nodular regenerative hyperplasia of the liver in hepatocellular carcinoma. J Clin Gastroenterol 1993, **16**: 155–159.

675 Naber AH, Van Haelst U, Yap SH. Nodular regenerative hyperplasia of the liver. An important cause of portal hypertension in non-cirrhotic patients. J Hepatol 1991, **12**: 94–99.

676 Roskams T, Baptista A, Bianchi L, Burt A, Callea F, Denk H, De Groote J, Desmet V, Hübscher S, Ishak K, MacSween R, Portmann B, Poulsen H, Scheuer P, Terracciano L, Thaler H. Histopathology of portal hypertension. A practical guideline. Histopathology 2002, **42**: 2–13.

677 Wanless IR. Micronodular transformation (nodular regenerative hyperplasia) of the liver: a report of 64 cases among 2.500 autopsies and a new classification of benign hepatocellular nodules. Hepatology 1990, **11**: 787–797.

Partial nodular transformation

678 Hoso M, Terada T, Nakanuma Y. Partial nodular transformation of liver developing around intrahepatic portal venous emboli of hepatocellular carcinoma. Histopathology 1996, **29**: 580–582.

679 Wanless IR, Lentz JS, Roberts EA. Partial nodular transformation of liver in an adult with persistent ductus venosus. Arch Pathol Lab Med 1985, **109**: 427–432.

Focal nodular hyperplasia

680 Butron Vila MM, Haot J, Desmet VJ. Cholestatic features in focal nodular hyperplasia of the liver. Liver 1984, **4**: 387–395.

681 Wanless JR, Mawdsley C, Adams R. On the pathogenesis of focal nodular hyperplasia of the liver. Hepatology 1985, **5**: 1194–1200.

Liver disease in pregnancy

682 Rolfes DB, Ishak KG. Liver disease in pregnancy. Histopathology 1986, **10**: 555–570.

Liver disease unique to pregnancy
Acute fatty liver of pregnancy

683 Riely CA. Acute fatty liver of pregnancy. Semin Liver Dis 1987, **7**: 47–54.

684 Rinaldo P. Fatty acid transport and mitochondrial oxidation disorders. Semin Liver Dis 2001, **21**: 489–500.

685 Rolfes DB, Ishak KG. Acute fatty liver of pregnancy: a clinicopathologic study of 35 cases. Hepatology 1985, **5**: 1149–1158.

686 Rolfes DB, Ishak KG. Liver disease in pregnancy. Histopathology 1986, **10**: 555–570.

687 Schoeman MN, Batey RG, Wilcken B. Recurrent acute fatty liver of pregnancy associated with a fatty-acid oxidation defect in the offspring. Gastroenterology 1991, **100**: 544–548.

Toxemia of pregnancy (preeclampsia/eclampsia)

688 Riely CA. Acute fatty liver of pregnancy. Semin Liver Dis 1987, **7**: 47–54.

689　Rolfes DB, Ishak KG. Liver disease in pregnancy. Histopathology 1986, **10**: 555–570.

690　Rolfes DB, Ishak KG. Liver disease in toxemia of pregnancy. Am J Gastroenterol 1986, **81**: 1138–1144.

HELLP syndrome

691　Barton JR, Riely CA, Adamec TA, Shanklin DR, Khoury AD, Sibai BM. Hepatic histopathologic condition does not correlate with laboratory abnormalities in HELLP syndrome (hemolysis, elevated liver enzymes, and low platelet count). Am J Obstet Gynecol 1992, **167**: 1538–1543.

Intrahepatic cholestasis of pregnancy

692　Jacquemin E. Role of multidrug resistance 3 deficiency in pediatric and adult liver disease: one gene for three diseases. Semin Liver Dis 2001, **21**: 551–562.

693　Lammert F, Marschall HU, Glantz A, Matern S. Review. Intrahepatic cholestasis of pregnancy: molecular pathogenesis, diagnosis and management. J Hepatol 2000, **33**: 1012–1021.

694　Rolfes DB, Ishak KG. Liver disease in pregnancy. Histopathology 1986, **10**: 555–570.

Liver involvement in other organ and systemic diseases

Granulomas

695　Denk H, Scheuer PJ, Baptista A, Bianchi L, Callea F, De Groote J, Desmet VJ, Gudat F, Ishak KG, Korb G, MacSween RNM, Phillips MJ, Portmann B, Poulsen H, Schmid M, Thaler H. Guidelines for the diagnosis and interpretation of hepatic granulomas. Histopathology 1994, **25**: 209–218.

696　Devaney K, Goodman ZD, Epstein MS, Zimmerman HJ, Ishak KG. Hepatic sarcoidosis. Clinicopathologic features in 100 patients. Am J Surg Pathol 1993, **17**: 1272–1280.

697　Guckian JG, Perry JE. Granulomatous hepatitis. Analysis of 63 cases and review of the literature. Ann Intern Med 1966, **65**: 1081–1100.

698　Maddrey WC. Sarcoidosis and primary biliary cirrhosis. Associated disorders? N Engl J Med 1983, **308**: 588–590.

699　Murphy E, Griffiths MR, Hunter JA, Burt AD. Fibrin-ring granulomas: a non-specific reaction to liver injury? Histopathology 1991, **19**: 91–93.

700　Murphy JR, Sjogren MH, Kikendall JW, Peura DA, Goodman Z. Small bile duct abnormalities in sarcoidosis. J Clin Gastroenterol 1990, **12**: 555–561.

701　Pellegrin M, Delsol G, Auvergnat JC, Familiades J, Faure H, Guiu M. Granulomatous hepatitis in Q fever. Hum Pathol 1980, **11**: 51–57.

702　Rudzki C, Ishak KG, Zimmerman HJ. Chronic intrahepatic cholestasis of sarcoidosis. Am J Med 1975, **59**: 373–387.

703　Sartin JS, Walker RC. Granulomatous hepatitis. A retrospective review of 58 cases at the Mayo Clinic. Mayo Clin Proc 1991, **66**: 914–918.

704　Satti MB, al-Freihi H, Ibrahim EM, Abu-Melha A, al-Ghassab G, al-Idrissi HI, al-Sohaibani MO. Hepatic granuloma in Saudi-Arabia. A clinicopathological study of 59 cases. Am J Gastroenterol 1990, **85**: 669–674.

705　Sherlock S. The liver in sarcoidosis. Semin Respir Med 1992, **13**: 450–454.

706　Valla D, Pessegueiro-Miranda H, Degott C, Lebrec D, Rueff B, Benhamou JP. Hepatic sarcoidosis with portal hypertension. A report of seven cases with a review of the literature. Q J Med 1987, **63**: 531–544.

Cytomegalovirus infection

707　Chang MH, Huang HH, Huang ES, Kao CL, Hsu HY, Lee CY. Polymerase chain reaction to detect human cytomegalovirus in livers of infants with neonatal hepatitis. Gastroenterology 1992, **103**: 1022–1025.

708　Clarke J, Craig RM, Saffro R, Murphy P, Yokoo H. Cytomegalovirus granulomatous hepatitis. Am J Med 1979, **66**: 264–269.

709　Snover DC, Horwitz CA. Liver disease in cytomegalovirus mononucleosis: a light microscopical and immunoperoxidase study of six cases. Hepatology 1984, **4**: 408–412.

710　Strickler JG, Manivel JC, Copenhaver CM, Kubic VL. Comparison of in situ hybridization and immunohistochemistry for detection of cytomegalovirus and herpes simplex virus. Hum Pathol 1990, **21**: 443–448.

711　Theise ND, Conn M, Thung SN. Localization of cytomegalovirus antigens in liver allografts over time. Hum Pathol 1993, **24**: 103–108.

712　Vanstapel MJ, Desmet VJ. Cytomegalovirus hepatitis: a histological and immunohistochemical study. Appl Pathol 1983, **1**: 41–49.

Infectious mononucleosis

713　White NJ, Juel-Jensen BE. Infectious mononucleosis hepatitis. Semin Liver Dis 1984, **4**: 301–306.

Acquired immune deficiency syndrome

714　Beral V, Peterman T, Berkelman R, Jaffe H. AIDS-associated non-Hodgkin lymphoma. Lancet 1991, **337**: 805–809.

715　Cello JP. Human immunodeficiency virus-associated biliary tract disease. Semin Liver Dis 1992, **12**: 213–218.

716　Dupon M, Kosaifi T, Le Bail B, Lacut Y, Balabaud C, Bioulac-Sage P. Lipid-laden perisinusoidal cells in patients with acquired immunodeficiency syndrome. Liver 1991, **11**: 211–219.

717　Hasan FA, Jeffers LJ, Welsh SW. Hepatic involvement as the primary manifestation of Kaposi's sarcoma in the acquired immune deficiency syndrome. Am J Gastroenterol 1989, **84**: 1449–1451.

718　Housset C, Pol S, Carnot F, Dubois F, Nalpas B, Housset B, Berthelot P, Brechot C. Interactions between human immunodeficiency virus-1, hepatitis delta virus and hepatitis B virus infections in 260 chronic carriers of hepatitis B virus. Hepatology 1992, **15**: 578–583.

719　Jeffers LJ, Alzate I, Aguilar H, Reddy KR, Idrovo V, Cheinquer H, Hasan FA, Parker T, Montero C, Dickinson G, Schiff ER. Laparoscopic and histologic findings in patients with the human immunodeficiency virus. Gastrointest Endosc 1994, **40**: 160–164.

720　Kennedy M, O'reily M, Bergin CJ, McDonald GS. Liver biopsy pathology in human immunodeficiency virus infection. Eur J Gastroenterol Hepatol 1998, **10**: 255–258.

721　Lafon ME, Kirn A. Human immunodeficiency virus infection of the liver. Semin Liver Dis 1992, **12**: 197–204.

722　Lefkowitch J. The liver in AIDS. Semin Liver Dis 1997, **17**: 335–344.

723　Nakanuma Y, Liew CT, Peters RL, Govindarajan S. Pathologic features of the liver in acquired immune deficiency syndrome (AIDS). Liver 1986, **6**: 158–166.

724　Perkocha LA, Geaghan SM, Yen TS, Nishimura SL, Chan SP, Garcia-Kennedy R, Honda G, Stoloff AC, Klein HZ, Goldman RL, Van Meter S, Ferrell LD, LeBoit P. Clinical and pathological features of bacillary peliosis hepatis in association with human immunodeficiency virus infection. N Engl J Med 1990, **323**: 1581–1586.

725　Poblete RB, Rodriguez K, Foust RT, Reddy R, Saldana MJ. Pneumocystis carinii hepatitis in the acquired immunodeficiency syndrome (AIDS). Ann Intern Med 1989, **110**: 737–738.

726　Pol S, Romana CA, Richard S, Amouyal P, Desportes-Livage I, Carnot F, Pays JF, Berthelot P. Microsporidia infection in patients with the human immunodeficiency virus and unexplained cholangitis. N Engl J Med 1993, **328**: 95–99.

727　Romeo R, Rumi MG, Donato MF, Cargnel MA, Vigano P, Mondelli M, Cesana B, Colombo M. Hepatitis C is more severe in drug users with human immunodeficiency virus infection. J Viral Hep 2000, **7**: 297–301.

728 Scoazec JY, Marche C, Girard PM, Houtmann J, Durand-Schneider AM, Saimot AG, Benhamou JP, Feldmann G. Peliosis hepatis and sinusoidal dilatation during infection by the human immunodeficiency virus (HIV). Am J Pathol 1988, **131**: 38–47.

729 Spengler U, Rockstroh JK. Review. Hepatitis C in the patient with human immunodeficiency virus infection. J Hepatol 1998, **29**: 1023–1030.

730 Wilkins MJ, Lindley R, Dourakis SP, Goldin RD. Surgical pathology of the liver in HIV infection. Histopathology 1991, **18**: 459–464.

Malaria

731 Pounder DJ. Malarial pigment and hepatic anthracosis. Am J Surg Pathol 1983, **7**: 501–502.

Total parenteral nutrition

732 Body JJ, Bleiberg H, Bron D, Maurage H, Birigimana V, Heimann R. Total parenteral nutrition-induced cholestasis mimicking large bile duct obstruction. Histopathology 1982, **6**: 787–792.

733 Cohen C, Olsen MM. Pediatric total parenteral nutrition: liver histopathology. Arch Pathol Lab Med 1981, **105**: 152–156.

734 Mullick FG, Moran CA, Ishak KG. Total parenteral nutrition. A histopathologic analysis of the liver changes in 20 children. Mod Pathol 1994, **7**: 190–194.

735 Quigley EM, Marsh MN, Shaffer JL, Markin RS. Hepatobiliary complications of total parenteral nutrition. Gastroenterology 1993, **104**: 286–301.

736 Wolfe BM, Walker BK, Shaul DB, Wong L, Ruebner BH. Effect of total parenteral nutrition on hepatic histology. Arch Surg 1988, **123**: 1084–1090.

Amyloidosis and light chain deposition disease

737 Buck FS, Koss MN. Hepatic amyloidosis: morphologic differences between systemic AL and AA types. Hum Pathol 1991, **22**: 904–907.

738 Faa G, Van Eyken P, De Vos R, Fevery J, Van Damme B, De Groote J, Desmet VJ. Light chain deposition disease of the liver associated with AL-type amyloidosis and severe cholestasis. J Hepatol 1991, **12**: 75–82.

739 Finkelstein SD, Fornasier VL, Pruzanski W. Intrahepatic cholestasis with predominant pericentral deposition in systemic amyloidosis. Hum Pathol 1981, **12**: 470–472.

740 Hoffman MS, Stein BE, Davidian MN, Rosenthal WS. Hepatic amyloidosis presenting as severe intrahepatic cholestasis. A case report and review of the literature. Am J Gastroenterol 1988, **83**: 783–786.

741 Kanel GC, Uchida T, Peters RL. Globular hepatic amyloid – an unusual morphologic presentation. Hepatology 1981, **1**: 647–652.

742 Wright JR, Calkins E, Humphrey RL. Potassium permanganate reaction in amyloidosis. A histologic method to assist in differentiating forms of this disease. Lab Invest 1977, **36**: 274–281.

Nonspecific reactive changes

743 Gerber MA, Thung SN. Histology of the liver. Am J Surg Pathol 1987, **11**: 709–722.

744 Schaffner F, Popper H. Nonspecific reactive hepatitis in aged and infirm people. Am J Dig Dis 1959, **4**: 389–399.

Liver pathology in organ transplantation
Liver transplantation

745 Bzeizi KI, Jalan R, Plevris JN, Hayes PC. Primary graft dysfunction after liver transplantation: from pathogenesis to prevention. Liver Transplant Surg 1997, **3**: 137–148.

746 Eggink HF, Hofstee N, Gips CH, Krom RA, Houthoff HJ. Histopathology of serial graft biopsies from liver transplant recipients. Am J Pathol 1984, **114**: 18–31.

747 Fishbein TM, Fiel MI, Emre S, Cubukcu O, Guy SR, Schwartz ME, Miller CM, Sheiner PA. Use of livers with microvesicular fat safely expands the donor pool. Transplantation 1977, **64**: 248–251.

748 Hertzler GL, Millikan WJ. The surgical pathologist's role in liver transplantation. Arch Pathol Lab Med 1991, **115**: 273–282.

749 Kubota K, Ericzon BG, Reinholt FP. Comparison of fine-needle aspiration biopsy and histology in human liver transplants. Transplantation 1991, **51**: 1010–1013.

750 Lucey MR. Editorial. Serial liver biopsies: a gateway into understanding the long-term health of the liver allograft. J Hepatol 2001, **34**: 762–763.

751 Selzner M, Clavien PA. Fatty liver in liver transplantation and surgery. Semin Liver Dis 2001, **21**: 105–113.

752 Trevisani F, Colantoni A, Caraceni P, Van Thiel DH. The use of donor fatty liver for liver transplantation: a challenge or a quagmire? J Hepatol 1996, **24**: 114–121.

Preservation injury

753 Bilzer M, Gerbes AL. Review. Preservation injury of the liver: mechanisms and novel therapeutic strategies. J Hepatol 2000, **32**: 508–515.

754 Christoffersen P, Poulsen H, Skeie E. Focal liver cell necrosis accompanied by infiltration of granulocytes arising during operation. Acta Hepatosplenol 1970, **17**: 240–245.

755 Gaffey MJ, Boyd JC, Traweek ST, Ali MA, Rezeig M, Caldwell SH, Iezzoni JC, McCullough C, Stevenson WC, Khuroo S, Nezamuddin N, Ishitani MB, Pruett TL. Predictive value of intraoperative biopsies and liver function test for preservation injury in orthotopic liver transplantation. Hepatology 1997, **25**: 184–189.

756 Goldstein NS, Hart J, Lewin KJ. Diffuse hepatocyte ballooning in liver biopsies from orthotopic liver transplant patients. Histopathology 1991, **18**: 331–338.

757 Ludwig J, Gross JB, Perkins JD, Moore SB. Persistent centrilobular necroses in hepatic allografts. Hum Pathol 1990, **21**: 656–661.

758 Ng IOL, Burroughs AK, Rolles K, Belli LS, Scheuer PJ. Hepatocellular ballooning after liver transplantation: a light and electronmicroscopic study with clinicopathological correlation. Histopathology 1991, **18**: 323–330.

759 Tillery W, Demetris J, Watkins D, Goldstein R, Poplawski S, Husberg B, Klintmalm G. Pathologic recognition of preservation injury in hepatic allograft with six month's follow-up. Transplant Proc 1989, **21**: 1330–1331.

760 Williams JW, Vera S, Peters TG, Van Voorst S, Britt LG, Dean PJ, Hagitt R, Massie JD. Cholestatic jaundice after hepatic transplantation. A nonimmunologically mediated event. Am J Surg 1986, **151**: 65–70.

Allograft rejection

761 Batts KP. Acute and chronic hepatic allograft rejection: pathology and classification. Liver Transplant Surg 1999, **5** (Suppl 1): S21–S29.

762 Demetris AJ. Editorial. Central venulitis in liver allografts: considerations of differential diagnosis. Hepatology 2001, **33**: 1329–1330.

763 Demetris AJ. The pathology of liver transplantation. In Popper H, Schaffner F (eds): Progress in liver diseases, vol. IX. Philadelphia, 1990, W.B. Saunders, pp. 687–709.

764 Demetris AJ, Jaffe R, Tzakis A, Ramsey G, Todo S, Belle S, Esquivel C, Shapiro R, Markus B, Mroczek E, Van Thiel DH, Sysyn G, Gordon R, Makowka L, Starzl T. Antibody-mediated rejection of human orthotopic liver allograft. A study of liver transplantation across ABO blood group barriers. Am J Pathol 1988, **132**: 489–502.

765 Demetris AJ, Lasky S, Van Thiel D, Starzl TE, Dekker A. Pathology of hepatic transplantation. A review of 62 adult allograft recipients immunosuppressed with a cyclosporin/steroid regimen. Am J Pathol 1985, **118**: 151–161.

766 Hübscher SG. Histological findings in liver allograft rejection – new insights into the pathogenesis of hepatocellular damage in liver allografts. Histopathology 1991, **18**: 377–383.

767 International Panel. Banff schema for grading liver allograft rejection: an international consensus document. Hepatology 1997, **25**: 658–663.

768 International Panel. Update of the international Banff schema for liver allograft rejection: working recommendations for the histopathologic staging and reporting of chronic rejection. Hepatology 2000, **31**: 792–799.

769 International Working Party. Terminology for hepatic allograft rejection. Hepatology 1995, **22**: 648–654.

770 Jones KD, Ferell LD. Interpretation of biopsy findings in the transplant liver. Semin Diagn Pathol 1998, **15**: 306–317.

771 Krasinskas AM, Ruchelli ED, Rand EB, Chittams JL, Furth EE. Central venulitis in pediatric liver allografts. Hepatology 2001, **33**: 1141–1147.

772 Mor E, Solomon H, Gibbs JF, Holman MJ, Goldstein RM, Husberg BS, Gonwa TA, Klintmalm GB. Acute cellular rejection following liver transplantation: clinical pathologic features and effect on outcome. Semin Liver Dis 1992, **12**: 28–40.

773 Nagral A, Ben-Ari Z, Dhillon AP, Burroughs AK. Eosinophils in acute cellular rejection in liver allografts. Liver Transplant Surg 1998, **4**: 355–362.

774 Quaglia AF, Del Vecchio Blanco G, Greaves R, Burroughs AK, Dhillon AP. Development of ductopaenic liver allograft rejection includes a "hepatitic" phase prior to duct loss. J Hepatol 2000, **33**: 773–780.

775 Sebagh M, Debette M, Samuel D, Emile JF, Falissard B, Cailliez V, Shouval D, Bismuth H, Reynes M. "Silent" presentation of veno-occlusive disease after liver transplantation as part of the process of cellular rejection with endothelial predilection. Hepatology 1999, **30**: 1144–1150.

776 Snover DC, Sibley RK, Freese DK, Sharp HL, Bloomer JR, Najarian JS. Orthotopic liver transplantation: a pathological study of 63 serial liver biopsies from 17 patients with special reference to the diagnostic features and natural history of rejection. Hepatology 1984, **4**: 1212–1222.

777 Vierling JM. Immunology of acute and chronic hepatic allograft rejection. Liver Transplant Surg 1999, **5** (Suppl 1): S1–S20.

778 Wiesner RH, Demetris AJ, Belle SH, Seaberg EC, Lake JR, Zetterman RK, Everhart J, Detre KM. Acute hepatic allograft rejection: in incidence, risk factors and impact on outcome. Hepatology 1998, **28**: 638–645.

Other complications

779 Sterneck M, Wiesner R, Ascher N, Roberts J, Ferrell L, Ludwig J, Lake J. Azathioprine hepatotoxicity after liver transplantation. Hepatology 1991, **14**: 806–810.

780 Wisecarver JL, Earl RA, Haven MC, Timmins PW, Shaw BW, Stratta RJ, Langnas AN, Zetterman RK, Donovan JP, Shaefer MS, Markin RS. Histologic changes in liver allograft biopsies associated with elevated whole blood and tissue cyclosporine concentrations. Mod Pathol 1992, **5**: 611–616.

Recurrent disease

781 Berenguer M, Lopez-Labrador FX, Wright TL. Review. Hepatitis C and liver transplantation. J Hepatol 2001, **35**: 666–678.

782 Bernard PH, Le Bail B, Rullier A, Trimoulet P, Neau-Cransac M, Balabaud C, Bioulac-Sage P. Recurrence and accelerated progression of hepatitis C following liver transplantation. Semin Liver Dis 2000, **20**: 533–538.

783 Booth JCL, Goldin RD, Brown JL, Karayiannis P, Thomas HC.

784 Fibrosing cholestatic hepatitis in a renal transplant recipient associated with the hepatitis B virus precore mutant. J Hepatol 1995, **22**: 500–503.

784 Davies SE, Portmann BC, O'Grady JG, Aldis PM, Chaggar K, Alexander GJM, Williams R. Hepatic histological findings after transplantation for chronic hepatitis B virus infection, including a unique pattern of fibrosing cholestatic hepatitis. Hepatology 1991, **13**: 150–157.

785 Faust TW. Recurrent primary biliary cirrhosis, primary sclerosing cholangitis, and autoimmune hepatitis after transplantation. Semin Liver Dis 2000, **20**: 481–495.

786 Graziadei IW, Wiesner RH, Batts KP, Marotta PJ, Larusso NF, Porayko MK, Hay JE, Gores GJ, Charlton MR, Ludwig J, Poterucha JJ, Steers JL, Krom RAF. Recurrence of primary sclerosing cholangitis following liver transplantation. Hepatology 1999, **29**: 1050–1056.

787 Hoso M, Nakanuma Y, Kawano M, Oda K, Tsuneyama K, Van de Water J, Gershwin ME. Granulomatous cholangitis in chronic hepatitis C: a new diagnostic problem in liver pathology. Pathol Int 1996, **46**: 301–305.

788 Khettry U, Anand N, Gordon FD, Jenkins RL, Tahan SR, Loda M, Lewis WD. Recurrent hepatitis B, hepatitis C, and combined hepatitis B and C in liver allografts: a comparative pathological study. Hum Pathol 2000, **31**: 101–108.

789 Luketic VA, Shiffman ML, McCall JB, Posner MP, Mills AS, Carithers RL. Primary hepatocellular carcinoma after orthotopic liver transplantation for chronic hepatitis B infection. Ann Intern Med 1991, **114**: 212–213.

790 McPeake JR, O'Grady JG, Zaman S, Portmann B, Wight DG, Tan KC, Calne RY, Williams R. Liver transplantation for primary hepatocellular carcinoma: tumor size and number determine outcome. J Hepatol 1993, **18**: 226–234.

791 Petrovic LM, Villamil FG, Vierling JM, Makowka L, Geller SA. Comparison of histopathology in acute allograft rejection and recurrent hepatitis C infection after liver transplantation. Liver Transplant Surg 1997, **3**: 398–406.

792 Rosen HR, Martin P. Hepatitis B and C in the transplant recipient. Semin Liver Dis 2000, **20**: 465–480.

793 Saxena R, Ye MQ, Emre S, Klion F, Nalesnik MA, Thung SN. De novo hepatocellular carcinoma in a hepatic allograft with recurrent hepatitis C cirrhosis. Liver Transplant Surg 1999, **5**: 81–82.

794 Schluger LK, Sheiner PA, Thung SN, Lau JY, Min A, Wolf DC, Fiel I, Zhang D, Gerber MA, Miller CM, Bodenheimer HC. Severe recurrent cholestatic hepatitis C following orthotopic liver transplantation. Hepatology 1996, **23**: 971–976.

795 Sebagh M, Farges O, Dubel L, Samuel D, Bismuth H, Reynes M. Histological features predictive of recurrence of primary biliary cirrhosis after liver transplantation. Transplantation 1998, **65**: 1328–1333.

796 Sheiner P. Hepatitis C after liver transplantation. Semin Liver Dis 2000, **20**: 201–209.

797 Ye MQ, Thung SN. Hepatitis after transplantation. Liver Transplant Surg 1998, **4** (Suppl 1): S68–S72.

Bone marrow transplantation: graft-versus-host disease

798 Geubel A, Cnudde A, Ferrant A, Latinne D, Rahier J. Diffuse biliary tract involvement mimicking primary sclerosing cholangitis after bone marrow transplantation. J Hepatol 1990, **10**: 23–28.

799 McDonald GB, Shulman HW, Sullivan KM, Spencer GD. Intestinal and hepatic complications of human bone marrow transplantation. Part I. Gastroenterology 1986, **90**: 460–477.

800 Shulman HM, Fisher LB, Schoch HG, Henne KW, McDonald GB. Venoocclusive disease of the liver after marrow transplantation: histological correlates of clinical signs and symptoms. Hepatology 1994, **19**: 1171–1180.

801 Shulman HM, Sharma P, Amos D, Fenster F, McDonald GB. A coded histologic study of hepatic Graft-versus-Host disease after human bone marrow transplantation. Hepatology 1988, **8**: 463–470.

802 Sloane JP, Norton J. The pathology of bone marrow transplantation. Histopathology 1993, **22**: 201–209.

803 Snover DC. Biopsy interpretation in bone marrow transplantation. Pathol Annu 1989, **24**: 63–101.

804 Stechschulte DJ, Fishback JL, Emami A, Bhatia P. Secondary biliary cirrhosis as a consequence of graft-versus-host disease. Gastroenterology 1990, **98**: 223–225.

Echinococcus cyst (hydatid cyst)

805 Akinoglu A, Demiryurek H, Guzel C. Alveolar hydatid disease of the liver: a report on thirty-nine surgical cases in eastern Anatolia. Am J Trop Med Hyg 1991, **45**: 182–189.

806 Kalovidouris A, Voros D, Gouliamos A, Vlachos L, Papavasiliou C. Extracapsular (satellite) hydatid cysts. Gastrointest Radiol 1992, **17**: 353–356.

807 Langer JC, Rose DB, Keystone JS, Taylor BR, Langer B. Diagnosis and management of hydatid disease of the liver. A 15 year North American experience. Ann Surg 1984, **199**: 412–417.

808 Magistrelli P, Sasetti R, Coppola R, Messia A, Nuzzo G, Picciocchi A. Surgical treatment of hydatid disease of the liver. A 20-year experience. Arch Surg 1991, **126**: 518–523.

809 Munzer D. New perspectives in the diagnosis of Echinococcus disease. J Clin Gastroenterol 1991, **13**: 415–423.

810 William JF, Lopez AH, Trejos A. Current prevalence and distribution of hydatidosis with special reference to the Americas. Am J Trop Med Hyg 1971, **20**: 224–236.

811 Ammann R, Munch R, Largiader F, Akovbiantz A, Marincek B. Pancreatic and hepatic abscesses. A late complication in 10 patients with chronic pancreatitis. Gastroenterology 1992, **103**: 560–565.

Abscess

812 Barreda R, Ros PR. Diagnostic imaging of liver abscess. Crit Rev Diagn Imaging 1992, **33**: 29–58.

813 Bissada AA, Bateman J. Pyogenic liver abscess. A 7-year experience in a large community hospital. Hepatogastroenterology 1991, **38**: 317–320.

814 Brook I, Fraizer EH. Role of anaerobic bacteria in liver abscesses in children. Pediatr Infect Dis J 1993, **12**: 743–747.

815 Crippin JS, Wang KK. An unrecognised etiology for pyogenic hepatic abscesses in normal hosts. Dental disease. Am J Gastroenterol 1992, **87**: 1740–1743.

816 Do H, Lambiase RE, Deyoe L, Cronan JJ, Dorfman GS. Percutaneous drainage of hepatic abscesses. Comparison of results in ascesses with and without intrahepatic biliary communication. AJR Am J Roentgenol 1991, **157**: 1209–1212.

817 Georges RN, Deitch EA. Pyogenic hepatic abscess. South Med J 1993, **86**: 1233–1235.

818 Greenstein AJ, Barth J, Dicker A, Battone EJ, Aufses AH Jr. Amebic liver abscess. A study of 11 cases compared with a series of 38 patients with pyogenic liver abscess. Am J Gastroenterol 1985, **80**: 472–478.

819 Grois N, Mostbeck G, Scherrer R, Chott A, Schwarzinger I, Muhm M, Bettelheim P, Forstinger C, Laczika K, Kyrle P, et al. Hepatic and splenic abscesses – a common complication of intensive chemotherapy of acute myeloid leukaemia (AML). A prospective study. Ann Hematol 1991, **63**: 33–38.

820 Hughes MA, Petri WA Jr. Amebic liver abscess. Infect Dis Clin North Am 2000, **14**: 565–582.

821 Johannsen EC, Sifri CD, Madoff LC. Pyoenic liver abscesses. Infect Dis Clin North Am 2000, **14**: 547–563.

822 Johnson JL, Baird JS, Hulbert TV, Opas LM. Amebic liver abscess in infancy. Case report and review. Clin Infect Dis 1994, **19**: 765–767.

823 Lambiase RE, Deyoe L, Cronan JJ, Dorfman GS. Percutaneous drainage of 335 consecutive abscesses. Results of primary drainage with 1-year follow-up. Radiology 1992, **184**: 167–179.

824 Lupatkin H, Brau N, Flomenberg P, Simberkoff MS. Tuberculous abscesses in patients with AIDS. Clin Infect Dis 1992, **14**: 1040–1044.

825 Meng XY, Wu JX. Perforated amebic liver abscess. Clinical analysis of 110 cases. South Med 1994, **87**: 985–990.

826 Robert JH, Mirescu D, Ambrosetti P, Khoury G, Greenstein AJ, Rohner A. Critical review of the pyogenic hepatic abscess. Surg Gynecol Obstet 1992, **174**: 97–102.

827 Stanley SL Jr. Amobiasis. Lancet 2003, **361**: 1025–1034.

828 Weinberg RJ, Klish WJ, Brown MR, Smalley JR, Emmens RW. Hepatic abscess as a complication of Crohn's disease. J Pediatr Gastroenterol Nutr 1983, **2**: 171–174.

Heterotopia

829 Babu R, Van der Avoirt A. Ectopic intrathoracic liver. Pediatr Surg Int 2001, **17**: 461–462.

830 Boyle L, Galivan MV, Chun B, Lack EE. Heterotopia of gastric mucosa and liver involving the gallbladder. Report of two cases with literature review. Arch Pathol Lab Med 1992, **116**: 138–142.

831 Brustmann H. Heterotopic liver in the right cardiac auricle. Ann Diagn Pathol 2002, **6**: 248–249.

832 Buck FS, Koss MN. Heterotopic liver in an adrenal gland. Pediatr Pathol 1988, **8**: 535–540.

833 Mendoza A, Voland J, Wolf P, Benirschke K. Supradiaphragmatic liver in the lung. Arch Pathol Lab Med 1986, **110**: 1085–1086.

834 Newland JR, Markin RS, Wilson RB, Jones JW. Heterotopic liver of the jejunum. Report of a case and a review. J Clin Gastroenterol 1989, **11**: 461–463.

835 Shapiro Jl, Metlay LA. Heterotopic supradiaphragmatic liver formation in association with congenital cardiac anomalies. Arch Pathol Lab Med 1991, **115**: 238–240.

836 Tejada E, Danielson C. Ectopic or heterotopic liver (choristoma) associated with the gallbladder. Arch Pathol Lab Med 1989, **113**: 950–952.

Tumors and tumorlike conditions

Liver cell tumors and tumorlike conditions

Focal nodular hyperplasia

Focal nodular hyperplasia can occur in any age group, including childhood; most cases, however, are seen during the third to fifth decades of life. The female to male ratio has ranged from 2:1 to 8:1 in the various adult and pediatric series.[13,18] In approximately 80% of the cases, the lesion is asymptomatic.[13] In contrast with liver cell adenoma, hemoperitoneum is extremely rare.[17] The lesion is usually solitary; multicentricity has been described in 20% of the adult cases and in a higher percentage of the pediatric cases.[18] Multicentric cases may be associated with vascular malformations of various organs and neoplasms of brain.[12,20] A possible relationship to oral contraceptives has been postulated in many reports,[1] but it is not as clear-cut as for liver cell adenoma.[3,7,9] There is no question that this disease occurred prior to the widespread use of oral contraceptives and that it can occur in males, particularly in association with chronic alcohol abuse.[8]

The arteriographic appearance, characterized by a centrifugal filling pattern, is distinctive.[4] Grossly, the lesion usually presents as a subcapsular grayish white, solid mass that is sometimes pedunculated. On cut section, a white depressed area of fibrosis is often seen in the center, with broad strands radiating from it to the periphery in a stellate configuration (Figs 13.51 and 13.52). This can be detected in close to half of the cases by MRI techniques.[10,13,19] Microscopically, *all the components of the normal liver lobule are present*. The cellular morphology and relationship between hepatocytes and bile ducts are essentially those of normal liver, both by light and by electron microscopic criteria.

Some of the hepatocytes have increased amounts of glycogen and fat. In most of the cases, there is immunoreactivity for α_1-antitrypsin, a feature shared with liver cell adenoma and liver cell carcinoma.[14] Acute or chronic inflammatory cells are common. Fibrous septa contain-

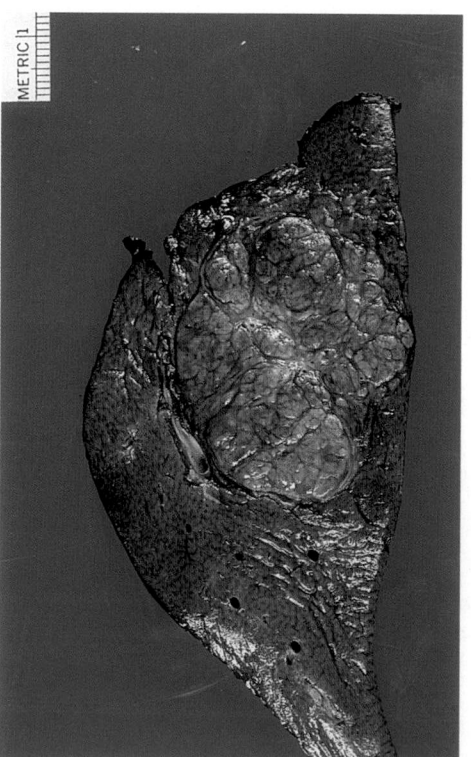

Fig. 13.51 Gross appearances of focal nodular hyperplasia. The resemblance to cirrhosis is striking.

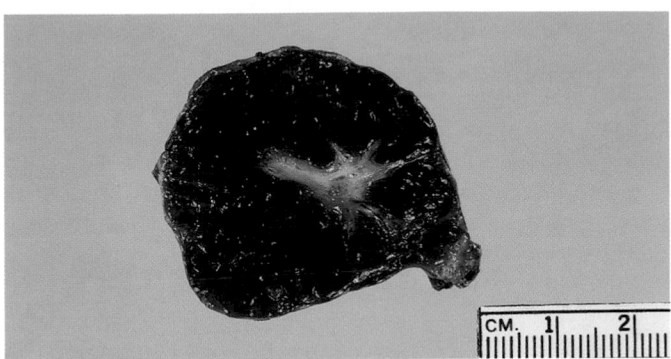

Fig. 13.52 Typical star-shaped central scar of radial shape in nodular hyperplasia.

ing eccentrically thickened vessels divide the lesion into (pseudo)lobules resembling those of cirrhosis and characterized by fibrovascular and ductular areas radiating from the septa, accompanied by an expanding periphery of normal-appearing hepatocytes (Fig. 13.53). The vessels can be prominent and have telangiectatic features.[13] Immunohistochemically, there is a continuous transition from the hepatocytes at the periphery (which express only keratins 8 and 18) to small hepatocytes and ductular aggregates in the center of the lobules (which also express keratins 7 and 19).[5] Strong immunoreactivity for the *ras* oncogene product p21 has been found, in contrast with its virtual absence in normal liver.[15] Immunostains for steroid hormone receptors have given negative results.[11] The differential diagnosis of focal nodular hyperplasia includes—at both the clinical and pathologic level—liver cell adenoma, well-differentiated liver cell

carcinoma, and the various types of "monoacinar" regenerative hepatocytic nodules discussed on p 961.[2] The pathogenesis of focal nodular hyperplasia is controversial. The general assumption is that it represents a cirrhosis-like hyperplastic/regenerative process following a localized insult to the liver parenchyma. As a matter of fact, sometimes lesions indistinguishable from nodular hyperplasia are seen in cirrhotic livers.[14a] The ductular structures present in the lesion are said to derive from activated undifferentiated progenitor cells.[16] Most of the cases investigated for the X chromosome with the Humara test have shown a clonal pattern of inactivation.[6]

Liver cell adenoma

True adenomas of the liver are rare. They have a striking predilection for females and are pathogenetically related to the use of oral contraceptives,[29,36,46] a fact supported by their occasional total regression following discontinuation of the hormones.[24,47] These neoplasms have also been reported following anabolic–androgenic steroid therapy,[25,50] following long-term carbamazepine therapy,[48] in association with glycogen storage diseases and other genetically determined diseases,[21,23,27,43] and in children with sex hormone disturbances.[37] When compared with focal nodular hyperplasia, the adenomas are more often symptomatic and can lead to severe and even fatal peritoneal hemorrhage.[22] Most of the patients are in the third to fifth decades of life, but cases have also been reported in children.[51] Approximately 70% of the lesions are solitary,[35] but on occasion there may be as many as 10 or more tumors, a condition known as *liver cell adenomatosis*.[31] They are usually visualized as defects on [99m]technetium–sulfur colloid liver scans and can occur anywhere in the liver, including the caudate lobe.[42] Grossly, they have a well-defined capsule and a different color from the surrounding liver. The typical central scar of nodular hyperplasia is absent (Fig. 13.54). Microscopically, the tumor is composed of well-differentiated hepatocytes

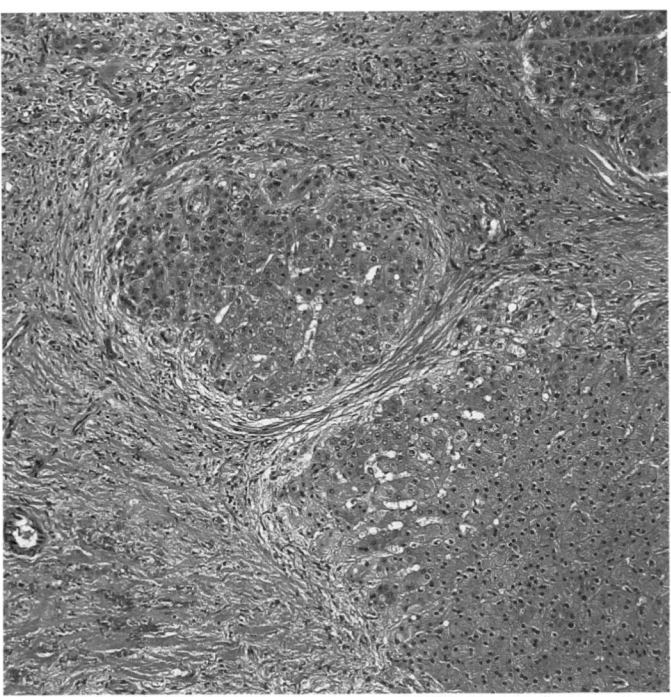

Fig. 13.53 Central portion of nodular hyperplasia showing the interphase between the fibrous scar and the hepatocytic nodules.

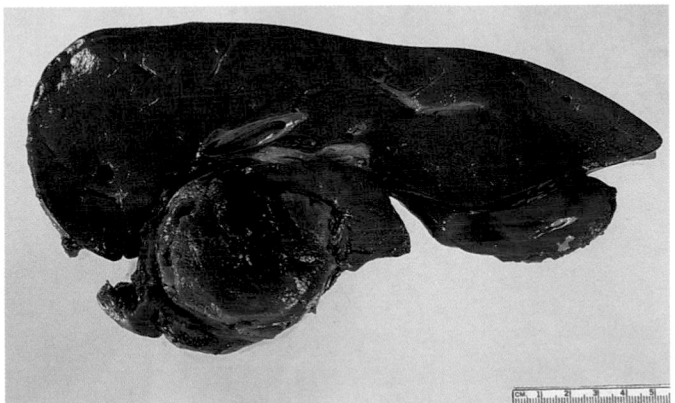

Fig. 13.54 Gross appearance of liver cell adenoma. The tumor, which is well circumscribed, has a large, central area of recent hemorrhage.

with abundant eosinophilic granular cytoplasm (Fig. 13.55). *There are no portal triads or central veins,* and there is no connection with the biliary system. Kupffer cells are always present, in a pattern comparable to that seen in normal liver.[32] Features occasionally seen in liver cell adenomas include oncocytic changes,[44] presence of Mallory's alcoholic hyaline,[34] pigmentation,[33] and secondary granulomatous reaction.[41] Sometimes there is a granulomatous hepatitis outside the adenoma.[38] Immunohistochemically, estrogen and progesterone receptors are present in about 75% of the adenomas, whereas androgen receptors are expressed in only 20% of the cases.[49] Immunohistochemical studies have also provided evidence of the presence of so-called "hepatic progenitor cells" in about half of the cases, suggesting that they play a role in the development of these tumors.[39] At the genetic level, β-catenin mutations have been found in about a third of these tumors.[26]

Multiple sections should be carefully evaluated in these cases to rule out a well-differentiated liver cell carcinoma. The search for blood vessel invasion in H&E sections or following immunostains for endothelial markers is particularly important.[45] Sometimes, the differential diagnosis between these two entities is impossible, and only the clinical course establishes the true nature of the lesion. Thus some of the androgen-induced tumors originally diagnosed as liver cell carcinoma have been reclassified as adenomas because of the benign long-term evolution.[40] Occasionally, an unequivocal focus of liver cell carcinoma is seen in a lesion having otherwise the features of adenoma,[30,36,45] or there may be coexistence of adenoma and carcinoma in the same liver.[28]

The most important differences between focal nodular hyperplasia and liver cell adenoma are listed in Table 13.10.

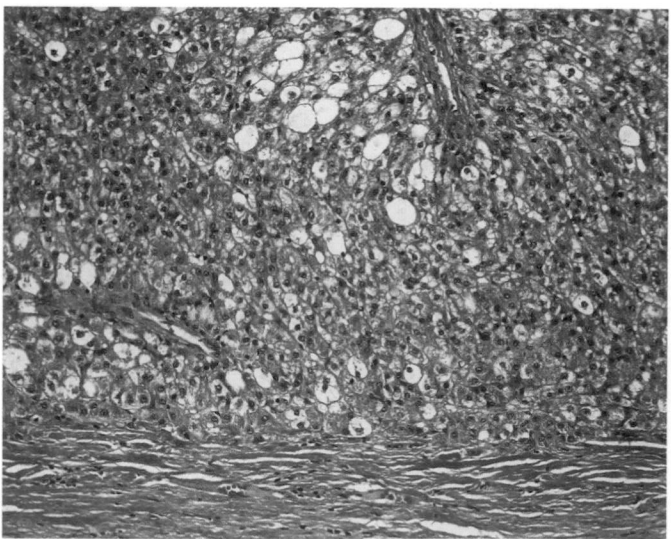

Fig. 13.55 Edge of a hepatic adenoma, showing encapsulation and a well-differentiated cytologic appearance, with some large vacuolated elements.

Liver cell carcinoma

General and clinical features

Liver cell carcinoma (hepatocellular carcinoma, hepatocarcinoma, hepatoma) remains relatively rare in the United States, although an alarming increase has been projected over the next 10 years, mostly attributable to hepatitis C (see below).[54] It is very common in all African countries south of the Sahara and in Southeast Asia.[57] In the People's Republic of China, this tumor is responsible for over 100,000 deaths per year. Most cases are seen in patients over the age of 50 years, but this tumor can also occur in younger individuals and even in children.[55,60,62,66] Some cases have occurred as second malignancies in successfully treated Wilms' tumor patients.[59]

Liver cell carcinoma is more common in males than in females, especially when associated with cirrhosis.[53] It usually presents with abdominal pain, ascites, and liver enlargement. Obstructive jaundice may result from tumor invasion into the common bile duct.[52] Liver cell carcinoma may be associated with systemic manifestations such as hypoglycemia, hypercholesterolemia, erythrocytosis, hypercalcemia, carcinoid syndrome, serum elevation of proline hydroxylase, ectopic production of chorionic gonadotropin and prostaglandin, dysfibrinogenemia, and several others.[58,61,64]

Serum elevation of α-fetoprotein (AFP) occurs in a large percentage of patients with liver cell carcinoma.[63] The incidence of positivity is higher in places in which the tumor is endemic (more than 75%) than in Europe or the United States (40% to 60%). This feature can also be seen with malignant germ cell tumors and, rarely, with metastatic carcinomas to the liver, hepatitis, and post-traumatic liver regeneration. However, increases over 100 times normal levels are virtually diagnostic of liver cell carcinoma if a malignant germ cell tumor can be excluded[65]; therefore, serial determinations of serum α-fetoprotein levels offer a good clue to early detection in high-risk populations. CT scan or MRI usually results in an accurate determination of the location of the tumor, the extent of its invasiveness, and the presence or absence of multicentricity.[56]

Predisposing and associated factors

A large proportion of liver cell carcinomas have been found to be associated with one or another of the factors subsequently listed, strongly suggesting a pathogenetic relationship.[69,71,83] Some of these parameters are clearly interrelated. A patient may have a hepatitis-induced cirrhosis accompanied by macroregenerative or borderline nodules that exhibit dysplastic changes, thus combining the first four (and most important) predisposing factors included in this section. For the purposes of discussion, these factors are listed separately.

1   *Hepatotropic viruses.* There is strong evidence of a pathogenetic role of hepatotropic viruses in the

Table 13.10 Comparison of clinical, radiologic, and pathologic characteristics of focal nodular hyperplasia and liver cell adenoma

Features	Focal nodular hyperplasia	Liver cell adenoma
Clinical		
Incidence	Uncommon	Rare
Age	All ages	Third, fourth decades
Sex	85% females	Nearly all females
Oral contraceptive use	Occasionally	Nearly always
Clinical presentation	Usually asymptomatic, 35% abdominal mass, abdominal discomfort	Often abdominal emergency, 45% abdominal mass, acute abdominal pain
Hemoperitoneum	Less than 1%	25%
Liver function tests	Nearly always normal	Nearly always normal
Malignant potential	None	Probably none
Therapy	Resection if operative risk negligible	Resection
Angiography		
Vascularity	Hypervascular with dense capillary blush	Hypovascular
Hematoma formation	Rare	Common
Necrosis	Rare	Common
Septation	Present in 50%	Absent
Liver scan		
Uptake	Normal or slightly decreased	None
Pathology		
Capsule	No capsule	Partial to ample encapsulation
Location	Usually subcapsular, 20% pedunculated, Often multiple	Usually subcapsular, 7% pedunculated, Usually solitary
Stellate scar	Present	Absent
Parenchyma	Nodular	Homogeneous
Hemorrhage, necrosis	Rare	Common
Bile stasis	Absent	Present
Hepatocytes	Cytologically normal	Glycogen rich, vacuolated
Bile ductules	Present	Absent
Kupffer cells	Present	Reduced or absent
Vascularity	Large thick-walled vessels	Thin-walled sinusoids
Ultrastructure	Normal	Simplified

From Knowles DM II, Casarella WJ, Johnson PM, Wolff M. The clinical, radiologic, and pathologic characterization of benign hepatic neoplasms. Alleged association with oral contraceptives. Medicine (Baltimore) 1978, **57**: 223–237.

development of liver cell carcinoma, not only through the production of cirrhosis but also in noncirrhotic livers.[104,110] This is true for both hepatitis B and hepatitis C viruses and for both adult and pediatric patients.[75,114] As a matter of fact, viral hepatitis is now regarded as the leading cause of hepatocellular carcinoma.[100] In one series from Japan, the development rate of hepatocellular carcinomas after a 15-year observation period was 27% in hepatitis B and 75% in hepatitis C.[95] The incidence of hepatitis B and/or hepatitis C surface antigenemia in patients with liver cell carcinoma is over 90%, both in the United States and overseas.[76,127,130] In a recent study involving almost 11,000 men from seven townships

in Taiwan, positivity for HBeAg was found to be definitely associated with an increased risk for the development of hepatocellular carcinoma.[133] Both surface and core antigens can be detected by immunohistochemistry in the cytoplasm of the tumor cells and the non-neoplastic hepatocytes in many of the cases.[91,96,120] Integration of hepatitis virus DNA into the genome of the tumor cells has also been documented.[74,97,117] The X antigen of the hepatitis B virus is thought to play an important role because of the fact that it stimulates virus gene expression and replication, and therefore it may be essential for the establishment and maintenance of the chronic carrier state.[88] The PCR technique can demonstrate transcriptionally active HBV genomes among patients with liver cell carcinoma who are negative for hepatitis B surface antigen.[112] In patients with hepatitis, increased proliferative indices and high AFP serum value represent risk markers for liver cell carcinoma.[84,128]

2 *Cirrhosis.* In the United States, 60% to 80% of the cases develop in livers affected by cirrhosis, which may be either clinically apparent or silent.[134] This is usually of the macronodular type, including that caused by hemochromatosis.[90] It has been estimated that the yearly incidence rate of hepatocellular carcinoma in patients with cirrhosis is 3%, both in the West and in Asia.[79] Cases of liver cell carcinoma have also been reported in association with biliary cirrhosis secondary to congenital bile duct atresia,[82] familial cholestatic cirrhosis of childhood,[81,129] cirrhosis caused by α_1-antitrypsin deficiency[103] or tyrosinemia,[131] and congenital hepatic fibrosis associated with adult polycystic kidneys.[105]

The liver cell carcinomas associated with cirrhosis have a greater tendency for widespread hepatic involvement than those arising in a previously normal liver.

3 *Liver cell dysplasia.* Two types of liver cell dysplasia have been identified.[116] In the traditional form (now known as *large cell dysplasia*), there is cellular enlargement, nuclear pleomorphism, and multinucleation, but the nucleocytoplasmic ratio remains normal. The presence of this change in the non-neoplastic portion of an organ harboring a liver cell carcinoma has been used as indirect evidence for viral participation in the process, and its presence in a liver without carcinoma has been viewed as a possible premalignant event.[80,109] Anthony et al.[70] studied the incidence of large cell dysplasia in a large group of patients from Uganda and found it in only 1% of patients with normal liver, in 6.9% of patients with liver cell carcinoma occurring in an otherwise normal liver, in 20.3% of patients with cirrhosis, and in 64.5% of patients with cirrhosis *and* liver cell carcinoma. They also documented a strong relationship between dysplasia and the presence of hepatitis B surface antigen and concluded that the presence of liver cell dysplasia identifies a group of patients who are at high risk for developing liver cell carcinoma. The statistical relation of hepatocytic dysplasia with both hepatitis B virus infection and the development of liver cell carcinoma has been confirmed by several other groups.[67,93,102] These dysplastic changes can also be seen in other forms of viral hepatitis[99] and in α_1-antitrypsin deficiency.[78] The fact that aneuploidy is common in liver cell dysplasia is an additional feature supporting its pathogenetic link with liver cell carcinoma.[126]

Small cell dysplasia is characterized by a decreased volume of hepatocytic cytoplasm associated with moderately enlarged nuclear size, resulting in an increased nucleocytoplasmic ratio. These nuclei are also characterized by an increased chromatin density. Some authors have suggested that this type of dysplasia represents a more important risk factor for liver cell carcinoma than large cell dysplasia,[80] but in the recent study by Libbrecht et al.,[101] the predictive value was statistically greater for large liver cell dysplasia (and for cirrhosis) than for small liver cell dysplasia.

4 *Adenomatous hyperplasia.* Adenomatous hyperplasia was the term traditionally applied to "atypical" nodular lesions occurring in liver with cirrhosis that did not fulfill the morphologic criteria for liver cell carcinomas but were thought to possibly represent precursors for them.[89,106,115,123] The terminology used for these lesions has been inconsistent and confusing and has included terms such as ordinary and atypical adenomatous hyperplasia, minimal deviation hepatoma, paraplasia, large regenerative nodule, and types I and II macroregenerative nodule. In a laudable attempt to standardize the diagnostic criteria and terminology for these lesions, a multinational panel of liver pathologists has proposed the following classification[89]:

a *Macroregenerative nodule (ordinary adenomatous hyperplasia).* This term is applied to a nodule measuring ≥0.8 cm with a generally intact reticular architecture, cell plates no more than two cells thick, and absence of infiltrative edge. Large cell dysplasia, iron deposits, fat, clear cell change, Mallory's hyaline, and bile can be present. This lesion is not thought to have a greater predisposition to the development of malignancy than the smaller nodules, seen in all cases of cirrhosis.

b *Borderline nodule (atypical adenomatous hyperplasia).* This term is used for a nodule that can contain foci of decreased reticulum staining, small cell dysplasia, Mallory's hyaline, isolated glandular structures ("pseudoglands"), liver cell plates up to three cells thick, and irregular edges. Morphologic, morphometric,[124] DNA ploidy,[111] cell proliferative,[121] and AgNOR[125] studies done on these lesions are all consistent with their presumed preneoplastic role. Foci of liver cell carcinoma may be identified within or in the vicinity of either macroregenerative or borderline nodules and should be identified as such.[85] Sometimes the borderline nodules are multiple, a possible explanation for some cases of multicentric hepatocellular carcinomas.[122]

5 *Thorium dioxide exposure.* Administration of thorium dioxide suspension (Thorotrast) as a radiographic contrast medium has resulted in the development of many liver cell carcinomas, the average latent period being 20 years.[119]

6   *Androgenic–anabolic steroids.* Several cases of liver tumors have been reported in males in association with long-term administration of androgenic–anabolic steroids.[73,87,98] Many of these are probably adenomas, analogous to those seen in females in association with contraceptive pills.[92,108] Others are clearly malignant, as evidenced by their metastasizing properties.[72]

7   *Progestational agents.* Several cases of liver cell carcinomas, either alone or in association with liver cell adenomas, have been reported in women taking contraceptive pills.[94,113,118]

8   *α_1-Antitrypsin deficiency.* Cases of cirrhosis caused by this inborn error of metabolism complicated by liver cell carcinoma are on record, but there is still controversy as to whether the deficiency per se is a preneoplastic condition.[77,86] Patients with the PIZ variant of antitrypsin deficiency seem to be particularly prone to this complication, and also to the development of cholangiocarcinoma.[135]

9   *Tyrosinemia.* The chronic form of this inborn error of metabolism is associated with a high incidence of liver cell carcinoma. In one series, 37% of 43 patients surviving beyond 2 years of age developed this malignancy.[131] All of the patients with tumor also had cirrhosis.

10 *Ataxia–telangiectasia.* A few cases of liver cell carcinomas have been observed in patients with this form of congenital immune deficiency.[132]

11 *Aflatoxins.* The peculiar geographic distribution of liver cell carcinoma has suggested to some a relationship with the ingestion of aflatoxins, which are metabolic products of the growth of the ubiquitous fungus *Aspergillus flavus.*[68] A good correlation exists between the level of contamination of foods with aflatoxins and the incidence of liver cancer; elimination of this contamination has resulted in a decrease in the number of tumors.

12 *Schistosomiasis.* There is no convincing evidence that schistosomiasis per se predisposes to liver cell carcinoma.[107]

Gross features

Grossly, liver cell carcinoma may present as a single mass, as multiple nodules, as diffuse liver involvement, or as a large mass replacing most of the liver; these have been referred to as solitary, multinodular, diffuse, and massive forms, respectively[142] (Figs 13.56 to 13.58). Livers with cirrhosis tend to develop liver cell carcinoma of the multinodular type.[145] Some lesions are surrounded by a grossly distinct capsule.[143,144] In rare cases, the tumor is pedunculated, presumably because it arises in an accessory lobe.[137,138] The tumor size varies a great deal from case to case. In recent years, progress in diagnostic procedures has led to the detection of an increased number of *small* or *minute* tumors, variously defined as measuring less than 3, 3.5, or 5 cm.[139–141]

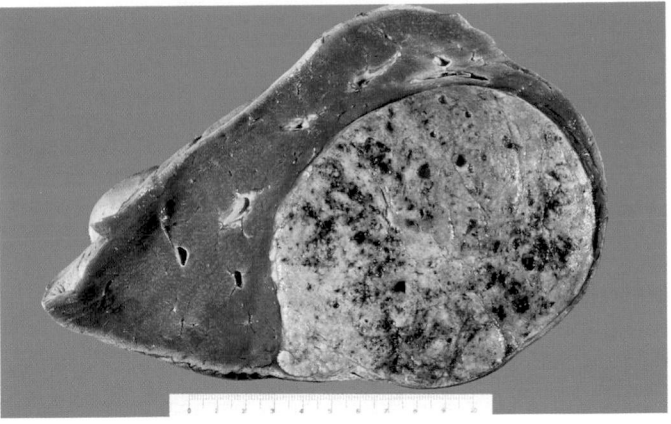

Fig. 13.56 Gross appearance of hepatocellular carcinoma. The tumor is well circumscribed and shows numerous small hemorrhagic foci. (Courtesy of Dr. RA Cooke, Brisbane, Australia; from Cooke RA, Stewart B: Colour Atlas of Anatomical Pathology. Edinburgh, Churchill Livingstone, 2004).

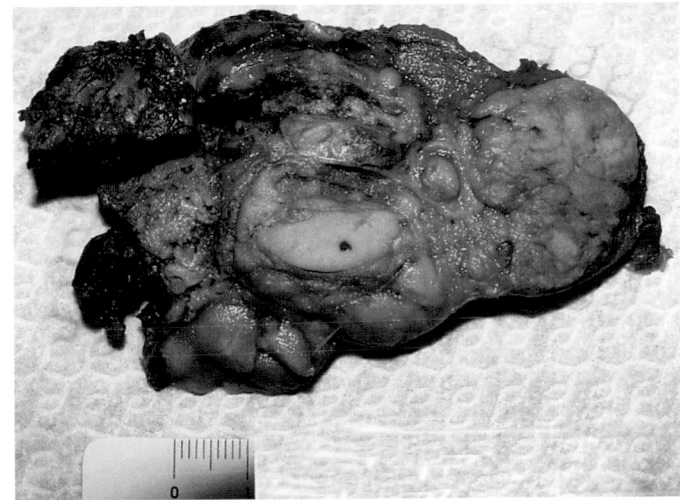

Fig. 13.57 Bile-stained hepatocellular carcinoma.

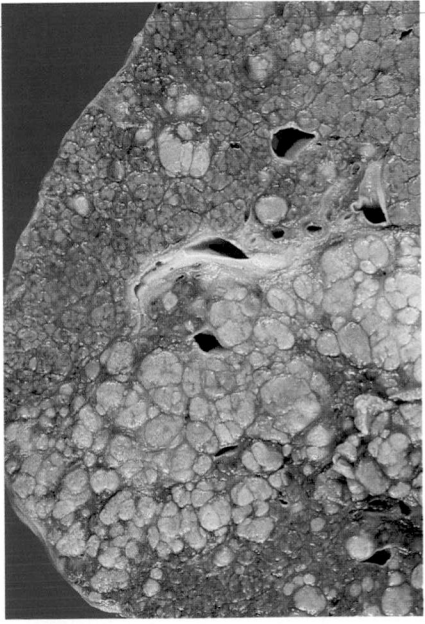

Fig. 13.58 Liver cell carcinoma. The tumor is multicentric and has arisen against a background of cirrhosis. (Courtesy of Dr. Richard Eisen, New Haven, CT)

Grossly evident portal vein thrombosis is found in a high proportion of the advanced cases.[136]

Microscopic features

Microscopically, the pattern of growth of liver cell carcinoma may be trabecular, solid, or tubular[155] (Figs 13.59 and 13.60). The latter, which has also been referred to as pseudoglandular or acinar, may result in papillary-like formations and can lead to diagnostic confusion with bile duct carcinoma.[155,156] A network of sinusoidal vessels surrounds the tumor cells, an important diagnostic feature; some of these sinusoids seem to be lined by tumor cells[157] (Fig. 13.61). A feature of great diagnostic significance is the thickness of the trabeculae, as estimated in the H&E sections but better evaluated in reticulin stains; the thicker the hepatocytic plates, the more likely the diagnosis of carcinoma. The stroma is usually scanty, in contrast to that of bile duct carcinoma (see, however, the sclerosing form, p. 1001). Invasion of veins in the portal tract is a frequent finding. Cytologically, there is a wide range of differentiation from tumor to tumor. The less well differentiated cases show great pleomorphism, bizarre mitotic figures, and tumor giant cells.[146,149] Nuclei and nucleoli are prominent, and the cytoplasm is scanty and basophilic. It may be difficult or impossible to identify these tumors with certainty as liver cell carcinomas. Conversely, the better differentiated tumors are easily recognized as being composed of hepatocytes but may be difficult to categorize as malignant. This is particularly true at the interphase between tumor and normal liver, in which the former may show a remarkably well-developed normotrabecular pattern.[154] An occasional cluster of enlarged hyperchromatic nuclei, an atypical mitotic figure, or a blood vessel with a thrombus may be the only clue to the malignant nature of the lesion.[153,160]

The tumor cells often exhibit intranuclear pseudoinclusions caused by cytoplasmic invaginations. The cytoplasm may contain Mallory's hyaline similar to that seen in alcoholic liver disease, round hyaline globules (some containing α-fetoprotein and others α_1-antitrypsin),[148,159] copper,[151,152] "pale bodies" (seen ultrastructurally as a membrane-bound mass of granular or fibrillary material that is immunoreactive for fibrinogen),[158,162] or bile pigment; the latter is an important diagnostic feature (Fig. 13.62). Both the copper and copper-binding proteins can be detected histochemically.[150] In one remarkable case, the tumor was black because of the accumulation of a Dubin–Johnson-like pigment.[161] The round hyaline bodies have been said to contain α-fetoprotein and α_1-antitrypsin,[148,159] but recently the interesting observation has been made that their major constituent is p62, a phosphotyrosine-independent ligand of p561ck kinase.[163]

A rare but well-documented event in hepatocellular carcinoma is the presence of focal neuroendocrine differentiation, a phenomenon analogous to that seen in most glandular epithelial tumors of other organs and not to be

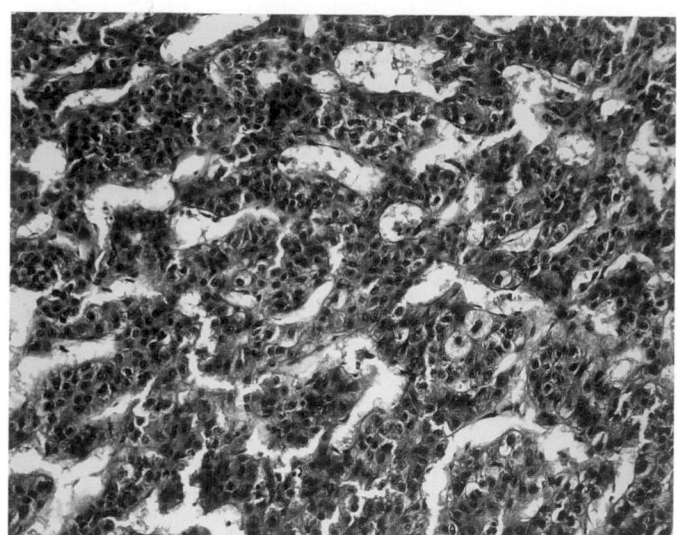

Fig. 13.59 Typical trabecular pattern of growth of hepatocellular carcinoma.

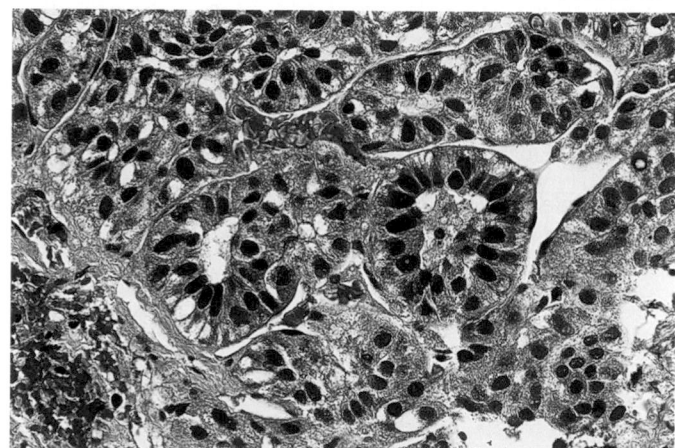

Fig. 13.60 Tubular formations in hepatocellular carcinoma. These should not be interpreted as evidence of a cholangiocarcinomatous component.

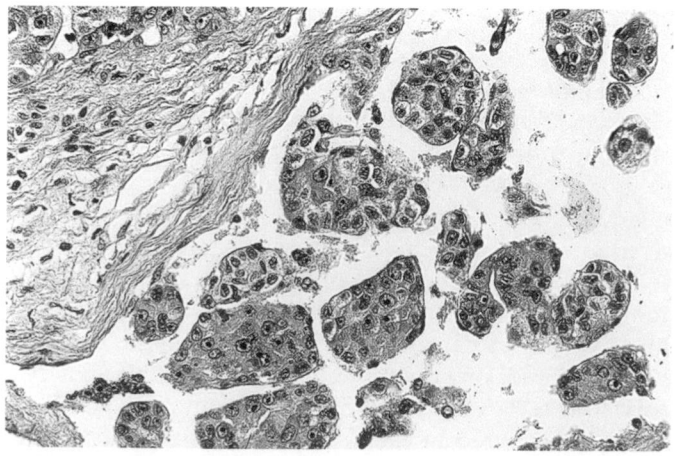

Fig. 13.61 The widely dilated sinusoids of this hepatocellular carcinoma result in sharply outlined tumor islands which are very typical of the entity.

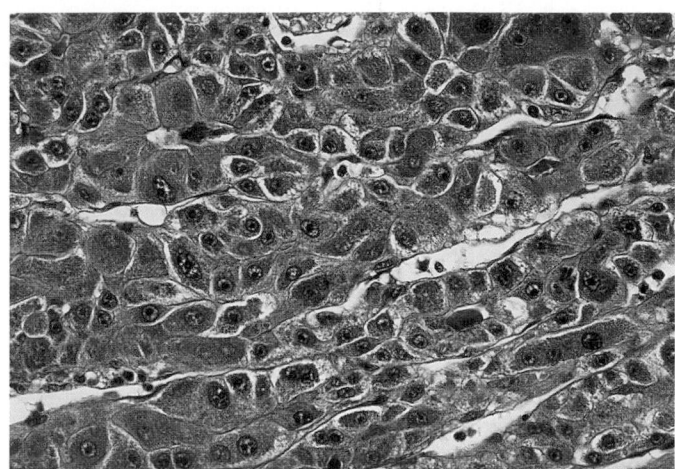

Fig. 13.62 Microscopic appearance of liver cell carcinoma. Note the trabecular pattern of growth, nuclear atypicality, and bile production by tumor cells.

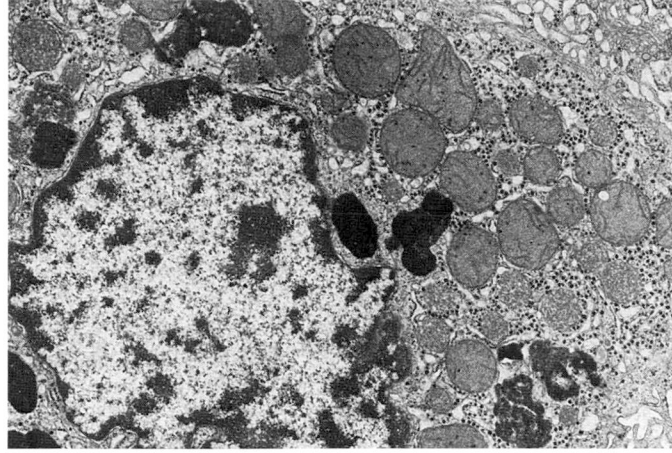

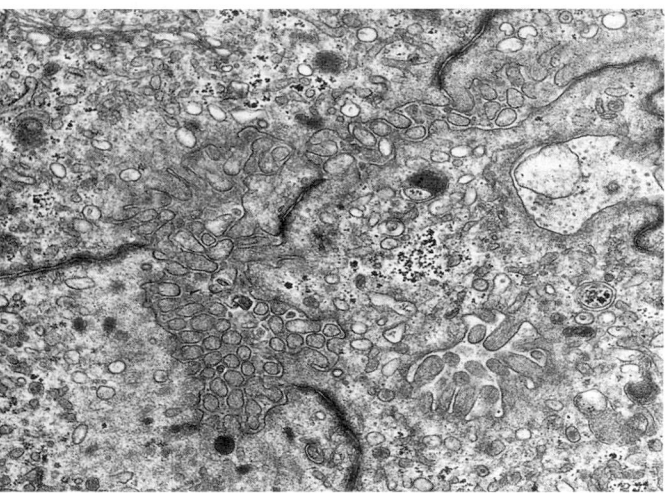

Fig. 13.63 Ultrastructural appearance of liver cell carcinoma. **A**, Malignant hepatocyte with numerous mitochondria, microbodies, and abundant glycogen. Cells also contain intracytoplasmic bile products. **B**, Electron microscopic appearance of liver cell carcinoma. Bile canaliculus with stubby microvilli and cell junctions of the tight and intermediate types. Clusters of electron-dense glycogen particles are also evident. (**A** X11,200; **B** X18,700) (**B** courtesy of Dr. Robert A. Erlandson, Memorial Sloan-Kettering Cancer Center)

equated with carcinoid tumor/neuroendocrine carcinoma.[147,164,165]

Kuppfer cells may be present in liver cell carcinomas, but they are usually scanty and irregularly distributed.

Electron microscopic and immunohistochemical features

The ultrastructure of liver cell carcinoma recapitulates in some respects that of the normal adult hepatocyte, and it differs in many ways from that of hepatoblastoma[182] (Fig. 13.63).

Immunohistochemically, liver cell carcinoma has been found to be immunoreactive for AFP,[175,187] keratin, EMA, α_1-antitrypsin,[177] fibrinogen, IgG, transferrin receptor,[201] ferritin,[172] Mallory body antigen,[169] albumin,[166] aromatase (an enzyme that converts androgen into estrogen),[212] integrins VLA-α_1 and VLA-β_1 (as in normal liver tissue),[210] CD15 (another adhesion molecule),[205] insulin-like growth factor II (more so than in normal liver),[190] epidermal growth factor receptor,[178] factor XIIIa,[177,183] villin[190a] and C-reactive protein.[183] Hep-Par-1 is a monoclonal antibody that reacts to an as yet unidentified cytoplasmic marker of normal and neoplastic hepatocytes.[211] It is very sensitive and reasonably specific[171,174a,191,196] (Fig. 13.64); as expected, it also stains hepatoid adenocarcinomas of the gastrointestinal tract and other sites.[194]

MOC31, a recently described antibody directed against a cell surface glycoprotein, could be viewed as the counterpart of Hep-Par-1, in the sense that it is said to be regularly expressed in cholangiocarcinoma and metastatic carcinoma but not in liver cell carcinomas.[196a,199]

The apparent expression of inhibin by liver cell carcinoma has been shown to be a spurious result due to the presence of endogenous biotin.[184]

TTF-1, which is present in the nuclei of thyroid and lung epithelial cells, is said to be expressed in the cytoplasm of the cells of hepatocellular carcinoma, a curious result that needs independent confirmation.[211a]

AFP is a relatively specific but rather insensitive marker for hepatocellular differentiation, being present in only one quarter of the cases.[168] On theoretical grounds, albumin ought to be an excellent marker of hepatocytic differentiation since this molecule is selectively produced by liver cells. However, it suffers from the fact that it is present in large amounts in the plasma, thus resulting in a high degree of diffuse tissue staining. Detection of albumin mRNA by in situ hybridization gets around this problem and has proved diagnostically useful, both for hepatocellular carcinomas and for extrahepatic hepatoid carcinomas[176,186a,188] (Fig. 13.65). CEA is usually negative or only focally positive (when detected with a monoclonal antibody, see later section), an important factor in the differential diagnosis with bile duct

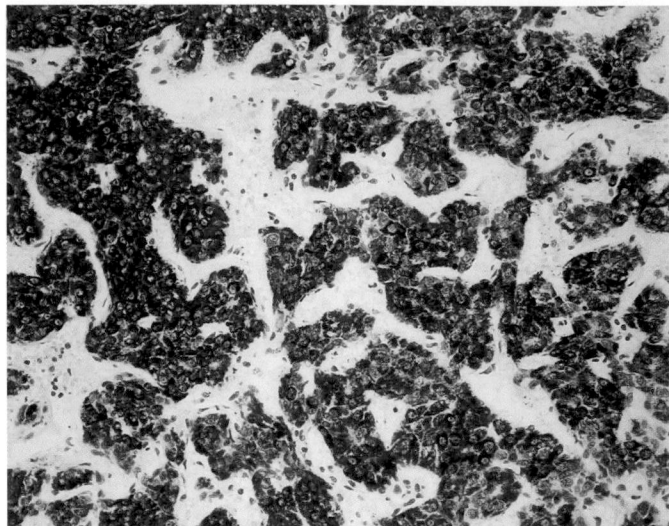

Fig. 13.64 Strong cytoplasmic positivity for Hep-Par-1 in hepatocellular carcinoma. The stain has a characteristically coarse granular quality.

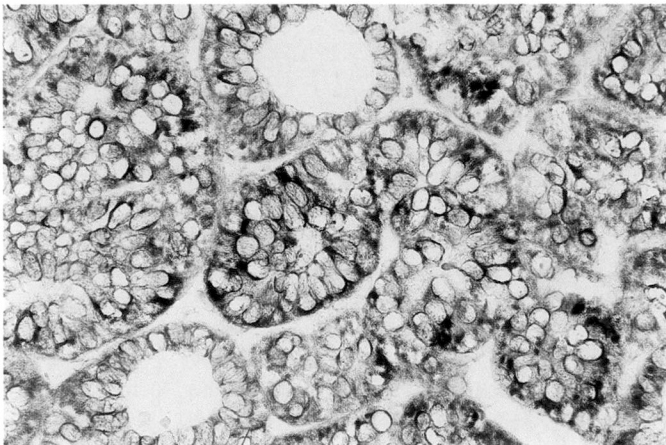

Fig. 13.65 Albumin production by the cells of hepatocellular carcinoma, as demonstrated by in situ hybridization.

carcinoma and metastatic carcinoma.[179,187] In regard to the keratins, it has been shown that most liver cell carcinomas are immunoreactive for monoclonal antibodies Cam 5.2 and 35βH11 (which recognize keratin 8) but not for monoclonal antibody AE1 (which recognizes keratins 10, 14, 15, 16, and 19).[186] Keratins 5/6, 18, and 20 are also absent, and keratin 7 is present in a small minority of cases.[193,209] This pattern, which recapitulates that of normal hepatocytes,[189] is maintained in most liver cell carcinomas. However, just as reactive or metaplastic hepatocytes can express "bile duct-type" keratins (such as keratin 7),[208] this can also be true of liver cell carcinoma.[193] We have seen several cases of primary neoplasms of the liver otherwise fulfilling all the criteria for this tumor type in which a wide range of keratin immunoreactivity was displayed. This finding is in keeping with the proposal that hepatocellular carcinoma and

cholangiocarcinoma arise from a common pluripotent stem cell.[195,202]

An important diagnostic feature of liver cell carcinoma is the production of bile canalicular structures between the tumor cells. These can be demonstrated in cytologic or histologic preparations with stains for alkaline phosphatase, biliary glycoprotein (using a polyclonal antibody for CEA, which cross reacts with this marker), CD10 (neprilysin), or low-molecular-weight keratin[167,170,187,192] (Fig. 13.66). The claim that this canalicular staining pattern as demonstrated by alkaline phosphatase staining is present in the benign but not in the malignant hepatocytic tumors[173] seems to us to be of doubtful validity. Unfortunately, this statement also applies to most if not all of the markers mentioned in this section. Many of them are useful in segregating hepatocellular (and hepatoid) carcinomas from cholangiocarcinomas and from carcinomas metastatic to the liver, but are of little or no use in the differential diagnosis with liver cell adenoma or the various forms of adenomatous hyperplasia.[207]

The cells of liver cell carcinoma have also been found to possess both estrogen and androgen receptors.[197,198] The better differentiated tumors show deposition of basement membrane components (laminin, type IV collagen, and fibronectin) in a peritrabecular or periacinar pattern.[174,180,185] The expression of laminin is coordinated with the expression of integrin,[206] and the expression of fibronectin is abnormally high.[204] The vessels of liver cell carcinomas show ultrastructural and immunohistochemical features of true capillaries (such as *Ulex* EA1 binding and CD34 staining), which are different from the sinusoids of normal liver.[181,200]

AgNOR counts are significantly higher in liver cell carcinomas than in benign or "borderline" hepatocytic lesions.[203]

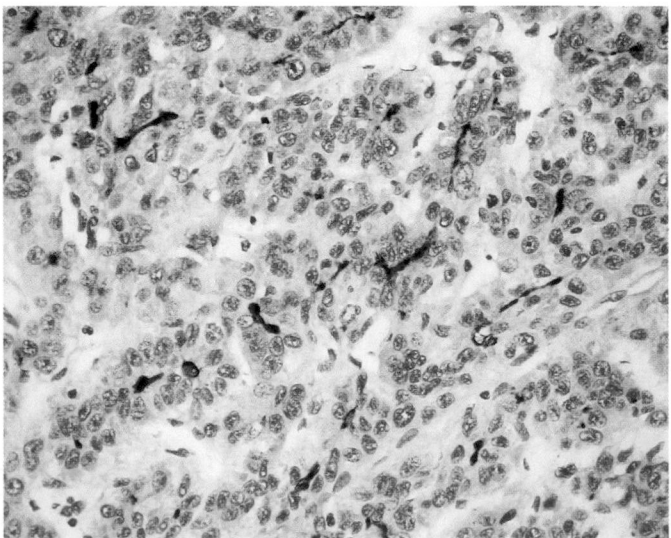

Fig. 13.66 Canalicular formations in hepatocellular carcinoma demonstrated immunohistochemically with polyclonal CEA.

Molecular genetic features

Alterations of the *p53* gene have often been found, particularly in areas of the world where hepatitis B infection and aflatoxin ingestion are common,[213,219,220] much less so in the Mediterranean basin.[214] One particular mutation of this gene (G-to-T transversion at codon 249) seems to be unusually well represented.[215,218] Bcl-2 protein is present in a minority of liver cell carcinomas but apparently not in liver cell dysplasia.[223] Aberrations of genes involved in the cell cycle are also common.[221] The technique of comparative genomic hybridization has shown a high correlation between hepatocellular carcinoma and high-grade dysplastic nodules, strongly supporting the preneoplastic nature of the latter.[222] Aneuploidy, as determined by flow or image cytometry, is present in about half of the cases and it correlates with the microscopic grade of the tumor.[216,217]

The molecular profile of hepatocellular carcinoma is beginning to get defined.[220a]

Other microscopic types

Clear cell hepatocellular carcinoma comprises about 9% of all malignant hepatocellular neoplasms.[260] The tumor shows a marked female predominance and a high association with cirrhosis.[261] The cytoplasmic clearing, which is due to the accumulation of glycogen and/or fat, may result in an appearance closely resembling that of renal or adrenal cortical carcinoma.[228] The differential diagnosis is facilitated by the performance of special techniques such as immunostaining for Hep-Par-1 and polyclonal CEA[247] and FISH for albumin mRNA.[249] As in most other organs (such as lung, thyroid, and breast), clear cell carcinoma is not a distinct entity but rather a clinically inconsequential morphologic variant of one of the major tumor types.[231]

Sclerosing hepatocellular carcinoma has been described, especially following therapy.[241] A case has been documented associated with secretion of a PTH-like protein.[225]

Small cell hepatocellular carcinoma is composed of small cells growing in broad nests and showing positivity for low-molecular-weight keratin and AFP.[262]

Lymphoepithelioma-like carcinoma of the hepatobiliary region resembles its counterpart in the nasopharyngeal region and seems similarly related to EBV.[259] This tumor type is probably identical to the neoplasm that has been reported as hepatocellular carcinoma with lymphoid stroma.[230]

Sarcomatoid (spindle) cell hepatocellular carcinoma contains spindle and/or multinucleated cells of mesenchymal appearance.[237,240,246] There may be also osteoclast-like giant cells,[238,242] bone and cartilage, and skeletal muscle.[224] As in other organs, the term *carcinosarcoma* has been used when the carcinomatous and the sarcoma-like areas are sharply segregated.[234]

Mixed hepatocarcinoma–cholangiocarcinoma is now rec-ognized as a bona fide entity exhibiting dual differentiation into liver cell and bile duct lines, both at the morphologic and the immunohistochemical level.[236,239,242,253,257] This is a different phenomenon from the presence of concomitant hepatocellular carcinoma and cholangiocarcinoma in the same liver or even in the same mass ("collision tumor").[235,243] It is also different from the phenomenon of focal ductular differentiation in liver cell carcinoma. In this morphologic variant of hepatocellular carcinoma, the ductular formations are lined by tumor cells resembling hepatocytes rather than bile duct cells at both the light and the electron microscopic level, and the luminal content is mucin negative.[250]

Fibrolamellar carcinoma (also known as polygonal cell type hepatocellular carcinoma with fibrous stroma and oncocytic hepatocellular tumor) is a distinctive morphologic variant of liver cell carcinoma seen predominantly in young patients without cirrhosis and associated with a generally favorable prognosis[227,229] (Fig. 13.67). Almost half of the liver cell carcinomas seen in the United States in patients younger than 35 years belong to this type.[232] A case has been reported associated with Fanconi anemia.[244] The most characteristic microscopic feature is fibrosis arranged in a lamellar fashion around the neoplastic hepatocytes. The tumor cells are polygonal and deeply eosinophilic, possibly as a secondary effect from the fibrosis (Fig. 13.68).[226] These features can also be appreciated in material from fine needle aspiration.[256]

Ultrastructurally, the tumor cells have numerous mitochondria, in keeping with their oncocytic appearance at the light microscopic level.[233,251] Bile canaliculi-like lumina can also be appreciated.[254] Dense-core granules of neurosecretory type have been reported in some cases.[245,252]

Immunohistochemically, the tumor cells express cytokeratins 8 and 18 (like those of conventional liver cell carcinoma) but also 7 and (to a lesser extent) 19.[258] The collagen deposited around the tumor cells is predominantly composed of types I, III, and V.[248]

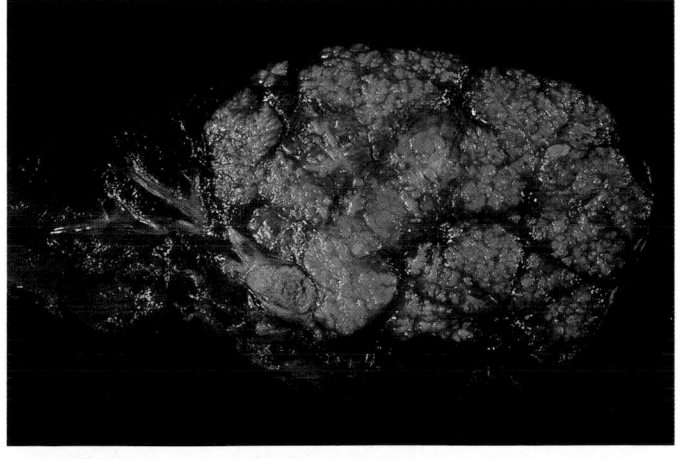

Fig. 13.67 Gross appearance of fibrolamellar carcinoma. The tumor is large, well circumscribed, multinodular, and yellow.

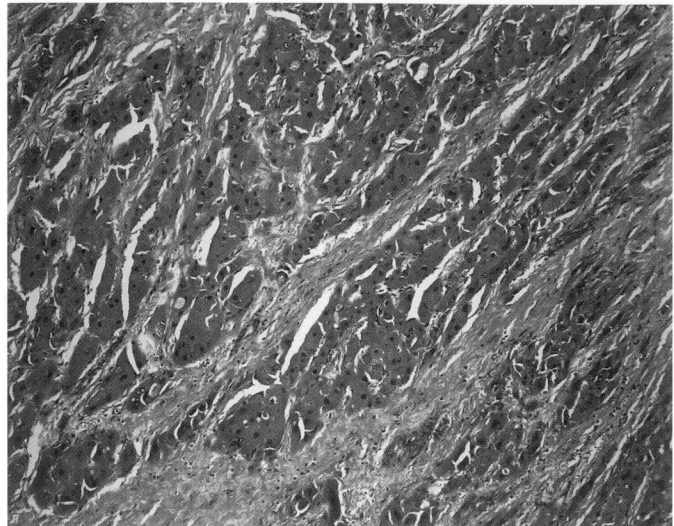

Fig. 13.68 Fibrolamellar carcinoma showing tumor lobules separated by wide fibrous bands. Note the oncocytic appearance of the tumor cells.

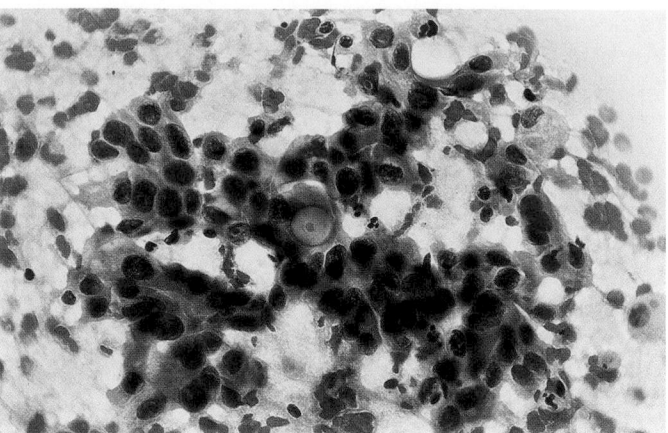

Fig. 13.69 Cytologic appearance of hepatocellular carcinoma. Note the pleomorphism and lack of an inflammatory component.

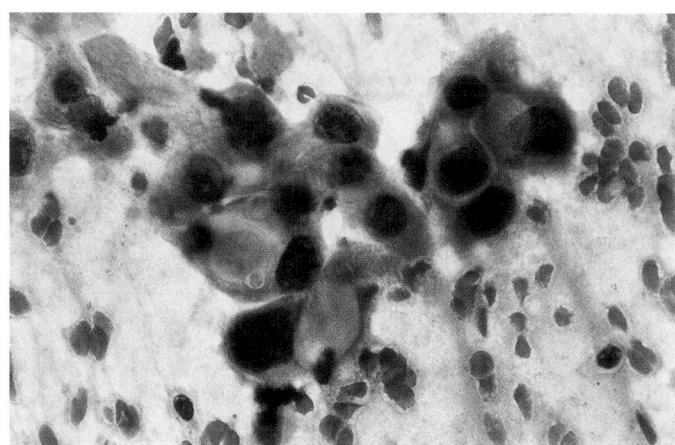

Fig. 13.70 High-power view of a fine needle aspiration specimen from hepatocellular carcinoma (same case as Fig. 13.69).

The architectural similarities between fibrolamellar carcinoma and focal nodular hyperplasia, and the occasional coexistence of the two entities, have suggested to some authors that these two disorders may be pathogenetically related.[255]

Over half of the fibrolamellar carcinomas are resectable, and the cure rate is about 50%. Children, however, do not have a better prognosis than those affected by hepatocellular carcinoma of the conventional type.[240a]

Biopsy and cytology

The diagnosis of liver cell carcinoma can be made by core or fine needle biopsy[265,266,270,272] or a combination of both.[269,273] The better differentiated the tumor, the more difficult the diagnosis of malignancy. In fine needle material, the most useful diagnostic criteria are similarity of tumor cells to liver cells, the prominence of nucleoli, a trabecular pattern of growth, and the presence of a sinusoidal stroma.[267,269]

At the cytologic level, features favoring the diagnosis of liver cell carcinoma over cirrhosis are absence of bile duct epithelial cells and chronic inflammatory cells, increased nucleocytoplasmic ratio, trabecular pattern, and atypical naked hepatocytic nuclei[264] (Figs 13.69 and 13.70). Features favoring liver cell carcinoma over metastatic carcinoma include polygonal cells with centrally placed nuclei, cells separated by sinusoidal stroma, nuclear pseudoinclusions, eosinophilic cytoplasmic globules, and bile secretion.[264,269] As with histologic preparations, the diagnosis can be aided by performing immunocytochemical stains on the fine needle aspiration material.[263,268]

Two rare but well-documented complications of needle biopsy are implantation along the tract and intra-abdominal hemorrhage.[271]

Spread and metastases

Liver cell carcinomas quickly permeate the liver through the portal venous system, to spread first within the liver itself[277] and then into the lung to grow into the pulmonary arterial tree. They may also grow into the hepatic vein and from there reach the inferior vena cava and the right atrium.[276] Gross tumor invasion of the biliary tree is less common but it does occur.[275] Local invasion of the diaphragm and metastases to regional lymph nodes also are common.[282] In rare cases, wide dissemination through the bloodstream takes place, with the development of adrenal and extensive bone metastases.[274,279,280] In some of the cases, a pathologic fracture or some other sign attributable to bone metastasis is the first sign of the disease.[278,280] Metastases to the ovary need to be distinguished from primary hepatoid tumors of this organ.[281] Hematogenous metastases are less common in the solitary (nodular) form of liver cell carcinoma and very frequent in the massive and diffuse types.[282]

Treatment and prognosis

The overall median survival of untreated liver cell carcinoma is about 4 months,[289,305] and the overall 5-year survival rate in the United States is only 3%.[287] The major causes of death are hepatic failure and gastrointestinal bleeding.[314] Sometimes the terminal event is spontaneous rupture[288] or localized submassive liver cell necrosis.[312] Under exceptional circumstances, hepatocellular carcinomas have been found to undergo spontaneous regression.[298]

The most effective treatment of liver cell carcinoma is complete resection, the only long-term (5 to 10 years) survivors being in this group.[315,317,319,321] Numerous reports from Japan indicate that if the tumor is diagnosed and excised at an early stage, good chances of cure exist.[313] The Japan Liver Cancer Study Group reported that, as of the end of 1974, 25 of 297 patients who had had hepatectomy had survived for more than 5 years, the longest survival being more than 17 years.[297] Other centers have reported 5-year survival rates ranging from 25% to 65%.[285,296] Currently, a large number of tumors have been treated with liver transplantation; the best results with this technique have been obtained with small solitary tumors.[286,304,318]

Systemic or arterial chemotherapy can offer a modest degree of palliation in inoperable or recurrent tumors.[290] Transcatheter hepatic arterial embolization is also employed and can result in extensive tumor necrosis, especially for small lesions; the tumors successfully treated also develop a markedly thickened capsule.[294]

Factors to be mentioned in relation to the prognosis of liver cell carcinoma include the following:

1 *Stage.* This constitutes the most important prognostic determinator.[300,314,316]
2 *Size.* In most series, patients with "small" tumors (anywhere from 2 to 5 cm in diameter) have had a significantly better prognosis.[285,293,320] Some authors, however, have not found size per se to be an important prognostic determinator.[295,296]
3 *Encapsulation.* The liver cell carcinomas that are totally surrounded by a capsule behave in a less aggressive fashion than those lacking this feature.[295,307]
4 *Number of tumors.* As expected, single lesions are associated with a longer survival rate than multiple tumors.[285,296,303,317]
5 *Portal vein involvement.* This finding constitutes an important adverse prognostic sign.[284,285,293,317]
6 *Microscopic type.* As already indicated, the fibrolamellar variant is associated with a definitely better prognosis (see p. 1002). No consistent correlations have been found between prognosis and the other morphologic variants of liver cell carcinoma.[285]
7 *Microscopic features.* In a multi-institutional study of 425 patients with hepatocellular carcinomas resected for cure, the microscopic features that proved to be independent predictors of survival were vascular invasion, high nuclear grade, and mitotic activity.[301] The prognostic value of the mitotic index in this situation has also been shown by other studies.[293]
8 *Presence of cirrhosis.* Carcinomas associated with cirrhosis have a worsened prognosis, probably because of the combination of a lesser functional defense and frequent widespread tumor involvement.[302,306,311]
9 *Serum AFP levels.* High AFP levels at presentation are said to have not only a diagnostic but also an adverse prognostic significance.[310,317]
10 *Viral antigenemia.* No significant prognostic differences exist between hepatitis B antigen-positive and hepatitis B antigen-negative cases.[291,292]
11 *Use of progestational hormones.* It has been stated that tumors in patients who have taken contraceptive pills have a better prognosis than the others.
12 *Sex and age.* In most series, these parameters have not been found to correlate with tumor prognosis. However, a recent study showed a better survival for females and attributed it to the fact that the tumor is more often encapsulated in them.[309]
13 *c-myc amplification.* It has been stated that the presence of this feature in hepatocellular carcinoma predicts an unfavorable prognosis.[283]
14 *Heat shock protein.* Expression of HSP-27 is related to tumor grade and survival, but it remains to be seen whether it constitutes an independent prognostic determinator.[299]
15 *P-glycoprotein.* In one study, the chemotherapy response of hepatocellular carcinoma was inversely related to Pgp expression, the difference being statistically significant.[308]

Hepatoblastoma

Hepatoblastoma occurs primarily in infants, but isolated instances in older children and adults have been reported.[323,338,341] The tumor has been seen in association with a variety of congenital abnormalities (particularly hemihypertrophy), Wilms' tumor of kidney, glycogen storage disease, and familial colonic polyposis.[324,335,341,342] In contrast with liver cell carcinoma, hepatoblastoma does not have a relationship with cirrhosis. Some patients present with virilization as a result of ectopic sex hormone production.[347] Serum levels of α-fetoprotein are often elevated. Hepatic angiography and CT scans provide the most valuable preoperative assessment of the tumor location and extent.[334] Grossly, hepatoblastoma is solid, well circumscribed, and more often solitary than multiple. Microscopically, most of the tumors are composed exclusively of immature hepatocytic elements and are referred to as *pure* or epithelial[365] (Figs 13.71 and 13.72). Some of these, known as *fetal*, consist of hepatocytes arranged in irregular laminae two cells thick, recapitulating those of the fetal liver. Others, designated as *embryonal*, have a more immature appearance and a pattern of growth that is predominantly solid but that may also exhibit ribbons, rosettes, and papillary formations.[360,368] Some tumors are largely made up of anaplastic small cells.[336,346,365] Others show a tubular

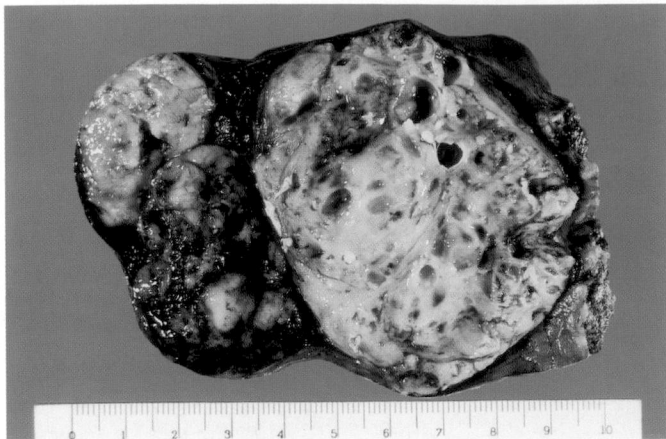

Fig.13.71 Gross appearance of hepatoblastoma occurring in a 12-week-old infant. The tumor is well circumscribed and has a variegated appearance. (Courtesy of Dr. RA Cooke, Brisbane, Australia; from Cooke RA, Stewart B: Colour Atlas of Anatomical Pathology. Edinburgh, Churchill Livingstone, 2004).

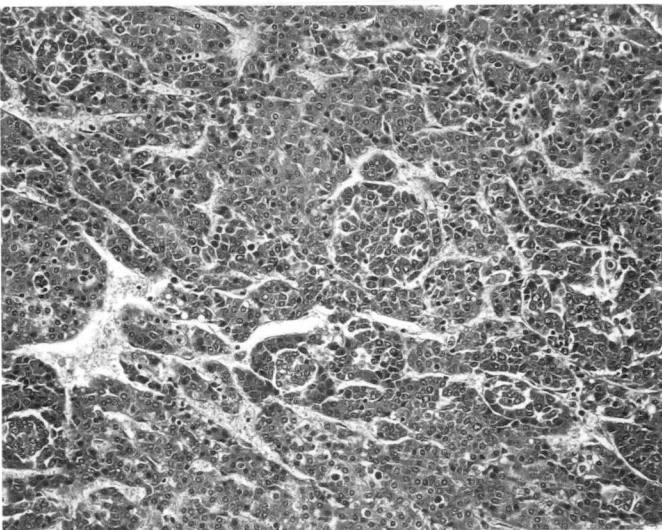

A

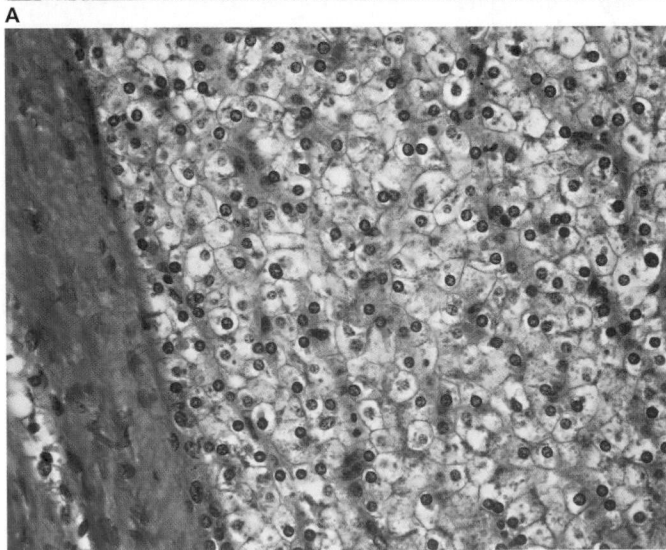

B

Fig. 13.72 A and B, Pure epithelial hepatoblastoma. A, Nesting pattern of growth combining embryonal and fetal features. B, An area with more mature hepatocytes exhibiting cytoplasmic clearing.

component with cholangiolar features ("cholangioblastic hepatoblastoma").[369] The number of mitoses varies widely, but in general it is higher in the embryonal forms. Foci of extramedullary hematopoiesis are often seen, these being invariably associated with the fetal pattern.[329] Multinucleated giant cells may be present, particularly in the tumors associated with hormone production.[349,351] Transitions between the fetal and the embryonal patterns are common. A *macrotrabecular type* of hepatoblastoma resembling liver cell carcinoma has been described[337] (Fig. 13.73). The main light microscopic differences between hepatoblastoma and liver cell carcinoma are listed in Table 13.11. Some of the primary malignant liver cell tumors developing in older children and adolescents have an appearance intermediate between that of hepatoblastomas and hepatocellular carcinomas; these have been referred to as *transitional liver cell tumors*.[353]

About a fourth of hepatoblastomas (referred to as *mixed*) contain, in addition to the epithelial cells, a stromal component that may be undifferentiated or develop into bone or cartilage, resulting in an appearance reminiscent of Wilms' tumor. This feature supports the interpretation that these tumors arise from a multipotential blastema capable of both epithelial and mesenchymal differentiation, sometimes reaching teratoma-like features.[326] Indeed, the distinction between hepatoblastoma with teratoid features and teratoma of the liver can be as difficult on conceptual and practical grounds as the one between teratoid Wilms' tumor and teratoma of the kidney.

Ultrastructurally, the epithelial tumor cells of hepatoblastoma have features of immature hepatocytes.[343,363] Immunohistochemically, reactivity has been found for keratin, EMA, vimentin, polyclonal CEA, Hep-Par-1, α-fetoprotein, hCG, and transferrin receptor.[322,330,350,362]

As in liver cell carcinoma, the keratins expressed in hepatoblastoma are generally of low-molecular-weight

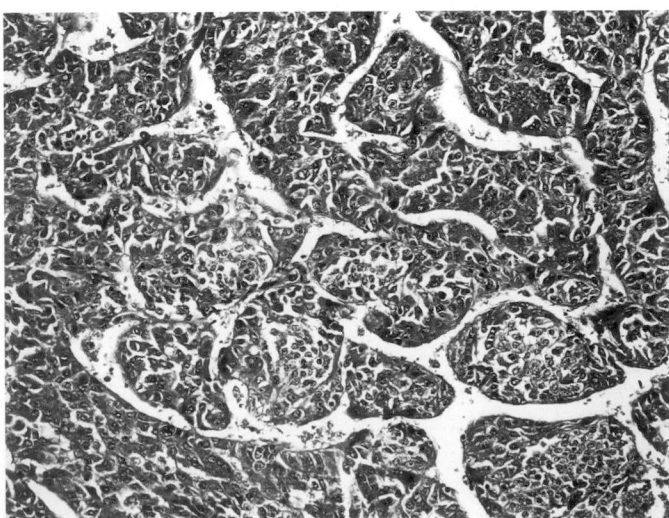

Fig. 13.73 So-called "macrotrabecular variant" of hepatoblastoma.

Table 13.11 Morphologic comparison between epithelial type of hepatoblastoma and liver cell carcinoma

Histologic findings	Hepatoblastoma	Liver cell carcinoma
Tumor mass	Single	Single or multiple
Pseudocapsule	Present	Usually absent
Trabeculae	Usually two cells thick	Usually many cells thick
Canaliculi	Present	Present
"Light and dark" pattern	Present	Usually absent
Size of cells compared to uninvolved hepatocytes	Smaller	Larger
Pleomorphism	Absent to minimal	Present
Tumor giant cells	Absent	Present
Multinucleated tumor cells	Absent	Present
Bile formation	Present	Present
Glycogen	Present	Present or absent
Fat	Present	Present or absent
Cytoplasmic globular and other inclusions	Absent	Present or absent
Extramedullary hematopoiesis	Present	Absent
Associated cirrhosis	Absent	Present or absent

From Ishak KG, Glunz PR. Hepatoblastoma and hepatocarcinoma in infancy and childhood. Cancer 1967, **20**: 396–422.

type (8 and 18, but sometimes also 19 and 7).[366] The expression of keratin 7 (together with albumin) in a small cell epithelial component of hepatoblastoma has been interpreted as documenting the presence of bipotential hepatic stem cells capable of differentiating into hepatocytes and bile duct cells.[358] The CEA staining pattern is also similar in the sense of being demonstrable only with a polyclonal antiserum and featuring a canalicular pattern; this is more likely to be present in the fetal than in the embryonal subtype.[330] Hepatoblastomas with focal neuroendocrine differentiation exist, this representing yet another analogy between this tumor and liver cell carcinoma. Such tumors may be found to be immunoreactive for neuron-specific enolase (NSE), chromogranin, somatostatin, and serotonin[355,367]; some have also been found to contain melanin and to express immunoreactivity for HMB-45.[357] The extracellular material in hepatoblastoma (like that of liver cell carcinoma) stains for basement membrane components such as laminin, type IV collagen, and fibronectin.[356]

Cytogenetically, the most consistent alterations are trisomies 2, 8, and 20, and rearrangements of 1q,[325,352] some of these abnormalities being also common in embryonal rhabdomyosarcoma.[332,365] The DNA content as evaluated by flow cytometry is usually diploid in the fetal type but aneuploid in about 50% of the tumors of embryonal and small anaplastic types.[340] Overexpression of p53 is often detected immunohistochemically, but this does not seem to be caused by gene mutations.[344] CGH analysis has shown a high frequency of X-chromosome gains, and has demonstrated that the epithelial and stromal components of the tumor are genetically similar.[365a]

Hepatoblastoma invades locally and gives rise to metastases in the regional nodes, lung, brain, and other organs. Some patients with hepatoblastoma have a peculiar adenomatoid transformation of the epithelium lining the Bowman's capsule of the renal glomeruli; the pathogenesis of this transformation is unknown.[345]

The treatment of choice of hepatoblastoma is surgical excision with adjuvant chemotherapy.[328,331] Liver transplantation is being increasingly used.[348,364] Preoperative chemotherapy can allow successful resection of an initially unresectable hepatoblastoma.[333,354] The morphologic effects of this therapy are necrosis and an apparent increase in the presence and amount of osteoid.[359] The survival rate is substantially better than for liver cell carcinoma and largely determined by the clinical stage.[327,337,361a] Among the histologic subtypes, it has been claimed that the fetal pattern is associated with a better prognosis than the embryonal variety[368] and that the macrotrabecular and small cell undifferentiated types are particularly aggressive tumors.[337,339,346] Several studies have concluded that aneuploidy as measured by either flow or image cytometry is associated with a poor prognosis.[340,361] However, in a study of 105 cases of hepatoblastoma,[327] neither histologic type nor ploidy had a prognostic impact.

Bile duct tumors and tumorlike conditions

Bile duct hamartoma

Bile duct hamartoma, also known as von Meyenburg or Moschcowitz complex and ductal plate anomaly, presents as multiple, small, whitish nodules scattered throughout the liver, which may be mistaken for metastatic carcinoma by the surgeon[377] (see also p. 959). If large enough, they may be detected ultrasonographically.[375] Microscopically, these nodules appear as a focal disorderly collection of bile ducts and ductules surrounded by abundant fibrous stroma.[370,376] Although the pattern of growth of the individual glands may be irregular, the outline of the lesion as seen on low-power view is sharp, and cellular atypia is nil.

Pathogenetic mechanisms that have been proposed include ischemia,[373] inflammation, and genetic anomalies. The fact that the latter play a role in at least some of the cases is suggested by their association with polycystic disease of kidney and/or liver; in one series, 97% of individuals with adult polycystic renal disease had von Meyenburg complexes in the liver.[374] Isolated instances of malignant transformation in the form of bile duct carcinomas have been reported.[371,372] A lesion having the general features of bile duct hamartoma but measuring 7 cm in diameter has been designated as *biliary adenofibroma*.[378]

Bile duct adenoma

Bile duct adenomas are solitary in over 80% of the cases. Grossly, they appear as well-circumscribed wedge-like white masses, sometimes with a central depression, closely resembling metastatic carcinoma. Most of the lesions are less than 1 cm in diameter and are located subcapsularly.[383] Microscopically, they are made up of small tubular structures with little or no lumen.[381] Inflammation and/or fibrosis are often present. A variant composed of clear cells and simulating metastatic renal cell carcinoma has been described,[379] as well as a type with prominent fibrous stroma (*biliary adenofibroma*).[384a] Immunohistochemically, there is bile duct adenoma reactivity for CEA, EMA, and keratin. Occasionally, a neuroendocrine component resembling pulmonary tumorlets may be seen.[384] The behavior is benign. The neoplastic versus hamartomatous nature of this process is disputed, and the distinction with von Meyenburg complexes is anything but sharp.[380] Consequently, some authors have made the sensible proposal of grouping these lesions into the category of *benign bile duct proliferations* (BPP).[382] Interestingly, a small percentage of these lesions (about 7%) harbor K-*ras* mutations.[382]

Biliary cystadenoma and cystadenocarcinoma

Benign and malignant cystic tumors of biliary origin can arise in the liver or, less frequently, in the extrahepatic biliary system (see Chapter 14).[390,396] Practically all patients are adult, and there is a great predominance of females.[385,388] Grossly, the neoplasms are multilocular and contain a mucinous or clear fluid. The benign tumors are lined by a single layer of cuboidal to tall columnar mucin-producing cells (similar to those of the intrahep-

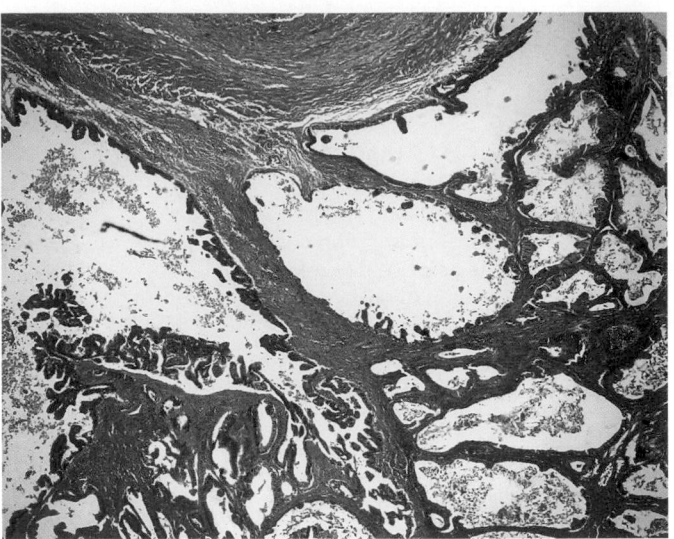

Fig. 13.74 Biliary cystadenocarcinoma showing variously sized cystic structures lined by atypical but well-differentiated mucin-producing glandular epithelium focally forming papillary structures.

atic bile ducts), whereas in the malignant variety the lining is usually of intestinal type (including goblet and Paneth cells),[386,392] associated with varying degrees of atypia and mitotic activity (Fig. 13.74). An endocrine cell component may be seen both in the benign and in the malignant types.[394] The cystadenocarcinomas may show areas of frank stromal invasion. Benign and malignant areas may coexist, emphasizing the need for thorough sampling. Oncocytic differentiation has also been described.[398] In some cases, occurring almost exclusively in females, the underlying layer of connective tissue is very cellular and closely resembles ovarian stroma.[385,397] These cells are immunoreactive for vimentin, smooth muscle actin, hormone receptors, and inhibin.[387,393] In rare cases, the malignant epithelial cells of cystadenocarcinoma acquire a spindle-shaped pseudosarcomatous appearance, as occurs in the analogous tumor of the pancreas.[395] Immunohistochemically, biliary cystadenocarcinoma exhibits consistent reactivity for keratin, CEA, and C 19-9.[391]

Cystadenocarcinomas accompanied by ovarian-like stroma in females follow an indolent course, whereas those lacking this distinctive stroma and seen in males follow a more aggressive course.[385]

Some of the cystic bile duct tumors are thought to be related to congenital abnormalities of the bile ducts, such as congenital cysts (see Chapter 14). The primary treatment of these tumors consists of surgical excision.[389]

Bile duct carcinoma (cholangiocarcinoma)

Malignant tumors of intrahepatic bile ducts are less common than those of hepatocytes. Although most cases seen in Western and African countries are unaccompanied by cirrhosis,[400] some Japanese series suggest that

HCV-related cirrhosis is a major risk factor for cholangio-carcinoma in that country.[417] Some cases have arisen within congenitally dilated intrahepatic bile ducts (Caroli's disease),[401,412] against a background of congenital hepatic fibrosis,[410] in association with multiple bile duct hamartomas[428] (von Meyenburg complexes, see p. 959), in patients with parasitic infestation of the liver (*Clonorchis sinensis* or *Opisthorchis viverrini*),[416,433] following Thorotrast administration[430] or anabolic steroid therapy,[434] or in association with intrahepatic lithiasis (hepatolithiasis).[404,407,418,425] In the latter condition, a precursor dysplastic change has been identified in the biliary ducts.[426]

Most cases of bile duct carcinoma occur after the age of 60 years. Clinically, abdominal pain and weight loss are the most common presenting features (as opposed to obstructive jaundice, which is the usual form of presentation for their extrahepatic counterpart).[399] Grossly, these tumors tend to be firmer and whiter than liver cell carcinomas because of their greater amount of fibrous stroma (Figs 13.75 and 13.76). Multicentricity is common.[435,442] Invasion of the portal vein or its branches is not as common as in liver cell carcinoma, but it can certainly occur.[439]

Microscopically, the tumor is an adenocarcinoma, the ductlike structures being lined by cuboidal or columnar cells (Fig. 13.77). A cribriform pattern may be present.[422] A common feature is the heterogeneity of the neoplastic epithelial cells within the same gland.[422,443] This peculiarity, which is of great diagnostic significance, is shared by adenocarcinomas of the entire biliary–pancreatic system, which ought to be viewed as belonging to a distinct category.[419] The tumor has a tendency to spread between hepatocyte plates, along duct walls, and in relation to nerves. In one series, perineurial invasion was found in 81% of the cases.[402] The stroma, usually abundant, is sometimes arranged circumferentially around the neoplastic glands.[415] The prominent sinusoidal pattern of liver cell carcinoma is absent. Mucin stains are nearly always positive.[443] Morphologic variations of cholangio-carcinoma include types with large amounts of mucin (mucinous cholangiocarcinoma),[409] with signet ring cells,[408] with a squamous component (adenosquamous carcinoma),[420,423] with clear cell and papillary features,[441] with oncocytic papillary features,[421a] with an osteoclast-like giant cell component,[413] with a lymphoepithelioma-like appearance,[406] (some associated with Epstein–Barr virus)[426a], and with a spindle cell component (spindle cell or sarcomatoid cholangiocarcinoma).[424]

Immunohistochemically, there is consistent reactivity for keratin, EMA, and CEA, features of importance in the differential diagnosis with liver cell carcinoma.[403,422] The positivity for keratin is seen with monoclonal antibody Cam 5.2 (as in liver cell carcinoma) *but also* with monoclonal antibody AE1, the latter indicating the presence of high-molecular-weight keratins.[414] There is an interesting and diagnostically useful difference in the keratin immunoprofile between intrahepatic and extrahepatic cholangiocarcinoma, in the sense that the former is usually CK27+/CK20+, whereas the latter is frequently CK7+/CK20–.[431,432] The positivity for CEA is not of the

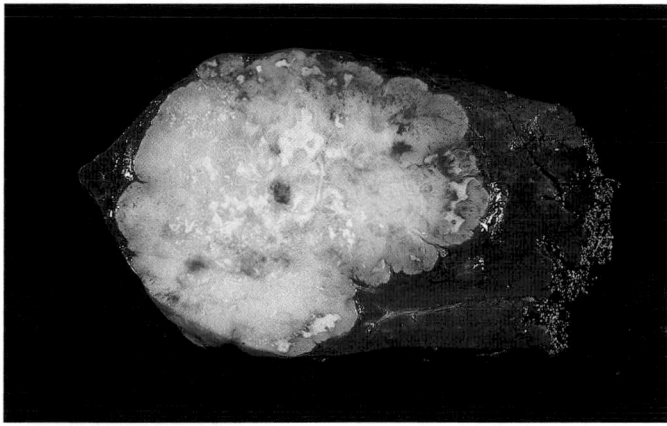

Fig. 13.75 Cholangiocarcinoma. The tumor has a lighter appearance than hepatocellular carcinoma.

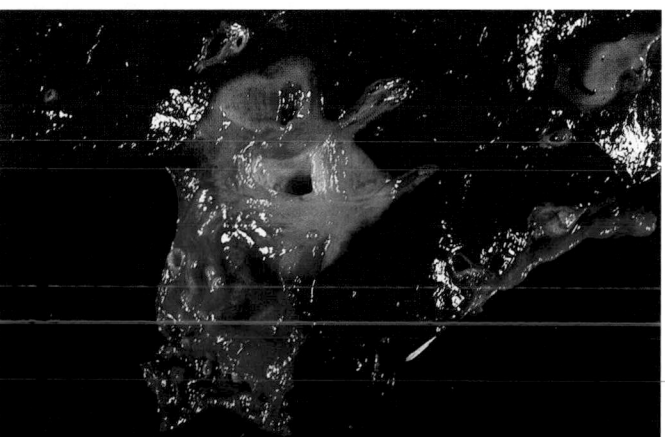

Fig. 13.76 Cholangiocarcinoma. The tumor had a firm consistency.

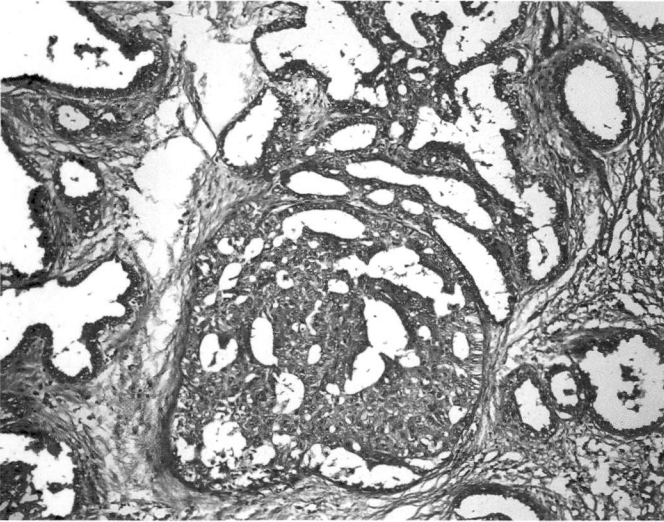

Fig. 13.77 Well-differentiated cholangiocarcinoma.

Table 13.12 Main clinical and pathologic differences between liver cell carcinoma and bile duct carcinoma

Features	Liver cell carcinoma	Bile duct carcinoma
Cell of origin	Hepatocyte	Bile duct cell
Geographic distribution	Marked variability	Worldwide
Age predilection	Young persons	Older persons
Sex predilection	Males	None
Presence of cirrhosis	Common	Exceptional
Liver cell dysplasia	May be present	Absent
α-Fetoprotein	Present	Absent
Bile production	May be present	Absent
Mucin secretion	Absent	Usually present
Gross appearance	Soft and hemorrhagic	Hard and whitish
Preferential spread	Through veins	Through lymphatics

canalicular type as seen in liver cell carcinoma when using polyclonal antisera (in reality representing a cross reaction to a biliary glycoprotein) but is rather cytoplasmic and luminal, as in most other digestive tract adenocarcinomas. The tumor has also been shown to stain for tissue polypeptide antigen,[427] amylase isoenzymes,[437] and PTH-related peptide[429] (in contrast with liver cell carcinoma, which is usually negative for all of these markers). Cholangiocarcinomas have been shown to overexpress MET/hepatocyte growth factor[440] and c-erbB-2.[438]

A high incidence of *ras* gene mutations has been detected, the incidence and spectrum being similar to those reported in large bowel carcinoma.[436] The occurrence of mixed liver cell–bile duct carcinomas has been mentioned on p. 998. The main clinical and pathologic differences between liver cell carcinoma and cholangiocarcinoma are listed in Table 13.12.

We have seen an extremely well-differentiated cholangiocarcinoma, originally diagnosed as bile duct adenoma, which in the course of 15 years replaced almost the entire liver and metastasized to the lung.[411]

The treatment of bile duct carcinoma is surgical, in the form of partial or total hepatic resection, the latter followed by liver transplantation.[421] The prognosis is poor, the overall mean survival time being less than 2 years.[405]

Mesenchymal tumors and tumorlike conditions

Vascular tumors

Hemangioma is the most common benign tumor of the liver. In most cases, it is found incidentally at laparotomy or autopsy. Occasionally, it grows large enough to form a clinically apparent mass. When this is the case, complications such as spontaneous bleeding with rupture and sequestration of platelets resulting in thrombocytopenic purpura may develop. The mass usually projects only slightly above the cut surface, but on occasion it may be pedunculated. On section, it has a characteristic spongy appearance and dark red color. Microscopically, most liver hemangiomas are of the cavernous type, constituted by widely dilated nonanastomotic vascular spaces lined by flat endothelial cells and supported by fibrous tissue. Thrombi in different stages of organization are often encountered (Fig. 13.78). Longstanding lesions can show extensive hyalinization or calcification.[454] Large and/or symptomatic hemangiomas need to be surgically excised; medical treatment or observation is justified in small or asymptomatic lesions.[444,462,481]

Lymphangioma is usually seen in infants or children; in most reported cases, the liver involvement is part of a multicentric process affecting other organs, particularly spleen (lymphangiomatosis).[455,471,477]

Benign (infantile) hemangioendothelioma is a highly cellular variant of hemangioma occurring almost exclusively in children and sometimes in neonates.[445,464] In the series reported by Dehner and Ishak,[448] 87% of the cases were diagnosed prior to 6 months of age. The tumors can be solitary or multiple. The latter are not infrequently associated with hemangiomas in other sites, particularly the skin.[468] They can also be seen as part of the Beckwith–Wiedemann syndrome.[451] There may be a serum elevation of α-fetoprotein. These tumors are associated with a high mortality rate, largely as a result of hepatic failure, congestive heart failure, or hyperconsumptive coagulopathy (Kasabach–Merritt syndrome).[448,474] Microscopically and ultrastructurally, the blood vessels of hemangioendothelioma are lined by one or more layers of plump endothelial cells and surrounded by equally prominent perithelial cells.[453] The lumen is small or collapsed in most vessels, but cavernous foci can sometimes be identified. A lobular configuration is focally apparent, and anastomosing channels are not a feature. Treatment includes radiation therapy, steroids, Endoxane, interferon, percutaneous catheter embolization, and surgical excision, depending on the size and clinical manifestations.[478]

Hemangioblastoma of the liver has been reported in a patient with von Hippel–Lindau syndrome, its appearance being identical to that of the homonymous cerebellar tumor.[469]

Epithelioid hemangioendothelioma is a distinctive type of endothelial vascular neoplasm.[456,461] Most patients are adult females, and there may be a relationship with oral contraceptive use.[447] Clinically, the tumor may simulate the Budd–Chiari syndrome.[479] Grossly, the

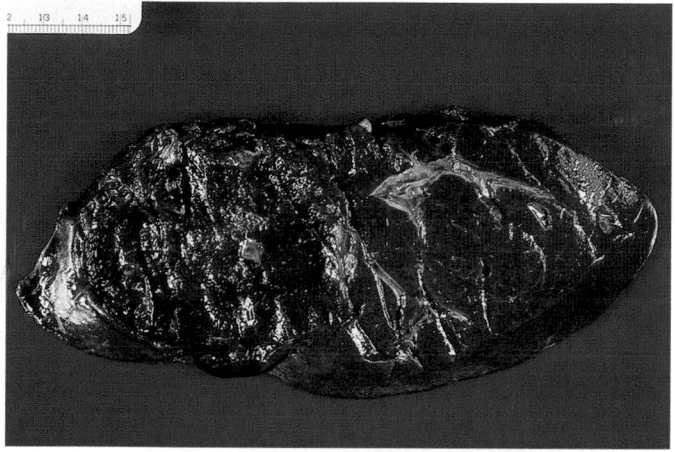

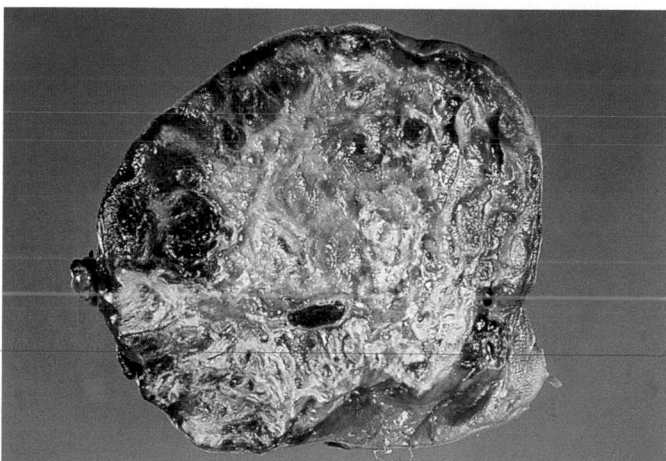

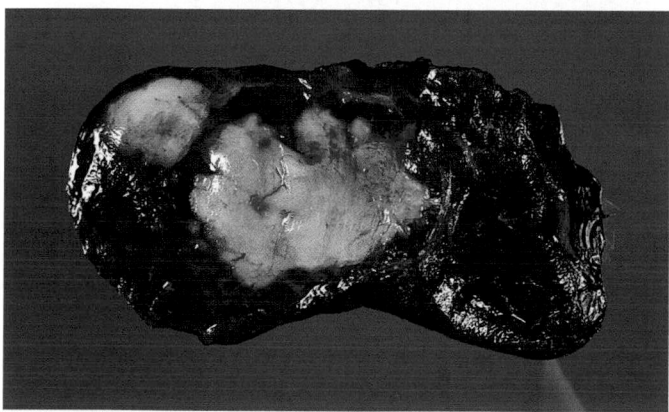

Fig. 13.78 A to C, Cavernous hemangioma of liver: **A**, typical deep red cut surface; **B**, tumor accompanied by large fibrin deposits secondary to thrombosis; **C**, an example with marked secondary fibrosis.

tumors are often multiple and involve both hepatic lobes. Microscopically, the neoplastic endothelial cells infiltrate sinusoids and veins, both as tuft-like intravascular proliferations and as fibrothrombotic occlusions.[450] These cells are plump, with an acidophilic cytoplasm that is often vacuolated (Fig. 13.79). Immunohistochemically, they exhibit focally positive staining for endothelial markers, and Weibel–Palade bodies may be seen ultrastructurally.[470,472] The stroma, usually abundant, may have myxoid, sclerotic, or calcifying features. The prognosis is much more favorable than for angiosarcoma, but extrahepatic metastases occurred in 27% of the 137 patients reported by Makhlouf et al.,[465] in what remains the largest series on this entity. The lung metastases closely simulate the appearance of primary epithelioid hemangioendothelioma of the lung, i.e., the lesion formerly known as intravascular bronchioloalveolar tumor (IV-BAT). The treatment is surgical; sometimes the extent of the tumor necessitates the performance of liver transplantation.[458] Exceptionally, the tumor will be seen recurring in the allograft.[449]

Angiosarcoma (hemangiosarcoma, malignant hemangioendothelioma) is characterized by the formation of freely anastomosing vascular channels (Fig. 13.80). The degree of differentiation varies a great deal from case to case, with the better differentiated examples simulating peliosis hepatis or other benign conditions[463] and the poorly differentiated types being difficult to distinguish from primary or metastatic epithelial neoplasms. Some of the tumors have an epithelioid appearance; they are distinguished from the epithelioid hemangioendotheliomas on the basis of their greater degree of atypia, mitotic activity, and necrosis.

Factor VIII-related antigen and other endothelial markers can be detected immunohistochemically in all

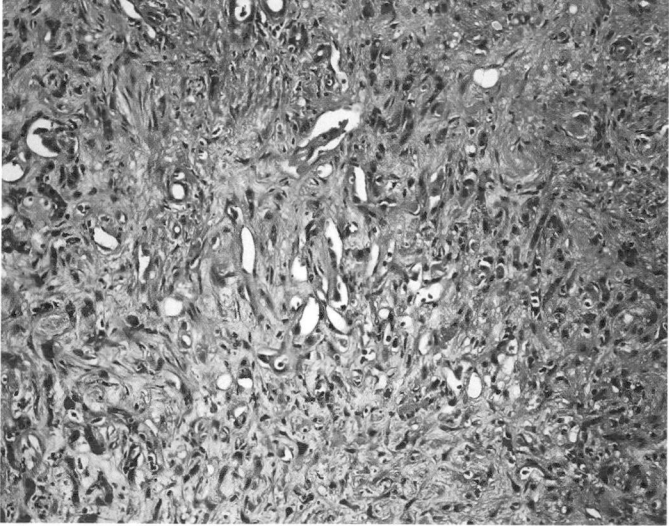

Fig. 13.79 Epithelioid hemangioendothelioma. The extensive fibrosis, entrapment of bile ducts, and epithelioid appearance of the tumor cells may lead to a mistaken diagnosis of cholangiocarcinoma.

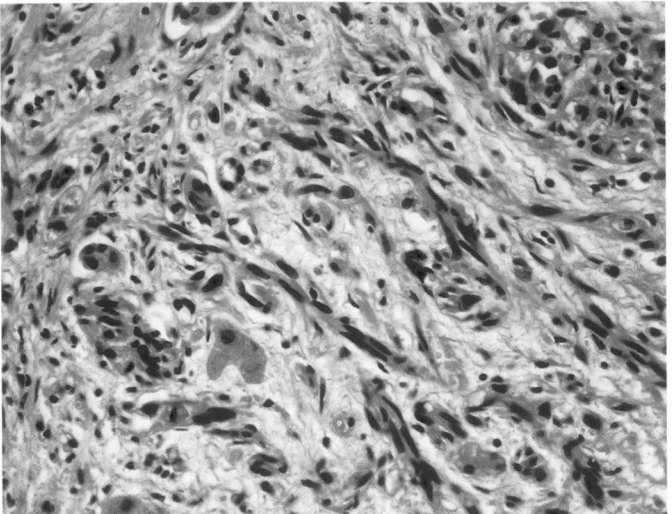

Fig. 13.80 Angiosarcoma of liver. Highly atypical spindle cells growing in thin cords, some surrounding a central lumen.

but the most undifferentiated neoplasms.[467] Most cases occur in adults, but well-documented cases in infants also are on record.[452,473]

An increased risk for the development of angiosarcoma of the liver in adults has been documented in the following conditions:

1 *Cirrhosis*. It is present in approximately one third of the adult cases and is usually of the macronodular (postnecrotic) type, including the variant that is caused by hemochromatosis.[475]

2 *Vinyl chloride exposure*. It has been shown that hepatic angiosarcoma occurs with undue frequency in workers at chemical plants that produce polyvinyl chloride (PVC), a component of most plastic products such as water pipes, wrapping materials, and building materials.[446] In the series of Makk et al.,[466] the average time of exposure was 16.9 years. Grossly, most tumors are multicentric, hemorrhagic, and necrotic, with areas of cystic degeneration and fibrosis. The non-neoplastic liver often exhibits subcapsular and portal fibrosis, sinusoidal dilatation, and endothelial hyperplasia.[476] The disease is invariably fatal; at autopsy, most of the cases are restricted to the liver or invade the local structures by direct extension; in contrast to the non-PVC-related hepatic angiosarcoma, distant metastases are rare.[466]

3 *Thorium dioxide exposure*. The administration of a suspension of thorium dioxide (Thorotrast) for radiographic purposes has been linked with the late development of hepatic angiosarcoma, the latent period ranging from 20 to 40 years.[457,460] As in the previous group, these tumors are often associated with sinusoidal dilatation and endothelial hyperplasia in the non-neoplastic areas.[460] In some of these patients, the angiosarcoma may be combined with liver cell carcinoma and/or cholangiocarcinoma.[459,480]

4 *Arsenic exposure*. Some cases of hepatic angiosarcomas have followed prolonged therapeutic administration of arsenic in the form of Fowler's solution.

Mesenchymal hamartoma

Mesenchymal hamartoma is a rare benign lesion with a predilection for infants, in whom it appears as a solitary, spherical, reddish nodule[485] (Fig. 13.81). It has also been reported in adults,[484,494] in whom it may be associated with distinct clinical features.[482] Some examples have a prominent cystic component[489] (Fig. 13.82). Most are asymptomatic and present during the first 2 years of life with abdominal swelling and a palpable abdominal

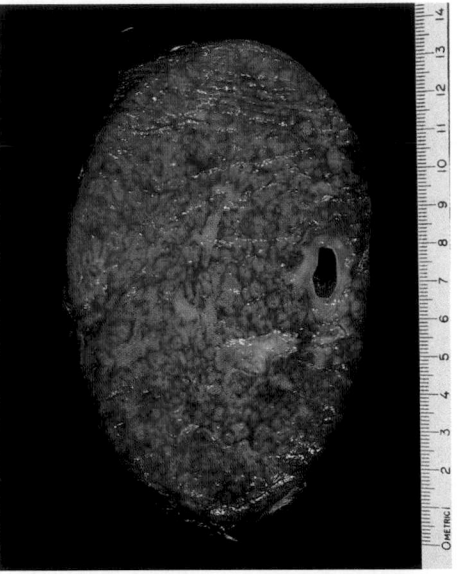

Fig. 13.81 Gross appearance of mesenchymal hamartoma of liver. The tumor shown has a solid micronodular appearance.

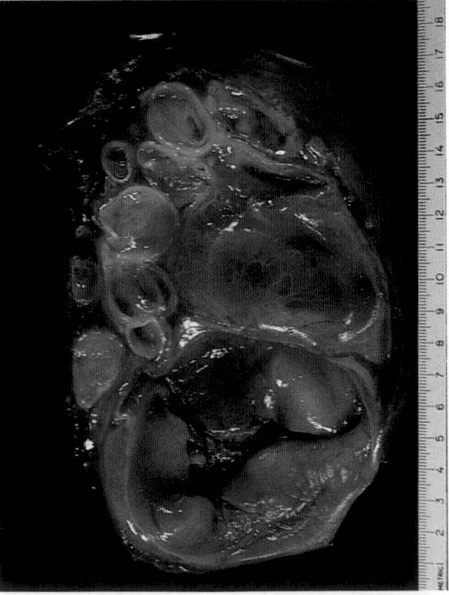

Fig. 13.82 Gross appearance of mesenchymal hamartoma of liver. The tumor shown is of multicystic type.

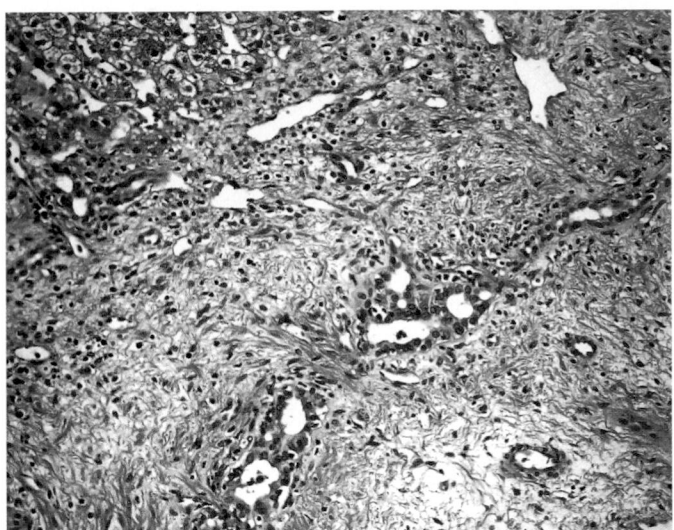

Fig. 13.83 Mesenchymal hamartoma of liver. The appearance is reminiscent of a mammary fibroadenoma.

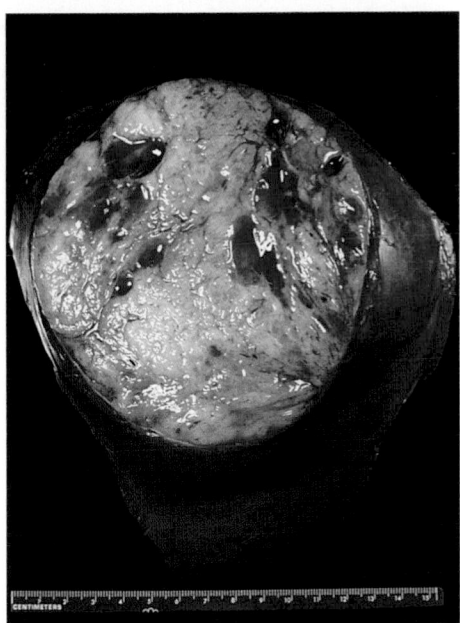

Fig. 13.84 Undifferentiated (embryonal) sarcoma. Gross appearance. The tumor is well circumscribed, largely solid, and with areas of cystic degeneration.

mass.[492] Sometimes the lesion grows to a huge size.[491] Microscopically, the main component is a well-vascularized mature connective tissue intermixed with elongated branching bile ducts. The low-power appearance is reminiscent of fibroadenoma of the breast[493] (Fig. 13.83). Ultrastructurally, the cells have a mesenchymal, fibroblast-like appearance.[483,490] It has been postulated that this lesion arises from the connective tissue of the portal tracts.[483] Its vascular pattern is similar to that seen in torsion of an accessory lobe of liver, which has suggested to some a related ischemic pathogenesis.[486] However, the detection of specific translocations involving chromosome 19[487] and the occasional occurrence of aneuploid lesions[488] speak in favor of a neoplastic nature for this lesion. Exceptionally, it may undergo malignant transformation into an undifferentiated (embryonal) sarcoma (see next section).

Undifferentiated (embryonal) sarcoma

Undifferentiated (embryonal) sarcoma, also known as malignant mesenchymoma, occurs predominantly in children but has also been seen in adults.[498,503a,506]

Grossly, it is usually large, solitary, and well circumscribed, with multiple areas of necrosis, hemorrhage, and cystic degeneration (Fig. 13.84). Microscopically, it is composed of a mixture of highly atypical spindle and giant cells, most of them having a sarcoma-like appearance (Fig. 13.85). The larger cells often contain numerous intracytoplasmic hyaline globules that are strongly PAS positive (Fig. 13.86). Scattered hyperplastic or degenerating bile ductlike structures surrounded by tumor cells are seen in most cases; since they show no clear-cut neoplastic features and are more numerous at the periphery of the tumor, they have been generally interpreted as entrapped elements (Fig. 13.87).

Ultrastructurally and immunohistochemically, most of

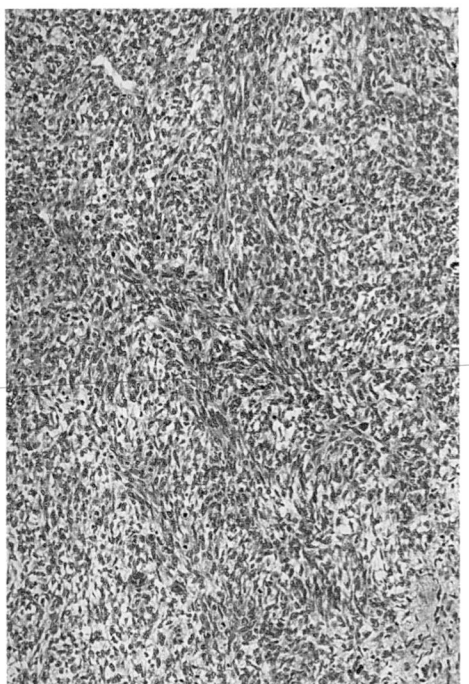

Fig. 13.85 Low-power microscopic appearance of an undifferentiated (embryonal) sarcoma showing marked cellularity and sarcomatous appearance.

the cells have features of undifferentiated mesenchymal cell, fibroblasts, and myofibroblasts, but others may show differentiation toward smooth and skeletal muscle elements on one hand and toward epithelial cells on the other.[503a] Thus immunoreactivity has been described for vimentin, α_1-antitrypsin, α_1-antichymotrypsin, lysozyme, smooth muscle actin, desmin, and keratin.[495,499,505] This peculiar combination of phenotypic features has led some authors to postulate a histogenetic relationship with primary hepatic embryonal rhabdomyosarcoma[505] and others to suggest that the tumor represents an anaplastic (sarcomatoid) variant of liver cell carcinoma.[503] The latter seems a most unlikely prospect. Several cases are on record arising in conjunction with a mesenchymal hamartoma.[497,501,504]

The treatment consists of a combined approach of radical resection and multiple-agent chemotherapy.[508,509] Unfortunately, the prognosis is generally poor, most of the patients dying of disease within 2 years.[500,502,507] However, a few cases of permanent cure are on record.[496]

Other mesenchymal tumors

Angiomyolipoma of liver is similar to its more common renal counterpart, being composed of tortuous blood vessels, smooth muscle, and fat.[519] As in other sites, a variant exists predominantly composed of epithelioid tumor cells (monotypic epithelioid angiomyolipoma or "PEComa")[533,546,552] (Fig. 13.88). Immunoreactivity for actin, desmin, S-100 protein, and—most important—HMB-45, is the rule.[545,550] Ultrastructurally, the features

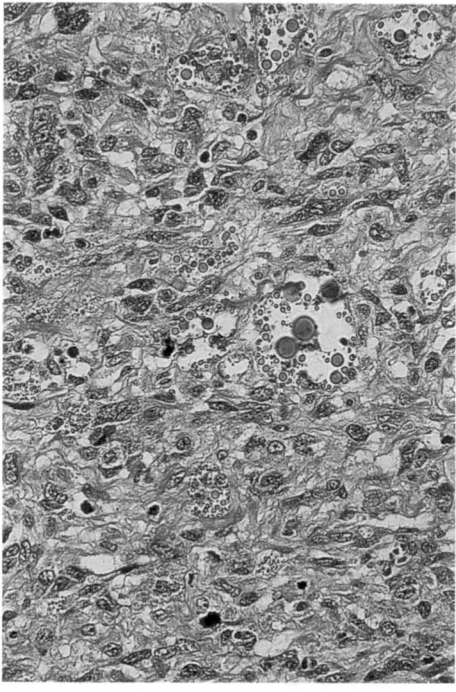

Fig. 13.86 Malignant mesenchymoma of liver. Large eosinophilic hyaline globules are present between the tumor cells.

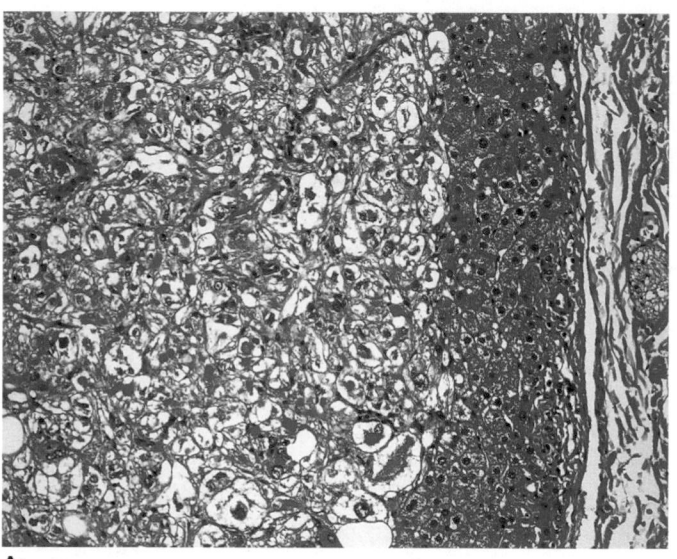

A

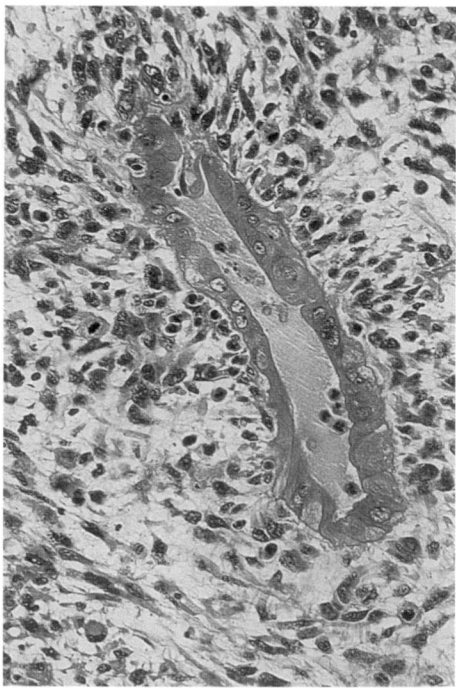

Fig. 13.87 Bile duct showing mild atypia of the epithelium, surrounded by sarcomatous elements.

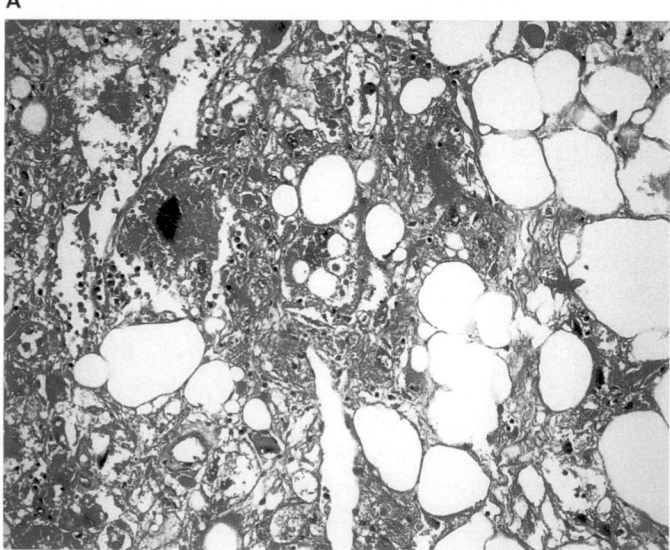

B

Fig. 13.88 A and **B**, Epithelioid angiomyolipoma of liver. **A**, The solid pattern of growth and the epithelioid appearance of the tumor cells may lead to a mistaken diagnosis of a hepatocellular neoplasm. **B**, Bizarre giant tumor cells are present, together with islands of adipose tissue.

are similar to those of the homonymous renal tumor.[535] In contrast to the renal tumors, the reported hepatic angiomyolipomas have not been associated with tuberous sclerosis. A variant of this tumor involves the ligamentum teres and has a prominent clear cell component, thus resembling clear cell ("sugar") tumor of the lung.[517,544]

The behavior of hepatic angiomyolipoma is generally benign, this also applying to most epithelioid cases; however, exceptional instances of clinical malignancy are on record.[515]

Myelolipoma of liver has an appearance similar to that of its more common adrenal counterpart, being composed of an admixture of fat and bone marrow-derived hematopoietic cells.[532,541]

Leiomyoma can present as a solitary hepatic nodule, the obvious differential diagnosis being a metastasis from a well-differentiated leiomyosarcoma.[520,539] Some hepatic smooth muscle neoplasms have occurred in HIV-infected patients or following organ transplantation and have been found to contain EBV by in situ hybridization.[525,526,538]

Lipoma presents as a single round intraparenchymal mass[523]; it should be distinguished from so-called *hepatic pseudolipoma*, which is a round nodule of fat attached to Glisson's capsule, probably representing entrapped, detached appendix epiploica.[524]

Solitary fibrous tumor (previously known as localized fibrous mesothelioma) may arise from beneath the liver capsule and the parenchyma[529] (Fig. 13.89); as in other sites, this tumor is immunoreactive for vimentin, CD4, and bcl-2.[512]

So-called **benign (multi)cystic mesothelioma** has been exceptionally seen to involve primarily the liver.

Benign schwannoma and **malignant peripheral nerve sheath tumor** have been reported in the liver, some of them developing in patients with von Recklinghausen's disease.[516,522,548]

Sarcomas primary in the liver are exceptional. Their differential diagnosis includes metastases from sarcomas of other sites and sarcomatoid liver cell carcinomas. Types of reported primary sarcoma of liver in adults include *fibrosarcoma*,[510,531] *leiomyosarcoma*[513,536,549] (some of them occurring in HIV-infected patients[540]), *rhabdomyosarcoma*[527] (one of them associated with long-term oral contraceptive use[514]), *malignant fibrous histiocytoma*,[511,528] *osteosarcoma*,[543,547] and *osteoclast-like giant cell tumor*.[521,530] In infants and children, there have been isolated reports of *embryonal rhabdomyosarcoma* and *rhabdoid tumor*.[518,534,537,542] One of the latter was associated with VIP secretion, suggesting that it represented a neuroendocrine carcinoma with rhabdoid features.[551] As in other sites (except perhaps the kidney), rhabdoid tumor of the liver is probably not a distinct entity but rather a morphologic and phenotypical pattern that can accompany a variety of cell types.

Malignant lymphoma and related lesions

Malignant lymphoma confined to the liver is a very rare occurrence.[554,572] Most cases occur in adults, but the disease may also affect children.[567]

In terms of relative frequency, the most common types of lymphoma involving the liver are diffuse large B-cell lymphoma, Hodgkin's lymphoma, peripheral T-cell lymphoma, follicle center lymphoma, and MALT-type marginal zone B-cell lymphomas.[558,559,564,579] A subset of the large B-cell lymphomas are rich in non-neoplastic T cells and histiocytes, and exhibit a distinctive diffuse pattern that can simulate inflammatory liver disease.[558,581] Some of the primary hepatic lymphomas have occurred in association with hepatitis C virus infection.[553,571]

Hepatosplenic gamma-delta T-cell lymphoma is a distinct entity characterized by occurrence in young adult males with hepatomegaly, B symptoms, peripheral blood cytopenias, absence of peripheral lymphadenopathy, presence of lymphoid infiltrates in the splenic red pulp, hepatic sinusoids and bone marrow sinuses, and an aggressive clinical course.[555,566] The *alpha-beta* variant of this tumor shows a female preponderance, and the liver infiltrates tend to be periportal.[566] An isochromosome 7q is often present. Cases have been reported in immunocompromised patients.[560,583] This disease is further discussed in Chapter 22.

Post-transplant lymphoproliferative disease is typically of B-cell type and associated with EBV. It usually presents between 6 and 17 months after transplantation as a systemic illness, with involvement of the hepatic graft in some of the cases.[570]

Hodgkin's lymphoma involvement of the liver is common in stage IV disease.[573]

Plasmacytoma and **multiple myeloma** can present as a space-occupying mass in the liver.[580,582]

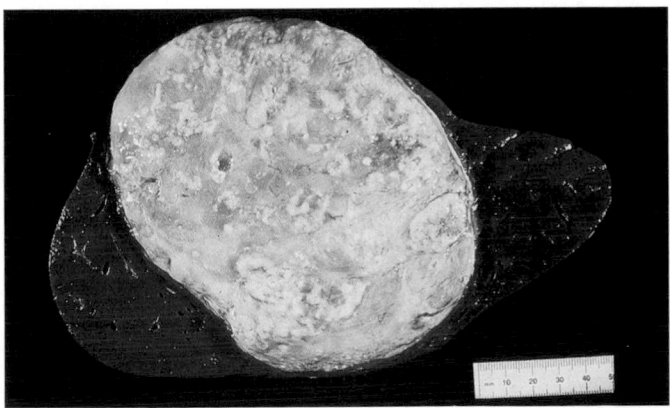

Fig. 13.89 Large solitary fibrous tumor of the liver. Microscopically, the tumor had malignant features.

Leukemic involvement of the liver is frequent in both chronic lymphocytic and chronic myelocytic leukemia.[573] In the former, the infiltrate is predominantly periportal and in the latter predominantly sinusoidal, but many exceptions to this rule exist.

Inflammatory myofibroblastic tumor was originally described as inflammatory pseudotumor but is now thought to be in most instances of neoplastic nature.[556,578] It presents in both adults and children with fever and upper abdominal pain.[562] Grossly, the lesions have a variegated appearance, accompanied by areas of necrosis and hemorrhage. Microscopically, they are composed of an inflammatory mononuclear component rich in mature plasma cells and abundant plump spindle cells[577] (Fig. 13.90). The latter have generally been identified as myofibroblasts, but the possibility of them being members of the accessory immune system (i.e., reticulum/ dendritic cells) needs to be considered. In some cases a proliferation of follicular dendritic cells associated with clonal EBV has been demonstrated.[574]

It is probable that several different conditions are currently included under the terms inflammatory myofibroblastic tumor and inflammatory pseudotumor. Some may be reactive, particularly those associated with occlusive phlebitis and chronic cholangitis,[563,568] as well as those exhibiting spontaneous regression.[561] Others, probably the majority, are or become a true neoplastic process. For these, surgical removal is the treatment of choice.[562]

Follicular dendritic cell tumor of the liver needs to be mentioned here, since it shares several morphologic features with inflammatory pseudotumor and may be pathogenetically related to it (Fig. 13.91). It is recognized because of the presence of a neoplastic component of cells bearing the markers of dendritic follicular cells, such as CD21 and CD35. In contrast to dendritic follicular cell tumors at other sites, there is usually evidence of EBV clonal proliferation.[557,576]

Reactive lymphoid hyperplasia and **nodular lymphoid lesion** are benign reactive lymphoid processes that can mimic follicle center cell lymphoma and MALT-type lymphoma, respectively.[569,575]

Langerhans' cell histiocytosis can involve the liver as an isolated event or as an expression of multisystem disease.[565]

Other primary tumors and tumorlike conditions

Squamous cell carcinoma of the liver has been reported as arising from congenital cyst, as a component of teratoma, and in association with intrahepatic lithiasis (hepatolithiasis).[592,606] Most of the latter cases probably represent the extreme expression of squamous metaplasia in cholangiocarcinoma.

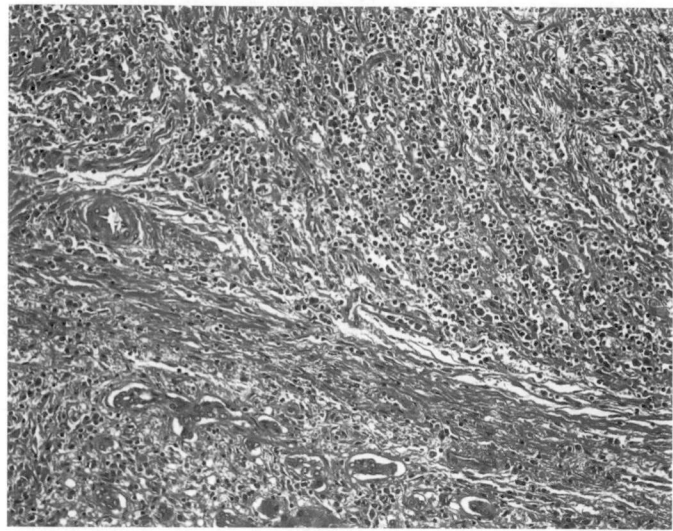

A

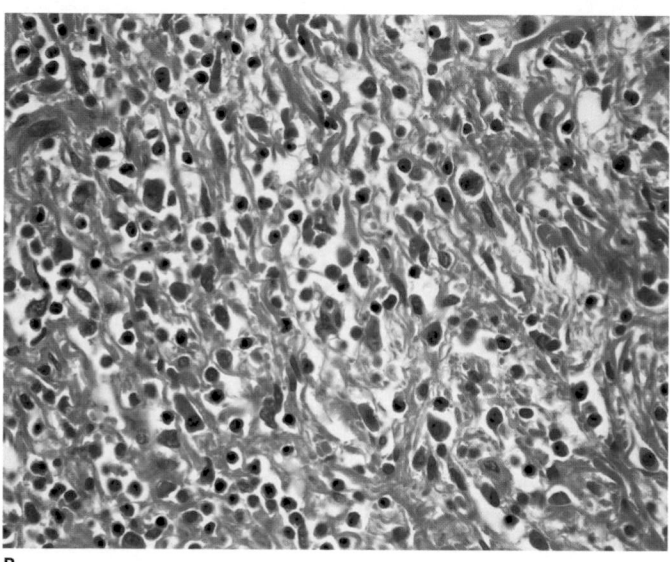

B

Fig. 13.90 A and **B**, Inflammatory myofibroblastic tumor: **A**, well-circumscribed nodule with a mixed cell composition; **B**, high-power view showing spindle cells admixed with lymphocytes, plasma cells, and histiocytes.

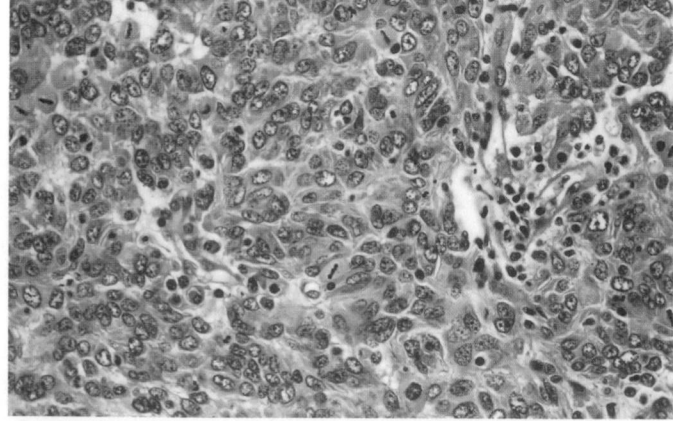

Fig. 13.91 Follicular dendritic cell tumor of liver. Note the sprinkling of lymphocytes.

Epithelial–myoepithelial carcinoma, exceptionally reported in the liver, may also be related to the bile duct system.[608]

Carcinoid tumor in the liver, whether solitary or multiple, represents in the overwhelming majority of cases the result of metastatic involvement from a primary tumor usually located in the gastrointestinal tract. However, on some occasions, a typical carcinoid tumor has been seen in the liver in the absence of a neoplasm in any other site after prolonged clinical search or at autopsy.[584,599,605] Primary carcinoid tumors of the small bowel can be extremely small, and it is difficult to dismiss entirely the possibility of their having been missed during the dissection. Yet, under these circumstances, it is appropriate to regard the carcinoid tumor as probably originating within the liver. Actually, this occurrence should be expected in view of the presence of neuroendocrine cells in the normal bile tract and the well-documented occurrence of carcinoid tumors in the gallbladder and extrahepatic biliary system. Indeed, one of the reported cases of carcinoid of the liver was located within an intrahepatic bile duct.[591] Some of the tumors have been immunoreactive for gastrin and have been accompanied by the Zollinger–Ellison syndrome.[597,601] Others have resulted in symptoms resulting from VIP hyperproduction.[585] Hepatic tumors having a less well differentiated appearance than carcinoids but still exhibiting neuroendocrine features have also been described.[596,611] These have often been referred to as neuroendocrine carcinomas.[602] The occasional occurrence of neuroendocrine differentiation in liver cell carcinoma was discussed on p. 994.

Paraganglioma confined to the liver and simulating hepatocellular carcinoma has been observed.[587]

Benign and malignant teratomas of the liver are exceptionally rare neoplasms seen predominantly in children but also described in adults.[604] The malignant should be distinguished from the mixed type of hepatoblastoma, which is a much more common occurrence[589,598] (see p. 1003). Cases of apparently primary *yolk sac tumor* of the liver have been reported,[593,609,610] sometimes combined with hepatoblastoma[588] or with hepatocellular carcinoma.[600] Primary pure *choriocarcinomas* and *malignant mixed germ cell tumors* have also been described.[590,595,607]

Tumorlike masses in the liver may result from abscesses (see p. 970), congenital hepatic fibrosis,[594] *solitary necrotic nodules* (possibly representing "ancient" sclerosing hemangiomas),[586] and *malakoplakia*.[603]

Metastatic tumors

Primary malignant tumors of the gallbladder, extrahepatic bile ducts, pancreas, and stomach frequently involve the liver by direct extension. Those from the gallbladder tend to follow the portal tract.[622] Carcinomas of the large bowel, lung, breast, pancreas, kidney, stomach, and other organs metastasize to the liver with appalling regularity. Sarcomas of soft tissues or internal organs and malignant melanomas also frequently metastasize to this organ. Within the highly receptive liver parenchyma, these metastases often grow to huge dimensions (Figs 13.92 to 13.95).

In a series of 8455 autopsies of adult patients with malignant tumors, 39% had liver metastases.[623] Only 6% of these were solitary. In 81 patients (2.5%), the metas-

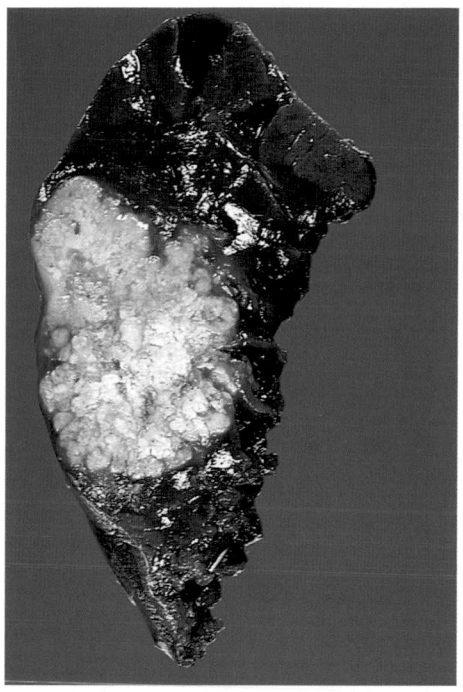

Fig. 13.92 Large bowel carcinoma metastatic to liver.

Fig 13.93 Leiomyosarcoma metastatic to liver. The primary tumor was located in the stomach.

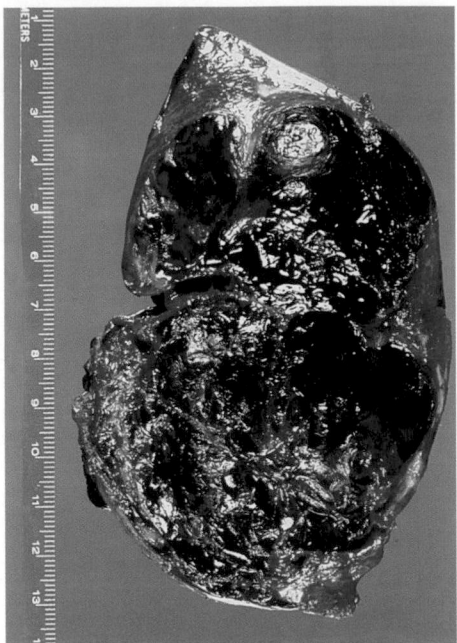

Fig. 13.94 Choriocarcinoma metastatic to liver. The tumor has the highly hemorrhagic appearance that is characteristic of this entity.

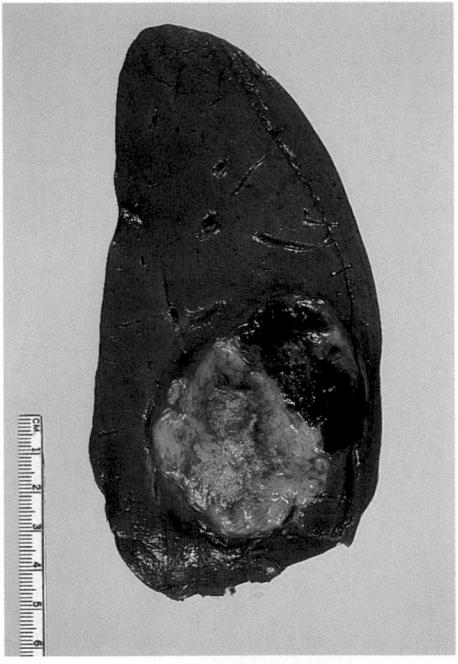

Fig. 13.95 Malignant melanoma metastatic to liver. Only a portion of the tumor shows black melanin pigmentation.

tases were confined to this organ; this phenomenon was seven times more frequent for tumors drained by the portal venous system than for the others.

Grossly, most metastatic tumors in the liver form discrete masses that may locally elevate the capsule. Central necrosis with umbilication occurs in the larger lesions. The absence of visible nodules on the external surface of the liver does not rule out the possibility of metastatic involvement. Sometimes large metastases are completely

hidden within the parenchyma.[626] In some instances, (particularly with colorectal carcinomas) the metastatic nodules are surrounded by a fibrous pseudocapsule.[622a]

A certain correlation exists between the site of the primary tumor and the gross appearance of the liver metastases. Metastases from carcinoma of the large bowel often result in a few large nodules with marked central umbilication; when mucin production is abundant, they tend to undergo marked calcification that may be apparent radiographically. Well-differentiated squamous cell carcinomas result in very soft nodules because of necrosis and keratinization. The nodules from lung or breast carcinoma are usually medium sized, without extensive necrosis or hemorrhage and with early central umbilication. The metastases from gallbladder carcinoma cluster around the gallbladder bed and progressively diminish in size as they move farther into the hepatic parenchyma. Occasionally, extremely small, almost miliary metastatic lesions are seen spreading throughout the liver and even simulating cirrhosis[613]; they are usually the result of tumors from the breast, prostate, or stomach.[625]

It is often said that liver metastases from carcinomas of the right colon tend to be located in the right lobe and those from the left colon and rectum in the left lobe,[628] but in some series the difference has not reached statistical significance.[627,630a] Metastatic breast carcinoma treated with chemotherapy can result in the coarsely lobulated liver appearance known as *hepar lobatum*, traditionally associated with syphilis.[624]

A review of over 10,000 autopsies from Trieste, Italy, and Tokyo-Chiba, Japan, confirmed the often quoted anecdotal observation that metastases are very rare in cirrhotic livers; whatever the reason for this may be (nonreceptive soil for the metastatic growth or simply the fact that most cirrhotic patients do not live long enough to develop them), the conclusion can be drawn that the large majority of malignant tumors occurring in cirrhotic livers are primary.[620]

Many benign lesions may have a gross appearance similar to that of metastatic carcinoma. This is true of fibrous scars, healed granulomas, bile duct hamartoma and adenoma, and nodular hyperplasia. Therefore *it is imperative that a microscopic confirmation be obtained in every patient in whom lesions suggestive of liver metastases are detected at laparotomy*, regardless of how typical they might seem grossly to the surgeon or the pathologist. The microscopic differential diagnosis with primary liver tumors can be difficult. Immunohistochemical keratin profiling can be of help in this regard[629] (see p. 999). A particularly treacherous but fortunately very rare situation is that of the hepatoid carcinoma of stomach or other sites that metastasizes to the liver.[628a]

A percutaneous liver biopsy will be positive in about 75% of the cases with widespread metastatic liver disease. For laparoscopically directed biopsies, the incidence of positivity is much higher. Fine needle biopsy aspiration is being increasingly used for the diagnosis of liver metastases, with excellent results.[615,616,618]

The finding of multiple hepatic metastases at exploration makes most surgical attempts of only temporary palliative value. However, in carefully selected patients with a single blood-borne metastatic lesion or with direct extension into the liver by a neighboring malignant tumor, partial hepatectomy may result in long-term palliation and, exceptionally, in cure.[619,631] Resection of hepatic metastases is particularly worthwhile in patients with metastatic carcinoid tumor because of the dramatic amelioration of the symptoms of the carcinoid syndrome often achieved.[621] It is also done frequently for metastases of colorectal carcinoma, the 5-year survival rates reaching figures in the neighborhood of 30%.[612,614,617,630]

References

Liver cell tumors and tumorlike conditions
Focal nodular hyperplasia

1 Baum JK, Bookstein JJ, Holtz F, Klein EW. Possible association between benign hepatomas and oral contraceptives. Lancet 1973, **2**: 926–929.

2 Bioulac-Sage P, Balabaud C, Wanless IR. Diagnosis of focal nodular hyperplasia: not so easy. Am J Surg Pathol 2001, **25**: 1322–1325.

3 Fechner RE. Benign hepatic lesions and orally administered contraceptives. A report of seven cases and a critical analysis of the literature. Hum Pathol 1977, **8**: 255–268.

4 Fechner RE, Roehm JOF Jr. Angiographic and pathologic correlations of hepatic focal nodular hyperplasia. Am J Surg Pathol 1977, **1**: 217–224.

5 Fischer HP, Lankes G. Morphologic correlation between liver epithelium and mesenchyme allows insight into histogenesis of focal nodular hyperplasia (FNH) of the liver. Virchows Arch [Cell Pathol] 1991, **60**: 373–380.

6 Gaffey MJ, Iezzoni JC, Weiss LM. Clonal analysis of focal nodular hyperplasia of the liver. Am J Pathol 1996, **148**: 1089–1096.

7 Gold JH, Guzman IJ, Rosai J. Benign tumors of the liver. Pathologic examination of 45 cases. Am J Clin Pathol 1978, **70**: 6–17.

8 Karhunen PJ, Penttilä A, Liesto K, Männikkö A, Möttönen MM. Occurrence of benign hepatocellular tumors in alcoholic men. Acta Pathol Microbiol Immunol Scand [A] 1986, **94**: 141–147.

9 Knowles DM II, Casarella WJ, Johnson PM, Wolff M. The clinical, radiologic, and pathologic characterization of benign hepatic neoplasms. Alleged association with oral contraceptives. Medicine (Baltimore) 1978, **57**: 223–237.

10 Mahfouz AE, Hamm B, Taupitz M, Wolf KJ. Hypervascular liver lesions. Differentiation of focal nodular hyperplasia from malignant tumors with dynamic gadolinium-enhanced MR imaging. Radiology 1993, **186**: 133–138.

11 Masood S, West AB, Barwick KW. Expression of steroid hormone receptors in benign hepatic tumors. An immunocytochemical study. Arch Pathol Lab Med 1992, **116**: 1355–1359.

12 Ndimbie OK, Goodman ZD, Chase RL, Ma CK, Lee MW. Hemangiomas with localized nodular proliferation of the liver. A suggestion on the pathogenesis of focal nodular hyperplasia. Am J Surg Pathol 1990, **14**: 142–150.

13 Nguyen BN, Flejou JF, Terris B, Belghiti J, Degott C. Focal nodular hyperplasia of the liver: a comprehensive pathologic study of 305 lesions and recognition of new histologic forms. Am J Surg Pathol 1999, **23**: 1441–1454.

14 Palmer PE, Christopherson WM, Wolfe HJ. Alpha-1-antitrypsin. Protein marker in oral contraceptive-associated hepatic tumors. Am J Clin Pathol 1977, **68**: 736–739.

14a Quaglia A, Tibals J, Grasso A, Prasad N, Nozza P, Davies SE, Burroughs AK,Watkinson A, Dhillon AP. Focal nodular hyperplasia-like areas in cirrhosis. Histopathology 2003, **42**: 14–21.

15 Radosevich JA, Gould KA, Koukoulis GK, Haines GK, Rosen ST, Lee I, Gould VE. Immunolocalization of *ras* oncogene p21 in human liver diseases. Ultrastruct Pathol 1993, **17**: 1–8.

16 Roskams T, De Vos R, Desmet V. 'Undifferentiated progenitor cells' in focal nodular hyperplasia of the liver. Histopathology 1996, **28**: 291–299.

17 Shortell CK, Schwartz SI. Hepatic adenoma and focal nodular hyperplasia. Surg Gynecol Obstet 1991, **173**: 426–431.

18 Stocker JT, Ishak KG. Focal nodular hyperplasia of the liver. A study of 21 pediatric cases. Cancer 1981, **48**: 336–345.

19 Vilgrain V, Flejou JF, Arrive L, Belghiti J, Najmark D, Menu Y, Zins M, Vullierme MP, Nahum H. Focal nodular hyperplasia of the liver. MR imaging and pathologic correlation in 37 patients. Radiology 1992, **184**: 699–703.

20 Wanless IR, Albrecht S, Bilbao J, Frei JV, Heathcote EJ, Roberts EA, Chiasson D. Multiple focal nodular hyperplasia of the liver associated with vascular malformations of various organs and neoplasia of the brain. A new syndrome. Mod Pathol 1989, **2**: 456–462.

Liver cell adenoma

21 Alshak NS, Cocjin J, Podesta L, van de Velde R, Makowka L, Rosenthal P, Geller SA. Hepatocellular adenoma in glycogen storage disease Type IV. Arch Pathol Lab Med 1994, **118**: 88–91.

22 Ameriks JA, Thompson NW, Frey CF, Appelman HD, Walter JF. Hepatic cell adenomas, spontaneous liver rupture, and oral contraceptives. Arch Surg 1975, **110**: 548–557.

23 Bianchi L. Glycogen storage disease I and hepatocellular tumors. Eur J Pediatr 1993, **152**: (Suppl 1): S63–70.

24 Bühler H, Pirovino M, Akovbiantz A, Altorfer J, Weitzel M, Maranta E, Schmid M. Regression of liver cell adenoma. A follow-up study of three consecutive patients after discontinuation of oral contraceptive use. Gastroenterology 1982, **2**: 775–782.

25 Chandra RS, Kapur SP, Kelleher J, Luban N, Patterson K. Benign hepatocellular tumors in the young. A clinicopathologic spectrum. Arch Pathol Lab Med 1984, **108**: 168–171.

26 Chen YW, Jeng YM, Yeh SH, Chen PJ. P53 gene and Wnt signaling in benign neoplasms: beta-catenin mutations in hepatic adenoma but not in focal nodular hyperplasia. Hepatology 2001, **36**: 927–935.

27 Coire CI, Qizilbash AH, Castelli MF. Hepatic adenomata in type Ia glycogen storage disease. Arch Pathol Lab Med 1987, **111**: 166–169.

28 Ding SF, Jalleh RP, Dooley J, Wood CB, Habib NA. Chromosome 17 allele loss in hepatocellular carcinoma but not in synchronous liver adenoma. Eur J Surg Oncol 1993, **19**: 195–197.

29 Edmondson HA, Henderson B, Benton B. Liver-cell adenomas associated with use of oral contraceptives. N Engl J Med 1976, **294**: 470–472.

30 Ferrell LD. Hepatocellular carcinoma arising in a focus of multilobular adenoma. A case report. Am J Surg Pathol 1993, **17**: 525–529.

31 Flejou JF, Barge J, Menu Y, Degott C, Bismuth H, Potet F, Benhamou JP. Liver adenomatosis. An entity distinct from liver adenoma? Gastroenterology 1985, **89**: 1132–1138.

32 Goodman ZD, Mikel UV, Lubbers PR, Ros PR, Langloss JM, Ishak KG. Kupffer cells in hepatocellular adenomas. Am J Surg Pathol 1987, **11**: 191–196.

33 Hasan N, Coutts M, Portmann B. Pigmented liver cell adenoma in two male patients. Am J Surg Pathol 2000, **24**: 1429–1432.

34 Heffelfinger S, Irani DR, Finegold MJ. "Alcoholic hepatitis" in a hepatic adenoma. Hum Pathol 1987, **18**: 751–754.

35 Ishak KG, Rabin L. Benign tumors of the liver. Med Clin North Am 1975, **59**: 995–1013.

36 Kerlin P, Davis GL, McGill DB, Weiland LH, Adson MA, Sheedy PF II. Hepatic adenoma and focal nodular hyperplasia. Clinical, pathologic, and radiologic features. Gastroenterology 1983, **84**: 994–1002.

37 Khoo US, Nicholls JM, Lee JSK, Saing H, Ng IOL. Cholestatic liver cell adenoma in a child with hirsutism and elevated serum levels of cortisol and ACTH. Histopathology 1994, **25**: 586–588.

38 Le Bail B, Jouhanole H, Deugnier Y, Salame G, Pellegrin JL, Saric J, Balabaud C, Bioulac-Sage P. Liver adenomatosis with granulomas in two patients on long-term oral contraceptives. Am J Surg Pathol 1992, **16**: 982–987.

39 Libbrecht L, De Vos R, Cassiman D, Desmet V, Aerts R, Roskams T. Hepatic progenitor cells in hepatocellular adenomas. Am J Surg Pathol 2001, **25**: 1388–1396.

40 McCaughan GW, Bilous MJ, Gallagher ND. Long-term survival with tumor regression in androgen-induced liver tumors. Cancer 1985, **56**: 2622–2626.

41 Malatjalian DA, Graham CH. Liver adenoma with granulomas. The appearance of granulomas in oral contraceptive-related hepatocellular adenoma and in the surrounding nontumorous liver. Arch Pathol Lab Med 1982, **106**: 244–246.

42 Miyagawa S, Makuuchi M, Chisuwa H, Lygidakis NJ. Resection of a large liver cell adenoma originating in the caudate lobe. Hepatogastroenterology 1992, **39**: 173–176.

43 Resnick MB, Kozakewich HPW, Perez-Atayde AR. Hepatic adenoma in the pediatric age group. Clinicopathological observations and assessment of cell proliferative activity. Am J Surg Pathol 1995, **19**: 1181–1190.

44 Salisbury JR, Portmann BC. Oncocytic liver cell adenoma. Histopathology 1987, **11**: 533–539.

45 Scott FR, El-Refaie A, More L, Scheuer PJ, Dhillon AP. Hepatocellular carcinoma arising in an adenoma: value of QBend 10 immunostaining in diagnosis of liver cell carcinoma. Histopathology 1996, **28**: 472–474.

46 Shortell CK, Schwartz SI. Hepatic adenoma and focal nodular hyperplasia. Surg Gynecol Obstet 1991, **173**: 426–431.

47 Tao LC. Oral contraceptive-associated liver cell adenoma and hepatocellular carcinoma. Cytomorphology and mechanism of malignant transformation. Cancer 1991, **68**: 341–347.

48 Tazawa K, Yasuda M, Ohtani Y, Makuuchi H, Osamura RY. Multiple hepatocellular adenomas associated with long-term carbamazepine. Histopathology 1999, **35**: 92–94.

49 Torbenson M, Lee JH, Choti M, Gage W, Abraham SC, Montgomery E, Boitnott J, Wu TT. Hepatic adenomas: analysis of sex steroid receptor status and the Wnt signaling pathway. Mod Pathol 2002, **15**: 189–196.

50 Westaby D, Portmann B, Williams R. Androgen related primary hepatic tumors in non-Fanconi patients. Cancer 1983, **51**: 1947–1952.

51 Wheeler DA, Edmondson HA, Reynolds TB. Spontaneous liver cell adenoma in children. Am J Clin Pathol 1986, **85**: 6–12.

Liver cell carcinoma

General and clinical features

52 Chen M-F, Jan Y-Y, Jeng L-B, Hwang T-L, Wang C-S, Chen S-C. Obstructive jaundice secondary to ruptured hepatocellular carcinoma into the common bile duct. Surgical experiences of 20 cases. Cancer 1994, **73**: 1335–1340.

53 Cong WM, Wu MC, Zhang XH, Chen H, Yuan JY. Primary hepatocellular carcinoma in women of mainland China. A clinicopathologic analysis of 104 patients. Cancer 1993, **71**: 2941–2945.

54 El-Serag HB, Mason AC. Rising incidence of hepatocellular carcinoma in the United States. N Engl J Med 1999, **340**: 745–750.

55 Farhi DC, Shikes RH, Murari PJ, Silverberg SG. Hepatocellular carcinoma in young people. Cancer 1983, **52**: 1516–1525.

56 Ferrucci JT. Liver tumor imaging. Cancer 1991, **67**(Suppl 4): 1189–1195.

57 Higginson J. The epidemiology of primary carcinoma of the liver. In Pack GT, Islami AH (eds): Tumors of the liver, vol. 26 of Recent results in cancer research. Heidelberg, 1970, Springer-Verlag.

58 Ikeda T, Tozuka S, Hasumura Y, Takeuchi J. Prostaglandin E-producing hepatocellular carcinoma with hypercalcemia. Cancer 1988, **61**: 1813–1814.

59 Kovalic JJ, Thomas PR, Beckwith JB, Feusner JH, Norkool PA. Hepatocellular carcinoma as second malignant neoplasms in successfully treated Wilms' tumor patients. A National Wilms' Tumor Study report. Cancer 1991, **67**: 342–344.

60 Lack EE, Neave C, Vawter GF. Hepatocellular carcinoma. Review of 32 cases in childhood and adolescence. Cancer 1983, **52**: 1510–1515.

61 Margolis S, Homey C. Systemic manifestations of hepatoma. Medicine (Baltimore) 1972, **51**: 381–391.

62 Ni YH, Chang MH, Hsu HY, Hsu HC, Chen CC, Chen WJ, Lee CY. Hepatocellular carcinoma in childhood. Clinical manifestations and prognosis. Cancer 1991, **68**: 1737–1741.

63 O'Conor GT, Tatarinov YS, Abelev GI, Uriel J. A collaborative study for the evaluation of a serologic test for primary liver cancer. Cancer 1970, **25**: 1091–1098.

64 Primack A, Wilson J, O'Conor GT, Engelman K, Canellos GP. Hepatocellular carcinoma with the carcinoid syndrome. Cancer 1971, **27**: 1182–1189.

65 Ruoslahti E, Seppala M, Vuopio P, Saksela E, Peltokallio P. Radioimmunoassay of alpha-fetoprotein in primary and secondary cancer of the liver. J Natl Cancer Inst 1972, **49**: 623–630.

66 Trevisani F, D'Intino PE, Grazi GL, Caraceni P, Gasbarrini A, Colantoni A, Stefanini GH, Mazziotti A, Gozzetti G, Gasbarrini G, Barnardi M. Clinical and pathologic features of hepatocellular carcinoma in young and older Italian patients. Cancer 1996, **77**: 2223–2232.

Predisposing and associated factors

67 Akagi G, Furuya K, Kanamura A, Chihara T, Otsuka H. Liver cell dysplasia and hepatitis B surface antigen in liver cirrhosis and hepatocellular carcinoma. Cancer 1984, **54**: 315–318.

68 Alpert ME, Davidson CS. Mycotoxins. A possible cause of primary carcinoma of the liver. Am J Med 1969, **46**: 325–327.

69 Anthony PP. Hepatocellular carcinoma: an overview. Histopathology 2001, **39**: 109–118.

70 Anthony PP, Vogel CL, Barker LF. Liver cell dysplasia. A premalignant condition. J Clin Pathol 1973, **26**: 217–223.

71 Aterman K. Hepatic neoplasia. Reflections and ruminations. Virchows Arch 1995, **427**: 1–18.

72 Balazs M. Primary hepatocellular tumours during long-term androgenic steroid therapy. A light and electron microscopic study of 11 cases with emphasis on microvasculature of the tumours. Acta Morphol Hung 1991, **39**: 201–216.

73 Boyd PR, Mark GJ. Multiple hepatic adenomas and a hepatocellular carcinoma in a man on oral methyl testosterone for eleven years. Cancer 1977, **40**: 1765–1770.

74 Brambilla C, Tackney C, Hirschman SZ, Colombo M, Dioguardi ML, Donato MF, Paronetto F. Varying nuclear staining intensity of hepatitis B virus DNA in human hepatocellular carcinoma. Lab Invest 1986, **55**: 475–481.

75 Cheah PL, Looi LM, Lin HP, Yap SF. Childhood primary hepatocellular carcinoma and hepatitis B virus infection. Cancer 1990, **65**: 174–176.

76 Chlebowski RT, Tong M, Weissman J, Block JB, Ramming KP,

Weiner JM, Bateman JR, Chlebowski JS. Hepatocellular carcinoma. Diagnostic and prognostic features in North American patients. Cancer 1984, **53:** 2701–2706.

77 Cohen C, Berson SD, Budgeon LR. Alpha-1-antitrypsin deficiency in southern African hepatocellular carcinoma patients. An immunoperoxidase and histochemical study. Cancer 1982, **49:** 2537–2540.

78 Cohen C, Derose PB. Liver cell dysplasia in α-1-antitrypsin deficiency. Mod Pathol 1994, **7:** 31–36.

79 Colombo M, de Franchis R, Del Ninno E, et al. Hepatocellular carcinoma in Italian patients with cirrhosis. N Engl J Med 1991, **325:** 675–680.

80 Crawford JM. Pathologic assessment of liver cell dysplasia and benign liver tumors. Differentiation from malignant tumors. Semin Diagn Pathol 1990, **7:** 115–128.

81 Dahms BB. Hepatoma in familial cholestatic cirrhosis of childhood. Its occurrence in twin brothers. Arch Pathol Lab Med 1979, **103:** 30–33.

82 Deoras MP, Dicus W. Hepatocarcinoma associated with biliary cirrhosis. A case due to congenital bile duct atresia. Arch Pathol 1968, **86:** 338–341.

83 Dominguez-Malagon H, Gaytan-Graham S. Hepatocellular carcinoma: an update. Ultrastruct Pathol 2001, **25:** 497–516.

84 Dutta U, Kench J, Byth K, Khan MH, Lin R, Liddle C, Farrell GC. Hepatocellular proliferation and development of hepatocellular carcinoma. A case-control study in chronic hepatitis C. Hum Pathol 1998, **29:** 1279–1284.

85 Eguchi A, Nakashima O, Okudaira S, Sugihara S, Kojiro M. Adenomatous hyperplasia in the vicinity of small hepatocellular carcinoma. Hepatology 1992, **15:** 843–848.

86 Eriksson S, Carlson J, Velez R. Risk of cirrhosis and primary liver cancer in α-1-antitrypsin deficiency. N Engl J Med 1986, **314:** 736–739.

87 Farrell GC, Uren RF, Perkins KW, Joshua DE, Baird PJ, Kronenberg H. Androgen-induced hepatoma. Lancet 1975, **1:** 430–432.

88 Feitelson MA, Duan LX. Hepatitis B virus x antigen in the pathogenesis of chronic infections and the development of hepatocellular carcinoma. Am J Pathol 1997, **150:** 1141–1157.

89 Ferrell LD, Crawford JM, Dhillon AP, Scheuer PJ, Nakanuma Y. Proposal for standardized criteria for the diagnosis of benign, borderline, and malignant hepatocellular lesions arising in chronic advanced liver disease. Am J Surg Pathol 1993, **17:** 1113–1123.

90 Gall EA. Primary and metastatic carcinoma of the liver. Relationship to hepatic cirrhosis. Arch Pathol 1960, **70:** 226–232.

91 Hamasaki K, Nakata K, Tsutsumi T, Tsuruta S, Nakao K, Kato Y, Shima M, Koji T, Nagataki S. Changes in the prevalence of hepatitis B and C infection in patients with hepatocellular carcinoma in the Nagasaki Prefecture, Japan. J Med Virol 1993, **40:** 146–149.

92 Hernandez-Nieto L, Bruguera M, Bombi JA, Camacho L, Rozman C. Benign liver-cell adenoma associated with long-term administration of an androgenic-anabolic steroid (methandienone). Cancer 1977, **40:** 1761–1764.

93 Ho JCI, Wu P-C, Mak T-K. Liver cell dysplasia in association with hepatocellular carcinoma, cirrhosis and hepatitis B surface antigen in Hong Kong. Int J Cancer 1981, **28:** 571–574.

94 Hromas RA, Srigley J, Murray JL. Clinical and pathological comparison of young adult women with hepatocellular carcinoma with and without exposure to oral contraceptives. Am J Gastroenterol 1985, **80:** 479–485.

95 Ikeda K, Saitoh S, Koida I, Arase Y, Tsubota A, Chayama K, Kumada H, Kawanishi M. A multivariate analysis of risk factors for hepatocellular carcinogenesis. A prospective observation of 795 patients with viral and alcoholic cirrhosis. Hepatology 1993, **18:** 47–53.

96 Ilardi CF, Ying YY, Ackerman LV, Elias JM. Hepatitis B surface antigen and hepatocellular carcinoma in the People's Republic of China. Cancer 1980, **46:** 1612–1616.

97 Imazeki F, Omata M, Yokosuka O, Okuda K. Integration of hepatitis B virus DNA in hepatocellular carcinoma. Cancer 1986, **58:** 1055–1060.

98 Johnson FL, Feagler JR, Lerner KG, Majerus PW, Siegel M, Hartman JR, Thomas ED. Association of androgenic-anabolic steroid therapy with development of hepatocellular carcinoma. Lancet 1972, **2:** 1273–1276.

99 Lefkowitch JH, Apfelbaum TF. Liver cell dysplasia and hepatocellular carcinoma in non-A, non-B hepatitis. Arch Pathol Lab Med 1987, **111:** 170–173.

100 Liang TJ, Ghany M. Hepatitis B e antigen—the dangerous endgame of hepatitis B. N Engl J Med 2002, **347:** 208–210.

101 Libbrecht L, Craninx M, Nevens F, Desmet V, Roskams T. Predictive value of liver cell dysplasia for development of hepatocellular carcinoma in patients with non-cirrhotic and cirrhotic chronic viral hepatitis. Histopathology 2001, **39:** 66–73.

102 Libbrecht L, De Vos R, Cassiman D, Desmet V, Aerts R, Roskams T. Hepatic progenitor cells in hepatocellular adenomas. Am J Surg Pathol 2001, **25:** 1388–1396.

103 Lieberman J, Silton RM, Agliozzo CM, McMahon J. Hepatocellular carcinoma and intermediate α-1-antitrypsin deficiency (MZ phenotype). Am J Clin Pathol 1975, **64:** 304–310.

104 London WT. Primary hepatocellular carcinoma. Etiology, pathogenesis, and prevention. Hum Pathol 1981, **12:** 1085–1097.

105 Manes JL, Kissane JM, Valdes AJ. Congenital hepatic fibrosis, liver cell carcinoma and adult polycystic kidneys. Cancer 1977, **39:** 2619–2623.

106 Nakanuma Y, Terada T, Ueda K, Terasaki S, Nonomura A, Matsui O. Adenomatous hyperplasia of the liver as a precancerous lesion. Liver 1993, **13:** 1–9.

107 Nakashima T, Okuda K, Kojiro M, Sakamoto K, Kubo Y, Shimokawa Y. Primary liver cancer coincident with schistosomiasis japonica. A study of 24 necropsies. Cancer 1975, **36:** 1483–1489.

108 Neuberger J, Nunnerley HB, Davis M, Portmann B, Laws JW, Williams R. Oral-contraceptive-associated liver tumours. Occurrence of malignancy and difficulties in diagnosis. Lancet 1980, **1:** 273–276.

109 Ojanguren I, Castella E, Ariza A, Santos J, Planas R, Bruguera M. Liver cell atypias: a comparative study in cirrhosis with and without hepatocellular carcinoma. Histopathology 1997, **30:** 106–112.

110 Okuda K, Nakashima T, Sakamoto K, Ikari T, Hidaka H, Kubo Y, Sakuma K, Motoike Y, Okuda H, Obata H. Hepatocellular carcinoma arising in noncirrhotic and highly cirrhotic livers. A comparative study of histopathology and frequency of hepatitis B markers. Cancer 1982, **49:** 450–455.

111 Orsatti G, Theise ND, Thung SN, Paronetto F. DNA image cytometric analysis of macroregenerative nodules (adenomatous hyperplasia) of the liver. Evidence in support of their preneoplastic nature. Hepatology 1993, **17:** 621–627.

112 Paterlini P, Gerken G, Nakajima E, Terre S, D'Errico A, Grigioni W, Nalpas B, Franco D, Wands J, Kew M, et al. Polymerase chain reaction to detect hepatitis B virus DNA and RNA sequences in primary liver cancers from patients negative for hepatitis B surface antigens. N Engl J Med 1990, **323:** 80–85.

113 Pryor AC, Cohen RJ, Goldman RL. Hepatocellular carcinoma in a woman on long-term oral contraceptives. Cancer 1977, **40:** 884–888.

114 Saito I, Miyamura T, Ohbayashi A, Harada H, Katayama T, Kikuchi S, Watanabe Y, Koi S, Onji M, Ohta Y, et al. Hepatitis C virus infection is associated with the development of hepatocellular carcinoma. Proc Natl Acad Sci U S A 1990, **87:** 6547–6549.

115 Sakamoto M, Hirohashi S, Shimosato Y. Early stages of multistep hepatocarcinogenesis. Adenomatous hyperplasia and early hepatocellular carcinoma. Hum Pathol 1991, **22**: 172–178.

116 Schwartz MR. Liver cell dysplasia and other atypical lesions: new insights and applications. Adv Anat Pathol 1998, **5**: 99–105.

117 Shafritz DA, Shouval D, Sherman HI, Hadziyannis SJ, Kew MC. Integration of hepatitis B virus DNA into the genome of liver cells in chronic liver disease and hepatocellular carcinoma. N Engl J Med 1981, **305**: 1067–1073.

118 Shar SR, Kew MC. Oral contraceptives and hepatocellular carcinoma. Cancer 1982, **49**: 407–410.

119 Smoron GL, Battifora HA. Thorotrast-induced hepatoma. Cancer 1972, **30**: 1252–1259.

120 Suzuki K, Uchida T, Horiuchi R, Shikata T. Localization of hepatitis B surface and core antigens in human hepatocellular carcinoma by immunoperoxidase methods. Replication of complete virions of carcinoma cells. Cancer 1985, **56**: 321–327.

121 Terada T, Nakanuma Y. Cell proliferative activity in adenomatous hyperplasia of the liver and small hepatocellular carcinoma. An immunohistochemical study demonstrating proliferating cell nuclear antigen. Cancer 1992, **70**: 591–598.

122 Terada T, Nakanuma Y, Sirica AE. Immunohistochemical demonstration of MET overexpression in human intrahepatic cholangiocarcinoma and in hepatolithiasis. Hum Pathol 1998, **29**: 175–180.

123 Terada T, Terasaki S, Nakanuma Y. A clinicopathologic study of adenomatous hyperplasia of the liver in 209 consecutive cirrhotic livers examined by autopsy. Cancer 1993, **72**: 1551–1561.

124 Terada T, Ueda K, Nakanuma Y. Histopathological and morphometric analysis of atypical adenomatous hyperplasia of human cirrhotic livers. Virchows Arch [A] 1993, **422**: 381–388.

125 Terasaki S, Terada T, Nakanuma Y, Nonomura A, Unoura M, Kobayashi K. Argyrophilic nucleolar organizer regions and alpha-fetoprotein in adenomatous hyperplasia in human cirrhotic livers. Am J Clin Pathol 1991, **95**: 850–857.

126 Thomas RM, Berman JJ, Yetter RA, Moore GW, Hutchins GM. Liver cell dysplasia. A DNA aneuploid lesion with distinct morphologic features. Hum Pathol 1992, **23**: 496–503.

127 Tong MJ, Sun SC, Schaeffer BT, Chang NK, Lo KJ, Peters RL. Hepatitis-associated antigen and hepatocellular carcinoma in Taiwan. Ann Intern Med 1971, **75**: 687–691.

128 Tsukuma H, Hiyama T, Tanaka S, Nakao M, Yabuuchi T, Kitamura T, Nakanishi K, Fujimoto I, Inoue A, Yamazaki H, et al. Risk factors for hepatocellular carcinoma among patients with chronic liver disease. N Engl J Med 1993, **328**: 1797–1801.

129 Ugarte N, Gonzalez-Crussi F. Hepatoma in siblings with progressive familial cholestatic cirrhosis of childhood. Am J Clin Pathol 1981, **76**: 172–177.

130 Vogel CL, Mody N, Anthony PP, Barker LF. Hepatitis-associated antigen in Ugandan patients with hepatocellular carcinoma. Lancet 1970, **2**: 621–624.

131 Weinberg AG, Mize CE, Worthen HG. The occurrence of hepatoma in the chronic form of hereditary tyrosinemia. J Pediatr 1976, **88**: 434–438.

132 Weinstein S, Scottolini AG, Loo SYT, Caldwell PC, Bhagavan NV. Ataxia telangiectasia with hepatocellular carcinoma in a 15-year-old girl and studies of her kindred. Arch Pathol Lab Med 1985, **109**: 1000–1004.

133 Yang HI, Lu SN, Liaw YF, You SL, Sun CA, Wang LY, Hsiao CK, Chen PJ, Chen DS, Chen CJ. Hepatitis B e antigen and the risk of hepatocellular carcinoma. N Engl J Med 2002, **347**: 168–174.

134 Zaman SN, Johnson PJ, Williams R. Silent cirrhosis in patients with hepatocellular carcinoma. Implications for screening in high-incidence and low-incidence areas. Cancer 1990, **65**: 1607–1610.

135 Zhou H, Fischer HP. Liver carcinoma in PiZ alpha-1-antitrypsin deficiency. Am J Surg Pathol 1998, **22**: 742–748.

Gross features

136 Albacete RA, Matthews MJ, Saini N. Portal vein thromboses in malignant hepatoma. Ann Intern Med 1967, **67**: 337–348.

137 Anthony PP, James K. Pedunculated hepatocellular carcinoma. Is it an entity? Histopathology 1987, **11**: 403–414.

138 Horie Y, Katoh S, Yoshida H, Imaoka T, Suou T, Hirayama C. Pedunculated hepatocellular carcinoma. Report of three cases and review of literature. Cancer 1983, **51**: 746–751.

139 Hsu H-C, Sheu J-C, Lin Y-H, Chen D-S, Lee C-S, Hwang L-Y, Beasley RP. Prognostic histologic features of resected small hepatocellular carcinoma (HCC) in Taiwan. A comparison with resected large HCC. Cancer 1985, **56**: 672–680.

140 Kanai T, Hirohashi S, Upton MP, Noguchi M, Kishi K, Makuuchi M, Yamasaki S, Hasegawa H, Takayasu K, Moriyama N, Shimosato Y. Pathology of small hepatocellular carcinoma. A proposal for a new gross classification. Cancer 1987, **60**: 810–819.

141 Kondo Y, Niwa Y, Akikusa B, Takazawa H, Okabayashi A. A histopathologic study of early hepatocellular carcinoma. Cancer 1983, **52**: 687–692.

142 Nagasue N, Yukaya H, Hamada T, Hirose S, Kanashima R, Inokuchi K. The natural history of hepatocellular carcinoma. A study of 100 untreated cases. Cancer 1984, **54**: 1461–1465.

143 Okuda K, Musha H, Nakajima Y, Kubo Y, Shimokawa Y, Nagaski Y, Sawa Y, Junnouchi S, Kaneko T, Obata H, Hisamitsu T, Motoike S, Okazaki N, Kojiro M, Sakamoto K, Nakashima T. Clinicopathologic features of encapsulated hepatocellular carcinoma. A study of 26 cases. Cancer 1977, **40**: 1240–1245.

144 Torimura T, Ueno T, Inuzuka S, Tanaka M, Abe H, Tanikawa K. Mechanism of fibrous capsule formation surrounding hepatocellular carcinoma. Immunohistochemical study. Arch Pathol Lab Med 1991, **115**: 365–371.

145 Trevisani F, Caraceni P, Bernardi M, D'Intino PE, Arienti V, Amorati P, Stefanini GF, Grazi G, Mazziotti A, Fornale L, et al. Gross pathologic types of hepatocellular carcinoma in Italian patients. Relationship with demographic, environmental, and clinical factors. Cancer 1993, **72**: 1557–1563.

Microscopic features

146 Anthony PP. Primary carcinoma of the liver. A study of 282 cases in Ugandan Africans. J Pathol 1973, **110**: 37–48.

147 Barsky SH, Linnoila I, Triche TJ, Costa J. Hepatocellular carcinoma with carcinoid features. Hum Pathol 1984, **15**: 892–894.

148 Cohen C. Intracytoplasmic hyaline globules in hepatocellular carcinomas. Cancer 1976, **37**: 1754–1758.

149 Edmonson HA, Steiner PE. Primary carcinoma of the liver. A study of 100 cases among 48,900 necropsies. Cancer 1954, **7**: 462–503.

150 Guigui B, Mavier P, Lescs M-C, Pinaudeau Y, Dhumeaux D, Zafrani ES. Copper and copper-binding protein in liver tumors. Cancer 1988, **61**: 1155–1158.

151 Haratake J, Horie A, Nakashima A, Takeda S, Mori A. Minute hepatoma with excessive copper accumulation. Report of two cases with resection. Arch Pathol Lab Med 1986, **110**: 192–194.

152 Haratake J, Horie A, Takeda S, Kobori K, Sato H, Tokudome S. Tissue copper content in primary and metastatic liver cancers. Acta Pathol Jpn 1987, **37**: 231–238.

153 Hytiroglou P, Theise ND. Differential diagnosis of hepatocellular nodular lesions. Semin Diagn Pathol 1998, **15**: 285–299.

154 Komatsu T, Kondo Y, Yamamoto Y, Isono K. Hepatocellular carcinoma presenting well differentiated, normotrabecular patterns in peripheral or metastatic loci. Analysis of 103 resected cases. Acta Pathol Jpn 1990, **40**: 887–893.

155 Kondo Y. Histologic features of hepatocellular carcinoma and allied disorders. Pathol Annu 1985, **20**(Pt 2): 405–430.

156 Kondo Y, Nakajima T. Pseudoglandular hepatocellular carcinoma. A morphogenetic study. Cancer 1987, **60**: 1032–1037.

157 Nakashima T, Kojiro M, Kawano Y, Shirai F, Takemoto N, Tomimatsu H, Kawasaki H, Okuda K. Histologic growth pattern of hepatocellular carcinoma. Relationship to orcein (hepatitis B surface antigen)-positive cells in cancer tissue. Hum Pathol 1982, **13**: 563–568.

158 Nakashima O, Sugihara S, Eguchi A, Taguchi J, Watanabe J, Kojiro M. Pathomorphologic study of pale bodies in hepatocellular carcinoma. Acta Pathol Jpn 1992, **42**: 414–418.

159 Palmer PE, Wolfe HJ. α-1-Antitrypsin deposition in primary hepatic carcinomas. Arch Pathol Lab Med 1976, **100**: 232–236.

160 Quaglia A, Bhattacharjya S, Dhillon AP. Limitations of the histopathological diagnosis and prognostic assessment of hepatocellular carcinoma. Histopathology 2001, **38**: 167–174.

161 Roth JA, Berman E, Befeler D, Johnson FB. A black hepatocellular carcinoma with Dubin-Johnson-like pigment and Mallory bodies. A histochemical and ultrastructural study. Am J Surg Pathol 1982, **6**: 375–382.

162 Stromeyer FW, Ishak KG, Gerber MA, Mathew T. Ground-glass cells in hepatocellular carcinoma. Am J Clin Pathol 1980, **74**: 254–258.

163 Stumptner C, Heid H, Fuchsbichler A, Hauser H, Mischinger HJ, Zatloukal K, Denk H. Analysis of intracytoplasmic hyaline bodies in a hepatocellular carcinoma. Demonstration of p62 as major constituent. Am J Pathol 1999, **154**: 1701–1710.

164 Subramony C, Herrera GA, Lockard V. Neuroendocrine differentiation in hepatic neoplasms. Report of four cases. Surg Pathol 1993, **5**: 17–33.

165 Tajima Y, Nakajima T, Sugano I, Nagao K, Kondo Y, Saito J. Hepatocellular carcinoma containing endocrine cells. An autopsy report of triple cancer involving the liver, kidney and thyroid. Acta Pathol Jpn 1992, **42**: 904–910.

Electron microscopic and immunohistochemical features

166 Alpino G, Aragona E, Dabeva M, Salvi R, Shafritz DA, Tavoloni N. Distribution of albumin and alpha-fetoprotein mRNAs in normal, hyperplastic, and preneoplastic rat liver. Am J Pathol 1992, **141**: 623–632.

167 Borscheri N, Roessner A, Rocken C. Canalicular immunostaining of neprilysin (CD10) as a diagnostic marker for hepatocellular carcinomas. Am J Surg Pathol 2001, **25**: 1297–1303.

168 Brumm C, Schulze C, Charels K, Morohoshi T, Kloppel G. The significance of alpha-fetoprotein and other tumor markers in differential immunocytochemistry of primary liver tumors. Histopathology 1989, **14**: 503–513.

169 Chedid A, Chejfec G, Eichorst M, Villamil F, Terg R, Telenta M, Hojman R. Antigenic markers of hepatocellular carcinoma. Cancer 1990, **65**: 84–87.

170 Christensen WN, Boitnott JK, Kuhajda FP. Immunoperoxidase staining as a diagnostic aid for hepatocellular carcinoma. Mod Pathol 1989, **2**: 8–12.

171 Chu PG, Ishizawa S, Wu E, Weiss LM. Hepatocyte antigen as a marker of hepatocellular carcinoma: an immunohistochemical comparison to carciembryonic antigen, CD10, and alpha-fetoprotein. Am J Surg Pathol 2002, **26**: 978–988.

172 Cohen C, Berson SD, Shulman G, Budgeon LR. Immunohistochemical ferritin in hepatocellular carcinoma. Cancer 1984, **53**: 1931–1935.

173 Cohen MB, Beckstead JH, Ferrell LD, Yen TSB. Enzyme histochemistry of hepatocellular neoplasms. Am J Surg Pathol 1986, **10**: 789–794.

174 Donato MF, Colombo M, Matarazzo M, Paronetto F. Distribution of basement membrane components in human hepatocellular carcinoma. Cancer 1989, **63**: 272–279.

174a Fan Z, Van de Rijn M, Montgomery K, Rouse RV. Hep Par 1 antibody stain for the differential diagnosis of hepatocellular carcinoma: 676 tumors tested using tissue microarrays and conventional tissue sections. Mod Pathol 2003, **16**: 137–144.

175 Ferrandez-Izquierdo A, Llombart-Bosch A. Immunohistochemical characterization of 130 cases of primary hepatic carcinomas. Pathol Res Pract 1987, **182**: 783–791.

176 Foschini MP, Baccarini P, Dal Monte PR, Sinard J, Eusebi V, Rosai J. Albumin gene expression in adenocarcinomas with hepatoid differentiation. Virchows Arch 1998, **433**: 537–541.

177 Fucich LF, Cheles MK, Thung SN, Gerber MA, Marrogi AJ. Primary vs metastatic hepatic carcinoma. An immunohistochemical study of 34 cases. Arch Pathol Lab Med 1994, **118**: 927–930.

178 Fukusato T, Mori S, Kawamoto T, Taniguchi S, Machinami R. Immunohistochemical and ultrastructural localization of epidermal growth factor receptor in human liver and hepatocellular carcinoma tissues. Acta Pathol Jpn 1990, **40**: 22–29.

179 Goodman ZD, Ishak KG, Langloss JM, Sesterhenn IA, Rabin L. Combined hepatocellular-cholangiocarcinoma. A histologic and immunohistochemical study. Cancer 1985, **55**: 124–135.

180 Grigioni WF, Garbisa S, D'Errico A, Baccarini P, Stetler-Stevenson WG, Liotta LA, Mancini AM. Evaluation of hepatocellular carcinoma aggressiveness by a panel of extracellular matrix antigens. Am J Pathol 1991, **138**: 647–654.

181 Haratake J, Scheuer PJ. An immunohistochemical and ultrastructural study of the sinusoids of hepatocellular carcinoma. Cancer 1990, **65**: 1985–1993.

182 Horie A, Kotoo Y, Hayashi I. Ultrastructural comparison of hepatoblastoma and hepatocellular carcinoma. Cancer 1979, **44**: 2184–2193.

183 Hurlimann J, Gardiol D. Immunohistochemistry in the differential diagnosis of liver carcinomas. Am J Surg Pathol 1991, **15**: 280–288.

184 Iezzoni JC, Mills SE, Pelkey TJ, Stoler MH. Inhibin is not immunohistochemical marker for hepatocellular carcinoma, an example of the potential pitfall in diagnostic immunohistochemistry caused by endogenous biotin. Am J Clin Pathol 1999, **111**: 229–234.

185 Jagirdar J, Ishak KG, Colombo M, Brambilla C, Paronetto F. Fibronectin patterns in hepatocellular carcinoma and its clinical significance. Cancer 1985, **56**: 1643–1648.

186 Johnson DE, Herndier BG, Medeiros LJ, Warnke RA, Rouse RV. The diagnostic utility of the keratin profiles of hepatocellular carcinoma and cholangiocarcinoma. Am J Surg Pathol 1988, **12**: 187–197.

186a Kakar S, Muir T, Murphy LM, Lloyd RV, Burgart J. Immunoreactivity of Hep Par 1 in hepatic and extrahepatic tumors and its correlation with albumin in situ hybridisation in hepatocellular carcinoma. Am J Clin Pathol 2003, **119**: 361–366.

187 Koelma IA, Nap M, Huitema S, Krom RAF, Houthoff HJ. Hepatocellular carcinoma, adenoma, and focal nodular hyperplasia. Comparative histopathologic study with immunohistochemical parameters. Arch Pathol Lab Med 1986, **110**: 1035–1040.

188 Krishna M, Lloyd RV, Batts KP. Detection of albumin messenger RNA in hepatic and extrahepatic neoplasms: a marker of hepatocellular differentiation. Am J Surg Pathol 1997, **21**: 147–152.

189 Lai YS, Thung SN, Gerber MA, Chen ML, Schaffner F. Expression of cytokeratins in normal and diseased livers and in primary liver carcinomas. Arch Pathol Lab Med 1989, **113**: 134–138.

190 Lamas E, Le Bail B, Housset C, Boucher O, Brechot C. Localization of insulin-like growth factor-II and hepatitis B virus mRNAs and proteins in human hepatocellular carcinomas. Lab Invest 1991, **64**: 98–104.

190a Lau SK, Prakash S, Geller SA, Alsabeh R. Comparative immunohistochemical profile of hepatocellular carcinoma, cholangiocarcinoma, and metastatic adenocarcinoma. Hum Pathol 2002, **33**: 1175–1181.

191 Leong AS, Sormunen RT, Tsui WM, Liew CT. Hep Par 1 and

selected antibodies in the immunohistological distinction of hepatocellular carcinoma from cholangiocarcinoma, combined tumours and metastatic carcinoma. Histopathology 1998, **33**: 318–324.

192 Ma CK, Zarbo RJ, Frierson HF Jr, Lee MW. Comparative immunohistochemical study of primary and metastatic carcinomas of the liver. Am J Clin Pathol 1993, **99**: 530–532.

193 Maeda T, Kajiyama K, Adachi E, Takenaka K, Sugimachi K, Tsuneyoshi M. The expression of cytokeratins 7, 19, and 20 in primary and metastatic carcinomas of the liver. Mod Pathol 1996, **9**: 901–909.

194 Maitra A, Murakata LA, Albores-Saavedra J. Immunoreactivity for hepatocyte paraffin 1 antibody in hepatoid adenocarcinomas of the gastrointestinal tract. Am J Clin Pathol 2001, **115**: 689–694.

195 Marceau N. Cell lineages and differentiation programs in epidermal, urothelial and hepatic tissues and their neoplasms. Lab Invest 1990, **63**: 4–20.

196 Minervini MI, Demetris AJ, Lee RG, Carr BI, Madariaga J, Nalesnik MA. Utilization of hepatocyte-specific antibody in the immunocytochemical evaluation of liver tumors. Mod Pathol 1997, **10**: 686–692.

196a Morrison C, Marsh W, Frankel WL. A comparison of CD10 to pCEA, MOC-31, and hepatocyte for the distinction of malignant tumors in the liver. Mod Pathol 2002, **15**: 1279–1287.

197 Nagasue N, Kohno H, Yamanoi A, Kimoto T, Chang YC, Nakamura T. Progesterone receptor in hepatocellular carcinoma. Correlation with androgen and estrogen receptors. Cancer 1991, **15**: 2501–2505.

198 Nagasue N, Yukaya H, Chang Y-C, Ogawa Y, Kohno H, Ito A. Active uptake of testosterone by androgen receptors of hepatocellular carcinoma in humans. Cancer 1986, **57**: 2162–2167.

199 Porcell AI, De Young BR, Proca DM, Frankel WL. Immunohistochemical analysis of hepatocellular and adenocarcinoma in the liver: MOC31 compare favorably with other putative markers. Mod Pathol 2000, **13**: 773–778.

200 Ruck P, Xiao JC, Kaiserling E. Immunoreactivity of sinusoids in hepatocellular carcinoma. An immunohistochemical study using lectin UEA-1 and antibodies against endothelial markers, including CD34. Arch Pathol Lab Med 1995, **119**: 173–178.

201 Sciot R, Paterson AC, Van Eyken P, Callea F, Kew MC, Desmet VJ. Transferrin receptor expression in human hepatocellular carcinoma. An immunohistochemical study of 34 cases. Histopathology 1988, **12**: 53–63.

202 Sell S, Dunsford HA. Evidence for the stem cell origin of hepatocellular carcinoma and cholangiocarcinoma. Am J Pathol 1989, **134**: 1347–1363.

203 Shiro T, Seki T, Naitoh Y, Inoue K, Okamura A. A correlation of argyrophilic nucleolar organizer regions with stages of hepatocellular carcinoma. Cancer 1993, **71**: 44–49.

204 Torbenson M, Wang J, Choti M, Ashfaq R, Maitra A, Wilentz RE, Boitnott J. Hepatocellular carcinomas show abnormal expression of fibronectin protein. Mod Pathol 2002, **15**: 826–830.

205 Torii A, Nakayama A, Harada A, Nakao A, Nonami T, Sakamoto J, Watanabe T, Ito M, Takagi H. Expression of the CD15 antigen in hepatocellular carcinoma. Cancer 1993, **71**: 3864–3867.

206 Torimura T, Ueno T, Kin M, Inuzuka S, Sugawara H, Tamaki S, Tsuji R, Sujaku K, Sata M, Tanikawa K. Coordinated expression of integrin alpha 6 beta 1 and laminin in hepatocellular carcinoma. Hum Pathol 1997, **28**: 1131–1138.

207 Tsuji M, Kashihara T, Terada N, Mori H. An immunohistochemical study of hepatic atypical adenomatous hyperplasia, hepatocellular carcinoma, and cholangiocarcinoma with alpha-fetoprotein, carcinoembryonic antigen, CA19-9, epithelial membrane antigen, and cytokeratins 18 and 19. Pathol Int 1999, **49**: 310–317.

208 Van Eyken P, Sciot R, Desmet VJ. A cytokeratin immunohistochemical study of cholestatic liver disease. Evidence that hepatocytes can express "bile duct-type" cytokeratins. Histopathology 1989, **15**: 125–135.

209 Vlasoff DM, Baschinsky DY, Frankel WL. Cytokeratin 5/6 immunostaining in hepatobiliary and pancreatic neoplasms. Appl Immunohistochem Mol Morphol 2002, **10**: 147–151.

210 Volpes R, van den Oord JJ, Desmet VJ. Integrins as differential cell lineage markers of primary liver tumors. Am J Pathol 1993, **142**: 1483–1492.

211 Wennerberg AE, Nalesnik MA, Coleman WB. Hepatocyte paraffin 1. A monoclonal antibody that reacts with hepatocytes and can be used for differential diagnosis of hepatic tumors. Am J Pathol 1993, **143**: 1050–1054.

211a Wiezorek TJ, Pinkus JL, Glickman JN, Pinkus GS. Comparison of thyroid transcription factor-1 and hepatocyte antigen immunohistochemical analysis in the differential diagnosis of hepatocellular carcinoma, metastatic adenocarcinoma, renal cell carcinoma, and adrenal cortical carcinoma. Am J Clin Pathol 2002, **118**: 911–921.

212 Yabuuchi I, Kawata S, Tamura S, Ito N, Matsuda Y, Nishioka M, Moriwaki K, Matsuzawa Y, Tarui S. Aromatase activity in human hepatocellular carcinoma. Relationship with the degree of histologic differentiation. Cancer 1993, **71**: 56–61.

Molecular genetic features

213 Aguilar F, Harris CC, Sun T, Hollstein M, Cerutti P. Geographic variation of p53 mutational profile in nonmalignant human liver. Science 1994, **264**: 1317–1319.

214 Boix-Ferrero J, Pellin A, Blesa R, Adrados M, Llombard-Bosch A. Absence of p53 gene mutations in hepatocarcinomas from a Mediterranean area of Spain. A study of 129 archival tumour samples. Virchows Arch 1999, **434**: 497–501.

215 Bressac B, Galvin KM, Liang TJ, Isselbacher KJ, Wands JR, Ozturk M. Abnormal structure and expression of p53 gene in human hepatocellular carcinoma. Proc Natl Acad Sci U S A 1990, **87**: 1973–1977.

216 Ezaki T, Kanematsu T, Okamura T, Sonoda T, Sugimachi K. DNA analysis of hepatocellular carcinoma and clinicopathologic implications. Cancer 1988, **61**: 106–109.

217 Fujimoto J, Okamoto E, Yamanaka N, Toyosaka A, Mitsunobu M. Flow cytometric DNA analysis of hepatocellular carcinoma. Cancer 1991, **67**: 939–944.

218 Goldblum JR, Bartos RE, Carr KA, Frank TS. Hepatitis B and alterations of the p53 tumor suppressor gene in hepatocellular carcinoma. Am J Surg Pathol 1993, **17**: 1244–1251.

219 Nagao T, Kondo F, Sato T, Nagato Y, Kondo Y. Immunohistochemical detection of aberrant p53 expression in hepatocellular carcinoma. Correlation with cell proliferative activity indices, including mitotic index and MIB-1 immunostaining. Hum Pathol 1995, **26**: 326–333.

220 Ojanguren I, Ariza A, Castella EM, Fernandez-Vasalo A, Mate JL, Navas-Palacios JJ. p53 immunoreactivity in hepatocellular adenoma, focal nodular hyperplasia, cirrhosis and hepatocellular carcinoma. Histopathology 1995, **26**: 63–68.

220a Paradis V, Bièche I, Dargère D, Laurendeau I, Laurent C, Bioulac Sage P, Degott C, Belghiti J, Vidaud M, Bedossa P. Molecular profiling of hepatocellular carcinomas (HCC) using a large-scale real-time RT-PCR approach. Am J Pathol 2003, **163**: 733–741.

221 Tannapfel A, Witteking C. Genes involved in hepatocellular carcinomas: deregulation in cell cycling and apoptosis. Virchows Arch 2002, **440**: 345–352.

222 Tornillo L, Carafa V, Sauter G, Moch H, Minola E, Gambacorta M, Vecchione R, Bianchi L, Terracciano LM. Chromosomal alterations in hepatocellular nodules by comparative genomic hybridization: high-grade dysplastic nodules represent early stages of hepatocellular carcinoma. Lab Invest 2002, **82**: 547–553.

223 Zhao M, Zhang NX, Economou M, Blaha I, Laissue JA, Zimmermann A. Immunohistochemical detection of bcl-2 protein

in liver lesions. Bcl-2 protein is expressed in hepatocellular carcinomas but not in liver cell dysplasia. Histopathology 1994, **25:** 237–245.

Other microscopic types

224 Akasofu M, Kawahara E, Kaji K, Nakanishi I. Sarcomatoid hepatocellular-carcinoma showing rhabdomyoblastic differentiation in the adult cirrhotic liver. Virchows Arch 1999, **434:** 511–515.

225 Albar JP, De Miguel F, Esbrit P, Miranda R, Fernandez-Flores A, Sarasa JL. Immunohistochemical detection of parathyroid hormone-related protein in a rare variant of hepatic neoplasm (sclerosing hepatic carcinoma). Hum Pathol 1996, **27:** 728–731.

226 Altmann HW. Some histological remarks on the fibrolamellar carcinoma of the liver. Pathol Res Pract 1990, **186:** 63–69.

227 Berman MM, Libbey NP, Foster JH. Hepatocellular carcinoma. Polygonal cell type with fibrous stroma. An atypical variant with a favorable prognosis. Cancer 1980, **46:** 1448–1455.

228 Buchanan TF Jr, Huvos AG. Clear-cell carcinoma of the liver. A clinicopathologic study of 13 patients. Am J Clin Pathol 1974, **61:** 529–539.

229 Craig JR, Peters RL, Edmondson HA, Omata M. Fibrolamellar carcinoma of the liver. A tumor of adolescents and young adults with distinctive clinicopathologic features. Cancer 1980, **46:** 372–379.

230 Emile J-F, Adam R, Sebagh M, Marchadier E, Falissard B, Dussaix E, Bismuth H, Reynes M. Hepatocellular carcinoma with lymphoid stroma: a tumour with good prognosis after liver transplantation. Histopathology 2001, **37:** 523–529.

231 Emile J-F, Lemoine A, Azoulay D, Debuire B, Bismuth H, Reynes M. Histological, genomic and clinical heterogeneity of clear cell hepatocellular carcinoma. Histopathology 2001, **38:** 225–231.

232 Farhi DC, Shikes RH, Murari PJ, Silverberg SG. Hepatocellular carcinoma in young people. Cancer 1983, **52:** 1516–1525.

233 Farhi DC, Shikes RH, Silverberg SG. Ultrastructure of fibrolamellar oncocytic hepatoma. Cancer 1982, **50:** 702–709.

234 Fayyazi A, Nolte W, Oestmann JW, Sattler B, Ramadori G, Radzun HJ. Carcinosarcoma of the liver. Histopathology 1998, **32:** 385–387.

235 Fujii H, Zhu XG, Matsumoto T, Inagaki M, Tokusashi Y, Miyokawa N, Fukusato T, Uekusa T, Takegaki T, Kadowaki N, Shirai T. Genetic classification of combined hepatocellular-cholangiocarcinoma. Hum Pathol 2000, **31:** 1011–1017.

236 Goodman ZK, Ishak KG, Langloss JM, Sesterhenn IA, Rabin L. Combined hepatocellular-cholangiocarcinoma. A histologic and immunohistochemical study. Cancer 1985, **55:** 124–135.

237 Haratake J, Horie A. An immunohistochemical study of sarcomatoid liver carcinoma. Cancer 1991, **68:** 93–97.

238 Hood DL, Bauer TW, Leibel SA, McMahon JT. Hepatic giant cell carcinoma. An ultrastructural and immunohistochemical study. Am J Clin Pathol 1990, **93:** 111–116.

239 Jarnagin WR, Weber S, Tickoo SK, Koea JB, Obiekwe S, Fong Y, DeMatteo RP, Blumgart LH, Klimstra D. Combined hepatocellular and cholangiocarcinoma: demographic, clinical, and prognostic factors. Cancer 2002, **94:** 2040–2046.

240 Kakizoe S, Kojiro M, Nakashima T. Hepatocellular carcinoma with sarcomatous change. Clinicopathologic and immunohistochemical studies of 14 autopsy cases. Cancer 1987, **59:** 310–316.

240a Katzenstein HM, Krailo MD, Malogolowkin MH, Ortega JA, Qu W, Douglass EC, Feusner JH, Reynolds M, Quinn JJ, Newman K, Finegold MJ, Haas JE, Sensel MG, Castleberry RP, Bowman LC. Fibrolamellar hepatocellular carcinoma in children and adolescents. Cancer 2003, **97:** 2006–2012.

241 Kondo Y. Histologic features of hepatocellular carcinoma and allied disorders. Pathol Annu 1985, **20**(Pt 2): 405–430.

242 Kuwano H, Sonoda T, Hashimoto H, Enjoji M. Hepatocellular

243 Kwon Y, Lee SK, Kim JS, Ro JY, Yu E. Synchronous hepatocellular carcinoma and cholangiocarcinoma arising in two different dysplastic nodules. Mod Pathol 2002, **15:** 1096–1101.

244 LeBrun DP, Silver MM, Freedman MH, Phillips MJ. Fibrolamellar carcinoma of the liver in a patient with Fanconi anemia. Hum Pathol 1991, **22:** 396–398.

245 Lloreta J, Vadell C, Fabregat X, Serrano S. Fibrolamellar hepatic tumor with neurosecretory features and systemic deposition of AA amyloid. Ultrastruct Pathol 1994, **18:** 287–292.

246 Maeda T, Adachi E, Kajiyama K, Takenaka K, Sugimachi K, Tsuneyoshi M. Spindle cell hepatocellular carcinoma: a clinicopathologic and immunohistochemical analysis of 15 cases. Cancer 1996, **77:** 51–57.

247 Murakata LA, Ishak K, Nzeako UC. Clear cell carcinoma of the liver: a comparative immunohistochemical study with renal cell carcinoma. Mod Pathol 2000, **13:** 874–881.

248 Nerlich AG, Majewski S, Hunzelmann N, Brenner RE, Wiebecke B, Müller PK, Krieg T, Remberger K. Excessive collagen formation in fibrolamellar carcinoma of the liver. A morphological and biochemical study. Mod Pathol 1992, **5:** 580–585.

249 Oliveira AM, Erickson LA, Bugart LJ, Lloyd RV. Differentiation of primary and metastatic clear cell tumors in the liver by in situ hybridization for albumin messenger RNA. Am J Surg Pathol 2000, **24:** 177–182.

250 Ordóñez NG, Mackay B. Ultrastructure of liver cell and bile duct carcinomas. Ultrastruct Pathol 1983, **5:** 201–241.

251 Papotti M, Cassoni P, Taraglio S, Bussolati G. Oncocytic and oncocytoid tumors of the exocrine pancreas, liver, and gastrointestinal tract. Semin Diagn Pathol 1999, **16:** 126–134.

252 Payne CM, Nagle RB, Paplanus SH, Graham AR, Berman MM. Fibrolamellar carcinoma of liver. A primary malignant oncocytic carcinoid? Ultrastruct Pathol 1986, **10:** 539–552.

253 Sasaki M, Nakanuma Y, Ho SB, Kim YS. Cholangiocarcinomas arising in cirrhosis and combined hepatocellular-cholangiocellular carcinomas share apomucin profiles. Am J Clin Pathol 1998, **109:** 302–308.

254 Sato S-I, Masuda T, Oikawa H, Satodate R, Suzuki K, Sato S, Suzuki A, Monma N. Bile canaliculi-like lumina in fibrolamellar carcinoma of the liver: a light- and electron-microscopic study and three-dimensional examination of serial sections. Pathol Int 1997, **47:** 763–768.

255 Saul SH, Titelbaum DS, Gansler TS, Varello M, Burke DR, Atkinson BF, Rosato EF. The fibrolamellar variant of hepatocellular carcinoma. Its association with focal nodular hyperplasia. Cancer 1987, **60:** 3049–3055.

256 Suen KC, Magee JF, Halparin LS, Chan NH, Greene C-A. Fine needle aspiration cytology of fibrolamellar hepatocellular carcinoma. Acta Cytol (Baltimore) 1984, **29:** 867–872.

257 Tickoo SK, Zee SY, Obiekwe S, Xiao H, Koea J, Robiou C, Blumgart LH, Jarnagin W, Ladanyi M, Klimstra DS. Combined hepatocellular-cholangiocarcinoma: A histopathologic, immunohistochemical, and in situ hybridization study. Am J Surg Pathol 2002, **26:** 989–997.

258 Van Eyken P, Sciot R, Brock P, Casteels-Van Daele M, Ramaekers FC, Desmet VJ. Abundant expression of cytokeratin 7 in fibrolamellar carcinoma of the liver. Histopathology 1990, **17:** 101–107.

259 Vortmeyer AO, Kingma DW, Fenton RG, Curti BD, Jaffe ES, Duray PH. Hepatobiliary lymphoepithelioma-like carcinoma associated with Epstein-Barr virus. Am J Clin Pathol 1998, **109:** 90–95.

260 Wu PC, Lai CL, Lam KC, Lok ASF, Lin HJ. Clear cell carcinoma of liver. An ultrastructural study. Cancer 1983, **52:** 504–507.

261 Yang SH, Watanabe J, Nakashima O, Kojiro M. Clinicopathologic

carcinoma with osteoclast-like giant cells. Cancer 1984, **54:** 837–842.

study on clear cell hepatocellular carcinoma. Pathol Int 1996, **46**: 503–509.

262 Zanconati F, Falconieri G, Lamovec J, Zidar A. Small cell carcinoma of the liver: a hitherto unreported variant of hepatocellular carcinoma. Histopathology 1996, **29**: 449–453.

Biopsy and cytology

263 Bedrossian CW, Davila RM, Merenda G. Immunocytochemical evaluation of liver fine-needle aspirations. Arch Pathol Lab Med 1989, **113**: 1225–1230.

264 Bottles K, Cohen MB. An approach to fine-needle aspiration biopsy diagnosis of hepatic masses. Diagn Cytopathol 1991, **7**: 204–210.

265 Chlebowski RT, Tong M, Weissman J, Block JB, Ramming KP, Weiner JM, Bateman JR, Chlebowski JS. Hepatocellular carcinoma. Diagnostic and prognostic features in North American patients. Cancer 1984, **53**: 2701–2706.

266 Glenthoj A, Sehested M, Torp-Pedersen S. Diagnostic reliability of histological and cytological fine needle biopsies from focal liver lesions. Histopathology 1989, **15**: 375–383.

267 Greene C-A, Suen KC. Some cytologic features of hepatocellular carcinoma as seen in fine needle aspirates. Acta Cytol (Baltimore) 1986, **28**: 713–725.

268 Johnson DE, Powers CN, Rupp G, Frable WJ. Immunocytochemical staining of fine-needle aspiration biopsies of the liver as a diagnostic tool for hepatocellular carcinoma. Mod Pathol 1992, **5**: 117–123.

269 Kung IT, Chan SK, Fung KH. Fine-needle aspiration in hepatocellular carcinoma. Combined cytologic and histologic approach. Cancer 1991, **67**: 673–680.

270 Noguchi S, Yamamoto R, Tatsuta M, Kasugai H, Okuda S, Wada A, Tamura H. Cell features and patterns in fine-needle aspirates of hepatocellular carcinoma. Cancer 1986, **58**: 321–328.

271 Sakurai M, Okamura J, Seki K, Kuroda C. Needle tract implantation of hepatocellular carcinoma after percutaneous liver biopsy. Am J Surg Pathol 1983, **7**: 191–195.

272 Tao LC, Ho CS, McLoughlin MJ, Evans WK, Donat EE. Cytologic diagnosis of hepatocellular carcinoma by fine-needle aspiration biopsy. Cancer 1984, **53**: 547–552.

273 Zainol H, Sumithran E. Combined cytological and histological diagnosis of hepatocellular carcinoma in ultrasonically guided fine needle biopsy specimens. Histopathology 1993, **22**: 581–586.

Spread and metastases

274 Becker FF. Hepatoma. Nature's model tumor. A review. Am J Pathol 1974, **74**: 179–200.

275 Kojiro M, Kawabata K, Kawano Y, Shirai F, Takemoto N, Nakashima T. Hepatocellular carcinoma presenting as intrabile duct tumor growth. A clinicopathologic study of 24 cases. Cancer 1982, **49**: 2144–2147.

276 Kojiro M, Nakahara H, Sugihara S, Murakami T, Nakashima T, Kawasaki H. Hepatocellular carcinoma with intra-atrial tumor growth. A clinicopathologic study of 18 autopsy cases. Arch Pathol Lab Med 1984, **108**: 989–992.

277 Kondo Y, Wada K. Intrahepatic metastasis of hepatocellular carcinoma. A histopathologic study. Hum Pathol 1991, **22**: 125–130.

278 Liaw CC, Ng KT, Chen TJ, Liaw YF. Hepatocellular carcinoma presenting as bone metastasis. Cancer 1989, **64**: 1753–1757.

279 Linder GT, Crook JN, Cohn I Jr. Primary liver carcinoma. Cancer 1974, **33**: 1624–1629.

280 Okazaki N, Yoshino M, Yoshida T, Hirohashi S, Kishi K, Shimosato Y. Bone metastasis in hepatocellular carcinoma. Cancer 1985, **55**: 1991–1994.

281 Young RH, Gersell DJ, Clement PB, Scully RE. Hepatocellular carcinoma metastatic to the ovary. A report of three cases discovered during life with discussion of the differential

282 diagnosis of hepatoid tumors of the ovary. Hum Pathol 1992, **23**: 574–580.

282 Yuki K, Hirohashi S, Sakamoto M, Kanai T, Shimosato Y. Growth and spread of hepatocellular carcinoma. A review of 240 consecutive autopsy cases. Cancer 1990, **66**: 2174–2179.

Treatment and prognosis

283 Abou-Elella A, Gramlich T, Fritsch C, Gansler T. C-myc amplification in hepatocellular carcinoma predicts unfavorable prognosis. Mod Pathol 1996, **9**: 95–98.

284 Adachi E, Maeda T, Kajiyama K, Kinukawa N, Matsumata T, Sugimachi K, Tsuneyoshi M. Factors correlated with portal venous invasion by hepatocellular carcinoma: Univariate and multivariate analyses of 232 resected cases without preoperative treatments. Cancer 1996, **77**: 2022–2031.

285 Arii S, Tanaka J, Yamazoe Y, Minematsu S, Morino T, Fujita K, Maetani S, Tobe T. Predictive factors for intrahepatic recurrence of hepatocellular carcinoma after partial hepatectomy. Cancer 1992, **69**: 913–919.

286 Bismuth H, Chichie L, Adam R, Castaing D, Diamond T, Dennison A. Liver resection versus transplantation for hepatocellular carcinoma in cirrhotic patients. Ann Surg 1993, **218**: 145–151.

287 Carriaga MT, Henson DE. Liver, gallbladder, extrahepatic bile ducts, and pancreas. Cancer 1995, **75**: 171–190.

288 Chearanai O, Plengvanit U, Asavanich C, Damrongsak D, Sindhvananda K, Boonyapisit S. Spontaneous rupture of primary hepatoma. Report of 63 cases with particular reference to the pathogenesis and rationale treatment by hepatic artery ligation. Cancer 1983, **51**: 1532–1536.

289 Chlebowski RT, Tong M, Weissman J, Block JB, Ramming KP, Weiner JM, Bateman JR, Chlebowski JS. Hepatocellular carcinoma. Diagnostic and prognostic features in North American patients. Cancer 1984, **53**: 2701–2706.

290 Colleoni M, Bajetta E, Nelli P, Boni L, Bochicchio AM, Nole F, Buzzoni R, Celio L, Mazzaferro V, Bonfanti G, et al. Prognostic factors in patients affected by hepatocellular carcinoma treated with systemic chemotherapy. The experience of the National Cancer Institute of Milan. Ann Oncol 1993, **4**: 489–493.

291 Falkson G, Böhmer RH, Adam M, Coetzer BJ. Hepatitis-B as a prognostic discriminant in patients with primary liver cancer. Cancer 1986, **57**: 812–815.

292 Fisher RL, Scheuer PJ, Sherlock S. Primary liver cell carcinoma in the presence or absence of hepatitis B antigen. Cancer 1976, **38**: 901–905.

293 Haratake J, Takeda S, Kasai T, Nakano S, Tokui N. Predictable factors for estimating prognosis of patients after resection of hepatocellular carcinoma. Cancer 1993, **72**: 1178–1183.

294 Higuchi T, Kikuchi M, Okazaki M. Hepatocellular carcinoma after transcatheter hepatic arterial embolization. A histopathologic study of 84 resected cases. Cancer 1994, **73**: 2259–2267.

295 Hsu H-C, Sheu J-C, Lin Y-H, Chen D-S, Lee C-S, Hwang L-Y, Beasley RP. Prognostic histologic features of resected small hepatocellular carcinoma (HCC) in Taiwan. A comparison with resected large HCC. Cancer 1985, **56**: 672–680.

296 Ikeda K, Saitoh S, Tsubota A, Arase Y, Chayama K, Kumada H, Watanabe G, Tsurumaru M. Risk factors for tumor recurrence and prognosis after curative resection of hepatocellular carcinoma. Cancer 1993, **71**: 19–25.

297 Ishikawa K, et al. Statistics of liver surgery in Japan. III. A study by Japan Liver Cancer Study Group. Acta Hepatol Jpn 1976, **17**: 460–465.

298 Kaczynski J, Hansson G, Remotti H, Wallerstedt S. Spontaneous regression of hepatocellular carcinoma. Histopathology 1998, **32**: 147–150.

299 King KL, Li AF, Chau GY, Chi CW, Wu CW, Huang CL, Lui WY.

Prognostic significance of heat shock protein-27 expression in hepatacellular carcinoma and its relation to histologic grading and survival. Cancer 2000, **88**: 2464–2470.

300 Lau H, Fan ST, Ng IO, Wong J. Long term prognosis after hepatectomy for hepatocellular carcinoma: A survival analysis of 204 consecutive patients. Cancer 1998, **83**: 2302–2311.

301 Lauwers GY, Terris B, Balis UJ, Batts KP, Regimbeau J-M, Chang Y, Graeme-Cook F, Yamabe H, Ikai I, Cleary KR, Fujita S, Flejou JF, Zukerberg LR, Nagorney DM, Belghiti J, Yamoaka Y, Vauthey J-N. Prognostic histologic indicators of curatively resected hepatocellular carcinomas: a multi-institutional analysis of 425 patients with definition of a histologic prognostic index. Am J Surg Pathol 2002, **26**: 25–34.

302 Lin DY, Liaw Y-F, Chu CM, Chang-Chien CS, Wu CS, Chen PC, Sheen IS. Hepatocellular carcinoma in noncirrhotic patients. A laparoscopic study of 92 cases in Taiwan. Cancer 1984, **54**: 1466–1468.

303 Lise M, Bacchetti S, Da Pian P, Nitti D, Pilati PL, Pigato P. Prognostic factors affecting long term outcome after liver resection for hepatocellular carcinoma: results in a series of 100 Italian patients. Cancer 1998, **82**: 1028–1036.

304 Mazzaferro V, Regalia E, Doci R, Andreola S, Pulvirenti A, Bozzetti F, Montalto F, Ammatuna M, Morabito A, Gennari I. Liver transplantation for the treatment of small hepatocellular carcinomas in patients with cirrhosis. N Engl J Med 1996, **334**: 693–699.

305 Nagasue N, Yukaya H, Hamada T, Hirose S, Kanashima R, Inokuchi K. The natural history of hepatocellular carcinoma. A study of 100 untreated cases. Cancer 1984, **54**: 1461–1465.

306 Nagasue N, Yukaya H, Ogawa Y, Sasaki Y, Chang Y-C, Niimi K. Clinical experience with 118 hepatic resections for hepatocellular carcinoma. Surgery 1986, **99**: 694–702.

307 Ng IO, Lai EC, Ng MM, Fan ST. Tumor encapsulation in hepatocellular carcinoma. A pathologic study of 189 cases. Cancer 1992, **70**: 45–49.

308 Ng IO, Liu CL, Fan SF, Ng M. Expression of P-glycoprotein in hepatocellular carcinoma. A determinant of chemotherapy response. Am J Clin Pathol 2000, **113**: 355–363.

309 Ng IO, Ng MM, Lai EC, Fan ST. Better survival in female patients with hepatocellular carcinoma. Possible causes from a pathologic approach. Cancer 1995, **75**: 18–22.

310 Nomura F, Ohnishi K, Tanabe Y. Clinical features and prognosis of hepatocellular carcinoma with reference to serum alpha-fetoprotein levels. Analysis of 606 patients. Cancer 1989, **64**: 1700–1707.

311 Nzeako UC, Goodman ZD, Ishak KG. Hepatocellular carcinoma in cirrhotic and noncirrhotic livers. A clinico-histopathologic study of 804 North American patients. Am J Clin Pathol 1996, **105**: 65–75.

312 Okuda K, Musha H, Kanno H, Kojiro M, Sakamoto K, Nakashima T, Igarashi M, Nakano M, Shimokawa Y, Kubo Y, Arishima T, Hashimoto M, Nagata P. Localized submassive liver cell necrosis as a terminal event of liver carcinoma. Cancer 1976, **37**: 1965–1972.

313 Okuda K, Nakashima T, Obata H, Kubo Y. Clinicopathological studies of minute hepatocellular carcinoma. Analysis of 20 cases, including 4 with hepatic resection. Gastroenterology 1977, **73**: 109–115.

314 Okuda K, Ohtsuki T, Obata H, Tomimatsu M, Okazaki N, Hasegawa H, Nakajima Y, Ohnishi K. Natural history of hepatocellular carcinoma and prognosis in relation to treatment. Study of 850 patients. Cancer 1985, **56**: 918–928.

315 Patt YZ, Claghorn L, Charnsangavej C, Soski M, Cleary K, Mavligit GM. Hepatocellular carcinoma. A retrospective analysis of treatments to manage disease confined to the liver. Cancer 1988, **61**: 1884–1888.

316 Stuart KE, Anand AJ, Jenkins RL. Hepatocellular carcinoma in the United States: Prognostic features, treatment outcome, and survival. Cancer 1996, **77**: 2217–2222.

317 The Liver Cancer Study Group of Japan. Predictive factors for long term prognosis after partial hepatectomy for patients with hepatocellular carcinoma in Japan. Cancer 1994, **74**: 2772–2780.

318 Yamamoto J, Iwatsuki S, Kosuge T, Dvorchik I, Shimada K, Marsh JW, Yamasaki S, Starzl TE. Should hepatomas be treated with hepatic resection or transplantation? Cancer 1999, **86**: 1151–1158.

319 Yamanaka N, Okamoto E, Toyosaka A, Mitunobu M, Fujihara S, Kato T, Fujimoto J, Ohiyama T, Funukawa K, Kawamura E. Prognostic factors after hepatectomy for hepatocellular carcinomas. A univariate and multivariate analysis. Cancer 1990, **65**: 1104–1110.

320 Zhou XD, Tang ZY, Yang BH, Lin ZY, Ma ZC, Ye SL, Wu ZQ, Fan J, Qin LX, Zheng BH. Experience of 1000 patients who underwent hepatectomy for small hepatocellular carcinoma. Cancer 2001, **91**: 1479–1486.

321 Zhou XD, Tang ZY, Yu YQ, Yang BH, Lin ZY, Lu JZ, Ma ZC, Tang CL. Long term survivors after resection for primary liver cancer. Clinical analysis of 19 patients surviving more than ten years. Cancer 1989, **63**: 2201–2206.

Hepatoblastoma

322 Abenoza P, Manivel JC, Wick MR, Hagen K, Dehner LP. Hepatoblastoma. An immunohistochemical and ultrastructural study. Hum Pathol 1987, **18**: 1025–1035.

323 Altmann HW. Epithelial and mixed hepatoblastoma in the adult. Histological observations and general considerations. Pathol Res Pract 1992, **188**: 16–26.

324 Baggenstoss AH. Pathology of tumors of liver in infancy and childhood. In Pack GT, Islami AH (eds): Tumors of the liver. Vol. 26 of Recent results in cancer research. Heidelberg, 1970, Springer-Verlag.

325 Buendia MA. Genetic alterations in hepatoblastoma and hepatocellular carcinoma: common and distinctive aspects. Med Pediatr Oncol 2002, **39**: 530–535.

326 Conrad RJ, Gribbin D, Walker NI, Ong TH. Combined cystic teratoma and hepatoblastoma of the liver. Probable divergent differentiation of an uncommited hepatic precursor cell. Cancer 1993, **72**: 2910–2913.

327 Conran RM, Hitchcock CL, Waclawiw MA, Stocker JT, Ishak KG. Hepatoblastoma. The prognostic significance of histologic type. Pediatr Pathol 1992, **12**: 167–183.

328 Douglass EC, Reynolds M, Finegold M, Cantor AB, Glicksman A. Cisplatin, vincristine, and fluorouracil therapy for hepatoblastoma. A Pediatric Oncology Group study. J Clin Oncol 1993, **11**: 96–99.

329 Emura I, Ohnishi Y, Yamashita Y, Iwafuchi M. Immunohistochemical and ultrastructural study on erythropoiesis in hepatoblastoma. Acta Pathol Jpn 1985, **35**: 79–86.

330 Fasano M, Theise ND, Nalesnik M, Goswami S, Garcia de Davila MT, Finegold MJ, Greco MA. Immunohistochemical evaluation of hepatoblastomas with use of the hepatocyte-specific marker, hepatocyte paraffin 1, and the polyclonal anti-carcinoembryonic antigen. Mod Pathol 1998, **11**: 934–938.

331 Filler RM, Ehrlich PF, Greenberg ML, Babyn PS. Preoperative chemotherapy in hepatoblastoma. Surgery 1991, **110**: 591–596.

332 Fletcher JA, Kozakewich HP, Pavelka K, Grier HE, Shamberger RC, Korf B, Morton CC. Consistent cytogenetic aberrations in hepatoblastoma. A common pathway of genetic alterations in embryonal liver and skeletal muscle malignancies? Genes Chromosom Cancer 1991, **3**: 37–43.

333 Fuchs J, Rydzynski J, Hecker H, Mildenberger H, Burger D, Harms D, V Schweinitz D. The influence of preoperative chemotherapy and surgical technique in the treatment of

hepatoblastoma—a report from the German Co-operative Liver Tumour Studies HB 89 and HB 94. Eur J Pediatr Surg 2002, **12:** 255–261.

334 Giacomantonio M, Ein SH, Mancer K, Stephens CA. Thirty years of experience with pediatric primary malignant liver tumors. J Pediatr Surg 1984, **19:** 523–526.

335 Giardiello FM, Offerhaus GJ, Krush AJ, Booker SV, Tersmette AC, Mulder JW, Kelley CN, Hamilton SR. Risk of hepatoblastoma in familial adenomatous polyposis. J Pediatr 1991, **119:** 766–768.

336 Gonzalez-Crussi F. Undifferentiated small cell (anaplastic) hepatoblastoma. Pediatr Pathol 1991, **11:** 155–161.

337 Gonzalez-Crussi F, Upton MP, Maurer HS. Hepatoblastoma. Attempt at characterization of histologic subtypes. Am J Surg Pathol 1982, **6:** 599–612.

338 Green LK, Silva EG. Hepatoblastoma in an adult with metastasis to the ovaries. Am J Clin Pathol 1989, **92:** 110–115.

339 Haas JE, Feusner JH, Finegold MJ. Small cell undifferentiated histology in hepatoblastoma may be unfavorable. Cancer 2001, **92:** 3130–3134.

340 Hata Y, Ishizu HY, Ohmori K, Hamada H, Sasaki F, Uchino J, Inoue K, Naitoh H, Fujita M, Kobayashi T, et al. Flow cytometric analysis of the nuclear DNA content of hepatoblastoma. Cancer 1991, **88:** 2566–2570.

341 Ishak KG, Glunz PR. Hepatoblastoma and hepatocarcinoma in infancy and childhood. Cancer 1967, **20:** 396–422.

342 Ito E, Sato Y, Kawauchi K, Munakata H, Kamata Y, Yodono H, Yokoyama M. Type Ia glycogen storage disease with hepatoblastoma in siblings. Cancer 1987, **59:** 1776–1780.

343 Ito J, Johnson WW. Hepatoblastoma and hepatoma in infancy and childhood, light and electron microscopic studies. Arch Pathol 1969, **87:** 259–266.

344 Kennedy SM, Macgeogh C, Jaffe R, Spurr NK. Overexpression of the oncoprotein p53 in primary hepatic tumors of childhood does not correlate with gene mutations. Hum Pathol 1994, **25:** 438–442.

345 Knowlson GTG, Cameron AH. Hepatoblastoma with adenomatoid renal epithelium. Histopathology 1979, **3:** 201–208.

346 Lack EE, Neave C, Vawter GF. Hepatoblastoma. A clinical and pathologic study of 54 cases. Am J Surg Pathol 1982, **6:** 693–705.

347 McArthur JW, Toll GD, Russfield AB, Reiss AM, Quinby WC, Baker WH. Sexual precocity attributable to ectopic gonadotropin secretion by hepatoblastoma. Am J Med 1973, **54:** 390–403.

348 Molmenti EP, Wilkinson K, Molmenti H, Roden JS, Squires RH, Fasola CG, Tomlinson G, Nagata DE, D'Amico L, Lopez MJ, Savino LM, Marubashi S, Sanchez EQ, Goldstein RM, Levy MF, Andrews W, Andersen JA, Klintmalm GB. Treatment of unresectable hepatoblastoma with liver transplantation in the pediatric population. Am J Transplant 2002, **2:** 535–538.

349 Morinaga S, Yamaguchi M, Watanabe I, Kasai M, Ojima M, Sasano N. An immunohistochemical study of hepatoblastoma producing human chorionic gonadotropin. Cancer 1983, **51:** 1647–1652.

350 Nakagawara A, Ikeda K, Hayashida Y, Tsuneyoshi M, Enjoji M, Kawaoi A. Immunocytochemical identification of human chorionic gonadotropin- and alpha-fetoprotein-producing cells of hepatoblastoma associated with precocious puberty. Virchows Arch [A] 1982, **398:** 45–51.

351 Nakagawara A, Ikeda K, Tsuneyoshi M, Daimaru Y, Enjoji M, Watanabe I, Iwafuchi M, Sawada T. Hepatoblastoma producing both alpha-fetoprotein and human chorionic gonadotropin. Clinicopathologic analysis of four cases and a review of the literature. Cancer 1985, **56:** 1636–1642.

352 Parada LA, Limon J, Iliszko M, Czauderna P, Gisselsson D, Hoglund M, Kullendorff CM, Wiebe T, Mertens F, Johansson B. Cytogenetics of hepatoblastoma: further characterization of 1q rearrangements by fluorescence in situ hybridization: an internal collaborative study. Med Pediatr Oncol 2000, **34:** 165–170.

353 Prokurat A, Kluge P, Kosciesza A, Perek D, Kappeler A, Zimmermann A. Transitional liver cell tumors (TLCT) in older children and adolescents: a novel group of aggressive hepatic tumors expressing beta-catenin. Med Pediatr Oncol 2002, **39:** 510–518.

354 Reynolds M, Douglass EC, Finegold M, Cantor A, Glicksman A. Chemotherapy can convert unresectable hepatoblastoma. J Pediatr Surg 1992, **27:** 1080–1083.

355 Ruck P, Harms D, Kaiserling E. Neuroendocrine differentiation in hepatoblastoma. An immunohistochemical investigation. Am J Surg Pathol 1990, **14:** 847–855.

356 Ruck P, Kaiserling E. Extracellular matrix in hepatoblastoma. An immunohistochemical investigation. Histopathology 1992, **21:** 115–126.

357 Ruck P, Kaiserling E. Melanin-containing hepatoblastoma with endocrine differentiation. An immunohistochemical and ultrastructural study. Cancer 1993, **72:** 361–368.

358 Ruck P, Xiao JC, Pietsch T, Von Schweinitz D, Kaiserling E. Hepatic stem-like cells in hepatoblastoma: expression of cytokeratin 7, albumin and oval cell associated antigens detected by OV-1 and OV-6. Histopathology 1997, **31:** 324–329.

359 Saxena R, Leake JL, Shafford EA, Davenport M, Mowat AP, Pritchard J, Mieli-Vergani G, Howard ER, Spitz L, Malone M et al. Chemotherapy effects on hepatoblastoma. A histological study. Am J Surg Pathol 1993, **17:** 1266–1271.

360 Schmidt D, Harms D, Lang W. Primary malignant hepatic tumours in childhood. Virchows Arch [A] 1985, **407:** 387–403.

361 Schmidt D, Wischmeyer P, Lauschner I, Sprenger E, Langenau E, von Schweinitz D, Harms D. DNA analysis in hepatoblastoma by flow and image cytometry. Cancer 1993, **72:** 2914–2919.

361a Schnater JM, Köhler SE, Lamers WH, Von Schweinitz D, Aronson DC. Where do we stand with hepatoblastomas? Cancer 2003, **98:** 668–678.

362 Sciot R, Van Eyken P, Desmet VJ. Transferrin receptor expression in benign tumours and in hepatoblastoma of the liver. Histopathology 1990, **16:** 59–62.

363 Silverman JF, Fu Y-S, McWilliams NB, Kay S. An ultrastructural study of mixed hepatoblastoma with osteoid elements. Cancer 1975, **36:** 1436–1443.

364 Srinivasan P, McCall J, Pritchard J, Dhawan A, Baker A, Vergani GM, Muiesan P, Rela M, David Heaton N. Transplantation 2002, **74:** 652–655.

365 Stocker JT. Hepatoblastoma. Semin Diagn Pathol 1994, **11:** 136–143.

365a Terracciano LM, Bernasconi B, Ruck P, Stallmach T, Riner J, Sauter G, Moch H, Vecchione R, Pollice L, Pettinato G, Gürtl B, Ratschek M, De Krijger R, Tornillo L, Bruder E. Comparative genomic hybridisation analysis of hepatoblastoma reveals high frequency of X-chromosome gains and similarities between epithelial and stromal components. Hum Pathol 2003, **34:** 864–871.

366 Van Eyken P, Sciot R, Callea F, Ramaekers F, Schaart G, Desmet VJ. A cytokeratin-immunohistochemical study of hepatoblastoma. Hum Pathol 1990, **21:** 302–308.

367 Warfel KA, Hull MT. Hepatoblastomas. An ultrastructural and immunohistochemical study. Ultrastruct Pathol 1992, **16:** 451–461.

368 Weinberg AG, Finegold MJ. Primary hepatic tumors of childhood. Hum Pathol 1983, **14:** 512–537.

369 Zimmermann A. Hepatoblastoma with cholangioblastic features ('cholangioblastic hepatoblastoma') and other liver tumors with bimodal differentiation in young patients. Med Pediatr Oncol 2002, **39:** 487–491.

Bile duct tumors and tumorlike conditions
Bile duct hamartoma

370 Chung EB. Multiple bile-duct hamartomas. Cancer 1970, **26:** 287–296.

371 Honda N, Cobb C, Lechago J. Bile duct carcinoma associated with multiple von Meyenburg complexes in the liver. Hum Pathol 1986, **17**: 1287–1290.

372 Jain D, Sarode VR, Abdul-Karim FW, Homer R, Robert ME. Evidence for the neoplastic transformation of Von-Meyenburg complexes. Am J Surg Pathol 2000, **24**: 1131–1139.

373 Popovsky MA, Costa JC, Doppman JL. Meyenburg complexes of the liver and bile cysts as a consequence of hepatic ischemia. Hum Pathol 1979, **10**: 425–432.

374 Redston MS, Wanless IR. The hepatic von Meyenburg complex: prevalence and association with hepatic and renal cysts among 2843 autopsies. Mod Pathol 1996, **9**: 233–237.

375 Salo J, Bru C, Vilella A, Gines P, Gilabert R, Castells A, Bruguera M, Rodes J. Bile-duct hamartomas presenting as multiple focal lesions on hepatic ultrasonography. Am J Gastroenterol 1992, **87**: 221–223.

376 Thommesen N. Biliary hamartomas (von Meyenburg complexes) in liver needle biopsies. Acta Pathol Microbiol Scand [A] 1978, **86**: 93–99.

377 Tsui WM. How many types of biliary hamartomas and adenomas are there? Adv Anat Pathol 1998, **5**: 16–20.

378 Tsui WM, Loo KT, Chow LT, Tse CC. Biliary adenofibroma. A heretofore unrecognized benign biliary tumor of the liver. Am J Surg Pathol 1993, **17**: 186–192.

Bile duct adenoma

379 Albores-Saavedra J, Hoang MP, Murakata LA, Sinkre P, Yaziji H. Atypical bile duct adenoma, clear cell type: a previously undescribed tumor of the liver. Am J Surg Pathol 2001, **25**: 956–960.

380 Bhathal PS, Hughes NR, Goodman ZD. The so-called bile duct adenoma is a peribiliary gland hamartoma. Am J Surg Pathol 1996, **20**: 858–864.

381 Govindarajan S, Peters RL. The bile duct adenoma. A lesion distinct from Meyenburg complex. Arch Pathol Lab Med 1984, **108**: 922–924.

382 Hruban RH, Sturm PD, Slebos RJ, Wilentz RE, Musler AR, Yeo CJ, Sohn TA, van Velthuysen ML, Offerhaus GLA. Can K-ras codon 12 mutations be used to distinguish benign bile duct proliferations from metastases in the liver? A molecular analysis of 101 liver lesions from 93 patients. Am J Pathol 1997, **151**: 943–949.

383 Ishak KG, Rabin L. Benign tumors of the liver. Med Clin North Am 1975, **59**: 995–1013.

384 O'Hara BJ, McCue PA, Miettinen M. Bile duct adenomas with endocrine component. Immunohistochemical study and comparison with conventional bile duct adenomas. Am J Surg Pathol 1992, **16**: 21–25.

384a Varnhold H, Vaughey J-N, Dal Cin P, De W Marsh R, Bhathal PS, Hughes NR, Lauwers GY. Biliary adenofibroma. Am J Surg Pathol 2003, **27**: 693–698.

Biliary cystadenoma and cystadenocarcinoma

385 Devaney K, Goodman ZD, Ishak KG. Hepatobiliary cystadenoma and cystadenocarcinoma. A light microscopic and immunohistochemical study of 70 patients. Am J Surg Pathol 1994, **18**: 1078–1091.

386 Gourley WK, Kumar D, Bouton MS, Fish JC, Nealon W. Cystadenoma and cystadenocarcinoma with mesenchymal stroma of the liver. Immunohistochemical analysis. Arch Pathol Lab Med 1992, **116**: 1047–1050.

387 Grayson W, Teare J, Myburgh JA, Paterson AC. Immunohistochemical demonstration of progesterone receptor in hepatobiliary cystadenoma with mesenchymal stroma. Histopathology 1996, **29**: 461–463.

388 Ishak KG, Willis GW, Cummins SD, Bullock AA. Biliary cystadenoma and cystadenocarcinoma. Report of 14 cases and review of the literature. Cancer 1977, **38**: 322–338.

389 Kosuge T, Andersson R, Yamazaki S, Makuuchi M, Takayama T, Mukai K, Hasegawa H. Surgical management of biliary cystadenocarcinoma. Hepatogastroenterology 1992, **39**: 417–419.

390 Mizumoto R, Kawarada Y, Taoka H. A new classification of cystic malignant tumours of the liver. Classification of 65 cases reported at the 26th annual meeting of the Liver Cancer Society of Japan. J Gastroenterol Hepatol 1991, **6**: 400–407.

391 Nakajima T, Sugano I, Matsuzaki O, Nagao K, Kondo Y, Miyazaki M, Wada K. Biliary cystadenocarcinoma of the liver. A clinicopathologic and histochemical evaluation of nine cases. Cancer 1992, **69**: 2426–2432.

392 Shimonishi T, Zen Y, Chen TC, Chen MF, Jan YY, Yeh TS, Nimura Y, Nakanuma Y. Increasing expression of gastrointestinal phenotypes and p53 along with histologic progression of intraductal papillary neoplasia of the liver. Hum Pathol 2002, **33**: 503–511.

393 Subramony C, Herrera GA, Turbat-Herrera EA. Hepatobiliary cystadenoma. A study of five cases with reference to histogenesis. Arch Pathol Lab Med 1993, **117**: 1036–1042.

394 Terada T, Kitabura Y, Ohta T, Nakanuma Y. Endocrine cells in hepatobiliary cystadenomas and cystadenocarcinomas. Virchows Arch 1997, **430**: 37–40.

395 Unger PD, Thung SN, Kaneko M. Pseudosarcomatous cystadenocarcinoma of the liver. Hum Pathol 1987, **18**: 521–523.

396 Wang YJ, Lee SD, Lai KH, Wang SS, Lo KJ. Primary biliary cystic tumors of the liver. Am J Gastroenterol 1993, **88**: 599–603.

397 Wheeler DA, Edmondson HA. Cystadenoma with mesenchymal stroma (CMS) in the liver and bile ducts. A clinicopathologic study of 17 cases, 4 with malignant change. Cancer 1985, **56**: 1434–1445.

398 Wolf H, Garcia J, Bossen E. Oncocytic differentiation in intrahepatic biliary cystadenocarcinoma. Mod Pathol 1992, **5**: 665–668.

Bile duct carcinoma (cholangiocarcinoma)

399 Altaee MY, Johnson PJ, Farrant JM, Williams R. Etiologic and clinical characteristics of peripheral and hilar cholangiocarcinoma. Cancer 1991, **68**: 2051–2055.

400 Anthony PP. Primary carcinoma of the liver. A study of 282 cases in Ugandan Africans. J Pathol 1973, **110**: 37–48.

401 Azizah N, Paradinas FJ. Cholangiocarcinoma coexisting with developmental liver cysts. A distinct entity different from liver cystadenocarcinoma. Histopathology 1980, **4**: 391–400.

402 Bhuiya MR, Nimura Y, Kamiya J, Kondo S, Fukata S, Hayakawa N, Shionoya S. Clinicopathologic studies on perineural invasion of bile duct carcinoma. Ann Surg 1992, **215**: 344–349.

403 Bonetti F, Chilosi M, Pisa R, Novelli P, Zamboni G, Menestrina F. Epithelial membrane antigen expression in cholangiocarcinoma. A useful immunohistochemical tool for differential diagnosis with hepatocarcinoma. Virchows Arch [A] 1983, **401**: 307–313.

404 Chen MF, Jan YY, Wang CS, Hwang TL, Jeng LB, Chen SC, Chen TJ. A reappraisal of cholangiocarcinoma in patient with hepatolithiasis. Cancer 1993, **71**: 2461–2465.

405 Chen MF, Jan YY, Wang CS, Jeng LB, Hwang TL. Clinical experience in 20 hepatic resections for peripheral cholangiocarcinoma. Cancer 1989, **64**: 2226–2232.

406 Chen TC, Ng KF, Kuo T. Intrahepatic cholangiocarcinoma with lymphoepithelioma-like component. Mod Pathol 2001, **14**: 527–532.

407 Chijiiwa K, Ichimiya H, Kuroki S, Koga A, Nakayama F. Late development of cholangiocarcinoma after the treatment of hepatolithiasis. Surg Gynecol Obstet 1993, **177**: 279–282.

408 Chou ST, Chan CW, Ng WL. Mucin histochemistry of human cholangiocarcinoma. J Pathol 1976, **118**: 165–170.

409 Chow LT, Ahuja AT, Kwong KH, Fung KS, Lai CK, Lau JW. Mucinous cholangiocarcinoma: an unusual complication of

hepatholithiasis and recurrent pyogenic cholangitis. Histopathology 1997, **30**: 491–494.

410 Daroca PJ Jr, Tuthill R, Reed RJ. Cholangiocarcinoma arising in congenital hepatic fibrosis. A case report. Arch Pathol 1975, **99**: 592–595.

411 Foucar E, Kaplan LR, Gold JH, Kiang DT, Sibley RK, Bosl G. Well differentiated peripheral cholangiocarcinoma with an unusual clinical course. Gastroenterology 1979, **77**: 347–353.

412 Gallagher PJ, Millis RR, Mitchinson MJ. Congenital dilatation of the intrahepatic bile ducts with cholangiocarcinoma. J Clin Pathol 1972, **25**: 804–808.

413 Haratake J, Yamada H, Horie A, Inokuma T. Giant cell tumor-like cholangiocarcinoma associated with systemic cholelithiasis. Cancer 1992, **69**: 2444–2448.

414 Johnson DE, Herndier BG, Medeiros LJ, Warnke RA, Rouse RV. The diagnostic utility of the keratin profiles of hepatocellular carcinoma and cholangiocarcinoma. Am J Surg Pathol 1988, **12**: 187–197.

415 Kajiyama K, Maeda T, Takenaka K, Sugimachi K, Tsuneyoshi M. The significance of stromal desmoplasia in intrahepatic cholangiocarcinoma: a special reference of 'scirrhous-type' and 'nonscirrhous-type' growth. Am J Surg Pathol 1999, **23**: 892–902.

416 Kim YI, Yu ES, Kim ST. Intraductal variant of peripheral cholangiocarcinoma of the liver with *Clonorchis sinensis* infection. Cancer 1989, **63**: 1562–1566.

417 Kobayashi M, Ikeda K, Saitoh S, Suzuki F, Tsubota A, Suzuki Y, Arase Y, Murashima N, Chayama K, Kumada H. Incidence of primary cholangiocellular carcinoma of the liver in japanese patients with hepatitis C virus-related cirrhosis. Cancer 2000, **88**: 2470–2477.

418 Koga A, Ichimiya H, Yamaguchi K, Miyazaki K, Nakayama F. Hepatolithiasis associated with cholangiocarcinoma. Possible etiologic significance. Cancer 1985, **55**: 2826–2829.

419 Longnecker DS, Terhune PG. The case for parallel classification of biliary tract and pancreatic neoplasms. Mod Pathol 1996, **9**: 828–837.

420 Maeda T, Takenaka K, Taguchi K, Kajiyama K, Shirabe K, Shimada M, Tsuneyoshi M, Sugimachi K. Adenosquamous carcinoma of the liver: clinicopathologic characteristics and cytokeratin profile. Cancer 1997, **80**: 364–371.

421 Nagorney DM, Donohue JH, Farnell MB, Schleck CD, Ilstrup DM. Outcomes after curative resections of cholangiocarcinoma. Arch Surg 1993, **128**: 871–877.

421a Martin RCG, Klimstra DS, Schwartz L, Yilmaz A, Blumgart LH, Jarnagin W. Hepatic intraductal oncocytic papillary carcinoma. Cancer 2002, **95**: 2180–2187.

422 Nakajima T, Kondo Y. Well-differentiated cholangiocarcinoma. Diagnostic significance of morphologic and immunohistochemical parameters. Am J Surg Pathol 1989, **13**: 569–573.

423 Nakajima T, Kondo Y. A clinicopathologic study of intrahepatic cholangiocarcinoma containing a component of squamous cell carcinoma. Cancer 1990, **65**: 1401–1404.

424 Nakajima T, Tajima Y, Sugano I, Nagao K, Kondo Y, Wada K. Intrahepatic cholangiocarcinoma with sarcomatous change. Clinicopathologic and immunohistochemical evaluation of seven cases. Cancer 1993, **72**: 1872–1877.

425 Nakanuma Y, Terada T, Tanaka Y, Ohta G. Are hepatolithiasis and cholangiocarcinoma aetiologically related? A morphological study of 12 cases of hepatolithiasis associated with cholangiocarcinoma. Virchows Arch [A] 1985, **406**: 45–58.

426 Ohta T, Nagakawa T, Ueda N, Nakamura T, Akiyama T, Ueno K, Miyazaki I. Mucosal dysplasia of the liver and the intraductal variant of peripheral cholangiocarcinoma in hepatolithiasis. Cancer 1991, **68**: 2217–2223.

426a Ortiz MR, Garijo G, Adrados M, López-Bonet E, Acero D, Bernadó L. Epstein–Barr virus-associated cholangiocarcinoma

with lymphoepithelioma-like component. Int J Surg Pathol 2000, **8**: 347–351.

427 Pastolero GC, Wakabayashi T, Oka T, Mori S. Tissue polypeptide antigen. A marker antigen differentiating cholangiolar tumors from other hepatic tumors. Am J Clin Pathol 1987, **87**: 168–173.

428 Rocken C, Pross M, Brucks U, Ridwelski K, Roessner A. Cholangiocarcinoma occurring in a liver with multiple bile duct hamartomas (von Meyenburg complexes). Arch Pathol Lab Med 2000, **124**: 1704–1706.

429 Roskams T, Willems M, Campos RV, Drucker DJ, Yap SH, Desmet VJ. Parathyroid hormone-related peptide expression in primary and metastatic liver tumours. Histopathology 1993, **23**: 519–525.

430 Rubel LR, Ishak KG. Thorotrast-associated cholangiocarcinoma. An epidemiologic and clinicopathologic study. Cancer 1982, **50**: 1408–1415.

431 Rullier A, Le Bail B, Fawaz R, Blanc JF, Saric J, Bioulac-Sage P. Cytokeratin 7 and 20 expression in cholangiocarcinomas varies along the biliary tract but still differs from that in colorectal carcinoma metastases. Am J Surg Pathol 2000, **24**: 870–876.

432 Shimonishi T, Miyazaki K, Nakanuma Y. Cytokeratin profile relates to histological subtypes and the intrahepatic location of intrahepatic cholangiocarcinoma and primary sites of metastatic adenocarcinoma of liver. Histopathology 2000, **37**: 55–63.

433 Shirai T, Pairojkul C, Ogawa K, Naito H, Thamavit W, Bhudhisawat W, Ito N. Histomorphological characteristics of cholangiocellular carcinomas in northeast Thailand, where a region infection with the liver fluke, *Opisthorchis viverrini*, is endemic. Acta Pathol Jpn 1992, **42**: 734–739.

434 Stromeyer FW, Smith DH, Ishak KG. Anabolic steroid therapy and intrahepatic cholangiocarcinoma. Cancer 1979, **43**: 440–443.

435 Suzuki M, Takahashi T, Ouchi K, Matsuno S. The development and extension of hepatohilar bile duct carcinoma. A three-dimensional tumor mapping in the intrahepatic biliary tree visualized with the aid of a graphics computer system. Cancer 1989, **64**: 658–666.

436 Tada M, Omata M, Ohto M. High incidence of *ras* gene mutation in intrahepatic cholangiocarcinoma. Cancer 1992, **69**: 1115–1118.

437 Terada T, Nakanuma Y. An immunohistochemical survey of amylase isoenzymes in cholangiocarcinoma and hepatocellular carcinoma. Arch Pathol Lab Med 1993, **117**: 160–162.

438 Terada T, Ashida K, Endo K, Horie S, Maeta H, Matsunaga Y, Takashima K, Ohta T, Kitamura Y. c-erB-2 protein is expressed in hepatolithiasis and cholangiocarcinoma. Histopathology 1998, **33**: 325–331.

439 Terada T, Kida T, Nakanuma Y, Noguchi T. Extensive portal tumor thrombi with portal hypertension in an autopsy case of intrahepatic cholangiocarcinoma. Am J Gastroenterol 1992, **87**: 1513–1518.

440 Terada T, Nakanuma Y, Sirica AE. Immunohistochemical demonstration of MET overexpression in human intrahepatic cholangiocarcinoma and in hepatolithiasis. Hum Pathol 1998, **29**: 175–180.

441 Tihan T, Blumbart L, Klimstra DS. Clear cell papillary carcinoma of the liver: an unusual variant of peripheral cholangiocarcinoma. Hum Pathol 1998, **29**: 196–200.

442 Yamamoto M, Takasaki K, Nakano M, Saito A. Minute nodular intrahepatic cholangiocarcinoma. Cancer 1998, **82**: 2145–2149.

443 Weinbren K, Mutum SS. Pathological aspects of cholangiocarcinoma. J Pathol 1983, **139**: 217–238.

Mesenchymal tumors and tumorlike conditions
Vascular tumors

444 Belli L, De Carlis L, Beati C, Rondinara G, Sansalone V, Brambilla G. Surgical treatment of symptomatic giant hemangiomas of the liver. Surg Gynecol Obstet 1992, **174**: 474–478.

445 Cerar A, Dolenc-Strazar ZD, Bartenjev D. Infantile hemangioendothelioma of the liver in a neonate: Immunohistochemical observations. Am J Surg Pathol 1996, **20**: 871–876.

446 Dannaher CL, Tamburro CH, Yam LT. Occupational carcinogenesis. The Louisville experience with vinyl chloride-associated hepatic angiosarcoma. Am J Med 1981, **70**: 279–287.

447 Dean PJ, Haggitt RC, O'Hara CJ. Malignant epithelioid hemangioendothelioma of the liver in young women. Relationship to oral contraceptive use. Am J Surg Pathol 1985, **10**: 695–704.

448 Dehner LP, Ishak KG. Vascular tumors of the liver in infants and children. A study of 30 cases and review of the literature. Arch Pathol 1971, **92**: 101–111.

449 Demetris AJ, Minervini M, Raikow RB, Lee RG. Hepatic epithelioid hemangioendothelioma: Biological questions based on pattern of recurrence in an allograft and tumor immunophenotype. Am J Surg Pathol 1997, **21**: 263–270.

450 Dietze O, Davies SE, Williams R, Portmann B. Malignant epithelioid haemangioendothelioma of the liver. A clinicopathological and histochemical study of 12 cases. Histopathology 1989, **15**: 225–237.

451 Drut R, Drut RM, Toulouse JC. Hepatic hemangioendotheliomas, placental chorioangiomas, and dysmorphic kidneys in Beckwith-Wiedemann syndrome. Pediatr Pathol 1992, **12**: 197–203.

452 Falk H, Herbert JT, Edmonds L, Heath CW Jr, Thomas LB, Popper H. Review of four cases of childhood hepatic angiosarcoma. Elevated environmental arsenic exposure in one case. Cancer 1981, **47**: 382–391.

453 Feldman PS, Shneidman D, Kaplan C. Ultrastructure of infantile hemangioendothelioma of the liver. Cancer 1978, **42**: 521–527.

454 Haratake J, Horie A, Nagafuchi Y. Hyalinized hemangioma of the liver. Am J Gastroenterol 1992, **87**: 234–236.

455 Haratake J, Koide O, Takeshita H. Hepatic lymphangiomatosis. Report of two cases, with an immunohistochemical study. Am J Gastroenterol 1992, **87**: 906–909.

456 Ishak KG, Sesterhenn IA, Goodman MZD, Rabin L, Stromeyer FW. Epithelioid hemangioendothelioma of the liver. A clinicopathologic and follow-up study of 32 cases. Hum Pathol 1984, **15**: 839–852.

457 Ito Y, Kojiro M, Nakashima T, Mori T. Pathomorphologic characteristics of 102 cases of Thorotrast-related hepatocellular carcinoma, cholangiocarcinoma, and hepatic angiosarcoma. Cancer 1988, **62**: 1153–1162.

458 Kelleher MB, Iwatsuki S, Sheahan DG. Epithelioid hemangioendothelioma of liver. Clinicopathological correlation of 10 cases treated by orthotopic liver transplantation. Am J Surg Pathol 1989, **13**: 999–1008.

459 Kojiro M, Kawano Y, Kawasaki H, Nakashima T, Ikezaki H. Thorotrast-induced hepatic angiosarcoma, and combined hepatocellular and cholangiocarcinoma in a single patient. Cancer 1982, **49**: 2161–2164.

460 Kojiro M, Nakashima T, Ito Y, Ikezaki H, Mori T, Kido C. Thorium dioxide-related angiosarcoma of the liver. Pathomorphologic study of 29 autopsy cases. Arch Pathol Lab Med 1985, **109**: 853–857.

461 Lauffer JM, Zimmermann A, Krahenbuhl L, Triller J, Baer HU. Epithelioid hemangioendothelioma of the liver: A rare hepatic tumor. Cancer 1996, **78**: 2318–2327.

462 Lise M, Feltrin G, Da Pian PP, Miotto D, Pilati PL, Rubaltelli L, Zane D. Giant cavernous hemangiomas. Diagnosis and surgical strategies. World J Surg 1992, **16**: 516–520.

463 Ludwig J, Hoffman HN II. Hemangiosarcoma of the liver. Spectrum of morphologic changes and clinical findings. Mayo Clin Proc 1975, **50**: 255–263.

464 Luks FI, Yazbeck S, Brandt ML, Bensoussan AL, Brochu P, Blanchard H. Benign liver tumors in children. A 25-year experience. J Pediatr Surg 1991, **26**: 1326–1330.

465 Makhiouf HR, Ishak KG, Goodman ZD. Epithelioid hemangioendothelioma of the liver. A clinicopathologic study of 137 cases. Cancer 1999, **85**: 562–582.

466 Makk L, Delmore F, Creech JL Jr, Ogden LL, Fadell EH, Songster CL, Clanton J, Johnson MN, Christopherson WM. Clinical and morphologic features of hepatic angiosarcoma in vinyl chloride workers. Cancer 1976, **37**: 149–163.

467 Manning JT Jr, Ordóñez NG, Barton JH. Endothelial cell origin of thorium oxide-induced angiosarcoma of liver. Arch Pathol Lab Med 1983, **107**: 456–458.

468 McLean RH, Moller JH, Warwick WJ, Satran L, Lucas RV Jr. Multinodular hemangiomatosis of the liver in infancy. Pediatrics 1972, **49**: 563–573.

469 Rojiani AM, Owen DA, Berry K, Woodhurst B, Anderson FH, Scudamore CH, Erb S. Hepatic hemangioblastoma. An unusual presentation in a patient with von Hippel–Lindau disease. Am J Surg Pathol 1991, **15**: 81–86.

470 Ruebner BH, Eggleston JC. What is new in epithelioid hemangioendothelioma of the liver? Pathol Res Pract 1987, **182**: 110–112.

471 Schmid C, Beham A, Uranus S, Melzer G, Aubock L, Seewann HL, Klimpfinger M. Non-systemic diffuse lymphangiomatosis of spleen and liver. Histopathology 1991, **18**: 478–480.

472 Scoazec JY, Degott C, Reynes M, Benhamou JP, Feldmann G. Epithelioid hemangioendothelioma of the liver. An ultrastructural study. Hum Pathol 1989, **20**: 673–681.

473 Selby DM, Stocker JT, Ishak KG. Angiosarcoma of the liver in childhood. A clinicopathologic and follow-up study of 10 cases. Pediatr Pathol 1992, **12**: 485–498.

474 Stanley P, Geer GD, Miller JH, Gilsanz V, Landing BH, Boechat IM. Infantile hepatic hemangiomas. Clinical features, radiologic investigations, and treatment of 20 patients. Cancer 1989, **64**: 936–949.

475 Sussman EB, Nydick I, Gray GF. Hemangioendothelial sarcoma of the liver and hemochromatosis. Arch Pathol 1974, **97**: 39–42.

476 Thomas LB, Popper H, Berk PD, Selikoff I, Falk H. Vinyl-chloride-induced liver disease. From idiopathic portal hypertension (Banti's syndrome) to angiosarcomas. N Engl J Med 1975, **292**: 17–22.

477 Van Steenbergen W, Joosten E, Marchal G, Baert A, Vanstapel MJ, Desmet V, Wijnants P, DeGroote J. Hepatic lymphangiomatosis. Report of a case and review of the literature. Gastroenterology 1985, **88**: 1968–1972.

478 Waldschmidt J, Schier F, Bein U, Soerensen M. The use of the laser in the treatment of arterio-venous malformations and vascular tumours of the liver. Eur J Pediatr Surg 1993, **3**: 217–223.

479 Walsh MM, Hytiroglou P, Thung SN, Fiel MI, Siegel D, Emre S, Ishak KG. Epithelioid hemangioendothelioma of the liver mimicking Budd-Chiari syndrome. Arch Pathol Lab Med 1998, **122**: 846–948.

480 Winberg CD, Ranchod M. Thorotrast induced hepatic cholangiocarcinoma and angiosarcoma. Hum Pathol 1979, **10**: 108–112.

481 Yamagata M, Kanematsu T, Matsumata T, Utsunomiya T, Ikeda Y, Sugimachi K. Management of haemangioma of the liver. Comparison of results between surgery and observation. Br J Surg 1991, **78**: 1223–1225.

Mesenchymal hamartoma

482 Cook JR, Pfeifer JD, Dehner LP. Mesenchymal hamartoma of the liver in the adult: association with distinct clinical features and histological changes. Hum Pathol 2002, **33**: 893–898.

483 Dehner LP, Ewing SL, Sumner HW. Infantile mesenchymal hamartoma of the liver. Histologic and ultrastructural observations. Arch Pathol 1975, **99**: 379–382.

484 Drachenberg CB, Papadimitriou JC, Rivero MA, Wood C. Adult mesenchymal hamartoma of the liver. Report of a case with light

microscopic, FNA cytology, immunohistochemistry, and ultrastructural studies and review of the literature. Mod Pathol 1991, **4**: 392–395.

485 Lack EE. Mesenchymal hamartoma of the liver. A clinical and pathologic study of nine cases. Am J Pediatr Hematol/Oncol 1986, **8**: 91–98.

486 Lennington WJ, Gray GF Jr, Page DL. Mesenchymal hamartoma of liver. A regional ischemic lesion of a sequestered lobe. Am J Dis Child 1993, **147**: 193–196.

487 Mascarello JT, Krous HF. Second report of a translocation involving 19q13.4 in a mesenchymal hamartoma of the liver. Cancer Genet Cytogenet 1992, **58**: 141–142.

488 Otal TM, Hendricks JB, Pharis P, Donnelly WH. Mesenchymal hamartoma of the liver. DNA flow cytometric analysis of eight cases. Cancer 1994, **74**: 1237–1242.

489 Raffensperger JG, Gonzalez-Crussi F, Skeehan T. Mesenchymal hamartoma of the liver. J Pediatr Surg 1983, **18**: 585–587.

490 Rhodes RH, Marchildon MB, Luebke DC, Edmondson HA, Mikitz VG. A mixed hamartoma of the liver. Light and electron microscopy. Hum Pathol 1978, **9**: 211–221.

491 Shuto T, Kinoshita H, Yamada C, Hirohashi K, Shiokawa C, Kubo S, Fujio N, Kobayashi Y. Bilateral lobectomy excluding the caudate lobe for giant mesenchymal hamartoma for the liver. Surgery 1993, **113**: 215–222.

492 Srouji MN, Chatten J, Schulman WM, Ziegler MM, Koop CE. Mesenchymal hamartoma of the liver in infants. Cancer 1978, **42**: 2483–2489.

493 Sutton CA, Eller JL. Mesenchymal hamartoma of the liver. Cancer 1968, **22**: 29–34.

494 Wada M, Ohashi E, Jin H, Nishikawa M, Shintani S, Yamashita M, Kano M, Yamanaka N, Nishigami T, Shimoyama T. Mesenchymal hamartoma of the liver. Report of an adult case and review of the literature. Intern Med 1992, **31**: 1370–1375.

Undifferentiated (embryonal) sarcoma

495 Aoyama C, Hachitanda Y, Sato JK, Said JW, Shimada H. Undifferentiated (embryonal) sarcoma of the liver. A tumor of uncertain histogenesis showing divergent differentiation. Am J Surg Pathol 1991, **15**: 615–624.

496 Bisogno G, Pilz T, Perilongo G, Ferrari A, Harms D, Ninfo V, Treuner J, Carli M. Undifferentiated sarcoma of the liver in childhood: a curable disease. Cancer 2002, **94**: 252–257.

497 de Chadarevian JP, Pawel BR, Faerber EN, Weintraub WH. Undifferentiated (embryonal) sarcoma arising in conjunction with mesenchymal hamartoma of the liver. Mod Pathol 1994, **7**: 490–493.

498 Dehner LP. Hepatic tumors in the pediatric age group. A distinctive clinicopathologic spectrum. Perspect Pediatr Pathol 1978, **4**: 217–268.

499 Keating S, Taylor GP. Undifferentiated (embryonal) sarcoma of the liver. Ultrastructural and immunohistochemical similarities with malignant fibrous histiocytoma. Hum Pathol 1985, **16**: 693–699.

500 Lack EE, Schloo BL, Azumi N, Travis WD, Grier HE, Kozakewich HP. Undifferentiated (embryonal) sarcoma of the liver. Clinical and pathologic study of 16 cases with emphasis on immunohistochemical features. Am J Surg Pathol 1991, **15**: 1–16.

501 Lauwers GY, Grant LD, Donnelly WH, Meloni AM, Foss RM, Sanberg AA, Langham MR Jr. Hepatic undifferentiated (embryonal) sarcoma arising in a mesenchymal hamartoma. Am J Surg Pathol 1997, **21**: 1248–1254.

502 Leuschner I, Schmidt D, Harms D. Undifferentiated sarcoma of the liver in childhood. Morphology, flow cytometry, and literature review. Hum Pathol 1990, **21**: 68–76.

503 Miettinen M, Kahlos T. Undifferentiated (embryonal) sarcoma of the liver. Epithelial features as shown by immunohistochemical

analysis and electron microscopic examination. Cancer 1989, **64**: 2096–2103.

503a Nishio J, Iwasaki H, Sakashita N, Haraoka S, Isayama T, Naito M, Miyayama H, Yamashita Y, Kikuchi M. Undifferentiated (embryonal) sarcoma of the liver in middle-aged adults: smooth muscle differentiation determined by immunohistochemistry and electron microscopy. Hum Pathol 2003, **34**: 246–252.

504 O'Sullivan MJ, Swanson PE, Knoll J, Taboada EM, Dehner LP. Undifferentiated embryonal sarcoma with unusual features arising within mesenchymal hamartoma of the liver: report of a case and review of the literature. Pediatr Dev Pathol 2001, **4**: 482–489.

505 Parham DM, Kelly DR, Donnelly WH, Douglass EC. Immunohistochemical and ultrastructural spectrum of hepatic sarcomas of childhood. Evidence for a common histogenesis. Mod Pathol 1991, **4**: 648–653.

506 Stanley RJ, Dehner LP, Hesker AE. Primary malignant mesenchymal tumors (mesenchymoma) of the liver in childhood. An angiographic-pathologic study of three cases. Cancer 1973, **32**: 973–984.

507 Stocker JT, Ishak KG. Undifferentiated (embryonal) sarcoma of the liver. Report of 31 cases. Cancer 1978, **42**: 336–348.

508 Urban CE, Mache CJ, Schwinger W, Pakisch B, Ranner G, Riccabona M, Schimpl G, Brandesky G, Messner H, Pobegen W, et al. Undifferentiated (embryonal) sarcoma of the liver in childhood. Successful combined-modality therapy in four patients. Cancer 1993, **72**: 2511–2516.

509 Ware R, Friedman HS, Filston HC, Chaffee S, Kurtzberg J, Kinney TR, Falletta JM. Childhood hepatic mesenchymoma. Successful treatment with surgery and multiple-agent chemotherapy. Med Pediatr Oncol 1988, **16**: 62–65.

Other mesenchymal tumors

510 Alrenga DP. Primary fibrosarcoma of the liver. Case report and review of the literature. Cancer 1975, **36**: 446–449.

511 Arends JW, Willebrand D, Blaauw AMM, Bosman FT. Primary malignant fibrous histiocytoma of the liver. A case report with immunocytochemical observations. Histopathology 1987, **11**: 427–431.

512 Barnoud R, Arvieux C, Pasquier D, Pasquier B, Letoublon C. Solitary fibrous tumour of the liver with CD34 expression. Histopathology 1996, **28**: 551–554.

513 Bloustein PA. Hepatic leiomyosarcoma. Ultrastructural study and review of the differential diagnosis. Hum Pathol 1978, **9**: 713–715.

514 Cote RJ, Urmacher C. Rhabdomyosarcoma of the liver associated with long-term oral contraceptive use. Possible role of estrogens in the genesis of embryologically distinct liver tumors. Am J Surg Pathol 1990, **14**: 784–790.

515 Dalle I, Sciot R, de Vos R, Aerts R, van Damme B, Desmet V, Roskams T. Malignant angiomyolipoma of the liver: a hitherto unreported variant. Histopathology 2000, **36**: 443–450.

515a Di Blasi A, Boscaino A, De Dominicis G, Marsilia GM, D'Antonio A, Nappi O. Multicystic mesothelioma of the liver with secondary involvement of peritoneum and inguinal region. Int J Surg Pathol 2003 (in press).

516 Fiel MI, Schwartz M, Min AD, Sung MW, Thung SN. Malignant schwannoma of the liver in a patient without neurofibromatosis: a case report and review of the literature. Arch Pathol Lab Med 1996, **120**: 1145–1147.

516a Flemming P, Becker T, Klempnauer J, Högemann D, Kreft A, Kreipe HH. Benign cystic mesothelioma of the liver. Int J Surg Pathol 2002, **26**: 1523–1527.

517 Folpe AL, Goodman ZD, Ishak KG, Paulino AF, Taboada EM, Meehan SA, Weiss SW. Clear cell myomelanocytic tumor of the falciform ligament/ligamentum teres: A novel member of the perivascular epithelioid clear cell family of tumors with a

predilection for children and young adults. Am J Surg Pathol 2000, **24:** 1239–1246.

518 Foschini MP, Van Eyken P, Brock PR, Casteels-Van Daele M, De Vos R, Dal Cin P, Van den Berghe H, Desmet VJ. Malignant rhabdoid tumour of the liver. A case report. Histopathology 1992, **20:** 157–165.

519 Goodman ZD, Ishak KG. Angiomyolipomas of the liver. Am J Surg Pathol 1984, **8:** 745–750.

520 Hawkins EP, Jordan GL, McGavran MH. Primary leiomyoma of the liver. Successful treatment by lobectomy and presentation of criteria for diagnosis. Am J Surg Pathol 1980, **4:** 301–304.

521 Horie Y, Hori T, Hirayama C, Hashimoto K, Yumoto T, Tanikawa K. Osteoclast-like giant cell tumor of the liver. Acta Pathol Jpn 1987, **37:** 1327–1335.

522 Hytiroglou P, Linton P, Klion F, Schwartz M, Miller C, Thung SN. Benign schwannoma of the liver. Arch Pathol Lab Med 1993, **117:** 216–218.

523 Ishak KG, Rabin L. Benign tumors of the liver. Med Clin North Am 1975, **59:** 995–1013.

524 Karhunen PJ. Hepatic pseudolipoma. J Clin Pathol 1985, **38:** 877–879.

525 Le Bail B, Morel D, Merel P, Corneau F, Merlio JP, Carles J, Trillaud H, Bioulac-Sage P. Cystic smooth-muscle tumor of the liver and spleen associated with Epstein-Barr virus after renal transplantation. Am J Surg Pathol 1996, **20:** 1418–1425.

526 Lee ES, Locker J, Nalesnik M, Reyes J, Jaffe R, Alashari M, Nour B, Tzakis A, Dickman PS. The association of Epstein-Barr virus with smooth-muscle tumors occurring after organ transplantation. N Engl J Med 1995, **332:** 19–25.

527 McArdle JP, Hawley I, Shevland J, Brain T. Primary rhabdomyosarcoma of the adult liver. Am J Surg Pathol 1989, **13:** 961–965.

528 McGrady BJ, Mirakhur MM. Recurrent malignant fibrous histiocytoma of the liver. Histopathology 1992, **21:** 290–292.

529 Moran CA, Ishak KG, Goodman ZD. Solitary fibrous tumor of the liver: a clinicopathologic and immunohistochemical study of nine cases. Ann Diagn Pathol 1998, **2:** 19–24.

530 Munoz PA, Rao MS, Reddy JK. Osteoclastoma-like giant cell tumor of the liver. Cancer 1980, **46:** 771–779.

531 Nakahama M, Takanashi R, Yamazaki I, Machinami R. Primary fibrosarcoma of the liver. Immunohistochemical and electron microscopic studies. Acta Pathol Jpn 1989, **39:** 814–820.

532 Nishizaki T, Kanematsu T, Matsumata T, Yasunaga C, Kakizoe S, Sugimachi K. Myelolipoma of the liver. A case report. Cancer 1989, **63:** 930–934.

533 Nonomura A, Mizukami Y, Muraoka K, Yajima M, Oda K. Angiomyolipoma of the liver with pleomorphic histological features. Histopathology 1994, **24:** 279–281.

534 Ohyama M, Ijjri R, Tanaka Y, Kato K, Aida N, Ohnuma K, Sho N, Masano M, Misugi K. Congenital primitive epithelial tumor of the liver showing focal rhabdoid features, placental involvement, and clinical features mimicking multifocal hemangioma or stage 4S neuroblastoma. Hum Pathol 2000, **31:** 259–263.

535 Okada K, Yokoyama S, Nakayama I, Tada I, Kobayashi M. An electron microscopic study of hepatic angiomyolipoma. Acta Pathol Jpn 1989, **39:** 743–749.

536 O'Leary MR, Hill RB, Levine RA. Peritoneoscopic diagnosis of primary leiomyosarcoma of liver. Hum Pathol 1982, **13:** 76–78.

537 Parham DM, Peiper SC, Robicheaux G, Ribeiro RC, Douglass EC. Malignant rhabdoid tumor of the liver. Evidence for epithelial differentiation. Arch Pathol Lab Med 1988, **112:** 61–64.

538 Prevot S, Neris J, de Saint Maur PP. Detection of Epstein-Barr virus in an hepatic leiomyomatous neoplasm in an adult human immunodeficiency virus 1-infected patient. Virchows Arch 1994, **425:** 321–325.

539 Reinertson TE, Fortune JB, Peters JC, Pagnotta I, Balint JA. Primary leiomyoma of the liver. A case report and review of the literature. Dig Dis Sci 1992, **37:** 622–627.

540 Ross JS, Del Rosario A, Bui HX, Sonbati H, Solis O. Primary hepatic leiomyosarcoma in a child with the acquired immunodeficiency syndrome. Hum Pathol 1992, **23:** 69–72.

541 Rubin E, Russinovich NAE, Luna RF, Tishler JMA, Wilkerson JA. Myelolipoma of the liver. Cancer 1984, **54:** 2043–2046.

542 Scheimberg I, Cullinane C, Kelsey A, Malone M. Primary hepatic malignant tumor with rhabdoid features: A histological immunocytochemical, and electron microscopic study of four cases and a review of the literature. Am J Surg Pathol 1996, **20:** 1394–1400.

543 Sumiyoshi A, Niho Y. Primary osteogenic sarcoma of the liver. Report of an autopsy case. Acta Pathol Jpn 1971, **21:** 305–312.

544 Tanaka Y, Ijiri R, Kato K, Kato Y, Misugi K, Nakatani Y, Hara M. HMB 45/melan-A and smooth muscle actin-positive clear-cell epithelioid tumor arising in the ligament teres hepatis: additional example of clear cell "sugar" tumors. Am J Surg Pathol 2000, **24:** 1295–1299.

545 Tsui WM, Yuen AK, Ma KF, Tse CC. Hepatic angiomyolipomas with a deceptive trabecular pattern and HMB-45 reactivity. Histopathology 1992, **21:** 569–573.

546 Tsui WMS, Colombari R, Portmann BC, Bonetti F, Thung SN, Ferrell LD, Nakanuma Y, Snover DC, Bioulac-Sage P, Dhillon AP. Hepatic angiomyolipoma: A clinicopathologic study of 30 cases and delineation of unusual morphologic variants. Am J Surg Pathol 1999, **23:** 34–48.

547 von Hochstetter AR, Hättenschwiler J, Vogt M. Primary osteosarcoma of the liver. Cancer 1987, **60:** 2312–2317.

548 Wada Y, Jimi A, Nakashima O, Kojiro M, Kurohiji T, Sai K. Schwannoma of the liver: report of two surgical cases. Pathol Int 1998, **48:** 611–617.

549 Watanabe K, Saito A, Wakabayashi H, Kawaguchi T, Suzuki T. Two autopsy cases of primary leiomyosarcoma of the liver. Superiority of muscle-specific actin immunoreactivity in diagnosis. Acta Pathol Jpn 1991, **41:** 461–465.

550 Weeks DA, Malott RL, Arnesen M, Zuppan C, Aitken D, Mierau G. Hepatic angiomyolipoma with striated granules and positivity with melanoma-specific antibody (HMB-45). A report of two cases. Ultrastruct Pathol 1991, **15:** 563–571.

551 Weyman C, Dolson L, Kedar A. Secretion of vasointestinal peptide by a primary liver tumor with rhabdoid features. J Surg Oncol 1993, **54:** 267–270.

552 Yamasaki S, Tanaka S, Fujii H, Matsumoto T, Okuda C, Watanabe G, Suda K. Monotypic epithelioid angiomyolipoma of the liver. Histopathology 2000, **36:** 451–456.

Malignant lymphoma and related lesions

553 Ascoli V, Lo Coco F, Artini M, Levrero M, Martelli M, Negro F. Extranodal lymphomas associated with hepatitis C virus infection. Am J Clin Pathol 1998, **109:** 600–609.

554 Bagley CM Jr, Thomas LB, Johnson RE, Chretien PB, De Vita T Jr. Diagnosis of liver involvement by lymphoma. Results in 96 consecutive peritoneoscopies. Cancer 1973, **31:** 840–847.

555 Chang KL, Arber DA. Hepatosplenic gamma delta T-cell lymphoma – not just alphabet soup. Adv Anat Pathol 1998, **5:** 21–29.

556 Chen KTK. Inflammatory pseudotumor of the liver. Hum Pathol 1984, **15:** 694–696.

557 Chen TC, Kuo TT, Ng KF. Follicular dendritic cell tumor of the liver: a clinicopathologic and Epstein-Barr virus study of two cases. Mod Pathol 2001, **14:** 354–360.

558 Dargent J-L, De Wolf-Peeters C. Liver involvement by lymphoma: identification of a distinctive pattern of infiltration related to T-cell/histiocyte-rich-B-cell lymphoma. Ann Diagn Pathol 1998, **2:** 363–369.

559 DeMent SH, Mann RB, Staal SP, Kuhajda FP, Boitnott JK. Primary lymphomas of the liver. Report of six cases and review of the literature. Am J Clin Pathol 1987, **88:** 255–263.

560 Francois A, Lesesve J-F, Stamatoullas A, Comoz F, Lenormand B, Etienne I, Mendel I, Hémet J, Bastard C, Tilly H. Hepatosplenic gamma/delta T-cell lymphoma: A report of two cases in immunocompromised patients, associated with isochromosome 7q. Am J Surg Pathol 1997, **21**: 781–790.

561 Gollapudi P, Chejfec G, Zarling EJ. Spontaneous regression of hepatic pseudotumor. Am J Gastroenterol 1992, **87**: 214–217.

562 Hata Y, Sasaki F, Matuoka S, Hamada H, Taguchi K, Hasumi T, Manabe K, Uchino J, Nojima T, Hujioka Y et al. Inflammatory pseudotumor of the liver in children. Report of cases and review of the literature. J Pediatr Surg 1992, **27**: 1549–1552.

563 Horiuchi R, Uchida T, Kojima T, Shikata T. Inflammatory pseudotumor of the liver. Clinicopathologic study and review of the literature. Cancer 1990, **65**: 1583–1590.

564 Isaacson PG, Banks PM, Best PV, McLure SP, Muller-Hermelink HK, Wyatt JI. Primary low-grade hepatic B-cell lymphoma of mucosa-associated lymphoid tissue (MALT)-type. Am J Surg Pathol 1995, **19**: 571–575.

565 Kaplan KJ, Goodman ZD, Ishak KG. Liver involvement in Langerhans' cell histiocytosis: a study of nine cases. Mod Pathol 1999, **12**: 370–378.

566 Macon WR, Levy NB, Kurtin PJ, Salhany KE, Elkhalifa MY, Casey TT, Craig FE, Vnencak-Jones CL, Gulley ML, Park JP, Cousar JB. Hepatosplenic alfa beta T-cell lymphomas: A report of 14 cases and comparison with hepatosplenic gamma delta T-cell lymphomas. Am J Surg Pathol 2001, **25**: 285–296.

567 Miller ST, Wollner N, Meyers PA, Exelby P, Jereb B, Miller DR. Primary hepatic or hepatosplenic non-Hodgkin's lymphoma in children. Cancer 1983, **52**: 2285–2288.

568 Nakanuma Y, Tsuneyama K, Masuda S, Tomioka T. Hepatic inflammatory pseudotumor associated with chronic cholangitis. Report of three cases. Hum Pathol 1994, **25**: 86–91.

569 Nonomura A, Minato H, Shimizu K, Kadoya M, Matsui O, Sawasaki A, Nakamura S. Pseudolymphoma (reactive lymphoid hyperplasia) of the liver containing epithelioid cell granulomas and Schaumann's bodies in giant cells: a case report. Int J Surg Pathol 1998, **6**: 101–108.

570 Nuckols JD, Baron PW, Stenzel TT, Olatidoye BA, Tuttle-Newhall JE, Clavien PA, Howell DN. The pathology of liver-localized post-transplant lymphoproliferative disease: A report of three cases and a review of the literature. Am J Surg Pathol 2000, **24**: 733–741.

571 Rubbia-Brandt L, Brundler MA, Kerl K, Negro F, Nador RG, Scherrer A, Kurt AM, Mentha G, Borisch B. Primary hepatic diffuse large B-cell lymphoma in a patient with chronic hepatitis C. Am J Surg Pathol 1999, **23**: 1124–1130.

572 Ryan J, Straus DJ, Lange C, Filippa DA, Botet JF, Sanders LM, Shiu MH, Fortner JG. Primary lymphoma of the liver. Cancer 1988, **61**: 370–375.

573 Scheimberg IB, Pollock DJ, Collins PW, Doran HM, Newland AC, van der Walt JD. Pathology of the liver in leukaemia and lymphoma. A study of 110 autopsies. Histopathology 1995, **26**: 311–322.

574 Selves J, Meggetto F, Brousset P, Voigt JJ, Pradere B, Grasset D, Icart J, Mariame B, Knecht H, Delsol G. Inflammatory pseudotumor of the liver: Evidence for follicular dendritic reticulum cell proliferation associated with clonal Epstein-Barr virus. Am J Surg Pathol 1996, **20**: 747–753.

575 Sharifi S, Murphy M, Loda M, Pinkus GS, Khettry U. Nodular lymphoid lesion of the liver: An immune-mediated disorder mimicking low-grade malignant lymphoma. Am J Surg Pathol 1999, **23**: 302–308.

576 Shek TW, Ho FC, Ng IO, Chan AC, Ma L, Srivastava G. Follicular dendritic cell tumor of the liver: Evidence for an Epstein-Barr virus-related clonal proliferation of follicular dendritic cells. Am J Surg Pathol 1996, **20**: 313–324.

577 Shek TW, Ng IO, Chan KW. Inflammatory pseudotumor of the liver. Report of four cases and review of the literature. Am J Surg Pathol 1993, **17**: 231–238.

578 Someren A. "Inflammatory pseudotumor" of liver with occlusive phlebitis. Report of a case in a child and review of the literature. Am J Clin Pathol 1978, **69**: 176–181.

579 Strayer DS, Reppum TS, Levin M, Deschryver-Kecskemeti K. Primary lymphoma of the liver. J Gastroenterol 1980, **78**: 1571–1576.

580 Thiruvengadam R, Penetrante RB, Goolsby HJ, Silk YN, Bernstein ZP. Multiple myeloma presenting as space-occupying lesions of the liver. Cancer 1990, **65**: 2784–2786.

581 Trudel M, Aramendi T, Caplan S. Large-cell lymphoma presenting with hepatic sinusoidal infiltration. Arch Pathol Lab Med 1991, **115**: 821–824.

582 Weichhold W, Labouyrie E, Merlio J Ph, Masson B, de Mascarel A. Primary extramedullary plasmacytoma of the liver. A case report. Am J Surg Pathol 1995, **19**: 1197–1202.

583 Wu H, Wasik MA, Przybylski G, Finan J, Haynes B, Moore H, Leonard DG, Montone KT, Naji A, Nowell PC, Kamoun M, Tomaszewski JE, Salhany KE. Hepatosplenic gamma-delta T-cell lymphoma as a late-onset posttransplant lymphoproliferative disorder in renal transplant recipients. Am J Clin Pathol 2000, **113**: 487–496.

Other primary tumors and tumorlike conditions

584 Andreola S, Lombardi L, Audisio RA, Mazzaferro V, Koukouras D, Doci R, Gennari L, Makowka L, Starzl TE, van Thiel DH. A clinicopathologic study of primary hepatic carcinoid tumors. Cancer 1990, **65**: 1211–1218.

585 Ayub A, Zafar M, Abdulkareem A, Ali MA, Lingawi T, Harbi A. Primary hepatic vipoma. Am J Gastroenterol 1993, **88**: 958–961.

586 Berry CL. Solitary "necrotic nodule" of the liver. A probable pathogenesis. J Clin Pathol 1985, **38**: 1278–1280.

587 Corti B, D'Errico A, Pierangeli F, Fiorentino M, Altimari A, Grigioni WF. Primary paraganglioma strictly confined to the liver and mimicking hepatocellular carcinoma: An immunohistochemical and in situ hybridization study. Am J Surg Pathol 2002, **26**: 945–949.

588 Cross SS, Variend S. Combined hepatoblastoma and yolk sac tumor of the liver. Cancer 1992, **69**: 1323–1326.

589 Edmondson HA. Tumors of the liver and intrahepatic bile ducts. In Atlas of human pathology, section 4, fascicle 25. Washington, D.C., 1958, Armed Forces Institute of Pathology.

590 Fernandez Alonso J, Saez C, Perez P, Montano A, Japon MA. Primary pure choriocarcinoma of the liver. Pathol Res Pract 1992, **188**: 375–377.

591 Gembala RB, Arsuaga JE, Friedman AC, Radecki PD, Ball DS, Hartman GG, Rabin L, Caroline DF. Carcinoid of the intrahepatic ducts. Abdom Imaging 1993, **18**: 242–244.

592 Gresham GA, Rue LW III. Squamous cell carcinoma of the liver. Hum Pathol 1985, **16**: 413–416.

593 Hart WR. Primary endodermal sinus (yolk sac) tumor of the liver. First reported case. Cancer 1975, **35**: 1453–1458.

594 Hausner RJ, Alexander RW. Localized congenital hepatic fibrosis presenting as an abdominal mass. Hum Pathol 1978, **9**: 473–476.

595 Heaton GE, Matthews TH, Christopherson WM. Malignant trophoblastic tumors with massive hemorrhage presenting as liver primary. A report of two cases. Am J Surg Pathol 1986, **10**: 342–347.

596 Hsueh C, Tan XD, Gonzalez-Crussi F. Primary hepatic neuroendocrine carcinoma in a child. Morphologic, immunocytochemical, and molecular biologic studies. Cancer 1993, **71**: 2660–2665.

597 Larriva-Sahd J, Angeles-Angeles A, Hernandez-Pando R, Munoz Fernandez L, Rondan A, Orozco Estevez H, Campuzano Fernandez M. Ultrastructural and immunocytochemical study of a primary gastrinoma of the liver. Ultrastruct Pathol 1992, **16**: 667–672.

598 Misugi K, Reiner CB. A malignant true teratoma of liver in childhood. Arch Pathol 1965, **80**: 409–412.

599 Miura K, Shirasawa H. Primary carcinoid tumor of the liver. Am J Clin Pathol 1988, **89**: 561–564.

600 Morinaga S, Nishiya H, Inafuku T. Yolk sac tumor of the liver combined with hepatocellular carcinoma. Arch Pathol Lab Med 1996, **120**: 687–690.

601 Moriura S, Ikeda S, Hirai M, Naiki K, Fujioka T, Yokochi K, Gotou S. Hepatic gastrinoma. Cancer 1993, **72**: 1547–1550.

602 Pilichowska M, Kimura N, Ouchi A, Lin H, Mizuno Y, Nagura H. Primary hepatic carcinoid and neuroendocrine carcinoma: clinicopathological and immunohistochemical study of five cases. Pathol Int 1999, **49**: 318–324.

603 Robertson SJ, Higgins RB, Powell C. Malacoplakia of liver. A case report. Hum Pathol 1991, **22**: 1294–1295.

604 Robinson RA, Nelson L. Hepatic teratoma in an anencephalic fetus. Arch Pathol Lab Med 1986, **10**: 655–657.

605 Sioutos N, Virta S, Kessimian N. Primary hepatic carcinoid tumor. An electron microscopic and immunohistochemical study. Am J Clin Pathol 1991, **95**: 172–175.

606 Song E, Kew MC, Grieve T, Isaacson C, Myburgh JA. Primary squamous cell carcinoma of the liver occurring in association with hepatolithiasis. Cancer 1984, **53**: 542–546.

607 Theegarten D, Reinacher A, Graeven U, Philippou S. Mixed malignant germ cell tumour of the liver. Virchows Arch 1998, **433**: 93–96.

608 Tsuneyama K, Hoso M, Kono N, Kitagawa M, Masuda S, Matsuki N, Nakanuma Y. An unusual case of epithelial-myoepithelial carcinoma of the liver. Am J Surg Pathol 1999, **23**: 349–353.

609 Villaschi S, Balistreri P. Endodermal sinus tumour of the liver. Histopathology 1991, **18**: 86–88.

610 Wakely PE Jr, Krummel TM, Johnson DE. Yolk sac tumor of the liver. Mod Pathol 1991, **4**: 121–125.

611 Yu-Ping X, Ji-yao Y. Primary neuroendocrine carcinoma of the liver. Ultrastruct Pathol 1986, **10**: 331–336.

Metastatic tumors

612 Ballantyne GH, Quin J. Surgical treatment of liver metastases in patients with colorectal cancer. Cancer 1993, **71**: 4252–4266.

613 Borja ER, Hori JM, Pugh RP. Metastatic carcinomatosis of the liver mimicking cirrhosis. Case report and review of the literature. Cancer 1975, **35**: 445–449.

614 Fong Y, Cohen AM, Fortner JG, Enker WE, Turnbull AD, Coit DG, Marrero AM, Prasad M, Blumgart LH, Brennan MF. Liver resection for colorectal metastases. J Clin Oncol 1997, **15**: 938–946.

615 Hajdu SI, D'Ambrosio FG, Fields V, Lightdale CJ. Aspiration and brush cytology of the liver. Semin Diagn Pathol 1986, **3**: 227–238.

616 Johansen P, Svendsen KN. Scan-guided fine needle aspiration biopsy in malignant hepatic disease. Acta Cytol (Baltimore) 1978, **22**: 292–296.

617 Lind DS, Parker GA, Horsley JS, Kornstein MJ, Neifeld JP, Bear HD, Lawrence W Jr. Formal hepatic resection of colorectal liver metastases. Ploidy and prognosis. Ann Surg 1992, **215**: 677–683.

618 Lundquist A. Fine needle aspiration biopsy for cytodiagnosis of malignant tumor in the liver. Acta Med Scand 1970, **188**: 465–470.

619 McKenzie AD, Wilson JW. Hepatic resection for blood borne metastases from large bowel carcinoma. Case report and review of literature. Can J Surg 1970, **13**: 159–162.

620 Melato M, Laurino L, Mucli E, Valente M, Okuda K. Relationship between cirrhosis, liver cancer, and hepatic metastases. An autopsy study. Cancer 1989, **64**: 455–459.

621 Mosenthal WT. Resection of massive liver metastases in the malignant carcinoid syndrome. Surg Clin North Am 1963, **43**: 1253–1262.

622 Ohtsuka M, Miyazaki M, Itoh H, Nakagawa K, Ambiru S, Shimizu H, Nakajima N, Akikusa B, Kondo Y. Routes of hepatic metastasis of gallbladder carcinoma. Am J Clin Pathol 1998, **109**: 62–68.

622a Okano T, Niinobu T, Ogata N, Takami M. Fibrous pseudocapsule of metastatic liver tumors from colorectal carcinoma: clinicopathologic study of 152 first resection cases. Cancer 2000, **89**: 267–275.

623 Pikren JW, Tsukada Y, Lane WW. Liver metastases. Analysis of autopsy data. In Weiss L, Gilber HA (eds): Liver metastases. Boston, 1982, G.K. Hall & Co.

624 Qizilbash A, Kontozoglou T, Sianos J, Scully K. Hepar lobatum associated with chemotherapy and metastatic breast cancer. Arch Pathol Lab Med 1987, **111**: 58–61.

625 Sawabe M, Kato Y, Ohashi I, Kitagawa T. Diffuse intrasinusoidal metastasis of gastric carcinoma to the liver leading to fulminant hepatic failure. A case report. Cancer 1990, **65**: 169–173.

626 Schulz W, Hort W. The distribution of metastases in the liver. A quantitative postmortem study. Virchows Arch [A] 1981, **394**: 89–96.

627 Schulz W, Hagen CH, Hort W. The distribution of liver metastases from colonic cancer. A quantitative postmortem study. Virchows Arch [A] 1985, **406**: 279–284.

628 Shirai Y, Wakai T, Ohtani T, Sakai Y, Tsukada K, Hatakeyama K. Colorectal carcinoma metastases to the liver: Does primary tumor location affect its lobar distribution? Cancer 1996, **77**: 2213–2216.

628a Terracciano LM, Glatz K, Mhawech P, Vasei M, Lehmann FS, Vecchione R, Tornillo L. Hepatoid adenocarcinoma with liver metastatasis mimicking hepatocellular carcinoma. Am J Surg Pathol 2003, **27**: 1302–1312.

629 Tot T. Adenocarcinomas metastatic to the liver. The value of cytokeratins 20 and 7 in the search for unknown primary tumors. Cancer 1999, **85**: 171–177.

630 van Ooijen B, Wiggers T, Meijer S, van der Heijde MN, Slooff MJ, van de Velde CJ, Obertop H, Gouma DJ, Bruggink ED, Lange JF. Hepatic resections for colorectal metastases in The Netherlands. A multiinstitutional 10-year study. Cancer 1992, **70**: 28–34.

630a Wigmore SJ, Madhavan K, Redhead DN, Currie EJ, Garden J. Distribution of colorectal liver metastases in patients referred for hepatic resection. Cancer 2000, **89**: 285–287.

631 Wilson SM, Adson MA. Surgical treatment of hepatic metastases from colorectal cancers. Arch Surg 1976, **111**: 330–334.

14 Gallbladder and extrahepatic bile ducts

Normal anatomy

The gallbladder is a pear-shaped sac attached to the posterior aspect of the right hepatic lobe. In the adult, it measures up to 10 cm in length and 3 to 4 cm in width. The free surface is covered by serosa that is continuous with that on the hepatic surface. The gallbladder is divided into the following regions: fundus, body, and neck. The portion of the body that joins the neck is referred to as the infundibulum; sometimes there is a small bulge in this portion, known as Hartmann's pouch.

The gallbladder is supplied by the cystic artery, which is usually a branch of the right hepatic artery (see later section). Lymph drains to the node(s) at the gallbladder neck or cystic duct, from which it flows to nodes near the hepatic hilum and in the inferior portion of the hepato-duodenal ligament, the latter reaching nodes on the celiac axis.

The wall of the gallbladder is composed of three layers: mucosa, muscularis, and serosa (the latter only on the free surface). There is no muscularis mucosae or submucosa. The mucosa is made up of variably sized branching folds lined by a single layer of columnar cells having a pale cytoplasm with occasional small apical vacuoles and basally located nuclei.[3] Ultrastructurally, these cells have numerous apical microvilli with filamentous glycocalyx and core rootlets.[7] Smaller, darkly staining columnar cells have been called "pencil-like" cells. Ultrastructurally, these cells have a dense, organelle-packed cytoplasm and basal cytoplasmic extensions that project into the basal lamina. Basal cells are inconspicuous, and myoepithelial cells are absent. In the gallbladder, true glands are present only in the neck. They are of the tubuloalveolar mucous type and differ from the antral-type metaplastic glands found throughout the gallbladder in cases of chronic cholecystitis or cholelithiasis[1,6] (see p. 1041).

Histochemically, the mucin produced by both the lining cells and the neck mucous glands is mainly of sulfated acid types (in contrast to that of metaplastic glands). Immunohistochemically, both cell types are reactive for EMA and low-molecular-weight keratin. Scattered neuroendocrine cells may be found in the mucous glands of the neck.

The lamina propria encompasses loose connective tissue, vessels, nerves, and a scattering of IgA-containing plasma cells.[4] The muscle layer is made up of haphazardly distributed bundles of smooth muscle fibers. Ganglion cells may be found anywhere in the wall of the gallbladder. Minute paraganglia are present in the subserosal region and are occasionally detected in a random section of the organ.[2] Rokitansky–Aschoff sinuses and Luschka's ducts are discussed on p. 1041.

The other components of the extrahepatic biliary system are the cystic, hepatic (right, left, and common), and common bile ducts. Their general organization is similar, except for the fact that the lining of the cystic duct is pleated, with large oblique folds containing smooth muscle (spiral valve of Heister). Numerous variations in the anatomy of these ducts and their blood supply occur (see next section and Fig. 14.1).[8] The lymph drainage from the common bile duct is to nodes located along the duct, near the porta hepatis, around the pancreas, and ultimately into the celiac axis group.

Microscopically, the lining of all the extrahepatic ducts is made up of a single layer of columnar cells resting on dense connective tissue. This epithelium penetrates into the stroma to form pits known as the *sacculi of Beale*, the larger of which can be seen grossly. Surrounding these saccules are small glands that are surrounded by dense stroma and may mimic well-differentiated carcinoma; their lobular architecture seen on low-power microscopy is the most important distinguishing feature. Different patterns of smooth muscle distribution are seen in different portions of the extrahepatic biliary system, which may influence the estimation of depth of invasion of tumors at this site; specifically, the muscle coat is inconspicuous or absent in the upper third of the tract.[5]

Ultrastructurally, histochemically, and immunohistochemically, the lining epithelium of the extrahepatic lobe ducts is qualitatively similar to that of the gallbladder.

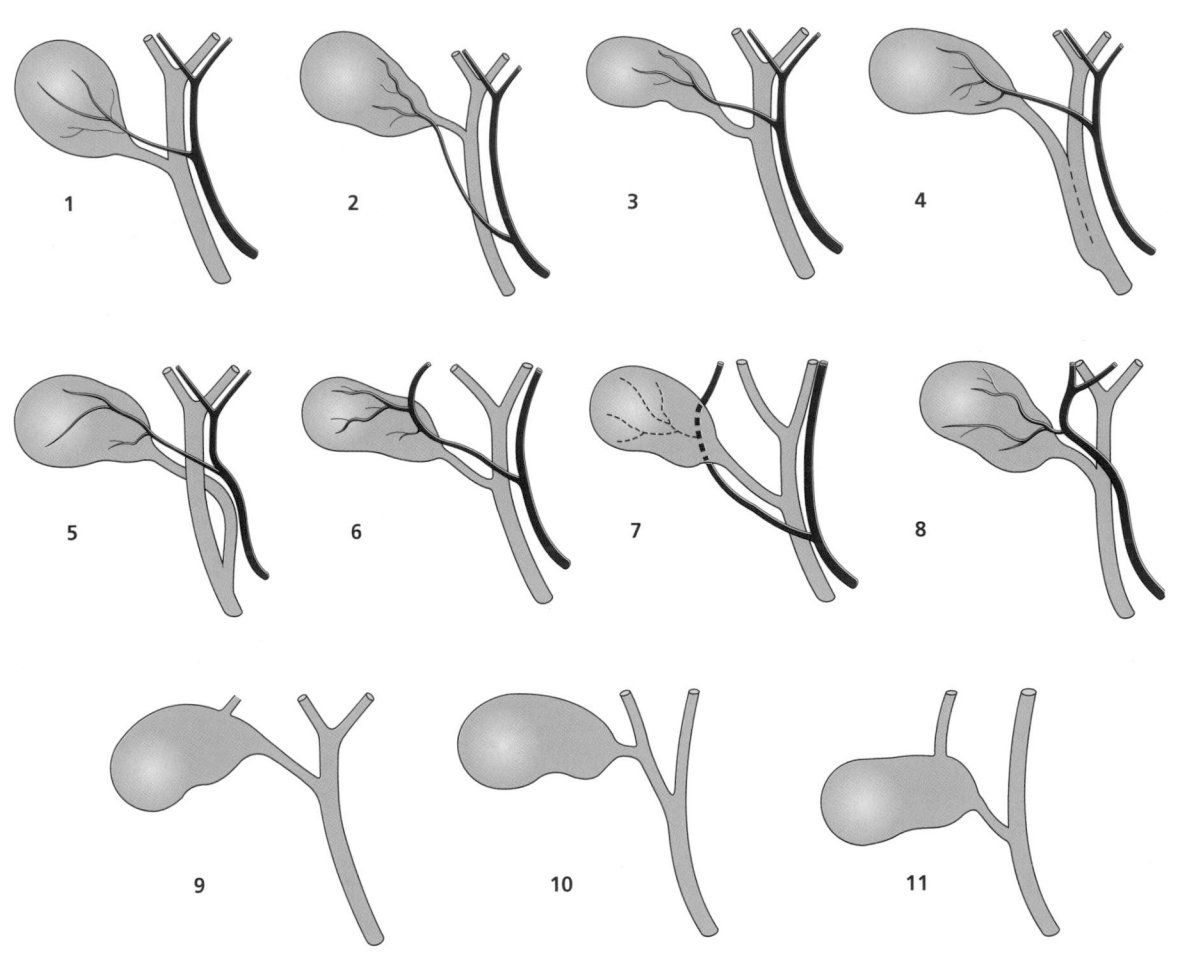

Fig. 14.1 Normal and anomalous arrangements of extrahepatic bile ducts and their adjoining arteries. **1**, Normal arrangement. **2**, Caudad origin of cystic artery (frequent variation). **3**, Placement of cystic artery posterior to common hepatic duct. **4**, Long cystic duct attached to common hepatic duct for some distance before confluence to form common bile duct. **5**, Long cystic duct passing behind common hepatic duct and joining it medially at lower level. **6**, Normal ductal system with anomalous right hepatic artery reaching the gallbladder wall, where it gives off cystic artery and then turns into liver. In this anomaly, which is not rare, the right hepatic artery is often ligated either with the cystic duct or as a separate structure erroneously identified as the cystic artery. **7**, Anomalous right hepatic artery in posterior position presenting the same dangers mentioned in 6. **8**, Very dangerous anomaly of entire hepatic artery that follows cystic duct to gallbladder before turning into liver. Accidental ligation on entire hepatic artery was almost always fatal before the advent of antibiotics, and it is still hazardous. **9**, Anomalous bile duct entering gallbladder through its bed in liver. Cholecystectomy in such instances is usually followed by profuse drainage of bile and is likely to result in fatal peritonitis unless external drainage is afforded. **10**, Anomalous insertion of cystic duct into right hepatic duct. The section of right hepatic duct caudad to its junction with cystic duct can easily be mistaken for cystic duct and ligated, thus shutting off drainage of right lobe of liver into intestine. **11**, Anomalous arrangement of right hepatic duct in which it enters gallbladder so that all the bile from right lobe of liver must drain through cystic duct.

Congenital abnormalities

Congenital abnormalities of the gallbladder include duplication, absence (agenesis), multiseptation, anomalous positions, and the presence of heterotopic tissues.[18,40] Agenesis of the bladder is usually associated with biliary atresia (see later discussion) and sometimes with duodenal atresia.[20] There are many anomalous arrangements of the extrahepatic bile ducts and their adjoining arteries (Fig. 14.1). The "phrygian cap" deformity represents an inversion of the fundus into the body of the organ, to which it may become adherent.[13,31] A localized area of adenomyomatosis (adenomyoma) is often present at the apex of the inverted fundus[13] (see p. 1042).

In **biliary atresia**, the gallbladder and extrahepatic ducts may be completely absent or may be represented by a fibrous cord without a lumen. The etiology, which remains unknown, may be multifactorial.[30] About 20% of the patients have associated anomalies.[15] The microscopic appearance suggests the occurrence of a widespread (possibly viral) injury to the extrahepatic biliary tree and liver; the changes in the biliary tree are characterized by damage to the epithelium, inflammation, lumen loss, and fibrosis.[22,38,46] Increased deposition of type IV collagen (a major component of the perisinusoidal wall of the liver) has been documented, and this has been correlated with increased serum levels of this marker.[37] Hypertrophic and hyperplastic changes of the hepatic artery and its branches are common.[23]

Biliary atresia has been divided into two types: (1) *correctable* (10% of the cases), with patency of the proximal bile duct system, which is treatable by biliary–enteric anastomosis; and (2) *noncorrectable* (90% of the cases), in which there is no patent portion of the extrahepatic bile system that communicates with the intrahepatic portion. In two thirds of patients with noncorrectable biliary atresia, the entire extrahepatic system, including the gallbladder, is atretic; in the other third, the gallbladder and common bile duct are patent, but the system proximal to the cystic duct is atretic. The noncorrectable form can be treated by portoenterostomy, i.e., the Kasai operation (which is primarily palliative) or by liver transplantation (which is primarily curative).[32] In portoenterostomy, the fibrous tissue at the porta hepatis is transected and the open area anastomosed to a limb of jejunum (or to the gallbladder when present).[9] Long-term survival after liver transplantation is excellent.[10,25] Frozen section can be useful at the time of surgery to determine whether bile ducts are present at the hilum and, if so, what their caliber is.[29]

Choledochal cyst is the most common cause of obstructive jaundice in children beyond infancy,[34,42] but it may also first present in adulthood.[45] It is not a cyst but rather a focal fusiform or spherical dilatation of the common bile duct, which may secondarily obstruct the other extrahepatic biliary ducts or even the duodenum. It is more common in females and characteristically presents with pain, jaundice, and a mass. The pathogenesis is unknown.[36] It may be associated with other congenital abnormalities of the biliary tract and other sites.[36] Ultrasonography is a rapid and accurate method to diagnose this abnormality. Grossly, the cyst wall is fibrous and sometimes calcified, and the average amount of bile in the cavity is 1 to 2 liters (Fig. 14.2). The bile duct distal to the cyst is frequently narrowed.[39] Four major gross variations of choledochal cyst have been described.[16,28]

The microscopic appearance depends on the age of the patient at the time of excision.[26] In infants, an intact columnar epithelium is usually present, and inflammation is scanty. In older children, there is more pronounced inflammation, and the epithelial lining is often discontinuous. In adults, there is even greater inflammation as well as destruction of the lining. Intramural glandular structures with metaplastic features are present. Chronic cholecystitis is often present. In some of the cases excised from adult patients, papillomas and adenocarcinomas have been found in the cyst wall.[11,26,33] Other tumor types have been reported within choledochal cysts, including carcinoid tumor[43] and embryonal rhabdomyosarcoma.[35]

The treatment of choice of choledochal cysts is excision with Roux-en-Y hepaticojejunostomy. Technical modifications such as interposition of a short segment of jejunum are said to improve the results.[19]

In a classic article, Landing[27] proposed grouping the conditions of biliary atresia, choledochal cyst, and neonatal hepatitis under the designation "infantile obstructive cholangiopathy" in view of their probably related pathogenesis. Neonatal hepatitis is discussed in Chapter 13.

Heterotopic tissues occurring in the gallbladder include gastric and intestinal mucosa,[24,44] pancreas,[24] liver,[12,41] adrenal,[14] and thyroid follicles.[21] Most cases of

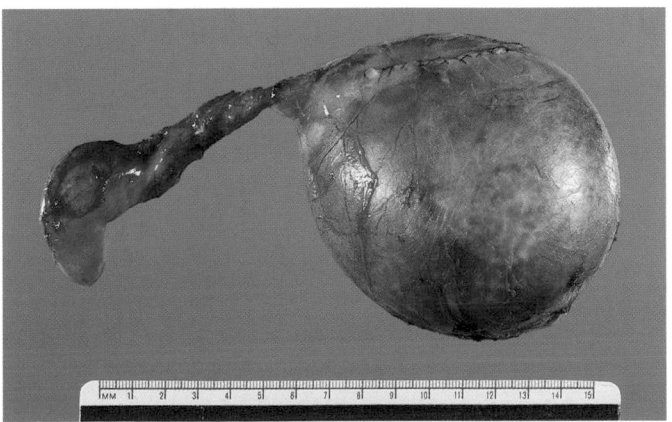

Fig. 14.2 Choledochal cyst in a 5-year-old female. The structure to the left is the attached gallbladder. (Courtesy of Dr. RA Cooke, Brisbane, Australia; from Cooke RA, Stewart B: Colour Atlas of Anatomical Pathology. Edinburgh, Churchill Livingstone, 2004).

heterotopic gastric mucosa occur in the gallbladder neck or in the adjacent cystic duct as a small well-defined intramural nodule.[17] Heterotopic liver should be anatomically separate from the main organ, in contrast to an accessory lobe.[12]

Cholelithiasis

The proposed pathogenesis of cholelithiasis, based on human studies and experimental animal models, is bile supersaturation, nucleation and precipitation of cholesterol monohydrate crystals, and growth to stone-sized aggregates.[50,62] Before the appearance of stones, there is always the formation of a "biliary sludge" containing mucus gel, hydrophobic bile pigments, cholesterol–lecithin liquid crystals, and solid cholesterol monohydrate crystals. The cholesterol crystal nucleation seems to occur in the mucus gel on the epithelial surface. Gallstone-containing bile is characterized by supersaturation with cholesterol and rapid in vitro nucleation of cholesterol crystals.[62]

Approximately 20% of the stones contain sufficient calcium to be radiopaque. Of the nonopaque stones, about 50% are manifest only by nonvisualization of the gallbladder by cholecystography. The others show as a negative shadow when the gallbladder concentrates the dye. The technique of sonography has been successfully used to identify gallbladder stones, and it has become the method of choice for their detection.[66]

The incidence of stones in the general population of the United States is 11%, as determined by the Framingham study.[48] Torvik and Höivik[64] report a frequency of 19.5% in autopsy material from Scandinavia. The incidence is four times higher in women than in males. A roughly linear relation has been found between body weight and the risk of gallstones.[52] There is also a definite increase with age until, at 60 years, about one of every four women has stones. However, stones can occur in any age group, including infants and newborns.[63]

Gallstones vary considerably in chemical composition, the basic constituents being cholesterol, calcium bilirubinate, and calcium carbonate, either alone or in combination.[61]

Pure gallstones (10%) are composed of only one of the substances mentioned. *Cholesterol stones* are single, spheroidal, and coarsely nodular; they have a translucent bluish white color. On fracture, they show large, flat crystals. Most cholesterol stones are found in multiparous women; this is probably related to the fact that cholesterol metabolism is altered during pregnancy and to the clinical observation that the first signs and symptoms of cholelithiasis often develop shortly after pregnancy.[49] However, no correlation exists between the presence of cholesterol stones in the gallbladder and the level of cholesterol in the blood.

Calcium bilirubinate stones are multiple, small, brown to jet black, and faceted; they measure 2 to 5 mm in diameter (Fig. 14.3). They are associated with cirrhosis and with hemolytic disorders, such as sickle cell anemia, thalassemia, hereditary spherocytosis, and artificial cardiac valves.[55,59] *Calcium carbonate stones* are amorphous and grayish white.

The gallbladder containing pure gallstones shows little or no inflammatory reaction if the cystic duct is not obstructed.

Mixed gallstones (80%) consist of various combinations of cholesterol, calcium bilirubinate, and calcium carbonate. Their size and number vary. They are usually multiple, faceted, and laminated. Chronic cholecystitis is almost always present (Figs 14.4 and 14.5). Several crops may be present, suggesting that the causes for their formation may operate at different times.

Combined gallstones (10%) are characteristically large and single. They may have a pure nucleus with a mixed shell or the reverse. *Barrel stones*, a type of combined stone, are usually two in number, large, and faceted on one surface, and the thick-walled gallbladder is closely wrapped around them (Fig. 14.4). Combined stones are always accompanied by chronic inflammation of the gallbladder and occasionally by biliary fistulas.

Sequential cholecystographic studies and carbon-14 dating suggest that gallbladder stones grow at a rate of approximately 1 to 2 mm per year and that they are usually present for 5 to 20 years before they are removed.[54]

Gallstones are formed in the gallbladder, from which they may escape into the cystic and other extrahepatic

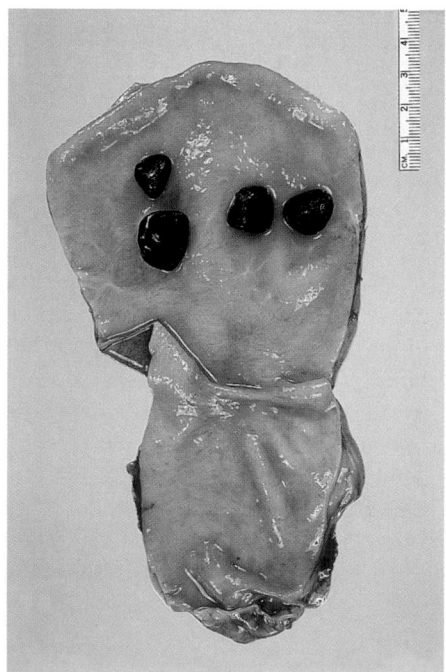

Fig. 14.3 Dilated gallbladder containing four mixed stones predominantly composed of calcium bilirubinate, having a characteristic jet black color.

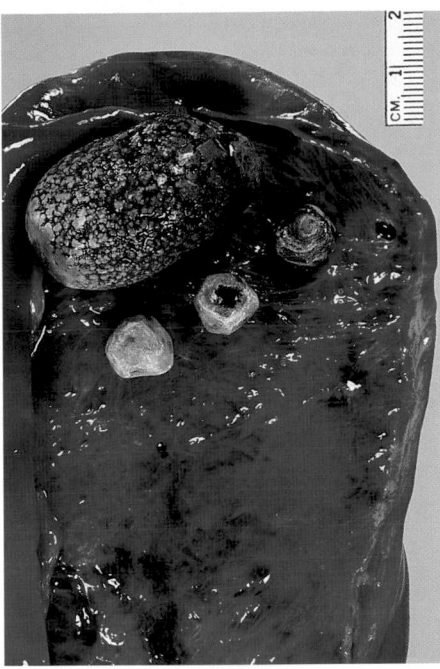

Fig. 14.4 Gallbladder with acute and chronic cholecystitis containing three mixed stones and one large combined stone.

Fig. 14.5 Gallbladder containing numerous stones of mixed type. There is a mild thickening of the wall due to chronic cholecystitis.

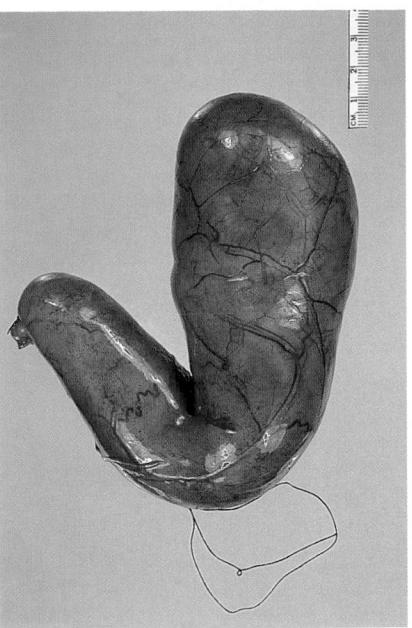

Fig. 14.6 Hydrops of gallbladder resulting from a stone impacted in the cystic duct.

ducts. Their independent formation in the extrahepatic ducts is rare.[53] Choledocholithiasis, with or without obstruction, is nearly always secondary to cholelithiasis.[51] The appearance of symptoms of choledocholithiasis some time after cholecystectomy for stones is usually caused by stones that were overlooked at the time of surgery. However, the occasional finding of multiple small intrahepatic stones indicates that they can also form in the hepatic duct system outside the gallbladder.

Impaction of the stone in the cystic duct may lead to cystic dilatation of the gallbladder (hydrops) (Fig. 14.6) or to acute cholecystitis, and impaction in the terminal third of the common duct or ampulla of Vater will result in severe, colicky pain and obstructive jaundice. Sometimes an impacted cystic duct stone causes edema and compression of the adjacent common hepatic duct, a condition known as *Mirizzi's syndrome*.[56] The standard treatment for symptomatic cholelithiasis is cholecystectomy, which at present is usually done laparoscopically.[47] Spillage of gallstones into the peritoneal cavity occurs not infrequently during this procedure and is generally of little consequence; however, sometimes it leads to intraperitoneal abscess, foreign body granuloma, and (exceptionally) implantation of the gallstones in the ovary.[65] Lithotripsy is an attractive alternative to cholecystectomy because of its noninvasive character and the fact that it can be performed in an ambulatory setting; however, it is applicable in only a small percentage of the patients and the recurrence rate is as high as 50% within 5 years.[60] The approach to individuals with asymptomatic gallstones remains controversial.[58] Endoscopic sphincterotomy is being increasingly performed for the treatment of cholelithiasis.[57]

Cholesterosis

Cholesterosis of the gallbladder occurs, for the most part, in multiparous women. The gross appearance is characteristic; linear yellow streaks are seen in the prominences of the ridges, surrounded by a congested mucosa ("strawberry gallbladder") (Fig. 14.7). Sometimes one or more of the deposits grow larger and protrude into the lumen, in which case they are referred to as *cholesterol polyps* (see p. 1043).

The bile within the gallbladder with cholesterosis is usually dark and thick, and it shows a high concentration of cholesterol by chemical analysis.

Microscopically, collections of lipid-filled foamy cells are present in the tips of the villi (Fig. 14.8). Inflammatory changes are usually insignificant, unless the cholesterosis is accompanied by stones in the cystic duct. The rarity of the coexistence of cholesterosis with advanced cholecystitis has suggested that the inflammatory process induces in some way the resorption of the lipid deposits.

Although cholesterosis of the gallbladder is in all likelihood a morphologic marker for a functional abnormality of bile metabolism, it is probably erroneous to ascribe the symptoms that these patients might have to the mere presence of the foamy histiocytes, especially in view of the fact that these changes are restricted to the gallbladder mucosa and do not ordinarily extend to the mucosa of the extrahepatic bile ducts.

Acute cholecystitis

The main clinical symptoms of acute cholecystitis are pain in the right upper quadrant, nausea and vomiting, and fever. Grossly, the gallbladder wall is markedly edematous and the mucosa has an angry red color[87] (Fig. 14.9A). Focal or extensive ulceration may be present. When stones are present (95% of the cases), the disease is known as **acute calculous cholecystitis**. The luminal content often has a yellow, grumous appearance; this may appear grossly as empyema, but in reality the material is not pus but an emulsion of calcium carbonate and/or cholesterol. Often, the acute changes are superimposed on an organ with chronic cholecystitis. Microscopically, the tissue response is characterized in most cases by edema, hyperemia, extravasation of red blood cells, and widespread fibroblastic proliferation rather than the customary polymorphonuclear infiltrate seen in other acutely inflamed organs (Fig. 14.9B). However, in cases associated with common bile duct obstruction, one can see intraepithelial aggregates of neutrophils in the mucosa, these formations having been likened to the reaction seen in the wall of the common bile duct and liver as part of the process of ascending cholangitis.[70] Marked reactive changes can be present in the epithelium, which should not be confused with dysplasia or carcinoma in situ (Fig. 14.9C). Fresh thrombi are often found within small veins in the gallbladder wall.[87]

The pathogenesis of most cases of acute calculous cholecystitis is probably chemical or ischemic rather than infectious, and it is nearly always related to a stone impacted in the cystic duct.[73,75] Such impaction is thought to lead to changes in the concentration and composition of the bile and possibly also to interference with the venous supply of the gallbladder by obstructing the tortuous venous channels surrounding the cystic duct. The hypothesis that most cases of acute cholecystitis have a chemical rather than an infectious pathogenesis is supported by the experimental production of acute cholecystitis by injecting concentrated bile into the gallbladder,[88] by the fact that 25% to 50% of bile cultures from acutely inflamed gallbladders are sterile, and by the observation that free perforation of these gallbladders is only rarely followed by bacterial peritonitis.

The chemical agents that have been proposed as mediators of acute cholecystitis are trypsin from pancreatic juice, unconjugated bile salts, and the phospholipid lysolecithin.[84] In an acutely distended gallbladder, these agents may leak through the intact wall and cause *bile*

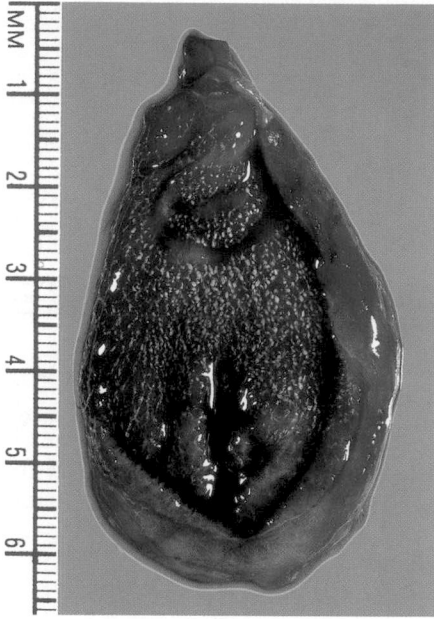

Fig. 14.7 Cholesterosis of gallbladder. (Reproduced with permission from RA Cooke and taken from, Colour Atlas of Anatomical Pathology, 3E, published by Churchill Livingstone.)

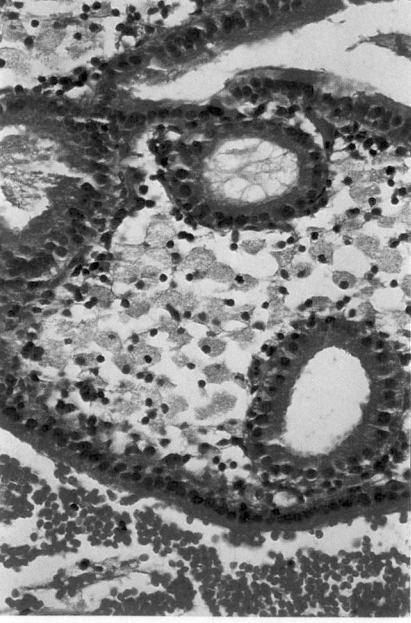

Fig. 14.8 Microscopic appearance of cholesterosis of gallbladder. Foamy macrophages are seen in the stroma separating the glands.

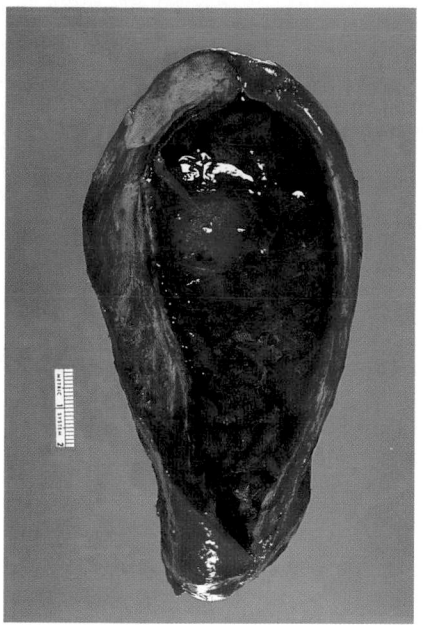
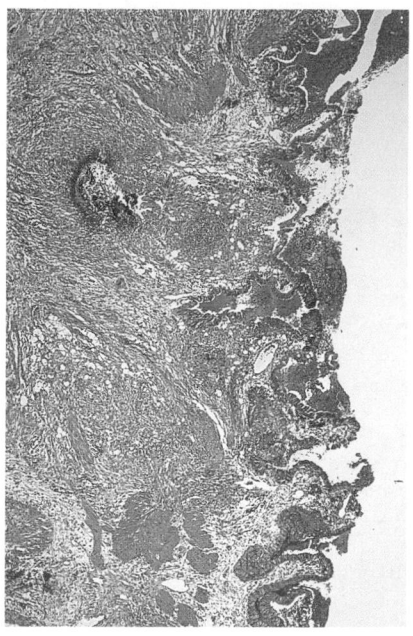
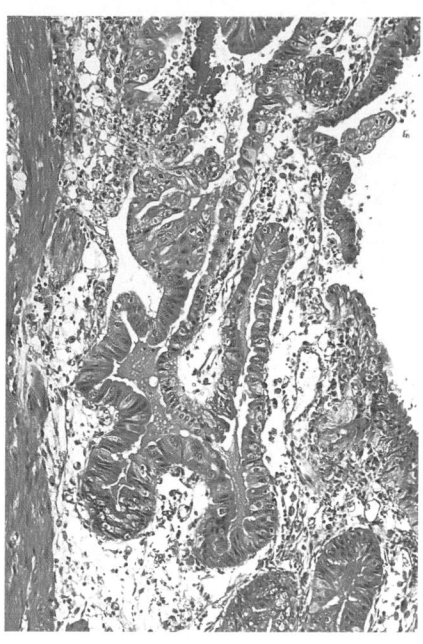

A　　　　　　　　　　B　　　　　　　　　　C

Fig. 14.9 A, Acute cholecystitis superimposed on a chronically inflamed gallbladder. The mucosa has a characteristic "angry red" color. Note the marked edema of the wall and the serosal hyperemia. **B,** Acute cholecystitis showing extensive ulceration, hemorrhage, and edema but only scanty inflammation. **C,** Reactive epithelial atypia associated with acute cholecystitis. This change should not be overdiagnosed as dysplasia or carcinoma in situ.

peritonitis, a condition associated with an ominous prognosis.[80]

Free perforation into the peritoneal cavity has become a relatively rare occurrence because of surgeons' awareness of importance of an operation promptly after onset of symptoms of gallbladder disease. In one oft-quoted study,[86] half of 140 patients with acute cholecystitis had early operation (within 24 hours), whereas the remaining had delayed operation (2 months later). The patients in the latter group had more protracted fever, longer hospital stay, and greater loss of time from work. The cholecystectomy is being increasingly done through a laparoscopic route.[85,89]

Bacterial invasion in acute calculous cholecystitis is usually a secondary event. If the organisms are of the gas-forming type, the condition known as *emphysematous* or *acute gaseous cholecystitis* may result[69]; this complication is particularly common in diabetics.

Acute acalculous cholecystitis accounts for about 5% of all cases of acute cholecystitis and a higher proportion of cases in children.[72,74,76] It may follow systemic infections such as hemolytic streptococcal septicemia, or typhoid fever. Increasingly, cases of cytomegalovirus (CMV) acalculous cholecystitis in HIV-infected patients have been reported.[67,68,77] Cases of chemical acalculous cholecystitis have also been seen after open heart surgery, in bone marrow transplant recipients, and after the administration of hepatic arterial chemotherapy.[79,82,83]

Occasionally a gallbladder removed because of acute inflammation shows fibrinoid necrosis of the muscular arteries, indistinguishable from that seen in polyarteritis nodosa.[71,78] On follow-up, some of these patients develop evidence of a multisystem disorder, but others remain asymptomatic, indicating that the vascular changes are not always part of a systemic disease.[81]

Chronic cholecystitis and cholangitis

Chronic cholecystitis is rarely seen in the absence of lithiasis, although pure stones of the cholesterol and calcium bilirubinate types may be present without inflammation. Thickening of the wall is always present, sometimes to a striking degree. Occasionally this is associated with diffuse calcification, a condition known as "porcelain gallbladder". In most instances, stones are of the mixed or combined type (see Fig. 14.4). Ulceration of the mucosa may result from pressure by the stones.

Microscopically, the mucosa of a chronically inflamed gallbladder shows varying degrees of mononuclear infiltration and fibrosis (Figs 14.4). The epithelium may be relatively normal or atrophic or show hyperplastic and metaplastic changes.[102]† The metaplasia can be of goblet cell ("intestinal") or pyloric ("antral") type, the former being accompanied by the appearance of Paneth cells and endocrine cells (Fig. 14.10).[114,134] In contrast to the normal glands in the gallbladder neck, the cells of metaplastic glands contain nonsulfated acid mucin and neutral mucin but little sulfated acid mucin.[106] The endocrine cells can exhibit immunocytochemical

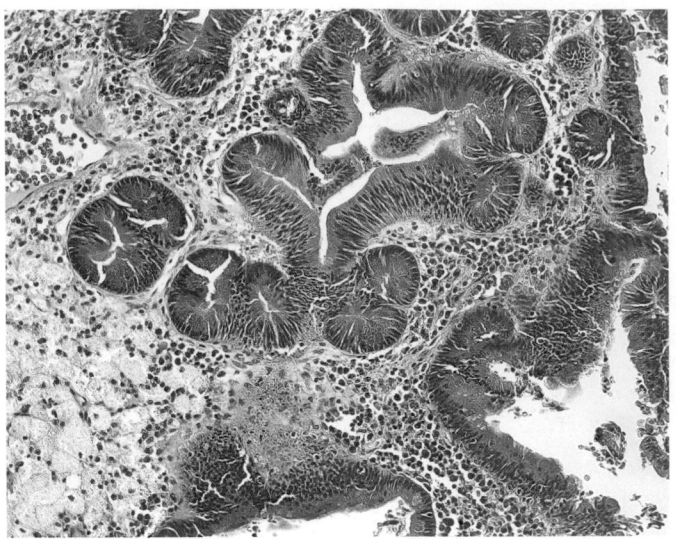

Fig. 14.10 Intestinal metaplasia of gallbladder with numerous Paneth cells.

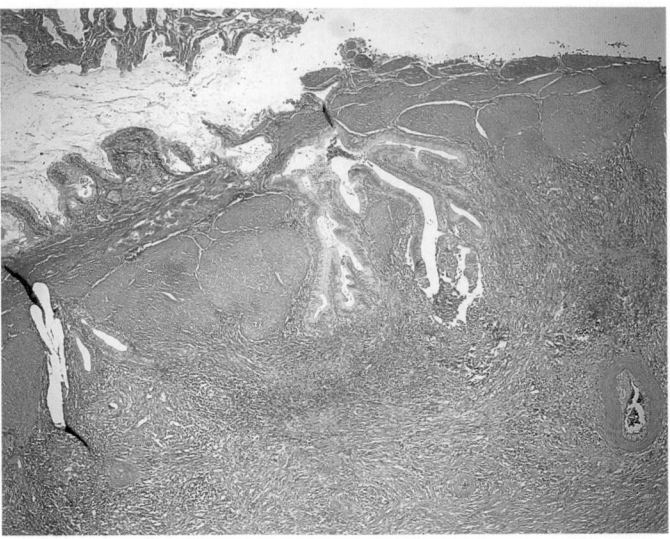

Fig. 14.11 Rokitansky–Aschoff sinus associated with hyperplasia of the muscle wall. Exaggerated examples of this phenomenon are designated as adenomyomatosis.

reactivity for serotonin, somatostatin, cholecystokinin, gastrin, and pancreatic polypeptide.[92] The incidence of these metaplastic changes increases steadily with age.[112]

The gallbladder wall may show fibrosis, muscle hypertrophy, encrusted stones, or nodular collections of foamy macrophages. Irregularly shaped tubular structures are present within the wall in over half of cases. They are lined by columnar or cuboidal epithelium and may contain bile or stones. These tubular structures, traditionally known as *Rokitansky–Aschoff* sinuses, are thought to represent herniations or diverticula resulting from increased intraluminal pressure.[101] Similar but smaller tubular formations are sometimes found in the subserosal layer (usually on the hepatic side) and are known as *Luschka's ducts*.[129] Some authors believe that they have a similar origin, but that their communication with the lumen has been cut off so that they have become cysts with bud-like branches.[129] Others believe them to be embryonic remnants because of their lack of communication with Rokitansky–Aschoff sinuses, the fact that sometimes they have been found to communicate with intrahepatic bile ducts, and the occasional presence of small foci of hepatic parenchyma adjacent to them.

Exaggerated examples of gallbladder diverticulosis associated with muscular hypertrophy have been dignified with the impressive but inaccurate names of *adenomyoma* (when focal) and *adenomyomatosis* (when diffuse).[111] The localized form may involve any segment of the organ but in most cases is located in the fundus (especially if inverted, see p. 1037), where it results in a sharply circumscribed lesion[94] (Figs 14.11 and 14.12).

The occurrence of intra- and perineural invasion in gallbladders affected by chronic cholecystitis with pyloric gland metaplasia has been reported, thus adding the gallbladder to the increasing list of organs in which

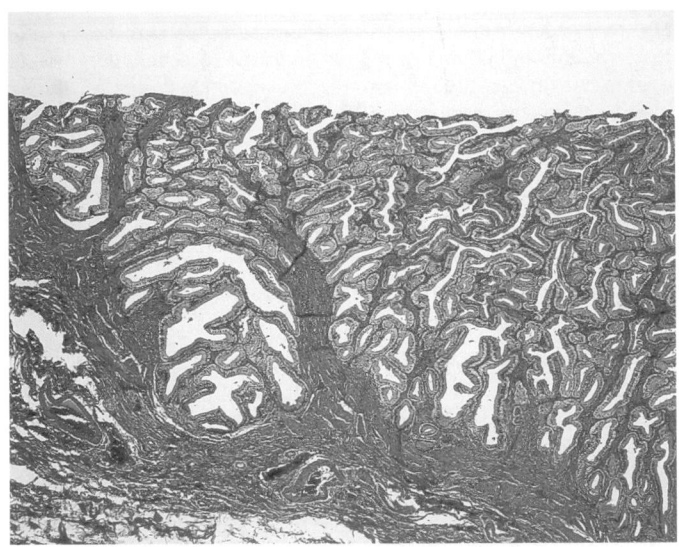

Fig. 14.12 Adenomyomatosis of gallbladder. In this area the proliferative change is mainly of the mucosal glandular component.

this phenomenon can occur in the absence of malignant disease.[91]

Several morphologic variants of chronic cholecystitis have been described. *Follicular cholecystitis* is characterized by widespread formation of lymphoid follicles in all layers of the gallbladder.[103] *Diffuse lymphoplasmacytic cholecystitis* has been described in association with primary sclerosing cholangitis,[110] but it is not specific for it[90a] (see below). *Eosinophilic cholecystitis* (which is usually acalculous) shows a massive outpouring of mature eosinophils.[98,136] *Xanthogranulomatous cholecystitis*,[105,107] *cholecystic granuloma*,[108] and *ceroid granuloma*[93] refer to the presence in the wall of diffuse or nodular collections of macrophages containing neutral fat and lipofuscin (ceroid) pigment. Some of these lesions are probably the result of the rupture of Rokitansky–Aschoff sinuses. Antigens directed against *E. coli* have been identified immunohistochemically, suggesting an infectious etiology.[123] A few of the reported cases have been associated with gallbladder adenocarcinoma.[117] *Malakoplakia* may rarely involve the gallbladder; it is identified by the presence of calcium- and iron-positive Michaelis–Gutmann bodies in the cytoplasm of histiocytes.[97]

Other rare inflammatory gallbladder diseases include *schistosomiasis*,[128] *amebiasis*,[136] and *Crohn's disease*.[122,126] CMV acalculous cholecystitis was mentioned on p. 1041.

It has often been argued that all gallbladders containing stones should be removed surgically because of the risk of cancer, this risk being greater than the operative mortality. This argument lacks validity, since the incidence of carcinoma in gallbladders with lithiasis is less than 1%.[99] A more valid reason for removing gallbladders containing stones relates to the serious inflammatory and obstructive complications that may arise from them.[137] Lund[120] followed 526 nonoperated cases of cholelithiasis and found that one third to one half of the patients subsequently developed severe symptoms or complications from the disease; he therefore concluded that prophylactic removal of the gallbladder containing stones is indicated in all patients who are good surgical risks. Similar conclusions were drawn in the National Cooperative Gallstone Study, which involved 305 patients.[132]

Gallstones may lead to **internal biliary fistulas**.[90] Over 90% of these fistulas are located between the gallbladder and the duodenum, the gallbladder and the colon, or the common bile duct and the duodenum. These fistulas are created by the formation of inflammatory adhesions between the biliary tree and adjacent organs and the subsequent erosion of a stone through the gallbladder or the common duct into the gastrointestinal tract. Continuing choledochal obstruction contributes to the persistence of the fistula. Biliary fistulas may become evident by the patient vomiting or passing per rectum a large gallstone, by detecting air in the biliary tree in a plain abdominal roentgenogram, or by seeing the outline of the biliary tree in an upper gastrointestinal series or a barium enema. With cholecystocolic fistulas, infection is often severe. Repair of these fistulas requires cholecystectomy and closure or resection of the involved portion of bowel.

Strictures of the common duct are usually caused by surgical trauma in which the duct is inadvertently injured or ligated.[113] Anatomic variations of the ducts and blood vessels are often responsible for this complication.

The goal of therapy is to establish a wide, tension-free anastomosis between the normal portion of the bile duct and the bowel, with mucosa-to-mucosa apposition. This is usually accomplished by an end-to-end choledochoduodenostomy or a Roux-en-Y hepaticojejunostomy.[125,135]

Cholangitis may be seen in conjunction with calculous cholecystitis, secondarily to stone impaction in the duct. Chronically inflamed extrahepatic bile ducts may show metaplastic changes in the mucosa analogous to those more commonly seen in the gallbladder, i.e., pyloric, intestinal and squamous.[109]

Sclerosing cholangitis is a relatively rare disorder of unknown etiology characterized by diffuse thickening of the wall, which, if severe enough, will lead to obstruction of the lumen.[95,121,138] Microscopically, there are dense fibrosis, a sparse mixed inflammatory infiltrate (sometimes containing eosinophils), and a relatively intact epithelium.[115] The most typical microscopic changes seen in the early stages of the disease are not in the extrahepatic bile ducts but in the liver biopsy and are characterized by a fibrous obliterative cholangitis leading to replacement of duct segments by solid cords of connective tissue and eventually to complete loss of bile ducts.[115,118] Sometimes the disease is associated with diffuse lymphoplasmacytic cholecystitis, but the latter is not a specific marker for it.[90a]

Sclerosing cholangitis shows a striking association with HLA-DRw52a antigen; in one series, this haplotype was present in 100% of the patients, whereas it occurs in only 35% of the population.[127] Sclerosing cholangitis has been reported in association with Riedel's thyroiditis, retroperitoneal or mediastinal fibrosis, orbital pseudotumor, Crohn's disease, sclerosing pancreatitis, and, in particular, ulcerative colitis.[116,123a,124,130,133] In recent times, many cases have been documented in HIV-infected patients[104]; the mechanism is unknown but is suspected to be related to infectious pathogens such as CMV and cryptosporidia. Patients with primary sclerosing cholangitis associated with ulcerative colitis have a marked increase in the frequency of serum anticolon antibodies.[96] The possibility of sclerosing, well-differentiated adenocarcinoma should always be considered before making the diagnosis of sclerosing cholangitis. The relation between the two disorders is controversial, but we believe that sclerosing cholangitis may undergo dysplastic changes, which in turn may lead to the development of bile duct carcinoma (see p. 1049).[119] Some cases of sclerosing cholangitis have been found associated with gallbladder carcinoma.[100] In rare cases a metastatic tumor to the area may simulate a sclerosing cholangitis.[131]

Tumors

Benign tumors and tumorlike conditions

Cholesterol polyps are multilobular yellow formations composed of aggregates of foamy histiocytes in the lamina propria covered by an intact epithelium; they represent a morphologic variation in the theme of cholesterosis (see p. 1039).[159,162] *Inflammatory polyps* are always associated with chronic cholecystitis.[143] *Adenomatous hyperplasia* and the already mentioned *adenomyomatous hyperplasia* (see p. 1042) are also reactive mucosal changes secondary to inflammation and/or lithiasis.[143] *Villous papillomas* of the gallbladder (not to be confused with villous adenomas) have been seen in infants and adults with metachromatic leukodystrophy and may result in massive hemobilia.[141,157] *Adenomas* resemble their homologues in the gastrointestinal tract; they may be sessile or pedunculated and can exhibit tubular, tubulovillous (tubulopapillary), or villous (papillary) patterns of growth.[140,154] Squamoid spindle cell metaplasia ("morules") may be found focally in them.[152] Most tubular adenomas are composed of pyloric-type gland, but others resemble those found in the large bowel. Some degree of atypia is often present (particularly in the latter), and a few will show changes of carcinoma in situ or focal invasive carcinoma. As in the colorectum, the larger the adenoma, the more likely that an area of malignant change will be found.[147] However, on the whole they do not seem to represent an important precursor of gallbladder carcinoma (see next section). Estrogen receptors have been detected in over half of adenomas and have been interpreted as a manifestation of a metaplastic change in the mucosa.[161]

Paragangliomas arise from small paraganglia known to occur in the gallbladder serosa.[150] *Granular cell tumors* present as small nodules in the gallbladder wall, sometimes in association with similar lesions in the extrahepatic biliary tree.[160]

Benign tumors of the extrahepatic bile duct are exceptional. Those of epithelial nature have been designated as *adenomas, cystadenomas,* and *papillomas,* depending on their configuration.[139,146,155] The cystadenomas resemble their pancreatic counterpart in the sense that the epithelium is often surrounded by a cellular spindle cell mesenchymal component resembling ovarian stroma.[158] *Multiple papillomas* (papillomatosis) may involve extensive portions of the extrahepatic bile duct system; they have a tendency to recur and to undergo malignant transformation.[149,151] *Granular cell tumors* may occur anywhere along the intrahepatic and extrahepatic biliary system[142,144] (Fig. 14.13). As in other sites, they may be associated with pseudocarcinomatous changes of the overlying epithelium.[144] *Traumatic neuromas* occur most often after operations in the area[145]; their most common site is the stump of the cystic duct following a cholecystectomy. They may cause postcholecystectomy pain or obstructive jaundice.[148] Some cases have occurred in the gallbladder and/or in the absence of previous surgery, perhaps as an expression of a hyperplastic reactive change.[153] There are also isolated cases of *neurofibroma* involving the common bile duct.[156]

Carcinoma of gallbladder

General and clinical features

Carcinoma of the gallbladder is more frequent in females than males (3 to 4:1 ratio); over 90% of the patients are 50 years of age or older at the time of diagnosis.[167] It is more common in some Latin American countries than in the United States.[164,170] In this country, there is a concentration of cases in the South-west, North Central, and Appalachian regions.[166] The incidence is high in American Indians, relatively low in whites of European

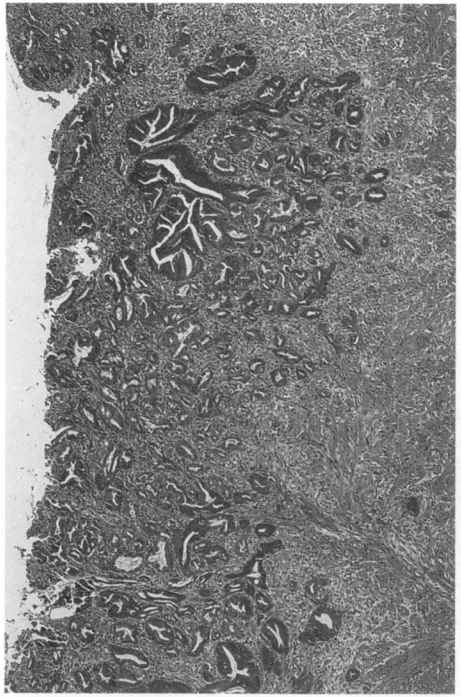

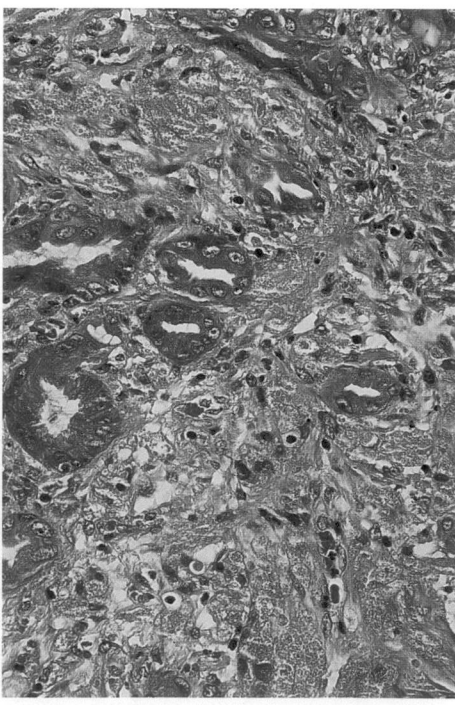

A   B

Fig. 14.13 A and **B**, Granular cell tumor of common bile duct associated with hyperplasia of the overlying epithelium. (Courtesy of Dr. Richard Eisen, New Haven, CT)

extraction, and very rare in blacks. In Europe, the rate is very high in Germany and surrounding central countries, low in Mediterranean countries, and low and declining in Britain and Ireland.[175]

A definite epidemiologic parallel exists between gallbladder carcinoma and cholelithiasis, but the pathogenetic relationship between them remains obscure. In the non-Indian, non-Hispanic population of the United States, the incidence of carcinoma in gallbladders with lithiasis is less than 1%.[170]

Other conditions associated with an increased risk of gallbladder carcinoma are cholecystoenteric fistula, porcelain gallbladder, ulcerative colitis, adenomyomatosis,[169,172] polyposis coli,[163] Gardner's syndrome,[174] and anomalous connection between the common bile duct and the pancreatic duct.[165,168,171] Many of the latter cases present at an advanced stage.[173] The most common clinical manifestations of gallbladder carcinoma are right upper quadrant abdominal pain and anorexia, and the most common abnormal laboratory finding is elevated alkaline phosphatase levels.

Gross features

Grossly, gallbladder carcinoma may present as a diffusely growing (70%) or polypoid (30%) mass[176] (Figs 14.14 and 14.15). When diffuse, the gross distinction from chronic cholecystitis may be difficult. Gallbladders with carcinomas usually also contain calculi (80% to 90% of the cases) and exhibit marked fibrosis of the wall. The latter may represent a reaction to the tumor or the expression of a preexisting chronic cholecystitis. The fact that some gallbladder carcinomas are not obvious on gross examination indicates the need for microscopic

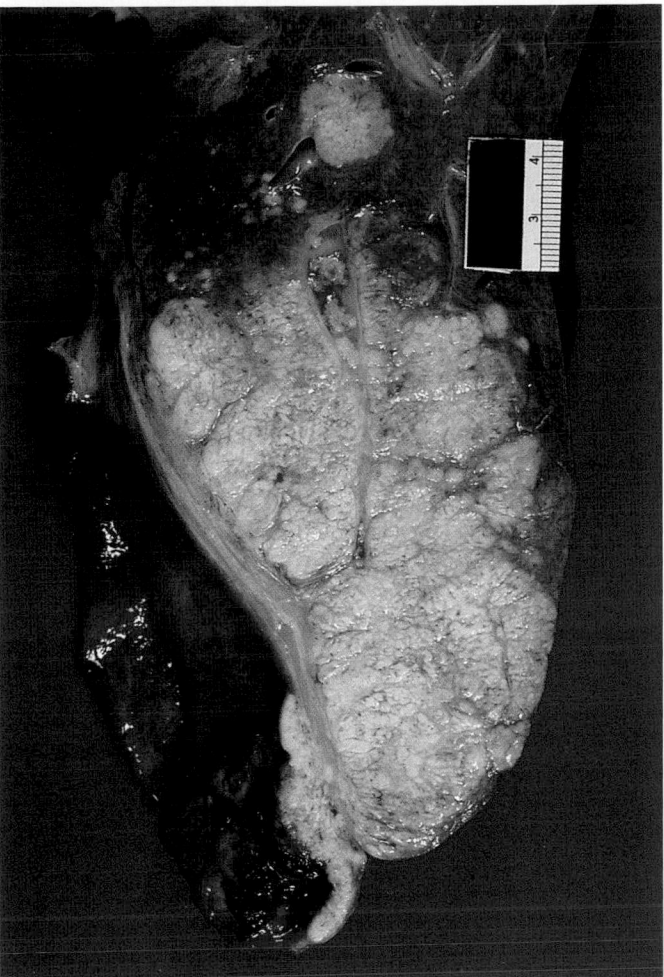

Fig. 14.15 Adenocarcinoma growing in diffuse fashion in the distal wall of the gallbladder, associated with extensive involvement of the liver. It was interpreted as being primary in the gallbladder.

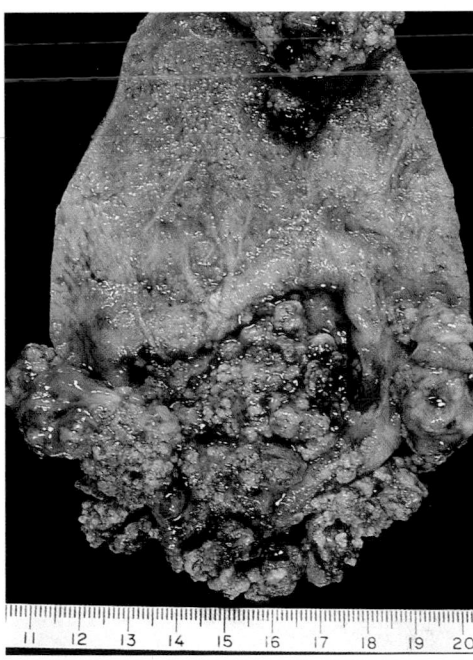

Fig. 14.14 Adenocarcinoma of the gallbladder having a predominantly papillary configuration.

examination of every excised gallbladder. We have seen several patients in whom an unexpected metastatic tumor was found in the liver some time after the removal of a gallbladder thought to have only lithiasis and inflammation on gross examination by the surgeon and therefore discarded.

Microscopic features

Microscopically, most gallbladder cancers are adenocarcinomas showing varying degrees of differentiation (Figs 14.16 and 14.17). Many have a papillary surface, but they may also be deeply invasive. Most tumors have a morphologic appearance that is common to adenocarcinomas of the pancreatobiliary region—well-formed glands with wide lumina lined by one or a few rows of highly atypical cuboidal cells, surrounded by a cellular stroma often arranged concentrically.[181] It is characteristic for these glands to seem well differentiated at an architectural level but poorly differentiated at a cytologic level. Sometimes the adenocarcinoma extends to Rokitansky–Aschoff sinuses in a manner analogous to endometrial

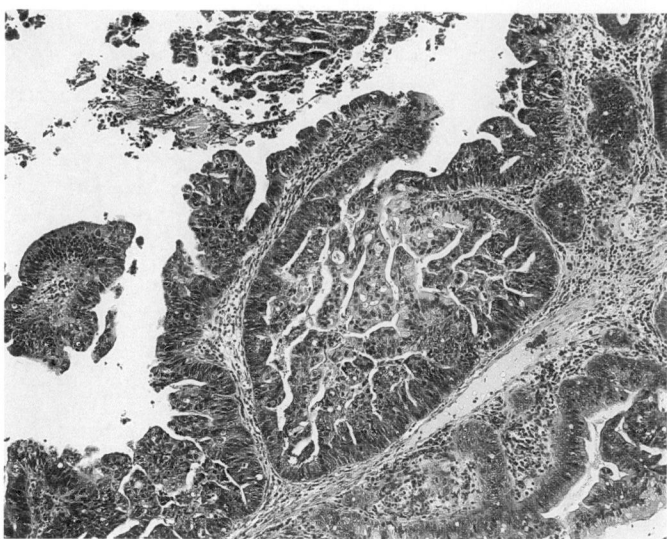

Fig. 14.16 Well-differentiated gallbladder adenocarcinoma.

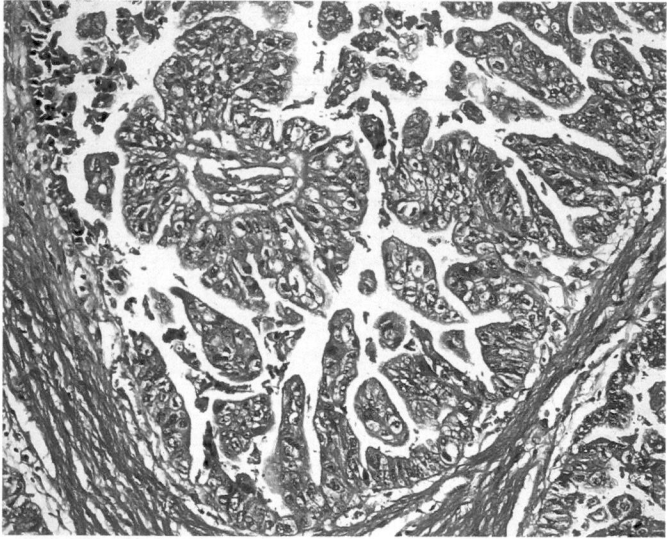

Fig. 14.17 Well-differentiated gallbladder adenocarcinoma with a papillary pattern of growth.

adenocarcinoma extending to foci of adenomyosis; it is important not to misinterpret this finding as a sign of deep infiltration by the tumor.[182] Evidence of perineural invasion is common (however, see p. 1042).

Foci of intestinal differentiation are common, with the appearance of goblet cells, endocrine cells, and even Paneth cells. Occasionally, the entire tumor is of intestinal type on morphologic, histochemical, and immunohistochemical grounds.[178,180] In other instances the differentiation or metaplasia proceeds along gastric foveolar and mucopeptic lines.[179] Sometimes the pattern of growth of the tumor is predominantly cribriform.[177]

Histochemical, immunohistochemical & electron microscopic features

The mucin produced by gallbladder adenocarcinoma is variable in amount and typically of the sialomucin type,

in contrast to the predominantly sulfomucin type secreted by the normal, inflamed, or obstructed gallbladder.[185,187,190]

Keratin immunostains are strongly positive.[183] The usual keratin profile for carcinoma of the gallbladder and extrahepatic bile ducts is CK7+/CK20+, whereas peripheral (intrahepatic) cholangiocarcinoma is usually CK7+/CK20–.[184,188]

Other markers found in gallbladder adenocarcinoma are EMA, CEA, and, exceptionally, alpha-fetoprotein.[189]

Ultrastructurally, the adenocarcinoma cells show pleomorphic microvilli, mucin vacuoles, and abundant lysosomes.[186]

Molecular genetic features

Overexpression of p53 has been found in approximately half of gallbladder carcinomas.[197,200] It is more common in high-grade tumors,[194,198,198a] and apparently more common than in adenocarcinomas of the extrahepatic bile duct,[199] especially those of the proximal portion of the system.[191,199]

K-ras mutations also occur[195]; they were detected by Itoi et al.[193] in biopsy specimens and bile in about half of the cases of biliary tract cancer, an intriguing result in terms of its possible diagnostic applications. Telomerase is usually highly activated,[196] whereas the FHIT gene is often inactivated.[199a] There is no overexpression of bcl-2.[192]

Other microscopic types

Adenocarcinomas of the gallbladder may exhibit varying degrees of squamous metaplasia; terms such as *adenoacanthoma* and *adenosquamous carcinoma* have been used for them, depending on whether the squamous component was, respectively, well or poorly differentiated[224] (Fig. 14.18). Pure *squamous cell carcinomas* are exceptional.[217] *Clear cell* and *signet ring* variants of adenocarcinoma have also been described, some of the latter being in situ.[203,226]

Lymphoepithelioma-like carcinoma can be seen in the gallbladder or extrahepatic bile ducts; some of the cases were associated with Epstein–Barr virus but others were not.[215,218,225]

Undifferentiated (anaplastic, pleomorphic, spindle, sarcomatoid) carcinomas occur in various morphologic presentations (giant cell, spindle cell, pseudoangiosarcomatous), many of them closely simulating sarcomas.[201–203,205,209,210,222] The tumors in which the carcinomatous and sarcoma-like components segregate in a biphasic pattern and/or show differentiation toward a specific mesenchymal line (i.e., rhabdomyoblastic)[213] have also been called malignant mixed tumor and carcinosarcoma,[212,227] but most evidence suggests that the sarcoma-like component is also of epithelial derivation (Fig. 14.19). In exceptional cases, gallbladder adenocarcinomas or adenosquamous carcinomas have a component of osteoclast-like giant cells, similar to those seen more

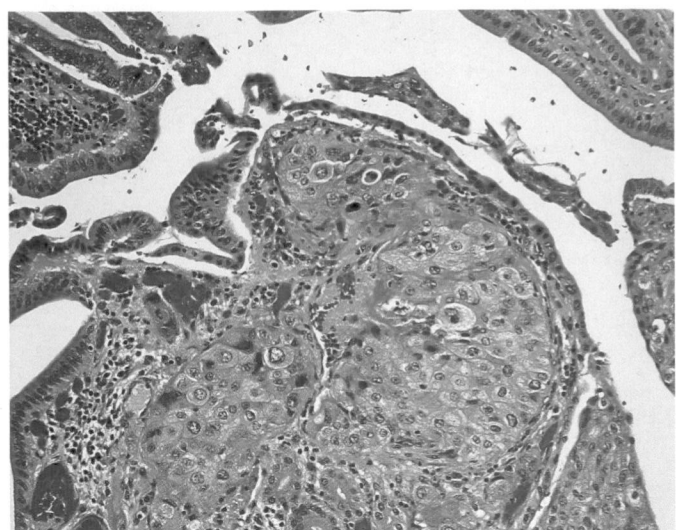

Fig. 14.18 Adenosquamous carcinoma of gallbladder growing beneath atrophic residual mucosa. In this area only the squamous component of the tumor is evident.

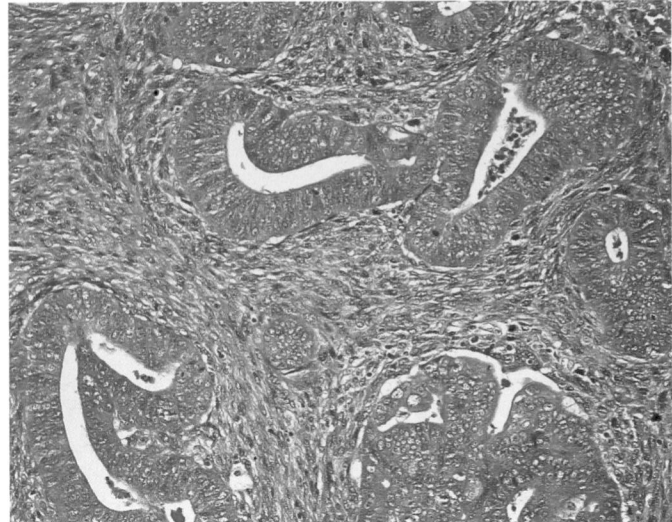

Fig. 14.19 Sarcomatoid carcinoma of gallbladder. In cases like this, in which there is a sharp segregation of the carcinomatous and sarcoma-like components, the term carcinosarcoma is often used.

often in pancreatic adenocarcinoma.[208,214] Others are accompanied by a heavy neutrophilic infiltrate, due to the production of granulocyte colony-stimulating factor, resulting in an inflammatory MFH-like appearance.[217]

Some gallbladder adenocarcinomas have *choriocarcinoma-like areas*.[201] *Small cell neuroendocrine carcinoma* is a high-grade neoplasm morphologically analogous to the homonymous tumor in the lung and other sites.[202,216,220] Ultrastructurally, dense core secretory granules can be found. Virtually all cases of small cell carcinoma inactivate the p16/pRB pathway, usually by retinoblastoma

protein loss.[223a] This is a highly aggressive neoplasm, which metastasizes early and causes death shortly after diagnosis.[204] As in other organs, neuroendocrine differentiation in gallbladder carcinoma may manifest in several other ways: as a large cell neuroendocrine carcinoma,[223] as an immunohistochemical or ultrastructural finding in a tumor with the morphologic features of ordinary adenocarcinoma, or as one of the components of a biphasic tumor having elsewhere the appearance of an adenocarcinoma (Fig. 14.20). Depending on the features of the neuroendocrine component and the bias of the

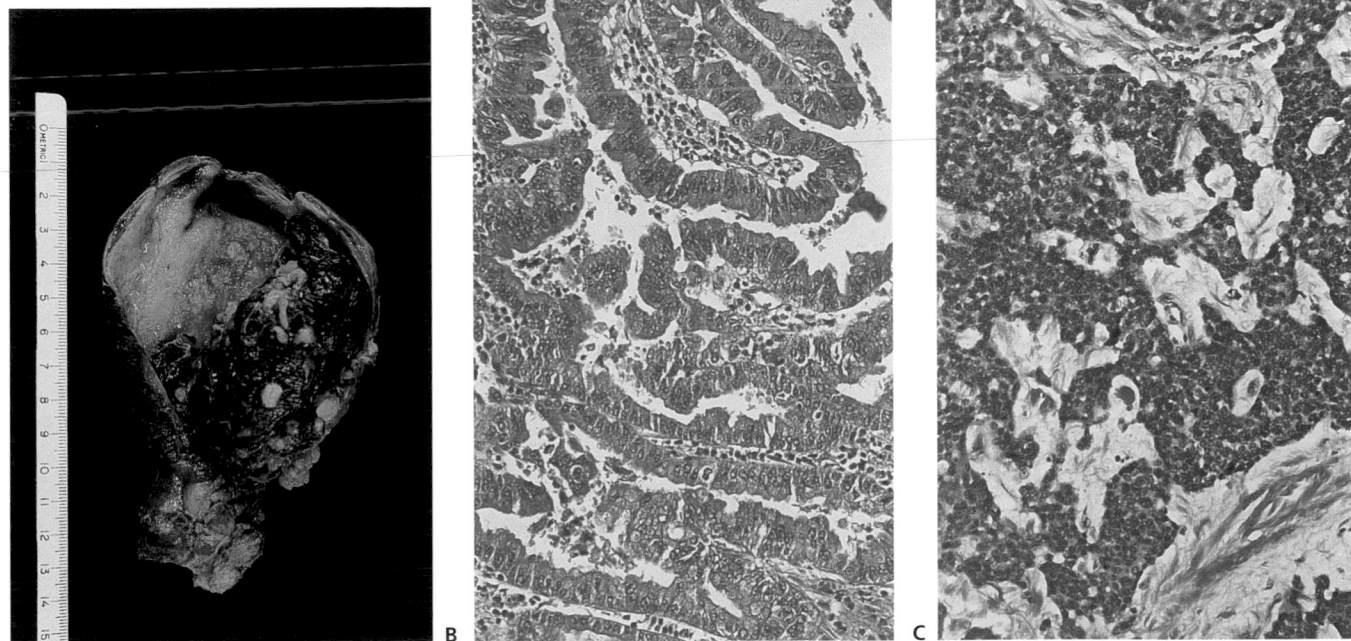

Fig. 14.20 Mixed adenocarcinoma–small cell carcinoma of gallbladder. **A,** Gross appearance showing massive involvement of the gallbladder by tumor. **B,** Well-differentiated adenocarcinomatous component. **C,** Small cell component. This was strongly reactive with the Grimelius stain, and it contained neurosecretory granules on ultrastructural examination.

observer, this combined tumor has been variously designated small cell neuroendocrine carcinoma– adenocarcinoma, adenocarcinoid tumor, and combined endocrine cell carcinoma–adenocarcinoma.[206,211,219,221] Pure carcinoid tumor of the gallbladder is discussed on p. 1050.

Dysplasia and carcinoma in situ

As in the stomach, it is believed that most cases of gallbladder adenocarcinoma are preceded by a sequence of intestinal metaplasia, dysplasia (atypical hyperplasia), and carcinoma in situ[228,229,231,233,234,237] (Figs 14.21 and 14.22). Instead, only a minority of the cases arise from malignant transformation of adenomas, a fact supported by the observation that beta-catenin mutations and other molecular abnormalities found in the latter are different from those of adenocarcinoma.[231a,236] Intestinal metaplasia is a very common finding in the gallbladder mucosa adjacent to an invasive adenocarcinoma. In a study done in Mexico City (a place with a very high incidence of gallbladder carcinoma), lesions interpreted as carcinoma in situ were found in the mucosa adjacent to invasive carcinoma in 79% of 39 cases.[228] Also, mucosal lesions interpreted as atypical hyperplasia and carcinoma in situ were observed in 13.5% and 3.5%, respectively, of 200 consecutive specimens of cholecystectomy performed for cholelithiasis or cholecystitis. In a subsequent study from the same group, 18 cases of carcinoma in situ were reported.[229] Grossly, the lesions could not be distinguished from chronic cholecystitis. Two of the tumors had a papillary configuration, and four exhibited beginning invasion of the underlying lamina propria (i.e., they had become microinvasive carcinomas). One of these four patients died with liver metastases; the others were cured by cholecystectomy.

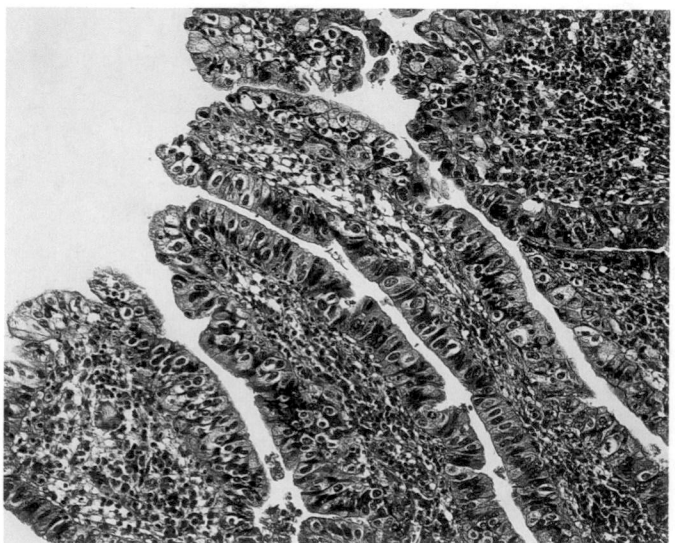

Fig. 14.21 Severe dysplasia of gallbladder with a villous pattern of growth.

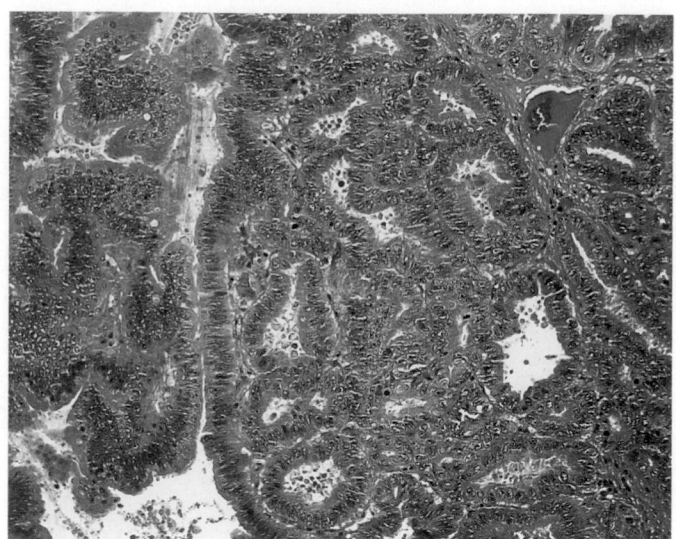

Fig. 14.22 Area of severe dysplasia/carcinoma in situ in the gallbladder mucosa.

The mucin phenotype of dysplastic gallbladder mucosa is both of intestinal and gastric type (whereas the gastric surface phenotype predominates in invasive carcinoma).[235]

The pattern of CEA distribution is similar to that of other mucosae in the digestive tract; whereas in the normal epithelium it is limited to the apical surface, in dysplasias and carcinomas it is abundantly present both in the cytoplasm and the lumen.[230] Overexpression of p53 and LOH in 5q have been found in gallbladder dysplasia, suggesting that they represent early events in the evolution of gallbladder carcinoma.[232,234] Whenever an invasive carcinoma is present, the in situ component usually harbors the same genetic alterations as the former.[234a]

Spread and metastases

Gallbladder carcinoma has a great propensity to invade the liver directly and to a lesser extent the stomach and duodenum; it also metastasizes frequently to liver (often through the portal tracts), cystic and pericholedochal lymph nodes in the lesser omentum, and lymph nodes behind the first portion of the duodenum.[238,240,242] The frequency of lymph node involvement is highly dependent on the depth of invasion of the primary tumor.[243] Almost half of the patients already have metastatic disease at the time of surgery.[239] Ovarian metastases from carcinoma of the gallbladder may simulate primary tumors of the ovary.[241,244]

Treatment and prognosis

The treatment of gallbladder carcinoma is primarily surgical, its extent depending on the stage of the disease (see Appendix C). Nevin et al.[252] recommend cholecystectomy alone for stages I and II, radical surgery (including right hepatic lobectomy and lymphadenectomy) for stages III and IV, and palliation alone for stage V. Other authors have recommended a more aggressive approach for stage II disease because of the high incidence of locoregional disease after cholecystectomy alone.[253,259,263] The importance of a systematic dissection of the various lymph node groups has been emphasized.[258] It has been claimed that the addition of adjuvant chemotherapy or radiation therapy in patients treated surgically lengthens the survival time.[251]

Factors that have been evaluated as possible predictors of prognosis in gallbladder carcinoma are the following:

1 **Stage**. As in most other organs, the stage of the tumor is the most important prognostic determinant.[252,254] The 5-year survival rate is over 90% for stages I and II, 11% for stages III and IV, and zero for stage V.[252] By the time the diagnosis of carcinoma of the gallbladder can be made clinically, the tumor is advanced and usually inoperable (stage V).[249,255] Under such circumstances, the chances of cure—even after heroic surgical measures—are minimal.[261] Even when the carcinoma becomes apparent to the surgeon at the time of exploration of the gallbladder for chronic cholecystitis and/or cholelithiasis, it is often incurable because of its tendency to spread through the wall of the gallbladder and its propensity to invade the liver, pericolic tissues, and lymph nodes and even infiltrate the duodenum. In a series of 80 cases, there was only one long-term survivor.[247] The best possibility of cure is when the cancer is found incidentally by the pathologist on gross or microscopic examination.[246] Most such cases are stage I or II disease.

2 **Surgical margins**. This factor, which is obviously related to the stage of the disease, was found in one series to be the main determinant of prognosis in early stage disease.[260]

3 **Grading**. Histologic grading has been found to be related to prognosis in several series.[245,248,252] As expected, well-differentiated papillary tumors have the most favorable prognosis.[245] The combination of staging and microscopic grading seems to offer the best prognostic evaluation in gallbladder carcinoma.[252]

4 **DNA content**. The value of DNA content as an independent prognostic marker in gallbladder carcinoma remains to be demonstrated.[256,257]

5 **K-Ras**. The claim has been made that the presence of K-Ras codon 12 mutations is an independent prognostic factor in these tumors.[250]

6 **c-erbB-2 oncogene**. Neither amplification of this gene nor overexpression of the corresponding protein product seems to correlate with prognosis, microscopic grade, or lymph node metastases.[262]

7 **Angiogenesis**. It has been claimed that angiogenesis or their surrogate markers (such as thymidine phasphorylase expression) correlate with prognosis in multivariate analysis.[246a]

Carcinoma of extrahepatic bile ducts

Bile duct carcinoma (cholangiocarcinoma) occurs with equal frequency in males and females[299] (in contrast with the female predominance for gallbladder carcinoma); the average age of presentation is 60 years. About 90% of patients present with jaundice. An increased incidence of this disease has been reported in patients with ulcerative colitis,[264,297] sclerosing cholangitis (see p. 1043), *Clonorchis sinensis* infestation,[299] and in a variety of congenital abnormalities of the intrahepatic and extrahepatic bile ducts, such as congenital dilatation of the bile duct (including choledochal cyst), Caroli's disease, congenital hepatic fibrosis, polycystic disease, and abnormal pancreaticocholedochal junction.[278,298,300]

These tumors can develop at any level of the biliary tree. They have been divided anatomically into those of the upper third, including the hilum (50% to 75%); those of the middle third (10% to 25%); and those of the lower third (10% to 20%).[267,295,307] A more refined anatomic classification is that proposed by Bismuth, nicely illustrated in the review by de Groen[274]: *type I*: below the confluence of the left and right hepatic ducts; *type II*: reaching the confluence; *type III*: occluding the common hepatic duct and either the right (*type IIIa*) or left (*type IIIb*) hepatic duct; *type IV*: multicentric or involving the confluence and both the right and left hepatic ducts. Tumors arising from the intrahepatic bile ducts are discussed in Chapter 14 and those located in the ampulla of Vater in Chapter 16. The presence and location of these tumors are best shown by retrograde endoscopic cholangiography or percutaneous transhepatic cholangiography. Using the latter technique, Elias et al.[276] demonstrated the site of the extrahepatic obstruction in 95% of cases. Cytologic procedures (fine needle aspiration, brushing, or bile aspiration) yield diagnostic material in about 70% of cases.[270,275]

Grossly, bile duct carcinomas can be polypoid and superficial, but most are nodular or sclerosing, with deep

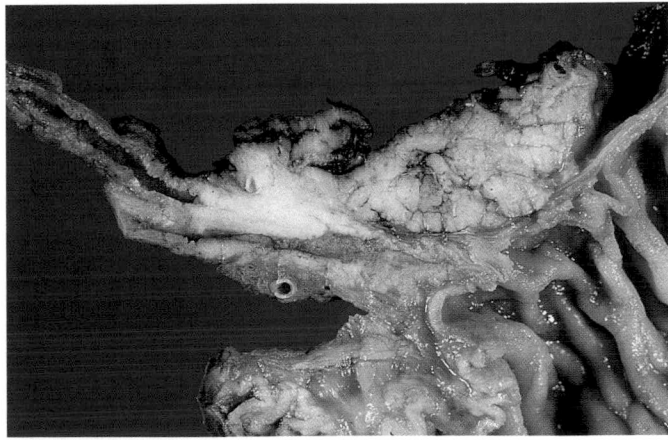

Fig. 14.23 Gross appearance of carcinoma of extrahepatic bile ducts. The tumor extends from the junction of the cystic and hepatic ducts to the ampulla of Vater.

penetration into the wall[306] (Fig. 14.23). Occasionally, they are multicentric and/or associated with carcinoma of the gallbladder.[287] Direct extension to the liver is common in upper third lesions.[272,279] Metastases to regional and peripancreatic nodes are also frequent; the lymph node groups most commonly affected are those around the lower portion of the hepatoduodenal ligament, the superoposterior pancreaticoduodenal group, and the superior mesenteric artery group.[283]

Microscopically, the large majority of bile duct malignancies are well-differentiated, mucin-secreting adenocarcinomas.[306] A papillary surface may be seen in the more distal lesions. Sometimes the entire tumor is a well-differentiated papillary adenocarcinoma with minimal or no invasion.[266] The tumors can be so well differentiated— even in metastatic sites—that their identification as malignant is very difficult. Heterogeneity of cells within the same gland, increased nucleocytoplasmic ratio, nucleolar prominence, stromal and *perineurial* invasion, and concentric layering of cellular stroma around the neoplastic glands are the most important identifying features (Fig. 14.24). As Weinbren and Mutum have emphasized,[306] the juxtaposition of normal-appearing cells with cells having large nuclei with prominent nucleoli is a particularly important diagnostic clue. Clusters of small acini, normally present in the wall and known as periluminal sacculi of Beale, should not be misinterpreted as invasive carcinoma.

In addition to these morphologic features, bile duct carcinoma resembles gallbladder carcinoma in its expression of mucosubstances and CEA,[291,293,306] common detection of metaplastic and dysplastic changes in the adjacent epithelium,[288] and the occasional occurrence of variants with squamous metaplasia,[286] clear cell changes,[304] or neuroendocrine features[294,308] (including small cell neuroendocrine carcinoma).[303] A type of extremely well differentiated adenocarcinoma featuring gastric foveolar type epithelium and simulating adenoma has been described.[265]

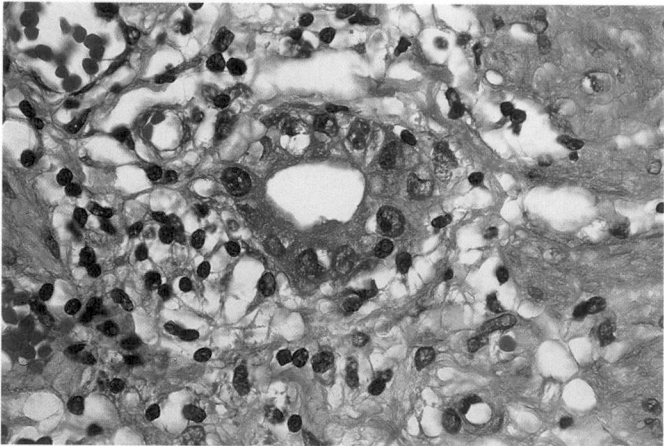

Fig. 14.24 Single neoplastic gland from gallbladder adenocarcinoma. The gland is architecturally well formed but the nuclear atypia is marked. This discrepancy is typical of tumors of this region.

A somewhat distinct variant of bile duct carcinoma is *sclerosing carcinoma* (Altemeier–Klatskin's tumor).[268,284] It begins at the hepatic duct junction and spreads from there to long segments of the biliary tree; it is characterized by a long clinical course and a well-differentiated microscopic appearance, associated with extensive fibrosis. The main differential diagnosis, both radiographically and pathologically, is with sclerosing cholangitis.[296] It is likely that some cases of sclerosing carcinomas actually arise in a background of sclerosing cholangitis and that this is the reason for the striking similarities between the two entities.[290,305] A lifetime risk of approximately 10% is mentioned in most studies of the subject.[274]

An interesting difference in the immunohistochemical overexpression of p53 (present in 94% of bile duct carcinomas but in none of the cases of primary sclerosing cholangitis) has been reported[271]; if independently confirmed, this finding could provide much needed help in the often difficult differential diagnosis between the two entities. Argani et al.[269] have shown that expression of p53 and *DPC4* (another tumor-suppressor gene) is significantly higher in distal than in proximal bile duct carcinoma. They conjectured that these differences reflect different pathways of carcinogenesis, which in turn suggest different etiologies.

Surgical resection offers the only possibility of cure for bile duct carcinoma.[289] Proximal lesions are treated with resection (which may include hepatic lobectomy) and Roux-en-Y hepaticojejunostomy; distal lesions are treated by the Whipple procedure.[282] Often only palliative treatment is warranted in the form of biliary drainage[273] or radiation therapy.[277] A modest improvement in the results has been obtained with a combined modality approach consisting of surgery, radiation therapy, and chemotherapy.[292] The overall survival rate is 10%. Stage of disease (particularly absence or presence of lymph node metastases), location (upper, middle, or lower third), histologic grade and histologic type are the most important prognostic indicators.[280,285] The survival for patients with tumor of the lower third is about 25%.[302] Among papillary tumors, separation of invasive from non-invasive/minimally invasive tumors is critical in predicting the patient's outcome.[280a] Carcinomas with exclusive or predominant neuroendocrine differentiation have a shorter survival time than those lacking this feature.[281] It has also been claimed that tumors associated with mucin core protein expression are associated with a higher incidence of liver metastases and poorer prognosis.[301]

Other malignant tumors

Carcinoid tumors of either insular or tubular types can occur in the gallbladder and extrahepatic bile ducts.[310,314,337] (Fig. 14.25). The latter can present with biliary obstruction.[313,326] One such tumor, located in the cystic duct, had the immunohistochemical features of

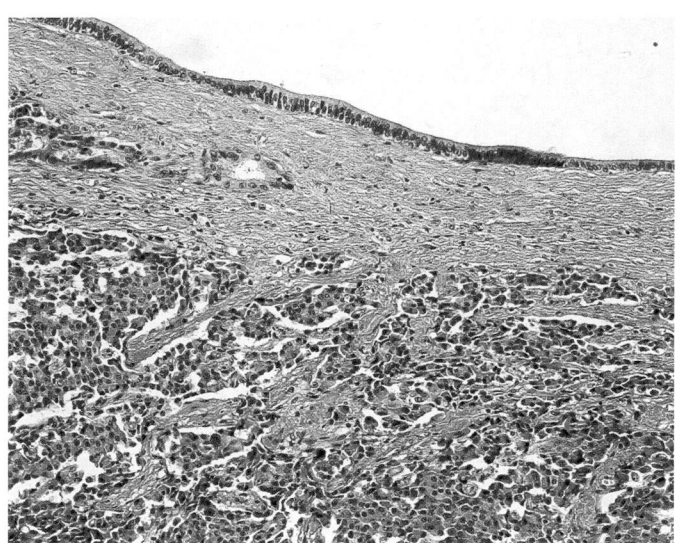

Fig. 14.25 Carcinoid tumor of gallbladder. The artifactual crushing may lead to overdiagnosis as a higher grade tumor.

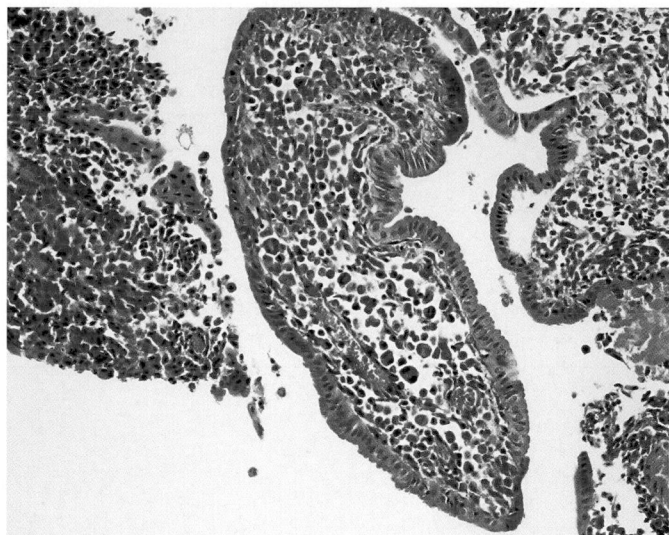

Fig. 14.27 Microscopic appearance of malignant melanoma metastatic to gallbladder mucosa.

somatostatinoma[322]; another, presenting as a polyp in the gallbladder neck, was immunoreactive for pancreatic polypeptide.[341] A *signet ring cell* variety has also been seen,[333] as has a *clear cell variant*, sometimes in the setting of von Hippel–Lindau disease.[323a,339]

Primary malignant melanoma may present as a mass inside the gallbladder[311,317,334] or the extrahepatic bile ducts.[312,316,342] Some of the cases have occurred in the setting of the dysplastic nevus syndrome.[335] Most tumors have already metastasized by the time of diagnosis. Before making the diagnosis of primary melanoma of this organ, the more likely possibility of a metastasis from a cutaneous or ocular source must be ruled out (Figs 14.26 and 14.27).

Malignant lymphoma and *leukemia* can involve the gallbladder or extrahepatic bile ducts as part of a systemic disease; their initial presentation in these sites is exceptional but has been recorded.[319,323,331] As in most other mucosa-lined organs, it has been postulated that some gallbladder lymphomas are of mucosa-associated lymphoid tissue (MALT) types.[325,329]

Botryoid rhabdomyosarcoma is the most common malignant tumor of extrahepatic bile ducts in children.[315] It can also involve the gallbladder,[328] and a few cases have been described in adults.[309] Obstructive jaundice is the usual presenting sign. Grossly, it has a deceptively soft polypoid appearance. Microscopically, small undifferentiated spindle cells concentrate beneath an intact epithelium ("cambium layer"). Cross striations may or may not be present in them (Fig. 14.28). The combination of surgery, radiation therapy, and chemotherapy has resulted in many long-term survivals.[338] Metastases occur in about 40% of cases, but death is usually due to the local effects of the tumor.[324]

Other *mesenchymal neoplasms* of the gallbladder occur in adults, such as benign and malignant forms of

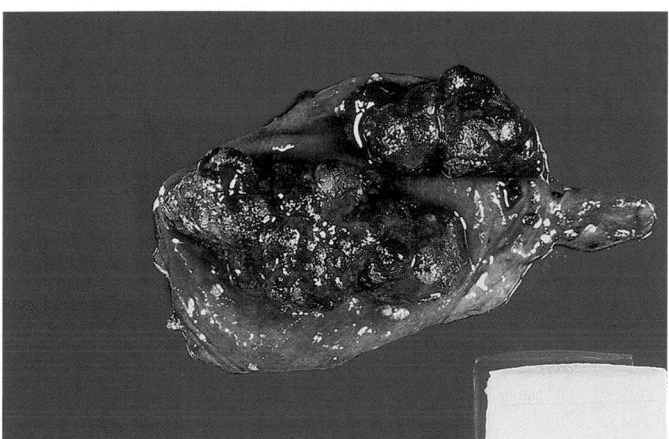

Fig. 14.26 Malignant melanoma metastatic to the gallbladder. The tumor nodules are heavily pigmented.

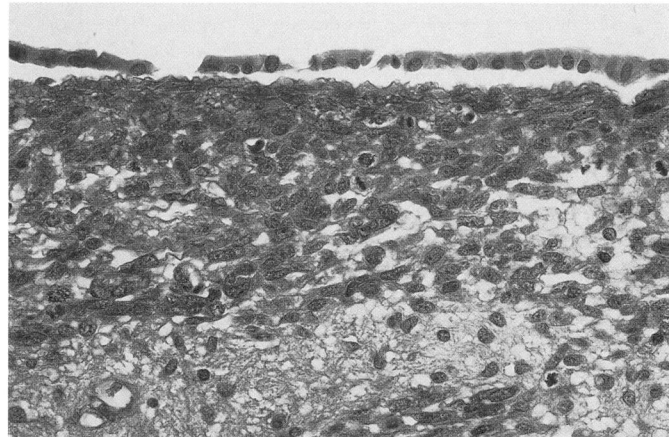

Fig. 14.28 Embryonal rhabdomyosarcoma of botryoid subtype. There is a prominent cambium layer beneath the biliary epithelium.

Fig. 14.29 Gallbladder with metastatic breast carcinoma presenting in the form of multiple nodules protruding through the mucosa and associated with inflammatory changes.

GIST,[327,332] *leiomyosarcoma*,[330,344,345] *angiosarcoma*[344] (including the epithelioid variety[343]) and *malignant fibrous histiocytoma*,[340] but before the latter diagnosis is made, the alternative possibility of sarcomatoid carcinoma should always be considered. Kaposi's sarcoma of gallbladder has been seen in the setting of HIV infection.[318]

Metastatic tumors to the gallbladder are exceptionally rare; most of the reported cases were malignant melanomas (see earlier discussion), renal cell carcinoma, or breast carcinoma[320,321] (Fig. 14.29). Intrabiliary growth of colonic adenocarcinoma mimicking primary neoplasia at this site has also been observed.[336]

References

Normal anatomy

1 Albores-Saavedra J, Nadji M, Henson DE, Ziegels-Weissman J, Mones JM. Intestinal metaplasia of the gallbladder. A morphologic and immunocytochemical study. Hum Pathol 1986, **17**: 614–620.
2 Fine G, Raju UB. Paraganglia in the human gallbladder. Arch Pathol Lab Med 1980, **104**: 265–268.
3 Frierson H. Gallbladder and extrahepatic billiary system. In Sternberg S (ed.): Histology for pathologists, ed. 2. Philadelphia, 1997, Lippincott-Raven Publishers, pp. 593–612.
4 Green FHY, Fox H. An immunofluorescent study of the distribution of immunoglobulin-containing cells in the normal and the inflamed human gallbladder. Gut 1972, **13**: 379–384.
5 Hong SM, Kang GH, Lee HY, Ro JY. Smooth muscle distribution in the extrahepatic bile duct: Histologic and immunohistochemical studies of 122 cases. Am J Surg Pathol 2000, **24**: 660–667.
6 Laitio M. Morphology and histochemistry of non-tumorous gallbladder epithelium. A series of 103 cases. Pathol Res Pract 1980, **167**: 335–345.
7 Laitio M, Nevalainen T. Gland ultrastructure in human gallbladder. J Anat 1975, **120**: 105–112.
8 Lamah M, Karanjia ND, Dickson GH. Anatomical variations of the extrahepatic biliary tree: review of the world literature. Clin Anat 2001, **14**: 167–172.

Congenital abnormalities

9 Altman RP. The portoenterostomy procedure for biliary atresia. A five-year experience. Ann Surg 1978, **188**: 351–362.
10 Beath S, Pearmain G, Kelly D, McMaster P, Mayer A, Buckels J. Liver transplantation in babies and children with extrahepatic biliary atresia. J Pediatr Surg 1993, **28**: 1044–1047.
11 Bloustein PA. Association of carcinoma with congenital cystic conditions of the liver and bile ducts. Am J Gastroenterol 1977, **67**: 40–46.
12 Boyle L, Gallivan MV, Chun B, Lack EE. Heterotopia of gastric mucosa and liver involving the gallbladder. Report of two cases with literature review. Arch Pathol Lab Med 1992, **116**: 138–142.
13 Burnett RA, McKay AJ. Inversion of the gallbladder. Am J Clin Pathol 1989, **91**: 594–596.
14 Busuttil A. Ectopic adrenal within the gall-bladder wall. J Pathol 1974, **113**: 231–233.
15 Carmi R, Magee CA, Neill CA, Karrer FM. Extrahepatic biliary atresia and associated anomalies. Etiologic heterogeneity suggested by distinctive patterns of associations. Am J Med Genet 1993, **45**: 683–693.
16 Chijiiwa K, Koga A. Surgical management and long-term follow-up of patients with choledochal cysts. Am J Surg 1993, **165**: 238–242.
17 Christensen AH, Ishak KG. Benign tumors and pseudotumors of the gallbladder. Report of 180 cases. Arch Pathol 1970, **90**: 423–432.
18 Corcoran DB, Wallace KK. Congenital anomalies of the gallbladder. Am Surg 1954, **20**: 709–725.
19 Cosentino CM, Luck SR, Raffensperger JG, Reynolds M. Choledochal duct cyst. Resection with physiologic reconstruction. Surgery 1992, **112**: 740–747.
20 Coughlin JP, Rector FE, Klein MD. Agenesis of the gallbladder in duodenal atresia. Two case reports. J Pediatr Surg 1992, **27**: 1304.
21 Curtis LE, Shehan DG. Heterotopic tissues in the gallbladder. Arch Pathol 1969, **88**: 677–683.
22 Gautier M, Eliot N. Extrahepatic biliary atresia. Morphological study of 98 biliary remnants. Arch Pathol Lab Med 1981, **105**: 397–402.
23 Ho CW, Shioda K, Shirasaki K, Takahashi S, Tokimatsu S, Maeda K. The pathogenesis of biliary atresia. A morphological study of the hepatobiliary system and the hepatic artery. J Pediatr Gastroenterol Nutr 1993, **16**: 53–60.
24 Järvi O, Meurman L. Heterotopic gastric mucosa and pancreas in the gallbladder with reference to the question of heterotopias in general. Ann Acad Sci Fenn 1964, **106**(suppl 22): 1–42.
25 Kalayoglu M, D'Alessandro AM, Knechtle SJ, Eckhoff DE, Pirsch JD, Judd R, Sollinger HW, Hoffmann RM, Belzer FO. Long-term results of liver transplantation for biliary atresia. Surgery 1993, **114**: 711–717.
26 Komi N, Tamura T, Tsuge S, Miyoshi Y, Udaka H, Takehara H. Relation of patient age to premalignant alterations in choledochal cyst epithelium. Histochemical and immunohistochemical studies. J Pediatr Surg 1986, **21**: 430–433.
27 Landing B. Considerations on the pathogenesis of neonatal hepatitis, biliary atresia, and choledochal cyst—the concept of infantile obstructive cholangiopathy. In Bill AH, Kasai M (eds): Progress in pediatric surgery, vol. 6. Baltimore, 1974, University Park Press.
28 Matsumoto Y, Uchida K, Nakase A, Houjo I. Clinicopathologic classification of congenital cystic dilatation of the common bile duct. Am J Surg 1977, **134**: 569–574.

29 Miyano T, Suruga K, Tsuchiya H, Suda K. A histopathological study of the remnant of extrahepatic bile duct in so-called uncorrectable biliary atresia. J Pediatr Surg 1977, **12**: 19–25.

30 Narkewicz MR. Biliary atresia: an update on our understanding of the disorder. Curr Opin Pediatr 2001, **13**: 435–440.

31 Ober WB, Wharton RN. On the "phrygian cap." N Engl J Med 1956, **255**: 571–572.

32 Ohi R. Surgery for biliary atresia. Liver 2001, **21**: 175–182.

33 Ohita H, Yamaguchi Y, Yamakawa O, Watanabe H, Satomura Y, Motoo Y, Okai T, Terada T, Sawabu N. Biliary papillomatosis with the point mutation of K-*ras* gene arising in congenital choledochal cyst. Gastroenterology 1993, **105**: 1209–1212.

34 Olbourne NA. Choledochal cysts. A review of the cystic anomalies of the biliary tree. Ann R Coll Surg Engl 1975, **56**: 26–32.

35 Patil KK, Omojola MF, Khurana P, Iyengar JK. Embryonal rhabdomyosarcoma within a choledochal cyst. Can Assoc Radiol J 1992, **43**: 145–148.

36 Schweizer P, Schweizer M. Pancreaticobiliary long common channel syndrome and congenital anomalous dilatation of the choledochal duct—study of 46 patients. Eur J Pediatr Surg 1993, **3**: 15–21.

37 Shirahase I, Ooshima A, Tanaka K, Ozawa K, Yamabe H, Yamamoto T. Increased deposition and serum level of type IV collagen in patients with extrahepatic biliary atresia. J Pediatr Surg 1993, **28**: 847–850.

38 Sokol RJ, Mack C. Etiopathogenesis of biliary atresia. Semin Liver Dis 2001, **21**: 517–524.

39 Suda K, Matsumoto Y, Miyano T. Narrow duct segment distal to choledochal cyst. Am J Gastroenterol 1991, **86**: 1259–1263.

40 Tan CE, Howard ER, Driver M, Murray-Lyon IM. Non-communicating multiseptate gall bladder and choledochal cyst. A case report and review of publications. Gut 1993, **34**: 853–856.

41 Tejada E, Danielson C. Ectopic or heterotopic liver (choristoma) associated with the gallbladder. Arch Pathol Lab Med 1989, **113**: 950–952.

42 Trout HH III, Longmire WP Jr. Long-term follow-up study of patients with congenital cystic dilatation of the common bile duct. Am J Surg 1971, **121**: 68–86.

43 Ueyama T, Ding J, Hashimoto H, Tsuneyoshi M, Enjoji M. Carcinoid tumor arising in the wall of a congenital bile duct cyst. Arch Pathol Lab Med 1992, **116**: 291–293.

44 Vallera DU, Dawson PJ, Path FR. Gastric heterotopia in the gallbladder. Case report and review of literature. Pathol Res Pract 1992, **188**: 49–52.

45 Weyant MJ, Maluccio MA, Bertagnolli MM, Daly JM. Choledochal cysts in adults: a report of two cases and review of the literature. Am J Gastroenterol 1998, **93**: 2580–2583.

46 Witzleben CL, Buck BE, Schnaufer L, Brzosko WJ. Studies on the pathogenesis of biliary atresia. Lab Invest 1978, **38**: 525–532.

Cholelithiasis

47 Donohue JH, Farnell MB, Grant CS, van Heerden JA, Wahlstrom HE, Sarr MG, Weaver AL, Ilstrup DM. Laparoscopic cholecystectomy. Early Mayo Clinic experience. Mayo Clin Proc 1992, **67**: 449–455.

48 Friedman GD, Kannel WF, Dawber TR. The epidemiology of gallbladder diseases. Observations in the Framingham study. J Chronic Dis 1966, **19**: 273–292.

49 Gerwig WH, Thistlethwaite JR. Cholecystitis and cholelithiasis in young women following pregnancy. Surgery 1950, **28**: 983–996.

50 Johnston DE, Kaplan MM. Pathogenesis and treatment of gallstones. N Engl J Med 1993, **328**: 412–421.

51 Jordan GL Jr. Choledocholithiasis. Curr Probl Surg 1982, **19**: 723–798.

52 Maclure KM, Hayes KC, Colditz GA, Stampfer MJ, Speizer FE, Willett WC. Weight, diet, and the risk of symptomatic gallstones in middle-aged women. N Engl J Med 1989, **321**: 563–569.

53 Madden JL, Vanderheyden L, Kandalaft S. The nature and surgical significance of common duct stones. Surg Gynecol Obstet 1968, **126**: 2–8.

54 Mok HYI, Druffel ERM, Rampone WM. Chronology of cholelithiasis. Dating gallstones from atmospheric radiocarbon produced by nuclear bomb explosions. N Engl J Med 1986, **314**: 1075–1077.

55 Ostrow JD. The etiology of pigment gallstones. Hepatology 1984, **4**: 215S–222S.

56 Paul MG, Burris DG, McGuire AM, Thorfinnson HD, Schonekas H. Laparoscopic surgery in the treatment of Mirizzi's syndrome. J Laparoendosc Surg 1992, **2**: 157–163.

57 Persson GE, Thelin AG, Thulin AJ. Changes in the surgical treatment of gallstones during a 10 year period. Eur J Surg 1993, **159**: 409–413.

58 Ranshoff DF, Gracie WA. Treatment of gallstones. Ann Intern Med 1993, **119**: 606–619.

59 Rudolph R, Williams JS. Cholecystectomy in patients with sickle cell disease. Experience at a regional hospital in southeast Georgia. J Natl Med Assoc 1992, **84**: 692–696.

60 Schirmer BD. Gallstone lithotripsy. Surg Annu 1991, **23**(Pt 1): 91–114.

61 Small DM. Gallstones. N Engl J Med 1968, **279**: 588–592.

62 Smith BF, LaMont JT. The sequence of events in gallstone formation. Lab Invest 1987, **56**: 125–126.

63 St-Vil D, Yazbeck S, Luks FI, Hancock BJ, Filiatrault D, Youssef S. Cholelithiasis in newborns and infants. J Pediatr Surg 1992, **27**: 1305–1307.

64 Torvik A, Höivik B. Gallstones in an autopsy series. Acta Chir Scand 1960, **120**: 168–174.

65 Vadlamudi G, Graebe R, Khoo M, Schinella R. Gallstones implanting in the ovary: a complication of laparoscopic cholecystectomy. Arch Pathol Lab Med 1997, **121**: 155–158.

66 Van Leeuwen DJ. The imager replacing the pathologist in the diagnosis of hepatobiliary and pancreatic disease. Ann Diagn Pathol 2001, **5**: 57–66.

Acute cholecystitis

67 Adolph MD, Bass SN, Lee SK, Blum JM, Schreiber H. Cytomegaloviral acalculous cholecystitis in acquired immunodeficiency syndrome patients. Am J Surg 1993, **59**: 679–684.

68 Bigio EH, Haque AK. Disseminated cytomegalovirus infection presenting with calculous cholecystitis and acute pancreatitis. Arch Pathol Lab Med 1989, **113**: 1287–1289.

69 Bigler FC. Acute gaseous cholecystitis. Am J Med 1960, **29**: 181–186.

70 Chitkara YK. Pathology of the gallbladder in common bile duct obstruction. The concept of ascending cholecystitis. Hum Pathol 1993, **24**: 279–283.

71 Fish DE, Evans DJ, Pusey CD. Gallbladder vasculitis. A report of two cases. Histopathology 1993, **23**: 584–585.

72 Frazee RC, Nagorney DM, Mucha P Jr. Acute acalculous cholecystitis. Mayo Clin Proc 1989, **64**: 163–167.

73 Glenn F. Acute cholecystitis. Surg Gynecol Obstet 1976, **143**: 56–60.

74 Glenn F, Becker CG. Acute acalculous cholecystitis. An increasing entity. Ann Surg 1982, **195**: 131–136.

75 Hallendorf LC, Dockerty MB, Waugh JM. Gangrenous cholecystitis. A clinical and pathologic study of 100 cases. Surg Clin North Am 1948, **28**: 979–998.

76 Hanson BA, Mahour GH, Woolley MM. Diseases of the gallbladder in infancy and childhood. J Pediatr Surg 1971, **6**: 277–283.

77 Hinnant K, Schwartz A, Rotterdam H, Rudski C. Cytomegaloviral and cryptosporidial cholecystitis in two patients with AIDS. Am J Surg Pathol 1989, **13**: 57–60.

78 Ito M, Sano K, Inaba H, Hotchi M. Localized necrotizing arteritis. A report of two cases involving the gallbladder and pancreas. Arch Pathol Lab Med 1991, **115**: 780–783.

79 Jardines LA, O'Donnell MR, Johnson DL, Terz JJ, Forman SJ. Acalculous cholecystitis in bone marrow transplant patients. Cancer 1993, **15:** 354–358.

80 Kent SJS, Menzies-Gow N. Biliary peritonitis without perforation of the gallbladder in acute cholecystitis. Br J Surg 1974, **61:** 960–962.

81 LiVolsi VA, Perzin KH, Porter M. Polyarteritis nodosa of the gallbladder, presenting as acute cholecystitis. Gastroenterology 1973, **65:** 115–123.

82 Marymont JV, Dakhil SR, Travers H, Housholder DF. Chemical cholecystitis associated with hepatic arterial chemotherapy delivered by a permanently implanted pump. Hum Pathol 1985, **16:** 986–990.

83 Sessions SC, Scoma RS, Sheikh FA, McGeehin WH, Smink RD Jr. Acute acalculous cholecystitis following open heart surgery. Am Surg 1993, **59:** 74–77.

84 Sjödahl R, Tagesson C, Wetterfors J. On the pathogenesis of acute cholecystitis. Surg Gynecol Obstet 1976, **146:** 199–202.

85 Svanvik J. Laparoscopic cholecystectomy for acute cholecystitis. Eur J Surg Suppl 2000, **585:** 16–17.

86 van der Linden W, Sunzel H. Early versus delayed operation for acute cholecystitis. A controlled clinical trial. Am J Surg 1970, **120:** 7–13.

87 Weedon D. Pathology of the gallbladder. New York, 1984, Masson Publishing USA.

88 Womack NA, Bricker EM. Pathogenesis of cholecystitis. Arch Surg 1942, **44:** 658–676.

89 Zucker KA, Flowers JL, Bailey RW, Graham SM, Buell J, Imbembo AL. Laparoscopic management of acute cholecystitis. Am J Surg 1993, **165:** 508–514.

Chronic cholecystitis and cholangitis

90 Abou-Saif A, Al-Kawas FH. Complications of gallstone disease: Mirizzi syndrome, cholecystocholedochal fistula, and gallstone ileus. Am J Gastroenterol 2002, **97:** 249–254.

90a Abraham SC, Cruz-Correa M, Argani P, Furth EE, Hruban RH, Boitnott JK. Diffuse lymphoplasmacytic chronic cholecystitis is highly specific for extrahepatic billiary tract disease but does not distinguish between primary and secondary cholangiopathy. Am J Surg Pathol 2003, **27:** 1313–1320.

91 Albores-Saavedra J, Henson DE. Pyloric gland metaplasia with perineural invasion of the gallbladder: a lesion that can be confused with adenocarcinoma. Cancer 1999, **86:** 2625–2631.

92 Albores-Saavedra J, Nadji M, Henson DE, Ziegels-Weissman J, Mones JM. Intestinal metaplasia of the gallbladder. A morphologic and immunocytochemical study. Hum Pathol 1986, **17:** 614–620.

93 Amazon F, Rywlin AM. Ceroid granulomas of the gallbladder. Am J Clin Pathol 1980, **73:** 123–127.

94 Beilby JO. Diverticulosis of the gall bladder. The fundal adenoma. Br J Exp Pathol 1967, **48:** 455–461.

95 Cameron JL, Gayler BW, Sanfey H, Milligan F, Kaufman S, Maddrey WC, Herlong HF. Sclerosing cholangitis. Anatomical distribution of obstructive lesions. Ann Surg 1984, **200:** 54–60.

96 Chapman RW, Cottone M, Selby WS, Shepherd HA, Sherlock S, Jewell DP. Serum autoantibodies, ulcerative colitis and primary sclerosing cholangitis. Gut 1986, **27:** 86–91.

97 Charpentier P, Prade M, Bognel C, Gadenne C, Duvillard P. Malacoplakia of the gallbladder. Hum Pathol 1983, **14:** 827–828.

98 Dabbs DJ. Eosinophilic and lymphoeosinophilic cholecystitis. Am J Surg Pathol 1993, **17:** 497–501.

99 De Groen PC, Gores GJ, LaRusso NF, Gunderson LL, Nagorney DM. Biliary tract cancers. N Engl J Med 1999, **341:** 1368–1378.

100 Dorudi S, Chapman RW, Kettlewell MG. Carcinoma of the gallbladder in ulcerative colitis and primary sclerosing cholangitis. Report of two cases. Dis Colon Rectum 1991, **34:** 827–828.

101 Elfving G. Crypts and ducts in the gallbladder wall. Acta Pathol Microbiol Immunol Scand (Suppl) 1960, **49:** 1–45.

102 Elfving G, Silvonen E, Tier H. Mucosal hyperplasia of the gallbladder in cases of cholecystolithiasis. Acta Chir Scand 1969, **135:** 519–522.

103 Estrada RL, Brown NM, James CE. Chronic follicular cholecystitis. Radiological, pathological, and surgical aspects. Br J Surg 1958, **48:** 205–209.

104 Forbes A, Blanshard C, Gazzard B. Natural history of AIDS related sclerosing cholangitis. A study of 20 cases. Gut 1993, **34:** 116–121.

105 Franco V, Aragona F, Genova G, Florena AM, Stella M, Campesi G. Xanthogranulomatous cholecystitis. Histopathological study and classification. Pathol Res Pract 1990, **186:** 383–390.

106 Frierson HF Jr. The gross anatomy and histology of the gallbladder, extrahepatic bile ducts, Vaterian system, and minor papilla. Am J Surg Pathol 1989, **13:** 146–162.

107 Goodman ZD, Ishak KG. Xanthogranulomatous cholecystitis. Am J Surg Pathol 1981, **5:** 653–659.

108 Hanada M, Tujimura T, Kimura M. Cholecystic granulomas in gallstone disease. A clinicopathologic study of 17 cases. Acta Pathol Jpn 1981, **31:** 221–231.

109 Hoang MP, Murakata LA, Padilla-Rodriguez AL, Albores-Saavedra J. Metaplastic lesions of the extrahepatic bile ducts: a morphologic and immunohistochemical study. Mod Pathol 2001, **14:** 1119–1125.

110 Jessurun J, Bolio-Solis A, Manivel JC. Diffuse lymphoplasmacytic acalculous cholecystitis: a distinctive form of chronic cholecystitis associated with primary sclerosing cholangitis. Hum Pathol 1998, **29:** 512–517.

111 Jutras JA, Levesque HP. Adenomyoma and adenomyomatosis of gallbladder. Radiologic and pathologic correlations. Radiol Clin North Am 1966, **4:** 483–500.

112 Kozuka S, Hackisuka K. Incidence by age and sex of intestinal metaplasia in the gallbladder. Hum Pathol 1984, **15:** 779–784.

113 Lahey RH, Pyrtek LJ. Experience with the operative management of 280 strictures of the bile ducts. Surg Gynecol Obstet 1950, **91:** 25–56.

114 Laitio M, Nevalainen T. Ultrastructure of endocrine cells in metaplastic epithelium of human gall bladder. J Anat 1975, **120:** 219–225.

115 LaRusso NF, Wiesner RH, Ludwig J, MacCarty RL. Primary sclerosing cholangitis. N Engl J Med 1984, **310:** 899–903.

116 Lee YM, Kaplan MM. Primary sclerosing cholangitis. N Engl J Med 1995, **332:** 924–933.

117 Lopez JI, Elizalde JM, Calvo MA. Xanthogranulomatous cholecystitis associated with gallbladder adenocarcinoma. A clinicopathological study of 5 cases. Tumori 1991, **77:** 358–360.

118 Ludwig J. Surgical pathology of the syndrome of primary sclerosing cholangitis. Am J Surg Pathol 1989, **13**(Suppl 1): 43–49.

119 Ludwig T, Wahlstrom HE, Batts KP, Wiesner RH. Papillary bile duct dysplasia in primary sclerosing cholangitis. Gastroenterology 1992, **102:** 2134–2138.

120 Lund J. Surgical indication in cholelithiasis. Prophylactic cholecystectomy elucidated on the basis of long-term follow up on 526 nonoperated cases. Ann Surg 1960, **151:** 153–162.

121 Martin M. Primary sclerosing cholangitis. Annu Rev Med 1993, **44:** 221–227.

122 McClure J, Banerjee SS, Schofield PS. Crohn's disease of the gall bladder. J Clin Pathol 1984, **37:** 516–518.

123 Mori M, Watanabe M, Sakuma M, Tsutsumi Y. Infectious etiology of xanthogranulomatous cholecystitis: Immunohistochemical identification of bacterial antigens in the xanthogranulomatous lesions. Pathol Int 1999, **49:** 849–852.

123a Notohara K, Smyrk TC, Burgart LJ. Benign localized strictures of the large bile ducts; a clinicopathological study. (Abstract) Mod Pathol 2003, **16**: 283A.

124 Nuako KW, Ahlquist DA, Sandborn WJ, Mahoney DW, Siems DM, Zinsmeister AR. Primary sclerosing cholangitis and colorectal carcinoma in patients with chronic ulcerative colitis: a case-control study. Cancer 1998, **82**: 822–826.

125 Pitt HA, Miyamoto T, Parapatis SK, Tompkins RK, Longmire WP Jr. Factors influencing outcome in patients with postoperative biliary strictures. Am J Surg 1982, **144**: 14–21.

126 Post AB, van Stolk R, Broughan TA, Tuthill RJ. Crohn's disease of the gallbladder. J Clin Gastroenterol 1993, **16**: 139–142.

127 Prochazka EJ, Terasaki PI, Park MS, Goldstein LI, Busutti RW. Association of primary sclerosing cholangitis with HLA-DRw52a. N Engl J Med 1990, **322**: 1842–1844.

128 Rappaport I, Albukerk J, Schneider IJ. Schistosomal cholecystitis. Arch Pathol 1975, **99**: 227–228.

129 Robertson HE, Ferguson WJ. The diverticula (Luschka's crypts) of the gallbladder. Arch Pathol 1945, **40**: 312–333.

130 Sivak MV Jr, Farmer RG, Lalli AF. Sclerosing cholangitis. Its increasing frequency of recognition and association with inflammatory bowel disease. J Clin Gastroenterol 1981, **3**: 261–266.

131 Taylor J, Lindor K. Metastatic prostate cancer simulating sclerosing cholangitis. J Clin Gastroenterol 1993, **16**: 143–145.

132 Thistle JL, Cleary PA, Lachin JM, Tyor MP, Hersh T. The natural history of cholelithiasis. The National Cooperative Gallstone Study. Ann Intern Med 1984, **101**: 171–175.

133 Thompson HH, Pitt HA, Tompkins RK, Longmire WP Jr. Primary sclerosing cholangitis. A heterogenous disease. Ann Surg 1982, **196**: 127–136.

134 Tsutsumi Y, Nagura H, Osamura RY, Watanabe K, Yanaihara N. Histochemical studies of metaplastic lesions in the human gallbladder. Arch Pathol Lab Med 1984, **108**: 917–921.

135 Warren KW, Mountain JC, Midell AL. Management of strictures of the biliary tract. Surg Clin North Am 1971, **51**: 711–731.

136 Weedon D. Pathology of the gallbladder. New York, 1984, Masson Publishing USA.

137 Wenchert A, Robertson B. The natural course of gallstone disease. Eleven-year review of 781 nonoperated cases. Gastroenterology 1966, **50**: 376–381.

138 Wiesner RH, LaRusso NF. Clinicopathologic features of the syndrome of primary sclerosing cholangitis. Gastroenterology 1980, **79**: 200–206.

Tumors

Benign tumors and tumorlike conditions

139 Albores-Saavedra J, Defortuna SM, Smothermon WE. Primary papillary hyperplasia of the gallbladder and cystic and common bile ducts. Hum Pathol 1990, **21**: 228–231.

140 Albores-Saavedra J, Vardaman CJ, Vuitch F. Non-neoplastic polypoid lesions and adenomas of the gallbladder. Pathol Annu 1993, **28**: 145–178.

141 Cappell MS, Marks M, Kirschenbaum H. Massive hemobilia and acalculous cholecystitis due to benign gallbladder polyp. Dig Dis Sci 1993, **38**: 1156–1161.

142 Chandrasoma P, Fitzgibbons P. Granular cell tumor of the intrapancreatic common bile duct. Cancer 1984, **53**: 2178–2182.

143 Christensen AH, Ishak KG. Benign tumors and pseudotumors of the gallbladder. Report of 180 cases. Arch Pathol 1970, **90**: 423–432.

144 Eisen RN, Kirby WM, O'Quinn JL. Granular cell tumor of the biliary tree. A report of two cases and a review of the literature. Am J Surg Pathol 1991, **15**: 460–465.

145 Elhag AM, Al Awadi NZ. Amputation neuroma of the gallbladder. Histopathology 1992, **21**: 586–587.

146 Ishak KG, Willis GW, Cummins SD, Bullock AA. Biliary

cystadenoma and cystadenocarcinoma. Report of 14 cases and review of the literature. Cancer 1977, **39**: 322–338.

147 Kozuka S, Tsubone M, Yasui A, Hachisuka K. Relation of adenoma to carcinoma in the gallbladder. Cancer 1982, **50**: 2226–2234.

148 Larson DM, Storsteen KA. Traumatic neuroma of the bile ducts with intrahepatic extension causing obstructive jaundice. Hum Pathol 1984, **15**: 287–290.

149 Madden JJ Jr, Smith GW. Multiple biliary papillomatosis. Cancer 1974, **34**: 1316–1320.

150 Miller TA, Weber TR, Appelman HD. Paraganglioma of the gallbladder. Arch Surg 1972, **105**: 637–639.

151 Neumann RD, LiVolsi VA, Rosenthal NS, Burrell M, Ball TJ. Adenocarcinoma in biliary papillomatosis. Gastroenterology 1976, **70**: 779–782.

152 Nishihara K, Yamaguchi K, Hashimoto H, Enjoji M. Tubular adenoma of the gallbladder with squamoid spindle cell metaplasia. Report of three cases with immunohistochemical study. Acta Pathol Jpn 1991, **41**: 41–45.

153 Peison B, Benisch B. Traumatic neuroma of the cystic duct in the absence of previous surgery. Hum Pathol 1985, **16**: 1168–1169.

154 Sato H, Mizushima M, Ito J, Doi K. Sessile adenoma of the gallbladder. Reappraisal of its importance as a precancerous lesion. Arch Pathol Lab Med 1985, **109**: 65–69.

155 Taguchi J, Yasunaga M, Kojiro M, Arita T, Nakayama T, Simokobe T. Intrahepatic and extrahepatic biliary papillomatosis. Arch Pathol Lab Med 1993, **117**: 944–947.

156 Walsh MM, Drew M, Bleiweiss IJ. Neurofibroma of the common bile duct: a case report and review of the literature. Int J Surg Pathol 1996–1997, **4**: 245–248.

157 Warfel KA, Hull MT. Villous papilloma of the gallbladder in association with leukodystrophy. Hum Pathol 1984, **15**: 1192–1194.

158 Wheeler DA, Edmondson HA. Cystadenoma with mesenchymal stroma in the liver and bile ducts. A clinico-pathologic study of 17 cases, 4 with malignant change. Cancer 1985, **56**: 1434–1439.

159 Yamaguchi K, Enjoji M. Gallbladder polyps. Inflammatory, hyperplastic and neoplastic types. Surg Pathol 1988, **1**: 203–213.

160 Yamaguchi K, Kuroki S, Daimaru Y, Hashimoto H, Enjoji M. Granular cell tumor of the gallbladder. Report of a case. Acta Pathol Jpn 1985, **35**: 687–691.

161 Yamamoto M, Nakajo S, Tahara E. Immunohistochemical analysis of estrogen receptors in human gallbladder. Acta Pathol Jpn 1990, **40**: 14–21.

162 Yang HL, Sun YG, Wang Z. Polypoid lesions of the gallbladder. Diagnosis and indications for surgery. Br J Surg 1992, **79**: 227–229.

Carcinoma of gallbladder

General and clinical features

163 Bombi JA, Rives A, Astudillo E, Pera C, Cardesa A. Polyposis coli associated with adenocarcinoma of the gallbladder. Report of a case. Cancer 1984, **53**: 2561–2563.

164 Carriaga MT, Henson DE. Liver, gallbladder, extrahepatic bile ducts, and pancreas. Cancer 1995, **75**: 175–190.

165 Chijiwa K, Tanaka M, Nakayama F. Adenocarcinoma of the gallbladder associated with anomalous pancreaticobiliary ductal junction. Am Surg 1993, **594**: 30–434.

166 Diehl AK. Epidemiology of gallbladder cancer. A synthesis of recent data. J Natl Cancer Inst 1980, **65**: 1209–1214.

167 Donohue JH, Stewart AK, Menck HR. The National Cancer Data Base report on carcinoma of the gallbladder, 1989–1995. Cancer 1998, **83**: 2618–2629.

168 Kinoshita H, Nagata E, Hirohashi K, Sakai K, Kobayashi Y. Carcinoma of the gallbladder with an anomalous connection between the choledochus and the pancreatic duct. Report of 10

cases and review of the literature in Japan. Cancer 1984, **54:** 762–769.

169 Kurihara K, Mizuseki K, Ninomiya T, Shoji I, Kajiwara S. Carcinoma of the gallbladder arising in adenomyomatosis. Acta Pathol Jpn 1993, **43:** 82–85.

170 Lazcano-Ponce EC, Miquel JF, Munoz N, Herrero R, Ferrecio C, Wistuba II, Alonso de Ruiz P, Aristi Urista G, Nervi F. Epidemiology and molecular pathology of gallbladder cancer. CA 2001, **51:** 349–364.

171 Morohoshi T, Kunimura T, Kanda M, Takahashi H, Yagi H, Shimizu K, Nakayoshi A, Asanuma K. Multiple carcinomata associated with anomalous arrangement of the biliary and pancreatic duct system. A report of two cases with a literature survey. Acta Pathol Jpn 1990, **60:** 755–763.

172 Ootani T, Shirai Y, Tsukada K, Muto T. Relationship between gallbladder carcinoma and the segmental type of adenomyomatosis of the gallbladder. Cancer 1992, **69:** 2647–2652.

173 Tanaka K, Nishimura A, Yamada K, Ishibe R, Ishizaki N, Yoshimine M, Hamada M, Taira A. Cancer of the gallbladder associated with anomalous junction of the pancreatobiliary duct system without bile duct dilatation. Br J Surg 1993, **80:** 622–624.

174 Walsh N, Qizilbash A, Banerjee R, Waugh GA. Biliary neoplasia in Gardner's syndrome. Arch Pathol Lab Med 1987, **111:** 76–77.

175 Zatonski W, La Vecchia C, Levi F, Negri E, Lucchini F. Descriptive epidemiology of gall-bladder cancer in Europe. J Cancer Res Clin Oncol 1993, **119:** 165–171.

Gross features

176 Sons HU, Borchard F, Joel BS. Carcinoma of the gallbladder. Autopsy findings in 287 cases and review of the literature. J Surg Oncol 1985, **28:** 199–206.

Microscopic features

177 Albores-Saavedra J, Molberg K, Henson DE. Unusual malignant epithelial tumors of the gallbladder. Semin Diagn Pathol 1996, **13:** 326–338.

178 Albores-Saavedra J, Nadji M, Henson DE. Intestinal-type adenocarcinoma of the gallbladder. A clinicopathologic and immunocytochemical study of seven cases. Am J Surg Pathol 1986, **10:** 19–25.

179 Kushima R, Lohe B, Borchard F. Differentiation towards gastric foveolar, mucopeptic and intestinal goblet cells in gallbladder adenocarcinoma. Histopathology 1996, **29:** 443–448.

180 Laitio M, Käkkinen I. Intestinal-type carcinoma of gallbladder. A histochemical and immunologic study. Cancer 1975, **36:** 1668–1674.

181 Longnecker DS, Terhune PG. The case for parallel classification of biliary tract and pancreatic neoplasms. Mod Pathol 1996, **9:** 828–837.

182 Yamaguchi A, Hachisuka K, Isogai M, Tsubone M. Carcinoma in situ of the gallbladder with superficial extension into the Rokitansky-Aschoff sinuses and mucous glands. Gastroenterol Jpn 1992, **27:** 765–772.

Histochemical, immunohistochemical & electron microscopic

183 Albores-Saavedra J, Nadji M, Morales AR, Henson DE. Carcinoembryonic antigen in normal, preneoplastic and neoplastic gallbladder epithelium. Cancer 1983, **52:** 1069–1072.

184 Alexander J, Krishnamurthy S, Kovacs D, Dayal Y. Cytokeratin profile of extrahepatic pancreaticobiliary epithelia and their carcinomas: diagnostic application. Appl Immunohistochem 1997, **5:** 216–222.

185 Esterly JR, Spicer SS. Mucin histochemistry of human gallbladder. Changes in adenocarcinoma, cystic fibrosis, and cholecystitis. J Natl Cancer Inst 1968, **40:** 1–10.

186 Koga A, Momii S, Eguchi M, Makino T. Ultrastructure of well-differentiated adenocarcinoma of the gallbladder. Ultrastruct Pathol 1991, **15:** 41–48.

187 Laitio M. Histogenesis of epithelial neoplasms of human gallbladder. II. Classification of carcinoma on the basis of morphological features. Pathol Res Pract 1983, **178:** 57–66.

188 Rullier A, Le Bail B, Fawaz R, Blanc JF, Saric J, Bioulac-Sage P. Cytokeratin 7 and 20 expression in cholangiocarcinomas varies along the biliary tract but still differs from that in colorectal carcinomas metastases. Am J Surg Pathol 2000, **24:** 870–876.

189 Watanabe M, Hori Y, Nojima T, Kato H, Takata K, Isogawa S, Yokoyama K, Nakagawa S. Alpha-fetoprotein-producing carcinoma of the gallbladder. Dig Dis Sci 1993, **38:** 561–564.

190 Yonezawa S, Sato E. Expression of mucin antigens in human cancers and its relationship with malignancy potential. Pathol Int 1997, **47:** 813–830.

Molecular genetic features

191 Argani P, Shaukat A, Kaushal M, Wilentz RE, Su GH, Sohn TA, Yeo CJ, Cameron JK, Kern SE, Hruban RH. Differing rates of loss of DPC4 expression and of p53 overexpression among carcinomas of the proximal and distal bile ducts. Cancer 2001, **91:** 1332–1341.

192 Arora DS, Ramsdale J, Lodge JPA, Wyatt JI. p53 but not bcl-2 is expressed by most cholangiocarcinomas: a study of 28 cases. Histopathology 1999, **34:** 497–501.

193 Itoi T, Takei K, Shinohara Y, Takeda K, Nakamura K, Horibe T, Sanada A, Ohno H, Matsubayashi H, Saito T, Watanabe H. K-ras codon 12 and p53 mutations in biopsy specimens and bile from biliary tract cancers. Pathol Int 1999, **49:** 30–37.

194 Kamel D, Paakko P, Nuorva K, Vahakangas K, Soini Y. p53 and c-erbB-2 protein expression in adenocarcinomas and epithelial dysplasias of the gallbladder. J Pathol 1993, **170:** 67–72.

195 Lazcano-Ponce EC, Miquel JF, Munoz N, Herrero R, Ferrecio C, Wistuba II, Alonso de Ruiz P, Aristi Urista G, Nervi F. Epidemiology and molecular pathology of gallbladder cancer. CA Cancer J Clin 2001, **51:** 349–364.

196 Niiyama H, Mizumoto K, Kusumoto M, Ogawa T, Suehara N, Shimura H, Tanaka M. Activation of telomerase and its diagnostic application in biopsy specimens from biliary tract neoplasms. Cancer 1999, **85:** 2138–2143.

197 Oohashi Y, Watanabe H, Ajioka Y, Hatakeyama K. p53 immunostaining distinguishes malignant from benign lesions of the gallbladder. Pathol Int 1995, **45:** 58–65.

198 Roa I, Villaseca M, Araya J, Roa J, De Aretxabala X, Melo A, Ibacache G. p53 tumour suppressor gene protein expression in early and advanced gallbladder carcinoma. Histopathology 1997, **31:** 226–230.

198a Sessa F, Furlan D, Genasetti A, Billo P, Feltri M, Capella C. Microsatellite instability and p53 expression in gallbladder carcinomas. Diagn Mol Pathol 2003, **12:** 96–102.

199 Teh M, Wee A, Raju GC. An immunohistochemical study of p53 protein in gallbladder and extrahepatic bile duct/ampullary carcinomas. Cancer 1994, **74:** 1542–1545.

199a Wistuba I, Ashfaq R, Maitra A, Alvarez H, Riquelme E, Gazdar A. Fragile histidine triad gene abnormalities in the pathogenesis of gallbladder carcinoma. Am J Pathol 2002, **160:** 2073.

200 Wistuba II, Gazdar AF, Roa I, Albores-Saavedra J. p53 protein overexpression in gallbladder carcinoma and its precursor lesions: an immunohistochemical study. Hum Pathol 1996, **27:** 360–365.

Other microscopic types

201 Albores-Saavedra J, Cruz-Ortiz H, Alcantara-Vazques A, Henson DE. Unusual types of gallbladder carcinoma. A report of 16 cases. Arch Pathol Lab Med 1981, **105:** 287–293.

202 Albores-Saavedra J, Henson DE, Sobin LH. The WHO Histological Classification of Tumors of the Gallbladder and Extrahepatic Bile Ducts. A commentary on the second edition. Cancer 1992, **70:** 410–414.

203 Albores-Saavedra J, Molberg K, Henson DE. Unusual malignant epithelial tumors of the gallbladder. Semin Diagn Pathol 1996, 13: 326–338.

204 Albores-Saavedra J, Soriano J, Larraza-Hernandez O, Aguirre J, Henson DE. Oat cell carcinoma of the gallbladder. Hum Pathol 1984, 15: 639–646.

205 Appelman HD, Coopersmith N. Pleomorphic spindle-cell carcinoma of the gall-bladder. Relation to sarcoma of the gallbladder. Cancer 1970, 25: 535–541.

206 Fish DE, Al-Izzi M, George PP, Whitaker B. Combined endocrine cell carcinoma and adenocarcinoma of the gallbladder. Histopathology 1990, 17: 471–472.

207 Furihata M, Sonobe H, Ohtsuki Y, Enzan H, Tokuoka H, Nakanuma Y. An immunohistochemical study on a case of granulocyte-colony stimulating factor-producing gall-bladder carcinoma. Pathol Int 1999, 49: 1010–1013.

208 Grosso LE, Gonzalez JG. Stromal osteoclast-like giant cells in an adenosquamous carcinoma of the gallbladder. Hum Pathol 1992, 32: 703–706.

209 Guo K-J, Yamaguchi K, Enjoji M. Undifferentiated carcinoma of the gallbladder. A clinicopathologic, histochemical, and immunohistochemical study of 21 patients with a poor prognosis. Cancer 1988, 61: 1872–1879.

210 Iezzoni JC, Mills SE. Sarcomatoid carcinomas (carcinosarcomas) of the gastrointestinal tract. A review. Semin Diagn Pathol 1993, 10: 176–187.

211 Iida Y, Tsutumi Y. Small cell (endocrine cell) carcinoma of the gallbladder with squamous and adenocarcinomatous components. Acta Pathol Jpn 1992, 42: 119–125.

212 Inoshita S, Iwashita A, Enjoji M. Carcinosarcoma of the gallbladder. Report of a case and review of the literature. Acta Pathol Jpn 1986, 36: 913–920.

213 Ishihara T, Kawano H, Takahashi M, Yokota T, Uchino F, Matsumoto N, Fukuyama N. Carcinosarcoma of the gallbladder. A case report with immunohistochemical and ultrastructural studies. Cancer 1990, 66: 992–997.

214 Ito M, Hsu CT, Naito S, Matsuo T, Onizuka S, Sekine I, Fujii H, Matsuoka Y. Osteoclast-like giant cell tumour of the gallbladder. Virchows Arch [A] 1992, 420: 359–366.

215 Jeng YM, Chen CL, Hsu HC. Lymphoepithelioma-like cholangiocarcinoma: an Epstein-Barr virus-associated tumor. Am J Surg Pathol 2001, 25: 516–520.

216 Johnstone AK, Zuch RH, Anders KH. Oat cell carcinoma of the gallbladder. A rare and highly lethal neoplasm. Arch Pathol Lab Med 1993, 117: 1009–1012.

217 Karasawa T, Itoh K, Komukai M, Ozawa U, Sakurai I, Shikata T. Squamous cell carcinoma of gallbladder. Report of two cases and review of literatures. Acta Pathol Jpn 1981, 31: 299–308.

218 Kim YB, Park YN, Han JY, Hong KC, Hwang TS. Biliary lymphoepithelioma-like carcinoma not associated with Epstein-Barr virus. Arch Pathol Lab Med 1999, 123: 441–443.

219 McLean CA, Pedersen JS. Endocrine cell carcinoma of the gallbladder. Histopathology 1991, 19: 173–176.

220 Maitra A, Tascilar M, Hruban RH, Albores-Saavedra J. Small cell carcinoma of the gallbladder: a clinicopathologic, immunohistochemical and molecular pathology study of 12 cases. Am J Surg Pathol 2001, 25: 595–601.

221 Nishihara K, Nagai E, Tsuneyoshi M, Nagashima M. Small-cell carcinoma combined with adenocarcinoma of the gallbladder. A case report with immunohistochemical and flow cytometric studies. Arch Pathol Lab Med 1994, 118: 177–181.

222 Nishihara K, Tsuneyoshi M. Undifferentiated spindle cell carcinoma of the gallbladder. A clinicopathologic, immunohistochemical, and flow cytometric study of 11 cases. Hum Pathol 1993, 24: 1298–1305.

223 Papotti M, Cassoni P, Sapino A, Passarino G, Krueger JE, Albores-Saavedra J. Large cell neuroendocrine carcinoma of the gallbladder: report of two cases. Am J Surg Pathol 2000, 24: 1424–1428.

223a Parwani A, Geradts J, Caspers E, Offerhaus J, Yeo C, Cameron J, Klimstra D, Maitra A, Hruban R, Argani P. Immunohistochemical and genetic analysis of non-small cell and small cell gallbladder carcinoma and their precursor lesions. Mod Pathol 2003, 16: 299–308.

224 Suster S, Huszar M, Herczeg E, Bubis JJ. Adenosquamous carcinoma of the gallbladder with spindle cell features. A light microscopic and immunocytochemical study of a case. Histopathology 1987, 11: 209–214.

225 Todd DL, Ro JY, Gulley ML, Ayala AG. Lymphoepithelioma like carcinoma of the gallbladder. Int J Surg Pathol 1996–1997, 4: 183–188.

226 Vardaman C, Albores-Saavedra J. Clear cell carcinomas of the gallbladder and extrahepatic bile ducts. Am J Surg Pathol 1995, 19: 91–99.

227 Von Kuster LC, Cohen C. Malignant mixed tumor of the gallbladder. Report of two cases and a review of the literature. Cancer 1982, 50: 1166–1170.

Dysplasia and carcinoma in situ

228 Albores-Saavedra J, Alcantara-Vazquez A, Cruz Ortiz H, Herrera-Goepfert R. The precursor lesions of invasive gallbladder carcinoma. Hyperplasia, atypical hyperplasia and carcinoma in situ. Cancer 1980, 45: 919–927.

229 Albores-Saavedra J, de Jesus Manrique J, Angeles-Angeles A, Henson DE. Carcinoma in situ of the gallbladder. A clinicopathologic study of 18 cases. Am J Surg Pathol 1984, 8: 323–333.

230 Albores-Saavedra J, Nadji M, Morales AR, Henson DE. Carcinoembryonic antigen in normal, preneoplastic and neoplastic gallbladder epithelium. Cancer 1983, 52: 1069–1072.

231 Black WC. The morphogenesis of gallbladder carcinoma. Prog Surg Pathol 1980, 2: 207–223.

231a Chang HJ, Jee, CD, Kim WH. Mutation and altered expression of β-catenin during gallbladder carcinogenesis. Am J Surg Pathol 2002, 26: 758–766.

232 Chang HJ, Kim SW, Kim YT, Kim WH. Loss of heterozygosity in dysplasia and carcinoma of the gallbladder. Mod Pathol 1999, 12: 763–769.

233 Duarte I, Llanos O, Domke H, Harz C, Valdivieso V. Metaplasia and precursor lesions of gallbladder carcinoma. Frequency, distribution, and probability of detection in routine histologic samples. Cancer 1993, 72: 1878–1884.

234 Kamel D, Paakko P, Nuorva K, Vahakangas K, Soini Y. p53 and c-erbB-2 protein expression in adenocarcinomas and epithelial dysplasias of the gallbladder. J Pathol 1993, 170: 67–72.

234a Parwani A, Geradts J, Caspers E, Offerhaus J, Yeo C, Cameron J, Klimstra D, Maitra A, Hruban R, Argani P. Immunohistochemical and genetic analysis of non-small cell and small cell gallbladder carcinoma and their precursor lesions. Mod Pathol 2003, 16: 299–308.

235 Sasaki M, Yamato T, Nakanuma Y, Ho SB, Kim YS. Expression of MUC2, MUC5AC and MUC6 apomucins in carcinoma, dysplasia and non-dysplastic epithelia of the gallbladder. Pathol Int 1999, 49: 38–44.

236 Wisuba II, Miquel JF, Gazdar AF, Albores-Saavedra J. Gallbladder adenomas have molecular abnormalities different from those present in gallbladder carcinomas. Hum Pathol 1999, 30: 21–25.

237 Yamamoto M, Nakajo S, Tahara E. Dysplasia of the gallbladder. Its histogenesis and correlation to gallbladder adenocarcinoma. Pathol Res Pract 1989, 185: 454–460.

Spread and metastases

238 Fahim RB, McDonald JR, Richards JC, Ferris DO. Carcinoma of the gallbladder. A study of its modes of spread. Ann Surg 1982, 156: 114–124.

239 Hamrick RE Jr, Liner FJ, Hastings PR, Cohn I Jr. Primary carcinoma of the gallbladder. Ann Surg 1982, **195**: 270–273.

240 Ohtsuka M, Miyazaki M, Itoh H, Nakagawa K, Ambiru S, Shimizu H, Nakajima N, Akikusa B, Kondo Y. Routes of hepatic metastasis of gallbladder carcinoma. Am J Clin Pathol 1998, **109**: 62–68.

241 Petru E, Pickel H, Heydarfadai M, Lahousen M, Haas J, Schaider H, Tamussino K. Nongenital cancers metastatic to the ovary. Gynecol Oncol 1992, **44**: 83–86.

242 Shirai Y, Tsukada K, Ohtani T, Watanabe H, Hatakeyama K. Hepatic metastases from carcinoma of the gallbladder. Cancer 1995, **75**: 2063–2068.

243 Tsukada K, Kurosaki I, Uchida K, Shirai Y, Oohashi Y, Yokoyama N, Watanabe H, Hatakeyama K. Lymph node spread from carcinoma of the gallbladder. Cancer 1997, **80**: 661–667.

244 Young RH, Scully RE. Ovarian metastases from carcinoma of the gallbladder and extrahepatic bile ducts simulating primary tumors of the ovary. A report of six cases. Int J Gynecol Pathol 1990, **9**: 60–72.

Treatment and prognosis

245 Appelman RM, Morlock CG, Dahlin DC, Adson MA. Long term survival in carcinoma of the gallbladder. Surg Gynecol Obstet 1963, **117**: 459–464.

246 Frank SA, Spjut HJ. Inapparent carcinoma of the gallbladder. Am Surg 1967, **33**: 367–372.

246a Giatromanolaki A, Sivridis E, Simopoulos C, Polychronidis A, Gatter K, Harris A, Koukourakis M. Thymidine phosphorylase expression in gallbladder adenocarcinomas. Int J Surg Pathol 2002, **10**: 181–188.

247 Hamrick RE Jr, Liner FJ, Hastings PR, Cohn I Jr. Primary carcinoma of the gallbladder. Ann Surg 1982, **195**: 270–273.

248 Henson DE, Albores-Saavedra J, Corle D. Carcinoma of the gallbladder. Histologic types, stage of disease, grade, and survival rates. Cancer 1992, **70**: 1493–1497.

249 Kimura W, Nagai H, Kuroda A, Morioka Y. Clinicopathologic study of asymptomatic gallbladder carcinoma found at autopsy. Cancer 1989, **64**: 98–103.

250 Malats N, Porta M, Piñol JL, Corominas JM, Rifà J, Real FX for the PANK-*ras* I Project Investigators. *Ki-ras* mutations as a prognostic factor in extrahepatic bile system cancer. J Clin Oncol 1995, **13**: 1679–1686.

251 Nadler LH, McSherry CK. Carcinoma of the gallbladder. Review of the literature and report on 56 cases at the Beth Israel Medical Center. Mt Sinai J Med 1992, **59**: 47–52.

252 Nevin JE, Moran TJ, Ray S, King R. Carcinoma of the gallbladder. Staging, treatment and prognosis. Cancer 1976, **37**: 141–148.

253 Oertli D, Herzog U, Tondelli P. Primary carcinoma of the gallbladder. Operative experience during a 16 year period. Eur J Surg 1993, **159**: 415–420.

254 Ouchi K, Suzuki M, Saijo S, Ito K, Matsuno S. Do recent advances in diagnosis and operative management improve the outcome of gallbladder carcinoma? Surgery 1993, **113**: 324–329.

255 Piehler JM, Crichlow RW. Primary carcinoma of the gallbladder. Surg Gynecol Obstet 1978, **147**: 929–942.

256 Roa I, Araya JC, Shiraishi T, Yatani R, Wistuba I, Villaseca M, De Aretxabala X. DNA content in gallbladder carcinoma. A flow cytometric study of 96 cases. Histopathology 1993, **23**: 459–464.

257 Sato Y, Tanaka J, Koyama K, van Gulik TM, Lygidakis NJ, van der Heyde MN. Tumor DNA content in gallbladder carcinoma. Hepatogastroenterology 1993, **40**: 375–379.

258 Shimada H, Endo I, Togo S, Nakano A, Izumi T, Nakagawara G. The role of lymph node dissection in the treatment of gallbladder carcinoma. Cancer 1997, **79**: 892–899.

259 Shirai Y, Yoshida K, Tsukada K, Muto T. Inapparent carcinoma of the gallbladder. An appraisal of a radical second operation after simple cholecystectomy. Ann Surg 1992, **215**: 326–331.

260 Shirai Y, Yoshida K, Tsukada K, Muto T, Watanabe H. Early carcinoma of the gallbladder. Eur J Surg 1992, **158**: 545–548.

261 Solan MJ, Jackson BT. Carcinoma of the gall-bladder. A clinical appraisal and review of 57 cases. Br J Surg 1971, **58**: 593–597.

262 Suzuki T, Takano Y, Kakita A, Okudaira M. An immunohistochemical and molecular biological study of c-erbB-2 amplification and prognostic relevance in gallbladder cancer. Pathol Res Pract 1993, **189**: 283–292.

263 Yamaguchi K, Tsuneyoshi M. Subclinical gallbladder carcinoma. Am J Surg 1992, **163**: 382–386.

Carcinoma of extrahepatic bile ducts

264 Akwari OE, Van Heerden JA, Foulk WT, Baggenstoss AH. Cancer of the bile ducts associated with ulcerative colitis. Ann Surg 1975, **181**: 303–309.

265 Albores-Saavedra J, Delgado R, Henson DE. Well-differentiated adenocarcinoma, gastric foveolar type, of the extrahepatic bile ducts: a previously unrecognized and distinctive morphologic variant of bile duct carcinoma. Ann Diagn Pathol 1999, **3**: 75–80.

266 Albores-Saavedra J, Murakata L, Krueger JE, Henson DE. Noninvasive and minimally invasive papillary carcinomas of the extrahepatic bile ducts. Cancer 2000, **89**: 508–515.

267 Alexander F, Rossi RL, O'Bryan M, Khettry U, Braasch JW, Walkins E Jr. Biliary carcinoma. A review of 109 cases. Am J Surg 1984, **147**: 503–509.

268 Altemeier WA, Gall EA, Zinninger MM, Hoxworth PI. Sclerosing carcinoma of the major intrahepatic bile ducts. Arch Surg 1957, **75**: 450–461.

269 Argani P, Shaukat A, Kaushal M, Wilentz RE, Su GH, Sohn TA, Yeo CJ, Cameron JK, Kern SE, Hruban RH. Differing rates of loss of dpc4 expression and of p53 overexpression among carcinomas of the proximal and distal bile ducts: evidence for a biologic distinction. Cancer 2001, **91**: 1332–1341.

270 Bardales RGH, Stanley MW, Simpson DD, Baker SJ, Steele CT, Schaefer RF, Powers CN. Diagnostic value of brush cytology in the diagnosis of duodenal, biliary and ampullary neoplasms. Am J Clin Pathol 1998, **109**: 540–548.

271 Batheja N, Suriawinata A, Saxena R, Ionescu G, Schwartz M, Thung SN. Expression of p53 and PCNA in cholangiocarcinoma and primary sclerosing cholangitis. Mod Pathol 2000, **13**: 1265–1268.

272 Beazley RM, Hadjis N, Benjamin IS, Blumgart LH. Clinicopathological aspects of high bile duct cancer. Experience with resection and bypass surgical treatments. Ann Surg 1984, **199**: 623–636.

273 Cucchiara G, Gandini G, Simonetti G, Bracci F, Daffina A. Palliative treatment of extrahepatic bile duct tumors. J Surg Oncol Suppl 1993, **3**: 154–157.

274 De Groen PC, Gores GJ, LaRusso NF, Gunderson LL, Nagorney DM. Biliary tract cancers. N Engl J Med 1999, **341**: 1368–1378.

275 Desa LA, Akosa AB, Lazzara S, Domizio P, Krausz T, Benjamin IS. Cytodiagnosis in the management of extrahepatic biliary stricture. Gut 1991, **32**: 1188–1191.

276 Elias E, Hamlyn AN, Jain S, Long RG, Summerfield JA, Sherlock S. A randomized trial of percutaneous transhepatic cholangiography with the Chiba needle versus endoscopic retrograde cholangiography for bile duct visualization in jaundice. Gastroenterology 1976, **71**: 439–443.

277 Flickinger JC, Epstein AH, Iwatsuki S, Carr BI, Starzl TE. Radiation therapy for primary carcinoma of the extrahepatic biliary system. An analysis of 63 cases. Cancer 1991, **68**: 289–294.

278 Gallagher PJ, Millis RR, Mitchinson MJ. Congenital dilatation of the intrahepatic bile ducts with cholangiocarcinoma. J Clin Pathol 1972, **25**: 804–808.

279 Hayashi S, Miyazaki M, Kondo Y, Nakajima N. Invasive growth patterns of hepatic hilar ductal carcinoma. A histologic analysis of 18 surgical cases. Cancer 1994, **73**: 2922–2929.

280 Henson DE, Albores-Saavedra J, Corle D. Carcinoma of the extrahepatic bile ducts. Histologic types, stage of disease, grade, and survival rates. Cancer 1992, **70**: 1498–1501.

280a Hoang M, Murakata L, Katabi N, Henson D, Albores-Saavedra J. Invasive papillary carcinomas of the extrahepatic bile ducts: a clinicopathologic and immunohistochemical study of 13 cases. Mod Pathol 2002, **15**: 1251–1258.

281 Hsu W, Deziel DJ, Gould VE, Warren WH, Gooch GT, Staren ED. Neuroendocrine differentiation and prognosis of extrahepatic biliary tract carcinomas. Surgery 1991, **110**: 604–610.

282 Iida S, Tsuzuki T, Ogata Y, Yoneyama K, Iri H, Watanabe K. The long-term survival of patients with carcinoma of the main hepatic duct junction. Cancer 1987, **60**: 1612–1619.

283 Kayahara M, Nagakawa T, Ueno K, Ohta T, Takeda T, Miyazaki I. Lymphatic flow in carcinoma of the distal bile duct based on a clinicopathologic study. Cancer 1993, **72**: 2112–2117.

284 Klatskin G. Adenocarcinoma of the hepatic duct at its bifurcation within the porta hepatis. An unusual tumor with distinctive clinical and pathological features. Am J Med 1965, **38**: 241–256.

285 Klempnauer J, Ridder GJ, von Wasielewski R, Werner M, Weimann A, Pichlmayr R. Resectional surgery of hilar cholangiocarcinoma: a multivariate analysis of prognostic factors. J Clin Oncol 1997, **15**: 947–954.

286 Koo J, Ho J, Wong J, Ong GB. Mucoepidermoid carcinoma of the bile duct. Ann Surg 1982, **196**: 140–148.

287 Kozuka S, Tsubone M, Hachisuka K. Evolution of carcinoma in the extrahepatic bile ducts. Cancer 1984, **54**: 65–72.

288 Laitio M. Carcinoma of extrahepatic bile ducts. A histopathologic study. Pathol Res Pract 1983, **178**: 67–72.

289 Langer JC, Langer B, Taylor BR, Zeldin R, Cummings B. Carcinoma of the extrahepatic bile ducts. Results of an aggressive surgical approach. Surgery 1985, **98**: 752–759.

290 MacCarty RL, LaRusso NF, May GR, Bender CE, Wiesner RH, King JE, Coffey RJ. Cholangiocarcinoma complicating primary sclerosing cholangitis. Cholangiographic appearances. Radiology 1985, **156**: 43–46.

291 Maxwell P, Davis RI, Sloan JM. Carcinoembryonic antigen (CEA) in benign and malignant epithelium of the gallbladder, extrahepatic bile ducts, and ampullae of Vater. J Pathol 1993, **170**: 73–76.

292 Minsky BD, Kemeny N, Armstrong JG, Reichman B, Botet J. Extrahepatic biliary system cancer. An update of a combined modality approach. Am J Clin Oncol 1991, **14**: 433–437.

293 Nagura H, Tsutsumi Y, Watanabe K, Hasegawa H, Fujimoto T, Sugita T, Mitomi T. Immunohistochemistry of carcinoembryonic antigen, secretory component and lysozyme in benign and malignant common bile duct tissues. Virchows Arch [A] 1984, **403**: 271–280.

294 Nishihara K, Tsuneyoshi M, Niyama H, Ichimiya H. Composite glandular-endocrine cell carcinoma of the extrahepatic bile duct. Immunohistochemical study. Pathology 1993, **25**: 90–94.

295 Okuda K, Kubo Y, Okazaki N, Arishima T, Hashimoto M, Jinnouchi S, Sawa Y, Shimokawa Y, Nakajima Y, Noguchi T, Nakano M, Kojiro M, Nakashima T. Clinical aspects of intrahepatic bile duct carcinoma including hilar carcinoma. A study of 57 autopsy-proven cases. Cancer 1977, **39**: 232–246.

296 Qualman SJ, Haupt HM, Bauer TW, Taxy JB. Adenocarcinoma of the hepatic duct junction. A reappraisal of the histologic criteria of malignancy. Cancer 1984, **53**: 1545–1551.

297 Ritchie JK, Allan RM, Macartney J, Thompson H, Hawley PR, Cooke WT. Biliary tract carcinoma associated with ulcerative colitis. Q J Med 1974, **43**: 263–279.

298 Sameshima Y, Uchimura M, Muto Y, Maeda J, Tsuchiyama H. Coexistent carcinoma in congenital dilatation of the bile duct and anomalous arrangement of the pancreatico-bile duct. Carcinogenesis of coexistent gallbladder carcinoma. Cancer 1987, **60**: 1883–1890.

299 Strom BL, Hibberd PL, Soper KA, Stolley PD, Nelson WL. International variations in epidemiology of cancers of the extrahepatic biliary tract. Cancer Res 1985, **45**: 5165–5168.

300 Suda K, Matsumoto Y, Miyano T. An extended common channel in patients with biliary tract carcinoma and congenital biliary dilatation. Surg Pathol 1988, **1**: 65–69.

301 Takao S, Uchikura K, Yonezawa S, Shinchi Haikou T. Mucin core protein expression in extrahepatic bile duct carcinoma is associated with metastases to the liver and poor prognosis. Cancer 1999, **86**: 1966–1975.

302 Tompkins RK, Thomas D, Wile A, Longmire WP Jr. Prognostic factors in bile duct carcinoma. Analysis of 96 cases. Ann Surg 1981, **194**: 447–457.

303 van der Wal AC, van Leeuwen DJ, Walford N. Small cell neuroendocrine (oat cell) tumour of the common bile duct. Histopathology 1990, **16**: 398–400.

304 Vardaman C, Albores-Saavedra J. Clear cell carcinomas of the gallbladder and extrahepatic bile ducts. Am J Surg Pathol 1995, **19**: 91–99.

305 Wee A, Ludwig J, Coffey RJ, LaRusso NF, Wiesner RH. Hepatobiliary carcinoma associated with primary sclerosing cholangitis and chronic ulcerative colitis. Hum Pathol 1985, **16**: 719–726.

306 Weinbren K, Mutum SS. Pathological aspects of cholangiocarcinoma. J Pathol 1983, **139**: 217–238.

307 Whelton MJ, Petrelli M, George P, Young WB, Sherlock S. Carcinoma of the junction of the main hepatic ducts. Q J Med 1969, **38**: 211–230.

308 Yamamoto M, Nakajo S, Tahara E, Miyoshi N. Endocrine cell carcinoma of extrahepatic bile duct. Acta Pathol Jpn 1986, **36**: 587–593.

Other malignant tumors

309 Aldabagh SM, Shibata CS, Taxy JB. Rhabdomyosarcoma of the common bile duct in an adult. Arch Pathol Lab Med 1986, **110**: 547–550.

310 Angeles-Angeles A, Quintanilla L, Larriva J. Primary carcinoid of the common bile duct. Immunohistochemical characterization of a case and review of the literature. Am J Clin Pathol 1991, **96**: 3341–3444.

311 Borja SR, Meyer WR, Cahill JP. Malignant melanoma of the gallbladder. Report of a case. Cancer 1984, **54**: 929–931.

312 Carstens PHB, Ghazi C, Carnighan RH, Brewer MS. Primary malignant melanoma of the common bile duct. Hum Pathol 1986, **17**: 1282–1285.

313 Chamberlain RS, Blumgart LH. Carcinoid tumors of the extrahepatic bile duct. A rare cause of malignant biliary obstruction. Cancer 1999, **86**: 1959–1965.

314 Chittal SM, Ra PM. Carcinoid of the cystic duct. Histopathology 1989, **15**: 643–646.

315 Davis GL, Kissane JM, Ishak KG. Embryonal rhabdomyosarcoma (sarcoma botryoides) of the biliary tree. Report of five cases and review of the literature. Cancer 1969, **24**: 333–342.

316 Deugnier Y, Turlin B, Lehry D, Pennarun JR, Verger P, Launois B, Ramee MP. Malignant melanoma of the hepatic and common bile ducts. A case report and review of the literature. Arch Pathol Lab Med 1991, **115**: 915–917.

317 Dong XD, DeMatos P, Prieto VG, Seigler HF. Melanoma of the gallbladder: a review of cases seen at Duke University Medical Center. Cancer 1999, **85**: 32–39.

318 Enad JG, Lapa JC, Jaklic B, Nellestein ME, Ghosh BC. Kaposi's sarcoma of the gallbladder. Mil Med 1992, **157**: 559–561.

319 Fidias P, Carey RW, Grossbard ML. Non-Hodgkin's lymphoma presenting with biliary tract obstruction. A discussion of seven patients and a review of the literature. Cancer 1995, **75**: 2063–2068.

320 Fullarton GM, Burgoyne M. Gallbladder and pancreatic

metastases from bilateral renal carcinoma presenting with hematobilia and anemia. Urology 1991, 38: 184–186.

321 Golbey S, Gerard PS, Frank RG. Metastatic hypernephroma masquerading as acute cholecystitis. Clin Imaging 1991, 15: 293–295.

322 Goodman ZD, Albores-Saavedra J, Lundblad DM. Somatostatinoma of the cystic duct. Cancer 1984, 53: 498–502.

323 King DK, Ewen SWB, Sewell HF, Dawson AA. Obstructive jaundice. An unusual presentation of granulocytic sarcoma. Cancer 1987, 60: 114–117.

323a Konishi E, Nakashima Y, Smyrk T, Masuda S. Clear cell carcinoid tumor of the gallbladder: a case without von Hippel-Lindau disease. Arch Pathol Lab Med 2003, 127: 745.

324 Lack EE, Perez-Atayde AR, Schuster SR. Botryoid rhabdomyosarcoma of the biliary tract. Report of five cases with ultrastructural observations and literature review. Am J Surg Pathol 1981, 5: 643–652.

325 McCluggage WG, Mackel E, McCusker G. Primary low grade malignant lymphoma of mucosa-associated lymphoid tissue of gallbladder. Histopathology 1996, 29: 285–288.

326 Maitra A, Krueger JE, Tascilar M, Offerhaus GJ, Angeles-Angeles A, Klimstra DS, Hruban RH, Albores-Saavedra J. Carcinoid tumors of the extrahepatic bile ducts: a study of seven cases. Am J Surg Pathol 2000, 24: 1501–1510.

327 Mendoza-Marin M, Hoang MP, Albores-Saavedra J. Malignant stromal tumor of the gallbladder with interstitial cells of Cajal phenotype. Arch Pathol Lab Med 2002, 126: 481–483.

328 Mihara S, Matsumoto H, Tokunaga E, Yano H, Ota M, Yamashita S. Botryoid rhabdomyosarcoma of the gallbladder in a child. Cancer 1982, 49: 812–818.

329 Mosnier JF, Brousse N, Sevestre C, Fléjou JF, Delteil C, Hénin D, Potet F. Primary low-grade B-cell lymphoma of the mucosa-associated lymphoid tissue arising in the gallbladder. Histopathology 1992, 20: 273–275.

330 Newmark H III, Kliewer K, Curtis A, DenBesten L, Enenstein W. Primary leiomyosarcoma of gallbladder seen on computed tomography and ultrasound. Am J Gastroenterol 1986, 81: 202–204.

331 Nguyen G. Primary extranodal non-Hodgkin's lymphoma of the extrahepatic bile ducts. Report of a case. Cancer 1982, 50: 2218–2222.

332 Ortiz-Hidalgo C, de Leon Bojorge B, Albores-Saavedra J. Stromal tumor of the gallbladder with phenotype of interstitial cells of

Cajal: a previously unrecognized neoplasm. Am J Surg Pathol 2000, 24: 1420–1423.

333 Papotti M, Galliano D, Monga G. Signet-ring cell carcinoid of the gallbladder. Histopathology 1990, 17: 255–259.

334 Peison B, Rabin L. Malignant melanoma of the gallbladder. Report of three cases and review of the literature. Cancer 1976, 37: 2448–2454.

335 Ricci R, Maggiano N, Martini M, Mulé AMA, Pierconti F, Capelli A, Larocca LM. Primary malignant melanoma of the gall bladder in dysplastic naevus syndrome. Virchows Arch 2001, 438: 159–165.

336 Riopel MA, Klimstra DS, Godellas CV, Blumgart LH, Westra WH. Intrabiliary growth of metastatic colonic adenocarcinoma: a pattern of intrahepatic spread easily confused with primary neoplasia of the biliary tract. Am J Surg Pathol 1997, 21: 1030–1036.

337 Rugge M, Sonego F, Militello C, Guido M, Ninfo V. Primary carcinoid tumor of the cystic and common bile ducts. Am J Surg Pathol 1992, 16: 802–807.

338 Ruymann FB, Raney B Jr, Crist WM, Lawrence W Jr, Lindberg RD, Soule EH. Rhabdomyosarcoma of the biliary tree in childhood. A report from the Intergroup Rhabdomyosarcoma Study. Cancer 1985, 56: 575–581.

339 Sinkre PA, Murakata L, Rabin L, Hoang MP, Albores-Saavedra J. Clear cell carcinoid tumor of the gallbladder another distinctive manifestation of Von Hippel-Lindau disease. Am J Surg Pathol 2001, 25: 1334–1339.

340 Sreekantaiah C, Rao UN, Karakousis CP, Sandberg AA. Cytogenetic findings in a malignant fibrous histiocytoma of the gallbladder. Cancer Genet Cytogenet 1992, 59: 30–34.

341 Tanaka K, Iida Y, Tsutsumi Y. Pancreatic polypeptide-immunoreactive gallbladder carcinoid tumor. Acta Pathol Jpn 1992, 42: 115–118.

342 Wagner MS, Shoup M, Pickleman J, Yong S. Primary malignant melanoma of the common bile duct: a case report and review of the literature. Arch Pathol Lab Med 2000, 124: 419–422.

343 White J, Chan Y-F. Epithelioid angiosarcoma of the gallbladder. Histopathology 1994, 24: 269–271.

344 Willen R, Willen H. Primary sarcoma of the gallbladder. A light and electron-microscopical study. Virchows Arch [A] 1982, 396: 91–102.

345 Yasuma T, Yanaka M. Primary sarcoma of the gallbladder. Report of three cases. Acta Pathol Jpn 1971, 21: 285–304.

15 Pancreas and ampullary region

Pancreas

Normal anatomy

The pancreas forms from two separate buds or *Anlagen*, which later rotate and fuse. The ventral bud, which appears as a part of the developing hepatic duct, forms the posterior and inferior parts of the head and the uncinate process; the larger dorsal bud, which develops from the other side of the foregut and extends into the dorsal mesentery, forms the body, tail, and anterior part of the head. Abnormalities in this process result in annular pancreas (see p. 1062) and most types of heterotopic pancreas (see p. 1063).

The normal adult pancreas has a dual composition.

The **exocrine component** is made of lobular units of acini, which empty into ducts of increasingly larger size that finally merge into the main pancreatic duct (of Wirsung) and the accessory pancreatic duct (of Santorini). The duct of Wirsung ends in the papilla of Vater, usually in conjunction with the common bile duct (see Chapter 14). The duct of Santorini ends separately in a minor duodenal papilla. Normally, the Wirsung and Santorini ducts are joined by numerous anastomotic connections; when this is not the case, and the duct of Santorini constitutes the principal drainage for the organ, the condition known as *pancreas divisum* results. This occurs in approximately 10% of individuals. It has been claimed to predispose to the development of pancreatitis, but the evidence for this is less than conclusive.[4,11]

Acinar cells are large, pyramidally shaped, and highly polarized. The luminal border has prominent microvilli, the apical cytoplasm is filled with markedly eosinophilic PAS-positive zymogen granules, and the basilar cytoplasm is intensely basophilic because of the abundance of granular endoplasmic reticulum. Centroacinar cells have a paler cytoplasm and oval nuclei; as their name indicates, they are located in the central portion of the acinus. They blend with the cells of the intercalated duct, which drains the acinus. Focal collections of centroacinar cells sometimes occur and should not be confused with Langerhans' islets.[12] The merging of intercalated ducts forms the intralobular ducts, which are lined by small cuboidal cells with pale cytoplasm.[9] These are continued by the much larger interlobular ducts, which are lined by mucin-producing columnar cells. The microscopic composition of Wirsung and Santorini ducts is similar to that of the interlobular ducts, except for a greater representation of goblet cells.[9]

The **endocrine component** of the pancreas is mainly represented by the Langerhans' islets.[3] These constitute 1% to 2% of the adult pancreas but a much larger proportion of the organ at the time of birth. Most islets are round and compact structures that are highly vascularized but with only scanty amounts of connective tissue. Their average diameter is 225 µm; individual variations in size exist, but any islet measuring over 400 µm should be regarded as abnormal. In humans, islets are composed of the following main cell types:

1 *B cells*. The insulin-secreting cells constitute two thirds to three fourths of the islet population and tend to concentrate in the central portions. The insulin granules have a typical crystalline appearance on ultrastructural examination. B cells also secrete islet cell amyloid polypeptide (IAPP), a putative hormone that is thought to be co-released with insulin.[16]

2 *A cells*. The glucagon-secreting cells make up one fifth to one fourth of the total islet population and are mainly located at their periphery. Ultrastructurally, the secretory granules are characterized by an eccentric electron-dense core.

3 *D cells*. The somatostatin-secreting cells are scattered throughout the islets, and their number is rather small. Ultrastructurally, the content of the granules has a very low electron density.

4 *PP cells*. The pancreatic polypeptide-secreting cells are very scarce in most islets and are typically located at their periphery.

It should be pointed out that all of the endocrine cells present in the pancreas are of endodermal rather than neural crest derivation, as formerly believed.[14] All of them stain for chromogranin A and B, except beta cells (however, beta cell tumors are often positive for this marker). They are also immunoreactive for synaptophysin, neuron-specific enolase, and neurofilaments.[13]

The islets located in the portion of the pancreatic head derived from the ventral bud differ from the others by virtue of their highly irregular outlines, trabecular arrangement, and very high content of PP cells.[15]

In addition to the Langerhans' islets, endocrine cells can be found in connection with ducts and acini.[2] Most of these cells are of Kultschitsky (serotonin-producing) and PP type. It should be noted that G (gastrin-producing) cells are not normally present in the normal adult pancreas, a remarkable fact considering that this organ is the most common site for the occurrence of G cell tumors (gastrinomas) (see p. 1089). However, progastrin expression has been detected in mammalian (including human) pancreas. The processing of the molecule is more complete in the fetal than in the adult pancreas but always less complete than in the adult antral mucosa.[1]

Nesidioblastosis is the name given to the presence of islets in intimate association with ducts, with formation of so-called *ductulo-insular complexes*.[5,7] Focal and diffuse forms of this condition have been described.[6] This process is interpreted as an indicator of active formation of endocrine cells by the multipotential cells located in the basal portion in these ducts. A mild degree of nesidioblastosis is normal in infants,[10] although an exaggerated form of this condition has been described in cases of neonatal hypoglycemia, with or without associated hyperplasia of Langerhans' islets.[5] It has also been occasionally reported in adult patients with persistent hyperinsulinemic hypoglycemia, but the correlation between the morphologic and functional abnormalities is poor.[8]

Congenital abnormalities

Annular pancreas

Annular pancreas is a rare embryologic abnormality in which the ventral primordium of the pancreas fails to rotate properly.[19,21] It can be seen by itself or in combination with other congenital abnormalities of the gastrointestinal tract.[17,18] Down syndrome is a predisposing condition for this anomaly.[20] Grossly, there is encirclement of the duodenum by pancreatic parenchyma, which may lead to constriction of the duodenal lumen.[17] The duct in the annular pancreas originates anteriorly and courses to the right over the duodenum and then posteriorly and to the left behind the duodenum, passing near the common duct and finally joining the main pancreatic duct.[23] These anatomic variations have to be kept in mind when surgery is contemplated.[18] Pancreatitis may develop in association with this anomaly.

Microscopically, the annular pancreas contains a large number of PP cells in its many irregularly shaped islets, in keeping with its origin from the ventral bud.[22,23]

Heterotopic pancreas

Heterotopia of pancreatic tissue is a relatively frequent congenital anomaly. It is most common in the duodenum (particularly the second portion), stomach, and jejunum but also occurs in the ileum, Meckel's diverticulum, gastric and intestinal diverticula, gallbladder and bile ducts, large bowel, spleen (usually within or immediately beneath the capsule), omentum, abdominal wall, and several other locations.[32,34]

Grossly, the heterotopic tissue resembles normal pancreas. Firm, yellow, lobulated nodules measuring up to 4 cm are seen sharply circumscribed from the surrounding tissues (Fig. 15.1). Central umbilication is often present in the cases located beneath a mucosa, corresponding to a central duct that opens into the lumen; both the umbilication and the duct can be demonstrated radiographically and constitute an important diagnostic sign.[26] Microscopically, acinar and ductal tissues are always present, whereas islet tissue is found in only one third of the cases. In some cases, there is also a component of pyloric-type mucous glands. The islet component contains all the major types of endocrine cells, but their relative number varies a great deal from case to case. In most instances, the islets are rich in alpha cells and poor in PP cells (dorsal type), but in others the reverse is true (ventral type).[28] Heterotopic pancreas in the stomach should be distinguished from pancreatic metaplasia of the gastric mucosa[35] (see Chapter 11).

Every pathologic change that occurs in the pancreas can occur in its heterotopic counterpart, including acute pancreatitis and neoplasms of either exocrine or endocrine type.[24,25,31,33] Heterotopic pancreas in the stomach may cause hemorrhage, ulceration, or pyloric obstruction.[27] When located in the area of the ampulla of Vater, it may result in obstructive jaundice. It has been postulated that some of the reported cases of intrasplenic mucinous cystadenomas have arisen in heterotopic pancreatic tissue.[25,29,30]

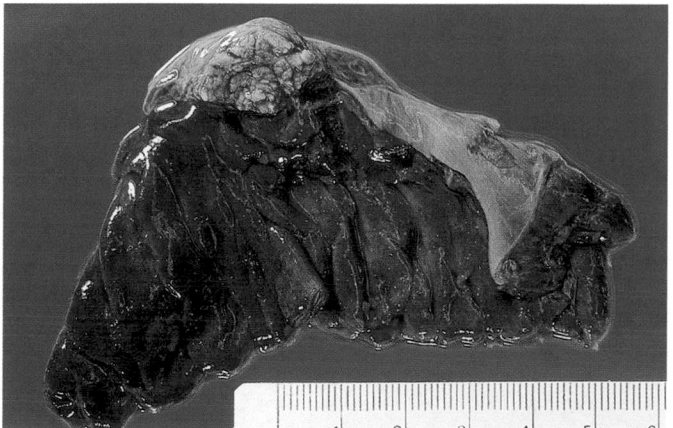

Fig. 15.1 Ectopic pancreas in the wall of the jejunum. (Courtesy of Dr. RA Cooke, Brisbane, Australia: From Cooke RA, Stewart B: Colour Atlas of Anatomical Pathology, Edinburgh, Churchill Livingstone, 2004)

Pancreatitis

Acute pancreatitis

The pathogenesis of acute pancreatitis remains controversial.[40,55,67,68] Experimental work has been hampered by the fact that most laboratory animals do not suffer naturally from this illness. Opie[60] postulated an obstructive mechanism in a classic work published in 1901 after demonstrating in his famous case of pancreatitis the presence of a small stone lodged in the ampulla, which had converted the common bile duct and the main pancreatic duct (duct of Wirsung) into a "common channel." The assumption was that the bile had passed from the common bile duct into the pancreatic duct and activated trypsinogen, thus beginning a series of events that included the digestion of the duct wall, adjacent parenchyma, and vessel walls by trypsin, as well as the splitting of fat and formation of calcium soaps by lipase. Theoretically, fibrosis of the sphincter of Oddi or a neoplasm in this region could induce a similar process. Indeed, cases of acute pancreatitis secondary to tumors of the ampullary area or to primary or metastatic tumors in the head of the pancreas have been recorded.[49]

The difficulty with this theory is that the formation of a common channel with a stone impacted in the ampulla or another clearly identifiable anatomic cause occurs in less than 5% of patients with acute pancreatitis. This discrepancy could be explained by postulating a transient blockage of the ampulla of Vater by a migrating gallstone, by biliary sludge, or by a spasm of the sphincter of Oddi, all of which could produce a common channel in the absence of an identifiable impacted stone. Acosta and Ledesma[36] recovered gallstones in the feces of 34 of 36 patients with pancreatitis but in only 3 of 36 control subjects (patients with lithiasis of the gallbladder but no pancreatitis). Biliary sludge (a suspension of cholesterol monohydrate crystals or calcium bilirubinate granules) was found by Lee et al.[54] in 23 of 31 patients with "idiopathic" acute pancreatitis. Sphincter spasm can be demonstrated in experimental animals and in humans by chemical and radiographic studies performed under various conditions, including the administration of drugs resulting in muscle contraction (such as morphine) and relaxation (such as nitrites). The pancreatic duct is visualized in about 25% of the patients having postoperative T-tube cholangiograms. If the common duct T tube is in place and pancreatic secretion is injected intravenously, almost pure pancreatic juice is recovered from the T tube.[43] If spasm of the sphincter of Oddi is produced by morphine and radiopaque material is injected through the T tube into the common duct, the whole pancreatic system may be visualized. Bile taken from the common duct or gallbladder often contains pancreatic enzymes. Conversely, bile may be found in the peripancreatic tissues of patients operated on for pancreatitis, possibly because of rupture of a pancreatic duct.

All these experiments demonstrate that a common channel may indeed occur under physiologic circumstances and that the relative secretory pressures of the gallbladder, bile ducts, and pancreatic ducts (which fluctuate greatly under different conditions) and the status of the sphincter of Oddi will determine the type and direction of the flow.

A related approach to the problem is a careful anatomic examination of the system in an attempt to determine how often a common channel is possible on anatomic grounds alone. Several autopsy studies have shown that there are many anatomic variations in the ampullary area that preclude such an occurrence. These include separation of common and pancreatic ducts by a septum and independent emptying of the main pancreatic duct into the duodenum. The consensus reached from these anatomic studies is that a common channel is anatomically present in 50% to 60% of all individuals.[50]

The anatomic arrangement of the accessory (Santorini's) pancreatic duct is also important because this duct has no sphincter; therefore if it communicates with the duct of Wirsung and the latter in turn communicates with the common bile duct, the biliary duct pressure will predominate. In the study of Howard and Jones,[50] the duct of Santorini communicated with the duct of Wirsung in 54 (36%) of the 150 cases. Interestingly enough, this communication was present in almost 50% of the cases in which reflux could be demonstrated but in less than 15% of those in whom no reflux occurred.

A variation of the obstructive theory for the pathogenesis of pancreatitis postulates that partial or total obstruction of the pancreatic duct *alone* is enough to induce the production of pancreatitis, through a mechanism of increased secretion, rupture of ductules and acini, and liberation of pancreatic enzymes into the parenchyma. In another classic study, Rich and Duff[64] postulated that squamous metaplasia of the pancreatic duct might result in such an obstruction. Such a type of metaplasia, however, can be found at autopsy in at least 6% of otherwise normal pancreases.[42] Interestingly, if a patient with heterotopic pancreas develops acute pancreatitis, the inflammatory process will also affect the heterotopic foci. It has also been postulated that butyl cholinesterase, normally present in large amounts in the pancreatic acinar cells, may be directly involved in the production of pancreatitis.[45,46] Regardless of what the precise pathogenetic mechanism will prove to be, it is a fact that the large majority of cases of acute pancreatitis are associated with biliary tract disease (63%), alcoholism (8%), and trauma. Some cases—especially in the AIDS population—have been associated with specific infections such as toxoplasmosis[37,44] or adenovirus.[59]

The gross changes vary from a swollen and edematous but otherwise well-preserved organ to a hemorrhagic and necrotic mass of tissue (Fig. 15.2). Yellow plaques and nodules representing fat necrosis are seen within the pancreas as well as throughout the mesenteric and peritoneal fat (Fig. 15.3). The process sometimes spreads to the neighboring colon, and it may result in localized ileus, stenosis, perforation, fistulous formations, and ischemic necrosis.[53]

Microscopically, the earlier changes in the pancreas are represented by acinar cell homogenization, ductal dilatation with epithelial degeneration, diffuse interstitial edema, leukocytic infiltration, and fibroblastic reaction.[63] Whether the pancreatitis is initiated in the acinar cell or in the interstitial space is controversial. If the disease progresses, extensive necrosis and hemorrhage of pancreatic tissue supervene. This may occur within hours, as shown by contrast-enhanced CT scan.[51,56]

The foci of peritoneal fat necrosis become almost immediately surrounded and infiltrated by neutrophils;

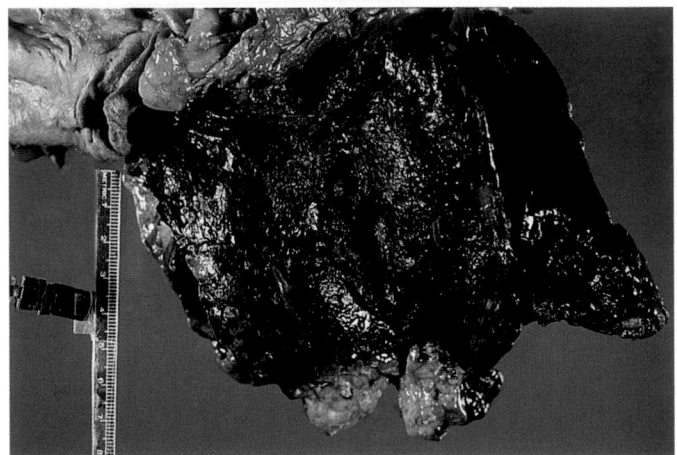

Fig. 15.2 Gross appearance of acute pancreatitis. Extensive hemorrhagic necrosis of the pancreas extends into the surrounding mesentery.

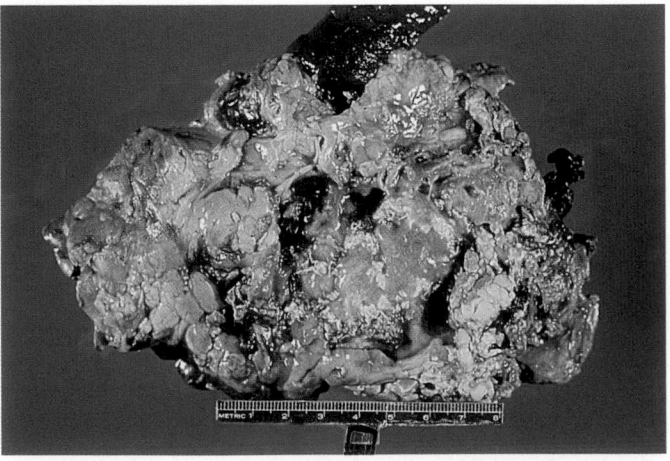

Fig. 15.3 Gross appearance of acute pancreatitis. Massive fat necrosis of the pancreas and mesenteric fat.

this population later changes to foamy histiocytes and lymphocytes. Calcification occurs early and extensively in these areas. The pancreatic necrotic foci can undergo secondary infection; this condition, termed *infected pancreatic necrosis*, is currently regarded as the most common, most severe, and most lethal of the infectious complications of acute pancreatitis.[39,58]

Acute pancreatitis can evolve into a chronic form, but the large majority of the cases of chronic pancreatitis are not preceded by an acute phase.[52,65,69]

Acute pancreatitis is characteristically associated with serum elevation of amylase, an alteration that can also be found with duodenal ulcer, volvulus, gangrenous cholecystitis, ruptured aortic aneurysm, and mesenteric thrombosis.[62,71] Serum lipase is also elevated; this elevation is more sustained than that of amylase and its determination is particularly useful in cases of alcoholic pancreatitis.[66,71] Serum C-reactive protein is a reliable marker for the presence of pancreatic necrosis.[51]

The overall mortality rate for acute pancreatitis is about 20%.[41] It is higher (about 50%) when the pancreas is hemorrhagic and necrotic than when it is swollen and edematous but viable (10% to 15%). The most widely used therapeutic approach is to treat medically suspected cases of acute pancreatitis vigorously for 4 to 6 hours; if the diagnosis is in doubt and the patient is deteriorating despite therapy, emergency laparotomy is indicated. Others have suggested emergency endoscopic retrograde cholangiopancreatography with or without endoscopic papillotomy.[48,56] The presence of an upper abdominal mass suspected of being a pseudocyst and persistent rising jaundice are also indications for surgical intervention.[57] The development of diabetes is more common in patients with acute pancreatitis who had pancreatic resections than in those treated with pancreatic lavage.[47]

Postoperative pancreatitis is in most, but not all, cases the result of direct operative trauma to the pancreatic region.[61] Of 70 cases reported by White et al.,[70] the original operation had included exploration of the common bile duct in 28 and gastric resection in 17. In 16 patients, the surgical procedure was such that the possibility of local trauma could be excluded. Asbun et al.[38] reported on cases of acute relapsing pancreatitis as a complication of papillary stenosis after endoscopic sphincterotomy.

Chronic pancreatitis

Etiologic factors for chronic pancreatitis include obstruction of the ductal system by carcinoma or stones,[82] alcoholism (present in up to 75% of the cases in some series),[108,109] hyperparathyroidism (as a result of the hypercalcemia),[93,106] genetic factors (in the hereditary form manifested during childhood and inherited as an autosomal mendelian dominant trait),[92,113] polyarteritis nodosa, mumps infection,[78] a "tropical" form,[75] tuberculosis,[104] sarcoidosis,[76] malakoplakia,[115] secondary exten-

sion of primary sclerosing cholangitis,[86,87] and HIV infection (in which the morphologic changes are usually mild). Other unusual forms of chronic pancreatitis are mentioned below. In some cases the chronic inflammation seems to be a sequela of acute pancreatitis.[105a]

A strong association has been found between chronic pancreatitis and mutations of the cystic fibrosis gene, suggesting that the latter aberration may be an important predisposing factor.[79,102]

At the molecular level, K-*ras* mutations have been found in close to half of the cases of chronic pancreatitis, indicating that this alteration should not be viewed as a marker of malignancy but that it can also occur in the self-limited pancreatic lesions that accompany chronic inflammation.[95] Acidic and basic fibroblast growth factors have been found to be abundant in ductal and acinar cells in cases of chronic pancreatitis, suggesting that they may be involved in the pathogenesis of this disorder.[84]

Clinically, chronic pancreatitis characteristically presents with abdominal pain, which can be very severe and which constitutes the most common indication for surgery.[72,105] When the pancreatitis is fully developed, it leads to severe deficiency of both exocrine and endocrine function.[90]

Morphologically, two major forms of chronic pancreatitis have been described, one associated with obstruction of the major pancreatic ducts and the other accompanied by extensive parenchymal calcification[100,101] (Figs 15.4 and 15.5).

Obstructive chronic pancreatitis is the result of narrowing or occlusion of the pancreatic ducts, the most common causes being carcinoma and stones. In the latter condition, known as *chronic pancreatitis with lithiasis*, most of the stones are found in the duct of Wirsung within 2 to 4 cm of the ampulla of Vater, and often restricted to a small portion of the gland.[80,106]

Chronic calcifying pancreatitis (which constitutes about 95% of the cases) is characterized grossly by a pancreas that is nodular, hard, and misshapen, and which may be either enlarged or atrophic. Microscopically, the main features are dilatation of ducts and acini, squamous metaplasia, intraluminal eosinophilic mucoprotein plugs (which often calcify), acinar atrophy, and perilobular and intralobular sclerosis (Fig. 15.6).[99] Proliferative changes in the ductal epithelium are frequent.[111] Sometimes, a scar plate develops between the head of the pancreas and the duodenum, a condition that has been dignified by the term *groove pancreatitis*.[74,114] Unusual forms of chronic pancreatitis include *eosinophilic pancreatitis* (to be distinguished from other causes of eosinophilic infiltration of the pancreas),[71a] *lymphoplasmacytic sclerosing pancreatitis* (which can be accompanied by lymphoplasmacytic chronic cholecystitis and biliary tract disease, and which may be the pancreatic component of inflammatory fibrosclerosis),[71b, 96a] (Fig. 15.7), *idiopathic duct-centric chronic pancreatitis* (an ill-defined condition),[96a] and

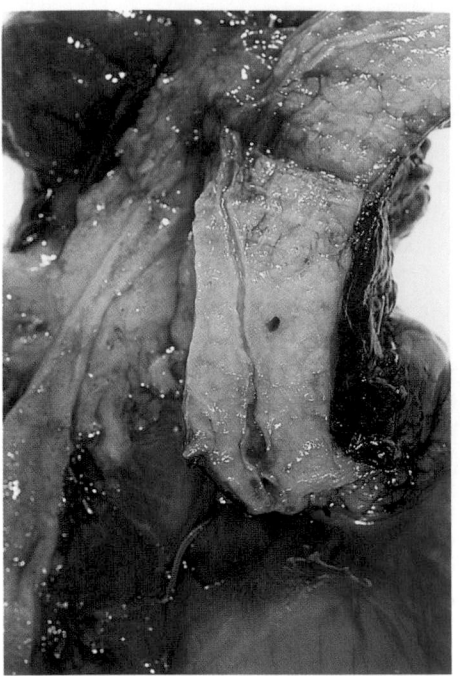

Fig. 15.4 Gross appearance of chronic pancreatitis. There is diffuse fibrosis of the pancreas, associated with stenosis and increased tortuosity of the main pancreatic duct.

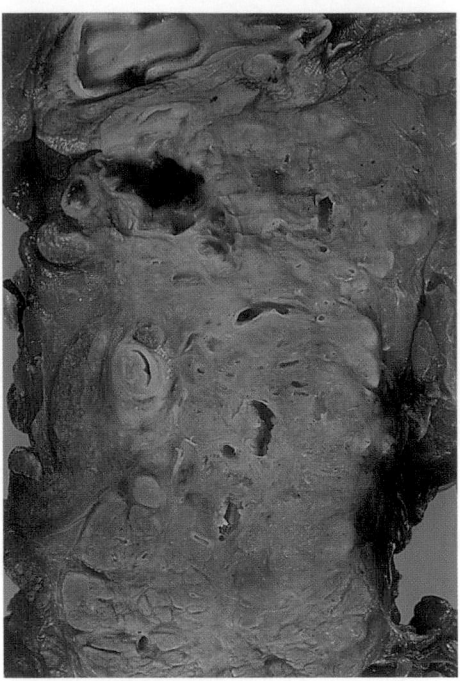

Fig. 15.5 Close-up of another case of chronic pancreatitis, showing fibrosis and cystic dilatation of ducts, some of which are occupied by a grumous secretory material.

Fig. 15.6 Chronic pancreatitis, showing a proteinaceous stone in a cystically dilated duct.

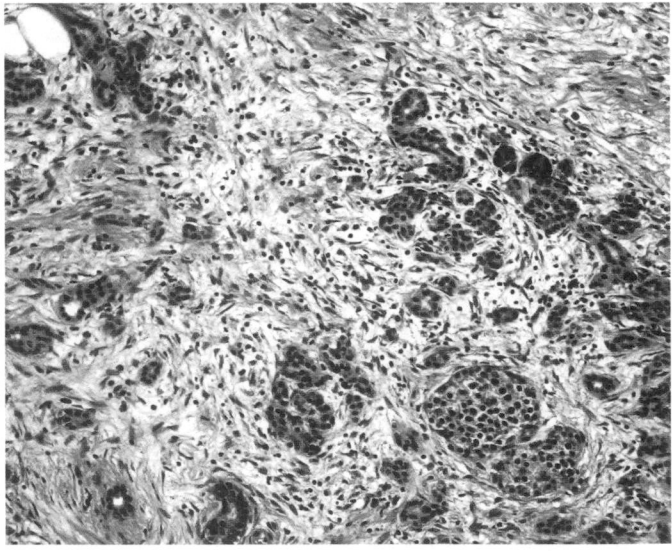

Fig. 15.7 Sclerosing lymphoplasmacytic pancreatitis. There is marked atrophy of the acinar component.

paraduodenal pancreatitis (a pseudoneoplastic form, presumably secondary to obstruction of an accessory pancreatic duct).[109a]

The appearance of Langerhans' islets in chronic pancreatitis varies considerably from case to case. Often, there is atrophy and distortion, with a relative decrease in the number of B cells.[91] Conversely, other cases show a marked proliferation of islet cells, which may grow in cords and small clusters.[88] Sometimes they may even simulate a malignant neoplasm (Figs 15.8 and 15.9).[73] Immunohistochemical stains have shown that all major types of islet cells are represented.[73] Concomitant hyper-

plasia of Brunner's glands in the duodenum is a common finding in chronic pancreatitis.[107]

A good correlation exists between the severity of the histologic alterations and pancreatic exocrine function tests.[85] Acinar necrosis and acute inflammation are seen more often in patients with persistent pain than in those who are free of pain.[97] However, cases exist in which severe abdominal pain of pancreatic origin is accompanied by minimal morphologic changes.[112]

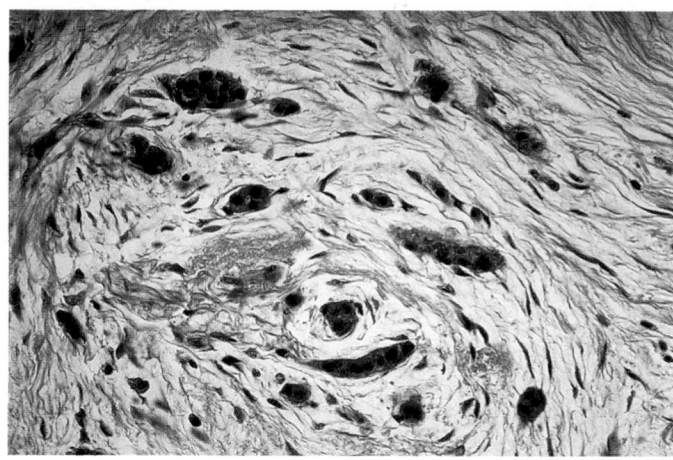

Fig. 15.8 Pseudoneoplastic proliferation of pancreatic endocrine cells in chronic pancreatitis.

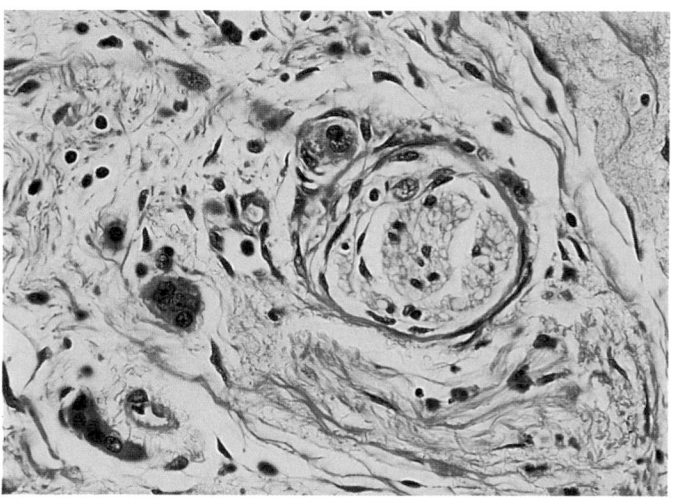

Fig. 15.9 Perineurial extension of pancreatic endocrine cells in a case of chronic pancreatitis associated with extensive fibrosis. These cells were immunoreactive for insulin.

Complications of chronic pancreatitis include pseudocyst and pseudoaneurysm formation which can lead to exsanguinating acute hemorrhage.[77,81,89] A rare complication of both acute and chronic pancreatitis is the occurrence of widespread metastatic fat necrosis, presumably as a consequence of the liberation of lipase by the damaged organ. Subcutaneous tissue (particularly in the legs), mediastinum, pleura, pericardium, bone marrow, periarticular fat, and liver can be involved.[96] Erythema nodosum-like lesions of the skin, polyarthropathy, and avascular bone necrosis are some of the alterations that may develop as a result.[96]

The treatment of chronic pancreatitis includes pancreatic duct drainage (through pancreaticojejunostomy or endoscopic removal of ductal stones), partial pancreatic resection, and near-total pancreatectomy with or without islet autotransplantation.[72,83,94,98,103,110]

Pancreatic transplantation

The two main indications for pancreatic transplantation are chronic pancreatitis and insulin-resistant diabetes mellitus.[116,123,124] At present, pancreatic graft survival rates approach 90% at 1 year.[119] Two important complications of the procedure are "graft pancreatitis" and pancreatic thrombosis; both of these occur in the early postoperative period and are thought to be related to donor factor, procurement and preservation variables, and postimplantation recipient management.[117,118] The two other important complications, which tend to occur at a later stage, are recurrence of the original disease and rejection. Microscopic changes specific for rejection are vascular alterations such as "endothelialitis," vasculitis, and obliterative endarteritis. Another common abnormality is a periductal lymphocytic or mixed infiltrate.[121] Morphologic features found to correlate strongly with a negative outcome include moderate to severe inflammation of acinar tissue, acinar tissue loss and fibrosis, and vascular luminal narrowing.[122] Vasculitis is a more aggressive and clinically more significant lesion than endothelialitis and defines the existence of severe rejection.[122]

Transplanted pancreases show a significant increase in glucagon-producing islet cells and a corresponding decrease in insulin-producing cells.[120]

Recurrent diabetes in the graft is detected by selective loss of B cells and by the presence of "isleitis." Identification of the latter is aided by staining for CD45 and CD45RO.[121]

Abscess

Pancreatic abscesses are most often seen as complications of acute pancreatitis. They are bona fide infections, characterized by the presence of pus and the microbiologic identification of bacteria in over 90% of the cases.[126] They have different presentation, clinical course, and outcome than infected pseudocysts and necrosis, from which they should be distinguished.[125]

Pseudocysts

Pseudocysts are related to pancreatitis, trauma, and, rarely, to neoplastic obstruction of large ducts.[131] They can become very large, spread beyond the substance of the pancreas into the lesser peritoneal cavity, and present through the gastrocolic or gastrohepatic ligament. They are multiple in about 15% of the cases.[128] Grossly, the wall is thick and irregular. The inner surface is ragged, and the intraluminal content is cloudy or bloody. Microscopically, the lack of epithelial lining is the main distinguishing feature with true cysts and cystic neoplasms. The intraluminal fluid has a high amylase content. Communication with the ductal system may or may not be present.[127]

Complications of pancreatic pseudocyst include perforation and hemorrhage. The splenic artery is the most common source of the latter, which can be massive and result in sudden death.[129]

Small pseudocysts located in the body or tail of the pancreas can be treated with excision. Most of the others are treated by external drainage (preferred for the infected cysts) or internal drainage, in the form of transgastric cystgastrostomy or cystojejunostomy to a Roux-en-Y loop of jejunum.[130] External drainage is contraindicated if the pseudocyst connects with the ductal system.[127]

True cysts

Cysts lined by non-neoplastic glandular epithelium are usually congenital and associated with similar cysts of other viscera such as liver or kidney (Fig. 15.10). They may be seen as a component of von Hippel–Lindau disease or of oral–facial–digital syndrome type I.[134] The condition is also referred to as *pancreatic cystic dysplasia*.[133a]

Other epithelial-lined cysts of the pancreas are retention cysts, cystic acinar transformation, para-ampullary duodenal wall cysts (which may be derived from the ductal component of ectopic pancreatic tissue), enterogenous cysts, dermoid cysts, and parasitic cysts.[132,135,138]

Lymphoepithelial cyst is a distinctive variant of pancreatic cyst that is morphologically similar to the homonymous cyst of branchial pouch-derived structures. It is often multilocular and lined by squamous epithelium, and it features abundant lymphocytes in the wall, usually accompanied by germinal center forma-

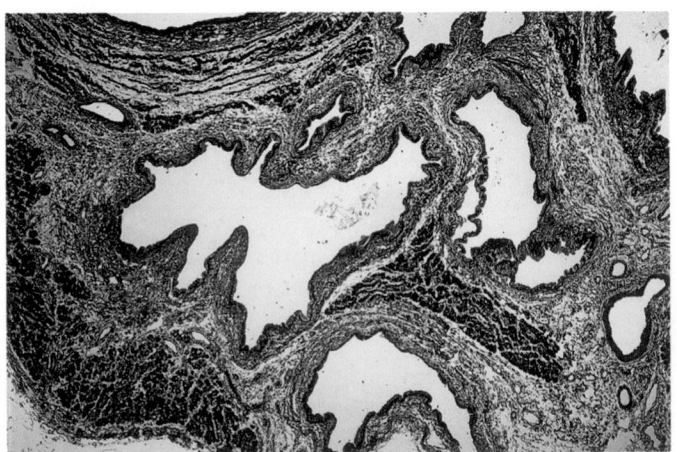

Fig. 15.10 Congenital cystic change in the pancreas ("pancreatic cystic dysplasia").

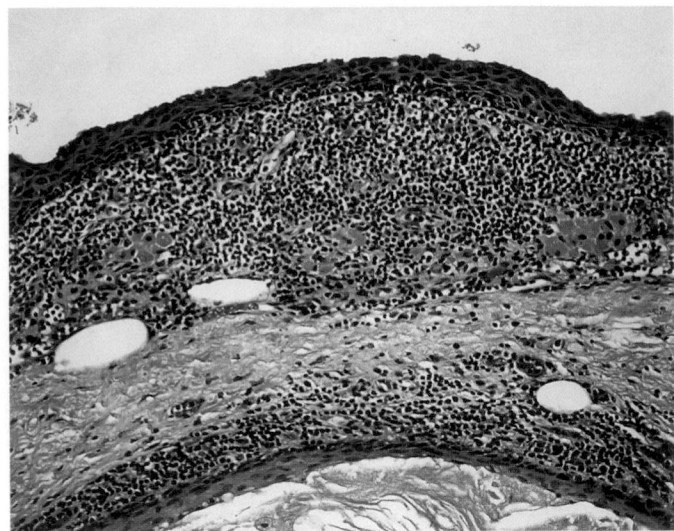

Fig. 15.11 Lymphoepithelial cyst of pancreas. The cyst lining is of squamous type.

tion.[133,137,141] It has been suggested that these pancreatic lymphoepithelial cysts develop from pancreatic ducts protruding into a lymph node or an intrapancreatic accessory spleen[132,140] (Fig. 15.11). If true, this would render them anatomically and perhaps pathogenetically related to the branchial cleft-related lymphoepithelial cysts of the head, neck and mediastinum.[139]

Mucinous non-neoplastic cyst is the latest addition to the list of cystic lesions of the pancreas.[136] It can be uni- or multilocular, and it may represent the benign extreme of the spectrum of mucinous cystadenoma.

Tumors

Ductal adenocarcinoma

General and clinical features

Ductal adenocarcinoma of the exocrine pancreas comprises about 85% of all cases of pancreatic malignancy.[144,154,161] It constitutes the fourth most common cause of death from cancer in the United States, and its incidence is increasing, particularly in women.[168] Cases have been reported in the past in workers exposed to β-naphthylamine or benzidine.[155] Cigarette smoking has also been cited as a risk factor.[142,151,159]

It is estimated that about 10% of pancreatic cancers show familial aggregation consistent with a genetic susceptibility.[150a] At least five such syndromes have been identified, to wit: 1) Familial breast cancer with germline mutation of BRCA2; (2) Familial atypical multiple mole melanoma syndrome with germline mutation in the p16 gene; (3) Peutz–Jeghers syndrome with germline mutations in the STK11/LKB1 gene; (4) Hereditary nonpolyposis colorectal cancer with germline mutations in one of the DNA mismatch repair genes; (5) Hereditary pancreatitis with germline mutations in the cationic trypsinogen gene.[143,150a,157,158,160] It has been claimed that chronic pancreatitis is positively associated with an increased risk for pancreatic cancer, but the cause–effect relationship between the two diseases is often difficult to ascertain.[151,156,169] It has also been suggested that variations in pancreaticobiliary ductal anatomy may be related to the incidence of carcinoma, in view of the fact that lack of a common channel has been found at autopsy to be associated with microscopic abnormalities of the ductal epithelium.[146] There is an increase in the incidence of diabetes in patients with pancreatic carcinoma, but this usually develops within a short time after the diagnosis of cancer, suggesting that in most instances it represents a secondary event.[150] Overproduction of islet amyloid polypeptide by beta cells may contribute to this complication.[163]

Most patients with pancreatic carcinoma are elderly, and there is a slight male preponderance (1.6:1 ratio).[159] Because of its strategic location in relation to the extrahepatic bile ducts, carcinoma of the head of the pancreas usually causes progressive jaundice that is associated with pain in at least half of the patients; however, the diagnosis in most cases is made when the tumor is relatively large (about 5 cm) and has extended beyond the pancreas (85% of the cases).[167] The rare microscopic or grossly detectable but minute carcinomas that are found incidentally at autopsy also tend to be invasive and to be accompanied by perineurial spread.[148,152] Carcinomas of the body and tail of the pancreas grow insidiously and often have already metastasized at the time of diagnosis. They are associated with peripheral venous thrombi in about 25% of the patients[153]; these may be a late development in patients with overt carcinoma or may be present in patients with clinically silent tumor.[162,164] The syndrome is thought to be due to the release by the macrophages present in the stroma of tumor necrosis factor, interleukin-1, and interleukin-6. Another mechanism may be production of substances with a procoagulant activity by the tumor cells themselves.[142a]

Several techniques have been used with various degrees of success to detect pancreatic carcinoma at an early stage.[166] These include CT scan, nuclear magnetic resonance, celiac angiography, sonography, endoscopic retrograde cholangiopancreatography (ERCP), selenomethionine scan, duodenal aspiration, and serum tests.[147] The latter use monoclonal antibodies against various cancer-related antigens. Those measuring levels of SPan-1 and CA19-9 antigen seem more effective than those measuring CEA or other markers.[145,149,165]

Location and gross features

Pancreatic carcinoma is located in the head of the pancreas in two thirds of the patients and in the body or tail in the other third. Multiple tumors are found in about 20% of the cases. Most are poorly delineated and firm,

Fig. 15.12 Gross appearance of typical invasive ductal carcinoma of the head of the pancreas. The tumor is protruding into the duodenal lumen.

with a yellowish gray cut surface (Fig. 15.12). Rarely, the tumor undergoes massive cystic degeneration.[170a] The duodenal wall is invaded by direct extension in one fourth of the tumors arising from the pancreatic head. The involved pancreatic ducts frequently become greatly dilated and plugged with necrotic tumor. This dilatation may extend for a considerable distance beyond the main mass of the tumor. Extrapancreatic extension is common; when extensive, it may be very difficult to determine whether or not a given tumor is of pancreatic origin. Cubilla and Fitzgerald[170] found that one third of the cases clinically regarded as pancreatic carcinomas were not of pancreatic origin but rather of duodenal (ampullary), retroperitoneal, or metastatic nature. Of 28 patients in whom the carcinoma was grossly located in the area of the head of the pancreas, an origin from the pancreatic ducts could be proved in only 14. In 5, the site of origin could not be determined; in the others, the tumors originated in the ampulla, bile ducts, or duodenum.

The non-neoplastic pancreas distal to the tumor may show extensive atrophy, chronic inflammation, and fibrosis, plus the ductal dilatation previously mentioned.

Microscopic features

Pancreatic duct adenocarcinomas are graded microscopically into well differentiated, moderately differentiated, and poorly differentiated (Fig. 15.13A). Their pattern of growth is papillary in only a minority of the cases once the intraductal papillary mucinous tumors are excluded (see later section).[173] In the well-differentiated tumors, the microscopic diagnosis can be extremely difficult.[179] Close attention must be given to cytologic details. At low-power examination, the glands are often well formed, have a large lumen, and are lined by one or a few

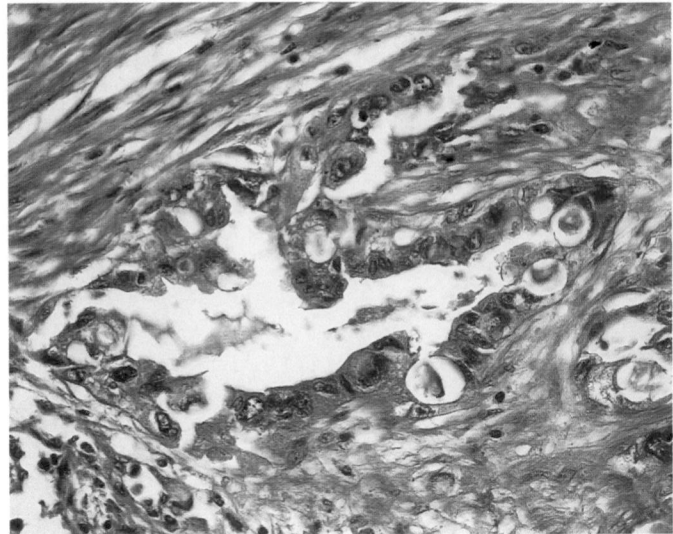

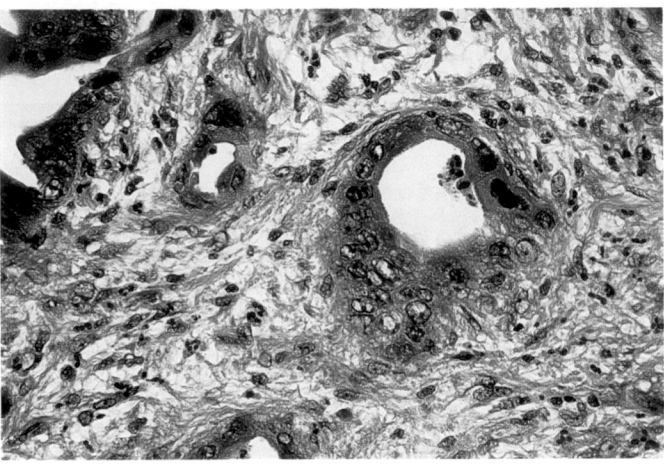

A

B

Fig. 15.13 A and **B,** Pancreatic ductal adenocarcinoma. It is typical of this tumor type to be well differentiated architecturally but to show marked cytologic atypia.

layers of cylindrical or cuboidal epithelium. Their overall low-power appearance may not be particularly suggestive of carcinoma, except for the irregularities in the shape and distribution of the glands and the peculiar concentric desmoplastic stroma that surrounds them[180]; however, high-power examination of the lining epithelium will show one or more features that, in this location, are indicative of malignancy: marked nuclear pleomorphism, loss of polarity, prominent nucleoli, and mitotic activity. This disparity between the high degree of cytologic atypia and the low level of architectural atypia is typical of tumors of the pancreaticobiliary region[183] (Fig. 15.13B). Perineurial invasion, which is present in 90% of the cases, constitutes an additional important diagnostic sign. However, there are two caveats: benign epithelial inclusions have been observed in pancreatic nerves,[175] and perineurial extension of islet cells can occur in chronic pancreatitis.[171] The perineurial invasion by carcinoma can extend from the intrapancreatic nerves into the

extrapancreatic neural plexus, a fact that might have some bearing on the surgical procedure.[184,186] Invasion of blood vessels, particularly veins, is seen in half of the tumors.

Carcinoma in situ is found in the duct epithelium adjacent to the carcinoma in about 20% to 30% of the cases, sometimes at a distance from the main tumor mass and even at the point of surgical transection.[177,187] Atypia and papillary hyperplasia of duct epithelium are present in one third of the cases with carcinoma, whereas the incidence of these abnormalities in the pancreases of control subjects is very low[172,174,176,182,185] (Fig. 15.14). Conversely, the prevalence of squamous metaplasia, pyloric gland metaplasia, mucous hypertrophy, and focal epithelial hyperplasia is not significantly different between the two groups.[176,181] Because of these facts, carcinoma in situ and atypical hyperplasia (now grouped under the term pancreatic intraepithelial neoplasia or PanIN) are regarded as precursors of invasive ductal adenocarcinomas.[170b] This belief is supported by the realization that some of these lesions have been identified in pancreases years before the development of invasive carcinoma, the fact that molecular genetic analysis has revealed that they frequently harbor many of the same genetic alterations present in invasive cancer (see later section), and the nearly universal detection in them of telomere shortening.[187a]

The lobular tissue may be completely destroyed because of ductal occlusion by the invasive carcinoma. The islet tissue is usually well preserved, resulting in an appearance designated as *insular pancreas*; however, both atrophic and hypertrophic changes can occur in the islets. Most commonly, destruction of a variable amount of islet tissue mass results in a subclinical or overt diabetic picture. Rarely, hypertrophy of the islets occurs distal to a ductal adenocarcinoma and produces hypoglycemia. Gambill[178] found significant pancreatitis in 26 (10%) of 255 patients with pancreatic or ampullary

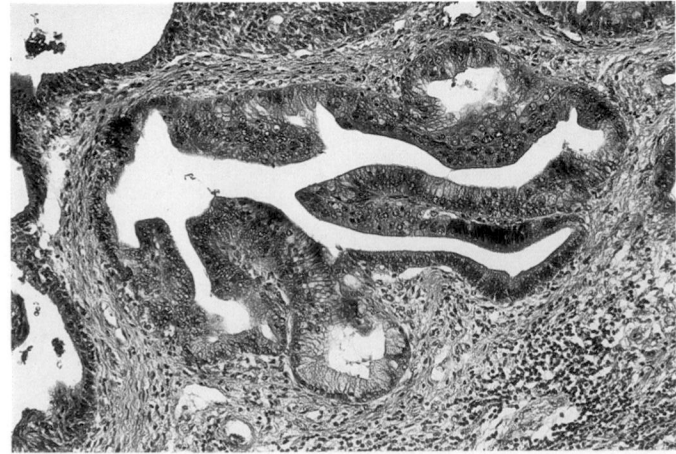

Fig. 15.14 Atypical hyperplastic ductal changes (PanIN) in pancreas affected elsewhere by invasive ductal adenocarcinoma.

carcinoma. The presence of pancreatitis resulted in a considerable delay in the diagnosis of carcinoma.

Histochemical and immunohistochemical features

Most pancreatic ductal adenocarcinomas are positive for mucin stains. These mucins are of gastric and small intestinal types and usually lack 8-0-acetyl-*N*-acetyl-neuraminic acid (a marker of large intestinal-type mucin).[201,212,213]

Immunohistochemically, there is consistent reactivity for keratin and EMA. The keratins expressed are those of simple epithelia such as 7, 8, 18, and 19 (as normal ductal cells) but also 15/16, 17, 20, and—in a lesser percentage—5/6, 10, and 13.[204,211] Keratin 20 is expressed less frequently in pancreatic ductal than in ampullary adenocarcinomas,[188] but the difference is not such as to be of diagnostic help.[193] The glycoprotein MUC1 is expressed in over 60% of conventional invasive ductal carcinomas and in a similar percentage of the in situ carcinomas (PanINs), supporting a pathogenetic relationship between the two; this is in contrast to the intraductal papillary carcinomas discussed below, mucinous (colloid) carcinomas, ampullary carcinomas, and colorectal carcinomas, which are more often positive for MUC2.[187b,213a] Other markers usually expressed by ductal adenocarcinoma cells are CEA, CA19-9, B72.3, other "pancreatic cancer-associated antigens" such as DU-PAN-2, YPan-1 and SPan-1, the Tn and sialosyl-Tn antigens, and the DF3 antigen (mammary-type apomucin).[190,195,203] Unfortunately, ducts in cases of chronic pancreatitis also exhibit immunoreactivity for most of these markers, thus greatly diminishing their differential diagnostic utility.[197,199,208,209] Additional substances often detected in these tumors include M1 and cathepsin E (markers of gastric surface–foveolar epithelial cells) and pepsinogen II (a marker of gastroduodenal mucopeptic cells), indicating that gastrointestinal differentiation is common in them.[207] There is also expression of villin (a cytoskeletal protein associated with axial microfilament bundles of brush border microvilli), epidermal growth factor receptor,[189,198] maspin,[202] and sea urchin fascin homolog, the latter having been identified by global expression microarrays.[200] Laminin is present at the interphase between neoplastic glands and stroma.[194]

A high proportion of ductal-type adenocarcinomas contain a minor population of endocrine cells, demonstrable with silver stains or with immunostains for chromogranin or for one or another of the islet cell hormones.[192,196,206,210] There is also frequent expression of the neural cell adhesion molecule Nr-CAM.[191] In rarer instances, a distinct admixture of immunohistochemically detectable ductal and endocrine components is seen in the same tumor.[205]

Molecular genetic features

Cytogenetically, structural rearrangements (or loss) of genes located on 1p, 3p, 6p, 8p, and 17p are often found and seem to be of importance in pancreatic carcinogenesis.[226] Mutations and/or accumulation of p53 are detected in about half of the cases,[215,218,227] mutations of the K-*ras* oncogene in over 90% of the cases,[224] inactivation of p16 in over 95% of the cases,[216,224] and overexpression of HER2/*neu* oncogene in approximately half of the cases.[233] Accumulation of p53 is present in the in situ component in two thirds of the positive cases, suggesting that it represents an early genetic event in pancreatic carcinogenesis.[222] Similarly, HER2/*neu* is present in the large majority of the intraductal atypical proliferative lesions that accompany the invasive component, in keeping with its presumed role as a mediator of growth factor-related signal transduction.[217,229] Along these lines, it is worth mentioning that the search for genetic molecular alterations in the invasive component of pancreatic ductal carcinoma and in the accompanying (and presumably preceding) in situ lesions of the same specimen have provided key information on the genetic progression of pancreatic carcinoma.[214,223,225,234]

It is important to point out that patients with chronic pancreatitis lacking microscopic features of invasive or in situ adenocarcinoma or ductal atypia often show K-*ras* mutations, indicating that this genetic alteration is not specific for malignancy or even premalignant conditions but that it can also be present in self-limited conditions.[228,230] Obviously, this limits greatly the diagnostic utility of this marker in histologic or cytologic material. The *DPC4* suppressor gene[221] is inactivated in approximately half of pancreatic ductal carcinomas but practically never in benign conditions; therefore, the immunohistochemical *absence* of the protein product in the ductal epithelium of a pancreatic biopsy specimen is strongly suggestive of carcinoma.[232]

Another molecular alteration that has been found in a subset of pancreatic ductal adenocarcinoma is a set of DNA replication errors; interestingly, tumors with this alterations tend to have wild K-*ras*, pushing borders, and a syncytial growth pattern (i.e., a medullary carcinoma-type morphology).[220]

Amplification of the nuclear receptor co-activator AIB 1 (which maps to chromosome 20q12) has been found in over half of pancreatic adenocarcinomas, the significance of this finding being obscure.[219]

DNA ploidy analyses have yielded aneuploid patterns in about half of the tumors, the incidence being higher with the poorly differentiated forms.[231,235] Whether this determination will be useful as an independent prognostic variable remains to be seen.

Other microscopic types

Uncommon but reasonably distinctive variants of pancreatic adenocarcinoma include *adenosquamous carcinoma* (a term more accurate than mucoepidermoid carcinoma or adenoacanthoma),[243] *oncocytic carcinoma* (to be distinguished from other oncocytic tumors of pancreas, see

p. 1078) (Fig. 15.15),[241,246] *clear cell carcinoma*,[242,245] *hepatoid carcinoma*,[247,249] *signet ring carcinoma*, and *mucinous (colloid) carcinoma* (to be distinguished from mucinous cystadenocarcinoma and intraductal papillary mucinous neoplasm, see pp. 1076 and 1078, respectively)[236,240] (Fig. 15.16). Mucinous (colloid) carcinoma, which may result in pseudomyxoma peritonei, has been said to result from the combined effect of the production of MUC2 (a gelforming mucin), altered cell polarity, and abnormal cell-stroma interaction.[235a] The few reported cases of pure *squamous cell carcinoma* of the pancreas probably represent a variant of adenosquamous carcinoma in which the squamous component has overrun the glandular elements; this tumor type can be associated with hypercalcemia.[238]

Adsay[237] has described a subtype of ductal adenocarcinoma with a *foamy gland pattern* having a deceptively benign appearance, and Wilentz et al.[248] have identified a *medullary carcinoma* characterized by a solid, sometimes lymphoepithelioma-like pattern of growth, usually wild-type (nonmutated) *ras*, and occasional multicentricity.

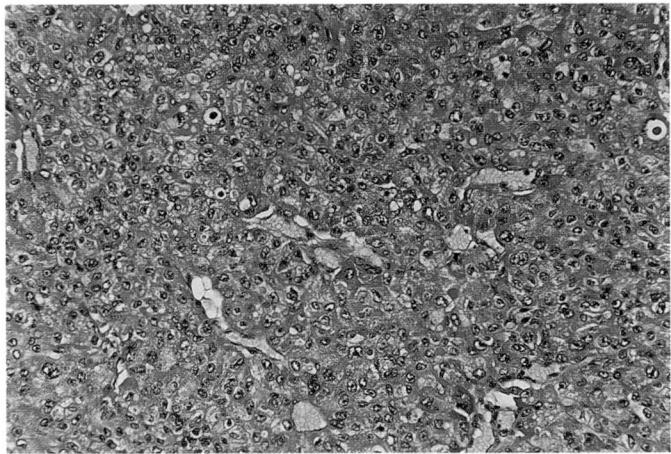

Fig. 15.15 Oncocytic carcinoma of the pancreas. The tumor grows in a solid fashion, without evidence of glandular differentiation. Stains for endocrine markers were negative.

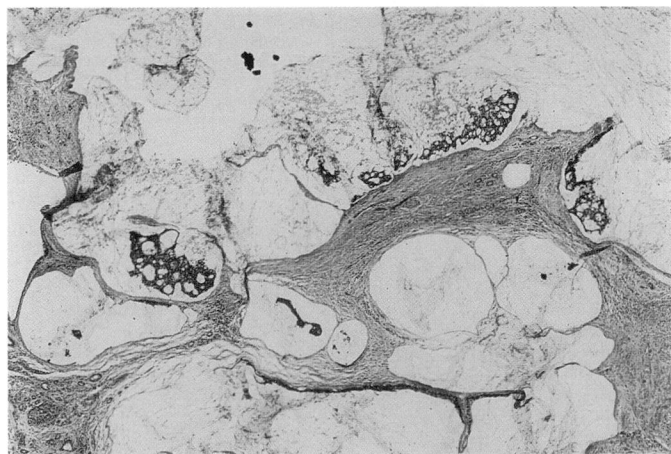

Fig. 15.16 Mucin-producing adenocarcinoma of the pancreas associated with large pools of extracellular mucin.

Microadenocarcinoma had originally been described as a distinct type of pancreatic ductal adenocarcinoma characterized by a microglandular appearance but reevaluation of the original and new cases has led to the conclusion that it represents instead a pattern of growth associated with an aggressive clinical course rather than a distinctive morphologic entity.[244]

Spread and metastases

Pancreatic duct adenocarcinoma tends to metastasize to multiple lymph nodes located around the organ. The lymph node groups most often involved in carcinoma of the head of the pancreas are those around the common hepatic artery, hepatoduodenal ligament, posterior pancreaticoduodenal, around the superior mesenteric artery, para-aortic, and anterior pancreaticoduodenal.[251,252,255] Cubilla et al.[250] found that in 33% of patients with pancreatic carcinoma, nodal metastases were present in groups of nodes not usually removed with the standard Whipple's procedure. Some of these metastases occur very early in the course of the disease.[254,256] Microscopic metastases have been found in 75% of T1 and T2 lesions.[254,257]

The most common sites of distant metastases are liver, peritoneum, lung, adrenal, bone, distant lymph node groups, skin, and central nervous system.[253] Sometimes, a distant nodal metastasis (particularly in the supraclavicular region) is the first manifestation of pancreatic carcinoma.

Cytology

Cytologic material for the diagnosis of pancreatic and periampullary carcinoma can be obtained from different sources, with various degrees of success.

1 Duodenal secretion. The reported success rate for identifying pancreatic carcinoma is 66% overall, 79% for tumors of the head, and 33% for those of the tail.[261,264]
2 Pancreatic juice obtained during the performance of an endoscopic retrograde cholangiopancreatography (ERCP). The yield rate has ranged from 50% to 85% in the reported series.[262,266]
3 Percutaneous fine needle aspiration with ultrasonic, angiographic, or CT guidance.[259,263,265,268] The accuracy of this method is over 90%.[259]
4 Intraoperative fine needle aspiration. The accuracy of this technique is well over 90% (see next section).

It should be pointed out that these cytologic techniques can also successfully identify intraductal carcinomas,[269] and that cytologic material is suitable for immunohistochemical and molecular evaluation, such as search for mutation of K-*ras*,[258,267] p53,[260] or *DPC4*.[270]

Exploration and frozen section

At the time of exploration for a presumptive diagnosis of carcinoma of the pancreas or ampullary region, evidence of metastatic disease in the peripancreatic nodes, liver, and peritoneum should be searched for and a frozen section requested if a lesion in any of these sites is encountered. In the absence of detectable metastases, the search for the primary tumor should then be undertaken. If a mass is palpated in the pancreas, this should be examined microscopically by an incisional biopsy, core needle biopsy, or fine needle aspiration. The last technique has become popular because it minimizes the possibilities of hemorrhage, pancreatitis, and tumor seeding that exist with the biopsy procedures.[271,273] When the pancreatic head is biopsied, experience is required to avoid the common bile duct, the gastroduodenal artery, and the portal vein.

During exploration of the jaundiced patient in whom no obvious pancreatic tumor is detected, the head of the pancreas should be mobilized and carefully palpated, and the common bile duct should be exposed. If the latter is dilated, it should be explored. If no tumor or stones are found in it, duodenotomy should follow, and the ampullary region should be inspected; in the presence of a mass in the area, a biopsy should be submitted for frozen section. In papillary lesions, the biopsy specimen should be deep to detect the invasive component if present. One should remember that dilatation of the common duct and of the gallbladder in the presence of jaundice and in the absence of biliary tract stones is almost always caused by carcinoma.

Frozen section interpretation of pancreatic lesions can be very difficult because of the well-differentiated nature of many carcinomas on one hand and the architectural distortion resulting from chronic pancreatitis on the other.[276,277] One should search for perineurial invasion and also evaluate carefully the cytologic features of the glandular formations.[274] When examining sections from the terminal portion of the common bile duct or the ampullary region, one should be careful not to misinterpret accessory pancreatic ducts or Beale's periluminal sacculi as malignant.[275] If all of these precautions are taken, it will be found that the accuracy of the procedure is very high, and that the percentage of cases in which the diagnosis needs to be deferred is low.[272]

Treatment

The curative treatment of pancreatic carcinoma is primarily surgical, its extent depending on the site and size of the tumor.[283] Neoplasms of the body and tail are treated with a distal pancreatectomy.[280] Neoplasms of the pancreatic head and ampullary region are generally treated with the Whipple operation, the alternative being total pancreatectomy.[278,279,282,284] These operations have traditionally carried a 10% to 20% mortality rate,[287,290] but this has decreased to less than 2% in recent times in specialized centers.[289,291] A plea has been made to include a retroperitoneal resection (with removal of nerve plexuses and lymph nodes) in curative resections for patients with stage I or II pancreatic carcinoma to diminish the frequency of retroperitoneal recurrence.[281,286]

Unfortunately, most tumors have already extended outside the pancreas at the time of laparotomy and are therefore not amenable to curative surgery. Such tumors are better treated with palliative bypass operations, which result in similar overall survival times with much less operative morbidity and mortality. Locally unresectable pancreatic carcinomas can also be treated with radiation therapy (sometimes administered intraoperatively) and/or chemotherapy.[285,288] Combination regimens result in longer survival than radiation alone.[285]

A certain number of Whipple operations (almost 10% in some large centers) performed under the clinical impression of pancreatic carcinoma will reveal only inflammatory and fibrotic changes upon microscopic examination of the resected specimen; this occurrence should be reduced to a minimum, but at the current stage of knowledge it must be accepted as one of the inevitable occasional outcomes of the procedure.[227a]

Prognosis

In most series of pancreatic carcinoma, the overall 5-year survival rate has been 4% or less, with over 90% of the patients dying within 1 year of diagnosis and with a mean survival of 3 months for untreated patients.[293,295] Even when the tumor seems confined to the pancreas at the time of surgery, the 5-year survival rate does not exceed 15%.[293,301]

Factors related to prognosis are the following:

1 *Tumor stage.* As in most other organs, stage is the most important prognostic determinator.[292,299]
2 *Microscopic grade.* Better differentiated tumors are associated with a longer median survival time.[296,300]
3 *Tumor size.* Small tumors (less than 4.5 cm in diameter) have the greatest chance of curative operation and the longest survival.[298,302] However, size does not affect survival for the unresectable tumors.[298]
4 *Blood vessel invasion* and *retroperitoneal margin of resection.* Both parameters are associated with a decreased survival.[297]
5 *Lymph node metastases.* This factor, which is included in the staging system, is of great significance. The determination is usually made on microscopic grounds, but it has been claimed that the detection of mutated k-*ras* by molecular techniques can be used as a surrogate marker.[297a]
6 *DNA ploidy.* The independent prognostic value of this parameter is very limited.[300]
7 *TGF-β1 expression.* The expression of this marker is related to better differentiated tumors and is therefore associated with a better outcome, but it probably has no independent prognostic value.[294]

Anaplastic carcinoma

Anaplastic carcinomas, also known as pleomorphic, sarcomatoid, or undifferentiated carcinomas, are in most cases variants of duct-derived carcinomas; however, their appearance is so distinctive and their behavior so aggressive that a distinction from the ordinary ductal adenocarcinoma is warranted.[316] They comprise about 7% of all nonendocrine pancreatic malignancies. Most involve the body or tail of the pancreas rather than the head. Most patients are above the age of 50 at the time of diagnosis, and there is a distinct male predilection. Three morphologic types can be recognized, which sometimes are seen in combination[303]:

1 Pleomorphic carcinomas that contain a large number of bizarre, multinucleated tumor cells (Fig. 15.17). These can be confused with amelanotic melanoma, hepatocellular carcinoma, and some types of sarcomas. Both lymph-borne and hematogenous metastases are very common.[321]
2 Tumors that are largely composed of spindle-shaped cells and that can be easily confused with sarcomas (Fig. 15.18). The diagnosis of primary sarcoma of the pancreas therefore should be regarded with a high degree of skepticism.
3 Tumors that are composed of small, monotonous round cells growing in a solid fashion, somewhat reminiscent of malignant lymphoma. Some of these tumors exhibit features of neuroendocrine differentiation and should be viewed as examples of extrapulmonary small cell neuroendocrine carcinomas[313,315] (see p. 1090). Others may show focal or extensive rhabdoid features.[312]

Any of these varieties can be accompanied by areas of ductal adenocarcinoma or a mucinous cystic neoplasm.[309,312] The presence in both components of the same K-*ras* mutations suggests a common origin[308] (Fig. 15.17).

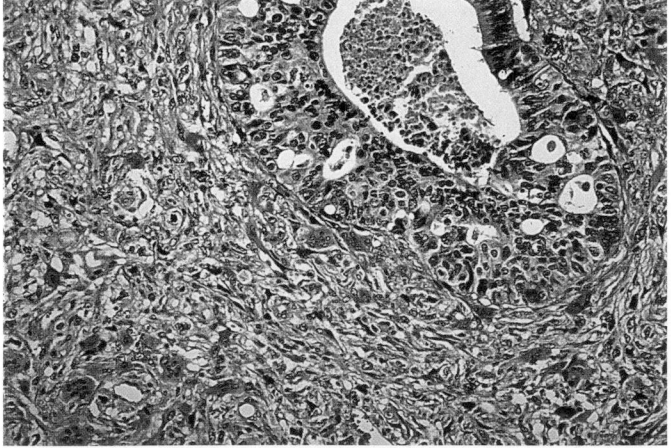

Fig. 15.17 Sarcomatoid carcinoma of the pancreas associated with areas of clear-cut glandular differentiation. The two components are sharply separated, resulting in a carcinosarcoma-type appearance.

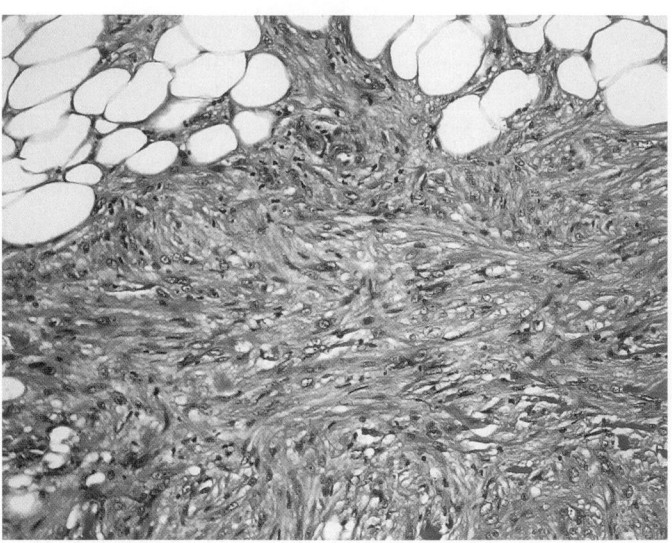

Fig. 15.18 Spindle cell carcinoma of pancreas closely simulating the appearance of a sarcoma.

Immunohistochemically, stains for keratin, EMA, and CEA are positive in the obvious epithelial component and sometimes also in the sarcoma-like areas (Fig. 15.19).

The prognosis for all of these varieties of anaplastic carcinoma is extremely poor.

Giant cell tumor of the pancreas is included in some series as another variant of anaplastic carcinoma, but it should be kept separate from it because of its different morphologic appearance and better prognosis. Grossly, it is usually large and hemorrhagic (Fig. 15.20). Occasionally, it may grow in a fashion simulating a pseudocyst.[314] Microscopically, the tumor has a dual population: relatively uniform spindle cells of mesenchymal appearance and atypical cytologic features (such as nuclear hyperchromasia and high mitotic activity) alternate with multinucleated giant cells having an appearance and a histochemical profile indistinguishable from that of normal osteoclasts.[304,307,318] The nuclei of these osteoclast-like cells are uniformly small, and mitoses are absent. Bizarre giant cells with atypical nuclei are not

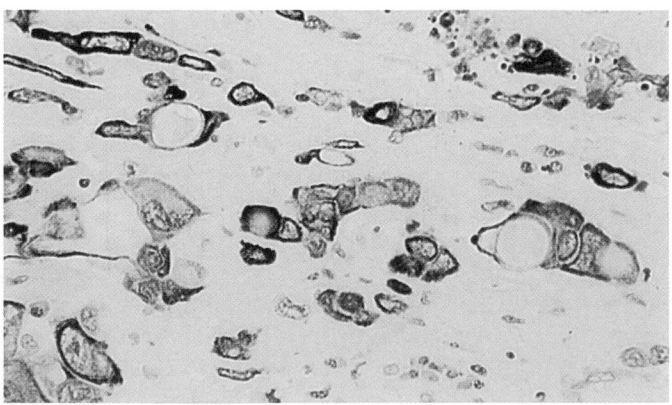

Fig. 15.19 Anaplastic carcinoma of pancreas showing immunoreactivity for keratin.

found (Fig. 15.21). In some cases, areas of clear-cut epithelial glandular appearance are seen, suggesting that giant cell tumor is yet another variant of carcinoma of ductal derivation.[311,317,320] Also in keeping with this interpretation is the occasional coexistence of giant cell tumor and anaplastic carcinoma of the pleomorphic type[305,310] and the fact that the same K-*ras* mutations have been found in the neoplastic mesenchymal-like mononuclear cells and in the intraductal atypical epithelial proliferations of mucinous cystic neoplasms, whenever present.[322] More difficult to explain is the claim by the same authors that these mutations are also present in the osteoclast-like multinucleated giant cells, inasmuch as these cells are widely regarded as of non-neoplastic nature and histiocytic derivation.[306,319]

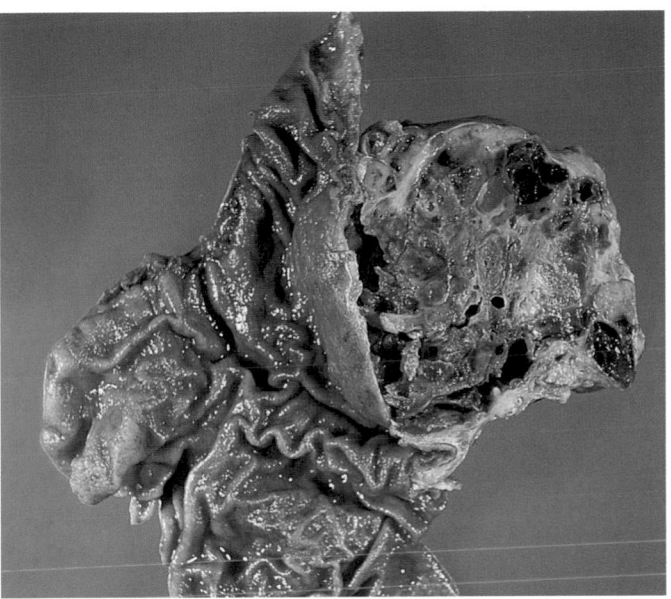

Fig. 15.20 Gross appearance of giant cell tumor of pancreas. There is a large hemorrhagic mass in the head of the pancreas that is protruding into the stomach.

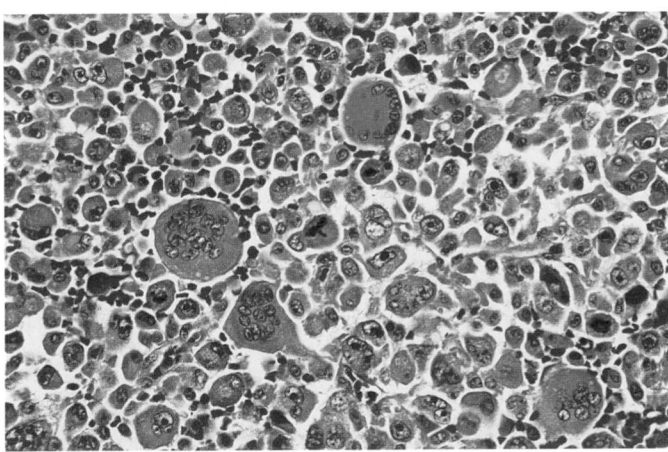

Fig. 15.21 Microscopic appearance of giant cell tumor of the pancreas. Osteoclast-like multinucleated giant cells are seen scattered among mononuclear neoplastic elements showing a high degree of atypia.

Cystic pancreatic neoplasms

Secondary cystic changes can be seen in most types of pancreatic neoplasms, whether of exocrine or endocrine nature.[326] These are to be distinguished from the tumors in which a cystic configuration is universally present and part of their definition (i.e., cystadenomas and cystadenocarcinomas).[323] It is just as important for these to be clearly separated from the non-neoplastic cysts previously described, and it is recommended that confusing terms such as proliferative pancreatic cysts be avoided for them.[325] The large majority of cystic pancreatic neoplasms fall into two distinct categories—microcystic and mucinous—while acknowledging the fact that occasional examples are difficult to classify.[324]

Microcystic cystadenoma and cystadenocarcinoma

Microcystic cystadenoma, also known as glycogen-rich or serous cystadenoma, usually presents grossly as a large multiloculated mass, the individual cystic cavities being small and filled with a clear ("serous") fluid[330] (Fig. 15.22). The spongy appearance of the cut surface is reminiscent of that of infantile polycystic kidney.

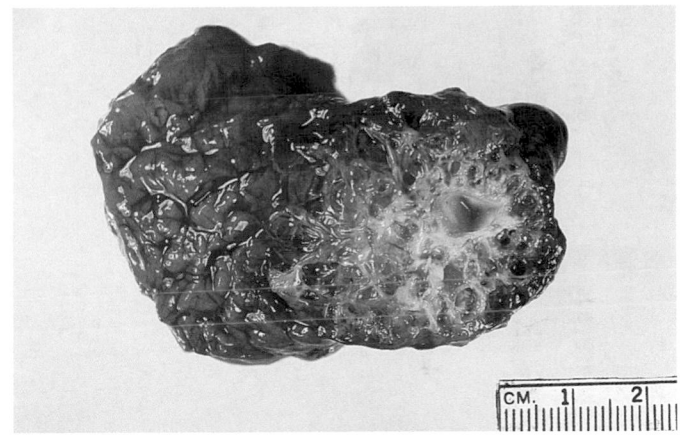

B

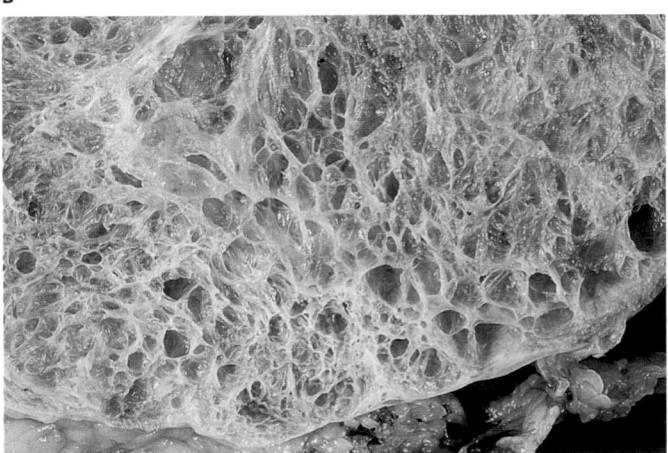

B

Fig. 15.22 A and **B**, Microcystic adenoma of pancreas. **A**, The tumor, which is sharply outlined, shows numerous small cysts. **B**, Close-up of another case showing innumerable cystic cavities separated by a thin fibrous wall.

Occasionally, the gross appearance is macrocystic and oligo- or unilocular[331,337] (Fig. 15.23). Most cases are solitary, but a few multicentric examples are on record.[335] A central scar is present in nearly half of the cases.[347] Microscopically, they are composed of multiple small

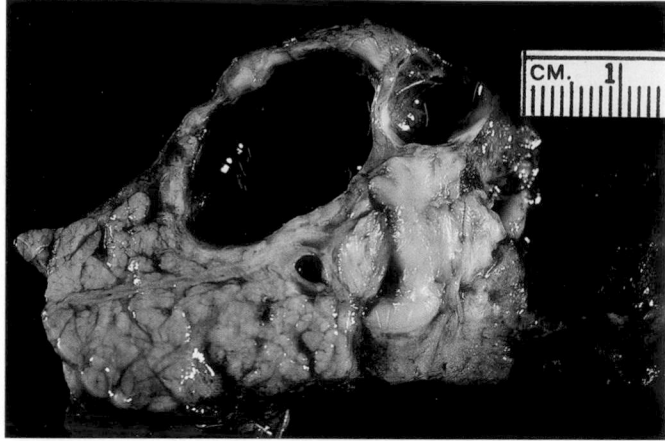

Fig. 15.23 Variant of microcystic cystadenoma showing a large unilocular cavity.

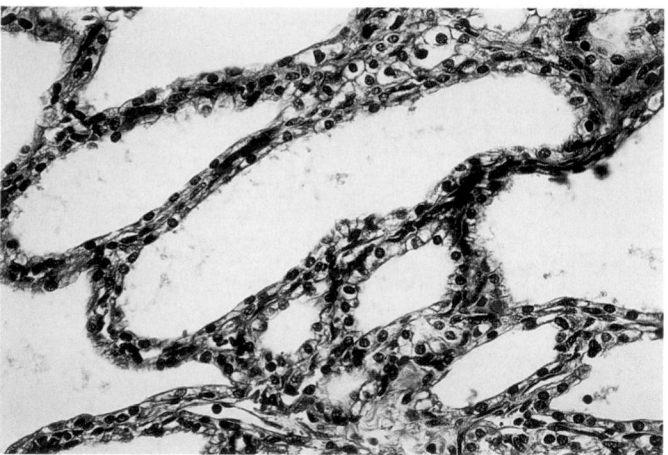

Fig. 15.24 Microcystic cystadenoma showing typical multilocular appearance.

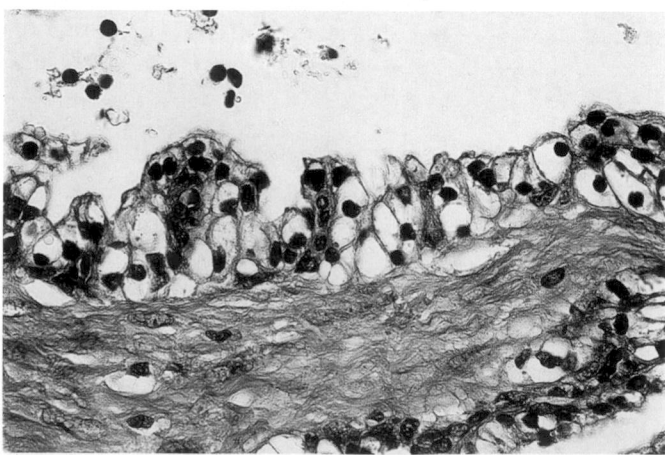

Fig. 15.25 High-power view of microcystic cystadenoma showing lining of cuboidal epithelium with optically clear cytoplasm.

cysts lined by small, flat or cuboidal cells containing abundant glycogen but only an insignificant amount of mucin[329,333] (Figs 15.24 and 15.25). A layer of myoepithelial cells is present beneath this epithelium.[340] Papillae are absent or inconspicuous. Exceptionally, the stroma of the tumor is found to contain amyloid deposits.[344] Ultrastructural studies have shown prominent microvilli and other features comparable to those of normal centroacinar cells.[328,343] A few cells with dense-core endocrine granules may also be found. Immunohistochemically, there is reactivity for EMA and low-molecular-weight keratin. The trabeculae between the locules may contain numerous Langerhans' islets. These trabeculae may also show calcification, which appears radiographically in a radiating pattern. The fluid contained in the cyst lumen has a low CEA level, in contrast to mucinous neoplasms.[336] The prominent vascularization that is typical of these tumors can be well appreciated by selective angiography.

The patients are usually elderly, and there is no sex predilection. The disease either is discovered incidentally or manifests as an abdominal mass with local discomfort or pain. Some of the cases occur in the context of von Hippel–Lindau disease,[339] and sporadic cases have been found to harbor allelic deletions and mutations of the von Hippel–Lindau tumor suppressor gene.[346] Other cases have been seen in pancreases harboring a ductal adenocarcinoma elsewhere.[338] Diabetes may be associated with these lesions if sufficient islet cell tissue is destroyed by the tumor. When located in the head of the pancreas, which is often the case, these tumors may result in gastrointestinal or biliary obstruction.[327] Excision is curative.[342]

A malignant counterpart of this tumor has been described as *serous* or *microcystic adenocarcinoma*. In one case, the microscopic appearance was similar to that of microcystic adenoma, but metastases were present in stomach and liver.[332,348] Other cases have exhibited nuclear atypia, perineurial invasion, and aneuploid DNA pattern.[334,345] Interestingly, aneuploidy has also been found in several morphologically unremarkable microcystic adenomas.[345]

Another variation on the theme is represented by the benign pancreatic tumor composed of the same cells as serous cystadenoma but having a solid instead of a microcystic pattern of growth; such a tumor has been referred to as *solid serous adenoma*.[341]

Mucinous cystic neoplasms

Mucinous cystic tumors of the pancreas are seen in a younger age group than the preceding type, predominate in women, and are characterized by the formation of large multilocular or, in rare cases, unilocular cysts lined by tall, mucin-producing cells, often forming papillae[349,363,367] (Figs 15.26 to 15.28). Most are found in the body and tail rather than in the head. Calcification in the

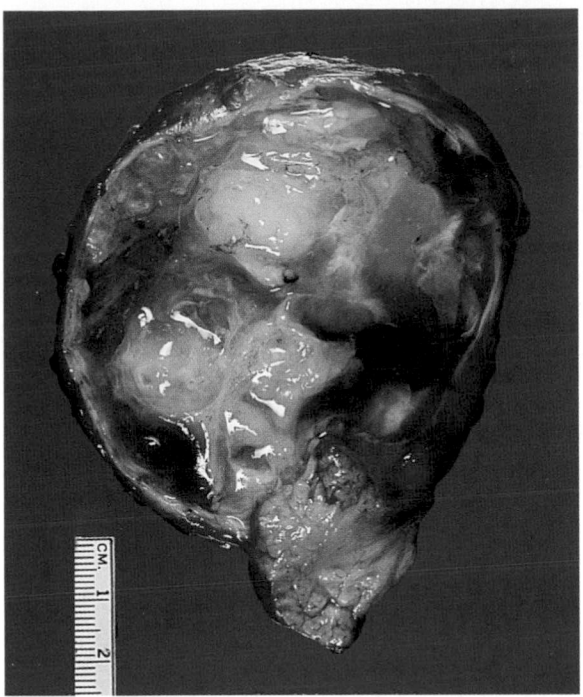

Fig. 15.26 Mucinous cystadenoma of pancreas. The lesion is unilocular and contains abundant inspissated mucin.

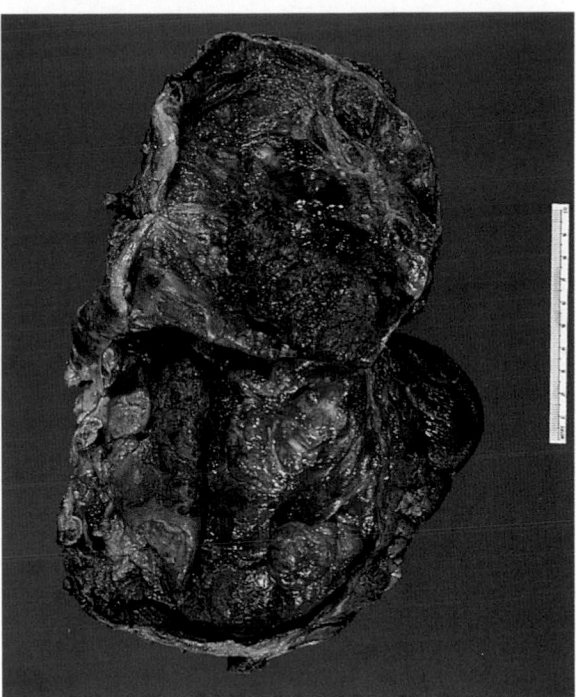

Fig. 15.27 Mucinous cystadenocarcinoma. This tumor, which was invasive at the microscopic level, shows areas of hemorrhage and solid growth.

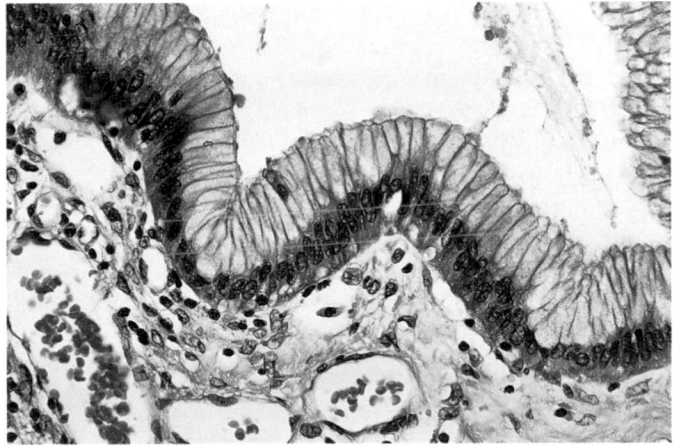

Fig. 15.28 Mucinous cystadenoma of pancreas. The lining is monolayered and made up of well-differentiated mucinous epithelium.

wall is a common finding. The underlying stroma is often very cellular, its appearance closely resembling that of ovarian stroma (Fig. 15.29A). This similarity persists at the immunophenotypic level, in the sense that this stroma is reactive for estrogen and progesterone receptors and for inhibin[361] (Fig. 15.29B and C). Interestingly, this type of stroma is also present in neoplasms developing in male patients.[365] The clinical presentation is similar to that of the microcystic adenomas and pancreatic pseudocysts. Aspiration of the fluid can be useful in the differential diagnosis. In the mucinous tumors, tall columnar mucin-producing cells are present, and the

fluid contains higher levels of CEA and lower levels of elastase I than the fluid of pseudocysts.[355,357] These *cystic* mucinous neoplasms should be distinguished from the *intraductal* tumors associated with increased mucin production described in the next section, some of which may exhibit a cystlike fusiform dilatation of the involved ducts.

Mucinous cystic tumors have been divided into a benign (mucinous cystadenoma) and a malignant (mucinous cystadenocarcinoma) category. Actually, if one were to use criteria analogous to those employed to assess mucinous tumors of the ovary, these pancreatic tumors could also be divided into benign, borderline, and malignant. The diagnosis of malignancy is based on the presence of invasion of the wall by neoplastic glands or frank anaplasia of the superficial component. The distinction is not always clear-cut, and extensive sampling of the specimen is required. Because of this fact, and the belief by some authors that all of these mucinous cystomas are potentially malignant, a total excision (rather than incomplete excision or marsupialization) should be carried out whenever possible.[350,351] However, it should be made clear that the general rules of mucinous tumors in other organs (such as the ovary) apply, i.e., a thorough pathologic evaluation with special emphasis on the presence or absence of invasion accurately predicts prognosis.[364] Therefore, we do not subscribe to the extreme view that all mucinous cystic neoplasms should be regarded as mucinous cystadenocarcinomas of low-grade malignant potential.[358] The evolution of mucinous cystomas—including malignant ones—is very slow; metastases, when present, are usually restricted to the abdominal cavity. Metastases of this tumor to the ovary may simulate a primary mucinous tumor of this organ.[366]

Histochemically, the mucin profile of the noninvasive tumors is similar to that of ductal adenocarcinomas and

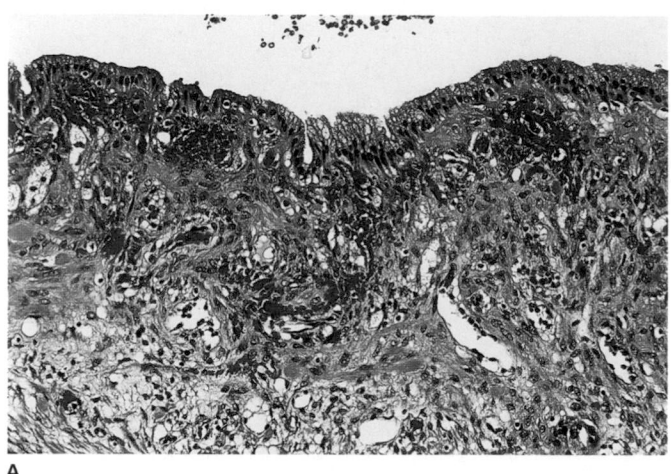

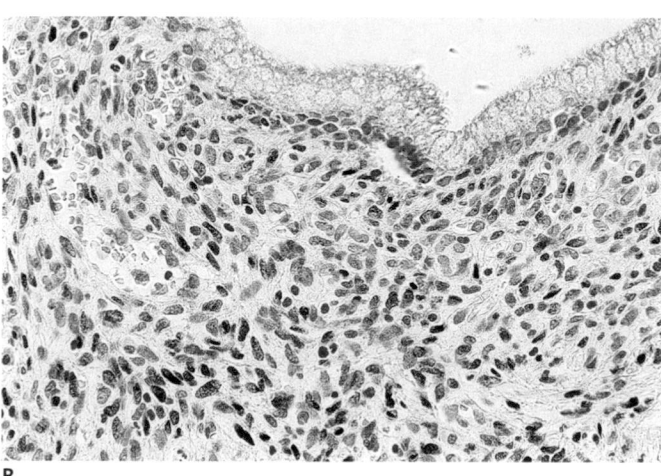

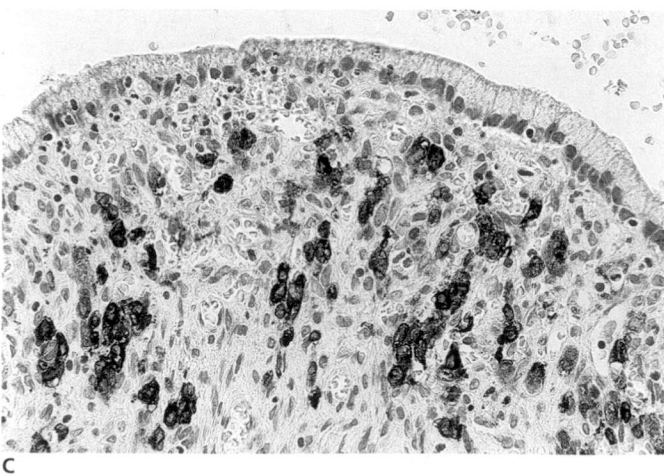

Fig. 15.29 A to **C,** Mucinous cystadenoma with underlying ovarian-type stroma: **A,** hematoxylin–eosin; **B,** progesterone receptor; **C,** inhibin.

intraductal papillary mucinous neoplasms regarding the expression of MUC5AC; however, they usually express MUC2 and they are said to lack expression of MUC1, except when they become invasive.[356] Malignant cases also tend to express p53, HER2/neu, high MIB-1 and EGFR,[369] whereas they lose expression of the DPC4 protein.[354] At the molecular level, they are usually microsatellite stable.[382a]

A morphologic variation on the theme of pancreatic mucinous cystoma (which is again analogous to that having been reported more frequently in mucinous ovarian neoplasms) is represented by the occasional finding of a *mural nodule* with the features of a giant cell tumor, a pleomorphic sarcoma, or an anaplastic carcinoma.[352,359,362] As in the ovary, the nature of these various types of proliferation is debatable,[353] but we regard all of them as neoplastic and of epithelial nature, as supported by the molecular evidence of a monoclonal origin.[360]

Mucinous cystic neoplasms of the pancreas rarely show positive nuclear immunostaining for p53, in contrast to ordinary ductal adenocarcinomas.[368] Cell proliferation markers (such as MIB-1) can be abundantly expressed.

Intraductal papillary mucinous neoplasms

Intraductal papillary mucinous neoplasm (IPMN) is a distinct type of intraductal pancreatic tumor that has been defined and segregated from other neoplasms of this organ (particularly mucinous cystic neoplasms) only recently,[372,389] cases being reported with increasing frequency from Japan,[377,396] and also from Europe and the United States.[392] The gross and microscopic appearance of these tumors is dependent upon the interplay of two factors: epithelial proliferation and mucinous secretion (Fig. 15.30). When the former predominates, the result is a multicentric involvement of major ducts by a predominantly papillary lesion sometimes combined with cribriform features and varying degrees of cytologic atypia.[382,384,386] This atypia, which can also be detected in cytologic preparations from pancreatic juice,[404] tends to be less pronounced in tumors confined to secondary ducts than in those involving the main pancreatic ducts.[403] A variant of this tumor is represented by the *intraductal oncocytic papillary neoplasm*, characterized by arborizing papillary structures with a focal cribriform pattern lined by stratified and pseudostratified oncocytic cells[370,390] which are uniformly immunoreactive for B72.3 but only rarely and focally for CEA.[370]

When there is instead a predominance of the mucinous secretion, the result is a gross dilatation of the ducts, which appear filled with mucus.[379,384] When fully developed, the lesion shows cystic formations somewhat reminiscent of bronchiectasis in the lung. This variant has been variously designated mucus-hypersecreting, mucin-producing, or duct ectatic tumor.[371,387,391,405] Microscopically, the epithelium is columnar, mucin secreting,

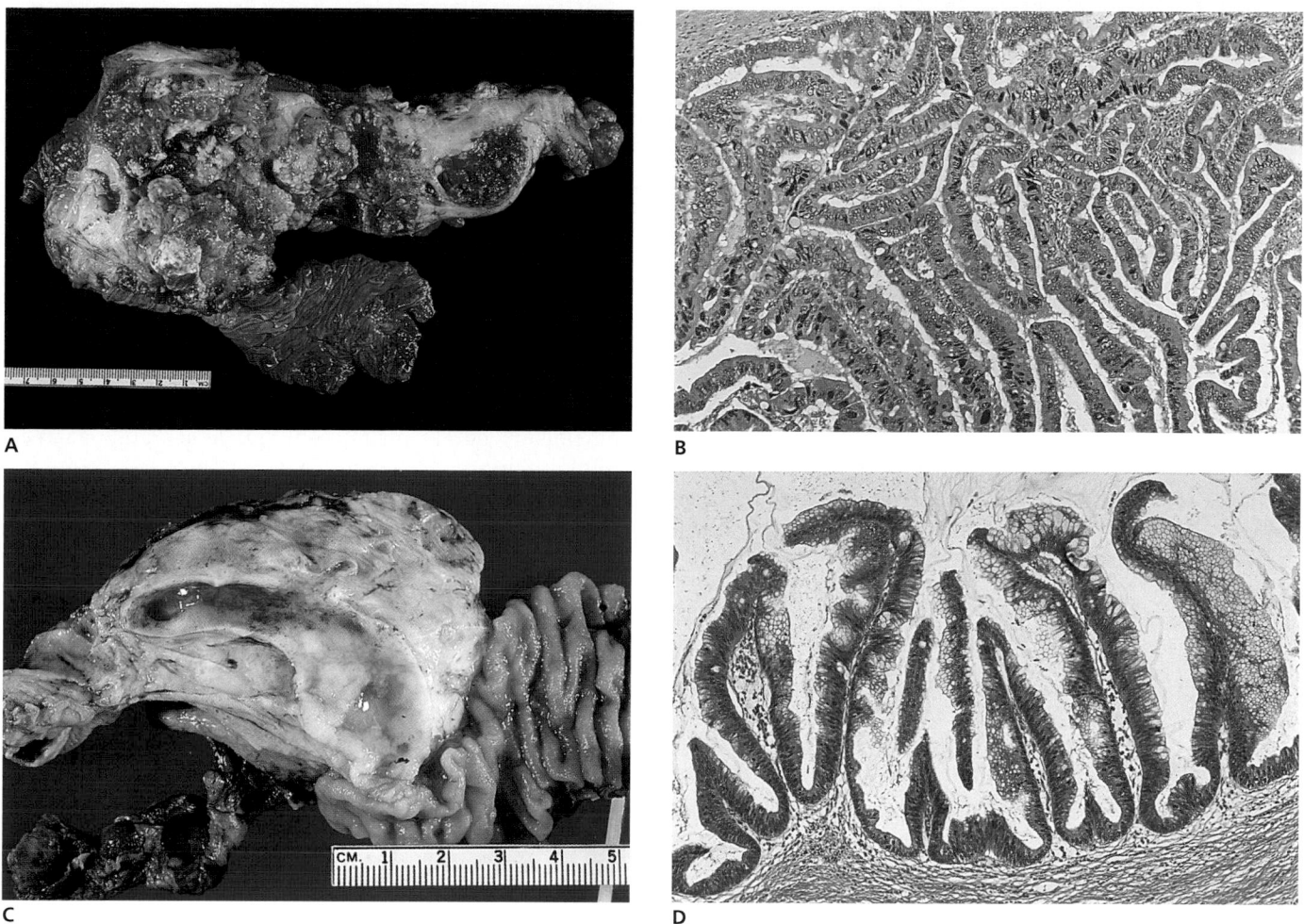

Fig. 15.30 A, Gross appearance of intraductal papillary carcinoma. The tumor massively involves several major pancreatic ducts. **B,** Microscopic appearance of the same case, showing a complex papillary architecture. **C,** Mucus-hypersecreting intraductal carcinoma. There is marked dilatation of a major pancreatic duct accompanied by fibrosis and atrophy of the surrounding parenchyma. This duct contained large amounts of mucin in its lumen. **D,** Microscopic appearance of the same case showing a papillary configuration associated with mucin hypersecretion. (**A** and **C** courtesy of Dr. David S. Klimstra, Memorial Sloan-Kettering Cancer Center)

and well differentiated, sometimes accompanied by a minor component of endocrine cells.[401]

It is better to think of these lesions as variations on a theme and group them under the term *intraductal papillary mucinous neoplasm* (IPMN), reserving the term carcinoma only for those tumors accompanied by an invasive component. The alternative is to use for the entire spectrum of noninvasive proliferative ductal lesions the term *pancreatic intraepithelial neoplasia* (PANIN), as recently recommended by a pathology panel.[380]

The natural history of these lesions is to spread slowly over the ductal system, with eventual progression in some cases to invasive adenocarcinoma, in which case they may be accompanied by lymph node metastases.[371] The invasive component may be of the garden-variety type or have a mucinous (colloid) appearance[374]; it has been stated that nearly all invasive mucinous (colloid) carcinomas arise from in situ papillary neoplasms.[395] Histochemically, the mucin expression pattern is hetero-

geneous, suggesting the existence of several tumor subtypes.[383] However, gastric-type differentiation tends to prevail among the better differentiated noninvasive tumors, whereas intestinal-type markers are present in most carcinomas.[385,397] Tumor progression is also marked by a steady increase in MYC expression.[398]

Cytogenetically, these tumors are very heterogeneous, this being at least partially due to their slow growth rate.[375] At the molecular level, mutations of the *ras* gene are common.[399,400] Overexpression of the HER2/*neu* product is also frequently found, in contrast to its rarity in ordinary ductal adenocarcinoma.[394] The protein product of the *DPC4* gene is present in virtually all cases, in contrast to its frequent absence in ordinary ductal carcinoma, suggesting a substantial difference in the pathogenesis of these two neoplasms.[381] Inactivation of the Peutz–Jeghers gene has been found in some cases of IPMN, suggesting that it may play a role in their pathogenesis.[393] Gene expression profiles have shown that the most highly upregulated genes in IPMNs correspond to members of the trefoil factor family.[402]

The prognosis of these tumors is largely dependent upon the presence and extent of the invasive component. It should be noted that patients with IPMNs with invasion still have a better survival than those with ordinary ductal adenocarcinoma without an in situ component.[378]

The main differential diagnosis of IPMN is with mucinous cystic neoplasms. The latter are more common in females, do not communicate with the ductal system, and usually have ovarian-type stroma beneath the epithelium.[376]

Other types of intraductal pancreatic neoplasms exist, including adenomas composed of pyloric-type glands.[373]

Acinar cell tumors and tumorlike conditions

Acinar cell hyperplasia is a common incidental microscopic finding. On low-power examination, these hyperplastic nodules may be confused with Langerhans' islets[413] (Fig. 15.31). They may exhibit mild atypical changes, and it has been suggested that they might be precursors of acinar cell carcinoma.[419,424]

Acinar cell adenoma having a solid pattern of growth is an entity of very doubtful existence.[428] Most of the cases in which this diagnosis has been entertained represent extremely well-differentiated forms of either acinar cell carcinoma (in adults) or pancreatoblastoma (in children).[420]

Acinar cell cystadenoma has instead emerged as a reasonably distinct entity.[409,430] It is a uni- or multicystic lesion lined by well-differentiated acinar cells, usually not connected with the pancreatic ductal system. It is regarded as the benign counterpart of acinar cell cystadenocarcinoma (see below).

Acinar cell carcinoma usually occurs in adults but may also develop in children.[411,417] In most cases it presents as an intra-abdominal mass with or without jaundice, but several cases have been reported associated with widespread subcutaneous fat necrosis and arthralgia, as a result of the secretion of lipase by the tumor (see later section).[407] Parenthetically, amylase secretion has also been occasionally observed with extrapancreatic neoplasms.[414] Acinar cell carcinoma presents grossly as a relatively well-circumscribed fleshy mass, averaging 11 cm in greatest diameter, with sometimes extensive hemorrhage and necrosis (Fig. 15.32). Exceptionally, its pattern of growth is primarily intraductal.[412] Microscopically, it is a cellular neoplasm that characteristically lacks the desmoplastic stroma commonly seen with the ductal carcinomas. The pattern of growth may be solid, trabecular, or glandular, or it may reproduce the normal acinar structure, sometimes to the point of simulating normal pancreas[416] (Fig. 15.33). The nuclei are round to oval, with only mild pleomorphism, single prominent nucleoli, and variable mitotic activity. The cytoplasm tends to be abundant, eosinophilic, and granular, but in the solid tumors it may be scanty. PAS-positive, diastase-resistant cytoplasmic granules are common, and the butyrate esterase histochemical stain for lipase activity is usually positive. There is immunoreactivity for trypsin, lipase, and (less commonly) chymotrypsin and amylase[417,421,425] (Fig. 15.34). A minor endocrine component (identifiable with chromogranin and/or islet cell hormones) is present in one third to one half of the cases.[415,417] Occasional examples of acinar cell carcinoma (and of pancreatoblastoma, which can be considered its infantile counterpart) can be accompanied by production of AFP and elevated serum levels of this marker.[410] Ultrastructurally, the cells are polarized, with well-developed microvilli on the luminal border, abundant granular endoplasmic reticulum, and zymogen-like granules[423] (Fig. 15.35). In addition, pleomorphic membrane-bound inclusions containing filaments (presumably representing abnormal zymogen granules) are often found.[417,427]

At the molecular genetic level, acinar cell carcinomas show a high frequency of allelic loss on 11p and mutations in the APC/β catenin pathway, a pattern similar to that of pancreatoblastoma and distinct from pancreatic ductal adenocarcinoma.[406]

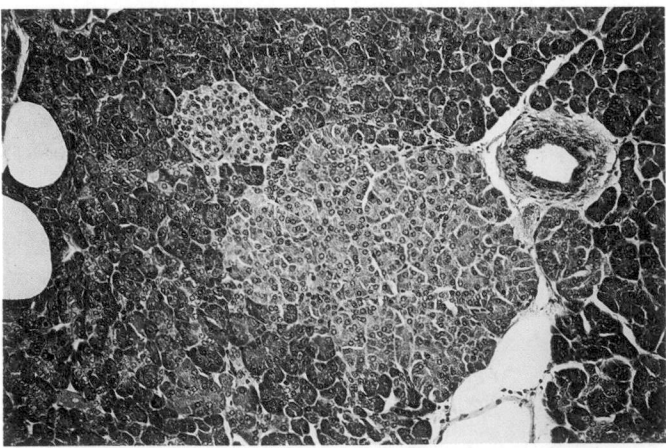

Fig. 15.31 Incidental acinar cell hyperplasia of pancreas. These formations are sometimes confused with hyperplastic islets.

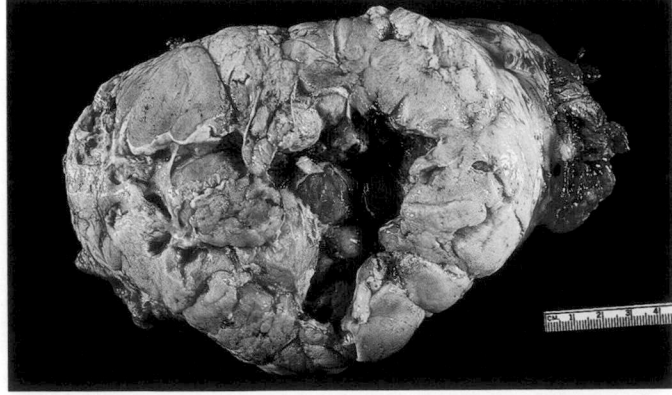

Fig. 15.32 Acinar cell carcinoma. The cut surface is solid and has a necrotic center. It lacks the fibrous component usually seen in ductal adenocarcinoma.

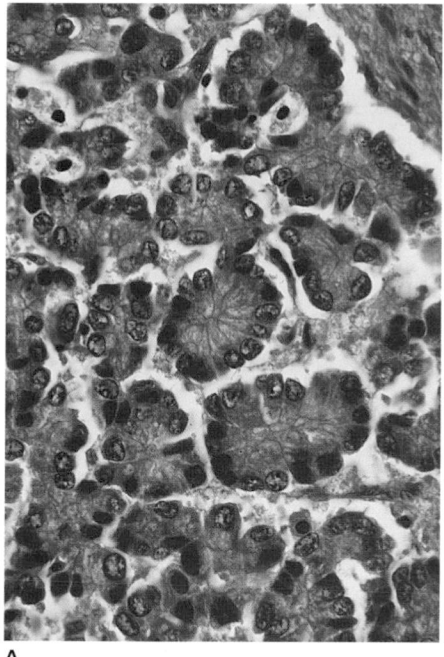 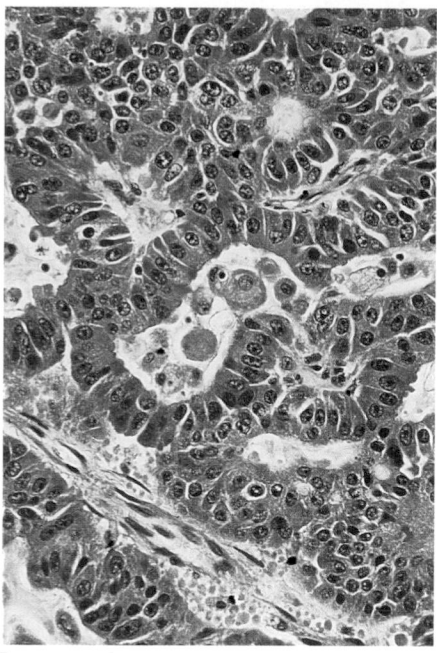

A   B

Fig. 15.33 A, Acinar cell carcinoma of the pancreas showing a well-differentiated acinar arrangement of the tumor cells. A minute central lumen is identifiable in some of the acini. **B**, Acinar cell carcinoma showing a trabecular pattern of growth that may be confused with that of an endocrine tumor.

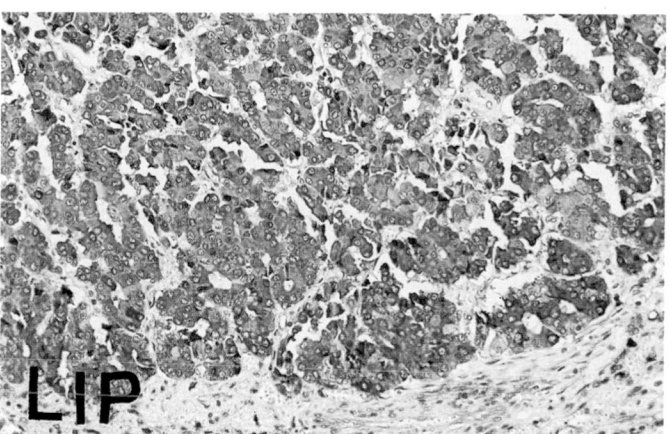

Fig. 15.34 Strong immunoreactivity for lipase in acinar cell carcinoma.

In one series, metastases were already present at the time of diagnosis in half of the cases and developed later in an additional quarter; they were usually restricted to the regional lymph nodes and liver.[417]

A variant known as *acinar cell cystadenocarcinoma* is predominantly cystic and resembles grossly the appearance of a microcystic adenoma[408,415,426] (Fig. 15.36). Another variant, described as *mixed acinar–endocrine tumor*, displays an even admixture of acinar and endocrine cells.[418] Yet another variant on the theme is represented by the rare tumor combining ductal, acinar, and islet cell components.[422] It ought to be pointed out that one or more markers of acinar differentiation (such as lipase, chymotrypsin, or trypsin) are present in about two thirds of pancreatic tumors having otherwise the

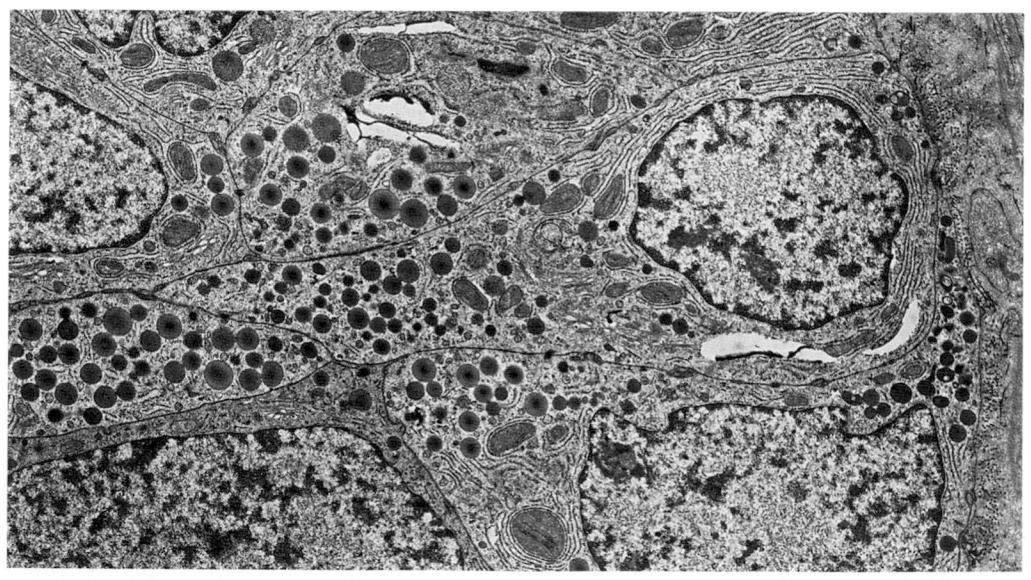

Fig. 15.35 Electron micrograph of pancreatic acinar cell carcinoma metastatic to omentum. Portion of a cluster of epithelial tumor cells showing perinuclear stacked rough endoplasmic reticulum cisternae (right) and numerous electron-dense zymogen granules. (×9000; courtesy of Dr. Robert A. Erlandson, Memorial Sloan-Kettering Cancer Center)

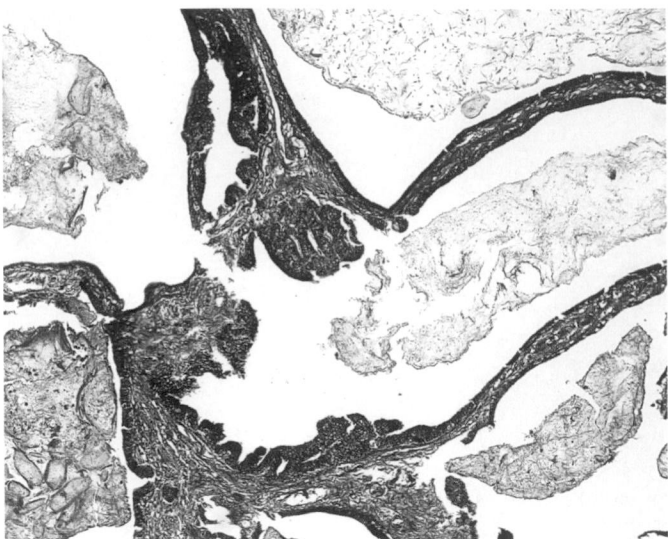

Fig. 15.36 Acinar cystadenocarcinoma, a rare tumor that may be confused with microcystic cystadenoma.

typical features of pancreatic endocrine neoplasms; this feature is of no prognostic significance and should not alter the tumor designation.[429]

Solid–pseudopapillary tumor

Solid–pseudopapillary tumor (SPPT) is the preferred term for a distinctive type of pancreatic tumor also known as papillary and solid epithelial neoplasm, papillary–cystic neoplasm, and cystic–solid papillary carcinoma. Most cases are found in young women, and the most common clinical sign is a palpable abdominal mass.[435,442] Grossly, it is usually large and on cross section it often contains areas of hemorrhage and necrosis. Most cases are surrounded by a well-developed capsule, but in some instances the edges are those of a solid infiltrative neoplasm.[443] Other cases are predominantly cystic. Multicentricity is exceptionally rare.[449] A few cases have been found adjacent to but anatomically separate from the pancreas.[438]

Microscopically, SPPT is very cellular and simulates somewhat the appearance of a pancreatic endocrine neoplasm. Its most distinctive feature is the presence of pseudopapillae covered by several layers of epithelial cells. The nuclei are ovoid and folded, with indistinct nucleoli and few mitoses. Hyaline globules and collections of foamy cells may be present.[441] The thick fibrovascular core often shows prominent mucinous changes, a feature of diagnostic importance (Fig. 15.37). Ultrastructurally, evidence of acinar, ductal, and (sometimes) endocrine cell differentiation has been found.[433,436,441] Immunohistochemically, there is reactivity for keratin, desmoplakin, trypsin, chymotrypsin, amylase, and vimentin.[441,444,452] In addition, focal positivity has been found for neuron-specific enolase and other neuroendocrine markers[444,445] and—at least in some studies—for various islet cell hormones, such as insulin and glucagon.[444] These results suggest that SPPT is a tumor of primitive pancreatic epithelial cells with predominance of exocrine features but having the capacity for dual (exocrine and endocrine) differentiation.[444,450] Another marker consistently expressed in SPPT and therefore of diagnostic utility is CD10.[448] Progesterone receptors have been detected both immunohistochemically and by the standard biochemical method.[447,453] These results, which are consistent with its well-known predilection for females, suggest that this is a hormone-dependent neoplasm and therefore potentially susceptible to hormonal therapeutic manipulation. This staining pattern has also led to the odd suggestion that SPPT might be derived from genital ridge/ovarian anlage related cells which were attached to the pancreatic tissue during early embryogenesis.[439]

Genetically, SPPTs of the pancreas are different from ordinary ductal adenocarcinomas and almost always exhibit β-catenin mutations.[431] The translocation der(17)t(13;17)(q14;p11) has been detected in a case.[434]

The treatment is surgical, and the overall prognosis is excellent.[435] However, several cases resulting in

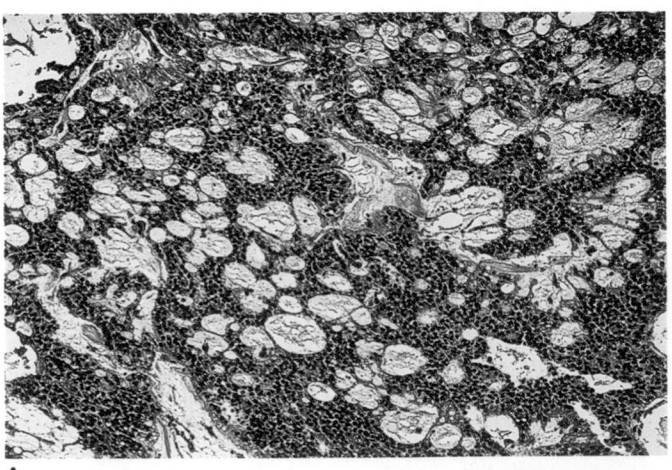

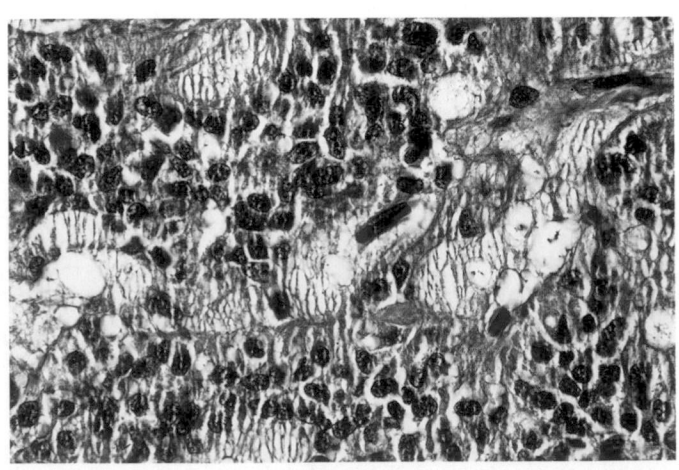

A   B

Fig. 15.37 A and **B**, Solid and pseudopapillary tumor of pancreas. Note the accumulation of myxoid material around the vessels.

local recurrence and liver metastases have been reported.[432,440–442,451] Therefore, SPPT should be regarded as a carcinoma of low malignant potential.[437] In one series, the metastasizing tumors exhibited a greater incidence of venous invasion, high nuclear grade, and necrosis than the others.[446]

Pancreatoblastoma

Pancreatoblastoma is the most common form of pancreatic neoplasia in childhood,[466] but it can also occur in adults.[458] Isolated cases have been reported in patients with the Beckwith–Wiedemann syndrome and with familiar adenomatous polyposis of the colon.[454] In the series of Klimstra et al.,[462] there was a bimodal age distribution, the mean ages being 2.4 and 33 years, respectively. In contrast with SPPN (a tumor with which it has often been confused), there is no sex predilection. The mean tumor size is 10 cm, and partial encapsulation is the rule. Microscopically, these are very cellular tumors, made up of uniform epithelial cells arranged in solid sheets and nests, admixed with well-formed acinar structures and occasional dilated ductular formations (Fig. 15.38). "Squamoid corpuscles" are a constant and characteristic finding[459] (Fig. 15.39). The tumor cells present within these corpuscles often have optically clear nuclei, apparently due to the accumulation of biotin.[465] The stroma may be abundant and occasionally hypercellular.

Immunohistochemically, these tumors show evidence of acinar, endocrine, and ductal differentiation, with positivity for pancreatic enzymes, endocrine markers, and CEA[457,464] (Fig. 15.40). α-Fetoprotein may be produced by the tumor, in keeping with its primitive nature.[456] Ultrastructurally, features consistent with acinar cell differentiation have been detected.[460] Indeed, pancreatoblastoma could be regarded as the infantile version of acinar cell carcinoma, just as hepatoblastoma is the infantile version of hepatocellular carcinoma. The prognosis in infants is relatively favorable.[455,461] In the series of Klimstra et al.,[462] half of the pediatric patients were cured by the resection, whereas three of the four adult patients died of tumor.

It should be kept in mind that not all pancreatic tumors in childhood are examples of pancreatoblastoma; ductal, ordinary acinar, and islet cell tumors also occur[463]; because of this fact, it is better to avoid using the term infantile pancreatic carcinoma as a synonym for pancreatoblastoma.

Endocrine tumors

General and clinical features

Endocrine tumors of the pancreas have been traditionally designated *islet cell tumors*. However, it has been pointed out that this term is properly applied only to tumors composed of cells that are normally present in the pancreatic islets and that a more generic term such as *pancreatic*

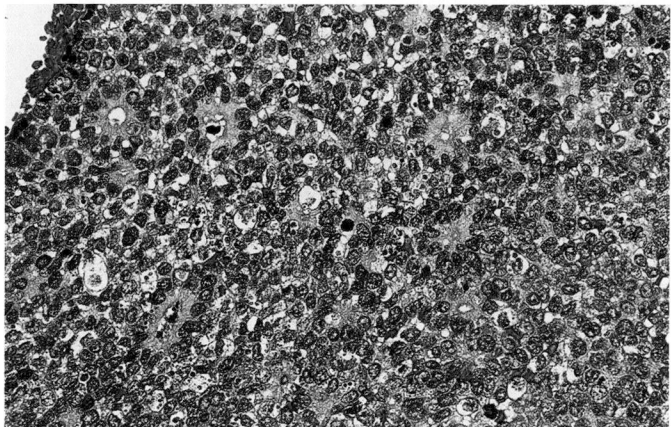

Fig. 15.38 Pancreatoblastoma showing a predominantly solid pattern of growth but also small rosette-like glandular formations.

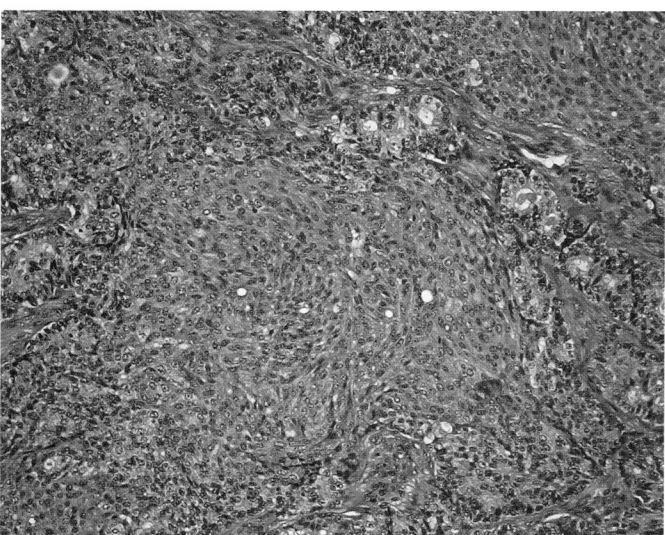

Fig. 15.39 Pancreatoblastoma showing a large squamoid corpuscle surrounded by small glands.

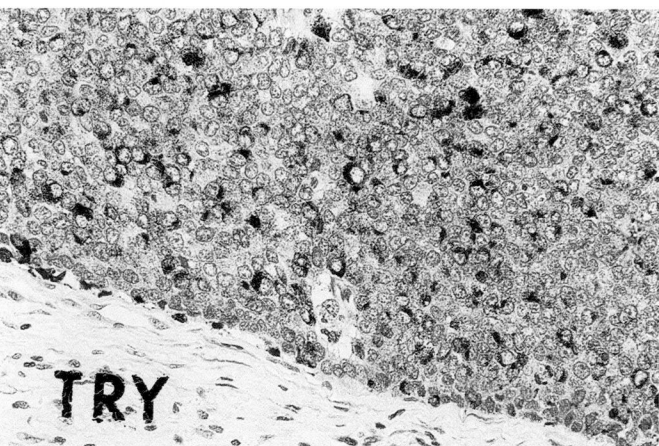

Fig. 15.40 Immunoreactivity for trypsin in pancreatoblastoma.

endocrine neoplasm is preferable for the group as a whole.[476] Actually, it is possible that all of these neoplasms arise from primitive multipotential cells located within ducts rather than from the islets themselves.[468,473,517]

Endocrine tumors make up a small fraction of all pancreatic neoplasms. Most occur in adults, although a few have been described in children and even in newborn infants.[470,477]

Morphologic features

The most common location is the body and tail of the organ, correlating with a greater islet concentration in these locations. A few cases have been reported in association with chronic pancreatitis,[518] but caution should be exercised not to overdiagnose as neoplastic the proliferating islet cells often seen in that condition (see p. 1066). Grossly, the more cellular tumors have a pinkish cast and may resemble spleen or a congested lymph node (Fig. 15.41). They do not have a well-defined capsule. Other, presumably longer-standing tumors have a large amount of fibrous tissue and may even contain calcium and bone. A few have a predominantly cystic appearance.[504] This secondary, probably degenerative change is to be distinguished from the exceptional pancreatic endocrine tumor arising in a mucinous cystic neoplasm.[494]

Microscopically, these tumors are usually composed of small, relatively uniform cuboidal cells with centrally located nuclei and acidophilic or amphophilic, finely granular cytoplasm. However, nuclear enlargement and other aberrations are common.

Depending on their pattern of growth, endocrine tumors of the pancreas have been divided into solid, gyriform (with ribbons and festoons), glandular, and nondescript types.[487,508,509] These have also been referred to as A, B, C, and D, or as I, II, III, and IV, respectively, and these patterns have been related to the various endocrine cell types that may be present in them. Predominantly gyriform tumors are often of beta or alpha cell type, and glandular tumors are often composed of G or VIP cells; solid tumors, which are the majority, can be of any cell type.

The stroma of pancreatic endocrine tumors is highly vascular. In some cases, an abundant hyaline material separates the tumor cells into scattered nests. Amyloid may be encountered, particularly in insulin-secreting neoplasms,[533] but also in other tumor types.[527] The material deposited in these areas, which may have a crystalline configuration, has been designated islet amyloid polypeptide (IAPP) and can be detected immunohistochemically.[528,534] Unusual features of pancreatic endocrine tumors include mucin production, black pigmentation, clear cell, vacuolated or oncocytic change, psammoma body formation, rhabdoid features,[515a] and sarcomatoid transformation.[484,488,520,530] The latter may include the presence of skeletal muscle cells.[485] The cytoplasmic vacuolization is due to the accumulation of cytoplasmic lipid,[513] and the pigmentation to the presence of lipofuscin-type granules.[525] The clear cell change tends to occur in tumors associated with von Hippel–Lindau disease and may mimic renal cell carcinoma.[491]

Pancreatic endocrine tumors may be nonfunctioning, at least at the level of clinical detection.[474,495] In other instances they present with an endocrine abnormality resulting from the secretion of one or more hormones.[500] Pancreatic endocrine tumors (as well as other extrahepatic endocrine neoplasms) can also secrete the alpha

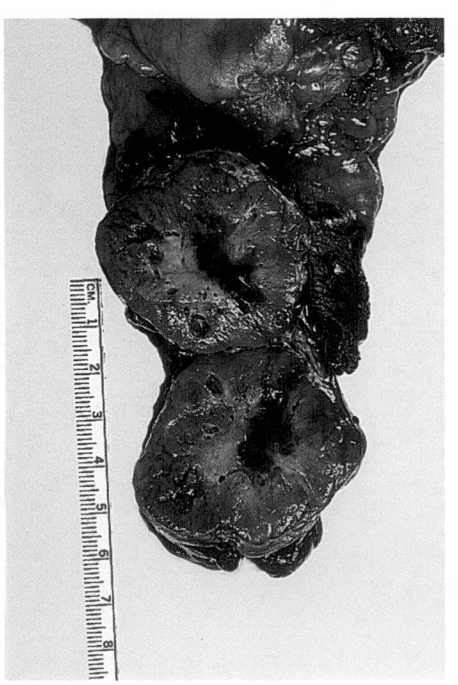 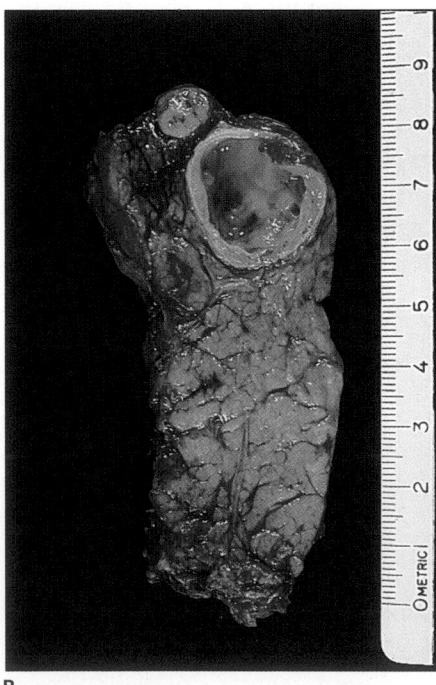 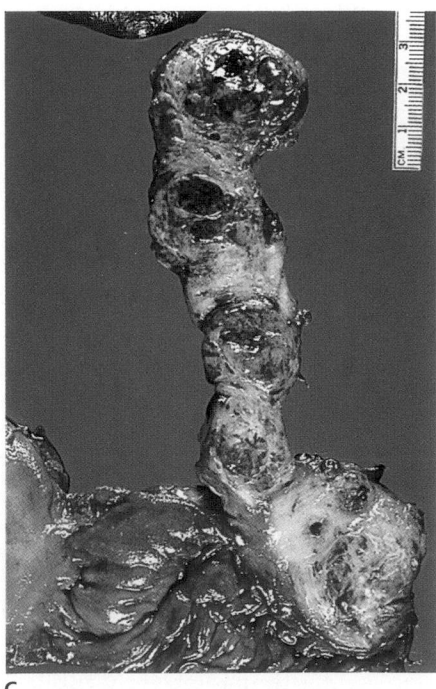

A   B   C

Fig. 15.41 A to C, Three different cases of pancreatic endocrine tumor. The neoplasms shown in **A** and **B** are partially cystic. The tumor shown in **C** is multicentric.

and/or beta subunits of hCG, particularly the former. This phenomenon, which can be detected by serum assays or immunohistochemical staining of the tumor, is more common with the malignant than the benign neoplasms, although the difference among them is not as pronounced as originally claimed.[486,493,521] Studies of pancreatic endocrine tumors with immunocytochemical techniques have shown that multihormonal examples are common and that these can occur in a variety of forms: as a single tumor with multiple cell types; as multiple tumors, each of a single cell type; and as multiple tumors, each of multiple cell types.[469] Sometimes, two different peptide hormones have been found within the same tumor cell and even within the same secretory granule.[503,511]

The nature of the predominant cell determines the type of clinical syndrome and the name given to the tumor.[500,501] Tumors associated with multihormone production of a type that can be detected clinically or by serum determinations are often malignant.[489]

Examination of hematoxylin–eosin sections simply allows the generic diagnosis of pancreatic endocrine tumor. As previously stated, some correlations can be made between the pattern of growth and the cell type, but many exceptions occur. Traditional special stains for islet cells, including silver techniques, give consistent results in normal tissue but are less predictable when applied to neoplasms.[535] Electron microscopy will readily and consistently demonstrate cytoplasmic secretory granules of endocrine type in all but the most undifferentiated members of this group, categorizing the tumor as endocrine and often also allowing the identification of the specific cell type involved (Fig. 15.42). However, the latter is not always the case, because in some instances the tumor cell granules have a nondescript appearance.

Immunohistochemically, the cells of pancreatic endocrine neoplasms stain for epithelial markers (such as keratin 7),[475] for "panendocrine" markers, and (depending on the cell types) for those specific for the various peptide hormones. The former include neuron-specific enolase, chromogranin A and B, synaptophysin, and opioid peptides.[471,478,505,524] Positivity for chromogranin, which is seen in some tumor types but not in others, is said to correlate with the presence of argyrophilia.[505] Production of chromogranin and other substances by these tumors can result in a corresponding serum level elevation, a feature that is of diagnostic importance.[510,519] Other substances that have been found in some of these tumors are neurofilaments, α_1-antitrypsin,[512] transthyretin,[492] myosin XVA,[497] and progesterone receptor (but not estrogen receptor).[532]

Studies performed with the second group of markers have demonstrated that these tumors can secrete any of the hormones known to be present in the pancreatic islets, including insulin, glucagon, somatostatin, and pancreatic polypeptide.[490,507] They have also been found to secrete gastrin,[490,507,508] VIP,[490,507,508] ACTH,[479] ADH, MSH, calcitonin, neurotensin, secretoneurin,[523] a PTH-like peptide,[506] the alpha subunit of hCG (as already mentioned),[531] growth hormone and growth hormone-releasing factor,[468,472,482] secretogranin II,[502] inhibin/activin,[499] prohormone convertases 2 and 3,[496] metallothionein,[529] and somatostatin receptors.[514]

About half of the pancreatic endocrine tumors exhibit an aneuploid DNA pattern; this does not allow a distinction between benign and malignant tumors but seems to correlate with clinical aggressiveness in the malignant group.[467,483] The degree of cell proliferation as determined by Ki-67 immunostaining has been found to be an independent predictor of malignancy in several series.[480,498,515,516]

At the genetic level, the pattern is heterogeneous but with some apparent correlations with cell types, such as 6q loss in malignant insulinoma.[526] Furthermore, loss of heterozygosity at the MEN I gene locus at 11q13 has been found in about half of the sporadic endocrine neoplasms of foregut derivation (including pancreatic ones), but not in those of midgut or hindgut origin.[481] In contrast to pancreatic ductal neoplasms, endocrine neoplasms practically never show inactivation of DPC4, indicating that the tumorigenetic pathways of these two lesions are very different.[522]

Specific types

Beta cell tumors constitute the most common and better known variety of pancreatic endocrine neoplasms, which—when functioning—are referred to as insulinomas.[568] Most occur in adults, and the incidence is equal in both sexes.[594] Only a minority of the patients (less than 10%) are affected by MEN I. The Whipple triad thought to be characteristic of this tumor consists of: (1) mental confusion, weakness, fatigue, and convulsions; (2) fasting blood glucose levels below 50 mg%; and (3) relief of symptoms by the administration of glucose.[595] Intravenous tolbutamide administration and determinations of circulating insulin levels are useful tests for the diagnosis of insulinomas.[576] Circulating proinsulin-like material can be detected in the serum.[560] Celiac arteriography is extremely useful in the localization of these neoplasms, which may otherwise prove quite elusive at surgical exploration.[539] The reported success rate of angiographic localization is between 60% and 75%. Another highly sensitive technique is that of endoscopic ultrasonography, which in one series was often successful in locating the tumor in cases in which angiography and CT had failed.[591]

Over 90% of beta cell tumors are solitary.[570] Practically all of them are located within the substance of the pancreas; only 2% of the cases are seen in adjacent areas, such as the duodenal wall. About 70% of them measure 1.5 cm or less, sometimes as little as 3 or 4 mm. Microscopically, the tumor may grow in a solid or

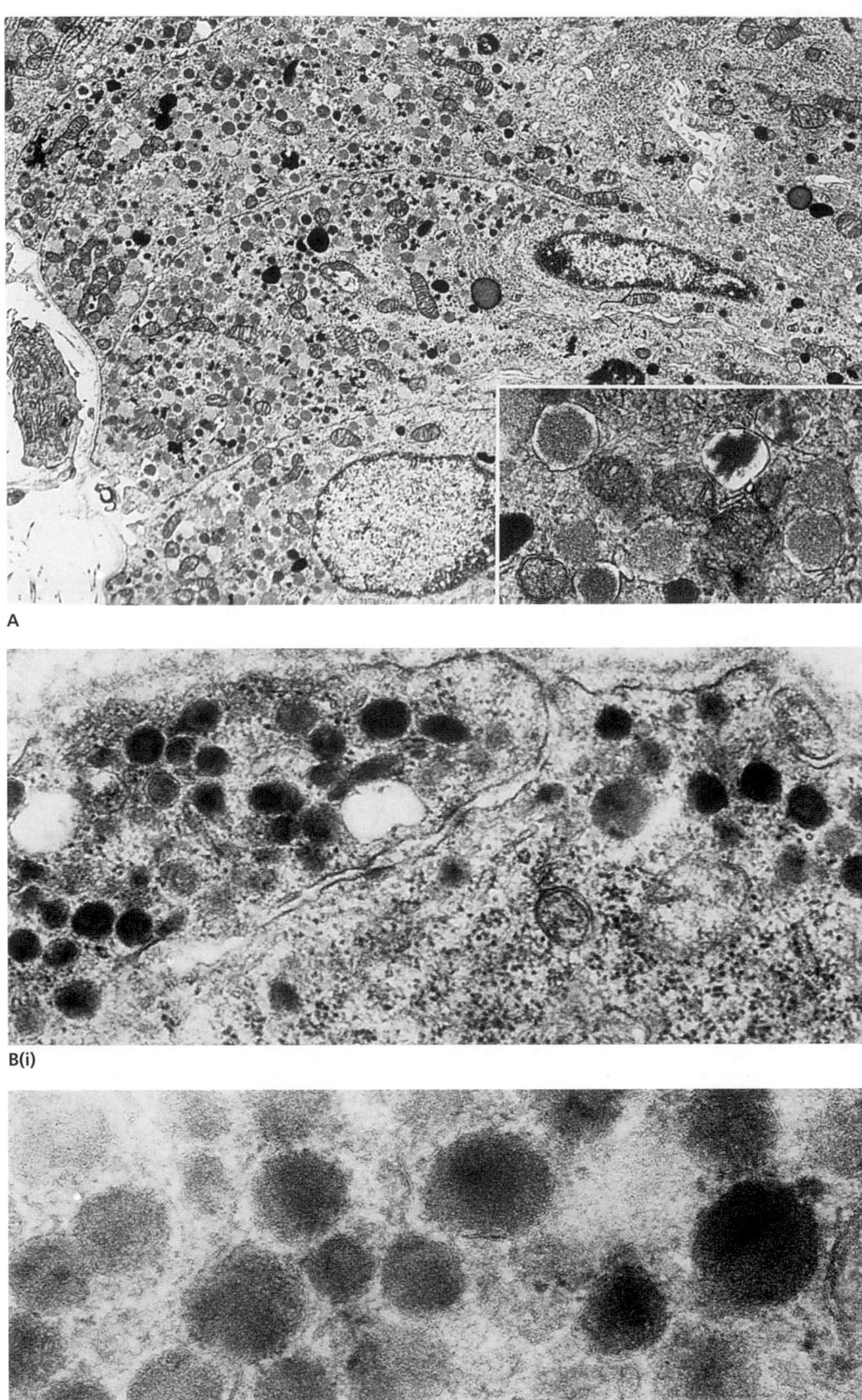

A

B(i)

B(ii)

Fig. 15.42 A to **D**, Electron microscopic appearance of different types of pancreatic endocrine tumors. **A**, Beta cell tumor. Many of the granules have irregular or crystalline content. **B**, Alpha cell tumor. Granules are large and have dense peripheral nucleoid. *(continued)*

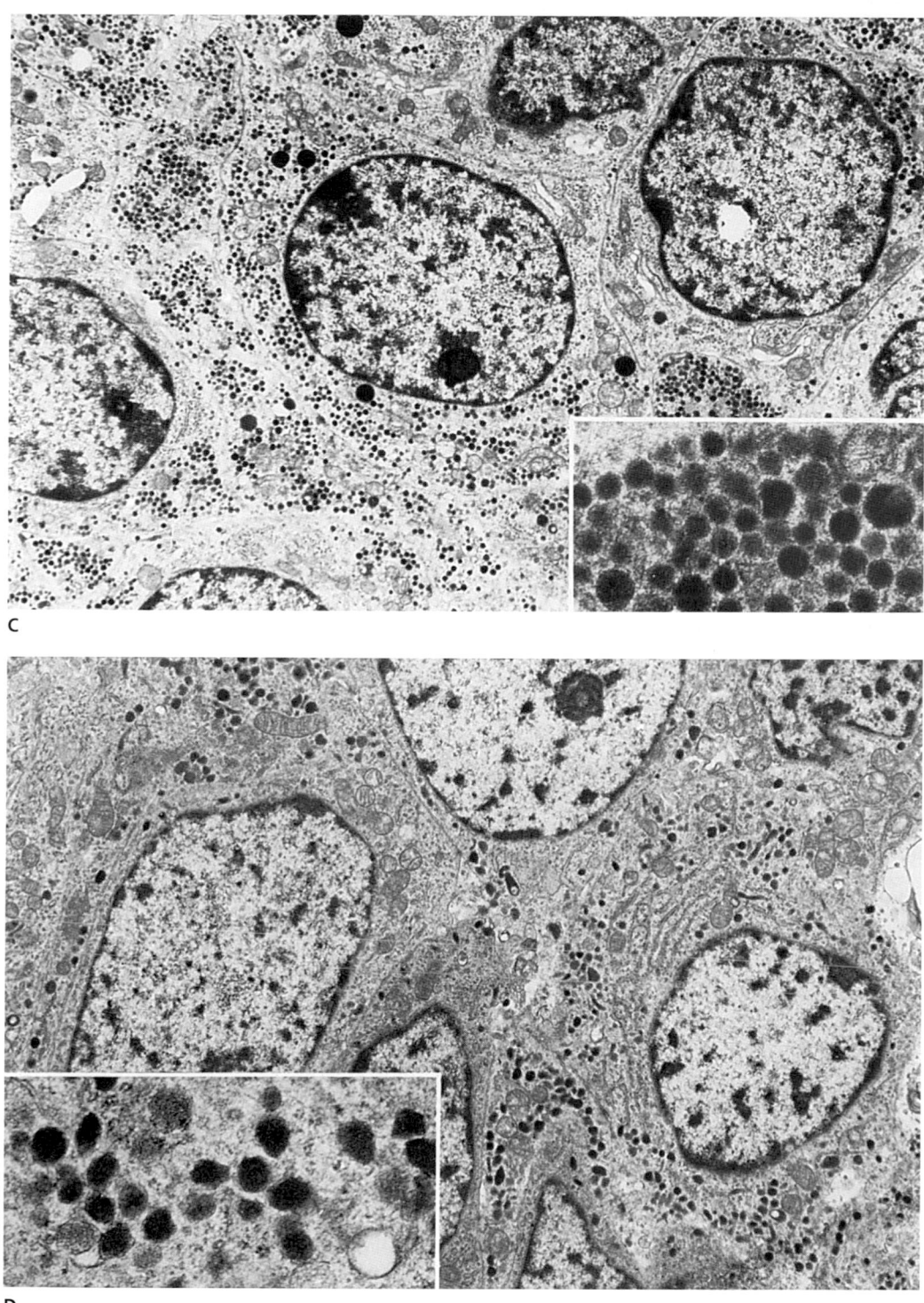

C

D

Fig. 15.42 A to **D,** *(continued)* Electron microscopic appearance of different types of pancreatic endocrine tumors. **C,** G-cell tumor. Granules are similar to those of VIP-producing tumor and of normal gastrin cells. Most tumors from patients with Zollinger–Ellison syndrome have this appearance. **D,** VIP-producing tumor having larger and more pleomorphic granules. This variety is uncommon in our experience. (Courtesy of Dr. M. Greider, St. Louis, and Dr. M.H. McGavran, Houston)

gyriform pattern; glands are usually absent. Exceptional cases have been described with a ductal or acinar component[583,589] and with hepatoid differentiation.[569] Ultrastructurally, dense-core secretory granules are invariably present, but they do not always have the crystalline material that identifies them as being of beta cell type in the normal islets.[588] Immunohistochemically, there is reactivity for insulin, although this is usually of a lesser degree than in the normal beta cells.[572] About half of the cases also show diffuse labeling for proinsulin.[536,592] Beta cell tumors show a lesser degree of reactivity for chromogranin than other islet cell neoplasms.[574] Another peptide often detected in beta cell tumors (although not specific for them) is amylin.[555]

In children with beta cell tumors, there may be evidence of direct transformation of ductal epithelium into neoplastic islet tissue in the form of nesidioblastosis[542,548] (see p. 1062).

Only 7% to 10% of beta cell tumors are malignant if the criteria of infiltration and/or metastases are adhered to.[594] In general, the malignant variety is associated with a shorter history and more pronounced hypoglycemia.[549] Neither conventional morphology nor DNA ploidy patterns are good predictors of behavior.[557]

The treatment of beta cell tumors is surgical. If the diagnosis of hyperinsulinism is reasonably certain and surgical exploration fails to reveal a neoplasm, a subtotal pancreatectomy is justified. Of 33 patients reported by Laroche et al.[570] in whom this operation was performed, the tumor was found in the resected specimen in 15.

Extrapancreatic neoplasms may rarely be associated with hypoglycemia that disappears on removal of the tumor.[573] Most have been liver cell carcinomas or mesenchymal neoplasms. The latter have received diagnoses such as leiomyosarcoma, hemangiopericytoma, and fibrosarcoma, but the evidence strongly suggests that the large majority have the morphologic features of either benign or malignant solitary fibrous tumor. Most are found in the pleura or retroperitoneum, and they tend to attain a very large size.[597] The hypoglycemia has been found to be caused by the secretion of insulin-like growth factor II by the tumor cells.[550]

Alpha cell tumors can be divided into two distinct types. Those associated with the glucagonoma syndrome (glucagonomas) are usually solitary and large, with a nondescript microscopic pattern, atypical granules ultrastructurally, few cells positive for glucagon immunohistochemically, and high incidence of malignancy[561] (Figs 15.43 and 15.44). These ultrastructural and immunohistochemical aberrations may be caused by abnormalities in the biosynthesis and secretion of glucagon, sometimes with alternative production of the related precursor peptides glycentin and oxyntomodulin.[554] The alpha cell tumors not associated with the glucagonoma syndrome are often multiple and small, have a gyriform pattern of growth, are strongly immunoreactive for glucagon,

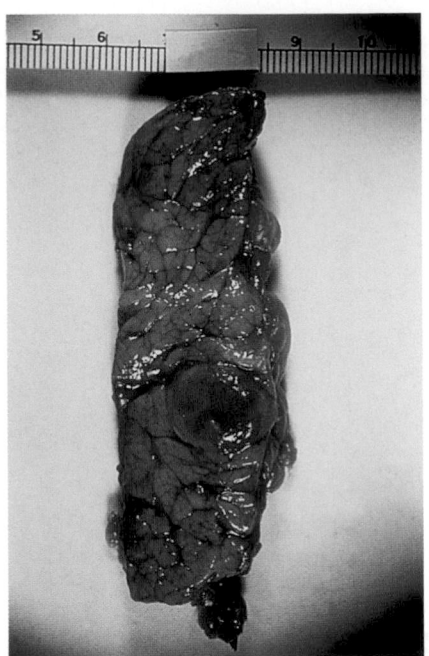

Fig.15.43 Gross appearance of alpha cell tumor. The tumor shown, required the performance of a near-total pancreatectomy.

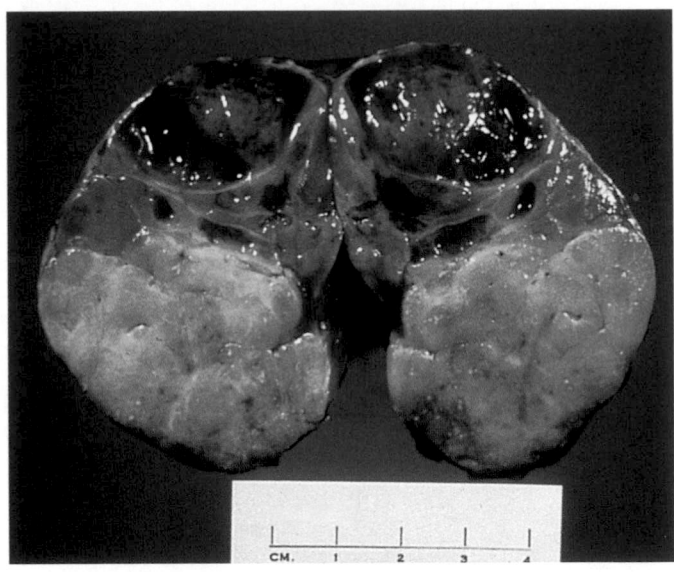

Fig. 15.44 Gross appearance of alpha cell tumor (glucagonoma). The tumor shown, exhibits foci of hemorrhage and necrosis.

exhibit typical alpha cell granules ultrastructurally, and are nearly always benign (Fig. 15.45). Argyrophilia can be demonstrated with the Grimelius technique. The glucagonoma syndrome, seen mainly in adult females, is thought to be the direct or indirect result of the hypersecretion of glucagon.[602] Its components are an abnormal glucose tolerance test, normocytic normochromic anemia, a skin rash known as necrolytic migratory erythema, sore red tongue, angular stomatitis, severe weight loss, depression, deep vein thrombosis, and tendency to develop overwhelming infection. The skin rash involves mainly the legs, perineum, and groin; it starts as

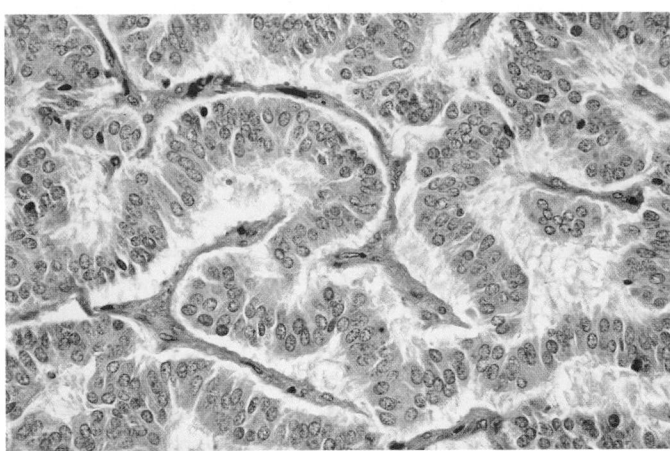

Fig.15.45 Alpha cell tumor showing a prominent gyriform arrangement of the tumor cells. Tumors with this pattern are usually composed of either alpha or beta cells.

erythema, progresses to superficial blisters, and gradually spreads with central clearing. It heals without scarring but with hyperpigmentation in 7 to 14 days. Microscopically, the main features are epidermal necrolysis, with liquefaction necrosis of the granular cell layer and subcorneal clefting or blister formation.[567]

G-cell tumors can produce the Zollinger–Ellison syndrome as a result of excessive production of gastrin and are then referred to as gastrinomas.[566,607,610] The tumors are most often found in the pancreas, followed by duodenal wall and gastric antrum (see Chapter 11) (Fig. 15.46). This distribution pattern is most peculiar, because it is exactly the opposite of what one would expect to find on the basis of G-cell distribution in the normal tissues. Cases of Zollinger–Ellison syndrome have also been reported in association with tumors of the ovary, mesentery, liver, and intra-abdominal (usually peripancreatic) lymph nodes.[538,579,599,606] It is not clear whether the

latter arise in ectopic islet tissue in the lymph nodes or whether they represent metastases from undetected small primary neoplasms.[564]

The Zollinger–Ellison syndrome is characterized by gastric hyperacidity with gastric, duodenal, or jejunal ulcers.[545] Diarrhea is seen in one third of the patients as a result of the excessive gastric secretion. Although the original reports emphasized the atypical location of the ulcers, this has not been substantiated in subsequent series. Radioimmunoassay of gastrin is the most useful test to confirm the diagnosis.[575]

Cases of *sporadic* G-cell tumor associated with the Zollinger–Ellison syndrome are nearly always solitary, located in either the pancreas (slightly more often) or the duodenal wall, and often clinically malignant; cases presenting as a component of *MEN I* (see later section) tend to be multicentric, are usually located in the duodenal wall (and very rarely in the pancreas), and are less likely to be clinically malignant.[537,553,559,604,609] Microscopically, the pattern of growth is usually solid and/or glandular.

Some authors claim to obtain positivity in the majority of these tumors with the Grimelius argyrophilic stain,[547] but others have found it very difficult to duplicate these results. Gastrin production by the neoplastic cells is readily demonstrable by immunohistochemistry. The phenotypical features of the neoplastic cells correlate better with those of the gastrin-producing G cells of the gastric antrum than with any of the known normal human islet cells.[547,558,559]

The non-neoplastic pancreas in patients with G-cell tumors often shows large islets and nesidioblastosis. Immunohistochemically, there is a hyperplasia of all islet cell types[571] and particularly of PP cells in the ventrally derived portion of the pancreas.[577]

The conventional therapy for G-cell tumor associated with the Zollinger–Ellison syndrome has been the removal of the target organ through the performance of a total gastrectomy. In some instances, this is said to have led to a regression of the tumor.[580] This therapy is still advocated for patients whose tumors are not amenable to resection (undetectable, multicentric, or metastatic) and in whom medical therapy with H_2-receptor blocking agents is unsuccessful.[540,607] In cases of solitary nonmetastasizing tumors, total excision of the tumor is the treatment of choice, since at present the tumor growth is the main single determinant of long-term survival.[551,562,608]

VIP-producing tumors are associated with a diarrheogenic or cholera-like syndrome in the absence of gastric hypersecretion.[556,597] This is caused by the secretion of vasoactive intestinal peptide (VIP).[578,593]

The morphologic, histochemical, and ultrastructural features of these tumors are indistinguishable from those of G-cell tumors[559]; however, immunocytochemical techniques will show absence of gastrin production by the tumor cells. In addition to VIP, many of these tumors also contain PP, calcitonin, and the alpha chain of hCG.[541,582]

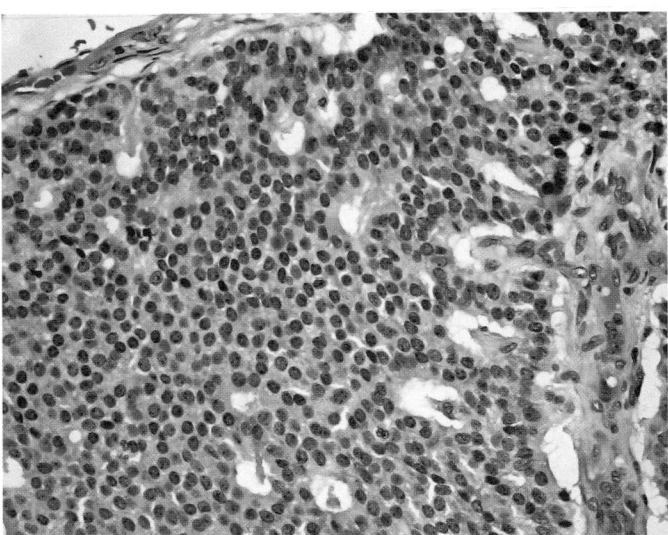

Fig. 15.46 Rosette-like gland formation in G-cell tumor (gastrinoma).

Delta cell tumors seem generally nonfunctioning at the clinical level because of the fact that somatostatin is an inhibitory hormone.[590,603] However, as a result of these inhibitory properties, patients may present with diabetes, cholecystolithiasis, steatorrhea, indigestion, hypochlorhydria, and occasionally anemia, a clinical complex sometimes referred to as the somatostatinoma syndrome.[587] Some delta cell tumors are located in the duodenal wall instead of in the pancreas.[598] Psammoma bodies are commonly found among the tumor cells. Like other endocrine tumors of the pancreas, it may be associated with a ductal component.[544]

PP cell tumors are rare if one restricts the definition of the term to neoplasms composed exclusively or predominantly of this cell type.[581,600] However, a secondary and minor component of PP cells is found in a high proportion of pancreatic endocrine neoplasms of other cell types, including their metastases.[563,601] Sometimes, the non-neoplastic islets of pancreases with islet cell tumor show a prominent hyperplasia of PP cells.[571]

Carcinoid tumors analogous in every way to those more commonly seen in the gastrointestinal tract can occur in the pancreas.[584,585] They probably arise from Kulchitsky's (serotonin-secreting) cells, which are normally present in this organ in connection with the exocrine ducts. In contrast with all other types of pancreatic endocrine neoplasms, they exhibit strong argentaffinity. Serotonin can be demonstrated immunohistochemically.[605] Some tumors have been associated with the carcinoid syndrome, sometimes together with hyperinsulinism.[552,586] One reported case had prominent oncocytic features.[543]

Small cell carcinoma also occurs in the pancreas. It is morphologically similar to its more common pulmonary counterpart and as such it exhibits abortive features of neuroendocrine differentiation. In the WHO scheme, it is coupled with the poorly differentiated neuroendocrine carcinoma (see later section). It is sometimes associated with ectopic ACTH secretion[546] or hypercalcemia.[565] It should be distinguished from primitive neuroectodermal tumor (PNET), which has also been described in an intrapancreatic location (see p. 1091).

Malignancy

The morphologic features that correlate with behavior in pancreatic endocrine tumors are size, extrapancreatic spread, vascular invasion, mitotic activity, and degree of Ki-67 immunostaining.[611,613] On the basis of these features, the WHO Committee for the Histological Typing of Endocrine Tumours has proposed to classify pancreatic endocrine neoplasms into the following categories[615]

1. Well differentiated endocrine tumor
   1.1 Benign behavior (without extrapancreatic spread or vascular invasion, <2 cm in size, £2 mitoses/10 HPF, and <2% Ki-67+ cells).
   1.2 Uncertain behavior (without extrapancreatic extension but with one or more of these features: ≥2 cm in size,

angioinvasive <2 mitoses/10 HPF, and/or ≥2% Ki-67+ cells.

2. Well differentiated (low grade malignant) carcinoma (any tumor with gross local invasion and/or metastases).

In this scheme, all of these tumors are further subdivided into nonfunctioning and functioning, the latter being named according to the syndrome they cause, i.e., gastrinoma, insulinoma, etc. In other words, a pancreatic endocrine tumor composed of G cells as determined by immunohistochemistry will be called a gastrinoma *only* if it is associated with clinical and laboratory evidence of gastrin hypersecretion (Zollinger–Ellison syndrome).

The third member of the group is the poorly differentiated endocrine carcinoma, which includes the small cell neuroendocrine carcinoma.

In terms of other predictors of clinical malignancy, nuclear pleomorphism is a particularly unreliable criterion. Tumors with a glandular or solid pattern of growth are more likely to behave in a malignant fashion than those with a gyriform pattern. As already indicated, these morphologic features are somewhat related to the cell type, which is another predictor of behavior. Beta cell tumors are malignant in about 7% to 10% of the cases, whereas all other cell types are malignant in a much higher percentage. High AgNOR counts and immunoreactivity for the alpha chain of hCG correlate statistically with malignancy, especially if they coexist.[614] The clinical factors that correlate more closely with prognosis in malignant pancreatic endocrine neoplasms are age of the patient and extent of the disease at presentation; survival does not differ significantly among the functioning or nonfunctioning tumors.[616]

Malignant endocrine neoplasms of the pancreas are generally slow growing. In the first reported case of nonfunctioning tumor, liver metastases were first detected 5 years after the original operation, and the patient lived another 5 years following this event.[617] Metastases are restricted to peripancreatic lymph nodes and liver in the majority of the cases. Resection is justified even in incurable cases because of the long-term symptomatic relief that can be achieved.[612] Specific chemotherapeutic agents, such as streptozocin, have resulted in long-term palliation in several instances.[612]

Multiple endocrine neoplasia

Multiple endocrine neoplasia (MEN) syndromes are inherited in an autosomal dominant fashion and are characterized by hyperplastic or neoplastic proliferation of more than one endocrine gland.[618,639,646] They are discussed here because of the frequent occurrence in some of them of a clinically important pancreatic endocrine component.[623] Three distinct types have been described.

MEN type I (Werner's syndrome) is characterized by involvement of the anterior pituitary gland (adenomas), pancreas, and parathyroid glands (chief cell hyperplasia).[619,629,632,647] The pancreatic abnormalities are represented by G-cell tumors in 50% of the cases, beta cell tumors in 30%, VIP cell tumors in 12%, and alpha cell tumors in less than 5%.[631,633]

Thus the main clinical manifestations are primary hyperparathyroidism, the Zollinger–Ellison syndrome, and acromegaly or hypopituitarism.[641] Other abnormalities, although less constant, involve the adrenal cortex and thyroid gland (in the form of nodular hyperplasia or adenomas), carcinoid tumors of various locations but mainly of foregut derivatives (lung, thymus, and gastrointestinal tract), multiple soft tissue lipomas, multiple leiomyomas at various sites, and Menetrier's disease of the stomach.[635] We have seen cases of MEN type I with thymic carcinoid tumors[640] and others associated with multiple carcinoid tumors of the gastric fundus.[644] The disease is due to a variety of germline mutations of the *MEN1* gene, located on chromosome 11q13.[618,628,647] It has also been noted that mutations and allelic deletions of the *MEN1* gene are seen in a subset of sporadic endocrine neoplasms.[626,643]

MEN II is formed by three variants, all of them caused by germline mutations in the *RET* proto-oncogene, located on chromosome 10q11.2,[622,636] and all sharing medullary thyroid carcinoma as part of the disease: MEN IIA, MEN IIB, and familial medullary thyroid carcinoma (FMTC). Parenthetically, the *RET* oncogene is also commonly mutated in Hirschsprung's disease[637,648] and frequently rearranged in papillary thyroid carcinoma (see Chapter 9).

MEN IIA (Sipple's syndrome) is characterized by C-cell hyperplasia and medullary carcinoma of the thyroid gland (often multiple and/or bilateral), pheochromocytoma of the adrenal glands (often bilateral and accompanied by adrenal medullary hyperplasia), and parathyroid chief cell hyperplasia.[624] Thus the overlap between MEN types I and IIA is represented by the parathyroid involvement, which is morphologically and functionally similar in these two disorders.

MEN IIB (Gorlin's syndrome) comprises medullary carcinoma of the thyroid, adrenal pheochromocytoma (with features similar to those seen in MEN IIA), so-called "mucosal neuromas" (resulting in hypertrophied corneal nerves, bumpy lips, and enlarged nodular tongue), skeletal abnormalities, and a marfanoid habitus.[625,634] Mucosal neuromas (which Carney et al.[621] prefer to designate as mucosal ganglioneuromas or ganglioneuromatosis) represent the most constant feature of this syndrome. In many cases, there is extensive ganglioneuromatosis of the digestive tract, which may result in constipation, diarrhea, and even the production of megacolon.[620] Sometimes the gastrointestinal manifestations represent the initial manifestation of the disease. Some patients with MEN IIB also have polyposis coli.[638] Parathyroid disease is distinctly unusual in MEN IIB.

Parenthetically, it should be noted that in older reports MEN IIB was referred to as MEN II.[630]

Familial medullary thyroid carcinoma (FMTC) is characterized by the development of medullary thyroid carcinoma in at least four family members.[648] Other combinations have been found, suggesting the existence of additional types or varieties of MEN. These include the coexistence of pancreatic endocrine tumors and paraganglioma, paraganglioma and thyroid papillary carcinoma, and others.[627,642,645]

Lymphoid tumors and tumorlike conditions

Most **malignant lymphomas** involving the pancreas originate in peripancreatic or retroperitoneal lymph nodes.[650,653] Cases have been reported of pancreatic *lymphoblastic lymphoma* of natural killer cell origin,[655] *posttransplant lymphoproliferative disease*,[652] *plasmacytoma*,[651] and *plasma cell granuloma*.[649] A case of localized *lymphoid hyperplasia* ("pseudolymphoma") of the pancreas presenting with obstructive jaundice is also on record.[654]

Mesenchymal and other primary tumors

Benign mesenchymal tumors of pancreas, all extremely rare, include lymphangioma (not to be confused with the more common microcystic cystadenoma),[665,666] adenomatoid tumor,[665a] hemangioma,[661] schwannoma,[656] solitary fibrous tumor,[663] and clear cell ("sugar") tumor, i.e., a neoplasm of HMB-45-positive epithelioid smooth muscle cells.[671]

Primary **sarcomas** of the pancreas are also rare, most malignant tumors of sarcomatous appearance involving this organ being anaplastic carcinomas or pancreatic extensions of retroperitoneal sarcomas. Primary liposarcomas,[659] leiomyosarcomas,[658,662,662a] malignant peripheral nerve sheath tumors,[660] and malignant fibrous histiocytomas of pancreas[667,668] have been described. Some cases are convincing enough, but in others one has the suspicion that additional sections or special studies might have shown evidence of epithelial differentiation and placed the tumor in an undifferentiated (sarcomatoid) carcinoma category. Ewing's sarcoma/PNET can present as a primary pancreatic mass; most of the reported cases have been in children or young adults.[664]

Isolated examples of pancreatic **choriocarcinoma**[657] and **inflammatory myofibroblastic tumor**[669,670] of the pancreas have been reported.

Metastatic tumors

Most tumors metastatic to the pancreas involve the organ by direct extension, either from an adjacent viscus or peripancreatic lymph nodes; the large bowel and kidney are the most common sites for the primary tumor.[672,675] Blood-borne metastases are sometimes found at autopsy in carcinomatosis, but a pancreatic metastasis will only exceptionally manifest itself clinically.[674] In some cases, the metastatic tumor has been seen to involve the epithelium of the pancreatic ducts and even to exhibit pagetoid features.[673]

Ampullary region

Ampullary carcinoma and precursor lesions

Ampullary carcinoma is the term employed for any malignant epithelial tumor centered in the ampulla of Vater. Although originally defined on topographic grounds, the term ampullary carcinoma also carries a histogenetic significance, in the sense that it implies origin from the intestinal-type mucosa of the ampullary region, often on the basis of a preexisting villous adenoma or villoglandular polyp.[679,701] It should therefore be distinguished from carcinomas of pancreas, terminal third of common bile duct, and other portions of duodenal mucosa with secondary involvement of the ampulla. Such a distinction may not be possible in advanced cases, in which the only diagnosis that can be rendered is that of "carcinoma of the pancreato-biliary-ampullary region."

Clinically, most individuals are over the age of 60, and there is a slight male predominance; several cases have been described in patients with neurofibromatosis type I.[682]

Grossly, ampullary carcinoma usually bulges into the duodenal lumen (Fig. 15.47). On duodenostomy, the duodenal mucosa appears stretched but otherwise normal if the entire tumor is confined to the ampullary lumen (intra-ampullary carcinoma). In other instances, the tumor presents mainly as a circumferential growth around the ampulla (periampullary carcinoma) (Figs

15.48 and 15.49). In still others, a combined intra-ampullary and periampullary pattern of growth exists (mixed carcinoma).[683] Those tumors with a prominent component of residual villous adenoma present as soft, sessile, papillary masses projecting into the duodenal lumen, which may not be felt through the unopened duodenum because of their softness.

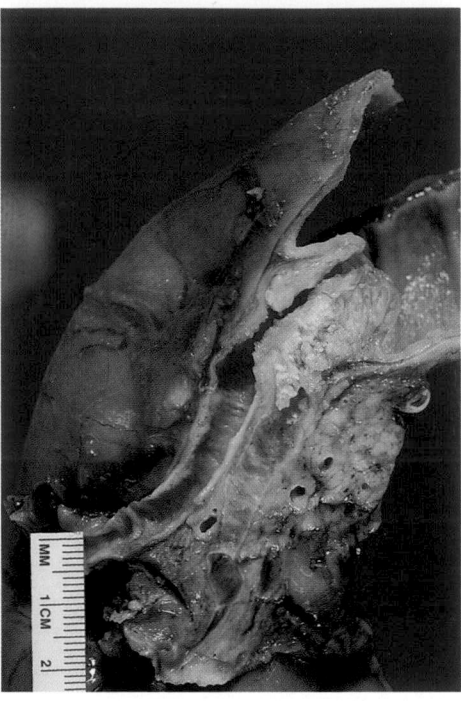

Fig. 15.48 Gross appearance of ampullary adenocarcinoma. The tumor is centered in the ampulla of Vater and has a papillary configuration.

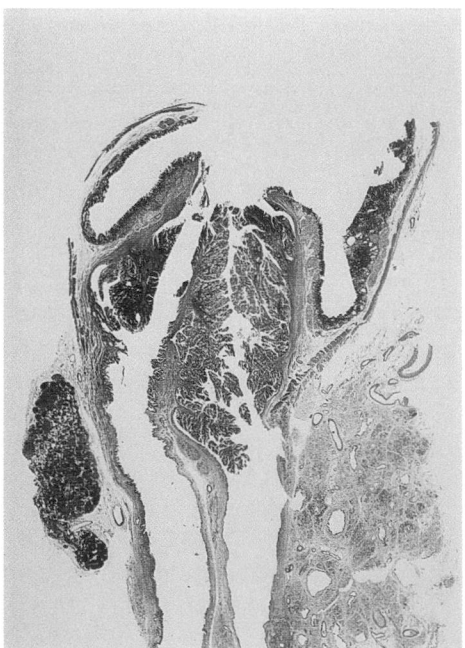

Fig. 15.49 Whole-mount appearance of ampullary carcinoma. The tumor obliterates the ampulla almost completely, and it has a distinctly papillary appearance.

Fig. 15.47 Typical bulging into the duodenal mucosa of an ampullary carcinoma.

When the tumor is small and confined to the ampulla, both the endoscopic and radiographic appearances may be normal.[681] CT and ultrasound usually show dilatation of the common bile duct or pancreatic duct, but the mass itself may be inapparent. Endoscopic ultrasound is said to be the best technique for staging purposes.[681]

Microscopically, nearly all ampullary malignant tumors are adenocarcinomas (Fig. 15.50), often poorly differentiated. Many of them have a superficial papillary component with the appearance of villous adenoma or villoglandular polyp[697] (Fig. 15.51). In the past, by the time exploration was carried out, an invasive carcinoma was almost invariably present at the base. As a result, the whole lesion was regarded as malignant, the superficial

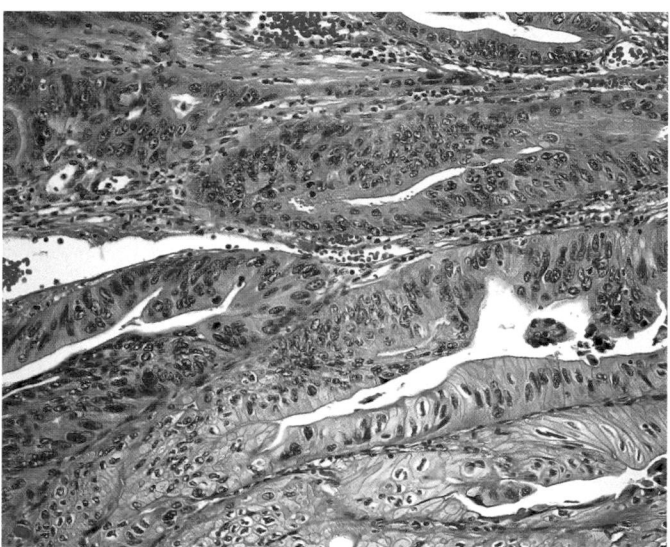

Fig. 15.50 Well-differentiated adenocarcinoma of ampulla. The tumor is of intestinal type by virtue of the elongated architecture of the gland and the highly stratified lining.

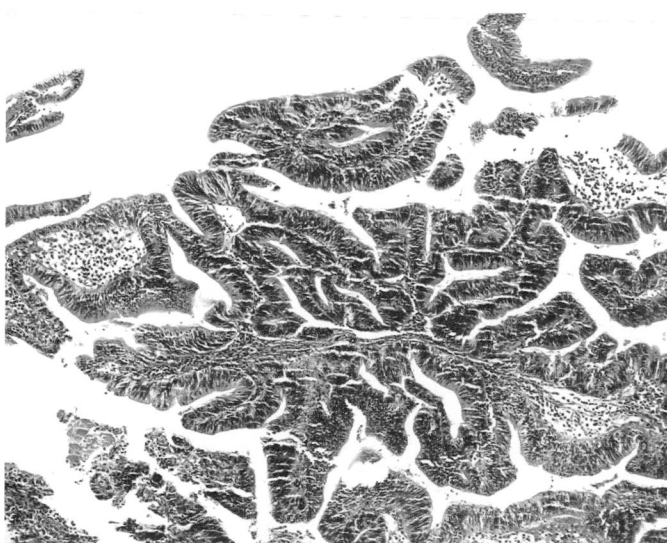

Fig. 15.51 Well-differentiated papillary proliferation in ampulla with morphologic features analogous to those of villous adenoma of large bowel.

portion being interpreted as its better differentiated component. With the increased use of endoscopic procedures for the early detection of these lesions, it has become obvious that a papillary lesion can exist in this area in the absence of stromal invasion.[693] This lesion has morphologic and biologic characteristics akin to those of colorectal *villous adenoma* and, less commonly, of a *villoglandular polyp*, including an association with familial colonic polyposis and a high propensity for malignant transformation.[691] This tendency is of particularly ominous significance in the ampulla because of difficulties in detection in the period preceding the malignant change.

Morphologic variations on the theme of ampullary carcinoma include examples with a prominent Paneth cell component,[685] cases exhibiting hepatoid differentiation,[686] and small cell (neuroendocrine) carcinomas.[689,694,702] We have also seen several cases of ampullary carcinoma with the typical cytoarchitectural features previously described (with or without a villous adenoma component) blending with a deeper component in the head of the pancreas having the cytoarchitectural features of pancreatobiliary-type tumors (see p. 1069). Sometimes the pancreatic component of the tumor has been entirely in situ.[676] Whether these regional differences are the result of microenvironmental influences or the expression of a field effect we are unable to say. Some differences in the keratin immunoprofile between ampullary and pancreatic ductal adenocarcinomas have been described,[677] but they do not seem to be sufficiently consistent to be of great utility in the differential diagnosis.[687]

Mutations of p53 have been detected in the majority of ampullary carcinomas, with a corresponding accumulation of the abnormal product as detected immunohistochemically.[695,697] Ampullary carcinomas are less likely to show loss of Dpc4 expression and of K-*ras* gene mutations than pancreatic ductal carcinomas.[690]

Ampullary carcinoma may invade the adjacent duodenal mucosa, duodenal wall, pancreas, and common bile duct by direct extension. Perineurial invasion may also be present. Regional lymph node metastases are found in 35% to 50% of the cases; in general, they are restricted to one adjacent periampullary group.[684,700]

As already stated, the differential diagnosis of ampullary carcinoma includes several other types of carcinoma of this region. Carcinoma of the terminal third of the *common bile duct* shows great longitudinal thickening of this structure and a granular appearance of the mucosa; it may infiltrate deeply and extend upward beneath the bile duct mucosa and downward into the ampullary region. Microscopically, it is usually a well-differentiated adenocarcinoma formed by small glands, with or without a papillary component, and often accompanied by an intense desmoplastic reaction (see Chapter 14). The rare *nonampullary duodenal carcinomas* do not greatly differ microscopically from those that originate in the ampulla; like the latter, they often arise on the basis of a lesion with the features of villous adenoma (see Chapter 11, small bowel). Therefore the differential diagnosis is largely based on topographic considerations as seen endoscopically and in the gross specimen.

The diagnosis of ampullary carcinoma may be made by cytologic examination (see p. 1072), endoscopic biopsy, or transduodenal biopsy.[680] The latter may be examined as a frozen section procedure. The biopsy should not be too superficial, or else areas of malignant change may be missed. The biopsy preferably should be

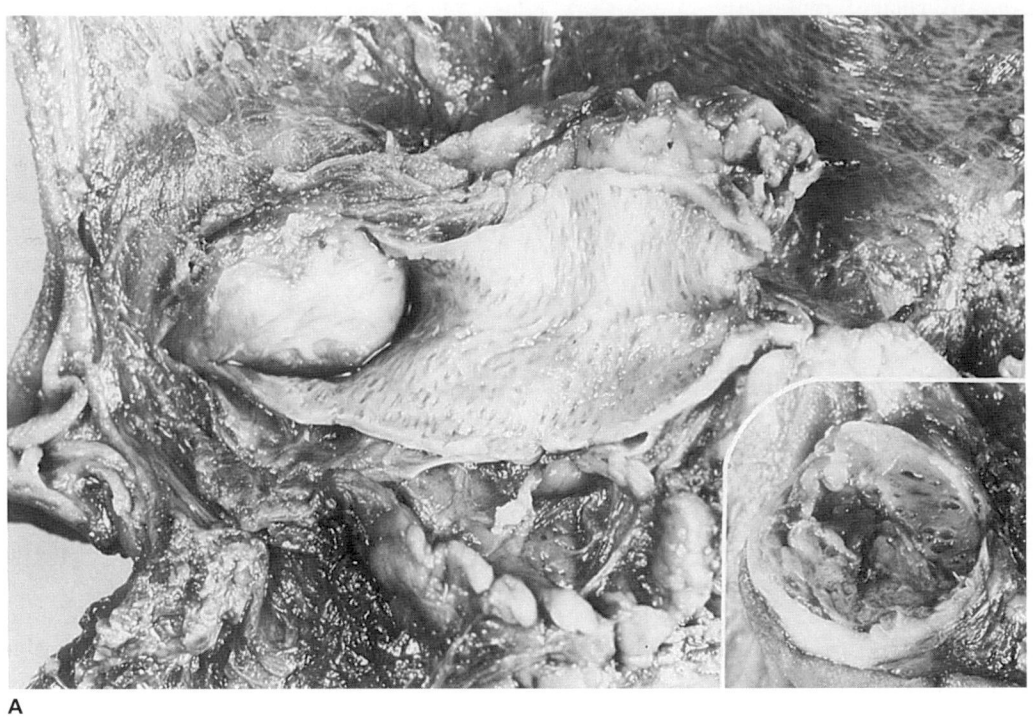

A

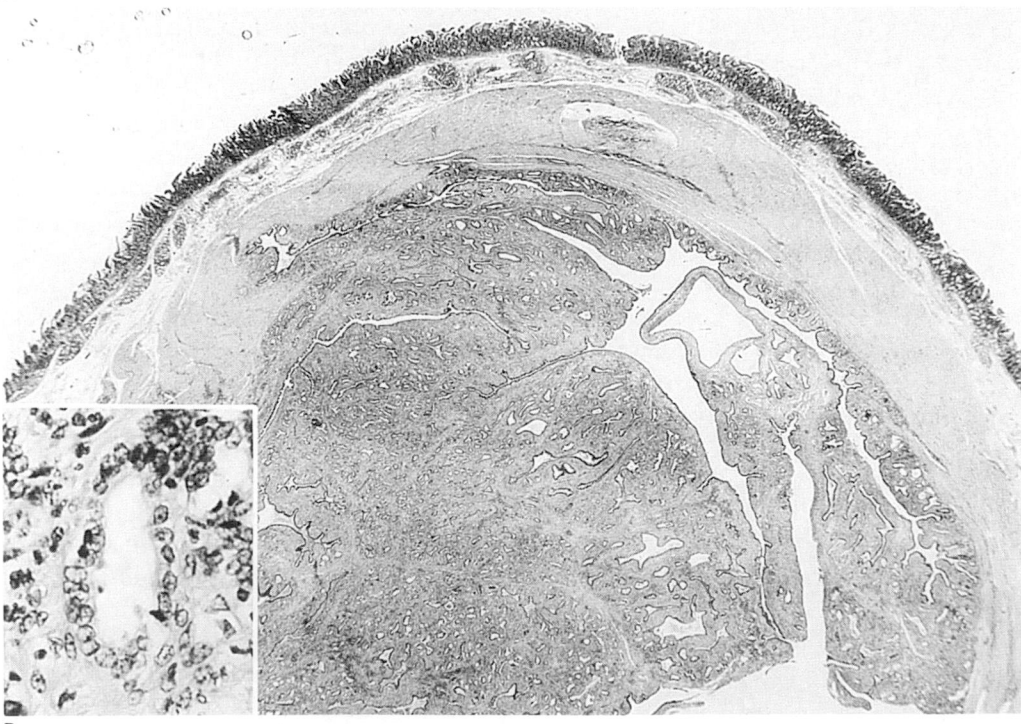

B

Fig. 15.52 A and **B,** Adenomyoma of ampulla of Vater resulting in obstructive jaundice. **A,** The common bile duct shows marked dilatation. Inset shows a cross section of the lesion demonstrating its well-encapsulated nature. It could have been easily enucleated. Instead, Whipple's procedure was carried out under the clinical impression that it was a malignant neoplasm. **B,** Photomicrograph of the same specimen. Glands and stroma intermingle in a manner reminiscent of breast fibroadenoma. Inset demonstrates the benign appearance of the glands.

in the form of step-sectioned multiple fragments, a procedure with a diagnostic reliability greater than 90%.[688]

The treatment of choice of ampullary carcinoma is the Whipple procedure. Transduodenal resection represents adequate treatment for the noninvasive papillary or villoglandular lesions but not when an invasive component has developed unless extremely superficial.[678,692]

The prognosis of ampullary carcinoma is significantly better than that of pancreatic carcinoma and bile duct carcinoma, hence the importance of the separation. The overall 5-year survival rate, which was around 25% in former series, has risen to 50% or above in more recent studies.[696,699] As expected, this figure is even higher (up to almost 80%) in the absence of lymph node metastases.[699] The prognosis is also directly related to the local extent of the disease, as determined grossly and microscopically.[683,698,701] In one series, patients with tumors restricted to within the muscle of Oddi (defined as stage I lesions) had a 5-year survival rate of 85%.[701]

The prognosis of ampullary villous adenoma or villoglandular polyp without malignant transformation is excellent if complete excision has been carried out.

Other lesions

The diagnosis of **fibrosis** of the papilla of Vater is sometimes made in patients with right upper abdominal pain in whom a "pinpoint ampullary opening" is found at surgery.[703,714] More often than not, the microscopic sections show no significant abnormalities. In our experience, clear-cut inflammatory or fibrotic changes in the papilla of Vater have always been associated with chronic gallbladder or pancreatic disease. The morphologic substratum of the nebulous condition referred to as "sphincter of Oddi dysfunction" remains to be determined; endoscopic or sham sphincterotomies are often carried out (with allegedly excellent results), but tissue is rarely obtained for microscopic examination.[705]

Benign tumors and tumorlike conditions of the ampulla other than the already mentioned villous adenomas and villoglandular polyps are extremely rare. They include conditions of probable non-neoplastic nature such as *adenomyoma*[705a,716] (Fig. 15.52), *adenomyomatous hyperplasia* (thought to be a sequela of chronic papillitis),[711] and *inflammatory polyp*. These lesions can cause partial biliary obstruction and are best treated by local resection. *Gangliocytic paraganglioma* is discussed in Chapter 11. *Carcinoid tumors* can also occur in this location, including the adenocarcinoid types.[704,706,707,715] A precursor lesion of carcinoid tumor, which has also been reported in this location, is represented by endocrine cell "micronests."[712] Most of the carcinoid tumors located in the ampulla are immunoreactive for somatostatin and/or PP.[712] In contrast to their counterparts in the rest of the duodenum, ampullary carcinoid tumors practically never express gastrin and are more likely to be associated with neurofibromatosis type I.[708] A case has been seen admixed with a pancreatic acinar component.[710] Primary *malignant lymphoma* of the ampulla has also been described.[709,713]

References

PANCREAS
Normal anatomy

1 Bardram L, Hilsted L, Rehfeld JF. Progastrin expression in mammalian pancreas. Proc Natl Acad Sci U S A 1990, **87**: 298–302.
2 Bendayan M. Presence of endocrine cells in pancreatic ducts. Pancreas 1987, **2**: 393–397.
3 Bloodworth JMB Jr. The pancreatic islet and its relationship to the general endocrine system. Endocr Pathol Update 1990, **1**: 49–84.
4 Delhaye M, Cremer M. Clinical significance of pancreas divisum. Acta Gastroenterol Belg 1992, **55**: 306–313.
5 Goossens A, Gepts W, Saudubray JM, Bonnefont JP, Nihoul-Fekete, Heitz PU, Kloppel G. Diffuse and focal nesidioblastosis. A clinicopathological study of 24 patients with persistent neonatal hyperinsulinemic hypoglycemia. Am J Surg Pathol 1989, **13**: 766–775.
6 Gould VE, Memoli VA, Dardi LE, Gould NS. Nesidiodysplasia and nesidioblastosis of infancy. Ultrastructural and immunohistochemical analysis of islet cell alterations with and without associated hyperinsulinaemic hypoglycaemia. Scand J Gastroenterol 1981, **16**(Suppl 70): 129–142.
7 Jaffe R, Hashida Y, Yunis EJ. The endocrine pancreas of the neonate and infant. In Rosenberg HS, Bernstein J (eds): Perspectives in pediatric pathology, vol. 7. Chicago, 1982, Year Book Medical Publishers.
8 Karnauchow PN. Nesidioblastosis in adults without insular hyperfunction. Am J Clin Pathol 1982, **78**: 511–513.
9 Klimstra DS. Pancreas. In Sternberg SS (ed.): Histology for pathologists, ed. 2. Philadelphia, 1997, Lippincott-Raven, pp. 613–647.
10 Lebenthal E, Lev R, Lee PC. Prenatal and postnatal development of the human exocrine pancreas. In Go VLW, Brooks FP, DiMagno EP, Gardner JD, Lebenthal E, Scheele GA (eds): The exocrine pancreas. Biology, pathobiology, and diseases. New York, 1986, Raven Press.
11 Lehman GA, Sherman S, Nisi R, Hawes RH. Pancreas divisum. Results of minor papilla sphincterotomy. Gastrointest Endosc 1993, **39**: 1–8.
12 Oertel JE. The pancreas. Nonneoplastic alterations. Am J Surg Pathol 1989, **13**(Suppl 1): 50–65.
13 Perez MA, Saul SH, Trojanowski JQ. Neurofilament and chromogranin expression in normal and neoplastic neuroendocrine cells of the human gastrointestinal tract and pancreas. Cancer 1990, **65**: 1219–1227.
14 Peters J, Jurgensen A, Kloppel G. Ontogeny, differentiation and growth of the endocrine pancreas. Virchows Arch 2000, **436**: 527–538.
15 Stefan Y, Grasso S, Perrelet A, Orci L. The pancreatic polypeptide-rich lobe of the human pancreas. Definitive identification of its derivation from the ventral pancreatic primordium. Diabetologia 1982, **23**: 141–142.
16 Westermark P, Engstrom U, Westermark GT, Johnson KH, Permerth J, Betsholtz C. Islet amyloid polypeptide (IAPP) and pro-IAPP immunoreactivity in human islets of Langerhans. Diabetes Res Clin Pract 1989, **7**: 219–226.

Congenital abnormalities
Annular pancreas

17 Bailey PV, Tracy TF Jr, Connors RH, Mooney DP, Lewis JE, Weber TR. Congenital duodenal obstruction. A 32-year review. J Pediatr Surg 1993, **28**: 92–95.

18 Grosfeld JL, Rescorla FJ. Duodenal atresia and stenosis. Reassessment of treatment and outcome based on antenatal diagnosis, pathologic variance, and long-term follow-up. World J Surg 1993, **17**: 301–309.

19 Kiernan PD, ReMine SG, Kiernan PC, ReMine WH. Annular pancreas. Mayo Clinic experience from 1957 to 1976 with review of the literature. Arch Surg 1980, **115**: 46–50.

20 Levy J. The gastrointestinal tract in Down syndrome. Prog Clin Biol Res 1991, **373**: 245–256.

21 Paraskevas G, Papaziogas B, Lazardis C, Gigis P, Papaziogas T. Annular pancreas in adults: embryological development, morphology and clinical significance. Surg Radiol Anat 2001, **23**: 437–442.

22 Sessa F, Fiocca R, Tenti P, Solcia E, Tavani E, Pliteri S. Pancreatic polypeptide rich tissue in the annular pancreas. A distinctive feature of ventral primordium derivatives. Virchows Arch [A] 1983, **399**: 227–232.

23 Suda K. Immunohistochemical and gross dissection studies of annular pancreas. Acta Pathol Jpn 1990, **40**: 505–508.

Heterotopic pancreas

24 Brotman SJ, Pan W, Pozner J, Weiss M, Bleiweiss IJ. Ductal adenocarcinoma arising in duodeno-pyloric heterotopic pancreas. Int J Surg Pathol 1994, **2**: 37–42.

25 Carp NZ, Paul AR, Kowalyshyn MJ, Petersen RO, Hoffman JP. Heterotopic mucinous cystadenoma of the pancreas. Dig Dis Sci 1992, **37**: 1297–1301.

26 Dolan RV, ReMine WH, Dockerty MB. The fate of heterotopic pancreatic tissue. A study of 212 cases. Arch Surg 1974, **109**: 762–765.

27 Haj M, Shiller M, Loberant N, Cohen I, Kerner H. Obstructing gastric heterotopic pancreas: case report and literature review. Clin Imaging 2002, **26**: 267–269.

28 Hara M, Tsutsumi Y. Immunohistochemical studies of endocrine cells in heterotopic pancreas. Virchows Arch [A] 1986, **408**: 385–394.

29 Morinaga S, Ohyama R, Koizumi J. Low-grade mucinous cystadenocarcinoma in the spleen. Am J Surg Pathol 1992, **16**: 903–908.

30 Nisar PJ, Zaitoun AM, Lobo DN, Rowlands BJ. Heterotopic pancreas in the spleen: malignant degeneration to mucinous cystadenocarcinoma. Eur J Gastroenterol Hepatol 2002, **14**: 793–796.

31 Sapino A, Pietribiasi F, Papotti M, Bussolati G. Ectopic endocrine pancreatic tumour simulating splenic angiosarcoma. Pathol Res Pract 1989, **184**: 292–296.

32 Shim YT, Kim SY. Heterotopic gastric mucosa and pancreatic tissue in the skin of the abdominal wall. J Pediatr Surg 1992, **27**: 1539–1540.

33 Tanaka K, Tsunoda T, Eto T, Yamada M, Tajima Y, Shimogama H, Yamaguchi T, Matsuo S, Izawa K. Diagnosis and management of heterotopic pancreas. Int Surg 1993, **78**: 32–35.

34 Tanigawa K, Yamashita S, Tezuka H, Morita S, Ohtsubo T, Maeda R. Diagnostic difficulty in a case of heterotopic pancreatic tissue of the ileum. Am J Gastroenterol 1993, **88**: 451–453.

35 Yamagiwa H, Onishi N, Nishii M. Heterotopic pancreas of the stomach. Histogenesis and immunohistochemistry. Acta Pathol Jpn 1992, **42**: 249–254.

Pancreatitis

Acute pancreatitis

36 Acosta JM, Ledesma CL. Gallstone migration as a cause of acute pancreatitis. N Engl J Med 1974, **290**: 484–488.

37 Ahuja SK, Ahuja SS, Thelmo W, Seymour A, Phelps KR. Necrotizing pancreatitis and multisystem organ failure associated with toxoplasmosis in a patient with AIDS. Clin Infect Dis 1993, **16**: 432–434.

38 Asbun HJ, Rossi RL, Heiss FW, Shea JA. Acute relapsing pancreatitis as a complication of papillary stenosis after endoscopic sphincterotomy. Gastroenterology 1993, **104**: 1814–1817.

39 Bradley EL III. A fifteen year experience with open drainage for infected pancreatic necrosis. Surg Gynecol Obstet 1993, **177**: 215–222.

40 Calleja GA, Barkin JS. Acute pancreatitis. Med Clin North Am 1993, **77**: 1037–1056.

41 Corfield AP, Cooper MJ, Williamson RCN. Acute pancreatitis. A lethal disease of increasing incidence. Gut 1985, **26**: 724–729.

42 Cubilla AL, Fitzgerald PJ. Morphological lesions associated with human primary invasive nonendocrine pancreas cancer. Cancer Res 1976, **36**: 2690–2698.

43 Doubilet H. Pancreatic reflux deliberately produced. Surg Gynecol Obstet 1947, **84**: 710–715.

44 Dowell SF, Moore GW, Hutchins GM. The spectrum of pancreatic pathology in patients with AIDS. Mod Pathol 1990, **3**: 49–53.

45 Dressel TD, Goodale RL Jr, Arneson MA, Borner JW. Pancreatitis as a complication of anticholinesterase insecticide intoxication. Ann Surg 1979, **189**: 199–204.

46 Dressel TD, Goodale RL Jr, Hunninghake DB, Borner JW. Sensitivity of the canine pancreatic intraductal pressure to subclinical reduction in cholinesterase activity. Ann Surg 1979, **190**: 6–12.

47 Eriksson J, Doepel M, Widen E, Halme L, Ekstrand A, Groop L, Hockerstedt K. Pancreatic surgery, not pancreatitis, is the primary cause of diabetes after acute fulminant pancreatitis. Gut 1992, **33**: 843–847.

48 Fan ST, Lai EC, Mok FP, Lo CM, Zheng SS, Wong J. Early treatment of acute biliary pancreatitis by endoscopic papillotomy. N Engl J Med 1993, **328**: 228–232.

49 Gutman M, Inbar M, Klausner JM. Metastases-induced acute pancreatitis. A rare presentation of cancer. Eur J Surg Oncol 1993, **19**: 302–304.

50 Howard J, Jones R. The anatomy of the pancreatic ducts. The etiology of acute pancreatitis. Am J Med Sci 1947, **214**: 617–622.

51 Isenmann R, Buchler M, Uhl W, Malfertheiner P, Martini M, Beger HG. Pancreatic necrosis. An early finding in severe acute pancreatitis. Pancreas 1993, **8**: 358–361.

52 Klöppel G, Maillet B. Chronic pancreatitis. Evolution of the disease. Hepatogastroenterology 1991, **38**: 408–412.

53 Kukora JS. Extensive colonic necrosis complicating acute pancreatitis. Surgery 1985, **97**: 290–294.

54 Lee SP, Nicholls JF, Park HZ. Biliary sludge as a cause of acute pancreatitis. N Engl J Med 1992, **326**: 589–593.

55 Longnecker DS. Pathology and pathogenesis of diseases of pancreas. Am J Pathol 1982, **107**: 103–121.

56 Marshall JB. Acute pancreatitis. A review with an emphasis on new developments. Arch Intern Med 1993, **153**: 1185–1198.

57 Martin JK, VanHeerden JA, Bess MA. Surgical management of acute pancreatitis. Mayo Clin Proc 1984, **59**: 259–267.

58 Medich DS, Lee TK, Melhem MF, Rowe MI, Schraut WH, Lee KK. Pathogenesis of pancreatic sepsis. Am J Surg 1993, **165**: 46–50.

59 Niemann TH, Trigg ME, Winick N, Penick GD. Disseminated adenoviral infection presenting as acute pancreatitis. Hum Pathol 1993, **24**: 1145–1148.

60 Opie EL. The etiology of acute hemorrhagic pancreatitis. Bull Hopkins Hosp 1901, **12**: 182–188.

61 Paloyan D (ed.). Pancreatitis. New Hyde Park, NY, 1983, Medical Examination Publishing.

62 Pezzilli R, Billi P, Miglioli M, Gullo L. Serum amylase and lipase concentrations and lipase/amylase ratio in assessment of etiology and severity of acute pancreatitis. Dig Dis Sci 1993, **38**: 1265–1269.

63 Phat VN, Guerrieri MT, Alexandre JH, Camilleri JP. Early histological changes in acute necrotizing hemorrhagic

pancreatitis. A retrospective pathological study of 20 total pancreatectomy specimens. Pathol Res Pract 1984, **178**: 273–279.

64 Rich AR, Duff GL. Experimental and pathologic studies on the pathogenesis of acute hemorrhagic pancreatitis. Bull Hopkins Hosp 1936, **58**: 212–260.

65 Sarles H, Camarena-Trabous J, Gomez-Santana C, Choux R, Iovanna J. Acute pancreatitis is not a cause of chronic pancreatitis in the absence of residual duct strictures. Pancreas 1993, **8**: 354–357.

66 Smotkin J, Tenner S. Laboratory diagnostic tests in acute pancreatitis. J Clin Gastroenterol 2002, **34**: 459–462.

67 Steer ML, Meldolesi J. The cell biology of experimental pancreatitis. N Engl J Med 1987, **316**: 144–150.

68 Steinberg W, Tenner S. Acute pancreatitis. N Engl J Med 1994, **330**: 1198–1210.

69 Suda K, Tsukahara M. Histopathological and immunohistochemical studies on apparently uninvolved areas of pancreas in patients with acute pancreatitis. Arch Pathol Lab Med 1992, **116**: 934–937.

70 White TT, Morgan A, Hopton D. Postoperative pancreatitis. A study of seventy cases. Am J Surg 1970, **120**: 132–137.

71 Yadav D, Agarwal N, Pitchumoni CS. A critical evaluation of laboratory tests in acute pancreatitis. Am J Gastroenterol 2002, **97**: 1309–1318.

Chronic pancreatitis

71a Abraham SC, Leach S, Yeo CJ, Cameron JL, Murakata LA, Boitnott JK, Albores-Saavedra J, Hruban RH. Eosinophilic pancreatitis and increased eosinophils in the pancreas. Am J Surg Pathol 2003, **27**: 334–342.

71b Abraham SC, Cruz-Correa M, Argani, Furth EE, Hruan RH, Boitnott JK. Lymphoplasmacytic chronic cholecystitis and biliary tract disease in patients with lymphoplasmacytic sclerosing pancreatitis. Am J Surg Pathol 2003, **27**: 441–451.

72 Alvarez C, Widdison AL, Reber HA. New perspectives in the surgical management of chronic pancreatitis. Pancreas 1991, **6** (Suppl 1): S76–S81.

73 Bartow S, Mukai K, Rosai J. Pseudoneoplastic proliferation of endocrine cells in pancreatic fibrosis. Cancer 1981, **47**: 2627–2633.

74 Becker V, Mischke U. Groove pancreatitis. Int J Pancreatol 1991, **10**: 173–182.

75 Bhatia E, Choudhuri G, Sikora SS, Landt O, Kage A, Becker M, Witt H. Tropical calcific pancreatitis: strong association with SPINK1 trypsin inhibitor mutations. Gastroenterology 2002, **123**: 1020–1025.

76 Brady MS, Garfein CF, Klimstra D, Brennan MF. Sarcoidosis of the pancreas. J Surg Oncol 1993, **54**: 132–137.

77 Bresler L, Boissel P, Grosdidier J. Major hemorrhage from pseudocysts and pseudoaneurysms caused by chronic pancreatitis. Surgical therapy. World J Surg 1991, **15**: 649–652.

78 Brown M, Smiley RK. Chronic pancreatitis with steatorrhea following mumps with acute pancreatitis. Am J Dig Dis 1950, **17**: 280–282.

79 Cohn JA, Friedman KJ, Noone PG, Knowles MR, Silverman LM, Jowell PS. Relation between mutations of the cystic fibrosis gene and idiopathic pancreatitis. N Engl J Med 1998, **339**: 653–658.

80 Edmondson HA, Bullock WK, Mehl JW. Chronic pancreatitis and lithiasis. Am J Pathol 1950, **26**: 37–55.

81 el Hamel A, Parc R, Adda G, Bouteloup PY, Huguet C, Malafosse M. Bleeding pseudocysts and pseudoaneurysms in chronic pancreatitis. Br J Surg 1991, **78**: 1059–1063.

82 Farnbacher MJ, Schoen C, Rabenstein T, Benninger J, Hahn EG, Schneider HT. Pancreatic duct stones in chronic pancreatitis: Criteria for treatment intensity and success. Gastrointest Endosc 2002, **56**: 501–506.

83 Friess H, Berberat PO, Wirtz M, Buchler MW. Surgical treatment and long-term follow-up in chronic pancreatitis. Eur J Gastroenterol Hepatol 2002, **14**: 971–977.

84 Friess H, Yamanaka Y, Büchler M, Beger HG, Do DA, Kobrin MS, Korc M. Increased expression of acidic and basic fibroblast growth factors in chronic pancreatitis. Am J Pathol 1994, **144**: 117–128.

85 Hayakawa T, Kondo T, Shibata T, Noda A, Suzuki T, Nakano S. Relationship between pancreatic exocrine function and histological changes in chronic pancreatitis. Am J Gastroenterol 1992, **87**: 1170–1174.

86 Ichimura T, Kondo S, Ambo Y, Hirano S, Ohmi M, Okushiba S, Morikawa T, Shimizu M, Katoh H. Primary sclerosing cholangitis associated with autoimmune pancreatitis. Hepatogastroenterology 2002, **49**: 1221–1224.

87 Kawaguchi K, Koike M, Tsuruta K, Okamoto A, Tabata I, Fujita N. Lymphoplasmacytic sclerosing pancreatitis with cholangitis. A variant of primary sclerosing cholangitis extensively involving pancreas. Hum Pathol 1991, **22**: 387–395.

88 Klöppel G, Bommer G, Commandeur G, Heitz P. The endocrine pancreas in chronic pancreatitis. Virchows Arch [A] 1978, **377**: 157–174.

89 Lankisch PG. Natural course of chronic pancreatitis. Pancreatology 2001, **1**: 3–14.

90 Lankisch PG, Lohr-Happe A, Otto J, Creutzfeldt W. Natural course in chronic pancreatitis. Pain, exocrine and endocrine pancreatic insufficiency and prognosis of the disease. Digestion 1993, **54**: 148–155.

91 Laszik Z, Pap A, Farkas G, Ormos J. Endocrine pancreas in chronic pancreatitis. A qualitative and quantitative study. Arch Pathol Lab Med 1989, **113**: 47–51.

92 Miller AR, Nagorney DM, Sarr MG. The surgical spectrum of hereditary pancreatitis in adults. Ann Surg 1992, **215**: 39–43.

93 Mixter CG Jr, Keynes M, Cope O. Further experience with pancreatitis as a diagnostic clue to hyperparathyroidism. N Engl J Med 1962, **266**: 265–272.

94 Morrow CE, Cohen JI, Sutherland DER, Najarian JS. Chronic pancreatitis. Long-term surgical results of pancreatic duct drainage, pancreatic resection, and near-total pancreatectomy and islet autotransplantation. Surgery 1984, **96**: 608–616.

95 Mulligan NJ, Yang S, Andry C, Klein M, O'Brien MJ. The role of p21 RAS in pancreatic neoplasia and chronic pancreatitis. Hum Pathol 1999, **30**: 602–610.

96 Mullin GT, Caperton EM Jr, Crespin SR, Williams RC Jr. Arthritis and skin lesions resembling erythema nodosum in pancreatic disease. Ann Intern Med 1968, **68**: 75–87.

96a Notohara K, Burgart LJ, Yadav D, Chari S, Smyrk TC. Idiopathic chronic pancreatitis with periductal lymphoplasmacytic infiltration. Am J Surg Pathol 2003, **27**: 1119–1127.

97 Proca DM, Ellison EC, Hibbert D, Frankel WL. Major pancreatic resections for chronic pancreatitis. Arch Pathol Lab Med 2001, **125**: 1051–1054.

98 Rosch T, Daniel S, Scholz M, Huibregtse K, Smits M, Schneider T, Ell C, Haber G, Riemann JF, Jakobs R, Hintze R, Adler A, Neuhaus H, Zavoral M, Zavada F, Schusdziarra V, Soehendra N. Endoscopic treatment of chronic pancreatitis: a multicenter study of 1000 patients with long-term follow-up. Endoscopy 2002, **34**: 765–771.

99 Sarles H. Chronic calcifying pancreatitis—chronic alcoholic pancreatitis. Gastroenterology 1974, **66**: 604–616.

100 Sarles H. Chronic pancreatitis and diabetes. Baillieres Clin Endocrinol Metab 1992, **6**: 745–775.

101 Sarner M, Cotton PB. Classification of pancreatitis. Gut 1984, **25**: 756–759.

102 Sharer N, Schwarz M, Malone G, Howarth A, Painter J, Super M, Braganza J. Mutations of the cystic fibrosis gene in patients with chronic pancreatitis. N Engl J Med 1998, **339**: 645–652.

103 Sherman S, Lehman GA, Hawes RH, Ponich T, Miller LS, Cohen LB, Kortan P, Haber GB. Pancreatic ductal stones. Frequency of successful endoscopic removal and improvement in symptoms. Gastrointest Endosc 1991, **37**: 511–517.

104 Stambler JB, Klibaner MI, Bliss CM, LaMont JT. Tuberculous abscess of the pancreas. Gastroenterology 1982, **83**: 922–925.

105 Steer ML, Waxman I, Freedman S. Chronic pancreatitis. N Engl J Med 1995, **332**: 1482–1490.

105a Standop J, Standop S, Itami A, Nozawa F, Brand RE, Büchler MW, Pour PM. ErbB2 oncogene expression supports the acute pancreatitis-chronic pancreatitis sequence. Virchows Arch 2002, **441**: 385–391.

106 Stobbe KC, ReMine WH, Baggenstoss AH. Pancreatic lithiasis. Surg Gynecol Obstet 1970, **131**: 1090–1099.

107 Stolte M, Schwabe H, Prestele H. Relationship between diseases of the pancreas and hyperplasia of Brunner's glands. Virchows Arch [A] 1981, **394**: 75–87.

108 Strate T, Yekebas E, Knoefel WT, Bloechle C, Izbicki JR. Pathogenesis and the natural course of chronic pancreatitis. Eur J Gastroenterol Hepatol 2002, **14**: 929–934.

109 Strum WB, Spiro HM. Chronic pancreatitis. Ann Intern Med 1971, **74**: 264–277.

109a Tranchida P, Taylor JP, Weaver DW, Klimstra DS, Cheng JD, Adsay NV. Paraduodenal pancreatitis: a clinically and pathologically distinct form of pseudotumoral chronic pancreatitis associated with abnormalities of accessory duct, accessory ampulla or duodenal wall. Mod Pathol 2003, **16**: 286–287a.

110 Traverso LW, Kozarek R. The Whipple procedure for severe complications of chronic pancreatitis. Arch Surg 1993, **128**: 1047–1050.

111 Volkholz H, Stolte M, Becker V. Epithelial dysplasias in chronic pancreatitis. Virchows Arch [A] 1982, **396**: 331–349.

112 Walsh TN, Rode J, Theis BA, Russell RC. Minimal change chronic pancreatitis. Gut 1992, **33**: 1566–1571.

113 Whitcomb DC. Hereditary pancreatitis: a model for understanding the genetic basis of acute and chronic pancreatitis. Pancreatology 2001, **1**: 565–570.

114 Yamaguchi K, Tanaka M. Groove pancreatitis masquerading as pancreatic carcinoma. Am J Surg 1992, **163**: 312–316.

115 Zuk RJ, Neal JW, Baithun SI. Malakoplakia of the pancreas. Virchows Arch [A] 1990, **417**: 181–184.

Pancreatic transplantation

116 Barker CF, Naji A. Perspectives in pancreatic and islet transplantation. N Engl J Med 1992, **327**: 271–273.

117 Busing M, Hopt UT, Quacken M, Becker HD, Morgenroth K. Morphological studies of graft pancreatitis following pancreas transplantation. Br J Surg 1993, **80**: 1170–1173.

118 Grewal HP, Garland L, Novak K, Gaber L, Tolley EA, Gaber AO. Risk factors for postimplantation pancreatitis and pancreatic thrombosis in pancreas transplant recipients. Transplantation 1993, **56**: 609–612.

119 Krishnamurthi V, Philosophe B, Bartlett ST. Pancreas transplantation: contemporary surgical techniques. Urol Clin North Am 2001, **28**: 833–838.

120 Lloyd RV, Dafoe DC, Campbell DA Jr, Merion RM, Turcotte JG, Vinik AI. Pancreas transplantation. An immunohistochemical analysis of pancreatic hormones and HLA-DR expression. Mod Pathol 1989, **2**: 323–330.

121 Nakhleh RE, Gruessner RW, Swanson PE, Tzardis PJ, Brayman K, Dunn DL, Sutherland DE. Pancreas transplant pathology. A morphologic, immunohistochemical, and electron microscopic comparison of allogeneic grafts with rejection, syngeneic grafts, and chronic pancreatitis. Am J Surg Pathol 1991, **15**: 246–256.

122 Nakhleh RE, Sutherland DE. Pancreas rejection. Significance of histopathologic findings with implications for classification of rejection. Am J Surg Pathol 1992, **16**: 1098–1107.

123 Robertson RP. Pancreatic islet transplantation for diabetes: successes, limitations, and challenges for the future. Mol Genet Metab 2001, **74**: 200–205.

124 Shapiro AM, Ryan EA, Lakey JR. Pancreatic islet transplantation in the treatment of diabetes mellitus. Best Pract Res Clin Endocrinol Metab 2001, **15**: 241–264.

Abscess

125 Fedorak IJ, Ko TC, Djuricin G, McMahon M, Thompson K, Prinz RA. Secondary pancreatic infections. Are they distinct clinical entities? Surgery 1992, **112**: 824–830.

126 Warshaw AL. Pancreatic abscesses. Current concepts. N Engl J Med 1972, **287**: 1234–1236.

Pseudocysts

127 D'Egidio A, Schein M. Pancreatic pseudocysts. A proposed classification and its management implications. Br J Surg 1991, **78**: 981–984.

128 Goulet RJ, Goodman J, Schaffer R, Dallemand S, Andersen DK. Multiple pancreatic pseudocyst disease. Ann Surg 1984, **199**: 6–13.

129 Greenstein A, DeMaio E, Nabsetch DC. Acute hemorrhage associated with pancreatic pseudocysts. Surgery 1971, **69**: 56–62.

130 Huizinga WK, Baker LW. Treatment of persistent and complicated pancreatic pseudocysts. J R Coll Surg Edinb 1992, **37**: 373–376.

131 Kloppel G. Pseudocysts and other non-neoplastic cysts of the pancreas. Semin Diagn Pathol 2000, **17**: 7–15.

True cysts

132 Adsay NV, Hasteh F, Cheng JD, Klimstra DS. Squamous-lined cysts of the pancreas: lymphoepithelial cysts, dermoid cysts (teratomas) and accessory-splenic epidermoid cysts. Semin Diagn Pathol 2000, **17**: 56–65.

133 Di Corato MP, Schned AR. A rare lymphoepithelial cyst of the pancreas. Am J Clin Pathol 1992, **98**: 188–191.

133a Drut R, Drut M. Pancreatic cystic dysplasia (dysgenesis) presenting as a surgical pathology specimen in a patient with multiple malformations and familial ear pits. Int J Surg Pathol 2002, **10**: 303–308.

134 Kennedy SM, Hashida Y, Malatack JJ. Polycystic kidneys, pancreatic cysts, and cystadenomatous bile ducts in the oral-facial-digital syndrome type I. Arch Pathol Lab Med 1991, **115**: 519–523.

135 Kloppel G. Pseudocysts and other non-neoplastic cysts of the pancreas. Semin Diagn Pathol 2000, **17**: 7–15.

136 Kosmahl M, Egawa N, Schroder S, Carneiro F, Luttges J, Kloppel G. Mucinous nonneoplastic cyst of the pancreas: a novel nonneoplastic cystic change? Mod Pathol 2002, **15**: 154–158.

137 Ramsden KL, Newman J. Lymphoepithelial cyst of the pancreas. Histopathology 1991, **18**: 267–268.

138 Suda K, Takase M, Shiono S, Yamasaki S, Nobukawa B, Kasamaki S, Arakawa A, Suzuki F. Duodenal wall cysts may be derived from a ductal component of ectopic pancreatic tissue. Histopathology 2002, **41**: 351–356.

139 Suster S, Rosai J. Multilocular thymic cyst. An acquired reactive process: study of 18 cases. Am J Surg Pathol 1991, **15**: 388–398.

140 Tateyama H, Tada T, Murase T, Fujitake S, Eimoto T. Lymphoepithelial cyst and epidermoid cyst of the accessory spleen in the pancreas. Mod Pathol 1999, **11**: 1171–1177.

141 Truong LD, Rangdaeng S, Jordan PH Jr. Lymphoepithelial cyst of the pancreas. Am J Surg Pathol 1987, **11**: 899–903.

Tumors
Ductal adenocarcinoma
General and clinical features

142 Ahlgren JD. Epidemiology and risk factors in pancreatic cancer. Semin Oncol 1996, **23**: 241–250.

142a Bick RL. Cancer-associated thrombosis. N Engl J Med 2003, **349**: 109–111.

143 Bowlby LS. Pancreatic adenocarcinoma in an adolescent male with Peutz-Jeghers syndrome. Hum Pathol 1986, **17:** 97–99.

144 Cubilla AL, Fitzgerald PJ. Cancer of the exocrine pancreas. The pathologic aspects. Cancer 1985, **35:** 2–18.

145 DelFavero G, Fabris C, Plebani M, Panucci A, Piccoli A, Perobelli L, Pedrazzoli S, Baccaglini U, Burlina A, Naccarato R. CA 19-9 and carcinoembryonic antigen in pancreatic carcinoma diagnosis. Cancer 1986, **57:** 1576–1579.

146 DiMagno EP, Shorter RG, Taylor WF, Go VLW. Relationships between pancreaticobiliary ductal anatomy and pancreatic ductal and parenchymal histology. Cancer 1982, **49:** 361–368.

147 Fitzgerald PJ, Fortner JG, Watson RC, Schwartz MK, Sherlock P, Benua RS, Cubilla AL, Schottenfeld D, Miller D, Winawer SJ, Lightdale CJ, Leidner SD, Nisselbaum JS, Menendez-Botet CJ, Poleski MH. The value of diagnostic aids in detecting pancreas cancer. Cancer 1978, **41:** 868–879.

148 Furukawa H, Okada S, Saisho H, Ariyama J, Karasawa E, Nakaizumi A, Nakazawa S, Murakami K, Kakizoe T. Clinicopathologic features of small pancreatic adenocarcinoma: A collective study. Cancer 1996, **78:** 986–990.

149 Gattani AM, Mandeli J, Bruckner HW. Tumor markers in patients with pancreatic carcinoma. Cancer 1996, **78:** 57–62.

150 Gullo L, Pezzilli R, Morselli-Labate AM. Diabetes and the risk of pancreatic cancer. Italian Pancreatic Cancer Study Group. N Engl J Med 1994, **331:** 81–84.

150a Hruban RH, Petersen GM, Ha PK, Kern SE. Genetics of pancreatic cancer. From genes to families. Surg Oncol Clin N Am 1998, **7:** 1–23.

151 Kalapothaki V, Tzonou A, Hsieh CC, Toupadaki N, Karakatsani A, Trichopoulos D. Tobacco, ethanol, coffee, pancreatitis, diabetes mellitus, and cholelithiasis as risk factors for pancreatic carcinoma. Cancer Causes Control 1993, **4:** 375–382.

152 Kimura W, Morikane K, Esaki Y, Chan WC, Pour PM. Histologic and biologic patterns of microscopic pancreatic ductal adenocarcinomas detected incidentally at autopsy. Cancer 1998, **82:** 1839–1849.

153 Lafler CJ, Hinerman DL. A morphologic study of pancreatic carcinoma with reference to multiple thrombi. Cancer 1961, **14:** 944–952.

154 Levison DA. Carcinoma of the pancreas. J Pathol 1979, **129:** 203–223.

155 Longnecker DS. Pathology and pathogenesis of diseases of the pancreas. Am J Pathol 1982, **107:** 103–121.

156 Lowenfels AB, Maisonneuve P, Cavallini G, Ammann RW, Lankisch PG, Andersen JR, Dimagno EP, Andren-Sandberg A, Domellof L. Pancreatitis and the risk of pancreatic cancer. International Pancreatitis Study Group. N Engl J Med 1993, **328:** 1433–1437.

157 Lynch HT, Brand RE, Hogg D, Deters CA, Fusaro RM, Lynch JF, Liu L, Knezetic H, Lassam NJ, Goggins M, Kern S. Phenotypic variation in eight extended CDKN2A germline mutation familial atypical multiple mole melanoma-pancreatic carcinoma-prone families: the familial atypical multiple mole melanoma-pancreatic carcinoma syndrome. Cancer 2002, **94:** 84–96.

158 Lynch HT, Smyrk T, Kern SE, Hruban RH, Lightdale CJ, Lemon SJ, Lynch JF, Fusaro LR, Fusaro RM, Ghadirian P. Familial pancreatic cancer: A review. Semin Oncol 1996, **23:** 251–275.

159 MacMahon B. Risk factors for cancer of the pancreas. Cancer 1982, **50:** 2676–2680.

160 Meckler KA, Brentnall TA, Haggitt RC, Crispin D, Byrd DR, Kimmey MB, Bronner MP. Familial fibrocystic pancreatic atrophy with endocrine cell hyperplasia and pancreatic carcinoma. Am J Surg Pathol 2001, **25:** 1047–1053.

161 Morohoshi T, Held G, Klöppel G. Exocrine pancreatic tumours and their histological classification. A study based on 167 autopsy and 97 surgical cases. Histopathology 1983, **7:** 645–661.

162 Naschitz JE, Yeshurun D, Eldar S, Lev LM. Diagnosis of cancer-associated vascular disorders. Cancer 1996, **77:** 1759–1767.

163 Permert J, Larsson J, Westermark GT, Herrington MK, Christmanson L, Pour PM, Westermark P, Adrian TE. Islet amyloid polypeptide in patients with pancreatic cancer and diabetes. N Engl J Med 1994, **330:** 313–318.

164 Prandoni P, Lensing AW, Buller HR, Cogo A, Prins MH, Cattelan AM, Cuppini S, Noventa F, ten Cate JW. Deep-vein thrombosis and the incidence of subsequent symptomatic cancer. N Engl J Med 1992, **327:** 1128–1133.

165 Safi F, Berger HG, Bittner R, Büchler M, Krautzberger W. CA 19-9 and pancreatic adenocarcinoma. Cancer 1986, **57:** 779–783.

166 Van Riel JMGH, Giaccone G, Pinedo HM. Pancreaticobiliary cancer: the future aspects of medical oncology. Annal of Oncology 2000, **10:** S296–S299.

167 Wanebo HJ, Vezeridis MP. Pancreatic carcinoma in perspective: A continuing challenge. Cancer 1996, **78:** 580–591.

168 Warshaw AL, Fernandez-del Castillo C. Pancreatic carcinoma. N Engl J Med 1992, **326:** 455–465.

169 Yamaguchi K. Pancreatic carcinoma associated with chronic calcifying pancreatitis. Int J Pancreatol 1992, **12:** 297–303.

Location and gross features

170 Cubilla AL, Fitzgerald PJ. Morphological patterns of primary nonendocrine human pancreas carcinoma. Cancer Res 1975, **35:** 2234–2248.

170a Lee L-Y, Hsu H-L, Chen H-M, Hsueh C. Ductal adenocarcinoma of the pancreas with huge cystic degeneration: a lesion to be distinguished from pseudocyst and mucinous cystadenocarcinoma. Int J Surg Pathol 2003, **11:** 235–239.

Microscopic features

170b Andea A, Sarkar F, Adsay VN. Clinicopathological correlates of pancreatic intraepithelial neoplasia: a comparative analysis of 82 cases with and 152 cases without pancreatic ductal adenocarcinoma. Mod Pathol 2003; **16:** 996–1006.

171 Bartow S, Mukai K, Rosai J. Pseudoneoplastic proliferation of endocrine cells in pancreatic fibrosis. Cancer 1981, **47:** 2627–2633.

172 Brockie E, Anand A, Albores-Saavedra J. Progression of atypical ductal hyperplasia/carcinoma in situ of the pancreas to invasive adenocarcinoma. Ann Diagn Pathol 1998, **2:** 286–292.

173 Chen J, Baithun SI. Morphological study of 391 cases of exocrine pancreatic tumours with special reference to the classification of exocrine pancreatic carcinoma. J Pathol 1985, **146:** 17–29.

174 Chen J, Baithun SI, Ramsay MA. Histogenesis of pancreatic carcinomas. A study based on 248 cases. J Pathol 1985, **146:** 65–76.

175 Costa J. Benign epithelial inclusions in pancreatic nerves. Am J Clin Pathol 1977, **67:** 306–307.

176 Cubilla AL, Fitzgerald PJ. Morphological lesions associated with human primary invasive nonendocrine pancreas cancer. Cancer Res 1976, **36:** 2690–2698.

177 Edis AJ, Kiernan PD, Taylor WF. Attempted curative resection of ductal carcinoma of the pancreas. Review of Mayo Clinic experience, 1951–1975. Mayo Clin Proc 1980, **55:** 531–540.

178 Gambill EE. Pancreatitis associated with pancreatic carcinoma. A study of 26 cases. Mayo Clin Proc 1971, **46:** 173–177.

179 Hyland C, Kheir SM, Kashlan NB. An evaluation of pancreatic biopsy with the Vim-Silverman needle. Am J Surg Pathol 1981, **5:** 179–191.

180 Iacobuzio-Donahue CA, Ryu B, Hruban RH, Kern SE. Exploring the host desmoplastic response to pancreatic carcinoma. Gene expression of stromal and neoplastic cells at the site of primary invasion. Am J Pathol 2002, **160:** 91–99.

181 Kodama T, Mori W. Morphological lesions of the pancreatic ducts. Significance of pyloric gland metaplasia in carcinogenesis of exocrine and endocrine pancreas. Acta Pathol Jpn 1983, **33:** 645–660.

182 Kozuka S, Sassa R, Taki T, Masamoto K, Nagasawa S, Saga S, Hasegawa K, Takeuchi M. Relation of pancreatic duct hyperplasia to carcinoma. Cancer 1979, **43:** 1418–1428.

183 Longnecker DS, Terhune PG. The case for parallel classification of biliary tract and pancreatic neoplasms. Mod Pathol 1996, 9: 828–837.

184 Nagakawa T, Kayahara M, Ueno K, Ohta T, Konishi I, Ueda N, Miyazaki I. A clinicopathologic study on neural invasion in cancer of the pancreatic head. Cancer 1992, 69: 930–935.

185 Pour PM, Sayed S, Sayed G. Hyperplastic, preneoplastic and neoplastic lesions found in 83 human pancreases. Am J Clin Pathol 1982, 77: 137–152.

186 Takahashi T, Ishikura H, Kato H, Tanabe T, Yoshiki T. Intra-pancreatic, extra-tumoral perineural invasion (nex). An indicator for the presence of retroperitoneal neural plexus invasion by pancreas carcinoma. Acta Pathol Jpn 1992, 42: 99–103.

187 Tryka AF, Brooks JR. Histopathology in the evaluation of total pancreatectomy for ductal carcinoma. Ann Surg 1979, 190: 373–381.

187a Van Heek NT, Meeker AK, Kern SE, Yeo CJ, Lillemoe KD, Cameron JL, Johan G, Offerhaus A, Hicks JL, Wilentz RE, Goggins MG, De Marzo AM, Hruban RH, Maitra A. Telomere shortening is nearly universal in pancreatic intraepithelial neoplasia. Am J Pathol 2002, 161: 1541–1547.

Histochemical and immunohistochemical features

187b Adsay NV, Merati K, Andea A, Sarkar F, Hruban RH, Wilentz RE, Goggins M, Iocobuzio-Donahue C, Longnecker DS, Klimstra DS. The dichotomy in the preinvasive neoplasia to invasive carcinoma sequence in the pancreas: differential expression of MUC1 and MUC2 supports the existence of two separate pathways of carcinogenesis. Mod Pathol 2002, 15: 1087–1095.

188 Alexander J, Krishnamurthy S, Kovacs D, Dayal Y. Cytokeratin profile of extrahepatic pancreaticobiliary epithelia and their carcinomas. Appl Immunohistochem 1997, 5: 216–222.

189 Bacchi CE, Gown AM. Distribution and pattern of expression of villin, a gastrointestinal-associated cytoskeletal protein, in human carcinomas. A study employing paraffin-embedded tissue. Lab Invest 1991, 64: 418–424.

190 Bätge B, Bosslet K, Sedlacek HH, Kern HF, Klöppel G. Monoclonal antibodies against CEA-related components discriminate between pancreatic duct type carcinomas and nonneoplastic duct lesions as well as nonduct type neoplasias. Virchows Arch [A] 1986, 408: 361–374.

191 Dhodapkar KM, Friedlander D, Scholes J, Grumet M. Differential expression of the cell-adhesion molecule Nr-CAM in hyperplastic and neoplastic human pancreatic tissue. Hum Pathol 2001, 32: 396–400.

192 Eusebi V, Capella C, Bondi A, Sessa F, Vezzadini P, Mancini AM. Endocrine-paracrine cells in pancreatic exocrine carcinomas. Histopathology 1981, 5: 599–613.

193 Goldstein NS, Bassi D. Cytokeratins 7, 17 and 20 reactivity in pancreatic and ampulla of vater adenocarcinomas. Percentage of positivity and distribution is affected by the cut-point threshold. Am J Clin Pathol 2001, 115: 695–702.

194 Haglund C, Roberts PJ, Nordling S, Ekblom P. Expression of laminin in pancreatic neoplasms and in chronic pancreatitis. Am J Surg Pathol 1984, 8: 669–676.

195 Ichihara T, Nagura H, Nakao A, Sakamoto J, Watanabe T, Takagi H. Immunohistochemical localization of CA19-9 and CEA in pancreatic carcinoma and associated diseases. Cancer 1988, 61: 324–333.

196 Kamisawa T, Fukayama M, Tabata I, Isawa T, Tsuruta K, Okamoto A, Koike M. Neuroendocrine differentiation in pancreatic duct carcinoma. Special emphasis on duct-endocrine cell carcinoma of the pancreas. Pathol Res Pract 1996, 192: 901–908.

197 Kim JH, Ho SB, Montgomery CK, Kim YS. Cell lineage markers in human pancreatic cancer. Cancer 1990, 66: 2134–2143.

198 Lemoine NR, Hughes CM, Barton CM, Poulsom R, Jeffery RE, Kloppel G, Hall PA, Gullick WJ. The epidermal growth factor receptor in human pancreatic cancer. J Pathol 1992, 166: 7–12.

199 Loy TS, Springer D, Chapman RK, Diaz-Arias AA, Bulatao IS, Bickel JT. Lack of specificity of monoclonal antibody B72.3 in distinguishing chronic pancreatitis from pancreatic adenocarcinoma. Am J Clin Pathol 1991, 96: 684–688.

200 Maitra A, Iacobuzio-Donahue C, Rahman A, Sohn TA, Argani P, Meyer R, Yeo CJ, Cameron JL, Goggins M, Kern SE, Ashfaq R, Hruban RH, Wilentz RE. Immunohistochemical validation of a novel epithelial and a novel stromal marker of pancreatic ductal adenocarcinoma identified by global expression microarrays. Sea urchin fascin homolog and heat shock protein 47. Am J Clin Pathol 2002, 118: 52–59.

201 Matsuzawa K, Akamatsu T, Katsuyama T. Mucin histochemistry of pancreatic duct cell carcinoma, with special reference to organoid differentiation simulating gastric pyloric mucosa. Hum Pathol 1992, 23: 925–933.

202 Oh YL, Song SY, Ahn G. Expression of maspin in pancreatic neoplasms: application of maspin immunohistochemistry to the differential diagnosis. Appl Immunohistochem Mol Morphol 2002, 10: 62–66.

203 Osako M, Yonezawa S, Siddiki B, Huang J, Ho JJ, Kim YS, Sato E. Immunohistochemical study of mucin carbohydrates and core proteins in human pancreatic tumors. Cancer 1993, 71: 2191–2199.

204 Real FX, Vila MR, Skoudy A, Ramaekers FC, Corominas JM. Intermediate filaments as differentiation markers of exocrine pancreas. II. Expression of cytokeratins of complex and stratified epithelia in normal pancreas and in pancreas cancer. Int J Cancer 1993, 54: 720–727.

205 Reid JD, Yuh S-L, Petrelli M, Jaffe R. Ductuloinsular tumors of the pancreas. A light, electron microscopic and immunohistochemical study. Cancer 1982, 49: 908–915.

206 Sakaki M, Sano T, Hirokawa M, Takahashi M, Kiyoku H. Immunohistochemical study of endocrine cells in ductal adenocarcinoma of the pancreas. Virchows Arch 2002, 441: 249–255.

207 Sessa F, Bonato M, Frigerio B, Capella C, Solcia E, Prat M, Bara J, Samloff IM. Ductal cancers of the pancreas frequently express markers of gastrointestinal epithelial cells. Gastroenterology 1990, 98: 1655–1665.

208 Shimizu M, Saitoh Y, Ohyanagi H, Itoh H. Immunohistochemical staining of pancreatic cancer with CA19-9, KM01, unabsorbed CEA, and absorbed CEA. A comparison with normal pancreas and chronic pancreatitis. Arch Pathol Lab Med 1990, 114: 195–200.

209 Tempero M, Takasaki H, Uchida E, Takiyama Y, Colcher D, Metzgar RS, Pour PM. Co-expression of CA 19-9, DU-PAN-2, CA 125, and TAG-72 in pancreatic adenocarcinoma. Am J Surg Pathol 1989, 13(Suppl 1): 89–95.

210 Tezel E, Nagasaka T, Nomoto S, Sugimoto H, Nakao A. Neuroendocrine-like differentiation in patients with pancreatic carcinoma. Cancer 2001, 89: 2230–2236.

211 Vlasoff DM, Baschinsky DY, Frankel WL. Cytokeratin 5/6 immunostaining in hepatobiliary and pancreatic neoplasms. Appl Immunohistochem Mol Morphol 2002, 10: 147–151.

212 Xerri L, Payan MJ, Choux R, Gros N, Figarella-Branger D, Sarles H. Predominance of sialomucin secretion in malignant and premalignant pancreatic lesions. Hum Pathol 1990, 21: 927–931.

213 Yonezawa S, Sato E. Expression of mucin antigens in human cancers and its relationship with malignancy potential. Pathol Int 1998, 47: 813–830.

213a Zhang H, Maitra A, Tabacka P, Wilentz RE, Hruban RH, Adsay NV. Differential MUC1, MUC2 and MUC5AC expression in colorectal, ampullary and pancreatobiliary carcinomas: potential biologic and diagnostic implications (Abstract). Mod Pathol 2003, 16: 138a.

Molecular genetic features

214 Apple SK, Hecht JR, Lewin DN, Jahromi SA, Grody WW, Nieberg RK. Immunohistochemical evaluation of K-ras, P53 and HER-2/neu expression in hyperplastic, dysplastic, and

carcinomatous lesions of the pancreas: evidence for multistep carcinogenesis. Hum Pathol 1999, **30:** 123–129.

215 Boschman CR, Stryker S, Reddy JK, Rao MS. Expression of p53 protein in precursor lesions and adenocarcinoma of human pancreas. Am J Pathol 1994, **145:** 1291–1295.

216 Caldas C, Hahn SA, Da Costa LT, Redston MC, Schutte M, Seymour AB, Weinstein CL, Hruban RH, Yeo CJ, Kern SE. Frequent somatic mutations and homozygous deletions of the p16 (MTS1) gene in pancreatic adenocarcinoma. Nat Genet 1994, **8:** 27–32.

217 Day JD, Di Giuseppe JA, Yeo C, Lai-Goldman M, Anderson SM, Goodman SN, Kern SE, Hruban RH. Immunohistochemical evaluation of HER-2/neu expression in pancreatic adenocarcinoma and pancreatic intraepithelial neoplasms. Hum Pathol 1996, **27:** 119–124.

218 Di Giuseppe JA, Hruban RH, Goodman SN, Polak M, van den Berg FM, Allison DC, Cameron JL, Offerhaus GJ. Overexpression of p53 protein in adenocarcinoma of the pancreas. Am J Clin Pathol 1994, **101:** 684–688.

219 Ghadimi BM, Schrock E, Walker RL, Wangsa D, Jauho A, Meltzer PS, Ried T. Specific chromosomal aberrations and amplification of the AIB1 nuclear receptor coactivator gene in pancreatic carcinomas. Am J Pathol 1999, **154:** 525–536.

220 Goggins M, Offerhaus GJ, Hilgers W, Griffin CA, Shekher M, Tang D, Sohn TA, Yeo CJ, Kern SE, Hruban RH. Pancreatic adenocarcinomas with DNA replication errors (RER+) are associated with wild-type K-ras and characteristic histopathology. Poor differentiation, a syncytial growth pattern, and pushing borders suggests RER+. Am J Pathol 1998, **152:** 1501–1507.

221 Hahn SA, Schutte M, Hoque S, Moskaluk CA, daCosta LT, Rozenblum E, Weinstein CL, Fischer A, Yeo CJ, Hruban RH, Kern SE. DPC4, a candidate tumor suppressor gene at human chromosome 18q21.1. Science 1996, **271:** 350–353.

222 Hameed M, Marero AM, Conlon KC, Brennan MF, Klimstra DS. Expression of p53 nucleophosphoprotein in *in situ* pancreatic ductal adenocarcinoma. An immunohistochemical analysis of 100 cases. (Abstract.) Lab Invest 1994, **70:** 132A.

223 Heinmoller E, Dietmaier W, Zirngibl H, Heinmoller P, Scaringe W, Jauch KW, Hofstadter F, Ruschoff J. Molecular analysis of microdissected tumors and preneoplastic intraductal lesions in pancreatic carcinoma. Am J Pathol 2000, **157:** 83–92.

224 Hruban RH, van Mansfeld AD, Offerhaus GJ, van Weering DH, Allison DC, Goodman SN, Kensler TW, Bose KK, Cameron JL, Bos JL. K-*ras* oncogene activation in adenocarcinoma of the human pancreas. A study of 82 carcinomas using a combination of mutant-enriched polymerase chain reaction analysis and allele-specific oligonucleotide hybridization. Am J Pathol 1993, **143:** 545–554.

225 Hruban RH, Wilentz RE, Kern SE. Genetic progression in pancreatic ducts. Am J Pathol 2000, **156:** 1821–1825.

226 Johansson B, Bardi G, Heim S, Mandahl N, Mertens F, Bak-Jensen E, Andren-Sandberg A, Mitelman F. Nonrandom chromosomal rearrangements in pancreatic carcinomas. Cancer 1992, **69:** 1674–1681.

227 Li Y, Bhuiyan M, Vaitkevicius VK, Sarkar FH. Molecular analysis of the p53 gene in pancreatic adenocarcinoma. Diagn Mol Pathol 1998, **7:** 4–9.

228 Luttges L, Diederichs A, Menke MA, Vogel I, Kremer B, Kloppel G. Ductal lesions in patients with chronic pancreatitis show K-ras mutations in a frequency similar to that in the normal pancreas and lack nuclear immunoreactivity for p53. Cancer 2000, **88:** 2495–2504.

229 Luttges J, Feyerabend B, Buchelt T, Pacena M, Kloppel G. The mucin profile of noninvasive and invasive mucinous cystic neoplasms of the pancreas. Am J Surg Pathol 2002, **26:** 466–471.

230 Luttges J, Schlehe B, Menke MA, Vogel I, Henne-Bruns D,

Kloppel G. The K-ras mutation pattern in pancreatic ductal adenocarcinoma usually is identical to that in associated normal, hyperplastic, and metaplastic ductal epithelium. Cancer 1999, **85:** 1703–1710.

231 Porschen R, Remy U, Bevers G, Schauseil S, Hengels KJ, Borchard F. Prognostic significance of DNA ploidy in adenocarcinoma of the pancreas. A flow cytometric study of paraffin-embedded specimens. Cancer 1993, **71:** 3846–3850.

232 Tascilar M, Offerhaus JA, Altink R, Argani P, Sohn TA, Yeo CJ, Cameron JL, Goggins M, Hruban RH, Wilentz RE. Immunohistochemical labeling for the Dpc4 gene product is a specific marker for adenocarcinoma in biopsy specimens of the pancreas and bile duct. Am J Clin Pathol 2001, **116:** 831–837.

233 Yamanaka Y, Friess H, Kobrin MS, Buchler M, Kunz J, Beger HG, Korc M. Overexpression of HER2/neu oncogene in human pancreatic carcinoma. Hum Pathol 1993, **24:** 1127–1134.

234 Yamano M, Fujii H, Takagaki T, Kadowaki N, Watanabe H, Shirai T. Genetic progression and divergence in pancreatic carcinoma. Am J Pathol 2000, **156:** 2123–2133.

235 Yoshimura T, Manabe T, Imamura T, Imanishi K, Ohshio G, Yamabe H, Kitamura O, Matsumoto M, Ogasahara K, Takasan H, et al. Flow cytometric analysis of nuclear DNA content of duct cell carcinoma of the pancreas. Cancer 1992, **70:** 1069–1074.

Other microscopic types

235a Adsay NV, Merati K, Nassar H, Shia J, Sarker F, Pierson CR, Cheng JD, Visscher DW, Hruban RH, Klimstra DS. Pathogenesis of colloid (pure mucinous) carcinoma of exocrine organs. Am J Surg Pathol 2003, **27:** 571–578.

236 Adsay NV, Pierson C, Sarkar F, Abrams J, Weaver D, Conlon KC, Brennan MF, Klimstra DS. Colloid (mucinous noncystic) carcinoma of the pancreas. Am J Surg Pathol 2001, **25:** 26–42.

237 Adsay V, Logani S, Sarkar F, Crissman J, Vaitkevicius V. Foamy gland pattern of pancreatic ductal adenocarcinoma: A deceptively benign-appearing variant. Am J Surg Pathol 2000, **24:** 493–504.

238 Brayko CM, Doll DC. Squamous cell carcinoma of the pancreas associated with hypercalcemia. Gastroenterology 1982, **83:** 1297–1299.

239 Chejfec G, Rieker WJ, Jablokow VR, Gould VE. Pseudomyxoma peritonei associated with colloid carcinoma of the pancreas. Gastroenterology 1986, **90:** 202–205.

240 Cubilla AL, Fitzgerald PJ. Morphological patterns of primary nonendocrine human pancreas carcinoma. Cancer Res 1975, **35:** 2234–2248.

241 Huntrakoon M. Oncocytic carcinoma of the pancreas. Cancer 1983, **51:** 332–336.

242 Kanai N, Nagaki S, Tanaka T. Clear cell carcinoma of the pancreas. Acta Pathol Jpn 1987, **37:** 1521–1526.

243 Kardon DE, Thompson LD, Przygodzki RM, Heffess CS. Adenosquamous carcinoma of the pancreas: a clinicopathologic series of 25 cases. Mod Pathol 2001, **14:** 443–451.

244 Lonardo F, Cubilla AL, Klimstra DS. Microadenocarcinoma of the pancreas—morphologic pattern or pathologic entity? A reevaluation of the original series. Am J Surg Pathol 1996, **20:** 1385–1393.

245 Luttges J, Vogel I, Menke M, Henne-Bruns D, Kremer B, Kloppel G. Clear cell carcinoma of the pancreas: an adenocarcinoma with ductal phenotype. Histopathology 1998, **32:** 444–448.

246 Nozawa Y, Abe M, Sakuma H, Ogata M, Haga J, Sakuma H, Wakasa H. A case of pancreatic oncocytic tumor. Acta Pathol Jpn 1990, **40:** 367–370.

247 Paner GP, Thompson KS, Reyes CV. Hepatoid carcinoma of the pancreas. Cancer 2000, **88:** 1582–1589.

248 Wilentz RE, Goggins M, Redston M, Marcus VA, Adsay VN, Shon TA, Kadkol SS, Yeo CJ, Choti M, Zahurak M, Johnson K, Tascilar M, Offerhaus GJ, Hruban RH, Kern SE. Genetic, immunohistochemical, and clinical features of medullary

carcinoma of the pancreas. A newly described and characterized entity. Am J Pathol 2000, **156**: 1641–1651.

249 Yano T, Ishikura H, Wada T, Kishimoto T, Kondo S, Katoh H, Yoshiki T. Hepatoid adenocarcinoma of the pancreas. Histopathology 1999, **35**: 90–92.

Spread and metastases

250 Cubilla AL, Fortner J, Fitzgerald PJ. Lymph node involvement in carcinoma of the head of the pancreas area. Cancer 1978, **41**: 880–887.

251 Kayahara M, Nagakawa T, Kobayashi H, Mori K, Nakano T, Kadoya N, Ohta T, Ueno K, Miyazaki I. Lymphatic flow in carcinoma of the head of the pancreas. Cancer 1992, **70**: 2061–2066.

252 Kayahara M, Nagakawa T, Ohta T, Kitagawa H, Ueno K, Tajima H, Elnemr A, Miwa K. Analysis of paraaortic lymph node involvement in pancreatic carcinoma. A significant indication for surgery? Cancer 1999, **85**: 583–590.

253 Lee Y-TN, Tatter D. Carcinoma of the pancreas and periampullary structures. Pattern of metastasis at autopsy. Arch Pathol Lab Med 1984, **108**: 584–587.

254 Nagai H, Kuroda A, Morioka Y. Lymphatic and local spread of T1 and T2 pancreatic cancer. A study of autopsy material. Ann Surg 1986, **204**: 65–71.

255 Nagakawa T, Kobayashi H, Ueno K, Ohta T, Kayahara M, Miyazaki I. Clinical study of lymphatic flow to the paraaortic lymph nodes in carcinoma of the head of the pancreas. Cancer 1994, **73**: 1155–1162.

256 Tsuchiya R, Oribe T, Noda T. Size of the tumor and other factors influencing prognosis of carcinoma of the head of the pancreas. Am J Gastroenterol 1985, **80**: 459–462.

257 Tsuchiya R, Tsunoda T, Yamaguchi T. Operation of choice for resectable carcinoma of the head of the pancreas. Int J Pancreatol 1990, **6**: 295–306.

Cytology

258 Apple SK, Hecht JR, Novak JM, Nieberg RK, Rosenthal DL, Grody WW. Polymerase chain reaction-based K-ras mutation detection of pancreatic adenocarcinoma in routine cytology smears. Am J Clin Pathol 1996, **105**: 321–326.

259 Hajdu EO, Kumari-Subaiya S, Phillips G. Ultrasonically guided percutaneous aspiration biopsy of the pancreas. Semin Diagn Pathol 1986, **3**: 166–175.

260 Iwao T, Hanada K, Tsuchida A, Hirata M, Eguchi N, Kajiyama G. The establishment of a preoperative diagnosis of pancreatic carcinoma using cell specimens from pancreatic duct brushing with special attention to p53 mutations. Cancer 1998, **82**: 1487–1494.

261 Kline TS, Joshi LP, Goldstein F. Preoperative diagnosis of pancreatic malignancy by the cytologic examination of duodenal secretions. Am J Clin Pathol 1978, **70**: 851–854.

262 Nakaizumi A, Tatsuta M, Uehara H, Yamamoto R, Takenaka A, Kishigami Y, Takemura K, Kitamura T, Okuda S. Cytologic examination of pure pancreatic juice in the diagnosis of pancreatic carcinoma. The endoscopic retrograde intraductal catheter aspiration cytologic technique. Cancer 1992, **70**: 610–614.

263 Nguyen G-K. Percutaneous fine-needle aspiration cytology of the pancreas. Pathol Annu 1985, **20**(Pt 1): 221–238.

264 Nieburgs HE, Dreiling DA, Rubio C, Reisman H. The morphology of cells in duodenal-drainage smears. Histologic origin and pathologic significance. Am J Dig Dis 1962, **7**: 489–505.

265 Smith EH, Bartrum RJ Jr, Chang YC, Orsi CJ, Lokich J, Abbruzzese A, Dantono J. Percutaneous aspiration biopsy of the pancreas under ultrasonic guidance. N Engl J Med 1975, **292**: 825–828.

266 Smithies A, Hatfield ARW, Brown BE. The cytodiagnostic aspects of pure pancreatic juice obtained at the time of endoscopic

retrograde cholangiopancreatography (ERCP). Acta Cytol (Baltimore) 1977, **21**: 191–195.

267 Tada M, Komatsu Y, Kawabe T, Sasahira N, Isayama H, Toda N, Shiratori Y, Omata M. Quantitative analysis of K-ras gene mutation in pancreatic tissue obtained by endoscopic ultrasonography-guided fine needle aspiration: clinical utility for diagnosis of pancreatic tumor. Am J Gastroenterol 2002, **97**: 2263–2270.

268 Tao L-C, Ho C-S, McLoughlin MJ, McHattie J. Percutaneous fine needle aspiration biopsy of the pancreas. Cytodiagnosis of pancreatic carcinoma. Acta Cytol [Baltimore] 1978, **22**: 215–220.

269 Uehara H, Nakaizumi A, Tatsuta M, Iishi H, Kitamura T, Ohigashi H, Ishikawa O, Takenaka A. Diagnosis of carcinoma in situ of the pancreas by peroral pancreatoscopy and pancreatoscopic cytology. Cancer 1997, **79**: 454–461.

270 van Heek T, Rader AE, Offerhaus GJ, McCarthy DM, Goggins M, Hruban RH, Wilentz RE. K-ras, and DPC4 (MAD4) alterations in fine-needle aspirates of the pancreas. A molecular panel correlates with and supplements cytologic diagnosis. Am J Clin Pathol 2002, **117**: 755–765.

Exploration and frozen section

271 Beazley RM. Needle biopsy diagnosis of pancreatic cancer. Cancer 1981, **47**: 1685–1687.

272 Cioc AM, Ellison EC, Proca DM, Lucas JG, Frankel WL. Frozen section diagnosis of pancreatic lesions. Arch Pathol Lab Med 2002, **126**: 1169–1173.

273 Forsgren L, Orell S. Aspiration cytology in carcinoma of the pancreas. Surgery 1973, **73**: 38–42.

274 Hyland C, Kheir SM, Kashlan MB. Frozen section diagnosis of pancreatic carcinoma. A prospective study of 64 biopsies. Am J Surg Pathol 1981, **5**: 179–191.

275 Loquvam GS, Russell WO. Accessory pancreatic ducts of the major duodenal papilla. Am J Clin Pathol 1950, **20**: 305–313.

276 Spjut HJ, Ramos AJ. An evaluation of biopsy-frozen section of the ampullary region and pancreas. A report of 68 consecutive patients. Ann Surg 1957, **146**: 923–930.

277 Weiland LH. Frozen section diagnosis in tumors of the pancreas. Semin Diagn Pathol 1984, **1**: 54–58.

Treatment

277a Abraham SC, Wilentz RE, Yeo CJ, Sohn TA, Cameron JL, Boitnott JK, Hruban RH. Pancreaticoduodenectomy (Whipple resections) in patients without malignancy. Am J Surg Pathol 2003, **27**: 110–120.

278 Fortner JG. Surgical principles for pancreatic cancer. Regional total and subtotal pancreatectomy. Cancer 1981, **47**: 1712–1718.

279 Holyoke ED. New surgical approaches to pancreatic cancer. Cancer 1981, **47**: 1719–1723.

280 Johnson CD, Schwall G, Flechtenmacher J, Trede M. Resection for adenocarcinoma of the body and tail of the pancreas. Br J Surg 1993, **80**: 1177–1179.

281 Kayahara M, Nagakawa T, Ueno K, Ohta T, Takeda T, Miyazaki I. An evaluation of radical resection for pancreatic cancer based on the mode of recurrence as determined by autopsy and diagnostic imaging. Cancer 1993, **72**: 2118–2123.

282 Longmire WP Jr, Traverso LW. The Whipple procedure and other standard operative approaches to pancreatic cancer. Cancer 1981, **47**: 1706–1711.

283 McGrath PC, Sloan DA, Kenady DE. Surgical management of pancreatic carcinoma. Semin Oncol 1996, **23**: 200–212.

284 Manabe T, Ohshio G, Baba N, Miyashita T, Asano N, Tamura K, Yamaki K, Nonaka A, Tobe T. Radical pancreatectomy for ductal cell carcinoma of the head of the pancreas. Cancer 1989, **64**: 1132–1137.

285 Moertel CG, Frytak S, Hahn RF, O'Connell MJ, Reitemeier RJ, Rubin J, Schutt AJ, Weiland LH, Childs DS, Holbrook MA, Lavin

PT, Livstone E, Spiro H, Knowlton A, Kalser M, Barkin J, Lessner H, Mann-Kaplan R, Ramming K, Douglas HO Jr, Thomas P, Nave H, Bateman J, Lokich J, Brooks J, Chaffey J, Corson JM, Zamcheck N, Novak JW. Therapy of locally unresectable pancreatic carcinoma. A randomized comparison of high dose (6000 rad) radiation alone, moderate dose radiation (4000 rad+5-fluorouracil), and high dose radiation+5-fluorouracil. The Gastrointestinal Tumor Study Group. Cancer 1981, **48**: 1705–1710.

286 Nagakawa T, Nagamori M, Futakami F, Tsukioka Y, Kayahara M, Ohta T, Veno K, Miyazaki I. Results of extensive surgery for pancreatic carcinoma. Cancer 1996, **77**: 640–645.

287 Newton WT. Mortality and morbidity associated with resection of pancreaticoduodenal cancers. Am Surg 1961, **27**: 74–79.

288 Nishimura A, Nakano M, Otsu H, Nakano K, Iida K, Sakata S, Iwabuchi K, Maruyama K, Kihara M, Okamura T, Todoroki T, Iwasaki Y. Intraoperative radiotherapy for advanced carcinoma of the pancreas. Cancer 1984, **54**: 2375–2384.

289 Rattner DW. Pancreatic cancer in 1991. Has any progress been noted? (editorial). Mayo Clin Proc 1992, **67**: 907–909.

290 Tepper J, Nardi G, Suit H. Carcinoma of the pancreas. Review of MGH experience from 1963 to 1973. Analysis of surgical failure and implications for radiation therapy. Cancer 1976, **37**: 1519–1524.

291 Trede M, Schwall G, Saeger H-D. Survival after pancreatoduodenectomy. 118 consecutive resections without an operative mortality. Ann Surg 1990, **211**: 447–458.

Prognosis

292 Allema JH, Reinders ME, van Gulik TM, Koelemay MJ, Van Leeuwen DJ, de Wit LT, Gouma DJ, Obertop H. Prognostic factors for survival after pancreaticoduodenectomy for patients with carcinoma of the pancreatic head region. Cancer 1995, **75**: 2069–2076.

293 Baylor SM, Berg JW. Cross-classification and survival characteristics of 5,000 cases of cancer of the pancreas. J Surg Oncol 1973, **5**: 335–358.

294 Coppola D, Lu L, Fruehauf JP, Kyshtoobayeva A, Karl RC, Nicosia SV, Yeatman TJ. Analysis of p53, p21^{WAFI}, and TGF-β1 in human ductal adenocarcinoma of the pancreas. TGF-β1 protein expression predicts longer survival. Am J Clin Pathol 1998, **110**: 16–23.

295 Gudjonsson B. Cancer of the pancreas. 50 years of surgery. Cancer 1987, **60**: 2284–2303.

296 Klöppel G, Lingenthal G, Von Bülow M, Kern HF. Histological and fine structural features of pancreatic ductal adenocarcinomas in relation to growth and prognosis. Studies in xenografted tumours and clinico-histopathological correlation in a series of 75 cases. Histopathology 1985, **9**: 841–856.

297 Luttges J, Vogel I, Menke M, Henne-Bruns D, Kremer B, Kloppel G. The retroperitoneal resection margin and vessel involvement are important factors determining survival after pancreaticoduodenectomy for ductal adenocarcinoma of the head of the pancreas. Virchows Arch 1998, **433**: 237–242.

297a Niedergethmann M, Rexin M, Hildenbrand R, Knob S, Sturm JW, Richter A, Post S. Prognostic implications of routine, immunohistochemical, and molecular staging in resectable pancreatic adenocarcinoma. Am J Surg Pathol 2002, **26**: 1578–1587.

298 Nix GA, Dubbelman C, Wilson JH, Schutte HE, Jeekel J, Postema RR. Prognostic implications of tumor diameter in carcinoma of the head of the pancreas. Cancer 1991, **67**: 529–535.

299 Pollard HM, Anderson WAD, Brooks FP, Cohn I Jr, Copeland MM, Connelly RR, Fortner JG, Kissane JM, Lemon HM, Palmer PES, Thomas LB, Webster PD III, Carter S. Staging of cancer of the pancreas. Cancer 1981, **47**: 1631–1637.

300 Rugge M, Sonego F, Sessa F, Leandro G, Capella C, Sperti C, Pasquali C, Di Mario F, Pedrazzoli S, Ninfo V. Nuclear DNA content and pathology in radically treated pancreatic carcinoma: The prognostic significance of DNA ploidy, histology and nuclear grade. Cancer 1996, **77**: 459–466.

301 Tepper J, Nardi G, Suit H. Carcinoma of the pancreas. Review of MGH experience from 1963 to 1973. Analysis of surgical failure and implications for radiation therapy. Cancer 1976, **37**: 1519–1524.

302 Tsuchiya R, Oribe T, Noda T. Size of the tumor and other factors influencing prognosis of carcinoma of the head of the pancreas. Am J Gastroenterol 1985, **80**: 459–462.

Anaplastic carcinoma

303 Alguacil-Garcia A, Weiland LH. The histologic spectrum, prognosis, and histogenesis of the sarcomatoid carcinoma of the pancreas. Cancer 1977, **39**: 1181–1189.

304 Berendt RC, Shnitka TK, Wiens E, Manickavel V, Jewell LD. The osteoclast-type giant cell tumor of the pancreas. Arch Pathol Lab Med 1987, **111**: 43–48.

305 Deckard-Janatpour K, Kragel S, Teplitz RL, Min BH, Gumerlock PH, Frey CF, Ruebner BH. Tumors of the pancreas with osteoclast-like and pleomorphic giant cells: an immunohistochemical and ploidy study. Arch Pathol Lab Med 1998, **122**: 266–272.

306 Dizon MA, Multhaupt HAB, Paskin DL, Warhol MJ. Osteoclastic giant cell tumor of the pancreas: an immunohistochemical study. Arch Pathol Lab Med 1996, **120**: 306–309.

307 Dworak O, Wittekind C, Koerfgen HP, Gall FP. Osteoclastic giant cell tumor of the pancreas. An immunohistological study and review of the literature. Pathol Res Pract 1993, **189**: 228–231.

308 Gocke CD, Dabbs DJ, Benko FA, Silverman JF. KRAS oncogene mutations suggest a common histogenetic origin for pleomorphic giant cell tumor of the pancreas, osteoclastoma of the pancreas and pancreatic duct adenocarcinoma. Hum Pathol 1997, **28**: 80–83.

309 Lane RB Jr, Sangueza OP. Anaplastic carcinoma occurring in association with a mucinous cystic neoplasm of the pancreas. Arch Pathol Lab Med 1997, **121**: 533–541.

310 Lewandrowski KB, Weston L, Dickersin GR, Rattner DW, Compton CC. Giant cell tumor of the pancreas of mixed osteoclastic and pleomorphic cell type. Evidence for a histogenetic relationship and mesenchymal differentiation. Hum Pathol 1990, **21**: 1184–1187.

311 Molberg KH, Heffess C, Delgado R, Albores-Saavedra J. Undifferentiated carcinoma with osteoclast-like giant cells of the pancreas and periampullary region. Cancer 1998, **82**: 1279–1287.

312 Nishihara K, Katsumoto F, Kurokawa Y, Toyoshima S, Takeda S, Abe R. Anaplastic carcinoma showing rhabdoid features combined with mucinous cystadenocarcinoma of the pancreas. Arch Pathol Lab Med 1997, **121**: 1104–1107.

313 O'Connor TP, Wade TP, Sunwoo YC, Reimers HJ, Palmer DC, Silverberg AB, Johnson FE. Small cell undifferentiated carcinoma of the pancreas. Report of a patient with tumor marker studies. Cancer 1992, **70**: 1514–1519.

314 Oehler I, Jürs M, Klöppel G, Helpap B. Osteoclast-like giant cell tumour of the pancreas presenting as a pseudocyst-like lesion. Virchows Arch 1997, **431**: 215–218.

315 Ordóñez NR, Cleary KR, Mackay B. Small cell undifferentiated carcinoma of the pancreas. Ultrastruct Pathol 1997, **21**: 467–474.

316 Paal E, Thompson LD, Frommelt RA, Przygodzki RM, Heffess CS. A clinicopathologic and immunohistochemical study of 35 anaplastic carcinomas of the pancreas with a review of the literature. Ann Diagn Pathol 2001, **5**: 129–140.

317 Posen JA. Giant cell tumor of the pancreas of the osteoclastic type associated with a mucous secreting cystadenocarcinoma. Hum Pathol 1981, **12**: 944–947.

318 Rosai J. Carcinoma of pancreas simulating giant cell tumor of bone. Electron microscopic evidence of its acinar cell origin. Cancer 1968, **22**: 333–344.

319 Sakai Y, Kupelioglu AA, Yanagisawa A, Yamaguchi K, Hidaka E, Matsuya S, Ohbuchi T, Tada Y, Saisho H, Kato Y. Origin of giant cells in osteoclast-like giant cell tumors of the pancreas. Hum Pathol 2000, **31**: 1223–1229.

320 Trepeta RW, Mathur B, Lagin S, LiVolsi VA. Giant cell tumor ("osteoclastoma") of the pancreas. A tumor of epithelial origin. Cancer 1981, **48**: 2022–2028.

321 Tschang T, Garza-Garza R, Kissane JM. Pleomorphic carcinoma of the pancreas. An analysis of 15 cases. Cancer 1977, **39**: 2114–2126.

322 Westra WH, Sturm P, Drillenburg P, Choti MA, Klimstra DS, Albores-Saavedra J, Montag A, Offerhaus GJ, Hruban RH. K-ras oncogene mutations in osteoclast-like giant cell tumors of the pancreas and liver: genetic evidence to support origin from the duct epithelium. Am J Surg Pathol 1998, **22**: 1247–1254.

Cystic pancreatic neoplasms

323 Albores-Saavedra J, Gould EW, Angeles-Angeles A, Henson DE. Cystic tumors of the pancreas. Pathol Annu 1990, **25**(Pt 2): 19–50.

324 Friedman HD. Nonmucinous, glycogen-poor cystadenocarcinoma of the pancreas. Arch Pathol Lab Med 1990, **114**: 888–891.

325 Hoover E, Natesha R, Dao A, Adams CZ Jr, Barnwell S. Proliferative pancreatic cysts. Pathogenesis and treatment options. Am J Surg 1991, **162**: 274–277.

326 Iacono C, Serio G, Fugazzola C, Zamboni G, Bergamo Andreis IA, Jannucci A, Zicari M, Dagradi A. Cystic islet cell tumors of the pancreas. A clinico-pathological report of two nonfunctioning cases and review of the literature. Int J Pancreatol 1992, **11**: 199–208.

Microcystic cystadenoma and cystadenocarcinoma

327 Alpert LC, Truong LD, Bossart MI, Spjut HJ. Microcystic adenoma (serous cystadenoma) of the pancreas. A study of 14 cases with immunohistochemical and electron-microscopic correlation. Am J Surg Pathol 1988, **12**: 251–263.

328 Bogomoletz WV, Adnet JJ, Widgren S, Stavrou M, McLaughlin JE. Cystadenoma of the pancreas. A histological, histochemical and ultrastructural study of seven cases. Histopathology 1980, **4**: 309–320.

329 Compagno J, Oertel JE. Microcystic adenomas of the pancreas (glycogen-rich cystadenomas). A clinicopathologic study of 34 cases. Am J Clin Pathol 1978, **69**: 289–298.

330 Compton CC. Serous cystic tumors of the pancreas. Semin Diagn Pathol 2000, **17**: 43–55.

331 Egawa N, Maillet B, Schroder S, Mukai K, Kloppel G. Serous oligocystic and ill-demarcated adenoma of the pancreas. A variant of serous cystic adenoma. Virchows Arch 1994, **424**: 13–17.

332 George DH, Murphy F, Michalski R, Ulmer BG. Serous cystadenocarcinoma of the pancreas. A new entity? Am J Surg Pathol 1989, **13**: 61–66.

333 Hodgkinson DJ, ReMine WH, Weiland LH. Pancreatic cystadenoma. A clinicopathologic study of 45 cases. Arch Surg 1978, **113**: 512–519.

334 Kamei K, Funabiki T, Ochiai M, Amano H, Marugami Y, Kasahara M, Sakamoto T. Some considerations on the biology of pancreatic serous cystadenoma. Int J Pancreatol 1991, **11**: 97–104.

335 Kim YI, Seo JW, Suh JS, Lee KU, Choe KJ. Microcystic adenomas of the pancreas. Report of three cases with two of multicentric origin. Am J Clin Pathol 1990, **94**: 150–156.

336 Lewandrowski KB, Southern JF, Pins MR, Compton CC, Warshaw AL. Cyst fluid analysis in the differential diagnosis of pancreatic cysts. A comparison of pseudocysts, serous cystadenomas, mucinous cystic neoplasms, and mucinous cystadenocarcinoma. Ann Surg 1993, **217**: 41–47.

337 Lewandrowski K, Warshaw A, Compton C. Macrocystic serous cystadenoma of the pancreas. A morphologic variant differing from microcystic adenoma. Hum Pathol 1992, **23**: 871–875.

338 Montag AG, Fossati N, Michelassi F. Pancreatic microcystic adenoma coexistent with pancreatic ductal carcinoma. A report of two cases. Am J Surg Pathol 1990, **14**: 352–355.

339 Neumann HP, Dinkel E, Brambs H, Wimmer B, Friedburg H, Volk B, Sigmund G, Riegler P, Haag K, Schollmeyer P. Pancreatic lesions in the von Hippel–Lindau syndrome. Gastroenterology 1991, **101**: 465–471.

340 Nyongo A, Huntrakoon M. Microcystic adenoma of the pancreas with myoepithelial cells. Am J Clin Pathol 1985, **84**: 114–120.

341 Perez-Ordonez B, Naseem A, Lieberman PH, Klimstra DS. Solid serous adenoma of the pancreas: The solid variant of serous cystadenoma? Am J Surg Pathol 1996, **20**: 1401–1405.

342 Pyke CM, van Heerden JA, Colby TV, Sarr MG, Weaver AL. The spectrum of serous cystadenoma of the pancreas. Clinical, pathologic, and surgical aspects. Ann Surg 1992, **215**: 132–139.

343 Shorten SD, Hart WR, Petras RE. Microcystic adenomas (serous cystadenomas) of pancreas. A clinicopathologic investigation of eight cases with immunohistochemical and ultrastructural studies. Am J Surg Pathol 1986, **10**: 365–372.

344 Tripodi SA, Civitelli S, Schurfeld K, Cintorino M. Microcystic adenoma of the pancreas (glycogen-rich cystadenoma) with stromal amyloid deposits. Histopathology 2000, **37**: 147–149.

345 Unger PD, Danque PO, Fuchs A, Kaneko M. DNA flow cytometric evaluation of serous and mucinous cystic neoplasms of the pancreas. Arch Pathol Lab Med 1991, **115**: 563–565.

346 Vortmeyer AO, Lubensky IA, Fogt F, Linehan WM, Khettry U, Zhuang Z. Allelic deletion and mutation of the von Hippel-Lindau (VHL) tumor suppressor gene and pancreatic microcystic adenomas. Am J Pathol 1997, **151**: 951–956.

347 Yasuhara Y, Sakaida N, Uemura Y, Senzaki H, Shikata N, Tsubura A. Serous microcystic adenoma (glycogen-rich cystadenoma) of the pancreas: Study of 11 cases showing clinicopathological and immunohistochemical correlations. Pathol Int 2002, **52**: 307–312.

348 Yoshimi N, Sugie S, Tanaka T, Aijin W, Bunai Y, Tatematsu A, Okada T, Mori H. A rare case of serous cystadenocarcinoma of the pancreas. Cancer 1992, **69**: 2449–2453.

Mucinous cystic neoplasms

349 Albores-Saavedra J, Gould EW, Angeles-Angeles A, Henson DE. Cystic tumors of the pancreas. Pathol Annu 1990, **25**(Pt 2): 19–50.

350 Compagno J, Oertel JE. Mucinous cystic neoplasms of the pancreas with overt and latent malignancy (cystadenocarcinoma and cystadenoma). A clinicopathologic study of 41 cases. Am J Clin Pathol 1978, **69**: 573–580.

351 Delcore R, Thomas JH, Forster J, Hermreck AS. Characteristics of cystic neoplasms of the pancreas and results of aggressive surgical treatment. Am J Surg 1992, **164**: 437–441.

352 Garcia Rego JA, Valbuena Ruvira L, Alvarez Garcia A, Santiago Freijanes MP, Suarez Penaranda JM, Rois Soto JM. Pancreatic mucinous cystadenocarcinoma with pseudosarcomatous mural nodules. A report of a case with immunohistochemical study. Cancer 1991, **67**: 494–498.

353 Hunt JL, Gannon FH, Rosato EF, Siegelman ES, Tomaszewski JE, LiVolsi VA. A non-epithelial pseudosarcomatous mural nodule in a mucinous cystic neoplasm of the pancreas: immunohistochemistry, electron microscopy, and imaging studies. Int J Surg Pathol 1997, **5**: 43–48.

354 Iacobuzio-Donahue CA, Wilentz RE, Argani P, Yeo CJ, Cameron JL, Kern SE, Hruban RH. Dpc-4 protein in mucinous cystic neoplasms of the pancreas: frequent loss of expression in invasive carcinomas suggests a role in genetic progression. Am J Surg Pathol 2000, **24**: 1544–1548.

355 Lewandrowski KB, Southern JF, Pins MR, Compton CC, Warshaw AL. Cyst fluid analysis in the differential diagnosis of

pancreatic cysts. A comparison of pseudocysts, serous cystadenomas, mucinous cystic neoplasms, and mucinous cystadenocarcinoma. Ann Surg 1993, **217:** 41–47.

356 Luttges J, Feyerabend B, Buchelt T, Pacena M, Kloppel G. The mucin profile of noninvasive and invasive mucinous cystic neoplasms of the pancreas. Am J Surg Pathol 2002, **26:** 466–471.

357 Tatsuta M, Iishi H, Ichii M, Noguchi S, Yamamoto R, Yamamura H, Okuda S. Values of carcinoembryonic antigen, elastase 1, and carbohydrate antigen determinant in aspirated pancreatic cystic fluid in the diagnosis of cysts of the pancreas. Cancer 1986, **57:** 1836–1839.

358 Thompson LDR, Becker RC, Przygodzki RM, Adair CF, Heffess CS. Mucinous cystic neoplasm (mucinous cystadenocarcinoma of low-grade malignant potential) of the pancreas: a clinicopathologic study of 130 cases. Am J Surg Pathol 1999, **23:** 1–16.

359 Tsujimura T, Kawano K, Taniguchi M, Yoshikawa K, Tsukaguchi I. Malignant fibrous histiocytoma coexistent with mucinous cystadenoma of the pancreas. Cancer 1992, **70:** 2792–2796.

360 Van den Berg W, Tascilar M, Offerhaus GJ, Albores-Saavedra J, Wenig BM, Hruban RH, Gabrielson E. Pancreatic mucinous cystic neoplasms with sarcomatous stroma: molecular evidence for monoclonal origin with subsequent divergence of the epithelial and sarcomatous components. Mod Pathol 2000, **13:** 86–91.

361 Weihing RR, Shintaku IP, Geller SA, Petrovic LM. Hepatobiliary and pancreatic mucinous cystadenocarcinomas with mesenchymal stroma: analysis of estrogen receptors/ progesterone receptors and expression of tumor-associated antigens. Mod Pathol 1997, **10:** 372–379.

362 Wenig B, Albores-Saavedra J, Buetow P, Heffess C. Pancreatic mucinous cystic neoplasm with sarcomatous stroma: a report of three cases. Am J Surg Pathol 1997, **21:** 70–80.

363 Wilentz RE, Albores-Saavedra J, Hruban RH. Mucinous cystic neoplasms of the pancreas. Semin Diagn Pathol 2000, **17:** 31–42.

364 Wilentz RE, Albores-Saavedra J, Zahurak M, Talamini MA, Yeo CJ, Cameron JL, Hruban RH. Pathologic examination accurately predicts prognosis in mucinous cystic neoplasms of the pancreas. Am J Surg Pathol 1999, **23:** 1320–1327.

365 Wouters K, Ectors N, Van Steenbergen W, Aerts R, Driessen A, Van Hoe L, Geboes K. A pancreatic mucinous cystadenoma in a man with mesenchymal stroma, expressing oestrogen and progesterone receptors. Virchows Arch 1998, **432:** 187–189.

366 Young RH, Hart WR. Metastases from carcinoma of the pancreas simulating primary mucinous tumors of the ovary. A report of seven cases. Am J Surg Pathol 1989, **18:** 748–756.

367 Zamboni G, Scarpa A, Bogina G, Iacono C, Bassi C, Talamini G, Sessa F, Capella C, Solcia E, Rickaert F, Mariuzzi GM, Kloppel G. Mucinous cystic tumors of the pancreas: clinicopathological features, prognosis, and relationship to other mucinous cystic tumors. Am J Surg Pathol 1999, **23:** 410–422.

368 Zhang SY, Ruggeri B, Agarwal P, Sorling AF, Obara T, Ura H, Namiki M, Klein-Szanto AJ. Immunohistochemical analysis of p53 expression in human pancreatic carcinomas. Arch Pathol Lab Med 1994, **118:** 150–154.

369 Zhao J, Liang SX, Savas L, Banner BF. An immunostaining panel for diagnosis of malignancy in mucinous tumors of the pancreas. Arch Pathol Lab Med 2001, **125:** 765–769.

Intraductal papillary mucinous neoplasms (IPMNs)

370 Adsay NV, Adair C, Heffess CS, Klimstra DS. Intraductal oncocytic papillary neoplasm of the pancreas. Am J Surg Pathol 1996, **20:** 980–994.

371 Adsay NV, Conlon KC, Zee SY, Brennan MF, Klimstra DS. Intraductal papillary-mucinous neoplasms of the pancreas: an analysis of in situ and invasive carcinomas in 28 patients. Cancer 2002, **94:** 62–77.

372 Adsay NV, Longnecker DS, Klimstra DS. Pancreatic tumors with

cystic dilatation of the ducts: Intraductal papillary mucinous neoplasms and intraductal oncocytic papillary neoplasms. Semin Diagn Pathol 2000, **17:** 16–30.

373 Bakotic BW, Robinson MJ, Sturm PD, Hruban RH, Offerhaus JA, Albores-Saavedra J. Pyloric gland adenoma of the main pancreatic duct. Am J Surg Pathol 1999, **23:** 227–231.

374 Brat DJ, Lillemoe KD, Yeo CJ, Warfield PB, Hruban RH. Progression of pancreatic intraductal neoplasias to infiltrating adenocarcinoma of the pancreas. Am J Surg Pathol 1998, **22:** 163–169.

375 Fujii H, Inagaki M, Kasai S, Miyokawa N, Tokusashi Y, Gabrielson E, Hruban RH. Genetic progression and heterogeneity in intraductal papillary-mucinous neoplasms of the pancreas. Am J Pathol 1997, **151:** 1447–1454.

376 Fukushima N, Mukai K. Differential diagnosis between intraductal papillary-mucinous tumors and mucinous cystic tumors of the pancreas. Int J Surg Pathol 2001, **8:** 271–278.

377 Fukushima N, Mukai K, Kanai Y, Hasebe T, Shimada K, Ozaki H, Kinoshta T, Kosuge T. Intraductal papillary tumors and mucinous cystic tumors of the pancreas: clinicopathologic study of 38 cases. Hum Pathol 1997, **28:** 1010–1017.

378 Fukushima N, Sakamoto M, Mukai K, Kanai Y, Shimada K, Kosuge T, Hirohashi S. Intraductal papillary components in invasive ductal carcinoma of the pancreas are associated with long-term survival of patients. Hum Pathol 2001, **32:** 834–841.

379 Furukawa T, Takahashi T, Kobari M, Matsuno S. The mucus-hypersecreting tumor of the pancreas. Development and extension visualized by three-dimensional computerized mapping. Cancer 1992, **70:** 1505–1513.

380 Hruban RH, Adsay NV, Albores-Saavedra J, Compton C, Garret ES, Goodman SN, Kern SE, Klimstra DS, Klopper G, Longnecker DS, Luttges J, Offerhaus GJ. Pancreatic intraepithelial neoplasia: a new nomenclature and classification system for pancreatic duct lesions. Am J Surg Pathol 2001, **25:** 579–586.

381 Iacobuzio-Donahue CA, Klimstra SD, Adsay NV, Wilentz RE, Argani P, Sohn TA, Yeo CJ, Cameron JL, Kern SE, Hruban RH. Dpc-4 protein is expressed in virtually all human intraductal papillary mucinous neoplasms of the pancreas: Comparison with conventional ductal adenocarcinomas. Am J Pathol 2000, **157:** 755–761.

382 Longnecker DS. Intraductal papillary-mucinous tumors of the pancreas (editorial). Arch Pathol Lab Med 1995, **119:** 197–198.

382a Lüttges J, Beyser K, Pust S, Paulus A, Rüschoff J, Klöppel G. Pancreatic mucinous noncystic (colloid) carcinomas and intraductal papillary mucinous carcinomas are usually microsatellite stable. Mod Pathol 2003, **16:** 537–542.

383 Luttges J, Zamponi G, Longnecker D, Kloppel G. The immunohistochemical mucin expression pattern distinguishes different types of intraductal papillary mucinous neoplasms of the pancreas and determines their relationship to mucinous noncystic carcinoma and ductal adenocarcinoma. Am J Surg Pathol 2001, **25:** 942–948.

384 Milchgrub S, Campuzano M, Casillas J, Albores-Saavedra J. Intraductal carcinoma of the pancreas. Cancer, **69:** 651–656.

385 Nagai E, Ueki T, Chijiiwa K, Tanaka M, Tsuneyoshi M. Intraductal papillary mucinous neoplasms of the pancreas associated with so-called "mucinous ductal ectasia." Histochemical and immunohistochemical analysis of 29 cases. Am J Surg Pathol 1995, **19:** 576–589.

386 Nishihara K, Fukuda T, Tsuneyoshi M, Kominami T, Maeda S, Saku M. Intraductal papillary neoplasm of the pancreas. Cancer 1993, **72:** 689–696.

387 Obara T, Maguchi H, Saitoh Y, Itoh A, Arisato S, Ashida T, Nishino N, Ura H, Namiki M. Mucin-producing tumor of the pancreas. Natural history and serial pancreatogram changes. Am J Gastroenterol 1993, **88:** 564–569.

388 Ohta T, Nagakawa T, Akiyama T, Fukushima W, Ueno K,

Miyazaki I, Suzuki M, Matsui O, Terada T, Nakanuma Y. The "duct-ectatic" variant of mucinous cystic neoplasm of the pancreas. Clinical and radiologic studies of seven cases. Am J Gastroenterol 1992, **87**: 300–304.

389 Paal E, Thompson LD, Przygodzki RM, Bratthauer GL, Heffess CS. A clinicopathologic and immunohistochemical study of 22 intraductal papillary mucinous neoplasms of the pancreas, with a review of the literature. Mod Pathol 1999, **12**: 518–528.

390 Papotti M, Cassoni P, Taraglio S, Bussolati G. Oncocytic and oncocytoid tumors of the exocrine pancreas, liver and gastrointestinal tract. Semin Diagn Pathol 1999, **16**: 126–134.

391 Rickaert F, Cremer M, Deviere J, Tavares L, Lambilliotte JP, Schroder S, Wurbs D, Kloppel G. Intraductal mucin-hypersecreting neoplasms of the pancreas. A clinicopathologic study of eight patients. Gastroenterology 1991, **101**: 512–519.

392 Santini D, Campione O, Salerno A, Gullo L, Mazzoleni G, Leone O, Martinelli G, Marrano D. Intraductal papillary-mucinous neoplasm of the pancreas. A clinicopathologic entity. Arch Pathol Lab Med 1995, **119**: 209–213.

393 Sato N, Rosty C, Jansen M, Fukushima N, Ueki T, Yeo CJ, Cameron JL, Iacobuzio-Donahue CA, Hruban RH, Goggins M. STK11/LKB1 Peutz-Jeghers gene inactivation in intraductal papillary-mucinous neoplasms of the pancreas. Am J Pathol 2001, **159**: 2017–2022.

394 Satoh K, Sasano H, Shimosegawa T, Koizumi M, Yamazaki T, Mochizuki F, Kobayashi N, Okano T, Toyota T, Sawai T. An immunohistochemical study of the c-*erbB*-2 oncogene product in intraductal mucin-hypersecreting neoplasms and in ductal cell carcinomas of the pancreas. Cancer 1993, **72**: 51–56.

395 Seidel G, Zahurak M, Iacobuzio-Donahue C, Sohn TA, Adsay V, Yeo CJ, Lillemoe KD, Cameron JL, Hruban RH, Wilentz RE. Almost all infiltrating colloid carcinomas of the pancreas and periampullary region arise in in situ papillary neoplasms: a study of 39 cases. Am J Surg Pathol 2002, **26**: 56–63.

396 Sessa F, Solcia E, Capella C, Bonato M, Scarpa A, Zamboni G, Pellegata NS, Ranzani GN, Rickaert F, Kloppel G. Intraductal papillary-mucinous tumors represent a distinct group of pancreatic neoplasms. An investigation of tumour cell differentiation and K-*ras*, p53 and c-*erb*B-2 abnormalities in 26 patients. Virchows Arch 1994, **425**: 357–367.

397 Shimizu M, Manabe T. Mucin-producing pancreatic tumors. Historical review of its nosological concept. Zentralbl Pathol 1994, **140**: 211–223.

398 Swartz MJ, Batra SK, Varshney GC, Hollingsworth MA, Yeo CJ, Cameron JL, Wilentz RE, Hruban RH, Argani P. MUC4 expression increases progressively in pancreatic intraepithelial neoplasia. Am J Clin Pathol 2002, **117**: 791–796.

399 Tada M, Omata M, Ohto M. *Ras* gene mutations in intraductal papillary neoplasms of the pancreas. Analysis in five cases. Cancer 1991, **67**: 634–647.

400 Terada T, Ohta T, Nakanuma Y. Expression of oncogene products, anti-oncogene products and oncofetal antigens in intraductal papillary-mucinous neoplasm of the pancreas. Histopathology 1996, **29**: 355–361.

401 Terada T, Ohta T, Kitamura Y, Ashida K, Matsunaga Y, Kato M. Endocrine cells in intraductal papillary-mucinous neoplasms of the pancreas. A histochemical and immunohistochemical study. Virchows Arch 1997, **431**: 31–36.

402 Terris B, Blaveri E, Crnogorac-Jurcevic T, Jones M, Missiaglia E, Ruszniewski P, Sauvanet A, Lemoine NR. Characterization of gene expression profiles in intraductal papillary-mucinous tumors of the pancreas. Am J Pathol 2002, **160**: 1745–1754.

403 Terris B, Ponsot P, Paye F, Hammel P, Sauvanet A, Molas G, Benades P, Belghiti J, Ruszniewski P, Flejou JF. Intraductal papillary mucinous tumors of the pancreas confined to secondary ducts show less aggressive pathologic features as compared with those involving the main pancreatic duct. Am J Surg Pathol 2000, **24**: 1372–1377.

404 Uehara H, Nakaizumi A, Iishi H, Tatsuta M, Kitamra T, Okuda S, Ohigashi H, Ishikawa O, Takenaka A, Ishiguro S. Cytologic examination of pancreatic juice for differential diagnosis of benign and malignant mucin-producing tumors of the pancreas. Cancer 1994, **74**: 826–833.

405 Yamada M, Kozuka S, Yamao K, Nakazawa S, Naitoh Y, Tsukamoto Y. Mucin-producing tumor of the pancreas. Cancer 1991, **68**: 159–168.

Acinar cell tumors and tumorlike conditions

406 Abraham SC, Wu T-T, Hruban RH, Lee J-H, Yeo CJ, Conlon K, Brennan M, Cameron JL, Klimstra DS. Genetic and immunohistochemical analysis of pancreatic acinar cell carcinoma. Frequent allelic loss on chromosome 11p and alteration in the APC/beta-catenin pathway. Am J Pathol 2002, **160**: 953–962.

407 Burns WA, Matthews MJ, Hamosh M, vander Weider G, Blum R, Johnson FB. Lipase-secreting acinar cell carcinoma of the pancreas with polyarthropathy. A light and electron microscopic, histochemical, and biochemical study. Cancer 1974, **33**: 1002–1009.

408 Cantrell BB, Cubilla AL, Erlandson RA, Fortner J, Fitzgerald PJ. Acinar cell cystadenocarcinoma of human pancreas. Cancer 1981, **47**: 410–416.

409 Chatelain D, Paye F, Mourra N, Scoazec JY, Baudrimont M, Parc R, Flejou J-F. Unilocular acinar cell cystadenoma of the pancreas. An unusual acinar cell tumor. Am J Clin Pathol 2002, **118**: 211–214.

410 Cingolani N, Shaco-Levy R, Farruggio A, Klimstra DS, Rosai J. Alpha-fetoprotein production by pancreatic tumors exhibiting acinar cell differentiation: study of five cases, one arising in a mediastinal teratoma. Hum Pathol 2000, **31**: 938–944.

411 Cubilla AL, Fitzgerald PJ. Morphological patterns of primary nonendocrine human pancreas carcinoma. Cancer Res 1975, **35**: 2234–2248.

412 Fabre A, Sauvanet A, Flejou JF, Belghiti J, Palazzo L, Ruzniewski P, Degott C, Terris B. Intraductal acinar carcinoma of the pancreas. Virchows Arch 2001, **438**: 312–315.

413 Glenner GG, Mallory GK. The cystadenoma and related non-functional tumors of the pancreas. Pathogenesis, classification and significance. Cancer 1956, **9**: 980–996.

414 Gomi K, Kameya T, Tsumuraya M, Shimosato Y, Zeze F, Abe K, Yoneyama T. Ultrastructural, histochemical, and biochemical studies of two cases with amylase, ACTH, and B-MSH producing tumor. Cancer 1976, **38**: 1645–1654.

415 Hoorens A, Lemoine NR, McLellan E, Morohoshi T, Kamisawa T, Heitz PU, Stamm B, Ruschoff J, Wiedenmann B, Klöppel G. Pancreatic acinar cell carcinoma. An analysis of cell lineage markers, p53 expression, and Ki-*ras* mutation. Am J Pathol 1993, **143**: 685–698.

416 Hsueh C, Kuo TT. Acinar cell carcinoma of the pancreas. Report of two cases with complex histomorphologic features causing diagnostic problems. Int J Pancreatol 1992, **12**: 305–313.

417 Klimstra DS, Heffess CS, Oertel JE, Rosai J. Acinar cell carcinoma of the pancreas. A clinicopathologic study of 28 cases. Am J Surg Pathol 1992, **16**: 815–837.

418 Klimstra DS, Rosai J, Heffess CS. Mixed acinar-endocrine carcinomas of the pancreas. Am J Surg Pathol 1994, **18**: 765–778.

419 Kodama T, Mori W. Atypical acinar cell nodules of the human pancreas. Acta Pathol Jpn 1983, **33**: 701–714.

420 Lack EE, Cassady JR, Levey R, Vawter GF. Tumors of the exocrine pancreas in children and adolescents. A clinical and pathologic study of eight cases. Am J Surg Pathol 1983, **7**: 319–327.

421 Morohoshi T, Kanda M, Horie A, Chott A, Dreyer T, Klöppel G,

Heitz PU. Immunocytochemical markers of uncommon pancreatic tumors. Acinar cell carcinoma, pancreatoblastoma, and solid cystic (papillary-cystic) tumor. Cancer 1987, 59: 739–747.

422 Nonomura A, Kono N, Mizukami Y, Nakanuma Y, Matsubara F. Duct-acinar-islet cell tumor of the pancreas. Ultrastruct Pathol 1992, 16: 317–329.

423 Ordonez NG, Mackay B. Acinar cell carcinoma of the pancreas. Ultrastruct Pathol 2000, 24: 227–241.

424 Shinozuka H, Lee RE, Dunn JL, Longnecker DS. Multiple atypical acinar cell nodules of the pancreas. Hum Pathol 1980, 11: 389–391.

425 Skacel M, Ormsby AH, Petras RE, McMahon JT, Henricks WH. Immunohistochemistry in the differential diagnosis of acinar and endocrine pancreatic neoplasms. Appl Immunohistochem Mol Morphol 2000, 8: 203–209.

426 Stamm B, Burger H, Hollinger A. Acinar cell cystadenocarcinoma of the pancreas. Cancer 1987, 60: 2542–2547.

427 Tucker JA, Shelburne JD, Benning TL, Yacoub L, Federman M. Filamentous inclusions in acinar cell carcinoma of the pancreas. Ultrastruct Pathol 1994, 18: 279–286.

428 Webb JN. Acinar cell neoplasms of the exocrine pancreas. J Clin Pathol 1977, 30: 103–112.

429 Yantiss RK, Chang HK, Farraye FA, Compton CC, Odze RD. Prevalence and prognostic significance of acinar cell differentiation in pancreatic endocrine tumors. Am J Surg Pathol 2002, 26: 893–901.

430 Zamboni G, Terris B, Scarpa A, Kosmahl M, Capelli P, Klimstra DA, Lam PW, Klopper G. Acinar cell cystadenoma of the pancreas: A new entity? Am J Surg Pathol 2002, 26: 698–704.

Solid–pseudopapillary tumor

431 Abraham SC, Klimstra DS, Wilentz RE, Yeo CJ, Conlon K, Brennan M, Cameron JL, Wu T-T, Hruban RH. Solid-pseudopapillary tumors of the pancreas are genetically distinct from pancreatic ductal adenocarcinomas and almost always harbor beta-catenin mutations. Am J Pathol 2002, 160: 1361–1369.

432 Cappelari JO, Geisinger KR, Albertson DA, Wolfman NT, Kute TE. Malignant papillary cystic tumor of the pancreas. Cancer 1990, 66: 193–198.

433 de la Roza G, Cleary KR, Ordóñez NG, El-Naggar A, Mackay B, Romsdahl MM. Solid and papillary tumor of the pancreas: Ultrastructural observations on two contrasting cases. Ultrastruct Pathol 1997, 21: 439–447.

434 Grant LD, Lauwers GY, Meloni AM, Stone JF, Betz JL, Vogel S, Sandberg AA. Unbalanced chromosomal translocation, der(17)t(13;17)(q14;p11) in a solid and cystic papillary epithelial neoplasm of the pancreas. Am J Surg Pathol 1996, 20: 339–345.

435 Jeng LB, Chen MF, Tang RP. Solid and papillary neoplasm of the pancreas. Emphasis on surgical treatment. Arch Surg 1993, 128: 433–436.

436 Jorgensen LJ, Hansen AB, Burcharth F, Philipsen E, Horn T. Solid and papillary neoplasm of the pancreas. Ultrastruct Pathol 1992, 16: 659–666.

437 Klimstra DS, Wenig BM, Heffess CS. Solid-pseudopapillary tumor of the pancreas: a typically cystic carcinoma of low malignant potential. Semin Diagn Pathol 2000, 17: 66–80.

438 Klöppel G, Maurer R, Hofmann E, Luthold K, Oscarson J, Forsby N, Ihse I, Ljungberg O, Heitz PU. Solid-cystic (papillary-cystic) tumours within and outside the pancreas in men. Report of two patients. Virchows Arch [A] 1991, 418: 179–183.

439 Kosmahl M, Seada LS, Janig U, Harms D, Kloppel G. Solid-pseudopapillary tumor of the pancreas: its origin revisited. Virchows Arch 2000, 436: 473–480.

440 Kuo T-t, Su I-J, Chien C-h. Solid and papillary neoplasm of the pancreas. Report of three cases from Taiwan. Cancer 1984, 54: 1469–1474.

441 Lieber MR, Lack EE, Roberts JR Jr, Merino MJ, Patterson K, Restrepo C, Solomon D, Chandra R, Triche TJ. Solid and papillary epithelial neoplasm of the pancreas. An ultrastructural and immunocytochemical study of six cases. Am J Surg Pathol 1987, 11: 85–93.

442 Matsunou H, Konishi F. Papillary-cystic neoplasm of the pancreas. A clinicopathologic study concerning the tumor aging and malignancy of nine cases. Cancer 1990, 65: 283–291.

443 Matsunou H, Konishi F, Yamamichi N, Takayanagi N, Mukai M. Solid, infiltrating variety of papillary cystic neoplasm of the pancreas. Cancer 1990, 65: 2747–2757.

444 Miettinen M, Partanen S, Fräki O, Kivilaakso E. Papillary cystic tumor of the pancreas. An analysis of cellular differentiation by electron microscopy and immunohistochemistry. Am J Surg Pathol 1987, 11: 885–865.

445 Morohoshi T, Kanda M, Horie A, Chott A, Dreyer T, Klöppel G, Heitz PU. Immunocytochemical markers of uncommon pancreatic tumors. Acinar cell carcinoma, pancreatoblastoma, and solid cystic (papillary-cystic) tumor. Cancer 1987, 59: 739–747.

446 Nishihara K, Nagoshi M, Tsuneyoshi M, Yamaguchi K, Hayashi I. Papillary cystic tumors of the pancreas. Assessment of their malignant potential. Cancer 1993, 71: 82–92.

447 Nishihara K, Tsuneyoshi M, Ohshima A, Yamaguchi K. Papillary cystic tumor of the pancreas. Is it a hormone-dependent neoplasm? Pathol Res Pract 1993, 189: 521–526.

448 Notohara K, Hamazaki S, Tsukayama C, Nakamoto S, Kawabata K, Mizobuchi K, Sakamoto K, Okada S. Solid-pseudopapillary tumor of the pancreas: immunohistochemical localization of neuroendocrine markers and CD10. Am J Surg Pathol 2000, 24: 1361–1371.

449 Orlando CA, Bowman RL, Loose JH. Multicentric papillary-cystic neoplasm of the pancreas. Arch Pathol Lab Med 1991, 115: 958–960.

450 Pettinato G, Manivel JC, Ravetto C, Terracciano LM, Gould EW, di Tuoro A, Jaszcz W, Albores-Saavedra J. Papillary cystic tumor of the pancreas. A clinicopathologic study of 20 cases with cytologic, immunohistochemical, ultrastructural, and flow cytometric observations, and a review of the literature. Am J Clin Pathol 1992, 98: 478–488.

451 Sclafani LM, Reuter VE, Coit DG, Brennan MF. The malignant nature of papillary and cystic neoplasm of the pancreas. Cancer 1991, 68: 153–158.

452 Stommer P, Kraus J, Stotlte M, Giedl J. Solid and cystic pancreatic tumors. Clinical, histochemical, and electron microscopic features in ten cases. Cancer 1991, 67: 1635–1641.

453 Zamboni G, Bonetti F, Scarpa A, Pelos G, Doglioni C, Iannucci A, Castelli P, Balercia G, Aldovini D, Bellomi A, et al. Expression of progesterone receptors in solid-cystic tumour of the pancreas. A clinicopathological and immunohistochemical study of ten cases. Virchows Arch [A] 1993, 423: 425–431.

Pancreatoblastoma

454 Abraham SC, Wu T-T, Klimstra DS, Finn LS, Lee JH, Yeo CJ, Cameron JL, Hruban RH. Distinctive molecular genetic alterations in sporadic and familial adenomatous polyposis-associated pancreatoblastomas: frequent alterations in the APC/beta-catenin pathway and chromosome 11p. Am J Pathol 2001, 159: 1619–1627.

455 Buchino JJ, Castello FM, Nagaraj HS. Pancreatoblastoma. A histochemical and ultrastructural analysis. Cancer 1984, 53: 963–969.

456 Cingolani N, Shaco-Levy R, Farruggio A, Klimstra DS, Rosai J. Alpha-fetoprotein production by pancreatic tumors exhibiting acinar cell differentiation: study of five cases, one arising in a mediastinal teratoma. Hum Pathol 2000, 31: 938–944.

457 Cooper JE, Lake BD. Use of enzyme histochemistry in the

diagnosis of pancreatoblastoma. Histopathology 1989, **15**: 407–414.

458 Dunn JL, Longnecker DS. Pancreatoblastoma in an older adult. Arch Pathol Lab Med 1995, **119**: 547–550.

459 Horie A, Yano Y, Kotoo Y, Miwa A. Morphogenesis of pancreatoblastoma, infantile carcinoma of the pancreas. Report of two cases. Cancer 1977, **39**: 247–254.

460 Kakudo K, Sakurai M, Miyaji T, Ikeda Y, Satani M, Manabe H. Pancreatic carcinoma in infancy. An electron microscopic study. Acta Pathol Jpn 1976, **26**: 719–726.

461 Kissane JM. Pancreatoblastoma and solid and cystic papillary tumor. Two tumors related to pancreatic ontogeny. Semin Diagn Pathol 1994, **11**: 152–164.

462 Klimstra DS, Wenig BM, Adair CF, Heffess CS. Pancreatoblastoma. A clinicopathologic study and review of literature. Am J Surg Pathol 1995, **19**: 1371–1389.

463 Lack EE, Cassady JR, Levey R, Vawter GF. Tumors of the exocrine pancreas in children and adolescents. A clinical and pathologic study of eight cases. Am J Surg Pathol 1983, **7**: 319–327.

464 Morohoshi T, Kanda M, Horie A, Chott A, Dreyer T, Klöppel G, Heitz PU. Immunocytochemical markers of uncommon pancreatic tumors. Acinar cell carcinoma, pancreatoblastoma, and solid cystic (papillary-cystic) tumor. Cancer 1987, **59**: 739–747.

465 Tanaka Y, Ijiri R, Yamananka S, Kato K, Nishihira H, Nishi T, Misugi K. Pancreatoblastoma: optically clear nuclei in squamoid corpuscles are rich in biotin. Mod Pathol 1998, **11**: 945–949.

466 Taxy JB. Adenocarcinoma of the pancreas in childhood. Report of a case and a review of the English language literature. Cancer 1976, **37**: 1508–1518.

Endocrine tumors

General and clinical features; Morphologic features

467 Alanen KA, Joensuu H, Klemi PJ, Marin S, Åvaikko M, Nevalainen TJ. DNA ploidy in pancreatic neuroendocrine tumors. Am J Clin Pathol 1990, **93**: 784–788.

468 Berger G, Trouillas J, Bloch B, Sassolas G, Berger F, Partensky C, Chayvialle J-A, Brazeau P, Claustrat B, Lesbros F, Girod C. Multihormonal carcinoid tumor of the pancreas. Secreting growth hormone-releasing factor as a cause of acromegaly. Cancer 1984, **54**: 2097–2108.

469 Bordi C, De Vita O, Pilato FP, Carfagna G, D'Adda T, Missale G, Peracchia A. Multiple islet cell tumors with predominance of glucagon-producing cells and ulcer disease. Am J Clin Pathol 1987, **88**: 153–161.

470 Bordi C, Ravazzola M, Pollak A, Lubec G, Orci L. Neonatal islet cell adenoma. A distinct type of islet cell tumor? Diabetes Care 1982, **5**: 122–125.

471 Bostwick DG, Null WE, Holmes D, Weber E, Barchas JD, Bensch KG. Expression of opioid peptides in tumors. N Engl J Med 1987, **317**: 1439–1443.

472 Bostwick DG, Quan R, Hoffman AR, Webber RJ, Chang JK, Bensch KG. Growth-hormone-releasing factor immunoreactivity in human endocrine tumors. Am J Pathol 1984, **117**: 167–170.

473 Bouwens L, Kloppel G. Islet cell neogenesis in the pancreas. Virchows Arch 1996, **427**: 553–560.

474 Broughan TA, Leslie JD, Soto JM, Hermann RE. Pancreatic islet cell tumors. Surgery 1986, **99**: 671–678.

475 Cai Y-C, Banner B, Glickman J, Odze RD. Cytokeratin 7 and 20 and thyroid transcription factor 1 can help distinguish pulmonary from gastrointestinal carcinoid and pancreatic endocrine tumors. Hum Pathol 2001, **32**: 1087–1093.

476 Capella C, Heitz PU, Hofler H, Solcia E, Klöppel G. Revised classification of neuroendocrine tumours of the lung, pancreas and gut. Virchows Arch 1995, **425**: 547–560.

477 Carney CN. Congenital insulinoma (nesidioblastoma).

Ultrastructural evidence for histogenesis from pancreatic ductal epithelium. Arch Pathol Lab Med 1976, **100**: 352–356.

478 Chejfec G, Falkmer S, Grimelius L, Jacobsson B, Rodensjö M, Wiedenmann B, Franke WW, Lee I, Gould VE. Synaptophysin. A new marker for pancreatic neuroendocrine tumors. Am J Surg Pathol 1987, **11**: 241–247.

479 Clark ES, Carney JA. Pancreatic islet cell tumor associated with Cushing's syndrome. Am J Surg Pathol 1984, **8**: 917–924.

480 Clarke MR, Baker EE, Weyant RJ, Hill L, Carty SE. Proliferative activity in pancreatic endocrine tumors: association with function, metastases, and survival. Endocr Pathol 2002, **8**: 181–187.

481 D'Adda T, Pizzi S, Azzoni C, Bottarelli L, Crafa P, Pasquali C, Davoli C, Corleto VD, Delle Fave G, Bordi C. Different patterns of 11q allelic losses in digestive endocrine tumors. Hum Pathol 2002, **33**: 322–329.

482 Dayal Y, Lin HD, Tallberg K, Reichlin S, DeLellis RA, Wolfe HJ. Immunocytochemical demonstration of growth hormone-releasing factor in gastrointestinal and pancreatic endocrine tumors. Am J Clin Pathol 1986, **85**: 13–20.

483 Donow C, Baisch H, Heitz PU, Klöppel G. Nuclear DNA content in 27 pancreatic endocrine tumours: Correlation with malignancy, survival and expression of glycoprotein hormone alpha chain. Virchows Arch [A] 1991, **419**: 463–468.

484 Emerson L, Layfield LJ, Reiss R, Mulvihill S, Holden J. Malignant islet cell tumor with sarcomatous differentiation. Mod Pathol 2001, **14**: 1187–1191.

485 Ferreiro J, Lewin K, Herron RM, Bhuta S. Malignant islet cell tumor with rhabdomyosarcomatous differentiation. Am J Surg Pathol 1989, **13**: 422–427.

486 Graeme-Cook F, Nardi G, Compton CC. Immunocytochemical staining for human chorionic gonadotropin subunits does not predict malignancy in insulinomas. Am J Clin Pathol 1990, **93**: 273–276.

487 Greider MH, Rosai J, McGuigan JE. The human pancreatic islet cells and their tumors. II. Ulcerogenic and diarrheogenic tumors. Cancer 1974, **33**: 1423–1443.

488 Guarda LA, Silva EG, Ordóñez NG, Mackay B, Ibanez ML. Clear cell islet cell tumor. Am J Clin Pathol 1983, **79**: 512–517.

489 Hammar S, Sale G. Multiple hormone producing islet cell carcinomas of the pancreas. A morphological and biochemical investigation. Hum Pathol 1975, **6**: 349–362.

490 Heitz PU, Kasper M, Polak JM, Klöppel G. Pancreatic endocrine tumors. Immunocytochemical analysis of 125 tumors. Hum Pathol 1982, **13**: 263–271.

491 Hoang MP, Hruban RH, Albores-Saavedra J. Clear cell endocrine pancreatic tumor mimicking renal cell carcinoma: a distinctive neoplasm of Von Hippel-Lindau disease. Am J Surg Pathol 2001, **25**: 602–609.

492 Jacobsson B, Carlstrom A, Collins VP, Grimelius L. Transthyretin in endocrine pancreatic tumors. Am J Pathol 1989, **134**: 466–471.

493 Kahn CR, Rosen SW, Weintraub BD, Fajans SS, Gorden P. Ectopic production of chorionic gonadotropin and its sub-units by islet cell tumors. N Engl J Med 1977, **297**: 565–569.

494 Keel SB, Zukerberg L, Graeme-Cook F, Compton CC. A pancreatic endocrine tumor arising within a serous cystadenoma of the pancreas. Am J Surg Pathol 1996, **20**: 471–475.

495 Kent RB III, Van Heerden JA, Weiland LH. Nonfunctioning islet cell tumors. Ann Surg 1981, **193**: 185–190.

496 Kimura N, Pilichowska M, Okamoto H, Kimura I, Aunis D. Immunohistochemical expression of chromogranins A and B, prohormone convertases 2 and 3, and amidating enzyme in carcinoid tumors and pancreatic endocrine tumors. Mod Pathol 2000, **13**: 140–146.

497 La Rosa S, Capella C, Lloyd RV. Localization of myosin XVA in endocrine tumors of gut and pancreas. Endocr Pathol 2002, **13**: 29–37.

498 La Rosa S, Sessa F, Capella C, Riva C, Leone BE, Klersy C, Rindi G, Solcia E. Prognostic criteria in nonfunctioning pancreatic endocrine tumours. Virchows Arch 1997, **429**: 323–334.

499 La Rosa S, Uccella S, Billo P, Facco C, Sessa F, Capella C. Immunohistochemical localization of alpha- and beta-subunits of inhibin/activin in human normal endocrine cells and related tumors of the digestive system. Virchows Arch 1999, **434**: 29–36.

500 Larsson LI. Endocrine pancreatic tumors. Hum Pathol 1978, **9**: 401–416.

501 Larsson LI, Grimelius L, Hakanson R, Rehfeld JF, Stadil F, Holst J, Angervall L, Sundler F. Mixed endocrine pancreatic tumors producing several peptide hormones. Am J Pathol 1975, **79**: 271–284.

502 Le Gall F, Vallet VS, Thomas D, De Monti M, Duval J, Ramee MP. Immunohistochemical study of secretogranin II in 62 neuroendocrine tumours of the digestive tract and of the pancreas in comparison with other granins. Pathol Res Pract 1997, **193**: 179–185.

503 Leone BE, Mangili F, Vagani A, Taccagni GL. Coexpression of insulin and somatostatin in single secretory granules of a pancreatic endocrine tumor. Pathol Res Pract 1993, **189**: 458–462.

504 Ligneau B, Lombard-Bohas C, Partensky C, Valette P-J, Calender A, Dumortier J, Gouysse G, Boulez J, Napoleon B, Berger F, Chayvialle JA, Scoazec JY. Cystic endocrine tumors of the pancreas: clinical, radiologic, and histopathologic features in 13 cases. Am J Surg Pathol 2001, **25**: 742–760.

505 Lloyd RV, Mervak T, Schmidt K, Warner TFCS, Wilson BS. Immunohistochemical detection of chromogranin and neuron-specific enolase in pancreatic endocrine neoplasms. Am J Surg Pathol 1984, **8**: 607–614.

506 Miraliakbari BA, Asa SL, Boudreau SF. Parathyroid hormone-like peptide in pancreatic endocrine carcinoma and adenocarcinoma associated with hypercalcemia. Hum Pathol 1992, **23**: 884–887.

507 Mukai K. Functional pathology of pancreatic islets. Immunocytochemical exploration. Pathol Annu 1983, **18**(Pt 2): 87–107.

508 Mukai K, Grotting JC, Greider MH, Rosai J. Retrospective study of 77 pancreatic endocrine tumors using the immunoperoxidase method. Am J Surg Pathol 1982, **6**: 387–399.

509 Nieuwenhuijzen Kruseman AC, Knijnenburg G, Brutel de la Riviere G, Bosman FT. Morphology and immunohistochemically-defined endocrine function of pancreatic islet cell tumours. Histopathology 1978, **2**: 389–399.

510 O'Connor DT, Deftos LJ. Secretion of chromogranin A by peptide-producing endocrine neoplasms. N Engl J Med 1986, **314**: 1145–1151.

511 Ooi A, Katsuda S, Nakanishi I, Kameya T, Yamaguchi K, Kitamura H, Hayakawa Y. Electron microscopic and immunoelectron microscopic demonstration of pancreatic polypeptide cells in glucagonoma. Colocalization of pancreatic peptide and glucagon in single secretory granules. Ultrastruct Pathol 1989, **13**: 15–22.

512 Ordóñez NG, Manning JT, Hanssen G. Alpha-1-antitrypsin in islet cell tumors of the pancreas. Am J Clin Pathol 1983, **80**: 277–282.

513 Ordóñez NG, Silva EG. Islet cell tumour with vacuolated lipid-rich cytoplasm: a new histological variant of islet cell tumour. Histopathology 1997, **31**: 157–160.

514 Papotti M, Bongiovanni M, Volante M, Allia E, Landolfi S, Helboe L, Schindler M, Cole SL, Bussolati G. Expression of somatostatin receptor types 1-5 in 81 cases of gastrointestinal and pancreatic endocrine tumors. A correlative immunohistochemical and reverse-transcriptase polymerase chain reaction analysis. Virchows Arch 2002, **440**: 461–475.

515 Pelosi G, Bresaola E, Bogina G, Pasini F, Rodella S, Castelli P, Iacono C, Serio G, Zamboni G. Endocrine tumors of the pancreas: Ki-67 immunoreactivity on paraffin sections is an independent predictor for malignancy: A comparative study with proliferating-cell nuclear antigen and progesterone receptor protein immunostaining, mitotic index, and other clinicopathologic variables. Hum Pathol 1996, **27**: 1124–1134.

515a Perez-Montiel MD, Frankel WL, Suster S. Neuroendocrine carcinomas of the pancreas with 'rhabdoid' features. Am J Surg Pathol 2003, **27**: 642–649.

516 Perret AG, Mosnier JF, Buono JP, Berthelot P, Chipponi J, Balique JG, Cuilleret J, Dechelotte P, Boucheron S. The relationship between MIB-1 proliferation index and outcome in pancreatic neuroendocrine tumors. Am J Clin Pathol 1998, **109**: 286–293.

517 Pour P. Islet cells as a component of pancreatic ductal neoplasms. I. Experimental study. Ductular cells, including islet cell precursors, as primary progenitor cells of tumors. Am J Pathol 1978, **90**: 295–316.

518 Prescott RJ, Manson J, Haboubi NY. Malignant islet cell tumour arising in chronic pancreatitis. Histopathology 1993, **22**: 499–501.

519 Prinz RA, Bermes EW Jr, Kimmel JR, Marangos PJ. Serum markers for pancreatic islet cell and intestinal carcinoid tumors. A comparison of neuron-specific enolase β-human chorionic gonadotropin and pancreatic polypeptide. Surgery 1983, **94**: 1019–1023.

520 Radi MJ, Fenoglio-Preiser CM, Chiffelle T. Functioning oncocytic islet-cell carcinoma. Report of a case with electron-microscopic and immunohistochemical confirmation. Am J Surg Pathol 1985, **9**: 517–524.

521 Ruschoff J, Willemer S, Brunzel M, Trautmann ME, Frank M, Arnold R, Kloppel G. Nucleolar organizer regions and glycoprotein-hormone alpha-chain reaction as markers of malignancy in endocrine tumours of the pancreas. Histopathology 1993, **22**: 51–57.

522 Scarpa A, Orlandini S, Moore PS, Lemoine NR, Beghelli S, Baron A, Falconi M, Zamboni G. Dpc4 is expressed in virtually all primary and metastatic pancreatic endocrine carcinomas. Virchows Arch 2002, **440**: 155–159.

523 Schmid KW, Brink M, Freytag G, Kirchmair R, Bocker W, Fischer-Colbrie R, Heitz PU, Kloppel G. Expression of chromogranin A and B and secretoneurin immunoreactivity in neoplastic and nonneoplastic pancreatic alpha cells. Virchows Arch 1994, **425**: 127–132.

524 Simpson S, Vinik AI, Marangos PJ, Lloyd RV. Immunohistochemical localization of neuron-specific enolase in gastroenteropancreatic neuroendocrine tumors. Correlation with tissue and serum levels of neuron-specific enolase. Cancer 1984, **54**: 1364–1369.

525 Smith AE, Levi AW, Nadasdy T, Campbell KA, Fishman EK, Hruban RH. The pigmented "black" neuroendocrine tumor of the pancreas: a question of origin. Cancer 2001, **92**: 1984–1991.

526 Speel EJ, Richter J, Moch H, Egenter C, Saremaslani P, Rutimann K, Zhao J, Barghorn A, Roth J, Heitz PU, Komminoth P. Genetic differences in endocrine pancreatic tumor subtypes detected by comparative genomic hybridization. Am J Pathol 1999, **155**: 1787–1794.

527 Takahashi M, Hoshii Y, Kawano H, Setoguchi M, Gondo T, Yamashita Y, Nakayasu K, Kamei T, Ishihara T. Multihormone-producing islet cell tumor of the pancreas associated with somatostatin-immunoreactive amyloid: immunohistochemical and immunoelectron microscopic studies. Am J Surg Pathol 1998, **22**: 360–367.

528 Tischler AS, Compagno J. Crystal-like deposits of amyloid in pancreatic islet cell tumors. Arch Pathol Lab Med 1979, **103**: 247–251.

529 Tomita T. Metallothionein in pancreatic endocrine neoplasms. Mod Pathol 2000, **13**: 389–395.

530 Tomita T, Bhatia P, Gourley W. Mucin producing islet cell adenoma. Hum Pathol 1981, **12**: 850–853.

531 Tsutsumi Y. Expression of the alpha subunit of human chorionic gonadotropin in normal and neoplastic neuroendocrine cells. An immunohistochemical study. Acta Pathol Jpn 1989, **39**: 413–419.

532 Viale G, Doglioni C, Gambacorta M, Zamboni G, Coggi G, Bordi C. Progesterone receptor immunoreactivity in pancreatic endocrine tumors. An immunocytochemical study of 156 neuroendocrine tumors of the pancreas, gastrointestinal and respiratory tracts, and skin. Cancer 1992, **70**: 2268–2277.

533 Westermark P, Grimelius L, Polak JM, Larsson LT, van Noorden S, Wilander E, Pearse AGE. Amyloid in polypeptide hormone-producing tumors. Lab Invest 1977, **37**: 212–215.

534 Williams AJ, Coates PJ, Lowe DG, McLean C, Gale EA. Immunochemical investigation of insulinomas for islet amyloid polypeptide and insulin. Evidence for differential synthesis and storage. Histopathology 1992, **21**: 215–223.

535 Woodtli W, Hedinger C. Histologic characteristics of insulinomas and gastrinomas. Value of argyrophilia, metachromasia, immunohistology, and electron microscopy for the identification of gastrointestinal and pancreatic endocrine cells and their tumors. Virchows Arch [A] 1976, **371**: 331–350.

Specific types

536 Azzoni C, D'adda T, Tamburrano G, Coscelli C, Madsen OD, Scopsi L, Bordi C. Functioning human insulinomas. An immunohistochemical analysis of intracellular insulin processing. Virchows Arch 1998, **433**: 495–504.

537 Ballard HS, Frame B, Hartsock RJ. Familial multiple endocrine adenoma-peptic ulcer complex. Medicine (Baltimore) 1964, **43**: 481–516.

538 Bhagavan BS, Slavin RE, Goldberg J, Rao RN. Ectopic gastrinoma and Zollinger-Ellison syndrome. Hum Pathol 1986, **17**: 584–592.

539 Boden G. Insulinoma and glucagonoma. Semin Oncol 1987, **14**: 253–262.

540 Bonfils S, Landor JH, Mignon M, Hervoir P. Results of surgical management of 92 consecutive patients with Zollinger-Ellison syndrome. Ann Surg 1981, **194**: 692–697.

541 Capella C, Polak JM, Buffa R, Tapia FJ, Heitz P, Usellini L, Bloom SR, Solcia E. Morphologic patterns and diagnostic criteria of VIP-producing endocrine tumors. A histologic, histochemical, ultrastructural, and biochemical study of 32 cases. Cancer 1983, **52**: 1860–1874.

542 Carney CN. Congenital insulinoma (nesidioblastoma). Ultrastructural evidence for histogenesis from pancreatic ductal epithelium. Arch Pathol Lab Med 1976, **100**: 352–356.

543 Carstens PH, Cressman FK Jr. Malignant oncocytic carcinoid of the pancreas. Ultrastruct Pathol 1989, **13**: 69–75.

544 Chatelain D, Parc Y, Christin-Maitre S, Parc R, Flejou J-F. Mixed ductal–pancreatic polypeptide-cell carcinoma of the pancreas. Histopathology 2002, **41**: 122–126.

545 Christlieb AR, Schuster MM. Zollinger-Ellison syndrome. A clinical appraisal based on a review of the literature. Arch Intern Med 1964, **114**: 381–388.

546 Corrin B, Gilby ED, Jones NF, Patrick J. Oat cell carcinoma of the pancreas with ectopic ACTH secretion. Cancer 1973, **31**: 1523–1527.

547 Creutzfeldt W, Arnold R, Creutzfeldt C, Track NS. Pathomorphologic, biochemical, and diagnostic aspects of gastrinomas (Zollinger-Ellison syndrome). Hum Pathol 1975, **6**: 47–76.

548 Dahms BB, Lippe BM, Dakake C, Fonkalsrud EW, Mirra JM. The occurrence in a neonate of a pancreatic adenoma with nesidioblastosis in the tumor. Am J Clin Pathol 1976, **65**: 462–466.

549 Danforth DN Jr, Gorden P, Brennan MF. Metastatic insulin-secreting carcinoma of the pancreas. Clinical course and the role of surgery. Surgery 1984, **96**: 1027–1037.

550 Daughaday WH, Emanuele MA, Brooks MH, Barbato AL, Kapadia M, Rotwin P. Synthesis and secretion of insulin-like

growth factor II by a leiomyosarcoma with associated hypoglycemia. N Engl J Med 1988, **319**: 1434–1440.

551 Deveney CW, Deveney KE, Stark D, Moss A, Stein S, Way LW. Resection of gastrinomas. Ann Surg 1983, **198**: 546–553.

552 Dollinger MR, Ratner LH, Shamoian CA, Blackbourne BD. Carcinoid syndrome associated with pancreatic tumors. Arch Intern Med 1967, **120**: 575–580.

553 Donow C, Pipeleers-Marichal M, Schroder S, Stamm B, Heitz PU, Kloppel G. Surgical pathology of gastrinoma. Site, size, multicentricity, association with multiple endocrine neoplasia type 1, and malignancy. Cancer 1991, **68**: 1329–1334.

554 Drucker DJ, Asa SL, Silverberg J, Brubaker PL. Molecular and cellular analysis of a neoplastic pancreatic A cell tumor. Cancer 1990, **65**: 1762–1770.

555 Eissele R, Neuhaus C, Trautmann ME, Funk A, Arnold R, Hofler H. Immunoreactivity and expression of amylin in gastroenteropancreatic endocrine tumors. Am J Pathol 1993, **143**: 283–291.

556 Field M, Chang EB. Pancreatic cholera. N Engl J Med 1983, **309**: 1513–1515.

557 Graeme-Cook F, Bell DA, Flotte TJ, Preffer F, Pastel-Levy C, Nardi G, Compton C. Aneuploidy in pancreatic insulinomas does not predict malignancy. Cancer 1990, **66**: 2365–2368.

558 Greider MU, McGuigan JE. Electron microscopic identification of the gastrin cell of the human antral mucosa by means of immunocytochemistry. Gastroenterology 1972, **63**: 572–583.

559 Greider MH, Rosai J, McGuigan JE. The human pancreatic islet cells and their tumors. II. Ulcerogenic and diarrheogenic tumors. Cancer 1974, **33**: 1423–1443.

560 Gutman RA, Lazarus NR, Penhos JC, Fajans S, Recant L. Circulating proinsulin-like material in patients with functioning insulinomas. N Engl J Med 1971, **284**: 1003–1008.

561 Hamid QA, Bishop AE, Sikri KL, Varndell IM, Bloom SR, Polak JM. Immunocytochemical characterization of 10 pancreatic tumours, associated with the glucagonoma syndrome, using antibodies to separate regions of the proglucagon molecule and other neuroendocrine markers. Histopathology 1986, **10**: 119–133.

562 Harmon JW, Norton JA, Collin MJ, Krudy AG, Shawker TH, Doppman JL, D'Avis J, Jensen RT. Removal of gastrinomas for control of Zollinger-Ellison syndrome. Ann Surg 1984, **200**: 396–404.

563 Heitz P, Polak JM, Bloom SR, Adrian TE, Pearse AGE. Cellular origin of human pancreatic polypeptide (HPP) in endocrine tumours of the pancreas. Virchows Arch [Cell Pathol] 1976, **21**: 259–265.

564 Herrmann ME, Ciesla MC, Chejfec D, Dejong SA, Yong SL. Primary nodal gastrinomas. Arch Pathol Lab Med 2000, **124**: 832–835.

565 Hobbs RD, Stewart AF, Ravin ND, Carter D. Hypercalcemia in small cell carcinoma of the pancreas. Cancer 1984, **53**: 1552–1554.

566 Isenberg JI, Walsh JH, Grossman MI. Zollinger-Ellison syndrome. Gastroenterology 1973, **65**: 140–165.

567 Kheir SM, Omura EF, Grizzle WE, Herrera GA, Lee I. Histologic variation in the skin lesions of the glucagonoma syndrome. Am J Surg Pathol 1986, **10**: 445–453.

568 Komminoth P, Heitz PU, Roth J. Human insulinomas: clinical, cellular, and molecular aspects. Endocr Pathol 2002, **10**: 269–282.

569 Lam K-Y, Lo C-Y, Wat M-S, Fan S-T. Malignant insulinoma with hepatoid differentiation: a unique case with alpha-fetoprotein production. Endocr Pathol 2001, **12**: 351–354.

570 Laroche GP, Ferris DO, Priestley JT, Scholz DA, Dockerty MB. Hyperinsulinism. Surgical results and management of occult functioning islet cell tumor. Review of 154 cases. Arch Surg 1968, **96**: 763–771.

571 Larsson L. Two distinct types of islet abnormalities associated with endocrine pancreatic tumours. Virchows Arch [A] 1977, **376**: 209–219.

572 Liu T-H, Tseng H-C, Zhu Y, Zhong S-X, Chen J, Cui Q-C. Insulinoma. An immunocytochemical and morphologic analysis of 95 cases. Cancer 1985, **56**: 1420–1429.

573 Lloyd RV, Erickson LA, Nascimento AG, Kloppel G. Neoplasms causing nonhyperinsulinemic hypoglycemia. Endocr Pathol 2002, **10**: 291–297.

574 Lloyd RV, Mervak T, Schmidt K, Warner TFCS, Wilson BS. Immunohistochemical detection of chromogranin and neuron-specific enolase in pancreatic endocrine neoplasms. Am J Surg Pathol 1984, **8**: 607–614.

575 McGuigan JE, Trudeau WL. Immunochemical measurement of elevated levels of gastrin in the serum of patients with pancreatic tumors of the Zollinger-Ellison variety. N Engl J Med 1968, **278**: 1308–1313.

576 McMahon MM, O'Brien PC, Service FJ. Diagnostic interpretation of the intravenous tolbutamide test for insulinoma. Mayo Clin Proc 1989, **64**: 1481–1488.

577 Martella EM, Ferraro G, Azzoni C, Marignani M, Bordi C. Pancreatic-polypeptide cell hyperplasia associated with pancreatic or duodenal gastrinomas. Hum Pathol 1997, **28**: 149–153.

578 Mekhjian HS, O'Dorisio TM. VIPoma syndrome. Semin Oncol 1987, **14**: 282–291.

579 Moriura S, Ikeda S, Hirai M, Naiki K, Fujioka T, Yokochi K, Gotou S. Hepatic gastrinoma. Cancer 1993, **72**: 1547–1550.

580 Morowitz DA, Levine AE. Malignant Zollinger-Ellison syndrome. Remission of primary and metastatic pancreatic tumor after gastrectomy. Report of a case and review of the literature. Am J Gastroenterol 1986, **81**: 471–473.

581 Nobin A, Berg M, Ericsson M, Ingemansson S, Olsson E, Sundler F. Pancreatic polypeptide-producing tumors. Report on two cases. Cancer 1984, **53**: 2688–2691.

582 Ooi A, Kameya T, Tsumuraya M, Yamaguchi K, Abe K, Shimosato Y, Yanaihara N. Pancreatic endocrine tumours associated with WDHA syndrome. An immunohistochemical and electron microscopic study. Virchows Arch [A] 1985, **405**: 311–323.

583 Ordóñez NG. Insulinoma with fibrillar inclusions and acinar cell elements. Ultrastruct Pathol 2002, **25**: 485–495.

584 Ordóñez NG, Manning JT Jr, Raymond AK. Argentaffin endocrine carcinoma (carcinoid) of the pancreas with concomitant breast metastasis. An immunohistochemical and electron microscopic study. Hum Pathol 1985, **16**: 746–751.

585 Patchefsky AS, Gordon G, Harrer WV, Hoch WS. Carcinoid tumor of the pancreas. Ultrastructural observations of a lymph note metastasis and comparison with bronchial carcinoid. Cancer 1974, **33**: 1349–1354.

586 Patchefsky AS, Solit R, Phillips LD, Craddock M, Harrer WV, Cohn HE, Kowlessar OD. Hydroxyindole-producing tumors of the pancreas. Carcinoid-islet cell tumor and oat cell carcinoma. Ann Intern Med 1972, **77**: 53–61.

587 Pipeleers D, Couturier E, Gepts W, Reynders J, Somers G. Five cases of somatostatinoma. Clinical heterogeneity and diagnostic usefulness of basal and tolbutamide-induced hypersomatostatinemia. J Clin Endocrinol Metab 1983, **56**: 1236–1242.

588 Rawlinson DG, Christiansen RO. Light and electron microscopic observations on a congenital insulinoma. Cancer 1973, **32**: 1470–1476.

589 Regitnig P, Spuller E, Denk H. Insulinoma of the pancreas with insular-ductal differentiation in its liver metastasis–indication of a common stem-cell origin of the exocrine and endocrine components. Virchows Arch 2001, **438**: 624–628.

590 Reichlin S. Somatostatin. N Engl J Med 1983, **309**: 1495–1563.

591 Rosch T, Lightdale CJ, Botet JF, Boyce GA, Sivak MV Jr, Yasuda K, Heyder N, Palazzo L, Dancygler H, Schusdziarra V, et al. Localization of pancreatic endocrine tumors by endoscopic ultrasonography. N Engl J Med 1992, **326**: 1721–1726.

592 Roth J, Klöppel G, Madsen OD, Storch MJ, Heitz PU. Distribution patterns of proinsulin and insulin in human insulinomas. An immunohistochemical analysis in 76 tumors. Virchows Arch [Cell Pathol] 1992, **63**: 51–61.

593 Said SI, Faloona GR. Elevated plasma and tissue levels of vasoactive intestinal polypeptide in the watery-diarrhea syndrome due to pancreatic, bronchogenic and other tumors. N Engl J Med 1975, **293**: 155–160.

594 Service FJ, McMahon MM, O'Brien PC, Ballard DJ. Functioning insulinoma–incidence, recurrence, and long-term survival of patients. A 60-year study. Mayo Clin Proc 1991, **66**: 711–719.

595 Shetty MR, Boghossian HM, Duffell D, Freel R, Gonzales JC. Tumor-induced hypoglycemia. A result of ectopic insulin production. Cancer 1982, **49**: 1920–1923.

596 Silverstein MN. Tumor hypoglycemia. Cancer 1969, **23**: 142–144.

597 Stoker DJ, Wynn V. Pancreatic islet cell tumour with watery diarrhea and hypokalaemia. Gut 1970, **11**: 911–920.

598 Tanaka S, Yamasaki S, Matsushita H, Osawa Y, Kurosaki A, Takeuchi K, Hoshihara Y, Doi T, Watanabe G, Kawaminami K. Duodenal somatostatinoma: a case report and review of 31 cases with special reference to the relationship between tumor size and metastasis. Pathol Int 2000, **50**: 146–152.

599 Thompson NW, Vinik AI, Eckhauser FE, Strodel WE. Extrapancreatic gastrinomas. Surgery 1985, **98**: 1113–1120.

600 Tomita T, Friesen SR, Kimmel JR, Doull V, Pollock HG. Pancreatic polypeptide-secreting islet-cell tumors. Am J Pathol 1983, **113**: 134–142.

601 Tomita T, Kimmel JR, Friesen SR, Doull V, Pollock HG. Pancreatic polypeptide in islet cell tumors. Morphologic and functional correlations. Cancer 1985, **56**: 1649–1657.

602 Unger RH, Orci L. Glucagon and the A cell. Physiology and pathophysiology. N Engl J Med 1981, **304**: 1518–1524.

603 Vinik AI, Strodel WE, Eckhauser FE, Moattari AR, Lloyd R. Somatostatinomas, PPomas, neurotensinomas. Semin Oncol 1987, **14**: 263–281.

604 Wermer P. Duality of pancreatogenous peptic ulcer. N Engl J Med 1968, **278**: 397–398.

605 Wilson RW, Gal AA, Cohen C, De Rose PB, Millikan WJ. Serotonin immunoreactivity in pancreatic endocrine neoplasms (carcinoid tumors). Mod Pathol 1991, **4**: 727–732.

606 Wolfe MM, Alexander RW, McGuigan JE. Extrapancreatic, extraintestinal gastrinoma. Effective treatment by surgery. N Engl J Med 1982, **306**: 1533–1536.

607 Wolfe MM, Jensen RT. Zollinger-Ellison syndrome. Current concepts in diagnosis and management. N Engl J Med 1987, **317**: 1200–1209.

608 Yu F, Venzon DJ, Serrano J, Goebel SU, Doppman JL, Gibril F, Jensen RT. Prospective study of the clinical course, prognostic factors, causes of death, and survival in patients with long standing Zollinger-Ellison syndrome. J Clin Oncol 1999, **17**: 615–630.

609 Zollinger RM. Gastrinoma. Factors influencing prognosis. Surgery 1985, **97**: 49–54.

610 Zollinger RM. Gastrinoma. The Zollinger-Ellison syndrome. Semin Oncol 1987, **14**: 247–252.

Malignancy

611 Capella C, La Rosa S, Solcia E. Criteria for malignancy in pancreatic endocrine tumors. Endocr Pathol 1997, **8**: 87–90.

612 Freisen SR. Tumors of the endocrine pancreas. N Engl J Med 1982, **306**: 580–590.

613 Heymann MF, Joubert M, Nemeth J, Franc B, Visset J, Hamy A, le Borgne J, le Neel JC, Murat A, Cordel S, le Bodic MF. Prognostic and immunohistochemical validation of the Capella classification of pancreatic neuroendocrine tumors: an analysis of 82 sporadic cases. Histopathology 2000, **36**: 421–432.

614 Ruschoff J, Willemer S, Brunzel M, Trautmann ME, Frank M,

Arnold R, Kloppel G. Nucleolar organizer regions and glycoprotein-hormone alpha-chain reaction as markers of malignancy in endocrine tumours of the pancreas. Histopathology 1993, **22:** 51–57.

615 Solcia E, Klöppel G, Sobin LH. Histological typing of endocrine tumors. Berlin, 2000, Springer.

616 Venkatesh S, Ordonez NG, Ajani J, Schultz PN, Hickey RC, Johnston DA, Samaan NA. Islet cell carcinoma of the pancreas. A study of 98 patients. Cancer 1990, **65:** 354–357.

617 Whipple AO. Pancreatoduodenectomy for islet cell carcinoma. Ann Surg 1945, **121:** 847–852.

Multiple endocrine neoplasia

618 Brandi ML. Multiple endocrine neoplasia type 1. Rev Endocr Metab Disord 2000, **1:** 275–282.

619 Brandi ML, Gagel RF, Angeli A, Bilezikian JP, Beck-Peccoz P, Bordi C, Conte-Devolx B, Falchetti A, Gheri RG, Libroia A, Lips CJ, Lombardi G, Mannelli M, Pacini F, Ponder BA, Raue F, Skogseid B, Tamburrano G, Thakker RV, Thompson NW, Tomassetti P, Tonelli F, Wells SA Jr, Marx SJ. Guidelines for diagnosis and therapy of MEN type 1 and type 2. J Clin Endocrinol Metab 2001, **86:** 5658–5671.

620 Carney JA, Go VLW, Sizemore GW, Hayles AB. Alimentary-tract ganglioneuromatosis. A major component of the syndrome of multiple endocrine neoplasia, type 2b. N Engl J Med 1976, **295:** 1287–1291.

621 Carney JA, Sizemore GW, Lovestedt SA. Mucosal ganglioneuromatosis, medullary thyroid carcinoma, and pheochromocytoma. Multiple endocrine neoplasia, type 2b. Oral Surg 1976, **41:** 739–752.

622 Decker RA, Peacock ML. Update on the profile of multiple endocrine neoplasia type 2a RET mutations: practical issues and implications for genetic testing. Cancer 1997, **80:** 557–568.

623 DeLellis RA. The hereditary forms of pancreatic neuroendocrine tumors. Adv Anat Pathol 1999, **6:** 149–153.

624 Eng C. Multiple endocrine neoplasia type 2 and the practice of molecular medicine. Rev Endocr Metab Disord 2000, **1:** 283–290.

625 Gorlin RJ, Sedano HO, Vickers RA, Cervenka J. Multiple mucosal neuromas, pheochromocytoma and medullary carcinoma of thyroid. A syndrome. Cancer 1968, **22:** 293–299.

626 Gortz B, Roth J, Krahenmann A, de Krijger RR, Muletta-Feurer S, Rutimann K, Saremaslani P, Speel EJ, Heitz PU, Komminoth P. Mutations and allelic deletions of the MEN1 gene are associated with a subset of sporadic endocrine pancreatic and neuroendocrine tumors and not restricted to foregut neoplasms. Am J Pathol 1999, **154:** 429–436.

627 Gould E, Albores-Saavedra J, Shuman J. Pituitary prolactinoma, pancreatic glucagonomas, and aldosterone-producing adrenal cortical adenoma. A suggested variant of multiple endocrine neoplasia type I. Hum Pathol 1987, **18:** 1290–1293.

628 Guo SS, Sawicki MP. Molecular and genetic mechanisms of tumorigenesis in multiple endocrine neoplasia type-1. Mol Endocrinol 2001, **15:** 1653–1664.

629 Karges W, Schaaf L, Dralle H, Boehm BO. Clinical and molecular diagnosis of multiple endocrine neoplasia type 1. Langenbecks Arch Surg 2002, **386:** 547–552.

630 Khairi MRA, Dexter RN, Burzynski NJ, Johnson CC Jr. Mucosal neuroma, pheochromocytoma and medullary thyroid carcinoma. Multiple endocrine neoplasia type 3. Medicine (Baltimore) 1975, **54:** 89–112.

631 Klöppel G, Willemer S, Stamm B, Häcki WH, Heitz PU. Pancreatic lesions and hormonal profile of pancreatic tumors in multiple endocrine neoplasia type I. An immunocytochemical study of nine patients. Cancer 1986, **57:** 1824–1832.

632 Komminoth P. Review: multiple endocrine neoplasia type 1, sporadic neuroendocrine tumors, and MENIN. Diagn Mol Pathol 1999, **8:** 107–112.

633 Le Bodic MF, Heymann MF, Lecomte M, Berger N, Berger F, Louvel A, De Micco C, Patey M, De Mascarel A, Burtin F, Saint-Andre J-P. Immunohistochemical study of 100 pancreatic tumors in 28 patients with multiple endocrine neoplasia, type 1. Am J Surg Pathol 1996, **20:** 1378–1384.

634 Lee NC, Norton JA. Multiple endocrine neoplasia type 2B–genetic basis and clinical expression. Surg Oncol 2000, **9:** 111–118.

635 McKeeby JL, Li X, Zhuang Z, Vortmeyer AO, Huang S, Pirner M, Skarulis MC, James-Newton L, Marx SJ, Lubensky IA. Multiple leiomyomas of the oesophagus, lung, and uterus in multiple endocrine neoplasia type 1. Am J Pathol 2001, **159:** 1121–1127.

636 Pasini B, Ceccherini I, Romeo G. RET mutations in human disease. Trends Genet 1996, **12:** 138–144.

637 Pasini B, Rossi R, Ambrosio MR, Zatelli MC, Gullo M, Gobbo M, Collini P, Aiello A, Pansini G, Trasforini G, degli Uberti EC. RET mutation profile and variable clinical manifestations in a family with multiple endocrine neoplasia type 2A and Hirschsprung's disease. Surgery 2002, **131:** 373–381.

638 Perkins JT, Blackstone MO, Riddell RH. Adenomatous polyposis coli and multiple endocrine neoplasia type 2b. A pathogenetic relationship. Cancer 1985, **55:** 375–381.

639 Phay JE, Moley JF, Lairmore TC. Multiple endocrine neoplasias. Semin Surg Oncol 2000, **18:** 324–332.

640 Rosai J, Higa E, Davie J. Mediastinal endocrine neoplasm in patients with multiple endocrine adenomatosis. A previously unrecognized association. Cancer 1972, **29:** 1075–1083.

641 Samaan NA, Ouais S, Ordóñez NG, Choksi UA, Sellin RV, Hickey RC. Multiple endocrine syndrome type I. Clinical, laboratory findings, and management in five families. Cancer 1989, **64:** 741–752.

642 Schneider NR, Cubilla AL, Chaganti RSK. Association of endocrine neoplasia with multiple polyposis of the colon. Cancer 1983, **51:** 1171–1175.

643 Shan L, Nakamura Y, Nakamura M, Yokoi T, Tsujimoto M, Arima R, Kameya T, Kakudo K. Somatic mutations of multiple endocrine neoplasia type 1 gene in the sporadic endocrine tumors. Lab Invest 1998, **78:** 471–475.

644 Solcia E, Capella C, Fiocca R, Rindi G, Rosai J. Gastric argyrophil carcinoidosis in patients with Zollinger-Ellison syndrome due to type 1 multiple endocrine neoplasia. A newly recognized association. Am J Surg Pathol 1990, **14:** 503–513.

645 Tateishi R, Wada A, Ishiguro S, Ehara M, Sakamoto H, Miki T, Mori Y, Matsui Y, Ishikawa O. Coexistence of bilateral pheochromocytoma and pancreatic islet cell tumor. Cancer 1978, **42:** 2928–2934.

646 Thakker RV. Multiple endocrine neoplasia. Horm Res 2001, **56:** 67–72.

647 Tsukada T, Yamaguchi K, Kameya T. The MEN1 gene and associated diseases: an update. Endocr Pathol 2001, **12:** 259–273.

648 van Heyningen V. One gene. Four syndromes. Nature 1994, **367:** 319–320.

Lymphoid tumors and tumorlike conditions

649 Abrebanel P, Sarfaty S, Gal R, Chaimoff C, Kessler E. Plasma cell granuloma of the pancreas. Arch Pathol Lab Med 1984, **108:** 531–532.

650 Bern'ardeau M, Auroux J, Cavicchi M, Haioun C, Tsakiris L, Delchier JC. Secondary pancreatic involvement by diffuse large B-cell lymphoma presenting as acute pancreatitis: treatment and outcome. Pancreatology 2002, **2:** 427–430.

651 Borgia G, Ciampi R, Nappa S, Iovinella V, Crowell J. Pancreatic plasmacytoma. An unusual cause of obstructive jaundice. Arch Pathol Lab Med 1984, **108:** 773–774.

652 Drachenberg CB, Abruzzo LV, Klassen DK, Bartlett ST, Johnson LB, Kuo PC, Kumar D, Papadimitriou JC. Epstein-Barr virus-related posttransplantation lymphoproliferative disorder

involving pancreas allografts: histological differential diagnosis from acute allograft rejection. Hum Pathol 1998, **29**: 569–577.

653 Hirata S, Yamaguchi K, Bandai S, Izumo A, Chijiiwa K, Tanaka M. Secondary extramedullary plasmacytoma involving the pancreas. J Hepatobiliary Pancreat Surg 2002, **9**: 111–115.

654 Nakashiro H, Tokunaga O, Watanabe T, Ishibashi K, Kuwaki T. Localized lymphoid hyperplasia (pseudolymphoma) of the pancreas presenting with obstructive jaundice. Hum Pathol 1991, **22**: 724–726.

655 Tamura H, Ogata K, Mori S, An E, Tajika K, Sugisaki Y, Dan K. Lymphoblastic lymphoma of natural killer cell origin, presenting as pancreatic tumour. Histopathology 1998, **32**: 508–511.

Mesenchymal and other primary tumors

656 Brown SZ, Owen DA, O'Connell JX, Scudamore CH. Schwannoma of the pancreas: a report of two cases and a review of the literature. Mod Pathol 1999, **11**: 1178–1182.

657 Childs CC, Korsten MA, Choi H-SH, Schwarz R, Fisse RD. Pancreatic choriocarcinoma presenting as inflammatory pseudocyst. Gastroenterology 1985, **89**: 426–431.

658 de Alava E, Torramade J, Vazquez JJ. Leiomyosarcoma of the pancreas. Virchows Arch [A] 1993, **422**: 419–422.

659 Elliott TE, Albertazzi VJ, Danto LA. Pancreatic liposarcoma. Case report with review of retroperitoneal liposarcomas. Cancer 1980, **45**: 1720–1723.

660 Hirose T, Maeda T, Furuya K, Kiyasu Y, Kawasaki H. Malignant peripheral nerve sheath tumor of the pancreas with perineurial cell differentiation. Ultrastruct Pathol 1998, **22**: 227–231.

661 Horie H, Iwasaki I, Iida H, Takizawa J, Itoh F, Kohda S. Benign hemangioendothelioma of the pancreas with obstructive jaundice. Acta Pathol Jpn 1985, **35**: 975–979.

662 Ishikawa O, Matsui Y, Aoki Y, Iwanaga T, Terasawa T, Wada A. Leiomyosarcoma of the pancreas. Report of a case and review of the literature. Am J Surg Pathol 1981, **5**: 597–602.

662a Khanani F, Kilinc N, Nassar H, Othman M, Bejarano P, Cheng J, Adsay NV. Mesenchymal lesions involving the pancreas (Abstract). Mod Pathol 2003, **16**: 279a.

663 Luttges J, Mentzel T, Hubner G, Kloppel G. Solitary fibrous tumour of the pancreas: a new member of the small group of mesenchymal pancreatic tumours. Virchows Arch 1999, **435**: 37–42.

664 Movahedi-Lankarani S, Hruban RH, Westra WH, Klimstra DS. Primitive neuroectodermal tumors of the pancreas: A report of seven cases of a rare neoplasm. Am J Surg Pathol 2002, **26**: 1040–1047.

665 Murao T, Toda K, Tomiyama Y. Lymphangioma of the pancreas. A case report with electron microscopic observations. Acta Pathol Jpn 1987, **37**: 503–510.

665a Overstreet K, Wixom C, Shabaik A, Bouvet M, Herndier B. Adenomatoid tumor of the pancreas: a case report with comparison of histology and aspiration cytology. Mod Pathol 2003, **16**: 613–617.

666 Paal E, Thompson LD, Heffess CS. A clinicopathologic and immunohistochemical study of ten pancreatic lymphangiomas and a review of the literature. Cancer 1998, **82**: 2150–2158.

667 Pascal RR, Sullivan L, Hauser L, Ferzli G. Primary malignant fibrous histiocytoma of the pancreas. Hum Pathol 1989, **20**: 1215–1217.

668 Suster S, Phillips M, Robinson MJ. Malignant fibrous histiocytoma (giant cell type) of the pancreas. A distinctive variant of osteoclast-type giant cell tumor of the pancreas. Cancer 1989, **64**: 2303–2308.

669 Walsh SV, Evangelista F, Khettry U. Inflammatory myofibroblastic tumor of the pancreaticobiliary region: Morphologic and immunocytochemical study of three cases. Am J Surg Pathol 1998, **22**: 412–418.

670 Wreesmann V, Van Eijck CH, Naus DC, Van Velthuysen ML, Jeekel J, Mooi WJ. Inflammatory pseudotumor (inflammatory myofibroblastic tumour) of the pancreas: a report of six cases associated with obliterative phlebitis. Histopathology 2001, **38**: 105–110.

671 Zamboni G, Pea M, Martignoni G, Zancanaro C, Faccioli G, Gilioli E, Pederzoli P, Bonetti F. Clear cell "sugar" tumor of the pancreas: A novel member of the family of lesions characterized by the presence of perivascular epithelioid cells. Am J Surg Pathol 1996, **20**: 722–730.

Metastatic tumors

672 Charnsangavej C, Whitley NO. Metastases to the pancreas and peripancreatic lymph nodes from carcinoma of the right side of the colon. CT findings in 12 patients. AJR Am J Roentgenol 1993, **160**: 49–52.

673 Matsukuma S, Suda K, Abe H, Ogata S, Wada R. Metastatic cancer involving pancreatic duct epithelium and its mimicry of primary pancreatic cancer. Histopathology 1997, **30**: 208–213.

674 Tanabe S-I, Soeda S, Mukai T, Oki S, Yun K, Miyahara S-I. A case report of pancreatic metastasis of an intracranial angioblastic meningioma (hemangiopericytoma) and a review of metastatic tumor to the pancreas. J Surg Oncol 1984, **26**: 63–68.

675 Thompson LD, Heffess CS. Renal cell carcinoma to the pancreas in surgical pathology material. Cancer 2000, **89**: 1076–1088.

Ampullary region
Ampullary carcinoma and precursor lesions

676 Agoff SN, Crispin DA, Bronner MP, Dail DH, Hawes SE, Haggit RC. Neoplasms of the ampulla of Vater with concurrent pancreatic intraductal neoplasia: a histological and molecular study. Mod Pathol 2001, **14**: 139–146.

677 Alexander J, Krishnamurthy S, Kovacs D, Dayal Y. Cytokeratin profile of extrahepatic pancreaticobiliary epithelia and their carcinomas. Appl Immunohistochem 1997, **5**: 216–222.

678 Asbun HJ, Rossi RL, Munson JL. Local resection for ampullary tumors. Is there a place for it? Arch Surg 1993, **128**: 515–520.

679 Baczako K, Büchler M, Beger H-G, Kirkpatrick CJ, Haferkamp O. Morphogenesis and possible precursor lesions of invasive carcinoma of the papilla of Vater. Epithelial dysplasia and adenoma. Hum Pathol 1985, **16**: 305–310.

680 Bardales RH, Stanley MW, Simpson DD, Baker SJ, Steele CT, Schaefer RF, Powers CN. Diagnostic value of brush cytology in the diagnosis of duodenal, biliary, and ampullary neoplasms. Am J Clin Pathol 1998, **109**: 540–548.

681 Buck JL, Elsayed AM. Ampullary tumors. Radiologic-pathologic correlation. Radiographics 1993, **13**: 193–212.

682 Costi R, Caruana P, Sarli L, Violi V, Roncoroni L, Bordi C. Ampullary adenocarcinoma in neurofibromatosis type 1. Case report and literature review. Mod Pathol 2001, **14**: 1169–1174.

683 Cubilla AL, Fitzgerald PJ. Cancer of the exocrine pancreas. The pathologic aspects. Cancer 1985, **35**: 2–18.

684 Cubilla AL, Fortner J, Fitzgerald PJ. Lymph node involvement in carcinoma of the head of the pancreas area. Cancer 1978, **41**: 880–887.

685 Ferrell LD, Beckstead JH. Paneth-like cells in an adenoma and adenocarcinoma in the ampulla of Vater. Arch Pathol Lab Med 1991, **115**: 956–958.

686 Gardiner GW, Lajoie G, Keith R. Hepatoid adenocarcinoma of the papilla of Vater. Histopathology 1992, **20**: 541–544.

687 Goldstein NS, Bassi D. Cytokeratins 7, 17, and 20 reactivity in pancreatic and ampulla of vater adenocarcinomas. Percentage of positivity and distribution is affected by the cut-point threshold. Am J Clin Pathol 2001, **115**: 695–702.

688 Komorowski RA, Beggs BK, Geenan JE, Venu RP. Assessment of ampulla of Vater pathology. An endoscopic approach. Am J Surg Pathol 1991, **15**: 1188–1196.

689 Lee CS, Machet D, Rode J. Small cell carcinoma of the ampulla of Vater. Cancer 1992, **70**: 1502–1504.

690 McCarthy DM, Hruban RH, Argani P, Howe JR, Conlon KC, Brennan MF, Zahurak M, Wilentz RE, Cameron JL, Yeo CJ, Kern SE, Klimstra DS. Role of the DPC4 tumor suppressor gene in adenocarcinoma of the ampulla of vater: analysis of 140 cases. Mod Pathol 2003, **16**: 272–278.

691 Noda Y, Watanabe H, Iida M, Narisawa R, Kurosaki I, Iwafuchi M, Satoh, Ajioka Y. Histologic follow-up of ampullary adenomas in patients with familial adenomatosis coli. Cancer 1992, **70**: 1847–1856.

692 Ponchon T, Berger F, Chavaillon A, Bony R, Lambert R. Contribution of endoscopy to diagnosis and treatment of tumors of the ampulla of Vater. Cancer 1989, **64**: 161–167.

693 Rosenberg J, Welch JP, Pyrtek LJ, Walker M, Trowbridge P. Benign villous adenomas of the ampulla of Vater. Cancer 1986, **58**: 1563–1568.

694 Sarker AB, Hoshida Y, Akagi S, Hayashi K, Murakami I, Jeon HJ, Takahashi K, Akagi T. An immunohistochemical and ultrastructural study of a case of small-cell neuroendocrine carcinoma in the ampullary region of the duodenum. Acta Pathol Jpn 1992, **42**: 529–535.

695 Scarpa A, Capelli P, Zamboni G, Oda T, Mukai K, Bonetti F, Martignoni G, Iacono C, Serio G, Hirohashi S. Neoplasia of the ampulla of Vater. Ki-*ras* and p53 mutations. Am J Pathol 1993, **142**: 1163–1172.

696 Shutze WP, Sack J, Aldrete JS. Long-term follow-up of 24 patients undergoing radical resection for ampullary carcinoma, 1953 to 1988. Cancer 1990, **66**: 1717–1720.

697 Takashima M, Ueki T, Nagai E, Yao T, Yamaguchi K, Tanaka M, Tsuneyoshi M. Carcinoma of the ampulla of Vater associated with or without adenoma: a clinicopathologic analysis of 198 cases with reference to p53 and Ki-67 immunohistochemical expression. Mod Pathol 2000, **13**: 1300–1307.

698 Talbot IC, Neoptolemos JP, Shaw DE, Carr-Locke D. The histopathology and staging of carcinoma of the ampulla of Vater. Histopathology 1988, **12**: 155–165.

699 Willett CG, Warshaw AL, Convery K, Compton CC. Patterns of failure after pancreaticoduodenectomy for ampullary carcinoma. Surg Gynecol Obstet 1993, **176**: 33–38.

700 Wise L, Pizzimbono C, Dehner LP. Periampullary cancer. A clinicopathologic study of sixty-two patients. Am J Surg 1976, **131**: 141–148.

701 Yamaguchi K, Enjoji M. Carcinoma of the ampulla of Vater. A clinicopathologic study and pathologic staging of 109 cases of carcinoma and 5 cases of adenoma. Cancer 1987, **59**: 506–515.

702 Zamboni G, Franzin G, Bonetti F, Scarpa A, Chilosi M, Colombari R, Menestrina F, Pea M, Iacono C, Serio G, et al. Small-cell neuroendocrine carcinoma of the ampullary region. A clinicopathologic, immunohistochemical, and ultrastructural study of three cases. Am J Surg Pathol 1990, **14**: 703–713.

Other lesions

703 Acosta JM, Civantos F, Nardi GL, Castleman B. Fibrosis of the papilla of Vater. Surg Gynecol Obstet 1967, **124**: 787–794.

704 Bornstein-Quevedo L, Gamboa-Dominguez A. Carcinoid tumors of the duodenum and ampulla of Vater: a clinicomorphologic, immunohistochemical, and cell kinetic comparison. Hum Pathol 2001, **32**: 1252–1256.

705 Geenan JE, Hogan WJ, Dodds WJ, Toouli J, Venu RP. The efficacy of endoscopic sphincterotomy after cholecystectomy in patients with sphincter-of-Oddi dysfunction. N Engl J Med 1989, **320**: 82–87.

705a Handra-Luca A, Terris B, Couvelard A, Bonte H, Flejou J-F. Adenomyoma and adenomyomatous hyperplasia of the vaterian system: clinical, pathological, and new immunohistochemical features of 13 cases. Mod Pathol 2003, **16**: 530–536.

706 Hatzitheoklitos E, Buchler MW, Friess H, Poch B, Ebert M, Mohr W, Imaizumi T, Beger HG. Carcinoid of the ampulla of Vater. Clinical characteristics and morphologic features. Cancer 1994, **73**: 1580–1588.

707 Jones MA, Griffith LM, West AB. Adenocarcinoid tumor of the periampullary region. A novel duodenal neoplasm presenting as biliary tract obstruction. Hum Pathol 1990, **21**: 1188–1190.

708 Makhlouf HR, Burke AP, Sobin LH. Carcinoid tumors of the ampulla of Vater: a comparison with duodenal carcinoid tumors. Cancer 1999, **85**: 1241–1249.

709 Misdraji J, Fernandez del Castillo C, Ferry JA. Follicle center lymphoma of the ampulla of Vater presenting with jaundice: report of a case. Am J Surg Pathol 1997, **21**: 484–488.

710 Moncur JT, Lacy BE, Longnecker DS. Mixed acinar-endocrine carcinoma arising in the ampulla of Vater. Hum Pathol 2002, **33**: 449–451.

711 Narita T, Yokoyama M. Adenomyomatous hyperplasia of the papilla of Vater: a sequela of chronic papillitis? Ann Diagn Pathol 1999, **3**: 174–177.

712 Noda Y, Watanabe H, Iwafuchi M, Furuta K, Ishihara N, Satoh M, Ajioka Y. Carcinoids and endocrine cell micronests of the minor and major duodenal papillae. Their incidence and characteristics. Cancer 1992, **70**: 1825–1833.

713 Pawade J, Lee CS, Ellis DW, Vellar ID, Rode J. Primary lymphoma of the ampulla of Vater. Cancer 1994, **73**: 2083–2086.

714 Shingleton WW, Gamburg D. Stenosis of the sphincter of Oddi. Am J Surg 1970, **119**: 35–37.

715 Stamm B, Hedinger Chr E, Saremaslani P. Duodenal and ampullary carcinoid tumors. A report of 12 cases with pathological characteristics, polypeptide content and relation to the MEN I syndrome and von Recklinghausen's disease (neurofibromatosis). Virchows Arch [A] 1986, **408**: 475–489.

716 Ulich TR, Kollin M, Simmons GE, Wilczynski SP, Waxman K. Adenomyoma of the papilla of Vater. Arch Pathol Lab Med 1987, **111**: 388–390.

16 Adrenal gland and other paraganglia

Normal anatomy

Adrenal gland

The adrenal gland is a composite of two endocrine organs, one mesodermally derived (cortex) and the other neuroectodermally derived (medulla).[2,3,5] The function of the adrenal cortex is to secrete several steroid hormones known as corticosteroids, all of which are produced by a series of complicated enzymatic steps from cholesterol (Fig. 16.1). They are classified into three groups—glucocorticoids, mineralocorticoids, and sex hormones (adrenal androgens)—depending on their biologic action. The enzymes responsible for their production can be assayed biochemically and detected immunohistochemically.[4]

The adrenal glands are located in the retroperitoneum, superomedial to the kidneys. The combined adrenal weight in normal adult individuals should not exceed 6 g; there are no apparent sex differences.

The complete fibrous capsule surrounding the gland sometimes fuses with the capsules of the kidneys and (on the right side) the liver. The adrenal cortex is divided into three zones, all of which are under the influence of adrenocorticotropic hormone (ACTH): glomerulosa, fasciculata, and reticularis (Fig. 16.2). The zona glomerulosa, which lies immediately beneath the capsule and is the site of mineralocorticoid (aldosterone) production, is

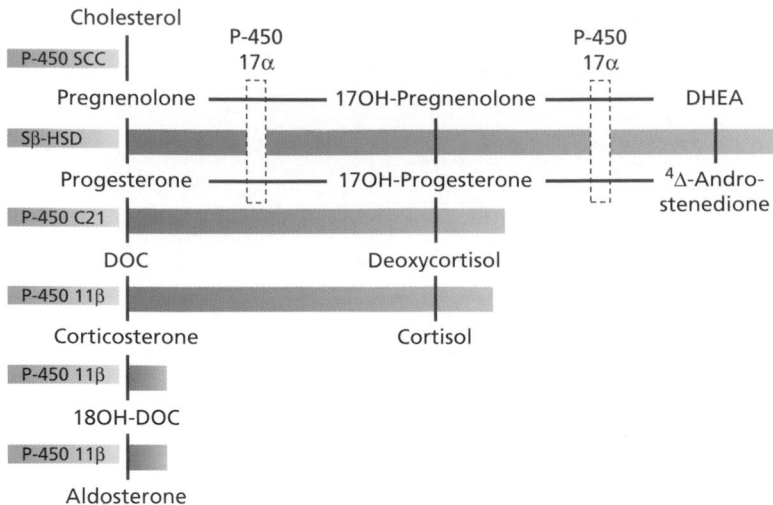

Fig. 16.1 Pathways of corticosteroidogenesis.

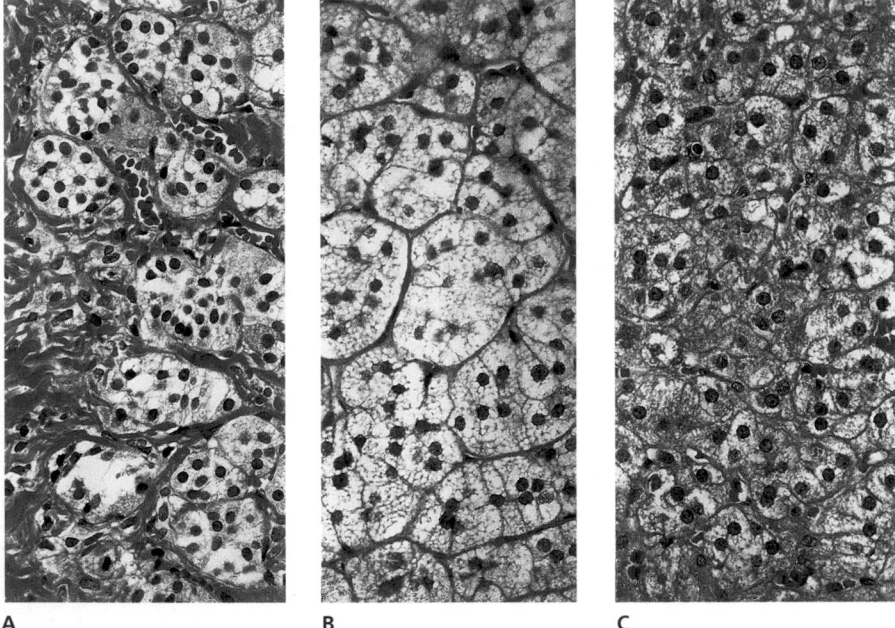

A   B   C

Fig. 16.2 The three layers of the normal adrenal cortex: **A**, glomerulosa; **B**, fasciculata; **C**, reticularis.

composed of well-outlined cells aggregated into small clusters and short trabeculae. The zona fasciculata, which is the site of glucocorticoid and sex hormone production, forms a broad band made up of large cells with distinct membranes arranged in two cell-wide cords. The cytoplasm is characterized by the presence of innumerable small lipid-containing vacuoles, some of which indent the centrally located nucleus in a fashion similar to that seen in sebaceous cells and lipoblasts; these cells are sometimes referred to as spongiocytes or clear cells. The zona reticularis is also involved in the secretion of glucocorticoids and sex hormones (particularly the latter). Its cells, which are arranged in a haphazard fashion, are smaller than those in the zona fasciculata and have a cytoplasm that is granular and acidophilic, with little or no lipid ("compact cells"). Some of these cells contain lipofuscin in their cytoplasm.[2]

The predominant cell type in the medulla is the pheochromocyte (medullary cell or chromaffin cell), which is admixed with scattered cortical cells and ganglion cells. The pheochromocyte is a rather large cell of polygonal shape and poorly outlined borders. Its abundant cytoplasm is distinctly granular and usually basophilic, although it may be amphophilic or even eosinophilic. Occasional cells feature cytoplasmic hyaline ("colloid") droplets, which are strongly positive with periodic acid–Schiff (PAS) stain.[2] A second cell population of the medullary region is represented by the sustentacular cells, which are located at the periphery of the nests and trabeculae; they are difficult to identify in routinely stained preparations but are readily demonstrated by immunostaining for S-100 protein.[2]

Ultrastructurally, the cells of the adrenal cortex share two important features that are common to all steroid-producing cells: abundant smooth endoplasmic reticulum and numerous mitochondria. The latter have lamellar cristae in the zona glomerulosa and tubulovesicular cristae in the zona fasciculata and reticularis.[1] The medullary cells can be divided into two types on the basis of the size of the cytoplasmic dense-core neurosecretory granules they contain: norepinephrine containing (electron opaque, often eccentrically located within a dilated sac, about 250 nm in diameter) and epinephrine containing (finely granular, filling the enclosing membrane, about 190 nm in diameter).

The immunohistochemical features of the cells are discussed in connection with the respective neoplasms.

Paraganglion system

The paraganglion system is formed by numerous collections of neuroepithelial cells ("chief cells") scattered throughout the body,[7] their common morphologic denominator being the presence of numerous cytoplasmic neurosecretory granules containing catecholamines.[6,9a] Microscopically, all paraganglia have a similar morphologic appearance characterized by chief cells arranged in well-defined nests ("Zellballen") encircled by a thin layer of S-100 protein-positive sustentacular cells. The most conspicuous member of the paraganglion system is the already described adrenal medulla, a neuroeffector system connected with the orthosympathetic system. Extra-adrenal paraganglia can be divided into two broad categories: those related to the parasympathetic system (ninth, tenth, and possibly third and fifth nerves) and those connected with the orthosympathetic system. The former are usually nonchromaffin, are concentrated in the head, neck, and mediastinum, and are thought to have a chemoreceptor function. The latter are chromaffin, predominate in the retroperitoneum along the thoracolumbar para-aortic region, and probably represent lesser homologues of the adrenal medulla (Fig. 16.3). Sometimes small paraganglia are found incidentally in sites such as the bladder, prostate, gallbladder, splenic capsule, and mesosigmoid.[8] Special care should be exercised not to confuse them with foci of metastatic carcinoma.[9]

Biopsy and cytology

The specimens from adrenal gland received in the laboratory usually consist of the entire organ, but in selected cases the diagnosis can be achieved through the performance of an ultrasonically or computed tomography-guided (CT-guided) biopsy[10,13] or fine needle aspiration cytology (Fig. 16.4).[11,12,14,16] The latter procedure is particularly useful for the diagnosis of metastatic tumors to this organ. In the series of Suen et al.,[15] a success rate of 86% was achieved in obtaining cellular material for diagnosis. A high rate of diagnostic accuracy for adrenal core biopsy (an overall sensitivity for malignancy of 94.6% and a specificity of 95.3%) was reported in a recently concluded multiinstitutional trial of 220 consecutive patients.[14a]

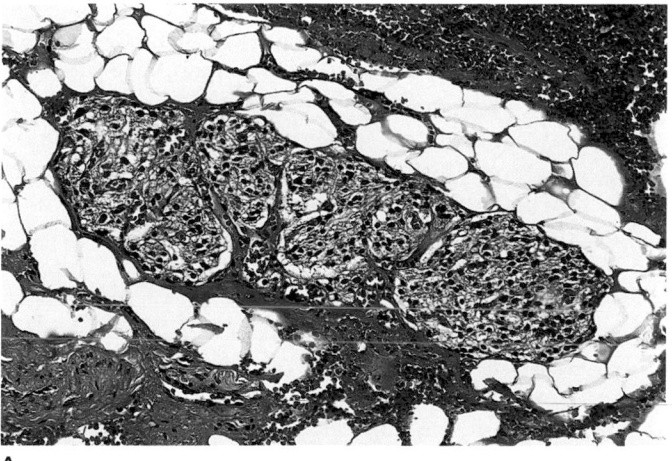

A

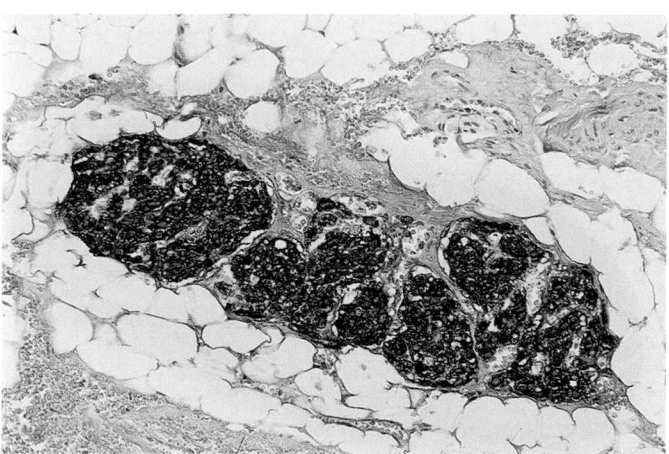

B

Fig. 16.3 Normal paraganglion found incidentally in the retroperitoneal region. **A**, Hematoxylin–eosin; **B**, chromogranin.

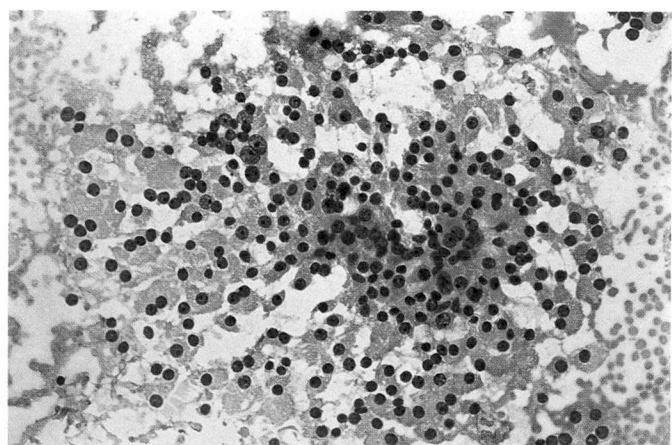

Fig. 16.4 Fine needle aspiration specimen from an adrenal cortical adenoma.

Lesions of adrenal cortex

Heterotopia

Heterotopic (accessory) adrenal cortical tissue has been reported in numerous locations, many of them resulting from some cells of the adrenocortical primordium becoming associated with and migrating alongside the gonads. The most common site is the retroperitoneal fat close to the adrenal gland. Other described sites include the region of the celiac plexus, the kidney, along the course of the spermatic and ovarian veins, the testis, adjacent to the tail of the epididymis, the broad ligament near the ovary, the ovary itself (but only exceptionally), the canal of Nuck, hernial and hydrocele sacs, the mesoappendix, and the liver. It has also been rarely reported in distant sites such as lung, intradural space, and brain.[17,18,22,23,25] The epididymis associated with the ectopic adrenal tissue may show various types of malformation.[19] The ectopic cortical tissue is almost never accompanied by a medullary component.

These ectopic nests may undergo marked hyperplasia in patients with Nelson's syndrome or other conditions associated with increased ACTH production,[20] and they occasionally give rise to ectopic adrenal cortical adenomas and carcinomas.[21,22,24] This includes the testicular "tumors" occurring in patients with congenital adrenal cortical hyperplasia; these are discussed in Chapter 19.

Cortical nodule

Small nodules ("micronodules") composed of microscopically normal adrenocortical tissue are often found within the adrenal cortex or protruding through the capsule into the adjacent fat. They are roughly spherical, unencapsulated, usually multiple, and range in size from microscopic to grossly apparent. Commons and Callaway[26] found nodules greater than 3 mm in 216 (3%) of 7437 consecutive autopsies. These nodules do not have clinical significance.[27] They increase in number with age but are not correlated with hypertension, diabetes, or cardiovascular disease. They should be distinguished from the nodules of true cortical hyperplasia and from cortical adenomas (see below). Sasano et al.[28] found intense immunoreactivity for cytochrome P-450 11β-hydroxylase in these cortical nodules.

Congenital hyperplasia

Congenital hyperplasia, an inborn error of metabolism, occurs with equal frequency in males and females and is transmitted by an autosomal recessive gene.[33,35] It is responsible for the large majority of cases of adrenogenital syndrome developing within the first year of life, but it can also first present clinically during adulthood.[30] The inherited defect may be in any of the five enzymatic steps required to synthesize cortisol from cholesterol.[38]

In approximately 95% of the cases, the basic defect is an absence of the enzyme 21-hydroxylase, which results in the accumulation of 17OH-progesterone and its catabolite pregnanetriol and in a deficiency of cortisol. The clinical picture is usually that of a pure virilizing syndrome, although in approximately 30% of patients electrolyte disturbances also occur.[36] The second most frequent form is due to a deficiency of 11β-hydroxylase and is characterized by virilization and hypertension. Several other variants, all exceptionally rare, have been described.[37] The genes encoding each of the steroid biosynthetic enzymes have been cloned, and the mutations in these genes that cause the various forms of congenital adrenal hyperplasia are being determined.[34] The most important of these is the *CYP21* gene on chromosome 6p21.3.[29,32] The pathologic change is the same in all types and is characterized by diffuse cortical hyperplasia, especially of the zona reticularis. The treatment consists of replacement with cortisol and surgical correction of the external sex organs.[31] The testicular "tumors" occurring in patients with adrenal cortical hyperplasia, which probably arise from ectopic adrenal cortical nests, are discussed in Chapter 19.

Acquired hyperplasia

Acquired hyperplasia, which is always bilateral, may result in a diffuse or a nodular ("adenomatous" or "adenomatoid") enlargement of the adrenal gland (Fig. 16.5). An adrenal gland in an adult can be regarded as hyperplastic if it weighs over 6 g, provided that a careful dissection of the fat has been carried out. Most cases of *diffuse* cortical hyperplasia are due to ACTH hyperproduction by either the pituitary gland or an ACTH-producing neoplasm in the lung or some other organ. Thus they are referred to as ACTH dependent or—in the former instance—pituitary dependent. In some cases, however, the pathogenesis remains obscure.

Microscopically, an increased thickness of the zona reticularis and fasciculata is observed, the relative

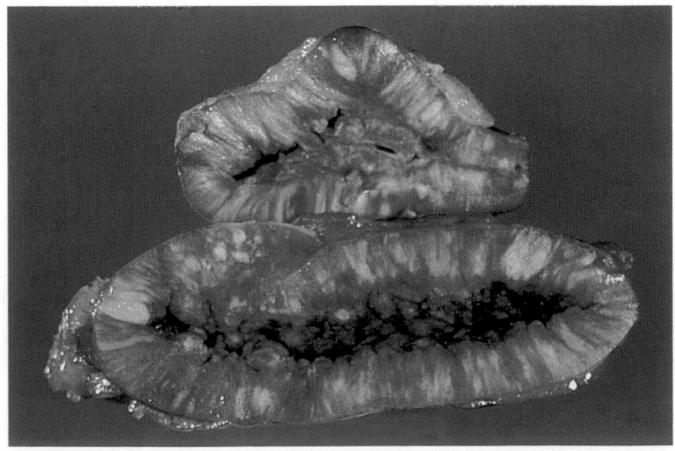

Fig. 16.5 Adrenal cortical hyperplasia showing multinodular pattern of growth.

proportions varying from case to case. Occasionally, cells with large hyperchromatic nuclei are seen in some of the nodules. Many of the cells in the fasciculata layer appear compact and lipid depleted. Ultrastructurally, these cells have abundant smooth endoplasmic reticulum and long microvilli that interdigitate with the microvilli of adjacent cells.[43] Flow cytometric and image analysis studies have shown the presence of aneuploid and polyploid cell populations.[43]

Most cases of *nodular* cortical hyperplasia are unrelated to ACTH production and are therefore referred to as ACTH independent or adrenal dependent.[45] In some instances, however, they represent a later stage of diffuse hyperplasia, in which the lesion has undergone a transition from pituitary dependent to adrenal dependent.[40,41]

A morphologically distinct **primary pigmented nodular adrenal cortical hyperplasia (dysplasia)** has been described as part of Carney's syndrome or complex. This is clinically characterized by Cushing's disease and also includes spotty cutaneous pigmentation, cutaneous and cardiac myxomas, growth hormone-secreting pituitary adenomas, and psammomatous melanotic schwannomas. In addition, females may have multiple myxoid fibroadenomas of the breast, and males may be affected by large cell calcifying Sertoli cell tumors of the testis.[39,42,46]

The adrenal glands, which may be small, normal sized, or slightly enlarged, show multiple pigmented cortical nodules with atrophy of the intervening cortex. These nodules are primarily composed of eosinophilic, lipid-poor cells similar to those of the normal zona reticularis (Fig. 16.6). These cells show intense immunoreactivity for all the steroidogenic enzymes.[44] Occasional additional features include microscopic foci of necrosis, mitoses, and a trabecular pattern of growth.[47]

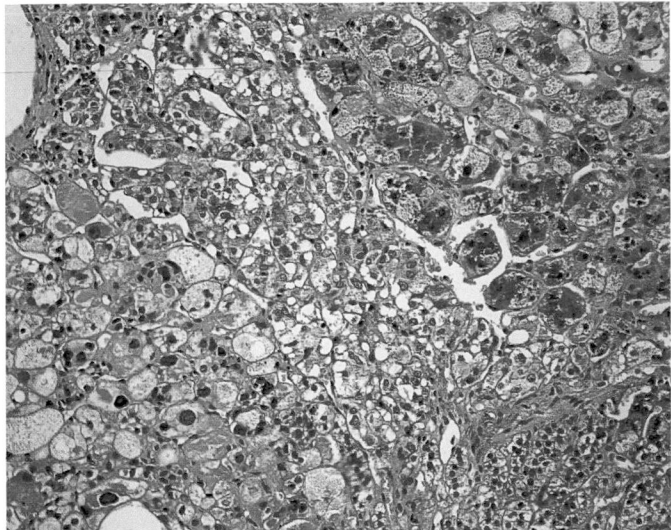

Fig. 16.6 Primary pigmented nodular adrenal cortical hyperplasia. Nodules of eosinophilic cells containing abundant brown pigment are seen, together with others showing clear cytoplasm and nuclear aberrations.

Adrenocortical tumors

Traditionally, adrenocortical neoplasms have been divided into adenomas and carcinomas. Many tumors can be easily placed into one category or another, but cases exist for which the distinction is difficult and to some extent arbitrary. Because of this fact, and also because these tumors share a large number of phenotypic features, they are discussed as a single nosologic entity, pointing out the differences between the two whenever they exist.

Clinical features

Most patients with adrenocortical neoplasms are adults (with an average age of about 50 years for the carcinomas[49,51,55]), but many pediatric cases are also on record.[48,52,53,56] The sex distribution is equal. These tumors can be found incidentally at autopsy[57] or as a result of radiographic investigations done for other reasons, or they may be detected because of symptoms or signs related to hormonal dysfunction (about 50% of the carcinomas[49,51,58]), or may be evident because of a mass effect.[50] Highly necrotic carcinomas may result in fever and thus simulate an infectious disease clinically.[59] Palpable adrenocortical neoplasms are malignant in practically every instance. Computed tomography is the most useful technique for the detection, pretreatment staging, and determination of resectability of these tumors.[54] Some of these tumors develop at the sites of ectopic adrenal cortical tissue including the spinal cord[48a] (see p. 1118).

Morphologic features

Grossly, both adenomas and carcinomas are usually solitary. Adenomas are characteristically small, rarely exceeding 5 cm in greatest diameter or 50 g in weight, whereas most carcinomas weigh more than 10 g, and some may reach 1000 g or more before being discovered.[80] Adenomas are thoroughly encapsulated; a capsule may also be present around carcinomas, but this is often infiltrated by tumor. The cut surface of an adenoma usually has a solid homogeneous yellow appearance (Fig. 16.7), whereas that of a carcinoma shows a variegated pattern, with soft and friable intratumoral nodules (Fig. 16.8). Areas of necrosis and hemorrhage are frequent in carcinomas and very rare in adenomas, although on rare occasions they can be so extensive in the latter as to simulate an angiosarcoma.[72] Invasion of major veins is a frequent finding in carcinoma and often leads to total occlusion, thrombosis, and embolism.

Microscopically, the adenomas may recapitulate the appearance of the zona fasciculata, the zona glomerulosa, or, more commonly, a combination of both (Fig. 16.9). Occasional bizarre nuclear forms can be seen, as in most other endocrine neoplasms. However, *mitoses are exceptionally rare or absent.*[68] The carcinomas exhibit a wide range of differentiation, from tumors that are so

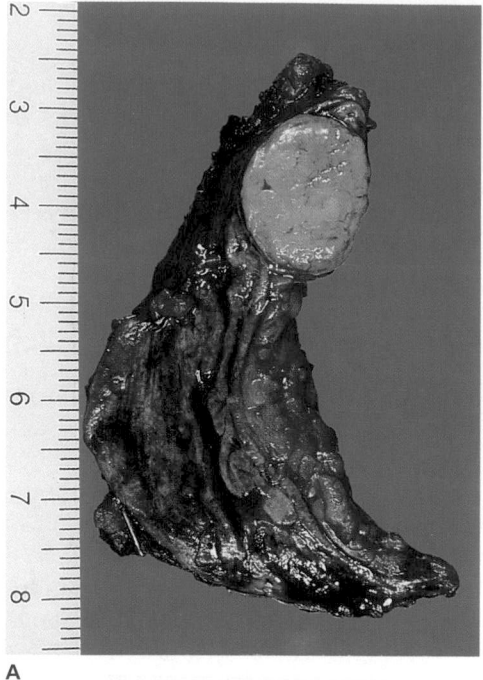

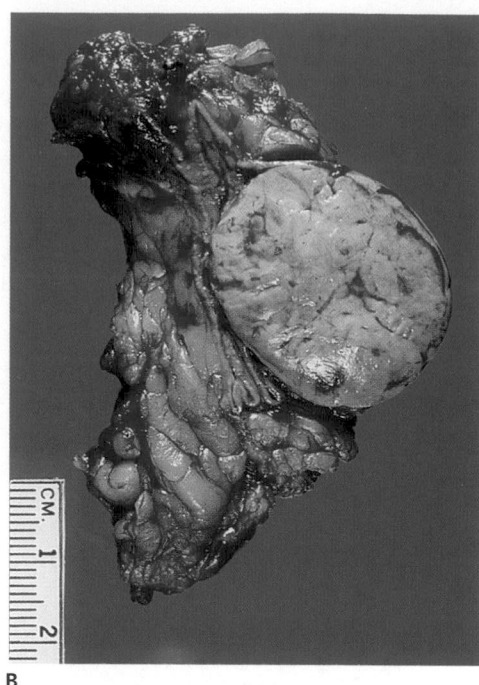

Fig. 16.7 A and **B**, Gross appearance of adrenal cortical adenoma. Both tumors are well circumscribed, of homogeneous appearance, without hemorrhage or necrosis. The tumor in **A** has the typical golden yellow color associated with aldosterone secretion.

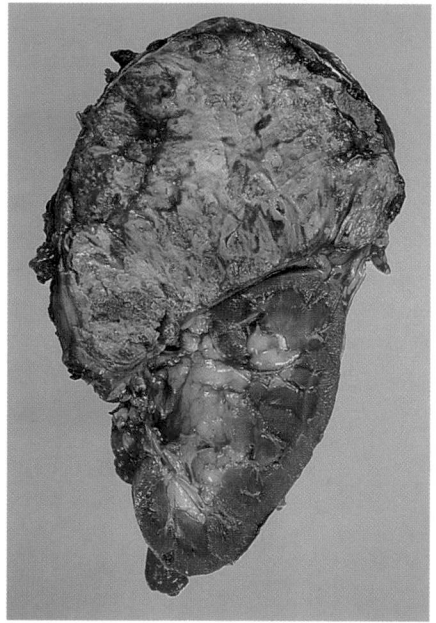

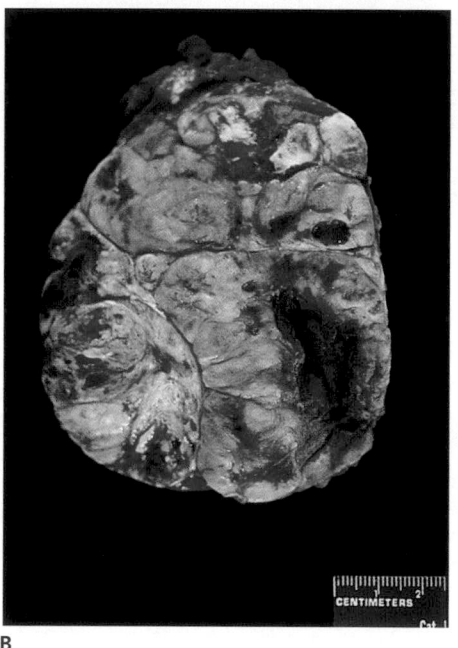

Fig. 16.8 A and **B**, Gross appearance of adrenal cortical carcinoma. Both tumors are large and exhibit areas of hemorrhage and necrosis. The tumor shown in **A** has destroyed the upper pole of the kidney.

well differentiated as to be almost impossible to distinguish from adenoma to totally undifferentiated neoplasms composed of giant cells with abundant acidophilic cytoplasm and bizarre hyperchromatic nuclei, sometimes multiple (Fig. 16.10). Occasionally, the tumor is heavily infiltrated by neutrophils, with some of the latter located within the cytoplasm of the tumor cells.

The principal morphologic distinguishing features between adenoma and carcinoma are discussed in a later section. Morphologic variants of adrenocortical neoplasms include:

1 Adrenocortical adenoma containing foci of *myelolipoma* (Fig. 16.10).[83]
2 *Black adenoma*.[74] Occasionally, adenomas (as well as hyperplastic nodules) have a dark brown to black color because of the presence of pigment, thought to represent either lipofuscin[76] or neuromelanin.[63] The former interpretation is more likely, the pathogenesis being probably related to alterations of lipid metabolism induced by the abnormal mitochondria present in the cells of these lesions. Most of these "black adenomas" or "black nodules" are nonfunctioning and

found incidentally at autopsy, but on occasion they have been associated with primary aldosteronism[82] or Cushing's syndrome.[73] These nodules have a higher radiologic density than the ordinary yellow cortical tumors.[73]

3 *Corticomedullary mixed tumor.* This refers to the association within the same mass (or possibly even within the

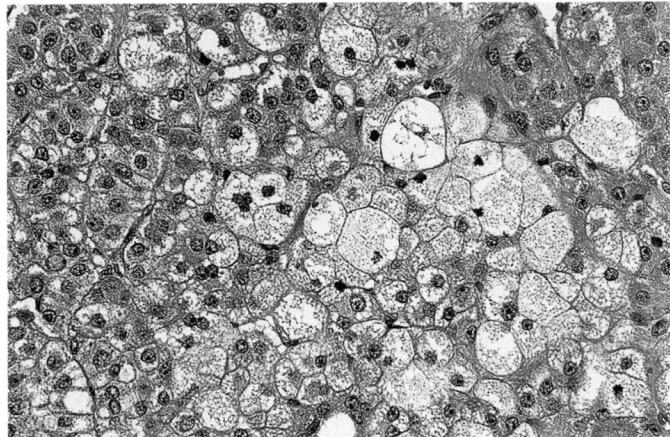

Fig. 16.9 Adrenal cortical adenoma showing numerous lipid-laden clear cells similar to those of the normal fasciculata layer.

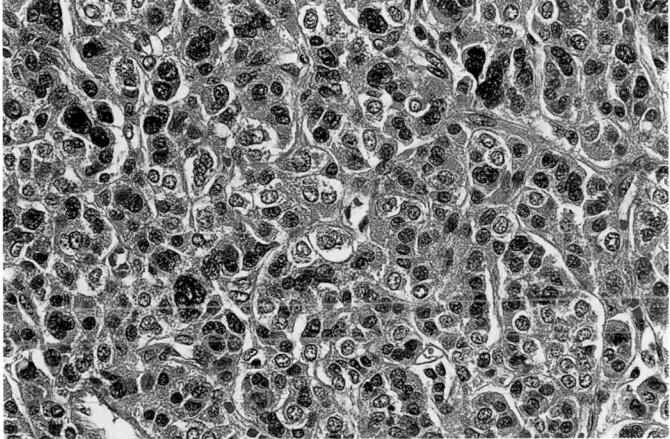

Fig. 16.10 Adrenal cortical carcinoma. There is nuclear hyperchromasia, diffuse pattern of growth, and mitotic activity.

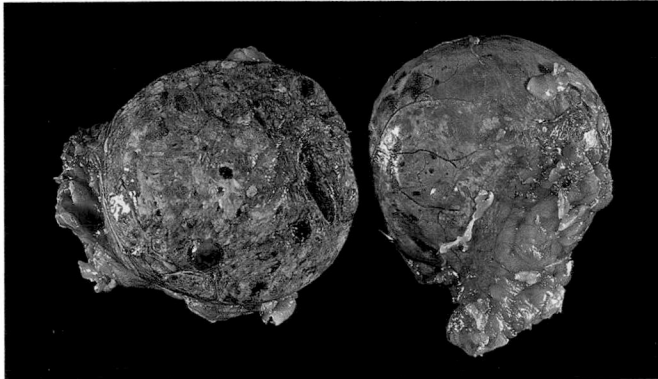

Fig. 16.11 Gross appearance of adrenal cortical adenoma with myelolipomatous component, represented by the small hemorrhagic foci.

same cell) of features indicative of adrenocortical *and* adrenomedullary differentiation.[72b,77] Most of the reported cases have been of benign nature.[77]

4 *Adrenocortical oncocytoma.* As the name indicates, this is a neoplasm in which the tumor cells are packed with mitochondria (Fig. 16.12). Both benign and malignant forms exist, the former predominating.[61,61a,66,79] Most are nonfunctioning.[72a,75] Interestingly, the mitochondria retain at the ultrastructural level the tubulovesicular cristae which are typical of steroid-producing cells.[67] These cells also contain peculiar cytoplasmic crystalline inclusions.[81]

5 *Myxoid adrenocortical neoplasms.* Both adenomas and carcinomas can have prominent myxoid features, their features being otherwise typical of their respective types.[62]

6 *Lipoadenoma.* Cases have been reported of adrenocortical adenomas (as well as nodular cortical hyperplasias) containing abundant mature adipose tissue.[69,70,78]

7 *Sarcomatoid carcinoma*, a self-explanatory designation. As in other sites, when the carcinomatous and the sarcoma-like elements are sharply segregated, the alternative term *carcinosarcoma* has been used.[60,64,71]

8 *Adenosquamous carcinoma.* Another self-explanatory name, and the rarest of all variants.[65]

Electron microscopic, histochemical, immunohistochemical, and molecular genetic features

A broad range of ultrastructural appearances is present among adrenocortical neoplasms, the differences relating to the amount of cytoplasmic lipid, number of lysosomes, and quantity and architecture of the mitochondria (many of which contain tubulovesicular cristae) and smooth endoplasmic reticulum. Further variations include tumors with lipid-rich, oncocytic, and glycogen-rich cells.[99,106]

Immunohistochemically, the cells of adrenocortical neoplasms are immunoreactive for vimentin, synaptophysin (but no chromogranin), inhibin, A103, and Melan-A (Mart-1) (Fig. 16.13).[84–86,98] They also stain for bcl-2,[89] calretinin (usually in a focal fashion),[92] and keratin (especially the adenomas, but only focally and erratically). They are negative for EMA, CEA, B72.3, and Lewis blood group antigens.[87,96,97,104,105]

Various steroid hormones and the enzymes involved in their synthesis (such as cytochrome P-450$_{C21}$) have been demonstrated in these tumors immunohistochemically and by in situ hybridization techniques.[102,103] They have also been found to express insulin-like growth factor I and epidermal growth factor and their receptors, suggesting the existence of an autocrine/paracrine regulation.[88,91,93,94] The presence of neural/neuroendocrine markers such as neurofilaments, synaptophysin, and NSE, has been correlated with the presence of dense-core granules at the electron microscopic level.[90,95,100]

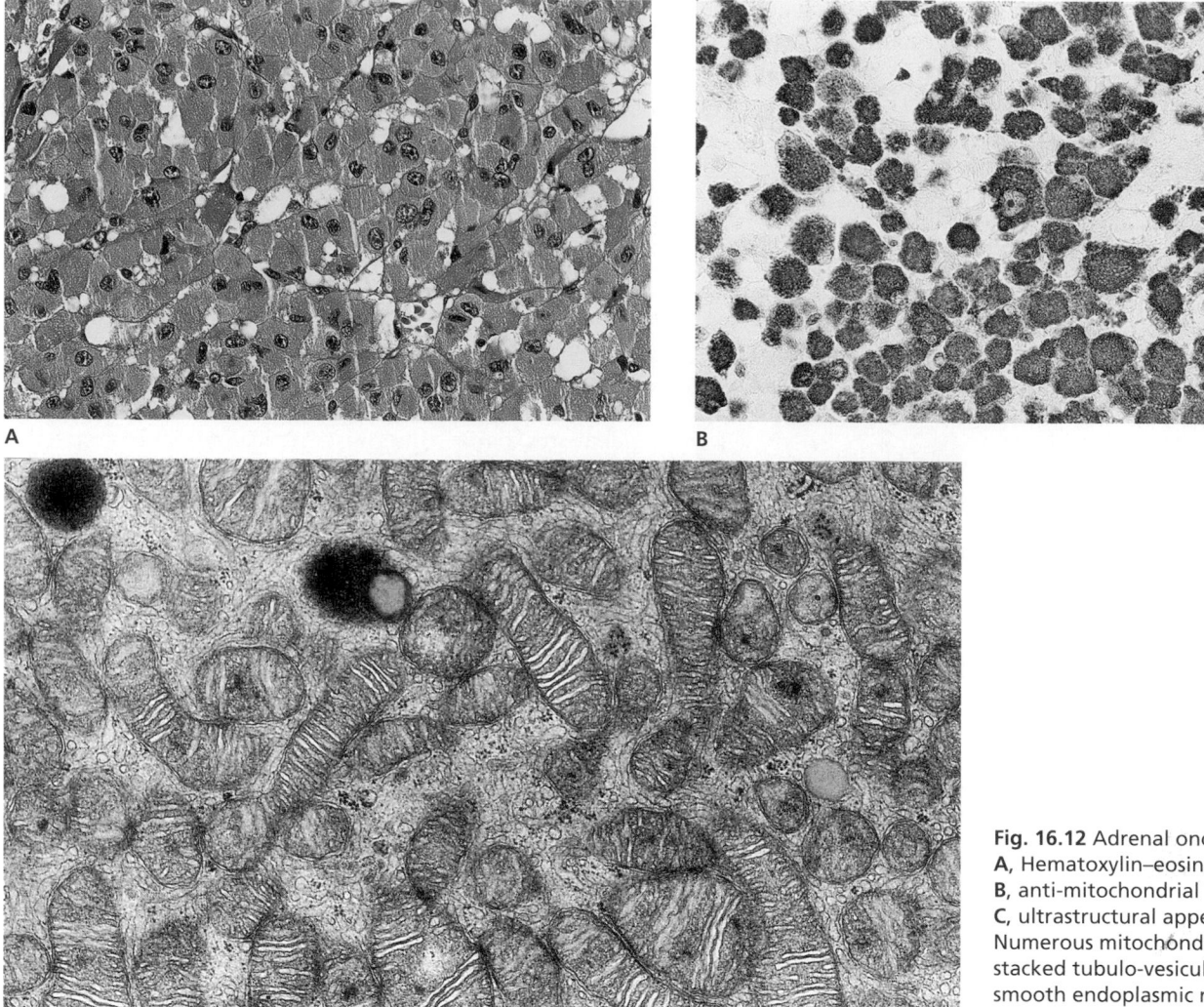

A

B

C

Fig. 16.12 Adrenal oncocytoma. **A**, Hematoxylin–eosin; **B**, anti-mitochondrial immunostain; **C**, ultrastructural appearance. Numerous mitochondria with stacked tubulo-vesicular cristae, smooth endoplasmic reticulum, and two lysosomes are illustrated. (×31,200; courtesy of Dr. Robert E. Erlandson, Memorial Sloan-Kettering Cancer Center)

Cytogenetically, gain of chromosome 17 seems to be an early event in adrenocortical neoplastic development.[107] Mutations of p53 occur in a minority of the cases (mainly malignant ones, see later section), and *ras* mutations have not been detected.[101]

An allegedly distinct transcriptional profile of adrenocortical tumors as determined by DNA microarray analysis has been described. This includes a several-fold differential expression of insulin-like growth factor, osteopontin and serine threonine kinase 15 genes in adrenocortical carcinomas when compared with normal adrenal cortex and adrenocortical adenomas.[89a]

Differential diagnosis

The principal differential diagnostic problems in this area are (1) between adrenocortical adenoma and carcinoma; (2) between adrenocortical carcinoma and renal cell carcinoma; (3) between adrenocortical and adrenomedullary tumors. Regarding the first, adenomas tend to

be smaller, more homogeneous, and lacking hemorrhage and necrosis.[109,131] Specifically, lesions under 50 g are generally cured by excision, even if exceptions occur.[117] Microscopically, mitotic activity (especially if accompanied by atypical forms) and venous invasion correlate best with recurrence or metastasis.[113,129,131,132,134] Weiss[134] listed the following microscopic criteria as suggestive of malignancy in an adrenocortical tumor (particularly when seen together): nuclear grade III or IV, mitotic rate greater than 5 per 50 high-power fields, atypical mitoses, paucity or absence of clear cells, diffuse architecture, necrosis, capsular invasion, and vascular (venous or sinusoidal) invasion. In his series, none of the 24 tumors with two or less of these criteria metastasized or recurred, whereas all but one of the 19 tumors with four or more of these criteria did. The value of this approach has been proven by independent observers, both in adults[107a,131a] and in children.[136a] Another feature suggestive of malignancy is spindling of the tumor cells.[122]

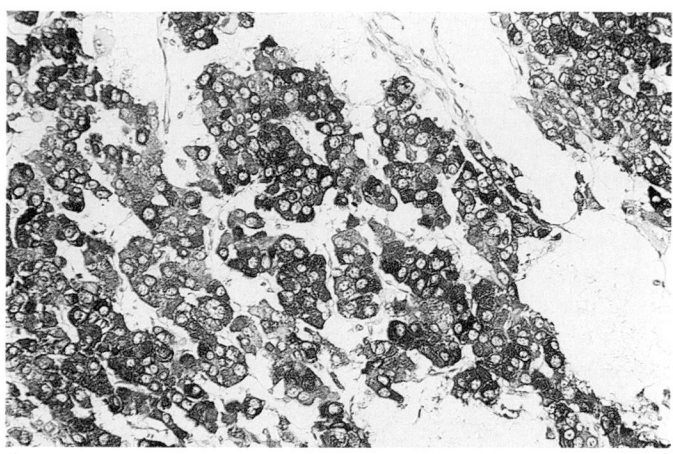

A

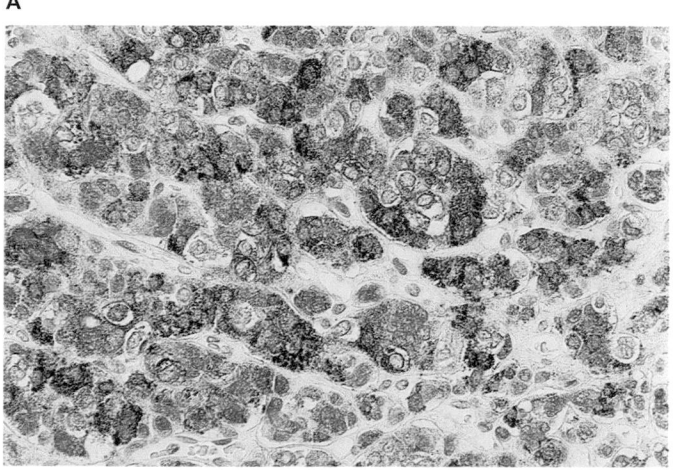

B

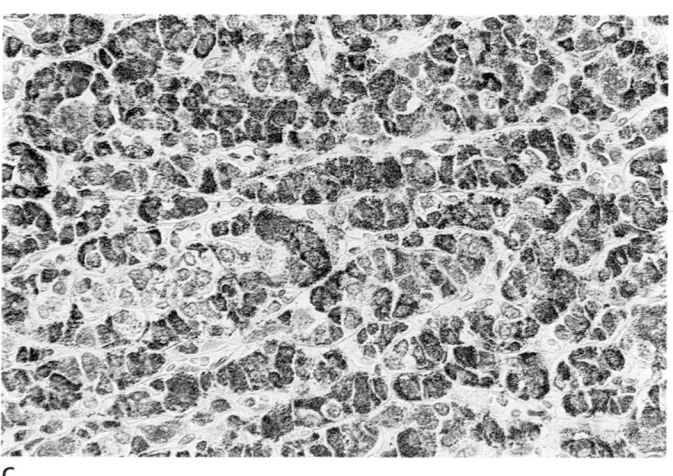

C

Fig. 16.13 Immunohistochemical reactivity of adrenal cortical neoplasm. **A**, Inhibin; **B**, Aloz; **C**, Melan-A.

Immunohistochemically, adrenal cortical adenomas show a greater expression of low-molecular-weight keratins and a lesser expression of vimentin than adrenal cortical carcinomas. Therefore an adrenocortical tumor that is strongly positive for vimentin and negative or only weakly positive for keratin is likely to be a carcinoma.[112,116]

Special techniques that have been tested as possible ancillary aids to this differential diagnosis include the search for aneuploidy by flow cytometry or cytophotometry (20% in adenomas versus almost 70% in carcinomas in one series[111,125]); AgNOR counts (of little practical value)[128]; Ki-67 (MIB-1) and DNA topoisomerase II alpha (higher in carcinoma than adenoma[107a,118,121,124]); overexpression of p53 (more frequent in carcinoma than adenoma[118,133]); telomerase activity (allegedly higher in the carcinomas[119]); and loss of heterozygosity (LOH) at the site of various gene markers.[115]

The fact that so many parameters have been evaluated for this purpose provides indirect evidence that none—short of detection of metastases—discriminates in an absolute fashion between adenomas and carcinomas, particularly in pediatric cases.[108,110,123] A combined evaluation of clinical features, size or weight, microscopic appearance, and immunohistochemical/molecular genetic data is necessary.[120,126,131,134] Even so, the pathologist and the clinician should accept the fact that a sharp distinction between adenomas and carcinomas may be impossible at the practical level and unsound at the conceptual level. Except for the cases situated at the two extremes, it may be more honest and accurate to designate the tumors as *adrenocortical neoplasms*, followed by an estimate of the risk of the tumor recurring or metastasizing on the basis of all the evaluable parameters, the list of which is likely to increase further in the next few years.

The second important differential diagnosis is between adrenocortical carcinoma and renal cell carcinoma, which can invade the adrenal gland directly or metastasize to it, either ipsilaterally or contralaterally.[137] Microscopically, these two tumors resemble each other a great deal. Two features favoring the diagnosis of renal cell carcinoma are the presence of glands (particularly if they contain numerous red blood cells) and abundant cytoplasmic glycogen, but neither is pathognomonic. Immunohistochemically, strong positivity for cytokeratin, EMA, CD10, and Lewis blood group isoantigen favors renal cell carcinoma,[136] whereas positivity for inhibin, A103, Melan-A (Mart-1), and synaptophysin favors adrenocortical carcinoma.[127] This also applies to fine needle aspiration specimens.[114,130]

Regarding the differential diagnosis between adrenocortical and adrenomedullary tumors (which can be very difficult but for some reason is rarely mentioned), the former should be favored in the presence of inhibin, Melan-A and calretinin positivity, whereas the latter is more likely if chromogranin reactivity is present; synaptophysin is of no help since it stains both tumor types.[137a]

Spread and metastases

Whereas adrenocortical adenoma is encapsulated, adrenocortical carcinoma often spreads to the retroperitoneum and infiltrates the kidney. Lymph node metastases are rare, but blood-borne metastases are frequent. They are already present at the time of the diagnosis in half of cases.[139] The most common sites of metastatic involvement are liver (60%), regional lymph nodes (40%), lungs (40%), peritoneal and pleural surfaces, and bone.[138,144] Poorly differentiated ("anaplastic") tumors also tend to metastasize to skin.[140] Some of these may masquerade as primary tumors in these sites.[142,143,145] Solitary lung metastases may benefit from surgical resection.[141]

Treatment and prognosis

The primary treatment of adrenocortical neoplasms is surgical excision.[149] Unfortunately, the carcinoma often recurs, and its radiosensitivity is usually poor.[146,151] Palliative results have been obtained with o,p-DDD and mitotane therapy, the latter being sometimes effective in controlling endocrine symptoms.[150,153,156] In most series, half of the patients are dead within 2 years of the onset of the symptoms, and the 5-year survival rate is between 20% and 35%.[150]

Some correlation exists between microscopic degree of differentiation in carcinoma and survival.[148] Proliferative activity—whether measured by counting mitoses or through other means—seems to be the pathologic feature of greatest prognostic significance.[157] In contrast with early reports, it would seem that flow cytometric DNA analysis is not a very effective predictor of clinical outcome in these tumors.[147,154,158]

Functional manifestations

Acquired hyperplasia, adenoma, and carcinoma may be "nonfunctioning," at least at a clinical level, or be the cause of various syndromes resulting from the secretion of excessive amounts of corticosteroid hormones.[160]

Sometimes, an adrenal lesion that is initially silent may later clinically result in hormonal manifestations.[159] A fairly accurate prediction regarding the morphologic type of abnormality in the adrenal gland can be made by knowing the clinical syndrome plus the age and sex of the patient.

Nonfunctioning lesions

Whereas instances of cortical hyperplasia and adenomas are found commonly at post mortem examination of asymptomatic individuals,[163] most of the nonfunctioning adrenal cortical lesions seen in the past as surgical specimens were carcinomas.[164] This has changed markedly since the advent of ultrasonography, CT, and MRI, which have allowed the detection of a large number of benign asymptomatic adrenocortical tumors.[161,166,167]

The lack of endocrine manifestations in some adrenocortical tumors—particularly carcinomas—has been explained by the fact that the malignant process is often accompanied by a deletion in some of the enzymes required for cortisol synthesis. It results in the production and release of steroid precursors such as dehydroepiandrosterone and 11-deoxycortisol (compound S). The presence of the latter is a consequence of a deficiency of the 11β-hydroxylase enzyme, which is a characteristic feature of adrenal carcinoma.[162,165]

The finding of a cortical adenoma in a hypertensive patient does not, in itself, imply any causal relationship.

Aldosteronism

In primary aldosteronism (Conn's syndrome), the excessive amount of secreted aldosterone results in urinary loss of potassium, retention of sodium, suppressed renin levels, hypertension, and muscle weakness.[172,173,187] The diagnosis should be suspected when hypokalemia is found in a patient with hypertension and is confirmed by demonstrating nonsuppressible aldosterone excretion in conjunction with normal cortisol excretion.[189] The adrenal lesion is an adenoma in over 70% of cases, cortical hyperplasia being responsible for most of the remaining, and carcinoma for exceedingly few.[185] The adenomas can usually be distinguished from the hyperplasias by a combination of clinical and laboratory parameters (including the ratio of plasma aldosterone to plasma renin activity),[174,186] but sometimes the morphologic features of one are associated with the biochemical features of the other.[170,179] A familial variety of primary aldosteronism has been described and includes both adrenocortical hyperplasia and adenoma.[175,176] Adrenal surgery is more likely to be beneficial in patients with adenoma than in those with hyperplasia. The adenoma is usually unilateral, solitary (91%), and small.[181] The cut surface has a homogeneous golden yellow or yellow–brown color. Only exceptionally is the tumor grossly of the so-called "black adenoma" type.[171]

Microscopically, one would expect these adenomas to have an appearance similar to that of the zona glomerulosa, since this is the area in which aldosterone is produced in the normal adrenal gland. Although this is sometimes the case, most of the tumor cells resemble those of the zona fasciculata or have characteristics intermediate between zona glomerulosa and zona fasciculata cells (so-called "hybrid cells") (Fig. 16.14). Ultrastructurally, most of the mitochondria in the tumor cells have lamellar cristae (characteristic of the zona glomerulosa),[180] but mitochondria with cristae of the tubulovesicular type (as in the normal zona fasciculata) also can be found.[183] The zona glomerulosa of the nontumoral gland is often atrophic, although it may be normal or even hyperplastic.[182] In patients who have been treated with spironolactone, a characteristic cytoplasmic structure may appear in the tumor cells, as well as in the cells of the adjacent zona glomerulosa. It is a whorled, multilaminar collection of membranes, as large as 20 μm in diameter, and is thought to derive from the smooth endoplasmic reticulum[168,184] (Fig. 16.15). Immunohistochemical positivity for aldosterone has been found in these bodies, suggesting that the hormone is bound to them.[178]

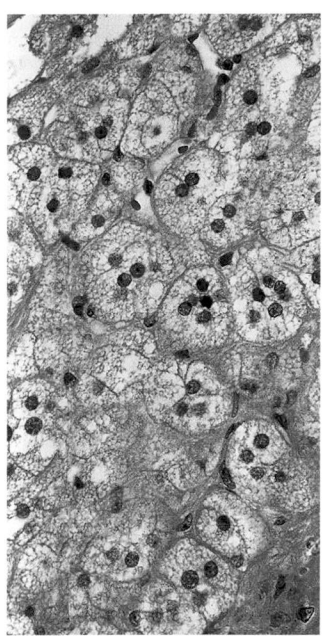 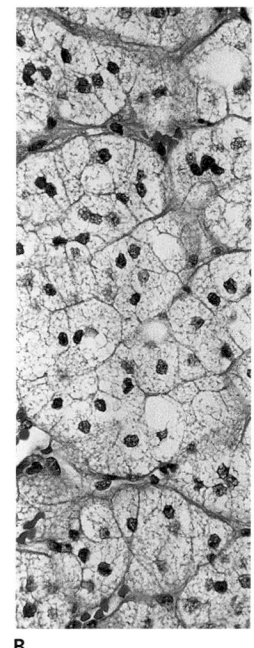 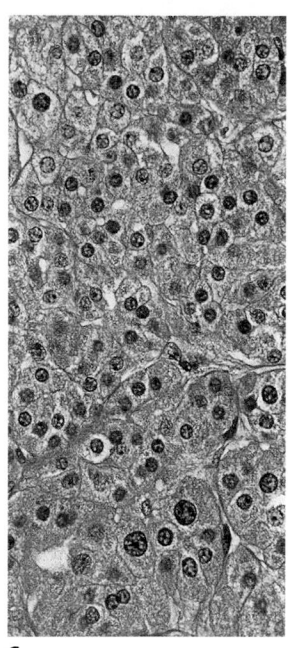

A   B   C

Fig. 16.14 A to **C**, Various morphologic patterns within the same aldosterone-secreting adrenal cortical adenoma.

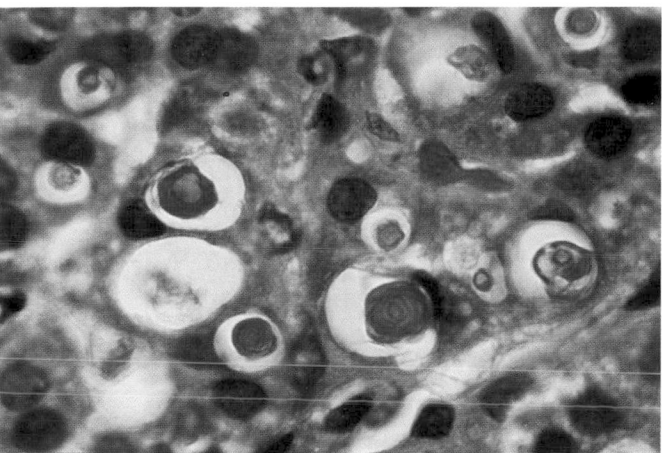

Fig. 16.15 So-called "spironolactone bodies." They appear as concentric laminated eosinophilic structures.

In most of the reported cases in which a cortical adrenal carcinoma has resulted in increased aldosterone production, secretion of other steroid hormones (such as deoxycorticosterone) was also found, thus excluding them as cases of pure primary aldosteronism.[169,185,188]

Proper evaluation of a patient suspected of having primary aldosteronism includes pharmacologic exploration of the renin–angiotensin–aldosterone system[6] and radiographic examination of the adrenal glands to distinguish primary aldosteronism from cases of renovascular and essential hypertension. A radioisotopic technique has been devised for visualization of the adrenal glands, based on the uptake and esterification of [131]I-19-iodocholesterol by the adrenal glands, which has led to the successful localization of aldosterone-producing adenomas.[177]

Cushing's syndrome

Cushing's syndrome is the result of hyperproduction of cortisol.[199] It has a primary adrenal cause in only 20% of cases.[200] Approximately 80% of patients are females. In only 20% of the cases does the syndrome occur before puberty. The abnormality encountered in the adrenal gland in cases of Cushing's syndrome may be (diffuse or nodular) hyperplasia, adenoma, or carcinoma (in that order of frequency), in both adults and children.[194,198,206] The hyperplasias are always bilateral. The adenomas and carcinomas are usually unilateral, although bilateral cases are on record.[191] In rare cases the adrenal neoplasm associated with Cushing's syndrome is not of cortical origin but rather a pheochromocytoma (see p. 1136).[195]

In cases of Cushing's syndrome-associated adrenal cortical tumor, the remaining adrenal cortex often shows signs of atrophy. The presence of a large adrenal mass in a patient with Cushing's syndrome is practically always indicative of carcinoma. Similarly, cases of Cushing's syndrome associated with obvious changes of virilization ("mixed" type) and markedly increased excretion of 17-ketosteroids are almost always the result of cortical carcinoma.[197,203]

Most carcinomas are easily demonstrated by routine intravenous pyelography because of their large size. In contrast, adenomas usually require a CT scan, MRI, or arteriography for their demonstration. CT is currently regarded as the most accurate imaging modality for the preoperative localization of these tumors.[204]

Most of the cases of *diffuse* cortical hyperplasia associated with Cushing's syndrome are the result of pituitary hyperfunction (ACTH dependent) and are referred to as *Cushing's disease*.[192] Other cases of diffuse cortical hyperplasia are secondary to the presence of nonpituitary

ACTH-producing neoplasms. A critical review of the pathology of these neoplasms was made in a classic article by Azzopardi and Williams.[193] In contrast to the then prevailing opinion that almost any type of tumor may result in the production of Cushing's syndrome, these authors showed that nearly all acceptable cases fall into four main categories: (1) small cell carcinoma of the lung; (2) endocrine tumors of foregut origin, such as carcinoid tumor of the lung, medullary carcinoma of the thyroid gland, and carcinoid tumor of the thymus; (3) pheochromocytoma and related tumors; and (4) certain ovarian tumors. The first two account for more than 90% of the acceptable cases. In this group of patients, hypokalemic alkalosis, very high urinary excretion of free cortisol, skin pigmentation, edema, and severe diabetes mellitus occur more frequently than in the cases caused by a primary adrenal lesion. Confirmation that the tumor is related to Cushing's syndrome requires remission of the syndrome after tumor resection and demonstration of an ACTH-like substance by immunocytochemistry or biochemical assay. Some of these tumors secrete not only ectopic ACTH but also a group of tumor peptides that stimulate the secretion of ACTH from the pituitary gland, thus contributing to the ectopic ACTH syndrome.[207]

As already indicated, cases of *nodular* adrenal hyperplasia are independent of ACTH production[190,196,205,209]; some of these are a component of Carney's syndrome[208] (see p. 1119).

Electron microscopic studies of cells from hyperplastic adrenal glands associated with Cushing's syndrome have shown mitochondria with tubulovesicular configuration of the cristae, consistent with elements of the zona fasciculata.[201] The treatment of choice of Cushing's syndrome resulting from primary adrenal disease is surgical. It consists of removal of the tumor in cases of adenoma or carcinoma and bilateral adrenalectomy in cases of hyperplasia.[202]

In patients without identifiable tumor preoperatively, adrenal exploration should be transabdominal. If one adrenal gland is found to be atrophic, there is probably a tumor on the opposite side. However, if one adrenal gland is normal or hyperplastic, the other gland may still contain a tumor. Frozen section examination is not a particularly helpful technique in determining whether a given adrenal gland is normal or atrophic.

Adrenogenital syndrome

Excess androgens secreted by an adrenal lesion bring about changes toward adult masculinity in male or female children and toward masculinity in female adults.[218] About 50% of the cases occur before puberty, and 80% of the patients are female.[215] In 1947 Patterson[217] devised a simple chemical test, the principle of which is still valid in differentiating virilizing adrenal tumors from cases of adrenal hyperplasia, interstitial cell tumor of the testis, and Sertoli–Leydig cell tumor of the ovary. It is based on the finding of the 17-ketosteroid hormone known as dehydroisoandrosterone. The rarest form of endocrine abnormality caused by an adrenal cortical lesion is feminization in a male adult accompanied by increased output of 17-ketosteroids.

The most common cause of virilization in childhood is congenital adrenal hyperplasia. However, if an adrenal neoplasm is present, it will be a carcinoma in most instances.[210,216] Virilization of adrenal origin in female adults is usually the result of secretion by the tumor of dehydroepiandrosterone and dehydroepiandrosterone sulfate (rather than testosterone, as usually seen with virilizing ovarian tumors)[212]; only exceptionally will adrenal tumors secrete testosterone in the absence of other assessable androgens.[211]

The probability that an adrenal cortical tumor is of a malignant nature is about 70% if it results in virilization in an adult woman, and even higher if the virilization is accompanied by Cushing's syndrome.[211,213] In adult male patients with feminization, the incidence of malignancy is nearly 100%.[214] In general, the adrenocortical carcinomas run a more aggressive clinical course in younger patients.

Other functional manifestations

Less common manifestations of adrenal cortical lesions (particularly carcinomas) include hypoglycemia,[221] polycythemia,[220] and inappropriate secretion of antidiuretic hormone.[219]

Lesions of adrenal medulla

Tumors and tumorlike conditions of the adrenal medulla segregate into two distinct categories, acknowledging the existence of hybrid and transitional forms:

1 **Embryonal neural (sympathetic system) tumors,** histologically represented by the categories of neuroblastoma, ganglioneuroblastoma and neuroblastoma. These are characteristically seen in infants and children, but they can also present in adults (particularly the more mature forms).
2 **Adult neuroendocrine tumors and tumorlike conditions,** represented by pheochromocytoma and adrenal medullary hyperplasia. These are characteristically seen in adults, although they can also appear in children (particularly if part of a genetically determined syndrome).

The first group of tumors, i.e., those belonging to the embryonal neural line, should be sharply distinguished from peripheral neuroectodermal tumors (PNETs)/ Ewing's sarcomas.[222] They exhibit a broad range of differentiation from neuroblastomas at one end, ganglioneuroma at the other, and ganglioneuroblastoma in between.[225,227] It should be realized that there is a continuum between these categories, both morphologically and at the level of developmental gene expression, so that a precise boundary line between them is difficult to draw.[223,224,226] These tumors can be found anywhere along the sympathetic chain, including the neck, mediastinum, and retroperitoneum. They are discussed here because many of them, particularly the poorly differentiated members of this family, arise within or close to the adrenal gland. The better differentiated the tumor and the older the patient, the less likely that the lesion will be located in the adrenal gland.

Neuroblastoma

General and clinical features

Neuroblastomas usually are seen in young children of both sexes; over 80% are detected in those under the age of 4 years, and the median age at diagnosis is 21 months. Typical examples in adults occur, but are exceptional.[228,232] Neuroblastomas can exhibit familial incidence[233]; be associated with the Beckwith–Wiedemann syndrome,[230] Hirschsprung's disease,[231] and other congenital abnormalities (especially if the tumor itself is congenital[229,236]); present in patients with neurofibromatosis[237]; or occur as a complication of fetal hydantoin syndrome.[234] The usual presentation of neuroblastoma is in the form of an abdominal mass first noted by the parents. Rare cases have been reported associated with watery diarrhea (although not nearly as commonly as with ganglioneuroma), Cushing's syndrome, heterochromia iridis and Horner's syndrome (in cervical or mediastinal tumors), opsoclonus/myoclonus (thought to be a paraneoplastic, perhaps autoimmune syndrome), and several other manifestations.[231a] About 70% of the neuroblastomas occur in the retroperitoneum, and the majority of these involve the adrenal gland. Synchronous or metachronous bilaterality is extremely unusual.[235]

Morphologic features

Grossly, neuroblastomas are usually large, soft, gray, and relatively well circumscribed; areas of hemorrhage, necrosis, and calcification are often present (Fig. 16.16). Sometimes the hemorrhage is so extensive as to mimic a hematoma. Cystic degeneration can also occur, to the point of simulating the appearance of an adrenal cyst. Multifocality is present in less than 10% of the cases.[240]

Microscopically, the pattern of growth is vaguely nodular as a result of the presence of delicate, incomplete fibrous septa. Hemorrhage, which is common, occasionally leads to the formation of pseudovascular or alveolar structures. Calcification may be a prominent feature; it may appear as a dustlike basophilic stippling, as closely aggregated round concretions, or surrounding individual tumor cells in a "chicken wire" fashion. Necrosis is also a rather constant feature, sometimes leaving viable tumor cells grouped around blood vessels. The tumor cells are small and regular, with round, deeply staining

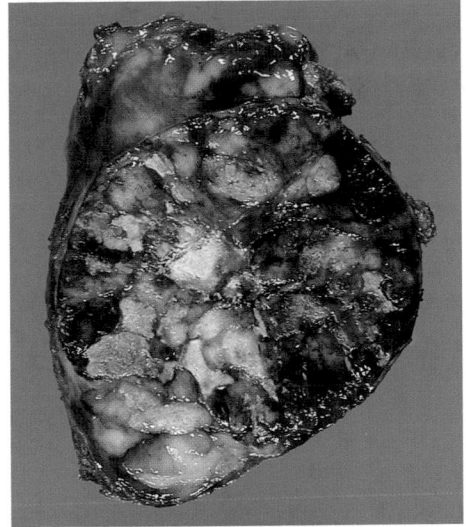

A

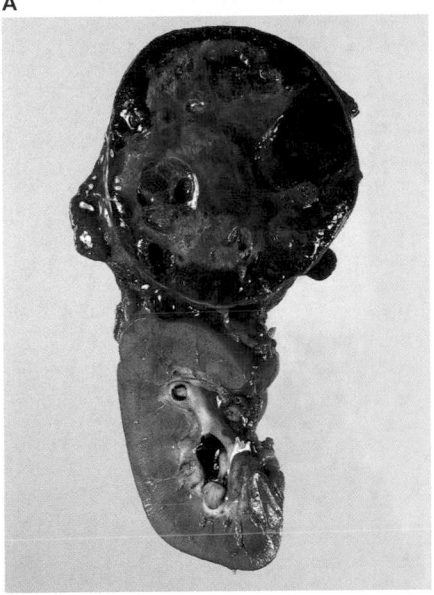

B

Fig. 16.16 A and B, Gross appearance of adrenal neuroblastoma. The tumor shown in A exhibits a variegated appearance resulting from hemorrhage and necrosis. The tumor displayed in B shows the typical location above the upper pole of the kidney, which is uninvolved. (B, Courtesy of Dr RA Cooke, Brisbane, Australia; From Cooke RA, Stewart B: Colour Atlas of Anatomical Pathology, Edinburgh, Churchill Livingstone, 2004)

nuclei slightly larger than lymphocytes. There is little cytoplasm, and cytoplasmic outlines are poorly defined. Homer Wright's rosettes are present in about a fourth to a third of the cases; they are characterized by collections of tumor cells not related to blood vessels, arranged around a central area filled with a fibrillary material[241] (Fig. 16.17). The latter is composed of a tangled mass of neurites as revealed by silver stains, immunohistochemistry, or electron microscopy. In contrast to the structures formed by retinoblastomas, ependymomas, and carcinoid tumors, the rosettes of neuroblastomas do not have a central lumen. On occasion, the lobular pattern just described becomes prominent, the tumor nests being

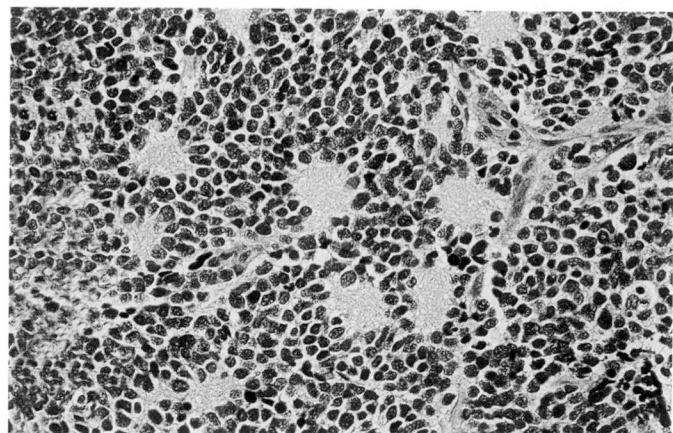

Fig. 16.17 Homer Wright rosettes in neuroblastoma. Note the absence of a central lumen.

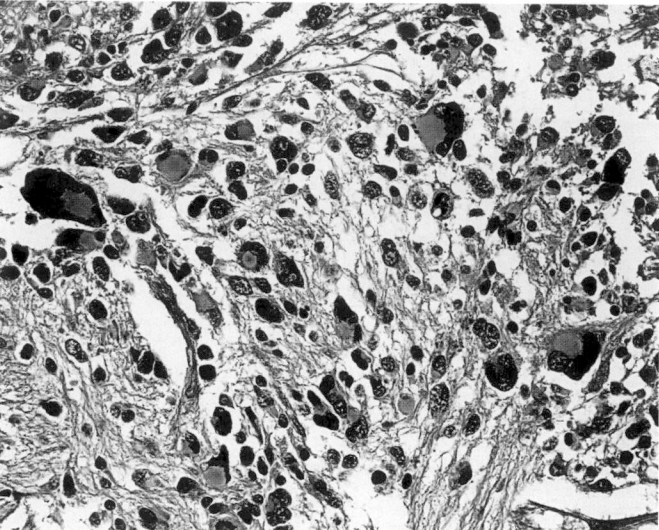

Fig. 16.18 So-called "anaplastic neuroblastoma."

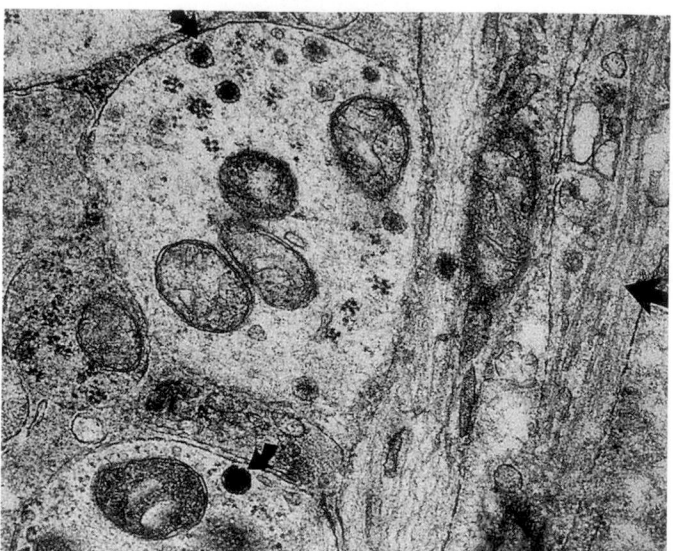

Fig. 16.19 Electron micrograph of adrenal neuroblastoma, removed from a 3-year-old male. These are 100-nm neurosecretory granules (short arrows) and microtubules (large arrow). (×36,400; courtesy of Dr. Robert E. Erlandson, Memorial Sloan-Kettering Cancer Center)

surrounded by elongated S-100 protein-positive cells in a "Zellballen" configuration reminiscent of that seen in paraganglia and paragangliomas.[239] A rare pleomorphic form of neuroblastoma characterized by the presence of bizarre giant tumor cells has been described (Fig. 16.18).[238]

Morphologic variations and subtypes of neuroblastoma that relate to the degree of differentiation of the tumor and have a bearing on prognosis are discussed on p. 1129.

Electron microscopic, histochemical, immunohistochemical, and molecular genetic features

Ultrastructurally, neuroblastoma cells are characterized by the presence of neurites, neurosecretory granules, and synaptic endings (Fig. 16.19).[255,258] The neurites form a complex interdigitating meshwork in the center of the Homer Wright rosettes.

Immunohistochemically, neuroblastoma cells express neuron-specific enolase, neurofilaments, neurofilament-66/α-internexin, peripherin, chromogranin, synaptophysin, secretogranin II, vasoactive intestinal peptide, microtubule-associated proteins, NB-84, nerve growth factor receptors, and other neural-related antigens,[242,250,254,259,263,265,267,268–271,276–278,280] including the cell surface ganglioside GD_2.[274] These, together with molecular techniques, are of great use in the differential diagnosis between neuroblastoma and other small cell (blue cell, round cell) tumors of infancy, such as rhabdomyosarcoma, Ewing's sarcoma/PNET, and malignant lymphoma.[268,276] Caution should be exercised in the interpretation of results obtained using polyclonal antibodies against neuron-specific enolase[249]; we have obtained somewhat more satisfactory results with a set of monoclonal antibodies against this marker.[275] The anti-neuroblastoma antibody NB-84 has also proved less than specific, in that it also stains several other types of small blue round cell tumors.[251,264] Expression of insulin-like growth factor 2 in neuroblastomas seems associated with a lobular growth pattern and good cytologic differentiation.[257]

The recently described Trk receptor protein has been found in neuroblastomas (especially those with favorable histology) by Northern analysis and immunohistochemistry.[243a,248] Neuroblastomas produce catecholamines, which can be demonstrated in sections or touch preparations by the technique of formaldehyde-induced fluorescence.[247,273] Along similar lines, expression of genes involved in catecholamine biosynthesis can be demonstrated with the PCR technique.[253]

Two characteristic genetic events in neuroblastomas are the loss of a critical region on the distal short arm of chromosome 1 and amplification of the N-*myc* oncogene[244,246,256]; these two events are related, with LOH for chromosome 1p preceding the development of amplification.[243,243a,252] Other genetic abnormalities sometimes found in this tumor include gain of chromosome 17, hyperploidy or near triploidy, and defects in expression or function of the nerve growth factor receptor.[245,262,272] Mutations of the p53 and *ras* genes are found only rarely.[260,266,279] Curiously, most neuroblastoma cell lines that have been tested have shown to express *ALK* transcripts and ALK protein.[261]

In situ, regressing, and maturing neuroblastoma

Collections of neuroblasts resembling small neuroblastomas are often seen as incidental findings at autopsy and have been regarded by some authors as in situ neoplasms.[283,286] The fact that in most reported cases the infants were less than 3 months of age suggests either that the process was not neoplastic[291] or, if it was, that it resolved spontaneously.[281,282]

Neuroblastomas can undergo extensive necrosis, to the point of rendering the microscopic diagnosis impossible. At least in some cases this seems to be the result of massive apoptosis.[285]

In other instances, typical symptomatic neuroblastomas, even accompanied by metastatic disease, are seen to undergo complete maturation that results in a spontaneous cure. In vitro maturation of neuroblastoma is a well-documented phenomenon that has been used sometimes as a diagnostic aid. Neurites may develop spontaneously within 24 hours[287,288] or may be induced with chemical agents such as retinoic acid.[289,290] Neuroblastomas can also be maintained in a functional state when xenotransplanted in nude mice.[284]

Spread and metastases

Adrenal neuroblastomas locally invade the surrounding tissues. They may show intraspinal (dumbbell) extension[294] or spread into the kidney. The most common sites of distant metastases are liver (so-called "Pepper's syndrome"), skeletal system (particularly skull and orbit; so-called "Hutchison's syndrome"), lymph nodes, ovary, testis and paratesticular region, and central nervous system.[295,297,298] Bone metastases are usually multiple and sometimes symmetrical, a point to remember in the differential diagnosis with Ewing's sarcoma (Fig. 16.20). Lung metastases are rare. Most recurrences and metastases develop within 2 years after excision of the primary tumor, but occasional instances of very late recurrences are on record.[292] The pattern of tumor metastases is altered by the therapy.[293]

Morphologic evaluation of bone marrow for neuroblastoma cells is a routine component of clinical staging. The use of immunostains to increase the yield of detection has been advocated.[296]

Therapy and prognosis

The treatment of neuroblastoma depends on the stage of the disease, and it includes surgical excision, multiagent chemotherapy, and bone marrow transplantation.[301,316] The overall 3-year survival rate for patients with neuroblastoma is around 30%[350] and has changed relatively little during the past two decades. The prognosis is related to several factors, many of which are clearly interrelated.[307,317,327,339]

1   *Age of the patient.* Children under 2 years of age at the time of diagnosis have the best prognosis.[311,324] The rare neuroblastomas occurring in adolescents and adults tend to run an indolent course, but their ultimate prognosis is poor.[318]

2   *Location of the tumor.* Extra-adrenal tumors have a better outlook; this is probably related to the fact that they tend to be better differentiated.

3   *Surgical staging* (see Appendix C). The prognosis is directly related to the stage of the disease. It decreases from 90% in stage I to 2.4% in stage IV, except for a subtype of stage IV known as *S* (for *special*). This subtype, which apparently lacks the chromosomal abnormalities of other stage IV neuroblastomas, is associated with frequent spontaneous remissions and a 60% to 90% survival rate.[348,349] It is defined as having distant metastases in liver, skin, and/or bone marrow without radiologic or other evidence of bone metastases, and it accounts for 8% to 12% of all cases.[321] However, even within this group there is a subset with poor prognosis.[329]

4   *Microscopic grading.* Several grading systems have been proposed for neuroblastoma over the years, largely based on microscopic criteria but sometimes also incorporating clinical parameters (e.g., age at the time of diagnosis)[323,324a,325,326,330,331,343,346] (Table 16.1). Since one of the most important microscopic items is the degree of differentiation, all of these grading schemes inevitably overlap with the classification scheme of these tumors in relation to the neuroblastoma–ganglioneuroblastoma–ganglioneuroma spectrum.[345] Thus, in the typical neuroblastoma, differentiation as judged by standard light microscopic features is either absent or limited to less than 5% of the tumor. This neoplasm has been designated in the various grading schemes as undifferentiated, classic, grade III to IV, or stroma-poor neuroblastoma.[346] Neuroblastomas having a neuropil background are referred to as *poorly differentiated* if only 5% or less of the tumor cell population shows features of differentiation toward ganglion cells, and as *differentiating* if the neuropil is more abundant and, more importantly, if over 5% of the tumor cells show differentiation toward ganglion cells.[344,346,347] Differentiating neuroblasts are recognized because of their enlarged, eccentric nucleus with a vesicular chromatin pattern and usually a single prominent nucleolus, and a conspicuous, acidophilic or amphophilic cytoplasm. The differentiating form of

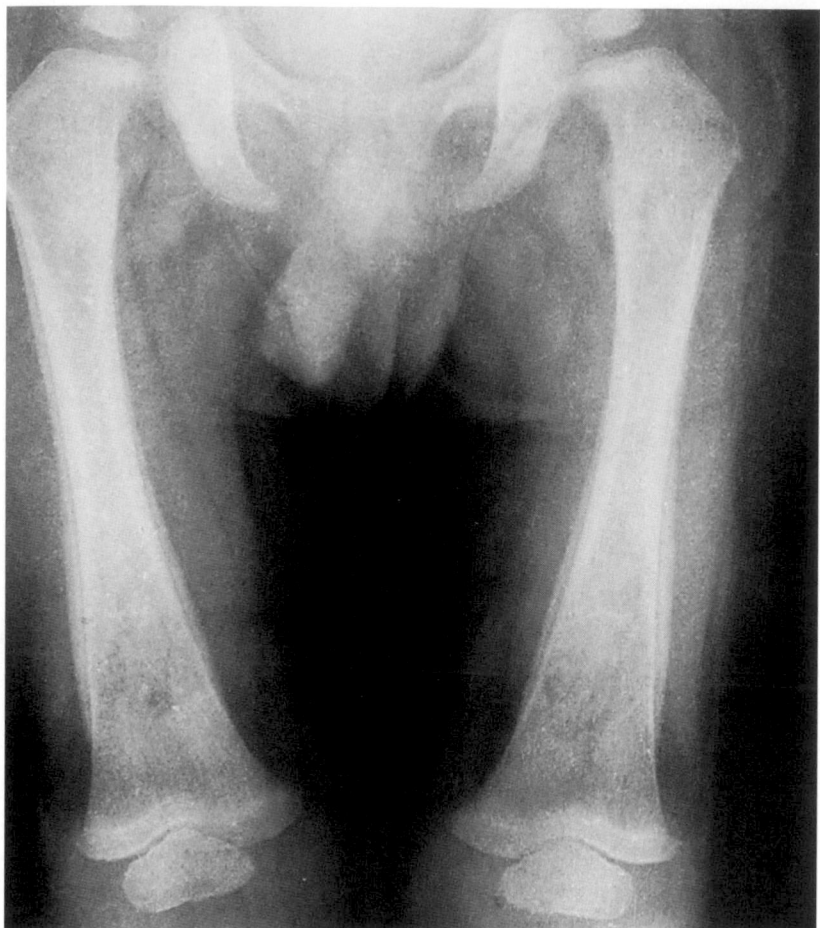

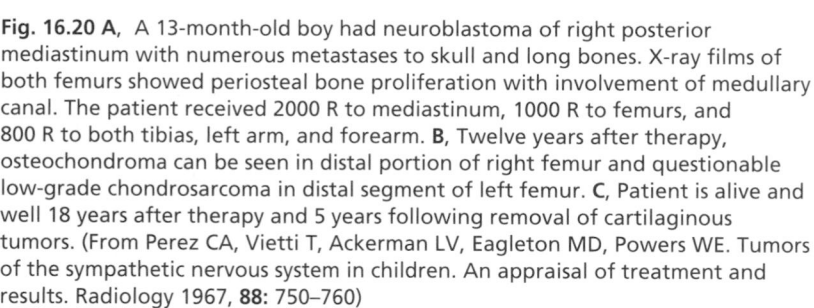

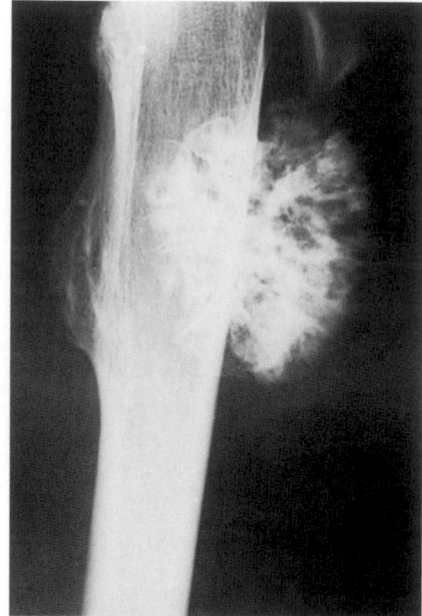

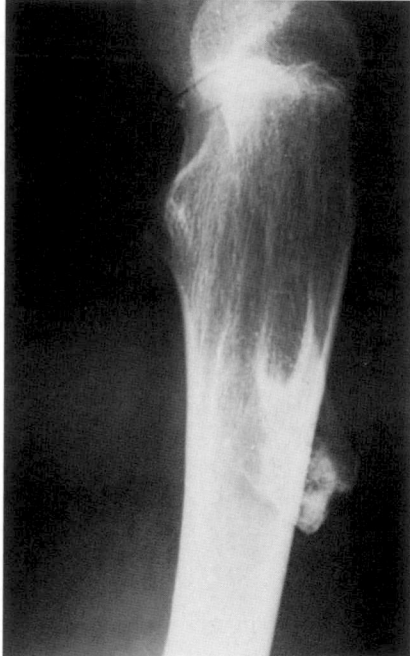

Fig. 16.20 A, A 13-month-old boy had neuroblastoma of right posterior mediastinum with numerous metastases to skull and long bones. X-ray films of both femurs showed periosteal bone proliferation with involvement of medullary canal. The patient received 2000 R to mediastinum, 1000 R to femurs, and 800 R to both tibias, left arm, and forearm. **B,** Twelve years after therapy, osteochondroma can be seen in distal portion of right femur and questionable low-grade chondrosarcoma in distal segment of left femur. **C,** Patient is alive and well 18 years after therapy and 5 years following removal of cartilaginous tumors. (From Perez CA, Vietti T, Ackerman LV, Eagleton MD, Powers WE. Tumors of the sympathetic nervous system in children. An appraisal of treatment and results. Radiology 1967, **88:** 750–760)

neuroblastoma clearly merges with the ganglioneuroblastoma (see later section). All of the three grades of neuroblastoma above described are regarded as schwannian stroma-poor tumors.[344] Several series have shown a good correlation between the degree of microscopic differentiation in neuroblastoma as defined above and the prognosis.[300,320,323,331,347] Neuroblastoma and the neuroblastomatous areas of the nodular subtype of ganglioneuroblastoma should be further evaluated for prognostic purposes by either counting mitoses (10 contiguous HPFs at ×400 magnification) or by determining the mitosis–karyorrhexis index (MKI), using 5000 tumor cells as the denominator. Both of these measurements have been shown to correlate with outcome.[328,344,346,352a]

5 *Proliferative activity.* Ki-67 (MIB-1) scores have been shown to have statistically significant prognostic value in multivariate analysis.[338]

6 *Tumor angiogenesis.* The claim has been made that the degree of vascularization of neuroblastoma correlates with N-*myc* amplification, metastatic disease, and poor outcome,[333] but others have failed to validate these results.[306]

7 *CD44.* The presence of this cell surface glycoprotein is a marker of aggressiveness in neuroblastoma that usually correlates with N-*myc* amplification.[314]

Table 16.1 Major grading systems proposed for neuroblastoma

Beckwith and Martin (1968)[302]

Grade	Percentage of differentiated elements	Survival
I	Over 50%	100%
II	5 to 50%	75%
III	Under 5%	32%
IV	Zero	4%

Hughes, Marsden, and Palmer (1974)[323]

Grade	Description	Survival
I	Mixed pattern of undifferentiated cells and fully differentiated (mature) ganglion cells	69%
II	Mixed pattern of undifferentiated cells and cells with partial ganglionic differentiation	14%
III	Undifferentiated cells without any evidence of differentiation	10%

Shimada et al. (1984)[347]

Stroma-rich

Type	Description	Survival
Well-differentiated	Few randomly distributed aggregated of immature neuroblastic cells that do not form nests	100%
Intermixed	Immature neuroblastic cells arranged in sharply defined nests	92%
Nodular	Nodules of undifferentiated neuroblastic cells	18%

Stroma-rich

Age	Differentiation*	MKI†	Prognostic group	Survival
<1.5 yr	Any	<200	Favorable	84%
		>200	Unfavorable	4.5%
	Differentiated	<100	Favorable	84%
1.5–4 yr		>100	Unfavorable	4.5%
	Undifferentiated	Any	Unfavorable	4.5%
>5 yr	Any	Any	Unfavorable	4.5%

*Micosis karyorrhectic index (MKI): number of karyorrhectic cells based on 5000 cell counts in random fields: low (<100), intermediate (100–200), high (>200), †Undifferentiated (<5% differentiated elements); differentiated (>5% differentiated elements).

Joshi et al. (1992)[325,326]

Grade	Description	Age	Prognostic group
I	Low mitotic rate (<10/10 HPF) and calcification	Any	Low
II	Low mitotic rate (<10/10 HPF) or calcification	<1 yr	Low
III	High mitotic rate (>10/10 HPF) and no calcification	Any	High

International Neuroblastoma Pathology Committee (1999)[344,345]

Schwannian (ganglioneuromatous) development	Category and subtype (see text)
	Neuroblastoma (Schwannian stroma-poor)
None to minimal	Undifferentiated
	Poorly differentiated
None to minimal to <50% of the tumor tissue	Differentiating
>50% of the tumor tissue	Ganglioneuroblastoma, intermixed (Schwannian stroma-rich)
	Ganglioneuroma (Schwannian stroma-dominant)
Dominant	Maturing[a]
	Mature
Proportion of Schwannian stroma-rich/stroma dominant and stroma-poor (nodular) areas, variable	Ganglioneuroblastoma, nodular (Composite Schwannian stroma-rich/stroma-dominant and stroma-poor)

[a]This subtype is termed "borderline" ganglioneuroblastoma, according to the Joshi classification.[325,326]

8 *Telomerase activity.* There is a significant association between telomerase activity and poor outcome.[337]

9 *Lymphocytic infiltration.* Infiltration by mature lymphocytes around the tumor is a seemingly favorable prognostic sign.

10 *S-100 protein-positive cells.* In the undifferentiated neuroblastoma, the total absence of these cells (which are presumably a component of the immune system and evidence of host reaction to the tumor) is said to be associated with a decreased survival.[334,346]

11 *Low urinary VMA/HVA ratio.* A VMA/HVA ratio of less than 1 is an unfavorable prognostic sign. This is related to a reported relative deficiency of dopamine β-hydroxylase activity in the more primitive and aggressive neoplasms.

12 *Tumor-associated serum markers.* Increased serum levels of NSE, ferritin, lactate dehydrogenase, chromogranin A, and creatine kinase BB are associated with advanced stage disease and adverse outcome.[354]

13 *Ganglioside composition.* The absence of the ganglioside known as Gt1b seems to indicate a poor prognosis.[340,353]

14 *Flow cytometric DNA pattern.* A favorable clinical outcome has been found in association with an aneuploid stem line and a low percentage of tumor cells in the S, G_2, and M phases of the cell cycle.[308,319] The non-aneuploid tumors secrete higher levels of DOPA, dopamine, and HVA and are more likely to present in higher clinical stages.[299] Diploid tumors tend to exhibit an unfavorable histology and high proliferative activity.[313]

15 *Cytogenetic aberrations.* Allelic loss of chromosome 1p and gain of chromosome arm 17q are strong predictors of unfavorable outcome.[305,309]

16 *N-myc amplification.* Amplification of the N-*myc* oncogene, which occurs in approximately 25% of the cases, is associated with rapid clinical progression.[303,332,341,352] This also applies to stage IV cases[304] but not to stage IVS patients.[351] This amplification can be rapidly detected by fluorescent in situ hybridization or with the PCR technique,[315,342] and the N-*myc* protein product can be detected immunohistochemically.[322]

17 *Expression of bcl-2.* Expression of the apoptosis-suppressing protein bcl-2 is associated with unfavorable histology, N-*myc* amplification, and poor prognosis.[310]

18 *P-glycoprotein.* High expression of this multidrug resistance protein is a predictor of poor outcome in neuroblastoma.[312,336]

19 Trk *gene expression.* High levels of expression of the *Trk* gene, which encodes the nerve growth factor receptor, have been found to correlate with favorable outcome.[335]

20 Factors that do not significantly influence prognosis are the patient's sex, and nodal status at diagnosis.[350]

Ganglioneuroblastoma

Ganglioneuroblastomas (formerly also known as malignant ganglioneuromas) are tumors exhibiting a degree of differentiation that is intermediate between neuroblastoma and ganglioneuroma. Most of them are seen in young children, but typical examples in adults are on record. In contrast to neuroblastomas, most of the neoplasms are located in the retroperitoneum or mediastinum rather than in the adrenal gland; thus their distribution approaches that of ganglioneuroma (Fig. 16.21). Their gross appearance varies, depending on the subtype and extent of differentiation; in general, they have a more homogeneous appearance and firmer consistency than neuroblastomas. Calcification is very common.

Microscopically, two distinct varieties can be recognized. In one, sometimes designated as *intermixed, schwannian stroma-rich,* or imperfect, there are all stages of neuronal differentiation throughout the neoplasm. This may lead to the formation of collections of ganglion cells, many of them immature, multinucleated, or otherwise abnormal. A fine, fibrillary, cobwebby network is seen between masses of cells (Figs 16.22 and 16.23); this material, which represents an important diagnostic feature of ganglioneuroblastomas, is made up of large numbers of neurites emanating from the tumor cells, with occasional formation of synaptic junctions.[359] As already indicated, it is likely that this variety of ganglioneuroblastoma and the previously mentioned "differentiating neuroblastoma" represent slightly different stages of the maturing process undergone by some neuroblastomas. The authors who prefer to draw a distinction between the two tumors will designate as differentiating neuroblastomas the tumors that show

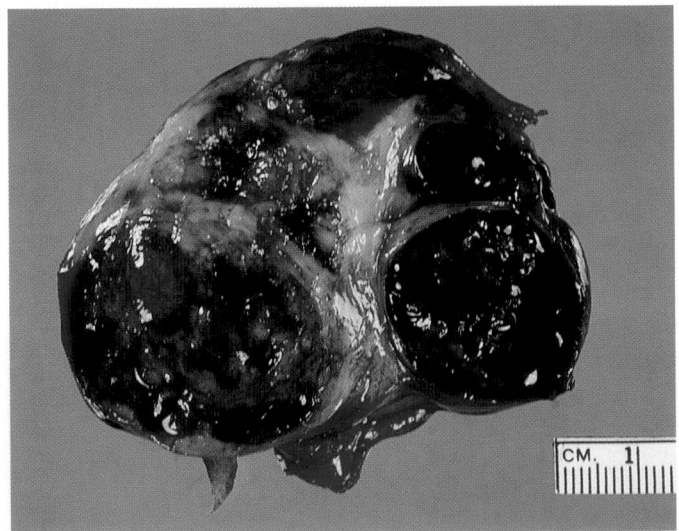

Fig. 16.21 Gross appearance of ganglioneuroblastoma. The dark red hemorrhagic areas represent poorly differentiated foci, whereas the intervening whitish areas correspond to better differentiated ganglioneuroma-like elements.

more than 5% ganglion cells but no *predominant* (over 50%) ganglioneuromatous component, and as ganglioneuromas the tumors in which such a component is present.[357]

The second variety of ganglioneuroblastoma (known as *nodular, composite schwannian stroma-rich/stroma dominant and stroma poor*), or *immature*, is easier to define and recognize. Basically, it has the gross and microscopic appearance of a ganglioneuroma except for the presence of well-defined, highly cellular areas of neuroblastoma. In contrast to the neuronal cells, the Schwann cell elements are cytogenetically normal, and are therefore thought to be non-neoplastic in nature.[355] One should be careful not to confuse perivascular collections of lymphocytes (often present in these neoplasms) with foci of neuroblasts. The boundaries between the two patterns tend to be quite sharp. The difference between these two varieties could be expressed by saying that the first is overwhelmingly formed by cells of intermediate differentiation, whereas the second is largely made up of the two extremes of the differentiation sequence.

Ultrastructural studies of ganglioneuroblastomas confirm the better differentiated nature of this tumor as compared with neuroblastoma. Tangled unmyelinated cell processes are seen running through a maze of Schwann cells; neurosecretory granules and neurotubules are easily found in the cytoplasm and in extensions of the tumor cells.[359] Immunohistochemically, ganglion cell differentiation correlates with the presence of cathepsin D as detected immunohistochemically.[358]

The prognosis for ganglioneuroblastoma is appreciably better than that for (undifferentiated) neuroblastoma.

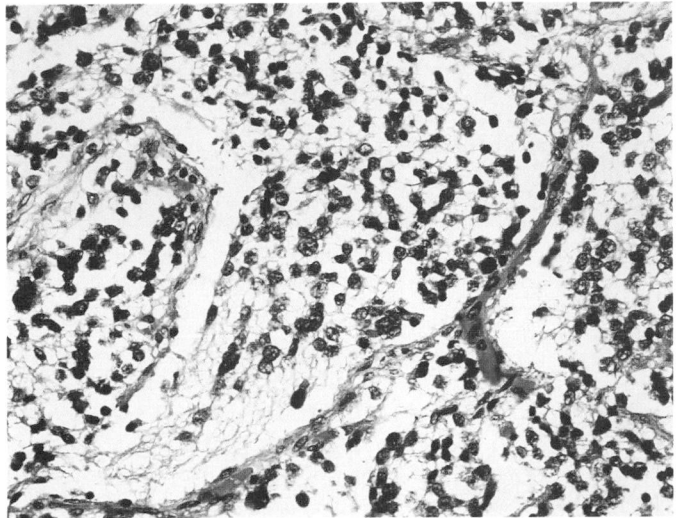

Fig. 16.22 The differentiating quality of this neuroblastoma is manifested through the formation of a fine eosinophilic network between the tumor cell nuclei ("neuropil").

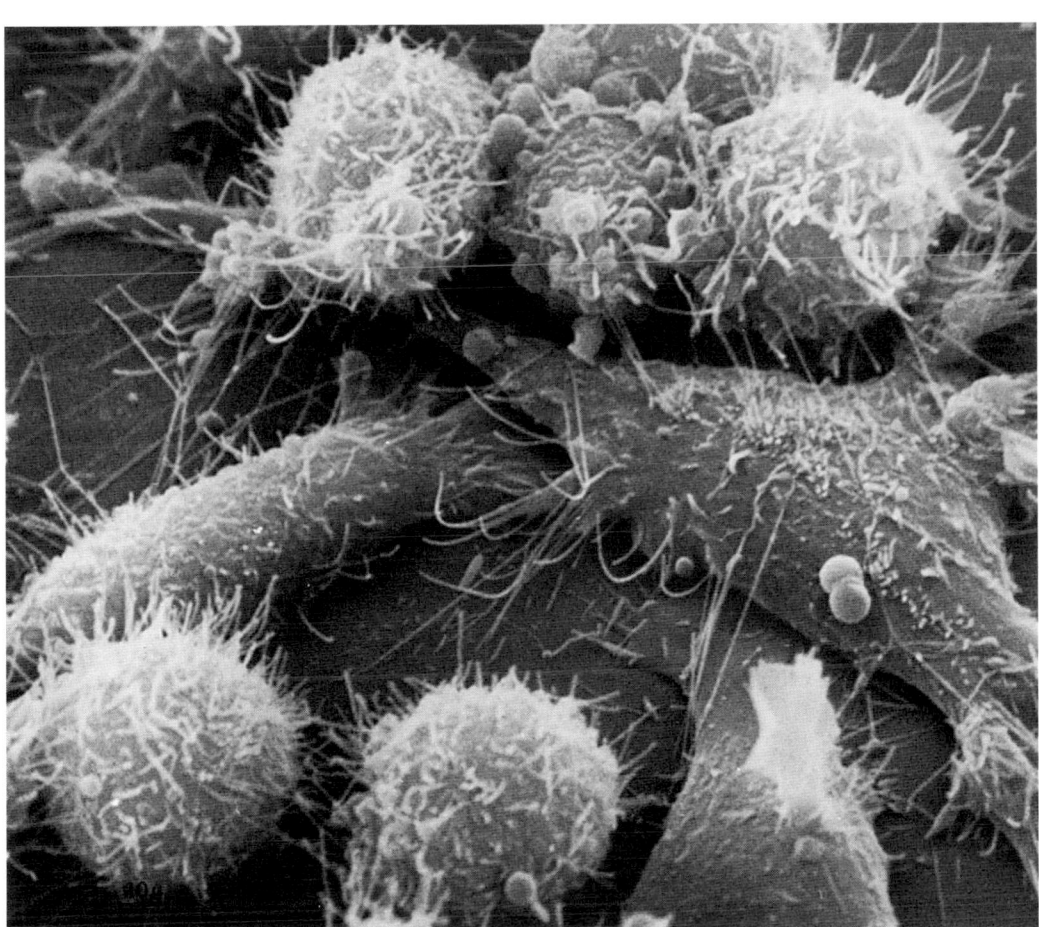

Fig. 16.23 Scanning electron micrograph of established line of mouse neuroblastoma that first appeared in sympathetic ganglion of A/J mouse. Spherical cells are probably in G_1 phase of cell cycle. Others are in late G, or S. Filiform cytoplasmic prolongations are extremely numerous. Some probably correspond to dendrites and axons. (Courtesy of Dr. V. Fonte and Dr. K. Porter, Boulder, CO)

Among the ganglioneuroblastomas, the prognosis is worse for the immature (composite) than for the imperfect variety, especially when the neuroblastoma component is in the form of nodular aggregates.[356] Not surprisingly, these ganglioneuroblastomas are amenable to the same prognostic evaluation employed for neuroblastoma, i.e., by taking into account the patient's age, the degree of neuroblastic differentiation, and the mitosis–karyorrhexis index.[360]

Ganglioneuroma

Ganglioneuromas represent the fully differentiated members of the group and are invariably benign. They are seen in an older age group than the preceding tumors and constitute the most common neoplasm of the sympathetic nervous system in adults. They can be multiple and/or associated with other independent types of neural/neuroendocrine neoplasms, such as neuroblastoma and pheochromocytoma. They are only rarely found in the adrenal gland, their most common location being the posterior mediastinum and retroperitoneum. Grossly, they are large, encapsulated masses of firm consistency with a homogeneous, solid, grayish white cut surface having a focally edematous appearance (Fig. 16.24). Thorough sampling for microscopic examination is crucial; areas of different color or consistency, especially if friable or hemorrhagic, are particularly suspicious for harboring less differentiated foci, which, if present, would place the tumor into a ganglioneuroblastoma category. Microscopically, the overall appearance of a ganglioneuroma resembles that of a neurofibroma (hence its designation as a schwannian stroma-dominant tumor) except for the presence of numerous collections of abnormal but fully mature ganglion cells, often having more than one nucleus (Fig. 16.25). If every single ganglion cell is mature, the ganglioneuroma is designated as the *mature* subtype; if, instead, there is a minor component of scattered collections of differentiating neuroblasts and/or maturing ganglion cells, the tumor is named the *maturing* subtype. It should be obvious that the latter blends with the intermixed subtype of ganglioneuroblastoma, from which it differs in that the immature foci do not form distinct microscopic nests.[368] Ultrastructurally, the resemblance to normal sympathetic ganglion cells is striking[369] (Fig. 16.26).

Exceptionally, the Schwann cell component of the ganglioneuroma may show features of a malignant nerve sheath tumor.[362]

Catecholamine synthesis is an almost constant feature of all the tumors in this series. It rarely leads to hypertension but has provided very sensitive tests for their detection. Most of the production is in the form of catecholamine precursors, leading to the excretion of vanilmandelic acid, homovanillic acid, and other products in the urine. There is considerable variation in the relative production of these substances by a given tumor,

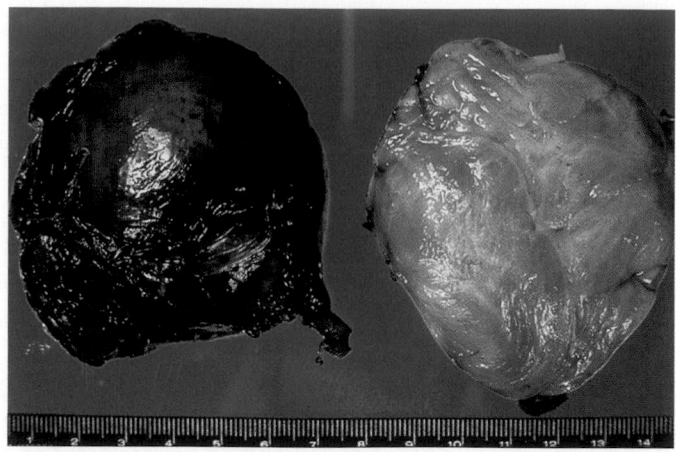

Fig. 16.24 Outer aspect and cut surface of ganglioneuroma. The tumor is well circumscribed and has a whitish, slightly mucoid appearance.

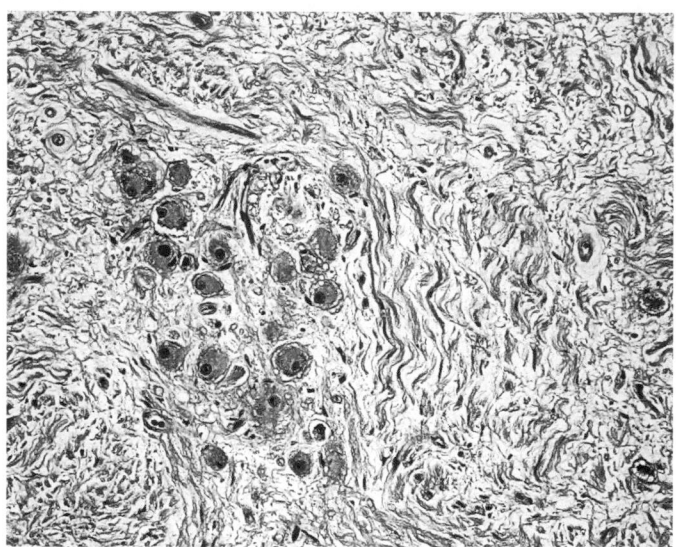

Fig. 16.25 Ganglioneuroma of adrenal gland showing clusters of mature ganglion cells surrounded by fascicles of Schwann-like cells.

but some abnormality will be detected in over 95% of the patients. Occasionally, severe diarrhea is found in association with these tumors and disappears on their removal[365]; it is more commonly seen with ganglioneuroma than with either ganglioneuroblastoma or neuroblastoma and results from the secretion of vasoactive intestinal peptide.[361] This product can be identified by immunohistochemistry in the differentiating and mature ganglion cells.[366]

Primary **malignant melanocytic tumors** arising from cervical, posterior mediastinal, and lumbar sympathetic ganglia occur.[363] They arise from neural crest derivatives that can produce melanin pigment, in a manner equivalent to that sometimes exhibited by neurofibroma, schwannoma, malignant peripheral nerve sheath tumor, neuroblastoma,[367] ganglioneuroblastoma,[364] and "melanotic meningioma." Most of these primary melanocytic

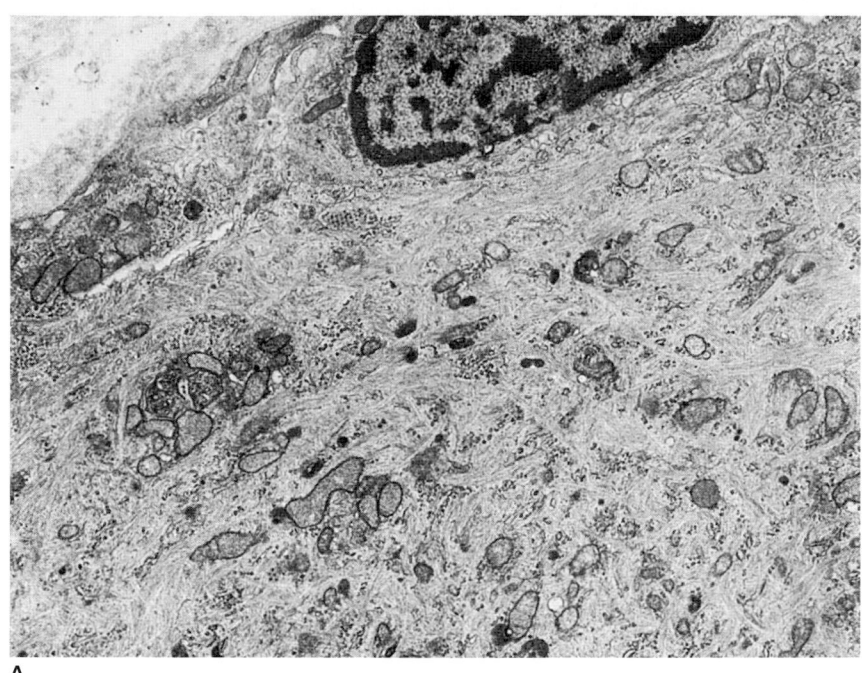

A

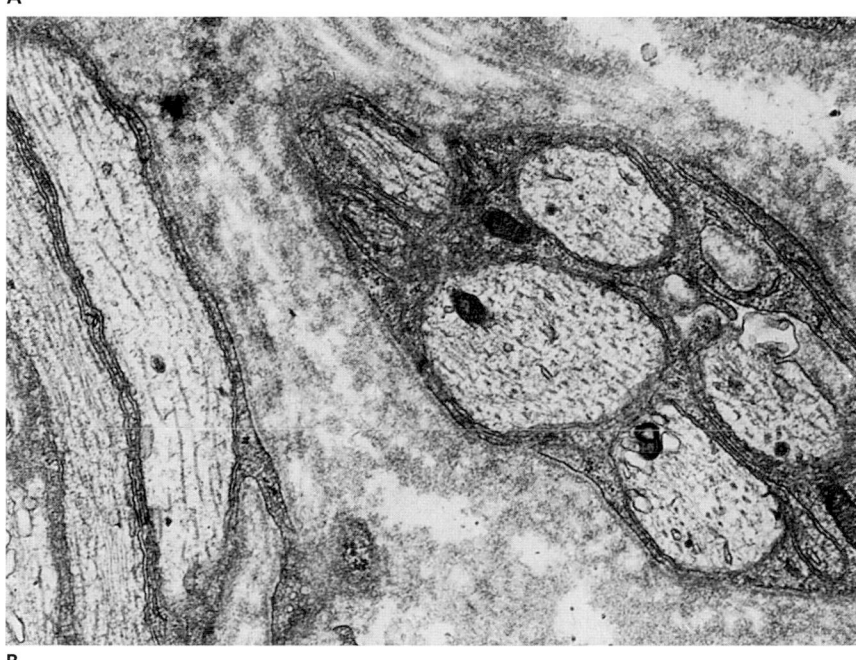

B

Fig. 16.26 Ganglioneuroma of retroperitoneum. **A**, Huge ganglion cell with eccentrically placed nucleus containing large numbers of cytoplasmic organelles, including microfilaments. This cell is separated from surrounding stroma by basal lamina. **B**, Neural bundles are surrounded by basal lamina; they contain numerous microtubules and other cytoplasmic organelles. (**A**, ×7450; **B**, ×16,850.)

neoplasms of ganglia behave as low-grade malignancies, with a tendency for local recurrence and eventual distant metastases.

Adrenal medullary hyperplasia

Hyperplasia of the adrenal medulla is a distinct entity, which may result in symptoms similar to those of pheochromocytoma.[376] It may be nodular or diffuse and is always bilateral. Ultrastructurally and immunohistochemically, the features are similar to those of normal medullary cells: chromogranin, synaptophysin, neuron-specific enolase, and Leu-enkephalin reactivity can be consistently demonstrated.[371]

Advanced cases of medullary hyperplasia are easy to recognize, but earlier phases may need morphometric studies to detect minor increases in medullary volume and weight, inasmuch as random sectioning techniques are grossly inadequate for this purpose.[372,373] In most cases the medullary hyperplasia is a component of multiple endocrine neoplasia type IIb (also known as MEN III), together with medullary thyroid carcinoma and parathyroid chief cell hyperplasia, and is the background against which both benign and malignant pheochromocytomas (sometimes multiple and bilateral) develop in these patients.[370,374] It has also been reported in association with von Recklinghausen's disease, somatostatin-rich duodenal carcinoid,[377] and the Beckwith–Wiedemann syndrome.[375]

Pheochromocytoma

General and clinical features

Pheochromocytoma can be defined as a paraganglioma of the adrenal medulla (see p. 1142). As such, it is the better known and more common member of the paraganglioma family, which is discussed in a later section. The term *extra-adrenal pheochromocytoma* has been traditionally used for extra-adrenal paragangliomas that are either functioning and/or connected with the orthosympathetic (rather than the parasympathetic) system, such as those arising in the bladder or in Zuckerkandl's body. It is probably better to avoid the term altogether. Pheochromocytoma has been called *the 10% tumor*— approximately 10% are bilateral, 10% are extra-adrenal (i.e., they are paragangliomas), 10% occur in children, and 10% are malignant. Pheochromocytomas in children are less likely to be malignant but more likely to be bilateral, or associated with MEN.[379,382] Both pheochromocytomas and paragangliomas secrete norepinephrine, but only the former have the capacity to also secrete epinephrine, since the adrenal cortex is necessary for the needed methylation step. Indeed, the pure norepinephrine-producing adrenal pheochromocytomas have been found to have a deficiency of phenylethanolamine *N*-methyltransferase.[383]

Pheochromocytomas may be associated with neurofibromatosis,[385] renal artery stenosis resulting from dysplasia of this vessel,[380,386] paragangliomas of other sites, adrenal cortical tumors,[392] or von Hippel–Lindau disease.[388,389] Many familial cases have been described.[381] When compared with the sporadic examples, they tend to occur in a younger age group, are more commonly bilateral, and are more frequently associated with other primary neoplasms.[393] Familial cases of pheochromocytoma may be seen as a component of MEN type IIA (Sipple's syndrome) or type IIB (III; Gorlin's syndrome).[378] At present, it is believed that the susceptibility genes for pheochromocytoma include *ret* (associated with MEN II), *VHL* (associated with von Hippel–Lindau disease), *SDHD* (the gene for succinate dehydrogenase subunit D), and *SDHB* (the corresponding gene for the subunit B). Interestingly, almost one fourth of patients with apparently sporadic pheochromocytoma are carriers of germline mutations in one or another of these genes.[378a]

The clinical signs and symptoms of hormonally active pheochromocytomas derive from the catecholamines they secrete (predominantly epinephrine) and from their relative stimulation of alpha- or beta-adrenergic receptors. Hypertensive attacks are usually intermittent but at times may be sustained, particularly in children. They may be precipitated by drugs, anesthetic agents, parturition, surgery for an unrelated condition, or massaging of the tumor.[378] The symptomatic triad of sweating attacks, tachycardia, and headaches is virtually diagnostic of pheochromocytoma. The high secretion of catecholamines by these tumors may result in myocarditis and noncardiac pulmonary edema.[384] Confirmation of the diagnosis is usually obtained by measuring urinary catecholamines or their catabolites, vanilmandelic acid, and total metanephrines.[390,391] Provocative pharmacologic tests are used only when the biochemical results are

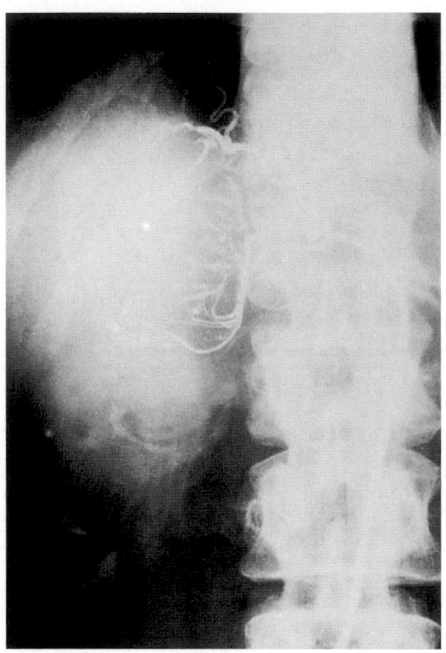

A

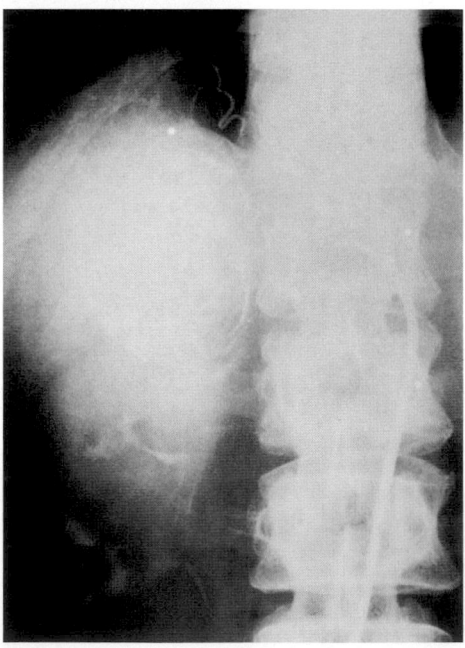

B

Fig. 16.27 Arteriographic demonstration of adrenal pheochromocytoma, early and late arterial phases. Latter shows a typical "tumor stain." (From Meaney TF, Buonocore E. Selective arteriography as a localizing and provocative test in the diagnosis of pheochromocytoma. Radiology 1966, **87**: 309–314)

equivocal.[378] Because of the high vascularization of pheochromocytomas, selective arteriography has been used successfully for years to detect them (Fig. 16.27). However, the advent of CT has largely replaced it as the method of choice for the preoperative detection of these tumors.

Morphologic features

The weight of pheochromocytomas ranges from a few grams to over 2000 g. They are encapsulated, usually soft, and, on section, yellowish white to reddish brown (Fig. 16.28). The larger tumors often have areas of necrosis, hemorrhage, and cyst formation. The adrenal gland usually is compressed or incorporated within the tumor.

Microscopically, the tumor cells are characteristically arranged in well-defined nests ("Zellballen") bound by a delicate fibrovascular stroma, which may contain amyloid (Fig. 16.29).[415] The cells vary considerably in size and shape and have a finely granular basophilic or amphophilic cytoplasm. The nuclei are usually round or oval with prominent nucleoli and may contain inclusion-like structures resulting from deep cytoplasmic invaginations.[397] Intracytoplasmic hyaline globules are common.[406] Lipid accumulation may develop in the cytoplasm and lead to confusion with adrenal cortical tumors

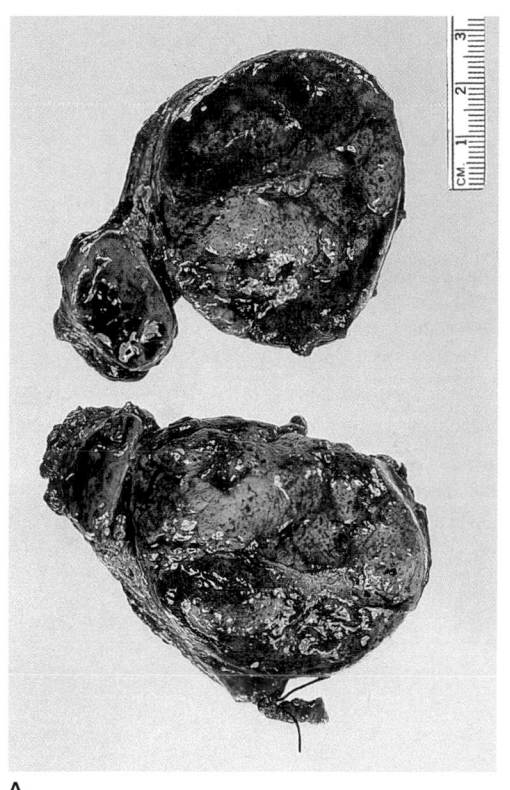

A

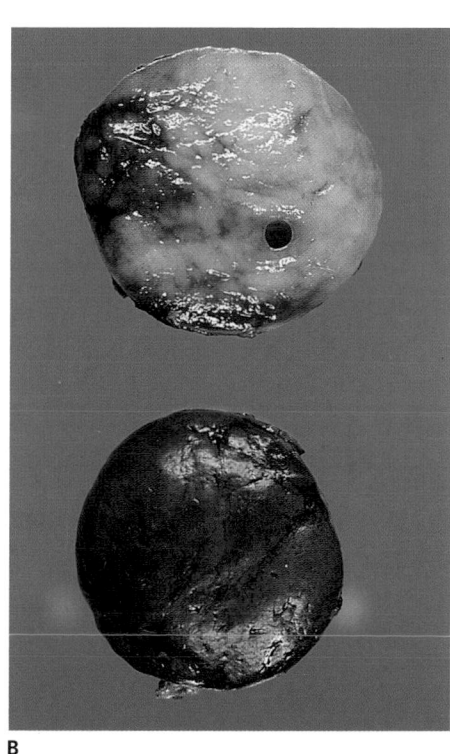

B

Fig. 16.28 A and **B**, Gross appearance of adrenal pheochromocytoma. The tumor shown in **A** has a markedly variegated appearance. The lower half of the specimen shown in **B** was fixed in Zenker fluid and has acquired the typical dark brown color indicative of a positive chromaffin reaction.

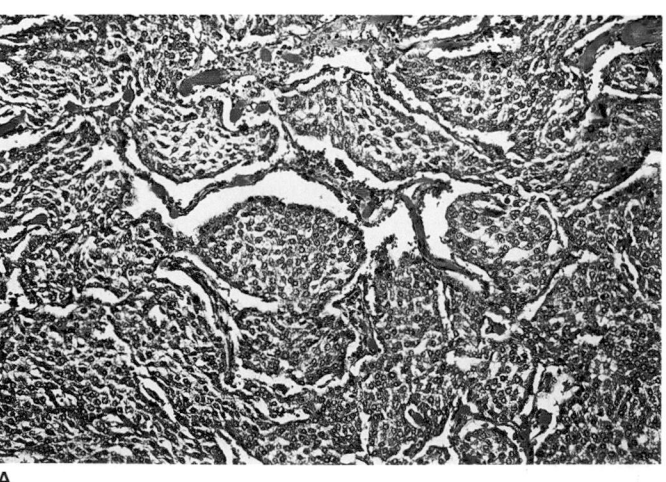

A

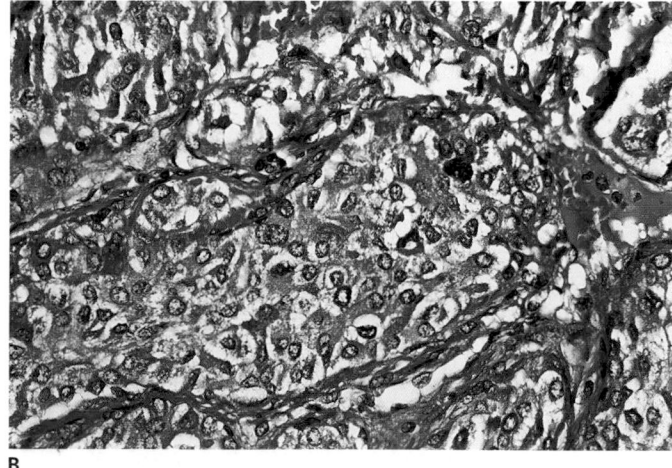

B

Fig. 16.29 A and **B**, Adrenal pheochromocytoma. **A** shows the typical "Zellballen" configuration, whereas **B** makes evident the abundant granular amphophilic cytoplasm of the tumor cells.

on both gross and light microscopic examination.[407,413,417] Melanin pigment is occasionally present.[395,404] Nuclear gigantism and hyperchromasia are common and *are not an expression of malignancy*. As a matter of fact, we know of no reliable morphologic markers of malignancy for this tumor other than the presence of metastases. As a group, however, malignant pheochromocytomas are usually larger, have more necrosis, and are composed of smaller cells than their benign counterparts.[409] Pheochromocytomas presenting in the setting of von Hippel–Lindau disease are said to differ morphologically in some subtle respects from the others, including the absence of hyaline globules and nuclear atypia.[402]

Exceptionally, the cells of pheochromocytomas are found to contain a large number of mitochondria (in addition to the neurosecretory granules) and thus acquire an oncocytic appearance.[405,418] Adipose tissue of the brown (hibernating) type is often found surrounding the capsule of pheochromocytoma,[410] but there is some question as to whether the two processes are related.[408]

Isolated ganglion cells are sometimes found in pheochromocytoma. More rarely, a tumor will be found to be composed of a mixture of pheochromocytoma and ganglioneuroma, ganglioneuroblastoma, or neuroblastoma, a finding not surprising in view of the close histogenetic relationship of the cell lines.[396,401,403,412] The immunohistochemical features correspond to those of the respective cell types and can therefore be of help in identifying the two components[398,416] (see later discussion). Some of these combined tumors have occurred in the setting of MEN IIA.[394]

Other combinations that have been described are pheochromocytoma with spindle cell sarcoma,[399,411] some of possibly malignant peripheral nerve sheath nature,[414] pheochromocytoma with cortical adenoma (see p. 1121), and pheochromocytoma with neuroendocrine carcinoma.[400]

Electron microscopic, histochemical, immunohistochemical, and molecular genetic features

Ultrastructurally, the cells of pheochromocytoma contain numerous dense-core granules of neurosecretory type; in the typical case they segregate into two size categories, corresponding to their respective content of norepinephrine and epinephrine.[420,423,449]

When pheochromocytoma is immersed in dichromate solution, it takes on a characteristic dark brown appearance. This is the basis of the time-honored chromaffin reaction. It should be emphasized that to obtain consistent results, the tumor tissue should be fresh and the pH of the dichromate solution kept between 5 and 6.[425]

Immunohistochemically, pheochromocytoma cells are always reactive for catecholamines, catecholamine-synthesizing enzymes, neuron-specific enolase, chromogranins, synaptophysin, and opioid peptides (metenkephalin, Leu-enkephalin, β-endorphin, dynorphin B, and others).[421,435,438,445] They can also show positivity for neurofilaments, serotonin, somatostatin, calcitonin, CGRP, gastrin, substance P, neuropeptide Y, galanin, cholecystokinin, calbindin, renin, vasoactive intestinal peptide, corticotropin and growth hormone-releasing factors, neurotrophins and neurotrophin receptors, and other neuron-related markers.[419,422,424,426,430,433,434,437,439–442,444,450,451] Kimura et al.[427] found cytokeratin and vimentin in approximately one quarter of their pheochromocytoma cases; curiously, keratin was detectable in adrenal but not extra-adrenal tumors. Sasaki et al. found a similar pattern for corticotropin and growth hormone-releasing factors and for the peptide histidine methionine.[444]

Occasionally the tumor may secrete ACTH and result in Cushing's syndrome,[429] or it may produce parathormone and result in hypercalcemia.[447] In one series, one third of the cases were found to contain HMB-45-positive cells, a not too surprising finding in view of the close histogenetic link between adrenal medullary cells and melanocytes.[453]

A second cell component of pheochromocytoma is represented by the sustentacular cells, which form a peripheral coat around the "Zellballen" and are strongly reactive for S-100 protein. These cells are more numerous in the pheochromocytomas associated with MEN than in the sporadic examples of this tumor, and more common in the benign than in the malignant forms.[431,452]

The previously mentioned chromogranin composes a group of acidic polypeptides of various sizes that form a major part of the soluble proteins in the secretory granules of the adrenal medulla: A, B, and C (also known as secretogranin II).[432,446] The largest of these polypeptides is chromogranin A[455]; the plasma concentration of this substance is usually elevated in pheochromocytoma and other peptide-producing neoplasms, a feature of great diagnostic utility.[436]

Cytogenetically, LOH on the long arm of chromosome 22 has been detected in many cases of pheochromocytoma, particularly those occurring in a familial setting,[448] whereas LOH on the short arm of chromosomes 1 and 3 has been detected in approximately half of sporadic pheochromocytomas (but not in paragangliomas).[454]

The various gene mutations that are associated with pheochromocytoma (see p. 1136) can be detected in paraffin-embedded material by single-strand conformation polymorphism analysis and direct sequencing.[428,443]

Spread, metastases, treatment, and prognosis

Although the statement is often made that only 10% of pheochromocytomas are malignant, several series in adults with long-term follow-up suggest that the real incidence is much higher.[460,466] Malignant pheochromocytomas have a marked tendency to metastasize to the skeletal system, particularly ribs and spine, often to the exclusion of other organs. Because of this feature, a preoperative bone scan is recommended in all patients suspected of having a pheochromocytoma.

The primary treatment of pheochromocytoma is surgical excision. Most patients with metastatic tumor die within 1 year of diagnosis, but long-term relapse-free survival is possible for locally invasive neoplasms.[460,461]

Morphologic parameters such as pleomorphism, necrosis, and vascular invasion have proved to be poor prognostic determinants in this tumor, at least when evaluated independently. Combining them in a scoring system in a way similar to the one that has been successfully employed for adrenocortical tumors may prove more effective.[467]

Flow cytometric DNA analysis seems to be an important and independent prognostic variable in pheochromocytoma.[459,463,464] In one series, 84% of the tumors that invaded blood vessels and all cases associated with metastases had a tetraploid or aneuploid pattern.

Other alleged unfavorable prognostic factors are high proliferative index (as measured with MIB-1 or topoisomerase alpha II staining)[456–458,462,465a]; absence of S-100 protein-positive sustentacular cells[468]; and increased expression of tenascin, and human telomerase reverse transcriptase (hTERT) gene expression.[457a,465]

Other adrenal lesions

Adrenal hemorrhage of massive proportions can occur in infants within the first few days after delivery; it may present as an abdominal or retroperitoneal mass, septicemia, or adrenal insufficiency.[487] In the first instance, surgery is indicated to rule out the possibility of neuroblastoma.[494] This differential diagnosis also applies to the surgical and pathologic findings, since neuroblastoma can undergo marked hemorrhagic necrosis. Massive adrenal hemorrhage also must be distinguished from renal vein thrombosis. This hemorrhage can be unilateral (more commonly on the right side) or affect both glands; if the patient survives, calcification rapidly develops around its periphery[476] (Fig. 16.30). The postulated causes include fetal hypoxia, septicemia, thrombocytopenia, coagulopathies, and disseminated thromboembolic disease.

Adrenal cysts can be clinically confused with retroperitoneal neoplasms because of their occasionally large size (up to 30 cm in diameter)[482] (Fig. 16.31). They are sometimes bilateral. Microscopically, the wall is composed of partially calcified fibrous tissue without an epithelial lining.[509] In some instances, intracystic mature adipose tissue or myelolipomatous metaplasia is encountered.[492] The content may be serous or blood-colored fluid. The mechanism of formation remains controversial. It would seem that two main variants exist.[469,491,493,497] The first, known as *endothelial (vascular) cyst*, contains serous fluid, is multiloculated, has an endothelial lining,

and often contains adrenal cortex in the wall. The second, known as *hemorrhagic cyst* or *pseudocyst*, contains clotted blood and hyalinized thrombus with attenuated adrenal cortex in the outer fibrous wall.[501] It has been suggested that both cyst types arise on the basis of a vascular anomaly,[531] perhaps of lymphatic nature in the first instance and of blood vessel type in the second.[491] Hemorrhagic cysts can occur as a component of the Beckwith–Wiedemann syndrome.[507,533] In rare cases, *epithelial-lined ("true") adrenal cysts* are seen; their histogenesis is probably similar to that of epithelial-lined cysts of the spleen and possibly derived from mesothelial structures.[510] These should be distinguished from *bronchogenic cysts*, which sometimes present as adrenal masses.[512,530]

Adrenal cytomegaly refers to the presence in the adrenal cortex of foci of bizarre polyhedral cells with eosinophilic granular cytoplasm and large hyperchromatic nuclei with pseudoinclusions. This condition is usually detected in infancy, often as a component of Beckwith's syndrome; it is not likely to be seen as a surgical specimen.[515]

Heterotopic tissue in the adrenal gland is highly unusual. This includes *liver tissue* (usually resulting from adrenohepatic fusion but sometimes occurring as a separate nodule),[498] *thyroid tissue*,[527] and stromal spindle cell foci resembling *ovarian stroma* or *theca*. The latter appear as multiple, often bilateral, wedge-shaped microscopic and occasionally grossly visible nodules in the adrenal cortex.[481] Most patients are postmenopausal women, and no clinical significance is attributed to the nodules,[489] except for their possible role in the genesis of a questionable theca–granulosa cell tumor.[519] A case of ovarian stroma-

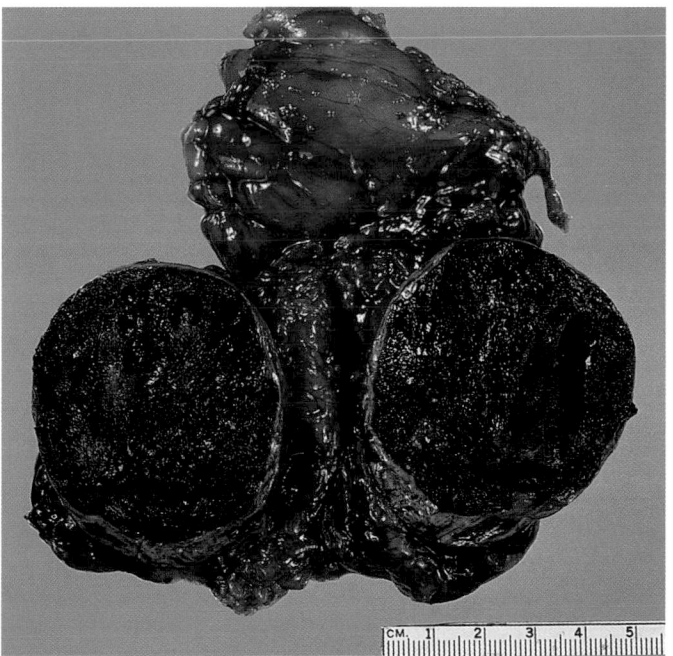

Fig. 16.30 Adrenal gland massively replaced by hemorrhage. There was no evidence of a tumor in any of the many sections taken.

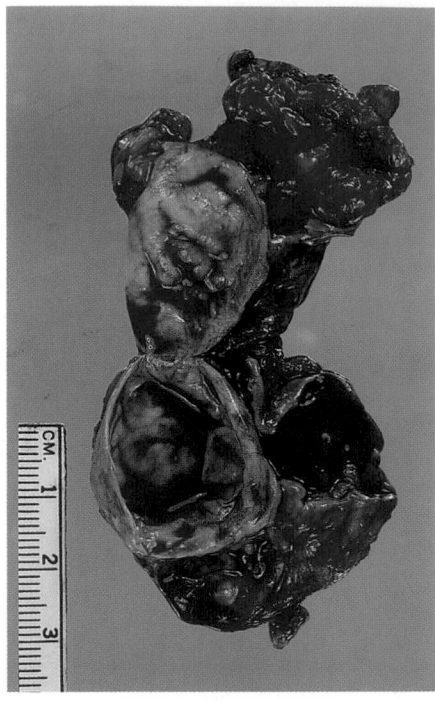

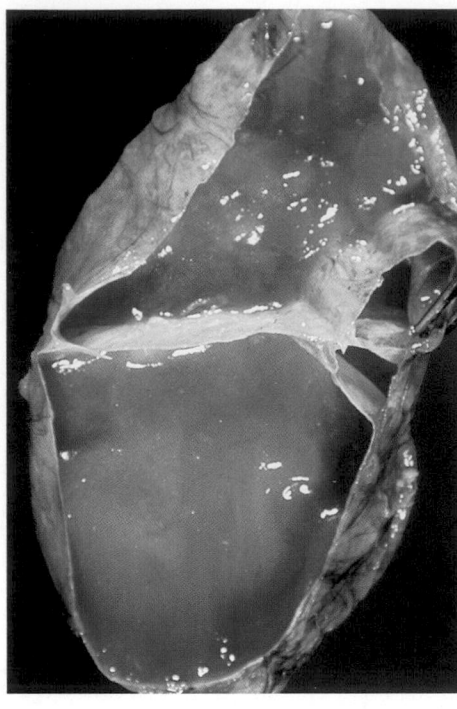

Fig. 16.31 A and **B**, Gross appearance of adrenal cyst. The cyst shown in **A** has a unilocular appearance, whereas that shown in **B** is divided into two portions by a prominent septum.

like metaplasia has been reported in a man with acquired bilateral testicular atrophy.[523] *Leydig cells* containing Reinke's crystalloids have also been described in several adrenal disorders,[498] and a few cases of adrenal *Leydig cell tumor* accompanied by virilization are on record.[520]

Tuberculosis of the adrenal glands is one of the classic causes of Addison's disease[517]; the glands are enlarged, calcified, and massively replaced by granulomatous inflammation.[508]

Malakoplakia involving the adrenal gland has been reported in infants[529] and adults.[473]

Myelolipoma is a lesion characterized by the presence within the adrenal gland of adult fat containing active bone marrow elements[506,516] (Figs 16.32 and 16.33). Most cases are found incidentally, either at autopsy or through

CT scanning done for other reasons. Only occasionally will the lesion attain a size large enough to become clinically apparent.[479,535] Bilaterality is rare.[503] The tumors are hormonally inactive, most of the patients being obese adults. Traumatic rupture leading to hemoperitoneum may supervene.[511] Myelolipoma has been seen in association with adrenal cortical tumors accompanied by Cushing's syndrome[475] (see p. 1120) with congenital adrenal hyperplasia,[485] and with adrenal ganglioneuroma.[512] Cases of pure adrenal myelolipoma associated with Cushing's disease have also been reported.[475,478] In contrast to other extramedullary foci of hematopoiesis in adults (which are usually the expression of a hematologic disease), adrenal myelolipoma is practically always accompanied by a normal bone marrow.[500]

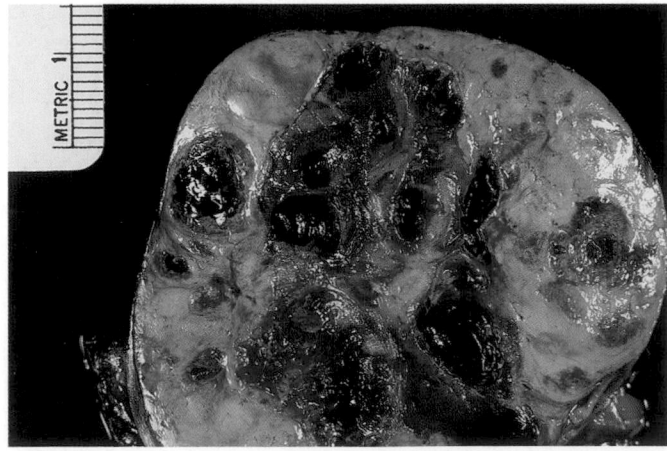

Fig. 16.32 Gross appearance of adrenal myelolipoma. Yellow areas with the appearance of adipose tissue alternate with hemorrhagic foci composed of bone marrow tissue.

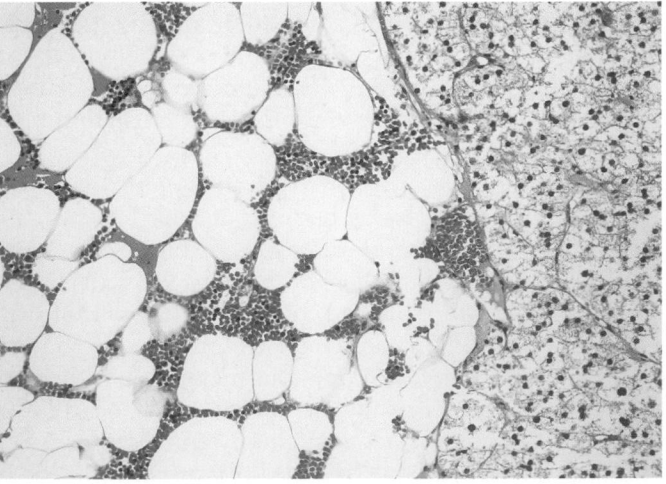

Fig. 16.33 Adrenal myelolipoma composed of bone marrow elements and mature fat.

Benign mesenchymal tumors of the adrenal gland, all exceptionally rare, include lipoma, angioma, solitary fibrous tumor, and schwannoma.[470,472,477,521]

Adenomatoid tumor has been reported in a primary adrenal location; as in other sites, its nature is in all likelihood mesothelial. The behaviour is benign.[500a,522,528,532]

Adrenocortical blastoma is the term proposed by Molberg et al.[514] for a virilizing malignant adrenocortical tumor occurring in infancy and having morphologic features reminiscent of the normal embryologic development of the adrenal cortex.

Sarcomas primary in the adrenal gland are exceptionally rare. They include leiomyosarcoma,[505] (some in association with HIV infection[488]), malignant peripheral nerve sheath tumor,[471,495] and angiosarcoma (Figs 16.35 and 16.36). The latter characteristically exhibits an epithelioid morphology and immunoreactivity for

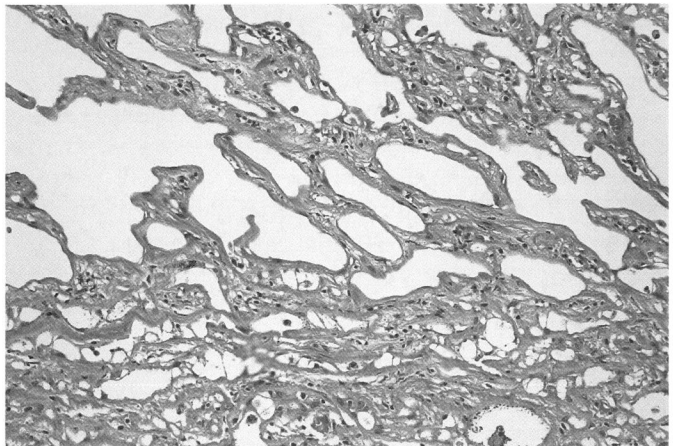

Fig. 16.34 Adenomatoid tumor of adrenal gland. The appearance closely simulates that of a lymphangioma.

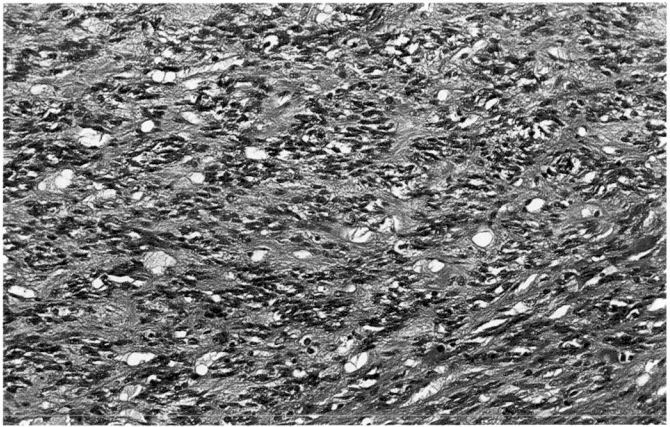

Fig. 16.35 Malignant peripheral nerve sheath tumor. It was immunohistochemically reactive for S-100 protein and the individual cells were surrounded by basement membrane material.

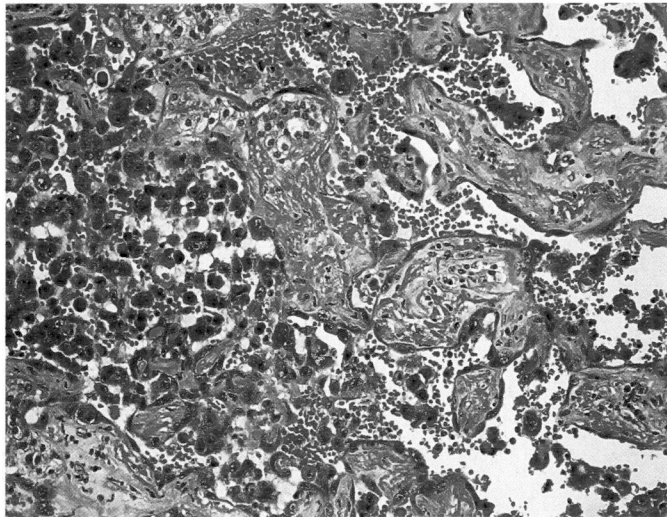

Fig. 16.36 Adrenal angiosarcoma with epithelioid component.

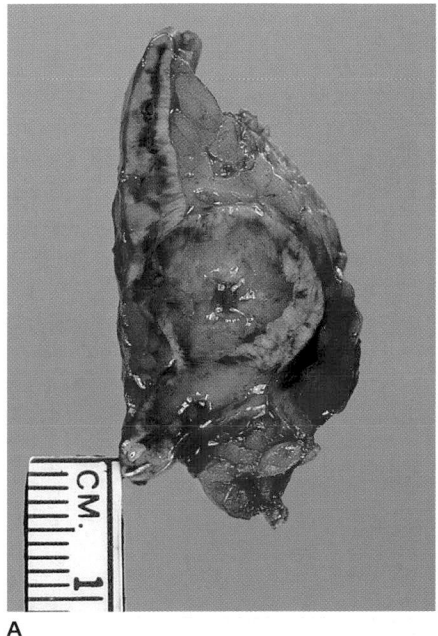

A

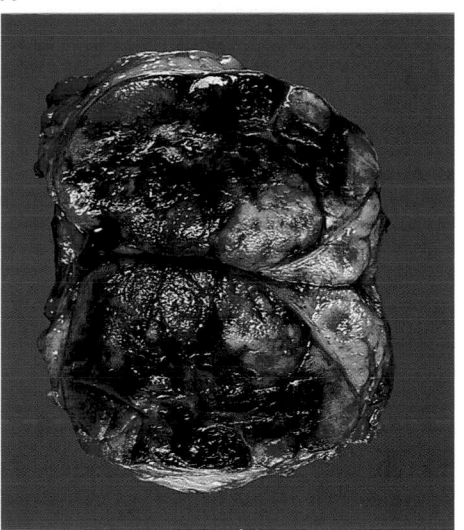

B

Fig. 16.37 Metastatic carcinoma to adrenal gland. **A,** The whitish, ill-defined mass present in the center of the gland represents metastatic squamous cell carcinoma from the esophagus. **B,** Enlargement of the gland by a markedly hemorrhagic tumor representing metastatic breast carcinoma.

keratin (in addition to endothelial markers).[474, 534] There have also been isolated reports of *Ewing's sarcoma/PNET* arising in the adrenal gland, to be distinguished from the considerably more common neuroblastomas,[502] and a case of an intra-adrenal neoplasm indistinguishable from renal *Wilms' tumor*.[524]

Malignant lymphoma involving the adrenal gland is usually a manifestation of widespread disease. Only a few cases have been reported as having an apparently primary adrenal location.[483,496] Most of the cases have been of B-cell type, and several of these were EBV associated.[518] There have also been cases of T-cell lymphoma,[518] anaplastic large cell lymphoma,[490] and angiotropic lymphoma[484]; actually, a good number of cases of the latter disease are accompanied by adrenal involvement. If the adrenal replacement is extensive bilaterally, adrenal insufficiency may result.[480,525]

Malignant melanoma as a primary adrenal tumor is now accepted as an entity; the differential diagnosis includes melanotic pheochromocytoma and metastatic melanoma, both of which are considerably more common.[486]

Metastatic tumors to the adrenal glands are very common at autopsy but sometimes also present as surgical specimens simulating a primary adrenal neoplasm (Fig. 16.37). Bilaterality is the rule. CT scanning is the method of choice for their detection. If extensive enough, they will lead to Addison's disease.[504,526] The most common sites of the primary tumor are lung, breast, skin (melanoma), and kidney. Renal metastases can be contralateral and simulate grossly and microscopically the appearance of adrenocortical carcinoma (Fig. 16.38).[499]

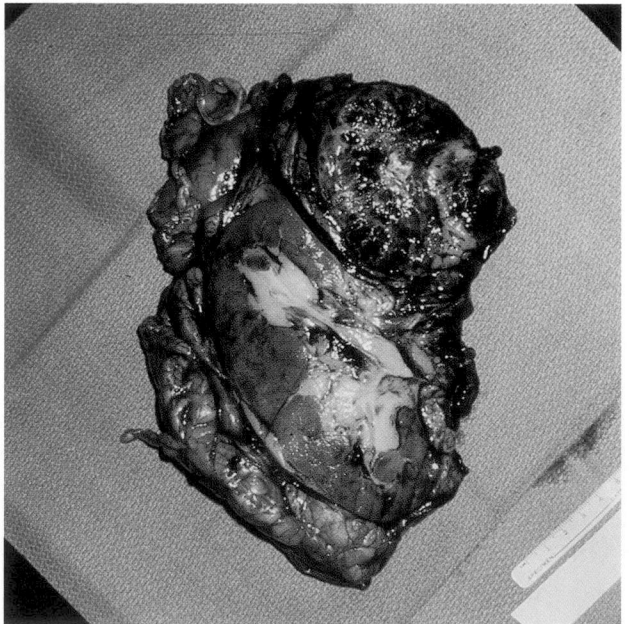

Fig. 16.38 Renal cell carcinoma metastatic to contralateral adrenal gland and simulating a primary adrenal cortical tumor at the gross and microscopic level.

Tumors and tumorlike lesions of other paraganglia

Generalities

Paraganglioma is the generic term applied to tumors of paraganglia regardless of location.[536,544] The only exception, largely on the basis of tradition, is the already discussed paraganglioma of the adrenal medulla, which is rarely designated as such but universally known as *pheochromocytoma* (see p. 1136). By extension, paragangliomas located outside the adrenal gland that are obviously chromaffin and associated with clinical evidence of norepinephrine and/or epinephrine secretion also have been designated as *extra-adrenal pheochromocytomas*. Most of these arise from orthosympathetic-related paraganglia, whereas most of the nonchromaffin, nonfunctioning paragangliomas originate from parasympathetic-related organs. It is not possible on morphologic grounds to distinguish between these two types or to predict whether a tumor is functioning at the clinical level or not.

The alternative term *chemodectoma*, which was once in vogue to designate these tumors, is too restrictive, since it can be properly applied only to carotid and aortic body tumors (i.e., tumors of the only paraganglia for which a chemoreceptor function has been demonstrated physiologically).

Paragangliomas have been found in practically every site in which normal paraganglia are known to occur, their description sometimes preceding that of the corresponding normal structure. Paragangliomas of the head and neck (particularly carotid body tumors) are about ten times more frequent in persons living at high altitudes than in those at sea level[547,548]; these have been invariably benign and may actually represent exaggerated examples of the well-known hyperplastic changes that consistently occur in these organs when they are exposed to prolonged and severe hypoxic stimulation (see below).[537,545] A definite familial incidence has been documented.[541] Paragangliomas occurring bilaterally, affecting two or more paraganglia simultaneously, involving a given area in a diffuse or multicentric fashion ("paragangliomatosis"), associated with von Hippel–Lindau disease, or as a component of multiple endocrine neoplasia have been reported.[542,543,549] Carney et al.[538,540] have identified a disease complex characterized by the exotic association of extra-adrenal paraganglioma, gastric malignant stromal tumors, and pulmonary chondroma. Most of the cases have occurred in young females.[546] This process, which is referred to as *Carney's triad*, is only rarely seen in a familial setting and it can be accompanied by adrenocortical tumors. It should be distinguished both from the recently described autosomal dominantly inherited combination of paraganglioma and gastric stromal sarcoma,[539] and from Carney's *syndrome* (see p. 1119).

Morphologic features

The gross and microscopic appearance of paragangliomas is practically the same regardless of location and indistinguishable from that of adrenal pheochromocytoma (Fig. 16.39). Well-defined nests of cuboidal cells ("Zellballen") are separated by highly vascularized fibrous septa (Fig. 16.40). The individual cells have a moderately abundant granular basophilic cytoplasm. On occasion, a brown melanin-like pigment is present (*pigmented* or *black* paraganglioma).[550,551] As with many other endocrine tumors, bizarre nuclei and vascular invasion are sometimes found, neither of which should be taken as evidence of malignancy. Mitoses are exceptional, except in the obviously malignant cases. The stroma can be very abundant; it often has a hyalinized quality and it may undergo osseous metaplasia.[552]

Histochemical, immunohistochemical, electron microscopic, and molecular genetic features

Argentaffin cells can be regularly demonstrated by the del Rio Hortega techniques in frozen sections[553] (if one wants to bother doing so) but only rarely with the Fontana–Masson or Masson–Hamperl methods as applied to paraffin-embedded material. Conversely, argyrophilia is easily demonstrable in routinely processed material.[558] Treatment of freeze-dried preparations or tumor imprints with formaldehyde vapors or glyoxylic acid induces a bright fluorescence indicative of catecholamines,[563] but this is yet another technique that has been rendered obsolete by immunohistochemistry. As in pheochromocytoma, the sustentacular cells can be demonstrated with S-100 protein.[560]

Ultrastructurally, the tumor ("chief") cells contain large numbers of cytoplasmic neurosecretory granules whose appearance is similar to those seen in normal paraganglia[555,567] (Fig. 16.41). Giant mitochondria with paracrystalline inclusions may also be present.[561] The second cell type present in these tumors is the sustentacular cell, which wraps around the chief cells and lacks dense-core granules. Biochemical assays of the tumor have confirmed the presence of norepinephrine and sometimes also of epinephrine and dopamine.[554,562] Immunohistochemically, positivity has been found for neuron-specific enolase, chromogranin, synaptophysin, galanin, neurofilaments, opioid peptides, serotonin, somatostatin, galanin, and various other peptide hormones (Fig. 16.42).[556,557,559,564,565a,567] Keratin is almost always negative, a fact of importance in the differential diagnosis with neuroendocrine carcinomas, the curious exceptions being paraganglioma of the filum terminale (see p. 1146) and the already mentioned

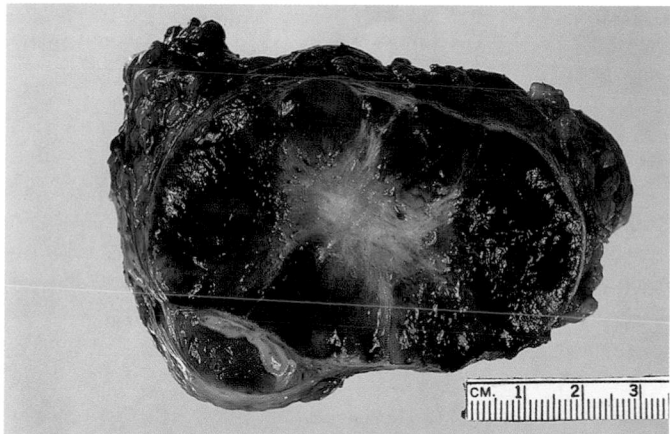

Fig. 16.39 Gross appearance of paraganglioma. The brown appearance of the cut surface is characteristic. A large central scar is present.

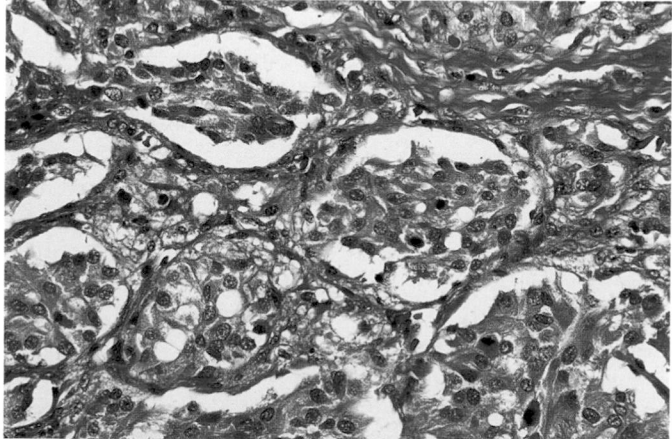

Fig. 16.40 "Zellballen" formation in paraganglioma.

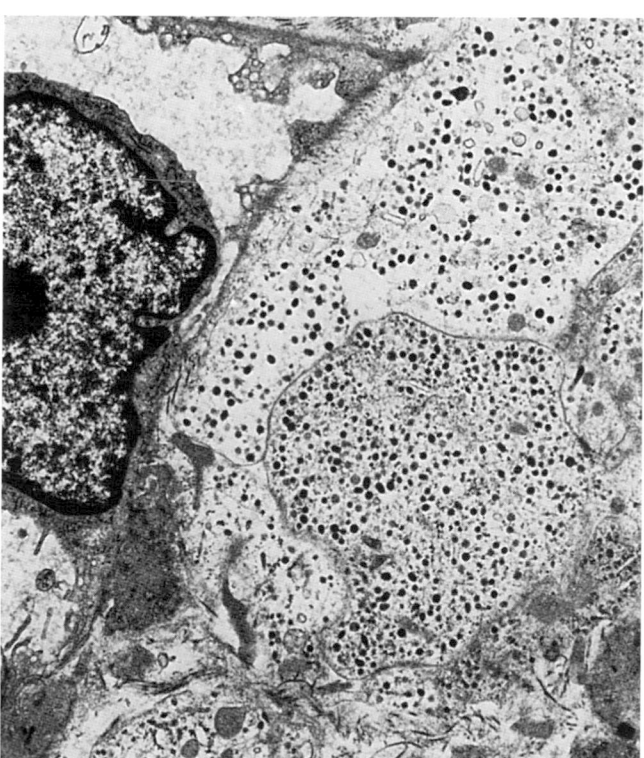

Fig. 16.41 Electron microscopic appearance of retroperitoneal paraganglioma, characterized by tumor cells with uniform, small, dense-core granules. Tumor cells are in close proximity to capillary vessels.

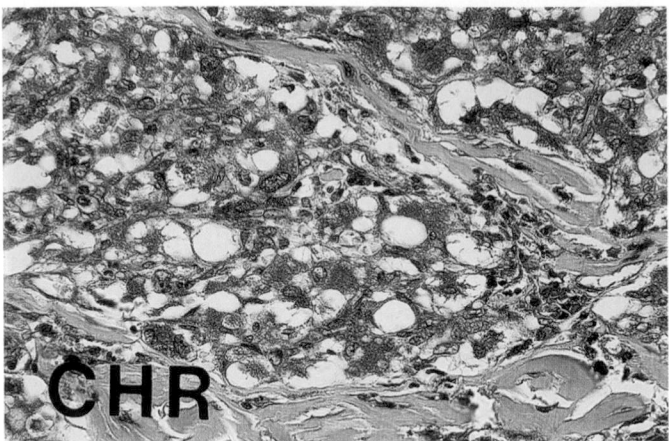

Fig. 16.42 Intense immunoreactivity for chromogranin in the tumor cells of paraganglioma.

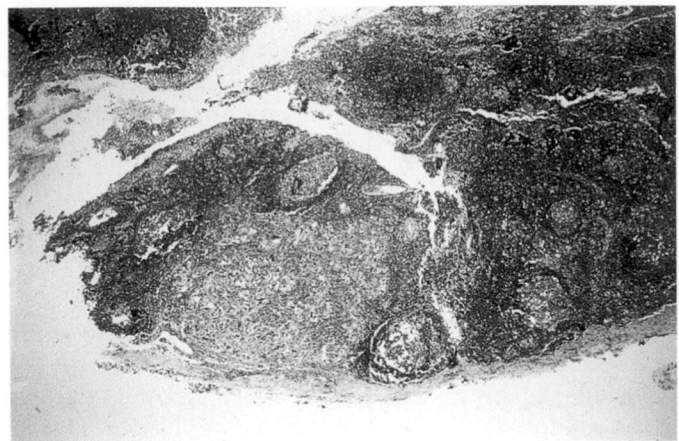

Fig. 16.44 Lymph node metastasis of paraganglioma. This is a very unusual event.

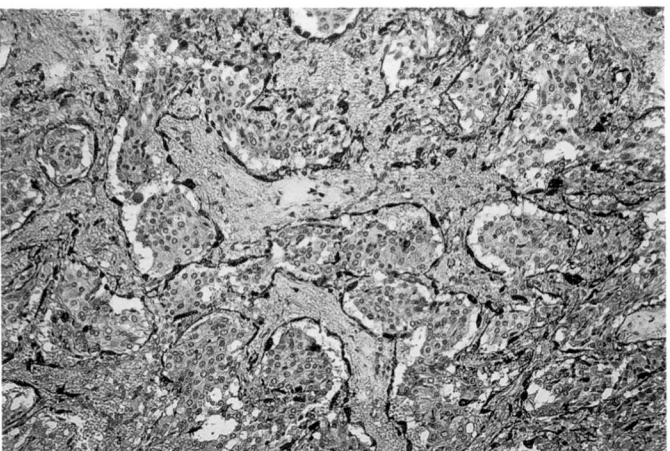

Fig. 16.43 Sustentacular cells immunostained for S-100 protein at the periphery of the tumor nests of paraganglioma.

pheochromocytoma. The sustentacular cells can be demonstrated with S-100 protein, another feature of importance in the differential diagnosis from other endocrine neoplasms (Fig. 16.43).[565] Paragangliomas of the head and neck (and probably those of other sites as well) show complete LOH in the 11q22–q23 region, where the gene *PGL1* is located.[566]

Spread and metastases, treatment, and prognosis

Most paragangliomas follow a benign clinical course. The quoted incidence of malignancy is in the range of 10%—similar to that of adrenal pheochromocytomas.[576] However, as in the latter, long-term follow-up studies suggest that the real incidence of malignancy may be higher, at least for some locations.[574,575] Metastases occur most commonly to regional lymph nodes, lungs and skeletal system, with the primary tumor occasionally being occult (Fig. 16.44).[569] There are no reliable morphologic criteria by which to separate the benign from the malignant forms, although high mitotic activity and decreased immunohistochemical reactivity for neuropeptides correlate with clinical malignancy.[572,573] It has

also been shown that paragangliomas associated with a benign clinical course have a greater representation of S-100 protein-positive sustentacular cells than those with aggressive behavior.[568]

AgNor counts are higher in the malignant tumors, but the considerable degree of overlap limits the usefulness of the technique.[570] Whether DNA ploidy patterns will prove of prognostic use (as they have in adrenal pheochromocytoma) remains to be demonstrated.[571]

Specific paraganglioma types

Carotid body paragangliomas constitute the most common and important group of extra-adrenal paragangliomas.[582,599,613,618] They are located at the bifurcation of the common carotid artery and become closely adherent to it (Fig. 16.45). This firm adherence is often misinterpreted by the surgeon as a sign of malignancy. Arteriography demonstrates them particularly well because of their rich vascularity. Often the clinical diagnosis is not made until the characteristic location of the paraganglioma is determined at surgery. The high operative risk and morbidity formerly associated with the removal of a carotid body tumor have been markedly reduced as a result of improved surgical techniques and the use of arterial substitutes.[606] Consequently, early surgical resection is currently advocated.[611]

Approximately 10% of carotid body tumors have behaved malignantly. This may be manifested as local invasion or metastatic spread, particularly to lymph nodes and lung.[605,616] The possibility of multicentric paragangliomas should always be considered before concluding that a given tumor has metastasized.[624] *Carotid body hyperplasia* is an almost universal finding among people living in high altitude regions such as Peru, presumably as an adaptation mechanism.[578] It has also been described in association with cirrhosis of the liver.[588]

Jugulotympanic paragangliomas are often referred to as *glomus jugulare tumors*. It is better to avoid the term "glomus tumor" to prevent confusion with the totally

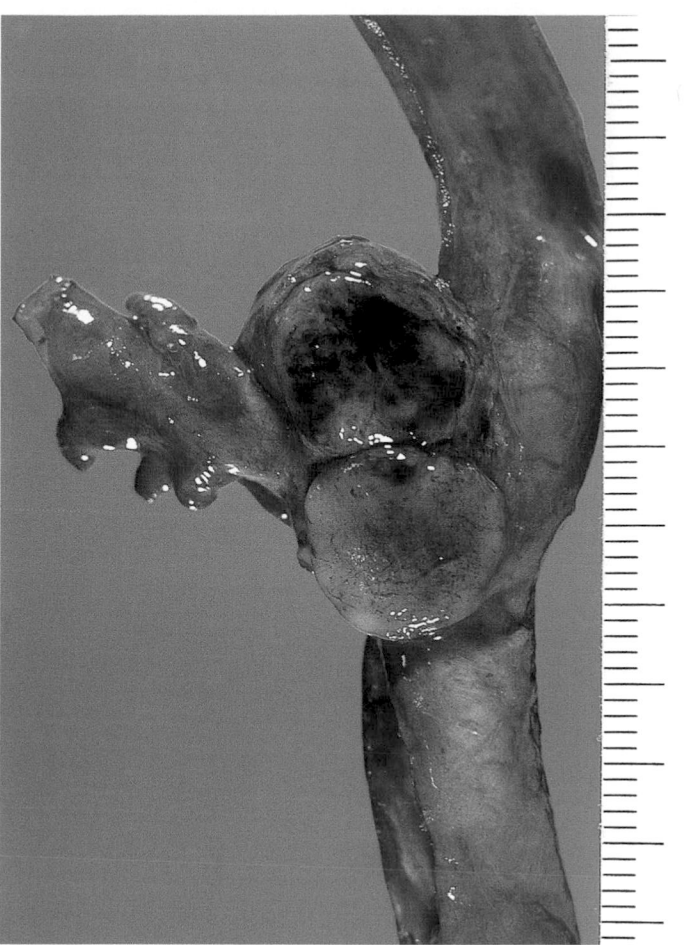

Fig. 16.45 Typical location of carotid body tumor at the bifurcation of the carotid artery. (Courtesy of Dr RA Cooke, Brisbane, Australia; From Cooke RA, Stewart B: Colour Atlas of Anatomical Pathology, Edinburgh, Churchill Livingstone, 2004)

unrelated neoplasm that goes by this name and that arises from specialized smooth muscle cells of the blood vessel wall. Jugulotympanic paragangliomas usually arise laterally in the temporal bones and, through erosion of the floor of the hypotympanum, present as a mass in the middle ear or the external auditory canal.[594,617,619] In other instances, they are located in the adventitia of the jugular bulb and present as a mass at the base of the skull, causing enlargement of the jugular foramen. Rarely, these tumors appear as pedunculated middle ear polyps arising from the cochlear promontory. Extension into the cranial cavity occurs in about 40% of cases. Most cases occur in adults. There is a striking predilection for females, a fact not apparent for paragangliomas in other locations. Angiographic examination is of great diagnostic value; at surgery, marked bleeding may be encountered. Microscopically, the appearance is similar to that of other paragangliomas, but since these tumors are often removed in small fragments, the artifacts present may render the diagnosis difficult or even impossible. We have seen several cases misdiagnosed as hemangiomas. The recommended treatment is surgical

removal followed by external megavoltage radiation.[587] Radiation therapy alone has led to long-term control in some cases.[603,622]

Vagal (intravagal) paragangliomas are characteristically located in the anterolateral portion of the neck, near the jugular foramen, and are thought to arise from the paraganglion intravagale, adjacent to the ganglion nodosum.[581,589,595,597,610] They also can occur at other points along the peripheral distribution of the vagus nerve. The majority are well circumscribed and easily removable, but others may invade locally and even result in intracranial infiltration through the jugular foramen. Hyalinized fibrous septa, continuous with the perineurium of the vagus nerve, are often prominent. A few cases with regional lymph node and/or distant metastases have been observed.[621]

Mediastinal paragangliomas, for the most part, originate in the supra-aortic or aorticopulmonary bodies and are therefore found in the anterosuperior portion of the mediastinum, in the area of the aortic arch.[604,609,626] Others arise from aorticosympathetic paraganglia and are located in the costovertebral sulcus. Olson and Salyer[614] reviewed the literature on aortic body tumors and found a high incidence of aggressive tumor growth in the mediastinum, with resultant important morbidity or death in 16 of 35 cases.

Retroperitoneal paragangliomas can occur anywhere along the paravertebral chain, sometimes close to the adrenal gland[601,615] (Fig. 16.46).

Zuckerkandl's body paragangliomas are found in the normal location of this structure, i.e., close to the angle formed by the anterior wall of the aorta and the origin of the inferior mesenteric artery[577,583,612] (and not at the aortic

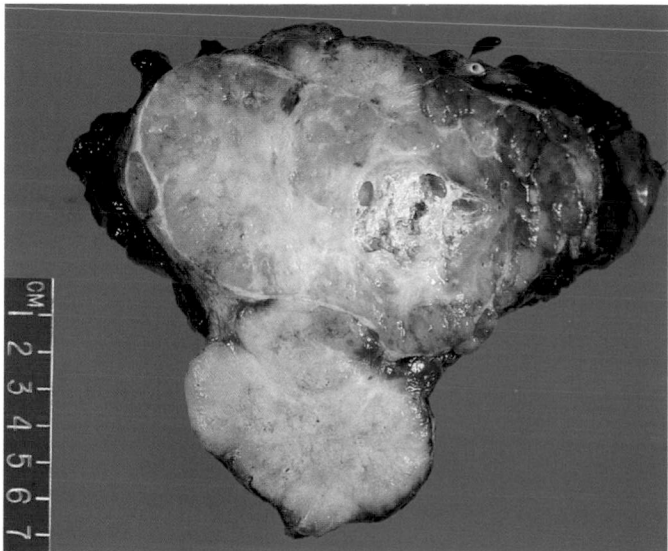

Fig. 16.46 Malignant paraganglioma of the retroperitoneum. Partial encapsulation is present on the left, but the rest of the tumor grows in an invasive multinodular fashion. Foci of fibrosis, cystic degeneration, and hemorrhage are seen. The adrenal gland was not involved. (Courtesy of Dr. Christopher Otis, Springfield, MA)

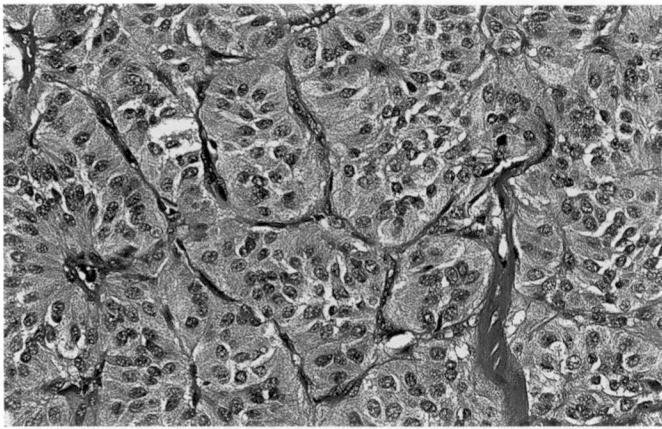

A

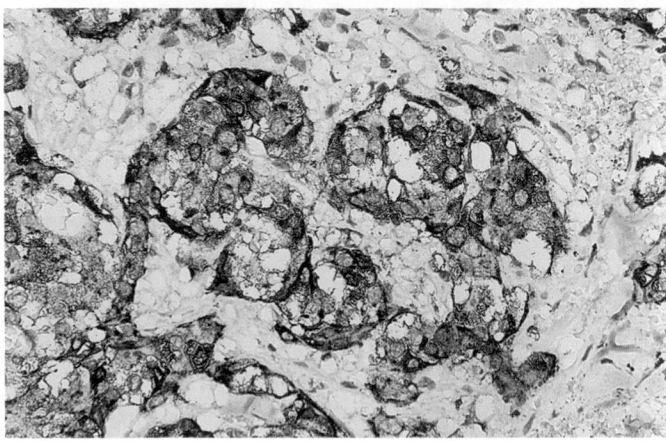

B

Fig. 16.47 A and **B,** Paraganglioma of cauda equina.
A, Hematoxylin–eosin; **B,** chromogranin.

bifurcation, a peculiarly common misconception). They may secondarily invade the inferior vena cava.[586]

Other locations where paragangliomas have been described include cavernous sinus,[591] orbit,[623] tongue,[580] nose and paranasal cavities,[600,625] larynx and trachea,[600,628] thyroid,[602] heart,[593] gallbladder,[607] urinary bladder (one of the most frequent),[584,585] uterus,[579,627] and spinal cord (especially lumbar region and cauda equina) (Fig. 16.47).[592,608] As already mentioned, the latter are the only paragangliomas likely to show immunoreactivity for keratin. Some of these tumors are discussed with their respective organs. Paragangliomas have also been described in the duodenum,[596] lung,[590,598] and pineal gland,[620] but the placement of these tumors in this category is highly questionable. Alveolar soft part sarcoma, a tumor once designated as malignant nonchromaffin paraganglioma, is clearly unrelated to this group of tumors (see Chapter 26).

REFERENCES

Normal anatomy
Adrenal gland

1 Belloni AS, Mazzocchi G, Mantero F, Nussdorfer GG. The human adrenal cortex. Ultrastructure and base-line morphometric data. J Submicrosc Cytol 1987, **19:** 657–668.

2 Carney JA. Adrenal gland. In Sternberg SS (ed.): Histology for pathologists, ed. 2. Baltimore, 1997, Lippincott Williams and Wilkins pp. 1107–1132.

3 Cooper MJ, Hutchins GM, Israel MA. Histogenesis of the human adrenal medulla. An evaluation of the ontogeny of chromaffin and nonchromaffin lineages. Am J Pathol 1990, **137:** 605–615.

4 Sasano H. New approaches in human adrenocortical pathology. Assessment of adrenocortical function in surgical specimen of human adrenal glands. Endocr Pathol 1992, **3:** 4–13.

5 Symington T. Functional pathology of the human adrenal gland. Baltimore, 1969, Williams & Wilkins.

Paraganglion system

6 Bloom FE. Electron microscopy of catecholamine-containing structures. In Blaschko H, Muschall E (eds): Handbook of experimental pharmacology, vol. 33. Catecholamines. New York, 1972, Springer-Verlag.

7 Coupland RE. The chromaffin system. In Blaschko H, Muschall E (eds): Handbook of experimental pharmacology, vol. 33. Catecholamines. New York, 1972, Springer-Verlag.

8 Freedman SR, Goldman RL. Normal paraganglion in the mesosigmoid. Hum Pathol 1981, **12:** 1037–1038.

9 Mäkinen J, Nickels J. Paraganglion cells mimicking metastatic clear cell carcinoma. Histopathology 1979, **3:** 459–465.

9a Tischler AS. Paraganglia. In Sternberg S (ed.): Histology for pathologists. ed. 2. Philadelphia, 1997, Lippincott-Raven Publishers, pp. 1153–1172.

Biopsy and cytology

10 Berkman WA, Bernardino ME, Sewell CW, Price RB, Sones PJ Jr. The computed tomography-guided adrenal biopsy. An alternative to surgery in adrenal mass diagnosis. Cancer 1984, **53:** 2098–2103.

11 Hoda SA, Zaman MB, Burt M. Aspiration cytology in the evaluation of adrenal masses. Acta Cytol 1991, **35:** 594.

12 Hoon V, Saigo PE. Fine needle aspiration of the adrenal gland. A review of 141 cases. Acta Cytol (Baltimore) (in press).

13 Karstrup S, Torp-Pedersen S, Nolsoe C, Horn T, Hegedus L. Ultrasonically guided fine-needle biopsies from adrenal tumors. Scand J Urol Nephrol Suppl 1991, **137:** 31–34.

14 Katz RL, Patel S, Mackay B, Zornoza J. Fine needle aspiration cytology of the adrenal gland. Acta Cytol (Baltimore) 1984, **28:** 269–282.

14a Saeger W, Fassnacht M, Chita R, Prager G, Nies C, Lorenz K, Barlehner E, Simon D, Niederle B, Beuschlein F, Allolio B, Reincke M. High diagnostic accuracy of adrenal core biopsy: results of the German and Austrian adrenal network multicenter trial in 220 consecutive patients. Hum Pathol 2003, **34:** 180–186.

15 Suen KC, Chan NH. Fine needle aspiration biopsy of the adrenal gland. Cytological features and clinical applications. Endocr Pathol 1992, **3:** 173–181.

16 Wadih GE, Nance KV, Silverman JF. Fine-needle aspiration cytology of the adrenal gland. Fifty biopsies in 48 patients. Arch Pathol Lab Med 1992, **116:** 841–846.

Lesions of adrenal cortex
Heterotopia

17 Dahl EV, Bahn RC. Aberrant adrenal cortical tissue near the testis in human infants. Am J Pathol 1962, **40:** 587–598.

18 Graham LS. Celiac accessory adrenal glands. Cancer 1953, **6:** 149–152.

19 Habuchi T, Mizutani Y, Miyakawa M. Ectopic aberrant adrenals with epididymal abnormality. Urology 1992, **39:** 251–253.

20 Johnson RE, Scheithauer B. Massive hyperplasia of testicular adrenal rests in a patient with Nelson's syndrome. Am J Clin Pathol 1982, **77:** 501–507.

21 Kepes JJ, O'Boynick P, Jones S, Baum D, McMillan J, Adams ME.

Adrenal cortical adenoma in the spinal canal of an 8-year-old girl. Am J Surg Pathol 1990, **14**: 481–484.

22 Mitchell A, Scheithauer BW, Sasano H, Hubbard EW, Ebersold MJ. Symptomatic intradural adenoma of the spinal nerve root. Report of two cases. Neurosurgery 1993, **332**: 658–661.

23 Nelson AA. Accessory adrenal cortical tissue. Arch Pathol 1939, **27**: 955–965.

24 Nguyen GK, Vriend R, Ronaghan D, Lakey WH. Heterotopic adrenocortical oncocytoma. A case report with light and electron microscopic studies. Cancer 1992, **70**: 2681–2684.

25 Vestfrid MA. Ectopic adrenal cortex in neonatal liver. Histopathology 1980, **4**: 669–672.

Cortical nodule

26 Commons RR, Callaway CP. Adenomas of the adrenal cortex. Arch Intern Med 1948, **81**: 37–41.

27 Nevile A. The nodular adrenal. Invest Cell Pathol 1978, **1**: 99–111.

28 Sasano H, Okamoto M, Sasano N. Immunohistochemical study of cytochrome P-450 11 beta hydroxylase in human adrenal cortex with mineralo- and glucocorticoid excess. Virchows Arch [A] 1988, **413**: 313–318.

Congenital hyperplasia

29 Dacou-Voutetakis C, Maniati-Christidi M, Dracopoulou-Vabouli M. Genetic aspects of congenital adrenal hyperplasia. J Pediatr Endocrinol Metab 2001, **14** (Suppl 5): 1303–1308.

30 Georgitis WJ. Clinically silent congenital adrenal hyperplasia masquerading as ectopic adrenocorticotropic hormone syndrome. Am J Med 1986, **80**: 703–708.

31 Jones HW Jr, Verkauf BS. Surgical treatment in congenital adrenal hyperplasia. Age at operation and other prognostic factors. Obstet Gynecol 1970, **36**: 1–10.

32 Lee H. CYP21 mutations and congenital adrenal hyperplasia. Clin Genet 2001, **59**: 293–301.

33 Merke DP, Camacho CA. Novel basic and clinical aspects of congenital adrenal hyperplasia. Rev Endocr Metab Disord 2001, **2**: 289–296.

34 Miller WL. Congenital adrenal hyperplasias. Endocrinol Metab Clin North Am 1991, **20**: 721–749.

35 Mininberg DT, Levine LS, New MI. Current concepts in congenital hyperplasia. Pathol Annu 1982, **17**(Pt 2): 179–195.

36 New MI. Congenital adrenal hyperplasia. Pediatr Clin North Am 1968, **15**: 395–407.

37 Sasano H, Masuda T, Ojima M, Fukuchi S, Sasano N. Congenital 17 β-hydroxylase deficiency. A clinicopathologic study. Hum Pathol 1987, **18**: 1002–1007.

38 White PC, New MI, Dupont B. Congenital adrenal hyperplasia. N Engl J Med 1987, **316**: 1519–1586.

Acquired hyperplasia

39 Carney JA, Hruska LS, Beauchamp GD, Gordon H. Dominant inheritance of the complex of myxomas, spotty pigmentation, and endocrine overactivity. Mayo Clin Proc 1986, **61**: 165–172.

40 Hermus AR, Pieters GF, Smals AG, Pesman GJ, Lamberts SW, Benraad TJ, van Haelst UJ, Kloppenborg PW. Transition from pituitary-dependent to adrenal-dependent Cushing's syndrome. N Engl J Med 1988, **38**: 966–970.

41 Hocher B, Bahr V, Dorfmuller S, Oelkers W. Hypercortisolism with non-pigmented micronodular adrenal hyperplasia. Transition from pituitary dependent to adrenal-dependent Cushing's syndrome. Acta Endocrinol 1993, **128**: 120–125.

42 Iseli BE, Hedinger Chr E. Histopathology and ultrastructure of primary adrenocortical nodular dysplasia with Cushing's syndrome. Histopathology 1985, **9**: 1171–1193.

43 Li KH, Asa SL, Kovacs K, Murray D, Singer W. The adrenal cortex in ectopic adrenocorticotropic hormone syndrome. A morphological study with histology, transmission and scanning electron microscopy, flow cytometry, and image analysis. Endocr Pathol 1990, **1**: 183–191.

44 Sasano H, Miyazaki S, Sawai T, Sasano N, Nagura H, Funahashi H, Aiba M, Demura H. Primary pigmented nodular adrenocortical disease (PPNAD). Immunohistochemical and in situ hybridization analysis of steroidogenic enzymes in eight cases. Mod Pathol 1992, **5**: 23–29.

45 Sasano H, Suzuki T, Nagura H. ACTH-independent macronodular adrenocortical hyperplasia. Immunohistochemical and in situ hybridization studies of steroidogenic enzymes. Mod Pathol 1994, **7**: 215–219.

46 Shenoy BV, Carpenter PC, Carney JA. Bilateral primary pigmented nodular adrenocortical disease. Rare cause of the Cushing syndrome. Am J Surg Pathol 1984, **8**: 335–344.

47 Travis WD, Tsokos M, Doppman JL, Nieman L, Chrousos GP, Cutler GB Jr, Loriaux DL, Norton JA. Primary pigmented nodular adrenocortical disease. A light and electron microscopic study of eight cases. Am J Surg Pathol 1989, **13**: 921–930.

Adrenocortical tumors

Clinical features

48 Bergada I, Venara M, Maglio S, Ciaccio M, Diez B, Bergada C, Chemes H. Functional adrenal cortical tumors in pediatric patients: A clinicopathologic and immunohistochemical study of a long term follow-up series. Cancer 1996, **77**: 771–777.

48a Cassarino DS, Santi M, Arruda A, Tsokos M, Ghatak N, Quezado M. Spinal adrenal cortical adenoma with oncocytic features: report of the first intramedullary case and review of the literature. Int J Surg Pathol (in press).

49 Henley DJ, van Heerden JA, Grant CS, Carney JA, Carpenter PC. Adrenal cortical carcinoma—a continuing challenge. Surgery 1983, **94**: 926–931.

50 Hensen J, Buhl M, Oelkers W. The functional spectrum of adrenocortical adenomas. Med Hypotheses 1993, **40**: 217–222.

51 Icard P, Chapuis Y, Adreassian B, Bernard A, Proye C. Adrenocortical carcinoma in surgically treated patients. A retrospective study on 156 cases by the French Association of Endocrine Surgery. Surgery 1992, **112**: 972–979.

52 Kay R, Schumacher OP, Tank ES. Adrenocortical carcinoma in children. J Urol 1983, **130**: 1130–1132.

53 Lack EE, Mulvihill JJ, Travis WD, Kozakewich HP. Adrenal cortical neoplasms in the pediatric and adolescent age group. Clinicopathologic study of 30 cases with emphasis on epidemiological and prognostic factors. Pathol Annu 1992, **27**(Pt 1): 1–53.

54 McClennan BL. Oncologic imaging. Staging and follow-up of renal and adrenal carcinoma. Cancer 1991, **67**: 1199–1208.

55 Nader S, Hickey RC, Sellin RV, Samaan NA. Adrenal cortical carcinoma. A study of 77 cases. Cancer 1983, **52**: 707–711.

56 Riberiro RC, Sandrini Neto RS, Schell MJ, Lacerda L, Sambaio GA, Cat I. Adrenocortical carcinoma in children. A study of 40 cases. J Clin Oncol 1990, **8**: 67–74.

57 Saeger W, Reinhard K, Reinhard C. Hyperplastic and tumorous lesions of the adrenals in an unselected autopsy series. Endocr Pathol 1998, **9**: 235–240.

58 Samaan NA, Hickey RC. Adrenal cortical carcinoma. Semin Oncol 1987, **14**: 292–296.

59 Wood KF, Lus F, Rosenthal FD. Carcinoma of the adrenal cortex without endocrine effects. Br J Surg 1957, **45**: 41–50.

Morphologic features

60 Barksdale SK, Marincola FM, Jaffe G. Carcinosarcoma of the adrenal cortex presenting with mineralocorticoid excess. Am J Surg Pathol 1993, **17**: 941–945.

61 Begin LR. Adrenocortical oncocytoma. Case report with immunocytochemical and ultrastructural study. Virchows Arch [A] 1992, **421**: 533–537.

61a Bisceglia M, Ludovico O, Di Mattia A, Ben-Dor D, Sandbank J, Pasquinelli G, Lau SK, Weiss IM. Adrenocortical oncocytic tumors. An account of ten additional cases and a review of the literature. Int J Surg Pathol (In press, 2004).

62 Brown FM, Gaffey TA, Wold LE, Lloyd RV. Myxoid neoplasms of the adrenal cortex: a rare histologic variant. Am J Surg Pathol 2000, 24: 396–401.

63 Damron TA, Schelper RL, Sorensen L. Cytochemical demonstration of neuromelanin in black pigmented adrenal nodules. Am J Clin Pathol 1987, 87: 334–341.

64 Decorato JW, Gruber H, Petti M, Levowitz BS. Adrenal carcinosarcoma. J Surg Oncol 1990, 45: 134–136.

65 Drachenberg CB, Lee HK, Gann DS, Wong-You-Cheong J, Papadimitriou JC. Adrenal cortical carcinoma with adenosquamous differentiation. Report of a case with immunohistochemical and ultrastructural studies. Arch Pathol Lab Med 1995, 119: 260–265.

66 el-Naggar AK, Evans DB, Mackay B. Oncocytic adrenal cortical carcinoma. Ultrastruct Pathol 1991, 15: 549–556.

67 Erlandson RA, Reuter VE. Oncocytic adrenal cortical adenoma. Ultrastruct Pathol 1991, 15: 539–547.

68 Evans HL, Vassilopoulou-Sellin R. Adrenal cortical neoplasms. A study of 56 cases. Am J Clin Pathol 1996, 105: 76–86.

69 Feldberg E, Guy M, Eisenkraft S, Czernobilsky B. Adrenal cortical adenoma with extensive fat cell metaplasia. Pathol Res Pract 1996, 192: 62–65.

70 Finch C, Davis R, Truong LD. Extensive lipomatous metaplasia in bilateral macronodular adrenocortical hyperplasia. Arch Pathol Lab Med 1999, 123: 167–169.

71 Fischler DF, Nunez C, Levin HS, McMahon JT, Sheeler LR, Adelstein DJ. Adrenal carcinosarcoma presenting in a woman with clinical signs of virilization. A case report with immunohistochemical and ultrastructural findings. Am J Surg Pathol 1992, 16: 626–631.

72 Granger JK, Houn HY, Collins C. Massive hemorrhagic functional adrenal adenoma histologically mimicking angiosarcoma. Report of a case with immunohistochemical study. Am J Surg Pathol 1991, 15: 699–704.

72a Hoang MP, Ayala AG, Albores–Saavedra J. Oncocytic adrenocortical carcinoma: a morphologic, immunohistochemical and ultrastructural study of four cases. Mod Pathol 2002, 15: 973–978.

72b Ivsic T, Komorowski RA, Sudakoff GS, Wilson SD, Datta MW. Adrenal cortical adenoma with adrenalin-type neurosecretory granules clinically mimicking a pheochromocytoma. Arch Pathol Lab Med 2002, 126: 1530.

73 Komiya I, Takasu N, Aizawa T, Yamada T, Koizumi Y, Hashizume K, Ishihara M, Hiramatsu K, Ichikawa K, Katakura M, Kobayashi M, Yamauchi K, Yanagisawa K, Naka M, Miyamoto T. Black (or brown) adrenal cortical adenoma. Its characteristic features on computed tomography and endocrine data. J Clin Endocrinol Metab 1985, 61: 711–717.

74 Lam K-Y, Wat M-S. Adrenal cortical black adenoma: Report of two cases and review of the literature. J Urol Pathol 1996, 4: 183–190.

75 Lin BT, Bonsib SM, Mierau GW, Weiss LM, Medeiros LJ. Oncocytic adrenocortical neoplasms: a report of seven cases and review of the literature. Am J Surg Pathol 1998, 22: 603–614.

76 Macadam RF. Black adenoma of the human adrenal cortex. Cancer 1971, 27: 116–119.

77 Ohta TI, Motoyama T, Imai T, Komeyama T, Watanabe H. Cortico-medullary mixed tumor (pheochromocytoma and cortical adenoma) of the adrenal gland. J Urol Pathol 1995, 3: 157–164.

78 Papotti M, Sapino A, Mazza E, Sandrucci S, Volante M, Bussolati G. Lipomatous changes in adrenocortical adenomas: Report of two cases. Endocr Pathol 1996, 7: 223–228.

79 Sasano H, Suzuki T, Sano T, Kameya T, Sasano N, Nagura H. Adrenocortical oncocytoma. A true nonfunctioning adrenocortical tumor. Am J Surg Pathol 1991, 15: 949–956.

80 Schteingart DE, Oberman HA, Friedman BA, Conn JW. Adrenal cortical neoplasms producing cushing's syndrome. A clinicopathologic study. Cancer 1968, 22: 1005–1013.

81 Seo S, Henley JD, Min K-W. Peculiar cytoplasmic inclusions in oncocytic adrenal cortical tumors: an electron microscopic observation. Ultrastruct Pathol 2002, 26: 229–235.

82 Sienkowski IK, Watkins RM, Anderson VER. Primary tumours aldosteronism due to a black adrenal adenoma. A light and electron microscopic study. J Clin Pathol 1984, 37: 143–149.

83 Vyberg M, Sestoft L. Combined adrenal myelolipoma and adenoma associated with Cushing's syndrome. Am J Clin Pathol 1986, 86: 541–545.

Electron microscopic, histochemical, immunohistochemical, and molecular genetic features

84 Busam KJ, Iversen K, Coplan KA, Old LJ, Stockert E, Chen Y-T, McGregor D, Jungbluth A. Immunoreactivity for A103, and antibody to Melan-A (Mart-1), in adrenocortical and other steroid tumors. Am J Surg Pathol 1998, 22: 57–63.

85 Chivite A, Matias-Guiu X, Pons C, Algaba F, Prat J. Inhibin A expression in adrenal neoplasms: a new immunohistochemical marker for adrenocortical tumors. Appl Immunohistochem 1998, 6: 42–49.

86 Cho EY, Ahn GH. Immunoexpression of inhibin alpha subunit in adrenal neoplasms. AIMM 2001, 9: 222–228.

87 Cote RJ, Cordon-Cardo C, Reuter VE, Rosen PP. Immunopathology of adrenal and renal cortical tumors. Coordinated change in antigen expression is associated with neoplastic conversion in the adrenal cortex. Am J Pathol 1990, 136: 1077–1084.

88 Faical S, Maciel RM, Nose-Alberti V, Santos MC, Kater CE. Immunodetection of insulin-like growth factor I (IGF-I) in normal and pathological adrenocortical tissue. Endocr Pathol 1998, 9: 63–70.

89 Fogt F, Vortmeyer AO, Poremba C, Minda M, Harris CA, Tomaszewski JE. Bcl-2 expression in normal adrenal glands and in adrenal neoplasms. Mod Pathol 1998, 11: 716–720.

89a Giordano TJ, Thomas DG, Kuick R, Lizyness M, Misek DE, Smith AL, Sanders D, Aljundi RT, Gauger PG, Thompson NW, Taylor JMG, Hanash SM. Distinct transcriptional profiles of adrenocortical tumors uncovered by DNA microarray analysis. Am J Pathol 2003, 162: 251–531.

90 Haak HR, Fleuren G-J. Neuroendocrine differentiation of adrenocortical tumors. Cancer 1995, 75: 860–864.

91 Ilvesmaki V, Kahri AI, Miettinen PJ, Voutilainen R. Insulin-like growth factors (IGFs) and their receptors in adrenal tumors. High IGF-II expression in functional adrenocortical carcinomas. J Clin Endocrinol Metab 1993, 77: 852–858.

92 Jorda M, De Madeiros B, Nadji M. Calretinin and inhibin are useful in separating adrenocortical neoplasms from pheochromocytomas. AIMM 2002, 10: 67–70.

93 Kamio T, Shigematsu K, Kawai K, Tsuchiyama H. Immunoreactivity and receptor expression of insulinlike growth factor I and insulin in human adrenal tumors. An immunohistochemical study of 94 cases. Am J Pathol 1991, 138: 83–91.

94 Kamio T, Shigematsu K, Sou H, Kawai K, Tsuchiyama H. Immunohistochemical expression of epidermal growth factor receptors in human adrenocortical carcinoma. Hum Pathol 1990, 21: 277–282.

95 Komminoth P, Roth J, Schroder S, Saremaslani P, Heitz PU. Overlapping expression of immunohistochemical markers and synaptophysin mRNA in pheochromocytomas and adrenocortical carcinomas. Implications for the differential

diagnosis of adrenal gland tumors. Lab Invest 1995, **72:** 424–431.

96 Kumar D, Kumar S. Adrenal cortical adenoma and adrenal metastasis of renal cell carcinoma. Immunohistochemical and DNA ploidy analysis. Mod Pathol 1993, **6:** 36–41.

97 Loy TS, Nashelsky MB. Reactivity of B72.3 with adenocarcinomas. An immunohistochemical study of 476 cases. Cancer 1993, **72:** 2495–2498.

98 Loy TS, Phillips RW, Linder CL. A103 immunostaining in the diagnosis of adrenal cortical tumors: an immunohistochemical study of 316 cases. Arch Pathol Lab Med 2002, **126:** 170–172.

99 Mackay B, El-Naggar A, Ordonez NG. Ultrastructure of adrenal cortical carcinoma. Ultrastruct Pathol 1994, **18:** 181–190.

100 Miettinen M. Neuroendocrine differentiation in adrenocortical carcinoma. New immunohistochemical findings by electron microscopy. Lab Invest 1992, **66:** 169–174.

101 Ohgaki H, Kleihues P, Heitz PU. p53 mutations in sporadic adrenocortical tumors. Int J Cancer 1993, **54:** 408–410.

102 Sasano H, Suzuki T, Nagura H, Nishikawa T. Steroidogenesis in human adrenocortical carcinoma. Biochemical activities, immunohistochemistry, and in situ hybridization of steroidogenic enzymes and histopathologic study in nine cases. Hum Pathol 1993, **24:** 397–404.

103 Sasano H, White PC, New MI, Sasano N. Immunohistochemical localization of cytochrome P-450$_{C21}$ in human adrenal cortex and its relation to endocrine function. Hum Pathol 1988, **19:** 181–185.

104 Schroder S, Padberg BC, Achilles E, Holl K, Dralle H, Kloppel G. Immunocytochemistry in adrenocortical tumours. A clinicomorphological study of 72 neoplasms. Virchows Arch [A] 1992, **420:** 65–70.

105 Sheahan K, O'Brien MJ, Burke B, Dervan PA, O'Keane JC, Gottlieb LS, Zamcheck N. Differential reactivities of carcinoembryonic antigen (CEA) and CEA-related monoclonal and polyclonal antibodies in common epithelial malignancies. Am J Clin Pathol 1990, **94:** 157–164.

106 Silva EG, Mackay B, Samaan NA, Hickey RC. Adrenocortical carcinomas. An ultrastructural study of 22 cases. Ultrastruct Pathol 1982, **3:** 1–7.

107 Zhao J, Speel EJ, Muletta-Feurer S, Rutimann K, Saremaslani P, Roth J, Heitz PU, Komminoth P. Analysis of genomic alterations in sporadic adrenocortical lesions. Gain of chromosome 17 is an early event in adrenocortical tumorigenesis. Am J Pathol 1999, **155:** 1039–1045.

Differential diagnosis

107a Aubert S, Wacrenier A, Leroy X, Devos P, Carnaille B, Proye C, Wemeau JL, Lecomte-Houcke M, Leteurtre E. Weiss system revisited: a clinicopathologic and immunohistochemical study of 49 adrenocortical tumors. Am J Surg Pathol 2002, **26:** 1612–1619.

108 Bergada I, Venara M, Maglio S, Ciaccio M, Diez B, Bergada C, Chemes H. Functional adrenal cortical tumors in pediatric patients: A clinicopathologic and immunohistochemical study of a long term follow-up series. Cancer 1996, **77:** 771–777.

109 Bugg MF, Ribeiro RC, Roberson PK, Lloyd RV, Sandrini R, Silva JB, Epelman S, Shapiro DN, Parham DM. Correlation of pathologic features with clinical outcome in pediatric adrenocortical neoplasia. A study of a Brazilian population. Brazilian Group for Treatment of Childhood Adrenocortical Tumors. Am J Clin Pathol 1994, **101:** 625–629.

110 Cagle PT, Hough AJ, Pysher TJ, Page DL, Johnson EH, Kirkland RT, Holcombe JH, Hawkins EP. Comparison of adrenal cortical tumors in children and adults. Cancer 1986, **57:** 2235–2237.

111 Cibas ES, Medeiros LJ, Weinberg DS, Gelb AB, Weiss LM. Cellular DNA profiles of benign and malignant adrenocortical tumors. Am J Surg Pathol 1990, **14:** 948–955.

112 Cote RJ, Cordon-Cardo C, Reuter VE, Rosen PP. Immunopathology of adrenal and renal cortical tumors.

Coordinated change in antigen expression is associated with neoplastic conversion in the adrenal cortex. Am J Pathol 1990, **136:** 1077–1084.

113 Evans HL, Vassilopoulou-Sellin R. Adrenal cortical neoplasms. A study of 56 cases. Am J Clin Pathol 1996, **105:** 76–86.

114 Fetsch PA, Powers CN, Zakowski MF, Abati A. Anti-α-inhibin: marker of choice for the consistent distinction between adrenocortical carcinoma and renal cell carcinoma in fine-needle aspiration. Cancer Cytopathol 1999, **87:** 168–172.

115 Fogt F, Vargas MP, Zhuang Z, Merino MJ. Utilization of molecular genetics in the differentiation between adrenal cortical adenomas and carcinomas. Hum Pathol 1998, **29:** 518–521.

116 Gaffey MJ, Traweek ST, Mills SE, Travis WD, Lack EE, Medeiros LJ, Weiss LM. Cytokeratin expression in adrenocortical neoplasia. An immunohistochemical and biochemical study with implications for the differential diagnosis of adrenocortical, hepatocellular, and renal cell carcinoma. Hum Pathol 1992, **23:** 144–153.

117 Gandour MJ, Grizzle WE. A small adrenocortical carcinoma with aggressive behavior. An evaluation of criteria for malignancy. Arch Pathol Lab Med 1986, **110:** 1076–1079.

118 Gupta D, Shidham V, Holden J, Layfield L. Value of topoisomerase II alpha, MIB-1, p53, E-cadherin, retinoblastoma gene protein product, and HER-2/neu immunohistochemical expression for the predication of biologic behavior in adrenocortical neoplasms. AIMM 2001, **9:** 215–221.

119 Hirano Y, Fujita K, Suzuki K, Ushiyama T, Ohtawara Y, Tsuda F. Telomerase activity as an indicator of potential malignant adrenal tumors. Cancer 1998, **83:** 772–776.

120 Hough AJ, Hollifield HW, Page DL, Hartmann WH. Prognostic factors in adrenal cortical tumors. Am J Clin Pathol 1979, **72:** 390–399.

121 Iino K, Sasano H, Yabuki N, Oki Y, Kikuchi A, Yoshimi T, Nagura H. DNA topoisomerase IIα and Ki-67 in human adrenocortical neoplasms: a possible marker of differentiation between adenomas and carcinomas. Mod Pathol 1997, **10:** 901–907.

122 Kay S. Hyperplasia and neoplasia of the adrenal gland. Pathol Annu 1976, **11:** 103–139.

123 Medeiros LJ, Weiss LM. New developments in the pathologic diagnosis of adrenal cortical neoplasms. A review. Am J Clin 1992, **97:** 73–83.

124 Nakazumi H, Sasano H, Iino K, Ohashi Y, Orikasa S. Expression of cell cycle inhibitor p27 and Ki-67 in human adrenocortical neoplasms. Mod Pathol 1998, **11:** 1165–1170.

125 Padberg BC, Lauritzen I, Achilles E, Holl K, Bressel M, Kloppel G, Dralle H, Schroder S. DNA cytophotometry in adrenocortical tumours. A clinicomorphological study of 66 cases. Virchows Arch [A] 1991, **419:** 167–170.

126 Page DL, Hough AJ, Gray GF. Diagnosis and prognosis of adrenocortical neoplasm. Arch Pathol Lab Med 1986, **110:** 993–994.

127 Renshaw AA, Granter SR. A comparison of A103 and inhibin reactivity in adrenal cortical tumors: distinction from hepatocellular carcinoma and renal tumors. Mod Pathol 1998, **11:** 1160–1164.

128 Sasano H, Saito Y, Sato I, Sasano N, Nagura H. Nucleolar organizer regions in human adrenocortical disorders. Mod Pathol 1990, **3:** 591–595.

129 Sasano H, Suzuki T, Moriya T. Discerning malignancy in resected adrenocortical neoplasms. Endocr Pathol 2002, **12:** 397–406.

130 Shin SJ, Hoda RS, Ying L, DeLellis RA. Diagnostic utility of the monoclonal antibody A103 in fine needle aspiration biopsies of the adrenal. Am J Clin Pathol 2000, **113:** 295–302.

131 Slooten HV, Schaberg A, Smeenk D, Moolenaar AJ. Morphologic characteristics of benign and malignant adrenocortical tumors. Cancer 1985, **55:** 766–773.

131a Stojadinovic A, Brennan MF, Hoos A, Omeroglu A, Leung DHY, Dudas ME, Nissan A, Cordon-Cardo C, Ghossein RA. Adrenocortical adenoma and carcinoma: histopathological and molecular comparative analysis. Mod Pathol 2003, **16**: 742–751.

132 Tang CL, Gray GF. Adrenocortical neoplasms. Prognosis and morphology. Urology 1975, **5**: 691–695.

133 Vargas MP, Vargas HI, Kleiner DE, Merino MJ. Adrenocortical neoplasms: role of prognostic markers MIB-1, P53, and RB. Am J Surg Pathol 1997, **21**: 556–562.

134 Weiss LM. Comparative histologic study of 43 metastasizing and nonmetastasizing adrenocortical tumors. Am J Surg Pathol 1984, **8**: 163–169.

135 Weiss LM, Medeiros LJ, Vickery AL Jr. Pathologic features of prognostic significance in adrenocortical carcinoma. Am J Surg Pathol 1989, **13**: 202–206.

136 Wick MR, Cherwitz DL, McGlennen RC, Dehner LP. Adrenocortical carcinoma. An immunohistochemical comparison with renal cell carcinoma. Am J Pathol 1986, **122**: 343–352.

136a Wieneke JA, Thompson IDR, Heffess CS. Adrenal cortical neoplasms in the pediatric population: a clinicopathologic and immunophenotypic analysis of 83 patients. Am J Surg Pathol 2003, **24**: 867–881.

137 Winter P, Miersch WD, Vogel J, Jaeger N. On the necessity of adrenal extirpation combined with radical nephrectomy. J Urol 1990, **144**: 842–843.

137a Zhang PJ, Genega EM, Tomaszewski JE, Pasha TL, Livolsi VA. The role of calretinin, inhibin, melan-a, bcl-2, and c-kit in differentiating adrenal cortical and medullary tumors: an immunohistochemical study. Mod Pathol 2003, **16**: 591–597.

Spread and metastases

138 Didolkar MS, Bescher RA, Elias EG, Moore RH. Natural history of adrenal cortical carcinoma. A clinicopathologic study of 42 patients. Cancer 1981, **47**: 2153–2161.

139 Grondal S, Cedermark B, Eriksson B, Grimelius L, Harach R, Kristoffersson A, Rastad J, Uden P, Akerstrom G. Adrenocortical carcinoma. A retrospective study of a rare tumor with a poor prognosis. Eur J Surg Oncol 1990, **16**: 500–506.

140 Hogan TF, Gilchrist KW, Westring DW, Citrin DL. A clinical and pathological study of adrenocortical carcinoma. Cancer 1980, **45**: 2880–2883.

141 Kwauk S, Burt M. Pulmonary metastases from adrenal cortical carcinoma. Results of resection. J Surg Oncol 1993, **53**: 243–246.

142 McCartney ACE. Metastatic adrenal carcinoma masquerading as primary bronchial carcinoma. Report of two cases. Thorax 1984, **39**: 315–316.

143 Milchgrub S, Wiley EL. Adrenal carcinoma presenting as a lesion resembling cutaneous angiosarcoma. Cancer 1991, **67**: 3087–3092.

144 Nader S, Hickey RC, Sellin RV, Samaan NA. Adrenal cortical carcinoma. A study of 77 cases. Cancer 1983, **52**: 707–711.

145 Pommier RF, Brennan MF. An eleven-year experience with adrenocortical carcinoma. Surgery 1992, **112**: 963–970.

Treatment and prognosis

146 Brennan MF. Adrenocortical carcinoma. Cancer 1988, **37**: 348–365.

147 Camuto P, Schinella R, Gilchrist K, Citrin D, Fredrickson G. Adrenal cortical carcinoma. Flow cytometric study of 22 cases, an ECOG study. Urology 1991, **37**: 380–384.

148 Karakousis CP, Rao U, Moore R. Adrenal adenocarcinomas. Histologic grading and survival. J Surg Oncol 1985, **29**: 105–111.

149 Kasperlik-Zaluska AA, Migdalska BM, Zgliczynski S, Makowska AM. Adrenocortical carcinoma. A clinical study and treatment results of 52 patients. Cancer 1995, **75**: 2587–2591.

150 Luton JP, Cerdas S, Billaud L, Thomas G, Guilhaume B, Bertagna X, Laudat MH, Louvel A, Chapuis Y, Blondeau P, et al. Clinical features of adrenocortical carcinoma, prognostic factors, and the effect of mitotane therapy. N Engl J Med 1990, **322**: 1195–1201.

151 Markoe AM, Serber W, Micaily B, Brady LW. Radiation therapy for adjunctive treatment of adrenal cortical carcinoma. Am J Clin Oncol 1991, **14**: 170–174.

152 McNicol AM, Struthers AJ, Nolan CE, Hermans J, Haak HR. Proliferation in adrenocortical tumors: correlation with clinical outcome and p53 status. Endocr Pathol 1997, **8**: 29–36.

153 Pommier RF, Brennan MF. An eleven-year experience with adrenocortical carcinoma. Surgery 1992, **112**: 963–970.

154 Suzuki T, Sasano H, Nisikawa T, Rhame J, Wilkinson DS, Nagura H. Discerning malignancy in human adrenocortical neoplasms. Utility of DNA flow cytometry and immunohistochemistry. Mod Pathol 1992, **5**: 224–231.

155 Vargas MP, Vargas HI, Kleiner DE, Merino MJ. Adrenocortical neoplasms: role of prognostic markers MIB-1, P53, and RB. Am J Surg Pathol 1997, **21**: 556–562.

156 Vassilopoulou-Sellin R, Guinee VF, Klein MJ, Taylor SH, Hess KR, Schultz PN, Samaan NA. Impact of adjuvant mitotane on the clinical course of patients with adrenocortical cancer. Cancer 1993, **71**: 3119–3123.

157 Weiss LM, Medeiros LJ, Vickery AL Jr. Pathologic features of prognostic significance in adrenocortical carcinoma. Am J Surg Pathol 1989, **13**: 202–206.

158 Zerbini C, Kozakewich HP, Weinberg DS, Mundt DJ, Edwards JA III, Lack EE. Adrenocortical neoplasms in childhood and adolescence. Analysis of prognostic factors including DNA content. Endocr Pathol 1992, **3**: 116–128.

Functional manifestations

159 Grunberg SM. Development of Cushing's syndrome and virilization after presentation of a nonfunctioning adrenocortical carcinoma. Cancer 1982, **50**: 815–816.

160 O'Hare MJ, Monaghan P, Neville A. The pathology of adrenocortical neoplasia. A correlated structural and functional approach to the diagnosis of malignant disease. Hum Pathol 1979, **10**: 137–154.

Nonfunctioning lesions

161 Corsello SM, Della Casa S, Bollanti L, Rufini V, Rota CA, Danza F, Colasanti S, Vellante C, Troncone L, Barbarino A. Incidentally discovered adrenal masses. A functional and morphological study. Exp Clin Endocrinol 1993, **101**: 131–137.

162 Doerr HG, Sippell WG, Drop SLS, Bidlingmaier F, Knorr D. Evidence of 11 beta-hydroxylase deficiency in childhood adrenocortical tumors. The plasma corticosterone/11-deoxycorticosterone ratio as a possible marker for malignancy. Cancer 1987, **60**: 1625–1629.

163 Hedeland H, Östberg G, Hokfelt B. On the prevalence of adrenocortical adenomas in an autopsy material in relation to hypertension and diabetes. Acta Med Scand 1968, **184**: 211–214.

164 Lewinsky BS, Grigor KM, Symington T, Neville AM. The clinical and pathologic features of "nonhormonal" adrenocortical tumors. Report of twenty new cases and review of the literature. Cancer 1974, **33**: 778–790.

165 Nicolis GL, Gabrilove JL. Studies on the efficiency of adrenocortical II β-hydroxylation in the human subject. J Clin Endocrinol Metab 1969, **29**: 831–836.

166 Suzuki T, Sasano H, Sawai T, Tsunoda K, Nisikawa T, Abe K, Yoshinaga K, Nagura H. Small adrenocortical tumors without apparent clinical endocrine abnormalities. Immunolocalization of steroidogenic enzymes. Pathol Res Pract 1992, **188**: 883–889.

167 Yamakita N, Saitoh M, Mercado-Asis LB, Kitada M, Morita H, Yasuda K, Miura K. Asymptomatic adrenal tumor; 386 cases in Japan including our 7 cases. Endocrinol Jpn 1990, **37**: 671–684.

Aldosteronism

168 Aiba M, Suzuki H, Kageyama K, Murai M, Tazaki H, Abe O, Saruta T. Spironolactone bodies in aldosteromas and in the attached adrenals. Enzyme histochemical study of 19 cases of primary aldosteronism and a case of aldosteronism due to bilateral diffuse hyperplasia of the zona glomerulosa. Am J Pathol 1981, **103**: 404–410.

169 Alterman SL, Dominguez C, Lopez-Gomez A, Lieber AL. Primary adrenocortical carcinoma causing aldosteronism. Cancer 1969, **24**: 602–609.

170 Banks WA, Kastin AJ, Biglieri EG, Ruiz AE. Primary adrenal hyperplasia. A new subset of primary hyperaldosteronism. J Clin Endocrinol Metab 1984, **58**: 783–785.

171 Cohen RJ, Brits R, Phillips JI, Both JP. Primary hyperaldosteronism due to a functional black (pigmented) adenoma of the adrenal cortex. Arch Pathol Lab Med 1991, **115**: 813–815.

172 Ganguly A. Primary aldosteronism. N Engl J Med 1998, **339**: 1828–1834.

173 Ganguly A, Donohue JP. Primary aldosteronism. Pathophysiology, diagnosis and treatment. J Urol 1983, **129**: 241–247.

174 Gleason PE, Weinberger MH, Pratt JH, Bihrle R, Dugan J, Eller D, Donohue JP. Evaluation of diagnostic tests in the differential diagnosis of primary aldosteronism. Unilateral adenoma versus bilateral micronodular hyperplasia. J Urol 1993, **150**: 1365–1368.

175 Gordon RD, Klemm SA, Tunny TJ, Stowasser M. Primary aldosteronism. Hypertension with a genetic basis. Lancet 1992, **340**: 159–161.

176 Gordon RD, Stowasser M, Tunny TJ, Klemm SA, Finn WL, Krek AL. Clinical and pathological diversity of primary aldosteronism, including a new familial variety. Clin Exp Pharmacol Physiol 1991, **18**: 283–286.

177 Hogan MJ, McRae J, Schambelan M, Biglieri EG. Location of aldosterone-producing adenomas with ^{131}I-19-iodocholesterol. N Engl J Med 1976, **294**: 410–414.

178 Hsu S-M, Raine L, Martin HF. Spironolactone bodies. An immunoperoxidase study with biochemical correlation. Am J Clin Pathol 1981, **75**: 92–95.

179 Imai T, Seo H, Murata Y, Funahashi H, Satoh Y, Sasano H, Matsui N, Takagi H. Dexamethasone-nonsuppressible cortisol in two cases with aldosterone-producing adenoma. J Clin Endocrinol Metab 1991, **72**: 575–581.

180 Kano K, Sato S, Hama H. Adrenal adenomata causing primary aldosteronism. An ultrastructural study of twenty-five cases. Virchows Arch [A] 1979, **384**: 93–102.

181 Neville AM, Symington T. Pathology of primary aldosteronism. Cancer 1966, **19**: 1854–1868.

182 O'Neal LW, Kissane JM, Hartroft PM. The kidney in endocrine hypertension. Cushing's syndrome, pheochromocytoma and aldosteronism. Arch Surg 1970, **100**: 498–505.

183 Reidbord H, Fisher ER. Aldosteronoma and nonfunctioning adrenal cortical adenoma. Comparative ultrastructural study. Arch Pathol 1969, **88**: 155–161.

184 Shrago SS, Waisman J, Cooper PH. Spironolactone bodies in an adrenal adenoma. Arch Pathol 1975, **99**: 416–420.

185 Slee PH, Schaberg A, Van Brummelen P. Carcinoma of the adrenal cortex causing primary hyperaldosteronism. A case report and review of the literature. Cancer 1983, **51**: 2341–2345.

186 Weinberger MH, Fineberg NS. The diagnosis of primary aldosteronism and separation of two major subtypes. Arch Intern Med 1993, **153**: 2125–2129.

187 White PC. Disorders of aldosterone biosynthesis and action. N Engl J Med 1994, **331**: 250–258.

188 Yamamoto A, Naroda T, Kagawa S, Umaki Y, Shintani Y, Sano T, Sasano H. Deoxycorticosterone-secreting adrenocortical carcinoma. Endocr Pathol 1993, **4**: 165–168.

189 Young WF Jr, Hogan MJ, Klee GG, Grant CS, van Heerden JA. Primary aldosteronism. Diagnosis and treatment. Mayo Clin Proc 1990, **65**: 96–110.

Cushing's syndrome

190 Aiba M, Hirayama A, Iri H, Ito Y, Fujimoto Y, Mabuchi G, Murai M, Tazaki H, Maruyama H, Saruta T, et al. Adrenocorticotropic hormone-independent bilateral adrenocortical macronodular hyperplasia as a distinct subtype of Cushing's syndrome. Enzyme histochemical and ultrastructural study of four cases with a review of the literature. Am J Clin Pathol 1991, **96**: 334–340.

191 Aiba M, Kawakami M, Ito Y, Fujimoto Y, Suda T, Demura H. Bilateral adrenocortical adenomas causing Cushing's syndrome. Report of two cases with enzyme histochemical and ultrastructural studies and a review of the literature. Arch Pathol Lab Med 1992, **116**: 146–150.

192 Aron DC, Tyrrell JB, Fitzgerald PA, Findling JW, Forsham PH. Cushing's syndrome. Problems in diagnosis. Medicine (Baltimore) 1981, **60**: 25–33.

193 Azzopardi JG, Williams ED. Pathology of "nonendocrine" tumors associated with Cushing's syndrome. Cancer 1968, **22**: 274–286.

194 Gilbert MG, Cleveland WW. Cushing's syndrome in infancy. Pediatrics 1970, **46**: 217–229.

195 Hartmann CA, Gross U, Stein H. Cushing syndrome-associated pheochromocytoma and adrenal carcinoma. An immunohistological investigation. Pathol Res Pract 1992, **188**: 287–295.

196 Joffe SN, Brown C. Nodular adrenal hyperplasia and Cushing's syndrome. Surgery 1983, **17**: 919–925.

197 Neville AM, Symington T. The pathology of the adrenal gland in Cushing's syndrome. J Pathol Bacteriol 1967, **93**: 19–35.

198 Neville AM, Symington T. Bilateral adrenocortical hyperplasia in children with Cushing's syndrome. J Pathol 1972, **107**: 95–106.

199 Orth DN. Cushing's syndrome. N Engl J Med 1995, **332**: 791–803.

200 Perry RR, Nieman LK, Cutler GB Jr, Chrousos GP, Loriaux DL, Doppman JL, Travis WD, Norton JA. Primary adrenal causes of Cushing's syndrome. Diagnosis and surgical management. Ann Surg 1989, **210**: 59–68.

201 Reidbord H, Fisher ER. Electron microscopic study of adrenal cortical hyperplasia in Cushing's syndrome. Arch Pathol 1968, **86**: 419–426.

202 Sarkar R, Thompson NW, McLeod MK. The role of adrenalectomy in Cushing's syndrome. Surgery 1990, **108**: 1079–1084.

203 Schteingart DE, Oberman HA, Friedman BA, Conn JW. Adrenal cortical neoplasms producing Cushing's syndrome. A clinicopathologic study. Cancer 1968, **22**: 1005–1013.

204 Scott HW, Abumrad NN, Orth DN. Tumors of the adrenal cortex and Cushing's syndrome. Ann Surg 1985, **201**: 586–594.

205 Smals AGH, Pieters GFFM, Van Haelst UJG, Kloppenborg PWC. Macronodular adrenocortical hyperplasia on long-standing Cushing's disease. J Clin Endocrinol Metab 1984, **58**: 25–31.

206 Thomas CG Jr, Smith AT, Griffith JM, Askin FB. Hyperadrenalism in childhood and adolescence. Ann Surg 1984, **199**: 538–548.

207 Upton GV, Amatruda TT Jr. Evidence for the presence of tumor peptides with corticotropin-releasing-factor-like activity in the ectopic ACTH syndrome. N Engl J Med 1971, **285**: 419–424.

208 Young WF Jr, Carney JA, Musa BU, Wulffraat NM, Lens JW, Drexhage HA. Familial Cushing's syndrome due to primary pigmented nodular adrenocortical disease. Reinvestigation 50 years later. N Engl J Med 1989, **321**: 1677–1678.

209 Zeiger MA, Nieman LK, Cutler GB, Chrousos GP, Doppman JL, Travis WD, Norton JA. Primary bilateral adrenocortical causes of Cushing's syndrome. Surgery 1991, **110**: 1106–1115.

Adrenogenital syndrome

210 Burrington JD, Stephens CA. Virilizing tumors of the adrenal gland in childhood. Report of eight cases. J Pediatr Surg 1969, **4**: 291–302.

211 Del Gaudio AD, Del Gaudio GA. Virilizing adrenocortical tumors in adult women. Report of 10 patients, 2 of whom each had a tumor secreting only testosterone. Cancer 1993, **72**: 1997–2003.

212 Derksen J, Nagesser SK, Meinders AE, Haak HR, van de Velde CJ. Identification of virilizing adrenal tumors in hirsute women. N Engl J Med 1994, **331**: 968–973.

213 Fischler DF, Nunez C, Levin HS, McMahon JT, Sheeler LR, Adelstein DJ. Adrenal carcinosarcoma presenting in a woman with clinical signs of virilization. A case report with immunohistochemical and ultrastructural findings. Am J Surg Pathol 1992, **16**: 626–631.

214 Gabrilove JL, Sharma DC, Wotiz HH, Dorfman RI. Feminizing adrenocortical tumors in the male. A review of 52 cases including a case report. Medicine (Baltimore) 1965, **44**: 37–79.

215 Heinbecker P, O'Neal LW, Ackerman LV. Functioning and nonfunctioning adrenal cortical tumors. Surg Gynecol Obstet 1957, **105**: 21–33.

216 Kenny FM, Hashida Y, Askari HA, Sieber WH, Fetterman GH. Virilizing tumors of the adrenal cortex. Am J Dis Child 1968, **115**: 445–458.

217 Patterson J. Diagnosis of adrenal tumours. A new chemical test. Lancet 1947, **2**: 580–581.

218 Sakai Y, Yanase T, Hara T, Takayanagi R, Haji M, Nawata H. Mechanism of abnormal production of adrenal androgens in patients with adrenocortical adenomas and carcinomas. J Clin Endocrinol Metab 1994, **78**: 36–40.

Other functional manifestations

219 Falchuk KR. Inappropriate antidiuretic hormone-like syndrome associated with an adrenal carcinoma. Am J Med Sci 1973, **266**: 393–395.

220 Lipsett MB, Hertz R, Ross GT. Clinical and pathophysiologic aspects of adrenocortical carcinoma. Am J Med 1963, **35**: 374–383.

221 Williams R, Kellie AE, Wade AP, Williams ED, Chalmers TM. Hypoglycaemia and abnormal steroid metabolism in adrenal tumours. Q J Med 1961, **30**: 269–284.

Lesions of adrenal medulla

222 Askin FB, Perlman EJ. Neuroblastoma and peripheral neuroectodermal tumors. Am J Clin Pathol 1998, **109**: S23–S30.

223 Gestblom C, Grynfeld A, Ora I, Ortoft E, Larsson C, Axelson H, Sandstedt B, Cserjesi P, Olson EN, Pahlman S. The basic helix-loop-helix transcription factor dHAND, a marker gene for the developing human sympathetic nervous system, is expressed in both high- and low-stage neuroblastomas. Lab Invest 1999, **79**: 67–79.

224 Hoehner JC, Hedborg F, Eriksson L, Sandstedt B, Grimelius L, Olsen L, Pahlman S. Development gene expression of sympathetic nervous system tumors reflects their histogenesis. Lab Invest 1998, **78**: 29–45.

225 Lack EE. Pathology of adrenal and extra-adrenal paraganglia. Major problems in pathology, vol. 29. Philadelphia, 1994, WB Saunders.

226 Magno G, Grasso S. Glial cells in the ontogenesis of the human peripheral sympathetic nervous system and in neuroblastoma. Pathologica 2001, **93**: 505–516.

227 Shimada H. Neuroblastoma. Pathology and biology. Acta Pathol Jpn 1992, **42**: 229–241.

Neuroblastoma
General and clinical features

228 Allan SG, Cornbleet MA, Carmichael J, Arnott SJ, Smyth JF. Adult neuroblastoma. Report of three cases and review of the literature. Cancer 1986, **57**: 2419–2421.

229 Anderson HJ, Hariri J. Congenital neuroblastoma in a fetus with multiple malformations. Metastasis in the umbilical cord as a cause of intrauterine death. Virchows Arch [A] 1983, **400**: 219–222.

230 Emery LG, Shields M, Shah NR, Garbes A. Neuroblastoma associated with Beckwith-Wiedemann syndrome. Cancer 1983, **52**: 176–179.

231 Gaisie G, Oh KS, Young LW. Coexistent neuroblastoma and Hirschsprung's disease. Another manifestation of the neurocristopathy. Pediatr Radiol 1979, **8**: 161–163.

231a Gambini C, Conte M, Bernini G, Angelini P, Pession A, Paolucci P, Donfrancesco A, Veneselli W, Nlazzocco K, Tonini GP, Raffaghello I, Dominici C, Morando A, Negri F, Favre A, De Bernardi B, Pistoia V. Neuroblastic tumors associated with opsoclonus-myoclonus syndrome: Histological, immunohistochemical and molecular features of 15 Italian cases. Virchows Arch 2003, **442**: 555–562.

232 Kaye JA, Warhol MJ, Kretschmar C, Landsberg L, Frei E III. Neuroblastoma in adults. Three case reports and a review of the literature. Cancer 1986, **58**: 1149–1157.

233 Kushner BH, Gilbert F, Helson L. Familial neuroblastoma. Case reports, literature review, and etiologic considerations. Cancer 1986, **57**: 1887–1893.

234 Sherman S, Roizen N. Fetal hydantoin syndrome and neuroblastoma. Lancet 1976, **2**: 517.

235 Suzuki H, Honzumi M, Funada M, Tomiyama H. Metachronous bilateral adrenal neuroblastoma. Cancer 1985, **56**: 1490–1492.

236 Sy WM, Edmonson JH. The developmental defects associated with neuroblastoma. Etiologic implications. Cancer 1968, **22**: 234–238.

237 Witzleben CL, Landy RA. Disseminated neuroblastoma in a child with von Recklinghausen's disease. Cancer 1974, **34**: 786–790.

Morphologic features

238 Cozzuto C, Carbone A. Pleomorphic (anaplastic) neuroblastoma. Arch Pathol Lab Med 1988, **112**: 621–625.

239 Hachitanda Y, Tsuneyoshi M. Neuroblastoma with a distinct organoid pattern. A clinicopathologic, immunohistochemical and ultrastructural study. Hum Pathol 1994, **25**: 67–72.

240 Hiyama E, Yokoyama T, Hiyama K, Yamaoka H, Matsuura Y, Nishimura S, Ueda K. Multifocal neuroblastoma: Biologic behaviour and surgical aspects. Cancer 2000, **88**: 1955–1963.

241 Joshi VV, Silverman JF. Pathology of neuroblastic tumors. Semin Diagn Pathol 1994, **11**: 107–117.

Electron microscopic, histochemical, immunohistochemical, and molecular genetic features

242 Artlieb U, Krepler R, Wiche G. Expression of microtubule-associated proteins, Map-1 and Map-2, in human neuroblastomas and differential diagnosis of immature neuroblasts. Lab Invest 1985, **53**: 684–691.

243 Brodeur GM. Neuroblastoma. Clinical significance of genetic abnormalities. Cancer Surv 1990, **9**: 673–688.

243a Brodeur GM. Neuroblastoma: biological insights into a clinical enigma. Cancer 2003, **3**: 203–216.

244 Brodeur GM. Molecular pathology of human neuroblastomas. Semin Diagn Pathol 1994, **11**: 118–125.

245 Brodeur GM, Azar C, Brother M, Hiemstra J, Kaufman B, Marshall H, Moley J, Nakagawara A, Saylors R, Scavarda N, et al. Neuroblastoma. Effect of genetic factors on prognosis and treatment. Cancer 1992, **70**: 1685–1694.

246 Christiansen H, Schestag J, Christiansen NM, Grzeschik KH, Lampert L. Clinical impact of chromosome 1 aberrations in neuroblastoma. A metaphase and interphase cytogenetic study. Genes Chromosomes Cancer 1992, **5**: 1141–1149.

247 DeLellis RA. Formaldehyde-induced fluorescence technique for the demonstration of biogenic amines in diagnostic histopathology. Cancer 1971, **28**: 1704–1710.

248 Donovan MJ, Hempstead BL, Horvath C, Chao MV, Schofield D.

Immunohistochemical localization of Trk receptor protein in pediatric small round blue cell tumors. Am J Pathol 1993, **1143:** 1560–1567.

249 Dranoff G, Bigner DD. A word of caution in the use of neuron-specific enolase expression in tumor diagnosis. Arch Pathol Lab Med 1984, **108:** 535.

250 Foley J, Witte D, Chiu FC, Parysek LM. Expression of the neural intermediate filament proteins peripherin and neurofilament-66/alpha-internexin in neuroblastoma. Lab Invest 1994, **71:** 193–199.

251 Folpe AL, Patterson K, Gown AM. Antineuroblastoma antibody NB-84 also identifies a significant subset of other small blue round cell tumors. Appl Immunohistochem 1997, **5:** 239–245.

252 Gilbert F, Feder M, Balaban G, Brangman D, Lurie DK, Podolsky R, Rinaldt V, Vinikoor N, Weisband J. Human neuroblastomas and abnormalities of chromosomes 1 and 17. Cancer Res 1984, **44:** 5444–5449.

253 Gilbert J, Haber M, Bordow SB, Marshall GM, Norris MD. Use of tumor-specific gene expression for the differential diagnosis of neuroblastoma from other pediatric small round-cell malignancies. Am J Pathol 1999, **155:** 17–21.

254 Grossman DB, Jin L, Heidelberger KP, Lloyd RV. Expression of chromogranin A protein and messenger RNA and tyrosine hydroxylase protein in paraffin-embedded sections of neuroendocrine neoplasms. Endocr Pathol 1991, **2:** 148–154.

255 Hachitanda Y, Tsuneyoshi M, Enjoji M. An ultrastructural and immunohistochemical evaluation of cytodifferentiation in neuroblastic tumors. Mod Pathol 1989, **2:** 13–19.

256 Hayashi Y, Kanda N, Inaba T, Hanada R, Nagahara N, Muchi H, Yamamoto K. Cytogenetic findings and prognosis in neuroblastoma with emphasis on marker chromosome 1. Cancer 1989, **63:** 126–132.

257 Hedborg F, Ohlsson R, Sandstedt B, Grimelius L, Hoehner JC, Pahlman S. IGF2 expression is a marker for paraganglionic/SIF cell differentiation in neuroblastoma. Am J Pathol 1995, **146:** 833–847.

258 Kay S. Hyperplasia and neoplasia of the adrenal gland. Pathol Annu 1976, **11:** 103–139.

259 Kimura N, Nakamura M, Kimura I, Nagura H. Tissue localization of nerve growth factor receptors: trk A and low-affinity nerve growth factor receptor in neuroblastoma, pheochromocytoma and retinoblastoma. Endocr Pathol 1996, **7:** 281–290.

260 Komuro H, Hayashi Y, Kawamura M, Hayashi K, Kaneko Y, Kamoshita S, Hanada R, Yamamoto K, Hongo T, Yamada M, et al. Mutations of the p53 gene are involved in Ewing's sarcomas but not in neuroblastomas. Cancer Res 1993, **53:** 5284–5288.

261 Lamant L, Pulford K, Bischof D, Morris SW, Mason DY, Delsol G, Mariame B. Expression of the ALK tyrosine kinase gene in neuroblastoma. Am J Pathol 2000, **156:** 1711–1721.

262 Maris JM, Matthay KK. Molecular biology of neuroblastoma. J Clin Oncol 1999, **17:** 2264–2279.

263 Mendelsohn G, Eggleston JC, Olson JL, Said SI, Baylin SB. Vasoactive intestinal peptide and its relationship to ganglion cell differentiation in neuroblastic tumors. Lab Invest 1979, **41:** 144–149.

264 Miettinen M, Chatten J, Paetau A, Stevenson A. Monoclonal antibody NB84 in a differential diagnosis of neuroblastoma and other small round cell tumors. Am J Surg Pathol 1998, **22:** 327–332.

265 Molenaar WM, Baker DL, Pleasure D, Lee VM, Trojanowski JQ. The neuroendocrine and neural profiles of neuroblastomas, ganglioneuroblastomas, and ganglioneuromas. Am J Pathol 1990, **136:** 375–382.

266 Moley JF, Brother MB, Wells SA, Spengler BA, Biedler JL, Brodeur GM. Low frequency of *ras* gene mutations in neuroblastomas, pheochromocytomas, and medullary thyroid

cancers. Cancer Res 1991, **51:** 1596–1599.

267 Mukai M, Torikata C, Iri H, Morikawa Y, Shimizu K, Shimoda T, Nukina N, Ihara Y, Kageyama K. Expression of neurofilament triplet proteins in human neural tumors. Am J Pathol 1986, **122:** 28–35.

268 Oppedal BR, Brandtzaeg P, Kemshead T. Immunohistochemical differentiation of neuroblastomas from other small round cell neoplasms of childhood using a panel of mono- and polyclonal antibodies. Histopathology 1987, **11:** 363–374.

269 Osborn M, Dirk T, Kaser H, Weber K, Altmannsberger M. Immunohistochemical localization of neurofilaments and neuron-specific enolase in 29 cases of neuroblastoma. Am J Pathol 1986, **122:** 433–442.

270 Pagani A, Fischer-Colbrie R, Sanfilippo B, Winkler H, Cerrato M, Bussolati G. Secretogranin II expression in Ewing's sarcomas and primitive neuroectodermal tumors. Diagn Mol Pathol 1992, **1:** 165–172.

271 Pagani A, Forni M, Tonini GP, Papotti M, Bussolati G. Expression of members of the chromogranin family in primary neuroblastomas. Diagn Mol Pathol 1992, **1:** 16–24.

272 Plantaz D, Mohapatra G, Matthay KK, Pellarin M, Seeger RC, Feuerstein BG. Gain of chromosome 17 is the most frequent abnormality detected in neuroblastoma by comparative genomic hybridization. Am J Pathol 1997, **150:** 81–89.

273 Reynolds CP, German DC, Weinberg AG, Smith RG. Catecholamine fluorescence and tissue culture morphology. Am J Clin Pathol 1981, **75:** 275–282.

274 Sariola H, Terava H, Rapola J, Saarinen UM. Cell-surface ganglioside GD$_2$ in the immunohistochemical detection and differential diagnosis of neuroblastoma. Am J Clin Pathol 1991, **96:** 248–252.

275 Seshi B, True L, Carter D, Rosai J. Immunohistochemical characterization of a set of monoclonal antibodies to human neuron-specific enolase. Am J Pathol 1988, **131:** 258–269.

276 Triche TJ, Askin FB. Neuroblastoma and the differential diagnosis of small-, round-, blue-cell tumors. Hum Pathol 1983, **14:** 569–595.

277 Tsokos M, Linnoila RI, Chandra RS, Triche TJ. Neuron-specific enolase in the diagnosis of neuroblastoma and other small, round-cell tumors in children. Hum Pathol 1984, **15:** 575–584.

278 Vinores SA, Bonnin YM, Rubinstein LY, Marangos PY. Immunohistochemical demonstration of neuron-specific enolase in neoplasms of the CNS and other tissues. Arch Pathol Lab Med 1984, **108:** 536–540.

279 Vogan K, Bernstein M, Leclerc JM, Brisson L, Brossard J, Brodeur GM, Pelletier J, Gros P. Absence of p53 gene mutations in primary neuroblastomas. Cancer Res 1993, **53:** 5269–5273.

280 Wirnsberger GH, Becker H, Ziervogel K, Hofler H. Diagnostic immunohistochemistry of neuroblastic tumors. Am J Surg Pathol 1992, **16:** 49–57.

In situ, regressing, and maturing neuroblastoma

281 Bolande RP. The spontaneous regression of neuroblastoma. Experimental evidence for a natural host immunity. Pathol Annu 1991, **26**(Pt 2): 187–199.

282 Carlsen NL. How frequent is spontaneous remission of neuroblastomas? Implications for screening. Br J Cancer 1990, **61:** 441–446.

283 Guin GH, Gilbert EF, Jones B. Incidental neuroblastoma in infants. Am J Clin Pathol 1969, **51:** 126–136.

284 Hata J-I, Ueyama Y, Nozi H, Tamaoki N, Akatsuka A, Shimizu K, Morikawa Y, Sato K. Morphology and function of human neuroblastoma xenotransplanted in nude mice. Cancer 1984, **53:** 2497–2506.

285 Ikeda H, Hirato J, Akami M, Suzuki N, Takahashi A, Kuroiwa M, Matsuyama S. Massive apoptosis detected by in situ DNA nick end labeling in neuroblastoma. Am J Surg Pathol 1996, **20:** 649–655.

286   Ikeda Y, Lister J, Bouton JM, Buyukpamukcu M. Congenital neuroblastoma, neuroblastoma in situ, and the normal fetal development of the adrenal. J Pediatr Surg 1981, **16**: 636–644.

287   Murray MR, Stout AP. Distinctive characteristics of the sympathicoblastoma cultivated in vitro. Am J Pathol 1947, **23**: 429–442.

288   Reynolds CP, Smith RG, Frenkel EP. The diagnostic dilemma of the "small round cell neoplasm." Catecholamine fluorescence and tissue culture morphology as markers for neuroblastoma. Cancer 1981, **48**: 2088–2094.

289   Robson JA, Sidell N. Ultrastructural features of a human neuroblastoma cell line treated with retinoic acid. Neuroscience 1985, **14**: 1149–1162.

290   Tsokos M, Scarpa S, Ross RA, Triche TJ. Differentiation of human neuroblastoma recapitulates neural crest development. Study of morphology, neurotransmitter enzymes, and extracellular matrix proteins. Am J Pathol 1987, **128**: 484–496.

291   Turkel SB, Itabashi HH. The natural history of neuroblastic cells in the fetal adrenal gland. Am J Pathol 1974, **76**: 225–244.

Spread and metastases

292   Dannecker G, Leidig F, Treuner J, Niethammer D. Late recurrence of neuroblastoma. A reason for prolonged follow-up? Am J Pediatr Hematol Oncol 1983, **5**: 271–274.

293   De La Monte SM, Moore GW, Hutchins GM. Nonrandom distribution of metastases in neuroblastic tumors. Cancer 1983, **52**: 915–925.

294   Holgersen LO, Santulli TV, Schullinger JN, Berdon WE. Neuroblastoma with intraspinal (dumbbell) extension. J Pediatr Surg 1983, **18**: 406–411.

295   Kramer K, Kushner B, Heller G, Cheung NK. Neuroblastoma metastatic to the central nervous system: the Memorial Sloan-Kettering Cancer Center experience and a literature review. Cancer 2001, **91**: 1510–1519.

296   Moss TJ, Reynolds CP, Sather HN, Romansky SG, Hammond GD, Seeger RC. Prognostic value of immunocytologic detection of bone marrow metastases in neuroblastoma. N Engl J Med 1991, **324**: 219–226.

297   Simon T, Hero B, Berthold F. Testicular and paratesticular involvement by metastatic neuroblastoma. Cancer 2000, **88**: 2636–2641.

298   Young RH, Kozakewich HP, Scully RE. Metastatic ovarian tumors in children. A report of 14 cases and review of the literature. Int J Gynecol Pathol 1993, **12**: 8–19.

Therapy and prognosis

299   Abramowsky CR, Taylor SR, Anton AH, Berk AI, Roederer M, Murphy RF. Flow cytometry DNA ploidy analysis and catecholamine secretion profiles in neuroblastoma. Cancer 1989, **63**: 1752–1756.

300   Ambros IM, Hata J, Joshi VV, Roald B, Dehner LP, Tuchler H, Potschger U, Shimada H. Morphologic features of neuroblastoma (schwannian stroma-poor tumors) in clinically favorable and unfavorable groups. Cancer 2002, **94**: 1574–1583.

301   Azizkhan RG, Haase GM. Current biologic and therapeutic implications in the surgery of neuroblastoma. Semin Surg Oncol 1993, **9**: 493–501.

302   Beckwith JB, Martin RF. Observations on the histopathology of neuroblastoma. J Pediatr Surg 1968, **3**: 106–110.

303   Bordow SB, Norris MD, Haber PS, Marshall GM, Haber M. Prognostic significance of MYCN oncogene expression in childhood neuroblastoma. J Clin Oncol 1998, **16**: 3286–3294.

304   Bourhis J, Dominici C, McDowell H, Raschella G, Wilson G, Castello MA, Plouvier E, Lemerle J, Riou G, Benard J, et al. N-*myc* genomic content and DNA ploidy in stage IVS neuroblastoma. J Clin Oncol 1991, **9**: 1371–1375.

305   Bown N, Cotterill S, Lastowska M, O'Neill S, Pearson AD, Plantaz D, Meddeb M, Danglot G, Brinkschmidt C, Christiansen H, Laureys G, Speleman F. Gain of chromosome arm 17Q and adverse outcome in patients with neuroblastoma. N Engl J Med 1999, **340**: 1954–1961.

306   Canete A, Navarro S, Bermudez J, Pellin A, Castel V, Llombart-Bosch A. Angiogenesis in neuroblastoma: relationship to survival and other prognostic factors in a cohort of neuroblastoma patients. J Clin Oncol 2000, **18**: 27–34.

307   Carlsen NLT, Christensen IJ, Schroeder H, Bro PV, Erichsen G, Hamborg-Pedersen B, Jensen KB, Nielsen OH. Prognostic factors in neuroblastomas treated in Denmark from 1943 to 1980. A statistical estimate of prognosis based on 253 cases. Cancer 1986, **58**: 2726–2735.

308   Carlsen NL, Ornvold K, Christensen IJ, Laursen H, Larsen JK. Prognostic importance of DNA flow cytometrical, histopathological and immunohistochemical parameters in neuroblastomas. Virchows Arch [A] 1992, **420**: 411–418.

309   Caron H, van Sluis P, de Kraker J, Bokkerink J, Egeler M, Laureys G, Slater R, Westerveld A, Voute PA, Versteeg R. Allelic loss of chromosome 1p as a predictor of unfavorable outcome in patients with neuroblastoma. N Engl J Med 1996, **334**: 225–230.

310   Castle VP, Heidelberger KP, Bromberg J, Ou X, Dole M, Nunez G. Expression of the apoptosis-suppressing protein bcl-2, in neuroblastoma is associated with unfavorable histology and N-*myc* amplification. Am J Pathol 1993, **143**: 1543–1550.

311   Castleberry RP, Shuster JJ, Smith EI. The Pediatric Oncology Group experience with the international staging system criteria for neuroblastoma. Member Institutions of the Pediatric Oncology Group. J Clin Oncol 1994, **12**: 2378–2381.

312   Chan HS, Haddad G, Thorner PS, De Boer G, Lin YP, Ondrusek N, Yeger H, Ling V. P-glycoprotein expression as a predictor of the outcome of therapy for neuroblastoma. N Engl J Med 1991, **325**: 1608–1614.

313   Cohn SL, Rademaker AW, Salwen HR, Franklin WA, Gonzales-Crussi F, Rosen ST, Bauer KD. Analysis of DNA ploidy and proliferative activity in relation to histology and N-*myc* amplification in neuroblastoma. Am J Pathol 1990, **136**: 1043–1052.

314   Combaret V, Gross N, Lasset C, Frappaz D, Peruisseau G, Philip T, Beck D, Favrot MC. Clinical relevance of CD44 cell-surface expression and n-myc gene amplification in a multicentric analysis of 121 pediatric neuroblastomas. J Clin Oncol 1996, **14**: 25–34.

315   Crabbe DC, Peters J, Seeger RC. Rapid detection of MYCN gene amplification in neuroblastomas using the polymerase chain reaction. Diagn Mol Pathol 1992, **1**: 229–234.

316   De Bernardi B, Conte M, Mancini A, Donfrancesco A, Alvisi P, Toma P, Casale F, Cordero di Montezemolo L, Cornelli PE, Carli M, Tonini GP, Pession A, Giaretti W, Garaventa A, Marchese N, Magillo P, Nigro M, Kotitsa Z, Tamaro P, Tamburini A, Rogers D, Bruzzi P. Localized resectable neuroblastoma. Results of the second study of the Italian Cooperative Group for Neuroblastoma. J Clin Oncol 1995, **13**: 884–893.

317   Evans AE, D'Angio GJ, Koop CE. Diagnosis and treatment of neuroblastoma. Pediatr Clin North Am 1976, **23**: 161–170.

318   Franks LM, Bollen A, Seeger RC, Stram DO, Matthay KK. Neuroblastoma in adults and adolescents: an indolent course with poor survival. Cancer 1997, **79**: 2028–2035.

319   Gansler T, Chatten J, Varello M, Bunin GR, Atkinson B. Flow cytometric DNA analysis of neuroblastoma. Correlation with histology and clinical outcome. Cancer 1986, **58**: 2453–2458.

320   Goto S, Umehara S, Gerbing RB, Stram DO, Brodeur GM, Seeger RC, Lukens JN, Matthay KK, Shimada H. Histopathology (international neuroblastoma pathology classification) and MYCN status in patients with peripheral neuroblastic tumors:

a report from the Children's Cancer Group. Cancer 2001, **92:** 2699–2708.

321 Hachitanda Y, Hata J. Stage IVS neuroblastoma: A clinical, histological, and biological analysis of 45 cases. Hum Pathol 1996, **27:** 1135–1138.

322 Hiyama E, Hiyama K, Yokoyama T, Ishii T. Immunohistochemical analysis of N-*myc* protein expression in neuroblastoma. Correlation with prognosis of patients. J Pediatr Surg 1991, **26:** 838–843.

323 Hughes M, Marsden HB, Palmer MK. Histologic patterns of neuroblastoma related to prognosis and clinical staging. Cancer 1974, **34:** 1706–1711.

324 Jereb B, Bretsky SS, Vogel R, Helson L. Age and prognosis in neuroblastoma. Review of 112 patients younger than 2 years. Am J Pediatr Hematol Oncol 1984, **6:** 233–243.

324a Joshi VV. Peripheral neuroblastic tumors: pathologic classification based on recommendations of international neuroblastoma pathology committee (Modification of Shimada Classification). Pediatr Dev Pathol 2000; **3:** 184–199.

325 Joshi VV, Cantor AB, Altshuler G, Larkin EW, Neill JS, Shuster JJ, Holbrook CT, Hayes FA, Castleberry RP. Recommendations for modification of terminology of neuroblastic tumors and prognostic significance of Shimada classification. A clinicopathologic study of 213 cases from the Pediatric Oncology Group. Cancer 1992, **69:** 2183–2196.

326 Joshi VV, Cantor AB, Altshuler G, Larkin EW, Neill JS, Shuster JJ, Holbrook CT, Hayes FA, Nitschke R, Duncan MH, et al. Age-linked prognostic categorization based on a new histologic grading system of neuroblastomas. A clinicopathologic study of 211 cases from the Pediatric Oncology Group. Cancer 1992, **69:** 2197–2112.

327 Joshi VV, Cantor AB, Brodeur GM, Look AT, Shuster JJ, Altshuler G, Larkin EW, Holbrook CT, Silverman JF, Norris HT, et al. Correlation between morphologic and other prognostic markers of neuroblastoma. A study of histologic grade, DNA index, N-*myc* gene copy number, and lactic dehydrogenase in patients in the Pediatric Oncology Group. Cancer 1993, **71:** 3173–3181.

328 Joshi VV, Rao PV, Cantor AB, Altshuler G, Shuster JJ, Castleberry RP. Modified histologic grading of neuroblastomas by replacement of mitotic rate with mitosis karyorrhexis index: a clinicopathologic study of 223 cases from the Pediatric Oncology Group. Cancer 1996, **77:** 1582–1588.

329 Katzenstein HM, Bowman LC, Brodeur GM, Thorner PS, Joshi VV, Smith EI, Look AT, Rowe ST, Nash MB, Holbrook T, Alvarado C, Rao PV, Castleberry RP, Cohn SL. Prognostic significance of age, MYCN oncogene amplification, tumor cell ploidy, and histology in 110 infants with stage D(S) neuroblastoma: the Pediatric Oncology group experience—a Pediatric Oncology Group study. J Clin Oncol 1998, **16:** 2007–2017.

330 Lack EE. Pathology of adrenal and extra-adrenal paraganglia. Major problems in pathology, vol. 29. Philadelphia, 1994, WB Saunders.

331 Mäkinen J. Microscopic patterns as a guide to prognosis of neuroblastoma in childhood. Cancer 1972, **29:** 219–228.

332 Maris JM, Matthay KK. Molecular biology of neuroblastoma. J Clin Oncol 1999, **17:** 2264–2279.

333 Meitar D, Crawford SE, Rademaker AW, Cohn SL. Tumor angiogenesis correlates with metastatic disease, N-myc amplification and poor outcome in human neuroblastoma. J Clin Oncol 1996, **14:** 405–414.

334 Nagoshi M, Tsuneyoshi M, Enjoji M. S-100 positive undifferentiated neuroblastomas with a special reference to the tumor stroma related to favorable prognosis. Pathol Res Pract 1992, **188:** 273–283.

335 Nakagawara A, Arima-Nakagawara M, Scavarda NJ, Azar CG, Cantor AB, Brodeur GM. Association between high levels of expression of the TRK gene and favorable outcome in human neuroblastoma. N Engl J Med 1993, **328:** 847–854.

336 Norris MD, Bordow SN, Marshall GM, Haber PS, Cohn SL, Haber M. Expression of the gene for multidrug-resistance-associated protein and outcome in patients with neuroblastoma. N Engl J Med 1996, **334:** 231–238.

337 Poremba C, Scheel C, Hero B, Christiansen H, Schafer KL, Nakayama J, Berthold F, Juergens H, Boecker W, Dockhorn-Dworniczack B. Telomerase activity and telomerase subunits gene expression patterns in neuroblastoma: a molecular and immunohistochemical study establishing prognostic tools for fresh-frozen and paraffin embedded tissues. J Clin Oncol 2000, **18:** 2582–2592.

338 Rudolph P, Lappe T, Hero B, Berthold F, Parwaresch R, Harms D, Schmidt D. Prognostic significance of the proliferative activity in neuroblastoma. Am J Pathol 1997, **150:** 133–145.

339 Sandstedt B, Jereb B, Eklund G. Prognostic factors in neuroblastomas. Acta Pathol Microbiol Immunol Scand [A] 1983, **91:** 365–371.

340 Schengrund C-L, Repman MA, Shochat SJ. Ganglioside composition of human neuroblastomas. Correlation with prognosis. A pediatric oncology group study. Cancer 1985, **56:** 2640–2646.

341 Seeger RC, Brodeur GM, Sather H, Dalton A, Siegel SE, Wong KY, Hammond D. Association of multiple copies of the N-*myc* oncogene with rapid progression of neuroblastomas. N Engl J Med 1985, **313:** 1111–1116.

342 Shapiro DN, Valentine MB, Rowe ST, Sinclair AE, Sublett JE, Roberts WM, Look AT. Detection of N-*myc* gene amplification by fluorescence in situ hybridization. Diagnostic utility for neuroblastoma. Am J Pathol 1993, **142:** 1339–1346.

343 Shimada H. Neuroblastoma. Pathology and biology. Acta Pathol Jpn 1992, **42:** 229–241.

344 Shimada H, Ambros IM, Dehner LP, Hata J, Joshi VV, Roald B. Terminology and morphologic criteria of neuroblastic tumors: Recommendations by the International Neuroblastoma Pathology Committee. Cancer 1999, **86:** 349–363.

345 Shimada H, Ambros IM, Dehner LP, Hata J, Joshi VV, Roald B, Stram DO, Gerbing RB, Lukens JN, Matthay KK, Castleberry RP. The International Neuroblastoma Pathology Classification (the Shimada system). Cancer 1999, 86: 364–372.

346 Shimada H, Aoyama C, Chiba T, Newton WA Jr. Prognostic subgroups for undifferentiated neuroblastoma: immunohistochemical study with anti-S-100 antibody. Hum Pathol 1985, **16:** 471–476.

347 Shimada H, Chatten J, Newton JA Jr, Sachs N, Hamoudi AB, Chiba T, Marsden HB, Misugi K. Histopathologic prognostic factors in neuroblastic tumors. Definition of subtypes of ganglioneuroblastoma and an age-linked classification of neuroblastomas. J Natl Cancer Inst 1984, **73:** 405–416.

348 Stephenson SR, Cook BA, Mease AD, Ruymann FB. The prognostic significance of age and pattern of metastases in stage IV-S neuroblastoma. Cancer 1986, **58:** 372–375.

349 Stokes SH, Thomas PRM, Perez CA, Vietti TJ. Stage IV-S neuroblastoma. Results with definitive therapy. Cancer 1984, **53:** 2083–2086.

350 Thomas PRM, Lee JY, Fineberg BB, Razek AA, Ferez CA, Land VJ, Vietti TJ. An analysis of neuroblastoma at a single institution. Cancer 1984, **53:** 2079–2082.

351 Tonini GP, Boni L, Pession A, Rogers D, Iolascon A, Basso G, Cordero di Montezemolo L, Casale F, Pession A, Perri P, Mazzocco K, Scaruffi P, Lo Cunsolo C, Marchese N, Milanaccio C, Conte M, Bruzzi P, De Bernardi B. MYCN oncogene amplification in neuroblastoma in associated with worse prognosis, except in stage 4s: The Italian experience with 295 children. J Clin Oncol 1997, **15:** 85–93.

352 Tsuda T, Obara M, Hirano H, Gotoh S, Kubomura S, Higashi K, Kuroiwa A, Nakagawara A, Nagahara N, Shimizu K. Analysis of N-*myc* amplification in relation to disease stage and histologic types in human neuroblastomas. Cancer 1987, **60:** 820–826.

352a Umehara S, Nakagawa A, Matthay KK, Leukens JN, Seeger RC, Stram DO, Gerbing RB, Shimada H. Histopathology defines prognostic subsets of ganglioneuroblastoma, nodular. Cancer 2000, **89**: 1150–1161.

353 Wu Z-L, Schwartz E, Seeger R, Ladisch S. Expression of G$_{D2}$ ganglioside by untreated primary human neuroblastomas. Cancer Res 1986, **46**: 440–443.

354 Zeltzer PM, Marangos PJ, Evans AE, Schneider SL. Serum neuron-specific enolase in children with neuroblastoma. Relationship to stage and disease course. Cancer 1986, **57**: 1230–1234.

Ganglioneuroblastoma

355 Ambros IM, Zellner A, Roald B, Amann G, Ladenstein R, Printz D, Gadner H, Ambros PF. Role of ploidy, chromosome 1p, and schwann cells in the maturation of neuroblastoma. N Engl Med 1996, **334**: 1505–1511.

356 Aoyama C, Qualman SJ, Shimada H, Newton WA. Composite ganglioneuroblastoma (C-GNB). Immunohistochemical distinction of stromal components correlates with prognosis (abstract). Lab Invest 1988, **58**: 5A.

357 Joshi VV, Cantor AB, Altshuler G, Cohen LJ, Larkin EW, Shuster JJ, Rao PV, Holbrook CT, Hayes FA, Castleberry RP. Conventional versus modified morphologic criteria for ganglioneuroblastoma: A review of cases from the Pediatric Oncology Group. Arch Pathol Lab Med 1996, **120**: 859–865.

358 Magro A, Ruggieri M, Fraggetta F, Grasso S, Viale G. Cathepsin D is a marker of ganglion cell differentiation in the developing and neoplastic human peripheral sympathetic nervous system. Virchows Arch 2000, **437**: 406–412.

359 Misugi K, Misugi N, Newton WA Jr. Fine structural study of neuroblastoma, ganglioneuroblastoma and pheochromocytoma. Arch Pathol 1968, **86**: 160–170.

360 Umehara S, Nakagawa A, Matthay KK, Lukens JN, Seeger RC, Stram DO, Gerbing RB, Shimada H. Histopathology defines prognostic subsets of ganglioneuroblastoma, nodular: a report from the children's cancer group. Cancer 2000, **89**: 1150–1161.

Ganglioneuroma

361 Bunnett N, Reeve JR, Dimaline R, Shively JE, Hawke D, Walsh JH. The isolation and sequence analysis of vasoactive intestinal peptide from a ganglioneuroblastoma. J Clin Endocrinol Metab 1984, **59**: 1133–1137.

362 Chandrasoma P, Shibata D, Radin R, Brown LP, Koss M. Malignant peripheral nerve sheath tumor arising in an adrenal ganglioneuroma in an adult male homosexual. Cancer 1986, **57**: 2022–2025.

363 Fu Y, Kaye GI, Lattes R. Primary malignant melanocytic tumors of the sympathetic ganglia, with an ultrastructural study of one. Cancer 1975, **36**: 2029–2041.

364 Gonzalez-Crussi F, Hsueh W. Bilateral adrenal ganglioneuroblastoma with neuromelanin. Clinical and pathologic observations. Cancer 1988, **61**: 1159–1166.

365 Hamilton JR, Radde IC, Johnson G. Diarrhea associated with adrenal ganglioneuroma. New findings related to the pathogenesis of diarrhea. Am J Med 1968, **44**: 453–463.

366 Mendelsohn G, Eggleston JC, Olson JL, Said SI, Baylin SB. Vasoactive intestinal peptide and its relationship to ganglion cell differentiation in neuroblastic tumors. Lab Invest 1979, **41**: 144–149.

367 Mullins JD. A pigmented differentiating neuroblastoma. A light and ultrastructural study. Cancer 1980, **46**: 522–528.

368 Shimada H, Ambros IM, Dehner LP, Hata J-I, Joshi VV, Roald B. Terminology and morphologic criteria of neuroblastic tumors: Recommendations by the International Neuroblastoma Pathology Committee. Cancer 1999, **86**: 349–363.

369 Yokoyama M, Okada K, Tokue A, Takayesu H. Ultrastructural and biochemical study of benign ganglioneuroma. Virchows Arch [A] 1973, **361**: 195–209.

Adrenal medullary hyperplasia

370 Carney JA, Sizemore GW, Sheps SG. Adrenal medullary disease in multiple endocrine neoplasia, type 2. Pheochromocytoma and its precursors. Am J Clin Pathol 1976, **66**: 279–290.

371 DeLellis RA, Tischler AS, Lee AK, Blount M, Wolfe HJ. Leu-enkephalin-like immunoreactivity in proliferative lesions of the human adrenal medulla and extra-adrenal paraganglia. Am J Surg Pathol 1983, **7**: 29–37.

372 DeLellis RA, Wolfe HJ, Gagel RF, Feldman ZT, Miller HH, Gang DL, Reichlin S. Adrenal medullary hyperplasia. A morphometric analysis in patients with familial medullary thyroid carcinoma. Am J Pathol 1976, **83**: 117–196.

373 Kreiner E. Weight and shape of the human adrenal medulla in various age groups. Virchows Arch [A] 1982, **397**: 7–15.

374 Kurihara K, Mizuseki K, Kondo T, Ohoka H, Mannami M, Kawai K. Adrenal medullary hyperplasia. Hyperplasia-pheochromocytoma sequence. Acta Pathol Jpn 1990, **40**: 683–686.

375 Tischler AS, Semple J. Adrenal medullary nodules in Beckwith-Wiedemann syndrome resembling extra-adrenal paraganglia. Endocr Pathol 1996, **7**: 265–272.

376 Visser JW, Axt R. Bilateral adrenal medullary hyperplasia. A clinicopathological entity. J Clin Pathol 1975, **28**: 298–304.

377 Yoshida A, Hatanaka S, Ohi Y, Umekita Y, Yoshida H. von Recklinghausen's disease associated with somatostatin-rich duodenal carcinoid (somatostatinoma), medullary thyroid carcinoma and diffuse adrenal medullary hyperplasia. Acta Pathol Jpn 1991, **41**: 847–856.

Pheochromocytoma

General and clinical features

378 Bravo EL, Gifford RW. Pheochromocytoma. Diagnosis, localization and management. N Engl J Med 1984, **311**: 1298–1303.

378a Bryant J, Farmer J, Kessler LJ, Townsend RR, Nathanson KL. Pheochromocytoma: the expanding genetic differential diagnosis. J Natl Cancer Inst 2003; **95**: 1196–1204.

379 Caty MG, Coran AG, Geagen M, Thompson NW. Current diagnosis and treatment of pheochromocytoma in children. Experience with 22 consecutive tumors in 14 patients. Arch Surg 1990, **125**: 978–981.

380 de Mendonca WC, Espat PA. Pheochromocytoma associated with arterial fibromuscular dysplasia. Am J Clin Pathol 1981, **75**: 749–754.

381 Irvin GL III, Fishman LM, Sher JA. Familial pheochromocytoma. Surgery 1983, **96**: 938–940.

382 Kaufman BH, Telander RL, van Heerden JA, Zimmerman D, Sheps SG, Dawson B. Pheochromocytoma in the pediatric age group. Current status. J Pediatr Surg 1983, **18**: 879–884.

383 Kimura N, Togo A, Sugimoto T, Nata K, Okamoto H, Nagatsu I, Hagura H. Deficiency of phenylethanolamine N-methyltransferase in norepinephrine-producing pheochromocytoma. Endocr Pathol 1996, **7**: 131–136.

384 Kline IK. Myocardial alterations associated with pheochromocytomas. Am J Pathol 1961, **38**: 539–551.

385 Lamovec J, Frkovic-Grazio S, Bracko M. Nonsporadic cases and unusual morphological features in pheochromocytoma and paraganglioma. Arch Pathol Lab Med 1998, **122**: 63–68.

386 Melicow MM. One hundred cases of pheochromocytoma (107 tumors) at the Columbia-Presbyterian Medical Center, 1926–1976. A clinicopathological analysis. Cancer 1977, **40**: 1987–2004.

387 Neumann HP, Bausch B, McWhinney SR, Bender BU, Gimm O, Franke G, Schipper J, Klisch J, Altehoefer C, Zerres K, Januszwicz A, Eng C, for the Freiburg-Warsaw-Columbus pheochromocytoma study group. Germ-line mutations in nonsyndromic pheochromocytoma. N Engl J Med 2002, **346**: 1459–1488.

388 Neumann HP, Berger DP, Sigmund G, Blum U, Schmidt D, Parmer RJ, Volk B, Kirste G. Pheochromocytomas, multiple endocrine neoplasia type 2, and von Hippel-Lindau disease. N Engl J Med 1993, **329:** 1531–1538.

389 Nibbelink DW, Peters BH, McCormick WF. On the association of pheochromocytoma and cerebellar hemangioblastoma. Neurology 1969, **19:** 455–460.

390 Samaan NA, Hickey RC. Pheochromocytoma. Semin Oncol 1987, **14:** 297–305.

391 Sheps SG, Jiang NS, Klee GG, van Heerden JA. Recent developments in the diagnosis and treatment of pheochromocytoma. Mayo Clin Proc 1990, **65:** 88–95.

392 Sparagana M, Feldman JM, Molnar Z. An unusual pheochromocytoma associated with an androgen-secreting adrenocortical adenoma. Evaluation of its polypeptide hormone, catecholamine, and enzyme characteristics. Cancer 1987, **60:** 223–231.

393 Wilson RA, Ibanez ML. A comparative study of 14 cases of familial and nonfamilial pheochromocytomas. Hum Pathol 1978, **9:** 181–188.

Morphologic features

394 Brady S, Lechan RM, Schwaitzberg SD, Dayal Y, Ziar J, Tischler AS. Composite pheochromocytoma/ganglioneuroma of the adrenal gland associated with multiple endocrine neoplasia 2A: case report with immunohistochemical analysis. Am J Surg Pathol 1997, **21:** 102–108.

395 Chetty R, Clark SP, Taylor DA. Pigmented pheochromocytomas of the adrenal medulla. Hum Pathol 1993, **24:** 420–423.

396 Chetty R, Duhig JD. Bilateral pheochromocytoma-ganglioneuroma of the adrenal in type 1 neurofibromatosis. Am J Surg Pathol 1993, **17:** 837–841.

397 DeLellis RA, Suchow E, Wolfe HJ. Ultrastructure of nuclear "inclusions" in pheochromocytoma and paraganglioma. Hum Pathol 1980, **11:** 205–207.

398 Franquemont DW, Mills SE, Lack EE. Immunohistochemical detection of neuroblastomatous foci in composite adrenal pheochromocytoma-neuroblastoma. Am J Clin Pathol 1994, **102:** 163–170.

399 Harach HR, Laidler P. Combined spindle cell sarcoma/phaeochromocytoma of the adrenal. Histopathology 1993, **23:** 567–569.

400 Juarez D, Brown RW, Ostrowski M, Reardon MJ, Lechago J, Truong LD. Pheochromocytoma associated with neuroendocrine carcinoma: a new type of composite pheochromocytoma. Arch Pathol Lab Med 1999, **123:** 1274–1279.

401 Kimura N, Miura Y, Miura K, Takahashi N, Osamura Y, Nagatsu I, Nagura H. Adrenal and retroperitoneal mixed neuroendocrine-neural tumors. Endocr Pathol 1991, **2:** 139–147.

402 Koch CA, Mauro D, Walther MM, Linehan WM, Vortmeyer AO, Jaffe R, Pacak K, Chrousos GP, Zhuang Z, Lubensky IA. Pheochromocytoma in von Hippel-Lindau disease: distinct histopathologic phenotype compared to pheochromocytoma in multiple endocrine neoplasia type 2. Endocr Pathol 2002, **13:** 17–27.

403 Lam K-Y, Lo C-Y. Composite pheochromocytoma-ganglioneuroma of the adrenal gland: an uncommon entity with distinctive clinicopathologic features. Endocr Pathol 1999, **10:** 343–352.

404 Landas SK, Leigh C, Bonsib SM, Layne K. Occurrence of melanin in pheochromocytoma. Mod Pathol 1993, **6:** 175–178.

405 Li M, Wenig BM. Adrenal oncocytic pheochromocytoma. Am J Surg Pathol 2000, **24:** 1552–1557.

406 Linnoila RI, Keiser HR, Steinberg SM, Lack EE. Histopathology of benign versus malignant sympathoadrenal paragangliomas. Clinicopathologic study of 120 cases including unusual histologic features. Hum Pathol 1990, **21:** 1168–1180.

407 McNicol AM. Differential diagnosis of pheochromocytomas and paragangliomas. Endocr Pathol 2002, **12:** 407–416.

408 Medeiros LJ, Katsas GG, Balogh K. Brown fat and adrenal pheochromocytoma. Association or coincidence? Hum Pathol 1985, **16:** 970–972.

409 Medeiros LJ, Wolf BC, Balogh K, Federman M. Adrenal pheochromocytoma. A clinicopathologic review of 60 cases. Hum Pathol 1985, **16:** 580–589.

410 Melicow MM. One hundred cases of pheochromocytoma (107 tumors) at the Columbia-Presbyterian Medical Center, 1926–1976. A clinicopathological analysis. Cancer 1977, **40:** 1987–2004.

411 Michal M, Havlicek F. Corticomedullary tumors of the adrenal glands—report of two cases. Association of corticomedullary tumor with spindly cell sarcoma. Pathol Res Pract 1997, **192:** 1082–1091.

412 Nakagawara A, Ikeda K, Tsuneyoshi M, Daimaru Y, Enjoji M. Malignant pheochromocytoma with ganglioneuroblastomatous elements in a patient with von Recklinghausen's disease. Cancer 1985, **55:** 2794–2798.

413 Ramsay JA, Asa SL, van Nostrand AWP, Hassaram ST, de Harven EP. Lipid degeneration in pheochromocytomas mimicking adrenal cortical tumors. Am J Surg Pathol 1987, **11:** 480–486.

414 Sakaguchi N, Sano K, Ito M, Baba T, Fukuzawa M, Hotchi M. A case of von Recklinghausen's disease with bilateral pheochromocytoma-malignant peripheral nerve sheath tumors of the adrenal and gastrointestinal autonomic nerve tumors. Am J Surg Pathol 1996, **20:** 889–897.

415 Steinhoff MM, Wells SA Jr, De Schryver-Kecskemeti K. Stromal amyloid in pheochromocytomas. Hum Pathol 1992, **23:** 33–36.

416 Tischler AS, Dayal Y, Balogh K, Cohen RB, Connolly JL, Tallberg K. The distribution of immunoreactive chromogranins, S-100 protein, and vasoactive intestinal peptide in compound tumors of the adrenal medulla. Hum Pathol 1987, **18:** 909–917.

417 Unger PD, Cohen JM, Thung SN, Gordon R, Pertsemlidis D, Dikman SH. Lipid degeneration in a pheochromocytoma histologically mimicking an adrenal cortical tumor. Arch Pathol Lab Med 1990, **114:** 892–894.

418 Wang BY, Gabrilove L, Pertsemlidis D, Gordon RE, Unger PD. Oncocytic pheochromocytoma with cytokeratin reactivity: a case report with immunohistochemical and ultrastructural studies. Int J Surg Pathol 1997, **5:** 61–67.

Electron microscopic, histochemical, immunohistochemical, and molecular genetic features

419 Berelowitz M, Szabo M, Barowsky H, Arbel ER, Frohman LA. Somatostatin-like immunoactivity and biological activity is present in a human pheochromocytoma. J Clin Endocrinol Metab 1983, **56:** 134–138.

420 Bloom FE. Electron microscopy of catecholamine-containing structures. In Blaschko H, Muschall E (eds): Handbook of experimental pharmacology, vol. 33. Catecholamines. New York, 1972, Springer-Verlag.

421 Bostwick DG, Null WE, Holmes D, Weber E, Barchas JD, Bensch KG. Expression of opioid peptides in tumors. N Engl J Med 1987, **317:** 1439–1443.

422 Fried G, Wikstrom LM, Hoog A, Arver S, Cedermark B, Hamberger B, Grimelius L, Meister B. Multiple neuropeptide immunoreactivities in a renin-producing human paraganglioma. Cancer 1994, **74:** 142–151.

423 Gomez RR, Osborne BM, Ordonez NG, Mackay B. Pheochromocytoma. Ultrastruct Pathol 1991, **15:** 557–562.

424 Hassoun J, Monges G, Giraud P, Henry JF, Charpin C, Payan H, Toga M. Immunohistochemical study of pheochromocytomas. An investigation of methionine-enkephalin, vasoactive intestinal peptide, somatostatin, corticotropin, β-endorphin, and calcitonin in 16 tumors. Am J Pathol 1984, **114:** 56–63.

425 Kennedy JS, Symington T, Woodger BA. Chemical and histochemical observations in benign and malignant phaeochromocytoma. J Pathol Bacteriol 1961, **81**: 409–418.

426 Kimura N. Functioning and nonfunctioning adrenal medullary tumors. Endocr Pathol 1991, **2**: 64–73.

427 Kimura N, Nakazato Y, Nagura H, Sasano N. Expression of intermediate filaments in neuroendocrine tumors. Arch Pathol Lab Med 1990, **114**: 506–510.

428 Komminoth P, Kunz E, Hiort O, Schroder S, Matias-Guiu X, Christiansen G, Roth J, Heitz PU. Detection of RET proto-oncogene point mutations in paraffin-embedded pheochromocytoma specimens by nonradioactive single-strand conformation polymorphism analysis and direct sequencing. Am J Pathol 1994, **145**: 922–929.

429 Lamovec J, Memoli VA, Terzakis JA, Sommers SC, Gould VE. Pheochromocytoma producing immunoreactive ACTH with Cushing's syndrome. Ultrastruct Pathol 1984, **7**: 41–48.

430 Lehto V-P, Virtanen I, Miettinen M, Dahl D, Kahri A. Neurofilaments in adrenal and extra-adrenal pheochromocytoma. Arch Pathol Lab Med 1983, **107**: 492–494.

431 Lloyd RV, Blaivas M, Wilson BS. Distribution of chromogranin and S 100 protein in normal and abnormal adrenal medullary tissues. Arch Pathol Lab Med 1985, **109**: 633–635.

432 Lloyd RV, Jin L, Kulig E, Fields E. Molecular approaches for the analysis of chromogranins and secretogranins. Diagn Mol Pathol 1992, **2**: 2–15.

433 Lloyd RV, Shapiro B, Sisson JC, Kalff V, Thompson NW, Beierwaltes WA. An immunohistochemical study of pheochromocytomas. Arch Pathol Lab Med 1984, **108**: 541–544.

434 Lloyd RV, Shapiro B, Sisson JC, Verhofstad AAJ. Immunohistochemical localization of epinephrine, norepinephrine, catecholamine-synthesizing enzymes, and chromogranin in neuroendocrine cells and tumors. Am J Pathol 1986, **125**: 45–54.

435 Miettinen M. Synaptophysin and neurofilament proteins as markers for neuroendocrine tumors. Arch Pathol Lab Med 1987, **111**: 813–818.

436 O'Connor DT, Deftos LJ. Secretion of chromogranin A by peptide-producing endocrine neoplasms. N Engl J Med 1986, **314**: 1145–1151.

437 O'Connor DT, Frigon RP, Deftos LJ. Immunoreactive calcitonin in catecholamine storage vesicles of human pheochromocytoma. J Clin Endocrinol Metab 1983, **56**: 582–585.

438 Osamura RY, Yasuda O, Kawai K, Hori S, Suemizu H, Onoda N, Joh TH. Immunohistochemical localization of catecholamine-synthesizing enzymes in human pheochromocytomas. Endocr Pathol 1990, **1**: 102–108.

439 Pello JM, Guate JL, Naves FJ, Escaf S, Vega JA. Neurotrophins and neurotrophin receptors in some neural crest-derived tumours (ganglioneuroma, phaeochromocytoma and paraganglioma). Histopathology 1999, **34**: 216–225.

440 Sano T, Saito H, Inaba H, Hizawa K, Saito S, Yamanoi A, Mizunuma Y, Matsumura M, Yuasa M, Hiraishi K. Immunoreactive somatostatin and vasoactive intestinal polypeptide in adrenal pheochromocytoma. Cancer 1983, **52**: 282–289.

441 Sano T, Saito H, Yamasaki R, Hosoi E, Kameyama K, Saito S, Hirose T, Hizawa K. Production and secretion of immunoreactive growth hormone-releasing factor by pheochromocytomas. Cancer 1986, **57**: 1788–1793.

442 Sano T, Vrontakis ME, Kovacs K, Asa SL, Friesen HG. Galanin immunoreactivity in neuroendocrine tumors. Arch Pathol Lab Med 1991, **115**: 926–929.

443 Santoro M, Rosati R, Grieco M, Berlingieri MT, D'Amato GL, de Franciscis V, Fusco A. The ret proto-oncogene is consistently expressed in human pheochromocytomas and thyroid medullary carcinomas. Oncogene 1990, **5**: 1595–1598.

444 Sasaki A, Yumita S, Kimura S, Miura Y, Yoshinaga K. Immunoreactive corticotropin-releasing hormone, growth hormone-releasing hormone, somatostatin, and peptide histidine methionine are present in adrenal pheochromocytomas, but not in extra-adrenal pheochromocytoma. J Clin Endocrinol Metab 1990, **70**: 996–999.

445 Schmid KW, Dockhorn-Dworniczak B, Fahrenkamp A, Kirchmair R, Totsch M, Fischer-Colbrie R, Bocker W, Winkler H. Chromogranin A, secretogranin II and vasoactive intestinal peptide in phaeochromocytomas and ganglioneuromas. Histopathology 1993, **22**: 527–533.

446 Schober M, Fischer-Colbrie R, Schmid KW, Bussolati G, O'Connor DT, Winkler H. Comparison of chromogranins A, B, and secretogranin II in human adrenal medulla and pheochromocytoma. Lab Invest 1987, **57**: 385–391.

447 Shanberg AM, Baghdassarian R, Tansey LA, Bacon D, Greenberg P, Perley M. Pheochromocytoma with hypercalcemia. Case report and review of literature. J Urol 1985, **133**: 258–259.

448 Tanaka N, Nishisho I, Yamamoto M, Miya A, Shin E, Karakawa K, Fujita S, Kobayashi T, Rouleau GA, Mori T, et al. Loss of heterozygosity on the long arm of chromosome 22 in pheochromocytoma. Genes Chromosomes Cancer 1992, **5**: 399–403.

449 Tannenbaum M. Ultrastructural pathology of adrenal medullary tumors. In Sommers SC (ed.): Pathology annual. New York, 1970, Appleton-Century-Crofts.

450 Tischler AS, Dayal Y, Balogh K, Cohen RB, Connolly JL, Tallberg K. The distribution of immunoreactive chromogranins, S-100 protein, and vasoactive intestinal peptide in compound tumors of the adrenal medulla. Hum Pathol 1987, **18**: 909–917.

451 Trojanowski JQ, Lee VM-Y. Expression of neurofilament antigens by normal and neoplastic human adrenal chromaffin cells. N Engl J Med 1985, **313**: 101–104.

452 Unger P, Hoffman K, Persemlidis D, Thung S, Wolfe D, Kaneko M. S100 protein-positive sustentacular cells in malignant and locally aggressive adrenal pheochromocytomas. Arch Pathol Lab Med 1991, **115**: 484–487.

453 Unger PD, Hoffman K, Thung SN, Pertsemlides D, Wolfe D, Kaneko M. HMB-45 reactivity in adrenal pheochromocytomas. Arch Pathol Lab Med 1992, **116**: 151–153.

454 Vargas MP, Zhuang Z, Wang C, Vortmeyer A, Linehan WM, Merino MJ. Loss of heterozygosity on the short arm of chromosomes 1 and 3 in sporadic pheochromocytoma and extra-adrenal paraganglioma. Hum Pathol 1997, **28**: 411–415.

455 Wilson BS, Lloyd RV. Detection of chromogranin in neuroendocrine cells with a monoclonal antibody. Am J Pathol 1984, **115**: 458–468.

Spread, metastases, treatment, and prognosis

456 Brown HM, Komorowski RA, Wilson SD, Demeure MJ, Zhu Y. Predicting metastasis of pheochromocytomas using DNA flow cytometry and immunohistochemical markers of cell proliferation: a positive correlation between MIB-1 staining and malignant tumor behavior. Cancer 1999, **86**: 1583–1589.

457 Clarke MR, Weyant RJ, Watson CG, Carty SE. Prognostic markers in pheochromocytoma. Hum Pathol 1998, **29**: 522–526.

457a Elder EE, Xu D, Höög A, Enberg U, Hou M, Pisa P, Gruber A, Larsson C, Bäckdahl M. Ki-67 and HTERT expression can aid in the distinction between malignant and benign heochromocytoma and paraganglioma. Mod Pathol 2003, **16**: 246–255.

458 Gupta D, Shidham V, Holden J, Layfield L. Prognostic value of immunohistochemical expression of topoisomerase alpha II MIB-1, p53, E-cadherin, retinoblastoma gene protein product, and HER-2/neu in adrenal and extra-adrenal pheochromocytomas. AIMM 2000, **8**: 267–274.

459 Hosaka Y, Rainwater LM, Grant CS, Farrow GM, van Heerden JA, Lieber MM. Pheochromocytoma. Nuclear deoxyribonucleic

acid patterns studied by flow cytometry. Surgery 1986, **10:** 1003–1009.

460 Lewi HJE, Reid R, Mucci B, Davidson JK, Kyle KF, MacPherson SG, Semple P, Kaye S. Malignant pheochromocytoma. Br J Urol 1985, **57:** 394–398.

461 Medeiros LJ, Wolf BC, Balogh K, Federman M. Adrenal pheochromocytoma. A clinicopathologic review of 60 cases. Hum Pathol 1985, **16:** 580–589.

462 Nagura S, Katoh R, Kawaoi A, Kobayashi M, Ocara T, Omata K. Immunohistochemical estimations of growth activity to predict biological behaviour of pheochromocytomas. Mod Pathol 1999, **12:** 1107–1123.

463 Nativ O, Grant CS, Sheps SG, O'Fallon JR, Farrow GM, van Heerden JA, Lieber MM. The clinical significance of nuclear DNA ploidy pattern in 184 patients with pheochromocytoma. Cancer 1992, **69:** 2683–2687.

464 Pang LC, Tsao KC. Flow cytometric DNA analysis for the determination of malignant potential in adrenal and extra-adrenal pheochromocytomas or paragangliomas. Arch Pathol Lab Med 1993, **117:** 1142–1147.

465 Salmenkivi K, Haglund C, Arola J, Heikkila P. Increased expression of tenascin in pheochromocytomas correlates with malignancy. Am J Surg Pathol 2001, **25:** 1419–1423.

465a Salmenkivi K, Heikkila P, Haglund C, Louhimol I, Arola J. Lack of histologically suspicious features, proliferative activity, and p53 expression suggests benign diagnosis in phaeochromocytomas. Histopathology 2003, **43:** 62–71.

466 Scott HW, Halter SA. Oncologic aspects of pheochromocytoma. The importance of follow-up. Surgery 1984, **96:** 1061–1066.

467 Thompson LD. Pheochromocytoma of the adrenal gland scaled score (PASS) to separate benign from malignant neoplasms: a clinicopathologic and immunophenotypic study of 100 cases. Am J Surg Pathol 2002, **26:** 551–566.

468 Unger P, Hoffman K, Persemlidis D, Thung S, Wolfe D, Kaneko M. S100 protein-positive sustentacular cells in malignant and locally aggressive adrenal pheochromocytomas. Arch Pathol Lab Med 1991, **115:** 484–487.

Other adrenal lesions

469 Abell MR, Hart WR, Olson JR. Tumors of the peripheral nervous system. Hum Pathol 1970, **1:** 503–551.

470 Avinoach I, Robinson CR, Avinoah E, Peiser J. Adrenal lipoma. A rare tumour of the adrenal gland. Histopathology 1989, **15:** 195–196.

471 Ayala GE, Ettinghausen SE, Epstein AH, Travis WD, Lack EE. Primary malignant peripheral nerve sheath tumor of the adrenal gland. Case report and literature review. J Urol Pathol 1994, **2:** 265–272.

472 Bedard YC, Horvath E, Kovacs K. Adrenal schwannoma with apparent uptake of immunoglobulins. Ultrastruct Pathol 1986, **10:** 505–513.

473 Benjamin E, Fox H. Malakoplakia of the adrenal gland. J Clin Pathol 1981, **34:** 606–611.

474 Ben-Izhak O, Auslander L, Rabinson S, Lichtig C, Sternberg A. Epithelioid angiosarcoma of the adrenal gland with cytokeratin expression. Report of a case with accompanying mesenteric fibromatosis. Cancer 1992, **69:** 1808–1812.

475 Bennett BD, McKenna TJ, Hough AJ, Dean R, Page DL. Adrenal myelolipoma associated with Cushing's disease. Am J Clin Pathol 1980, **73:** 443–447.

476 Black J, Williams DI. Natural history of adrenal haemorrhage in the newborn. Arch Dis Child 1973, **48:** 183–190.

477 Bongiovanni M, Viberti L, Giraudo G, Morino M, Papotti M. Solitary fibrous tumor of the adrenal gland associated with pregnancy. Virchows Arch 2000, **437:** 445–449.

478 Boronat M, Moreno A, Rámon y Cajal S, Pineda E, Lucas T, Estrada J. Subclinical Cushing's syndrome due to adrenal myelolipoma. Arch Pathol Lab Med 1997, **121:** 735–737.

479 Boudreaux D, Waisman J, Skinner DG, Low R. Giant adrenal myelolipoma and testicular interstitial cell tumor in a man with congenital 21-hydroxylase deficiency. Am J Surg Pathol 1979, **3:** 109–123.

480 Carey RW, Harris N, Kliman B. Addison's disease secondary to lymphomatous infiltration of the adrenal glands. Cancer 1987, **59:** 1087–1090.

481 Carney JA. Unusual tumefactive spindle-cell lesions in the adrenal glands. Hum Pathol 1987, **18:** 980–985.

482 Cheema P, Cartagena R, Staubitz W. Adrenal cysts. Diagnosis and treatment. J Urol 1981, **126:** 396–399.

483 Choi CH, Durishin M, Garbadawala ST, Richard J. Non-Hodgkin's lymphoma of the adrenal gland. Arch Pathol Lab Med 1990, **114:** 883–885.

484 Chu P, Costa J, Lachman MF. Angiotropic large cell lymphoma presenting as primary adrenal insufficiency. Hum Pathol 1996, **27:** 209–211.

485 Condom E, Villabona CM, Gomez JM, Carrera M. Adrenal myelolipoma in a woman with congenital 17-hydroxylase deficiency. Arch Pathol Lab Med 1985, **109:** 1116–1118.

486 Dao AH, Page DL, Reynolds VH, Adkins RB Jr. Primary malignant melanoma of the adrenal gland. A report of two cases and review of the literature. Am Surg 1990, **56:** 199–203.

487 DeSa DJ, Nicholls S. Haemorrhagic necrosis of the adrenal gland in perinatal infants. A clinico-pathological study. J Pathol 1972, **106:** 133–149.

488 Dugan MC. Primary adrenal leiomyosarcoma in acquired immunodeficiency syndrome. Arch Pathol Lab Med 1996, **120:** 797–798.

489 Fidler WJ. Ovarian thecal metaplasia in adrenal glands. Am J Clin Pathol 1977, **67:** 318–323.

490 Frankel WL, Shapiro P, Weidner N. Primary anaplastic large cell lymphoma of the adrenal gland. Ann Diagn Pathol 2000, **4:** 158–164.

491 Gaffey MJ, Mills SE, Fechner RE, Bertholf MF, Allen MS Jr. Vascular adrenal cysts. A clinicopathologic and immunohistochemical study of endothelial and hemorrhagic (pseudocystic) variants. Am J Surg Pathol 1989, **13:** 740–747.

492 Gaffey MJ, Mills SE, Medeiros LJ, Weiss LM. Unusual variants of adrenal pseudocysts with intracystic fat, myelolipomatous metaplasia, and metastatic carcinoma. Am J Clin Pathol 1990, **94:** 706–713.

493 Groben PA, Roberson JB Jr, Anger SR, Askin FB, Price WG, Siegal GP. Immunohistochemical evidence for the vascular origin of primary adrenal pseudocysts. Arch Pathol Lab Med 1986, **110:** 121–123.

494 Gross M, Kottmeier PK, Waterhouse K. Diagnosis and treatment of neonatal adrenal hemorrhage. J Pediatr Surg 1967, **2:** 308–312.

495 Harach HR, Laidler P. Adrenal spindle-cell sarcoma with features of malignant peripheral nerve sheath tumor. Endocr Pathol 1993, **4:** 222–225.

496 Harris GJ, Tio FO, Von Hoff DD. Primary adrenal lymphoma. Cancer 1989, **63:** 799–803.

497 Hodges FV, Ellis FR. Cystic lesions of the adrenal glands. Arch Pathol 1958, **66:** 53–58.

498 Honore LH. Intra-adrenal hepatic heterotopia. J Urol 1985, **133:** 652–654.

499 Huisman TK, Sands JP Jr. Renal cell carcinoma with solitary metachronous contralateral adrenal metastasis. Experience with 2 cases and review of the literature. Urology 1991, **38:** 364–368.

500 Hunter SB, Schemankewitz EH, Patterson C, Varma VA. Extraadrenal myelolipoma. A report of two cases. Am J Clin Pathol 1992, **997:** 402–404.

500a Isotalo PA, Keeney GL, Sebo TI, Riehle DL, Cheville JC. Adenomatoid tumor of the adrenal gland: a clinicopathologic study of five cases and review of the literature. Am J Surg Pathol 2003, **27:** 969–977.

501 Jennings TA, Ng B, Boguniewicz A, Khan M, Rice D, Figge J. Adrenal pseudocysts: evidence of their posthemorragic nature. Endocr Pathol 1999, **9**: 353–362.

502 Kato K, Kato Y, Ijiri R, Misugi K, Nanba I, Nagai J, Nagahara N, Kigasawa H, Toyoda Y, Nishi T, Tanaka Y. Ewing's sarcoma family of tumor arising in the adrenal gland—possible diagnostic pitfall in pediatric pathology: histologic, immunohistochemical, ultrastructural, and molecular study. Hum Pathol 2001, **32**: 1012–1016.

503 Kraimps JL, Marechaud R, Levillain P, Lacour JF, Barbier J. Bilateral symptomatic adrenal myelipoma. Surgery 1992, **111**: 114–117.

504 Kung AWC, Pun KK, Lam K, Wang C, Leung CY. Addisonian crisis as presenting feature in malignancies. Cancer 1990, **65**: 177–179.

505 Lack EE, Graham CW, Azumi N, Bitterman P, Rusnock EJ, O'Brien W, Lynch JH. Primary leiomyosarcoma of adrenal gland. Case report with immunohistochemical and ultrastructural study. Am J Surg Pathol 1991, **15**: 899–905.

506 Lam KY. Lipomatous tumors of the adrenal gland. Clinicopathologic study of eight cases. J Urol Pathol 1995, **3**: 95–106.

507 McCauley RG, Beckwith JB, Elias ER, Faerber EN, Prewitt LH Jr, Berdon WE. Benign hemorrhagic adrenocortical macrocysts in Beckwith-Wiedemann syndrome. AJR 1991, **157**: 549–552.

508 McMurry JF Jr, Long D, McClure R, Kotchen T. Addison's disease with adrenal enlargement on computed tomographic scanning (report of two cases of tuberculosis and review of the literature). Am J Med 1984, **77**: 365–368.

509 Medeiros LJ, Lewandrowski KB, Vickery AL Jr. Adrenal pseudocyst. A clinical and pathologic study of eight cases. Hum Pathol 1989, **20**: 660–665.

510 Medeiros LJ, Weiss LM, Vickery AL Jr. Epithelial-lined (true) cyst of the adrenal gland. A case report. Hum Pathol 1989, **20**: 491–492.

511 Medeiros LJ, Wolf BC. Traumatic rupture of an adrenal myelolipoma (letter to the editor). Arch Pathol Lab Med 1983, **107**: 500.

512 Meehan SM, Scully RE. Para-adrenal bronchogenic cyst: clinical dilemma, pathologic curiosity. J Urol Pathol 1996, **4**: 51–56.

513 Merchant SH, Herman CM, Amin MB, Ro JY, Troncoso P. Myelolipoma associated with adrenal ganglioneuroma. Arch Pathol Lab Med 2002, **126**: 736–737.

514 Molberg K, Vuitch F, Stewart D, Albores-Saavedra J. Adrenocortical blastoma. Hum Pathol 1992, **23**: 1187–1190.

515 Nakamura Y, Yano H, Nakashima T. False intranuclear inclusions in adrenal cytomegaly. Arch Pathol Lab Med 1981, **105**: 358–360.

516 Noble MJ, Montague DK, Levin HS. Myelolipoma. An unusual surgical lesion of the adrenal gland. Cancer 1982, **49**: 952–958.

517 Oelkers W. Adrenal insufficiency. N Engl J Med 1996, **335**: 1206–1212.

518 Ohsawa M, Tomita Y, Hashimoto M, Tasunaga Y, Kanno H, Aozasa K. Malignant lymphoma of the adrenal gland: Its possible correlation with the Epstein-Barr virus. Mod Pathol 1996, **9**: 534–543.

519 Orselli R, Bassler TJ. Theca granulosa cell tumor arising in adrenal. Cancer 1973, **31**: 474–477.

520 Pollock WJ, McConnell CF, Hilton C, Lavine RL. Virilizing Leydig cell adenoma of adrenal gland. Am J Surg Pathol 1986, **10**: 816–822.

521 Prevot S, Penna C, Imbert JC, Wendum D, de Saint-Maur PP. Solitary fibrous tumor of the adrenal gland. Mod Pathol 1996, **9**: 1170–1174.

522 Raaf HN, Grant LD, Santoscoy C, Levin HS, Abdul-Karim FW. Adenomatoid tumor of the adrenal gland: A report of four new cases and a review of the literature. Mod Pathol 1996, **9**: 1046–1051.

523 Romberger CF, Wong TW. Thecal metaplasia in the adrenal gland of a man with acquired bilateral testicular atrophy. Arch Pathol Lab Med 1989, **113**: 1071–1075.

524 Santonja C, Diaz MA, Dehner LP. A unique dysembryonic neoplasm of the adrenal gland composed of nephrogenic rests in a child. Am J Surg Pathol 1996, **20**: 118–124.

525 Schnitzer B, Smid D, Lloyd RV. Primary T-cell lymphoma of the adrenal glands with adrenal insufficiency. Hum Pathol 1986, **17**: 634–636.

526 Seidenwurm DJ, Elmer EB, Kaplan LM, Williams EK, Morris DG, Hoffman AR. Metastases to the adrenal glands and the development of Addison's disease. Cancer 1984, **54**: 552–557.

527 Shiraishi T, Imai H, Fukutome K, Watanabe M, Yatani R. Ectopic thyroid in the adrenal gland. Hum Pathol 1999, **30**: 105–108.

528 Simpson PR. Adenomatoid tumor of the adrenal gland. Arch Pathol Lab Med 1990, **114**: 725–727.

529 Sinclair-Smith C, Kahn LB, Cywes S. Malacoplakia in childhood. Arch Pathol 1975, **99**: 198–203.

530 Swanson SJ III, Skoog SJ, Garcia V, Wahl RC. Pseudoadrenal mass. Unusual presentation of bronchogenic cyst. J Pediatr Surg 1991, **26**: 1401–1403.

531 Torres C, Ro JY, Batt MA, Park YW, Ordonez NG, Ayala AG. Vascular adrenal cysts: a clinicopathologic and immunohistochemical study of six cases and a review of the literature. Mod Pathol 1997, **10**: 530–536.

532 Travis WD, Lack EE, Azumi N, Tsokos M, Norton J. Adenomatoid tumor of the adrenal gland with ultrastructural and immunohistochemical demonstration of a mesothelial origin. Arch Pathol Lab Med 1990, **114**: 722–724.

533 Walton GR, Peng BC, Berdon WE, Collins MH, Hensle TW. Cystic adrenal masses in the neonate associated with hemihypertrophy and the relation to the Beckwith-Wiedemann syndrome. J Urol 1991, **146**: 580–582.

534 Wenig BM, Abbondanzo SL, Heffess CS. Epithelioid angiosarcoma of the adrenal glands. A clinicopathologic study of nine cases with a discussion of the implications of finding "epithelial-specific" markers. Am J Surg Pathol 1994, **18**: 62–73.

535 Wilhelmus JL, Schrodt R, Alberhasky MT, Alcorn MO. Giant adrenal myelolipoma. Arch Pathol Lab Med 1981, **105**: 532–535.

Tumors and tumorlike lesions of other paraganglia
Generalities

536 Abell MR, Hart WR, Olson JR. Tumors of the peripheral nervous system. Hum Pathol 1970, **1**: 503–551.

537 Arias-Stella J, Valcarcel J. Chief cell hyperplasia in the human carotid body at high altitudes. Physiologic and pathologic significance. Hum Pathol 1976, **7**: 361–373.

538 Carney JA. Gastric stromal sarcoma, pulmonary chondroma, and extra-adrenal paraganglioma (Carney Triad): natural history, adrenocortical component, and possible familial occurrence. Mayo Clin Proc 1999, **74**: 543–552.

539 Carney JA, Stratakis CA. Familial paraganglioma and gastric stromal sarcoma: a new syndrome distinct from the Carney triad. Am J Med Genet 2002, **108**: 132–139.

540 Carney JA, Sheps SG, Co VLW, Gordon H. The triad of gastric leiomyosarcoma, functioning extraadrenal paraganglioma and pulmonary chondroma. N Engl J Med 1977, **296**: 1517–1518.

541 Chedid A, Jao W. Hereditary tumors of the carotid bodies and chronic obstructive pulmonary disease. Cancer 1974, **33**: 1635–1641.

542 Hull MT, Roth LM, Glover JL, Walker PD. Metastatic carotid body paraganglioma in von Hippel-Lindau disease. Arch Pathol Lab Med 1982, **106**: 235–239.

543 Kipkie GF. Simultaneous chromaffin tumors of the carotid body and the glomus jugularis. Arch Pathol 1947, **44**: 113–118.

544 Kliewer KE, Cochran AJ. A review of the histology, ultrastructure, immunohistology, and molecular biology of extra-adrenal paragangliomas. Arch Pathol Lab Med 1989, **113:** 1209–1218.

545 Lack EE. Hyperplasia of vagal and carotid body paraganglia in patients with chronic hypoxemia. Am J Pathol 1978, **91:** 497–516.

546 Raafat F, Salman WD, Roberts K, Ingram L, Rees R, Mann JR. Carney's triad. Gastric leiomyosarcoma, pulmonary chondroma and extra-adrenal paraganglioma in young females. Histopathology 1986, **10:** 1325–1333.

547 Rodriguez-Cuevas H, Lau I, Rodriguez HP. High-altitude paragangliomas. Diagnostic and therapeutic considerations. Cancer 1986, **57:** 672–676.

548 Saldana MJ, Salem LE, Travezan R. High altitude hypoxia and chemodectomas. Hum Pathol 1973, **4:** 251–263.

549 Zanelli M, van der Walt JD. Carotid body paraganglioma in von Hippel-Lindau disease: a rare association. Histopathology 1996, **29:** 178–180.

Morphologic features

550 Lack EE, Kim H, Reed K. Pigmented ("black") extraadrenal paraganglioma. Am J Surg Pathol 1998, **22:** 265–269.

551 Moran CA, Albores-Saavedra J, Wenig BM, Mena H. Pigmented extraadrenal paragangliomas: a clinicopathologic and immunohistochemical study of five cases. Cancer 1997, **79/2:** 398–402.

552 Reddy VB, Norris J, Waters B, Gattus P. Extraadrenal retroperitoneal paraganglioma with osseous metaplasia. Int J Surg Pathol 1996–1997, **4:** 193–196.

Histochemical, immunohistochemical, electron microscopic, and molecular genetic features

553 Barroso-Moguel R, Costero I. Argentaffin cells of the carotid body tumor. Am J Pathol 1962, **41:** 389–402.

554 Crowell WT, Grizzle WE, Siegel AL. Functional carotid paragangliomas. Arch Pathol Lab Med 1982, **106:** 599–603.

555 Grimley PM, Glenner GG. Histology and ultrastructure of carotid body paragangliomas. Comparison with the normal gland. Cancer 1967, **20:** 1473–1488.

556 Hamid Q, Varndell IM, Ibrahim NB, Mingazzini P, Polak JM. Extraadrenal paragangliomas. An immunocytochemical and ultrastructural report. Cancer 1987, **60:** 1776–1781.

557 Kliewer KE, Wen DR, Cancilla PA, Cochran AJ. Paragangliomas. Assessment of prognosis by histologic, immunohistochemical, and ultrastructural techniques. Hum Pathol 1989, **20:** 29–39.

558 Lack EE, Cubilla AL, Woodruff JM, Lieberman PH. Extra-adrenal paragangliomas of the retroperitoneum. A clinicopathologic study of 12 tumors. Am J Surg Pathol 1980, **4:** 109–120.

559 Martinez-Madrigal F, Bosq J, Micheau C, Nivet P, Luboinski B. Paragangliomas of the head and neck. Immunohistochemical analysis of 16 cases in comparison with neuro-endocrine carcinomas. Pathol Res Pract 1991, **187:** 814–823.

560 Min KW. Diagnostic usefulness of sustentacular cells in paragangliomas: immunocytochemical and ultrastructural investigation. Ultrastruct Pathol 1998, **22:** 369–376.

561 Papadimitriou JC, Drachenberg CB. Giant mitochondria with paracrystalline inclusions in paraganglioma of the urinary bladder. Correlation with mitochondrial abnormalities in paragangliomas of other sites. Ultrastruct Pathol 1994, **18:** 559–564.

562 Pryse-Davies J, Dawson IMP, Westbury G. Some morphologic, histochemical and chemical observations on chemodectomas and the normal carotid body, including a study of the chromaffin reaction and possible ganglion cell elements. Cancer 1964, **17:** 185–202.

563 Reynolds CP, German DC, Weinberg AG, Smith RG.

Catecholamine fluorescence and tissue culture morphology. Technics in the diagnosis of neuroblastoma. Am J Clin Pathol 1981, **75:** 275–282.

564 Saito H, Saito S, Sano T, Kagawa N, Hizawa K, Tatara K. Immunoreactive somatostatin in catecholamine-producing extra-adrenal paraganglioma. Cancer 1982, **50:** 560–565.

565 Schroder HD, Johannsen L. Demonstration of S-100 protein in sustentacular cells of phaeochromocytomas and paragangliomas. Histopathology 1986, **10:** 1023–1033.

565a Tadros TS, Strauss RM, Cohen C, Gal AA. Galanin immunoreactivity in paragangliomas but not in carcinoid tumors. Appl Immuno Mol Morphol 2003, **11:** 250–252.

566 Van Schothorst EM, Beekman M, Torremans P, Kuipers-Dijkshoorn NJ, Wessels HW, Bardoel AFJ, van der Mey AG, van der Vijver MJ, van Ommen GJ, Devilee P, Cornelisse CJ. Paragangliomas of the head and neck region show complete loss of heterozygosity at 11q22-q23 in chief cells and the flow-sorted DNA aneuploid fraction. Hum Pathol 1998, **29:** 1045–1049.

567 Warren WH, Lee I, Gould VE, Memoli VA, Jao W. Paragangliomas of the head and neck. Ultrastructural and immunohistochemical analysis. Ultrastruct Pathol 1985, **8:** 333–343.

Spread and metastases, treatment, and prognosis

568 Achilles E, Padberg BC, Holl K, Kloppel G, Schroder S. Immunocytochemistry of paragangliomas—value of staining for S-100 protein and glial fibrillary acid protein in diagnosis and prognosis. Histopathology 1991, **18:** 453–458.

569 Au WY, Chan AC, Wong KK, Leung CY, Liang R, Kwong YL. Multiple osseous metastases from occult paraganglioma: a diagnostic pitfall. Histopathology 1998, **33:** 287–288.

570 Gee MS, Kliewer KE, Hinton DR. Nucleolar organizer regions in paragangliomas of the head and neck. Arch Otolaryngol Head Neck Surg 1992, **118:** 380–383.

571 Jovanovic R, Hacker GW, Falkmer UG, Falkmer S, Mendel L, Graf AH, Hoog A, Kanjuh V, Silfversward C, Grimelius L. Paragangliomas. Neuroendocrine features and cytometric DNA distribution patterns. A clinico-pathological study of 22 cases. Virchows Arch [A] 1991, **419:** 455–461.

572 Lack EE, Cubilla AL, Woodruff JM, Lieberman PH. Extra-adrenal paragangliomas of the retroperitoneum. A clinicopathologic study of 12 tumors. Am J Surg Pathol 1980, **4:** 109–120.

573 Linnoila RJ, Lack EE, Steinberg SM, Keiser HR. Decreased expression of neuropeptides in malignant paragangliomas. An immunohistochemical study. Hum Pathol 1988, **19:** 41–50.

574 Olson JL, Salyer WR. Mediastinal paragangliomas (aortic body tumor). A report of four cases and a review of the literature. Cancer 1978, **41:** 2405–2412.

575 Vidal S, Kovacs K, Lloyd RV, Meyer FB, Scheithauer BW. National cancer data base report on malignant paragangliomas of the head and neck. Cancer 2002, **94:** 730–737.

576 Whimster WF, Masson AF. Malignant carotid body tumor with extradural metastases. Cancer 1970, **26:** 239–244.

Specific paraganglioma types

577 Altergott R, Barbato A, Lawrence A, Paloyan E, Freeark RJ, Prinz RA. Spectrum of catecholamine-secreting tumors of the organ of Zuckerkandl. Surgery 1985, **98:** 1121–1126.

578 Arias-Stella J, Valcarcel J. Chief cell hyperplasia in the human carotid body at high altitudes. Physiologic and pathologic significance. Hum Pathol 1976, **7:** 361–373.

579 Beham A, Schmid C, Fletcher CD, Aubock L, Pickel H. Malignant paraganglioma of the uterus. Virchows Arch [A] 1992, **420:** 453–457.

580 Bertogalli D, Calearo C, Pignataro O. Les paragangliomes non-cromatophiles à siège rare. A propos de deux observations personnelles (paragangliome du pneumogastrique cervical et

paragangliome de la base de la langue). Ann Otolaryngol (Paris) 1959, **76**: 688–699.

581 Eriksen C, Girdhar-Gopal H, Lowry LD. Vagal paragangliomas. A report of nine cases. Am J Otolaryngol 1991, **12**: 278–287.

582 Farr HW. Carotid body tumors. A 30 year experience at Memorial Hospital. Am J Surg 1967, **114**: 614–619.

583 Glenn F, Gray GF. Functional tumors of the organ of Zuckerkandl. Ann Surg 1976, **9**: 578–585.

584 Glucksman MA, Persinger CP. Malignant non-chromaffin paraganglioma of the bladder. J Urol 1963, **89**: 822–825.

585 Grignon DJ, Ro JY, Mackay B, Ordonez NG, el-Naggar A, Molina TJ, Shum DT, Ayala AG. Paraganglioma of the urinary bladder. Immunohistochemical, ultrastructural and DNA flow cytometric studies. Hum Pathol 1991, **22**: 1162–1169.

586 Harach HR, Wheatley T, Smellie WA, Brown MJ. Phaeochromocytoma of the organ of Zuckerkandl invading inferior vena cava. Histopathology 1996, **28**: 556–559.

587 Hatfield PM, James AE, Schulz MD. Chemodectomas of the glomus jugulare. Cancer 1972, **30**: 1164–1168.

588 Heath D, Smith P. Enlargement of the carotid bodies in cirrhosis of the liver. Histopathology 1994, **25**: 159–164.

589 Heinrich MC, Harris AE, Bell WR. Metastatic intravagal paraganglioma. Case report and review of the literature. Am J Med 1985, **78**: 1017–1024.

590 Heppleston AG. A carotid-body-like tumour in the lung. J Pathol Bacteriol 1958, **75**: 461–464.

591 Ho K-C, Meyer G, Garancis J, Hanna J. Chemodectoma involving the cavernous sinus and semilunar ganglion. Hum Pathol 1982, **13**: 942–943.

592 Horoupian DS, Kerson LA, Saiontz H, Valsamis M. Paraganglioma of cauda equina. Clinicopathologic and ultrastructural studies of an unusual case. Cancer 1974, **33**: 1337–1348.

593 Johnson TL, Shapiro B, Beierwaltes WH, Orringer MB, Lloyd RV, Sisson JC, Thompson NW. Cardiac paragangliomas. A clinicopathologic and immunohistochemical study of four cases. Am J Surg Pathol 1985, **9**: 827–834.

594 Johnstone PA, Foss RD, Desilets DJ. Malignant jugulotympanic paraganglioma. Arch Pathol Lab Med 1990, **114**: 976–979.

595 Kahn LB. Vagal body tumor (nonchromaffin paraganglioma, chemodectoma, and carotid body-like tumor) with cervical node metastasis and familial association. Ultrastructural study and review. Cancer 1976, **38**: 2367–2377.

596 Kepes JJ, Zacharias DL. Gangliocytic paragangliomas of the duodenum. Report of two cases with light and electron microscopy examination. Cancer 1971, **27**: 61–70.

597 Kipkie GF. Simultaneous chromaffin tumors of the carotid body and the glomus jugularis. Arch Pathol 1947, **44**: 113–118.

598 Korn D, Bensch K, Liebow AA, Castleman B. Multiple minute pulmonary tumors resembling chemodectomas. Am J Pathol 1960, **37**: 641–672.

599 Lack EE, Cubilla AL, Woodruff JM. Paragangliomas of the head and neck region. A pathologic study of tumors from 71 patients. Hum Pathol 1979, **10**: 191–218.

600 Lack EE, Cubilla AL, Woodruff JM, Farr HW. Paragangliomas of the head and neck region. A clinical study of 69 patients. Cancer 1977, **39**: 397–409.

601 Lack EE, Cubilla AL, Woodruff JM, Lieberman PH. Extra-adrenal paragangliomas of the retroperitoneum. A clinicopathologic study of 12 tumors. Am J Surg Pathol 1980, **4**: 109–120.

602 LaGuette J, Matias-Guiu X, Rosai J. Thyroid paraganglioma: a clinicopathologic and immunohistochemical study of three cases. Am J Surg Pathol 1997, **21**: 748–753.

603 Larner JM, Hahn SS, Spaulding CA, Constable WC. Glomus jugulare tumors. Long-term control by radiation therapy. Cancer 1992, **69**: 1813–1817.

604 Lattes R. Nonchromaffin paraganglioma of ganglion nodosum, carotid body and aortic arch bodies. Cancer 1950, **3**: 667–694.

605 Merino MJ, Livolsi VA. Malignant carotid body tumors. Report of two cases and review of the literature. Cancer 1981, **47**: 1403–1414.

606 Meyer FB, Sundt TM Jr, Pearson BW. Carotid body tumors. A subject review and suggested surgical approach. J Neurosurg 1986, **64**: 377–385.

607 Miller TA, Weber TR, Appelman HD. Paraganglioma of the gallbladder. Arch Surg 1972, **105**: 637–639.

608 Moran CA, Rush W, Mena H. Primary spinal paragangliomas: a clinicopathological and immunohistochemical study of 30 cases. Histopathology 1997, **31**: 167–173.

609 Moran CA, Suster S, Fishback N, Koss MN. Mediastinal paragangliomas. A clinicopathologic and immunohistochemical study of 16 cases. Cancer 1993, **72**: 2358–2364.

610 Murphy TE, Huvos AG, Frazell EL. Chemodectomas of the glomus intravagale. Vagal body tumors, nonchromaffin paragangliomas of the nodose ganglion of the vagus nerve. Ann Surg 1970, **172**: 246–255.

611 Nora JD, Hallett JW Jr, O'Brien PC, Naessens JM, Cherry KJ Jr, Pairolero PC. Surgical resection of carotid body tumors. Long-term survival, recurrence, and metastasis. Mayo Clin Proc 1988, **63**: 348–352.

612 Ober WB. Emil Zuckerkandl and his delightful little organ. Pathol Annu 1983, **18**(Pt 1): 103–119.

613 Oberman HA, Holtz F, Sheffer LA, Magielski JE. Chemodectomas (nonchromaffin paragangliomas) of the head and neck. A clinicopathologic study. Cancer 1968, **21**: 838–851.

614 Olson JL, Salyer WR. Mediastinal paragangliomas (aortic body tumor). A report of four cases and a review of the literature. Cancer 1978, **41**: 2405–2412.

615 Olson JR, Abell MR. Nonfunctional, nonchromaffin paragangliomas of the retroperitoneum. Cancer 1969, **23**: 1358–1367.

616 Robertson DI, Cooney TP. Malignant carotid body paraganglioma. Light and electron microscopic study of the tumor and its metastases. Cancer 1980, **46**: 2623–2633.

617 Rosenwasser H. Glomus jugulare tumors. Arch Otolaryngol 1968, **88**: 1–40.

618 Shamblin WR, ReMine WH, Sheps SG, Harrison EG. Carotid body tumor (chemodectoma). Clinicopathologic analysis of 90 cases. Am J Surg 1971, **122**: 732–739.

619 Shermer KL, Pantius EE, Dziabis MD, McQuistan RJ. Tumors of the glomus jugulare and glomus tympanicum. Cancer 1966, **19**: 1273–1280.

620 Smith WT, Hughes B, Ermocilla R. Chemodectoma of the pineal region, with observations of the pineal body and chemoreceptor tissue. J Pathol Bacteriol 1966, **92**: 69–76.

621 Someren A, Karcioglu Z. Malignant vagal paraganglioma. Report of a case and review of the literature. Am J Clin Pathol 1977, **68**: 400–408.

622 Spector GJ, Compagno J, Perez CA, Maisel RH, Ogura JH. Glomus jugulare tumors. Effects of radiotherapy. Cancer 1975, **35**: 1316–1321.

623 Thacker WC, Duckworth JK. Chemodectoma of the orbit. Cancer 1969, **23**: 1233–1238.

624 Tu H, Bottomley RH. Malignant chemodectoma presenting as a miliary pulmonary infiltrate. Cancer 1974, **33**: 244–249.

625 Ueda N, Yoshida A, Fukunishi R, Fujita H, Yanagihara N. Nonchromaffin paraganglioma in the nose and paranasal sinuses. Acta Pathol Jpn 1985, **35**: 489–495.

626 Wilkinson R, Forgan-Smith R. Chemodectoma in relation to the aortic arch (aortic body tumour). Thorax 1969, **24**: 488–491.

627 Young TW, Thrasher TV. Nonchromaffin paraganglioma of the uterus. A case report. Arch Pathol Lab Med 1982, **106**: 608–609.

628 Zeman MS. Carotid body tumor of the trachea, glomus jugularis tumor, tympanic body tumor, nonchromaffin paraganglioma. Ann Otol Rhinol Laryngol 1956, **65**: 960–962.

17 Urinary tract

Nelson G. Ordóñez* and Juan Rosai

Kidney, renal pelvis, and ureter
Bladder

* Author of the section on "Non-neoplastic diseases"

Kidney, renal pelvis, and ureter

Non-neoplastic diseases

The renal biopsy

The renal biopsy is an invaluable method used in the evaluation of patients with renal disease.[1,2] By this procedure, it is possible to establish an accurate diagnosis, obtain critical information on the evolution and prognosis of the disease process, and develop a rational approach to the treatment of renal disorders. Even in advanced stages of kidney damage, a biopsy can provide clues regarding the possibility of recurrence of the disease following transplantation. The renal biopsy is also important in the management of the transplant recipient, representing the most accurate method for determining the presence of cellular or humoral rejection, acute tubular necrosis, cyclosporine nephrotoxicity, or the development of de novo or recurrent glomerulonephritis in the allograft.

Renal disease is usually manifested by a limited number of symptoms which are often grouped in clinical syndromes, i.e., nephrotic syndrome, persistent proteinuria, acute nephritis, persistent or recurrent hematuria, asymptomatic renal insufficiency, hypertension, rapidly progressive renal failure, acute renal failure, and chronic renal failure. Also, the kidney reacts to a variety of injurious agents with a limited number of histopathologic patterns of injury. Thus, a given clinical syndrome can be associated with several histopathologic patterns, while a single histopathologic pattern may be linked to more than one syndrome. The accurate interpretation of a renal biopsy requires detailed knowledge of the structure and function of the normal kidney, as well as an understanding of the clinical, morphologic, and histopathogenic aspects of renal disease. In order to evaluate a kidney biopsy, the pathologist should correlate complete clinical and laboratory information with light microscopic, immunofluorescence, and ultrastructural findings.

Handling of the biopsy

Most renal biopsies are done by either the percutaneous route using a cutting needle or by direct exposure of the kidney (open biopsy). The specimen should be divided for light microscopy, immunofluorescence, and electron microscopy. Ideally, two biopsy cores should be obtained when a needle biopsy is performed. From the first core, two or more samples measuring 0.5 to 1 mm in thickness are taken from each end with a fresh razor or scalpel blade and placed in a cold solution of 2% glutaraldehyde in phosphate or cacodylate buffer for electron microscopy studies while the remaining tissue is placed in saline. If the second core is adequate, samples should also be taken from each end for electron microscopy, while the remainder is snap frozen in liquid nitrogen or in isopentane cooled on dry ice for immunofluorescence. For light microscopy, the tissue that was placed in saline should be transferred to a fixative. If only one core is obtained, material should be taken from each end for electron microscopy, and the remainder divided longitudinally for light microscopy and immunofluorescence. If the core is too small, the specimen should be divided for electron microscopy and immunofluorescence studies since most of the light microscopic information can be obtained from the study of semi-thin sections of the plastic-embedded tissue processed for electron microscopy.

Light microscopy

A variety of fixatives have been recommended for the light microscopic study of renal biopsies. Most pathologists feel that mercuric solutions provide the best architectural and cytologic detail. Zenker's, Helly's, Bouin's, and Van der Griff's fixatives are widely used, but 10% neutral formalin can also provide good morphologic detail. Tissue should be fixed in ethanol to search for glycogen or crystals of urate, uric acid, and other water-soluble substances. Although a variety of special stains have been recommended for the routine evaluation of renal biopsies, from the practical point of view periodic acid–Schiff (PAS) is the most useful, easiest to perform, and can also provide most of the information obtained from silver preparations and Masson trichrome stain. It is recommended that the biopsy core be serially sectioned through its full thickness and that 3 to 4 tissue sections be placed on each slide. At intervals of every 5 slides, one slide is stained with hematoxylin and eosin, and another with PAS. By following this procedure, the maximum number of glomeruli can be examined. The remaining unstained slides are saved in the event that special stains are needed.[5]

Electron microscopy

There is a general misconception that electron microscopy is a complex and time-consuming procedure. In fact, satisfactory processing methods have been developed that require less than 5 hours.[4] Many fixatives have been developed for this procedure, each of which has specific advantages. Some pathologists prefer a primary fixation in osmium tetroxide for optimal demonstration of deposits in the basement membrane, but glutaraldehyde fixation with post-osmification is more convenient and is suitable as a routine procedure. For tissue embedding, various epoxy resins with comparable characteristics are available and their selection is a matter of personal preference. Semi-thin (1 µm thick) sections obtained from the plastic-embedded tissue blocks are stained with toluidine blue or methylene blue and

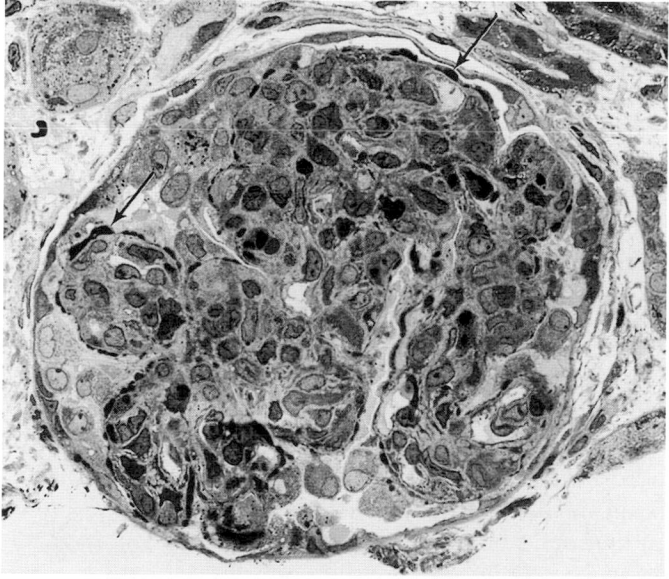

Fig. 17.1 Plastic-embedded semi-thin section stained with toluidine blue showing numerous humps along the capillary walls (arrows) and obliteration of the glomerular capillary loops by endocapillary cell proliferation in a case of poststreptococcal glomerulonephritis.

carefully studied as they can yield a great deal of information, especially when examined at high magnification (Fig. 17.1).[3,5] Thin sections from the blocks selected for ultrastructural study are double-stained with uranyl acetate and lead citrate for electron microscopic examination.

Immunohistochemistry

Direct immunofluorescence performed on frozen tissue sections is the most satisfactory method for the routine assessment of a renal biopsy. The antisera most commonly used are for IgG, IgA, IgM, C1q, C3, C4, fibrinogen, and fibrin. Immunofluorescence for a variety of other complement factors, light chains, and various cell markers is performed for selected diagnostic purposes. Immunoperoxidase studies can also be successfully done on formalin-fixed, paraffin-embedded tissues, but these immunohistochemical methods, which are commonly used in oncologic surgical pathology, have not had the same degree of acceptance in the routine study of kidney biopsies. This is largely due to the fact that the different patterns of reactivity in glomerular disease are easier to recognize by immunofluorescence microscopy.

Biopsy interpretation

Many pathologists believe that the interpretation of renal biopsies is extremely difficult. Admittedly, it has become more complex over the years due to changing approaches to the classification of glomerular diseases and to the added need to perform immunofluorescence and electron microscopy, but the diagnosis of renal biopsy specimens is based on the same foundation of careful observation and clinicopathologic correlation used in other areas of pathology. Knowledge of normal morphology is essential for the recognition of any alteration that may occur in the various components of the kidney. A checklist that can be used during the biopsy evaluation is provided in Table 17.1.

A renal biopsy must contain glomeruli to be considered adequate, but there is disagreement over the number of glomeruli required to make a diagnosis. The definition of adequacy largely depends on the disease under consideration. In disorders characterized by irregular or crescentic proliferation, the assessment should be based on a minimum of 10 glomeruli, whereas in diffuse lesions (such as membranous glomerulonephritis) the identification of specific features in a single glomerulus may be sufficient to allow the diagnosis, especially if ultrastructural studies are also performed. Even in these diffuse processes, there is often a variation in the severity of a particular lesion among different glomeruli: therefore, a good rule of thumb is that at least 5 to 10 glomeruli should be examined in order to assess properly the extent and severity of the disease.

Table 17.1 Biopsy evaluation checklist

	Light microscopy	Electron microscopy	Immunofluorescence
Glomeruli	Size and cellularity	Basement membrane (thickness, density, contours)	Positive/negative reaction
	Segmental or global changes	Cellular changes	Reagent Igs, complement, fibrin, etc.
	Mesangium	Mesangium	Pattern (linear or granular)
	Leukocytes	Deposits (type and location)	Intensity
	Capillary walls	Inclusions	
	Necrosis		
	Thrombi (type)		
	Adhesions to Bowman's capsule		
	Deposits (type and location)		
	Crescents (type and %)		
	Sclerosis (distribution and %)		
Tubules	Necrosis	Cellular changes	Reactions and pattern
	Reparative changes	Inclusions	Intensity
	Dilation	Basement membrane	
	Casts (type)	Deposits (type and location)	
	Crystals		
	Cellular inclusions		
	Vacuolization		
	Basement membrane		
Blood vessels	Intimal thickening (type)	Intimal and medial changes	Reactions and distribution
	Elastica changes	Deposits	
	Media hypertrophy		
	Hyalinosis		
	Thrombosis and embolism		
	Necrosis		
	Inflammation		
	Juxtaglomerular apparatus		
Interstitium	Edema	Cellular infiltrates	Reactions and distribution
	Inflammation and fibrosis (type and %)	Deposits	

Normal structure of the glomerulus

Since most of the changes seen in renal biopsies occur in the glomerulus, we will briefly review the morphology of this structure. The glomerulus is a vascular structure composed of a tuft of specialized capillaries that arise from the afferent arteriole to form lobules then rejoin the vascular pole to drain into the efferent arteriole. Normally, the lobules are poorly defined, but they are highlighted in some disease processes. Each lobule consists of a cluster of capillaries supported by a branching framework, the mesangium. The tuft of capillaries lies within the lumen of the expanded proximal end of the nephron, or Bowman's space, which is lined on its parietal aspect by a layer of attenuated epithelial cells overlying a thick basement membrane. Together, the latter two structures make up **Bowman's capsule**, which is continuous at the vascular pole of the glomerulus with

the adventitia of the afferent and efferent arterioles. At the urinary pole, the basement membrane of the Bowman's capsule merges with that of the proximal tubule. Each glomerulus measures approximately 200 μm in diameter, but they are not all of the same size. Those located in the juxtamedullary area are about 20% larger than those elsewhere in the cortex. The cellularity of the glomerulus varies in different diseases, and an accurate assessment requires histologic preparations 2 to 4 μm thick. The presence of more than three cells in an individual glomerular mesangial region away from the vascular pole is considered hypercellularity.

The walls of the glomerular capillaries are clothed by a reflected layer of cells of Bowman's capsule. These highly specialized epithelial cells are known as podocytes because they have many tiny foot processes that rest on the basement membrane that separates them from the attenuated, fenestrated endothelium of the capillaries. The **glomerular basement membrane (GBM)** is a trilaminar structure composed of a central electron-dense zone, or lamina densa, bordered by two narrow electron-lucent layers, the lamina rara interna and the lamina rara externa. The major components of the GBM are type IV collagen, laminin, heparan sulfate proteoglycans, and entactin, but small amounts of other proteins have also been found.[13]

The principal function of the glomerulus is filtration, and the GBM is the main component of the filtration barrier. In normal adults, the GBM measures 310 to 380 nm in thickness; it is somewhat thinner in children, and slightly thicker in males than in females.[6] The GBM does not completely surround the capillary lumen since the vessel is attached to the mesangium, which consists of mesangial cells embedded in a basement membrane-like material, the mesangial matrix (Fig. 17.2). By electron microscopy, the mesangial matrix appears more fibrillar than the GBM. It is composed of collagen types IV, V, and VI, fibronectin, laminin, entactin, and sulfated glycosaminoglycans, including heparan sulfate, and chondroitin sulfate.[11] The mesangial cells have cytoplasmic processes which contain α-smooth muscle actin and myosin filaments, characteristics shared by smooth muscle cells, pericytes, and myofibroblasts.[7,8] Mesangial cells thus possess contractile properties and are probably involved in the regulation of the flow of blood through the glomeruli and modulation of the filtration process.[9] They produce growth factors that allow normal cell turnover.[8] Mesangial cells may also have some phagocytic activity and play a role in the clearance of debris from the mesangium.[10] Although obvious ultrastructural differences exist between the endothelial and mesangial cells, these differences are not always evident in glomerular diseases, and differentiation between endothelium and mesangium is usually based on the location of these structures in the glomerulus.

The visceral epithelial cells are involved in basement membrane synthesis and, by their unique structure, play an important role in glomerular permeability. These cells cover the GBM on its urinary side and are attached to it by cytoplasmic extensions or foot processes that, under the scanning electron microscope, appear as a complex of interdigitating structures originating from different epithelial cells (Fig. 17.3). The foot processes are approximately 25 to 60 nm apart, with a connecting slit-pore diaphragm 4 to 7 nm thick whose function remains unclear. Bowman's capsule limits the urinary space and is lined by a layer of flattened parietal epithelial cells which express cytokeratin proteins. In contrast, the visceral epithelial cells are not immunoreactive for cytokeratin, but are for vimentin and desmin.[12]

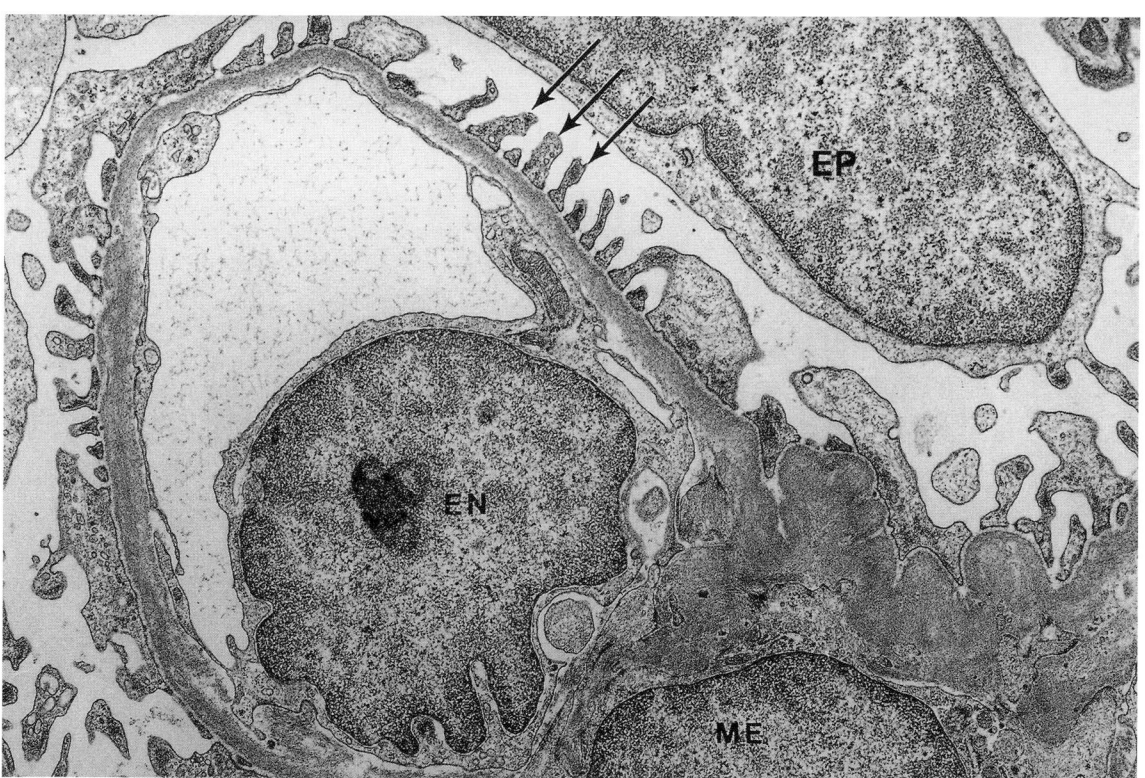

Fig. 17.2 Electron micrograph of normal glomerulus showing the relationship of different cell types. The epithelial aspect of the basement membrane is covered by foot processes (arrows) and the capillary lumen is lined by attenuated endothelium. EP = epithelial cell; ME = mesangium; EN = endothelial cell. (× 13,000)

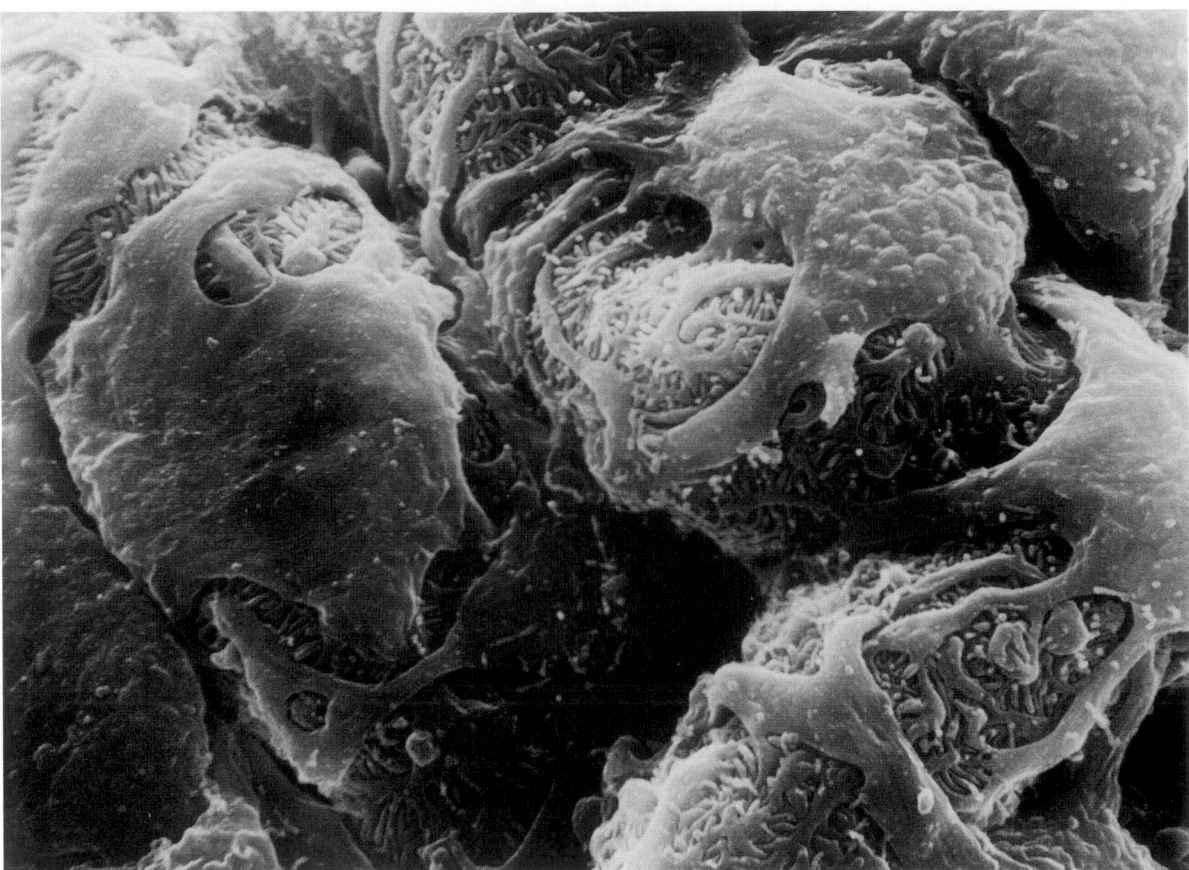

Fig. 17.3 Scanning electron micrograph showing the capillary loops covered by epithelial cells and interdigitating foot processes. (× 8000)

Classification of glomerular disease

Glomerulonephritis is an inflammation of the glomerulus, while **glomerulopathy** is an all-embracing term for disorders affecting this structure. In glomerular diseases, other parts of the nephron may also be involved, but the diagnosis hinges on the identification of derangement of the normal glomerular configuration. The changes may be recognizable by routine light microscopy, though the findings from immunofluorescence are often significant. Electron microscopy is always informative and it is sometimes the only means whereby the structural changes can be detected and defined. The damage to the glomeruli may take the form of definable morphologic patterns, and subdivisions in the character or distribution of the glomerular lesions are used to classify glomerulonephritis. Although there is general agreement on the definitions applied to the distribution of glomerular lesions (Table 17.2), categorizations that are more specific are sometimes controversial. Over the years, there have been numerous attempts to classify glomerulonephritis, both by individuals, as well as by committee. Of the latter efforts, the most notable was sponsored by the World Health Organization (WHO).[14] This classification is based on a primary subdivision according to the overall pattern of glomerular change, and a second categorization by the type and distribution of superimposed lesions.

In this chapter, glomerular lesions are subdivided into those associated with the nephrotic syndrome or persistent proteinuria, those seen in acute nephritis or hematuria, and lesions associated with vascular diseases such as systemic vasculitis, hemolytic uremic syndrome, and systemic sclerosis. Separate sections, including those describing tubulointerstitial lesions, renal vascular disorders, cystic diseases, and the interpretation of biopsies of transplanted kidneys, will be presented.

Table 17.2 Classification of glomerular disease by distribution

Classification of disease distribution when many glomeruli are considered:
    Focal: disease affecting only some of the glomeruli
    Diffuse: disease affecting most or all glomeruli
Classification of disease distribution when single glomeruli are considered:
    Segmental: a lesion involving only a part of the glomerulus
    Global: a lesion involving the entire glomerulus

Glomerular lesions associated with the nephrotic syndrome

The nephrotic syndrome is clinically characterized by the occurrence of massive proteinuria, hypoproteinemia, edema, and hyperlipidemia. Damage to the filtration barrier of the glomerulus allows proteins, particularly albumin, to be filtered into the urine. The criterion for the syndrome is the excretion of more than 3.5 g of protein in a 24-hour period. A spectrum of morphology has been correlated with the syndrome, but some glomerular lesions are not accompanied by significant inflammatory or proliferative response within the glomerulus: they include primary nephrotic syndrome with minimal change glomerulopathy, membranous glomerulonephritis, diabetes mellitus, amyloidosis, and various forms of congenital nephrotic syndrome. The major histologic, electron microscopic, and immunofluorescence findings in each of these conditions are summarized in Table 17.3.

Minimal change glomerulopathy

Minimal change glomerulopathy (MCG) accounts for approximately 80% of all cases of the idiopathic nephrotic syndrome in childhood,[21,22] and 20% to 30% of adult cases.[17,18] Most of the children are under the age of 6 when first seen, the majority being 3 or 4 years old.[21,22] There is a male predominance of about 2.5:1 in children, but no sex difference is seen in adults.[17,21] In 80% to 90% of children, MCG is idiopathic. It has been associated with infectious diseases, recent immunizations, ingestion of heavy metals, such as mercury or lead, allergies, and drug reactions in a minority of cases.[25,26] In adult patients, especially the elderly, MCG has been related to the use of nonsteroidal anti-inflammatory drugs.[26] In these cases, this disease is often accompanied by interstitial nephritis

Table 17.3 Glomerular lesions associated with the nephrotic syndrome

Disease	Light microscopy	Electron microscopy	Immunofluorescence
Minimal change glomerulopathy	Minimal or no mesangial prominence	Extensive foot process obliteration	Usually negative for Igs and C3
Diffuse mesangial hypercellularity with nephrotic syndrome	Mild mesangial hypercellularity	Obliteration of foot processes, sparse mesangial deposits	IgM with or without C3
Focal and segmental glomerulosclerosis	Focal and segmental mesangial sclerosis	Extensive foot process obliteration	Nonspecific trapping of IgM and C3
Membranous glomerulonephritis	Uniform capillary wall thickening, sometimes with spiked dome pattern	Four stages of subepithelial and intramembranous deposits	Granular deposits along capillary wall of IgG and C3, sometimes IgM, IgA
Diabetic nephropathy	Nodular and diffuse mesangial sclerosis; insudative lesions	Diffuse thickening of basement membranes. Increased mesangial matrix.	Linear staining for IgG along capillary walls
Amyloidosis	Mesangial and vascular deposits of Congo red-positive material with green birefringence	Fibrils 8 to 10 nm in diameter	Amyloid AA and light chains
Light chain deposition disease	Mesangial widening and deposition of PAS-positive material	Granular, dense material along the basement membranes	Peripheral and mesangial kappa and lambda-light chains
Fibrillary glomerulonephritis	Mesangial widening and occasional hypercellularity, capillary wall thickening	Fibrils 20 nm in diameter	Variable IgG, C3, occasional IgM, IgA
Immunotactoid glomerulopathy	Mesangial widening and occasional hypercellularity, capillary wall thickening	Fibrils 30 to 50 nm in diameter, often in parallel bundles	Variable IgG, C3, occasional IgM, IgA
Congenital nephrotic syndrome:			
Finnish type	Tubular ectasia, microcysts, glomerular sclerosis	Obliteration of foot processes	Nonspecific trapping of IgM and C3
Diffuse mesangial sclerosis	Diffuse mesangial sclerosis	Obliteration of foot processes	Negative

and acute renal failure.[20,31] It has also been found in association with lymphoproliferative disorders, especially Hodgkin's lymphoma.[27]

A full-blown nephrotic syndrome with heavy proteinuria, often of selective type, is the most common presentation. Nephritic features, such as hematuria, hypertension, and reduced renal function, are uncommon.[26] Complete remission is common within 8 weeks of starting corticosteroid therapy,[21,22,28] but after withdrawal of the steroids, about half of the patients enter into a period in which there are intermittent relapses; this phase may last for up to 10 years. The relapses are usually steroid-responsive and the disease does not progress to chronic renal failure. The development of azotemia should suggest an incorrect diagnosis. Relapse is uncommon after a disease-free interval of 2 years. Patients who achieve only a partial remission with corticosteroid therapy may benefit from immunosuppressive drugs.[23,29,30] The factors responsible for this disorder are not known, and the mechanism underlying the glomerular permeability defect is also unclear, but the association with T-cell lymphoma and responsiveness to steroids and immunosuppressive agents that interfere with T-lymphocyte function provide direct evidence that immune-mediated mechanisms might be involved in the pathogenesis of this condition.[19,26]

On routine light microscopy, changes are seen in the convoluted tubules where large amounts of lipid and protein transport droplets accumulate in the cell cytoplasm. In contrast, all the glomeruli appear normal (Fig. 17.4). The finding of lipid droplets in the urine led Munk in 1913 to introduce the term lipoid nephrosis for this condition.[24] Other common synonyms are minimal change disease, nil lesion, and minimal change nephrotic syndrome, all of which reflect the lack of significant morphologic alternations on light microscopy.

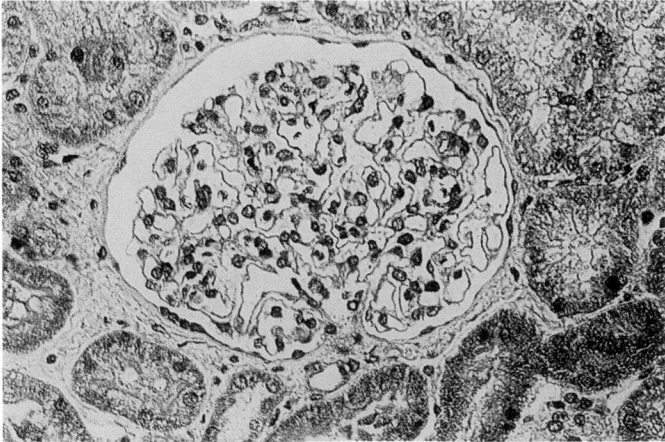

Fig. 17.4 Glomerulus from a patient with minimal change glomerulopathy. The glomerulus is normocellular, the capillary loops are patent, and the basement membrane is normal in thickness.

Only after biopsies could be studied by electron microscopy was it established that the glomeruli, not the tubules, were the primary site of the pathology. The observation of an extensive loss of epithelial foot processes led to yet another designation, epithelial cell disease. This type of structural change was initially viewed as true fusion of the foot processes, but scanning electron microscopy showed that swelling of the cells caused the foot processes to retract into the cell bodies.[15,16] Foot process effacement is not restricted to MCG. It can be found in other conditions associated with heavy proteinuria or the nephrotic syndrome, and there may be an accompanying increase in cytoplasmic organelles, cyst formation, and the development of numerous microvilli (Fig. 17.5). Although there is increased electron density in the epithelial cell cytoplasm adjacent to the basement membrane, immune complex deposits are not seen, and all the changes are reversible; biopsy specimens taken during remission look normal. The mesangium usually shows little or no change, but a mild increase in mesangial cells and matrix may be found. Immunofluorescence studies are almost invariably negative for immunoglobulin and complement, but small amounts of IgM and C3 are occasionally detected in cases with mesangial prominence. Albumin may be seen as fine droplets in the cytoplasm of proximal tubule cells when the tissue is stained for this protein (Fig. 17.6).

A biopsy is susceptible to sampling error and it therefore should be kept in mind that lesions that affect only some glomeruli, such as focal and segmental glomerulosclerosis, may be misdiagnosed as MCG. Conversely, since tubular atrophy and interstitial scarring are not features of MCG, focal and segmental glomerulosclerosis should enter into the differential diagnosis if these findings are seen on a biopsy.

Diffuse mesangial hypercellularity with nephrotic syndrome

It has been estimated that 2% to 10% of the renal biopsies from patients with idiopathic nephrotic syndrome may present some degree of mesangial hypercellularity.[33,36] Diffuse mesangial hypercellularity (DMH) has been described in some patients with MCG who frequently are steroid resistant or steroid dependent.[41,42] DMH has also been found in association with focal and segmental glomerulosclerosis, and with mesangial deposits of IgM.[38,39] Some authors considered that cases with significant deposition of IgM in the mesangium constituted a separate clinicopathologic entity which they referred to as IgM nephropathy or IgM glomerulonephritis.[34,35,37] Others, however, have concluded that the finding of mesangial IgM is not of major significance.[39,40] At present, the relationship between DMH, MCG, and focal and segmental glomerulosclerosis remains unclear. Similarly unsettled is the issue of whether DMH with deposition of IgM in patients with

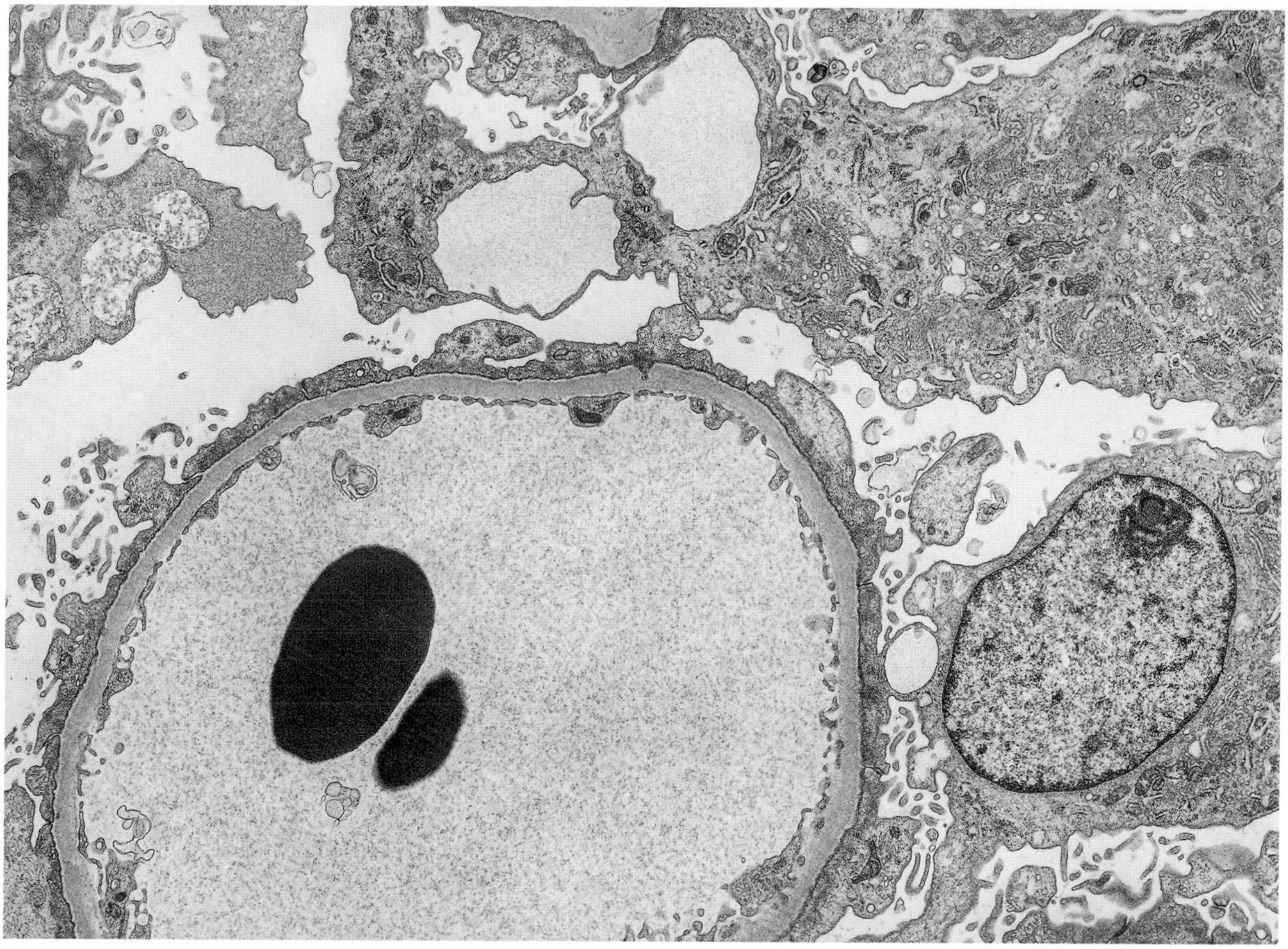

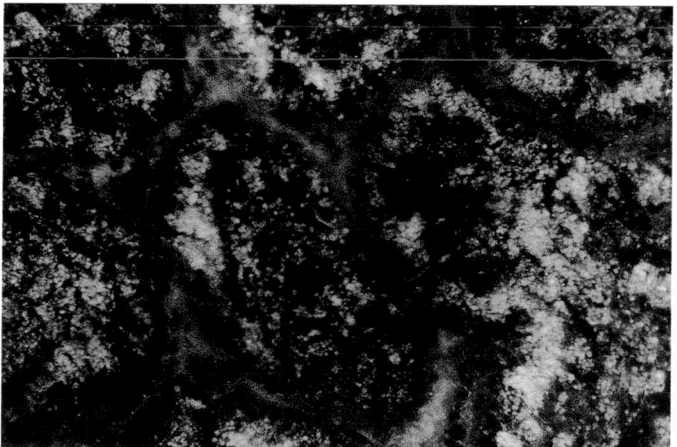

Fig. 17.5 Portion of a glomerulus from a patient with minimal change glomerulopathy showing obliteration of foot processes. The epithelial cell cytoplasm is hyperactive and shows microvillus and cyst formation. (× 8400)

Fig. 17.6 Immunofluorescence preparation demonstrating numerous albumin-positive resorption lipid droplets in the proximal tubular epithelial cells.

idiopathic nephrotic syndrome is part of the spectrum of MCG, an early stage of focal and segmental glomerulosclerosis, or a specific form of immune trapping glomerulonephritis, such as IgA nephropathy.[32,33]

Focal and segmental glomerulosclerosis

Focal and segmental glomerulosclerosis (FSGS) is a clinicopathologic syndrome characterized by proteinuria, commonly in the nephrotic range, a high incidence of progressive renal failure, and focal and segmental sclerotic glomerular lesions. FSGS may be primary (idiopathic) or secondary to various etiologies and pathogenic mechanisms. The pathogenesis of primary FSGS is unknown but it appears to be the result of circulating "permeability" factor(s), possibly a lymphokine or a cytokine, which leads to epithelial cell injury resulting in segmental scar formation and ultimately glomerular obsolescence.[66] The glomerular lesion of secondary FSGS is histologically similar to that of primary FSGS and can occur in a variety of clinical settings with a clinical presentation indistinguishable from that of primary FSGS. Since the pathogenetic mechanisms involved in these disorders and their treatment differ significantly from those of primary FSGS, it is of paramount importance that they be excluded before a diagnosis of primary FSGS is made.[56] Table 17.4 lists the conditions most commonly associated with FSGS which should be excluded before making the diagnosis of primary FSGS.

Table 17.4 Classification of focal and segmental glomerulosclerosis

Primary (idiopathic)
    Typical FSGS
    Collapsing glomerulopathy
    Glomerular tip lesion
Secondary
    Unilateral renal agenesis
    Renal ablation–remnant kidney
    HIV infection
    Heroin addiction
    Morbid obesity
    Sickle cell disease
    Cyanotic congenital heart disease
    Reflux and obstructive nephropathy
    Glycogen storage disease
    Hypertensive nephropathy
    Healed focal proliferative or necrotizing glomerulonephritis

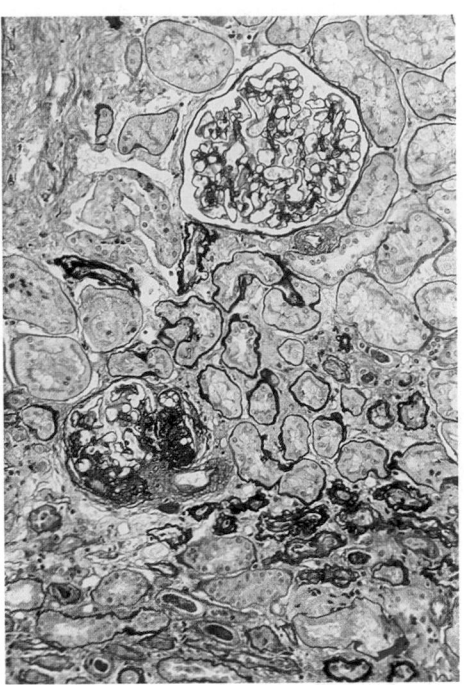

Fig. 17.7 Biopsy from a patient with focal and segmental glomerulosclerosis. One of the glomeruli shows segmental sclerosis, while the other appears unremarkable. Tubular atrophy is also seen.

Primary FSGS is responsible for approximately 10% to 15% of the cases of nephrotic syndrome in children and 20% to 30% in adults. It constitutes the predominant cause of idiopathic nephrotic syndrome in adult patients, especially in the African-American population.[45] Although FSGS generally occurs as a sporadic disease, rare familial cases inherited by autosomal dominant and recessive modes of inheritance have been described.[51,60,71,74] The greatest prevalence of the disease is in children under 5 years of age and in adults in the third and fourth decades.[59] The onset is insidious, and the nephrotic syndrome is the primary clinical manifestation, although 10% to 30% of patients have asymptomatic proteinuria which is typically nonselective. Examination of the urinary sediment will often lead to the detection of microscopic hematuria. Forty to 60% of patients have been shown to develop end-stage renal disease within 10 to 20 years,[44,62] and recurrence following transplantation has been reported in 15% to 50% of the patients.[43,70] A de novo form of FSGS in transplanted kidneys in which the patient's original disease was not FSGS has also been reported.[75]

Since the renal involvement usually begins in the corticomedullary region and spreads toward the periphery, the lesion can be missed if this population of glomeruli is not included in the biopsy. Segmental sclerosis usually affects one or more lobules of the glomerular tuft near the axial region, often appearing to adhere to Bowman's capsule. Early lesions show an increased mesangial matrix and mild mesangial hypercellularity: only when the sclerosis is advanced do these areas become hypocellular (Fig. 17.7). On occasion, sclerosis is seen in the portion of the glomerulus opposite the hilus, forming an adhesion in the vicinity of the opening of the Bowman's space into the proximal tubule (glomerular tip lesion).[52,54] The loops in the sclerosed areas are distorted and may contain hyaline material, which is thought to represent plasmatic insudation and lipid-laden cells (Fig. 17.8).[67] The frequent presence of hyalinosis has led some investigators to use the term "FSGS and hyalinosis" to designate the disease; however, it should be emphasized that hyalinosis is neither a specific nor a constant feature of FSGS. Areas of tubular atrophy are common, and while this finding is not by itself diagnostic of FSGS, it should raise the possibility in biopsies which otherwise show minimal change glomerulopathy.[59] Interstitial fibrosis accompanies tubular loss and atrophy, and it has been shown that the extent of the tubulointerstitial damage is a prognostic indicator of the disease.[56,64,68,73]

As in minimal change glomerulopathy, the most significant ultrastructural feature is the presence of extensive foot process obliteration, which is not confined to the glomeruli having sclerosed areas; glomeruli that look normal by light microscopy can also be affected. A variable increase in mesangial matrix is customary in all glomeruli, and some degree of mesangial hypercellularity is not uncommon. The glomerular basement membranes are often folded and focally thickened. On occasion, there are areas of detachment of the epithelial lining and these spaces can be quite wide and can accumulate multilayered basement membrane-like material and cellular debris. The hyaline deposits are composed of finely granular material that has an appearance and electron density similar to that of the insudative material seen in diabetic nephropathy. These deposits are predominantly subendothelial and located in the areas of

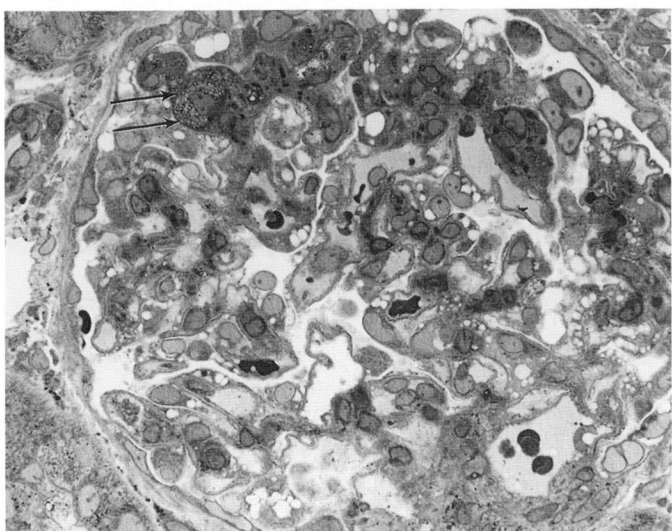

Fig. 17.8 Plastic-embedded semi-thin section from a biopsy of a patient with early focal and segmental glomerulosclerosis. There is mild segmental prominence of the mesangium (upper third) and vacuolization of the epithelial cell cytoplasm. A lipid-laden intracapillary cell with foamy cytoplasm is also present (arrows).

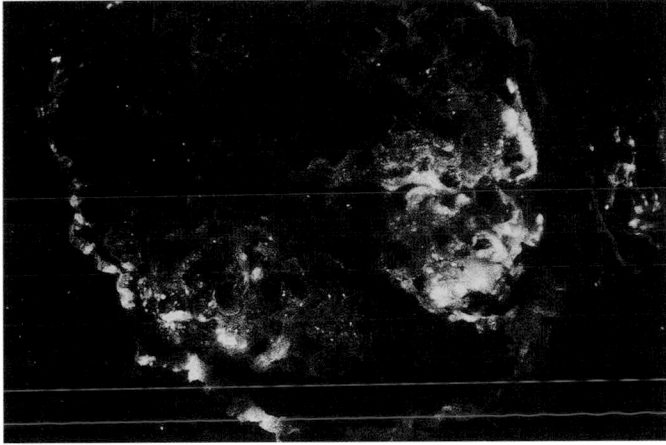

Fig. 17.9 Immunofluorescence microscopy demonstrating segmental deposition of IgM in a biopsy from a patient with focal and segmental glomerulosclerosis.

segmental sclerosis. Immunofluorescence studies show that they contain IgM and C3 (Fig. 17.9).

Collapsing glomerulopathy

Collapsing glomerulopathy is a clinically and pathologically distinct variant of FSGS characterized by widespread collapse of glomerular capillary loops, a male and an African-American racial predominance, and a poor prognosis with rapid loss of renal function and virtually no response to therapy. It can occur as an idiopathic disease[50,69,72] or as a secondary process associated with intravenous drug abuse and/or human immunodeficiency virus (HIV) infection.[50,53,55,65] This variant of FSGS constitutes about 80% to 85% of the glomerular changes reported in the latter group of patients.[63] Collapsing glomerulopathy has, on occasion, also been reported in

association with some autoimmune diseases, lymphoproliferative disorders, and non-HIV viral infections, such as hepatitis C virus infection.[58] In renal transplants, it can occur as recurrent or de novo disease.[48,61]

The characteristic histologic feature is a predominantly collapsing type of focal glomerulosclerosis that is segmental and often global. The segmental sclerosis is characterized by localized hypertrophy and hyperplasia of the epithelial cells overlying the sclerotic segment.[57] These cells are often swollen and vacuolated, and may contain abundant resorption droplets. Relative to the extent of glomerular sclerosis, tubulointerstitial injury is more severe in collapsing glomerulopathy than in typical FSGS. The tubular epithelial cells may present degenerative changes and the tubular lumina are often markedly dilated and show extensive proteinaceous cast formation. The interstitium often exhibits a prominent inflammatory infiltrate mainly composed of lymphocytes.

The most common immunofluorescence finding in the glomeruli in patients with collapsing glomerulopathy is IgM and C3 in a segmental distribution. Less commonly, other immunoglobulin classes may also be localized. The changes seen by electron microscopy are generally similar to those of typical FSGS. A distinctive but nonspecific feature is the finding of endothelial tubuloreticular inclusions in over 90% of patients with HIV-associated collapsing glomerulopathy.[47,58] These structures are rarely seen in idiopathic collapsing glomerulopathy or in collapsing glomerulopathy associated with intravenous drug abuse. Numerous endothelial tubuloreticular inclusions are often seen in patients with systemic lupus erythematosus or in patients treated with interferon alpha.

Glomerular tip lesion

This morphologic variant of FSGS was first described by Howie and Brewer in 1984.[52] It is characterized by a consolidation of the glomerular segment adjacent to the origin of the proximal tubule. The capillary lumina of sclerotic loops may appear obliterated by swelling of endothelial cells and the presence of foamy cells. The epithelial cells adjacent to the involved segment are enlarged, vacuolated, and often contain intracytoplasmic hyaline droplets. Some lesions are less cellular with an increase in mesangial matrix. Although early studies[52,54,76] suggested that the tip lesion variant had a better response to corticosteroid therapy and a more benign clinical course than typical FSGS, later investigations were unable to confirm an improved long-term renal survival for this variant of FSGS.[46,68] At present, there is no evidence to justify considering glomerular tip lesion as a distinct form of FSGS.[46]

C1q nephropathy

C1q nephropathy is a relatively rare, immune complex-mediated glomerulopathy characterized by the presence of prominent C1q deposition in the mesangium. Patients with this condition often present with nephrotic-range proteinuria that responds poorly to steroid treatment.[78,79] The disease usually occurs in adolescents and young adults, and it affects blacks and males more often, with a black to white ratio of 4.7:1 and a male to female ratio of 1.8:1. Progression to renal failure is slow and it has been estimated that the 3-year renal survival is approximately 85%.[77]

The light microscopic findings vary from slight to marked mesangial hypercellularity with an increase in mesangial matrix, with or without segmental glomerulosclerosis. Electron microscopy studies invariably demonstrate mesangial immune complex deposits. Subendothelial or subepithelial deposits are uncommon. On immunofluorescence, C1q is usually accompanied by IgG, IgM, and C3 immunoreactivity. IgA can be found in about 60% of the cases. The main differential diagnosis of C1q nephropathy is with lupus nephritis, which also can have prominent C1q deposition in the mesangium together with immunoglobulins and C3.

Membranous glomerulonephritis

Membranous glomerulonephritis (MGN; also termed membranous nephropathy, membranous glomerulonephropathy, extramembranous glomerulonephropathy, and epimembranous nephropathy) is a glomerular disease of diverse etiology characterized by epimembranous immune complex deposits and variable basement membrane thickening, without mesangial cell proliferation or infiltration by inflammatory cells. MGN accounts for 20% to 30% of all cases of idiopathic nephrotic syndrome in adults[89] and 1% to 9% in children.[100,103] In the large majority of the cases, this condition occurs as an idiopathic (primary) form, but the disease has been related to a wide variety of conditions (secondary) in approximately 25% of the adults and 80% of the children (Table 17.5).[113] Over 85% of the cases of secondary MGN are caused by infection, neoplasia, or systemic lupus erythematosus (SLE).[107] The most common causes worldwide are malaria and schistosomiasis, while SLE, neoplasia, hepatitis B infection, and drugs are the most frequent in the United States.[113] Rare familial cases of MGN, probably related to a genetically transmitted mechanism, have been reported.[109]

The pathogenetic mechanism that leads to the immune complex localization in the subepithelial aspect of the GBM is not fully understood and the nature and source of the antigens involved in the immune complexes remain largely unknown. Two mechanisms that have been considered to be responsible for the development and localization of the deposits along the GBM are that the immune complexes are formed in situ at the subepithelial capillary wall, or that circulating immune complexes are deposited in that location. Experimental studies suggest that in most cases the immune com-

Table 17.5 Entities associated with secondary membranous glomerulonephritis

Infectious:
Hepatitis B, hepatitis C, syphilis, malaria, leprosy, schistosomiasis, filariasis, hydatid disease, enterococcal endocarditis, brucellosis
Neoplastic diseases:
Carcinoma (lung, gastrointestinal tract, breast, kidney), seminoma, lymphoma (especially non-Hodgkin's), leukemia, melanoma
Immunologic disorders:
Systemic lupus erythematosus, mixed connective tissue disease, Sjögren's syndrome, rheumatoid arthritis, sarcoid, Hashimoto's thyroiditis, Graves' disease, Weber–Christian panniculitis, myasthenia gravis, bullous pemphigoid, autoimmune enteropathy, primary biliary cirrhosis
Medications:
Organic gold, D-penicillamine, bucillamine, mercury, probenecid, captopril, trimethadione, lithium, clomethiazole, diclofenac
Miscellaneous:
De novo renal allografts, sickle cell disease, diabetes, Kimura's disease, sclerosing cholangitis, renal vein thrombosis, anti-GBM disease, cryoglobulinemia, Guillain–Barré syndrome

plexes are probably formed in situ by the binding of circulating antibodies with antigens that are normally present in the glomerulus or with extrinsic antigens that have previously been planted as free antigens in the subepithelial area. The antigen(s) involved in primary human MGN are unknown. However, in some instances of secondary MGN, hepatitis B surface and e antigens have been identified in the immune deposits. In both primary and secondary forms, complement is activated at the capillary wall site and appears to be related to the development of the proteinuria.

The incidence of MGN in different populations varies; there is a particularly high frequency in Japanese children[111] and in certain African populations,[110,114] probably related to a high incidence of hepatitis B infection and parasitic infestations. Although MGN may occur at any age, it is rare in children and adolescents. Eighty to 90% of the patients are over the age of 30 at the time of diagnosis, with a peak in the fourth and fifth decades.[85,87,99] The disease is twice as common in males.[104] Sixty to 80% of patients have the nephrotic syndrome at onset and others are usually referred for investigation of asymptomatic proteinuria or an abnormal urinalysis.[87,103,107] The proteinuria is usually nonselective, but a highly selective proteinuria is seen in as many as 20% of cases.[85,89] Macroscopic hematuria is rare, but as many as 90% of patients have microscopic hematuria at some time during the course of the disease.[85,107] Hypertension is usually found after renal insufficiency has developed, but it can occur in 30% of the patients at presentation.[113] Circulating immune complexes can be demonstrated in some patients,[80] but attempts to identify a specific antigen have been unsuccessful. Rare cases with circulating anti-GBM antibody and/or anti-neutrophil cytoplasmic antibody (ANCA) have also been reported.[98] Serum levels of C3, as well as other components of the complement, are usually normal. If they are reduced, it suggests a secondary form of the disease. Urinary excretion of the C5b–C9 terminal complement complex is elevated in some patients and can be correlated with disease activity and prognosis.[81,94]

The natural history and overall prognosis of MGN can be significantly affected by the underlying disease and the way it was treated. When the MGN is secondary to drugs, toxic substances, or infections, removal of the etiologic agent will often result in the disappearance of the clinical symptoms and resolution of the renal lesion. The nephrotic syndrome may abate and the glomerular changes regress after resection and treatment of a malignant tumor.[83,115] In patients with membranous lupus nephritis, the course is indolent, whereas those who develop a superimposed anti-glomerular basement membrane antibody disease undergo rapid progression to renal failure. Most patients with idiopathic MGN present with chronic proteinuria and recurrent episodes of the nephrotic syndrome persisting over many years. Only 20% to 25% of these patients progress to renal fail-

ure terminating in end-stage renal disease.[106] Partial or complete spontaneous remission has been reported in 20% to 65% of cases.[87,106] The likelihood of spontaneous remission is greatly increased in children[84,103] and in patients who presented with proteinuria without the nephrotic syndrome and in whom the biopsy demonstrated a stage I glomerular lesion.[101] Recurrence or de novo development of MGN after renal transplantation can occur, but it is a rare event.[90,98,108,112]

The structural features of the glomerular capillary wall have been used to define four histopathologic stages of the disease.[88] In **stage I**, the glomeruli appear normal by light microscopy, and there are no significant changes in the thickness of the basement membrane. At this early stage, an incorrect diagnosis of minimal change disease is possible if the biopsy is studied only by light microscopy. With the electron microscope, these cases show sparse immune complex deposits between the epithelial cell cytoplasm and the lamina densa of the basement membrane, but the latter appears homogeneous and uniform in thickness. The deposits can be irregular, dome-shaped, or appear as small humps with a well-defined line between the lamina densa and the epithelial cell. Foot processes over the deposits are obliterated, but they often appear normal elsewhere (Fig. 17.10).

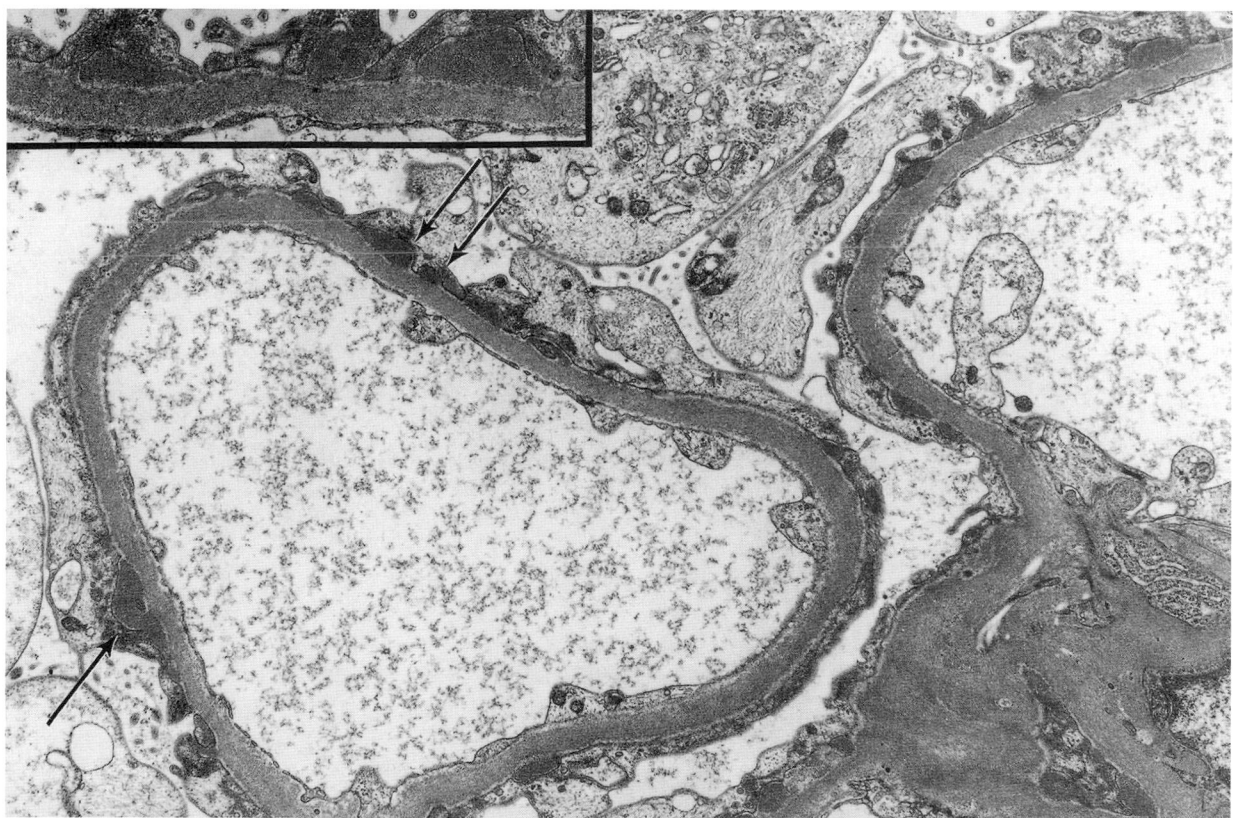

Fig. 17.10 Membranous glomerulonephritis, stage I. The basement membrane is normal in thickness. Small, sparse subepithelial deposits (arrows) are separated from the basement membrane by a thin clear zone (inset). The epithelial foot processes are obliterated. (× 6000; inset, × 9100)

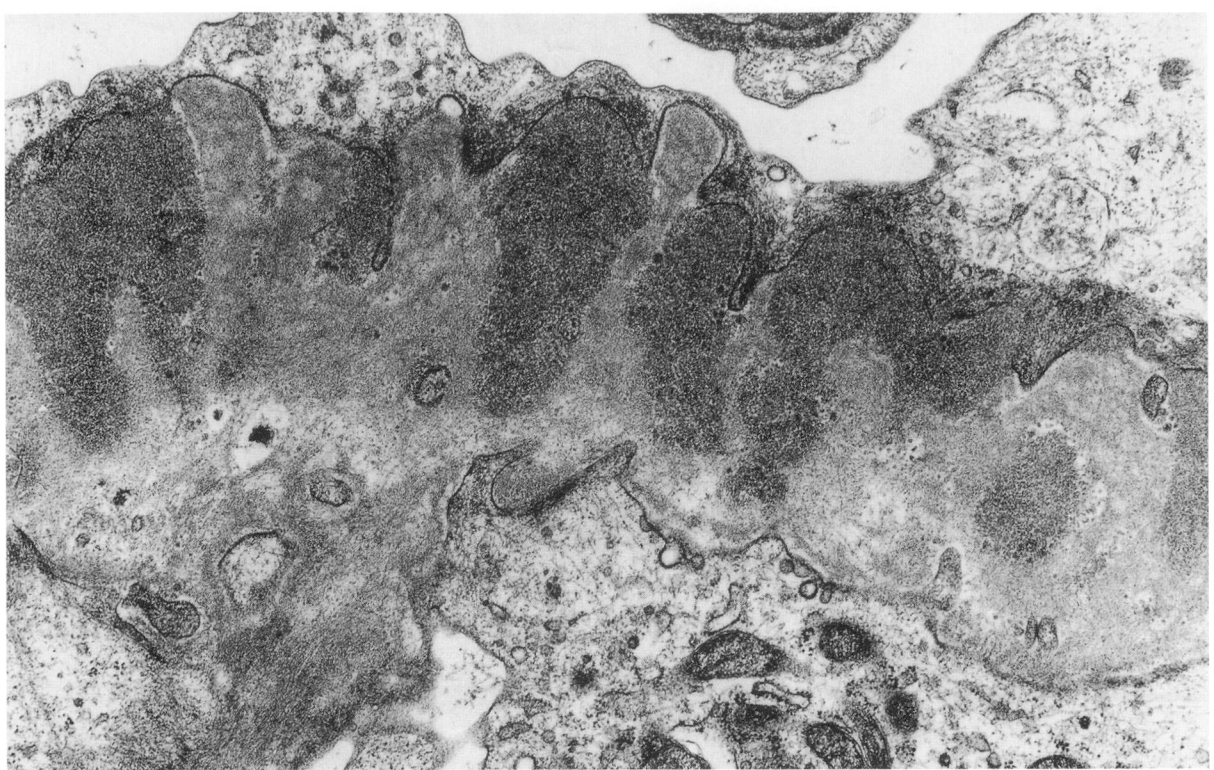

Fig. 17.11 Membranous glomerulonephritis, stage II. Subepithelial deposits are separated by projections of the basement membrane. (× 18,000)

In **stage II**, the capillary walls are thickened, and many subepithelial deposits are present separated by extensions of basement membrane (Fig. 17.11). The deposits do not stain with silver impregnation techniques, but the extensions of basement membrane do, thus creating the impression that the capillary loop is covered by spikes (Fig. 17.12). These spikes have been shown to be composed of type IV collagen and noncollagenous extracellular matrix components, including laminin, heparan sulfate, proteoglycans, and vitronectin.[83] The epithelial foot processes are extensively obliterated throughout the loops.

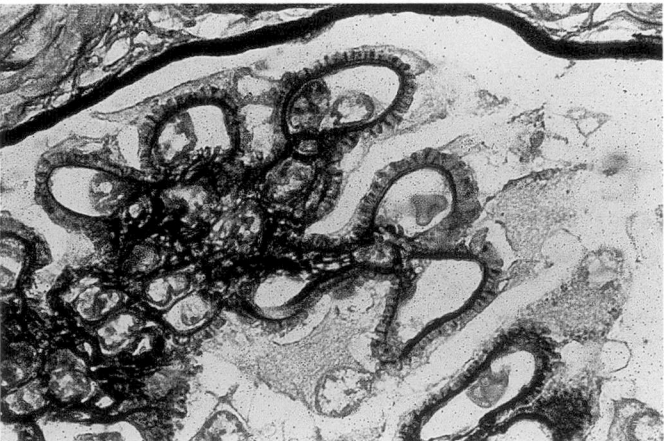

Fig. 17.12 Silver preparation showing spike formation along the thickened basement membrane.

When the disease is more advanced (**stage III**), the deposits are encircled by a newly formed basement membrane (Fig. 17.13). The capillary walls are markedly thickened and the capillary lumina narrowed. The basement membrane shows a reduplicated or moth-eaten appearance with PAS and silver stains. By electron microscopy, many of the deposits in stage III disease have a rarefied appearance that indicates resolution, and small spherical structures, which have been confused with virus particles, may be present during dissolution of the deposits. Individual deposits may also contain striated membranous bodies, which are probably formed by degeneration of entrapped cellular components.

During the late stage of the disease (**stage IV**), deposits gradually lose their electron density and the basement membrane becomes vacuolated, folded, and thickened. Deposits may no longer be evident (Fig. 17.14). Capillary lumina become obliterated and the glomerular tufts show segmental or total sclerosis. Severe tubular atrophy and vascular sclerosis can be prominent making the diagnosis difficult. In the end stage of the disease, the differential diagnosis includes various types of chronic glomerulonephritis. Although the degree of proteinuria does not parallel the stages of the renal lesion, stage I carries a better prognosis than more advanced disease, and spontaneous remission is more likely. However, there seems to be no difference in prognosis between stages II, III, and IV. Histologic progression can occur without clinical progression, and

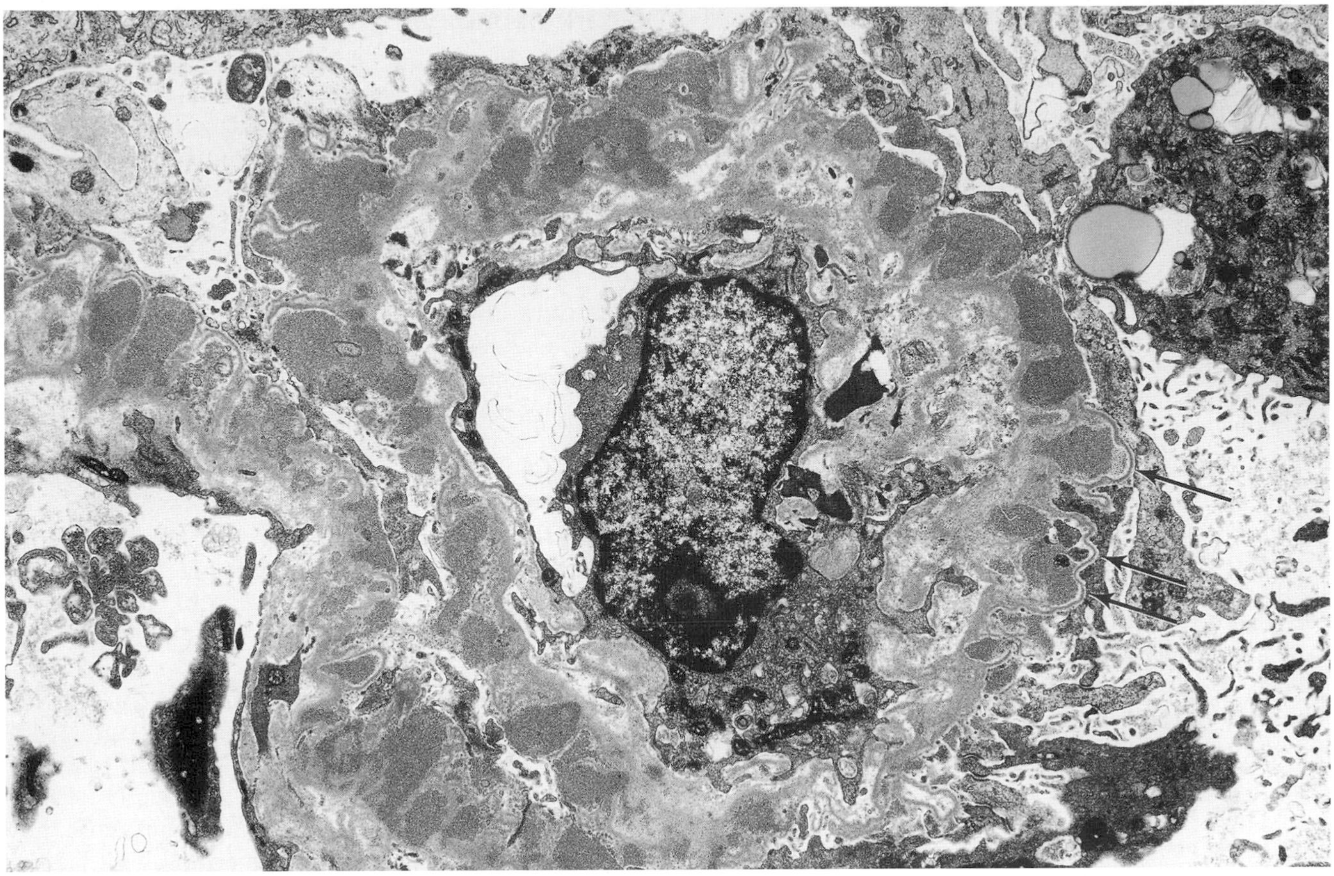

Fig. 17.13 Membranous glomerulonephritis, stage III. The basement membrane is markedly thickened and the deposits appear surrounded by a newly formed basement membrane (arrows). (× 6900)

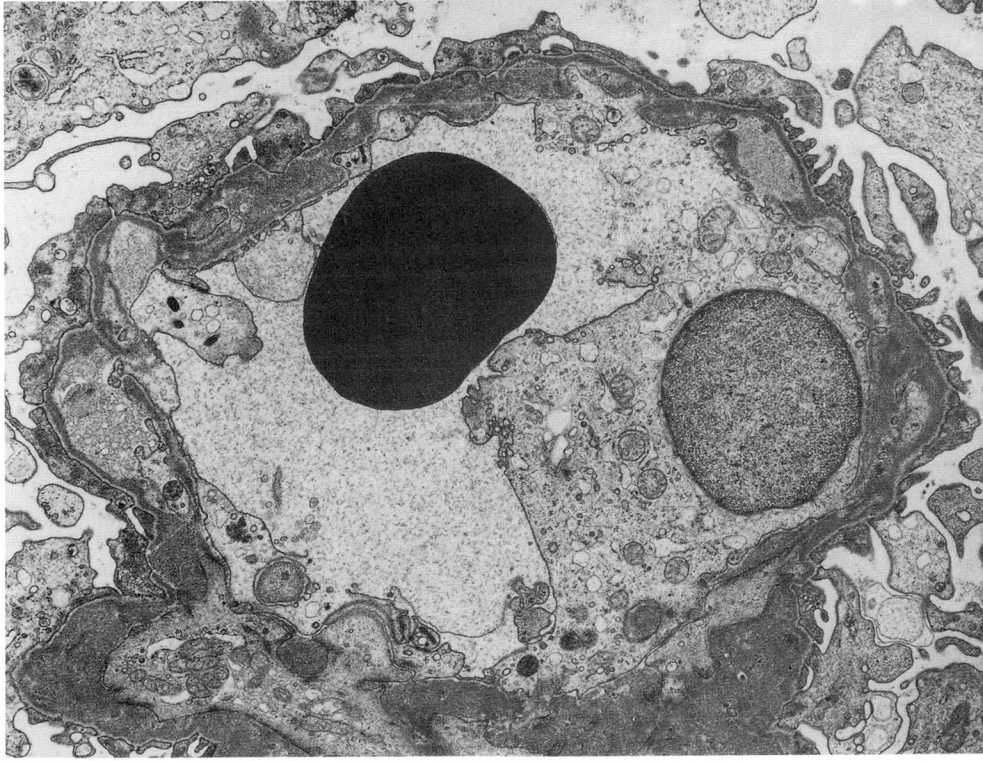

Fig. 17.14 Membranous glomerulonephritis, stage IV. The basement membrane is markedly irregular and most of the deposits have been reabsorbed, leaving large electron-lucent areas. (× 9360)

clinical remission can occur in the absence of histologic regression.[113]

Notable morphologic characteristics of MGN throughout its evolution are the absence of mesangial hypercellularity and a lack of inflammatory cells within the glomeruli. On occasion, however, a mild to moderate increase in mesangial cells can occur, especially in patients with secondary forms of MGN, such as SLE, hepatitis B, or disease associated with gold or penicillamine. In addition to epimembranous and intramembranous deposits, small amounts of immune complex deposition may be seen in the mesangial and/or subendothelial areas.[105] Similar changes can also occur in idiopathic MGN and it has been suggested that they may confer a more favorable prognosis.[86] Margination of leukocytes in the glomerular capillaries may be an indication of renal vein thrombosis.[96] Focal crescent formation can occur in MGN, but it is uncommon. Diffuse fulminant crescentic disease is a rare and late consequence of the superimposition of anti-GBM or ANCA disease.[93,95,97,98,102] Rarely, patients with MGN have tubulointerstitial nephritis because of anti-tubular basement membrane antibodies. These patients are almost invariably male children and progress to end-stage renal disease.[92]

Immunofluorescence microscopy in all stages of MGN reveals a generalized, peripheral granular pattern of IgG and C3, sometimes with C1q, C4, IgM, and IgA (Fig. 17.15). The reaction for IgA is usually not intense, and if it is strong and associated with the early components of complement (C1q and C4), the possibility of lupus MGN must be considered. Although not evaluated on routine diagnostic studies, there is strong reactivity for terminal complement components (i.e., C5b–C9 membrane attack complex). Extraglomerular deposits have only rarely been reported in idiopathic MGN.[91,107] The finding of deposits along the tubular basement membrane should always raise the possibility of membranous lupus nephritis since they occur in 30% to 50% of these cases.[91]

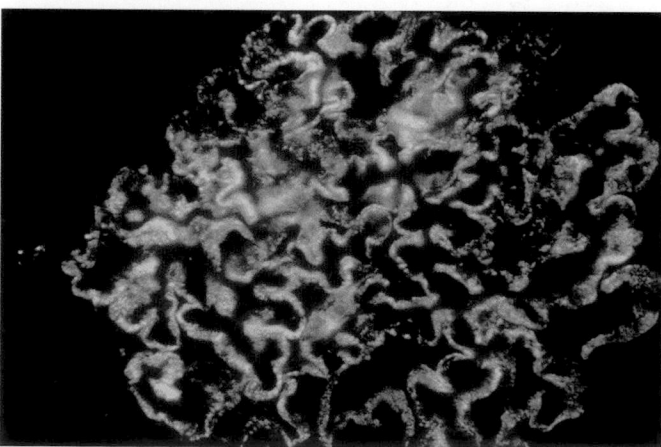

Fig. 17.15 Immunofluorescence preparation of membranous glomerulonephritis showing peripheral granular deposits of IgG.

Diabetic nephropathy

Renal disease is a frequent complication of diabetes mellitus and by far the most common cause of end-stage renal disease in the United States, accounting for more than one third of the patients who undergo long-term dialysis.[132] Of all diabetics, 30% die as a result of chronic renal failure.[117] Proteinuria, usually of nonselective type, is the most consistent clinical manifestation of diabetic nephropathy. The nephrotic syndrome has been reported in 6% to 40% of the cases[119,120] and moderate microscopic hematuria can be found in 28% to 48% of diabetics with renal disease.[125] Hypertension is a late complication seen with advanced renal failure. Most of the patients who develop diabetic nephropathy have had diabetes for at least 10 years, so it is more frequent in type I diabetes than in the type II form of the disease.

Diabetic microangiopathy occurring throughout the body is the most characteristic morphologic change in the diabetic patient, and its hallmark is an increase in the amount of vascular basement membrane material. There are no significant morphologic differences in the renal lesions caused by type I and type II diabetes.[128,130] The most striking renal lesions are found in the glomeruli and blood vessels, and they include diffuse glomerulosclerosis, nodular glomerulosclerosis, and the so-called "insudative lesions" (fibrin caps, capsular drops, and arteriolar hyalinosis). Diabetic glomerulosclerosis is the general term for all of these lesions, and they are considered to be an expression of the microangiopathy, though it is uncertain whether they are variants of a single pathologic process or independent events.

Diffuse glomerulosclerosis, the most common lesion in diabetic nephropathy, is characterized by a diffuse increase in the mesangial matrix and thickening of the capillary walls (Fig. 17.16).[133] Thickening of the GBM is the most consistent finding in diabetic nephropathy, and it is often seen in both diffuse and nodular glomerulosclerosis. Although minor degrees of basement membrane thickening are not specific to diabetes, measurement of the basement membrane width is the most effective way to quantitate early diabetic glomerular lesions.[118,126] In advanced stages, the GBM may be many times its normal thickness, often with accentuation of the normal fibrillar structure. The GBM and mesangial changes can be seen by electron microscopy before the damage is visible by light microscopy. Whether or not the mesangial lesion precedes abnormalities in the GBM remains controversial. However, morphometric electron microscopic studies in short-term type I (insulin-dependent) diabetics indicate that the earliest structural alteration in diabetic glomerulopathy that can be quantitated is an increase in the thickness of the GBM, which can be documented as early as 1½ to 2½ years after onset of the disease.[126] Increases in the relative area of the mesangium appear to develop later. The difficulty in

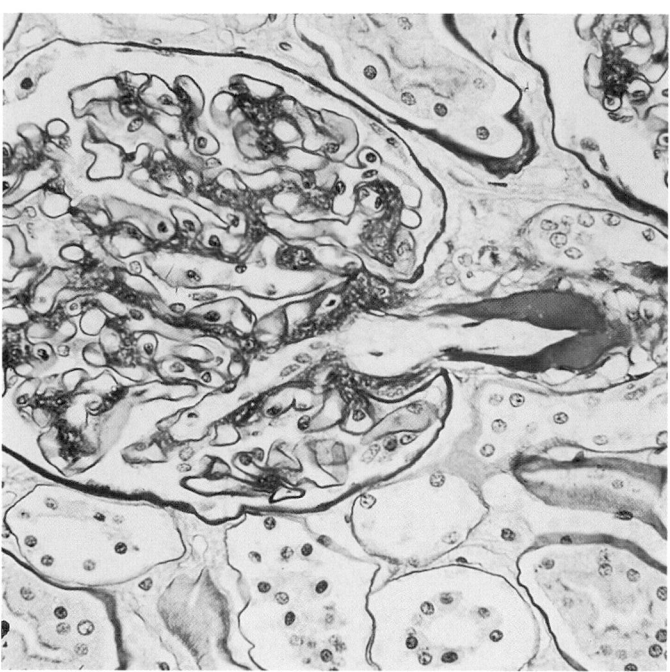

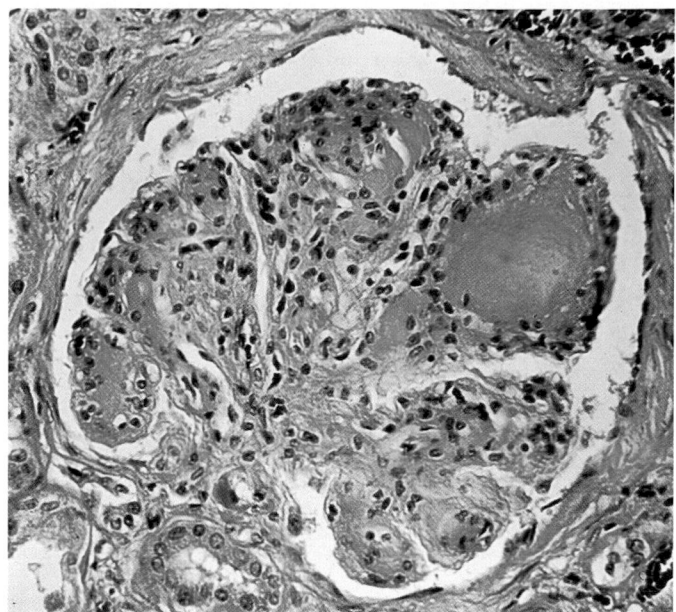

Fig. 17.17 Nodule of diabetic glomerulosclerosis.

Fig. 17.16 Early diffuse diabetic glomerulosclerosis showing a mild increase in mesangial matrix and thickened capillary walls. The arteriole shows the typical hyaline appearance of an insudative lesion.

detecting early changes may be due to the great variations in this structure that exist in normal individuals. Nevertheless, clear increases in mesangial matrix and cellularity can be detected as early as 5 to 7 years after the onset of diabetes mellitus[124,126] or within 2 to 5 years following transplantation.[123] Several studies have indicated that, while there is a correlation between the mesangial expansion and clinical renal parameters, no correlation is found between the duration of the diabetes or urinary albumin excretion and the thickness of the GBM.[124,129] A lack of correlation between the mesangial changes and the thickness of the GBM was also found, suggesting that the alterations in these structures may occur by different mechanisms.[124,127]

Nodular glomerulosclerosis (Kimmelstiel–Wilson lesion) is the characteristic histopathologic lesion of diabetic glomerulosclerosis. It consists of largely acellular nodules that are located in the intercapillary regions (Fig. 17.17). These nodules vary in size and often have a laminated appearance. They are eosinophilic, argyrophilic, and PAS positive, and stain green with Masson's trichrome stain, and blue with Mallory's stain. Ultrastructurally, they are composed of masses of extracellular mesangial matrix (Fig. 17.18). Both the mesangial widening and the nodules are the result of an increase in the synthesis, as well as a decrease in the degradation, of the mesangial matrix.[122] The capillary loops surrounding the nodules may have narrowed lumina because of expansion of the mesangium, but they can also be aneurysmally dilated, and some have peripheral mesan-

gial extensions. Focal areas of mesangiolysis may also be present.[131] Diffuse and nodular diabetic glomerulosclerosis can be found together, not only in the same patient, but also in the same glomerulus. Although nodular glomerulosclerosis is virtually pathognomonic of diabetic nephropathy, identical light microscopic lesions can be found in cases of light chain nephropathy. In this condition, however, the nodules are composed of granular electron-dense material that stains with antibodies against kappa or lambda light chains, and they lack the basement membrane-like appearance that is characteristic of diabetic nodular glomerulosclerosis. Nodular glomerulosclerosis has rarely been reported in patients without manifested diabetes or light chain disease.[121] Diffuse or nodular deposits of amyloid can sometimes be confused with diabetic glomerulosclerosis by light microscopy, but ultrastructural identification of the amyloid fibrils will establish the diagnosis.

The **insudative lesions** are the least specific of the glomerular changes in diabetes. Ultrastructurally, they are seen to be masses of finely granular, electron-dense material, often containing lipid droplets. Common locations for these lesions are the periphery of the loop in a subendothelial location (fibrin caps), within the basement membrane of Bowman's capsule (capsular drops), or in the mesangium or glomerular basement membrane (Figs 17.18 and 17.19). In blood vessels, they are more extensive in the subintima and media, but they can also involve the adventitia (Fig. 17.16). Afferent and efferent arterioles are often affected. Histochemical and immunofluorescence studies indicate that this insudative material represents infiltration by constituents of the plasma, including protein, lipids, and mucopolysaccharides.

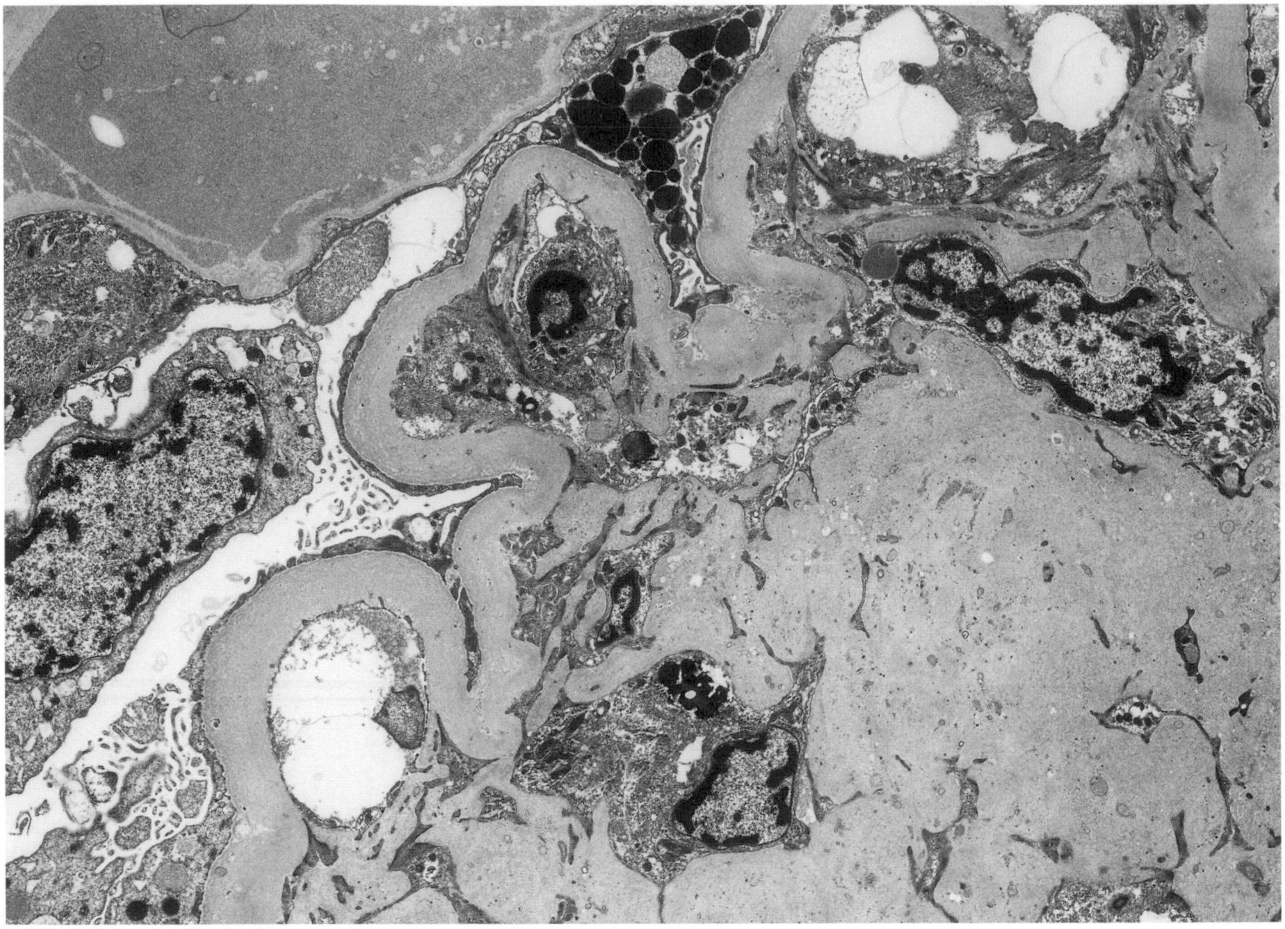

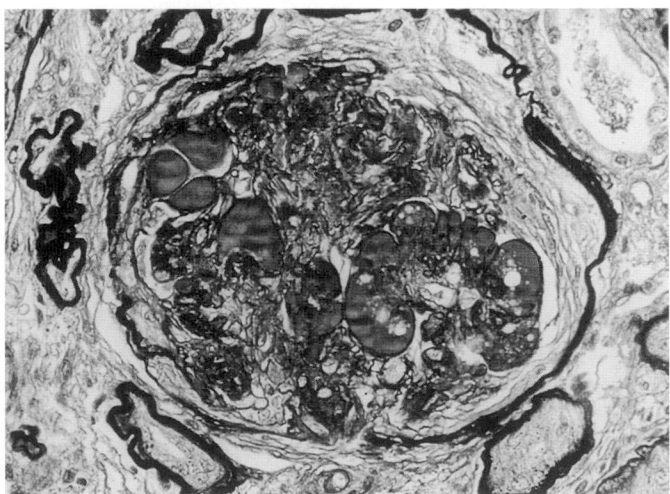

Fig. 17.18 Nodular diabetic glomerulosclerosis. The massive enlargement of the mesangium is due to an increase in mesangial matrix. The basement membrane is markedly thickened and a capsular drop is present at the left upper corner of the figure. (× 4400)

Active **epithelial crescents** are rare in diabetic glomerulosclerosis, but foci of organizing fibroepithelial crescents occur and their presence can be associated with

Fig. 17.19 Glomerulus in advanced diabetic glomerulosclerosis with fibrous crescent and numerous "fibrin caps" containing abundant lipid.

an unusually aggressive clinical course (Fig. 17.19).[116] The most characteristic tubular change is diffuse thickening of the tubular basement membrane. When the disease is advanced, there is also tubular atrophy and interstitial scarring. Glycogen vacuolization of the renal tubular epithelial cells (Armanni–Ebstein lesion), associated with uncontrolled hyperglycemia, was common in the past but is rarely seen today.

Diffuse linear localization of IgG along glomerular and tubular basement membranes and Bowman's capsule is the most common immunofluorescence finding in diabetic nephropathy (Fig. 17.20). IgG deposition can be accompanied by linear localization of other plasma components, including IgM, IgA, albumin, and ceruloplasmin. In contrast with anti-glomerular basement membrane antibody disease, eluates obtained from diabetic kidneys do not show specific antibody activity to basement membrane antigens, and it is thought that the immunoglobulin and complement localization in diabetic kidneys represents a nonspecific trapping of plasma protein secondary to mesangial or basement membrane dysfunction.

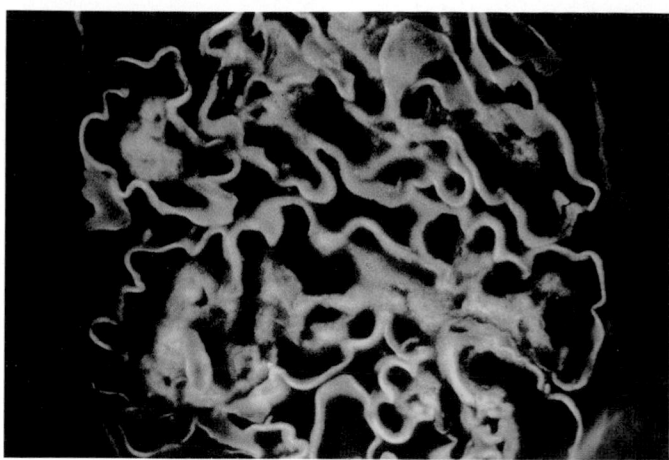

Fig. 17.20 Diabetic glomerulosclerosis with linear staining for IgG along the glomerular basement membrane.

Amyloidosis

The term amyloidosis designates a group of conditions characterized by extracellular deposition of fibrillar proteins that have a β-pleated sheet configuration on x-ray diffraction analysis. It is this physical property that is responsible for the tinctorial and optical characteristics seen with Congo red staining, which produces an apple-green birefringence when the tissue sections are examined under polarized light. Amyloid does not have a constant chemical composition, but is instead a group of proteins that share certain common physical characteristics. Its insolubility and relative resistance to proteolytic digestion under physiologic conditions cause amyloid to accumulate within tissues and interfere with their functions, causing the gradual destruction of vital organs and eventually leading to death.

Although there is a general tendency among pathologists to consider amyloidosis a histopathologic entity typified by deposits of hyaline material, the disease process itself is diverse in terms of its clinical manifestations, pathogenesis, and biochemical and immunologic aspects. When the deposits involve many organs and tissues, the condition is designated systemic amyloidosis, whereas when it is limited to a single site it is called localized amyloidosis.

AL or "primary" amyloidosis represents a plasma cell dyscrasia characterized by a systemic deposition of amyloid and a mild increase in monoclonal plasma cells in the bone marrow. About 20% of these patients have overt multiple myeloma or some other lymphoproliferative disorder. In AL amyloidosis, the deposits have often been found to be made of the NH_2-terminal fragment of the variable region of monoclonal immunoglobulin light chains. The amyloidogenic light chains are more frequently lambda than kappa in type, in contrast to normal or myeloma light chains.[142,158] Immunoglobulin heavy chains can be involved in amyloid formation (amyloid AH), however, this is less common.[160]

The term **secondary or AA amyloidosis** is used when the disease is associated with chronic inflammatory conditions such as osteomyelitis, bronchiectasis, decubitus ulcers, leprosy, Crohn's disease, and rheumatoid arthritis. In this form, the main component of the amyloid fibril is protein A, which is derived from serum amyloid A protein, an acute phase reactant. In familial amyloidosis, the amyloid fibrils often consist of transthyretin (amyloid TTR). More than 60 mutations of the transthyretin molecule have been described,[141] many of which result in distinct clinical syndromes.[136] Fibrinogen, apolipoprotein A-I, gelsolin, lysozyme, cystatin-C, and β protein have also been associated with familial amyloidosis but these forms are rare.[137,139,141,147,156,161,162] In familial Mediterranean fever, the deposits of amyloid consist of amyloid AA and, in contrast to other forms of familial amyloidosis which are autosomal dominant, this disorder exhibits a recessive pattern of inheritance.[159] Prior to the time that amyloid fibrils and their precursors were identified, familial amyloidoses were classified into two major groups based on their clinical and pathologic phenotype: neuropathic and non-neuropathic (or nephropathic) forms. Amyloid deposits, however, can also be found in the kidney in neuropathic amyloidosis.

Another form of amyloidosis is that which has been described in patients undergoing long-term hemodialysis or peritoneal dialysis.[134,145,152,154,167] This amyloid protein is composed of intact and modified $β_2$-microglobulin (amyloid $β_2$M).[148] In these instances, the amyloid deposits occur in perineural and periarterial tissues, and in bone, joint, skin, and subcutaneous tissues.[152] $β_2$M amyloid can cause carpal tunnel syndrome and a destructive arthropathy of medium-sized and large joints, especially the shoulders and knees. It is also responsible for the development of bone cysts, especially in the femur and femoral heads, that have been related to the high prevalence of pathologic femoral head fracture in hemodialysis patients.[154,155] With the use of standardized procedures, it has been possible to extract purified fibrils from involved tissues. These fibrils have been chemically characterized and a total of 18 proteins have definitively been identified as amyloid precursors associated with human disease (Table 17.6).[165] In addition to fibrillary protein, all amyloid deposits contain nonfibrillary glycoproteins, such as amyloid P component, glycosaminoglycans, and apolipoprotein E (Apo E). The amyloid P component is identical to serum amyloid P (SAP), which is a proteinase-resistant circulating glycoprotein.[157] SAP binds to amyloid fibrils and may contribute to the relative stability of the amyloid deposits. Due to its high affinity for amyloid fibrils, ^{123}I-labeled SAP has been used in scintigraphic studies for assessing the extent of amyloid deposition.[149,150]

Nonselective proteinuria, with or without the nephrotic syndrome, is the most common manifestation of renal involvement by amyloidosis. Approximately

Table 17.6 Amyloid fibril proteins and their precursors in humans

Amyloid protein	Precursor	Systemic (S) or localized (L)	Syndrome or involved tissues
AL	Immunoglobulin light chain	S, L	Primary Myeloma-associated
AH	Immunoglobulin heavy chain	S, L	Primary Myeloma-associated
ATTR	Transthyretin	S	Familial (prototype Portuguese, Japanese, Swedish) Senile systemic
		L?	Tenosynovium
AA	(Apo)serum AA	S	Secondary, reactive
$A\beta_2M$	B_2-microglobulin	S	Chronic hemodialysis
		L?	Joints
AApoAI	Apolipoprotein AI	S	Familial
		L	Aortic
AGel	Gelsolin	S	Familial (prototype Finnish)
ALys	Lysozyme	S	Familial
AFib	Fibrinogen α-chain	S	Familial
ACys	Cystatin C	S	Familial (prototype Icelandic)
$A\beta$	$A\beta$ protein precursor ($A\beta PP$)	L	Alzheimer's disease, aging familial (prototype Dutch)
APrP^{SC}	Prion protein	L	Spongiform encephalopathies
ACal	(Pro)calcitonin	L	C-cell thyroid tumors
AIAPP	Islet amyloid polypeptide	L	Islet of Langerhans insulinomas
AANF	Atrial natriuretic factor	L	Cardiac atria
APro	Prolactin	L	Aging pituitary prolactinomas
AIns	Insulin	L	Iatrogenic
ALac*	Lactoferrin	L	Cornea

*Preliminary; awaiting confirmation. With permission from Westermark et al. and Parthenon Publishing.

25% of patients with AL amyloidosis have the nephrotic syndrome at diagnosis and a total of about 40% will develop the syndrome during the course of the disease.[146,153] Over 90% of the patients with AA amyloidosis have renal insufficiency or the nephrotic syndrome at diagnosis, however, the degree of proteinuria does not correlate with the extent of amyloid deposition in the kidney.[153] The prognosis for patients with renal amyloidosis is poor, especially in those with the primary form.[138,153]

The most significant deposition of amyloid in the kidneys is in the glomeruli, but it also takes place around tubules, within the interstitium, and in the walls of blood vessels (Fig. 17.21). In about 10% of patients with AL amyloidosis, the deposits are restricted to nonglomerular areas.[151] The morphologic features of the deposits do not differ in AL and AA amyloidosis. Intra- or extracapillary glomerular cell proliferations are uncommon and when present in a presumptively affected case make a diagnosis of amyloidosis unlikely. Small fibrous epithelial crescents can be seen on occasion, but this is an uncommon finding. In rare instances, multinucleated giant cells may be seen at the periphery of the deposits.[164] Several histochemical techniques have been used to detect amyloid (crystal violet, thioflavin T or S, and Congo red), but none is absolutely specific, and all require a critical amount of amyloid before a positive reaction can be

elicited (Fig. 17.22). The production of an apple-green color by polarized light in Congo red-stained sections is probably the most reliable light microscopic method for diagnosing amyloidosis. It should be mentioned, however, that the staining procedure must be performed on sections that are at least 8 μm thick in order to obtain optimal results. The fibrils of primary AL and secondary AA amyloidosis can be distinguished by pretreating

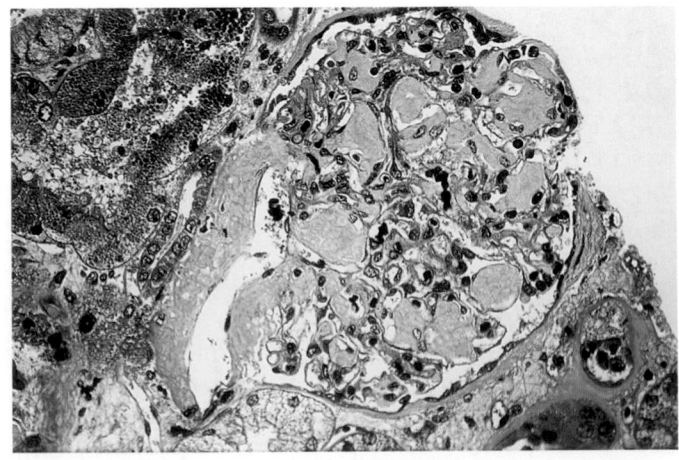

Fig. 17.21 Glomerulus with prominent mesangial and vascular deposition of amyloid.

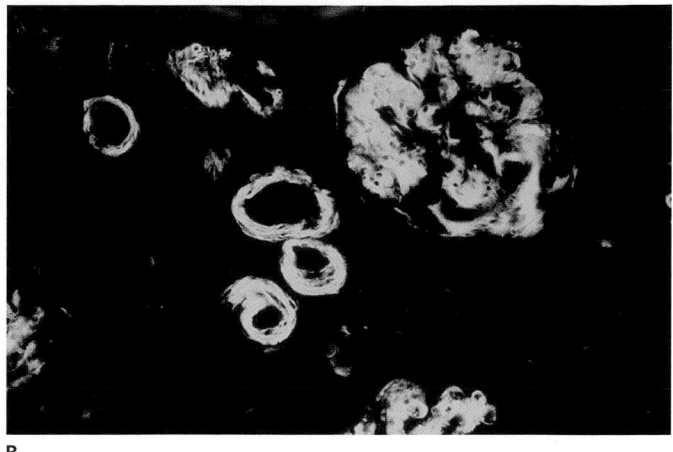

A **B**

Fig. 17.22 A, Deposits of amyloid exhibiting birefringence under polarized light (Congo red stain). **B**, Fluorescence of amyloid under ultraviolet light (thioflavin T stain).

tissue sections with potassium permanganate before Congo red staining. Under these conditions, AA amyloid fibrils lose their affinity for the Congo red stain and the birefringence is lost, whereas AL amyloid is not affected.[163]

In the early stages of renal involvement when histochemical preparations fail to detect the deposits of amyloid, electron microscopy is the only method available to establish the diagnosis. Ultrastructurally, the amyloid fibrils in tissue sections form random aggregates of rigid, nonbranching rods measuring 8 to 10 nm in diameter, and from 30 to over 1000 nm in length. At times a beaded structure with a periodicity of 5 nm can be seen, and on cross section at high magnification, the fibrils appear hollow (Fig. 17.23). Initially, the amyloid is seen in the mesangium around mesangial cells, between the mesangial and endothelial cells, and between the mesangial cells and the basement membrane. From the mesangium, amyloid deposition extends into the subendothelial zone and throughout the basement membrane. A spicular appearance is sometimes produced and it can, by light microscopy, resemble membranous nephropathy.[135] Epithelial foot processes adjacent to deposits of amyloid are usually obliterated.

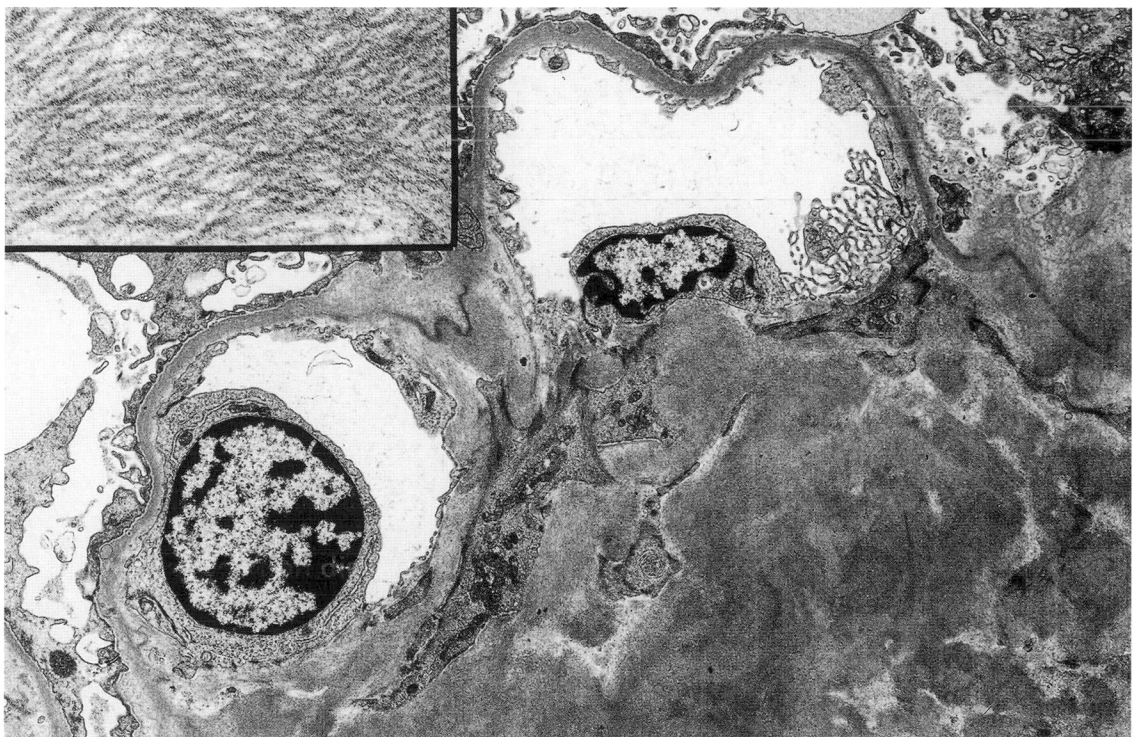

Fig. 17.23 Portion of a glomerulus with large amounts of mesangial deposits of amyloid. The typical ultrastructural appearance of the amyloid fibrils is shown at high magnification. (× 5400; inset, × 64,000)

Immunofluorescence may reveal the accumulation of immunoglobulins in a nonspecific pattern. By using antibodies specific for amyloid AA and light chains, it is possible to differentiate between amyloids AA and AL.[143,144] Amyloid P component can be demonstrated using immunohistochemical methods in all types of amyloidosis. However, amyloid P component is not specific for amyloid since it can be present in the organized deposits of immunotactoid glomerulopathy[166] and normal GBM and blood vessels.[140]

Fibrillary glomerulonephritis and immunotactoid glomerulopathy

Fibrillary glomerulonephritis and immunotactoid glomerulopathy are two rare variants of glomerulonephritis which are primarily defined by electron microscopy. Although the term immunotactoid glomerulopathy has been used as a synonym of fibrillary glomerulopathy, the latter designation is used for a glomerular disease characterized by extracellular deposition of nonbranching, randomly arrayed fibrils approximately 20 nm in diameter, while the former is commonly used when the deposits consist of organized microtubular structures ranging from 30 to 50 nm in width (Fig. 17.24).[168] Other important characteristics of the deposits in both types of lesions are that they do not stain with Congo red or thioflavin T stains (thus differentiating them from amyloid fibrils) and they are observed in the absence of circulating cryoglobulins or parapro-

tein. Although at present there is a heated debate as to whether fibrillary glomerulonephritis and immunotactoid glomerulopathy represent a single entity or two separate conditions, the prevalent belief is that they are probably two distinct entities.[169,173,177]

Fibrillary glomerulonephritis most commonly affects middle-aged adults, but it may also occur in older individuals and children as young as 10 years of age.[170,173] It is more common in Caucasians than in blacks (ratio of 9:1) and there is a slight female predominance.[173,175] The usual presentation is heavy proteinuria, often in the nephrotic range.[173] Microscopic hematuria is common, but on occasion gross hematuria may occur. About 70% of the patients develop hypertension, sometimes severe. No specific serum or urine protein abnormalities have been recorded, and the patients have a low incidence of associated lymphoproliferative malignancy. With the exception of a single patient who developed pulmonary hemorrhage one year after the diagnosis of fibrillary glomerulonephritis and who was found to have fibrillary material in the interstitium of the lungs,[174] no other cases have been documented showing any evidence of extrarenal fibrillary deposits even after many years of follow-up. Roughly half of the patients with fibrillary glomerulonephritis progress to end-stage renal disease within 2 years of the initial diagnosis[173] and the disease can recur after renal transplantation.[175]

Although the clinical presentation of immunotactoid glomerulopathy is quite similar to that of fibrillary

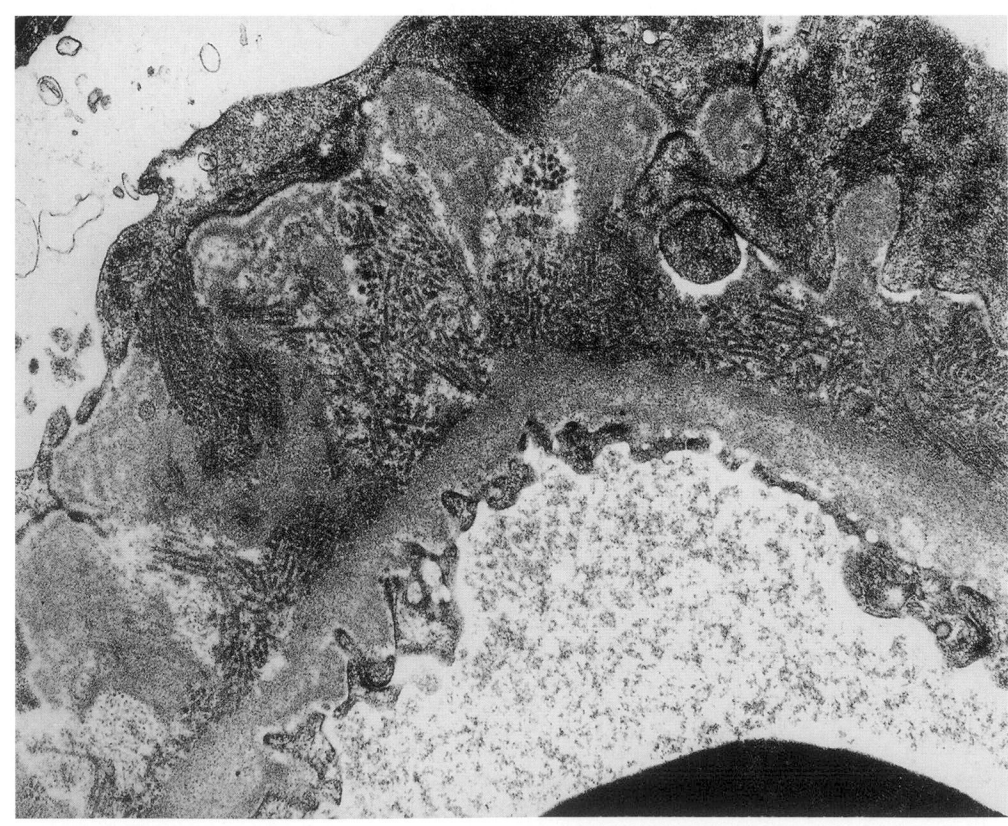

Fig. 17.24 Immunotactoid glomerulopathy showing intramembranous fibrils with a diameter of around 45 nm. (× 20,000)

glomerulonephritis, these conditions differ in that immunotactoid glomerulopathy tends to occur in older individuals, is more likely to have an associated lymphoproliferative malignancy, and has a poor long-term survival.[172] As in fibrillary glomerulonephritis, the occurrence of extrarenal deposits in immunotactoid glomerulopathy is rare with only one example having been reported in the literature.[176] In that case, the deposits occurred in the liver and bone.

The light microscopic findings of both fibrillary glomerulonephritis and immunotactoid glomerulopathy are similar and nonspecific. Common features include mesangial hypercellularity, mesangial expansion with amorphous PAS-positive material, and thickening of the glomerular capillary wall. The overall appearance of the lesions can resemble mesangial proliferative, membranoproliferative, focal and diffuse proliferative, and membranous glomerulonephritis. Crescents are not uncommon and can occur in about one fourth to one third of the cases.

Ultrastructurally, the deposits can be found in all of the glomerular compartments including the mesangium, GBM, and the subendothelial and subepithelial areas. In rare cases of fibrillary glomerulonephritis, fibrils have been reported in the peritubular capillary walls and in the tubular basement membranes.[169,171] In contrast to the random array of the fibrils seen in fibrillary glomerulonephritis, the microtubular structures in immunotactoid glomerulopathy are usually organized in parallel bundles. Although at routine magnifications the fibrils in fibrillary glomerulonephritis do not appear to have lumina, they become apparent in most fibrils under higher magnifications. Patients with fibrillary glomerulonephritis usually exhibit extensive effacement of the epithelial foot processes, a finding that correlates with the often severe proteinuria observed in these patients. Immunofluorescence microscopy most often reveals IgG and C3 in a distribution that corresponds with the deposits of fibrils and microtubules. On occasion, small amounts of IgM and IgA can also be seen.[173,177] Among patients with fibrillary glomerulonephritis, IgG4 is the dominant subclass.[173] Kappa and lambda light chains are detected in both fibrillary glomerulonephritis and immunotactoid glomerulopathy, indicating that the deposits of IgG are polyclonal in both lesions. The current belief is that the fibrils and microtubules represent highly structured immune deposits.

Light chain deposition disease

Light chain deposition disease (LCDD) is an uncommon systemic condition characterized by the overproduction and extracellular deposition of a monoclonal immunoglobulin light chain. A minority of cases may also have heavy chain determinants.[186] Although the principal clinical manifestations are dominated by renal disease, patients may present secondary symptoms produced by

cardiac, hepatic, or neural damage.[180] In addition, light chains can be deposited in many other organs, including the skin, spleen, thyroid, adrenal glands, gastrointestinal tract, and large blood vessels.[180,189] LCDD has many features in common with AL amyloidosis; however, in contrast to amyloidosis in which the deposits of amyloid are fibrillar, in LCDD the deposits are granular, do not bind Congo red stain or thioflavin T, and are not associated with amyloid P protein.[178,188,190] Also, while the deposits in amyloidosis mainly consist of lambda light chains, in 80% of the cases of LCDD, they are composed of kappa light chains.[193] Males are more frequently affected than females in a ratio of approximately 4:1.[181] Approximately 60% of the reported patients with LCDD have had well-documented multiple myeloma or another lymphoplasmacytic disorder at the time of or subsequent to discovery of the nephropathy.[178,191] LCDD occurs more frequently in older individuals, but it has been reported in children.[192] Most patients present with renal failure associated with heavy and nonselective proteinuria, often in the nephrotic range.[178,181,182] In patients with secretory myeloma, the urine may contain large amounts of free immunoglobulin light chains. Hematuria is uncommon. Renal insufficiency can progress to end-stage kidney disease, at which time the patient will require dialysis or a renal transplant. Recurrence in a renal transplant has been reported.[179,183] The prognosis for patients with LCDD is generally poor and death is often attributed to cardiac disease or complications of infection.[184,187] The 5-year survival rate is approximately 70%, but it is less if there is a coexistent myeloma.[184,191]

Affected glomeruli are enlarged and the deposition of the markedly PAS-positive material produces capillary wall thickening and nodular expansion of the mesangium. The extent of glomerular involvement can vary in a biopsy from mild mesangial expansion to a fully developed nodular glomerulosclerosis that resembles diabetic glomerulosclerosis,[188] but other morphologic features characteristic of diabetes such as severe arteriolar hyalinosis, fibrin caps, and capsular drops are absent (Fig. 17.25). The pathogenesis of glomerulosclerosis in LCDD is not clear, but experimental studies have shown that mesangial cells exposed to light chains obtained from a patient with LCDD produce transforming growth factor β, which acts as an entactoid to stimulate those cells to produce matrix proteins such as type IV collagen, laminin, and fibronectin.[185,194] Fibroepithelial crescents may, on occasion, be present.[193] The tubular basement membranes are thickened and present a homogeneous glassy appearance. Myeloma casts are rarely found.[193]

Electron microscopy studies reveal continuous deposition of an electron-dense material in the GBM, the mesangium, and along the tubular and vascular basement membranes. Ultrastructurally, the material differs from dense deposit disease in that it is finely granular, relatively homogeneous in thickness, and distributed along the inner aspect of the GBM and the outer aspect of the tubular basement membrane (Fig. 17.26). Immunofluorescence microscopy demonstrates staining of the abnormal light chain along the glomerular and tubular basement membranes, as well as in the mesangium, vessel walls, and interstitium (Fig. 17.27).

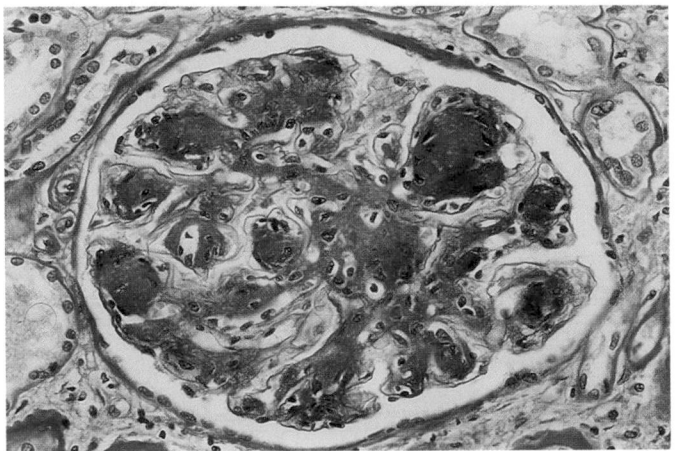

Fig. 17.25 Biopsy from a patient with light chain deposition disease showing nodular mesangial lesions resembling those of diabetes mellitus.

Heavy chain deposition disease

Heavy chain deposition disease (HCDD) is less common than LCDD. It is characterized by the systemic deposition of a monoclonal truncated heavy chain. The clinical manifestations and histologic features of HCDD are similar to those of LCDD.[195–199] The diagnosis of HCDD can be done by immunofluorescence demonstrating positivity for heavy chains of immunoglobulins (usually gamma) and negativity for both kappa and lambda light chains. The reactivity for the heavy chain occurs along the glomerular, tubular, and vascular basement membranes and in the mesangium.[195]

Congenital nephrotic syndrome

The nephrotic syndrome is uncommon in the first year of life.[201] The term congenital nephrotic syndrome encompasses a heterogeneous group of conditions but it is reserved for patients who present clinical symptoms at birth or within the first three months of life. Two distinct types have been recognized: congenital nephrotic syndrome of the Finnish type and diffuse mesangial sclerosis. Neither form responds to steroid or immunosuppressive therapy; renal transplantation is the only way to prolong and improve the quality of life. A renal biopsy is essential in order to differentiate these two

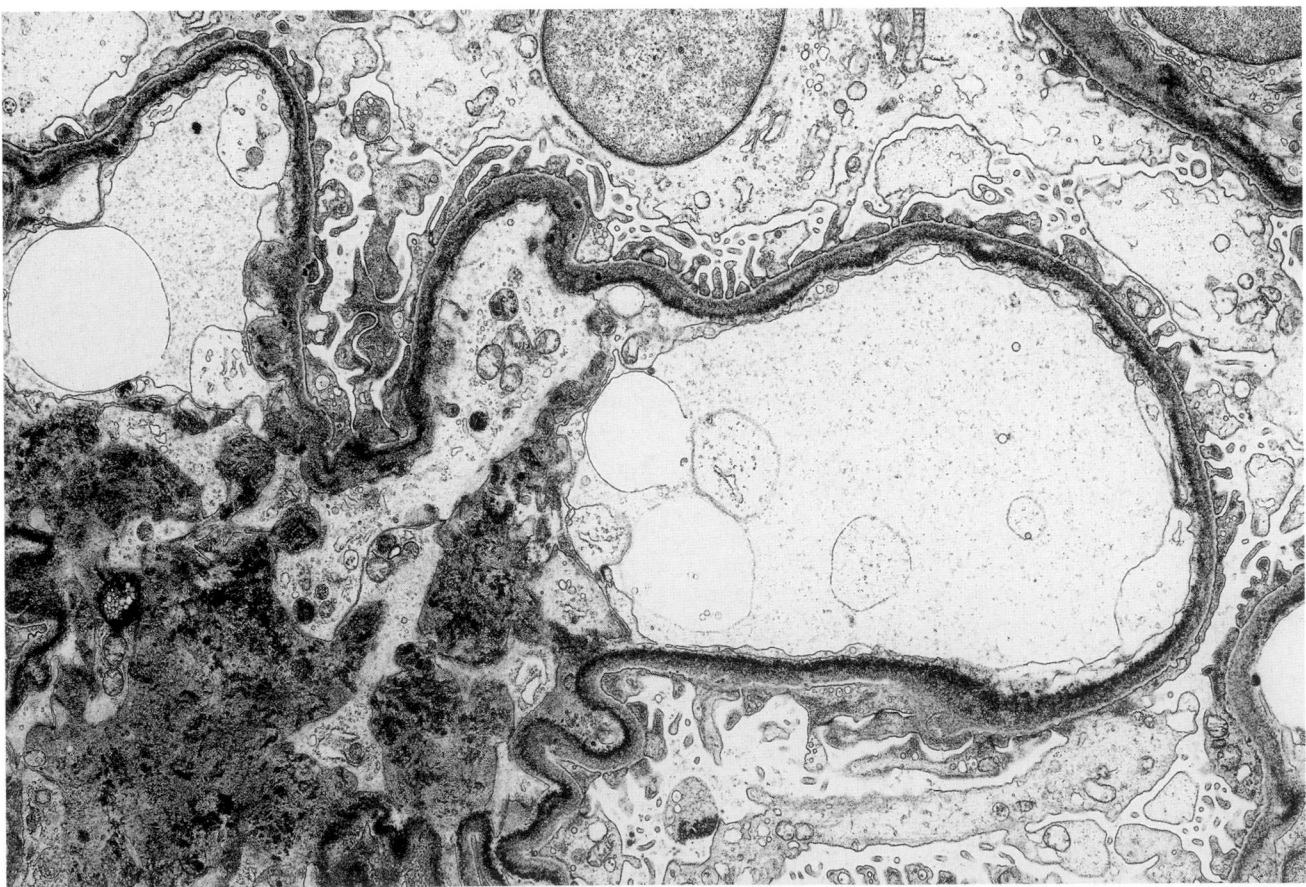

Fig. 17.26 Subendothelial and mesangial deposition of electron-dense material in light chain deposition disease. (× 7000)

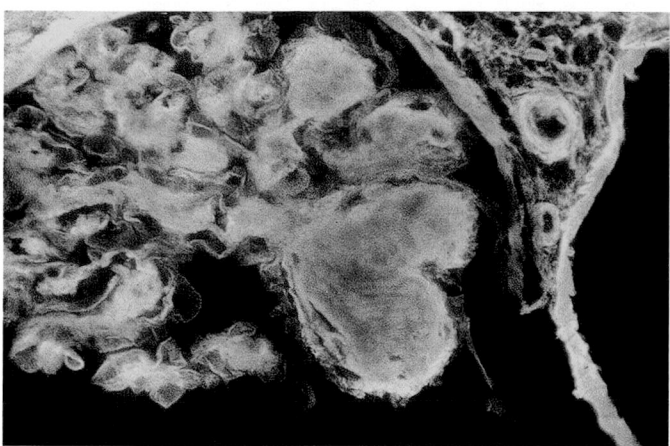

Fig. 17.27 Immunofluorescence preparation demonstrating reactivity for kappa light chain along the glomerular basement membrane, mesangium, Bowman's capsule, and vessel walls.

types of congenital nephrotic syndrome from other renal disorders of the neonatal period, including membranous glomerulonephritis (associated with congenital syphilis or mercury intoxication), congenital toxoplasmosis, HIV (especially in the offspring of narcotic addicts), malaria, cytomegalic inclusion disease, and minimal change glomerulopathy.[217]

Congenital nephrotic syndrome of the Finnish type

Congenital nephrotic syndrome of the Finnish type is inherited as an autosomal recessive trait and makes up fewer than 1.5% of the cases of nephrotic syndrome in childhood.[202] The estimated incidence of the disease in the genetically isolated population of Finland is approximately 1:10,000 newborns, but it has been reported, though with much less frequency, throughout the world in families with no known Finnish origin.[200,211,214,215] The affected gene has been localized to the chromosome 19q13.1 region and has been designated *NPHS1*.[208] This gene encodes a 1241 amino acid transmembrane protein named nephrin.[207] This protein is localized at the slit diaphragm of the glomerular podocyte and although its function remains unclear, it is believed that it plays an essential role in the normal glomerular filtration barrier.[213] Recent studies have shown that nephrin is often absent from the glomerular podocytes of patients with mutations of the *NPHS1* gene and the severe form of Finnish-type congenital nephrotic syndrome.[212]

The diagnosis may be suspected in utero from the characteristic family history and the finding of elevated α-fetoprotein levels in the amniotic fluid and maternal serum[216] but this is neither highly specific nor sensitive. Recently, linkage and haplotype analyses have successfully been used in the prenatal diagnosis of the disease.[210] Direct genetic testing is now possible since the gene and the mutations have been identified. The disease manifests in the fetal stage with heavy proteinuria in utero. At birth, the patients have large placentas, proteinuria,

edema, and a high susceptibility to infections.[205] Premature birth, mild abnormalities in face and limbs, and poor somatic development are common findings. The nephrotic syndrome often makes its appearance during the first days of life and it does not respond to steroid therapy. The proteinuria is initially highly selective, but becomes nonselective with advancing glomerular damage. The disease is progressive during the first two years of life and kidney transplantation is the only life-saving treatment that is successful for this condition. Patients who receive transplants usually show dramatic improvement in their psychomotor development but the nephrotic syndrome has been reported to recur in 20% of the patients.[204,209]

The most striking histologic feature is ectasia of the proximal and distal tubules with flattening of the tubular epithelium. The glomeruli show varying degrees of mesangial proliferation, sclerosis, and dilation of Bowman's capsule. There may also be an increased number of immature glomeruli (Fig. 17.28). Obliteration of epithelial foot processes and other changes seen in minimal change disease are observed by electron microscopy. Immunofluorescence is usually negative for immunoglobulins and complement components, but mesangial and capillary staining for immunoglobulins, usually IgM and C3, has been reported.

Diffuse mesangial sclerosis

Diffuse mesangial sclerosis (DMS) is a rare condition characterized by the early onset of severe proteinuria, and rapid progression to end-stage renal failure before the age of 3 years.[201,217] DMS can occur in an isolated form or associated with the Denys–Drash syndrome (DDS), a rare disorder in the development of the urogenital tract characterized by early onset of the nephrotic syndrome, male pseudohermaphroditism, and Wilms' tumor. Incomplete forms of the syndrome consisting of the glomerulopathy associated with either genital abnormality or Wilms' tumor, which can be unilateral or bilateral, have also been described. Constitutional heterogeneous intragenic mutations of the *WT1* suppressor gene located on chromosome 11p13 have been demonstrated in nearly all patients with the complete or incomplete forms of the syndrome.[218] Mutations identical to those found in DDS have also been observed in some patients, usually female, with the isolated form of DMS.[206] This finding, together with that of isolated mesangial sclerosis in males with normal genitalia and the frequent familial incidence, indicate that isolated DMS could be a heterogeneous entity with some of the cases having an autosomal recessive inheritance.[214]

In patients with DMS, the nephrotic syndrome develops as early as the first week of life, but it is more likely to appear after the third month. In contrast to the Finnish type, the nephrotic syndrome in DMS is not associated with a large placenta, premature birth, or low birth

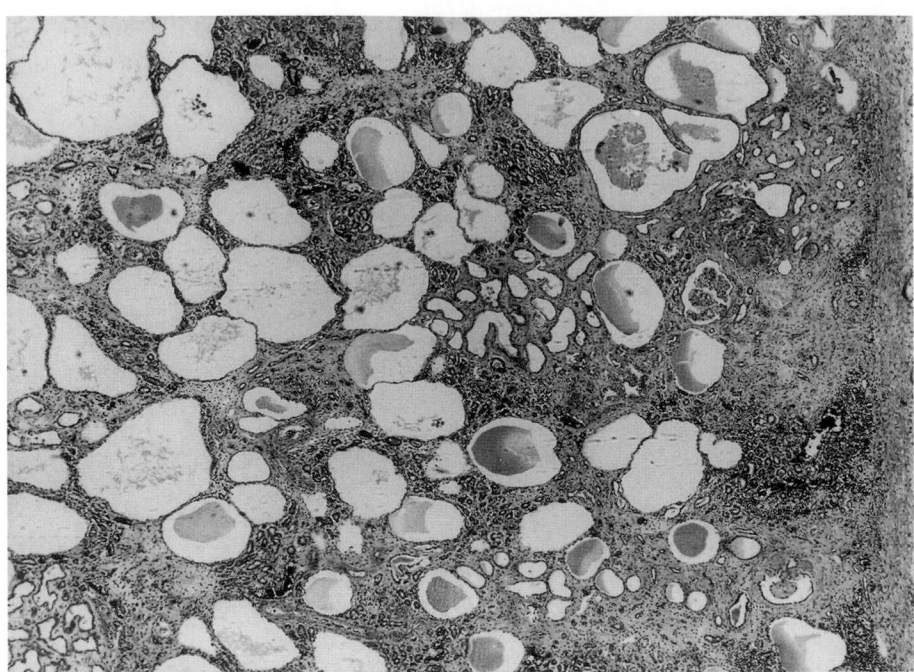

Fig. 17.28 Microcystic dilation of proximal tubules and interstitial scarring in a 1-year-old child with congenital nephrotic syndrome, Finnish type.

weight. Other abnormalities that have been reported in patients with DMS, whether associated with DDS or not, include cataract and corneal clouding, aniridia, microencephaly, mental retardation, and hypertelorism.[217] The condition does not recur after transplantation.[203]

By light microscopy, the glomeruli in diffuse mesangial sclerosis do not as a rule show cellular proliferation, although occasional instances of crescent formation have been recorded. In advanced stages, there is marked tubular atrophy with interstitial fibrosis. The findings by electron microscopy are extensive obliteration of the epithelial foot processes, basement membrane thickening, and an increase in the mesangial matrix. By immunofluorescence, mesangial deposits of IgM, C3, and C1q are present in the least affected glomeruli, while deposits of IgM and C3 outline the periphery of the sclerosed glomeruli.

Glomerular lesions associated with the syndrome of acute nephritis

Another major clinical presentation of patients with glomerular lesions is the acute nephritis syndrome. Patients with this syndrome present with hematuria, azotemia, oliguria, and mild to moderate hypertension. Urinalysis reveals an "active" sediment, which consists of red blood cells, leukocytes, and red blood cell casts. Proteinuria is common but it is rarely in the nephrotic range. Edema, when present, is usually mild and is frequently manifested by facial puffiness. Variants of the clinical syndrome include milder forms that are identified by the presence of microscopic hematuria and non-nephrotic proteinuria that is occasionally associated with mild hypertension, and a fulminant form known as rapidly progressive glomerulonephritis. As with the nephrotic syndrome, the histopathologic lesions that can give rise to this clinical presentation are varied.

Diffuse endocapillary proliferative glomerulonephritis

Diffuse endocapillary (or intracapillary) proliferative glomerulonephritis is a term used to describe lesions characterized by both mesangial and endothelial proliferation. Although this category has become virtually synonymous with acute poststreptococcal glomerulonephritis, it may occur after infections by other bacteria including staphylococci, meningococci, pneumococci, Klebsiella, salmonella, enterococci, brucella, leptospira, and mycobacteria.[225,228,229] It can also arise as a complication of rickettsial infections; viral diseases including hepatitis B, varicella, mumps, measles, cytomegalovirus, and infectious mononucleosis; and parasitic conditions such as malaria, trichinosis, and toxoplasmosis.[220,222,230]

Acute poststreptococcal glomerulonephritis

Poststreptococcal glomerulonephritis is primarily a disease of childhood, usually occurring between the ages of 5 and 15 years, but it can affect individuals of any age. Approximately 5% of the patients are younger than 2 years of age and about 10% are older than 40 years of age.[226] There is no predilection for either sex. In the classic form, the disease occurs within 1 to 4 weeks after infection with a nephritogenic strain of group A β-hemolytic streptococci. Primary infections may be either pharyngeal or cutaneous. The principal serotypes implicated are streptococci of group M types 1, 2, 12, 49, 55, 57, and 60. The risk for developing glomerulonephritis after infection with a nephritogenic streptococcus is variable, depending on a variety of factors, including the site of infection. For example, throat infection with streptococcus M type 49 carries a 5% risk of glomerulonephritis while the same infection in the skin carries a 5 times greater risk.[226] The overall risk for developing glomerulonephritis after a nephritogenic streptococcus infection has been estimated to be about 15%. Although clinical, morphologic, and serologic findings indicate that poststreptococcal glomerulonephritis is an immune complex disease, the exact nature of the antigens involved in the formation of nephritogenic immune complexes is unknown. Attempts to localize soluble antigenic products in the glomeruli have been difficult to reproduce, inconclusive, or have failed.[222]

Clinically, this disease is manifested by a rather abrupt onset of gross hematuria, edema, proteinuria, hypertension, and impaired renal function. The serum levels of hemolytic complement activity and C3 protein are abnormally reduced early in the course of the disease, but the values return to normal in less than 8 weeks. Two to 5% of the patients die during the acute episode of poststreptococcal glomerulonephritis as a result of complications such as pulmonary edema, hypertensive encephalopathy, or rapidly progressive renal failure due to crescentic glomerulonephritis.[226,230] These figures are much higher in elderly patients.[224] The long-term prognosis of patients with acute poststreptococcal glomerulonephritis is good, especially in children, with only a small number of patients progressing to chronic renal failure many years after the acute episode.[221,226–228] Recovery in adults is less predictable than in children, especially when the initial episode is associated with severe renal impairment, persistent proteinuria, or the nephrotic syndrome.[230,231] Progression is more common in patients who develop crescentic glomerulonephritis. Since the clinical syndrome of acute poststreptococcal glomerulonephritis may be quite distinctive and the overall prognosis is excellent, biopsies are not commonly performed unless some atypical feature complicates the presentation, such as the nephrotic syndrome, anuria, persistent or severe hypertension, or no sign of recovery after 6 weeks.

Light microscopic examination of biopsies taken within a few weeks of the onset of the glomerulonephritis shows diffuse enlargement of the glomerular tufts which tend to fill the Bowman's space. Glomerular intracapillary cellularity is increased due to mesangial proliferation and, to a lesser extent, to an increase in the number and size of the endothelial cells. As a result, there is a narrowing of the capillary lumina and accentuation of the lobular glomerular pattern. Infiltration by leukocytes can contribute to the capillary obstruction and when this is prominent the term exudative glomerulonephritis has been used (Fig. 17.29). Accompanying the

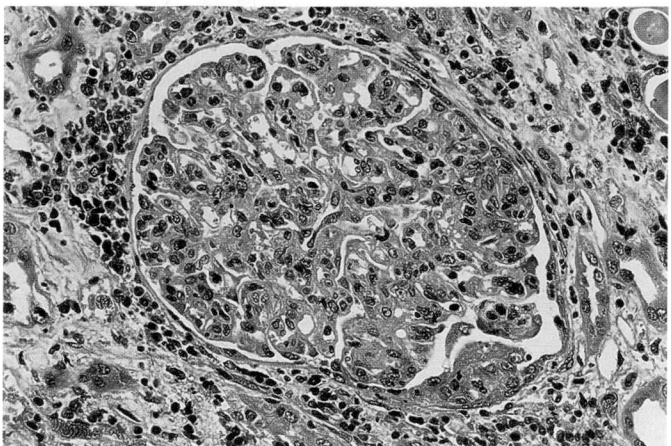

Fig. 17.29 Diffuse endocapillary glomerulonephritis. There is marked hypercellularity due to an increase in mesangial and endothelial cells and infiltration by inflammatory cells.

polymorphonuclear leukocytes are mononuclear cells and, on occasion, eosinophils. Segmental necrosis and thrombosis with crescent formation are uncommon findings but when they occur, they are considered to be an indication of poor prognosis. Necrotizing vasculitis has been reported in rare instances.[219]

The most characteristic ultrastructural feature in the early stages of the disease is the presence of subepithelial, finely granular, dome-shaped, electron-dense deposits called humps (Fig. 17.30). The deposits are separated from the lamina densa by a recognizable lamina rara externa and are surrounded by epithelial cell cytoplasm that contains a zone of increased density adjacent to the deposits. The foot processes of the epithelial cells overlying the humps are usually obliterated. In general, there is a correlation between the number of humps and the degree of polymorphonuclear cell infiltration, but the humps may occur in loops devoid of leukocytes. Humps of atypical shape and size, with varying texture, may be seen and have been associated with severe inflammation and delayed resolution.[223] In some loops, the humps may become confluent or they may be separated by extensions of basement membrane which simulate the spikes of membranous nephropathy. Intramembranous deposits, some of them in continuity with the humps, and small subendothelial and mesangial deposits are not uncommon.

Immunofluorescence studies during the acute phase of the disease typically reveal granular staining for IgG and C3 along the capillary loop where the humps are located (Fig. 17.31). Small amounts of IgM and IgA may be found. Properdin is frequently present, and this, coupled with the strong reactivity for C3 and the absence of C1q and C4 in the deposits, suggests involvement of the alternative complement pathway.

Serial biopsies show a gradual resolution of the glomerular changes. Cellularity decreases and the humps

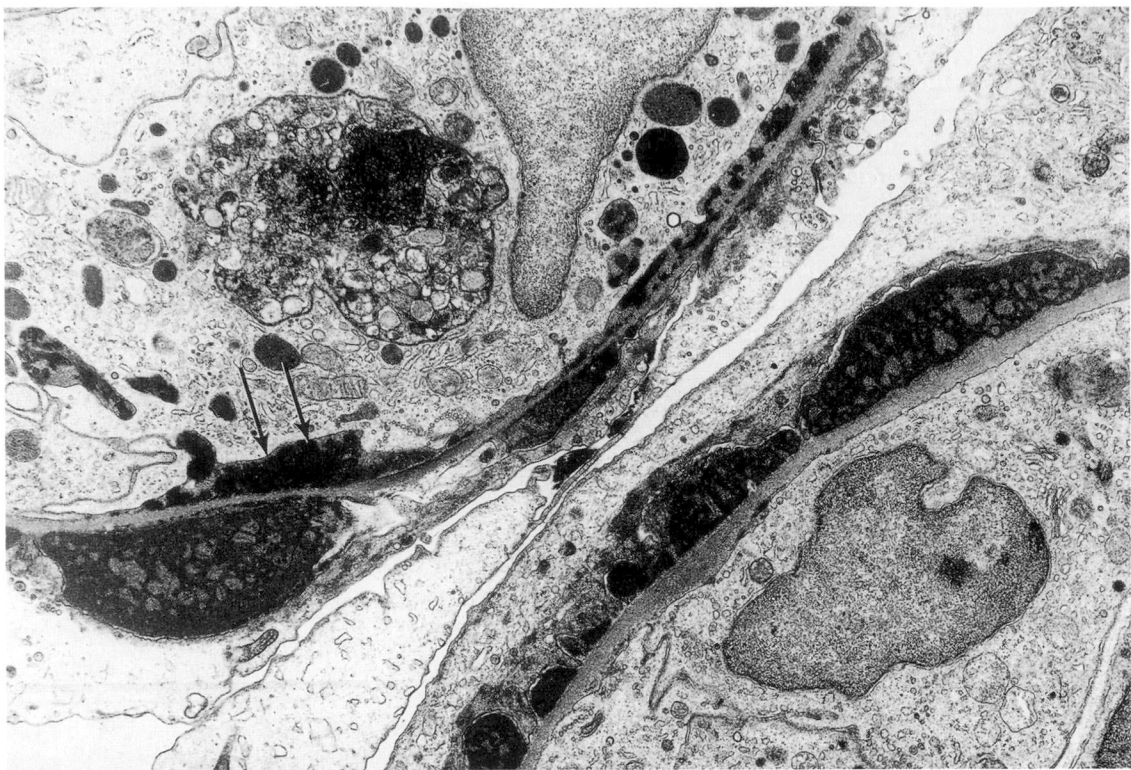

Fig. 17.30 Biopsy from a patient with acute poststreptococcal glomerulonephritis. There are numerous humps along the basement membrane. The capillary loops are obliterated by cell proliferation and inflammatory cells. Small amounts of fibrin are present in the subendothelial areas (arrows). (× 9800)

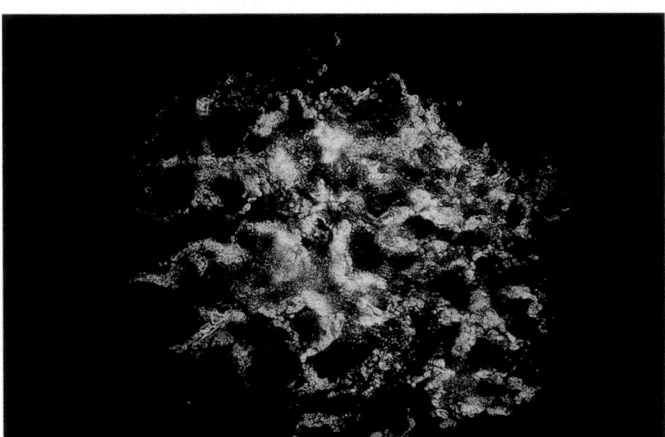

Fig. 17.31 Poststreptococcal glomerulonephritis. The coarse granular immunostaining for C3 along the capillary loops corresponds to the humps seen by electron microscopy.

generally disappear in 6 to 8 weeks, although they have been identified as long as 6 months after the onset of the disease. During the resolving phase, the basement membrane may show focal irregularities with decreased electron density, the capillary lumen becomes patent, and the endothelial swelling and polymorphonuclear leukocytic infiltration disappear. Electron-dense deposits either are no longer visible or are confined to the mesangium. IgG may not be demonstrable, and C3 staining gradually disappears from the periphery and becomes restricted to the mesangial areas. Complete restoration to normal histology may be seen as early as 6 months and certainly within 2 to 3 years. In a small percentage of cases, mesangial hypercellularity, mesangial deposits, and increased mesangial matrix may persist for years after the acute episode, and the mesangial prominence can be focal and segmental.

Membranoproliferative (mesangiocapillary) glomerulonephritis

The terms *membranoproliferative glomerulonephritis (MPGN)* and *mesangiocapillary glomerulonephritis* are used to designate a glomerular lesion with a distinctive pattern characterized by a combination of mesangial cell proliferation and capillary wall thickening which is the result of extension of the mesangium into the periphery of the loop. Hypocomplementemic persistent glomerulonephritis was once used to designate this condition because patients with this form of glomerulonephritis often have a persistent decrease of the serum levels of C3 and of the total hemolytic complement activity, but it was later found that the lesion can also occur without hypocomplementemia, and the terms given above are now the preferred terms for the condition.

Based on the morphology and distribution of the deposits, MPGN has been subdivided into two major types. In the first (type I), the deposits are primarily subendothelial, whereas in the second (type II) they are extremely dense and lie within the basement membrane. Due to these characteristics, the latter form has also been designated dense deposit disease (DDD). In addition, other variants, sometimes termed type III, have been described, but they are distinguished almost exclusively on the basis of their electron microscopic features.[232,236,255,258] Although this subdivision of MPGN implies various patterns of a single clinicopathologic entity, the conditions do not in fact share a common pathogenesis and they are linked only by the morphologic similarities that are seen in routine light microscopic preparations. Currently, it is believed that type I and type III MPGN (which some authors include in the former group) represent chronic immune complex diseases, whereas type II MPGN is a specific entity characterized by a unique dense transformation of the glomerular and tubular basement membranes. Membranoproliferative (mesangiocapillary) glomerulonephritis is thus not a pure entity.

Type I membranoproliferative glomerulonephritis

Although most cases of MPGN are idiopathic (primary), the glomerular lesion can be secondary to various infectious, neoplastic, systemic autoimmune, and hereditary diseases. Some of the conditions most commonly associated with MPGN are listed in Table 17.7.

Type I MPGN accounts for approximately 5% of the cases of end-stage renal disease secondary to glomerulonephritis. In the primary form of the disease, children and young adults are most frequently affected, with 90% of all patients being between 8 and 16 years of age at the time of diagnosis.[242,250,258] Onset before the age of 4 years is rare. There does not appear to be a male or female predominance. Rare familial cases, probably inherited as an autosomal dominant or X-linked trait, have been reported.[235] Patients may present with overt signs of nephritis, gross hematuria only, or asymptomatic proteinuria and/or microscopic hematuria. Approximately one third of the patients present with the nephritic syndrome and although some may have a history of upper respiratory infection, there is no clear association with streptococcal infection. Approximately two thirds of the patients develop hypocomplementemia with marked variation of the complement during the course of the disease. The predominant complement depletion is C3 but early acting components are also depressed. The hypocomplementemia is primarily the result of hypercatabolism of C3, although a diminished C3 synthesis often serves to intensify it.[258] The clinical course is usually indolent but relentless, progressing to renal failure over a period of 10 or more years.[252] The disease has been reported to recur in 30% to 50% of the patients.[233,243,248]

On light microscopy, the glomeruli appear diffusely enlarged with thickening of the capillary walls and prominent mesangial proliferation that produces lobulation of the tuft (Fig. 17.32). Mesangial matrix accumulates in the center of the lobule, sometimes forming nodules similar to those seen in diabetic glomerulosclerosis. This pattern was previously termed lobular glomerulonephritis, but it is now recognized to be part of the MPGN lesion, not a separate condition. In addition to the lobular

Table 17.7 Classification of membranoproliferative glomerulonephritis

Primary idiopathic
Type I With subendothelial mesangial immune complex deposits
Type II Dense deposit disease
Type III With mixed features of type I MPGN with either MGN[236] or with massive intramembranous immune deposits[232,255]

Secondary
Infections
Hepatitis B and C, endocarditis, visceral abscesses, shunt nephritis, malaria, schistosomiasis, mycoplasma, HIV and Epstein–Barr virus infections

Immunologic and systemic disorders
Systemic lupus erythematosus, scleroderma, Sjögren's syndrome, rheumatoid arthritis, sarcoidosis, mixed essential cryoglobulinemia with or without hepatitis C infection, ulcerative colitis, sickle cell disease

Neoplastic diseases
Carcinoma, chronic lymphocytic leukemia, non-Hodgkin's lymphoma, melanoma

Hereditary diseases
α_1Antitrypsin deficiency, complement deficiency (C1q, C2, C3, or C4) with or without partial lipodystrophy, hereditary angioedema, Wiskott–Aldrich syndrome, Sherwood–Proesmans syndrome, autosomal recessive MPGN type I

Miscellaneous
Drug abuse (heroin, pentazocine), Kartagener's syndrome, Turner's syndrome, Down's syndrome

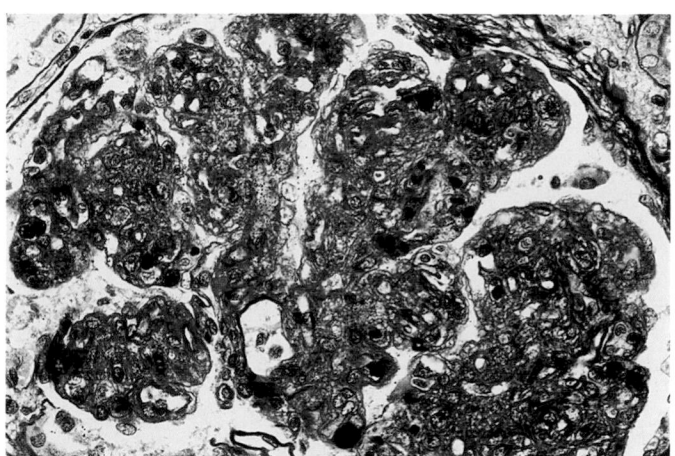

Fig. 17.32 Type I membranoproliferative glomerulonephritis. There is an increase in lobulation, diffuse mesangial hypercellularity, and thickening of the capillary walls.

pattern, exudative, crescentic, and focal segmental histologic variants have been described.[238] The capillary wall thickening in MPGN is due to interposition of the mesangial cells and matrix throughout the subendothelial zone producing a "tram-track" appearance in the periphery of the loop which can be visualized with PAS and silver stains (Fig. 17.33). The presence of hyaline thrombi within the capillary lumina should raise the possibility of cryo-

globulinemia or lupus nephritis. Hyaline thrombi are not true thrombi but rather represent aggregates of immune complexes filling capillary lumina.

Electron microscopy reveals an intact basement membrane and a continuous layer of mesangial cytoplasm around the entire capillary with an irregular layer of new matrix beneath the basement membrane. Electron-dense deposits are typically present in the subendothelial and mesangial areas (Fig. 17.34). Immunofluorescence usually shows a granular reaction for C3 and IgG along the capillary walls and mesangium (Fig. 17.35). In addition, IgM, C1q, and C4 can sometimes be found. A minority of cases of type I MPGN have staining of the immune complexes along the tubular basement membranes or in extraglomerular vessels or both.[240,253]

Type II membranoproliferative glomerulonephritis (dense deposit disease)

Type II membranoproliferative glomerulonephritis, or dense deposit disease, is a specific clinicopathologic entity characterized by a unique morphologic appearance of the basement membrane that is best seen by electron microscopy, but usually discernible with the light microscope. It is much more rare than MPGN type I, constituting approximately 10% of all cases of idiopathic MPGN. The clinical presentation and age distribution of patients with MPGN type II is similar to that of type I MPGN.[237,241,247] There is a nearly equal sex ratio. Even though there are clinical similarities between both types of MPGN, there are also some differences.

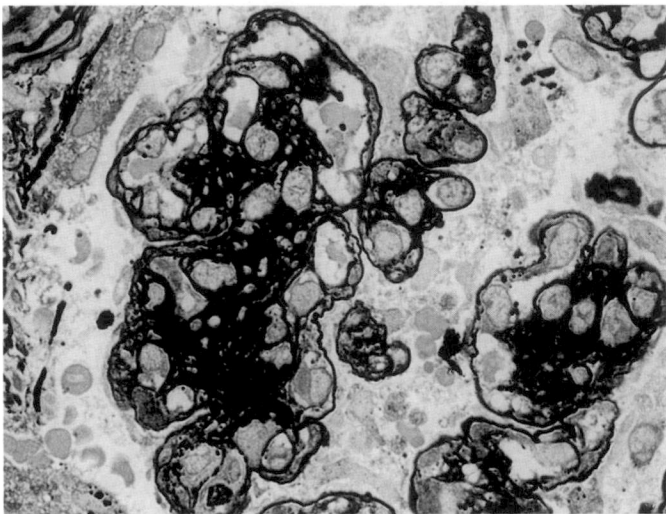

Fig. 17.33 Silver preparation showing marked increase in mesangial matrix in the centrolobular areas with peripheral extension of the mesangium producing a double contour pattern in the loops.

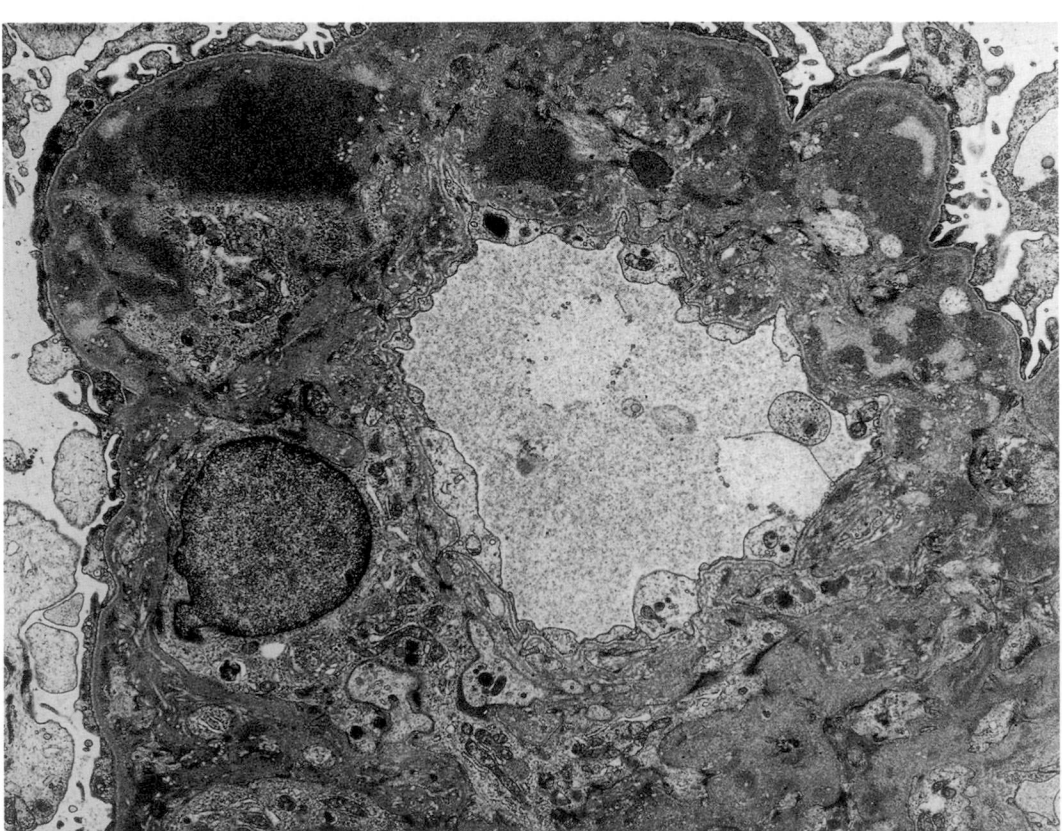

Fig. 17.34 Glomerular capillary loop from a patient with type I membranoproliferative glomerulonephritis showing peripheral extension of the mesangium and subendothelial deposits.

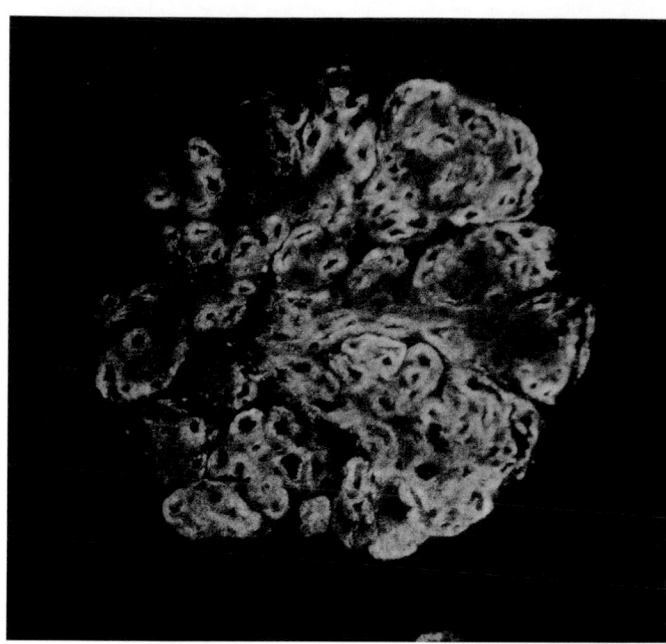

Fig. 17.35 Immunofluorescence preparation demonstrating immunoreactivity for C3 along the capillary loops.

Type II MPGN tends to present with nephritis, whereas MPGN type I presents more often with nephrotic features.[253] Serum levels of C3 are more frequently and severely depressed and they remain low for a longer period of time in patients with type II MPGN than in those with type I disease, while serum levels of early acting components such as C1q and C4 are normal or only slightly reduced. Serum concentrations of factor B and properdin of the alternative pathway are low. These complement profiles suggest that complement is activated in MPGN type II primarily through the alternative pathway, whereas in MPGN type I it occurs through the classical pathway. Over 60% of patients with MPGN type II have an IgG autoantibody in their serum called C3 nephritic factor (C3NeF); this binds to the alternative pathway C3 convertase, protecting it from activation by factor H and thereby causing continuous breakdown of C3. However, C3NeF is not a specific serologic marker because it also occurs, though less frequently, with MPGN type I.[253] Another unusual aspect of MPGN type II is its association with partial lipodystrophy, a condition characterized by the loss of subcutaneous fat from the face and upper portions of the body. These patients have been found to have hypocomplementemia and C3NeF regardless of whether or not they also have MPGN.[234,251,254] Type II MPGN has a poorer prognosis than type I disease. Progressive renal destruction and decline of renal function can be slow and steady, or occur abruptly with the development of crescentic disease. On rare occasions, there have been reports of morphologic regression.[244,249] In approximately 50% of the cases, the lesion progresses to end-stage kidney disease within 10 years of the diagnosis. Recurrence after renal transplan-

tation has been reported in 80% to 100% of the cases.[243] This observation, together with the finding of deposits in the sinusoidal basement membranes of the spleen,[257] and in the choroid and Bruch's membrane of the eye,[239,245] which are similar to those seen in the kidney, supports the recent suggestion that MPGN type II is a systemic disease.[258] However, the mechanism of deposit formation and the exact nature of the deposits remain unknown. That this condition invariably recurs in a renal allograft is compelling evidence that a circulating systemic factor plays a role in its pathogenesis.[253]

On light microscopy, the general morphologic features are similar to those seen in type I MPGN, but the cellular proliferation, and especially the circumferential mesangial interposition, is much less prominent. A feature which will establish the diagnosis is an eosinophilic refractile and ribbon-like thickening of the basement membrane which is usually most pronounced along the GBM, although it can be seen in Bowman's capsule and in the tubular basement membrane. The material producing this effect is strongly PAS positive, stains green with the Masson trichrome stain, and can be easily recognized by its dark color on toluidine blue-stained plastic-embedded tissue sections (Fig. 17.36). It produces a bright fluorescent effect with thioflavin T, and is light brown in color, sometimes with thin peripheral black bands, in silver-stained sections. Ultrastructurally, the material is extremely electron dense, and it lacks the prominent granularity of immune complex deposits. It is centrally positioned within the basement membrane in a ribbon-like manner, but it may vary in thickness or be focally discontinuous. Similar deposits can usually be found in the mesangium as homogeneous nodules or, less frequently, subepithelial humps (Fig. 17.37).[241] The immunofluorescence pattern is typical and diagnostic. Linear or double-contoured staining for C3 along the

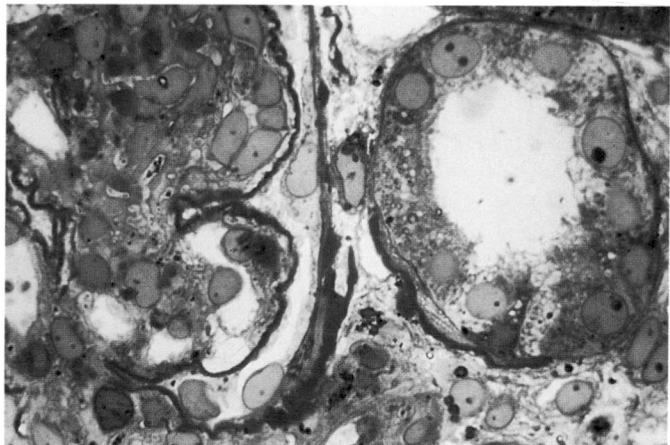

Fig. 17.36 Plastic-embedded toluidine blue-stained tissue section of type II membranoproliferative glomerulonephritis. There is hypercellularity and a continuous ribbon-like thickening of the glomerular basement membrane. Intramembranous dark material is also present in Bowman's capsule.

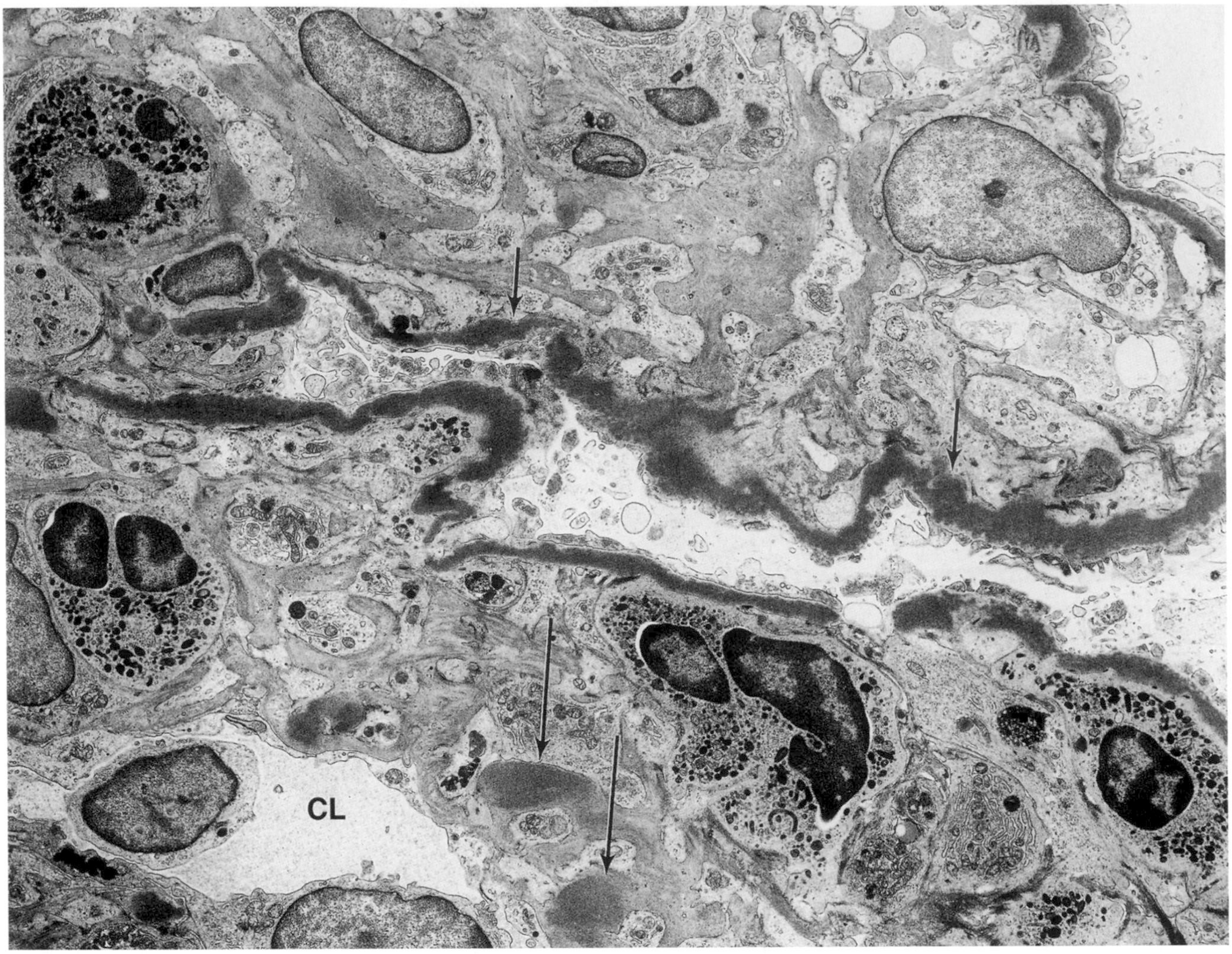

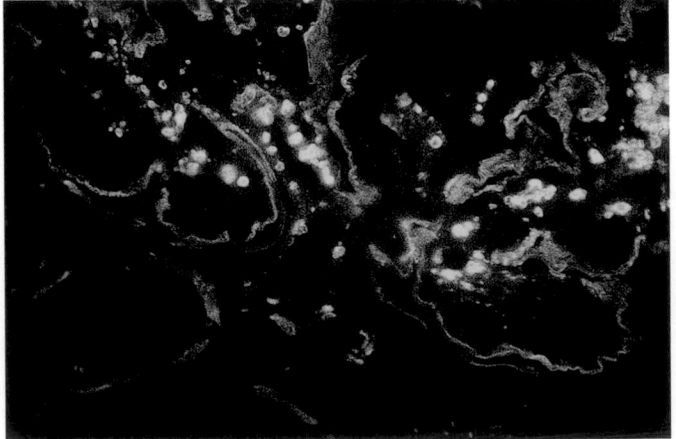

Fig. 17.37 Type II membranoproliferative glomerulonephritis. There is homogeneous, highly dense material within the lamina densa (short arrows) and nodular deposits (long arrows) of the same electron density in the mesangium. The capillary lumen in the left lower portion of the figure is narrowed due to peripheral extension of the mesangium. Numerous neutrophils are also present. CL = capillary lumen. (× 4000)

glomerular capillary walls is associated with a bright nodular or ringlike reaction in the mesangium (Fig. 17.38). A more focal and often discontinuous linear C3 reaction can be seen in Bowman's capsule and in some tubular basement membranes. Immunoglobulin and early components of the complement are usually absent. Using phase-contrast microscopy, it has been found that complement and immunoglobulins are localized at the edges between the dense deposit and the adjacent lamina densa of the GBM but not within the deposits themselves.[246]

Type III membranoproliferative glomerulonephritis

Type III MPGN is a very uncommon and controversial variant of MPGN of which two morphologic subtypes have been defined. In the first subtype, sometimes referred to as the Burkholder variant, the glomerular lesion presents combined features of MPGN type I and membranous glomerulonephritis.[236] Ultrastructural

Fig. 17.38 Immunofluorescent staining for C3 showing weak linear staining along glomerular capillary and tubular basement membranes (right lower corner) and bright granular deposits in the mesangium, some of which have a ringlike pattern.

examination of the capillary walls demonstrates mesangial interposition, subendothelial deposits, and numerous subepithelial deposits associated with basement membrane spikes. In the second subtype described by Anders and associates in 1977, the glomerular lesion resembles a hybrid between type I and type II MPGN.[232,255,256] In these cases, electron microscopy shows a characteristic pattern of membranous disruption produced by a massive accumulation within the basement membrane and on either side of the granular deposits.[232,256,259] The extent of the membranous disruption can be best demonstrated by silver impregnation of the ultra-thin sections examined by electron microscopy since this technique distinguishes the silver-negative deposits of the variant from the argyrophilic density of MPGN type II. Despite the pathologic differences, both variants of type III MPGN are clinically similar and do not differ significantly from MPGN type I.

Diffuse mesangioproliferative glomerulonephritis

Diffuse proliferation of the mesangial cells and matrix without significant involvement of capillary walls or lumina occurs in a variety of renal diseases, including IgA nephropathy, Henoch–Schönlein (anaphylactoid) purpura, systemic lupus erythematosus, IgM nephropathy, and the resolving stage of postinfectious glomerulonephritis. The differential diagnosis of these conditions requires correlation of the light, electron, and immunofluorescent microscopic findings with the patient's clinical data. Only IgA nephropathy is discussed in this section.

IgA nephropathy

In 1968, Berger and Hinglais described a renal disease primarily characterized by mesangial proliferative changes as seen by light microscopy, and diffuse mesangial deposits of IgA, often associated with IgG and C3, by immunofluorescence.[260]

The clinical presentation was that of repeated episodes of microscopic or gross hematuria, frequently associated with nonspecific respiratory tract infections but without other evidence of systemic disease. This condition, which became known as IgA/IgG glomerulonephropathy, Berger's disease, or simply IgA nephropathy, is now recognized as the most common form of primary glomerulonephritis worldwide, accounting for about 10% of the patients reaching end-stage renal failure in many countries. The disease is more common in southern Europe and Asia, and among Native Americans.[264] Familial clustering has been reported but this is rare.[266,274] Since the diagnosis is primarily based on the demonstration of IgA deposits in the mesangium, the boundaries of this entity are not well defined. In fact, it has become evident that several different conditions share this common immunohistochemical finding. Thus, it would be better to regard IgA nephropathy as a syndrome rather than a specific renal disease.[271] Henoch–Schönlein purpura nephritis and IgA nephropathy are two closely related conditions that may well form part of the syndrome. The secondary forms include an increasing number of diseases associated with glomerular deposits of IgA, such as chronic liver disease,[272] celiac disease,[264,269] dermatitis herpetiformis,[269] HIV infection,[268] Crohn's disease,[267] ankylosing spondylitis,[275] carcinomas of various sites,[264,270] mycosis fungoides,[273] and Sjögren's syndrome.[264] The pathogenesis of IgA nephropathy is not fully understood, but it is believed that multiple factors, including immunologic abnormalities leading to increased mucosal IgA synthesis in response to respiratory and gastrointestinal exposure to infectious antigens, inability to clear IgA-containing deposits from the mesangium, and a hereditary predisposition, are likely to play a role in the development of the disease.[261,264,266,276] Only the primary form of IgA nephropathy (Berger's disease) will be discussed in this section.

IgA nephropathy can occur at any age but it is more common in the second and third decades.[262] It is uncommon in children under the age of 10. Males are affected 2 to 6 times more often than females.[261] Approximately 75% of the patients have a history of recurrent episodes of macroscopic hematuria which, in one third of the cases, occurred a few days after a respiratory or, less commonly, gastrointestinal or urinary tract infection.[271] Other patients are diagnosed upon detection of microscopic hematuria during routine physical examination. Patients often have proteinuria, which is usually mild although it can on occasion be severe. Roughly 5% to 10% develop the nephrotic syndrome.[271] The disease is not nearly as benign as was emphasized in early reports, and it is currently estimated that 25% to 40% of the cases slowly progress to chronic renal failure over a period of 20 years.[263] About half of the patients who receive transplants experience a recurrence of the disease in the donor kidney.

It is now recognized that IgA nephropathy may display a wide variety of histologic patterns, ranging from normal or nearly normal to a diffuse necrotizing crescentic glomerulonephritis.[264,265] Widening of the mesangium by increased matrix and hypercellularity is the most common microscopic finding (Fig. 17.39). The mesangial involvement is often uneven and it varies among the glomeruli and glomerular lobules giving the impression of a focal segmental glomerulonephritis. Healing of the focal proliferative lesion may lead to focal segmental glomerulosclerosis. By electron microscopy, it is possible to demonstrate mesangial deposits in all glomeruli, indicating that the lesion is diffuse, not focal (Fig. 17.40). On occasion, small subendothelial or subepithelial deposits may also be found, especially in patients with more severe disease.

The immunofluorescence pattern parallels the distribution of the deposits seen by electron microscopy. There is strong diffuse mesangial reactivity for IgA and it can extend into the capillary loops (Fig. 17.41). IgG is also common and may rival IgA in intensity. Approximately one third of the cases show weak reactivity for IgM and fibrinogen. C3 reactivity is strong with a pattern similar to that of the immunoglobulins, but no reactivity for either C1q or C4 is seen, indicating that the complement is activated via the alternate pathway. Deposits of IgA are not limited to the glomeruli in IgA nephropathy. They

can also be demonstrated in capillaries of the dermis, lung, liver, and intestine.[261] These findings have prompted some authors to propose that the disease is systemic in nature and probably an immune complex-mediated disease, and that the IgA is polymeric and predominantly of the IgA1 subclass.[261] There are similarities in the immunohistochemical patterns of IgA nephropathy and Henoch–Schönlein purpura, and it is conceivable that Berger's disease may represent a localized form of anaphylactoid purpura. However, until more information regarding the pathogenesis of both conditions becomes available, we believe that IgA nephropathy and Henoch–Schönlein purpura should be viewed as separate conditions.

Crescentic glomerulonephritis

Crescentic glomerulonephritis is a histopathologic term used to designate a severe form of glomerulonephritis in which the majority of the glomeruli are involved by epithelial crescents. This type of glomerular injury is associated with a clinical syndrome known as rapidly progressive glomerulonephritis that is characterized by the rapid and progressive loss of renal function accompanied by hematuria, erythrocyte cylindruria, variable degrees of proteinuria, and severe oliguria. Untreated, this disease can result in death within weeks. The terms

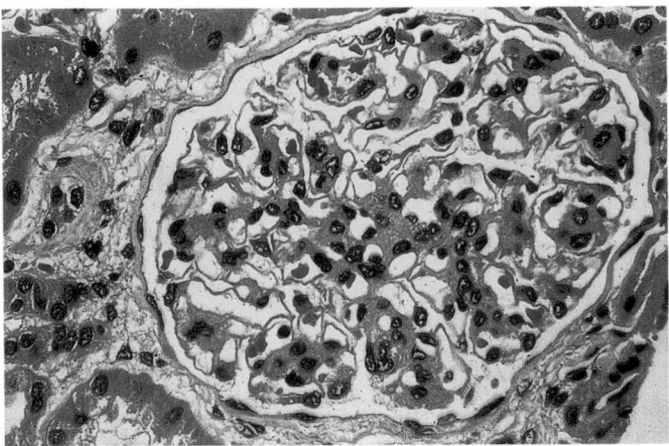

Fig. 17.39 Mesangial enlargement with increase in mesangial matrix and mesangial hypercellularity in IgA nephropathy.

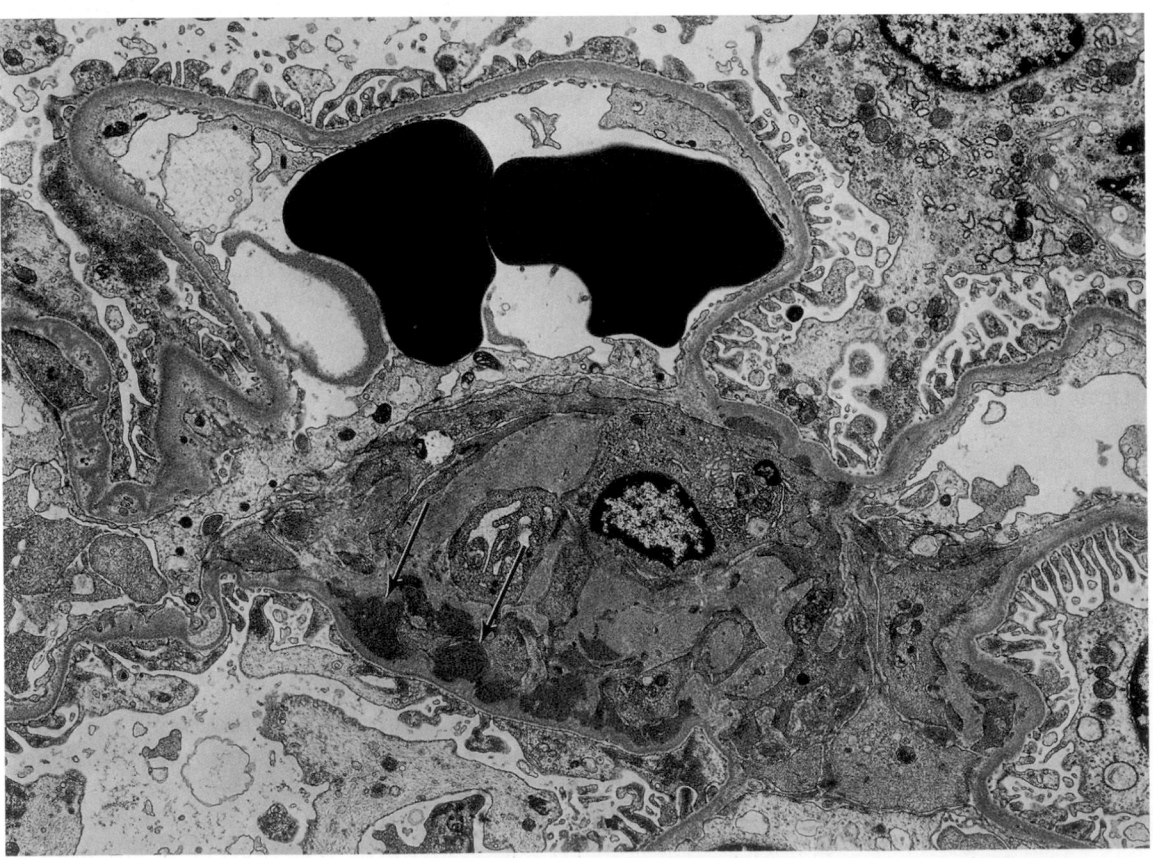

Fig. 17.40 Portion of a glomerulus from a patient with IgA nephropathy showing electron-dense mesangial deposits (arrows). (× 6000)

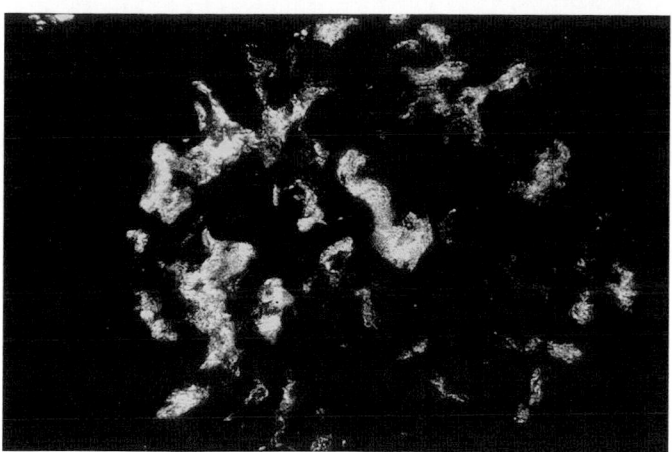

Fig. 17.41 Immunofluorescence preparation of a glomerulus demonstrating mesangial deposits of IgA.

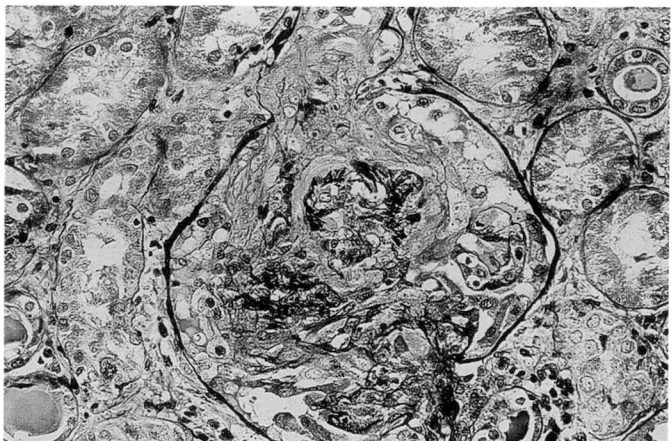

Fig. 17.42 Silver-stained histologic preparation of a glomerulus with epithelial crescent obliterating Bowman's space and extending into the proximal tubule. The glomerular tuft is collapsed.

crescentic glomerulonephritis and *rapidly progressive glomerulonephritis* are often used interchangeably. Like crescentic glomerulonephritis, *extracapillary proliferative glomerulonephritis* is a pathologic term for this lesion which is used to emphasize that the cell proliferation is primarily in Bowman's space. All three of the above terms are considered proper designations for this form of glomerular injury.

Early investigators believed that the crescents were composed exclusively of a proliferation of cells mainly derived from the glomerular capsular epithelial cells; however, later studies using cell markers showed that the crescents were composed of a mixed population of cells primarily consisting of glomerular epithelial cells and macrophages.[283] It has been postulated that crescent formation results from disruption of the glomerular capillaries which allows leukocytes, fibrin, and other plasma proteins to enter Bowman's space where they induce epithelial cell proliferation and macrophage maturation that together produce cellular crescents (Fig. 17.42).[280] This is supported by the invariable immunofluorescent finding of fibrin in active crescentic glomerulonephritis and the demonstration of ruptures of the GBM which can be better seen on silver-stained histologic preparations or by electron microscopy (Figs 17.43 and 17.44). As the disease progresses, the extracapillary proliferating cells are transformed into fibroepithelial crescents which incorporate fibroblasts and collagen. Over time, the sclerosis progresses and the glomeruli become completely scarred.

Crescentic glomerulonephritis can be caused by a wide variety of diseases which can be either restricted to the kidney or systemic. Using immunofluorescence and electron microscopy techniques, three main categories that may reflect different pathogenic mechanisms have been identified: (a) anti-GBM glomerulonephritis; (b) immune complex crescentic glomerulonephritis; and (c) pauci-immune crescentic glomerulonephritis. In each

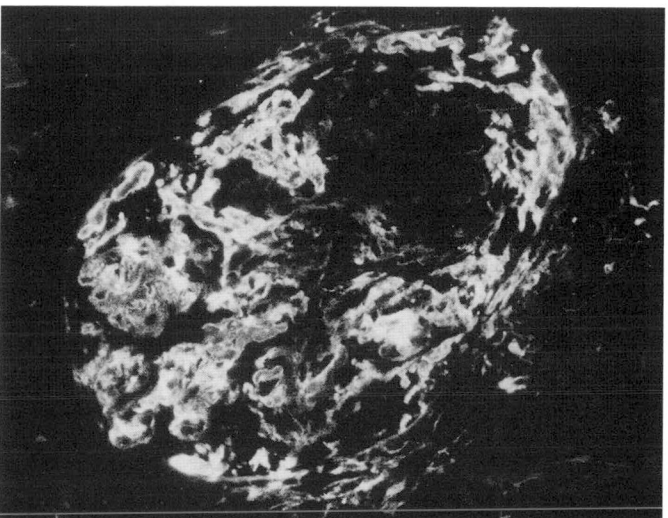

Fig. 17.43 Immunofluorescent preparation showing massive fibrin deposition within the crescent and glomerular capillary tuft.

group, the disease may be associated with a known disorder or may be idiopathic.

Anti-glomerular basement membrane disease

Anti-glomerular basement membrane disease is characterized by the immunofluorescent demonstration of linear deposits of IgG and, in many instances, C3 along the GBM (Fig. 17.45).[283] Anti-GBM disease accounts for 10% to 20% of the cases of crescentic glomerulonephritis.[280] It can be limited to the kidney or occur as a pulmonary–renal syndrome as a result of a cross-reaction of the anti-GBM antibodies with pulmonary basement membranes (Goodpasture's syndrome). The incidence of anti-GBM disease has two peaks with respect to patient age.[280] The first is in the second and third decades of life and has a male predominance and a higher frequency of pulmonary involvement (Goodpasture's syndrome). The second occurs in the sixth and seventh decades, has a

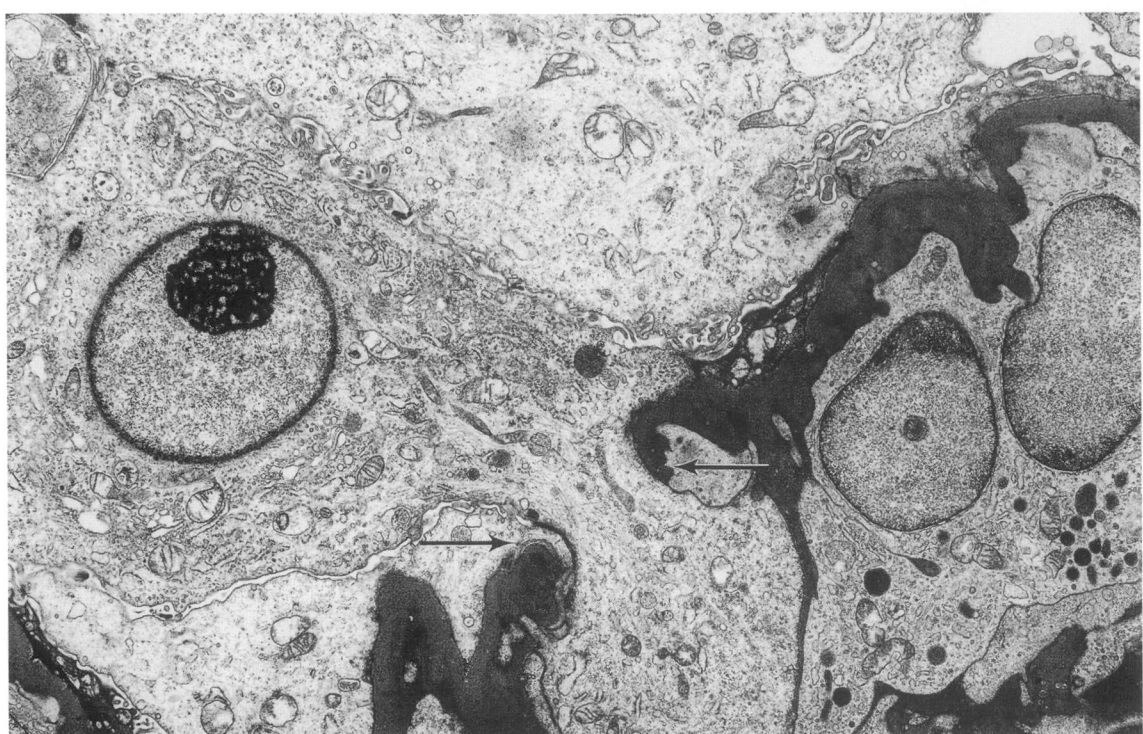

Fig. 17.44 Disruption of the glomerular basement membrane (arrows) in a case of crescentic glomerulonephritis. (× 9000)

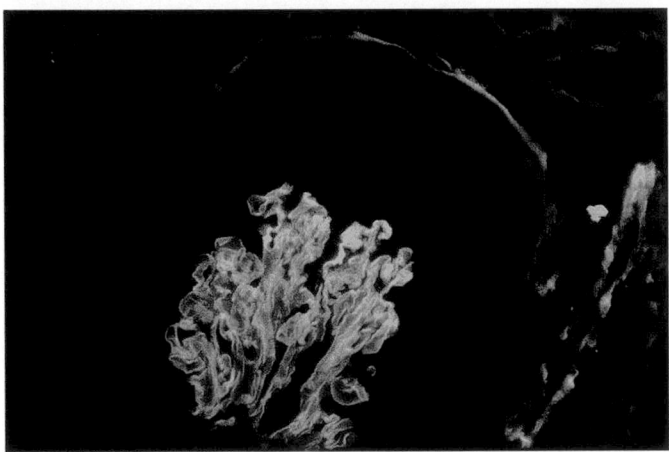

Fig. 17.45 Continuous linear IgG reactivity along the capillary walls in a case of anti-GBM glomerulonephritis. The tuft is compressed by an epithelial crescent.

female predominance, and is more often limited to the kidney. The principal antigen to which anti-GBM antibodies react is localized to the carboxyl terminus of the NC1 domain of the α3 chain of type IV collagen (Goodpasture epitope).[282,285]

Renal anti-GBM disease is typically characterized by the abrupt onset of acute glomerulonephritis with severe oliguria or anuria. On rare occasions, however, the onset is more insidious and the patient may remain essentially asymptomatic until uremic symptoms develop.[280] Patients with Goodpasture's syndrome present with glomerulonephritis and pulmonary involvement, which is more often in the form of severe pulmonary hemorrhage. A preceding upper respiratory infection has been documented in approximately one fourth of these patients. Pulmonary hemorrhage has also been observed after exposure to various inhalants, particularly hydrocarbons. Anti-GBM disease can complicate other diseases. It can arise de novo following renal transplantation in patients with Alport's syndrome and it has been reported in patients with crescentic transformation of membranous glomerulonephritis. Up to one third of the patients with anti-GBM disease have circulating antineutrophil cytoplasmic antibodies (ANCA), especially ANCA with specificity for myeloperoxidase.[277,286,287] The presence of ANCA in patients with anti-GBM disease is associated with small vessel vasculitis in various organs in addition to lung and kidney.[280]

The typical light microscopic lesion in renal anti-GBM disease is that of a necrotizing glomerulonephritis with crescent formation which can be focal or diffuse. In the involved areas, the glomerular capillaries are disrupted and clusters of granulocytes are often present, but there is minimal intracapillary cell proliferation. The uninvolved segments may appear normal or slightly infiltrated by leukocytes or mononuclear inflammatory cells. The most severely involved glomeruli may exhibit extensive necrosis, disruption of Bowman's capsule, and intense periglomerular inflammation. Electron microscopy may demonstrate the presence of a subendothelial lucent zone but this is not a constant or specific feature. Disruptions of the GBM and fibrin deposition can also be seen. An important negative ultrastructural finding in anti-GBM disease is the absence of immune complex deposits. Immunofluorescence studies demonstrate continuous linear immunostaining of the glomerular capillaries for IgG that is often accompanied by focal linear staining for C3 (Fig. 17.45). While this finding strongly indicates anti-GBM disease, it must be kept in mind that a similar immunofluorescence pattern can be seen in other glomerular lesions, including diabetic nephropathy and systemic lupus erythematosus, so it is necessary to confirm the diagnostic impression with the demonstration of circulating anti-GBM antibodies by radioimmunoassay or enzyme immunoassay. Although indirect immunofluorescence microscopy assays can also be used, they are not sensitive enough to be adequate serologic tests for demonstrating anti-GBM antibodies.[280]

Immune complex crescentic glomerulonephritis

Immune complex crescentic glomerulonephritis represents approximately 40% of all of the cases of crescentic glomerulonephritis. It occurs most frequently as a complication of any of the immune complex glomerulonephritides, including postinfectious glomerulonephritis, types I and II MPGN, cryoglobulinemic glomerulonephritis, systemic lupus erythematosus, IgA nephropathy, and Henoch–Schönlein purpura (Fig. 17.46). In a minority of the cases of immune complex crescentic glomerulonephritis, the underlying cause cannot be determined. These patients are diagnosed as having idiopathic immune complex glomerulonephritis. Immune complex crescentic glomerulonephritis occurs more frequently in children, which reflects the general tendency of many types of immune complex glomerulonephritides to affect more commonly this patient population group. The prognosis of idiopathic immune complex crescentic glomerulonephritis, although poor, is better than that of anti-GBM disease. Patients with the secondary form may have a somewhat better outcome,

particularly those with crescentic postinfectious glomerulonephritis.[280,283]

The light microscopic features of immune complex crescentic glomerulonephritis depend upon the underlying glomerular disease. The glomerular segments adjacent to the crescents usually present some degree of necrosis, but this is not as extensive as that seen in anti-GBM or pauci-immune glomerulonephritis. An important finding that can help to distinguish immune complex crescentic glomerulonephritis from both anti-GBM and pauci-immune crescentic glomerulonephritis is the presence of various combinations of capillary wall thickening and endocapillary cell proliferation, features that are typically absent in the latter two types of crescentic glomerulonephritis.[283] Electron microscopy and immunofluorescence allow the presence of immune complex deposits to be determined, thus establishing the diagnosis of immune complex crescentic glomerulonephritis. The differential diagnosis of the different categories of immune complex crescentic glomerulonephritis can usually be achieved by the careful correlation of the patient's clinical and laboratory data with light, immunofluorescence, and electron microscopic findings.

Pauci-immune crescentic glomerulonephritis

Pauci-immune crescentic glomerulonephritis is characterized by the absence of or minimal staining for immunoglobulin by immunofluorescence. It is the most common form of crescentic glomerulonephritis diagnosed by renal biopsy (40% to 50% of the cases) and it more frequently affects elderly individuals. Pauci-immune crescentic glomerulonephritis can occur as a disease limited to the kidney or as a component of systemic necrotizing small vessel vasculitis. Patients with pauci-immune crescentic glomerulonephritis tend to respond better to treatment than those with anti-GBM glomerulonephritis and therefore have a better prognosis.

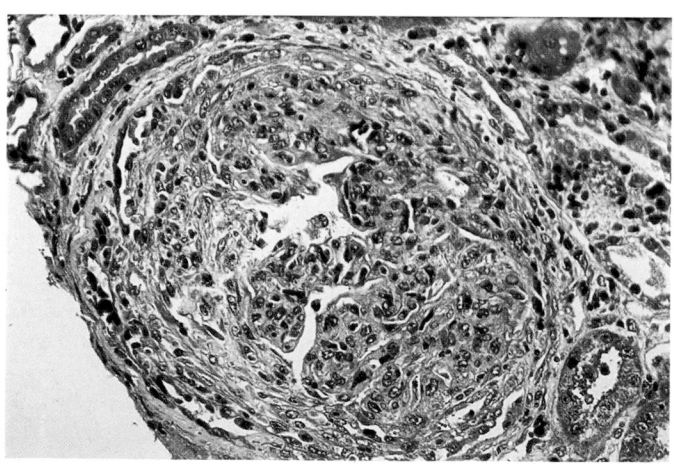
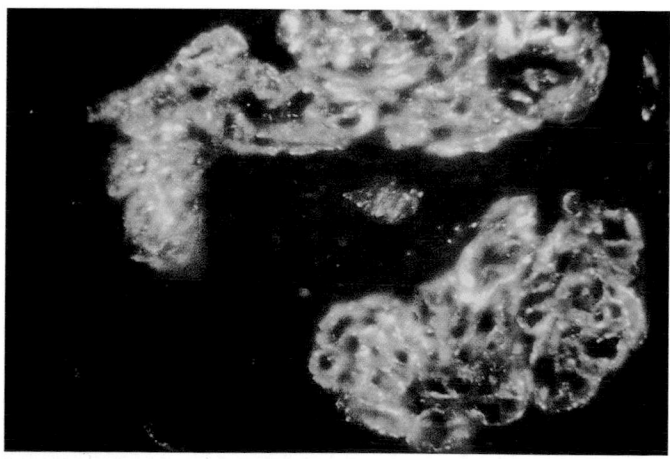

A

B

Fig. 17.46 A, Acute postinfectious glomerulonephritis with intracapillary proliferation and crescent formation. **B,** The glomerular tuft is compressed by an epithelial crescent. Coarse granular deposits of IgG are prominent along the capillary walls.

Anti-neutrophil cytoplasmic antibodies (ANCA) have been recognized as serologic markers for pauci-immune glomerulonephritis with or without evidence of extrarenal disease.[278,279,281,284] By indirect immunofluorescence with ethanol-fixed neutrophils as substrate, two distinct immunostaining patterns have been recognized: cytoplasmic (c-ANCA) and perinuclear (p-ANCA). Enzyme-linked immunoabsorbent assay (ELISA) has shown that most c-ANCA- and p-ANCA-positive sera recognize proteinase 3 (PR3), which is a serine protease of 29 kDa, and myeloperoxidase (MPO), respectively. Both are localized in the azurophilic granules of the neutrophils and monocytes, are translocated to the cell surface during cell activation, and are thus able to interact directly with ANCA. Patients with pauci-immune crescentic glomerulonephritis without evidence of extrarenal vasculitis most often have p-ANCA/MPO-ANCA. Those with Wegener's granulomatosis most often have c-ANCA/PR3-ANCA, while those with microscopic polyangiitis have an approximately equal incidence of p-ANCA and c-ANCA.[283]

The light microscopic appearance of pauci-immune crescentic glomerulonephritis is indistinguishable from that of anti-GBM disease. Immunofluorescence studies may reveal small irregular focal staining for C3. Fibrinogen is frequently found in the crescents or in the necrotic areas of the glomerular tuft. Electron microscopy often demonstrates ruptures of the GBM as well as fibrin deposition. The absence of immune complex deposits differentiates pauci-immune crescentic glomerulonephritis from immune complex crescentic glomerulonephritis.

Lupus nephritis

Systemic lupus erythematosus (SLE) is an autoimmune disease with a wide range of clinical manifestations. The American Rheumatism Association has established diagnostic criteria for this condition based on clinical and serologic manifestations.[310] SLE can affect adults as well as children; two thirds of patients present symptoms between 16 and 30 years of age. The onset of lupus before puberty is rare.[295,302] It is ten times more common in females than in males, with black females being more frequently affected than white. A drug-induced lupus-like disease, most commonly linked with hydralazine, procainamide, isoniazid, methyldopa, chlorpromazine, and quinidine, has also been recognized.[298] The renal lesions in these cases are similar to those seen in spontaneous SLE.

Immune-mediated nephritis is a common complication of SLE. The pathogenesis of this lesion is likely to be related to the inflammation response resulting from the presence of immune aggregates at the site of injury. Whether these aggregates are derived from circulating complexes or from an in situ combination of antigen and antibody still remains unclear. Clinical evidence of renal involvement, as determined by urinalysis, or impaired renal function is seen in approximately 40% to 80% of unselected patients with SLE. It is likely, however, that clinical assessment underestimates the actual frequency since histologic evidence of renal disease may be present even when the urinalysis is essentially normal. The clinical spectrum of lupus nephritis is wide, encompassing the acute nephritic syndrome, the nephrotic syndrome, acute and chronic renal failure, and isolated abnormalities in the urinary sediment. The most constant feature, which is found in nearly all patients with clinical lupus nephritis, is proteinuria. Microscopic hematuria is almost always present, but rarely does it develop in isolation; macroscopic hematuria is rare.

A kidney biopsy is essential in the renal assessment of patients with SLE and it is indicated in all patients having abnormalities of the urine sediment or renal function. This is because it is not possible to predict with accuracy the histopathology based on the clinical presentation even though, in general, more severe histology tends to correlate with more severe clinical disease. Furthermore, it has been shown that in untreated patients the histopathologic features of the renal disease can provide an indication of the subsequent clinical course, thus the renal biopsy can aid in planning treatment.

The pathologic findings of lupus nephritis are extremely diverse and may occur in any or all four renal compartments: glomeruli, tubules, interstitium, and blood vessels. This diversity may be the result of differences in the immune response in different patients or in the same individual over a period of time. Because the renal lesions are so diverse, the World Health Organization (WHO) has developed a classification of lupus nephritis that uses information obtained from light, immunofluorescent, and electron microscopic evaluation.[292] The six major categories of this classification, together with the clinicopathologic correlations, are shown in Table 17.8.

According to the WHO classification, class I lupus nephritis cases are those in which the renal biopsy appears essentially normal by light, electron, and immunofluorescence microscopy, although minor nonspecific changes can occasionally be seen by electron microscopy. It is therefore questionable whether class I represents a true class of renal disease.

Class II (10% to 20% of the cases), which is restricted to pure glomerular mesangial lesions, has been subdivided into classes IIA and IIB. In class IIA, the changes seen by light microscopy are at most minimal, but immune deposits are evident in the mesangium by immunofluorescence and electron microscopy. Unequivocal evidence of glomerular mesangial hypercellularity is seen by light microscopy in class IIB. It involves the center of the lobules away from the vascular pole (Fig. 17.47); the peripheral capillary walls do not appear to be affected. Immune deposits are demonstrated by immunofluorescence and electron microscopy but only in the mesangial

Table 17.8 WHO classification of lupus nephritis with clinicopathologic correlation

Class	Pathology findings	Clinical renal manifestations
I. Normal or minimal abnormality	Kidney is normal by light, electron, and immunofluorescence microscopy	Usually asymptomatic
II. Pure mesangial alterations	Mesangial expansion but mostly patent capillaries Mesangial immune deposits	Low-grade proteinuria with or without hematuria Normal renal function
III. Focal proliferative glomerulonephritis	Focal and segmental proliferative intra- and/or extracapillary necrotizing and/or sclerosing lesions in <50% of glomeruli Predominantly mesangial and subendothelial immune deposits	Nephritic urinary sediment Variable but usually non-nephrotic proteinuria
IV. Diffuse proliferative glomerulonephritis	Predominantly global proliferative lesions, necrosis, crescents in >50% of glomeruli Variable sclerosis, prominent inflammatory interstitial infiltrate Predominantly mesangial and subendothelial immune deposits	Nephritic and nephrotic syndromes, hypertension, variable degree of renal insufficiency
V. Membranous glomerulonephritis	Diffuse thickening of capillary walls Subepithelial (and mesangial) immune deposits	Nephrotic syndrome or severe proteinuria
VI. Advanced sclerosing glomerulonephritis	Glomerular obsolescence and segmental glomerulosclerosis, tubular atrophy, and interstitial fibrosis Few, if any, immune deposits	Chronic renal failure

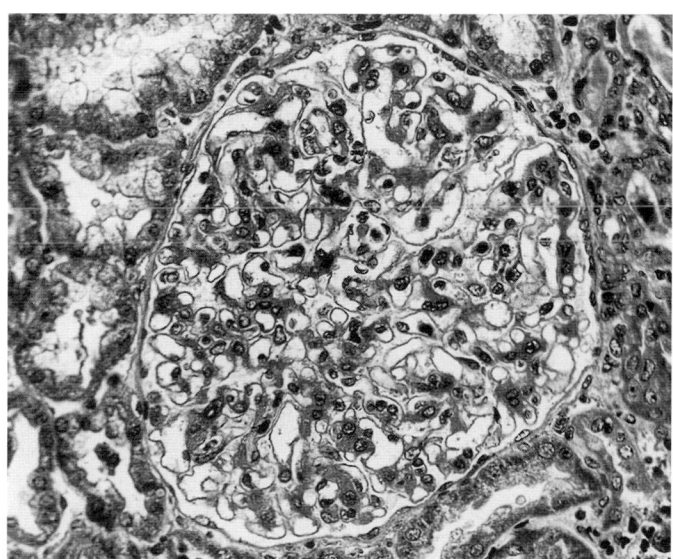

Fig. 17.47 Lupus nephritis, WHO Class II. There is mild diffuse mesangial hypercellularity and an increase in matrix. Mesangial deposits may be identified by immunofluorescence and electron microscopy.

region. Tubular, interstitial, and vascular changes are insignificant. Clinically, the majority of patients have mild to moderate evidence of renal involvement and generally have a good prognosis with a 5-year renal survival rate of more than 90%.

Class III disease (30% to 40% of the cases) is characterized by focal and segmental endocapillary proliferative glomerulonephritis that affects less than 50% of the glomeruli. The biopsy may reveal a variable admixture of proliferative, necrotizing, and sclerosing lesions. The less affected glomeruli usually exhibit a diffuse mesangial prominence similar to that seen in class II. The segmental proliferative lesions may be associated with leukocyte infiltration, fibrinoid material, and necrotic debris (Fig. 17.48). Focal areas of necrosis containing fragmented nuclei known as hematoxylin bodies may be present (Fig. 17.49). These structures are considered pathognomonic of lupus nephritis but are found in only 1% to 2% of renal biopsies from these patients. They range considerably in size from minute fragments to rounded masses approximating the size of the nucleus and have a characteristic lilac tinge in hematoxylin and eosin sections.[294,305] The segmental necrotic lesions may be associated with cellular crescent formation and tend to resolve by segmental sclerosis with focal capsular adhesions or the development of fibrous crescents. Despite the focal nature of the lesions by light microscopy, immunofluorescence generally reveals a more diffuse deposition of immunoglobulins and complement. Electron microscopy often demonstrates deposits in the mesangial and subendothelial regions and, less frequently, in the subepithelial areas. Focal interstitial inflammation and edema, which in lesions

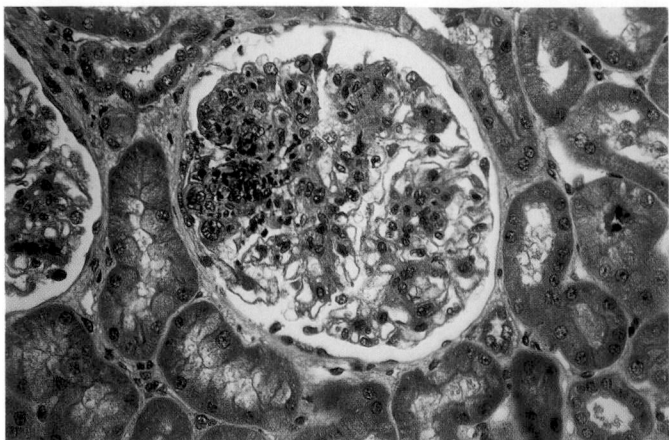

Fig. 17.48 Lupus nephritis, WHO Class III. There is focal and segmental glomerulonephritis characterized by segmental necrosis, adhesions to Bowman's capsule, and leukocytic infiltration.

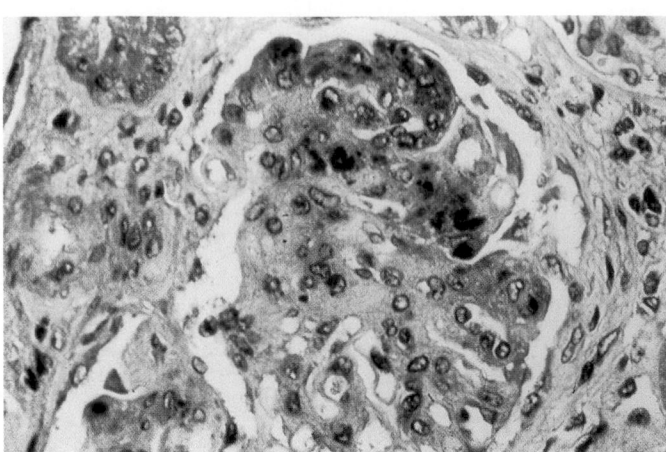

Fig. 17.49 Glomerulus from a patient with WHO Class IV lupus nephritis showing a well-circumscribed area of necrosis containing numerous small hematoxylin bodies.

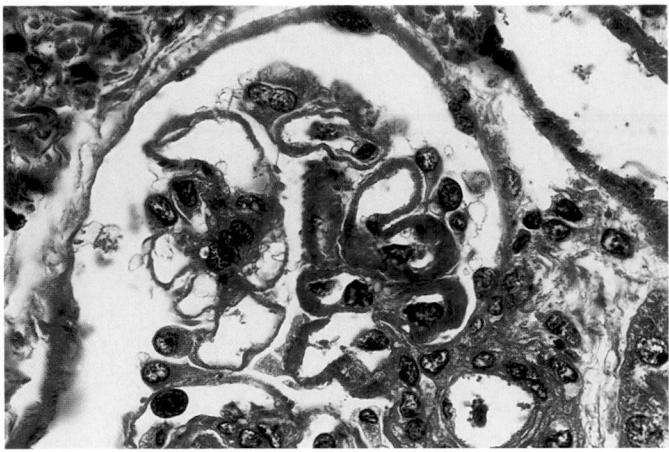

A

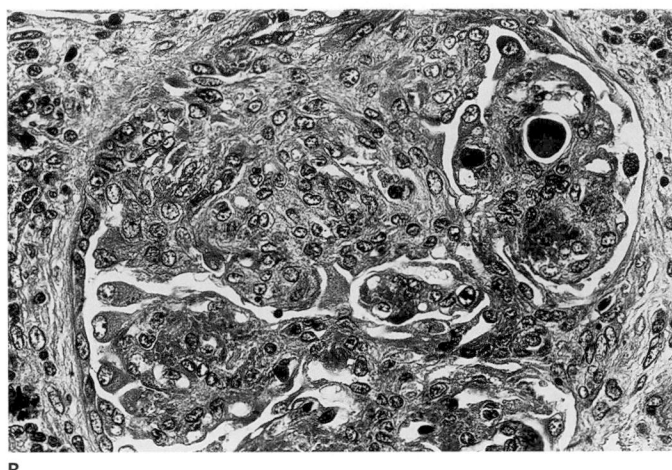

B

Fig. 17.50 A, Glomerulus from a patient with Class IV lupus nephritis showing several wire-loop lesions. **B,** Glomerulus with an epithelial crescent showing two hyaline thrombi.

that are more chronic may coexist with scarring and tubular atrophy, are not uncommon findings.

The designation of class IV (40% to 60% of the cases) is given in those instances in which over 50% of the glomeruli are affected by endocapillary proliferation. The lesions in this class are similar to those in class III, but tend to be diffuse and more global, and the immune deposits are more abundant. It has been suggested that classes III and IV lupus nephritis are ends of a pathologic continuum since the differences between these classes are quantitative rather than qualitative. The immune deposits in the subendothelial areas may produce marked thickening of the capillary walls to form the characteristic "wire loop" lesions (Fig. 17.50A). On occasion, the capillary lumina can be occluded by massive deposition of immune complexes ("hyaline thrombi") (Fig. 17.50B). The glomerular damage ranges from a diffuse mesangial hypercellularity without necrosis, sclerosis, or wire loops to a severe necrotizing and crescentic glomerulonephritis. In some cases, there is accentuation of the glomerular lobules, with extension of the mesangium into the periphery of the loops in a manner similar to that seen in membranoproliferative glomerulonephritis. Immunofluorescence studies often reveal more than one class of immunoglobulin in a coarse granular pattern in the mesangium and peripheral capillary walls in all glomeruli. IgG is almost invariably present, but IgM and IgA also are frequently found. When all three immunoglobulins are present, the pattern is often referred to as a "full house," an immunofluorescent profile which is considered characteristic of lupus nephritis (Fig. 17.51). Both C3 and C1q are frequently found and the staining for C1q is particularly strong. Reactivity for fibrin and fibrinogen is commonly seen in crescentic and necrotizing lesions. Electron microscopy demonstrates large subendothelial electron-dense deposits, accompanied usually by mesangial and sometimes by subepithelial and/or intramembranous deposits (Fig. 17.52). Subendothelial deposits are primarily found in proliferative lupus nephritis (classes III and

IV) and are considered a marker of activity.[293,297] On occasion, the electron-dense deposits may show a distinctive fingerprint-like crystalline pattern that has been proposed to be the result of DNA crystallization (Fig. 17.53).[301] These deposits, although nonspecific for lupus nephritis, are usually associated with this lesion.[300] The endothelial cells may be swollen and may contain tubulovesicular structures that resemble myxovirus-like particles (Fig. 17.54). These structures are similar to those seen in the endothelial cells of patients with HIV-

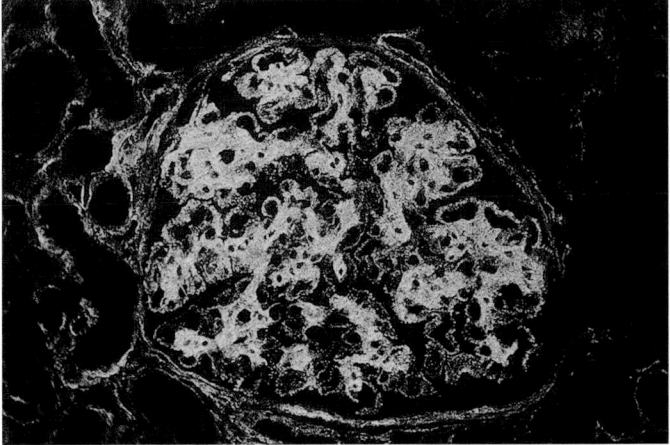

Fig. 17.51 Immunofluorescence preparation for IgG showing large amounts of immune complex deposits not only in the mesangium and along the glomerular capillary loops, but also around tubular basement membranes, interstitium, blood vessels, and in the Bowman's capsule.

associated nephropathy. The symptoms in class IV lesions are fairly severe and may include nephrotic-range proteinuria and active urinary sediment. Without therapy, these patients are considered to have the worst prognosis since a high percentage progress rapidly to renal failure.

Class V disease (10% to 15% of the cases) is characterized by a diffuse membranous glomerulonephritis that is essentially identical to that seen in idiopathic MGN. By light microscopy, there is a generalized diffuse thickening of the peripheral capillary walls, and the so-called "spike and dome" pattern may be demonstrated on silver methenamine stain (Fig. 17.55). Mesangial hypercellularity is seen in some cases but this does not appear to affect the prognosis when these cases are compared with those without any evidence of mesangial proliferation.[306] Immunofluorescence demonstrates a confluent peripheral granular deposition of immunoglobulin, which is sometimes accompanied by mesangial granular deposits. Electron microscopy reveals numerous epimembranous and intramembranous deposits and, less frequently, mesangial deposits. Proteinuria is common and can be in the nephrotic range, but the lesions tend to progress in a somewhat indolent fashion, similar to that of idiopathic MGN.

Class VI lesions are characterized by advanced glomerulosclerosis, interstitial fibrosis, inflammation, and tubular atrophy. In the less advanced lesions, mesangial or endocapillary hypercellularity may be seen, and small amounts of immune deposits can be detected by

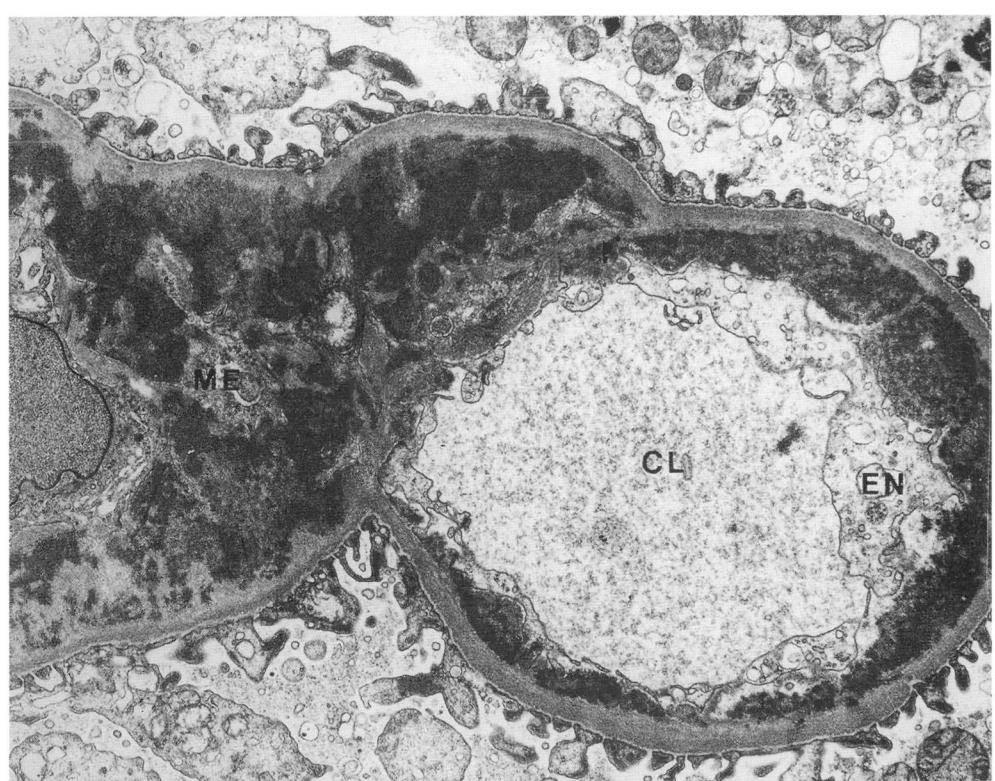

Fig. 17.52 Capillary loop showing marked accumulation of deposits in the mesangium and subendothelial regions. The deposits in the latter location represent the wire-loop lesion seen by light microscopy. CL = capillary lumen; EN = endothelial cell; ME = mesangium. (× 7000)

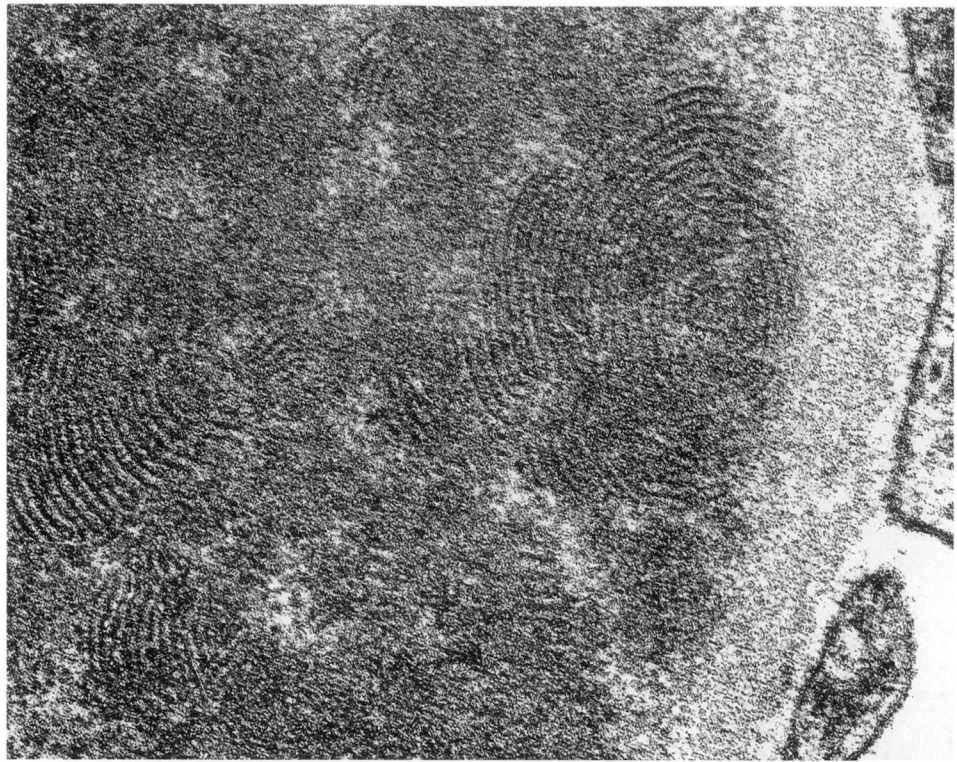

Fig. 17.53 Subendothelial deposits displaying a fingerprint-like pattern. (× 77,000)

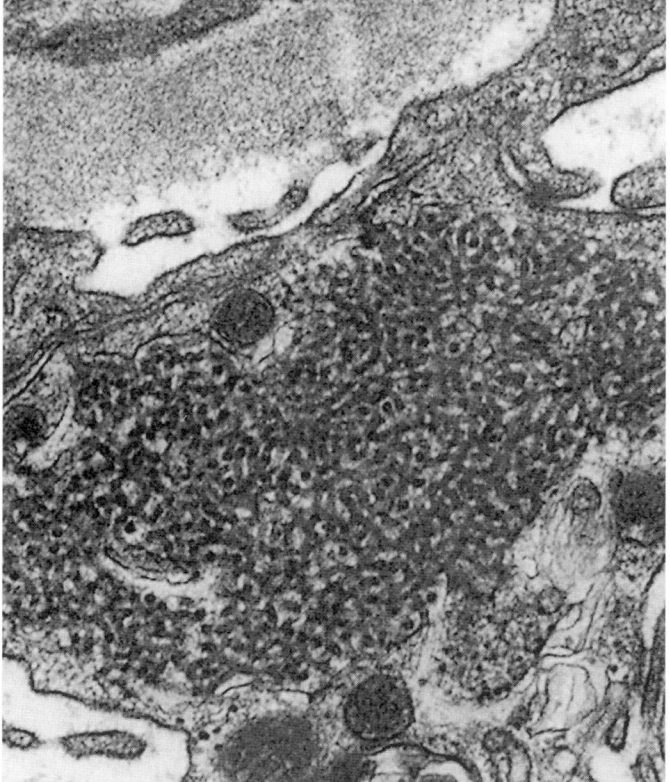

Fig. 17.54 Tubulovesicular particles in an endothelial cell. (× 34,250)

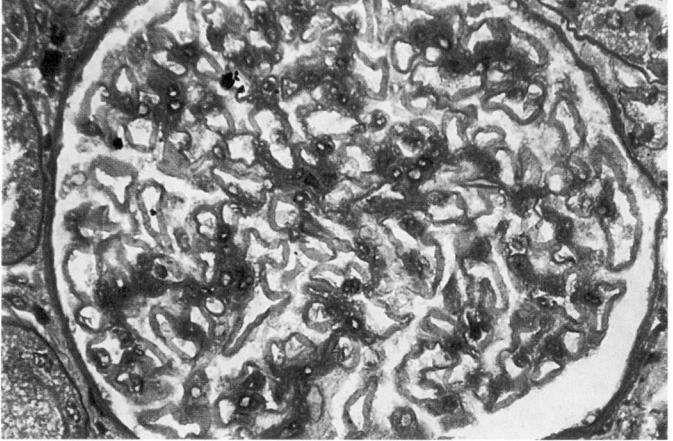

Fig. 17.55 Lupus nephritis, WHO class V. The capillary walls are thickened and the mesangial matrix increased.

immunofluorescence or electron microscopy in the mesangium and thickened capillary walls. Patients with class VI lesions usually have significant proteinuria and renal insufficiency and are unlikely to respond to therapy.

While most cases of lupus nephritis fall into the above categories, some overlapping between classifications exists. The most common of these involve classes III and V, and IV and V, and have been designated as combined classes III+V, and IV+V, respectively. The transformation of lupus nephritis lesions from one class to another is not uncommon during the course of the disease. It has been reported in 10% to 50% of the patients who undergo successive renal biopsies[288,291,303,304] and has occurred between all morphologic types: focal to diffuse,[311] focal to membranous,[304] diffuse to membranous,[296] membranous to diffuse proliferative,[299,307] and membranous to membranous with focal proliferative lesions.[288]

Tubulointerstitial disease can be encountered in all classes of lupus nephritis, even in those with minimal glomerular lesions.[294,303] Severe active tubulointerstitial nephritis is most frequently seen in patients with classes III or IV lupus nephritis. In most instances, the interstitial inflammatory infiltrate is comprised of mononuclear leukocytes, including lymphocytes, monocytes, and plasma cells, although neutrophils and eosinophils can sometimes be seen and may reflect a more active lesion. In severe cases, there is inflammatory infiltration of the tubules, and the tubular epithelial cells present degenerative and regenerative changes. Tubular casts made of neutrophils, erythrocytes, and shed tubular epithelial cells may be seen in the more severe cases. In approximately 50% of the patients, immunofluorescence and electron microscopy can demonstrate granular immune deposits along the peritubular capillaries, basement membranes of proximal convoluted tubules, and interstitium (Fig. 17.51). These deposits occur more frequently in diffuse proliferative lupus nephritis than in the focal proliferative variant, but may also be found in some patients with the membranous and mesangial proliferative forms.[294] Lupus nephritis is one of the few renal diseases in which immune deposits can be found not only in the glomeruli, but also in extraglomerular sites. The severity of the tubulointerstitial inflammation roughly correlates with the glomerular proliferative lesions; however, a few cases of severe tubular interstitial damage without the significant glomerular disease that has sometimes led to acute renal failure have been reported.[309]

Renal vascular lesions are relatively common in SLE and can assume a variety of morphologic forms, including uncomplicated vascular immune deposits, noninflammatory necrotizing vasculopathy, true vasculitis with leukocyte infiltration and necrosis of the vascular walls, thrombotic microangiopathy, and nonspecific arteriosclerosis.[294] All of these vascular changes are signs of poor prognosis and thus it is important that they be recognized.

Some authors have proposed that histologic indices derived from the semiquantitative analysis of activity and chronicity in renal biopsies of patients with SLE have a prognostic value and can serve as a therapeutic guide.[289,290] According to this system, the activity index is calculated by the assessment of the following six histologic parameters: glomerular endocapillary proliferation; glomerular neutrophil infiltration; wire-loop deposits and hyaline thrombi; glomerular fibrinoid necrosis and karyorrhexis; cellular crescents; and interstitial inflammation. The severity of each of these features is scored on a scale of 0 to 3+ and the fibrinoid necrosis/karyorrhexis and cellular crescents scores are multiplied by 2. Thus, the maximum activity score is 24. The chronicity index is computed by the sum of individual scores (0 to 3+) of the following four parameters:

glomerular sclerosis, fibrous crescents, tubular atrophy, and interstitial fibrosis. Thus, the maximum chronicity score is 12. Although the validity and reproducibility of the activity and chronicity indices have been questioned,[308] these indices can be useful in guiding the management of individual cases since they can provide a rough estimate of the potential reversibility of the renal lesions.

Glomerular lesions associated with vascular diseases

Systemic vasculitis

Vasculitis may occur in a variety of conditions, particularly in connective tissue diseases such as systemic lupus erythematosus and rheumatoid arthritis, and in hypersensitivity reactions caused by infections and drug reactions. Vasculitis may also occur as the primary manifestation of a variety of clinical conditions known as idiopathic systemic vasculitides. Clinical symptoms depend on the organ distribution, the size of the affected vessels, and the severity of the inflammation. The kidneys can be affected in different ways in systemic vasculitis. Large vessel vasculitides, such as giant cell (temporal) arteritis and Takayasu disease, can produce narrowing of the renal arteries resulting in renal ischemia and hypertension. Medium-sized vessel vasculitides, such as polyarteritis nodosa and Kawasaki disease, can affect intrarenal arteries and cause infarction and hemorrhage, whereas, in small vessel vasculitides, such as microscopic polyangiitis (microscopic polyarteritis), Wegener's granulomatosis, Henoch–Schönlein purpura, and cryoglobulinemic vasculitis, the renal involvement is often manifested by glomerulonephritis.

The pathogenesis of these disorders is poorly understood and, until recently, the diagnosis was exclusively based on clinical and histopathologic characteristics. Recent investigations have shown that ANCA constitute reliable serologic markers for various types of vasculitis. There is also strong evidence that ANCA and their target antigens may play a role in the pathogenesis of these diseases.[312] It is important to emphasize that, even though ANCA are regularly found in primary vasculitis, they cannot always be detected; therefore, their absence does not rule out such a diagnosis.[313] Some of the conditions in which vasculitis appears to be the primary histopathologic lesion will be discussed in this section.

Polyarteritis nodosa

Polyarteritis nodosa (PAN) is a primary vasculitis of unknown etiology that affects muscular arteries at the branch points, and produces lesions of varying stages of evolution (acute and healed) and aneurysm formation. The kidneys and gastrointestinal tract are among the organs most commonly affected, while the lungs are usually spared. The estimated incidence is 2 to 3 cases per million.[314] Males are affected twice as often as females, and the peak incidence is in the sixth decade of life. Approximately one third of the patients may be carriers of the hepatitis B virus.[316] There is no serum marker for PAN. Only a minority (<20%) of patients have positive ANCA, particularly p-ANCA, titers in their sera. The kidneys are involved in 80% to 90% of the cases. Renal infarctions occur frequently and may be manifested by loin pain and hematuria. Hypertension is common and may be severe or malignant. The renal lesion in PAN is a necrotizing vasculitis that involves medium-sized muscular arteries such as the renal, interlobar, and arcuate arteries (Fig. 17.56). The lesions are

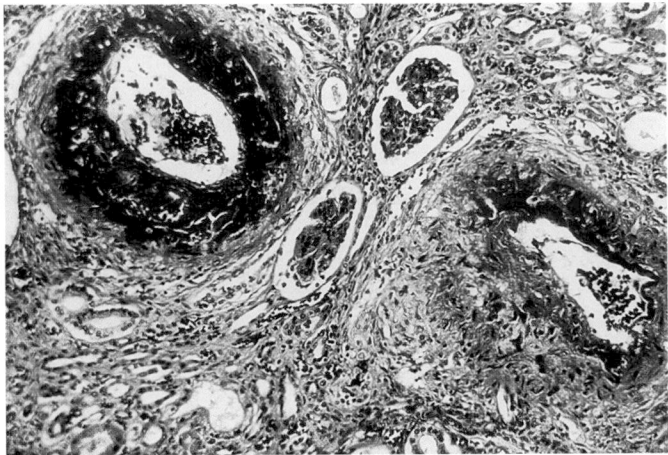

Fig. 17.56 Fibrinoid necrosis involving two medium-sized arteries in polyarteritis nodosa.

usually focal, and tend to localize to the bifurcations. Weakening of the vessel wall leads to the formation of aneurysmal dilatations. The inflammatory process may involve part of or the entire vessel wall and is characterized by fibrinoid necrosis and leukocytic infiltration, sometimes associated with intraluminal thrombosis. The acute phase evolves into a healing phase in which the necrosis subsides and the leukocytic inflammation is replaced by mononuclear infiltrate. In the healed stage, there is fibrosis of the media and perivascular tissue and recanalization of the thrombosed vessels.[315,317] The focal nature of the vessel lesion means that evidence of vasculitis may not be seen on a needle biopsy. The glomeruli show changes associated with ischemia consisting of variable degrees of collapse and sclerosis of the tufts. Immunofluorescence and electron microscopy typically do not reveal evidence of immune complex deposits.[317]

Microscopic polyangiitis

Microscopic polyangiitis, formerly known as microscopic polyarteritis nodosa, is a necrotizing systemic vasculitis with few or no immune complexes (pauci-immune) that affects small vessels (capillaries, venules, and arterioles) (Fig. 17.57). Involvement of small and medium sized arteries can also occur, but this is not a constant feature. Because of the absence of arterial involvement in many cases and the frequent involvement of venules, arterioles, and capillaries, the term microscopic polyangiitis is now considered more appropriate for this form of vasculitis than the designation of microscopic polyarteritis.[322,323] Although microscopic polyangiitis was initially considered a category of

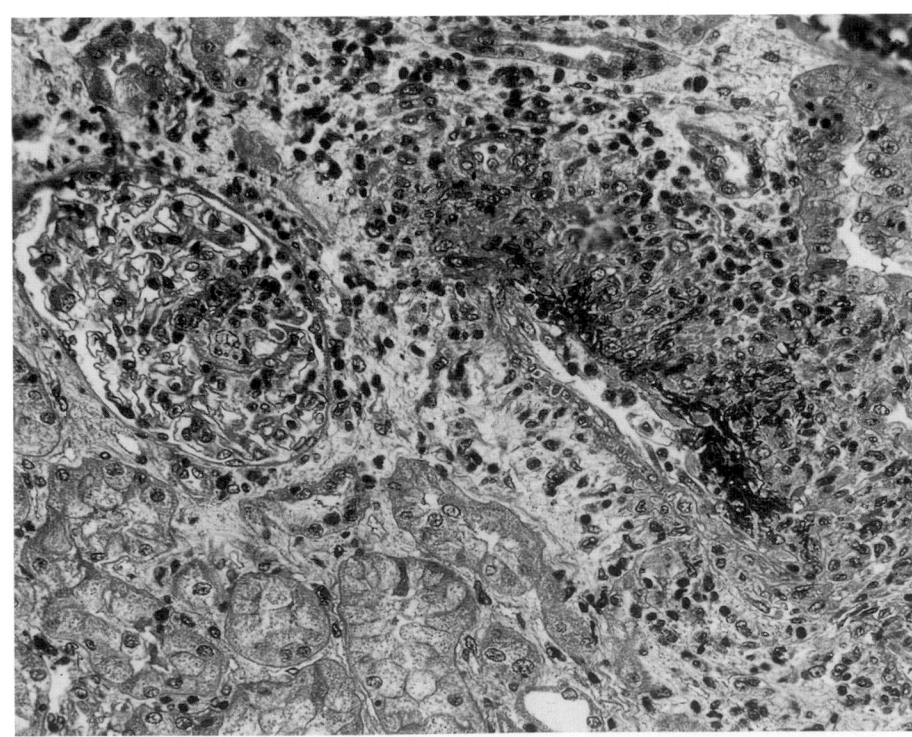

Fig. 17.57 Renal biopsy from a patient with microscopic polyongiitis showing small vessel with necrosis and inflammatory infiltrate. The glomerulus has segmental capillary collapse, necrosis, and inflammation.

polyarteritis nodosa, it is now believed to represent a separate category of vasculitis.[322,324]

The incidence of microscopic polyangiitis is approximately 1 per 100,000.[324] Males are affected slightly more than females and although it can occur at any age, it is more frequent during the sixth decade of life. Clinical manifestations are quite varied and nonspecific. Depending upon the organ(s) affected, the most common clinical features are hematuria and proteinuria, hemoptysis, palpable purpura, abdominal pain, myalgias, and arthralgias. Hypertension may occur, but it is usually mild. Approximately 90% of the patients have renal involvement. In contrast to polyarteritis nodosa, however, the lungs are commonly affected in microscopic polyangiitis. A frequent clinical presentation of microscopic polyangiitis is as pulmonary–renal syndrome. This syndrome raises the possibility of anti-GBM disease (Goodpasture's syndrome); however, the demonstration of ANCA in microscopic polyangiitis or anti-GBM antibodies in anti-GBM disease will establish the differential diagnosis. Over 80% of patients present detectable ANCA, most often p-ANCA. In the kidney, the most frequent lesion is glomerulonephritis, and the glomerular involvement ranges from a focal and segmental necrotizing glomerulonephritis to a severe diffuse crescentic glomerulonephritis.[321,324] When present, necrotizing arteritis most often affects the interlobular and arcuate arteries.[324] Histologically, these lesions are indistinguishable from those seen in PAN. In contrast to the lesions seen in PAN, however, which are usually in varying stages of evolution, those in microscopic polyangiitis almost invariably appear to be in the same stage.[318] Healed and healing lesions are seen as focal and segmental areas of glomerular sclerosis. A tubulointerstitial infiltrate including eosinophils is frequently present. Immune complex deposits are not usually seen in the glomeruli, although there have been reports of sparse deposits containing IgG or IgM with C3 in various intraglomerular locations.[319,320]

Wegener's granulomatosis

Wegener's granulomatosis (WG) is a multisystem disease of unknown etiology characterized by the triad of: (1) necrotizing granulomatous inflammation involving the upper respiratory tract (ear, nose, throat, and sinuses) and/or lungs; (2) necrotizing vasculitis affecting small to medium-sized vessels (capillaries, venules, arterioles, and arteries) most prominently in the lungs and upper airways but also involving other sites as well; and (3) renal disease, most often manifested in the form of focal necrotizing glomerulonephritis. Those patients who do not manifest the full triad are considered to have limited WG. In these cases, involvement is limited to the respiratory tract and the kidneys are unaffected. The prevalence of WG in the United States has been estimated to be 3 per 100,000 with a male to female ratio of 1:1.[326] It may occur

at any age but is more common in the fourth and fifth decades.[327,331] The first clinical indication is usually upper respiratory symptoms which are followed by systemic phenomena related to the vasculitis.[335] Approximately 80% to 85% of patients present some signs of renal involvement, usually simultaneously with other clinical features[331]; fewer than 20% actually present with renal impairment. Patients with renal involvement, if untreated, usually have a rapidly progressive and fatal disease. Therapy with cyclophosphamide and corticosteroids has produced remission in most patients, but approximately 50% of the patients may relapse.[331]

The differentiation of WG from other types of vasculitis can be difficult clinically or morphologically. A positive ANCA test, especially c-ANCA, can be extremely helpful in establishing or supporting the diagnosis of WG. The specificity of c-ANCA in biopsy proven WG has been shown to be about 90%. The sensitivity depends upon the extent and activity of the disease. It is 50% in the initial phase of the disease and close to 100% for patients with active and generalized disease.[329] C-ANCA is not detectable in most patients in complete remission, and it can be very low in those in partial remission. Although it has been shown that serum levels parallel the clinical activity of the disease[325] and that rising levels may be used as a predictor of relapse, there are some patients in whom c-ANCA titers do not follow disease activity.[330,331]

The most common renal lesion is focal necrotizing glomerulonephritis, often with crescents.[333,334] Granulomatous glomerulonephritis occurs but it is uncommon, even in autopsy series, and is usually accompanied by necrosis of the hilar arterioles.[336] Renal papillary necrosis complicates up to 20% of cases of WG and it is possibly caused by the vasculitis leading to thrombotic occlusions of the vasa recta.[332] Necrotizing vasculitis involving the arterioles and small arteries occurs but it is not a common finding in kidney biopsies. Interstitial inflammatory infiltrates are common, but necrotizing granulomas are rarely seen in renal biopsy specimens.[331]

As a rule, immune complex deposits cannot be detected in WG by electron microscopy, though there have been reports of the occurrence of sparse electron-dense deposits at different sites in the glomerulus.[328,333] Immunofluorescence shows fibrinogen in glomeruli and the walls of involved vessels, and small amounts of IgM and/or IgG and C3 have been reported in glomeruli and vessels.

Henoch–Schönlein purpura

Henoch–Schönlein (anaphylactoid) purpura is a distinct systemic vasculitis syndrome that is characterized by palpable purpura (most commonly distributed over the lower extremities and buttocks), migratory arthralgias, abdominal manifestations, including pain, vomiting, and intestinal bleeding, and renal abnormalities. The clinical manifestations of the syndrome are caused by a systemic small vessel vasculitis of the leukocytoclastic type. The inflammatory reaction seen in the skin, kidney, and other organs is caused by deposition of IgA-containing immune complexes. Seventy five per cent of the patients are between the ages of 2 and 11 years. The disease is rare in adults, in whom the renal manifestations are usually more severe, and in infants under the age of 1 year. Henoch–Schönlein purpura is uncommon in blacks, and familial cases have rarely been reported.[339] Approximately one fourth of the patients have a history of allergies. Renal symptoms occur in as many as 70% of patients and they range from mild hematuria and proteinuria with no reduction of renal function to the nephrotic syndrome and severe renal insufficiency. The disease undergoes complete, spontaneous remission in half of the patients, usually within a year of onset, but many others progress to end-stage renal disease over a period of 5 to 10 years. In general, there is a good correlation between the severity of the lesion and the clinical manifestations, and patients with the nephrotic syndrome usually progress to chronic renal failure. Recurrence can occur in allografts.[337,340,341]

By light microscopy, the most characteristic feature is a mesangial proliferative glomerulonephritis with a variable degree of crescent formation. The mesangial changes, which may be focal or diffuse, include both mesangial hypercellularity and an increase in mesangial matrix. Occasional cases may show a membranoproliferative pattern. In the most severe cases, the glomerular tufts may be infiltrated by polymorphonuclear leukocytes and mononuclear cells, and may exhibit areas of necrosis. Inflammatory changes in the glomerular arterioles and interlobular arteries can also occur but this is not a common finding on renal biopsies. Electron microscopy shows mesangial deposits that may extend into the subendothelial area. Subepithelial deposits similar to those in membranous nephropathy or resembling the humps of postinfectious glomerulonephritis may also be seen.[338,342] The most distinctive feature is the demonstration of IgA by immunofluorescence. As in IgA nephropathy, the deposits can also contain IgG, IgM, C3, and properdin, but not C4 or C1q. This had led to the notion that IgA nephropathy and Henoch–Schönlein purpura are spectra of the same disease.

Mixed cryoglobulinemia

Cryoglobulins are complexes of one or more different classes of immunoglobulins that precipitate at low temperatures (4°C) and become soluble again when the temperature is elevated (30°C). Three types of cryoglobulinemia are recognized.[343] In type I, the cryoglobulin is a single monoclonal immunoglobulin class usually generated by a lymphoproliferative malignancy such as multiple myeloma or Waldenström's macroglobulinemia. Type II is a mixture of at least two immunoglobulins, one

of them a monoclonal antibody directed against polyclonal IgG. The most common combination is IgG–IgM in which the monoclonal IgM usually possesses rheumatoid factor activity. In type III, both immunoglobulin components are polyclonal IgG and IgM in most cases. Mixed cryoglobulins (types II and III) can be found in the serum of patients with a variety of clinical conditions including some lymphoproliferative disorders, chronic infections, chronic liver disease, and autoimmune diseases, particularly systemic lupus erythematosus.[343,345,346,349,350] In the past, there was no clear cause in approximately 30% of all mixed cryoglobulinemias; these were termed "essential," "primary," or "idiopathic" mixed cryoglobulinemia. However, recent studies have clearly documented the hepatitis C virus as a major cause of cryoglobulin production in most patients previously believed to have essential mixed cryoglobulinemia.[349,351,352]

A distinctive clinical syndrome characterized by a variable combination of fatigue, purpura, arthralgias, hepatosplenomegaly, lymphadenopathy, Raynaud's phenomenon, and glomerulonephritis has been observed in patients with mixed cryoglobulinemia. Both sexes are affected, although it is most common in women in the fourth and fifth decades.[344] Purpura is almost always present and is usually distributed over the lower extremities. Renal disease occurs in about 50% of the patients and becomes apparent 1 to 3 years after the purpura, but it can be a presenting symptom.[350] Typical clinical manifestations are nephrotic-range proteinuria, microscopic hematuria, and hypertension. Acute nephritic syndrome occurs in 20% to 30% of the cases, and oliguric acute renal failure in approximately 5% of patients with renal disease.

The most common finding in renal biopsies from patients with mixed cryoglobulinemia is a diffuse proliferative glomerulonephritis (often with a membranoproliferative pattern). Focal and segmental glomerulonephritis, and, less frequently, membranous or crescentic glomerulonephritis, can also occur. In more acute cases, the deposits produce the appearance of thrombi or wire loops comparable to what is seen in lupus glomerulonephritis. Vasculitis is the basic pathologic lesion in every affected tissue including the kidney, where it tends to involve the interlobular arteries and afferent arterioles. Electron microscopy often demonstrates large amounts of subendothelial immune complex deposits and, less frequently, mesangial, intramembranous, or subepithelial deposits. In approximately half of the cases, the glomerular deposits present a fibrillary or tubular structure forming bundles or arranged in a fingerprint-like array (Fig. 17.58).[347,348] In some cases, it is possible to find rhomboid or needle-shaped crystals in the cytoplasm of endothelial and mesangial cells.[353,354] Immunofluorescence usually demonstrates positivity for the immunoglobulins present in the cryoglobulins in the glomeruli and vessels. C3 is often found in these loca-

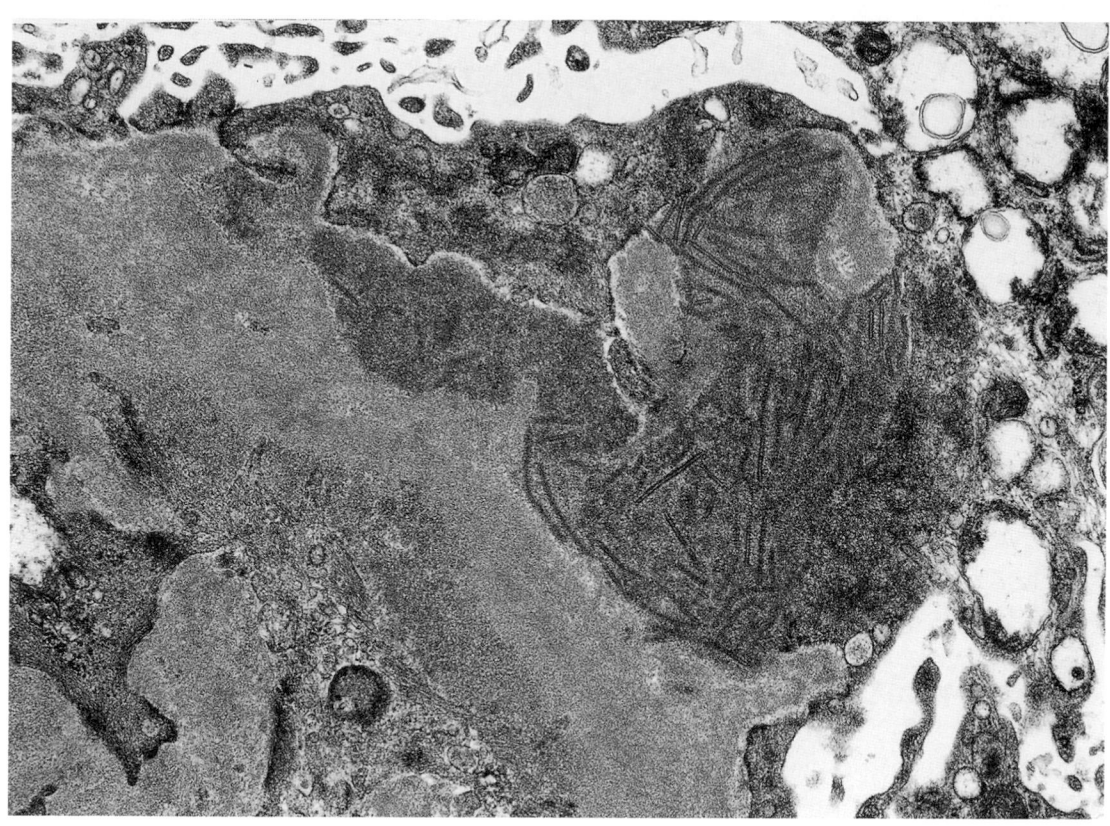

Fig. 17.58 Subepithelial deposits demonstrating fibrillary configuration in a case of cryoglobulinemia. (× 21,500)

tions, whereas C1q and C4 occur in only about one third of the cases.

Hemolytic uremic syndrome and thrombotic thrombocytopenic purpura

Hemolytic uremic syndrome (HUS) and thrombotic thrombocytopenic purpura (TTP) encompass a group of conditions characterized by microangiopathic hemolytic anemia, thrombocytopenia, and variable organ impairment. Traditionally, the diagnosis of HUS is made when renal failure is the predominant feature and children are primarily affected, whereas the term TTP is used for adult patients having predominantly central nervous system impairment. It is now recognized, however, that HUS and TTP are part of a clinical spectrum in which the manifestations of the disease depend on the distribution of the microangiopathy. The overlapping of clinical features and difficulty in distinguishing between both syndromes have led to the terms TTP/HUS, microangiopathic hemolytic anemia, and thrombotic microangiopathy being used sometimes to avoid an uncertain differential diagnosis. *Thrombotic microangiopathy* is the designation given to the vascular lesion that is characterized by widening of the subendothelial space and intraluminal platelet microthrombi typically found in arterioles and capillaries of the kidney, as well as in a variety of other organs, including the brain, gastrointestinal tract, pancreas, skin, heart, spleen, and adrenal glands.

The underlying causes of HUS have been broadly divided into diarrhea-associated (D+ HUS), also known as classic HUS, and nondiarrheal forms (D− HUS).[368] The classic form occurs primarily in infants and young children but may appear at any age, and both sexes are equally affected. It accounts for most of the cases of HUS in North America and is characterized by occasional occurrence in small epidemics after exposure to contaminated foods, especially undercooked ground beef, unpasteurized apple juice, and dairy products with verotoxin-producing *Escherichia coli* 0157:H7 and, less commonly, with *Shigella dysenteriae* type I.[359,362] Patients usually present with prodromal diarrhea (often bloody) followed by acute renal failure. Approximately one third of the patients may present symptoms of neurologic involvement, commonly manifested by seizures, altered consciousness, and focal neurologic signs. Because the thrombotic microangiopathy is most often confined to the glomeruli, patients with classic HUS usually have a good prognosis and recovery occurs in about 80% to 90% of the cases. Approximately 5% of the patients, however, die of disease, usually of cerebral causes.

Nondiarrheal (D−) HUS is much less common than the classic type. It most frequently affects older children and adults and has a less favorable prognosis than D+ HUS.[365] The etiology of D− HUS is heterogeneous. It can be associated with nonenteric infections caused by bacteria such as *Streptococcus pneumoniae*, or viruses such as influenza A virus and human immunodeficiency virus (HIV).[355,357,361] Some forms of D− HUS are hereditary, can occur at any age, follow a relapsing pattern, and are transmitted either as an autosomal recessive or an autosomal

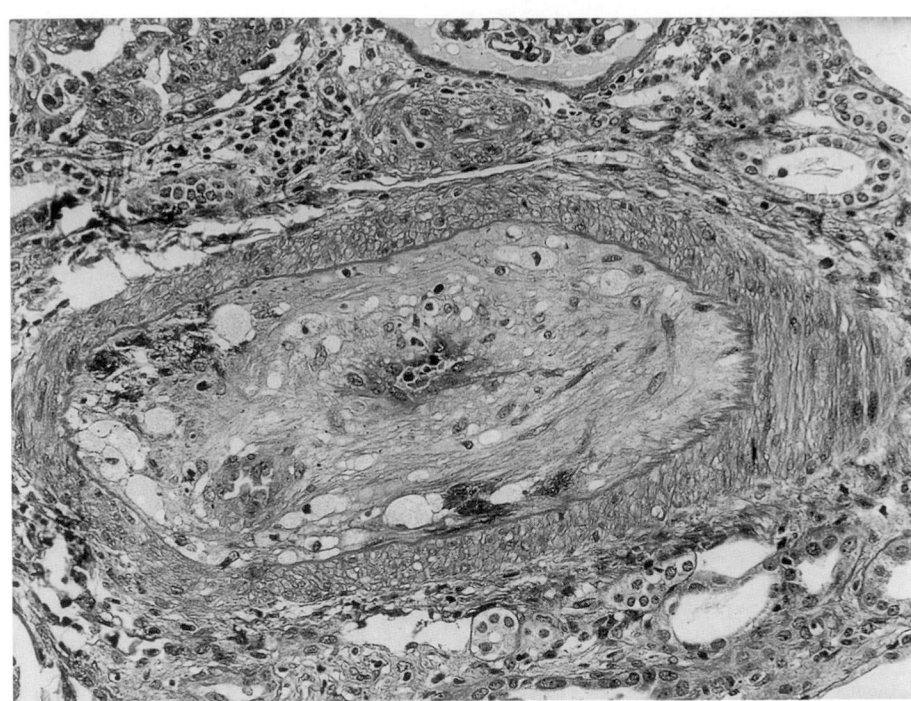

Fig. 17.59 Interlobular artery with prominent mucinous subintimal proliferation in hemolytic uremic syndrome. The lumen is almost completely occluded and some cells have foamy cytoplasm.

dominant trait.[367] They can also occur in association with disorders such as systemic lupus erythematosus, systemic sclerosis, and malignant hypertension, or various forms of cancer, especially prostatic, gastric, breast, and pancreatic carcinomas.[360,368,369] HUS can be induced by total body irradiation, chemotherapy, or immunosuppressive drugs (mitomycin C, cisplatin, cyclosporine), quinine, and oral contraceptives.[358,360,365,369,370] A severe form occurs in association with pregnancy, especially in the postpartum period.[363,364] The prognosis of these patients is poor with a high mortality rate from central nervous system disease or uncontrollable bleeding; if they survive, they usually develop chronic renal failure.

The pathogenesis of HUS is complex and not completely understood; however, it is best explained as local endothelial damage caused by toxins such as verotoxins and Shiga toxins, by lytic anti-endothelial cell antibodies, or by agents such as cyclosporine and mitomycin C, in the nonclassic forms. Damage to the endothelium induces the release of von Willebrand multimers, causes platelet aggregation, and affects prostacyclin (PGI$_2$) synthesis by the endothelial cells. This leads to the formation of thrombi in the glomeruli and arterioles, intimal proliferation of the interlobular arteries, microangiopathic hemolytic anemia, thrombocytopenia, and acute renal failure.[356,366,369]

A biopsy taken early in the course of the disease shows fibrinoid necrosis, intimal and subintimal fibrin deposits with red cell insudation, thrombosis, and endothelial cell proliferation in small arteries and arterioles. The glomeruli exhibit acute ischemic changes, and some may be infarcted. There is endothelial swelling with narrow-ing of the capillary lumen. The mesangium is expanded and, in severe cases, mesangiolysis may occur. As the lesion progresses, there is an intense basophilic intimal thickening in the small arteries and arterioles which greatly restricts the vascular lumen. These mucoid intimal changes usually develop over several weeks, although they may be seen very early in the course of the disease (Fig. 17.59). Aneurysmal dilatation, accompanied by proliferation of some arterioles, particularly at the hilus of the glomerulus (glomeruloid body) is a typical finding (Fig. 17.60).

Electron microscopy reveals the most characteristic feature of HUS: narrowing of the capillary lumen as a result of marked widening of the subendothelial space,

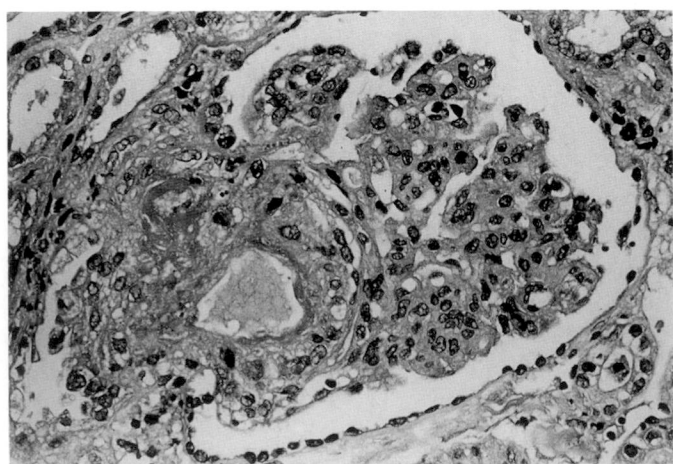

Fig. 17.60 Glomerulus from a patient with hemolytic uremic syndrome showing aneurysmal dilation, endothelial proliferation, and thrombosis of the afferent arteriole.

which becomes filled with a pale, finely particulate or fibrillar material that stains positively for fibrinogen by immunohistochemical methods (Fig. 17.61). An irregular, thin layer of basement membrane-like substance is present between the endothelial cell cytoplasm and the electron-lucent area. Because of its argyrophilic characteristics, this material can produce a double contour on light microscopy, thus simulating a membranoprolifera-

tive pattern. Fibrin and platelet aggregates may occlude the capillary lumen, and the endothelium is often disrupted in these thrombosed areas. The mesangial cells are swollen and hypertrophic and contain many phagolysosomes. Extensive foot process obliteration is seen in the areas of collapse. In the later stages, interlobular arteries and arterioles are affected by a mucinous, onionskin-like obliterating endarteritis (Fig. 17.62). The

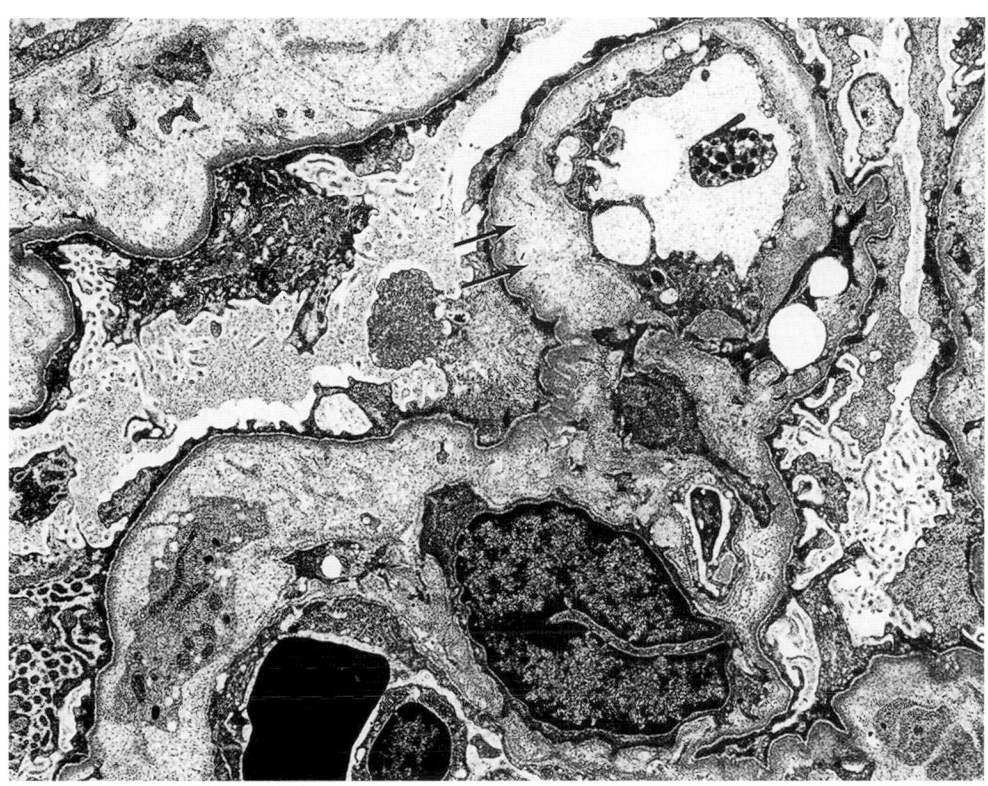

Fig. 17.61 Portion of a glomerulus showing a prominent subendothelial electron-lucent zone (arrows) in a case of hemolytic uremic syndrome. (× 9000)

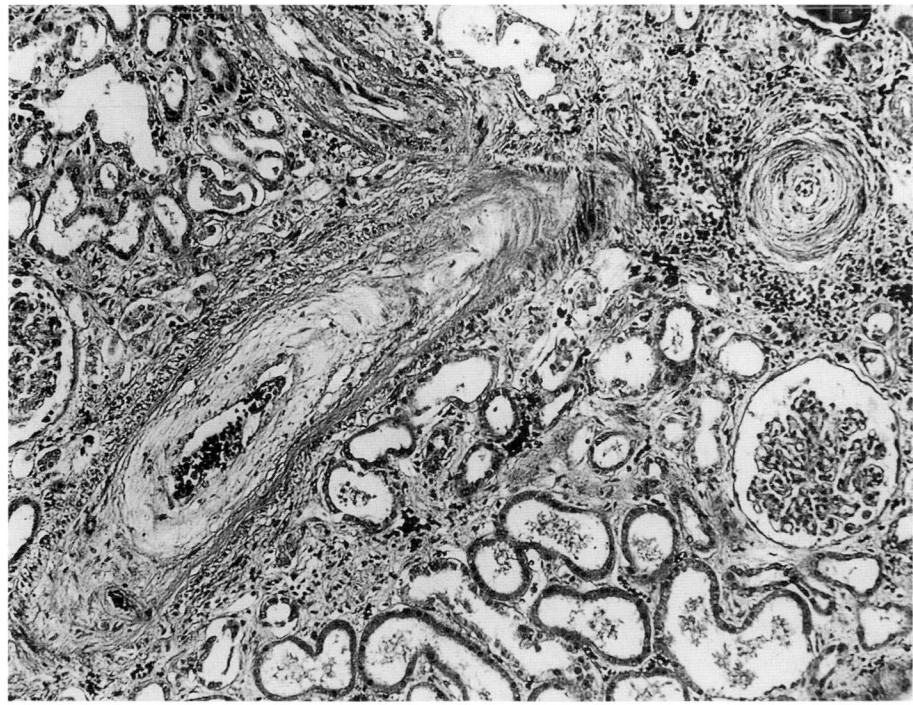

Fig. 17.62 Interlobular arteries showing stenosing intimal proliferation in hemolytic uremic syndrome.

vascular lesions are similar to those of systemic sclerosis and malignant hypertension, so careful analysis of the clinical data is required.

Systemic sclerosis

Systemic sclerosis, progressive systemic sclerosis, and systemic scleroderma are terms used to designate a connective tissue disorder of unknown etiology characterized by multiple organ system involvement. The clinical features of the disease are produced by differing combinations of excessive collagen deposition and vascular disease, the former causing deformity and morbidity, and the latter being the mechanism of most of the systemic complications. Raynaud's syndrome, skin thickening, digital pulp atrophy, and telangiectasia are the primary clinical manifestations of systemic sclerosis. Musculoskeletal involvement includes periarticular tendon and nerve entrapment, flexion contractures, acral osteolysis, and myopathy. In the alimentary tract, the disease can cause esophageal dysmotility and malabsorption. Pulmonary hypertension and interstitial fibrosis, cardiomyopathy, and scleroderma renal crisis are the major causes of mortality. Systemic sclerosis predominantly affects women, in a ratio of approximately 3:1.[372] It may occur at any age, but is more common between the fourth and sixth decades of life. The disease is rare in children.[373] Renal involvement occurs in 60% to 70% of the patients.[371] Two clinical forms of renal involvement have been recognized: an acute and rapidly progressive form of renal failure often associated with malignant hypertension, systemic vasoconstriction, and microangiopathic hemolytic anemia; and a more common, slowly progressive chronic form which is manifested by varying combinations of proteinuria, hypertension, and azotemia.

The main morphologic changes in the acute form of renal failure are in the interlobular arteries which show intimal thickening by loose, myxoid fibrous tissue. Subendothelial fibrin deposition and intimal hemorrhage may also be seen. Arterioles frequently exhibit fibrinoid necrosis and thrombosis. The glomeruli show varying degrees of acute ischemic changes and, on occasion, intracapillary fibrin thrombi. By electron microscopy, affected blood vessels show intimal widening by amorphous electron-lucent material corresponding to the myxoid ground substance seen by light microscopy. The glomeruli present basement membrane wrinkling with focal widening of the subendothelial area, which may contain fibrin strands. In the chronic form, the vascular lumina of the arteries are narrowed by dense concentric intimal fibroelastosis. In addition, there are varying degrees of glomerulosclerosis, tubular atrophy, and interstitial scarring. Immunofluorescence studies often demonstrate reactivity for fibrinogen, with or without IgM and C3, in the intima of blood vessels and along the glomerular capillaries. The pathogenesis of the vascular lesions in systemic sclerosis is not well understood.

Increased vascular reactivity to vasoconstrictor agents and intravascular coagulation are believed to play an important role in the pathogenesis of the accelerated form of the disease. Since the renal lesions in systemic sclerosis, HUS, and malignant hypertension can be identical, careful evaluation of the patient's clinical history and laboratory data are essential in establishing the differential diagnosis.

Renal diseases of pregnancy

Renal disease may be initiated or exacerbated during pregnancy. Because of the extent and complexity of the topic and space limitations, only preeclampsia will be discussed here.

Preeclampsia

Preeclampsia is a pregnancy-induced disease characterized by hypertension, proteinuria, and edema, and at times, coagulation and liver disorders. It develops in 5% to 7% of first pregnancies, usually appearing after the 20th gestational week, and accounts for over 50% of the hypertensive disorders complicating pregnancy. When the disease progresses to a convulsive stage, it is termed eclampsia. Preeclampsia is six to eight times more common in primiparas than in multiparas and it occurs most commonly at the extremes of reproductive age.[376] When it occurs in multiparas, it is likely to be associated with multifetal pregnancy, or fetal hydrops, or to coexist with essential hypertension or renal disease. The etiology of preeclampsia is unknown. Coagulation abnormalities, hormonal factors, uteroplacental ischemia, and immune mechanisms have all been implicated in the pathogenesis of this condition.[374] Current evidence indicates that some type of endothelial cell injury with local activation of intravascular coagulation is likely to be the cause of the renal lesions.[377,378]

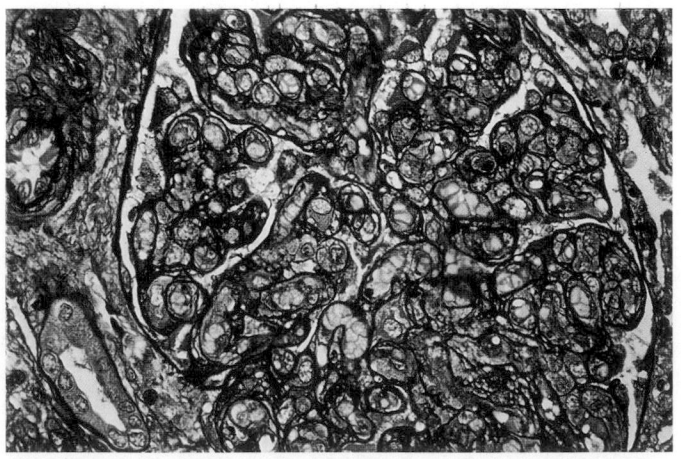

Fig. 17.63 Preeclamptic nephropathy. The capillary lumina are obliterated by swollen endothelial cells.

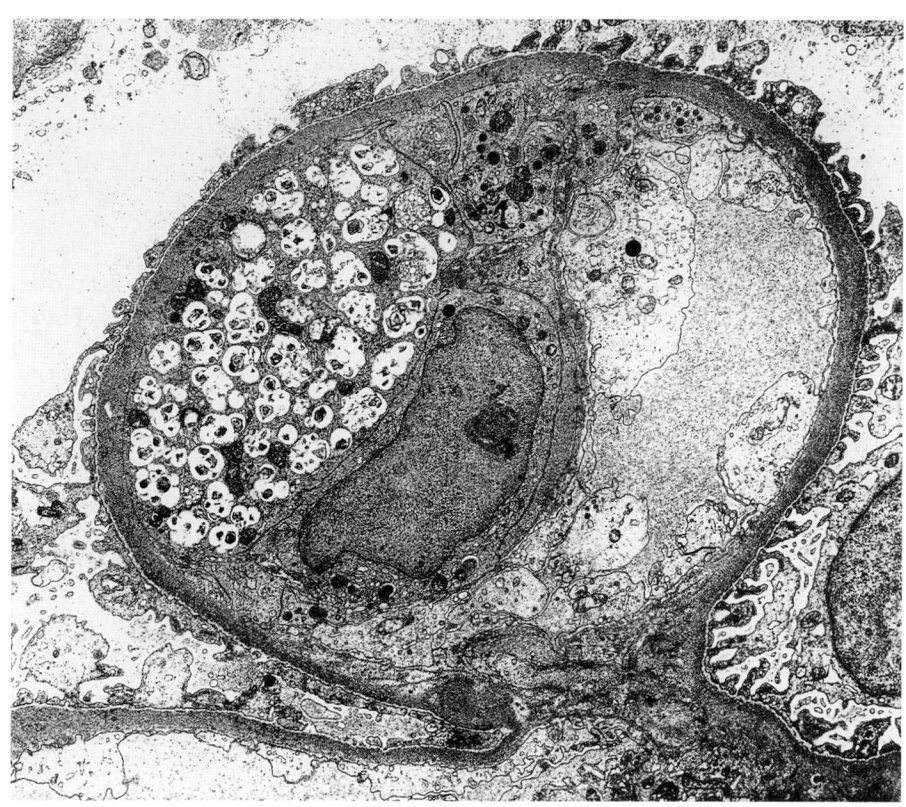

Fig. 17.64 The capillary lumen is narrowed by swollen cytoplasm containing membranous structures, some of which have the appearance of myelin-like figures. (× 7200)

The changes in preeclamptic nephropathy occur primarily in the glomeruli, which characteristically appear enlarged, swollen, and bloodless, with little or no hypercellularity (Fig. 17.63). On occasion, glomerular swelling results in herniation of the capillary tuft into the neck of the proximal tubule ("pouting"). Crescent formation is rare and only occurs in the most severe cases.[375] With the electron microscope, various types of vacuoles can be seen in the cytoplasm of the reactive endothelial and mesangial cells. The most prominent endothelial cell vacuoles are clear and limited by a single membrane. The capillary lumen may be narrowed or obliterated by swollen cytoplasm: early descriptions of this change were labeled endotheliosis, but the mesangial cells are actually more involved. The mesangial change is more variable and consists of a wide variety of lysosomal structures, some of which have a myeloid figure appearance, while others appear as bland lipids of varying electron density (Fig. 17.64). When mesangial cell hypertrophy is severe, the mesangium may become interposed between the endothelium and the basement membrane. In many instances, an amorphous extracellular electron-dense material separates the swollen cells at points where there is severe narrowing of the capillary lumen. Distinct strands of fibrin are present in the most severe cases. Translucent subendothelial zones containing loose fibrillar material can occasionally be seen.[379] Immunofluorescence studies have shown that the deposits in the glomeruli consist mainly of fibrinogen. Immunoglobulins, especially IgM, may on occasion be present

and it is believed that this is the result of nonspecific trapping in injured glomeruli. The afferent arterioles are not sclerotic and their endothelial cells retain a normal appearance that is in striking contrast to the swollen, vacuolated glomerular endothelial cells. Patients in whom preeclamptic nephropathy is superimposed on essential hypertension have hypertensive arterial and arteriolar changes in addition to the glomerular lesion. Preeclampsia usually carries a good prognosis. The changes in the glomerular capillaries disappear in a few weeks following delivery, and blood pressure falls to normal levels within a month.

Hereditary glomerular diseases

Alport's syndrome (hereditary nephritis)

Alport's syndrome is an inherited type IV collagen disorder of the basement membranes manifested by hematuria, progressive nephritis with proteinuria and declining renal function, deafness, and ocular abnormalities.[392,396,397] Bilateral, high-frequency, sensorineural hearing loss occurs in approximately 55% of males and females with the disease.[406] The severity of the deafness is variable and in some patients it is only detectable by audiometric testing.[406] Hearing impairment is always accompanied by renal involvement but there is no relationship between the severity of the hearing loss and renal disease. Ocular abnormalities occur in 15% to 30%

of the patients and appear to be confined to juvenile kindreds.[385] Anterior lenticonus, a forward central protrusion of the anterior surface of the ocular lens resulting from a weakness in the type IV collagen forming the anterior lens capsule, is virtually pathognomonic of Alport's syndrome.[403] Other ocular abnormalities include keratoconus, spherophakia, myopia, retinal flecks, cataracts, retinitis pigmentosa, and amaurosis.[385] Other uncommon variants of Alport's syndrome include the association of hereditary nephritis with megathrombocytopenia (Epstein syndrome),[386] inclusions in leukocytes (Fechtner syndrome),[402] diffuse leiomyomatosis (esophagus, tracheobronchial tree, and urogenital tract),[380,381] ichthyosis, and hyperprolinuria.[388] Alport's syndrome is a genetically heterogeneous disorder. Approximately 80% to 85% of the patients have the X-linked form of the syndrome resulting from a mutation of *COL4A5*, the gene located at Xq22 that codes for the α5 chain of type IV collagen.[382,399] Most of the remaining patients have autosomal recessive Alport's syndrome due to mutations in either *COL4A3* or *COL4A4*, while a minority of families exhibit autosomal dominant disease that may also arise from mutations in these genes.[394] To date, approximately 300 different mutations have been identified in X-linked Alport's syndrome by different groups of investigators in various parts of the world.[392]

Hereditary nephritis with and without deafness has been reported in patients from a wide variety of geographic regions and different ethnic groups. In the United States, Alport's syndrome accounts for 2.5% of children and 0.3% of adults with end-stage renal disease (ESRD).[387] Males are more commonly affected than females. The disorder is usually manifested in children and young adults by recurrent microscopic or gross hematuria. Proteinuria is usually mild, but in advanced stages of the disease it can become sufficiently severe to cause the nephrotic syndrome. In males, the disease is usually progressive. Females may also progress to end-stage renal failure, but it is much less common. In families with autosomal inheritance, females are affected as severely and as early as males. Based on the progression to ESRD within affected families, two main clinical variants of Alport's syndrome have been recognized: a "juvenile" form in which ESRD occurs in males before the age of 31 years, and an "adult" variant in which ESRD occurs in males at a mean age greater than 31 years.[389] The clinical course of patients in the former group tends to be highly stereotypical, whereas the course of those in the latter group is more diverse and the prognosis in individual cases is more difficult to predict.[390] Patients with Alport's syndrome lack a component of the glomerular basement membrane. After transplantation, 3% to 4% of male patients develop anti-GBM nephritis, presumably because tolerance to the normal antigen has not been acquired.[392,397,400] The target(s) of the anti-GBM antibody in some patients has been established with variable results. Most patients with X-linked Alport's syndrome show antibodies against the NC1 domain of the α5 chain of collagen IV, but antibodies to the NC1 domain of the α3 chain have also been described.[384,395]

The light microscopic features in the kidney are nonspecific and the diagnosis depends on the electron microscopic and immunofluorescence findings. Most biopsies exhibit both glomerular and tubulointerstitial changes. In biopsies taken in the early stage of the disease, the glomeruli appear normal or may show mild mesangial hypercellularity with minor thickening of the capillary walls. As the disease progresses, however, the glomeruli undergo segmental and global sclerosis. Tubular interstitial changes appear relatively early, and consist of irregular areas of nonspecific sclerosis. The presence of interstitial foamy cells in the absence of nephrotic-range proteinuria is a characteristic but nonspecific feature of Alport's syndrome.

The most significant morphologic finding of Alport's syndrome can only be seen by electron microscopic examination of the glomeruli.[383] The typical lesion is thickening of the GBM with transformation of the lamina densa into multiple interwoven lamellae 30 to 100 nm wide which enclose electron-lucent areas containing round granules of variable density measuring 20 to 50 nm in diameter (Fig. 17.65). The nature of these granules is unknown but they may represent degenerating islands of visceral epithelial cell cytoplasm.[405] The epithelial aspect of the basement membrane often has a scalloped appearance, whereas the endothelial surface is usually smooth. Similar lesions can occur in the basement membranes of the Bowman's capsule and tubules; however, they do not have the same diagnostic value when seen in these locations. The typical lesion of the GBM occurs in most, but not all, patients with Alport's syndrome. Affected young males, heterozygous females of any age, and affected adult males may have attenuated GBM which can measure as little as 100 nm or even less.[396] Studies of males with human or canine Alport's syndrome have shown that the earliest manifestation of the GBM lesion is thinning of the GBM and that the extent and severity of the multilamellation increases with age.[393] Heterozygous females may have normal appearing GBM or, at the other end of the spectrum, diffuse GBM thickening with multilamellation, but most will exhibit mild to moderate abnormalities.[401] Some authors have found a correlation between the percentage of the GBM having a splitting of the lamina densa and the degree of proteinuria in patients with Alport's syndrome, which suggests that the increased permeability of the GBM to protein is the functional consequence of the GBM alteration.[404] Although multilamellation of the GBM suggests hereditary nephritis, it can also be seen in other conditions, such as in the resolving stages of membranous glomerulonephritis.[391]

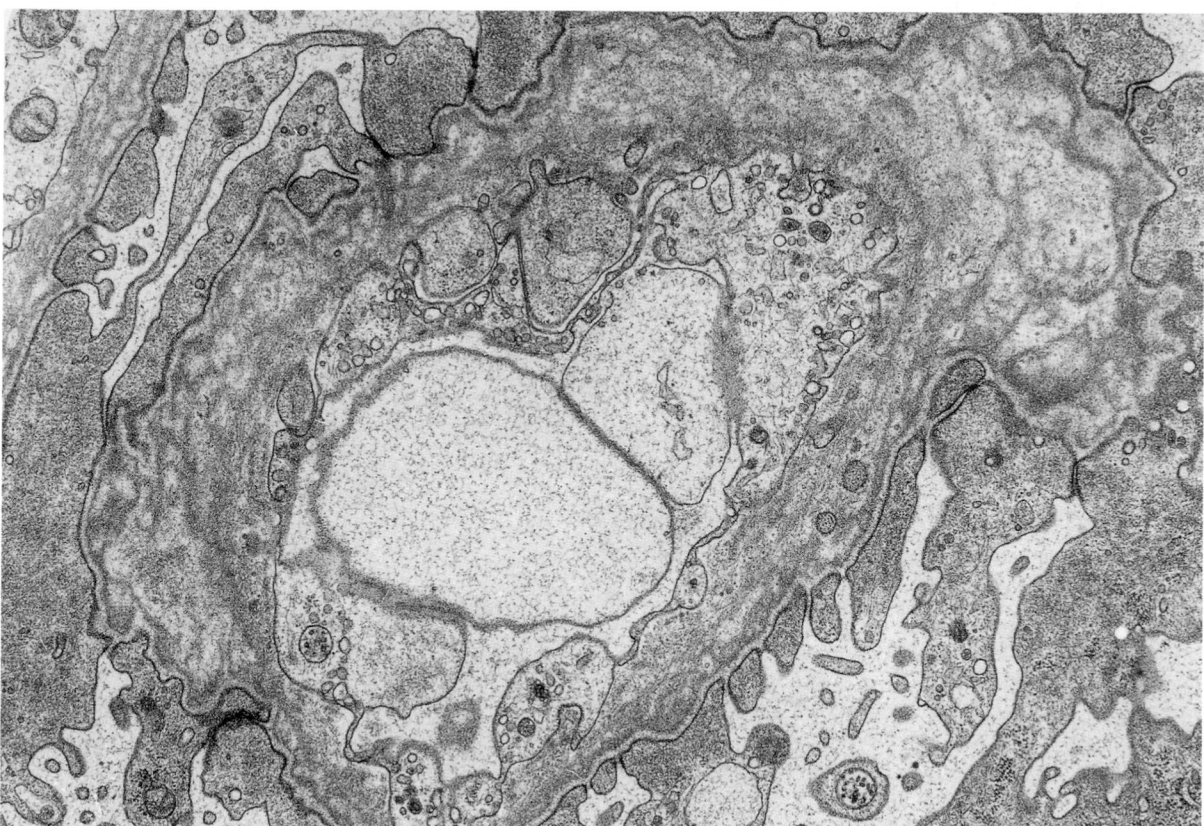

Fig. 17.65 Glomerular capillary loop showing diffuse, irregular, thickening of the GBM. The lamina densa is split into multiple interwoven lamellae. (× 11,400)

The panel of antibodies used in routine immunofluorescence studies usually fails to show any reactivity, although small and scattered deposits of IgM and C3 can sometimes be seen. The recent commercial availability of specific monoclonal antibodies directed against different subunits of type IV collagen has greatly facilitated the diagnosis of Alport's syndrome. Kidneys from individuals who are not affected by Alport's syndrome show strong continuous immunostaining with antibodies to the α3, α4, and α5 chains along the GBM, and the basement membrane of Bowman's capsule and the distal convoluted tubules. This reactivity is absent in male patients with X-linked Alport's syndrome. Skin biopsies examined by immunofluorescence can also be an important diagnostic tool since the α5 chain is expressed in the normal epidermal basement membrane but not in X-linked Alport's syndrome patients. Therefore, in male patients with a clinical and familial history suggestive of X-linked Alport's syndrome, skin examination for α5 chain may obviate the necessity for a kidney biopsy. It should be kept in mind, however, that some affected males will express α5 chain in their basement membranes.[398] A mosaic staining pattern (interrupted or segmentally weaker staining) for α5 chain is frequently seen in the epidermal and renal basement membranes of heterozygous females. While this finding is diagnostic of the carrier state, a normal result does not exclude heterozygosity.

The immunohistochemical findings in the basement membranes of patients with Alport's syndrome are summarized in Table 17.9. Immunofluorescence studies of patients suspected to have Alport's syndrome should include staining with anti-GBM antibodies obtained from patients with anti-GBM disease or from patients with Alport's syndrome who had developed anti-GBM disease after transplantation. Because these antibodies stain the GBM of patients with familial thin GBM disease, but not that of patients with Alport's syndrome, they assist in discriminating between the two conditions.

When the diagnosis of Alport's syndrome cannot be unequivocally excluded or if it cannot be determined based on a careful analysis of the family history, molecular genetic studies may be considered. The only way to determine with certainty whether a female relative of a patient with X-linked Alport's syndrome is a carrier of the disease is by molecular genetic analysis, either through linkage analysis or by mutation identification. This is also the only method of prenatal diagnosis for Alport's syndrome.

Thin glomerular basement membrane disease

The descriptive term thin glomerular basement membrane disease is used to designate a hereditary renal disease that is characterized by uniform thinning of the GBM and normal patient survival without deterioration

Table 17.9 Immunohistochemical findings in the basement membranes of patients with Alport syndrome using antibodies to α3, α4, and α5 chains of type IV collagen

	Glomerular basement membrane	Bowman's capsule	Distal tubular basement membrane	Epidermal basement membrane
Normal (both sexes)				
α3	Present	Present	Present	Absent
α4	Present	Present	Present	Absent
α5	Present	Present	Present	Present
X-linked (males)				
α3	Absent	Absent	Absent	Absent
α4	Absent	Absent	Absent	Absent
α5	Absent	Absent	Absent	Absent
X-linked (females)				
α3	Mosaic	—	—	Absent
α4	Mosaic	—	—	Absent
α5	Mosaic	—	—	Absent
Autosomal recessive (both sexes)				
α3	Absent	Absent	Absent	Absent
α4	Absent	Absent	Absent	Absent
α5	Absent	Present	Present	Present

Modified from: Kashtan CE. Alport syndrome: An inherited disorder of renal, ocular, and cochlear basement membranes. Medicine 1999, **78**: 338–360.

of renal function. Benign familial hematuria is another designation that has also been used for this condition; however, it is now considered inappropriate since it could embrace other pathologic entities, such as familial cases of IgA nephropathy, in which the prognosis is not always "benign." Although thin basement membrane disease (TBMD) has generally been considered an autosomal dominant hereditary condition, recent genetic studies suggest that it is a heterogeneous disease and that in some cases it may be autosomal recessive related to mutations of the *COL4A3* and *COL4A4* genes.[409,414,418] It has been suggested that patients with TBMD exhibiting these mutations are carriers of autosomal recessive Alport's syndrome and that TBMD falls within the spectrum of type IV collagen diseases.[409,414,418]

The true incidence of TBMD is unknown but some studies have estimated that 20% to 25% of patients with isolated hematuria have the disease.[417,420,423] Both sexes are equally affected and the condition may occur in children and adults, but it is seldom reported after 50 years of age. The onset of the hematuria is usually in childhood and it is typically microscopic and persistent; on occasion, however, it may be macroscopic and recurrent. Mild proteinuria is not uncommon and has been described in up to 60% of the reported cases.[419] Heavy proteinuria in the nephrotic range has been documented in rare instances.[413,419] It has been suggested, however, that the nephrotic syndrome in these cases is probably unrelated to TBMD per se, but rather represents a manifestation of its coexistence with other glomerular lesions, such as minimal change disease, IgA nephropathy, focal glomerulosclerosis, or membranous glomerulonephritis.[410,419] In contrast to patients with Alport's syndrome, those with TBMD have only rarely been reported to exhibit any of the extrarenal manifestations of Alport's syndrome.[407,415] Nonfamilial cases of TBMD have been reported, but these studies often lack rigorous testing of family members.

Aside from the finding of erythrocytes in the Bowman's space and renal tubules, renal biopsies appear normal by light microscopy. The diagnosis is made by ultrastructural demonstration of uniform thinning of the lamina densa of the GBM (Fig. 17.66). The overall width of the GBM is reduced to one third or approximately 200 nm,[408,411,417] and, on occasion, ruptures of the GBM may be found.[422] Immunofluorescence studies are usually negative for immunoglobulins and complement components, but deposits of IgM and IgG, with and without C3, have occasionally been reported.[414] Immunohistochemical evaluation for type IV collagen may assist in distinguishing TBMD from Alport's syndrome.[415] A normal distribution of type IV collagen α chains is supportive of the diagnosis of TBMD. In contrast to Alport's syndrome, antibodies to the NC1 domain react with the GBM from patients with TBMD, a finding that could also assist in the differential diagnosis between these two conditions.[412,416,421]

Angiokeratoma corporis diffusum universale

Angiokeratoma corporis diffusum universale, better known as Fabry's disease, is an X-linked inborn disorder of glycosphingolipid metabolism caused by the absence

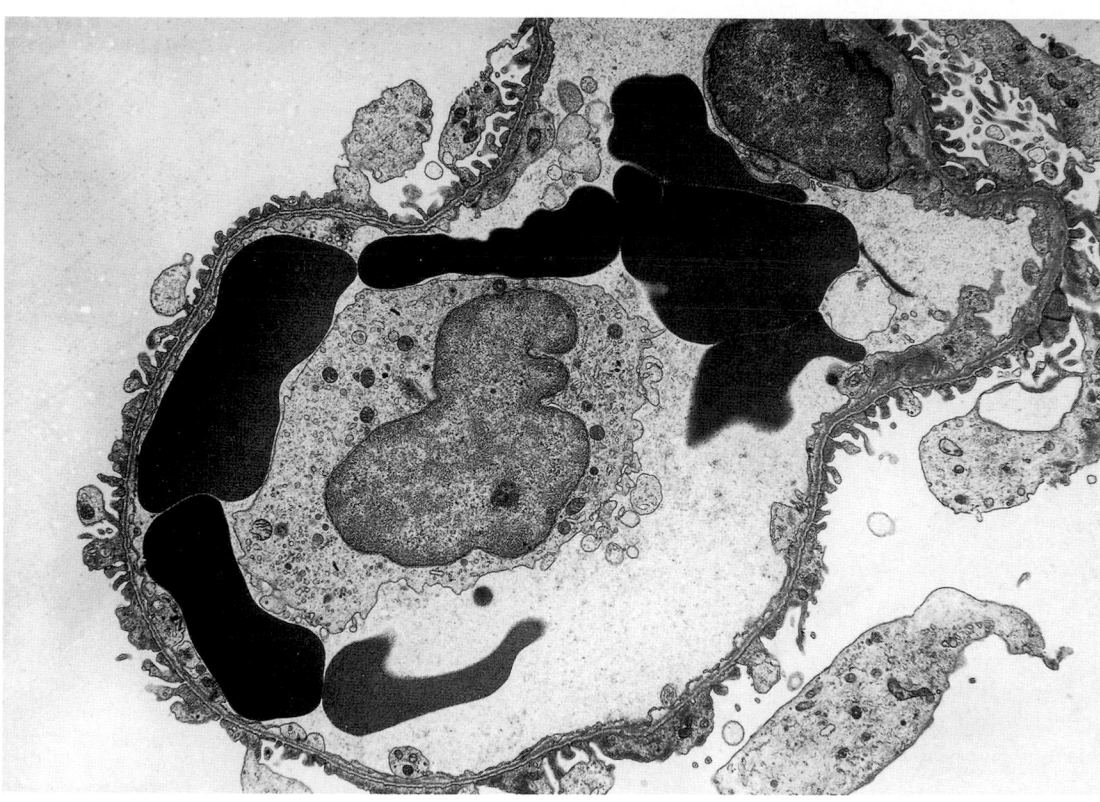

Fig. 17.66 Capillary loop showing marked uniform thinning of the GBM. (× 4200) (Reproduced from Spargo BH, Seymour AE, Ordóñez NG. Introduction. In: Renal biopsy pathology with diagnostic and therapeutic implications. New York, 1980, John Wiley & Sons, pp. 1–13. By permission of John Wiley & Sons, Inc.)

of α-galactosidase A, a lysosomal enzyme whose gene is located on the long arm of the X chromosome q21–22.[426,431] The entire gene has been coded.[427] Specific molecular defects vary from family to family and include rearrangement, deletions, and point mutations.[424,425,432] The consequence of the deficiency is that neutral glycosphingolipids, predominantly ceramide trihexoside and cerebroside dihexoside, accumulate in many tissues and organs, including the kidney. Progressive lysosomal storage of these glycosphingolipids causes a characteristic, albeit protean, clinical syndrome of punctate skin lesions, renal disease, and recurrent "shooting" pains in the lower extremities. The skin lesions consist of innumerable small angiokeratomas scattered over the body, especially the abdomen, buttocks, lips, genitalia, and upper thighs. Systemic manifestations result from deposition of glycosphingolipids in blood vessels, heart, and kidney. Female carriers, being heterozygous for the genetic abnormality, are usually only mildly affected.

Renal involvement is often manifested by hematuria and proteinuria in the second decade of life, followed by gradual deterioration of renal function in the third and fourth decades. Death occurs around the fifth decade from renal, cardiac, or cerebrovascular involvement. Early reports suggested that renal transplantation might provide a source for the missing enzyme, but subsequent studies have shown no significant release of the renally

generated enzyme into general circulation. Thus, little overall lipid can be mobilized once it has accumulated and the disease continues to progress in the majority of patients despite a successful renal transplant.[428] Recurrence in the transplanted kidney has been reported,[430] but there is no indication that this event has a

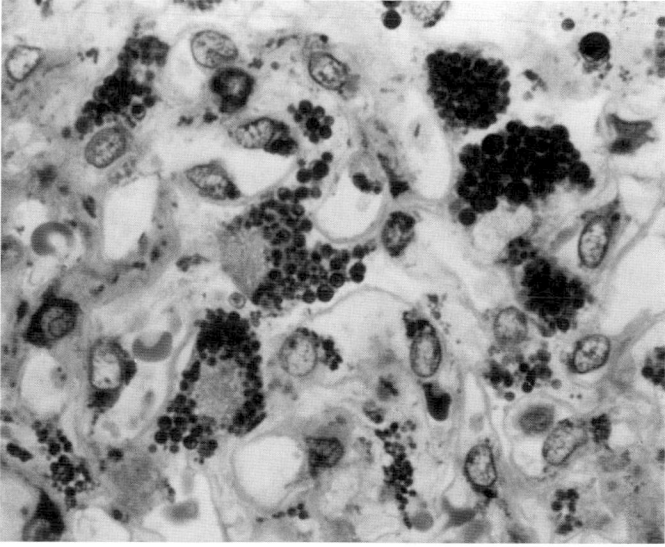

Fig. 17.67 Plastic-embedded semi-thin section of a portion of a glomerulus stained with toluidine blue showing numerous deeply stained epithelial cell inclusions in a case of Fabry's disease.

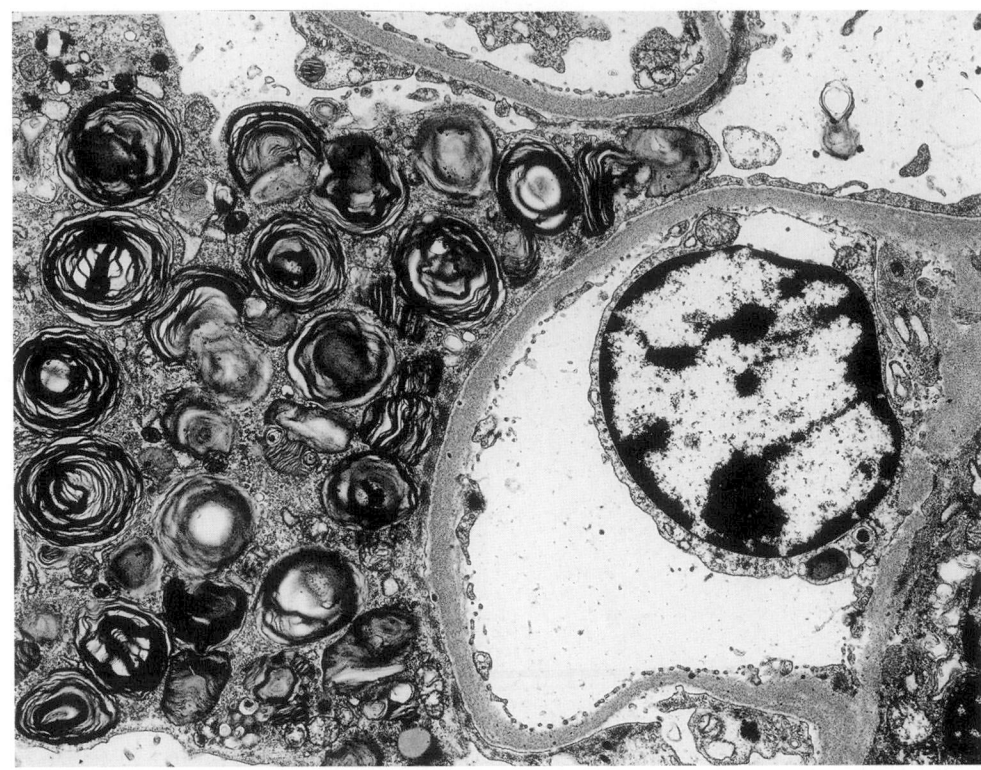

Fig. 17.68 Portion of a glomerulus from a patient with Fabry's disease demonstrating numerous laminated inclusions in the epithelial cell cytoplasm. (× 7750)

significant impact on long-term allograft survival in most patients.[429]

On light microscopy, the visceral epithelial cells are enlarged and vacuolated, giving a honeycomb appearance to the glomeruli. Similar changes are seen in the parietal epithelium of Bowman's capsule, and in mesangial and endothelial cells (Fig. 17.67). By electron microscopy, a vast number of laminated inclusion bodies are present in the cytoplasm of the affected cells. Each is surrounded by a single unit membrane and they measure up to 5 μm in diameter. They are either round with a concentric myelin-like structure, or ovoid with parallel layers ("zebra" bodies; Fig. 17.68). Similar inclusions are present outside the glomeruli in endothelial and smooth muscle cells of blood vessels and in the tubule cells, especially those of the distal convoluted tubule and loop of Henle. This ultrastructural pattern is virtually diagnostic of the disease, but since similar inclusions can occur in other disorders, biochemical studies are required to confirm the diagnosis.

Hereditary onycho-osteodysplasia

Onycho-osteodysplasia, also known as the nail–patella syndrome, Turner–Keiser syndrome, and Fog's syndrome, is an uncommon autosomal dominant disorder characterized by aplasia or dysplasia of the fingernails, especially those of the first fingers, absence or hypoplasia of the patellae, subluxation of the radial head, iliac horns, and less often, certain other skeletal and ocular abnormalities. Molecular studies have linked the syndrome to chromosome 9q34 and identified point mutations in the

LMX1B gene.[434–436] Other kindreds have been linked to chromosome 17q21–22.[437] The incidence of the disease has been estimated at 1 per 50,000 live births.[436] Renal involvement occurs in approximately 30% to 55% of patients. Asymptomatic proteinuria is the most common event but the nephrotic syndrome can occur and some patients progress to renal failure.[438] Light microscopy of the kidney shows nonspecific changes such as focal thickening of the glomerular capillary walls and some glomerular sclerosis. By electron microscopy, the GBM appears irregularly thickened and often exhibits electron-lucent areas, giving it the so-called "moth eaten" appearance. Collagen-like fibers are seen in the electron-lucent areas and in the mesangium (Fig. 17.69).[431] It has been postulated that an enzymatic defect in collagen metabolism plays a role in the pathogenesis of this condition.[433] No recurrence of the renal changes has been seen after transplantation.

Collagen type III glomerulopathy

Due to some ultrastructural similarities with hereditary onycho-osteodysplasia, patients with collagen type III glomerulopathy were initially regarded as having an incomplete, purely renal form of the nail–patella syndrome. However, it is now considered to be a separate clinicopathologic entity which has also been reported under the designations primary glomerular fibrosis[443] and collagenofibrotic glomerulopathy.[440,445] Collagen type III glomerulopathy occurs in both familial and sporadic forms; the familial cases show an autosomal recessive pattern of inheritance. The disease affects both

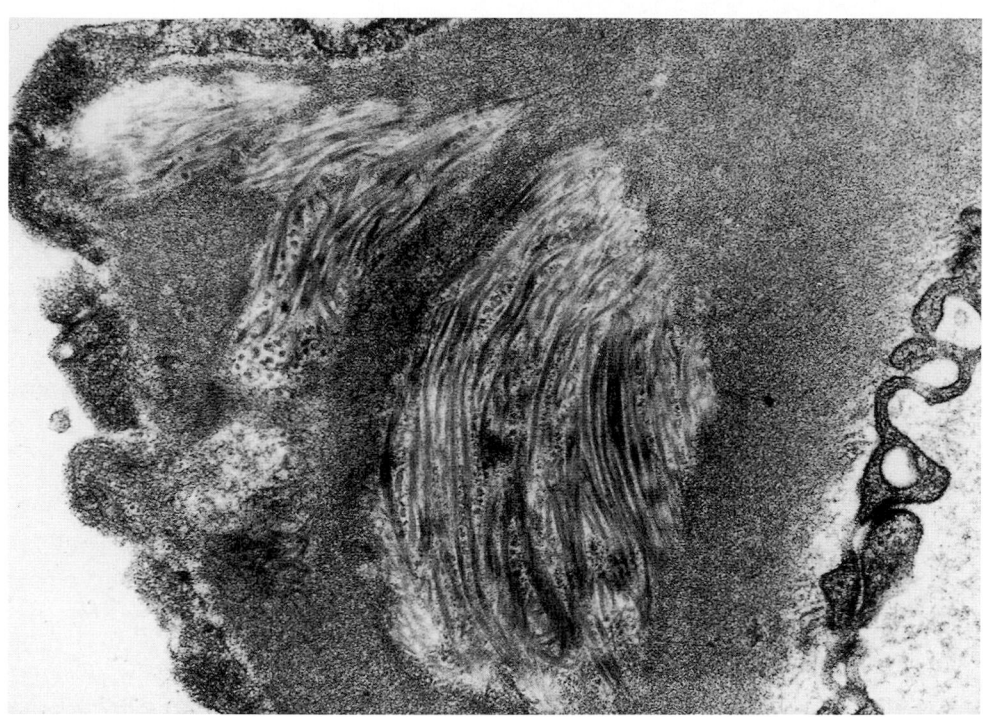

Fig. 17.69 Collagen-like fibers in the GBM in nail–patella syndrome. (× 35,000) (Reproduced from Spargo BH, Seymour AE, Ordóñez NG. Introduction. In: Renal biopsy pathology with diagnostic and therapeutic implications. New York, 1980, John Wiley & Sons, pp. 1–13. By permission of John Wiley & Sons, Inc.)

sexes and can manifest during childhood or adulthood. Children often present with increasing proteinuria leading to the nephrotic syndrome, hypertension, and progressive renal failure. The important feature in these patients is that they can develop superimposed hemolytic uremic syndrome.[441] In adults, the disease often has a more indolent course.[443,444] There are reports in which the disease has been associated with inherited factor H deficiency[447] and hepatic perisinusoidal fibrosis.[445] Elevated serum concentrations of procollagen III may be a useful marker for this condition.[442,443,446]

Light microscopy shows a diffuse increase in the mesangial matrix and generalized widening of the glomerular capillary walls sometimes associated with mesangial interposition. By electron microscopy, there is a large accumulation of collagen fibrils in the glomeruli, particularly in the subendothelial aspect of the GBM and in the mesangial matrix. Conventional immunofluorescence studies are either negative or show focal nonspecific deposits of immunoglobulins, especially IgM and complement components.[442] The most important diagnostic feature is the presence of strong mesangial and capillary loop reactivity with anti-collagen type III antibodies. This type of collagen is absent in normal human kidneys.

Fibronectin glomerulopathy

Fibronectin glomerulopathy is a recently described hereditary kidney disease that is characterized by massive fibronectin deposition in the glomeruli.[448–451] Clinically, it is manifested by proteinuria (often within the nephrotic range), microscopic hematuria, hypertension, and a slow deterioration of renal function that occurs over a period of several years. This condition affects both sexes and exhibits an autosomal dominant pattern of inheritance. The gene locus for fibronectin glomerulopathy has been localized on chromosome 1q32.[452]

By light microscopy, the glomeruli show pronounced lobular accentuation and a minimal degree of hypercellularity. The most characteristic feature is a marked enlargement of the mesangium and subendothelial space resulting from the massive deposition of a homogeneous, PAS-positive, Congo red-negative material which, by electron microscopy, has a dense granular appearance. Intermixed within the deposits are fibrils 12 to 16 nm in diameter that, on occasion, may constitute the dominant component of the deposits. Immunofluorescence studies demonstrate strong reactivity for fibronectin in the areas corresponding to the deposits. Scanty amounts of immunoglobulins and complement factors may occasionally be seen but this is an inconsistent finding. The disease has been reported to recur after renal transplantation,[451,452] and an underlying abnormality in the metabolism of circulating fibronectin has been suggested in the pathogenesis of this condition.[451]

Renal transplant rejection

Renal biopsies on transplanted kidneys are performed to determine: (1) whether the failure of the graft is due to rejection, nephrotoxicity caused by immunosuppressive drugs (i.e., cyclosporin A, tacrolimus), or other causes, such as acute tubular necrosis, acute infectious pyelonephritis, obstruction of the vasculature or urinary outflow tract, or recurrent or de novo glomerular disease; or, (2) if rejection is present, to evaluate the intensity and nature of the rejection, and to predict the potential reversibility of the lesions with therapy. Rejection has been classified as hyperacute, acute, and chronic.

Hyperacute rejection

Hyperacute rejection may occur within minutes or hours after revascularization, with the immediate result being the abrupt cessation of urine flow. The diagnosis may be obvious to the surgeon when he sees mottling cyanosis and diminished turgor in the graft. The reaction is produced by the interaction of preformed circulating antibodies in the recipient with antigens on donor endothelial cells. The antibodies are often related to previous pregnancies, blood transfusions, or a previous kidney transplant.[454–456] The introduction of routine transplant screening and cross-matching techniques has made this a rare complication.[453,455]

In hyperacute rejection, fibrin thrombi are present in all the renal vessels including the glomerular capillaries and peritubular venules. The thrombosis is associated with infarction and tubular necrosis, and there is a variable infiltrate of leukocytes within the glomeruli, peritubular capillaries, and interstitium. Immunofluorescence may show linear staining for IgM or IgG and C3 along the glomerular and peritubular capillaries. Electron microscopy shows platelets, fibrin, sludged red blood cells, and evidence of necrosis of the endothelial cells of glomerular capillaries and other vessels (Fig. 17.70).

Acute rejection

Acute rejection, despite the name, can occur at any time during the course of transplantation. It is most often seen in the months following grafting and becomes less common after the first year. Two reaction patterns can be seen: vascular and interstitial.

In **acute vascular rejection**, also termed acute humoral rejection, the most severe changes occur in the small arteries, veins, and arterioles. The earliest morphologic indication of acute vascular rejection is swelling and vacuolization of the endothelial cells with areas of ulceration. This is usually associated with intimal infiltration by mononuclear inflammatory cells and by changes in the media. Individual smooth muscle cells show vacuolization caused by dilatation of the endoplastic reticulum. The intimal changes can be accompanied by either thrombosis or intimal proliferation (Fig. 17.71). Thromboses are often small and nonocclusive, but in those cases progressing to irreversible rejection they become obliterative and widespread with necrosis of the vessel walls. Occasionally, a pattern of acute necrotizing vasculitis may be seen. The glomeruli show endothelial cell swelling, an increase in cellularity, and occasional thrombosis.[461] Interstitial hemorrhage, tubular necrosis, and infarctions are also seen. Immunofluorescence microscopy will occasionally reveal the presence of complement components in vessel walls and in glomeruli and, rarely, the presence of immunoglobulins. Electron microscopy demonstrates endothelial cell swelling associated with separation of the endothelium from the basement membrane by fluffy fibrillar material, which

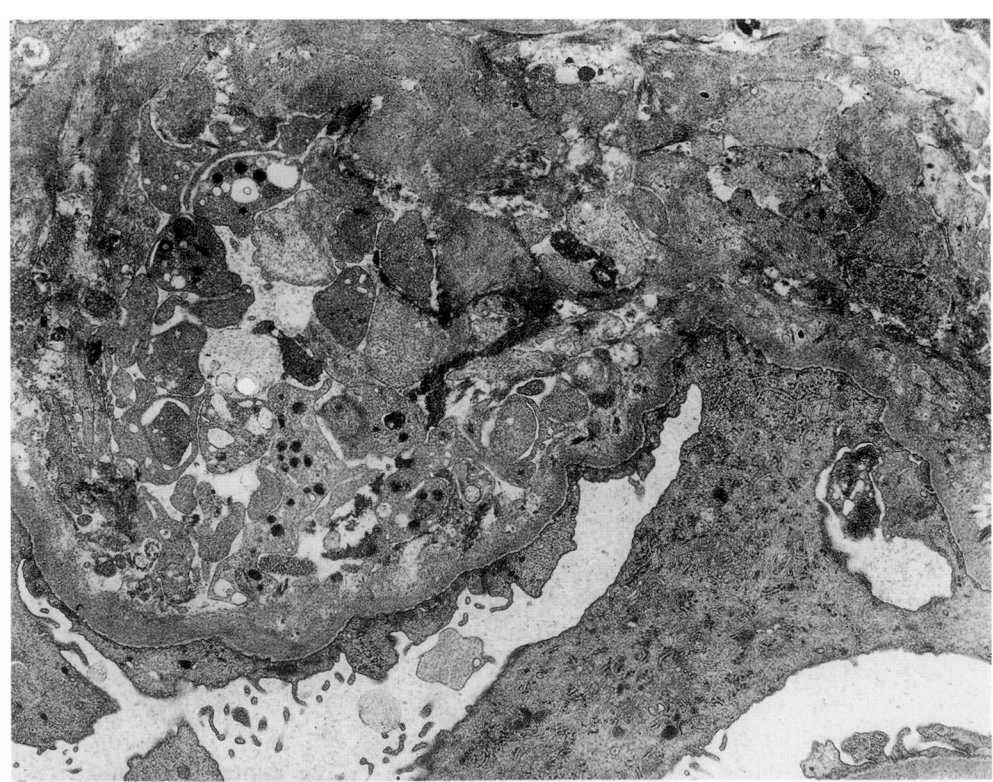

Fig. 17.70 Hyperacute rejection. There is endothelial denudation of the GBM and capillary occlusion by degranulated platelets. (× 7980)

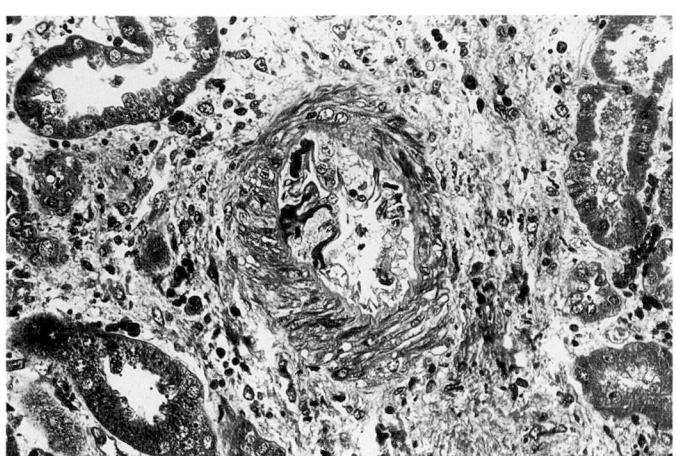

Fig. 17.71 Acute vascular rejection. The endothelium is swollen and focally detached. The darker material in contact with the endothelium represents fibrin.

occasionally contains fibrin strands and platelet fragments.

Acute interstitial allograft rejection has also been called cellular rejection, acute tubulointerstitial or acute reversible rejection.[459,460] In the early stages, light microscopy reveals edema and focal infiltration of the interstitium and peritubular capillaries by lymphocytes (Fig. 17.72). As the rejection progresses, the inflammatory infiltrate becomes more diffuse and the lymphocytes, many of them immunoblasts, are accompanied by plasma cells, monocytes, and macrophages (Fig. 17.73). Granulocytes may be present, but they are not numerous. When they are abundant, the possibility of humoral rejection or pyelonephritis should be considered.[458]

Eosinophils can also be present, but rarely in large numbers. A characteristic finding in acute interstitial rejection is invasion of the tubular epithelial cells by lymphocytes producing a lesion referred to as tubulitis. Tubulitis has been regarded as a reliable marker for acute rejection even though it can be seen in other forms of interstitial nephritis.[457,458] The intensity of the infiltrate and tubular injury are features often used to grade the rejection. The infiltrate is more concentrated in the cortex than in the renal medulla. Immunophenotyping shows that most of the lymphoid cells are T lymphocytes, and that as many as 60% to 80% are CD8-positive cells, the remainder being CD4-positive T lymphocytes, plasma cells, and monocyte/macrophages.[459] Immunofluorescence is generally negative, with the exception of some reaction for fibrin in affected vessels and immunoglobulins in inflammatory cells. Electron microscopy shows tubular damage and regeneration, and many inflammatory cells in the interstitium. Glomerular and vascular changes are invariably present, but may be mild. Rejection that is predominantly cellular is considered to be readily reversible with therapy.

Although it is convenient for descriptive purposes to consider the two types of allograft rejection reaction separately, every case is really a combination of interstitial and vascular changes. Since the interstitial component of allograft rejection is more responsive to some forms of therapy than the vascular form, it is important to identify and as far as possible quantitate the relative contributions of the two types. This is essential in assisting the clinician in determining whether or not the rejection episode should be treated with steroids or a complete

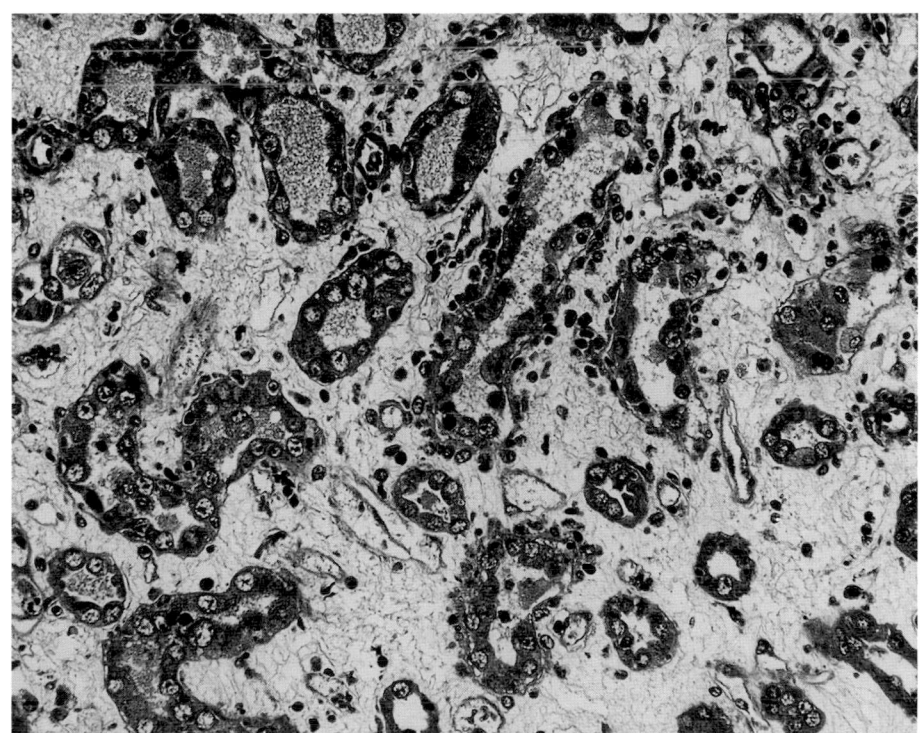

Fig. 17.72 Severe interstitial edema in acute rejection. Some tubules show focal necrosis with detachment of epithelial cells. There is also a peritubular mononuclear inflammatory infiltrate and dilatation of interstitial capillaries. Some inflammatory cells are located between the epithelial cells and the tubular basement membrane.

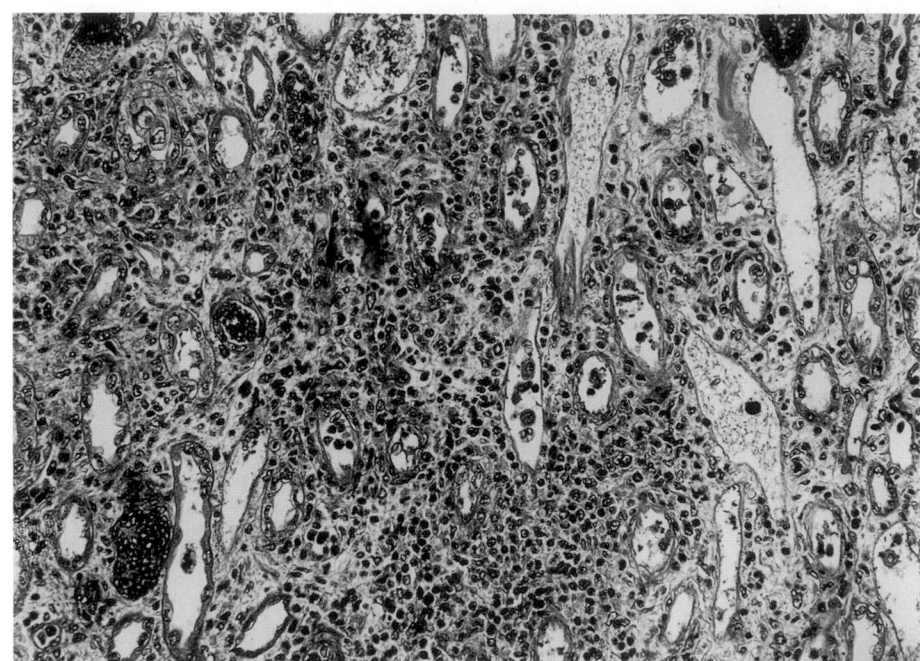

Fig. 17.73 Acute interstitial rejection. There is dilatation of peritubular capillaries and prominent infiltration of the interstitium by lymphocytes.

change in the immunosuppressive approach. It is also of importance in studying follow-up biopsies after therapy, particularly when the therapeutic response has not been favorable.

Chronic rejection

Chronic rejection may occur at any time from several months to several years after transplantation and, once initiated, is irreversible. It constitutes the most common cause of graft failure after the initial 6 to 12 months. Chronic rejection is not a distinct entity with a specific pathogenesis, but rather the end stage of repeated episodes of acute vascular or interstitial rejection.[463] In addition, long-term administration of cyclosporin A or tacrolimus probably contributes to the development of some of the changes seen in chronic rejection. Clinically, there is a gradual decrease in renal function. The deterioration may be preceded by proteinuria, sometimes with the nephrotic syndrome,[467] and it is commonly associated with hypertension. Microscopically, the picture is similar to that seen in nephrosclerosis. The blood vessels, especially the interlobular and arcuate arteries, show severe obliterative fibrointimal proliferation or mucoid widening of the intima (Fig. 17.74).[465,466] Reduplication or disruption of the elastic lamina and irregular fibrosis of the media are also common. The distribution of the vascular lesions is irregular and some blood vessels appear normal while others present lesions of variable degrees of severity. Small thrombi in various stages of organization can be found. Tubules are atrophic and the interstitium is diffusely scarred.[462] The glomerular lesions consist of ischemic glomerular capillary collapse, thickening of the capillary walls, and segmental and global sclerosis.[464,468] On occasion, however, segmental

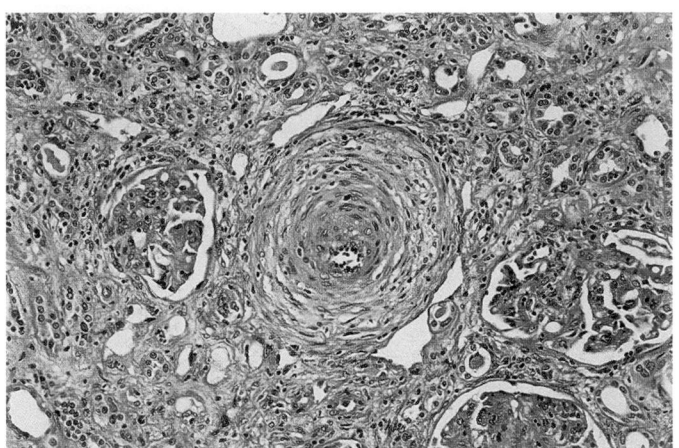

Fig. 17.74 Chronic allograft rejection. Interlobular artery showing marked fibrointimal proliferation. The glomerular tufts are condensed, and the capillary loops present a variable degree of collapse. The interstitium is scarred and contains sparse mononuclear inflammatory cells.

sclerosis can occur in the absence of vascular changes (transplant glomerulopathy). The capillary walls may be thickened due to marked widening of the subendothelial space or mesangial interposition, which is better demonstrated by electron microscopy (Fig. 17.75). No immune complexes are seen, although immunofluorescent studies occasionally show linear or granular deposition of IgM, IgG, and complement components (Fig. 17.76).

The Banff classification

Over the past decade, in order to help to establish uniform therapeutic guidelines to clinical management and to provide an objective evaluation of clinical trials of new antirejection agents, several classification systems for the

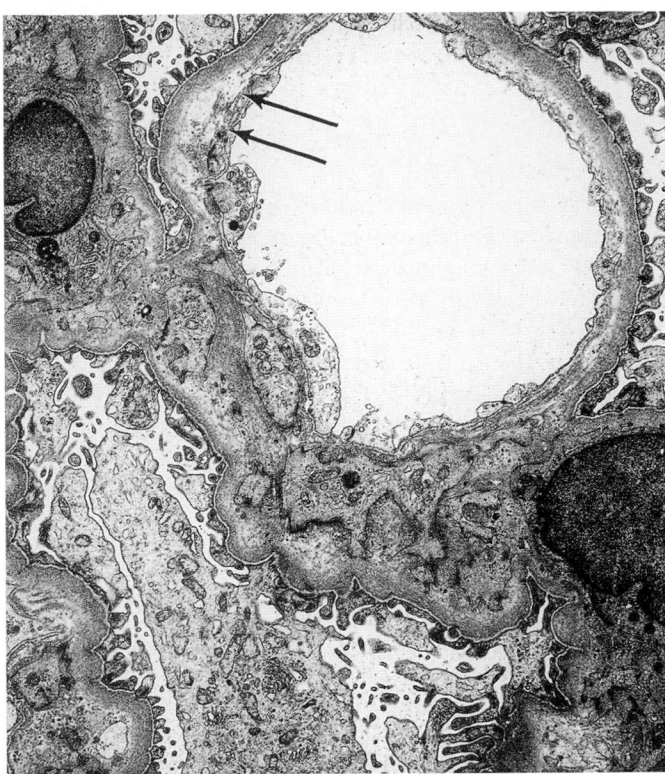

Fig. 17.75 Chronic allograft rejection. Portion of a glomerulus showing prominent widening of the subendothelial region (arrows). (× 3500)

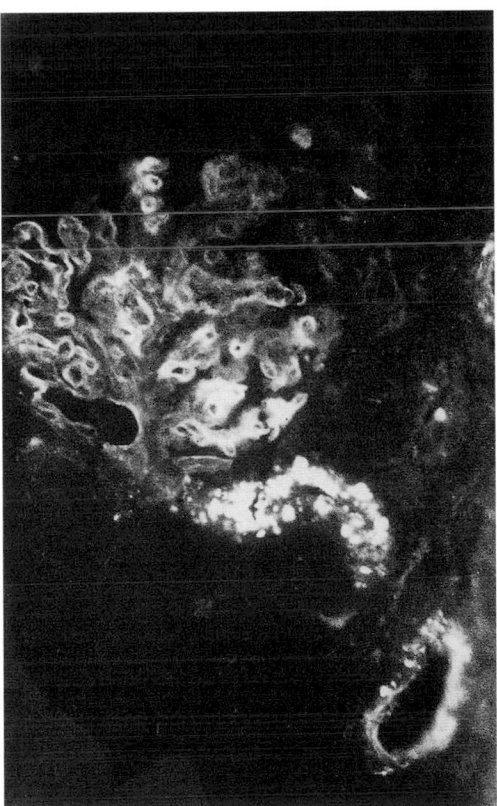

Fig. 17.76 Chronic allograft rejection. Granular deposits of C3 are present in the glomerular arterioles and there is linear staining along the glomerular capillary loops.

evaluation of the histologic appearance of renal allograft biopsies have been developed.[469–472] The best known is the Banff Working Classification of Renal Allograft Pathology which was formulated by an international group of renal pathologists, nephrologists, and transplant surgeons who met in Banff, Canada, in August, 1991, and which was published in 1993.[472] This classification has undergone several revisions, the latest in March, 1997, which was published in 1999.[471] There are six diagnostic categories in the Banff classification: normal, antibody-mediated rejection, borderline changes, acute rejection, chronic rejection, and other changes not related to rejection. The details of the Banff 97 classification are shown in Table 17.10. In this classification, an adequate core biopsy must contain a minimum of 10 glomeruli and at least 2 arteries; a marginal sample is that with 7 to 10 glomeruli and 1 artery; and an unsatisfactory biopsy is a core with less than 7 glomeruli or no arteries. At present,

Table 17.10 Banff 97 diagnostic categories for renal allograft biopsies

1. Normal
2. Antibody-mediated rejection
   A. Immediate (hyperacute)
   B. Delayed (accelerated acute)
3. Borderline changes: "Suspicious" for acute rejection
   Cases with foci of mild tubulitis (1 to 4 mononuclear cells/tubular cross section) and interstitial inflammation (10% to 25% of parenchyma affected)
4. Acute/active rejection
   Type IA: Cases with significant interstitial inflammation (>25% of parenchyma affected) and foci of moderate tubulitis (>4 mononuclear cells/tubular cross section or group of 10 tubular cells)
   Type IB: Cases with significant interstitial inflammation (>25% of parenchyma affected) and foci of severe tubulitis (>10 mononuclear cells/tubular cross section or group of 10 tubular cells)
   Type IIA: Cases with mild to moderate intimal arteritis (v1)
   Type IIB: Cases with severe intimal arteritis comprising >25% of the luminal ares (v2)
   Type III: Cases with "transmural" arteritis and/or arterial fibrinoid change and necrosis of medial smooth muscle cells (v3 with accompanying lymphocytic inflammation)
5. Chronic/sclerosing allograft nephropathy
   Grade I: Mild interstitial fibrosis and tubular atrophy without (a) or with (b) specific changes suggesting chronic rejection
   Grade II: Moderate interstitial fibrosis and tubular atrophy (a) or (b)
   Grade III: Severe interstitial fibrosis and tubular atrophy and tubular loss (a) or (b)
6. Changes unrelated to rejection

Adapted from Racusen, Solez, Colvin, et al. The Banff 97 working classification of renal allograft pathology. Kidney Int 1999, **55**: 713–723.

the Banff classification is considered to be a working model and its reproducibility among pathologists, as well as its clinical utility, is still being evaluated.

Cyclosporin A toxicity

Cyclosporin A (CsA, cyclosporine, ciclosporin) is an immunosuppressant drug that is extremely effective in controlling transplant rejection; unfortunately, however, it is nephrotoxic. Other CsA effects include hepatotoxicity, neurotoxicity, gingival hyperplasia, hypertrichosis, and malignancies, particularly lymphomas.[473,474,476] Nephrotoxicity can occur not only in patients receiving renal transplants, but also in those receiving the drug for any other reason. CsA nephrotoxicity is dose related and has been classified into functional toxicity in which there are no structural changes, and morphologic forms in which the toxicity is manifested by a variety of lesions affecting tubules, vessels, and renal interstitium. Three major morphologic forms are recognized: acute nephrotoxicity, chronic nephrotoxicity, and thrombotic microangiopathy.[475]

Functional toxicity

Functional CsA toxicity probably affects every patient who receives this medication. A mild decrease in renal function and a mild elevation of serum creatinine levels are seen soon after therapy starts, but both are reversible if the dosage is reduced. Hypertension is seen in up to 50% of the patients.[477] Renal biopsies in these patients appear normal or at most show some dilatation and congestion of peritubular capillaries. The pathogenesis is an alteration of intrarenal hemodynamics that results from the ability of CsA to induce intense renal vasoconstriction.

Acute toxicity

The clinical manifestations of acute CsA toxicity are similar to those of functional toxicity, but tend to be more severe. Histologically, the lesion is characterized by vacuolization of the proximal tubules, often in an isometric pattern, with giant mitochondria, large lysosomes, and microcalcifications.[477] Electron microscopic studies have demonstrated that the vacuolization is the result of dilatation of the endoplasmic reticulum. In addition, the arterioles may show individual medial smooth muscle cell degeneration, necrosis/apoptosis and myocyte dropout, endothelial cell swelling, intimal thickening, variable hyalinosis, and mucoid or insudative deposits which together may result in significant narrowing of the vascular lumen. Acute nephrotoxicity is usually dose dependent and reversible.

Thrombotic microangiopathy

Patients with CsA toxicity can develop symptoms similar to those of hemolytic uremic syndrome a few days or weeks after transplantation. The histologic findings are those of thrombotic microangiopathy with platelet and fibrin thrombi in the glomeruli and vessels, and minimal inflammatory infiltrate.[475] The prognosis of these patients is generally poor, but in some instances the lesions have resolved after the drug has been withdrawn.

Chronic toxicity

Chronic CsA toxicity is clinically manifested by slow progression to renal failure and hypertension. Biopsies show arteriolopathy and interstitial fibrosis with tubular atrophy. The arteriolopathy consists of nodular or diffuse hyalinosis of the vessel walls, or mucoid thickening of the intima, resulting in narrowing or complete occlusion of the vascular lumen.[475] The changes are usually accompanied by focal interstitial fibrosis and tubular atrophy which are best seen in the cortex. The glomeruli are usually spared in the early stages, although the capillaries may contain aggregates of platelets and fibrin. When the process is advanced, focal and segmental glomerulosclerosis or global scarring of the glomeruli may be seen.[478] In contrast to acute nephrotoxicity, the changes in chronic nephrotoxicity are irreversible.

Tacrolimus (FK506) toxicity

Tacrolimus is a new immunosuppressant drug used in the control of transplant rejection. The morphologic changes associated with tacrolimus toxicity are similar to those of CsA toxicity.[479]

Tubulointerstitial nephritis

Tubulointerstitial nephritis is a heterogeneous group of disorders that primarily affect the renal interstitium and tubules, and only secondarily involve the other structures of the kidney. The frequency with which tubular interstitial diseases affect the kidney is difficult to determine; however, it is believed that primary tubulointerstitial disease is the cause of renal failure in an estimated 20% to 40% of all patients undergoing treatment for end-stage renal disease.[480] The clinical presentations are usually very similar, but the etiologies are quite different and include infection, obstruction, and immune-mediated and toxic tubulointerstitial diseases (Table 17.11). The functional manifestations include impaired concentrating ability, impaired ability to secrete acid, diminished reabsorption of sodium, hyperkalemia, and azotemia. Symptoms may be acute or chronic with corresponding morphologic changes.

Acute tubular necrosis

Acute tubular necrosis (ATN) is a clinicopathologic syndrome that is characterized by the acute suppression of renal function accompanied by morphologic evidence of tubular epithelial cell injury. Two subtypes of ATN have been recognized: ischemic and toxic.

Table 17.11 Classification of tubulointerstitial diseases

Infections
  Acute pyelonephritis
    Ascending infection
    Hematogenous spread
    Bacterial; fungal; other
  Chronic pyelonephritis
    Nonobstructive (reflux associated)
    Obstructive
    Xanthogranulomatous
    Malakoplakia
Obstructive uropathy
  Hydronephrosis without infection
  Hydronephrosis with infection
  Reflux-associated nephropathy
Allergic tubulointerstitial nephritis
  Drug induced (antibiotics, diuretics, nonsteroidals)
  Associated with systemic vasculitis
  Lupus associated
  Anti-tubular basement membrane
Toxic tubulointerstitial nephritis
  Drug induced
    Aminoglycosides
    Cyclosporine
    Lithium
    Analgesics
  Heavy metal toxicity
    Cisplatin
    Lead, mercury, and others
  Other
  Radiation
  Sarcoid
  Idiopathic

Ischemic acute tubular necrosis, also known as acute vasomotor nephropathy, is the most common form and results from hypoperfusion of the kidney. It is usually associated with hypotension, which can occur as a result of a wide variety of conditions such as severe traumatic lesions and burns, shock after a surgical operation, septic shock, pancreatitis, and dehydration after diarrhea, vomiting, or extensive sweating. The nephrotoxic form is a chemically induced injury of the tubular epithelial cells that can be caused by a wide variety of substances including organic solvents (e.g., carbon tetrachloride, ethylene glycol), heavy metals (e.g., mercury, lead), antibiotics (e.g., amphotericin B, gentamycin), chemotherapeutic agents (e.g., methotrexate, cisplatin), and radiographic contrast agents. Hemoglobin and myoglobin are considered endogenous toxins capable of causing ATN when present in urine in high concentrations. Hemoglobulinuria can be due to incompatible blood transfusion, malaria, and paroxysmal hemoglobulinuria. Myoglobinuric acute renal failure can be caused by the liberation of myoglobin from muscles by trauma (crush injury), myositis, ischemia, excessive exertion, or exposure to toxins (snake venom, alcohol, cocaine). It is believed that, while the toxicity of the hemoglobin and myoglobin may contribute to the pathogenesis of the ATN, ischemia and microcirculatory disturbances probably play a greater role in its development.[481] Clinically, ATN is manifested by rapidly increasing serum creatinine levels associated with oliguria or anuria. Less frequently, ATN induces nonoliguric renal failure. Urinalysis typically demonstrates sloughed degenerated epithelial cells and granular casts. The clinical course of ATN is highly variable and the prognosis largely depends on the clinical setting in which it occurs.

The morphologic changes in ischemic ATN depend on the severity of the renal failure and the evolution of the lesion.[481] In the early stages, the cellular changes can range from minimal cell swelling to individual cell necrosis accompanied by focal denudation of the basement membrane and desquamation of the necrotic cells into the tubular lumen (Fig. 17.77A). The proximal tubules may appear dilated and their PAS-positive brush border thinned or absent. Hyaline, granular, and pigmented casts are common, especially in the distal and collecting ducts. These casts consist mainly of

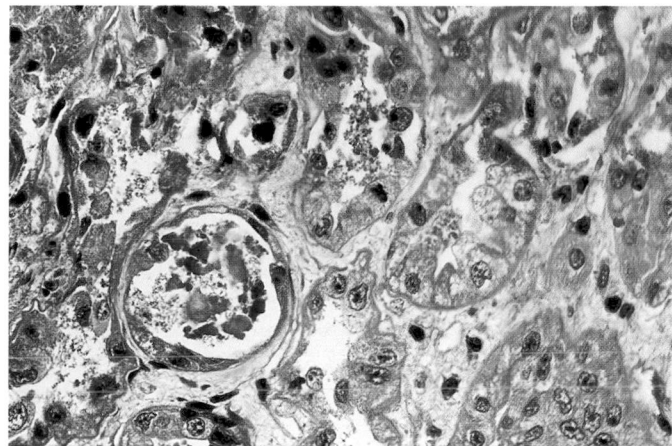

A

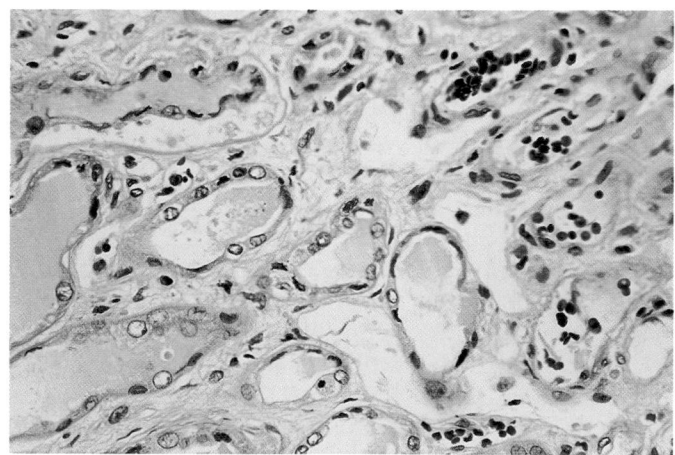

B

Fig. 17.77 Acute tubular necrosis. **A,** There is focal necrosis and desquamation of the cells into the tubular lumen. **B,** The tubules are dilated and lined by flattened epithelium.

Tamm–Horsfall protein mixed with cellular necrotic debris. Other findings in ischemic ATN are interstitial edema and the accumulation of mononuclear leukocytes within the vasa recta of the outer medulla. As the disease progresses after the initial injury, evidence of tubular regeneration can be seen. Changes believed to represent regeneration include flattened epithelium with dilatation of the tubular lumen, the presence of large nuclei with prominent nucleoli, and mitotic activity (Fig. 17.77B).

Toxic ATN is characterized by extensive necrosis of the tubular cells along segments of the proximal tubule. Depending on the type of poisoning, several patterns of injury have been recognized.[481,483] For example, ethylene glycol produces marked ballooning and hydropic or vacuolar degeneration of the proximal convoluted tubules, and extensive deposition of oxalate crystals in the tubular lumina, whereas carbon tetrachloride poisoning is characterized by the accumulation of neutral lipids in the injured cells followed by necrosis.[483] In acute lead nephropathy, dark intranuclear inclusions are seen in addition to the cellular necrosis. Hemoglobinuric and myoglobinuric ATN following hemolysis or severe muscle damage show histologic features similar to those of ischemic ATN, with numerous deeply pigmented, red–brown casts in the distal and collecting ducts.[482]

Acute and chronic pyelonephritis

Infectious tubulointerstitial nephritis is generally designated as pyelonephritis, implying that the inflammatory process involves the collecting system as well as the renal parenchyma.[498] There are three peaks of incidence: infancy and early childhood, women of child-bearing age, and both men and women older than 60 years of age. Both acute and chronic pyelonephritis are frequently associated with congenital or acquired obstructive lesions of the lower urinary tract or are associated with conditions resulting in residual retention of urine in the bladder.[497] Congenital lesions are often the cause of pyelonephritis in infancy and early childhood. In older adults, obstruction by nodular hyperplasia of the prostate gland in men and the development of cystoceles in women are important etiologic factors. In addition, conditions such as cancer of the cervix and nephrolithiasis are also commonly associated with renal infection.

In acute pyelonephritis associated with an ascending infection, an acute inflammatory infiltrate involves the renal cortex and medulla (Fig. 17.78). The cells are mostly polymorphonuclear leukocytes and they are present in the interstitium and within the tubular lumina. Foci of necrosis and abscess formation are also present in the cortex. The kidney can become infected by organisms arriving via the hematogenous route, resulting in the formation of many small cortical abscesses with little involvement of the medulla. Special stains may reveal the responsible pathogens. Ascending infections are usually caused by gram-negative organisms that are

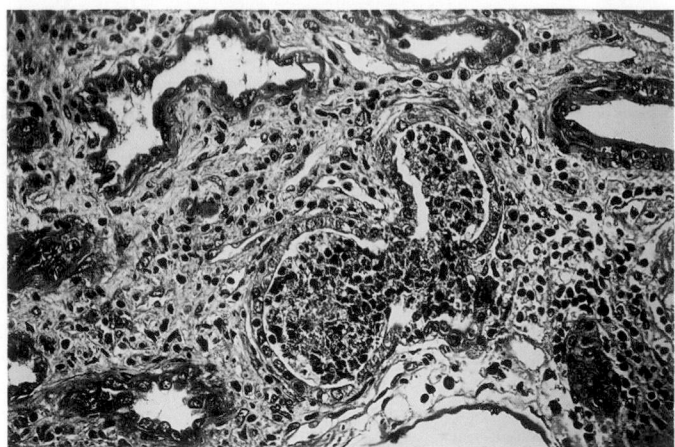

Fig. 17.78 Acute pyelonephritis in a patient presenting with fever and elevated creatinine. There is an acute inflammatory infiltrate in the interstitium and tubular lumina.

normally present in the intestinal tract. By far the most common is *Escherichia coli*, followed by Klebsiella, and Enterobacter. *Staphylococcus aureus* or fungal organisms, including Candida and Aspergillus, may be the cause of hematogenous infections and they are seen more often in immunosuppressed individuals.

Chronic pyelonephritis produces a coarse fibrosis of the kidney parenchyma which is distinctly focal in its distribution.[496] Cortical and papillary scars overlie dilated, blunted, deformed calyces. The architecture of the medulla is distorted, and papillae may be flattened. Light microscopy shows tubular damage, interstitial inflammation, and fibrosis (Fig. 17.79). The tubules are

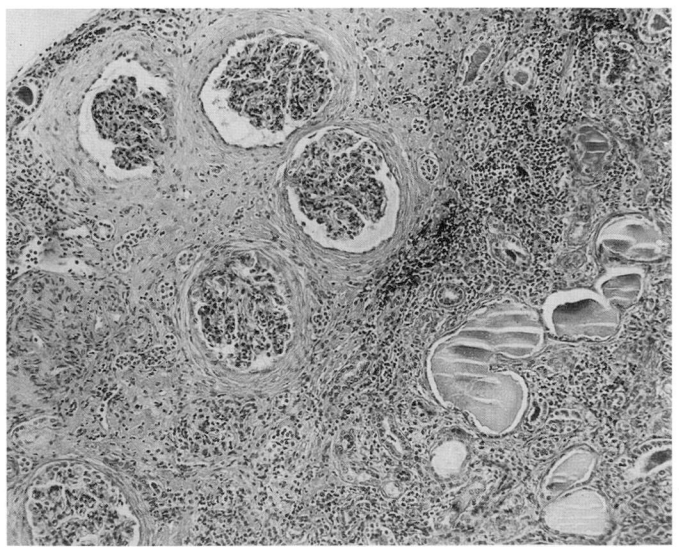

Fig. 17.79 Nephrectomy specimen from a patient with obstructive hydronephrosis. There is interstitial scarring with periglomerular fibrosis and mononuclear inflammatory cell infiltration. The tubules are atrophic and contain hyaline casts. (Reproduced from Spargo BH, Seymour AE, Ordóñez NG. Introduction. In: Renal biopsy pathology with diagnostic and therapeutic implications. New York, 1980, John Wiley & Sons, pp. 1–13. By permission of John Wiley & Sons, Inc.)

atrophic or dilated, and they are lined by flattened epithelium and filled with colloid casts, a pattern that has been called thyroidization. Lymphocytes, histiocytes, and plasma cells form the bulk of the inflammatory infiltrate. In chronic pyelonephritis associated with reflux or obstruction, Tamm–Horsfall protein can be identified in the interstitium as small bodies of amorphous fibrillary material that are strongly PAS positive and surrounded by inflammatory cells. The glomeruli are not primarily involved, but they can be affected by periglomerular fibrosis. Ischemic changes consisting of focal and segmental sclerosis and hyalinosis may also occur.

The histopathologic changes associated with chronic pyelonephritis have also been described in vesicoureteral reflux and chronic urinary obstruction.[485] An extreme form of localized scarring is seen in the so-called "Ask–Upmark" kidney[489] where total fibrosis of a lobule produces an appearance of segmental hypoplasia.

Xanthogranulomatous pyelonephritis is an uncommon and distinct type of chronic infectious pyelonephritis in which yellow, lobulated masses diffusely replace the renal architecture.[487] There are cases in which only a portion of the kidney, such as one pole, is involved. The condition is usually unilateral, although rare bilateral cases have been reported.[495] This disease can occur at any age: it has been reported in patients as young as 11 months to as old as 89 years, but it is more common in adults in the fifth through the seventh decades.[488,498] It is twice as common in women as in men.[498] Urinary obstruction is almost invariably present and is most often caused by stones. Other causes of obstruction include postradiation strictures, congenital pelviureteric stenosis, and tumors.[490,494] The mass-occupying nature of this lesion frequently mimics that of a renal cell carcinoma, resulting in unnecessary nephrectomies. A correct preoperative diagnosis is rarely made. Microscopically, there is a diffuse granulomatous inflammatory infiltrate that includes large numbers of foamy histiocytes and some multinucleated giant cells, as well as lymphocytes, plasma cells, and neutrophils (Fig. 17.80). Electron microscopy shows that the foamy macrophages initially contain bacteria and subsequently contain numerous phagolysosomes with a myeloid configuration and amorphous material.[491] The lesion is destructive, tending to obliterate renal parenchyma within the affected areas. *Escherichia coli* is the usual etiologic agent, but *Proteus mirabilis* and *Staphylococcus aureus* have also been found to be responsible.[498,499]

The gross and microscopic appearances of malakoplakia resemble those of xanthogranulomatous pyelonephritis. Confluent nodules of homogeneous yellow–tan tissue replace large areas of renal parenchyma. Fibrosis is also prominent. The inflammatory infiltrate consists largely of histiocytes with relatively few lymphocytes and plasma cells. The distinctive Michaelis–Gutmann bodies are found both within the histiocytes and extracellularly in the stroma (Fig. 17.81).[492] Ultrastructurally, these bodies are round with a core of concentric membranes, amorphous material, or foci of calcification, and they show up well with the PAS stain (Figs 17.81 inset, and 17.82).[486] The pathogenesis of this cellular accumulation is unknown, but there is suggestive evidence that the lesions result from a defect in macrophage function that blocks the lysosomal degradation of engulfed bacteria and overloads the cytoplasm with undigested cellular debris.[484,493]

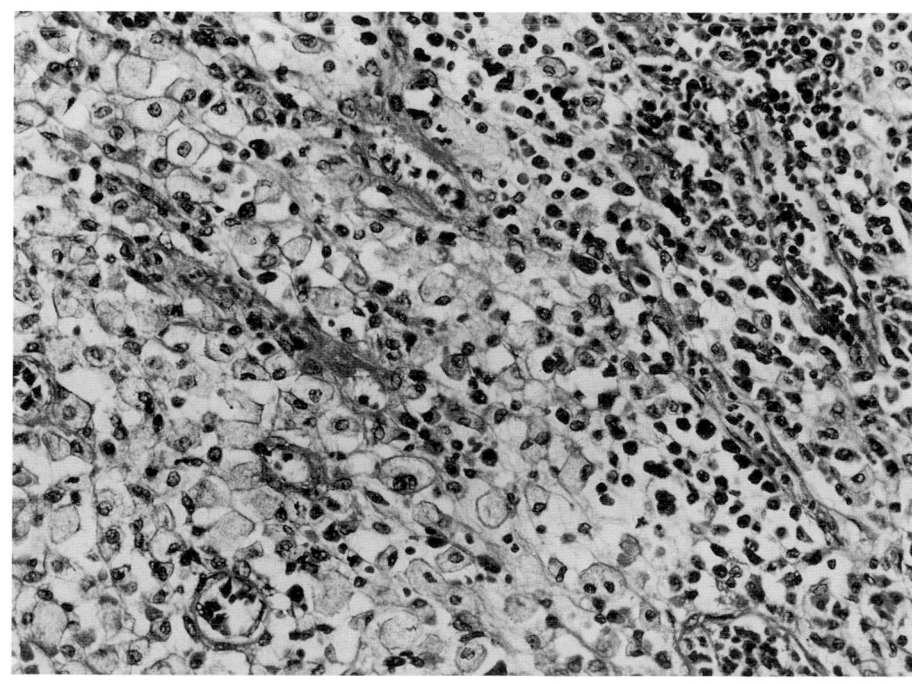

Fig. 17.80 Foamy histiocytes in xanthogranulomatous pyelonephritis. Lymphocytes and plasma cells are also present.

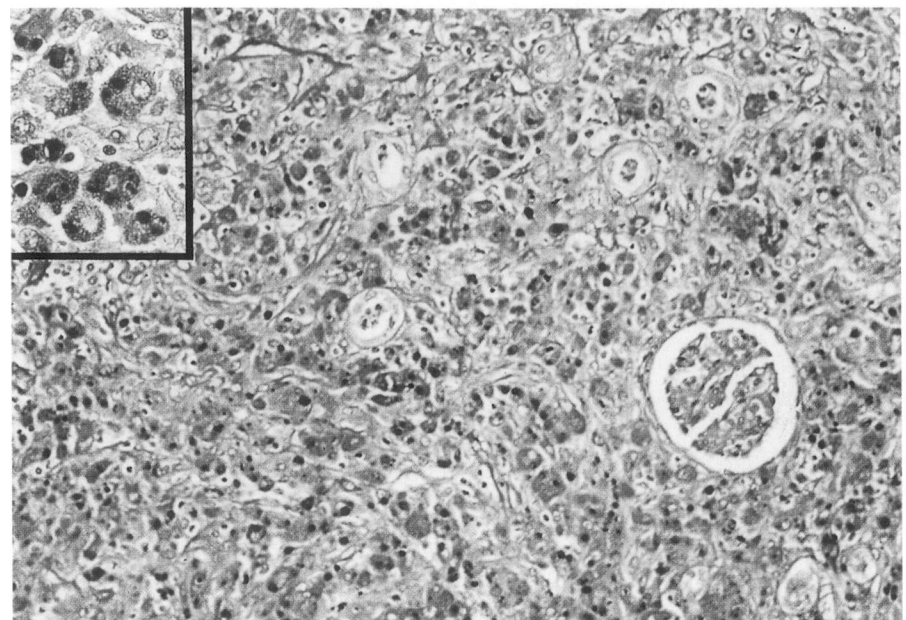

Fig. 17.81 Nephrectomy specimen from a patient with malakoplakia. The interstitium is infiltrated by numerous macrophages with granular cytoplasm. Inset: Several Michaelis–Gutmann bodies are seen in the cytoplasm.

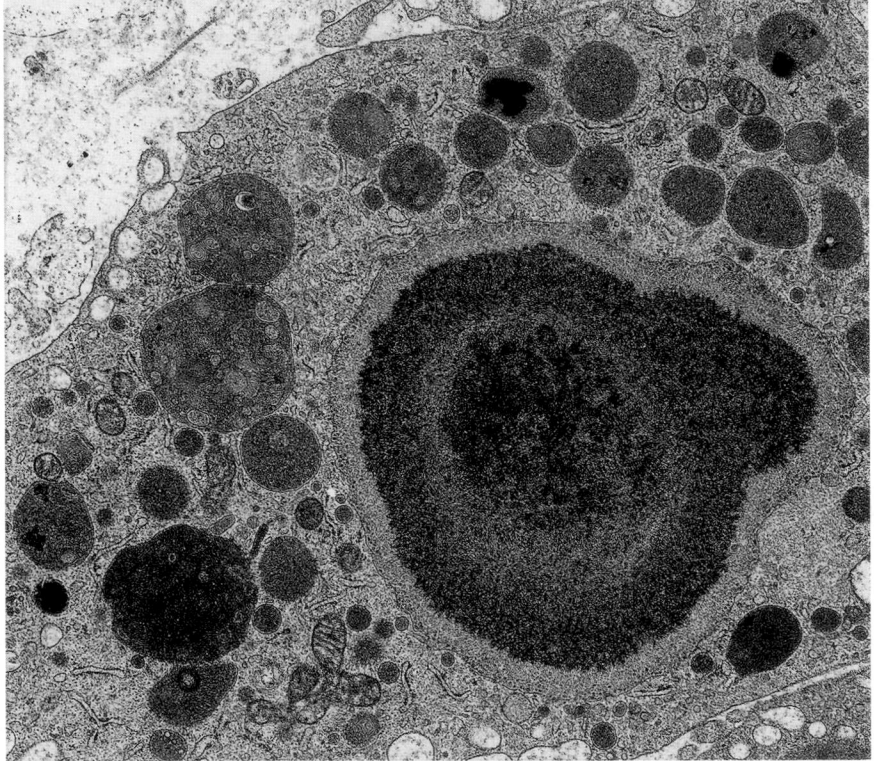

Fig. 17.82 Electron micrograph of a histiocyte showing numerous phagolysosomes and a Michaelis–Gutmann body with calcified central core. (× 11,400)

Acute allergic tubulointerstitial nephritis

Many drugs, including β-lactam antibiotics, nonsteroidal anti-inflammatory drugs, diuretics, and diverse other substances, can be responsible for acute tubulointerstitial nephritis.[505,507] The clinical presentation is quite variable but fever, hematuria, and azotemia are common, and eosinophilia occurs in a majority of cases. Urinalysis reveals hematuria, sterile pyuria, and moderate proteinuria, and eosinophils may be detected in the sediment.[503] Acute interstitial nephritis combined with a glomeru-lopathy producing nephrotic-range proteinuria has been described.[511] A skin rash, usually described as maculopapular, is sometimes seen.

Light microscopy reveals generalized interstitial edema and infiltration of the interstitium by lymphocytes, macrophages, plasma cells, and eosinophils.[502,508] Damage to tubular epithelial cells with evidence of regeneration is always found, and leukocytes can lie within the lumen. The glomeruli and vessels are not usually involved. Occasionally, granulomas with giant cells can be seen.[502,506]

Although bacterial infection and drugs are the most common causes of acute interstitial nephritis, a similar picture can be found in patients with systemic lupus erythematosus and, rarely, in association with anti-tubular basement membrane antibodies.[501,504] The clinical and pathologic findings are similar to those of allergic tubulointerstitial nephritis. Biopsy-proven instances of acute oliguric tubulointerstitial nephritis without any known cause have also been reported. A syndrome of acute interstitial nephritis with anterior uveitis and bone marrow and lymph node granulomas has been reported to occur, usually in adolescent and young adult women.[509,510] The etiology is unknown, but recent reports have suggested an association with Chlamydia infection.[500,512]

Analgesic abuse nephropathy

Analgesic abuse nephropathy is a bilateral renal disease characterized by papillary necrosis and chronic tubulointerstitial nephritis that results from the excessive intake of analgesic mixtures containing aspirin or antipyrine, combined with phenacetin, acetaminophen (paracetamol), or salicylamide, and caffeine or codeine.[515] The incidence of analgesic nephropathy varies in different countries. In the early 1990s, the reported incidence of analgesic nephropathy among patients receiving dialysis was estimated to be 0.8% in the United States, 3% in Europe, and 9% in Australia.[514,517] The condition is more common in women than in men. The most important diagnostic feature is a history of chronic pain syndromes and analgesic abuse over several years or decades. Renal function abnormalities include impaired urine concentration defects and impaired sodium conservation. Urinary infection is a complication in about 50% of the cases. On occasion, fragments of necrotic papillae are excreted. This may cause gross hematuria or renal colic due to obstruction of the ureter by the necrotic tissue. Renal imaging studies are helpful in detecting papillary necrosis and calcification. Progressive impairment of renal function may lead to chronic renal failure. An important association in analgesic nephropathy is the increased risk for developing transitional cell carcinoma.[513]

The pathologic features develop in three stages. In the early stage, the weight of the kidneys is unchanged and the cortex is normal, but the papillae are firmer than normal and show gray streaks. Microscopically, there is interstitial homogenization, and thickening of the basement membranes of the loops of Henle and peritubular capillaries. Foci of necrotic epithelial, endothelial, and interstitial cells are associated with fine calcification. In the second stage, the papillae are shrunken and they have a brown coloration. Microscopically, confluent zones of necrosis within the inner medulla involve the loops of Henle, peritubular capillaries, and vasa recta, and the cortex may contain foci of tubular atrophy, interstitial fibrosis, and patches of chronic inflammation.

In the third stage, the kidneys are reduced in weight and the gross changes are similar to those seen in chronic pyelonephritis. Total papillary necrosis occurs, extensive calcification is usually present, and in rare instances there may even be metaplastic bone formation. If the necrotic papillae have not been sloughed, the overlying cortex will show marked degrees of tubular atrophy, interstitial fibrosis and inflammation, and glomerular sclerosis, which are thought to be secondary to obstruction of the urine flow. If the papillae have been sloughed, minor cortical changes similar to those seen in the second stage are found. Papillary necrosis is not specific for analgesic nephropathy. It can also occur in a variety of other conditions including diabetes mellitus, urinary tract obstruction, and sickle cell disease.[516]

Heavy metals nephrotoxicity

Renal damage can result from environmental or occupational exposure to heavy metals, such as lead, cadmium, mercury, uranium, chromium, copper and arsenic,[518,522,523,526–528] or the administration of therapeutic forms of platinum,[519,520] gold,[521] and bismuth.[524] Only the changes in the kidney produced by lead exposure will be discussed due to their characteristic morphologic features and clinical importance.

Lead nephropathy

Lead poisoning may be the result of occupational or environmental exposure. Workers at risk include electric storage battery makers, painters, welders, foundrymen, and jewelers. Children may be exposed by eating flaking lead paint. Inadvertent ingestion of lead can occur from drinking water contaminated by lead pipes, earthenware, or from adulterated wine or moonshine liquor. Lead is also present as an atmospheric contaminant resulting from the use of lead-containing gasoline and various industrial processes.

The organs most commonly affected by lead exposure are the central and peripheral nervous systems, gastrointestinal tract, and kidney. The most striking morphologic changes in lead exposure occur in the tubules and consist of eosinophilic intranuclear or cytoplasmic acid-fast inclusions that stain red with Giemsa stain. These inclusions consist of a lead–protein complex and by electron microscopy appear as compact cores surrounded by a loose meshwork of fibrils (Fig. 17.83). They may be seen in tubular epithelial cells in urinary sediment during acute poisoning.[525] Lead-containing inclusions have also been found in the liver and neural tissue.[527]

Renal biopsies in chronic lead nephropathy often show tubular atrophy and interstitial fibrosis with minimal inflammatory reaction. Arteriolar changes similar to those of nephrosclerosis may be present even in the absence of hypertension.[527] The inclusions are often absent when the disease is of long standing or after the administration of chelating agents.

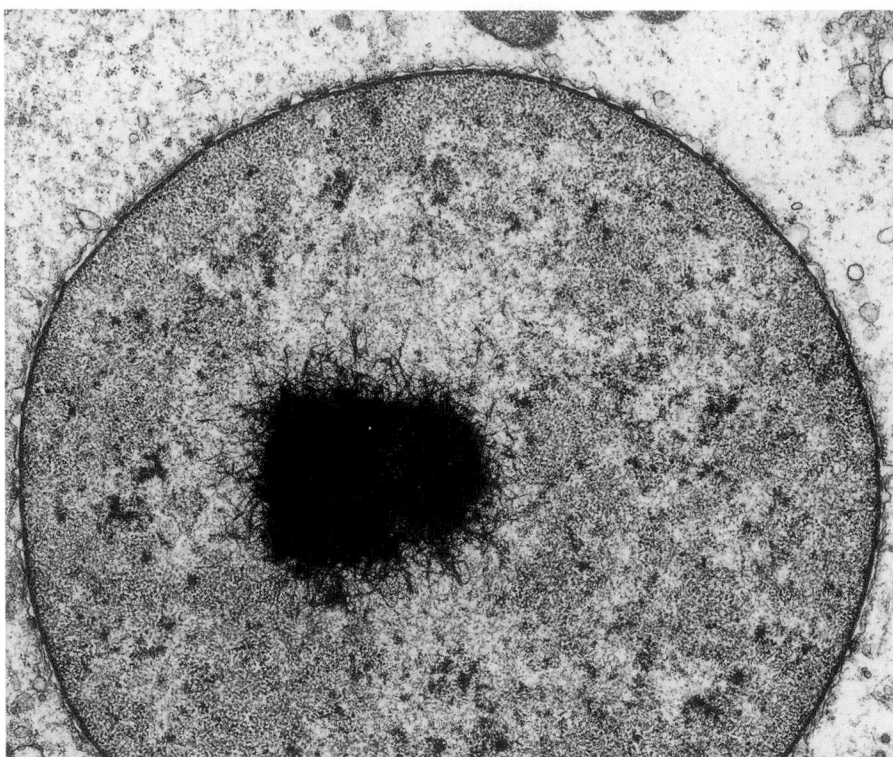

Fig. 17.83 Intranuclear lead inclusions showing dense central cores surrounded by fibrillar material. (× 15,600)

Pyelitis and ureteritis cystica

Hinman and Cordonnier[529] have shown that pyelitis and ureteritis cystica result from downward proliferation of the surface epithelium in chronically inflamed mucosa. Buds of epithelium become pinched off to form detached cell nests that degenerate centrally to form cystic structures (Fig. 17.84). Mottled bubble-like defects are seen in the ureterogram.

Pelvic lipomatosis

Pelvic lipomatosis must be distinguished from a true lipoma of the kidney. The fatty replacement seen in lipomatosis develops whenever atrophy of the kidney occurs, and it is seen quite frequently with chronic pyelonephritis and renal lithiasis.[530,531] Diffuse adipose tissue is present in the vicinity of the renal hilus, and the remainder of the kidney is atrophic. Microscopic sections show mature fat. Extensive lipomatosis associated with lithiasis may simulate a renal neoplasm by producing filling defects on pyelography.

Nephrolithiasis and nephrocalcinosis

Nephrolithiasis is a common disorder defined as the development and accumulation of stones within the collecting system of the kidney. The estimated incidence in the United States ranges from 7 to 21 cases per 10,000 population.[540] Men are affected approximately four times more frequently than women and the predominant age at onset is in the third to the fifth decades. The most characteristic symptoms of nephrolithiasis are pain and

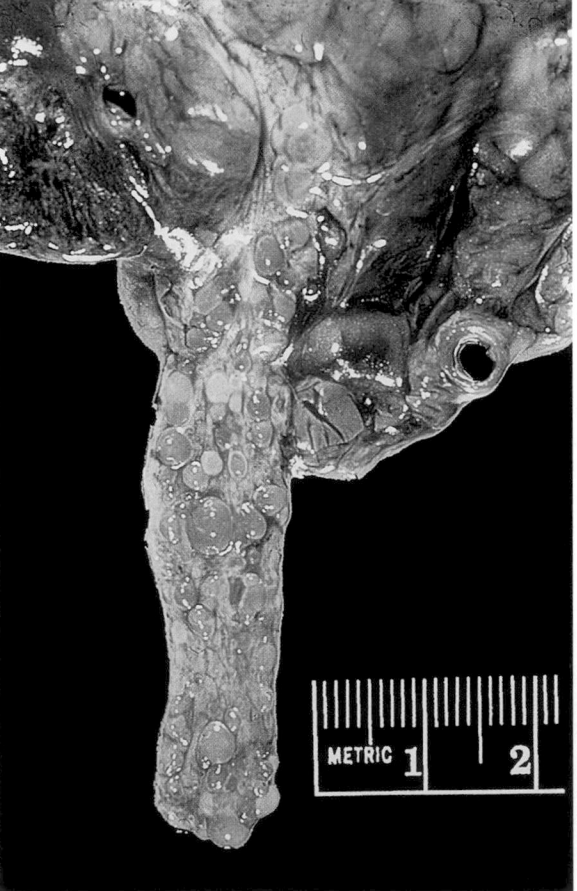

Fig. 17.84 Ureter covered by numerous vesicle-like lesions in a case of ureteritis cystica.

hematuria. The classic pain is that of severe, abrupt, flank pain (renal colic) which only resolves after the passage or removal of the stone. The hematuria can be gross or microscopic and most commonly occurs with large calculi during infection or colic. Approximately 75% of the stones are composed of calcium oxalate or calcium oxalate mixed with calcium phosphate; 15% are the so-called "struvite stones" that are composed of magnesium ammonium phosphate, and which are often associated with urea-splitting bacterial infections; 6% to 10% consist of uric acid, and 1% to 2% of cystine. Renal stones within the pelvic caliceal system can cause gross and microscopic changes in the renal parenchyma that are identical to those seen in pyelonephritis and hydronephrosis.

The presence of calcium within the renal parenchyma is known as nephrocalcinosis. Calcium deposition occurs on tubular basement membranes and in the interstitium. Tubular atrophy, interstitial fibrosis, and periglomerular fibrosis are also present. Some of the glomeruli may be sclerosed. A number of systemic disorders are associated with nephrocalcinosis and the formation of stones. Calcium phosphate and oxalate stones occur in hyperparathyroidism, sarcoidosis, the milk–alkali syndrome, excessive dietary intake of vitamin D, multiple myeloma, and renal tubular acidosis.

Uric acid stone formation takes place in an acid urine in the presence of hyperuricosuria, which may result from an inborn error of metabolism such as gout or the Lesch–Nyhan syndrome, glycogen storage disease following treatment of hematopoietic malignancies, overindulgence in dietary proteins, or the use of uricosuric drugs.[534,542] Uric acid stones are usually radiolucent. They are often small and may be passed, but larger ones in the renal pelvis can grow and become staghorn calculi. Uric acid crystals are also deposited within the renal parenchyma and can be seen within the collecting tubules as elongated or rectangular crystals or as doubly refractile crystals in the interstitium surrounded by a giant cell reaction.[535,536]

A clinical sign of cystinuria is calculi in the urinary tract. The stones are formed in acid urine. They are typically yellow–brown and radiopaque. Cystine crystals appear as microscopic, flat hexagons in the urine and this feature constitutes the clue for the diagnosis. The disorder is characterized by the defective transport of cystine, lysine, arginine, and ornithine by epithelial cells of the renal tubules and the gastrointestinal tract; it is transmitted as an autosomal recessive trait with an incidence of 1 in 20,000.[532,539] Complications of calculi formation include urinary tract obstruction and infection, which may result in renal failure.

Hyperoxaluria is characterized by recurring calcium oxalate nephrolithiasis and/or nephrocalcinosis often terminating in chronic renal failure (Fig. 17.85). Type 1 and type 2 hyperoxaluria are two rare genetic disorders of glycoxalate metabolism resulting in hyperox-

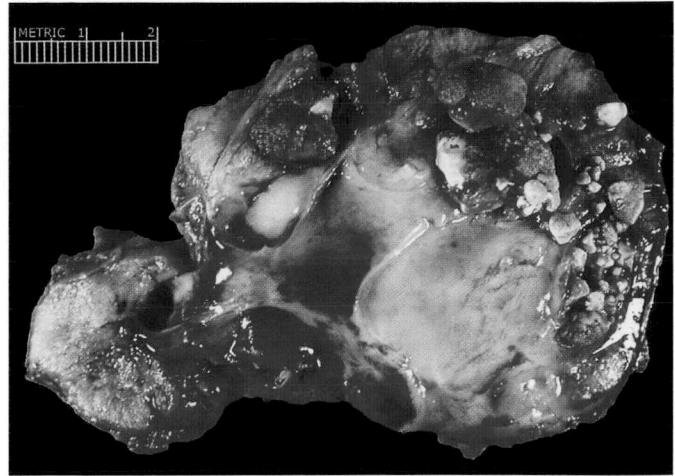

Fig. 17.85 Severely distorted kidney with dilated pelvicaliceal system containing numerous stones in a case of primary oxalosis.

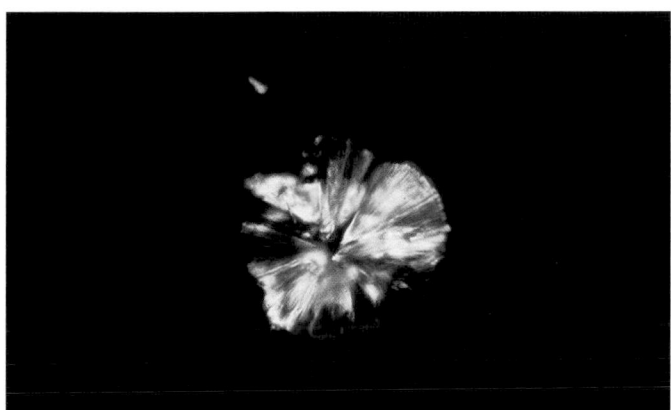

Fig. 17.86 Oxalate crystal under polarized light.

aluria.[537,538] Ethylene glycol poisoning, methoxyflurane anesthesia, pyridoxine deficiency, and various chronic gastrointestinal disorders (including Crohn's disease, chronic pancreatitis, and status post jejunoileal bypass procedure) have been associated with oxalosis.[533,537] In the kidney, oxalate crystals are deposited in the interstitium, tubules, and, rarely, glomeruli. They have radial striations that show up particularly well with polarized light (Fig. 17.86). The results are tubular atrophy, interstitial fibrosis and inflammation, and glomerular sclerosis.

Xanthinuria is a rare hereditary condition transmitted as an autosomal recessive trait. The enzyme xanthine oxidase, which is responsible for the conversion of xanthine and hypoxanthine to uric acid, is deficient. Xanthine stone formation occurs in one third of patients with this disorder. Similar stones are seen as a complication of allopurinol therapy since this drug blocks xanthine oxidase activity.[541]

Myeloma cast nephropathy

Myeloma cast nephropathy, also known as Bence Jones cast nephropathy or myeloma kidney, is the most common form of renal disease associated with multiple myeloma. Clinically, it may present as progressive renal insufficiency or acute renal failure, which may be precipitated by dehydration, hypercalcemia, intravenous infusion of contrast media, or antibiotic toxicity. Proteinuria is found, although not usually in the nephrotic range, and it most often consists predominantly of immunoglobulin light chains (Bence Jones protein). Light chains are normally filtered by the glomeruli, and reabsorbed and metabolized by proximal tubular cells. In patients with multiple myeloma, the excess monoclonal light chains overwhelm the catabolic capacity of the proximal tubules, thus allowing them to reach the distal nephron where the presence of Tamm–Horsfall protein may facilitate their precipitation in the form of voluminous casts. It is believed that these light chains in some way damage the renal tubules and ultimately damage the entire nephron resulting in renal failure.

By light microscopy, the distal and collecting tubules appear occluded by numerous dense, markedly eosinophilic, lamellated casts sometimes surrounded by multinucleated giant cells which are derived from interstitial macrophages that invade the tubules through breaks in the basement membrane (Fig. 17.87).[544,545] Some casts may exhibit Congo red and thioflavin T positivity. The tubular cells may appear flattened or show varying degrees of degeneration with necrosis and denudation of the tubular basement membranes. Depending on the staging of the disease, there is a variable degree of interstitial fibrosis, usually associated with acute and/or chronic inflammatory cell infiltrates. The casts may sometimes contain rhomboid or needle-shaped crystalline structures which may also be found in the tubular epithelium and, on rare occasions, in the glomeruli.[543] By electron microscopy, the crystals show a characteristic lattice-like pattern with a periodicity of 8 to 11 nm. Immunofluorescence studies demonstrate that the casts are largely made of the pathogenic light chain, either

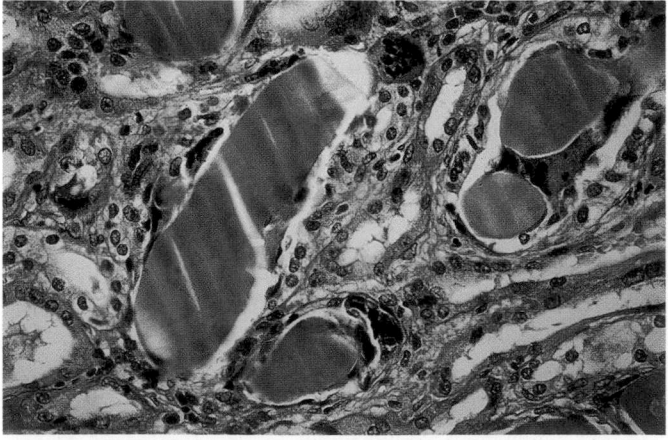

Fig. 17.87 Light chain cast nephropathy. Large laminated tubular casts surrounded by multinucleated giant cells.

kappa or lambda. Tamm–Horsfall protein is invariably present.

Renal vascular disease

Renal arteriolar disease

The kidney plays an essential role in hypertension, and the vessels of the kidney are susceptible to a variety of pathologic changes directly related to increased pressure.[546] The most susceptible vessels are small arteries and arterioles, with preglomerular vessels being more prominently affected. Narrowing of these intrarenal vessels eventually leads to glomerular sclerosis, tubular atrophy, and interstitial fibrosis (nephrosclerosis). The changes in the small vessels of the kidney fall into three general categories: hyaline arteriolosclerosis, myointimal hypertrophy and hyperplasia, and fibrinoid necrosis.[547]

In **hyaline arteriolosclerosis**, the outer part of the wall of affected vessels is thickened by deposition of a homogeneous, eosinophilic, PAS-positive material (Fig. 17.88). Associated changes are atrophy of the smooth muscle cells in the vessel walls and uniform thickening of the basement membrane. Hyaline arteriolosclerosis is most marked in the afferent arteriole and in vessels lacking an internal elastic lamina. Mild hyaline arteriolosclerosis is often seen with increasing age but it is more prominent in patients with hypertension or diabetes. The effects are more marked in hypertension where the arteriolar lumina become severely narrowed causing diffuse renal ischemia and symmetric shrinking of the kidneys. It is believed that the hyalin results from leakage of plasma components across the vascular endothelium and increasing extracellular matrix production by smooth muscle cells. The hyalinized arterioles are usually immunoreactive for IgM and complement components, especially C3 (Fig. 17.88 inset). Hyaline arteriolosclerosis is a major morphologic feature in benign nephrosclerosis in which, in addition to arteriolar hyalinization, the interlobular and arcuate arteries may exhibit medial hypertrophy and reduplication of the elastic lamina.

The second type of vascular abnormality seen in hypertension is that of **myointimal hypertrophy and hyperplasia**. The hyperplastic lesions involve the smooth muscle and intima of small arteries and arterioles. Hyperplastic arteriolosclerosis is generally associated with acute or persistent severe high blood pressure and, therefore, is seen more often in malignant than benign hypertension. In the early stages, the lesions are characterized by profuse intimal thickening by myxoid and sparse cellular connective tissue, which drastically reduces the vascular lumen. Over time, this acute change shows progressive scarring and uniform concentric thickening of the vessel wall by a proliferation of myointimal cells, and deposition of basement membrane-like material. The microscopic appearance of this lesion has led to

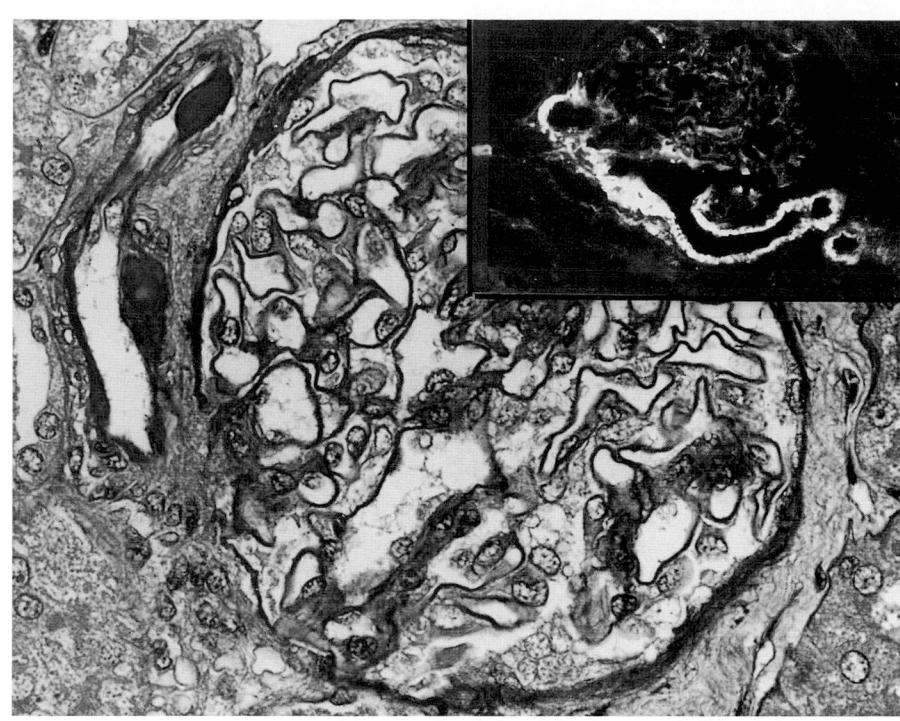

Fig. 17.88 Afferent arteriole with subintimal homogeneous hyaline material. Inset: Immunofluorescence preparation showing reaction for C3. (Reproduced from Spargo BH, Seymour AE, Ordóñez NG. Introduction. In: Renal biopsy pathology with diagnostic and therapeutic implications. New York, 1980, John Wiley & Sons, pp. 1–13. By permission of John Wiley & Sons, Inc.)

the descriptive term of "onion skinning" (Fig. 17.89). These changes are more pronounced in arcuate and interlobular arteries, but they extend into the arterioles where they may coexist with hyalinosis from longstanding hypertension.

The third and most dramatic renal vascular lesion in hypertension is necrotizing arteriolitis.[548] **Fibrinoid necrosis** of the afferent arteriole has been regarded as the hallmark of accelerated (malignant) hypertension (Fig. 17.90). The necrosis is usually superimposed on a pre-existing hyperplastic or hyaline lesion but it can be the initial event in young patients with severe acute malignant hypertension. The architecture of the media of affected vessels is obliterated by the necrotizing process and further obscured by the deposition of deeply eosinophilic, fibrillar material which, by histochemical and immunofluorescent techniques, has been demonstrated to be fibrin and fibrinogen.[549] The arteriolar lumen may be reduced in size as a result of wall thickening, extravasation of red blood cells, and intraluminal

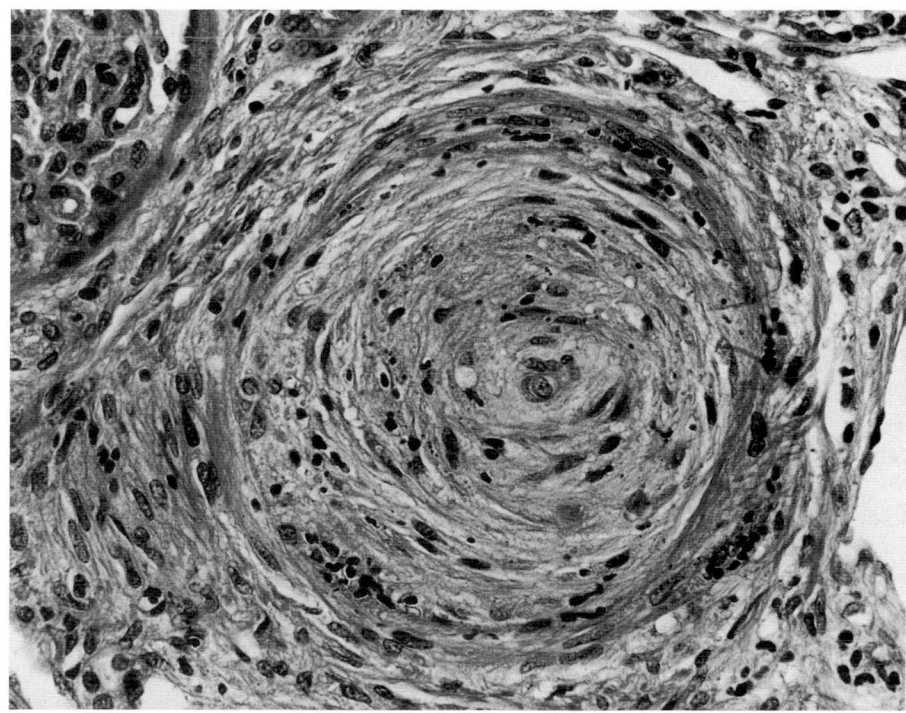

Fig. 17.89 Malignant hypertension. Interlobular artery with thinning of the media and marked intimal hyperplasia with hemorrhage. (Reproduced from Spargo BH, Seymour AE, Ordóñez NG. Introduction. In: Renal biopsy pathology with diagnostic and therapeutic implications. New York, 1980, John Wiley & Sons, pp. 1–13. By permission of John Wiley & Sons, Inc.)

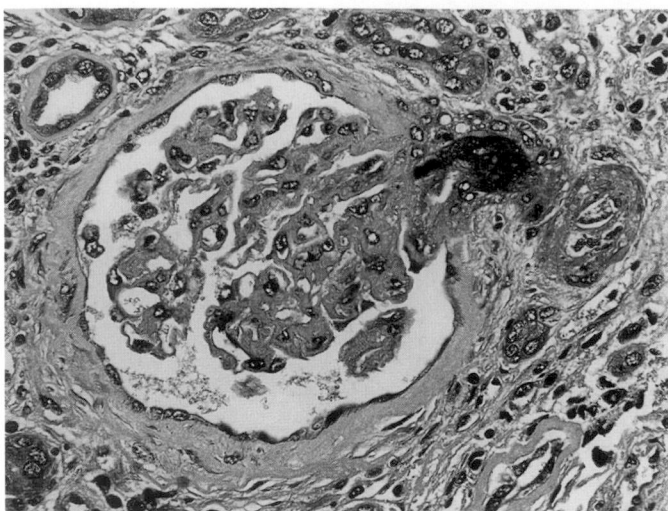

Fig. 17.90 Malignant hypertension. Necrosis of the afferent arteriole with ischemic shrinkage of the tuft. (Reproduced from Spargo BH, Seymour AE, Ordóñez NG. Introduction. In: Renal biopsy pathology with diagnostic and therapeutic implications. New York, 1980, John Wiley & Sons, pp. 1–13. By permission of John Wiley & Sons, Inc.)

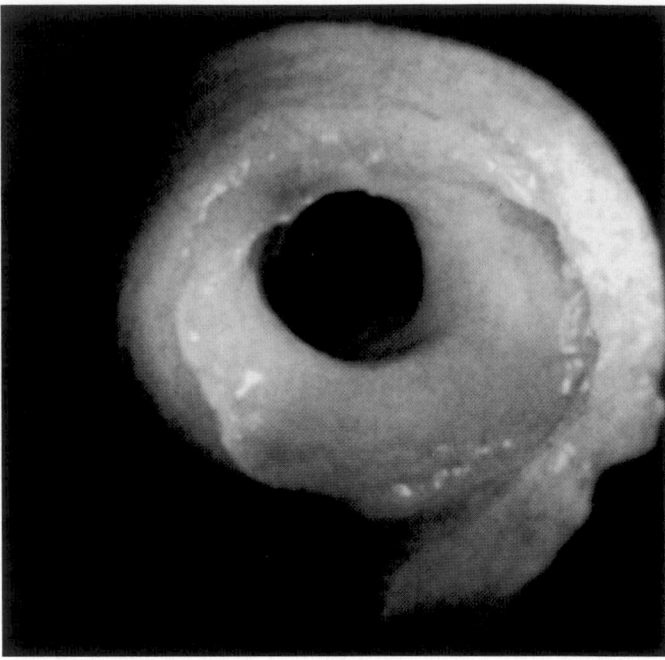

Fig. 17.91 Eccentric arteriosclerotic plaque in renal artery causing almost complete obstruction and hypertension. This was resected and arterial continuity reestablished.

thrombosis. Occasionally, leukocytes may be present in the wall, suggesting an inflammatory arteriolitis.

In malignant hypertension, the glomeruli often show a variable degree of ischemic changes characterized by wrinkling and collapse of the capillary walls (Fig. 17.90). In addition to this diffuse pattern of ischemic damage, segmental lesions may occur. There are either areas of apparent necrosis in direct continuity with arteriolar lesions or of proliferation, which may simulate segmental glomerulonephritis. Small epithelial or fibroepithelial crescents may be seen. By electron microscopy, the endothelium often appears swollen and sometimes focally disrupted or separated from the GBM by the accumulation of electron-lucent material. On occasion, subendothelial or intracapillary strands of fibrin may be seen. Immunofluorescence microscopy may reveal fibrin, fibrinogen, IgM, and complement components in a segmental distribution.

Renal arterial disease

The larger arteries in the kidney can also be the site of renal vascular disease. Atheromatous involvement is accelerated in patients with hypertension. It may be a source of atheromatous emboli and give rise to renal parenchymal infarcts. Arteries down to the arcuate size can show arteriosclerotic changes, but smaller vessels are more commonly involved by intimal thickening of the hyperplastic type, similar to that seen in the small arteries. Disease of the major arteries becomes particularly important when it involves a main renal artery and causes significant stenosis, resulting in secondary hypertension (Fig. 17.91).[550,557] The lesions involving the main renal artery can be broken down into three categories:

arteriosclerosis, dysplastic diseases of the fibromuscular vessels, and a miscellaneous group that includes congenital anomalies, Takayasu's aortitis, and radiation injury.

The most common cause of renal artery stenosis is obstruction of the lumen by an **atheromatous plaque** at the orifice of the main renal artery.[556] It is usually associated with severe atheromatous disease of the aorta and is seen more often in males and in patients with diabetes mellitus. The lesion is frequently associated with aneurysmal dilatation of the aorta distal to the renal arteries.

The second group of conditions that lead to stenosis are the so-called **dysplastic lesions of the renal artery**.[553,554] These lesions can involve other systemic vessels, suggesting that there may be an underlying defect in vessel structure, and can become clinically important when they cause obstruction of a major renal artery, thereby leading to severe hypertension which is not responsive to antihypertensive drugs. Typically, these lesions occur in the distal two thirds of the artery and are bilateral in 50% of the cases. The disorders that fall within this group can be subdivided into six subtypes: intimal fibroplasia, medial fibroplasia, medial hyperplasia, perimedial fibroplasia, medial dissection, and periarterial fibroplasia. As the terms indicate, the differences may be somewhat subtle, and fibromuscular dysplasia has been coined as an umbrella term. There is, however, some value in subtyping since different patient populations may be affected (Table 17.12).

The lesion in *intimal fibroplasia* is hyperplasia of the intima. Microscopically, it is virtually indistinguishable

Table 17.12 Dysplastic lesions of the renal artery

Diagnosis	Age incidence	Sex incidence	Relative frequency	Lesion
Intimal fibroplasia	1–50	M = F	1–2%	Narrowing by intimal proliferation without lipid
Medial fibroplasia with aneurysms	30–60	F > M	60–70%	"String of beads," alternating stenosis and mural thinning
Medial hyperplasia	30–60	F > M	5–15%	Smooth muscle hyperplasia and thickening
Perimedial fibroplasia	30–60	F > M	15–24%	Fibrosis of outer media, occasionally aneurysms
Medial dissection	30–60	F > M	5–15%	Fibrosis of media with dissecting aneurysms
Periarterial fibroplasia	15–50	F > M	1%	Perivascular fibrosis and inflammation

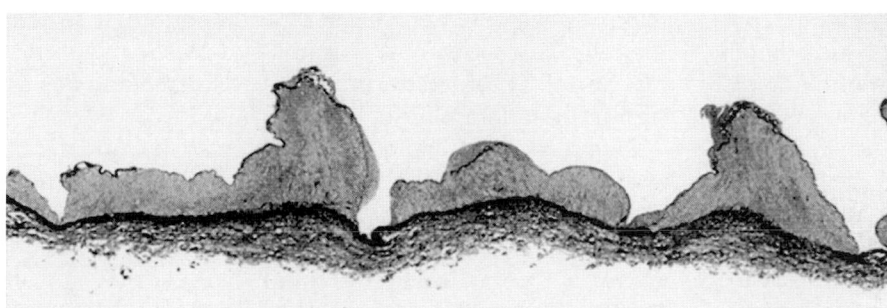

Fig. 17.92 Fibromuscular dysplasia in a young woman with hypertension. Note aneurysmal formations in this longitudinally sectioned artery demonstrating medial fibrodysplasia with mural aneurysms.

from the proliferative stage of atherosclerosis, although it is not associated with increased deposition of lipids. The architecture of the elastica and media are preserved so the only abnormality in the vessel wall is intimal hyperplasia. Individuals as young as 1 year of age have been affected, but it is seen more often in the third and fourth decades. The most common of the dysplastic lesions is *medial fibroplasia*. In this condition, multiple foci of stenosis alternate with microaneurysms to produce a "string of beads" appearance (Fig. 17.92).[555] Microscopically, atrophy of the muscle coat and fibrosis of the media in the vicinity of small aneurysms alternate with foci of muscular hypertrophy and fibrosis in the stenotic areas. The second in frequency is *perimedial fibroplasia* (Fig. 17.93). In this variant, segmental aneurysmal dilatation does not occur, and the outer half of the media, elastica, and intima maintain their normal architecture. Medial hyperplasia is seen less frequently. Hyperplasia of the muscle produces a uniform circumferential thickening of the vessel wall with narrowing of the lumen. *Periarterial fibroplasia* is a rare lesion in which fibrosis of the adventitia extends into the surrounding adipose and connective tissue, causing constriction of the vessel from without rather than from thickening within the wall.

Among the **miscellaneous causes** of renal artery stenosis, *radiation injury* is of particular interest.[552] The lesion is characterized by a loss of muscle and intense fibrosis in all layers of the vessel wall. It is usually a distant event that follows radiation therapy for a malignant tumor where the renal artery was included in the irradi-

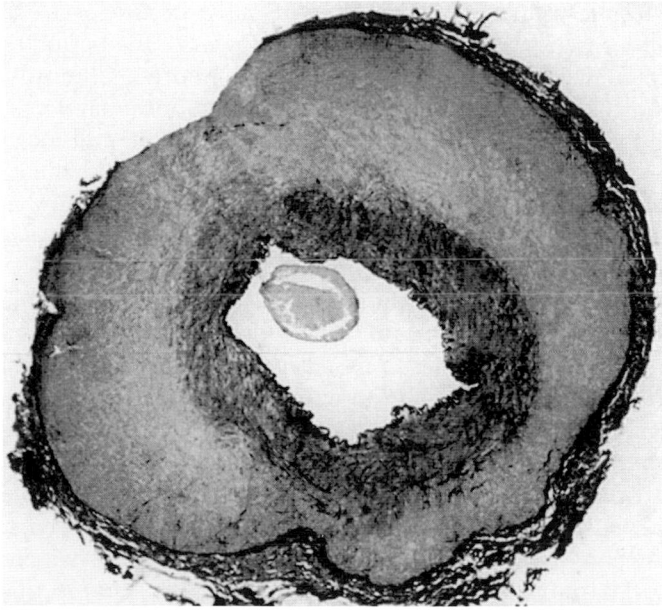

Fig. 17.93 Fibromuscular dysplasia in a 23-year-old woman with hypertension. Segmental resection revealed an artery with the perimedial variety of fibrodysplasia.

ated area. *Takayasu's aortitis* or pulseless disease is a chronic sclerosing aortitis of unknown etiology that can cause renal artery stenosis from narrowing of the ostium.[551] An inflammatory infiltrate is frequently present, suggesting an immunologic mechanism.

An ischemic kidney is smaller than the contralateral kidney, irrespective of the etiology. Glomeruli are small and the tubules are atrophic. Interstitial fibrosis is present, and the hyperplastic juxtaglomerular apparatus shows increased granulation with special stains. The small vessels are protected from the hypertension, in contrast to the contralateral kidney where biopsy may show hypertensive microvascular disease.

Radiation nephropathy

Radiation nephropathy is the term used to designate the renal disease that occurs as a result of irradiation of the abdomen during the treatment of malignant tumors. Although the term acute radiation nephritis has also been used for this disease, the terms acute and chronic radiation nephropathy, rather than nephritis, are preferred since no acute inflammation occurs immediately after kidney irradiation, and histologic examination of the radiation-damaged kidneys usually reveals only minimal proliferation and inflammatory changes.[558,559] The severity of the pathologic changes in the damaged kidney depends upon multiple factors including radiation dosage, method of irradiation, age of the patient, amount of perirenal fat, preexistence of renal disease, and the concomitant use of chemotherapeutic agents, as well as individual susceptibility.

Acute radiation nephropathy usually occurs 6 to 12 months after radiation exposure. However, the period of latency can be shorter, especially in children. Clinically, the disease is manifested by the gradual onset of edema, hypertension, dyspnea on exercise, pleural and peritoneal serous effusions, anemia, headaches, and urinary changes which include proteinuria and the presence of casts. Rare cases of radiation nephropathy causing nephrotic syndrome have been reported.[560] The glomerular filtration rate decreases and over half of the patients progress to renal failure. Those who recover from the acute episode usually have persistent proteinuria and renal impairment. On occasion, malignant hypertension may develop during the acute radiation syndrome. The mortality of patients with this complication is high.

Chronic radiation nephropathy either follows the acute phase or develops insidiously over a period of years. Although no specific threshold has been established for total accumulative radiation exposure that leads to this form of injury, it appears that relatively small doses of radiation (500 to 1000 rads) may, in susceptible individuals, cause renal damage.[559] In most patients, the findings of mild proteinuria and moderate hypertension are not detected until many years after radiation exposure.

Depending on the severity and stage of the disease, biopsies from patients with radiation nephropathy will show a wide range of glomerulosclerosis.[558] Some glomeruli may appear segmentally or completely scarred, while others may show no significant changes. Segmental areas of fibrinoid necrosis of the tuft in continuity with similar changes in the arterioles may be seen. The glomerular capillary walls may be thickened, and a double contour may be demonstrated by silver impregnation techniques.[561] The mesangium may be prominent as a result of an increase in mesangial matrix. Mesangiolysis, adhesions to Bowman's capsule, and occasional crescents may be seen. Vascular injury is manifested by fibrinoid necrosis of arterioles and small arteries, sometimes accompanied by thrombosis. Loose intimal thickening involving arterioles and interlobular arteries is a frequent feature. The arterial lumina may also be narrowed by foamy cells.[559] Swelling of the tubular epithelium with desquamation of the cells, and basement membrane thickening and splitting followed by tubular loss and atrophy are common findings and may be severe. Regeneration is often abnormal so that the cells may have poorly formed cytoplasm and abnormal nuclei. The interstitium is focally scarred and has no significant inflammation.

Electron microscopic examination of the glomeruli shows widening of the subendothelial zone which may contain flocculent material or strands of fibrin. Focal extension of the mesangium into the subendothelial space may also be seen. The endothelial cells may appear swollen or focally detached from the endothelial aspect of the GBM. Immunofluorescence may show focal deposition of IgM and fibrinogen in glomeruli and blood vessels.

Bone marrow transplant nephropathy

Bone marrow transplant nephropathy is the term used to designate a syndrome of late onset renal insufficiency that has been reported to occur in up to 20% of patients who have received a bone marrow transplant.[563] Total body irradiation is the main factor in the development of bone marrow transplant nephropathy, but it is possible that other factors, such as drug therapy and infections, may also contribute to this syndrome.[562,563] The renal insufficiency usually manifests 9 to 12 months after the transplant. In some patients, the clinical picture can be similar to that of hemolytic uremic syndrome with a rapid decline of renal function, while in others there may be a slow decline in renal function without apparent ongoing hemolysis.[564] The renal lesions, regardless of whether or not the patient has clinical evidence of hemolytic uremic syndrome, typically affect the glomeruli and small arterial and arteriolar vessels, and are histologically similar to those reported in radiation nephropathy and hemolytic uremic syndrome.[562]

Cystic diseases of the kidney

Due to space limitations, only the most common cystic diseases will be discussed in this section.

Multicystic renal dysplasia

In multicystic renal dysplasia the development of the kidney is disorganized because of anomalous differentiation of the metanephros (Fig. 17.94). The disorder is the most common form of cystic renal disease in children and the most common cause of abdominal masses in newborns. The dysplasia is usually unilateral, but can be bilateral, segmental, or focal.[565] Abnormalities of the collecting system are common and they include obstruction of the uretero-pelvic junction, ureteral atresia, and urethral obstruction. Malformations of other organs, especially of the heart, can occur in conjunction with renal dysplasia. The clinical presentation largely depends on the extent of the dysplastic involvement and the degree of associated urinary obstruction. Most dysplastic kidneys arise sporadically, but a few are familial or occur in syndromes of multiple malformations. A large reniform mass of cysts of various sizes obscures any renal parenchyma that may be present. In focal and segmental dysplasia, only part of the kidney is involved by the dysplasia and cyst formation. Microscopically, the findings are quite characteristic.[566,567] The cysts are lined by cuboidal epithelial cells and surrounded by immature stromal elements. Primitive tubules and glomerular structures may be present, as may islands of dysplastic mesenchyme including cartilage and fibromuscular tissue (Fig. 17.95).

Fig. 17.94 Dysplastic kidney of an infant. The opposite kidney appeared normal by pyelogram.

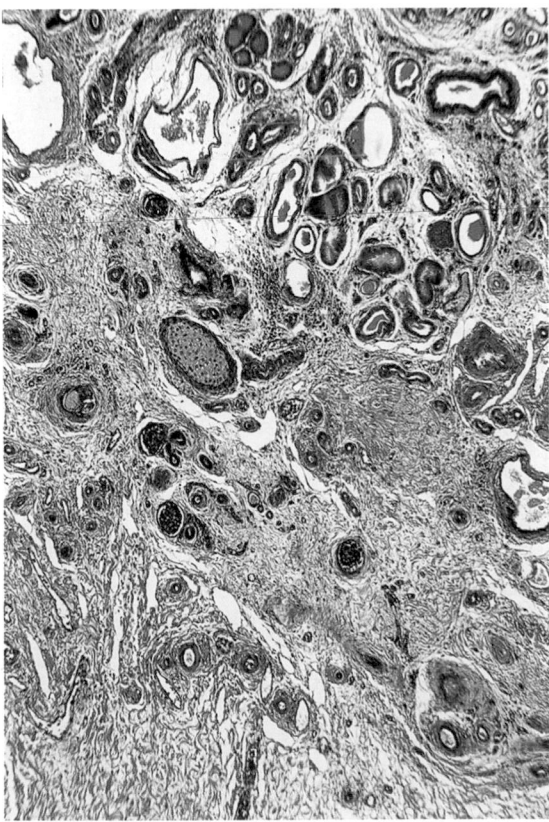

Fig. 17.95 Same kidney illustrated in Fig. 17.94 showing embryonic-like connective tissue and tubules.

Autosomal dominant (adult) polycystic kidney disease

Autosomal dominant polycystic kidney disease (ADPKD) is a hereditary condition characterized by expanding cysts that progressively destroy the renal parenchyma of both kidneys, ultimately causing renal failure. It is one of the most common hereditary human disorders, occurring in approximately 1 or 2 per 1000 live births and accounting for approximately 10% of cases requiring dialysis or renal transplantation.[571,573] The pattern of inheritance is autosomal dominant with almost complete penetrance. The disease is genetically heterogeneous and is caused by a mutation in two genes, *PKD1* and *PKD2*, that are located on chromosomes 16p13.3 and 4q13–23, respectively.[576,579] Mutations in the *PKD1* gene are responsible for 85% to 90% of all cases of ADPKD; mutations in *PKD2* cause the disease in the large majority of the remaining patients. The absence of a linkage to *PKD1* or *PKD2* in a few families with the ADPKD phenotype has been seen as evidence of the existence of *PKD3*, a third gene for this condition. This gene, however, has not yet been mapped. Approximately 10% of the patients do not have a family history and are considered to have new mutations. Males and females are equally affected. ADPKD can present at any time during life but most frequently becomes symptomatic during the fourth and fifth decades with a gradual onset of renal failure. Clinical manifestations include flank pain, flank masses, hematuria, hypertension, and renal failure. Approximately 20% of the patients with ADPKD develop nephrolithiasis.[578] Radiographic findings are usually diagnostic, sonography and computed tomography are reliable procedures for the demonstration of early involvement, and gene linkage analysis allows prenatal diagnosis.[568,578,583] The disease is bilateral, but significant asynchrony of involvement of the kidneys may be noted on occasion.[577] The kidneys are markedly enlarged and have a bosselated outer cortical surface which is produced by multiple cysts of

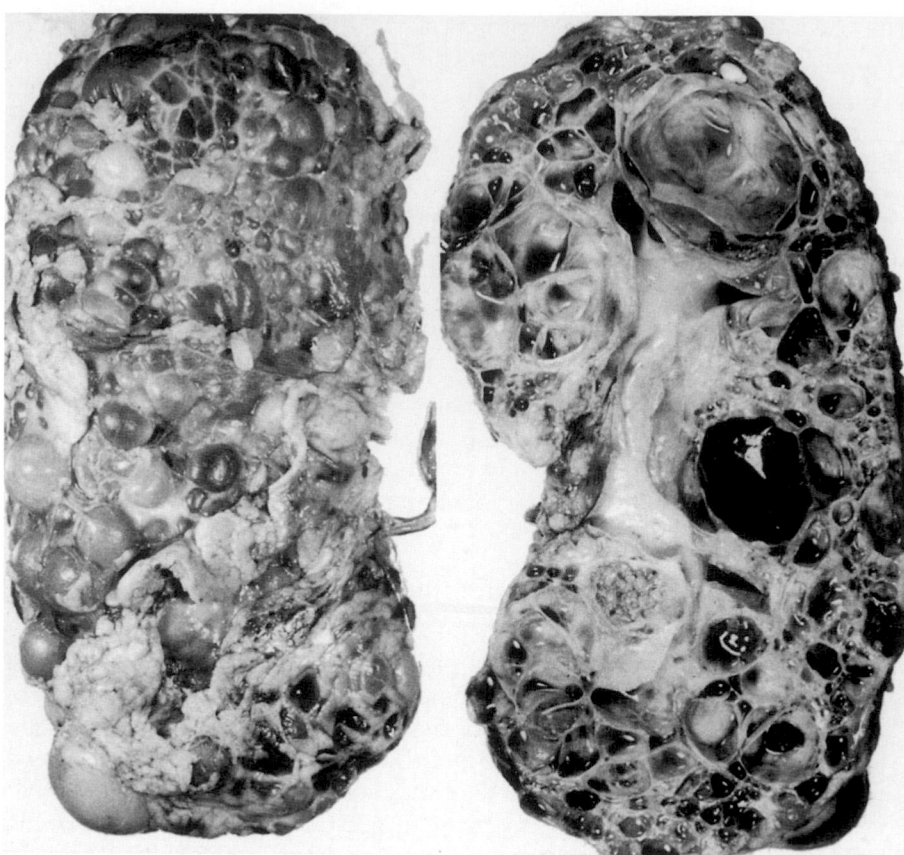

Fig. 17.96 External and cut surface of a nephrectomy specimen from a patient with autosomal dominant polycystic kidney disease.

varying sizes (Fig. 17.96). When the disease is severe, normal renal parenchyma is apparent only on microscopy. The cysts develop in all segments of the renal tubule and glomerular capsule as saccular expansions or diverticula. In the early stages, the fluid of the cysts is derived from glomerular filtrate. As the cysts enlarge, however, they commonly become disconnected from the tubule of origin, thereafter filling with fluid exclusively by transepithelial secretion.[573] On light microscopy, the cysts are lined by cuboidal, flattened epithelium, and hyperplastic polypoid foci are often found. The intervening renal parenchyma appears relatively normal although foci of interstitial scarring, tubular atrophy, and pyelonephritis are common. Renal adenomas have been reported to develop in approximately 20% of the patients with ADPKD.[574]

ADPKD is considered a systemic condition since over half of the patients develop cysts in other organs including the liver, pancreas, spleen, pineal gland, seminal vesicles, and lungs.[571,572,578] Other abnormalities include the presence of cerebral[570,582] and coronary[569,581] artery aneurysms, mitral valve prolapse, abnormal aortic valves,[570,575] colonic diverticula,[580] and skeletal malformations.[583]

Autosomal recessive (infantile) polycystic kidney disease

Autosomal recessive polycystic kidney disease is a rare disorder with an estimated incidence of 1 per 20,000 live births. The genetic defect has been localized to the short arm of chromosome 6.[585,586,588] The liver and both kidneys are invariably affected, but the severity of involvement varies, thus creating a spectrum of clinical presentation. In the neonatal period, the renal symptoms usually predominate. Later in life, patients seek medical attention because of hepatic disease, which consists of congenital hepatic fibrosis with a variable degree of biliary dysgenesis and bile duct ectasia.[584] These patients may also develop hepatic portal hypertension with hepatosplenomegaly and esophageal varices. Occasional patients may present with liver cysts, but cysts in other viscera aside from the kidneys and liver are rare and their presence may suggest a different disease.

Patients with autosomal recessive polycystic kidney disease present with large abdominal masses at birth. They may also have the "Potter" phenotype with its characteristic facies secondary to oligohydramnios, joint deformities, and pulmonary hypoplasia. Newborns who have the severe form of the disease die shortly after birth, usually due to respiratory failure. Patients who survive the perinatal period usually develop renal failure, hypertension, and portal hypertension. The estimated perinatal mortality is 30% to 50%; for those who survive the first month of life, the reported mean 5-year survival rate is 80% to 95%.[587,589]

The kidneys are markedly enlarged bilaterally but retain their reniform configuration. The cysts tend to be linear and radiate from the medulla to the outer cortex. They develop in the collecting ducts, which expand to a large size due to fluid accumulation within the cyst cavity. Microscopically, the cysts appear as dilated tubular structures lined by cuboidal or flattened epithelium. The intervening tissue may contain uninvolved nephrons, but this depends on the severity of the disorder.

Medullary sponge kidney

Medullary sponge kidney (MSK) is a renal cystic disorder characterized by dilated medullary and papillary collecting ducts which give the renal medulla a sponge-like appearance. The true incidence of MSK is unknown, although it has been estimated at 1 per 5000 population.[595] The disease is asymptomatic unless it is complicated by nephrolithiasis, hematuria, or infections. In these instances, the diagnosis is established when the patient undergoes radiographic examination.[595,596] Typically, symptoms start between the fourth and fifth decades of life, but presentation in adolescence has been reported.[591] Both sexes are equally affected. Most cases appear sporadically and, while occurrences in siblings or in the same family have been documented in rare instances, no clear family transmission has been established.[593,594] A curious association with hemihypertrophy of the body has been reported in as many as 25% of the patients.[592]

The involved kidneys are usually normal in size, but they can be slightly enlarged in those cases presenting pronounced sponge-like changes. The cysts are multiple, small, and limited to the medullary pyramids and papillae. They usually affect all pyramids in both kidneys but, on occasion, only one or two pyramids or only one kidney may be affected. The cysts are lined by collecting duct epithelium and usually communicate with collecting tubules.[590] Concretions adherent to the walls of the cysts and the dilated collecting ducts may be seen. The interstitium often shows severe inflammation and scarring, often accompanied by tubular atrophy, especially near the papillary tips. In instances where there is nephrolithiasis and pyelonephritis, the cortex may show significant cortical scarring.

Nephronophthisis–medullary cystic kidney disease complex

Nephronophthisis–medullary cystic kidney disease (NPH-MCKD) complex encompasses several renal disorders that, although they are genetically heterogeneous, share some clinical features and have a similar macroscopic pathology and renal histology.[603,604] The diseases of the NPH-MCKD complex have been divided into two major groups based on their mode of inheritance and the age of onset of the end-stage renal disease. The term nephronophthisis (NPH) is used to designate those variants transmitted by an autosomal recessive mode of inheritance, whereas the term medullary cystic kidney disease (MCKD) is used for those transmitted as an autosomal dominant trait. Three forms of NPH, referred to as juvenile (NPH1),[601] infantile (NPH2),[602] and adolescent (NPH3),[608] with a median age for the onset of end-stage renal disease of 13 years, 1 to 3 years, and 19 years, respectively, have been recognized. In MCKD, terminal renal failure occurs only in adulthood; two variants, known as MCKD1 and MCKD2, with a median age of onset of end-stage renal disease of 62 and 32 years, respectively, have been identified.

Juvenile NPH constitutes the most common genetic cause of end-stage renal disease in children. Both sexes are equally affected. The clinical presentation usually occurs at approximately 4 years of age. It consists of polydipsia, polyuria, anuresis, decrease in urinary concentration, severe anemia, and growth retardation. The disease occurs in a pure renal form in approximately 85% of the patients. Approximately 12% of the cases are associated with retinitis pigmentosa (Senior–Loken syndrome).[606,611] Other less common renal associations that have been described include hepatic fibrosis, skeletal malformations, and various defects of the central nervous system.[597,598,603,607,609] The gene responsible for the purely renal form of NPH1 (*NPHP1*) has recently been identified on chromosome 2q13.[605] This gene encodes a novel protein called nephrocystin whose function remains unclear. The genes for NPH2 and NPH3 are localized on chromosomes 9q22–q31 and 3q21–q22, respectively.[602,608] Neither of these two variants is associated with extrarenal disease.

The clinical presentation of **MCKD** typically occurs in the third and fourth decades of life and is similar to that of juvenile NPH except that the growth retardation and long history of anemia may not be found. MCKD is not associated with any of the extrarenal disorders that are found in NPH1; however, in both MCKD1 and MCKD2 there is an association with hyperuricemia and gout that is not present in any of the variants of NPH. The gene loci for MCKD1 and MCKD2 are on chromosomes 1q21 and 16p13, respectively.[599,610]

All variants of the NPH-MCKD complex have similar microscopic and histopathologic features. The kidneys are normal or moderately reduced in size and exhibit a granular surface. Renal involvement is always bilateral. On cut sections, the cortex and medulla are both thinned. The corticomedullary junction is indistinct and typically the site of a variable number of thin-walled, fluid-filled cysts ranging in size from barely visible up to 2.0 cm in diameter. The cysts may also occur deeper in the renal medulla and occasionally in the papillae. Microdissection studies have shown that the cysts arise from the loop of Henle, distal convoluted tubules, and collecting ducts. Histologic findings are nonspecific and depend upon the severity of the disease. Tubulointerstitial fibrosis with lymphocytic inflammatory infiltrate, tubular atrophy, and cyst formation is seen. The tubular atrophy is often accompanied by a marked thickening of the tubular basement membrane that is better seen on PAS-stained sections. By electron microscopy, these basement membranes can appear homogeneously thickened, split into thin lamellae, reticulated, or completely disintegrated.[600,612] It has been suggested that these findings, as well as that of a reduction or absence of certain antigens, indicate a primary biochemical or structural abnormality of the tubular basement membrane.

Acquired renal cystic disease

Although acquired renal cystic disease (ARCD) was initially reported in patients undergoing long-term dialysis, similar changes can also occur in uremic nondialyzed patients.[615,616] ARCD has been reported to occur in 7% to 22% of patients with renal failure who are not on dialysis, 40% of patients who have been on dialysis for 3 years, and 80% to 90% of patients who have been on dialysis for 10 years.[613] The etiology of ARCD has not yet been well established and it has been suggested that the cysts found in this condition result from obstruction of the renal tubules by local fibrosis, oxalate deposition, or epithelial hyperplasia. In most cases, the disease is asymptomatic but sometimes the cysts bleed, rupture, or become infected causing fever, hematuria, and flank pain. The most serious complication, however, is the development of renal carcinomas in the walls of the cysts. It has been estimated that renal cell carcinoma is found 50 times more frequently in dialysis patients with ARCD than in the general population.

The cysts in ARCD are usually bilateral and occur both in the renal cortex and medulla. Their number can vary from a few subcapsular cysts to diffuse involvement of almost the entire renal parenchyma. The cysts are filled with straw-colored or hemorrhagic fluid and often contain calcium oxalate crystals. Most cysts are less than 0.5 cm, but they can measure up to 2 to 3 cm in diameter. Microscopically, most cysts are lined by flattened epithelium, while some are lined by hyperplastic cuboidal or columnar cells. Some of these hyperplastic cysts may also have papillary projections that may on occasion exhibit cellular atypia. Most of the tumors found in ARCD are papillary adenomas that have no clinical importance for the patient. Renal cell carcinomas have been reported to occur in approximately 6% of the dialyzed patients with ARCD. They can be multicentric in approximately 50% of the cases, and bilateral in approximately 10%, and although they are predominantly papillary, they can also be of the nonpapillary clear cell type.[614]

Simple cysts

Simple cysts are the most common cystic abnormality encountered in the kidneys. Their occurrence increases with age, with an incidence of less than 0.1% in children and up to 20% in individuals over 50 years of age.[617] They are usually asymptomatic and are often detected at autopsy or as an incidental finding in the radiologic evaluation for other diseases. On occasion, however, when complicated by hemorrhage or infection, they can cause pain. Simple cysts can be solitary or multiple and bilateral. They occur more commonly in the renal cortex, and although their etiology has not been well established, it is believed that they are derived from preexisting tubules. Most are under 5 cm in diameter, but larger cysts have been documented. They are usually unilocular, but on occasion bilocular or multilocular. The cysts are normally translucent, filled with clear serous fluid, and lined by a single layer of cuboidal or flattened epithelium. Cases complicated by hemorrhage or infection can have thick capsular walls with hemosiderin-laden macrophages and atrophic lining epithelium.

Pediatric tumors and tumorlike conditions

Wilms' tumor

General features

Wilms' tumor is also known as nephroblastoma (currently the preferred term), embryoma, carcinosarcoma, adenosarcoma, and adenomyosarcoma. It constitutes the prototypical example of a neoplastic process that faithfully recapitulates embryogenesis at the morphologic and molecular levels.[622,631a,651] It is seen primarily in infants, 50% of the cases occurring before the age of 3 years and 90% before the age of 6 years.[624,630,649] However, Wilms' tumor is only exceptionally seen as a congenital neoplasm, a point of great importance in the differential diagnosis with mesoblastic nephroma.[627] There are also well-documented cases of Wilms' tumors in adolescents[634] and adults.[625,628,650] The latter should be investigated and treated according to the same guidelines used for the pediatric neoplasms.[618] There is no appreciable sex predilection. The risk in whites is lower than in Orientals but higher than in blacks.

The classic location for Wilms' tumor is the kidney. Both kidneys are equally affected, the incidence of synchronous or metachronous bilateral involvement being 5% to 10%.[639,640,644] However, cases with the typical morphologic features of Wilms' tumor have been recorded in extrarenal sites, including the retroperitoneum, sacrococcygeal region, testis, uterus (sometimes presenting as a cervical polyp), inguinal canal, and mediastinum.[619,626,632,636,642,647,648] Some of them have arisen within a teratoma, and even those in which this feature was not evident have been viewed by some as teratomas with a predominant or exclusive nephroblastic component. A putative precursor lesion and expression of *WT1* gene (see later section) have been detected in some of these extrarenal cases.[642,643]

Wilms' tumor has been reported in monozygous twins and other familial settings.[629] Conditions associated with a *definite* increased risk of Wilms' tumor are Wilms–aniridia genital anomaly–retardation (WAGR) syndrome, omphalocele–macroglossia (Beckwith–Wiedemann syndrome), hemihypertrophy, and Denys–Drash syndrome.[623,633,635,645] Conditions associated with *possible* increased risk of Wilms' tumor are renal and genital malformations, cutaneous nevi and angiomas, trisomy 18, Klippel–Trenaunay syndrome, neurofibromatosis, Bloom syndrome, and cerebral gigantism.[620,638,641,646] The incidence of urogenital congenital abnormalities is particularly high for Wilms' tumors occurring during the first year of life and/or involving both kidneys. Wilms' tumor has also been encountered in association with other malignancies, such as osteosarcoma, botryoid rhabdomyosarcoma, retinoblastoma, hepatocellular carcinoma and neuroblastoma.[619a,621,631,637]

Clinical features

The classic clinical presentation of Wilms' tumor is in the form of an abdominal mass felt by the mother when handling the child. Hematuria and pain are rare. Hypertension, present in a minority of the cases, has been shown to be caused by renin secretion by the tumor.[656] Proteinuria may be caused by the presence of tumor-associated glomerular disease in the non-neoplastic kidney.[658] Sometimes the first symptoms are related to traumatic rupture. Cases have been reported presenting as sudden death resulting from tumor embolism.[659]

Intravenous pyelogram shows an intrarenal mass that displaces and distorts the pelvis. Ultrasonography, CT scan, and MRI are used to further define the tumor extent.

Several potential tumor markers have been described in association with Wilms' tumor.[652] These include increased circulating levels of hyaluronic acid,[657] acquired von Willebrand's factor (which may be associated with severe coagulopathies),[653] inactive renin,[654] and elevated serum levels of erythropoietin.[655] Unfortunately, none of them is specific or consistently present, and therefore their practical utility is not great.

Morphologic features

Grossly, most Wilms' tumors are solitary, well circumscribed, rounded, and of soft consistency. Their size is extremely variable, with a median of 550 g. The cut section is predominantly solid and pale gray or tan and often exhibits areas of cystic change, necrosis, and hemorrhage (Fig. 17.97). A lobular pattern resulting from fibrous septation is common. Multicentric foci are appreciable in 7% of the cases.

Microscopically, three major components are identified: undifferentiated blastema, mesenchymal (stromal) tissue, and epithelial tissue.[662,663,679] Most Wilms' tumors show a representation of all three components, but the proportions vary widely. Some tumors are biphasic, and still others are monophasic (monomorphous). The *blastematous* areas are extremely cellular and composed of small round-to-oval primitive cells; the cytoplasm is usually very scanty, but sometimes it exhibits an oncocytoid appearance. The pattern of growth may be diffuse, nodular, cordlike (serpentine), or basaloid (with peripheral palisading). Wilms' tumors in which the blastematous component predominates can be confused with any of the small round cell tumors, including neuroblastoma. The *mesenchymal* elements usually have a spindle cell fibroblast-like configuration but may also exhibit differentiation toward various cell types, particularly smooth

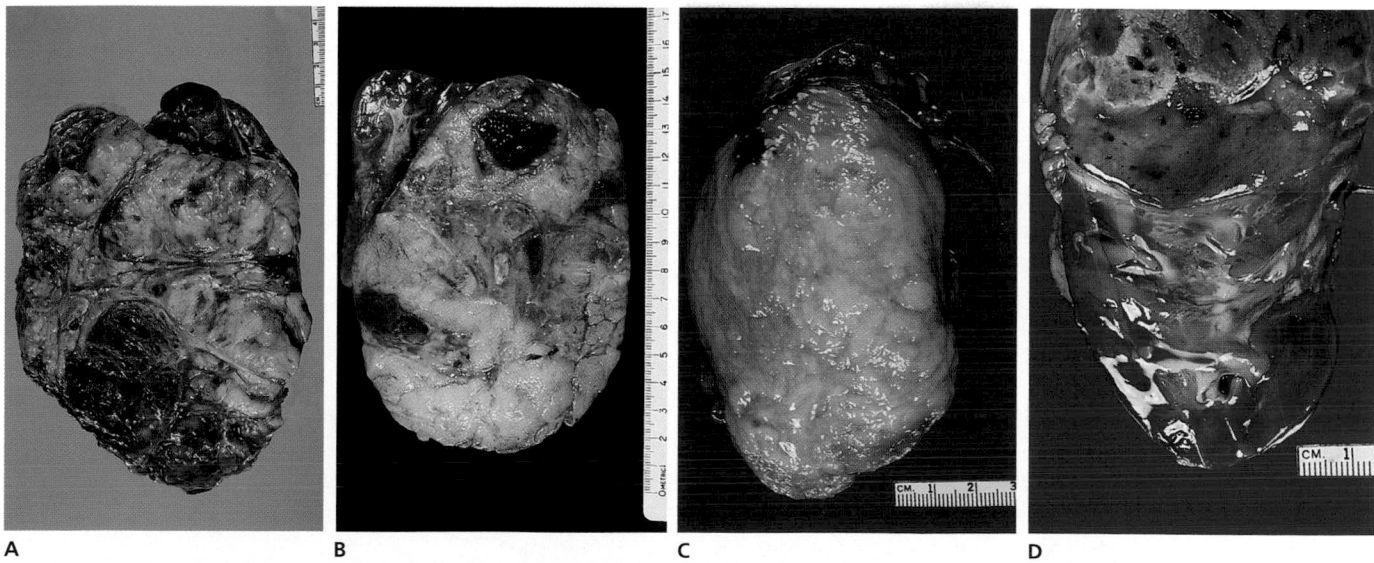

Fig. 17.97 A to D, Various gross appearances of Wilms' tumor. The lesions shown in **A** and **B** have a variegated appearance, that shown in **C** is more homogeneous and nodular, and that shown in **D** has extensive areas of infarct-like necrosis.

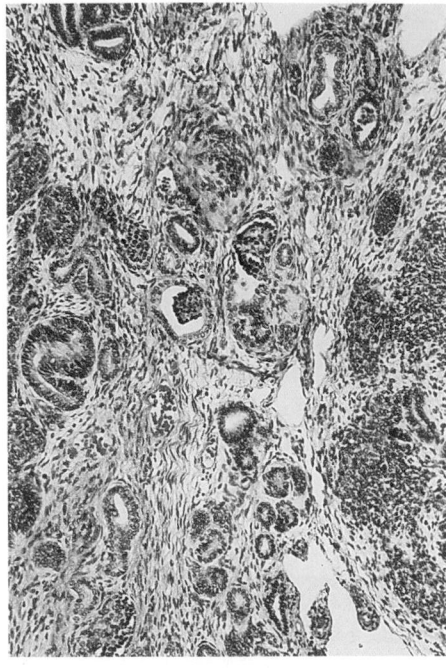
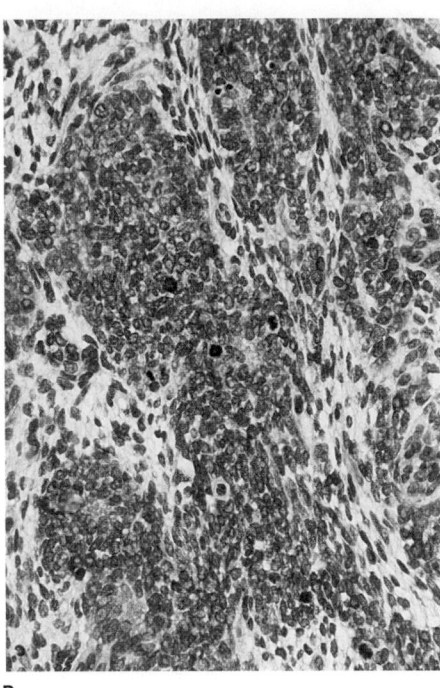

A   **B**

Fig. 17.98 A and **B**, Microscopic appearance of Wilms' tumor. **A**, Low-power microscopic view showing a combination of blastema, stroma, epithelial tubular formation, and immature glomeruli. **B**, High-power view showing blastema, stroma, and immature tubular formations.

muscle and skeletal muscle.[667] Sometimes this mesenchymal component predominates almost to the exclusion of others.[685] Wilms' tumors with an extensive skeletal muscle component are invariably seen in young children and are bilateral in over half of the cases.[668] Predominantly rhabdomyosarcomatous Wilms' tumors involving the renal pelvis or supernumerary ureteropelvic structures acquire morphologic features very similar to those of botryoid rhabdomyosarcoma.[678,682,684] In some instances, these largely mesenchymal neoplasms are seen in the opposite kidney of patients with typical Wilms' tumor.[672]

The *epithelial* component is characterized by the formation of embryonic tubular (and sometimes glomerular) structures that closely recapitulate the appearance of normal developing metanephric tubules (and glomeruli) at the light microscopic, ultrastructural, and lectin histochemistry levels[661,664,681,686] (Fig. 17.98). The differentiation can be so pronounced that tumor analogs of nearly all segments of the normal nephron can be formed.[670] These tubular structures can be small and round, thus simulating the rosettes of neuroblastoma. Features favoring tubules over basal lamina are the presence of a lumen, single cell layer, distinct basal lamina, and surrounding fibromyxoid stroma.[662] The differential diagnosis of predominantly epithelial Wilms' tumors also includes multicystic nephroma and renal cell carcinoma.[662,675] Exceptionally, marked hydropic changes are seen in the tubular epithelium.[666]

In the type known as *papillonodular*, grossly evident projections are seen extending from the septa into the cyst lumina.[674] The resulting appearance on low power may be fibroadenoma like.[665]

Anaplastic features may be present focally or exten-sively in Wilms' tumors; they are discussed in the section on prognosis.

Additional morphologic features that can be encountered in Wilms' tumor include ciliated, mucinous, squamous, or transitional epithelium[662,671] (Fig. 17.99); endocrine cells of various types[671]; renin-producing cells[676]; neuroepithelium, neuroblasts, and mature ganglion cells[669,680] (Fig. 17.100); neuroglia[673]; adipose tissue;

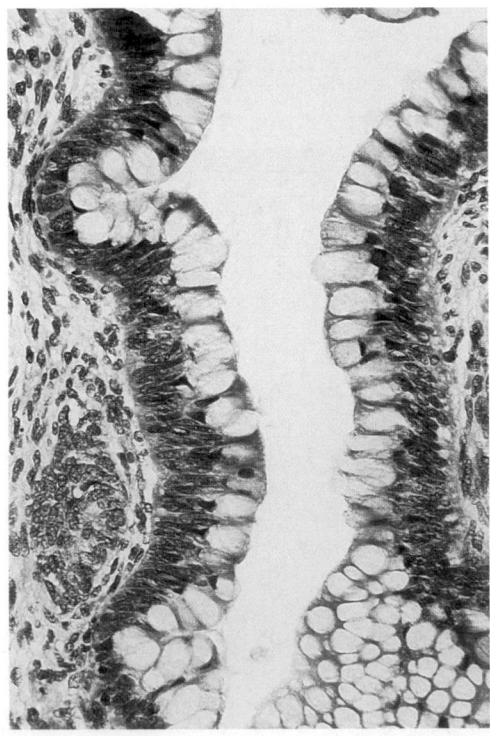

Fig. 17.99 Mucinous epithelium in Wilms' tumor.

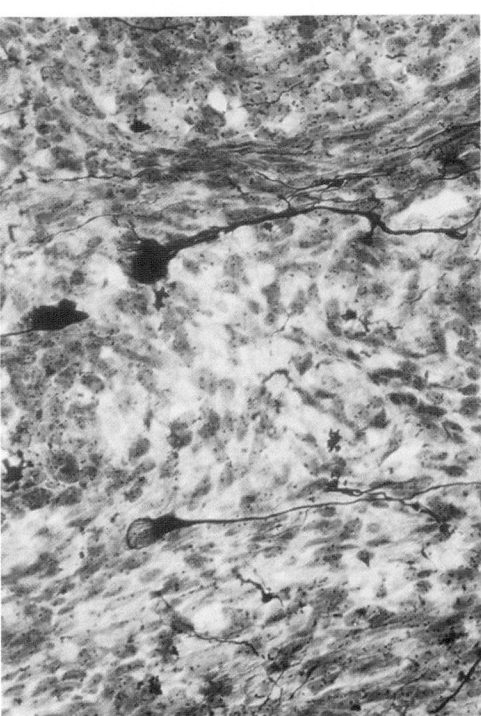

Fig. 17.100 Neural differentiation in Wilms' tumor. Several neuron-like structures with prominent dendritic extensions are well appreciated in this slide, stained with the Del-Rio Hortega technique. (Courtesy of Dr. Hugo Cejas, Cordoba, Argentina)

and cartilage, bone, and hematopoietic cells.[671] Sometimes the variety of tissues present is such that the distinction between Wilms' tumor and teratoma becomes blurred[662]; the term *teratoid Wilms' tumor* is sometimes used for these cases.[677,683] On other occasions, foci of renal cell carcinoma occur in otherwise typical Wilms' tumor.[660,675]

Histochemical and immunohistochemical features

The immunohistochemical profile of the various components of Wilms' tumor mirrors that of their counterparts in the developing kidney, including highly specialized compounds such as transport mediators.[688,691]

The blastematous elements show only focal positivity for vimentin; the epithelial elements react for keratin, EMA, various lectins, and the various components of the basement membrane[688,694]; the mesenchymal elements show a reactivity pattern consonant with their morphologic appearance (such as positivity for myogenin and desmin in the rhabdomyoblastomatous foci)[689]; and the neural elements—when present—exhibit reactivity for neuron-specific enolase, glial fibrillary acidic protein, and S-100 protein.[692]

Type I insulin-like growth factor receptors have been found in Wilms' tumor, which may be responsible for increased proliferation and inhibition of differentiation.[687,690,693]

Electron microscopic features

Ultrastructurally, the cells of Wilms' tumor closely resemble those of the developing metanephros.[695,698]

Features that, if found in poorly differentiated neoplasms of this region, favor the diagnosis of Wilms' tumor include well-developed cell junctions, microvillous differentiation, and a layer of thick, flocculent coating around the cell surface.[695,696] The latter is a dense lamina formed of highly sialylated neural cell adhesion molecules.[697]

Molecular genetic features

The genetic loci predisposing to Wilms' tumor are *WT1* (located in 11p13 and encoding a zinc finger transcription factor that is expressed in the early development of the urogenital system)[699,712,713] and *WT2* (located in 11p15.5).[700,705,709,710] A relationship has been shown between the level of expression of these genes and the microscopic features of the tumor.[702,704,706,714]

Abnormalities in other chromosomes—1, 7q, 8, 12 and 16—have also been encountered.[703,707,708] These genetic changes are identical in the various histologic components of the tumor.[715] Mutations of *p53* and/or overexpression of the protein are found in only 5% of the cases of Wilms' tumor. They are largely restricted to the anaplastic foci and carry an unfavorable prognostic connotation.[701,711]

Cytology

The role of diagnostic cytology in Wilms' tumor has been very limited, but its use has been advocated for some subsets of patients, such as those with stage IV disease.[717] All three major cell components of the tumor can be recognized with this technique.[716]

Spread and metastases

In advanced cases, local spread occurs in the perirenal soft tissues. From here, the tumor may involve the adrenal glands, bowel, liver, vertebrae, and paraspinal region; the latter may result in spinal cord compression.[718] Invasion of the renal vein is common, but extension into the renal pelvis or ureter is a rare and late event. When present, the resulting polypoid masses protruding into the pyelocalyceal system may resemble those of botryoid rhabdomyosarcoma.[719] Metastases in regional lymph nodes are found in 15% of the cases. The most common sites of distant metastases are lungs, liver, and peritoneum, but several other organs can be involved, including the central nervous system.[720] The presence of lung metastases in a child with a retroperitoneal neoplasm strongly favors a diagnosis of Wilms' tumor over that of neuroblastoma. Conversely, the presence of bone metastases suggests a diagnosis other than Wilms' tumor, since they occur in only 1% of the cases.

Therapy

The therapy for Wilms' tumor has been relatively standardized, largely through the results of the National Wilms' Tumor Study instituted in 1969.[723,724,726,730] The current choice of therapy depends on surgical and pathologic staging. All stage I tumors regardless of histology and stage II tumors with "favorable histology" (i.e., without anaplastic features) are treated with nephrectomy and two-agent chemotherapy (actinomycin D and vincristine) for no longer than 6 months without radiation therapy.[723] Other chemotherapeutic agents and radiation therapy are added to tumors of higher staging. Bilateral Wilms' tumors are usually treated by biopsy followed by chemotherapy, with subsequent operation to resect the remaining tumor.[729] Nephrectomy for Wilms' tumor is done via a wide transperitoneal route, which allows visualization of the opposite kidney and regional lymph nodes. During the operation, it is important to examine the contralateral kidney, examine and sample suspicious lymph nodes, and carefully explore the other infradiaphragmatic structures. Lately, it has been suggested that nephrectomy alone may be sufficient for small stage I, favorable-histology Wilms' tumors in patients less than 2 years of age.[727,728]

The effects of chemotherapy and radiation therapy are more pronounced in the blastematous component than in the mesenchymal or epithelial areas.[721,722,731] The incidence of anaplasia does not seem to be affected by this treatment modality.[731]

It remains essential to obtain a histologic diagnosis through laparotomy before embarking on radiation therapy or chemotherapy, inasmuch as the percentage of incorrect clinicoradiographic diagnoses is as high as 5%.[725]

Prognosis

The overall cure rate for unilateral Wilms' tumor is 80% to 90%.[740] A small percentage of long-term survivors of Wilms' tumor develop a second malignant neoplasm, either because of a genetic predisposition to neoplasia or secondary to therapy.[732]

The prognostic connotations of various clinical and morphologic parameters are as follows:

1 *Age*. Patients under 2 years of age have significantly fewer metastases and a better 5-year survival rate than those over 2 years.[733,736]
2 *Stage*. Clinicopathologic staging of Wilms' tumor is the most important prognostic determinator (see Appendix C). Capsular invasion, rupture at surgery, extrarenal vein invasion, tumor implants, lymph node metastases, distant metastases, and bilaterality are the main criteria used.[743] Unfortunately, staging of Wilms' tumor by the pathologist is fraught with pitfalls. The tumor "capsule" (or pseudocapsule) can be confused with the renal capsule; the renal sinus and surgical margins may be difficult to evaluate; and the renal vein may retract considerably, giving a false impression—when invaded—that tumor is present at the margin. It is important for sections to be taken from the renal sinus, the junction between tumor and normal kidney, tumor capsule, and the uninvolved renal parenchyma.

In a study of stage I cases, the following four features were found to be associated with increased rate of relapse: presence of an inflammatory pseudocapsule, invasion of the renal sinus, extensive infiltration of the renal capsule, and tumor infiltration of intrarenal vessels.[748]
3 *Size*. Tumor mass, as measured by the weight of the excised specimen, is an important determinator of outcome, especially in stage I tumors.[737]
4 *Anaplasia*. For a case of Wilms' tumor to be placed into the anaplastic category, it should meet the following three criteria: (a) marked enlargement of nuclei within the blastemal, epithelial, or stromal cell lines (excepting skeletal muscle cells) to at least three times the diameter of adjacent nuclei of the same cell type; (b) obvious hyperchromasia of the enlarged nuclei; and (c) multipolar mitotic figures (Fig. 17.101).[738]

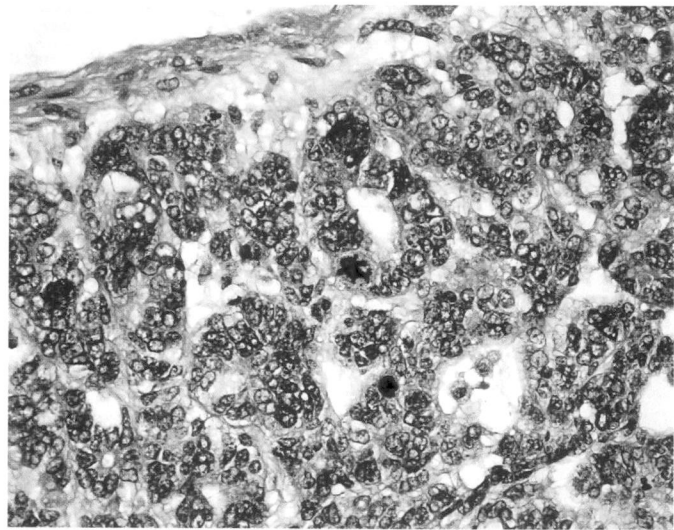

A

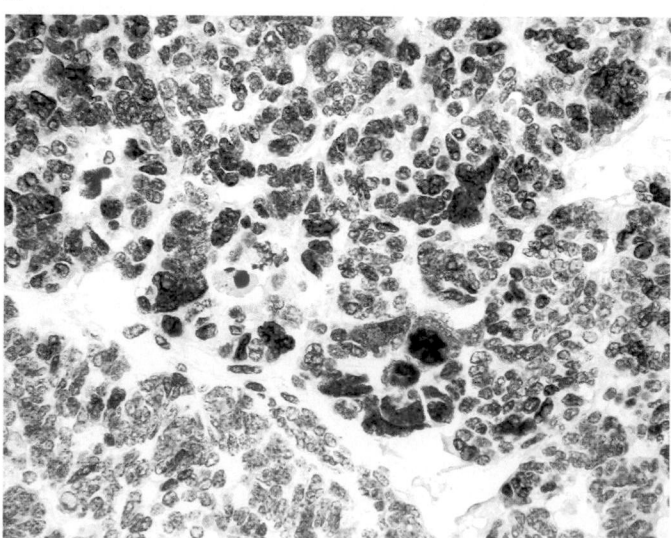

B

Fig. 17.101 A and **B,** Anaplastic ("unfavorable histology") Wilms' tumor. **A,** Marked pleomorphism with giant hyperchromatic nuclei and atypical mitoses. **B,** Strong nuclear immunoreactivity for p53.

Anaplasia thus defined is present in about 4% of the cases, the incidence being higher in blacks and in older patients.[735] It is very uncommon in tumors from patients under 2 years of age; this is probably the reason for the better prognosis exhibited by this age group. Sometimes it is found in the metastases and not in the primary tumor.

In an early proposal, the cases with anaplasia were divided into diffuse and focal based on quantitative criteria, but this scheme was subsequently changed to incorporate topographic criteria. Currently, *focal* anaplasia applies only to cases in which the above defined changes are restricted *to one or a few discrete loci within the primary tumor, with no anaplasia or marked nuclear atypia elsewhere.*[741] Thorough tumor sampling (one section for each centimeter of tumor diameter) is obviously needed to properly evaluate this feature.[750] Wilms' tumors with anaplasia are referred to as having "unfavorable histology" in the sense of exhibiting a lesser response to chemotherapy. This predictive connotation is greater when the anaplasia is diffuse rather than focal, and it does not apply to stage I tumors.[751]

5 *Extensive tubular differentiation.* This is said to be a good prognostic sign. According to some authors, this is also true for cases with extensive glomerular differentiation.[744,746]

6 *Skeletal muscle differentiation.* This feature does not seem to have a significant effect on prognosis except when present in massive amounts. In the latter instance it is said to be associated with a better prognosis.[742,749]

7 *Mucin production.* It has been suggested that the rare patients with Wilms' tumors in whom mucin is detected in the serum have a poor prognosis.[734]

8 *DNA ploidy.* Some studies have suggested that evaluation of DNA ploidy may give information of prognostic utility.[747]

9 *p53 mutation.* Mutations of the *p53* gene, evaluated indirectly through the immunohistochemical detection of p53 protein overexpression, correlate with the presence of anaplasia at the histologic level and therefore with an unfavorable outcome.[739,745]

Mesoblastic nephroma

Mesoblastic nephroma, also known as fetal, mesenchymal, or leiomyomatous hamartoma, is a congenital renal neoplasm that is usually discovered before the patient reaches 6 months of age. Examples in adults have been reported, exhibiting a morphologic spectrum similar to their pediatric congeners.[770,771] Grossly, the tumor is solid, yellowish gray to tan, with a whorled configuration reminiscent of uterine leiomyoma (Fig. 17.102). Most are

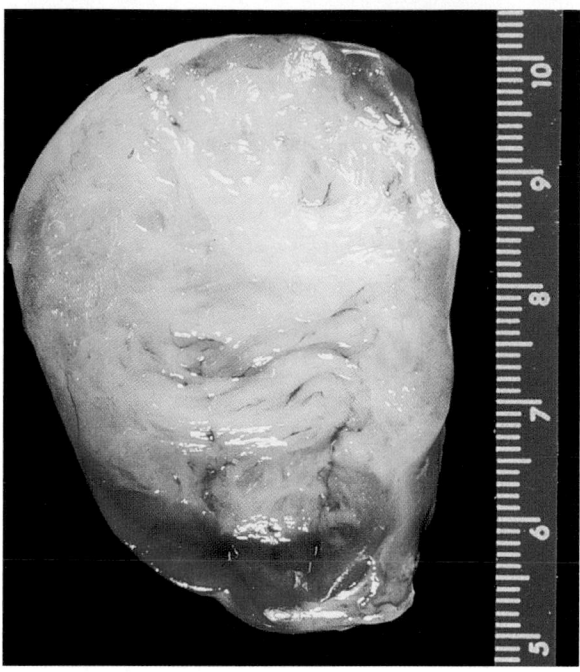

Fig. 17.102 Mesoblastic nephroma. Gross appearance. The well-circumscribed character of this tumor and its white fibrous cut surface are well illustrated.

centered near the hilus of the kidney. The tumor is usually well circumscribed, but it may be seen infiltrating the renal parenchyma and even the perirenal fat. Areas of hemorrhage and necrosis are usually absent. A cystic variant of this tumor has been described.[755a,756]

Microscopically, a variably cellular growth of spindle cells is the predominant feature[769] (Fig. 17.103). Wigger[773] believes that these cells have the features of secondary mesenchyme, which, in contrast with those of primary mesenchyme or mesoblast, lack the capacity to form epithelial structures. Instead, the proliferating cells acquire the features of fibroblasts, myofibroblasts, or smooth muscle cells.[754,763] As such, they contain vimentin, fibronectin, and sometimes actin, but not keratin or laminin.[762] Tubules and glomeruli may be seen surrounded by the spindle cells. Some of them exhibit hyperplastic and metaplastic changes. Most are located at the periphery and are probably the result of entrapment; others, more centrally located and with a complex and variegated appearance, may be a component of the tumor. Small islands of hyaline cartilage and foci of extramedullary hematopoiesis may be present. There is no capsule separating the tumor from the uninvolved parenchyma. In some instances the tumors are very cellular and mitotically active; these have a tendency to infiltrate the renal pelvis or perirenal tissue and may contain areas of hemorrhage and necrosis.[767] At the ultrastructural level, they are similar to infantile fibrosarcomas.[764] These tumors have been referred to as *cellular* or *atypical mesoblastic nephromas*[761,765] (Fig. 17.104).

Mesoblastic nephromas lack the abnormalities in chromosome 11 that characterize Wilms' tumor and are associated instead with polysomies for chromosomes 8, 11, 17 and 20.[755,766,768] Recently, it has been found that they contain the t(12;15)(p13;q25) translocation, which results

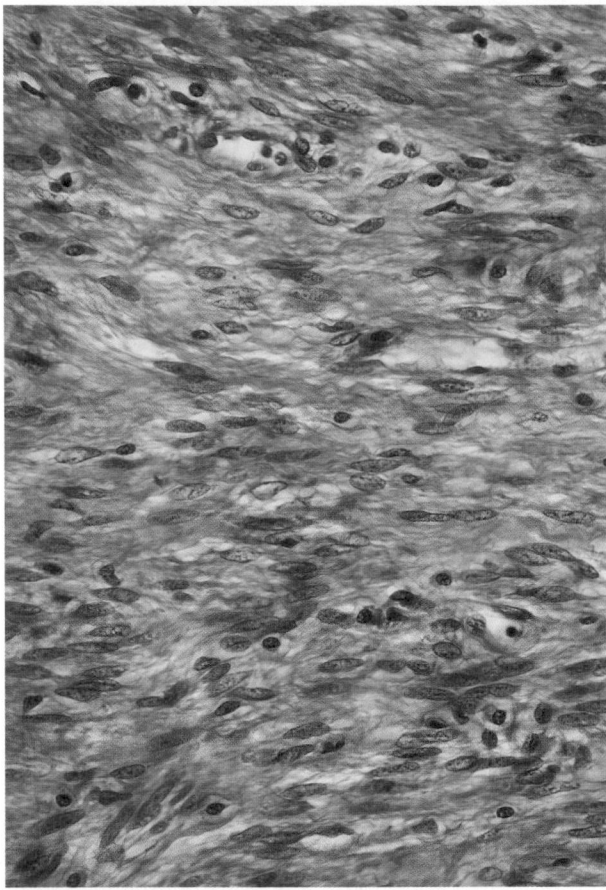

Fig. 17.103 Mesoblastic nephroma. Microscopic appearance showing a monotonous proliferation of spindle cells with bland nuclei and abundant fibrillary acidophilic cytoplasm.

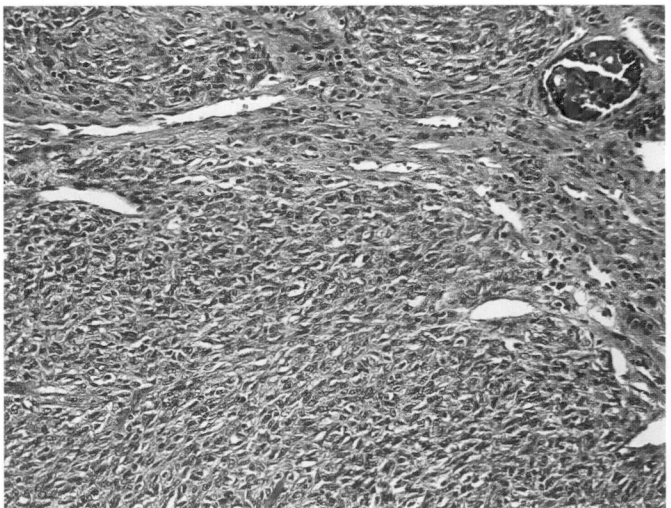

Fig. 17.104 Cellular mesoblastic nephroma accompanied by mitotic activity. An entrapped glomerulus is present in a corner. Some of these tumors behave in an aggressive fashion.

in the *ETV6–NTRK3* gene fusion, the latter being detectable in paraffin-embedded material.[752] This is the same genetic abnormality that is found in infantile fibrosarcoma, supporting the notion that these two tumors represent a single neoplastic entity.[766]

The large majority of mesoblastic nephromas are cured following nephrectomy.[760] Therefore radiation therapy or chemotherapy is not indicated. In up to 7% of the cases, recurrence with local invasion of retroperitoneum will occur and may prove fatal.[758,761] Cases associated with distant metastases to lung and brain have also been reported[759,772]; most of these aggressive tumors have had atypical morphologic features, as previously defined.[757,761] Beckwith and Weeks[753] have pointed out that in all but one of the recurrent mesoblastic nephromas the patients were over 3 months of age at the time of the original nephrectomy; they believe that age at diagnosis and adequacy of excision may be more important prognostic factors than the morphologic features.

Multicystic nephroma

Multicystic nephroma (multilocular cystic nephroma, multilocular cyst) is an uncommon but distinctive lesion that arises in early infancy but that may present clinically at any age.[781,783] Clinical manifestations result from the presence of a mass or, not uncommonly, from ureteral obstruction by one of the daughter locules.

Grossly, the lesion is usually solitary, unilateral, and sharply delineated from the uninvolved renal parenchyma.[775] The usual size range is between 5 and 15 cm, and the outer surface is coarsely nodular. The cut surface shows a multilocular appearance, the individual cysts measuring from 1 mm to 3 cm or more (Fig. 17.105). The wall of these cysts is thin and sometimes translucent and lacks papillary projections. The fluid within the cavity is usually serous. The cysts do not communicate with each other or with the pelvis. The remaining renal parenchyma is normal. Extension of the lesion beyond the renal capsule may occur.

Microscopically, the cysts are lined by tubular epithelium which ranges in height from columnar to extremely flat, resembling endothelium and simulating the appearance of lymphangioma (Fig. 17.106). A "hobnail" pattern is common. Ultrastructurally, this epithelium displays long cilia and other features suggestive of differentiation toward collecting tubule cells.[785] The stroma between the cysts usually has a fibroblastic nondescript nature, but it may contain smooth muscle, skeletal muscle, or cartilage[778] (Fig. 17.107). Sometimes it also contains immature blastematous or abortive tubular elements with an appearance indistinguishable from that of Wilms' tumor. The fact that there is a nonrandom X chromosome inactivation in this condition goes along with its presumed neoplastic nature.[782] Some authors prefer to designate

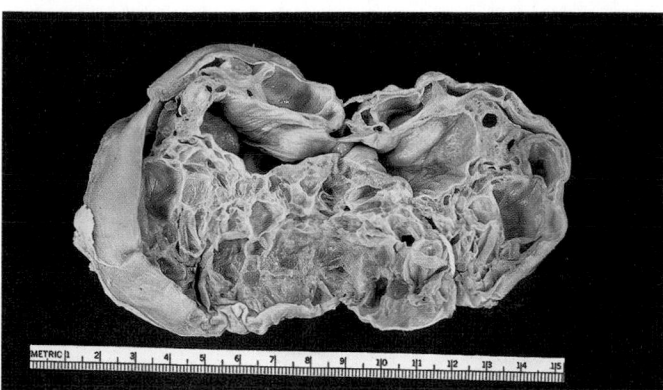

Fig. 17.105 Gross appearance of multicystic nephroma involving most of the kidney.

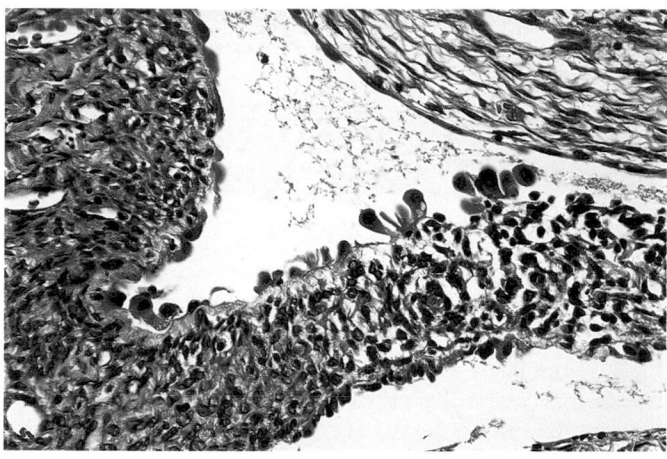

A

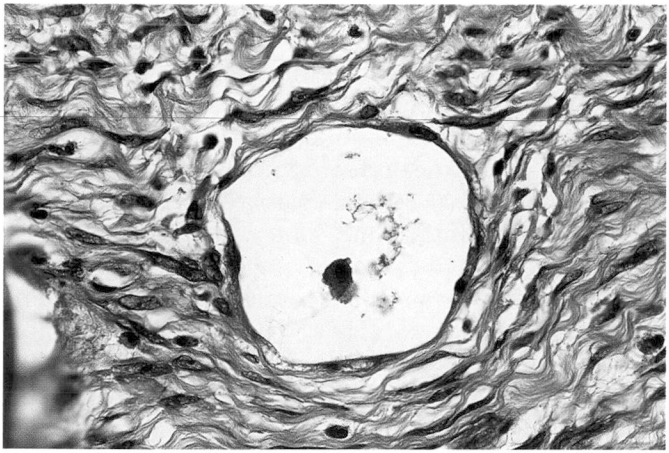

B

Fig. 17.106 A and **B**, Multicystic nephroma. **A**, The epithelial lining of the cyst has a hobnail quality. **B**, In this instance the cyst lining is flat, simulating endothelium.

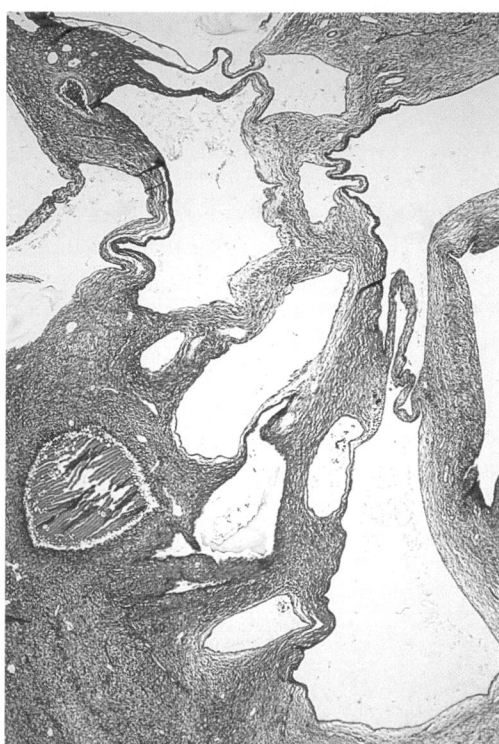

Fig. 17.107 Low-power microscopic appearance of multicystic nephroma showing multiple cysts lined by flattened epithelium and separated by a cellular spindle cell stroma.

tumor.[777,779] The occasional coexistence of Wilms' tumor and multicystic nephroma and the fact that their phenotypes are very similar would seem to support this concept.[774,776,787] From a practical standpoint, however, it is important for these entities to be kept separate because of the fact that multicystic nephroma/multilocular cyst is a benign process that can be cured by nephrectomy alone. The main feature favoring Wilms' tumor in a multicystic lesion is the presence of expansile solid regions of nephroblastomatous tissue not molded by the cystic spaces.

A few cases of multicystic nephroma have been reported in adult patients to contain clusters of clear cells with the appearance of renal cell carcinoma, suggesting that this entity may have a potential for malignant degeneration. However, no metastases have so far been encountered in any of those cases.[784,786]

Nephroblastomatosis and nephrogenic rests

Nephroblastomatosis and nephrogenic rests are congenital dysontogenetic rather than neoplastic disorders, but they are discussed here because of their frequent confusion and possible histogenetic relationship with Wilms' tumor.[790,793,797] These lesions appear as single or multifocal, unilateral or bilateral subcapsular aggregates of

this entity as *multilocular cyst* when nephroblastomatous tissue is absent and as *multicystic nephroma* when it is present, but it is doubtful whether this distinction is conceptually valid or practically useful.[779,780] It has been further suggested that this entity represents the end of a spectrum of differentiation of Wilms' tumor and that it could be viewed as a fully differentiated variant of this primitive metanephric tissue. When microscopic in size, they are referred to as nephrogenic rests, (persistent) nodular renal blastema, or metanephric hamartomas; when massive, they are designated as nephroblastomatosis. However, a morphologic continuum between them exists.[798]

Nephrogenic rests have been divided into perilobar and intralobar forms (Fig. 17.108). The former, which is more common, is located peripherally, has sharply demarcated margins, is composed of blastema and tubules with scanty (or sclerotic) stroma, and is often solitary. The intralobar form is randomly distributed in the cortex and medulla and has irregular margins. It shows a predominance of stroma over blastema and tubules and is usually multifocal.[788,789,794] A panlobar form has also been described.[792,799]

Foci of nephroblastomatosis are found in 1% of neonatal kidneys and in 30% of kidneys containing Wilms'

tumors.[790] In its most florid form, the process is often associated with a variety of congenital anomalies and with hypertension.[796]

Nephroblastomatosis can be diagnosed by arteriography, CT scan, MRI, or ultrasound.[800] Grossly, the most exuberant examples of this disease can be distinguished from Wilms' tumor because of the diffuse nature of the process and the involvement of the entire subcapsular region. Microscopically, the mass is composed of tightly packed nephrogenic epithelial cells that have a primitive but not anaplastic appearance. Stromal tissue is scanty; cartilage, striated cells, and primitive mesenchyme are absent.

In cases associated with Wilms' tumor, they have been found to share the same mutation of *WT1*.[795]

A conservative therapeutic approach is indicated in cases of nephrogenic rests and nephroblastomatosis.[791]

Intrarenal neuroblastoma and peripheral neuroectodermal tumor

Neuroblastoma can invade the kidney secondarily from an adrenal or some other retroperitoneal site, or it may initially present as a primary intrarenal tumor.[806] When the latter occurs, a misdiagnosis of Wilms' tumor is likely. This issue is further complicated by the fact that the embryonal tubules of Wilms' tumor can simulate rosettes and that true neuroblastic elements can occur in Wilms' tumor (see p. 1242). Ultrastructural, immunohistochemical, and molecular genetic evaluation, and determination of catecholamines in serum and urine are of help in this differential diagnosis.[801,805] Metastases from intrarenal neuroblastoma tend to be in orbit and bone, as for their more common adrenal counterparts.[810]

Peripheral neuroectodermal tumor (PNET) can also occur as a primary renal mass.[803] Its morphologic, immunohistochemical, and molecular genetic features are analogous to those of Ewing's sarcoma/PNET of other sites. Most patients are young adults and the clinical course is very aggressive.[802] Many of the cases are centered in the medullary/pelvic region (Fig. 17.109). The main differential diagnosis is with blastema-predominant Wilms' tumor, from which it is distinguished by its positivity for CD99 and the carboxy terminus of FLI-1 and its negativity for WT1. If needed, the diagnosis can be confirmed by the demonstration by cytogenetics, FISH, or RT-PCR of the t(11;22) translocation or the *EWS–FLI* gene fusion that results from it.[808,809] Some of the reported cases have been associated with adenomatoid hyperplasia of the Bowman's capsule epithelium, a peculiar morphologic change in the non-neoplastic kidney which has also been described in cases of hepatoblastoma.[804]

A recent analysis of 146 cases of primary malignant neuroepithelial tumors of the kidney from the NWTSG

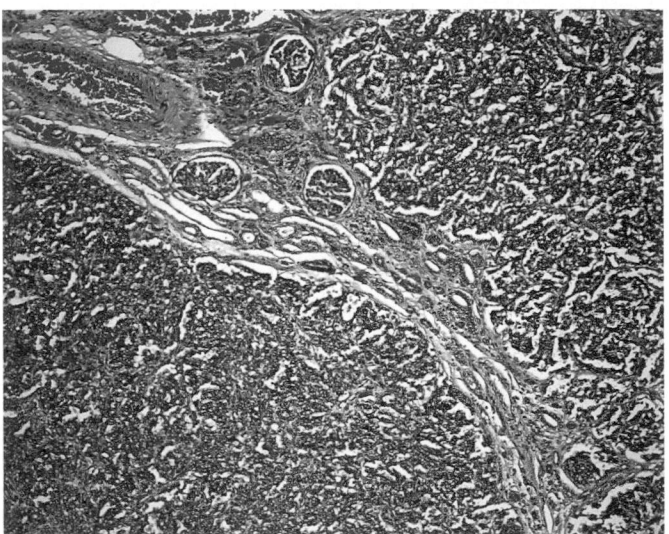

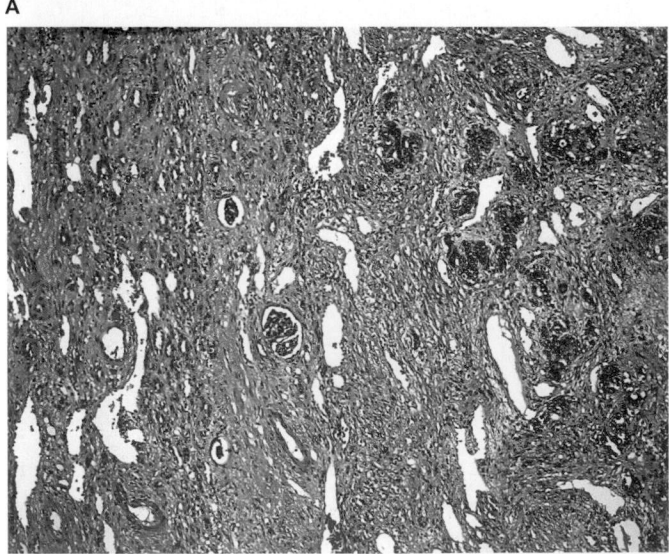

Fig. 17.108 Nephroblastomatosis: **A**, perilobar type; **B**, intralobar type.

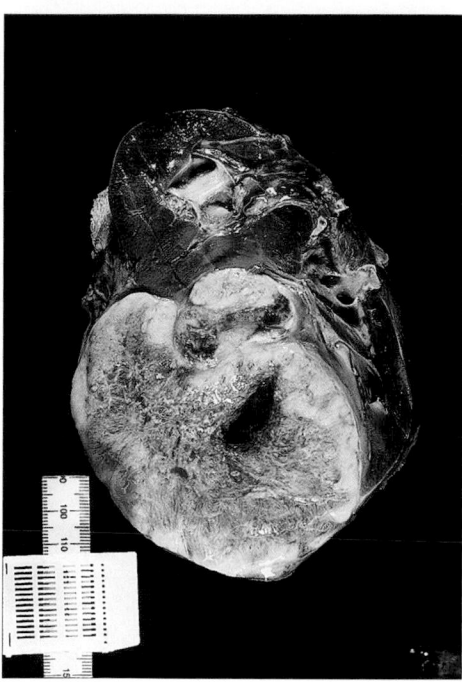

Fig. 17.109 Gross appearance of Ewing's sarcoma/PNET primary in the kidney.

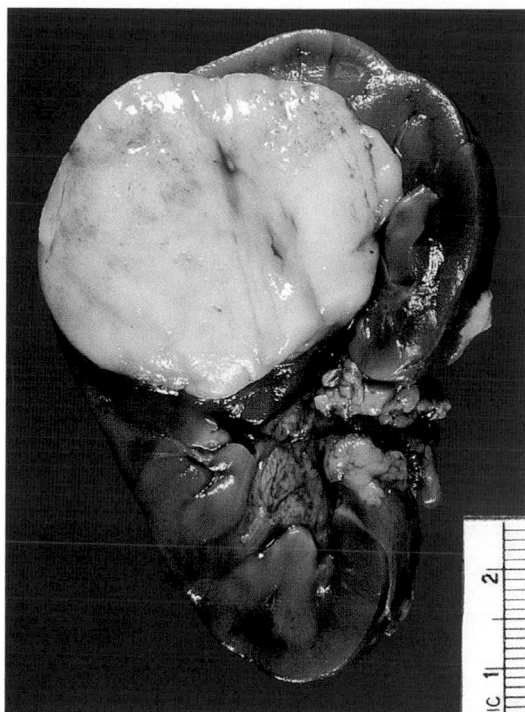

Fig. 17.110 Gross appearance of clear cell sarcoma of kidney. The tumor is well circumscribed and whitish, and it bulges on the cut surface.

Pathology Center files led the authors to the conclusion that these represent a diverse group of high-grade tumors which are not always easy to place in a specific category, even after their evaluation with immunohistochemical and molecular genetic tools.[807]

Clear cell sarcoma

Clear cell sarcoma, also known as bone-metastasizing renal tumor, is a distinctive renal malignancy formerly regarded as a morphologic variant of Wilms' tumor.[815,816,821] It comprises approximately 4% of childhood renal tumors; its incidence peaks during the second year of life. Isolated cases have been described in adults,[817] in extrarenal sites,[824] and in association with familial colonic polyposis.[823] Grossly, the tumor tends to be large, sharply outlined, and centered in the medullary or central region of the kidney, with a homogeneous cut surface of light brownish gray color and myxoid appearance (Fig. 17.110). The consistency is usually hard, and cystic formations are common.

Microscopically, the most common pattern is that of a diffuse growth of relatively small cells with round normochromatic nuclei, inconspicuous nucleoli, light-staining (sometimes vacuolated) cytoplasm, and indistinct cell margins. Despite the tumor name, a clear cytoplasm is a prominent feature in only 20% of the cases. Nuclear grooves are common, and mitoses are infrequent. The fibrovascular stroma may result in arrangements of the tumor cells in nests, palisades, cords, or trabeculae (Fig. 17.111). The latter should not be confused with the tubules or the serpentine arrangement of Wilms' tumor. Myxoid changes, fibrosis, and hyalinization may be present, the appearance of the hyalinized tissue sometimes simulating osteoid. Cysts may result from dilatation of entrapped tubules or from stromal degeneration. It has been remarked that the distinctive alveolar and arborizing vascular stroma is a more reliable diagnostic feature than the clear cells or the sclerosis.[818] As many as nine histologic patterns of this tumor have been described, i.e., classic, myxoid, sclerosing, cellular, epithelioid, palisading, spindle, storiform, and anaplastic.[812]

Ultrastructurally, the cells of clear cell sarcoma have scanty organelles, generally sparse cytoplasmic filaments, primitive cell junctions, and complex cytoplasmic processes.[813] Immunohistochemically, only focal reactivity for vimentin has been encountered.[814,822] The DNA pattern, as evaluated by flow cytometry, is usually diploid.[811] No specific genetic abnormalities have been detected.[819a]

The origin of this neoplasm remains uncertain. It may be histogenetically related to Wilms' tumor,[818,819] but it should be kept in a separate category because of its substantially different natural history. It expresses insulin-like growth factor (like Wilms' tumor) but not *WT1* transcripts.[820,825] p53 gene mutations are rare.[813a] Untreated clear cell sarcoma is a very malignant tumor, with a high tendency for relapse and a propensity for skeletal metastases, particularly skull.[821] In this regard, it should be noted that skeletal metastases are extraordinarily rare in

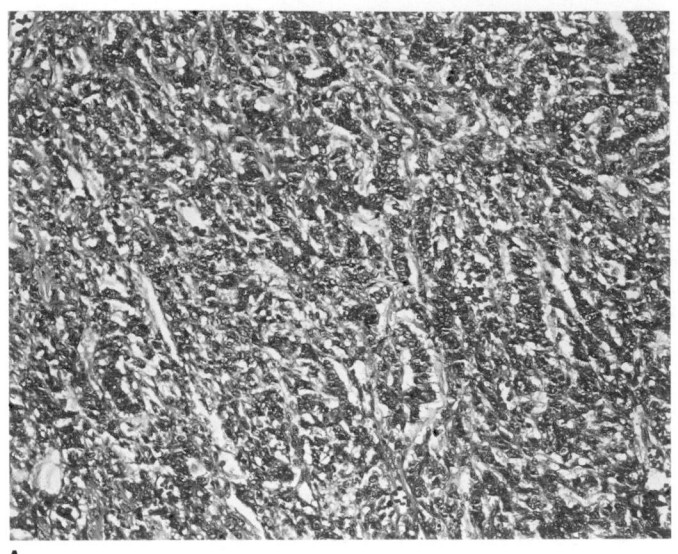
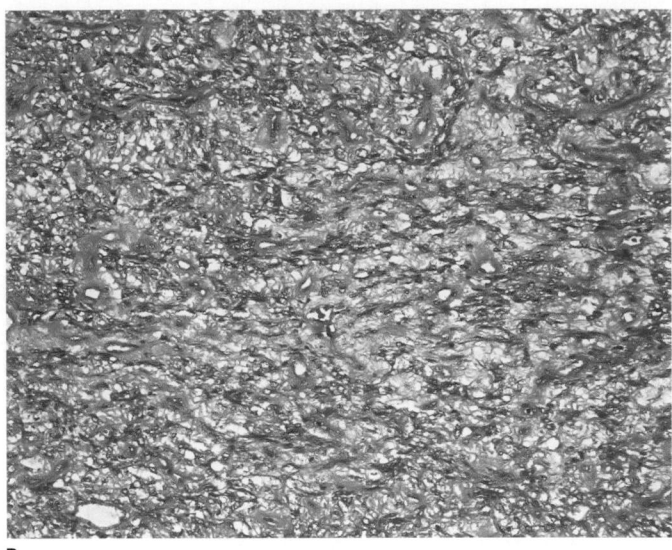

A   B

Fig. 17.111 A and **B,** Clear cell sarcoma of kidney. **A,** Trabecular pattern of growth. **B,** Another area from the same case shows a hypocellular spindle cell appearance.

conventional Wilms' tumors. Metastases also occur to regional lymph nodes, brain, lung, and liver. In contrast to Wilms' tumor, these metastases tend to develop after long intervals following the removal of the primary tumor (5 years or more).

The overall survival rate in a series of 351 cases entered in a NWTSG trial was 69%. Multivariate analysis showed that treatment with doxorubicin, stage, age at diagnosis, and tumor necrosis were independent prognostic factors. Of note, stage I patients had a 98% survival rate.[812]

Rhabdoid tumor

Rhabdoid tumor was regarded for many years as a solid, monophasic, or rhabdomyosarcomatoid variant of Wilms' tumor but is now thought of as a separate tumor type.[826] Most cases occur in young infants, the median age at diagnosis being 18 months.[839] Some of the cases have resulted in hypercalcemia.[833,837] Renal rhabdoid tumor is associated in about 15% of the cases with primary embryonal tumors in the midline posterior fossa, particularly medulloblastoma.[827,831] A notable case has been seen occurring two decades after irradiation of a Wilms' tumor.[832]

Grossly, rhabdoid tumor is solid, soft, and relatively well circumscribed. Microscopically, it is a monomorphic neoplasm that always involves the medullary region and has a generally diffuse but sometimes alveolar or trabecular pattern of growth. The tumor cells are medium sized and generally round or oval. However, they can also be spindle, prompting the possibility of confusion with mesoblastic nephroma. The most characteristic feature is the presence of a large cytoplasmic eosinophilic hyaline

globule that displaces the nucleus laterally to result in a plasmacytoid appearance (Fig. 17.112). Ultrastructurally, this globule is made up of a tangle of intermediate filaments.[830] Immunohistochemically, there is strong reactivity for vimentin and usually also for keratin but generally not muscle or neural markers. However, cases with desmin and myofilament reactivity have been described.[828] It should be remarked that focal rhabdoid features resulting from accumulation of cytoplasmic filaments can be seen in many other renal tumors, including Wilms' tumor, mesoblastic nephroma, and renal cell carcinoma.[840]

The histogenesis of rhabdoid tumor remains controversial; an origin from primitive cells located in the renal

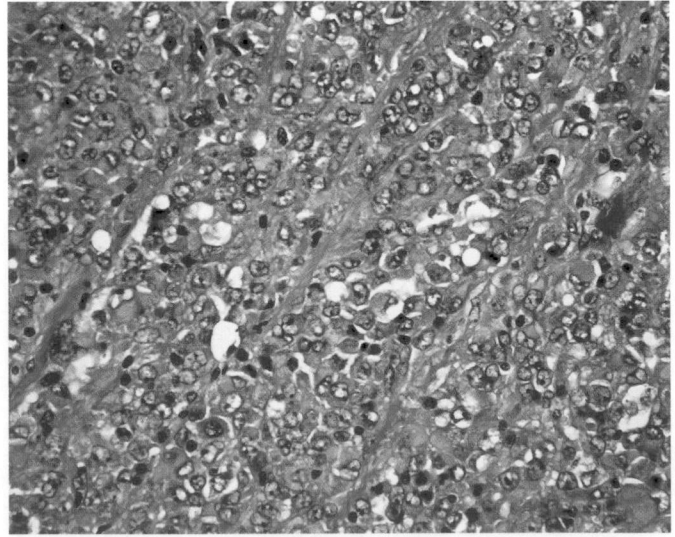

Fig. 17.112 Rhabdoid tumor of kidney. The nuclear grade is high. An eosinophilic amorphous ("hyaline") material fills the scanty cytoplasm and pushes the nucleus aside.

medulla seems the most likely. The behavior is extremely aggressive, even when occurring in young infants. The death rate is over 75%. High tumor stage and male sex are unfavorable prognostic signs.[840]

Tumors morphologically indistinguishable from rhabdoid tumor of kidney have been reported in many other sites, including the soft tissue, pelvis, bladder, and thymus.[829,834-836] Doubts have been expressed about the identity of the two lesions, and the suggestion has been made that extrarenal rhabdoid tumor is the expression of a phenotype rather than a specific entity.[838]

Metanephric stromal tumor

Metanephric stromal tumor is a recently described pediatric renal neoplasm. It typically presents grossly as a fibrous lesion centered in the renal medulla that contains smooth-walled cysts. Microscopically, it is identical to the stromal component of metanephric adenofibroma (see p. 1264). The neoplastic cells are spindle shaped, with onionskin cuffing around entrapped tubules. There may be heterologous differentiation in the form of glia or cartilage and various types of associated vascular alterations. Immunohistochemically, most cases are reactive for CD34. Surgical excision is curative.[841]

Other pediatric tumor types

Isolated examples of pediatric neoplasms not clearly belonging to any of the previous categories have been described. They include *ossifying renal tumor of infancy* (presenting as a calcified mass in the renal pelvis and composed of spindle cells in a partially calcified osteoid matrix),[844] *embryonal sarcoma* (often associated with prominent cystic formations),[843,846] *intrarenal teratoma* (to be distinguished from teratoid Wilms' tumor),[845] and an *HMB-45-positive epithelioid tumor* (also characterized by abundant basement membrane formation and a specific chromosomal translocation).[842]

Adult tumors and tumorlike conditions

Renal cell carcinoma

General features
Renal cell carcinoma is generally a tumor of adults (average age at diagnosis: 55 to 60 years).[869] The rare renal cell carcinomas occurring in children have an appearance and behavior equivalent to those developing in adults,[854,858,865] although there is an increased incidence of papillary architecture and other unusual subtypes.[872] The male to female ratio is about 2:1, and the incidence of bilaterality is 1%. Cigarette smoking and high blood pressure are said to increase the risk for development of the disease.[853] A rare familial form of the disease has been described.[847]

Conditions that may be complicated by renal cell carcinoma are the following:

1 *von Hippel–Lindau (VHL) disease.* Renal cell carcinoma occurs in 50% or more of individuals with this autosomal dominant syndrome, which is also characterized by the presence of CNS (usually cerebellar) and retinal hemangioblastomas, cysts of kidney, liver, and pancreas, clear cell tumors in a variety of sites (including inner ear), and pheochromocytomas.[856,873] Renal cell carcinomas in these patients tend to be multiple and associated with cysts, some of which show atypical changes.[864,867,875] The cysts, atypical cysts, and renal tumors have a similar immunohistochemical profile.[871] The VHL disease gene has been identified at chromosome 3p25.5. This tumor-suppressor gene is thought to exercise its action through the mechanism of transcription elongation instead of the usual transcription initiation. It is mutated in the germline of affected individuals, and in VHL-associated renal cell carcinomas it is associated with a chromosomal deletion of the inherited wild-type allele. Furthermore, the VHL gene is also frequently mutated in sporadic (nonpapillary) renal cell carcinoma, especially in the familial form,[857] an alteration that can be detected in formalin-fixed, paraffin-embedded material.[878] The marked degree of vascularization that often accompanies renal cell carcinoma (and other pVHL-defective tumors, such as cerebellar hemangioblastoma) is probably explained by the overproduction by the tumor cells of hypoxia-inducible factor (HIV) and the products of genes targeted by HIV, such as vascular endothelial growth factor (VEGF) (a potent endothelial-cell mitogen), platelet derived growth factor (PDGF), transforming growth factor α (TGF-α), and erythropoietin.[856a]

2 *Acquired cystic disease.* Half of the patients on long-term dialysis develop an acquired form of polycystic renal disease, which in a few cases has been complicated by the appearance of renal cell adenomas and carcinomas. The tumors tend to be small, multiple, bilateral, and have a generally lower proliferative rate than conventional tumors[861] (see also below) and a metastatic rate of 5% to 7%.[850,852,876] They have also been described in the kidneys with acquired cystic disease of patients who have not had dialysis. Papillary hyperplasia of the epithelium of cysts is a consistent feature in these cases and the likely pathogenetic basis for tumor development.[860] Along these lines, a high proportion of these tumors are of the papillary type, even if their cytogenetic features do not completely

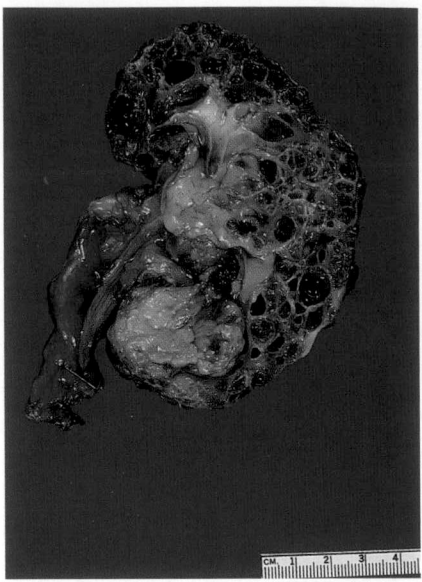

Fig. 17.113 Renal cell carcinoma developing in the adult form of polycystic renal disease. The tumor was multicentric.

duplicate those of the corresponding sporadic tumors.[859]

3 *Adult form of polycystic kidney disease* and *multicystic nephroma (multilocular cyst)* (see p. 1246) (Fig. 17.113). As with the preceding entity, the carcinoma is accompanied and probably preceded by foci of papillary hyperplasia.[848]

4 *Tuberous sclerosis.* Although the classic renal tumor associated with this neurologic syndrome is angiomyolipoma, there is also an increased incidence of renal cell carcinoma, sometimes seen in intimate connection with the former (see p. 1266).[849]

5 *Neuroblastoma.* Several cases have been reported of renal cell carcinoma developing in children who had been previously treated for neuroblastoma. Cytologically, these tumors had oncocytoid features and architecturally they displayed solid and papillary growth patterns.[868]

6 *Familial cutaneous leiomyomatosis.* It has been postulated that individuals affected by this rare hereditary condition have an increased risk for the development of renal cell carcinoma, which tends to have highly papillary features.[863]

7 *Malignant lymphoma.* There have been enough reported cases of coexistent renal cell carcinoma and malignant lymphoma to suggest the possibility of a causal relationship between them.[870,877]

One of the many peculiarities of renal cell carcinoma is its occasional regression in the absence of all treatment, a phenomenon found also with gestational choriocarcinoma, malignant melanoma, neuroblastoma, and—in lesser proportion—with several other tumors.[855,862]

Renal cell carcinoma is the most common "recipient" of the curious phenomenon of metastasis of a cancer into another cancer.[871a] Lung carcinoma is the most common "donor," the resulting microscopic appearance leading to interesting problems of interpretation.[851,866,874]

Clinical features

Renal carcinoma usually presents with hematuria (59%), flank pain (41%), or abdominal mass (45%). However, the combination of these three features, classically regarded as the diagnostic triad of renal cell carcinoma, occurs in only 9% of the patients.[894] Other manifestations are weight loss (28%), anemia (21%), fever (7%), and symptoms caused by a metastatic deposit (10%). Rare systemic/paraneoplastic manifestations include leukemoid reaction, systemic amyloidosis, polyneuromyopathy, gastrointestinal disturbances, hepatosplenomegaly, and hepatic dysfunction.[882,884,890,893,895] Hepatomegaly associated with hepatic dysfunction in patients with renal cell carcinoma is known as *Stauffer syndrome*; it is not due to metastatic deposits, and the main morphologic change detected in the liver is sinusoidal dilatation.[880] Renal cell carcinoma can produce hypercalcemia as a result of the production of a parathormone-like hormone or some other substance,[883,886] hypertension caused by renin secretion,[888] polycythemia secondary to the secretion of an erythropoietic-stimulating substance,[892] gynecomastia as a result of gonadotropin and placental lactogen production,[887] and Cushing's syndrome resulting from the secretion of an ACTH-like substance.[891] Secretion of prolactin, enteroglucagon, insulin-like substance, and prostaglandin A has also been reported.[879]

In general, the investigation of a suspected renal mass begins with intravenous pyelography and is followed by ultrasonography, CT scan, or MRI.[885] Following the advent of the latter three techniques, the role of renal arteriography and inferior vena cavogram has greatly diminished, and their use is reserved for special circumstances. With the increasing use of these modalities, the number of incidentally found renal cell carcinomas has increased substantially.[881,889]

Morphologic features

Grossly, most renal cell carcinomas are well delineated and centered on the cortex (Figs 17.114 and 17.115A and B). On occasion, only a small portion is connected with the cortex, the bulk of the tumor appearing as an extrarenal mass (Fig. 17.115C). Extension to the renal pelvis occurs only late in the course of the disease. In approximately 5% of the cases, multiple tumor nodules are seen scattered throughout the organ[906] (Fig. 17.115D). The larger the tumor, the more likely it is that there will be satellite nodules.[912]

In a typical case of renal cell carcinoma the cut surface shows a solid golden yellow tumor sharply separated from the surrounding tissues by a fibrous pseudocapsule (Fig. 17.114A). The common occurrences of hemorrhage, necrosis, calcification, and cystic change result in the

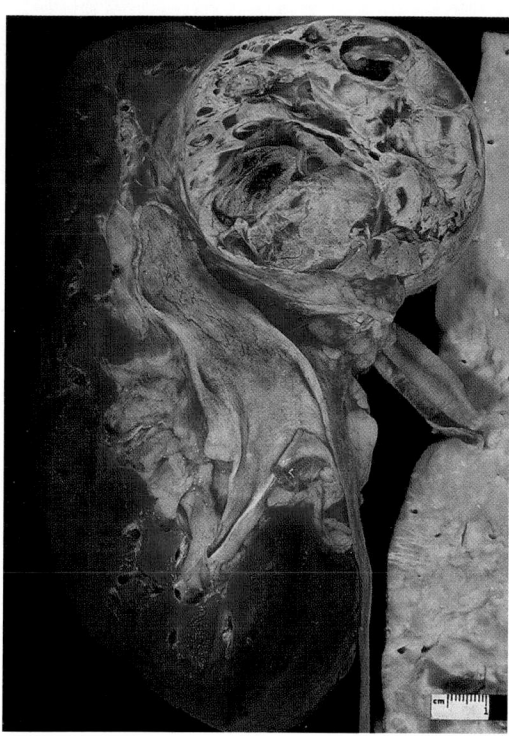

A

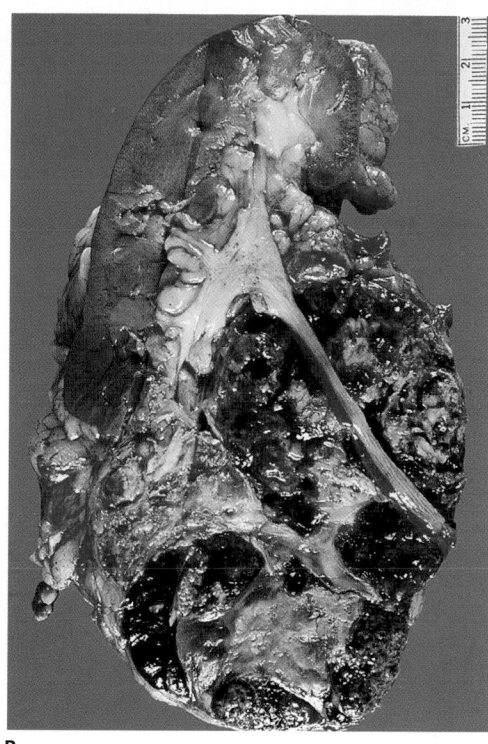

B

Fig. 17.114 A and **B**, Gross appearances of renal cell carcinoma. Both tumors are relatively well circumscribed and variegated, with a combination of cystic, solid, and hemorrhagic areas. The tumor shown in **A** has a bright yellow color, whereas that portrayed in **B** has extensive areas of hemorrhage.

variegated appearance that is very characteristic of this neoplasm (Fig. 17.114B). A remarkable range of color may be seen; however, in the presence of a white, finely granular tumor in the kidney, the diagnosis is likely to be something other than renal cell carcinoma. On occasion, the cystic degeneration is so advanced that a mural nodule remains as the only evidence of the real nature of the lesion. Sometimes even this disappears, and the diagnosis is made only on microscopic examination.[896] Cortical cysts composed of a thick fibrous (often partially calcified) capsule and containing a grumous, yellow, necrotic material represent, in most cases, necrotic renal cell carcinomas. Renal cell carcinomas with extensive cystic degeneration are designated by some as *cystadenocarcinomas*, but they should not be viewed as a special tumor type.[911]

More distinct are the low-grade tumors described as *multilocular cystic renal cell carcinomas*, which are well-demarcated multicystic lesions containing variably sized aggregates of tumor cells[896,909] (Fig. 17.116).

Microscopically, the tumor cells are large, the appearance of the cytoplasm ranging from optically clear, with sharply outlined boundaries ("vegetable cells"), to deeply granular, with many transitional forms[900,904,908,914] (Fig. 17.117). Some authors have divided renal cell carcinomas into clear cell and granular cell types on this basis, but it is doubtful whether the distinction is warranted. Tumors predominantly composed of granular cells are sometimes also called "chromophilic," in contrast with the "chromophobe" tumors discussed in the next section. Since practically all types of renal cell

tumors can exhibit a granular cytoplasm[910] and since other authors have used the term "chromophyl" as a synonym for papillary renal cell carcinomas, it is probably best to avoid the qualifier "chromophyl" altogether. The cytoplasm may also contain hyaline droplets, phagocytosed blood pigment, other lysosomal granules (resulting in brown pigmentation), and—exceptionally—Mallory-like bodies or melanin.[901–903,905,907] The clear cell appearance of the tumor cells results from the accumulation of glycogen (because of abnormalities of carbohydrate metabolism[913]) and also of fat, which can be easily demonstrated with PAS and oil red O stains, respectively. Cytoplasmic mucin is nearly always absent. Tubular, papillary, and cystic formations may be present. The nuclei are generally centrally located; their size, chromatin pattern, and nucleolar appearance vary notably from case to case, this constituting the main basis for microscopic grading (see p. 1262). Occasionally, scattered bizarre nuclear forms are seen in otherwise typical tumors, a phenomenon similar to that more commonly seen in endocrine neoplasms and which should not be equated to sarcomatoid or anaplastic transformation.[899]

Architecturally, most renal cell carcinomas show evidence of glandular (tubular) differentiation, hence their alternative designation as renal adenocarcinomas. In the usual case, however, the pattern of growth is predominantly solid, with formation of large nests of tumor cells separated by a stroma that is characteristically endowed with prominent sinusoid-like vessels. Large sections or multiple sections usually show diverse patterns in the

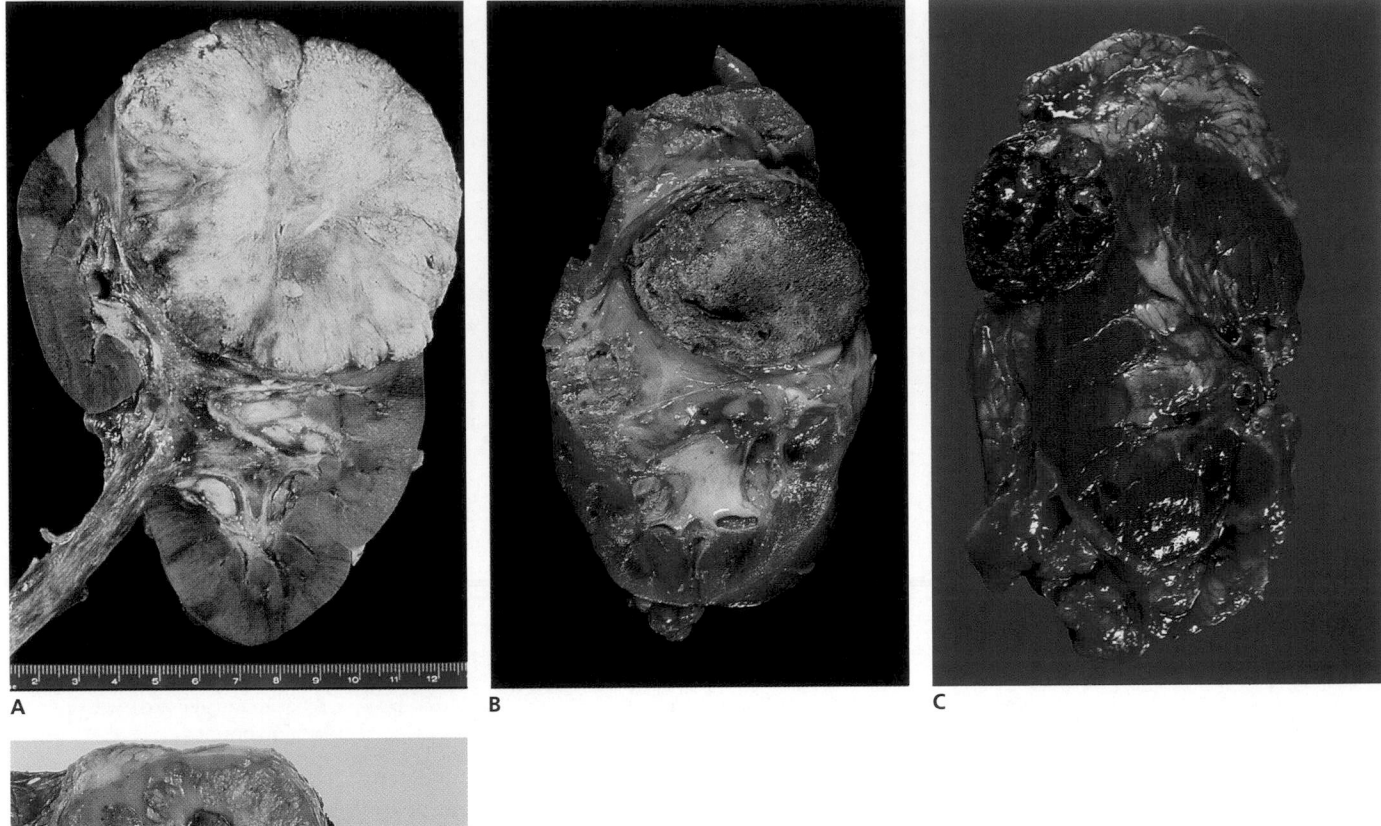

Fig. 17.115 A to **D**, Other gross appearances of renal cell carcinoma. The tumor shown in **A** is well circumscribed and relatively homogeneous, that shown in **B** is almost entirely necrotic, that shown in **C** grows outside the kidney and is markedly hemorrhagic, and that shown in **D** involves almost the entire kidney and extends into the renal vein. (**D** courtesy of Dr. Juan Jose Segura, San Jose, Costa Rica)

same tumor, a feature that renders subclassifications based on morphologic pattern of little significance, except for the types described in the following discussion.

The stroma of renal cell carcinoma is nondescript and, in general, not as abundant as in collecting duct carcinoma or transitional cell carcinoma. A lymphocytic infiltrate (mainly composed of T cells) of variable degree is present. We have seen several cases in which the renal cell carcinoma was surrounded and closely intermingled with abundant smooth muscle bundles; a similar case has been reported in association with a separate angiomyolipoma.[897] Cases have also been described in

which the red blood cells in the stroma arrange in clusters, resulting in a myospherulosis-like appearance.[898]

Electron microscopic features

Ultrastructurally, the clear cells are seen to contain abundant glycogen, variable amounts of fat, scanty organelles, long microvilli on the apical surface, and numerous cell junctions.[918] In the granular cells, organelles are more numerous, and glycogen and fat are more scanty.[915,917] Rarely, myelinoid lamellated cytoplasmic inclusions are found.[916,918] Variable numbers of mitochondria are seen, reaching their highest concentration in tumors with oncocytic features.[918]

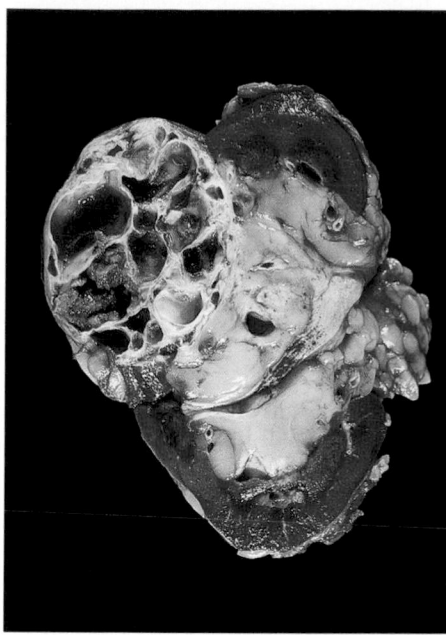

Fig. 17.116 Renal cell carcinoma with multilocular gross appearance.

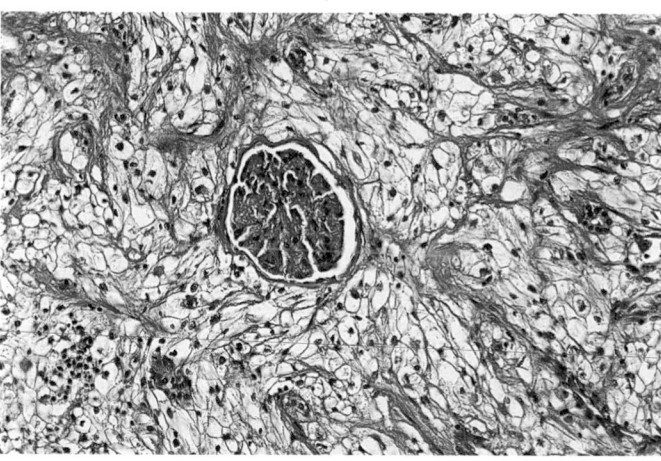

A

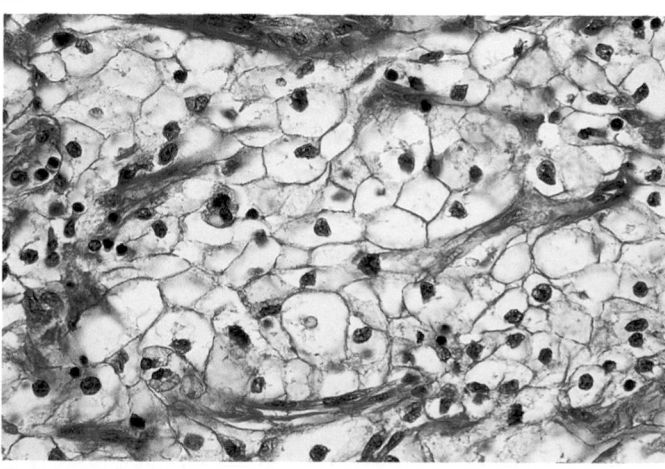

B

Fig. 17.117 A and **B**, Renal cell carcinoma, clear cell type. **A**, Diffuse pattern of growth with entrapment of glomerulus. **B**, High-power view showing optically clear cytoplasm and sharply outlined cell membrane.

Histochemical and immunohistochemical features

The features here described apply mainly to the prototypical renal cell carcinoma (generally known as common or conventional), i.e., that composed of clear and/or granular cells, whereas those associated with the variants are mentioned in the subsequent section in connection with them. Immunohistochemically, renal cell carcinoma shows reactivity for epithelial markers such as keratin, EMA, and CEA.[921,925,933,952,955] The keratins usually expressed are 8 and 18 (i.e., of simple epithelial type). Coexpression of keratins and vimentin is the rule, a feature not present in normal tubular cells.[939,941a,961] Other antigens detected in the cells of renal cell carcinoma are brush border membrane/villin,[937,939,962] α_1-antitrypsin and a_1-antichymotrypsin,[932] S-100 protein (particularly the alpha subunit),[958] Lewis' blood group isoantigens,[928] aldolase C isozyme,[957] two forms of enolase isozymes,[938] angiotensin-converting enzyme,[956] angiopoietin-like 4,[942a] Tamm–Horsfall protein,[940] galectin-1 and -3,[934] CD10,[920] several CD44 isoforms,[929,959] CD68,[954] epidermal growth factor receptor,[948] hormone receptors (erratically),[923] MUC1 mucins and trefoil factor 1 protein,[942,943] beta-defensin-1,[962a] parvalbumin,[962a] and MUC3 parathormone-related protein,[936] erythropoietin,[924] prealbumin (transthyretin),[919,935] and the von Hippel–Lindau gene product.[927] The lectin-binding pattern is similar to that of normal proximal tubules.[960] There is an altered pattern of major histocompatibility complex expression.[940a] In addition, a variety of monoclonal antibodies against various defined and undefined epitopes of renal cell carcinoma (such as the "RCC marker" and human γ-glutamyl transpeptidase) have been evaluated for their potential diagnostic utility.[920,922,941,944,945,951]

From the standpoint of differential diagnosis, the utility of most of these markers is relatively limited. Their choice depends on the specific situation at hand, i.e., whether one is trying to decide to which subtype a given renal cell carcinoma belongs (to be discussed below) or whether a given clear cell carcinoma in an extrarenal site represents a metastasis of a renal cell carcinoma or not. In regard to the latter, the most useful *positive* markers are the coexpression of keratin and vimentin and the positivity for CD10. It is, however, the *negative* markers that are of greatest use depending on the circumstance, to wit: (1) in the differential diagnosis with adrenal cortical carcinoma, the fact that renal cell carcinoma is negative for inhibin and A103[931,953]; (2) in the differential diagnosis with clear cell carcinoma of the ovary, the fact that renal cell carcinoma is usually negative for keratin 34 βE12 and CA-125[950]; (3) in the differential diagnosis with clear cell carcinoma of the thyroid, the fact that renal cell carcinoma is negative for thyroglobulin and TTF-1, and so forth.[947,949] It is actually embarrassing that, for a tumor arising from a cell type that produces so many proteins, a truly specific and sensitive marker is still wanting.

From a histogenetic standpoint, the application of

these various markers to renal cell carcinoma has by and large supported the long-held impression that most examples of this tumor differentiate in the direction of proximal renal tubules.[926,930,946]

Molecular genetic features

The notable aspect of the genetic aspects of renal cell carcinoma is that, in contrast to epithelial neoplasms in most other organs, there is a very close relationship with the various morphologic subtypes,[947a,971] which can be investigated by conventional cytogenetics, PCR-based RFLP screening techniques, or microsatellite analysis.[963,964]

The most common cytogenetic abnormality in renal cell carcinoma is a terminal deletion of the short arm of chromosome 3, beginning at 3p13.[968,969,977,979,981] This alteration is seen in most cases of nonpapillary renal cell carcinoma of all types, but is absent in oncocytic and most papillary tumors (see next section).[966,973,978,980]

Overexpression of p53 is present in 10% to 35% of renal cell carcinomas depending on the series; it has also been found in morphologically normal renal tubules adjacent to the tumor, possibly indicating the presence of a precursor lesion.[970,972,974] Renal cell carcinoma shows loss of *Rb* gene function in about 20% of the cases,[975] and loss of *Fhit* gene expression in about 90%, the incidence being particularly higher with the clear cell type.[967] Pax-2 protein, which is usually expressed, seems to correlate with the proliferation index.[965] Cyclin-D1 can be detected in about half of the cases.[976]

As already indicated in the section on General features (p. 1251), the VHL gene is frequently mutated in renal cell carcinoma, including the sporadic form.

Other microscopic types

Several subsets of renal cell carcinomas exist that deserve to be segregated from the common or conventional type on the basis of their cytoarchitectural features, especially when these are associated with distinct cytogenetic and behavioral properties.[1043c] However, it remains to be seen whether these differences are as sharp and consistent as implied by some of the currently proposed classification schemes[987,1033] or whether—as has happened before many times in too many other organs—further studies reveal an array of hybrid and transitional forms.

Papillary renal cell carcinoma comprises about 15% of all cases of renal cell carcinoma. It is sometimes also called chromophil but—as already discussed—it is better to avoid this synonym. Renal tumors arising in patients on chronic hemodialysis tend to be of papillary type.[1027] Some cases of papillary renal cell carcinoma are hereditary, and these have been found to be associated with germline mutations of the c-*met* oncogene.[1038]

Papillary renal cell carcinoma is characteristically hypovascular on radiographic studies, and grossly it may exhibit extensive areas of necrosis.[1045] It is more likely than conventional renal cell carcinoma to be localized to the kidney, but also more likely to be multicentric or bilateral.[986,1026,1032]

Microscopically, complex papillary formations are seen, often accompanied by prominent stromal infiltration by neutrophils or foamy macrophages[1040,1044] (Fig. 17.118). Psammoma bodies may be numerous. The nuclear grade is variable (but see below). Immunohistochemically (and in contrast with conventional renal cell carcinoma) there is consistent expression of keratin 7.[1018,1021] Cytogenetically, the most consistent aberrations are trisomy of chromosomes 3q, 7, 8, 12, 16, 17, and 20, and loss of Y chromosome.[1000,1028,1029] In contrast to conventional renal cell carcinoma, there is no loss of 3p13.

It has been proposed that papillary renal cell carcinoma can be further subdivided into two types: *type 1*, in which the papillae are lined by a single layer of cells with scanty pale cytoplasm; and *type 2*, in which the papillae are lined by a pseudostratified epithelium composed of cells with abundant acidophilic cytoplasm.[1005,1006] According to this scheme, it is the type 1 tumors that are accompanied by foamy macrophages and psammoma bodies and that are immunoreactive for keratin 7 and MUC1.[1036a,1041a] They may also have different cytogenetic abnormalities,[1028,1052a] but their clinical outcome is similar. It is questionable whether these are truly two distinct subtypes or different grades of the same tumor (lower for type 1 and higher for grade II). As a group, papillary renal cell carcinoma has a better prognosis than conventional renal cell carcinoma.[985a,986]

Although papillary renal cell carcinoma is currently regarded as a distinct subtype, it is far from being an homogeneous entity at any level. Morphologically (in addition to the alleged two subtypes above described), there are solid variants,[1049] variants with rare papillae similar to collecting duct carcinoma,[1047] and variants in which the tumor cells have clear cell cytoplasm (and

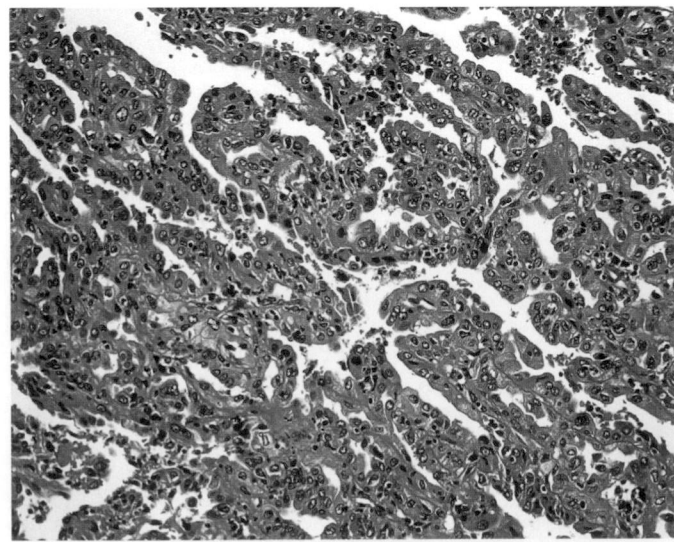

Fig. 17.118 Renal cell carcinoma of papillary type. Note the neutrophilic infiltration.

chromosomal loss of 3p).[1020] The latter should probably be regarded as a conventional (clear cell) renal cell carcinoma with a papillary pattern of growth rather than a papillary renal cell carcinoma with clear cells.

It should also be realized that papillary renal cell carcinoma (like all other types) can undergo anaplastic or sarcomatoid changes (see below).[991,999,1048]

Collecting duct carcinoma (1% to 2% of all cases) is the name given to a form of renal cell carcinoma that, in contrast, to the usual type, is thought to arise from or differentiate toward collecting (Bellini's) ducts, hence its alternate designation as *Bellini duct carcinoma*.[1052] These tumors, which are more common in males, are centered in the medulla, have a tubulopapillary architecture, and are surrounded by a desmoplastic reaction.[1016,1042] (Fig. 17.119 to 17.121). The latter is an important diagnostic clue.[988,1055] Atypical changes in the adjacent ducts are common. The ultrastructural appearance, lectin-binding pattern, and expression of high-molecular-weight keratins recapitulate those of the lower nephron.[1017,1030] A case producing α-fetoprotein has been reported.[1002] Mucin stains are usually positive, in stark contrast with conventional renal cell carcinoma,[1030] and cases with signet ring features have been reported.[1037] Vinculin has been proposed as an immunohistochemical marker for this tumor type.[1035] It is likely that some of the cases formerly described as papillary renal cell carcinoma belong to this category.[1040]

Cytogenetically, the few cases studied have shown monosomies for chromosomes 1, 6, 14, 15, and 22 and have lacked the changes seen in either conventional or papillary renal cell carcinoma.[1019]

The behavior of collecting duct carcinoma is generally aggressive, many of the patients having distant metastases at the time of presentation.[1055]

Rare renal tumors have been reported featuring parallel or paired sheets of cuboidal cells, possibly recapitulating loops of Henle.[1043]

Renal medullary carcinoma is very rare malignant renal neoplasm occurring in young black patients with sickle cell disease.[982,995] It is centered in the medulla and microscopically exhibits a reticular, yolk sac-like or adenoid cystic appearance, often with poorly differentiated areas in a highly desmoplastic stroma admixed with neutrophils and usually marginated by lymphocytes (Fig. 17.122).[1012,1051] Metastases are usually present at the time of the diagnosis. The behavior is very aggressive.[1003]

Chromophobe renal cell carcinoma (5% of all cases) is grossly well circumscribed, solitary, with a homogeneous

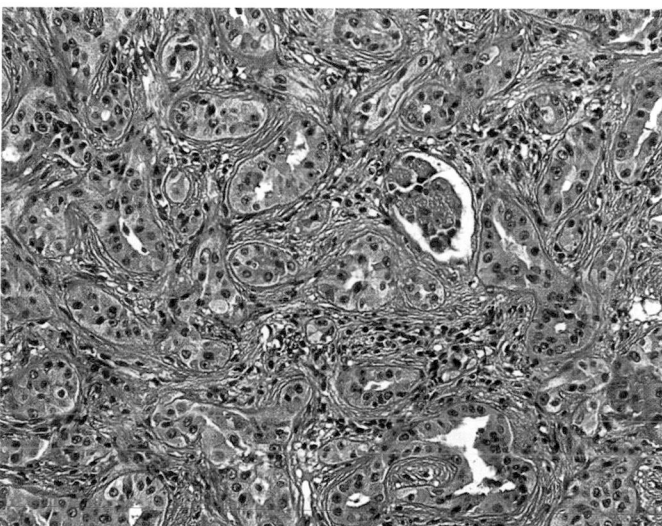

Fig. 17.120 Collecting duct carcinoma. A cellular stroma separates the well-differentiated tubules.

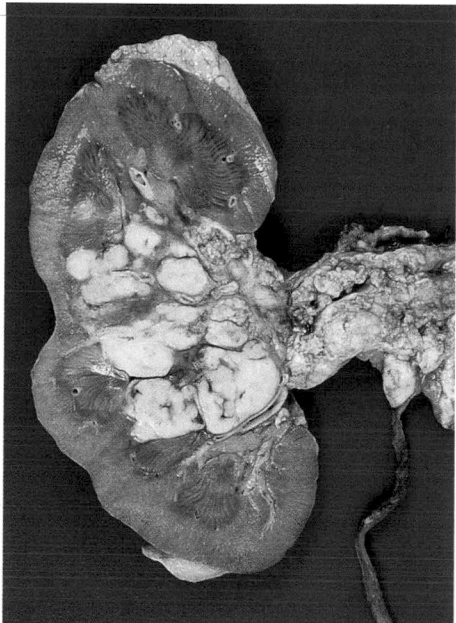

Fig. 17.119 Gross appearance of collecting duct carcinoma which is centered in the medullary portion of the kidney and extends into the renal pelvis.

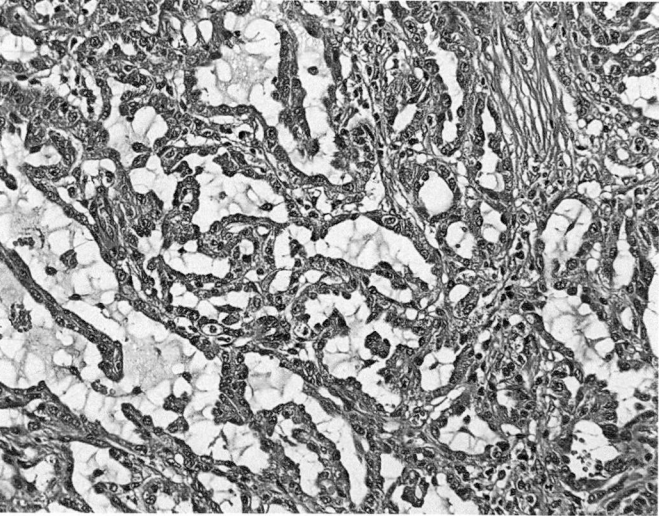

Fig. 17.121 Collecting duct carcinoma showing branching tubules lined by cuboidal cells.

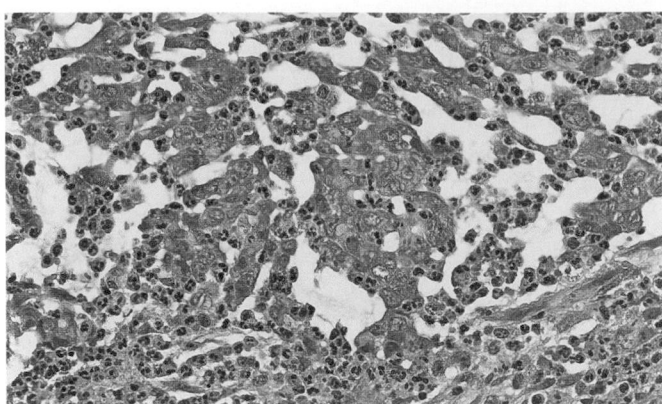

Fig. 17.122 Renal medullary carcinoma in a patient with sickle cell disease. The tumor is poorly differentiated and is heavily infiltrated by neutrophils. (Courtesy of Dr. Victor E. Reuter, Memorial Sloan-Kettering Cancer Center)

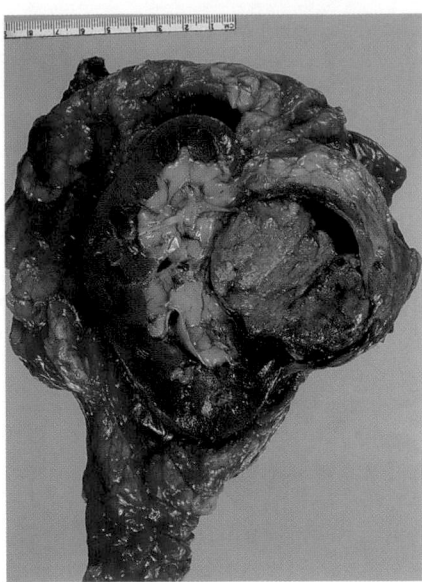

Fig. 17.123 Gross appearance of renal chromophobe cell carcinoma. The tumor is well circumscribed and has a light brown color.

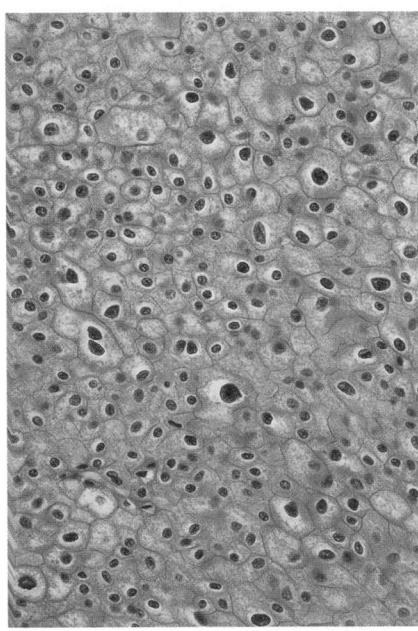

Fig. 17.124 Microscopic appearance of chromophobe cell carcinoma. The cells have a well-defined cell membrane, faintly granular cytoplasm, and perinuclear clear halo. The pattern of growth is solid.

gray to brown cut surface devoid of hemorrhage or necrosis[994] (Fig. 17.123). Microscopically, there is a characteristic nesting ("alveolar") arrangement of the tumor cells, which have sharply defined borders and abundant cytoplasm[984] (Fig. 17.124). The latter has a pale, acidophilic quality, and there is often a clear perinuclear region.[1011] This cytoplasmic appearance is due to the presence of numerous cytoplasmic vesicles that are well appreciated by electron microscopy (Fig. 17.125). These vesicles stain for Hale's colloidal iron, indicating the presence of acidic mucins[993,1053,1057,1059] (Fig. 17.126). Calcification is present in nearly half of the cases.[1048a] Immunohistochemically, chromophobe renal cell carcinoma is positive for EMA, keratin, CD9, paxillin, and E-cadherin, but not N-cadherin or vimentin.[1008,1030a,1034a,1056] The characteristic cytoplasmic features of the tumor can be recognized in fine needle aspiration specimens.[1023,1063]

Chromophobe renal cell carcinoma is also consistently positive for parvalbumin, a calcium-binding protein expressed in the distal nephron, a feature further suggesting a histogenetic relationship between this tumor and the intercalated ducts.[1041] The proliferation index is generally similar to that of oncocytoma, and lower than that of conventional renal cell carcinoma.[1001] By DNA flow cytometry, most chromophobe renal cell carcinomas are hypodiploid, in contrast with conventional renal cell carcinomas.[983]

Loss of chromosomes 1, 2, 6, 10, 13, 17, and 21 has been found by comparative genomic hybridization[1054] and microsatellite markers.[996,1054]

Chromophobe renal cell carcinoma can undergo sarcomatoid transformation; as a matter of fact, it may have a greater tendency to this prognostically unfavorable event than other types.[985,1064]

The histogenetically most interesting and practically most important issue with chromophobe renal cell carcinoma is that of its relationship with oncocytoma. We strongly suspect that these two tumors are closely related, based on the following observations:

1 The fact that at least some of the cytoplasmic vacuoles that characterize chromophobe renal cell carcinoma have ultrastructural features indicative of their mitochondrial nature.[1014,1036,1061]
2 The occurrence of the reciprocal phenomenon, i.e., renal oncocytomas with prominent intracytoplasmic vacuoles of mitochondrial origin.[1031]

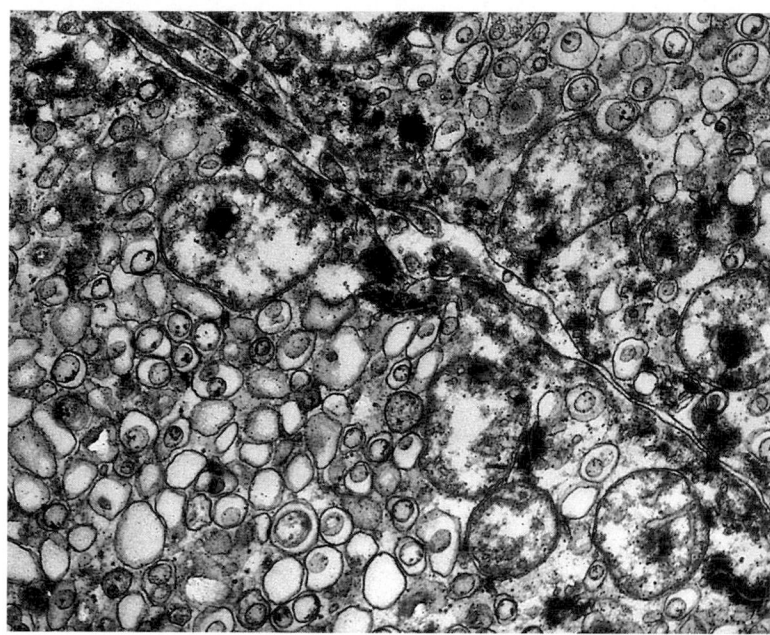

Fig. 17.125 Electron microscopic appearance of chromophobe cell carcinoma of the kidney. Portions of two tubular epithelial tumor cells that contain numerous small cytoplasmic vesicles. The larger structures with the double membranes are mitochondria. (×22,900; courtesy of Dr. Robert A. Erlandson, Memorial Sloan-Kettering Cancer Center)

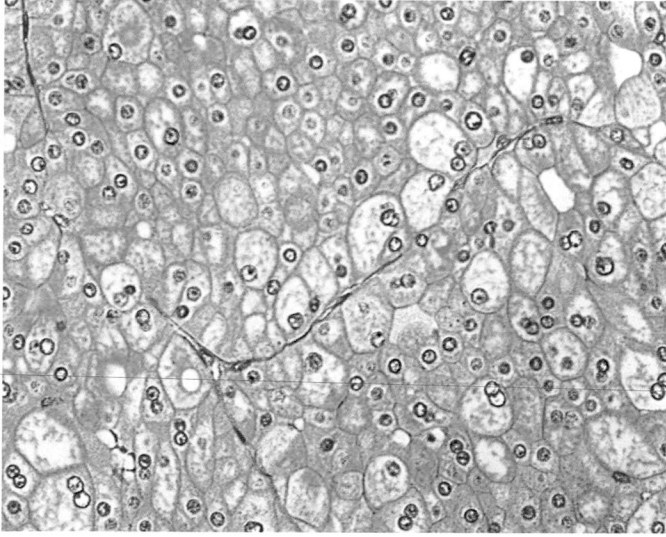

Fig. 17.126 Positive Hale's colloidal iron stain in chromophobe carcinoma.

3   The existence of transitional forms between the two tumors, represented by chromophobe renal cell carcinoma with a more granular cytoplasmic appearance than the norm, resulting from greater richness of mitochondria (so-called "eosinophilic subtype").[1025]

4   The fact that the "dominant nodule" in some cases of renal oncocytosis is not an oncocytoma but a chromophobe cell carcinoma.[1060]

5   The fact that several immunohistochemical markers (such as paxillin and parvalbumin) are shared by chromophobe renal cell carcinoma and oncocytoma but not by other renal tumors.[1035,1041]

6   The fact that patients with the Birt-Hogg-Dubé syndrome (an autosomal dominant genodermatosis

may develop chromophobe renal cell carcinoma and hybrid chromophobe-oncocytic neoplasms.[1043a]

Having said this, we hasten to add that the distinction between chromophobe renal cell carcinoma and oncocytoma should always be attempted in view of the different clinical outcome associated with the two lesions.[998] This distinction will be possible in the large majority of the cases on the basis of the morphologic features coupled with the Hale's colloidal iron stain. Regarding the former, it should be pointed out that the differences are not only cytoplasmic but also nuclear. The cells of chromophobe renal cell carcinoma have wrinkled, raisin-like hyperchromatic nuclei, whereas those of oncocytoma tend to be perfectly round. Also, bi- and multinucleated tumor cells are more common in chromophobe renal cell carcinoma than in oncocytoma.[1058]

As a whole, the prognosis of chromophobe renal cell carcinoma is more favorable than that of conventional renal cell carcinoma, but distant metastases can develop (liver, lungs), especially when the tumors are large and/or there is a coexistent papillary component.[1046] Needless to say, if a sarcomatoid transformation has developed, the prognosis becomes very poor.

Sarcomatoid renal cell carcinoma (also known as spindle-cell carcinoma, anaplastic carcinoma, or carcinosarcoma) makes up about 1% of all renal tumors in adults[1062] (Fig. 17.127). It is largely composed of spindle and/or pleomorphic tumor giant cells, and its appearance may simulate malignant fibrous histiocytoma, fibrosarcoma, rhabdomyosarcoma, or angiosarcoma[1009,1015,1050] (Figs 17.128 and 17.129). The sarcomatoid component may also differentiate in the direction of cartilage and bone[992] and it may contain osteoclast-like multinucleated giant cells.[1013] Numerous sections may be necessary to find

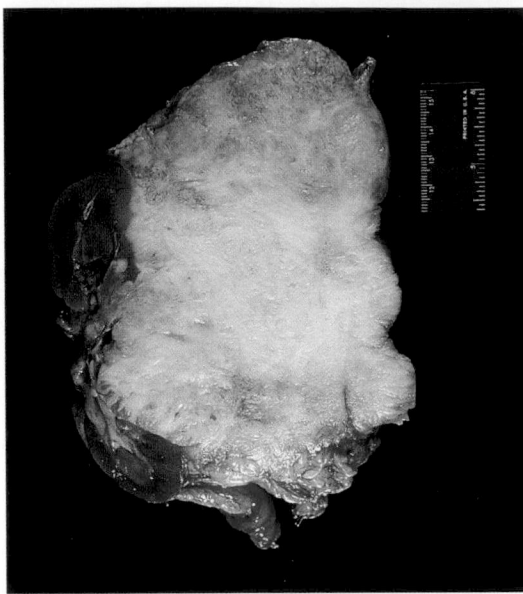

Fig. 17.127 Gross appearance of sarcomatoid renal cell carcinoma. The tumor, which has a white fibrous appearance and ill-defined edges, is replacing most of the organ.

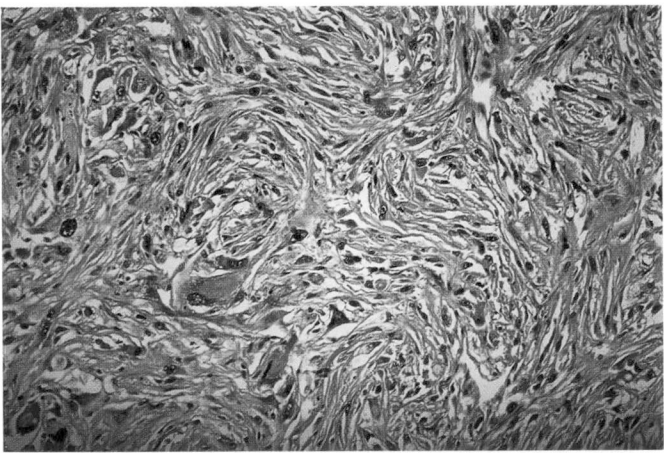

Fig. 17.128 Sarcomatoid renal cell carcinoma composed of spindle cells and simulating a mesenchymal neoplasm.

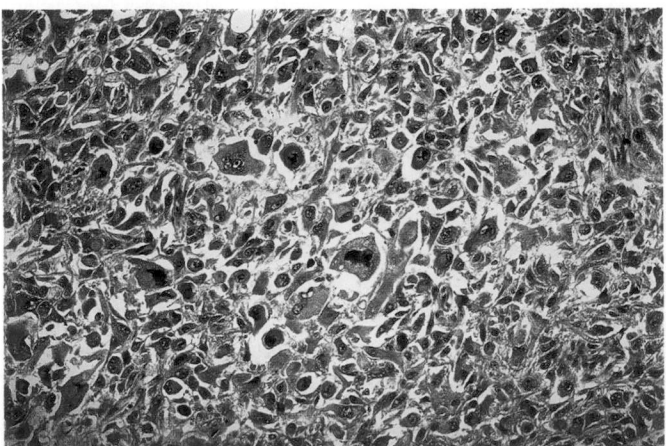

Fig. 17.129 Sarcomatoid renal cell carcinoma with pleomorphic giant cell appearance.

areas of recognizable carcinoma. Conversely, the sarcomatoid component can be very focal in an otherwise typical renal cell carcinoma.[1039] The nuclear grade is usually (but not always) high.[1009] By immunohistochemistry and electron microscopy, epithelial markers may or may not be found in the sarcomatoid cells,[1004,1007] which show consistent strong reactivity for vimentin.[1010]

The morphologic appearance of the identifiable epithelial component (when present) and the lectin-binding pattern are usually in keeping with a proximal tubular origin (as in conventional renal cell carcinoma),[1024,1034] but some of the cases represent sarcomatoid variants of collecting duct carcinomas, papillary carcinomas, or chromophobe cell carcinomas (see under respective sections).

Sarcomatoid carcinoma, which can be identified by fine needle aspiration,[990] is an extremely aggressive neoplasm, in keeping with its generally grade IV cytology.[997] Cases in which the sarcomatoid component is very focal do better than the others.[1039] Extrarenal invasion is usually present at operation.[1062] Multiple metastases of this tumor in the skeletal system have been known to simulate the entity of multicentric osseous fibrosarcoma. When a sarcomatoid pattern is found in a metastatic site, this will usually also be present in the primary renal tumor in nearly every instance.

Two other types of renal cell carcinomas will be mentioned in this section because of the fact that they have sarcoma-like features, although they are rather unique and quite different from the sarcomatoid renal cell carcinomas above described. One is the *renal cell carcinoma with rhabdoid features*, which—as the name indicates—contains a high-grade component of rhabdoid tumor cells and which (like rhabdoid tumors elsewhere) behaves in a very aggressive fashion.[1022,1035a]

The other lesion is a renal neoplasm occurring in young people and having the overall features of renal cell carcinoma but also exhibiting light microscopic and ultrastructural traits reminiscent of alveolar soft part sarcoma. Notably, this tumor has the *ASPL–TFE3* gene fusion of alveolar soft part sarcoma, but with the peculiarity that—in contrast to the latter tumor—the t(x;17) translocation responsible for this fusion is cytogenetically balanced.[989] Other gene fusions involving the *TFE3* gene have been described, including *PRCC–TFE3* and *PSF–TFE3*.[988a,989a] Aberrant nuclear immunoreactivity for TFE3 has been detected in these cases.[989a]

Two other peculiar forms of renal cell carcinoma that have been recently described are a low-grade tubular mucinous variety,[1043b] and a spindle and cuboidal cell type.[1026a]

Cytology

Cytologic examination of voided urine or bladder washing is an inefficient method for the diagnosis of renal cell carcinoma, the detection rate in most series being no

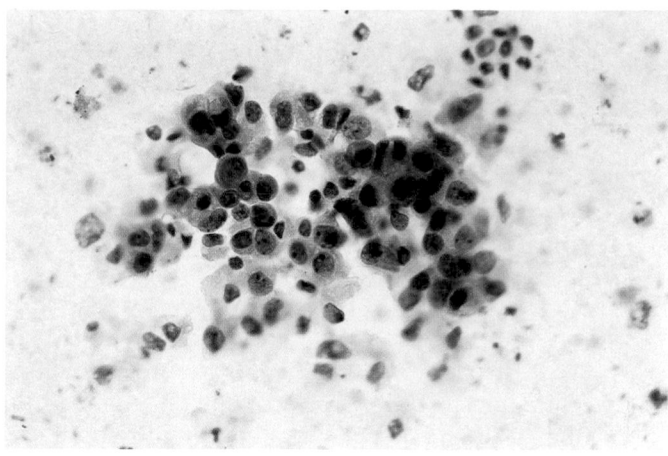

A

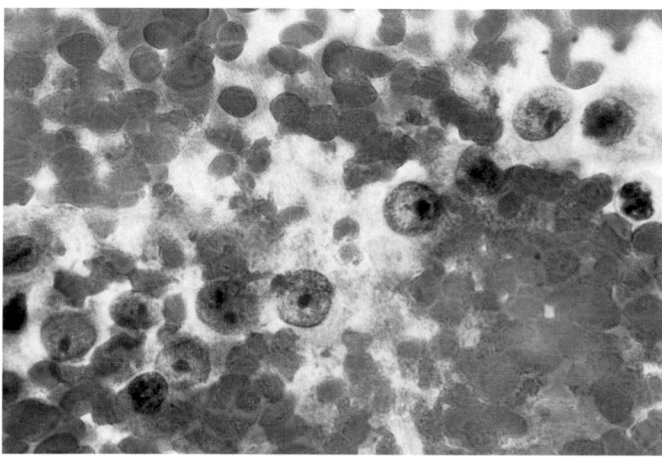

B

Fig. 17.130 Cytologic appearance of renal cell carcinoma as seen in low- and high-power.

higher than 25%. Better results have been obtained by using retrograde brushing cytology in pyelocalyceal carcinomas and renal cell carcinomas that have invaded the collecting system.[1065]

Percutaneous fine needle aspiration is a safe and accurate technique[1067,1068] (Fig. 17.130). Its main use is in the differential diagnosis between a renal cyst and an avascular or hypovascular renal tumor and in confirmation of tumor recurrence in the renal fossa after nephrectomy.[1067]

The degree of concordance in nuclear grading between cytologic and histologic preparations is high.[1066]

Spread and metastases

Approximately one third of renal cell carcinomas are found to invade perinephric fat and/or regional lymph nodes at the time of operation.[1090] Invasion of the main renal vein used to be a common finding, but now it is seen in less than 10% of the cases. From the renal vein, the tumor may extend into the inferior vena cava and occasionally even into the right atrium. Renal cell carcinoma, like Wilms' tumor, can invade the renal sinus (the adipose tissue compartment located within the confines of the kidney and containing numerous veins and lymphatics), a fact which theoretically should increase the risk for metastatic spread.[1070] Satellite tumors, which may represent intrarenal tumor spread or independent primaries, are seen in approximately 6% of the cases.[1077]

Approximately one third of patients with renal cell carcinoma already have distant metastases at the time they seek medical attention.[1076] The most common sites of distant metastases are the lung and skeleton. The bones most often involved are the pelvis and femur, but there is also a predilection for the sternum, scapula, and small bones of the hands and feet.[1075,1091] Metastases can also develop in the adrenal gland, liver, skin, soft tissue, central nervous system, ovary, and almost any other site.[1076a] Renal cell carcinoma is actually notorious (together with malignant melanoma and choriocarcinoma) for metastasizing to the most unusual places, such as the nasal cavity, oral cavity, larynx, parotid, thyroid, heart, bladder, testis, prostate, and pituitary gland.[1071,1078,1081-1084,1089] These metastases are often solitary, at least at the clinical level.[1086] Even at autopsy, 8% of the patients have metastatic involvement of only one or two organs.[1087] Because of this and the fact that the primary tumor is often clinically silent, these metastases tend to be confused with primary tumors of the organs in which they lodge. That may be the case when renal cell carcinoma metastasizes to the ovary,[1093] and even more so when it metastasizes to the *contralateral* adrenal gland.[1073,1085] In these instances, detection of EMA and keratin positivity favors a diagnosis of renal cell carcinoma.[1092] An additional source of misinterpretation stems from the fact that sometimes these metastases develop years or decades after the removal of the primary tumor.[1079,1088] Several cases have been documented in which these metastases have undergone spontaneous regression.[1072,1074]

Metastases are extremely rare in tumors that measure 3 cm or less, but they can certainly occur, indicating that the time-honored practice of separating renal cell carcinoma from adenoma on the basis of size alone is unreliable.[1069]

Therapy

The primary treatment of renal cell carcinoma is surgical excision. The preferred approach is a transabdominal or thoracoabdominal radical nephrectomy, with removal of the entire kidney, surrounding fat, Gerota's fascia, and adrenal gland.[1096,1097,1110,1114] Some authors advocate node dissection in continuity with nephrectomy or after the renal mass has been removed. The dissection should include a minimum distance of 4 to 6 cm above and below the renal vessel; however, the indication for the performance of this regional lymphadenectomy remains controversial.[1101,1106] No consistent benefits have yet been demonstrated for administration of adjunctive radiation therapy or chemotherapy.

Renal cell carcinomas that are bilateral, that develop in the setting of von Hippel–Lindau disease, or that occur in a solitary kidney are treated with partial nephrectomy, if technically feasible.[1098,1100,1102,1104,1113] Some authors have proposed this approach for small renal cell carcinomas in general.[1111,1112] Lately, laparoscopic nephrectomy has been proposed for small renal tumors in selected patients; this iconoclastic approach results in the kidney being morcellated into small fragments while still in situ, which may make it very difficult or impossible for the pathologist to determine the tumor stage, renal capsule involvement, and renal vein involvement.[1109]

Limited surgical resection of the lung is justified in patients with unilateral pulmonary metastases. A relatively long survival can be expected if the metastasis is found to be solitary on pathologic examination, if it shows extensive necrosis, and if the hilar lymph nodes are negative.[1094,1099,1107,1108]

Various immune-based therapeutic approaches (such as interleukin-2 and α-interferon) are currently being tried in metastatic renal cell carcinoma; these have met with erratic if occasionally impressive results.[1095,1103,1105]

Prognosis

The overall 5-year survival rate for renal cell carcinoma is approximately 70%. The prognosis is related to several clinicopathologic parameters.

1. *Sex and race.* These factors carry little if any prognostic connotation by themselves.
2. *Age.* The relationship between age and prognosis is minimal.[1148] Even the rare renal carcinomas occurring in patients below the age of 40 years seem to follow the same course as in older patients.[1135]
3. *Staging.* Patients who do not have distant metastases at diagnosis are given a stage on the basis of surgical findings. There are four stages: stage I, confined to the kidney; stage II, extension to perirenal fat but within Gerota's fascia; stage III, renal vein or vena caval involvement or regional lymph node metastases; and stage IV, extension to adjacent organs other than adrenal or distant metastases. There is a close correlation between this staging system, which was revised in 1997, and outcome.[1116,1119,1122,1134a,1139,1141] The 5-year survival rate following nephrectomy is 60% to 80% in stage I, 40% to 70% in stage II, 10% to 40% in stage III, and 5% or less in stage IV.[1149,1150]
4. *Distant metastases.* The presence of distant metastatic disease at the time of operation is, not surprisingly, the single most important prognostic parameter.[1148]
5. *Tumor size.* Size of the primary tumor relates to prognosis for the very small (less than 3 cm) and the very large (over 12 cm) tumors but not for those between these extremes, which represent the large majority.[1118,1130,1138] For such tumors (3–12 cm), size seems to be a continuous and therefore relative variable.[1116] Out of necessity, an arbitrary size cut-off is needed,

and this cut-off has been established to be 7 cm between T1 and T2 tumors in the 1997 TNM staging system; however, it has been suggested that a tumor size cut-off of 5.0 or 5.5 cm is more predictive of the survival of stage I patients after radical nephrectomy.[1117a,1131]

6. *Renal vein invasion.* Traditionally, gross invasion of the renal vein has been regarded as a poor prognostic sign and has therefore constituted a criterion for the surgical staging. However, some recent series have shown that this factor has little prognostic significance by itself[1145,1148] or that it affects outcome only in the high-grade tumors.[1138] In contrast, microscopic vein invasion has been found to be an important predictor of relapse.[1143,1146]
7. *Invasion of renal pelvis.* This feature does not seem to be of prognostic significance.[1138]
8. *Microscopic grade.* Nuclear grade of the tumor as determined in microscopic sections is an important predictor of survival.[1133,1140,1148] It is strongly correlated with surgical staging, but it also maintains statistical validity independently from it.[1118,1120] Four grades are generally used. In one series, the incidence of metastases was 0% for grade I tumors and 50% for the others.[1118] In other series, the incidence of metastases for low-grade tumors has been higher.[1152] It would seem that the most marked prognostic difference is between grades I and II tumors on one side and grades III and IV on the other.[1116,1137,1138,1148] It is possible that the use of standardized nuclear and nucleolar features and of nuclear morphometry may further refine the criteria for nuclear grading.[1136a,1142,1147]
9. *Clear versus granular cytoplasm.* Clear cell tumors are, as a group, less aggressive than granular cell tumors, but this is largely a function of the nuclear grade.[1118,1148]
10. *Microscopic variants.* The prognostic significance associated with the various microscopic variants of renal cell carcinoma is discussed in connection with those variants[1114a] (see p. 1256).
11. *Lymphocytic infiltration.* A correlation has been found between increased T-cell infiltration and both high clinical stage and pathologic grade.[1132] Whether the presence of these cells is of prognostic value by itself remains to be seen.
12. *DNA ploidy.* A close correlation has been found between DNA ploidy and morphologic nuclear grading.[1117,1136] However, whether DNA ploidy provides prognostic information that is independent from the grading remains controversial.[1125,1126,1144]
13. *Cell proliferation.* A correlation has been found between cell proliferation (as evaluated by flow cytometry or MIB-1 immunostaining) and prognosis.[1115,1124,1128,1129,1134,1151]
14. *p53 overexpression.* It has been claimed that positive p53 immunostaining in renal cell carcinoma is associ-

ated with metastatic disease and poor survival in patients with early stage disease.[1127,1153]

15 *CD44S expression.* The suggestion has been made that the expression of CD44S (the standard isomorph of CD44) as demonstrated immunohistochemically correlates with progression and recurrence of renal cell carcinoma.[1123]

16 *Vessel density.* There is no convincing evidence that the degree of intratumoral microvessel density contributes additional prognostic information to these tumors.[1121]

17 *MUC1 expression.* This immunohistochemically detectable feature has been found to correlate with nuclear grade and tumor progression.[1134b]

18 *Insulin-like growth factor-I receptor.* High expression levels of this molecule are said to predict poor survival among women with renal cell carcinoma.[1145a]

19 *Neural cell adhesion molecule.* The expression of this marker is associated with a higher risk of metastases and a lower survival rate.[1114b]

Adenomas

Tubulo-papillary adenomas, defined as minute cortical foci of tubular or (more commonly) papillary epithelium, are present in approximately 20% or more of adult kidneys; most of them measure 1 to 3 mm in diameter and rarely exceed 1 cm.[1160,1164,1169] The cytoplasm of the proliferating cells is acidophilic rather than clear and not particularly abundant.[1174] Psammoma bodies may be present. The ultrastructural appearance of these tumors does not indicate an origin from a special segment of the nephron.[1165] They seem to be associated with arteriolonephrosclerosis and other forms of renal scarring[1157] and are particularly common and numerous in end-stage kidneys in patients on long-term dialysis (renal adenomatosis).[1166,1168] Three cases studied cytogenetically lacked the 3p alteration that is characteristic of renal cell carcinoma and showed instead a different and consistent chromosome pattern.[1158]

In the past, some authors have designated as adenoma any renal epithelial neoplasm measuring 3 cm or less. We do not agree with this practice and regard renal tumors having a solid pattern of growth and/or predominantly composed of clear cells as carcinomas regardless of their size. The facts that DNA aneuploid cell populations are common in these tumors[1161] and that distant metastases from neoplasms as small as 1 cm have been documented[1154] support this interpretation.

Metanephric adenoma tends to occur in young or middle-aged female patients. Grossly, these tumors tend to be considerably larger than the tubulo-papillary adenomas. Microscopically, they are mostly composed of tiny tubules and papillae accompanied by very scanty stroma[1159,1167,1173] (Figs 17.131 and 17.132). The nuclear fea-

tures are bland. The overall appearance is very reminiscent of developing metanephric tubular epithelium.[1162]

Secondary changes such as hemorrhage or cyst formation are common. Some of these features are also apparent on cytologic examination.[1163]

The behavior of metanephric adenoma is generally benign, but a few cases having a compatible microscopic appearance have resulted in metastases; it is possible that some represent papillary renal cell carcinomas with a solid pattern of growth (having more abundant cytoplasm and atypical nuclear features),[1171] but in at least two instances the tumors were said to have all the architectural, cytologic, immunohistochemical, and cytogenetic features of the entity.[1172] The relationship between these two entities remains controversial. The cytogenetic differences between them suggest that they are different processes,[1156a] but the occasional occurrence of focal papillary carcinoma in an otherwise typical metanephric carcinoma points to a possible relationship between them.[1160a]

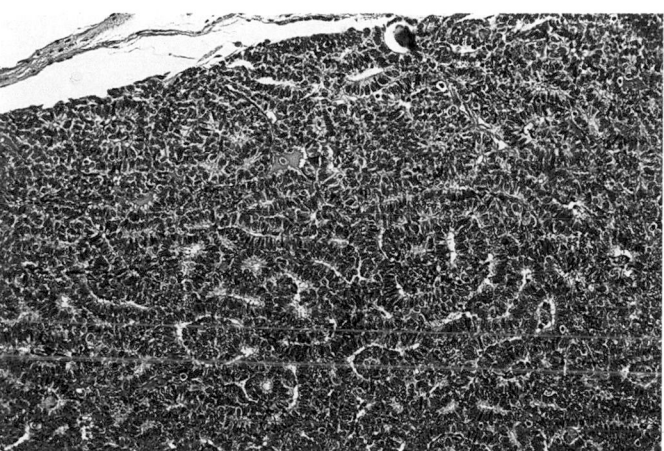

Fig. 17.131 Low-power view of metanephric adenoma. The lesion is extremely cellular.

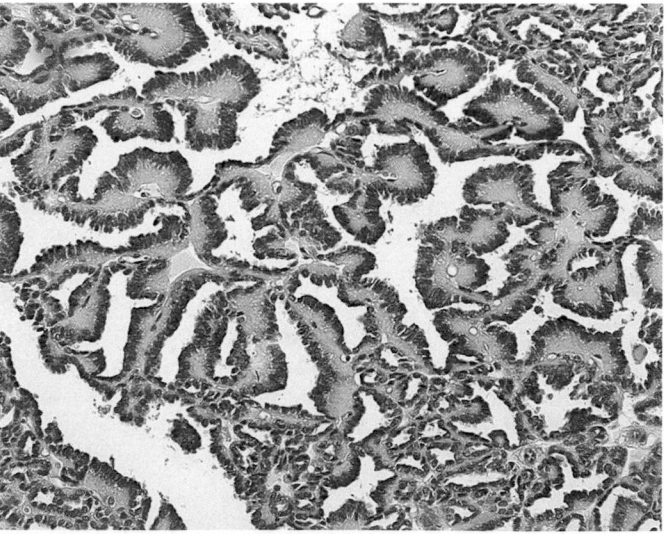

Fig. 17.132 Papillary pattern of growth of metanephric adenoma.

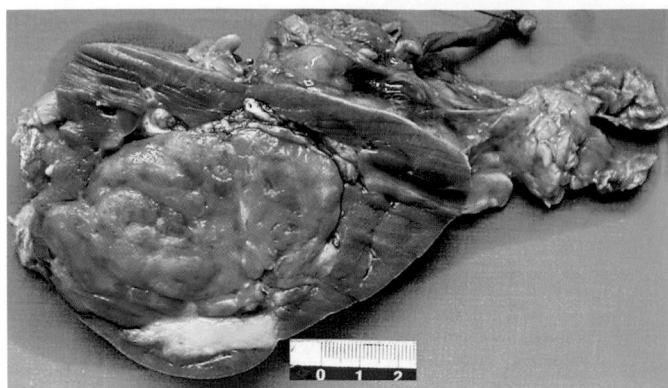

Fig. 17.133 Gross appearance of renal adenofibroma. The tumor is solid and vaguely nodular.

The suggestion has been made that metanephric adenoma represents the mature differentiated counterpart of Wilms' tumor (and nephrogenic rests) on the basis of the considerable morphologic, lectin histochemical, and immunohistochemical similarities.[1156,1164,1170] In contrast to Wilms' tumor, however, the karyotype of the tested cases of metanephric adenoma has been normal.[1162]

Metanephric adenofibroma (previously termed nephrogenic adenofibroma) is a biphasic tumor in which an epithelial component similar to that of metanephric adenoma is intimately admixed with a bland spindle cell stroma similar to that of metanephric stromal tumor[1155] (Fig. 17.133). In some of the reported cases, part of the epithelial component was indistinguishable from that of Wilms' tumor and in others it closely resembled papillary renal cell carcinoma, supporting again the concept that these are all related lesions.[1155]

Oncocytoma and oncocytosis

Renal oncocytomas make up approximately 7% of all primary nonurothelial epithelial renal neoplasms.[1198] Grossly, they are typically solid and mahogany brown, often have a central stellate scar, and can reach huge sizes (Fig. 17.134).[1180] They can be multicentric and bilateral.[1188,1205,1207] Invasion of the renal capsule or renal vein may be encountered.[1198] Some of these gross features (particularly the central scar) have been used to distinguish oncocytomas from renal cell carcinoma on CT scan, but the level of accuracy is poor.[1183] The diagnosis can be reliably made in fine needle aspiration specimens, particularly if supplemented with immunocytochemical evaluation.[1193] Microscopically, oncocytomas are composed entirely of cells with abundant acidophilic granular cytoplasm, growing in a nesting ("alveolar") or tubular fashion (Figs 17.135 and 17.136). The nuclei are usually small, round, and regular, and therefore most of these tumors qualify as grade I lesions.[1192] Focal nuclear pleomorphism can occur, but the typical case of oncocytoma should not

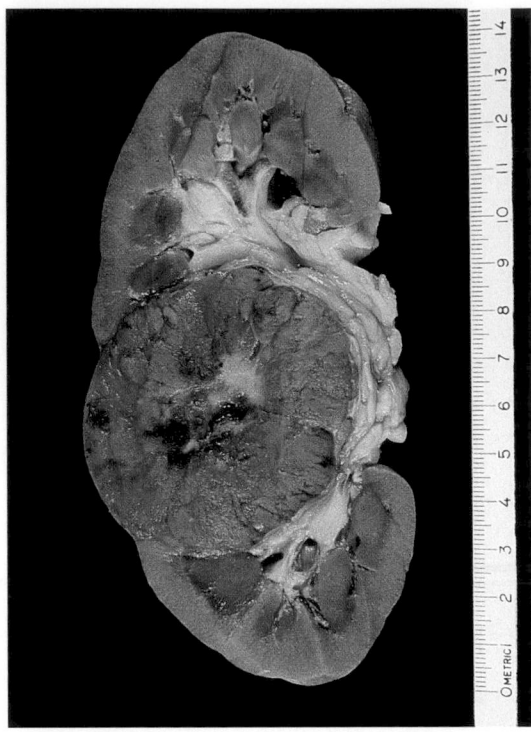

Fig. 17.134 Gross appearance of oncocytoma of kidney. The tumor is characteristically well circumscribed, mahogany brown, and has a central fibrous scar.

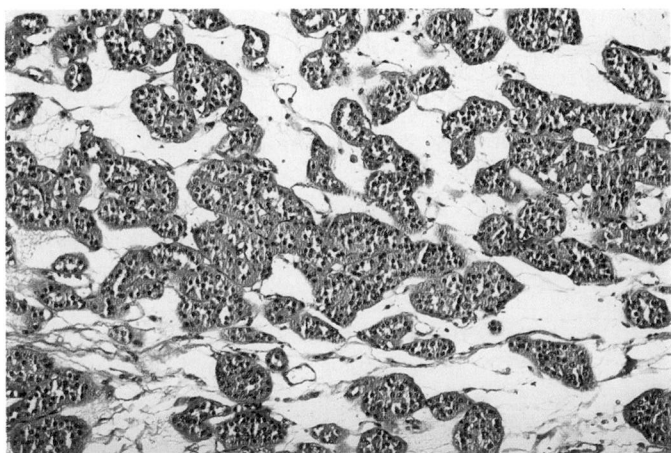

Fig. 17.135 Typical nesting pattern of renal oncocytoma.

contain prominent papillary formations, clear cells, or necrosis.[1177,1197] Psammoma bodies can be present, most of them in an intraluminal location (a phenomenon analogous to that of intrafollicular psammoma bodies in oncocytic thyroid tumors). A variant of oncocytoma has been described composed of small cells, which can be easily misinterpreted.[1187a] Immunohistochemically, the tumor cells express keratins 8 and 18 but, in contrast to the conventional renal cell carcinomas, do not show reactivity for vimentin.[1199] They also express keratin 14, CD3,[1176a] and mitochondrial markers such as the ones demonstrated with the antibodies mES-13 and 113-1.[1181,1203] Keratin 7 is usually negative, and keratin 20 always so.[1206a] Ultra-

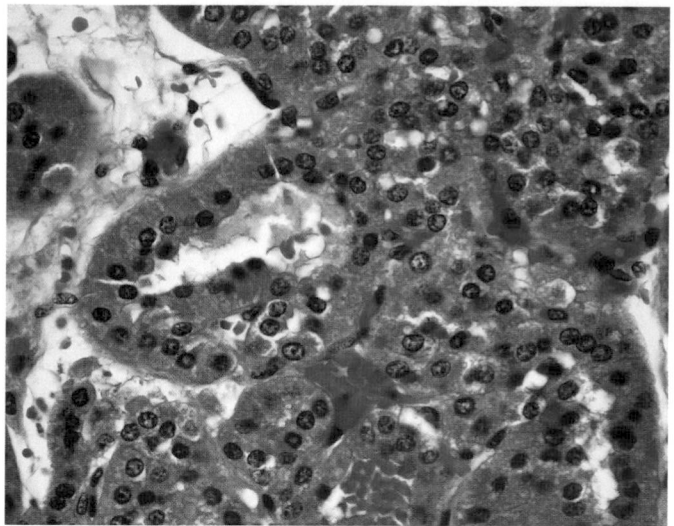

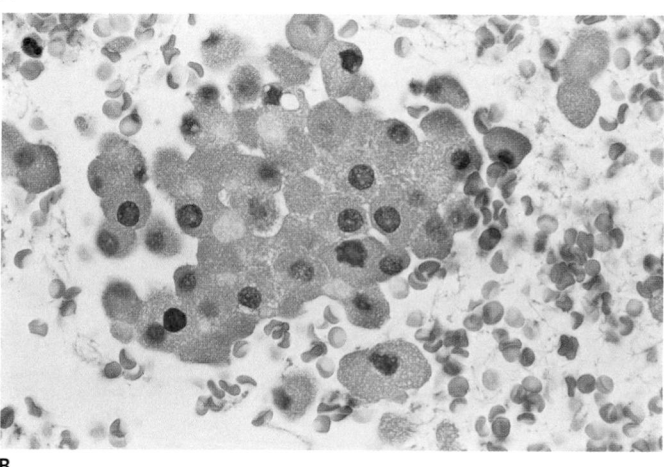

Fig. 17.136 Appearance of the cells of renal oncocytoma as seen microscopically (**A**) and in a cytologic preparation (**B**).

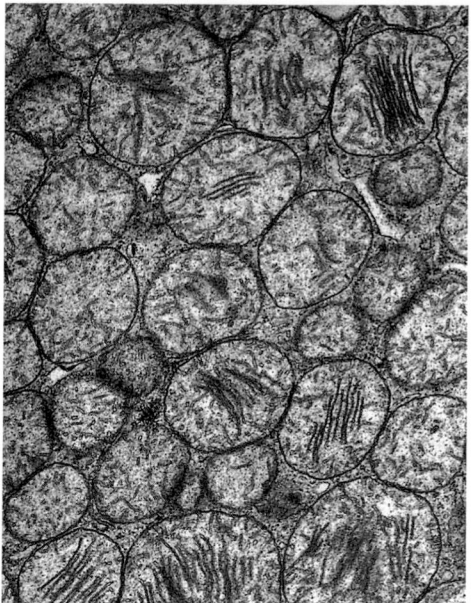

Fig. 17.137 Electron microscopic appearance of renal oncocytoma. The cytoplasm of the tumor cells is characteristically filled with mitochondria, many of which have stacked cristae. (×17,700; courtesy of Dr. Robert A. Erlandson, Memorial Sloan-Kettering Cancer Center)

structurally, packing of the cytoplasm by mitochondria is the most striking feature[1179,1186,1194,1201] (Fig. 17.137). Some of these mitochondria are entangled with intermediate filaments, the complex resulting in "globular filamentous bodies" that are responsible for the dot-like positivity seen immunohistochemically for keratins 8 and 18.[1178] The ultrastructural finding of intracytoplasmic lumina has led to the suggestion of an origin from intercalated cells of the collecting duct.[1195] Tumor cells with scanty cytoplasm and only a moderate number of small mitochondria have been called *oncoblasts* and regarded as precursors of the oncocytes, but others believe that they are simply damaged or involuted oncocytes.[1200] Cytogenetically, oncocytomas lack the 3p abnormalities of renal cell carcinoma and display different chromosomal alterations, particularly allelic deletions at 10q. Some authors have reported a tumor-associated mitDNA restriction fragment length polymorphism, but we and others have failed to confirm these results.[1182,1185,1202] The *Ron* proto-oncogene product (a receptor for macrophage stimulation protein, is characteristically expressed.[1199a]

DNA levels are almost always in the diploid range,[1187,1206] and there is a fivefold increase in the amount of mitochondrial DNA.[1202]

If strict morphologic criteria are employed, it will found that the overwhelming majority of oncocytomas will be cured by nephrectomy regardless of size.[1175,1176,1184,1189,1190,1192,1196] However, well-documented cases that have resulted in distant metastases exist.[1198]

The main differential diagnosis of renal oncocytoma is with conventional renal cell carcinoma (particularly the type predominantly composed of granular cells) and chromophobe cell carcinoma. Although oncocytoma and renal cell carcinoma are considered separate entities on both conceptual and practical grounds, a relationship between these two lesions undoubtedly exists. This is manifested by the presence of renal cell carcinomas with oncocytic features, the frequent coexistence of renal cell carcinoma in the same or contralateral kidney of patients with oncocytoma (as high as 32% in one series[1191]), and the fact that sometimes a renal cell carcinoma is found "buried" within an oncocytoma.[1184] This relationship is particularly close with chromophobe cell carcinoma, as discussed on p. 1257.

Oncocytosis is the term proposed for a condition characterized by the presence of innumerable oncocytic nodules in one or both kidneys, usually associated with the presence of a dominant nodule. The disease can affect adults and children.[1179a] Microscopically, the oncocytic tubules intermingle with the normal parenchyma and may be associated with diffuse oncocytic change in the renal tubules and oncocytic cortical cysts.[1204]

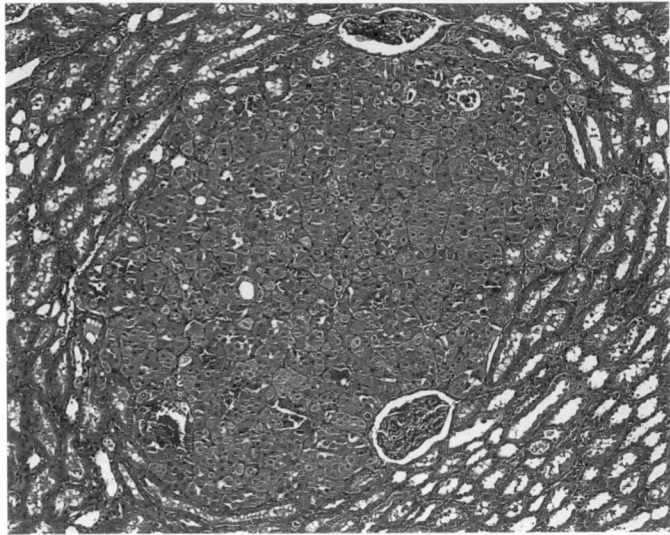

Fig. 17.138 So-called "renal oncocytosis." Many similar nodules were scattered throughout the kidney.

Neuroendocrine tumors

Small cell neuroendocrine carcinoma of the kidney with features similar to those of the homonymous pulmonary tumor has been described.[1209,1212] Evidence of neuroendocrine differentiation has been found in it ultrastructurally and immunohistochemically.[1209,1217,1220] Some of the cases have appeared to arise from pelvic epithelium and to be admixed with a component of transitional cell carcinoma.[1210,1216] The behavior of the few reported cases has been very aggressive.

Carcinoid tumor, which should be sharply segregated from small cell carcinoma, has been reported in a pure form[1208,1221,1222] and as a component of cystic teratoma.[1211,1215,1221a] Microscopically, the tumor cells are well differentiated at the morphologic, immunohistochemical, and ultrastructural levels.[1214,1218] The pattern of growth is often trabecular, and therefore similar to that seen in rectal carcinoid and in the carcinoid component of strumal carcinoid of the ovary.[1214,1219] The cytoplasm of the tumor cells may have an oncocytic quality.[1213] Stage at presentation is the most important factor in determining outcome.[1218]

Other epithelial tumors

Very unusual and as yet not fully characterized morphologic types of renal epithelial neoplasms include the *low-grade myxoid renal epithelial neoplasm with distal nephron differentiation* (forming interconnecting tubules and cord-like structures in a bubbly myxoid stroma)[1223a,1224]; the *mixed epithelial and stromal tumor of the kidney* (usually seen in women and characterized by an admixture of epithelial and stromal elements with solid and cystic growth patterns)[1223,1225] (Fig. 17.139); *spiradenocylindroma*

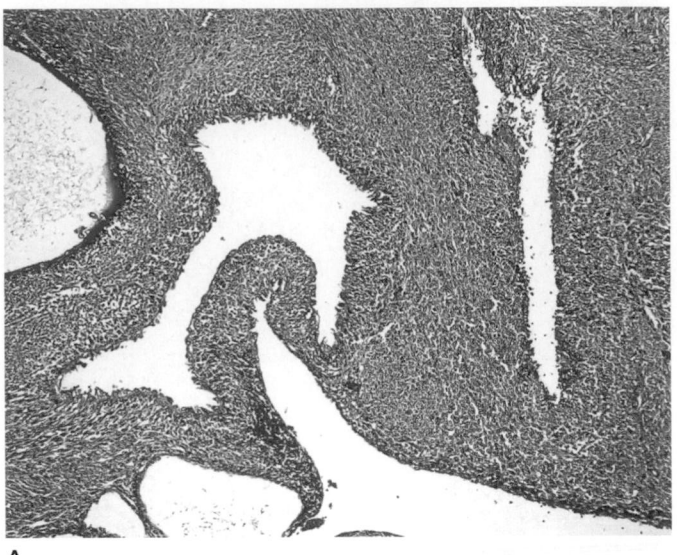

A

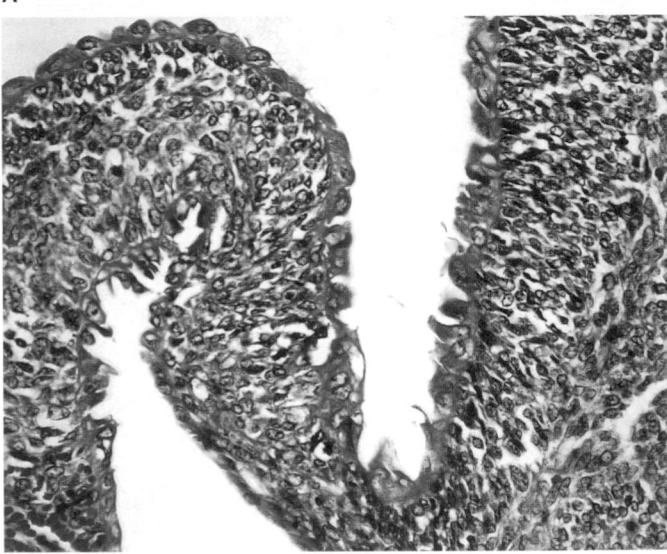

B

Fig. 17.139 So-called "mixed epithelial–stromal tumor of the kidney," as seen on low (**A**) and high power (**B**).

(a sweat gland tumorlike renal neoplasm developing in the wall of a renal cyst and having a somatic mutation in the *CYLD1* gene)[1227]; and the *papillary tumor of the renal medulla* (a type of carcinoma that is different morphologically and cytogenetically from the usual papillary renal cell carcinoma and from collecting duct carcinoma).[1226]

Angiomyolipoma

Angiomyolipoma has undergone a remarkable transformation in recent years, from a rare and rather pedestrian tumor type restricted to the kidney to a biologically fascinating and morphologically heterogeneous entity which can occur in a wide variety of sites. In its conventional form, it is composed of an intimate admixture of vessels, smooth muscle and fat, hence its name.[1245,1252]

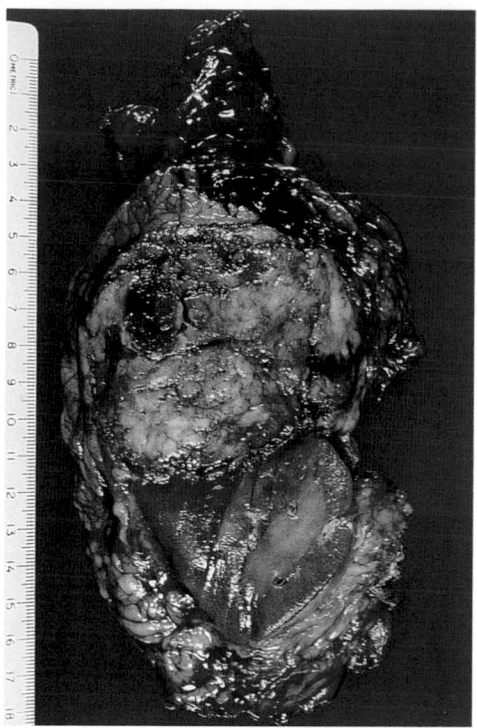 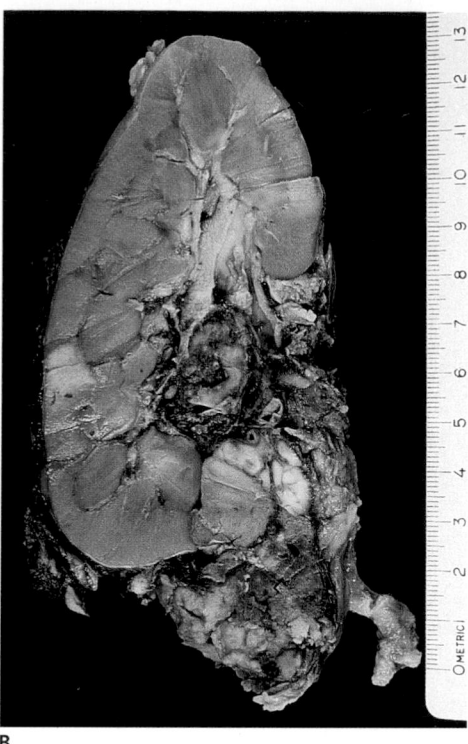

A   B

Fig. 17.140 A and **B**, Gross appearances of angiomyolipoma of kidney. Both tumors are variegated, with a predominance of yellowish areas, admixed with hemorrhagic foci.

Most patients are adults. The tumor may be found incidentally or result in retroperitoneal hemorrhage, which can be massive and even fatal.[1286] Approximately one third of the patients with renal angiomyolipoma suffer from tuberous sclerosis, the incidence being higher if the tumors are multiple or bilateral. Tuberous sclerosis is an autosomal dominant complex characterized by seizures, mental retardation, and hamartomatous tumors in multiple organs, which in addition to angiomyolipomas include subependymal giant astrocytomas and cardiac rhabdomyomas. The disease is associated with mutations in two genes: *TSC1* (whose product is hamartin) and *TSC2* (whose product is tuberin).[1284] It has been estimated that approximately 80% of the patients with the complete or severe form of tuberous sclerosis have renal angiomyolipomas.[1233] It has been shown that patients with the closely related genetic disease known as *TSC2/PKD1 contiguous gene syndrome* also have an increased incidence of renal angiomyolipoma.[1271]

The appearance of angiomyolipoma on ultrasonography and CT scan is highly characteristic,[1242] and the diagnosis can be confirmed by fine needle aspiration, preferably supplemented by immunocytochemistry.[1235,1250]

The gross appearance of the tumor depends on the relative amounts of the various components and may closely simulate renal cell carcinoma because of the admixture of yellow areas (fat) and hemorrhagic areas (vessels) (Fig. 17.140). Capsular invasion is present in a fourth of the cases, and there can be extension into the perirenal soft tissues. The tumors are multiple in approximately one third of the cases, and bilateral in approxi-

mately 15%.[1247] Microscopically, the typical case shows mature adipose tissue, tortuous thick-walled blood vessels lacking elastic tissue lamina, and bundles of smooth muscle that seem to emanate from the vessel walls (Fig. 17.141). A fourth component, which in reality is a variation of the third, is represented by a cell type with epithelioid features originally described by Apitz[1230] and currently known as the *perivascular epithelioid cell* (PEC).[1234] This cell, which often has an intimate relationship with blood vessel walls, may have a clear (due to abundant glycogen content) or acidophilic cytoplasm and a large hyperchromatic bizarre nucleus (Fig. 17.142). Multinucleation may be present (Fig. 17.143). Some of the tumor cells (particularly the large ones) contain a grumous basophilic cytoplasmic material

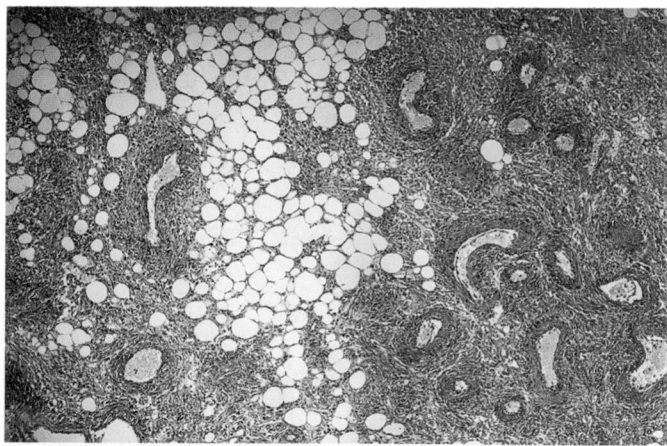

Fig. 17.141 Typical renal angiomyolipoma. The tumor is composed of adipose tissue, smooth muscle, and vessels.

vaguely resembling the Nissl's substance of neurons and the Mallory's alcoholic hyalin of hepatocytes. Immunohistochemically, PECs are notable because in addition to the expected smooth muscle markers (such as actin) they regularly contain melanocytic markers such as HMB-45, Mart-1/Melan-1, gp-100, microphthalmia transcription factor, tyrosinase, and dopaoxidase[1231,1254,1258,1269,1283,1286,1287,1290,1292] (Fig. 17.144). At the ultrastructural level, this immunohistochemical profile is associated with the presence of unique cytoplasmic crystalloids[1278] and of organelles consistent with premelanosomes.[1232,1260,1266] Some of the above markers have also been demonstrated by RT-PCR.[1259] A high proportion of angiomyolipomas are also immunoreactive for CD117 (c-kit)[1270] and hormone receptors.[1241,1253] Tuberous sclerosis patients with mutation of the *TSC1* and *TSC2* genes have been found to have loss of expression of hamartin and tuberin, respectively,[1284] but other studies have given con-

flicting results.[1257] Aneuploidy has been found in some of these tumors by flow cytometry.[1228] CGH and Humara analysis have shown that the various cell components are clonal populations, but that they do not necessarily belong to the same clone.[1238,1261,1281]

The many morphologic variants of angiomyolipoma are related to the variations in the relative proportions of the various components and/or the presence of atypical/pleomorphic cytologic features. When multiple tumors are present, one nodule may be composed almost entirely of fat and another of smooth muscle.[1239] Multicentric microscopic foci are common; exceptionally, they may be seen involving the glomeruli.[1263]

Tumors in which spindle cells of smooth muscle type predominate may look like leiomyomas, leiomyosarcomas, or gastrointestinal stromal tumors (Fig. 17.145).[1246,1291] As a matter of fact, it is not clear whether *pure* benign-looking smooth muscle tumors of the kidney that exhibit HMB-45 immunoreactivity should be called predominantly leiomyomatous angiomyolipomas or HMB-45-positive leiomyomas.[1279] Tumors in which the adipose tissue is predominant and accompanied by atypical cells and lipoblasts can be easily confused with an atypical lipoma-

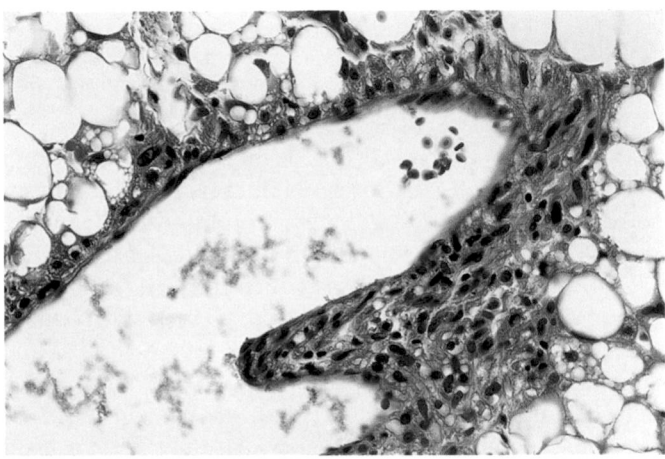

Fig. 17.142 Intimate relationship of the epithelioid smooth muscle of angiomyolipoma with a large vessel. This is an important diagnostic clue.

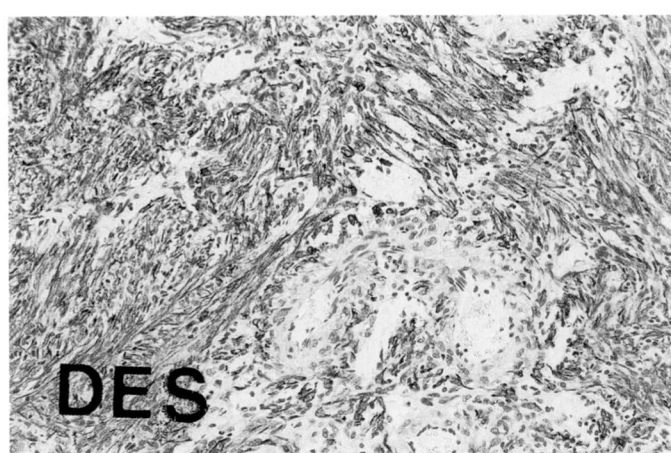

A

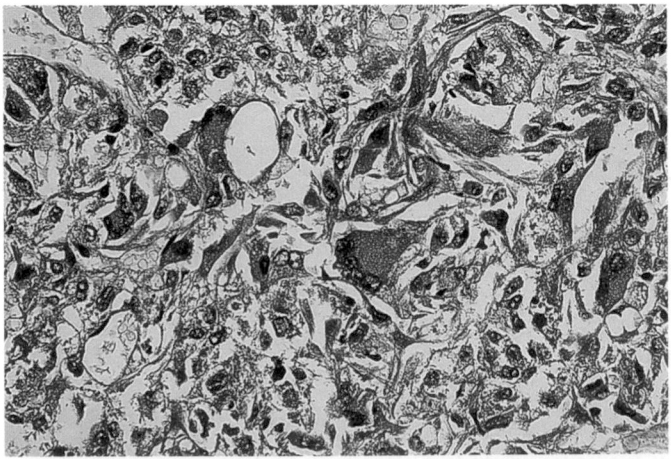

Fig. 17.143 Angiomyolipoma of the kidney showing marked pleomorphism of the tumor cells. This tumor recurred locally and later metastasized to lung.

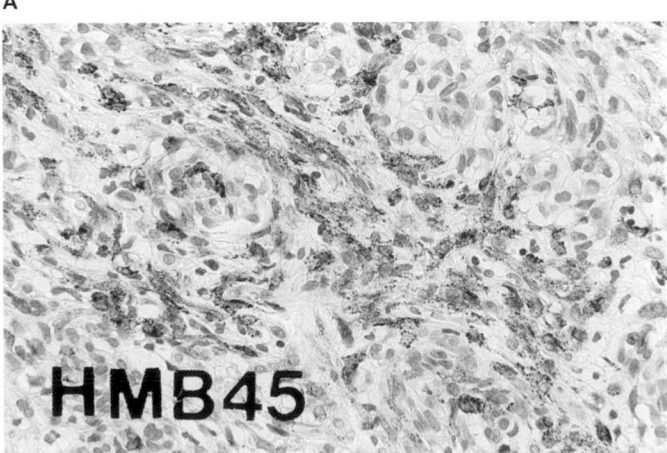

B

Fig. 17.144 Renal angiomyolipoma showing immunoreactivity for desmin (**A**) and HMB-45 (**B**).

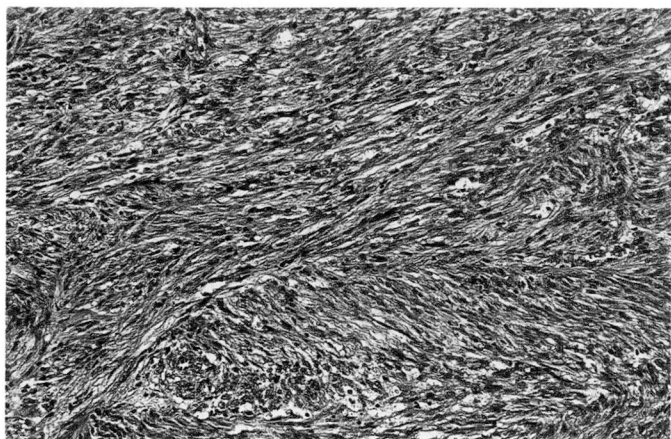

Fig. 17.145 Renal angiomyolipoma showing great predominance of the smooth muscle component.

tous tumor (well-differentiated liposarcoma). Highly pleomorphic tumors with epithelioid cells closely resemble sarcomatoid renal cell carcinomas and malignant fibrous histiocytomas.[1243,1267] Tumors composed of monomorphic epithelioid cells with homogeneous acidophilic cytoplasm may be mistaken for oncocytomas.[1272,1285a] In all of these instances, clues to the recognition of this entity include: (1) presence of islands of mature fat among the other cell components; (2) collections of epithelioid clear cells in intimate relation to vessel walls; and (3) presence in the cytoplasm of the more pleomorphic cells of the grumous basophilic material above mentioned. Needless to say, an HMB-45 stain should be carried out to confirm the suspicion of angiomyolipoma in any of these circumstances.

The treatment of renal angiomyolipoma is surgical, and excision is usually curative.[1280] However, cases resulting in death from massive local recurrence are on record.[1264] It is also now abundantly clear that angiomyolipoma is capable of distant metastases. Perhaps it is true that the regional lymph node involvement that sometimes accompanies renal angiomyolipoma is an expression of multicentricity rather than true embolic metastases,[1229,1236,1285] but cases with indisputable metastatic spread in the form of huge retroperitoneal deposits or nodules in the lung and other organs have been documented.[1240,1248,1262,1274] Practically all of these biologically malignant cases had highly atypical features morphologically, which leads to the question as to whether it is possible to make a diagnosis of malignant angiomyolipoma on morphologic grounds. Strict criteria for doing so have not yet been established, but it is obvious that a potential for malignant behavior should be anticipated for angiomyolipomas which are highly pleomorphic, mitotically active, and which contain areas of necrosis. A subject pertinent to the themes of histogenesis and malignancy in this tumor is the occasional coexistence of angiomyolipoma with renal cell carcinoma, collecting duct carcinoma, adenoma, or oncocytoma.[1251,1265,1275,1289] It is true that some such cases may simply have been oncocytoid or clear cell variants of angiomyolipomas that have been misinterpreted,[1273,1282] but there is no question that bona fide renal cell carcinoma (usually of the clear cell type) can be encountered within a renal angiomyolipoma, apparently arising from it (Fig. 17.146.[1256,1268]

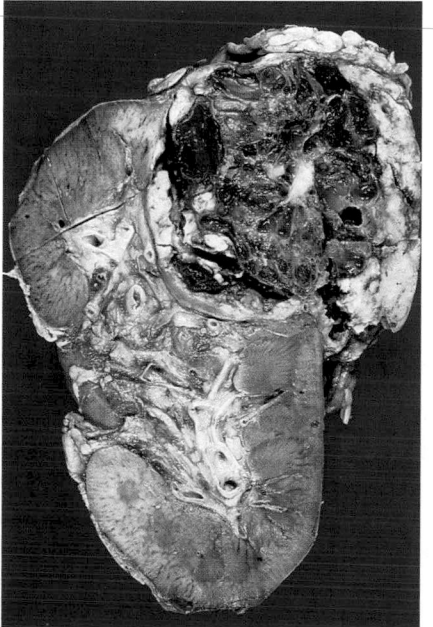

A

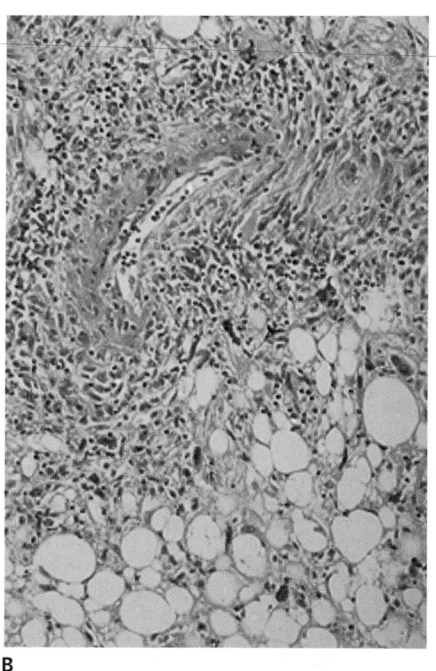

B

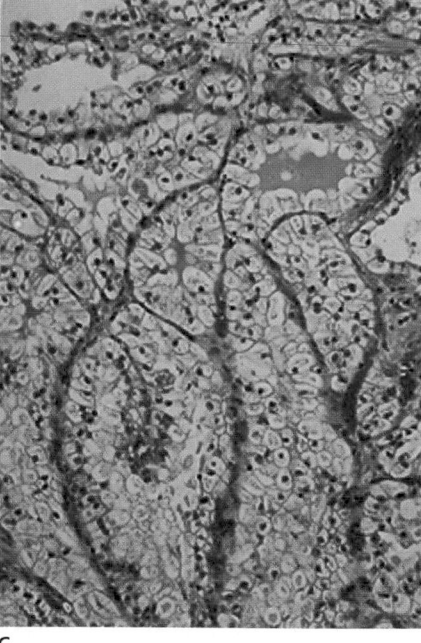

C

Fig. 17.146 A to **C**, Combined angiomyolipoma and renal cell carcinoma. **A**, Gross appearance. The renal cell carcinoma component is in the central portion of the mass. **B**, Angiomyolipoma component. **C**, Renal cell component showing characteristic glandular architecture and clear cells. (Courtesy of Dr. Christopher Otis, Springfield, MA)

The identification of the HMB-45-positive PEC as the defining feature of angiomyolipoma and all of its variants has led to two important conclusions:

1 That renal angiomyolipoma is a member of a family of phenotypically similar tumors which includes lymphangiomyoma(tosis) of lung and lymph nodes and so-called "clear cell tumor" ("sugar tumor") of lung,[1237,1249,1277] with which it may coexist.[1277]

2 That angiomyolipoma and all of its variants can occur in a wide variety of extrarenal sites, including liver, pelvic region, retroperitoneum (unconnected to the kidney), soft tissue of the back and chest region, large bowel, nasal cavity, and bone.[1244,1255] Once again, renal angiomyolipoma can coexist with these extrarenal tumors.[1276]

Juxtaglomerular cell tumor

Patients with juxtaglomerular cell tumor usually present clinically with hypertension because of excessive renin production,[1295] but some cases are nonfunctioning.[1296] Most patients are adult, but cases have also been reported in children.[1300] Grossly, all reported cases have been unilateral and solitary. Most have been less than 3 cm in diameter and located in the cortex, but occasional examples have reached 8 cm.[1303] They are solid and well circumscribed, with a grayish-white to light yellow cut surface.

The light microscopic appearance is reminiscent of hemangiopericytoma and glomus tumor.[1297,1303] The tumor cells are uniform and round to polyhedral and have a granular acidophilic cytoplasm (Fig. 17.147). Mast cells are numerous. In some cases the tumor cells were spindle, and the pattern of growth may be papillary.[1306] The intracytoplasmic renin granules may be demonstrated with PAS and Bowie stains and with immunohistochemical tech-

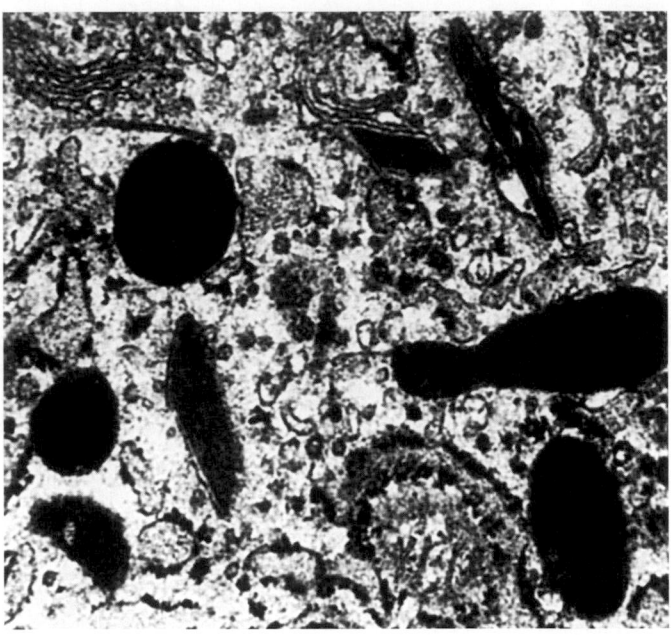

Fig. 17.148 Secretory granules of juxtaglomerular cell tumor as seen ultrastructurally. Some of them are diamond shaped, identical to those seen in normal juxtaglomerular cells. This case has been reported by Conn et al.[1295] (Courtesy of Dr. M.R. Abell, Ann Arbor, MI)

niques.[1294,1295,1297] In contrast to conventional or epithelioid angioleiomyoma, juxtaglomerular cell tumor is negative for HMB-45.[1293] Ultrastructurally, adrenergic or nerve terminals are seen in contact with the tumor cells, which have various types of secretory granules, some of them containing a rhomboid crystalline material thought to be renin protogranules.[1294,1298,1299,1302] (Fig. 17.148). All of the reported cases have behaved in a benign fashion, but some patients have remained hypertensive following nephrectomy.[1303,1305]

It should be noted that renin secretion can be associated with other renal and extrarenal neoplasms, such as renal cell carcinoma, Wilms' tumor, and pancreatic adenocarcinoma.[1301,1304,1307]

Other benign tumors and tumorlike conditions

Teratoma of the kidney is exceptionally rare.[1320] Most cases in which this diagnosis has been considered represent either retroperitoneal teratomas with renal extension or Wilms' tumors with teratoid features.[1312]

Medullary fibroma is also referred to as *renomedullary interstitial cell tumor*, under the assumption that it arises from the medullary interstitial cell.[1318] The latter is a specialized stromal element that produces prostaglandins and is believed to be involved in the regulation of intrarenal blood pressure.[1321] The tumors are asymptomatic and invariably found incidentally as minute (3 mm

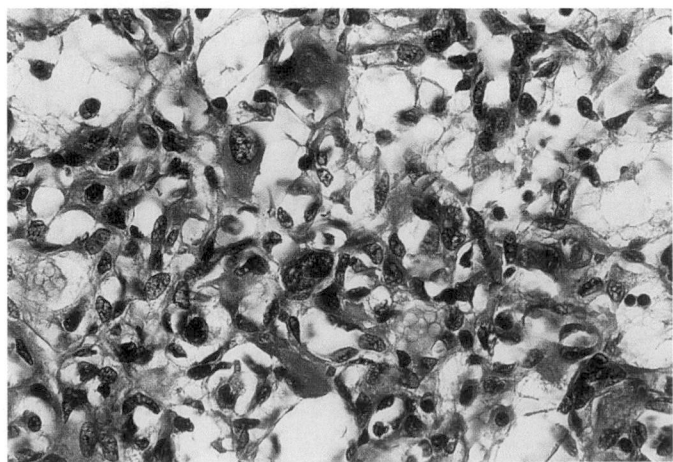

Fig. 17.147 Microscopic appearance of juxtaglomerular cell tumor. The lesion has a distinct vascular background.

or less) white nodules in the midportion of the medullary pyramids.[1329] Microscopically, they are composed of small, stellate, or polygonal cells in a loose stromal background, with entrapped tubules at the periphery. Ultrastructurally, large lipid droplets may be found in the cytoplasm.

Leiomyoma is usually located in the cortex or capsule, and it represents, in most instances, an incidental finding, inasmuch as these lesions tend to measure 1 to 3 mm in diameter.[1329] However, occasionally they become large and symptomatic.[1313] The differential diagnosis includes angiomyolipoma in adults and mesoblastic nephroma in infants.

Lipoma is also a predominantly cortical or capsular tumor, which in most cases is found incidentally. Larger examples exist,[1314,1328] but before the diagnosis of renal lipoma is made, three alternative possibilities should be considered: angiomyolipoma predominantly composed of fat, atypical lipomatous tumor of the retroperitoneum (most of which are centered in the perirenal region and which can look very lipoma-like), and pelvic/parapelvic lipomatosis (see p. 1275).

Myxoma presents as a gelatinous intraparenchymal tumor; its appearance is identical to that of myxoma of soft tissue.[1325]

Benign peripheral nerve tumors of both schwannoma[1309,1324] and perineurioma type[1319] have been described.

Hemangioma is frequently located in the medullary portion, where it can give rise to copious hematuria (see p. 1275).[1329] **Lymphangioma** can involve the kidney,[1310,1322] but before this diagnosis is made, the more likely possibility of multicystic nephroma should be considered (see p. 1246).

Solitary fibrous tumor has been seen involving the renal parenchyma or the renal capsule; some of the cases have been associated with hypoglycemia.[1316,1317,1330] The cases reported as hemangiopericytoma are very closely related to the former entity, if not identical.[1326]

Inflammatory myofibroblastic tumor may affect primarily the kidney; the behavior is generally indolent.[1319a]

Hydatid cyst can present as an intrarenal mass in countries where this parasitosis is endemic (Fig. 17.149).

Hematomas can develop in the kidney or perirenal tissues as a result of trauma, from rupture of hemangiomas, and sometimes for no apparent cause. Hematomas of the pelvic region are discussed on p. 1276. Some perirenal hematomas may contain peculiar periodic formations ("Liesegang structures") with radial striations that can simulate the appearance of parasites and that have been confused with such.[1327]

Rosai–Dorfman disease (sinus histiocytosis with massive lymphadenopathy) and **malakoplakia** can result in pseudoneoplastic renal masses (see p. 1276)[1308,1311,1323,1315] (Fig. 17.150).

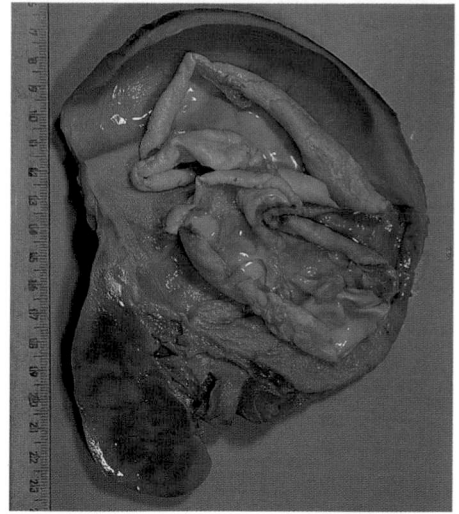

A

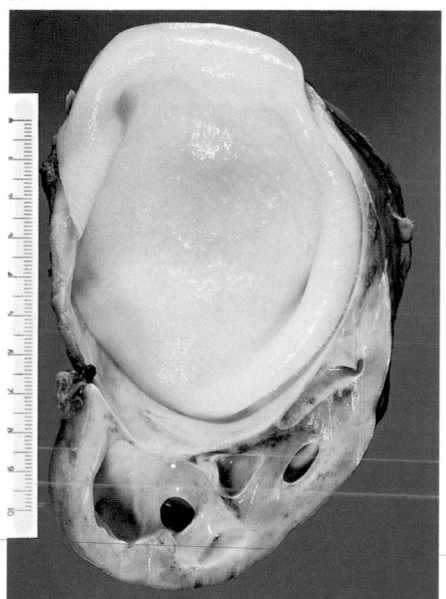

B

Fig. 17.149 A, Gross appearance of hydatid cyst of the kidney in a patient from Mar del Plata, Argentina. **B,** Another case of hydatid cyst of the kidney, this one originating from Australia. (Courtesy of Dr RA Cooke, Brisbane, Australia; From Cooke RA, Stewart B: Colour Atlas of Anatomical Pathology, Edinburgh, Churchill Livingstone, 2004)

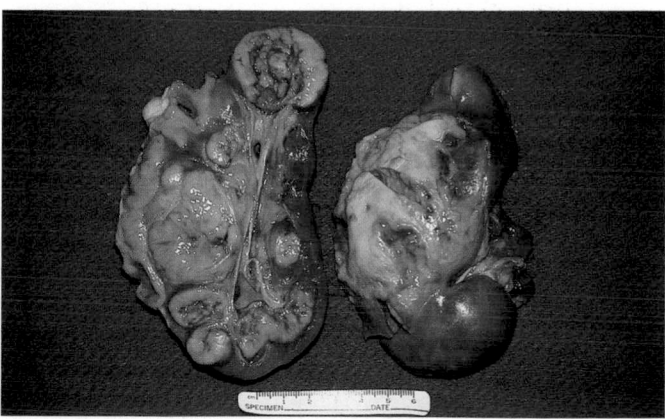

Fig. 17.150 Massive renal involvement by malakoplakia.

Sarcomas

Sarcomas of various types can arise in the adult kidney.[1335,1336,1349] These include *leiomyosarcoma* (including the myxoid variety),[1350] *fibrosarcoma, synovial sarcoma,*[1331,1332a,1337] *rhabdomyosarcoma, malignant fibrous histiocytoma,*[1347] *liposarcoma,*[1339] *malignant hemangiopericytoma, angiosarcoma,*[1332,1348] *osteosarcoma,*[1334,1341,1344] *chondrosarcoma,*[1342] *malignant mesenchymoma,*[1340,1345] and *clear cell sarcoma* (malignant melanoma of soft parts), discussed in the section on Pediatric renal tumors).[1346] Some of the chondrosarcomas have been of the mesenchymal variety.[1338] Some of the smooth muscle tumors have occurred in immunosuppressed patients in association with Epstein–Barr virus (EBV) infection.[1333] The synovial sarcomas, before the possibility of their intrarenal occurrence was realized and documented by molecular studies, were probably included in the heterogeneous group of embryonal sarcomas of the kidney.[1331] The reported cases have been of the monophasic type. Along these lines, it is well to remember that the entrapment of cystically dilated tubules lined by hobnail epithelium can simulate a biphasic appearance (just as the entrapment of bronchioloalveolar epithelium can result in a similar appearance in primary or metastatic monophasic synovial sarcoma in the lung).

Some of the renal sarcomas have been seen to arise from the renal capsule.[1343] Before a diagnosis of primary sarcoma of the kidney is made, the more common possibilities of sarcomatoid renal cell carcinoma and primary retroperitoneal soft tissue sarcoma (particularly liposarcoma) with secondary renal invasion should be considered.

Malignant lymphoma and related lymphoid lesions

Malignant lymphoma of the kidney is usually the expression of generalized disease,[1360,1361a] but sometimes the kidney is the only site of tumor.[1353,1355,1356] (Fig. 17.151). Bilaterality is common.[1361a] Renal failure may result from diffuse involvement of the organ.[1352,1359] The majority of the cases are of large cell type. Other types have been described, including low-grade B-cell lymphoma of so-called "MALT" type (containing lymphoepithelial lesions within renal tubules)[1357] and small noncleaved (undifferentiated) lymphoma.[1361] One such case has been reported in the setting of AIDS[1362] and others in organ transplant recipients,[1363] sometimes with involvement of the renal allograft.[1358]

Two varieties of lymphoma with a predilection for secondary renal involvement are thymic large B-cell lymphoma with sclerosis (see Chapter 8) and lymphomatoid granulomatosis/angiotrophic large cell lymphoma (see Chapter 7).[1351]

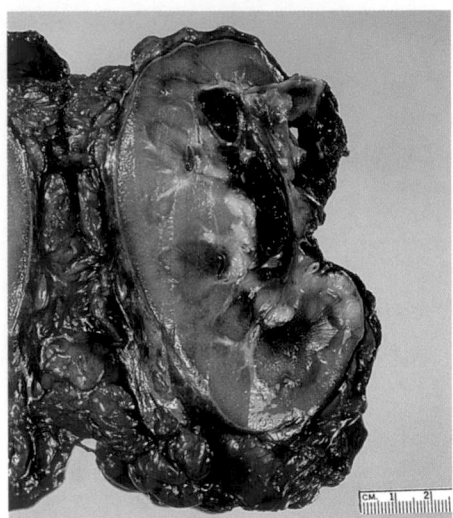

Fig. 17.151 Involvement of the kidney by large cell lymphoma. The tumor is centered in the pelvic region.

Plasmacytomas may be found within the kidney, usually as a result of dissemination in multiple myeloma but sometimes as an expression of extramedullary tumor.[1354]

Metastatic tumors

Metastatic carcinoma can affect the kidney as a part of a disseminated process, but the renal involvement is only rarely of clinical significance.[1366,1368] The metastasis may appear years or decades after the removal of the primary tumor.[1370] On CT scan, renal metastases tend to be small, multiple, bilateral, wedge shaped, intracortical, and less exophytic than primary renal cell carcinoma.[1369] In contrast to renal cell carcinoma, metastatic tumors are bilateral in over 50% of the cases.[1372] A total of 31% of the 81 patients reported by Wagle et al.[1372] had microscopic hematuria. Sometimes the metastases are exclusively limited to the renal glomeruli, in an intracapillary or extracapillary fashion, and may be diagnosed by needle biopsy.[1364,1371] The most common primary sites are the lung, skin (malignant melanoma), breast, gastrointestinal tract, pancreas, ovary, and testis.[1363a,1370a] Odd examples of metastatic tumors to the kidney simulating primary renal tumors include SETTLE (see Chapter 9), adenoid cystic carcinoma of breast,[1365] and the follicular variant of papillary thyroid carcinoma.[1367]

Tumors of renal pelvis and ureter

Transitional cell carcinoma

Most transitional cell carcinomas of the renal pelvis occur in adults (in whom they constitute about 7% of all primary carcinoma), but pediatric cases also have been documented.[1382,1390] There is a history of analgesic abuse and/or coexistence of renal papillary necrosis in approximately one fourth of the cases.[1388,1389] Cases have been seen following administration of Thorotrast for radiographic purposes,[1410] and as a complication of cyclophosphamide therapy.[1393] These tumors have also been reported in horseshoe kidneys; their incidence may actually be increased in this congenital abnormality.[1399] Some cases have developed as a manifestation of the hereditary nonpolyposis colorectal cancer syndrome.[1378a] Hematuria is the most common clinical presentation.[1406,1408] Synchronous or metachronous tumors elsewhere in the urinary tract are found in almost 40% of the patients[1388]; exceptionally, an independent renal cell carcinoma may be found in the same kidney.[1384,1412,1414] Even more unusual is the single tumor combining features of transitional cell carcinoma and renal cell carcinoma, possibly representing an example of collision tumor.[1374] Intravenous and retrograde pyelography provides the most accurate means of diagnosis.[1406] The sensitivity and accuracy of cytologic examination are higher than for renal cell carcinoma, particularly for the high-grade tumors.[1405]

Grossly, these tumors form soft, grayish red masses with smooth, glistening surfaces that resemble the transitional cell tumors of the bladder[1389] (Fig. 17.152). They often diffusely involve the entire renal pelvis and form arborescent masses that may extend down the ureter. Occasionally they are circumscribed to a calix or even to the inside of a calyceal cyst.[1396] Grade III and grade IV lesions can spread massively into the renal parenchyma and even reach the renal capsule. They can be distin-guished grossly from renal cell carcinoma because of their whitish or gray color, granular appearance, and extensive pelvic involvement. Invasion of the renal vein is common, and several cases of tumor extension into the inferior vena cava are on record.[1391] A rare form has been described with a solid fleshy appearance that simulates grossly amyloidosis.[1386a]

Transitional cell carcinomas of the ureter may be located anywhere along the length of the organ and usually result in dilatation of the proximal portion[1379,1394] (Figs 17.153).

The microscopic appearance of these transitional carcinomas, whether located in the renal pelvis or ureter, is identical to that of their more common homologs in the bladder (Fig. 17.154). The majority are grade II or grade III neoplasms. The pelvic neoplasms sometimes extend proximally along the collecting tubules, a pattern that should not be confused with adenocarcinoma.[1377] The adjacent urothelium is often abnormal, the changes ranging from hyperplasia to carcinoma in situ.[1395] The presence of fibrous thickening of small stromal vessels has been found to correlate with a history of long-term analgesic ingestion.[1403] The similarities with transitional cell carcinomas of the bladder also apply to their immunohistochemical features, including coexpression of keratins 7 and 20,[1383] overexpression of p53 protein (particularly in the high-grade tumors),[1407] and expression of p27 (a negative regulator of the cell cycle).[1401]

The standard treatment of pyeloureteral transitional cell carcinoma is nephroureterectomy. Segmental resection has sometimes been employed for midureteral

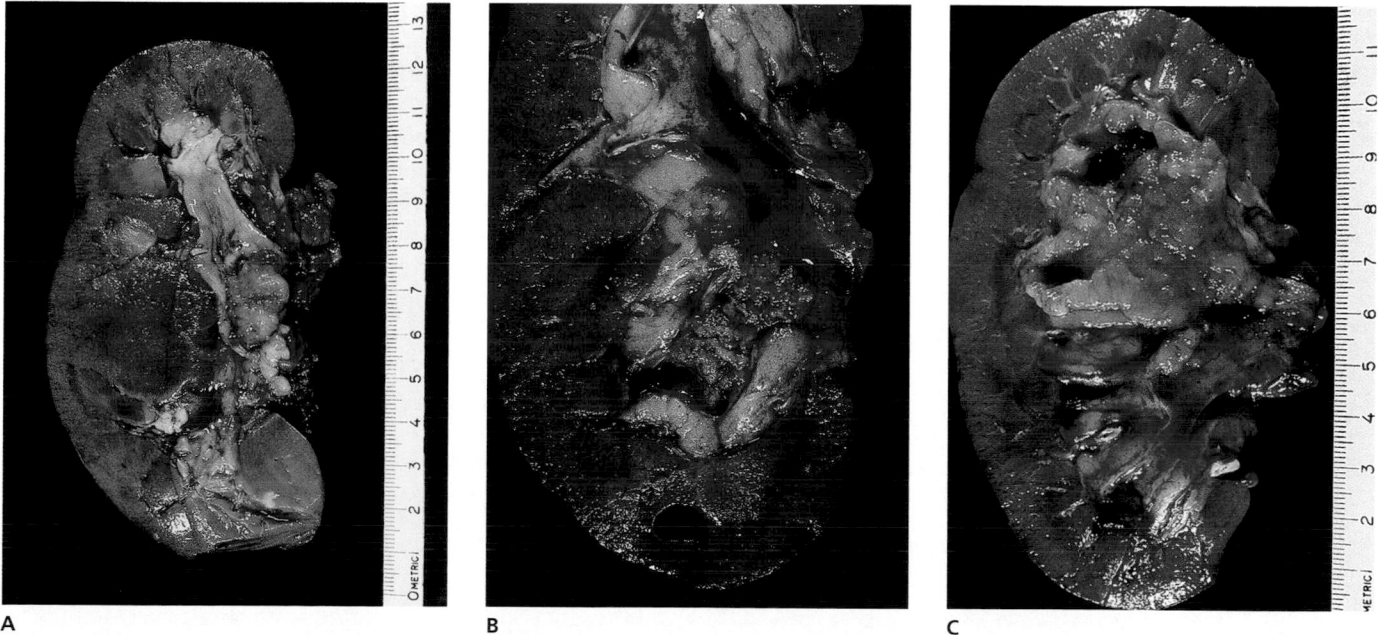

Fig. 17.152 Gross appearances of transitional cell carcinoma of renal pelvis. The tumor protrudes into the pelvic cavity and has a granular surface. The tumor shown in **C** coats the pelvis and calyces.

A   B   C

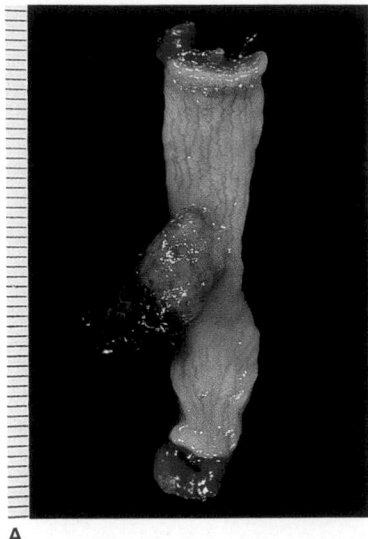

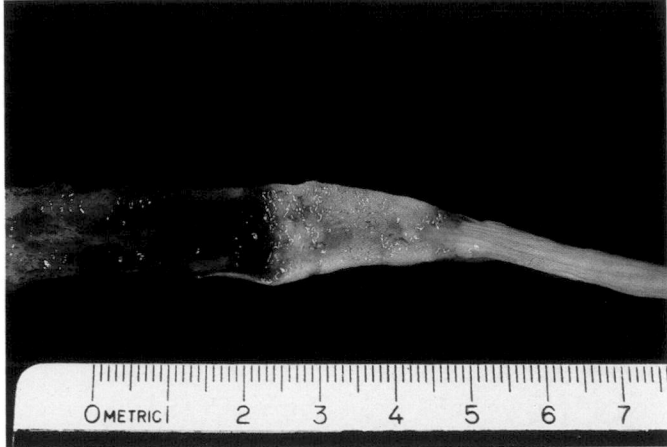

Fig. 17.153 A and **B**, Transitional cell carcinoma of ureter. The tumor shown in **A** is highly polypoid, whereas that present in **B** has a more diffuse and sessile quality.

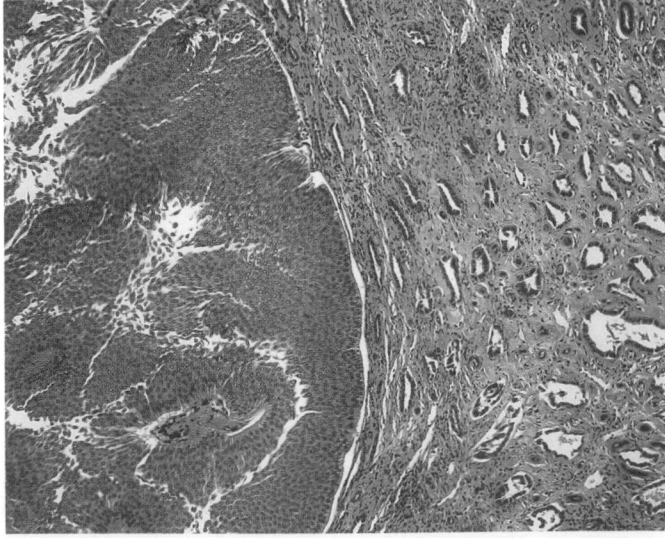

Fig. 17.154 Low-grade transitional cell carcinoma of renal pelvis growing in a pushing fashion around the medullary renal tubules.

lesions,[1396] and endoscopic removal has been done for low-grade noninvasive lesions,[1387] but the high incidence of multicentricity and coexistent dysplasia (particularly with the high-grade tumors) indicates that radical surgery is the treatment of choice for the large majority of the cases.[1376,1392] Furthermore, these tumors have a tendency to implant along the ureter, especially in its terminal (intramural) portion. Therefore it is important for a resection of the bladder cuff to be performed to avoid tumor recurrence.[1409,1411] For tumors occurring in solitary kidneys or for bilateral tumors, nephroureterectomy with renal autotransplantation and pyelocystostomy has been advocated.[1404] The overall 5-year survival rate in the surgically resected cases is about 50%.[1382,1388] The prognosis is largely determined by the stage of the lesion for both the pelvic and ureteral lesions.[1373,1378,1382,1397,1398,1413]

DNA ploidy levels, as measured by flow cytometry, have been found to provide valuable prognostic information in several independent studies.[1375,1380,1381,1402] Vascular invasion, present in approximately 35% of the cases, is also said to be of prognostic significance.[1385]

Carcinoma in situ of the renal pelvis and ureter also occurs, but its detection at this stage has only rarely been achieved.[1400]

Other carcinoma types

Adenocarcinoma of the pyelocalyceal and ureteral system is usually preceded by glandular metaplasia of the transitional epithelium at these sites (pyelitis or ureteritis glandularis and cystica) induced by long-standing chronic inflammation, sometimes secondary to renal stones.[1424] As in the bladder, the term adenocarcinoma should be reserved for the rare tumors that form unequivocal glandular structures, and not applied to transitional cell carcinomas that have small pools of mucin in between the tumor cells.[1416] Adenocarcinomas at this site have been subdivided into tubulovillous, mucinous, papillary nonintestinal, and signet-ring cell types.[1430,1431] A case has been reported having hepatoid features and secreting α-fetoprotein.[1423]

Squamous cell carcinoma of the renal pelvis is often associated with squamous metaplasia ("leukoplakia"), renal calculi, and pyelonephritis.[1422,1428] Cases have also been reported developing years after retrograde pyelography in which Thorotrast was used.[1435] Grossly, the tumor is usually large, necrotic, and ulcerated (Fig. 17.155). Most of the tumors have high-grade microscopic features.[1428] Invasion of the renal parenchyma and retroperitoneal soft tissues is common. In one series, 84% of the tumors were found at operation to be locally advanced and/or metastatic.[1428] The prognosis is very poor.[1428,1432]

Verrucous carcinoma has been reported in the pelvis of a horseshoe kidney associated with staghorn calculi.[1429]

Lymphoepithelioma-like carcinoma of the pelvis has a morphologic appearance similar to that of its

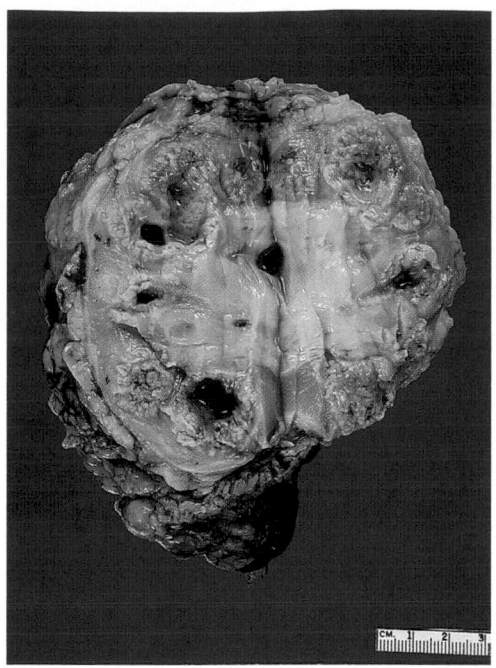
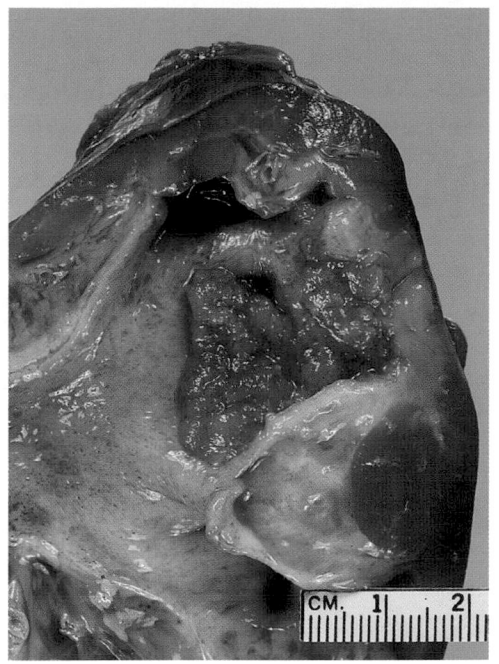

A   **B**

Fig. 17.155 A and **B**, Gross appearance of squamous cell carcinoma of the renal pelvis. The tumor shown in **A** is extensive and associated with marked pyelonephritis, whereas that shown in **B** is smaller and has a granular polypoid appearance.

nasopharyngeal counterpart, but no EBV genomic sequences have been detected in it[1418] (Fig. 17.156).

Sarcomatoid carcinoma (spindle cell carcinoma; carcinosarcoma) has a predominantly spindle cell and/or pleomorphic appearance, sometimes combined with foci of conventional transitional cell carcinoma[1419,1433,1436] (Fig. 17.157).

Giant cell carcinoma is a malignant tumor that is morphologically similar to giant cell tumor of bone and (even more so) giant cell tumor of soft tissues. It may be seen in a pure form or in association with papillary transitional, in situ, or sarcomatoid carcinoma.[1415,1427,1437]

Small cell neuroendocrine carcinoma has been described in the pelvis in association with transitional cell carcinoma.[1421,1426]

Carcinoma with trophoblastic features can be seen admixed with a conventional transitional cell carcinoma or in a pure form, in which case the tumor looks indistinguishable from a choriocarcinoma (although it probably still is a carcinoma rather than a germ cell tumor).[1417,1420,1434,1437a]

Rhabdoid features can be seen focally or extensively in primary carcinomas at this site; as in other locations, this phenotype is an indicator of a very aggressive behavior.[1425]

Other tumors and tumorlike conditions

Fibroepithelial polyp[1455,1462] (Fig. 17.158) and **hypertrophic infundibular stenosis of the calyces**[1456] are two rare tumorlike masses of the pelvic region. **Pelvic lipomatosis** or **fibrolipomatosis** results from excessive proliferation of peripelvic fat, and it may simulate a neoplasm radiographically.[1450] **Amyloidosis** can present as a localized nodule in the wall of one or both ureters

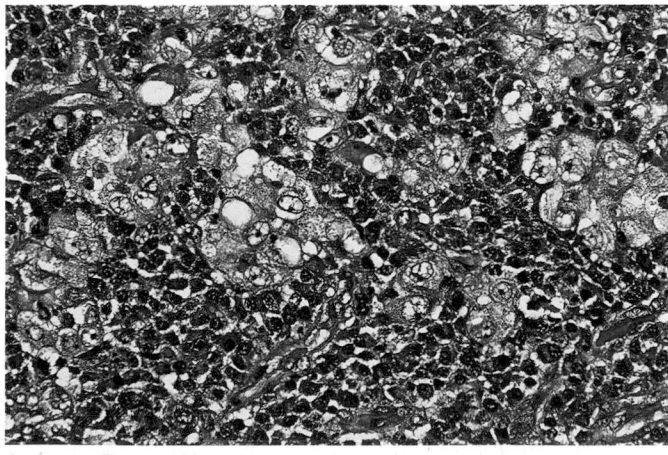
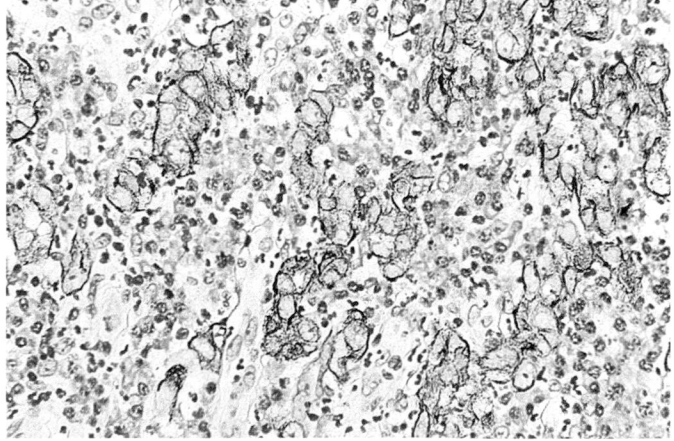

A   **B**

Fig. 17.156 A and **B**, Lymphoepithelioma-like carcinoma of the ureter. The tumor cells are strongly positive for keratin (**B**).

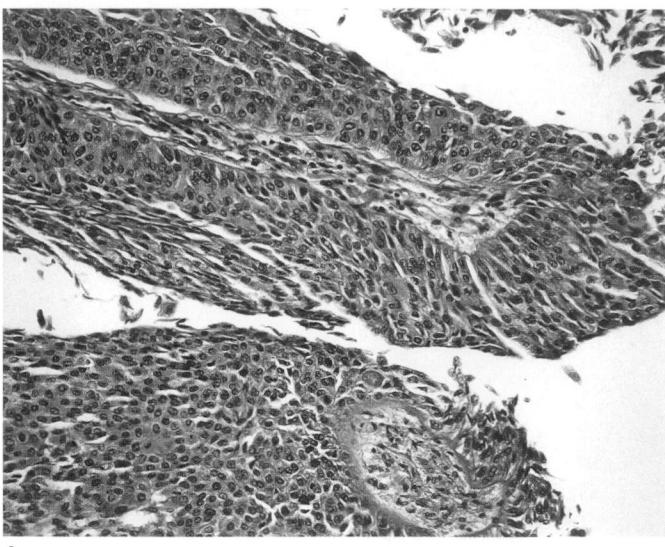

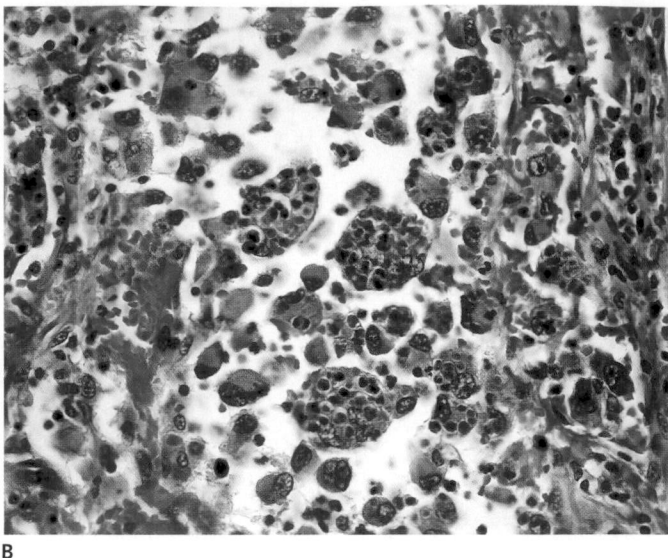

Fig. 17.157 A and **B**, Transitional cell carcinoma of pelvis with a sarcomatoid (dedifferentiated) component. The morphologic difference between the well-differentiated (**A**) and the anaplastic areas (**B**) is striking. Note the numerous neutrophils within the cytoplasm of the giant tumor cells in the anaplastic component.

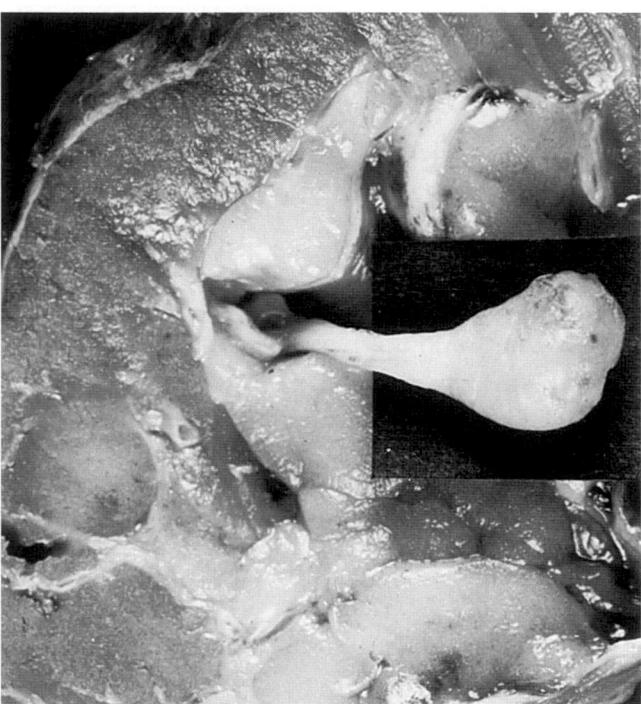

Fig. 17.158 Benign fibroepithelial polyp emerging from lower calyx of the left kidney in a 61-year-old woman. The tumor caused hematuria, and total nephrectomy was performed.

(so-called "amyloid tumor").[1445] **Myelolipoma** morphologically similar to its more common adrenal counterpart can present as a mass in the renal sinus.[1438] **Malakoplakia** of the pelvis or ureter may result in obstruction and hydronephrosis.[1459,1467] **Stone granuloma** is a complication of ureteroscopy and ureteral stone fragmentation; it is characterized by the presence of embedded particles of calcium oxalate associated with macrophages and foreign body giant cells, with surrounding fibrosis and dilatation of the proximal ureter.[1443]

Subepithelial hematoma of the renal pelvis (Antopol–Goldman lesion) can present with gross hematuria and simulate radiographically a malignant tumor. The etiology is unknown.[1442,1451]

"Urinoma" results from the extravasation of urine into the renal perihilar and peripelvic fat; in the early stages there is lipolysis with foamy macrophages and multinucleated giant cells, followed by fibrosis and deposition of "urinary precipitates." Demonstration of Tamm–Horsfall protein by immunostaining confirms the fact that the amorphous extracellular precipitates are derived from uroprotein.[1439]

Benign pyeloureteral tumors include inverted papilloma (sometimes multiple),[1447,1454] so-called "nephrogenic adenoma,"[1446,1449a,1453,1458] villous adenoma,[1469] hemangioma,[1441] leiomyoma,[1471] solitary fibrous tumor,[1448] and neurofibroma. The hemangiomas are often located at the tips of the papillae, are multiple in about 10% of the cases, and may result in recurrent episodes of hemorrhage.[1440,1444] Owing to their small size, extensive sectioning may be needed to find the lesion. The nephrogenic adenoma may show gastric metaplasia.[1461]

Cystic hamartoma is a lesion of the renal pelvis that presents grossly as an intrarenal multicystic mass situated adjacent to the pyelocalyceal system. Microscopically, a biphasic proliferation of epithelial cells (tubules and cysts lined by cuboidal and columnar epithelium) and mesenchymal cells (predominantly fibroblastic but with scattered bundles of smooth muscle) is seen.[1460,1463]

Malignant tumors of nonepithelial type are exceptional. A few cases of leiomyosarcoma have been reported.[1472] Non-Hodgkin's malignant lymphoma of the retroperitoneum can involve the ureter secondarily.[1468] A case of primary malignant lymphoma has been reported in the pelvis of a transplanted kidney.[1457]

Ureterosigmoidoscopy, an operation no longer practiced, can be complicated by the appearance of a tumor at a site of anastomosis many years following the operation.[1466] The tumor, which is usually of an **adenocarcinoma** type, develops on the colonic side, usually on a background of hyperplastic mucosa of the so-called "transitional type."[1470] A few cases of benign and malignant tumors have been reported in ureteroileal conduits.[1452,1464]

Carcinomas **metastatic** to the retroperitoneum can invade the ureteral wall and result in obstruction; the breast and lung are the most common sites for the primary tumors.[1449,1465]

References

NON-NEOPLASTIC DISEASES
The renal biopsy

1   Habib R. A story of glomerulopathies: a pathologist's experience. Pediatr Nephrol 1993, **7**: 336–346.
2   Pirani CL. Evaluation of kidney biopsy specimens. In Tisher CC, Brenner BM (eds): Renal pathology: With clinical and functional correlations, ed. 2, vol. I. Philadelphia, 1994, J.B. Lippincott, pp. 85–115.

Handling of the biopsy

3   Hoffmann EO, Flores TR. High resolution light microscopy in renal pathology. Am J Clin Pathol 1981, **76**: 636–643.
4   Johanssen JR. Rapid processing of kidney biopsies for electron microscopy. Kidney Int 1973, **3**: 46–50.
5   Spargo BH, Seymour AE, Ordóñez NG. Introduction. In: Renal biopsy pathology with diagnostic and therapeutic implications. New York, 1980, John Wiley & Sons, pp. 1–13.

Normal structure of the glomerulus

6   Clapp WL, Croker BP. Adult kidney. In Sternberg SS (ed.): Histology for pathologists, ed. 2. New York, 1997, Raven Press, pp. 799–834.
7   Drenckhahn D, Schnittler H, Nobiling R, Kriz W. Ultrastructural organization of contractile proteins in rat glomerular mesangial cells. Am J Pathol 1990, **137**: 1343–1351.
8   Johnson RJ, Floege J, Yoshimura A, Iida H, Couser WG, Alpers CE. The activated mesangial cell: A glomerular "myofibroblast"? J Am Soc Nephrol 1992, **2**: S190–S197.
9   Mené P, Simonson MS, Dunn MJ. Physiology of the mesangial cell. Physiol Rev 1989, **69**: 1347–1424.
10 Michael AF, Keane WF, Raij L, Vernier RC, Mauer SM. The glomerular mesangium. Kidney Int 1980, **17**: 141–154.
11 Sraer JD, Adida C, Peraldi M-N, Rondeau E, Kanfer A. Species-specific properties of the glomerular mesangium. J Am Soc Nephrol 1993, **3**: 1342–1350.
12 Stamenkovic I, Skalli O, Gabliani G. Distribution of intermediate filament proteins in normal and diseased human glomeruli. Am J Pathol 1986, **125**: 465–475.
13 Weber M. Basement membrane proteins. Kidney Int 1992, **41**: 620–628.

Classification of glomerular disease

14 Churg J, Bernstein J, Glassock RJ. Renal disease: Classification and atlas of glomerular diseases, ed. 2. New York, 1995, Igaku-Shoin, pp. 3–21.

Glomerular lesions associated with the nephrotic syndrome
Minimal change glomerulopathy

15 Andrews PM. A scanning and transmission electron microscopic comparison of puromycin aminonucleoside-induced nephrosis to hyperalbuminemia-induced proteinuria with emphasis on kidney podocyte pedicel loss. Lab Invest 1977, **36**: 183–197.
16 Arakawa M. A scanning electron microscope study of the human glomerulus. Am J Pathol 1971, **64**: 457–462.
17 Cameron JS, Glassock R (eds). The nephrotic syndrome. New York, 1988, Marcel Dekker.
18 Coggins CH. Minimal change nephrosis in adults. In: Proceedings of the 8th International Congress of Nephrology. Basel, 1981, S Karger, pp. 336–344.
19 Daniel V, Trautmann Y, Konrad M, Nayir A, Schärer K. T-lymphocyte populations, cytokines and other growth factors in serum and urine of children with idiopathic nephrotic syndrome. Clin Nephrol 1997, **47**: 289–297.
20 Finkelstein A, Fraley DS, Stachura I, Feldman HA, Gandy DR, Bourke E. Fenoprofen nephropathy: Lipoid nephrosis and interstitial nephritis: A possible T-lymphocyte disorder. Am J Med 1982, **72**: 81–87.
21 Habib R, Kleinknecht C. The primary nephrotic syndrome in children. Classification and clinicopathologic study of 406 cases. In Sommers SC (ed.): Kidney pathology decennial, 1966–1976. New York, 1975, Appleton-Century-Crofts, pp. 165–224.
22 International Study of Kidney Disease in Children. Primary nephrotic syndrome in children: Clinical significance of histopathologic variants of minimal change and of diffuse mesangial hypercellularity. Kidney Int 1981, **20**: 765–771.
23 Korbet SM, Schwartz MM, Lewis EJ. Minimal change glomerulopathy of adulthood. Am J Nephrol 1988, **8**: 291–297.
24 Munk F. Klinische Diagnostik der degenerativen Nierenerkrankungen. Z Klin Med 1913, **78**: 1–52.
25 Nadasdy T, Silva FG, Hogg RJ. Minimal change nephrotic syndrome – focal sclerosis complex (including IgM nephropathy and diffuse mesangial hypercellularity). In Tisher CC, Brenner BM (eds): Renal pathology: With clinical and functional correlations, ed. 2, vol. I. Philadelphia, 1994, J.B. Lippincott, pp. 330–389.
26 Olson JL, Schwartz MM. The nephrotic syndrome: Minimal change disease, focal segmental glomerulosclerosis and miscellaneous causes. In Jennette JC, Olson JL, Schwartz MM, Silva FG (eds): Heptinstall's Pathology of the kidney, ed. 5. Philadelphia, 1998, Lippincott-Raven, pp. 187–257.
27 Peces R, Sanchez L, Gorostidi M, Alvarez J. Minimal change nephrotic syndrome associated with Hodgkin's lymphoma. Nephrol Dial Transplant 1991, **6**: 155–158.
28 Schnaper HW, Robson AM. Nephrotic syndrome: Minimal change disease, focal glomerulosclerosis, and related disorders. In Schrier RW, Gottschalk CW (eds): Diseases of the kidney, ed. 5, vol. II. Boston, 1993, Little, Brown and Co., pp. 1731–1784.
29 Siegel NJ, Gaudio KM, Krassner LS, McDonald BM, Anderson FP, Kashgarian M. Steroid-dependent nephrotic syndrome in children: Histopathology and relapses after cyclophosphamide treatment. Kidney Int 1981, **19**: 454–459.
30 Tanaka R, Yoshikawa N, Kitano Y, Ito H, Nakamura H. Long-term cyclosporine treatment in children with steroid-dependent nephrotic syndrome. Pediatr Nephrol 1993, **7**: 249–252.
31 Warren GV, Korbet SM, Schwartz MM, Lewis EJ. Minimal change glomerulopathy associated with nonsteroidal antiinflammatory drugs. Am J Kidney Dis 1989, **13**: 127–130.

Diffuse mesangial hypercellularity with nephrotic syndrome

32 Al-Eisa A, Carter JE, Lirenman DS, Magil AB. Childhood IgM nephropathy: comparison with minimal change disease. Nephron 1996, **72**: 37–43.

33 Alexopoulos E, Papagianni A, Stangou M, Pantzaki A, Papadimitriou M. Adult-onset idiopathic nephrotic syndrome associated with pure diffuse mesangial hypercellularity. Nephrol Dial Transplant 2000, **15**: 981–987.

34 Border WA. Distinguishing minimal-change disease from mesangial disorders. Kidney Int 1988, **34**: 419–434.

35 Cavallo T, Johnson MP. Immunopathologic study of minimal-change glomerular disease with mesangial IgM deposits. Nephron 1981, **2**: 281–284.

36 Cohen AH, Adler SG. Mesangial proliferative glomerulonephritis. In Massry SG, Glassock RJ (eds): Textbook of nephrology, ed. 3, vol. 1. Baltimore, 1995, Williams & Wilkins, pp. 739–742.

37 Cohen AH, Border WA, Glassock RJ. Nephrotic syndrome with glomerular mesangial IgM deposits. Lab Invest 1978, **38**: 610–619.

38 D'Agati V. The many masks of focal segmental glomerulosclerosis. Kidney Int 1994, **46**: 1223–1241.

39 Hirszel P, Yamase HT, Carney WR, Galen MA, Graeber CW, Johnson KJ, Kennedy TL, Lapkin RA, McLean RH, Rosenworcel E. Mesangial proliferative glomerulonephritis with IgM deposits. Clinicopathologic analysis and evidence for morphologic transitions. Nephron 1984, **38**: 100–108.

40 Hsu HC, Chen WY, Lin GJ, Kao SL, Huang CC, Lin CY. Clinical and immunopathologic study of mesangial IgM nephropathy: Report of 41 cases. Histopathology 1984, **8**: 435–466.

41 International Study of Kidney Disease in Children. Primary nephrotic syndrome in children: Clinical significance of histopathologic variants of minimal change and of diffuse mesangial hypercellularity. Kidney Int 1981, **20**: 765–771.

42 Waldherr R, Gubler ME, Levy M, Broyer M, Habib R. The significance of pure diffuse mesangial proliferation in idiopathic nephrotic syndrome. Clin Nephrol 1978, **10**: 171–179.

Focal and segmental glomerulosclerosis

43 Artero M, Biava C, Amend W, Tomlanovich S, Vincenti F. Recurrent focal glomerulosclerosis: natural history and response to therapy. Am J Med 1992, **92**: 375–383.

44 Beaufils H, Alphonse JC, Guedon J, Legrain M. Focal glomerulosclerosis: Natural history and treatment. Report of 70 cases. Nephron 1978, **21**: 75–85.

45 Braden GL, Mulhern JG, O'Shea MH, Nash SV, Ucci AA Jr, Germain MJ. Changing incidence of glomerular diseases in adults. Am J Kidney Dis 2000, **35**: 878–883.

46 Cameron JS. The enigma of focal segmental glomerulosclerosis. Kidney Int 1996, **50**: S119–S131.

47 Chawder P, Soni A, Suri A, Bhagwat R, Yoo J, Treser G. Renal ultrastructural markers in AIDS associated nephropathy. Am J Pathol 1987, **126**: 513–526.

48 Clarkson MR, O'Meara YM, Murphy B, Rennke HG, Brady HR. Collapsing glomerulopathy – Recurrence in a renal allograft. Nephrol Dial Transplant 1998, **13**: 503–506.

49 D'Agati V, Appel GB. Renal pathology of human immunodeficiency virus infection. Semin Nephrol 1998, **18**: 378–395.

50 Detwiler RK, Falk RJ, Hogan SL, Jennette JC. Collapsing glomerulopathy: a clinically and pathologically distinct variant of focal segmental glomerulosclerosis. Kidney Int 1994, **45**: 1416–1424.

51 Faubert PF, Porush JG. Familial focal segmental glomerulosclerosis: Nine cases in four families and review of the literature. Am J Kidney Dis 1997, **30**: 265–270.

52 Howie AJ, Brewer DB. Further studies on the glomerular tip lesion: early and late stages and life table analysis. J Pathol 1985, **147**: 245–255.

53 Ingulli E, Tejani A, Fikrig S, Nicastri A, Chen CK, Pomrantz A. Nephrotic syndrome associated with acquired immunodeficiency syndrome in children. J Pediatr 1991, **119**: 710–716.

54 Ito H, Yoshikawa N, Aozai F, Hazikano H, Sakaguchi H, Akamatsu R, Matsuo T, Matsuyama S. Twenty-seven children with focal segmental glomerulosclerosis: Correlation between the segmental location of the glomerular lesions and prognosis. Clin Nephrol 1984, **22**: 9–14.

55 Klotman PE. HIV-associated nephropathy. Kidney Int 1999, **56**: 1161–1176.

56 Korbet SM. Clinical picture and outcome of primary focal segmental glomerulosclerosis. Nephrol Dial Transplant 1999, **14**: 68–73.

57 Kriz W, Lemley KV. The role of the podocyte in glomerulosclerosis. Curr Opin Nephrol Hyperten 1999, **8**: 489–497.

58 Laurinavicius A, Hurwitz S, Rennke HG. Collapsing glomerulopathy in HIV and non-HIV patients: A clinicopathological and follow-up study. Kidney Int 1999, **56**: 2203–2213.

59 Magil AB. Focal and segmental glomerulosclerosis. Mod Pathol 1991, **4**: 383–391.

60 Mathis BJ, Kim SH, Calabrese K, Haas M, Seidman JG, Seidman CE, Pollak MR. A locus for inherited focal segmental glomerulosclerosis maps to chromosome 19q13. Kidney Int 1998, **53**: 282–286.

61 Meehan SM, Pascual M, Williams WW, Tolkoff-Rubin N, Delmonico FL, Cosimi AB, Colvin RB. De novo collapsing glomerulopathy in renal allografts. Transplantation 1998, **65**: 1192–1197.

62 Mongeau JG, Robitaille PO, Glermont MJ, Merovani A, Russo P. Focal segmental glomerulosclerosis (FSG) 20 years later. From toddler to grown-up. Clin Nephrol 1993, **40**: 1–6.

63 Nochy D, Glotz D, Dosquet P, Pruna A, Lemoine R, Guettier C, Weiss L, Hinglais N, Idatte JM, Mery JP, et al. Renal lesions associated with human immunodeficiency virus infection: North American vs. European experience. Adv Nephrol Necker Hosp 1993, **22**: 269–286.

64 Olson JL, Schwartz MM. The nephrotic syndrome: Minimal change disease, focal segmental glomerulosclerosis and miscellaneous causes. In Jennette JC, Olson JL, Schwartz MM, Silva FG (eds): Heptinstall's Pathology of the kidney, ed. 5. Philadelphia, 1998, Lippincott-Raven, pp. 187–257.

65 Pardo V, Meneses R, Ossa L, Jaffe DJ, Strauss J, Roth D, Bourgoignie JJ. AIDS-related glomerulopathy. Occurrence in specific risk groups. Kidney Int 1987, **31**: 1167–1173.

66 Savin VJ, Sharma R, Sharma M, McCarthy ET, Swan SK, Ellis E, Lovell H, Warady B, Gunwar S, Chonko AM, Artero M, Vincenti F. Circulating factor associated with increased glomerular permeability to albumin in recurrent focal segmental glomerulosclerosis. N Engl J Med 1996, **334**: 878–883.

67 Schönholzer KW, Waldron M, Magil AB. Intraglomerular foam cells and human focal glomerulosclerosis. Nephron 1992, **62**: 130–136.

68 Schwartz MM, Korbet SM, Rydel J, Borok R, Genchi R. Primary focal segmental glomerular sclerosis in adults: Prognostic value of histologic variants. Am J Kidney Dis 1995, **25**: 845–852.

69 Singh HK, Baldree LA, McKenney DW, Hogan SL, Jennette JC. Idiopathic collapsing glomerulopathy in children. Pediatr Nephrol 2000, **14**: 132–137.

70 Stephanian E, Matas AJ, Mauer SM, Chavers B, Nevins T, Kashtan C, Sutherland DE, Gores P, Najarian JS. Recurrence of disease in patients retransplanted for focal segmental glomerulosclerosis. Transplantation 1992, **53**: 755–757.

71 Tsukaguchi H, Yager H, Dawborn J, Jost L, Cohlmia J, Abreu PF, Pereira AB, Pollak MR. A locus for adolescent and adult onset familial focal segmental glomerulosclerosis on chromosome 1q25–31. J Am Soc Nephrol 2000, **11**: 1674–1680.

72 Valeri A, Barisoni L, Appel GB, Seigle R, D'Agati V. Idiopathic collapsing focal segmental glomerulosclerosis: a clinicopathologic study. Kidney Int 1996, **50**: 1734–1746.

73 Wehrmann M, Bohle A, Held H, Schumm G, Kendziorra H, Pressler H. Long-term prognosis of focal sclerosing glomerulonephritis: an analysis of 250 cases with particular regard to tubulointerstitial changes. Clin Nephrol 1990, **33**: 115–122.

74 Winn MP, Conlon PJ, Lynn KL, Howell DN, Slotterbeck BD, Smith AH, Graham FL, Bembe ML, Quarles LD, Pericak-Vance MA, Vance JM. Linkage of a gene causing familial focal segmental glomerulosclerosis to chromosome 11 and further evidence of genetic heterogeneity. Genomics 1999, **58**: 113–120.

75 Woolley AC, Rosenberg ME, Burke BA, Nath KA. De novo focal glomerulosclerosis after kidney transplantation. Am J Med 1988, **84**: 310–314.

76 Yoshikawa N, Ito H, Akamatsu R, Matsuyama S, Hasegawa O, Nakahara C, Matsuo T. Focal segmental glomerulosclerosis with and without nephrotic syndrome in children. J Pediatr 1986, **109**: 65–70.

C1q nephropathy

77 Falk RJ, Jennette JC, Nachman PH. C1q nephropathy. In Brenner BM (ed.): Brenner and Rector's The kidney, ed. 6. Philadelphia, 2000, W.B. Saunders, pp. 1283–1284.

78 Iskandar SS, Browning MC, Lorentz WB. C1q nephropathy: A pediatric clinicopathological study. Am J Kidney Dis 1991, **18**: 459–465.

79 Jennette JC, Hipp CG. C1q nephropathy: A distinct pathologic entity usually causing nephrotic syndrome. Am J Kidney Dis 1985, **6**: 103–110.

Membranous glomerulonephritis

80 Abrass CK, Hall CL, Border WA, Brown CA, Glassock RJ, Coggins CH. Circulating immune complexes in adults with idiopathic nephrotic syndrome. Collaborative study of the adult idiopathic nephrotic syndrome. Kidney Int 1980, **17**: 545–553.

81 Brenchley PE, Coupes B, Short CD, O'Donoghue DJ, Ballardie FW, Mallick NP. Urinary C3dg and C5b-9 indicate active immune disease in human membranous nephropathy. Kidney Int 1992, **41**: 933–937.

82 Burstein DM, Korbet SM, Schwartz MM. Membranous glomerulonephritis and malignancy. Am J Kidney Dis 1993, **22**: 5–10.

83 Buyukbabani N, Droz D. Distribution of the extracellular matrix components in human glomerular lesions. J Pathol 1994, **172**: 199–207.

84 Cameron JS. Membranous nephropathy in childhood and its treatment. Pediatr Nephrol 1990, **4**: 193–198.

85 Coggins CH, Frommer JP, Glassock RJ. Membranous nephropathy. Semin Nephrol 1982, **2**: 264–273.

86 Davenport A, Maciver AG, Hall CL, MacKenzie JC. Do mesangial immune complex deposits affect the renal prognosis in membranous glomerulonephritis? Clin Nephrol 1994, **41**: 271–276.

87 Donadio JV Jr, Torres VE, Velosa JA, Wagoner RD, Holley KE, Okamkura M, Ilstrup DM, Chu CP. Idiopathic membranous nephropathy: the natural history of untreated patients. Kidney Int 1988, **33**: 708–715.

88 Ehrenreich T, Churg J. Pathology of membranous nephropathy. Pathol Annu 1968, **3**: 145–186.

89 Hayslett JP, Kashgarian M, Bensch KG, Spargo BH, Freedman LR, Epstein FH. Clinicopathological correlations in the nephrotic syndrome due to primary renal disease. Medicine [Baltimore] 1973, **52**: 93–120.

90 Heidet L, Gagnadoux ME, Beziau A, Niaudet P, Broyer M, Habib R. Recurrence of de novo membranous glomerulonephritis on renal grafts. Clin Nephrol 1994, **41**: 314–318.

91 Jennette JC, Iskandar SS, Dalldorf FG. Pathologic differentiation between lupus and nonlupus membranous glomerulopathy. Kidney Int 1983, **24**: 377–385.

92 Katz A, Fish AJ, Santamaria P, Nevins TE, Kim Y, Butkowski RJ. Role of antibodies to tubulointerstitial nephritis antigen in human anti-tubular basement membrane nephritis associated with membranous nephropathy. Am J Med 1992, **93**: 691–698.

93 Koethe J, Gerig J, Glickman J, Sturgill BC, Bolton WK. Progression of membranous nephropathy to acute crescentic rapidly progressive glomerulonephritis and response to pulse methylprednisolone. Am J Nephrol 1986, **6**: 224–228.

94 Kon SP, Coupes B, Short CD, Solomon LR, Raftery MJ, Mallick NP, Brenchley PE. Urinary C5b-9 excretion and clinical course in idiopathic human membranous nephropathy. Kidney Int 1995, **48**: 1953–1958.

95 Levy M, Gagnadoux M-F, Beziau A, Habib R. Membranous glomerulonephritis associated with anti-tubular and anti-alveolar basement membrane antibodies. Clin Nephrol 1978, **10**: 158–165.

96 Llach F, Arieff AI, Massry SG. Renal vein thrombosis and nephrotic syndrome: A prospective study of 36 adult patients. Ann Intern Med 1975, **83**: 8–14.

97 Mathieson PW, Peat DS, Short A, Watts RA. Coexistent membranous nephropathy and ANCA-positive crescentic glomerulonephritis in association with penicillamine. Nephrol Dial Transplant 1996, **11**: 863–866.

98 Meisels IS, Stillman IS, Kuhlik AB. Anti-glomerular basement membrane disease and dual positivity for antineutrophil cytoplasmic antibody in a patient with membranous nephropathy. Am J Kidney Dis 1998, **32**: 646–648.

99 Monga G, Mazzucco G, Basolo B, Quaranta S, Motta M, Segoloni G, Amoroso A. Membranous glomerulonephritis (MGN) in transplanted kidneys: Morphologic investigation on 256 renal allografts. Mod Pathol 1993, **6**: 249–258.

100 Nephrotic syndrome in children. Prediction of histopathology from clinical and laboratory characteristics at time of diagnosis: A report of the International Study of Kidney Disease in Children. Kidney Int 1978, **13**: 159–165.

101 Noel LH, Zanetti M, Droz DS, Barbanel C. Long-term prognosis of idiopathic membranous glomerulonephritis. Study of 116 untreated patients. Am J Med 1979, **66**: 82–90.

102 Pettersson E, Tornroth T, Miettinen A. Simultaneous anti-glomerular basement membrane and membranous glomerulonephritis: case report and literature review. Clin Immunol Immunopathol 1984, **31**: 171–180.

103 Ramirez F, Brouhard BH, Travis LB, Ellis EN. Idiopathic membranous nephropathy in children. J Pediatr 1982, **5**: 677–681.

104 Reichert LJM, Koene RAP, Wetzels JFM. Prognostic factors in idiopathic membranous nephropathy. Am J Kidney Dis 1998, **31**: 1–11.

105 Report of the Southwest Pediatric Nephrology Study Group. Comparison of idiopathic and systemic lupus erythematosus-associated membranous glomerulonephropathy in children. Am J Kidney Dis 1986, **7**: 115–124.

106 Schieppati A, Mosconi L, Perna A, Mecca G, Bertani T, Garattini S, Remuzzi G. Prognosis of untreated patients with idiopathic membranous nephropathy. N Engl J Med 1993, **329**: 85–89.

107 Schwartz MM. Membranous glomerulonephritis. In Jennette JC, Olson JL, Schwartz MM, Silva FG (eds): Heptinstall's Pathology of the kidney, ed. 5, vol. 1. Philadelphia, 1998, Lippincott-Raven, pp. 259–307.

108 Schwarz A, Krause PH, Offermann G, Keller F. Impact of de novo membranous glomerulonephritis on the clinical course after kidney transplantation. Transplantation 1994, **58**: 650–654.

109 Scolari F, Amoroso A, Savoldi S, Borelli I, Valzorio B, Costantino E, Bracchi M, Usberti M, Prati E, Maiorca R. Familial membranous nephropathy. J Nephrol 1998, **11**: 35–39.

110 Seggie J, Nathoo K, Davies PB. Association of hepatitis B (HBs) antigenemia and membranous glomerulonephritis in Zimbabwean children. Nephron 1984, **38**: 115–119.

111 Takekoshi Y, Tanaka M, Shida N, Satake Y, Saheki Y, Matsumoto S. Strong association between membranous nephropathy and hepatitis-B surface antigenaemia in Japanese children. Lancet 1978, **2**: 1065–1068.

112 Truong LD, Gelfand J, D'Agati V, Tomaszewski J, Appel G, Hardy M, Pirani CL. De novo membranous glomerulonephropathy in renal allografts: a report of ten cases and review of the literature. Am J Kidney Dis 1989, **14**: 131–144.

113 Wasserstein AG. Membranous glomerulonephritis. J Am Soc Nephrol 1997, **8**: 664–674.

114 Wing AJ, Hutt MS, Kibukamusoke JW. Progression and remission in the nephrotic syndrome associated with quartan malaria in Uganda. Q J Med 1972, **163**: 273–289.

115 Yamauchi H, Linsey MS, Biava CG, Hopper J Jr. Cure of membranous nephropathy after resection of carcinoma. Arch Intern Med 1985, **145**: 2061–2063.

Diabetic nephropathy

116 Elfenbein IB, Reyes JW. Crescents in diabetic glomerulopathy. Incidence and clinical significance. Lab Invest 1975, **33**: 687–695.

117 Grenfell A, Watkins PJ. Clinical diabetic nephropathy: natural history and complications. J Clin Endocrinol Metab 1986, **15**: 783–805.

118 Gundersen JH, Gotzsche O, Hirose K, Droustrup JP, Mogensen CE, Seyer-Hansen K, Osterby R. Early structural changes in glomerular capillaries and their relationship to long-term diabetic nephropathy. Acta Endocrinol 1981, **97**(Suppl): 19–21.

119 Hatch FE, Watt MF, Kramer NC, Parrish AE, Howe JS. Diabetic glomerulosclerosis: A long-term follow-up based on renal biopsies. Am J Med 1961, **31**: 216–230.

120 Henderson LL, Spargue RB, Wagner HP. Intercapillary glomerulosclerosis. Am J Med 1947, **3**: 131–144.

121 Jensen R, Larsen VS. Nodular mesangial glomerulosclerosis in patients without manifest diabetes mellitus. Int Urol Nephrol 1990, **22**: 95–103.

122 McLennan SV, Death AK, Fisher EJ, Williams PF, Yue DK, Turtle JR. The role of the mesangial cell and its matrix in the pathogenesis of diabetic nephropathy. Cell Mol Biol 1999, **45**: 123–135.

123 Mauer SM, Steffes MW, Connett J, Najarian JS, Sutherland DER, Barbosa J. The development of lesions in the glomerular basement membrane and mesangium after transplantation of normal kidneys into diabetic patients. Diabetes 1983, **32**: 948–952.

124 Mauer SM, Steffes MW, Ellis EN, Sutherland DER, Brown DM, Goetz FC. Structural functional relationships in diabetic nephropathy. J Clin Invest 1984, **74**: 1143–1155.

125 Mogensen CE, Schmitz O. The diabetic kidney: from hyperfiltration and microalbuminuria to end-stage renal failure. Med Clin North Am 1988, **72**: 1465–1492.

126 Osterby R. Early phases in the development of diabetic glomerulopathy. Acta Med Scand 1975, **574**(Suppl): 1–85.

127 Osterby R. Structural changes in the diabetic kidney. Clin Endocrinol Metab 1986, **15**: 733–751.

128 Osterby R. Glomerular structural changes in type I (insulin-dependent) diabetes mellitus: causes, consequences, and prevention. Diabetologia 1992, **35**: 803–812.

129 Osterby R, Parving HH, Nyberg G, Hommel E, Jorgensen HE, Lokkegaard H, Svalander C. A strong correlation between glomerular filtration rate and filtration surface in diabetic nephropathy. Diabetologia 1988, **31**: 265–270.

130 Ritz E, Stefanski A. Diabetic nephropathy in type II diabetes. Am J Kidney Dis 1996, **27**: 167–194.

131 Stout LC, Kumar S, Whorton EB. Focal mesangiolysis and the pathogenesis of the Kimmelstiel-Wilson nodule. Hum Pathol 1993, **24**: 77–89.

132 United States Renal Data Study. USRDS 1995 annual data report. Bethesda, MD: National Institutes of Health, National Institutes of Diabetes and Digestive and Kidney Diseases, 1995.

133 Watkins PJ, Blainey JD, Brewer DB, Fitzgerald MG, Malins JM, O'Sullivan DJ, Pinto JA. The natural history of diabetic renal disease: A follow-up study of a series of renal biopsies. Q J Med 1972, **41**: 437–456.

Amyloidosis

134 Akash N. Dialysis-related amyloidosis: Pathogenesis and promoting factors (a review). Dialysis Transplant 2000, **29**: 325–329.

135 Ansell ID, Joekes AM. Spicular arrangement of amyloid in renal biopsy. J Clin Pathol 1972, **25**: 1056–1062.

136 Benson MD, Uemichi T. Transthyretin amyloidosis. Amyloid 1996, **3**: 44–56.

137 Benson MD, Liepnieks J, Uemichi T, Wheeler G, Correa R. Hereditary renal amyloidosis associated with a mutant fibrinogen α-chain. Nat Genet 1993, **3**: 252–255.

138 Bohle A, Wehrmann M, Eissele R, Gise HV, Mackensen-Haen S, Müller C, Müller GA. The long-term prognosis of AA and AL renal amyloidosis and the pathogenesis of chronic renal failure in renal amyloidosis. Path Res Pract 1993, **189**: 316–331.

139 Buxbaum JN, Tagoe CE. The genetics of the amyloidoses. Annu Rev Med 2000, **51**: 543–569.

140 Dyck RF, Lockwood CM, Kershaw M, McHugh N, Duance VC, Baltz ML, Pepys MB. Amyloid P component is a constituent of normal human glomerular basement membrane. J Exp Med 1980, **152**: 1162–1174.

141 Falk RH, Skinner M. The systemic amyloidoses: An overview. Adv Intern Med 2000, **45**: 107–137.

142 Falk RH, Comenzo RL, Skinner M. The systemic amyloidoses. N Engl J Med 1997, **337**: 898–909.

143 Fitzmaurice RJ, Bartley C, McClure J, Ackrill P. Immunohistological characterisation of amyloid deposits in renal biopsy specimens. J Clin Pathol 1991, **44**: 200–204.

144 Gallo GR, Feiner HD, Chuba JV, Beneck D, Marion P, Cohen DH. Characterization of tissue amyloid by immunofluorescence microscopy. Clin Immunol Immunopathol 1986, **39**: 479–490.

145 Gejyo F, Homma N, Arakawa M. Long-term complications of dialysis: Pathogenic factors with special reference to amyloidosis. Kidney Int 1993, **43**(Suppl 41): S78–S82.

146 Gertz MG, Kyle RA. Primary systemic amyloidosis: A diagnostic primer. Mayo Clin Proc 1989, **64**: 1505–1519.

147 Gillmore JD, Booth DR, Madhoo S, Pepys MB, Hawkins PN. Hereditary renal amyloidosis associated with variant lysozyme in a large English family. Nephrol Dial Transplant 1999, **14**: 2639–2644.

148 Gorevic PD, Munoz PC, Casey TT, DiRaimondo CR, Stone WJ, Prelli FC, Rodrigues MM, Poulik MD, Frangione B. Polymerization of intact beta-2-microglobulin in tissue causes amyloidosis in patients on chronic hemodialysis. Proc Natl Acad Sci U S A 1986, **83**: 7908–7912.

149 Hachulla E, Maulin L, Deveaux M, Facon T, Blétry O, Vanhille Ph, Wechsler B, Godeau P, Levesque H, Hatron PY, Devulder B, Marchandise X. Prospective and serial study of primary amyloidosis with serum amyloid P component scintigraphy: From diagnosis to prognosis. Am J Med 1996, **101**: 77–87.

150 Hawkins PN, Lavender JP, Pepys MB. Evaluation of systemic amyloidosis by scintigraphy with ^{123}I-labeled serum amyloid P component. N Engl J Med 1990, **323**: 508–513.

151 Honma K, Azuma M, Yamada T. Amyloid vascular disease and

contracted kidneys: Report of a case with review of literature. Wien Klin Wochenschr 1984, **96:** 629–633.

152 Kleinman KS, Coburn JW. Amyloid syndromes associated with hemodialysis. Kidney Int 1989, **35:** 567–575.

153 Kyle RA, Gertz MA. Primary systemic amyloidosis: Clinical and laboratory features of 474 cases. Semin Hematol 1995, **32:** 45–59.

154 Manske CL. Dialysis-related amyloidosis. J Lab Clin Med 1994, **123:** 458–459.

155 Onishi S, Andress DL, Maloney NA, Coburn JW, Sherrard DJ. Beta-2-microglobulin deposition in bone in chronic renal failure. Kidney Int 1991, **39:** 990–995.

156 Pepys MB, Hawkins PN, Booth DR, Vigushin DM, Tennent GA, Soutar AK, Totty N, Nguyen O, Blake CCF, Terry CJ, Feest TG, Zalin AM, Hsuan JJ. Human lysozyme gene mutations cause hereditary systemic amyloidosis. Nature 1993, **362:** 553–557.

157 Pepys MB, Rademacher TW, Amatayakul-Chantler S, Williams P, Noble GE, Hutchinson WL, Hawkins PN, Nelson SR, Gallimore JR, Herbert J, Hutton T, Dwek RA. Human serum amyloid P component is an invariant constituent of amyloid deposits and has a uniquely homogeneous glycostructure. Proc Natl Acad Sci U S A 1994, **91:** 5602–5606.

158 Perfetti V, Ubbiali P, Vignarelli MC, Diegoli M, Fasani R, Stoppini M, Lisa A, Mangione P, Obici L, Arbustini E, Merlini G. Evidence that amyloidogenic light chains undergo antigen-driven selection. Blood 1998, **91:** 2948–2954.

159 Sohar E, Gafni J, Pras M, Heller H. Familial Mediterranean fever: A survey of 470 cases and review of the literature. Am J Med 1967, **43:** 227–253.

160 Solomon A, Weiss DT, Murphy C. Primary amyloidosis associated with a novel heavy-chain fragment (AH amyloidosis). Am J Hematol 1994, **45:** 171–176.

161 Soutar AK, Hawkins PN, Vigushin DM, Tennent GA, Booth SE, Hutton T, Nguyen O, Totty NF, Feest TG, Hsuan JJ, Pepys MB. Apolipoprotein AI mutation Arg-60 causes autosomal dominant amyloidosis. Proc Natl Acad Sci U S A 1992, **89:** 7389–7393.

162 Uemichi T, Liepnieks JJ, Benson MD. Hereditary renal amyloidosis with a novel variant fibrinogen. J Clin Invest 1994, **93:** 731–736.

163 Van Rijswijk MH, van Heusden CW. The potassium permanganate method: a reliable method for differentiating amyloid AA from other forms of amyloid in routine laboratory practice. Am J Pathol 1979, **97:** 43–58.

164 Weiss SW, Page DL. Amyloid nephropathy of Ostertag with special reference to renal glomerular giant cells. Am J Pathol 1973, **72:** 447–460.

165 Westermark P, Araki S, Benson MD, Cohen AS, Frangione B, Masters CL, Saraiva MJ, Sipe JD, Husby G, Kyle RA, Selkoe D. Nomenclature of amyloid fibril proteins. Report from the meeting of the International Nomenclature Committee on Amyloidosis, August 8–9, 1998, Part 1. Amyloid 1999, **6:** 63–66.

166 Yang GC, Nieto R, Stachura I, Gallo GR. Ultrastructural immunohistochemical localization of polyclonal IgG, C3, and amyloid P component on the Congo red-negative amyloid-like fibrils of fibrillary glomerulopathy. Am J Pathol 1992, **141:** 409–419.

167 Zingraff J, Drueke T. Beta2-microglobulin amyloidosis: past and future. Artificial Organs 1998, **22:** 581–584.

Fibrillary glomerulonephritis and immunotactoid glomerulopathy

168 Brady HR. Fibrillary glomerulopathy. Kidney Int 1998, **53:** 1421–1429.

169 Churg J, Venkataseshan VS. Fibrillary glomerulonephritis without immunoglobulin deposits in the kidney. Kidney Int 1993, **44:** 837–842.

170 Devaney K, Sabnis SG, Antonovych TT. Nonamyloidotic fibrillary glomerulopathy, immunotactoid glomerulopathy, and the differential diagnosis of filamentous glomerulopathies. Mod Pathol 1991, **4:** 36–45.

171 Duffy JL, Khurana E, Susin M, Gomez-Leon G, Churg J. Fibrillary renal deposits and nephritis. Am J Pathol 1983, **113:** 279–280.

172 Fogo A, Qureshi N, Horn RG. Morphologic and clinical features of fibrillary glomerulonephritis versus immunotactoid glomerulopathy. Am J Kidney Dis 1993, **22:** 367–377.

173 Iskandar SS, Falk RJ, Jennette JC. Clinical and pathologic features of fibrillary glomerulonephritis. Kidney Int 1992, **42:** 1401–1407.

174 Masson RG, Rennke HG, Gottlieb MN. Pulmonary hemorrhage in a patient with fibrillary glomerulonephritis. N Engl J Med 1992, **326:** 36–39.

175 Pronovost PH, Brady HR, Gunning ME, Espinoza O, Rennke HG. Clinical features, predictors of disease progression and results of renal transplantation in fibrillary/immunotactoid glomerulopathy. Nephrol Dial Transplant 1996, **11:** 837–842.

176 Wallner M, Prischl FC, Hobling W, Haidenthaler A, Regele H, Ulrich W, Kramar R. Immunotactoid glomerulopathy with extrarenal deposits in the bone, and chronic cholestatic liver disease. Nephrol Dial Transplant 1996, **11:** 1619–1624.

177 Yang GC, Nieto R, Stachura I, Gallo GR. Ultrastructural immunohistochemical localization of polyclonal IgG, C3, and amyloid P component on the Congo red-negative amyloid-like fibrils of fibrillary glomerulopathy. Am J Pathol 1992, **141:** 409–419.

Light chain deposition disease

178 Alpers CE. Glomerulopathies of dysproteinurias, abnormal immunoglobulin deposition, and lymphoproliferative disorders. Curr Opin Nephrol Hypertens 1994, **3:** 349–355.

179 Alpers CE, Marchioro TRL, Johnson RJ. Monoclonal immunoglobulin deposition disease in a renal allograft: Probable recurrent disease in a patient without myeloma. Am J Kidney Dis 1989, **13:** 418–423.

180 Buxbaum J, Gallo G. Nonamyloidotic monoclonal immunoglobulin deposition disease. Light-chain, heavy-chain, and light- and heavy-chain deposition disease. Hematol Oncol Clin NA 1999, **13:** 1235–1248.

181 Buxbaum JN, Chuba JV, Hellman GC, Solomon A, Gallo GR. Monoclonal immunoglobulin deposition disease: Light chain and light and heavy chain deposition diseases and their relation to light chain amyloidosis. Ann Intern Med 1990, **112:** 455–464.

182 Confalonieri R, Barbiano di Belgiojoso G, Banfi G, Ferrario F, Bertani T, Pozzi C, Casanova S, Lupo A, De Ferrari G, Minetti L. Light chain nephropathy: histological and clinical aspects in 15 cases. Nephrol Dial Transplant 1988, **3:** 150–156.

183 Gerlag PG, Koene RA, Berden JH. Renal transplantation in light chain nephropathy: Case report and review of the literature. Clin Nephrol 1986, **25:** 101–104.

184 Heilman RI, Velosa JA, Holley KE, Offord KP, Kyle RA. Long-term follow-up and response to chemotherapy in patients with light-chain deposition disease. Am J Kidney Dis 1992, **20:** 34–41.

185 Herrera GA, Russell WJ, Isaac J, Turbat-Herrera EA, Tagouri YM, Sanders PW, Picken MM, Dempsey S. Glomerulopathic light chain-mesangial cell interactions modulate in vitro extracellular matrix remodeling and reproduce mesangiopathic findings documented in vivo. Ultrastruct Pathol 1999, **23:** 107–126.

186 Morel-Maroger S LJ, Preud'homme J-L, D'Amico G, Striker GE. Monoclonal gammopathies, mixed cryoglobulinemias, and lymphomas. In Tisher CC, Brenner BM (eds): Renal pathology: With clinical and functional correlations, ed. 2, vol. II. Philadelphia, 1994, J.B. Lippincott, pp. 1442–1490.

187 Pozzi C, Fogazzi GB, Banfi G, Strom EH, Ponticelli C, Locatelli

F. Renal disease and patient survival in LCDD. Clin Nephrol 1995, **43**: 281–287.

188 Preud'homme JL, Aucouturier P, Touchard G, Striker L, Khamlichi AA, Rocca A, Denoroy L, Cogné M. Monoclonal immunoglobulin deposition disease (Randall type): Relationship with structural abnormalities of immunoglobulin chains. Kidney Int 1994, **46**: 965–972.

189 Randall RE, Williamson WC, Mullinax F, Tung MY, Still WJS. Manifestations of systemic light chain deposition. Am J Med 1976, **60**: 293–299.

190 Sanders PW, Herrera GA. Monoclonal immunoglobulin light chain-related renal disease. Semin Nephrol 1993, **13**: 324–341.

191 Schwartz MM. The dysproteinemias and amyloidosis. In Jennette JC, Olson JL, Schwartz MM, Silva FG (eds): Heptinstall's Pathology of the kidney, ed. 5, vol. 2. Philadelphia, 1998, Lippincott-Raven, pp. 1321–1369.

192 Shimamura T, Weiss LS, Walker JA, Sherman RA, Eisinger RP. Light chain nephropathy in a 19-month-old boy with AIDS. Acta Pathol Jpn 1992, **42**: 500–503.

193 Strom EH, Fogazzi GB, Banfi G, Pozzi C, Mihatsch MJ. Light chain deposition disease of the kidney. Morphological aspects in 24 patients. Virchows Arch 1994, **425**: 271–280.

194 Zhu L, Herrera GA, Murphy-Ulrich JE, Huang Z-O, Sanders PW. Pathogenesis of glomerulosclerosis in light chain deposition disease: Role for transforming growth factor-beta. Am J Pathol 1995, **147**: 375–385.

Heavy chain deposition disease

195 Aucouturier P, Khamlichi AA, Touchard G, Justrabo E, Cogne M, Chauffert B, Martin F, Preud'homme J-L. Heavy-chain deposition disease. N Engl J Med 1993, **329**: 1389–1393.

196 Herzenberg AM, Kiaii M, Magil AB. Heavy chain deposition disease: Recurrence in a renal transplant and report of IgG(2) subtype. Am J Kidney Dis 2000, **35**: E251–E255.

197 Liapis H, Papadakis I, Nakopoulou L. Nodular glomerulosclerosis secondary to μ heavy chain deposits. Hum Pathol 2000, **31**: 122–125.

198 Rott T, Vizjak A, Lindic J, Hvala A, Perkovic T, Cernelc P. IgG heavy-chain deposition disease affecting kidney, skin, and skeletal muscle. Nephrol Dial Transplant 1998, **13**: 1825–1828.

199 Yasuda T, Fujita K, Imai H, Morita K, Nakamoto Y, Miura AB. Gamma-heavy chain deposition disease showing nodular glomerulosclerosis. Clin Nephrol 1995, **44**: 394–399.

Congenital nephrotic syndrome

200 Aya K, Tanaka H, Seino Y. Novel mutation in the nephrin gene of a Japanese patient with congenital nephrotic syndrome of the Finnish type. Kidney Int 2000, **57**: 401–404.

201 Habib R. Nephrotic syndrome in the 1st year of life. Pediatr Nephrol 1993, **7**: 347–353.

202 Habib R, Kleinknecht C. Primary nephrotic syndrome of childhood: Classification and clinicopathologic study of 406 cases. Pathol Annu 1977, **6**: 417–474.

203 Habib R, Gubler MC, Antignac C, Gagnadoux MF. Diffuse mesangial sclerosis: A congenital glomerulopathy with nephrotic syndrome. Adv Nephrol Necker Hosp 1993, **22**: 43–57.

204 Holmberg C, Antikainen M, Rönnholm K, Ala-Houhala M, Jalanko H. Management of congenital nephrotic syndrome of the Finnish type. Pediatr Nephrol 1995, **9**: 87–93.

205 Huttunen N-P. Congenital nephrotic syndrome of Finnish type. Study of 75 patients. Arch Dis Child 1976, **51**: 344–348.

206 Jeanpierre C, Denamur E, Henry I, Cabanis M-O, Luce S, Cécille A, Elion J, Peuchmaur M, Loirat C, Niaudet P, Gubler M-C, Junien C. Identification of constitutional WT1 mutations, in patients with isolated diffuse mesangial sclerosis, and analysis of genotype/phenotype correlations by use of a computerized mutation database. Am J Hum Genet 1998, **62**: 824–833.

207 Kestilä M, Lenkkeri U, Männikkö M, Lamerdin J, McCready P, Putaala H, Ruotsalainen V, Morita T, Nissinen M, Herva R, Kashtan CE, Peltonen L, Holmberg C, Olsen A, Tryggvason K. Positionally cloned gene for a novel glomerular protein – nephrin – is mutated in congenital nephrotic syndrome. Mol Cell 1998, **1**: 575–582.

208 Kestilä M, Männikkö M, Holmberg C, Gyapay G, Weissenbach J, Savolainen E-R, Peltonen L, Tryggvason K. Congenital nephrotic syndrome of the Finnish type maps to the long arm of chromosome 19. Am J Hum Genet 1994, **54**: 757–764.

209 Laine J, Jalanko H, Holthöfer H, Krogerus L, Rapola J, von Willebrand E, Lautenschlager I, Salmela K, Holmberg C. Post-transplantation nephrosis in congenital nephrotic syndrome of the Finnish type. Kidney Int 1993, **44**: 867–874.

210 Männikkö M, Kestilä M, Lenkkeri U, Alakurtti H, Holmberg C, Leisti J, Salonen R, Aula P, Mustonen A, Peltonen L, Tryggvason K. Improved prenatal diagnosis of the congenital nephrotic syndrome of the Finnish type based on DNA analysis. Kidney Int 1997, **51**: 868–872.

211 Männikkö M, Lenkkeri U, Kashtan CE, Kestila M, Holmberg C, Tryggvason K. Haplotype analysis of congenital nephrotic syndrome of the Finnish type in non-Finnish families. J Am Soc Nephrol 1996, **7**: 2700–2703.

212 Patrakka J, Kestilä M, Wartiovaara J, Ruotsalainen V, Tissari P, Lenkkeri U, Männikkö M, Visapää I, Holmberg C, Rapola J, Tryggvason K, Jalanko H. Congenital nephrotic syndrome (NPHS1): Features resulting from different mutations in Finnish patients. Kidney Int 2000, **58**: 972–980.

213 Ruotsalainen V, Ljungberg P, Wartiovaara J, Lenkkeri U, Kestila M, Jalanko H, Holmberg C, Tryggvason K. Nephrin is specifically located at the slit diaphragm of glomerular podocytes. Proc Natl Acad Sci U S A 1999, **96**: 7962–7967.

214 Salomon R, Gubler MC, Niaudet P. Genetics of the nephrotic syndrome. Curr Opin Pediatr 2000, **12**: 129–134.

215 Savage JM, Jefferson JA, Maxwell AP, Hughes AE, Shanks JH, Gill D. Improved prognosis for congenital nephrotic syndrome of the Finnish type in Irish families. Arch Dis Child 1999, **80**: 466–469.

216 Seppälä M, Rapola J, Huttunen N-P, Aula P, Karjalainen O, Ruoslahti E. Congenital syndrome. Prenatal diagnosis and genetic counselling by estimation of amniotic fluid and maternal serum alpha-fetoprotein. Lancet 1976, **II**: 123–125.

217 Sibley RK, Striegel J. Nephrotic syndrome in the first year of life. In Fisher CC, Brenner BM (eds): Renal pathology: With clinical and functional correlations, vol. II. Philadelphia, 1994, J.B. Lippincott, pp. 1291–1311.

218 Yang Y, Jeanpierre C, Dressler GR, Lacoste M, Niaudet P, Gubler M-C. WT1 and PAX-2 podocyte expression in Denys-Drash syndrome and isolated diffuse mesangial sclerosis. Am J Pathol 1999, **154**: 181–192.

Glomerular lesions associated with the syndrome of acute nephritis
Diffuse endocapillary proliferative glomerulonephritis

219 Bodaghi E, Kheradpir KM, Maddah M. Vasculitis in acute streptococcal glomerulonephritis. Int J Pediatr Nephrol 1987, **8**: 69–74.

220 Brzosko WJ, Krawczynski K, Nazarewicz T, Morzycka M, Nowoslawski A. Glomerulonephritis associated with hepatitis-B surface antigen immune complexes in children. Lancet 1974, **2**: 477–481.

221 Dodge WF, Spargo BH, Bass JA, Travis LB. The relationship between the clinical and pathologic features of poststreptococcal glomerulonephritis. A study of the early natural history. Medicine [Baltimore] 1986, **47**: 227–267.

222 Glassock RJ, Adler SG, Ward HJ, Cohen AH. Primary

glomerular diseases. In Brenner BM, Rector FC (eds): The kidney, ed. 4, vol. 1. Philadelphia, 1991, W.B. Saunders, pp. 1182–1368.

223 Hinglais N, Garcia-Torres R, Kleinknecht C. Long-term prognosis in acute glomerulonephritis. Am J Med 1974, **56:** 52–60.

224 Melby PC, Musick WD, Luger AM, Khanna R. Poststreptococcal glomerulonephritis in the elderly. Am J Nephrol 1987, **7:** 235–240.

225 Montseny JJ, Meyrier A, Kleinknecht D, Callard P. The current spectrum of infectious glomerulonephritis. Experience with 76 patients and review of the literature. Medicine 1995, **74:** 63–73.

226 Rodríguez-Iturbe B. Acute poststreptococcal glomerulonephritis. In Schrier RW, Gottschalk CW (eds): Diseases of the kidney, ed. 5, vol. II. Boston, 1993, Little, Brown and Co., pp. 1715–1730.

227 Schacht RG, Gluck MC, Gallo GR, Baldwin DS. Progression to uremia after remission of acute poststreptococcal glomerulonephritis. N Engl J Med 1976, **295:** 977–981.

228 Schachter J, Pomeranz A, Berger I, Wolach B. Acute glomerulonephritis secondary to lobar pneumonia. Int J Pediatr Nephrol 1987, **8:** 211–214.

229 Schoeneman M, Bennett B, Greifer I. Shunt nephritis progressing to chronic renal failure. Am J Kidney Dis 1982, **2:** 375–377.

230 Silva FG. Acute postinfectious glomerulonephritis and glomerulonephritis complicating persistent bacterial infection. In Jennette JC, Olson JL, Schwartz MM, Silva FG (eds): Heptinstall's Pathology of the kidney, ed. 5, vol. I. Philadelphia, 1998, Lippincott-Raven, pp. 389–453.

231 Vogl W, Renke M, Mayer-Eichberger D, Schmitt H, Bohle A. Long-term prognosis for endocapillary glomerulonephritis of post streptococcal type in children and adults. Nephron 1986, **44:** 58–65.

Membranoproliferative (mesangiocapillary) glomerulonephritis

232 Anders D, Agricola B, Sippel M, Thoenes W. Basement membrane changes in membranoproliferative glomerulonephritis: II. Characterization of a third type by silver impregnation of ultrathin sections. Virchows Arch [A] Pathol Anat Histopathol 1977, **376:** 1–19.

233 Andresdottir MB, Assmann KJ, Hoitsma AJ, Koene RA, Wetzels JF. Recurrence of type I membranoproliferative glomerulonephritis after renal transplantation: analysis of the incidence, risk factors, and impact on graft survival. Transplantation 1997, **63:** 1628–1633.

234 Bennett WM, Bardana EJ, Wuepper K, Houghton D, Border WA, Götze O, Schreiber R. Partial lipodystrophy, C3 nephritic factor and clinically inapparent mesangiocapillary glomerulonephritis. Am J Med 1977, **62:** 757–760.

235 Bogdanovic RM, Dimitrijevic JZ, Nikolic VN, Ognjanovic MV, Rodic BD, Slavkovic BV. Membranoproliferative glomerulonephritis in two siblings: report and literature review. Pediatr Nephrol 2000, **14:** 400–405.

236 Burkholder PM, Marchand A, Krueger RP. Mixed membranous and proliferative glomerulonephritis: A correlative light, immunofluorescence and electron microscopic study. Lab Invest 1970, **23:** 459–479.

237 Cameron JS, Turner DR, Heaton J, Williams DG, Ogg CS, Chantler C, Haycock GB, Hicks J. Idiopathic mesangiocapillary glomerulonephritis: Comparison of types I and II in children and adults and long-term prognosis. Am J Med 1983, **74:** 175–192.

238 D'Amico G, Ferrario F. Mesangiocapillary glomerulonephritis. J Am Soc Nephrol 1992, **2**(10 Suppl): S159–S166.

239 Duval-Young J, MacDonald MK. Fundus changes in (type II)

mesangiocapillary glomerulonephritis simulating drusen: a histopathological report. Br J Ophthalmol 1989, **73:** 297–302.

240 Falk RJ, Jennette JC, Nachman PH. C1q nephropathy. In Brenner BM (ed.): Brenner and Rector's The kidney, ed. 6. Philadelphia, 2000, W.B. Saunders, pp. 1283–1284.

241 Habib R, Gubler MC, Loirat C, Maiz HB, Levy M. Dense deposit disease: A variant of membranoproliferative glomerulonephritis. Kidney Int 1975, **7:** 204–215.

242 Habib R, Kleinknecht C, Gubler MC, Levy M. Idiopathic membranoproliferative glomerulonephritis in children: Report of 105 cases. Clin Nephrol 1973, **1:** 194–214.

243 Hariharan S. Recurrent and de novo diseases after renal transplantation. Semin Dialysis 2000, **13:** 195–199.

244 Kher KK, Makker S, Aikawa M, Kirson IJ. Regression of dense deposits in type II membranoproliferative glomerulonephritis. A case report of clinical course in a child. Clin Nephrol 1982, **17:** 100–103.

245 Kim DD, Mieler WF, Wolf MD. Posterior segment changes in membranoproliferative glomerulonephritis. Am J Ophthalmol 1992, **114:** 593–599.

246 Kim Y, Vernier RL, Fish AJ, Michael AF. Immunofluorescence studies of dense-deposit disease: the presence of railroad tracks and mesangial rings. Lab Invest 1979, **40:** 474–480.

247 Lamb V, Tisher CC, McCoy RC, Robinson RR. Membranoproliferative glomerulonephritis with dense intramembranous alterations: A clinicopathologic study. Lab Invest 1977, **36:** 607–617.

248 Lien Y-HH, Scott K. Long-term cyclophosphamide treatment for recurrent type I membranoproliferative glomerulonephritis after transplantation. Am J Kidney Dis 2000, **35:** 539–543.

249 McEnery PT, McAdams AJ. Regression of membranoproliferative glomerulonephritis type II (dense deposit disease): observation in six children. Am J Kidney Dis 1988, **12:** 138–146.

250 Magil AB, Price JD, Bower G, Rance CP, Huber J, Chase WH. Membranoproliferative glomerulonephritis type 1: Comparison of natural history in children and adults. Clin Nephrol 1979, **11:** 239–244.

251 Mathieson PW, Peters DK. Lipodystrophy in MCGN type II: the clue to links between the adipocyte and the complement system. Nephrol Dial Transplant 1997, **12:** 1804–1806.

252 Schmitt H, Bohle A, Reineke T, Mayer-Eichberger D, Vogl W. Long term prognosis of membranoproliferative glomerulonephritis. Nephron 1990, **55:** 242–250.

253 Silva FG. Membranoproliferative glomerulonephritis. In Jennette JC, Olson JL, Schwartz MM, Silva FG (eds): Heptinstall's Pathology of the kidney, ed. 5, vol. I. Philadelphia, 1998, Lippincott-Raven, pp. 309–368.

254 Sissons JGP, West RJ, Fallows J, Williams DG, Boucher BJ, Amos N, Peters DK. The complement abnormalities of lipodystrophy. N Engl J Med 1976, **294:** 461–465.

255 Strife CF, Jackson EC, McAdams AJ. Type III membranoproliferative glomerulonephritis: long-term clinical and morphologic evaluation. Clin Nephrol 1984, **21:** 323–334.

256 Strife CF, McEnery PT, McAdams AJ, West CD. Membranoproliferative glomerulonephritis with disruption of the glomerular basement membrane. Clin Nephrol 1977, **7:** 65–72.

257 Thorner P, Baumal R. Extraglomerular dense deposits in dense deposit disease. Arch Pathol Lab Med 1982, **106:** 628–631.

258 West CD. Idiopathic membranoproliferative glomerulonephritis in childhood. Pediatr Nephrol 1992, **6:** 96–103.

259 West CD, McAdams AJ. Glomerular paramesangial deposits: Association with hypocomplementemia in membranoproliferative glomerulonephritis types I and III. Am J Kidney Dis 1998, **31:** 427–434.

Diffuse mesangioproliferative glomerulonephritis

260   Berger J, Hinglais N. Les depots intercapillaires d'IgA-IgG. J Urol Nephrol (Paris) 1968, **74**: 694–695.

261   Clarkson AR, Woodroffe AJ, Aarons I. IgA nephropathy and Henoch-Schönlein purpura. In Schrier RW, Gottschalk CW (eds): Diseases of the kidney, ed. 5, vol. II. Boston, 1993, Little, Brown and Co., pp. 1839–1864.

262   D'Amico G. Natural history of idiopathic IgA nephropathy: role for clinical and histological prognostic factors. Am J Kidney Dis 2000, **36**: 227–237.

263   Donadio JV, Grande JP. Immunoglobulin A nephropathy: A clinical perspective. J Am Soc Nephrol 1997, **8**: 1324–1332.

264   Emancipator SN. IgA nephropathy and Henoch-Schönlein syndrome. In Jennette JC, Olson JL, Schwartz MM, Silva FG (eds): Heptinstall's Pathology of the kidney, ed. 5. Philadelphia, 1998, Lippincott-Raven, pp. 479–539.

265   Haas M. Histologic subclassification of IgA nephropathy: a clinicopathologic study of 244 cases. Am J Kidney Dis 1997, **29**: 829–842.

266   Hsu SI, Ramirez SB, Winn MP, Bonventre JV, Owen WF. Evidence for genetic factors in the development and progression of IgA nephropathy. Kidney Int 2000, **57**: 1818–1835.

267   Hubert D, Beaufils M, Meyrier A. Néphropathie glomérulaire à immunoglobulines A associée à une colite inflammatoire. A propos de deux observations. Presse Med 1984, **13**: 1083–1085.

268   Kimmel PL, Phillips TM, Ferreira-Centeno A, Farkas-Szallasi T, Abraham AA, Garrett CT. Idiotypic IgA nephropathy in patients with human immunodeficiency virus infection. N Engl J Med 1992, **327**: 702–706.

269   Moorthy AV, Zimmerman SW, Maxim PE. Dermatitis herpetiformis and celiac disease: Association with glomerulonephritis, hypocomplementaemia and circulating immune complexes. JAMA 1978, **239**: 2019–2020.

270   Mustonen J, Pasternack A, Helin H. IgA mesangial nephropathy in neoplastic diseases. Contrib Nephrol 1984, **40**: 283–291.

271   Niaudet P, Murcia I, Beaufils H, Broyer M, Habib R. Primary IgA nephropathies in children: Prognosis and treatment. Adv Nephrol Necker Hosp 1993, **2**: 121–140.

272   Nochy D, Callard P, Bellon B, Barrety J, Druet P. Association of overt glomerulonephritis and liver disease: A study of 34 patients. Clin Nephrol 1976, **6**: 422–427.

273   Ramirez G, Stinson JB, Zawada ET, Moatamed F. IgA nephritis associated with mycosis fungoides. Report of two cases. Arch Intern Med 1981, **141**: 1287–1291.

274   Scolari F. Familial IgA nephropathy. J Nephrol 1999, **12**: 213–219.

275   Shu KH, Lian JD, Yang YF, Lu YS, Wang JY, Lan JL, Chou G. Glomerulonephritis in ankylosing spondylitis. Clin Nephrol 1986, **25**: 169–174.

276   Williams DG. Pathogenesis of idiopathic IgA nephropathy. Pediatr Nephrol 1993, **7**: 303–311.

Crescentic glomerulonephritis

277   Bonsib SM, Goeken JA, Kemp JD, Chandran P, Shadur C, Wilson L. Coexistent anti-neutrophil cytoplasmic antibody and antiglomerular basement membrane antibody associated disease: Report of six cases. Mod Pathol 1993, **6**: 526–530.

278   Falk RJ, Jennette JC. Proceedings of the Third International Workshop on ANCA. Am J Kidney Dis 1991, **18**: 145–193.

279   Falk RJ, Hogan S, Carey TS, Jennette JC. The Glomerular Disease Collaborative Network: Clinical course of anti-neutrophil cytoplasmic autoantibody-associated glomerulonephritis and systemic vasculitis. Ann Intern Med 1990, **113**: 656–663.

280   Falk RJ, Jennette JC, Nachman PH. C1q nephropathy. In Brenner BM (ed.): Brenner and Rector's The kidney, ed. 6. Philadelphia, 2000, W.B. Saunders, pp. 1283–1284.

281   Goeken JA. Antineutrophil cytoplasmic antibody – A useful serological marker for vasculitis. J Clin Immunol 1991, **11**: 161–174.

282   Hudson BG, Kalluri R, Gunwar S, Noelken ME, Mariyama M, Readers ST. Molecular characteristics of the Goodpasture autoantigen. Kidney Int 1993, **43**: 135–139.

283   Jennette JC. Crescentic glomerulonephritis. In Jennette JC, Olson JL, Schwartz MM, Silva FG (eds): Heptinstall's Pathology of the kidney, ed. 5. Philadelphia, 1998, Lippincott-Raven, pp. 625–656.

284   Kallenberg CG, Brouwer E, Weening JJ, Tervaert JW. Anti-neutrophil cytoplasmic antibodies. Current diagnostic and pathophysiological potential. Kidney Int 1994, **46**: 1–15.

285   Kalluri R, Gunwar S, Readers ST, Morrison KE, Mariyama M, Ebner KE, Noelken ME, Hudson BG. Goodpasture syndrome: Localization of the epitope for the autoantibodies to the carboxyl-terminal region of the α3(IV) chain of basement membrane collagen. J Biol Chem 1991, **266**: 24018–24024.

286   Lockwood CM, Jayne DRW, Marshall P, Jones SJ. A prospective study of the incidence of anti-GBM and anti-neutrophil cytoplasm antibodies in patients with rapidly progressive nephritis. Kidney Int 1988, **33**: 329.

287   Noël LH, Geffriaud C, Chauveau D, Houhou S, Landais P, Kirhaoui F, Nusbaum P, Gouarin C, O'Donoghue D, Halbwachs-Mecarelli L, Grünfeld J-P. Antineutrophil cytoplasm antibodies: Diversity and clinical applications. Adv Nephrol Necker Hosp 1993, **22**: 237–267.

Lupus nephritis

288   Appel GB, Silva FG, Pirani CI, Meltzer JI, Estes D. Renal involvement in systemic lupus erythematosus (SLE): A study of 56 patients emphasizing histologic classification. Medicine [Baltimore] 1978, **57**: 371–410.

289   Austin HA III, Muenz LR, Joyce KM, Antonovych TT, Balow JE. Diffuse proliferative lupus nephritis. Identification of specific pathologic features affecting renal outcome. Kidney Int 1984, **25**: 689–695.

290   Austin HA III, Muenz LR, Joyce KM, Antonovych TT, Kullick ME, Klippel JH, Decker JL, Balow JE. Prognostic factors in Lupus Nephritis. Contribution of renal histologic data. Am J Med 1983, **75**: 382–391.

291   Baldwin DS, Gluck MC, Lowenstein J, Gallo GR. Lupus nephritis: Clinical course as related to morphologic forms and their transitions. Am J Med 1977, **62**: 12–30.

292   Churg J, Bernstein J, Glassock RJ. Renal disease: Classification and atlas of glomerular diseases, ed. 2. New York, 1995, Igaku-Shoin, pp. 151–179.

293   Comerford FR, Cohen AS. The nephropathy of systemic lupus erythematosus. An assessment of clinical, light and electron microscopic criteria. Medicine [Baltimore] 1967, **46**: 425–473.

294   D'Agati VD. Renal disease in systemic lupus erythematosus, mixed connective tissue disease, Sjögren's syndrome, and rheumatoid arthritis. In Jennette JC, Olson JL, Schwartz MM, Silva FG (eds): Heptinstall's Pathology of the kidney, ed. 5. Philadelphia, 1998, Lippincott-Raven, pp. 541–620.

295   Gloor JM. Lupus nephritis in children. Lupus 1998, **7**: 639–643.

296   Hecht B, Siegel N, Adler M, Kashgarian MD, Hayslett JP. Prognostic indices in lupus nephritis. Medicine [Baltimore] 1976, **55**: 163–181.

297   Herrera GA. The value of electron microscopy in the diagnosis and clinical management of lupus nephritis. Ultrastruct Pathol 1999, **23**: 63–77.

298   Hess E. Drug-related lupus. N Engl J Med 1988, **318**: 1460–1462.

299   Hill GS, Hinglais N, Tron F, Bach JF. Systemic lupus

erythematosus: Morphologic correlations with immunologic and clinical data at the time of biopsy. Am J Med 1978, **64:** 61–79.

300 Hvala A, Kobenter T, Ferluga D. Fingerprint and other organised deposits in lupus nephritis. Wien Klin Wochenschr 2000, **112:** 711–715.

301 Kim Y, Choi Y, Reiner L. Ultrastructural fingerprint in cryoprecipitate and glomerular deposits. A case report of systemic lupus erythematosus. Hum Pathol 1991, **12:** 86–90.

302 Lehman TJA, McCurdy DK, Bernstein BH, King KK, Hanson V. Systemic lupus erythematosus in the first decade of life. Pediatrics 1989, **83:** 235–239.

303 Le Thi Huong D, Papo T, Beaufils H, Wechsler B, Blétry O, Baumelou A, Godeau P, Piette J-C. Renal involvement in systemic lupus erythematosus: A study of 180 patients from a single center. Medicine 1999, **78:** 148–166.

304 Mahajan SK, Ordóñez NG, Spargo BH, Katz AI. Changing histopathology patterns in lupus nephropathy. Clin Nephrol 1978, **10:** 1–8.

305 Ordóñez NG, Gomez LG. The ultrastructure of glomerular haematoxylin bodies. J Pathol 1981, **135:** 259–265.

306 Pasquali S, Banfi G, Zucchelli A, Moroni G, Ponticelli C, Zucchelli P. Lupus membranous nephropathy: long-term outcome. Clin Nephrol 1993, **39:** 175–182.

307 Schwartz MM, Kawala K, Roberts JL, Humes C, Lewis EJ. Clinical and pathological features of membranous glomerulonephritis of systemic lupus erythematosus. Am J Nephrol 1984, **4:** 301–311.

308 Schwartz MM, Lan S-P, Bernstein J, Hill GS, Holley K, Lewis EJ. The Lupus Nephritis Collaborative Study Group. Irreproducibility of the activity and chronicity indices limits their utility in the management of lupus nephritis. Am J Kidney Dis 1993, **21:** 374–377.

309 Singh AK, Ucci A, Madias NE. Predominant tubulointerstitial lupus nephritis. Am J Kidney Dis 1996, **27:** 273–278.

310 Tan EM, Cohen AS, Fries JF, Masi AT, McShane DJ, Rothfield NF, Schaller JG, Talal N, Winchester RJ. The 1982 revised criteria for the classification of systemic lupus erythematosus. Arthritis Rheum 1982, **25:** 1271–1277.

311 Zimmerman SW, Jenkins PG, Shelf WD, Bloodworth JMB Jr, Burkholder PM. Progression from minimal or focal to diffuse proliferative lupus nephritis. Lab Invest 1975, **32:** 665–679.

Glomerular lesions associated with vascular diseases
Systemic vasculitis

312 Gross WL, Schmitt WH, Csernok E. ANCA and associated diseases: immunodiagnostic and pathogenetic aspects. Clin Exp Immunol 1993, **91:** 1–12.

313 Noël LH, Geffriaud C, Chauveau D, Houhou S, Landais P, Kirhaoui F, Nusbaum P, Gouarin C, O'Donoghue D, Halbwachs-Mecarelli L, Grünfeld J-P. Antineutrophil cytoplasm antibodies: Diversity and clinical applications. Adv Nephrol Necker Hosp 1993, **22:** 237–267.

Polyarteritis nodosa

314 Bonsib SM. Polyarteritis nodosa. Semin Diagn Pathol 2001, **18:** 14–23.

315 D'Agati VD, Appel GB. Polyarteritis nodosa, Wegener granulomatosis, Churg-Strauss syndrome, temporal arteritis, Takayasu arteritis, and lymphomatoid granulomatosis. In Tisher CC, Brenner BM (eds): Renal pathology: With clinical and functional correlations, ed. 2, vol. II. Philadelphia, 1994, J.B. Lippincott, pp. 1087–1153.

316 Drueke T, Barbanel C, Jungers P, Didgeon M, Poisson M, Brivet F. Hepatitis B antigen-associated periarteritis nodosa in patients undergoing long-term hemodialysis. Am J Med 1980, **68:** 86–90.

317 Jennette JC. Renal involvement in systemic vasculitis. In

Jennette JC, Olson JL, Schwartz MM, Silva FG (eds): Heptinstall's Pathology of the kidney, ed. 5. Philadelphia, 1998, Lippincott-Raven, pp. 1059–1095.

Microscopic polyangiitis

318 D'Agati VD, Appel GB. Polyarteritis nodosa, Wegener granulomatosis, Churg-Strauss syndrome, temporal arteritis, Takayasu arteritis, and lymphomatoid granulomatosis. In Tisher CC, Brenner BM (eds): Renal pathology: With clinical and functional correlations, ed. 2, vol. II. Philadelphia, 1994, J.B. Lippincott, pp. 1087–1153.

319 D'Agati V, Chander P, Nash M, Mancilla-Jimenez R. Idiopathic microscopic polyarteritis nodosa: Ultrastructural observations on the renal vascular and glomerular lesions. Am J Kidney Dis 1986, **7:** 95–110.

320 Droz D, Noel LH, Leibowitch N, Barbanel C. Glomerulonephritis and necrotizing angiitis. Adv Nephrol 1979, **8:** 343–363.

321 Guillevin L, Durand-Gasselin B, Cevallos R, Gayraud M, Lhote F, Callard P, Amouroux J, Casassus P, Jarrousse B. Microscopic polyangiitis: Clinical and laboratory findings in eighty-five patients. Arthritis Rheum 1999, **42:** 421–430.

322 Jennette JC, Falk RJ. Small-vessel vasculitis. N Engl J Med 1997, **337:** 1512–1522.

323 Jennette JC, Falk RJ, Andrassy K, Bacon PA, Churg J, Gross WL, Hagen EC, Hoffman GS, Hunder GG, Kallenberg CG, et al. Nomenclature of systemic vasculitides: The proposal of an international consensus conference. Arthritis Rheum 1994, **37:** 187–192.

324 Jennette JC, Thomas DB, Falk RJ. Microscopic polyangiitis (microscopic polyarteritis). Semin Diagn Pathol 2001, **18:** 3–13.

Wegener's granulomatosis

325 Cohen Tervaert JW, Huitem MG, Hene RJ, Sluiter WJ. Prevention of relapses in Wegener's granulomatosis by treatment based on anti-neutrophil cytoplasmic antibody titer. Lancet 1990, **336:** 709–711.

326 Cotch MF, Hoffman GS, Yerg DE, Kaufman GI, Targonski P, Kaslow RA. The epidemiology of Wegener's granulomatosis. Estimates of the five-year period prevalence, annual mortality, and geographic disease distribution from population-based data sources. Arthritis Rheum 1996, **39:** 87–92.

327 Fauci AS, Haynes BF, Katz P, Wolff SM. Wegener's granulomatosis: Prospective clinical and therapeutic experience with 85 patients for 21 years. Ann Intern Med 1983, **98:** 76–95.

328 Gaber LW, Wall BM, Cooke CR. Coexistence of anti-neutrophil cytoplasmic antibody-associated glomerulonephritis and membranous glomerulopathy. Am J Clin Pathol 1993, **99:** 211–215.

329 Gross WL, Schmitt WH, Csernok E. ANCA and associated diseases: immunodiagnostic and pathogenetic aspects. Clin Exp Immunol 1993, **91:** 1–12.

330 Hoffman GS. Wegener's granulomatosis. Curr Opin Rheumatol 1993, **5:** 11–17.

331 Hoffman GS, Kerr GS, Leavitt RY, Hallahan CW, Lebovics RS, Travis WD, Rottem M, Fauci AS. Wegener granulomatosis: An analysis of 158 patients. Ann Intern Med 1992, **116:** 488–498.

332 Watanabe T, Nagafuchi Y, Yoshikawa Y, Toyoshima H. Renal papillary necrosis associated with Wegener's granulomatosis. Hum Pathol 1983, **14:** 551–557.

333 Weiss MA, Crissman JD. Renal biopsy findings in Wegener's granulomatosis: Segmental necrotizing glomerulonephritis with glomerular thrombosis. Hum Pathol 1984, **15:** 943–956.

334 Woodworth TG, Abuelo JG, Austin HA, Esparza A. Severe glomerulonephritis with late emergence of classic Wegener's granulomatosis: Report of 4 cases and review of the literature. Medicine [Baltimore] 1987, **66:** 181–191.

335 Yi ES, Colby TV. Wegener's granulomatosis. Semin Diagn Pathol 2001, **18**: 34–46.

336 Yoshikawa Y, Watanabe T. Granulomatous glomerulonephritis in Wegener's granulomatosis. Virchows Arch [A] 1984, **402**: 361–372.

Henoch–Schönlein purpura

337 Hasegawa A, Kawamura T, Ito FL, Hasegawa O, Ogawa O, Honda M, Ohara T, Hajikano H. Fate of renal grafts with recurrent Henoch Schönlein purpura nephritis in children. Transplant Proc 1989, **21**: 2130–2133.

338 Kim CK, Aikawa M, Makker SP. Electron dense subepithelial glomerular deposits in Henoch-Schönlein purpura syndrome. Arch Pathol Lab Med 1979, **103**: 595.

339 Lofters WS, Penco GF, Luke KH, Yaworsky RG. Henoch-Schönlein purpura occurring in three members of a family. Can Med Assoc J 1973, **109**: 46.

340 Meulders Q, Pirson Y, Cosyns JP, Squifflet JP, van Ypersele de Strihou C. Course of Henoch-Schönlein nephritis after renal transplantation. Report on ten patients and review of the literature. Transplantation 1994, **58**: 1179–1186.

341 Nast CC, Ward FU, Koyle MA, Cohen AH. Recurrent Henoch-Schönlein purpura following renal transplantation. Am J Kidney Dis 1987, **9**: 39.

342 Urizar EE, Singh JK, Muhammad T, Hines O. Henoch-Schönlein anaphylactoid purpura nephropathy. Electron microscopic lesions mimicking acute post-streptococcal nephritis. Hum Pathol 1978, **9**: 223.

Mixed cryoglobulinemia

343 Brouet JC, Clauvel JP, Danon F, Klein M, Seligman M. Biological and clinical significance of cryoglobulins. A report of 86 cases. Am J Med 1974, **57**: 775–788.

344 D'Amico G, Colasanti G, Ferrario F, Sinico RA. Renal involvement in essential mixed cryoglobulinemia. Kidney Int 1989, **35**: 1004–1014.

345 Dispenzieri A, Gorevic PD. Cryoglobulinemia. Hematol Oncol Clin North Am 1999, **13**: 1315–1349.

346 Doutrelepont JM, Adler M, Willems M, Durez P, Yap SH. Hepatitis C infection and membranoproliferative glomerulonephritis (letter). Lancet 1993, **341**: 317.

347 Faraggiana T, Parolini C, Previato G, Lupo A. Light and electron microscopic findings in five cases of cryoglobulinemic glomerulonephritis. Virchows Arch [A] 1979, **384**: 29–44.

348 Feiner H, Gallo G. Ultrastructure in glomerulonephritis associated with cryoglobulinemia. A report of six cases and review of the literature. Am J Pathol 1977, **88**: 145–154.

349 Ferri C, Greco F, Longombardo G, Palla P, Moretti A, Marzo E, Mazzoni A, Pasero G, Bombardieri S, Highfield P. Association between hepatitis C virus and mixed cryoglobulinemia. Clin Exp Rheumatol 1991, **9**: 621–624.

350 Gorevic PD, Kassab HJ, Levo Y, Kohn R, Meltzer M, Prose P, Franklin EC. Mixed cryoglobulinemia: Clinical aspects and long-term follow-up of 40 patients. Am J Med 1980, **69**: 287–308.

351 Johnson RJ, Willson R, Yamabe K, Couser W, Alpers CE, Wener MH, Davis C, Gretch DR. Renal manifestations of hepatitis C virus infection. Kidney Int 1994, **46**: 1255–1263.

352 Misiani R, Bellavita P, Fenili D, Borelli G, Marchesi D, Massazza M, Vendramin G, Comotti B, Tanzi E, Scudeller G. Hepatitis C virus infection in patients with essential mixed cryoglobulinemia. Ann Intern Med 1992, **117**: 573–577.

353 Porush JG, Grishman E, Alter AA, Mandelbaum H, Churg J. Paraproteinemia and cryoglobulinemia associated with atypical glomerulonephritis and the nephrotic syndrome. Am J Med 1969, **47**: 957–964.

354 Rossmann P, Hornych A, Englis M. Histology and ultrastructure of crystalloid inclusions in the podocytes in a case of paraproteinemia. Virchows Arch [A] 1968, **344**: 151–158.

Hemolytic uremic syndrome and thrombotic thrombocytopenic purpura

355 Asaka M, Ishikawa I, Nakazawa T, Tomosugi N, Yuri T, Suzuki K. Hemolytic uremic syndrome associated with influenza A virus infection in an adult renal allograft recipient: Case report and review of the literature. Nephron 2000, **84**: 258–266.

356 Ashkenazi S. Role of bacterial cytotoxins in hemolytic uremic syndrome and thrombotic thrombocytopenic purpura. Annu Rev Med 1993, **44**: 11–18.

357 Cabrera GR, Fortenberry JD, Warshaw BL, Chambliss CR, Butler JC, Cooperstone BG. Hemolytic uremic syndrome associated with invasive Streptococcus pneumoniae infection. Pediatrics 1998, **101**: 699–703.

358 Glynne P, Salama A, Chaudhry A, Swirsky D, Lightstone L. Quinine-induced immune thrombocytopenic purpura followed by hemolytic uremic syndrome. Am J Kidney Dis 1999, **33**: 133–137.

359 Gordjani N, Sutor AH, Zimmerhackl LB, Brandis M. Hemolytic uremic syndromes in childhood. Semin Thromb Hemost 1997, **23**: 281–293.

360 Gordon LI, Kwaan HC. Thrombotic microangiopathy manifesting as thrombotic thrombocytopenic purpura/hemolytic uremic syndrome in the cancer patient. Semin Thromb Hemost 1999, **25**: 217–221.

361 Hymes KB, Karpatkin S. Human immunodeficiency virus infection and thrombotic microangiopathy. Semin Hematol 1997, **34**: 117–125.

362 Keusch GT, Acheson DWK. Thrombotic thrombocytopenic purpura associated with Shiga toxins. Semin Hematol 1997, **34**: 106–116.

363 Li PK, Lai FM, Tam JS, Lai KN. Acute renal failure due to postpartum haemolytic uraemic syndrome. Aust N Z J Obstet Gynaecol 1988, **28**: 228–230.

364 McCrae KR, Cines DB. Thrombotic microangiopathy during pregnancy. Semin Hematol 1997, **34**: 148–158.

365 Melnyk AMS, Solez K, Kjellstrand CM. Adult hemolytic-uremic syndrome: A review of 37 cases. Arch Intern Med 1995, **155**: 2077–2084.

366 Moake JL. Studies on the pathophysiology of thrombotic thrombocytopenic purpura. Semin Hematol 1997, **34**: 83–89.

367 Niaudet P, Gagnadoux MF, Broyer M, Salomon R. Hemolytic-uremic syndrome: Hereditary forms and forms associated with hereditary diseases. Adv Nephrol 2000, **30**: 261–280.

368 Remuzzi G, Ruggenenti P. The hemolytic uremic syndrome. Kidney Int 1998, **53**(Suppl 66): S54–S57.

369 Ring GH, Lakkis FG, Badr KF. Microvascular diseases of the kidney. In Brenner BM (ed.): Brenner and Rector's The kidney, ed. 6. Philadelphia, 2000, W.B. Saunders, pp. 1597–1620.

370 van der Heijden M, Ackland SP, Deveridge S. Haemolytic uraemic syndrome associated with bleomycin, epirubicin and cisplatin chemotherapy: A case report and review of the literature. Acta Oncol 1998, **37**: 107–109.

Systemic sclerosis

371 Eknoyan G, Suki WN. Renal vascular phenomena in systemic sclerosis (scleroderma). Semin Nephrol 1985, **5**: 34–45.

372 Rocco VK, Hurd ER. Scleroderma and scleroderma-like disorders. Semin Arthritis Rheum 1986, **16**: 22–69.

373 Uziel Y, Miller ML, Laxer RM. Scleroderma in children. Pediatr Clin North Am 1995, **42**: 1171–1203.

Renal diseases of pregnancy
Preeclampsia

374 Branch DW, Porter TF. Hypertensive disorders of pregnancy. In Scott JR, Di Saia PJ, Hammond CB, Spellacy WN (eds):

Danforth's Obstetrics and gynecology, ed. 8. Philadelphia, 1999, Lippincott, Williams, and Wilkins, pp. 309–326.

375 Fogo AB. Renal diseases in pregnancy. In Jennette JC, Olson JL, Schwartz MM, Silva FG. Heptinstall's Pathology of the kidney, ed. 5. Philadelphia, 1998, Lippincott-Raven, pp. 1097–1130.

376 Gant NF, Pritchard JA. Pregnancy-induced hypertension. Semin Nephrol 1984, **4:** 260–269.

377 Paller MS. The kidney and hypertension in pregnancy. In Brenner BM (ed.): The kidney, ed. 6. Philadelphia, 2000, Sanders, pp. 1621–1655.

378 Roberts JM, Taylor RN, Musci TJ, Rodgers GM, Hubel CA, McLaughlin MK. Preeclampsia: an endothelial cell disorder. Am J Obstet Gynecol 1989, **161:** 1200–1204.

379 Sheehan HL. Renal morphology in preeclampsia. Kidney Int 1980, **18:** 241–252.

Hereditary glomerular diseases
Alport's syndrome (hereditary nephritis)

380 Antignac C, Heidet L. Mutations in Alport syndrome associated with diffuse esophageal leiomyomatosis. Contrib Nephrol 1996, **117:** 172–182.

381 Antignac C, Zhou J, Sanak M, Cochat P, Roussel B, Deschenes G, Gros F, Knebelmann B, Hors-Cayla MC, Tryggvason K. Alport syndrome and diffuse leiomyomatosis: Deletions in the 5′ end of the COL4A5 collagen gene. Kidney Int 1992, **42:** 1178–1183.

382 Barker D, Hostikka SL, Zhou J, Chow LT, Oliphant AR, Gerken SC, Gregory MC, Skolnick MH, Atkin CL, Tryggvason K. Identification of mutations in the COL4A5 collagen gene in Alport syndrome. Science 1990, **248:** 1224–1227.

383 Bernstein J. The glomerular basement membrane abnormality in Alport's syndrome. Am J Kidney Dis 1987, **10:** 222–229.

384 Brainwood D, Kashtan C, Gubler MC, Turner AN. Targets of alloantibodies in Alport anti-glomerular basement membrane disease after renal transplantation. Kidney Int 1998, **53:** 762–766.

385 Colville DJ, Savige J. Alport syndrome: a review of the ocular manifestations. Ophthalmic Genet 1997, **18:** 161–173.

386 Epstein CJ, Sahud MA, Piel CF, Goodman JR, Bernfield MR, Kushner JH, Ablin AR. Hereditary macrothrombocytopenia, nephritis and deafness. Am J Med 1972, **52:** 299–310.

387 Excerpts from United States Renal Data System 1997 Annual Report: Incidence and prevalence of ESRD. Am J Kidney Dis 1997, **30:** S40–S53.

388 Goyer RA, Reynolds J Jr, Burke J, Burkholder P. Hereditary renal disease with neurosensory hearing loss, prolinuria and ichthyosis. Am J Med Sci 1968, **256:** 166–179.

389 Gregory MC, Atkin CL. Alport syndrome. In Schrier RW, Gottschalk CW (eds): Diseases of the kidney, ed. 5, vol. I. Boston, 1993, Little, Brown and Company, pp. 571–591.

390 Gubler M-C, Antignac C, Deschênes G, Knebelmann B, Hors-Cayla MC, Grünfeld J-P, Broyer M, Habib R. Genetic, clinical, and morphologic heterogeneity in Alport's syndrome. Adv Nephrol Necker Hosp 1993, **22:** 15–35.

391 Hill GS, Jenis EH, Goodloe S Jr. The nonspecificity of the ultrastructural alterations in hereditary nephritis: With additional observations on benign familial hematuria. Lab Invest 1974, **31:** 516–532.

392 Jais JP, Knebelmann B, Giatras I, De Marchi M, Rizzoni G, Renieri A, Weber M, Gross O, Netzer K-O, Flinter F, Pirson Y, Verellen C, Wieslander J, Persson U, Tryggvason K, Martin P, Hertz JM, Schroder C, Sanak M, Krejcova S, Carvalho MF, Saus J, Antignac C, Smeets H, Gubler MC. X-linked Alport syndrome: Natural history in 195 families and genotype-phenotype correlations in males. J Am Soc Nephrol 2000, **11:** 649–657.

393 Jansen B, Thorner P, Baumal R, Valli V, Maxie MG, Singh A. Samoyed hereditary glomerulopathy (SHG): Evolution of

splitting of glomerular capillary basement membranes. Am J Pathol 1986, **125:** 536–545.

394 Jefferson JA, Lemmink HH, Hughes AE, Hill CM, Smeets HJ, Doherty CC, Maxwell AP. Autosomal dominant Alport syndrome linked to the type IV collagen alpha 3 and alpha 4 genes (COL4A3 and COL4A4). Nephrol Dial Transplant 1997, **12:** 1595–1599.

395 Kalluri R, Webber M, Netzer K-O, Sun MJ, Neilson EG, Hudson BG. COL4A5 gene deletion and production of post-transplant anti-α3(IV) collagen alloantibodies in Alport syndrome. Kidney Int 1994, **45:** 721–726.

396 Kashtan CE. Alport syndrome: An inherited disorder of renal, ocular, and cochlear basement membranes. Medicine 1999, **78:** 338–360.

397 Kashtan CE. Alport syndrome: phenotypic heterogeneity of progressive hereditary nephritis. Pediatr Nephrol 2000, **14:** 502–512.

398 Kashtan CE, Michael AF. Alport syndrome. Kidney Int 1996, **50:** 1445–1463.

399 Lemmink HH, Schröder CH, Monnens LAH, Smeets HJM. The clinical spectrum of type IV collagen mutations. Hum Mutat 1997, **9:** 477–499.

400 McCoy RC, Johnson HK, Stone WJ, Wilson CB. Absence of nephritogenic GMB antigen(s) in some patients with hereditary nephritis. Kidney Int 1982, **21:** 642–652.

401 Meleg-Smith S, Magliato S, Cheles M, Garola RE, Kashtan CE. X-linked Alport syndrome in females. Hum Pathol 1998, **29:** 404–408.

402 Moxey-Mims MM, Young G, Silverman A, Selby DM, White JG, Kher KK. End-stage renal disease in two pediatric patients with Fechtner syndrome. Ped Nephrol 1999, **13:** 782–786.

403 Nielsen CE. Lenticonus anterior and Alport's syndrome. Arch Ophthalmol 1978, **56:** 518–530.

404 Rumpelt H-J. Hereditary nephropathy (Alport syndrome): Correlation of clinical data with glomerular basement membrane alterations. Clin Nephrol 1980, **13:** 203–207.

405 Rumpelt H-J. Alport's syndrome: Specificity and pathogenesis of glomerular basement membrane alterations. Pediatr Nephrol 1987, **1:** 422–427.

406 Wester DC, Atkin CL, Gregory MC. Alport syndrome: clinical update. J Am Acad Audiol 1995, **6:** 73–79.

Thin glomerular basement membrane disease

407 Aarons I, Smith PS, Davies RA, Woodroffe AJ, Clarkson AR. Thin membrane nephropathy: a clinicopathological study. Clin Nephrol 1989, **32:** 151–158.

408 Basta-Jovanovic G, Venkataseshan VS, Gil J, Kim DU, Dikman SH, Churg J. Morphometric analysis of glomerular basement membranes (GBM) in thin basement membrane disease (TBMD). Clin Nephrol 1990, **33:** 110–114.

409 Boye E, Mollet GF, Cohen-Solal L, Heidet L, Cochat P, Grunfeld J-P, Palcoux J-B, Gubler M-C, Antignac C. Determination of the genomic structure of the COL4A4 gene and of novel mutations causing autosomal recessive Alport syndrome. Am J Hum Genet 1998, **63:** 1329–1340.

410 Cosio FG, Falkenhain ME, Sedmak DD. Association of thin glomerular basement membrane with other glomerulopathies. Kidney Int 1994, **46:** 471–474.

411 Dische FE. Measurement of glomerular basement membrane thickness and its application to the diagnosis of thin-membrane nephropathy. Arch Pathol Lab Med 1992, **116:** 43–49.

412 Dische FE, Brooke IP, Cashman SJ, Severn A, Taube D, Parsons V, Kershaw M, Reed A, Pusey CD. Reactivity of monoclonal antibody P1 with glomerular basement membrane in thin-membrane nephropathy. Nephrol Dial Transplant 1989, **4:** 611–617.

413 Dische FE, Weston MJ, Parson V. Abnormally thin glomerular

basement membranes associated with hematuria, proteinuria or renal failure in adults. Am J Nephrol 1985, **5:** 103–109.

414 Frasca GM, Onetti-Muda A, Renieri A. Thin glomerular basement membrane disease. J Nephrol 2000, **13:** 15–19.

415 Kashtan CE. Alport syndrome and thin glomerular basement membrane disease. J Am Soc Nephrol 1998, **9:** 1736–1750.

416 Kiyatake I, Tomino Y, Shirato I, Nakayama S, Koide H. Alport syndrome diagnosed by immunofluorescence using a new monoclonal antibody. Intern Med 1993, **32:** 26–30.

417 Lang S, Stevenson B, Risdon RA. Thin basement membrane nephropathy as a cause of recurrent haematuria in childhood. Histopathology 1990, **16:** 331–337.

418 Lemmink HH, Nillesen WN, Mochizuki T, Schroder CH, Brunner HG, van Oost BA, Monnens LAH, Smeets HJM. Benign familial hematuria due to mutation of the type IV collagen [alpha]4 gene. J Clin Invest 1996, **98:** 1114–1118.

419 Nogueira M, Cartwright J Jr, Horn K, Doe N, Shappell S, Barrios R, Coroneos E, Truong LD. Thin basement membrane disease with heavy proteinuria or nephrotic syndrome at presentation. Am J Kidney Dis 2000, **35:** 1–8.

420 Perry GJ, George CRP, Field MJ, Collett PV, Karowski S, Wynonram RN, Newland RC, Lin BPC, Kneale KL, Lawrence JR. Thin-membrane nephropathy: A common cause of glomerular haematuria. Med J Aust 1989, **151:** 638–642.

421 Pettersson E, Tornroth T, Wieslander J. Abnormally thin glomerular basement membrane and the Goodpasture epitope. Clin Nephrol 1990, **33:** 105–109.

422 Rogers PW, Kurtzman NA, Bunn SM Jr, White MG. Familial benign essential hematuria. Arch Intern Med 1973, **131:** 257–262.

423 Schroder CH, Bontemps CM, Assmann KJM, Schuurmans Stekhoven JH, Foidart JM, Monnens LA, Veerkamp JH. Renal biopsy and family studies in 65 children with isolated hematuria. Acta Paediatr Scand 1990, **79:** 630–636.

Angiokeratoma corporis diffusum universale

424 Ashton-Prolla P, Tong BZ, Shabbeer J, Astrin KH, Eng CM, Desnick RJ. Fabry disease: Twenty-two novel mutations in the alpha-galactosidase A gene and genotype/phenotype correlations in severely and mildly affected hemizygotes and heterozygotes. J Invest Med 2000, **48:** 227–235.

425 Bernstein HS, Bishop DF, Astrin KH, Kornreich R, Eng CM, Sakuraba H, Desnick RJ. Fabry disease: Six gene rearrangements and an exonic point mutation in the alpha-galactosidase gene. J Clin Invest 1989, **83:** 1390–1399.

426 Desnick RJ, Astrin KH, Bishop DF. Fabry's disease: Molecular genetics of the inherited nephropathy. Adv Nephrol 1989, **18:** 113–128.

427 Kornreich R, Desnic RJ, Bishop DF. Nucleotide sequences of the human alpha-galactosidase A gene. Nucleic Acids Res 1989, **17:** 3301–3302.

428 Kramer W, Thorman J, Mueller K, Frenzel H. Progressive cardiac involvement by Fabry's disease despite successful renal allotransplantation. Int J Cardiol 1985, **7:** 72–75.

429 Ojo A, Meier-Kriesche H-U, Friedman G, Hanson J, Cibrik D, Leichtman A, Kaplan B. Excellent outcome of renal transplantation in patients with Fabry's disease. Transplantation 2000, **69:** 2337–2339.

430 Popli S, Molnar ZV, Leehey DJ, Daugirdas JT, Roth DA, Adams MB, Cheng JC, Ing TS. Involvement of renal allograft by Fabry's disease. Am J Nephrol 1987, **7:** 316–318.

431 Savi M, Olivetti G, Neri T, Curtoni C. Clinical, histopathological, and biochemical findings of Fabry's disease: A case report and family study. Arch Pathol Lab Med 1977, **101:** 536–539.

432 Topaloglu AK, Ashley GA, Tong BZ, Shabbeer J, Astrin KH, Eng CM, Desnick RJ. Twenty novel mutations in the alpha-

galactosidase A gene causing Fabry disease. Mol Med 1999, **5:** 806–811.

Hereditary onycho-osteodysplasia

433 Chan PC, Chan KW, Cheng IK, Chan MK. Living-related renal transplantation in a patient with nail-patella syndrome. Nephron 1988, **50:** 164–166.

434 Dreyer SD, Zhou G, Baldini A, Winterpacht A, Zabel B, Cole W, Johnson RL, Lee B. Mutations in LMX1B cause abnormal skeletal patterning and renal dysplasia in nail patella syndrome. Nat Genet 1998, **19:** 47–50.

435 Knoers NVAM, Bongers EMHF, van Beersum SEC, Lommen EJP, van Bokhoven H, Hol FA. Nail-patella syndrome: Identification of mutations in the LMX1B gene in Dutch families. J Am Soc Nephrol 2000, **11:** 1762–1766.

436 McIntosh I, Clough MV, Schaffer AA, Puffenberger EG, Horton VK, Peters K, Abbott MH, Roig CM, Cutone S, Ozelius L, Kwiatkowski DJ, Pyeritz RE, Brown LJ, Pauli RM, McCormick MK, Francomano CA. Fine mapping of the nail-patella syndrome locus at 9q34. Am J Hum Genet 1997, **60:** 133–142.

437 Mangino M, Sanchez O, Torrente I, De Luca A, Capon F, Novelli G, Dallapiccola B. Localization of a gene for familial patella aplasia-hypoplasia (PTLAH) to chromosome 17q21–22. Am J Hum Genet 1999, **65:** 441–447.

438 Meyrier A, Rizzo R, Gubler MC. The nail-patella syndrome. A review. J Nephrol 1990, **2:** 133–140.

439 Morita T, Laughlin LO, Kawano K, Kimmelstiel P, Suzuki Y, Churg J. Nail-patella syndrome. Light and electron microscopic studies in the kidney. Arch Intern Med 1973, **131:** 271–277.

Collagen type III glomerulopathy

440 Arakawa M, Yamanaka N. Collagenofibrinotic glomerulonephropathy. Nishimura, Smith-Gordon, Niigata, 1991, pp. 3–92.

441 Gubler M-C, Dommergues JP, Foulard M, Bensman A, Leroy JP, Broyer M, Habib R. Collagen type III glomerulopathy: a new type of hereditary nephropathy. Pediatr Nephrol 1993, **7:** 354–360.

442 Gubler M-C, Heidet L, Antignac C. Alport's syndrome, thin basement membrane nephropathy, nail-patella syndrome, and type III collagen glomerulopathy. In Jennette JC, Olson JL, Schwartz MM, Silva FG (eds): Heptinstall's Pathology of the kidney, ed. 5. Philadelphia, Lippincott-Raven, 1998, pp. 1207–1230.

443 Ikeda K, Yokoyama H, Tomosugi N, Kida H, Ooshima A, Kobayashi K. Primary glomerular fibrosis: a new nephropathy caused by diffuse intraglomerular increase in atypical type III collagen fibers. Clin Nephrol 1990, **33:** 155–159.

444 Imbasciati E, Gherardi G, Morozumi K, Gudat F, Epper R, Basler V, Mihatsch MJ. Collagen type III glomerulopathy: a new idiopathic glomerular disease. Am J Nephrol 1991, **11:** 422–429.

445 Mizuiri S, Hasegawa A, Kikuchi A, Amagasaki Y, Nakamura N, Sakaguchi H. A case of collagenofibrotic glomerulopathy associated with hepatic perisinusoidal fibrosis. Nephron 1993, **63:** 183–187.

446 Tamura H, Matsuda A, Kidoguchi N, Matsumura O, Mitarai T, Isoda K. A family with two sisters with collagenofibrotic glomerulonephropathy. Am J Kidney Dis 1996, **27:** 588–595.

447 Vogt BA, Wyatt RJ, Burke BA, Simonton SC, Kashtan CE. Inherited factor H deficiency and collagen type III glomerulopathy. Ped Nephrol 1995, **9:** 11–15.

Fibronectin glomerulopathy

448 Abt AB, Wassner SJ, Moran JJ. Familial lobular glomerulopathy. Hum Pathol 1991, **22:** 825–829.

449 Assmann KJ, Koene RA, Wetzels JF. Familial glomerulonephritis characterised by massive deposits of fibronectin. Am J Kidney Dis 1995, **25:** 781–791.

450 Mazzucco G, Maran E, Rollino C, Monga G. Glomerulonephritis with organized deposits: A mesangiopathic, not immune complex-mediated disease? A pathologic study of two cases in the same family. Hum Pathol 1992, **23:** 63–68.

451 Strom EH, Banfi G, Krapf R, Abt AB, Mazzucco G, Monga G, Gloor F, Neuweiler J, Riess R, Stosiek P, Hebert LA, Sedmak DD, Gudat F, Mihatsch MJ. Glomerulopathy associated with predominant fibronectin deposits: A newly recognized hereditary disease. Kidney Int 1995, **48:** 163–170.

452 Vollmer M, Jung M, Rüschendorf F, Ruf R, Wienker T, Reis A, Krapf R, Hildebrandt F. The gene for human fibronectin glomerulopathy maps to 1q32, in the region of the regulation of complement activation gene cluster. Am J Hum Genet 1998, **63:** 1724–1731.

Renal transplant rejection
Hyperacute rejection

453 Iwaki Y, Terasaki PI. Primary nonfunction in human cadaver kidney transplantation: Evidence for hidden hyperacute rejection. Clin Transplant 1987, **1:** 125–131.

454 Opelz G, Graver B, Mickey MR, Terasaki PI. Lymphocytotoxic antibody responses to transfusions in potential kidney transplant recipients. Transplantation 1981, **32:** 177–185.

455 Pardo-Mindán FJ, Salinas-Madrigal L, Idoate M, Garola R, Sola I, French M. Pathology of renal transplantation. Semin Diagn Pathol 1992, **9:** 185–199.

456 Scornik JC, Ireland JE, Howard RJ, Pfaff WW. Assessment of the risk for broad sensitization by blood transfusions. Transplantation 1984, **37:** 49–53.

Acute rejection

457 Colvin RB. The renal allograft biopsy. Kidney Int 1996, **50:** 1069–1082.

458 Colvin RB. Renal transplant pathology. In Jennette JC, Olson JL, Schwartz MM, Silva FG (eds): Heptinstall's Pathology of the kidney, ed. 5. Philadelphia, 1998, Lippincott-Raven, pp. 1409–1540.

459 Croker BP, Ramos EL. Pathology of the renal allograft. In Tisher CC, Brenner BM (eds): Renal pathology with clinical and functional correlations, ed. 2, vol. II. Philadelphia, 1994, J.B. Lippincott, pp. 1591–1640.

460 Olsen S. Pathology of the renal allograft rejection. In Churg J, Spargo BJ, Mostofi F (eds): Kidney disease. Present status. Baltimore, 1979, Williams & Wilkins, pp. 327–355.

461 Verani RR, Bergman D, Kerman RH. Glomerulopathy in acute and chronic rejection. Relationship of ultrastructure to graft survival. Am J Nephrol 1983, **3:** 253–263.

Chronic rejection

462 Busch GJ, Galvanek EG, Reynolds ES Jr. Human renal allografts. Analysis of lesions in long-term survivors. Hum Pathol 1971, **2:** 253–298.

463 Croker BP, Ramos EL. Pathology of the renal allograft. In Tisher CC, Brenner BM (eds): Renal pathology with clinical and functional correlations, ed. 2, vol. II. Philadelphia, 1994, J.B. Lippincott, pp. 1591–1640.

464 Maryniak BK, First MR, Weiss MA. Transplant glomerulopathy. Evolution of morphologically distinct changes. Kidney Int 1985, **27:** 799–806.

465 Olsen S. Pathology of the renal allograft rejection. In Churg J, Spargo BJ, Mostofi F (eds): Kidney disease. Present status. Baltimore, 1979, Williams & Wilkins, pp. 327–355.

466 Paul LC, Foegh HM, Dennis MJ, Mihatsch MJ, Larsson E, Fellström B. Diagnostic criteria for chronic rejection/accelerated graft atherosclerosis in heart and kidney transplants: Joint proposal from the Fourth Alexis Carrel Conference on Chronic Rejection and Accelerated Arteriosclerosis in Transplanted Organs. Transplant Proc 1993, **25:** 2022–2023.

467 Petersen VP, Olsen TS, Kissmeyer-Nielsen F, Bohman SO, Hansen HE, Hansen ES, Skov PE, Solling K. Late failure of human renal transplants: an analysis of transplant disease and graft failure among 125 recipients surviving from one to eight years. Medicine [Baltimore] 1975, **54:** 45–71.

468 Verani RR, Bergman D, Kerman RH. Glomerulopathy in acute and chronic rejection. Relationship of ultrastructure to graft survival. Am J Nephrol 1983, **3:** 253–263.

The Banff classification

469 Colvin RB. The renal allograft biopsy. Kidney Int 1996, **50:** 1069–1082.

470 Colvin RB, Cohen AH, Saiontz C, Bonsib S, Buick M, Burke B, Carter S, Cavallo T, Haas M, Lindblad A, Manivel JC, Nast CC, Salomon D, Weaver C, Weiss M. Evaluation of pathologic criteria for acute renal allograft rejection: reproducibility, sensitivity and clinical correlation. J Am Soc Nephrol 1997, **8:** 1930–1941.

471 Racusen LC, Solez K, Colvin RB, Bonsib SM, Castro MC, Cavallo T, Croker BP, Demetris AJ, Drachenberg CB, Fogo AB, Furness P, Gaber LW, Gibson IW, Glotz D, Goldberg JC, Grande J, Halloran PF, Hansen HE, Hartley B, Hayry PJ, Hill CM, Hoffman EO, Hunsicker LG, Lindblad AS, Marcussen N, Mihatsch MJ, Nadasdy T, Nickerson P, Olsen TS, Papadimitriou JC, Randhawa PS, Rayner DC, Roberts I, Rose S, Rush D, Salinas-Madrigal L, Salomon DR, Sund S, Taskinen E, Trpkov K, Yamaguchi Y. The Banff 97 working classification of renal allograft pathology. Kidney Int 1999, **55:** 713–723.

472 Solez K, Axelsen RA, Benediktsson H, Burdick JF, Cohen AH, Colvin RB, Croker BP, Droz D, Dunnil MS, Halloran PF, Häyry P, Jennette JC, Keown PA, Marcussen N, Mihatsch MJ, Morozumi K, Myers BD, Nast CC, Olsen S, Racusen LC, Ramos E, Rosen S, Sachs DH, Salomon DR, Sanfilippo F, Verani R, Willenbrand E, Yamaguchi Y. International standardization of criteria for the histologic diagnosis of renal allograft rejection: The Banff working classification of kidney transplant pathology. Kidney Int 1993, **44:** 411–422.

Cyclosporin A toxicity

473 Atkinson A, Biggs J, Dodds A, Concannon A. Cyclosporine-associated hepatotoxicity after allogeneic marrow transplantation in man: Differentiation from other causes of posttransplant liver disease. Transplant Proc 1983, **15:** 2761–2767.

474 Cockburn I. Assessment of risks of malignancy and lymphomas developing in patients using Sandimmune. Transplant Proc 1988, **19:** 1804–1807.

475 Colvin RB. Renal transplant pathology. In Jennette JC, Olson JL, Schwartz MM, Silva FG (eds): Heptinstall's Pathology of the kidney, ed. 5. Philadelphia, 1998, Lippincott-Raven, pp. 1409–1540.

476 Graham RM. Cyclosporine: Mechanisms of action and toxicity. Cleve Clin J Med 1994, **61:** 308–313.

477 Mihatsch MJ, Thiel G, Ryffel B. Morphologic diagnosis of cyclosporine nephrotoxicity. Semin Diagn Pathol 1988, **5:** 104–121.

478 Takeda A, Morozumi K, Uchida K, Yokoyama I, Takagi H, Yoshida A, Fujinami T, Thiel G, Gudat F, Mihatsch MJ. Is cyclosporine-associated glomerulopathy a new glomerular lesion in renal allografts using CyA? Transplant Proc 1993, **25:** 515–517.

Tacrolimus (FK506) toxicity

479 Randhawa P, Shapiro R, Jordan ML, Starzl TE, Demetis AJ. The histopathological changes associated with allograft rejection

and drug toxicity in renal transplant recipients maintained on FK506. Clinical significance and comparison with cyclosporine. Am J Surg Pathol 1993, **17**: 60–68.

Tubulointerstitial nephritis

480 Eknoyan G. Chronic tubulointerstitial nephropathies. In Schrier RW, Gottschalk CW (eds): Diseases of the kidney, ed. 5, vol. II. Boston, 1993, Little, Brown and Company, pp. 1959–1990.

Acute tubular necrosis

481 Kashgarian M. Acute tubular necrosis and ischemic renal injury. In Jennette JC, Olson JL, Schwartz MM, Silva FG (eds): Heptinstall's Pathology of the kidney, ed. 5, vol. 2. Philadelphia, 1998, Lippincott-Raven, pp. 863–889.

482 Olsen S, Solez K. Acute tubular necrosis and toxic renal injury. In Tisher CC, Brenner BM (eds): Renal pathology: With clinical and functional correlations, ed. 2, vol. I. Philadelphia, 1994, J.B. Lippincott, pp. 769–809.

483 Seshan SV, D'Agati VD, Appel GA, Churg J. Acute vasomotor injury/toxic tubular necrosis. In: Renal disease: Classification and atlas of tubulo-interstitial and vascular diseases. Baltimore, 1999, Williams & Wilkins, pp. 133–154.

Acute and chronic pyelonephritis

484 Abdou NI, NaPombejara C, Sagawa A, Ragland C, Stechschulte DJ, Nilsson U, Gousley W, Watanabe I, Lindsey NJ, Allen MS. Malakoplakia evidence of monocyte lysosome abnormality correctable by cholinergic agonist in vitro and in vivo. N Engl J Med 1977, **297**: 1413–1419.

485 Becker GJ, Kincaid-Smith P. Reflux nephropathy: the glomerular lesion and progression of renal failure. Pediatr Nephrol 1993, **7**: 365–369.

486 Esparza AR, McKay DB, Cronan JJ, Chazan JA. Renal parenchymal malakoplakia. Histologic spectrum and its relationship to megalocytic interstitial nephritis and xanthogranulomatous pyelonephritis. Am J Surg Pathol 1989, **13**: 225–236.

487 Goodman M, Curry T, Russel T. Xanthogranulomatous pyelonephritis (XGP). A local disease with systemic manifestations. Report of 23 patients and review of the literature. Medicine [Baltimore] 1979, **58**: 171–181.

488 Hammadah MY, Nicholls CJ, Calder JC, Buick RG, Gornall P, Corkery JJ. Xanthomatous pyelonephritis in childhood: Pre-operatory diagnosis is possible. Br J Urol 1994, **73**: 83–86.

489 Hodson CJ, Cotran RS. Vesicoureteral reflux, reflux nephropathy and chronic pyelonephritis. In Brenner B, Stein J (series eds), Cotran RS (guest ed.): Tubulo-interstitial nephropathies. Contemporary issues in nephrology, vol. 10. New York, 1983, Churchill Livingstone, pp. 83–102.

490 Huisman TK, Sands JP. Focal xanthogranulomatous pyelonephritis associated with renal cell carcinoma. Urology 1992, **39**: 281–284.

491 Khalyl-Mawad J, Greco MA, Schinella RA. Ultrastructural demonstration of intracellular bacteria in xanthogranulomatous pyelonephritis. Hum Pathol 1982, **13**: 41.

492 Lambrid PA, Yardley JH. Urinary tract malakoplakia. Johns Hopkins Med J 1970, **126**: 1–14.

493 Lou TY, Teplitz C. Malakoplakia: Pathogenesis and ultrastructural morphogenesis. A problem of altered macrophage (phagolysosomal) response. Hum Pathol 1974, **5**: 191–207.

494 Parsons MA, Harris SC, Longstaff AJ, Grainger RG. Xanthogranulomatous pyelonephritis: A pathological, clinical and aetiological analysis of 87 cases. Diagn Histopathol 1983, **6**: 203–219.

495 Perez LM, Thrasher JB, Anderson EE. Successful management of bilateral xanthogranulomatous pyelonephritis by bilateral partial nephrectomy. J Urol 1993, **149**: 100–102.

496 Ransley PG, Risdon RA. The renal papilla, intrarenal reflux and chronic pyelonephritis. In Hodson CJ, Kincaid-Smith P (eds): Reflux nephropathy. New York, 1979, Masson Publishing, pp. 126–133.

497 Stamey TA. Pathogenesis and treatment of urinary tract infection. Baltimore, 1980, Williams & Wilkins.

498 Tolkoff-Rubin NE, Cotran RS, Rubin RH. Urinary tract infection, pyelonephritis and reflux nephropathy. In Brenner BM (ed.): The kidney, ed. 6. Philadelphia, 2000, W.B. Saunders, pp. 1449–1508.

499 Treadwell TS, Craven DE, Delfin H, Stilmant MM, McCabe WR. Xanthogranulomatous pyelonephritis caused by methicillin-resistant Staphylococcus aureus. Am J Med 1984, **76**: 533–537.

Acute allergic tubulointerstitial nephritis

500 Branley P, Speed B. Acute interstitial nephritis due to Chlamydia psittaci. Aust NZ J Med 1995, **25**: 365.

501 Cameron JS. Immunologically mediated interstitial nephritis: Primary and secondary. Adv Nephrol 1989, **18**: 207–248.

502 Colvin RB, Fang LST. Interstitial nephritis. In Tisher CC, Brenner BM (eds): Renal pathology: With clinical and functional correlations, ed. 2, vol. I. Philadelphia, 1994, J.B. Lippincott, pp. 723–768.

503 Corwin HL, Korbet SM, Schwartz MM. Clinical correlates of eosinophiluria. Arch Intern Med 1985, **145**: 1097–1099.

504 Katz A, Fish AJ, Santamaria P, Nevins TE, Kim Y, Butkowski RJ. Role of antibodies to tubulointerstitial nephritis antigen in human anti-tubular basement membrane nephritis associated with membranous nephropathy. Am J Med 1992, **93**: 691–698.

505 Kelly CJ, Nielsen EG. Tubulointerstitial diseases. In Brenner BM (ed.): The kidney, ed. 6. Philadelphia, 2000, W.B. Saunders, pp. 1509–1536.

506 Magil AB. Drug-induced acute interstitial nephritis with granulomas. Hum Pathol 1983, **14**: 36–41.

507 Murray KM, Keane WR. Review of drug-induced acute interstitial nephritis. Pharmacotherapy 1992, **12**: 462–467.

508 Nadasdy T, Racusen L. Renal injury caused by therapeutic and diagnostic agents, and abuse of analgesics and narcotics. In Jennette JC, Olson JL, Schwartz MM, Silva FG (eds): Heptinstall's Pathology of the kidney, ed. 5. New York, 1998, Lippincott-Raven, pp. 811–861.

509 Okada K, Okamoto Y, Kagami S, Funai M, Morimoto Y, Yasutomo K, Kuroda Y. Acute interstitial nephritis and uveitis with bone marrow granulomas and anti-neutrophil cytoplasmic antibodies. Am J Nephrol 1995, **15**: 337–342.

510 Riminton S, O'Donnell J. Tubulo-interstitial nephritis and uveitis (TINU) syndrome in an adult. Aust NZ J Med 1993, **23**: 57.

511 Soffer O, Nassar VH, Campbell WG, Bourke E. Light chain nephropathy and acute renal failure associated with rifampin therapy. Am J Med 1987, **82**: 1052–1056.

512 Stupp R, Mihatsch MJ, Matter L, Streuli RA. Acute tubulo-interstitial nephritis with uveitis (TINU syndrome) in a patient with serologic evidence for Chlamydia infection. Klin Wochenschr 1990, **68**: 971–975.

Analgesic abuse nephropathy

513 Bokemeyer C, Thon WF, Brunkhorst T, Kuczyk MA, Pichlmayr R, Kliem V. High frequency of urothelial cancers in patients with kidney transplantations for end-stage analgesic nephropathy. Eur J Cancer 1996, **32A**: 175–176.

514 De Broe ME, Elseviers MM. Analgesic nephropathy. N Engl J Med 1998, **338**: 446–452.

515 Gault MH, Barrett BJ. Analgesic nephropathy. Am J Kidney Dis 1998, **32**: 351–360.

516 Griffin MD, Bergstralh EJ, Larson TS. Renal papillary necrosis: a sixteen-year clinical experience. J Am Soc Nephrol 1995, **6**: 248–256.

517 United States Renal Data System. 1996 Annual Data Report. Bethesda, MD, 1996, U.S. Department of Health and Human Services, National Institutes of Health, p. 25.

Heavy metals nephrotoxicity

518 Fowler BA. Mechanisms of kidney cell injury from metals. Environ Health Perspect 1992, **100**: 57–63.

519 Friedman AC, Lautin EM. *Cis*-platinum (II) diaminedichloride: another cause of bilateral small kidney. Urology 1980, **16**: 584–586.

520 Gonzalez-Vitale JC, Hayes DM, Cvitrovic E, Sternberg SS. The renal pathology in clinical trials of cis-platinum (II) diamminedichloride. Cancer 1977, **39**: 1362–1371.

521 Hall CL, Fothergill NG, Blackwell MM, Harrison PR, Mackenzie JC. The natural course of gold nephropathy: Long term study of 21 patients. Br Med J 1987, **295**: 745–748.

522 Hocher B, Keller F, Krause PH, Gollnick H, Oelkers W. Interstitial nephritis with reversible renal failure due to a copper-containing intrauterine device. Nephron 1992, **61**: 111–113.

523 Prasad GVR, Rossi NF. Arsenic intoxication associated with tubulointerstitial nephritis. Am J Kidney Dis 1995, **26**: 373–376.

524 Randall RE, Osheroff RJ, Bakerman S, Setter JG. Bismuth nephrotoxicity. Ann Intern Med 1972, **77**: 481–482.

525 Schumann GB, Lerner SI, Weiss MA, Gawronski L, Lohiya GK. Inclusion-bearing cells in industrial workers exposed to lead. Am J Clin Pathol 1980, **74**: 192–196.

526 Sözeri E, Feist D, Ruder H, Schärer K. Proteinuria and other renal functions in Wilson's disease. Pediatr Nephrol 1997, **11**: 307–311.

527 Wedeen RP. Heavy metals. In Schrier RW, Gottschalk CW (eds): Diseases of the kidney, ed. 5, vol. II. Boston, 1993, Little, Brown and Company, pp. 1237–1253.

528 Yasuda M, Miwa A, Kitagawa M. Morphometric studies of renal lesions in itai-itai disease: chronic cadmium nephropathy. Nephron 1995, **69**: 14–19.

Pyelitis and ureteritis cystica

529 Hinman F, Cordonnier J. Cystitis follicularis. J Urol 1935, **34**: 302–308.

Pelvic lipomatosis

530 Hamm FC, DeVeer JA. Fatty replacement following renal atrophy or destruction. J Urol 1939, **41**: 850–866.

531 Young HH. Lipomatosis or destructive fat replacement of renal cortex. Report of 11 cases. J Urol 1933, **29**: 631–644.

Nephrolithiasis and nephrocalcinosis

532 Crawhall JC, Purkiss P, Watts RWE, Young EP. The excretion of amino acids by cystinuric patients and their relatives. Ann Hum Genet 1969, **33**: 149–169.

533 Gelbart GR, Brewer LL, Fajardo LF. Oxalosis and chronic renal failure after intestinal bypass. Arch Intern Med 1977, **137**: 239–243.

534 Gutman AB, Yu T-F. Uric acid nephrolithiasis. Am J Med 1968, **45**: 756–779.

535 Johnson RJ, Kivlighu S, Kim YK, Suga S, Fogo A. A reappraisal of the pathogenesis and consequences of hyperuricemia in hypertension. Am J Kidney Dis 1999, **33**: 224–234.

536 Nickeleit V, Mihatsch MJ. Uric acid nephropathy and the end stage renal disease – review of a non-disease. Nephrol Dial Transplant 1997, **12**: 1832–1838.

537 Polinsky MS, Kaiser BA, Baluarte HJ, Gruskin AB. Renal stones and hypercalciuria. Adv Pediatr 1993, **40**: 353–384.

538 Sergeant LE, deGroot GW, Dilling LA, Mallory CJ, Haworth JC. Primary oxaluria type 2 (L-glyceric aciduria): A rare cause of nephrolithiasis in children. J Pediatr 1991, **118**: 912–914.

539 Shakhaee K. Pathogenesis and medical management of cystinuria. Semin Nephrol 1996, **16**: 435–437.

540 Smith LH. The medical aspects of urolithiasis: an overview. J Urol 1989, **141**: 707–710.

541 Smith LH. The pathophysiology and medical treatment of urolithiasis. Semin Nephrol 1990, **10**: 31–52.

542 Talbott JH. Gout. Med Clin North Am 1970, **54**: 431–441.

Myeloma cast nephropathy

543 Carstens PHB, Woo D. Crystalline glomerular inclusions in multiple myeloma. Am J Kidney Dis 1989, **14**: 56–60.

544 Sedmak DD, Tubbs RR. The macrophagic origin of multinucleated giant cells in myeloma kidney: An immunohistochemical study. Hum Pathol 1987, **18**: 304–306.

545 Start DA, Silva FG, Davis L, D'Agati V, Pirani CL. Myeloma cast nephropathy: Immunohistochemical and lectin studies. Mod Pathol 1988, **1**: 336–347.

Renal vascular disease
Renal arteriolar disease

546 Bohle A, Ratschek M. The compensated and decompensated form of benign nephrosclerosis. Pathol Res Pract 1982, **174**: 357–367.

547 Kashgarian M. Pathology of the kidney in hypertension. In Kaplan NM, Brenner BM, Laragh JH (eds): The kidney in hypertension. New York, 1987, Raven Press, pp. 77–89.

548 Kincaid-Smith P. Malignant hypertension. Mechanisms and management. Pharmacol Ther 1980, **9**: 245–269.

549 Valenzuela R, Gogate PA, Deodar SD, Gifford RW. Hyaline arteriolonephrosclerosis. Immunofluorescent findings in vascular lesions. Lab Invest 1980, **43**: 530–534.

Renal arterial disease

550 Breslin DJ, Swinton NW, Libertino JA, Zinman L. Renovascular hypertension. Baltimore, 1982, Williams & Wilkins.

551 Chugh KS, Jain S, Sakhuja V, Malik N, Gupta A, Sengal S, Jha V, Gupta KL. Renovascular hypertension due to Takayasu's arteritis among Indian patients. Q J Med 1992, **85**: 833–843.

552 Gerlock AJ Jr, Goncharenko VA, Ekelund L. Radiation-induced stenosis of the renal artery causing hypertension: Case report. J Urol 1977, **118**: 1064–1065.

553 Harrison EG, McCormack LV. Pathologic classification of renal arterial disease in renovascular hypertension. Mayo Clin Proc 1971, **46**: 161–166.

554 Luscher TF, Lie JT, Stanson AW, Houser OW, Hollier CH, Sheps SG. Arterial fibromuscular dysplasia. Mayo Clin Proc 1987, **62**: 931–952.

555 McCormack LJ, Poutasse EF, Meaney TF, Noto TJ, Duston HP. Arteriographic correlations of renal artery disease. Am Heart J 1966, **72**: 188–198.

556 Ram CV. Current concepts in renovascular hypertension. Am J Med Sci 1992, **304**: 53–71.

557 Stanley JC, Ernst CB, Fry WJ. Renovascular hypertension. Philadelphia, 1984, W.B. Saunders.

Radiation nephropathy

558 Alpers CE. Irradiation injury. In Jennette JC, Olson JL, Schwartz MM, Silva FG (eds): Heptinstall's Pathology of the kidney, ed. 5. Philadelphia, 1998, Lippincott-Raven, pp. 1131–1148.

559 Crosson JT, Keane WF, Anderson WR. Radiation nephropathy. In Tisher CC, Brenner BM (eds): Renal pathology: With clinical and functional correlations, ed. 2, vol. I. Philadelphia, 1994, J.B. Lippincott, pp. 937–947.

560 Jennette JC, Ordóñez NG. Radiation nephritis causing nephrotic syndrome. Urology 1983, **22**: 631–634.

561 Keane WF, Crosson JT, Staley NA, Anderson WR, Shapiro FL. Radiation-induced renal disease: A clinicopathologic study. Am J Med 1976, **60**: 127–137.

Bone marrow transplant nephropathy

562 Alpers CE. Irradiation injury. In Jennette JC, Olson JL, Schwartz MM, Silva FG (eds): Heptinstall's Pathology of the kidney, ed. 5. Philadelphia, 1998, Lippincott-Raven, pp. 1131–1148.

563 Cohen EP, Lawton CA, Moulder JE. Bone marrow transplant nephropathy: radiation nephritis revisited. Nephron 1995, **70**: 217–222.

564 Cohen EP, Lawton CA, Moulder JE, Becker CG, Ash RC. Clinical course of late-onset bone marrow transplant nephropathy. Nephron 1993, **64**: 626–635.

Cystic diseases of the kidney
Multicystic renal dysplasia

565 Bernstein J, Gardner KD Jr. Cystic disease and dysplasia of the kidneys. In Williams MM (ed.): Urological pathology, ed. 2. Philadelphia, 1997, W.B. Saunders, pp. 503–538.

566 Okayasu I, Kaijita A. Histopathological study of congenital cystic kidneys with special reference to the multicystic, dysplastic type. Acta Pathol Jpn 1978, **28**: 427–434.

567 Risdon RA. Renal dysplasia. Part I. A clinical pathologic study of 76 cases. Part II. A necroscopy study of 41 cases. J Clin Pathol 1971, **24**: 57–71.

Autosomal dominant (adult) polycystic kidney disease

568 Ceccherini I, Lituania M, Cordone MS, Perfumo F, Gusmano R, Callea F, Archidiacono N, Romeo G. Autosomal dominant polycystic kidney disease: Prenatal diagnosis by DNA analysis and sonography at 14 weeks. Prenat Diagn 1989, **9**: 751–758.

569 Christ M, Bechtel U, Schnaack S, Theisen K, Wehling M. Aneurysms of coronary arteries in a patient with adult polycystic kidney disease: arteriosclerosis or involvement by the primary disease? Clin Invest 1993, **71**: 150–152.

570 Gabow P. Autosomal dominant polycystic kidney disease – more than just a renal disease. Am J Kidney Dis 1990, **14**: 403–413.

571 Gabow PA. Definition and natural history of autosomal dominant polycystic kidney disease. In Watson ML, Torres VE (eds): Polycystic kidney disease. Oxford, 1996, Oxford University Press, pp. 333–355.

572 Gabow P, Johnson AM, Kaehny WD, Manco-Johnson ML, Duley IT, Everson GT. Risk factors for the development of hepatic cysts in autosomal dominant polycystic kidney disease. Hepatology 1990, **11**: 1033–1037.

573 Grantham JJ. Polycystic kidney disease: hereditary and acquired. Adv Intern Med 1993, **38**: 409–420.

574 Gregoire JR, Torres VE, Holley KE, Farrow GM. Renal epithelial hyperplastic and neoplastic proliferations in autosomal dominant polycystic kidney disease. Am J Kidney Dis 1987, **9**: 27–38.

575 Hossack KF, Leddy CL, Johnson AM, Schrier RW, Gabow PA. Echocardiographic findings in autosomal dominant polycystic disease. N Engl J Med 1988, **319**: 907–912.

576 Kimberling WJ, Kumar S, Gabow PA, Kenyon JB, Connolly CJ, Somlo S. Autosomal dominant polycystic kidney disease: localization of the second gene to chromosome 4q13–q23. Genomics 1993, **18**: 467–472.

577 Kossow AS, Meek JM. Unilateral adult polycystic kidney disease. J Urol 1982, **127**: 297–300.

578 O'Sullivan DA, Torres VE. Autosomal dominant polycystic kidney disease. In Johnson RJ, Feehally J (eds): Comprehensive clinical nephrology. London, 2000, Harcourt, pp. 9.49.1–9.49.12.

579 Reeders ST, Breuning MH, Davies KE, Nichols RD, Jarman AP, Higgs DR, Pearson PL, Weatherall DJ. A highly polymorphic DNA marker linked to adult polycystic kidney disease on chromosome 16. Nature 1985, **317**: 542–544.

580 Sheff RT, Zuckerman G, Harter H, Delmez J, Koehler R. Diverticular disease in patients with chronic renal failure due to polycystic kidney disease. Ann Intern Med 1980, **92**: 202–204.

581 Torra R, Nicolau C, Badenas C, Bru C, Perez L, Estivill X, Darnell A. Abdominal aortic aneurysms and autosomal dominant polycystic kidney disease. J Am Soc Nephrol 1996, **7**: 2483–2486.

582 Torres VE, Wiehers DO, Forbes GS. Cranial computed tomography and magnetic resonance imaging in autosomal dominant polycystic kidney disease. J Am Soc Nephrol 1990, **1**: 84–90.

583 Turco AE, Padovani EM, Chiaffoni GP, Peissel B, Rossetti S, Marcolongo A, Gammaro L, Maschio G, Pignatti PF. Molecular genetic diagnosis of autosomal dominant polycystic kidney disease in a newborn with bilateral cystic kidneys detected prenatally and multiple skeletal malformations. J Med Genet 1993, **30**: 419–422.

Autosomal recessive (infantile) polycystic kidney disease

584 Bernstein J. Hepatic and renal involvement in malformation syndromes. Mt Sinai J Med 1986, **53**: 421–428.

585 Guay-Woodford LM, Muecher G, Hopkins SD, Avner ED, Germino GG, Guillot AP, Herrin J, Holleman R, Irons DA, Primack W. The severe perinatal form of autosomal recessive polycystic kidney disease (ARPKD) maps to chromosome 6p21.1–p12: implications for genetic counseling. Am J Hum Genet 1995, **56**: 1101–1107.

586 Mücher G, Becker J, Knapp M, Buettner R, Moser M, Rudnik-Schöneborn S, Somlo S, Germino G, Onuchic L, Avner E, Guay-Woodford L, Zerres K. Fine mapping of the autosomal recessive polycystic kidney disease locus (PKHD1) and the genes MUT, RDS, CSNK2β, and GSTA1 at 6p21.1–p12. Genomics 1998, **48**: 40–45.

587 Roy S, Dillon M, Trompeter R, Barratt T. Autosomal recessive polycystic kidney disease: long-term outcome of neonatal survivors. Pediatr Nephrol 1997, **11**: 302–306.

588 Zerres K, Mücher G, Bachner L, Deschennes G, Eggermann T, Kääriäinen H, Knapp M, Lennert T, Misselwitz J, von Mühlendahl KE, Neumann HPH, Pirson Y, Rudnik-Schöneborn S, Steinbicker V, Wirth B, Schärer K. Mapping of the gene for autosomal recessive polycystic kidney disease (ARPKD) to chromosome 6p21-cen. Nat Genet 1994, **7**: 429–432.

589 Zerres K, Rudnik-Schöneborn S, Deget F, Holtkamp U, Brodehl J, Geisert J, Scharer K. Autosomal recessive polycystic kidney disease in 115 children: clinical presentation, course and influence of gender. Acta Paediatr 1996, **85**: 437–445.

Medullary sponge kidney

590 Bernstein J, Gardner KD Jr. Cystic disease and dysplasia of the kidneys. In Williams MM (ed.): Urological pathology, ed. 2. Philadelphia, 1997, W.B. Saunders, pp. 503–538.

591 Ginalski J, Portmann L, Jaeger P. Does medullary sponge kidney really cause nephrolithiasis. Am J Roentgenol 1990, **155**: 299–302.

592 Harrison AR, Rose GA. Medullary sponge kidney. Urol Res 1979, **7**: 197–207.

593 Kliger AS, Scheer RL. Familial disease of the renal medulla. A study of progeny in a family with medullary cystic disease. Ann Intern Med 1976, **85**: 190–194.

594 Kuiper JJ. Medullary sponge kidney in three generations. NY State J Med 1971, **71**: 2665–2669.

595 Kuiper JJ. Medullary sponge kidney. In Gardner KD Jr (ed.): Cystic disease of the kidney. New York, 1976, John Wiley & Sons, pp. 151–172.

596 Yendt ER. Medullary sponge kidney and nephrolithiasis. N Engl J Med 1982, **306:** 1106–1107.

Nephronophthisis–medullary cystic kidney disease complex

597 Betz R, Rensing C, Otto E, Mincheva A, Zehnder D, Lichter P, Hildebrandt F. Children with ocular motor apraxia type Cogan carry deletions in the gene (NPHP1) for juvenile nephronophthisis. J Pediatr 2000, **136:** 828–831.

598 Boichis H, Passwell J, David R, Miller H. Congenital hepatic fibrosis and nephronophthisis. A family study. Q J Med 1973, **42:** 221–233.

599 Christodoulou K, Tsingis M, Stavrou C, Elftheriou A, Papapavlou P, Patsalis PC, Ioannou P, Pierides A, Constantinou Deltas C. Chromosome 1 localization of a gene for autosomal dominant medullary cystic kidney disease (ADMCKD). Hum Mol Genet 1998, **7:** 905–911.

600 Cohen AH, Hoyer JR. Nephronophthisis. A primary tubular basement membrane defect. Lab Invest 1986, **55:** 564–572.

601 Fanconi G, Hanhart E, Albertini A. Die familiare juvenile Nephronophthise. Hel Pediatr Acta 1951, **6:** 1–49.

602 Haider NB, Carmi R, Shalev H, Sheffield VC, Landau D. A Bedouin kindred with infantile nephronophthisis demonstrates linkage to chromosome 9 by homozygosity mapping. Am J Hum Genet 1998, **63:** 1404–1410.

603 Hildebrandt F, Omram H. New insights: nephronophthisis-medullary cystic kidney disease. Pediatr Nephrol 2001, **16:** 168–176.

604 Hildebrandt F, Otto E. Molecular genetics of nephronophthisis and medullary cystic kidney disease. J Am Soc Nephrol 2000, **11:** 1753–1761.

605 Hildebrandt F, Otto E, Rensing C, Nothwang HG, Vollmer M, Adolphs J, Hanusch H, Brandis M. A novel gene encoding an SH3 domain protein is mutated in nephronophthisis type 1. Nat Genet 1997, **17:** 149–153.

606 Loken A, Hanssen O, Halvorsen S, Jolster N. Hereditary renal dysplasia and blindness. Acta Pediatr 1961, **50:** 177–184.

607 Mainzer F, Saldino RM, Ozonoff MB, Minagi H. Familial nephropathy associated with retinitis pigmentosa, cerebellar ataxia and skeletal abnormalities. Am J Med 1970, **49:** 556–562.

608 Omran H, Fernandez C, Jung M, Häffner K, Fargier B, Villaquiran A, Waldherr R, Gretz N, Brandis M, Rüschendorf F, Reis A, Hildebrandt F. Identification of a new gene locus for adolescent nephronophthisis, on chromosome 3q22 in a large Venezuelan pedigree. Am J Hum Genet 2000, **66:** 118–127.

609 Saraiva JM, Baraitser M. Joubert syndrome: A review. Am J Med Genet 1992, **43:** 726–731.

610 Scolari F, Puzzer D, Amoroso A, Caridi G, Ghiggeri GM, Maiorca R, Aridon P, De Fusco M, Ballabio A, Casari G. Identification of a new locus for medullary cystic disease, on chromosome 16p12. Am J Hum Genet 1999, **64:** 1655–1660.

611 Senior B, Friedmann A, Braudo J. Juvenile familial nephropathy with tapetoretinal degeneration: A new oculorenal dystrophy. Am J Ophthalmol 1961, **52:** 625–633.

612 Welling LW, Grantham JJ. Cystic diseases of the kidney. In Tisher CC, Brenner BM (eds): Renal pathology: With clinical and functional correlations, ed. 2, vol II. Philadelphia, 1994, J.B. Lippincott, pp. 1312–1354.

Acquired cystic renal disease

613 Gabow PA. Polycystic and acquired cystic diseases. In Greenberg A (ed.): Primer on kidney diseases, ed. 2. San Diego, 1998, Academic Press, pp. 313–318.

614 Hughson MD. End-stage renal disease. In Jennette JC, Olson JL, Schwartz MM, Silva FG (eds): Heptinstall's Pathology of the kidney, ed. 5. Philadelphia, 1998, Lippincott-Raven, pp. 1371–1408.

615 Mickisch O, Bommer J, Bachmann S, Waldherr R, Mann JFE, Ritz E. Multicystic transformation of kidneys in chronic renal failure. Nephron 1984, **38:** 93–99.

616 Yamaguchi S, Fujii H, Kaneko S, Yachiku S, Anzai T, Inada F, Kobayashi T, Furuta K, Ishida H. Ultrasonographic study on kidneys in patients with chronic renal failure. Part II. Acquired cystic disease of the kidneys. Nippon Hinyokika Gakkai Zasshi 1990, **81:** 1183–1189.

Simple cysts

617 Gabow PA. Polycystic and acquired cystic diseases. In Greenberg A (ed.): Primer on kidney diseases, ed. 2. San Diego, 1998, Academic Press, pp. 313–318.

PEDIATRIC TUMORS AND TUMORLIKE CONDITIONS
Wilms' tumor
General features

618 Babaian RJ, Skinner DG, Waisman J. Wilms' tumor in the adult patient. Diagnosis, management, and review of the world medical literature. Cancer 1980, **45:** 1713–1719.

619 Benatar B, Wright C, Freinkel AL, Cooper K. Primary extrarenal Wilms' tumor of the uterus presenting as a cervical polyp. Int J Gynecol Pathol 1998, **17:** 277–280.

619a Bissig H, Staehelin F, Tolnay M, Avoledo P, Richter J, Betts D, Bruder E, Kühne T. Co-occurrence of neuroblastoma and nephroblastoma in an infant with Fanconi's anemia. Hum Pathol 2002, **33:** 1047–1051.

620 Bolande RP. Neoplasia of early life and its relationships to teratogenesis. Perspect Pediatr Pathol 1976, **3:** 145–183.

621 Breslow NE, Takashima JR, Whitton JA, Moksness J, D'Angio GJ, Green DM. Second malignant neoplasms following treatment for Wilms' tumor. A report from the National Wilms' Tumor Study Group. J Clin Oncol 1995, **13:** 1851–1859.

622 Chevalier G, Yeger H, Martinerie C, Laurent M, Alami J, Schofield PN, Perbal B. novH: Differential expression in developing kidney and Wilms' tumors. Am J Pathol 1998, **152:** 1563–1575.

623 Clericuzio CL. Clinical phenotypes and Wilms tumor. Med Pediatr Oncol 1993, **21:** 182–187.

624 Crist WM, Kun LE. Common solid tumors of childhood. N Engl J Med 1991, **324:** 461–471.

625 Hentrich MU, Meister P, Brack NG, Lutz LL, Hartenstein RC. Adult Wilms' tumor. Report of two cases and review of the literature. Cancer 1995, **75:** 545–551.

626 Ho J, Ma L, Wong KC. An extrarenal Wilms' tumor arising from an undescended testis. Pathology 1981, **13:** 619–624.

627 Hrabovsky EE, Othersen HB Jr, deLorimier A, Kelalis P, Beckwith JB, Takashima J. Wilms' tumor in the neonate. A report from the National Wilms' Tumor Study. J Pediatr Surg 1986, **21:** 385–387.

628 Huser J, Grignon DJ, Ro JY, Ayala AG, Shannon RL, Papadopoulos NJ. Adult Wilms' tumor. A clinicopathologic study of 11 cases. Mod Pathol 1990, **3:** 321–326.

629 Juberg RC, St. Martin EC, Hundley JR. Familial occurrence of Wilms' tumor. Nephroblastoma in one of monozygous twins and in other sibling. Am J Hum Genet 1975, **27:** 155–164.

630 Kissane JM, Dehner LP. Renal tumors and tumor-like lesions in pediatric patients. Pediatr Nephrol 1992, **6:** 365–382.

631 Kovalic JJ, Thomas PR, Beckwith JB, Feusner JH, Norkool PA. Hepatocellular carcinoma as second malignant neoplasms in successfully treated Wilms' tumor patients. A National Wilms' Tumor Study report. Cancer 1991, **67:** 342–344.

631a Li C-M, Guo M, Borczuk A, Powell CA, Wei M, Thaker HM, Friedman R, Klein U, Tycko B. Gene expression in Wilms' tumor mimics the earliest committed stage in the metanephric mesenchymal-epithelial transition. Am J Pathol 2002, **160:** 2181–2190.

632 Luchtrath H, deLeon F, Giesen H, Gok Y. Inguinal nephroblastoma. Virchows Arch [A] 1984, **405**: 113–118.

633 Manivel JC, Sibley RK, Dehner LP. Complete and incomplete Drash syndrome. A clinicopathologic study of five cases of a dysontogenetic-neoplastic complex. Hum Pathol 1987, **18**: 80–89.

634 Merten DF, Yang SS, Bernstein J. Wilms' tumor in adolescence. Cancer 1976, **37**: 1532–1538.

635 Miller RW, Fraumeni JF, Manning MD. Association of Wilms' tumor with aniridia, hemihypertrophy and other congenital malformations. N Engl J Med 1964, **270**: 922–927.

636 Mount SL, Dickerman JD, Taatjes DJ. Extrarenal Wilm's tumor: An ultrastructural and immunoelectron microscopic case report. Ultrastruct Pathol 1996, **20**: 155–166.

637 Nakamura Y, Nakashima T, Nakashima H, Hashimoto T. Bilateral cystic nephroblastomas and botryoid sarcoma involving vagina and urinary bladder in a child with microcephaly, arhinencephaly, and bilateral cataracts. Cancer 1981, **48**: 1012–1015.

638 Olshan AF, Breslow NE, Falletta JM, Grufferman S, Pendergrass T, Robison LL, Waskerwitz M, Woods WG, Vietti TJ, Hammond GD. Risk factors for Wilms tumor. Report from the National Wilms Tumor Study. Cancer 1993, **72**: 938–944.

639 Paulino AC, Thakkar B, Henderson WG. Metachronous bilateral Wilms' tumor: the importance of time interval to the development of a second tumor. Cancer 1998, **82**: 415–420.

640 Ragab AH, Vietti TJ, Crist W, Perez C, McAllister W. Bilateral Wilms' tumor. A review. Cancer 1972, **30**: 983–988.

641 Rajfer J. Association between Wilms' tumor and gonadal dysgenesis. J Urol 1981, **125**: 388–390.

642 Roberts DJ, Haber D, Sklar J, Crum CP. Extrarenal Wilms' tumors. A study of their relationship with classical renal Wilms' tumor using expression of WT1 as a molecular marker. Lab Invest 1993, **68**: 528–536.

643 Sarode VR, Savitri K, Banerjee CK, Narasimharao KL, Khajuria A. Primary extrarenal Wilms' tumor. Identification of a putative precursor lesion. Histopathology 1992, **21**: 76–78.

644 Shearer P, Parham DM, Fontanesi J, Kumar M, Lobe TE, Fairclough D, Douglass EC, Wilimas J. Bilateral Wilms tumor. Review of outcome, associated abnormalities, and late effects in 36 pediatric patients treated at a single institution. Cancer 1993, **72**: 1422–1426.

645 Sotelo-Avila C, Gooch WM III. Neoplasms associated with the Beckwith-Wiedemann syndrome. Perspect Pediatr Pathol 1976, **3**: 255–272.

646 Stay EJ, Vawter G. The relationship between nephroblastoma and neurofibromatosis (von Recklinghausen's disease). Cancer 1977, **39**: 2550–2555.

647 Wakely PE Jr, Sprague RI, Kornstein MJ. Extrarenal Wilms' tumor. An analysis of four cases. Hum Pathol 1989, **20**: 691–695.

648 Ward SP, Dehner LP. Sacrococcygeal teratoma with nephroblastoma (Wilms' tumor). A variant of extragonadal teratoma in childhood. A histologic and ultrastructural study. Cancer 1974, **33**: 1355–1363.

649 Webber BL, Parham DM, Drake LG, Wilimas JA. Renal tumors in childhood. Pathol Annu 1992, **27**(Pt 1): 191–232.

650 Williams G, Colbeck RA, Gowing NF. Adult Wilms' tumour. Review of 14 patients. Br J Urol 1992, **70**: 230–235.

651 Yashima K, Maitra A, Timmons CF, Rogers BB, Pinar H, Shay JW, Gazday AF. Expression of the RNA component of the telomerase in Wilms' tumor and nephrogenic rest recapitulates renal embryogenesis. Hum Pathol 1998, **29**: 536–542.

Clinical features

652 Coppes MJ. Serum biological markers and paraneoplastic syndromes in Wilms tumor. Med Pediatr Oncol 1993, **21**: 213–221.

653 Coppes MJ, Zandvoort SW, Sparling CR, Poon AO, Weitzman S, Blanchette VS. Acquired von Willebrand disease in Wilms' tumor patients. J Clin Oncol 1992, **10**: 422–427.

654 Johnston MA, Carachi R, Lindop GB, Leckie B. Inactive renin levels in recurrent nephroblastoma. J Pediatr Surg 1991, **26**: 613–614.

655 Murphy GP, Mirand EA, Johnston GS, Gibbons RP, Jones RL, Scott WW. Erythropoietin release associated with Wilms' tumor. Johns Hopkins Med J 1967, **120**: 26–32.

656 Sheth KJ, Tang TT, Blaedel ME, Good TA. Polydipsia, polyuria, and hypertension associated with renin-secreting Wilms' tumor. J Pediatr 1978, **92**: 921–924.

657 Stern M, Longaker MT, Adzick NS, Harrison MR, Stern R. Hyaluronidase levels in urine from Wilms' tumor patients. J Natl Cancer Inst 1991, **83**: 1569–1574.

658 Thorner P, McGraw M, Weitzman S, Balfe JW, Klein M, Baumal R. Wilms' tumor and glomerular disease. Occurrence with features of membranoproliferative glomerulonephritis and secondary focal, segmented glomerulosclerosis. Arch Pathol Lab Med 1984, **108**: 141–146.

659 Zakowski MF, Edwards RH, McDonough ET. Wilms' tumor presenting as sudden death due to tumor embolism. Arch Pathol Lab Med 1990, **114**: 605–608.

Morphologic features

660 Allsbrook WC, Boswell WC, Takahashi R, Pantazis CG, Howell CG Jr, Martinez JE, Beck JR. Recurrent renal cell carcinoma arising in Wilms' tumor. Cancer 1991, **67**: 690–695.

661 Balsaver AM, Gibley CW Jr, Tessmer CF. Ultrastructural studies in Wilms' tumor. Cancer 1968, **22**: 417–427.

662 Beckwith JB. Wilms' tumor and other renal tumors of childhood. A selective review from the National Wilms' Study Pathology Center. Hum Pathol 1983, **14**: 481–492.

663 Charles AK, Vujanic GM, Berry PJ. Review: renal tumours of childhood. Histopathology 1998, **32**: 293–309.

664 Chatten J. Epithelial differentiation in Wilms' tumor. A clinicopathologic appraisal. Perspect Pediatr Pathol 1976, **3**: 225–254.

665 Delemarre JFM, Sandstedt B, Tournade MF. Nephroblastoma with fibroadenomatous-like structures. Histopathology 1984, **8**: 55–62.

666 Edwards O, Chatten J. Hydropic cell variant (clear cell variant) of Wilms' tumor. Arch Pathol Lab Med 1985, **109**: 956–958.

667 Garvin AJ, Surrette F, Hintz DS, Rudisill MT, Sens MA, Sens DA. The in vitro growth and characterization of the skeletal muscle component of Wilms' tumor. Am J Pathol 1985, **121**: 298–310.

668 Gonzalez-Crussi F, Hsueh W, Ugarte N. Rhabdomyogenesis in renal neoplasia of childhood. Am J Surg Pathol 1981, **5**: 525–532.

669 Grimes MM, Wolff M, Wolff JA, Jaretzki A III, Blanc WA. Ganglion cells in metastatic Wilms' tumor. Review of a histogenetic controversy. Am J Surg Pathol 1982, **6**: 565–571.

670 Hennigar RA, Spice SA, Sens DA, Othersen JB Jr, Garvin JA. Histochemical evidence for tubule segmentation in a case of Wilms' tumor. Am J Clin Pathol 1986, **85**: 724–731.

671 Hou LT, Azzopardi JG. Muco-epidermoid metaplasia and argentaffin cells in nephroblastoma. J Pathol Bacteriol 1967, **93**: 477–481.

672 Hughson MD, Hennigar GR, Othersen HB Jr. Cyto-differentiated renal tumors occurring with Wilms' tumor of the opposite kidneys. Report of two cases. Am J Clin Pathol 1976, **66**: 376–389.

673 Jenkins MC, Allibone EB, Berry PJ. Neuroglial tissue in partially cystic Wilms' tumour. Histopathology 1991, **18**: 309–313.

674 Joshi VV, Beckwith JB. Pathologic delineation of the papillonodular type of cystic partially differentiated nephroblastoma. A review of 11 cases. Cancer 1990, **66**: 1568–1577.

675 Kodet R, Marsden HB. Papillary Wilms' tumour with carcinoma-like foci and renal cell carcinoma in childhood. Histopathology 1985, **9**: 1091–1102.

676 Lindop GBM, Fleming S, Gibson AAM. Immunocytochemical localisation of renin in nephroblastoma. J Clin Pathol 1984, **37**: 738–742.

677 Magee JF, Ansari S, McFadden DE, Dimmick J. Teratoid Wilms' tumour. A report of two cases. Histopathology 1992, **20**: 427–431.

678 Mahoney JP, Saffos RO. Fetal rhabdomyomatous nephroblastoma with a renal pelvic mass simulating sarcoma botryoides. Am J Surg Pathol 1981, **5**: 297–306.

679 Marsden HB. The pathology and natural history of childhood tumours. Recent Results Cancer Res 1983, **88**: 11–25.

680 Masson P. The role of the neural crest in the embryonal adenosarcomas of the kidney. Am J Cancer 1938, **33**: 1–32.

681 Mierau GW, Beckwith JB, Weeks DA. Ultrastructure and histogenesis of the renal tumors of childhood. An overview. Ultrastruct Pathol 1987, **11**: 313–333.

682 Pawel BR, de Chadarevian J-P, Smergel EM, Weintraub WH. Teratoid Wilms' tumor arising as a botryoid growth within a supernumerary ectopic ureteropelvic structure. Arch Pathol Lab Med 1998, **122**: 925–928.

683 Variend S, Spicer RD, Mackinnon AE. Teratoid Wilms' tumor. Cancer 1984, **53**: 1936–1942.

684 Weinberg AG, Currarino G, Hurt GE Jr. Botryoid Wilms' tumor of the renal pelvis. Arch Pathol Lab Med 1984, **108**: 147–148.

685 Wigger HJ. Fetal rhabdomyomatous nephroblastoma. A variant of Wilms' tumor. Hum Pathol 1976, **7**: 613–632.

686 Yeger H, Baumal R, Harason P, Phillips MJ. Lectin histochemistry of Wilms' tumor. Comparison with normal adult and fetal kidney. Am J Clin Pathol 1987, **88**: 278–285.

Immunohistochemical and other special techniques

687 Baccarini P, Fiorentino M, D'Errico A, Mancini AM, Grigioni WF. Detection of anti-sense transcripts of the insulin-like growth factor-2 gene in Wilms' tumor. Am J Pathol 1993, **143**: 1535–1542.

688 Droz D, Rousseau-Merck MF, Jaubert F, Diebold N, Nezelof C, Adafer E, Mouly H. Cell differentiation in Wilms' tumor (nephroblastoma). An immunohistochemical study. Hum Pathol 1990, **21**: 536–544.

689 Folpe AL, Patterson K, Gown AM. Antibodies to desmin identify the blastemal component of nephroblastoma. Mod Pathol 1997, **10**: 895–900.

690 Gansler T, Allen KD, Burant DF, Inabnett T, Scott A, Buse MG, Sens DA, Garvin AJ. Detection of type 1 insulinlike growth factor (IGF) receptors in Wilms' tumors. Am J Pathol 1988, **130**: 431–435.

691 Hennigar RA, Garvin AJ, Hazen-Martin DJ, Schulte BA. Immunohistochemical localization of transport mediators in Wilms' tumor. Comparison with fetal and mature human kidney. Lab Invest 1989, **61**: 192–201.

692 Magee F, Mah RG, Taylor GP, Dimmick JE. Neural differentiation in Wilms' tumor. Hum Pathol 1987, **18**: 33–37.

693 Paik S, Rosen N, Jung W, You JM, Lippman ME, Perdue JF, Yee D. Expression of insulin-like growth factor-II mRNA in fetal kidney and Wilms' tumor. An in situ hybridization study. Lab Invest 1989, **61**: 522–526.

694 Sariola H, Ekblom P, Rapola J, Vaheri A, Timpl R. Extracellular matrix and epithelial differentiation of Wilms' tumor. Am J Pathol 1985, **118**: 96–107.

Electron microscopic features

695 Mierau GW, Beckwith JB, Weeks DA. Ultrastructure and histogenesis of the renal tumors of childhood. An overview. Ultrastruct Pathol 1987, **11**: 313–333.

696 Mierau GW, Weeks DA, Beckwith JB. Anaplastic Wilms' tumor and other clinically aggressive childhood renal neoplasms. Ultrastructural and immunocytochemical features. Ultrastruct Pathol 1989, **13**: 225–248.

697 Roth J, Zuber C. Immunoelectron microscopic investigation of surface coat of Wilms tumor cells. Dense lamina is composed of highly sialylated neural cell adhesion molecule. Lab Invest 1990, **62**: 55–60.

698 Weeks DA, Mierau GW, Malott RL, Beckwith JB. Practical electron microscopy of pediatric renal tumors. Ultrastruct Pathol 1996, **20**: 31–34.

Molecular genetic features

699 Coppes MJ, Haber DA, Grundy PE. Genetic events in the development of Wilms' tumor. N Engl J Med 1994, **331**: 586–590.

700 Dowdy SF, Fasching CL, Araujo D, Lai KM, Livanos E, Weissman BE, Stanbridge EJ. Suppression of tumorigenicity in Wilms tumor by the p15.5–p14 region of chromosome 11. Science 1991, **254**: 293–295.

701 El Bahtimi R, Hazen-Martin DJ, Re GG, Willingham MC, Garvin AJ. Immunophenotype, mRNA expression, and gene structure of p53 in Wilms' tumors. Mod Pathol 1996, **9**: 238–244.

702 Gerald WL, Gramling TS, Sens DA, Garvin AJ. Expression of the 11p13 Wilms' tumor gene, WT1, correlates with histologic category of Wilms' tumor. Am J Pathol 1992, **140**: 1031–1037.

703 Govender D. The genetics of Wilms tumor. Adv Anat Pathol 1997, **4**: 202–206.

704 Kikuchi H, Akasaka Y, Nagai T, Umezawa A, Iri H, Kato S, Hata J. Genomic changes in the WT-gene (WT1) in Wilms' tumors and their correlation with histology. Am J Pathol 1992, **140**: 781–786.

705 Malik K, Yan P, Huang THM, Brown KW. Wilms' tumor: a paradigm for the new genetics. Oncol Res 2001, **12**: 441–449.

706 Re GG, Hazen-Martin DJ, Sens DA, Garvin AJ. Nephroblastoma (Wilms' tumor). A model system of aberrant renal development. Semin Diagn Pathol 1994, **11**: 126–135.

707 Rubin BP, Pins MR, Neilsen GP, Rosen S, Hsi B-L, Fletcher JA, Renshaw AA. Isochromosome 7q in adult Wilms' tumors: diagnostic and pathogenetic implications. Am J Surg Pathol 2000, **24**: 1663–1669.

708 Sheng WW, Soukup S, Bove K, Gotwals G, Lampkin B. Chromosome analysis of 31 Wilms' tumors. Cancer Res 1990, **50**: 2786–2793.

709 Slater RM, deKraker J. Chromosome number 11 and Wilms' tumor. Cancer Genet Cytogenet 1982, **5**: 237–246.

710 Slater RM, Mannens MM. Cytogenetics and molecular genetics of Wilms' tumor of childhood. Cancer Genet Cytogenet 1992, **61**: 111–121.

711 Takeuchi S, Bartram CR, Ludwig R, Royer-Pokora B, Schneider S, Imamura J, Koeffler HP. Mutations of p53 in Wilms' tumors. Mod Pathol 1995, **8**: 483–487.

712 Telerman A, Dodemont H, Degraef C, Galand P, Bauwens S, Van Oostveldt P, Amson RB. Identification of the cellular protein encoded by the human Wilms' tumor (WT1) gene. Oncogene 1992, **7**: 2545–2548.

713 van Heyningen V, Bickmore WA, Seawright A, Fletcher JM, Maule J, Fekete G, Gessler M, Bruns GA, Huerre-Jeanpierre C, Junien C, et al. Role for the Wilms tumor gene in genital development? Proc Natl Acad Sci U S A 1990, **87**: 5383–5386.

714 Yeger H, Cullinane C, Flenniken A, Chilton-MacNeil S, Campbell C, Huang A, Bonetta L, Coppes MJ, Thorner P, Williams BR. Coordinate expression of Wilms' tumor genes correlates with Wilms' tumor phenotypes. Cell Growth Differ 1992, **3**: 855–864.

715 Zhuang Z, Merino MJ, Vortmeyer AO, Bryant B, Lash AE, Wang C, Deavers MT, Shelton WF, Kapur S, Chandra RS.

Identical genetic changes in different histologic components of Wilms' tumors. J Natl Cancer Inst 1997, **89:** 1148–1152.

Cytology

716 Dey P, Radhika S, Rajwanshi A, Rao KL, Khajuria A, Nijhawan R, Banarjee CK. Aspiration cytology of Wilms' tumor. Acta Cytol 1993, **37:** 477–482.

717 Geisinger KR, Wakely PE Jr, Wofford MM. Unresectable stage IV nephroblastoma. A potential indication for fine-needle aspiration biopsy in children. Diagn Cytopathol 1993, **9:** 197–201.

Spread and metastases

718 Ebb DH, Kerasidis H, Vezina G, Packer RJ, Carabell S, Ivy P. Spinal cord compression in widely metastatic Wilms' tumor. Paraplegia in two children with anaplastic Wilms' tumor. Cancer 1992, **69:** 2726–2730.

719 Losty P, Kierce B. Botryoid Wilms' tumor – an unusual variant. Br J Urol 1993, **72:** 251–252.

720 Lowis SP, Foot A, Gerrard MP, Charles A, Imeson J, Middleton H, Coakham H, Bouffet E. Central nervous system metastasis in Wilms' tumor: a review of three consecutive United Kingdom trials. Cancer 1998, **83:** 2023–2029.

Therapy

721 Becht EW, Rumpelt HJ, Frohneberg D, Gutjahr P, Thoenes W. Angioma-like pseudometamorphosis in Wilms' tumors subjected to preoperative radio- and chemotherapy. Pathol Res Pract 1983, **177:** 22–31.

722 Brisigotti M, Cozzutto C, Fabbretti G, Caliendo L, Haupt R, Cornaglia-Ferraris P, Callea F. Wilms' tumor after treatment. Pediatr Pathol 1992, **12:** 397–406.

723 D'Angio GJ, Breslow N, Beckwith JB, Evans A, Baum H, de Lorimier A, Fernbach D, Hrabovsky E, Jones B, Kelalis P, et al. Treatment of Wilms' tumor. Results of the Third National Wilms' Tumor Study. Cancer 1989, **64:** 349–360.

724 D'Angio GJ, Evans A, Breslow N, Beckwith B, Bishop H, Farewell V, Goodwin W, Leape L, Palmer N, Sinks L, Sutow W, Tefft M, Wolff J. The treatment of Wilms' tumor. Results of the second National Wilms' Tumor Study. Cancer 1981, **47:** 2302–2311.

725 Ehrlich RM, Bloomberg SD, Gyepes MT, Levitt SB, Kogan S, Hanna M, Goodwin WE. Wilms' tumor, misdiagnosed preoperatively. A review of 19 National Wilms' Tumor Study I cases. J Urol 1979, **122:** 790–792.

726 Green DM, Beckwith JB, Breslow NE, Faria P, Moksness J, Finklestein JZ, Grundy P, Thomas PR, Kim T, Shochat S, et al. Treatment of children with stages II to IV anaplastic Wilms' tumor. A report from the National Wilms' Tumor Study Group. J Clin Oncol 1994, **12:** 2126–2131.

727 Green DM, Breslow NE, Beckwith JB, Takashima J, Kelalis P, D'Angio GJ. Treatment outcomes in patients less than 2 years of age with small, stage I, favorable-histology Wilms' tumors. A report from the National Wilms' Tumor Study. J Clin Oncol 1993, **11:** 91–95.

728 Larsen E, Perez-Atayde A, Green DM, Retik A, Clavell LA, Sallan SE. Surgery only for the treatment of patients with stage I (Cassady) Wilms' tumor. Cancer 1990, **66:** 264–266.

729 Shaul DB, Srikanth MM, Ortega JA, Mahour GH. Treatment of bilateral Wilms' tumor. Comparison of initial biopsy and chemotherapy to initial surgical resection in the preservation of renal mass and function. J Pediatr Surg 1992, **27:** 1009–1014.

730 Tournade MF, Com-Nougue C, Voute PA, Lemerle J, de Kraker J, Delemarre JF, Burgers M, Habrand JL, Moorman CG, Burger D, et al. Results of the Sixth International Society of Pediatric Oncology Wilms' Tumor Trial and Study. A risk-adapted therapeutic approach in Wilms' tumor. J Clin Oncol 1993, **11:** 1014–1023.

731 Zuppan CW, Beckwith JB, Weeks DA, Lackey DW, Pringle KC. The effect of preoperative therapy on the histologic features of Wilms' tumor. An analysis of cases from the Third National Wilms' Tumor Study. Cancer 1991, **68:** 385–394.

Prognosis

732 Antman KH, Ruxer RL Jr, Aisner J, Vawter G. Mesothelioma following Wilms' tumor in childhood. Cancer 1984, **54:** 367–369.

733 Arrigo S, Beckwith JB, Sharples K, D'Angio G, Haase G. Better survival after combined modality care for adults with Wilms' tumor. A report from the National Wilms' Tumor Study. Cancer 1990, **66:** 827–830.

734 Ater JL, Gooch WM III, Bybee BL, O'Brien RT. Poor prognosis for mucin-producing Wilms' tumor. Cancer 1984, **53:** 319–323.

735 Bonadio JF, Storer B, Norkool P, Farewell VT, Beckwith JB, D'Angio GJ. Anaplastic Wilms' tumor. Clinical and pathologic studies. J Clin Oncol 1985, **3:** 513–520.

736 Breslow NE, Palmer NF, Hill LR, Buring J, D'Angio GJ. Wilms' tumor. Prognostic factors for patients without metastases at diagnosis. Results of the National Wilms' Tumor Study. Cancer 1978, **41:** 1577–1589.

737 Breslow N, Sharples K, Beckwith JB, Takashima J, Kelalis PP, Green DM, D'Angio GJ. Prognostic factors in nonmetastatic, favorable histology Wilms' tumor. Results of the Third National Wilms' Tumor Study. Cancer 1991, **68:** 2345–2353.

738 Buchino JJ. Wilms' tumor – the continuing search for the true meaning of anaplasia. Adv Anat Pathol 1997, **4:** 239–243.

739 Cheah PL, Looi LM, Chan LL. Immunohistochemical expression of p53 proteins in Wilms' tumour: a possible association with the histological prognostic parameter of anaplasia. Histopathology 1996, **28:** 49–54.

740 D'Angio GJ. Oncology seen through the prism of Wilms' tumor. Med Pediatr Oncol 1985, **13:** 53–58.

741 Faria P, Beckwith JB, Mishra K, Zuppan C, Weeks DA, Breslow N, Green DM. Focal versus diffuse anaplasia in Wilms tumor – new definitions with prognostic significance: a report from the National Wilms Tumor Study Group. Am J Surg Pathol 1996, **20:** 909–920.

742 Gonzalez-Crussi F, Hsueh W, Ugarte N. Rhabdomyogenesis in renal neoplasia of childhood. Am J Surg Pathol 1981, **5:** 525–532.

743 Jereb B, Tournade MF, Lemerle J, Voute PA, Delemarte JF, Ahstrom L, Flamant R, Gerard-Marchant R, Sandstedt B. Lymph node invasion and prognosis in nephroblastoma. Cancer 1980, **45:** 1632–1636.

744 Khair S, Pritchett PS, Moreno H, Robinson CA. Histologic grading of Wilms' tumor as a potential prognosis factor. Results of a retrospective study of 26 patients. Cancer 1978, **41:** 1199–1207.

745 Lahoti C, Thorner P, Malkin D, Yeger H. Immunohistochemical detection of p53 in Wilms' tumors correlates with unfavorable outcome. Am J Pathol 1996, **148:** 1577–1589.

746 Lawler W, Marsden HB, Palmer MK. Wilms' tumor. Histologic variation and prognosis. Cancer 1975, **36:** 1122–1126.

747 Schmidt D, Wiedemann B, Keil W, Sprenger E, Harms D. Flow cytometric analysis of nephroblastomas and related neoplasms. Cancer 1986, **58:** 2494–2500.

748 Weeks DA, Beckwith JB, Luckey DW. Relapse-associated variables in stage I favorable histology Wilms' tumor. A report of the National Wilms' Tumor Study. Cancer 1987, **60:** 1204–1212.

749 Wigger HJ. Fetal rhabdomyomatous nephroblastoma. A variant of Wilms' tumor. Hum Pathol 1976, **7:** 613–623.

750 Zuppan CW. Handling and evaluation of pediatric renal tumors. Am J Clin Pathol 1998, **109:** S31–S37.

751 Zuppan CW, Beckwith JB, Luckey DW. Anaplasia in unilateral

Wilms' tumor. A report from the National Wilms' Tumor Study pathology center. Hum Pathol 1988, **19**: 1199–1209.

Mesoblastic nephroma

752 Argani P, Fritsch M, Kadkol S, Schuster A, Beckwith JB, Perlman EJ. Detection of the ETV6-NTRK3 chimeric RNA of infantile fibrosarcoma/cellular congenital mesoblastic nephroma in paraffin-embedded tissue: application to challenging pediatric renal stromal tumors. Mod Pathol 2000, **13**: 29–36.

753 Beckwith JB, Weeks DA. Congenital mesoblastic nephroma. When should we worry? Arch Pathol Lab Med 1986, **110**: 98–99.

754 Bogdan R, Taylor DEM, Mostofi FK. Leiomyomatous hamartoma of the kidney. A clinical and pathologic analysis of 20 cases from the Kidney Tumor Registry. Cancer 1973, **31**: 462–467.

755 Carpenter PM, Mascarello JT, Krous HF, Kaplan GW. Congenital mesoblastic nephroma. Cytogenetic comparison to leiomyoma. Pediatr Pathol 1993, **13**: 435–441.

755a Drut R. Multicystic congenital mesoblastic nephroma. Int J Surg Pathol 2002, **10**: 59–63.

756 Ganick DJ, Gilbert EF, Beckwith JB, Kiviat N. Congenital cystic mesoblastic nephroma. Hum Pathol 1981, **12**: 1039–1043.

757 Gonzalez-Crussi F, Sotelo-Avila C, Kidd JM. Malignant mesenchymal nephroma of infancy. Report of a case with pulmonary metastases. Am J Surg Pathol 1980, **4**: 185–190.

758 Gonzalez-Crussi F, Sotelo-Avila C, Kidd JM. Mesenchymal renal tumors in infancy. A reappraisal. Hum Pathol 1981, **12**: 78–85.

759 Heidelberger KP, Ritchey ML, Dauser RC, McKeever PE, Beckwith JB. Congenital mesoblastic nephroma metastatic to the brain. Cancer 1993, **72**: 2499–2502.

760 Howell CG, Othersen HB, Kiviat NE, Norkool P, Beckwith JB, D'Angio GJ. Therapy and outcome in 51 children with mesoblastic nephroma. A report of the National Wilms' Tumor Study. J Pediatr Surg 1982, **17**: 826–831.

761 Joshi VV, Kasznica J, Walters TR. Atypical mesoblastic nephroma. Pathologic characterization of a potentially aggressive variant of conventional congenital mesoblastic nephroma. Arch Pathol Lab Med 1986, **110**: 100–106.

762 Kumar S, Marsden HB, Carr T, Kodet R. Mesoblastic nephroma contains fibronectin but lacks laminin. J Clin Pathol 1985, **38**: 507–511.

763 Nadasdy T, Roth J, Johnson DL, Bane BL, Weinberg A, Verani R, Silva FG. Congenital mesoblastic nephroma. An immunohistochemical and lectin study. Hum Pathol 1993, **24**: 413–419.

764 O'Malley DP, Mierau GW, Beckwith JB, Weeks DA. Ultrastructure of cellular congenital mesoblastic nephroma. Ultrastruct Pathol 1996, **20**: 417–428.

765 Pettinato G, Manivel JC, Wick MR, Dehner LP. Classical and cellular (atypical) congenital mesoblastic nephroma. A clinicopathologic, ultrastructural, immunohistochemical, and flow cytometric study. Hum Pathol 1989, **20**: 682–690.

766 Rubin BP, Chen C-J, Morgan TW, Xiao S, Grier H, Kozakewich HP, Perez-Atayde AR, Fletcher JA. Congenital mesoblastic nephroma t(12;15) is associated with ETV6-NTRK3 gene fusion. Cytogenetic and molecular relationship to congenital (infantile) fibrosarcoma. Am J Pathol 1998, **153**: 1451–1458.

767 Sandstedt B, Delemarre JFM, Krul EJ, Tournade MF. Mesoblastic nephromas. A study of 29 tumours from the SIOP nephroblastoma file. Histopathology 1985, **9**: 741–750.

768 Schofield DE, Yunis EJ, Fletcher JA. Chromosome aberrations in mesoblastic nephroma. Am J Pathol 1993, **143**: 714–724.

769 Shen SC, Yunis EJ. A study of the cellularity and ultrastructure of congenital mesoblastic nephroma. Cancer 1980, **45**: 306–314.

770 Truong LD, Williams R, Ngo T, Cawood C, Chevez-Barrios P,

Awalt HL, Brown RW, Younes M, Ro JY. Adult mesoblastic nephroma: expansion of the morphologic spectrum and review of literature. Am J Surg Pathol 1998, **22**: 827–839.

771 Tulbah A, Kardar AH, Akhtar M. Mesoblastic nephroma in an adult. J Urol Pathol 1997, **6**: 67–74.

772 Vujanic GM, Delemarre JF, Moeslichan S, Lam J, Harms D, Sandstedt B, Voute PA. Mesoblastic nephroma metastatic to the lungs and heart – another face of this peculiar lesion. Case report and review of the literature. Pediatr Pathol 1993, **13**: 143–153.

773 Wigger HG. Fetal mesenchymal hamartoma of kidney. A tumor of secondary mesenchyme. Cancer 1975, **36**: 1002–1008.

Multicystic nephroma

774 Andrews MJ Jr, Askin FB, Fried FA, McMillan CW, Mandell J. Cystic partially differentiated nephroblastoma and polycystic Wilms' tumor. A spectrum of related clinical and pathologic entities. J Urol 1983, **129**: 577–580.

775 Baldauf MC, Schulz DM. Multilocular cyst of the kidney. Report of three cases with review of the literature. Am J Clin Pathol 1976, **65**: 93–102.

776 Domizio P, Risdon RA. Cystic renal neoplasms of infancy and childhood. A light microscopical, lectin histochemical and immunohistochemical study. Histopathology 1991, **19**: 199–209.

777 Eble JN, Bonsib SM. Extensively cystic renal neoplasms: cystic nephroma, cystic partially differentiated nephroblastoma, multilocular cystic renal cell carcinoma, and cystic hamartoma of renal pelvis. Semin Diagn Pathol 1998, **15**: 2–20.

778 Gallo GE, Penchansky L. Cystic nephroma. Cancer 1977, **39**: 1322–1327.

779 Joshi VV, Banerjee AK, Yadav K, Pathak IC. Cystic partially differentiated nephroblastoma. A clinicopathologic entity in the spectrum of infantile renal neoplasia. Cancer 1977, **40**: 789–795.

780 Joshi VV, Beckwith JB. Multilocular cyst of the kidney (cystic nephroma) and cystic, partially differentiated nephroblastoma. Terminology and criteria for diagnosis. Cancer 1989, **64**: 466–479.

781 Kajani N, Rosenberg BF, Bernstein J. Multilocular cystic nephroma. J Urol Pathol 1993, **1**: 33–42.

782 Kanomata N, Eble JN, Halling KC. Nonrandom X chromosome inactivation in cystic nephroma demonstrates the neoplastic nature of these tumors. J Urol Pathol 1997, **7**: 81–88.

783 Nagao T, Sugano I, Ishida Y, Tajima Y, Masai M, Nagakura K, Matsuzaki O, Kondo Y, Nagao K. Cystic partially differentiated nephroblastoma in an adult: an immunohistochemical, lectin histochemical, and ultrastructural study. Histopathology 1999, **35**: 65–73.

784 Sherman ME, Silverman ML, Balogh K, Tan SS-G. Multilocular renal cyst. A hamartoma with potential for neoplastic transformation? Arch Pathol Lab Med 1987, **111**: 732–736.

785 Tang TT, Harb JM, Oechler HW, Camitta BM. Multilocular renal cyst. Electron microscopic evidence of pathogenesis. Am J Pediatr Hematol Oncol 1984, **6**: 27–32.

786 Taxy JB, Marshall FF. Multilocular renal cysts in adults. Possible relationship to renal adenocarcinoma. Arch Pathol Lab Med 1983, **107**: 633–637.

787 Walford N, Delemarre JF. Wilms' tumour associated with deep cystic nephroma-like changes. Three cases of a putative Wilms' tumour precursor. Histopathology 1991, **18**: 123–131.

Nephroblastomatosis and nephrogenic rests

788 Beckwith JB. Precursor lesions of Wilms' tumor. Clinical and biological implications. Med Pediatr Oncol 1993, **21**: 158–168.

789 Beckwith JB, Kiviat NB, Bonadio FJ. Nephrogenic nests, nephroblastomatosis, and the pathogenesis of Wilms' tumor. Pediatr Pathol 1990, **10**: 1–30.

790 Bove KE, McAdams AJ. The nephroblastomatosis complex and

its relationship to Wilms' tumor. A clinico-pathologic treatise. Perspect Pediatr Pathol 1976, **3**: 185–223.

791   de Chadarevian J-P, Fletcher BD, Chatten J, Rabinovitch HH. Massive infantile nephroblastomatosis. A clinical, radiological, and pathological analysis of four cases. Cancer 1977, **39**: 2294–2305.

792   Gaulier A, Boccon-Gibod L, Sabatier P, Lucas G. Panlobar nephroblastomatosis with cystic dysplasia. An unusual case with diffuse renal involvement studied by immunohistochemistry. Pediatr Pathol 1993, **13**: 741–749.

793   Heideman RL, Haase GM, Foley CL, Wilson HL, Bailey WC. Nephroblastomatosis and Wilms' tumors. Clinical experience and management of seven patients. Cancer 1985, **55**: 1446–1451.

794   Machin GA, McCaughey WTE. A new precursor lesion of Wilms' tumor (nephroblastoma). Intralobar multifocal nephroblastomatosis. Histopathology 1984, **8**: 35–53.

795   Park S, Bernard A, Bove KE, Sens DA, Hazen-Martin DJ, Garvin AJ, Haber DA. Inactivation of WT1 in nephrogenic nests, genetic precursors to Wilms' tumour. Nat Genet 1993, **5**: 363–367.

796   Perlman M, Levin M, Wittels B. Syndrome of fetal gigantism, renal hamartomas, and nephroblastomatosis with Wilms' tumor. Cancer 1975, **35**: 1212–1217.

797   Stambolis C. Benign epithelial nephroblastoma. A contribution to its histogenesis. Virchows Arch [A] 1977, **376**: 267–272.

798   Vogler CA, Sotelo-Avila C, Ramón-García G, Salinas-Madrigal L. Nodular renal blastema and metanephric hamartomas in children with urinary tract malformations. A morphologic spectrum of abnormal metanephric differentiation. Semin Diagn Pathol 1988, **5**: 122–131.

799   Walford N. Panlobar nephroblastomatosis. A distinctive form of renal dysplasia associated with Wilms' tumour. Histopathology 1990, **17**: 37–44.

800   White KS, Kirks DR, Bove KE. Imaging of nephroblastomatosis. An overview. Radiology 1992, **182**: 1–5.

Intrarenal neuroblastoma and peripheral neuroectodermal tumor

801   Beckwith JB. Wilms' tumor and other renal tumors of childhood. A selective review from the National Wilms' Tumor Study Pathology Center. Hum Pathol 1983, **14**: 481–492.

802   Jimenez RE, Folpe AL, Lapham RL, Ro JY, O'Shea PA, Weiss SW, Amin MB. Primary Ewing's sarcoma/primitive neuroectodermal tumor of the kidney: A clinicopathologic and immunohistochemical analysis of 11 cases. Am J Surg Pathol 2002, **26**: 320–327.

803   Marley EF, Liapis H, Humphrey P, Nadler RB, Siegel CL, Zhu X, Brandt JM, Dehner LP. Primitive neuroectodermal tumor of the kidney – another enigma: A pathologic, immunohistochemical, and molecular diagnostic study. Am J Surg Pathol 1997, **21**: 354–359.

804   Mikami Y, Manabe T. Adenomatoid hyperplasia of the Bowman's capsule epithelium in association with primary pulmonary primitive neuroectodermal tumor. Histopathology 2000, **36**: 281–282.

805   Nisen PH, Rich MA, Gloster E, Valderrama E, Saric O, Shende A, Lanzkowsky P, Alt FW. N-*myc* oncogene expression in histopathologically unrelated bilateral pediatric renal tumors. Cancer 1987, **61**: 1821–1826.

806   Panuel M, Bourliere-Najean B, Gentet JC, Scheiner C, Delarue A, Faure F, Devred P. Aggressive neuroblastoma with initial pulmonary metastases and kidney involvement simulating Wilms' tumor. Eur J Radiol 1992, **14**: 201–203.

807   Parham DM, Roloson GJ, Feeley M, Green DM, Bridge JA, Beckwith JB. Primary malignant neuroepithelial tumors of the kidney: a clinicopathologic analysis of 146 adult and pediatric cases from the National Wilms' Tumor Study Group Pathology Center. Am J Surg Pathol 2001, **25**: 133–146.

808   Quezado M, Benjamin DR, Tsokos M. EWS/FLI-1 fusion transcripts in three peripheral primitive neuroectodermal tumors of the kidney. Hum Pathol 1997, **28**: 767–771.

809   Sheaff M, McManus A, Scheimberg I, Paris A, Shipley J, Baithun S. Primitive neuroectodermal tumor of the kidney confirmed by fluorescence in situ hybridisation. Am J Surg Pathol 1997, **21**: 461–468.

810   Verma L, Sandramouli S, Garg SP, Vashishi S. Intrarenal neuroblastoma presenting as orbital and multiple skeletal metastases. Indian Pediatr 1993, **30**: 673–676.

Clear cell sarcoma

811   Amin MB, De Peralta-Venturina MN, Ro JY, El-Naggar A, Backay B, Ordenez N, Mani A, Ayala A. Clear cell sarcoma of kidney in an adolescent and in young adults: A report of four cases with ultrastructural, immunohistochemical, and DNA flow cytometric analysis. Am J Surg Pathol 1999, **23**: 1455–1463.

812   Argani P, Perlman E, Breslow N, Browing NG, Green DM, D'Angio GJ, Beckwith BJ. Clear cell sarcoma of the kidney: A review of 351 cases from the National Wilms Tumor Study Group Pathology Center. Am J Surg Pathol 2000, **24**: 4–18.

813   Haas JE, Bonadio JF, Beckwith JB. Clear cell sarcoma of the kidney with emphasis on ultrastructural studies. Cancer 1984, **54**: 2978–2987.

813a Hsueh C, Wang H, Gonzalez-Crussi F, Lin J-N, Hung I-J, Yang C-P, Jiang T-H. Infrequent p53 gene mutations and lack of p53 protein expression in clear cell sarcoma of the kidney: Immunohistochemical study and mutation analysis of p53 in renal tumors of unfavorable prognosis. Mod Pathol 2002, **15**: 606–610.

814   Looi LM, Cheah PL. An immunohistochemical study comparing clear cell sarcoma of the kidney and Wilms' tumor. Pathology 1993, **25**: 106–109.

815   Marsden HB, Lawler W, Kumar PM. Bone metastasizing renal tumor of childhood. Morphological and clinical features and differences from Wilms' tumor. Cancer 1978, **42**: 1922–1928.

816   Morgan E, Kidd JM. Undifferentiated sarcoma of the kidney. A tumor of childhood with histopathologic and clinical characteristics distinct from Wilms' tumor. Cancer 1978, **42**: 1916–1921.

817   Oda H, Shiga J, Machinami R. Clear cell sarcoma of kidney. Two cases in adults. Cancer 1993, **71**: 2286–2291.

818   Sandstedt BE, Delemarre JFM, Harms D, Tournade MF. Sarcomatous Wilms' tumour with clear cells and hyalinization. A study of 38 tumours in children from the SIOP nephroblastoma file. Histopathology 1987, **11**: 273–285.

819   Schmidt D, Harms D, Evers KG, Bliesener JA, Beckwith JB. Bone metastasizing renal tumor (clear cell sarcoma) of childhood with epithelioid elements. Cancer 1985, **56**: 609–613.

819a Schuster AE, Schneider DT, Fritsch MK, Grundy P, Perlman EJ, The National Wilms Tumor Study Group. Genetic and genetic expression analyses of clear cell sarcoma of the kidney. Lab Invest 2003, **83**: 1293–1299.

820   Sohda T, Soejima H, Matsumoto T, Yun K. Insulin-like growth factor 2 gene imprinting in clear cell sarcoma of the kidney. Hum Pathol 1997, **28**: 1315–1317.

821   Sotelo-Avila C, Gonzalez-Crussi F, Sadowinski S, Gooch WM III, Pena R. Clear cell sarcoma of the kidney. A clinicopathologic study of 21 patients with long-term follow-up evaluation. Hum Pathol 1986, **16**: 1219–1230.

822   Takagi M, Takakuwa T, Ushigome S, Nakata K, Fujioka T, Watanabe A. Sarcomatous variants of Wilms' tumor. Immunohistochemical and ultrastructural comparison with classical Wilms' tumor. Cancer 1987, **59**: 963–971.

823   Uzoaru I, Podbielski FJ, Chou P, Raffensperger JG, Gonzalez-Crussi F. Familial adenomatous polyposis coli and clear cell sarcoma of the kidney. Pediatr Pathol 1993, **13**: 133–141.

824 Weeks DA, Malott RL, Zuppan C, Mierau GW, Beckwith JB. Primitive pelvic sarcoma resembling clear cell sarcoma of kidney. Ultrastruct Pathol 1991, **15**: 403–408.

825 Yun K. Clear cell sarcoma of the kidney expresses insulinlike growth factor-II but not WT1 transcripts. Am J Pathol 1993, **142**: 39–47.

Rhabdoid tumor

826 Berry PJ, Vujanic GM. Malignant rhabdoid tumour. Histopathology 1992, **20**: 189–193.

827 Bonnin JM, Rubinstein LJ, Palmer NF, Beckwith JB. The association of embryonal tumors originating in the kidney and in the brain. A report of seven cases. Cancer 1984, **54**: 2137–2146.

828 Fischer HP, Thomsen H, Altmannsberger M, Bertram U. Malignant rhabdoid tumour of the kidney expressing neurofilament proteins. Immunohistochemical findings and histogenetic aspects. Pathol Res Pract 1989, **184**: 541–547.

829 Frierson HF Jr, Mills SE, Innes DJ Jr. Malignant rhabdoid tumor of the pelvis. Cancer 1985, **55**: 1963–1967.

830 Haas JE, Palmer NF, Weinberg AG, Beckwith JB. Ultrastructure of malignant rhabdoid tumor of the kidney. A distinctive renal tumor of children. Hum Pathol 1981, **12**: 646–657.

831 Howat AJ, Gonzales MF, Waters KD, Campbell PE. Primitive neuroectodermal tumour of the central nervous system associated with malignant rhabdoid tumour of the kidney. Report of a case. Histopathology 1986, **10**: 643–650.

832 Litman DA, Bhuta S, Barsky SH. Synchronous occurrence of malignant rhabdoid tumor two decades after Wilms' tumor irradiation. Am J Surg Pathol 1993, **17**: 729–737.

833 Mayes LC, Kasselberg AG, Roloff JS, Lukens JN. Hypercalcemia associated with immunoreactive parathyroid hormone in a malignant rhabdoid tumor of the kidney (rhabdoid Wilms' tumor). Cancer 1984, **54**: 882–884.

834 Sotelo-Avila C, Gonzalez-Crussi F, deMello D, Vogler C, Gooch WM III, Gale G, Pena R. Renal and extrarenal rhabdoid tumors in children. A clinicopathologic study of 14 patients. Semin Diagn Pathol 1986, **3**: 151–163.

835 Tsokos M, Kouradlis G, Chandra RS, Bhagavan BS, Triche TJ. Malignant rhabdoid tumor of the kidney and soft tissues. Evidence for a diverse morphological and immunocytochemical phenotype. Arch Pathol Lab Med 1989, **113**: 115–120.

836 Tsuneyoshi M, Daimaru Y, Hashimoto H, Enjoji M. Malignant soft tissue neoplasms with the histologic features of renal rhabdoid tumors. An ultrastructural and immunohistochemical study. Hum Pathol 1985, **16**: 1235–1242.

837 Vujanic GM, Sandstedt B, Harms D, Boccon-Gibod L, Delemarre JFM. Rhabdoid tumour of the kidney: a clinicopathologic study of 22 patients from the International Society of Paediatric Oncology (SIOP) nephroblastoma file. Histopathology 1996, **28**: 333–340.

838 Weeks DA, Beckwith JB, Mierau GW. Rhabdoid tumor. An entity or a phenotype? Arch Pathol Lab Med 1989, **113**: 113–114.

839 Weeks DA, Beckwith JB, Mierau GW, Luckey DW. Rhabdoid tumor of kidney. A report of 111 cases from the National Wilms' Tumor Study Pathology Center. Am J Surg Pathol 1989, **13**: 439–458.

840 Weeks DA, Beckwith JB, Mierau GW, Zuppan CW. Renal neoplasms mimicking rhabdoid tumor of kidney. A report from the National Wilms' Tumor Study Pathology Center. Am J Surg Pathol 1991, **15**: 1042–1054.

Metanephric stromal tumor

841 Argani P, Beckwith JB. Metanephric stromal tumor: report of 31 cases of a distinctive pediatric renal neoplasm. Am J Surg Pathol 2000, **24**: 927–937.

Other pediatric tumor types

842 Argani P, Hawkins A, Griffin CA, Goldstein JD, Haas M, Beckwith JB, Mankinen CB, Perlman EJ. A distinctive pediatric renal neoplasm characterized by epithelioid morphology, basement membrane production, focal HMB45 immunoreactivity, and t(6;11)(p21.1;q12) chromosome translocation. Am J Pathol 2001, **158**: 2089–2096.

843 Arnold MM, Beckwith JB, Faris P, Weeks DA. Embryonal sarcoma of adult and pediatric kidneys (abstract). Mod Pathol 1995, **8**: 72a.

844 Chatten J, Cromie WJ, Dockett JW. Ossifying tumor of infantile kidney. Report of two cases. Cancer 1980, **45**: 609–612.

845 Dehner LP. Intrarenal teratoma occurring in infancy. Report of a case with discussion of extragonadal germ cell tumors in infancy. J Pediatr Surg 1973, **8**: 369–378.

846 Delahunt B, Beckwith JB, Eble JN, Fraundorfer MR, Sutton TD, Trotter GE. Cystic embryonal sarcoma of kidney: a case report. Cancer 1998, **82**: 2427–2433.

ADULT TUMORS AND TUMORLIKE CONDITIONS
Renal cell carcinoma
General features

847 Berg S, Jacobs SC, Cohen AJ, Li F, Marchetto D, Brown RS. The surgical management of hereditary multifocal renal carcinoma. J Urol 1981, **126**: 313–315.

848 Bernstein J, Evan AP, Gardner KD Jr. Epithelial hyperplasia in human polycystic kidney diseases. Its role in pathogenesis and risk of neoplasia. Am J Pathol 1987, **129**: 92–101.

849 Bjornsson J, Short MP, Kwiatkowski DJ, Henske EP. Tuberous sclerosis-associated renal cell carcinoma. Clinical, pathological, and genetic features. Am J Pathol 1996, **149**: 1201–1208.

850 Bretan PN Jr, Busch MP, Hricak H, Williams RD. Chronic renal failure. A significant risk factor in the development of acquired renal cysts and renal cell carcinoma. Case reports and review of the literature. Cancer 1986, **57**: 1871–1879.

851 Campbell LV Jr, Gilbert E, Chamberlain CR Jr, Watne AL. Metastases of cancer to cancer. Cancer 1968, **22**: 635–643.

852 Chung-Park M, Ricanati E, Lankerani M, Kedia K. Acquired renal cysts and multiple renal cell and urothelial tumors. Am J Clin Pathol 1983, **79**: 238–242.

853 Coughlin SS, Neaton JD, Randall B, Sengupta A, for the Multiple Risk Factor Intervention Trial Research Group. Predictors of mortality from kidney cancer in 333,547 men screened for the Multiple Risk Factor Intervention Trial. Cancer 1997, **79**: 2171–2177.

854 Dehner LP, Leestma JE, Price EB Jr. Renal cell carcinoma in children. A clinicopathologic study of 15 cases and review of the literature. J Pediatr 1970, **76**: 358–368.

855 Everson TC. Spontaneous regression of cancer. Ann NY Acad Sci 1964, **114**: 721–735.

856 Friedrich CA. Von Hippel-Lindau syndrome: a pleomorphic condition. Cancer 1999, **86**: 2478–2482.

856a George DJ, Kaelin WG. The von Hippel-Lindau protein, vascular endothelial growth factor, and kidney cancer. New Engl J Med 2003, **349**: 419–421.

857 Gnarra JR, Lerman MI, Zbar B, Linehan WM. Genetics of renal-cell carcinoma and evidence for a critical role for von Hippel–Lindau in renal tumorigenesis. Semin Oncol 1995, **22**: 3–8.

858 Hartman DS, Davis CJ Jr, Madewell JE, Friedman AC. Primary malignant renal tumors in the second decade of life. Wilms' tumor versus renal cell carcinoma. J Urol 1982, **127**: 888–891.

859 Hughson MC, Bigler S, Dickman K, Kovacs G. Renal cell carcinoma of end-stage renal disease: an analysis of chromosome 3, 7, and 17 abnormalities by microsatellite amplification. Mod Pathol 1999, **12**: 301–309.

860 Hughson MD, Buchwald D, Fox M. Renal neoplasia and acquired cystic kidney disease in patients receiving long-term dialysis. Arch Pathol Lab Med 1986, **110:** 592–601.

861 Ikeda R, Tanaka T, Moriyama MT, Kawamura K, Miyazawa K, Suzuki K. Proliferative activity of renal cell carcinoma associated with acquired cystic disease of the kidney: comparison with typical renal cell carcinoma. Hum Pathol 2002, **33:** 230–235.

862 Katz SE, Schapira HE. Spontaneous regression of genitourinary cancer. An update. J Urol 1982, **128:** 1–4.

863 Kiuru M, Launonen V, Hietala M, Aittomaki K, Vierimaa O, Salovaara R, Arola J, Pukkala E, Sistonen P, Herva R, Aaltonen LA. Familial cutaneous leiomyomatosis is a two-hit condition associated with renal cell cancer of characteristic histopathology. Am J Pathol 2001, **159:** 825–829.

864 Kragel PJ, Walther MM, Pestaner JP, Filling-Katz MR. Simple renal cysts, atypical renal cysts, and renal cell carcinoma in von Hippel–Lindau disease. A lectin and immunohistochemical study in six patients. Mod Pathol 1991, **4:** 210–214.

865 Lack EE, Cassady R, Sallan SE. Renal cell carcinoma in childhood and adolescence. A clinical and pathological study of 17 cases. J Urol 1985, **133:** 822–828.

866 Mai KT, Veinot JP, Collins JP. Renal cell carcinoma with regression. J Urol Pathol 1998, **9:** 129–140.

867 Malek RS, Omess PJ, Benson RC Jr, Zincke H. Renal cell carcinoma in von Hippel–Lindau syndrome. Am J Med 1987, **82:** 236–238.

868 Medeiros LJ, Palmedo G, Krigman HR, Kovacs G, Beckwith JB. Oncocytoid renal cell carcinoma after neuroblastoma: a report of four cases of a distinct clinicopathologic entity. Am J Surg Pathol 1999, **23:** 772–780.

869 Motzer RJ, Bander NH, Nanus DM. Renal cell carcinoma. N Engl J Med 1996, **335:** 865–875.

870 Nishikubo CY, Kunkel LA, Figlin R, Belldegrun A, Rosen P, Elashoff R, Wang H, Territo MC. An association between renal cell carcinoma and lymphoid malignancies: A case series of eight patients. Cancer 1996, **78:** 2421–2426.

871 Paraf F, Chauveau D, Chretien Y, Richard S, Grunfeld J-P, Droz D. Renal lesions in von Hippel-Lindau disease: immunohistochemical expression of nephron differentiation molecules, adhesion molecules and apoptosis proteins. Histopathology 2000, **36:** 457–465.

871a Petraki C, Vaslamatzis M, Argyrakos T, Petraki K, Strataki M, Alexopoulos C, Sotsiou F. Tumor to tumor metastasis: report of two cases and review of the literature. Int J Surg Pathol 2003, **11:** 127–135.

872 Renshaw AA, Granter SR, Fletcher JA, Kozakewich HP, Corless CL, Perez Atayde AR. Renal cell carcinomas in children and young adults: increased incidence of papillary architecture and unique subtypes. Am J Surg Pathol 1999, **23:** 795–802.

873 Shen T, Zhuang Z, Gersell DJ, Tavassoli FA. Allelic deletion of VHL gene detected in papillary tumors of the broad ligament, epididymis, and retroperitoneum in von Hippel-Lindau disease patients. Int J Surg Pathol 2000, **8:** 207–212.

874 Singh EO, Benson RC Jr, Wold LE. Cancer-to-cancer metastasis. J Urol 1984, **132:** 340–342.

875 Stornes I, Jorgensen TM. Renal malignancy in von Hippel–Lindau's disease. Case reports. Scand J Urol Nephrol 1993, **27:** 139–142.

876 Takahashi S, Shirai T, Ogawa K, Imaida K, Yamazaki C, Ito A, Masuko K, Ito N. Renal cell adenomas and carcinomas in hemodialysis patients. Relationship between hemodialysis period and development of lesions. Acta Pathol Jpn 1993, **43:** 674–682.

877 Tihan T, Filippa DA. Coexistence of renal cell carcinoma and malignant lymphoma: A causal relationship or coincidental occurrence? Cancer 1996, **77:** 2325–2331.

878 Zhuang Z, Gnarra JR, Dudley CF, Zbar B, Linehan WM, Lubensky IA. Detection of von Hippel-Lindau disease gene mutations in paraffin-embedded sporadic renal cell carcinoma specimens. Mod Pathol 1996, **9:** 838–842.

Clinical features

879 Altaffer LF III, Chenault DW Jr. Paraneoplastic endocrinopathies associated with renal tumors. J Urol 1979, **122:** 573–577.

880 Aoyagi T, Mori I, Ueyama Y, Tamaoki N. Sinusoidal dilatation of the liver as a paraneoplastic manifestation of renal cell carcinoma. Hum Pathol 1989, **20:** 1193–1197.

881 Aso Y, Homma Y. A survey on incidental renal cell carcinoma in Japan. J Urol 1992, **147:** 340–343.

882 Dalakas MC, Fujihara S, Askanas V, Engel WK, Glenner GG. Nature of amyloid deposits in hypernephroma. Immunocytochemical studies in 2 cases associated with amyloid polyneuropathy. Am J Pathol 1984, **116:** 447–454.

883 Fan K, Smith DJ. Hypercalcemia associated with renal cell carcinoma. Probable role of neoplastic stromal cells. Hum Pathol 1983, **14:** 168–173.

884 Fletcher MS, Packham DA, Pryor JP, Yates-Bell AJ. Hepatic dysfunction in renal carcinoma. Br J Urol 1981, **53:** 533–536.

885 Frohmuller HG, Grups JW, Heller V. Comparative value of ultrasonography, computerized tomography, angiography and excretory urography in the staging of renal cell carcinoma. J Urol 1987, **138:** 482–484.

886 Goldberg MF, Tashjian AH Jr, Order SE, Dammin GJ. Renal adenocarcinoma containing a parathyroid hormone-like substance and associated with marked hypercalcemia. Am J Med 1964, **36:** 805–814.

887 Golde DW, Schambelan M, Weintraub BD, Rosen SW. Gonadotropin-secreting renal carcinoma. Cancer 1974, **33:** 1048–1053.

888 Hollifield JW, Page DL, Smith C, Michelakis AM, Staab E, Rhamy R. Renin-secreting clear cell carcinoma of the kidney. Arch Intern Med 1975, **135:** 859–864.

889 Konnak JW, Grossman HB. Renal cell carcinoma as an incidental finding. J Urol 1985, **134:** 1094–1096.

890 Maesaka JK, Mittal SK, Fishbane S. Paraneoplastic syndromes of the kidney. Semin Oncol 1997, **24:** 373–381.

891 Marshall FF, Walsh PC. Extrarenal manifestations of renal cell carcinoma. J Urol 1977, **117:** 439–440.

892 Okabe T, Urabe A, Kato T, Chiba S, Takaku F. Production of erythropoietinlike activity by human renal and hepatic carcinomas in cell culture. Cancer 1985, **55:** 1918–1923.

893 Ramos CV, Taylor HB. Hepatic dysfunction associated with renal carcinoma. Cancer 1972, **29:** 1287–1292.

894 Skinner DG, Colvin RB, Vermillion CD, Pfister RC, Leadbetter WF. Diagnosis and management of renal cell carcinoma. A clinical and pathologic study of 309 cases. Cancer 1971, **28:** 1165–1177.

895 Vanatta PR, Silva FG, Taylor WE, Costa JC. Renal cell carcinoma and systemic amyloidosis. Demonstration of AA protein and review of the literature. Hum Pathol 1983, **14:** 195–201.

Morphologic features

896 Brinker DA, Amin MB, de Peralta-Venturina M, Reuter VG, Chan TY, Epstein JI. Extensively necrotic cystic renal cell carcinoma: a clinicopathologic study with comparison to other cystic and necrotic renal cancers. Am J Surg Pathol 2000, **24:** 988–995.

897 Canzonieri V, Volpe R, Gloghini A, Carbone A, Merlo A. Mixed renal tumor with carcinomatous and fibroleiomyomatous components, associated with angiomyolipoma in the same kidney. Pathol Res Pract 1993, **189:** 951–956.

898 Chau KY, Pretorius JM, Stewart AW. Myospherulosis in renal cell carcinoma. Arch Pathol Lab Med 2000, **124:** 1476–1480.

899 Chetty R, Cvijan D. Giant (bizarre) cell variant of renal carcinoma. Histopathology 1997, **30:** 585–587.

900 Fleming S, O'Donnell M. Surgical pathology of renal epithelial neoplasms: recent advances and current status. Histopathology 2000, **36:** 195–202.

901 Fukuda T, Kamishima T, Emura I, Takastuka H, Suzuki T. Pigmented renal cell carcinoma: accumulation of abnormal lysosomal granules. Histopathology 1997, **34:** 38–46.

902 Gatalica Z, Miettinen M, Kovatich A, McCue PA. Hyaline globules in renal cell carcinomas and oncocytomas. Hum Pathol 1997, **28:** 400–403.

903 Hes O, Michal M, Sulc M, Kocova L, Hora M, Rousarova M. Glassy hyaline globules in granular cell carcinoma, chromophobe cell carcinoma, and oncocytoma of the kidney. Ann Diagn Pathol 1998, **2:** 12–18.

904 Humphrey PA. Clear cell neoplasms of the urinary tract and male reproductive system. Semin Diagn Pathol 1997, **14:** 240–252.

905 Jagirdar J, Irie T, French SW, Patil J, Schwarz R, Paronetto F. Globular Mallory-like bodies in renal cell carcinoma. Report of a case and review of cytoplasmic eosinophilic globules. Hum Pathol 1985, **16:** 949–952.

906 Kinouchi T, Mano M, Saiki S, Meguro N, Maeda O, Kuroda M, Usami M, Kotake T. Incidence rate of satellite tumors in renal cell carcinoma. Cancer 1999, **86:** 2331–2337.

907 Lei JY, Middleton LP, Guo XD, Duray PH, McWilliams G, Linehan WM, Merino MJ. Pigmented renal clear cell carcinoma with melanocytic differentiation. Hum Pathol 2001, **32:** 233–236.

908 Montironi R, Mikuz G, Algaba F, Lopez-Beltran A, Hamilton PW, Parkinson C. Epithelial tumours of the adult kidney. Virchows Arch 1999, **434:** 281–290.

909 Murad T, Komaiko W, Oyasu R, Bauer K. Multilocular cystic renal cell carcinoma. Am J Clin Pathol 1991, **95:** 633–637.

910 Reuter VE. Renal tumors exhibiting granular cytoplasm. Semin Diagn Pathol 1999, **16:** 135–145.

911 Reznicek SB, Narayana AS, Culp DA. Cystadenocarcinoma of the kidney. A profile of 13 cases. J Urol 1985, **134:** 256–259.

912 Stein A, Sova Y, Abu-Maaruf A. Characteristics of the predominant renal tumor and their impact on the incidental findings of multifocal renal cell carcinoma: a study of 96% nephrectomy specimens. J Urol Pathol 1998, **8:** 149–156.

913 Steinberg P, Storkel S, Oesch F, Thoenes W. Carbohydrate metabolism in human renal clear cell carcinoma. Lab Invest 1992, **67:** 506–511.

914 Thoenes W, Störkel S, Rumpelt HJ. Histopathology and classification of renal cell tumors (adenomas, oncocytomas and carcinomas). The basic cytological and histopathological elements and their use for diagnostics. Pathol Res Pract 1986, **181:** 125–143.

Electron microscopic features

915 Herrera GA, Turbat-Herrera EA. The role of ultrastructural pathology in the diagnosis of epithelial and unusual renal tumors. Ultrastruct Pathol 1996, **20:** 7–26.

916 Hull MT, Eble JN. Myelinoid lamellated cytoplasmic inclusions in human renal adenocarcinomas. An ultrastructural study. Ultrastruct Pathol 1988, **12:** 41–48.

917 Krishnan B, Truong LD. Renal epithelial neoplasms: the diagnostic implications of electron microscopic study in 55 cases. Hum Pathol 2002, **33:** 68–79.

918 Mackay B, Ordóñez NG, Khoursand J. The ultrastructure and immunocytochemistry of renal cell carcinoma. Ultrastruct Pathol 1987, **11:** 483–502.

Histochemical and immunohistochemical features

919 Ang LC, Debowski T, Michalski R. Immunolocalization of prealbumin (transthyretin) in renal cell carcinoma. Histopathology 1991, **18:** 565–568.

920 Avery AK, Beckstead J, Renshaw AA, Corless CI. Use of antibodies to RCC and CD10 in the differential diagnosis of renal neoplasms. Am J Surg Pathol 2000, **24:** 203–210.

921 Banner BF, Burnham JA, Bahnson RR, Ernstoff MS, Auerbach HE. Immunophenotypic markers in renal cell carcinoma. Mod Pathol 1990, **3:** 129–134.

922 Borowitz MJ, Weiss MA, Bossen EH, Metzgar RS. Characterization of renal neoplasms with monoclonal antibodies to leukocyte differentiation antigens. Cancer 1986, **57:** 251–256.

923 Brown DF, Dababo MA, Hladik CL, Eagan KP, White CL III, Rushing EJ. Hormone receptor immunoreactivity in hemangioblastomas and clear cell renal cell carcinomas. Mod Pathol 1998, **11:** 55–59.

924 Clark D, Kersting R, Rojiani AM. Erythropoietin immunolocalization in renal cell carcinoma. Mod Pathol 1998, **11:** 24–28.

925 Cohen C, McCue PA, DeRose PB. Immunohistochemistry of renal adenomas and carcinomas. J Urol Pathol 1995, **3:** 61–72.

926 Cordon-Cardo C, Finstad CL, Bander NH, Melamed MF. Immunoanatomic distribution of cytostructural and tissue-associated antigens in the human urinary tract. Am J Pathol 1987, **126:** 269–284.

927 Corless CL, Kibel AS, Lliopoulos O, Kaelin WG Jr. Immunostaining of the von Hippel-Lindau gene product in normal and neoplastic human tissues. Hum Pathol 1997, **28:** 459–464.

928 Cote RJ, Cordon-Cardo C, Reuter V, Rosen PP. Immunopathology of adrenal and renal cortical tumors. Coordinated change in antigen expression is associated with neoplastic conversion in the adrenal cortex. Am J Pathol 1990, **136:** 1077–1084.

929 de Alava E, Panizo A, Sola I, Rodriguez-Rubio FI, Javier Paro-Mindan F. CD44v6 expression is related to progression in renal epithelial tumours. Histopathology 1998, **33:** 39–45.

930 Droz D, Zachar D, Charbit L, Gogusev J, Chretein Y, Iris L. Expression of the human nephron differentiation molecules in renal cell carcinomas. Am J Pathol 1990, **137:** 895–905.

931 Fetsch PA, Powers CN, Zakowski MF, Abati A. Anti-α-inhibin: marker of choice for the consistent distinction between adrenocortical carcinoma and renal cell carcinoma in fine-needle aspiration. Cancer Cytopathol 1999, **87:** 168–172.

932 Fleming S, Gibson AAM. Proteinase inhibitors in the kidney and its tumours. Histopathology 1986, **10:** 1303–1313.

933 Fleming S, Lindop GBM, Gibson AAM. The distribution of epithelial membrane antigen in the kidney and its tumours. Histopathology 1985, **9:** 729–739.

934 Francois C, van Veithoven R, De Lathouwer O, Moreno C, Peltier A, Kaltner H, Salmon I, Gavius H-J, Danguy A, Decaestecker C, Kiss R. Galectin-1 and galectin-3 binding pattern expression in renal cell carcinomas. Am J Clin Pathol 1999, **112:** 194–203.

935 Giordano TJ, Medeiros LJ, Monterroso V, Linehan WM, Merino MJ. Transthyretin (prealbumin) immunoreactivity in renal cell carcinoma and other neoplasms. Int J Surg Pathol 1996, **4:** 1–8.

936 Gotoh A, Kitazawa S, Mizuno Y, Takenaka A, Arakawa S, Matsumoto O, Kitazawa R, Fujimori T, Maeda S, Kamidono S. Common expression of parathyroid hormone-related protein and no correlation of calcium level in renal cell carcinomas. Cancer 1993, **71:** 2803–2806.

937 Gröne H-J, Weber K, Helmchen U, Osborn M. Villin. A marker of brush border differentiation and cellular origin in human renal cell carcinoma. Am J Pathol 1986, **124:** 294–302.

938 Haimoto H, Takashi M, Koshikawa T, Asai J, Kato K. Enolase isozymes in renal tubules and renal cell carcinoma. Am J Pathol 1986, **124**: 488–495.

939 Holthöfer H, Miettinen A, Passivuo R, Lehto V-P, Linder E, Alfthan O, Virtanen I. Cellular origin and differentiation of renal carcinomas. A fluorescence microscopic study with kidney-specific antibodies, antiintermediate filament antibodies, and lectins. Lab Invest 1983, **49**: 317–326.

940 Howie AJ, Smithson N, Raafat F. Distinctive patterns of renal neoplasms containing Tamm-Horsfall protein. Virchows Arch [A] 1993, **422**: 361–365.

940a Ibrahim EC, Allory Y, Commo F, Gattegno B, Callard P, Paul P. Altered pattern of major histocompatibility complex expression in renal carcinoma. Tumor-specific expression of the nonclassical human leukocyte antigen-G molecule is restricted to clear cell carcinoma while up-regulation of other major histocompatibility complex antigens is primarily distributed in all subtyes of renal carcinoma. Am J Pathol 2003, **162**: 501–508.

941 Kaufmann O, Dietel M, Scherberich JE, Gaedicke G, Fischer P. Immunohistochemical differentiation of metastases of renal carcinomas versus other carcinomas with anti-γGT monoclonal antibody 138H11. Histopathology 1997, **31**: 31–37.

941a Kim M-K, Kim S. Immunohistochemical profile of common epithelial neoplasms arising in the kidney. Appl Immuno Mol Morphol 2002, **10**: 332–338.

942 Kraus S, Abel PD, Nachtmann C, Linsenmann H-J, Weidner W, Stamp GWH, Chaudhary KS, Mitchell SE, Franke FE, Lalani E-N. MUC1 mucin and trefoil factor 1 protein expression in renal cell carcinoma: correlation with prognosis. Hum Pathol 2002, **33**: 60–67.

942a Le Jan S, Amy C, Cazes A, Monnot C, Lamande N, Favier J, Philippe J, Sibony M, Gasc J-M, Corvol P, Germain S. Angiopoietin-like 4 is a proangiogenic factor produced during ischemia and in conventional renal cell carcinoma. Am J Pathol 2003, **16**: 1521–1528.

943 Leroy X, Copin M-C, Devisme L, Buisine M-P, Aubert J-P, Gosselin B, Porchet N. Expression of human mucin genes in normal kidney and renal cell carcinoma. Histopathology 2002, **40**: 450–457.

944 Liebert M, Jaffe R, Taylor RJ, Ballou BT, Solter D, Hakala TR. Detection of SSEA-1 on human renal tumors. Cancer 1987, **59**: 1404–1408.

945 McGregor DK, Khurana KK, Cao C, Tsao CC, Ayala G, Krishnan B, Ro JY, Lechago J, Truong LD. Diagnosing primary and metastatic renal cell carcinoma: the use of the monoclonal antibody "renal cell carcinoma marker." Am J Surg Pathol 2001, **25**: 1485–1492.

946 Mackay B, Ordóñez NG, Khoursand J. The ultrastructure and immunocytochemistry of renal cell carcinoma. Ultrastruct Pathol 1987, **11**: 483–502.

947 MacLennan GT, Farrow GM, Gostwick DG. Immunohistochemistry in the evaluation of renal cell carcinoma: a critical appraisal. J Urol Pathol 1997, **6**: 195–204.

947a Moch H, Mihatsch MJ. Genetic progression of renal cell carcinoma. Virchows Arch 2002, **441**: 320–327.

948 Moch H, Sauter G, Buchholz N, Gasser TC, Bubendorf L, Waldman FM, Mihatsch MJ. Epidermal growth factor receptor expression is associated with rapid tumor cell proliferation in renal cell carcinoma. Hum Pathol 1997, **28**: 1255–1259.

949 Nappi O, Mills SE, Swanson PE, Wick MR. Clear cell tumors of unknown nature and origin: a systematic approach to diagnosis. Semin Diagn Pathol 1997, **14**: 164–174.

950 Nolan LP, Heatley MK. The value of immunohistochemistry in distinguishing between clear cell carcinoma of the kidney and ovary. Int J Gynecol Pathol 2001, **20**: 155–159.

951 Oosterwijk E, Ruiter DJ, Wakka JC, Meij JWH-VD, Jonas U, Fleuren G-J, Zwartendijk J, Hoedemaeker P, Warnaar SO.

Immunohistochemical analysis of monoclonal antibodies to renal antigens. Application in the diagnosis of renal cell carcinoma. Am J Pathol 1986, **123**: 301–309.

952 Pitz S, Moll R, Störkel S, Thoenes W. Expression of intermediate filament proteins in subtypes of renal cell carcinomas and in renal oncocytomas. Distinction of two classes of renal cell tumors. Lab Invest 1987, **56**: 642–653.

953 Renshaw AA, Granter SR. A comparison of A103 and inhibin reactivity in adrenal cortical tumors: distinction from hepatocellular carcinoma and renal tumors. Mod Pathol 1998, **11**: 1160–1164.

954 Shah IA, Mellstrom M, Wheeler L, Haddad FS. CD68 immunoreactivity in renal cell carcinoma: an aid to diagnosis and histogenesis. J Urol Pathol 1996, **5**: 193–206.

955 Shazizadeh M, Kagawa S, Kurokawa K. Immunohistochemical studies of human renal cell carcinoma for ABO(H) blood group antigens, T antigen-like substance and carcinoembryonic antigen. J Urol 1985, **133**: 762–766.

956 Takada Y, Hiwada K, Yokoyama M, Ochi K, Takeuchi M, Kokubu T. Angiotensin converting enzyme. A possible histologic indicator for human renal cell carcinoma. Cancer 1988, **61**: 889–895.

957 Takashi M, Haimoto H, Koshikawa T, Kato K. Expression of aldolase C isozyme in renal cell carcinoma. Am J Clin Pathol 1990, **93**: 631–636.

958 Takashi M, Haimoto H, Murase T, Mitsuya H, Kato K. An immunochemical and immunohistochemical study of S 100 protein in renal cell carcinoma. Cancer 1988, **61**: 889–895.

959 Terpe HJ, Storkel S, Zimmer U, Anquez V, Fischer C, Pantel K, Gunthert U. Expression of CD44 isoforms in renal cell tumors. Positive correlation to tumor differentiation. Am J Pathol 1996, **148**: 453–463.

960 Ulrich W, Horvat R, Krisch K. Lectin histochemistry of kidney tumours and its pathomorphological relevance. Histopathology 1985, **9**: 1037–1050.

961 Waldherr R, Schwechheimer K. Co-expression of cytokeratin and vimentin intermediate-sized filaments in renal cell carcinomas. Comparative study of the intermediate-sized filament distribution in renal cell carcinomas and normal human kidney. Virchows Arch [A] 1985, **408**: 15–27.

962 Yoshida SO, Iman A, Olson CA, Taylor CR. Proximal renal tubular surface membrane antigens identified in primary and metastatic renal cell carcinomas. Arch Pathol Lab Med 1986, **110**: 825–832.

962a Young AN, de Oliveira Salles P, Lim SD, Cohen C, Petros JA, Marshall FF, Neish AS, Amin MB. Beta defensin-1, parvalbumin, and vimentin. A panel of diagnostic immunohistochemical markers for renal tumors derived from gene expression profiling studies using cDNA microarrays. Am J Surg Pathol 2003, **27**: 199–205.

Molecular genetic features

963 Amo-Takyi BK, Handt S, Gunawan B, Hollweg H-G, Fuzesi L. A cytogenetic approach to the differential diagnosis of metastatic clear cell renal carcinoma. Histopathology 1998, **32**: 436–443.

964 Bugert P, Kovacs G. Molecular differential diagnosis of renal cell carcinomas by microsatellite analysis. Am J Pathol 1996, **149**: 2081–2088.

965 Daniel L, Lechevallier E, Giorgi R, Sichez H, Zattara-Cannoni H, Figarella-Branger D, Coulange C. Pax-2 expression in adult renal tumors. Hum Pathol 2001, **32**: 282–287.

966 El-Naggar AK, Batsakis JG, Wang G, Lee M-S. PCR-based RFLP screening of the commonly deleted 3p loci in renal cortical neoplasms. Diagn Mol Pathol 1993, **2**: 269–276.

967 Eyzaguirre EJ, Miettinen M, Norris BA, Gatalica Z. Different immunohistochemical patterns of Fhit protein expression in renal neoplasms. Mod Pathol 1999, **12**: 979–983.

968 Fleming S. The impact of genetics on the classification of renal carcinoma. Histopathology 1993, **22:** 89–92.

969 Hadeczek P, Podolski J, Toloczko A, Kurzawski G, Sikorski A, Rabbitts P, Huebner K, Lubinski J. Losses at 3p common deletion sites in subtypes of kidney tumours: histopathological correlations. Virchows Arch 1996, **429:** 37–42.

970 Haitel A, Wiener HG, Blaschitz U, Marberger M, Susani M. Biologic behavior of and p53 overexpression in multifocal renal cell carcinoma of clear cell type: an immunohistochemical study correlating grading, staging, and proliferation markers. Cancer 1999, **85:** 1593–1598.

971 Iqbal MA, Akhtar M, Ali MA. Cytogenetic findings in renal cell carcinoma. Hum Pathol 1996, **27:** 949–954.

972 Kattar MM, Grignon DJ, Sarkar FH, Flaherty LE, Shimoyama RK, Tabaczka PM, Sakr WA, Crissman JD. p53 gene expression in renal cell carcinoma: a clinicopathologic analysis and immunohistochemical study with review of the literature. J Urol Pathol 1997, **5:** 207–222.

973 Kovacs G. Molecular differential pathology of renal cell tumours. Histopathology 1993, **22:** 1–8.

974 Lai R, el Dabbagh L, Mourad WA. Mutant p53 expression in kidney tubules adjacent to renal cell carcinoma: Evidence of a precursor lesion. Mod Pathol 1996, **9:** 690–695.

975 Lai S, Benedict WF, Silver SA, El-Naggar AK. Loss of retinoblastoma gene function and heterozygosity at the RB locus in renal cortical neoplasms. Hum Pathol 1997, **28:** 693–697.

976 Lin BT-Y, Brynes RK, Gelb AB, McCourty A, Amin MB, Medeiros LJ. Cyclin D1 expression in renal carcinomas and oncocytomas: An immunohistochemical study. Mod Pathol 1998, **11:** 1075–1081.

977 McCue PA, Gorstein F. Genetic markers in renal cell carcinomas. Hum Pathol 2001, **32:** 1027–1028.

978 Presti JC, Reuter VE, Cordon-Cardo C, Mazumdar M, Fair WR, Jhanwar SC. Allelic deletions in renal tumors. Histopathological correlations. Cancer Res 1993, **53:** 5780–5783.

979 Teyssier JR, Henry I, Dozier C, Ferre D, Adnet JJ, Pluot M. Recurrent deletion of the short arm of chromosome 3 in human renal cell carcinoma. Shift of the c-raf 1 locus. J Natl Cancer Inst 1986, **77:** 1187–1195.

980 van der Hout AH, van den Berg E, van der Vlies P, Dijkhuizen T, Storkel S, Oosterhuis JW, de Jong B, Buys CH. Loss of heterozygosity at the short arm of chromosome 3 in renal-cell cancer correlates with the cytological tumour type. Int J Cancer 1993, **53:** 353–357.

981 Weiss LM, Gelb AB, Medeiros LJ. Adult renal epithelial neoplasms. Am J Clin Pathol 1995, **103:** 624–635.

Other microscopic types

982 Adsay VN, De Roux SJ, Sakr W, Grignon D. Cancer as a marker of genetic medical disease: An unusual case of medullary carcinoma of the kidney. Am J Surg Pathol 1998, **22:** 260–264.

983 Akhtar M, Chantziantoniou N. Flow cytometric and quantitative image cell analysis of DNA ploidy in renal chromophobe cell carcinoma. Hum Pathol 1998, **29:** 1181–1188.

984 Akhtar M, Kardar H, Linjawi T, McClintock J, Ali MA. Chromophobe cell carcinoma of the kidney. A clinicopathologic study of 21 cases. Am J Surg Pathol 1995, **19:** 1245–1256.

985 Akhtar T, Tulbah A, Kardar AH, Ali MA. Sarcomatoid renal cell carcinoma: The chromophobe connection. Am J Surg Pathol 1997, **21:** 1188–1195.

985a Allory Y, Ouazana D, Boucher E, Thiounn N, Vieillefond A. Papillary renal cell carcinoma: prognostic value of morphological subtypes in a clinicopathologic study of 43 cases. Virchows Arch 2003, **442:** 336–342.

986 Amin MB, Corless CL, Renshaw AA, Tickoo SK, Kubus J, Schultz DS. Papillary (chromophil) renal cell carcinoma: Histomorphologic characteristics and evaluation of conventional pathologic prognostic parameters in 62 cases. Am J Surg Pathol 1997, **21:** 621–635.

987 Amin MB, Tamboli P, Javidan J, Stricker H, De Peralta-Venturina M, Deshpande A, Menon M. Prognostic impact of histologic subtyping of adult renal epithelial neoplasms: an experience of 405 cases. Am J Surg Pathol 2002, **26:** 281–291.

988 Amin MB, Varma MD, Tickoo SK, Ro JY. Collecting duct carcinoma of the kidney. Adv Anat Pathol 1997, **4:** 85–94.

988a Argani P, Antonescu CR, Couturier J, Fournet J-C, Sciot R, Debiec-Rychter M, Hutchinson B, Reuter VE, Boccon-Gibod L, Timmons C, Hafez N, Ladanyi M. PRCC-TFE3 renal carcinomas: morphologic, immunohistochemical, ultrastructural, and molecular analysis of an entity associated with +(X;1)(p11; q21). Am J Surg Pathol 2002, **26:** 1553–1566.

989 Argani P, Antonescu CR, Illei PB, Lui MY, Timmons CF, Newbury R, Reuter VE, Garvin AJ, Perez-Atayde AR, Fletcher JA, Beckwith JB, Bridge JA, Ladanyi M. Primary renal neoplasms with the ASPL-TFE3 gene fusion of alveolar soft part sarcoma: a distinctive tumor entity previously included among renal cell carcinomas of children and adolescents. Am J Pathol 2001, **159:** 179–192.

989a Argani P, Lal P, Hutchinson B, Lui MY, Reuter VE, Ladanyi. Aberrant nuclear immunoreactivity for TFE3 in neoplasms with TFE3 gene fusions: a sensitive and specific immunohistochemical assay. Am J Surg Pathol 2003, **27:** 750–761.

990 Auger M, Katz RL, Sella A, Ordóñez NG, Lawrence DD, Ro JY. Fine-needle aspiration cytology of sarcomatoid renal cell carcinoma. A morphologic and immunocytochemical study of 15 cases. Diagn Cytopathol 1993, **9:** 46–51.

991 Baer SC, Ro JY, Ordóñez NG, Maiese RL, Loose JH, Grignon DG, Ayala AG. Sarcomatoid collecting duct carcinoma. A clinicopathologic and immunohistochemical study of five cases. Hum Pathol 1993, **24:** 1017–1022.

992 Bastacky S, McBee A, Fusca F, Beicich MJ. Sarcomatoid renal carcinoma with malignant osseous and chondroid differentiation: case reports and review of the literature. J Urol Pathol 1997, **5:** 119–138.

993 Bonsib SM. Renal chromophobe cell carcinoma : The relationship between cytoplasmic vesicles and colloidal iron stain. J Urol Pathol 1996, **4:** 9–14.

994 Bonsib SM, Lager DJ. Chromophobe cell carcinoma. Analysis of 5 cases. Am J Surg Pathol 1990, **14:** 260–267.

995 Bruno D, Wigfall DR, Zimmerman SA, Rosoff PM, Wiener JS. Genitourinary complications of sickle cell disease. J Urol 2001, **166:** 803–811.

996 Bugert P, Gaul C, Weber K, Hebers J, Akhtar M, Ljungberg B, Kovacs G. Specific genetic changes of diagnostic importance in chromophobe renal cell carcinomas. Lab Invest 1997, **76:** 203–208.

997 Cangiano T, Liao J, Naitoh J, Dorey F, Figlin R, Belldegrun A. Sarcomatoid renal cell carcinoma: biologic behavior, prognosis, and response to combined surgical resection and immunotherapy. J Clin Oncol 1999, **17:** 523–529.

998 Cochand-Priollet B, Molinié V, Bougaran J, Bouvier R, Dauge-Geffroy MC, Deslignieres S, Fournet JC, Gros P, Lesourd A, Saint-Andre JP, Toublanc M, Vieillefond A, Wassef M, Fontaine A, Groleau L. Renal chromophobe cell carcinoma and oncocytoma: a comparative morphologic, histochemical, and immunohistochemical study of 124 cases. Arch Pathol Lab Med 1997, **121:** 1081–1086.

999 Cohen RJ, McNeal JE, Susman M, Sellner LN, Iacopetta BJ, Weinstein SL, Dawkins HJ. Sarcomatoid renal cell carcinoma of papillary origin: a case report and cytogenetic evaluation. Arch Pathol Med Lab 2000, **124:** 1830–1833.

1000 Corless CL, Aburatani H, Fletcher JA, Housman DE, Amin MB, Weinberg DS. Papillary renal cell carcinoma: Quantitation of chromosomes 7 and 17 by FISH, analysis of chromosome 3p for LOH, and DNA ploidy. Diagn Mol Pathol 1996, **5:** 53–64.

1001 Dabbs DJ, Davis AT, Bonsib SM, Jones EC. Comparison of MIB-1 proliferation rates for eosinophilic renal tumors: oncocytoma, chromophobe renal carcinoma, and eosinophilic variant of renal carcinoma. Appl Immunohistochem 1998, **6:** 187–190.

1002 Davies JH, Fisher C. Alpha-fetoprotein-producing collecting duct carcinoma of the kidney. Int J Surg Pathol 1994, **1:** 239–244.

1003 Davis CJ Jr, Mostofi FK, Sesterhenn IA. Renal medullary carcinoma. The seventh sickle cell nephropathy. Am J Surg Pathol 1995, **19:** 1–11.

1004 Deitchman B, Sidhu GS. Ultrastructural study of a sarcomatoid variant of renal cell carcinoma. Cancer 1980, **46:** 1152–1157.

1005 Delahunt B, Eble JN. Papillary renal cell carcinoma: A clinicopathologic and immunohistochemical study of 105 tumors. Mod Pathol 1997, **10:** 537–544.

1006 Delahunt B, Eble JN, McCredie MRE, Bethwaite PB, Stewart JH, Bilous AM. Morphologic typing of papillary renal cell carcinoma: comparison of growth kinetics and patient survival 66 cases. Hum Pathol 2001, **32:** 590–595.

1007 De Long W, Grignon DJ, Eberwein P, Shum DT, Wyatt JK. Sarcomatoid renal cell carcinoma. An immunohistochemical study of 18 cases. Arch Pathol Lab Med 1993, **117:** 636–640.

1008 DeLong WH, Sakr W, Grignon DJ. Chromophobe renal cell carcinoma: a comparative histochemical and immunohistochemical study. J Urol Pathol 1996, **4:** 1–8.

1009 de Peralta-Venturina M, Moch H, Amin M, Tamboli P, Hailemariam S, Mihatsch M, Javidan J, Stricker H, Ro JY, Amin MB. Sarcomatoid differentiation in renal cell carcinoma: a study of 101 cases. Am J Surg Pathol 2001, **25:** 275–284.

1010 Dierick AM, Praet M, Roels H, Verbeeck P, Robyns C, Oosterlinck W. Vimentin expression of renal cell carcinoma in relation to DNA content and histological grading. A combined light microscopic, immunocytochemical and cytophotometrical analysis. Histopathology 1991, **18:** 315–322.

1011 Durham JR, Keohane M, Amin MB. Chromophobe renal cell carcinoma. Adv Anat Pathol 1996, **3:** 336–342.

1012 Eble JN. Renal medullary carcinoma: A distinct entity emerges from the confusion of "collecting duct carcinoma." Adv Anat Pathol 1996, **3:** 233–238.

1013 el-Naggar AK, Gaber K, Ordóñez NG. Renal cell carcinoma with osteoclast-like giant cells. Virchows Arch [A] 1993, **422:** 427–431.

1014 Erlandson RA, Shek TWH, Reuter VE. Diagnostic significance of mitochondria in four types of renal epithelial neoplasms: an ultrastructural study of 60 tumors. Ultrastruct Pathol 1997, **21:** 409–418.

1015 Farrow GM, Harrison EG Jr, Utz DC. Sarcomas and sarcomatoid and mixed malignant tumors of the kidney in adults. Cancer 1968, **22:** 545–563.

1016 Fleming S, Lewi HJE. Collecting duct carcinoma of the kidney. Histopathology 1986, **10:** 1131–1141.

1017 Fleming S, Symes CE. The distribution of cytokeratin antigens in the kidney and in renal tumours. Histopathology 1987, **11:** 157–170.

1018 Fleming S, Lindop GBM, Gibson AAM. The distribution of epithelial membrane antigen in the kidney and its tumours. Histopathology 1985, **9:** 729–739.

1019 Fuzesi L, Cober M, Mittermayer C. Collecting duct carcinoma. Cytogenetic characterization. Histopathology 1992, **21:** 155–160.

1020 Fuzesi L, Gunawan B, Bergmann F, Tack S, Braun S, Jakse G. Papillary renal cell carcinoma with clear cell cytomorphology and chromosomal loss of 3p. Histopathology 1999, **35:** 157–161.

1021 Gatalica Z, Kovatich A, Miettinen M. Consistent expression of cytokeratin 7 in papillary renal-cell carcinoma. An

immunohistochemical study in formalin-fixed, paraffin-embedded tissues. J Urol Pathol 1995, **3:** 205–211.

1022 Gokden N, Nappi O, Swanson PE, Pfeifer JD, Vollmer RT, Wick MR, Humphrey PA. Renal cell carcinoma with rhabdoid features. Am J Surg Pathol 2000, **24:** 1329–1338.

1023 Granter SR, Renshaw AA. Fine-needle aspiration of chromophobe renal cell carcinoma: analysis of six cases. Cancer Cytopathol 1997, **81:** 122–128.

1024 Harris SC, Hird PM, Shortland JR. Immunohistochemistry and lectin histochemistry in sarcomatoid renal cell carcinoma. A comparison with classical renal cell carcinoma. Histopathology 1989, **15:** 607–616.

1025 Henn W, Welter C, Wullich B, Zang KD, Blin N, Seitz G. Chromophobe renal cell carcinoma and renal oncocytoma. A cytogenetic and cytological comparison. J Urol Pathol 1993, **1:** 145–155.

1026 Henn W, Zwergel T, Wullich B, Thonnes M, Zang KD, Seitz G. Bilateral multicentric papillary renal tumors with heteroclonal origin based on tissue-specific karyotype instability. Cancer 1993, **72:** 1315–1318.

1026a Hes O, Hora M, Perez-Montiel DM, Suster S, Curik R, Sokol L, Ondic O, Mikulastik J, Betlach J, Peychl L, Hrabl P, Kodet R, Straka L, Ferak I, Vraec V, Michal M. Spindle and cuboidal renal cell carcinoma, a tumour having frequent association with nephrolithiasis: report of 11 cases including a case with hybrid conventional renal cell carcinoma spindle and cuboidal renal cell carcinoma components. Histopathology 2002, **41:** 549–555.

1027 Ishikawa I, Kovacs G. High incidence of papillary renal cell tumours in patients on chronic haemodialysis. Histopathology 1993, **22:** 135–139.

1028 Jiang F, Richter J, Schraml P, Bubendorf L, Gasser T, Sauter G, Mihatsch M, Moch H. Chromosomal imbalances in papillary renal cell carcinoma. Genetic differences between histological subtypes. Am J Pathol 1998, **153:** 1467–1473.

1029 Kattar MM, Grignon DJ, Wallis T, Haas GP, Sakr WA, Pontes JE, Visscher DW. Clinicopathologic and interphase cytogenetic analysis of papillary (chromophilic) renal cell carcinoma. Mod Pathol 1997, **10:** 1143–1150.

1030 Kennedy SM, Merino MJ, Linehan WM, Roberts JR, Robertson CN, Neumann RD. Collecting duct carcinoma of the kidney. Hum Pathol 1990, **21:** 449–456.

1030a Khoury JD, Abrahams NA, Levin HS, MacLennan GT. The utility of epithelial membrane antigen and vementin in the diagnosis of chromophobe renal cell carcinoma. Ann Diagn Pathol 2002, **6:** 154–158.

1031 Koller A, Kain R, Haitel A, Mazal PR, Asboth F, Susani M. Renal oncocytoma with prominent intracytoplasmic vacuoles of mitochondrial origin. Histopathology 2000, **37:** 264–268.

1032 Kovacs G, Kovacs A. Parenchymal abnormalities associated with papillary renal cell tumors. A morphological study. J Urol Pathol 1993, **1:** 301–312.

1033 Kovacs G, Akhtar M, Beckwith BJ, Bugert P, Cooper CS, Delahunt B, Eble JN, Fleming S, Ljungberg B, Medeiros LJ, Moch H, Reuter VE, Ritz E, Roos G, Schmidt D, Srigley JR, Storkel S, van den Berg E, Zbar B. The Heidelberg classification of renal cell tumors. J Pathol 1997, **183:** 131–133.

1034 Kragel PJ, Walther MM, Pestaner JP, Merino MJ. Sarcomatoid renal cell carcinoma. Five cases with immuno- and lectin histochemistry supporting proximal tubular origin. Int J Surg Pathol 1993, **1:** 107–110.

1034a Kuroda N, Inoue K, Guo L, Miyazaki E, Hayashi Y, Naruse K, Toi M, Hiroi M, Shuin T, Enzan H. Expression of CD9/motility-related protein 1 (MRP-1) in renal parenchymal neoplasms: consistent expression in papillary and chromopobe renal cell carcinomas. Hum Pathol 2001, **32:** 1071–1077.

1035 Kuroda N, Naruse K, Miyazaki E, Hayashi Y, Yoshikawa C,

Ashida S, Moriki T, Yamasaki Y, Numoto S, Yamamoto Y, Yamasaki I, Hiroi M, Shuin T, Enzan H. Vinculin: its possible use as a marker of normal collecting ducts and renal neoplasms with collecting duct system phenotype. Mod Pathol 2000, **13**: 1109–1114.

1035a Kuroiwa K, Kinoshita Y, Shiratsuchi H, Oshiro Y, Tamiya S, Oda Y, Naito S, Tsuneyoshi M. Renal cell carcinoma with rhabdoid features: an aggressive neoplasm. Histopathology 2002, **41**: 538–548.

1036 Latham B, Dickersin GR, Oliva E. Subtypes of chromophobe cell renal carcinoma: an ultrastructural and histochemical study of 13 cases. Am J Surg Pathol 1999, **23**: 530–536.

1036a Leroy X, Zini L, Leteurtre E, Zerimech F, Porchet N, Aubert J-P, Gosselin B, Copin M-C. Morphologic subtyping of papillary renal cell carcinoma: correlation with prognosis and differential expression of MUC1 between the two subtypes. Mod Pathol 2002, **15**: 1126–1130.

1037 Li M, Vuolo MA, Weidenheim KM, Minsky LS. Collecting-duct carcinoma of the kidney with prominent signet ring cell features. Mod Pathol 2001, **14**: 623–628.

1038 Lubensky IA, Schmidt L, Zhuang Z, Weirich G, Pack S, Zambrano N, Walther MM, Choyke P, Linehan MW, Zbar B. Hereditary and sporadic papillary renal carcinomas with c-met mutations share a distinct morphological phenotype. Am J Pathol 1999, **155**: 517–526.

1039 Mai KT, Blew B, Collins JP. Renal cell carcinoma with extensive and minimal sarcomatoid change: prognostic significance and relationship with subtypes of renal cell carcinoma. J Urol Pathol 1999, **11**: 35–46.

1040 Mancilla-Jimenez R, Stanley RJ, Blath RA. Papillary renal cell carcinoma. A clinical, radiologic and pathologic study of 34 cases. Cancer 1976, **38**: 2469–2480.

1040a Martignoni G, Eble JN, Brunelli M, Cheng L, Pea M, Delahunt B. Chromophobe renal cell carcinoma: a clinicopathologic study of 100 cases (Abstract). Mod Pathol 2003, **16**: 161a.

1041 Martignoni G, Pea M, Chilosi M, Brunelli M, Scarpa A, Colato C, Tardanico R, Zamboni G, Bonetti F. Parvalbumin is constantly expressed in chromophobe renal carcinoma. Mod Pathol 2001, **14**: 760–767.

1041a Mathers ME, Pollock AM, Marsh C, O'Donnell M. Cytokeratin 7: a useful adjunct in the diagnosis of chromophobe renal cell carcinoma. Histopathology 2002, **40**: 563–567.

1042 Morell-Quadreny L, Gregori-Romero A, Carda-Batalla C, Llombart-Bosch A. Collecting duct carcinoma of the kidney: a morphologic and DNA flow cytometric study of seven cases. J Urol Pathol 1998, **8**: 69–84.

1043 Ordonez NG, Mackay B, Swanson DA. Renal cell carcinoma with unusual differentiation. Ultrastruct Pathol 1996, **20**: 27–30.

1043a Pavlovich CP, Walther MM, Eyler RA, Hewitt SM, Zbar B, Linehan WM, Merino MJ. Renal tumors in the Birt-Hogg-Dubé syndrome. Am J Surg Pathol 2002, **26**: 1542–1552.

1043b Rakozy C, Schmahl GE, Bogner S, Störkel S. Low-grade tubular-mucinous renal neoplasm: morphologic, immunohistochemical, and genetic features. Mod Pathol 2002, **15**: 1162–1171.

1043c Renshaw AA. Subclassification of renal cell neoplasms: an update for the practising pathologist. Histopathology 2002, **41**: 283–300.

1044 Renshaw AA, Corless CL. Papillary renal cell carcinoma. Histology and immunohistochemistry. Am J Surg Pathol 1995, **19**: 842–849.

1045 Renshaw AA, Corless CL. Papillary renal cell carcinoma: gross features and histologic correlates. J Urol Pathol 1997, **7**: 9–20.

1046 Renshaw AA, Henske EP, Loughlin KR, Shipiro C, Weinberg DS. Aggressive variants of chromophobe renal cell carcinoma. Cancer 1996, **78**: 1756–1761.

1047 Renshaw AA, Maurici D, Fletcher JA. Papillary renal cell carcinoma with rare papillae histologically resembling collecting duct carcinoma. J Urol Pathol 1996, **5**: 65–74.

1048 Renshaw AA, Morgan IW, Fletcher JA. A sarcomatoid renal cell carcinoma with a "hobnail pattern" and immunohistochemical and cytogenetic features of papillary carcinoma. J Urol Pathol 1998, **9**: 93–102.

1049 Renshaw AA, Zhang H, Corless CL, Fletcher JA, Pins MR. Solid variants of papillary (chromophil) renal cell carcinoma: Clinicopathologic and genetic features. Am J Surg Pathol 1997, **21**: 1203–1209.

1050 Ro JY, Ayala AG, Sella A, Samuels ML, Swanson DA. Sarcomatoid renal cell carcinoma. Clinicopathologic. A study of 42 cases. Cancer 1987, **59**: 516–526.

1051 Rodriguez-Jurado R, Gonzalez-Crussi F. Renal medullary carcinoma: Immunohistochemical and ultrastructural observations. J Urol Pathol 1996, **4**: 191–203.

1052 Rumpelt HJ, Störkel S, Moll R, Scharfe T, Thoenes W. Bellini duct carcinoma. Further evidence for this rare variant of renal cell carcinoma. Histopathology 1991, **18**: 115–122.

1052a Sanders ME, Mick R, Tomaszewski JE, Barr FG. Unique patterns of allelic imbalance distinguish Type 1 from Type 2 sporadic papillary renal cell carcinoma. Am J Pathol 2002, **161**: 997–1005.

1053 Skinnider BF, Jones EC. Renal oncocytoma and chromophobe renal cell carcinoma: A comparison of colloidal iron staining and electron microscopy. Am J Clin Pathol 1999, **111**: 796–803.

1054 Speicher MR, Schoell B, du Manoir S, Schrock E, Ried T, Cremer T, Störkel S, Kovacs A, Kovacs G. Specific loss of chromosomes 1, 2, 6, 10, 13, 17, and 21 in chromophobe renal carcinomas revealed by comparative genomic hybridization. Am J Pathol 1994, **145**: 356–364.

1055 Srigley JR, Eble JN. Collecting duct carcinoma of kidney. Semin Diagn Pathol 1998, **15**: 54–67.

1056 Taki A, Nakatani Y, Misugi K, Yao M, Nagashima Y. Chromophobe renal cell carcinoma: an immunohistochemical study of 21 Japanese cases. Mod Pathol 1999, **12**: 310–317.

1057 Thoenes W, Störkel S, Rumpelt HJ. Human chromophobe cell renal carcinoma. Virchows Arch [Cell Pathol] 1985, **48**: 207–217.

1058 Tickoo SK, Amin MB. Discriminant nuclear features of renal oncocytoma and chromophobe renal cell carcinoma. Analysis of their potential utility in the differential diagnosis. Am J Clin Pathol 1998, **110**: 782–787.

1059 Tickoo SK, Amin MB, Zarbo RJ. Colloidal iron staining in renal epithelial neoplasms, including chromophobe renal cell carcinoma: Emphasis on technique and patterns of staining. Am J Surg Pathol 1998, **22**: 419–424.

1060 Tickoo SK, Reuter VE, Amin MB, Srigley JR, Epstein JI, Min KW, Rubin MA, Ro JY. Renal oncocytosis: a morphologic study of fourteen cases. Am J Surg Pathol 1999, **23**: 1094–1101.

1061 Tickoo ST, Lee MW, Eble JN, Amin M, Christopherson T, Zarbo RJ, Amin MB. Ultrastructural observations on mitochondria and microvesicles in renal oncocytoma, chromophobe renal cell carcinoma, and eosinophilic variant of conventional (clear cell) renal cell carcinoma. Am J Surg Pathol 2000, **24**: 1247–1256.

1062 Tomera KM, Farrow GM, Lieber MM. Sarcomatoid renal carcinoma. J Urol 1983, **130**: 657–659.

1063 Wiatrowska BA, Zakowski MF. Fine-needle aspiration biopsy of chromophobe renal cell carcinoma and oncocytoma: comparison of cytomorphologic features. Cancer Cytopathol 1999, **87**: 161–167.

1064 Wilson EJ, Resnick MI, Jacobs G. Sarcomatoid chromophobe renal cell carcinoma: report of an additional case with ultrastructural findings. J Urol Pathol 1999, **11**: 113–122.

Cytology

1065 Bibbo M, Gill WB, Harris MJ, Lu C-T, Thomsen S, Wied GL. Retrograde brushing as a diagnostic procedure of ureteral, renal pelvic and renal calyceal lesions. A preliminary report. Acta Cytol (Baltimore) 1974, **18**: 137–141.

1066 Cajulis RS, Katz RL, Dekmezian R, el-Naggar A, Ro JY. Fine needle aspiration biopsy of renal cell carcinoma. Cytologic parameters and their concordance with histology and flow cytometric data. Acta Cytol 1993, **37**: 367–372.

1067 Nguyen G-K. Percutaneous fine-needle aspiration biopsy cytology of the kidney and adrenal. Pathol Annu 1987, **22**(Pt 1): 163–191.

1068 Renshaw AA, Granter SR, Cibas ES. Fine-needle aspiration of the adult kidney. Cancer Cytopathol 1997, **81**: 71–88.

Spread and metastases

1069 Aizawa F, Suzuki M, Kikuchi Y, Nikaido T, Matsumoto K. Clinicopathological study on small renal cell carcinomas with metastases. Acta Pathol Jpn 1987, **37**: 947–954.

1070 Bonsib SM, Gibson D, Mhoon M, Greene GF. Renal sinus involvement in renal cell carcinomas. Am J Surg Pathol 2000, **24**: 451–458.

1071 Datta MW, Ulbright TM, Young RH. Renal cell carcinoma metastatic to the testis and its adnexa: a report of five cases including three that accounted for the initial clinical presentation. Int J Surg Pathol 2001, **9**: 49–56.

1072 Fairlamb DJ. Spontaneous regression of metastases of renal cancer. A report of two cases including the first recorded regression following irradiation of a dominant metastasis and review of the world literature. Cancer 1981, **47**: 2102–2106.

1073 Foucar E, Dehner LP. Renal cell carcinoma occurring with contralateral adrenal metastasis. A clinical and pathological trap. Arch Surg 1979, **114**: 959–963.

1074 Garfield DH, Kennedy BJ. Regression of metastatic renal cell carcinoma following nephrectomy. Cancer 1972, **30**: 190–196.

1075 Gurney H, Larcos G, McKay M, Kefford R, Langlands A. Bone metastases in hypernephroma. Frequency of scapular involvement. Cancer 1989, **64**: 1429–1431.

1076 Holland JM. Cancer of the kidney. Natural history and staging. Cancer 1973, **32**: 1030–1042.

1076a Insabato L, De Rosa G, Franco R, D'Onofrio V, Di Vizio D. Ovarian metastasis from renal cell carcinoma : a report of three cases. Int J Surg Pathol (In press).

1077 Kinouchi T, Mano M, Saiki S, Meguro N, Maeda O, Kuroda M, Usami M, Kotake I. Incidence rate of satellite tumors in renal cell carcinoma. Cancer 1999, **86**: 2331–2337.

1078 Leung CS, Srigley JR, Robertson AR. Metastatic renal cell carcinoma presenting as solitary bleeding prostatic metastasis. J Urol Pathol 1997, **7**: 127–132.

1079 McNichols DW, Segura JW, DeWeerd JH. Renal cell carcinoma. Long-term survival and late recurrence. J Urol 1981, **126**: 17–23.

1080 Marlowe SD, Swartz JD, Koenigsberg R, Zwillenberg S, Marlowe FI, Looby C. Metastatic hypernephroma to the larynx. An unusual presentation. Neuroradiology 1993, **35**: 242–243.

1081 Matias-Guiu X, Garcia A, Curell R, Prat J. Renal cell carcinoma metastatic to the thyroid gland. A comparative molecular study between the primary and the metastatic tumor. Endocr Pathol 1998, **9**: 255–260.

1082 Melnick SJ, Amazon K, Dembrow V. Metastatic renal cell carcinoma presenting as a parotid tumor. A case report with immunohistochemical findings and a review of the literature. Hum Pathol 1989, **20**: 195–197.

1083 Nishio S, Tsukamoto H, Fukui M, Matsubara T. Hypophyseal metastatic hypernephroma mimicking a pituitary adenoma. Case report. Neurosurg Rev 1992, **15**: 319–322.

1084 Okabe Y, Ohoka H, Miwa T, Nagayama I, Furukawa M. View from beneath. Pathology in focus. Renal cell carcinoma metastasis to the tongue. J Laryngol Otol 1992, **106**: 282–284.

1085 Previte SR, Willscher MK, Burke CR. Renal cell carcinoma with solitary contralateral adrenal metastasis. Experience with 2 cases. J Urol 1982, **128**: 132–134.

1086 Radley MG, McDonald JV, Pilcher WH, Wilbur DC. Late solitary cerebral metastases from renal cell carcinoma. Report of two cases. Surg Neurol 1993, **39**: 230–234.

1087 Saitoh H, Hida M, Nakamura K, Takao S, Shiramizu T, Satoh H. Metastatic processes and a potential indication of treatment for metastatic lesions of renal adenocarcinoma. J Urol 1982, **128**: 916–918.

1088 Shah IA, Haddad FS, Wheeler L, Chinichian A. Metastatic renal cell carcinoma: Late recurrence and prolonged survival. J Urol Pathol 1996, **4**: 289–298.

1089 Sim SJ, Ro JY, Ordonez NG, Park YW, Kee KH, Ayala AG. Metastatic renal cell carcinoma to the bladder: A clinicopathologic and immunohistochemical study. Mod Pathol 1999, **12**: 351–355.

1090 Skinner DG, Colvin RB, Vermillion CD, Pfister RC, Leadbetter WF. Diagnosis and management of renal cell carcinoma. A clinical and pathologic study of 309 cases. Cancer 1971, **28**: 1165–1177.

1091 Troncoso A, Ro JY, Grignon DJ, Han WS, Wexler H, von Eschenbach A, Ayala AG. Renal cell carcinoma with acrometastasis. Report of two cases and review of the literature. Mod Pathol 1991, **4**: 66–69.

1092 Wick MR, Cherwitz DL, McGlennen RC, Dehner LP. Adrenocortical carcinoma. An immunohistochemical comparison with renal cell carcinoma. Am J Pathol 1986, **122**: 343–352.

1093 Young RH, Hart WR. Renal cell carcinoma metastatic to the ovary. A report of three cases emphasizing possible confusion with ovarian clear cell adenocarcinoma. Int J Gynecol Pathol 1992, **11**: 96–104.

Therapy

1094 Appelqvist P. The role and value of surgery in metastatic renal adenocarcinoma. A retrospective clinical study of 106 nephrectomized cases. J Surg Oncol 1984, **26**: 138–145.

1095 Atkins MB, Dutcher J, Weiss G, Margolin K, Clark J, Sosman J, Logan T, Aronson F, Mier J, Cytokine Working Group. Kidney cancer: the Cytokine Working Group experience (1986-2001): part 1. IL-2-based clinical trials. Med Oncol 2001, **18**: 197–207.

1096 Bissada NK. Renal cell adenocarcinoma. Surg Gynecol Obstet 1977, **145**: 97–104.

1097 DeKernion JB, Berry D. The diagnosis and treatment of renal cell carcinoma. Cancer 1980, **45**: 1947–1956.

1098 Frydenberg M, Malek RS, Zincke H. Conservative renal surgery for renal cell carcinoma in von Hippel–Lindau's disease. J Urol 1993, **149**: 461–464.

1099 Katzenstein A-L, Purvis R Jr, Gmelich J, Askin F. Pulmonary resection for metastatic renal adenocarcinoma. Pathologic findings and therapeutic value. Cancer 1978, **41**: 712–723.

1100 Lund GO, Fallon B, Curtis MA, Williams RD. Conservative surgical therapy of localized renal cell carcinoma in von Hippel–Lindau disease. Cancer 1994, **74**: 2541–2545.

1101 Marshall FF, Powell KC. Lymphadenectomy for renal cell carcinoma. Anatomical and therapeutic considerations. J Urol 1982, **128**: 677–681.

1102 Marshall FF, Walsh PC. In situ management of renal tumors. Renal cell carcinoma and transitional cell carcinoma. J Urol 1984, **131**: 1045–1049.

1103 Nathan PD, Eisen TG. The biological treatment of renal-cell carcinoma and melanoma. Lancet Oncol 2002, **3**: 89–96.

1104 Novick AC. Partial nephrectomy for renal cell carcinoma. Urol Clin North Am 1987, **14**: 419–433.

1105 Pantuck AJ, Zisman A, Belldegrun A. Gene and immune therapy for renal cell carcinoma. Int J Urol 2001, **8**: S1–4.

1106 Phillips E, Messing EM. Role of lymphadenectomy in the treatment of renal cell carcinoma. Urology 1993, **41**: 9–15.

1107 Piltz S, Meimarakis G, Wichmann MW, Hatz R, Schildberg FW, Fuerst H. Long-term results after pulmonary resection of renal cell carcinoma metastases. Ann Thorac Surg 2002, **73**: 1082–1087.

1108 Pogrebniak HW, Haas G, Linehan WM, Rosenberg SA, Pass HI. Renal cell carcinoma. Resection of solitary and multiple metastases. Ann Thorac Surg 1992, **54**: 33–38.

1109 Rabban JT, Meng MV, Yeh B, Koppie T, Ferrell L, Stoller ML. Kidney morcellation in laparoscopic nephrectomy for tumor: recommendations for specimen sampling and pathologic tumor staging. Am J Surg Pathol 2001, **25**: 1158–1166.

1110 Robson CJ, Churchill BM, Anderson W. The results of radical nephrectomy for renal cell carcinoma. Trans Am Assoc Genitourin Surg 1968, **60**: 122–126.

1111 Steinbach F, Stockle M, Muller SC, Thuroff JW, Melchior SW, Stein R, Hohenfellner R. Conservative surgery of renal cell tumors in 140 patients. 21 years of experience. J Urol 1992, **148**: 24–29.

1112 Stephens R, Graham SD Jr. Enucleation of tumor versus partial nephrectomy as conservative treatment of renal cell carcinoma. Cancer 1990, **65**: 2663–2667.

1113 Topley M, Novick AC, Montie JE. Long-term results following partial nephrectomy for localized renal adenocarcinoma. J Urol 1984, **131**: 1050–1052.

1114 Waters WB, Richie JP. Aggressive surgical approach to renal cell carcinoma. Review of 130 cases. J Urol 1979, **122**: 306–309.

Prognosis

1114a Cheville JC, Lohse CM, Zincke H, Weaver AL, Blute ML. Comparisons of outcome and prognostic features among histologic subtypes of renal cell carcinoma. Am J Surg Pathol 2003, **27**: 612–624.

1114b Daniel L, Bouvier C, Chetaille B, Gouvernet J, Luccioni A, Rossi D, Lechevallier E, Muracciole X, Coulange C, Figarella-Branger D. Neural cell adhesion molecular expression in renal cell carcinomas: relation to metastatic behaviour. Hum Pathol 2003, **34**: 528–532.

1115 Delahunt B. Histopathologic prognostic indicators for renal cell carcinoma. Semin Diagn Pathol 1998, **15**: 68–76.

1116 Delahunt B, Kittelson JM, McCredie MRE, Reeve AE, Stewart JH, Bilous AM. Prognostic importance of tumor size for localized conventional (clear cell) renal cell carcinoma: assessment of TNM T1 and T2 tumor categories and comparison with other prognostic parameters. Cancer 2002, **94**: 658–664.

1117 Ekfors TO, Lipasti J, Nurmi MJ, Eerola E. Flow cytometric analysis of the DNA profile of renal cell carcinoma. Pathol Res Pract 1987, **182**: 58–62.

1117a Elmore JM, Kadesky KT, Koeneman KS, Sagalowsky AI. Reassessment of the 1997 TNM classification system for renal cell carcinoma: A 5-cm T1/T2 cutoff is a better predictor of clinical outcome. American Cancer Society 2003, 2329–2334.

1118 Fuhrman SA, Lasky LC, Limas C. Prognostic significance of morphologic parameters in renal cell carcinoma. Am J Surg Pathol 1982, **6**: 655–663.

1119 Gelb AB. Renal cell carcinoma: current prognostic factors. Cancer 1997, **80**: 981–986.

1120 Gelb AB, Shibuya RB, Weiss LM, Medeiros LJ. Stage I renal cell carcinoma. A clinicopathologic study of 82 cases. Am J Surg Pathol 1993, **17**: 275–286.

1121 Gelb AB, Sudilovsky D, Wu CD, Weiss LM, Medeiros LJ. Appraisal of intratumoral microvessel density, MIB-1 score, DNA content, and p53 protein expression as prognostic indicators in patients with locally confined renal cell carcinoma. Cancer 1997, **80**: 1758–1775.

1122 Gettman MT, Blute ML, Spotts B, Bryant SC, Zinche H. Pathologic staging of renal cell carcinoma: significance of tumor classification with the 1997 TNM staging system. Cancer 2001, **91**: 354–361.

1123 Gilcrease MZ, Guzman-Paz M, Niehans G, Cherwitz D, McCarthy JB, Albores-Saavedra J. Correlation of CD44S expression in renal clear cell carcinomas with subsequent tumor progression of recurrence. Cancer 1999, **86**: 2320–2326.

1124 Grignon DJ, Abdel-Malak M, Mertens W, Koster J, Keeney M, Sakr W, Shepherd RR. Prognostic significance of cellular proliferation in renal cell carcinoma. A comparison of synthesis-phase fraction and proliferating cell nuclear antigen index. Mod Pathol 1995, **8**: 18–24.

1125 Grignon DJ, Ayala AG, el-Naggar A, Wishnow KI, Ro JY, Swanson DA, McLemore D, Giacco GG, Guinee VF. Renal cell carcinoma. A clinicopathologic and DNA flow cytometric analysis of 103 cases. Cancer 1989, **64**: 2133–2140.

1126 Grignon DJ, el-Naggar A, Green LK, Ayala AG, Ro JY, Swanson DA, Troncoso P, McLemore D, Giacco GG, Guinee VF. DNA flow cytometry as a predictor of outcome of stage I renal cell carcinoma. Cancer 1989, **63**: 1161–1165.

1127 Haitel A, Wiener HG, Blaschitz U, Marberger M, Susani M. Biologic behavior of and p53 overexpression in multifocal renal cell carcinoma of clear cell type: an immunohistochemical study correlating grading, staging, and proliferation markers. Cancer 1999, **85**: 1593–1598.

1128 Haitel A, Wiener HG, Migschitz B, Marberger M, Susani M. Proliferating cell nuclear antigen and MIB-1; An alternative to classic prognostic indicators in renal cell carcinomas? Am J Clin Pathol 1997, **107**: 229–235.

1129 Jochum W, Schroder S, Al-Taha R, August C, Gross AJ, Berger J, Padberg BC. Prognostic significance of nuclear DNA content and proliferative activity in renal cell carcinomas: A clinicopathologic study of 58 patients using mitotic count, MIB-1 staining, and DNA cytophotometry. Cancer 1996, **77**: 514–521.

1130 Kay S. Renal carcinoma. A 10-year study. Am J Clin Pathol 1968, **50**: 428–432.

1131 Kinouchi T, Saiki S, Meguro N, Maeda O, Kuroda M, Usami M, Kotake T. Impact of tumor size on the clinical outcomes of patients with Robson Stage 1 renal cell carcinoma. Cancer 1999, **85**: 689–695.

1132 Kolbeck PC, Kaveggia FF, Johansson SL, Grune MT, Taylor RJ. The relationships among tumor-infiltrating lymphocytes, histopathologic findings, and long-term clinical follow-up in renal cell carcinoma. Mod Pathol 1992, **5**: 420–425.

1133 Lanigan D, Conroy R, Barry-Walsh C, Loftus B, Royston D, Leader M. A comparative analysis of grading systems in renal adenocarcinoma. Histopathology 1994, **24**: 473–476.

1134 Larsson P, Roos G, Stenling R, Ljungberg B. Tumor-cell proliferation and prognosis in renal-cell carcinoma. Int J Cancer 1993, **55**: 566–570.

1134a Leibovich BC, Blute ML, Cheville JC, Lohse CM, Frank I, Kwon ED, Weaver AL, Parker AS, Zincke H. Prediction of progression after radical nephrectomy for patients with clear cell renal cell carcinoma. A stratification tool for prospective clinical trials. Cancer 2003, **97**: 1663–1671.

1134b Leroy X, Zerimech F, Zini L, Copin M-C, Buisine M-P, Gosselin B, Aubert J-P, Porchet N. MUC1 expression is correlated with nuclear grade and tumor progression in pT1 renal clear cell carcinoma. Am J Clin Pathol 2002, **118**: 47–51.

1135 Lieber MM, Tomera FM, Taylor WF, Farrow GM. Renal adenocarcinoma in young adults. Survival and variables affecting prognosis. J Urol 1981, **125**: 164–168.

1136 Ljungberg B, Stenling R, Roos G. DNA content and prognosis in renal cell carcinoma. A comparison between primary tumors and metastases. Cancer 1986, **57**: 2346–2350.

1136a Lohse CM, Blute ML, Zincke H, Weaver AL, Cheville JC. Comparison of standardized and nonstandardized nuclear grade of renal cell carcinoma to predict outcome among 2,042 patients. Am J Clin Pathol 2002, **118**: 877–886.

1137 Medeiros LJ, Gelb AB, Weiss LM. Low-grade renal cell carcinoma. A clinicopathologic study of 53 cases. Am J Surg Pathol 1987, **11**: 633–642.

1138 Medeiros LJ, Gelb AB, Weiss LM. Renal cell carcinoma. Prognostic significance of morphologic parameters in 21 cases. Cancer 1988, **61**: 1639–1651.

1139 Medeiros LJ, Jones EC, Aizawa S, Aldape HC, Cheville JC, Goldstein NS, Lubensky IA, Ro J, Shanks J, Pacelli A, Jung S-H. Grading of renal cell carcinoma: workgroup no. 2. Cancer 1997, **80**: 990–991.

1140 Minervini A, Lilas L, Minervini R, Selli C. Prognostic value of nuclear grading in patients with intracapsular (pT1–pT2) renal cell carcinoma: long term analysis in 213 patients. Cancer 2002, **94**: 2590–2595.

1141 Moch H, Gasser T, Amin MB, Torhorst J, Sauter G, Mihatsch MJ. Prognostic utility of the recently recommended histologic classification and revised TNM staging system of renal cell carcinoma: A swiss experience with 588 tumors. Cancer 2000, **89**: 604–614.

1142 Montironi R, Santinelli A, Pomante R, Mazzuchelli R, Colanzi P, LongattoFilho A, Scarpelli M. Morphometric index of adult renal cell carcinoma. Comparison with the Fuhrman grading system. Virchows Arch 2000, **437**: 82–89.

1143 Mrstik C, Salamon J, Weber R, Stogermayer F. Microscopic venous infiltration as predictor of relapse in renal cell carcinoma. J Urol 1992, **148**: 271–274.

1144 Nakano E, Kondoh M, Okatani K, Seguchi T, Sugao H. Flow cytometric analysis of nuclear DNA content of renal cell carcinoma correlated with histologic and clinical features. Cancer 1993, **72**: 1319–1323.

1145 Nurmi MJ. Prognostic factors in renal carcinoma. An evaluation of operative findings. Br J Urol 1984, **56**: 270–275.

1145a Parker AS, Cheville JC, Janney CA, Cerhan JR. High expression levels of insulin-like growth Factor-1 receptor predict poor survival among women with clear-cell renal cell carcinomas. Hum Pathol 2002, **33**: 801–805.

1146 Poppel HV, Vandendriessche H, Boel K, Mertens V, Goethuys H, Haustermans K, Van Damme B, Baert L. Microscopic vascular invasion is the most relevant prognosticator after radical nephrectomy for clinically nonmetastatic renal cell carcinoma. J Urol 1997, **158**: 45–49.

1147 Pound CR, Partin AW, Epstein JI, Simons JW, Marshall FF. Nuclear morphometry accurately predicts recurrence in clinically localized renal cell carcinoma. Urology 1993, **42**: 243–248.

1148 Selli C, Hinshaw WM, Woodard BH, Paulson DF. Stratification of risk factors in renal cell carcinoma. Cancer 1984, **52**: 270–275.

1149 Sene AP, Hunt L, McMahon RF, Carroll RN. Renal carcinoma in patients undergoing nephrectomy. Analysis of survival and prognostic factors. Br J Urol 1992, **70**: 125–134.

1150 Thrasher JB, Paulson DF. Prognostic factors in renal cancer. Urol Clin North Am 1993, **20**: 247–262.

1151 Tickoo SK, Amin MB, Linden MD, Zarbo RJ. The MIB-1 tumor proliferation index in adult renal epithelial tumors with granular cytoplasm: biologic implications and differential diagnostic potential. Mod Pathol 1998, **11**: 1115–1121.

1152 Tomera KM, Farrow GM, Lieber MM. Well differentiated (grade I) clear cell renal carcinoma. J Urol 1983, **129**: 933–937.

1153 Uhlman DL, Nguyen PL, Manivel JC, Aeppli D, Resnick JM, Fraley EE, Zhang G, Niehans GA. Association of immunohistochemical staining for p53 with metastatic progression and poor survival in patients with renal cell carcinoma. J Natl Cancer Inst 1994, **86**: 1470–1475.

Adenomas

1154 Aizawa S, Suzuki M, Kikuchi Y, Nikaido T, Matsumoto K. Clinicopathological study on small renal cell carcinomas with metastases. Acta Pathol Jpn 1987, **37**: 947–954.

1155 Arroyo MR, Green DM, Perlman E, Beckwith JB, Argani P. The spectrum of metanephric adenofibroma and related lesions: clinicopathologic study of 25 cases from the National Wilms Tumor Study Group Pathology Center. Am J Surg Pathol 2001, **25**: 433–444.

1156 Ban S, Yoshii S, Tsuruta A, Gotoh Y, Onda T, Shimizu Y, Shibata T. Metanephric adenoma of the kidney: Ultrastructural, immunohistochemical and lectin histochemical studies. Pathol Int 1996, **46**: 661–666.

1156a Brunelli M, Eble JN, Zhang S, Martignoni G, Cheng L. Metanephric adenoma lacks the gains of chromosomes 7 and 17 and loss of Y which are typical of papillary renal cell carcinoma and adenoma. Mod Pathol 2003, **16**: 1060–1063.

1157 Budin RE, McDonnell PJ. Renal cell neoplasms. Their relationship to arteriolonephrosclerosis. Arch Pathol Lab Med 1984, **108**: 138–140.

1158 Dal Cin P, Gaeta J, Huban R, Li FP, Prout GR Jr, Sandberg AA. Renal cortical tumors. Cytogenetic characterization. Am J Clin Pathol 1989, **92**: 408–414.

1159 Davis CJ Jr, Barton JH, Sesterhenn IA, Mostofi FK. Metanephric adenoma. Clinicopathological study of fifty patients. Am J Surg Pathol 1995, **19**: 1101–1114.

1160 Delahunt B, Eble JN. Papillary adenoma of the kidney: An evolving concept. J Urol Pathol 1997, **7**: 99–112.

1160a Drut R, Drut RM, Ortolani C. Metastatic metanephric adenoma with foci of papillary carcinoma in a child. A combined histologic, immunohistochemical, and FISH study. Int J Surg Pathol 2001, **9**: 241–247.

1161 Ellis WJ, Bauer KD, Oyasu R, McVary KT. Flow cytometric analysis of small renal tumors. J Urol 1992, **148**: 1774–1777.

1162 Gatalica Z, Grujic S, Kovatich A, Petersen RO. Metanephric adenoma: Histology, immunophenotype, cytogenetics, ultrastructure. Mod Pathol 1996, **9**: 329–333.

1163 Granter SR, Fletcher JA, Renshaw AA. Cytologic and cytogenetic analysis of metanephric adenoma of the kidney: A report of two cases. Am J Clin Pathol 1997, **108**: 544–549.

1164 Grignon DJ, Eble JN. Papillary and metanephric adenomas of the kidney. Semin Diagn Pathol 1998, **15**: 41–53.

1165 Holm-Nielsen P, Olsen TS. Ultrastructure of renal adenoma. Ultrastruct Pathol 1988, **12**: 27–39.

1166 Hughson MD, Hennigar GR, McManus JFA. Atypical cysts, acquired renal cystic disease, and renal cell tumors in end stage dialysis kidneys. Lab Invest 1980, **42**: 475–480.

1167 Jones EC, Pins M, Dickersin GR, Young RH. Metanephric adenoma of the kidney. A clinicopathological, immunohistochemical, flow cytometric, cytogenetic, and electron microscopic study of seven cases. Am J Surg Pathol 1995, **19**: 615–626.

1168 Kobs DG III, Crotty K, Orihuela E, Cowan DF. Renal adenomatosis in acquired renal cystic disease without dialysis. J Urol Pathol 1996, **4**: 273–282.

1169 Ligato S, Ro JY, Tamboli P, Amin MB, Ayala AG. Benign tumors and tumor-like lesions of the adult kidney. Part 1: Benign renal epithelial neoplasms. Adv Anat Pathol 1999, **6**: 1–11.

1170 Muir TE, Cheville JC, Lager DJ. Metanephric adenoma, nephrogenic rests, and Wilms' tumor: A histologic and immunophenotypic comparison. Am J Surg Pathol 2001, **25**: 1290–1296.

1171 Pins MR, Jones EC, Martul EV, Kamat BR, Umlas J, Renshaw AA. Metanephric adenoma-like tumors of the kidney: report of 3 malignancies with emphasis on discriminating features. Arch Pathol Lab Med 1999, **123**: 415–420.

1172 Renshaw AA, Fryer DR, Hammers YA. Metastatic metanephric adenoma in a child. Am J Surg Pathol 2000, **24**: 570–574.

1173 Strong JW, Ro JY. Metanephric adenoma of the kidney: A newly characterized entity. Adv Anat Pathol 1996, **3**: 172–178.

1174 Suzuki M, Nikaido T, Ikegami M, Kikuchi Y, Takasaki S, Furusato M, Aizawa S. Renal adenoma. Clinicopathological and histochemical studies. Acta Pathol Jpn 1989, **39**: 731–736.

Oncocytoma and oncocytosis

1175 Alanen KA, Ekfors TO, Lipasti JA, Nurmi MJ. Renal oncocytoma. The incidence of 18 surgical and 12 autopsy cases. Histopathology 1984, **8**: 731–737.

1176 Amin MB, Crotty T, Tickoo S, Farrow G. Renal oncocytoma: a reappraisal of morphologic features with clinicopathologic findings in 80 cases. Am J Surg Pathol 1997, **21**: 1–12.

1176a Baiyee D, Jiang Z, Banner B. CD3 is a good marker for renal oncocytomas (Abstract). Mod Pathol 2003, **16**: 265a.

1177 Barnes CA, Beckman EN. Renal oncocytoma and its congeners. Am J Clin Pathol 1983, **79**: 312–318.

1178 Bonsib SM, Bromley C, Lager DJ. Renal oncocytoma. Diagnostic utility of cytokeratin-containing globular filamentous bodies. Mod Pathol 1991, **4**: 16–23.

1179 Chang A, Harawi SJ. Oncocytes, oncocytosis, and oncocytic tumors. Pathol Annu 1992, **27**(Pt 1): 263–304.

1179a Chen TS, McNally M, Hulbert W, Di Sant'Agnese PA, Huang J. Renal oncocytosis presenting in childhood: a case report. Int J Surg Pathol 2003, **11**: 325–329.

1180 Choi H, Almagro UA, McManus JT, Norback DH, Jacobs SC. Renal oncocytoma. A clinicopathologic study. Cancer 1983, **51**: 1887–1896.

1181 Chu PG, Weiss LM. Cytokeratin 14 immunoreactivity distinguishes oncocytic tumour from its renal mimics: an immunohistochemical study of 63 cases. Histopathology 2001, **39**: 455–462.

1182 Crotty TB, Lawrence KM, Moertel CA, Bartelt DH Jr, Batts KP, Dewald GW, Farrow GM, Jenkins RB. Cytogenetic analysis of six renal oncocytomas and a chromophobe cell renal carcinoma. Evidence that -Y, -1 may be a characteristic anomaly in renal oncocytomas. Cancer Genet Cytogenet 1992, **61**: 61–66.

1183 Davidson AJ, Hayes WS, Hartman DS, McCarthy WF, Davis CJ Jr. Renal oncocytoma and carcinoma. Failure of differentiation with CT. Radiology 1993, **186**: 693–696.

1184 Davis CJ Jr, Sesterhenn IA, Mostofi FK, Ho CK. Renal oncocytoma. Clinicopathological study of 166 patients. J Urogen Pathol 1991, **1**: 41–52.

1185 Dobin SM, Harris CP, Reynolds JA, Coffield KS, Klugo RC, Peterson RF, Speights VO. Cytogenetic abnormalities in renal oncocytic neoplasms. Genes Chromosom Cancer 1992, **4**: 25–31.

1186 Eble JN, Hull MT. Morphologic features of renal oncocytoma. A light and electron microscopic study. Hum Pathol 1984, **15**: 1054–1061.

1187 Hartwick RW, el-Naggar AK, Ro JY, Srigley JR, McLemore DD, Jones EC, Grignon DJ, Thomas MJ, Ayala AG. Renal oncocytoma and granular renal cell carcinoma. A comparative clinicopathologic and DNA flow cytometric study. Am J Clin Pathol 1992, **98**: 587–593.

1187a Hes O, Michal M, Buodova L, Mukensnable P, Kindor Z, Miculka P. Small cell variant of renal oncocytoma – a rare and misleading type of benign renal tumor. Int J Surg Pathol 2001, **9**: 215–222.

1188 Kadesky KT, Fulgham PF. Bilateral multifocal renal oncocytoma. Case report and review of the literature. J Urol 1993, **150**: 1227–1228.

1189 Klein MJ, Valensi QJ. Proximal tubular adenomas of kidney with so-called oncocytic features. A clinicopathologic study of 13 cases of a rarely reported neoplasm. Cancer 1976, **38**: 906–914.

1190 Lewi HJE, Alexander CA, Fleming S. Renal oncocytoma. Br J Urol 1986, **58**: 12–15.

1191 Licht MR, Novick AC, Tubbs RR, Klein EA, Levin HS, Streem SB. Renal oncocytoma. Clinical and biological correlates. J Urol 1993, **150**: 1380–1383.

1192 Lieber MM, Tomera KM, Farrow GM. Renal oncocytoma. J Urol 1981, **125**: 481–485.

1193 Liu J, Fanning CV. Can renal oncocytomas be distinguished from renal cell carcinoma on fine-needle aspiration specimens?: a study of conventional smears in conjunction with ancillary studies. Cancer Cytopathol 2001, **93**: 390–397.

1194 Lloreta-Trull J, Serrano S. Biology and pathology of the mitochondrion. Ultrastruct Pathol 1998, **22**: 357–368.

1195 Lyzak JS, Farhood A, Verani R. Intracytoplasmic lumens in renal oncocytoma and possible origin from intercalated cells of the collecting duct. J Urol Pathol 1994, **2**: 135–152.

1196 Medeiros LJ, Gelb AB, Weiss LM. Low-grade renal cell carcinoma. A clinicopathologic study of 53 cases. Am J Surg Pathol 1987, **11**: 633–642.

1197 Merino MJ, LiVolsi VA. Oncocytomas of the kidney. Cancer 1982, **50**: 1852–1856.

1198 Perez-Ordonez B, Hamed G, Campbell S, Erlandson RA, Russo P, Gaudin PB, Reuter VE. Renal oncocytoma: A clinicopathologic study of 70 cases. Am J Surg Pathol 1997, **21**: 871–883.

1199 Pitz S, Moll R, Störkel S, Thoenes W. Expression of intermediate filament proteins in subtypes of renal cell carcinomas and in renal oncocytomas. Distinction of two classes of renal cell tumors. Lab Invest 1987, **56**: 642–653.

1199a Rampino T, Gregorini M, Soccio G, Maggio M, Rosso R, Malvezzi P, Collesi C, Dal Canton A. The Ron proto-oncogene product is a phenotype marker of renal oncocytoma. Am J Surg Pathol 2003, **27**: 779–785.

1200 Shimazaki H, Tanaka K, Aida S, Tamai S, Segusci K, Hayakawa M. Renal oncocytoma with intracytoplasmic lumina: a case report with ultrastructural findings of "oncoblasts". Ultrastruct Pathol 2001, **25**: 153–158.

1201 Tallini G. Oncocytic tumours. Virchows Arch 1998, **433** : 5–12.

1202 Tallini G, Ladanyi M, Rosai J, Jhanwar SC. Analysis of nuclear and mitochondrial DNA alterations in thyroid and renal oncocytic tumors. Cytogenet Cell Genet 1994, **66**: 253–259.

1203 Tickoo SK, Amin MB, Linden MD, Lee MW, Zarbo RJ. Antimitochondrial antibody (113-1) in the differential diagnosis of granular renal cell tumors. Am J Surg Pathol 1997, **21**: 922–930.

1204 Tickoo SK, Reuter VE, Amin MB, Srigley JR, Epstein JI, Min K-W, Rubin MA, Ro JY. Renal oncocytosis: A morphologic study of fourteen cases. Am J Surg Pathol 1999, **23**: 1094–1101.

1205 van der Walt JD, Reid HAS, Risdon RA, Shaw JHF. Renal oncocytoma. A review of the literature and report of an unusual multicentric case. Virchows Arch [A] 1983, **398**: 291–304.

1206 Veloso JD, Solis OG, Barada JH, Fisher HA, Ross JS. DNA ploidy of oncocytic-granular renal cell carcinomas and renal oncocytomas by image analysis. Arch Pathol Lab Med 1992, **116**: 154–158.

1206a Wu SL, Kothari P, Wheeler TM, Reese T, Connelly JH. Cytokeratins 7 and 20 immunoreactivity in chromophobe renal cell carcinomas and renal oncocytomas. Mod Pathol 2002, **15**: 712–717.

1207 Zhang G, Monda L, Wasserman NF, Fraley EE. Bilateral renal oncocytoma. Report of 2 cases and literature review. J Urol 1985, **133**: 84–86.

Neuroendocrine tumors

1208 Bégin LR, Jamison BM. Renal carcinoid – a tumor of probable hindgut neuroendocrine phenotype. Report of a case and literature review. J Urol Pathol 1993, **3**: 269–382.

1209 Capella C, Eusebi V, Rosai J. Primary oat cell carcinoma of the kidney. Am J Surg Pathol 1984, **8**: 855–861.

1210 Essenfeld H, Manivel JC, Benedette P, Albores-Saavedra J. Small cell carcinoma of the renal pelvis. A clinicopathologic, morphologic and histochemical study of 2 cases. J Urol 1991, **144**: 344–347.

1211 Fetissof F, Benatre A, Dubois MP, Lanson Y, Arbeille-Brassart B, Jobard P. Carcinoid tumor occurring in a teratoid malformation of the kidney. An immunohistochemical study. Cancer 1984, 54: 2305–2308.

1212 Gonzàlez-Lois C, Madero S, Redondo P, Alonso I, Salas A, Montalbàn MA. Small cell carcinoma of the kidney: a case report and review of the literature. Arch Pathol Lab Med 2001, 125: 796–798.

1213 Hannah J, Lippe B, Lai-Goldman M, Bhuta S. Oncocytic carcinoid of the kidney associated with periodic Cushing's syndrome. Cancer 1988, 61: 2136–2140.

1214 Huettner PC, Bird DJ, Chang YC, Seiler MW. Carcinoid tumor of the kidney with morphologic and immunohistochemical profile of a hindgut endocrine tumor. Report of a case. Ultrastruct Pathol 1991, 15: 655–661.

1215 Kojiro M, Ohishi H, Isobe H. Carcinoid tumor occurring in cystic teratoma of the kidney. A case report. Cancer 1976, 38: 1636–1640.

1216 Mills SE, Weiss MA, Swanson PE, Wick MR. Small cell undifferentiated carcinoma of the renal pelvis. A light microscopic, immunocytochemical, and ultrastructural study. Surg Pathol 1988, 1: 83–88.

1217 Morgan KG, Banerjee SS, Eyden BP, Barnard RJ. Primary small cell neuroendocrine carcinoma of the kidney. Ultrastruct Pathol 1996, 20: 141–144.

1218 Raslan WF, Ro JY, Ordóñez NG, Amin MB, Troncoso P, Sella A, Ayala AG. Primary carcinoid of the kidney. Immunohistochemical and ultrastructural studies of five patients. Cancer 1993, 72: 2660–2666.

1219 Takeshima Y, Inai K, Yonedi K. Primary carcinoid tumor of the kidney with special reference to its histogenesis. Pathol Int 1996, 46: 894–900.

1220 Tétu B, Ro JY, Ayala AG, Ordóñez NG, Johnson DE. Small cell carcinoma of the kidney. A clinicopathologic, immunohistochemical, and ultrastructural study. Cancer 1987, 60: 1809–1814.

1221 Unger PD, Russell A, Thung SN, Gordon RE. Primary renal carcinoid. Arch Pathol Lab Med 1990, 114: 68–71.

1221a Yoo J, Park S, Lee Hg, Kang SJ, Kim BK. Primary carcinoid tumor arising in a mature teratoma of the kidney. A case report and review of the literature. Arch Pathol Lab Med 2002, 126: 979–981.

1222 Zak FG, Jindrak K, Capozzi F. Carcinoidal tumor of the kidney. Ultrastruct Pathol 1983, 4: 51–59.

Other epithelial tumors

1223 Adsay NV, Eble JN, Srigley JR, Grignon DJ. Mixed epithelial and stromal tumor of the kidney. Am J Surg Pathol 2000, 24: 958–970.

1223a Aubert S, Duchene F, Augusto D, Llinares K, Lemaitre L, Gosselin B, Leroy X. Low-grade tubular myxoid renal tumours: a clinicopathological study of 3 cases. Int J Surg Pathol (in press).

1224 Parwani AV, Husain AN, Epstein JI, Beckwith JB, Argani P. Low-grade myxoid renal epithelial neoplasms with distal nephron differentiation. Hum Pathol 2001, 32: 506–512.

1225 Pierson CR, Schober MS, Wallis T, Sarkar FH, Sorenson PHB, Eble JN, Srigley JR, Jones EC, Grignon DJ, Adsay V. Mixed epithelial and stromal tumor of the kidney lacks the genetic alterations of cellular congenital mesoblastic nephroma. Hum Pathol 2001, 32: 513–520.

1226 Renshaw AA, Shapiro C, Fletcher JA, Pins MR. An unusual papillary tumor of the renal medulla. Distinction from usual papillary renal cell carcinoma and collecting duct carcinoma. J Urol Pathol 1998, 8: 121–133.

1227 Strobel P, Zettl A, Ren Z, Starostik P, Riedmiller H, Storkel S, Muller-Hermelink HK, Marx A. Spiradenocylindroma of the kidney: Clinical and genetic findings suggesting a role of

somatic mutation of the CYLD1 gene in the oncogenesis of an unusual renal neoplasm. Am J Surg Pathol 2002, 26: 119–124.

Angiomyolipoma

1228 Abdulla M, Bui HX, del Rosario AD, Wolf BC, Ross JS. Renal angiomyolipoma. DNA content and immunohistochemical study of classic and multicentric variants. Arch Pathol Lab Med 1994, 118: 735–739.

1229 Ansari SJ, Stephenson RA, Mackay B. Angiomyolipoma of the kidney with lymph node involvement. Ultrastruct Pathol 1991, 15: 531–538.

1230 Apitz K. Die Geschwülste und Gewebsmissbildungen der Nierenrinde. II. Die mesenchymalen Neubildungen. Virchows Arch 1914, 311: 306–327.

1231 Ashfaq R, Weinberg AG, Albores-Saavedra J. Renal angiomyolipomas and HMB-45 reactivity. Cancer 1993, 71: 3091–3097.

1232 Barnard M, Lajoie G. Angiomyolipoma: Immunohistochemical and ultrastructural study of 14 cases. Ultrastruct Pathol 2001, 25: 21–30.

1233 Bernstein J, Robbins TO, Kissane JM. The renal lesions of tuberous sclerosis. Semin Diagn Pathol 1986, 3: 97–105.

1234 Bonetti F, Pea M, Martignoni G, Zamboni G, Manfrin E, Colombari R, Mariuzzi GM. The perivascular epithelioid cell and related lesions. Adv Anat Pathol 1997, 4: 343–358.

1235 Bonzanini M, Pea M, Martignoni G, Zamboni G, Capelli P, Bernardello F, Bonetti F. Preoperative diagnosis of renal angiomyolipoma. Fine needle aspiration cytology and immunocytochemical characterization. Pathology 1994, 26: 170–175.

1236 Brecher ME, Gill WB, Straus FH II. Angiomyolipoma with regional lymph node involvement and long-term follow-up study. Hum Pathol 1986, 17: 962–963.

1237 Chan JK, Tsang WY, Pau MY, Tang MC, Pang SW, Fletcher CD. Lymphangiomyomatosis and angiomyolipoma. Closely related entities characterized by hamartomatous proliferation of HMB-45-positive smooth muscle. Histopathology 1993, 22: 445–455.

1238 Cheng L, Gu J, Eble JN, Bostwick DG, Younger C, MacLennan GT, Abdul-Karim FW, Geary WA, Koch MO, Zhang S, Ulbright TM. Molecular genetic evidence of different clonal origin of components of human renal angiomyolipomas. Am J Surg Pathol 2001, 25: 1231–1236.

1239 Chowdhury PR, Tsuda N, Anami M, Hayashi T, Iseki M, Kishikawa M, Matsuya F, Kanetake H, Saito Y. A histopathologic and immunohistochemical study of small nodules of renal angiomyolipomas: A comparison of small nodules with angiomyolipoma. Mod Pathol 1996, 9: 1081–1088.

1240 Cibas ES, Goss GA, Kulke MH, Demetri GD, Fletcher CDM. Malignant epithelioid angiomyolipoma ('sarcoma ex angiomyolipoma') of the kidney: a case report and review of the literature. Am J Surg Pathol 2001, 25: 121–126.

1241 Colombat M, Boccon-Gibot L, Carton S. An unusual renal angiomyolipoma with morphological lymphangioleiomyomatosis feature and coexpression of oestrogen and progesterone receptors. Virchows Arch 2002, 440: 102–104.

1242 Daughtry JD, Rodan BA. Renal angiomyolipoma. Definitive diagnosis by ultrasonography and computerized tomography. South Med J 1985, 78: 195–197.

1243 Delgado R, de Leon Bojorge B, Albores-Saavedra J. Atypical angiomyolipoma of the kidney: a distinct morphologic variant that is easily confused with a variety of malignant neoplasms. Cancer 1998, 83: 1581–1592.

1244 Ditonno P, Smith RB, Koyle MA, Hannah J, Belldegrun A. Extrarenal angiomyolipomas of the perinephric space. J Urol 1992, 147: 447–450.

1245 Eble JN. Angiomyolipoma of kidney. Semin Diagn Pathol 1998, **15**: 21–40.

1246 Eble JN, Amin MB, Young RH. Epithelioid angiomyolipoma of the kidney: A report of five cases with a prominent and diagnostically confusing epithelioid smooth muscle component. Am J Surg Pathol 1997, **21**: 1123–1130.

1247 Farrow GM, Harrison EG Jr, Utz DC, Jones DR. Renal angiomyolipoma. A clinicopathologic study of 32 cases. Cancer 1968, **22**: 564–570.

1248 Ferry JA, Malt RA, Young RH. Renal angiomyolipoma with sarcomatous transformation and pulmonary metastases. Am J Surg Pathol 1991, **5**: 1083–1088.

1249 Fetsch PA, Fetsch JF, Marincola FM, Travis W, Batts KP, Abati A. Comparison of melanoma antigen recognized by T cells (MART-1) to HMB-45: additional evidence to support a common lineage for angiomyolipoma, lymphangiomyomatosis, and clear cell sugar tumor. Mod Pathol 1998, **11**: 699–703.

1250 Granter SR, Renshaw AA. Cytologic analysis of renal angiomyolipoma: a comparison of radiologically classic and challenging cases. Cancer Cytopathol 1999, **87**: 135–140.

1251 Graves N, Barnes WF. Renal cell carcinoma and angiomyolipoma in tuberous sclerosis. Case report. J Urol 1986, **135**: 122–123.

1252 Hayashi T, Tsuda N, Chowdhury PR, Iseki M, Anami M, Matsuya F, Kanetake H, Saito Y. Renal angiomyolipoma: clinicopathologic features and differential diagnosis. J Urol Pathol 1999, **10**: 121–140.

1253 Henske EP, Ao X, Short P, Greenberg R, Neumann HPH, Kwiatkowski DJ, Russo I. Frequent progesterone receptor immunoreactivity in tuberous sclerosis-associated renal angiomyolipomas. Mod Pathol 1998, **11**: 665–668.

1254 Hoon V, Thung SN, Kaneko M, Unger PD. HMB-45 reactivity in renal angiomyolipoma and lymphangioleiomyomatosis. Arch Pathol Lab Med 1994, **118**: 732–734.

1255 Hruban RH, Bhagavan BS, Epstein JI. Massive retroperitoneal angiomyolipoma. A lesion that may be confused with well-differentiated liposarcoma. Am J Clin Pathol 1989, **92**: 805–808.

1256 Jimenez RE, Eble JN, Reuter VE, Epstein JI, Folpe AL, de Peralta-Venturina M, Tamboli P, Ansell ID, Grignon DJ, Young RH, Amin MB. Concurrent angiomyolipoma and renal cell neoplasms: a study of 36 cases. Mod Pathol 2001, **14**: 157–163.

1257 Johnson SR, Clelland CA, Ronan J, Tattersfield AE, Knox AJ. The TSC-2 product tuberin is expressed in lymphangioleiomyomatosis and angiomyolipoma. Histopathology 2002, **40**: 458–463.

1258 Jungbluth AA, Iversen K, Coplan K, Williamson B, Chen Y-T, Stockert E, Old LJ, Busam KJ. Expression of melanocyte-associated markers gp-100 and Melan-A/MART-1 in angiomyolipomas. An immunohistochemical and rt-PCR analysis. Virchows Arch 1999, **434**: 429–436.

1259 Jungbluth AA, King R, Fiscel DE, Iversen K, Coplan K, Kolb D, Williamson B, Chen YT, Stockert E, Old LB, Busam KJ. Immunohistochemical and reverse transcription-polymerase chain reaction expression analysis of tyrosinase and microphthalmia-associated transcription factor in angiomyolipomas. AIMM 2001, **9**: 29–34.

1260 Kaiserling E, Kröber S, Xiao J-C, Schaumburg-Lever G. Angiomyolipoma of the kidney. Immunoreactivity with HMB-45. Light- and electron-microscopic findings. Histopathology 1994, **25**: 41–48.

1261 Kattar MM, Grignon DJ, Eble JN, Hurley PM, Lewis PE, Sakr WE, Cher ML. Chromosomal analysis of renal angiomyolipoma by comparative genomic hybridization: evidence for clonal origin. Hum Pathol 1999, **30**: 295–299.

1262 Kawaguchi K-I, Oda Y, Nakanishi K, Saito T, Tamiya S, Nakahara K, Matsuoka H, Tsuneyoshi M. Malignant transformation of renal angiomyolipoma: A case report. Am J Surg Pathol 2002, **26**: 523–529.

1263 Kilicaslan I, Gulluoglu MG, Dogan O, Uysal V. Intraglomerular microlesions in renal angiomyolipoma. Hum Pathol 2000, **31**: 1325–1327.

1264 Kragel PJ, Toker C. Infiltrating recurrent renal angiomyolipoma with fatal outcome. J Urol 1985, **133**: 90–91.

1265 L'Hostis H, DeMiniere C, Ferriere J-M, Coindre J-M. Renal angiomyolipoma: A clinicopathologic, immunohistochemical, and follow-up study of 46 cases. Am J Surg Pathol 1999, **23**: 1011–1020.

1266 Liwnicz BH, Weeks DA, Zuppan CW. Extrarenal angiomyolipoma with melanocytic and hibernoma-like features. Ultrastruct Pathol 1994, **18**: 443–448.

1267 Mai KT, Perkins DG, Collins JP. Epithelioid cell variant of renal angiomyolipoma. Histopathology 1996, **28**: 277–280.

1268 Mai KT, Perkins DG, Robertson S, Thomas J, Morrash C, Collins JP. Composite renal cell carcinoma and angiomyolipoma: A study of the histogenetic relationship of the two lesions. Pathol Int 1999, **49**: 1–8.

1269 Makhlouf HR, Ishak KG, Shekar R, Sesterhenn IA, Young DY, Fanburg-Smith JC. Melanoma markers in angiomyolipoma of the liver and kidney: a comparative study. Arch Pathol Lab Med 2002, **126**: 49–55.

1270 Makhlouf HR, Remotti HE, Ishak KG. Expression of KIT (CD117) in angiomyolipoma. Am J Surg Pathol 2002, **26**: 493–497.

1271 Martignoni G, Bonetti F, Pea M, Tardanico R, Brunelli M, Eble JN. Renal disease in adults with TSC2/PKD1 contiguous gene syndrome. Am J Surg Pathol 2002, **26**: 198–205.

1272 Martignoni G, Pea M, Bonetti F, Brunelli M, Eble JN. Oncocytoma-like angiomyolipoma: A clinicopathologic and immunohistochemical study of 2 cases. Arch Pathol Lab Med 2002, **126**: 610–612.

1273 Martignoni G, Pea M, Bonetti F, Zamboni G, Carbonara C, Longa L, Zancanaro C, Maran M, Brisigotti M, Mariuzzi GM. Carcinomalike monotypic epithelioid angiomyolipoma in patients without evidence of tuberous sclerosis: A clinicopathologic and genetic study. Am J Surg Pathol 1998, **22**: 663–672.

1274 Martignoni G, Pea M, Rigaud G, Manfrin E, Colato C, Zamboni G, Scarpa A, Tardanico R, Roncalli M, Bonetti F. Renal angiomyolipoma with epithelioid sarcomatous transformation and metastases: Demonstration of the same genetic defects in the primary and metastatic lesions. Am J Surg Pathol 2000, **24**: 889–894.

1275 Michal M, Hes O, Havlicek F. Benign renal angiomyoadenomatous tumor: a previously unreported renal tumor. Ann Diagn Pathol 2000, **4**: 311–315.

1276 Monga G, Ramponi A, Falzoni PU, Boldorini R. Renal and hepatic angiomyolipomas in a child without evidence of tuberous sclerosis. Pathol Res Pract 1994, **190**: 1208–1211.

1277 Monteforte WJ Jr, Kohnen PW. Angiomyolipomas in a case of lymphangiomyomatosis syndrome. Relationships to tuberous sclerosis. Cancer 1974, **34**: 317–321.

1278 Mukai M, Torikata C, Iri H, Tamai S, Sugiura H, Tanaka Y, Sakamoto M, Hirohashi S. Crystalloids in angiomyolipoma. 1. A previously unnoticed phenomenon of renal angiomyolipoma occurring at a high frequency. Am J Surg Pathol 1992, **16**: 1–10.

1279 Nonomura A, Minato H, Kurumaya H. Angiomyolipoma predominantly composed of smooth muscle cells: problems in histological diagnosis. Histopathology 1998, **33**: 20–27.

1280 Oesterling JE, Fishman EK, Goldman SM, Marshall FF. The management of renal angiomyolipoma. J Urol 1986, **135**: 1121–1124.

1281 Paradis V, Laurendeau I, Vieillefond A, Blanchet P, Eschwege P, Benoit F, Vidaud M, Jardin A, Bedossa P. Clonal analysis of renal sporadic angiomyolipomas. Hum Pathol 1998, **29:** 1063–1067.

1282 Pea M, Bonetti F, Martignoni G, Henske EP, Manfrin E, Colato C, Bernstein J. Apparent renal cell carcinomas in tuberous sclerosis are heterogeneous: The identification of malignant epithelioid angiomyolipoma. Am J Surg Pathol 1998, **22:** 180–187.

1283 Pea M, Bonetti F, Zamboni G, Martignoni G, Riva M, Colombari R, Mombello A, Bonzanini M, Scarpa A, Ghimenton C, et al. Melanocyte-marker HMB-45 is regularly expressed in angiomyolipoma of the kidney. Pathology 1991, **23:** 185–188.

1284 Plank TL, Logginidou H, Klein-Szanto A, Henske EP. The expression of hamartin, the product of the TSC1 gene in normal human tissues and in TSC1- and TSC2-linked angiomyolipomas. Mod Pathol 1999, **12:** 539–545.

1285 Ro JY, Ayala AG, el-Naggar A, Grignon DJ, Hogan SF, Howard DR. Angiomyolipoma of kidney with lymph node involvement. DNA flow cytometric analysis. Arch Pathol Lab Med 1990, **114:** 65–67.

1285a Sironi M, Spinelli M. Oncocytic angiomyolipoma of the kidney. A case report. Int J Surg Pathol 2003, **11:** 229–234.

1286 Steiner MS, Goldman SM, Fishman EK, Marshall FF. The natural history of renal angiomyolipoma. J Urol 1993, **150:** 1782–1786.

1287 Stone CH, Lee MW, Amin MB, Yaziji H, Gown AM, Ro JY, Tetu B, Paraf F, Zarbo RJ. Renal angiomyolipoma: further immunophenotypic characterization of an expanding morphologic spectrum. Arch Pathol Lab Med 2001, **125:** 751–758.

1288 Sturtz CL, Dabbs DJ. Angiomyolipomas. The nature and expression of the HMB-45 antigen. Mod Pathol 1994, **7:** 842–845.

1289 Waters DJ, Holt SA, Andres DF. Unilateral simultaneous renal angiomyolipoma and oncocytoma. J Urol 1986, **135:** 568–570.

1290 Weeks DA, Chase DR, Malott RL, Chase RL, Zuppan CW, Beckwith JB, Mierau GW. HMB-45 staining in angiomyolipoma, cardiac rhabdomyoma, other mesenchymal processes, and tuberous sclerosis-associated brain lesions. Int J Surg Pathol 1994, **1:** 191–198.

1291 Zamecnik M, Majercik M, Gomolcak P. Renal angiomyolipoma resembling gastrointestinal stromal tumor with skenoid fibers. Ann Diagn Pathol 1999, **3:** 88–91.

1292 Zavala-Pompa A, Folpe AL, Jimenez RE, Lim SD, Cohen C, Elbe JN, Amin MB. Immunohistochemical study of microphthalmia transcription factor and tyrosinase in angiomyolipoma of the kidney, renal cell carcinoma, and renal and retroperitoneal sarcomas: Comparative evaluation with traditional diagnostic markers. Am J Surg Pathol 2001, **25:** 65–70.

Juxtaglomerular cell tumor

1293 Bonsib SM, Hansen KK. Juxtaglomerular cell tumors: a report of two cases with HMB-45 immunostaining. J Urol Pathol 1998, **9:** 61–72.

1294 Camilleri J-P, Hinglais N, Bruneval P, Bariety J, Tricottet V, Rouchon M, Mancilla-Jimenez R, Corvol P, Menard J. Renin storage and cell differentiation in juxtaglomerular cell tumors. An immunohistochemical and ultrastructural study of three cases. Hum Pathol 1984, **15:** 1069–1079.

1295 Conn JW, Cohen EL, Lucas CP, McDonald WJ, Mayor GH, Blough WM Jr, Eveland WC, Bookstin JJ, Lapides J. Primary reninism. Hypertension, hyperreninemia, and secondary aldosteronism due to renin-producing juxtaglomerular cell tumors. Arch Intern Med 1972, **130:** 682–696.

1296 Endoh Y, Motoyama T, Hayami S, Kihara I. Juxtaglomerular cell tumor of the kidney: Report of a non-functioning variant. Pathol Int 1997, **47:** 393–396.

1297 Gherardi GJ, Arya S, Hickler RB. Juxtaglomerular body tumor.

A rare occult but curable cause of lethal hypertension. Hum Pathol 1974, **5:** 236–240.

1298 Hasegawa A. Juxtaglomerular cell tumor of the kidney: a case report with electron microscopic and flow cytometric investigation. Ultrastruct Pathol 1997, **21:** 201–208.

1299 Kim CH, Park YW, Ordonez NG, Ayala AG, Burroughs JF, Ro JY. Juxtaglomerular cell tumor of the kidney: case report with immunohistochemical and electron microscopic investigations and review of the literature. Int J Surg Pathol 1999, **7:** 115–123.

1300 Kodet R, Taylor M, Vachalova H, Pycha K. Juxtaglomerular cell tumor. An immunohistochemical, electron-microscopic, and in situ hybridization study. Am J Surg Pathol 1994, **18:** 837–842.

1301 Lindop GBM, Leckie B, Winearls CG. Malignant hypertension due to a renin-secreting renal cell carcinoma. An ultrastructural and immunocytochemical study. Histopathology 1986, **10:** 1077–1088.

1302 Lindop GBM, Stewart JA, Downie TT. The immunocytochemical demonstration of renin in a juxtaglomerular cell tumor by light and electron microscopy. Histopathology 1983, **7:** 421–431.

1303 Martin SA, Mynderse LA, Lager DJ, Cheville JC. Juxtaglomerular cell tumor. A clinicopathologic study of four cases and review of the literature. Am J Clin Pathol 2001, **116:** 854–863.

1304 Ruddy MC, Atlas SA, Salerno FG. Hypertension associated with a renin-secreting adenocarcinoma of the pancreas. N Engl J Med 1982, **307:** 993–997.

1305 Squires JP, Ulbright TM, DeSchryver-Kecskemeti K, Engleman W. Juxtaglomerular cell tumor of the kidney. Cancer 1984, **53:** 516–523.

1306 Tetu B, Vaillancourt L, Camilleri JP, Bruneval P, Bernier L, Tourigny R. Juxtaglomerular cell tumor of the kidney. Report of two cases with a papillary pattern. Hum Pathol 1993, **24:** 1168–1174.

1307 Tomita T, Poisner A, Inagami T. Immunohistochemical localization of renin in renal tumors. Am J Pathol 1987, **126:** 73–80.

Other benign tumors and tumorlike conditions

1308 Afzal M, Baez-Giangreco A, al Jaser AN, Onuora VC. Unusual bilateral renal histiocytosis. Extranodal variant of Rosai-Dorfman disease. Arch Pathol Lab Med 1992, **116:** 1366–1367.

1309 Alvarado-Cabrero I, Folpe AL, Srigley JR, Gaudin P, Philip AT, Reuter VE, Amin MB. Intrarenal schwannoma: a report of four cases including three cellular variants. Mod Pathol 2000, **13:** 851–856.

1310 Anderson C, Knibbs DR, Ludwig ME, Ely MG III. Lymphangioma of the kidney. A pathologic entity distinct from solitary multilocular cyst. Hum Pathol 1992, **23:** 465–468.

1311 August C, Holzhausen HJ, Schroder S. Renal parenchymal malakoplakia. Ultrastructural findings in different stages of morphogenesis. Ultrastruct Pathol 1994, **18:** 483–491.

1312 Beckwith JB. Wilms' tumor and other renal tumors of childhood. A selective review from the National Wilms' Tumor Study Pathology Center. Hum Pathol 1983, **14:** 481–492.

1313 Bossart MI, Spjut HJ, Wright JE, Pranke DW. Multilocular cystic leiomyoma of the kidney. Ultrastruct Pathol 1982, **3:** 367–374.

1314 Dineen MK, Venable DD, Misra RP. Pure intrarenal lipoma. Report of a case and review of the literature. J Urol 1984, **132:** 104–107.

1315 Esparza AR, McKay DB, Cronan JJ, Chazan JA. Renal parenchymal malakoplakia. Histologic spectrum and its relationship to megalocytic interstitial nephritis and xanthogranulomatous pyelonephritis. Am J Surg Pathol 1989, **13:** 225–236.

1316 Fain JS, Eble J, Nascimento AG, Farrow GM, Bostwick DG.

Solitary fibrous tumor of the kidney: Report of three cases. J Urol Pathol 1996, **4**: 227–238.

1317 Gelb AB, Simmons ML, Weidner N. Solitary fibrous tumor involving the renal capsule. Am J Surg Pathol 1996, **20**: 1288–1295.

1318 Glover SD, Buck AC. Renal medullary fibroma. A case report. J Urol 1982, **127**: 758–760.

1319 Kahn DG, Duckett T, Bhuta SM. Perineurioma of the kidney. Report of a case with histologic, immunohistochemical, and ultrastructural studies. Arch Pathol Lab Med 1993, **117**: 654–657.

1319a Kapusta LR, Weiss MA, Ramsay J, Lopez-Beltran A, Srigley JR. Inflammatory myofibroblastic tumors of the kidney. A clinicopathologic and immunohistochemical study of 12 cases. Am J Surg Pathol 2003, **27**: 658–666.

1320 Kojiro M, Ohishi H, Isobe H. Carcinoid tumor occurring in cystic teratoma of the kidney. A case report. Cancer 1976, **38**: 1636–1640.

1321 Lerman RJ, Pitcock JA, Stephenson P, Muirhead EE. Renomedullary interstitial cell tumor (formerly fibroma of the renal medulla). Hum Pathol 1972, **3**: 559–568.

1322 Levine E. Lymphangioma presenting as a small renal mass during childhood. Urol Radiol 1992, **14**: 155–158.

1323 Lloreta J, Angels Cañas M, Munné A, Arumi M, Bielsa O, Gelabert A, Serrano S. Renal malakoplakia: report of a case with multifocal involvement. Ultrastruct Pathol 1997, **21**: 575–586.

1324 Ma KF, Tse CH, Tsui MS. Neurilemmoma of kidney – a rare occurrence. Histopathology 1990, **17**: 378–380.

1325 Melamed J, Reuter VE, Erlandson RA, Rosai J. Renal myxoma. A report of two cases and review of the literature. Am J Surg Pathol 1994, **18**: 187–194.

1326 Richard GK, Freeborn WA, Zaatari GS. Hemangiopericytoma of the renal capsule. J Urol Pathol 1996, **4**: 85–98.

1327 Sneige N, Dekmezian RH, Silva EG, Cartwright J Jr, Ayala AG. Pseudoparasitic Liesegang structures in perirenal hemorrhagic cysts. Am Clin Pathol 1988, **89**: 148–153.

1328 Stone NN, Cherry J. Renal capsular lipoma. J Urol 1985, **134**: 118–119.

1329 Tamboli P, Ro JY, Amin MB, Ligato S, Ayala AG. Benign tumors and tumor-like lesions of the adult kidney part II: Benign mesenchymal and mixed neoplasms, and tumor-like lesions. Adv Anat Pathol 2000, **7**: 47–68.

1330 Wang J, Arber DA, Frankel K, Weiss LM. Large solitary fibrous tumor of the kidney: report of two cases and review of the literature. Am J Surg Pathol 2001, **25**: 1194–1199.

Sarcomas

1331 Argani P, Faria PA, Epstein JI, Reuter VE, Perlman EJ, Beckwith JB, Ladanyi M. Primary renal synovial sarcoma: Molecular and morphologic delineation of an entity previously included among embryonal sarcomas of the kidney. Am J Surg Pathol 2000, **24**: 1087–1097.

1332 Cerilli LA, Huffman HT, Anand A. Primary renal angiosarcoma: A case report with immunohistochemical, ultrastructural, and cytogenetic features and review of the literature. Arch Pathol Lab Med 1998, **122**: 929–935.

1332a Chen S, Bhuiya T, Liatsikos EN, Alexianu MD, Weiss GH, Kahn LB. Primary synovial sarcoma of the kidney. A case report with literature review. Int J Surg Pathol 2001, **9**: 335–339.

1333 Creager AJ, Maia DM, Funkhouser WK. Epstein-Barr virus-associated renal smooth muscle neoplasm: Report of a case with review of the literature. Arch Pathol Lab Med 1998, **122**: 277–281.

1334 Eble JN, Young RHJ, Störkel CS, Thoenes W. Primary osteosarcoma of the kidney. A report of three cases. J Urogen Pathol 1991, **1**: 83–88.

1335 Farrow GM, Harrison EG Jr, Utz DC. Sarcomas and sarcomatoid and mixed malignant tumors of the kidney in adults. Cancer 1968, **22**: 545–563.

1336 Grignon DJ, Ayala AG, Ro JY, el-Naggar A, Papadopoulos NJ. Primary sarcomas of the kidney. A clinicopathologic and DNA flow cytometric study of 17 cases. Cancer 1990, **65**: 1611–1618.

1337 Kim D-H, Sohn JH, Lee MC, Lee G, Yoon G-S, Hashimoto H, Sonobe H, Ro JY. Primary synovial sarcoma of the kidney. Am J Surg Pathol 2000, **24**: 1097–1104.

1338 Malhotra CM, Doolittle CH, Rodil JV, Vezeridis MP. Mesenchymal chondrosarcoma of the kidney. Cancer 1984, **54**: 2495–2499.

1339 Mayes DC, Fechner RE, Gillenwater JY. Renal liposarcoma. Am J Surg Pathol 1990, **14**: 268–273.

1340 Mead JH, Herrera GA, Kaufman MF, Herz JH. Case report of a primary cystic sarcoma of the kidney, demonstrating fibrohistiocytic, osteoid, and cartilaginous components (malignant mesenchymoma). Cancer 1982, **50**: 2211–2214.

1341 Micolonghi TS, Liang D, Schwartz S. Primary osteogenic sarcoma of the kidney. J Urol 1984, **131**: 1164–1166.

1342 Nativ O, Horowitz A, Lindner A, Many M. Primary chondrosarcoma of the kidney. J Urol 1985, **134**: 120–121.

1343 Ng WD, Chan KW, Chan YT. Primary leiomyosarcoma of renal capsule. J Urol 1985, **133**: 834–835.

1344 O'Malley FP, Grignon DJ, Shepherd RR, Harker LA. Primary osteosarcoma of the kidney. Report of a case studied by immunohistochemistry, electron microscopy, and DNA flow cytometry. Arch Pathol Lab Med 1991, **115**: 1262–1265.

1345 Quinn CM, Day DW, Waxman J, Krausz T. Malignant mesenchymoma of the kidney. Histopathology 1993, **23**: 86–88.

1346 Rubin BP, Fletcher JA, Renshaw AA. Clear cell sarcoma of soft parts: Report of a case primary in the kidney with cytogenetic confirmation. Am J Surg Pathol 1999, **23**: 589–594.

1347 Scriven RR, Thrasher TV, Smith DC, Stewart SC. Primary renal malignant fibrous histiocytoma. A case report and literature review. J Urol 1984, **131**: 948–949.

1348 Tsuda N, Chowdhury PR, Hayashi T, Anami M, Iseki M, Koga S, Matsuya F, Kanetake H, Saito Y, Horita Y. Primary renal angiosarcoma: A case report and review of the literature. Pathol Int 1997, **47**: 778–783.

1349 Vogelzang NJ, Fremgen AM, Guinan PD, Chmiel JS, Sylvester JL, Sener SF. Primary renal sarcoma in adults. A natural history and management study by the American Cancer Society, Illinois Division. Cancer 1993, **71**: 804–810.

1350 Yokose T, Fukuda H, Ogiwara A, Sakai K, Saitoh K. Myxoid leiomyosarcoma of the kidney accompanying ipsilateral ureteral transitional cell carcinoma. A case report with cytological, immunohistochemical and ultrastructural study. Acta Pathol Jpn 1991, **41**: 694–700.

Malignant lymphoma and related lymphoid lesions

1351 D'Agati V, Sablay LB, Knowles DM, Walter L. Angiotropic large cell lymphoma (intravascular malignant lymphomatosis) of the kidney. Presentation as minimal change disease. Hum Pathol 1989, **20**: 263–268.

1352 Ellman L, Davis J, Lichtenstein NS. Uremia due to occult lymphomatous infiltration of the kidneys. Cancer 1974, **33**: 203–205.

1353 Ferry JA, Harris NL, Papanicolaou N, Young RH. Lymphoma of the kidney. A report of 11 cases. Am J Surg Pathol 1995, **19**: 134–144.

1354 Kandel LB, Harrison LH, Woodruff RD, Williams CD, Ahl ET Jr. Renal plasmacytoma. A case report and summary of reported cases. J Urol 1984, **132**: 1167–1169.

1355 Okuno SH, Hoyer JD, Ristow K, Witzig TE. Primary renal non-Hodgkin's lymphoma. An unusual extranodal site. Cancer 1995, **75**: 2258–2261.

1356 Osborne BM, Brenner M, Weitzmer S, Butler JJ. Malignant lymphoma presenting as a renal mass. Four cases. Am J Surg Pathol 1987, **11**: 375–382.

1357 Parveen T, Navarro-Roman L, Medeiros LJ, Raffeld M, Jaffe ES. Low-grade B-cell lymphoma of mucosa-associated lymphoid tissue arising in the kidney. Arch Pathol Lab Med 1993, **117:** 780–783.

1358 Randhawa PS, Magnone M, Jordan M, Shapiro R, Demetris AJ, Nalesnik M. Renal allograft involvement by Epstein-Barr virus associated post-transplant lymphoproliferative disease. Am J Surg Pathol 1996, **20:** 563–571.

1359 Randolph VL, Hall W, Bramson W. Renal failure due to lymphomatous infiltration of the kidneys. Cancer 1983, **52:** 1120–1121.

1360 Richmond J, Sherman RS, Diamond HD, Craver LF. Renal lesions associated with malignant lymphomas. Am J Med 1962, **32:** 184–207.

1361 Salem Y, Pagliaro LC, Manyaki MJ. Primary small noncleaved cell lymphoma of kidney. Urology 1993, **42:** 331–335.

1361a Smith MJ, Caraway N, Truong LD. Renal lymphoma: the morphologic spectrum and clinical correlates in 23 cases. A case report with literature review (Abstract). Mod Pathol 2003, **16:** 171a-172a.

1362 Tsang K, Kneafsey P, Gill MJ. Primary lymphoma of the kidney in the acquired immunodeficiency syndrome. Arch Pathol Lab Med 1993, **117:** 541–543.

1363 Weissman DJ, Ferry JA, Harris NL, Louis DN, Delmonico F, Spiro I. Post-transplantation lymphoproliferative disorders in solid organ recipients are predominantly aggressive tumors of host origin. Am J Clin Pathol 1995, **103:** 748–755.

Metastatic tumors

1363a Bates AW, Baithun SI. The significance of secondary neoplasms of the urinary and male genital tract. Virchows Arch 2002, **440:** 640–647.

1364 Belghiti D, Hirbec G, Bernaudin JF, Pariente EA, Martin N. Intraglomerular metastases. Report of two cases. Cancer 1984, **54:** 2309–2312.

1365 Colome MI, Ro JY, Ayala AG, El-Naggar AK, Siddiqui RT, Ordonez NG. Adenoid cystic carcinoma of the breast metastatic to the kidney: an unusual site of initial distant metastasis, mimicking a primary renal tumor. J Urol Pathol 1996, **4:** 69–78.

1366 Davis RI, Corson JM. Renal metastases from well-differentiated follicular thyroid carcinoma. A case report with light and electron microscopic findings. Cancer 1979, **43:** 265–268.

1367 Gamboa-Dominguez A, Tenorio-Villalvazo A. Metastatic follicular variant of papillary thyroid carcinoma manifested as a renal neoplasm. Endocr Pathol 1999, **10:** 265–268.

1368 Herzberg AJ, Bossen EH, Walther PJ. Adenoid cystic carcinoma of the breast metastatic to the kidney. A clinically symptomatic lesion requiring surgical management. Cancer 1991, **68:** 1015–1020.

1369 Honda H, Coffman CE, Berbaum KS, Barloon TJ, Masuda K. CT analysis of metastatic neoplasms of the kidney. Comparison with primary renal cell carcinoma. Acta Radiol 1992, **33:** 39–44.

1370 Johnson MW, Morettin LB, Sarles HE, Zaharopoulos P. Follicular carcinoma of the thyroid metastatic to the kidney 37 years after resection of the primary tumor. J Urol 1982, **127:** 114–116.

1370a Tamboli P, Abrahams NA, Wright ET, Ro JY, Ayala AG. Metastases to the kidney: a clinicopathologic analysis of 50 cases (Abstract). Mod Pathol 2003, **16:** 172a.

1371 Toth T. Extracapillary tumorous metastatic crescents in glomeruli of the kidney. Pathol Res Pract 1987, **182:** 240–243.

1372 Wagle DG, Moore RH, Murphy GP. Secondary carcinomas of the kidney. J Urol 1975, **114:** 30–32.

Tumors of renal pelvis and ureter
Transitional cell carcinoma

1373 Akaza H, Koiso K, Niijima T. Clinical evaluation of urothelial tumors of the renal pelvis and ureter based on a new classification system. Cancer 1987, **59:** 1369–1375.

1374 Akhtar M, Kardar AH, Chudek J, Ali MA, Kovacs G. Mixed renal cell and transitional cell carcinoma of the kidney: Genetic and morphologic studies of an unusual case. J Urol Pathol 1998, **8:** 103–110.

1375 al-Abadi H, Nagel R. Transitional cell carcinoma of the renal pelvis and ureter. Prognostic relevance of nuclear deoxyribonucleic acid ploidy studied by slide cytometry. An 8-year survival time study. J Urol 1992, **148:** 31–37.

1376 Auld D, Grigor KM, Fowler JW. Histopathological review of transitional cell carcinoma of the upper urinary tract. Br J Urol 1984, **56:** 485–489.

1377 Balslev E, Fischer S. Transitional cell carcinoma of the renal collecting tubules (renal urothelioma). Acta Pathol Microbiol Immunol Scand (A) 1983, **91:** 419–424.

1378 Batata MA, Whitmore WF Jr, Hilaris BS, Tokita N, Grabstald H. Primary carcinoma of the ureter. A prognostic study. Cancer 1975, **35:** 1626–1632.

1378a Blaszyk H, Wang L, Dietmaier W, Hofstädter F, Burgart LJ, Cheville JC, Hartmann A. Upper tract urothelial carcinoma: a clinicopathologic study including microsatellite instability analysis. Mod Pathol 2002, **15:** 790–797.

1379 Bloom NA, Vidone RA, Lytton B. Primary carcinoma of the ureter. A report of 102 new cases. J Urol 1970, **103:** 590–598.

1380 Chiang PH, Huang MS, Tsai CJ, Tsai EM, Huang CH, Chiang CP. Transitional cell carcinoma of the renal pelvis and ureter in Taiwan. DNA analysis by flow cytometry. Cancer 1993, **71:** 3988–3992.

1381 Corrado F, Mannini D, Ferri C, Corrado G, Bertoni F, Bacchini P, Lieber MM, Song JM. The prognostic significance of DNA ploidy pattern in transitional cell cancer of the renal pelvis and ureter. Continuing follow-up. Eur Urol 1992, **21:** 48–50.

1382 Guinan P, Vogelzang NJ, Randazzo R, Sener S, Chmiel J, Fremgen A, Sylvester J. Renal pelvic cancer. A review of 611 patients treated in Illinois 1975–1985. Cancer Incidence and End Results Committee. Urology 1992, **40:** 393–399.

1383 Han AC, Duszak R Jr. Coexpression of cytokeratins 7 and 20 confirms urothelial carcinoma presenting as an intrarenal tumor. Cancer 1999, **86:** 2327–2330.

1384 Hart AP, Brown R, Lechago J, Truong LD. Collision of transitional cell carcinoma and renal cell carcinoma. An immunohistochemical study and review of the literature. Cancer 1994, **73:** 154–159.

1385 Hasui Y, Nishi S, Kitada S, Osada Y, Asada Y. The prognostic significance of vascular invasion in upper urinary tract transitional cell carcinoma. J Urol 1992, **148:** 1783–1785.

1386 Heney NM, Nocks BN, Daly JJ, Blitzer PH, Parkhurst EC. Prognostic factors in carcinoma of the ureter. J Urol 1981, **125:** 632–636.

1386a Hes O, Michal M, Kinkor Z, Čuřík R, Baumruk L. Renal pelvic carcinoma with unusual appearance simulating amyloidosis(myeloma kidney). A report of five cases. Int J Surg Pathol 2002, **10:** 41–45.

1387 Huffman JL, Bagley DH, Lyon ES, Morse MJ, Herr HW, Whitmore WF Jr. Endoscopic diagnosis and treatment of upper-tract urothelial tumors. A preliminary report. Cancer 1985, **55:** 1422–1428.

1388 Johansson S, Angervall L, Bengtsson U, Wahlqvist L. Uroepithelial tumors of the renal pelvis associated with abuse of phenacetin-containing analgesics. Cancer 1974, **33:** 743–753.

1389 Johansson S, Angervall L, Bengtsson U, Wahlqvist L. A clinicopathologic and prognostic study of epithelial tumors of the renal pelvis. Cancer 1976, **37:** 1376–1383.

1390 Koyanagi T, Sasaki K, Arikado K, Hirano T, Tsuji I. Transitional cell carcinoma of the renal pelvis in an infant. J Urol 1975, **113:** 114–117.

1391 Leo ME, Petrou SP, Barrett DM. Transitional cell carcinoma of the kidney with vena caval involvement. Report of 3 cases and a review of the literature. J Urol 1992, **148**: 398–400.

1392 McCarron JP Jr, Chasko SB, Gray GF Jr. Systematic mapping of nephroureterectomy specimens removed for urothelial cancer. Pathological findings and clinical correlations. J Urol 1982, **128**: 243–246.

1393 McDougal WS, Cramer SF, Miller R. Invasive carcinoma of the renal pelvis following cyclophosphamide therapy for nonmalignant disease. Cancer 1981, **48**: 691–695.

1394 McIntyre D, Pyrah LN, Raper FP. Primary ureteric neoplasms. Report of 40 cases. Br J Urol 1965, **37**: 160–191.

1395 Mahadevia PS, Karwa GL, Koss LG. Mapping of urothelium in carcinomas of the renal pelvis and ureter. A report of nine cases. Cancer 1983, **51**: 890–897.

1396 Mai KT, Gerridzen RG, Millward SF. Papillary transitional cell carcinoma arising in a calyceal cyst and masquerading as a renal cyst. Arch Pathol Lab Med 1996, **120**: 879–882.

1397 Melamed MR, Reuter VE. Pathology and staging of urothelial tumors of the kidney and ureter. Urol Clin North Am 1993, **20**: 333–347.

1398 Mills C, Vaughan ED Jr. Carcinoma of the ureter. Natural history, management and 5-year survival. J Urol 1983, **129**: 275–277.

1399 Murphy DM, Zincke H. Transitional cell carcinoma in the horseshoe kidney. Report of 3 cases and review of the literature. Br J Urol 1982, **54**: 484–485.

1400 Murphy WM, von Buedingen RP, Poley RW. Primary carcinoma in situ of renal pelvis and ureter. Cancer 1974, **34**: 1126–1130.

1401 Nakanishi K, Kawai T, Aida S, Kasamatsu H, Aurues T, Ikeda T. Expression of P27Kip1 protein in transitional cell carcinoma of the upper urinary tract. Mod Pathol 2001, **14**: 371–376.

1402 Oldbring J, Hellsten S, Lindholm K, Mikulowski P, Tribukait B. Flow DNA analysis in the characterization of carcinoma of the renal pelvis and ureter. Cancer 1989, **64**: 2141–2145.

1403 Palvio DHB, Andersen JC, Falk E. Transitional cell tumors of the renal pelvis and ureter associated with capillarosclerosis indicating analgesic abuse. Cancer 1987, **59**: 972–976.

1404 Pettersson S, Brynger H, Henriksson C, Johansson SL, Nilson AE, Ranch T. Treatment of urothelial tumors of the upper urinary tract by nephroureterectomy, renal autotransplantation, and pyelocystostomy. Cancer 1984, **54**: 379–386.

1405 Potts SA, Thomas PA, Cohen MB, Raab SS. Diagnostic accuracy and key cytologic features of high-grade transitional cell carcinoma in the upper urinary tract. Mod Pathol 1997, **10**: 657–662.

1406 Raabe NK, Fossa SD, Bjerkehagen B. Carcinoma of the renal pelvis. Experience of 80 cases. Scand J Urol Nephrol 1992, **26**: 357–361.

1407 Rey A, Lara PC, Redondo E, Valdes E, Apolinario R. Overexpression of p53 in transitional cell carcinoma of the renal pelvis and ureter. Relations to tumor proliferation and survival. Cancer 1997, **79**: 2178–2185.

1408 Strobel SL, Jasper WS, Gogate SA, Sharma HM. Primary carcinoma of the renal pelvis and ureter. Evaluation of clinical and pathologic features. Arch Pathol Lab Med 1984, **108**: 697–700.

1409 Strong DW, Pearse HD. Recurrent urothelial tumors following surgery for transitional cell carcinoma of the upper urinary tract. Cancer 1976, **38**: 2178–2183.

1410 Verhaak RLOM, Harmsen AE, van Unnik AJM. On the frequency of tumor induction in a Thorotrast kidney. Cancer 1974, **34**: 2061–2068.

1411 Wagle DG, Moore RH, Murphy GP. Primary carcinoma of the renal pelvis. Cancer 1974, **33**: 1642–1648.

1412 Wegner HE, Bornhoft G, Dieckmann KP. Renal cell cancer and concomitant transitional cell cancer of the renal pelvis and

ureter in the same kidney – report of 4 cases and review of the literature. Urol Int 1993, **51**: 158–163.

1413 Werth DD, Weigel JW, Mebust WK. Primary neoplasms of the ureter. J Urol 1981, **125**: 628–631.

1414 Yokoyama I, Berman E, Rickert RR, Bastidas J. Simultaneous occurrence of renal cell adenocarcinoma and urothelial carcinoma of the renal pelvis in the same kidney diagnosed by preoperative angiography. Cancer 1981, **48**: 2762–2766.

Other carcinoma types

1415 Akhtar M, Aslam M, Lindstedt E, Pesti T, Kovacs G. Osteoclast-like giant cell tumor of renal pelvis. J Urol Pathol 1999, **11**: 181–194.

1416 Aufderheide AC, Streitz JM. Mucinous adenocarcinoma of the renal pelvis. Report of two cases. Cancer 1974, **33**: 167–173.

1417 Deodhare S, Leung CS, Bullock M. Choriocarcinoma associated with transitional cell carcinoma in-situ of the ureter. Histopathology 1996, **28**: 363–364.

1418 Fukunaga M, Ushigome S. Lymphoepithelioma-like carcinoma of the renal pelvis: a case report with immunohistochemical analysis and in situ hybridization for the Epstein-Barr viral genome. Mod Pathol 1998, **11**: 1252–1256.

1419 Genega E, Ittmann M, Wieczorek R, Sidhu G. Carcinosarcoma of the renal pelvis with immunohistochemistry and review of the literature. J Urol Pathol 1997, **6**: 205–212.

1420 Grammatico D, Grignon DJ, Eberwein P, Shepherd RR, Hearn SA, Walton JC. Transitional cell carcinoma of the renal pelvis with choriocarcinomatous differentiation. Immunohistochemical and immunoelectron microscopic assessment of human chorionic gonadotropin production by transitional cell carcinoma of the urinary bladder. Cancer 1993, **71**: 1835–1841.

1421 Guillou L, Duvoisin B, Chobaz C, Chapuis G, Costa J. Combined small-cell and transitional cell carcinoma of the renal pelvis. A light microscopic, immunohistochemical, and ultrastructural study of a case with literature review. Arch Pathol Lab Med 1993, **117**: 239–243.

1422 Hertle L, Androulakakis P. Keratinizing desquamative squamous metaplasia of the upper urinary tract. Leukoplakia–cholesteatoma. J Urol 1982, **127**: 631–635.

1423 Ishikura H, Ishiguro T, Enatsu C, Fujii H, Kakuta Y, Kanda M, Yoshiki T. Hepatoid adenocarcinoma of the renal pelvis producing alpha-fetoprotein of hepatic type and bile pigment. Cancer 1991, **67**: 3051–3056.

1424 Kobayashi S, Ohmori M, Akaeda T, Ohmori H, Miyaji Y. Primary adenocarcinoma of the renal pelvis. Report of two cases and brief review of literature. Acta Pathol Jpn 1983, **33**: 589–597.

1425 Kumar S, Kumar D, Cowan DF. Transitional cell carcinoma with rhabdoid features. Am J Surg Pathol 1992, **16**: 515–521.

1426 Mills SE, Weiss MA, Swanson PE, Wick MR. Small cell undifferentiated carcinoma of the renal pelvis. A light microscopic, immunocytochemical, and ultrastructural study. Surg Pathol 1988, **1**: 83–88.

1427 Molinie V, Pouchot J, Vinceneux P, Barge J. Osteoclastoma-like giant cell tumor of the renal pelvis associated with papillary transitional cell carcinoma. Arch Pathol Lab Med 1997, **121**: 162–166.

1428 Nativ O, Reiman HM, Lieber MM, Zincke H. Treatment of primary squamous cell carcinoma of the upper urinary tract. Cancer 1991, **68**: 2575–2578.

1429 Sheaff M, Fociani P, Badenoch D, Baithun S. Verrucous carcinoma of the renal pelvis: case presentation and review of the literature. Virchows Arch 1996, **428**: 375–380.

1430 Shibihara N, Okada S, Onishi S, Hamada K, Takasaki N, Miyazaki S, Ito Y, Mori H. Primary mucinous carcinoma of the renal pelvis. Pathol Res Pract 1993, **189**: 946–949.

1431 Spires SE, Banks ER, Cibull ML, Munch L, Delworth M, Alexander NJ. Adenocarcinoma of renal pelvis. Arch Pathol Lab Med 1993, 117: 1156–1160.

1432 Strobel SL, Jasper WS, Gogate SA, Sharma HM. Primary carcinoma of the renal pelvis and ureter. Evaluation of clinical and pathologic features. Arch Pathol Lab Med 1984, 108: 697–700.

1433 Suster S, Robinson MJ. Spindle cell carcinoma of the renal pelvis. Immunohistochemical and ultrastructural study of a case demonstrating coexpression of keratin and vimentin intermediate filaments. Arch Pathol Lab Med 1989, 113: 404–408.

1434 Vahlensieck W Jr, Riede U, Wimmer B, Ihling C. Beta-human chorionic gonadotropin-positive extragonadal germ cell neoplasia of the renal pelvis. Cancer 1991, 67: 3146–3149.

1435 Verhaak RLOM, Harmsen AE, van Unnik AJM. On the frequency of tumor induction in a Thorotrast kidney. Cancer 1974, 34: 2061–2068.

1436 Wick MR, Perrone TL, Burke BA. Sarcomatoid transitional cell carcinoma of the renal pelvis. An ultrastructural and immunohistochemical study. Arch Pathol Lab Med 1985, 109: 55–58.

1437 Zanella M, Falconieri G. Sarcomatoid urothelial carcinoma of the renal pelvis: report of two cases with extensive osteoclast-like giant cell component. J Urol Pathol 2000, 12: 13–28.

1437a Zettl A, Konrad MA, Polzin S, Ehsan A, Riedmiller H, Müller-Hermelink HK, Ott G. Urethelial carcinoma of the renal pelvis with choriocarcinomatous features: genetic evidence of clonal evolution. Hum Pathol 2002, 35: 1234–1237.

Other tumors and tumorlike conditions

1438 Amin MB, Tickoo SK, Schultz D. Myelolipoma of the renal sinus: an unusual site for a rare extra-adrenal lesion. Arch Pathol Lab Med 1999, 123: 631–634.

1439 Carr RA, Newman J, Antonakapulos GN, Parkinson MC. Lesions produced by the extravasation of urine from the upper urinary tract. Histopathology 1997, 30: 335–340.

1440 Chabrel CM, Hickey BB, Parkinson C. Pericaliceal hemangioma. A cause of papillary necrosis? Case report and review of 7 similar vascular lesions. Br J Urol 1982, 54: 334–340.

1441 Cubilla E, Hesker AE, Stanley RJ. Cavernous hemangioma of the kidney. An angiographic-pathologic correlation. J Can Assoc Radiol 1973, 24: 254–256.

1442 Demirkan NC, Tuncay L, Duzcan E, Atahan O, Pakdermirli E. Subepithelial haematoma of the renal pelvis (Antopol-Goldman lesion). Histopathology 1999, 35: 282–283.

1443 Dretler SP, Young RH. Stone granuloma. A cause of ureteral stricture. J Urol 1993, 150: 1800–1802.

1444 Edward HG, Deweerd JH, Woolner LB. Renal hemangiomas. Proc Staff Meetings Mayo Clin 1962, 37: 545–551.

1445 Farrands PA, Tribe CR, Slade N. Localized amyloid of the ureter. Case report and review of the literature. Histopathology 1983, 7: 613–622.

1446 Fernandez PL, Nogales FF, Zuluaga A. Nephrogenic adenoma of the ureter. Br J Urol 1991, 68: 104–105.

1447 Fromowitz FB, Steinbook ML, Lautin EM, Friedman AC, Kahan N, Bennett MJ, Koss LG. Inverted papilloma of the ureter. J Urol 1981, 126: 113–116.

1448 Fukunaga M, Nikaido T. Solitary fibrous tumour of the renal peripelvis. Histopathology 1997, 30: 451–456.

1449 Geller SA, Lin C-S. Ureteral obstruction from metastatic breast carcinoma. Arch Pathol 1975, 99: 476–478.

1449a Gokaslan ST, Krueger JE, Albores-Saavedra J. Symptomatic nephrogenic metaplasia of ureter: a morphologic and immunohistochemical study of four cases. Mod Pathol 2002, 15: 765–770.

1450 Hurwitz RS, Benjamin JA, Cooper JF. Excessive proliferation of peripelvic fat of the kidney. Urology 1978, 11: 448–456.

1451 Kim SJ, Ahn HS, Chung DY, Kim YS, Lee EJ, Park KH. Subepithelial hematoma of the renal pelvis simulating neoplasm (Antopol-Goldman) lesion. Urol Int 1997, 59: 260–262.

1452 Kochevar J. Adenocarcinoid tumor, goblet cell type, arising in a ureteroileal conduit. A case report. J Urol 1984, 131: 957–959.

1453 Kunze E, Fischer G, Dembowski J. Tubulo-papillary adenoma (so-called nephrogenic adenoma) arising in the renal pelvis. Report of a case with a critical consideration of histogenesis and terminology. Pathol Res Pract 1993, 189: 217–225.

1454 Kyriakos M, Royce RK. Multiple simultaneous inverted papillomas of the upper urinary tract. A case report with a review of ureteral and renal pelvic inverted papillomas. Cancer 1989, 63: 368–380.

1455 Macksood MJ, Roth DR, Chang C-H, Perlmutter AD. Benign fibroepithelial polyps as a cause of intermittent ureteropelvic junction obstruction in a child. A case report and review of the literature. J Pathol 1985, 134: 951–952.

1456 MacMahon HE. Hypertrophic infundibular stenosis of the calyces of the kidney. Hum Pathol 1974, 5: 363–364.

1457 Maeda K, Hawkins ET, Oh HK, Kini SR, Van Dyke DL. Malignant lymphoma in transplanted renal pelvis. Arch Pathol Lab Med 1986, 110: 626–629.

1458 Martinez-Pineiro L, Hidalgo L, Picazo ML, Cozar JM, Martinez-Pineiro JA. Nephrogenic adenoma of the renal pelvis. Br J Urol 1991, 67: 101.

1459 Matthews PN, Greenwood RN, Hendry WF, Cattell WR. Extensive pelvis malacoplakia. Observations on management. J Urol 1986, 135: 132–134.

1460 Mensch LS, Trainer TD, Plante MK. Cystic hamartoma of the renal pelvis: a rare pathologic entity. Mod Pathol 1999, 12: 417–421.

1461 Nasu M, Hamasaki K, Kishi H, Matsubara O. Nephrogenic adenoma of the ureter with gastric metaplasia. J Urol Pathol 1997, 7: 63–69.

1462 Nowak MA, Marzich CS, Scheetz KL, McElroy JB. Benign fibroepithelial polyps of the renal pelvis. Arch Pathol Lab Med 1999, 123: 850–852.

1463 Pawade J, Soosay GN, Delprado W, Parkinson MC, Rode J. Cystic hamartoma of the renal pelvis. Am J Surg Pathol 1993, 17: 1169–1175.

1464 Peterson NE. Adenoma of ileal urinary conduit. J Urol 1984, 131: 1171–1172.

1465 Recloux P, Weiser M, Piccart M, Sculier J-P. Ureteral obstruction in patients with breast cancer. Cancer 1988, 61: 1904–1907.

1466 Rivard JY, Bedard A, Dionne L. Colonic neoplasms following ureterosigmoidostomy. J Urol 1975, 113: 781–786.

1467 Rudd EG, Matthews MD. Malacoplakia. An unusual etiology of ureteral obstruction. Obstet Gynecol 1982, 60: 134–136.

1468 Scharifker D, Chalasani A. Ureteral involvement by malignant lymphoma. Ten years' experience. Arch Pathol Lab Med 1978, 102: 541–542.

1469 Seibel L, Prasad S, Weiss RE, Bancila E, Epstein JI. Villous adenoma of the urinary tract: a lesion frequently associated with malignancy. Hum Pathol 2002, 33: 236–241.

1470 Strachan JR, Rees HC, Willams G. Histochemical changes after ureterosigmoidostomies and colonic diversion. Br J Urol 1985, 57: 700–702.

1471 Uchida M, Watanabe H, Mishina T, Shimada N. Leiomyoma of the renal pelvis. J Urol 1981, 125: 572–574.

1472 Werner JR, Klingersmith W, Denko JV. Leiomyosarcoma of the ureter. Case report and review of literature. J Urol 1959, 82: 68–71.

Bladder

Normal anatomy

The bladder is a hollow viscus with the shape of a four-sided inverted pyramid when empty and of a rounded structure when distended. It is divided into the following portions: *superior surface* (also known as *dome* and covered by the pelvic parietal peritoneum), *posterior surface* (also known as *base*), and the two *inferolateral surfaces*.[2] The *trigone* is located at the base of the bladder and is continuous with the *bladder neck*, in which the posterior and inferolateral wall converge to open into the urethra. The structure on which the bladder neck rests (rectum in males and vagina in females) is known as the *bladder bed*. The lymphatic drainage of the bladder is primarily through the external and internal iliac nodes; portions of the bladder neck region may drain to the sacral or common iliac nodes.

The layers of the bladder are the mucosa, muscularis propria, and adventitia. The latter is covered by serosa at the dome. The mucosa is formed by the epithelium, lamina propria, and (rarely) a continuous or discontinuous muscularis mucosae. The epithelium of the bladder has been traditionally referred to as *transitional*, but the term *urothelium* is more informative and accurate. It is 6 to 7 cells thick in the contracted bladder but only 2 or 3 cells thick in the distended bladder. It has three layers: superficial, intermediate, and basal. The superficial layer is made up of a single row of large, elliptical cells having abundant eosinophilic cytoplasm and referred to as *umbrella cells*. The ultrastructural appearance of the luminal surface of these cells is characteristic.[2] The intermediate cells have a cuboidal to low columnar shape, oval nuclei with finely stippled chromatin, moderately abundant cytoplasm, and well-defined margins. The basal layer is made up of a row of cuboidal cells that lie on a thin continuous basal lamina.

The lamina propria is composed of loose connective tissue containing a rich vascular network, lymph vessels, and a few elastic fibers. A rather prominent collection of arteries and veins is present in the midportion of the lamina propria and divides this layer into an inner and an outer zone. Smooth muscle cells are present in association with these vessels, usually as isolated bundles, sometimes as a discontinuous thin layer, and rarely as a continuous layer (muscularis mucosae).[2] These muscle bundles should not be confused with those of the muscularis propria when evaluating the depth of invasion of a bladder neoplasm.

The muscularis propria is vaguely divided into inner and outer longitudinal layers and a central circular layer; these are best individualized in the bladder neck region.

Islands of mature adipose tissue are commonly present in the wall of the bladder, particularly in the deep portion of the lamina propria.[1]

Small paraganglia may be found in the adjacent connective tissue, usually in association with neural structures.

Congenital abnormalities

Urachal lesions

The urachus is a 5 to 6 cm vestigial structure located between the dome of the bladder and the umbilicus which results from the involution of the allantoic duct and the cloaca.[3] During development, it connects the bladder with the allantois. At birth the urachus retracts from the bladder, but its lumen may persist within the bladder wall and be continuous with the bladder cavity. The lining may be of transitional or columnar type. Schubert et al.[16] found tubular urachal remnants in 32% of 122 bladders studied at autopsy.

Anomalies related to urachal remnants most often occur in children, but they can also first present in adults.[15] They include the following: *patent urachus* through which urine may pass, *blind sinuses* in the anterior abdominal wall, *abscesses, granulomatous omphalitis*, and intravesical polypoid multicystic masses ("*hamarotomas*").[5,7,11,14,17]

Tumors may also develop from this structure, of which *adenocarcinoma* is the most common; the majority of these cases are well-differentiated mucin-producing tumors, but signet ring carcinomas also occur[4] (Fig. 17.159). Other tumor types include *villous adenoma, "fibroadenoma," transitional cell carcinoma*, and *squamous cell carcinoma*.[6,8,12,13] Most of these tumors arise from the intramural portion of the urachus and grow into the wall of the bladder, sometimes in the absence of mucosal involvement. Others occur beneath the peritoneum of the anterior abdominal wall between the umbilicus and the bladder dome. The overall prognosis is poor, the main reason being that the location of the tumor does not result in early symptoms and precludes a timely diagnosis. Depending on the extent of the disease, the treatment can be either umbilectomy with partial cystectomy or en bloc radical cystoprostatectomy/umbilectomy.[9,10]

Exstrophy

Bladder (cloacal) exstrophy is a congenital abnormality characterized by absence of the anterior vesicle and lower abdominal wall, with eversion of the posterior bladder wall. These changes may be partial or complete and are often associated with other anomalies of the urogenital tract. Malignant change was found in 3 (7.5%) of 42 patients with exstrophic bladder reported by Engel and Wilkinson.[19] It has been calculated that the risk of neoplasia in adults born with exstrophy is 17.5%, and that the highest risk (38%) is for those patients who have been exposed to mixing of urine and feces in a colorectal reservoir.[22] The tumor type in most series has usually been adenocarcinoma, occasionally admixed with squamous elements.[18,19]

The treatment of bladder exstrophy depends on the specific features of the malformation and may consist of reapproximating or closing the defect, in addition to

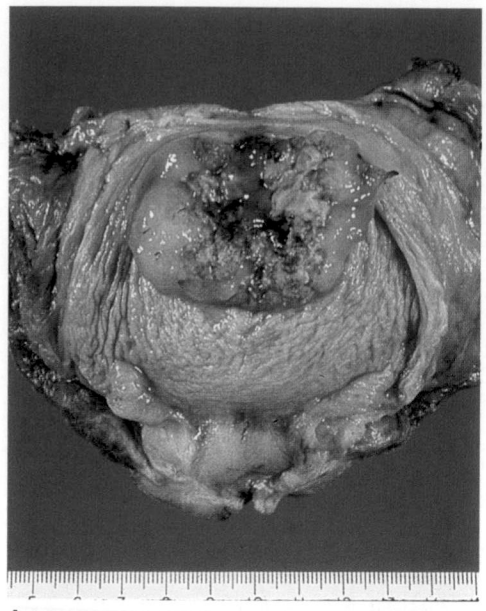

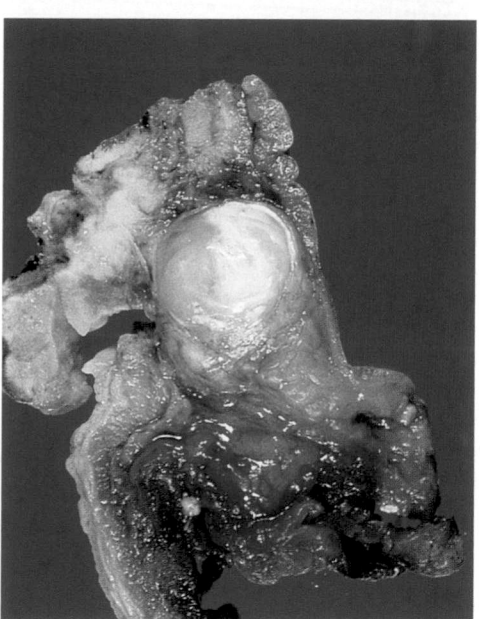

Fig. 17.159 A and **B**, Gross appearance of adenocarcinoma arising from urachal remnants. **A**, The tumor protrudes as a polypoid ulcerated mass from the dome of the bladder. **B**, The cut surface shows a large intramural mass of mucinous appearance.

repairing the other abnormalities that often accompany this condition.[20,21]

Diverticulosis

Most diverticula of the bladder are acquired and develop because of partial urinary obstruction in the urethra or bladder neck, usually as a result of prostatic nodular hyperplasia.[24,25] The longstanding increased muscular contractions required to empty the bladder cause thickening of the wall and mucosal herniation in areas of weakness. Other diverticula are thought to be congenital.[30]

Bladder diverticula are most commonly located in the posterior wall above the trigone, the region of the ureteral orifices, and the dome at the site of an obliterated urachus. The communication into the bladder is usually large but may be pinpoint in size. The wall of the diverticulum usually consists of fibrous tissue with little or no muscle. Squamous metaplasia of the lining epithelium often occurs if there is associated inflammation.

Complications of bladder diverticula include lithiasis, free perforation into the peritoneal cavity, and tumor development.[28] The tumors are usually transitional cell carcinomas[23,29] but may be glandular (adenocarcinomas) or of other types.[26,27] They may grow to a large size before detection because of their hidden location. The development of neoplasia may be related to the obstruction, chronic inflammation, epithelial hyperplasia, and squamous metaplasia to which these diverticula are prone.

Lithiasis

Bladder calculi occur much more often in male than in female individuals; most of the patients are elderly. They represent a frequent complication in paraplegics and quadriplegics. The majority of these stones are solitary and composed of phosphate salts; others are made up of urate and oxalate salts.[33] The most common associated abnormality is nodular hyperplasia of the prostate gland.

Treatment modalities include removal by cystostomy, mechanical (endoscopic) cystolithotripsy, and extracorporeal shock wave therapy. The latter has been found to be a simple, effective, and safe modality for the treatment of most cases and is becoming the therapy of choice.[31,32] Recurrence develops in about 10% of the patients.

Endometriosis and related müllerian-type changes

Endometriosis may involve the bladder as an isolated focus or in association with similar lesions in other sites[40] (Fig. 17.160). In most instances, there is a history of a previous operation in the area or of symptoms related to the female genital tract.[45] The disease can also occur in men following estrogen therapy for prostatic carcinoma. In the most florid cases, a mass can be palpated at the base of the bladder. Serosal foci are the most common and are usually asymptomatic. Foci occurring in the bladder wall, beneath an intact mucosa, result in a bluish cast on cystoscopic examination and may be accompanied by marked hyperplasia of the vesical muscle in a fashion analogous to that seen in uterine adenomyosis[39]; these

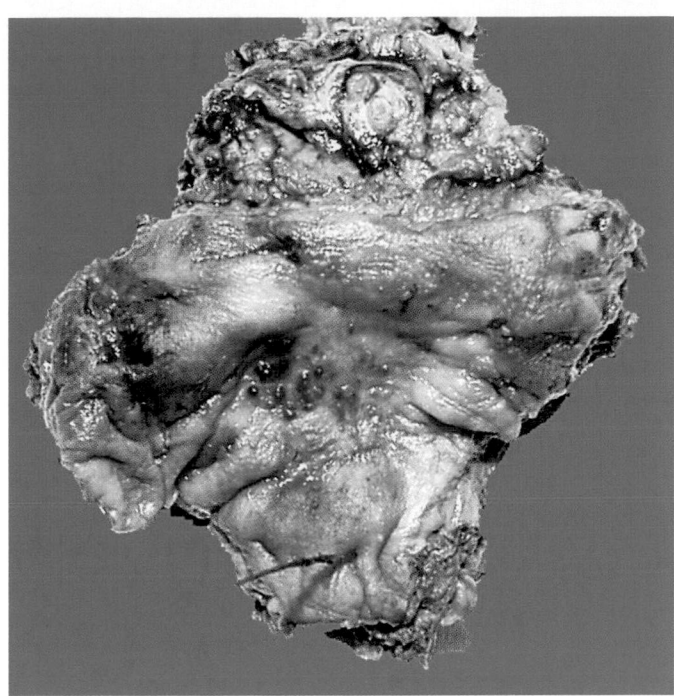

Fig. 17.160 Gross appearance of endometriosis of bladder. Multiple small reddish spots protrude from the bladder surface.

can present with persistent hematuria during menstruation. Radiographically, the lesion may be indistinguishable from an intravesical neoplasm.[43]

In addition to classical endometriosis composed of endometrial glands and stroma (the latter sometimes partially or completely replaced by hemosiderin-laden macrophages), one can encounter tubal-type epithelium (including ciliated cells, peg cells, and intercalated cells) and endocervical-type epithelium (columnar mucinous cells). The former change is referred to as *endosalpingiosis* and the latter as *endocervicosis*. When they occur in combination, the picturesque term *müllerianosis* is sometimes used.[38,47] Florid cases of endocervicosis may simulate adenocarcinoma.[36,37,41] True malignant tumors can develop in this setting, including endometrioid adenocarcinoma,[34] clear cell carcinoma,[42] and endometrioid adenosarcoma.[44]

The treatment of endometriosis of the bladder includes hormonal manipulation and resection; depending on the location, the latter may be carried out laparoscopically.[35,46]

Amyloidosis

Amyloidosis of the bladder may be the expression of a generalized process or present as a nodular localized mass ("amyloid tumor").[52] The latter are often misinterpreted as neoplasms both clinically and cystoscopically.[50] The histologic appearance is diagnostic; as in other sites, a florid secondary histiocytic and foreign body-type giant cell reaction may be present.[50] The material is made up in most instances of AL protein (immunoglobulin light chain), but some cases have been found to be transthyretin related.[48,49,53] Most reported patients with adequate follow-up have remained free of disease following local excision of the mass. Therefore the presence of an amyloid tumor should not be regarded as a manifestation of myeloma or plasmacytoma.[51,53]

Cystitis

Interstitial (Hunner's) cystitis

The classic clinical description of interstitial (Hunner's) cystitis is that of an adult or elderly female with ulceration and marked submucosal edema of the bladder resulting in prominent lower abdominal, suprapubic, or perineal pain and urinary frequency, unresponsive to medical therapy.[58] Because of the consistent presence of ulceration, the disease is also known as *Hunner's ulcer*.

The lesion can be located anywhere in the bladder. Microscopically, there is mucosal ulceration covered by fibrin and necrotic material. The underlying lamina propria and muscularis show edema, hemorrhage, granulation tissue, and a mononuclear inflammatory infiltrate that sometimes exhibits a predominantly perineurial location.[68,72] Mast cells are usually present and sometimes numerous; they are found beneath the ulcer, within the detrusor muscle bundles, and between the epithelial cells in the adjacent mucosa.[59,67] None of these microscopic features is pathognomonic.[62] The suggestion that adherence of Tamm–Horsfall protein to bladder epithelium may constitute a diagnostic test for interstitial cystitis has not materialized.[70,71,73] Cases lacking ulceration are considered by some authors to represent a different condition affecting a younger patient population.[64]

The etiology of this disorder remains obscure.[65] The search for infectious organisms has been unrewarding.[55] Hyperexpression of HLA class I molecules,[54,60] strong urothelial staining for IgA,[66] and increased sympathetic outflow into the bladder[56,61] suggest the participation of autoimmune mechanisms, whereas the finding of a reduction in the expression of heat shock protein 60 suggests a defect in the proliferative response of the urothelium.[69] The treatment is usually medical, but surgical intervention (including supratrigonal or total cystectomy) may be necessary in severe cases.[57,63]

Eosinophilic cystitis

Eosinophilic cystitis can occur in two different clinical settings. The first is seen in women and children and is often associated with allergic disorders and eosinophilia.[82] The second presents in older men and is usually associated with bladder injury related to other disorders of the bladder and prostate.[76,77] Exceptionally, the disease is due to parasitic infestation.[80]

Clinically, eosinophilic cystitis presents with dramatic and recurrent episodes of dysuria and hematuria.[79] Rarely, it may result in ureteral obstruction.[78] The cystoscopic appearance is that of a diffusely edematous and erythematous mucosa, with broad-based polypoid growths that may simulate a neoplastic process.[75] Microscopically, a dense inflammatory infiltrate rich in eosinophils, often accompanied by fibrosis and muscle necrosis and sometimes by giant cells, is present.[74] This condition is not related to Langerhans' cell histiocytosis. The treatment of choice is transurethral resection of the bladder lesions and a combination of steroids and antihistaminics.[81]

Polypoid cystitis

Polypoid cystitis is a benign process of a reactive nature which may simulate a neoplasm grossly. The typical site of involvement is the posterior wall above the trigone, but on occasion the entire bladder is affected. Gross variants of this condition include *bullous cystitis*, in which the elevations are broad and rounded, and *papillary cystitis*, in which they are thin and filiform.[84] The latter term should be used cautiously, lest it be misinterpreted as a neoplastic epithelial condition.

The better known cause of polypoid cystitis is catheterization of the bladder; the more frequent the procedure, the greater the frequency and severity of the condition, which reaches its peak at 3 months.[83]

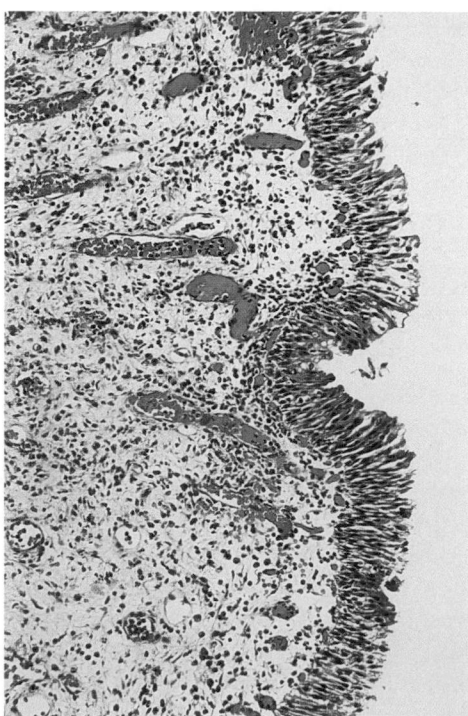

Fig. 17.161 Chronic cystitis exhibiting marked hyperemia, edema, and mixed mononuclear cell infiltrate.

However, in only a minority of reported cases of polypoid cystitis is there a history of recent catheterization.[84] It has also been seen in association with radiation therapy and malignant tumors.

Microscopically, stromal edema and congestion are the main features. Inflammation is scanty, and epithelial atypia is absent[83] (Fig. 17.161). Stellate mononuclear or multinucleated fibroblasts may be present; these are similar to those seen in analogous reactive conditions beneath other epithelium-covered surfaces, such as the nasal cavity, oral cavity, and vagina.

Emphysematous cystitis

Emphysematous cystitis (cystitis emphysematosa) is an inflammatory condition caused by gas-forming bacteria (such as *Clostridium perfringens*) and characterized by the presence of gas-filled vesicles in the bladder wall. Patients with diabetes, neurogenic bladder, chronic urinary infection, and malignant hematologic conditions are predisposed to the disease.[85–88] In some series, as many as half of the patients with emphysematous cystitis suffered from diabetes. Microscopically, multinucleated giant cells are seen partially lining the cysts.[88] The treatment consists of antibiotic therapy and relief of bladder outlet obstruction.[86]

Tuberculosis and BCG-induced granulomas

Tuberculosis remains the most frequent cause of granulomatous inflammation of the bladder in many parts of the world. It invariably develops from secondary foci, most often located in the kidney, as demonstrated in the classic study by Auerbach in 1940.[89] Most bladder lesions are found in the region of the trigone, especially around the ureteral orifices. Early lesions are superficial and small, with a floor of soft caseous material and a peripheral hyperemic zone. As the disease progresses, multiple ulcers coalesce to form larger ones that produce much fibrosis and involve the underlying musculature. In males, there may be secondary involvement of the prostate, whereas in females the disease may be complicated by vesico-vaginal fistula.[90]

Intravesical administration of bacillus Calmette–Guerin (BCG), as used for the treatment of superficial carcinoma of the bladder, can result in granulomatous inflammation of this organ, which may be detected microscopically or on cytologic examination of bladder wash specimens[91,92] (Fig. 17.162). The changes can extend to the prostate[93] and sometimes even to the lungs.[94]

Malakoplakia

Malakoplakia of the bladder is characterized by the appearance of multiple nodular thickenings of the mucosa and submucosa, usually in the region of the trigone, that may be mistaken for carcinoma.[99,105] It has been associated with immune deficiency states and has been reported on several occasions in renal transplant recipients.[96,106]

Microscopically, collections of histiocytes with granular acidophilic cytoplasm accumulate beneath the surface epithelium. In some of these cells, rounded, concentrically layered intracytoplasmic inclusions known as Michaelis–Gutmann bodies or calcospherites are seen (Fig. 17.163); these are basophilic and PAS positive and stain for iron and calcium. Ultrastructurally and immunohistochemically, intracellular bacteria can be identified.[101,102,104] The presence of transitional forms between these bacteria, lipid inclusions, and Michaelis–Gutmann bodies suggests that the latter represent the result of

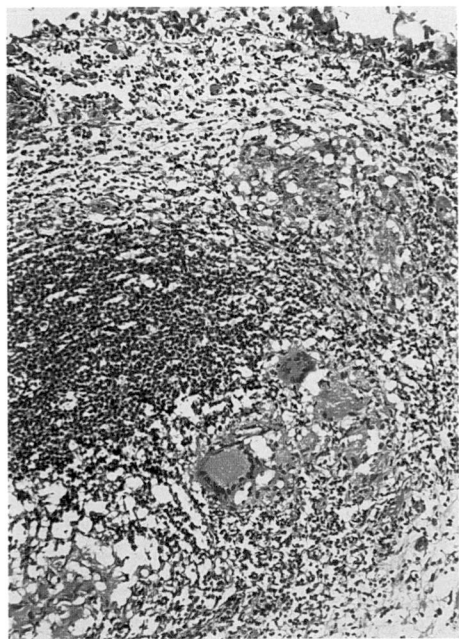

Fig. 17.162 Granulomas induced by BCG therapy for transitional cell carcinoma. (Courtesy of Dr. Victor E. Reuter, Memorial Sloan-Kettering Cancer Center)

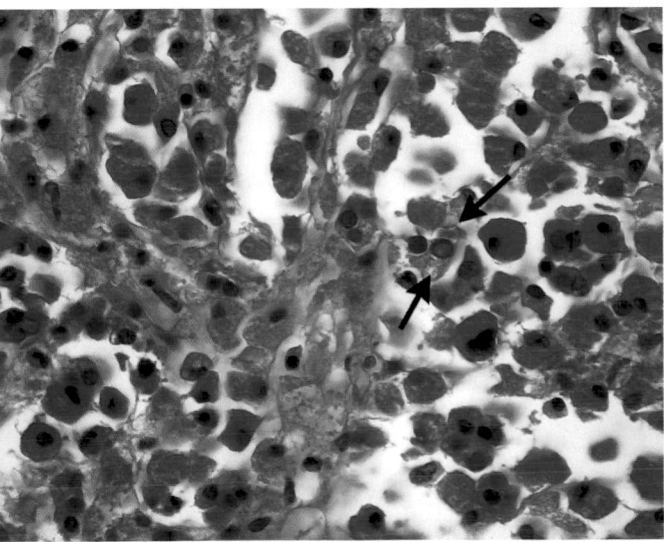

Fig. 17.163 High-power view of malakoplakia of bladder, showing Michaelis–Gutmann bodies and numerous histiocytes.

bacterial degradation.[100] Accordingly, malakoplakia is presently regarded as a defect in the host macrophage (phagolysosomal) response to a bacterial infection, usually from gram-negative coliform bacilli.[98,100,108] **Xanthogranulomatous cystitis** is morphologically and probably pathogenetically similar to malakoplakia, but it lacks Michaelis–Gutmann bodies.[109] Some of the reported cases have been associated with malignant tumors.[95]

Malakoplakia may also involve the renal pelvis and parenchyma, ureter, prostate gland, testis, epididymis, broad ligament, endometrium, retroperitoneal structures, colon, stomach, appendix, lymph nodes, brain, lungs, bones, skin, and several other sites.[97,103,107,110]

Other forms of cystitis

Other reasonably distinct types of cystitis that have been described are hemorrhagic cystitis, giant cell cystitis, follicular cystitis, radiation cystitis, gangrenous cystitis,[112] xanthogranulomatous cystitis,[120] and encrusted cystitis.[121]

Hemorrhagic cystitis is a well-recognized complication of cyclophosphamide therapy for bone marrow transplantation or systemic vasculitis,[114,117,119] but it has also been seen in the absence of medication.[111] Some cases of hemorrhagic cystitis have been found to result from herpes simplex virus or cytomegalovirus.[115,118] Severe cases of hemorrhagic cystitis may necessitate the performance of a total cystectomy.[116]

HIV-infected and other immunosuppressed patients may develop cystitis of various types, including malakoplakia (see previous section) and *Toxoplasma* cystitis.[113]

Metaplastic conditions

The bladder epithelium is prone to a remarkably wide range of metaplastic changes, most of them induced by chronic inflammation. Although clearly related to each other and often coexisting, they have traditionally been regarded as distinct entities of either inflammatory or neoplastic nature.

Intestinal (glandular) metaplasia and/or cystic changes result from chronic inflammation or other causes of mucosal irritation, such as ureteral reimplantation, neurogenic bladder, or bladder exstrophy.[133,139] They may regress completely if the underlying pathogenetic factor is removed. Grossly, they usually present as irregular mamillated lesions that may be confused cystoscopically with carcinoma. The trigone is the area most commonly affected, but rare instances of involvement of the entire bladder mucosa have been reported.[122] Similar lesions may be present in the ureter and renal pelvis.

Microscopically, the initial change is focal proliferation of the basal layer of the transitional epithelium, which produces buds that later become solid nodules (*von Brunn's nests or islands*) located within the lamina propria. Some of these nodules develop a central cystic area

caused by the accumulation of mucin (Fig. 17.164). When the cells lining the cyst maintain a transitional appearance, the condition is called *cystitis cystica*; when they acquire morphologic features analogous to those of colonic epithelium, the process is designated either as *cystitis glandularis* or as *intestinal (glandular, colonic) metaplasia*[125,134,141] (Fig. 17.165). The common occurrence of transitional forms suggests that these represent various stages or manifestations of the same basic process. When very florid, these metaplastic changes can mimic urothelial carcinoma, particularly the nested variant.[138a] Some forms of inverted papilloma may be related to this process (see p. 1326).

Immunohistochemically, neuroendocrine cells may be found in von Brunn's nests and cystitis cystica.[132] Ultrastructurally, the lining in cystitis cystica is made up of cells with short microvilli on the luminal surface; the taller cells contain numerous membrane-bound electron-dense secretory granules.[130] Immunohistochemically, reactivity for PSA and/or PSAP has been found in the metaplastic foci in 35% of the cases, including some in female patients; this finding has been interpreted as indicating the occurrence of prostate-like metaplasia,

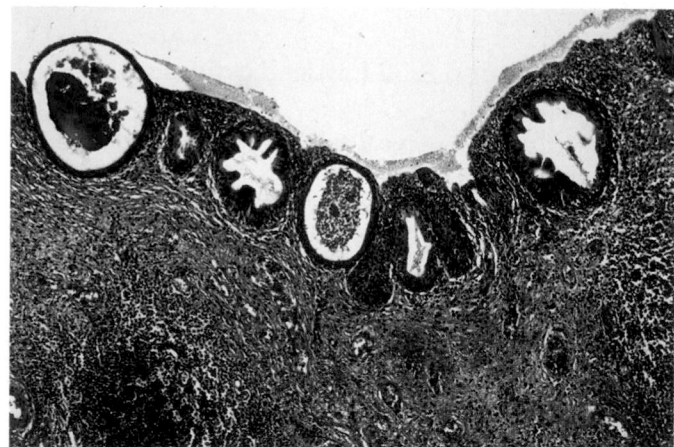

A

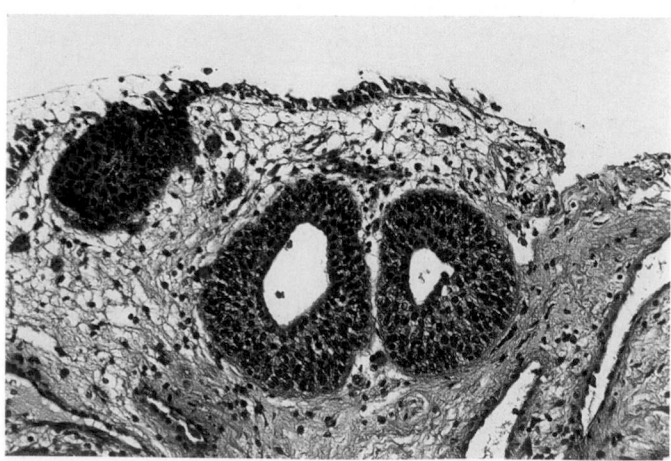

B

Fig. 17.164 Low- and high-power views of cystitis cystica. Most of the epithelial nests have a central lumen.

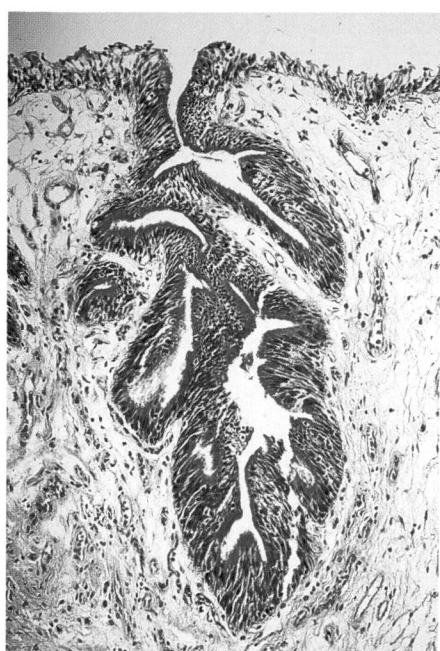

Fig. 17.165 Cystitis glandularis. A complex glandular structure lined by mucin-producing cells connects with the overlying transitional epithelium.

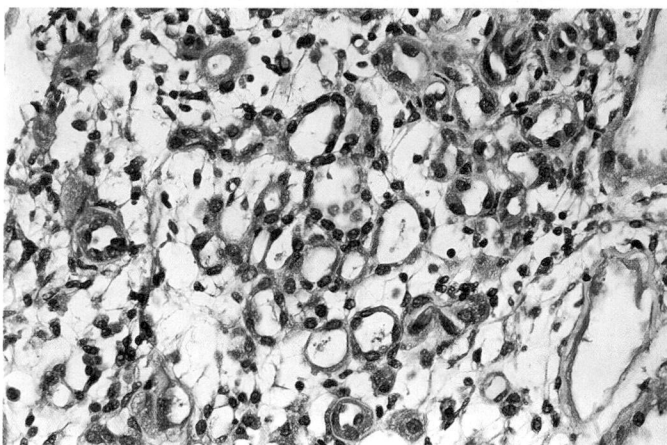

Fig. 17.166 So-called mesonephroid hyperplasia. A complex clustering of gland-like formations lined by cuboidal to flattened cells is seen surrounded by an edematous stroma.

possibly induced by the adult bladder stroma closest to the prostate.[126a,135]

Patients in whom the intestinal metaplasia is very extensive are at a high risk for the development of adenocarcinoma.[125]

Mesonephroid (adenomatoid, nephrogenic) metaplasia has been regarded in the past as a benign neoplasm and designated as nephrogenic adenoma, but most authors correctly favor the interpretation that it represents a localized or diffuse metaplastic change of the urothelium in response to chronic infection, calculi, or prolonged catheterization.[128] As such, it is often seen in association with cystitis cystica or glandularis, is associated with bladder conditions that predispose to metaplasia (such as exstrophy),[129] and exhibits a diploid DNA pattern.[129] However, the startling claim has been recently made, backed by very convincing cytogenetic data, that at least some of these lesions—as seen in renal transplant recipients—represent implants into eroded bladder mucosa of tubular cells from the kidney.[134a] Most cases of this condition are seen in adults, but children can also be affected.[131] Grossly, these lesions can be papillary, polypoid, or sessile; approximately 20% are multiple.[142] Their microscopic appearance is that of small tubular formations lined by cuboidal and hobnail cells having a light microscopic, ultrastructural, and lectin-binding appearance that is remarkably similar to those of mesonephric tubules[124,127,137] (Fig. 17.166). Immunohistochemically, they are always positive for keratin 7 and often positive for keratin 20 and CA-125.[136a] Some cases are associated with some degree of nuclear enlargement, hyperchroma-

sia, and pleomorphism; there is no evidence that these cases, referred to as *atypical*, have a precancerous potential.[126] The main differential diagnosis is with adenocarcinoma of mesonephroid (clear cell) type (see p. 1338). In the rare cases in which the pattern of growth is papillary, the lesion may simulate a papilloma or papillary carcinoma of transitional cell type.

Squamous metaplasia refers to the replacement of urothelium by stratified squamous epithelium. This has been subdivided into a *vaginal* and a *keratinizing* type.[140,141] The former, seen only in females, is so common as to be regarded as normal. The keratinizing type, traditionally known as leukoplakia, is more common in males and is usually associated with chronic irritation.[123,136] The L1 antigen (as detected by the monoclonal antibody Mac387) has been used as a marker of squamous differentiation, since it is absent in normal urothelium and in transitional cell carcinoma.[138]

Tumorlike conditions

Postoperative granulomas can develop following catheterization and diathermy. The microscopic appearance may be that of a foreign-body granuloma or resemble a rheumatoid nodule by virtue of central necrosis surrounded by a palisading of histiocytes and scattered giant cells.[161,162] These lesions heal by fibrous scarring. The usual assumption is that they represent a local reaction to tissue necrosis, but the metals deposited from the diathermy instruments (such as tungsten, nickel, chromium, and zinc) may play a pathogenetic role.[147]

Postoperative spindle cell nodule is another lesion that may follow surgical interventions in the area, particularly transurethral resection (TUR).[166] Microscopically, it closely simulates the appearance of a sarcoma (particularly leiomyosarcoma) because of its marked cellularity and high mitotic activity[155,158] (Figs 17.167 and 17.168). It appears a few weeks following a TUR procedure and is characteristically located in the operative area. Cystoscopically, it typically presents as a small sessile friable nodule that bleeds easily. The fascicular pattern of

growth, ulcerated surface, red blood cell extravasation, and lack of significant pleomorphism, together with the history of a recent surgical procedure, distinguish this lesion from true sarcoma. The proliferating spindle cells are thought to be of mesenchymal nature and probably akin to myofibroblasts; however, they show a strong and as yet unexplained reactivity for low-molecular-weight keratin[164] (Fig. 17.169A); they also stain for vimentin, actin, and desmin but are negative for EMA[164] (Fig. 17.169B).

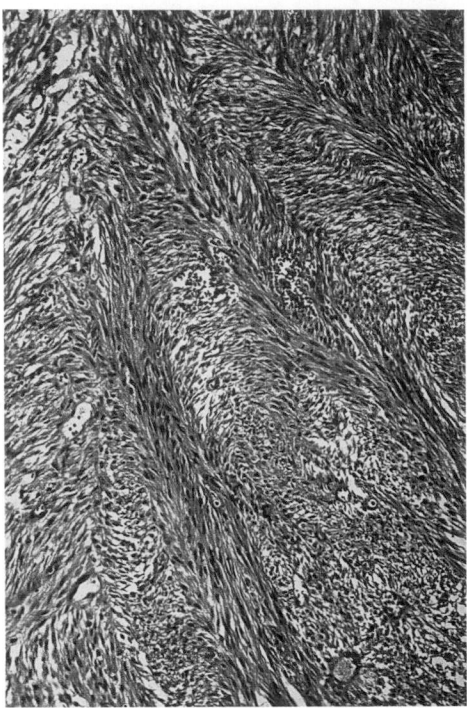

Fig. 17.167 Postoperative spindle cell nodule. Low-power microscopic view showing well-developed fascicular arrangement of the proliferating cells.

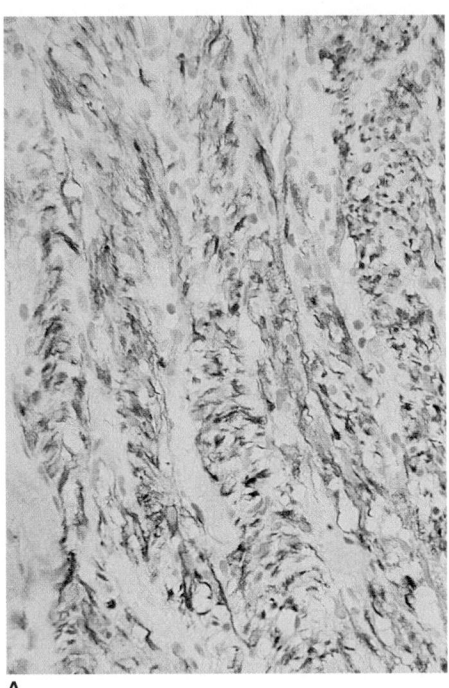

A

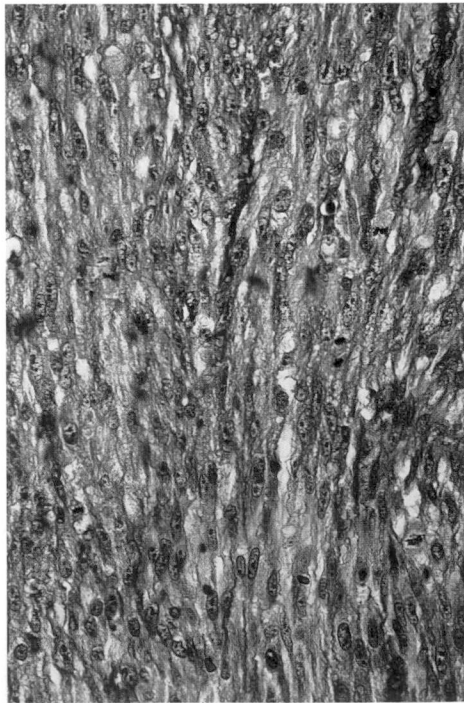

Fig. 17.168 Postoperative spindle cell nodule. High-power view showing extreme cellularity and numerous mitotic figures.

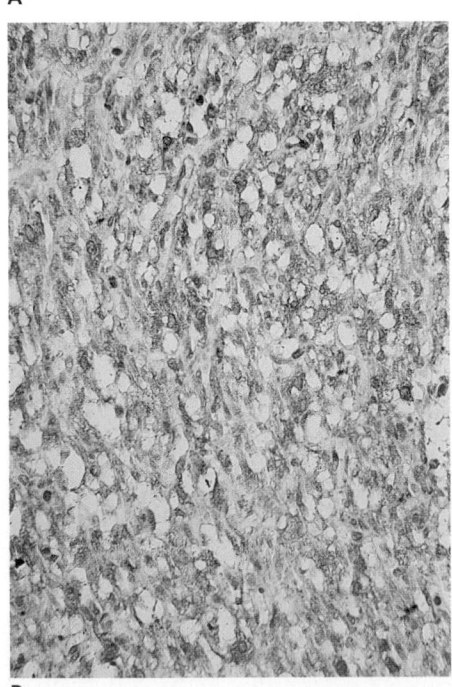

B

Fig. 17.169 Postoperative spindle cell nodule. Strong immunoreactivity for **A** keratin, **B** actin.

Inflammatory pseudotumor is the term traditionally used for a polypoid bladder growth, most commonly seen in children, characterized by the proliferation of generally spindle cells in a myxoid and inflammatory background[143,151] (Fig. 17.170). The main differences with postoperative spindle cell nodule are a tendency to reach a larger size, greater prominence of the myxoid stroma, lesser degree of cellularity, greater pleomorphism, and lesser tendency for keratin immunoreactivity (which, however, may still be present).[143,152,153] Fibrosclerotic areas may be present.[154,159] The differential diagnosis includes

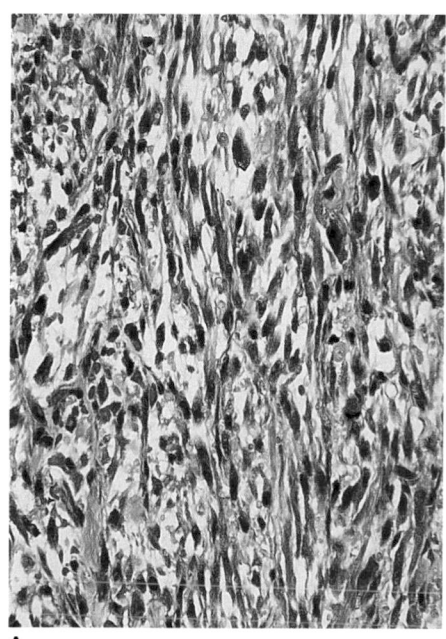

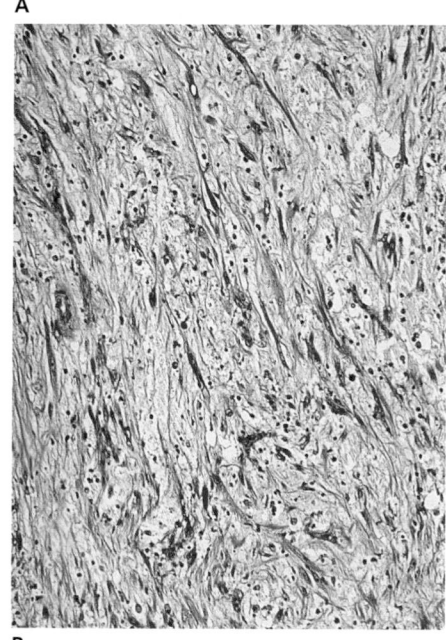

Fig. 17.170 So-called "inflammatory pseudotumor." Highly cellular spindle cell proliferation showing a moderate degree of atypia and somewhat edematous stroma. There is an associated inflammatory mononuclear component.

embryonal/botryoid rhabdomyosarcoma in children, and leiomyosarcoma and sarcomatoid carcinoma in adults. Immunohistochemical evaluation can be of help, in the sense that myogenin is expressed only by rhabdomyosarcoma, whereas high-molecular-weight caldesmon is preferentially expressed by leiomyosarcoma.[163]

Inflammatory pseudotumor has been generally regarded as a reactive condition, as implied by its name.[166,167] Its distinction from ordinary sarcomas and carcinomas is certainly of importance because of its generally indolent nature.[149] However, several pieces of evidence have accumulated in recent years that suggest that this entity is of neoplastic nature, albeit of a low-grade nature. This includes the occurrence of cases with deep infiltration of the wall and extension into the perivesical soft tissue,[143] and the demonstration of a non-random chromosomal translocation involving 2p23 that results in the expression of anaplastic lymphoma kinase (ALK).[146,147a] Accordingly, it has been proposed that this entity be renamed *inflammatory myofibroblastic tumor*.

Pseudosarcomatous stromal reactions have been described adjacent to transitional cell carcinomas, the reactive tissue having a nodular fasciitis-like appearance.[148,156] The distinction with sarcomatoid (spindle) transitional cell carcinoma is often difficult, and it may be impossible.

Pseudocarcinomatous proliferation can occur as a result of radiation therapy, with or without associated ulceration. The atypical epithelium may be of transitional or squamous type (Fig. 17.171). The presence of vascular ectasia and atypical fibroblasts in the stroma represent important diagnostic clues.[144,144a]

Prostatic-type polyps similar to those more commonly occurring in the prostatic urethra have been seen in the bladder neck and around the ureteral orifices.[145]

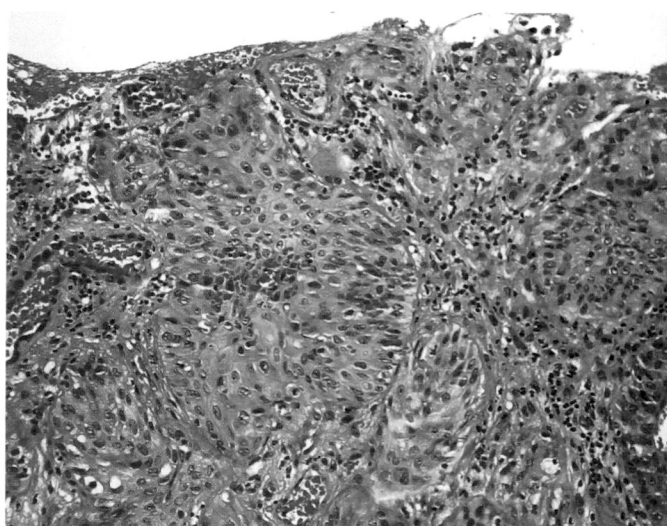

Fig. 17.171 Postradiation architectural and cytologic atypia of bladder epithelium. These changes are sometimes overinterpreted as carcinoma.

Collagen polyps result from the injection of collagen into the bladder or urethral wall as treatment of urinary stress incontinence. Microscopically, the polyps show a submucosal accumulation of degraded collagen surrounded by a modest inflammatory reaction.[160]

Other reported types of tumorlike conditions of the bladder include **xanthoma**,[157] **extramedullary hematopoiesis**,[150] and **hamartoma** (occurring in association with the Beckwith–Wiedemann syndrome).[165]

Benign tumors

Inverted papilloma (brunnian adenoma) is thought to represent a benign epithelial tumor. It is more commonly seen in adult and elderly males and is almost always located in the trigone, bladder neck, or prostatic urethra.[174,190] It is usually solitary and presents with hematuria and/or obstruction. Cystoscopy reveals a polypoid and usually pedunculated lesion of smooth contours (Fig. 17.172). Microscopically, the most characteristic feature is the invagination of the epithelium, which shows no atypical features (Fig. 17.173). Papillae are absent, and connective tissue is very scanty.

In some lesions, there is a distinct trabecular arrangement, with peripheral palisading of the tumor cells; in

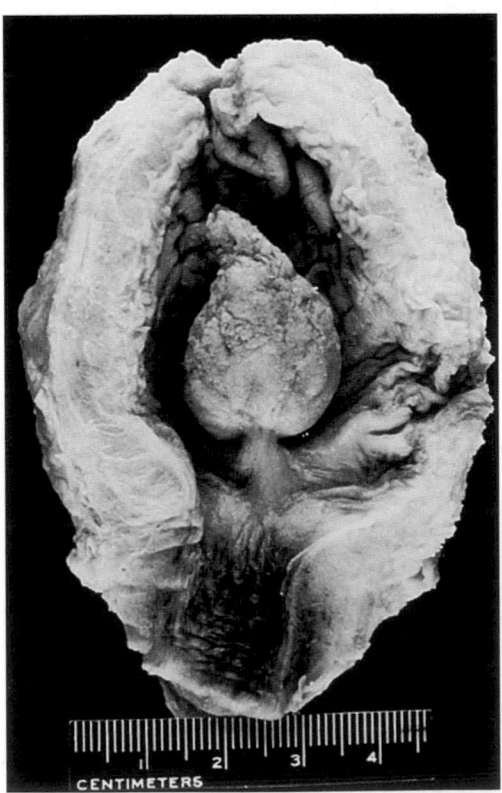

Fig. 17.172 Inverted papilloma of bladder. A large polypoid, but not papillary, mass protrudes in the trigone. (From Kim YH, Reiner L. Brunnian adenoma [inverted papilloma] of the urinary bladder. Report of a case. Hum Pathol 1978, 9: 229–231)

others, there are islands of urothelial cells accompanied by gland-like and mucin-secreting structures.[191] The latter type may actually represent an unduly proliferative form of cystitis glandularis or cystica.[184,191] Exceptionally, a neuroendocrine component made up of granular eosinophilic cells is present.[206] There is no evidence that inverted papilloma predisposes to the development of carcinoma, but the occasional coexistence of the two lesions suggests a pathogenetic relationship.[170,193] Unfortunately, morphology, ploidy, MIB-1 proliferative activity, and p53 immunostaining have not proved useful in separating those inverted papillomas that are associated with transitional cell carcinomas from those that are not.[181]

Papilloma of exophytic type is discussed together with the urothelial carcinomas (see p. 1331).

Inverted papilloma should be distinguished from transitional cell carcinoma spreading into Brunn's islands and growing in an inverted fashion. Simple excision is adequate treatment.

Villous adenoma is microscopically similar to its colorectal counterpart.[196] As in the latter location, it can be pure or associated with a tubular component (tubulo-villous adenoma).[168] It is often associated with cystitis glandularis and cystica,[175] and it should be distinguished from bladder extension of well-differentiated colorectal carcinoma.[204] As is also the case in other locations, villous adenoma of the bladder has a tendency to undergo malignant transformation in the form of invasive adenocarcinoma.[178,202]

Condyloma acuminatum can involve the bladder, often in conjunction with similar lesions in the external genitalia and adjacent areas.[183] Koilocytosis is seen microscopically, and HPV antigen can be detected immunohistochemically.[203]

Squamous papilloma is architecturally similar to condyloma acuminatum but it lacks cytopathic epithelial changes and is negative for HPV DNA, suggesting a lack of relation between the two lesions; most occur in elderly women and follow a benign clinical course, with occasional local recurrences.[176]

Paraganglioma (extra-adrenal pheochromocytoma) can present as a primary bladder neoplasm localized within the wall[182] (Fig. 17.174). Most patients are young adult women.[177] Its histologic appearance and immunohistochemical profile are the same as for paragangliomas in other sites.[197] Morphologic variants include *oncocytic paraganglioma*[173] and *composite paraganglioma–ganglioneuroma*.[192] Approximately half of the patients have symptoms produced by the excessive secretion of catecholamines, sometimes associated with voiding.[169] Multicentricity is rare. Local recurrence and metastases may supervene, an indication that these tumors should not be necessarily regarded as benign. As usual, clinical stage is the most useful prognostic indicator.[177] Their DNA pattern is often abnormal.[188]

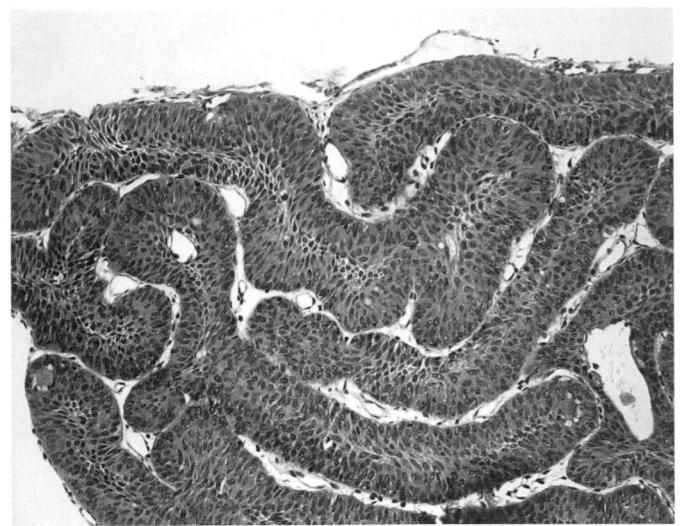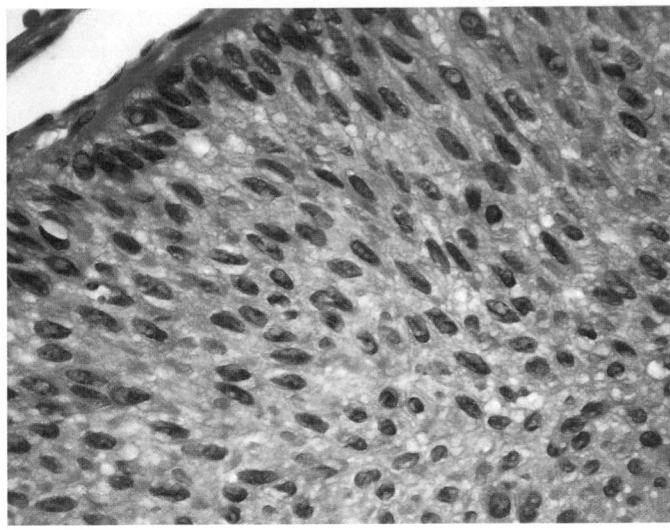

A

B

Fig. 17.173 A and **B,** Inverted papilloma of bladder. **A,** The proliferation has a festoon-like quality and is located below a flat epithelium. **B,** High-power view showing the oval to spindle shape of the cells and their total lack of atypia.

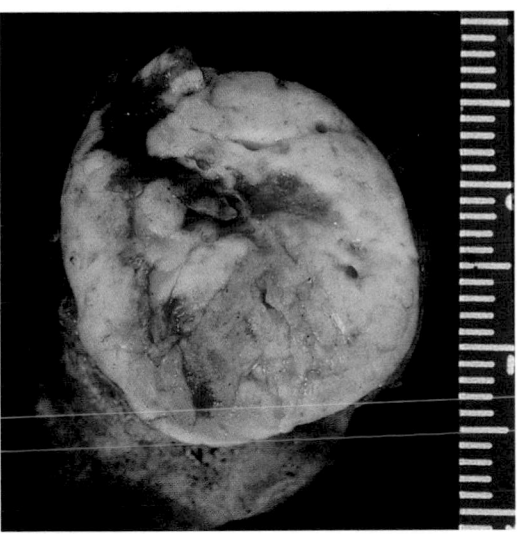

Fig. 17.174 Gross appearance of paraganglioma of bladder. The tumor is well circumscribed and yellowish. It turned a deep brown color when immersed in bichromate solution.

Solitary fibrous tumor can present as a mass in the bladder wall. CD34 and bcl-2 immunoreactivity are the rule, as in other sites. Most reported cases have behaved in a benign fashion.[171,207]

Other rare **benign tumors** of the bladder include *mucin-secreting "cystadenoma" of possible müllerian origin,*[187,205] *leiomyoma,*[194] *hemangioma,*[179,189] *arteriovenous malformation,*[199] *lymphangioma,*[172] *chondroma,*[200] *granular cell tumor,*[185] *schwannoma,*[198] *neurofibroma(tosis),*[180,186,208] *angiomyolipoma,*[189a] and the related *clear cell myomelanocytic tumor.*[199a] The hemangiomas are usually seen in children; they are usually located in the lateral or posterior walls, are sessile, are sometimes associated with cutaneous hemangiomas, and may be the cause of gross painless hematuria.[201] The diagnosis of leiomyoma

should be reserved for those smooth muscle tumors that are noninfiltrative and lack mitotic activity, cytologic atypia, and necrosis.[195]

Transitional cell (urothelial) carcinoma

General and clinical features

Transitional cell carcinoma (also known as urothelial carcinoma, a synonym which is currently favored) comprises approximately 90% of all primary tumors of this organ. As with most other carcinomas, its development seems to depend on a combination of genetic and environmental factors.[219] Among the latter, chemical factors are thought to be of great importance.[221] Bladder tumors are more common in industrial areas (especially in those associated with petrochemicals), and their incidence is increased with exposure to cigarette smoke and arylamines.[209,214,215,222] Auerbach et al.[210] showed in a classic study a sharp correlation between smoking habits and the occurrence of nuclear atypia in the transitional epithelium, complementing the epidemiologic evidence of a dose-response of cigarette smoking and urinary bladder carcinoma.

Other environmental factors include aniline dyes (particularly benzidine and β-naphthylamine),[226,229] auramines, phenacetin, and cyclophosphamide.[216,223,225] It has been postulated that urinary tryptophan metabolites may be the endogenous counterparts of the carcinogenic dyes.[212] *Schistosoma haematobium* is also thought to be pathogenetically related to transitional cell (and squamous cell) carcinoma of the bladder, being that the greatest concentration of carcinoma of this organ occurs in areas of the world infested by this parasite.[217,223] The role of HPV remains controversial, but most of the available evidence suggests that it does not play a significant role in the genesis of this tumor.[213,218,228] It is believed that there is a slight increased risk for the development of bladder carcinomas in patients who had been treated with radiation therapy for prostatic carcinoma.[224] A curious event is the isolated case of transitional cell carcinoma arising in the gastric remnant following gastrocystoplasty.[225a] Along similar lines, cases have been reported of adenocarcinoma[225b] and leiomyosarcoma[228a] arising at the site of an ileal neo-bladder.

Most cases of transitional cell carcinoma of the bladder present in patients over the age of 50 years, but they can also occur in younger adults and children.[211,220,230] The latter tend to be low-grade, indolent neoplasms, but occasional highly aggressive examples in this age group are on record.[227]

Men are affected more often than women, and whites more often than blacks. Gross or microscopic hematuria is the most common form of presentation, followed by symptoms related to associated urinary tract infection. Dysuria is more often seen with high-grade tumors, perhaps because of involvement of the bladder wall.

Morphologic features

Transitional cell tumors can arise anywhere in the bladder. In a series of approximately 1000 cases, the location was listed as follows: lateral walls, 37%; posterior wall, 18%; trigone, 12%; neck, 11%; ureteric orifices, 10%; dome, 8%; and anterior wall, 4%[254] (Fig. 17.175). They

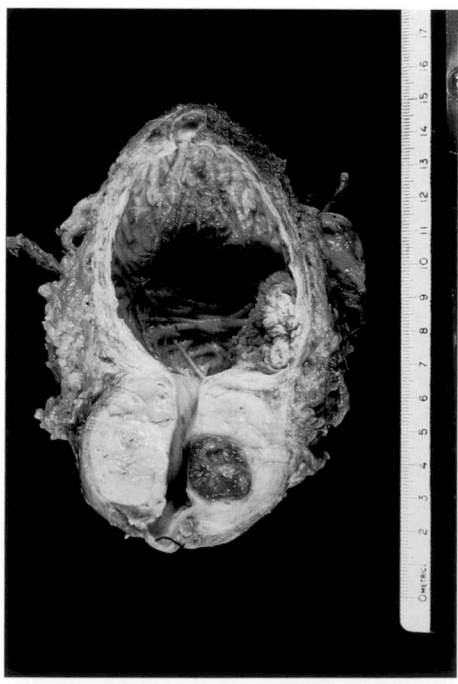

Fig. 17.175 Exophytic and papillary pattern of growth of a transitional cell carcinoma arising in a bladder with hypertrophy of the wall due to prostatic nodular hyperplasia. The tumor, which is located in the left lateral wall, was treated by total cystoprostatectomy. The prostate shows an incidental infarct.

have also been reported within diverticula (see p. 1318) and even arising from regenerated urothelium over a lyophilized dura patch,[253] or within the gastric remnant following gastrocystoplasty.[249] When located around the ureteral orifices, they may produce partial or complete blockage of one or both ureters, with resulting hydronephrosis and pyelonephritis. Synchronous or metachronous multicentricity is common. Most clinical and molecular genetic evidence suggests that in the large majority of cases the tumors arise from a common clone, and that therefore they are the consequence of intramucosal seeding of a single tumor rather than true multicentric neoplasms.[244]

The pattern of growth may be exophytic or endophytic, or a combination of both.[237,239,246] When exophytic, the tumor may adopt a papillary configuration (with central fibrovascular cores) or a solid (nodular) appearance. When growing endophytically (especially if well-differentiated), it may result in clusters of tumor cells in the lamina propria, which may be underdiagnosed as von Brunn's nests or cystitis glandularis or cystica.[231,247,251,255] This is referred to as the *nested variant* of transitional cell carcinoma.[234]

Stromal invasion by transitional cell carcinoma proceeds in two stages: invasion of the lamina propria and invasion of the muscle layer (Fig. 17.176). Detection of the former is a difficult and somewhat subjective exercise.[240] Conversely, detection of muscle invasion is of great consequence because of its influence on therapy and prognosis[231,232] (Fig. 17.177). It has even been suggested that evaluation of this feature be standardized through its objective measurement with a micrometer.[235] Care should be exercised not to misinterpret the inconsistent but sometimes prominent fascicles of muscularis mucosae (particularly common in women) as belonging to the muscularis propria.[238,241,258,259] Lymphovascular invasion may be present, but immunohistochemical studies for endothelial markers suggest that this feature

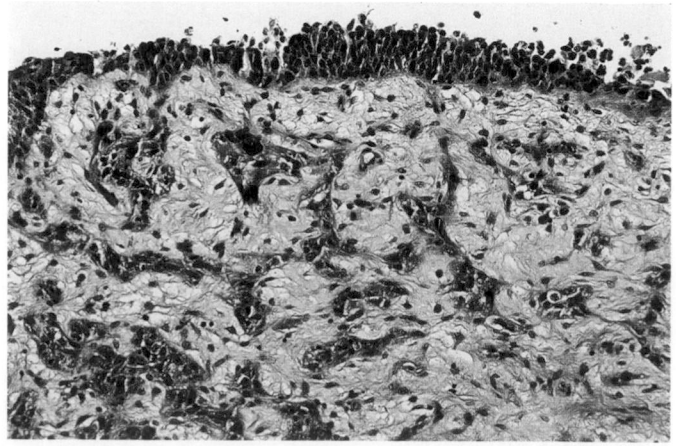

Fig. 17.176 Lamina propria invasion by transitional cell carcinoma of bladder.

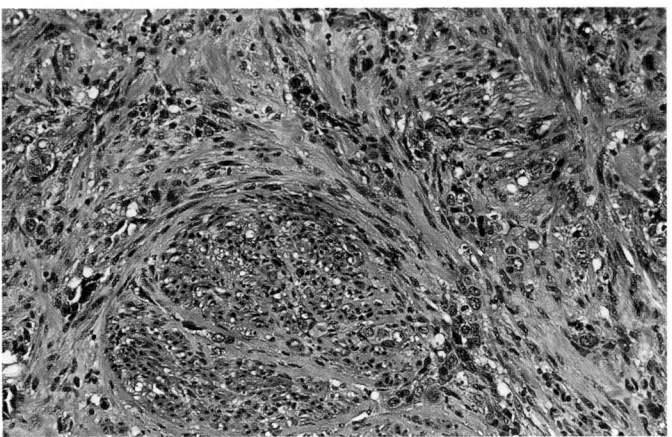

Fig. 17.177 Muscle invasion by transitional cell carcinoma of bladder.

can be closely simulated by retraction artifact.[243,250] It is also important not to misinterpret the mature adipose tissue commonly present in the lamina propria or muscularis propria as perivesical soft tissue, in order to avoid a tumor adjacent to fat in a biopsy specimen being badly overstaged.[248]

Several cytoarchitectural variations of transitional cell carcinoma exist. Foci of glandular metaplasia are common, usually in the form of intracytoplasmic mucin-containing vacuoles.[236] Exceptionally, a microcystic pattern develops as the result of enlargement of the mucin-filled cavities, which can reach a diameter of 1 mm or more.[260] Ward[257] found that 25% to 30% of transitional cell carcinomas had evidence of focal mucin production and that a similar number (but not necessarily the same cases) showed some glandular formation. These tumors, sometimes incorrectly designated as "mixed carcinomas," behave as conventional transitional cell carcinomas of equivalent grades. A clear distinction should be made between them and the pure adenocarcinomas of the bladder (see p. 1337). Similarly, many otherwise typical transitional cell carcinomas (especially grade III and grade IV lesions) show foci of squamous differentiation. These tumors should still be regarded as of transitional origin and clearly separated from pure squamous cell carcinomas (see p. 1338). Clear cells may be prominent in transitional cell carcinoma and simulate adenocarcinoma.[242] A micropapillary pattern has been described that resembles that of ovarian serous papillary carcinoma.[233] An exceptional variant of transitional cell carcinoma is characterized by a plasmacytoid appearance that mimics myeloma.[252]

Lymphocytic infiltration is sometimes seen at the interphase between the transitional cell tumor and the underlying stroma. Exceptionally, this lymphocytic infiltrate is so intense as to obscure the epithelial component and to simulate a malignant lymphoma.[261] In other instances, a heavy infiltration by eosinophils is present;

this seems to be particularly common in tumors with squamous features.[245] Deposition of Tamm–Horsfall protein may be seen in connection with necrosis and inflammation.[256]

Histochemical and immunohistochemical features

Immunohistochemically, transitional cell carcinomas express various keratin types, a difference in pattern having been noted among basal cells, transitional cells, and umbrella cells (when present).[263] There is consistent expression of CK20, in stark contrast with the morphologically similar transitional cell carcinomas of the ovary.[276] This CK20 positivity is particularly common and strong in the high-grade tumors.[267] The coordinate expression of CK7 and CK20 is a particularly reproducible feature of transitional cell carcinoma,[264] and is usually maintained in the metastatic foci.[271] An increased expression of CK8 and CK18 has been found at the interface between tumor and stroma.[277] In general, the expression of CK18 is decreased in higher-grade and higher-stage tumors, but many exceptions occur.[277] Two relatively new useful markers for transitional cell carcinoma are thrombomodulin and uroplakin III. The former is very sensitive but not very specific (in that it also stains most squamous cell carcinomas and mesotheliomas), whereas the latter has a high degree of specificity but is only moderately sensitive.[272,275,276a] Other markers commonly expressed by these tumors are CEA and cathepsin B (particularly in high-grade lesions),[270,280,282] CA19-9,[274] CD15 (Leu-M1),[269] survivin,[272a] and androgen receptors.[283] If one is confronted with a high-grade malignant tumor for which the differential diagnosis is between transitional cell and prostatic carcinoma, an useful immunohistochemical panel to use is the following: CK34-β-12, CK7, p53, PSA, PSAP, and Leu7; the first three stains are likely to be positive in the former, and the last three stains in the latter.[268,274a,281a]

Some tumors are also immunoreactive for hCG, human placental lactogen, and SP-1, especially in the most pleomorphic areas[266,278]; this can occur in the absence of morphologic evidence of trophoblastic differentiation by the tumor (see p. 1341).

Deletion of ABO blood group antigens is a common finding in transitional cell carcinomas, particularly in those having high-grade microscopic features. This alteration can only be evaluated in "secretor" individuals, whose urothelium normally expresses these markers.[279] A related abnormality is the neoexpression of Lewis X antigen (which is absent in normal urothelium) in over 85% of transitional cell carcinomas regardless of tumor stage and grade.[279] Interestingly, the loss of blood group antigens is often associated with an overexpression of the epidermal growth factor receptor.[273]

Staining for the basal lamina component laminin has been advocated for the detection of early stromal invasion.[262] Tenascin, an extracellular matrix protein, is strongly expressed in invasive, high-grade carcinomas with abundant stroma and is thought to reflect both the severity of the inflammatory infiltrate and the extent of stromal remodeling.[281]

AgNOR counts are generally elevated in transitional cell carcinoma, but the degree of overlap between inflammatory, dysplastic, and neoplastic epithelium is such as to severely limit the diagnostic utility of the technique.[265]

Electron microscopic features

Ultrastructurally, high-grade transitional cell carcinomas are accompanied by a decrease of specialized junctions[284]; pleomorphic microvilli are apparent by scanning electron microscopy regardless of tumor grade.[285]

Molecular genetic features

Several types of nonrandom chromosomal alterations have been described in transitional cell tumors.[302] Loss of heterozygosity of chromosome 9 occurs in both superficial and invasive tumors, whereas loss of heterozygosity of 3p, 5q, and 17p is commonly found only in invasive tumors.[292,296,299,300] Other markers frequently exhibiting loss of heterozygosity in transitional cell carcinomas of bladder are located in chromosomes 4, 8, and 11. Some brave authors are beginning to attempt the construction of a complex genetic model of human bladder carcinogenesis on the basis of these bewildering data.[291] Significantly, abnormalities of chromosome 9 have also been found in a high percentage of urothelial samples diagnosed as normal or hyperplastic without atypia on histologic grounds.[293] Genetic analyses have shown concordant changes between superficial papillary tumors and the invasive tumors that followed, supporting the time-honored belief of the tumor progression of one into the other.[303]

Overexpression of p53 occurs in a high proportion of transitional cell tumors (particularly the high-grade forms) and correlates well with prognosis (see p. 1337).[289,290] It is strongly associated with both loss of heterozygosity of 17p and mutations in the gene as detected by molecular techniques.[288] Abnormally high levels of MDM2, seen in approximately 30% of the cases, are associated with p53 overexpression.[295]

Increased expression of c-erbB-2 oncogene product has been found immunohistochemically in 10% of the grade II tumors, in 60% of the grade III tumors, and in 100% of the adenocarcinomas.[286,288] The expression of this oncogene is closely related to that of the epidermal growth factor receptor.[304]

Overexpression of bcl-2 is seen in approximately half of bladder transitional cell carcinomas, and is inversely correlated with tumor stage.[297]

Cyclin D1 overexpression correlates with tumor grade and stage, in the sense of being present in approximately half of grade I tumors but practically never in grade III tumors.[294,301]

Reduction or absence of *FHIT* (a tumor suppressor gene located at 3p14.2) has been found by immunohistochemical analysis in 61% of the bladder transitional cell carcinomas, and in a greater percentage of the high-stage tumors.[287]

Another gene frequently deleted in bladder transitional cell carcinoma is *INK4A*. This gene, located in chromosome 9p21, encodes proteins p16 and p19, which regulate the pRb and p53 pathways.[298]

Biopsy

Bladder tumors should be sampled or removed with a "cold" biopsy instrument. Ideally, the biopsy should include a portion of the underlying muscle. The urologist should not fulgurate a papillary tumor without biopsy simply because it appears benign. It is true that tumors wholly composed of delicate papillary fronds are usually well differentiated, but exceptions may occur. It is recommended that, in addition to the main tumor, biopsies be taken from apparently normal adjacent mucosa and from three other sites (one lateral to each ureteral orifice and one from the upper posterior wall).[305] These biopsies should be submitted separately and sectioned at various levels. The pathology report of a bladder biopsy that contains a tumor should include the following information (see also Appendix C):

1 Grade
2 Configuration (papillary or solid)
3 Depth of penetration
4 Presence of muscle
5 Lymphatic invasion
6 Blood vessel invasion
7 Changes in adjacent mucosa if present

Cytology

Exfoliative cytology is of little practical value in the initial evaluation of most bladder tumors because of their accessibility to formal biopsy. The technique is most useful in the following situations: detection of tumors associated with extensive chronic inflammation in which the biopsy may be negative because of sampling, carcinomas in situ, and carcinomas hidden in a bladder diverticulum. Specimens obtained from bladder irrigation are superior to those resulting from voided urine.[306,314] The diagnostic accuracy of urinary cytology is closely related to the histologic grade of the tumor and the pretreatment or posttreatment status and only minimally to the specific therapy mode.[321] Well-differentiated (grade I and some grade II) lesions are more likely to be overlooked because the cells are very similar to those of normal bladder mucosa.[312,317,322] Esposti et al.[307] recognized cytologically 68% of 124 cases of grade II to grade IV cancers from the first samples of urine and bladder washings. In 22 additional cases, "suspicious" cells were identified.

The greatest value of urinary bladder cytology is in

the follow-up evaluation of patients who have received surgical or radiotherapeutic treatment for bladder carcinoma.[316,323] In some cases, the recurrence may not become clinically apparent until more than a year after the malignant cells have been detected in the urine.[318,319]

The most distinctive cytologic features of transitional cell carcinoma (which can also be useful for their recognition at a metastatic site) are the spindle, pyramidal, and racquet-like shape of the tumor cells, the eccentric nuclei, and the cytoplasmic evidence of both squamous and glandular differentiation (including endo-ectoplasmic interfaces and intracytoplasmic vacuoles)[310] (Fig. 17.178). A recent description of the *cercariform cell* (a single tumor cell with a nucleated globular body and a unipolar cytoplasmic process with a nontapering, flattened, or bulbous end) as a quasi-specific cytologic feature of transitional cell carcinoma is not holding up, although the presence of a large number of these cells remains a good diagnostic clue.[309]

Although radiation therapy and chemotherapy may result in atypia of normal cells, an experienced pathologist provided with accurate clinical information is unlikely to confuse these changes with those of recurrent carcinoma.[307,316]

Flow cytometric and image analysis techniques have been developed for the evaluation of DNA abnormalities in cytologic specimens from the bladder; these have reached a degree of accuracy equivalent to that of conventional cytologic examination.[306,308,313,315] Identification

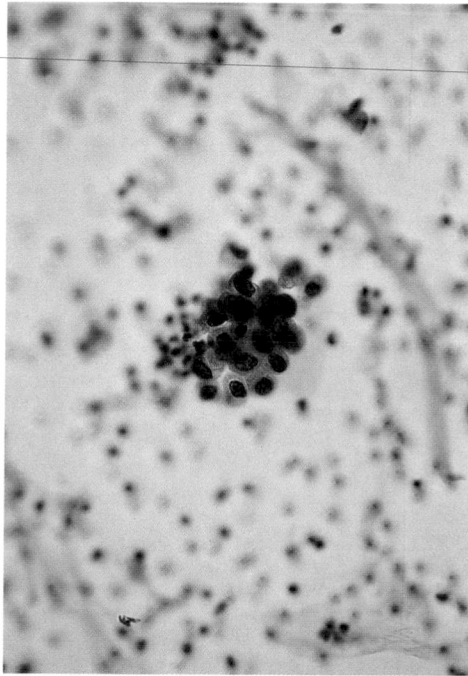

Fig. 17.178 Cytologic appearance of transitional cell carcinoma of bladder. The tumor cells, arranged in a tight cluster, show hyperchromatic nuclei and abnormal nucleocytoplasmic ratio.

of *p53* gene mutations in urine samples promises to become a useful tool for detecting neoplasms and for monitoring individuals following treatment.[320] Detection of CK20 by RT-PCR has been advocated as an adjunct for the cytologic diagnosis of transitional cell carcinoma, inasmuch as this marker is commonly expressed in tumors but not in normal urothelial cells.[311]

Classification

Several classification systems of bladder transitional cell carcinoma have been proposed over the years. These represent attempts at grading the increasing degrees of architectural and particularly *cytologic* disarrays of a single tumor type. The main such systems were those of Ash in 1940[324]; Mostofi in 1960,[336] adopted by the American Bladder Tumor Registry; Bergkvist et al. in 1965[325]; and Malmstrom et al. in 1987.[335] These have been superseded by the classification jointly proposed in 1998 by the World Health Organization and the International Society of Urological Pathology (WHO/ISUP).[331,339,341] While some authors have questioned the wisdom of simply assigning new names to basically the same categories without providing a convincing rationale for doing so,[339] the fact of the matter is that this "new" classification scheme is likely to be adopted on a worldwide basis because of the authority of its proponents. Its main features are the division of the neoplastic lesions into flat and papillary, and the separate evaluation of the papillary neoplasms for grade (based on architecture and cytology) and invasiveness (divided into lamina propria and muscularis propria levels). The types of papillary neoplasms recognized in this classification are the following: *papilloma* (with the variant *inverted papilloma*, already discussed on p. 1326); *papillary neoplasm of low malignant potential; low-grade papillary carcinoma*; and *high-grade papillary carcinoma* (Fig. 17.179). The criteria used to place the tumors into these categories are listed in Table 17.13.

The grading of transitional cell tumors of the bladder by this or any of the preceding schemes is of great prognostic significance. Thus, the tumors at the lower end of the spectrum (called papillomas in the WHO/ISUP scheme) have a low incidence of recurrence and a negligible incidence of in situ or invasive carcinoma.[326,335a] Cystoscopic examination by an experienced urologist is a very useful tool for predicting the neoplastic versus non-neoplastic nature of a bladder lesion, but not a very accurate one for the differentiation of low-grade and high-grade lesions or the assessment of invasion.[329]

It should be kept in mind that the differentiation of a neoplasm may vary from area to area,[327] and that therefore a biopsy or TUR may show a lower grade than what will be found in the surgical specimen.[328,332] It is also well to remember that this grading system has been devised for its application to noninvasive lesions and the noninvasive (superficial) component of invasive tumor, and

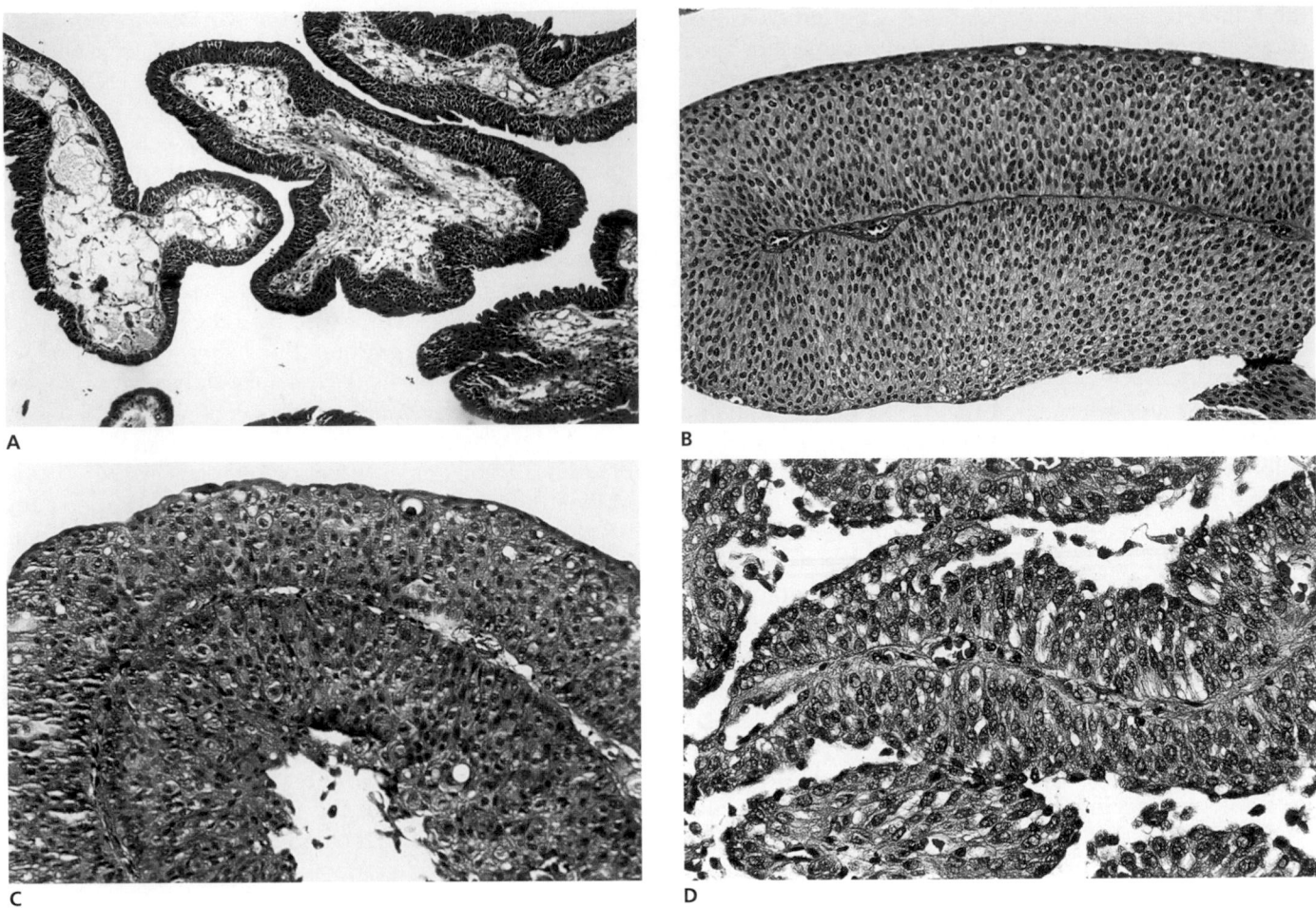

Fig. 17.179 A to **D**, Various types of transitional cell neoplasms of the bladder: **A**, papilloma; **B**, papillary neoplasm of low malignant potential; **C**, low-grade transitional cell carcinoma; **D**, high-grade transitional cell carcinoma.

that it does not have much discriminatory power when applied to the invasive component of these tumors.[333]

As expected, there is some degree of inter- and intraobserver variability in the evaluation of these lesions.[337] However, the basic soundness of this morphologically-based distinction is supported by the correlation with several independent parameters, such as proliferative activity and oncogene expression.[330,340] Whether quantitative morphometric grading will prove superior to the subjective methods currently used remains to be seen.[334,338]

Local spread and metastases

Invasive bladder carcinomas (especially high-grade tumors) are often associated with zones of atypical proliferation, carcinoma in situ, and early invasive carcinomas in areas remote from the main tumor mass. As already stated, molecular studies analyzing the *p53* tumor-suppressor gene and the pattern of X-chromosome inactivation suggest that in most instances these apparently multifocal urothelial tumors are derived from a single progenitor cell.[345,356] In some instances, this atypical proliferation spreads from the bladder into the ureters or renal pelvices.[346] Thus Sharma et al.[355] detected ureteral lesions that they interpreted as carcinoma in situ in 17 (8.5%) of 205 patients undergoing cystectomy for bladder carcinoma. The incidence was highest in patients with multifocal tumors and in those with high-stage and high-grade neoplasms. In a similar study, Schade et al.[354] found ureteral changes varying from mild atypia to early invasive carcinoma in many of the cases (Fig. 17.180). In another study, of 307 patients with high-risk superficial bladder tumors treated by a bladder-sparing strategy, 78 (25%) developed tumors in the upper urinary tract.[346]

Bladder carcinoma also may extend into the neck of the bladder, urethra, prostatic ducts, and seminal vesicle, perhaps even more commonly than to the ureters.[342,348,350,351] This is responsible for the occasional instances of urethral recurrence following cystectomy for carcinoma of the bladder.[357] In view of this finding, a routine diagnostic transurethral biopsy has been recommended in the workup of patients with in situ and high-grade bladder carcinoma,[350] and a routine ureterectomy is carried out in female patients with invasive bladder carcinoma.[343]

Table 17.13 Histologic features used to classify urothelial papillary lesions according to the scheme proposed by the WHO/ISUP

	Papilloma	Papillary neoplasm of low malignant potential	Low-grade papillary carcinoma	High-grade papillary carcinoma
Architecture				
Papillae	Delicate	Delicate: occasionally fused	Fused, branching, and delicate	Fused, branching, and delicate
Organization of cells	Identical to normal	Polarity identical to normal; any thickness; cohesive	Predominantly ordered, yet minimal crowding and minimal loss of polarity; any thickness; cohesive	Predominantly disordered with frequent loss of polarity; any thickness; often dyscohesive
Cytology				
Nuclear size	Identical to normal	May be uniformly enlarged	Enlarged with variation in size	Enlarged with variation in size
Nuclear shape	Identical to normal	Elongated, round–oval, uniform	Round–oval; slight variation in shape and contour	Moderate–marked pleomorphism
Nuclear chromatin	Fine	Fine	Mild variation within and between cells	Moderate–marked variation both within and between cells with hyperchromasia
Nucleoli	Absent	Absent to inconspicuous	Usually inconspicuous*	Multiple prominent nucleoli may be present
Mitoses	Absent	Rare, basal	Occasional, at any level	Usually frequent, at any level
Umbrella cells	Uniformly present	Present	Usually present	May be absent

* If present, small and regular and not accompanied by other features of high-grade carcinoma.
(From Epstein JI, Amin MB, Reuter VR, Mostofi FK, and the Bladder Consensus Conference Committee. The World Health Organization/International Society of Urological Pathology Consensus Classification of Urothelial (Transitional Cell) Neoplasms of the Urinary Bladder. Am J Surg Pathol 1998, **22**: 1435–1448)

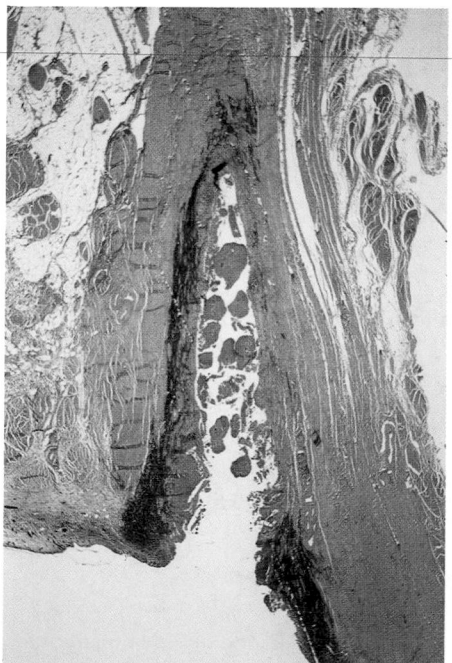

Fig. 17.180 Spread of low-grade transitional cell carcinoma of bladder into lower end of ureter.

Sakamoto et al.[353] showed that a TUR biopsy containing prostatic tissue at the 5 and/or 7 o'clock position of the verumontanum portion is the best specimen to detect involvement of prostatic ducts and acini by bladder carcinoma in men.

Lymph node metastases in the pelvic chains are found in 25% of the invasive tumors.[347] Thorough examination of H&E-stained sections remains the best method for detecting these metastases; there is no evidence that immunohistochemical staining or RT-PCR for keratin plays a useful role in this situation.[358]

The most common sites of distant metastases are the lungs, liver, bone, and central nervous system.[344,349,352]

Carcinoma in situ and dysplasia

Most cases of *carcinoma in situ* (CIS) and *dysplasia* of the bladder (also known, respectively, as low-grade and high-grade intraurothelial neoplasia) are seen in association with conventional transitional cell carcinoma and are especially common in high-grade lesions[358a,367,370,379,381]; in these instances, the invasive component tends to be multifocal.[365,382] In a study using giant histologic sections, Soto et al.[382] found that almost two thirds of 45 patients with invasive carcinoma had adjacent carcinoma in situ.

Sometimes CIS is found in the bladder in the absence of an invasive component, nearly always associated with various degrees of hyperplasia and dysplasia.[359,366,374,384] The lesion may be asymptomatic but often presents with irritative bladder symptoms. Grossly, it has a slightly raised, granular, or cobblestone appearance, and it may be accompanied by marked hyperemia. The lesion, which is often multicentric, has a predilection for the trigone, lateral walls, and dome.[362] The diagnosis is made through urinary cytology and/or multiple random cold biopsies.

The microscopic criteria are essentially the same as for CIS of other locations (notably the uterine cervix) and are generally defined as a partial or total replacement of the urothelial surface by cells having the morphologic features of carcinoma but lacking architectural alterations other than an increase in the number of cell layers[364,371] (Fig. 17.181). Thus by convention, the term carcinoma in situ (Tis) of the bladder is reserved for high-grade lesions showing pronounced cytologic atypia but lacking a papillary configuration. One should realize that papillary transitional cell carcinomas that do not invade the stroma are also carcinomas in situ (Ta), but they are not designated as such to avoid lumping together two conditions with markedly different morphologic features, natural history, and probably molecular pathways.[359,383]

It is also important for the term CIS not to be equated with *superficial carcinoma*; the latter is used by urologists for tumors that have not invaded into the muscularis propria regardless of their type and grade, and therefore it does not represent a pathologic entity.

Morphologic variations of bladder CIS include a large cell type with nuclear pleomorphism, a large cell type without nuclear pleomorphism, and a small cell type.[373]

Sometimes the tumor cells of CIS spread along the basement membrane and lift up the normal transitional cells, resulting in a pagetoid pattern of growth.[369,371a,378] They also have a great tendency to detach from the stroma; this results in a typical cystoscopic appearance ("*denuding cystitis*") and is also the cause of false-negative biopsies[377] (Fig. 17.182). If the clinical suspicion is high, multiple repeat biopsies are imperative.

Of 25 cases of CIS of the bladder included in the classic study by Melamed et al.,[374] 8 patients subsequently developed invasive carcinoma after intervals ranging from 8 to 67 months. Of 36 patients with localized urothelial dysplasia reviewed by Cheng et al.,[361] 7 (19%) developed biopsy-proven progression in the form of CIS (4) or invasive carcinoma (3). Seemayer et al.[380] have shown that a high proportion of patients with carcinoma in situ of the bladder have extensive intraductal prostatic involvement, a feature with obvious prognostic and therapeutic implications.

The abnormalities of lectin expression,[375] blood group antigen expression,[363] and DNA ploidy[368,376] that exist in invasive bladder carcinoma have also been documented in CIS; it is doubtful whether the minor differences among these parameters that have been detected between in situ and invasive lesions will be of help in the differential diagnosis between these two conditions.[375] Instead, immunostaining for CK20, cadherin, p53 and CD44 (standard isoform) has proved useful in the differential diagnosis between CIS and reactive atypia, in the sense that the first three markers tend to be positive in the former, whereas CD44 is mainly expressed in the latter.[371b,372,383a,b] Another interesting observation along these lines is that CIS lesions with synchronous carcinomas tend to show chromosome 9 loss whereas predominantly isolated CIS lesions do not.[368a]

In situ adenocarcinoma is an extremely rare form of intraepithelial bladder malignancy, which is frequently

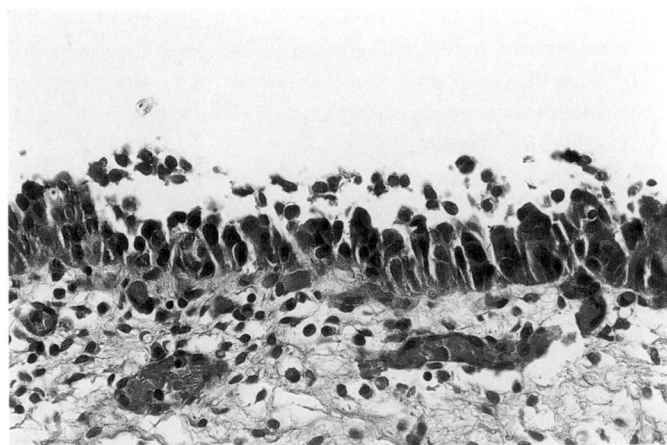

Fig. 17.181 Carcinoma in situ of bladder. Note the lack of maturation and the detachment of the tumor cells on the superficial portion.

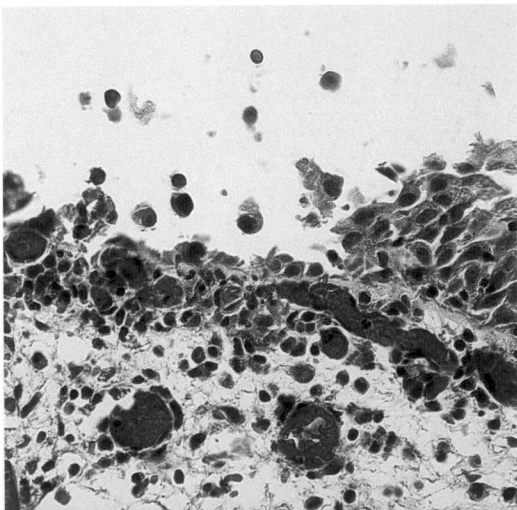

Fig. 17.182 Carcinoma in situ of bladder. The tumor has detached from the underlying stroma, only a few residual malignant cells remaining. The underlying stroma is markedly inflamed and hyperemic, resulting in the picture known as "denuding cystitis."

associated with invasive small cell carcinoma and micropapillary transitional cell carcinoma.[360]

Atypical papillary urothelial hyperplasia is a recent addition to the family of precursor bladder lesions.

It consists of undulating folds of urothelium that lack both the cytologic atypia and the well-developed branching fibrovascular cases of papillary neoplasms.[380a]

Treatment

The therapy of bladder carcinoma needs to be individualized, taking into account the age of the patient and the surgical risk; the extent, stage, and microscopic grade of the tumor; and the presence of dysplasia or carcinoma in situ elsewhere in the bladder.[402]

The recommended treatment for carcinoma in situ is total cystectomy, except for small and apparently localized lesions; for these, intravesical chemotherapy may induce temporary and sometimes complete remission[390,400,406]; however, in 40% to 70% of the cases, new tumors will develop, usually within a 6- to 12-month period.[404]

Grades I and II transitional cell tumors without muscle invasion usually are treated initially with transurethral resection; this is sometimes supplemented with intravesical chemotherapy or radiation therapy, especially in cases of multiple or recurrent tumors.[386,392,393,401,405] Grades III and IV transitional cell tumors, tumors with muscle invasion irrespective of grade, and tumors resistant to conservative therapy are generally best treated by radical cystectomy, with or without preoperative radiation therapy or chemotherapy.[385,398,403,406,408] In some centers, they have also been treated by radiation alone.[389,409] The radiation tends to obliterate the superficial papillary component of the tumor but has little discernible effect in the invasive component; parenthetically, it also leads to an increased degree of nuclear pleomorphism and induces metaplastic squamous changes.[399]

Radical cystectomy in the male includes the bladder, prostate, seminal vesicles, and adjacent perivesical tissues; in the female, it includes the bladder, uterus, tubes, ovaries, anterior vagina, and urethra. Argument persists as to whether a total urethrectomy should be part of the procedure in males.[388] In some centers, the radical cystectomy is combined with en bloc pelvic lymph node dissection.[397,407] At present, operative mortality for radical cystectomy is low, and pyelonephritis is no longer a frequent complication.

The addition of neoadjuvant chemotherapy to the cystectomy has improved the survival of patients with advanced bladder carcinoma.[390a]

Segmental (partial) cystectomy has fallen into disfavor because of the high rate of recurrence in the residual bladder. An initially controversial but now widely accepted therapy for superficial bladder carcinomas of either papillary or in situ type is intravesical immunotherapy with the Calmette–Guerin bacillus (BCG), which in some series has shown remarkable reduction of the tumor recurrence rate[387,391,394,396]; microscopically, this therapy results in superficial mucosal erosion, submucosal granulomatous inflammation, and reactive epithelial atypia[395] (see p. 1321).

Prognosis

The prognosis of bladder carcinoma is related to many parameters:

1 *Stage.* This is by far the most important prognostic determinator, as the pioneer studies of Jewett and others have demonstrated[434,435,452] (Fig. 17.183). Several staging systems have been proposed as modifications of Jewett's original scheme. The sharp decrease in survival associated with invasion of the muscle wall is possibly a result of the access that the tumor thus gains into the rich vascular network present at this level. The importance of this feature makes it imperative for the pathologist to state whether there is muscle in a biopsy specimen and, if so, whether it is invaded by tumor.[429] Although extension of tumor in perivesical tissues is a very poor prognostic sign, long-term cures have been achieved in some of these patients.[423] The current overall 5-year survival rate for small superficial bladder cancer is over 90%, whereas for deeply invasive bladder cancer (B_2 and C) it is between 45% and 55%.[418,467]

2 *Lymph node involvement.* This has been incorporated into the staging scheme and is an ominous prognostic sign. The long-term survival rate of these patients is nearly zero, particularly if several nodes are involved.[423,427a]

3 *Microscopic grade.* This is related to the stage, in the sense that most grade I and II tumors are superficial, whereas many grade III and IV tumors are deeply invasive[440]; however, grading has independent prognostic value within a given stage.[430,431,436,442] For the grade I lesions ("papillomas"), the recurrence rate following local excision is approximately 30% to 45% if tumors are solitary, and 65% to 90% if they are multiple.[444,455] In approximately 10% to 30% of the cases, the recurrence shows a higher grade than the original lesion.[463] These "recurrences," which may be the result of implantation or multicentric growth, are particularly common in the bladder vault. In a series of 1012 cases of superficial (mostly low-grade) bladder neoplasms, the cumulative risk of invasive carcinoma was 7%, 13%, and 16% after 5, 10, and 15 years, respectively.[445] It should be pointed out that, important as these low-grade noninvasive tumors are in the development of invasive high-grade neoplasms, in the large majority of the latter there is no history of a preceding noninvasive malignancy.[416,439]

4 *Patient's age.* The few tumors presenting during the first two decades of life are usually well differentiated and noninvasive and are therefore associated with an excellent prognosis.[433]

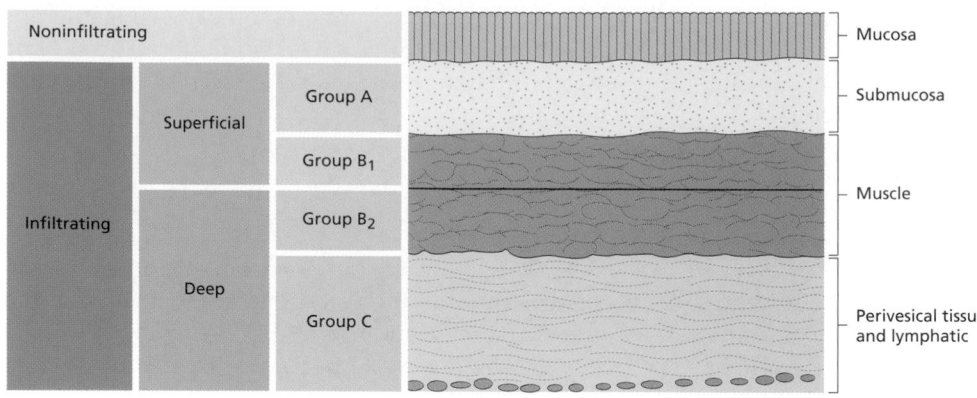

Fig. 17.183 Schematic representation of depth of invasion of bladder cancer according to the classic Jewett scheme. The more superficial the tumor, the better the prognosis. (From Jewett HJ. Carcinoma of the bladder. Influence of depth of infiltration on the five-year results following complete extirpation of the primary growth. J Urol 1952, 67: 672–680)

5 *Location.* Tumors of the bladder neck are associated with a poorer prognosis. Tumors of the bladder dome tend to present as higher-grade lesions, whereas tumors of the ureteric orifices and lateral walls tend to be of lower grade.[471]

6 *Abnormalities in the remaining bladder mucosa.* The presence of smaller, independent tumors or dysplastic changes away from the main tumor mass is related to a high recurrence rate.[425,428,431,442,455,468,476]

7 *Vascular invasion.* This feature, as determined microscopically in either lymph vessels or blood vessels, is associated with an increased rate of recurrence.[413,432,442]

8 *Type of tumor margin* and *inflammatory response.* Tumors with pushing margins associated with lymphocytic reaction have a better prognosis.[466]

9 *Tumor size.* For stage II tumors, the size of the tumor is a better predictor of the risk of metastases and probability of survival than the depth of muscle invasion.[417]

10 *Tumor-infiltrating lymphocytes (TIL).* The density of TIL correlates with tumor grade and with progression in Ta-T1 tumors, but in a multivariate analysis they have shown no independent predictive value.[450]

11 *Microvessel density.* This feature is alleged to be an independent prognostic indicator,[415] but its value still needs to be proven.

12 *Status of blood group antigens.* As already indicated, ABH and Lewis antigens are normally expressed by the urothelial mucosa but may be markedly reduced or absent in tumors, particularly high-grade ones.[438,447,449,461] This deletion can be evaluated by the red cell adherence test, or immunohistochemistry.[421,449,475] It appears to correlate with an aggressive clinical course, in the form of increased probability of recurrence and the acquisition of invasive features.[437,449,470] Some of the conflicting results among different series may be attributed to methodologic factors.[446] Radiation therapy has been found to induce false-positive results.[411,477] Along related lines, expression of T (Thomsen–Friedenreich) antigen as a result of unmasking has been found to correlate with the presence of invasion and a higher risk of lymph node involvement.[443,448,472]

13 *DNA ploidy.* This parameter, as determined by flow cytometry or static techniques, has proved to have independent prognostic value in bladder carcinomas, particularly in grade II tumors.[410,414,420,457] A high degree of correlation between DNA ploidy, microscopic grade, and clinical outcome has been observed.[458] Flow cytometry has also been used for the detection of Ca antigen, a cell surface determinant associated with invasive bladder tumors.[424]

14 *Cell proliferation.* Markers of cell proliferation correlate with tumor grade but not with stage.[419] In some series, the presence of a high mitotic count or a high S phase fraction was shown to be an independent predictor of prognosis, particularly with the low-stage tumors.[451,453,460,462,473] Similar results have been obtained in grade II tumors by determining the number of Ki-67 positive cells immunohistochemically.[456]

15 *Chromosomal aberrations.* Various types of karyotypic aberration have been said to correlate with increased risk of progression, such as Y losses and polysomies of 1 and 17.[459]

16 *p53 overexpression.* The nuclear overexpression of p53, as detected immunohistochemically and as a likely indicator of a mutation, has been found to show a high statistical correlation with disease progression in T1 and T2a bladder carcinomas.[464,465] Both grade and stage of bladder carcinoma seem to be related to this alteration.[427,469]

17 *Altered expression of Rb gene.* Tumors exhibiting decreased expression of the Rb protein have a more aggressive behavior than the others, but it is not clear whether this constitutes an independent prognostic parameter.[422,454]

18 *Loss of E-cadherin.* In one study, patients whose bladder tumor had loss of E-cadherin had a much worse prognosis than those in which this surface antigen was present.[462]

19 *Loss of CD44 variant protein.* Focal loss of CD44 variant protein as evaluated immunohistochemically has been found to have a high correlation with a short recurrence-free interval in superficial bladder carcinoma.[474]

20 *Loss of p27 (Kip1) and cyclin E.* The loss of these two cell cycle regulators correlates with increased histologic aggressiveness and decreased patient survival.[426] Along similar lines, it has been shown that expression of WAF1/p21, an inhibitor of cyclin-dependent kinases, is a predictor of shortened disease-free survival.[441]

21 *Cytokeratin 20.* In one study, tumors that showed an abnormal pattern of CK20 immunostain were more likely to recur than the others, but the differences were not statistically significant.[412]

Other primary carcinomas

Adenocarcinoma and related tumors

Bladder adenocarcinomas constitute approximately 2% of the malignant tumors of this organ.[486] Most develop from sequential changes in the surface transitional epithelium initiated by chronic inflammation—from Brunn's islands, to cystitis glandularis and cystica, and, finally, to adenocarcinoma, which is usually mucin secreting.[509] The tumors arising on this basis are usually located in the trigone area.[494] Other adenocarcinomas arise in bladders with exstrophy[483] (Fig. 17.184), in diverticula,[491] or at the dome of the bladder from urachal remnants[494,496] (see p. 1318). The subject of in situ adenocarcinoma is discussed on p. 1335.

Grossly, advanced cases appear as fungating masses that ulcerate the mucosa and invade the bladder wall. The surface of the mucin-producing tumors is covered with thick, slimy, gelatinous material.[505] Microscopically, there is a wide range of glandular differentiation, the better differentiated examples eliciting the differential diagnosis with intestinal metaplasia[479,489] (Figs 17.185 and 17.186). Deep invasion of the muscle is the rule, but very superficial examples of this tumor have been observed.[497] The mucin histochemical profile is similar to that of colorectal adenocarcinoma.[478,487,495,510] Some tumors have been found to contain both Paneth cells and endocrine cells.[499,502]

Immunohistochemically, primary bladder adenocarcinoma differs from colorectal carcinoma by the fact that the pattern of staining for β-catenin, if present, is primarily membranous (and some cytoplasmic) rather than nuclear.[508] It is also more commonly positive for keratin 7 (6.5% vs. 0%) and less commonly for keratin 20 (53% vs. 94%).[503a,508] In contrast with ovarian and cervical carcinoma, it is usually negative for OC125, and—in contrast with endometrial adenocarcinoma—it is negative for vimentin.[506]

Occasional bladder adenocarcinomas show immunoreactivity for PSA and prostatic acid phosphatase.[484] It is possible that some of these represent primary bladder carcinomas arising from prostatic-type tissue in this

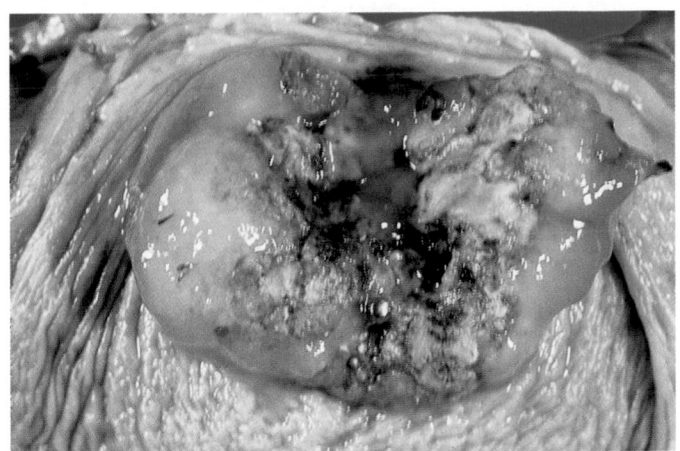

Fig. 17.184 Mucinous adenocarcinoma located in the dome of the bladder, probably arising from urachal remnants.

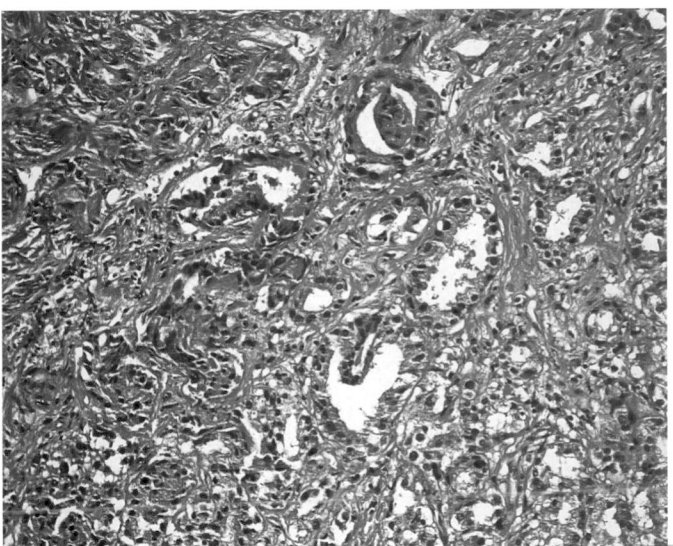

Fig. 17.185 Non-mucinous adenocarcinoma of bladder.

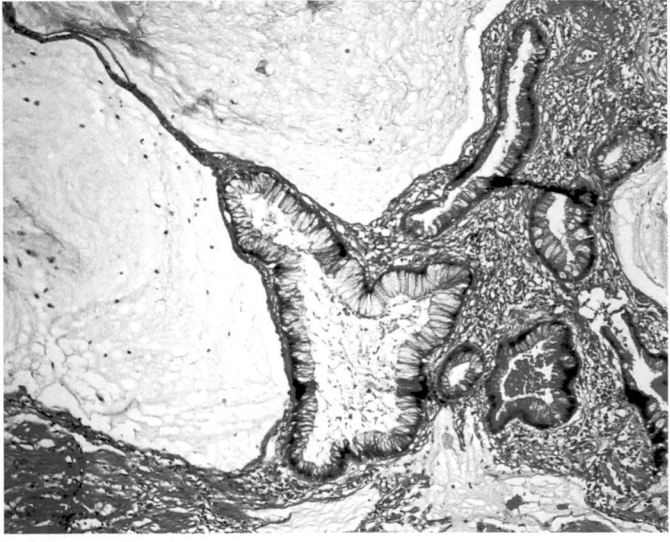

Fig. 17.186 Well-differentiated mucinous adenocarcinoma of bladder. Some of the mucin has extravasated into the stroma.

organ, but the majority will have concurrent or precedent adenocarcinoma in the prostate.[493]

It should be pointed out that focal positivity for mucin and MUC5AC apomucin is not unusual in transitional cell carcinoma, probably as a result of the embryologic origin of the bladder from the pluripotent tissues of the cloacal endoderm and the mesodermal wolffian ducts[490]; the term *adenocarcinoma* should be reserved for those malignant tumors in which the glandular component predominates.[479] The overall prognosis is poor: in one series of 64 cases, the 5-year survival was only 18%.[479] As in the case of transitional cell carcinoma, stage is the most important prognostic factor.[484] The pattern and frequency of metastases are also similar to those of high-grade, conventional transitional cell carcinoma.

A distinct variant of bladder adenocarcinoma is the **clear cell (mesonephric, mesonephroid) type**,[488,512] a tumor type that can also occur in the urethra (Fig. 17.187). It is usually papillary and is characterized microscopically by a mixture of tubular glands, papillae, cysts, and areas of solid growth. Two of its most distinctive features are the presence of hobnail cells and abundant cytoplasmic glycogen.[511,512] This lesion is distinguished from the more common mesonephroid metaplasia ("nephrogenic adenoma"; see p. 1323) on the basis of clinical, gross, and microscopic features; sheets of clear cells, marked pleomorphism, mitotic activity, and necrosis favor a diagnosis of malignancy.[512,513] Corroborating features include high MIB-1 positivity and strong immunostaining for p53.[498] On occasions, clear cell carcinoma is seen admixed with transitional cell carcinoma.[481] Nearly all of these tumors arise from the transitional epithelium of the bladder by a process of metaplasia, as

also suggested by their similar immunohistochemical profile.[492,498] However, some are probably of müllerian origin and related to endometriosis, as suggested by the great female preponderance and the presence in some of these tumors of benign müllerian components.[498] Metastases can develop in regional lymph nodes and distally (Fig. 17.188).

Another distinct type of adenocarcinoma is **signet ring carcinoma**.[501,504] The pattern of infiltration of the bladder wall is diffuse, similar to that seen in signet ring carcinoma (linitis plastica) of the stomach.[500] In some instances there is no cystoscopically visible mucosal lesion.[485] Microscopically, the tumor cells are usually small and uniform, but on occasion they exhibit considerable pleomorphism.[507] The clinical course of the disease has been rapidly progressive and fatal in nearly all the reported cases with follow-up information.[482]

Yet another variant of this tumor type is **hepatoid adenocarcinoma**, thus adding the bladder to the increasingly long list of organs in which this tumor type—which mimics the morphologic and immunohistochemical features of hepatocellular carcinoma—can occur.[480,491a,503]

Small cell carcinoma and related neuroendocrine tumors

Like most other epithelium-lined organs, the urinary bladder can be the site of tumors exhibiting various degrees of endocrine differentiation. The most common manifestation of this phenomenon is the presence of scattered endocrine cells in otherwise typical adenocarcinomas; these tumors behave like adenocarcinomas lacking these elements and should be labeled as such. Another is the exceptionally rare **carcinoid tumor** of the bladder,

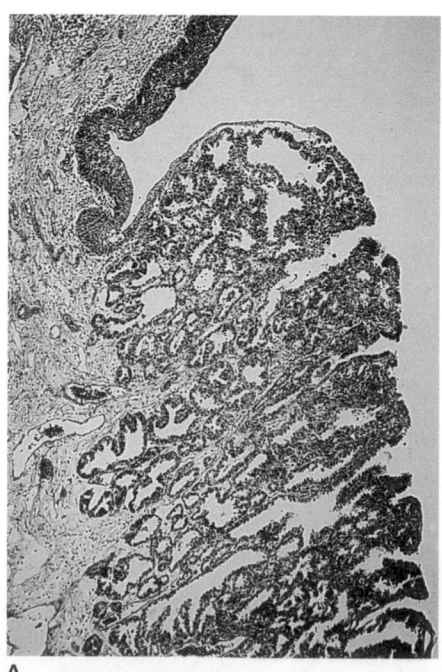
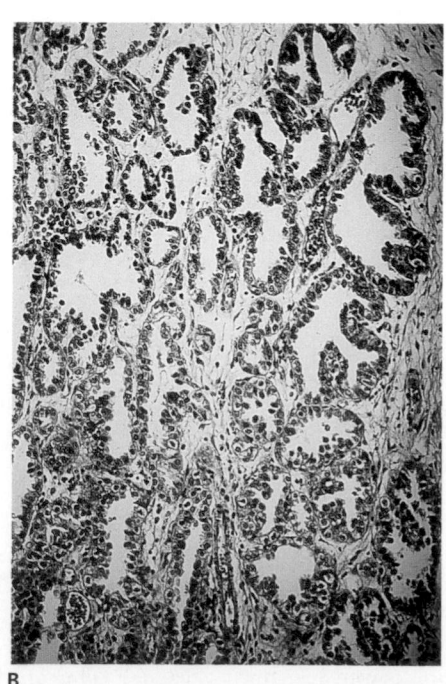

Fig. 17.187 Low-power (**A**) and high-power (**B**) views of clear cell (mesonephroid) carcinoma of bladder. This very rare tumor should be distinguished from the much more common mesonephroid metaplasia.

A

B

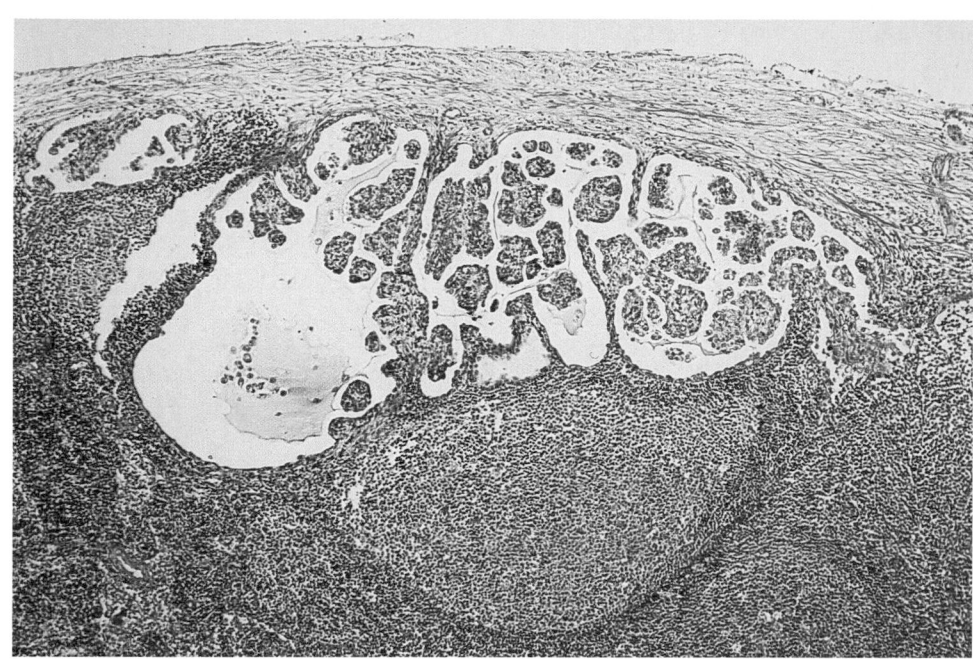

Fig. 17.188 Clear cell (mesonephroid) carcinoma of bladder metastatic to regional lymph node (same case as Fig. 17.187).

which exhibits typical architectural features at the light microscopic level and numerous dense-core granules on ultrastructural examination.[517,518,529] Yet another is the highly malignant bladder tumor known as **small cell carcinoma**, which is morphologically similar to its homonyms in the lung and other organs (Fig. 17.189).[522,525] This may be seen in a pure form or combined with in situ or invasive transitional cell carcinoma, adenocarcinoma, squamous cell carcinoma, or sarcomatoid carcinoma.[514,524,525] Age, sex, and symptoms at presentation are comparable to those of transitional cell carcinoma.[516] Most cases are already advanced (stages C or D) when first diagnosed.[520] Microscopically, small cells with very hyperchromatic nuclei and extremely scanty cytoplasm are seen growing in a predominantly solid fashion, sometimes associated with occasional rosette formation.

Dense-core granules can be demonstrated ultrastructurally but usually in small numbers and with some difficulty.[519,525] Immunohistochemically, there is reactivity for NSE, chromogranin, and/or synaptophysin. The staining pattern for low-molecular-weight keratin (Cam 5.2) has a dot-like perinuclear pattern, and CD44 v6 is usually absent (in contrast to transitional cell carcinoma).[523] Some of these cases have been associated with hypercalcemia[528] or ectopic ACTH production.[526] The diagnosis can be suspected on cytologic preparations[515] and the behavior is extremely aggressive.[516,524] Metastatic spread occurs quickly, the most frequent sites of involvement being regional lymph nodes, liver, bones, and peritoneal cavity.[516] Similar to other types of bladder carcinoma, the prognosis is largely dependent on the stage.[527]

Large cell neuroendocrine carcinoma is defined in the

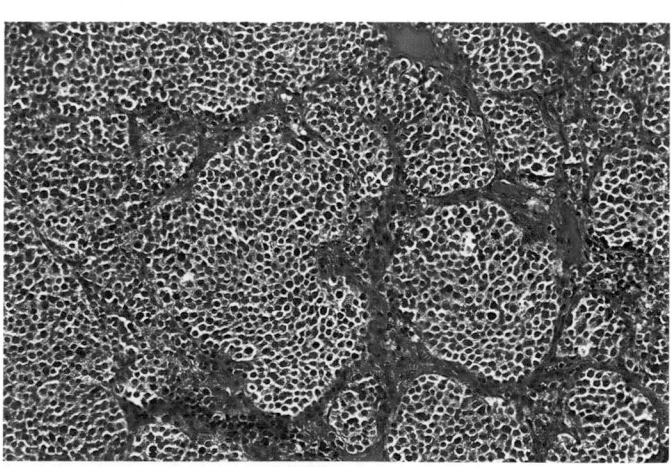

A   B

Fig. 17.189 **A** and **B**, Small cell neuroendocrine carcinoma of bladder. **A**, Low-power view showing a solid mass of small cell carcinoma covered by mucosa with carcinoma in situ. **B**, High-power view of the invasive small cell component.

bladder, as in other sites, as a high-grade neoplasm exhibiting neuroendocrine features at the H&E level, high mitotic activity, and evidence of neuroendocrine differentiation at the immunohistochemical level.[519a,521]

Squamous cell carcinoma and related tumors

Squamous cell carcinoma comprises approximately 5% of all malignant bladder tumors. Some of these neoplasms arise on a background of chronic cystitis with marked squamous metaplasia[531,539,540] (see p. 1323). Cases have also been reported in association with exstrophy, defunctionalized bladder, chronic infection, lithiasis, chronic indwelling catheters, and prolonged medication with cyclophosphamide.[545] Another well-known association, reported from Egypt, Sudan, and other countries, is with schistosomiasis.[532,534,543] Some squamous cell carcinomas of the bladder probably represent metaplastic changes in tumors that were originally of transitional cell type[542] (Fig. 17.190).

Since focal squamous cell changes are common in high-grade transitional cell tumors, the term *squamous cell carcinoma* should be reserved for those tumors that are squamous throughout (Fig. 17.191).

Grossly, these tumors are usually large, ulcerated, and necrotic. Microscopically, most are poorly differentiated and have nearly always invaded the muscle at the time of diagnosis.[538,541] The prognosis is very poor regardless of the degree of differentiation.[530] Death within the first year occurred in 59% of the patients reviewed by Newman et al.[538]; in another series, the 5-year survival rate was 37% for patients with submucosal or muscular invasion and 13% for those with perivesical invasion.[533]

A high frequency of chromosome 9p allelic loss and *CDKN2* tumor-suppressor gene alterations have been found in squamous cell carcinoma of the bladder, in contrast with transitional cell carcinomas.[535]

Basaloid squamous cell carcinoma morphologically similar to its counterpart in the upper aerodigestive tract occurs exceptionally in the bladder.[544]

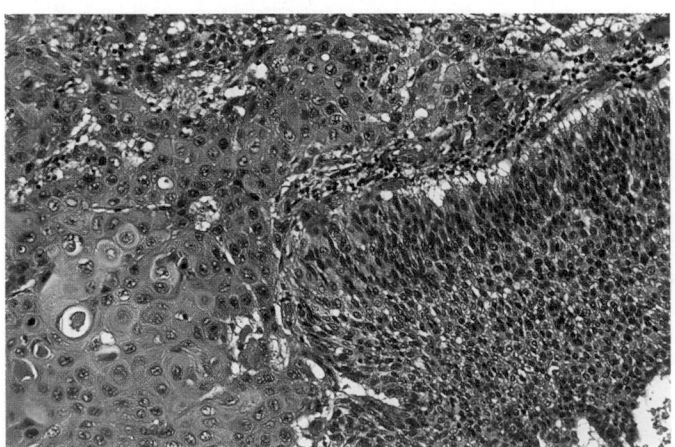

Fig. 17.190 Squamous cell carcinoma of bladder merging with a transitional cell (urothelial) pattern.

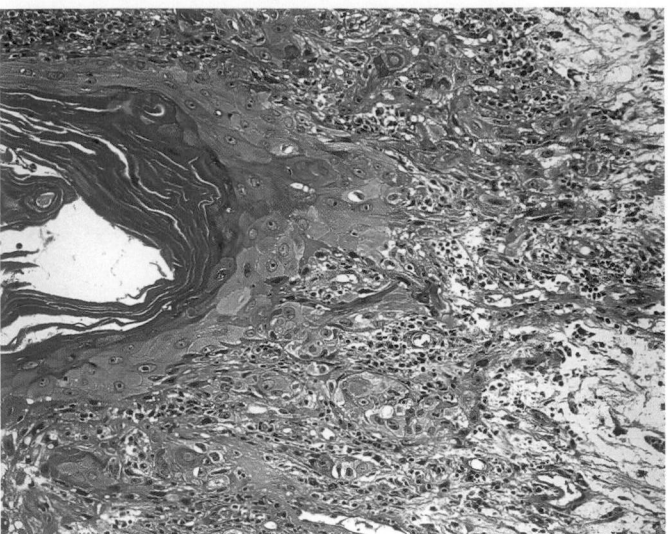

Fig. 17.191 Pure squamous cell carcinoma of bladder. The tumor is heavily keratinized.

Verrucous carcinoma of the bladder has been diagnosed mainly in Egypt, in association with schistosomiasis.[536] A bizarre case has been reported of a verrucous carcinoma associated with sebaceous and glandular differentiation.[537]

Warty carcinoma arising from condyloma, morphologically similar to the homonymous penile tumor, has been described in the bladder.[530a]

Lymphoepithelioma-like carcinoma

Lymphoepithelioma-like carcinoma has only recently been described at this site; its appearance is that of a nonkeratinizing carcinoma associated with a heavy inflammatory infiltrate.[546,547,549] Some cases are pure, but most represent a focal or extensive change in a tumor having otherwise the appearance of a transitional cell carcinoma.[548]

Sarcomatoid carcinoma and related tumors

Sarcomatoid carcinoma (spindle cell, metaplastic) carcinoma is a high-grade neoplasm of the bladder in which a malignant epithelial component, clearly identifiable as such (of transitional, glandular, squamous, or undifferentiated type), coexists with areas having a sarcoma-like appearance[558,559,572,573,581] (Fig. 17.192). The latter may have a nonspecific spindle cell or pleomorphic look (sometimes admixed with osteoclast-like giant cells)[550,556,564,583] or may exhibit specific features of mesenchymal differentiation, such as rhabdomyosarcoma, chondrosarcoma, osteosarcoma, liposarcoma, or malignant fibrous histiocytoma.[552,567,570,579] When such specific features are present, the tumor may be designated as carcinosarcoma,[554,571] but we view this as a variation of the same basic process. Whether areas of specific mesenchymal differentiation occur or not, transitions may be seen between the two major components, suggesting that the sarcoma-like areas are also of epithelial nature.[561] Further evidence of the epithelial nature

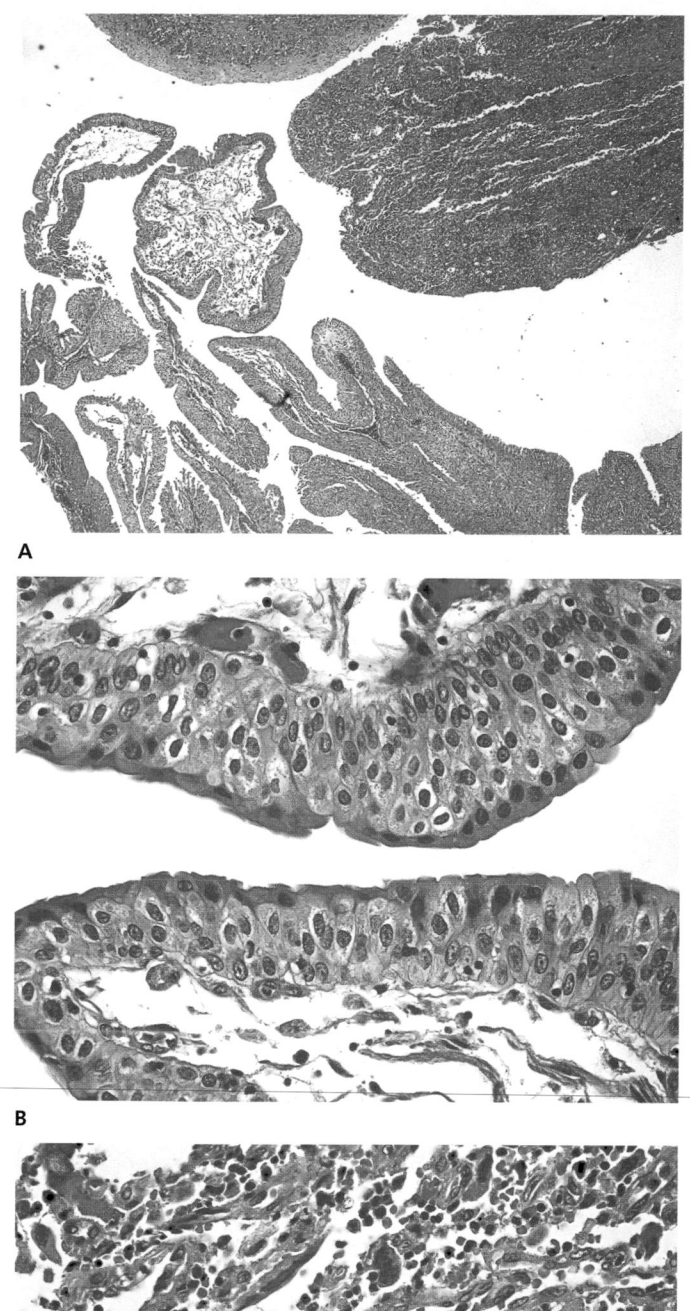

Fig. 17.192 A to **C**, Transitional cell carcinoma of bladder with sarcomatoid features. **A**, Low-power view of the two components. **B**, Low-grade transitional cell component. **C**, High-grade sarcomatoid component. The tumor has a markedly pleomorphic appearance.

of these proliferations is provided by the immunoreactivity for keratin often detected in the sarcoma-like component.[551,576,577] Exceptionally, the epithelial component is made up of small cells with neuroendocrine features.[565] On other occasions, the tumor has prominent myxoid or sclerosing features.[562]

Grossly, these tumors are often large and polypoid. They are equivalent in most respects to their more common counterparts located in the upper aerodigestive tract[561]; as in those, the obvious epithelial component is sometimes present only in the form of carcinoma in situ on the surface and at the periphery of the invasive sarcoma-like tumor.[557] The differential diagnosis includes true sarcomas, inflammatory myofibroblastic tumor, and transitional cell carcinomas with reactive stroma.[580]

Most patients with sarcomatoid carcinoma are elderly males, and the death rate is about 50%.[579] Sequential involvement of ureter and renal pelvis may occur.[569] Metastases develop in regional lymph nodes and distantly; they may consist of only the epithelial or the sarcoma-like component.[575] The treatment of this tumor should be the same as for high-grade transitional cell carcinoma of equivalent stage.[559]

Another bladder malignancy characterized by the presence of heterologous elements is the rare transitional cell carcinoma having areas with morphologic and immunohistochemical features indicative of trophoblastic differentiation and sometimes accompanied by serum elevations of hCG.[553,568,574] Occasionally the entire lesion has the appearance of *choriocarcinoma*, in which case it needs to be distinguished from a metastatic tumor.[560,578] Some transitional cell carcinomas are associated with immunohistochemical reactivity for hCG and other placental glycoproteins even if they lack identifiable foci of choriocarcinoma.[563,566] This feature is particularly common in the high-grade tumors.[555]

A much more unusual phenomenon is the presence of foci of *yolk sac tumor* in an otherwise typical transitional cell carcinoma.[582]

Other malignant tumors

Embryonal rhabdomyosarcoma (particularly the botryoid subtype) is the most common malignant tumor of the bladder in children. Sporadic cases have been seen in association with Wilms' tumor; one such case was reported in a child with Dandy–Walker syndrome.[603] The trigone is the most common location. Grossly, the tumor has a myxoid appearance and polypoid shape (Fig. 17.193). It infiltrates surrounding tissues, but distant metastases are rare. Microscopically, it shows myxoid tissue in which small malignant cells are seen (Fig. 17.194A). These are characteristically grouped beneath the epithelium ("cambium layer") (Fig. 17.194B). Cross striations may or may not be present. In the past, the

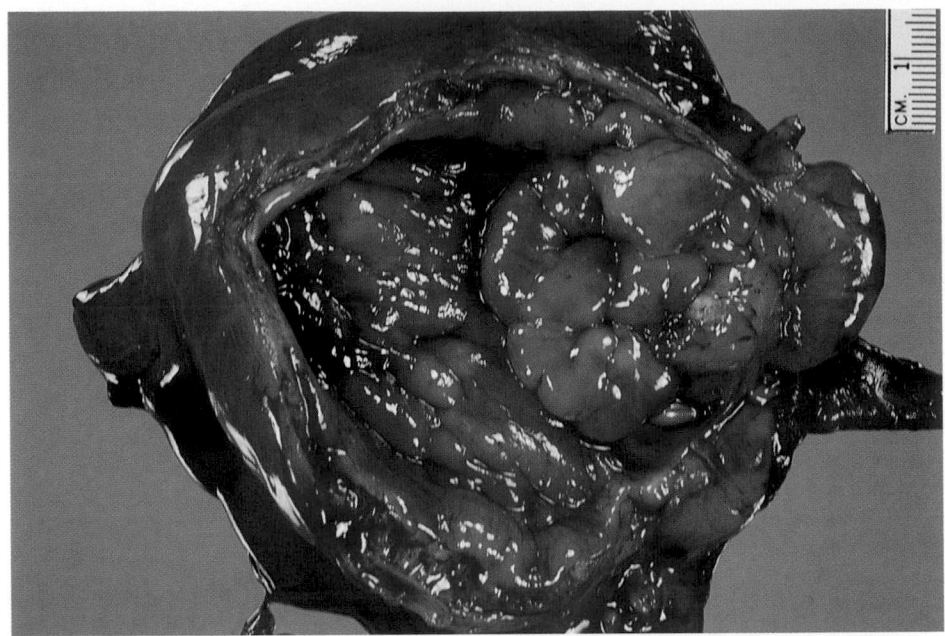

Fig. 17.193 Gross appearance of botryoid rhabdomyosarcoma of bladder. A huge tumor mass is seen filling the lumen of the organ.

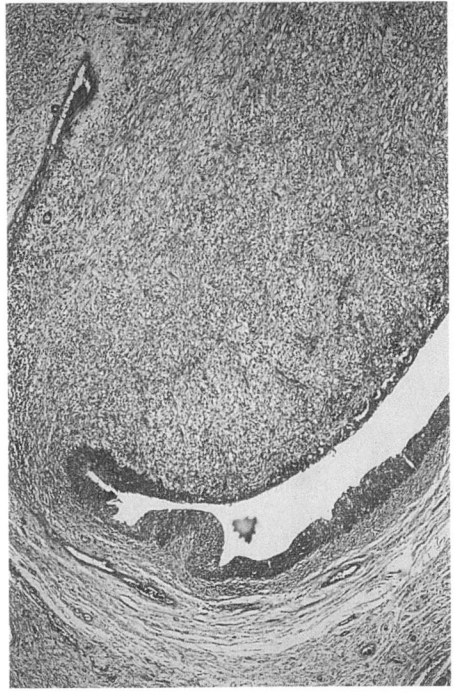

A

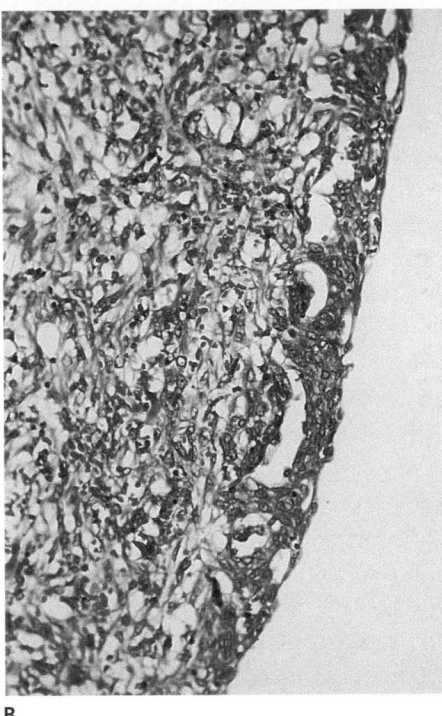

B

Fig. 17.194 A and **B,** Microscopic appearance of botryoid rhabdomyosarcoma. **A,** Low-power view showing polypoid mass protruding beneath a flattened epithelium. **B,** High-power view showing "cambium layer." Clusters of tumor cells present immediately beneath the epithelium result in a nevoid appearance.

prognosis was poor, with isolated cures being achieved with radical cystectomy or radiation therapy. The addition of multidrug chemotherapy to these modalities has notably increased the survival rates, even when the surgical resection was incomplete.[598] The prognosis is better for tumors exhibiting the classic polypoid pattern of growth than for those with diffuse intramural spread. Specimens from recurrences often show a marked maturation of the rhabdomyosarcomatous elements, presumably induced by chemotherapy.[608]

Leiomyosarcoma is most commonly seen in adults.

Approximately half of the cases are located in the bladder dome.[614,622] They infiltrate the bladder muscle, an important feature in the differential diagnosis with leiomyoma. Microscopic grading of the tumor based on nuclear atypia, mitotic activity, and tumor necrosis correlates closely with outcome.[611] Some of these tumors are partially or extensively myxoid, resembling inflammatory pseudotumor (inflammatory myofibroblastic tumor) to such a degree that the distinction may become impossible.[614,628] Immunohistochemically, they are reactive for vimentin, actin, and (often) desmin.[614]

Other sarcomas of the adult bladder include *rhabdomyosarcoma*,[605,613] *rhabdoid tumor*,[590,597,609] *malignant fibrous histiocytoma*[595,606] (including its inflammatory[600] and myxoid[617] variants), *osteosarcoma*,[588,629] *soft tissue-type clear cell sarcoma*,[592] *GIST-type tumors* (questionably),[607] and *malignant mesenchymoma*.[624] Care should be exercised to rule out by appropriate sampling and immunohistochemical testing the alternative possibility of a sarcomatoid carcinoma (carcinosarcoma)[599,600] (see p. 1341).

Primary **malignant melanoma** can occur in the bladder,[584,585,604] although not as commonly as in the urethra or as metastases in the bladder from a melanoma arisen elsewhere.[612] Variants have been described having clear cell features,[616] or associated with melanosis (i.e., pigmentation of the basal layer of the non-neoplastic transitional epithelium).[604]

Primitive neuroectodermal tumor (PNET) has been described presenting as a bladder mass. It is immunoreactive for CD99, is associated with the *EWS–FLI1* gene fusion, and should not be confused with small cell neuroendocrine carcinoma.[586,593]

Malignant lymphoma can involve the bladder as a primary site.[618] Grossly, it may appear as a solitary mass, as multiple masses, or as a diffuse lesion with mass formation.[618] Often the lesions are covered by normal mucosa. Microscopically, they are nearly always of non-Hodgkin type, and most are low-grade small lymphocytic tumors (of the so-called "MALT type").[602,610,618,619] Accordingly, they tend to remain localized for a long period of time. The bladder also can be involved by **leukemia, plasmacytoma,**[601,626] **multiple myeloma,**[625] **peripheral T-cell lymphoma,**[615] and *Hodgkin's lymphoma*.[589]

A case of **yolk sac tumor** (endodermal sinus tumor) of the bladder has been described in a 1-year-old child.[623]

Most cases of **metastatic tumor** in the bladder are from breast carcinoma[594,596,620] and malignant melanoma,[612] but they have also been reported from several other sites, including lung, kidney, stomach, pancreas, and ovary.[587,591,621] The latter may closely mimic a primary bladder neoplasm.[627] The large majority of these metastatic deposits are solitary.[587] Direct extension into the bladder can occur with carcinomas of large bowel, prostate, and cervix.[587,587a]

References

Normal anatomy

1 Philip AT, Amin MB, Tamboli P, Lee TJ, Hill CE, Ro JY. Intravesical adipose tissue: a quantitative study of its presence and location with implications for therapy and prognosis. Am J Surg Pathol 2000, **24:** 1286–1290.

2 Reuter VE. Urinary bladder, ureter, and renal pelvis. In Sternberg SS (ed.): Histology for pathologists, ed. 2. Philadelphia, 1997, Lippincott-Raven, pp. 835–847.

Congenital abnormalities
Urachal lesions

3 Cappele O, Sibert L, Descargues J, Delmas V, Grise P. A study of the anatomic features of the duct of the urachus. Surg Radiol Anat 2001, **23:** 229–235.

4 Chen KT, Workman RD, Rainwater G. Urachal signet-ring cell carcinoma. Urology 1990, **36:** 339–340.

5 Chen WJ, Hsieh HH, Wan YL. Abscess of urachal remnant mimicking urinary bladder neoplasm. Br J Urol 1992, **69:** 510–512.

6 Chow YC, Lin WC, Tzen CY, Chow YK, Lo KY. Squamous cell carcinoma of the urachus. J Urol 2000, **163:** 903–904.

7 Di Santis DJ, Siegel MJ, Katz ME. Simplified approach to umbilical remnant abnormalities. Radiographics 1991, **11:** 59–66.

8 Eble JN, Hull MT, Rowland RG, Hostetter M. Villous adenoma of the urachus with mucusuria. A light and electron microscopic study. J Urol 1986, **135:** 1240–1244.

9 Henly DR, Farrow GM, Zincke H. Urachal cancer. Role of conservative surgery. Urology 1993, **42:** 635–639.

10 Herr HW. Urachal carcinoma. The case for extended partial cystectomy. J Urol 1994, **151:** 365–366.

11 Iuchtman M, Rahav S, Zer M, Mogilner J, Siplovich L. Management of urachal anomalies in children and adults. Urology 1993, **42:** 426–430.

12 Jimi A, Munaoka H, Sato S, Iwata Y. Squamous cell carcinoma of the urachus. A case report and review of literature. Acta Pathol Jpn 1986, **36:** 945–952.

13 Lucas DR, Lawrence WD, McDevitt WJ, Giacomelli F. Mucinous papillary adenocarcinoma of the bladder arising within a villous adenoma of urachal remnants. An immunohistochemical and ultrastructural study. J Urol Pathol 1994, **2:** 173–182.

14 Park C, Kim H, Lee YB, Song JM, Ro JY. Hamartoma of the urachal remnant. Arch Pathol Lab Med 1989, **113:** 1393–1395.

15 Risher WH, Sardi A, Bolton J. Urachal abnormalities in adults. The Ochsner experience. South Med J 1990, **83:** 1036–1039.

16 Schubert GE, Pavkovic MB, Bethke-Bedürftig BA. Tubular urachal remnants in adult bladders. J Urol 1982, **127:** 40–42.

17 Steck WD, Helwig EB. Umbilical granulomas, pilonidal disease, and the urachus. Surg Gynecol Obstet 1965, **120:** 1043–1057.

Exstrophy

18 Davillas N, Thanos A, Liakatas J, Davillas E. Bladder exstrophy complicated by adenocarcinoma. Br J Urol 1991, **68:** 107.

19 Engel RM, Wilkinson HA. Bladder exstrophy. J Urol 1970, **104:** 699–704.

20 Lund DP, Hendren WH. Cloacal exstrophy: a 25-year experience with 50 cases. J Pediatr Surg 2001, **36:** 68–75.

21 Ricketts RR, Woodard JR, Zwiren GT, Andrews HG, Broecker BH. Modern treatment of cloacal exstrophy. J Pediatr Surg 1991, **26:** 444–448.

22 Smeulders N, Woodhouse CR. Neoplasia in adult exstrophy patients. BJU Int 2001, **87:** 623–628.

Diverticulosis

23 Faysal MH, Freiha FS. Primary neoplasm in vesical diverticula. A report of 12 cases. Br J Urol 1981, **53:** 141–143.

24 Fox M, Power RF, Bruce AW. Diverticulum of the bladder. Presentation and evaluation of treatment of 115 cases. Br J Urol 1962, **34:** 286–298.

25 Kretschmer HL. Diverticula of the urinary bladder. A clinical study of 236 cases. Surg Gynecol Obstet 1940, **71:** 491–503.

26 Lam KY, Ma L, Nicholls J. Adenocarcinoma arising in a diverticulum of the urinary bladder. Pathology 1992, **24:** 40–42.

27 McCormick SR, Dodds PR, Kraus PA, Lowell DM. Nonepithelial neoplasms arising within vesical diverticula. Urology 1985, **25:** 405–408.

28 Mitchell RJ, Hamilton SG. Spontaneous perforation of bladder diverticula. Br J Surg 1971, **58:** 712.

29 Shirai T, Arai M, Sakata T, Fukushima S, Ito N. Primary carcinomas of urinary bladder diverticula. Acta Pathol Jpn 1984, **34:** 417–424.

30 Stage KH, Tank ES. Primary congenital bladder diverticula in boys. Urology 1992, **40:** 536–538.

Lithiasis

31 Bhatia V, Biyani CS. Vesical lithiasis. Open surgery versus cystolithotripsy versus extracorporeal shock wave therapy. J Urol 1994, **151:** 660–662.

32 Kojima Y, Yoshimura M, Hayashi Y, Asaka H, Ando Y, Kohri K. Extracorporeal shock wave lithotripsy for vesical lithiasis. Urol Int 1998, **61:** 35–38.

33 Wishard WN, Nourse MH. Vesical calculus with report of a gigantic stone in the female bladder. J Urol 1950, **63:** 794–801.

Endometriosis and related müllerian-type changes

34 al-Izzi MS, Horton LW, Kelleher J, Fawcett D. Malignant transformation in endometriosis of the urinary bladder. Histopathology 1989, **14:** 191–198.

35 Chapron C, Dubuisson JB. Laparoscopic management of bladder endometriosis. Acta Obstet Gynecol Scand 1999, **78:** 887–890.

36 Chitale SV, Whymark A, Wadood SU, Webb RJ, Gaches CGC, Roberts PF, Ball RY. Tumor-like mullerianosis of the urinary bladder. J Urol Pathol 1999, **10:** 169–176.

37 Clement PB, Young RH. Endocervicosis of the urinary bladder. A report of six cases of a benign mullerian lesion that may mimic adenocarcinoma. Am J Surg Pathol 1992, **16:** 533–542.

38 Donne C, Vidal M, Buttin X, Becerra P, Carvia R, Zuluaga A, Nogales FF. Mullerianosis of the urinary bladder: clinical and immunohistochemical findings. Histopathology 1998, **33:** 290–292.

39 Donnez J, Spada F, Squifflet J, Nisolle M. Bladder endometriosis must be considered as bladder adenomyosis. Fertil Steril 2000, **74:** 1175–1181.

40 Lichtenheld FR, McCauley RT, Staples PP. Endometriosis involving the urinary tract. A collective review. Obstet Gynecol 1961, **17:** 762–768.

41 New NE, Roberts PF. Mucinous metaplasia in endometriosis of the bladder. Histopathology 1990, **16:** 307–308.

42 Oliva E, Amin MB, Jimenez R, Young RH. Clear cell carcinoma of the urinary bladder: a report and comparison of four tumors of mullerian origin and nine of probable urothelial origin with discussion of histogenesis and diagnostic problems. Am J Surg Pathol 2002, **26:** 190–197.

43 Schwartzwald D, Mooppan UM, Ohm HK, Kim H. Endometriosis of bladder. Urology 1992, **39:** 219–222.

44 Vara AR, Ruzics EP, Moussabeck O, Martin DC. Endometrioid adenosarcoma of the bladder arising from endometriosis. J Urol 1990, **143:** 813–815.

45 Vermesh M, Zbella EA, Menchaca A, Confino E, Lipshitz S. Vesical endometriosis following bladder injury. Am J Obstet Gynecol 1985, **153:** 894–895.

46 Westney OL, Amundsen CL, McGuire EJ. Bladder endometriosis: conservative management. J Urol 2000, **163:** 1814–1817.

47 Young RH, Clement PB. Mullerianosis of the urinary bladder. Mod Pathol 1996, **9:** 731–737.

Amyloidosis

48 Ehara H, Deguchi T, Yanagihara M, Yokota T, Uchino F, Kawada Y. Primary localized amyloidosis of the bladder. An immunohistochemical study of a case. J Urol 1992, **147:** 458–460.

49 Fujihara S, Glenner GG. Primary localized amyloidosis of the genitourinary tract. Immunohistochemical study on eleven cases. Lab Invest 1981, **44:** 55–60.

50 Khan SM, Birch PJ, Bass PS, Williams JH, Theaker JM. Localized amyloidosis of the lower genitourinary tract.

A clinicopathological and immunohistochemical study of nine cases. Histopathology 1992, **21:** 143–147.

51 Lipper S, Kahn LB. Amyloid tumor. A clinicopathologic study of four cases. Am J Surg Pathol 1978, **2:** 141–145.

52 Malek RS, Greene LF, Farrow GM. Amyloidosis of the urinary bladder. Br J Urol 1971, **43:** 189–200.

53 Tirzaman O, Wahner-Roedler DL, Malek RS, Sebo TJ, Li CY, Kyle RA. Primary localized amyloidosis of the urinary bladder: a case series of 31 patients. Mayo Clin Proc 2000, **75:** 1264–1268.

Cystitis
Interstitial (Hunner's) cystitis

54 Christmas TJ, Bottazzo GF. Abnormal urothelial HLA-DR expression in interstitial cystitis. Clin Exp Immunol 1992, **87:** 450–454.

55 Hampson SJ, Christmas TJ, Moss MT. Search for mycobacteria in interstitial cystitis using mycobacteria-specific DNA probes with signal amplification by polymerase chain reaction. Br J Urol 1993, **72:** 303–306.

56 Hohenfellner M, Nunes L, Schmidt RA, Lampel A, Thuroff JW, Tanagho EA. Interstitial cystitis. Increased sympathetic innervation and related neuropeptide synthesis. J Urol 1992, **147:** 587–591.

57 Irwin PP, Galloway NT. Surgical management of interstitial cystitis. Urol Clin North Am 1994, **21:** 145–151.

58 Koziol JA, Clark DC, Gittes RF, Tan EM. The natural history of interstitial cystitis. A survey of 374 patients. J Urol 1993, **149:** 465–469.

59 Larsen S, Thompson SA, Hald T, Barnard RJ, Gilpin CJ, Dixon JS, Gosling JA. Mast cells in interstitial cystitis. Br J Urol 1982, **54:** 283–286.

60 Liebert M, Wedemeyer G, Stein JA, Washington R Jr, Faerber G, Flint A, Grossman HB. Evidence for urothelial cell activation in interstitial cystitis. J Urol 1993, **149:** 470–475.

61 Lundeberg T, Liedberg H, Nordling L, Theodorsson E, Owzarski A, Ekman P. Interstitial cystitis. Correlation with nerve fibres, mast cells and histamine. Br J Urol 1993, **71:** 427–429.

62 Lynes WL, Flynn SD, Shortliffe LD, Stamey TA. The histology of interstitial cystitis. Am J Surg Pathol 1990, **14:** 969–976.

63 Moldwin RM, Sant GR. Interstitial cystitis: a pathophysiology and treatment update. Clin Obstet Gynecol 2002, **45:** 259–272.

64 Peeker R, Fall M. Toward a precise definition of interstitial cystitis: further evidence of differences in classic and nonulcer disease. J Urol 2002, **167:** 2470–2472.

65 Ratliff TL, Klutke CG, McDougall EM. The etiology of interstitial cystitis. Urol Clin North Am 1994, **21:** 21–30.

66 Said JW, Van de Velde R, Gillespie L. Immunopathology of interstitial cystitis. Mod Pathol 1989, **2:** 593–602.

67 Sant GR, Theoharides TC. The role of the mast cell in interstitial cystitis. Urol Clin North Am 1994, **21:** 41–53.

68 Smith BH, Dehner LP. Chronic ulcerating interstitial cystitis (Hunner's ulcer). A study of 28 cases. Arch Pathol 1972, **93:** 76–81.

69 Somji S, Sens DA, Todd JH, Garrett SH, Nseyo UO, Sens MA. Expression of heat shock protein 60 is reduced in the bladder of patients with interstitial cystitis. J Urol Pathol 1999, **10:** 97–108.

70 Stein PC, Santamaria PJ, Kurtz SB, Parsons CL. Evaluation of urothelial Tamm-Horsfall protein and serum antibody as a potential diagnostic marker for interstitial cystitis. J Urol 1993, **150:** 1405–1408.

71 Stone AR, Vogelsang P, Miller CH, Mac Dermott JP. Tamm-Horsfall protein as a marker in interstitial cystitis. J Urol 1992, **148:** 1406–1408.

72 Tomaszewski JE, Landis JR, Russack V, Williams TM, Wang LP, Hardy C, Brensinger C, Matthews YL, Abele ST, Kusek JW, Nyberg LM; The International Cystitis Database Study Group. Biopsy features are associated with primary symptoms in interstitial cystitis: results from the interstitial cystitis database study. Urology 2001, **57:** 67–81.

73 Warren JW, Keay SK. Interstitial cystitis. Curr Opin Urol 2002, **12:** 69–74.

Eosinophilic cystitis

74 Antonakopoulos GN, Newman J. Eosinophilic cystitis with giant cells. A light microscopic and ultrastructural study. Arch Pathol Lab Med 1984, **108:** 728–731.

75 Hansen MV, Kristensen PB. Eosinophilic cystitis simulating invasive bladder carcinoma. Scand J Urol Nephrol 1993, **27:** 275–277.

76 Hellstrom HR, David BK, Shonnard JW. Eosinophilic cystitis. A study of 16 cases. Am J Clin Pathol 1979, **72:** 777–784.

77 Itano NM, Malek RS. Eosinophilic cystitis in adults. J Urol 2001, **165:** 805–807.

78 Johansson SL, Smout MS, Taylor RJ. Eosinophilic cystitis associated with symptomatic ureteral involvement. A report of two cases. J Urol Pathol 1993, **1:** 69–77.

79 Marshall FF, Middleton AW Jr. Eosinophilic cystitis. J Urol 1974, **112:** 335–337.

80 Oh SJ, Chi JG, Lee SE. Eosinophilic cystitis caused by vesical sparganosis. A case report. J Urol 1993, **149:** 581–583.

81 van den Ouden D. Diagnosis and management of eosinophilic cystitis: a pooled analysis of 135 cases. Eur Urol 2000, **37:** 386–394.

82 Verhagen PC, Nikkels PG, de Jong TP. Eosinophilic cystitis. Arch Dis Child 2001, **84:** 344–346.

Polypoid cystitis

83 Ekelund P, Johansson S. Polypoid cystitis. A catheter associated lesion of the human bladder. Acta Pathol Microbiol Scand (A) 1979, **87:** 179–184.

84 Young RH. Papillary and polypoid cystitis. A report of eight cases. Am J Surg Pathol 1988, **12:** 542–546.

Emphysematous cystitis

85 Greene MH. Emphysematous cystitis due to *Clostridium perfringens* and *Candida albicans* in two patients with hematologic malignant conditions. Cancer 1992, **70:** 2658–2663.

86 Patel NP, Lavengood RW, Fernandes M, Ward JN, Walzak MP. Gas-forming infections in genitourinary tract. Urology 1992, **39:** 341–345.

87 Quint HJ, Drach GW, Rappaport WD, Hoffman CJ. Emphysematous cystitis. A review of the spectrum of disease. J Urol 1992, **147:** 134–137.

88 Rocca JM, McClure J. Cystitis emphysematosa. Br J Urol 1985, **57:** 585–596.

Tuberculosis and BCG-induced granulomas

89 Auerbach O. The pathology of urogenital tuberculosis. Int Clin 1940, **3:** 21–61.

90 Ba-Thike K, Than-Aye, Nan-Oo. Tuberculous vesico-vaginal fistula. Int J Gynaecol Obstet 1992, **37:** 127–130.

91 Betz SA, See WA, Cohen MB. Granulomatous inflammation in bladder wash specimens after intravesical bacillus Calmette-Guerin therapy for transitional cell carcinoma of the bladder. Am J Clin Pathol 1993, **99:** 244–248.

92 Lamm DL. Complications of bacillus Calmette-Guerin immunotherapy. Urol Clin North Am 1992, **19:** 565–572.

93 Miyashita H, Troncoso P, Babaian RJ. BCG-induced granulomatous prostatitis. A comparative ultrasound and pathologic study. Urology 1992, **39:** 364–367.

94 Smith RL, Alexander RF, Aranda CP. Pulmonary granulomata. A complication of intravesical administration of bacillus Calmette-Guerin for superficial bladder carcinoma. Cancer 1993, **71:** 1846–1847.

Malakoplakia

95 Bates AW, Fegan AW, Baithun SI. Xanthogranulomatous cystitis associated with malignant neoplasms of the bladder. Histopathology 1998, **33:** 212–215.

96 Biggar WD, Crawford L, Cardella C, Bear RA, Gladman D, Reynolds WJ. Malakoplakia and immunosuppressive therapy. Reversal of clinical and leukocyte abnormalities after withdrawal of prednisone and azathioprine. Am J Pathol 1985, **119:** 5–11.

97 Brown RC, Smith BH. Malakoplakia of the testis. Am J Clin Pathol 1967, **47:** 135–147.

98 Lewin KJ, Fair WR, Steigbigel RT, Winberg CD, Drolier MJ. Clinical and laboratory studies into the pathogenesis of malacoplakia. J Clin Pathol 1976, **29:** 354–363.

99 Long JP Jr, Althausen AF. Malacoplakia. A 25-year experience with a review of the literature. J Urol 1989, **141:** 1328–1331.

100 Lou TY, Teplitz C. Malakoplakia. Pathogenesis and ultrastructural morphogenesis. A problem of altered macrophage (phagolysosomal) response. Hum Pathol 1974, **5:** 191–207.

101 McClure J, Cameron CHS, Garrett R. The ultrastructural features of malakoplakia. J Pathol 1981, **134:** 13–25.

102 McClurg FV, D'Agostino AN, Martin JH, Race GJ. Ultrastructural demonstration of intracellular bacteria in three cases of malakoplakia of the bladder. Am J Clin Pathol 1973, **60:** 780–788.

103 Moore WM III, Stokes TL, Cabanas VY. Malakoplakia of the skin. Report of a case. Am J Clin Pathol 1973, **59:** 218–221.

104 Qualman SJ, Gupta PK, Mendelsohn G. Intracellular *Escherichia coli* in urinary malakoplakia. A reservoir of infection and its therapeutic implications. Am J Clin Pathol 1984, **81:** 35–42.

105 Stanton MJ, Maxted W. Malacoplakia. A study of the literature and current concepts of pathogenesis, diagnosis and treatment. J Urol 1981, **125:** 139–146.

106 Streem SB. Genitourinary malacoplakia in renal transplant recipients. Pathogenic, prognostic and therapeutic considerations. J Urol 1984, **132:** 10–12.

107 Terner JH, Lattes R. Malakoplakia of the colon and retroperitoneum. Am J Clin Pathol 1965, **44:** 20–31.

108 Thorning D, Vracko R. Malakoplakia. Defect in digestion of phagocytized material due to impaired vacuolar acidification? Arch Pathol 1975, **99:** 456–460.

109 Walther M, Glenn JF, Vellinos F. Xanthogranulomatous cystitis. J Urol 1985, **134:** 745–746.

110 Yunis EJ, Estevez J, Pinzon GJ, Moran TJ. Malakoplakia. Discussion of pathogenesis and report of three cases including one of fatal gastric and colonic involvement. Arch Pathol 1967, **83:** 180–187.

Other forms of cystitis

111 Block JA. Hemorrhagic cystitis complicating untreated necrotizing vasculitis. Arthritis Rheum 1993, **36:** 857–859.

112 Devitt AT, Sethia KK. Gangrenous cystitis. Case report and review of the literature. J Urol 1993, **149:** 1544–1545.

113 Hofman P, Quintens H, Michiels JF, Taillan B, Thyss A. *Toxoplasma* cystitis associated with acquired immunodeficiency syndrome. Urology 1993, **42:** 589–592.

114 Letendre L, Hoagland HC, Gertz MA. Hemorrhagic cystitis complicating bone marrow transplantation. Mayo Clin Proc 1992, **67:** 128–130.

115 McClanahan C, Grimes MM, Callaghan E, Stewart J. Hemorrhagic cystitis associated with herpes simplex virus. J Urol 1994, **151:** 152–153.

116 Okaneya T, Kontani K, Komiyama I, Takezaki T. Severe cyclophosphamide-induced hemorrhagic cystitis successfully treated by total cystectomy with ileal neobladder substitution. A case report. J Urol 1993, **150:** 1909–1910.

117 Sencer SF, Haake RJ, Weisdorf DJ. Hemorrhagic cystitis after bone marrow transplantation. Risk factors and complications. Transplantation 1993, **56:** 875–879.

118 Spach DH, Bauwens JE, Myerson D, Mustafa MM, Bowden RA. Cytomegalovirus-induced hemorrhagic cystitis following bone marrow transplantation. Clin Infect Dis 1993, **16:** 142–144.

119 Stillwell TJ, Benson RC Jr. Cyclophosphamide-induced

hemorrhagic cystitis. A review of 100 patients. Cancer 1988, **61:** 451–457.

120 Walther M, Glenn JF, Vellios F. Xanthogranulomatous cystitis. J Urol 1985, **134:** 745–746.

121 Young RH. Pseudoneoplastic lesions of the urinary bladder. Pathol Annu 1988, **23**(Pt 1): 67–104.

Metaplastic conditions

122 Bell TE, Wendel RG. Cystitis glandularis. Benign or malignant? J Urol 1968, **100:** 462–465.

123 Benson RC Jr, Swanson SK, Farrow GM. Relationship of leukoplakia to urothelial malignancy. J Urol 1984, **131:** 507–511.

124 Bhagavan BS, Tiamson EM, Wenk RE, Berger BW, Hamamoto G, Eggleston JC. Nephrogenic adenoma of the urinary bladder and urethra. Hum Pathol 1981, **12:** 907–916.

125 Bullock PS, Thoni DE, Murphy WM. The significance of colonic mucosa (intestinal metaplasia) involving the urinary tract. Cancer 1987, **59:** 2086–2090.

126 Cheng L, Cheville JC, Sebo TJ, Eble JN, Bostwick DG. Atypical nephrogenic metaplasia of the urinary tract: A precursor lesion? Cancer 2000, **88:** 853–861.

126a Cohen RJ, Garrett K, Golding JL, Thomas RB, McNeal JE. Epithelial differentiation of the lower urinary tract with recognition of the minor prostatic glands. Hum Pathol 2002, **33:** 905–909.

127 Devine P, Ucci AA, Krain H, Gavris VE, Bhagavan BS, Heaney JA, Alroy J. Nephrogenic adenoma and embryonic kidney tubules share PNA receptor sites. Am J Clin Pathol 1984, **81:** 728–732.

128 Ford TF, Watson GM, Cameron KM. Adenomatous metaplasia (nephrogenic adenoma) of urothelium. An analysis of 70 cases. J Urol 1985, **57:** 427–433.

129 Gaylis FD, Keer HN, Bauer KD, Kozlowski JM, Grayhack JT. DNA profile of nephrogenic adenoma assessed by flow cytometry. Urology 1993, **41:** 160–161.

130 Jost SP, Dixon JS, Gosling JA. Ultrastructural observations on cystitis cystica in human bladder urothelium. Br J Urol 1993, **71:** 28–33.

131 Kay R, Lattanzi C. Nephrogenic adenoma in children. J Urol 1985, **133:** 99–101.

132 Kiernan M, Gaffney EF. The endocrine-paracrine cells of von Brunn's nests and glandular metaplasia in the supramontanal prostatic urethra. Histopathology 1990, **16:** 365–369.

133 Kroovand RL, Chang C-H, Broecker BH, Perrin EV, Oldford J, Perlmutter AD. Epithelial lesions of bladder mucosa following ureteral reimplantation. J Urol 1981, **126:** 822–823.

134 Lapertosa G, Baracchini P, Fulcheri E, Tanzi R. O-acetylated sialic acid variants in intestinal glandular metaplasia of the urinary tract. Histopathology 1986, **10:** 707–712.

134a Mazal PR, Schaufler R, Altenhuber-Muller R, Haitel A, Watschinger B, Kratzik C, Krupitza G, Regele H, Meisl FT, Zechner O, Kerjaschki D, Susani M. Derivation of nephrogenic adenomas from renal tubular cells in kidney-transplant recipients. N Engl J Med 2002, **347:** 653–659.

135 Nowels K, Kent E, Rinsho K, Oyasu R. Prostate specific antigen and acid phosphatase-reactive cells in cystitis cystica and glandularis. Arch Pathol Lab Med 1988, **112:** 734–737.

136 O'Flynn JD, Mullaney J. Leukoplakia of the bladder. A report on 20 cases, including 2 cases progressing to squamous cell carcinoma. Br J Urol 1967, **39:** 461–471.

136a Oliva E, Moch H, Cabrera R, Young RH, Reuter V, Amin MB. Nephrogenic adenoma (NA): an immunohistochemical (ICH) study of 40 cases (Abstract). Mod Pathol 2003, **16:** 172a.

137 Oliva E, Young RH. Nephrogenic adenoma of the urinary tract. A review of the microscopic appearance of 80 cases with emphasis on unusual features. Mod Pathol 1995, **8:** 722–730.

138 Tungekar MF, Heryet A, Gatter KC. The L1 antigen and squamous metaplasia in the bladder. Histopathology 1991, **19:** 245–250.

138a Volmar KE, Chan TY, De Marzo AM, Epstein JI. Florid von Brunn nests mimicking urothelial carcinoma. A morphologic and immunohistochemical comparison to the nested variant of urothelial carcinoma. Am J Surg Pathol 2003, **27:** 1243–1252.

139 Walther MM, Campbell WG Jr, O'Brien DP III, Wheatley JK, Graham SD Jr. Cystitis cystica. An electron and immunofluorescence microscopic study. J Urol 1987, **137:** 764–768.

140 Widran J, Sanchez R, Gruhn J. Squamous metaplasia of the bladder. A study of 450 patients. J Urol 1974, **112:** 479–482.

141 Wiener DP, Koss LG, Sablay B, Freed SZ. The prevalence and significance of Brunn's nests, cystitis cystica and squamous metaplasia in normal bladders. J Urol 1979, **122:** 317–321.

142 Young RH, Scully RE. Nephrogenic adenoma. A report of 15 cases, review of the literature, and comparison with clear cell adenocarcinoma of the urinary tract. Am J Surg Pathol 1986, **10:** 268–275.

Tumorlike conditions

143 Albores-Saavedra J, Manivel JC, Essenfeld H, Dehner LP, Drut R, Gould E, Rosai J. Pseudosarcomatous myofibroblastic proliferations in the urinary bladder of children. Cancer 1990, **66:** 1234–1241.

144 Baker PM, Young RH. Radiation-induced pseudocarcinomatous proliferations of the urinary bladder: a report of 4 cases. Hum Pathol 2000, **31:** 678–683.

144a Chan TY, Epstein JI. Radiation cystitis with "pseudocarcinomatous" features (Abstract). Mod Pathol 2003, **16:** 145a.

145 Chan JK, Chow TC, Tsui MS. Prostatic-type polyps of the lower urinary tract. Three histogenetic types? Histopathology 1987, **11:** 789–801.

146 Cheuk W, Chan JK. Timely topic: anaplastic lymphoma kinase (ALK) spreads its influence. Pathology 2001, **33:** 7–12.

147 Henry L, Wagner B, Faulkner MK, Slater DN, Ansell ID. Metal deposition in post-surgical granulomas of the urinary tract. Histopathology 1993, **22:** 457–465.

147a Hirsch MS, Cin PD, Fletcher CDM. ALK expression in reactive pseudosarcomatous myofibroblastic proliferations of the genitourinary tract (Abstract). Mod Pathol 2003, **16:** 153a.

148 Hughes DF, Biggart JD, Hayes D. Pseudosarcomatous lesions of the urinary bladder. Histopathology 1991, **18:** 67–71.

149 Iczkowski KA, Shanks JH, Gadaleanu V, Cheng L, Jones EC, Neumann R, Nascimento AG, Bostwick DG. Inflammatory pseudotumor and sarcoma of urinary bladder: differential diagnosis and outcome in thirty-eight spindle cell neoplasms. Mod Pathol 2001, **14:** 1043–1051.

150 Iyengar V, Smith DK, Jablonski DV, Gallivan MV. Extramedullary hematopoiesis in the urinary bladder in a case of agnogenic myeloid metaplasia. J Urol Pathol 1993, **1:** 419–423.

151 Jones EC, Clement PB, Young RH. Inflammatory pseudotumor of the urinary bladder. A clinicopathological, immunohistochemical, ultrastructural, and flow cytometric study of 13 cases. Am J Surg Pathol 1993, **17:** 264–274.

152 Jones EC, Young RH. Nonneoplastic and neoplastic spindle cell proliferations and mixed tumors of the urinary bladder. J Urol Pathol 1994, **2:** 105–134.

153 Koirala TR, Hayashi K, Ohara N, Sarker AB, Yoshino T, Takahashi K, Akagi T, Nasu Y, Murakami T. Inflammatory pseudotumor of the urinary bladder with an aberrant expression of cytokeratin. Pathol Int 1994, **44:** 73–79.

154 Lamovec J, Zidar A, Trsinar B, Jancar J. Sclerosing inflammatory pseudotumor of the urinary bladder in a child. Am J Surg Pathol 1992, **16:** 1233–1238.

155 Lundgren L, Aldenborg F, Angerval L, Kindblom LG. Pseudomalignant spindle cell proliferations of the urinary bladder. Hum Pathol 1994, **25:** 181–191.

156 Mahadevia PS, Alexander JE, Rojas-Corona R, Koss LG.

Pseudosarcomatous stromal reaction in primary and metastatic urothelial carcinoma. A source of diagnostic difficulty. Am J Surg Pathol 1989, **13**: 782–790.

157 Miliauskas JR. Bladder xanthoma. Histopathology 1992, **21**: 177–178.

158 Proppe KH, Scully RE, Rosai J. Postoperative spindle cell nodules of genitourinary tract resembling sarcomas. A report of eight cases. Am J Surg Pathol 1984, **8**: 101–108.

159 Ro JY, el-Naggar AK, Amin MB, Sahin AA, Ordóñez NG, Ayala AG. Pseudosarcomatous fibromyxoid tumor of the urinary bladder and prostate. Immunohistochemical, ultrastructural, and DNA flow cytometric analyses of nine cases. Hum Pathol 1993, **24**: 1203–1210.

160 Smith VC, Boone TB, Truong LD. Collagen polyp of the urinary tract: A report of two cases. Mod Pathol 1999, **12**: 1090–1093.

161 Sorensen FB, Marcussen N. Iatrogenic granulomas of the prostate and the urinary bladder. Pathol Res Pract 1987, **182**: 822–830.

162 Spagnolo DV, Waring PM. Bladder granulomata after bladder surgery. Am J Clin Pathol 1986, **86**: 430–437.

163 Watanabe K, Baba K, Saito A, Hoshi N, Suzuki T. Pseudosarcomatous myofibroblastic tumor and myosarcoma of the urogenital tract: immunohistochemical characteristics and differential diagnosis. Arch Pathol Lab Med 2001, **125**: 1070–1073.

164 Wick MR, Brown BA, Young RH, Mills SE. Spindle-cell proliferations of the urinary tract. An immunohistochemical study. Am J Surg Pathol 1988, **112**: 379–389.

165 Williams MP, Ibrahim SK, Rickwood AM. Hamartoma of the urinary bladder in an infant with Beckwith-Wiedemann syndrome. Br J Urol 1990, **65**: 106–107.

166 Young RH. Pseudoneoplastic lesions of the urinary bladder and urethra: a selective review with emphasis on recent information. Semin Diagn Pathol 1997, **14**: 133–146.

167 Young RH, Scully RE. Pseudosarcomatous lesions of the urinary bladder, prostate gland, and urethra. A report of three cases and review of the literature. Arch Pathol Lab Med 1987, **111**: 354–358.

Benign tumors

168 Adegboyega PA, Adesokan A. Tubulovillous adenoma of the urinary bladder. Mod Pathol 1999, **12**: 735–738.

169 Albores-Saavedra J, Maldonado ME, Ibarra J, Rodriguez H. Pheochromocytoma of the urinary bladder. Cancer 1969, **23**: 1110–1118.

170 Anderström C, Johansson S, Pettersson S. Inverted papilloma of the urinary tract. J Urol 1982, **127**: 1132–1134.

171 Bainbridge TC, Singh RR, Mentzel T, Katenkamp D. Solitary fibrous tumor of urinary bladder: Report of two cases. Hum Pathol 1997, **28**: 1204–1206.

172 Bolkier M, Ginesin Y, Lichtig C, Levin DR. Lymphangioma of bladder. J Urol 1983, **129**: 1049–1050.

173 Camassei FD, Bosman C, Corsi A, de Matteis A. Oncocytic paraganglioma of the urinary bladder. J Urol Pathol 1998, **8**: 157–166.

174 Caro DJ, Tessler A. Inverted papilloma of the bladder. A distinct urological lesion. Cancer 1978, **42**: 708–713.

175 Channer JL, Williams JL, Henry L. Villous adenoma of the bladder. J Clin Pathol 1993, **46**: 450–452.

176 Cheng L, Leibovich BC, Cheville JC, Ramnani DM, Sebo TJ, Nehra A, Malek RS, Zincke H, Bostwick DG. Squamous papilloma of the urinary tract is unrelated to condyloma acuminata. Cancer 2000, **88**: 1679–1686.

177 Cheng L, Leibovich BC, Cheville JC, Ramnani DM, Sebo TJ, Neumann RM, Nascimento AG, Zincke H, Bostwick DG. Paraganglioma of the urinary bladder: Can biologic potential be predicted? Cancer 2000, **88**: 844–852.

178 Cheng L, Montironi R, Bostwick DG. Villous adenoma of the urinary tract: A report of 23 cases, including 8 with coexistent adenocarcinoma. Am J Surg Pathol 1999, **23**: 764–771.

179 Cheng L, Nascimento AG, Neumann RM, Nehra A, Cheville JC, Ramnani DM, Leibovich BC, Bostwick DG. Hemangioma of the urinary bladder. Cancer 1999, **86**: 498–504.

180 Cheng L, Scheithauer BW, Leibovich BC, Ramnani DM, Cheville JC, Bostwick DG. Neurofibroma of the urinary bladder. Cancer 1999, **86**: 505–513.

181 Cheville JC, Wu K, Sebo TJ, Cheng L, Riehle D, Lohse CM, Shane V. Inverted urothelial papilloma: Is ploidy, MIB-1 proliferative activity, or P53 protein accumulation predictive of urothelial carcinoma? Cancer 2000, **88**: 632–636.

182 Davaris P, Petraki K, Arvanitis D, Papacharalammpous N, Morakis A, Zorzos S. Urinary bladder paraganglioma (U.B.P.). Pathol Res Pract 1986, **181**: 101–105.

183 Del Mistro A, Koss LG, Braunstein J, Bennett B, Saccomano G, Simons KM. Condylomata acuminata of the urinary bladder. Natural history, viral typing, and DNA content. Am J Surg Pathol 1988, **12**: 205–215.

184 DeMeester L, Farrow GH, Utz DS. Inverted papilloma of the urinary bladder. Cancer 1975, **36**: 505–513.

185 Fletcher MS, Aker M, Hill JT, Pryor JP, Whimster WF. Granular cell myoblastoma of the bladder. Br J Urol 1985, **57**: 109–110.

186 Gersell DJ, Fulling KH. Localized neurofibromatosis of the female genitourinary tract. Am J Surg Pathol 1989, **13**: 873–878.

187 Goven ADT. A case of solitary mucus-secreting cystadenoma of the urinary bladder. J Pathol Bacteriol 1946, **58**: 293–295.

188 Grignon DJ, Ro JY, Mackay B, Ordóñez NG, el-Naggar A, Molina TJ, Shum DT, Ayala AG. Paraganglioma of the urinary bladder. Immunohistochemical, ultrastructural, and DNA flow cytometric studies. Hum Pathol 1991, **22**: 1162–1169.

189 Hendry WF, Vinnicombe J. Haemangioma of bladder in children and young adults. Br J Urol 1971, **43**: 209–216.

189a Huan Y, Dillon RW, Unger PD. Angiomyolipoma of the bladder. Ann Diagn Pathol 2002, **6**: 378–380.

190 Kim YH, Reiner L. Brunnian adenoma (inverted papilloma) of the urinary bladder. Report of a case. Hum Pathol 1978, **9**: 229–231.

191 Kunze E, Schauer A, Schmitt M. Histology and histogenesis of two different types of inverted urothelial papillomas. Cancer 1983, **51**: 348–358.

192 Lam KY, Loong F, Shek TWH, Chu SM. Composite paraganglioma-ganglioneuroma of the urinary bladder: a clinicopathologic, immunohistochemical, and ultrastructural study of a case and review of the literature. Endocr Pathol 1998, **9**: 353–361.

193 Lazarevic B, Garret R. Inverted papilloma and papillary transitional cell carcinoma of urinary bladder. Report of four cases of inverted papilloma, one showing papillary malignant transformation and review of the literature. Cancer 1978, **42**: 1904–1911.

194 McLucas B, Stein JJ. Bladder leiomyoma. A rare cause of pelvic pain. Am J Obstet Gynecol 1985, **153**: 896.

195 Martin SA, Sears DL, Sebo TJ, Lohse CM, Cheville JC. Smooth muscle neoplasms of the urinary bladder: A clinicopathologic comparison of leiomyoma and leiomyosarcoma. Am J Surg Pathol 2002, **26**: 292–300.

196 Miller DC, Gang DL, Gavris V, Alroy J, Ucci AA, Parkhurst EC. Villous adenoma of the urinary bladder. A morphologic or biologic entity? Am J Clin Pathol 1983, **79**: 728–731.

197 Moyana TN, Kontozoglou T. Urinary bladder paragangliomas. An immunohistochemical study. Arch Pathol Lab Med 1988, **112**: 70–72.

198 Ng KJ, Sherif A, McClinton S, Ewen SW. Giant ancient schwannoma of the urinary bladder presenting as a pelvic mass. Br J Urol 1993, **72**: 513–514.

199 Nuovo GJ, Nagler HM, Fenoglio JJ Jr. Arteriovenous malformation of the bladder presenting as gross hematuria. Hum Pathol 1986, **17**: 94–97.

199a Pan C-C, Yu I-T, Yang A-H, Chiang H. Clear cell myomelanocytic tumor of the urinary bladder. Am J Surg Pathol 2003, **27**: 689–692.

200 Pauwels CF, Van den Broecke C, Demeyer JM, De Potter CR. Chondroma of the bladder. Virchows Arch 1998, **432**: 299–300.

201 Sarma DP, Weiner M. Hemangioma of the urinary bladder. J Surg Oncol 1983, **24**: 142–144.

202 Seibel L, Prasad S, Weiss RE, Bancila E, Epstein JI. Villous adenoma of the urinary tract: A lesion frequently associated with malignancy. Hum Pathol 2002, **33**: 236–241.

203 Shirai T, Yamamoto K, Adachi T, Imaida K, Masui T, Ito N. Condyloma acuminatum of the bladder in two autopsy cases. Acta Pathol Jpn 1988, **38**: 399–405.

204 Silver SA, Epstein JI. Adenocarcinoma of the colon simulating primary urinary bladder neoplasia. A report of nine cases. Am J Surg Pathol 1993, **17**: 171–178.

205 Steele AA, Byrne AJ. Paramesonephric (müllerian) sinus of urinary bladder. Am J Surg Pathol 1982, **6**: 173–176.

206 Summers DE, Rushin JM, Frazier HA, Cotelingam JD. Inverted papilloma of the urinary bladder with granular eosinophilic cells. An unusual neuroendocrine variant. Arch Pathol Lab Med 1991, **115**: 802–806.

207 Westra WH, Grenko RT, Epstein J. Solitary fibrous tumor of the lower genital tract: A report of five cases involving the seminal vesicles, urinary bladder, and prostate. Hum Pathol 2000, **31**: 63–68.

208 Winfield HN, Catalona WJ. An isolated plexiform neurofibroma of the bladder. J Urol 1985, **134**: 542–543.

Transitional cell (urothelial) carcinoma

General and clinical features

209 Anton-Culver H, Lee-Feldstein A, Taylor TH. Occupation and bladder cancer risk. Am J Epidemiol 1992, **136**: 89–94.

210 Auerbach O, Garfinkel L. Histologic changes in the urinary bladder in relation to cigarette smoking and use of artificial sweeteners. Cancer 1989, **64**: 983–987.

211 Benson RC Jr, Tomera KM, Kelalis PP. Transitional cell carcinoma of the bladder in children and adolescents. J Urol 1983, **130**: 54–55.

212 Bryan GT. The role of urinary tryptophan metabolites in the etiology of bladder cancer. Am J Clin Nutr 1971, **24**: 841–847.

213 Chetsanga C, Malmstrom PU, Gyllensten U, Moreno-Lopez J, Dinter Z, Pettersson U. Low incidence of human papillomavirus type 16 DNA in bladder tumor detected by the polymerase chain reaction. Cancer 1992, **69**: 1208–1211.

214 Chowaniec J. Aetiology: epidemiological and experimental considerations. In Skrabanek P, Walsh A (eds): Bladder cancer. UICC Technical Report Series 1981, **60**: 118–143.

215 Friedell GH. National bladder cancer conference. Cancer Res 1977, **37**: 2737–2969.

216 Fuchs EF, Kay R, Poole R, Barry JM, Pearse HD. Uroepithelial carcinoma in association with cyclophosphamide ingestion. J Urol 1981, **126**: 544–545.

217 Fukushima S, Asamoto M, Imaida K, el-Bolkainy MN, Tawfik HN, Ito N. Comparative study of urinary bladder carcinomas in Japanese and Egyptians. Acta Pathol Jpn 1989, **39**: 176–179.

218 Knowles MA. Human papillomavirus sequences are not detectable by Southern blotting or general primer-mediated polymerase chain reaction in transitional cell tumors of the bladder. Urol Res 1992, **20**: 297–301.

219 Kroft SH, Oyasu R. Urinary bladder cancer. Mechanisms of development and progression. Lab Invest 1994, **71**: 158–174.

220 Kutarski PW, Padwell A. Transitional cell carcinoma of the bladder in young adults. Br J Urol 1993, **72**: 749–755.

221 Lower GM Jr. Concepts in causality. Chemically induced human urinary bladder cancer. Cancer 1982, **49**: 1056–1066.

222 Morrison AS, Buring JE, Verhoek WG, Aoki K, Leck I, Ohno Y, Obata K. An international study of smoking and bladder cancer. J Urol 1984, **131**: 650–654.

223 Murphy WM. Diseases of the urinary bladder, urethra, ureters, and renal pelves. In Murphy WM (ed.): Urological pathology. Philadelphia, 1989, W.B. Saunders, pp. 64–96.

224 Neugut AI, Ahsan H, Robinson E, Ennis ED. Bladder carcinoma and other second malignancies after radiotherapy for prostate carcinoma. Cancer 1997, **79**: 1600–1604.

225 Pedersen-Bjergaard J, Ersboll J, Hansen VL, Sorensen BL, Christoffersen K, Hou-Jensen K, Nissen NI, Knudsen JB, Hansen MM. Carcinoma of the urinary bladder after treatment with cyclophosphamide for nonHodgkin's lymphoma. N Engl J Med 1988, **318**: 1028–1032.

225a Qiu H, Kordunskaya S, Yantiss RK. Transitional cell carcinoma arising in the gastric remnant following gastrocystoplasty. Int J Surg Pathol 2003, **11**: 143–147.

225b Robles MW, Rutgers JKL, Shanberg AM. Adenocarcinoma and dysplasia in an ileal neobladder after ileo-cystoplasty for interstitial cystitis. Int J Surg Pathol (In press).

226 Schulte PA, Ringen K, Hemstreet GP, Altekruse EB, Gullen WH, Tillett S, Allsbrook WC Jr, Crosby JH, Witherington R, Stringer W, Brubaker MM. Risk factors for bladder cancer in a cohort exposed to aromatic amines. Cancer 1986, **58**: 2156–2162.

227 Scott AA, Stanley W, Worsham GF, Kirkland TA Jr, Gansler T, Garvin AJ. Aggressive bladder carcinoma in an adolescent. Report of a case with immunohistochemical cytogenetic, and flow cytometric characterization. Am J Surg Pathol 1989, **13**: 1057–1063.

228 Shibutani YF, Schoenberg MP, Carpiniello VL, Malloy TR. Human papillomavirus associated with bladder cancer. Urology 1992, **40**: 15–17.

228a Tumino R, Serrao A, Ninfo V. Leiomyosarcoma at the site of an ileal neobladder: a heretofore unreported occurrence. Int J Surg Pathol 2003, **11**: 149–151.

229 Vineis P, Magnani C. Occupation and bladder cancer in males. A case-control study. Int J Cancer 1985, **35**: 599–606.

230 Wan J, Grossman HB. Bladder carcinoma in patients age 40 years or younger. Cancer 1989, **64**: 178–181.

Morphologic features

231 Amin MB, Gómez JA, Young RH. Urothelial transitional cell carcinoma with endophytic growth patterns: A discussion of patterns of invasion and problems associated with assessment of invasion in 18 cases. Am J Surg Pathol 1997, **21**: 1057–1068.

232 Amin MB, Murphy WM, Reuter VE, Ro JY, Ayala AG, Weiss MA, Eble JN, Young RH. A symposium on controversies in the pathology of transitional cell carcinomas of the urinary bladder, Part II. Anat Pathol 1997, **2**: 71–110.

233 Amin MB, Ro JY, el-Sharkawy T, Lee KM, Troncoso P, Silva EG, Ordóñez NG, Ayala AG. Micropapillary variant of transitional cell carcinoma of the urinary bladder. Histologic pattern resembling ovarian papillary serous carcinoma. Am J Surg Pathol 1994, **18**: 1224–1232.

234 Billerey C, Martin L, Bittard H, Adessi GL, Carbillet JP. The nested variant of urothelial carcinoma of the urinary bladder: report of five cases and review of the literature. J Urol Pathol 1999, **11**: 89–100.

235 Cheng L, Weaver AL, Neumann RM, Scherer BG, Bostwick DG. Substaging of T1 bladder carcinoma based on the depth of invasion as measured by micrometer: A new proposal. Cancer 1999, **86**: 1035–1043.

236 Donhuijsen K, Schmidt U, Richter HJ, Leder LD. Mucoid cytoplasmic inclusions in urothelial carcinomas. Hum Pathol 1992, **23**: 860–864.

237 Eble JN, Young RH. Carcinoma of the urinary bladder: a review of its diverse morphology. Semin Diagn Pathol 1997, **14**: 98–108.

238 Engel P, Anagnostaki L, Braendstrup O. The muscularis mucosae of the human urinary bladder. Implications for tumor staging on biopsies. Scand J Urol Nephrol 1992, **26**: 249–252.

239 Goetsch SJ, Cooper K. An approach to papillary urothelial lesions, including a discussion of newly described papillary lesions of the urinary bladder. Adv Anat Pathol 1998, **5:** 329–345.

240 Jimenez RE, Keane TE, Hardy HT, Amin MB. pT1 urothelial carcinoma of the bladder: criteria for diagnosis, pitfalls, and clinical implications. Adv Anat Pathol 2000, **7:** 13–25.

241 Keep JC, Piehl M, Miller A, Oyasu R. Invasive carcinomas of the urinary bladder. Evaluation of tunica muscularis mucosae involvement. Am J Clin Pathol 1989, **91:** 575–579.

242 Kotliar SN, Wood CG, Schaeffer AJ, Oyasu R. Transitional cell carcinoma exhibiting clear cell features. A differential diagnosis for clear cell adenocarcinoma of the urinary tract. Arch Pathol Lab Med 1995, **119:** 79–81.

243 Larsen MP, Steinberg GD, Brendler CB, Epstein JI. Use of *Ulex europaeus* agglutinin (UEA) to distinguish vascular and "pseudovascular" invasion in transitional cell carcinoma of bladder with lamina propria invasion. Mod Pathol 1990, **3:** 83–88.

244 Li M, Cannizzaro LA. Identical clonal origin of synchronous and metachronous low-grade, noninvasive papillary transitional cell carcinomas of the urinary tract. Hum Pathol 1999, **30:** 1197–1200.

245 Lowe D, Fletcher CDM, Gower RL. Tumour-associated eosinophilia in the bladder. J Clin Pathol 1984, **37:** 500–502.

246 Murphy WM. Current topics in the pathology of bladder cancer. Pathol Annu 1983, **18**(Pt 1): 1–25.

247 Murphy WM, Deana DG. The nested variant of transitional cell carcinoma. A neoplasm resembling proliferation of Brunn's nests. Mod Pathol 1992, **5:** 240–243.

248 Philip AT, Amin MB, Tamboli P, Lee TJ, Hill CE, Ro JY. Intravesical adipose tissue: A quantitative study of its presence and location with implications for therapy and prognosis. Am J Surg Pathol 2000, **24:** 1286–1290.

249 Qiu H, Kordunskaya S, Yantiss RK. Transitional cell carcinoma arising in the gastric remnant following gastrocystoplasty: A case report and review of the literature. Int J Surg Pathol 2003, **11:** 143–147.

250 Ramani P, Birch BR, Harland SJ, Parkinson MC. Evaluation of endothelial markers in detecting blood and lymphatic channel invasion in pT1 transitional carcinoma of bladder. Histopathology 1991, **19:** 551–554.

251 Ro JY, Lapham RL, Amin MB. Deceptively bland transitional cell carcinoma of the urinary bladder – further characterization of subtle and diagnostically treacherous patterns of invasion in urothelial neoplasia. Adv Anat Pathol 1997, **4:** 244–251.

252 Sahin AA, Myhre M, Ro JY, Sneige N, Dekmezian RH, Ayala AG. Plasmacytoid transitional cell carcinoma. Report of a case with initial presentation mimicking multiple myeloma. Acta Cytol 1991, **35:** 277–280.

253 Selli C, Carcangiu ML, Carini M. Bladder carcinoma arising from regenerated urothelium over lyophilized dura patch. Urology 1986, **27:** 53–55.

254 Stephenson WT, Holmes FF, Noble MJ, Gerald KB. Analysis of bladder carcinoma by subsite. Cystoscopic location may have prognostic value. Cancer 1990, **66:** 1630–1635.

255 Talbert ML, Young RH. Carcinomas of the urinary bladder with deceptively benign-appearing foci. A report of three cases. Am J Surg Pathol 1989, **13:** 374–381.

256 Truong LD, Ostrowski ML, Wheeler TM. Tamm-Horsfall protein in bladder tissue. Morphologic spectrum and clinical significance. Am J Surg Pathol 1994, **18:** 615–622.

257 Ward AM. Glandular metaplasia and mucin production in transitional cell carcinomas of bladder. J Clin Pathol 1971, **24:** 481.

258 Weaver MG, Abdul-Karim FW. The prevalence and character of the muscularis mucosae of the human urinary bladder. Histopathology 1990, **17:** 563–566.

259 Younes M, Sussman J, True LD. The usefulness of the level of the muscularis mucosae in the staging of invasive transitional cell carcinoma of the urinary bladder. Cancer 1990, **66:** 543–548.

260 Young RH, Zukerberg LR. Microcystic transitional cell carcinomas of the urinary bladder. A report of four cases. Am J Clin Pathol 1991, **96:** 635–639.

261 Zukerberg LR, Harris NL, Young RH. Carcinomas of the urinary bladder simulating malignant lymphoma. A report of five cases. Am J Surg Pathol 1991, **15:** 569–576.

Histochemical and immunohistochemical features

262 Abou Farha KM, Janknegt RA, Kester AD, Arends JW. Value of immunohistochemical laminin staining in transitional cell carcinoma of human bladder. Urol Int 1993, **50:** 133–140.

263 Asamoto M, Fukishima S, Tatemoto Y, Yamada K, Fukui S, Mori M. Immunohistochemical expression of keratin proteins in urinary bladder carcinoma. Pathol Res Pract 1989, **184:** 194–201.

264 Bassily NH, Vallorosi CJ, Akdas G, Montie JE, Rubin MA. Coordinate expression of cytokeratins 7 and 20 in prostate adenocarcinoma and bladder urothelial carcinoma. Am J Clin Pathol 2000, **113:** 383–388.

265 Cairns P, Suarez V, Newman J, Crocker J. Nucleolar organizer regions in transitional cell tumors of the bladder. Arch Pathol Lab Med 1989, **113:** 1250–1252.

266 Campo E, Algaba F, Palacin A, Germa R, Sole-Balcells FJ, Cardesa A. Placental proteins in high-grade urothelial neoplasms. An immunohistochemical study of human chorionic gonadotropin, human placental lactogen, and pregnancy-specific beta-1-glycoprotein. Cancer 1989, **63:** 2497–2504.

267 Desai S, Lim SD, Jimenez RE, Chun T, Keane TE, McKenney JK, Zavala-Pompa A, Cohen C, Young RH, Amin MB. Relationship of cytokeratin 20 and CD44 protein expression with WHO/ISUP grade in pTa and pT1 papillary urothelial neoplasia. Mod Pathol 2000, **13:** 1315–1323.

268 Genega EM, Hutchinson B, Reuter VE, Gaudin PB. Immunophenotype of high-grade prostatic adenocarcinoma and urothelial carcinoma. Mod Pathol 2000, **13:** 1186–1191.

269 Hoshi S, Orikasa S, Numata I, Nose M. Expression of Leu-M1 antigens in carcinoma of the urinary bladder. J Urol 1986, **135:** 1075–1077.

270 Jautzke G, Altenaehr E. Immunohistochemical demonstration of carcinoembryonic antigen (CEA) and its correlation with grading and staging on tissue sections of urinary bladder carcinomas. Cancer 1982, **50:** 2052–2056.

271 Jiang J, Ulbright TM, Younger C, Sanchez K, Bostwick DG, Koch MO, Eble JN, Cheng L. Cytokeratin 7 and cytokeratin 20 in primary urinary bladder carcinoma and matched lymph node metastasis. Arch Pathol Lab Med 2001, **125:** 921–923.

272 Kaufmann O, Volmerig J, Dietel M. Uroplakin III is a highly specific and moderately sensitive immunohistochemical marker for primary and metastatic urothelial carcinomas. Am J Clin Pathol 2000, **113:** 683–687.

272a Lehner R, Lucia MS, Jarboe EA, Orlicky D, Shroyer AL, McGregor JA, Shroyer KR. Immunohistochemical localisation of the IAP protein surviving in bladder mucosa and transitional cell carcinoma. Appl Immuno Mol Morph 2002, **10:** 134–138.

273 Limas C. Relationship of epidermal growth factor receptor detectability with the A, B, H blood group antigens. Emphasis on normal and neoplastic urothelium. Am J Pathol 1991, **139:** 131–137.

274 Loy TS, Sharp SC, Andershock CJ, Craig SB. Distribution of CA 19-9 in adenocarcinomas and transitional cell carcinomas. An immunohistochemical study of 527 cases. Am J Clin Pathol 1993, **99:** 726–728.

274a Mhawech P, Uchida T, Pelte M-F. Immunohistochemical profile of high-grade urothelial bladder carcinoma and prostate adenocarcinoma. Hum Pathol 2002, **33:** 1136–1140.

275 Ordonez NG. Thrombomodulin expression in transitional cell carcinoma. Am J Clin Pathol 1998, **110:** 385–390.

276 Ordonez NG. Transitional cell carcinoma of the ovary and

bladder are immunophenotypically different. Histopathology 2000, **36**: 433–438.

276a Parker DC, Folpe AL, Bell J, Oliva E, Young RH, Cohen C, Amin MB. Potential utility of uroplakin III, thrombomodulin, high molecular weight cytokeratin, and cytokeratin 20 in non-invasive, invasive, and metastatic urothelial (transitional cell) carcinoma. Am J Surg Pathol 2003, **27**: 1–10.

277 Schaafsma HE, Ramaekers FC, van Muijen GN, Robben H, Lane EB, Leigh IM, Ooms EC, Schalken JA, van Moorselaar RJ, Ruiter DJ. Cytokeratin expression patterns in metastatic transitional cell carcinoma of the urinary tract. An immunohistochemical study comparing local tumor and autologous metastases. Am J Pathol 1991, **139**: 1389–1400.

278 Seidal T, Breborowicz J, Malmstrom PU, Busch C. Immunoreactivity to human chorionic gonadotropin in urothelial carcinoma. Correlation with tumor grade, stage, and prognosis. J Urol Pathol 1993, **1**: 397–410.

279 Sheinfeld J, Reuter VE, Fair WR, Cordon-Cardo C. Expression of blood group antigens in bladder cancer: Current concepts. Semin Surg Oncol 1992, **8**: 308–315.

280 Shevchuk MM, Fenoglio CM, Richart RM. Carcinoembryonic antigen localization in benign and malignant transitional epithelium. Cancer 1981, **47**: 899–905.

281 Tiitta O, Wahlstrom T, Virtanen I, Gould VE. Tenascin in inflammatory conditions and neoplasms of the urinary bladder. Virchows Arch [Cell Pathol] 1993, **63**: 283–287.

281a Varma M, Morgan M, Amin MB, Wozniak S, Jasani B. High molecular weight cytokeratin antibody (clone 34βE12): a sensitive marker for differentiation of high-grade invasive urothelial carcinoma from prostate cancer. Histopathology 2003, **42**: 167–172.

282 Visscher VW, Sloane BF, Sameni M, Babiarz JW, Jacobson J, Crissman JD. Clinicopathologic significance of cathepsin B immunostaining in transitional neoplasia. Mod Pathol 1994, **7**: 76–81.

283 Zhuang YH, Bläuer M, Tammela T, Tuohimaa P. Immunodetection of androgen receptor in human urinary bladder cancer. Histopathology 1997, **30**: 556–562.

Electron microscopic features

284 Alroy J, Pauli BU, Weinstein RS. Correlation between numbers of desmosomes and the aggressiveness of transitional cell carcinoma in human urinary bladder. Cancer 1981, **47**: 104–112.

285 Jacobs JB, Cohen SM, Farrow GM, Friedell GH. Scanning electron microscopic features of human urinary bladder cancer. Cancer 1981, **48**: 1399–1409.

Molecular genetic features

286 Asamoto M, Hasegawa R, Masuko T, Hashimoto Y, Ueda K, Ohtaguro K, Sasaki S, Washida H, Fukishima S. Immunohistochemical analysis of c-erbB-2 oncogene product and epidermal growth factor receptor expression in human urinary bladder carcinomas. Acta Pathol Jpn 1990, **40**: 322–326.

287 Baffa R, Gomella LG, Vecchione A, Bassi P, Mimori K, Sedor J, Calviello CM, Gardiman M, Minimo C, Strup SE, McCue PA, Kovatich AJ, Pagano F, Huebner K, Croce CM. Loss of FHIT expression in transitional cell carcinoma of the urinary bladder. Am J Pathol 2000, **156**: 419–424.

288 Coombs LM, Oliver S, Sweeney E, Knowles M. Immunocytochemical localization of c-erbB-2 protein in transitional cell carcinoma of the urinary bladder. J Pathol 1993, **169**: 35–42.

289 Cordon-Cardo C, Reuter VE. Alteration of tumor suppressor genes in bladder cancer. Semin Diagn Pathol 1997, **14**: 123–132.

290 Cordon-Cardo C, Dalbagni G, Saez GT, Oliva MR, Zhang ZF, Rosai J, Reuter VE, Pellicer A. p53 mutations in human bladder cancer. Genotypic versus phenotypic patterns. Int J Cancer 1994, **56**: 347–353.

291 Czerniak B, Li L, Chaturvedi V, Ro JY, Johnston DA, Hodges S, Benedict WF. Genetic modeling of human urinary bladder carcinogenesis. Genes Chromosomes Cancer 2000, **27**: 392–402.

292 Dalbagni G, Presti J, Reuter V, Fair WR, Cordon-Cardo C. Genetic alterations in bladder cancer. Lancet 1993, **342**: 469–471.

293 Hartmann A, Moser K, Kriegmair M, Hofstetter A, Hofstaedter F, Knuechel R. Frequent genetic alterations in simple urothelial hyperplasias of the bladder in patients with papillary urothelial carcinoma. Am J Pathol 1999, **154**: 721–727.

294 Lee CC, Yamamoto S, Morimura K, Wanibuchi H, Nishisaki N, Ikemoto S, Nakatani T, Wada S, Kishimoto T, Fukushima S. Significance of cyclin D1 overexpression in transitional cell carcinomas of the urinary bladder and its correlation with histopathologic features. Cancer 1997, **79**: 780–789.

295 Lianes P, Orlow I, Zhang ZF, Oliva MR, Sarkis AS, Reuter VE, Cordon-Cardo C. Altered patterns of MDM2 and TP53 expression in human bladder cancer. J Natl Cancer Inst 1994, **86**: 1325–1330.

296 Miyao N, Tsai YC, Lerner SP, Olumi AF, Spruck CH, Gonzalez-Zulueta M, Nichols PW, Skinner DG, Jones PA. Role of chromosome 9 in human bladder cancer. Cancer Res 1993, **53**: 4066–4070.

297 Nakopoulou L, Vourlakou C, Zervas A, Tzonou A, Gakiopoulou H, Dimopoulos MA. The prevalence of bcl-2, p53 and Ki-67 immunoreactivity in transitional cell bladder carcinoma and their clinicopathologic correlates. Hum Pathol 1998, **29**: 146–154.

298 Orlow I, LaRue H, Osman I, Lacombe L, Moore L, Rabbani F, Meyer F, Fradet Y, Cordon-Cardo C. Deletions of the INK4A gene in superficial bladder tumors. Association with recurrence. Am J Pathol 1999, **155**: 105–113.

299 Orlow I, Lianes P, Lacombe L, Dalbagni G, Reuter VE, Cordon-Cardo C. Chromosome 9 allelic losses and microsatellite alterations in human bladder tumors. Cancer Res 1994, **54**: 2848–2851.

300 Presti JC Jr, Reuter VE, Galan T, Fair WR, Cordon-Cardo C. Molecular genetic alterations in superficial and locally advanced human bladder cancer. Cancer Res 1991, **51**: 5405–5409.

301 Richter J, Wagner U, Kononen J, Kallionemi OP, Sauter G. High-throughput tissue microarray analysis of cyclin E gene amplification and overexpression in urinary bladder cancer. Am J Pathol 2000, **157**: 787–794.

302 Sandberg AA, Berger CS. Review of chromosome studies in urological tumors. II. Cytogenetics and molecular genetics of bladder cancer. J Urol 1994, **151**: 545–560.

303 Volante M, Tizzani A, Casetta G, Zitella A, Pacchioni D, Bussolati G. Progression from superficial to invasive carcinoma of the bladder: genetic evidence of either clonal or heterogeneous events. Hum Pathol 2001, **32**: 468–474.

304 Vollmer RT, Humphrey PA, Swanson PE, Wick MR, Hudson ML. Invasion of the bladder by transitional cell carcinoma: Its relation to histologic grade and expression of p53, MIB-1, c-erb B-2, epidermal growth factor receptor, and bcl-2. Cancer 1998, **82**: 715–723.

Biopsy

305 National Bladder Cancer Collaborative Group A. Development of a strategy for a longitudinal study of patients with bladder cancer. Cancer Res 1977, **37**: 2898–2906.

Cytology

306 Badalament RA, Kimmel M, Gay H, Cibas ES, Whitmore WF Jr, Herr HW, Fair WR, Melamed MR. The sensitivity of flow cytometry compared with conventional cytology in the detection of superficial bladder carcinoma. Cancer 1987, **59**: 2078–2085.

307 Esposti PL, Moberger G, Zajicek J. The cytologic diagnosis of transitional cell tumors of the urinary bladder and its histologic basis. Acta Cytol (Baltimore) 1970, **14**: 145–155.

308 Fuhr JE. Flow cytometry and cytopathology. Analysis of fine-needle aspirates, effusions, and urology specimens. Pathol Annu 1994, 29(Pt 1): 211–232.

309 Hida CA, Gupta PK. Cercariform cells: Are they specific for transitional cell carcinoma? Cancer 1999, 87: 69–74.

310 Johnson TL, Kini SR. Cytologic features of metastatic transitional cell carcinoma. Diagn Cytopathol 1993, 9: 270–278.

311 Klein A, Zemer R, Buchumensky V, Klaper R, Nissenkorn I. Expression of cytokeratin 20 in urinary cytology of patients with bladder carcinoma. Cancer 1998, 82: 349–354.

312 Koss LG, Deitch D, Ramanathan R, Sherman AB. Diagnostic value of cytology of voided urine. Acta Cytol (Baltimore) 1985, 29: 810–816.

313 Koss LG, Wersto RP, Simmons DA, Deitch D, Herz F, Freed SZ. Predictive value of DNA measurements in bladder washings. Comparison of flow cytometry, image cytophotometry, and cytology in patients with a past history of urothelial tumors. Cancer 1989, 64: 916–924.

314 Matzkin H, Moinuddin SM, Soloway MS. Value of urine cytology versus bladder washing in bladder cancer. Urology 1992, 39: 201–203.

315 Melamed MR, Klein FA. Flow cytometry of urinary bladder irrigation specimens. Hum Pathol 1984, 15: 302–305.

316 Murphy WM. Current status of urinary cytology in the evaluation of bladder neoplasms. Hum Pathol 1990, 21: 886–896.

317 National Bladder Cancer Collaborative Group A. Cytology and histopathology of bladder cancer cases in a prospective longitudinal study. Cancer Res 1977, 37: 2911–2915.

318 Orell SR. Transitional cell epithelioma of the bladder. Correlation of cytologic and histologic diagnosis. Scand J Urol Nephrol 1969, 3: 93–98.

319 Reichborn-Kjennerud S, Hoeg K. The value of urine cytology in the diagnosis of recurrent bladder tumors. Acta Cytol (Baltimore) 1972, 16: 269–272.

320 Sidransky D, Von Eschenbach A, Tsai YC, Jones P, Summerhayes I, Marshall F, Paul M, Green P, Hamilton SR, Frost P. Identification of p53 gene mutations in bladder cancers and urine samples. Science 1991, 252: 706–709.

321 Wiener HG, Vooijs GP, van't Hof-Grootenboer B. Accuracy of urinary cytology in the diagnosis of primary and recurrent bladder cancer. Acta Cytol 1993, 37: 163–169.

322 Wolinska WH, Melamed MR, Klein FA. Cytology of bladder papilloma. Acta Cytol (Baltimore) 1985, 29: 817–822.

323 Wolinska WH, Melamed MR, Schellhammer PF, Whitmore WF Jr. Urethral cytology following cystectomy for bladder carcinoma. Am J Surg Pathol 1977, 1: 225–233.

Classification

324 Ash JE. Epithelial tumors of the bladder. J Urol 1940, 44: 135–145.

325 Bergkvist A, Ljungqvist A, Moberger G. Classification of bladder tumours based on the cellular pattern. Acta Chir Scand 1965, 130: 371–378.

326 Cheng L, Darson M, Cheville JC, Neumann RM, Zincke H, Nehra A, Bostwick DG. Urothelial papilloma of the bladder: Clinical and biologic implications. Cancer 1999, 86: 2098–2101.

327 Cheng L, Neumann RM, Nehra A, Spotts BE, Weaver AL, Bostwick DG. Cancer heterogeneity and its biologic implications in the grading of urothelial carcinoma. Cancer 2000, 88: 1663–1670.

328 Cheng L, Neumann RM, Weaver AL, Cheville JC, Leibovich BC, Ramnani DM, Scherer BG, Nehra A, Zincke H, Bostwick DG. Grading and staging of bladder carcinoma in transurethral specimens. Correlation with 105 matched cystectomy specimens. Am J Clin Pathol 2000, 113: 275–279.

329 Cina SJ, Epstein JI, Endrizzi JM, Harmon WJ, Seay TM, Schoenberg MP. Correlation of cystoscopic impression with histologic diagnosis of biopsy specimens of the bladder. Hum Pathol 2001, 32: 630–637.

330 Cina SJ, Lancaster-Weiss KJ, Lecksell K, Epstein JI. Correlation of Ki-67 and p53 with the new World Health Organization/International Society of Urological Pathology classification system of urothelial neoplasia. Arch Pathol Lab Med 2001, 125: 646–651.

331 Epstein JI, Amin MB, Reuter VR, Mostofi FK. The World Health Organization/International Society of Urological Pathology consensus classification of urothelial (transitional cell) neoplasms of the urinary bladder. Bladder Consensus Conference Committee. Am J Surg Pathol 1998, 22: 1435–1448.

332 Jewett HJ, Blackman SS. Infiltrating carcinoma of the bladder. Histologic pattern and degree of cellular differentiation in 97 autopsy cases. J Urol 1946, 56: 200–210.

333 Jimenez RE, Gheiler E, Oskanian P, Tiguert R, Sakr W, Wood DP, Pontes JE, Grignon DJ. Grading the invasive component of urothelial carcinoma of the bladder and its relationship with progression-free survival. Am J Surg Pathol 2000, 24: 980–987.

334 Lipponen P, Simpanen H, Pesonen E, Eskelinen M, Sotarauta M, Collan Y. Potential of morphometry in grading transitional cell carcinoma of the urinary bladder. Pathol Res Pract 1989, 185: 617–620.

335 Malmstrom PU, Busch C, Morlen BJ. Recurrence, progression and survival in bladder cancer: a retrospective analysis of 232 patients with greater than or equal to 5-year follow-up. Scand J Urol Nephrol 1987, 21: 185–195.

335a McKenney JK, Amin MB, Young RH. Urothelial (transitional cell) papilloma of the urinary bladder: a clinicopathologic study of 26 cases. Mod Pathol 2003, 16: 623–629.

336 Mostofi FK. Standardization of nomenclature and criteria for diagnosis of epithelial tumors of urinary bladder. Acta Unio Int Contra Cancer 1960, 16: 310–314.

337 Olsen LH, Overgaard S, Frederiksen P, Ladefoged C, Ludwigsen E, Petri J, Poulsen JT. The reliability of staging and grading of bladder tumours. Impact of misinformation on the pathologist's diagnosis. Scand J Urol Nephrol 1993, 27: 349–353.

338 Ooms ECM, Kurver PHJ, Veldhuizen RW, Alons CL, Boon ME. Morphometric grading of bladder tumors in comparison with histologic grading by pathologists. Hum Pathol 1983, 14: 144–150.

339 Oyasu R. World Health Organization and International Society of Urological Pathology classification and two-number grading system of bladder tumors. Cancer 2000, 88: 1509–1512.

340 Pich A, Chiusa L, Formiconi A, Galliano D, Bortonin P, Navone R. Biologic differences between noninvasive papillary urothelial neoplasms of low malignant potential and low-grade (grade 1) papillary carcinomas of the bladder. Am J Surg Pathol 2001, 25: 1528–1533.

341 Reuter VR, Epstein JI, Amin MA, Mostofi FK, and the Bladder Consensus Conference Committee. A newly illustrated synopsis of the World Health Organization/International Society of Urological Pathology (WHO/ISUP) consensus classification of urothelial (transitional cell) neoplasms of the urinary bladder. J Urol Pathol 1999, 11: 1–28.

Local spread and metastases

342 Chibber PJ, McIntyre MA, Hindmarsh JR, Hargreave TB, Newsam JE, Chisholm GD. Transitional cell carcinoma involving the prostate. Br J Urol 1981, 53: 605–609.

343 De Paepe ME, Andre R, Mahadevia P. Urethral involvement in female patients with bladder cancer. A study of 22 cystectomy specimens. Cancer 1990, 65: 1237–1241.

344 Eng C, Cunningham D, Quade BJ, Schwamm L, Kantoff PW, Skarin AT. Meningeal carcinomatosis from transitional cell carcinoma of the bladder. Cancer 1993, 72: 553–557.

345 Habuchi T, Takahashi R, Yamada H, Kakehi Y, Sugiyama T,

Yoshida O. Metachronous multifocal development of urothelial cancers by intraluminal seeding. Lancet 1993, **342**: 1087–1088.

346 Herr HW. Extravesical tumor relapse in patients with superficial bladder tumors. J Clin Oncol 1998, **16**: 1099–1102.

347 Hopkins SC, Ford KS, Soloway MS. Invasive bladder cancer. Support for screening. J Urol 1983, **130**: 61–64.

348 Kirk D, Savage A, Makepeace AR, Gostelow BE. Transitional cell carcinoma involving the prostate. An unfavourable prognostic sign in the management of bladder cancer? Br J Urol 1981, **53**: 610–612.

349 Kishi K, Hirota T, Matsumoto K, Kakizoe T, Murase T, Fujita J. Carcinoma of the bladder. A clinical and pathological analysis of 87 autopsy cases. J Urol 1981, **125**: 36–39.

350 Mahadevia PS, Koss LG, Tar IJ. Prostatic involvement in bladder cancer. Prostate mapping in 20 cystoprostatectomy specimens. Cancer 1986, **58**: 2096–2102.

351 Ro JY, Ayala AG, el-Naggar A, Wishnow KI. Seminal vesicle involvement by in situ and invasive transitional cell carcinoma of the bladder. Am J Surg Pathol 1987, **11**: 951–958.

352 Rosenstein M, Wallner K, Scher H, Sternberg CN. Treatment of brain metastases from bladder cancer. J Urol 1993, **149**: 480–483.

353 Sakamoto N, Tsuneyoshi M, Naito S, Kumazawa J. An adequate sampling of the prostate to identify prostatic involvement by urothelial carcinoma in bladder cancer patients. J Urol 1993, **149**: 318–321.

354 Schade ROK, Serek-Hanssen A, Swinney J. Morphological changes in the ureter in cases of bladder carcinoma. Cancer 1971, **27**: 1267–1272.

355 Sharma TC, Melamed MR, Whitmore WF Jr. Carcinoma in situ of the ureter in patients with bladder carcinoma treated by cystectomy. Cancer 1970, **26**: 583–587.

356 Sidransky D, Frost P, Von Eschenbach A, Oyasu R, Preisinger AC, Vogelstein B. Clonal origin of bladder cancer. N Engl J Med 1992, **326**: 737–740.

357 Tongaonkar HB, Dalal AV, Kulkarni JN, Kamat MR. Urethral recurrences following radical cystectomy for invasive transitional cell carcinoma of the bladder. Br J Urol 1993, **72**: 910–914.

358 Yang XJ, Lecksell K, Epstein JI. Can immunohistochemistry enhance the detection of micrometastases in pelvic lymph nodes from patients with high-grade urothelial carcinoma of the bladder? Am J Clin Pathol 1999, **112**: 649–653.

Carcinoma in situ and dysplasia

358a Amin MB, McKenney JK. An approach to the diagnosis of flat intraepithelial lesions of the urinary bladder using the World Health Organization/International Society of Urological Pathology Consensus Classification System. Adv Anat Pathol 2002, **9**: 222–223.

359 Amin MB, Young RH. Intraepithelial lesions of the urinary bladder with a discussion of the histogenesis of urothelial neoplasia. Semin Diagn Pathol 1997, **14**: 84–97.

360 Chan TY, Epstein JI. In situ adenocarcinoma of the bladder. Am J Surg Pathol 2001, **25**: 892–899.

361 Cheng L, Cheville JC, Neumann RM, Bostwick DG. Natural history of urothelial dysplasia of the bladder. Am J Surg Pathol 1999, **23**: 443–447.

362 Cheng L, Cheville JC, Neumann RM, Leibovich BC, Egan KS, Spotts BE, Bostwick DG. Survival of patients with carcinoma in situ of the urinary bladder. Cancer 1999, **85**: 2469–2474.

363 Coon JS, McCall A, Miller AW III, Farrow GM, Weinstein RS. Expression of blood group-related antigens in carcinoma *in situ* of the urinary bladder. Cancer 1985, **56**: 797–804.

364 Farrow GM. Pathology of carcinoma in situ of the urinary bladder and related lesions. J Cell Biochem Suppl 1992, **161**: 39–43.

365 Farrow GM, Utz DC, Rife CC. Morphological and clinical observations of patients with early bladder cancer treated with total cystectomy. Cancer Res 1976, **36**: 2495–2501.

366 Friedell GH, Soloway MS, Hilgar AG, Farrow GM. Summary of workshop on carcinoma in situ of the bladder. J Urol 1986, **136**: 1047–1048.

367 Fukui I, Yokokawa M, Sekine H, Yamada T, Hosoda K, Ishiwata D, Oka K, Sarada T, Tohma T, Yamada T, Oshima H. Carcinoma in situ of the urinary bladder. Effect of associated neoplastic lesions on clinical course and treatment. Cancer 1987, **59**: 164–173.

368 Hofstädter F, Delgado R, Jakse G, Judmaier W. Urothelial dysplasia and carcinoma in situ of the bladder. Cancer 1986, **57**: 356–361.

368a Hopman AH, Kamps MA, Speel EJ, Schapers RF, Sauter G, Ramaekers FC. Identification of chromosome 9 alterations and p53 accumulation in isolated carcinoma *in situ* of the urinary ladder *versus* carcinoma *in situ* associated with carcinoma. Am J Pathol 2002, **161**: 1119–1125.

369 Iwasaki H, Enjoji M, Kano M. Nonpapillary carcinoma in situ of the urinary bladder. A histopathologic study and mapping of the urothelial lesions. Acta Pathol Jpn 1979, **29**: 623–633.

370 Kakizoe T, Matumoto K, Nishio Y, Ohtani M, Kishi K. Significance of carcinoma in situ and dysplasia in association with bladder cancer. J Urol 1985, **133**: 395–398.

371 Lopez-Beltran A, Cheng L, Andersson L, Brausi M, Montironi R, Sesterhenn I, van det Kwast KT, Mazerolles C. Preneoplastic non-papillary lesions and conditions of the urinary bladder: an update based on the Ancona International Consultation. Virchows Arch 2002, **440**: 3–11.

371a Lopez-Beltran A, Luque RJ, Moreno A, Bollito E, Carmona E, Montironi R. The pagetoid variant of bladder urothelial carcinoma in situ. A clinicopathological study of 11 cases. Virchows Arch 2002, **441**: 148–153.

371b Mallofré C, Castillo M, Morente V, Solé M. Immunohistochemical expression of CK20, p53 and Ki-67 as objective markers of urothelial dysplasia. Mod Pathol 2003, **16**: 187–191.

372 McKenney JK, Desai S, Cohen C, Amin MB. Discriminatory immunohistochemical staining of urothelial carcinoma in situ and non-neoplastic urothelium: an analysis of cytokeratin 20, p53, and CD44 antigens. Am J Surg Pathol 2001, **25**: 1074–1078.

373 McKenney JK, Gomez JA, Desai S, Lee MW, Amin MB. Morphologic expressions of urothelial carcinoma in situ: A detailed evaluation of its histologic patterns with emphasis on carcinoma in situ with microinvasion. Am J Surg Pathol 2001, **25**: 356–362.

374 Melamed MD, Voutsa NG, Grabstald H. Natural history and clinical behavior of in situ carcinoma of the human urinary bladder. Cancer 1964, **17**: 1533–1545.

375 Nakanishi K, Kawai T, Suzuki M. Lectin binding and expression of blood group-related antigens in carcinoma-in-situ and invasive carcinoma of urinary bladder. Histopathology 1993, **23**: 153–158.

376 Norming U, Tribukait B, Gustafson H, Nyman CR, Wang NN, Wijkstrom H. Deoxyribonucleic acid profile and tumor progression in primary carcinoma in situ of the bladder. A study of 63 patients with grade 3 lesions. J Urol 1992, **147**: 11–15.

377 Ooms ECM, Blomjous CEM, Zwartendijk J, Veldhuizen RW, Blok APR, Heinhuis RJ, Boon ME. Connective tissue stroma in bladder papillary transitional cell carcinoma, carcinoma *in situ* and benign cystitis. Histopathology 1986, **10**: 613–619.

378 Orozco RE, Vander Zwaag R, Murphy WM. The pagetoid variant of urothelial carcinoma in situ. Hum Pathol 1993, **24**: 1199–1202.

379 Prout GR Jr, Griffin PP, Daly JJ, Heney NM. Carcinoma *in situ* of the urinary bladder with and without associated vesical neoplasms. Cancer 1983, **52**: 524–532.

380 Seemayer TA, Knaack J, Thelmo WL, Wang N-S, Ahmed MN. Further observations on carcinoma in situ of the urinary bladder. Silent but extensive intraprostatic involvement. Cancer 1975, **36**: 514–520.

380a Swierczynski SL, Epstein JI. Prognostic significance of atypical papillary urothelial hyperplasia. Hum Pathol 2002, **33**: 512–517.

381 Skinner DG, Richie JP, Cooper PH, Waisman J, Kaufman JJ. The clinical significance of carcinoma in situ of the bladder and its association with overt carcinoma. J Urol 1974, **112**: 68–71.

382 Soto EA, Friedell GH, Tiltman AJ. Bladder cancer as seen in giant histologic sections. Cancer 1977, **39**: 447–455.

383 Spruck CH III, Ohneseit PF, Gonzalez-Zulueta M, Esrig D, Miyao N, Tsai YC, Lerner SP, Schmutte C, Yang AS, Cote R, et al. Two molecular pathways to transitional cell carcinoma of the bladder. Cancer Res 1994, **54**: 784–788.

383a Sun W, Herrera GA. E-cadherin expression in urothelial carcinoma in situ, superficial papillary transitional cell carcinoma, and invasive transitional cell carcinoma. Hum Pathol 2002, **33**: 996–1000.

383b Sun W, Zhang PL, Herrera GA. p53 protein and Ki-67 overexpression in urothelial dysplasia of bladder. Appl Immun Mol Morph 2002, **10**: 327–331.

384 Utz DC, Farrow GM, Rife CC, Segura JW, Zincke H. Carcinoma in situ of the bladder. Cancer 1980, **45**: 1842–1848.

Treatment

385 Amling CL, Thrasher JB, Frazier HA, Dodge RK, Robertson JE, Paulson DF. Radical cystectomy for stages Ta, Tis and T1 transitional cell carcinoma of the bladder. J Urol 1994, **151**: 31–36.

386 BLINST Italian Cooperative Group. Intravesical doxorubicin for the prophylaxis of superficial bladder tumors. A multicenter study. Cancer 1984, **54**: 756–761.

387 Cookson MS, Sarosdy MF. Management of stage T1 superficial bladder cancer with intravesical bacillus Calmette-Guerin therapy. J Urol 1992, **148**: 797–801.

388 Coutts AG, Grigor KM, Fowler JW. Urethral dysplasia and bladder cancer in cystectomy specimens. Br J Urol 1985, **57**: 535–541.

389 Fossa SD, Waehre H, Aass N, Jacobsen AB, Olsen DR, Ous S. Bladder cancer definitive radiation therapy of muscle-invasive bladder cancer. A retrospective analysis of 317 patients. Cancer 1993, **72**: 3036–3043.

390 Fukui I, Yokokawa M, Sekine H, Yamada T, Hosoda K, Ishiwata D, Oka K, Sarada T, Tohma T, Yamada T, Oshima H. Carcinoma in situ of the urinary bladder. Effect of associated neoplastic lesions on clinical course and treatment. Cancer 1987, **59**: 164–173.

390a Grossman HB, Natale RB, Tangen CM, Speights VO, Vogelzang NJ, Trump DL, DeVere White RW, Sarosdy MF, Wood DP, Raghaven D, Crawford ED. Neoadjuvant chemotherapy plus cystectomy compared with cystectomy alone for locally advanced bladder cancer. N Engl J Med 2003, **349**: 859–866.

391 Herr HW, Wartinger DD, Fair WR, Oettgen HF. Bacillus Calmette-Guerin therapy for superficial bladder cancer. A 10-year followup. J Urol 1992, **147**: 1020–1023.

392 Huland H, Otto U, Droese M, Klöppel G. Long-term mitomycin C instillation after transurethral resection of superficial bladder carcinoma. Influence on recurrence, progression and survival. J Urol 1984, **132**: 27–29.

393 Kaufman DS, Shipley WU, Griffin PP, Heney NM, Althausen AF, Efird JT. Selective bladder preservation by combination treatment of invasive bladder cancer. N Engl J Med 1993, **329**: 1377–1382.

394 Klein EA, Rogatko A, Herr HW. Management of local bacillus Calmette-Guerin failures in superficial bladder cancer. J Urol 1992, **147**: 601–605.

395 Lage JM, Bauer WC, Kelley DR, Ratliff TL, Catalona WJ. Histological parameters and pitfalls in the interpretation of bladder biopsies in bacillus Calmette-Guerin treatment of superficial bladder cancer. J Urol 1986, **135**: 916–919.

396 Lamm DL. Bacillus Calmette-Guerin immunotherapy for bladder cancer. J Urol 1985, **134**: 40–47.

397 Lerner SP, Skinner DG, Lieskovsky G, Boyd SD, Groshen SL, Ziogas A, Skinner E, Nichols P, Hopwood B. The rationale for en bloc pelvic lymph node dissection for bladder cancer patients with nodal metastases. Long-term results. J Urol 1993, **149**: 758–764.

398 Mameghan H, Fisher RJ, Watt WH, Meagher MJ, Rosen IM, Mameghan J, Brook S, Tynan AP, Korbel EI, Millard RJ, et al. The management of invasive transitional cell carcinoma of the bladder. Results of definitive and preoperative radiation therapy in 390 patients treated at the Prince of Wales Hospital, Sydney, Australia. Cancer 1992, **69**: 2771–2778.

399 Neumann MP, Limas C. Transitional cell carcinomas of the urinary bladder. Effects of preoperative irradiation on morphology. Cancer 1986, **58**: 2758–2763.

400 Pavone-Macaluso M, Tripi M, Ingargiola GD. Cooperative studies of chemoprophylaxis after transurethral resection of bladder tumors. Cancer Chemother Pharmacol 1983, **11**(Suppl): S16–S21.

401 Quilty PM, Duncan W. Treatment of superficial (T_1) tumours of the bladder by radical radiotherapy. Br J Urol 1986, **58**: 147–152.

402 Raghavan D, Shipley WU, Garnick MB, Russell PJ, Richie JP. Biology and management of bladder cancer. N Engl J Med 1990, **322**: 1129–1138.

403 Shipley WU, Prout GR Jr, Kaufman DS. Bladder cancer. Advances in laboratory innovations and clinical management, with emphasis on innovations allowing bladder-sparing approaches for patients with invasive tumors. Cancer 1990, **65**: 675–683.

404 Soloway MS. Rationale for intensive intravesical chemotherapy for superficial bladder cancer. J Urol 1980, **123**: 461–466.

405 Soloway MS. The management of superficial bladder cancer. Cancer 1980, **45**: 1856–1865.

406 Utz DC, Farrow GM, Rife CC, Segura JW, Zincke H. Carcinoma in situ of the bladder. Cancer 1980, **45**: 1842–1848.

407 Vieweg J, Whitmore WF Jr, Herr HW, Sogani PC, Russo P, Sheinfeld J, Fair WR. The role of pelvic lymphadenectomy and radical cystectomy for lymph node-positive bladder cancer. The Memorial Sloan-Kettering Cancer Center experience. Cancer 1994, **73**: 3020–3028.

408 Wishnow KI, Levinson AK, Johnson DE, Tenney DM, Grignon DJ, Ro JY, Ayala AJ, Logothetis CJ, Swanson DA, Babaian RJ, et al. Stage B (P2/3A/N0) transitional cell carcinoma of bladder highly curable by radical cystectomy. Urology 1992, **39**: 12–16.

409 Yu WS, Sagerman RH, Chung CT, Dalal PS, King GA. Bladder carcinoma. Experience with radical and preoperative radiotherapy in 421 patients. Cancer 1985, **56**: 1293–1299.

Prognosis

410 al-Abadi H, Nagel R. Deoxyribonucleic acid content and survival rates of patients with transitional cell carcinoma of the bladder. J Urol 1994, **151**: 37–42.

411 Alroy J, Teramura K, Miller AW III, Pauli BU, Gottesman JE, Flanagan M, Davidsohn I, Weinstein RS. Isoantigens A, B and H in urinary bladder carcinomas following radiotherapy. Cancer 1978, **41**: 1739–1745.

412 Alsheikh A, Mohamadali Z, Jones E, Masterson J, Gilks CB. Comparison of the WHO/ISUP classification and cytokeratin 20 expression in predicting the behavior of low-grade urothelial tumors. Mod Pathol 2001, **14**: 267–272.

413 Bell JT, Burney SW, Friedell GH. Blood vessel invasion in human bladder cancer. J Urol 1971, **105**: 675–678.

414 Blomjous EC, Schipper NW, Baak JP, Vos W, De Voogt HJ, Meijer CJ. The value of morphometry and DNA flow cytometry in addition to classic prognosticators in superficial urinary bladder carcinoma. Am J Clin Pathol 1989, **91**: 243–248.

415 Bochner BH, Cote RJ, Weidner N, Groshen S, Chen S-C, Skinner DG, Nichols PW. Angiogenesis in bladder cancer. Relationship between microvessel density and tumor prognosis. J Natl Cancer Inst 1995, **87**: 1603–1612.

416 Brawn PN. The origin of invasive carcinoma of the bladder. Cancer 1982, **50:** 515–519.

417 Cheng L, Neumann RM, Scherer BG, Weaver AL, Leibovich BC, Nehra A, Zincke H, Bostwick DG. Tumor size predicts the survival of patients with pathologic stage T2 bladder carcinoma: A critical evaluation of the depth of muscle invasion. Cancer 1999, **85:** 2638–2647.

418 Cheng L, Weaver AL, Leibovich BC, Ramnani DM, Neumann RM, Scherer BG, Nehra A, Zincke H, Bostwick DG. Predicting the survival of bladder carcinoma patients treated with radical cystectomy. Cancer 2000, **88:** 2326–2332.

419 Cohen MB, Waldman FM, Carroll PR, Kerschmann R, Chew K, Mayall BH. Comparison of five histopathologic methods to assess cellular proliferation in transitional cell carcinoma of the urinary bladder. Hum Pathol 1993, **24:** 772–778.

420 Coon JS, Schwartz D, Summers JL, Miller AW III, Weinstein RS. Flow cytometric analysis of deparaffinized nuclei in urinary bladder carcinoma. Comparison with cytogenetic analysis. Cancer 1986, **57:** 1594–1601.

421 Coon JS, Weinstein RS. Detection of ABH tissue isoantigens by immunoperoxidase methods in normal and neoplastic urothelium. Comparison with the erythrocyte adherence method. Am J Clin Pathol 1981, **8:** 163–171.

422 Cordon-Cardo C, Wartinger D, Petrylak D, Dalbagni G, Fair WR, Fuks Z, Reuter VE. Altered expression of the retinoblastoma gene product. Prognostic indicator in bladder cancer. J Natl Cancer Inst 1992, **84:** 1251–1256.

423 Cordonnier JJ. Cystectomy for carcinoma of the bladder. J Urol 1968, **99:** 172–173.

424 Czerniak B, Koss LG. Expression of Ca antigen on human urinary bladder tumors. Cancer 1985, **55:** 2380–2383.

425 Dalesio O, Schulman CC, Sylvester R, De Pauw M, Robinson M, Denis L, Smith P, Viggiano G, and Members of the European Organization for Research on Treatment of Cancer, Genitourinary Tract Cancer Cooperative Group. Prognostic factors in superficial bladder tumors. A study of the European Organization for Research on Treatment of Cancer. Genitourinary Tract Cancer Cooperative Group. J Urol 1983, **129:** 730–733.

426 Del Pizzo JJ, Borkowski A, Jacobs SC, Kyprianou N. Loss of cell cycle regulators p27[Kip 1] and cyclin E in transitional cell carcinoma of the bladder correlates with tumor grade and patient survival. Am J Pathol 1999, **155:** 1129–1136.

427 Esrig D, Spruck CH, Nichols PW, Chaiwun B, Steven K, Groshen S, Chen SC, Skinner DG, Jones PA, Cote RJ. p53 nuclear protein accumulation correlates with mutations in the p53 gene, tumor grade, and stage in bladder cancer. Am J Pathol 1993, **143:** 1389–1397.

427a Frank I, Cheville JC, Blute ML, Lohse CM, Nehra A, Weaver AL, Karnes R, Zincke H. Transitional cell carcinoma of the urinary bladder with regional lymph node involvement treated by cystectomy. Cancer 2003, **97:** 2425–2451.

428 Frazier HA, Robertson JE, Dodge RK, Paulson DF. The value of pathologic factors in predicting cancer-specific survival among patients treated with radical cystectomy for transitional cell carcinoma of the bladder and prostate. Cancer 1993, **71:** 3993–4001.

429 Friedell GH, Parija GC, Nagy GK, Soto EA. The pathology of human bladder cancer. Cancer 1980, **45:** 1823–1831.

430 Gilbert HA, Logan JL, Kagan AR, Friedman HA, Cove JK, Fox M, Muldoon TM, Lonni YW, Rowe JH, Cooper JF, Nussbaum H, Chan P, Rao A, Starr A. The natural history of papillary transitional cell carcinoma of the bladder and its treatment in an unselected population on the basis of histologic grading. J Urol 1978, **119:** 488–492.

431 Heney NM, Ahmed S, Flanagan MJ, Frable W, Corder MP, Hafermann MD, Hawkins IR for National Bladder Cancer Collaborative Group A. Superficial bladder cancer. Progression and recurrence. J Urol 1983, **130:** 1083–1086.

432 Heney NM, Proppe K, Prout GR Jr, Griffin PP, Shipley WU. Invasive bladder cancer. Tumor configuration, lymphatic invasion and survival. J Urol 1983, **130:** 895–897.

433 Javadpour N, Mostofi FK. Primary epithelial tumors of the bladder in the first two decades of life. J Urol 1969, **101:** 706–710.

434 Jewett HJ. Carcinoma of the bladder. Influence of depth of infiltration on the five-year results following complete extirpation of the primary growth. J Urol 1952, **67:** 672–680.

435 Jewett HJ, King LR, Shelley WM. A study of 365 cases of infiltrating bladder cancer. Relation of certain pathological characteristics to prognosis after extirpation. J Urol 1964, **92:** 668–678.

436 Jordan AM, Weingarten J, Murphy WM. Transitional cell neoplasms of the urinary bladder. Can biologic potential be predicted from histologic grading? Cancer 1987, **60:** 2766–2774.

437 Juhl BR, Hartzen SH, Hainau B. A, B, H antigen expression in transitional cell carcinomas of the urinary bladder. Cancer 1986, **57:** 1768–1775.

438 Juhl BR, Hartzen SH, Hainau B. Lewis a antigen in transitional cell tumors of the urinary bladder. Cancer 1986, **58:** 222–228.

439 Kaye KW, Lange PH. Mode of presentation of invasive bladder cancer. Reassessment of the problem. J Urol 1982, **128:** 31–33.

440 Kern WH. The grade and pathologic stage of bladder cancer. Cancer 1984, **53:** 1185–1189.

441 Korkolopoulou P, Konstantinidou A-E, Thomas-Tsagli E, Christadoulou P, Kapralos P, Davaris P. WAF1/p21 protein expression is an independent prognostic indicator in superficial and invasive bladder cancer. Appl Immunohistochem Mol Morphol 2000, **8:** 285–292.

442 Lapham RL, Grignon D, Ro JY. Pathologic prognostic parameters in bladder urothelial biopsy, transurethral resection, and cystectomy specimens. Semin Diagn Pathol 1997, **14:** 109–122.

443 Lehman TP, Cooper HS, Mulholland SG. Peanut lectin binding sites in transitional cell carcinoma of the urinary bladder. Cancer 1984, **53:** 272–277.

444 Lerman RI, Hutter RVP, Whitmore WF Jr. Papilloma of the urinary bladder. Cancer 1970, **25:** 333–342.

445 Levi F, La Vecchia C, Randimbison L, Franceschi S. Incidence of infiltrating cancer following superficial bladder carcinoma. Int J Cancer 1993, **55:** 419–421.

446 Limas C, Lange P. A, B, H antigen detectability in normal and neoplastic urothelium. Influence of methodologic factors. Cancer 1982, **49:** 2476–2484.

447 Limas C, Lange PH. Lewis antigens in normal and neoplastic urothelium. Am J Pathol 1985, **121:** 176–183.

448 Limas C, Lange P. T-antigen in normal and neoplastic urothelium. Cancer 1986, **58:** 1236–1245.

449 Limas C, Lange P, Fraley EE, Vessella RL. A, B, H antigens in transitional cell tumors of the urinary bladder. Correlation with the clinical course. Cancer 1979, **44:** 2099–2107.

450 Lipponen PK, Eskelinen MJ, Jauhiainen K, Harju E, Terho R. Tumour infiltrating lymphocytes as an independent prognostic factor in transitional cell bladder cancer. Eur J Cancer 1992, **29A:** 69–75.

451 Lipponen PK, Eskelinen MJ, Jauhiainen K, Harju E, Terho R, Haapasalo H. Grading of superficial bladder cancer by quantitative mitotic frequency analysis. J Urol 1993, **149:** 36–41.

452 Lipponen PK, Eskelinen M, Jauhianien K, Terho R, Harju E. Clinical prognostic factors in transitional cell cancer of the bladder. Urol Int 1993, **50:** 192–197.

453 Lipponen PK, Eskelinen MJ, Jauhiainen K, Terho R, Nordling S. Proliferation indices as independent prognostic factors in papillary Ta-T1 transitional cell bladder tumours. Br J Urol 1993, **72:** 451–457.

454 Logothetis CJ, Xu HJ, Ro JY, Hu SX, Sahin A, Ordóñez N,

Benedict WF. Altered expression of retinoblastoma protein and known prognostic variables in locally advanced bladder cancer. J Natl Cancer Inst 1992, **84**: 1256–1261.

455 Lund F, Lundwall F. Papillomas of the urinary bladder. Acta Pathol Microbiol Scand 1955, **105**(Suppl): 118–134.

456 Mulder AH, Van Hootegem JC, Sylvester R, ten Kate FJ, Kurth KH, Ooms EC, Van der Kwast TH. Prognostic factors in bladder carcinoma. Histologic parameters and expression of a cell cycle-related nuclear antigen (Ki-67). J Pathol 1992, **166**: 37–43.

457 Murphy WM. DNA flow cytometry in diagnostic pathology of the urinary tract. Hum Pathol 1987, **18**: 317–319.

458 Murphy WM, Chandler RW, Trafford RM. Flow cytometry of deparaffinized nuclei compared to histological grading for the pathological evaluation of transitional cell carcinomas. J Urol 1986, **135**: 694–697.

459 Neuhaus M, Wagner U, Schmid U, Ackermann D, Zellweger T, Maurer R, Alund G, Knonagel H, Rist M, Moch H, Mihatsch MJ, Gasser TC, Sauter G. Polysomies but not Y chromosome losses have prognostic significance in pTa/Pt1 urinary bladder cancer. Hum Pathol 1999, **30**: 81–86.

460 Oosterhuis JW, Schapers RF, Janssen-Heijnen ML, Smeets AW, Pauwels RPE. MIB-1 as a proliferative marker in transitional cell carcinoma of the bladder: Clinical significance and comparison with other prognostic factors. Cancer 2000, **88**: 2598–2605.

461 Orntoft TF, Nielsen MJS, Wolf H, Olsen S, Clausen H, Hakomori S-I, Dabelsteen E. Blood group ABO and Lewis antigen expression during neoplastic progression of human urothelium. Immunohistochemical study of type 1 chain structures. Cancer 1987, **60**: 2641–2648.

462 Otto T, Bex A, Schmidt U, Raz A, Rubben H. Improved prognosis assessment for patients with bladder carcinoma. Am J Pathol 1997, **150**: 1919–1923.

462a Pich A, Chiusa L, Formiconi A, Galliano D, Bortolin P, Comino A, Navone R. Proliferative activity is the most significant predictor of recurrence in non-invasive papillary urothelial neoplasms of low malignant potential and grade 1 papillary carcinomas of the bladder. Cancer 2002, **95**: 784–790.

463 Prout GR Jr, Barton BA, Griffin PP, Friedell GH. Treated history of noninvasive grade 1 transitional cell carcinoma. The National Bladder Cancer Group. J Urol 1992, **148**: 1413–1419.

464 Rodriguez-Alonso A, Pita-Fernandez S, Gonzalez-Correro J, Nogueira-March JL. Multivariate analysis of survival, recurrence, progression and development of metastasis in T1 and T2a transitional cell bladder carcinoma. Cancer 2002, **94**: 1677–1684.

465 Sarkis AS, Dalbagni G, Cordon-Cardo C, Zhang ZF, Sheinfeld J, Fair WR, Herr HW, Reuter VE. Nuclear overexpression of p53 protein in transitional cell bladder carcinoma. A marker for disease progression. J Natl Cancer Inst 1993, **85**: 53–59.

466 Sarma KP. The role of lymphoid reaction in bladder cancer. J Urol 1970, **104**: 843–849.

467 Skinner DG. Current perspectives in the management of high-grade invasive bladder cancer. Cancer 1980, **45**: 1866–1874.

468 Smith G, Elton RA, Beynon LL, Newsam JE, Chisholm GD, Hargreave TB. Prognostic significance of biopsy results of normal-looking mucosa in cases of superficial bladder cancer. Br J Urol 1983, **55**: 665–669.

469 Soini Y, Turpeenniemi-Hujanen T, Kamel D, Autio-Harmainen H, Risteli J, Risteli L, Nuorva K, Paakko P, Vahakangas K. p53 immunohistochemistry in transitional cell carcinoma and dysplasia of the urinary bladder correlates with disease progression. Br J Cancer 1993, **68**: 1029–1035.

470 Srinivas M, Orihuela E, Lloyd KO, Old LJ, Whitmore WF Jr. Estimation of ABO(H) isoantigen expression in bladder tumors. J Urol 1985, **133**: 25–28.

471 Stephenson WT, Holmes FF, Noble MJ, Gerald KB. Analysis of bladder carcinoma by subsite. Cystoscopic location may have prognostic value. Cancer 1990, **66**: 1630–1635.

472 Summers JL, Coon JS, Ward RM, Falor WH, Miller AW III, Weinstein RS. Prognosis in carcinoma of the urinary bladder based upon tissue blood group ABH and Thomsen-Friedenreich antigen status and karyotype of the initial tumor. Cancer Res 1983, **43**: 934–939.

473 Suwa Y, Takano Y, Iki M, Asakura T, Noguchi S, Masuda M. Prognostic significance of Ki-67 expression in transitional cell bladder carcinoma after radical cystectomy. Pathol Res Pract 1997, **193**: 551–556.

474 Toma V, Hauri D, Schmid U, Ackermann D, Maurer R, Alund G, Knonagel H, Rist M, Gasser TC, Sauter G, Roth J. Focal loss of CD44 variant protein expression is related to recurrence in superficial bladder carcinoma. Am J Pathol 1999, **155**: 1427–1432.

475 Vallancien G, Rouger PH, LeClerc JP, Kuss R. Immunofluorescence study of the distribution of A, B, and H cell surface antigens in bladder tumors. J Urol 1983, **130**: 67–70.

476 Wolf H, Hojgaard K. Prognostic factors in local surgical treatment of invasive bladder cancer, with special reference to the presence of urothelial dysplasia. Cancer 1983, **51**: 1710–1715.

477 Wolk FN, Bishop MC. The specific red cell adherence test in transitional cell carcinoma of the bladder before and after radiotherapy in patients with blood group A. J Urol 1983, **130**: 71–73.

Other primary carcinomas
Adenocarcinoma and related tumors

478 Alroy J, Roganovic D, Banner BF, Jacobs JB, Merk FB, Ucci AA, Kwan PWL, Coon JS IV, Miller AW III. Primary adenocarcinomas of the human urinary bladder. Histochemical, immunological, and ultrastructural studies. Virchows Arch [A] 1981, **393**: 165–181.

479 Anderström C, Johansson SL, von Schultz L. Primary adenocarcinoma of the urinary bladder. A clinicopathologic and prognostic study. Cancer 1983, **52**: 1273–1280.

480 Burgues O, Ferrer J, Navarro S, Ramos D, Botella E, Llombart-Bosch A. Hepatoid adenocarcinoma of the urinary bladder. An unusual neoplasm. Virchows Arch 1999, **435**: 71–75.

481 Butterworth DM, Haboubi NY, Lupton EW. Mixed mesonephric adenocarcinoma and transitional cell carcinoma of the bladder. Histopathology 1990, **16**: 601–604.

482 Choi H, Lamb S, Pintar K, Jacobs SC. Primary signet-ring cell carcinoma of the urinary bladder. Cancer 1984, **53**: 1985–1990.

483 Engel RM, Wilkinson HA. Bladder exstrophy. J Urol 1974, **104**: 699–704.

484 Epstein JI, Kuhajda FP, Lieberman PH. Prostate-specific acid phosphatase immunoreactivity in adenocarcinomas of the urinary bladder. Hum Pathol 1986, **17**: 939–942.

485 Grignon DJ, Ro JY, Ayala AG, Johnson DE. Primary signet-ring cell carcinoma of the urinary bladder. Am J Clin Pathol 1991, **95**: 13–20.

486 Grignon DJ, Ro JY, Ayala AG, Johnson DE, Ordóñez NG. Primary adenocarcinoma of the urinary bladder. A clinicopathologic analysis of 72 cases. Cancer 1991, **67**: 2165–2172.

487 Hasegawa R, Fukushima S, Hjirose M, Seki K, Takahashi M, Furukawa F, Toyoda K, Ito N. Histochemical demonstration of colonic type mucin in glandular metaplasia and adenocarcinoma of the human urinary bladder. Acta Pathol Jpn 1987, **37**: 1097–1103.

488 Humphrey PA. Clear cell neoplasms of the urinary tract and male reproductive system. Semin Diagn Pathol 1997, **14**: 240–252.

489 Jacobs LB, Brooks JD, Epstein JI. Differentiation of colonic metaplasia from adenocarcinoma of urinary bladder. Hum Pathol 1997, **28**: 1152–1157.

490 Kunze E, Francksen B, Schulz H. Expression of MUC5AC

apomucin in transitional cell carcinomas of the urinary bladder and its possible role in the development of mucus-secreting adenocarcinomas. Virchows Arch 2001, **439:** 609–615.

491 Lam KY, Ma L, Nicholls J. Adenocarcinoma arising in a diverticulum of the urinary bladder. Pathology 1992, **24:** 40–42.

491a Lopez-Beltran A, Luque RJ, Quintero A, Requena MJ, Montironi R. Hepatoid adenocarcinoma of the urinary bladder. Virchows Arch 2003, **442:** 381–387.

492 Loy TS. Distribution of 66.4.C2 immunoreactivity in adenocarcinomas and transitional cell carcinomas: an immunohistochemical study of 506 cases. Appl Immunohistochem 1998, **6:** 97–100.

493 Mai KT, Ford JC, Morash C, Gerridzen R. Primary and secondary prostatic adenocarcinoma of the urinary bladder. Hum Pathol 2001, **32:** 434–440.

494 Mostofi FK, Thomson RV, Dean AL Jr. Mucous adenocarcinoma of the urinary bladder. Cancer 1955, **8:** 741–758.

495 Newbould M, McWilliam LJ. A study of vesical adenocarcinoma, intestinal metaplasia and related lesions using mucin histochemistry. Histopathology 1990, **17:** 225–230.

496 Nocks BN, Heney NM, Daly JJ. Primary adenocarcinoma of urinary bladder. Urology 1983, **21:** 26–29.

497 O'Brien AME, Urbanski SJ. Papillary adenocarcinoma in situ of bladder. J Urol 1985, **134:** 544–546.

498 Oliva E, Amin MB, Jimenez R, Young RH. Clear cell carcinoma of the urinary bladder: a report and comparison of four tumors of mullerian origin and nine of probable urothelial origin with discussion of histogenesis and diagnostic problems. Am J Surg Pathol 2002, **26:** 190–197.

499 Pallesen G. Neoplastic Paneth cells in adenocarcinoma of the urinary bladder. A first case report. Cancer 1981, **47:** 1834–1837.

500 Poore TE, Egbert B, Jahnke R, Kraft JK. Signet ring cell adenocarcinoma of the bladder. Linitis plastica variant. Arch Pathol Lab Med 1981, **105:** 203–204.

501 Rosas-Uribe A, Luna MA. Primary signet ring cell carcinoma of the urinary bladder. Arch Pathol 1969, **88:** 294–297.

502 Satake T, Takeda A, Matsuyama M. Argyrophil cells in the urachal epithelium and urachal adenocarcinoma. Acta Pathol Jpn 1984, **34:** 1193–1199.

503 Sinard J, Macleary L, Melamed J. Hepatoid adenocarcinoma in the urinary bladder. Unusual localization of a newly recognized tumor type. Cancer 1994, **73:** 1919–1925.

503a Tamboli P, Mohsin SK, Hailemariam S, Amin MB. Colonic adenocarcinoma metastatic to the urinary tract versus primary tumors of the urinary tract with glandular differentiation: a report of 7 cases and investigation using a limited immunohistochemical panel. Arch Pathol Lab Med 2002, **126:** 1057–1063.

504 Tanaka T, Kanai N, Sugie S, Nakamura A, Hayashi H, Fujimoto Y, Takeuchi T. Primary signet-ring cell carcinoma of the urinary bladder. Pathol Res Pract 1987, **182:** 130–132.

505 Thomas DG. A study of 52 cases of adenocarcinoma of the bladder. Br J Urol 1971, **43:** 4–15.

506 Torenbeek R, Lagendijk JH, Van Diest PJ, Bril H, Van De Molengraft FJJM, Meijer CJL. Value of a panel of antibodies to identify the primary origin of adenocarcinomas presenting as bladder carcinoma. Histopathology 1998, **32:** 20–27.

507 Val-Bernal JF, Garcia-Arranz MP. Diffuse scirrhous undifferentiated pleomorphic carcinoma of the urinary bladder. J Urol Pathol 1999, **10:** 207–218.

508 Wang HL, Lu DW, Yerian LM, Alsikafi N, Steinberg G, Hart J, Yang XJ. Immunohistochemical distinction between primary adenocarcinoma of the bladder and secondary colorectal adenocarcinoma. Am J Surg Pathol 2001, **25:** 1380–1387.

509 Ward AM. Glandular neoplasia within the urinary tract. The aetiology of adenocarcinoma of the urothelium with a review of the literature. I. Introduction. The origin of glandular epithelium

in the renal pelvis, ureter, and bladder. Virchows Arch [A] 1971, **352:** 296–311.

510 Wells M, Anderson K. Mucin histochemistry of cystitis glandularis and primary adenocarcinoma of the urinary bladder. Arch Pathol Lab Med 1985, **109:** 59–61.

511 Young RH, Eble JN. Unusual forms of carcinoma of the urinary bladder. Hum Pathol 1991, **22:** 948–965.

512 Young RH, Scully RE. Clear cell adenocarcinoma of the bladder and urethra. A report of three cases and review of the literature. Am J Surg Pathol 1985, **9:** 816–826.

513 Young RH, Scully RE. Nephrogenic adenoma. A report of 15 cases, review of the literature, and comparison with clear cell adenocarcinoma of the urinary tract. Am J Surg Pathol 1986, **10:** 268–275.

Small cell carcinoma and related neuroendocrine tumors

514 Abenoza P, Manivel C, Sibley RK. Adenocarcinoma with neuroendocrine differentiation of the urinary bladder. Clinicopathologic, immunohistochemical, and ultrastructural study. Arch Pathol Lab Med 1986, **110:** 1062–1066.

515 Ali SZ, Reuter VE, Zakowski MF. Small cell neuroendocrine carcinoma of the urinary bladder: A clinicopathologic study with emphasis on cytologic features. Cancer 1997, **79:** 356–361.

516 Blomjous CE, Vos W, de Voogt HJ, Van der Valk P, Meijer CJ. Small cell carcinoma of the urinary bladder. A clinicopathologic, morphometric, immunohistochemical, and ultrastructural study of 18 cases. Cancer 1989, **64:** 1347–1357.

517 Burgess NA, Lewis DC, Matthews PN. Primary carcinoid of the bladder. Br J Urol 1992, **69:** 213–214.

518 Colby TV. Carcinoid tumor of the bladder. A case report. Arch Pathol Lab Med 1980, **104:** 199–200.

519 Cramer SF, Aikawa M, Cebelin M. Neurosecretory granules in small cell invasive carcinoma of the urinary bladder. Cancer 1981, **47:** 724–730.

519a Evans AJ, Al-Maghrabi J, Tsihlias J, Lajoie G, Sweet JM, Chapman WB. Primary large cell neuroendocrine carcinoma of the urinary bladder. Arch Pathol Lab Med 2002, **126:** 1229–1232.

520 Grignon DJ, Ro JY, Ayala AG, Shum DT, Ordóñez NG, Logothetis CJ, Johnson DE, Mackay B. Small cell carcinoma of the urinary bladder. A clinicopathologic analysis of 22 cases. Cancer 1992, **69:** 527–536.

521 Hailemariam S, Gaspert A, Komminoth P, Tamboli P, Amin M. Primary, pure, large-cell neuroendocrine carcinoma of the urinary bladder. Mod Pathol 1998, **11:** 1016–1020.

522 Helpap B, Kloppel G. Neuroendocrine carcinomas of the prostrate and urinary bladder: a diagnostic and therapeutic challenge. Virchows Arch 2002, **440:** 241–248.

523 Iczkowski KA, Shanks JH, Allsbrook WC, Lopez-Beltran A, Pantazis CG, Collins TR, Wetherington RW, Bostwick DG. Small cell carcinoma of urinary bladder is differentiated from urothelial carcinoma by chromogranin expression, absence of CD44 variant 6 expression, a unique pattern of cytokeratin expression, and more intense gamma-enolase expression. Histopathology 1999, **35:** 150–156.

524 Mills SE, Wolfe JT III, Weiss MA, Swanson PE, Wick MR, Fowler JE Jr, Young RH. Small cell undifferentiated carcinoma of the urinary bladder. A light-microscopic, immunocytochemical, and ultrastructural study of 12 cases. Am J Surg Pathol 1987, **11:** 606–617.

525 Ordóñez NG, Khorsand J, Ayala AG, Sneige N. Oat cell carcinoma of the urinary tract. An immunohistochemical and electron microscopic study. Cancer 1986, **58:** 2519–2530.

526 Partanen S, Asikainen U. Oat cell carcinoma of the urinary bladder with ectopic adrenocorticotropic hormone production. Hum Pathol 1985, **16:** 313–315.

527 Podesta AH, True LD. Small cell carcinoma of the bladder. Report of five cases with immunohistochemistry and review of

the literature with evaluation of prognosis according to stage. Cancer 1989, **64**: 710–714.

528 Reyes CV, Soneru I. Small cell carcinoma of the urinary bladder with hypercalcemia. Cancer 1985, **56**: 2530–2533.

529 Walker BF, Someren A, Kennedy JC, Nicholas EM. Primary carcinoid tumor of the urinary bladder. Arch Pathol Lab Med 1992, **116**: 1217–1220.

Squamous cell carcinoma and related tumors

530 Bessette PL, Abell MR, Herwig KR. A clinicopathologic study of squamous cell carcinoma of the bladder. J Urol 1974, **112**: 66–67.

530a Botella E, Burgués O, Navarro S, Ramos D, Ferrer J, Gimeno C, Llombart-Bosch A. Warty carcinoma arising in condyloma acuminatum of urinary bladder: a case report. Int J Surg Pathol 2000, **8**: 253–259.

531 DeKock MLS, Anderson CK, Clark PB. Vesical leukoplakia progressing to squamous cell carcinoma in women. Br J Urol 1981, **53**: 316–317.

532 El-Bolkainy MN, Mokhtar NM, Ghoneim MA, Hussein MH. The impact of schistosomiasis on the pathology of bladder carcinoma. Cancer 1981, **48**: 2643–2648.

533 Faysal MH. Squamous cell carcinoma of the bladder. J Urol 1981, **126**: 598–599.

534 Ghoneim MA, Ashamalla A, Gaballa MA, Ibrahim EI. Cystectomy for carcinoma of the bilharzial bladder. 126 patients 10 years later. Br J Urol 1985, **57**: 303–305.

535 Gonzalez-Zulueta M, Shibata A, Ohneseit Pf, Spruck CH III, Busch C, Shamaa M, Elbaz M, Nichols PW, Gonzalgo ML, Malmström P-U, Jones PA. High frequency of chromosome 9p allelic loss and CDkN2 tumor-suppressor gene alterations in squamous cell carcinoma of the bladder. J Natl Cancer Inst 1995, **87**: 1383–1393.

536 Mahran MR, el-Baz M. Verrucous carcinoma of the bilharzial bladder. Impact of invasiveness on survival. Scand J Urol Nephrol 1993, **27**: 189–192.

537 Michal M, Sulc M, Mukensnabl P. Verrucous carcinoma of the urinary bladder associated with sebaceous and glandular differentiation. J Urol Pathol 1997, **6**: 153–158.

538 Newman DM, Brown JR, Jay AC, Pontius EE. Squamous cell carcinoma of the bladder. J Urol 1968, **100**: 470–473.

539 O'Flynn JD, Mullaney J. Leukoplakia of the bladder. A report on 20 cases, including 2 cases progressing to squamous cell carcinoma. Br J Urol 1967, **39**: 461–471.

540 Royce RK, Ackerman LV. Carcinoma of the bladder. J Urol 1951, **65**: 66–86.

541 Rundle JSH, Hart AJL, McGeorge A, Smith JS, Malcolm AJ, Smith PM. Squamous cell carcinoma of bladder. A review of 114 patients. Br J Urol 1982, **54**: 522–526.

542 Sakamoto N, Tsuneyoshi M, Enjoji M. Urinary bladder carcinoma with a neoplastic squamous component. A mapping study of 31 cases. Histopathology 1992, **21**: 135–141.

543 Sharfi AR, el Sir S, Beleil O. Squamous cell carcinoma of the urinary bladder. Br J Urol 1992, **69**: 369–371.

544 Vakar-Lopez F, Abrams J. Basaloid squamous cell carcinoma occurring in the urinary bladder. Arch Pathol Lab Med 2000, **124**: 455–459.

545 Wall RL, Clausen KP. Carcinoma of the urinary bladder in patients receiving cyclophosphamide. N Engl J Med 1975, **293**: 271–273.

Lymphoepithelioma-like carcinoma

546 Amin MB, Ro JY, Lee KM, Ordóñez NG, Dinney CP, Gulley ML, Ayala AG. Lymphoepithelioma-like carcinoma of the urinary bladder. Am J Surg Pathol 1994, **18**: 466–473.

547 Dinney CP, Ro JY, Babaian RJ, Johnson DE. Lymphoepithelioma of the bladder. A clinicopathological study of 3 cases. J Urol 1993, **149**: 840–841.

548 Lopez-Beltràn A, Luque RJ, Vicioso L, Anglada F, Requena MJ, Quintero A, Montironi R. Lymphoepithelioma-like carcinoma of the urinary bladder: a clinicopathologic study of 13 cases. Virchows Arch 2001, **438**: 552–557.

549 Young RH, Eble J. Lymphoepithelioma-like carcinoma of the urinary bladder. J Urol Pathol 1993, **1**: 63–68.

Sarcomatoid carcinoma and related tumors

550 Amir G, Rosenmann E. Osteoclast-like giant cell tumour of the urinary bladder. Histopathology 1990, **17**: 413–418.

551 Bannach B, Grignon D, Shum D. Sarcomatoid transitional cell carcinoma vs pseudosarcomatous stromal reaction in bladder carcinoma. An immunohistochemical study. J Urol Pathol 1993, **1**: 105–120.

552 Baschinsky DY, Chen JH, Vadmal MS, Lucas JG, Bahnson RR, Niemann TH. Carcinosarcoma of the urinary bladder—an aggressive tumor with diverse histogenesis: a clinicopathologic study of 4 cases and review of the literature. Arch Pathol Lab Med 2000, **124**: 1171–1178.

553 Bastacky S, Dhir R, Nangia AK, Brufsky A, Bahnson RR, Becich MJ. Choriocarcinomatous differentiation in a high-grade urothelial carcinoma of the urinary bladder: case report and literature review. J Urol Pathol 1997, **6**: 223–234.

554 Bloxham CA, Bennett MK, Robinson MC. Bladder carcinosarcomas. Three cases with diverse histogenesis. Histopathology 1990, **16**: 63–67.

555 Dirnhofer S, Koessler P, Ensinger C, Feichtinger H, Madersbacher S, Berger P. Production of trophoblastic hormones by transitional cell carcinoma of the bladder: Association to tumor stage and grade. Hum Pathol 1998, **29**: 377–382.

556 Foschini MP, Pilato F, D'Aversa C, Scarpellini F, Cristofori E, Zuccoli E, Montironi R. Sarcomatoid carcinoma of the urinary bladder. J Urol Pathol 1997, **6**: 139–152.

557 Fromowitz FB, Bard RH, Koss LG. The epithelial origin of a malignant mixed tumor of the bladder. Report of a case with long-term survival. J Urol 1984, **132**: 978–981.

558 Holtz F, Fox JE, Abell MR. Carcinosarcoma of the urinary bladder. Cancer 1972, **29**: 294–304.

559 Ikegami H, Iwasaki H, Ohjimi Y, Takeuchi T, Ariyoshi A, Kikuchi M. Sarcomatoid carcinoma of the urinary bladder: A clinicopathologic and immunohistochemical analysis of 14 patients. Hum Pathol 2000, **31**: 332–340.

560 Ishikawa J, Nishimura R, Maeda S, Hamami G, Sugiyama T, Kamidono S. Primary choriocarcinoma of the urinary bladder. Acta Pathol Jpn 1988, **38**: 113–120.

561 Jao W, Soto JM, Gould VE. Squamous carcinoma of bladder with pseudosarcomatous stroma. Arch Pathol 1975, **99**: 461–466.

562 Jones EC, Young RH. Myxoid and sclerosing sarcomatoid transitional cell carcinoma of the urinary bladder: A clinicopathologic and immunohistochemical study of 25 cases. Mod Pathol 1997, **10**: 908–916.

563 Kawamura J, Machida S, Yoshida O, Osek F, Imura H, Hattori M. Bladder carcinoma associated with ectopic production of gonadotropin. Cancer 1978, **42**: 2773–2780.

564 Kitazawa M, Kobayashi H, Ohnishi Y, Kimura K, Sakurai S, Sekine S. Giant cell tumor of the bladder associated with transitional cell carcinoma. J Urol 1985, **133**: 472–475.

565 Mazzucchelli L, Kraft R, Gerber H, Egger C, Studer UE, Zimmermann A. Carcinosarcoma of the urinary bladder. A distinct variant characterized by small cell undifferentiated carcinoma with neuroendocrine features. Virchows Arch [A] 1992, **421**: 477–483.

566 Mostofi FK, Sesterhenn IA, Davis CJ Jr. Human chorionic gonadotropin and other placental glycoprotein production in nongerminal tumors of genitourinary tract (abstract). Lab Invest 1988, **58**: 65A.

567 Murao T, Tanahashi T. Carcinosarcoma of the urinary bladder.

Report of a case with electron microscopy and review of the literature. Acta Pathol Jpn 1985, **35:** 981–988.

568 Obe JA, Rosen N, Koss LG. Primary choriocarcinoma of the urinary bladder. Report of a case with probable epithelial origin. Cancer 1983, **52:** 1405–1409.

569 Orsatti G, Corgan FJ, Goldberg SA. Carcinosarcoma of urothelial organs. Sequential involvement of urinary bladder, ureter, and renal pelvis. Urology 1993, **41:** 289–291.

570 Pearson JM, Banerjee SS, Haboubi NY. Two cases of pseudosarcomatous invasive transitional cell carcinoma of the urinary bladder mimicking malignant fibrous histiocytoma. Histopathology 1989, **15:** 93–96.

571 Perret L, Chaubert P, Hessler D, Guillou L. Primary heterologous carcinosarcoma (metaplastic carcinoma) of the urinary bladder: A clinicopathologic, immunohistochemical, and ultrastructural analysis of eight cases and a review of the literature. Cancer 1998, **82:** 1535–1549.

572 Reuter VE. Sarcomatoid lesions of the urogenital tract. Semin Diagn Pathol 1993, **10:** 188–201.

573 Sen SE, Malek RS, Farrow GM, Lieber MM. Sarcoma and carcinosarcoma of the bladder in adults. J Urol 1985, **133:** 29–30.

574 Shah VM, Newman J, Crocker J, Chapple CR, Collard MJ, O'Brien JM, Considine J. Ectopic β-human chorionic gonadotropin production by bladder urothelial neoplasia. Arch Pathol Lab Med 1986, **110:** 107–111.

575 Smith JA Jr, Herr HW, Middleton RG. Bladder carcinosarcoma. Histologic variation in metastatic lesions. J Urol 1983, **129:** 829–831.

576 Torenbeek R, Blomjous CE, deBruin PC, Newling DW, Meifer CJ. Sarcomatoid carcinoma of the urinary bladder. Clinicopathologic analysis of 18 cases with immunohistochemical and electron microscopic findings. Am J Surg Pathol 1994, **18:** 241–249.

577 Wick MR, Brown BA, Young RH, Mills SE. Spindle-cell proliferations of the urinary tract. An immunohistochemical study. Am J Surg Pathol 1988, **12:** 379–389.

578 Yokoyama S, Hayashida Y, Nagahama J, Nakayama I, Kashima K, Ogata J. Primary and metaplastic choriocarcinoma of the bladder. A report of two cases. Acta Cytol 1992, **36:** 176–182.

579 Young RH. Carcinosarcoma of the urinary bladder. Cancer 1987, **59:** 1333–1339.

580 Young RH, Wick MR. Transitional cell carcinoma of the urinary bladder with pseudosarcomatous stroma. Am J Clin Pathol 1988, **90:** 216–219.

581 Young RH, Wick MR, Mills SE. Sarcomatoid carcinoma of the urinary bladder. A clinicopathologic analysis of 12 cases and review of the literature. Am J Clin Pathol 1988, **90:** 653–661.

582 Zamecnik M. Urothelial carcinoma of the bladder with foci of yolk sac tumor. J Urol Pathol 1999, **11:** 161–170.

583 Zukerberg LR, Armin AR, Pisharodi L, Young RH. Transitional cell carcinoma of the urinary bladder with osteoclast-type giant cells. A report of two cases and review of the literature. Histopathology 1990, **17:** 407–411.

Other malignant tumors

584 Ainsworth AM, Clark WH Jr, Mastrangelo M, Conger KB. Primary malignant melanoma of the urinary bladder. Cancer 1976, **37:** 1928–1936.

585 Anichkov NM, Nikonov AA. Primary malignant melanomas of the bladder. J Urol 1982, **128:** 813–815.

586 Banerjee SS, Eyden BP, McVey RJ, Bryden AA, Clarke NW. Primary peripheral primitive neuroectodermal tumour of urinary bladder. Histopathology 1997, **30:** 486–490.

587 Bates AW, Baithun SI. Secondary neoplasms of the bladder are histological mimics of nontransitional cell primary tumours: clinicopatholgical and histological features of 282 cases. Histopathology 2000, **36:** 32–40.

587a Bates AW, Baithun SI. The significance of secondary neoplasms

of the urinary and male genital tract. Virchows Arch 2002, **40:** 640–647.

588 Berenson RJ, Flynn S, Freiha FS, Kempson RL, Torti FM. Primary osteogenic sarcoma of the bladder. Case report and review of the literature. Cancer 1986, **57:** 350–355.

589 Bocian JJ, Flam MS, Mendoza CA. Hodgkin's disease involving the urinary bladder diagnosed by urinary cytology. A case report. Cancer 1982, **50:** 2482–2485.

590 Carter RL, McCarthy KP, al-Sam SZ, Monaghan P, Agrawal M, McElwain TJ. Malignant rhabdoid tumour of the bladder with immunohistochemical and ultrastructural evidence suggesting histiocytic origin. Histopathology 1989, **14:** 179–190.

591 Chiang KS, Lamki N, Athey PA. Metastasis to the bladder from pancreatic adenocarcinoma presenting with hematuria. Urol Radiol 1992, **13:** 187–189.

592 De Pinieux G, Chatelain D, Vieillefond A, Arrivets P, de Saint Maur PP. Clear cell sarcoma of tendons and aponeuroses presenting as a bladder mass: a case report. J Urol Pathol 1998, **9:** 239–246.

593 Desai S. Primary primitive neuroectodermal tumour of the urinary bladder. Histopathology 1998, **32:** 477–478.

594 Goldstein AG. Metastatic carcinoma to the bladder. J Urol 1967, **98:** 209–215.

595 Goodman AJ, Greaney MG. Malignant fibrous histiocytoma of the bladder. Br J Urol 1985, **57:** 106–107.

596 Haid M, Ignatoff J, Khandekar JD, Graham J, Holland J. Urinary bladder metastases from breast carcinoma. Cancer 1980, **46:** 229–232.

597 Harris M, Eyden BP, Joglekar VM. Rhabdoid tumour of the bladder. A histological, ultrastructural and immunohistochemical study. Histopathology 1987, **11:** 1083–1092.

598 Hays DM, Raney RB, Lawrence W, Soule EH, Gehan EA, Tefft M. Bladder and prostatic tumors in the Intergroup Rhabdomyosarcoma Study (IRS-1). Results of therapy. Cancer 1982, **50:** 1472–1482.

599 Helpap B. Nonepithelial neoplasms of the urinary bladder. Virchows Arch 2001, **439:** 497–503.

600 Henriksen OB, Mogensen P, Engelholm AJ. Inflammatory fibrous histiocytoma of the urinary bladder. Clinicopathological report of a case. Acta Pathol Microbiol Immunol Scand [A] 1982, **90:** 333–337.

601 Ho DS, Patterson AL, Orozco RE, Murphy WM. Extramedullary plasmacytoma of the bladder. Case report and review of the literature. J Urol 1993, **150:** 473–474.

602 Kempton CL, Kurtin PJ, Inwards DJ, Wollan P, Bostwick DG. Malignant lymphoma of the bladder: Evidence from 36 cases that low-grade lymphoma of the MALT-type is the most common primary bladder lymphoma. Am J Surg Pathol 1997, **21:** 1324–1333.

603 Kinoshita T, Nakamura Y, Kinoshita M, Fukuda S, Nakashima H, Hashimoto T. Bilateral cystic nephroblastomas and botryoid sarcoma in a child with Dandy-Walker syndrome. Arch Pathol Lab Med 1986, **110:** 150–152.

604 Kojima T, Tanaka T, Yoshimi N, Mori H. Primary malignant melanoma of the urinary bladder. Arch Pathol Lab Med 1992, **116:** 1213–1216.

605 Krumerman MS, Katatikarn V. Rhabdomyosarcoma of the urinary bladder with intraepithelial spread in an adult. Arch Pathol Lab Med 1976, **100:** 395–397.

606 Kunze E, Theuring F, Kruger G. Primary mesenchymal tumors of the urinary bladder. A histological and immunohistochemical study of 30 cases. Pathol Res Pract 1994, **190:** 311–332.

607 Lasota J, Carlson JA, Miettinen M. Spindle cell tumor of urinary bladder serosa with phenotypic and genotypic features of gastrointestinal stromal tumor. Arch Pathol Lab Med 2000, **124:** 894–897.

608 Leuschner I, Harms D, Mattke A, Koscielniak E, Treuner J. Rhabdomyosarcoma of the urinary bladder and vagina:

a clinicopathologic study with emphasis on recurrent disease: a report from the Kiel Pediatric Tumor Registry and the German CWS study. Am J Surg Pathol 2001, **25**: 856–864.

609 McBride JA, Ro JY, Hicks J, Ordóñez NG, Raney RB, Ayalia AG. Malignant rhabdoid tumor of the bladder in an adolescent. Case report and discussion of extrarenal rhabdoid tumor. J Urol Pathol 1994, **2**: 255–264.

610 Maghrabi JA, Reid SK, Jewett M, Gospdarowicz M, Wells W, Banerjee D. Primary low-grade B-cell lymphoma of mucosa-associated lymphoid tissue type arising in the urinary bladder: report of 4 cases with molecular genetic analysis. Arch Pathol Lab Med 2001, **125**: 332–336.

611 Martin SA, Sears DL, Sebo TJ, Lohse CM, Cheville JC. Smooth muscle neoplasms of the urinary bladder: A clinicopathologic comparison of leiomyoma and leiomyosarcoma. Am J Surg Pathol 2002, **26**: 292–300.

612 Meyer JE. Metastatic melanoma of the urinary bladder. Cancer 1974, **34**: 1822–1824.

613 Miettinen M. Rhabdomyosarcoma in patients older than 40 years of age. Cancer 1988, **62**: 2060–2065.

614 Mills E, Bova GS, Wick MR, Young RH. Leiomyosarcoma of the urinary bladder. A clinicopathologic and immunohistochemical study of 15 cases. Am J Surg Pathol 1989, **13**: 480–489.

615 Mourad WA, Khalil S, Radwi A, Peracha A, Ezzat A. Primary T-cell lymphoma of the urinary bladder. Am J Surg Pathol 1998, **22**: 373–377.

616 Mourad WA, Mackay B, Ordóñez NG, Ro JY, Swanson DA. Clear cell melanoma of the bladder. Ultrastruct Pathol 1993, **17**: 463–468.

617 Oesterling JE, Epstein JI, Brendler CB. Myxoid malignant fibrous histiocytoma of the bladder. Cancer 1990, **66**: 1836–1842.

618 Ohsawa M, Aozasa K, Horiuchi K, Kanamaru A. Malignant lymphoma of bladder. Report of three cases and review of the literature. Cancer 1993, **72**: 1969–1974.

619 Pawade J, Banerjee SS, Harris M, Isaacson P, Wright D. Lymphomas of mucosa-associated lymphoid tissue arising in the urinary bladder. Histopathology 1993, **23**: 147–151.

620 Perez-Mesa C, Pickren JW, Woodruff MN, Mohallatee A. Metastatic carcinoma of the urinary bladder from primary tumors in the mammary gland of female patients. Surg Gynecol Obstet 1965, **121**: 813–818.

621 Sim SJ, Ro JY, Ordonez NG, Park YW, Kee KH, Ayala AG. Metastatic renal cell carcinoma to the bladder: A clinicopathologic and immunohistochemical study. Mod Pathol 1999, **12**: 351–355.

622 Swartz DA, Johnson DE, Ayala AG, Watkins DL. Bladder leiomyosarcoma. A review of 10 cases with 5-year followup. J Urol 1985, **133**: 200–202.

623 Taylor G, Jordan M, Churchill B, Mancer K. Yolk sac tumor of the bladder. J Urol 1983, **129**: 591–594.

624 Terada Y, Saito I, Morohoshi T, Niijima T. Malignant mesenchymoma of the bladder. Cancer 1987, **60**: 858–863.

625 Weide R, Pfluger KH, Gorg C, Rohrmoser L, Neumann K, Havemann K. Multiple myeloma of the bladder and vagina. Cancer 1990, **66**: 989–991.

626 Yang C, Motteram R, Sandeman TF. Extramedullary plasmacytoma of the bladder. A case report and review of literature. Cancer 1982, **50**: 146–149.

627 Young RH, Johnston WH. Serous adenocarcinoma of the uterus metastatic to the urinary bladder mimicking primary bladder neoplasia. A report of a case. Am J Surg Pathol 1990, **14**: 877–880.

628 Young RH, Proppe KH, Dickersin GR, Scully RE. Myxoid leiomyosarcoma of the urinary bladder. Arch Pathol Lab Med 1987, **111**: 359–362.

629 Young RH, Rosenberg AE. Osteosarcoma of the urinary bladder. Report of a case and review of the literature. Cancer 1987, **59**: 174–178.

18 Male reproductive system

Prostate and seminal vesicles
Testis
Testicular adnexa
Penis and scrotum

Prostate and seminal vesicles

Prostate

Normal anatomy

The prostate is a pear-shaped glandular organ that weighs up to 20 g in the normal adult male and that depends for its differentiation and subsequent growth on androgenic hormones synthesized in the testis, acting through a poorly understood mesenchymal–epithelial interaction.[10] Traditionally, it has been divided into anterior, middle, posterior, and two lateral lobes by drawing divergent lines from the centrally located urethra. A division that correlates better with the physiologic and pathologic features of the organ is into an *inner (periurethral)* and an *outer (cortical)* zone. The inner zone is the primary site for nodular hyperplasia (and the rare carcinomas arising from large ducts), whereas the outer zone is the site of predilection for the ordinary adenocarcinoma arising from peripheral ducts and acini.[4,14] A modification of this scheme divides the prostate into peripheral, central, transitional, and periurethral gland regions.[17] According to this system, the transitional and periurethral regions are the exclusive sites of origin of nodular hyperplasia, whereas the peripheral zone is the one most susceptible to prostatitis and carcinoma.

The prostate is enveloped by a fibromuscular layer usually referred to as a capsule, but it has been pointed out that this is not a well-defined anatomic structure with constant features.[3] It is more evident along the base of the organ and less so along the anterior and apical surfaces.

The glandular component of the organ is composed of acini and ducts, the latter subdivided into large (primary, major, excretory) and peripheral (secondary, minor). Both acini and ducts contain secretory cells, basal cells, and scattered neuroendocrine cells. The secretory cells, which are located in the luminal side of the gland, contribute a wide variety of products to the seminal fluid. They produce prostatic acid phosphatase (PAP) and prostate-specific antigen (PSA), both of which can be readily identified immunohistochemically and have been proved of great diagnostic utility because of their organ-related specificity. PSA is a glycoprotein that has been identified as a kallikrein-like protease.[1] Secretory cells also coexpress various keratins and vimentin.[1,16] The keratins do not include high-molecular-weight types such as 34βF12, a fact of diagnostic significance.

The normal prostatic secretion is a neutral mucosubstance (a feature of some diagnostic significance because most adenocarcinomas secrete a mixture of acidic and neutral mucins). However, on occasion one encounters scattered columnar mucin-secreting cells in non-neoplastic prostatic epithelium, particularly in areas of atrophy.[1,12,20]

The complex secretory mechanism of normal prostatic glands is severely altered in neoplastic conditions, as evidenced through morphologic, histochemical, and immunohistochemical techniques.[9]

The basal cells form a thin continuous layer that separates the luminal secretory cells from the basement membrane. They characteristically contain keratins 34 βE12, CK8.12, and 312 C8-1 and stain strongly for antikeratin antibody 903, a fact that has been exploited in the differential diagnosis between well-differentiated carcinomas (in which basal cells are absent) and benign conditions that simulate it (in which they are generally present, although sometimes in a discontinuous fashion). Under normal conditions these basal cells do not have the phenotype of myoepithelial cells, in the sense that they lack immunoreactivity for S-100 protein or smooth muscle actin.[13,18,21] However, they can be viewed as being equivalent to the myoepithelial cells of the breast and other glandular organs. Support for this interpretation derives from the fact that they can undergo clearcut myoepithelial metaplasia in conditions such as sclerosing adenosis (see p. 1380). They do not express PSA or PAP, but they have been shown to exhibit strong immunoreactivity for androgen receptors focally.[5,8] They are thought to represent a multipotential population that gives rise to all epithelial lineages present in the normal, hyperplastic, and neoplastic prostate.[7]

The neuroendocrine cells express chromogranin A and B, secretogranin II, and various peptide hormones such as somatostatin, calcitonin, and bombesin[11,19]; they coexpress PSA, suggesting a common origin with the secretory cells.[2] However, they are negative for androgen receptors.[6]

The large prostatic ducts are lined by transitional epithelium that is continuous and indistinguishable from that lining the prostatic urethra. In contrast to bladder epithelium, its surface does not display umbrella cells but rather a single layer of columnar cells that are immunoreactive for PSA and PAP. On occasion, this epithelium undergoes squamous metaplastic changes; these were very common at the time that estrogen therapy was widely employed for prostatic carcinoma.[15]

The prostatic stroma is notable because of its large content of smooth muscle fibers, whose function is to squeeze out the prostatic secretion when properly stimulated; it has been pointed out that the presence of this muscular stroma duplicates the function of myoepithelial cells in other organs, such as breast, and makes the presence of myoepithelial cells in the prostate superfluous. Prostatic stromal cells have been found to contain androgen receptors.

Peripheral nerves are evenly distributed in the apex, mid gland, and base[22]; they are of importance to pathologists because of the high frequency with which the loose connective space that surrounds them (formerly thought to represent perineural lymph vessels) is involved by adenocarcinomas of this organ.

The prostatic lymph vessels drain into the pelvic lymph nodes and from there into the retroperitoneal chain.

Ectopia

Ectopia of prostatic tissue is a very rare event, save for the benign urethral polyps discussed in Chapter 17B. It has been described in the bladder, root of the penis, epididymis, testis, seminal vesicle, retrovesical space, submucosa of the anal canal, pericolic fat/pararectal space, and spleen.[23]

Nodular hyperplasia

Benign prostatic hypertrophy is the usual name applied to a common benign disorder of the prostate that, when extensive, results in varying degrees of urinary obstruction, sometimes requiring surgical intervention. The term *nodular hyperplasia*, as proposed by Moore[44] in his classic study, is a more exact designation. The disease represents a nodular enlargement of the gland caused by hyperplasia of both glandular and stromal components. This results in an increase in the weight of the organ well beyond the 20 g regarded as normal for adult individuals. The clinical incidence of this disease is only 8% during the fourth decade, but it reaches 50% in the fifth decade and 75% in the eighth decade. It has been estimated that the process begins before the age of 30 and that its doubling time progressively increases from 4.3 years in the early stage (third to fifth decade) to over 100 years in the late stage (patients beyond 70 years old).[28]

No predisposing or protecting factors (other than castration) have been identified. As Badenoch[26] put it, nodular hyperplasia of the prostate occurs "in saints and sinners, in fat men and thin, in parsons with large families and monks with none, in postmen and prime ministers." It has been established that prostatic nodular hyperplasia occurs only in individuals with intact testes and that it is an androgen-dependent disorder. Other possible contributing factors have been proposed, such as inflammation-induced release of platelet-derived growth factor[37] and human papilloma virus,[42] but it is difficult to escape from the conclusion that the disease is fundamentally the consequence of a hormonal imbalance which leads to an alteration of the delicate balance that exists both in the epithelium and the stroma between cell death and proliferation.[29,41] Specifically, it has been suggested that nodular hyperplasia may result from an initial activation of mesenchymal clones with embryonal functions that stimulate development of the glandular component.[24] In turn, this may result from dihydrotestosterone accumulation within the gland, resulting from decreased catabolism of the molecule and enhanced intracellular binding.[57] A peculiar immunohistochemical finding that may throw some light on this issue is the demonstration that p27 protein (a negative regulator of the cell cycle) is prominently expressed in the epithelial and stromal cells of the normal prostate but essentially negative in nodular hyperplasia.[32]

At autopsy the average weight of a prostate gland affected by nodular hyperplasia is 33 g ± 16 g. Specimens obtained surgically weigh 100 g on average, but on rare occasions weights of over 800 g have been recorded. Grossly, variously sized nodules with a gray to yellow color and a granular appearance are seen projecting above the cut surface (Fig. 18.1).

A cross section of an entire gland with early involvement clearly shows that nodular hyperplasia usually begins in the "inner" gland, i.e., the portions around the urethra and specifically where the ejaculatory ducts enter the urethra, which are also referred to as the periurethral and transitional zones. This fact supports the interpretation that this portion of the gland reacts differently to hormonal stimuli than the outer portion. In most instances the nodules congregate on both sides of the urethra, resulting in so-called *lateral lobe hyperplasia*. In others the disease results in a *midline dorsal nodule* at the bladder neck protruding into the bladder lumen. With increased growth, the periphery of the organ is pushed aside and compressed. In only about 5% will a focal lesion of nodular hyperplasia be found in the peripheral zone of the organ.[40,46,47,55]

Microscopically, the earliest change is a stromal proliferation about small sinusoidal spaces in the periurethral regions and, to a lesser degree, in the periductal and intralobular areas (Fig. 18.2). This stromal proliferation (which in the periductal areas may have a concentric or an eccentric quality) contains more smooth muscle and less elastic tissue than the normal stroma. This is

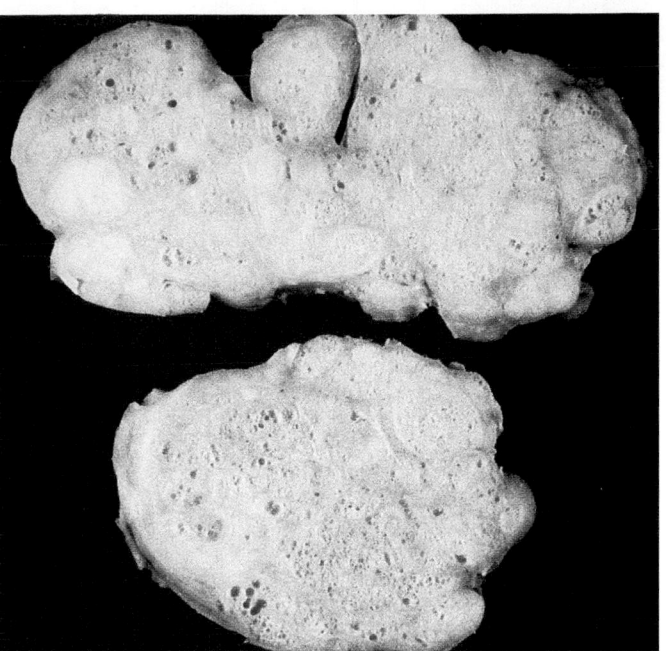

Fig. 18.1 Gross appearance of nodular hyperplasia in material obtained from suprapubic prostatectomy. Note the multinodular appearance and the admixture of solid and microcystic areas.

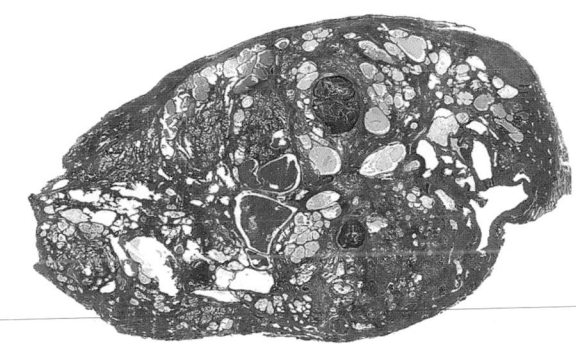

Fig. 18.2 Whole mount of nodular hyperplasia of prostate, showing nodular configuration and cystic changes.

followed by hyperplasia of the glandular component, so in the well-developed disease the nodules are composed of varying proportions of both elements.[49] These proportions are somewhat different in patients with symptomatic and those with asymptomatic nodular hyperplasia.[52] The glands are dilated or even cystic and often contain an inspissated secretion of glycoproteic nature (corpora amylacea), which is sometimes calcified.[53] The epithelium ranges from flat to columnar, sometimes facing each other in the same gland ("functional polarization"); the cytoplasm is pale, and the nuclei are regular and centrally located (Fig. 18.3). The nucleoli are inconspicuous. Papillary infoldings are common. A continuous basal cell layer is seen immediately above a well-developed basement membrane.

Small clusters of lymphocytes are common in the interstitium and around the ducts. They are probably the

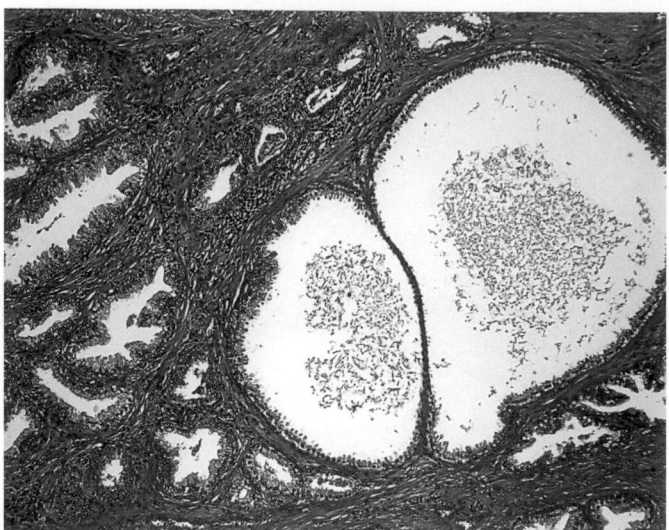

Fig. 18.3 Nodular hyperplasia of prostate, with cystic dilatation of the glands. Characteristically, the epithelium is tall on one side and flattened on the other.

result rather than the cause of the hyperplasia[54]; a diagnosis of chronic prostatitis is not warranted because of their mere presence.

Many morphologic variations of this basic theme exist, some of them resulting from the overgrowth of one component over the other and others from the emergence of distinctive patterns. Interestingly, many of the latter bear a notable resemblance to lesions of the breast (another organ characterized by a hormonally driven mesenchymal–epithelial interaction) and have been named accordingly. They include sclerosing adenosis (see p. 1380), fibroadenoma-like and phyllodes tumor-like hyperplasia[25,39] (adenomatoid tumor[31]), leiomyoma-like and fibromyxoid nodules, and the presence of bizarre cells in the stroma.[34,58]

It should be pointed out that there is little relation between a diagnosis of nodular hyperplasia made on a biopsy specimen and either the weight of the gland or the score system used to measure urinary obstructive symptoms.[55a]

The conventional treatment for nodular hyperplasia is surgical.[30] The involved area may be excised by various techniques, of which transurethral resection (TUR) and suprapubic prostatectomy are the most common.[27,56] It should be realized that these procedures remove *only the newly formed nodules*. The compressed peripheral portions of the gland remain; these expand by stromal growth to surround the prostatic urethra and may be the source of recurrent hyperplasia.[44] Not surprisingly, the chance of a patient undergoing a second operation for this disorder is substantially higher after a TUR than an open prostatectomy.[50] Adenocarcinoma can also develop in the residual gland many years after surgery.[51] Medical alternatives to surgery include various medications aimed at blocking the actions of androgens by prevent-

ing their secretion or their conversion to their tissue active form or at relaxing the stromal muscle cells.[33,36,38,45,47,48] Among these, the drug most widely used is finasteride, which works by inhibiting 5-α reductase, the enzyme that converts testosterone to the potent androgen dihydrotestosterone. The morphologic changes induced by this compound in the prostate are relatively minor and nonspecific. They include focal atrophy, increase in the stromal–epithelial ratio, squamous metaplasia, and transitional metaplasia.[35,43]

Infarct

Infarct of the prostate occurs predominantly in large prostates that exhibit nodular hyperplasia.[61] Its reported incidence is probably related to the thoroughness of the microscopic examination. In carefully studied glands, it has been found to be present in 18% to 25% of the cases.[62] It has been traditionally reported in TUR specimens, but it can also be recognized in prostatic needle biopsies.[61] The size and number of the infarcts are directly related to the degree of prostatic hyperplasia. True infarcts occurring on a vascular basis should be distinguished from necrotic changes involving a gland or group of glands but sparing the stroma, a change sometimes seen in nodular hyperplasia.

The mechanism of infarct is unknown but may be related to the presence of prostatic infection or trauma resulting from an indwelling catheter, cystitis, or prostatitis, all of which may result in thrombosis of the intraprostatic portion of the urethral arteries.[59]

Grossly, prostatic infarcts vary in size from a few millimeters up to 5 cm. They are speckled, grayish yellow, and often contain streaks of blood. The peripheral margins are usually sharp and hemorrhagic and may impinge on the urethra (Fig. 18.4). Microscopically, the infarcts are of ischemic type, with sharply outlined areas of coagulative necrosis involving glands *and stroma*. Prominent squamous metaplasia may develop in the ducts at the periphery of the infarct, a change that should not be confused with squamous cell carcinoma (Fig. 18.5). This metaplastic change is confined to the expanded ducts, keratinizes only rarely, and does not extend to the surrounding prostatic tissue.[63] It should be remembered that true squamous cell carcinomas of the prostate are exceptionally rare (see p. 1376).

Most prostatic infarcts are clinically silent. Occasionally, they cause acute urinary retention because of the accompanying edema.[60] Since they are often adjacent to the urethra, gross hematuria can also occur. Diffuse oozing of blood from the overlying mucosa may be seen cystoscopically. They may cause serum elevation of PAP and PSA.[64] Removal of the infarcted area promptly returns these levels to normal; if it does not, further workup is indicated.

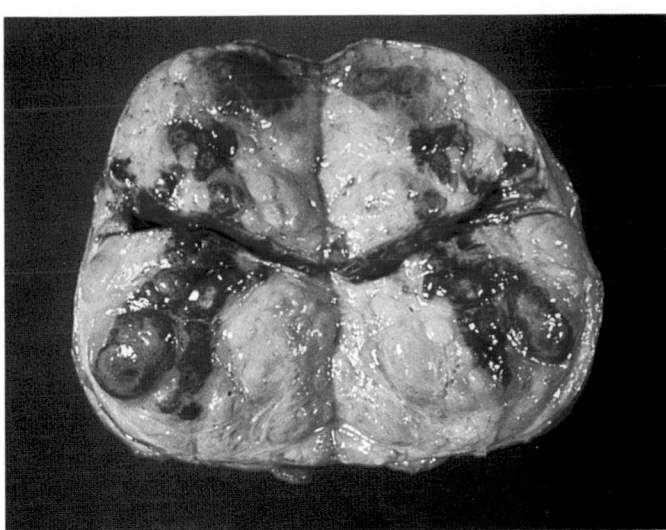

Fig. 18.4 Gross appearance of infarct of prostate. The lesion has a bright red color and bulges on the cut surface. Nodular hyperplasia is also present.

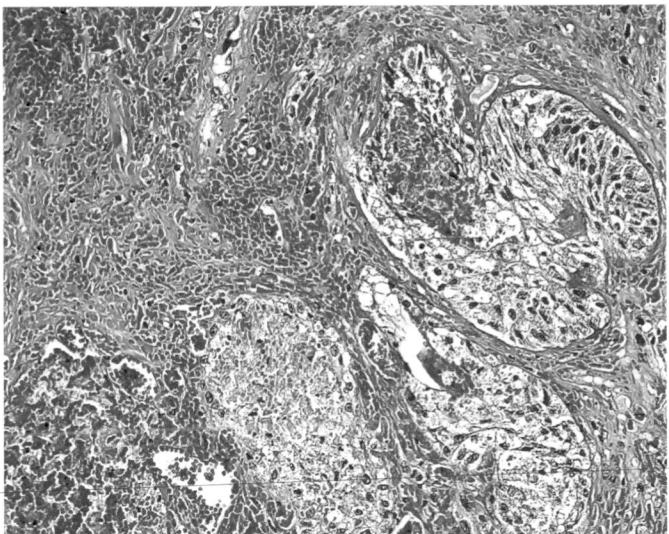

Fig. 18.5 Prominent metaplastic changes at the edge of a prostatic infarct. These are sometimes overdiagnosed as carcinoma.

Prostatitis

Acute prostatitis is rarely seen in surgical specimens. *Chronic prostatitis* is more common, but it is important to distinguish the true infectious processes of this organ from the inconsequential mononuclear infiltrates often seen accompanying nodular hyperplasia (see p. 1362). The latter phenomenon is sometimes dignified by terms such as "chronic nonbacterial prostatitis" or "lymphocytic prostatitis."[65,69] In bacterial prostatitis, the route of infection remains uncertain in most cases. Some cases follow gonococcal or nongonococcal urethritis, and others result from periurethral infection associated with indwelling urethral catheterization. Gram-positive

bacteria are the most common pathogens found in cultures from prostatic fluid.[66,68]

Microscopically, prostatitis usually appears as a *localized* process involving a small number of ducts or acini. The lumina are distended and filled with secretion mixed with inflammatory cells, among which neutrophils predominate. The stromal component, on the other hand, is mainly mononuclear and is composed of a mixture of lymphocytes, plasma cells, and histiocytes. In the presence of a monotonous infiltration of mature lymphocytes throughout the organ, the alternative diagnosis of involvement by chronic lymphocytic leukemia should be considered.

Prostatitis is often accompanied by elevation of serum PSA, which should return quickly to normal following successful antibiotic treatment.[67,70]

Abscess

In the past, the majority of prostatic abscesses resulted from gonorrhea. At present, most have an obstructive etiology and are the manifestation of secondary infection of the prostate from an infected pool of residual urine.[73] *Escherichia coli* is the organism usually responsible. In one series,[74] 36% presented with acute urinary retention and 31% with perineal or suprapubic pain. Prostatic fluctuation on digital rectal examination is the most characteristic sign, transrectal ultrasound is the most reliable diagnostic method, and transurethral drainage under antibiotic coverage is the treatment of choice.[71,72]

Tuberculosis and BCG-induced granulomas

The prostate is the organ most commonly involved in tuberculosis of the male genital system. Of 105 autopsy cases included in the classic study by Auerbach,[75] the prostate was involved in 100, and in 35 of the 105, it was the sole site in the system. In most cases, the infection is the result of hematogenous spread from the lungs (or, less often, from the skeletal system), but it may also result from direct invasion from the urethra.[77]

Early tuberculous lesions in the prostate are seldom detected on palpation. It is only when the disease is advanced that enlargement occurs and fluctuant, tender zones may be felt. Grossly, the lesions are usually bilateral. Confluent caseous zones occur with liquefaction and cavitation, until finally the prostate becomes an enlarged mass with multiple cavities. It may perforate into the urethra and extend into the urinary bladder.[76] With still further spread, sinus tracts may form into the rectum, perineum, and peritoneal cavity. Healing with calcification may supervene, a change detectable by radiographic examination. In the late stages, the prostate becomes shrunken, fibrotic, and hard, to the point that it may simulate carcinoma on palpation.

Microscopically, the initial lesion is in the stroma but quickly spreads to the acini. Well-developed lesions show confluent foci of caseation with incomplete fibrous encapsulation. There is little tendency for the formation of typical tubercles.

Patients treated with intravesical bacillus Calmette–Guerin (BCG) for bladder carcinoma may develop granulomas in the prostate similar to those seen more often in the bladder itself (see Chapter 17).[76] These granulomas may be of noncaseating or caseating type.[78] They may be located along the periurethral or transitional zone or involve the gland diffusely. Stains for acid-fast organisms are usually negative, although occasionally a few organisms are visualized.

Other specific infections

The prostate can be involved by blastomycosis,[81] coccidioidomycosis,[83,86] actinomycosis,[84] cryptococcosis,[80,87,89,90] histoplasmosis,[94] aspergillosis,[82] and candidiasis.[88,93] Many of these infections occur in the setting of immunosuppression resulting from AIDS or other disorders.[80,89,94]

Chlamydia trachomatis[91] and *Trichomonas vaginalis*[85] have been identified in the prostate gland, but their possible role as etiologic agents of prostatitis remains to be determined. The *Chlamydia* organism can be detected in tissue by immunohistochemical and in situ hybridization techniques.[79,92]

Granulomatous prostatitis

The term *granulomatous prostatitis*, sometimes preceded by qualifiers such as *nonspecific* or *idiopathic*, is applied to a rare prostatic disorder thought to represent an initially immune-mediated process accompanied by a reaction to the prostatic secretions released from obstructed ducts.[96,100] Most cases occur in glands affected by nodular hyperplasia in patients over 50 years of age. The clinical triad of high fever, symptoms of prostatitis, and a hard prostate on palpation is present in one fifth of cases and

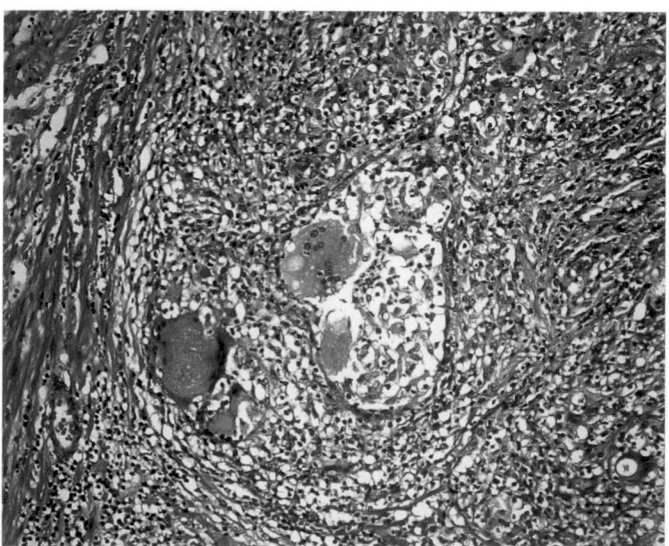

Fig. 18.6 Granulomatous prostatitis. The inflammatory infiltrate, which contains scattered multinucleated cells, is characteristically centered on a prostatic acinus.

should suggest the diagnosis.[97] A preoperative diagnosis of carcinoma is made in about 30% of cases because of the firmness of the lesion, caused by the dense fibrosis.

Grossly, the gland is firm to stony hard. The cut surface shows obliteration of the architecture, with formation of yellow granular nodules. Microscopically, large nodular aggregates of histiocytes, epithelioid cells, lymphocytes, and plasma cells are seen. Characteristically, these granuloma-like formations are centered in the lobules (Fig. 18.6). A tubercle-like reaction with multinucleated giant cells, as well as collections of neutrophils, eosinophils, and detritus within the ducts, also may be seen. Microorganisms and caseation necrosis are absent. The microscopic changes can simulate carcinoma in needle biopsy specimens.[98] Immunohistochemical studies have shown a concentration of T cells in and around damaged ducts and glands[95] and strong reactivity for lysozyme in the histiocytes.[99]

Prostatitis with eosinophils

Most cases of prostatitis associated with an eosinophilic infiltrate, sometimes intense, belong to one of the following categories[101,111]:

1 **(Nonspecific) granulomatous prostatitis** similar in all regards to the type described previously but for the presence of eosinophils diffusely admixed with the other inflammatory components.

2 **Eosinophilic prostatitis** (allergic prostatitis, allergic granuloma of prostate), characterized by small stellate necrobiotic nodules surrounded by palisading epithelioid histiocytes and eosinophils, resembling rheumatoid nodules.[106,109] Vasculitis may be found. Patients often have a history of allergy and asthma and usually exhibit peripheral eosinophilia; in some cases, systemic vasculitis is present. Elevation of serum PSA levels may occur in this disorder.[105]

3 **Iatrogenic granulomas**, a morphologically similar condition in patients lacking these systemic symptoms that develops after a surgical procedure to the area, usually a TUR but sometimes a prostatic needle biopsy.[101,102,104,107] The interval between the surgical procedure and the appearance of the prostatitis ranges from less than 1 month to several years; eosinophils are more numerous when this interval is shorter. The granulomas may represent a reaction to collagen altered as a result of the surgery or to the metal deposition from the instruments themselves.[103] Some of these granulomas are elongated and tortuous, whereas others are wedge shaped, with their base facing the cauterized tissue.[101,108]

4 A **parasitic infestation** resulting from metazoa.[110]

Other inflammations

Malakoplakia can involve the prostate, usually in association with bladder disease[115,116] (see Chapter 17). As in the latter site, it should be viewed as a peculiar form of tissue reaction to bacterial infection. The infiltrate is usually located around prostatic ducts and has a mixed composition. A similar condition but lacking Michaelis–Gutmann bodies has been described as **nodular histiocytic prostatitis**.[114]

Malakoplakia may simulate sonographically prostatic carcinoma.[112] It can also be seen in prostates having carcinoma in other portions of the gland.[117]

Vasculitis of either necrotizing, fibrinoid, or granulomatous type can involve the prostate as an isolated event.[118,119]

Hair granuloma, described exceptionally in TUR specimens, is thought to result from hair from the perineal area being introduced into the prostate by an earlier perineal prostatic needle biopsy.[113]

Calculi

Prostatic calculi are seen in about 7% of prostates with nodular hyperplasia.[120] They should be distinguished from those found in the prostatic urethra, which may have their origin in the bladder, ureter, or renal pelvis.

The corpora amylacea seen in glands with nodular hyperplasia may act as the nucleus for stone formation as a result of improper drainage, infection of the acini, and calcium deposition. Blood clots, epithelial detritus, and bacteria are also present in the stone nucleus. The main inorganic elements are phosphated salts (calcium, magnesium, aminomagnesium, potassium), calcium carbonate, and calcium oxalate.

Because of their extreme hardness, large prostatic calculi may be erroneously diagnosed as carcinoma on palpation. They are radiopaque and easily detectable in plain x-rays. If they are extremely large and numerous, a prostatectomy may be required.

Tumorlike conditions of prostate and prostatic urethra

Postoperative spindle cell nodules resembling sarcomas can develop as a result of an exuberant stromal reaction after a TUR procedure, the interval ranging from a few weeks to several months.[131,138] They present as friable reddish nodules in the prostatic bed and may be the source of postoperative bleeding. The superficial portion looks like granulation tissue, but the deep areas simulate sarcoma (particularly leiomyosarcoma) because of their extreme cellularity and high mitotic activity (Figs 18.7 and 18.8). Intersecting fascicles of spindle cells with extravasated red blood cells between are seen, resulting in a picture vaguely reminiscent of Kaposi's sarcoma. The proliferating cells, which in all likelihood are myofibroblastic, show immunohistochemically a strong and

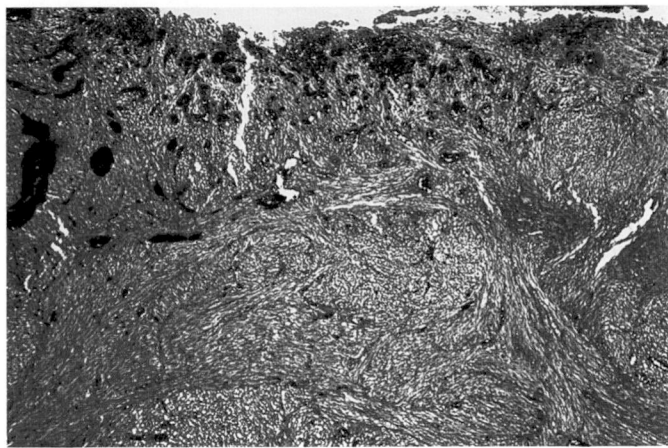

Fig. 18.7 Low-power appearance of a postoperative spindle cell nodule. The surface is ulcerated and covered by granulation tissue.

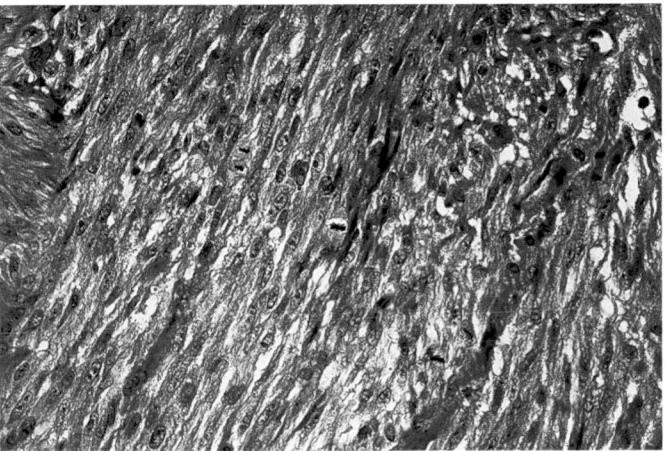

Fig. 18.8 Postoperative spindle cell nodule. The lesion is hypercellular, relatively monomorphic, and accompanied by high mitotic activity.

unexpected reactivity for keratin. They also express keratin and (inconstantly) actin and are EMA negative (Fig. 18.9). The temporal relationship of these changes with a surgical procedure and their benign evolution support a reactive pathogenesis.[138]

Inflammatory pseudotumor (pseudosarcomatous fibromyxoid tumor), similar to that more commonly seen in the bladder (see Chapter 17B), is sometimes seen in the prostate. Microscopically there is a proliferation of spindle cells of myoid (myofibroblastic) appearance in a well-vascularized and myxoid background.[139] As with its more common bladder counterpart, there is some question as to whether it should be regarded as a reactive pseudoneoplastic condition (as its original name implies) or as a low-grade neoplasm (as the alternative name *inflammatory myofibroblastic tumor* suggests).

Urethral polyps composed of tall columnar cells of prostatic origin are a common source of hematuria in young adults[124] (Fig. 18.10). They may have a villous configuration ("villous polyps") and tend to be found in the verumontanum but also along most of the posterior and

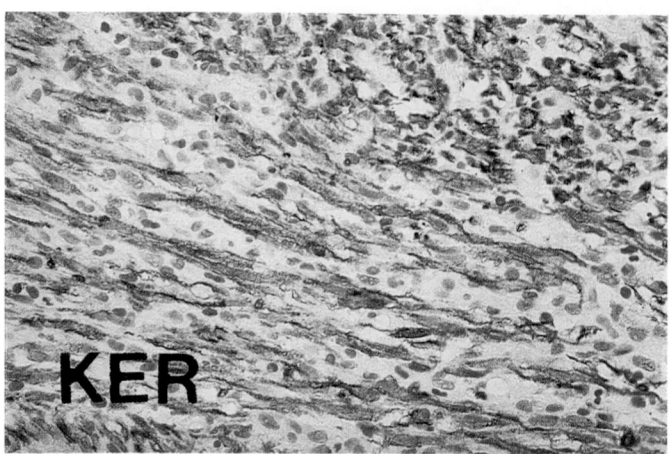

Fig. 18.9 Immunoreactivity for low-molecular-weight keratin (Cam 5.2) in the proliferating cells of a postoperative spindle cell nodule. This finding should not lead to a diagnosis of sarcomatoid carcinoma.

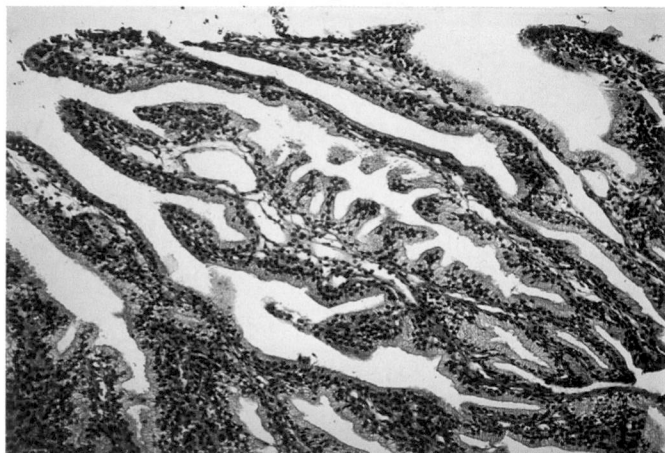

Fig. 18.10 Urethral polyp composed of well-differentiated prostatic glands. This is a common cause of hematuria in young males.

lateral surfaces of the prostatic urethra.[122,137,140] They have traditionally been thought to arise from ectopic prostatic tissue located in the prostatic urethra but are more likely of hyperplastic–metaplastic nature.[123] They stain intensely for both PAP and PSA.[143] Most are cured by transurethral fulguration, but instances of local recurrence have been described. Rarely, prostatic urethral polyps have an adenomatoid "nephrogenic" configuration,[125,135,143,144] and occasionally they may be the site of carcinoma.[142] Truly ectopic prostatic tissue has been seen in urachal remnants, bladder trigone, root of the penis, and pericolic fat.[128]

Other congenital and acquired non-neoplastic abnormalities of the prostatic utricle (verumontanum) include hyperplasia and hypertrophy, inflammation, cysts, and squamous metaplasia.[126,136] The latter change, which was common at the time that estrogen therapy for prostatic carcinoma was popular, may result in obstructive symptoms.[130]

Melanosis of the prostate refers to the presence of melanin-containing elongated cells in the prostatic stroma. The microscopic appearance is analogous to that of *blue nevus*.[127,133] The pigmented spindle cells are immunoreactive for S-100 protein,[134] and melanosomes can be demonstrated ultrastructurally.[140] This condition should be distinguished from lipofuscin pigmentation of the prostatic epithelium, which is equivalent to that more often seen in the seminal vesicle.[121,129]

Extramedullary hematopoiesis rarely involves the prostate in patients with myelofibrosis; the atypical megakaryocytes present in it should not be confused with malignant cells.[132]

Other tumorlike conditions of the prostate (such as basal cell hyperplasia and sclerosing adenosis) are discussed in connection with the differential diagnosis of prostatic carcinoma (see p. 1379).

Carcinoma

General features

Carcinoma of the prostate is the most common internal malignancy among men in the United States and is responsible for 10% of cancer deaths in this population[148a]. Each year in New York State more than 11,000 men are diagnosed with prostatic cancer, and more than 2300 die from it. Prostate cancer is the leading cause of new cancer in men and is second only to lung cancer as a leading cause of cancer-related deaths in men. Rates among black males are one and a half those of white males.[150] The age-adjusted incidence is on the increase in most countries. Hormonal factors appear to play a role in the development of prostatic carcinoma. The disease does not occur in eunuchs castrated before puberty, and its incidence is low in patients with hyperestrogenism resulting from liver cirrhosis. It has been estimated that 5% to 10% of prostatic carcinomas have a genetic link. If a man's brother or father had prostatic carcinoma, his own risk of developing the disease is two to three times greater than average. There is no demonstrable correlation with diet, venereal disease, sexual habits, smoking, or occupational exposure.[146] There is no convincing evidence that patients with nodular hyperplasia (or those who have had a transurethral resection for it) are at an increased risk for the development of prostatic carcinoma, although the two conditions often coexist.[145,147,148]

Almost 75% of the men diagnosed with prostatic cancer are age 65 or older, but the tumors can be seen in younger adults and even in children and adolescents.[149] Their frequency increases with age, a fact well substantiated by careful observations at autopsy. The frequency with which incidental carcinoma is found at post mortem examination varies between 15% and 70%[146] and is directly related to the age of the patient and the thoroughness of the sampling.

Clinical features

Skillful rectal examination remains a practical and efficient method for the detection of prostatic carcinoma[155,158,161]; however, pathologic confirmation is always necessary because early carcinomas cannot be distinguished with assurance from foci of nodular hyperplasia, granulomatous prostatitis, tuberculosis, infarct, or lithiasis.[159] Transrectal ultrasonography can detect carcinomas (which appear as hypoechoic lesions) as small as 5 mm in diameter[157]; however, it will miss up to 30% of the prostatic tumors that are isoechoic and has not proved an efficient tool for screening.[160]

PSA is secreted by all but the most undifferentiated prostatic tumors.[165] Gram for gram, the average prostatic carcinoma produces ten times or more the amount of PSA produced by normal tissue, and this is reflected in the circulatory levels of this marker. Serum determination of PSA has all but replaced the time-honored determination of PAP.[154,164] The test has a high sensitivity and specificity, is rapid and inexpensive, and is minimally invasive.[152,153,162] Mild serum elevations of PSA can be seen with nodular hyperplasia, but levels above 4 call for serial determination, with the performance of a biopsy if they continue to rise. Almost half of patients with prostatic carcinomas have levels over 10 mg/ml. Elevations of serum PSA also occur in prostatitis, prostatic infarct, and major trauma to the prostate, such as needle biopsy or TUR, but these elevations should be transitory and resolve with proper treatment.

The combination of digital rectal examination, transrectal ultrasonography, and serum PSA represents a powerful diagnostic triad for the detection of early prostatic carcinoma.[151,156] It is not clear whether measurement of the PSA density (PSA level as a function of prostatic volume) will provide a more specific test for carcinoma.[163]

Pathologic features

Prostatic carcinomas can be divided into two major categories: (1) adenocarcinoma of peripheral ("secondary") ducts and acini, and (2) carcinoma of large ("primary") ducts. This morphologic distinction has traditionally been based on the belief of a different site of origin for the two tumors. However (and as in the breast before), this histogenetic approach has been challenged by the observation that the two patterns are often seen together, and the alternative proposal has been advanced that it is the *site* of the growth rather than the *origin* that governs the tumor architecture.[166] Be that as it may, the majority of the tumors belong to the first category, and most studies dealing with grading, staging, prognosis, and therapy of prostatic carcinoma refer exclusively to them.

It should be pointed out that these two major tumor types may coexist in the same prostate, and that there are rare tumors with combined features in the same neoplasm.[166a]

Adenocarcinoma of peripheral ducts and acini

It is often emphasized that most prostatic carcinomas arise in the posterior lobe. Although this statement is basically correct, it is somewhat ambiguous because of the various definitions regarding the boundaries of this lobe.[204] More important than this is the fact that most prostatic carcinomas arise in the peripheral zone, whether posteriorly, laterally, or anteriorly, with sparing of the periurethral region except for the late stages of the disease[173,200] (Fig. 18.11).

Grossly, the tumor may be difficult to see but usually can be identified as a gray or yellowish, poorly delineated, firm area (Fig. 18.12).[199] Early detection efforts are resulting in the identification of increasingly smaller tumors. As a matter of fact, residual carcinoma may be

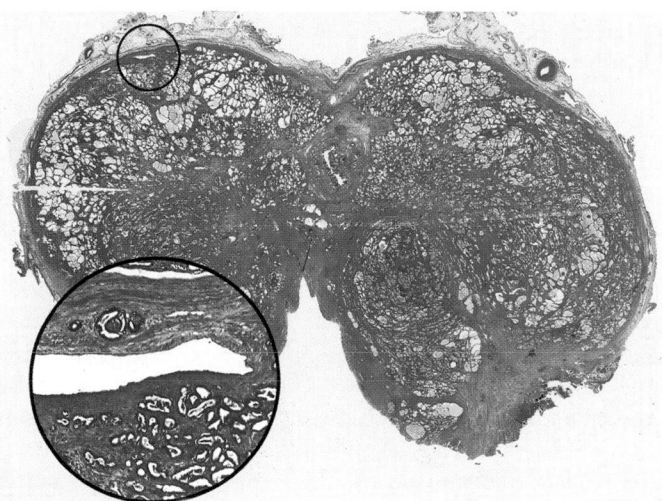

Fig. 18.11 Whole mount of radical prostatectomy specimen showing involvement by an extremely small prostatic carcinoma located at the periphery of the organ and accompanied by perineurial invasion, the latter better seen in the inset.

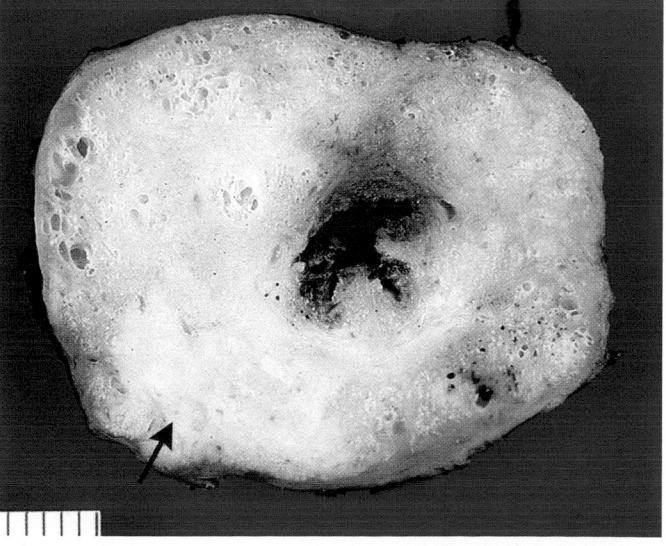

Fig. 18.12 Gross appearance of prostatic adenocarcinoma. The tumor appears as an irregularly shaped, yellowish mass with punctate foci of necrosis in a gland that is also involved by nodular hyperplasia.

unidentifiable grossly or even microscopically in a radical prostatectomy specimen performed because of a positive biopsy (so-called "vanishing cancer phenomenon" or "minimal residual cancer").[183] The frequency of this finding has increased in recent years, probably due to earlier diagnosis and therefore smaller size of the original tumors.[179]

Microscopically, prostatic adenocarcinomas exhibit a wide spectrum of appearances, ranging from anaplastic tumors to highly differentiated neoplasms that are distinguished from the non-neoplastic gland only with great difficulty.[185,196] Four major cytoarchitectural patterns occur, and these were well described in the classic article by Totten et al.[206]: medium-sized glands, small glands, diffuse individual cell infiltration, and cribriform. Carcinomas composed of *medium-sized glands* are detected on low-power examination by virtue of the closely spaced arrangement of those glands, irregular outline, smooth inner surface, and scanty intervening stroma (Fig. 18.13). Tumors made up of *small glands* appear as expansive nodules on low power, the individual glands having a regular round configuration and small size. Both of these architectural patterns (but particularly the latter) are accompanied by cytologic abnormalities in the form of nuclear enlargement, irregularity of contour, hyperchromasia, and—most important— prominent nucleoli ("macronucleoli", defined as measuring >1 μ in diameter).[181,192] These nucleoli tend to be marginated and are often multiple.[208] Mitoses are also of significance, but they are rarely found in well-differentiated tumors composed of either medium-sized or small glands. The pattern of *diffuse cell infiltration* resembles somewhat that of invasive lobular carcinoma of the breast (Fig. 18.14), whereas the *cribriform* pattern is highly reminiscent of that seen in the homonymous type of breast carcinoma. It has been stated that the cribriform pattern represents intraductal carcinoma, as evidenced by the preservation of the epithelial basal layer.[167,194] Although this observation is probably correct, it is as well to remember that this pattern is accompanied by clearcut invasive carcinoma in the overwhelming majority of cases; therefore use of the term "intraductal carcinoma" under these circumstances may be misleading.[202] An additional pattern of growth that has recently been described is that referred to as *glomeruloid* and characterized by the presence of intraluminal ball-like clusters of tumor cells.[198]

Two opposing but equally treacherous morphologic variations of prostatic adenocarcinoma are one in which the tumor simulates an atrophic process, and another in which it mimics a benign hyperplastic change. The first, described as *prostatic adenocarcinoma with atrophic features*, is formed by tumor cells with an attenuated cytoplasm, such that the nuclei occupy almost the entire cell height. These cells are identifiable as malignant because of their infiltrative pattern of growth, nuclear enlargement,

macronucleoli, and sometimes the presence of adjacent carcinoma of the ordinary type.[177,180,191]

The second variant, referred to as *pseudohyperplastic* prostatic adenocarcinoma, resembles benign glands at

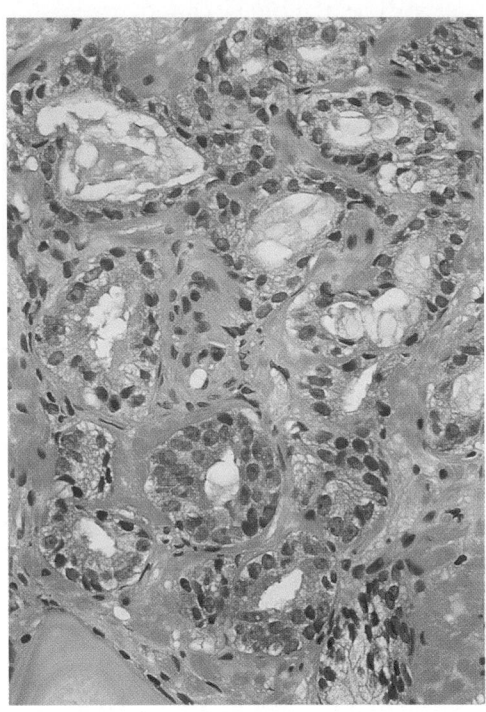

Fig. 18.13 Microscopic appearance of prostatic carcinoma. Well-differentiated tumor composed of medium-sized glands. Note the irregular shape of the glands and presence of intraluminal basophilic secretion. The contrast with the non-neoplastic glands present in the field is obvious.

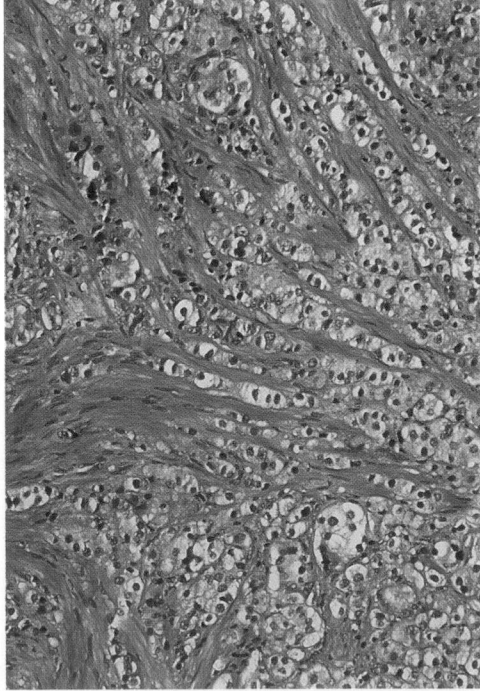

Fig. 18.14 Poorly differentiated tumor growing in a diffuse fashion. The appearance is reminiscent of that of invasive lobular carcinoma of breast.

the architectural level, including papillary infoldings, branching, and corpora amylacea. Features identifying the lesions as malignant are nuclear enlargement, macronucleoli, mitoses, intraluminal crystalloids, and sometimes the presence of adjacent PIN.[189,193]

The patterns just mentioned are often seen in combination, either synchronously or metachronously. For instance, a pattern of diffuse cell infiltration can be seen after the partial removal of a better differentiated neoplasm.[172] It should be mentioned here that it is on these patterns and their admixture, as seen on low-power examination, that the Gleason grading scheme is primarily based (see p. 1382).

Multiple tumor foci have been demonstrated in 75% to 85% of radical prostatectomy specimens studied by step-section or whole-mount techniques.[173,175,200] They are probably an expression of true multicentricity rather than intraglandular tumor spread, as supported by their frequent genetic heterogeneity.[176,205] Parenthetically, multicentricity is less common in centrally located tumors.

The presence of prostatic glands within perineural spaces is common in these tumors.[182] This finding is a strong indicator of malignancy but is not pathognomonic.[174] It does not represent permeation of perineurial lymphatic vessels, as formerly believed, but rather spread of glandular tissue along planes of lesser resistance.[184,201] Its presence in a needle biopsy specimen is a good predictor of capsular invasion by the tumor.[170]

The stroma surrounding the neoplastic glands may show a combination of hypercellularity and deposition of a basophilic ground substance ("mucinous fibroplasia" or "collagenous micronodules").[168a,169] Both intraluminal and stromal calcification may be seen in association with prostatic cancer, but the incidence of the latter is much lower than in benign prostates.[209]

Protein crystalloid structures morphologically and immunocytochemically similar to Bence Jones crystals are seen in the glandular lumina of 10% to 23% of prostatic carcinomas and are particularly common in tumors composed of medium-sized glands[187,190] (Fig. 18.15). Their presence usually indicates malignancy, but their occasional occurrence in benign glands has been documented.[171] When the latter is the case, their presence should not be viewed as indicating a significant risk factor for the subsequent development of cancer.[168,186] Electron probe x-ray microanalytic studies have shown that they are predominantly composed of inorganic sulfur.[178] Exceptionally, these crystalloids are also found in metastatic foci.[195] The presence of corpora amylacea in the glandular lumen is not necessarily a sign of benignancy, as formerly believed; these formations can also be found in association with malignant glands, particularly in examples of extensive, moderately differentiated tumor.[188]

The cytoplasm of the carcinoma cells usually has a nondescript finely granular appearance, but on occasion

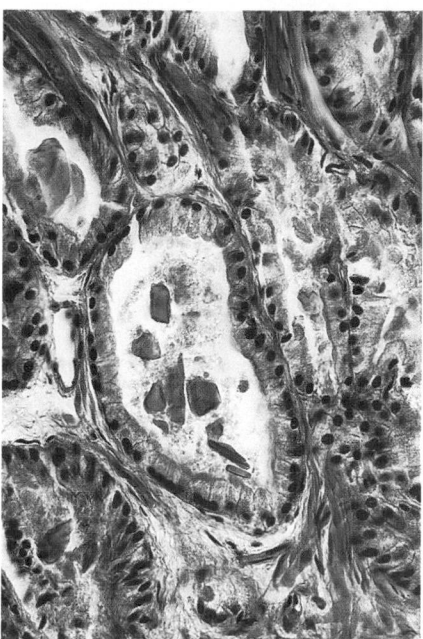

Fig. 18.15 Well-differentiated prostatic adenocarcinoma showing intraluminal crystalloids.

it is clear or foamy because of the massive accumulation of lipids ("foamy gland carcinoma").[197] When this feature is widespread, the tumor grossly acquires a bright yellow color and a soft consistency, making it difficult to detect on rectal palpation even when it is extensive. Its microscopic recognition can also be difficult, particularly at metastatic sites.[203] The behavior of these tumors is often aggressive despite the deceptively innocuous microscopic features.[207]

"Minimal adenocarcinoma" and atypical small acinar proliferation (ASAP)

A particularly vexing and increasingly frequent problem in the handling of prostatic needle biopsies is represented by the presence of foci of small atypical glands that are suspicious but not diagnostic of carcinoma. Minimal criteria for the unequivocal diagnosis of malignancy have been presented.[214,216,220] These criteria have been particularly well spelled out and illustrated by Grignon.[213] For the cases in which the recommended threshold is not reached, terms such as "atypical gland suspicious of malignancy" and "atypical small acinar proliferation (ASAP) suspicious of malignancy" have been proposed.[210,211,215,217] Alas, these terms are mired in controversy,[212,218] the main objection being that they do not represent morphologic entities. Semantics aside, the fact remains that a certain number of prostatic biopsies (about 4% to 6%) cannot be confidently placed into a benign or malignant category (with or without 34βE immunostainings[219]), and it seems to us wholly appropriate to express this uncertainty in the pathology report, whether using the ASAP acronym or with a descriptive "canned" text, as frustrating as this may be for the urologist and the patient.[212] One thing is certain: a patient with such a diagnosis warrants a second biopsy.[215]

Carcinoma of large ("primary") ducts

The other major (but numerically less significant) category of prostatic carcinoma originates from the large (primary) ducts that are normally found in a periurethral location[226,227,229,232] (Fig. 18.16). Cystoscopic examination often shows a polypoid villous or an infiltrative urethral component. Microscopically, the following types have been recognized:

1 **Large (prostatic) duct adenocarcinoma**. This tumor is characterized by malignant changes in large dilated ducts, often accompanied by papillary foci[233] and occasionally by a clear cell (mesonephroid) look[222] (Fig. 18.17). Sometimes the tumor is accompanied by pagetoid spread in the prostatic urethra.[240] Some cases of this entity have been reported in the past as Paget's

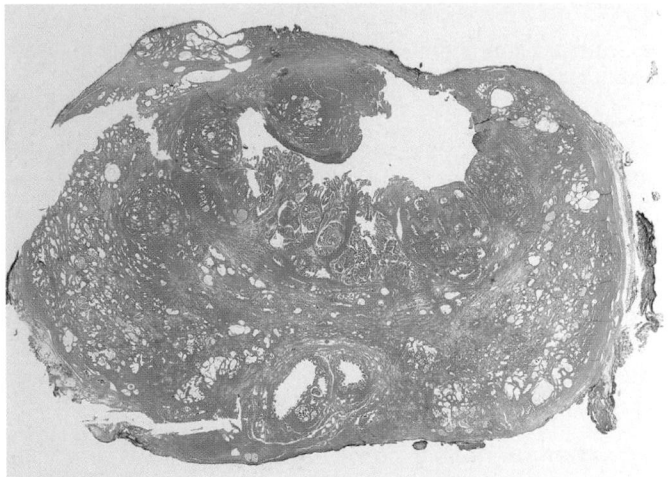

Fig. 18.16 Whole mount of large duct adenocarcinoma. The tumor is centrally located and has a distinctly papillary configuration.

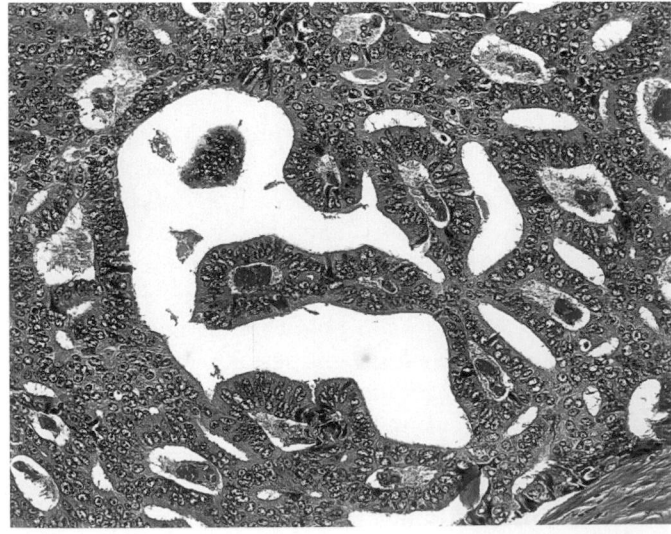

Fig. 18.17 Large duct adenocarcinoma of prostate with papillary features.

disease and Bowen's disease of this region. Positivity for PSA and PAP is the rule.[233] The tumors tend to have a more advanced stage at presentation and a higher short-term survival rate than peripheral duct–acinar carcinomas.[224] This comment also applies to the cases diagnosed on prostatic needle biopsy.[221]

Endometrial-type (endometrioid) adenocarcinoma was originally described as arising from the prostatic utricle (a müllerian remnant thought to represent the male homolog of the female uterus and vagina)[235] but is currently regarded as a variant of large duct prostatic adenocarcinoma.[236] Microscopically, glands and papillae are seen, lined by tall, pseudostratified columnar epithelium.[228] Microscopic studies, immunocytochemical determinations (positivity for PAP and PSA), and the response that has been observed after orchiectomy indicate that this tumor is truly of prostatic origin.[242,243,245,246]

2 **Primary transitional cell (urothelial) carcinoma** of the prostate.[223] The existence of this tumor type is explained by the fact that the outer portion of the prostatic (periurethral) ducts emptying into the urethra is lined by transitional epithelium.[230,231] This variant comprises less than 2% of all prostatic carcinomas. The microscopic appearance of this neoplasm is identical to that of the homonymous bladder tumor (Fig. 18.18). The diagnosis can be made in prostatic needle biopsies and in TUR specimens.[225,237] Before a diagnosis of primary transitional cell carcinoma of prostate is made, the possibility of prostatic extension from a bladder or urethral carcinoma should be excluded.[238,239]

3 **Mixed adenocarcinoma–transitional cell carcinoma**, exhibiting a combination of types 1 and 2.

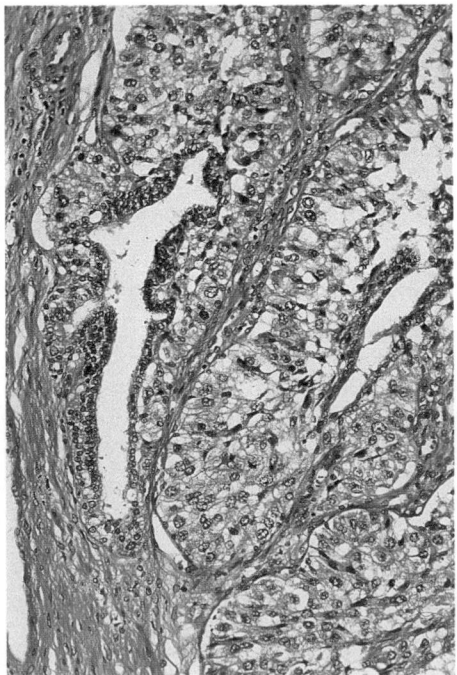

Fig. 18.18 Primary transitional cell carcinoma of prostate involving large suburethral prostatic ducts. The bladder was not affected.

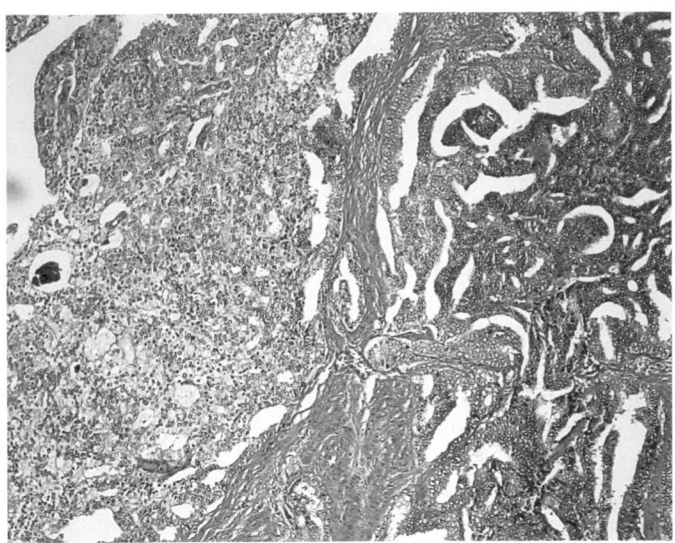

Fig. 18.19 Adenocarcinoma of prostate combining features of acinar and large duct type.

Sometimes, tumors having any of the appearances listed previously are seen associated with an ordinary prostatic adenocarcinoma or with an independent transitional cell tumor of the bladder[228,244] (Fig. 18.19). The mode of presentation, initial stage, and response to hormone therapy for the carcinomas arising from large ducts (with the possible exception of pure transitional cell carcinoma) are similar to those of the conventional prostatic adenocarcinoma.[234] Atypical hyperplasia and carcinoma in situ of periurethral glands, presumably representing the precursors of large duct carcinomas, have been observed.[241]

Histochemical & immunohistochemical features

It is generally believed that prostatic adenocarcinomas do not secrete mucin, this impression being based mainly on the use of the relatively insensitive Mayer's mucicarmine stain. On the contrary, it has been demonstrated that approximately two thirds of prostatic carcinomas produce acid mucosubstances (see also under mucinous (mucin-secreting) adenocarcinoma). The presence of this secretion should be suspected when the luminal content of the glands has a basophilic staining quality ("blue-tinged") in the routinely stained sections and can be easily confirmed with Alcian blue or colloidal iron.[260,268,274,285] This pattern of secretion is not found in normal prostatic epithelium (which secretes mucosubstances of neutral character) and therefore represents a valuable feature in the differential diagnosis. It is, however, not pathognomonic of malignancy, having also been detected in adenosis and following radiation therapy.

Two immunocytochemical markers for prostatic epithelium demonstrable in routinely processed material with polyclonal or monoclonal antisera are PAP and PSA.[280,282,288,290] They do not distinguish between benign and malignant processes in the prostate but are of great use in identifying the prostatic origin of metastatic tumors, since they are positive in all but the most undifferentiated cases[250,259,271] and in occasional advanced cases following hormonal therapy.[275] They are also useful in the differential diagnosis between poorly differentiated prostatic and transitional cell tumors, especially if used as part of a panel together with 34βE12, Leu7, CK7, and p53.[261,273] In several reported studies and in our experience, PSA has shown a more intense and extensive staining and a greater degree of specificity than PAP,[258,278,291] particularly when using monoclonal antibodies.[294a] This specificity, however, is not absolute, in the sense that PSA-like immunoreactivity has been detected in normal and neoplastic salivary glands, in some breast carcinomas, and in several normal human tissues.[247,293] Ultrastructurally, PAP has been localized to lysosomal granules and PSA to endoplasmic reticulum, vesicles, vacuoles, and glandular lumina.[296]

Another prostate-related marker is so-called "prostate-specific membrane antigen (PSMA)."[257] This is a membrane-bound glycoprotein that is expressed in all types of prostatic adenocarcinoma. Curiously, this expression *increases* from benign epithelium to high-grade PIN to adenocarcinoma.[253]

A brand-new marker touted to be highly sensitive and specific for prostatic carcinoma is P504S, a cytoplasmic protein that has been isolated through microarray screening.[270] It is an α-methylacyl-CoA racemase that plays a role in the beta-oxidation of branched-chain fatty acid and fatty acid derivatives.[270] It is related to tumor differentiation,[272a] it is not always present in carcinoma,[249a] and can also be detected in atypical adenomatous hyperplasia and PIN.[298a,298c] It is said to be particularly useful for the detection of small foci of carcinoma in needle biopsies,[270a] and for the confirmation of a diagnosis of malignancy in particularly difficult types of prostatic carcinoma, such as foamy gland and pseudohyperplastic.[298b]

Prostatic carcinoma cells are often immunoreactive for androgen and progesterone receptors, but much less so for estrogen receptors.[251,267,292,294] The latter is related to the Gleason grade and score.[323a] Her-2-neu protein is overexpressed in androgen-independent prostatic cancer, a situation somewhat analogous to that operating in breast carcinoma.[281]

Prostatic carcinoma cells are reactive for low-molecular-weight keratins.[297] In contrast to urothelial carcinoma, they stain only rarely for CK7 and CK20.[249,261] They are also positive for Leu7,[277,284] EMA (80%), carcinoembryonic antigen (CEA) (25%), B72.3, cathepsin D (50%),[254,276] glycoprotein A-80,[264] PTH-related protein,[248] and the gastric acid proteinase gastricsin (39%).[266,279,283]

Antibody 34βE12 identifies the high-molecular-weight keratin present in the basal cells in the prostatic glands and is therefore of considerable diagnostic use; it is invariably present (although sometimes discontinuously) in benign glands and absent in ordinary adenocarcinoma (of peripheral ducts and acini) regardless of

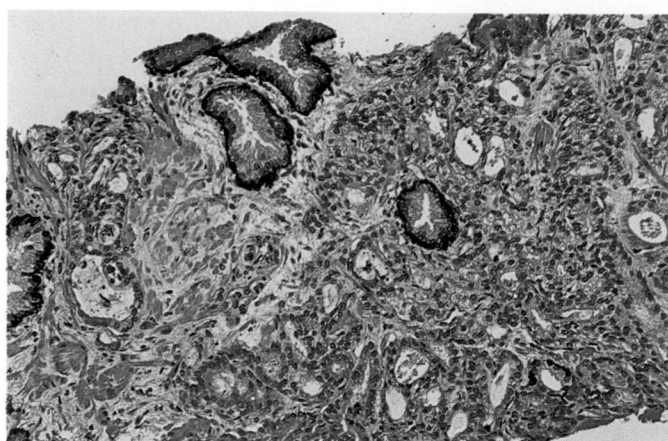

Fig. 18.20 Lack of basal cells around the neoplastic acini, as evidenced by immunostaining for high-molecular-weight keratin. The few residual non-neoplastic glands provide an internal control.

grade[262,263,298] (Fig. 18.20). Two caveats, however, are in order: this marker is often present, either as a continuous or discontinuous layer, in carcinoma of large ducts[286]; it may also be expressed, albeit exceptionally, in the carcinoma cells themselves.[295] Useful measures proposed to optimize the detection of this important marker include the use of antigen retrieval[269]; the systematic preparation of "intervening" unstained slides, in view of the fact that the lesion being evaluated may otherwise be no longer present in the residual block[265]; and the restaining of destained H&E sections if the above procedure had not been carried out.[256] Other markers that are being used for the same purpose are keratin 5/6 and p63,[246a,280a,289a] or combinations thereof.[298b]

Basement membrane components such as type IV collagen are often deposited at the interphase between tumor cells and stroma regardless of histologic pattern; therefore their detection is of no use in the differential diagnosis between prostatic intraepithelial neoplasia (see p. 1377) and invasive carcinoma.[252,287]

E-cadherin and other cell–cell adhesion proteins of the catenin/E-cadherin complex show a reduced expression in prostatic adenocarcinoma when compared to normal prostate. Among the carcinomas, the degree of immunoreactivity is inversely related to the degree of differentiation as determined by the Gleason grade.[255,272,289]

Molecular genetic features

Many cytogenetic and molecular alterations have been described in prostatic adenocarcinoma, but a consistent picture leading to a satisfying scheme for the genesis and progression of this tumor has yet to emerge.[299,312,313,315]

Allelic loss has been found in about half of the cases,[302,317,322] and the suggestion has been made that chromosomes 16q, 10q, and 8p may be the sites of tumor suppressor genes.[302,308] In one study, frequent loss of expression and loss of heterozygosity of the tumor suppressor gene *DCC* were found in the subset of the

prostatic carcinomas studied.[306] Numerical chromosomal aberrations are associated with advanced disease.[307]

Mutations of *p53* have been found in a subset of prostatic carcinomas characterized by a highly proliferative pattern and an aggressive behavior.[324] Conversely, alterations of *p53* and *MDM-2* genes are infrequent in clinically localized ordinary adenocarcinomas.[310,316] They are also seen more commonly in samples from metastatic sites than in those from primary tumors.[318] A good correlation has been found between the detection of mutations at the molecular level and the overexpression of the protein as detected immunohistochemically.[325] Immunohistochemically, the p53 reactivity in PIN is similar to that of invasive adenocarcinoma.[323] However, a microdissection study in cases of prostatic carcinoma associated with PIN showed different patterns of *p53* mutations, suggesting multiclonal development of the lesions.[326] Other similarities in molecular alterations between invasive adenocarcinoma and PIN have been documented.[300,301,304,319]

Alterations of the *Rb* tumor suppressor gene occur in a significant fraction of prostatic adenocarcinomas.[309]

p27, an inhibitor of cyclin and cyclin-dependent kinase complexes, shows decreased expression as the Gleason score, invasiveness and aneuploidy of the prostatic carcinoma increases.[303,305]

Her-2-neu gene amplification is seen in about one third of prostatic adenocarcinoma cases; it correlates with tumor grade, stage, and nondiploid DNA content.[321] As already stated, it also seems to correlate with androgen independence of the tumor.

Expression of several anti-apoptotic members of the *bcl-2* gene family (including *bcl-2*, *bcl-x*, and *mcl-1*) increases during progression of the prostatic carcinoma.[314]

Telomerase activity is detected in the majority of prostatic adenocarcinomas (in contrast to benign tissues) and seems to be independent of tumor stage, grade, or ploidy.[311]

Mutations of *BRCA1* and *BRCA2*, known to predispose to breast and ovarian carcinoma in women, do not seem to predispose men to prostatic cancer.[320]

Other microscopic types

Several distinct morphologic types of prostatic carcinoma exist, most of them probably representing variants of adenocarcinoma of the peripheral ducts and acini.[372] These include the following:

1   **Carcinoma with neuroendocrine features.** As already indicated, endocrine cells with argentaffin–argyrophil properties, serotonin, calcitonin, bombesin, and/or somatostatin immunoreactivity, and dense-core secretory granules on ultrastructural examination are present in 80% of normal or hyperplastic prostates[328,333,338,342,344,347,355,382] (Fig. 18.21). They have also been found in 10% to 33% of otherwise typical adenocarcinomas, supposedly arising by a

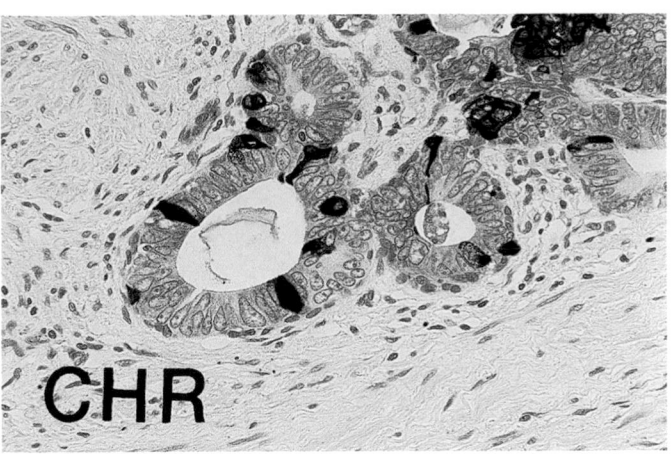

Fig. 18.21 Focal neuroendocrine differentiation in prostatic adenocarcinoma, as demonstrated with immunostaining for chromogranin.

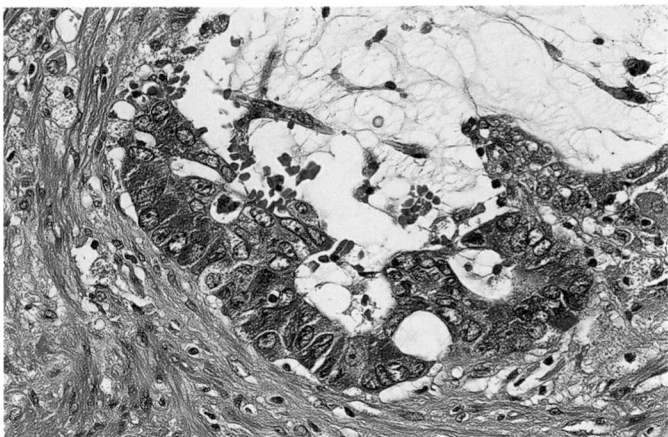

Fig. 18.22 Some of the neuroendocrine cells present in this prostatic adenocarcinoma show cytoplasmic coarse granules resembling those of intestinal Paneth cells.

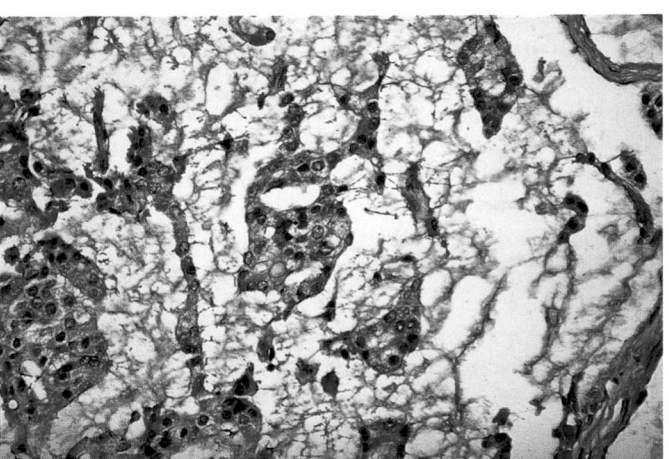

Fig. 18.23 Mucinous adenocarcinoma of prostate. Most of the mucin is located extracellularly.

process of divergent differentiation.[338] The presence of this neuroendocrine component has been demonstrated with silver stains, later by electron microscopy, later still by immunohistochemistry, and most recently with tissue microarrays.[366]

In some cases, the neuroendocrine cells simulate morphologically Paneth cells by virtue of the large size and eosinophilic staining quality of the granules[329] (Fig. 18.22). Neuroendocrine differentiation in all types of prostatic carcinoma appears to correlate with poor prognosis.[343,388] Furthermore, a relationship has been claimed to exist between the degree of neuroendocrine differentiation and tumor progression.[327] Parenthetically, prostatic carcinomas with neuroendocrine differentiation have a unique protein profile,[392] and express the estrogen-inducible pS2 protein.[337]

Some prostatic carcinomas have a morphologic appearance resembling in part or in toto that of a typical or atypical carcinoid tumor.[332,334] The fact that these tumors are generally strongly positive for PAP and PSA indicates that they are truly of prostatic glandular origin.[332,334] This is probably also true for the rare examples that are negative for prostatic markers.[370] The endocrine component is demonstrated ultrastructurally and by the fact that some of these tumors exhibit immunohistochemical reactivity for adrenocorticotropic hormone, β-endorphin, calcitonin, and other peptides.[338,348]

A histogenetically related neoplasm is **small cell carcinoma**, which is morphologically similar to the homonymous lung tumor.[367,389] This can present in a pure form or be associated with ordinary adenocarcinoma, either synchronously or metachronously.[336,379] Some of these tumors have resulted in Cushing's syndrome[352] or inappropriate antidiuretic hormone secretion.[353] Features of endocrine differentiation are demonstrable immunohistochemically and/or ultra-

structurally in some but not all of these cases.[355,376] These tumors feature a large number of apoptotic cells,[350] and their behavior is very aggressive.[367,383] On occasion, morphologically different forms of neuroendocrine differentiation (Paneth cell-like and small cell) are seen in the same neoplasm.[387]

2 **Mucinous (mucin-secreting) adenocarcinoma.** This tumor is accompanied by the formation of large amounts of intracellular and extracellular mucin, comprising 25% or more of the tumor[346,362] (Fig. 18.23). It is said to differ from the ordinary prostatic adenocarcinoma by the rarity of bone metastases, the lack of hormone dependency, and a lesser degree of response to radiation therapy. Its microscopic appearance is reminiscent of mucinous carcinoma of the breast. Microglandular, cribriform, "comedo," solid, and hypernephroid patterns may be present.[375] Whereas well-differentiated prostatic adenocarcinomas generally secrete non-O-acylated sialomucins and poorly differentiated adenocarcinomas contain mono-O-acylated sialomucins, mucinous

adenocarcinomas produce mono-, di- and tri-O-acy-lated sialoglycoproteins.[377] PAP and PSA staining is usually positive. The differential diagnosis includes extension of mucinous carcinoma from the large bowel and Cowper's gland carcinoma.[345,371] Most cases should probably be viewed as variants of peripheral adenocarcinoma, but others are related to large (periurethral) gland carcinoma.[381] Occasional mucin-secreting adenocarcinomas contain a population of neuroendocrine (including Paneth-like) cells.[385]

3 **Signet ring carcinoma.** This highly malignant neoplasm grows in a solid, acinar, or Indian file fashion and is composed primarily or exclusively of tumor cells with a signet ring configuration resulting from the intracellular accumulation of mucin.[339,357,359,384] Ultrastructurally, the cells have intracytoplasmic lumina lined by microvilli.[354] A treacherous artifact closely mimicking signet ring cells may be seen in the stromal cells and lymphocytes present in the stroma of TUR specimens[331] (see p. 1382).

4 **Adenosquamous carcinoma.** Some of these cases have been seen de novo, whereas others have occurred after radiation or hormonal therapy of ordinary adenocarcinomas.[341,351,365,370a,378]

5 **Squamous cell carcinoma.** Pure squamous cell carcinoma of the prostate is an extremely rare neoplasm. It can occur de novo or after hormonal therapy.[360,370a,386,390] It has also been seen presenting as a well-circumscribed nodule in the prostatic transition zone.[363] It is closely related to adenosquamous carcinoma and in most cases probably represents the extreme manifestation of a similar metaplastic squamous change.

6 **Adenoid basal cell tumor** (adenoid cystic-like tumor). This neoplastic process resembles adenoid cystic carcinoma of the salivary gland, to the point that some authors have regarded it as analogous to the latter.[349,356] However, no case of this lesion in the prostate has so far manifested evidence of progressive disease.[373] The key microscopic features are expansile pattern of growth, multinodularity, a surrounding fibromyxoid stroma, common occurrence of squamous differentiation, and merging with foci of basal cell hyperplasia (from which it may have arisen; Fig. 18.24). PAP and PSA staining is negative or focally positive.

If true adenoid cystic carcinoma of the prostate analogous in all regards to the homonymous salivary gland tumor exists, it must be a rare tumor indeed.

7 **Basaloid carcinoma.** This highly aggressive and extremely unusual neoplasm has morphologic features comparable to those of basaloid (cloacogenic) carcinoma of the anal canal and basaloid squamous cell carcinoma of the upper aerodigestive tract,[340] and should be clearly separated from adenoid basal cell tumor. Unfortunately, this is not always done and

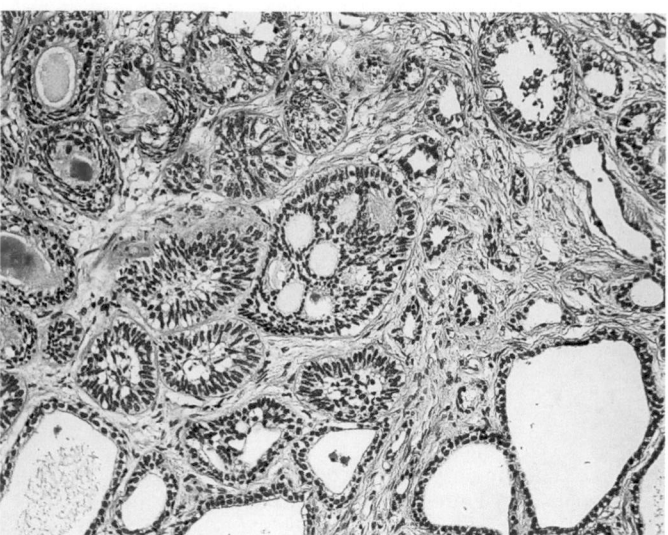

Fig. 18.24 So-called "adenoid basal cell tumor of prostate." The central tumor nest shows an appearance reminiscent of that seen in adenoid cystic carcinoma of salivary glands.

confusion ensues.[353a] Elevated expression of bcl-2 and high Ki-67 index are present, two features of help in the differential diagnosis with adenoid basal cell tumor.[393]

8 **Lymphoepithelioma-like carcinoma.** The appearance of this tumor is analogous to that of nasopharyngeal lymphoepithelioma.[330]

9 **Tubulocystic clear cell adenocarcinoma.** A unique case of a tumor resembling müllerian-type clear cell adenocarcinoma of the female genital tract has been reported in the prostate.[369] Another case has been described resembling the clear cell type of renal cell carcinoma.[381a]

10 **Sarcomatoid carcinoma.** This tumor combines features of recognizable carcinoma with sarcomatoid elements, the latter having either nonspecific spindle cell or giant cell features, or showing divergent differentiation toward cartilage, bone, and/or skeletal muscle.[358,361,364,368] The epithelial component is usually of adenocarcinoma type, but it may also have squamous features.[335] As in other sites, the distinction between carcinosarcoma and sarcomatoid carcinoma is arbitrary and probably unwarranted; most of the available evidence suggests that, whether a specific mesenchymal component is present or not, the tumor is in all likelihood of epithelial derivation.[358,374,380,391]

Intraepithelial proliferative lesions

The realization that the prostate may exhibit intraepithelial atypical proliferative changes possibly related to carcinoma and probably analogous to those long known to occur in the breast is a relatively new development. This is in part responsible for the confusion and uncertainties that still exist regarding their nature, terminology, and significance.[397,399,410] Two major categories have emerged, the first defined in terms of cytologic alterations occurring in architecturally normal structures and the second representing an architectural aberration of cytologically unremarkable glands.

Prostatic intraepithelial neoplasia (PIN) is the currently preferred term for a process involving prostatic ducts and acini, which has also been described as intraductal or ductal–acinar dysplasia.[404] It is often multicentric and may even extend to the prostatic utricle.[402,413,426] It has been divided into three grades, depending on the severity of the following alterations: cell crowding and stratification; nuclear enlargement, pleomorphism, and chromatin pattern; and nucleolar appearance. These three grades (I, II, and III) are currently grouped into two categories: low-grade PIN (corresponding to grades I and II) and high-grade PIN (corresponding to grade III)[411] (Fig. 18.25). The key feature in distinguishing high-grade from low-grade PIN is the nuclear (and particularly the nucleolar) appearance, regardless of architecture. Morphologic variations of PIN include micropapillary, cribriform and flat/atrophic (equivalent of "clinging" in the breast) patterns at the architectural level, and inverted (hobnail) and foamy types at the cytologic level.[394,396,427] Of these, the cribriform pattern is the most difficult to distinguish from invasive tumors, particularly in biopsy specimens.[420] The degree of cytologic (particularly nuclear and nucleolar) alterations in high-grade PIN (PIN III),[431] pattern of intraluminal mucin staining,[417] keratin immunoreactivity profile,[425] frequency of neuroendocrine cells,[401] frequency of erb-2 and erb-3 expression,[424] expression of EphA2 receptor tyrosine kinase,[433a] and expression (or lack thereof) of other molecular markers (see p. 1374) are analogous to those seen in invasive carcinoma, hence its alternate designation as carcinoma in situ.[400,422] AgNOR counts have not proved useful in the distinction between the three grades of PIN themselves or with adenocarcinoma.[406,425] The majority of low-grade PIN have a diploid DNA, whereas half of the high-grade PIN are aneuploid.[407]

Several studies have shown a statistical association between high-grade PIN and prostatic carcinoma, in the sense that PIN has been found in 59% to 100% of step-sectioned radical prostatectomy specimens. It has also been shown that in prostates containing both PIN and adenocarcinoma, there is a good degree of concordance in the DNA ploidy pattern of both lesions.[395,407,432] These findings have led to the suggestion that PIN may have a high predictive value as a marker for carcinoma and to the recommendation to follow closely patients in whom PIN is identified in a prostatic biopsy.[405,433] In this regard, it has been claimed that PIN in and of itself does not result in elevated PSA levels.[428] It has also been shown that low-grade PIN is a relatively common finding in young male patients.[429]

The questions raised by PIN are not too dissimilar from those raised in the breast by atypical hyperplasia/carcinoma in situ: Are patients with low-grade PIN (PIN I or PIN II) at an increased risk for the presence or subsequent development of carcinoma? Is high-grade PIN (PIN III) distinguishable at either the practical or the conceptual level from intraductal carcinoma? Some interesting data are beginning to emerge. In a study by Kronz et al.[419] repeat prostatic biopsy in patients with

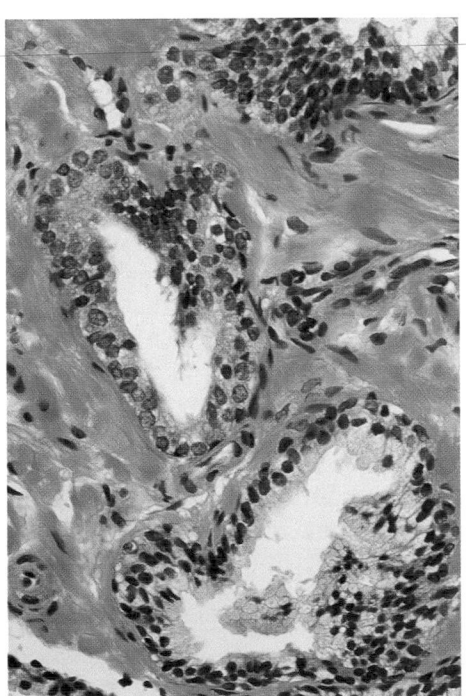

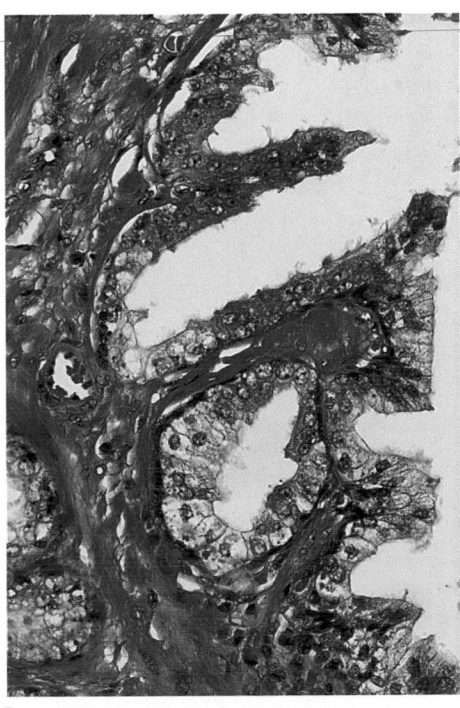

Fig. 18.25 A, Low-grade prostatic intraepithelial neoplasia (PIN I). **B,** High-grade prostatic intraepithelial neoplasia (PIN III).

A

B

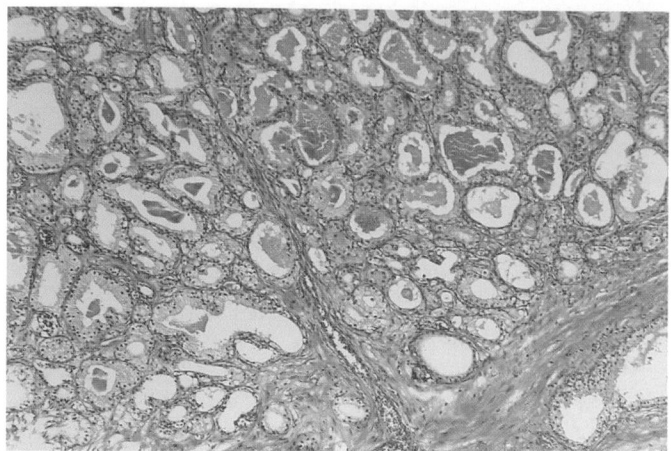

Fig. 18.26 Atypical adenomatous hyperplasia (adenosis) of prostate.

previous biopsy of high-grade PIN revealed cancer in 32.2% of the cases. The incidence was 30.2% if only 1 or 2 cores had showed PIN, 40% with 3 cores, and 75% with >3 cores. If cancer was not diagnosed on the first two follow-up biopsies, it was unlikely to develop later. If PIN was accompanied by the presence of adjacent small atypical glands, the risk of cancer on repeat biopsy was 46%.[421] Whereas the relationship between high-grade PIN and adenocarcinoma seems well established, this is not the case for low-grade PIN,[430] and it is therefore questionable whether the latter should be even mentioned in the pathology report.

Atypical adenomatous hyperplasia (also known as adenosis) has a low-power appearance similar to that of well-differentiated (Gleason grades 1 and 2) adenocarcinoma in the sense of featuring a complex and disorderly cluster of glands with an expansile margin, but lacking prominent nucleoli or other nuclear abnormalities[409,414] (Fig. 18.26). It is usually a microscopic finding, but occasionally it presents as a mass lesion.[418] Acidic mucin is often present in the lumen of the glands.[412,415] It involves the transition zone and is often accompanied by mucosal gland hyperplasia of the verumontanum.[423] Whether this lesion is a precursor of well-differentiated carcinoma (as some authors have proposed) or simply a microscopic simulator is not clear.[398] The fact that genetic and molecular aberrations in this condition are minor or absent favors the latter.[408,416] When the distinction between the two conditions is in doubt, a conservative approach is in order.[403]

Cytology

In experienced hands, the technique of fine needle aspiration cytology is very effective in detecting prostatic carcinoma.[434] Poorly and moderately differentiated tumors are diagnosed with ease, but there is some difficulty in identifying lesions at the better differentiated end of the spectrum.[435,436,442]

In a classic, oft quoted study, Esposti[439] examined 1110 patients at the Karolinska Institute with transrectal aspiration biopsy of the prostate. Satisfactory material was obtained in 98% of cases. Malignant cells were found in 336 cases, 162 of which could be checked by histologic examination. There were no false positives, but 10% were false negatives. In a subsequent study,[440] 469 cases of prostatic carcinoma were divided according to cytologic criteria into three grades. It was found that 73% of the 131 patients with grade I (highly differentiated) carcinoma, 61% of the 265 with grade II (moderately differentiated) carcinoma, and 29% of the 73 with grade III (poorly differentiated) carcinoma were alive after 3 years of hormone treatment. Epstein[438] correlated the findings of aspiration cytology with those of needle biopsy histology in 118 cases. The overall accuracy of the needle biopsy was 85.6%, and that of the aspirates was 86.6%; when considered together, the accuracy reached the remarkable figure of 95.8%. Despite these facts, aspiration cytology has fallen into disuse (especially in the United States) and has largely been replaced by the spring-loaded 18-gauge biopsy.

Atypical cells from the seminal vesicle can be present in the aspirate and constitute a pitfall in the cytologic diagnosis of carcinoma.[437,441,443]

Cytologic examination of prostatic secretion as a screening method for carcinoma has proved a futile exercise because of the large number of false-negative diagnoses.

Histologic examination

Many special types of needles and punches have been devised for obtaining prostatic tissue.[446] Traditionally, the 14-gauge needle has been the one most commonly used, but during the last decade the automated spring-loaded 18-gauge biopsy gun has gained in popularity. This provides less than half the amount of tissue supplied by the 14-gauge needle. The route may be either perineal or transrectal, the latter being currently favored. In the usual situation, six specimens are obtained ("sextant biopsies").[458] There is general agreement that adequate sampling of the core biopsy material entails cutting and staining three levels per core (step sections), with additional section to be taken if atypical features are found.[445,454,459,460] Specific recommendations on the amount of information to be included in the pathology reports of adenocarcinomas in core needle biopsy specimens are also available.[448] The risk of implantation following needle biopsy is extremely low.[444,453]

The presence of tumor in a TUR specimen may signify extensive spread by conventional carcinoma from the peripheral portion of the gland or may be a manifestation of the rare type of carcinoma from the central portion. The probability of detecting a carcinoma in a TUR specimen is directly related to the amount of sampling.[457] It has been estimated that if 5 blocks or 12 g of randomly selected chips are submitted, approximately 90% of the carcinomas will be detected.[456,464] With examination of 8 blocks, the probability of detection rises to 98%.[449,461] The need for submission of remaining tissue in the cases in which incidental carcinoma is found depends on whether the lesion is a T1a (recommended) or T1b (not needed).[455]

The accuracy of frozen section for the diagnosis of prostatic carcinoma is high. The main criteria used are architectural disarray and perineurial invasion. Frozen section examination and touch imprints are also useful for the diagnosis of lymph node metastases,[450,452,462] but both techniques suffer from a 10% to 15% incidence of false-negative results.

Radical prostatectomy specimens can be examined by performing whole-mount sections or by accurately mapping the organ with standard-size sections.[447,451,455a,463] The former produces material that is easier to evaluate and esthetically more pleasing, but at a considerable investment of time and money. The mapping with standard-size sections, if properly done, provides roughly the same amount of information. For small, nonpalpable tumors, it has been recommended to sample the entire posterior region of the organ and to take an additional section from the mid-anterior region of each lobe; if the latter is found to be positive, the entire ipsilateral region should be sampled.[463]

Microscopic differential diagnosis

In addition to the disorders discussed elsewhere in this chapter, a number of processes in the prostate must be considered in the differential diagnosis of adenocarcinoma.[488,501] **Lobular atrophy** (postatrophic hyperplasia) is an age-related phenomenon that occurs exclusively in the peripheral zone.[470] It may simulate carcinoma because of its complex arborization and surrounding fibrosis; however, the cytoplasm is scanty, and the lobular architecture is retained.[474,480,484,498] Gland size and shape are typically variable, including round, oval, elongated, slitlike and stellate forms. The nuclei are regular and devoid of hyperchromasia,[467] but the nucleoli may be prominent.[493] The stroma may show elastosis in addition to fibrosis.[471] Kinetic studies have shown that the proliferative activity is greater in this condition than in benign nonatrophic glands.[493] However, lobular atrophy is not associated with carcinoma and should not be viewed as a precancerous condition.[468]

A variant on the theme has been described as *partial atrophy*.[489] It features crowded glands, irregular nuclei, and visible nucleoli; keys to the diagnosis include scanty cytoplasm, distinct wrinkled nuclei, pale cytoplasm, and association with fully developed atrophic changes.

Cholesterol-laden microphages can appear in clusters ("xanthomas") and mimic prostatic carcinoma.[496]

Radiation changes are characterized by cytologic atypia associated with retention of the lobular architecture, squamous metaplasia, stromal fibrosis, atypical fibroblasts, and vascular alterations[472] (Fig. 18.27). These changes can be lost – lasting up to 72 months.[487b]

Basal cell hyperplasia is usually seen in the transition zone, but it may also occur in the peripheral portion of the gland.[497a] It appears as small, generally solid nests of benign-appearing epithelial cells with a somewhat clear cytoplasm (Fig. 18.28). There is always an accompanying nodular hyperplasia of the usual type, with frequent merging of the two processes.[476] In *florid* basal cell hyperplasia, the proliferation is unduly complex.[499] Nuclear enlargement, hyperchromasia, and nucleolar prominence are seen in the variant designated as *atypical basal hyperplasia*.[479] Other morphologic variations include the presence of intracytoplasmic globules (an allegedly diagnostic feature), psammomatous calcification, squamous changes, and cribriform pattern of growth.[491] Basal cell hyperplasia may be the progenitor of the so-called "adenoid basal cell tumor" described on p. 1376. The

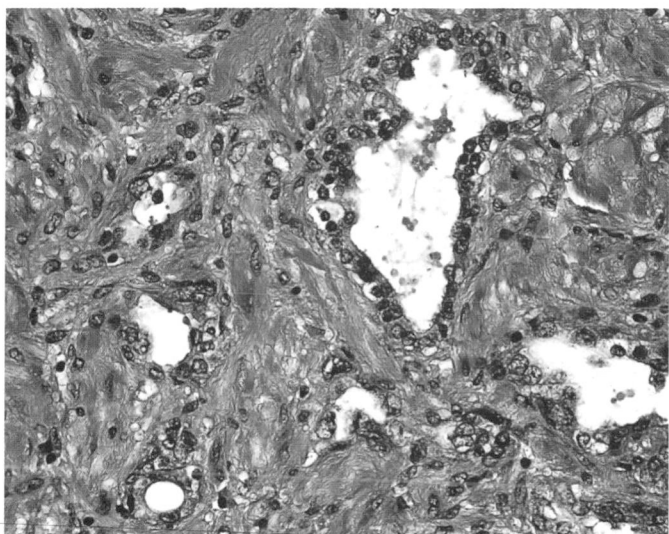

Fig. 18.27 Radiation changes in prostate. The acini show marked nuclear pleomorphism. On low power, the lobular architecture was retained.

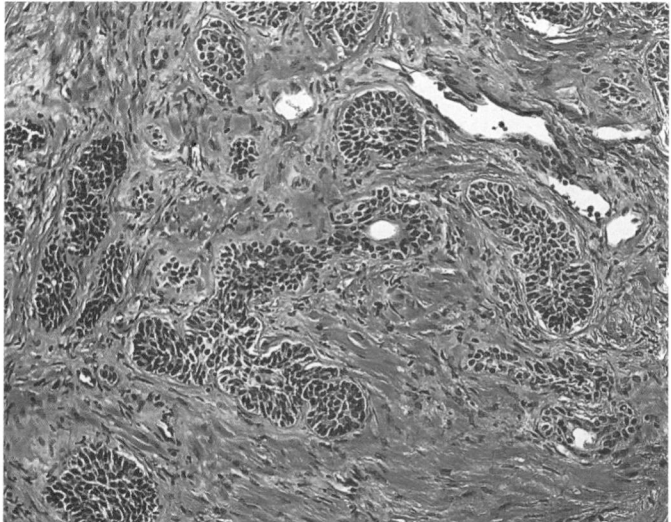

Fig. 18.28 Basal cell hyperplasia of prostate. The low-power architecture is characteristic of this benign process.

proliferating basal cells are immunoreactive for high-molecular-weight (34βE12) keratin and p63 but not for actin.[499a]

Transitional cell hyperplasia is characterized by the presence of a stratified epithelium composed of oval to spindle cells perpendicularly oriented to the lumina, and having scanty pale eosinophilic to clear cytoplasm. The nuclei are elongated, vesicular, often with longitudinal grooves and inconspicuous nucleoli.[500]

Squamous metaplasia can be seen at the periphery of infarcts (see p. 1364), after TUR, as a result of hormonal manipulation, or sometimes with no obvious predisposing cause.

Cribriform hyperplasia is an uncommon and controversial form of hyperplasia. The cytoplasm of the hyperplastic glandular cells often has a clear appearance, hence the original designation as *clear cell* cribriform hyperplasia[469] (Fig. 18.29). An important clue in the differential diagnosis with carcinoma is the presence of a prominent row of basal cells at the periphery of the lesion, which are highlighted by the 34βE12 keratin stain.[478] Nuclei are small, nucleoli are inconspicuous, and mitotic figures are absent.

Sclerosing adenosis has an appearance similar to the homonymous lesion in the breast. It appears as a well-circumscribed nodule composed of variably sized and shaped (often compressed) glands and small clusters of epithelial cells embedded in a cellular, often myxoid, stroma (Fig. 18.30). The clusters contain both a continuous basement membrane and a layer of basal cells. The latter are immunoreactive for keratin, S-100 protein, and smooth muscle actin, suggesting myoepithelial differentiation.[482,485,495]

Florid hyperplasia of mesonephric remnants can involve prostate and periprostatic tissues and mimic prostatic carcinoma.[472a,481,483]

Nephrogenic adenoma similar to its more common bladder counterpart can occur in the prostate urethra and be mistaken for prostatic adenocarcinoma.[465] The term is a misnomer, since the change probably represents a benign metaplastic response of the urothelium to injury.

Seminal vesicle and **ejaculatory duct** tissue, **Cowper's glands,** and **paraganglia** can be found incidentally in prostatic resection specimens and lead to diagnostic errors.[475,486,490,492,494,501] This is particularly true for the seminal vesicle because of its complex papillary arrangement and sometimes striking nuclear aberrations (Fig. 18.31). A clue to the nature of this epithelium is the presence of abundant lipofuscin granules in the cytoplasm.[487] It should be noted, however, that a similar pigment can be occasionally found in benign and malignant prostatic epithelium,[466] and that the distal seminal vesicle epithelium may show some immunoreactivity for

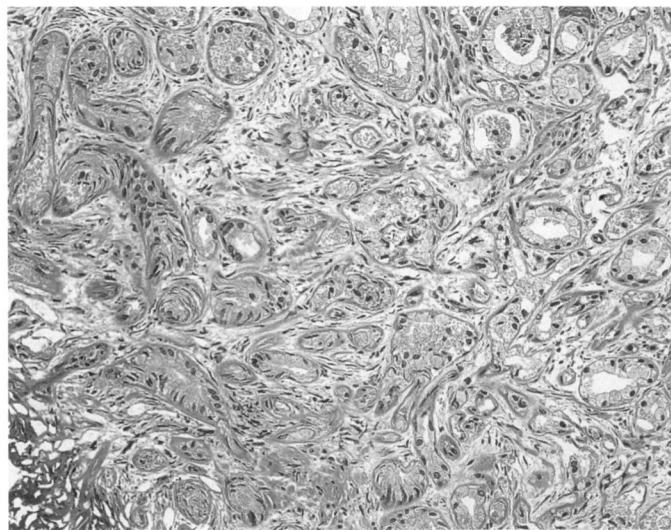

Fig. 18.30 Sclerosing adenosis of prostate. The features are similar to those of its better-known mammary counterpart.

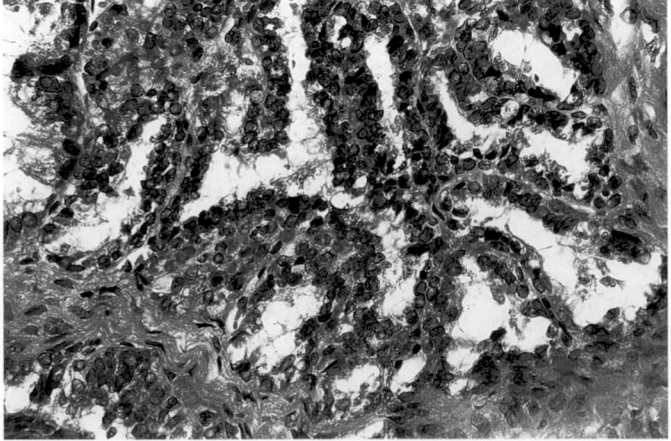

Fig. 18.31 Seminal vesicle epithelium present in a prostatic needle biopsy. The highly complex architecture may induce an overdiagnosis of carcinoma. Note the abundant intracytoplasmic pigment.

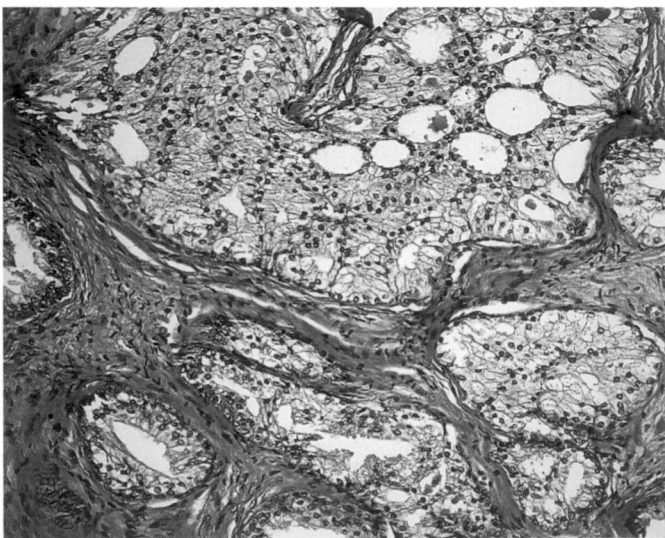

Fig. 18.29 Clear cell hyperplasia of prostate with a focally cribriform pattern of growth. This lesion is of controversial nature.

PSA.[497] Another clue is provided by the immunoreactivity of the seminal vesicle – ejaculatory duct epithelium for MUC6.[487a]

Signet-ring-like changes can develop in stromal cells and lymphocytes as a result of the effects of diathermy or other injuries and simulate signet ring adenocarcinoma. It is seen most often in TUR specimens but it has also been described in prostatectomy specimens.[501a]

In the interpretation of needle biopsies, it should be remembered that there are normally **bundles of striated muscle** within the prostate gland, especially in the apex and anterior aspects; therefore the presence of prostatic glands adjacent to a skeletal muscle fiber is not necessarily evidence of carcinoma, nor is the presence of skeletal muscle adjacent to a carcinoma evidence that the tumor has extended outside the gland. Similarly, it should be kept in mind that normal and hyperplastic prostatic glands may be seen in a **perineural location.**[473,477]

Spread and metastases

Prostatic carcinoma spreads initially within the various compartments of the prostate itself, including ducts and acini, fibromuscular stroma, perineural spaces, and blood vessels.[538,539]

Invasion of the "capsule" (i.e., the outer fibromuscular layer of the prostate) is very common. In one series, capsular invasion was found in 90% of specimens from radical prostatectomies studied with giant serial-step sections in patients with clinical stage A or B disease.[550] In another study, the probability of tumor having extended outside the prostate into the neurovascular bundles was found to be zero if the "capsular margin" was negative, 12% if it was equivocal, and 60% if it was positive.[518] Advanced tumor may extend into the seminal vesicles,[543,550] apex (distal aspect) of the gland, prostatic urethra (very rarely), and bladder.[542] Tumors should be listed as exhibiting seminal vesicle invasion only if the muscular wall of this organ is infiltrated by tumor.[519]

Rectal invasion is much less common, supposedly because of the resistance offered by the tough fibromuscular structure covering the posterior aspect of the prostate known as Denonvilliers' fascia.[556] This invasion can manifest in the form of an anterior rectal mass (with an intact or ulcerated mucosa), an annular rectal stricture resulting from circumferential infiltration, or subserosal implants.[521]

The most common sites of metastatic spread of prostatic carcinoma are the skeletal system and lymph nodes. Bone metastases are usually multiple but can be solitary.[509,527] They are characteristically osteoblastic and can radiographically simulate Paget's disease or even osteosarcoma,[535] but they can also be mixed or entirely osteolytic. Sometimes, the appearance of a bone metastasis precedes by several years the urologic manifestations. Lumbar spine, sacrum, and pelvis are the most common locations, supposedly as a result of tumor spread via Batson's vertebral venous system.[528] However, any other bone can be involved through the systemic circulation.[517] Metastases to the spine may result in epidural masses with spinal cord compression,[558] and metastases to the base of the skull may result in severe cranial nerve defects.[548]

Microscopically, clusters of malignant glands are seen surrounded by exuberant new bone formation. When the bone metastases are extensive, they can be accompanied by hypocalcemia, hypophosphatemia, and increased serum alkaline phosphatase levels.[510] Immunohistochemical reactions for PAP and PSA are usually positive, even after decalcification. The mechanism for the predominantly osteoblastic nature of bone metastases of prostatic carcinoma is not well understood, but it may be related to the production of bone growth factors by the tumor cells.[524]

The most common pathway of nodal involvement is to the pelvic chains, from which the tumor spreads to the retroperitoneal nodes. However, in some instances, retroperitoneal node metastases may occur in the absence of pelvic node metastases; these patients are less likely to have metastases to bladder and rectum but more likely to have them in lungs and liver.[551] Rarely, metastases are also found in periprostatic/periseminal vesicle lymph nodes.[533] The performance of surgical staging (including bilateral pelvic lymphadenectomy) has provided important information on the frequency of regional lymph node involvement and the pattern of spread of prostatic carcinoma.[503,544,552,559] The overall incidence of nodal metastases at the time of diagnosis has been in the neighborhood of 40% in the majority of published series,[520,549] but it has been considerably lower in most recent studies, suggesting a change in the stage at which prostatic carcinoma is currently diagnosed.[545] This incidence is related to the clinical staging, volume of tumor, PSA levels, microscopic degree of differentiation, and perhaps microvessel density.[520,540,549,557] Stage T1c tumors (nonpalpable, asymptomatic tumors) found because of serum PSA elevation (which accounts for close to 40% of prostatectomies at present) have a very low incidence (<5%) of positive nodes. Latent prostatic carcinomas detected at autopsy are almost never accompanied by nodal metastases.[506] A system has been proposed (the "Hamburg algorithm") for predicting the likelihood of lymph node metastases on the basis of the needle biopsy findings.[526a]

Nodal metastases in patients with clinically localized palpable prostatic carcinoma are most likely to be found on the same side as the tumor and are very unlikely to be present on the contralateral side alone.[529] Many patients with nodal metastases lack evidence of concurrent bony or visceral dissemination, thus contradicting the traditional concept that nodal metastases always represent a secondary phenomenon from skeletal metastases. Detection of nodal involvement by lymphangiography has proved notoriously inaccurate.[537] Instead, high-resolution MRI with magnetic nanoparticles seems extremely promising.[529a]

Metastases can also occur in supradiaphragmatic lymph node groups.[512] Sometimes, involvement of a left supraclavicular[508,531] or a mediastinal node[536] is the first manifestation of the disease (Fig. 18.32). Most of these tumors are poorly differentiated and not particularly suggestive of a prostatic origin on microscopic examination[505]; immunohistochemical staining for PSA or PAP is extremely valuable in establishing the prostatic origin of a metastatic adenocarcinoma, but it has not proved useful as a screening method for occult nodal metastases.[525,541] Conversely, reverse transcriptase PCR with primers specific for the PSA gene has successfully detected microscopic metastases in lymph nodes, even when these nodes appeared negative by histologic and immunohistochemical techniques.[514] We and others have been similarly successful in detecting circulating tumor cells with this technique, sometimes in patients with no clinicoradiographic evidence of metastatic disease.[523,553]

Lung metastases are not as rare as formerly believed; most of them exhibit a lymphangitic pattern of spread. Massive pleural effusion may be the initial symptom. On occasion, the process simulates primary lung carcinoma.[522] The pattern of growth may be microacinar, tubulopapillary, or carcinoid-like. Adenocarcinoma of large ducts may simulate metastatic colonic adenocarcinoma.[513]

Rarely, metastatic prostatic carcinoma is found unexpectedly in orchiectomy specimens.[555] Prostatic carcinoma also may metastasize to the breast, sometimes bilaterally, particularly in patients taking estrogens. This phenomenon is often confused clinically with gynecomastia and microscopically with primary breast carcinoma. In this regard, it is pertinent to note that several cases of primary breast carcinoma have been reported in patients treated with estrogen for prostatic carcinoma. PSA and PAP immunostains are important in this differential diagnosis.[526]

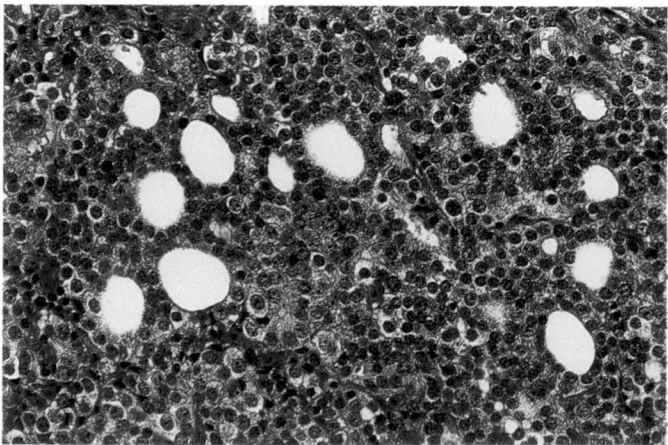

Fig. 18.32 Prostatic adenocarcinoma initially presenting as left supraclavicular adenopathy.

Other metastatic sites include liver, adrenal gland, central nervous system (including dura), eye, skin, and unusual locations such as penis and salivary gland.[502,507,515,516,530,532,546–548,554,554a,555] In general, the degree of microscopic differentiation of the metastases and of PSA expression follows quite closely that of the primary tumor.[504,534] However, in almost half of the cases the Gleason score is higher than in the primary tumor.[511]

Staging and grading

Carcinomas of the prostate have been traditionally divided into clinical, latent, and occult types. The *clinical* tumor produces local symptoms and signs; the *latent* (incidental) carcinoma is unsuspected clinically and found incidentally at autopsy or in prostatectomy specimens performed for nodular hyperplasia or some other condition; *occult* carcinomas result in distant metastases, whereas the primary tumor remains clinically undetected. Some of the criteria of this old-fashioned but eminently sound scheme have been incorporated into the currently used staging systems (see Appendix C). In the initial staging, stage A tumors correspond to the latent neoplasms of the previous classification; stage B carcinomas are clinically detectable but confined within the prostatic capsule; in stage C the disease has spread outside the capsule; and in stage D there are distant metastases.[580–582] Subdivisions within each category have been proposed, largely based on the amount or extent of tumor as determined clinically, serologically (PSA levels), and radiographically, sometimes incorporating technology such as MRI and ultrasonography[577,585,589,594,596] (Table 18.1). This must be distinguished from the pathologic staging done microscopically in biopsies, TUR, and radical prostatectomy specimens.[578] A particularly important subdivision which incorporates an element of grading (see below) exists in pathologic stage A tumors. Stage A1 tumors, which receive no additional therapy and have a good prognosis, are defined as small tumors that are well or moderately differentiated. Stage A2 tumors (large and/or poorly differentiated) require added therapy (often prostatectomy) and have a worse prognosis than stage B1 disease.[587]

Fowler et al.[572] studied the correlation between clinical and pathologic stages in prostatic carcinoma. They found that the carcinoma was confined microscopically to the prostate in 81% of clinical stages A2, 79% of B1N, 38% with B1, and 0% of B2 tumors. A similar degree of accord was encountered by Pontes et al.[592] A distressingly high incidence of clinical understaging was found by Epstein et al.[570]: in clinical stage T2 disease there was extension outside the gland in over 60% of the cases, and over 40% had positive margins. The proposal has been made to base staging on tumor volume, after showing that this parameter is a good predictor of all aspects of tumor progression. Thus there is a 10% possibility of capsular invasion in tumors measuring 0.5 ml, 10% probability of seminal

Table 18.1 Gleason's microscopic grading system of prostatic carcinoma

Stage	Description
1	Single, separate, uniform glands in closely packed masses with a definite, usually rounded, edge limiting the area of tumor
2	Single, separate, slightly less uniform glands, loosely packed (separated by small amounts of stroma), with less sharp edge
3a	Single, separate, much more variable glands, may be closely packed but usually irregularly separated; ragged, poorly defined edge
3b	Like 3a, but very small glands or tiny cell clusters
3c	Sharply and smoothly circumscribed rounded masses of papillary or loose cribriform tumor ("papillary intraductal tumor")
4a	Raggedly outlined, raggedly infiltrating, fused glandular tumor
4b	Like 4a, with large pale cells ("hypernephroid")
5a	Sharply circumscribed, rounded masses of almost solid cribriform tumor, usually with central necrosis ("comedocarcinoma")
5b	Ragged masses of anaplastic carcinoma with only enough gland formation or vacuoles to identify it as adenocarcinoma

From Gleason DF, The Veterans Administration Cooperative Urologic Research Group: Histological grading and clinical staging of prostatic carcinoma. In Tannenbaum M (ed.): Urologic pathology. The prostate. Philadelphia, 1977, Lea & Febiger, pp. 171–198.
Note: Tumor is assigned to a category according to grade in which tumor fits (as indicated by number), irrespective of its subgrade (as indicated by letter). Combined grade is obtained by adding predominant grade (primary grade) and the other grade (secondary grade) when present. When tumor has same grade throughout, its combined grade is obtained by doubling value of this grade.

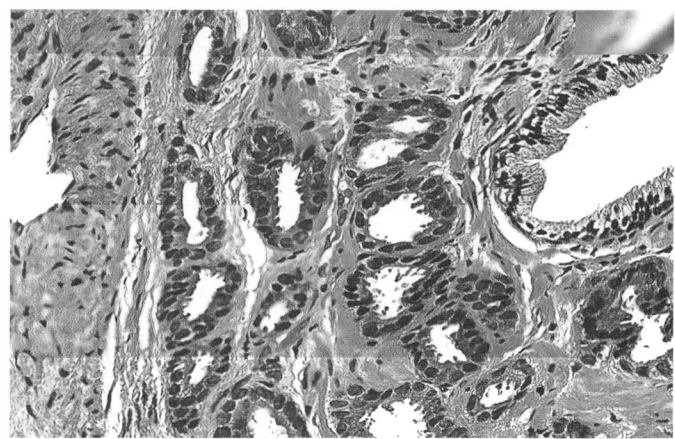

Fig. 18.33 Prostatic adenocarcinoma, Gleason's 3 + 3 = 6/10.

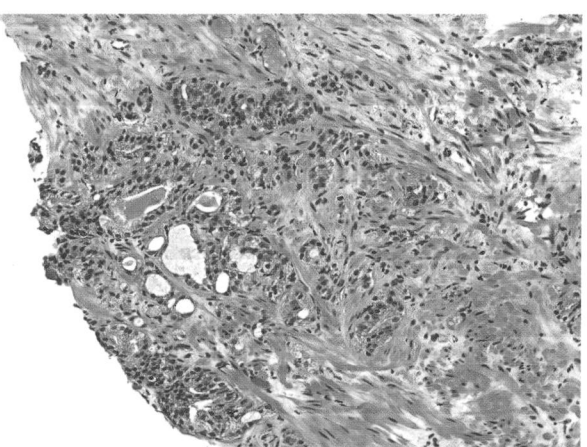

Fig. 18.34 Prostatic adenocarcinoma, Gleason's 3 + 4 = 7/10.

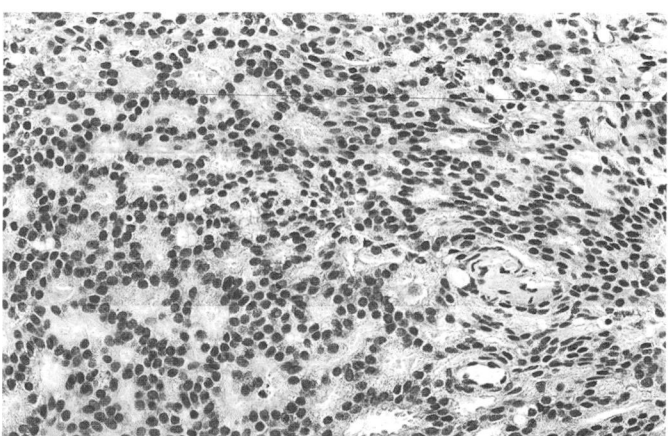

Fig. 18.35 Prostatic adenocarcinoma. Gleason's 4 + 4 = 8/10. The tumor has a cribriform pattern of growth.

vesicle invasion in tumors measuring 4 ml, and 10% probability of metastases in tumors measuring 5 ml.[568]

The microscopic grading system developed by Gleason in conjunction with the Veterans Administration Cooperative Urology Research Group[575,576] is currently preferred to the other grading systems that have been proposed over the years.[565,584,588,598] It is based on the degree of glandular differentiation and the growth pattern of the tumor in relation to the stroma as evaluated on low-power examination (Figs 18.33 to 18.37; Table 18.1). The predominant tumor pattern (referred to as "primary") is graded from 1 to 5, and the "secondary" pattern (if present) is graded similarly, with the two numbers being added to obtain the Gleason's *score* or *sum*. If the tumor has the same pattern throughout (i.e., it has only a "primary" pattern), the number is multiplied by 2 in order to obtain the final score.[563] The interobserver reproducibility has been found to be in an acceptable range both among urologic pathologists and among general pathologists.[561,562] A useful Web-based tutorial is available to train the uninitiated in the system.[583]

There is a reasonably good correlation between the tumor grade determined by biopsy and that in the prostatectomy specimen, but upgrading occurs in 30% to 45% of the cases and downgrading in about 5%.[564,567,573,585,597] As expected, the frequency and magnitude of this discrepancy are directly related to the quantity of tumor tissue present in the biopsy.[595] Parenthetically, the accuracy of the grading is similar whether one uses the traditional

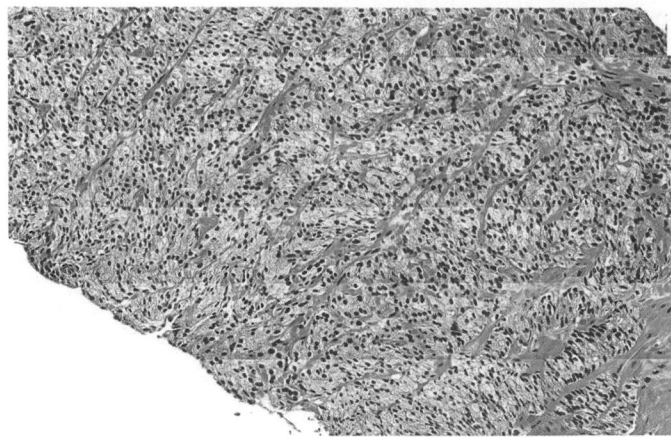

Fig. 18.36 Prostatic adenocarcinoma, Gleason's 4 + 4 = 8/10. This appearance is sometimes referred to as hypernephroid.

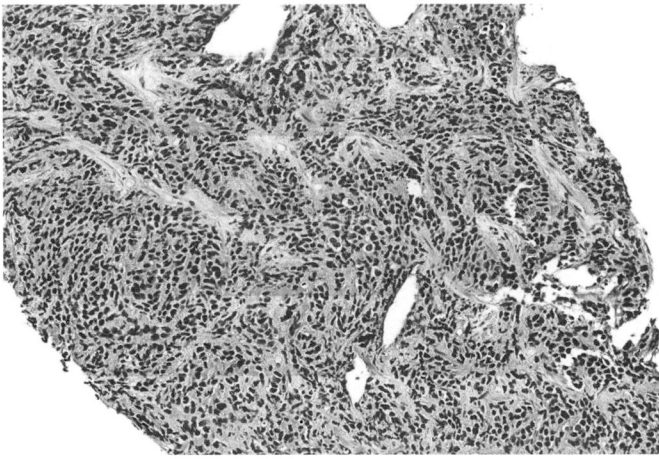

Fig. 18.37 Prostatic adenocarcinoma, Gleason's 5 + 5 = 10/10.

Deaths/ patient-year

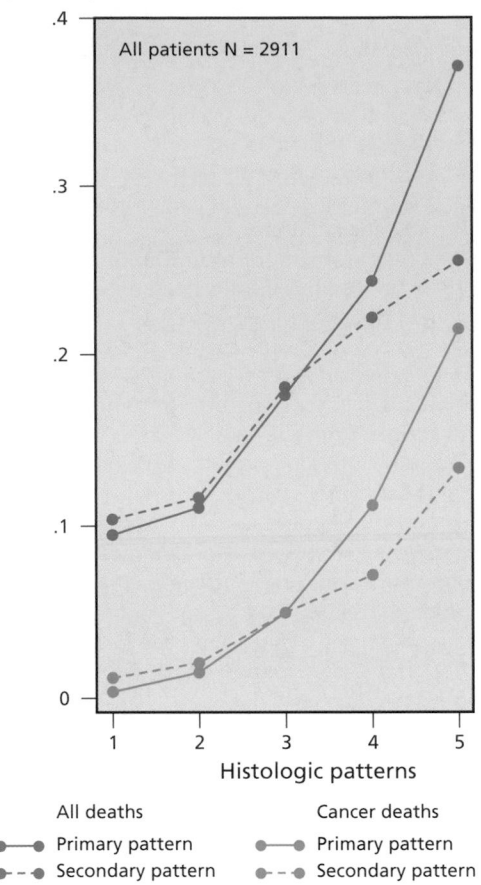

All patients N = 2911

Histologic patterns

All deaths		Cancer deaths	
●—● Primary pattern		●—● Primary pattern	
●--● Secondary pattern		●--● Secondary pattern	

Fig. 18.38 Relationship between microscopic pattern of prostatic carcinoma and mortality rates. "Primary" refers to the predominant microscopic pattern of a given tumor and "secondary" to a less extensive pattern that may be present in the same neoplasm. (From Gleason DF. The Veterans Administration Cooperative Urologic Research Group: Histologic grading and clinical staging of prostatic carcinoma. In Tannenbaum M (ed.): Urologic pathology. The prostate. Philadelphia, 1977, Lea & Febiger)

14-gauge needle biopsy or the automated spring-loaded 18-gauge biopsy gun.[566]

Microscopic grading of prostatic adenocarcinoma has been found to correlate well with PAP and PSA levels,[579,593] clinical and pathologic staging,[569,590] frequency of apoptotic bodies,[560] p53 overexpression,[581] incidence of lymph node and bone metastases,[571,600] survival rate, and response to therapy.[574,591,599] The correlation of the Gleason's grading system with the mortality rate is particularly impressive. Patients with a score of 2 to 4 almost never develop aggressive disease, whereas most patients with a score of 8 to 10 die of prostatic carcinoma.[586] This correlation of grading with mortality rates is maintained within each clinical stage[586] (Fig. 18.38). Thus, by combining staging and grading, the best predictive values are obtained.

Treatment

The management choices for localized prostatic carcinoma are radical prostatectomy, external radiation therapy, and "deferred" ("expectant") treatment.[651] There is still uncertainty (and therefore great controversy) as to which of these modalities is to be preferred.[611,622,635,648,652] After compiling data from the literature since 1980, Adolfson et al.[601] found that the weighted mean of disease-specific survival at 10 years was 93% for radical prostatectomy, 83% for deferred treatment, and 74% for external therapy. They concluded that clinically localized prostatic carcinoma often has a protracted course associated with a significant competing mortality, marginal benefit from radical prostatectomy, and no benefit from radiation therapy. In a similar study, Chodak et al.[611] concluded that the strategy of initial conservative management and delayed hormone therapy is a reasonable choice for patients with well-differentiated localized prostatic carcinoma, particularly those having an average life expectancy of 10 years or less. Very recently, a Scandinavian randomized trial showed that radical prostatectomy significantly reduced disease-specific mortality, but that there was no significant difference between surgery and "watchful waiting" in terms of overall survival.[627a]

Radical perineal prostatectomy, pioneered by Jewett at Johns Hopkins Hospital, has been improved technically so that the incidence of urinary incontinence has been markedly reduced.[606,608,620,624] The incidence of impotence has also fallen since the development of a nerve-sparing technique of radical retropubic prostatectomy.[617,649,650]

The results of radical prostatectomy are directly linked to tumor extent and degree of differentiation.[618] The extent of the operation varies from center to center, in some instances including retroperitoneal node dissection. Recurrent adenocarcinoma after radical prostatectomy may be difficult to detect in a needle biopsy because of its very focal nature.[638] Also difficult is the interpretation of specimens obtained after cryosurgery, which often show necrosis, hyalinization, granulomatous inflammation, and calcification.[605]

Radiation therapy has been applied in the form of external beam, interstitial implantation, or a combination.[614,619,636,639] Serum PSA levels are useful in monitoring the response of the tumor to this modality.[616] The routine performance of prostatic biopsy following radiation therapy is not felt to be necessary in the absence of a rising PSA level.[602] Radiation therapy has also been used as an adjuvant measure after radical prostatectomy.[631,634] Three-dimensional conformal external beam radiation therapy can induce marked cytologic atypia in the benign glandular epithelium that can be mistaken for carcinoma.[621,642] The changes in the tumor itself include the development of an abundant clear to finely granular cytoplasm which is PAS positive.[609,621,623] The incidence of PIN seems reduced in salvage radical prostatectomy specimens following radiation therapy when compared with prostatectomies without prior radiation.[610]

An important and difficult decision is whether there should be further therapy (usually in the form of radical prostatectomy) in patients with latent (incidental) carcinoma found unexpectedly in suprapubic enucleations or TUR specimens.[632] This is based on two criteria: amount of tumor and microscopic degree of differentiation. Small well-differentiated tumors (Gleason's combined scores of 2 to 4) generally receive no additional therapy.

Hormonal manipulation in the form of estrogens, LH, RH analogs and antiandrogens has replaced orchiectomy as a palliative measure in locally advanced and metastatic tumor, particularly to relieve the severe pain sometimes associated with skeletal disease.[615,630,633,640] Marked tumor regression can occur as the result of apoptosis, manifested microscopically by vacuolization of the cytoplasm, rupture of cell membranes, pyknosis, and naked nuclei.[625,627] Combined endocrine therapy (luteinizing hormone-releasing hormone agonist and flutamide) results in a striking vacuolization of the tumor cells, which may appear as isolated elements with a hemangiopericytoma-like appearance[603,612,613,621,643,644,646] (Fig. 18.39). Another

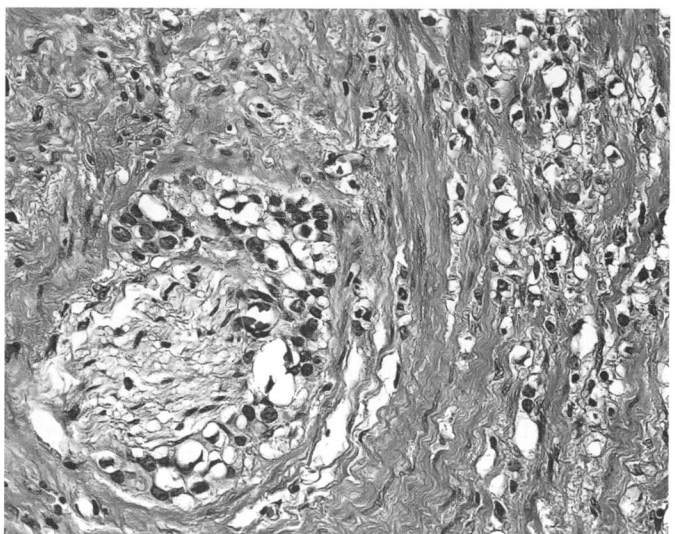

Fig. 18.39 Prominent cytoplasmic vacuolation in prostatic carcinoma as a result of hormonal treatment. The vacuolization is also present in the area of perineurial invasion.

alteration that has been described following neoadjuvant androgen ablation therapy is a peculiar pseudomyxoma-like change in the prostatic stroma resulting from mucin extravasation.[645]

It must be remembered that hormonal sensitivity of prostatic carcinomas is not an all-or-none phenomenon but varies in both the primary lesion and its metastases. Analysis of steroid receptors in the tumor may predict the value of endocrine therapy[604,629,637]; however, there is no apparent correlation between the content of androgen, estrogen, or progestin receptors and the microscopic grading of the tumor.[626,653] Side effects of hormonal therapy are squamous metaplasia of the non-neoplastic prostatic glands, testicular atrophy,[647] sore breasts, and nipple discharge. Microscopically, the breast shows intraductal hyperplasia, stromal proliferation, and occasionally lobular (acinar) formation.[641] As shown by randomized studies, excessive estrogen therapy increases the incidence of coronary artery disease and myocardial infarction.[607] These complications have been minimized by reducing the estrogen dosage and made less significant by the fact that estrogen therapy has been largely replaced by other medications.[628]

Systemic chemotherapy has proved so far of minimal benefit in hormone-refractory metastatic prostatic carcinoma.[654]

Prognosis

Many parameters have been evaluated for their ability to predict outcome in patients with prostatic carcinoma, as follows:

1 *Clinical stage.* This is a very important prognostic determinant, and it is likely to become even more so with the incorporation of newer technology (see p. 1369).

2　*Pathologic stage.* This represents the ultimate indicator of tumor extent and, as such, the most accurate predictor of prognosis currently available[709] (see Appendix C). Naturally, there is also a relationship between prognosis and the status of the individual factors that determine the stage, such as the prostatic capsule, the seminal vesicles, and the lymph nodes.[655] Thus, there is a strong association between the level of tumor invasion into or through the prostatic capsule and the grade, volume, and rate of recurrence of the tumor.[735] In cases with nodal metastases, the prognosis is worse when they are multiple rather than solitary, when they are detectable grossly rather than only microscopically, when their overall volume is large, and when they are accompanied by extracapsular extension.[666,669,688,728] Their prognostic significance seems to be the same regardless of whether they are found in the usual pelvic location or around the prostate/seminal vesicles.[700]

3　*Microscopic grading.* A direct correlation exists between clinical or pathologic staging and microscopic grading regardless of the grading system used.[694] In addition, there is convincing evidence that microscopic grading using Gleason's score system is superior to the others as an independent prognostic variable[679,702] (see Fig. 18.38). In a particularly impressive multivariate analysis of 185 cases of clinical stage B prostatic carcinoma treated by radical prostatectomy, Gleason's score was by far the best predictor of progression.[679] In another study involving 1143 consecutive patients who had radical prostatectomy for localized prostatic carcinoma, Gleason's tumor grade was found to be the only significant predictor of disease outcome.[738] Among Gleason's score 7 cases, there was no significant prognostic difference between 3 + 4 and 4 + 3 tumors.[691] A Gleason combined score of 7 is an indicator of clinically significant disease even if the disease is restricted to a single microscopic focus.[674] There is some suggestion that the predictive power of the Gleason scheme could be increased even further by taking into account the tertiary pattern whenever present.[714]

4　*Surgical margins.* In a multivariate analysis of over 500 retropubic prostatectomy specimens performed for clinical stages A and B prostatic carcinomas, positive margins strongly correlated with progression.[681] Several other studies have confirmed the value of margin status as an indicator of an increased risk of tumor progression.[658,668,698a]

5　*Tumor volume.* It has been shown that tumor volume, as measured in whole sections with morphometric techniques, correlates with Gleason's grade, capsular penetration, capsular margins of resection, seminal vesicle invasion, and lymph node metastases.[721] However, there is some question whether measurement of tumor volume provides additional prognostic information beyond that given by the parameters already listed (particularly Gleason's score), and it is therefore difficult to justify in routine practice the use of a technique which involves the performance of step sections of the whole specimen and the measurement of the tumor at 3 mm intervals with computer-assisted image analysis.[672,679] Some reasonable compromises have been proposed to make the determination more acceptable to the busy general surgical pathologist.[693,717,718] Parenthetically, a reasonably good prediction of tumor volume can be made from needle biopsy specimens by assessing a combination of morphologic and laboratory-based data.[722,734] It has even been proposed that a good estimate of tumor volume (referred to as *calculated* tumor volume) can be obtained by the following formula: cancer-specific serum PSA/amount of PSA leaking into the serum per cm^3 of cancer.[673] While on the subject of tumor volume or surface, it could be mentioned that even the roughest estimations of tumor amount in core needle biopsy material—such as percentage of cancer, number of positive cores, and bilaterality of the disease—bear a prognostic significance.[716] Therefore, it becomes important for the pathologist to provide a quantitative estimate of tumor amount in prostate needle biopsy specimens.[700a,700b]

6　*Age.* On the whole, the patient's age is not an important prognostic determinant. It is true that the few reported cases of prostatic carcinoma in men under 35 years of age have been usually characterized by poor differentiation and a very aggressive behavior.[720] However, statistical analysis of prostatic carcinomas occurring after the age of 40 years (the overwhelming majority) has not shown a definite relationship between age and survival.[656,690,725]

7　*Race.* Black males have a mortality from prostatic carcinoma that is almost twice that of white males. This is due, at least in part, to the fact that they are more likely to have a more advanced stage at presentation. When the disease is stratified for grade and stage, survival is similar in both races.[663]

8　*Method of initial diagnosis.* Patients in whom the prostatic carcinoma was diagnosed by TUR have a higher incidence of tumor dissemination than those diagnosed by needle biopsy[684]; it is not yet clear whether this is the result of the TUR procedure itself (unlikely) or a reflection of the fact that TUR-diagnosable tumors are usually more advanced.

9　*PSA serum levels.* The serum level of PSA is related to prognosis in prostatic carcinoma, as an indirect indicator of tumor volume, tumor extension, and response to therapy.[689]

10　*PSA and PAP immunoreactivity.* Prostatic carcinomas with areas of weak or negative reactivity for PSA or PAP behave as a group more aggressively than the others.[678]

11 *Perineural invasion.* Perineural invasion is a time-honored clue for the diagnosis of carcinoma, but its prognostic value remains controversial. Some studies have shown correlation with extraprostatic extension at resection[732] and with tumor progression after radical prostatectomy[723] (particularly if the diameter of the perineural invasion is quantitated[705]), but other authors have failed to find such an association.[676]

12 *Lymphovascular invasion.* Permeation of vascular channels as detected in whole-mount specimens of radical prostatectomy has been found to correlate with Gleason score, extraprostatic extension, seminal vesicle involvement, and likelihood of tumor progression.[692]

13 *Neovascularity.* It has been claimed that microvessel density is an independent predictor of pathologic stage and of progression in prostatic carcinoma.[661,662,726] Examination of CD34-immunostained sections has been found to be the most reliable in this regard.[675]

14 *Neuroendocrine features.* As already indicated, neuroendocrine features correlate with poor differentiation and poor prognosis. It is not clear, however, that they carry independent prognostic significance.[671]

15 *Androgen-receptor status.* Tumors in which the androgen receptor cannot be detected immunohistochemically have a worse prognosis than those in which this marker is present.[715] Mutations of the androgen-receptor gene have been detected in metastatic prostatic carcinoma and postulated to be the reason for the androgen independence of such tumors.[729]

16 *DNA ploidy.* Tumor aneuploidy, as determined by image or flow cytometry, correlates both with a higher Gleason score and with local and distant spread.[657,686,704,710,736] It also predicts an increased probability of grade shifting from the biopsy to the prostatectomy specimen.[719] However, there is still no agreement as to whether this technique provides independent prognostic information.[695,701,708,712,727] The Karolinska Institute authors, who have obtained the most impressive results with this technique,[685] believe that the controversies related to its use are largely related to methodologic inadequacies.[683]

17 *Proliferation index.* The Ki-67 labeling index of prostatic carcinoma has been said to predict tumor-specific mortality both in cases of limited disease and in cases associated with lymph node metastases.[665,706] The combined determination of histologic grade and proliferation index constitutes a particularly powerful prognostic tool.[670]

18 *Chromosomal abnormalities.* Patients with clonal karyotypic abnormalities are said to have shorter survival rates than those with normal karyotypes.[703]

19 *p53 expression.* The p53 tumor suppressor gene has been found to be mutated in a subset of advanced-stage prostatic carcinomas.[659,713,724,731] It remains to be seen whether this finding is of value independent of stage and grade.

20 ras *oncogene.* Expression of the *ras* oncogene p21 has also been found to correlate with the degree of nuclear anaplasia and therefore with microscopic grading, a feature closely related to prognosis.[733] However, there is no indication that the expression of this oncogene has independent prognostic value.

21 *bcl-2.* Positivity for this oncoprotein is statistically related to the probability of recurrence of prostatic carcinoma.[664,699]

22 *Circulating tumor cells.* The detection of circulating tumor cells through the measurement of PSA transcripts with the RT-PCR technique may indicate a greater likelihood of tumor recurrence.[677,687]

23 *Other molecular genetic markers.* In addition to the above, genetic molecular markers claimed to have prognostic relevance in prostatic carcinoma are gain of distal 8q, p21-waf1, p27-kip1, p34-cdc-2, p120, the various cyclins, and cathepsin-D.[682,696–698,707,730,731a]

The problem with these multitudinous markers, as in other areas of tumor pathology, is that most of them are indeed predictive of prognosis in an absolute sense, but their power diminishes considerably or disappears altogether when corrected for other factors, particularly stage and grade.[667,680,711,737] Several attempts have been made to combine some of these factors to produce multiple and hopefully more powerful prognostic indices.[716] In 1999, the College of American Pathologists (CAP) convened a group of clinicians, pathologists and statisticians to produce a consensus statement on the relative significance of these parameters, which were divided into the following categories[660]:

I   Proven to be of prognostic importance and useful in clinical patient management:
   Preoperative serum PSA level
   TNM stage grouping
   Histologic grade as Gleason score
   Surgical margin status

II Extensively studied but whose importance remains to be validated:
   Tumor volume
   Histologic type
   DNA ploidy

III Not sufficiently studied to demonstrate their prognostic value:
   Perineural invasion
   Neuroendocrine differentiation
   Microvessel density
   Nuclear roundness
   Chromatin texture
   Other karyometric factors
   Proliferation markers
   PSA derivates
   Other factors (oncogenes, tumor suppressor genes, apoptosis genes, etc.).

Other tumors

Embryonal rhabdomyosarcoma is by far the most common malignant prostatic tumor in infancy and childhood (Fig. 18.40). It produces a firm, smooth enlargement of the prostate. Extraprostatic extension is the rule; nodal metastases are less common than in rhabdomyosarcoma of head and neck.[761] Microscopically, these tumors are very cellular, especially around blood vessels. These hypercellular foci alternate with areas of myxoid or edematous change and with foci of necrosis. Most of the tumor cells are small, varying in shape from round to oval to spindle. Occasional bizarre forms with a more abundant, brightly acidophilic cytoplasm are also found. The microscopic appearance is distinctive, even in the absence of cross striations, but supportive evidence should be sought through immunocytochemical markers (see Chapter 25).

Tumors having a leiomyosarcoma-like appearance seem to be associated with a better prognosis. The current therapy for this tumor, which consists of multidrug chemotherapy combined with limited surgery and radiation, has proved highly effective; pelvic exenteration is reserved for the few unresponsive cases.[747,755]

Benign neoplasms of the adult prostate are practically nonexistent. Most cases diagnosed as leiomyoma are in reality foci of purely stromal overgrowth in nodular hyperplasia (see p. 1364).[752a]

Cystadenoma of the prostate presents as a large, multilocular mass composed of glands and cysts lined by prostatic-type epithelium lying in a hypocellular fibrous stroma.[759,760] It may extend into the retroperitoneum and be attached to the prostate by a small pedicle.[764]

Proliferative lesions of the specialized prostatic stroma comprise a number of entities with a wide range of morphologic appearances and clinical behavior. We have grouped them into two categories: *prostatic stromal proliferation of uncertain malignant potential (PSUMP) and stromal sarcoma*[749] (Figs 18.41 to 18.43) Four histologic patterns were identified in the PSUMP category, ranging from scattered atypical stromal cells (perhaps a regressive non-neoplastic disorder) to lesions having a pattern of growth resembling phyllodes tumor of breast.[768] Prostatic stromal sarcoma showed greater cellularity,

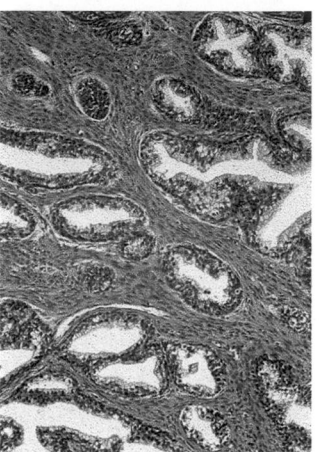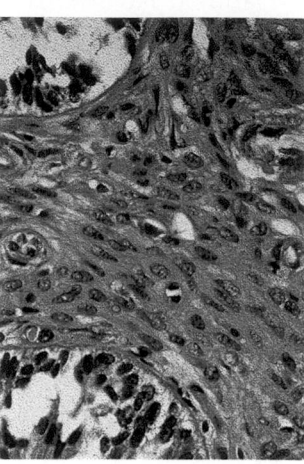

Fig. 18.41 Prostatic stromal proliferation of uncertain malignant potential (PSUMP).

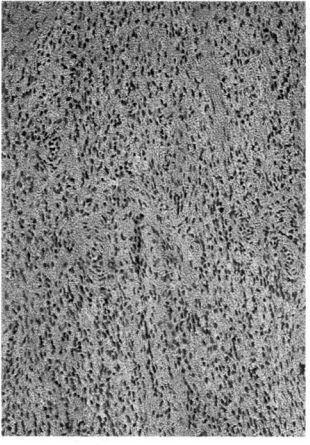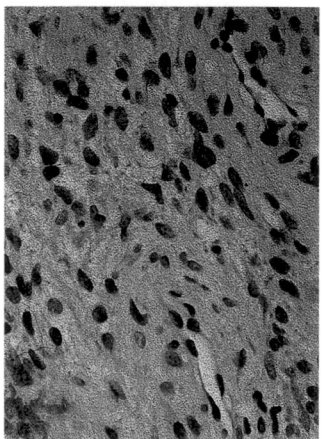

Fig. 18.42 Stromal sarcoma of prostate.

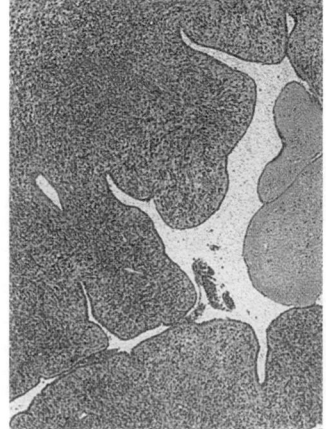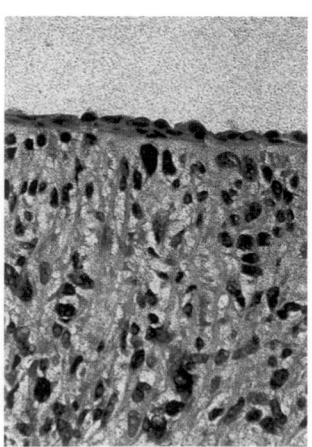

Fig. 18.43 Stromal sarcoma of prostate with an appearance reminiscent of phyllodes tumor of breast.

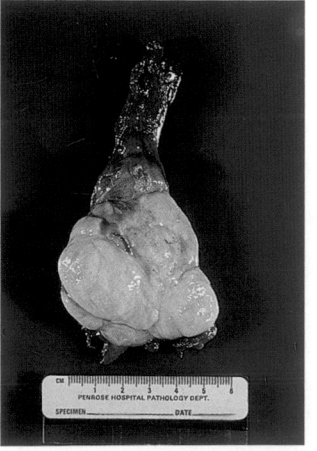

A   **B**

18.40 A and **B**, Outer aspect and cut surface of embryonal rhabdomyosarcoma of prostate in a child.

mitoses, necrosis, and stromal overgrowth. Immuno-histochemically, these lesions were positive for vimentin, CD34, actin (the latter in less than half of the cases) and progesterone receptors (but only rarely estrogen receptors). PSUMP lesions have a tendency to local recurrence, whereas stromal sarcomas have also the potential for distant metastases.[749]

Solitary fibrous tumor of the prostate, of which benign and malignant forms exist, shares many features with the above-described lesions (down to the positivity for progesterone but not for estrogen receptors), to the point of raising the question as to whether a separation among the two is warranted. However, a diagnosis of solitary fibrous tumor would seem justified for the lesions showing the classic alternation of hyper- and hypo-cellular areas, keloid-type collagen, and bcl immunoreactivity.[767,770]

Other sarcomas of the adult prostate include **leiomyosarcoma** (to be distinguished primarily from postoperative spindle cell nodule, an exercise of crucial importance, see p. 1367); **synovial sarcoma** (the existence of which in an intraprostatic location has been corroborated cytogenetically and molecularly[748,754]); **pleomorphic rhabdomyosarcoma; angiosarcoma** (Fig. 18.44); **fibrosarcoma;** and **malignant fibrous histiocytoma.**[744,752,762,769] The last two entities always remain diagnoses of exclusion and hardly of certainty in view of the lack of specific markers. Just as importantly, it is well to remember that—as in many other organs—one should consider the alternative and more likely possibility of sarcomatoid carcinoma/carcinosarcoma before making a diagnosis of primary sarcoma of one of those types.

Malignant mixed tumor, phyllodes tumor, Wilms' tumor, and **yolk sac tumor (endodermal sinus tumor),** morphologically analogous to those seen in the salivary

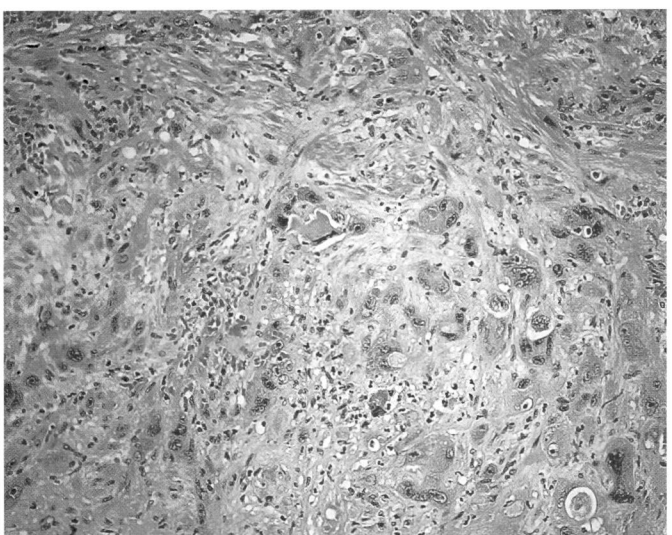

Fig. 18.44 Angiosarcoma with epithelioid features involving the prostate. Note the cytoplasmic vacuolization. The diagnosis was confirmed immunohistochemically.

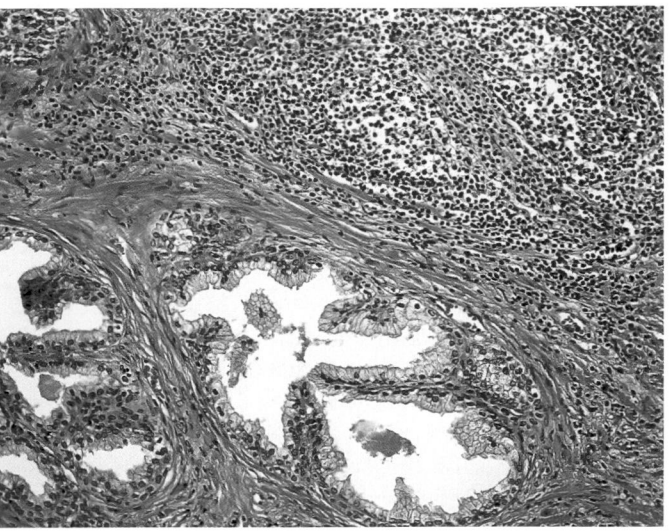

Fig. 18.45 Infiltration of the prostatic stroma by the cells of chronic lymphocytic leukemia. This was an incidental finding in an operation done for nodular hyperplasia.

glands, breast, kidney, and gonads, respectively, have been reported.[741,743,751,765,771]

Cystic epithelial–stromal tumor is the name given to a malignant prostatic neoplasm composed of an admixture of transitional, glandular, and mesenchymal-appearing spindle cells[753,756]; it probably represents a variation in the sarcomatoid carcinoma/carcinosarcoma spectrum.

Malignant lymphoma can involve the prostate. Most patients have previous or concurrent evidence of extraprostatic disease.[742,746] The majority of the cases are large B-cell lymphomas, but any other type can occur, including Hodgkin's lymphoma[757] and angiotropic lymphoma.[740] **Leukemic involvement** of the prostate is seen in about 8% of the cases.[766] This includes so-called "granulocytic sarcoma" and chronic lymphocytic leukemia, the incidence in the latter reaching 20%[745] (Fig. 18.45). Prostatic involvement by leukemia or lymphoma may result in acute urinary obstruction, which is quickly relieved by radiation therapy.

Secondary involvement of the prostate occurs through direct extension by carcinoma of the bladder and urethra,[763] colorectum and anus, and soft tissue tumors.[739,772] Distant metastases have been seen from lung carcinomas, melanomas, renal cell carcinomas, and other sites.[739,750,758]

Seminal vesicles and Cowper's glands

The seminal vesicles have a thick muscular wall and highly complex mucosal folds. The epithelium is composed of columnar and basal cells. The cytoplasm of the former characteristically contains large amounts of lipofuscin pigment.

"**Monstrous" cells** are a common feature of the epithelium of this organ, particularly in older individuals. They are thought to represent an involutionary phenomenon and should not be confused with a malignant process.[781] The presence of lipofuscin pigment in the cytoplasm is the most important clue to their nature.

Hyaline globules are often found in the muscular wall of the organ; they are thought to be of degenerative nature and have no clinical significance.

Amyloidosis is detected in the form of subepithelial deposits in about 10% of seminal vesicles.[777,790] It has been suggested that this abnormality may be more common in patients with hormonally treated prostatic adenocarcinoma.[794]

Tuberculosis of the seminal vesicle is usually secondary to infection in the prostate; therefore the greatest amount of involvement is in the portion of the glands immediately adjacent to this organ. In other cases, presumably of hematogenous origin, the disease is limited to the prostate.[773]

Cysts arising from the ducts of the seminal vesicle present as a soft cystic mass between the rectum and the base of the bladder. Congenital examples may be bilateral, associated with ipsilateral renal agenesis, ureteral anomalies, and oligospermia.[791,792] Acquired cysts result from obstruction secondary to chronic prostatitis.[776] Benign lesions of the seminal vesicles with a multilocular appearance have sometimes been designated as *cystadenomas*[787] or as *cystic epithelial–stromal tumors*[783] (Fig. 18.46).

Primary carcinomas of the seminal vesicle are pathologic curiosities.[793] Many of the reported cases probably represent secondary invasion from carcinoma originating in other sites, particularly the prostate. To make a diagnosis of primary carcinoma of the seminal vesicle, there must be no involvement of the prostate, and stains for PSA must be negative. They are instead immunoreactive for CA-125 and cytokeratin 7 (although not for cytokeratin 20).[786] Most cases have a prominent papillary configuration.[774]

Other reported types of primary malignant tumors of the seminal vesicles are **leiomyosarcoma**,[789] **phyllodes tumor**,[778] **choriocarcinoma**,[779] **müllerian adenosarcoma**,[782] **male adnexal tumor of probable wolffian origin**,[784] and **angiosarcoma**. In our experience, some of the latter have been of the epithelioid type.

Secondary involvement of seminal vesicles is common in prostatic carcinoma,[785] and it also occurs in in situ and invasive transitional cell carcinoma of the bladder.[788]

Normal Cowper's glands are sometimes seen in specimens from prostatic resections or needle biopsies.[775] They form well-demarcated lobules composed of small, compact glands radiating from a central excretory duct lined by pseudostratified epithelium. The best way to identify these glands is to remember that they have the appearance of mucinous minor salivary glands embedded within skeletal muscle.[775]

Adenocarcinomas of Cowper's gland are even less common than carcinomas of seminal vesicles, and the same care should be exercised in ruling out the alternative possibility of prostatic origin.[780] They are mucin producing and may ulcerate through the skin of the scrotum (Fig. 18.25).

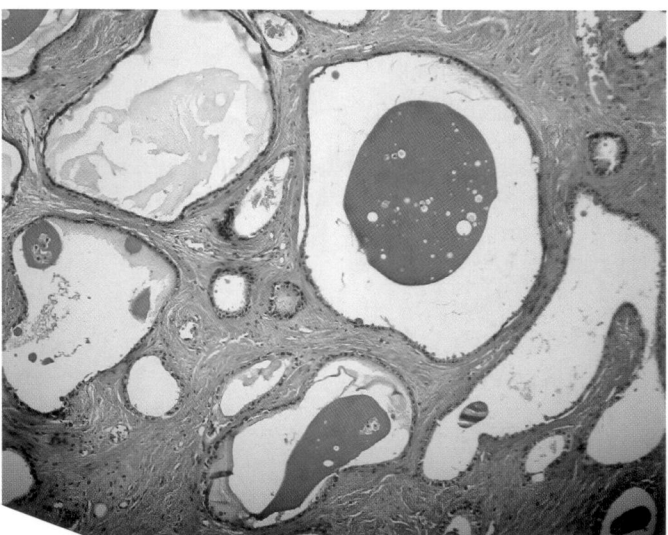

ó So-called "cystadenoma" of seminal vesicle.

References

PROSTATE
Normal anatomy

1   Allsbrook WC Jr, Simms WW. Histochemistry of the prostate. Hum Pathol 1992, **23**: 297–305.
2   Aprikian AG, Cordon-Cardo C, Fair WR, Reuter VE. Characterization of neuroendocrine differentiation in human benign prostate and prostatic adenocarcinoma. Cancer 1993, **71**: 3952–3965.
3   Ayala AG, Vae YR, Babaian R, Troncoso P, Grignon DJ. The prostatic capsule. Does it exist? Its importance in the staging and treatment of prostatic carcinoma. Am J Surg Pathol 1989, **13**: 21–27.
4   Blennerhassett JB, Vickery AL Jr. Carcinoma of the prostate gland. Cancer 1966, **19**: 980–984.
5   Bonkhoff H, Remberger K. Widespread distribution of nuclear androgen receptors in the basal cell layer of the normal and hyperplastic human prostate. Virchows Arch [A] 1993, **422**: 35–38.
6   Bonkhoff H, Stein U, Remberger K. Androgen receptor status in endocrine-paracrine cell types of the normal, hyperplastic, and neoplastic human prostate. Virchows Arch [A] 1993, **423**: 291–294.
7   Bonkhoff H, Stein U, Remberger K. Multidirectional differentiation in the normal, hyperplastic, and neoplastic human prostate. Simultaneous demonstration of cell-specific epithelial markers. Hum Pathol 1994, **25**: 42–46.
8   Chodak GW, Kranc DM, Puy LA, Takeda H, Johnson K, Chang C. Nuclear localization of androgen receptor in heterogeneous samples of normal, hyperplastic and neoplastic human prostate. J Urol 1992, **147**: 798–803.
9   Cohen RJ, McNeal JE, Redmond SL, Meehan K, Thomas R, Wilce M, Dawkins HJ. Luminal contents of benign and malignant prostatic glands: Correspondence to altered secretory mechanisms. Hum Pathol 2000, **31**: 94–100.

10 Cunha GR. Role of mesenchymal-epithelial interactions in normal and abnormal development of the mammary gland and prostate. Cancer 1994, **74:** 1030–1044.

11 di Sant'Agnese PA, de Mesy Jensen KL, Churkian CV. Human prostatic endocrine-paracrine (APUD) cells. Distributional analysis with a comparison of serotonin and neuron-specific enolase immunoreactivity and silver stains. Arch Pathol Lab Med 1985, **109:** 607–612.

12 Grignon DJ, O'Malley FP. Mucinous metaplasia in the prostate gland. Am J Surg Pathol 1993, **17:** 287–290.

13 Howatt AJ, Mills PM, Lyons TJ, Stephenson TJ. Absence of S-100 protein in prostatic glands. Histopathology 1988, **13:** 468–470.

14 Kirchheim D, Niles NR, Frankus E, Hodges CV. Correlative histochemical and histological studies on thirty radical prostatectomy specimens. Cancer 1966, **19:** 1683–1696.

15 Lager DJ, Goeken JA, Kemp JD, Robinson RA. Squamous metaplasia of the prostate. An immunohistochemical study. Am J Clin Pathol 1988, **90:** 597–601.

16 Leong AS, Gilham P, Milios J. Cytokeratin and vimentin intermediate filament proteins in benign and neoplastic prostatic epithelium. Histopathology 1988, **13:** 435–442.

17 McNeal JE. Prostate. In Sternberg S (ed.): Histology for pathologists, ed. 2. Philadelphia, 1997, Lippincott-Raven Publishers, p. 994.

18 Okada H, Tsubura A, Okamura A, Senzaki H, Naka Y, Komatz Y, Mori S. Keratin profiles in normal/hyperplastic prostates and prostate carcinoma. Virchows Arch [A] 1992, **421:** 157–161.

19 Schmid KW, Helpap B, Totsch M, Kirchmair R, Dockhorn-Dworniczak B, Bocker W, Fischer-Colbrie R. Immunohistochemical localization of chromogranins A and B and secretogranin II in normal, hyperplastic and neoplastic prostate. Histopathology 1994, **24:** 233–239.

20 Shiraishi T, Kusano I, Watanabe M, Yasani R, Liu PI. Mucous gland metaplasia of the prostate. Am J Surg Pathol 1993, **17:** 618–622.

21 Srigley JR, Dardick I, Hartwick RW, Klotz L. Basal epithelial cells of human prostate gland are not myoepithelial cells. A comparative immunohistochemical and ultrastructural study with the human salivary gland. Am J Pathol 1990, **136:** 957–966.

22 Zhou M, Patel A, Rubin MA. Prevalence and location of peripheral nerve found on prostate needle biopsy. Am J Clin Pathol 2001, **115:** 39–43.

Ectopia

23 Kanomata N, Eble JN, Ohbayashi C, Yasui N, Tanaka H, Matsumoto O. Ectopic prostate in the retrovesical space. J Urol Pathol 1997, **7:** 121–126.

Nodular hyperplasia

24 Algaba F. Bases morfológicas del desarrollo de la hiperplasia prostática. Patología 1993, **26:** 113–119.

25 Attah EB, Nkposong EO. Phylloides type of atypical prostatic hyperplasia. J Urol 1976, **115:** 762–764.

26 Badenoch A. Benign enlargement of the prostate. Trans Med Soc Lond 1970, **86:** 34–40.

27 Bennett AH, Harrison JH. A comparison of operative approach for prostatectomy, 1948 and 1968. Surg Gynecol Obstet 1969, **1281:** 969–974.

28 Berry SJ, Coffey DS, Walsh PC, Ewing LL. The development of human benign prostatic hyperplasia with age. J Urol 1984, **132:** 474–479.

29 Bonkhoff H, Remberger K. Morphogenetic concepts of normal and abnormal growth in the human prostate. Virchows Arch 1998, **433:** 195–202.

30 Brendler C, Schlegel P, Dowd J, Kirby R, Zattoni F. Surgical treatment for benign prostatic hyperplasia. Cancer 1992, **70:** 371–373.

31 Chen KTK, Schiff JJ. Adenomatoid prostatic tumor. Urology 1983, **21:** 88–89.

32 Cordon-Cardo C, Koff A, Drobnjak M, Capodieci P, Osman I, Millard SS, Gaudin PB, Fazzari M, Zhang ZF, Massague J, Scher HI. Distinct altered patterns of p27^{KIP1} gene expression in benign prostatic hyperplasia and prostatic carcinoma. J Natl Cancer Inst 1998, **90:** 1284–1291.

33 Denis L, Lepor H, Dowd J, Geller J, Griffiths K, Hald T, McConnell J. Alternatives to surgery for benign prostatic hyperplasia. Cancer 1992, **70:** 374–378.

34 Eble JN, Tejada E. Prostatic stromal hyperplasia with bizarre nuclei. Arch Pathol Lab Med 1991, **115:** 87–89.

35 Epstein JI, Partin AW, Shue M, Sherry ED, Marks LS. Histological changes in benign prostate biopsies following long-term finasteride therapy for prostatic hyperplasia. J Urol Pathol 1999, **10:** 87–96.

36 Eri LM, Tveter KJ. A prospective, placebo-controlled study of the luteinizing hormone-releasing hormone agonist leuprolide as treatment for patients with benign prostatic hyperplasia. J Urol 1993, **150:** 359–364.

37 Gleason PE, Jones JA, Regan JS, Salvas DB, Eble JN, Lamph WW, Vlahos CJ, Huang WL, Falcone JF, Hirsch KS. Platelet derived growth factor (PDGF), androgens and inflammation. Possible etiologic factors in the development of prostatic hyperplasia. J Urol 1993, **149:** 1586–1592.

38 Gormley GJ, Stoner E, Bruskewitz RC, Imperato-McGinley J, Walsh PC, McConnell JD, Andriole GL, Geller J, Bracken BR, Tenover JS, et al. The effect of finasteride in men with benign prostatic hyperplasia. The Finasteride Study Group. N Engl J Med 1992, **327:** 1185–1191.

39 Kafandaris PM, Polyzonis MB. Fibroadenoma-like foci in human prostatic nodular hyperplasia. Prostate 1983, **4:** 33–36.

40 Kerley SW, Corica FA, Qian J, Meyers RP, Bostwick DG. Peripheral zone involvement by prostatic hyperplasia. J Urol Pathol 1997, **6:** 87–94.

41 Kyprianou N, Tu H, Jacobs SC. Apoptotic versus proliferative activities in human benign prostatic hyperplasia. Hum Pathol 1996, **27:** 668–675.

42 McNicol PJ, Dodd JG. High prevalence of human papillomavirus in prostate tissues. J Urol 1991, **145:** 850–853.

43 Montironi R, Diamanti L. Morphologic changes in benign prostatic hyperplasia following chronic treatment with the 5-α reductase inhibitor finasteride: Comparison with the effect of combination endocrine therapy. J Urol Pathol 1996, **4:** 123–136.

44 Moore RA. Benign hypertrophy of the prostate. A morphological study. J Urol 1943, **50:** 680–710.

45 Oesterling JE. Benign prostatic hyperplasia. Medical and minimally invasive treatment options. N Engl J Med 1995, **332:** 99–109.

46 Ohori M, Egawa S, Wheeler TM. Nodules resembling nodular hyperplasia in the peripheral zone of the prostate gland. J Urol Pathol 1994, **2:** 223–234.

47 Oyen RH, Van de Voorde WM, Van Poppel HP, Brys PP, Ameye FE, Franssens YM, Baert AL, Baert LV. Benign hyperplastic nodules that originate in the peripheral zone of the prostate gland. Radiology 1993, **189:** 707–711.

48 Peters CA, Walsh P. The effect of nafarelin acetate, a luteinizing-hormone-releasing hormone agonist, on benign prostatic hyperplasia. N Engl J Med 1987, **317:** 599–604.

49 Price H, McNeal JE, Stamey TA. Evolving patterns of tissue composition in benign prostatic hyperplasia as a function of specimen size. Hum Pathol 1990, **21:** 578–585.

50 Roos NP, Wennberg JE, Malenka DJ, Fisher ES, McPherson K, Andersen TF, Cohen MM, Ramsey E. Mortality and reoperation after open and transurethral resection of the prostate for benign prostatic hyperplasia. N Engl J Med 1989, **320:** 1120–1124.

51 Schwartz I, Wein AJ, Malloy TR, Glick JH. Prostatic cancer after prostatectomy for benign disease. Cancer 1986, **58**: 994–996.

52 Shapiro E, Becich MJ, Hartanto V, Lepor H. The relative proportion of stromal and epithelial hyperplasia is related to the development of symptomatic benign prostate hyperplasia. J Urol 1992, **147**: 1293–1297.

53 Smith MJ. Prostatic corpora amylacea. Monogr Surg Sci 1966, **3**: 209–265.

54 Theyer G, Kramer G, Assmann I, Sherwood E, Preinfalk W, Marberger M, Zechner O, Steiner GE. Phenotypic characterization of infiltrating leukocytes in benign prostatic hyperplasia. Lab Invest 1992, **66**: 96–107.

55 Van de Voorde WM, Oyen RH, Van Poppel HP, Wouters K, Baert LV, Lauweryns JM. Peripherally localized benign hyperplastic nodules of the prostate. Mod Pathol 1995, **8**: 46–50.

55a Viglione MP, Potter S, Partin AW, Lesniak MS, Epstein JI. Should the diagnosis of benign prostatic hyperplasia be made on prostate needle biopsy? Hum Pathol 2002, **23**: 796–800.

56 Wasson JH, Reda DJ, Bruskewitz RC, Elinson J, Keller AM, Henderson WG for Veterans Affairs Cooperative Study Group on Transurethral Resection of the Prostate. A comparison of transurethral surgery with watchful waiting for moderate symptoms of benign prostatic hyperplasia. N Engl J Med 1995, **332**: 75–79.

57 Wilson JD. The pathogenesis of benign prostatic hyperplasia. Am J Med 1980, **68**: 745–756.

58 Young RH, Scully RE. Pseudosarcomatous lesions of the urinary bladder, prostate gland, and urethra. A report of three cases and review of the literature. Arch Pathol Lab Med 1987, **111**: 354–358.

Infarct

59 Flocks RH. The arterial distribution within the prostate gland. Its role in transurethral prostatic resection. J Urol 1937, **37**: 524–548.

60 Hubly JW, Thompson GJ. Infarction of the prostate and volumetric changes produced by the lesion. J Urol 1940, **43**: 459–467.

61 Milord RA, Kahane H, Epstein JI. Infarct of the prostatic gland: experience on needle biopsy specimens. Am J Surg Pathol 2000, **24**: 1378–1384.

62 Moore RA. Benign hypertrophy of the prostate. A morphological study. J Urol 1943, **50**: 680–710.

63 Mostofi FK, Morse WH. Epithelial metaplasia in "prostatic infarction." Arch Pathol 1951, **51**: 340–345.

64 Silber I, Rosai J, Cordonnier JJ. The incidence of elevated acid phosphatase in prostatic infarction. J Urol 1970, **103**: 765–766.

Prostatitis

65 Blumenfeld W, Tucci S, Narayan P. Incidental lymphocytic prostatitis. Selective involvement with nonmalignant glands. Am J Surg Pathol 1992, **16**: 975–981.

66 de la Rosette JJ, Hubregtse MR, Meuleman EJ, Stolk-Engelaar MV, Debruyne FM. Diagnosis and treatment of 409 patients with prostatitis syndromes. Urology 1993, **41**: 301–307.

67 Neal DE Jr, Clejan S, Sarma D, Moon TD. Prostate specific antigen and prostatitis. I. Effect of prostatitis on serum PSA in the human and nonhuman primate. Prostate 1992, **20**: 105–111.

68 Nickel JC, Costerton JW. Coagulase-negative staphylococcus in chronic prostatitis. J Urol 1992, **147**: 398–400.

69 Shortliffe LM, Sellers RG, Schachter J. The characterization of nonbacterial prostatitis. Search for an etiology. J Urol 1992, **148**: 1461–1466.

70 Thomson RD, Clejan S. Digital rectal examination-associated alterations in serum prostate-specific antigen. Am J Clin Pathol 1992, **97**: 466–467.

Abscess

....ni AM, O'Flynn JD. Prostatic abscess. A report of 25 cases. Urol 1968, **40**: 736–739.

72 Granados EA, Riley G, Salvador J, Vincente J. Prostatic abscess. Diagnosis and treatment. J Urol 1992, **148**: 80–82.

73 Jacobsen JD, Kvist E. Prostatic abscess. A review of literature and a presentation of 5 cases. Scand J Urol 1993, **27**: 281–284.

74 Trapnell J, Roberts M. Prostatic abscess. Br J Surg 1970, **57**: 565–569.

Tuberculosis and BCG-induced granulomas

75 Auerbach O. Tuberculosis of the genital system. Q Bull Sea View Hosp 1942, **7**: 188–207.

76 Miyashita H, Troncoso P, Babaian RJ. BCG-induced granulomatous prostatitis. A comparative ultrasound and pathologic study. Urology 1992, **39**: 364–367.

77 Moore RA. Tuberculosis of the prostate gland. J Urol 1937, **37**: 372–384.

78 Mukamel E, Konichezky M, Engelstein D, Cytron S, Abramovici A, Servadio C. Clinical and pathological findings in prostates following intravesical bacillus Calmette Guerin instillations. J Urol 1990, **144**: 1399–1400.

Other specific infections

79 Abdelatif OM, Chandler FW, McGuire BS Jr. Chlamydia trachomatis in chronic abacterial prostatitis. Demonstration by colorimetric in situ hybridization. Hum Pathol 1991, **22**: 41–44.

80 Adams JR Jr, Mata JA, Culkin DJ, Fowler M, Venable DD. Acquired immunodeficiency syndrome manifesting as prostate nodule secondary to cryptococcal infection. Urology 1992, **39**: 289–291.

81 Bergner DM, Kraus SD, Duck GB, Lewis R. Systemic blastomycosis presenting with acute prostate abscess. J Urol 1981, **126**: 132–133.

82 Campbell TB, Kaufman L, Cook JL. Aspergillosis of the prostate associated with an indwelling bladder catheter. Case report and review. Clin Infect Dis 1992, **14**: 942–944.

83 Chen KTK, Schiff JJ. Coccidioidomycosis of prostate. Urology 1985, **25**: 82–84.

84 de Souza E, Katz DA, Dworzack DL, Longo G. Actinomycosis of the prostate. J Urol 1985, **133**: 290–291.

85 Gardner WA, Culberson DE, Bennett BD. Trichomonas vaginalis in the prostate gland. Arch Pathol Lab Med 1986, **110**: 430–432.

86 Haddad FS. Coccidioidomycosis of the genitourinary tract with special emphasis on the epididymis and the prostate: Four case reports and review of the literature. J Urol Pathol 1996, **4**: 205–212.

87 Hinchey WW, Someren A. Cryptococcal prostatitis. Am J Clin Pathol 1981, **75**: 257–260.

88 Indudhara R, Singh SK, Vaidyanathan S, Banerjee CK. Isolated invasive candidal prostatitis. Urol Int 1992, **48**: 362–364.

89 Mamo GJ, Rivero MA, Jacobs SC. Cryptococcal prostatic abscess associated with the acquired immunodeficiency syndrome. J Urol 1992, **148**: 889–890.

90 Milchgrub S, Visconti E, Avellini J. Granulomatous prostatitis induced by capsule-deficient cryptococcal infection. J Urol 1990, **143**: 365–366.

91 Schachter J. Is chlamydia trachomatis a cause of prostatitis? J Urol 1985, **134**: 711.

92 Shurbaji MS, Gupta PK, Myers J. Immunohistochemical demonstration of chlamydial antigens in association with prostatitis. Mod Pathol 1988, **1**: 348–351.

93 Yu S, Provet J. Prostatic abscess due to *Candida tropicalis* in a nonacquired immunodeficiency syndrome patient. J Urol 1992, **148**: 1536–1538.

94 Zigelboim J, Goldfarb RA, Mody D, Williams TW, Bradshaw MW, Harris RL. Prostatic abscess due to *Histoplasma capsulatum* in a patient with the acquired immunodeficiency syndrome. J Urol 1992, **147**: 166–168.

Granulomatous prostatitis

95 Bryan RL, Newman J, Campbell A, Fitzgerald G, Kadow C, O'Brien JM. Granulomatous prostatitis. A clinicopathological study. Histopathology 1991, **19**: 453–457.

96 Dhundee J, Maciver AG. An immunohistological study of granulomatous prostatitis. Histopathology 1991, **18**: 435–441.

97 Kelalis PP, Greene LF, Harrison EG Jr. Granulomatous prostatitis. A mimic of carcinoma of the prostate. JAMA 1965, **191**: 111–113.

98 Oppenheimer JR, Kahane H, Epstein JI. Granulomatous prostatitis on needle biopsy. Arch Pathol Lab Med 1997, **121**: 724–729.

99 Presti B, Weidner N. Granulomatous prostatitis and poorly differentiated prostate carcinoma. Their distinction with the use of immunohistochemical methods. Am J Clin Pathol 1991, **95**: 330–334.

100 Tanner FH, McDonald JR. Granulomatous prostatitis. A histologic study of a group of granulomatous lesions collected from prostate glands. Arch Pathol 1943, **36**: 358–370.

Prostatitis with eosinophils

101 Epstein JI, Hutchins GM. Granulomatous prostatitis. Distinction among allergic, nonspecific, and posttransurethral resection lesions. Hum Pathol 1984, **15**: 818–825.

102 Helpap B, Vogel J. TUR-prostatitis. Histological and immunohistochemical observations on a special type of granulomatous prostatitis. Pathol Res Pract 1986, **181**: 301–307.

103 Henry L, Wagner B, Faulkner M, Slater D, Ansell I. Metal deposition in postsurgical granulomas of the urinary tract. Histopathology 1993, **22**: 457–466.

104 Lee G, Shepherd N. Necrotising granulomata in prostatic resection specimens—a sequel to previous operation. J Clin Pathol 1983, **36**: 1067–1070.

105 Liu S, Miller PD, Holmes SA, Christmas TJ, Kirby RS. Eosinophilic prostatitis and prostatic specific antigen. Br J Urol 1992, **69**: 61–63.

106 Melicow MMJ. Allergic granulomas of the prostate gland. J Urol 1951, **65**: 288–296.

107 Mies C, Balogh K, Stadecker M. Palisading prostate granulomas following surgery. Am J Surg Pathol 1984, **8**: 217–221.

108 Sorensen FB, Marcussen N. Iatrogenic granulomas of the prostate and the urinary bladder. Pathol Res Pract 1987, **182**: 822–830.

109 Stewart MJ, Wray S, Hall M. Allergic prostatitis in asthmatics. J Pathol Bacteriol 1954, **67**: 423–430.

110 Symmers W St C. Two cases of eosinophilic prostatitis due to metazoan infestation. J Pathol Bacteriol 1957, **73**: 549–555.

111 Towfighi J, Sadeghee S, Wheeler JE, Enterline HT. Granulomatous prostatitis with emphasis on the eosinophilic variety. Am J Clin Pathol 1972, **58**: 630–641.

Other inflammations

112 Chantelois AE, Parker SH, Sims JE, Horne DW. Malacoplakia of the prostate sonographically mimicking carcinoma. Radiology 1990, **177**: 193–195.

113 Day DS, Carpenter HD Jr, Allsbrook WC Jr. Hair granuloma of the prostate. Hum Pathol 1996, **27**: 196–197.

114 Fox H. Nodular histiocytic prostatitis. J Urol 1966, **96**: 372–374.

115 Rach JF, Kandzari SJ. Unusual site for an unusual disease. Malacoplakia of the prostate. W V Med J 1989, **85**: 90–91.

116 Shimizu S, Takimoto Y, Nimura T, Kaya H, Yamamoto T, Kawazoe K, Okada K. A case of prostatic malacoplakia. J Urol 1981, **126**: 277–279.

117 Sujka SK, Malin BT, Asirwatham JE. Prostatic malakoplakia associated with prostatic adenocarcinoma and multiple prostatic abscesses. Urology 1989, **34**: 159–161.

118 Val-Bernal JF, Garijo F. Isolated idiopathic granulomatous (giant cell) vasculitis of the prostate: a case report. Int J Surg Pathol 1999, **7**: 53–58.

119 Val-Bernal JF, Gonzalez-Vela C, Mayorga M, Garijo MF. Isolated fibrinoid arteritis of the prostate. Int J Surg Pathol 1997, **4**: 143–148.

Calculi

120 Klimas R, Bennett B, Gardner WA Jr. Prostatic calculi: a review. Prostate 1985, **7**: 91–96.

Tumorlike conditions of prostate and prostatic urethra

121 Brennick JB, O'Connell JX, Dickersin GR, Pilch BZ, Young RH. Lipofuscin pigmentation (so-called "melanosis") of the prostate. Am J Surg Pathol 1994, **18**: 446–454.

122 Butterick JD, Schnitzer B, Abell MR. Ectopic prostatic tissue in urethra. A clinicopathological entity and a significant cause of hematuria. J Urol 1971, **105**: 97–104.

123 Chan JK, Chow TC, Tsui MS. Prostatic-type polyps of the lower urinary tract: three histogenetic types? Histopathology 1987, **11**: 789–801.

124 Craig JR, Hart WR. Benign polyps with prostatic-type epithelium of the urethra. Am J Clin Pathol 1975, **63**: 343–347.

125 Daroca PJ Jr, Martin AA, Reed RJ, Krengel SS, Hellstrom WJ. Urethral nephrogenic adenoma. A report of three cases, including a case with infiltration of the prostatic stroma. J Urol Pathol 1993, **2**: 157–172.

126 Gagucas RJ, Brown RW, Wheeler TM. Verumontanum mucosal gland hyperplasia. Am J Surg Pathol 1995, **19**: 30–36.

127 Gardner WA Jr, Spitz WU. Melanosis of the prostate gland. Am J Clin Pathol 1971, **56**: 762–764.

128 Gledhill A. Ectopic prostatic tissue. J Urol 1985, **133**: 110–111.

129 Goldman RL. Melanogenic epithelium in the prostate gland. Am J Clin Pathol 1968, **49**: 75–78.

130 Goodwin WE, Cummings RH. Squamous metaplasia of the verumontanum with obstruction due to hypertrophy. Long-term effects of estrogen on the prostate in an aging male-to-female transsexual. J Urol 1984, **131**: 553–554.

131 Huang WL, Ro JY, Grignon DJ, Swanson D, Ordonez NG, Ayala AG. Postoperative spindle cell nodule of the prostate and bladder. J Urol 1990, **143**: 824–826.

132 Humphrey PA, Vollmer RT. Extramedullary hematopoiesis in the prostate. Am J Surg Pathol 1991, **15**: 486–490.

133 Jao W, Fretzin DF, Christ ML, Prinz LM. Blue nevus of the prostate gland. Arch Pathol 1971, **91**: 187–191.

134 Lew S, Richter S, Jelin N, Siegal A. A blue naevus of the prostate. A light microscopic study including an investigation of S-100 protein positive cells in the normal and in the diseased gland. Histopathology 1991, **18**: 443–448.

135 Malpica A, Ro JY, Troncoso P, Ordonez NG, Amin MB, Ayala AG. Nephrogenic adenoma of the prostatic urethra involving the prostate gland. A clinicopathologic and immunohistochemical study of eight cases. Hum Pathol 1994, **25**: 390–395.

136 Moore RA. Pathology of prostatic utricle. Arch Pathol 1937, **23**: 517–524.

137 Murad TM, Robinson LH, Bueschen AJ. Villous polyps of the urethra. A report of two cases. Hum Pathol 1979, **10**: 478–481.

138 Proppe KH, Scully RE, Rosai J. Postoperative spindle cell nodules of genitourinary tract resembling sarcomas. Am J Surg Pathol 1984, **8**: 101–108.

139 Ro JY, el-Naggar AK, Amin MB, Sahin AA, Ordonez NG, Ayala AG. Pseudosarcomatous fibromyxoid tumor of the urinary bladder and prostate. Immunohistochemical, ultrastructural, and DNA flow cytometric analyses of nine cases. Hum Pathol 1993, **24**: 1203–1210.

140 Ro JY, Grignon DJ, Ayala AG, Hogan SF, Tetu B, Ordonez NG. Blue nevus and melanosis of the prostate. Electron-microscopic and immunohistochemical studies. Am J Clin Pathol 1988, **90**: 530–535.

141 Stein AJ, Prioleau PG, Catalona WJ. Adenomatous polyps of the

prostatic urethra. A cause of hematospermia. J Urol 1980, **124:** 298–299.

142 Walker AN, Mills SE, Fechner RE, Perry JM. "Endometrial" adenocarcinoma of the prostatic urethra arising in a villous polyp. A light microscopic and immunoperoxidase study. Arch Pathol Lab Med 1982, **106:** 624–627.

143 Walker AN, Mills SE, Fechner RE, Perry JM. Epithelial polyps of the prostatic urethra. A light microscopic and immunohistochemical study. Am J Surg Pathol 1983, **7:** 351–356.

144 Young RH. Nephrogenic adenomas of the urethra involving the prostate gland. A report of two cases of a lesion that may be confused with prostatic adenocarcinoma. Mod Pathol 1992, **5:** 617–620.

Carcinoma

General features

145 Bostwick DG, Cooner WH, Denis L, Jones GW, Scardino PT, Murphy GP. The association of benign prostatic hyperplasia and cancer of the prostate. Cancer 1992, **70**(Suppl 1): 291–301.

146 Gittes RF. Carcinoma of the prostate. N Engl J Med 1991, **324:** 236–245.

147 Hammarsten J, Andersson S, Holmen A, Hogstedt B, Peeker R. Does transurethral resection of a clinically benign prostate gland increase the risk of developing clinical prostate cancer? A 10-year follow-up study. Cancer 1994, **74:** 2347–2351.

148 Kearse WS Jr, Seay TM, Thompson IM. The long-term risk of development of prostate cancer in patients with benign prostatic hyperplasia. Correlation with stage A1 disease. J Urol 1993, **150:** 1746–1748.

148a Nelson WG, de Marzo AM, Isaacs WB. Prostate cancer: mechanisms of disease. N Engl J Med 2003; **349:** 366–381.

149 Shimada H, Misugi K, Sasaki Y, Iizuka A, Nishihira H. Carcinoma of the prostate in childhood and adolescence. Report of a case and review of the literature. Cancer 1980, **46:** 2534–2542.

150 Zaridze DG, Boyle P, Smans M. International trends in prostatic cancer. Int J Cancer 1984, **33:** 223–230.

Clinical features

151 Babaian RJ, Mettlin C, Kane R, Murphy GP, Lee F, Drago JR, Chesley A. The relationship of prostate-specific antigen to digital rectal examination and transrectal ultrasonography. Findings of the American Cancer Society National Prostate Cancer Detection Project. Cancer 1992, **69:** 1195–1200.

152 Barry MJ. Prostate-specific-antigen testing for early diagnosis of prostate cancer. N Engl J Med 2001, **344:** 1373–1377.

153 Bostwick DG. Prostate-specific antigen. Current role in diagnostic pathology of prostate cancer. Am J Clin Pathol 1994, **102:** S31–S37.

154 Catalona WJ, Smith DS, Ratliff TL, Dodds KM, Coplen DE, Yuan JJ, Petros JA, Andriole GL. Measurement of prostate-specific antigen in serum as a screening test for prostate cancer. N Engl J Med 1991, **324:** 1156–1161.

155 Chodak GW, Wald V, Parmer E, Watanabe H, Ohe H, Saitoh M. Comparison of digital examination and transrectal ultrasonography for the diagnosis of prostatic cancer. J Urol 1986, **135:** 951–954.

156 Cupp MR, Oesterling JE. Prostate-specific antigen, digital rectal examination, and transrectal ultrasonography. Their roles in diagnosing early prostate cancer. Mayo Clin Proc 1993, **38:** 297–306.

157 Gittes RG. Carcinoma of the prostate. N Engl J Med 1994, **324:** 236–245.

158 Guinan P, Bush I, Ray V, Vieth R, Rao R, Bhatti R. The accuracy of the rectal examination in the diagnosis of prostate carcinoma. N Engl J Med 1980, **303:** 499–503.

⸱⸱t JH, Bridge RW, Gray GF Jr, Shelley WM. The palpable ⸱le of prostatic cancer. JAMA 1968, **203:** 403–406.

160 Kadow C, Gingell JC, Penry JB. Prostatic ultrasonography. A useful technique? Br J Urol 1985, **57:** 440–443.

161 Mettlin C, Murphy GP, Ray P, Shanberg A, Toi A, Chesley A, Babaian R, Badalament R, Kane RA, Lee F. American Cancer Society–National Prostate Cancer Detection Project. Results from multiple examinations using transrectal ultrasound, digital rectal examination, and prostate specific antigen. Cancer 1993, **71**(Suppl 3): 891–898.

162 Montironi R, Mazzucchelli R, Algaba F, Bostwick DG, Krongrad A. Prostate-specific antigen as a marker of prostatic disease. Virchows Arch 2000, **436:** 297–304.

163 Nishiya M, Miller GJ, Lookner DH, Crawford ED. Prostate specific antigen density in patients with histologically proven prostate carcinoma. Cancer 1994, **74:** 3002–3009.

164 Scardino PT, Weaver R, Hudson MA. Early detection of prostate cancer. Hum Pathol 1992, **23:** 211–222.

165 Stamey TA, Yang N, Hay AR, McNeal JE, Freiha FS, Redwine E. Prostate-specific antigen as a serum marker for adenocarcinoma of the prostate. N Engl J Med 1987, **317:** 909–916.

Pathologic features

166 Bock BJ, Bostwick DG. Does prostatic ductal adenocarcinoma exist? Am J Surg Pathol 1999, **23:** 781–785.

166a Mai KT, Collins JP, Veinot JP. Prostatic adenocarcinoma with urothelial (transitional cell) carcinoma features. Appl Immunohistochem Mol Morphol 2002, **10:** 231–236.

Adenocarcinoma of peripheral ducts and acini

167 Amin MB, Schultz DS, Zarbo RJ. Analysis of cribriform morphology in prostatic neoplasia using antibody to high-molecular-weight cytokeratins. Arch Pathol Lab Med 1994, **118:** 260–264.

168 Anton RC, Chakraborty S, Wheeler TM. The significance of intraluminal prostatic crystalloids in benign needle biopsies. Am J Surg Pathol 1998, **22:** 446–449.

168a Araugelovich V, Tretiakova M, Sengupta E, Krausz T, Yang XJ. Pathogenesis and significance of collagenous micronodules of the prostate. Appl Immunohistochem Mol Morphol 2003, **11:** 15–19.

169 Baisden BL, Kahane H, Epstein JI. Perineural invasion, mucinous fibroplasia, and glomerulations: diagnostic features of limited cancer on prostate needle biopsy. Am J Surg Pathol 1999, **23:** 918–924.

170 Bastacky SI, Walsh PC, Epstein JI. Relationship between perineural tumor invasion on needle biopsy and radical prostatectomy capsular penetration in clinical stage B adenocarcinoma of the prostate. Am J Surg Pathol 1993, **17:** 336–341.

171 Bennett BD, Gardner WA Jr. Crystalloids in prostatic hyperplasia. Prostate 1980, **1:** 31–35.

172 Brawn PN. The dedifferentiation of prostate carcinoma. Cancer 1983, **52:** 246–251.

173 Byar DP, Mostofi FK, The Veterans Administration Cooperative Urological Research Group: Carcinoma of the prostate. Prognostic evaluation of certain pathologic features in 208 radical prostatectomies. Examined by the step-section technique. Cancer 1972, **29:** 5–13.

174 Carstens PHB. Perineural glands in normal and hyperplastic prostates. J Urol 1980, **123:** 686–688.

175 Chen M, Johnston DA, Tang K, Babaian RJ, Troncoso P. Detailed mapping of prostate carcinoma foci: Biopsy strategy implications. Cancer 2000, **89:** 1800–1809.

176 Cheng L, Song SY, Pretlow TG, Abdul-Karim FW, Kung HJ, Dawson DV, Park WS, Moon YW, Tsai ML, Linehan WM, Emmert-Buck MR, Liotta LA, Zhuang Z. Evidence of independent origin of multiple tumors from patients with prostate cancer. J Natl Cancer Inst 1998, **90:** 233–237.

177 Cina SJ, Epstein JI. Adenocarcinoma of the prostate with atrophic features. Am J Surg Pathol 1997, **21:** 289–295.

178 Del Rosario AD, Bui HX, Abdulla M, Ross JS. Sulfur-rich prostatic intraluminal crystalloids. A surgical pathologic and electron probe x-ray microanalytic study. Hum Pathol 1993, **24**: 1159–1167.

179 DiGiuseppe JA, Sauvageot J, Epstein JI. Increasing incidence of minimal residual cancer in radical prostatectomy specimens. Am J Surg Pathol 1997, **21**: 174–178.

180 Egan AJM, Lopez-Beltran A, Bostwick DG. Prostatic adenocarcinoma with atrophic features: malignancy mimicking a benign process. Am J Surg Pathol 1997, **21**: 931–935.

181 Epstein JI. Diagnostic criteria of limited adenocarcinoma of the prostate on needle biopsy. Hum Pathol 1995, **26**: 223–229.

182 Franks LM. Latent carcinoma of the prostate. J Pathol Bacteriol 1954, **68**: 603–616.

183 Goldstein NS, Begin LR, Grody WW, Novak JM, Qian J, Bostwick DG. Minimal or no cancer in radical prostatectomy specimens. Report of 13 cases of the "vanishing cancer phenomenon." Am J Surg Pathol 1995, **19**: 1002–1009.

184 Hassan MO, Maksem J. The prostatic perineural space and its relation to tumor spread. Am J Surg Pathol 1980, **4**: 143–148.

185 Helpap B. Review of the morphology of prostatic carcinoma with special emphasis on subgrading and prognosis. J Urol Pathol 1993, **1**: 3–19.

186 Henneberry JM, Kahane H, Humphrey PA, Keetch DW, Epstein JI. The significance of intraluminal crystalloids in benign prostatic glands on needle biopsy. Am J Surg Pathol 1997, **21**: 725–728.

187 Holmes EJ. Crystalloids of prostatic carcinoma. Relationship to Bence-Jones crystals. Cancer 1977, **39**: 2073–2080.

188 Humphrey PA, Vollmer RT. Corpora amylacea in adenocarcinoma of the prostate. Prevalence in 100 prostatectomies and clinicopathologic correlations. Surg Pathol 1990, **3**: 133–141.

189 Humphrey PA, Kaleem Z, Swanson PE, Vollmer RT. Pseudohyperplastic prostatic adenocarcinoma. Am J Surg Pathol 1998, **22**: 1239–1246.

190 Jensen PE, Gardner WA Jr, Piserchia PV. Prostatic crystalloids. Association with adenocarcinoma. Prostate 1980, **1**: 25–30.

191 Kaleem Z, Swanson PE, Vollmer RT, Humphrey PA. Prostatic adenocarcinoma with atrophic features. A study of 202 consecutive completely embedded radical prostatectomy specimens. Am J Clin Pathol 1998, **109**: 695–703.

192 Kelemen PR, Buschmann RJ, Weisz-Carrington P. Nucleolar prominence as a diagnostic variable in prostatic carcinoma. Cancer 1990, **65**: 1017–1020.

193 Levi AW, Epstein JI. Pseudohyperplastic prostatic adenocarcinoma on needle biopsy and simple prostatectomy. Am J Surg Pathol 2000, **24**: 1039–1046.

194 McNeal JE, Reese JH, Redwin EA, Freiha FS, Stamey TA. Cribriform adenocarcinoma of the prostate. Cancer 1986, **58**: 1714–1719.

195 Molberg KH, Mikhail A, Vuitch F. Crystalloids in metastatic prostatic adenocarcinoma. Am J Clin Pathol 1994, **101**: 266–268.

196 Mostofi FK, Sesterhenn IA, Davis CJ Jr. A pathologist's view of prostatic carcinoma. Cancer 1993, **71**(Suppl 3): 906–932.

197 Nelson RS, Epstein JI. Prostatic carcinoma with abundant xanthomatous cytoplasm: Foamy gland carcinoma. Am J Surg Pathol 1996, **20**: 419–426.

198 Pacelli A, Lopez-Beltran A, Egan AJ, Bostwick DG. Prostatic adenocarcinoma with glomeruloid features. Hum Pathol 1998, **29**: 543–546.

199 Renshaw AA. Correlation of gross morphologic features with histologic features in radical prostatectomy specimens. Am J Clin Pathol 1998, **110**: 38–42.

200 Robinette MA, Robson CJ, Farrow GA, Kerr WK, Van Nostrand PA, Hobbs BB, Bulbul MM. Giant serial step sections of the prostate in assessment of the accuracy of clinical staging in patients with localized prostatic carcinoma (abstract). J Urol 1984, **131**(Suppl): 242A.

201 Rodin AE, Larson DL, Roberts DK. Nature of perineural space invaded by prostatic carcinoma. Cancer 1967, **20**: 1772–1779.

202 Rubin MA, de la Taille A, Bagiella E, Olsson CA, O'Toole KM. Cribriform carcinoma of the prostate and cribriform prostatic intraepithelial neoplasia: incidence and clinical implications. Am J Surg Pathol 1998, **22**: 840–848.

203 Samaratunga H, Williamson R. Metastatic foamy gland carcinoma of the prostate: a potential diagnostic pitfall. J Urol Pathol 1998, **9**: 155–162.

204 Strahan RW. Carcinoma of the prostate. Incidence, origin, pathology. J Urol 1963, **89**: 875–880.

205 Takimoto Y, Shimazui T, Akaza H, Sato N, Noguchi M. Genetic heterogeneity of surgically resected prostate carcinomas and their biopsy specimen is related to their histologic differentiation. Cancer 2001, **91**: 362–370.

206 Totten RS, Heinemann MW, Hudson PB, Sproul EE, Stout AP. Microscopic differential diagnosis of latent carcinoma of the prostate. Arch Pathol 1953, **55**: 131–141.

207 Tran TT, Sengupta E, Yang XJ. Prostatic foamy gland carcinoma with aggressive behavior: clinicopathologic, immunohistochemical, and ultrastructural analysis. Am J Surg Pathol 2001, **25**: 618–623.

208 Varma M, Lee MW, Tamboli P, Zarbo RJ, Jimerez RE, Salles PG, Amin MB. Morphologic criteria for the diagnosis of prostatic adenocarcinoma in needle biopsy specimens: a study of 250 consecutive cases in a routine surgical pathology practice. Arch Pathol Lab Med 2002, **126**: 554–561.

209 Woods JE, Soh S, Wheeler TM. Distribution and significance of microcalcifications in the neoplastic and non-neoplastic prostate. Arch Pathol Lab Med 1998, **122**: 152–155.

"Minimal adenocarcinoma" and atypical small acinar proliferation (ASAP)

210 Cheville JC, Reznicek MJ, Bostwick DG. The focus of "atypical glands, suspicious for malignancy" in prostatic needle biopsy specimens. Incidence, histologic features and clinical follow-up of cases diagnosed in a community practice. Am J Clin Pathol 1997, **108**: 633–640.

211 Dundore PA. Atypical small acinar proliferations (ASAP) suspicious for malignancy in prostate needle biopsies. J Urol Pathol 1998, **8**: 21–30.

212 Epstein JI. How should atypical prostate needle biopsy be reported? Controversies regarding the term "ASAP". Hum Pathol 1999, **30**: 1401–1402.

213 Grignon DJ. Minimal diagnostic criteria for adenocarcinoma of the prostate. J Urol Pathol 1998, **8**: 31–44.

214 Grignon DJ, Sakr WA. Pathologic staging of prostate carcinoma: What are the issues? Cancer 1996, **78**: 337–340.

215 Iczkowski KA, MacLennan GT, Bostwick DG. Atypical small acinar proliferation suspicious for malignancy in prostate needle biopsies: clinical significance in 33 cases. Am J Surg Pathol 1997, **21**: 1489–1495.

216 Iczkowski KA, Bostwick DG. Criteria for biopsy diagnosis of minimal volume prostatic adenocarcinoma: analytic comparison with nondiagnostic but suspicious atypical small acinar proliferation. Arch Pathol Lab Med 2000, **124**: 98–107.

217 Kambham N, Taylor JA, Troxel A, Rubin MA. Atypical small acinar proliferation in prostate needle biopsy: a clinically significant diagnostic category. J Urol Pathol 1999, **10**: 177–188.

218 Murphy WM. ASAP is a bad idea. Atypical small acinar proliferation. Hum Pathol 1999, **30**: 601.

219 Novis DA, Zarbo RJ, Valenstein PA. Diagnostic uncertainty expressed in prostate needle biopsies: a College of American Pathologists Q-probes study of 15753 prostate needle biopsies in 32 institutions. Arch Pathol Lab Med 1999, **123**: 687–692.

220 Thorson P, Humphrey PA. Minimal adenocarcinoma in prostate needle biopsy tissue. Am J Clin Pathol 2000, **114**: 896–909.

Carcinoma of large ("primary") ducts

221 Brinker DA, Potter SR, Epstein JI. Ductal adenocarcinoma of the prostate diagnosed on needle biopsy: correlation with clinical and radical prostatectomy findings and progression. Am J Surg Pathol 1999, **23**: 1471–1479.

222 Cantrell BB, Leifer G, DeKlerk DP, Eggleston JC. Papillary adenocarcinoma of the prostatic urethra with clear-cell appearance. Cancer 1981, **48**: 2661–2667.

223 Cheville JC, Dundore PA, Bostwick DG, Lieber MM, Batts KP, Sebo TJ, Farrow GM. Transitional cell carcinoma of the prostate: clinicopathologic study of 50 cases. Cancer 1998, **82**: 703–707.

224 Christensen WN, Steinberg G, Walsh PC, Epstein JI. Prostatic duct adenocarcinoma. Findings at radical prostatectomy. Cancer 1991, **67**: 2118–2124.

225 Cohen RJ, Nixon JM, Robinson E, Edgar SG, Allison L, McRae CU. Transitional cell carcinoma diagnosed at transurethral prostatectomy in patients with prostatic adenocarcinoma. J Urol Pathol 1996, **5**: 29–38.

226 Dube VE, Farrow GM, Greene LF. Prostatic adenocarcinoma of ductal origin. Cancer 1973, **32**: 402–409.

227 Ende N, Woods LP, Shelley HS. Carcinoma originating in ducts surrounding the prostatic urethra. Am J Clin Pathol 1963, **40**: 186–189.

228 Epstein JI, Woodruff JM. Adenocarcinoma of the prostate with endometrioid features. Cancer 1986, **57**: 111–119.

229 Greene LF, Farrow GM, Ravits JM, Tomera FM. Prostatic adenocarcinoma of ductal origin. J Urol 1979, **121**: 303–305.

230 Greene LF, O'Dea MJ, Dockerty MB. Primary transitional cell carcinoma of the prostate. J Urol 1976, **116**: 761–763.

231 Johnson DE, Hogan JM, Ayala AG. Transitional cell carcinoma of the prostate. A clinical morphological study. Cancer 1972, **29**: 287–293.

232 Kopelson G, Harisiadis L, Romas NA, Veenema RJ, Tannenbaum M. Periurethral prostatic duct carcinoma. Cancer 1978, **42**: 2894–2902.

233 Kuhajda FP, Gipson T, Mendelsohn G. Papillary adenocarcinomas of the prostate. Cancer 1984, **54**: 1328–1332.

234 Lemberger RJ, Bishop MC, Bates CP, Blundell W, Ansell ID. Carcinoma of the prostate of ductal origin. Br J Urol 1984, **56**: 706–709.

235 Melicow MM, Pachter MR. Endometrial carcinoma of the prostatic utricle (uterus masculinus). Cancer 1967, **20**: 1715–1722.

236 Millar EK, Sharma NK, Lessells AM. Ductal (endometrioid) adenocarcinoma of the prostate: A clinicopathological study of 16 cases. Histopathology 1996, **29**: 11–19.

237 Oliai BR, Kahane H, Epstein JI. A clinicopathologic analysis of urothelial carcinomas diagnosed on prostate needle biopsy. Am J Surg Pathol 2001, **25**: 794–801.

238 Reese JH, Freiha FS, Gelb AB, Lum BL, Torti FM. Transitional cell carcinoma of the prostate in patients undergoing radical cystoprostatectomy. J Urol 1992, **147**: 92–95.

239 Sawczuk I, Tannenbaum M, Olsson CA, de Vere White R. Primary transitional cell carcinoma of prostatic periurethral ducts. Urology 1985, **25**: 339–343.

240 Sleater JP, Ford MJ, Beers BB. Extramammary Paget's disease associated with prostate adenocarcinoma. Hum Pathol 1994, **25**: 615–617.

241 Ullmann AS, Ross OA. Hyperplasia, atypism, and carcinoma in situ in prostatic periurethral glands. Am J Clin Pathol 1967, **47**: 497–504.

242 Vale JA, Patel A, Ball AJ, Hendry WF, Chappel ME, Fisher C. Endometrioid carcinoma of the prostate. A misnomer? J R Soc Med 1992, **85**: 394–396.

243 Walther MM, Nassar V, Harruff RC, Mann BB Jr, Finnerty DP, Hewen-Lowe KO. Endometrial carcinoma of the prostatic utricle. ...mor of prostatic origin. J Urol 1985, **134**: 769–773.

... JHN, Lloyd-Davies RW. The management of transitional ...carcinoma in the prostate. Br J Urol 1981, **53**: 253–257.

245 Young BW, Lagios MD. Endometrial (papillary) carcinoma of the prostatic utricle—response to orchiectomy. A case report. Cancer 1973, **32**: 1293–1300.

246 Zaloudek C, Williams JW, Kempson RL. "Endometrial" adenocarcinoma of the prostate. A distinctive tumor of probable prostatic duct origin. Cancer 1976, **37**: 2255–2262.

Histochemical & immunohistochemical features

246a Abrahams NA, Ormsby AH, Brainard J. Validation of cytokeratin 5/6 as an effective substitute for keratin 903 in the differentiation of benign from malignant glands in prostate needle biopsies. Histopathology 2002, **41**: 35–41.

247 Alanen KA, Kuopio T, Koskinen PJ, Nevalainen TJ. Immunohistochemical labelling for prostate specific antigen in non-prostatic tissues. Pathol Res Pract 1996, **192**: 233–237.

248 Asadi F, Farraj M, Sharifi R, Malakouti S, Antar S, Kukreja S. Enhanced expression of parathyroid hormone-related protein in prostate cancer as compared with benign prostatic hyperplasia. Hum Pathol 1996, **27**: 1319–1323.

249 Bassily NH, Vallorosi CJ, Akdas G, Montie JE, Rubin MA. Coordinate expression of cytokeratins 7 and 20 in prostate adenocarcinoma and bladder urothelial carcinoma. Am J Clin Pathol 2000, **113**: 383–388.

249a Beach R, Gown AM, de Peralta-Venturina MN, Folpe AL, Yaziji H, Salles PG, Grignon DJ, Fanger GR, Amin MB. P504S immunohistochemical detection in 405 prostatic specimens including 376 18-gauge needle biopsies. Am J Surg Pathol 2002, **26**: 1588–1596.

250 Bentz MS, Cohen C, Demers LM, Budgeon LR. Immunohistochemical acid phosphatase level and tumor grade in prostatic carcinoma. Arch Pathol Lab Med 1982, **106**: 476–480.

251 Bonkhoff H, Fixemer T, Hunsicker I, Remberger K. Estrogen receptor expression in prostate cancer and premalignant prostatic lesions. Am J Pathol 1999, **155**: 641–647.

252 Bonkhoff H, Wernert N, Dhom G, Remberger K. Distribution of basement membranes in primary and metastatic carcinomas of the prostate. Hum Pathol 1992, **23**: 934–939.

253 Bostwick DG, Pacelli A, Blute M, Roche P, Murphy GP. Prostate specific membrane antigen expression in prostatic intraepithelial neoplasia and adenocarcinoma: a study of 184 cases. Cancer 1998, **82**: 2256–2261.

254 Cardillo MR, Petrangeli E, Ravenna L, Salvatori L, Chang C, Di Silverio F. Immunohistochemical quantification and determination of cathepsin D in prostatic neoplasia: correlation with steroid receptors. Appl Immunohistochem 1998, **6**: 133–139.

255 Cheng L, Nagabhushan M, Pretlow TP, Amini SB, Pretlow TG. Expression of E-cadherin in primary and metastatic prostate cancer. Am J Pathol 1996, **148**: 1375–1380.

256 Dardik M, Epstein JI. Efficacy of restaining prostate needle biopsies with high-molecular weight cytokeratin. Hum Pathol 2000, **31**: 1155–1161.

257 Elgamal AA, Holmes EH, Su SL, Tino WT, Simmons SJ, Peterson M, Greene TG, Boynton AL, Murphy GP. Prostate-specific membrane antigen (PSMA): current benefits and future value. Semin Surg Oncol 2000, **18**: 10–16.

258 Ellis DW, Leffers S, Davies JS, Ng ABP. Multiple immunoperoxidase markers in benign hyperplasia and adenocarcinoma of the prostate. Am J Clin Pathol 1984, **81**: 279–284.

259 Feiner HD, Gonzalez R. Carcinoma of the prostate with atypical immunohistological features. Clinical and histologic correlates. Am J Surg Pathol 1986, **10**: 765–770.

260 Franks LM, O'Shea JD, Thomson AER. Mucin in the prostate. A histochemical study in normal glands, latent, clinical, and colloid cancers. Cancer 1964, **17**: 983–991.

261 Genega EM, Hutchinson B, Reuter VE, Gaudin PB. Immunophenotype of high-grade prostatic adenocarcinoma and urothelial carcinoma. Mod Pathol 2000, **13**: 1186–1191.

262 Goldstein NS, Underhill J, Roszka J, Neill JS. Cytokeratin 34βE-12 immunoreactivity in benign prostatic acini. Quantitation, pattern assessment and electron microscopic study. Am J Clin Pathol 1999, **112**: 69–74.

263 Googe PB, McGinley KM, Fitzgibbon JF. Anticytokeratin antibody 34βE12 staining in prostate carcinoma. Am J Clin Pathol 1997, **107**: 219–223.

264 Gould VE, Doljanskaia V, Gooch G, Bostwick DG. Immunolocalization of glycoprotein A-80 in prostatic carcinoma and prostatic intraepithelial neoplasia. Hum Pathol 1996, **27**: 547–552.

265 Green R, Epstein JI. Use of intervening unstained slides for immunohistochemical stains for high molecular weight cytokeratin on prostate needle biopsies. Am J Surg Pathol 1999, **23**: 567–570.

266 Heyderman E, Brown BME, Richardson TC. Epithelial markers in prostatic, bladder, and colorectal cancer. An immunoperoxidase study of epithelial membrane antigen, carcinoembryonic antigen, and prostatic acid phosphatase. J Clin Pathol 1984, **37**: 1363–1369.

267 Hiramatsu M, Maehara I, Orikasa S, Sasano H. Immunolocalization of oestrogen and progesterone receptors in prostatic hyperplasia and carcinoma. Histopathology 1996, **28**: 163–168.

268 Hukill PB, Vidone RA. Histochemistry of mucus and other polysaccharides in tumors. II. Carcinoma of the prostate. Lab Invest 1967, **16**: 395–406.

269 Iczkowski KA, Cheng L, Crawford BG, Bostwick DG. Steam heat with an EDTA buffer and protease digestion optimizes immunohistochemical expression of basal cell-specific antikeratin 34BetaE12 to discriminate cancer in prostatic epithelium. Mod Pathol 1999, **12**: 1–4.

270 Jang Z, Woda BA, Rock KL, Xu Y, Savas L, Khan A, Pihan G, Cai F, Babcook JS, Rathanaswami P, Reed SG, Xu J, Fanger GR. P504S: a new molecular marker for the detection of prostate carcinoma. Am J Surg Pathol 2001, **25**: 1397–1404.

270a Jiang Z, Wu CL, Woda BA, Dresser K, Xu J, Fanger GR, Yang XJ. P504S/a-methylacyl-coA racemase: a useful marker for diagnosis of small foci of prostatic carcinoma on needle biopsy. Am J Surg Pathol 2002, **26**: 1169–1174.

271 Jobsis AC, De Vries GP, Anholt RRH, Sanders GTB. Demonstration of the prostatic origin of metastases. An immunohistochemical method for formalin-fixed embedded tissue. Cancer 1978, **41**: 1788–1793.

272 Kallakury BV, Sheehan CE, Winn-Deen E, Oliver J, Fisher HA, Kaufman RP Jr, Ross JS. Decreased expression of catenins (alpha and beta) p120 CTN, and E-cadherin cell adhesion proteins and E-cadherin gene promoter methylation in prostatic adenocarcinomas. Cancer 2001, **92**: 2786–2795.

272a Kuefer R, Varambatly S, Zhou M, Lucas PC, Loeffler M, Wolter H, Mattfeldt T, Hautmann RE, Gschwend JE, Barrette TR, Dunn RL, Chinnaiyan AM, Rubin MA. A-methylacyl-coA racemase: expression levels of this novel cancer biomarker depend on tumor differentiation. Am J Pathol 2002, **161**: 841.

273 Lindeman N, Weidner N. Immunohistochemical profile of prostatic and urothelial carcinoma: impact of heat-induced epitope retrieval and presentation of tumors with intermediate features. Appl Immunohistochem 1996, **4**: 264–275.

274 McMahon RF, McWilliam LJ, Mosley S. Evaluation of three techniques for differential diagnosis of prostatic needle biopsy specimens. J Clin Pathol 1992, **45**: 1094–1098.

275 Mai KT, Commons AS, Perkins DG, Yazdi HM, Collins JP. Absence of serum prostate-specific antigen and loss of tissue immunoreactive prostatic markers in advanced prostatic adenocarcinoma after hormonal therapy. A report of two cases. Hum Pathol 1996, **27**: 1377–1381.

276 Makar R, Mason A, Kittelson JM, Bowden GT, Cress AE, Nagle RB. Immunohistochemical analysis of cathepsin D in prostate carcinoma. Mod Pathol 1994, **7**: 747–751.

277 May EE, Perentes E. Anti-Leu 7 immunoreactivity with human tumours. Its value in the diagnosis of prostatic adenocarcinoma. Histopathology 1987, **11**: 295–304.

278 Maygarden SJ. Applications of immunohistochemistry to the diagnosis and prognostication of prostate carcinoma and prostatic intraepithelial neoplasia. Pathol Annu 1994, **29**(Pt I): 303–320.

279 Mazur MT, Shultz JJ. Prostatic adenocarcinoma. Evaluation of immunoreactivity to monoclonal antibody B72.3. Am J Clin Pathol 1990, **93**: 466–470.

280 Nadji M, Tabei SZ, Castro A, Chu TM, Murphy GP, Wang MC, Morales AR. Prostatic-specific antigen. An immunohistologic marker for prostatic neoplasms. Cancer 1984, **48**: 1229–1232.

280a Oliai BR, Kahane H, Epstein JI. Can basal cells be seen in adenocarcinoma of the prostate?: an immunohistochemical study using high molecular weight cytokeratin (clone 34βE12) Antibody. Am J Surg Pathol 2002, **26**: 1151–1160.

281 Osman I, Scher HI, Drobnjak M, Verbel D, Morris M, Agus D, Ross JS, Cordon-Cardo C. HER-2/neu (p185neu) protein expression in the natural or treated history of prostate cancer. Clin Cancer Res 2001, **7**: 2643–2647.

282 Papsidero LD, Croghan GA, Asirwatham J, Gaeta J, Abenoza P, Englander L, Valenzuela L. Immunohistochemical demonstration of prostate-specific antigen in metastases with the use of monoclonal antibody F5. Am J Pathol 1985, **121**: 451–454.

283 Reid WA, Liddle CN, Svasti J, Kay J. Gastricsin in benign and malignant prostate. J Clin Pathol 1985, **38**: 639–643.

284 Rusthoven JJ, Robinson JB, Kolin A, Pinkerton PH. The natural killer-cell-associated HNK-I (Leu-7) antibody reacts with hypertrophic and malignant prostatic epithelium. Cancer 1985, **56**: 289–293.

285 Saez C, Japon MA, Conde AF, Poveda MA, Luna-More S, Segura DI. Sialomucins are characteristically O-acylated in poorly differentiated and colloid prostatic adenocarcinomas. Mod Pathol 1998, **11**: 1193–1197.

286 Samaratunga H, Singh M. Distribution patterns of basal cells detected by cytokeratin 34 beta E12 in primary prostatic duct adenocarcinoma. Am J Surg Pathol 1997, **21**: 435–440.

287 Schultz DS, Amin MB, Zarbo RJ. Basement membrane type IV collagen immunohistochemical staining in prostatic neoplasia. Appl Immunohistochem 1993, **1**: 123–126.

287a Shah RB, Zhou M, Leblanc M, Snyder M, Rubin MA. Comparison of the basal cell-specific markers, 34βE12 and p63, in the diagnosis of prostate cancer. Am J Surg Pathol 2002, **26**: 1161–1168.

288 Shevchuk MM, Romas NA, Ng PY, Tannenbaum M, Olsson CA. Acid phosphatase localization in prostatic carcinoma. A comparison of monoclonal antibody to heteroantisera. Cancer 1983, **52**: 1642–1646.

289 Shim J-W, Lee Y-G, Kim S-S, Kim K-K, Park H-W, Ahn H-K, Park Y-E. Immunohistochemical evaluation of E-cadherin in prostatic adenocarcinoma. J Urol Pathol 1997, **6**: 185–194.

290 Stein BS, Vangore S, Petersen RO, Kendall AR. Immunoperoxidase localization of prostate-specific antigen. Am J Surg Pathol 1982, **6**: 553–557.

291 Svanholm H. Evaluation of commercial immunoperoxidase kits for prostatic specific antigen and prostatic specific acid phosphatase. Acta Pathol Microbiol Immunol Scand (A) 1986, **94**: 7–12.

292 Takeda H, Akakura K, Masai M, Akimoto S, Yatani R, Shimazaki J. Androgen receptor content of prostate carcinoma cells estimated by immunohistochemistry is related to prognosis of patients with stage D2 prostate carcinoma. Cancer 1996, **77**: 934–940.

293 Tazawa K, Kurihara Y, Kamoshida S, Tsukada K, Tsutsumi Y. Localization of prostate-specific antigen-like immunoreactivity in human salivary gland and salivary gland tumors. Pathol Int 1999, **49**: 500–505.

294 Trapman J, Brinkmann AO. The androgen receptor in prostate cancer. Pathol Res Pract 1996, **192:** 752–760.

294a Varma M, Morgan M, Jasani B, Tamboli P, Amin MB. Polyclonal anti-PSA is more sensitive but less specific than monoclonal anti-PSA. Implications for diagnostic prostatic pathology. Am J Clin Pathol 2002, **118:** 202–207.

295 Yang XJ, McEntee M, Epstein JI. Distinction of basaloid carcinoma of the prostate from benign basal cell lesions by using immunohistochemistry for bcl-2 and Ki-67. Hum Pathol 1998, **29:** 1447–1450.

296 Warhol MJ, Longtine JA. The ultrastructural localization of prostatic specific antigen and prostatic acid phosphatase in hyperplastic and neoplastic human prostates. J Urol 1985, **134:** 607–613.

296a Weinstein MH, Signoretti S, Loda M. Diagnostic utility of immunohistochemical staining for p63, a sensitive marker of prostatic basal cells. Mod Pathol 2002, **15:** 1302–1308.

297 Wernert N, Seitz G, Goebbels R, Dhom G. Immunohistochemical demonstration of cytokeratins in the human prostate. Pathol Res Pract 1986, **181:** 668–674.

298 Wojno KJ, Epstein JI. The utility of basal cell-specific anti-cytokeratin antibody (34 βE12) in the diagnosis of prostate cancer. A review of 228 cases. Am J Surg Pathol 1995, **19:** 251–260.

298a Yang MJ, Wu CL, Woda BA, Dresser K, Tretiakova M, Fanger GR, Jiang Z. Expression of α-methylacyl-coA racemase (P504S) in atypical adenomatous hyperplasia of the prostate. Am J Surg Pathol 2002, **26:** 921–925.

298b Zhou M, Chinnaiyan AM, Kleer CG, Lucas PC, Rubin MA. alpha-methylacyl-coA racemase: a novel tumor marker over-expressed in several human cancers and their precursor lesions. Am J Surg Pathol 2002, **26:** 926–931.

298c Zhou M, Jiang J, Epstein JI. Expression and diagnostic utility of alpha-methylacyl-coA-racemase (P504S) in foamy gland and pseudohyperplastic prostate cancer. Am J Surg Pathol 2003, **27:** 772–778.

298d Zhou M, Shah R, Shen R, Rubin MA. Basal cell cocktail (34β3E12 + p63) improves the detection of prostate basal cells. Am J Surg Pathol 2003, **27:** 365–371.

Molecular genetic features

299 Alers JC, Rochat J, Krijtenburg PJ, Hop WC, Kranse R, Rosenberg C, Tanke HJ, Schroder FH, van Dekken H. Identification of genetic markers for prostatic cancer progression. Lab Invest 2000, **80:** 931–942.

300 Allen MV, Smith GJ, Juliano R, Maygarden SJ, Mohler JL. Downregulation of the Beta4 integrin subunit in prostatic carcinoma and prostatic intraepithelial neoplasia. Hum Pathol 1998, **29:** 311–318.

301 Al-Maghrabi J, Vorobyova L, Toi A, Chapman W, Zielenska M, Squire JA. Identification of numerical chromosomal changes detected by interphase fluorescence in situ hybridization in high-grade prostate intraepithelial neoplasia as a predictor of carcinoma. Arch Pathol Lab Med 2002, **126:** 165–169.

302 Carter BS, Ewing CM, Ward WS, Treiger BF, Aalders TW, Schalken JA, Epstein JI, Isaacs WB. Allelic loss of chromosomes 16q and 10q in human prostate cancer. Proc Natl Acad Sci U S A 1990, **87:** 8751–8755.

303 Cheville JC, Lloyd RV, Sebo TJ, Cheng L, Erickson L, Bostwick DG, Lohse CM, Wollan P. Expression of p27kip1 in prostatic adenocarcinoma. Mod Pathol 1998, **11:** 324–328.

304 Erbersdobler A, Gurses N, Henke RP. Numerical chromosomal changes in high-grade prostatic intraepithelial neoplasia (PIN) and concomitant invasive carcinoma. Pathol Res Pract 1996, **192:** 418–423.

305 Erdamar S, Yang G, Harper JW, Lu X, Kattan MW, Thompson TC, Wheeler TM. Levels of expression of p27KIP1 protein in

human prostate and prostate cancer: an immunohistochemical analysis. Mod Pathol 1999, **12:** 751–755.

306 Gao X, Honn KV, Grignon D, Sakr W, Chen YQ. Frequent loss of expression and loss of heterozygosity of the putative tumor suppressor gene DCC in prostatic carcinomas. Cancer Res 1993, **53:** 2723–2727.

307 Henke RP, Kruger E, Ayhan N, Hubner D, Hammerer P. Frequency and distribution of numerical chromosomal aberrations in prostatic cancer. Hum Pathol 1994, **25:** 476–484.

308 Isaacs WB, Bova GS, Morton RA, Bussemakers MJ, Brooks JD, Ewing CM. Molecular biology of prostate cancer. Semin Oncol 1994, **21:** 514–521.

309 Ittmann MM, Wieczorek R. Alterations of the retinoblastoma gene in clinically localized, stage B prostate adenocarcinomas. Hum Pathol 1996, **27:** 28–34.

310 Ittmann M, Wieczorek R, Heller P, Dave A, Provet J, Krolewski J. Alterations in the p53 and MDM-2 genes are infrequent in clinically localized, stage B prostate adenocarcinomas. Am J Pathol 1994, **145:** 287–293.

311 Kallakury BV, Brien TP, Lowry CV, Muraca PJ, Fisher HA, Kaufman RP Jr, Ross JS. Telomerase activity in human benign prostate tissue and prostatic adenocarcinomas. Diagn Mol Pathol 1997, **6:** 192–198.

312 Konig JJ, Teubel W, Romijn JC, Schroder FH, Hagemeijer A. Gain and loss of chromosomes 1,7,8,10,18 and Y in 46 prostate cancers. Hum Pathol 1996, **27:** 720–727.

313 Konishi N, Cho M, Yamamoto K, Hiasa Y. Genetic changes in prostate cancer. Pathol Int 1997, **47:** 735–747.

314 Krajewska M, Krajewski S, Epstein JI, Shabaik A, Sauvageot J, Song K, Kitada S, Reed JC. Immunohistochemical analysis of bcl-2, bax, bcl-x and mcl-1 expression in prostate cancer. Am J Pathol 1996, **148:** 1567–1576.

315 Latil A, Lidereau R. Genetic aspects of prostate cancer. Virchows Arch 1998, **432:** 389–406.

316 Losi L, Di Gregorio C, Brausi M, Fante R, Hurlimann J. Expression of p53 protein in prostate cancers of different histologic types. Pathol Res Pract 1994, **190:** 384–388.

317 Lundgren R, Mandahl N, Heim S, Limon J, Henrikson H, Mitelman F. Cytogenetic analysis of 57 primary prostatic adenocarcinomas. Genes Chromosomes Cancer 1992, **4:** 16–24.

318 Meyers FJ, Gumerlock PH, Chi SG, Borchers H, Deitch AD, deVere White RW. Very frequent p53 mutations in metastatic prostate carcinoma and in matched primary tumors. Cancer 1998, **83:** 2534–2539.

319 Myers RB, Srivastava S, Oelschlager DK, Brown D, Grizzle WE. Expression of nm23-H1 in prostatic intraepithelial neoplasia and adenocarcinoma. Hum Pathol 1996, **27:** 1021–1024.

320 Nastiuk KL, Mansukhani M, Terry M-B, Kularatne P, Rubin MA, Melamed J, Gammon MD, Ittmann M, Krolewski JJ. Common mutations in BRCA1 and BRCA2 do not contribute to early prostate cancer in Jewish men. Prostate 1999, **40:** 172–177.

321 Ross JS, Sheehan C, Hayner-Buchan AM, Ambros RA, Kallakury BV, Kaufman R, Fisher HA, Muraca PJ. HER-2/neu gene amplification status in prostate cancer by fluorescence in situ hybridization. Hum Pathol 1997, **28:** 827–833.

322 Sandberg AA. Chromosomal abnormalities and related events in prostate cancer. Hum Pathol 1992, **23:** 368–380.

323 Tamboli P, Amin MB, Xu HJ, Linden MD. Immunohistochemical expression of retinoblastoma and p53 tumor suppressor genes in prostatic intraepithelial neoplasia: comparison with prostatic adenocarcinoma and benign prostate. Mod Pathol 1998, **11:** 247–252.

323a Torlakovic E, Lilleby W, Torlakovic G, Fosså SD, Chibbar R. Prostate carcinoma expression of estrogen receptor-β as detected by PPG5/10 antibody has positive association with primary Gleason grade and Gleason score. Hum Pathol 2002, **33:** 646.

324 Visakorpi T, Kallioniemi OP, Heikkinen A, Koivula T, Isola J. Small subgroup of aggressive, highly proliferative prostatic carcinomas defined by p53 accumulation. J Natl Cancer Inst 1992, **84**: 883–887.

325 Wertz IE, Deitch AD, Gumerlock PH, Gandour-Edwards R, Chi SG, DeVere White RW. Correlation of genetic and immunodetection of TP53 mutations in malignant and benign prostate tissues. Hum Pathol 1996, **27**: 573–580.

326 Yasunaga Y, Shin M, Fujita MQ, Nonomura N, Miki T, Okuyama A, Aozasa K. Different patterns of p53 mutations in prostatic intraepithelial neoplasia and concurrent carcinoma: analysis of microdissected specimens. Lab Invest 1998, **78**: 1275–1279.

Other microscopic types

327 Abrahamsson PA, Falkmer S, Falt K, Grimelius L. The course of neuroendocrine differentiation in prostatic carcinomas. An immunohistochemical study testing chromogranin A as an "endocrine marker." Pathol Res Pract 1989, **185**: 373–380.

328 Abrahamsson PA, Wadstrom LB, Alumets J, Falkmer S, Grimelius L. Peptide-hormone and serotonin-immunoreactive cells in normal and hyperplastic prostate glands. Pathol Res Pract 1986, **181**: 675–683.

329 Adlakha H, Bostwick DG. Paneth cell-like change in prostatic adenocarcinoma represents neuroendocrine differentiation. Report of 30 cases. Hum Pathol 1994, **25**: 135–139.

330 Adlakha K, Bostwick DG. Lymphoepithelioma-like carcinoma of the prostate. A new histologic variant of prostatic adenocarcinoma. J Urol Pathol 1994, **2**: 319–326.

331 Alguacil-Garcia A. Artifactual changes mimicking signet ring cell carcinoma in transurethral prostatectomy specimens. Am J Surg Pathol 1986, **10**: 795–800.

332 Almagro UA, Tieu TM, Remeniuk E, Kueck B, Strumpf K. Argyrophilic, "carcinoid-like" prostatic carcinoma. An immunocytochemical study. Arch Pathol Lab Med 1986, **110**: 916–919.

333 Aprikian AG, Cordon-Cardo C, Fair WR, Reuter VE. Characterization of neuroendocrine differentiation in human benign prostate and prostatic adenocarcinoma. Cancer 1993, **71**: 3952–3965.

334 Azumi N, Shibuya H, Ishikura M. Primary prostatic carcinoid tumor with intracytoplasmic prostatic acid phosphatase and prostate-specific antigen. Am J Surg Pathol 1984, **8**: 545–550.

335 Berney DM, Ravi R, Baitum SI. Prostatic carcinosarcoma with squamous cell differentiation: a consequence of hormonal therapy? Report of two cases and review of the literature. J Urol Pathol 1999, **11**: 123–132.

336 Bleichner JC, Chun B, Klappenbach RS. Pure small-cell carcinoma of the prostate with fatal liver metastasis. Arch Pathol Lab Med 1986, **110**: 1041–1044.

337 Bonkhoff H, Stein U, Welter C, Remberger K. Differential expression of the pS2 protein in the human prostate and prostate cancer. Association with premalignant changes and neuroendocrine differentiation. Hum Pathol 1995, **26**: 824–828.

338 Capella C, Usellini L, Buffa R, Frigerio B, Solcia E. The endocrine component of prostatic carcinomas, mixed adenocarcinoma-carcinoid tumours and non-tumour prostate. Histochemical and ultrastructural identification of the endocrine cells. Histopathology 1981, **5**: 175–192.

339 Das S, Brewer L, Bell S. Signet-ring cell carcinoma of the prostate. J Urol Pathol 1996, **5**: 149–156.

340 Denholm SW, Webb JN, Howard GC, Chisholm GD. Basaloid carcinoma of the prostate gland: Histogenesis and review of the literature. Histopathology 1992, **20**: 151–155.

341 Devaney DM, Dorman A, Leader M. Adenosquamous carcinoma of the prostate. A case report. Hum Pathol 1991, **22**: 1046–1050.

342 di Sant'Agnese PA. Neuroendocrine differentiation in prostatic

carcinoma. Recent findings and new concepts. Cancer 1995, **75**: 1850–1859.

343 di Sant'Agnese PA. Neuroendocrine differentiation in carcinoma of the prostate. Diagnostic, prognostic, and therapeutic implications. Cancer 1992, **70**: 254–268.

344 di Sant'Agnese PA, Cockett AT. Neuroendocrine differentiation in prostatic malignancy. Cancer 1996, **78**: 357–361.

345 Elbadawi A, Craig W, Linke CA, Cooper RA Jr. Prostatic mucinous carcinoma. Urology 1979, **13**: 658–666.

346 Epstein JI, Lieberman PH. Mucinous adenocarcinoma of the prostate gland. Am J Surg Pathol 1985, **9**: 299–308.

347 Faris G, Stein A, Sova Y, Lurie M, Lurie A. Chromogranin is a marker for neuroendocrine differentiation in prostate carcinoma of various grades and stages. J Urol Pathol 1995, **3**: 29–36.

348 Fetissof F, Bruandet P, Arbeille B, Penot J, Marboeuf Y, Le Roux J, Guilloteau D, Beaulieu J-L. Calcitonin-secreting carcinomas of the prostate. An immunohistochemical and ultrastructural analysis. Am J Surg Pathol 1986, **10**: 702–710.

349 Frankel K, Craig JR. Adenoid cystic carcinoma of the prostate. Report of a case. Am J Clin Pathol 1974, **62**: 639–645.

350 Gaffney EF. The extent of apoptosis in different types of high grade prostatic carcinoma. Histopathology 1994, **25**: 269–273.

351 Gattuso P, Carson HJ, Candel A, Castelli MJ. Adenosquamous carcinoma of the prostate. Hum Pathol 1995, **26**: 123–126.

352 Ghali VS, Garcia RL. Prostatic adenocarcinoma with carcinoidal features producing adrenocorticotropic syndrome. Cancer 1984, **54**: 1043–1048.

353 Ghandur-Mnaymneh L, Satterfield S, Block NL. Small cell carcinoma of the prostate gland with inappropriate antidiuretic hormone secretion. Morphological, immunohistochemical and clinical expressions. J Urol 1986, **135**: 1263–1266.

353a Grier DD, Bostwick DG, Houssain D, Banerjee SS, Iczkowski KA. Adenoid cystic/basal cell carcinoma of the prostate: clinical significance in 18 cases (Abstract). Mod Pathol 2003, **16**: 152A.

354 Guerin D, Hasan N, Keen CE. Signet ring cell differentiation in adenocarcinoma of the prostate. A study of five cases. Histopathology 1993, **22**: 367–371.

355 Helpap B, Kollermann J. Undifferentiated carcinoma of the prostate with small cell features: Immunohistochemical subtype and reflections on histogenesis. Virchows Arch 1999, **434**: 385–391.

356 Kuhajda FP, Mann RB. Adenoid cystic carcinoma of the prostate. A case report with immunoperoxidase staining for prostate-specific acid phosphatase and prostate-specific antigen. Am J Clin Pathol 1984, **81**: 257–260.

357 Kuroda N, Yamasaki I, Nakayama H, Tamura K, Yamamoto Y, Miyasazki E, Naruse K, Kiyoku H, Hiroi M, Enzan H. Protatic signet-ring cell carcinoma: Case report and literature review. Pathol Int 1999, **49**: 457–461.

358 Lauwers GY, Schevchuk M, Armenakas N, Reuter VE. Carcinoma of the prostate. Am J Surg Pathol 1993, **17**: 342–349.

359 Leong FJW-M, Leong AS-Y, Swift J. Signet-ring carcinoma of the prostate. Pathol Res Pract 1997, **192**: 1232–1238.

360 Little NA, Wiener JS, Walther PJ, Paulson DF, Anderson EE. Squamous cell carcinoma of the prostate. 2 cases of a rare malignancy and review of the literature. J Urol 1993, **149**: 137–139.

361 Ma TKF, Chapman WB, McLean M, Srigley J. Prostatic carcinosarcoma consisting of the unusual combination of ductal adenocarcinoma with osteogenic sarcoma: a report of a case and review of the literature. J Urol Pathol 1998, **8**: 111–120.

362 McNeal JE, Alroy J, Villers A, Redwine EA, Freiha FS, Stamey TA. Mucinous differentiation in prostatic adenocarcinoma. Hum Pathol 1991, **22**: 979–988.

363 Mai KT, Leahy CF. Squamous cell carcinoma occurring as a circumscribed nodule in the transition zone of the prostate: A case report and review of the literature. J Urol Pathol 1996, **5**: 85–92.

364 Mai KT, Burns BF, Morash C. Giant-cell carcinoma of the prostate. J Urol Pathol 1996, **5**: 167–174.

365 Moyana TN. Adenosquamous carcinoma of the prostate. Am J Surg Pathol 1987, **11**: 403–407.

366 Mucci NR, Akdas G, Manely S, Rubin MA. Neuroendocrine expression in metastatic prostate cancer: Evaluation of high throughput tissue microarrays to detect heterogeneous protein expression. Hum Pathol 2000, **31**: 406–414.

367 Oesterling JE, Hauzeur CG, Farrow GM. Small cell anaplastic carcinoma of the prostate: A clinical, pathological and immunohistological study of 27 patients. J Urol 1992, **147**: 804–807.

368 Ohtsuki Y, Ro JY, Ordonez NG, Kee KH, Richmond C, Ayala AG. Sarcomatoid carcinoma of the prostate with rhabdomyosarcomatous differentiation: case report and review of the literature. J Urol Pathol 1996, **5**: 157–166.

369 Pan CC, Chiang H, Chang YH, Epstein JI. Tubulocystic clear cell adenocarcinoma arising within the prostate. Am J Surg Pathol 2000, **24**: 1433–1436.

370 Papadimitriou JC, Weihing RR, Choi C, Drachenberg CB. Prostatic marker-negative amphicrine carcinoma of the prostate. Ultrastruct Pathol 1994, **18**: 357–363.

370a Parwani AV, Kronz JD, Genega EM, Gaudin P, Chang S, Epstein JI. Prostate carcinoma with squamous differentiation: an analysis of 33 cases (Abstract). Mod Pathol 2003, **16**: 165A.

371 Proia AD, McCarty KS Jr, Woodard BH. Prostatic mucinous adenocarcinoma. A Cowper gland carcinoma mimicker. Am J Surg Pathol 1981, **5**: 701–706.

372 Randolph TL, Amin MB, Ro JY, Ayala AG. Histologic variants of adenocarcinoma and other carcinomas of prostate: pathologic criteria and clinical significance. Mod Pathol 1997, **10**: 612–629.

373 Reed RJ. Consultation case. Am J Surg Pathol 1984, **8**: 699–704.

374 Reuter VE. Sarcomatoid lesions of the urogenital tract. Semin Diagn Pathol 1993, **10**: 188–201.

375 Ro JY, Grignon DJ, Ayala AG, Fernandez PL, Ordonéz NG, Wishnow KI. Mucinous adenocarcinoma of the prostate. Histochemical and immunohistochemical studies. Hum Pathol 1990, **21**: 593–600.

376 Ro JY, Tetu B, Ayala AG, Ordonéz NG. Small cell carcinoma of the prostate. II. Immunohistochemical and electron microscopic studies of 18 cases. Cancer 1987, **59**: 977–982.

377 Saez C, Japon MA, Conde AF, Poveda MA, Luna-More S, Segura DI. Sialomucins are characteristically O-acylated in poorly differentiated and colloid prostatic adenocarcinomas. Mod Pathol 1998, **11**: 1193–1197.

378 Saito R, Davis BK, Ollapally EP. Adenosquamous carcinoma of the prostate. Hum Pathol 1984, **15**: 87–89.

379 Schron DS, Gipson T, Mendelsohn G. The histogenesis of small cell carcinoma of the prostate. Cancer 1984, **53**: 2478–2480.

380 Shannon RL, Ro JY, Grignon DJ, Ordonez NG, Johnson DE, Mackay B, Tetu B, Ayala AG. Sarcomatoid carcinoma of the prostate. A clinicopathologic study of 12 patients. Cancer 1992, **69**: 2676–2682.

381 Silverman ML, Eyre RC, Zinman LA, Crosson AW. Mixed mucinous and papillary adenocarcinoma involving male urethra, probably originating in periurethral glands. Cancer 1981, **47**: 1398–1402.

381a Singh H, Flores-Sandoval N, Abrams J. Renal-type clear cell carcinoma occurring in the prostate. Am J Surg Pathol 2003, **27**: 407–410.

382 Speights VO Jr, Cohen MK, Coffield KS, Keegan GT, McClintock J, Arber DA. Neuroendocrine staining in malignant, hyperplastic, and atrophic prostate tissue. Appl Immunohistochem 1994, **2**: 212–217.

383 Tetu B, Ro JY, Ayala AG, Johnson DE, Logothetis CJ, Ordonéz NG. Small cell carcinoma of the prostate. I. A clinicopathologic study of 20 cases. Cancer 1987, **59**: 1803–1809.

384 Torbenson M, Dhir R, Nangia A, Becich MJ, Kapadia SB. Prostatic carcinoma with signet ring cells: a clinicopathologic and immunohistochemical analysis of 12 cases, with review of the literature. Mod Pathol 1998, **11**: 552–559.

385 van de Voorde W, Van Poppel H, Haustermans K, Baert L, Lauweryns J. Mucin-secreting adenocarcinoma of the prostate with neuroendocrine differentiation and Paneth-like cells. Am J Surg Pathol 1994, **18**: 200–207.

386 Wang I, Lin C-S, Unger PD. Squamous cell carcinoma arising in hormonally treated adenocarcinoma of the prostate. Int J Surg Pathol 1996, **4**: 13–16.

387 Weaver MG, Abdul-Karim FW, Srigley JR. Paneth cell-like change and small cell carcinoma of the prostate. Two divergent forms of prostatic neuroendocrine differentiation. Am J Surg Pathol 1992, **16**: 1013–1016.

388 Weinstein MH, Partin AW, Veltri RW, Epstein JI. Neuroendocrine differentiation in prostate cancer: Enhanced prediction of progression after radical prostatectomy. Hum Pathol 1996, **27**: 683–687.

389 Wenk RE, Bhagavan BS, Levy R, Miller D, Weisburger W. Ectopic ACTH, prostatic oat cell carcinoma, and marked hypernatremia. Cancer 1977, **40**: 773–778.

390 Wernert N, Goebbels R, Bonkhoff H, Dhom G. Squamous cell carcinoma of the prostate. Histopathology 1990, **17**: 339–344.

391 Wick MR, Young RH, Malvesta R, Beebe DS, Hansen JJ, Dehner LP. Prostatic carcinosarcomas. Clinical, histologic, and immunohistochemical data on two cases, with a review of the literature. Am J Clin Pathol 1989, **92**: 131–139.

392 Xue Y, Verhofstad A, Lange W, Smedts F, Debruyne F, de la Rosette J, Schalken J. Prostatic neuroendocrine cells have a unique keratin expression pattern and do not express bcl-2. Cell kinetic features of neuroendocrine cells in the human prostate. Am J Pathol 1997, **151**: 1759–1765.

393 Yang XJ, McEntee M, Epstein JI. Distinction of basaloid carcinoma of the prostate from benign basal cell lesions by using immunohistochemistry for bcl-2 and Ki-67. Hum Pathol 1998, **29**: 1447–1450.

Intraepithelial proliferative lesions

394 Argani P, Epstein JI. Inverted (hobnail) high-grade prostatic intraepithelial neoplasia (PIN): report of 15 cases of a previously undescribed pattern of high-grade PIN. Am J Surg Pathol 2001, **25**: 1534–1539.

395 Baretton GB, Vogt T, Blasenbreu S, Lohrs U. Comparison of DNA ploidy in prostatic intraepithelial neoplasia and invasive carcinoma of the prostate. An image cytometric study. Hum Pathol 1994, **25**: 506–513.

396 Berman DM, Yang J, Epstein JI. Foamy gland high-grade prostatic intraepithelial neoplasia. Am J Surg Pathol 2000, **24**: 140–144.

397 Bostwick DG, de la Roza G. Intraepithelial neoplasia. A call for standardized terminology. J Urol Pathol 1993, **1**: 95–103.

398 Bostwick DG, Qian J. Atypical adenomatous hyperplasia of the prostate. Relationship with carcinoma in 217 whole-mount radical prostatectomies. Am J Surg Pathol 1995, **19**: 506–518.

399 Bostwick DG, Algaba F, Amin MB, Ayala A, Eble J, Goldstein N, Helpap B, Humphrey P, Grignon D, Jones EC, et al. Consensus statement on terminology. Recommendation to use atypical adenomatous hyperplasia in place of adenosis of the prostate (letter). Am J Surg Pathol 1994, **18**: 1069–1070.

400 Bostwick DG, Amin MB, Dundore P, Marsh W, Schultz DS. Architectural patterns of high-grade prostatic intraepithelial neoplasia. Hum Pathol 1993, **24**: 298–310.

401 Bostwick DG, Dousa MK, Crawford BG, Wollan PC. Neuroendocrine differentiation in prostatic intraepithelial neoplasia and adenocarcinoma. Am J Surg Pathol 1994, **18**: 1240–1246.

402 Bostwick DG, Shan A, Qian J, Darson M, Maihle NJ, Jenkins RB, Cheng L. Independent origin of multiple foci of prostatic intraepithelial neoplasia: comparison with matched foci of prostate carcinoma. Cancer 1998, **83**: 1995–2002.

403 Bostwick DG, Srigley J, Grignon D, Maksem J, Humphrey P, van der Kwast TH, Bose D, Harrison J, Young RH. Atypical adenomatous hyperplasia of the prostate. Morphologic criteria for its distinction from well-differentiated carcinoma. Hum Pathol 1993, **24**: 819–832.

404 Brawer MK. Prostatic intraepithelial neoplasia: A premalignant lesion. Hum Pathol 1992, **23**: 242–248.

405 Brawer MK, Bigler SA, Sohlberg OE, Nagle RB, Lange PH. Significance of prostatic intraepithelial neoplasia on prostate needle biopsy. Urology 1991, **38**: 103–107.

406 Cheville JC, Clamon GH, Robinson RA. Silver-stained nucleolar organizer regions in the differentiation of prostatic hyperplasia, intraepithelial neoplasia, and adenocarcinoma. Mod Pathol 1990, **3**: 596–598.

407 Crissman JD, Sakr WA, Hussein ME, Pontes JE. DNA quantitation of intraepithelial neoplasia and invasive carcinoma of the prostate. Prostate 1993, **22**: 156–162.

408 Doll JA, Zhu X, Furman J, Kaleem Z, Torres C, Humphrey PA, Donis-Keller H. Genetic analysis of prostatic atypical adenomatous hyperplasia (adenosis). Am J Pathol 1999, **155**: 967–971.

409 Eble JN. Variants of prostatic hyperplasia that resemble carcinoma. J Urol Pathol 1998, **8**: 3–20.

410 Epstein JI. Controversies in prostate pathology. Dysplasia and carcinoma in situ. Monogr Pathol 1992, **34**: 149–182.

411 Epstein JI. Pathology of prostatic intraepithelial neoplasia and adenocarcinoma of the prostate. Prognostic influences of stage, tumor volume, grade, and margins of resection. Semin Oncol 1994, **21**: 527–541.

412 Epstein JI, Fynheer J. Acidic mucin in the prostate. Can it differentiate adenosis from adenocarcinoma? Hum Pathol 1992, **23**: 1321–1325.

413 Erdamar S, Slawin KM, Wheeler TM. High-grade prostatic intraepithelial neoplasia involving the prostatic utricle: a case report. J Urol Pathol 1998, **8**: 167–170.

414 Gaudin PB, Epstein JI. Adenosis of the prostate. Histologic features in transurethral resection specimens. Am J Surg Pathol 1994, **18**: 863–870.

415 Goldstein NS, Qian J, Bostwick DG. Mucin expression in atypical adenomatous hyperplasia of the prostate. Hum Pathol 1995, **26**: 887–891.

416 Haussler O, Epstein JI, Amin MB, Heitz PU, Hailemariam S. Cell proliferation, apoptosis, oncogene, and tumor suppressor gene status in adenosis with comparison to benign prostatic hyperplasia, prostatic intraepithelial neoplasia and cancer. Hum Pathol 1999, **30**: 1077–1086.

417 Humphrey PA. Mucin in severe dysplasia in the prostate. Surg Pathol 1991, **4**: 137–143.

418 Humphrey PA, Zhu X, Crouch EC, Carbone JM, Keetch DW. Mass-formative atypical adenomatous hyperplasia of prostate. J Urol Pathol 1998, **9**: 73–82.

419 Kronz JD, Allan CH, Shaikh AA, Epstein JI. Predicting cancer following a diagnosis of high-grade prostatic intraepithelial neoplasia on needle biopsy: data on men with more than one follow-up biopsy. Am J Surg Pathol 2001, **25**: 1079–1085.

420 Kronz JD, Shaikh AA, Epstein JI. Atypical cribriform lesions on prostate biopsy. Am J Surg Pathol 2001, **25**: 147–155.

421 Kronz JD, Shaikh AA, Epstein JI. High-grade prostatic intraepithelial neoplasia with adjacent small atypical glands on prostate biopsy. Hum Pathol 2001, **32**: 389–395.

422 Mostofi FK, Sesterhenn IA, Davis CJ Jr. Prostatic intraepithelial neoplasia (PIN). Morphological clinical significance. Prostate 1992, **4**(Suppl): 71–77.

423 Muezzinoglu B, Erdamar S, Chakraborty S, Wheeler TM. Verumontanum mucosal gland hyperplasia is associated with atypical adenomatous hyperplasia of the prostate. Arch Pathol Lab Med 2001, **125**: 358–360.

424 Myers RB, Srivastava S, Oelschlager DK, Grizzle WE. Expression of p160erbB-3 and p185erbB-2 in prostatic intraepithelial neoplasia and prostatic adenocarcinoma. J Natl Cancer Inst 1994, **86**: 1140–1145.

425 Nagle RB, Brawer MK, Kittelson J, Clark V. Phenotypic relationships of prostatic intraepithelial neoplasia to invasive prostatic carcinoma. Am J Pathol 1991, **138**: 119–128.

426 Qian J, Wollan P, Bostwick DG. The extent and multicentricity of high-grade prostatic intraepithelial neoplasia in clinically localized prostatic adenocarcinoma. Hum Pathol 1997, **28**: 143–148.

427 Reyes AO, Swanson PE, Carbone JM, Humphrey PA. Unusual histologic types of high-grade prostatic intraepithelial neoplasia. Am J Surg Pathol 1997, **21**: 1215–1222.

428 Ronnett BM, Carmichael MJ, Carter HB, Epstein JI. Does high grade prostatic intraepithelial neoplasia result in elevated serum prostate specific antigen levels? J Urol 1993, **150**: 386–389.

429 Sakr WA, Haas GP, Cassin BF, Pontes JE, Crissman JD. The frequency of carcinoma and intraepithelial neoplasia of the prostate in young male patients. J Urol 1993, **150**: 379–385.

430 Skjorten FJ, Berner A, Harvei S, Robsahm TE, Tretli S. Prostatic intraepithelial neoplasia in surgical resections: relationship to coexistent adenocarcinoma and atypical adenomatous hyperplasia of the prostate. Cancer 1997, **79**: 1172–1179.

431 Stesterhenn IA, Becker RL, Avallone FA, Mostofi FK, Lin TH, Davis CJ Jr. Image analysis of nucleoli and nucleolar organizer regions in prostatic hyperplasia, intraepithelial neoplasia, and prostatic carcinoma. J Urogen Pathol 1991, **1**: 61–74.

432 Weinberg DS, Weidner N. Concordance of DNA content between prostatic intraepithelial neoplasia and concomitant invasive carcinoma. Evidence that prostatic intraepithelial neoplasia is a precursor of invasive prostatic carcinoma. Arch Pathol Lab Med 1993, **117**: 1132–1137.

433 Weinstein MH, Epstein JI. Significance of high-grade prostatic intraepithelial neoplasia on needle biopsy. Hum Pathol 1993, **24**: 624–629.

433a Zeng G, Hu Z, Kinch MS, Pan C, Flockhart DA, Kao C, Gardner TA, Zhang S, Li L, Baldridge LE, Koch MO, Ulbright TM, Eble JN, Cheng L. High-level expression of EphA2 receptor tyrosine kinase in prostatic intraepithelial neoplasia. Am J Pathol 2003; **163**: 2271–2276.

Cytology

434 Andersson L, Hagmar B, Ljung BM, Skoog L. Fine needle aspiration biopsy for diagnosis and follow-up of prostate cancer. Consensus Conference on Diagnosis and Prognostic Parameters in Localized Prostate Cancer. Scand J Urol Nephrol Suppl 1994, **162**: 43–49, discussion 115–127.

435 Chodak GW, Bibbo M, Straus FH, Wied GL. Transrectal aspiration biopsy versus transperineal core biopsy for the diagnosis of carcinoma of the prostate. J Urol 1984, **132**: 480–482.

436 Cohen MB, Ljung BM. Fine-needle aspiration biopsy of the prostate. Pathol Annu 1991, **26**(Pt 2): 89–108.

437 Droese M, Voeth C. Cytologic features of seminal vesicle epithelium in aspiration biopsy smears of the prostate. Acta Cytol (Baltimore) 1976, **20**: 120–125.

438 Epstein NA. Prostatic biopsy. A morphologic correlation of aspiration cytology with needle biopsy histology. Cancer 1976, **38**: 2078–2087.

439 Esposti P-L. Cytologic diagnosis of prostatic tumors with the aid of transrectal aspiration biopsy. A critical review of 1,110 cases and a report of morphologic and cytochemical studies. Acta Cytol (Baltimore) 1966, **10**: 182–186.

440　Esposti P-L. Cytologic malignancy grading of prostatic carcinoma by transrectal aspiration biopsy. A five-year follow-up study of 469 hormone-treated patients. Scand J Urol Nephrol 1971, **5:** 199–209.

441　Koivuniemi A, Tyrkko J. Seminal vesicle epithelium in fine-needle aspiration biopsies of the prostate as a pitfall in the cytologic diagnosis of carcinoma. Acta Cytol (Baltimore) 1976, **20:** 116–119.

442　Ljung BM, Cherrie R, Kaufman JJ. Fine needle aspiration biopsy of the prostate gland. A study of 103 cases with histological followup. J Urol 1986, **135:** 955–958.

443　Mesonero CE, Oertel YC. Cells from ejaculatory ducts and seminal vesicles and diagnostic difficulties in prostatic aspirates. Mod Pathol 1991, **4:** 723–726.

Histologic examination

444　Bostwick DG, Vonk JB, Picado A. Pathologic changes in the prostate following contemporary 18-gauge needle biopsy. No apparent risk of local cancer seeding. J Urol Pathol 1994, **2:** 203–212.

445　Brat DJ, Wills ML, Lecksell KL, Epstein JI. How often are diagnostic features missed with less extensive histologic sampling of prostate needle biopsy specimens? Am J Surg Pathol 1999, **23:** 257–262.

446　Eble JN, Angermeier PA. The roles of fine needle aspiration and needle core biopsies in the diagnosis of primary prostatic cancer. Hum Pathol 1992, **23:** 1194–1195.

447　Egevad L, Engstrom K, Busch C. A new method for handling radical prostatectomies enabling fresh tissue harvesting, whole mount sections, and landmarks for alignment of sections. J Urol Pathol 1998, **9:** 17–28.

448　Epstein JI. The diagnosis and reporting of adenocarcinoma of the prostate in core needle biopsy specimens. Cancer 1996, **78:** 350–356.

449　Garborg I, Eide TJ. The probability of overlooking prostatic cancer in transurethrally resected material when different embedding practices are followed. Acta Pathol Microbiol Immunol Scand (A) 1985, **93:** 205–208.

450　Gentry JF. Pelvic lymph node metastases in prostatic carcinoma. The value of touch imprint cytology. Am J Surg Pathol 1986, **10:** 718–727.

451　Hoedemaeker RF, Ruijter ETG, Ruizeveld-de Winter JA, van der Kaa CA, The Biomed II MPC Study Group, van der Kwast Th H. Processing radical prostatectomy specimens: a comprehensive and standardized protocol. J Urol Pathol 1998, **9:** 211–222.

452　Kramolowsky EV, Narayana AS, Platz CE, Loening SA. The frozen section in lymphadenectomy for carcinoma of the prostate. J Urol 1984, **131:** 899–900.

453　Labardini MM, Nesbit RM. Perineal extension of adenocarcinoma of the prostate gland after punch biopsy. J Urol 1967, **97:** 891–893.

454　Lane RB Jr, Lane CG, Mangold KA, Johnson MH, Allsbrook WC Jr. Needle biopsies of the prostate: what constitutes adequate histologic sampling? Arch Pathol Lab Med 1998, 122: 833–835.

455　McDowell PR, Fox WM, Epstein JI. Is submission of remaining tissue necessary when incidental carcinoma of the prostate is found on transurethral resection? Hum Pathol 1994, **25:** 493–497.

455a　Montironi R, Mazzucchelli R, Kwast T. Morphological assessment of radical prostatectomy specimens. A protocol with clinical relevance. Virchows Arch 2003, **442:** 211–217.

456　Murphy WM, Dean PJ, Brasfield JA, Tatum L. Incidental carcinoma of the prostate. How much sampling is adequate? Am J Surg Pathol 1986, **10:** 170–174.

457　Newman AJ, Graham MA, Carlton CE Jr, Lieman S. Incidental carcinoma of the prostate at the time of transurethral resection. Importance of evaluating every chip. J Urol 1982, **128:** 948–950.

458　Peller PA, Young DC, Marmaduke DP, Marsh WL, Badalament RA. Sextant prostate biopsies. A histopathologic correlation with radical prostatectomy specimens. Cancer 1995, **75:** 530–538.

459　Renshaw AA. Adequate tissue sampling of prostate core needle biopsies. Am J Clin Pathol 1997, **107:** 26–29.

460　Reyes AO, Humphrey PA. Diagnostic effect of complete histologic sampling of prostate needle biopsy specimens. Am J Clin Pathol 1998, **109:** 416–422.

461　Rohr LR. Incidental adenocarcinoma in transurethral resections of the prostate. Partial versus complete microscopic examination. Am J Surg Pathol 1987, **11:** 53–58.

462　Sadlowski RW, Donahue DJ, Richman AV, Sharpe JR, Finney RP. Accuracy of frozen section diagnosis in pelvic lymph node staging biopsies for adenocarcinoma of the prostate. J Urol 1983, **129:** 324–326.

463　Sehdev AE, Pan C-C, Epstein JI. Comparative analysis of sampling methods for grossing radical prostatectomy specimens performed for nonpalpable (Stage T1C) prostatic adenocarcinoma. Hum Pathol 2001, **32:** 494–499.

464　Vollmer RT. Prostate cancer and chip specimens. Complete versus partial sampling. Hum Pathol 1986, **17:** 285–290.

Microscopic differential diagnosis

465　Allan CH, Epstein JI. Nephrogenic adenoma of the prostatic urethra: a mimicker of prostate adenocarcinoma. Am J Surg Pathol 2001, **25:** 802–808.

466　Amin MB, Bostwick DG. Pigment in prostatic epithelium and adenocarcinoma: A potential source of diagnostic confusion with seminal vesicular epithelium. Mod Pathol 1996, **9:** 791–795.

467　Amin MB, Tamboli P, Varma M, Srigley JR. Postatrophic hyperplasia of the prostate gland: a detailed analysis of its morphology in needle biopsy specimens. Am J Surg Pathol 1999, **23:** 925–931.

468　Anton RC, Kattan MW, Chakraborty S, Wheeler TM. Postatrophic hyperplasia of the prostate: lack of association with prostate cancer. Am J Surg Pathol 1999, **23:** 932–936.

469　Ayala AG, Srigley JR, Ro JY, Abdul-Karim FW, Johnson DE. Clear cell cribriform hyperplasia of prostate. Report of 10 cases. Am J Surg Pathol 1986, **10:** 665–671.

470　Billis A. Prostatic atrophy: an autopsy study of a histologic mimic of adenocarcinoma. Mod Pathol 1998, **11:** 47–54.

471　Billis A, Magna LA. Prostate elastosis: a microscopic feature useful for the diagnosis of postatrophic hyperplasia. Arch Pathol Lab Med 2000, **124:** 1306–1309.

472　Bostwick DG, Egbert BM, Fajardo LF. Radiation injury of the normal and neoplastic prostate. Am J Surg Pathol 1982, **6:** 541–551.

472a　Bostwick DG, Quan J, Ma J, Muir TE. Mesonephric remnants of the prostate: incidence and histologic spectrum. Mod Pathol 2003; **16:** 630–635.

473　Carstens PHB. Perineural glands in normal and hyperplastic prostates. J Urol 1980, **123:** 686–688.

474　Cheville JC, Bostwick DG. Postatrophic hyperplasia of the prostate. A histologic mimic of prostatic adenocarcinoma. Am J Surg Pathol 1995, **19:** 1068–1076.

475　Cina SJ, Silberman MA, Kahane H, Epstein JI. Diagnosis of Cowper's glands on prostate needle biopsy. Am J Surg Pathol 1997, **21:** 550–555.

476　Cleary KR, Choi HY, Ayala AG. Basal cell hyperplasia of the prostate. Am J Clin Pathol 1983, **80:** 850–854.

477　Cramer SF. Benign glandular inclusion in prostatic nerve. Am J Clin Pathol 1981, **75:** 854–855.

478　Eble JN. Variants of prostatic hyperplasia that resemble carcinoma. J Urol Pathol 1998, **8:** 3–20.

479　Epstein JI, Armas OA. Atypical basal cell hyperplasia of the prostate. Am J Surg Pathol 1992, **16:** 1205–1214.

480　Gaudin PB, Reuter VE. Benign mimics of prostatic adenocarcinoma on needle biopsy. Anat Pathol 1997, **2:** 111–134.

481　Gikas PW, Del Buono EA, Epstein JI. Florid hyperplasia of mesonephric remnants involving prostate and periprostatic tissue. Possible confusion with adenocarcinoma. Am J Surg Pathol 1993, **17**: 454–460.

482 Grignon DJ, Ro JY, Srigley JR, Troncoso P, Raymond AK, Ayala AG. Sclerosing adenosis of the prostate gland. A lesion showing myoepithelial differentiation. Am J Surg Pathol 1992, **16**: 383–391.

483 Jimenez RE, Raval MFT, Spanta R, Sakr W, Grignon DJ. Mesonephric remnants hyperplasia: a pitfall in the diagnosis of prostatic adenocarcinoma. J Urol Pathol 1998, **9**: 83–92.

484 Jones EC, Young RH. The differential diagnosis of prostatic carcinoma. Its distinction from premalignant and pseudocarcinomatous lesions of the prostate gland. Am J Clin Pathol 1994, **101**: 48–64.

485 Jones EC, Clement PB, Young RH. Sclerosing adenosis of the prostate gland. A clinicopathological and immunohistochemical study of 11 cases. Am J Surg Pathol 1991, **15**: 1171–1180.

486 Kawabata K. Paraganglion of the prostate in a needle biopsy: a potential diagnostic pitfall. Arch Pathol Lab Med 1997, **121**: 515–516.

487 Kuo T, Gomez LG. Monstrous epithelial cells in human epididymis and seminal vesicles. Am J Surg Pathol 1981, **5**: 483–490.

487a Leroy X, Ballereau C, Villers A, Saint F, Aubert S, Gosselin B, Porchet N, Copin MC. Muc6 is a marker of seminal vesicle-ejaculatory duct epithelium and is useful for the differential diagnosis with prostate adenocarcinoma. Am J Surg Pathol 2003, **27**: 519–521.

487b Magi-Galluzzi C, Sanderson H, Epstein JI. Atypia in nonneoplastic prostate glands after radiotherapy for prostate cancer: duration of atypia and relation to type of radiotherapy. Am J Surg Pathol 2003, **27**: 206–212.

488 Mostofi FK, Sesterhenn IA, Davis CJ Jr. Prostatic carcinoma. Problems in the interpretation of prostatic biopsies. Hum Pathol 1992, **23**: 223–241.

489 Oppenheimer JR, Wills ML, Epstein JI. Partial atrophy in prostate needle cores: another diagnostic pitfall for the surgical pathologist. Am J Surg Pathol 1998, **22**: 440–445.

490 Ostrowski ML, Wheeler TM. Paraganglia of the prostate. Location, frequency, and differentiation from prostatic adenocarcinoma. Am J Surg Pathol 1994, **18**: 412–420.

491 Rioux-Leclercq NC, Epstein JI. Unusual morphologic patterns of basal cell hyperplasia of the prostate. Am J Surg Pathol 2002, **26**: 237–243.

492 Rode J, Bentley A, Parkinson C. Paraganglial cells of urinary bladder and prostate. Potential diagnostic problem. J Clin Pathol 1990, **43**: 13–16.

493 Ruska KM, Sauvageot J, Epstein JI. Histology and cellular kinetics of prostatic atrophy. Am J Surg Pathol 1998, **22**: 1073–1077.

494 Saboorian MH, Huffman H, Ashfaq R, Ayala AG, Ro JY. Distinguishing Cowper's glands from neoplastic and pseudoneoplastic lesions of prostate: immunohistochemical and ultrastructural studies. Am J Surg Pathol 1997, **21**: 1069–1074.

495 Sakamonto N, Tsuneyoshi M, Enjoji M. Sclerosing adenosis of the prostate. Histopathologic and immunohistochemical analysis. Am J Surg Pathol 1991, **15**: 660–667.

496 Sebo TJ, Bostwick DG, Farrow GM, Eble JN. Prostatic xanthoma. A mimic of prostatic adenocarcinoma. Hum Pathol 1994, **25**: 386–389.

497 Shidham VB, Lindholm PF, Kajdacsy-Balla A, Basir Z, George V, Garcia FU. Prostate-specific antigen expression and lipochrome pigment granules in the differential diagnosis of prostatic adenocarcinoma versus seminal vesicle-ejaculatory duct epithelium. Arch Pathol Lab Med 1999, **123**: 1093–1097.

497a Thorson P, Swanson PE, Vollmer RT, Humphrey PA. Basal cell hyperplasia in the peripheral zone of the prostate. Mod Pathol 2003, **16**: 598–606.

498 Totten RS, Heinemann MW, Hudson PB, Sproul EE, Stout AP. Microscopic differential diagnosis of latent carcinoma of the prostate. Arch Pathol 1953, **55**: 131–141.

499 van de Voorde W, Baldewijns M, Lauweryns J. Florid basal cell hyperplasia of the prostate. Histopathology 1994, **24**: 341–348.

499a Yang XJ, Tretiakova MS, Sengupta E, Gong C, Jiang Z. Florid basal cell hyperplasia of the prostate: a histological, ultrastructural, and immunohistochemical analysis. Hum Pathol 2003, **34**: 462–470.

500 Yantiss RK, Young RH. Transitional cell "metaplasia" in the prostate gland: a survey of its frequency and features based on 103 consecutive prostatic biopsy specimens. J Urol Pathol 1997, **7**: 71–80.

501 Young RH. Tumor-like lesions of the urinary bladder and prostate. Pathol Annu 1988, **23**(Pt 1): 105–128.

501a Wang HL, Humphrey PA. Exaggerated signet-ring cell change in stromal nodule of prostate: a pseudoneoplastic proliferation. Am J Surg Pathol 2002, **26**: 1066–1070.

Spread and metastases

502 Baumann MA, Holoye PY, Choi H. Adenocarcinoma of prostate presenting as brain metastasis. Cancer 1984, **54**: 1723–1725.

503 Benson RC Jr, Tomera KM, Zincke H, Fleming TR, Utz DC. Bilateral pelvic lymphadenectomy and radical retropubic prostatectomy for adenocarcinoma confined to the prostate. J Urol 1984, **131**: 1103–1106.

504 Bovenberg SA, van der Zwet CJJ, van der Kwast TH, Marzella L, Bostwick DG. Prostate-specific antigen expression in prostate cancer and its metastases. J Urol Pathol 1993, **1**: 55–61.

505 Brawn P. Histologic features of metastatic prostate cancer. Hum Pathol 1992, **23**: 267–272.

506 Brawn PN, Kuhl D, Speights VO, Johnson CF III, Lind M. The incidence of unsuspected metastases from clinically benign prostate glands with latent prostate carcinoma. Arch Pathol Lab Med 1995, **119**: 731–733.

507 Bubendorf L, Schopfer A, Wagner U, Sauter G, Moch H, Willi N, Gasser TC, Mihatsch MJ. Metastatic patterns of prostate cancer: An autopsy study of 1,589 patients. Hum Pathol 2000, **31**: 578–583.

508 Butler JJ, Howe CD, Johnson DE. Enlargement of the supraclavicular lymph nodes as the initial sign of prostatic carcinoma. Cancer 1971, **27**: 1055–1063.

509 Carlin BI, Andriole GL. The natural history, skeletal complications, and management of bone metastases in patients with prostate carcinoma. Cancer 2000, **88**: 2989–2994.

510 Charhon SA, Chapuy MC, Delvin EE, Valentin-Opran A, Edouard CM, Meunier PJ. Histomorphometric analysis of sclerotic bone metastases from prostatic carcinoma with special reference to osteomalacia. Cancer 1983, **51**: 918–924.

511 Cheng L, Slezak J, Bergstralh EJ, Cheville JC, Sweat S, Zincke H, Bostwick DG. Dedifferentiation in the metastatic progression of prostate carcinoma. Cancer 1999, **86**: 657–663.

512 Cho KR, Epstein JI. Metastatic prostatic carcinoma to supradiaphragmatic lymph nodes. A clinicopathologic and immunohistochemical study. Am J Surg Pathol 1987, **11**: 457–463.

513 Copeland JN, Amin MB, Humphrey PA, Tamboli P, Ro JY, Gal AA. The morphologic spectrum of metastatic prostatic adenocarcinoma to the lung. Special emphasis on histologic features overlapping with other pulmonary neoplasms. Am J Clin Pathol 2002, **117**: 552–557.

514 Deguchi T, Doi T, Ehara H, Ito S, Takahashi Y, Nishino Y, Fujihiro S, Kawamura T, Komeda H, Horie M, et al. Detection of micrometastatic prostate cancer cells in lymph nodes by reverse transcriptase-polymerase chain reaction. Cancer Res 1993, **53**: 5350–5354.

515 de la Monte SM, Moore GW, Hutchins GM. Metastatic behavior of prostate cancer. Cancer 1986, **58**: 985–993.

516 De Potter P, Shields CL, Shields JA, Tardio DJ. Uveal metastasis from prostate carcinoma. Cancer 1993, **71**: 2791–2796.

517 Dodds PR, Caride VJ, Lytton B. The role of vertebral veins in the dissemination of prostatic carcinoma. J Urol 1981, **126**: 753–755.

518 Epstein JI. Evaluation of radical prostatectomy capsular margins of resection. The significance of margins designated as negative, closely approaching, and positive. Am J Surg Pathol 1990, **14**: 626–632.

519 Epstein JI, Carmichael M, Walsh PC. Adenocarcinoma of the prostate invading the seminal vesicle. Definition and relation of tumor volume, grade and margins of resection to prognosis. J Urol 1993, **149**: 1040–1045.

520 Fowler JE Jr, Whitmore WF. The incidence and extent of pelvic lymph node metastases in apparently localized prostatic cancer. Cancer 1981, **47**: 2941–2945.

521 Gengler L, Baer J, Finby N. Rectal and sigmoid involvement secondary to carcinoma of the prostate. Am J Roentgenol Radium Ther Nucl Med 1975, **125**: 910–917.

522 Gentile PS, Carloss HW, Huang TY, Yam LT, Lam WK. Disseminated prostatic carcinoma simulating primary lung cancer. Indications for immunodiagnostic studies. Cancer 1988, **62**: 711–715.

523 Ghossein RA, Scher HI, Gerald WL, Kelly WK, Curley T, Amsterdam A, Zhang Z-F, Rosai J. Detection of circulating tumor cells in patients with localized and metastatic prostatic carcinoma. Clinical implications. J Clin Oncol 1995, **13**: 1195–1200.

524 Goltzman D. Mechanisms of the development of osteoblastic metastases. Cancer 1997, **80**: 1581–1587.

525 Gomella LG, White JL, McCue PA, Byrne DS, Mulholland SG. Screening for occult nodal metastasis in localized carcinoma of the prostate. J Urol 1993, **149**: 776–778.

526 Green LK, Klima M. The use of immunohistochemistry in metastatic prostatic adenocarcinoma to the breast. Hum Pathol 1991, **22**: 242–246.

526a Haese A, Epstein JI, Huland H, Partin AW. Validation of a biopsy-based pathologic algorithm for predicting lymph node metastases in patients with clinically localized prostate carcinoma. Cancer 2002, **95**: 1016–1021.

527 Harada M, Iida M, Yamaguchi M, Shida K. Analysis of bone metastasis of prostatic adenocarcinoma in 137 autopsy cases. Adv Exp Med Biol 1992, **324**: 173–182.

528 Harada M, Shimizu A, Nakamura Y, Nemoto R. Role of the vertebral venous system in metastatic spread of cancer cells to the bone. Adv Exp Med Biol 1992, **324**: 83–92.

529 Harrison SH, Seale-Hawkins C, Schum CW, Dunn JK, Scardino PT. Correlation between side of palpable tumor and side of pelvic lymph node metastasis in clinically localized prostate cancer. Cancer 1992, **69**: 750–754.

529a Harisinghani MG, Barentsz J, Hahn PF, Deserno WM, Tabatabaei S, van de Kaa CH, de la Rosette J, Weissleder R. Noninvasive detection of clinically occult lymph-node metastases in prostate cancer. N Engl J Med 2003, **348**: 2491.

530 Hrebinko R, Taylor SR, Bahnson RR. Carcinoma of prostate metastatic to parotid gland. Urology 1993, **41**: 272–273.

531 Jones H, Anthony PP. Metastatic prostatic carcinoma presenting as left-sided cervical lymphadenopathy. A series of 11 cases. Histopathology 1992, **21**: 149–154.

532 Kasabian NG, Previte SR, Kaloustian HD, Ganem EJ. Adenocarcinoma of the prostate presenting initially as an intracerebral tumor. Cancer 1992, **70**: 2149–2151.

533 Kothari PS, Scardino PT, Ohori M, Kattan MW, Wheeler TM. Incidence, location, and significance of periprostatic and periseminal vesicle lymph nodes in prostate cancer. Am J Surg Pathol 2001, **25**: 1429–1432.

534 Kramer SA, Farnham R, Glenn JF, Paulson DF. Comparative morphology of primary and secondary deposits of prostatic adenocarcinoma. Cancer 1981, **48**: 271–273.

535 Legier JF, Tauber LN. Solitary metastasis of occult prostatic carcinoma simulating osteogenic sarcoma. Cancer 1968, **22**: 168–172.

536 Lindell MM, Doubleday LC, von Eschenbach AC, Libshitz HI. Mediastinal metastases from prostatic carcinoma. J Urol 1982, **128**: 331–334.

537 Loening SA, Schmidt JD, Brown RC, Hawtrey CE, Fallon B, Culp DA. A comparison between lymphangiography and pelvic node dissection in the staging of prostatic cancer. J Urol 1977, **117**: 752–756.

538 McNeal JE, Yemoto CE. Spread of adenocarcinoma within prostatic ducts and acini: Morphologic and clinical correlations. Am J Surg Pathol 1996, **20**: 802–814.

539 McNeal JE, Yemoto CE. Significance of demonstrable vascular space invasion for the progression of prostatic adenocarcinoma. Am J Surg Pathol 1996, **20**: 1351–1360.

540 McNeal JE, Villers AA, Redwine EA, Freiha FS, Stamey TA. Histologic differentiation, cancer volume, and pelvic lymph node metastasis in adenocarcinoma of the prostate. Cancer 1990, **66**: 1225–1233.

541 Moul JW, Lewis DJ, Ross AA, Kahn DG, Ho CK, McLeod DG. Immunohistologic detection of prostate cancer pelvic lymph node micrometastases. Correlation to preoperative serum prostate-specific antigen. Urology 1994, **43**: 68–73.

542 Mukamel E, deKernion JB, Hannah J, Smith RB, Skinner DG, Goodwin WE. The incidence and significance of seminal vesicle invasion in patients with adenocarcinoma of the prostate. Cancer 1987, **59**: 1535–1538.

543 Ohori M, Scardino PT, Lapin SL, Seale-Hawkins C, Link J, Wheeler TM. The mechanisms and prognostic significance of seminal vesicle involvement by prostate cancer. Am J Surg Pathol 1993, **17**: 1252–1261.

544 Olsson CA. Staging lymphadenectomy should be an antecedent to treatment in localized prostatic carcinoma. Urology 1985, **25**(Suppl): 4–6.

545 Petros JA, Catalona WJ. Lower incidence of unsuspected lymph node metastases in 521 consecutive patients with clinically localized prostate cancer. J Urol 1992, **147**: 1574–1575.

546 Pfister S, Kleinschmidt-DeMasters BK. Dural metastases from prostatic adenocarcinoma. Report of five cases and review of the literature. J Urol Pathol 1995, **3**: 119–128.

547 Powell FC, Venencie PY, Winkelmann RK. Metastatic prostate carcinoma manifesting as penile nodules. Arch Dermatol 1984, **120**: 1604–1606.

548 Ransom DT, Dinapoli RP, Richardson RL. Cranial nerve lesions due to base of the skull metastases in prostate carcinoma. Cancer 1990, **65**: 586–589.

549 Ray GR, Pistenma DA, Gastellino RA, Kempson RL, Meares E, Bagshaw MA. Operative staging of apparently localized adenocarcinoma of the prostate. Results in fifty unselected patients. I. Experimental design and preliminary results. Cancer 1976, **38**: 73–83.

550 Robinette MA, Robson CJ, Farrow GA, Kerr WK, Van Nostrand PA, Hobbs BB, Bulbul MM. Giant serial step sections of the prostate in assessment of the accuracy of clinical staging in patients with localized prostatic carcinoma (abstract). J Urol 1984, **133**(Suppl): 242A.

551 Saitoh H, Yoshida K, Uchijima Y, Kobayashi N, Suwata J, Kamata S. Two different lymph node metastatic patterns of a prostatic cancer. Cancer 1990, **65**: 1843–1846.

552 Saltzstein SL, McLaughlin AP III. Clinicopathologic features of unsuspected regional lymph node metastases in prostatic adenocarcinoma. Cancer 1977, **40**: 1212–1221.

553 Seiden MV, Kantoff PW, Krithivas K, Propert K, Bryant M, Haltom E, Gaynes L, Kaplan I, Bubley G, De Wolf W, et al. Detection of circulating tumor cells in men with localized prostate cancer. J Clin Oncol 1994, **12**: 2634–2639.

554 Simpson RH, Skalova A. Metastatic carcinoma of the prostate presenting as parotid tumour. Histopathology 1997, **30**: 70–74.

554a Tremont-Lukats IW, Bobustuc G, Lagos GK, Lolas K, Kyritsis AP, Puduvalli VK. Brain metastasis from prostate carcinoma. Cancer 2003, **98**: 363–368.

555 Tu SM, Reyes A, Maa A, Bhowmick D, Pisters LL, Pettaway CA, Lin SH, Troncoso P, Logothetis CJ. Prostate carcinoma with testicular or penile metastases: clinical, pathologic, and immunohistochemical features. Cancer 2002, **94**: 2610–2617.

556 Villers A, McNeal JE, Freiha FS, Boccon-Gibod L, Stamey TA. Invasion of Denonvilliers' fascia in radical prostatectomy specimens. J Urol 1993, **149**: 793–798.

557 Weidner N, Carroll PR, Flax J, Blumenfeld W, Folkman J. Tumor angiogenesis correlates with metastasis in invasive prostate carcinoma. Am J Pathol 1993, **143**: 401–409.

558 Zelefsky MJ, Scher HI, Krol G, Portenoy RK, Leibel SA, Fuks ZY. Spinal epidural tumor in patients with prostate cancer. Clinical and radiographic predictors of response to radiation therapy. Cancer 1992, **70**: 2319–2325.

559 Zincke H, Utz DC, Taylor WF. Bilateral pelvic lymphadenectomy and radical prostatectomy for clinical stage C prostatic cancer. Role of adjuvant treatment for residual cancer and in disease progression. J Urol 1986, **135**: 1199–1205.

Staging and grading

560 Aihara M, Truong LD, Dunn JK, Wheeler TM, Scardino PT, Thompson TC. Frequency of apoptotic bodies positively correlates with Gleason grade in prostate cancer. Hum Pathol 1994, **25**: 797–801.

561 Allsbrook WC Jr, Mangold KA, Johnson MH, Lane RB, Lane CG, Amin MB, Bostwick DG, Humphrey PA, Jones EC, Reuter VE, Sakr W, Sesterhenn IA, Troncoso P, Wheeler T, Epstein JI. Interobserver reproducibility of Gleason grading of prostatic carcinoma: urologic pathologists. Hum Pathol 2001, **32**: 74–80.

562 Allsbrook WC Jr, Mangold KA Jr, Johnson MH, Lane RB, Lane CG, Epstein JI. Interobserver reproducibility of Gleason grading of prostatic carcinoma: general pathologists. Hum Pathol 2001, **32**: 81–88.

563 Allsbrook WC, Mangold KA Jr, Yang X, Epstein JI. The Gleason grading system: an overview. J Urol Pathol 1999, **10**: 141–158.

564 Babaian RJ, Grunow WA. Reliability of Gleason grading system in comparing prostate biopsies with total prostatectomy specimens. Urology 1985, **25**: 564–567.

565 Bain GO, Koch M, Hanson J. Feasibility of grading prostatic carcinomas. Arch Pathol Lab Med 1982, **106**: 265–267.

566 Bostwick DG. Gleason grading of prostatic needle biopsies. Correlation with grade in 316 matched prostatectomies. Am J Surg Pathol 1994, **18**: 796–803.

567 Bostwick DG. Grading prostate cancer. Am J Clin Pathol 1994, **102**: S38–S56.

568 Bostwick DG, Graham SD Jr, Napalkov P, Abrahamsson PA, di Sant'agnese PA, Algaba F, Hoisaeter PA, Lee F, Littrup P, Mostofi FK, et al. Staging of early prostate cancer. A proposed tumor volume-based prognostic index. Urology 1993, **41**: 403–411.

569 Cantrell BB, DeKlerk DP, Eggleston JC, Boitnott JK, Walsh PC. Pathological factors that influence prognosis in stage A prostatic cancer. The influence of extent versus grade. J Urol 1981, **125**: 516–520.

570 Epstein JI, Walsh PC, Carmichael M, Brendler CB. Pathologic and clinical findings to predict tumor extent of nonpalpable (stage T1c) prostate cancer. JAMA 1994, **271**: 368–374.

571 Fan K, Peng C-F. Predicting the probability of bone metastasis through histological grading of prostate carcinoma. A retrospective correlative analysis of 81 autopsy cases with antemortem transurethral resection specimen. J Urol 1983, **130**: 708–711.

572 Fowler JE Jr, Mills SE. Operable prostatic carcinoma. Correlations among clinical stage, pathological stage, Gleason histological score and early disease-free survival. J Urol 1985, **133**: 49–52.

573 Garnett JE, Oyasu R, Grayhack JT. The accuracy of diagnostic biopsy specimens in predicting tumor grades by Gleason's classification of radical prostatectomy specimens. J Urol 1984, **131**: 690–693.

574 Gibbons RP, Correa RJ Jr, Brannen GE, Mason JT. Total prostatectomy for localized prostatic cancer. J Urol 1984, **131**: 73–76.

575 Gleason DF. Histologic grading of prostate cancer. A perspective. Hum Pathol 1992, **23**: 273–279.

576 Gleason DF, Mellinger GT. The Veterans Administration Cooperative Urological Research Group: Prediction of prognosis for prostatic adenocarcinoma by combined histological grading and clinical staging. J Urol 1974, **111**: 58–64.

577 Graham SD Jr. Critical assessment of prostate cancer staging. Cancer 1992, **70**: 269–274.

578 Grignon DJ, Sakr WA. Pathologic staging of prostate carcinoma: What are the issues? Cancer 1996, **78**: 337–340.

579 Humphrey PA, Frazier HA, Vollmer RT, Paulson DF. Stratification of pathologic features in radical prostatectomy specimens that are predictive of elevated initial postoperative serum prostate-specific antigen levels. Cancer 1993, **71**: 1821–1827.

580 Jewett HJ. Prostatic cancer. A personal view of the problem. J Urol 1984, **131**: 845–849.

581 Kallakury BV, Figge J, Ross JS, Fisher HA, Figge HL, Jennings TA. Association of p53 immunoreactivity with high Gleason tumor grade in prostatic adenocarcinoma. Hum Pathol 1994, **25**: 92–97.

582 Klein LA. Prostatic carcinoma. N Engl J Med 1979, **300**: 824–833.

583 Kronz JD, Silberman MA, Allsbrook WC, Epstein JI. A web-based tutorial improves practicing pathologists' Gleason grading of images of prostate carcinoma specimens obtained by needle biopsy: validation of a new medical education paradigm. Cancer 2000, **89**: 1818–1823.

584 Lilleby W, Torlakovic G, Torlakovic E, Skovlund E, Fossa SD. Prognostic significance of histologic grading in patients with prostate carcinoma who are assessed by the Gleason and World Health Organization grading systems in needle biopsies obtained prior to radiotherapy. Cancer 2001, **92**: 311–319.

585 Mills SE, Fowler JE Jr. Gleason histologic grading of prostatic carcinoma. Correlations between biopsy and prostatectomy specimens. Cancer 1986, **57**: 346–349.

586 Mills SE, Bostwick DG, Murphy WM, Weiss MA. A symposium on the surgical pathology of the prostate. Pathol Annu 1990, **25**(Pt 2): 109–158.

587 Montie JE. 1992 staging system for prostate cancer. Semin Urol 1986, **11**: 10–13.

588 Murphy GP, Whitmore WF Jr. A report of the workshops on the current status of the histologic grading of prostatic cancer. Cancer 1979, **44**: 1490–1494.

589 Ohori M, Wheeler TM, Scardino PT. The New American Joint Committee on Cancer and International Union Against Cancer TNM classification of prostate cancer. Clinicopathologic correlations. Cancer 1994, **74**: 104–114.

590 Partin AW, Yoo J, Carter HB, Pearson JD, Chan DW, Epstein JI, Walsh PC. The use of prostate specific antigen, clinical stage and Gleason score to predict pathological stage in men with localized prostate cancer. J Urol 1993, **150**: 110–114.

591 Perez CA, Bauer W, Garza R, Royce RK. Radiation therapy in the definitive treatment of localized carcinoma of the prostate. Cancer 1977, **40**: 1425–1433.

592 Pontes JE, Wajsman Z, Huben RP, Wolf RM, Englander LS. Prognostic factors in localized prostatic carcinoma. J Urol 1985, **134**: 1137–1139.

593 Pretlow TG, Harris BE, Bradley EL Jr, Bueschen AJ, Lloyd KL, Pretlow TP. Enzyme activities in prostatic carcinoma related to Gleason grades. Cancer Res 1985, **45**: 442–446.

594 Rifkin MD, Zerhouni EA, Gatsonis CA, Quint LE, Paushter DM, Epstein JI, Hamper U, Walsh PC, McNeil BJ. Comparison of magnetic resonance imaging and ultrasonography in staging early prostate cancer. Results of a multi-institutional cooperative trial. N Engl J Med 1990, **323**: 621–626.

595 Rubin MA, Dunn R, Kamblham N, Misik CP, O'Toole KM. Should a Gleason score be assigned to a minute focus of carcinoma on prostate biopsy? Am J Surg Pathol 2000, **24**: 1634–1640.

596 Ruckle HC, Klee GG, Oesterling JE. Prostate-specific antigen: Concepts for staging prostate cancer and monitoring response to therapy. Mayo Clin Proc 1994, **69**: 69–79.

597 Steinberg DM, Sauvageot J, Piantadosi S, Epstein JI. Correlation of prostate needle biopsy and radical prostatectomy Gleason grade in academic and community settings. Am J Surg Pathol 1997, **21**: 566–576.

598 Thomas R, Lewis RW, Sarma DP, Coker GB, Rao MK, Roberts JA. Aid to accurate clinical staging—histopathologic grading in prostatic cancer. J Urol 1982, **128**: 726–728.

599 Utz DC, Farrow GM. Pathologic differentiation and prognosis of prostatic carcinoma. JAMA 1969, **209**: 1701–1703.

600 Zincke H, Farrow GM, Myers RP, Benson RC Jr, Furlow WL, Utz DC. Relationship between grade and stage of adenocarcinoma of the prostate and regional pelvic lymph node metastases. J Urol 1982, **128**: 498–501.

Treatment

601 Adolfsson J, Steineck G, Whitmore WF Jr. Recent results of management of palpable clinically localized prostate cancer. Cancer 1993, **72**: 310–322.

602 American Society for Therapeutic Radiology and Oncology Consensus Panel. Consensus statements on radiation therapy of prostate cancer: guidelines for prostate re-biopsy after radiation and for radiation therapy with rising prostate-specific antigen levels after radical prostatectomy. J Clin Oncol 1999, **17**: 1155–1163.

603 Armas OA, Aprikian AG, Melamed J, Cordon-Cardo C, Cohen DW, Erlandson R, Fair WR, Reuter VE. Clinical and pathobiological effects of neoadjuvant total androgen ablation therapy on clinically localized prostatic adenocarcinoma. Am J Surg Pathol 1994, **18**: 979–991.

604 Benson RC Jr, Gorman PA, O'Brien PC, Holicky EL, Veneziale CM. Relationship between androgen receptor binding activity in human prostate cancer and clinical response to endocrine therapy. Cancer 1987, **59**: 1599–1606.

605 Borkowski P, Robinson MJ, Poppiti RJ Jr, Nash SC. Histologic findings in postcryosurgical prostatic biopsies. Mod Pathol 1996, **9**: 807–811.

606 Brendler CB, Walsh PC. The role of radical prostatectomy in the treatment of prostate cancer. CA Cancer J Clin 1992, **42**: 212–222.

607 Byar DP. Treatment of prostatic cancer. Studies by the Veterans Administration Cooperative Urological Research Group. Bull NY Acad Med 1972, **48**: 751–766.

608 Catalona WJ. Surgical management of prostate cancer: Contemporary results with anatomic radical prostatectomy. Cancer 1995, **75**: 1903–1908.

609 Cheng L, Cheville JC, Bostwick DG. Diagnosis of prostate cancer in needle biopsies after radiation therapy. Am J Surg Pathol 1999, **23**: 1173–1183.

610 Cheng L, Cheville JC, Pisansky TM, Sebo TJ, Slezak J, Bergstralh EJ, Neumann RM, Singh R, Pacelli A, Zincke H, Bostwick DG. Prevalence and distribution of prostatic intraepithelial neoplasia in salvage radical prostatectomy specimens after radiation therapy. Am J Surg Pathol 1999, **23**: 803–808.

611 Chodak GW, Thisted RA, Gerber GS, Johansson JE, Adolfsson J, Jones GW, Chisholm GD, Moskovitz B, Livne PM, Warner J. Results of conservative management of clinically localized prostate cancer. N Engl J Med 1994, **330**: 242–248.

612 Civantos F, Soloway MS. Prostatic pathology after androgen blockade: Effects on prostatic carcinoma and on nontumor prostate. Adv Anat Pathol 1996, **3**: 259–265.

613 Civantos F, Marcial MA, Banks ER, Ho CK, Speights VO, Drew PA, Murphy WM, Soloway MS. Pathology of androgen deprivation therapy in prostate carcinoma. A comparative study of 173 patients. Cancer 1995, **75**: 1634–1648.

614 D'Amico AV, Coleman CN. Role of interstitial radiotherapy in the management of clinically organ-confined prostate cancer: The jury is still out. J Clin Oncol 1996, **14**: 304–315.

615 Daneshgari F, Crawford ED. Endocrine therapy of advanced carcinoma of the prostate. Cancer 1993, **71**(Suppl 3): 1089–1097.

616 Dundas GS, Porter AT, Venner PM. Prostate-specific antigen. Monitoring the response of carcinoma of the prostate to radiotherapy with a new tumor marker. Cancer 1990, **66**: 45–48.

617 Eggleston JC, Walsh PC. Radical prostatectomy with preservation of sexual function. Pathological findings in the first 100 cases. J Urol 1985, **134**: 1146–1148.

618 Elder JS, Gibbons RP, Correa RJ Jr, Brannen GE. Efficacy of radical prostatectomy for stage A2 carcinoma of the prostate. Cancer 1985, **56**: 2151–2154.

619 Ennis RD, Peschel RE. Radiation therapy for prostate cancer. Long-term results and implications for future advances. Cancer 1993, **72**: 2644–2650.

620 Flocks RH, O'Donoghue EPN, Milleman LA, Culp DA. Surgery of prostatic carcinoma. Cancer 1975, **36**: 705–717.

621 Gaudin PB, Zelefsky MJ, Leibel SA, Fuks Z, Reuter VE. Histopathologic effects of three-dimensional conformal external beam radiation therapy on benign and malignant prostate tissues. Am J Surg Pathol 1999, **23**: 1021–1032.

622 Gibbons RP. Localized prostate carcinoma. Surgical management. Cancer 1993, **72**: 2865–2812.

623 Goldstein NS, Martinez A, Vicini F, Stromberg J. The histology of radiation therapy effect on prostate adenocarcinoma as assessed by needle biopsy after brachytherapy boost. Correlation with biochemical failure. Am J Clin Pathol 1998, **110**: 765–775.

624 Gomez CA, Soloway MS, Civantos F, Hachiya T. Bladder neck preservation and its impact on positive surgical margins during radical prostatectomy. Urology 1993, **42**: 689–694.

625 Grignon DJ, Sakr WA. Histologic effects of radiation therapy and total androgen blockade on prostate cancer. Cancer 1995, **75**: 1837–1841.

626 Habib FK, Odoma S, Busuttil A, Chisholm GD. Androgen receptors in cancer of the prostate. Cancer 1986, **57**: 2351–2356.

627 Hellstrom M, Haggman M, Brandstedt S, de la Torre M, Pedersen K, Jarlsfeldt I, Wijkstrom H, Busch C. Histopathological changes in androgen-deprived localized prostatic cancer. A study in total prostatectomy specimens. Eur Urol 1993, **24**: 461–465.

627a Holmberg I, Bill-Axelson A, Helgesen F, Salo JO, Folmerz P, Haggman M, Andersson SO, Spangberg A, Busch C, Nordling S, Palmgren J, Adami HO, Johansson IE, Norlén BJ. A randomized trial comparing radical prostatectomy with watchful waiting in early prostate cancer. N Engl J Med 2002, **347**: 781.

628 Huben RP, Murphy GP. Prostate cancer. An update. Cancer J Clin 1986, **36**: 274–292.

629 Koivisto P, Kolmer M, Visakorpi T, Kallioniemi OP. Androgen receptor gene and hormonal therapy failure of prostate cancer. Am J Pathol 1998, **152**: 1–9.

630 Labrie F. Endocrine therapy for prostate cancer. Endocrinol Metab Clin North Am 1991, **20**: 845–872.

631 Lee WRL, Ganks GE. Radiation therapy following radical prostatectomy. Cancer 1995, **75**: 1909–1913.

632 Matzkin H, Patel JP, Altwein JE, Soloway MS. Stage TIA carcinoma of prostate. Urology 1994, **43**: 11–21.

633 McLeod DG. Hormonal therapy in the treatment of carcinoma of the prostate. Cancer 1995, **75**: 1914–1919.

634 Meier R, Mark R, St. Royal L, Tran L, Colburn G, Parker R. Postoperative radiation therapy after radical prostatectomy for prostate carcinoma. Cancer 1992, **70**: 1960–1966.

635 Moul JW. Radical prostatectomy versus radiation therapy for clinically localized prostate carcinoma: the butcher and the baker selling their wares. Cancer 2002, **95**: 211–214.

636 Perez CA, Hanks GE, Leibel SA, Zietman AL, Fuks Z, Lee WR. Localized carcinoma of the prostate (stages TIB, TIC, T2, and T3). Review of management with external beam radiation therapy. Cancer 1993, **72**: 3156–3173.

637 Pertschuk LP, Rosenthal HE, Macchia RJ, Eisenberg KB, Feldman JG, Wax SH, Kim DS, Whitmore WF Jr, Abrahams JI, Gaetjens E, Wise GJ, Herr HW, Karr JP, Murphy GP, Sandberg AA. Correlation of histochemical and biochemical analyses of androgen binding in prostatic cancer. Relation to therapeutic response. Cancer 1982, **49**: 984–993.

638 Ripple MG, Potter SR, Partin AW, Epstein JI. Needle biopsy of recurrent adenocarcinoma of the prostate after radical prostatectomy. Mod Pathol 2000, **13**: 521–527.

639 Sagerman RH, Chun HC, King GA, Chung CT, Dalal PS. External beam radiotherapy for carcinoma of the prostate. Cancer 1989, **63**: 2468–2474.

640 Samson DJ, Seidenfeld J, Schmitt B, Hasselblad V, Albertsen PC, Bennett CL, Wilt TJ, Aronson N. Systematic review and meta-analysis of monotherapy compared with combined androgen blockade for patients with advanced prostate carcinoma. Cancer 2002, **95**: 361–376.

641 Schwartz IS, Wilens SL. The formation of acinar tissue in gynecomastia. Am J Pathol 1963, **43**: 797–807.

642 Sheaff MT, Baithun SI. Effects of radiation on the normal prostate gland. Histopathology 1997, **30**: 341–348.

643 Smith DM, Murphy WM. Histologic changes in prostate carcinomas treated with leuprolide (luteinizing hormone-releasing hormone effect). Distinction from poor tumor differentiation. Cancer 1994, **73**: 1472–1477.

644 Tetu B, Srigley JR, Boivin JC, Dupont A, Monfette G, Pinault S, Labrie F. Effect of combination endocrine therapy (LHRH agonist and flutamide) on normal prostate and prostatic adenocarcinoma. A histopathologic and immunohistochemical study. Am J Surg Pathol 1991, **15**: 111–120.

645 Tran TA, Jennings TA, Ross JS, Nazeer T. Pseudomyxoma ovariilike post-therapeutic alteration in prostatic adenocarcinoma: a distinctive pattern in patients receiving neoadjuvant androgen ablation therapy. Am J Surg Pathol 1998, **22**: 347–354.

646 Vailancourt L, Tetu B, Fradet Y, Dupont A, Gomez J, Cusan L, Suburu ER, Diamond P, Candas B, Labrie F. Effect of neoadjuvant endocrine therapy (combined androgen blockade) on normal prostate and prostatic carcinoma: a randomized study. Am J Surg Pathol 1996, **20**: 86–93.

647 Venizelos ID, Paradinas FJ. Testicular atrophy after oestrogen therapy. Histopathology 1988, **12**: 451–454.

648 von Eschenbach AC. The biologic dilemma of early carcinoma of the prostate. Cancer 1996, **78**: 326–329.

649 Walsh PC. Radical prostatectomy. A procedure in evolution. Semin Oncol 1994, **21**: 662–671.

650 Whitmore WF Jr. Locoregional prostatic cancer. Advances in management. Cancer 1990, **65**: 667–674.

651 Whitmore WF Jr. Expectant management of clinically localized prostatic cancer. Semin Oncol 1994, **21**: 560–568.

652 Whitmore WF Jr, Warner JA, Thompson IM Jr. Expectant management of localized prostatic cancer. Cancer 1991, **67**: 1091–1096.

653 Wolf RM, Schneider SL, Pontes JE, Englander L, Karr JP, Murphy GP, Sandberg AA. Estrogen and progestin receptors in human prostatic carcinoma. Cancer 1985, **55**: 2477–2481.

654 Wozniak AJ, Blumenstein BA, Crawford ED, Boileau M, Rivkin SE, Fletcher WS. Cyclophosphamide, methotrexate, and 5-fluorouracil in the treatment of metastatic prostate cancer. A Southwest Oncology Group study. Cancer 1993, **71**: 3975–3978.

Prognosis

655 Ahlering TE, Skarecky DW, McLaren CE, Weinberg AC. Seminal vesicle involvement in patients with D1 disease predicts early prostate specific antigen recurrence and metastasis after radical prostatectomy and early androgen ablation. Cancer 2002, **94**: 1648–1653.

656 Aprikian AG, Zhang ZF, Fair WR. Prostate adenocarcinoma in men younger than 50 years. A retrospective review of 151 patients. Cancer 1994, **74**: 1768–1777.

657 Benson MC, Walsh PC. The application of flow cytometry to the assessment of tumor cell heterogeneity and the grading of human prostatic cancer. Preliminary results. J Urol 1986, **135**: 1194–1198.

658 Blute ML, Bostwick DG, Seay TM, Martin SK, Slezak JM, Bergstralh EJ, Zincke H. Pathologic classification of prostate carcinoma: the impact of margin status. Cancer 1998, **82**: 902–908.

659 Bookstein R, Mac Grogan D, Hilsenbeck SG, Sharkey F, Allred DC. p53 is mutated in a subset of advanced-stage prostate cancers. Cancer Res 1993, **53**: 3369–3373.

660 Bostwick DG, Grignon DJ, Hammond ME, Amin MB, Cohen M, Crawford D, Gospadarowicz M, Kaplan RS, Miller DS, Montironi R, Pajak TF, Pollack A, Srigley JR, Yarbro JW. Prognostic factors in prostate cancer. College of American Pathologists Consensus Statement 1999. Arch Pathol Lab Med 2000, **124**: 995–1000.

661 Brawer M. Quantitative microvessel density: A staging and prognostic marker for human prostatic carcinoma. Cancer 1996, **78**: 345–349.

662 Brawer MK, Deering RE, Brown M, Preston SD, Bigler SA. Predictors of pathologic stage in prostatic carcinoma. The role of neovascularity. Cancer 1994, **73**: 678–687.

663 Brawn PN, Johnson EH, Kuhl DL, Riggs MW, Speights VO, Johnson CF, Pandya PP, Lind ML, Bell NF. Stage at presentation and survival of white and black patients with prostate carcinoma. Cancer 1993, **71**: 2569–2573.

664 Bubendorf L, Sauter G, Moch H, Jordan P, Blochlinger A, Gasser TC, Mihatsch MJ. Prognostic significance of Bcl-2 in clinically localized prostate cancer. Am J Pathol 1996, **148**: 1557–1565.

665 Bubendorf L, Tapia C, Gasser TC, Casella R, Grunder B, Moch H, Mihatsch MJ, Sauter G. Ki67 labeling index in core needle biopsies independently predicts tumor-specific survival in prostate cancer. Hum Pathol 1998, **29**: 949–954.

666 Cheng L, Bergstralh EJ, Cheville JC, Slezak J, Corcia FA, Zincke H, Blute ML, Bostwick DG. Cancer volume of lymph node metastasis predicts progression in prostate cancer. Am J Surg Pathol 1998, **22**: 1491–1500.

667 Cheng L, Bergstralh EJ, Scherer BG, Neumann RM, Blute ML, Zincke H, Bostwick DG. Predictors of cancer progression in T1a prostate adenocarcinoma. Cancer 1999, **85**: 1300–1304.

668 Cheng L, Darson MF, Bergstralh EJ, Slezak J, Myers RP, Bostwick DG. Correlation of margin status and extraprostatic extension with progression of prostate carcinoma. Cancer 1999, **86**: 1775–1782.

669 Cheng L, Pisansky TM, Ramnani DM, Leibovich BC, Cheville JC, Slezak J, Bergstralh EJ, Zincke H, Bostwick DG. Extranodal extension in lymph node-positive prostatic cancer. Mod Pathol 2000, **13**: 113–118.

670 Chiusa L, Galliano D, Formiconi A, Di Primio O, Pich A. High and low risk prostate carcinoma determined by histologic grade and proliferative activity. Cancer 1997, **79**: 1956–1963.

671 Cohen MB, Soloway MS, Murphy WM. Sampling of radical prostatectomy specimens. How much is adequate? Am J Clin Pathol 1994, **101**: 250–252.

672 Cohen MK, Arber DA, Coffield KS, Keegan GT, McClintock J, Speights VO Jr. Neuroendocrine differentiation in prostatic adenocarcinoma and its relationship to tumor progression. Cancer 1994, **74**: 1899–1903.

673 D'Amico AV, Whittington R, Kaplan I, Beard C, Schultz D, Malkowicz SB, Wein A, Tomaszewski JE, Coleman CN. Calculated prostate carcinoma volume: the optimal predictor of 3-year prostate specific antigen (PSA) failure free survival after surgery or radiation therapy of patients with pre-treatment PSA levels of 4–20 nanograms per milliliter. Cancer 1998, **82**: 334–341

674 D'Amico AV, Wu Y, Chen MH, Nash M, Renshaw AA, Richie JP. Pathologic findings and prostate specific antigen outcome after radical prostatectomy for patients diagnosed on the basis of a single microscopic focus of prostate carcinoma with a Gleason score </=7. Cancer 2000, **89**: 1810–1817.

675 de la Taille A, Katz AE, Bagiella E, Buttyan R, Sharir S, Olsson CA, Burchardt T, Ennis RD, Rubin MA. Microvessel density as a predictor of PSA recurrence after radical prostatectomy. A comparison of CD34 and CD31. Am J Clin Pathol 2000, **113**: 555–562.

676 Egan AJM, Bostwick DG. Prediction of extraprostatic extension of prostate cancer based on needle biopsy findings: perineural invasion lacks significance on multivariate analysis. Am J Surg Pathol 1997, **21**: 1496–1500.

677 Ennis RD, Katz AE, de Vries GM, Heitjan DF, O'Toole KM, Rubin M, Buttyan R, Benson MC, Schiff PB. Detection of circulating prostate carcinoma cells via an enhanced reverse transcriptase-polymerase chain reaction assay in patients with early stage prostate carcinoma: independence from other pre-treatment characteristics. Cancer 1997, **79**: 2402–2408.

678 Epstein JI, Eggleston JC. Immunohistochemical localization of prostate-specific acid phosphatase and prostate-specific antigen in stage A2 adenocarcinoma of the prostate. Prognostic implications. Hum Pathol 1984, **15**: 853–859.

679 Epstein JI, Carmichael M, Partin AW, Walsh PC. Is tumor volume an independent predictor of progression following radical prostatectomy? A multivariate analysis of 185 clinical stage B adenocarcinomas of the prostate with 5 years of followup. J Urol 1993, **149**: 1478–1481.

680 Epstein JI, Partin AW, Sauvageot J, Walsh PC. Prediction of progression following radical prostatectomy: a multivariate analysis of 721 men with long-term follow-up. Am J Surg Pathol 1996, **20**: 286–292.

681 Epstein JI, Pizov G, Walsh PC. Correlation of pathologic findings with progression after radical retropubic prostatectomy. Cancer 1993, **71**: 3582–3593.

682 Erdamar S, Yang G, Harper JW, Lu X, Kattan MW, Thompson TC, Wheeler TM. Levels of expression of p27^{KIP1} protein in human prostate and prostate cancer: an immunohistochemical analysis. Mod Pathol 1999, **12**: 751–755.

683 Falkmer UG. Methodologic sources of errors in image and flow cytometric DNA assessments of the malignancy potential of prostatic carcinoma. Hum Pathol 1993, **23**: 360–367.

684 Forman JD, Order SE, Zinreich ES, Lee D-J, Wharam MD, Mellits ED. The correlation of pretreatment transurethral resection of prostatic cancer with tumor dissemination and disease-free survival. A univariate and multivariate analysis. Cancer 1986, **58**: 1770–1778.

685 Forsslund G, Esposti PL, Nilsson B, Zetterberg A. The prognostic significance of nuclear DNA content in prostatic carcinoma. Cancer 1992, **69**: 1432–1439.

686 Frankfurt OS, Chin JL, Englander LS, Greco WR, Pontes JE, Rustum YM. Relationship between DNA ploidy, glandular differentiation, and tumor spread in human prostate cancer. Cancer Res 1985, **45**: 1418–1423.

687 Ghossein RA, Rosai J, Scher HI, Seiden M, Zhang ZF, Sun M, Chang G, Berlane K, Krithivas K, Kantoff PW. Prognostic significance of detection of prostate specific antigen transcripts in the peripheral blood of patients with metastatic androgen-independent prostatic carcinoma. Urology 1997, **50**: 100–105.

688 Griebling TL, Özkutlu D, See WA, Cohen MB. Prognostic implications of extracapsular extension of lymph node metastases in prostate cancer. Mod Pathol 1997, **10**: 804–809.

689 Hammond ME, Sause WT, Martz KL, Pilepich MV, Asbell SO, Rubin P, Myers RP, Farrow GM. Correlation of prostate-specific acid phosphatase and prostate-specific antigen immunocytochemistry with survival in prostate carcinoma. Cancer 1989, **63**: 461–466.

690 Harrison GSM. The prognosis of prostatic cancer in the younger man. Br J Urol 1983, **55**: 315–320.

691 Herman CM, Kattan MW, Ohori M, Scardino PT, Wheeler TM. Primary Gleason pattern as a predictor of disease progression in Gleason score 7 prostate cancer: a multivariate analysis of 823 men with radical prostatectomy. Am J Surg Pathol 2001, **25**: 657–660.

692 Herman CM, Wilcox GE, Kattan MW, Scardino PT, Wheeler TM. Lymphovascular invasion as a predictor of disease progression in prostate cancer. Am J Surg Pathol 2000, **24**: 859–863.

693 Humphrey PA, Vollmer RT. Percentage carcinoma as a measure of prostatic tumor size in radical prostatectomy tissues. Mod Pathol 1997, **10**: 326–333.

694 Humphrey PA, Walther PJ. Adenocarcinoma of the prostate. Part II: Tissue prognosticators. Am J Clin Pathol 1993, **100**: 256–269.

695 Hussain MH, Powell I, Zaki N, Maciorowski Z, Sakr W, Ku Kuruga M, Visscher D, Haas GP, Pontes JE, Ensley JF. Flow cytometric DNA analysis of fresh prostatic resections. Correlation with conventional prognostic parameters in patients with prostate cancer. Cancer 1993, **72**: 3012–3019.

696 Isaacs JT. Molecular markers for prostate cancer metastasis. Developing diagnostic methods for predicting the aggressiveness of prostate cancer. Am J Pathol 1997, **150**: 1511–1521.

697 Kallakury BV, Sheehan CE, Ambros RA, Fisher HA, Kaufman RP Jr, Ross JS. The prognostic significance of p34^{cdc2} and cyclin D1 protein expression in prostate adenocarcinoma. Cancer 1997, **80**: 753–763.

698 Kallakury BV, Sheehan CE, Rhee SJ, Fisher HA, Kaufman RP Jr, Rifkin MD, Ross JS. The prognostic significance of proliferation-associated nucleolar protein p120 expression in prostate adenocarcinoma: a comparison with cyclins A and B1, Ki-67, proliferating cell nuclear antigen, and p34^{cdc2}. Cancer 1999, **85**: 1569–1576.

698a Kausik SJ, Blute ML, Sebo TJ, Leibovich BC, Bergstralh EJ, Slezak J, Zincke H. Prognostic significance of positive surgical margins in patients with extraprostatic carcinoma after radical prostatectomy. Cancer 2002, **95**: 1215–1219.

699 Keshgegian AA, Johnston E, Cnaan A. Bcl-2 oncoprotein positivity and high MIB-1 (Ki-67) proliferative rate are independent predictive markers for recurrence in prostate carcinoma. Am J Clin Pathol 1998, **110**: 443–449.

700 Kothari PS, Scardino PT, Ohori M, Kattan MW, Wheeler TM. Incidence, location, and significance of periprostatic and periseminal vesicle lymph nodes in prostate cancer. Am J Surg Pathol 2001, **25**: 1429–1432.

700a Kunz GM, Epstein JI. Should each core with prostate cancer be assigned a separate Gleason score? Hum Pathol 2003; **34**: 911–914.

700b Lewis JS, Vollmer RT, Humphrey PA. Carcinoma extent in prostate needle biopsy tissue in the prediction of whole gland tumor volume in a screening population. Am J Clin Pathol 2002, **118**: 442–450.

701 Lieber MM, Murtaugh PA, Farrow GM, Myers RP, Blute ML.

DNA ploidy and surgically treated prostate cancer. Important independent association with prognosis for patients with prostate carcinoma treated by radical prostatectomy. Cancer 1995, **75**: 1935–1943.

702 Lilleby W, Torlakovic E, Skovlund E, Fossa SD. Prognostic significance of histologic grading in patients with prostate carcinoma who are assessed by the Gleason and World Health Organization grading systems in needle biopsies obtained prior to radiotherapy. Cancer 2001, **92**: 311–319.

703 Lundgren R, Heim S, Mandahl N, Anderson H, Mitelman F. Chromosome abnormalities are associated with unfavorable outcome in prostatic cancer patients. J Urol 1992, **147**: 784–788.

704 McIntire TL, Murphy WM, Coon JS, Chandler RW, Schwartz D, Conway S, Weinstein RS. The prognostic value of DNA ploidy combined with histologic substaging for incidental carcinoma of the prostate gland. Am J Clin Pathol 1988, **89**: 370–373.

705 Maru N, Ohori M, Kattan MW, Scardino PT, Wheeler TM. Prognostic significance of the diameter of perineural invasion in radical prostatectomy specimens. Hum Pathol 2001, **32**: 828–833.

706 Masuda M, Takano Y, Iki M, Asakura T, Hashiba T, Noguchi S, Hosaka M. Prognostic significance of Ki-67, p53 and Bcl-2 expression in prostate cancer patients with lymph node metastases: a retrospective immunohistochemical analysis. Pathol Int 1998, **48**: 41–46.

707 Matsushima H, Sasaki T, Goto T, Hosaka Y, Homma Y, Kitamura T, Kawabe K, Sakamoto A, Murakami T, Machinami R. Immunohistochemical study of p21^WAF1 and p53 proteins in prostatic cancer and their prognostic significance. Hum Pathol 1998, **29**: 778–783.

708 Mohler JL, Partin AW, Epstein JI, Becker RL, Mikel UV, Sesterhenn IA, Mostofi FK, Gleason DF, Sharief Y, Coffey DS. Prediction of prognosis in untreated stage A2 prostatic carcinoma. Cancer 1992, **69**: 511–519.

709 Montie JE. Staging of prostate cancer: Current TNM classification and future prospects for prognostic factors. Cancer 1995, **75**: 1814–1818.

710 Muller JG, Demel S, Wirth MP, Manseck A, Frohmuller HG, Muller HA. DNA-ploidy, G2M-fractions and prognosis of stages B and C prostate carcinoma. Virchows Arch 1994, **424**: 647–651.

711 Murphy WM. Prognostic factors in the pathological assessment of prostate cancer. Hum Pathol 1998, **29**: 427–430.

712 Nativ O, Winkler HZ, Raz Y, Themeau TM, Farrow GM, Myers RP, Zincke H, Lieber MM. Stage C prostatic adenocarcinoma: Flow cytometric nuclear DNA ploidy analysis. Mayo Clin Proc 1989, **64**: 911–919.

713 Navone NM, Troncoso P, Pisters LL, Goodrow TL, Palmer JL, Nichols WW, von Eschenbach AC, Conti CJ. p53 protein accumulation and gene mutation in the progression of human prostate carcinoma. J Natl Cancer Inst 1993, **85**: 1657–1669.

714 Pan CC, Potter SR, Partin AW, Epstein JI. The prognostic significance of tertiary Gleason patterns of higher grade in radical prostatectomy specimens: A proposal to modify the Gleason grading system. Am J Surg Pathol 2000, **24**: 563–569.

715 Pertschuk LP, Schaeffer H, Feldman JG, Macchia RJ, Kim Y-D, Eisenberg K, Braithwaite LV, Axiotis CA, Prins G, Greene GL. Immunostaining for prostate cancer androgen receptor in paraffin identifies a subset of men with a poor prognosis. Lab Invest 1995, **73**: 302–305.

716 Pisansky TM, Kahn MJ, Rasp GM, Cha SS, Haddock MG, Bostwick DG. A multiple prognostic index predictive of disease outcome after irradiation for clinically localized prostate carcinoma. Cancer 1997, **79**: 337–344.

716a Quinn DI, Henshall SM, Brenner PC, Kooner R, Golovsky D, O'Neill GF, Turner JJ, Delprado W, Grygiel JJ, Sutherland RL, Stricker PD. Prognostic significance of preoperative factors in localized prostate carcinoma treated with radical prostatectomy: Importance of percentage of biopsies that contain tumor and the presence of biopsy perineural invasion. Cancer 2003, **97**: 1884–1893.

717 Renshaw AA, Chang H, D'Amico AV. Estimation of tumor volume in radical prostatectomy specimens in routine clinical practice. Am J Clin Pathol 1997, **107**: 704–708.

718 Renshaw AA, Richie JP, Loughlin KR, Jiroutek M, Chung A, D'Amico AV. Maximum diameter of prostatic carcinoma is a simple, inexpensive, and independent predictor of prostate-specific antigen failure in radical prostatectomy specimens. Validation in a cohort of 434 patients. Am J Clin Pathol 1999, **111**: 641–644.

719 Ross JS, Sheehan CE, Ambros RA, Nazeer T, Jennings TA, Kaufman RP Jr, Fisher HA, Rifkin MD, Kallakury BV. Needle biopsy DNA ploidy status predicts grade shifting in prostate cancer. Am J Surg Pathol 1999, **23**: 296–301.

720 Sandhu DP, Munson KW, Benghiat A, Hopper IP. Natural history and prognosis of prostate carcinoma in adolescents and men under 35 years of age. Br J Urol 1992, **69**: 525–529.

721 Schmid HP, McNeal JE. An abbreviated standard procedure for accurate tumor volume estimation in prostate cancer. Am J Surg Pathol 1992, **16**: 184–191.

722 Sebo TJ, Cheville JC, Riehle DL, Lohse CM, Pankratz VS, Myers RP, Blute ML, Zincke H. Predicting prostate carcinoma volume and stage at radical prostatectomy by assessing needle biopsy specimens for percent surface area and cores positive for carcinoma, perineural invasion, Gleason score, DNA ploidy and proliferation, and preoperative serum prostate specific antigen: a report of 454 cases. Cancer 2001, **91**: 2196–2204.

723 Sebo TJ, Cheville JC, Riehle DL, Lohse CM, Pankratz VS, Myers RP, Blute ML, Zincke H. Perineural invasion and MIB-1 positivity in addition to Gleason score are significant preoperative predictors of progression after radical retropubic prostatectomy for prostate cancer. Am J Surg Pathol 2002, **26**: 431–439.

724 Shurbaji MS, Kalbfleisch JH, Thurmond TS. Immunohistochemical detection of p53 protein as a prognostic indicator in prostate cancer. Hum Pathol 1995, **26**: 106–109.

725 Silber I, McGavran M. Adenocarcinoma of the prostate in men less than 56 years old, a study of 65 cases. J Urol 1971, **105**: 283–285.

726 Silberman MA, Partin AW, Veltri RW, Epstein JI. Tumor angiogenesis correlates with progression after radical prostatectomy but not with pathologic stage in Gleason sum 5 to 7 adenocarcinoma of the prostate. Cancer 1997, **79**: 772–779.

727 Smith JA Jr. Management of localized prostate cancer. Cancer 1992, **70**: 302–306.

728 Smith JA Jr, Middleton RG. Implications of volume of nodal metastasis in patients with adenocarcinoma of the prostate. J Urol 1985, **133**: 617–619.

729 Taplin ME, Bubley GJ, Shuster TD, Frantz ME, Spooner AE, Ogata GK, Keer HN, Balk SP. Mutation of the androgen-receptor gene in metastatic androgen-independent prostate cancer. N Engl J Med 1995, **332**: 1393–1398.

730 Theodorescu D, Broder SR, Boyd JC, Mills SE, Frierson HF Jr. Cathepsin D and chromogranin A as predictors of long term disease specific survival after radical prostatectomy for localized carcinoma of the prostate. Cancer 1997, **80**: 2109–2119.

731 Thomas DJ, Robinson M, King P, Hasan T, Charlton R, Martin J, Carr TW, Neal DE. p53 expression and clinical outcome in prostate cancer. Br J Urol 1993, **72**: 778–781.

731a van Dekken H, Alers JC, Damen I, Vissers KJ, Krijtenburg PJ, Hoedemaeker RF, Wildhagen MF, Hop W, van der Kwast TH, Tanke HJ, Schröder FH. Genetic evaluation of localized prostate cancer in a cohort of forty patients: gain of distal 8q discriminates between progressors and nonprogressors. Lab Invest 2003, **83**: 789.

732 Vargas SO, Jiroutek M, Welch WR, Nucci MR, D'Amico AV, Renshaw AA. Perineural invasion in prostate needle biopsy specimens. Correlation with extraprostatic extension at resection. Am J Clin Pathol 1999, **111**: 223–228.

733 Viola MV, Fromowitz F, Oravez S, Deb S, Finkel G, Lundy J, Hand P, Thor A, Schlom J. Expression of *ras* oncogene p21 in prostate cancer. N Engl J Med 1986, **314:** 133–137.

734 Vollmer RT, Keetch DW, Humphrey PA. Predicting the pathology results of radical prostatectomy from preoperative information: A validation study. Cancer 1998, **83:** 1567–1580.

735 Wheeler TM, Dillioglugil Ö, Kattan MW, Arakawa A, Soh S, Suyama K, Ohori M, Scardino PT. Clinical and pathological significance of the level and extent of capsular invasion in clinical stage T1-2 prostate cancer. Hum Pathol 1998, **29:** 856–862.

736 Winkler HZ, Rainwater LM, Myers RP, Farrow GM, Therneau TM, Zincke H, Lieber MM. Stage D1 prostatic adenocarcinoma. Significance of nuclear DNA ploidy patterns studied by flow cytometry. Mayo Clin Proc 1988, **63:** 103–112.

737 Zagars GK, Pollack A, von Eschenbach AC. Prognostic factors for clinically localized prostate carcinoma: analysis of 938 patients irradiated in the prostate specific antigen era. Cancer 1997, **79:** 1370–1380.

738 Zincke H, Bergstralh EJ, Blute ML, Myers RP, Barrett DM, Lieber MM, Martin SK, Oesterling JE. Radical prostatectomy for clinically localized prostate cancer. Long-term results of 1,143 patients from a single institution. J Clin Oncol 1994, **12:** 2254–2263.

Other tumors

739 Bates AW, Baithun SI. Secondary solid neoplasms of the prostate: a clinico-pathological series of 51 cases. Virchows Arch 2002, **440:** 392–396.

740 Ben-Ezra J, Sheibani K, Kendrick FE, Winberg CD, Rappaport H. Angiotropic large cell lymphoma of the prostate gland. An immunohistochemical study. Hum Pathol 1986, **17:** 964–967.

741 Benson RC Jr, Segura JW, Carney JA. Primary yolk-sac (endodermal sinus) tumor of the prostate. Cancer 1978, **41:** 1395–1398.

742 Bostwick DG, Iczkowski KA, Amin MB, Discigil G, Osborne B. Malignant lymphoma involving the prostate: report of 62 cases. Cancer 1998, **83:** 732–738.

743 Casiraghi O, Martinez-Madrigal F, Mostofi FK, Micheau C, Caillou B, Tursz T. Primary prostatic Wilms' tumor. Am J Surg Pathol 1991, **15:** 885–890.

744 Chin W, Fay R, Ortega P. Malignant fibrous histiocytoma of prostate. Urology 1986, **27:** 363–365.

745 Dajani YF, Burke M. Leukemic infiltration of the prostate. A case study and clinicopathological review. Cancer 1976, **38:** 2442–2446.

746 Ferry JA, Young RH. Malignant lymphoma of the genitourinary tract. Curr Diagn Pathol 1997, **4:** 145–169.

747 Fleischmann J, Perinetti EP, Catalona WJ. Embryonal rhabdomyosarcoma of the genitourinary organs. J Urol 1980, **124:** 389–391.

748 Fritsch M, Epstein JI, Perlman EJ, Watts JC, Argani P. Molecularly confirmed primary prostatic synovial sarcoma. Hum Pathol 2000, **31:** 246–250.

749 Gaudin PB, Rosai J, Epstein JI. Sarcomas and related proliferative lesions of specialized prostatic stroma: a clinicopathologic study of 22 cases. Am J Surg Pathol 1998, **22:** 148–162.

750 Grignon DJ, Ro JY, Ayala AG. Malignant melanoma with metastasis to adenocarcinoma of the prostate. Cancer 1989, **63:** 196–198.

751 Gueft B, Walsh MA. Malignant prostatic cystosarcoma phyllodes. NY State J Med 1975, **75:** 2226–2228.

752 Hassan MO, Gogate PA, Hampel N. Malignant mesenchymoma of the prostate. Immunohistochemical and ultrastructural observations. Ultrastruct Pathol 1994, **18:** 449–456.

752a Helpap B. Nonepithelial tumor-like lesions of the prostate: a never-ending diagnostic problem. Virchows Arch 2002, **441:** 231–237.

753 Hessel RG, Reyes CV, Jensen J, Bayer R, Chinoy M, Bhoophalam M. Malignant cystic epithelial-stromal tumor of the prostate. Diagn Cytopathol 1993, **9:** 314–317.

754 Iwasaki H, Ishiguro M, Ohjimi Y, Ikegami H, Takeuchi T, Kikuchi M, Kaneko Y, Ariyoshi A. Synovial sarcoma of the prostate with t(X;18)(p11.2;q11.2). Am J Surg Pathol 1999, **23:** 220–226.

755 Kaplan WE, Firlit CF, Berger RM. Genitourinary rhabdomyosarcoma. J Urol 1983, **130:** 116–119.

756 Kevwitch MK, Walloch JL, Waters WB, Flanigan RC. Prostatic cystic epithelial-stromal tumors. A report of 2 new cases. J Urol 1993, **149:** 860–864.

757 Klotz LH, Herr HW. Hodgkin's disease of the prostate. A detailed case report. J Urol 1986, **135:** 1261–1262.

758 Leung CS, Srigley JR, Robertson AR. Metastatic renal cell carcinoma presenting as solitary bleeding prostatic metastasis. J Urol Pathol 1997, **7:** 127–132.

759 Levy DA, Gogate PA, Hampel N. Giant multilocular prostatic cystadenoma. A rare clinical entity and review of the literature. J Urol 1993, **150:** 1920–1922.

760 Lim DJ, Hayden RT, Murad T, Nemcek AA Jr, Dalton DP. Multilocular prostatic cystadenoma presenting as a large complex pelvic cystic mass. J Urol 1993, **149:** 856–859.

761 Loughlin KR, Retik AB, Weinstein HJ, Colodny AH, Shamberger RC, Delorey M, Tarbell N, Cassady JR, Hendren WH. Genitourinary rhabdomyosarcoma in children. Cancer 1989, **63:** 1600–1606.

762 Mackenzie AR, Whitmore WF Jr, Melamed MR. Myosarcomas of the bladder and prostate. Cancer 1968, **22:** 838–844.

763 Mahadevia PS, Koss LG, Tar IJ. Prostatic involvement in bladder cancer. Cancer 1986, **58:** 2096–2102.

764 Maluf HM, King ME, De Luca FR, Navarro J, Talerman A, Young RH. Giant multilocular prostatic cystadenoma. A distinctive lesion of the retroperitoneum in men. A report of two cases. Am J Surg Pathol 1991, **15:** 131–135.

765 Manrique JJ, Albores-Saavedra J, Orantes A, Brandt H. Malignant mixed tumor of the salivary-gland type primary in the prostate. Am J Clin Pathol 1978, **70:** 932–937.

766 Mitch WE Jr, Serpick AA. Leukemic infiltration of the prostate. A reversible form of urinary obstruction. Cancer 1970, **26:** 1361–1365.

767 Pins MR, Campbell SC, Laskin WB, Steinbronn K, Dalton DP. Solitary fibrous tumor of the prostate: a report of 2 cases and review of the literature. Arch Pathol Lab Med 2001, **125:** 274–277.

768 Wang X, Bostwick DG. Prostatic stromal hyperplasia with atypia: a study of 11 cases. J Urol Pathol 1997, **6:** 15–26.

769 Waring PM, Newland RC. Prostatic embryonal rhabdomyosarcoma in adults. A clinicopathologic review. Cancer 1992, **69:** 755–762.

770 Westra WH, Grenko RT, Epstein JI. Solitary fibrous tumor of the lower genital tract: A report of five cases involving the seminal vesicles, urinary bladder, and prostate. Hum Pathol 2000, **31:** 63–68.

771 Young JF, Jensen PE, Wiley CA. Malignant phyllodes tumor of the prostate. A case report with immunohistochemical and ultrastructural studies. Arch Pathol Lab Med 1992, **116:** 296–299.

772 Zein TA, Huben R, Lane W, Pontes JE, Englander LS. Secondary tumors of the prostate. J Urol 1985, **133:** 615–616.

SEMINAL VESICLES AND COWPER'S GLANDS

773 Auerbach O. Tuberculosis of the genital system. Q Bull Sea View Hosp 1942, **4:** 188–207.

774 Awadalla O, Hunt AC, Miller A. Primary carcinoma of the seminal vesicle. Br J Urol 1968, **40:** 574–579.

775 Cina SJ, Silberman MA, Kahane H, Epstein JI. Diagnosis of Cowper's gland on prostate needle biopsy. Am J Surg Pathol 1997, **21:** 550–555.

776 Conn IG, Peeling WB, Clements R. Complete resolution of a large

seminal vesicle cyst—evidence for an obstructive aetiology. Br J Urol 1992, **69:** 636–639.

777 Coyne JD, Kealy WF. Seminal vesicle amyloidosis. Morphological, histochemical and immunohistochemical observations. Histopathology 1993, **22:** 173–176.

778 Fain JS, Cosnow I, King BF, Zincke H, Bostwick DG. Cystosarcoma phyllodes of the seminal vesicle. Cancer 1993, **71:** 2055–2061.

779 Fairey AE, Mead GM, Murphy D, Theaker J. Primary seminal vesicle choriocarcinoma. Br J Urol 1993, **71:** 756–757.

780 Keen MR, Golden RL, Richardson JF, Melicow MM. Carcinoma of Cowper's gland treated with chemotherapy. J Urol 1970, **104:** 854–859.

781 Kuo T, Gomez LG. Monstrous epithelial cells in human epididymis and seminal vesicles. A pseudomalignant change. Am J Surg Pathol 1981, **5:** 483–490.

782 Laurila P, Leivo I, Makisalo H, Tuutu M, Miettinen M. Mullerian adenosarcoma-like tumor of the seminal vesicle. A case report with immunohistochemical and ultrastructural observations. Arch Pathol Lab Med 1992, **116:** 1072–1076.

783 Mazur MT, Myers JL, Maddox WA. Cystic epithelial-stromal tumor of the seminal vesicle. Am J Surg Pathol 1987, **11:** 210–217.

784 Middleton LP, Merino MJ, Popok SM, Ordonez NG, Ayala AG, Ro JY. Male adnexal tumor of probable Wolffian origin occurring in a seminal vesicle. Histopathology 1998, **33:** 269–274.

785 Ohori M, Scardino PT, Lapin SL, Seale-Hawkins C, Link J, Wheeler TM. The mechanisms and prognostic significance of seminal vesicle involvement by prostate cancer. Am J Surg Pathol 1993, **17:** 1252–1261.

786 Ormsby AH, Haskell R, Jones D, Goldblum JR. Primary seminal vesicle carcinoma: an immunohistochemical analysis of four cases. Mod Pathol 2000, **13:** 46–51.

787 Peker KR, Hellman BH Jr, McCammon KA, Bui TT, Schlossberg SM. Cystadenoma of the seminal vesicle: a case report and review of the literature. J Urol Pathol 1997, **6:** 213–222.

788 Ro JY, Ayala AG, el-Naggar A, Wishnow KI. Seminal vesicle involvement by in situ and invasive transitional cell carcinoma of the bladder. Am J Surg Pathol 1987, **11:** 951–958.

789 Schned AR, Ledbetter JS, Selikowitz SM. Primary leiomyosarcoma of the seminal vesicle. Cancer 1986, **57:** 2202–2206.

790 Seidman JD, Shmookler BM, Connolly B, Lack EE. Localized amyloidosis of seminal vesicles. Report of three cases in surgically obtained material. Mod Pathol 1989, **2:** 671–675.

791 Sharma TC, Dorman PS, Dorman HP. Bilateral seminal vesicular cysts. J Urol 1969, **102:** 741–744.

792 Sheih CP, Liao YJ, Li YW, Yang LY. Seminal vesicle cyst associated with ipsilateral renal malformation and hemivertebra. Report of 2 cases. J Urol 1993, **150:** 1214–1215.

793 Tanaka T, Takeuchi T, Oguchi K, Niwa K, Mori H. Primary adenocarcinoma of the seminal vesicle. Hum Pathol 1987, **18:** 200–202.

794 Unger PD, Wang QI, Gordon RE, Stock R, Stone N. Localized amyloidosis of the seminal vesicle: possible association with hormonally treated prostatic adenocarcinoma. Arch Pathol Lab Med 1997, **121:** 1265–1268.

Testis

Normal embryology and anatomy

The growth and development of the human testis can be divided into three major phases: (1) static, from birth to age 4 years; (2) growth, from age 4 to 10 years; and (3) developmental (maturation), from age 10 years to puberty.[1,11] At birth, the seminiferous tubules are compactly filled with small undifferentiated cuboidal cells. Leydig cells are seen in the newborn because of the influence of maternal hormones, but then disappear to reappear only later. Increases in tubule and cell size are slow and gradual, with barely perceptible growth from ages 4 to 10 years, increasing tortuosity, and lumen formation. At age 10 years, a definite spurt is noted, coinciding with the appearance of gonadotropins and 17-ketosteroids in urine. Mitotic figures appear in the tubular cells, and Leydig cells again become recognizable in the interstitium. At age 11 years, mitotic activity is pronounced, and primary and secondary spermatocytes appear. At age 12 years, spermatids are numerous. Finally, spermatozoa appear. The number of maturing tubules with active spermatogenesis increases gradually, until the adult stage is reached. Because of the great variation in the age at which puberty normally occurs, the age of the individual cannot be determined by histologic study of the testis after the twelfth year.[1]

The normal adult testis is a paired organ that lies within the scrotum suspended by the spermatic cord. The average weight of each testis is 15 to 19 g, the right usually being 10% heavier than the left.[3] The organ is covered by a capsule composed of three layers: the outer serosa or tunica vaginalis (covered by a flattened layer of mesothelial cells), the tunica albuginea, and the inner tunica vasculosa. The posterior portion of the capsule, called the mediastinum, contains blood and lymph vessels, nerves, and the mediastinal portion of the rete testis. The parenchyma is divided into approximately 250 lobules, each lobule containing up to four seminiferous tubules. The usual testicular biopsy is composed of three

to five lobules together with portions of the septa (which should not be misinterpreted as areas of fibrosis). The seminiferous tubules are bound by a limiting membrane made up of basal lamina and alternating layers of myoid cells and collagen fibers. These tubules contain germ cells in various stages of development and Sertoli cells.[10]

The maturation of germ cells in man covers a period of about 70 days and follows these steps: spermatogonium (of which two types have been described, known respectively as A and B), primary spermatocyte (further subdivided depending on the stage of meiosis into preleptotene, leptotene, zygotene, pachytene, and diplotene), secondary spermatocyte, spermatid, and (mature) spermatozoon (Fig. 18.47).[2] Until spermatozoa are formed, all progeny of a spermatogonium are held together by a narrow cytoplasmic bridge. This maturation proceeds in an orderly overlapping helical pattern along the length of the tubule[7]; as a consequence, not all stages of differentiation of germ cells are seen in any one cross-sectional view of a seminiferous tubule. *This normal pattern should not be confused with a maturation arrest.*

Several methods have been proposed for quantitatively assessing the germ cell elements and the relationship of spermatogenesis to seminal fluid sperm density. One of them[4] applies a score of 1 to 10 for each tubule cross section examined, according to the following criteria:

10 Complete spermatogenesis and perfect tubules
9 Many spermatozoa present but disorganized spermatogenesis
8 Only a few spermatozoa present
7 No spermatozoa but many spermatids present
6 Only a few spermatids present
5 No spermatozoa or spermatids present but many spermatocytes present
4 Only a few spermatocytes present
3 Only spermatogonia present
2 No germ cells present
1 No germ cells or Sertoli cells present.

In a normal adult testicle, the mean score count should be at least 8.90, with an average of 9.38, and 60% or more of the tubules should score at 10.

Two somewhat easier methods to estimate the degree of spermatogenesis in a testicular biopsy are the following:

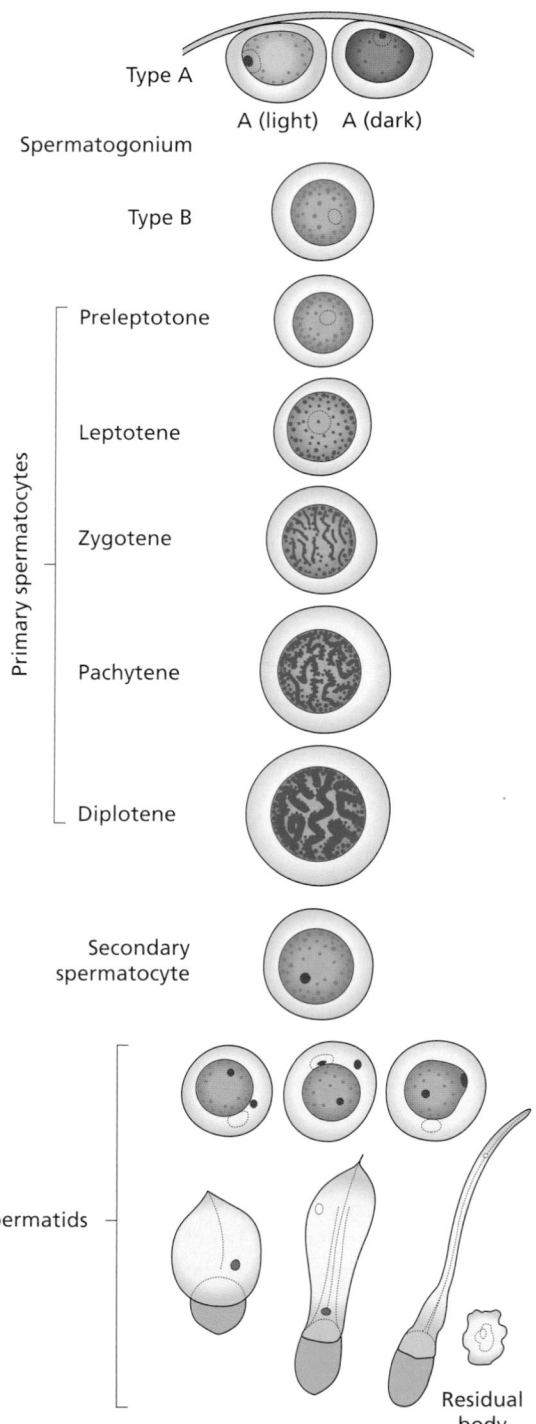

Type A

A (light)   A (dark)

Spermatogonium

Type B

Preleptotone

Leptotene

Zygotene

Pachytene

Diplotene

Primary spermatocytes

Secondary spermatocyte

Spermatids

Residual body

Fig. 18.47 Steps in spermatogenesis. (From Trainer TD. Testis and excretory duct system. In Sternberg SS (ed.): Histology for pathologists. Ed 2, New York, Lipincott–Raven, 1997, p. 1022)

1 Establishing the germ cell:Sertoli cell ratio by counting at least 30 tubule cross sections. This ratio is relatively constant at about 13:1 in young healthy men.[10] An average of 12 Sertoli cells per tubular cross section is considered normal; approximately half the germ cell elements should be in the spermatid stage.[9]

2 Counting spermatids per tubule cross section. Only the mature spermatids (i.e., those with oval, darkly staining nuclei) should be counted. The correlation with seminal fluid sperm count is excellent.[8]

Sertoli cells have a columnar shape, lie on the basement membrane of the tubule, and send cytoplasmic prolongations around the germ cell elements.[8] Their nuclei are irregularly shaped, are highly folded, and have a prominent nucleolus. The cytoplasm may contain Charcot–Bottcher crystalloids, which represent bundles of filaments. Immunohistochemically, the intermediate filament of Sertoli cells is vimentin, but coexpression of keratin and desmin is present in the fetal testis and can reappear in pathologic conditions.[5]

The interstitium contains stromal elements (including the already mentioned myoid cells) and Leydig cells. The latter occur either singly or in clusters and are often associated with nerve fibers.[6] Their cytoplasm contains lipid droplets, lipochrome pigment, and sometimes Reinke crystalloids, which appear ultrastructurally as hexagonal prisms.[10] Immunohistochemically, there is reactivity for inhibin and Melan-A (Mart-1). Leydig cells gradually decrease in number with aging.

Cryptorchidism

In one out of every ten males, the testis has not descended into the scrotum at the time of birth but has remained in the inguinal region or abdomen, the former being about four times as common as the latter.[14,20] Most of these "retained" or "retractile" testes descend into the scrotum during the first year of life. In only 1 in 100 individuals will a permanent retention of the testis outside the scrotum occur, a condition known as *cryptorchidism*. The exact pathogenesis is unknown, but most evidence favors a role for testosterone under the influence of the hypothalamic–pituitary axis.[29] If by the age of 2 or 3 years the testis has not spontaneously descended into the scrotum (or sooner, if the abnormality is bilateral), an open or laparoscopic orchiopexy should be carried out; otherwise permanent anatomic alterations will occur.[20,23] The usefulness of hormones such as chorionic gonadotropin in causing descent of true cryptorchid (as opposed to retractile) testes is questionable at best.[18,29]

Cryptorchidism is unilateral in 80% of the cases. Of patients with *bilateral* cryptorchid testes in whom repair is performed before the age of 5 years, 50% are fertile and 31% are normospermic.[17] The microscopic appearance of the prepuberal testicle as seen in a small biopsy at the time of orchiopexy is a good predictor of the degree of postpuberal spermatogenesis and therefore of fertility.[27]

Grossly, cryptorchid testes in adults are small and brown. The testicular tubules are atrophic, and their basement membrane is greatly thickened. The Leydig cells are prominent; some of them may be present inside the tubules.[26] Not infrequently, foci of hyperplastic Sertoli cells occur. They are usually multiple and may appear grossly as minute white nodules (see p. 1437). In some instances, atypical germ cells are seen at the base of the tubules; these are indicative of *intratubular germ cell neoplasia* and are the forerunner of malignancy (see p. 1431). Traditionally, the atrophy and infertility associated with cryptorchidism have been attributed to the higher intrascrotal temperature. However, the facts that boys with cryptorchidism have histologically abnormal seminiferous tubules also in the contralateral descended testis[25] and that men who had unilateral cryptorchidism corrected in childhood have lower sperm counts and higher serum concentrations of follicle-stimulating hormone as adults than do normal men[24] suggest that even unilateral cryptorchidism is associated with a bilateral testicular abnormality.

A cryptorchid testis is 30 to 50 times more likely to develop a malignant neoplasm than is a normally placed organ. Of 7000 cases of testicular germ cell tumors reviewed in a classic study by Gilbert and Hamilton[19] 10.9% occurred in cryptorchid organs. The incidence of malignancy is greater in the abdominal than in the inguinal testis. Seminoma is the most common type, but other germ cell tumors also occur.[12,13] The contralateral testis in patients with unilateral cryptorchidism also has an increased incidence of malignancy.[15,28] If a cryptorchid testis is surgically placed in the scrotum, it may still develop a germ cell neoplasm, especially if the operation has been done after 6 years of age.[22] Dow and Mostofi[16] reported 14 cases of such tumors occurring in patients who had had orchiopexy between the ages of 11 and 36 years. Because of these findings, it is recommended that high-positioned testes that have not been surgically placed into the scrotum before mid adolescence be removed.[18]

Atrophy and infertility

Atrophy of the testis may result from a large variety of causes: the already mentioned *cryptorchidism*; the orchitis of *mumps*, especially when the infection occurs at or after puberty[37]; liver *cirrhosis*, as a result of increased circulating endogenous estrogens not metabolized by the diseased liver[30]; administration of *estrogens* or *gonadotropin-releasing hormone analog* in the treatment of prostatic carcinoma[62]; *radiation exposure*; *chemotherapy*, particularly cyclophosphamide[34,48]; and exposure to an *environmental toxin*, the nematocide dibromochloropropane.

In advanced testicular atrophy of any of these etiologies, the tubules are small, with thick basement membranes and few or no germ cells. The interstitial tissue shows varying degree of fibrosis, and there may be an increased number of Leydig cells.

An extreme degree of testicular atrophy occurs in the *testicular regression ("vanishing testis") syndrome*, a condition characterized by a rudimentary epididymis and spermatic cord with no identifiable testicular tissue.[68] There is instead in this location a dense fibrovascular tissue ("nubbin") with foci of calcification and hemosiderin deposition.[59] The suggestion has been made that this condition results from testicular infarct, presumably caused by torsion occurring in utero.[63] It affects approximately 5% of patients with cryptorchidism.[68]

Various degrees of testicular atrophy occur frequently in AIDS-affected patients, the precise pathogenesis being unclear.[31,72]

The effect of vasectomy on testicular morphology is minimal but detectable; there is thickening of the tubular wall, reduction in the number of spermatids and Sertoli cells, and sometimes foci of interstitial fibrosis.[44]

The causes of male infertility fall into one of three categories: pretesticular, testicular, and post-testicular.[69-71] The pretesticular causes are extragonadal endocrine disorders, usually originating in the pituitary or adrenal gland. The testicular causes are primary diseases of the testes, and little treatment is available at the present time. The post-testicular causes consist mainly of obstructions of the ducts leading away from the testes. These obstructions may be congenital, postinflammatory, or postsurgical, and include *Young's syndrome*, in which the obstructive azoospermia is combined with chronic sinopulmonary infections.[41] These obstructions have generally little or no adverse effect on spermatogenesis. Treatment consists of epididymovasostomy or vasovasostomy to bypass the obstruction. Impaired sperm mobility, presumably because of faulty maturation or storage of spermatozoa in the epididymis, and immunologic factors are included among the post-testicular causes of infertility.[47]

The evaluation of the infertile male includes a thorough clinical history and examination, semen analysis, quantitation of leukocytes in semen, and search for anti-sperm antibodies. Tests of sperm function include evaluation of cervical mucus interaction, ova penetration, and the hemizonal assay. Additional tests, performed in selected cases, are transrectal ultrasonography, venography, and testicular biopsy.[36] The latter is particularly useful in the individual with azoospermia and normal endocrine findings.[35,49,56,57] Punch biopsy is not nearly as satisfactory as an open surgical biopsy. The material should be handled with extreme care.[58] Zenker's and Bouin's fixatives are preferred over formalin. Fine needle aspiration cytology has been proposed as an alternative to testicular biopsy,[57] some studies showing a high correlation between the two methods.[51]

Biopsy specimens from infertile men with total lack of spermatozoa (azoospermia) usually show one of the following conditions[52]:

1 *Germ cell aplasia* (Sertoli cell-only syndrome) (29%), in which the tubules are populated by only Sertoli cells, measure 100 to 150 μm in diameter, and may show some thickening of the tubular basement membrane; germ cells are completely absent[53]; Leydig cells are usually normal but on occasion are found to be reduced in size and number.
2 *Spermatocytic arrest* (26%), characterized by a halt of the maturation sequence, usually at the stage of the primary spermatocyte (presumably at the end of the meiotic prophase at late pachytene[66]); no spermatids or spermatozoa are present despite the presence of abundant cells in division; Leydig cells are normal.
3 *Generalized fibrosis* (18%).
4 *Normal spermatogenesis* (27%).

The last finding suggests the diagnosis of obstructive azoospermia and implies the bilateral obstruction or absence of some part of the duct system.[45] Meinhard et al.[50] have described microscopic features that they regard as virtually diagnostic of *testicular blockage* in patients with azoospermia: the tubular diameter is normal or slightly reduced, and all stages of spermatogenesis are present, but the normal orderly arrangement is lost, and the central lumen is absent. For a case to be assigned to this category, half or more of the tubules must be affected. In the series of Nistal et al.[54] of patients with obstructive azoospermia of known etiology, over half had a normal testicular biopsy, whereas most of the others exhibited subtle alterations of the adluminal compartment of the seminiferous tubules (early or late sloughing of primary spermatocytes), possibly induced by the increase in hydrostatic pressure.

In patients with a reduction in the number of spermatozoa (oligospermia), the following microscopic patterns are recognizable, often combined: (1) *incomplete spermatocytic arrest*, characterized by arrest of spermatogenesis in some of the tubules; (2) *regional or incomplete fibrosis*; (3) *spermatogenic hypoplasia* (hypospermatogenesis), characterized by tubules with a reduced population of germ cells and a poor order of spermatogenesis; (4) *tubular hyalinization*, a probably heterogeneous group that includes Klinefelter's syndrome, in which the tubules have a small diameter and a markedly thickened basement membrane, and Leydig cells are often increased in number; and (5) *normal* or *essentially normal spermatogenesis*, usually implying a partial occlusion of some part of the duct system.[64,65] Another pattern sometimes described is that of *sloughing and disorganization*, in which spermatogenesis has a disorderly appearance and the tubular lumina are filled with desquamated immature cells. We have found that this pattern is rather nonspecific, since it can be seen in spermatogenic hypoplasia as well as with testicular blockage; it also can be closely simulated by artifactual detachment of germ cells resulting from rough handling of the biopsy. The degree of spermatogenic hypoplasia, a very subjective evaluation, can be roughly estimated with the techniques described on p. 1412, or with quantitative techniques.[40,61]

Multinucleated giant stromal cells of reactive nature have been observed in cases of testicular atrophy after estrogen therapy.[60] In the presence of hyalinized tubules, it is useful to perform an elastic tissue stain. The finding of elastic fibers indicates that puberty has been reached and that the disease developed after this period. Meinhard et al.[50] found little correlation between clinical groupings of infertility and histology and even less between semen analysis and histology.

In the series of over 800 cases of azoospermia studied via testicular biopsy by Girgis et al.[38] the etiology was obstructive in about 55%. In more than half of these, epididymovasostomy proved beneficial. Patients with *varicocele* are often oligospermic and infertile. The most common patterns at biopsy are those of spermatogenic hypoplasia plus sloughing and disorganization.[33] The azoospermia commonly seen in patients with *cystic fibrosis* is obstructive, secondary to structural abnormalities of the epididymis and vas deferens.[46]

Biopsies are rarely done in patients with testicular failure involving primarily the endocrine function, since the diagnosis is usually established by hormonal determinations. Failure of pubertal maturation is the cardinal symptom if the disease is congenital or begins in childhood.[71] Three different patterns can be seen in testicular biopsies: (1) *hypogonadotrophic eunuchoidism* (60%) accompanied by low gonadotropin levels and characterized by small, infantile tubules with scattered spermatogonia and Sertoli cells but few or no Leydig cells; (2) *Klinefelter's syndrome* (30%), with fibrosis of tubules, prominent thickening of the basement membrane, and Leydig cell hyperplasia[39]; and (3) *testicular aplasia* (10%), characterized by the absence of testicular tissue and elevation of urinary gonadotropin levels. Patients with Klinefelter's syndrome have an increased incidence of breast carcinoma[43]; cases of Leydig cell tumor and testicular and extragonadal (mainly mediastinal) germ cell tumors also have been reported in this population.[32,42,67]

Other non-neoplastic lesions

Infarct of the testis is usually the result of torsion of the spermatic cord (see p. 1461), but it may also be due to venous thrombosis secondary to pyogenic epididymo-orchitis (see below) or, rarely, vasculitis of various causes, such as that accompanying Crohn's disease.[92]

Granulomatous orchitis is characterized grossly by a solid nodular enlargement of the testis (Fig. 18.48) and microscopically by granulomatous lesions centered in the seminiferous tubules, as described in the classic paper by Spjut et al.[96] (Fig. 18.49). Epithelioid cells, multinucleated giant cells, lymphocytes, and plasma cells are present. The granulomatous response is at least in part secondary to the products of disintegrated sperm. A history of trauma to the region is often obtained.[96] The clinical evolution is benign.[74,98]

Malakoplakia can involve the testis, either alone or accompanied by epididymal involvement.[80] It is associated with abscess formation, atrophy of tubules, and the characteristic Michaelis–Gutmann bodies. Thrombosed blood vessels are often found.[77] Bacteria (mainly coliform organisms) may be found on culture. Two other proliferative histiocytic disorders that occasionally involve the testis are **juvenile xanthogranuloma**[97] and **Rosai–Dorfman disease (sinus histiocytosis with massive lymphadenopathy)**.[85]

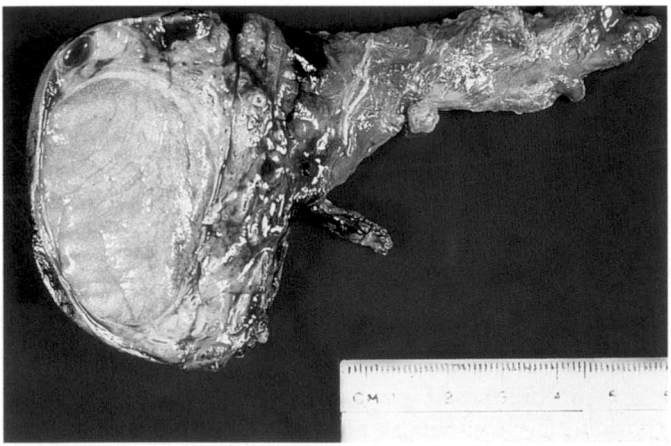

Fig. 18.48 Gross appearance of granulomatous orchitis. The testis is increased in consistency, enlarged, and vaguely nodular.

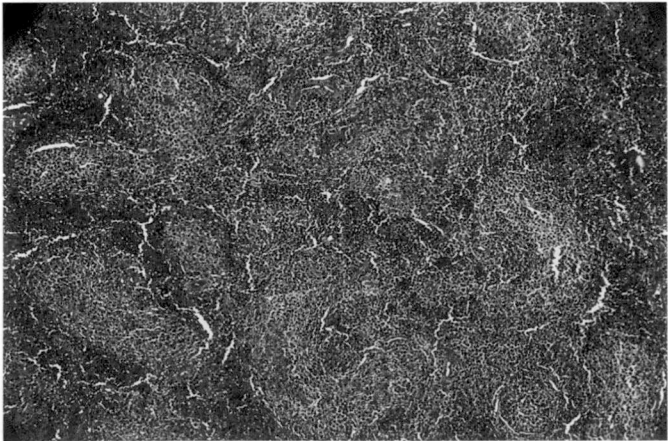

Fig. 18.49 Microscopic appearance of granulomatous orchitis. The inflammatory infiltrate is centered in the seminiferous tubules.

Pyogenic epididymo-orchitis may be complicated by venous thrombosis and septic infarct of the testis.[84] *E. coli* is the organism usually recovered. Microscopically, many similarities exist between this condition and granulomatous orchitis, suggesting a common ischemic background.

Tuberculosis, atypical mycobacteriosis,[83] **leprosy, sarcoidosis,**[82] **syphilis** and **Crohn's disease** can involve the testis.[75,92] Clinically, a syphilitic gumma can resemble a neoplasm.

Other infectious agents responsible for orchitis are *Toxoplasma* (in immunosuppressed patients), fungi, parasites, and *Brucella*. These are rarely seen as surgical specimens.[90]

Multinucleated stromal giant cells are a relatively common and clinically insignificant finding in the testis. They seem to be age related[79] and are said to be particularly common in cases of testicular atrophy due to estrogen therapy (see p. 1414).

Necrotizing vasculitis can involve the testis, either as a manifestation of polyarteritis nodosa or other systemic disease or as an isolated finding.[89,95]

Ectopic spleen in the scrotum (splenogonadal fusion syndrome) results from a congenital malformation occurring at a stage when the splenic and gonadal anlages are topographically close.[76] In the *continuous* variant, there is a fibrous or splenic tissue-containing cord that connects the spleen and the scrotal ectopic splenic tissue. In the *discontinuous* variant, the connection is lost, and the ectopic splenic tissue appears as a scrotal accessory spleen, which may clinically simulate a tumor. All of the reported cases have been on the left side.[87] An ovarian counterpart of this peculiar abnormality has been described (see also Chapter 22).

Cystic dysplasia of the testis is a rare congenital defect that results in the formation of numerous irregularly shaped cystic spaces within the mediastinum testis.[78] The cysts are lined by flattened cuboidal epithelium that morphologically and immunohistochemically resembles the epithelium of rete testis.[81] Thus this condition merges with those described in the section on rete testis (see p. 1457).

Cysts located within the testicular parenchyma away from the rete testis are lined by a similar flattened cuboidal (nonciliated) epithelium and may have a similar pathogenesis.[91]

Epidermoid cyst of the testis presents as an intraparenchymal lesion filled with keratin and lined by mature squamous epithelium (Figs 18.50 and 18.51). The histogenesis is controversial. Epidermal inclusions and squamous metaplasia of seminiferous tubules or rete testis have been proposed as possible pathogenetic mechanisms. We suspect that at least some of these lesions represent monodermal mature teratomas, despite the fact that intratubular germ cell neoplasm is practically never found in the remaining testis.[94] The recent

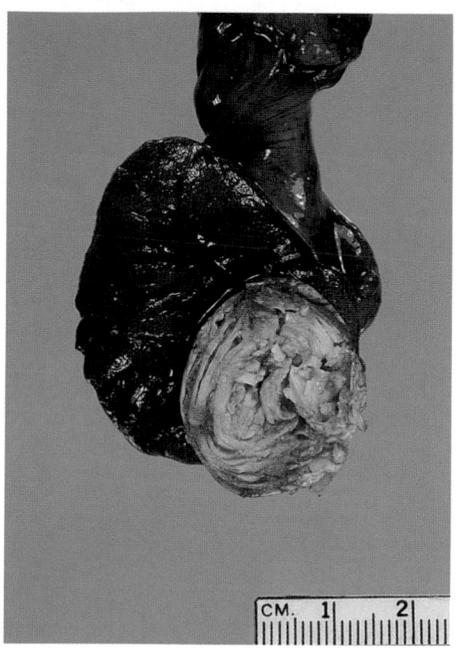

Fig. 18.50 Epidermoid cyst of testis. The lesion is sharply outlined and contains laminated layers of keratin.

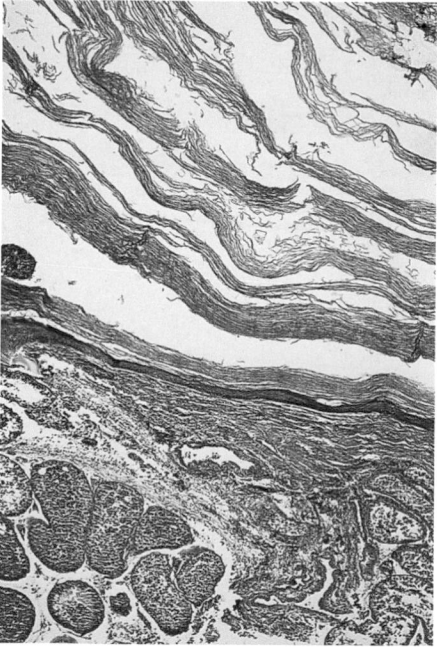

Fig. 18.51 Microscopic appearance of epidermoid cyst of testis. Keratin squames are laid down by well-differentiated squamous epithelium. There are no skin adnexal structures.

finding that these cysts harbor allelic loss at some of the same loci certainly suggests a neoplastic nature for at least some of them.[98a] From a practical standpoint, if no adnexal structures or other tissue types are identified on *thorough sampling*, a conservative surgical approach is indicated, since metastases never occur under these circumstances.[86,93] A variation in the theme is represented by *pilomatricoma* of the testis, having an appearance identical to that of its cutaneous counterpart.[88]

Testicular implants (silicone gel-filled) can elicit a tissue reaction similar to that seen in breast implants. Microscopically, it is characterized by a fibrous capsule infiltrated by lymphocytes and foamy macrophages, and occasionally featuring a synovial-like cleft at the interphase.[73]

Tumors

Testicular tumors are divided into five general categories: germ cell tumors (90%) arising from the germinal epithelium of the seminiferous tubules; sex cord–stromal tumors; mixed germ cell–sex cord–stromal tumors; primary tumors not specific to the testis; and metastatic tumors.

Germ cell tumors

Classification

The current classification of germ cell tumors represents an updating of the scheme originally proposed by Dixon and Moore[102] and colloquially known as the American classification. The alternative system, devised by Collins and Pugh[100] and commonly referred to as the British classification, is histogenetically more sound, but it was never widely accepted because of its lengthy and somewhat awkward terminology. Table 18.2 provides a comparison between these two major proposals and their updated versions.[109]

The first and most important division in germ cell tumors, both conceptually and practically, is between two major categories: *seminoma*, and all the others, which are collectively referred to as *nonseminomatous germ cell tumors (NSGCT)*. There is now general agreement that all of the tumor types in *both* groups arise from the germinal (seminiferous) epithelium of the mature or maturing testis.[112,113] Features in favor of this interpretation are their totipotential properties, their frequent admixtures and transitions, and the existence of lesions with similar cytologic features (usually resembling seminoma cells but occasionally having the appearance of NSGCT of one type or another) entirely confined within the seminiferous tubules (i.e., in an in situ location)[99,103,110] (see p. 1431).

NSGCT are thought to have a clonal origin (as demonstrated by the presence of identical allelic loss in their various components),[102a] and to recapitulate embryogenesis, their pattern of differentiation being directed toward the formation of one or more of the components of the embryo and/or related structures[104,105,108,112] (Fig. 18.52). The specific direction this differentiation takes will determine the morphologic appearance of a given tumor and hence its name (Fig. 18.53). Four basic patterns are recognized: **embryonal carcinoma**, wholly composed of primitive carcinoma-like cells with minimal or no signs of differentiation; **mature (adult) and immature teratoma**, in which the differentiation is toward structures of the embryo proper, usually a combination of endodermic,

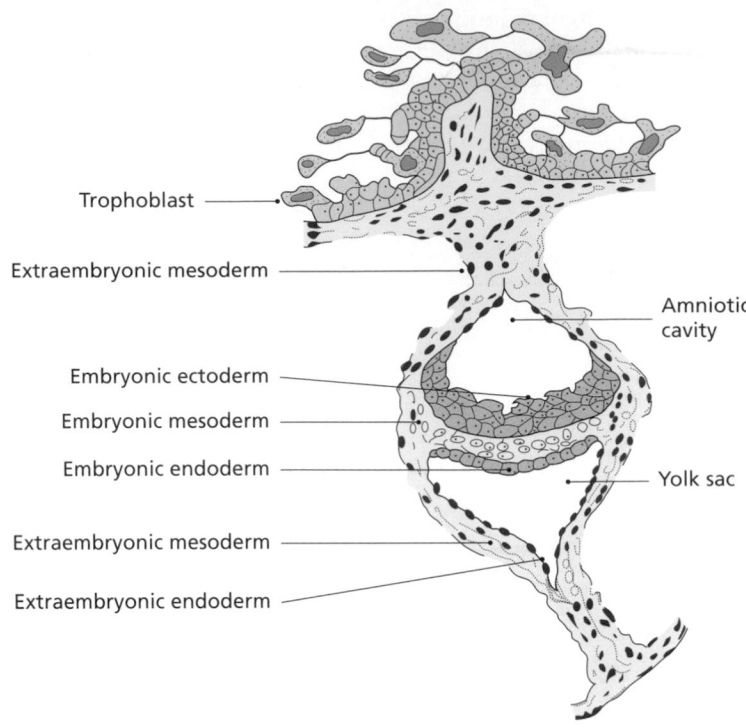

Trophoblast

Extraembryonic mesoderm

Amniotic cavity

Embryonic ectoderm

Embryonic mesoderm

Embryonic endoderm

Yolk sac

Extraembryonic mesoderm

Extraembryonic endoderm

Fig. 18.52 Scheme of components of normal human embryo. Testicular germ cell tumors attempt to differentiate toward one or more of these structures. (Slightly modified from Marin-Padilla M. Histopathology of the embryonal carcinoma of the testes. Embryological evaluation. Arch Pathol 1968, **85**: 614–622)

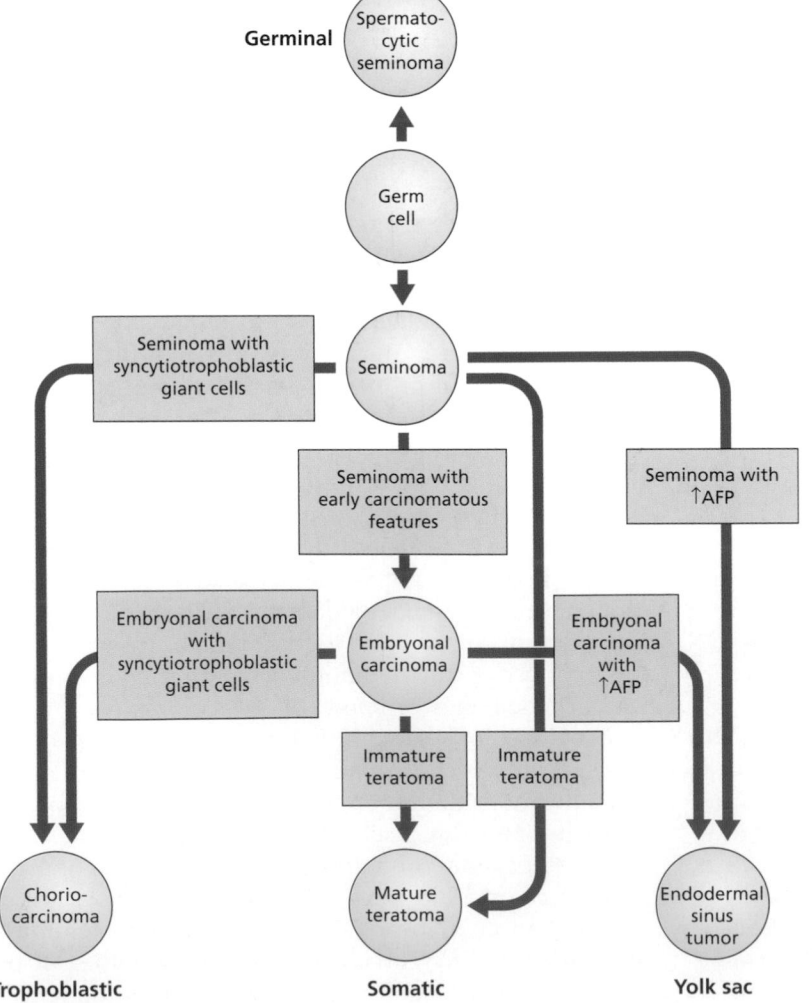

Fig. 18.53 Diagram showing relationships between various types of germ cell tumors. (From Srigley JR, Mackay B, Toth P, Ayala A. The ultrastructure and histogenesis of male germ neoplasia with emphasis on seminoma with early carcinomatous features. Ultrastruct Pathol 1988, **12**: 67–86)

Table 18.2 Comparison of classifications of testicular germ cell tumors

Dixon and Moore[102]	Collins and Pugh[100]	British Testicular Tumour Panel[109]	Mostofi and Price[107]	WHO[99]
Seminoma	Seminoma Classic Spermatocytic	Seminoma Classic Spermatocytic	Seminoma Typical Spermatocytic Anaplastic	Seminoma Spermatocytic seminoma
Embryonal carcinoma	Malignant teratoma, anaplastic (MTA) Malignant teratoma, intermediate, with no differentiated or organoid elements (MTIB)	Malignant teratoma, undifferentiated (MTU)	Embryonal carcinoma Adult Polyembryoma	Embryonal carcinoma Polyembryoma
Teratoma with embryonal carcinoma ("teratocarcinoma")	Malignant teratoma, intermediate, with differentiated or organoid elements (MTIA)	Malignant teratoma, intermediate	Embryonal carcinoma and teratoma ("teratocarcinoma")	Embryonal carcinoma and teratoma ("teratocarcinoma")
Teratoma, adult	Teratoma, differentiated (TD)	Teratoma, differentiated	Teratoma Mature Immature	Teratoma Mature Immature With malignant transformation
Choriocarcinoma	Malignant teratoma, trophoblastic (MTT) Orchioblastoma	Malignant teratoma, trophoblastic Yolk sac tumor	Choriocarcinoma Embryonal carcinoma, infantile (juvenile)	Choriocarcinoma Yolk sac tumor

From (with last two columns updated) Nochomovitz LE, De La Torre FE, Rosai J. Pathology of germ cell tumors of the testis. Urol Clin North Am 1977, **4**: 359–378.

mesodermic, and ectodermic tissues; **choriocarcinoma,** characterized by the presence of well-developed trophoblastic elements in an organoid fashion; and **yolk sac (endodermal sinus) tumor,** directed toward the formation of extraembryonic endoderm and mesoderm.

There are two factors complicating this scheme. First, differentiation may proceed in two or more different directions in the same lesion. Second, tumors in which the differentiation toward a given component is only partial are often seen.[111] The result is a bewildering combination of patterns. Tumors exhibiting two or more of them are best designated as **mixed NSGCT,** followed by a listing of the various patterns present and their relative amounts. The combination of embryonal carcinoma and (mature or immature) teratoma is also known as *teratocarcinoma*, but the term is falling into disuse.

Traditionally, seminoma has been regarded as not partaking of the properties of NSGCT but rather as an "endpoint" neoplasm incapable of differentiation in any of the previously described directions. Thus a sharp separation was drawn between it and the group of NSGCT, even to the point of suggesting a different histogenesis

for them.[100] Current morphologic, cytogenetic, and DNA ploidy data instead favor the interpretation that there is a very close link between the two and that seminoma (except for the spermatocytic type, which may be an endpoint lesion) probably serves a precursor role in the formation of NSGCT. Indeed, it is now recognized that some seminomas may show focal differentiation along the same lines described for the NSGCT, to wit: toward embryonic structures ("seminoma with early carcinomatous transformation," a lesion that overlaps with so-called "anaplastic seminoma", see p. 1423); toward trophoblastic tissue ("seminoma with trophoblastic giant cells"); and toward yolk sac structures ("seminoma with yolk sac elements").[101,106] Further evidence in favor of a link between these two major categories is the existence of tumors having *both* seminomatous and nonseminomatous components of one type or another (Fig. 18.54). The term proposed for them—*combined tumor*—is not informative enough. They should be called instead mixed seminoma and NSGCT, followed by the listing of the type(s) of NSGCT components and their relative amounts. Parenthetically, the NSGCT component can be

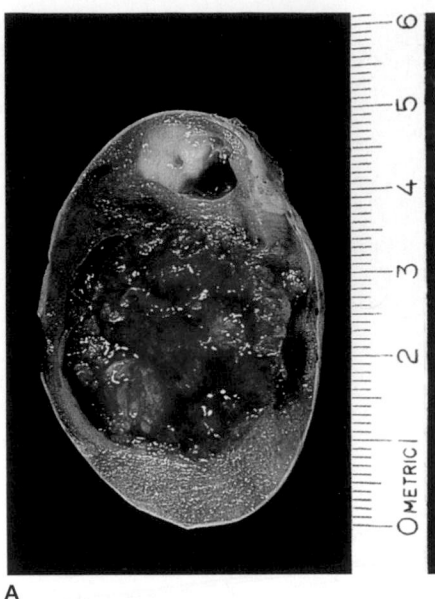
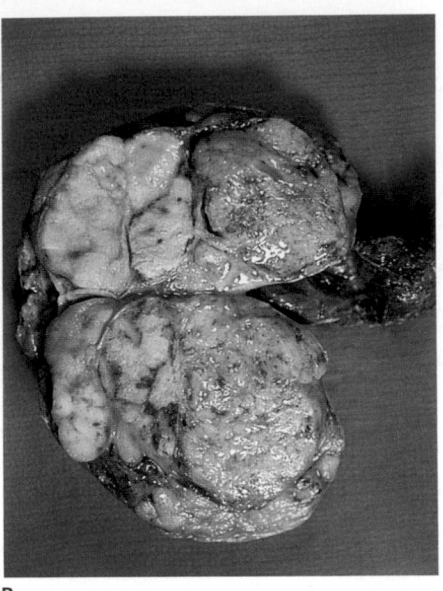

A   B

Fig. 18.54 A and **B**, Gross appearance of combined tumor of testis. In both instances, the solid homogeneous gray areas correspond to the seminoma, and the variegated foci with hemorrhage to the nonseminomatous component.

predominantly or exclusively monodermal, and composed of odd tissues such as prostate or myoid cells.[114]

Seminoma

Seminomas make up 30% to 40% of all testicular tumors (Fig. 18.55). They are divided into two major categories: classic and spermatocytic, the former including several variants.

Classic seminoma, which comprises approximately 93% of the cases of seminoma, has a characteristic gross appearance. It is usually of moderate size, solid, homogeneous, and light yellow, and it may contain sharply circumscribed zones of necrosis (Fig. 18.56). Areas of cystic change or hemorrhage are usually not seen. In their presence, the possibility of a nonseminomatous component should be suspected and the area thoroughly sampled.

Microscopically, the individual tumor cells are uniform, with abundant clear cytoplasm, sharply outlined cell membranes, a large centrally located nucleus, and clumped chromatin pattern (Fig. 18.57). The nucleolus has a characteristic appearance because of its prominence, amphophilic staining pattern, apparent multiplicity, elongated shape, and irregular contours (Fig. 18.58). The number of mitoses is highly variable. The tumor cells are typically arranged in nests outlined by fibrous bands; in 80% of the cases, these bands are infiltrated by lymphocytes (the large majority of T-cell type), plasma cells and histiocytes, possibly the expression of a host reaction to the tumor.[124,147,180] A granulomatous reaction containing Langhans-type multinucleated giant cells and epithelioid cells may also be present; occasionally it is so extensive as to obscure the neoplastic nature of the process (Fig. 18.59). Other sources of diagnostic difficulty are the sometimes excessive fibrosis; the exceptional occurrence of osseous metaplasia[143]; the fact that in some instances the tumor

cells arrange themselves in cribriform, Indian file, trabecular, or tubular patterns[126,163,181]; and the peculiar patterns that may result from extension into the rete testis (Fig. 18.60).

Number of cases

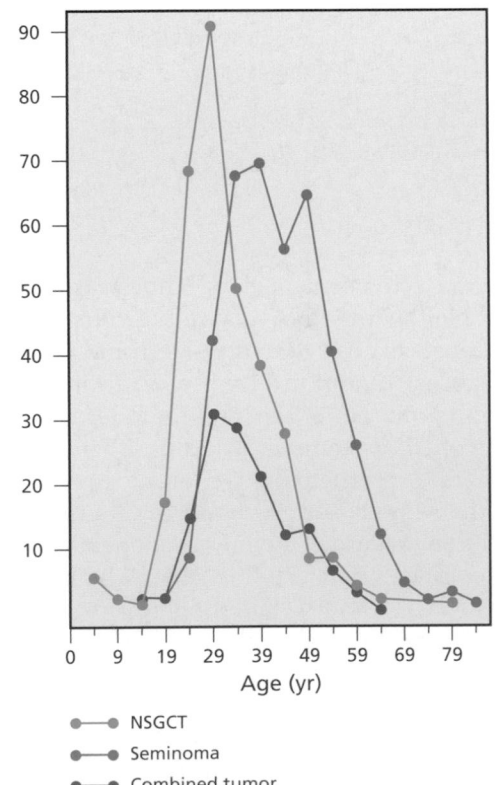

Fig. 18.55 Age distribution of patients at time of orchiectomy; 400 cases of seminoma, 322 cases of NSGCT, and 136 cases of combined tumor. Note how peak age of combined tumors occupies intermediate position between peaks for seminoma and NSGCT. (From Collins DH, Pugh RCP. Classification and frequency of testicular tumours. Br J Urol 1964, 36 (Suppl): 1–11)

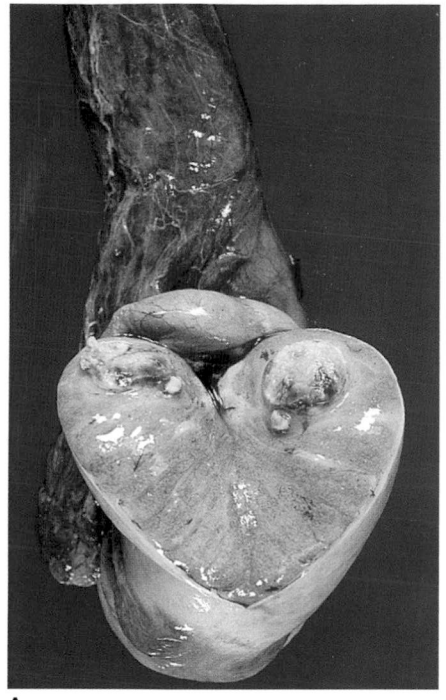

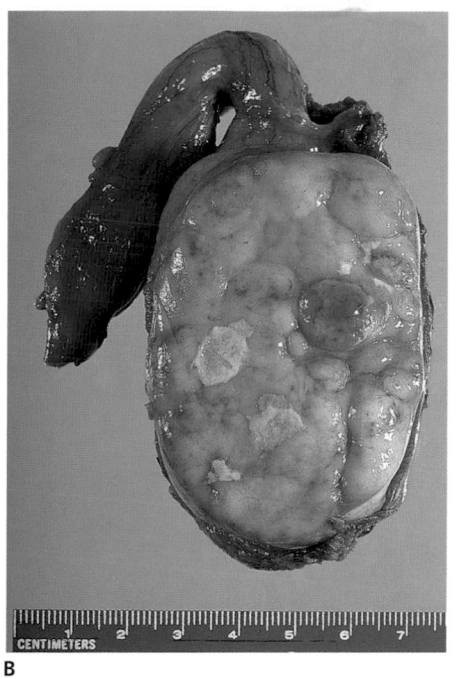

Fig. 18.56 A and **B**, Gross appearance of seminoma. The tumor in **A** is very small, whereas that in **B** has replaced most of the testis. (**B**, Courtesy of Dr RA Cooke, Brisbane, Australia; From Cooke RA, Stewart B: Colour Atlas of Anatomical Pathology, Edinburgh, Churchill Livingstone, 2004)

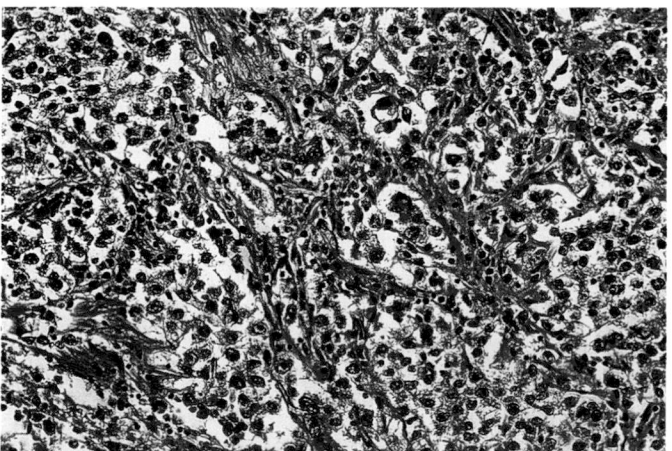

Fig. 18.57 Classic seminoma of testis. Compact nests of large tumor cells are separated by fibrous septa heavily infiltrated by lymphocytes.

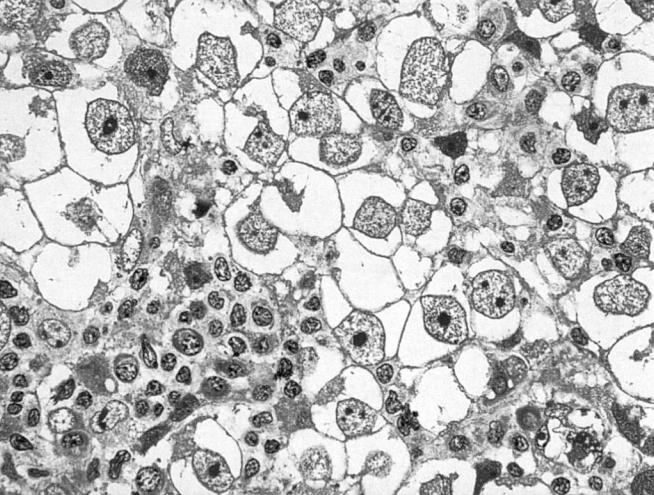

Fig. 18.58 Plastic-embedded section of classical seminoma. Notice the large nuclei, prominent nucleoli, abundant clear cytoplasm, sharply outlined cell membranes, and inflammatory infiltrate in the stroma.

Seminoma cells contain variable but usually abundant amounts of cytoplasmic glycogen, this being the reason for the ample amounts of clear cytoplasm (Fig. 18.61A,B). Immunohistochemically, they exhibit reactivity for placental alkaline phosphatase (PLAP), CD117 (c-kit) (Fig. 18.62), LDH, vimentin, ferritin, angiotensin I-converting enzyme, genes of the MAGE family, and Ki-A10 (a germ cell nuclear antigen), but are generally negative for high-molecular-weight keratin, EMA, and CD30, features of importance in the differential diagnosis with embryonal carcinoma.[116,117,119,121,132,137,138,146,159,164] However, positivity for low-molecular-weight and wide-spectrum keratin is seen frequently, and there may also be focal positivity for CD30 and EMA.[121] These "aberrant" findings call for caution in the use of immunostains to establish a diagnosis,

while providing further support to the existence of a close histogenetic link among these tumors.[133,149] Significantly, some of these immunomarkers are retained despite extensive tumor necrosis.[130] The presence of PLAP in the tumor cells as detected immunohistochemically is accompanied in about 40% of the cases with serum elevation of this marker.[139]

By electron microscopy, some of the seminoma cells have an undifferentiated appearance, with few cytoplasmic organelles; others have a more complex arrangement, indicative of some degree of differentiation[134,156] (Fig. 18.63). Cytoplasmic glycogen can usually

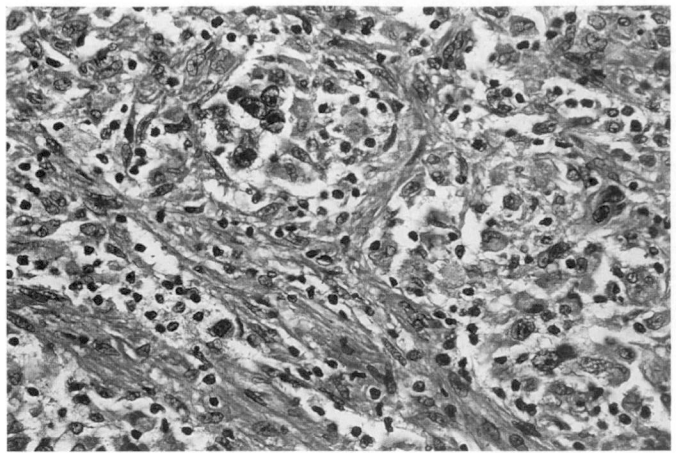

Fig. 18.59 Seminoma associated with marked granulomatous reaction. Only a few tumor cells are visible in this field.

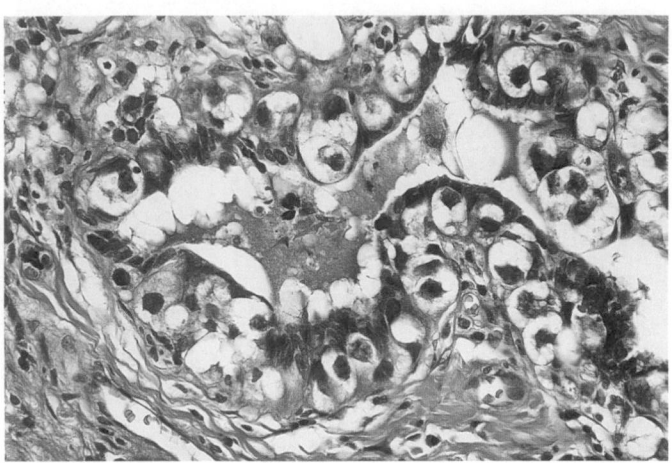

Fig. 18.60 Pagetoid extension of seminoma into rete testis. This should not be misinterpreted as a nonseminomatous component.

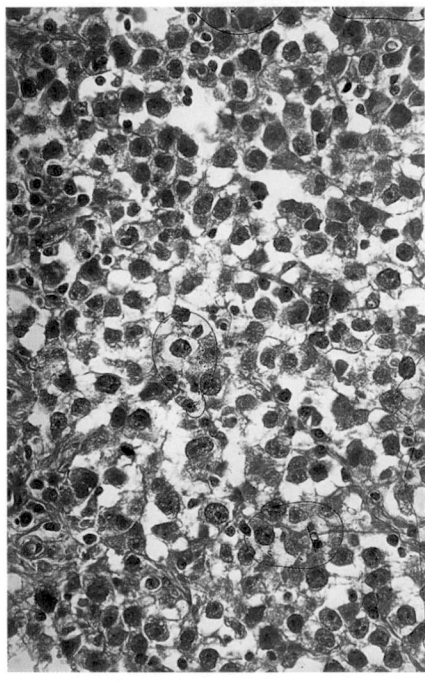

A

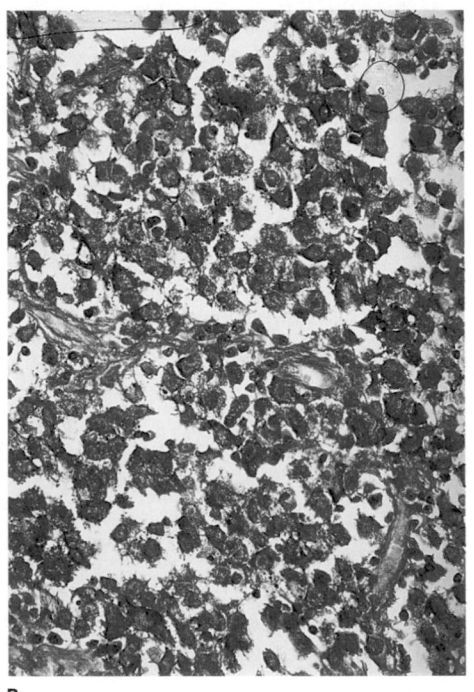

B

Fig. 18.61 A and **B**, Abundant glycogen present in the cytoplasm of seminoma cells, evidenced by the PAS reaction and removed by diastase digestion.

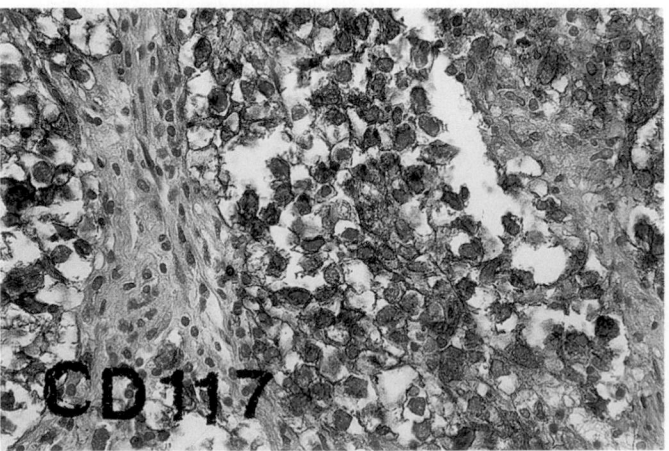

Fig. 18.62 CD117 immunoreactivity in classic seminoma.

be demonstrated. Annulate lamellae are common. There are also intranuclear membranous profiles, probably representing clefts of the nuclear envelope.[144] The characteristic nucleolar appearance is again evident at the ultrastructural level because of the dispersion of the prominent nucleolonema and the very inconspicuous pars amorpha.

As already mentioned in the section on classification (see p. 1417), a minority of otherwise classic seminomas exhibit their germ cell potentiality and differentiate focally along lines similar to those traditionally thought to occur only in the NSGCT.[127]

At the molecular level, 40% of seminomas are accompanied by *K-ras* mutations (usually of codon 12) and about a quarter have *p53* mutations.[157]

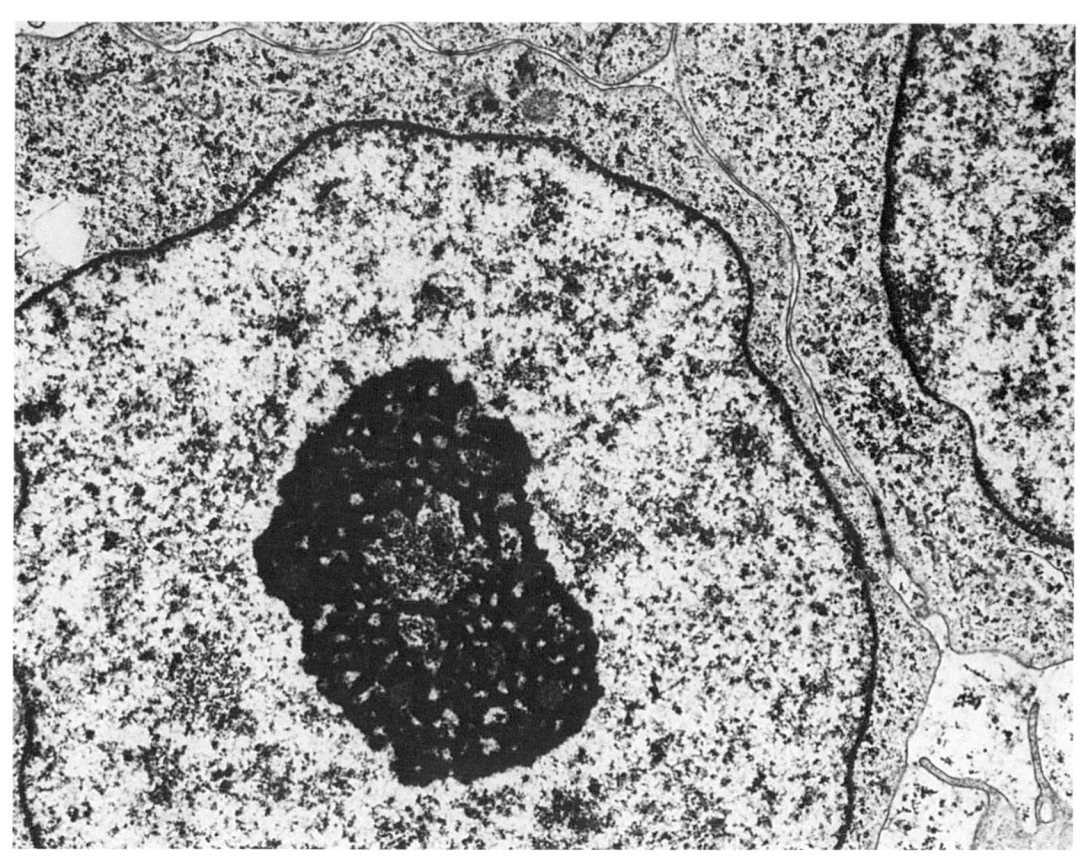

Fig. 18.63 Ultrastructural appearance of seminoma cells. Moderate amounts of cytoplasmic glycogen and characteristic nucleolus of germ cell tumors are demonstrated.

Anaplastic seminoma was originally defined by Mostofi[152,153] as a seminoma with features of the classic type having three or more mitoses per high-power field and characterized by a more aggressive clinical course. Several reports have subsequently appeared on this topic,[141,142,173] with a wide disparity of conclusions regarding the natural history of "anaplastic" seminoma as above defined. Some have found it to be more aggressive than classic seminoma regardless of stage; others have found it more likely to present as a high-stage lesion but not to be more aggressive than the classic tumor when matched stage by stage, and still others have not detected any prognostic differences with classic seminoma.[122,142] Obviously, the issue is in need of clarification. Part of the problem stems from the diagnostic criteria originally proposed for the definition of this entity. Since over 80% of all seminomas have three or more mitoses per high-power field, this criterion is clearly inadequate by itself.[176,182] Perhaps the mitotic threshold should be increased to six or more per high-power field and combined with other morphologic criteria, such as nuclear hyperchromasia, nucleolar size, pleomorphism, and amount of necrosis. Problems of definition notwithstanding, it seems clear that there exists a testicular tumor that is morphologically situated between classic seminoma and embryonal carcinoma that may represent a link between the two[176,177,179] (Fig. 18.64). Along these lines, there is a great deal of overlap—both conceptually and morphologically—between anaplastic seminoma and so-called *seminoma with atypical features,*[174] *seminoma with high mitotic index,*[154] and *seminoma with early carcinomatous transformation,*[150,167] the latter term better expressing the presumed transformation occurring in this tumor.

Seminoma with syncytiotrophoblastic giant cells results from focal differentiation of the tumor toward trophoblastic components and constitutes 10% to 20% of all classic seminomas. The giant cells are either isolated or in the form of syncytial masses; they are often closely related to blood vessels, and foci of hemorrhage are common around them[152] (Fig. 18.65A). They have been

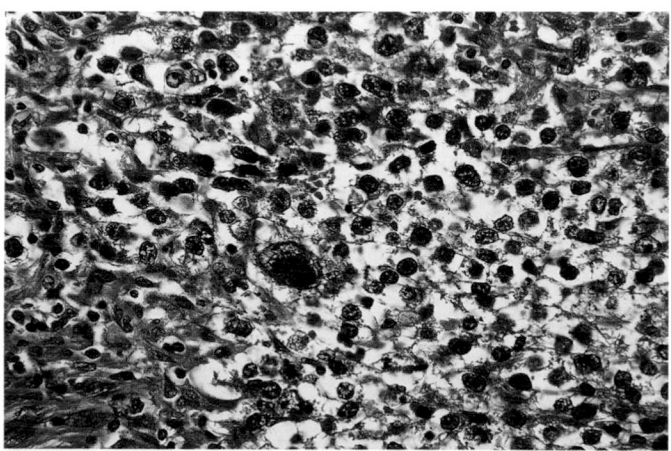

Fig. 18.64 Seminoma exhibiting pleomorphism and marked hyperchromasia. Some authors designate this neoplasm as "anaplastic seminoma."

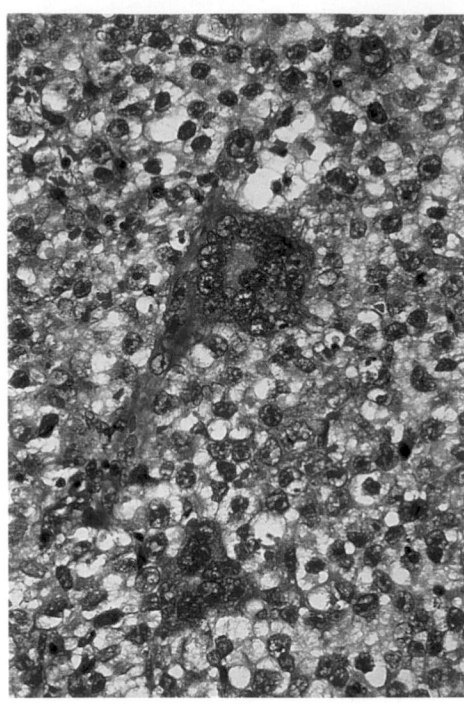
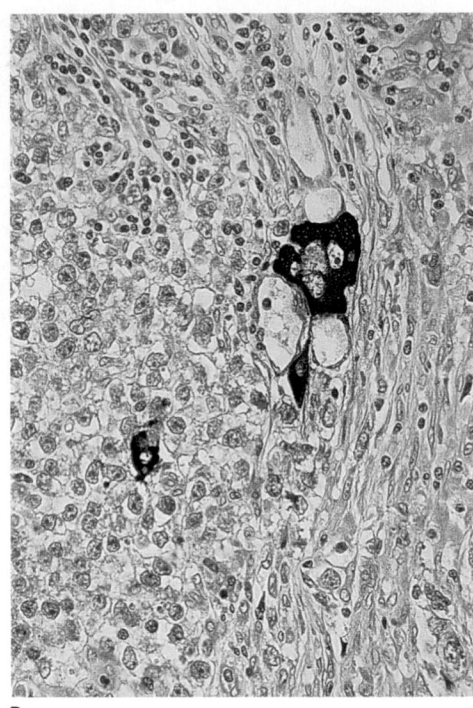

A   B

Fig. 18.65 Seminoma with trophoblastic giant cells. (**A**, Hematoxylin and eosin; **B**, hCG immunostain)

shown to contain human chorionic gonadotropin (hCG) (Fig. 18.65B), this explaining why some seminoma patients have serum elevations of this hormone in the absence of a fully developed choriocarcinomatous component. These trophoblastic giant cells should be distinguished from the already mentioned Langhans' giant cells seen as part of a granulomatous reaction, as well as from pleomorphic seminoma cells. Claims have been made that seminomas containing these cells and/or associated with elevated serum levels of hCG are more aggressive than the others, but this has not been confirmed in other studies.[135,140,151,178] Furthermore, no differences in the distribution of the DNA index have been found between them and the ordinary seminomas.[118] Therefore, it would seem appropriate to include these tumors in the classic seminoma category and to treat them as such.

Seminoma with yolk sac elements exhibits, as the name indicates, foci consistent with yolk sac differentiation by virtue of the architectural arrangement, hyaline globules, and immunoreactivity for α-fetoprotein (AFP). It is likely that the few reported cases of seminoma associated with serum AFP elevation[158] represent examples of this tumor type in which the yolk sac elements were missed because of insufficient sampling or simply because these foci were not identifiable at the morphologic level. On practical grounds, if high serum levels of AFP are found in a patient diagnosed as having a seminoma, the chances are very high that a nonseminomatous component exists, either in the primary lesion or in a metastatic focus.[136]

The three variations on the theme of seminoma previously described (which also occur in dysgerminoma, the ovarian equivalent of seminoma[155]), share with classic seminoma a similar background, morphologic appearance, and natural history. In all three instances the suggestion has been made that the behavior may be more aggressive, but conclusive evidence is still lacking. Because of this fact, it remains important to distinguish these phenomena from the admixture of classic seminoma with NSGCT (so-called "combined tumor") in which the nonseminomatous component is fully developed and sharply segregated from the seminomatous elements.[170]

Spermatocytic seminoma should be clearly separated from classic seminoma and its variants. It comprises 4% to 7% of all seminomas and occurs in an older age group.[123,171] Grossly, it has a soft, gelatinous appearance (Fig. 18.66). Microscopically, it is composed of cells with perfectly round nuclei and prominent variation in size.

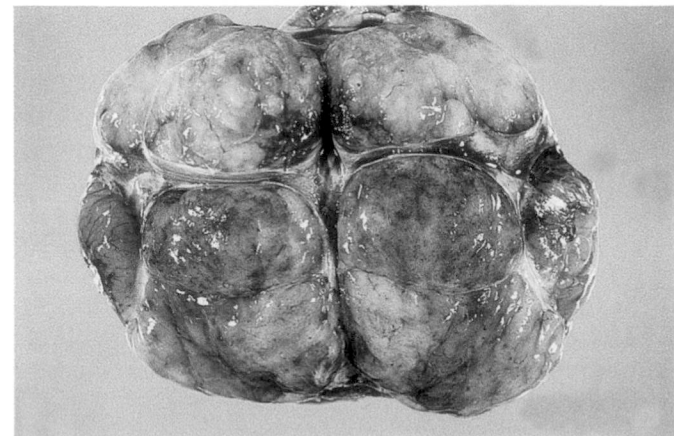

Fig. 18.66 Gross appearance of spermatocytic seminoma. A large tumor of myxoid appearance bulges on the cut surface.

Bizarre giant forms are common, together with small cells with a lymphocytic-like appearance (Fig. 18.67). Some of the nuclei have a filamentous appearance suggestive of an early stage of meiotic division (Fig. 18.68). Mitoses may be numerous. The cytoplasm is dense and devoid of glycogen.[120] Prominent intratubular growth is often seen at the periphery (Fig. 18.69). Areas of lymphocytic infiltration and granuloma formation are absent.[162]

In contrast to classic seminoma, immunoreactivity for placental alkaline phosphatase (PLAP) is usually absent.[125,128,169] Focal and inconstant positivity for keratin may be observed, as in classic seminoma.[125] Spermatocytic seminomas are also said to express NY-ESO-1 (the product of a "cancer-testis gene"), like normal spermatogonia, primary spermatocytes and the cells of ITGCN, and in contrast to classic seminoma and NSGCTs.[165] Ultrastructurally, the tumor cells show evidence of spermatocytic differentiation.[160,161,172] (Fig. 18.70). Although

cytometric and microspectrophotometric studies have not demonstrated the presence of haploid (postmeiotic) cells, it has been shown that the cells of spermatocytic (as opposed to classic) seminoma mature to the stage of

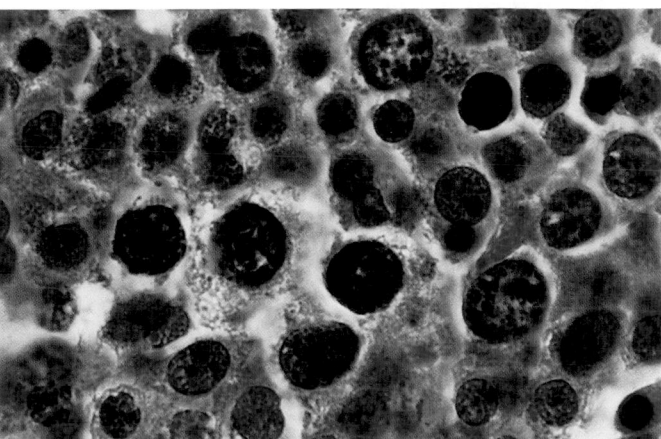

Fig. 18.68 Typical chromatin pattern of spermatocytic seminoma.

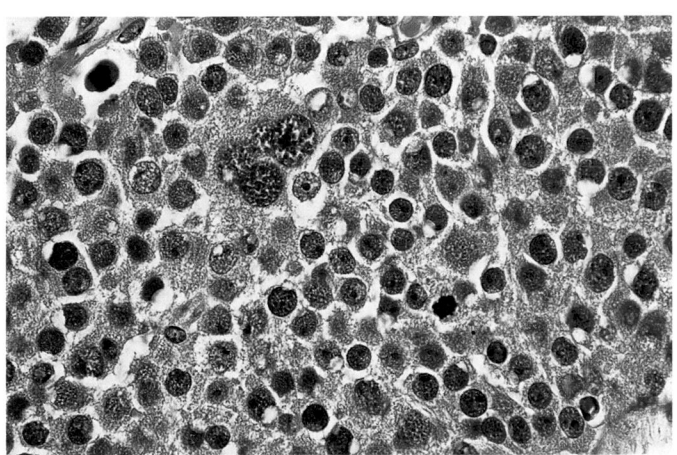

Fig. 18.67 Spermatocytic seminoma showing admixture of medium-sized cells (predominating), giant cells, and small lymphocyte-like cells.

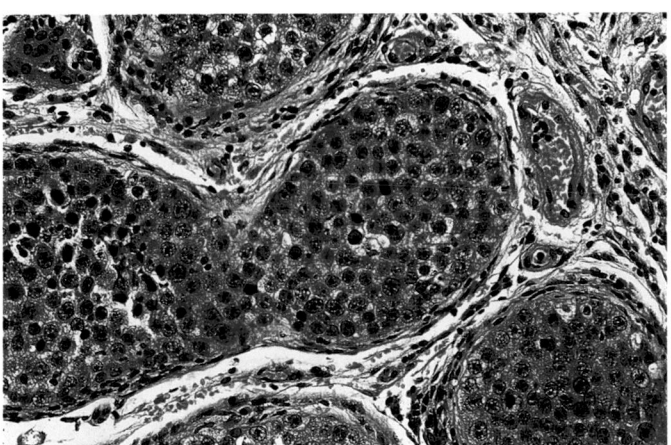

Fig. 18.69 Extensive intratubular growth of spermatocytic seminoma.

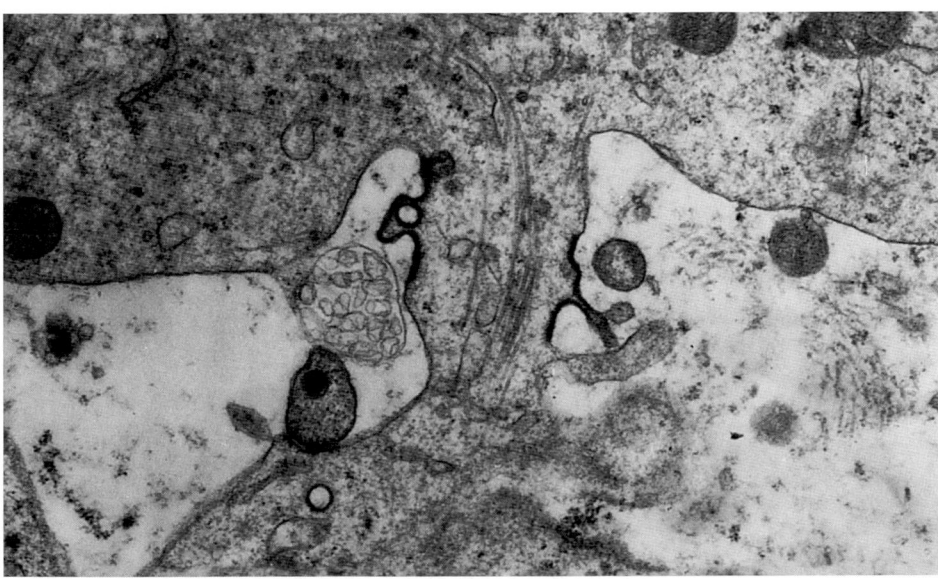

Fig. 8.70 Ultrastructural appearance of spermatocytic seminoma. An intercellular bridge joins two tumor cells in a manner analogous to that seen in normal spermatocytes. Note thickening of plasma membrane and microtubules running across bridge.

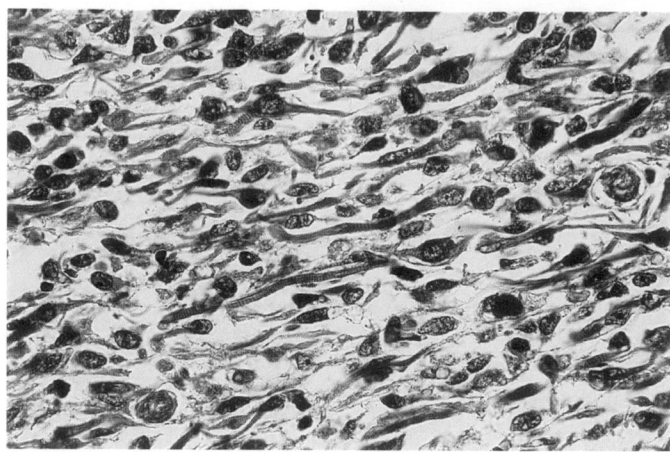

Fig.18.71 Sarcomatous focus in spermatocytic seminoma of testis, exhibiting rhabdomyoblastic differentiation. This section is from a lung metastasis.

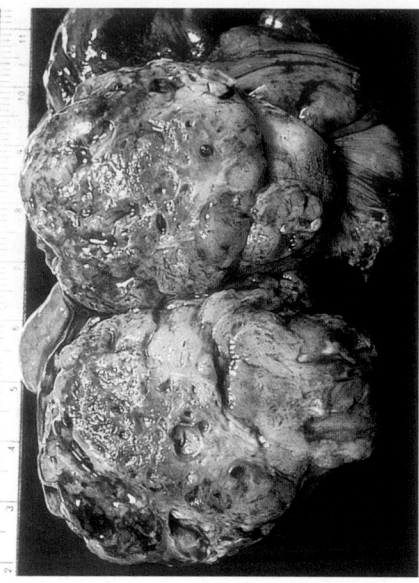

Fig. 18.72 Embryonal carcinoma showing solid nodular cut surface with numerous areas of necrosis and hemorrhage.

spermatogonia–pachytene spermatocyte, as demonstrated by the presence of SCP1 (synaptonemal complex protein 1) and other stage-specific markers.[168]

In contrast to the classic seminoma, the spermatocytic type occurs only in the testicle and is never seen in combination with NSGCT. It is more commonly bilateral, and the prognosis is excellent. Metastases are practically nonexistent, and therefore simple orchiectomy may be sufficient therapy.[120,129]

Spermatocytic seminoma may be complicated by a highly malignant component of *sarcomatous appearance*, sometimes exhibiting skeletal muscle differentiation (Fig. 18.71). This development is accompanied by an accelerated clinical course and the appearance of widespread distant metastases.[131,148,175] This is a different phenomenon from that seen in the *anaplastic variant* of spermatocytic seminoma, in which the highly atypical elements present retain the features of germ cells instead of having a sarcomatous character; the few reported cases of this variant have so far behaved no differently from spermatocytic seminomas lacking this feature.[115]

Interestingly, the testicular seminomas that develop not too infrequently in old dogs appear morphologically similar to human spermatocytic seminoma.[145,162,166]

Embryonal carcinoma

Embryonal carcinoma has a grossly more variegated appearance than seminoma (Fig. 18.72). It is mainly solid and gray or white, with foci of hemorrhage and necrosis. The latter may be so extensive as to render the diagnosis difficult. Microscopically, it may be composed wholly of solid sheets of undifferentiated cells or show signs of early differentiation toward embryonic structures, trophoblast, or extraembryonic endoderm or mesoderm in the form of papillary or glandular formations[184,187] (Fig. 18.73).

In the differential diagnosis with seminoma, it is important to remember that even in the solid, undiffer-

entiated form, the pattern of growth has a carcinomatous appearance. The cells are more anaplastic, with numerous mitoses (often atypical), and exhibit prominent variation in size and shape. Multiple large nucleoli are present, and overlapping of nuclei is frequent.[187] Immunohistochemically, embryonal carcinoma cells are reactive for keratin (including keratin 19 and high-molecular-weight forms) and CD30, but usually not for CD117.[185,186,188] Some of these reactions are useful in the differential diagnosis with seminoma, as already discussed on p. 1421. Of note, the reactivity for CD30 may disappear following chemotherapy.[183] Several other markers allegedly associated with embryonal carcinoma cells have been described (such as 43-9F), but their molecular nature is unknown and their specificity and utility remain to be established.[189,190]

Mature (adult) and immature teratoma

Mature teratoma comprises 5% to 10% of all testicular neoplasms.[199] Grossly, it is predominantly cystic and multiloculated (Fig. 18.74). Foci of cartilage are usually evident, but the presence of bone is infrequent.

All types of tissue can be seen microscopically in testicular teratoma, the most common being neural tissue, cartilage, and various types of epithelium (Fig. 18.75). The epithelial component can differentiate in the direction of gastrointestinal, respiratory, cutaneous, or virtually any other tissue type. All of the cells normally present in the corresponding somatic structures may be identified, including neuroendocrine cells in the case of gastrointestinal epithelium, and meningothelial cells (to the point of forming meningioma-like structures) in the case of neural tissue.[193,201,205] Sometimes one of the components of the teratoma (such as cartilage) predominates to the near exclusion of the others.[207]

A requisite for the diagnosis of *mature* teratoma is that all tissues be well differentiated, hence the synonym "differentiated" teratoma.

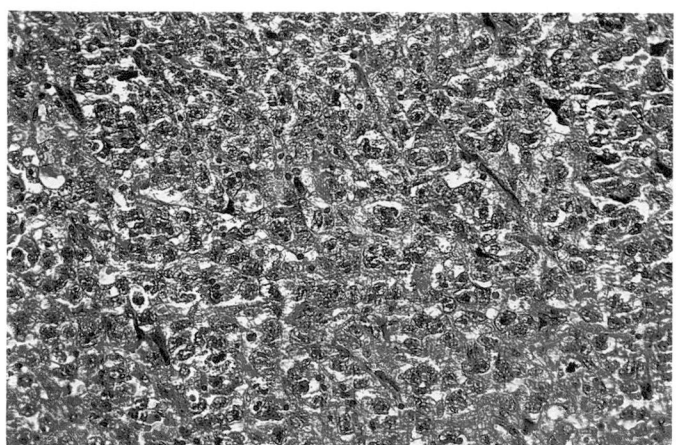

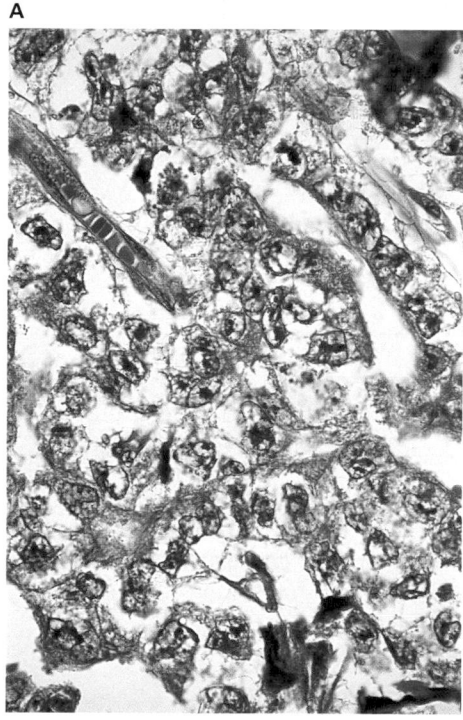

Fig. 18.73 A and **B,** Embryonal carcinoma. The pattern of growth is diffuse but without the nesting seen in classic seminoma. The high-power view shows the typical large, irregularly shaped, overlapping nuclei with multiple prominent nucleoli.

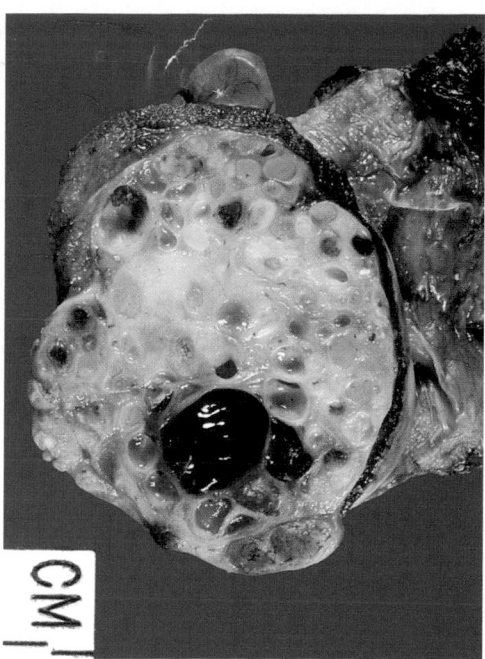

Fig. 18.74 Gross appearance of mature (adult) teratoma of testis. There are multiple cystic areas, lobules of mature adipose tissue, and shiny solid nodules corresponding to well-differentiated cartilage.

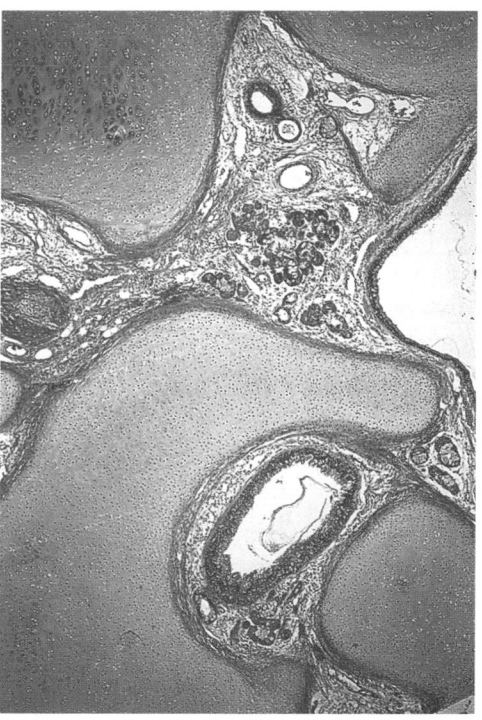

Fig. 18.75 Low-power microscopic view of mature teratoma. Large islands of cartilage are seen surrounding well-differentiated glandular structures.

It should be pointed out that the type of teratoma full of sebum, keratin and hairs ("dermoid cyst") so commonly seen in the ovary is extremely rare in the testis.[208] Curiously, the pilar component of this tumor may have a pilomatrixoma-like quality, and it is likely that the cases reported as pilomatrixoma of the testis are variations on the theme.[202]

A high proportion of testicular teratomas (particularly those seen in adult individuals) also exhibit some areas of tissue immaturity, which may reside in the stroma, epithelium, or neural component. This may range from a slight hypercellularity of the stroma around the glandular component to large foci of primitive glands, neuroepithelium, or even tissue with an appearance rem- iniscent of Wilms' tumor (Fig. 18.76). The World Health Organization (WHO) classification designates teratomas with these features as **immature,**[194,203] but the prognostic significance of this finding has yet to be determined, perhaps by using a grading system along the lines successfully applied to ovarian teratomas. It is

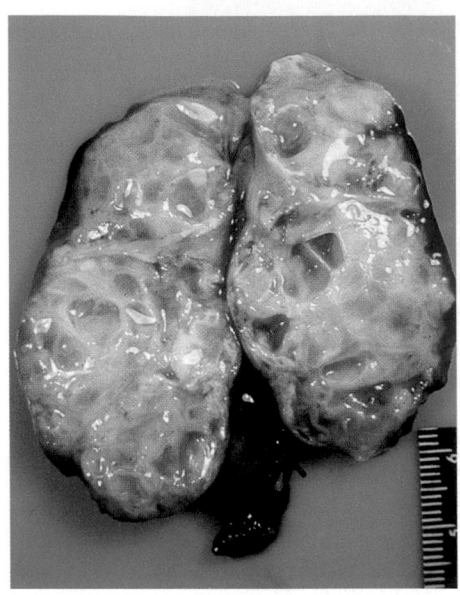

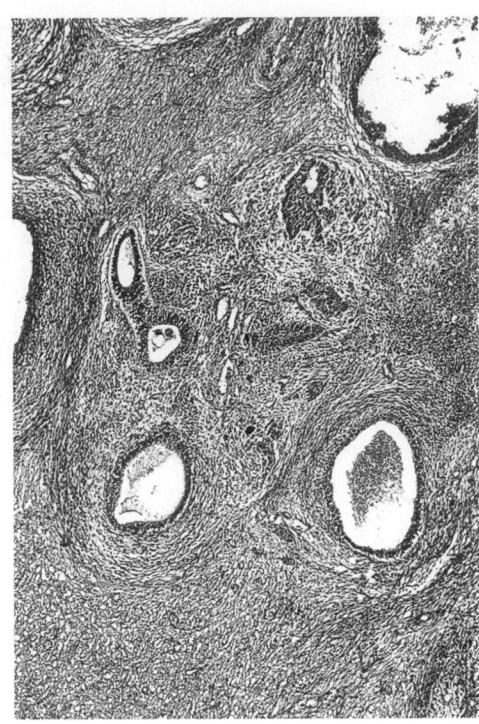

A

B

Fig. 18.76 Immature teratoma.
A, Gross appearance.
B, Microscopic appearance.
Hypercellular stroma is seen growing in a concentric fashion around glandular formations.

important, however, not to regard these areas of immaturity as indicative of embryonal carcinoma. A practical point to keep in mind is that in the evaluation of immature teratomas for prognostic purposes it is not so important to determine the extent and grade of the immaturity but to search for microscopic foci of yolk sac tumor.[197]

A much rarer occurrence is the development of a focal malignancy of somatic type in an otherwise mature teratoma, a phenomenon analogous to the malignant transformation of an ovarian benign cystic teratoma.[192,209] The malignant component is usually epithelial (often in the form of adenocarcinoma or squamous cell carcinoma), but it may also present in the form of sarcoma (such as rhabdomyosarcoma or angiosarcoma).[198,204] This phenomenon is designated as **teratoma with malignant transformation** (teratoma with malignant areas) in the WHO classification.[194,203]

Some immature germ cell tumors have a distinctive appearance resulting from their tissue composition. **Polyembryomas** are characterized by the presence of multiple embryoid bodies throughout the neoplasm. The term **diffuse embryoma** has been proposed for a testicular germ cell tumor featuring an orderly arrangement of embryonal, yolk sac, and trophoblastic elements.[195,196] Some immature teratomas are almost exclusively composed of primitive neuroepithelial tissue with the appearance of *neuroblastoma* or *peripheral neuroectodermal tumor*.[200,206] It is possible that the neoplasms reported as primitive neuroectodermal tumor of the testis represent the extreme manifestation of this phenomenon.[191]

Teratocarcinoma

Teratocarcinoma is composed of a mixture of teratoma and embryonal carcinoma. Its gross appearance depends on the relative amount of these two components: multicystic in the areas of teratoma; and solid, with hemorrhagic and necrotic foci, in the areas of embryonal carcinoma (Fig. 18.77). The appearance of the teratomatous foci ranges from mature to immature. Sometimes sarcomatous elements of non-germ cell type such as rhabdomyosarcoma, angiosarcoma, or chondrosarcoma are present.[210]

As already indicated, the term "teratocarcinoma" has fallen into disuse; current preference is to designate the lesion as a mixed NSGCT, followed by a listing and proportion of the relative components.

Choriocarcinoma

Choriocarcinomas account for about 5% of testicular tumors. These neoplasms are often small, with no enlargement of the testis. They are usually hemorrhagic and partially necrotic (Fig. 18.78). Rarely the primary tumor may completely regress, leaving only a scar containing hemosiderin pigment. Peculiar hematoxylin deposits may be present within the seminiferous tubules, probably representing remnants of preexisting neoplasm.[211] Microscopically, these tumors show giant syncytiotrophoblastic cells with large, atypical nuclei intermingled with cytotrophoblasts (Fig. 18.79). The syncytiotrophoblastic cells are consistently immunoreactive for hCG and keratin.[214,216] It has been noted that keratin 7 stains trophoblastic cells (whether in a choriocarcinoma

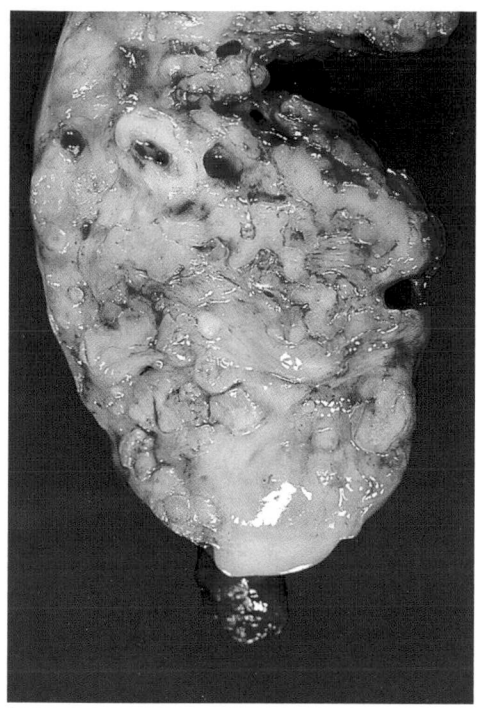

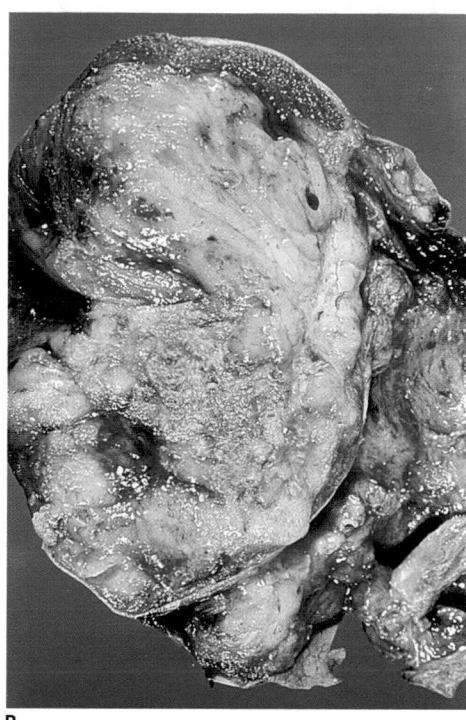

A

B

Fig. 18.77 **A** and **B**, Gross appearance of teratocarcinoma. The solid granular areas correspond to foci of embryonal carcinoma, whereas the pearly nodules correspond to well-differentiated cartilage.

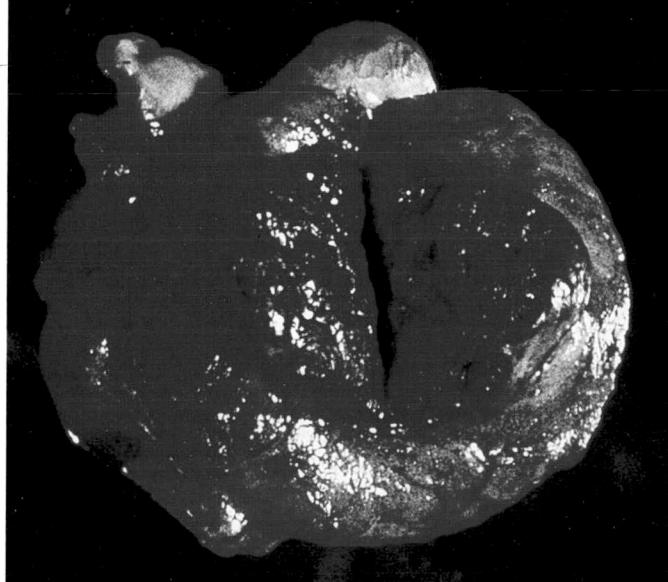

Fig. 18.78 Gross appearance of pure choriocarcinoma. The strikingly hemorrhagic appearance is characteristic of this tumor type.

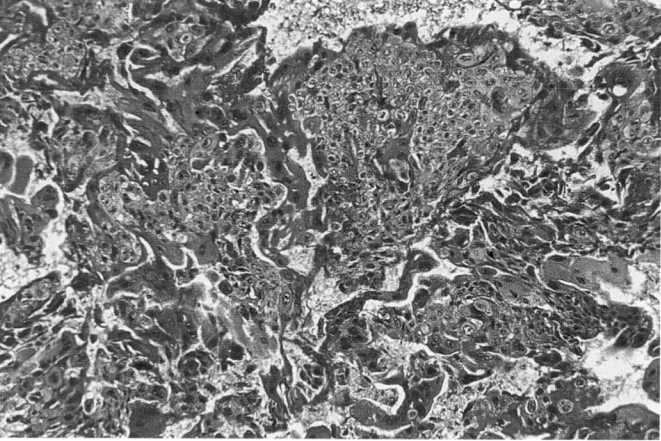

Fig. 18.79 Microscopic appearance of testicular choriocarcinoma. There is close intermingling of cytotrophoblast and syncytiotrophoblast, which recapitulates that seen in normal chorionic villi.

or in other germ cell tumors) but not any of the other tumor components in germ cell tumors.[212] Syncytiotropleoblastic cells also express the epidermal growth factor receptor. As already mentioned, cells with the morphologic appearance of syncytiotrophoblast can be seen in several other types of testicular tumors, including seminomas and NSGCT, particularly embryonal carcinoma. These cells have been shown to produce hCG, like those of choriocarcinoma, and there is no question that they are histogenetically related to the latter.[213,214]

However, their presence as isolated elements or even as syncytial clusters (with or without accompanying hemorrhage) in a testicular germ cell tumor should not be taken as evidence that a choriocarcinoma is present. It is only when these cells are intimately mixed with cytotrophoblastic elements in a biphasic plexiform pattern that the diagnosis of choriocarcinoma is justified. Something similar can be said concerning serum levels of chorionic gonadotropins. Although classically elevated in choriocarcinomas, they also may be increased in any other type of testicular germinal tumor. This finding, although of important prognostic value,[215] should not influence the morphologic typing of the tumor. The diagnosis of choriocarcinoma should be made on the basis of the microscopic pattern rather than on the basis of the hormone being produced.

It should also be mentioned that in exceptional circumstances one can find a trophoblastic testicular tumor formed exclusively of cytotrophoblast ("monophasic" choriocarcinoma) or of intermediate trophoblast (placental site trophoblastic tumor).[217]

Yolk sac tumor

Yolk sac tumor has also been designated over the years as endodermal sinus tumor, juvenile embryonal carcinoma, embryonal adenocarcinoma, distinctive adenocarcinoma of the infant testis, testicular adenocarcinoma with clear cells, and orchioblastoma.[218,233,239,240,243,245] Current evidence has conclusively proved Teilum's postulate that yolk sac tumor is a unilaterally developed teratoma mimicking embryonal yolk sac tissue.[220] Specifically, its appearance recapitulates that of the primary rather than the secondary yolk sac.[231]

A yolk sac pattern can be seen in testicular tumors under two distinct circumstances: (1) as a pure form—with the classic organoid appearance as described by Teilum—in infants and children (usually less than 2 years of age) and associated with an excellent prognosis[227]; and (2) as a component of a mixed germ cell tumor in adults, with a less differentiated and more malignant appearance and having a prognosis at least as guarded and possibly worse than embryonal carcinoma or teratocarcinoma.[229,237,244] Increased awareness of the different morphologic patterns that yolk sac differentiation may exhibit (as a result of correlative studies with immunocytochemical techniques) has led to an ever-increasing percentage of yolk sac elements being described in association with other germ cell components, particularly embryonal carcinoma and teratocarcinoma[238] but also seminoma.[236] In some series of NSGCT, the incidence of yolk sac elements is listed as high as 80%.[232]

Grossly, the pure yolk sac tumor of infancy has a soft consistency and a microcystic appearance on cross section (Fig. 18.80); yolk sac elements in germ cell tumors of adults are difficult to discern on gross inspection. Microscopically, the yolk sac component is recognized by the intermingling of epithelial and mesenchymal elements in a characteristic organoid fashion. Microcystic, glandular–alveolar, and papillary formations are common. Many of the cystic spaces are lined by a very flattened, endothelium-like layer of cells. The stroma can be quite cellular, spindle shaped, and reminiscent of smooth muscle. This mesenchyme-like component appears to represent a chemoresistant, pluripotential cell population, which in rare cases gives rise to a sarcoma after treatment.[230] This sarcoma is of spindle cell type and occurs against the background of a myxoid to collagenous stroma.[241]

Perivascular Schiller–Duval bodies are the most distinctive features of yolk sac tumor (Fig. 18.81). They have been compared to structures seen in the rat placenta[239] and represent an attempt to form yolk sacs. The similarity between the normal yolk sac and this tumor is maintained at the electron microscopic level.[221] Variants of yolk sac tumor that tend to be misinterpreted are those exhibiting an hepatoid pattern (featuring fetal-type liver cell cords), a solid pattern, or a well-differentiated glandular pattern (resembling fetal lung or intestine, the latter also referred to as primitive intestinal or enteric pattern).[223,223a,225,242]

Hyaline intracytoplasmic and extracytoplasmic round inclusions are consistently seen in yolk sac tumors

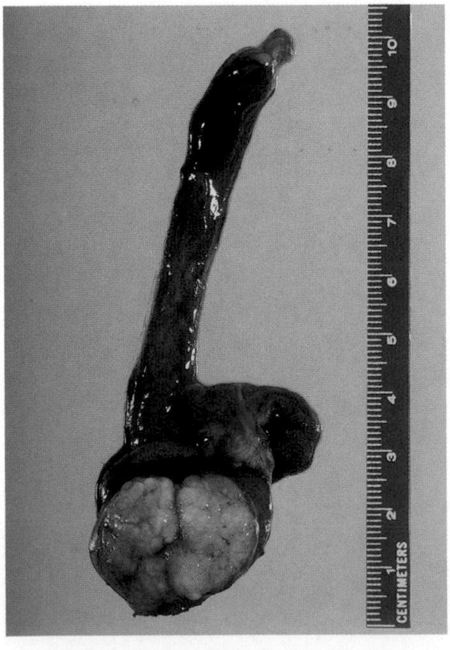

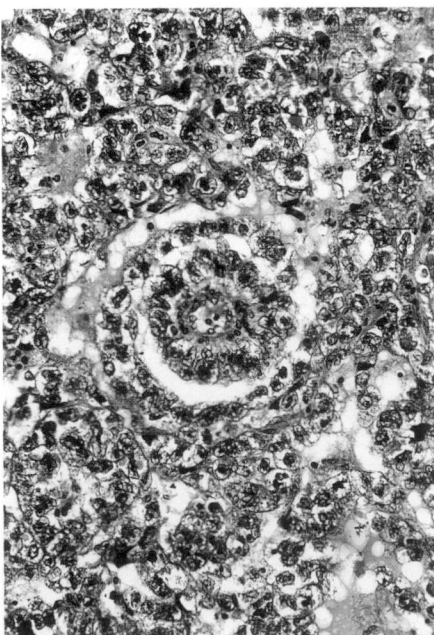

Fig. 18.80 Gross appearance of pure yolk sac tumor in an infant.

Fig. 18.81 Schiller–Duval body in yolk sac tumor of testis.

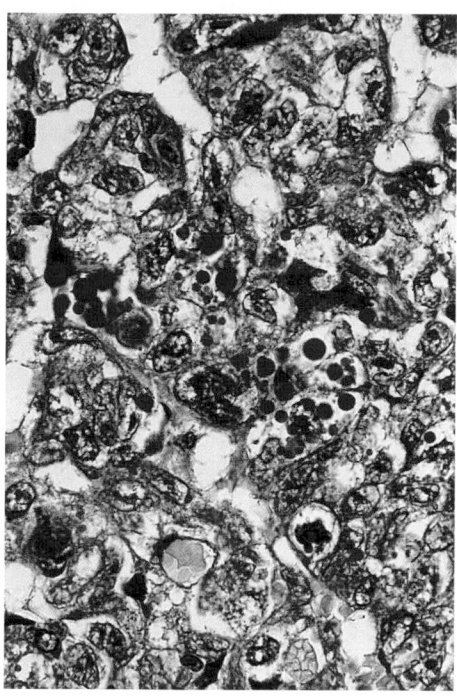

Fig. 18.82 Pleomorphism and hyaline globules in yolk sac tumor of testis.

(Fig. 18.82). They are eosinophilic, PAS positive, and diastase resistant; some have been shown by immunocytochemistry to contain AFP.[200] Others have been shown to be composed of other plasma proteins (such as albumin, α_1-antitrypsin, and transferrin) and of basal lamina material.[234] It should be pointed out that the production and release of AFP are not limited to yolk sac tumors as here defined; it is also commonly found, both in serum and in tissues, in embryonal carcinomas and teratocarcinomas containing only yolk sac elements and even in those without morphologically recognizable elements of this type.[222,224] It also needs to be remarked that most of the immunoreactivity for AFP is not in the hyaline globules but is rather seen diffusely or in granular fashion throughout the cytoplasm of the tumor cells.

The cells of yolk sac tumor are also consistently positive immunohistochemically for keratin.[219] The pediatric cases express GATA-4, a transcription factor that regulates the differentiation and function of murine yolk sac endoderm.[235] Hypermethylation of the RUNX3 gene promoter is thought to play a pathogenetic role in this neoplasm.[225a] Practically all cases of yolk sac tumor exhibit an aneuploid DNA pattern.[226]

Intratubular germ cell neoplasia

The in situ stage of germ cell neoplasia is generally designated as intratubular germ cell neoplasia (IGCN), but it is also known as in situ carcinoma and (somewhat inaccurately) as testicular intraepithelial neoplasia.[252,254,267] It is most often seen in the residual testis in organs harboring an invasive germ cell malignancy, the frequency being higher than 80% in some series.[259,262] It is also seen in the contra-lateral testicle in approximately 5% of patients with testicular tumors.[248,251] Interestingly, the appearance of IGCN is usually the same regardless of the nature of the invasive germ cell component. All types of postpubertal germ cell tumors have been found to be associated with IGCN. The incidence is substantially lower for mature teratoma[270]; it is also extremely low in pure yolk sac tumors and other germ cell neoplasms occurring in the prepubertal testis,[256,285] although it has also been reported in them.[258,282,286] IGCN of the testis has also been observed in association with primary germ cell tumors of the mediastinum.[255]

Although usually restricted to the seminiferous tubules, IGCN sometimes extends to the rete testis, where it results in a pagetoid appearance that can be very confusing to the unwary.[277]

Sometimes, IGCN is found incidentally in the absence of an obvious tumor, occasionally in children or adolescents with various intersex states,[281] but most often in the study of testicular biopsies performed for the study of infertility or in cases of current or corrected cryptorchidism.[265,284] It is important to recognize these changes because they represent the forerunners of clinically apparent neoplasms. Thus Skakkebaek[283] found foci of atypical germ cells in the testicular biopsy of 6 (1.1%) of 555 infertile men (in 2 of them bilateral); 4 of the 6 patients developed an invasive germ cell tumor within a follow-up period of 1.3 to 4.5 years. Similar experiences have been reported by other authors.[276,278]

A pathology panel that met in Minnesota in 1980, as part of an International Symposium on Testicular Germ Cell Cancer, accepted with slight modifications the following classification of IGCN as proposed by Dr. R.E. Scully:

1 IGCN, unclassified. This refers to the presence of atypical germ cells at the base of the seminiferous tubules, which otherwise contain a non-neoplastic population of germ cells and/or Sertoli cells (Fig. 18.83). Concomitant with the proliferation of atypical germ cells, the lamina propria of the tubule often becomes thickened and hyalinized. The atypical elements have a clear cytoplasm rich in glycogen, positive for PLAP, CD117 (c-kit), and other neoplastic germ cell markers,[247,257,269,274,279] and resembling that of seminoma cells (Figs 18.84 and 18.85). Their ploidy pattern and cytogenetic profile are also similar to those of seminoma.[250,287] However, the designation of "unclassified" was preferred because it was felt that at this stage the proliferation was still uncommitted as to specific tumor cell type. This lesion may be widespread throughout the testis but also focal[268,275]; it is least prominent in the region close to the epididymis.

Immunostaining for PLAP or CD117 is a very useful technique for detecting IGCN in the adult testis, inasmuch as the corresponding normal germ cells lack these markers[266,282b]; however, PLAP is expressed in a subset of normal infantile germ cells until the age of

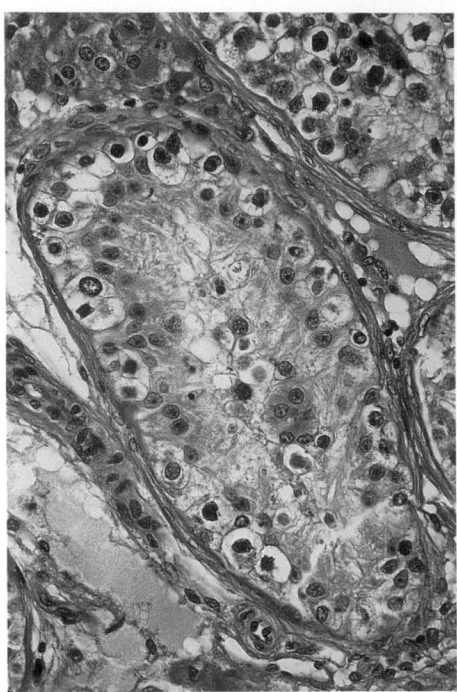

Fig. 18.83 Microscopic appearance of intratubular germ cell neoplasia in routinely stained section. A row of atypical germ cells with clear cytoplasm is seen against a thickened basement membrane. No spermatogenesis is occurring in this tubule.

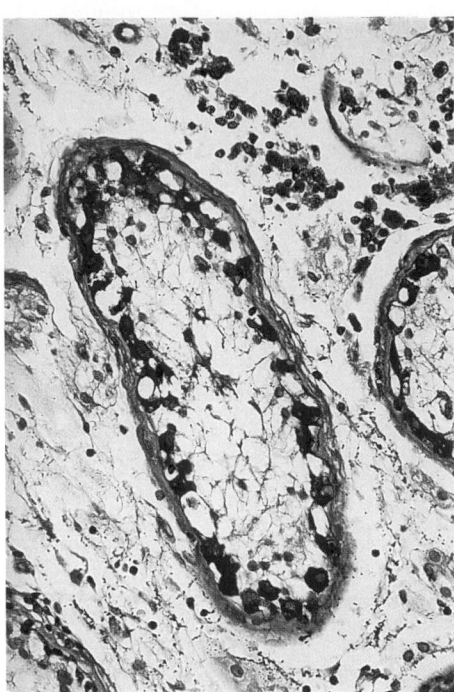

Fig. 18.84 PAS stain of intratubular germ cell neoplasia showing abundant intracytoplasmic glycogen in the neoplastic cells.

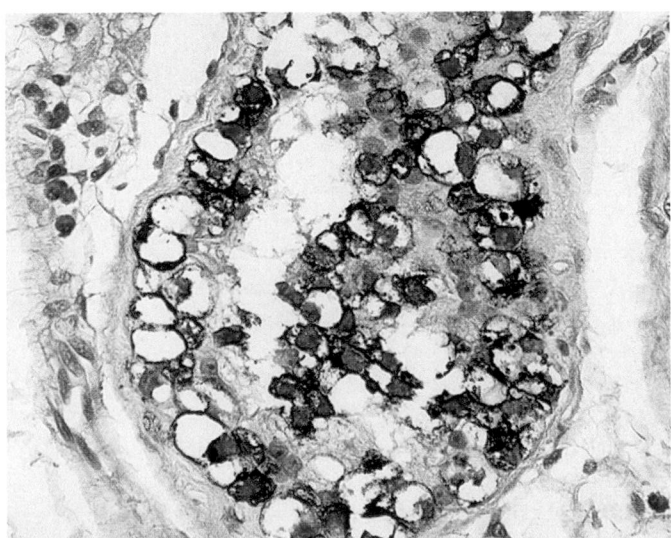

Fig. 18.85 PLAP immunoreactivity in the tumor cells of intratubular germ cell neoplasia.

1 year.[260] Overexpression of p53 often occurs in IGCN and represents another good diagnostic marker for this condition.[263,272] The cells of IGCN also differ from normal germ cells by the absence of RBM (RNA-binding motif) protein, encoded by a gene located in the human Y chromosome and expressed exclusively in the male germ cell line,[264] and by the loss of FHIT expression.[251a] Other markers, sometimes used on combination, have been proposed for the identification of this lesion.[282a] Interestingly, expression of NKX3.1 (a homeobox gene which exhibits prostate and testis specific expression) tends to get lost when the IGCN becomes an invasive germ cell tumor of one type of another.[248a]

2 **IGCN with extratubular extension.** In this category, which also may be called "microinvasive," an interstitial component of atypical germ cells is present, morphologically similar to what is seen within the tubules.[271] It has been shown that the transition from intratubular to invasive testicular germ cell neoplasia is associated with the loss of p21 and gain of mdm-2 expression.[249]

3 **Intratubular seminoma.** In this condition, atypical germ cells indistinguishable from those of seminoma are seen packing the tubules and totally replacing the normal Sertoli and germ cells. This type of neoplasia can be further subdivided into classic, spermatocytic, or with trophoblastic giant cells, using the same cytologic criteria as for the invasive tumors.

4 **Intratubular embryonal carcinoma.** The tubules contain highly malignant cells, identical to those seen in embryonal carcinoma. Foci of central necrosis are common in this lesion.[280]

5 **IGCN, other forms.** The possibility of other forms of germ cell neoplasia being identified in an intratubular phase exists. For instance, Mostofi[273] has described what he interpreted as an intratubular stage of yolk sac tumor and choriocarcinoma. On some occasions, all one sees is a collection of tubules with necrotic cells, often heavily calcified.[261] Azzopardi et al.[246] have convincingly shown that this often represents a burned-out stage of germ cell malignancy.

The obvious question is what to do if a focus of intratubular germ cell neoplasia is found in a testicular biopsy. One approach, based on the figures obtained from the studies mentioned earlier, is the performance of an orchiectomy plus a biopsy of the contralateral testis, if the latter was not already done. The alternative approach, depending on the circumstances, is careful follow-up, with clinical and ultrasonographic examination of the testes and serum determinations of hCG, AFP, and human placental lactogen (hPL). Localized radiation therapy has been administered for IGCN in the contralateral testis of patients who had had an orchiectomy for invasive germ cell tumor.[253]

Germ cell tumors—overview

Incidence. Testicular germ cell tumors make up only a small percentage of all malignant neoplasms but are the most common malignant tumors in young men between 25 and 29 years of age. Their incidence seems to be increasing, at least for the seminomas.[339a]

Predisposing factors. The great importance of cryptorchidism in the genesis of testicular germ cell tumors has already been mentioned (see p. 1414). A few cases of testicular germ cell tumor have occurred in a familial setting,[317,320,351] suggesting a genetic background.[335b] They are also thought to occur with a higher frequency in HIV-infected patients.[322] It has been claimed that multiple cutaneous atypical nevi occur with increased frequency in patients with testicular germ cell tumors and that they could represent a marker for this disease.[356] It has also been suggested that there is a greater than chance association between testicular germ cell tumors and sarcoidosis.[359]

A few cases of testicular germ cell tumors, all of nonseminomatous type, have been reported in association with the splenogonadal fusion syndrome.[326a]

Age. There is a good correlation between age and the incidence of the different types of testicular tumors. The peak is 41.9 years for classic seminoma, 65 years for spermatocytic seminoma, 30.4 years for the different types of NSGCT, and 35.1 years for the combination of seminoma and NSGCT.[303] In prepubertal children, seminomas and combined tumors are rare. Only NSGCT occur with some frequency, notably of the yolk sac tumor and the mature teratoma types.[288] The majority of pure yolk sac tumors occur in infants under 2 years of age.[378] In individuals over 60 years of age, NSGCT are extremely rare. Seminomas, either classic or spermatocytic, are the most common germ cell tumors in this age group, outnumbered only by malignant lymphomas.[289]

Presentation. Most testicular germ cell tumors present with progressive, painless enlargement of the testis. They may grow slowly or with appalling speed. Sometimes, the initial presentation is in the form of a metastatic deposit in the retroperitoneum, lung, or mediastinum. A small tumor may be found in a testis by palpation or ultrasonography. This form of presentation is very rare in seminoma but relatively common in choriocarcinoma, in which the patient may have gynecomastia, large mediastinal and/or pulmonary metastases, and markedly increased levels of serum hCG in the presence of a clinically normal testis.

Bilaterality. Bilateral testicular involvement by germ cell tumors is seen in 1.0% to 2.7% of the cases according to the different series.[292,302a,333,352] The risk of bilaterality rises to 15% if both testes are undescended. It can be seen as a synchronous or, more commonly, as a metachronous event. The tumors may have a different histology,[360] but the most common situation is bilateral spermatocytic or classic seminoma.[363] In the presence of bilateral testicular tumors in an elderly individual, the most likely diagnosis is malignant lymphoma.

DNA ploidy. The majority of testicular germ cell tumors manifest aneuploid DNA contents, with minimal intratumoral heterogeneity.[323] The mean DNA index of seminoma is significantly higher than that of NSGCT.[312,349]

Molecular genetic features. Germ cell tumors are almost always hyperdiploid and are frequently triploid or tetraploid. They have at least one X and one Y chromosome, indicating that the neoplastic transformation did occur before meiotic anaphase.[335a] Mature teratoma of the prepubertal testis is the only testicular germ cell tumor lacking gross chromosomal aberrations.[346]

Germ cell tumors of all other types (including IGCN) are characterized by two chromosome 12 abnormalities: an isochromosome for the short arm [i(12p)] (present in about 80% of cases) and deletions in the long arm [del (12q)].[297,347] These aberrations can be detected in paraffin-embedded tissue with the genetic technique known as interphase chromosome painting.[296] It has been postulated that these deletions represent the loss of one or more tumor suppressor genes whose products regulate the normal proliferation of spermatogonial germ cells. A comparison of the average number of copies of different chromosomes and of protein expression in seminoma and NSGCT has shown a marked similarity. In cases of combined seminoma–NSGCT in which the two components were evaluated separately from a genetic standpoint, some showed similar clonal abnormalities (suggesting an origin from the same stem cell) whereas others did not.[307,329a,376]

The role of *p53* in testicular germ cell neoplasia remains unclear. Although a certain number of cases exhibit mutations of this gene,[332,374] it would seem that the overexpression of the p53 protein that is the rule in these tumors is mainly of the wild type.[321]

Telomerase activity is present in all types of testicular germ cell tumors except for mature teratomas, a finding consistent with the expectation that there should be an inverse relationship between the level of this enzyme and the differentiation stage of the tumors.[290,308]

Cyclin E has a higher expression in embryonal carcinoma than in other NSGCTs and it also correlates with the tumor stage.[304]

Fas gene mutations are common, especially in embryonal carcinoma.[370a]

As expected, the expression of some genes that control cellular differentiation is related to the microscopic type of germ cell tumor.[290a]

Spread and metastases. It has been generally assumed that the first manifestation of local spread of testicular germ cell tumors is in the tunica albuginea, but invasion of the testicular hilum is actually a much more common event. Since this may be grossly inapparent, microscopic sampling of this region is mandatory.[310] Pagetoid spread of the tumor into the rete testis is discussed on p. 1458,[337] and spread into the spermatic cord (prone to be over-diagnosed because of specimen contamination)[348] is discussed on p. 1462.

In terms of lymph-borne metastases, testicular tumors spread first to periaortic and iliac lymph nodes and later to mediastinal and left supraclavicular nodes. Retroperitoneal lymph node metastases are on the side of the tumor in about 80% to 86% of cases and bilateral in about 13% to 20%. The presence of contralateral metastases in the absence of ipsilateral metastases is rare.[309,358] Characteristically, the first retroperitoneal metastases are highly placed, immediately below the renal vessels. In general, involvement of inguinal lymph nodes does not occur unless there is invasion of the skin of the scrotum, tumor recurrence in a cutaneous scar, or a history of previous operation in the area (such as correction of cryptorchidism, herniorrhaphy, or scrotal orchiectomy).[330] Blood-borne metastases occur most frequently in lungs, liver, brain, and bone.[357] There is a high incidence of brain metastases in choriocarcinoma and of bone metastases in seminoma.[300] Embryonal carcinoma frequently metastasizes early, and choriocarcinoma almost always has widespread metastases by the time the tumor is diagnosed. Mature teratoma occurring in the postpuberal testis can be accompanied by metastases no matter how well differentiated the primary tumor is. Conversely, mature teratoma of the prepubertal testis has never been shown to metastasize. Pure yolk sac tumors occurring in infants or children metastasize to periaortic or other lymph node groups only rarely,[378] whereas yolk sac tumor of adults combined with other NSGCT patterns metastasizes to these sites frequently.

The microscopic appearance of the metastases may differ from that of the primary tumor. Teratocarcinoma often metastasizes as embryonal carcinoma, and the reverse also occurs.[294] In general, classic seminoma metastasizes as classic seminoma, but it may also spread as embryonal carcinoma or choriocarcinoma.[300] In combined seminoma–NSGCT, the latter component is the one most likely to metastasize. Late metastases of testicular germ cell tumors often have a teratomatous appearance.[343] Mixed germ cell tumors with focal choriocarcinoma tend to metastasize as pure choriocarcinomas. Mature teratomas may give rise to metastases with the appearance of teratocarcinoma, whereas teratocarcinomas may be accompanied by completely mature metastases[324,344,366] (Fig. 18.86). The latter phenomenon, which occurs commonly in the retroperitoneal lymph nodes but also in the lungs,[306,368,369] has been explained by postulating in situ maturation of foci that were originally immature or anaplastic; it seems to be more common after chemotherapy, possibly as a result of selective destruction of the anaplastic components in tumors that have an inherent capacity for differentiation.[339] Indeed, sometimes the entire mass has a necrotic appearance (Fig. 18.87). Surgical removal of the postchemotherapy residual tumors is recommended.[354,364,367] In some instances, total spontaneous regression of the primary tumor or of the metastatic foci has been observed.[295,313] Sometimes, tumor foci with a "somatic" (rather than germ cell) appearance develop in these metastases. These include adenocarcinoma (occasionally having a clear cell appearance because of the abundance of cytoplasmic glycogen[326]), various forms of sarcoma,[341] and tumors with a blastomatous appearance, including some having a striking resemblance to Wilms' tumors (endowed with tubules, blastema, stroma, and sometimes even glomeruli).[342]

Fig. 18.86 Retroperitoneal metastasis of NSGCT. The mass is entirely composed of mature tissue, whereas the primary tumor had the features of a teratocarcinoma.

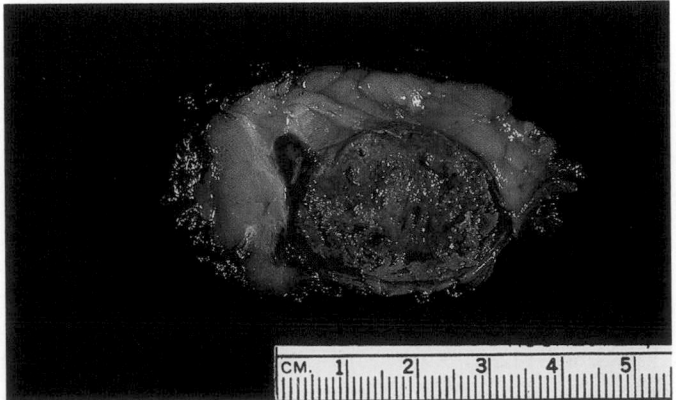

Fig. 18.87 Entirely necrotic retroperitoneal metastasis of NSGCT following chemotherapy.

The microscopic appearance of the lung metastases after chemotherapy correlates well with prognosis. The presence of total necrosis or fully mature elements is indicative of a good prognosis[336,350,354] (Fig. 18.88); viable immature or undifferentiated components are associated with a decreased survival, and the presence of sarcomatous elements is a particularly ominous sign.[372,373]

Treatment. The initial treatment for all testicular germ cell tumors is inguinal orchiectomy with high ligation of the spermatic cord ("radical orchiectomy").[365] The findings on pathologic examination determine the subsequent course. Patients with classic seminoma receive irradiation of the retroperitoneal and ipsilateral pelvic lymph nodes whether there is clinical or radiographic evidence of metastases or not.[299,301,325] Chemotherapy is given only to patients presenting with advanced disease or who have relapse after radiation therapy.[299,319,340] Until better information about the definition and natural history of anaplastic seminoma becomes available, it would seem appropriate to treat this tumor in the same fashion as classic seminoma. Whether to treat patients with spermatocytic seminoma with orchiectomy alone or to combine it with irradiation remains controversial.

The treatment of stages I and II NSGCT is controversial and constantly changing because of continuous advances in monitoring and chemotherapy. Depending on the institution, orchiectomy may be followed by retroperitoneal lymphadenectomy, radiation therapy, chemotherapy, a combination of them, or surveillance.[297,335,370,375] In the United States, the preference has been for nerve-sparing lymphadenectomy (with or without chemotherapy),[293,316] but some groups have recommended treating stage I seminoma or NSGCT with orchiectomy alone, with further therapy for only those cases that show relapse on close monitoring.[311,314,318,353] Along similar lines, it has been suggested that stage II NSGCT could be treated with orchiectomy and retroperitoneal lymphadenectomy, with chemotherapy reserved for those patients who develop relapse.[362,377] The

"surveillance only" approach is not indicated in cases with a predominance of the embryonal carcinoma pattern or in tumors exhibiting blood vessel invasion because of the high probability of distant metastases under these circumstances.[371]

The incidence of retroperitoneal spread in pure yolk sac tumors of infants is too low to justify a lymphadenectomy.[302] Similarly, mature teratomas occurring in infants or children should be treated by orchiectomy alone.

An increased incidence of sarcoma has been documented in patients with germ cell tumors treated with radiation therapy, with most of the sarcomas being located within the radiation field.[328]

Prognosis. At present, over 90% of patients with newly diagnosed germ cell tumors are cured.[299] The prognosis varies widely according to the clinical stage (see Appendix C) and tumor type.[315,331,361] It is excellent for classic seminoma. Over 95% of the patients with disease clinically limited to the testis (stage I) or to subdiaphragmatic lymph nodes (stage II) can be cured. It is even better for spermatocytic seminoma,[363] which practically never metastasizes.

In cases of NSGCT other than choriocarcinoma without clinically demonstrable lymph node involvement, the cure rate is over 95%, whether the patients are treated with retroperitoneal irradiation[375] or lymph node dissection[329]; in cases with metastatic disease, the current cure rate ranges from 40% to 95%. If restricted pulmonary metastases occur, 40% of patients may still be saved by radical pulmonary irradiation.[375] Extensive pulmonary disease is associated with a poor prognosis. Remarkable strides have been made in the chemotherapy of NSGCT, so cure is now possible even in stage III disease. Unfortunately, choriocarcinoma often remains a fatal disease. In yolk sac tumors, the prognosis is directly related to the age of the patient at the time of surgery: excellent for infants and children (in whom the tumor is usually pure) and similar to that of the other NSGCT in adults. In combined seminoma–NSGCT, the prognosis is related to the nature of the nonseminomatous component.

An International Germ Cell Cancer Collaborative Group, after evaluating almost 6000 cases of testicular germ cell tumors, identified the following *independent* prognostic factors: degree of elevation of hCG, AFP, and LDH, and presence of nonpulmonary visceral metastases.[327]

Morphologic factors that adversely influence the prognosis of testicular tumors, regardless of type, are extension of the tumor through the tunica vaginalis and into the spermatic cord, and vascular invasion.[291,338,345,355] In seminomas, the absence of lymphoid stroma is said to be a poor prognostic sign. Tumor size does not appear to correlate with metastatic rate.[355]

A very important tool in the monitoring of testicular germ cell tumor is the use of serum markers—largely hCG and AFP—for the purposes of diagnosis and selection of therapy.[298,305] hCG is elevated in about 72%

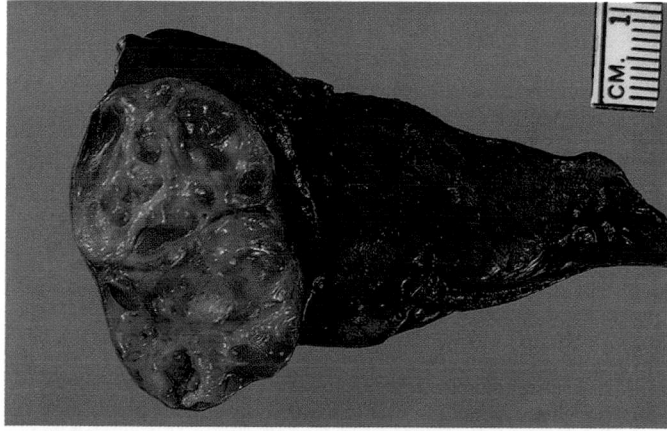

Fig. 18.88 Lung metastasis of NSGCT following chemotherapy. The mass was entirely composed of mature tissues.

and AFP in 75% of patients with NSGCT. The levels drop to normal values after successful therapy but reappear with tumor recurrence.[334]

Sex cord–stromal tumors

Leydig cell tumor and related lesions

Leydig (interstitial) cell tumors comprise between 1% and 3% of all testicular tumors. About 3% are bilateral, either synchronously or metachronously.[404] A few have been described in cryptorchid testes and others in patients with Klinefelter's syndrome. In rare cases, they occur in patients with a germ cell tumor in the contralateral testis, either synchronously or metachronously.[386] They may produce endocrine changes because of increased production of androgens and/or estrogens.[388,389] Most occur in adults, with a palpable testicular mass and gynecomastia being the most common symptoms. The few that occur in childhood cause precocious

pseudopuberty, with growth of pubic hair and penis but without spermatocytic maturation in the non-neoplastic testis (hence the prefix *pseudo*); these symptoms usually regress after removal of the tumor.[381]

Grossly, Leydig cell tumor presents as a generally small (average size, 3 cm), sharply delimited solid nodule embedded within the testicle (Fig. 18.89). The brown color it usually exhibits is one of its most distinguishing gross features. In rare cases Leydig cell tumor or other gonadal stromal tumors are found outside the testis proper.[397]

Microscopically, the tumor cells have well-defined outlines, deeply acidophilic but occasionally clear cytoplasm, and a round or oval (occasionally grooved) nucleus (Figs 18.90 and 18.91). Some of the cells have a plasmacytoid appearance. Lipochrome pigment and Reinke's crystalloids are sometimes present, the latter well demonstrated with Masson's trichrome stain. As with most other endocrine tumors, marked variation in

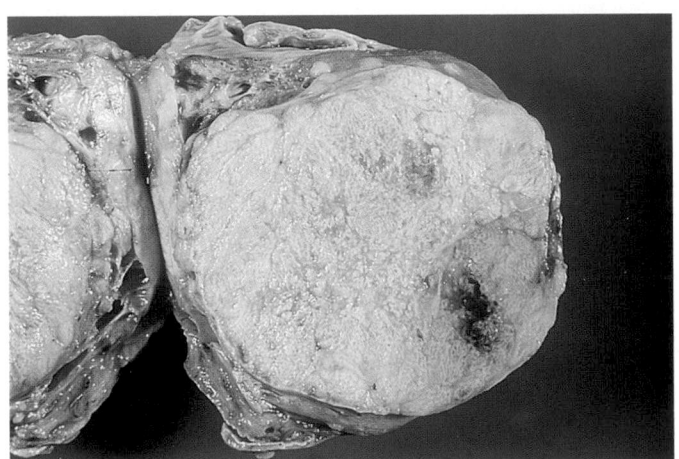
A

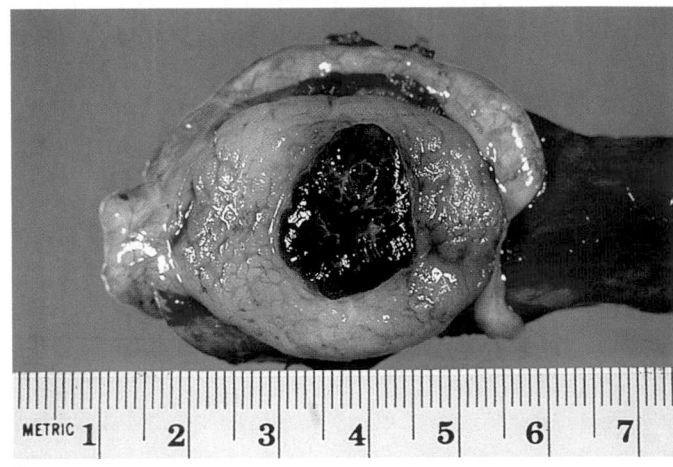
B

Fig. 18.89 Gross appearance of Leydig cell tumor. **A,** The tumor, which has replaced most of the testis, has a granular yellowish appearance. **B,** This tumor, occurring in a child, is solid, well circumscribed, and dark brown.

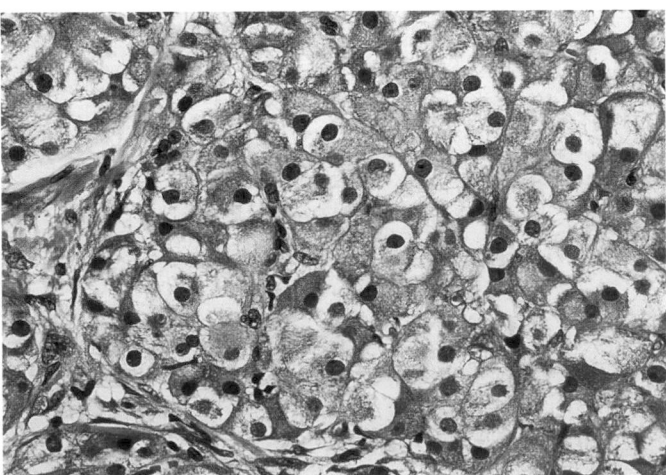

Fig. 18.90 Leydig cell tumor of testis. The neoplasm is characterized by solid growth of polygonal cells with abundant granular acidophilic cytoplasm.

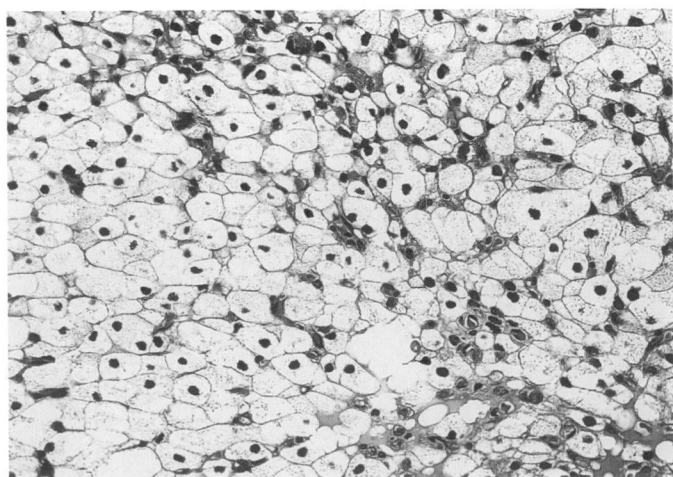

Fig. 18.91 Leydig cell tumor of testis. The tumor cells have a cytoplasmic clear quality, reminiscent of that seen in tumors of the adrenal cortex.

the size and shape of the tumor cells may occur, with the presence of bizarre forms with giant nuclei. The pattern of growth is generally solid, but trabecular, myxoid, pseudofollicular, and microcystic formations can be present[382,392] (Fig. 18.92). Occasionally, there is prominent spindling of tumor cells metaplastic ossification or adipose metaplasia.[380,402,404a] Ultrastructurally, the cells contain abundant smooth endoplasmic reticulum and mitochondria with tubulovesicular cristae, two features common to all steroid-producing cells[403] (Fig. 18.93); rarely, Reinke's crystalloids are identified (Fig. 18.93). On occasion, the ultrastructural appearance is reminiscent of fetal-type Leydig cells.[387] Immunohistochemically, various steroid hormones have been demonstrated in the cytoplasm, although with some difficulty.[394] Vimentin and S-100 protein are also expressed.[385,400]

The markers that have proved to be of the greatest utility for the evaluation of these tumors are inhibin and Mart-1 (also known as Melan-A and detected with the antibody A103).[379,383,399]

An activating mutation of the gene encoding the luteinizing hormone receptor has been detected in a case of Leydig cell tumor.[395]

About one tenth of all Leydig cell tumors show evidence of malignant behavior in the form of metastatic disease, particularly to lymph nodes, lung, and liver.[396] Malignant Leydig cell tumors occur exclusively in adults, are usually unaccompanied by endocrine changes, are larger than the benign variety (average size, 7.5 cm), are more commonly infiltrative, and tend to exhibit necrosis, blood vessel invasion, nuclear atypia, numerous mitoses, and lack of lipochrome pigment. Sarcomatoid (spindle cell) changes can be present in the metastatic foci.[391]

Metastasizing Leydig cell tumors have a higher MIB-1 index and a much higher incidence of aneuploidy than their non-metastasizing counterparts.[384,398]

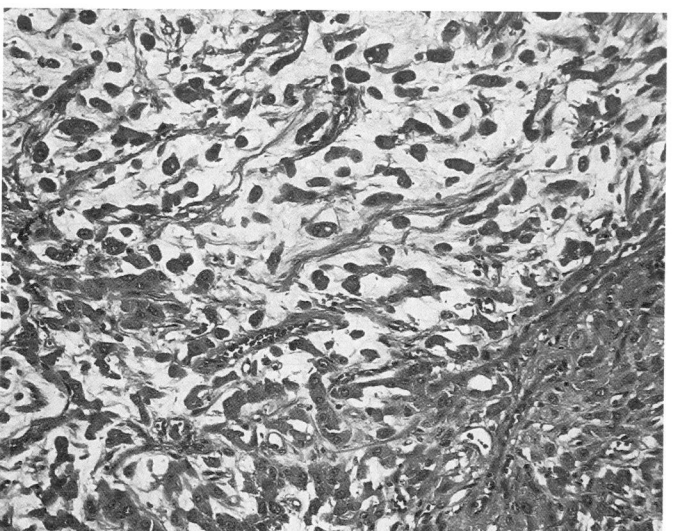

Fig. 18.92 Leydig cell tumor with myxoid features.

Leydig cell tumors are usually treated with simple orchiectomy. Malignant tumors may need retroperitoneal node dissection; some metastatic tumors have responded to o,p-DDD, a drug that is also occasionally effective with adrenal cortical carcinoma, another steroid-producing neoplasm.

The differential diagnosis of Leydig cell tumor includes the following conditions:

1 *Nodular Leydig cell hyperplasia*, as seen in cryptorchid testes and other conditions. The distinction is made on the basis of size (over 0.5 cm for the tumors) and the fact that, whereas nodular hyperplasia is characteristically multiple, true Leydig cell tumors are not accompanied by hyperplasia of Leydig cells in the remaining testis.[390]

2 *Large cell calcifying Sertoli cell tumor*, which may have a component with a Leydig cell-like appearance (see p. 1440).

3 *Testicular "tumor" of the adrenogenital syndrome.* This perhaps constitutes the most important and difficult differential diagnosis. This lesion is usually discovered during early adult life as a palpable mass; examples in children tend to be smaller and found incidentally. The adrenogenital syndrome is of the "salt-forming type" in two thirds of cases. The testicular masses are usually bilateral and located at the hilum. Grossly, they are well-circumscribed brown–green masses that are separated into lobules by prominent fibrous bands.[400] Microscopically, there are sheets, nests, and cords of cells with abundant eosinophilic cytoplasm (Fig. 18.94); these cells may contain lipochrome pigment, but Reinke's crystalloids are absent. Bilaterality of the lesions, associated clinical and laboratory features, and therapeutic response (decrease in size after corticosteroid therapy) are the most important features distinguishing these lesions—which may represent nodular hyperplasias of ectopic adrenal cortical cells rather than true neoplasms—from Leydig cell tumors.[393,400]

4 *Yolk sac tumor.* This is true for the cases of Leydig cell tumors exhibiting a prominent microcystic pattern of growth.[382]

Tumors and tumorlike conditions of Sertoli cells

Sertoli cell tumors and tumorlike conditions form a complex and poorly understood group of proliferative disorders composed of cells with morphologic features of Sertoli cells or related specialized gonadal stromal cells.[431]

Areas of **Sertoli cell hyperplasia** (also known as *hypoplastic tubules, dysgenetic zones*, and *tubular adenomas*) are seen in half of patients with cryptorchid testes, a finding that suggests that maldescent is a manifestation of abnormal sexual maturation. However, they have also been found in 20% of the non-neoplastic testes in patients with testicular tumors[425] and in about the same

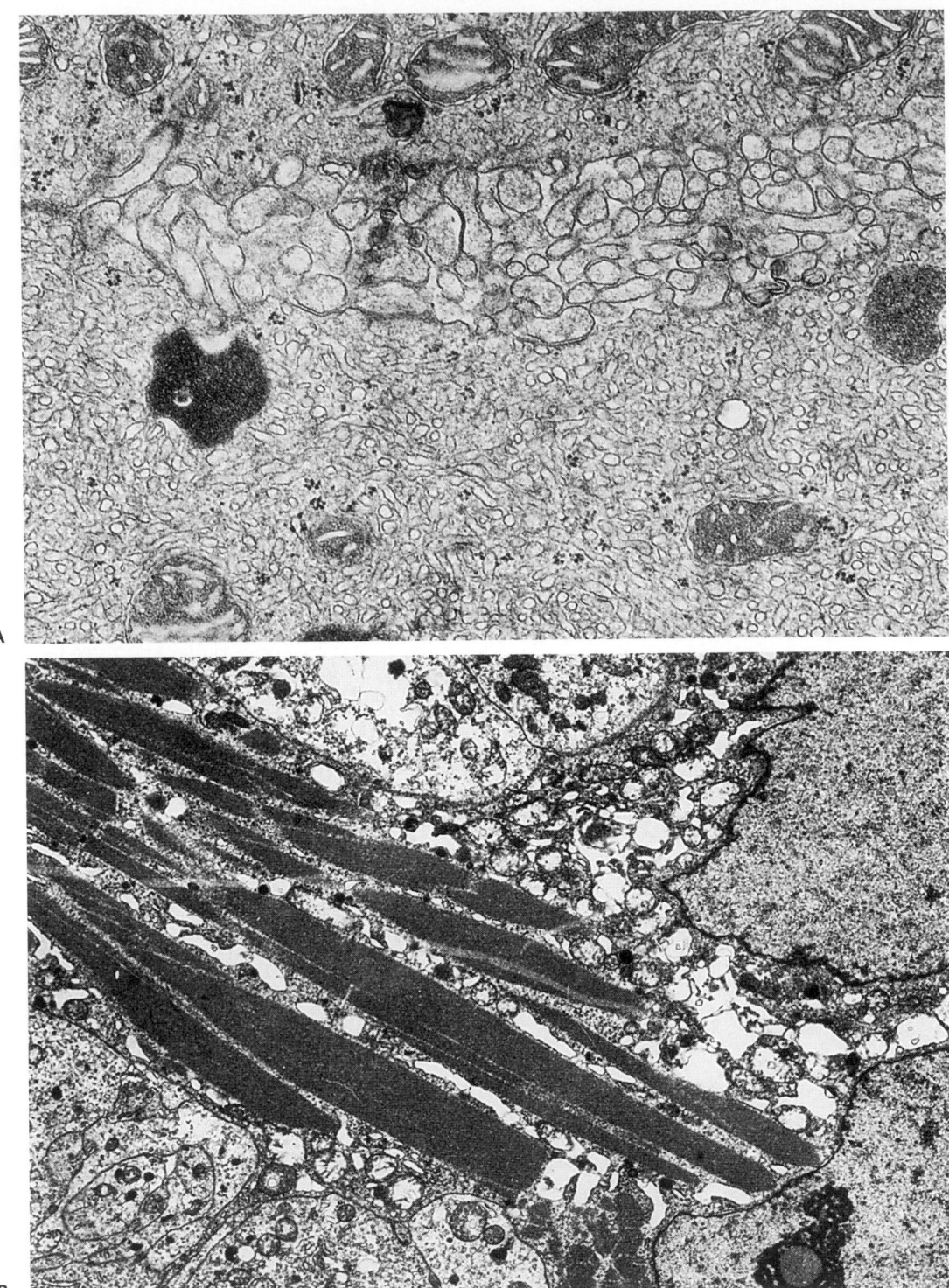

A

B

Fig. 18.93 Ultrastructural appearance of Leydig cell tumor. **A**, These steroid-producing cells contain prominent smooth endoplasmic reticulum. Cytoplasmic microvilli fill the intercellular space. **B**, Numerous Reinke's crystalloids are seen in the cytoplasm of a tumor cell. (Courtesy of Dr. J.H. Lin, East Meadow, NY)

proportion in an autopsy study of scrotal, otherwise normal testes; the frequency of these foci decreases with age.[409]

Sertoli cell adenomas are not uncommon in patients with the testicular feminization (androgen insensitivity) syndrome.[415,417,418] Microscopically, they are composed of elongated tubules lined by Sertoli-like cells (Fig. 18.95). A closely related tumor arising in patients with this background and in patients with the Peutz–Jeghers syndrome has morphologic features resembling those of the ovarian tumor known as *sex cord tumor with annular tubules*.[422,433] The Sertoli cell proliferations seen in children with

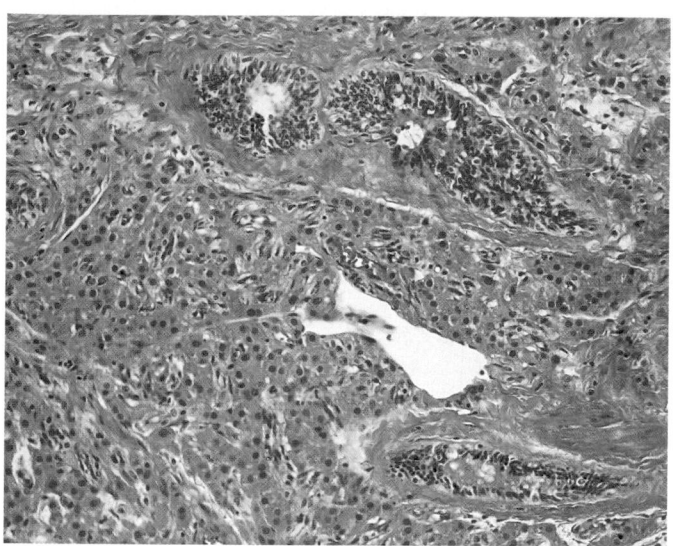

Fig.18.94 So-called "testicular tumor" of the adrenogenital syndrome. Multiple nodules are present, having an appearance compatible with adrenal cortical origin.

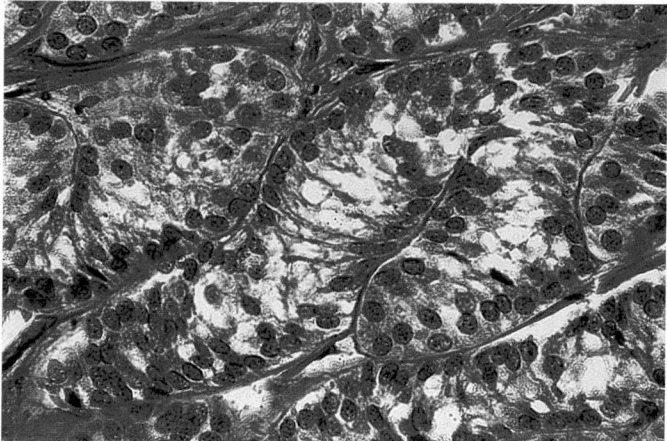

Fig. 18.95 Sertoli cell adenoma in a patient with testicular feminization syndrome.

Peutz–Jeghers syndrome are often multicentric and bilateral. It is not clear whether these represent nodular hyperplasias of Sertoli cells or intratubular forms of Sertoli cell tumor.[430]

Sertoli cell tumors (NOS, not otherwise specified) arise in the descended testis of normal individuals, and are sometimes associated with gynecomastia.[411,412,432] Grossly, the tumors are well circumscribed, white or yellow, and firm, with focal cystic areas. Microscopically, the diagnostic feature is the presence of tubular formations lined by elongated cells having the appearance of Sertoli cells. In other areas, the tumor is solid and can be confused with seminoma. The cytoplasm is moderate to abundant, with a pale to intense eosinophilic quality. Large cytoplasmic vacuoles are present in about half of the cases.[432] It seems likely that the testicular tumors reported as *androblastomas*[428] and as *tumors of specialized gonadal stroma*[416] belong to the same or a closely related category, the Sertoli cell features not being immediately apparent in some of them. When this is the case, terms such as *sex cord–stromal tumor* or *gonadal stromal tumor, not otherwise specified*, may be appropriate.[414] Exceptionally, Sertoli cell tumors are accompanied by a heterologous sarcomatous component[407] (Fig. 18.96). Immunohistochemically, Sertoli cell tumors show reactivity for vimentin, keratin, α_1-antitrypsin, and neuron-specific enolase.[413] Diagnostically more significant is their frequent positivity for inhibin, CD99, and anti-müllerian hormone, the latter substance being allegedly produced only by Sertoli cells and granulosa cells.[408,423] They are instead negative for PLAP and CD117 (c-kit).

About one tenth of Sertoli cell tumors behave in a malignant fashion, the most common site of metastatic involvement being the iliac and para-aortic lymph

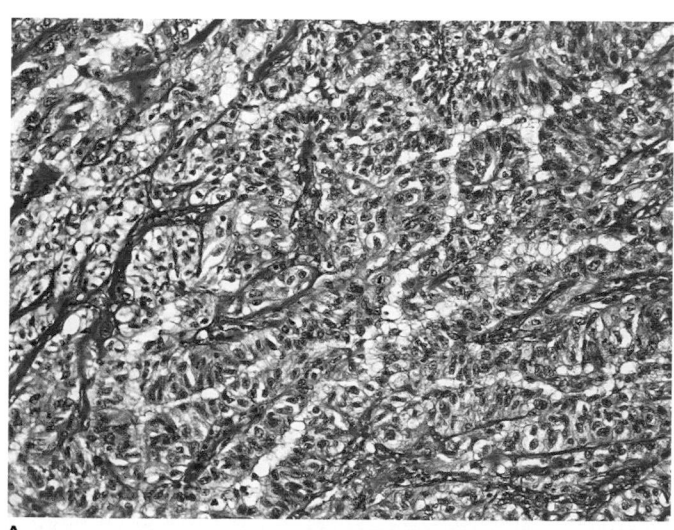

A

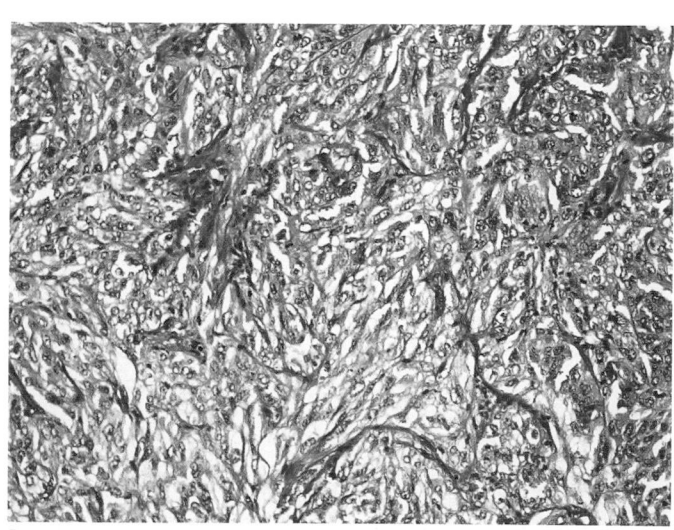

B

Fig. 18.96 A and B, Sertoli cell adenoma with sarcomatoid features. The latter are particularly evident in photograph **B**, whereas the Sertoli cell nature of the tumor is more apparent in **A**.

nodes.[426] Features that should raise the suspicion of malignancy in Sertoli cell tumors include mitotic figures, pleomorphism, large tumor size, and necrosis, particularly when occurring together.[413] Parenthetically, misinterpretation of a Sertoli cell tumor as seminoma is more likely to occur in these malignant forms.[410] The treatment of Sertoli cell tumor is orchiectomy. Surgical excision of metastatic lesions—when present—is recommended, inasmuch as radiation therapy and chemotherapy have not proved particularly effective.[413]

Sclerosing Sertoli cell tumor represents a distinct variant of this tumor type.[434] The patients are adults, and there is no evidence of estrogen production by the tumor. Grossly, they tend to be small, well-demarcated, hard, and yellow–white to tan. Microscopically, they are formed of simple and anastomosing tubules (some containing lumina), large nests, and thin cords of Sertoli cells in a prominent fibrohyaline background[424] (Fig. 18.97). No malignant behavior has been observed in any of the reported cases.[434]

Large cell calcifying Sertoli cell tumor is usually seen in patients under 20 years of age and is often part of the Carney syndrome, which may also include testicular Leydig cell tumors, pituitary tumors, pigmented nodular hyperplasia of the adrenal cortex, cardiac myxomas, spotty pigmentation of skin, and other abnormalities.[406,421] Bilaterality and multifocality are very common (Fig. 18.98). Microscopically, this lesion is characterized by sheets, cords, and solid tubules of cells with abundant acidophilic cytoplasm, separated by abundant fibrous tissue that contains large areas of calcification (Fig. 18.99).[419] Ultrastructurally, the features are those of Sertoli cells, including the presence of Charcot–Bottcher crystalloids.[405,420,429] Immunoreactivity for both the alpha and beta subunits of S-100 protein is the rule, a feature that may be functionally related to the characteristic calcification of this tumor (S-100 is a calcium-binding protein) and which represents a useful tool in the differential diagnosis with Leydig cell tumor.[427]

Other sex cord–stromal tumors

Some neoplasms belonging to this category have an appearance analogous to that of the adult or the juvenile forms of ovarian **granulosa cell tumor**.[443,446] The *adult* form, which is the more common, presents as a testicular mass without evidence of endocrine function, although isolated examples of gynecomastia are on record.[444] The pattern of growth may be solid, cystic, microfollicular, gyriform, circular, or trabecular, as in the ovarian counterpart[441] (Fig. 18.100). Similarly, Call–Exner bodies may be present. Immunohistochemically, there is reactivity for vimentin, inhibin, Mart-1 (Melan-A), and keratins 8 and 18, but not for EMA.[439] Steroid hormone receptors have been detected in the tumor cells.[439] Metastases have occurred in about 10% of the reported cases.[441]

The *juvenile* form occurs in infants younger than 6

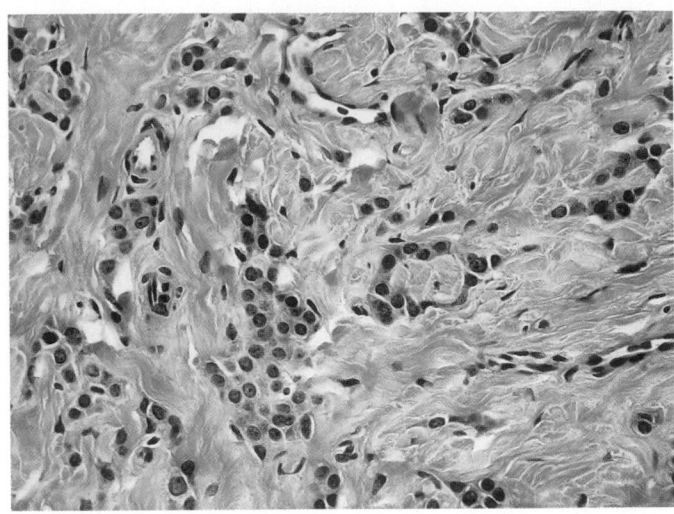

Fig. 18.97 Microscopic appearance of sclerosing Sertoli cell tumor.

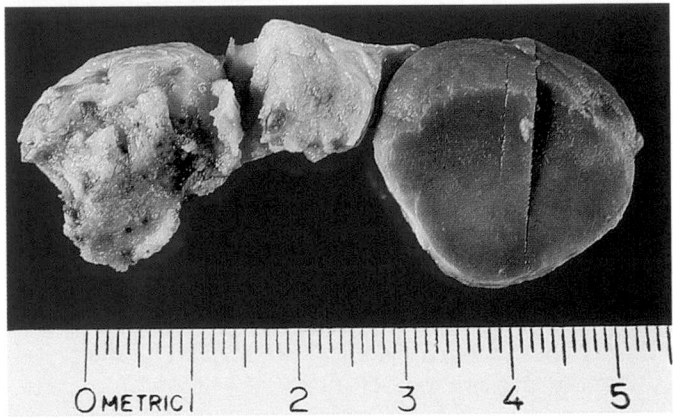

Fig. 18.98 Gross appearance of large cell calcifying Sertoli cell tumor of testis. The tumor is distinctly multinodular. The dark nodules had a prominent component of Leydig cells.

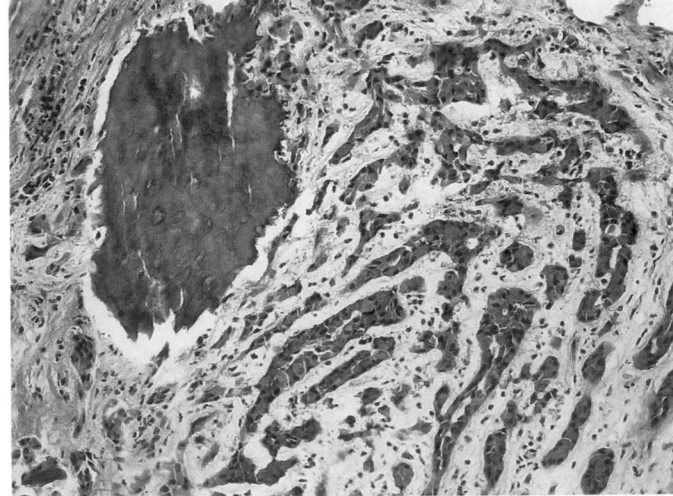

Fig. 18.99 Large cell calcifying Sertoli cell tumor.

months of age, and it may even be congenital[437,440] (Fig. 18.101). It is sometimes associated with cytogenetic abnormalities affecting the Y chromosome and with ambiguous genitalia.[452,455] Some of the tumors have developed in

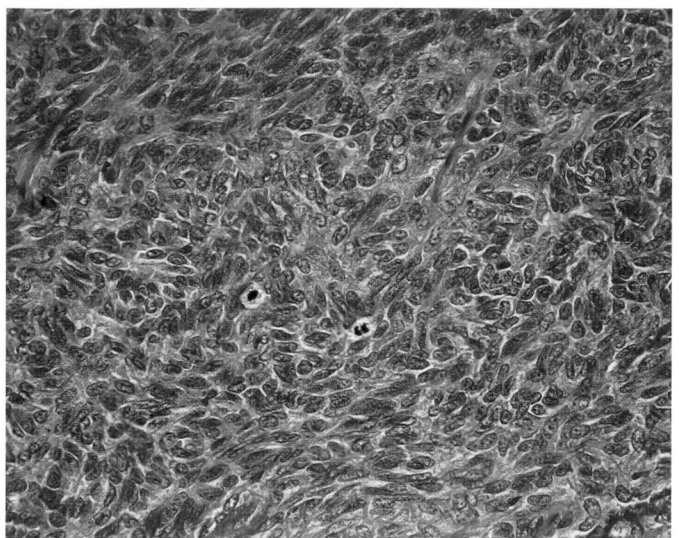

Fig. 18.100 Adult form of granulosa cell tumor involving testis. Note the occasional longitudinal grooves, the oval to spindle shape of the tumor cells, and the high mitotic activity.

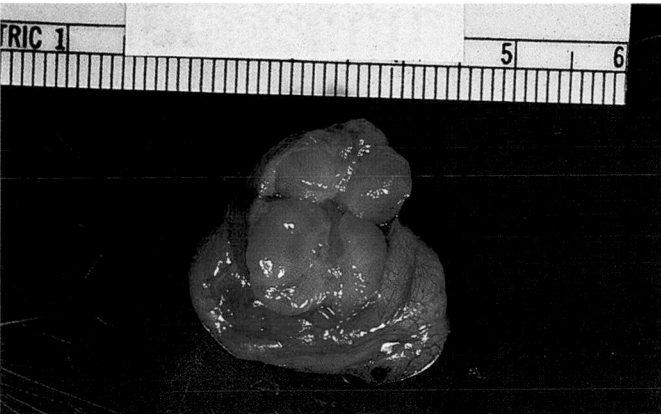

Fig. 18.101 Gross appearance of a juvenile granulosa cell tumor involving the testis of an infant.

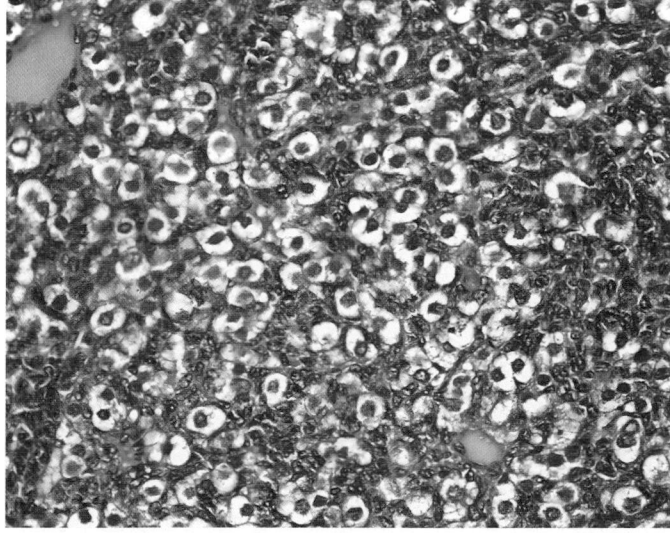

Fig. 18.102 Mixed germ cell–stromal tumor of the testis. This lesion is distinct from gonadoblastoma.

undescended testes. Evidence of dual differentiation along epithelial and smooth muscle lines has been found in these tumors at the ultrastructural and immunohistochemical level.[449]

Fibroma of gonadal stromal origin with an appearance similar to that of its vastly more common ovarian counterpart can occur in the testis and needs to be distinguished from fibroma of the testicular tunica.[442] Some of these tumors are grossly yellow–white, i.e., akin to ovarian fibrothecomas. Still others are analogous to the *ovarian fibroma with minor sex cord elements.*[438]

Other **spindle sex cord–stromal tumors** of the testis have a mesenchymal-like appearance at the light microscopic level but exhibit epithelial markers at the immunohistochemical level (sometimes associated with S-100 protein expression).[445,447,450,453] We have seen a case in which the spindle cells merged with islands of squamous epithelium.

As an aside, it could be mentioned that there are also testicular and paratesticular counterparts of ovarian tumors of surface epithelial derivation, including serous, mucinous, endometrioid, and clear cell cystoma, as well as Brenner types[435,436,448,451,452a,454] (see p. 1461).

Mixed germ cell–sex cord–stromal tumors

The better known member of this group is **gonadoblastoma**, a tumor that arises nearly always in individuals with an underlying gonadal disorder, either pure or mixed gonadal dysgenesis, or male pseudohermaphroditism,[458] and which is fully discussed in Chapter 20. Some cases, however, have developed in the testis of phenotypically and karyotypically normal males. Mixed germ cell–sex cord–stromal tumors with a morphology different from gonadoblastoma also exist[456,457] (Fig. 18.102). However, one should be careful not to misinterpret sex cord–stromal tumors of the testis with entrapped germ cells as mixed germ cell–sex cord–stromal tumors.[459]

Malignant lymphoma and related tumors

Malignant lymphoma comprises 5% of all testicular malignancies. It is the most common testicular tumor in elderly persons, but it can occur in any age group, including children.[466,474] It has a much greater tendency for bilaterality than germ cell tumors; as a matter of fact, about 50% of cases of bilateral testicular tumors are malignant lymphomas.[470]

Nearly all cases are of non-Hodgkin's type. By far the most common variety is diffuse large B-cell lymphoma, but small lymphocytic lymphoma and anaplastic large cell lymphoma (including the neutrophil-rich variety of the latter) NK/T-cell lymphoma, and intravascular (angiotropic) lymphoma[480a,480b] also occur.[460,462,464,481,482]

Grossly, large cell lymphoma results in a solid homogeneous replacement of the testicular parenchyma not too dissimilar from that of seminoma (Fig. 18.103). Microscopically, there is a predominantly interstitial

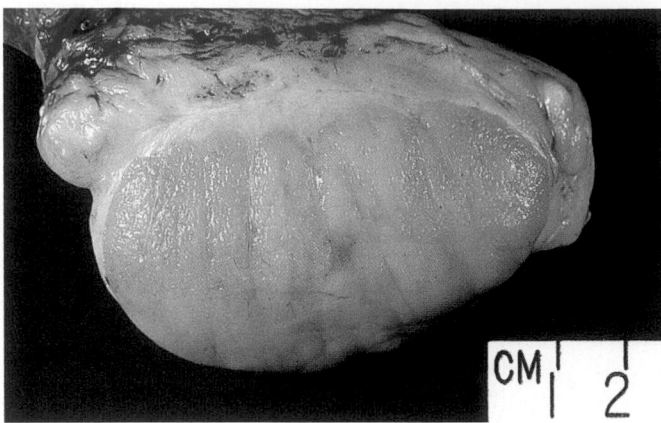

Fig. 18.103 Gross appearance of malignant lymphoma of large cell type, which completely replaces the testis.

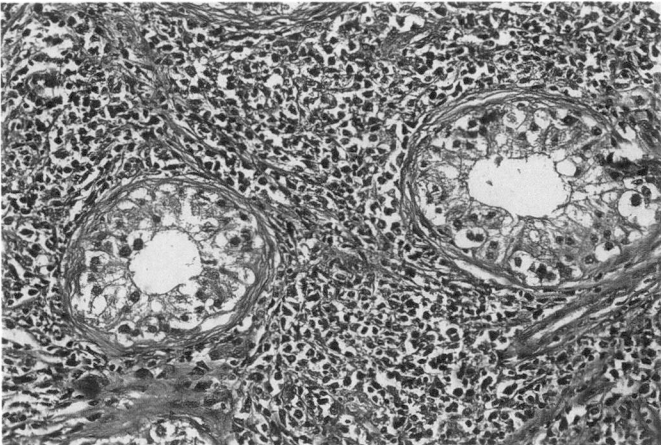

Fig. 18.104 Malignant lymphoma of testis. There is diffuse infiltration of the interstitium by neoplastic lymphocytes, which surround and separate atrophic tubules.

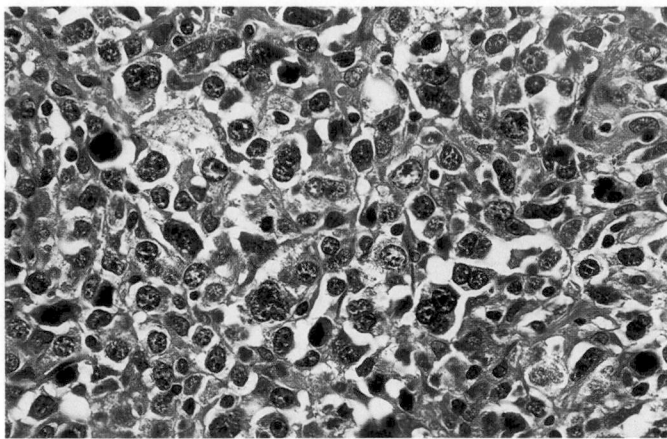

Fig. 18.105 Cases of large B-cell lymphoma with pleomorphic features such as that depicted in this photograph can be misdiagnosed as anaplastic or spermatocytic seminoma.

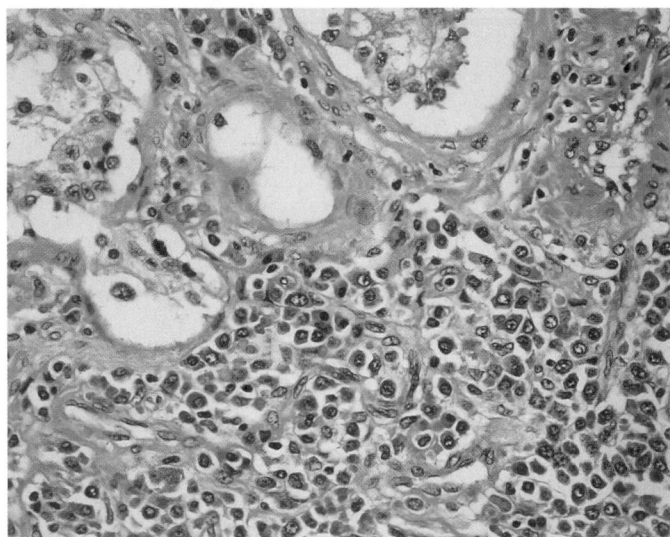

Fig. 18.106 Testicular involvement by granulocytic sarcoma. Most of the cells present in the interstitium are myeloid precursors.

proliferation of large tumor cells that surrounds and infiltrates the seminiferous tubules (Fig. 18.104). The presence of scattered malignant cells within the tubular epithelium should not be confused with intratubular germ cell neoplasia. There is a high incidence of vascular invasion.[477] Testicular lymphomas are sometimes misdiagnosed as spermatocytic or "anaplastic" seminomas, and anaplastic large cell lymphomas may be misinterpreted as embryonal carcinomas[464] (Fig. 18.105). Immunohistochemical (and, if needed, molecular) evaluation should establish the correct diagnosis without much difficulty.[469]

Diffuse large cell lymphoma of the testis is treated with orchiectomy and chemotherapy, sometimes combined with radiation therapy.[467] Nearly half of the patients are found to have systemic disease at the time of diagnosis and their prognosis is poor.[478,480] A high proportion of relapses occur in the CNS or contralateral testis.[467,480,483]

Plasmacytoma of testis may be seen as a manifestation of multiple myeloma or as an isolated lesion.[476] The latter is by far the most common situation, even if the testicular involvement may be the first clinical manifestation of the disease.[465,473]

Leukemic involvement of the testis is more commonly seen with lymphocytic leukemia, but it also may occur in the myelocytic types[468] (Fig. 18.106). It is not uncommon for the latter to be initially misdiagnosed as large cell lymphoma.[463] Children with acute lymphocytic leukemia develop clinical evidence of testicular involvement in about 8% of cases,[479] but the microscopic rate of involvement is over 20%.[471] Often the testis represents the first sign of relapse after bone marrow remission.[475] Assistance for the identification of residual disease can be obtained by the use of specific immunomarkers.[461] The diagnosis can be established by testicular needle biopsy. Radiotherapy is very effective in controlling the testicular involvement, but bone marrow relapse will develop in most cases.[472]

Other tumors

Carcinoid tumors in the testis may be seen as a component of a germ cell tumor (usually mature cystic teratoma), as a primary neoplasm arising from autochthonous neuroendocrine cells, or as a metastasis from a gastrointestinal tumor[487,492,508] (Fig. 18.107). Some of the reported cases have been in children.[497] The primary tumors present as well-circumscribed, solid masses of firm consistency and yellow to yellow–brown color.[486]

The tumor cells are argyrophil and sometimes argentaffin; they exhibit dense-core secretory granules ultrastructurally and contain serotonin, neuron-specific enolase, chromogranin, synaptophysin and various peptide hormones on immunocytochemical staining.[501,512] Most of them have been cured by orchiectomy, and they are usually not associated with the carcinoid syndrome.

Hemangioma and **hemangioendothelioma** can present as intratesticular masses both in children and adults. The varieties that have been reported include capillary (which can be multifocal), cavernous, and epithelioid (histiocytoid).[495,506,507] The latter needs to be distinguished from adenomatoid tumor.[484,493]

Juvenile xanthogranuloma can present as an intratesticular mass in children.[504]

Primary sarcoma of the testis is rare, both in children and in adults. Fibrosarcomas, leiomyosarcomas, Kaposi's sarcomas, angiosarcomas, osteosarcomas, and chondrosarcomas have been reported[491,499,510,514] (Fig. 18.108). In the presence of a tumor of sarcomatous appearance involving the testis of an infant, the possibility of sarcomatous transformation of a spermatocytic seminoma or a Sertoli cell tumor should be entertained (see corresponding sections).

Dendritic/reticulum cell tumor has been reported in the testis, its phenotypical features corresponding to the interdigitating dendritic cell subtype.[498]

Metastatic tumors in the testicle arise for the most part in the lung, prostate, kidney, stomach, or skin (melanoma) (Fig. 18.109).[485,488,489,500,502,509] It is very rare for them to be the first clinical sign of disease.[489,494] Historically, those originating in the prostate have usually been incidental findings in orchiectomy specimens[496] (Fig. 18.110).

The microscopic diagnosis is usually easy, but sometimes the tumor simulates the appearance of a primary sex cord–stromal tumor, particularly Leydig cell tumor; in case of doubt, stains for prostatic acid phosphatase or PSA should settle the issue. Secondary prostatic carcinoma in the testis appears to be associated with a better prognosis than secondary prostatic carcinoma in the penis.[511] Metastatic Merkel cell tumors to the testis can be confused with malignant lymphoma.[503] Metastatic signet ring carcinoma from the gastrointestinal tract may acquire features analogous to those of ovarian Krukenberg tumor.[513]

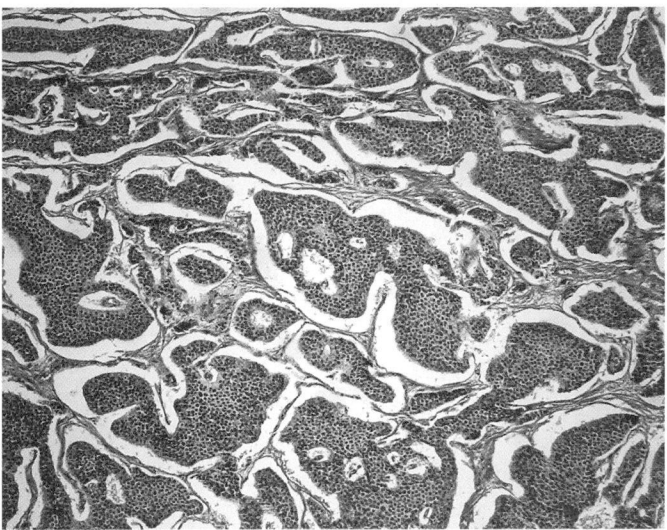

Fig. 18.107 Intratesticular carcinoid tumor showing the classic insular pattern.

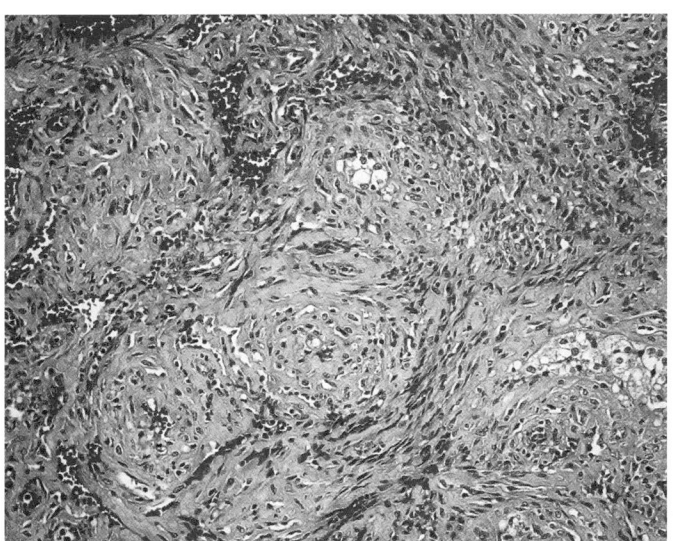

Fig. 18.108 Kaposi's sarcoma of the testis in an HIV-infected individual.

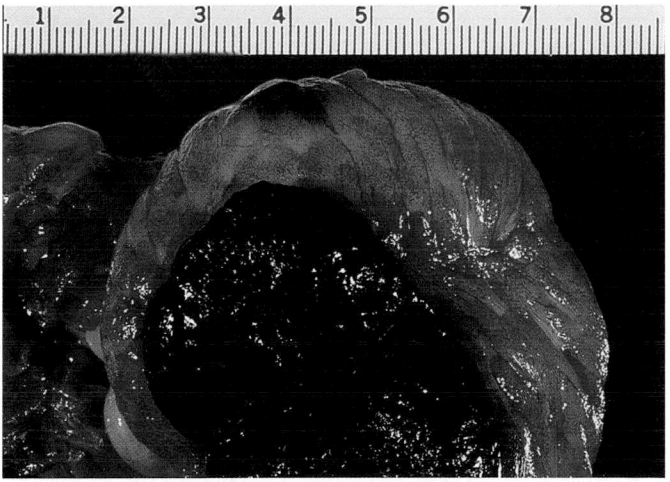

Fig. 18.109 Malignant melanoma metastatic to testis. The black color of the tumor is due to massive melanin deposition.

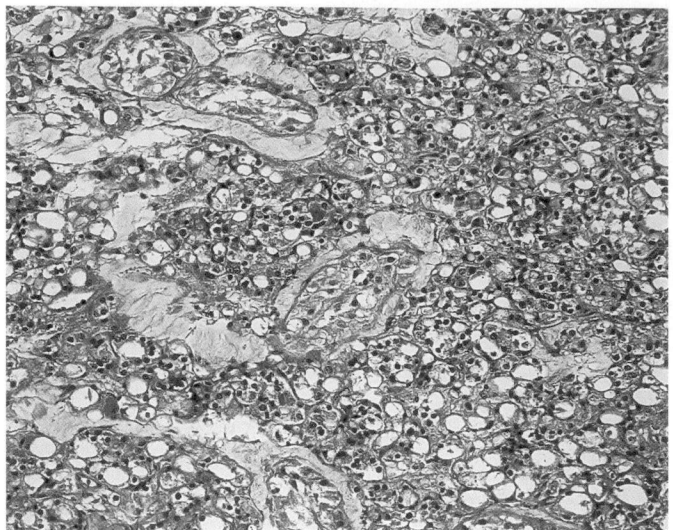

Fig. 18.110 Prostatic adenocarcinoma metastatic to testis. This not too rare occurrence is sometimes misdiagnosed as sex cord–stromal tumor.

In children, the testis can be involved by metastatic neuroblastoma from the adrenal or other sites.[490,505]

References

Normal embryology and anatomy

1 Charny CW, Conston AS, Meranze DR. Development of the testis. Fertil Steril 1952, **3:** 461–479.
2 Dym M. Spermatogonial stem cells of the testis (commentary). Proc Natl Acad Sci U S A 1994, **91:** 11287–11289.
3 Handelsman DJ, Stara S. Testicular size. The effects of aging, malnutrition, and illness. J Androl 1985, **6:** 144–151.
4 Johnson L, Petty CS, Neaves WB. The relationship of biopsy evaluations and testicular measurements to overall daily sperm production in human testes. Fertil Steril 1980, **34:** 36–40.
5 Rogatsch H, Jezek D, Hittmair A, Mijuz G, Feichtinger H. Expression of vimentin, cytokeratin, and desmin in Sertoli cells of human fetal, cryptorchid, and tumor-adjacent testicular tissue. Virchows Arch 1996, **427:** 497–502.
6 Schulze C. Sertoli cells and Leydig cells in man. Adv Anat Embryol Cell Biol 1984, **88:** 1–104.
7 Schulze W, Riemer M, Rehder U, Hohne K. Computer-aided three-dimensional reconstructions of the arrangement of primary spermatocytes in human seminiferous tubules. Cell Tissue Res 1986, **244:** 1–8.
8 Silber SJ, Rodriguez-Rigau LJ. Quantitative analysis of testicular biopsy. Determination of partial obstruction and prediction of sperm count after surgery for obstruction. Fertil Steril 1981, **36:** 480–485.
9 Skakkeback NE, Heller CG. Quantification of human seminiferous epithelium. J Reprod Fertil 1973, **32:** 379–389.
10 Trainer TD. Testis and excretory duct system. In Sternberg S (ed.): Histology for pathologists, ed. 2. Philadelphia, 1997, Lippincott-Raven Publishers, pp. 1019–1033.
11 Vilar O. Histology of the human testis from neonatal period to adolescence. Adv Exp Med Biol 1970, **10:** 95–111.

Cryptorchidism

12 Batata MA, Chu FCH, Hilaris BS, Whitmore WF, Golbey RB. Testicular cancer in cryptorchids. Cancer 1982, **49:** 1023–1030.
13 Batata MA, Whitmore WF Jr, Chu FCH, Hilaris BS, Loh J,

14 Grabstald H, Golbey R. Cryptorchidism and testicular cancer. J Urol 1980, **124:** 382–387.
14 Callaghan P. Undescended testis. Pediatr Rev 2000, **21:** 395.
15 Campbell HE. The incidence of malignant growth of the undescended testicle. A reply and re-evaluation. J Urol 1959, **81:** 663–668.
16 Dow JA, Mostofi FK. Testicular tumors following orchiopexy. South Med J 1967, **60:** 193–195.
17 Fonkalsrud EW. Current concepts in the management of the undescended testis. Surg Clin North Am 1970, **50:** 847–852.
18 Fonkalsrud EW. Current management of the undescended testis. Semin Pediatr Surg 1996, **5:** 2–7.
19 Gilbert JB, Hamilton JB. Studies in malignant testis tumors. Surg Gynecol Obstet 1940, **71:** 731–743.
20 Gill B, Kogan S. Cryptorchidism. Current concepts. Pediatr Clin North Am 1997, **44:** 1211–1227.
21 Gross RE, Jewett TC Jr. Surgical experiences from 1,222 operations for undescended testis. JAMA 1956, **160:** 634–641.
22 Hinman F Jr. The implications of testicular cytology in the treatment of cryptorchidism. Am J Surg 1955, **90:** 381–386.
23 Jordan GH. Laparoscopic management of the undescended testicle. Urol Clin North Am 2001, **28:** 23–29.
24 Lipschultz LI, Caminos-Torres R, Greenspan CS, Snyder PJ. Testicular function after orchiopexy for unilaterally undescended testis. N Engl J Med 1976, **295:** 15–18.
25 Mengel W, Hienz HA, Sippe WG II, Hecker WC. Studies on cryptorchidism. A comparison of histological findings in the germinative epithelium before and after the second year of life. J Pediatr Surg 1974, **9:** 445–450.
26 Mori H, Tamai M, Fushimi H, Fukuda H, Maeda T. Leydig cells within the aspermatogenic seminiferous tubules. Hum Pathol 1987, **18:** 1227–1231.
27 Nistal M, Paniagua R, Diez-Pardo JA. Histologic classification of undescended testes. Hum Pathol 1980, **11:** 666–674.
28 Palmer JM. The undescended testicle. Endocrinol Metab Clin North AM 1991, **20:** 231–240.
29 Rajfer J, Handelsman DJ, Swerdloff RS, Hurwitz R, Kaplan H, Vandergast T, Ehrlich RM. Hormonal therapy of cryptorchidism. A randomized, double-blind study comparing human chorionic gonadotropin and gonadotropin-releasing hormone. N Engl J Med 1986, **314:** 466–470.

Atrophy and infertility

30 Bennett HS, Baggenstoss AH, Butt HR. The testis and prostate of men who die of cirrhosis of the liver. Am J Clin Pathol 1950, **20:** 814–828.
31 De Paepe ME, Waxman M. Testicular atrophy in AIDS. A study of 57 autopsy cases. Hum Pathol 1989, **20:** 210–214.
32 Dodge OG, Jackson AW, Muldal S. Breast cancer and interstitial cell tumor in a patient with Klinefelter's syndrome. Cancer 1969, **24:** 1027–1032.
33 Durbin L, Hotchkiss RS. Testis biopsy in subfertile men with varicocele. Fertil Steril 1969, **20:** 50–57.
34 Fairley KF, Barrie JU, Johnson W. Sterility and testicular atrophy related to cyclophosphamide therapy. Lancet 1972, **1:** 568–569.
35 Federman DD. The assessment of organ function—the testis. N Engl J Med 1971, **285:** 901–904.
36 Fisch H, Lipshultz LI. Diagnosing male factors of infertility. Arch Pathol Lab Med 1992, **116:** 398–405.
37 Gall EA. The histopathology of acute mumps orchitis. Am J Pathol 1947, **23:** 637–652.
38 Girgis SM, Etriby A, Ibrahim AA, Kahil SA. Testicular biopsy in azoospermia. A review of the last ten years' experience of over 800 cases. Fertil Steril 1969, **20:** 467–477.
39 Gordon DL, Krmpotic E, Thomas W, Gandy HM, Paulsen CA. Pathologic testicular findings in Klinefelter's syndrome. 47, XXY vs 46,XY-47,XXY. Arch Intern Med 1972, **130:** 726–729.

40 Guarch R, Pesce C, Puras A, Lazaro J. A quantitative approach to the classification of hypospermatogenesis in testicular biopsies for infertility. Hum Pathol 1992, **23**: 1032–1037.

41 Handelman DJ, Conway AJ, Boylan LM, Turtle JR. Young's syndrome. Obstructive azoospermia and chronic sinopulmonary infections. N Engl J Med 1984, **310**: 3–9.

42 Isurugi K, Imao S, Hirose K, Aoki H. Seminoma in Klinefelter's syndrome with 47,XXY, 15s + karyotype. Cancer 1977, **39**: 2041–2047.

43 Jackson AW, Muldal S, Ockey CH, O'Connor PJ. Carcinoma of male breast in association with the Klinefelter syndrome. BMJ 1965, **1**: 223–225.

44 Jarow JP, Budin RE, Dym M, Zirkin BR, Noren S, Marshall FF. Quantitative pathologic changes in the human testis after vasectomy. A controlled study. N Engl J Med 1985, **313**: 1252–1256.

45 Jequier AM, Holmes SC. Aetiological factors in the production of obstructive azoospermia. Br J Urol 1984, **56**: 540–543.

46 Landing BH, Wells TR, Wang C-I. Abnormality of the epididymis and vas deferens in cystic fibrosis. Arch Pathol 1969, **88**: 569–580.

47 Lehmann D, Temminck B, Da Rugna D, Leibundgut B, Sulmoni A, Müller H. Role of immunological factors in male infertility. Immunohistochemical and serological evidence. Lab Invest 1987, **57**: 21–28.

48 Lendon M, Hann IM, Palmer MK, Shalet SM, Morris Jones PH. Testicular histology after combination chemotherapy in childhood for acute lymphoblastic leukaemia. Lancet 1978, **2**: 439–441.

49 Levin HS. Testicular biopsy in the study of male infertility. Its current usefulness, histologic techniques, and prospects for the future. Hum Pathol 1979, **10**: 569–584.

50 Meinhard E, McRae CU, Chisholm GD. Testicular biopsy in evaluation of male infertility. BMJ 1973, **3**: 577–581.

51 Meng MV, Cha I, Ljung BM, Turek PJ. Testicular fine-needle aspiration in infertile men: correlation of cytologic pattern with biopsy histology. Am J Surg Pathol 2001, **25**: 71–79.

52 Nelson WO. Testicular biopsy. In Tyler ET (ed.): Sterility—office management of the infertile couple. New York, 1961, McGraw-Hill.

53 Nistal M, Jimenez F, Paniagua R. Sertoli cell types in the Sertoli-cell-only syndrome. Relationships between Sertoli cell morphology and aetiology. Histopathology 1990, **16**: 173–180.

54 Nistal M, Riestra ML, Galmes-Belmonte I, Paniagua R. Testicular biopsy in patients with obstructive azoospermia. Am J Surg Pathol 1999, **23**: 1546–1554.

55 Palmer-Toy DE, McGovern F, Young RH. Granulomatous orchitis and vasculitis with testicular infarction complicating Crohn's disease: a hitherto undescribed tumor-like lesion of the testis. J Urol Pathol 1999, **11**: 143–150.

56 Pesce CM. The testicular biopsy in the evaluation of male infertility. Semin Diagn Pathol 1987, **4**: 264–274.

57 Piaton E, Fendler J-P, Berger N, Perrin P, Devonec M. Clinical value of fine-needle aspiration cytology and biopsy in the evaluation of male infertility. A comparative study of 48 infertile patients. Arch Pathol Lab Med 1995, **119**: 722–726.

58 Rowley MJ, Heller CG. The testicular biopsy. Surgical procedure, fixation, and staining technics. Fertil Steril 1966, **17**: 177–186.

59 Schned AR, Cendron M. Pathologic findings in the vanishing testis syndrome. J Urol Pathol 1997, **6**: 95–108.

60 Schofield JB, Evans DJ. Multinucleate giant stromal cells in testicular atrophy following oestrogen therapy. Histopathology 1990, **16**: 200–201.

61 Silber SJ, Rodriguez-Rigau LJ. Quantitative analysis of testicle biopsy. Determination of partial obstruction and prediction of sperm count after surgery for obstruction. Fertil Steril 1981, **36**: 480–485.

62 Smith JA Jr, Urry RL. Testicular histology after prolonged treatment with a gonadotropin-releasing hormone analogue. J Urol 1985, **133**: 612–614.

63 Smith NM, Byard RW, Bourne AJ. Testicular regression syndrome—a pathological study of 77 cases. Histopathology 1991, **19**: 269–272.

64 Sniffen RC. The testis. I. The normal testis. Arch Pathol 1950, **50**: 259–284.

65 Sniffen RC, Howard RP, Simmons FA. The testis. II. Abnormalities of spermatogenesis. Atresia of the excretory ducts. Arch Pathol 1950, **50**: 285–295.

66 Söderström K-O, Suominen J. Histopathology and ultrastructure of meiotic arrest in human spermatogenesis. Arch Pathol Lab Med 1980, **104**: 476–482.

67 Sogge MR, McDonald SD, Cofold PB. The malignant potential of the dysgenetic germ cell in Klinefelter's syndrome. Am J Med 1979, **66**: 515–518.

68 Spires SE, Woolums CS, Pulito AR, Spires SM. Testicular regression syndrome: a clinical and pathologic study of 11 cases. Arch Pathol Lab Med 2000, **124**: 694–698.

69 Wong TW, Straus FH II, Warner NE. Testicular biopsy in the study of male infertility. I. Testicular causes of infertility. Arch Pathol 1973, **95**: 151–159.

70 Wong TW, Straus FH II, Warner NE. Testicular biopsy in the study of male infertility. II. Posttesticular causes of infertility. Arch Pathol 1973, **95**: 160–164.

71 Wong TW, Straus FH II, Warner NE. Testicular biopsy in the study of male infertility. III. Pretesticular causes of infertility. Arch Pathol 1974, **98**: 1–8.

72 Yoshikawa Y, Truong LD, Fraire AE, Kim HS. The spectrum of histopathology of the testis in acquired immunodeficiency syndrome. Mod Pathol 1989, **2**: 233–238.

Other non-neoplastic lesions

73 Abbondanzo SL, Young VL, Wei MQ, Miller FW. Silicone gel-filled breast and testicular implant capsules: a histologic and immunophenotypic study. Mod Pathol 1999, **12**: 706–713.

74 Aitchison M, Mufti GR, Farrell J, Paterson PJ, Scott R. Granulomatous orchitis. Review of 15 cases. Br J Urol 1990, **66**: 312–314.

75 Akhtar M, Ali MA, Mackey DM. Lepromatous leprosy presenting as orchitis. Am J Clin Pathol 1980, **73**: 712–715.

76 Andrews RW, Copeland DD, Fried FA. Splenogonadal fusion. J Urol 1985, **133**: 1052–1053.

77 Brown RC, Smith BH. Malacoplakia of the testis. Am J Clin Pathol 1967, **47**: 135–147.

78 Camassei FD, Francalanci P, Ferro F, Capozza N, Boldrini R. Cystic dysplasia of the rete testis: report of two cases and review of the literature. Pediatr Dev Pathol 2002, **5**: 206–210.

79 Coyne JD, Dervan PA. Multinucleated stromal giant cells of testis. Histopathology 1997, **31**: 381–383.

80 Diaz Gonzalez R, Leiva O, Navas Palacios JJ, Usera G, Gonzalez Castillo P, Montalban MA, Borobia V. Testicular malacoplakia. J Urol 1982, **127**: 325–328.

81 Glantz L, Hansen K, Caldamone A, Medeiros LJ. Cystic dysplasia of the testis. Hum Pathol 1993, **24**: 1142–1145.

82 Haas GP, Badalament R, Wonnell DM, Miles BJ. Testicular sarcoidosis. Case report and review of the literature. J Urol 1986, **135**: 1254–1256.

83 Hepper NGG, Karlson AG, Leary FJ, Soule EH. Genitourinary infection due to *Mycobacterium kansasii*. Mayo Clin Proc 1971, **46**: 387–390.

84 Hourihane DO'B. Infected infarcts of the testis. A study of 18 cases preceded by pyogenic epididymoorchitis. J Clin Pathol 1970, **23**: 668–675.

85 Lossos IS, Okon E, Bogomolski-Yahalom V, Ron N, Polliack A. Sinus histiocytosis with massive lymphadenopathy (Rosai-Dorfman disease): report of a patient with isolated renotesticular involvement after cure of non-Hodgkin's lymphoma. Ann Hematol 1997, **74**: 41–44.

86 Malek RS, Rosen JS, Farrow GM. Epidermoid cysts of the testis. A critical analysis. Br J Urol 1985, **58**: 55–59.

87 Mendez R, Morrow JW. Ectopic spleen simulating testicular tumor. J Urol 1969, **102**: 598–601.

88 Minkowitz G, Lee M, Minkowitz S. Pilomatricoma of the testicle. An ossifying testicular tumor with hair matrix differentiation. Arch Pathol Lab Med 1995, **119**: 96–99.

89 Natarajan V, Gaches CGC, Scott DGI, Ball RY. Isolated vasculitis of the testis: distinction from generalized polyarteritis nodosa. J Urol Pathol 1996, **4**: 167–174.

90 Nistal M, Paniagua R. Inflammatory diseases of the epididymis and testis. In Nistal M, Paniagua R (eds): Testicular and epididymal pathology. New York, 1984, Thieme-Stratton, pp. 263–277.

91 Nistal M, Iniguez L, Paniagua R. Cysts of the testicular parenchyma and tunica albuginea. Arch Pathol Lab Med 1989, **113**: 902–906.

92 Palmer-Toy DE, McGovern F, Young RH. Granulomatous orchitis and vasculitis with testicular infarction complicating Crohn's disease: a hitherto undescribed tumor-like lesion of the testis. J Urol Pathol 1999, **11**: 143–150.

93 Price EB Jr. Epidermoid cysts of the testis. A clinical and pathologic analysis of 69 cases from the testicular tumor registry. J Urol 1969, **102**: 708–713.

94 Reinberg Y, Manivel JC, Llerena J, Niehans G, Fraley EE. Epidermoid cyst (monodermal teratoma) of the testis. Br J Urol 1990, **66**: 648–651.

95 Shurbaji MS, Epstein JI. Testicular vasculitis. Implications for systemic disease. Hum Pathol 1988, **19**: 186–189.

96 Spjut HJ, Thorpe JD. "Granulomatous orchitis." Am J Clin Pathol 1956, **26**: 136–145.

97 Townell NH, Gledhill A, Robinson T, Hopewell P. Juvenile xanthogranuloma of the testis. J Urol 1985, **133**: 1054–1055.

98 Wegner HE, Loy V, Dieckmann KP. Granulomatous orchitis—an analysis of clinical presentation, pathological anatomic features and possible etiologic factors. Eur Urol 1994, **26**: 56–60.

98a Younger C, Ulbright TM, Zhang S, Billings SD, Cummings OW, Foster RS, Eble JN, Cheng L. Molecular evidence supporting the neoplastic nature of some epidermoid cysts of the testis. Arch Pathol Lab Med 2003, **127**: 858.

Tumors
Germ cell tumors
Classification

99 Bar W, Hedinger E. Comparison of histologic types of primary testicular germ cell tumors with their metastases. Consequences for the WHO and the British nomenclatures? Virchows Arch [A] 1976, **370**: 41–54.

100 Collins DH, Pugh RCP. Classification and frequency of testicular tumours. Br J Urol 1964, **36**(Suppl):1–11.

101 Czaja JT, Ulbright TM. Evidence for the transformation of seminoma to yolk sac tumor, with histogenetic considerations. Am J Clin Pathol 1992, **97**: 468–477.

102 Dixon FJ, Moore RA. Tumors of the male sex organs. In Atlas of tumor pathology, series 1, section VIII, fascicles 31b and 32. Washington, D.C., 1952, Armed Forces Institute of Pathology.

102a Kernek KM, Ulbright TM, Zhang S, Billings SD, Cummings OW, Henley JD, Michael H, Brunelli M, Martignoni G, Foster RS, Eble JN, Cheng L. Identical allelic losses in mature teratoma and other histologic components of malignant mixed germ cell tumors of the testis. Am J Pathol 2003; **163**: 2477–2484.

103 Klein FA, Melamed MR, Whitmore WF. Intratubular malignant germ cells (carcinoma in situ) accompanying invasive testicular germ cell tumors. J Urol 1985, **133**: 413–415.

104 Marin-Padilla M. Origin, nature and significance of the "embryoids" of human teratomas. Virchows Arch [A] 1965, **340**: 105–121.

105 Marin-Padilla M. Histopathology of the embryonal carcinoma of the testes. Embryological evaluation. Arch Pathol 1968, **85**: 614–622.

106 Min KW, Scheithauer BW. Pineal germinomas and testicular seminoma. A comparative ultrastructural study with special references to early carcinomatous transformation. Ultrastruct Pathol 1990, **14**: 483–496.

107 Mostofi FK, Price EB Jr. Tumors of the male genital system. In Atlas of tumor pathology, series 2, fascicle 8. Washington, D.C., 1973, Armed Forces Institute of Pathology.

108 Pierce GB, Abell MR. Embryonal carcinoma of the testis. Pathol Annu 1970, **5**: 27–60.

109 Pugh RCB (ed.). Pathology of the testis. Oxford, 1976, Blackwell Scientific Publications.

110 Skakkebaek NE. Carcinoma in situ of the testis. Frequency and relationship to invasive germ cell tumours in infertile men. Histopathology 1978, **2**: 157–170.

111 Srigley JR, Mackay B, Toth P, Ayala A. The ultrastructure and histogenesis of male germ neoplasia with emphasis on seminoma with early carcinomatous features. Ultrastruct Pathol 1988, **12**: 67–86.

112 Stevens LC. Experimental production of testicular teratomas in mice. Proc Natl Acad Sci 1964, **52**: 654–661.

113 Ulbright TM, Roth LM. Recent developments in the pathology of germ cell tumors. Semin Diagn Pathol 1987, **4**: 304–319.

114 Unger PD, Cohen EL, Talerman A. Mized germ cell tumor of the testis: a unique combination of seminoma and teratoma composed predominantly of prostatic tissue. J Urol Pathol 1998, **9**: 257–264.

Seminoma

115 Albores-Saavedra J, Huffman H, Alvarado-Cabrero I, Ayala AG. Anaplastic variant of spermatocytic seminoma. Hum Pathol 1996, **27**: 650–655.

116 Aubry F, Satie A-P, Rioux-Leclercq N, Rajpert-De Myts E, Spagnoli GC, Chomez P, de Backer O, Jégou B, Samson M. MAGE-A4, a germ cell specific marker, is expressed differentially in testicular tumors. Cancer 2001, **92**: 2778–2785.

117 Battifora H, Sheibani K, Tubbs RR, Kopinski MI, Sun TT. Antikeratin antibodies in tumor diagnosis. Distinction between seminoma and embryonal carcinoma. Cancer 1984, **54**: 843–848.

118 Baretton G, Diebold J, De Pascale T, Bussar-Maatz R, Weissbach L, Lohrs U. Deoxyribonucleic acid ploidy in seminomas with and without syncytiotrophoblastic cells. J Urol 1994, **15**: 67–71.

119 Beckstead JH. Alkaline phosphatase histochemistry in human germ cell neoplasms. Am J Surg Pathol 1983, **7**: 341–349.

120 Burke AP, Mostofi FK. Spermatocytic seminoma. A clinicopathologic study of 79 cases. J Urol Pathol 1993, **1**: 21–32.

121 Cheville JC, Rao S, Iczkowski KA, Lohse CM, Pankratz UV. Cytokeratin expression in seminoma of the human testis. Am J Clin Pathol 2000, **113**: 583–588.

122 Cockburn AG, Vugrin D, Batata M, Hajdu S, Whitmore WF. Poorly differentiated (anaplastic) seminoma of the testis. Cancer 1984, **53**: 1991–1994.

123 Collins DH, Pugh RCP. Classification and frequency of testicular tumours. Br J Urol 1964, **36**(Suppl): 1–11.

124 Cope NJ, McCullagh P, Sarsfield PT. Tumour responding accessory cells in testicular seminoma: an immunohistochemical study. Histopathology 1999, **34**: 510–516.

125 Cummings OW, Ulbright TM, Eble JN, Roth LM. Spermatocytic seminoma. An immunohistochemical study. Hum Pathol 1994, **25**: 54–59.

126 Damjanov I, Niejadlik DC, Rabuffo JV, Donadio JA. Cribriform and sclerosing seminoma devoid of lymphoid infiltrates. Arch Pathol Lab Med 1980, **104**: 527–530.

127 De Jong B, Oosterhuis JW, Castedo SMMJ, Vos AM, te Meerman GJ. Pathogenesis of adult testicular germ cell tumors. A cytogenetic model. Cancer Genet Cytogenet 1990, **48**: 143–167.

128 Dekker I, Rozeboom T, Delemarre J, Dam A, Oosterhuis JW.

Placental-like alkaline phosphatase and DNA flow cytometry in spermatocytic seminoma. Cancer 1992, **69**: 993–996.

129 Eble JN. Spermatocytic seminoma. Hum Pathol 1994, **25**: 1035–1042.

130 Florentine BD, Roscher AA, Garrett J, Warner NE. Necrotic seminoma of the testis: establishing the diagnosis with masson trichrome stain and immunostains. Arch Pathol Lab Med 2002, **126**: 205–206.

131 Floyd C, Ayala AG, Logothetis CJ, Silva EG. Spermatocytic seminoma with associated sarcoma of the testis. Cancer 1988, **61**: 409–414.

132 Franke FE, Pauls K, Kerkman L, Steger K, Klonisch T, Metzger R, Alhenc-Gelas F, Burkhardt E, Bergmann M, Danilov SM. Somatic isoform of angiotensin I-converting enzyme in the pathology of testicular germ cell tumors. Hum Pathol 2000, **31**: 1466–1476.

133 Hittmair A, Rogatsch H, Hobisch A, Mikuz G, Feichtinger H. CD30 expression in seminoma. Hum Pathol 1996, **27**: 1166–1171.

134 Holstein AF, Körner F. Light and electron microscopical analysis of cell types in human seminoma. Virchows Arch [A] 1974, **363**: 97–112.

135 Hori K, Uematsu K, Yasoshima H, Yamada A, Sakurai K, Ohya M. Testicular seminoma with human chorionic gonadotropin production. Pathol Int 1997, **47**: 592–599.

136 Jacobsen GK. Alpha-fetoprotein (AFP) and human chorionic gonadotropin (HCG) in testicular germ cell tumors. A comparison of histologic and serologic occurrence of tumour markers. Acta Pathol Microbiol Immunol Scand (A) 1983, **91**: 183–190.

137 Jacobsen GK, Norgaard-Pedersen B. Placental alkaline phosphatase in testicular germ cell tumours and in carcinoma-in-situ of the testis. An immunohistochemical study. Acta Pathol Microbiol Immunol Scand (A) 1984, **92**: 323–329.

138 Jacobsen GK, Jacobsen M, Clausen PP. Distribution of tumor-associated antigens in the various histologic components of germ cell tumors of the testis. Am J Surg Pathol 1981, **5**: 257–266.

139 Javadpour N. Multiple biochemical tumor markers in seminoma. A double blind study. Cancer 1983, **52**: 887–889.

140 Javadpour N. Human chorionic gonadotropin in seminoma. J Urol 1984, **131**: 407.

141 Javadpour N, McIntire KR, Waldmann TA. Human chorionic gonadotropin (HCG) and alpha-fetoprotein (AFP) in sera and tumor cells of patients with testicular seminoma. Cancer 1978, **42**: 2768–2772.

142 Kademian M, Bosch A, Caldwell WL, Jaeschke W. Anaplastic seminoma. Cancer 1977, **40**: 3082–3086.

143 Kahn DG. Ossifying seminoma of the testis. Arch Pathol Lab Med 1993, **117**: 321–322.

144 Koide O, Iwai S, Matsumara H. Intranuclear membranous profiles in germinoma cells. A variant of nuclear pockets and intranuclear annulate lamellae. Acta Pathol Jpn 1985, **35**: 605–619.

145 Looijenga LH, Olie RA, van der Gagg I, van Sluijs FJ, Matoska J, Ploem-Zaaijer J, Knepfle C, Oosterhuis JW. Seminomas of the canine testis. Counterpart of spermatocytic seminoma of men? Lab Invest 1994, **71**: 490–496.

146 Manivel JC, Jessurun J, Wick MR, Dehner LP. Placental alkaline phosphatase immunoreactivity in testicular germ-cell neoplasms. Am J Surg Pathol 1987, **11**: 21–29.

147 Martin LSJ, Woodruff MW, Webster JH, Pickren JW. Testicular seminoma. A review of 179 patients treated over a 50-year period. Arch Surg 1965, **90**: 306–313.

148 Matoska J, Talerman A. Spermatocytic seminoma associated with rhabdomyosarcoma. Am J Clin Pathol 1990, **94**: 89–95.

149 Miettinen M, Virtanen I, Talerman A. Intermediate filament proteins in human testis and testicular germ-cell tumors. Am J Pathol 1985, **120**: 402–410.

150 Min KW, Scheithauer BW. Pineal germinomas and testicular seminoma. A comparative ultrastructural study with special

references to early carcinomatous transformation. Ultrastruct Pathol 1990, **14**: 483–496.

151 Mirimanoff RO, Shipley WU, Dosoretz DE, Meyer JE. Pure seminoma of the testis. The results of radiation therapy in patients with elevated human chorionic gonadotropin titers. J Urol 1985, **134**: 1124–1126.

152 Mostofi FK. Testicular tumors. Epidemiologic, etiologic, and pathologic features. Cancer 1973, **32**: 1186–1201.

153 Mostofi FK. Pathology of germ cell tumors of the testis. A progress report. Cancer 1980, **45**: 1735–1754.

154 Mostofi FK, Sesterhenn IA. Histological typing of testis tumours, ed. 2. Berlin, 1998, Springer.

155 Parkash V, Carcangiu ML. Transformation of ovarian dysgerminoma to yolk sac tumor. Evidence for a histogenetic continuum. Mod Pathol 1995, **8**: 881–887.

156 Pierce GB Jr. Ultrastructure of human testicular tumors. Cancer 1966, **19**: 1963–1983.

157 Przygodzki RM, Moran CA, Suster S, Khan MA, Swalsky PA, Bakker A, Koss MN, Finkelstein SD. Primary mediastinal and testicular seminomas: A comparison of K-ras-2 gene sequence and p53 immunoperoxidase analysis of 26 cases. Hum Pathol 1996, **27**: 975–979.

158 Raghavan D, Sullivan AL, Peckham MJ, Neville AM. Elevated serum alpha-fetoprotein and seminoma. Clinical evidence for a histologic continuum? Cancer 1982, **50**: 982–989.

159 Ramaekers F, Feitz W, Moesker O, Schaart G, Herman C, Debruyne F, Vooijs P. Antibodies to cytokeratin and vimentin in testicular tumour diagnosis. Virchows Arch [A] 1985, **408**: 127–142.

160 Romanenko AM, Persidsky YV, Mostofi FK. Ultrastructure and histogenesis of spermatocytic seminoma. J Urol Pathol 1993, **1**: 387–395.

161 Rosai J, Khodadoust K, Silber I. Spermatocytic seminoma. II. Ultrastructural study. Cancer 1969, **24**: 103–106.

162 Rosai J, Silber I, Khodadoust K. Spermatocytic seminoma. I. Clinicopathologic study of six cases and review of the literature. Cancer 1969, **24**: 92–102.

163 Rouse RV. Tubular seminoma: An addition to the short list of potentially confusing seminoma variants, with an addendum on the immunohistology of seminomas and dysgerminomas. Adv Anat Pathol 1996, **3**: 91–96.

164 Saint-Andre JP, Alhenc-Gelas F, Rohmer V, Chretien MF, Bigorgne JC, Corvol P. Angiotensin-I-converting enzyme in germinomas. Hum Pathol 1988, **19**: 208–213.

165 Satie A-P, Rajpert-De Meyts E, Spagnoli GC, Henno S, Olivo L, Jacobsen GK, Rioux-Leclercq N, Jégou B, Samson M. The cancer-testis gene, NY-ESO-1, is expressed in normal fetal and adult testes and in spermatocytic seminomas and testicular carcinoma in situ. Lab Invest 2002, **82**: 775.

166 Scully RE, Coffin DL. Canine testicular tumors. With special reference to their histogenesis, comparative morphology, and endocrinology. Cancer 1952, **5**: 592–605.

167 Srigley JR, Mackay B, Toth P, Ayala A. The ultrastructure and histogenesis of male germ cell neoplasia with emphasis on seminoma with early carcinomatous features. Ultrastruct Pathol 1988, **12**: 67–86.

168 Stoop H, van Gurp R, De Krijer R, Geurts van Kessel A, Koberle B, Oosterhuis W, Looijenga L. Reactivity of germ cell maturation stage-specific markers in spermatocytic seminoma: diagnostic and etiological implications. Lab Invest 2001, **81**: 919–928.

169 Suzuki T, Sasano H, Aoki H, Nagura H, Sasano N, Sano T, Saito M, Watanuki T, Kato H, Aizawa S. Immunohistochemical comparison between anaplastic seminoma and typical seminoma. Acta Pathol Jpn 1993, **43**: 751–757.

170 Talerman A. Yolk sac tumor associated with seminoma of the testis in adults. Cancer 1974, **33**: 1468–1473.

171 Talerman A. Spermatocytic seminoma. Clinicopathologic study of 22 cases. Cancer 1980, **45**: 2169–2176.

172 Talerman A, Fu YS, Okagaki T. Spermatocytic seminoma. Ultrastructural and microspectrophotometric observations. Lab Invest 1984, **51**: 343–349.

173 Teppo L. Testicular cancer in Finland. Acta Pathol Microbiol Scand (A) 1973, **238**(Suppl): 1–80.

174 Tickoo SK, Hutchinson B, Bacik J, Mazumdar M, Motzer RJ, Bajorin DF, Bosl GJ, Reuter VE. Testicular seminoma: a clinicopathologic and immunohistochemical study of 105 cases with special reference to seminomas with atypical features. Int J Surg Pathol 2002, **10**: 23–32.

175 True LD, Otis CN, Delprado W, Scully RE, Rosai J. Spermatocytic seminoma of testis with sarcomatous transformation. A report of five cases. Am J Surg Pathol 1988, **12**: 75–82.

176 von Hochstetter AR. Mitotic count in seminomas—an unreliable criterion for distinguishing between classical and anaplastic types. Virchows Arch [A] 1981, **390**: 63–69.

177 von Hochstetter AR, Hedinger ChE. The differential diagnosis of testicular germ cell tumors in theory and practice. Virchows Arch [A] 1982, **396**: 247–277.

178 von Hochstetter AR, Sigg Chr, Saremaslani P, Hedinger ChE. The significance of giant cells in human testicular seminomas. A clinico-pathological study. Virchows Arch [A] 1985, **407**: 309–322.

179 Walt H, Arrenbrecht S, Delozier-Blanchet CD, Keller PJ, Nauer R, Hedinger CE. A human testicular germ cell tumor with borderline histology between seminoma and embryonal carcinoma secreted beta-human chorionic gonadotropin and alpha-fetoprotein only as a xenograft. Cancer 1986, **58**: 139–146.

180 Wei YQ, Hang ZB, Liu KF. In situ observation of inflammatory cell–tumor cell interaction in human seminomas (germinomas). Light, electron microscopic, and immunohistochemical study. Hum Pathol 1992, **23**: 421–428.

181 Zavala-Pompa A, Ro JY, el-Naggar AK, Amin MB, Ordoñez NG, Sella A, Ayala AG. Tubular seminoma. An immunohistochemical and DNA flow-cytometric study of four cases. Am J Clin Pathol 1994, **102**: 397–401.

182 Zuckman MH, Williams G, Levin HS. Mitosis counting in seminoma. An exercise of questionable significance. Hum Pathol 1988, **19**: 329–335.

Embryonal carcinoma

183 Berney DM, Shamash J, Pieroni K, Oliver RT. Loss of CD30 expression in metastatic embryonal carcinoma: the effects of chemotherapy? Histopathology 2001, **39**: 382–385.

184 Jacobsen GK. Histogenetic considerations concerning germ cell tumours. Morphological and immunohistochemical comparative investigation of the human embryo and testicular germ cell tumors. Virchows Arch [A] 1986, **408**: 509–525.

185 Miettinen M, Virtanen I, Talerman A. Intermediate filament proteins in human testis and testicular germ-cell tumors. Am J Pathol 1985, **120**: 402–410.

186 Parkinson MC, Harland SJ, Harnden P, Sandison A. Review. The role of the histopathologist in the management of testicular germ cell tumour in adults. Histopathology 2001, **38**: 183–194.

187 Pierce GB Jr, Abell MR. Embryonal carcinoma of the testis. Pathol Annu 1970, **5**: 27–60.

188 Ramaekers F, Feitz W, Moesker O, Schaart G, Herman C, Debruyne LF, Vooijs P. Antibodies to cytokeratin and vimentin in testicular tumour diagnosis. Virchows Arch [A] 1985, **408**: 127–142.

189 Rinke de Wit TF, Wilson L, van den Elsen PJ, Thielen F, Brekhoff D, Oosterhuis JW, Pera MF, Stern PL. Monoclonal antibodies to human embryonal carcinoma cells. Antigenic relationships of germ cell tumors. Lab Invest 1991, **65**: 180–191.

190 Visfeldt J, Giwercman A, Skakkebaek NE. Monoclonal antibody 43-9F. An immunohistochemical marker of embryonal carcinoma of the testis. APMIS 1992, **100**: 63–70.

Mature (adult) and immature teratoma

191 Aguirre P, Scully RE. Primitive neuroectodermal tumor of the testis. Arch Pathol Lab Med 1983, **107**: 643–645.

192 Ahmed T, Bosl GJ, Hajdu SI. Teratoma with malignant transformation in germ cell tumors in men. Cancer 1985, **56**: 860–863.

193 Allen EA, Burger PC, Epstein JI. Microcystic meningioma arising in a mixed germ cell tumor of the testis: a case report. Am J Surg Pathol 1999, **23**: 1131–1135.

194 Bar W, Hedinger CE. Comparison of histologic types of primary testicular germ cell tumors with their metastases. Consequences for the WHO and the British nomenclatures? Virchows Arch [A] 1976, **370**: 41–54.

195 Cardoso de Almeida PC, Scully RE. Diffuse embryoma of the testis. A distinctive form of mixed germ cell tumor. Am J Surg Pathol 1983, **7**: 633–642.

196 de Peralta-Venturina MN, Ro JY, Ordóñez NG, Ayala AG. Diffuse embryoma of the testis. An immunohistochemical study of two cases. Am J Clin Pathol 1994, **101**: 402–405.

197 Heifetz SA, Cushing B, Giller R, Shuster JJ, Stolar CJ, Vinocur CD, Hawkins EP. Immature teratomas in children: pathologic consideration: a report from the combined Pediatric Oncology Group/ Children's Cancer Group. Am J Surg Pathol 1998, **22**: 1115–1124.

198 Hughes DF, Allen DC, O'Neill JJ. Angiosarcoma arising in a testicular teratoma. Histopathology 1991, **18**: 81–83.

199 Leibovitch I, Foster RS, Ulbright TM, Donohue JP. Adult primary pure teratoma of the testis. The Indiana experience. Cancer 1995, **75**: 2244–2250.

200 Michael H, Hull MT, Ulbright TM, Foster RS, Miller KD. Primitive neuroectodermal tumors arising in testicular germ cell neoplasms. Am J Surg Pathol 1997, **21**: 896–904.

201 Michal M. Meningeal nodules in teratoma of the testis. Virchows Arch 2001, **438**: 198–200.

202 Minkowitz G, Lee M, Minkowitz S. Pilomatricoma of the testicle. An ossifying testicular tumor with hair matrix differentiation. Arch Pathol Lab Med 1995, **119**: 96–99.

203 Mostofi FK, Sesterhenn IA. Histological typing of testis tumours, ed. 2. Berlin, 1998, Springer.

204 Nagahara N, Kitamura H, Kanisawa M, Ikeda A, Shirai K, Matsushita K. A testicular teratoma with rhabdomyosarcoma and seminoma. Acta Pathol Jpn 1991, **41**: 707–711.

205 Pichmann S, Mikuz G, Schmid KW. Chromogranins A and B in nonseminomatous testicular tumors. An immunohistochemical study. J Urol Pathol 1993, **1**: 43–54.

206 Serrano-Olmo J, Tang CK, Seidmon EJ, Ellison NE, Elfenbein IB, Ming PM. Neuroblastoma as a prominent component of a mixed germ cell tumor of testis. Cancer 1993, **72**: 3271–3276.

207 Singh N, Cumming J, Theaker JM. Pure cartilaginous teratoma differentiated of the testis. Histopathology 1997, **30**: 373–374.

208 Ulbright TM, Srigley JR. Dermoid cyst of the testis: a study of five postpubertal cases, including a pilomatrixoma-like variant, with evidence supporting its separate classification from mature testicular teratoma. Am J Surg Pathol 2001, **25**: 788–793.

209 Ulbright TM, Goheen MP, Roth LM, Gillespie JJ. The differentiation of carcinomas of teratomatous origin from embryonal carcinoma. A light and electron microscopic study. Cancer 1986, **57**: 257–263.

Teratocarcinoma

210 Ulbright TM, Loehrer PJ, Roth LM, Einhorn LH, Williams SD, Clark SA. The development of non-germ-cell malignancies within germ cell tumors. A clinicopathologic study of 11 cases. Cancer 1984, **54**: 1824–1833.

Choriocarcinoma

211 Azzopardi JG, Mostofi FK, Theiss EA. Lesions of testes observed in certain patients with widespread choriocarcinoma and related tumors. Am J Pathol 1961, **38**: 207–225.

212 Damjanov I, Osborn M, Miettinen M. Keratin 7 is a marker for a subset of trophoblastic cells in human germ cell tumors. Arch Pathol Lab Med 1990, **114**: 81–83.

212a Hechelhammer L, Störkel S, Odermatt B, Heitz PU, Jochum W. Epidermal growth factor receptor is a marker for syncytiotrophoblastic cells in testicular germ cell tumors. Virch Arch 2003; **443**: 28–31.

213 Javadpour N, McIntire KR, Waldmann TA. Human chorionic gonadotropin (HCG) and alpha-fetoprotein (AFP) in sera and tumor cells of patients with testicular seminoma. Cancer 1978, **42**: 2768–2772.

214 Kurman RJ, Scardino PT, McIntire KR, Waldmann TA, Javadpour N. Cellular localization of alpha-fetoprotein and human chorionic gonadotropin in germ cell tumors of the testis using an indirect immunoperoxidase technique. A new approach to classification utilizing tumor markers. Cancer 1977, **40**: 2136–2151.

215 McKendrick JJ, Theaker J, Mead GM. Nonseminomatous germ cell tumor with very high serum human chorionic gonadotropin. Cancer 1991, **67**: 684–689.

216 Mostofi FK, Sesterhenn IA, Davis CJ Jr. Immunopathology of germ cell tumors of the testis. Semin Diagn Pathol 1987, **4**: 320–341.

217 Ulbright TM, Young RH, Scully RE. Trophoblastic tumors of the testis other than classic choriocarcinoma: "monophasic" choriocarcinoma and placental site trophoblastic tumor; a report of two cases. Am J Surg Pathol 1997, **21**: 282–288.

Yolk sac tumor

218 Collins DH, Pugh RCP. Classification and frequency of testicular tumours. Br J Urol 1964, **36**(Suppl): 1–11.

219 Eglen DE, Ulbright TM. The differential diagnosis of yolk sac tumor and seminoma. Usefulness of cytokeratin, alpha-fetoprotein, and alpha-1-antitrypsin immunoperoxidase reactions. Am J Clin Pathol 1987, **88**: 328–332.

220 Gonzalez-Crussi F. The human yolk sac and yolk sac (endodermal sinus) tumors. A review. Perspect Pediatr Pathol 1979, **5**: 179–215.

221 Gonzalez-Crussi F, Roth LM. The human yolk sac and yolk sac carcinoma. An ultrastructural study. Hum Pathol 1976, **7**: 675–691.

222 Grigor KM, Detre SI, Kohn J, Neville AM. Serum alphafoetoprotein levels in 153 male patients with germ cell tumours. Br J Cancer 1977, **35**: 52–58.

223 Heifetz SA, Cushing B, Giller R, Shuster JJ, Stolar CJH, Vinocur CD, Hawkins EP. Immature teratomas in children: pathologic consideration: a report from the combined Pediatric Oncology Group/ Children's Cancer Group. Am J Surg Pathol 1998, **22**: 1115–1124.

223a Henley JD, Michael H, Young RH, Ulbright TM. Solid pattern of yolk sac tumor of the testis: A histologic and immunohistochemical study of 9 cases. Mod Pathol 2003, **16**: 153A.

224 Jacobsen GK, Jacobsen M. Alpha-fetoprotein (AFP) and human chorionic gonadotropin (HCG) in testicular germ cell tumours. Acta Pathol Microbiol Immunol Scand (A) 1983, **91**: 165–176.

225 Jacobsen GK, Jacobsen M. Possible liver cell differentiation in testicular germ cell tumours. Histopathology 1983, **7**: 537–548.

225a Kato N, Tamura G, Fukase M, Shibuya H, Motoyama T. Short communication. Hypermethylation of the RUNX3 gene promoter in testicular yolk sac tumor of infants. Am J Pathol 2003, **163**: 387–391.

226 Kommoss F, Bibbo M, Talerman A. Nuclear deoxyribonucleic acid content (ploidy) of endodermal sinus (yolk sac) tumor. Lab Invest 1990, **62**: 223–231.

227 Kramer SA, Wold LE, Gilchrist GS, Svensson J, Kelasis PP. Yolk sac carcinoma. An immunohistochemical and clinicopathologic review. J Urol 1984, **131**: 315–318.

228 Kurman RJ, Scardino PT, McIntire KR, Waldmann TA, Javadpour N. Cellular localization of alpha-fetoprotein and human chorionic gonadotropin in germ cell tumors of the testis using an indirect immunoperoxidase technique. A new approach to classification utilizing tumor markers. Cancer 1977, **40**: 2136–2151.

229 Logothetis CJ, Samuels ML, Trindade A, Grant C, Gomez L, Ayala A. The prognostic significance of endodermal sinus tumor histology among patients treated for stage III nonseminomatous germ cell tumors of the testes. Cancer 1984, **53**: 122–128.

230 Michael H, Ulbright TM, Brodhecker CA. The pluripotential nature of the mesenchyme-like component of yolk sac tumor. Arch Pathol Lab Med 1989, **113**: 1115–1119.

231 Nogales FF. Embryologic clues to human yolk sac tumors. A review. Int J Gynecol Pathol 1993, **12**: 101–107.

232 Parkinson C, Beilby JOW. Testicular germ cell tumours. Should current classification be revised? Invest Cell Pathol 1980, **3**: 135–140.

233 Pierce GB Jr, Bullock WK, Huntington RW Jr. Yolk sac tumors of the testis. Cancer 1970, **25**: 644–658.

234 Shirai T, Itoh T, Yoshiki T, Noro T, Tomino Y, Hayasaka T. Immunofluorescent demonstration of alpha-fetoprotein and other plasma proteins in yolk sac tumor. Cancer 1976, **38**: 1661–1667.

235 Siltanen S, Anttonen M, Heikkila P, Narita N, Laitinen M, Ritvos O, Wilson DB, Heikinheimo M. Transcription factor GATA-4 is expressed in pediatric yolk sac tumors. Am J Pathol 1999, **155**: 1823–1829.

236 Talerman A. Yolk sac tumor associated with seminoma of the testis in adults. Cancer 1974, **33**: 1468–1473.

237 Talerman A. The incidence of yolk sac tumor (endodermal sinus tumor) elements in germ cell tumors of the testis in adults. Cancer 1975, **36**: 211–215.

238 Talerman A. Endodermal sinus (yolk sac) tumor elements in testicular germ cell tumors in adults. Comparison of prospective and retrospective studies. Cancer 1980, **46**: 1213–1217.

239 Teilum G. Endodermal sinus tumor of the ovary and testis. Comparative morphogenesis of the so-called mesonephroma ovarii (Schiller) and of extraembryonic (yolk sac-allantoic) structures of the rat's placenta. Cancer 1959, **12**: 1092–1105.

240 Teoh TB, Steward JK, Willis RA. The distinctive adenocarcinoma of the infant's testis. An account of 15 cases. J Pathol Bacteriol 1960, **80**: 147–156.

241 Ulbright TM, Michael H, Loehrer PJ, Donohue JP. Spindle cell tumors resected from male patients with germ cell tumors. A clinicopathologic study of 14 cases. Cancer 1990, **65**: 148–156.

242 Ulbright TM, Roth LM, Brodhecker CA. Yolk sac differentiation in germ cell tumors. A morphologic study of 50 cases with emphasis on hepatic, enteric, and parietal yolk sac features. Am J Surg Pathol 1986, **10**: 151–164.

243 Woodtli W, Hedinger CE. Endodermal sinus tumor or orchioblastoma in children and adults. Virchows Arch [A] 1974, **364**: 93–110.

244 Wurster K, Hedinger CE, Meienberg O. Orchioblastomatous foci in testicular teratoma of adults. Virchows Arch [A] 1972, **357**: 231–242.

245 Young PG, Mount BM, Foote FW Jr, Whitmore WF Jr. Embryonal adenocarcinoma in the prepubertal testis. A clinicopathologic study of 18 cases. Cancer 1970, **26**: 1065–1075.

Intratubular germ cell neoplasia

246 Azzopardi JG, Mostofi FK, Theiss EA. Lesions of testes observed in certain patients with widespread choriocarcinoma and related tumors. Am J Pathol 1961, **38**: 207–225.

247 Bailey D, Marks A, Stratis M, Baumal R. Immunohistochemical staining of germ cell tumors and intratubular malignant germ cells of the testis using antibody to placental alkaline phosphatase and a monoclonal anti-seminoma antibody. Mod Pathol 1991, **4**: 167–171.

248 Berthelsen JG, Skakkebaek NE, Mogensen P, Sorensen BL. Incidence of carcinoma in situ of germ cells in contralateral testis of men with testicular tumours. BMJ 1979, **2**: 363–364.

249 Datta MW, Macri E, Signoretti S, Renshaw AA, Loda M. Transition from in situ to invasive testicular germ cell neoplasia

is associated with the loss of p21 and gain of mdm-2 expression. Mod Pathol 2001, **14**: 437–442.

250 de Graaff WE, Oosterhuis JW, de Jong B, Dam A, van Putten WL, Castedo SM, Sleijfer DT, Schraffordt Koops H. Ploidy of testicular carcinoma in situ. Lab Invest 1992, **66**: 166–168.

251 Dieckmann KP, Loy V. Prevalence of contralateral testicular intraepithelial neoplasia in patients with testicular germ cell neoplasms. J Clin Oncol 1996, **14**: 3126–3132.

251a Eyzaguirre E, Gatalica Z. Loss of fhit expression in testicular germ cell tumors and intratubular germ cell neoplasia. Mod Pathol 2002, **15**: 1068–1072.

252 Giwercman A, Hopman AH, Ramaekers FC, Skakkebaek NE. Carcinoma in situ of the testis. Possible origin, clinical significance, and diagnostic methods. Recent Results Cancer Res 1991, **123**: 21–36.

253 Giwercman A, von der Maase H, Berthelsen JG, Rorth M, Bertelsen A, Skakkebaek NE. Localized irradiation of testes with carcinoma in situ. Effects on Leydig cell function and eradication of malignant germ cells in 20 patients. J Clin Endocrinol Metab 1991, **73**: 596–603.

254 Gondos B, Migliozzi JA. Intratubular germ cell neoplasia. Semin Diagn Pathol 1987, **4**: 292–303.

255 Haiemariam S, Engeler DS, Bannwart F, Amin MB. Primary mediastinal germ cell tumor with intratubular germ cell neoplasia of the testis—further support for germ cell origin of these tumors: a case report. Cancer 1997, **79**: 1031–1036.

256 Hawkins E, Heifetz SA, Giller R, Cushing B. The prepubertal testis (prenatal and postnatal): its relationship to intratubular germ cell neoplasia: a combined Pediatric Oncology Group and Children's Cancer Study Group. Hum Pathol 1997, **28**: 404–410.

257 Hiraoka N, Yamada T, Abe H, Hata J. Establishment of three monoclonal antibodies specific for prespermatogonia and intratubular malignant germ cells in humans. Lab Invest 1997, **76**: 427–438.

258 Hu LM, Phillipson J, Barsky SH. Intratubular germ cell neoplasia in infantile yolk sac tumor. Verification by tandem repeat sequence in situ hybridization. Diagn Mol Pathol 1992, **1**: 118–128.

259 Jacobsen GK, Henriksen OB, Der Maase HV. Carcinoma in situ of testicular tissue adjacent to malignant germ-cell tumors. A study of 105 cases. Cancer 1981, **47**: 2660–2662.

260 Jorgensen N, Giwercman A, Muller J, Skakkebaek NE. Immunohistochemical markers of carcinoma in situ of the testis also expressed in normal infantile germ cells. Histopathology 1993, **22**: 373–378.

261 Kang J-L, Raipert-De Meyts E, Giwercman A, Skakkebaek NE. The association of testicular carcinoma in situ with intratubular microcalcifications. J Urol Pathol 1994, **2**: 235–242.

262 Klein FA, Melamed MR, Whitmore WF Jr. Intratubular malignant germ cells (carcinoma in situ) accompanying invasive testicular germ cell tumors. J Urol 1985, **133**: 413–415.

263 Kuczyk MA, Serth J, Bockemeyer C, Allhoff EP, Jonassen J, Kyczyk S, Jonas U. Overexpression of the p53 oncoprotein in carcinoma in situ of the testis. Pathol Res Pract 1994, **190**: 993–998.

264 Lifschitz-Mercer B, Elliott DJ, Leider-Trejo L, Schreiber-Bramante L, Hassner A, Eisenthal A, Maymon B. Absence of RBM expression as a marker of intratubular (in situ) germ cell neoplasia of the testis. Hum Pathol 2000, **31**: 1116–1120.

265 Lifschitz-Mercer B, Elliott DJ, Schreiber-Bramante L, Leider-Trejo L, Eisenthal A, Bar-Shira Maymon B. Intratubular germ cell neoplasia: associated infertility and review of the diagnostic modalities. Int J Surg Pathol 2001, **9**: 93–98.

266 Loftus BM, Gilmartin LG, O'Brien MJ, Carney DN, Dervan PA. Intratubular germ cell neoplasia of the testis. Identification by placental alkaline phosphatase immunostaining and argyrophilic nucleolar organizer region quantification. Hum Pathol 1990, **21**: 941–948.

267 Loy V, Dieckmann KP. Carcinoma in situ of the testis. Intratubular germ cell neoplasia or testicular intraepithelial neoplasia? Hum Pathol 1990, **21**: 457–458.

268 Loy V, Wigand I, Dieckmann KP. Incidence and distribution of carcinoma in situ in testes removed for germ cell tumour. Possible inadequacy of random testicular biopsy in detecting the condition. Histopathology 1990, **16**: 198–200.

269 Manivel JC, Jessurun J, Wick MR, Dehner LP. Placental alkaline phosphatase immunoreactivity in testicular germ-cell neoplasms. Am J Surg Pathol 1987, **11**: 21–29.

270 Manivel JC, Reinberg Y, Niehans GA, Fraley EE. Intratubular germ cell neoplasia in testicular teratomas and epidermoid cysts. Correlation with prognosis and possible biologic significance. Cancer 1989, **64**: 715–720.

271 Mikulowski P, Oldbring J. Microinvasive germ cell neoplasia of the testis. Cancer 1992, **70**: 659–664.

272 Moore BE, Banner BF, Gokden M, Woda B, Liu Y, Ayala A, Jiang Z. P53: a good diagnostic marker for intratubular germ cell neoplasia, unclassified. AIMM 2001, **9**: 203–206.

273 Mostofi FK. Pathology of germ cell tumors of the testis. A progress report. Cancer 1980, **45**: 1735–1754.

274 Niehans GA, Manivel JC, Wick MR, Dehner LP. Immunohistochemistry of intratubular germ cell neoplasia. Surg Pathol 1989, **2**: 213–230.

275 Nistal M, Codesal J, Paniagua R. Carcinoma in situ of the testis in infertile men. A histological, immunocytochemical, and cytophotometric study of DNA content. J Pathol 1989, **159**: 205–210.

276 Nuesch-Bachmann IH, Hedinger CE. Atypische Spermatogonien als präkanzerose. Schweiz Med Wochenschr 1977, **107**: 795–801.

277 Perry A, Wiley EL, Albores-Saavedra J. Pagetoid spread of intratubular germ cell neoplasia into rete testis. A morphologic and histochemical study of 100 orchiectomy specimens with invasive germ cell tumors. Hum Pathol 1994, **25**: 235–239.

278 Pryor JP, Cameron KM, Chilton CP, Ford TF, Parkinson MC, Sinokrot J, Westwood CA. Carcinoma in situ in testicular biopsies from men presenting with infertility. Br J Urol 1983, **55**: 780–784.

279 Rajpert-De Meyts E, Kvist M, Skakkebaek NE. Heterogeneity of expression of immunohistochemical tumour markers in testicular carcinoma in situ: pathogenetic relevance. Virchows Arch 1997, **428**: 133–140.

280 Rakheja D, Hoang MP, Sharma S, Albores-Saavedra J. Intratubular embryonal carcinoma. Arch Pathol Lab Med 2002, **126**: 487–490.

281 Ramani P, Yeung CK, Habeebu SS. Testicular intratubular germ cell neoplasia in children and adolescents with intersex. Am J Surg Pathol 1993, **17**: 1124–1133.

282 Renedo DE, Trainer TD. Intratubular germ cell neoplasia (ITGCN) with p53 and PCNA expression and adjacent mature teratoma in an infant testis. An immunohistochemical and morphologic study with a review of the literature. Am J Surg Pathol 1994, **18**: 947–952.

282a Schreiber L, Lifschitz-Mercer B, Paz G, Yavetz H, Elliott DJ, Kula K, Slowikowska-Hilczer J, Maymon B. Double immunolabeling by the RBM and the PLAP markers for identifying intratubular (in situ) germ cell neoplasia of the testis. Int J Surg Pathol 2003, **11**: 17–20.

282b Shah VI, Varma M, DePeralta M, Lim SD. Utility of CD117 (KIT) immunoreactivity (IR) in diagnostic histopathology of testicular germ cell tumor (Abstract). Mod Pathol 2003, **16**: 170A.

283 Skakkebaek NE. Atypical germ cells in the adjacent "normal" tissue of testicular tumours. Acta Pathol Microbiol Scand (A) 1975, **83**: 127–130.

284 Skakkebaek NE. Carcinoma in situ of the testis. Frequency and relationship to invasive germ cell tumours in infertile men. Histopathology 1978, **2**: 157–170.

284a Skotheim RI, Korkmaz KS, Klokk TI, Abeler VM, Korkmaz CG, Nesland JM, Fosså SD, Lothe RA, Saatcioglu F. NKX3.1

expression is lost in testicular germ cell tumors. Am J Pathol 2003; 163: 2149–2154.

285 Soosay GN, Bobrow L, Happerfield L, Parkinson MC. Morphology and immunohistochemistry of carcinoma in situ adjacent to testicular germ cell tumours in adults and children. Implications for histogenesis. Histopathology 1991, 19: 537–544.

286 Stamp IM, Barlebo H, Rix M, Jacobsen GK. Intratubular germ cell neoplasia in an infantile testis with immature teratoma. Histopathology 1993, 22: 69–72.

287 Walt H, Emmerich P, Cremer T, Hofmann MC, Bannwart F. Supernumerary chromosome 1 in interphase nuclei of atypical germ cells in paraffin-embedded human seminiferous tubules. Lab Invest 1989, 61: 527–531.

Germ cell tumors—overview

288 Abell MR, Holtz F. Testicular neoplasms in infants and children. I. Tumors of germ cell origin. Cancer 1963, 16: 965–981.

289 Abell MR, Holtz F. Testicular and paratesticular neoplasms in patients 60 years of age and older. Cancer 1968, 21: 852–870.

290 Albanell J, Bosl GJ, Reuter VE, Englehardt M, Franco S, Moore MA, Dmitrovsky E. Telomerase activity in germ cell cancers and mature teratomas. J Natl Cancer Inst 1999, 91: 1321–1326.

290a Albanese JM, Reuter VE, Bosl GJ, Houldsworth J, Chaganti RSK. Expression of id genes in differentiated elements of human male germ cell tumors. Diagn Mol Pathol 2001, 10: 248–254.

291 Alderdice JM, Merrett JD. Factors influencing the survival of patients with testicular teratoma. J Clin Pathol 1985, 38: 791–796.

292 Aristizabal S, Davis JR, Miller RC, Moore MJ, Boone MLM. Bilateral primary germ cell testicular tumors. Report of four cases and review of the literature. Cancer 1978, 42: 591–597.

293 Babaian RJ, Johnson DE. Management of stages I and II nonseminomatous germ cell tumors of the testis. Cancer 1980, 45: 1775–1781.

294 Bar W, Hedinger CE. Comparison of histologic types of primary testicular germ cell tumors with their metastases. Consequences for the WHO and the British nomenclatures? Virchows Arch [A] 1976, 370: 41–54.

295 Birkhead BM, Scott RM. Spontaneous regression of metastatic testicular cancer. Cancer 1973, 32: 125–129.

296 Blough RI, Heerema NA, Ulbright TM, Smolarek TA, Roth LM, Einhorn LH. Interphase chromosome painting of paraffin-embedded tissues in the differential diagnosis of possible germ cell tumors. Mod Pathol 1998, 11: 634–641.

297 Bosl GJ, Ilson DH, Rodriguez E, Motzer RJ, Reuter VE, Chaganti RS. Clinical relevance of the i(12p) marker chromosome in germ cell tumors. J Natl Cancer Inst 1994, 86: 349–355.

298 Bosl GJ, Lange PH, Fraley EE, Goldman A, Nochomovitz LE, Rosai J, Waldman TA, Johnson J, Kennedy BJ. Human chorionic gonadotropin and alphafetoprotein in the staging of nonseminomatous testicular cancer. Cancer 1981, 47: 328–332.

299 Bosl GJ, Motzer RJ. Testicular germ-cell cancer. N Engl J Med 1997, 337: 242–253.

300 Bredael JJ, Vugrin D, Whitmore WF Jr. Autopsy findings in 154 patients with germ cell tumors of the testis. Cancer 1982, 50: 548–551.

301 Caldwell WL, Kademian MT, Frias Z, Davis TE. The management of testicular seminomas, 1979. Cancer 1980, 45: 1768–1774.

302 Carroll WL, Kempson RL, Govan DE, Freiha FS, Shochat SJ, Link MP. Conservative management of testicular endodermal sinus tumors in childhood. J Urol 1985, 133: 1011–1014.

302a Che M, Tamboli P, Ro JY, Park DS, Ro JS, Amato RJ, Ayala AG. Bilateral testicular germ cell tumors: twenty-year experience at M.D. Anderson Cancer Center. Cancer 2002, 95: 1228–1233.

303 Collins DH, Pugh RCP. Classification and frequency of testicular tumours. Br J Urol 1964, 36(Suppl): 1–11.

304 Datta MW, Renshaw AA, Dutta A, Hoffman MA, Loughlin KR.

Evaluation of cyclin expression in testicular germ cell tumors: cyclin E correlates with tumor type, advanced clinical stage, and pulmonary metastasis. Mod Pathol 2000, 13: 667–672.

305 De Bruijn HWA, Sleijfer DTH, Koops HS, Suurmeijer AJH, Marrink J, Ockhuizen T. Significance of human chorionic gonadotropin, alpha-fetoprotein, and pregnancy-specific beta-1-glycoprotein in the detection of tumor relapse and partial remission in 126 patients with nonseminomatous testicular germ cell tumors. Cancer 1985, 55: 829–835.

306 de Graaff WE, Oosterhuis JW, van der Linden S, Homan van der Heide JN, Schraffordt Koops H, Sleijfer DT. Residual mature teratoma after chemotherapy for nonseminomatous germ cell tumors of the testis occurs significantly less often in lung than in retroperitoneal lymph node metastases. J Urogen Pathol 1991, 1: 75–81.

307 De Jong B, Oosterhuis JW, Castedo SMMJ, Vos AM, te Meerman GJ. Pathogenesis of adult testicular germ cell tumors. A cytogenetic model. Cancer Genet Cytogenet 1990, 48: 143–167.

308 Delgado R, Rathi A, Albores-Saavedra J, Gazdar AF. Expression of the RNA component of human telomerase in adult testicular germ cell neoplasia. Cancer 1999, 86: 1802–1811.

309 Donohue JP, Zachary JM, Maynard BR. Distribution of nodal metastases in nonseminomatous testis cancer. J Urol 1982, 128: 315–320.

310 Dry SM, Renshaw AA. Extratesticular extension of germ cell tumors preferentially occurs at the hilum. Am J Clin Pathol 1999, 111: 534–538.

311 Duchesne GM, Horwich A, Dearnaley DP, Nicholls J, Jay G, Peckham MJ, Hendry WF. Orchidectomy alone for stage I seminoma of the testis. Cancer 1990, 65: 1115–1118.

312 el-Naggar AK, Ro JY, McLemore D, Ayala AG, Batsakis JG. DNA ploidy in testicular germ cell neoplasms. Histogenetic and clinical implications. Am J Surg Pathol 1992, 16: 611–618.

313 Ferlicot S, Paradis V, Ladouch A, Ben Lagha N, Eschwege P, Benoit G, Bedossa P. "Burned out" testicular tumor: report of three cases. J Urol Pathol 1999, 11: 171–180.

314 Foster RS, Roth BJ. Clinical stage 1 nonseminoma: surgery versus surveillance. Semin Oncol 1998, 25: 145–153.

315 Fraley EE, Lange PH, Williams RD, Ortlip SA. Staging of early nonseminomatous germ-cell testicular cancer. Cancer 1980, 45: 1762–1767.

316 Fraley EE, Narayan P, Vogelzang NJ, Kennedy BJ, Lange PH. Surgical treatment of patients with stages I and II nonseminomatous testicular cancer. J Urol 1985, 124: 70–73.

317 Fuller DB, Plenk HP. Malignant germ cell tumors in a father and two sons. Case report and literature review. Cancer 1986, 58: 955–958.

318 Gelderman WAH, Koops HS, Sleijfer DTH, Oosterhuis JW, Marrink J, De Bruijn HWA, Oldhoff J. Orchidectomy alone in stage I nonseminomatous testicular germ cell tumors. Cancer 1987, 59: 578–580.

319 Gospodarowicz MK, Sturgeon JF, Jewett MA. Early stage and advanced seminoma: role of radiation therapy, surgery, and chemotherapy. Semin Oncol 1998, 25: 160–173.

320 Goss PE, Bulbul MA. Familial testicular cancer in five members of a cancer-prone kindred. Cancer 1990, 66: 2044–2046.

321 Guillou L, Estreicher A, Chaubert P, Hurlimann J, Kurt AM, Metthez G, Iggo R, Gray AC, Jichlinski P, Leisinger HJ, Benhattar J. Germ cell tumors of the testis overexpress wild-type p53. Am J Pathol 1996, 149: 1221–1228.

322 Hentrich MU, Brack NG, Schmid P, Schuster T, Clemm C, Hartenstein RC. Testicular germ cell tumors in patients with human immunodeficiency virus infection. Cancer 1996, 77: 2109–2116.

323 Hittmair A, Rogatsch H, Feichtinger H, Gobisch A, Miku G. Testicular seminomas are aneuploid tumors. Lab Invest 1995, 72: 70–74.

324 Hong WK, Wittes RE, Hajdu ST, Cvitkovic E, Whitmore WF,

Golbey RB. The evolution of mature teratoma from malignant testicular tumors. Cancer 1977, **40**: 2987–2992.

325 Horwich A, Dearnaley DP. Treatment of seminoma. Semin Oncol 1992, **19**: 171–180.

326 Hull MT, Warfel KA, Eble JN, Irons DA, Foster RS. Glycogen-rich clear cell adenocarcinomas arising in metastatic testicular germ cell tumors. J Urol Pathol 1994, **2**: 183–194.

326a Imperial SL, Sidhu JS. Nonseminomatous germ cell tumor arising in splenogonadal fusion. Arch Pathol Lab Med 2002, **126**: 1222.

327 International Germ Cell Cancer Collaborative Group. International germ cell consensus classification: a prognostic factor-based staging system for metastatic germ cell cancers. J Clin Oncol 1997, **15**: 594–603.

328 Jacobsen GK, Mellemgaard A, Engelholm SA, Moller H. Increased incidence of sarcoma in patients treated for testicular seminoma. Eur J Cancer 1993, **29A**: 664–668.

329 Johnson DE, Bracken RB, Blight EM. Prognosis for pathologic stage I non-seminomatous germ cell tumors of the testis managed by retroperitoneal lymphadenectomy. J Urol 1976, **116**: 63–65.

329a Kernek KM, Zhang S, Ulbright TM, Billings SD, Cummings OW, Henley JD, Michael H, Brunelli M, Martignoni G, Eble JN, Cheng L. Identical allelic loss in mature teratoma and different histologic components of malignant mixed germ cell tumors of the testis (Abstract). Mod Pathol 2003, **16**: 157A.

330 Klein FA, Whitmore WF Jr, Sogani PC, Batata M, Fisher H, Herr HW. Inguinal lymph node metastases from germ cell testicular tumors. J Urol 1984, **131**: 497–500.

331 Klepp O, Olsson AM, Henrikson H, Aass N, Dahl O, Stenwig AE, Persson BE, Cavallin-Stahl E, Fossa SD, Wahlqvist L. Prognostic factors in clinical stage I nonseminomatous germ cell tumors of the testis: Multivariate analysis of a prospective multicenter study. Swedish-Norwegian Testicular Cancer Group. J Clin Oncol 1990, **8**: 509–518.

332 Korman HJ, Schultz DS, Linden MD, Miles BJ, Peabody JO. Proliferating cell nuclear antigen and mutant p53 staining in testicular nonseminomatous germ-cell tumors. A pilot study. J Urol Pathol 1994, **2**: 327–336.

333 Kristainslund S, Fossa SD, Kjellevold K. Bilateral malignant testicular germ cell cancer. Br J Urol 1986, **58**: 60–63.

334 Lange PH, McIntire KR, Waldmann TA, Hakala TR, Fraley EE. Serum alphafetoprotein and human chorionic gonadotropin in the diagnosis and management of nonseminomatous germ-cell testicular cancer. N Engl J Med 1976, **295**: 1237–1240.

335 Logothetis CJ, Samuels ML, Selig DE, Johnson DE, Swanson DA, von Eschenbach AC. Primary chemotherapy followed by a selective retroperitoneal lymphadenectomy in the management of clinical stage II testicular carcinoma. A preliminary report. J Urol 1985, **134**: 1127–1130.

335a Looijenga LHJ, Oosterhuis JW. Pathobiology of testicular germ cell tumors. Analyt Quant Cytol Histol 2002, **24**: 263–279.

335b Lutke Holzik MF, Sijmons RH, Sleijfer DT, Sonneveld DJ, Hoekstra-Weebers J, van Echten-Arends J, Hoekstra HJ. Syndromic aspects of testicular carcinoma. Cancer 2003, **97**: 984–992.

336 Madden M, Goldstraw P, Corrin B. Effect of chemotherapy on the histological appearances of testicular teratoma metastatic to the lung. Correlation with patient survival. J Clin Pathol 1984, **37**: 1212–1214.

337 Mai KT, Yazdi HM, Rippstein P. Light and electron microscopy of the pagetoid spread of germ cell carcinoma in the rete testis: morphologic evidence suggestive of field effect as a mechanism of tumor spread. AIMM 2001, **9**: 335–339.

338 Marks LB, Rutgers JL, Shipley WU, Walker TG, Stracher MS, Waltman AC, Geller SC. Testicular seminoma. Clinical and pathological features that may predict para-aortic lymph node metastases. J Urol 1990, **143**: 524–527.

339 McCartney ACE, Paradinas FJ, Newlands ES. Significance of the "maturation" of metastases from germ cell tumours after intensive chemotherapy. Histopathology 1984, **8**: 457–467.

339a Mcglynn KA, Devesa SS, Sigurdson AJ, Brown LM, Tsao L, Tarone RE. Trends in the incidence of testicular germ cell tumors in the United States. Cancer 2003, **97**: 63–70.

340 Mencel PJ, Motzer RF, Mazumdar M, Vlamis V, Bajorin DF, Bosl GJ. Advanced seminoma. Treatment results, survival, and prognostic factors in 142 patients. J Clin Oncol 1994, **12**: 120–126.

341 Michael H. Nongerm cell tumors arising in patients with testicular germ cell tumors. J Urol Pathol 1998, **9**: 39–60.

342 Michael H, Hull MT, Foster RS, Sweeney CJ, Ulbright TM. Nephroblastoma-like tumors in patients with testicular germ cell tumors. Am J Surg Pathol 1998, **22**: 1107–1114.

343 Michael H, Lucia J, Foster RS, Ulbright TM. The pathology of late recurrence of testicular germ cell tumors. Am J Surg Pathol 2000, **24**: 257–273.

344 Moran CA, Travis WD, Carter D, Koss MN. Metastatic mature teratoma in lung following testicular embryonal carcinoma and teratocarcinoma. Arch Pathol Lab Med 1993, **117**: 641–644.

345 Moriyama N, Daly JJ, Keating MA, Lin C-W, Prout GR Jr. Vascular invasion as a prognosticator of metastatic disease in nonseminomatous germ cell tumors of the testis. Importance in "surveillance only" protocols. Cancer 1985, **56**: 2492–2498.

346 Mostert M, Rosenberg C, Stoop H, Schuyer M, Timmer A, Oosterhuis W, Looijenga L. Comparative genomic and in situ hybridization of germ cell tumors of the infantile testis. Lab Invest 2000, **80**: 1055–1064.

347 Murty VV, Houldsworth J, Baldwin S, Reuter V, Hunziker W, Besmer P, Bosl G, Chaganti RS. Allelic deletions in the long arm of chromosome 12 identify sites of candidate tumor suppressor genes in male germ cell tumors. Proc Natl Acad Sci U S A 1992, **89**: 11006–11010.

348 Nazeer T, Ro JY, Kee KH, Ayala AG. Spermatic cord contamination in testicular cancer. Mod Pathol 1996, **9**: 762–766.

349 Oosterhuis JW, Castedo SM, de Jong B, Cornelisse CJ, Dam A, Sleijfer DT, Schraffordt Koops H. Ploidy of primary germ cell tumors of the testis. Pathogenetic and clinical relevance. Lab Invest 1989, **60**: 14–21.

350 Panicek DM, Toner GC, Heelan RT, Bosl GJ. Nonseminomatous germ cell tumors: Enlarging masses despite chemotherapy. Radiology 1990, **175**: 499–502.

351 Patel SR, Kvols LK, Richardson RL. Familial testicular cancer. Report of six cases and review of the literature. Mayo Clin Proc 1990, **65**: 804–808.

352 Patel SR, Richardson RL, Kvols L. Synchronous and metachronous bilateral testicular tumors. Mayo Clinic experience. Cancer 1990, **65**: 1–4.

353 Peckham MJ, Barrett A, Horwich A, Hendry WF. Orchiectomy alone for stage I testicular nonseminoma. A progress report on the Royal Marsden Hospital Study. Br J Urol 1983, **55**: 754–759.

354 Qvist HL, Fossa SD, Ous S, Hoie J, Stenwig AE, Giercksky KE. Post-chemotherapy tumor residuals in patients with advanced nonseminomatous testicular cancer. Is it necessary to resect all residual masses? J Urol 1991, **145**: 300–302.

355 Raghavan D, Vogelzang NJ, Bosl GJ, Nochomovitz LE, Rosai J, Lange PH, Fraley EE, Goldman A, Torkelson J, Kennedy BJ. Tumor classification and size in germ-cell testicular cancer. Influence on the occurrence of metastases. Cancer 1982, **50**: 1591–1595.

356 Raghavan D, Zalcberg JR, Grygiel JJ, Teriana N, Cox KM, McCarthy W, Flynn M. Multiple atypical nevi. A cutaneous marker of germ cell tumors. J Clin Oncol 1994, **12**: 2284–2287.

357 Raina V, Singh SP, Kamble N, Tanwar R, Rao K, Dawar R, Rath GK. Brain metastasis as the site of relapse in germ cell tumor of testis. Cancer 1993, **72**: 2182–2185.

358 Ray B, Hajdu SI, Whitmore WF Jr. Distribution of retroperitoneal lymph node metastases in testicular germinal tumors. Cancer 1974, **33**: 340–348.

359 Rayson D, Burch PA, Richardson RL. Sarcoidosis and testicular carcinoma. Cancer 1998, **83**: 337–343.

360 Reinberg Y, Manivel JC, Zhang G, Reddy PK. Synchronous bilateral testicular germ cell tumors of different histologic type. Pathogenetic and practical implications of bilaterality in testicular germ cell tumors. Cancer 1991, **68**: 1082–1085.

361 Ro JY, Dexeus FH, el-Naggar A, Ayala AG. Testicular germ cell tumors. Clinically relevant pathologic findings. Pathol Annu 1991, **26**: (Pt2): 59–87.

362 Rorth M. Therapeutic alternatives in clinical stage I nonseminomatous disease. Semin Oncol 1992, **19**: 190–196.

363 Rosai J, Silber I, Khodadoust K. Spermatocytic seminoma. I. Clinicopathologic study of six cases and review of the literature. Cancer 1969, **24**: 92–102.

364 Sella A, el Naggar A, Ro JY, Dexeus FH, Amato RJ, Lee JS, Finn L, Logothetis CJ. Evidence of malignant features in histologically mature teratoma. J Urol 1991, **146**: 1025–1028.

365 Sheinfeld J, Herr HW. Role of surgery in management of germ cell tumor. Semin Oncol 1998, **25**: 203–209.

366 Snyder RN. Completely mature pulmonary metastasis from testicular teratocarcinoma. Case report and review of the literature. Cancer 1969, **24**: 810–819.

367 Sonnevald DJ, Sleijfer DT, Koops HS, Deemers-Gels ME, Molenaar WM, Hoekstra HJ. Mature teratoma identified after postchemotherapy surgery in patients with disseminated nonseminomatous testicular germ cell tumors: a plea for an aggressive surgical approach. Cancer 1998, **82**: 1343–1351.

368 Steyerberg EW, Keizer HJ, Fossa SD, Sleijfer DT, Toner GC, Schraffordt Koops H, Mulders PF, Messemer JE, Ney K, Donohue JP, et al. Prediction of residual retroperitoneal mass histology after chemotherapy for metastatic nonseminomatous germ cell tumor. Multivariate analysis of individual patient data from six study groups. J Clin Oncol 1995, **13**: 1177–1187.

369 Steyerberg EW, Keizer HJ, Messemer JE, Toner GC, Schraffordt Koops H, Fossa SD, Gerl A, Sleiffer DT, Donohue JP, Habbema JD. Residual pulmonary masses after chemotherapy for metastatic nonseminomatous germ cell tumor: prediction of histology. Cancer 1997, **79**: 345–355.

370 Sweeney CJ, Hermans BP, Heilman DK, Foster RS, Donohue JP, Einhorn LH. Results and outcome of retroperitoneal lymph node dissection for clinical stage 1 embryonal carcinoma-predominant testis cancer. J Clin Oncol 2000, **18**: 358–362.

370a Takayama H, Takakuwa T, Tsujimoto Y, Tani Y, Nonomura N, Okuyama A, Nagata S, Aozasa K. Frequent fas gene mutations in testicular germ cell tumors. Am J Pathol 2002, **161**: 635–641.

371 Ulbright TM. Germ cell neoplasms of the testis. Am J Surg Pathol 1993, **17**: 1075–1091.

372 Ulbright TM, Roth LM. A pathologic analysis of lesions following modern chemotherapy for metastatic germ-cell tumors. Pathol Annu 1990, **25**(Pt I): 313–340.

373 Ulbright TM, Loehrer PJ, Roth LM, Einhorn LH, Williams SD, Clark SA. The development of non-germ-cell malignancies within germ cell tumors. A clinicopathologic study of 11 cases. Cancer 1984, **54**: 1824–1833.

374 Ulbright TM, Orazi A, de Riese W, de Riese C, Messemer JE, Foster RS, Donohue JP, Eble JN. The correlation of p53 protein expression with proliferative activity and occult metastases in clinical stage I nonseminomatous germ cell tumors of the testis. Mod Pathol 1994, **7**: 64–68.

375 van der Werf-Messing B. Radiotherapeutic treatment of testicular tumors. Int J Radiat Oncol Biol Phys 1976, **1**: 235–248.

376 van Echten J, Oosterhuis JW, Looijenga LHJ, Dam A, Sleiffer DT, Schraffordt Koops H, de Jong B. Mixed testicular germ cell tumors: monoclonal or polyclonal. Mod Pathol 1996, **9**: 371–374.

377 Williams SD, Stablein DM, Einhorn LH, Muggia FM, Weiss RB, Donohue JP, Paulon DF, Brunner KW, Jacobs EM, Spaulding JT, DeWys WD, Crawford ED. Immediate adjuvant chemotherapy versus observation with treatment at relapse in pathological stage II testicular cancer. N Engl J Med 1987, **317**: 1433–1438.

378 Young PG, Mount BM, Foote FW Jr, Whitmore WF Jr. Embryonal adenocarcinoma in the prepubertal testis. A clinicopathologic study of 18 cases. Cancer 1970, **26**: 1065–1075.

Sex cord–stromal tumors
Leydig cell tumor and related lesions

379 Augusto D, Leteurtre E, de la Taille A, Gosselin B, Leroy X. Calretinin: a valuable marker of normal and neoplastic Leydig cells of the testis. Appl Immunohistochem Mol Morphol 2002, **10**: 159–162.

380 Balsitis M, Sokal M. Ossifying malignant Leydig (interstitial) cell tumour of the testis. Histopathology 1990, **16**: 599–601.

381 Bercovici JP, Nahoul K, Ducasse M, Tater D, Kerlan V, Scholler R. Leydig cell tumor with gynecomastia. Further studies—the recovery after unilateral orchidectomy. J Clin Endocrinol Metab 1985, **61**: 957–962.

382 Billings SD, Roth LM, Ulbright TM. Microcystic Leydig cell tumors mimicking yolk sac tumor: a report of four cases. Am J Surg Pathol 1999, **23**: 546–551.

383 Busam KJ, Iversen K, Coplan KA, Old LJ, Stockert E, Chen YT, McGregor D, Jungbluth A. Immunoreactivity for A103 and antibody to Melan-A (Mart-1) in adrenocortical and other steroid tumors. Am J Surg Pathol 1998, **22**: 57–63.

384 Cheville JC, Sebo TJ, Lager DJ, Bostwick DG, Farrow GM. Leydig cell tumor of the testis: a clinicopathologic, DNA content and MIB-1 comparison of nonmetastasizing and metastasizing tumors. Am J Surg Pathol 1998, **22**: 1361–1367.

385 Czernobilsky H, Czernobilsky B, Schneider HG, Franke WW, Ziegler R. Characterization of a feminizing testicular Leydig cell tumor by hormonal profile, immunocytochemistry, and tissue culture. Cancer 1985, **56**: 1667–1676.

386 Dieckmann KP, Loy V. Metachronous germ cell and Leydig cell tumors of the testis. Do testicular germ cell tumors and Leydig cell tumors share common etiologic factors? Cancer 1993, **72**: 1305–1307.

387 Ekfors TO, Martikainen P, Kuopio T, Malmi R, Nurmi MJ. Ultrastructure and immunohistochemistry of a fetal-type Leydig cell tumor. Ultrastruct Pathol 1992, **16**: 651–658.

388 Freeman DA. Steroid hormone-producing tumors of the adrenal, ovary, and testes. Endocrinol Metab Clin North Am 1991, **20**: 751–766.

389 Gabrilove JL, Nicolis GL, Mitty HA, Sohval AR. Feminizing interstitial cell tumor of the testis. Personal observations and a review of the literature. Cancer 1975, **35**: 1184–1202.

390 Grem JL, Robins HI, Wilson KS, Gilchrist K, Trump DL. Metastatic Leydig cell tumor of the testis. Report of three cases and review of the literature. Cancer 1986, **58**: 2116–2119.

391 Gulbahce HE, Lindeland AT, Engel W, Lillemoe TJ. Metastatic Leydig cell tumor with sarcomatoid differentiation. Arch Pathol Lab Med 1999, **123**: 1104–1107.

392 Kim I, Young RH, Scully RE. Leydig cell tumors of the testis. A clinicopathological analysis of 40 cases and review of the literature. Am J Surg Pathol 1985, **9**: 177–192.

393 Knudsen JL, Savage A, Mobb GE. The testicular "tumour" of adrenogenital syndrome—a persistent diagnostic pitfall. Histopathology 1991, **19**: 468–470.

394 Kurman RJ, Andrade D, Goebelsmann U, Taylor CR. An immunohistological study of steroid localization in Sertoli-Leydig tumors of the ovary and testis. Cancer 1978, **42**: 1772–1783.

395 Liu G, Duranteau L, Carel JC, Monroe J, Doyle DA, Shenker A.

Leydig-cell tumors caused by an activating mutation of the gene encoding the luteinizing hormone receptor. N Engl J Med 1999, **341**: 1731–1736.

396 Mahon FB Jr, Gosset F, Trinity RG, Madsen PO. Malignant interstitial cell testicular tumor. Cancer 1973, **31**: 1208–1212.

397 Maurer R, Taylor CR, Schmucki O, Hedinger CE. Extratesticular gonadal stromal tumor of the testis. A case report with immunoperoxidase findings. Cancer 1980, **45**: 985–990.

398 McCluggage WG, Shanks JH, Arthur K, Banerjee SS. Cellular proliferation and nuclear ploidy assessments augment established prognostic factors in predicting malignancy in testicular Leydig cell tumours. Histopathology 1998, **33**: 361–368.

399 McCluggage WG, Shanks JH, Whiteside C, Maxwell P, Banerjee SS, Biggart JD. Immunohistochemical study of testicular sex cord-stromal tumors, including staining with anti-inhibin antibody. Am J Surg Pathol 1998, **22**: 615–619.

400 McLaren K, Thomson D. Localization of S-100 protein in a Leydig and Sertoli cell tumour of testis. Histopathology 1989, **15**: 649–652.

401 Rutgers JL, Young RH, Scully RE. The testicular "tumor" of the adrenogenital syndrome. Am J Surg Pathol 1988, **12**: 503–513.

402 Santonja C, Varona C, Burgos FJ, Nistal M. Leydig cell tumor of testis with adipose metaplasia. Appl Pathol 1989, **7**: 201–204.

403 Sohval AR, Churg J, Gabrilove JL, Freiberg EK, Katz N. Ultrastructure of feminizing testicular Leydig cell tumors. Ultrastruct Pathol 1982, **3**: 335–345.

404 Sugimura J, Suzuki Y, Tamura G, Funaki H, Fujioka T, Satodate R. Metachronous development of malignant Leydig cell tumor. Hum Pathol 1997, **28**: 1318–1320.

404a Ulbright TM, Srigley JR, Hatzianastassiou DK, Young RH. Leydig cell tumors of the testis with unusual features: adipose differentiation, calcification with ossification, and spindle-shaped tumor cells. Am J Surg Pathol 2002, **26**: 1424–1433.

Tumors and tumorlike conditions of Sertoli cells

405 Cano-Valdez AM, Chanona-Vilchis J, Dominguez-Malagon H. Large cell calcifying Sertoli cell tumor of the testis: a clinicopathological immunohistochemical, and ultrastructural study of two cases. Ultrastruct Pathol 1999, **23**: 259–265.

406 Carney JA, Gordon H, Carpenter PC, Shenoy BV, Go VLW. The complex of myxomas, spotty pigmentation, and endocrine overactivity. Medicine 1985, **64**: 270–283.

407 Gilcrease MZ, Delgado R, Albores-Saavedra J. Testicular Sertoli cell tumor with a heterologous sarcomatous component: immunohistochemical assessment of Sertoli cell differentiation. Arch Pathol Lab Med 1998, **122**: 907–911.

408 Gordon MD, Corless C, Renshaw AA, Beckstead J. CD99, keratin, and vimentin staining of sex cord-stromal tumors, normal ovary, and testis. Mod Pathol 1998, **11**: 769–773.

409 Hedinger CE, Huber R, Weber E. Frequency of so-called hypoplastic or dysgenetic zones in scrotal and otherwise normal human testes. Virchows Arch [A] 1967, **342**: 165–168.

410 Henley JD, Young RH, Ulbright TM. Malignant Sertoli cell tumors of the testis: A study of 13 examples of a neoplasm frequently misinterpreted as a seminoma. Am J Surg Pathol 2002, **26**: 541–550.

411 Higgins JP, Rouse RV. Testicular Sertoli cell tumors NOS, the final word? Adv Anat Pathol 1999, **6**: 103–113.

412 Hopkins GB, Parry HD. Metastasizing Sertoli-cell tumor (androblastoma). Cancer 1969, **23**: 463–467.

413 Jacobsen GK. Malignant Sertoli cell tumors of the testis. J Urol Pathol 1993, **1**: 233–255.

414 Kaplan GW, Cromie WJ, Kelalis PP, Silber I, Tank ES Jr. Gonadal stromal tumors. A report of the prepubertal testicular tumor registry. J Urol 1986, **136**: 300–302.

415 Manuel M, Katayama KP, Jones HW Jr. The age of occurrence of gonadal tumor in intersex patients with a Y chromosome. Am J Obstet Gynecol 1976, **124**: 293–300.

416 Mostofi FK, Theiss EA, Ashley DJB. Tumors of specialized gonadal stroma in human male patients. Androblastoma. Sertoli cell tumor, granulosa-theca cell tumor of the testis, and gonadal stromal tumor. Cancer 1959, **12**: 944–957.

417 Neubecker RD, Theiss EA. Sertoli cell adenomas in patients with testicular feminization. Am J Clin Pathol 1962, **38**: 52–59.

418 O'Connell MJ, Ramsey HE, Whang-Peng J, Wiernik PH. Testicular feminization syndrome in three sibs. Emphasis on gonadal neoplasia. Am J Med Sci 1973, **265**: 321–333.

419 Plata C, Algaba F, Andujar M, Nistal M, Stocks P, Martinez JL, Nogales FF. Large cell calcifying Sertoli cell tumour of the testis. Histopathology 1995, **26**: 255–260.

420 Proppe KH, Dickersin GR. Large-cell calcifying Sertoli cell tumor of the testis. Light microscopic and ultrastructural study. Hum Pathol 1982, **13**: 1109–1114.

421 Proppe KH, Scully RE. Large-cell calcifying Sertoli cell tumor of the testis. Am J Clin Pathol 1980, **74**: 607–619.

422 Ramaswamy G, Jagadha V, Tcherkoff V. A testicular tumor resembling the sex cord with annular tubules in a case of the androgen insensitivity syndrome. Cancer 1985, **55**: 1607–1611.

423 Rey R, Sabourin J-C, Venara M, Long WQ, Jaubert F, Zeller WP, Duvillard P, Chemes H, Bidart J-M. Anti-Mullerian hormone is a specific marker of Sertoli- and granulosa-cell origin in gonadal tumors. Hum Pathol 2000, **31**: 1202–1208.

424 Samaratunga H, Spork MR, Cooritz D. Sclerosing Sertoli cell tumor of the testis. J Urol Pathol 2000, **12**: 39–50.

425 Sohval AR. Testicular dysgenesis in relation to neoplasm of the testicle. J Urol 1956, **75**: 285–291.

426 Talerman A. Malignant Sertoli cell tumor of the testis. Cancer 1971, **28**: 446–455.

427 Tanaka Y, Carney JA, Ijiri R, Kato K, Miyake T, Nakatani Y, Misugi K. Utility of immunostaining for S-100 protein subunits in gonadal sex cord-stromal tumors, with emphasis on the large-cell calcifying Sertoli cell tumor of the testis. Hum Pathol 2002, **33**: 285–289.

428 Teilum G. Classification of testicular and ovarian androblastoma and Sertoli cell tumors. Cancer 1958, **11**: 769–782.

429 Tetu B, Ro JY, Ayala AG. Large cell calcifying Sertoli cell tumor of the testis. A clinicopathologic, immunohistochemical, and ultrastructural study of two cases. Am J Clin Pathol 1991, **96**: 717–722.

430 Venara M, Rey R, Bergadà I, Mendilaharzu H, Campo S, Chemes H. Sertoli cell proliferations of the infantile testis: an intratubular form of Sertoli cell tumor? Am J Surg Pathol 2001, **25**: 1237–1244.

431 Young RH, Talerman A. Testicular tumors other than germ cell tumors. Semin Diagn Pathol 1987, **4**: 342–360.

432 Young RH, Koelliker DD, Scully RE. Sertoli cell tumors of the testis, not otherwise specified: a clinicopathologic analysis of 60 cases. Am J Surg Pathol 1998, 22: 709–721.

433 Young S, Gooneratne S, Straus FH, Zeller WP, Bulun SE, Rosenthal IM. Feminizing Sertoli cell tumors in boys with Peutz-Jeghers syndrome. Am J Surg Pathol 1995, **19**: 50–58.

434 Zukerberg LR, Young RH, Scully RE. Sclerosing Sertoli cell tumor of the testis. A report of 10 cases. Am J Surg Pathol 1991, **15**: 829–834.

Other sex cord–stromal tumors

435 Brennan MK, Srigley JR. Brenner tumor of the testis: case report and review of other intrascrotal examples. J Urol Pathol 1999, **10**: 219–228.

436 Caccamo D, Socias M, Truchet C. Malignant Brenner tumor of the testis and epididymis. Arch Pathol Lab Med 1991, **115**: 524–527.

437 Chan JK, Chan VS, Mak KL. Congenital juvenile granulosa cell tumour of the testis. Report of a case showing extensive degenerative changes. Histopathology 1990, **17**: 75–80.

438 De Pinieux G, Glaser C, Chatelain D, Perie G, Flam T, Vieillefond A. Testicular fibroma of gonadal stromal origin with minor sex cord elements: clinicopathologic and immunohistochemical study of 2 cases. Arch Pathol Lab Med 1999, **123**: 391–394.

439 Due W, Dieckmann KP, Niedobitek G, Bornhoft G, Loy V, Stein H. Testicular sex cord stromal tumour with granulosa cell differentiation. Detection of steroid hormone receptors as a possible basis for tumour development and therapeutic management. J Clin Pathol 1990, **43**: 732–737.

440 Harms D, Kock LR. Testicular juvenile granulosa cell and Sertoli cell tumours: a clinicopathologic study of 29 cases from the Kiel Paediatric Tumour Registry. Virchows Arch 1997, **430**: 301–310.

441 Jimenez-Quintero LP, Ro JY, Zavala-Pompa A, Amin MB, Tetu B, Ordonez NG, Ayala AG. Granulosa cell tumor of the adult testis. A clinicopathologic study of seven cases and a review of the literature. Hum Pathol 1994, **24**: 1120–1125.

442 Jones MA, Young RH, Scully RE. Benign fibromatous tumors of the testis and paratesticular region: a report of 9 cases with a proposed classification of fibromatous tumors and tumor-like lesions. Am J Surg Pathol 1997, **21**: 296–305.

443 Lawrence WD, Young RH, Scully RE. Juvenile granulosa cell tumor of the infantile testis. A report of 14 cases. Am J Surg Pathol 1985, **9**: 87–94.

444 Matoska J, Ondrus D, Talerman A. Malignant granulosa cell tumor of the testis associated with gynecomastia and long survival. Cancer 1992, **69**: 1769–1772.

445 Miettinen M, Salo J, Virtanen I. Testicular stromal tumor. Ultrastructural, immunohistochemical, and gel electrophoretic evidence of epithelial differentiation. Ultrastruct Pathol 1986, **10**: 515–528.

446 Mostofi FK, Theiss EA, Ashley DJB. Tumors of specialized gonadal stroma in human male patients. Androblastoma, Sertoli cell tumor, granulosa-theca cell tumor of the testis, and gonadal stromal tumor. Cancer 1959, **12**: 944–957.

447 Nistal M, Puras A, Perna C, Guarch R, Paniagua R. Fusocellular gonadal stromal tumour of the testis with epithelial and myoid differentiation. Histopathology 1996, **29**: 259–264.

448 Nogales FF Jr, Matilla A, Ortega I, Alvarez T. Mixed Brenner and adenomatoid tumor of the testis. Cancer 1979, **43**: 539–543.

449 Perez-Atayde AR, Joste N, Mulhern H. Juvenile granulosa cell tumor of the infantile testis: Evidence of a dual epithelial-smooth muscle differentiation. Am J Surg Pathol 1996, **20**: 72–79.

450 Renshaw AA, Gordon M, Corless CL. Immunohistochemistry of unclassified sex cord-stromal tumors of the testis with a predominance of spindle cells. Mod Pathol 1997, **10**: 693–700.

451 Ross L. Paratesticular Brenner-like tumor. Cancer 1968, **21**: 722–726.

452 Tanaka Y, Sasaki Y, Tachibana K, Suwa S, Terashima K, Nakatani Y. Testicular juvenile granulosa cell tumor in an infant with X/XY mosaicism clinically diagnosed as true hermaphroditism. Am J Surg Pathol 1994, **18**: 316–322.

452a Ulbright TM, Young RH. Primary mucinous tumors of the testis and paratestis: a report of nine cases. Am J Surg Pathol 2003; **27**: 1221–1228.

453 Weidner N. Myoid gonadal stromal tumor with epithelial differentiation (? testicular myoepithelioma). Ultrastruct Pathol 1991, **15**: 409–416.

454 Young RH, Scully RE. Testicular and paratesticular tumors and tumor-like lesions of ovarian common epithelial and müllerian types. A report of four cases and review of the literature. Am J Clin Pathol 1986, **86**: 146–152.

455 Young RH, Lawrence WD, Scully RE. Juvenile granulosa cell tumor. Another neoplasm associated with abnormal chromosomes and ambiguous genitalia. A report of three cases. Am J Surg Pathol 1985, **9**: 737–743.

Mixed germ cell–sex cord–stromal tumors

456 Bolen JW. Mixed germ cell–sex cord–stromal tumor. A gonadal tumor distinct from gonadoblastoma. Am J Clin Pathol 1981, **75**: 565–573.

457 Matoska J, Talerman A. Mixed germ cell–sex cord–stromal tumor of the testis. A report with ultrastructural findings. Cancer 1989, **64**: 2146–2153.

458 Scully RE. Gonadoblastoma. A review of 74 cases. Cancer 1970, **25**: 1340–1356.

459 Ulbright TM, Srigley JR, Reuter VE, Wojno K, Roth LM, Young RH. Sex cord-stromal tumors of the testis with entrapped germ cells: A lesion mimicking unclassified mixed germ cell sex cord-stromal tumors. Am J Surg Pathol 2000, 24: 535–542.

Malignant lymphoma and related tumors

460 Aktah M, Al-Dayel F, Siegrist K, Ezzat A. Neutrophil-rich Ki-1-positive anaplastic large cell lymphoma presenting as a testicular mass. Mod Pathol 1996, **9**: 812–815.

461 Brousset P, Imadalou K, Rubie H, Delsol-Tahou M, Selves J, Robert A, Delson G. Paraffin-section immunohistochemistry of residual disease in the testis in patients with acute lymphoblastic leukemia using anti-mb-1/CD79a (JCB117) monoclonal antibody. Appl Immunohistochem 1996, **4**: 56–60.

462 Ferry JA, Harris NL, Young RH, Coen J, Zietman A, Scully RE. Malignant lymphoma of the testis, epididymis, and spermatic cord. A clinicopathologic study of 69 cases with immuno-phenotypic analysis. Am J Surg Pathol 1994, **18**: 376–390.

463 Ferry JA, Srigley JR, Young RH. Granulocytic sarcoma of the testis: a report of two cases of a neoplasm prone to misinterpretation. Mod Pathol 1997, **10**: 320–325.

464 Ferry JA, Ulbright TM, Young RH. Anaplastic large-cell lymphoma presenting in the testis: a lesion that may be confused with embryonal carcinoma. J Urol Pathol 1996, **5**: 139–148.

465 Ferry JA, Young RH, Scully RE. Testicular and epididymal plasmacytoma: a report of 7 cases, including three that were the initial manifestation of plasma cell myeloma. Am J Surg Pathol 1997, **21**: 590–598.

466 Finn LS, Viswanatha DS, Belasco JB, Snyder H, Huebner D, Sorbara L, Raffeld M, Jaffe ES, Salhany KE. Primary follicular lymphoma of the testis in childhood. Cancer 1999, **85**: 1626–1635.

467 Fonseca R, Habermann TM, Colgan JP, O'Neill BP, White WL, Witzig TE, Egan KS, Marteson JA, Bugart LJ, Inwards DJ. Testicular lymphoma is associated with a high incidence of extranodal recurrence. Cancer 2000, **88**: 154–161.

468 Givler RL. Testicular involvement in leukemia and lymphoma. Cancer 1969, **23**: 1290–1295.

469 Hyland J, Lasota J, Jasinski M, Petersen RO, Nordling S, Miettinen M. Molecular pathological analysis of testicular diffuse large cell lymphomas. Hum Pathol 1998, **29**: 1231–1239.

470 Kiely IM, Massey BD Jr, Harrison EG Jr, Utz DC. Lymphoma of the testis. Cancer 1970, **26**: 847–852.

471 Kim TH, Hargreaves HK, Chan WC, Brynes RK, Alvarado C, Woodard J, Ragab AH. Sequential testicular biopsies in childhood acute lymphocytic leukemia. Cancer 1986, **57**: 1038–1041.

472 Kuo T-T, Tschang TP, Chu Y-Y. Testicular relapse in childhood acute lymphocytic leukemia during bone marrow remission. Cancer 1976, **38**: 2604–2612.

473 Levin HS, Mostofi FK. Symptomatic plasmacytoma of the testis. Cancer 1970, **25**: 1193–1203.

474 Lu D, Medeiros LJ, Eskenazi AE, Abruzzo LV. Primary follicular large cell lymphoma of the testis in a child. Arch Pathol Lab Med 2001, **125**: 551–554.

475 Nesbit ME Jr, Robison LL, Ortega JA, Sather HN, Donaldson M, Hammond D. Testicular relapse in childhood acute

lymphoblastic leukemia. Association with pretreatment patient characteristics and treatment. A report for Children's Cancer Study Group. Cancer 1980, **45**: 2009–2016.

476 Oppenheim PI, Cohen S, Anders KH. Testicular plasmacytoma. A case report with immunohistochemical studies and literature review. Arch Pathol Lab Med 1991, **115**: 629–632.

477 Paladugu RR, Bearman RM, Rappaport H. Malignant lymphoma with primary manifestation in the gonad. A clinicopathologic study of 38 patients. Cancer 1980, **45**: 561–571.

478 Shahab N, Doll DC. Testicular lymphoma. Semin Oncol 1999, **26**: 259–269.

479 Stoffel TJ, Nesbit ME, Levitt SH. Extramedullary involvement of the testes in childhood leukemia. Cancer 1975, **35**: 1203–1211.

480 Tondini C, Ferreri AJ, Siracusano L, Valagussa P, Giardini R, Rampinelli I, Bonadona G. Diffuse large-cell lymphoma of the testis. J Clin Oncol 1999, **17**: 2854–2858.

480a Totonchi KF, Engel G, Weisenberg E, Rhone DP, Macon WR. Testicular natural killer/t-cell lymphoma, nasal type, of true natural killer-cell origin. Arch Pathol Lab Med 2002, **126**: 1527.

480b Tranchida P, Bayerl M, Voelpel MJ, Plutke M. Testicular ischemia due to intravascular large B-cell lymphoma: a novel presentation in an immunosupressed individual. Int J Surg Pathol (in press).

481 Turner RR, Colby TV, MacKintosh FR. Testicular lymphomas. A clinicopathologic study of 35 cases. Cancer 1981, **48**: 2095–2102.

482 Wilkins BS, Williamson JM, O'Brien CJ. Morphological and immunohistological study of testicular lymphomas. Histopathology 1989, **15**: 147–156.

483 Woolley PV III, Osborne CK, Levi JA, Weirnik PH, Canelos GP. Extranodal presentation of non-Hodgkin's lymphomas in the testis. Cancer 1976, **38**: 1026–1035.

Other tumors

484 Banks ER, Mills SE. Histiocytoid (epithelioid) hemangioma of the testis. The so-called vascular variant of "adenomatoid tumor." Am J Surg Pathol 1990, **14**: 584–589.

485 Bates AW, Baithun SI. The significance of secondary neoplasms of the urinary and male genital tract. Virchows Arch 2002, **440**: 640–647.

486 Berdijs C, Mostofi FK. Carcinoid tumors of the testis. J Urol 1977, **118**: 777–782.

487 Collins DH, Pugh RCP. Classification and frequency of testicular tumours. Br J Urol 1964, **36**(Suppl): 1–11.

488 Datta MW, Young RH. Malignant melanoma metastatic to the testis: a report of three cases with clinically significant manifestations. Int J Surg Pathol 2000, **8**: 49–58.

489 Datta MW, Ulbright TM, Young RH. Renal cell carcinoma metastatic to the testis and its adnexa: a report of five cases including three that accounted for the initial clinical presentation. Int J Surg Pathol 2001, **9**: 49–56.

490 Dutt N, Bates AW, Baithun SI. Secondary neoplasms of the male genital tract with different patterns of involvement in adults and children. Histopathology 2000, **37**: 323–331.

491 Fuzesi L, Rixen H, Kirschner-Hermanns R. Cytogenetic findings in a metastasizing primary testicular chondrosarcoma. Am J Surg Pathol 1993, **17**: 738–742.

492 Gonzalez-Garcia JL, Kockelbergh RC, Roberts PF. Carcinoid tumors occurring in mature cystic teratoma of the testis: report of a case and review of the literature. J Urol Pathol 1997, **6**: 75–82.

493 Hargreaves HK, Scully RE, Richie JP. Benign

hemangioendothelioma of the testis. Case report with electron microscopic documentation and review of the literature. Am J Clin Pathol 1982, **77**: 637–642.

494 Haupt HM, Mann RB, Trump DL, Abeloff MD. Metastatic carcinoma involving the testis. Clinical and pathologic distinction from primary testicular neoplasms. Cancer 1984, **54**: 709–714.

495 Iczkowski KA, Kiviat J, Cheville JC, Bostwick DG. Multifocal capillary microangioma of the testis. J Urol Pathol 1997, **7**: 113–120.

496 Kay S, Hennigar GR, Hooper JW Jr. Carcinoma of the testes metastatic from carcinoma of the prostate. Arch Pathol 1954, **57**: 121–129.

497 Leake J, Levitt G, Ramani P. Primary carcinoid of the testis in a 10-year-old boy. Histopathology 1991, **19**: 373–375.

498 Luk ISC, Shek TW, Tang VW, Ng WF. Interdigitating dendritic cell tumor of the testis. A novel testicular spindle cell neoplasm. Am J Surg Pathol 1999, **23**: 1141–1148.

499 Masera A, Ovcak Z, Mikuz G. Angiosarcoma of the testis. Virchows Arch 1999, **434**: 351–353.

500 Nistal M, Gonzalez-Peramato P, Paniagua R. Secondary testicular tumors. Eur Urol 1989, **16**: 185–188.

501 Ordonez NG, Ayala AG, Sneige N, Mackay B. Immunohistochemical demonstration of multiple neurohormonal polypeptides in a case of pure testicular carcinoid. Am J Clin Pathol 1982, **78**: 860–864.

502 Price EB Jr, Mostofi FK. Secondary carcinoma of the testis. Cancer 1957, **10**: 592–595.

503 Ro JY, Ayala AG, Tetu B, Ordonez NG, el-Naggar A, Grignon DJ, Mackay B. Merkel cell carcinoma metastatic to the testis. Am J Clin Pathol 1990, **94**: 384–389.

504 Senger C, Gonzalez-Crussi F. Testicular juvenile xanthogranuloma: a case report. J Urol Pathol 1999, **10**: 159–168.

505 Simon T, Hero B, Berthold F. Testicular and paratesticular involvement by metastatic neuroblastoma. Cancer 2000, **88**: 2636–2641.

506 Slaughenhoupt BL, Cendron M, Al-Hindi HN, Wallace EC, Ucci A. Capillary hemangioma of the testis. J Urol Pathol 1996, **4**: 283–288.

507 Suriawinata A, Talerman A, Vapnek JM, Unger P. Hemangioma of the testis: report of unusual occurrences of cavernous hemangioma in a fetus and capillary hemangioma in an older man. Ann Diagn Pathol 2001, **5**: 80–83.

508 Talerman A, Gratama S, Miranda S, Okagaki T. Primary carcinoid tumor of the testis. Cancer 1978, **42**: 2696–2706.

509 Tiltman AJ. Metastatic tumours in the testis. Histopathology 1979, **3**: 31–37.

510 Washecka RM, Mariani AJ, Zuna RE, Honda SA, Chong CD. Primary intratesticular sarcoma: immunohistochemical, ultrastructural and DNA flow cytometric study of three cases with a review of the literature. Cancer 1996, **77**: 1524–1528.

511 Weitzner S. Survival of patients with secondary carcinoma of prostate in the testis. Cancer 1973, **32**: 447–449.

512 Zavala-Pompa A, Ro JY, el-Naggar A, Ordonez NG, Amin MB, Pierce PD, Ayala AG. Primary carcinoid tumor of testis. Immunohistochemical, ultrastructural, and DNA flow cytometric study of three cases with a review of the literature. Cancer 1993, **72**: 1726–1732.

513 Zuk RJ, Trotter SE, Baithun SI. "Krukenberg" tumour of the testis. Histopathology 1989, **14**: 214–216.

514 Zukerberg LR, Young RH. Primary testicular sarcoma. A report of two cases. Hum Pathol 1990, **21**: 932–935.

Testicular adnexa

Normal anatomy

The *rete testis*, located at the hilum of the testis, has a complex tubular architecture (particularly when undergoing reactive hyperplastic changes, see next section), which the uninitiated may confuse with a teratomatous lesion. It receives the luminal contents of the seminiferous tubules and is divided into three components: septal, mediastinal or tunical, and extratesticular (bullae retis).[4] The rete testis empties into the *ductuli efferentes*, which consist of 12 to 15 tubules aggregated in the region of the head of the epididymis; they are lined by pseudostratified ciliated and nonciliated epithelium.

The *epididymis* is a tubular structure connecting the ductuli efferentes to the vas deferens and composed anatomically of three portions: head (caput), body (corpus), and tail (cauda). The epididymal epithelium is composed of tall columnar (principal) cells; narrow, darker-staining columnar cells; basal cells; and clear cells. Prominent cilia are present in the tall columnar cells.[2] These cells may feature variously sized intranuclear eosinophilic PAS-positive inclusions, which are similar to those found in the vas deferens and seminal vesicles. They may also exhibit bright eosinophilic intracytoplasmic granules and globules, resulting in a Paneth cell-like appearance.[5]

The *vas deferens* is a 30 to 40 cm tubular structure arising from the caudal portion of the epididymis and emptying into the prostatic urethra at the level of the verumontanum. The distal portion joins the excretory duct of the seminal vesicle to form the ejaculatory duct. The vas is lined by pseudostratified epithelium composed of ciliated columnar and basal cells.[3] Prominent intranuclear inclusions may be seen.[1] The muscle coat, which is extremely thick, is composed of inner and outer longitudinal coats and a middle oblique or circular zone.

Four small *testicular appendages* of vestigial nature exist. Of these the most constant is the appendix testis or hydatid of Morgagni, which represents a remnant of the cranial portion of the müllerian duct. It is a round or oval, sessile or pedunculated, 1 to 10 mm structure attached to the tunica albuginea at the upper pole of the testis. The other appendages are the appendix epididymis (a remnant of the cranial portion of the mesonephric duct), the vas aberrans or organ of Haller (a remnant of mesonephric tubules), and the paradidymis or organ of Giraldes (also a remnant of mesonephric tubules).

Rete testis

Rete testis dysgenesis is the rule in cryptorchid testicles. Morphologically, it is characterized by underdevelopment of the rete, which is lined by columnar or large cuboidal cells.[17]

Calcifying nodules can be seen protruding into the rete testis channels; these probably represent dystrophic changes and are of no clinical significance.[20]

Cystic dilatation (transformation) of the rete testis can occur as a result of obstruction of the epididymis or of the intratesticular excretory ducts secondary to varicocele.[9,19] Other cases have been seen in the absence of obstruction in patients with renal failure treated with hemodialysis,[21] sometimes associated with deposits of calcium oxalate crystals.[18]

Inflammatory pseudotumor has been reported centered in the rete testis and accompanied by metaplastic changes of the epithelium.[11]

Adenomatous hyperplasia of rete testis may be confused with a malignant neoplasm. It may present in adult patients with a grossly evident solid or cystic mass in the testicular hilum. More commonly, the lesion is very small and detected as an incidental microscopic finding. Microscopically, there is a tubulopapillary and occasionally cribriform proliferation of rete testis epithelium with cytologic bland features.[6] Some cases of rete testis hyperplasia are accompanied by the deposition of hyaline globules, simulating the appearance of yolk sac tumor.[13,25]

Immunohistochemically, there is reactivity for keratin and EMA and negativity for vimentin, actin, desmin, and S-100 protein.[8] The behavior has been benign in all reported cases. The pathogenesis is unknown; in cases associated with germ cell tumor of the testis, it may represent a reaction to the invasion by the latter.[25]

Cystadenoma of the rete testis occurs, sometimes exhibiting *sertoliform* features.[10]

Adenocarcinoma of the rete testis is a very rare neoplasm, which may be difficult to distinguish from malignant mesothelioma of the tunica vaginalis.[22,24]

Some of these tumors have a distinctly papillary appearance.[7] Diagnostic criteria include involvement centered in the hilum of the testis, lack of direct extension through the parietal tunica, transitions from tumor to rete epithelium, no evidence of teratoma, and lack of any other primary tumor.[22] Intratubular invasion of the testis may occur.[23] The ultrastructural appearance of this tumor shows similarities with that of normal rete testis epithelium.[16] Cases have been described with a spindle (metaplastic) component,[26] and others having focal sertoliform differentiation similar to that also seen in the cystadenoma of this structure (see above).[27]

Secondary involvement of the rete testis by testicular germ cell tumors may occur in the form of pagetoid spread,[12] perhaps as a result of so-called "field effect".[15] This relatively common event (particularly with seminoma) should not be confused with a primary tumor of the epididymis.[14]

Epididymis

Non-neoplastic lesions

Nonspecific epididymitis may be caused by *Neisseria gonorrhoeae, Chlamydia trachomatis, E. coli*, or other organisms (Fig. 18.11). It may lead to testicular necrosis secondary to hypoperfusion caused by ischemia.[41] Chlamydial epididymitis is mainly proliferative, whereas bacterial epididymitis tends to be destructive and abscess forming.[33]

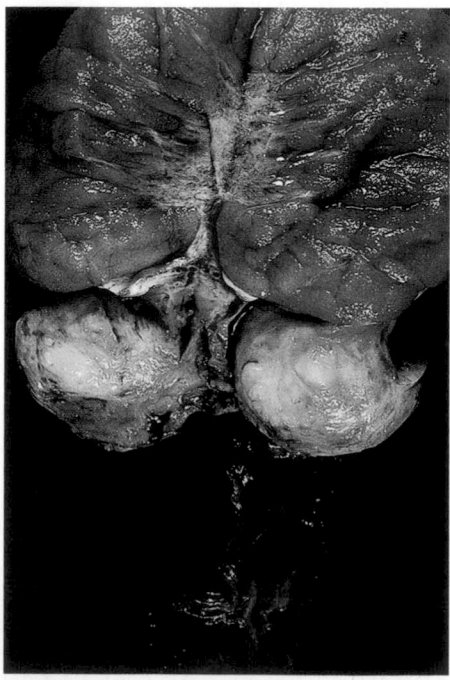

Fig. 18.111 Acute and chronic epididymitis. The inflammation has not spread to the testicle.

Tuberculosis of the epididymis may result in confluent caseation of this organ, as described by Auerbach in his classic work on urogenital tuberculosis.[28] When extensive, the infection can spread into the testis and clinically simulate a malignant tumor.[30] The source of infection may be hematogenous or through the prostate, the former being the more common. When the infection is hematogenous, the process begins in the epididymal interstitial tissue and preferentially involves the head, often with sparing of the vas deferens. When it originates in the prostate, there is involvement of the tail of the epididymis and the vas.

Fungal infections that can involve the epididymis include *coccidioidomycosis*[32] and *histoplasmosis*.[34]

Granulomatous ischemic lesion is the term proposed by Nistal et al.[37] for a granulomatous process involving the head of the epididymis accompanied by partial necrosis of the ductal wall, which they interpreted as of probable ischemic pathogenesis.[37]

Idiopathic granulomatous epididymitis is a diagnosis of exclusion, which is justified for cases of granulomatous inflammation lacking features that would place it in any of the specific categories mentioned in this section[43] (Fig. 18.112).

Spermatic granuloma of the epididymis (epididymitis nodosa) presents grossly as a nodule measuring up to 3 cm in diameter, most often located in the head (Fig. 18.113). Microscopically, a granulomatous reaction is seen around collections of spermatozoa. Caseation necrosis is absent. This lesion is thought to result from damage to the epithelium and basement membrane of epididymal ducts by inflammation or trauma,[31] with subsequent spillage of sperm into the interstitium. The granulomatous reaction is probably induced by an acid-fast fraction of lipid from the sperm, a hypothesis supported by the fact that this material has been found to provoke a granulomatous reaction when injected subcutaneously in hamsters.[29]

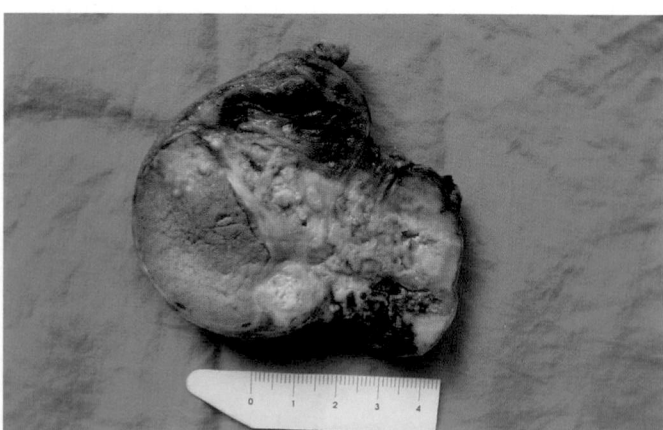

Fig. 18.112 Granulomatous epididymitis with focal extension into the testis. Some of the granulomas have a necrotic center. No microorganisms were identified on special stains.

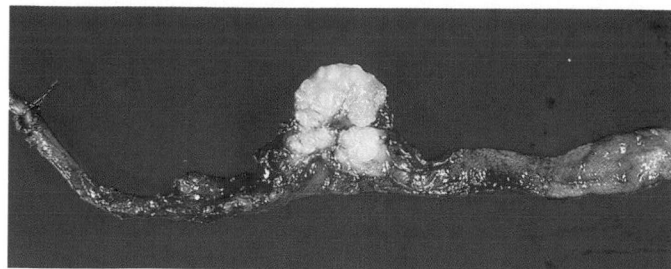

Fig. 18.113 Spermatic granuloma of epididymis.

Necrotizing vasculitis can occur in the epididymis as an isolated finding or as a manifestation of a systemic disease; since there are no apparent morphologic differences between the two forms, clinical evaluation and follow-up of these patients are indicated.[36,42]

Hyaline globules can be found in the cytoplasm of epithelial epididymal cells; their appearance is similar to that of the globules seen in cases of adenomatous hyperplasia of the rete testis (see later section).[39]

Monstrous epithelial cells similar to those commonly found in the seminal vesicles can be seen in the epididymis and should not be confused with a malignant process.[35,38]

Spermatocele represents a cystic dilatation of efferent ducts, with their lumina filled with masses of sperm. They are lined by ciliated tall columnar cells, and the wall is made up of loose connective tissue rather than smooth muscle. Secondary changes, such as cholesterol clefts and foreign body–giant cell reaction, are common.

Cribriform hyperplasia of the epididymis has a pattern reminiscent of cribriform intraductal carcinoma of the breast. It is apparently not associated with adenomatous hyperplasia of the rete testis.[38,40]

Tumors

Adenomatoid tumor and mesothelioma

Adenomatoid tumor is the most common neoplasm of the epididymis, most patients being in the third or fourth decade of life. It presents clinically as a mass, sometimes associated with pain. Grossly, it appears as a small (average size, 2 cm), solid, firm, grayish white nodule, occasionally containing small cysts (Fig. 18.114). Microscopically, the lesion is unencapsulated, and on rare occasions it may extend to the adjacent testis. There is a proliferation of cells ranging from cuboidal to flattened, which form solid cords with an epithelial appearance alternating with channels having dilated lumina simulating vascular structures (Figs 18.115 and 18.116). The prominent intervening stroma may contain abundant smooth muscle and elastic fibers[44]; it may also have a reactive desmoplastic quality and be infiltrated by inflammatory cells. The tumor cells may exhibit prominent cytoplasmic vacuolization. Histochemically, there is

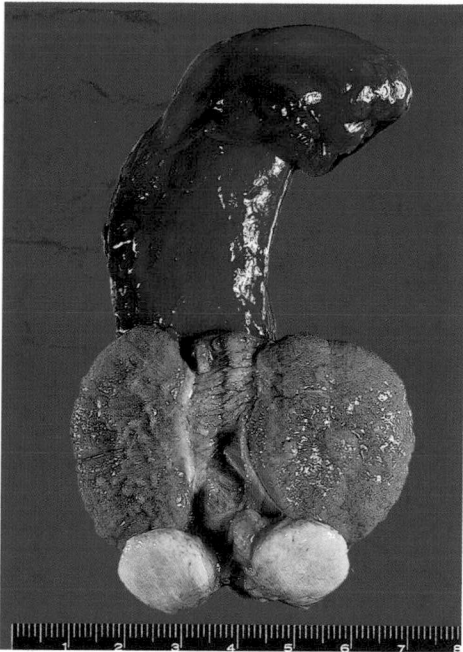

Fig. 18.114 Typical gross appearance of adenomatoid tumor of epididymis. (Courtesy of Dr RA Cooke, Brisbane, Australia; From Cooke RA, Stewart B: Colour Atlas of Anatomical Pathology, Edinburgh, Churchill Livingstone, 2004).

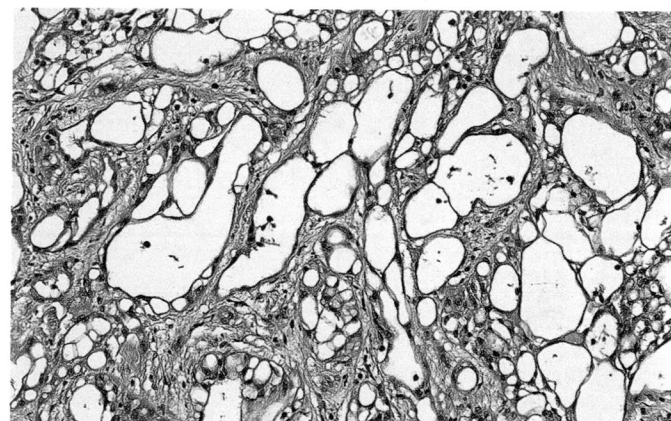

Fig. 18.115 Low-power appearance of adenomatoid tumor, showing typical conglomerate of cystically dilated spaces.

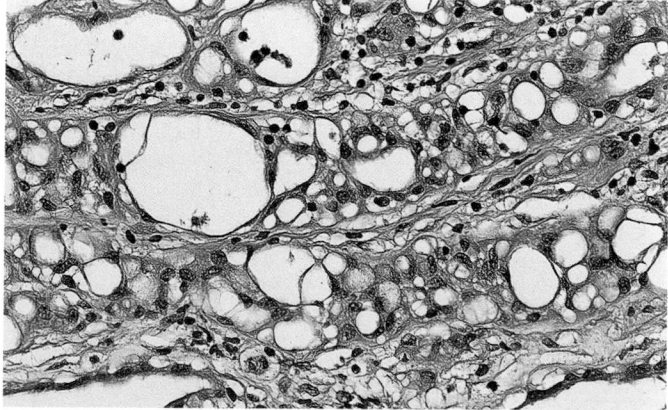

Fig. 18.116 On high power, some of the tubules of adenomatoid tumor are lined by cuboidal cells, whereas others are lined by flattened cells with the appearance of endothelial cells.

positivity for hyaluronidase-sensitive mucosubstances but negativity for lipids. Immunocytochemically, there is strong reactivity for keratin and EMA and negativity for CEA and factor VIII-related antigen[46,60] (Fig. 18.117). By electron microscopy, the tumor cells have prominent microvilli, desmosomes, and tonofilaments, and the intercellular spaces are dilated.[50,56,61]

This tumor also occurs in the testicular spermatic cord and ejaculatory duct in males and in the fallopian tube and uterus in females. Its histogenesis has been argued for years, the proposed candidates for the cell of origin being mesothelial, mesonephric, müllerian, and endothelial. The accumulated evidence obtained from the previously discussed techniques, the sporadic detection of a continuity between the peritoneal lining and the cells lining the tubular structures, and the occasional occurrence of these tumors in association with typical papillary mesotheliomas within the abdominal cavity[52] indicate that adenomatoid tumors are of mesothelial nature, as originally proposed by Masson et al.[57] Although they are generally regarded as benign neoplasms, the frequent coexistence of chronic inflammation and fibrosis suggests that at least some of the cases may represent instead a peculiar form of nodular mesothelial hyperplasia. This lesion should be distinguished from epithelioid hemangioma, which can also occur in this area and which can be so similar as to have been referred to (somewhat misleadingly) as the "vascular form" of adenomatoid tumor.[47,48] As expected, epithelioid hemangioma is immunoreactive for FVIII, *Ulex europaeus* I lectin, and CD34, but usually not for keratin. The behavior of true adenomatoid tumor is invariably benign, even when extending into the testis.

Mesothelioma of the usual type has also been described in this region, arising from the tunica vaginalis testis[53–55] (Fig. 18.118). Most cases are malignant, similar to those seen in the peritoneal cavity and—like them—are occasionally associated with asbestos exposure.[45,51] They exhibit a wide age range of occurrence (with occasional examples in children), a wide differentiation spectrum, and a generally aggressive behavior (with potential for late recurrence or metastasis).[53,58,59] It is not clear whether the few reported cases of "malignant fibrous mesothelioma" of this region[49] represent sarcomatoid mesotheliomas, malignant forms of solitary fibrous tumor, or other types of malignant tumor.

Other tumors and tumorlike conditions

Papillary cystadenoma of the epididymis may be unilateral or bilateral and exhibits a familial incidence.[83] It is regarded as the epididymal component of von Hippel–Lindau (VHL) disease and is often seen with other manifestations of the disease, especially when bilateral. Grossly, it measures 1 to 5 cm and is well circumscribed, either cystic or solid (Fig. 18.119). Microscopically, papillary infoldings lined by columnar

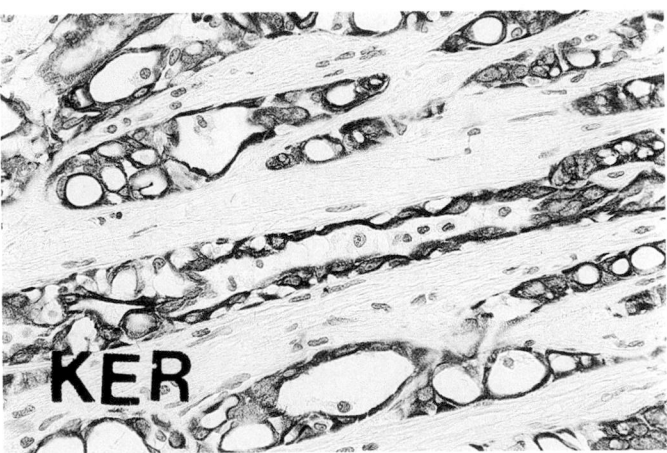

Fig. 18.117 Strong immunoreactivity for keratin in an adenomatoid tumor.

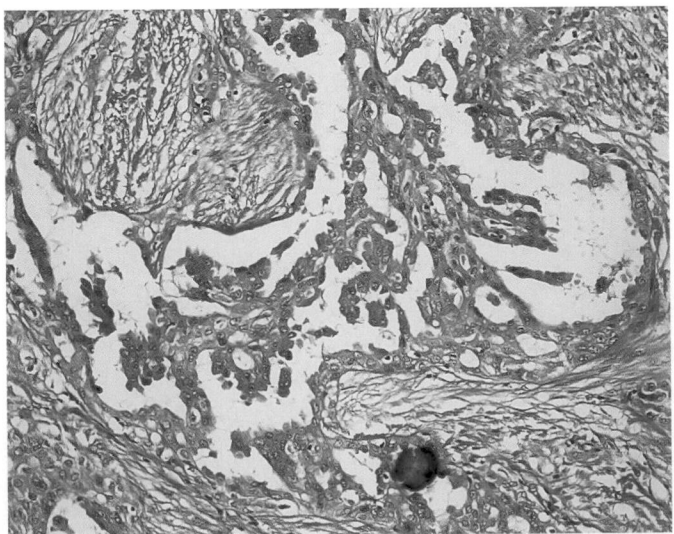

Fig. 18.118 Malignant mesothelioma involving the epididymis.

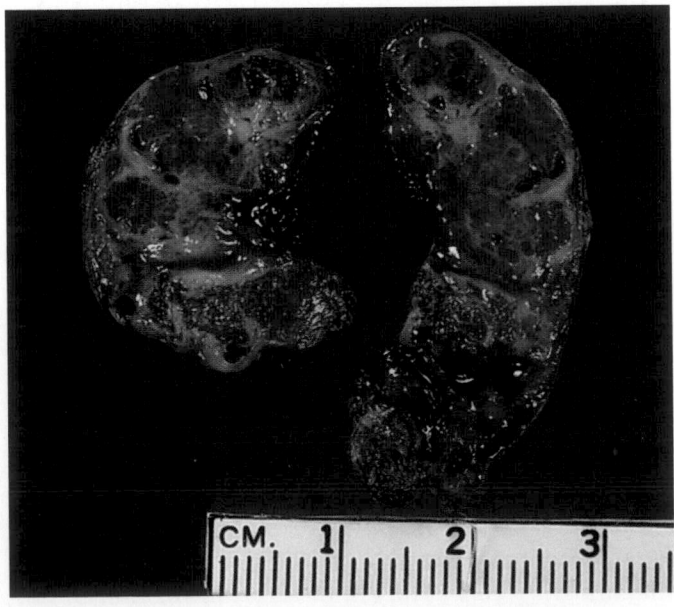

Fig. 18.119 Bilateral papillary cystadenoma of epididymis.

cells with abundant clear cytoplasm are the distinctive feature.[78] Immunohistochemically, they are reactive for keratin and CEA.[63] In contrast with renal cell carcinoma (which they morphologically resemble), they exhibit positivity for soybean agglutinin.[70] Allelic deletion of the VHL gene has been detected in these tumors,[81] as well as expression of vascular endothelial growth factor.[71] The latter probably explains the prominent vascular component that is such a common feature in practically all tumors occurring in the VHL syndrome.

Carcinoma of the epididymis is an extremely rare lesion; it has the microscopic appearance of either adenocarcinoma (more commonly) or undifferentiated carcinoma and is associated with a poor prognosis.[80] The pattern of growth of the adenocarcinoma can be tubular, tubulocystic or tubulopapillary, and there is often a conspicuous component of clear cells[68] (Fig. 18.120). Rare tumors combine epididymal-like cells and mucin-producing cells.[74]

Sometimes tumors develop in the paratesticular region or within the testis, having an appearance resembling that of various **ovarian tumors of epithelial type**, including serous, mucinous, endometrioid, clear cell, and Brenner varieties.[66,72,83a,87] They may be unilateral or bilateral.[75] Most of them have benign or borderline features, but some have the appearance of serous papillary carcinoma and can result in nodal and distal metastases.[62,69] The similarities with serous tumors of the female genital tract extend to the expression of estrogen and progesterone receptors.[64] Another example of the analogy between the male and female genital tracts is provided by the isolated examples of **endometriosis-like lesions** in the paratesticular region of males treated with estrogens.[87]

Other tumors of this region include **leiomyoma** and **leiomyosarcoma**[82] (Fig. 18.121), **hemangioma**[65] (includ-

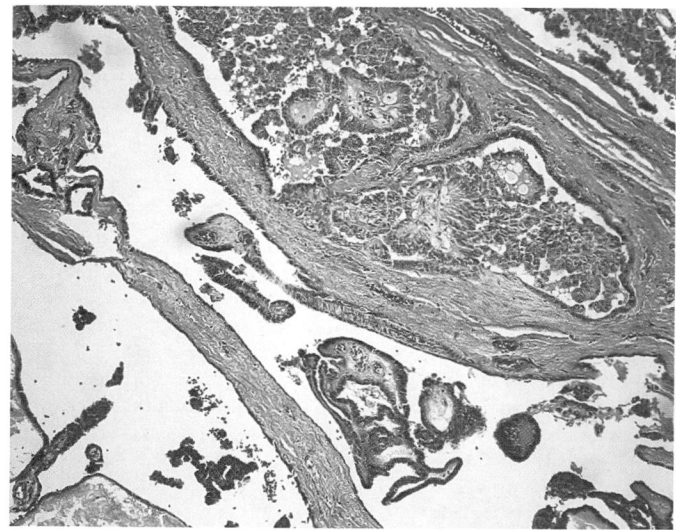

Fig. 18.120 Tumor interpreted as a primary papillary adenocarcinoma of the epididymis.

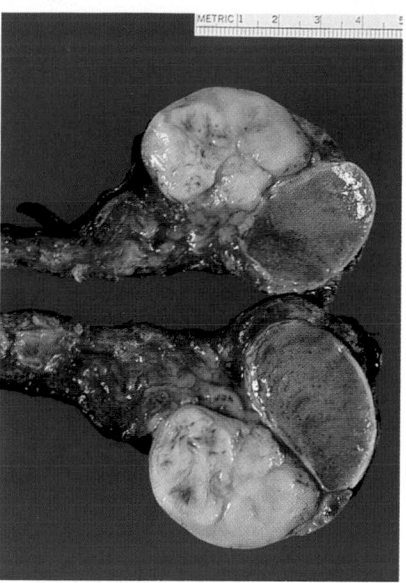

Fig. 18.121 Leiomyosarcoma of epididymal region.

ing the already-mentioned epithelioid type), **lymphangioma**,[77] **rhabdomyoma**,[85] **pigmented neuroectodermal tumor of infancy**,[79] **malignant lymphoma**,[73,76] and **plasmacytoma**.[67] In some cases of the latter, the epididymal involvement represents the first clinical manifestation of the disease.[67]

Secondary tumors, in the majority of instances, represent a direct extension from testicular lesions. Prostate, lung, and kidney account for most of the others.[84]

Pseudotumors centered in the epididymis and composed of reactive myofibroblasts may be encountered in children after testicular torsion.[86]

Spermatic cord (see also Scrotum p. 1475)

Torsion of the spermatic cord, if not treated promptly, may result in testicular infarct. Most cases occur in the first year of life, with a second peak toward puberty.[118] In 64% of the cases, the torsion is located in the intravaginal portion of the cord.[109] The adipose tissue around the cord may undergo fat necrosis, sometimes of the so-called "lipomembranous" type.[112] The treatment varies from untwisting of the torsion and fixation of the testis to orchiectomy, according to the viability of the testis as determined at surgery. Whatever procedure is carried out, the opposite testis should be fixed to the dartos musculature as a preventive measure.

The differential diagnosis of torsion of the spermatic cord includes *torsion of a testicular appendage*, a condition that results in a dramatic clinical picture out of proportion with the minute size and significance of this structure.[116,117] The appendix testis, a vestigial structure of müllerian derivation, is the one most often involved (92%) (see p. 1457). Parenthetically, tumors arising from this structure have been described.[104]

Giant cell vasculitis has been reported as an isolated event in the spermatic cord and presenting as a mass lesion.[94]

Vasitis nodosa is a granulomatous condition of the vas that resembles spermatic granuloma of the epididymis (Fig. 18.122) (see p. 1458).[121] Most of the reported cases have appeared after vasectomy or herniorrhaphy.[113] Perineurial invasion by the proliferating ductules may be found.[91]

Proliferative funiculitis is the name given to a pseudosarcomatous myofibroblastic proliferation of the spermatic cord.[102] Most of the reported cases have been incidental findings at inguinal herniorrhaphy. The microscopic appearance is similar to that of nodular fasciitis as seen in soft tissue. The pathogenesis is probably ischemic, sometimes resulting from torsion. These lesions are in all likelihood analogous to those sometimes seen under similar circumstances within the substance of the epididymis (see p. 1461).

Smooth muscle hyperplasia of testicular adnexa presents as a localized increase in mature smooth muscle of the spermatic cord or paratestis growing between or around vessels or efferent ducts.[92] It can reach a diameter of 7 cm and it may have an obstructive etiology.

Primary tumors of the spermatic cord can be of many types. Because of the intimate anatomic connection of the spermatic cord with the scrotum and the tunica vaginalis testis, it is often impossible to decide from which of these anatomic compartments these tumors have arisen. This is particularly true when the tumors in question are large, as is often the case. Indeed, one gets the impression that tumors are assigned into spermatic cord, tunica vaginalis, scrotal, epididymal and paratesticular categories on a very arbitrary basis.[101,119] From a topographic and surgical standpoint, it would perhaps be more appropriate to simply divide them into those of the scrotum and those of the inguinal canal, without attributing

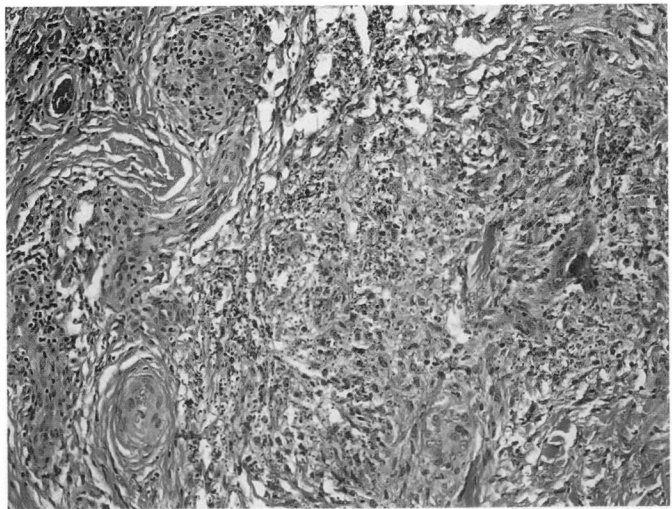

Fig. 18.122 Vasitis nodosa. Clumps of spermatozoa are present in the center of the granulomas.

them to a particular anatomic structure unless the gross and microscopic features of the case allow this to be done. In any event, the most common tumor of this region is the **lipoma**.[106] It is surrounded by tunica vaginalis and derives its blood supply from the vessels of the cord. The collections of mature fatty tissue seen in front of a hernia sac are not true lipomas.

Vascular myxolipoma (angiomyxolipoma) of the spermatic cord is a benign tumor to be distinguished from liposarcoma and aggressive angiomyxoma.[110]

Papillary cystadenoma of the spermatic cord may present as an inguinal mass.[103] The morphologic resemblance it bears with borderline ovarian serous tumors suggests a müllerian derivation.[108]

Other reported primary tumors of this region include **hemangioma, lymphangioma, leiomyoma, rhabdomyoma, solitary fibrous tumor,** and **paraganglioma**.[89,97,100,114,115,120]

The most common malignant tumor of this region in children is **embryonal rhabdomyosarcoma**, followed perhaps by **desmoplastic small cell tumor**.[95]

In adults, **atypical lipomatous tumor** (well-differentiated liposarcoma) predominate, but cases of **leiomyosarcoma, fibrosarcoma, epithelioid hemangioendothelioma** so-called **malignant fibrous histiocytoma** also occur.[88,99,105,107,107a,110a]

The standard treatment for the sarcomas occurring in adults consists of orchiectomy with high ligation of the cord. Since local recurrence is very common after this procedure, the administration of postoperative radiation therapy has been advocated.[90,98]

Secondary involvement of the spermatic cord by testicular germ cell tumors may occur as a result of direct extension or vascular invasion. It is important to distinguish this prognostically significant finding from contamination induced at the time of the gross dissection; the latter is particularly common with seminoma (probably because of its very friable nature) and it can be avoided with meticulous handling and processing.[111] Renal cell carcinoma has been seen metastasizing to the spermatic cord.[96]

References

Normal anatomy

1 Madara JL, Haggitt RC, Federman M. Intranuclear inclusions of the human vas deferens. Arch Pathol Lab Med 1978, **102:** 648–650.

2 Maneely RB. Epididymal structure and function. A historical and critical review. Acta Zool 1959, **40:** 1–21.

3 Paniagua R, Regadera J, Nistal M, Abaurrea MA. Histological, histochemical and ultrastructural variations along the length of the human vas deferens before and after puberty. Acta Anat 1981, **111:** 190–203.

4 Roosen-Runge EC, Holstein AF. The human rete testis. Cell Tissue Res 1978, **189:** 409–433.

5 Shah VI, Ro JY, Amin MB, Mullick S, Nazeer T, Ayala AG. Histologic variations in the epididymis: findings in 167 orchiectomy specimens. Am J Surg Pathol 1998, **22:** 990–996.

RETE TESTIS

6 Butterworth DM, Bisset DL. Cribriform intra-tubular epididymal change and adenomatous hyperplasia of the rete testis—a consequence of testicular atrophy? Histopathology 1992, **21**: 435–438.

7 Fukunaga M, Aizawa S, Furusato M, Akasaka Y, Machida T. Papillary adenocarcinoma of the rete testis. A case report. Cancer 1982, **50**: 134–138.

8 Hartwick RW, Ro JY, Srigley JR, Ordonez NG, Ayala AG. Adenomatous hyperplasia of the rete testis. A clinicopathologic study of nine cases. Am J Surg Pathol 1991, **15**: 350–357.

9 Jones EC, Murray SK, Young RH. Cysts and epithelial proliferations of the testicular collecting system (including rete testis). Semin Diagn Pathol 2000, **17**: 270–293.

10 Jones MA, Young RH. Sertoliform cystadenoma of the rete testes: a report of two cases. J Urol Pathol 1997, **7**: 47–54.

11 Khalil KH, Ball RY, Eardley I, Ashken MH. Inflammatory pseudotumor of the rete testis. J Urol Pathol 1996, **5**: 39–44.

12 Lee AH, Theaker JM. Pagetoid spread into the rete testis by testicular tumours. Histopathology 1994, **24**: 385–389.

13 Mai KT. Cytoplasmic eosinophilic granular change of the ductuli efferentes. A histological, immunohistochemical, and electron microscopic study. J Urol Pathol 1994, **2**: 273–282.

14 Mai KT, Carlier M, Lajeunesse C. Paratesticular composite tumour of epididymal-like and mucinous cells of low malignant potential. Histopathogy 1998, **33**: 193–194.

15 Mai KT, Yazdi HM, Rippstein P. Light and electron microscopy of the pagetoid spread of germ cell carcinoma in the rete testis: morphologic evidence suggestive of field effect as a mechanism of tumor spread. AIMM 2001, **9**: 335–339.

16 Mrak RE, Husain MM, Schaefer RF. Ultrastructure of metastatic rete testis adenocarcinoma. Arch Pathol Lab Med 1990, **114**: 84–88.

17 Nistal M, Jiménez-Heffernan JA. Rete testis dysgenesis: a characteristic lesion of undescended testes. Arch Pathol Lab Med 1997, **121**: 1259–1264.

18 Nistal M, Jiménez-Heffernan JA, Garcia-Viera M, Paniagua R. Cystic transformation and calcium oxalate deposits in rete testis and efferent ducts in dialysis patients. Hum Pathol 1996, **27**: 336–341.

19 Nistal M, Mate A, Paniagua R. Cystic transformation of the rete testis. Am J Surg Pathol 1996, **20**: 1231–1239.

20 Nistal M, Paniagua R. Nodular proliferation of calcifying connective tissue in the rete testis. A study of three cases. Hum Pathol 1989, **20**: 58–61.

21 Nistal M, Santamaria L, Paniagua R. Acquired cystic transformation of the rete testis secondary to renal failure. Hum Pathol 1989, **20**: 1065–1070.

22 Nochomovitz LE, Orenstein JM. Adenocarcinoma of the rete testis. Consolidation and analysis of 31 reported cases with a review of miscellaneous entities. J Urol Pathol 1994, **2**: 1–37.

23 Samaratunga H, Kanowski P, O'Loughlin B, Walker N, Searle J. Adenocarcinoma of the rete testis with intratubular invasion of the testis. J Urol Pathol 1994, **2**: 291–300.

24 Sarma DP, Weilbaecher TG. Adenocarcinoma of the rete testis. J Surg Oncol 1985, **30**: 67–71.

25 Ulbright TM, Gersell DJ. Rete testis hyperplasia with hyaline globule formation. A lesion simulating yolk sac tumor. Am J Surg Pathol 1991, **15**: 66–74.

26 Visscher DW, Talerman A, Rivera LR, Mazur MT. Adenocarcinoma of the rete testis with a spindle cell component. A possible metaplastic carcinoma. Cancer 1989, **64**: 770–775.

27 Watson PH, Jacob VC. Adenocarcinoma of the rete testis with sertoliform differentiation. Arch Pathol Lab Med 1989, **113**: 1169–1171.

EPIDIDYMIS

Non-neoplastic lesions

28 Auerbach O. The pathology of urogenital tuberculosis. Int Clin 1940, **3**: 21–61.

29 Berg JW. An acid-fast lipid from spermatozoa. Arch Pathol 1954, **57**: 115–120.

30 Ferrie SG, Rundle JSH. Tuberculous epididymo-orchitis. A review of 20 cases. Am J Urol 1983, **55**: 437–439.

31 Glassy FJ, Mostofi FK. Spermatic granulomas of the epididymis. Am J Clin Pathol 1956, **26**: 1303–1313.

32 Haddad FS. Coccidioidomycosis of the genitourinary tract with special emphasis on the epididymis and the prostate: four case reports and review of the literature. J Urol Pathol 1996, **4**: 205–212.

33 Hori S, Tsutsumi Y. Histological differentiation between chlamydial and bacterial epididymitis. Nondestructive and proliferative versus destructive and abscess forming. Immunohistochemical and clinicopathological findings. Hum Pathol 1995, **26**: 402–407.

34 Kanomata N, Eble JN. Fungal epididymitis caused by *Histoplasma capsulatum*: a case report. J Urol Pathol 1996, **5**: 229–234.

35 Kuo T-T, Gomez LG. Monstrous epithelial cells in human epididymis and seminal vesicles. A pseudomalignant change. Am J Surg Pathol 1981, **5**: 483–490.

36 Levine TS. Testicular and epididymal vasculitides. Is morphology of help in classification and prognosis? J Urol Pathol 1994, **2**: 81–88.

37 Nistal M, Mate A, Paniagua R. Granulomatous epididymal lesion of possible ischemic origin. Am J Surg Pathol 1997, **21**: 951–956.

38 Oliva E, Young RH. Paratesticular tumor-like lesions. Semin Diagn Pathol 2000, **17**: 340–358.

39 Schned AR, Memoli VA. Coarse granular cytoplasmic change of the epididymis. An immunohistochemical and ultrastructural study. J Urol Pathol 1994, **2**: 213–222.

40 Sharp SC, Batt MA, Lennington WJ. Epididymal cribriform hyperplasia. A variant of normal epididymal histology. Arch Pathol Lab Med 1994, **118**: 1020–1022.

41 Vordermark JS II, Favila MQ. Testicular necrosis. A preventable complication of epididymitis. J Urol 1982, **128**: 1322–1324.

42 Womack C, Ansell ID. Isolated arteritis of the epididymis. J Clin Pathol 1985, **38**: 797–800.

43 Yantiss RK, Young RH. Idiopathic granulomatous epididymitis: report of a case and review of the literature. J Urol Pathol 1998, **8**: 171–179.

Tumors

Adenomatoid tumor and mesothelioma

44 Akhtar M, Reyes F, Young I. Elastogenesis in adenomatoid tumor. Cancer 1976, **37**: 338–345.

45 Attanoos RL, Gibbs AR. Primary malignant gonadal mesotheliomas and asbestos. Histopathology 2000, **37**: 150–159.

46 Barwick KW, Madri JA. An immunohistochemical study of adenomatoid tumors utilizing keratin and factor VIII antibodies. Evidence for a mesothelial origin. Lab Invest 1982, **47**: 276–280.

47 Bell DA, Flotte TJ. Factor VIII related antigen in adenomatoid tumor. Implications for histogenesis. Cancer 1982, **50**: 932–938.

48 Davy CL, Tang CK. Are all adenomatoid tumors adenomatoid mesotheliomas? Hum Pathol 1981, **12**: 360–369.

49 Eimoto T, Inoue I. Malignant fibrous mesothelioma of the tunica vaginalis. A histologic and ultrastructural study. Cancer 1977, **39**: 2059–2066.

50 Ferenczy A, Fenoglio J, Richart RM. Observations on benign mesothelioma of the genital tract (adenomatoid tumor). A comparative ultrastructural study. Cancer 1972, **29**: 148–164.

51 Fligiel Z, Kaneko M. Malignant mesothelioma of the tunica vaginalis propria testis in a patient with asbestos exposure. A case report. Cancer 1976, **37**: 1478–1484.

52 Hanrahan JB. A combined papillary mesothelioma and adenomatoid tumor of the omentum. Report of a case. Cancer 1963, **16**: 1497–1500.

53 Jones MA, Young RH, Scully RE. Malignant mesothelioma of the

tunica vaginalis. A clinicopathologic analysis of 11 cases with review of the literature. Am J Surg Pathol 1995, **19**: 815–825.

54 Kamiya M, Eimoto T. Malignant mesothelioma of the tunica vaginalis. Pathol Res Pract 1990, **186**: 680–684.

55 Kasdon EJ. Malignant mesothelioma of the tunica vaginalis propria testis. Report of two cases. Cancer 1969, **23**: 1144–1150.

56 Mackay B, Bennington JL, Skoglund RW. The adenomatoid tumor. Fine structural evidence for a mesothelial origin. Cancer 1971, **27**: 109–115.

57 Masson P, Riopelle JL, Simard LC. Le mésothéliome bénin de la sphère génitale. Rev Can Biol 1942, **1**: 720–751.

58 Perez-Ordonez B, Srigley JR. Mesothelial lesions of the paratesticular region. Semin Diagn Pathol 2000, **17**: 294–306.

59 Plas E, Riedl CR, Pfuger H. Malignant mesothelioma of the tunica vaginalis testis: review of the literature and assessment of prognostic parameters. Cancer 1998, **83**: 2437–2446.

60 Said JW, Nash G, Lee M. Immunoperoxidase localization of keratin proteins, carcinoembryonic antigen, and factor VIII in adenomatoid tumors. Evidence for a mesothelial derivation. Hum Pathol 1982, **13**: 1106–1108.

61 Taxy JB, Battifora H, Oyasu R. Adenomatoid tumors. A light microscopic, histochemical, and ultrastructural study. Cancer 1974, **34**: 306–316.

Other tumors and tumorlike conditions

62 Blumberg HM, Hendrix LE. Serous papillary adenocarcinoma of the tunica vaginalis of the testis with metastasis. Cancer 1991, **67**: 1450–1453.

63 Calder CJ, Gregory J. Papillary cystadenoma of the epididymis. A report of two cases with an immunohistochemical study. Histopathology 1993, **23**: 89–91.

64 Carano KS, Soslow RA. Immunophenotypic analysis of ovarian and testicular mullerian papillary serous tumors. Mod Pathol 1997, **10**: 414–420.

65 Chetty R. Epididymal cavernous haemangiomas. Histopathology 1993, **22**: 396–398.

66 De Nictolis M, Tommasoni S, Fabris G, Prat J. Intratesticular serous cystadenoma of borderline malignancy. A pathological, histochemical and DNA content study of a case with long-term follow-up. Virchows Arch [A] 1993, **423**: 221–225.

67 Ferry JA, Young RH, Scully RE. Testicular and epididymal plasmacytoma: a report of 7 cases, including three that were the initial manifestation of plasma cell myeloma. Am J Surg Pathol 1997, **21**: 590–598.

68 Jones MA, Young RH, Scully RE. Adenocarcinoma of the epididymis: a report of four cases and review of the literature. Am J Surg Pathol 1997, **21**: 1474–1480.

69 Jones MA, Young RH, Srigley JR, Scully RE. Paratesticular serous papillary carcinoma. A report of six cases. Am J Surg Pathol 1995, **19**: 1359–1365.

70 Kragel PJ, Pestaner J, Travis WD, Linehan WM, Filling-Katz MR. Papillary cystadenoma of the epididymis. A report of three cases with lectin histochemistry. Arch Pathol Lab Med 1990, **114**: 672–675.

71 Leung SY, Chan AS, Wong MP, Yuen ST, Fan YW, Chung LP. Expression of vascular endothelial growth factor in von Hippel–Lindau syndrome-associated papillary cystadenoma of the epididymis. Hum Pathol 1998, **29**: 1322–1323.

72 McClure RF, Keeney GL, Sebo TJ, Cheville JC. Serous borderline tumor of the paratestis; a report of seven cases. Am J Surg Pathol 2001, **25**: 373–378.

73 McDermott MB, O'Briain DS, Shiels OM, Daly PA. Malignant lymphoma of the epididymis. A case report of bilateral involvement by a follicular large cell lymphoma. Cancer 1995, **75**: 2174–2179.

74 Mai KT, Carlier M, Lajeunesse C. Paratesticular composite tumour of epididymal-like and mucinous cells of low malignant potential. Histopathogy 1998, **33**: 193–194.

75 Nistal M, Revestido R, Paniagua R. Bilateral mucinous cystadenocarcinoma of the testis and epididymis. Arch Pathol Lab Med 1992, **116**: 1360–1363.

76 Novella G, Porcaro AB, Righetti R, Cavalleri S, Beltrami P, Ficarra V, Brunelli M, Martignoni G, Malossini G, Tallarigo C. Primary lymphoma of the epididymis: case report and review of the literature. Urol Int 2001, **67**: 97–99.

77 Postius J, Manzano C, Concepcion T, Castro D, Gutierrez P, Banares F. Epididymal lymphangioma. J Urol 2000, **163**: 550–551.

78 Price EB Jr. Papillary cystadenoma of the epididymis. Arch Pathol 1971, **91**: 456–470.

79 Ricketts RR, Majmudarr B. Epididymal melanotic neuroectodermal tumor of infancy. Hum Pathol 1985, **16**: 416–420.

80 Salm R. Papillary carcinoma of the epididymis. J Pathol 1969, **97**: 253–259.

81 Shen T, Zhuang Z, Gersell DJ, Tavassoli FA. Allelic deletion of VHL gene detected in papillary tumors of the broad ligament, epididymis, and retroperitoneum in von Hippel-Lindau disease patients. Int J Surg Pathol 2000, **8**: 207–212.

82 Spark RP. Leiomyoma of epididymis. Arch Pathol 1972, **93**: 18–21.

83 Tsuda H, Fukushima S, Takahashi M, Hikosaka Y, Hayashi K. Familial bilateral papillary cystadenoma of the epididymis. Report of three cases in siblings. Cancer 1976, **37**: 1831–1839.

83a Ulbright TM, Young RH. Primary mucinous tumors of the testis and paratestis: a report of nine cases. Am J Surg Pathol 2003; **27**: 1221–1228.

84 Wachtel TL, Mehan DG. Metastatic tumors of the epididymis. J Urol 1970, **103**: 624–627.

85 Wehner MS, Humphreys JL, Sharkey FE. Epididymal rhabdomyoma; a report of a case, including histologic and immunohistochemical findings. Arch Pathol Lab Med 2000, **124**: 1518–1519.

86 Yamashina M, Honma T, Uchijima Y. Myofibroblastic pseudotumor mimicking epididymal sarcoma. A clinicopathologic study of three cases. Pathol Res Pract 1992, **188**: 1054–1059.

87 Young RH, Scully RE. Testicular and paratesticular tumors and tumor-like lesions of ovarian common epithelial and müllerian types. A report of four cases and review of the literature. Am J Clin Pathol 1986, **86**: 146–152.

SPERMATIC CORD

88 Arlen M, Grabstald H, Whitmore WF Jr. Malignant tumors of the spermatic cord. Cancer 1969, **23**: 525–532.

89 Bacchi CE, Schmidt RA, Brandao M, Scapulatempo R, Costa JC, Schmitt FC. Paraganglioma of the spermatic cord. Report of a case with immunohistochemical and ultrastructural studies. Arch Pathol Lab Med 1990, **114**: 899–901.

90 Ballo MT, Zagars GK, Pisters PW, Feig BW, Patel SR, von Eschenbach AC. Spermatic cord sarcoma: outcome, patterns of failure and management. J Urol 2001, **166**: 1306–1310.

91 Balogh K, Travis WD. The frequency of perineurial ductules in vasitis nodosa. Am J Clin Pathol 1984, **82**: 710–713.

92 Barton JH, Davis CJ Jr., Sesterhenn IA, Mostofi FK. Smooth muscle hyperplasia of the testicular adnexa clinically mimicking neoplasia: clinicopathologic study of sixteen cases. Am J Surg Pathol 1999, **23**: 903–909.

93 Blitzer PH, Dosoretz DE, Proppe KH, Shipley WU. Treatment of malignant tumors of the spermatic cord. A study of 10 cases and a review of the literature. J Urol 1981, **126**: 611–614.

94 Corless CL, Daut D, Burke R. Localized giant cell vasculitis of the spermatic cord presenting as a mass lesion. J Urol Pathol 1997, **6**: 235–242.

95 Cummings OW, Ulbright TM, Young RH, Dei Tos AP, Fletcher CDM, Hull MT. Desmoplastic small round cell tumors of the

paratesticular region: a report of six cases. Am J Surg Pathol 1997, **21**: 219–225.

96 Datta MW, Ulbright TM, Young RH. Renal cell carcinoma metastatic to the testis and its adnexa: a report of five cases including three that accounted for the initial clinical presentation. Int J Surg Pathol 2001, **9**: 49–56.

97 Eusebi V, Massarelli G. Phaeochromocytoma of the spermatic cord. Report of a case. J Pathol 1971, **105**: 283–284.

98 Fagundes MA, Zietman AL, Althausen AF, Coen JJ, Shipley WU. The management of spermatic cord sarcoma. Cancer 1996, **77**: 1873–1876.

99 Fisher C, Goldblum JR, Epstein JI, Montgomery E. Leiomyosarcoma of the paratesticular region: a clinicopathologic study. Am J Surg Pathol 2001, **25**: 1143–1149.

100 Folpe AL, Weiss SW. Paratesticular soft tissue neoplasms. Semin Diagn Pathol 2000, **17**: 307–318.

101 Henley JD, Ferry J, Ulbright TM. Miscellaneous rare paratesticular tumors. Semin Diagn Pathol 2000, **17**: 319–339.

102 Hollowood K, Fletcher CD. Pseudosarcomatous myofibroblastic proliferations of the spermatic cord ("proliferative funiculitis"). Histologic and immunohistochemical analysis of a distinctive entity. Am J Surg Pathol 1992, **16**: 448–454.

103 Izhak OB. Solitary papillary cystadenoma of the spermatic cord presenting as an inguinal mass. J Urol Pathol 1997, **7**: 55–62.

104 Kernohan NM, Coutts AG, Best PV. Cystadenocarcinoma of the appendix testis. Histopathology 1990, **17**: 147–154.

105 Kinjo M, Hokamura K, Tanaka K, Fujisawa Y, Hara S. Leiomyosarcoma of the spermatic cord. A case report and a brief review of literature. Acta Pathol Jpn 1986, **36**: 929–934.

106 Lilly MC, Arregui ME. Lipomas of the cord and round ligament. Ann Surg 2002, **235**: 586–589.

107 Lin BT, Harvey DA, Medeiros LJ. Malignant fibrous histiocytoma of the spermatic cord: report of two cases and review of the literature. Mod Pathol 2002, **15**: 59–65.

107a McCluggage WG, Dolan S, Cameron CHS, Russell CFJ. Epithelioid hemangioendothelioma of the spermatic cord. Int J Surg Pathol 200, **8**: 75–78.

108 McCluggage WG, Shah V, Nott C, Clements B, Wilson B, Hill CM. Cystadenoma of spermatic cord resembling ovarian serous epithelial tumour of low malignant potential: immunohistochemical study suggesting Mullerian differentiation. Histopathology 1996, **28**: 77–80.

109 McFarland JB. Testicular strangulation in children. Br J Surg 1966, **53**: 110–114.

110 Mai KT, Yazdi HM, Collins JP. Vascular myxolipoma ("angiomyxolipoma") of the spermatic cord. Am J Surg Pathol 1996, **20**: 1145–1148.

110a Montgomery E, Fisher C. Paratesticular liposarcoma: A clinicopathologic study. Am J Surg Pathol 2003, **27**: 40–47.

111 Nazeer T, Ro JY, Kee KH, Ayala AG. Spermatic cord contamination in testicular cancer. Mod Pathol 1996, **9**: 762–766.

112 Nistal M, Gonzàlez-Peramato P, Paniagua R. Lipomembranous fat necrosis in three cases of testicular torsion. Histopathology 2001, **38**: 443–447.

113 Olson AL. Vasitis nodosa. Am J Clin Pathol 1971, **55**: 364–368.

114 Sarma DP, Weilbaecher TG. Leiomyoma of the spermatic cord. J Surg Oncol 1985, **28**: 318–320.

115 Shim JW, Ro JY, Yang I, Lee KW, Chung SY. Solitary fibrous tumor: a case report arising in the scrotum. J Urol Pathol 1999, **10**: 229–238.

116 Simon HB, Larkin PC. Torsion of the appendix testis. Report of 13 cases. JAMA 1967, **202**: 140–141.

117 Skoglund RW, McRoberts JW, Ragde H. Torsion of testicular appendages. Presentation of 43 new cases and a collective review. J Urol 1970, **104**: 598–600.

118 Skoglund RW, McRoberts JW, Ragde H. Torsion of the spermatic cord. A review of the literature and an analysis of 70 new cases. J Urol 1970, **104**: 604–607.

119 Srigley JR. The paratesticular region: histoanatomic and general considerations. Semin Diagn Pathol 2000, **17**: 258–269.

120 Tanda F, Rocca PC, Bosincu L, Massarelli G, Cossu A, Manca A. Rhabdomyoma of the tunica vaginalis of the testis: a histologic, immunohistochemical, and ultrastructural study. Mod Pathol 1997, **10**: 608–611.

121 Taxy JB. Vasitis nodosa. Arch Pathol Lab Med 1978, **102**: 643–647.

Penis and scrotum

Penis

Normal anatomy

The main anatomic components of the penis are the corpus (shaft), glans, and prepuce (foreskin). The corpus is composed of the corpora cavernosa (made up of a net of vascular spaces surrounded by the tunica albuginea) and the inferiorly located corpus spongiosus, in the center of which runs the penile urethra. All of these structures are covered by skin, a smooth discontinuous muscle layer known as *dartos*, and an elastic sheath designated as *Buck's fascia*. The latter separates the penis into dorsal (corpora cavernosa) and ventral (corpus spongiosum) portions, a distinction highlighted by computed tomography (CT) and magnetic resonance imaging (MRI) techniques.[2]

The skin of the glans is made up of nonkeratinized stratified squamous epithelium, five to six cell layers thick; this becomes keratinized after circumcision.[1] The glans is separated from the shaft by the *balanopreputial sulcus* in the dorsal and lateral aspects and by the *frenulum* in the ventral region. Modified sebaceous glands known as Tyson's glands and supposedly responsible for the production of smegma are said to occur along the balanopreputial sulcus, but if they truly occur in humans (as opposed to orangutans, as described by Tyson in 1699), they must be very rare indeed, since several studies have failed to demonstrate their presence.[1,3]

The male urethra is divided into three portions: prostatic (the short proximal segment surrounded by the prostate), membranous or bulbomembranous (extending from the lower pole of the prostate to the bulb of the corpus spongiosum), and penile (which passes longitudinally through the corpus spongiosum). The terminal enlarged portion of the penile urethra is known as the *fossa navicularis*. The penile urethra contains numerous IgA-positive plasma cells, and the epithelium expresses secretory component, indicating that this region is an active site of secretory IgA-mediated immune defense.[4]

Microscopically, the lining of the urethra is of transitional type in the proximal (prostatic) portion, of stratified squamous type in the distal portion corresponding to the fossa navicularis, and of stratified or pseudostratified columnar ciliated epithelium in the rest of the canal. Squamous metaplasia of this epithelium is a common occurrence after estrogen administration, as reported in a group of transsexual individuals before surgery.[5] Glandular structures associated with the urethra are the *intraepithelial glands* or Morgagni's lacunae (one-layer cylindrical intraepithelial glands), *Littré's glands* (tubuloacinar mucinous glands present along the full length of the corpus spongiosum), and the *bulbourethral* or *Cowper's glands* (mucous acinar structures located deeply at the level of the membranous urethra).[1]

The lymphatic drainage of the penis is to the superficial and deep inguinal nodes. There are centrally located anastomoses between lymph vessels that result in bilateral drainage.

Non-neoplastic lesions

Small accessory urethral canals or periurethral ducts may open in or about the fossa navicularis and produce symptoms because of secondary inflammation.[14] The *median raphe cyst* that has been described in the central aspect of the glans in young men probably represents a cystic dilatation of these structures[10] (Fig. 18.123).

Mucoid cyst can be found on the prepuce or glans penis. It has a lining of stratified columnar epithelium, often associated with intraepithelial mucous glands[8,22] (Fig. 18.124).

Mucinous metaplasia refers to the presence of mucin-producing cells in the surface epithelium in the prepuce or glans penis. It is seen in the elderly and appears to be a metaplastic change associated with severe chronic inflammation, particularly Zoon's balanitis (see below).[11,26]

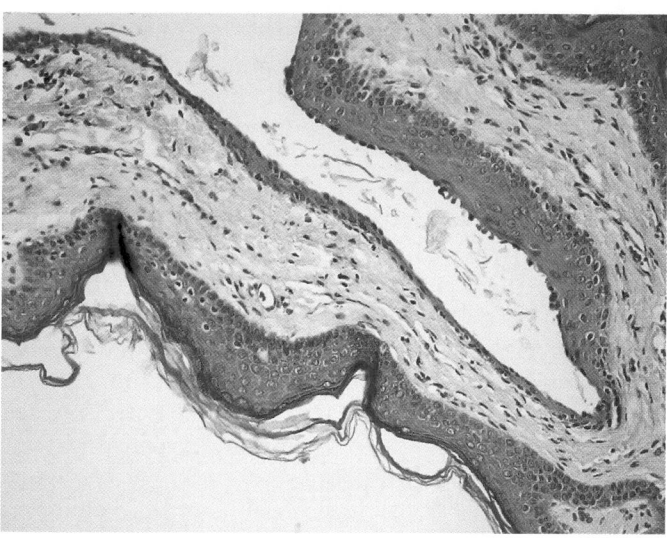

Fig. 18.123 Median raphe cyst. This probably results from cystic dilatation of accessory urethral canals or periurethral ducts.

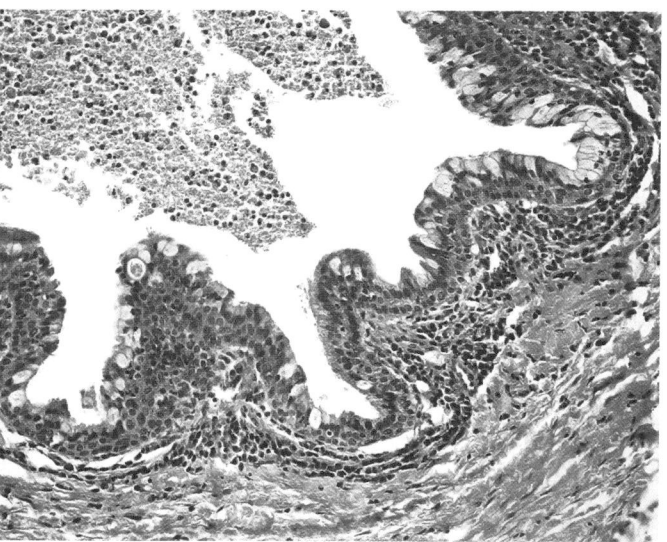

Fig. 18.124 Mucoid cyst of penis. The lesion is lined by stratified columnar epithelium containing mucin-secreting cells.

Inflammation of Littré's glands can simulate clinically a penile tumor.[15]

Dermatoses of various types can involve the skin of the penis. These include eczema, seborrheic dermatitis, fixed drug eruption, psoriasis, lichen planus, lichen nitidus, and lichen sclerosus et atrophicus. The latter condition, which in this location has traditionally been known as balanitis xerotica obliterans, is exceptionally accompanied by a lymphohistiocytic and granulomatous phlebitis.[7,9]

An inflammatory condition clinically resembling Bowen's disease is *balanitis circumscripta* (Zoon's balanitis), characterized microscopically by epidermal atrophy and a dense inflammatory infiltrate rich in plasma cells.[25,26a] Deep *granuloma annulare* can be localized to the penis.[16]

Amyloidosis presenting as a localized mass in the shaft of the penis has been reported.[17]

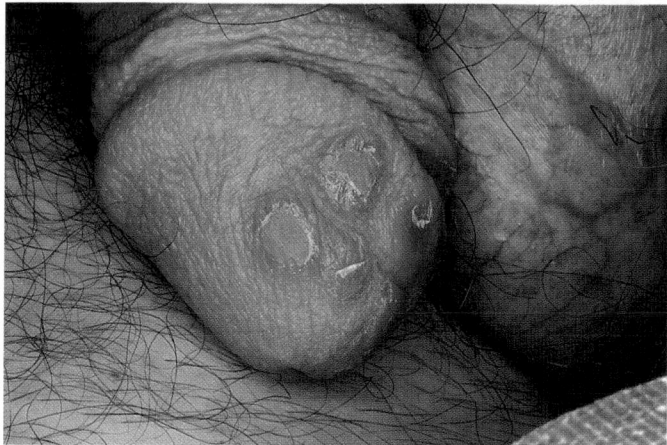

Fig. 18.125 Syphilitic chancre occurring on the glans penis. (Courtesy of Dr. N. Scott McNutt, New York)

Primary syphilis (chancre) (Fig. 18.125) consists microscopically of a thin and sometimes ulcerated epidermis accompanied by a dense dermal inflammatory infiltrate rich in plasma cells and lymphocytes. The blood vessels show marked endothelial cell swelling and proliferation as well as infiltration of the wall by inflammatory cells ("endarteritis obliterans"). Spirochetes can be demonstrated with the Warthin–Starry silver stain both in the epidermis and in the dermis (particularly in and around the proliferating vessels).

Chancroid, the most common cause of genital ulceration in Africa, is characterized microscopically by vasculitis in the deep dermis, manifested by perivascular and intramural lymphocytic and histiocytic infiltrates associated with swelling of endothelial cells, sometimes admixed with neutrophils and/or multinucleated giant cells. The overlying epidermis shows psoriasiform hyperplasia and spongiosis, sometimes accompanied by neutrophils in the malpighian and horny parakeratotic layers. It has been suggested that this infection may play a role in HIV transmission.[19]

Tuberculosis and other granulomatous inflammations can on rare occasions present as penile nodules.[6]

Abscess and **gangrene** of the penis are described, the clinical history sometimes revealing some rather lurid contributing factors.[13]

Wegener's granulomatosis can be localized to the penis and clinically simulate a carcinoma.[20]

Behçet's disease is a symptom complex of oral and genital ulcers and iritis. Microscopically, various types of vasculitis may be encountered (Fig. 18.126).

Peyronie's disease (plastic induration of the penis) is a circumscribed fibrous thickening arising in the connective tissue layer between the corpora cavernosa and the tunica albuginea. It causes pain and penile curvature toward the side of the lesion on penile erection.[18,21] Microscopically, the lesion is composed of hyalinized fibrous tissue, at times containing cartilage and bone[23]

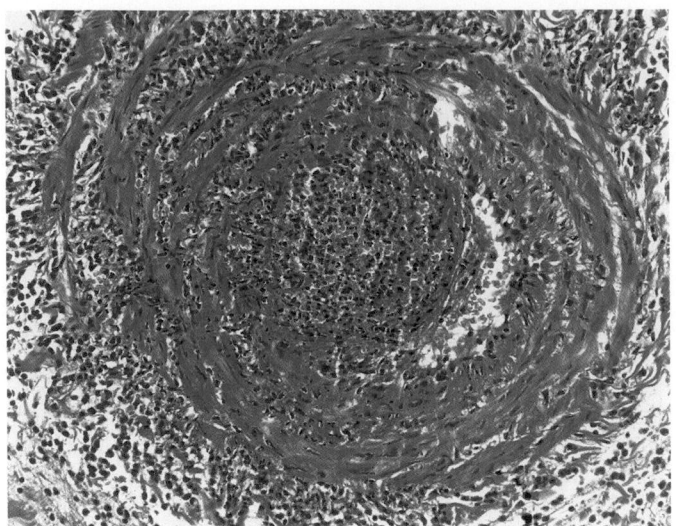

Fig. 18.126 Prominent arteritis in a case of Behçet's disease. (Courtesy of Dr. Fabio Facchetti, Brescia, Italy)

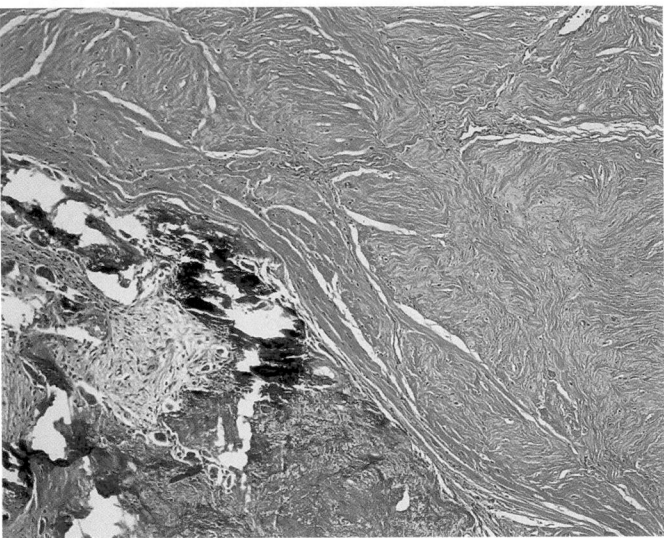

Fig. 18.127 Peyronie's disease. The lesion is composed of heavily sclerotized tissue that has undergone focal dystrophic calcification.

(Fig. 18.127). It may be associated with Dupuytren's contracture, and it may be alleviated by small amounts of irradiation, steroid administration, or excision. MRI is a very useful technique for planning therapy and for evaluating the response to medical treatment.[12]

Smith[24] described changes that he interpreted as subclinical examples of Peyronie's disease in 23 of 100 consecutive autopsies on adults. Because of the finding of associated urethritis in 7 of the 23 affected individuals, he suggested that Peyronie's disease results from a series of mild inflammatory and fibrosing reactions secondary to urethritis. If this concept is correct, the disease could be viewed as a sclerosing inflammatory process rather than as a form of fibromatosis, the latter being, however, the prevalent interpretation at present.

Condyloma acuminatum and related lesions

Condyloma acuminatum of the penis is a venereal disease caused by the human papilloma virus (HPV) and most commonly seen between the ages of 20 and 40 years. It presents as a papillary growth at the penile meatus or fossa navicularis or in other regions of the glans (Fig. 18.128). Almost 30% of the polypoid lesions of the male urethra are examples of this entity. Microscopically, there are complex papillary infoldings of squamous epithelium accompanied by vacuolization of keratinocytes and nuclear abnormalities ("koilocytosis") and a lymphocytic infiltrate in the stroma that is predominantly composed of CD4+ cells[30] (Fig. 18.129). The virus can be demonstrated by immunocytochemical and in situ hybridization techniques.[27,32]

Other benign HPV-induced lesions of this region are of a macular or papular rather than polypoid ("acuminate") nature. Their clinical detection is aided by the local application of acetic acid (causing so-called "acetowhitening"). In one study, "high-risk" HPV types (16, 18, 31, 33, 35) were demonstrated in 8% of acuminate, 24% of papular, and 56% of macular lesions, respectively.[29] Sometimes, HPV DNA is found in lesions lacking the microscopic features typically associated with this disorder and showing only focal thickening of the granular layer associated with epithelial crevices.[33,34] Immunohistochemically, HPV infection leads to a decrease in the expression of keratins 1 and 10 and in the appearance of keratin 13 and (to a lesser degree) keratin 4 in the affected squamous epithelium.[31]

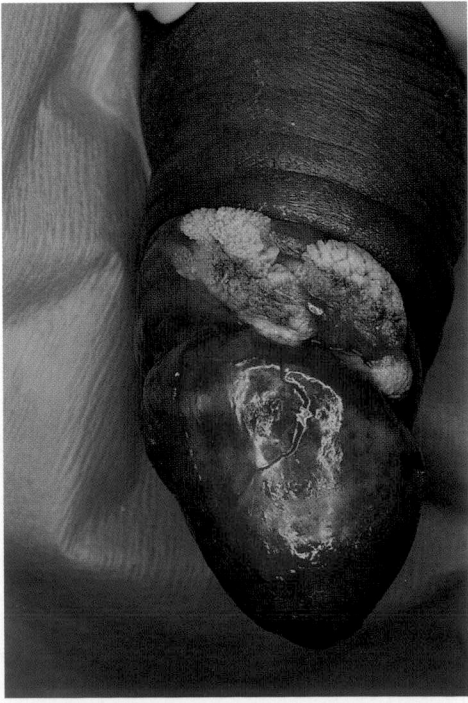

Fig. 18.128 Large lesions of condyloma acuminatum in an HIV-infected patient. The glans penis also shows herpesvirus infection.

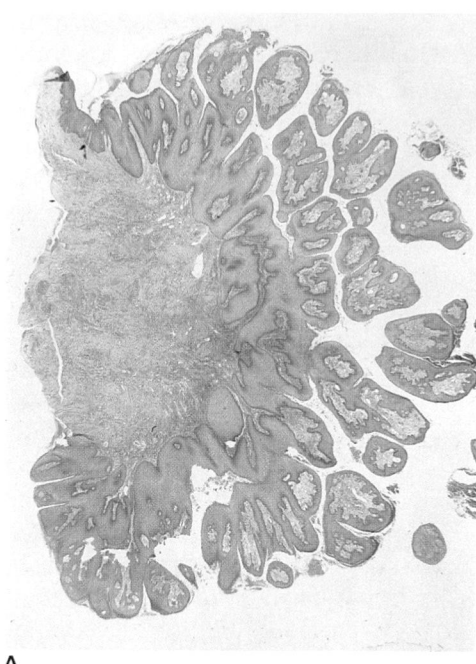

A

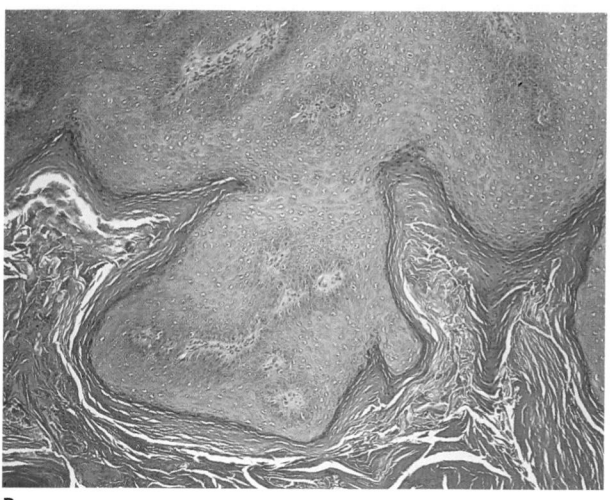

B

Fig. 18.129 A and **B**, Condyloma acuminatum. A complex papillary pattern composed of well-differentiated squamous epithelium is seen. Virus-induced cytopathic changes are not particularly prominent in this case, probably because of the longstanding nature of the lesion.

Pearly penile plaques (PPP) clinically resemble the papular type of condyloma but do not contain HPV DNA.[28] Microscopically, they show acanthosis and hyperkeratosis but no koilocytosis or significant stromal inflammation.

Tumors

Bowen's disease and related intraepithelial neoplasias

Bowen's disease is classically described as a sharply demarcated, scaly, erythematous plaque, whereas **erythroplasia of Queyrat** presents as a shiny, velvety, erythematous plaque.[42] Both processes typically arise in the glans or prepuce, usually in elderly individuals. They both represent *squamous cell carcinoma in situ* and are characterized by a full-thickness alteration of the epithelium (although associated with some degree of maturation), large hyperchromatic nuclei, multinucleated cells, dyskeratosis, vacuolization, and numerous typical and atypical mitoses (Fig. 18.130). Acanthosis and parakeratosis are also present. The underlying stroma shows chronic inflammation and vascular proliferation. The minor morphologic differences described between Bowen's disease and erythroplasia of Queyrat may result from anatomic variations in the area, and the two diseases should be regarded as one and the same for prognostic and therapeutic purposes.[45] HPV DNA has been consistently found in these lesions by in situ hybridization, Southern blotting, and PCR techniques.[40,41,43,46]

In about 5% of patients with penile squamous cell carcinoma in situ there is also an invasive component.[35]

Surgical excision is the treatment of choice for Bowen's disease, although electrodesiccation, laser therapy, curettage, topical fluorouracil, and imiquimod cream have also reportedly given satisfactory results.[48,50] Penectomy should be reserved for the few patients in whom an invasive carcinoma has developed.[42]

Bowenoid papulosis is the proposed term for a penile disease that has histologic features similar to those of Bowen's disease but an age distribution (young adults) and clinical appearance (multiple, reddish to violaceous papules on the shaft, glans, or scrotum) more in keeping with a virally induced lesion[51] (Fig. 18.131). Support for the viral etiology of bowenoid papulosis comes from the

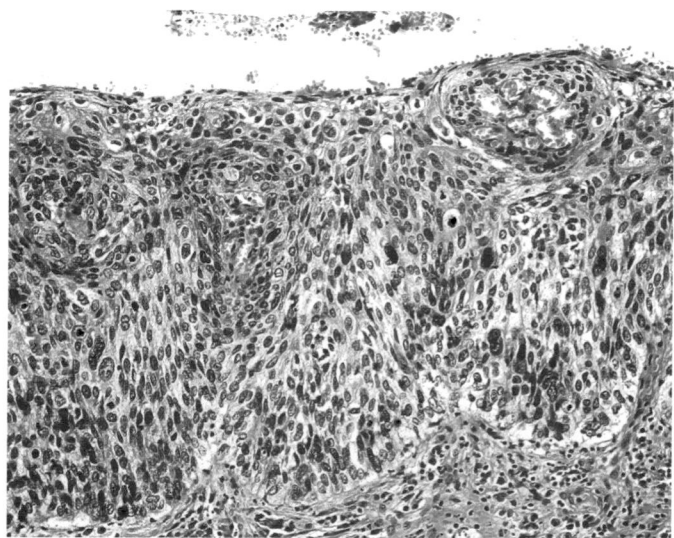

Fig. 18.130 Squamous cell carcinoma in situ (Bowen's disease) of penis. There is full-thickness atypia, with pleomorphism and high mitotic activity.

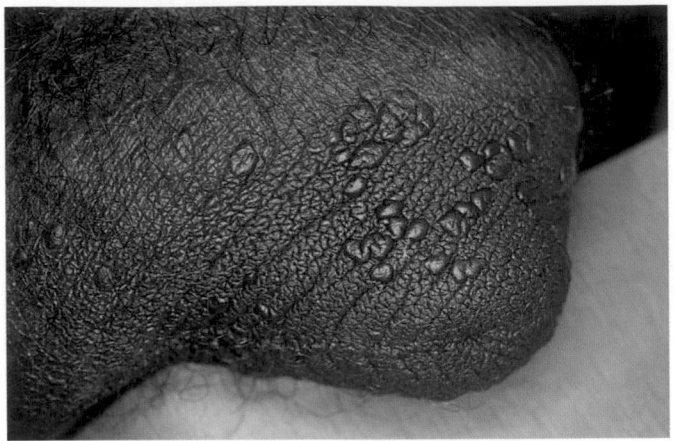

Fig. 18.131 Clinical appearance of bowenoid papulosis in the skin of the scrotum. The lesions are small, multiple, and hyperpigmented. (Courtesy of Dr. N. Scott McNutt, New York)

demonstration of HPV-16 in 80% of the cases in one series[44] and the occasional coexistence of this disease with typical condyloma acuminatum.[49] According to Patterson et al.,[47] bowenoid papulosis differs microscopically from Bowen's disease by virtue of a lesser degree of cytologic atypia, an orderly background of maturation, and a lesser number of dysplastic cells and mitotic figures. These authors also remarked that bowenoid papulosis tends to involve the upper portion of the sweat glands (acrosyringium) and to spare the upper portion of the pilosebaceous units (acrotrichium), a pattern they claim is reversed in Bowen's disease. The existence of a spectrum of morphologic changes, the common identification of HPV in both conditions, the fact that either one can be found in sexual partners of women with cervical intraepithelial neoplasia, and the report of cases of bowenoid papulosis associated with squamous cell carcinoma speak in favor of a common pathogenesis.[37,52] Some authors therefore prefer to group them under the designation of *bowenoid dysplasia* or *penile intraepithelial neoplasia*,[36,37] a practice that we find rather appealing. It has been further suggested that this penile intraepithelial neoplasia be subdivided into two or three grades, with a further subdivision depending on the pattern of growth into squamous or simplex, warty (condylomatous), and basaloid.[39]

Typically, the lesions of bowenoid papulosis undergo resolution, whether by limited surgery, by topical medication, or even spontaneously.[38] Whatever the ultimate relationship between this condition and Bowen's disease may prove to be, the importance of clinicopathologic correlation and a conservative therapeutic approach is obvious.

Squamous cell carcinoma

General features

Squamous cell carcinoma of the penis is relatively infrequent in the United States, accounting for fewer than 1% of all malignancies in males.[56] However, it is very common in some Asian, African, and Latin American countries, where it may constitute over 10% of all carcinomas.[58,61] It is largely a disease of the elderly, the rate increasing to a peak at about 80 years of age.[56]

If circumcision is done shortly after birth, as is the Jewish custom, carcinoma of the penis develops very rarely. If the operation is delayed until the age of 10 years, as is the Moslem custom, carcinoma is more likely to develop.[55] It is possible that carcinoma is related to personal hygiene and the carcinogenic effect of smegma, factors that might be enhanced by failure to circumcise.[54] In keeping with this assumption, an association has been found between penile cancer and long phimotic foreskins.[54,64a]

Cases have also been reported in association with lichen sclerosus et atrophicus (balanitis xerotica obliterans)[60] and lichen planus,[53] but these may simply be coincidental events. It has been found that psoriatic patients exposed to high levels of ultraviolet B radiation have a risk of genital tumors (including penile carcinoma) 4.6 times higher than the control population.[63]

The association of penile carcinoma with HPV has been well documented. McCance[57] found HPV-16 DNA sequences in 49% and HPV-18 DNA in 9% of 53 cases from Brazil. Studies from the United States have shown the presence of HPV DNA in over 80% of the cases, but with widely differing figures regarding the relative frequency of the various HPV types.[64,65] Rubin et al.[62] found evidence of HPV DNA in 42% of their cases of penile carcinoma (as opposed to 90% of the cases of intraepithelial neoplasia and 100% of the cases of condyloma); they also documented significant differences among the various microscopic subtypes (see below). Some of the cases of HPV-associated penile squamous cell carcinomas have occurred in HIV-positive patients.[59]

Morphologic features and types

Most squamous cell carcinomas of the penis arise in the glans, prepuce, and coronal sulcus, in this order of frequency. Their pattern of growth may be superficially spreading, predominantly exophytic (fungating, verruciform) or predominantly endophytic (infiltrative, ulcerating, vertical) (Figs 18.132 to 18.134). Mixtures of these patterns occur, and there may be multicentricity.[67] In general, the exophytic tumors are better differentiated than their endophytic counterparts. At the microscopic level, penile squamous cell carcinomas are divided into *usual type, warty (condylomatous), verrucous*, and *papillary NOS* (Figs 18.135 and 18.136). It should be emphasized that the last three categories are all characterized by a similar exophytic pattern of growth, and that the distinction among them is made on cytoarchitectural grounds. Only the warty (condylomatous) carcinoma exhibits prominent and diffuse koilocytotic atypia. All three tumors are for the most part well differentiated, but

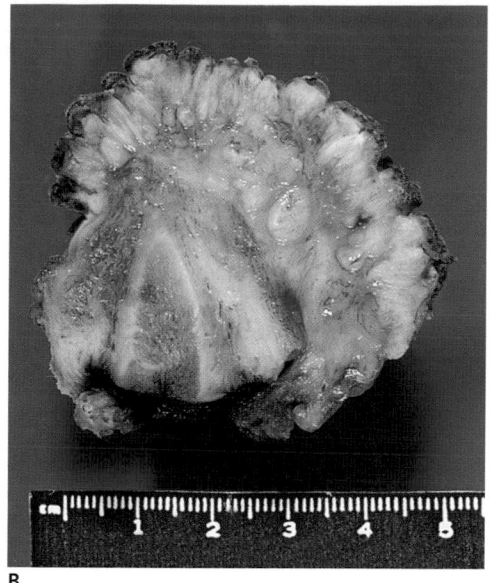

A

B

Fig. 18.132 Outer aspect and cut surface of squamous cell carcinoma of penis showing a papillomatous pattern of growth.

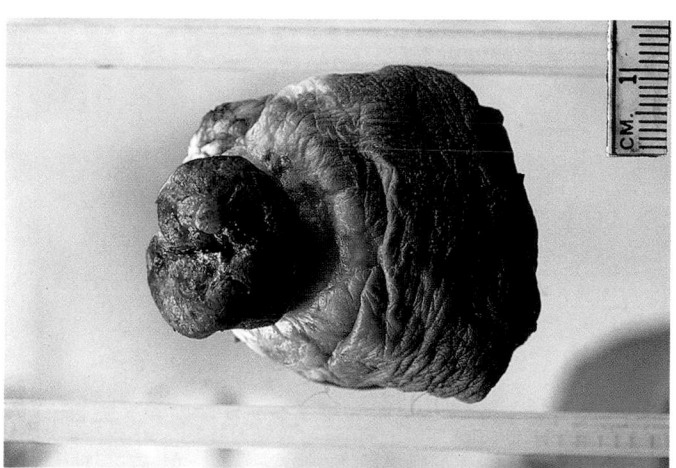

Fig. 18.133 Penile squamous cell carcinoma involving the glans in a vegetant fashion.

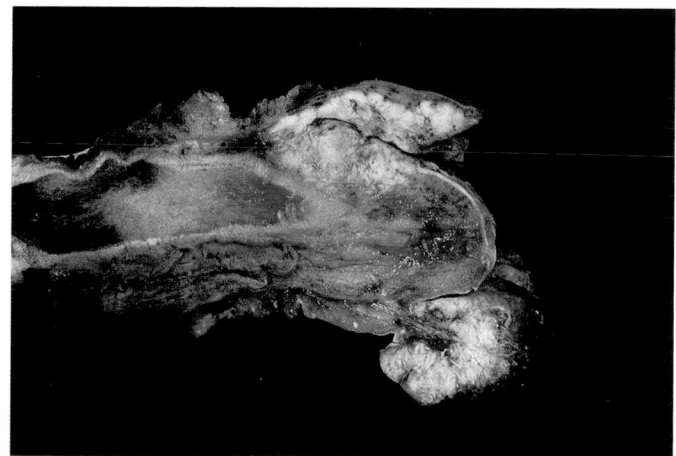

Fig. 18.134 Penile squamous cell carcinoma with extensive involvement of prepuce.

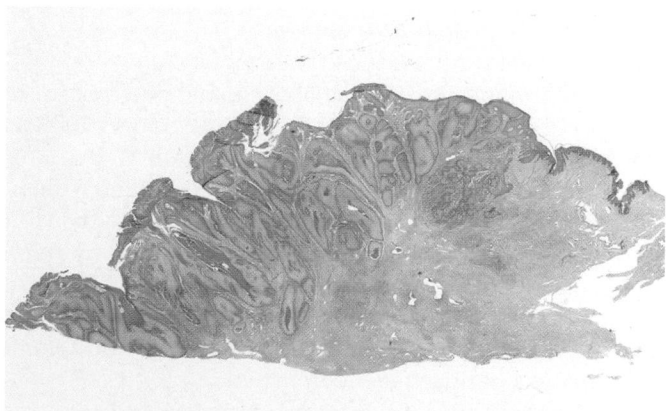

Fig. 18.135 Whole mount of well-differentiated squamous cell carcinoma showing pushing-type invasion into the underlying stroma, associated with a chronic inflammatory response.

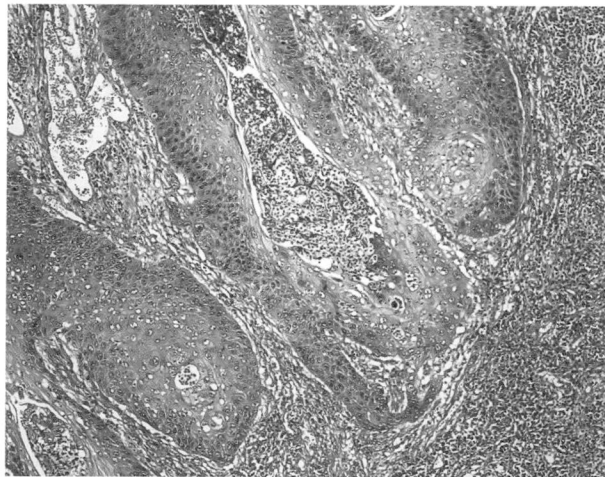

Fig. 18.136 Moderately differentiated invasive squamous cell carcinoma.

whereas verrucous carcinoma is by definition always a grade I tumor, warty and papillary carcinoma NOS can be either grade I or II. In others words, only tumors with an extremely well-differentiated cytologic appearance *throughout* should be designated as verrucous carcinomas.

Verrucous carcinoma, which constitutes about 5% of all penile cancers, has a more regular architecture than warty carcinoma, particularly at its base, where it features broad bulbous expansions of squamous epithelium lacking irregular stromal penetration[69,70] (Figs 18.137 and 18.138). Tumors combining features of squamous cell carcinoma of the usual and verrucous types are referred to as *hybrid tumors*.[70,73]

Other microscopic types of penile tumors related to squamous cell carcinoma are *basaloid carcinoma*[68] (Fig. 18.139), *adenoid (pseudoglandular) carcinoma*,[74] *surface adenosquamous carcinoma (mucoepidermoid carcinoma)*,[66,71] and *spindle cell (sarcomatoid) carcinoma*[72] (Fig. 18.140), and squamous cell carcinoma with rhabdoid features.[73a]

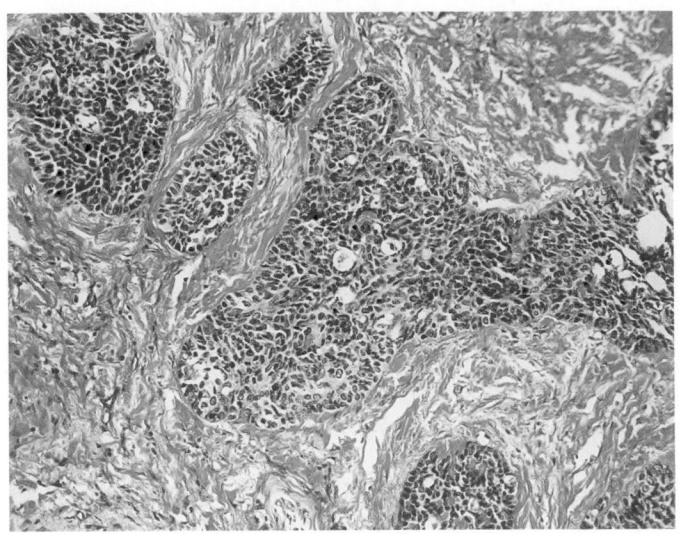

Fig. 18.139 Basaloid carcinoma of penis. This is regarded as a variant of squamous cell carcinoma.

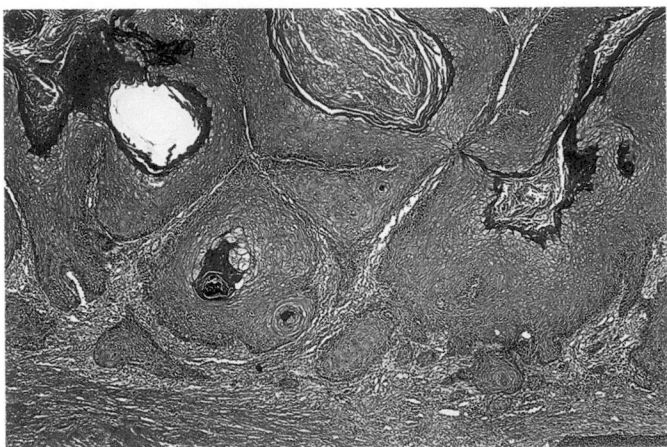

Fig. 18.137 Typical low-power appearance of verrucous carcinoma.

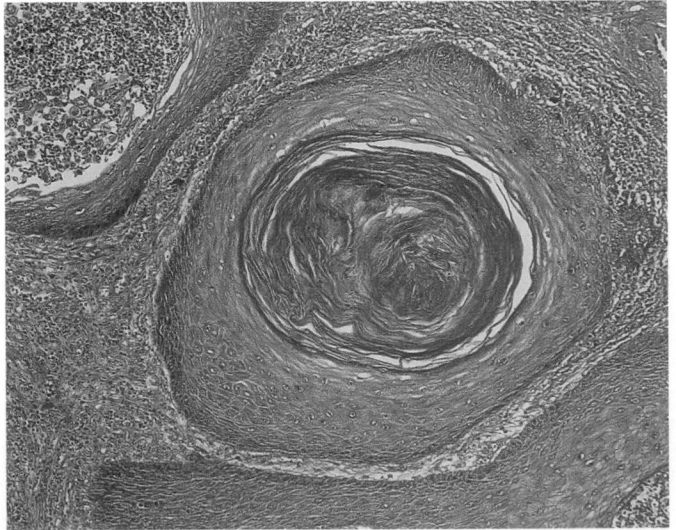

Fig. 18.138 Bulbous expansions of well-differentiated squamous epithelium in verrucous carcinoma.

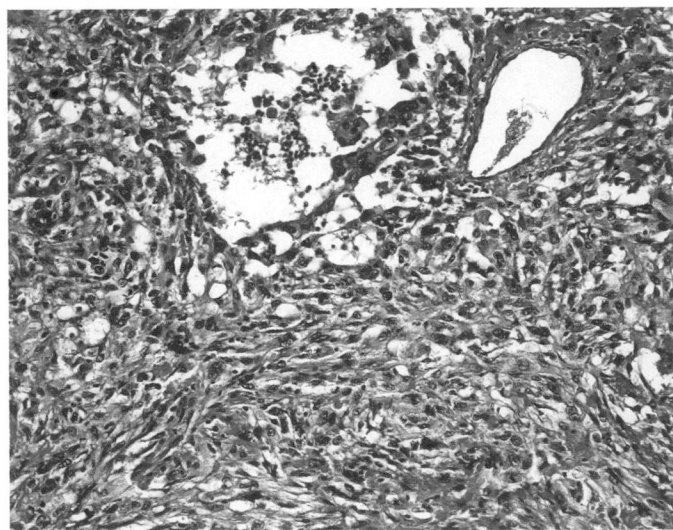

Fig. 18.140 Squamous cell carcinoma of penis with spindle cell (sarcomatoid) features. There is a blending of the carcinoma islands with the sarcoma-like component.

Molecular genetic features

Rubin et al.[79] found evidence of HPV DNA in about 33% of the squamous carcinomas of the usual and verrucous type, in 80% of the basaloid carcinomas, and in 100% of the warty carcinomas. The results obtained by other authors tend to confirm the high frequency of HPV DNA in basaloid and warty carcinoma,[75,76] and the low frequency in verrucous carcinoma.[78] The latter finding—plus some differences in morphology—has cast some doubts on the long-held assumption that verrucous carcinoma is identical to so-called "giant condyloma acuminatum of Buschke–Lowenstein."

DNA ploidy studies by flow cytometry have shown a uniform diploid population in verrucous carcinoma, and either a diploid or polypoid/aneuploid population in the other types of squamous cell carcinoma.[78]

Expression of p21 and p53 has been found in 40% and 80%, respectively, of penile squamous cell carcinomas, with often an inverse relation between them.[77]

Spread and metastases

Squamous cell carcinoma arising within a penile compartment (glans, prepuce, or coronal sulcus) often spreads to involve others. Early invasion of the Buck's fascia is common in carcinomas of the coronal sulcus. Local spread into the urethra is also a common finding, especially among the deeply invasive tumors.

The overall incidence of inguinal lymph node metastases is 15%. The first node usually involved ("sentinel node") belongs to the superficial epigastric group and is located medial to and above the epigastric–saphenous junction.[80] Because carcinomas are often associated with secondary infection, enlargement of inguinal nodes is very common and clinical appraisal is extremely inaccurate.[83] Lymph node metastases are uncommon in the exophytic tumors; when present, they usually appear late in the evolution of the disease. Conversely, they are common in the deeply invasive tumors, sometimes accompanied by spread to other lymph node groups. Metastases do not occur in verrucous carcinomas,[84] but may be present in hybrid carcinomas.[85] They are particularly common in basaloid and spindle cell carcinomas.[82] In the series of Cubilla et al.,[81] inguinal lymph node metastases were present in 82% of the deeply invasive tumors with minimal or no in situ component, 42% of the "superficially invasive" tumors, and 33% of the multicentric tumors. Nodal metastases were very rare in tumors that invaded only the lamina propria, and relatively common in the tumors that had invaded the urethra.

Treatment and prognosis

Carcinoma of the penis can be treated by local resection or by partial or total penectomy, according to the size and location of the lesion and its microscopic type.[91,93,102,105] Local recurrence is extremely rare if the surgical margins are negative, even if narrow (=10 mm).[95] Controversy still exists as to the role of elective inguinal lymphadenectomy. Most authors advocate it except for very small and early lesions,[90,91,96] but others have questioned the need for this procedure, which is associated with a significant morbidity.[103,104] Since lymph node metastases do not occur in verrucous carcinoma, this tumor is therefore treated with resection of the primary lesion only.[97] As in other sites, radiation therapy of this tumor type may result in anaplastic transformation.[92]

The overall 5- and 10-year survival rates for squamous cell carcinoma of the penis are 77% and 71%, respectively.[94] The prognosis is related to the following factors:

1 *Stage*. This is the most important parameter.[98] However, it should be noted that there is a considerable difference between clinical and pathologic stage, which is attributable to the difficulty of assessing corpora cavernosa invasion and inguinal lymph node metastases.[87,100] The close relationship that exists between the depth of invasion of the penile anatomic landmarks and prognosis renders essential an accurate anatomic dissection and sampling of the penectomy specimen.[88] If metastases are present in two or more nodes, the chances of cure are very small.[86]

2 *Microscopic type*. Verrucous carcinoma is associated with a much better prognosis, followed by warty carcinoma. Basaloid and sarcomatoid carcinomas are associated with high rate of nodal metastases and poor survival.[88a]

3 *Microscopic grade*. The grade of the tumor shows a very good correlation with prognosis.[89,90,101]

4 *Vascular invasion*. This is an indicator of poor prognosis, but it is not clear whether it retains its value independently of staging and microscopic grading.[89,90]

5 *p53 overexpression*. The overexpression of this marker as evaluated immunohistochemically is significantly associated with the presence of lymph node metastases.[99]

Other carcinoma types

Paget's disease is less common in the penis than in the scrotum or perineum; it may be purely intraepidermal or associated with an underlying adenocarcinoma.[107,108]

Basal cell carcinoma of the penis is microscopically similar to its counterpart elsewhere in the skin; to the best of our knowledge, no instances of metastatic behavior have been reported.[106] Obviously, a sharp distinction should be made between this tumor and basaloid squamous cell carcinoma (see p. 1472).

Tumors of penile urethra

Benign tumors of the penile urethra are extremely rare. Isolated cases of **inverted papilloma** similar to their bladder counterparts have been reported.[113] **Condyloma acuminatum** can extend into the distal portion of the urethra. **Leiomyoma** of the male urethra is much less common than in the female urethra, but its existence has been documented.[117]

Carcinoma of the male urethra is a rare disease. In some cases, it follows stricture produced by trauma or gonorrhea. In some series as many as 44% of the patients had a history of venereal disease.[115] The most common location of the tumor is the bulbomembranous portion, followed by the penile portion.[119] Microscopically, 75% of the tumors are *squamous cell carcinomas*; most of the others (usually located in the prostatic portion) are *transitional cell carcinomas* (Fig. 18.141). A few cases of *adenocarcinoma* have also been reported; possible sources for them are metaplastic urethral mucosa, bulbourethral (Cowper's) glands, and periurethral (Littré's) glands.[111] Some of these adenocarcinomas have been of mucinous (colloid) type.[116] Evidence of HPV infection has been found in some cases of urethral carcinoma.[112]

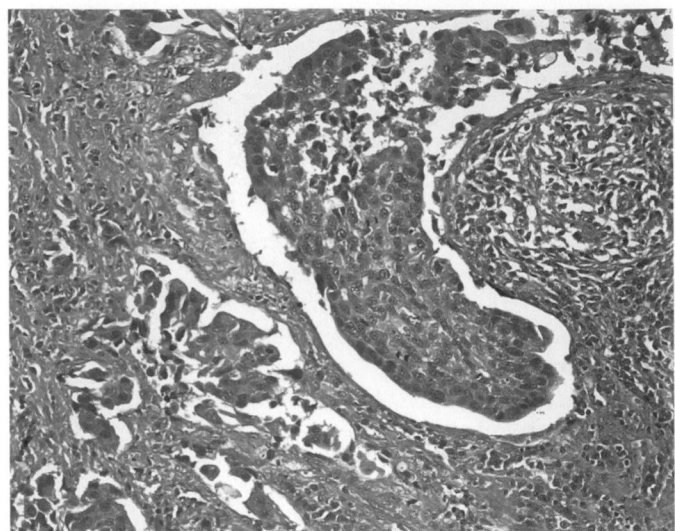

Fig. 18.141 Transitional cell carcinoma of penile urethra.

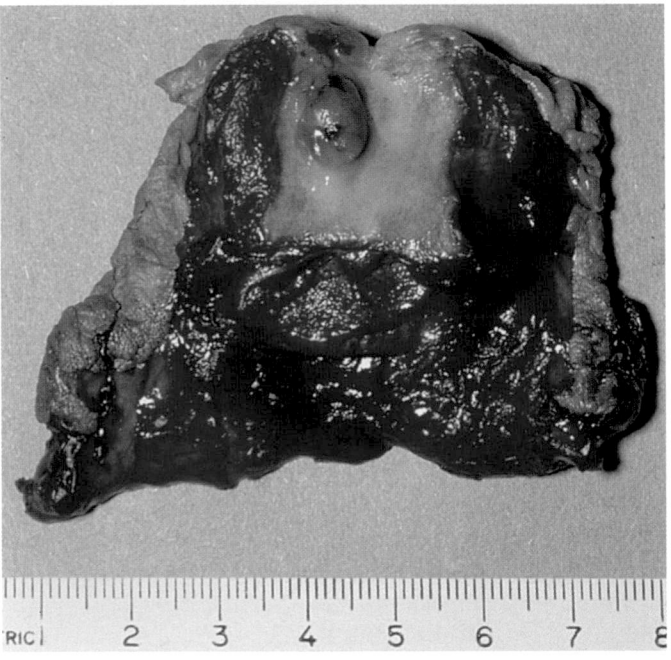

Fig. 18.142 Malignant melanoma presenting as a polypoid bluish mass protruding from the urethra.

The prognosis and treatment of urethral carcinoma depend more on location and stage than on microscopic type or grade.[110] Anterior or distal lesions have a much better prognosis than posterior or proximal lesions. In general, the anterior lesions drain to inguinal nodes, whereas posterior lesions drain into pelvic nodes.[115] The treatment is primarily surgical.

Primary **malignant melanoma** of the urethra also occurs; the shape of these tumors is typically polypoid and their prognosis is exceedingly poor[109,118] (Fig. 18.142).

Malignant lymphoma of T-cell type presenting in the urethra as the first manifestation of HIV infection has been described.[114]

Other tumors and tumorlike conditions

Hirsutoid papillomas (also known as papillomatosis corona penis or glans) appear as small, polypoid, 1 to 2 mm lesions in the corona of the glans, usually on its dorsal aspect. They can be solitary or multiple and have the microscopic appearance of fibroepithelial polyps.[159,162]

Adnexal tumors of sweat gland, sebaceous, or hair follicle type rarely occur in the penile skin.[142,149]

Melanocytic lesions of the penis can be of benign or malignant nature. **Lentigo** of the common variety occurs most commonly in the glans as a relatively large (up to 2 cm), multifocal, irregularly shaped lesion of variegated pigmentation. It is also known as (atypical) melanotic macule and is characterized microscopically by basal cell hyperpigmentation, epithelial hyperplasia, and lack of melanocytic atypia.[122,141] **Nevi** of various types also occur, including *blue nevus*.[161] **Malignant melanoma** may arise in the glans or prepuce; metastases to lymph nodes are common.[150,165]

Soft tissue tumors of the penis are located for the most part in the shaft. Among the benign tumors, those of vascular, neural, and smooth muscle derivation are the most common.[128,131a] These include, among others, hemangioma, epithelioid hemangioma,[157] Fordyce's angiokeratoma, lymphangioma,[136] schwannoma,[140] neurofibroma,[129,130] granular cell tumor,[126,158] leiomyoma,[123] myofibroma,[160] and verruciform xanthoma.[139] The list of malignant soft tissue tumors includes angiosarcoma,[134,152] Kaposi's sarcoma (some occurring in the setting of AIDS),[120,143,156] fibrosarcoma, malignant peripheral nerve sheath tumor, epithelioid sarcoma,[128,147] malignant fibrous histiocytoma,[132,148,163] clear cell sarcoma,[155] leiomyosarcoma,[137] and osteosarcoma.[121,154] *Myointimoma* is the term proposed by Fetsch et al.[131] for a peculiar vascular myointimal proliferation composed of cells with myoid features involving the corpus spongiosum of young men. The etiology is unknown and the evolution is benign.

Malignant lymphoma of penis usually represents secondary involvement by nodal lymphoma.[135,164] This includes involvement of penis, scrotum, and perineum by the type of malignant lymphoma formerly known as polymorphic reticulosis or idiopathic midline destructive disease[125] (see Chapter 7). *Langerhans' cell histiocytosis* can present in the male genitalia and lead to confusion microscopically with Paget's disease.[144]

Metastatic carcinoma to the penis is rare.[151,153] Priapism is one of the forms of presentation.[124] The most common sources are prostate, bladder, rectum, kidney, testis, and lung in that order of frequency.[127,133,138] Sometimes the tumor in the penile skin is epidermotropic and exhibits the features of extramammary Paget's disease, whether arising from an underlying sweat gland carcinoma[146] or a distant site, such as the bladder.[145]

Scrotum (see also Spermatic Cord, p. 1464)

Normal anatomy

The scrotal sac is a seven-layer structure that invests the testes, adnexa, and distal spermatic cord. The seven layers are the epidermis, dermis, tunica dartos (composed of smooth muscle bundles), the three layers of Colles' fascia (intercrural, cremasteric, and infundibuliform), and the parietal layer of the tunica vaginalis. The latter consists of a flattened layer of mesothelial cells resting on a well-developed basement membrane.[166]

The scrotal lymphatics drain into the ipsilateral superficial inguinal lymph nodes. Anastomotic connections to the lymphatics of the contralateral network across the raphe occur.

Non-neoplastic lesions

Hydrocele is the term given to the collection of serous fluid within the tunica vaginalis sac. Acquired and congenital forms exist, the former being associated with inflammatory processes of the scrotal contents (Fig. 18.143). The lining of the sac is made up of mesothelial cells. This condition should be distinguished from *spermatocele* of epididymal origin, which is identified by the presence of sperm in the cyst fluid.

Idiopathic calcinosis of the scrotum is characterized by multiple asymptomatic nodules in the scrotal skin that begin in childhood or adolescence and tend to increase in size and number (Fig. 18.144). Occasionally, they break down through the skin and discharge a chalky content. Microscopically, amorphous basophilic masses are seen in the corium, often associated with a prominent foreign body reaction[180] (Fig. 18.145).

The pathogenesis is obscure, but the presence in some cases of a layer of squamous epithelium surrounding the calcium deposits suggests that this lesion may be the result of massive calcification of keratinous cysts.[172]

Peritesticular fibrosis involving primarily the tunica albuginea can result in diffuse or nodular thickening that can simulate grossly the appearance of a tumor ("fibrous pseudotumor")[175] (Figs 18.146 and 18.147). It may be associated with fibrinous or hyalinized loose bodies in the cavity. Although it is conceivable that some of these lesions represent examples of the lesion currently known as solitary fibrous tumor,[170] most probably result from a smoldering nonspecific inflammatory process ("nodular periorchitis") (Fig. 18.148). Indeed, some of these lesions have appeared following the performance of a vasectomy.[173] In infants, intense periorchitis, associated with calcification and granulomatous inflammation, can be the result of perforation of the bowel wall in utero, with meconium gaining access to the tunica vaginalis ("meconium periorchitis").[171]

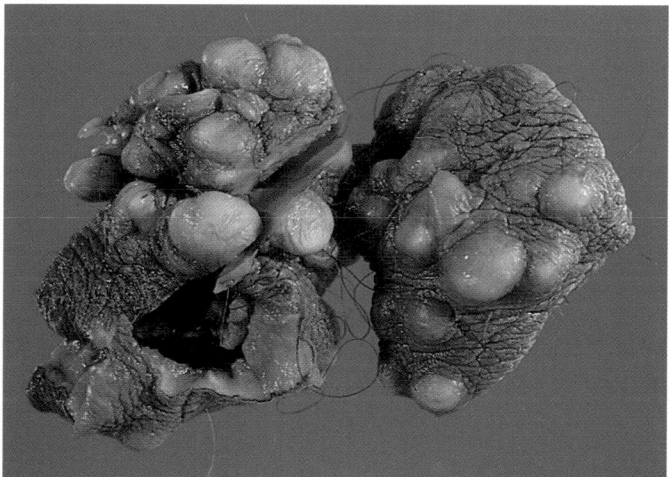

Fig. 18.144 Idiopathic calcinosis of scrotum. (Courtesy of Dr. Juan J. Segura, San Jose, Costa Rica)

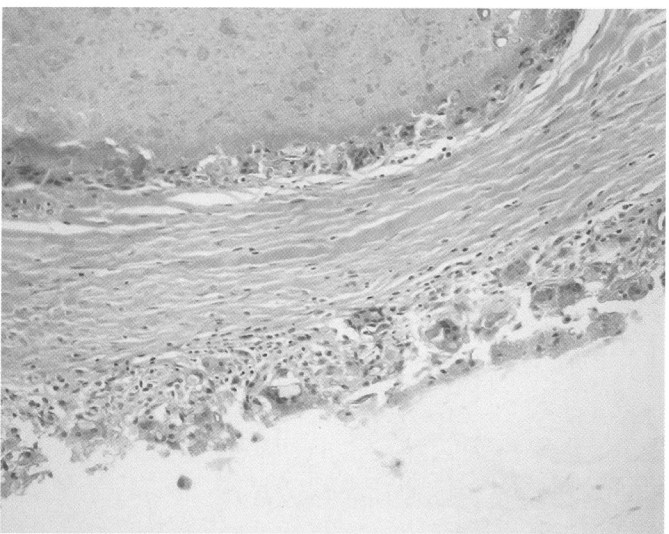

Fig. 18.145 Idiopathic calcinosis of scrotum, with accompanying foreign body-type giant cell reaction.

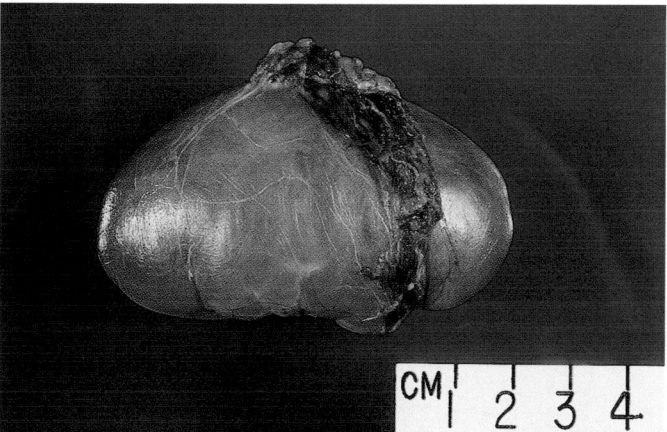

Fig. 18.143 Outer appearance of hydrocele. The wall is translucent and the content had a serous quality.

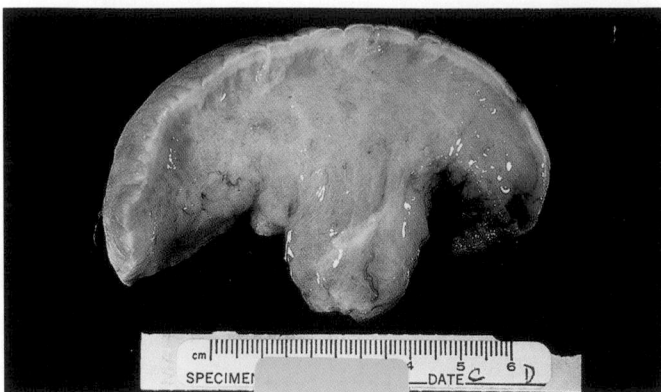

Fig. 18.146 Gross appearance of fibrous pseudotumor of scrotum. The mass has a fibrous quality and ill-defined margins.

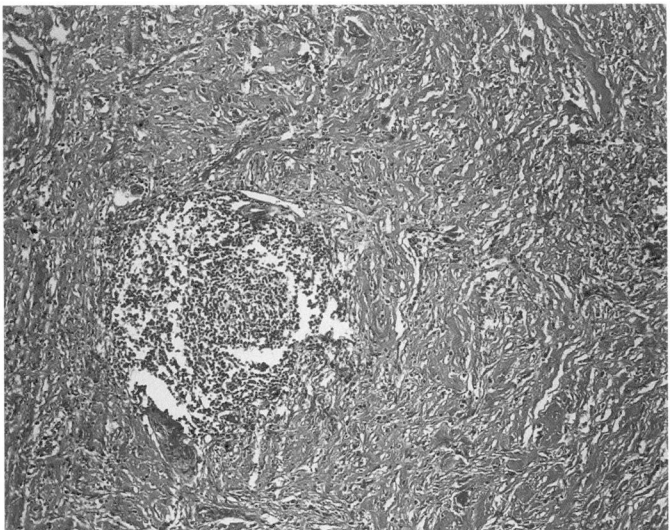

Fig. 18.147 Microscopic appearance of fibrous pseudotumor. Largely sclerotic hypocellular tissue with clusters of inflammatory cells.

Sclerosing lipogranuloma is a rare condition of the penis and scrotum that affects adults and is usually painless. Microscopically, foci of fat necrosis are intermingled with collections of histiocytes, foamy macrophages, and multinucleated giant cells, accompanied by extensive areas of fibrosis and hyalinization[181] (Fig. 18.149). A history of trauma is present in a minority of the cases. Oertel and Johnson[177] made the startling suggestion that the lesion is usually a sequel to injections of exogenous material ("paraffinoma"), after their demonstration of paraffin hydrocarbons by infrared spectrophotometry in nearly all of their cases. The microscopic differential diagnosis includes adenomatoid tumor, lymphangioma, and sclerosing well-differentiated liposarcoma (atypical lipomatous tumor).

Scrotal fat necrosis can result from exposure to cold; it usually presents as bilateral masses below the testis, in the lower portion of the scrotum.[174]

Cysts of the tunica albuginea are lined by a single row of low cuboidal to columnar cells, which may be ciliated. The cavity contains clear fluid. The pathogenesis is unknown.[176,183]

Accessory scrotum is the term generally used for the presence of a congenital perineal nodule adjacent to the scrotum composed of fat and smooth muscle. The condition is regarded by some authors as a hamartoma.[168]

Crohn's disease can involve the scrotum in the form of an erythematous non-tender swelling.[167]

Fournier's gangrene is a necrotizing subcutaneous (fascial) infection of the perineum and external genitalia.[182] It is usually characterized by an abrupt onset in previously healthy young males, but it can have an indolent onset and presents over a broad age range.[169,178]

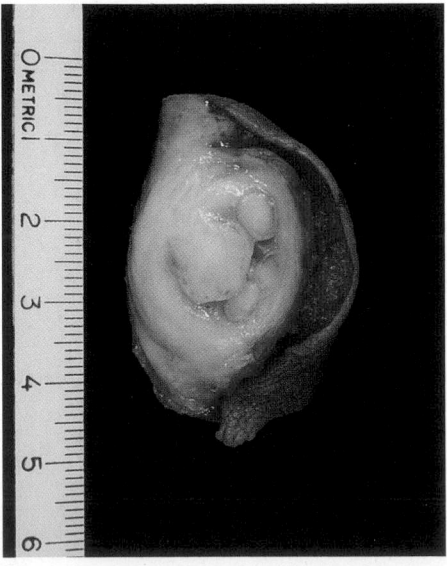

A

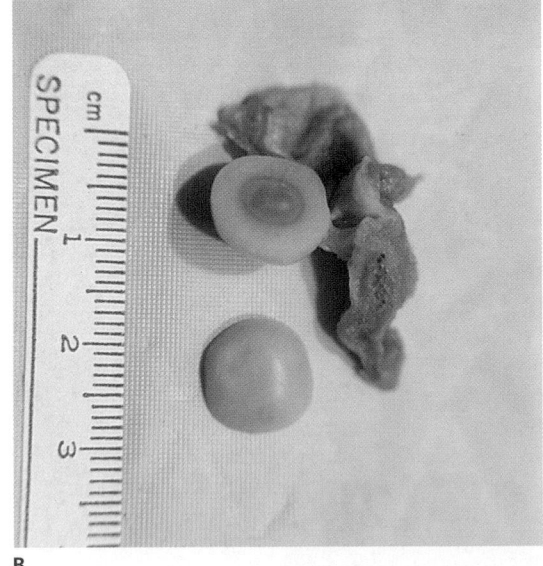

B

Fig. 18.148 A, Nodular periorchitis. A whitish mass of fibrous appearance is centered in the tunica albuginea, and compresses the adjacent testis. **B,** Loose bodies are present in the cavity.

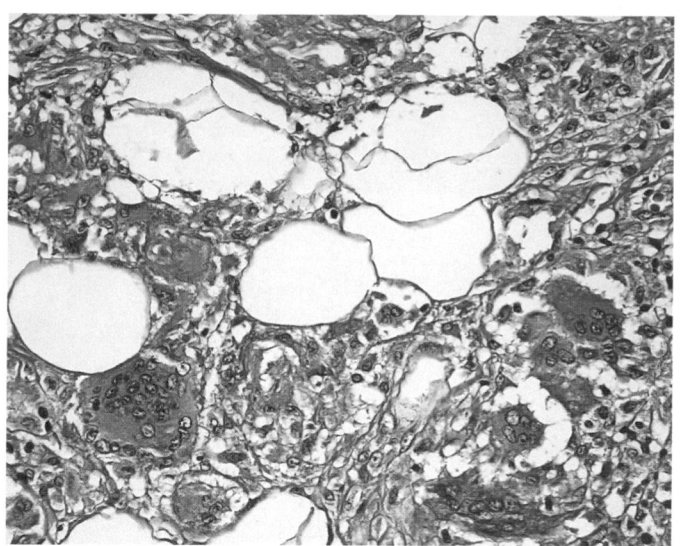

Fig. 18.149 Sclerosing lipogranuloma of scrotum. Prominent histiocytic and multinucleated giant cell reaction around empty spaces, which presumably contained lipid material.

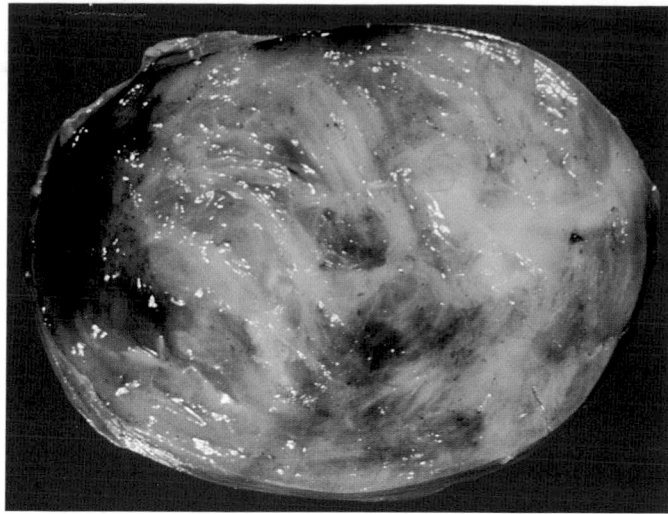

Fig. 18.150 Gross appearance of vascular leiomyoma of scrotum.

Some cases are idiopathic, others are secondary to urethral strictures with extravasation, and still others are seen as a complication of chemotherapy in patients with hematologic malignancies.[179]

Tumors

Both benign and malignant tumors of the scrotum are rare. Most of the benign tumors arise in the skin from cutaneous adnexa and have a morphologic appearance analogous to that of other cutaneous sites.

Leiomyoma is the most common benign mesenchymal tumor of this region (Figs 18.150 and 18.151)[194]; some of them have bizarre (symplasmic) nuclear features.[197]

Aggressive angiomyxoma, similar in all regards to its more common counterpart in the lower female genital tract, has been reported in the scrotum, spermatic cord, and inguinal region.[185,198] A related scrotal tumor, also microscopically similar to its female counterpart, is *angiomyofibroblastoma*; its appearance is sufficiently similar to that of spindle cell lipoma to suggest a common histogenesis.[190]

Squamous cell carcinoma is extremely rare in the general population but is notorious in the oncology literature for being the first malignancy linked to occupational exposure (found in chimney sweeps, paraffin workers, tar workers, and cotton mill workers).[184] Wide local excision with bilateral ilioinguinal lymphadenectomy is the treatment of choice, with more limited surgery advocated in early cases.[192]

Other malignant tumors of the scrotal skin are **basal cell carcinoma**[186] and **Paget's disease**.[195]

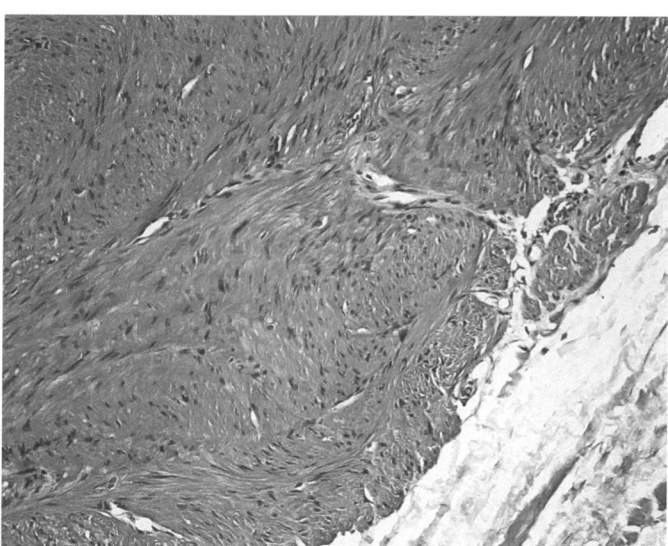

Fig. 18.151 Leiomyoma of tunica dartos.

The most common primary malignant tumor of the tunica vaginalis is **malignant mesothelioma**; this is nearly always of diffuse epithelial type and characterized by a combination of solid, papillary, and tubular foci.[187] Squamous metaplasia may be present in it.[193] It presents clinically as a swelling of the scrotum, often as a hydrocele. It may locally invade the testis, epididymis, tunica dartos and skin, and may metastasize to regional lymph nodes. This tumor is further discussed in the section on the epididymis (see p. 1460).

Sarcomas involving the scrotal wall are rare; most of the reported cases have been of smooth muscle derivation, i.e., *leiomyosarcomas*,[188,194] but other types have been reported, including *well-differentiated liposarcoma* (atypical lipomatous tumor) (Fig. 18.152), and *malignant fibrous histiocytoma*.[189]

Most malignant tumors involving the tunica vaginalis represent direct extension or metastases from other sites,

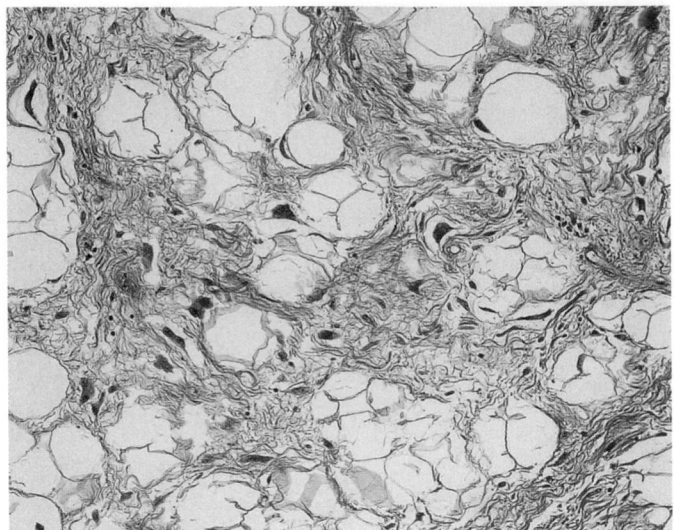

Fig. 18.152 Well-differentiated liposarcoma (atypical lipomatous tumor) involving the scrotum.

particularly the testis and kidney.[196] Carcinoid tumor of small bowel can metastasize to the scrotum and simulate a primary tumor at this site.[191]

References

PENIS
Normal anatomy

1 Barretto J, Caballero C, Cubilla A. Penis. In Sternberg SS (ed.): Histology for pathologists, ed. 2. Philadelphia, 1997, Lippincott-Raven, pp. 1039–1052.

2 Hricak H, Marotti M, Gilbert TJ, Lue T, Wetzel LH, Tanagho E. Normal penile anatomy and abnormal penile conditions. Evaluation with MR imaging. Radiology 1988, **169**: 683–690.

3 Hyman AB, Brownstein MH. "Tyson's glands." Ectopic and papillomatosis penis. Arch Dermatol 1969, **99**: 31–36.

4 Pudney J, Anderson DJ. Immunobiology of the human penile urethra. Am J Pathol 1995, **147**: 155–165.

5 Russell GA, Crowley T, Dalrymple JO. Squamous metaplasia in the penile urethra due to oestrogen therapy. Br J Urol 1992, **69**: 282–285.

Non-neoplastic lesions

6 Baskin LS, Mee S. Tuberculosis of the penis presenting as a subcutaneous nodule. J Urol 1989, **141**: 1430–1431.

7 Cabaleiro P, Drut RM, Drut R. Lymphohistiocytic and granulomatous phlebitis in penile lichen sclerosus. Am J Dermatopathol 2000, 22: 316–320.

8 Cole LA, Helwig EB. Mucoid cysts of the penile skin. J Urol 1976, **115**: 397–400.

9 Das S, Tunuguntla HS. Balanitis xerotica obliterans—a review. World J Urol 2000, **18**: 382–387.

10 Dini M, Baroni G, Colafranceschi M. Median raphe cyst of the penis: a report of two cases with Immunohistochemical Investigation. Am J Dermatopathol 2001, **23**: 320–324.

11 Fang AW, Whittaker MA, Theaker JM. Mucinous metaplasia of the penis. Histopathology 2002, **40**: 177–179.

12 Gholami SS, Lue TF. Peyronie's disease. Urol Clin North Am 2001, **28**: 377–390.

13 Haddad FS. Subcutaneous abscess and gangrene of the penis: report of four cases. J Urol Pathol 1996, **5**: 223–228.

14 Hinman F Jr. American pediatric urology. San Francisco, 1991, Norman.

15 Knowitt LN, Schechterman L. Inflammation of the periurethral glands of Littré simulating tumor. J Urol 1977, **118**: 685.

16 Kossard S, Collins AG, Wegman A, Hughes MR. Necrobiotic granulomas localised to the penis. A possible variant of subcutaneous granuloma annulare. J Cutan Pathol 1990, **17**: 101–104.

17 Leal SM, Novsam N, Zacks SI. Amyloidosis presenting as a penile mass. J Urol 1988, **140**: 830–831.

18 McRoberts JW. Peyronie's disease. Surg Gynecol Obstet 1969, **129**: 1291–1294.

19 Magro CM, Crowson AN, Alfa M, Nath A, Ronald A, Ndinya-Achola JO, Nasio J. A morphological study of penile chancroid lesions in human immunodeficiency virus (HIV)-positive and negative African men with a hypothesis concerning the role of chancroid in HIV transmission. Hum Pathol 1996, **27**: 1066–1070.

20 Nielsen GP, Pilch BZ, Black-Schaffer WS, Young RH. Wegener's granulomatosis of the penis clinically simulating carcinoma: Report of a case. J Urol Pathol 1996, **4**: 265–272.

21 Perimenis P, Athanasopoulos A, Gyftopoulos K, Katsenis G, Barbalias G. Peyronie's disease: epidemiology and clinical presentation of 134 cases. Int Urol Nephrol 2001, **32**: 691–694.

22 Shiraki JW. Parameatal cysts of the glans penis. A report of 9 cases. J Urol 1975, **114**: 544–548.

23 Smith BH. Peyronie's disease. Am J Clin Pathol 1966, **45**: 670–678.

24 Smith BH. Subclinical Peyronie's disease. Am J Clin Pathol 1969, **52**: 385–390.

25 Souteyrand P, Wong E, Macdonald DM. Zoon's balanitis (balanitis circumscripta plasmacellularis). Br J Dermatol 1981, **105**: 195–199.

26 Val-Bernal JF, Hernandez-Nieto E. Benign mucinous metaplasia of the penis. A lesion resembling extramammary Paget's disease. J Cutan Pathol 2000, **27**: 76–79.

26a Weyers W, Ende Y, Schalla W, Diaz-Cascajo C. Balanitis of Zoon:a clinicopathologic study of 45 cases. Am J Dermathopathol 2002, **24**: 459–467.

Condyloma acuminatum and related lesions

27 Del Mistro A, Braunstein JD, Halwer M, Koss LG. Identification of human papillomavirus types in male urethral condylomata acuminata by in situ hybridization. Hum Pathol 1987, **18**: 936–940.

28 Ferenczy A, Richart RM, Wright TC. Pearly penile papules. Absence of human papillomavirus DNA by the polymerase chain reaction. Obstet Gynecol 1991, **78**: 118–122.

29 Lowhagen GB, Bolmstedt A, Ryd W, Voog E. The prevalence of "high-risk" HPV types in penile condyloma-like lesions. Correlation between HPV type and morphology. Genitourin Med 1993, **69**: 87–90.

30 McMillan A, Bishop PE, Fletcher S. An immunohistological study of condylomata acuminata. Histopathology 1990, **17**: 45–52.

31 Mullink H, Jiwa NM, Walboomers JM, Horstman A, Vos W, Meijer CJ. Demonstration of changes in cytokeratin expression in condylomata acuminata in relation to the presence of human papilloma virus as shown by a combination of immunohistochemistry and in situ hybridization. Am J Dermatopathol 1991, **13**: 530–537.

32 Murphy WM, Fu YS, Lancaster WD, Jenson AB. Papillomavirus structural antigens in condyloma acuminatum of the male urethra. J Urol 1983, **130**: 84–85.

33 Nuovo GJ, Becker J, Margiotta M, MacConnell P, Comite S, Hochman H. Histological distribution of polymerase chain reaction-amplified human papillomavirus 6 and 11 DNA in penile lesions. Am J Surg Pathol 1992, **16**: 269–275.

34 Nuovo GJ, Hochman HA, Eliezri YD, Lastarria D, Comite SL, Silvers DN. Detection of human papillomavirus DNA in penile lesions histologically negative for condylomata. Analysis by in situ hybridization and the polymerase chain reaction. Am J Surg Pathol 1990, **14**: 829–836.

Tumors

Bowen's disease and related lesions

35 Andersson L, Jonsson G, Brehmer-Andersson E. Erythroplasia of Queyrat—carcinoma in situ. Scand J Urol Nephrol 1967, **1**: 303–306.

36 Aynaud O, Ionesco M, Barrasso R. Penile intraepithelial neoplasia. Specific clinical features correlate with histologic and virologic findings. Cancer 1994, **74**: 1762–1767.

37 Barrasso R, De Brux J, Croissant O, Orth G. High prevalence of papillomavirus-associated penile intraepithelial neoplasia in sexual partners of women with cervical intraepithelial neoplasia. N Engl J Med 1987, **317**: 916–923.

38 Berger BW, Hori Y. Multicentric Bowen's disease of the genitalia. Spontaneous regression of lesions. Arch Dermatol 1978, **114**: 1698–1699.

39 Cubilla AL, Meijer CJ, Young RH. Morphological features of epithelial abnormalities and precancerous lesions of the penis. Scand J Urol Nephrol Suppl 2000, **205**: 215–219.

40 Della Torre G, Donghi R, Longoni A, Pilotti S, Pasquini G, De Palo G, Pierotti MA, Rilke F, Della Porta G. HPV DNA in intraepithelial neoplasia and carcinoma of the vulva and penis. Diagn Mol Pathol 1992, **1**: 25–30.

41 Demeter LM, Stoler MH, Bonnez W, Corey L, Pappas P, Strussenberg J, Reichman RC. Penile intraepithelial neoplasia. Clinical presentation and an analysis of the physical state of human papillomavirus DNA. J Infect Dis 1993, **168**: 38–46.

42 Graham JH, Helwig EB. Erythroplasia of Queyrat. A clinicopathologic and histochemical study. Cancer 1973, **32**: 1396–1414.

43 Higgins GD, Uzelin DM, Phillips GE, Villa LL, Burrell CJ. Differing prevalence of human papillomavirus RNA in penile dysplasias and carcinomas may reflect differing etiologies. Am J Clin Pathol 1992, **97**: 272–278.

44 Ikenberg H, Gissmann L, Gross G, Grussendorf-Conen E-I, Zur Hausen H. Human papillomavirus type-16-related DNA in genital Bowen's disease and in bowenoid papulosis. Int J Cancer 1983, **32**: 563–565.

45 Kaye V, Zhang G, Dehner LP, Fraley EE. Carcinoma in situ of penis. Is distinction between erythroplasia of Queyrat and Bowen's disease relevant? Urology 1990, **36**: 479–482.

46 Malek RS, Goellner JR, Smith TF, Espy MJ, Cupp MR. Human papillomavirus infection and intraepithelial, in situ, and invasive carcinoma of penis. Urology 1993, **42**: 159–170.

47 Patterson JW, Kao GF, Graham JH, Helwig EB. Bowenoid papulosis. A clinicopathologic study with ultrastructural observations. Cancer 1986, **57**: 823–836.

48 Schroeder TL, Sengelmann RD. Squamous cell carcinoma in situ of the penis successfully treated with imiquimod 5% cream. J Am Acad Dermatol 2002, **46**: 545–548.

49 Steffen C. Concurrence of condylomata acuminata and bowenoid papulosis. Confirmation of the hypothesis that they are related conditions. Am J Dermatopathol 1982, **4**: 5–8.

50 von Krogh G, Horenblas S. Diagnosis and clinical presentation of premalignant lesions of the penis. Scand J Urol Nephrol Suppl 2000, **205**: 201–214.

51 Wade TR, Kopf AW, Ackerman AB. Bowenoid papulosis of the penis. Cancer 1978, **42**: 1890–1903.

52 Yoneta A, Yamashita T, Jin HY, Iwasawa A, Kondo S, Jimbow K. Development of squamous cell carcinoma by two high-risk human papillomaviruses (HPVs), a novel HPV-67 and HPV-31 from bowenoid papulosis. Br J Dermatol 2000, **143**: 604–608.

Squamous cell carcinoma

General features

53 Bain L, Geronemus R. The association of lichen planus of the penis with squamous cell carcinoma in situ and with verrucous squamous carcinoma. J Dermatol Surg Oncol 1989, **15**: 413–417.

54 Brinton LA, Li JY, Rong SD, Huang S, Xiao BS, Shi BG, Zhu ZJ, Schiffman MH, Dawsey S. Risk factors for penile cancer. Results from a case-control study in China. Int J Cancer 1991, **47**: 504–509.

55 Dillner J, von Krogh G, Horenblas S, Meijer CJ. Etiology of squamous cell carcinoma of the penis. Scand J Urol Nephrol Suppl 2000, **205**: 189–193.

56 Lucia MS, Miller GJ. Histopathology of malignant lesions of the penis. Urol Clin North Am 1992, **19**: 227–246.

57 McCance DJ, Kalache A, Ashdown K, Andrade L, Menezes F, Smith P, Doll R. Human papillomavirus types 16 and 18 in carcinomas of the penis from Brazil. Int J Cancer 1986, **37**: 55–59.

58 Merrin CE. Cancer of the penis. Cancer 1980, **45**: 1973–1979.

59 Poblet E, Alfaro L, Fernander-Sergoviano P, Jimenez-Reyes J, Salido EC. Human papillomavirus-associated penile squamous cell carcinoma in HIV-positive patients. Am J Surg Pathol 1999, **23**: 1119–1123.

60 Pride HB, Miller OF, Tyler WB. Penile squamous cell carcinoma arising from balanitis xerotica obliterans. J Am Acad Dermatol 1993, **29**: 469–473.

61 Riveros M, Lebron RF. Geographical pathology of cancer of the penis. Cancer 1963, **16**: 798–811.

62 Rubin MA, Kleter B, Zhou M, Ayala G, Cubilla AL, Quint WGV, Pirog EC. Detection and typing of human papillomavirus DNA in penile carcinoma. Evidence for multiple independent pathways of penile carcinogenesis. Am J Pathol 2001, **159**: 1211–1218.

63 Stern RS. Genital tumors among men with psoriasis exposed to psoralens and ultraviolet A radiation (PUVA) and ultraviolet B radiation. The Photochemotherapy Follow-up Study. N Engl J Med 1990, **322**: 1093–1097.

64 Varma VA, Sanchez-Lanier M, Unger ER, Clark C, Tickman R, Hewan-Lowe K, Chenggis ML, Swan DC. Association of human papillomavirus with penile carcinoma. A study using polymerase chain reaction and in situ hybridization. Hum Pathol 1991, **22**: 908–913.

64a Velazquez E, Bock A, Soskin A, Codas R, Arbo M, Cubilla AL. Preputial variability and preferential association of long phimotic foreskins with penile cancer: an anatomic comparative study of types of foreskin in a general population and cancer patients. Am J Surg Pathol 2003, **27**: 994–998.

65 Weaver MG, Abdul-Karim FW, Dale G, Sorensen K, Huang YT. Detection and localization of human papillomavirus in penile condylomas and squamous cell carcinomas using in situ hybridization with biotinylated DNA viral probes. Mod Pathol 1989, **2**: 94–100.

Morphologic features and types

66 Cubilla AL, Ayala MT, Barreto JE, Bellasai JG, Noel JC. Surface adenosquamous carcinoma of the penis: a report of three cases. Am J Surg Pathol 1996, **20**: 156–160.

67 Cubilla AL, Barreto J, Caballero C, Ayala G, Riveros M. Pathologic features of epidermoid carcinoma of the penis. A prospective study of 66 cases. Am J Surg Pathol 1993, **17**: 753–763.

68 Cubilla AL, Reuter VE, Gregoire L, Ayala G, Ocampos S, Lancaster WD, Fair W. Basaloid squamous cell carcinoma: a distinctive human papilloma virus-related penile neoplasm: a report of 20 cases. Am J Surg Pathol 1998, **22**: 755–761.

69 Cubilla AL, Velasquez EF, Reuter VE, Oliva E, Mihm MC, Young RH. Warty (condylomatous) squamous cell carcinoma of the penis: A report of 11 cases and proposed classification of "verruciform" penile tumors. Am J Surg Pathol 2000, **24**: 505–512.

70 Johnson DE, Lo RK, Srigley J, Ayala AG. Verrucous carcinoma of the penis. J Urol 1985, **133**: 216–218.

71 Layfield LJ, Liu K. Mucoepidermoid carcinoma arising in the glans penis. Arch Pathol Lab Med 2000, **124**: 148–151.

72 Manglani KS, Manaligod JR, Ray B. Spindle cell carcinoma of the glans penis. A light and electron microscopic study. Cancer 1980, **46**: 2266–2272.

73 Masih AS, Stoler MH, Farrow GM, Wooldridge TN, Johansson SL. Penile verrucous carcinoma: A clinicopathologic, human papillomavirus typing and flow cytometric analysis. Mod Pathol 1992, **5**: 48–55.

73a Urdiales-Viedma M, Fernandez-Rodriguez A, De Ham-Muñoz T, Pichardo-Pichardo S. Squamous cell carcinoma of the penis with rhabdoid features. Ann of Diagn Pathol 2002, **6**: 381–384.

74 Watanabe K, Mukawa A, Miyazaki K, Tsukahara K. Adenoid squamous cell carcinoma of the penis. Report of a surgical case clinically manifested with rapid lung metastasis. Acta Pathol Jpn 1983, **33**: 1243–1250.

Molecular genetic features

75 Bezerra AL, Lopes A, Landman G, Alencar GN, Torloni H, Villa LL. Clinicopathologic features and human papillomavirus Dna prevalence of warty and squamous cell carcinoma of the penis. Am J Surg Pathol 2001, **25**: 673–678.

76 Cubilla AL, Ayala MT, Barreto JE, Bellasai JG, Noel JC. Surface adenosquamous carcinoma of the penis: a report of three cases. Am J Surg Pathol 1996, **20**: 156–160.

77 Lam KY, Chan KW. Molecular pathology and clinicopathologic features of penile tumors: with special reference to analyses of p21 and p53 expression and unusual histologic features. Arch Pathol Lab Med 1999, **123**: 895–904.

78 Masih AS, Stoler MH, Farrow GM, Wooldridge TN, Johansson SL. Penile verrucous carcinoma: A clinicopathologic, human papillomavirus typing and flow cytometric analysis. Mod Pathol 1992, **5**: 48–55.

79 Rubin MA, Kleter B, Zhou M, Ayala G, Cubilla AL, Quint WGV, Pirog EC. Detection and typing of human papillomavirus DNA in penile carcinoma. Evidence for multiple independent pathways of penile carcinogenesis. Am J Pathol 2001, **159**: 1211–1218.

Spread and metastases

80 Cabanas RM. An approach for the treatment of penile carcinoma. Cancer 1977, **39**: 456–466.

81 Cubilla AL, Barreto J, Caballero C, Ayala G, Riveros M. Pathologic features of epidermoid carcinoma of the penis. A prospective study of 66 cases. Am J Surg Pathol 1993, **17**: 753–763.

82 Cubilla AL, Reuter V, Valazquez E, Piris A, Saito S, Young RH. Histologic classification of penile carcinoma and its relation to outcome in 61 patients with primary resection. Int J Surg Pathol 2001, **9**: 111–120.

83 Horenblas S, Van Tinteren H, Delemarre JF, Moonen LM, Lustig V, Kroger R. Squamous cell carcinoma of the penis. Accuracy of tumor, nodes and metastasis classification system, and role of lymphangiography, computerized tomography scan and fine needle aspiration cytology. J Urol 1991, **146**: 1279–1283.

84 Johnson DE, Lo RK, Srigley J, Ayala AG. Verrucous carcinoma of the penis. J Urol 1985, **133**: 216–218.

85 Kato N, Onozuka T, Yasukawa K, Kimura K, Sasaki K. Penile hybrid verrucous-squamous carcinoma associated with superficial inguinal lymph node metastasis. Am J Dermatopathol 2000, **22**: 339–343.

Treatment and prognosis

86 Baker BH, Spratt JS Jr, Perez-Mesa C, Leduc RJ, Watson FR. Carcinoma of the penis. J Urol 1976, **116**: 458–461.

87 Burgers JK, Badalament RA, Drago JR. Penile cancer. Clinical presentation, diagnosis, and staging. Urol Clin North Am 1992, **19**: 247–256.

88 Cubilla AL, Piris A, Pfannl R, Rodriguez I, Aguero F, Young RH. Anatomic levels: important landmarks in penectomy specimens: a detailed anatomic and histologic study based on examination of 44 cases. Am J Surg Pathol 2001, **25**: 1091–1094.

88a Cubilla AL, Reuter V, Velazquez E, Piris A, Saito S, Young RH. Histologic classification of penile carcinoma and its relation to outcome in 61 patients with primary resection. Int J Surg Pathol 2001, **9**: 111–120.

89 Emerson RE, Ulbright TM, Eble JN, Geary WA, Eckert GJ, Cheng L. Predicting cancer progression in patients with penile squamous cell carcinoma: the importance of depth of invasion and vascular invasion. Mod Pathol 2001, **14**: 963–968.

90 Fraley EE, Zhang G, Manivel C, Niehans GA. The role of ilioinguinal lymphadenectomy and significance of histological differentiation in treatment of carcinoma of the penis. J Urol 1989, **142**: 1478–1482.

91 Fraley EE, Zhang G, Sazama R, Lange PH. Cancer of the penis. Prognosis and treatment plans. Cancer 1985, **55**: 1618–1624.

92 Fukunaga M, Yokoi K, Miyazawa Y, Harada T, Ushigome S. Penile verrucous carcinoma with anaplastic transformation following radiotherapy. A case report with human papillomavirus typing and flow cytometric DNA studies. Am J Surg Pathol 1994, **18**: 501–505.

93 Hanash KA, Furlow WL, Utz DC, Harrison EG Jr. Carcinoma of the penis. A clinicopathologic study. J Urol 1970, **104**: 291–297.

94 Hayashi T, Tsuda N, Shimada O, Kishikawa M, Iseki M, Nishimura N, Taniguchi K, Saito Y. A clinicopathologic study of tumors and tumor-like lesions of the penis. Acta Pathol Jpn 1990, **40**: 343–351.

95 Hoffman MA, Renshaw AA, Loughlin KR. Squamous cell carcinoma of the penis and microscopic pathologic margins: how much margin is needed for local cure? Cancer 1999, **85**: 1565–1568.

96 Johnson DE, Lo RK. Management of regional lymph nodes in penile carcinoma. Five-year results following therapeutic groin dissections. Urology 1984, **24**: 308–311.

97 Johnson DE, Lo RK, Srigley J, Ayala AG. Verrucous carcinoma of the penis. J Urol 1985, **133**: 216–218.

98 Kaushal V, Sharma SC. Carcinoma of the penis. A 12-year review. Acta Oncol 1987, **26**: 413–417.

99 Lopes A, Bezerra AL, Pinto CA, Serrano SV, de Mello CA, Villa LL. P53 as a new prognostic factor for lymph node metastasis in penile carcinoma: analysis of 82 patients treated with amputation of bilateral lymphadenectomy. J Urol 2002, **168**: 81–86.

100 Maiche AG, Pyrhonen S. Clinical staging of cancer of the penis. By size? By localization? Or by depth of infiltration? Eur Urol 1990, **18**: 16–22.

101 Maiche AG, Pyrhonen S, Karkinen M. Histological grading of squamous cell carcinoma of the penis. A new scoring system. Br J Urol 1991, **67**: 522–526.

102 Narayana AS, Olney LE, Loening SA, Weimar GW, Culp DA. Carcinoma of the penis. Analysis of 219 cases. Cancer 1982, **49**: 2185–2191.

103 Ornellas AA, Seixas AL, de Moraes JR. Analyses of 200 lymphadenectomies in patients with penile carcinoma. J Urol 1991, **146**: 330–332.

104 Ravi R. Prophylactic lymphadenectomy vs observation vs inguinal biopsy in node-negative patients with invasive carcinoma of the penis. Jpn J Clin Oncol 1993, **23**: 53–58.

105 Young MJ, Reda DJ, Waters WB. Penile carcinoma. A twenty-five-year experience. Urology 1991, **38**: 529–532.

Other carcinoma types

106 Goldminz D, Scott G, Klaus S. Penile basal cell carcinoma. Report

of a case and review of the literature. J Am Acad Dermatol 1989, **20:** 1094–1097.

107 Kvist E, Osmundsen PE, Sjolin KE. Primary Paget's disease of the penis. Case report. Scand J Urol Nephrol 1992, **26:** 187–190.

108 Park S, Grossfeld GD, McAninch JW, Santucci R. Extramammary Paget's disease of the penis and scrotum: excision, reconstruction and evaluation of occult malignancy. J Urol 2001, **166:** 2112–2116.

Tumors of penile urethra

109 Begun FP, Grossman HB, Diokno AC, Sogani PC. Malignant melanoma of the penis and male urethra. J Urol 1984, **132:** 123–125.

110 Bolduan JP, Farah RN. Primary urethral neoplasms. Review of 30 cases. J Urol 1981, **125:** 198–200.

111 Bostwick DG, Lo R, Stamey TA. Papillary adenocarcinoma of the male urethra. Case report and review of the literature. Cancer 1984, **54:** 2556–2563.

112 Grussendorf-Conen E-I, Dentz FJ, de Villier EM. Detection of human papillomavirus-6 in primary carcinoma of the urethra in men. Cancer 1987, **60:** 1832–1835.

113 Heaton ND, Kadow C, Yates-Bell AJ. Inverted papilloma of the penile urethra. Br J Urol 1990, **66:** 661–662.

114 Kahn DG, Rothman PJ, Weisman JD. Urethral T-cell lymphoma as the initial manifestation of the acquired immune deficiency syndrome. Arch Pathol Lab Med 1991, **115:** 1169–1170.

115 Levine RL. Urethral cancer. Cancer 1980, **45:** 1965–1972.

116 Loo KT, Chan JK. Colloid adenocarcinoma of the urethra associated with mucosal in situ carcinoma. Arch Pathol Lab Med 1992, **116:** 976–977.

117 Mira JL, Fan G. Leiomyoma of the male urethra: a case report and review of the literature. Arch Pathol Lab Med 2000, **124:** 302–303.

118 Oliva E, Quinn TR, Amin MB, Eble JN, Epstein JI, Srigley JR, Young RH. Primary malignant melanoma of the urethra: A clinicopathologic analysis of 15 cases. Am J Surg Pathol 2000, **24:** 785–796.

119 Vernon HK, Wilkins RD. Primary carcinoma of the male urethra. Br J Urol 1950, **21:** 232–236.

Other tumors and tumorlike conditions

120 Angulo JC, Lopez JI, Unda-Urzaiz M, Larrinaga JR, Zubiaur CL, Flores NC. Kaposi's sarcoma of the penis as an initial urological manifestation of AIDS. A report of two cases. Urol Int 1991, **46:** 235–237.

121 Bacetic D, Knezevic M, Stojsic Z, Atanackovic M, Vujanic GM. Primary extraskeletal osteosarcoma of the penis with a malignant fibrous histiocytoma-like component. Histopathology 1998, **33:** 185–186.

122 Barnhill RL, Albert LS, Shama SK, Goldenhersh MA, Rhodes AR, Sober AJ. Genital lentiginosis. A clinical and histopathologic study. J Am Acad Dermatol 1990, **22:** 453–460.

123 Bartoletti R, Gacci M, Nesi G, Franchi A, Rizzo M. Leiomyoma of the corona glans penis. Urology 2002, **59:** 445.

124 Belville WD, Cohen JA. Secondary penile malignancies. The spectrum of presentation. J Surg Oncol 1992, **51:** 134–137.

125 Bostwick DG, Guthman DA, Letendre L, Banks PM, Texter JH Jr, Lieber MM. Polymorphic reticulosis (idiopathic midline destructive disease) of the penis, scrotum, and perineum. J Urol Pathol 1996, **5:** 57–64.

126 Carver BS, Venable DD, Eastham JA. Large granular cell tumor of the penis in a 53-year-old man with coexisting prostate cancer. Urology 2002, **59:** 602.

127 Daniels GF Jr, Schaeffer AJ. Renal cell carcinoma involving penis and testis. Unusual initial presentations of metastatic disease. Urology 1991, **37:** 369–373.

128 Dehner LP, Smith BH. Soft tissue tumors of the penis. A clinicopathologic study of 46 cases. Cancer 1970, **25:** 1431–1447.

129 Dwosh J, Mininberg DT, Schlossberg S, Peterson P. Neurofibroma involving the penis in a child. J Urol 1984, **132:** 988–989.

130 Fethiere W, Carter HW, Sturim HS. Elephantiasis neuromatosa of the penis. Arch Pathol 1974, **97:** 326–330.

131 Fetsch JF, Brinsko RW, Davis CJ Jr, Mostofi FK, Sesterhenn IA. A distinctive myointimal proliferation ("myointimoma") involving the corpus spongiosum of the glans penis: a clinicopathologic and immunohistochemical analysis of 10 cases. Am J Surg Pathol 2000, **24:** 1524–1530.

131a Fetsch JF, Sesterhenn IA, Davis CJ, Mostofi FK. Soft tissue tumors of the penis: A retrospective review of 114 cases (Abstract). Mod Pathol 2003, **16:** 149A.

132 Fletcher CDM, Lowe D. Inflammatory fibrous histiocytoma of the penis. Histopathology 1984, **8:** 1079–1084.

133 Fujimoto N, Hiraki A, Ueoka H, Harada M. Metastasis to the penis in a patient with squamous cell carcinoma of the lung with a review of reported cases. Lung Cancer 2001, **34:** 149–152.

134 Ghandur-Mnaymneh L, Gonzalez MS. Angiosarcoma of the penis with hepatic angiomas in a patient with low vinyl chloride exposure. Cancer 1981, **47:** 1318–1324.

135 Gonzalez-Campora R, Nogales FF, Lerma E, Navarro A, Matilla A. Lymphoma of the penis. J Urol 1981, **126:** 270–271.

136 Hayashi T, Tsuda N, Shimada O, Kishikawa M, Iseki M, Nishimura N, Taniguchi K, Saito Y. A clinicopathologic study of tumors and tumor-like lesions of the penis. Acta Pathol Jpn 1990, **40:** 343–351.

137 Isa SS, Almaraz R, Magovern J. Leiomyosarcoma of the penis. Case report and review of the literature. Cancer 1984, **54:** 939–942.

138 Kotake Y, Gohji K, Suzuki T, Watsuji T, Kusaka M, Takahara K, Ubai T, Noumi H, Inamoto T, Shibahara N, Ueda H, Katsuoka Y. Metastases to the penis from carcinoma of the prostate. Int J Urol 2001, **8:** 83–86.

139 Kraemer BB, Schmidt WA, Foucar E, Rosen T. Verruciform xanthoma of the penis. Arch Dermatol 1981, **117:** 516–518.

140 Kubota Y, Nakada T, Yaguchi H, Abe Y, Sasagawa I. Schwannoma of the penis. Urol Int 1993, **51:** 111–113.

141 Leicht S, Younberg G, Díaz-Miranda C. Atypical penile maculas. Arch Dermatol 1988, **124:** 1267–1270.

142 Lo JS, Dijkstra JW, Bergfeld WF. Syringomas on the penis (letter). Int J Dermatol 1990, **29:** 309–310.

143 Lowe FC, Lattimer DG, Metroka CE. Kaposi's sarcoma of the penis in patients with acquired immunodeficiency syndrome. J Urol 1989, **142:** 1475–1477.

144 Meehan SA, Smoller BR. Cutaneous Langerhans cell histiocytosis of the genitalia in the elderly: a report of three cases. J Cutan Pathol 1998, **25:** 370–374.

145 Metcalf JS, Lee RE, Maize JC. Epidermotropic urothelial carcinoma involving the glans penis. Arch Dermatol 1985, **121:** 532–534.

146 Mitsudo S, Nakanishi I, Koss LG. Paget's disease of the penis and adjacent skin. Its association with fatal sweat gland carcinoma. Arch Pathol Lab Med 1981, **105:** 518–520.

147 Moore SW, Wheeler JLE, Hefter LG. Epithelioid sarcoma masquerading as Peyronie's disease. Cancer 1975, **35:** 1706–1710.

148 Moran CA, Kaneko M. Malignant fibrous histiocytoma of the glans penis. Am J Dermatopathol 1990, **12:** 182–187.

149 Nomura M, Hata S. Sebaceous trichofolliculoma on scrotum and penis. Dermatologica 1990, **181:** 68–70.

150 Oldbring J, Mikulowski P. Malignant melanoma of the penis and male urethra. Report of nine cases and review of the literature. Cancer 1987, **59:** 581–587.

151 Perez-Mesa C, Oxenhandler R. Metastatic tumors of the penis. J Surg Oncol 1989, **42:** 11–15.

152 Rasbridge SA, Parry JR. Angiosarcoma of the penis. Br J Urol 1989, **63:** 440–441.

153 Robey EL, Schellhammer PF. Four cases of metastases to the penis and a review of the literature. J Urol 1984, **132:** 992–994.

154 Sacker AR, Oyama KK, Kessler S. Primary osteosarcoma of the penis. Am J Dermatopathol 1994, **16**: 285–287.

155 Saw D, Tse CH, Chan J, Watt CY, Ng CS, Poon YF. Clear cell sarcoma of the penis. Hum Pathol 1986, **17**: 423–425.

156 Seftel AD, Sadick NS, Waldbaum RS. Kaposi's sarcoma of the penis in a patient with the acquired immune deficiency syndrome. J Urol 1986, **136**: 673–675.

157 Srigley JR, Ayala AG, Ordonez NG, van Nostrand AWP. Epithelioid hemangioma of the penis. Arch Pathol Lab Med 1985, **109**: 51–54.

158 Tanaka Y, Sasaki Y, Kobayashi T, Terashima K. Granular cell tumor of the corpus cavernosum of the penis. J Urol 1991, **146**: 1596–1597.

159 Tanenbaum MH, Becker SW. Papillae of the corona of the glans penis. J Urol 1965, **93**: 391–395.

160 Val-Bernal JF, Garijo MF. Solitary cutaneous myofibroma of the glans penis. Am J Dermatopathol 1996, **18**: 317–321.

161 Val-Bernal JF, Hernando M. Blue nevus of the penis. J Urol Pathol 1997, **6**: 61–66.

162 Winer JH, Winer LH. Hirsutoid papillomas of the coronal margin of the glans penis. J Urol 1955, **74**: 375–378.

163 Yantiss RK, Althausen AF, Young RH. Malignant fibrous histiocytoma of the penis: report of a case and review of the literature. J Urol Pathol 1998, **9**: 171–180.

164 Yu GS, Nseyo UO, Carson JW. Primary penile lymphoma in a patient with Peyronie's disease. J Urol 1989, **142**: 1076–1077.

165 Zurrida S, Bartoli C, Clemente C, De Palo G. Malignant melanoma of the penis. A report of four cases. Tumori 1990, **76**: 599–602.

SCROTUM

Normal anatomy

166 Trainer TD. Histology of the normal testis. Am J Surg Pathol 1978, **11**: 797–809.

Non-neoplastic lesions

167 Acker AM, Sahn EE, Rogers HC, Maize JC, Moscatello SA, Frick KA. Genital cutaneous Crohn disease: two cases with unusual clinical and histopathologic features in young men. Am J Dermatopathol 2000, **22**: 443–446.

168 Amann G, Berger A, Rokitansky A. Accessory scrotum or perineal collision-hamartoma. A case report to illustrate a misnomer. Pathol Res Pract 1996, **192**: 1039–1043.

169 Bahlmann CM, Fourie IJvH, Arndt TCH. Fournier's gangrene. Necrotising fasciitis of the male genitalia. Br J Urol 1983, **55**: 85–88.

170 Benisch B, Peison B, Sobel HJ, Marquet E. Fibrous mesotheliomas (pseudofibroma) of the scrotal sac. A light and ultrastructural study. Cancer 1981, **47**: 731–735.

171 Dehner LP, Scott D, Stocker JT. Meconium periorchitis. A clinicopathologic study of four cases with a review of the literature. Hum Pathol 1986, **17**: 807–812.

172 Gormally S, Dorman T, Powell FC. Calcinosis of the scrotum. Int J Dermatol 1992, **31**: 75–79.

173 Hamilton FA, Persad RA, Webb RJ, Ball RU. Fibrous pseudotumor of the tunica vaginalis following vasectomy. J Urol Pathol 1997, **6**: 243–248.

174 Hollander JB, Begun FP, Lee RD. Scrotal fat necrosis. J Urol 1985, **134**: 150–151.

175 Honoré LH. Nonspecific peritesticular fibrosis manifested as testicular enlargement. Arch Surg 1978, **113**: 814–816.

176 Nistal M, Iniguez L, Paniagua R. Cysts of the testicular

parenchyma and tunica albuginea. Arch Pathol Lab Med 1989, **113**: 902–906.

177 Oertel YC, Johnson FB. Sclerosing lipogranuloma of male genitalia. Review of 23 cases. Arch Pathol 1977, **101**: 321–326.

178 Paty R, Smith AD. Gangrene and Fournier's gangrene. Urol Clin North Am 1992, **19**: 149–162.

179 Radaelli F, Della Volpe A, Colombi M, Bregani P, Polli EE. Acute gangrene of the scrotum and penis in four hematologic patients. The usefulness of hyperbaric therapy in one case. Cancer 1987, **60**: 1462–1464.

180 Shapiro L, Platt N, Torres-Rodriguez VM. Idiopathic calcinosis of the scrotum. Arch Dermatol 1970, **102**: 199–204.

181 Smetana HF, Bernhard W. Sclerosing lipogranuloma. Arch Pathol 1950, **50**: 296–325.

182 Spirnack PJ. Fournier's gangrene. Report of 20 patients. J Urol 1984, **131**: 289–291.

183 Warner KE, Noyes DT, Ross JS. Cysts of the tunica albuginea testis. A report of 3 cases with a review of the literature. J Urol 1984, **132**: 131–132.

Tumors

184 Castiglione FM, Selikowitz SM, Dimond RL. Mule spinner's disease. Arch Dermatol 1985, **121**: 370–372.

185 Clatch RJ, Drake WK, Gonzalez JG. Aggressive angiomyxoma in men. A report of two cases associated with inguinal hernias. Arch Pathol Lab Med 1993, **117**: 911–913.

186 Greider HD, Vernon SE. Basal cell carcinoma of the scrotum. A case report and literature review. J Urol 1982, **127**: 145–146.

187 Japko L, Horta AA, Schreiber K, Mitsudo S, Karwa GL, Singh G, Koss LG. Malignant mesothelioma of the tunica vaginalis testis. Report of first case with preoperative diagnosis. Cancer 1982, **49**: 119–127.

188 Johnson S, Rundell M, Platt W. Leiomyosarcoma of the scrotum. A case report with electron microscopy. Cancer 1978, **41**: 1830–1835.

189 Konety BR, Campanella SC, Hakam A, Becich MJ. Malignant fibrous histiocytoma of the scrotum. J Urol Pathol 1996, **5**: 51–56.

190 Laskin WB, Fetsch JF, Mostofi FK. Angiomyofibroblastomalike tumor of the male genital tract: analysis of 11 cases with comparison to female angiomyofibroblastoma and spindle cell lipoma. Am J Surg Pathol 1998, **22**: 6–16.

191 Lodato RF, Zentner GJ, Gomez CA, Nochomovitz LE. Scrotal carcinoid. Presenting manifestation of multiple lesions in the small intestine. Am J Clin Pathol 1991, **96**: 664–668.

192 Lowe FC. Squamous cell carcinoma of scrotum. Urology 1985, **25**: 63–65.

193 Morikawa Y, Ishuhara Y, Yanase Y, Takao T, Matsuura N, Kakudo K. Malignant mesothelioma of tunica vaginalis with squamous differentiation. J Urol Pathol 1994, **2**: 95–102.

194 Newman PL, Fletcher CD. Smooth muscle tumours of the external genitalia. Clinicopathological analysis of a series. Histopathology 1991, **18**: 523–529.

195 Perez MA, La Rossa DD, Tomaszewski JE. Paget's disease primarily involving the scrotum. Cancer 1989, **63**: 970–975.

196 Ribalta T, Ro J, Sahin A, Dexeus F, Ayala A. Intrascrotally metastatic renal cell carcinoma. Report of two cases and review of the literature. J Urol Pathol 1993, **1**: 201–210.

197 Slone S, O'Connor D. Scrotal leiomyomas with bizarre nuclei: a report of three cases. Mod Pathol 1998, **11**: 282–287.

198 Tsang WY, Chan JK, Lee KC, Fisher C, Fletcher CD. Aggressive angiomyxoma. A report of four cases occurring in men. Am J Surg Pathol 1992, **16**: 1059–1065.

Index

Page references in *italics* indicate figures. Page references followed by *t* or *b* indicate tables or boxes respectively.

ELSEVIER CD-ROM LICENSE AGREEMENT

PLEASE READ THE FOLLOWING AGREEMENT CAREFULLY BEFORE USING THIS CD-ROM PRODUCT. THIS CD-ROM PRODUCT IS LICENSED UNDER THE TERMS CONTAINED IN THIS CD-ROM LICENSE AGREEMENT ("Agreement"). BY USING THIS CD-ROM PRODUCT, YOU, AN INDIVIDUAL OR ENTITY INCLUDING EMPLOYEES, AGENTS AND REPRESENTATIVES ("You" or "Your"), ACKNOWLEDGE THAT YOU HAVE READ THIS AGREEMENT, THAT YOU UNDERSTAND IT, AND THAT YOU AGREE TO BE BOUND BY THE TERMS AND CONDITIONS OF THIS AGREEMENT. ELSEVIER INC. ("Elsevier") EXPRESSLY DOES NOT AGREE TO LICENSE THIS CD-ROM PRODUCT TO YOU UNLESS YOU ASSENT TO THIS AGREEMENT. IF YOU DO NOT AGREE WITH ANY OF THE FOLLOWING TERMS, YOU MAY, WITHIN THIRTY (30) DAYS AFTER YOUR RECEIPT OF THIS CD-ROM PRODUCT RETURN THE UNUSED, PIN NUMBER PROTECTED, CD-ROM PRODUCT, ALL ACCOMPANYING DOCUMENTATION TO ELSEVIER FOR A FULL REFUND.

DEFINITIONS As used in this Agreement, these terms shall have the following meanings:

"Proprietary Material" means the valuable and proprietary information content of this CD-ROM Product including all indexes and graphic materials and software used to access, index, search and retrieve the information content from this CD-ROM Product developed or licensed by Elsevier and/or its affiliates, suppliers and licensors.

"CD-ROM Product" means the copy of the Proprietary Material and any other material delivered on CD-ROM and any other human-readable or machine-readable materials enclosed with this Agreement, including without limitation documentation relating to the same.

OWNERSHIP This CD-ROM Product has been supplied by and is proprietary to Elsevier and/or its affiliates, suppliers and licensors. The copyright in the CD-ROM Product belongs to Elsevier and/or its affiliates, suppliers and licensors and is protected by the national and state copyright, trademark, trade secret and other intellectual property laws of the United States and international treaty provisions, including without limitation the Universal Copyright Convention and the Berne Copyright Convention. You have no ownership rights in this CD-ROM Product. Except as expressly set forth herein, no part of this CD-ROM Product, including without limitation the Proprietary Material, may be modified, copied or distributed in hardcopy or machine-readable form without prior written consent from Elsevier. All rights not expressly granted to You herein are expressly reserved. Any other use of this CD-ROM Product by any person or entity is strictly prohibited and a violation of this Agreement.

SCOPE OF RIGHTS LICENSED (PERMITTED USES) Elsevier is granting to You a limited, non-exclusive, non-transferable license to use this CD-ROM Product in accordance with the terms of this Agreement. You may use or provide access to this CD-ROM Product on a single computer or terminal physically located at Your premises and in a secure network or move this CD-ROM Product to and use it on another single computer or terminal at the same location for personal use only, but under no circumstances may You use or provide access to any part or parts of this CD-ROM Product on more than one computer or terminal simultaneously.

You shall not (a) copy, download, or otherwise reproduce the CD-ROM Product in any medium, including, without limitation, online transmissions, local area networks, wide area networks, intranets, extranets and the Internet, or in any way, in whole or in part, except for printing out or downloading nonsubstantial portions of the text and images in the CD-ROM Product for Your own personal use; (b) alter, modify, or adapt the CD-ROM Product, including but not limited to decompiling, disassembling, reverse engineering, or creating derivative works, without the prior written approval of Elsevier; (c) sell, license or otherwise distribute to third parties the CD-ROM Product or any part or parts thereof; or (d) alter, remove, obscure or obstruct the display of any copyright, trademark or other proprietary notice on or in the CD-ROM Product or on any printout or download of portions of the Proprietary Materials.

RESTRICTIONS ON TRANSFER This License is personal to You, and neither Your rights hereunder nor the tangible embodiments of this CD-ROM Product, including without limitation the Proprietary Material, may be sold, assigned, transferred or sublicensed to any other person, including without limitation by operation of law, without the prior written consent of Elsevier. Any purported sale, assignment, transfer or sublicense without the prior written consent of Elsevier will be void and will automatically terminate the License granted hereunder.

TERM This Agreement will remain in effect until terminated pursuant to the terms of this Agreement. You may terminate this Agreement at any time by removing from Your system and destroying the CD-ROM Product. Unauthorized copying of the CD-ROM Product, including without limitation, the Proprietary Material and documentation, or otherwise failing to comply with the terms and conditions of this Agreement shall result in automatic termination of this license and will make available to Elsevier legal remedies. Upon termination of this Agreement, the license granted herein will terminate and You must immediately destroy the CD-ROM Product and accompanying documentation. All provisions relating to proprietary rights shall survive termination of this Agreement.

LIMITED WARRANTY AND LIMITATION OF LIABILITY NEITHER ELSEVIER NOR ITS LICENSORS REPRESENT OR WARRANT THAT THE CD-ROM PRODUCT WILL MEET YOUR REQUIREMENTS OR THAT ITS OPERATION WILL BE UNINTERRUPTED OR ERROR-FREE. WE EXCLUDE AND EXPRESSLY DISCLAIM ALL EXPRESS AND IMPLIED WARRANTIES NOT STATED HEREIN, INCLUDING THE IMPLIED WARRANTIES OF MERCHANTABILITY AND FITNESS FOR A PARTICULAR PURPOSE. IN ADDITION, NEITHER ELSEVIER NOR ITS LICENSORS MAKE ANY REPRESENTATIONS OR WARRANTIES, EITHER EXPRESS OR IMPLIED, REGARDING THE PERFORMANCE OF YOUR NETWORK OR COMPUTER SYSTEM WHEN USED IN CONJUNCTION WITH THE CD-ROM PRODUCT. WE SHALL NOT BE LIABLE FOR ANY DAMAGE OR LOSS OF ANY KIND ARISING OUT OF OR RESULTING FROM YOUR POSSESSION OR USE OF THE SOFTWARE PRODUCT CAUSED BY ERRORS OR OMISSIONS, DATA LOSS OR CORRUPTION, ERRORS OR OMISSIONS IN THE PROPRIETARY MATERIAL, REGARDLESS OF WHETHER SUCH LIABILITY IS BASED IN TORT, CONTRACT OR OTHERWISE AND INCLUDING, BUT NOT LIMITED TO, ACTUAL, SPECIAL, INDIRECT, INCIDENTAL OR CONSEQUENTIAL DAMAGES. IF THE FOREGOING LIMITATION IS HELD TO BE UNENFORCEABLE, OUR MAXIMUM LIABILITY TO YOU SHALL NOT EXCEED THE AMOUNT OF THE LICENSE FEE PAID BY YOU FOR THE SOFTWARE PRODUCT. THE REMEDIES AVAILABLE TO YOU AGAINST US AND THE LICENSORS OF MATERIALS INCLUDED IN THE SOFTWARE PRODUCT ARE EXCLUSIVE.

If this CD-ROM Product is defective, Elsevier will replace it at no charge if the defective CD-ROM Product is returned to Elsevier within sixty (60) days (or the greatest period allowable by applicable law) from the date of shipment.

Elsevier warrants that the software embodied in this CD-ROM Product will perform in substantial compliance with the documentation supplied in this CD-ROM Product. If You report a significant defect in performance in writing to Elsevier, and Elsevier is not able to correct same within sixty (60) days after its receipt of Your notification, You may return this CD-ROM Product, including all copies and documentation, to Elsevier and Elsevier will refund Your money.

YOU UNDERSTAND THAT, EXCEPT FOR THE 60-DAY LIMITED WARRANTY RECITED ABOVE, ELSEVIER, ITS AFFILIATES, LICENSORS, SUPPLIERS AND AGENTS, MAKE NO WARRANTIES, EXPRESSED OR IMPLIED, WITH RESPECT TO THE CD-ROM PRODUCT, INCLUDING, WITHOUT LIMITATION THE PROPRIETARY MATERIAL, AND SPECIFICALLY DISCLAIM ANY WARRANTY OF MERCHANTABILITY OR FITNESS FOR A PARTICULAR PURPOSE.

If the information provided on this CD-ROM contains medical or health sciences information, it is intended for professional use within the medical field. Information about medical treatment or drug dosages is intended strictly for professional use, and because of rapid advances in the medical sciences, independent verification of diagnosis and drug dosages should be made.

IN NO EVENT WILL ELSEVIER, ITS AFFILIATES, LICENSORS, SUPPLIERS OR AGENTS, BE LIABLE TO YOU FOR ANY DAMAGES, INCLUDING, WITHOUT LIMITATION, ANY LOST PROFITS, LOST SAVINGS OR OTHER INCIDENTAL OR CONSEQUENTIAL DAMAGES, ARISING OUT OF YOUR USE OR INABILITY TO USE THE CD-ROM PRODUCT REGARDLESS OF WHETHER SUCH DAMAGES ARE FORESEEABLE OR WHETHER SUCH DAMAGES ARE DEEMED TO RESULT FROM THE FAILURE OR INADEQUACY OF ANY EXCLUSIVE OR OTHER REMEDY.

U.S. GOVERNMENT RESTRICTED RIGHTS The CD-ROM Product and documentation are provided with restricted rights. Use, duplication or disclosure by the U.S. Government is subject to restrictions as set forth in subparagraphs (a) through (d) of the Commercial Computer Restricted Rights clause at FAR 52.22719 or in subparagraph (c)(1)(ii) of the Rights in Technical Data and Computer Software clause at DFARS 252.2277013, or at 252.2117015, as applicable. Contractor/Manufacturer is Elsevier Inc., 360 Park Avenue South, New York, NY 10010 USA.

GOVERNING LAW This Agreement shall be governed by the laws of the State of New York, USA. In any dispute arising out of this Agreement, You and Elsevier each consent to the exclusive personal jurisdiction and venue in the state and federal courts within New York County, New York, USA.

AAP-2441

For Reference

Not to be taken from this room